Khc 1108

D1451318

Nations of the World

2009

Eighth Edition

Nations of the World

A Political, Economic & Business Handbook

Grey House Publishing

MILLERTON, NY 12546

Grey House Publishing

PUBLISHER: Leslie Mackenzie
EDITOR: Richard Gottlieb
EDITORIAL DIRECTOR: Laura Mars-Proietti
MARKETING DIRECTOR: Jessica Moody

Grey House Publishing, Inc.
185 Millerton Road
Millerton, NY 12546
518.789.8700
FAX 518.789.0545
www.greyhouse.com
e-mail: books @greyhouse.com

Central European Business Ltd

MANAGING DIRECTOR: Anthony Axon
PRODUCTION MANAGER: Elaine McCarthy
EDITORIAL: Ruth Davis, Anthony Griffin, Sue Hewitt, Patrick Ivory, Trevor Jones, Marianne Keating, Elaine McCarthy, Anthony Miller, Lena von Heimandahl, Sophie von Heimandahl

World of Information
11 Clarendon Street
Cambridge CB1 1JU, UK
Tel: +44 (0) 1223 351584

First edition published 2000
Eighth edition published 2008
Printed in the USA

Nations of the world: a political, economic & business handbook. – 8th ed. (2009) – 1836 p.

1. Almanacs, American. 2. Business travel – Handbooks, manuals, etc. 3. International trade – Handbooks, manuals. etc.

HF1010.N37
658-dc21 2001238305
ISBN: 978-1-59237-273-7 softcover

Contents

Country Profiles

World View

INTRODUCTION

This is the eighth edition of *Nations of the World: A Political, Economic & Business Handbook*. It profiles every nation and self-governing territory around the world in an easy-to-access, single-volume format. Political, economic and business information, supplemented by maps, charts and tables fill 1,836 pages.

Many nations of the post-9/11 world continue to be defined by volatility and violence. War, clashing political parties, opposing ethnic groups, economic insecurity, terrorist threats, and environmental catastrophes find world leaders and civilians alike immensely concerned at the state of the world. Many industry segments, such as safety and security, business and finance, and travel and tourism continue to be tremendously affected by fluctuations in global activity.

This 2009 edition of *Nations of the World* offers tremendous insight into the social conditions, political stability, and economic climates of 233 nations, one more than last edition, as Kosovo became a new country. Since the last edition, the world has seen 61 parliamentary elections and 20 presidential elections. The world has lost one king, as Nepal changed from a Monarchy to a Republic.

Every country profile in *Nations of the World* has been reviewed and updated. The thoughtful and comprehensive country essays have been prepared by 33 experts in their fields, international correspondents who have contributed to some of the most influential books and periodicals in the world; a detailed Contributor list follows this Introduction.

Nations of the World is a reliable, careful compilation of essential information that is presented in a useful, organized format, a reference that is critical for anyone doing business or traveling overseas. It has also proved to be an important reference tool for students from secondary school through college, as well as for professionals from the political arena to reconstruction.

COUNTRY CHAPTERS

Part One: Arranged in alphabetical order by nation or territory, each country chapter begins with a concise, independently written **Country Overview**. These overviews do not reflect the worldview of any particular government or intelligence agency. You will find current political and economic events, as well as an informed outlook toward the future. Most chapters include a **Map** with key places; some of the world's more obscure places are shown in relation to surrounding countries. All chapters include **Key Facts** — official country name(s), ruling parties, language, basic area, population, unemployment, inflation figures, **Key Indicators** — charted over five years and include population, GNP, imports/exports, foreign debt, exchange rate, and **Risk Assessment** — rates politics, economy and general stability of the region. Sources for this information follow the list of Contributors.

Part Two: This section of each chapter includes a **Country Profile**, with detailed historical information in easy-to-follow chronological order, political structure and parties, and a detailed look at the country's population, labor market, media, trade, industry, agriculture and energy. Business travelers will learn about that country's time zones, banking practices, entry requirements, dress codes, climate, health issues, hotels, working hours and the best way to travel to and from. ***Countries in political crises include warning and advice to visitors.***

Part Three: Each country chapter ends with a **Business Directory.** This includes contact numbers and web sites for hotels, travel information and chambers of commerce, plus dozens of other useful numbers and addresses.

WORLD VIEW

This section starts with **The World Today**, followed by five sections: **Africa; Americas; Asia; Europe; Middle East.** Like the individual country chapters, these regional chapters include **Maps,** expertly written **Overviews** on the political and economic climate, **Currencies,** and **Key Indicators.**

Nations of the World ends with a list of **US Embassies** with address, phone, fax, email and web sites.

Grey House Publishing is offering a CD-ROM companion to the print book. With the CD-ROM, users can quickly and easily view and print out Country Reports as ready-to-use resources. To add the CD-ROM to your order, simply fill out and return the coupon in the back of the book.

With 1,836 pages of critical political, economic and business information including narrative overviews, charts and maps, this newest edition of *Nations of the World: A Political, Economic & Business Handbook* — in both print and CD-ROM — is a timely and immensely valuable reference acquisition to all public, academic and special library collections.

Contributors

Guy Arnold is a freelance writer who specialises in north-south relations and African affairs. His most recent publications include *A Third World Handbook*, *Wars in the Third World Since 1945* and *The End of the Third World*.

Barry Baxter has spent most his working life in Africa. He has worked as a journalist for 45 years, reporting from Botswana, South Africa, Zambia (and northern Rhodesia), Zimbabwe (and Southern Rhodesia), Angola, Kenya, Tanzania and Uganda. Since 1994, he has operated NewsWorld, an Africa news agency serving Reuters, the South African Press Association, Agencia EFE and several magazines.

Gopal Chandra Bose is a freelance journalist based in India and contributes articles on political and economic themes for Asia. His work has been commissioned by the BBC.

Daniel Brett is a freelance journalist contributing articles on agricultural economics, protest movements and trade-related issues in Africa and Latin America as well as the politics and economics of other developing countries.

Ruth Davis has lived, worked and studied in south India and Japan. She has worked for the Department for International Development and is an analyst specialising in Asian countries.

Shanjukta Ghosh is a graduate of Delhi University and writes on socioeconomic themes of the Indian subcontinent, with emphasis on high-technology.

John Gorvett is based in Istanbul, and has written extensively on the politics and economies of Turkey and Greece.

Anthony Griffin is a UK-based journalist specialising in emerging markets, with an emphasis on Spanish speaking countries. He regularly contributes articles to British and international publications, on Europe and South America.

Aileen Herlihy, based in Australia, writes on health and welfare issues, with an emphasis on developing countries as well as Australia.

David Ivory has worked in various UK ministries and writes on governments and governance worldwide. His work includes analysis of elections and political leaderships results.

Niki Johnson is a research fellow at the Political Science Institute, Universidad de la República, Montevideo, Uruguay.

Trevor Jones is a freelance researcher and journalist, specialising in politico-economic developments in the Americas. He holds degrees from the University of Southampton, the London School of Economics and Darwin College, Cambridge.

Marianne Keating is a freelance writer contributing articles on various topics, in particular economic and political profiles, of Africa and Asia.

Ali Khalil is a business journalist at the UK-based *Asharq Al-Awsat* Arabic newspaper and writes on the Middle East.

Asbed Kotchikian is a doctoral student and lecturer at Boston University, US, specialising in the Middle East and the Caucasus. He has lectured at universities in Armenia, Georgia and Latvia.

Juma Kwayera is a sub-editor and writer for *The EastAfrican* newspaper and writes for *The Daily Nation* newspaper's KiSwahili edition in Kenya. He writes on east and central Africa

Marcela López Levy works as a researcher and editor at the UK-based Latin America Bureau, and writes on Latin America and the Caribbean.

Elaine McCarthy writes on agricultural and political trends within the European Union.

Ali Rafel al Mansour is an analyst based in the Middle East, who reports on the petroleum industry and OPEC.

Bhekie Matsebula is a Swaziland-based journalist and has written for the Pan-African News Agency and the BBC.

Meldun Mawson is a Swedish writer who specialises in travel and tourism issues, and the social and cultural implications of political change in Latin America, as well as northern Europe.

Dr Anthony Miller is a freelance journalist working in the NGO and thinktank sector, specialising in the Balkans, the Caucasus and the Middle East.

Marianne Morse is a freelance political and economic country analyst. She edited the *Organization of American States – the next 50 years*.

Neamat Nojumi is a former Afghani mujahideen soldier. Since 1991, he has been living in the US and works as a commentator on Central Asian affairs. He is author of *The Rise of the Taliban in Afghanistan*.

Gergana Noutcheva is a researcher specialising in Eastern Europe at the Centre for European Studies, based in Belgium.

Anita Parameswaran is a business analyst for a leading insurance company working on corporate strategy. She writes on North Africa and the Mediterranean.

Ibrahim Seaga Shaw is publisher and editor of www.expotimes.net which specialises in news and analysis of events in Africa and the African diaspora. He contributes to *New African* magazine and *The Guardian* newspaper.

Craig Stenhouse is a researcher specialising in Africa and the Middle East.

Bernadeta Tendyra specialises in Eastern Europe and has worked as a BBC World Service journalist.

Marian White is a freelance writer specialising in the politics and economics of the Pacific Rim with a particular interest in emerging economies.

William R Thomson is a former director and vice president in charge of the Asia Development Bank's lending programmes in over 25 Asian and Pacific countries. He advises both international investment houses and governments on regional economic developments and investment opportunities.

Damian Tobin is based in Ireland and the UK, lectures in economics and specialises in Europe and the Far East.

José Luis Velasco lectures in Mexican politics and holds a doctorate in political science from Boston University. He is the author of *El Debate Actual Sobre el Federalismo Mexicano*, published by Instituto Mora.

Main sources

It should be noted that the methodology used by the International Monetary Fund (IMF), World Bank, Organisation for Economic Co-operation and Development (OECD) and other main gatherers of international data can vary not only from each other but also from individual central banks and government departments. In order to ensure consistency and to allow like to be compared with like, *World of Information* uses the same single source for the Key Indicator data. Readers should be aware, however, that occasionally a more up to date figure is used in the body of the text that might not have been calculated in the same way. The principal sources used are: the IMF, World Bank, Asian Development Bank (ADB), African Development Bank (AfDB), Eastern Caribbean Central Bank (ECCB), Economic Commission for Latin America and the Caribbean (ECLAC), individual central bank reports and national statistics. Statistics have also been gathered from UN agencies including FAO, UNHCR and Unicef.

Afghanistan

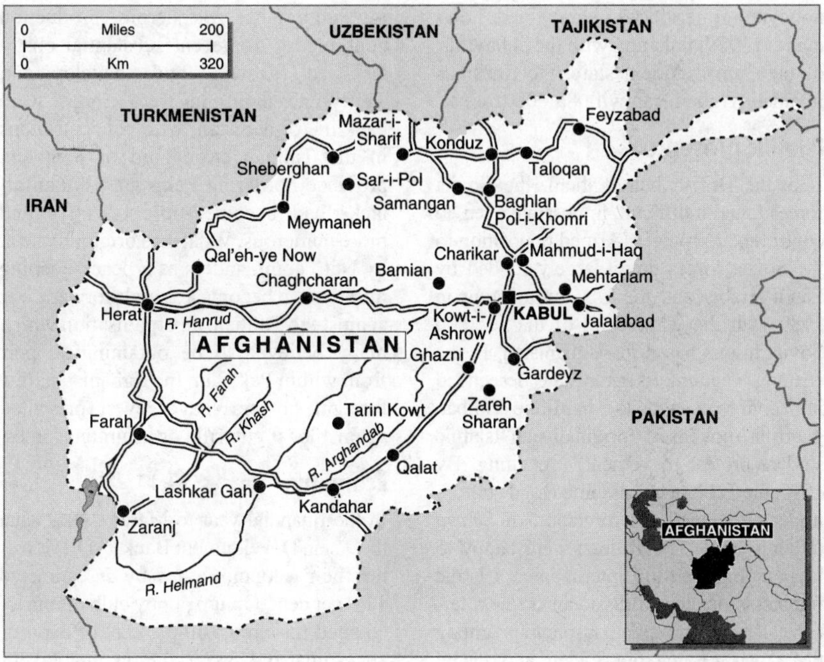

Afghanistan, before the advent of the steam engine and the jet engine, was seen as the crossroads between east and west. As a body politic, it is more an artificial creation than a natural entity. In many respects it resembles not so much a country, more a bone of territory chewed over and largely discarded by the imperial dogs of the day – more often than not neighbouring Tsarist Russia and the once Imperial Britain, seeking to protect the jewel of the imperial crown, India. Afghanistan's present boundaries were first fashioned, subsequently imposed, by Britain and Russia, who both saw the mountainous area as a natural – and probably the original – buffer state between them.

Tribal divisions

It is, none the less, simply impossible to comprehend Afghanistan and the problems that confront it in 2007 without an understanding of its history and the factors that not only lead to its creation, but also render it one of the world's most precarious democracies. Most students of world affairs are aware of the existence of the Taliban, and of Osama bin Laden and al Qaeda. How they affect, and are affected by, Afghanistan is often overlooked or misunderstood. First, there is no such person as an ethnic Afghani. The population is still a relatively loose grouping of tribes, making Afghanistan a traditionally difficult place to govern. To this day the tribes show varying degrees of loyalty – or a lack of it – to the central authority of Kabul. The principal common denominator between the Pashtuns (principally in the centre and the south-east) the Ghilzais (on the border with Pakistan, the Uzbeks (north lowlands) and the Tajiks or Parziwans of Persian origin, is their Islamic faith. Other tribes are the Nuristani (also known as Kefirs), Hazara and Chahar Aimak.

The tribes in Afghanistan were conquered and converted to Islam by the Arabs in the eleventh century. The Arabs were subsequently defeated by the Mongol forces of Genghis Khan in the thirteenth century, themselves to be followed by a succession of rulers – in some cases from Iran – and more or less constant civil war until the early nineteenth century. The British, by then in possession of India, took exception to the assumption of power

KEY FACTS

Official name: The Islamic Republic of Afghanistan

Head of State: President Hamid Karzai (since Jun 2002; elected 9 Oct 2004)

Head of government: President Hamid Karzai

Ruling party: Members of the national assembly are elected as independent candidates

Area: 647,497 square km

Population: 27.41 million (*2007) (some 1 million Afghanis are still in exile in Pakistan and Iran; the last census was in 1979)

Capital: Kabul

Official language: Pashtu and Dari (named as official languages in the constitution ratified 4 Jan 2004)

Currency: Afghani (Af) = 100 puls

Exchange rate: Af46.03 per US$ (Jul 2008)

GDP per capita: US$323 (2007)

GDP real growth: 6.10% (2007)

Labour force: 8.47 million (2004)

Unemployment: 10.80% (2004); 50% (2005, unofficial)

Inflation: 5.10% (2007)

Balance of trade: -US$3.40 billion (2005) (Aghanistan's highest export is opium, which is not included in the IMF export figure)

Foreign debt: US$8.50 billion (2004)

Annual FDI: US$100.00 million (2004)

* estimated figure

by Dost Mohammad, who they regarded as too close to the Russians. Attempts by the British to replace Dost Mohammad ended in ignominious defeat for the British in what came to be known as the First Afghan War in 1842, allowing Dost Mohammad to rule for a further 20 years. When his successor, Sher Ali sought to strengthen further his links with Russia, Britain again objected, and the second Afghan War broke out in 1878. This time the British enjoyed greater success, occupying the strategically important cities of Jalalabad and Kandahar.

The Great Game

Thus began a period of British influenced rule by Abdulrahman Khan (a grandson of Dost Mohammad). The strategically important Khyber Pass was surrendered to the British and the boundary between India (now Pakistan) and Afghanistan was accepted. Abdulrahman waged war on rebellious tribes in an attempt to enforce central authority. He was succeeded by his son, Habibullah, whose assassination in 1919 lead to a distancing from Britain and renewed overtures to what was now revolutionary Russia. Again, the British objected, leading to the third Afghan War – a political confrontation which became known as the Great Game, which ended with a muddled acceptance of Afghan independence.

Soviet influence

In the mid twentieth century, following Indian independence and the creation of Pakistan, British influence all but disappeared in the region. Moscow now had to compete with Washington for the region's hearts and minds. After a while, Washington began to lose interest, leaving Afghanistan overly dependent on Soviet aid and assistance. Gradually Moscow became more and more involved in Afghan affairs; Afghan army officers were now sent for training in Russia. This, almost inevitably, lead to a *coup d'etat*, led by Mohammed Daud, in 1973 in which the King (Afghanistan was by then a monarchy) was deposed and Afghanistan declared a republic. In 1978, General Daud was killed, making way for a regime that was more openly sympathetic to Moscow. The honeymoon period was short lived, however; in 1979, unhappy with the behaviour of their unruly client state, the Russians invaded Afghanistan with 85,000 troops.

Islamic presence

Like the British before them, the Soviet forces found it difficult, impossible even, to control their protégés. Armed opposition to the Soviet forces grew, largely funded by Saudi Arabia and the US, culminating in 1989 with the withdrawal of the 115,000 Soviet troops based in Afghanistan. In the ensuing vacuum, Afghanistan descended into civil war, with the hard-line Taliban guerrilla movement (originally an Islamic student protest movement) prevailing. By 1995, the Taliban had assumed total control, imposing a harsh interpretation of *Sharia* (Islamic law). The Taliban were happy to harbour high profile international Islamic figures associated to dissident or even terrorist Islamic groups. Conspicuous among these was Osama bin Laden and his al Qaeda network, sought by the US government on a number of charges. It was the Taliban refusal to extradite bin Laden and others that provoked a military response by the USA and the UK. A combination of air strikes and ground action brought about the eventual (but not as it turned out, total) defeat of the Taliban.

Failed state?

At the end of 2006 Afghanistan still had many of the attributes of a failed state. This is probably a mistaken description, since as a state, Afghanistan has never really succeeded. Following the defeat of the Taliban, Afghanistan was largely abandoned by an international community more than preoccupied with events in Iraq.

In 2006, tribal loyalties to tribal warlords, extensive corruption and the growing importance of heroin production continued to represent substantial obstacles to growth and development. Thirty-one thousand Nato troops were back in Afghanistan, with concentrations in the Taliban stronghold of Helmand province bordering Pakistan. Taliban attacks had become more effective and more numerous. What was originally seen by Nato commanders as a peace-keeping mission had become a straightforward war against the Taliban, an organisation which many believed to be obtaining support from within Pakistan. In Afghanistan, few foreign powers have ever prevailed against local guerrilla or insurgent forces.

Economy

In the financial year to March 2006, what the Asian Development Bank (ADB) terms the 'licit' economy grew by an estimated 13.8 per cent. Opium poppy cultivation accounted for almost 40 per cent of exports, an estimated US$2.7 billion in total, of which Afghanistan's farmers got US$560 million, the rest – US$2.1 billion – being pocketed by Afghan dealers. Drugs apart, the government estimates that a sustained growth rate of 9 per cent by the 'licit' economy is needed if living standards are to improve. Growth projections for the financial years 2006/07 and 2007/08 are put at 11.7 per cent and 10.6 per cent respectively. Forecast inflation for 2006 was 8.0 per cent, and for 2007, 5.0 per cent.

Afghanistan's trade deficit was estimated at US$2.5 billion for the fiscal year to March 2006. Goods imports increased to US$4.4 billion, exports to US$1.9 billion. Of the latter, US$566 million were actually exports, the balance re-exports. The current account deficit widened to US$3.0 billion (about 42 per cent of GDP). Including grants in aid, the current account recorded a surplus of US$123 million. Foreign direct investment (FDI) was US$253 million. All in all, the estimated balance of payments surplus of US$458 million meant that international reserves rose to US$1.73 billion at the end of fiscal year 2005/06.

Outlook

The failure to date of NATO troops to understand properly the nature of the war

KEY INDICATORS — Afghanistan

	Unit	2003	2004	2005	2006	2007
Population	m	25.25	25.79	24.32	*25.05	*25.80
Gross domestic product (GDP)	US$bn	4.60	5.76	7.31	7.05	*9.89
GDP per capita	US$	186	194	300	264	*323
GDP real growth	%	15.7	7.5	14.0	6.1	*5.5
Inflation	%	10.3	13.0	13.2	5.1	*13.0
Exports (fob) (goods)	US$m	100.0	144.0	471.0	430.0	–
Imports (cif) (goods)	US$m	2,452.0	2,101.0	3,870.0	2,960.0	–
Balance of trade	US$m	-2,352.0	-1,957.0	-3,399.0	-2,530.0	–
Current account	US$m	145.0	76.0	41.0	-145.0	*-379.0
Exchange rate	per US$	43.00	43.00	49.18	49.32	49.53

* estimated figure

they are fighting suggests that Afghanistan will continue to experience higher than acceptable levels of insecurity from the Taliban insurgent attacks. While the private sector continues to grow, in international terms that growth is small and the starting position very low. Furthermore, such growth depends on a stable economic and social environment, which – like Afghanistan's democracy – is very precarious.

Risk assessment

Politics	Poor
Economy	Poor/Improving
Regional stability	Poor

COUNTRY PROFILE

Historical profile

For centuries, Afghanistan's strategic location close to the heart of Central Asia made it the target of foreign powers. With its mixture of ethnic clans and feudal society ruled by powerful warlords, no foreign invader successfully managed to control Afghanistan for very long. In the nineteenth century, Afghanistan became the scene of the 'Great Game' as Britain tried to counter Russia's increasing influence in Central Asia.

In 1996, the Taliban, originally a group of Islamic scholars drawn from the Pashtun majority, seized Kabul after nearly two decades of conflict. Although its extreme version of Islam attracted widespread criticism, the Taliban remained in control of most of Afghanistan until its refusal to hand over Osama bin Laden led to air strikes by the US and Britain in 2001. By the end of the year, the Taliban had been defeated and Hamid Kazai became interim head of a power-sharing government. Although some visible progress has been made since the fall of the Taliban government, many problems remain unsolved: militants continue to fight; there has been a boom in the drugs trade and Afghanistan has become the world's leading producer of opium.

1838–42 First Afghan War. Britain invaded Afghanistan to counter the threat to British India from expanding Russian influence in Afghanistan and was defeated by fierce resistance from Afghanistan's many ethnic tribes.

1878–80 Second Afghan War. After Britain invaded Afghanistan for the second time, parts of the country were absorbed into British India. Russia also seized parts of Afghani territory.

1907 Russia signed an agreement with Britain, promising no further interference in Afghanistan.

1919 Third Afghan War, after which Britain recognised Afghanistan's independence.

1926 Amanullah proclaimed himself King.

1929 Amanullah fled after civil unrest over his reforms; Mohammed Nadir Shah was proclaimed King. He reunited a fragmented Afghanistan and took steps to modernise the country, though less obtrusively than Amanullah.

1933 Nadir Shah was assassinated and his son, Zahir Shah, became King; his reign lasted 40 years.

1956 Afghanistan built a close relationship with the Soviet Union, gaining arms supplies and undertaking trade.

1964 A constitutional monarchy was introduced, which led to political polarisation and power struggles.

1965 The Communist People's Democratic Party of Afghanistan (PDPA) was formed.

1973 General Mohammed Daud deposed King Zahir Shah, who moved into exile in Italy, and Afghanistan was declared a republic.

1978 General Daud was assassinated in the Saur (April) Revolution, a coup by the pro-Communists, led by the PDPA's leader, Noor Taraki, who was declared president.

1979 The Soviet Union invaded Afghanistan after the nationalist foreign minister, Hafizullah Amin, deposed Taraki. Amin was executed and replaced by the pro-Soviet Babrak Karmal. Numerous Afghan factions formed the Mujahidin and began a guerrilla war against the Soviet occupation forces. Backed by the US, Pakistan, China, Iran and Saudi Arabia, the Mujahidin inflicted heavy losses on Soviet troops.

1985 The Mujahidin gathered in Pakistan, forming an alliance against Soviet forces. Half of the Afghan population was displaced by the war.

1986 Babrak Karmal was replaced by Najibullah Ahmadzai, the head of the Afghani secret police, as head of the Soviet-backed regime.

1988 Afghanistan, USSR, the US and Pakistan signed peace accords.

1989 The Soviet Union withdrew its last troops from Afghanistan. Civil war continued as the Mujahidin refused to co-operate with the Najibullah regime.

1991 The US and Russia agreed to end military aid to both sides.

1992 Afghanistan was declared an Islamic republic after the capture of Kabul by Mujahidin factions and Najibullah was forced to seek the UN's protection in Kabul. Rival militias vied for power.

1993 Burhanuddin Rabbani, an ethnic Tajik, was proclaimed president, and Gulbuddin Hekmatyar, who was strongly backed by the US during the Soviet occupation, was appointed prime minister.

1994 The Pashtun-dominated Islamic fundamentalist Taliban, formed in Kandahar, south Afghanistan, emerged as the major challenge to the Rabbani government.

1995 The Taliban swept through southern Afghanistan.

1996 The Taliban captured Kabul and quickly imposed a strict version of sharia (Islamic law). President Rabbani fled to join the anti-Taliban alliance in the north.

1997 Only Pakistan and Saudi Arabia recognised the Taliban as legitimate rulers of Afghanistan. Hostilities increased in the north between the Taliban and the militias of the United National Islamic Front for the Salvation of Afghanistan (UNIFSA) (also known as the Northern Alliance).

1998 The Taliban captured Mazar-i-Sharif, the last major city outside Taliban control; around 6,000 civilians were massacred following the city's capture. The US launched cruise missiles at suspected bases of Osama bin Laden, accused of bombing US embassies in Africa.

1999 The UN introduced economic sanctions against Afghanistan for harbouring Bin Laden.

2001 The Afghan resistance leader, Commander Massoud, was assassinated. The giant statues of Buddha in Bamian were destroyed by the Taliban. The US and Britain launched air strikes against the Taliban and al Qaeda, following the Taliban's refusal to hand over Bin Laden, also blamed for masterminding the 11 September 2001 terrorist attacks in the US. Opposition forces seized Mazar-i-Sharif, then Kabul and other key cities. Afghan groups agreed an interim government in UN-sponsored talks in Bonn, Germany. The Taliban gave up Kandahar, its last stronghold, at the end of the year and Pashtun royalist, Hamid Karzai was sworn in as head of a 30-member interim power-sharing government.

2002 The first contingent of foreign peacekeepers arrived. Hamid Karzai was elected interim president by the Loya Jirga. Former monarch, Zahir Shah, returned to Kabul, but made no claim to the throne. The Interim President narrowly escaped an assassination attempt in his home town of Kandahar. After 23 years, the Asian Development Bank resumed lending to Afghanistan.

2003 The afghani was re-valued. Afghanistan introduced a law banning armed factions from politics. NATO forces took control of security in Kabul.

2004 Afghanistan ratified a new constitution including a presidential system. In presidential elections Hamid Karzai, won 55 per cent of the vote, Yunus Qanuni 16 per cent, Mohammad Mohaqeq 12 per cent and Abdul Rashid Dostum 12 per cent. President Karzai was sworn in as

Afghanistan's first democratically elected leader. Afghanistan was guaranteed US$8.2bn in aid until 2007.
2005 Parliamentary elections were held where the turnout was 36 per cent in Kabul and 53 per cent across the country.
2006 There was a resurgence of Taliban activity and fighting with coalition forces in the south, culminating in the fiercely-fought Operation Mountain Thrust. Responsibility for security in the south passed to NATO.
2007 The former King of Afghanistan, Zahir Shar, died in July. He had been in exile for 29 years before returning to Kabul in 2002. On 9 August a jirga (tribal council) began in Kabul to discuss means of combating the Taliban. President Musharraf of Pakistan was originally scheduled to inaugurate the jirga with President Kazai but withdrew the day before. In August, Russia cut around U$10 billion off Afghanistan's outstanding debt, accrued during the Soviet Union's occupation, 1979–89. The greater part of the country's external debt had been forgiven by the Paris Club of international creditors in 2006. The remaining debt to Russia is expected to by cancelled by 2010. On 20 September, 30 civilians were killed in Kabul by a suicide bomber belonging to the militant Taleban, which had rejected proposals by the president for peace talks. In October, the Asian Development Bank approved a loan of over US$170 million to complete the circular highway connecting Kabul and other major cities, in particular the section between Herat in the west and Mazar e Sharif in the north. The completed road will bypass the warring territory of the south, plus reduce travel times and transport costs. The highway will also facilitate trade with neighbouring countries in the north and west.
2008 In February the US reported that the Taliban was in control of about 10 per cent of Afghanistan and the government only controlled 30 per cent; the rest of the country was under the control of tribal chiefs. Government officials deny their control was so limited claiming the tribal chiefs supported central government and provided security in its stead.

Political structure

Constitution
On 4 January 2004, Afghanistan ratified a new constitution, which establishes an Islamic republic, in which the president rules with a national assembly; women are recognised as equal citizens and have one-fifth of the lower house seats.

Form of state
Islamic republic

The executive
The president is the Head of State, leading a cabinet, with two vice presidents and 29 ministers.

National legislature
The bicameral parliament consists of the Wolesi Jirga (House of the People) (lower) and Meshrano Jirga (House of Elders) (senate). The lower house has 249 members, elected for five-year terms; members of the senate are elected for four years. The Kuchi (nomad) community is allocated 10 seats in the lower house; women also have guaranteed seats.

Legal system
The new constitution guarantees an independent judiciary, consisting of a Stera Mahkama (supreme court), high courts and appeal courts.
The president appoints the members of the supreme court, with the approval of the Wolesi Jirga.

Last elections
9 October 2004 (presidential); 18 September 2005 (parliamentary).
Results: Presidential: incumbent Hamid Karzai won 55 per cent of the vote, Yunus Qanuni 16 per cent, Mohammad Mohaqeq 12 per cent and Abdul Rashid Dostum 12 per cent.
Parliamentary: Turnout was 36 per cent in Kabul and 53 per cent across the country. There is no party breakdown as candidates ran as independents.

Next elections
2009 (presidential); 2010 (parliamentary)

Political parties

Ruling party
Members of the national assembly are elected as independent candidates

Main opposition party
Jami'at e Islami (Islamic Society of Afghanistan) leads a loose alliance.

Population
*27.41 million (2007) (some 1 million Afghanis are still in exile in Pakistan and Iran; the last census was in 1979)
Last census: June 1979: 13,051,358 (excluding nomad population)
Population density: 36 inhabitants per square km; urban population 20.3 per cent (ADB 2006).
* estimate
Annual growth rate: 1.7 per cent 2005 (ADB)

Ethnic make-up
Pashtun (Pathan) (38 per cent), Tajik (25 per cent), Hazara (19 per cent), Uzbek (6 per cent), minority groups including Aimaks, Turkmen, Baluch and others (12 per cent).
The Pashtuns largely reside in south-eastern Afghanistan. Tajiks, Hazaras and Uzbeks are the main communities in northern and central Afghanistan.

Religions
Almost the entire population is Muslim (84 per cent Sunni Muslim, 15 per cent Shi'ite); Hindu, Sikh and Jewish minorities.

Education
The UN Educational, Scientific and Cultural Organisation (Unesco) assists the Afghan government in the education sector reconstruction by promoting universal primary education, especially for girls and the expansion of primary schooling with access to secondary education.
Unesco has extended its support for a computer centre at Kabul University, including Internet access for the young. It also funds the printing of text-books for all levels of education.
Literacy rate: 51.9 per cent and 21.9 per cent respectively for men and women; adult rates (Unesco 2000).
Enrolment rate: 15 per cent gross primary enrolment of relevant age group (including repeaters), rates for 2000–01 (Unesco 2002).

Health
Per capita total expenditure on health (2003) was US$26; of which per capita government spending was US$10, at the international dollar rate, (WHO 2006).
The World Health Organisation (Who) reported that since 2000, an estimated 180,000 internally displaced people (IDPs), mostly from Ghor and Badghis provinces had been living in the Maslakh camp outside the city of Herat, which has been the site of dire health conditions during the crisis. The mortality rate declined as international support enabled the establishment of more clinics inside the camp.
WHO continues to support the IDPs by providing essential medical supplies to clinics within the camps. There is provision for night health services and nutrition centres for malnourished children. Harsh winters in the region cause acute respiratory infections, while hot dry summers lead to diarrhoeal diseases.
Despite on-going security problems, UN relief agencies and the WHO provide emergency medical supplies and assistance to local hospitals.
Polio is endemic. In 2006, a large outbreak of the disease, in the volatile southern regions, followed a drop in overall numbers of cases in previous years. The UN undertook immunisation against polio of around 1.3 million children in the southern provinces of Kandahar and Helmand in September 2007. The week-long campaign took place within the war zones while 10,000 health workers were given safe passage to undertake the operation.
Life expectancy: 42 years, 2004 (WHO 2006)
Fertility rate/Maternal mortality rate: 7.4 births per woman, 2004 (WHO 2006)

Child (under 5 years) mortality rate (per 1,000): 165 per 1,000 live births (2002), 49 per cent of children aged under five were malnourished (World Bank).
Head of population per physician: 0.19 physicians per 1,000 people, 2001 (WHO 2006)

Welfare
Many Afghans fled the country due to war, drought and earthquakes. The UNHCR estimated that, at its peak, more than 3.7 million Afghans survive outside their homeland; between 1.1–1.5 million were internally displaced. Over 520,000 refugees returned in 2005, the largest group, of 453,000, came from camps in Pakistan. International agencies and the government have been working hard for their rehabilitation, as well as for the thousands who returned in previous years.
The WFP has been working with the Afghan government to rehabilitate irrigation systems and expand its activities to cover the reconstruction of schools, hospitals, roads and bridges.
In March 2005, Japan donated US$29 million to New Beginnings Programme that offers ex-militia soldiers the opportunity of joining the official army or retraining in peacetime occupations such as farming or tailoring. Japan had already donated US$90 million to the project that required US$140 million to fund.

Main cities
Kabul (capital, estimated population 2.4 million in 2008), Kandahar (347,253), Mazar-i-Sharif (277,302), Herat (350,154), Jalalabad (143,525).

Languages spoken
The languages spoken by Afghanistan's two largest ethnic groups are Dari (Afghan Persian) (50 per cent) and Pashtu (35 per cent). Turkic languages (primarily Uzbek and Turkmen) (11 per cent), 30 minor languages (primarily Baluchi and Pashai) (4 per cent). Farsi (Persian) is spoken by the Tajiks. Some speak a second language, including English, Russian, French or German.
Official language/s
Pashtu and Dari (named as official languages in the constitution ratified 4 Jan 2004)

Media
All material is subject to Sharia (Islamic law) and regulatory bodies are controlled by the government. However, since 2001 there has been a strong growth in broadcasting and print media, with five TV stations and over 300 newspapers published nationwide, although in a country with a low literacy rate the radio is the principal medium for news and information.
National news agency: BNA (Bakhtar News Agency)
Other news agencies: Pajhwok Afghan News: www.pajhwok.com
Afghan Islamic Press: www.afghanislamicpress.com
Press
Print journalism does not match broadcast journalism for professionalism and research with opinions offered instead of investigation and hard facts. Self-censorship is widely practiced by older writers and violence towards journalists has curbed the focus necessary for news gathering. The market for newspapers and advertising revenue is so small that private newspapers must rely on political factions and individuals for sponsorship.
Dailies: State-owned publications, in Dari and Pashtu, include Daily Anis Eslah (), Arman-e Melli and Eslah. In English the Karbul Times. Private newspapers in Dari and Pashtu, and Hewad, Eradeh, Shari'at, Daily Afghanistan (www.dailyafghanistan.com), Tolafghan (www.tolafghan.com) and Payam e Mojahed (www.payamemojahed.com). In English, the Daily Outlook Afghanistan (www.outlookafghanistan.net) and theDaily Cheragh (www.cheraghdaily.af).
Weeklies: In Dari and Pashtu, Aina-e-Zan (Women's Mirror). In English, Kabul Weekly is an independent newspaper funded by the UN. Omaid Weekly is published in the US and is one of the most widely read Afghani publications in the world.
Broadcasting
Radio: There are many radio stations broadcasting regionally. The government-owned Radio Afghanistan is national; it has competition from several foreign radio broadcasting services. Commercial radio stations including the popular Arman FM (www.arman.fm) with programmes in local languages and English, Radio Killid (www.thekillidgroup.com) and Rana FM (www.ranafm.org).
Television: The popularity for television is growing and some stations are providing local programming. The National Television Afghanistan (NRTA) is government run, other national, free-to-air private stations include Tolo TV (www.tolo.tv) which shows foreign and domestic programmes, Ariana TV (www.arianatelevision.com) with news in Pashtu, Dari and English and Ayna TV is based in the northern provinces and broadcasts in four local languages.
Television is also provided by foreign entities including the US-based satellite networks Noor TV (www.noor-tv.com) and Payame Afghan TV (www.payameafghantv.com). Khorasan TV, is a local satellite network with Shamshad and Afghan TV (http://afghanistantv.org).

Economy
The fall of the Taliban in 2001 left the government with extensive political, economic and social burdens. However, Afghanistan has been experiencing significant improvements in its economy – albeit from a low base – and political stability in its northern provinces. Extreme poverty is still estimated to affect 20 per cent of the population with a further 60 per cent being vulnerable. Long-term improvement will require substantial external financing, as well as government commitment to reform and to tackling the problems of an opium economy and the domestic security issues in the south.
The government's focus is on reviving the economy, particularly agriculture, energy, housing, education and export-related industries. Fuelled by an infusion of international assistance, the IMF reported GDP growth of 6.1 per cent in 2006 and 5.5 per cent in 2007. Domestic revenues have increased, mainly due to tax reforms. The repair and development of infrastructure remains heavily dependent on external backing.
An estimated 80 per cent of the population work in the agricultural sector, most of which is subsistence farming. Illicit opium production forms an increasing percentage of the country's GDP, accounting for just over half, with an estimated value of US$3 billion. Government and foreign donors are keen to tackle the illegal opium trade, but it is likely to be extremely challenging due to the scale of production and its economic importance. Some 15,000 hectares of opium poppy had been eradicated by June 2006. Even so, the US reported that depite efforts by the UN troops and Afghan government, poppy production increased by 25 per cent in 2006. It is estimated that Afghanistan accounts for around 90 per cent of the world's opium trade.

External trade
Much of the government's strategy for international trade is predicated on a future with secure, nationwide peace. It sees the future of Afghanistan as a hub for regional trade, with land links to surrounding countries and traditionally this, coupled with its low customs duties, has been an important distribution point for re-exports.
The Ministry of Commerce and Industry has undertaken negotiations in regional economic initiatives, which include the Economic Co-operation Organisation (ECO) and bilateral negotiations with neighbouring countries including Iran, India, Pakistan, Tajikistan and Uzbekistan. Future plans include participation in the South Asia Free Trade Area (Safta) and the Central Asian Regional Economic

Co-operation (Carec) programme. Afghanistan is also an observer member of the World Trade Organisation (WTO).
A suggested oil pipeline through Afghanistan to Pakistan would create an oil trade linking Central Asia with Pakistan.

Imports

Afghanistan mainly imports capital goods including construction items needed to repair its neglected infrastructure, foodstuffs, textiles and petroleum products.

Main sources: Pakistan (37.9 per cent of total imports, 2006), US (12.0 per cent), Germany (7.2 per cent).

Exports

Opium, Afghanistan's largest, albeit illegal, export is primarily transported north through the Central Asian republics and on to Europe. Measures by foreign governments have been introduced in an attempt to eradicate the crop. Around 10 per cent of Afghan families rely on its production and as opium represents a large proportion of the country's exports this could lead to a serious drop in income if the campaign is successful.
Principal non-opium exports include fruits and nuts, hand-woven carpet, small scale industrial products, pelts and hides and semi-precious and precious stones.

Main destinations: India (22.2 per cent of 2006 total goods exports), Pakistan (21.2 per cent), US (14.7 per cent).

Agriculture

Farming

The population is returning to the countryside and some rural areas have been transformed by the return of Afghan refugees from Pakistan and Iran. Development is impeded by the lack of finance for infrastructure repairs.
Twelve per cent of the total area is cultivated, another 10 per cent is pasture land and a further 5–6 per cent considered by some sources to have agricultural potential. Most cultivated land is situated in river valleys or plains, which are often fertile; an estimated two-thirds of cultivated land is irrigated. Food output is frequently below what is required to feed the population. In total more than 12,000 out of 22,000 farming villages were abandoned or destroyed during the fighting of the 1990s.
Apart from the opium poppy, the main crops are wheat, fruit and vegetables, maize, rice, barley, cotton, sugar beet, sugar cane, oil seeds.
The livestock herd needs rebuilding. Livestock includes sheep, cattle, goats and poultry, with donkeys, horses, camels, mules and buffaloes kept as draught animals. Sheep provide a major source of protein and animal fat. Some 70 per cent of wool production, along with hides from karakul sheep, is exported.
After the fall of the Taliban, the farmers started to sow poppies again. In 2002, President Karzai banned opium poppy cultivation and trafficking, and offered farmers US$350 for each 0.2 hectare (ha) to be replanted with alternative crops. This was only a fraction of what the farmers could earn from the poppy crop. Afghanistan recorded one of its highest opium harvests in 2006, accounting for about 90 per cent of global production and confirming its position as the world's leading producer.
The area under poppy cultivation in 2004 increased by 64 per cent and only crop disease prevented it from being the largest opium harvest ever recorded. Until economic and social alternatives are developed, the local population remains dependent on the opium economy. Despite government efforts, and those of the British army, a joint assessment survey carried out in December 2005 and January 2006 by the Ministry of Counter Narcotics and the UN Office on Drugs and Crime showed that plantings of poppy for 2006 was up on 2005.

Forestry

Wooded land is limited to the eastern Hindu Kush region and along the Pakistani border. Many forests in these areas have been severely reduced due to trees being cut down and the wood smuggled out to surrounding countries.

Tourism

Instability is an impediment to the development of a tourist sector in Afghanistan, although given the right conditions there is considerable potential. Some visitors are arriving and trekking trips have been arranged. Much work needs to be done to restore the necessary infrastructure. Accommodation in Kabul is limited to a few hotels and houses converted into guesthouses.

Mining

Natural resources include copper, chromite, lead, zinc, iron, salt, lapis lazuli, emeralds, talc and barium sulphate.
Long-term mineral development projects include copper mining and smelting at Ainak and high-grade iron ore mining at Hajigak in northern Afghanistan.
A Chinese-owned mining company won a tender in November 2007 to develop one of the world's largest copper mines sited in Logar Province. It is estimated that the site has 13 million tonnes of copper. Australia, Canada, China and Russia all contested the tender, ultimately won by China Metallurgical Group with an investment of US$3 billion. The mine is expected to be operational in 2012 and offer employment to thousands of Afghan workers.

Hydrocarbons

Prior to the 1979 Soviet invasion, Afghanistan's total oil and condensate reserves were estimated at around 95 million barrels. Oil production was almost entirely halted during the 1980s and 1990s. The sector will require foreign investment to return to its pre-1979 status. Petroleum products are imported mainly from Pakistan and Turkmenistan.
Afghanistan has natural gas reserves of around 125 billion cubic metres. Political and military problems have hindered further development of the sector. Proposals for a pipeline connecting Pakistan, Afghanistan and Turkmenistan have made little progress.
There are small deposits of coal. An estimated 73 million tonnes of coal are located mainly in northern Afghanistan in the region between Herat and Badashkah.

Energy

The energy sector was badly damaged during the years of upheaval. Afghanistan has installed capacity of 450 MW, generated by hydropower, of which only 271MW are available. Some border areas receive supplies from neighbouring countries. Electricity supply is only available to around 6 per cent of the population. Interruptions and blackouts are frequent.

Banking and insurance

Afghanistan has six banks (four of which have almost no assets) and two commercial banks – Pashtani and Milli – with assets. In September 2003, two banking laws were passed: the Central Banking Law and the Commercial Banking Law. The first laid the groundwork for the Central Bank to focus on monetary policy, pricing stability and oversight of the commercial markets; the second allowed for private ownership of commercial banks. By 2004 there were three commercial banks — Standard Chartered (UK), Microfinance Bank of Afghanistan and National Bank of Pakistan, with others being set up.

Central bank

Da Afghanistan Bank (re-opened January 2002).

Main financial centre

Kabul

Time

GMT plus 4.5 hours

Geography

Afghanistan is a landlocked country in south-western Asia. Its neighbours are Turkmenistan, Uzbekistan and Tajikistan to the north, Iran to the west, and Pakistan to the east and south. It also has a 76km border with the People's Republic of China to the north-east. The Hindu Kush mountains are in the north-east of the country.
There are three geographic areas: the central highlands (comprising over 60 per cent of the land), the arid southern region (25 per cent of the land) and the fertile northern plains.

Hemisphere
Northern

Climate
The climate is dry with large variations between day and night temperatures as well as swift seasonal changes. Maximum summer temperatures on the plains can reach 46 degrees Celsius (C), while the lowest winter temperatures, in the mountains, reach minus 26 degrees C; Kabul (at altitude 1,800 metres) has an average 16 to 33 degrees C in summer (July–August) and minus 8 to 2 degrees C in winter.
The rainy season is from October–April, although rainfall is very irregular; Kabul averages 335mm per annum.

Entry requirements
Passports
Required by all.
Visa
Required by all; application forms can be obtained via: www.embassyofafghanistan.org/main/consulate/visa.cfm or local embassies.
Business visas require a letter of introduction stating the purpose of visit and sponsorship information. A visa financial guarantee must be included with the application fee. For a multiply entry visa, a letter of introduction signed by the president of the organisation, must accompany the documentation.
Currency advice/regulations
Import and export of local currency is limited to Af500. Import of foreign currency is unlimited, although export of foreign currency is limited to the amount declared on arrival. US dollars circulate widely. Travellers cheques are not accepted.
Customs
Alcohol is permitted for personal consumption.
All antiquities, carpets, furs and photography films require an export permit.
Prohibited imports
Illegal drugs, pornography; pork products in any form.
Cameras require an import permit.

Health (for visitors)
Mandatory precautions
Vaccination certificate for yellow fever if travelling from an infected areas.
Advisable precautions
Hepatitis A, anti-malarial precautions, polio, tetanus, typhoid. Diphtheria, hepatitis B, TB immunisations are recommended in some circumstances – seek further advice. Water precautions are necessary. There is a risk of rabies.
Emergency medical care is limited and visitors should ensure they have medical insurance that includes emergency evacuation. Hospitals and doctors require immediate cash payment before commencing treatment. The German Medical Diagnostic Center (www.medical- kabul.com), operates in Kabul, offering treatment that includes medical, radiological and pharmacy services. It does not offer emergency, obstetric or dental treatment.
Public hospitals are not up to Western standards and should be avoided. There are a limited number of private hospitals and some international aid groups operate medical facilities in cities and villages. Visitors should travel with all their necessary medications.

Hotels
Accommodation tends to be scarce and spartan. There are only a few international hotels in Kabul, including the Intercontinental Hotel, Bagh-I-Balla, Kabul and the Serena Hotel, Froshgah Street, Kabul.

Credit cards
Only Visa branded credit and debit cards are accepted at very limited outlets.

Public holidays (national)
Afghanistan uses the Persian calendar, which differs from the Gregorian calendar: there are 31 days in each of the first six months of the Persian calendar, 30 days in each of the next five months and 29 days in the last month, except in leap years when it has 30 days.
Persian year 1385: 21 March 2006 to 20 March 2007 (year 1386: 21 March 2007 to 20 March 2008).
Dates of feasts vary according to the sighting of the new moon, so cannot be forecast exactly.
Fixed dates
21 Mar (Naw Roz/Persian New Year), 28 Apr (Islamic Revolution Day), 19 Aug (National Day).
Variable dates
Eid al Adha (three days), Ashura, Birth of the Prophet, First day of Ramadan, Eid al Fitr (three days).
Muslim holidays that occur on a Friday may be observed on Saturday.

Working hours
The weekend is Friday.
Banking
Sat–Wed: 0800–1200, 1300–1630; Thu: 0800–1330.
Business
Sat–Wed: 0800–1200, 1300–1630; Thu: 0800–1330.
Government
Sat–Thu: 0800–1600.
Shops
Commercial shops keep long but varying hours, usually Sat–Thu: 0700–2300.

Telecommunications
Mobile/cell phones
GSM 900/1800 services available in main cities only.

Electricity supply
220 volts AC, 60 cycle electrical system, using European round, two-prong plugs. Supplies may be seriously affected and power cuts frequent.

Weights and measures
Metric system (local units are also in use).

Social customs/useful tips
It is customary to shake hands on meeting and taking leave. Among men, embracing is a traditional form of greeting. Islamic conventions apply. When sitting cross-legged on sofas or cushions, soles of feet must not be shown.
Business meetings are usually conducted in English or Dari. Green or black tea, nuts and raisins are served. The form of greeting is Salaam Aleykum (peace be with you), followed by a firm handshake and placing the right hand over the heart. Several minutes are spent engaging in pleasantries about each other's countries. It is essential to build trust and to be patient.
Women should dress modestly in long skirts or trousers and avoid revealing tops and dresses.

Security
Foreign nationals are advised not to visit Afghanistan unless absolutely necessary. All visitors should register their presence with their diplomatic representative and keep up-to-date with local information on threat levels. Travel within the country should be kept to a minimum to lessen the risk of the threats posed by armed criminals and terrorists and between rival tribal armies.
Kidnapping, which is widespread, is the most serious threat to any visitor; seeking professional advice for security measures may be necessary.
Suicide-bombings have become more common and visitors must observe a high level of vigilance.
There is widespread danger from mines and unexploded ordinance throughout the country.
All street demonstrations and large gatherings should be avoided.

Getting there
Air
National airline: Ariana Afghan Airlines
International airport/s: Kabul airport (KBL), 16km from Kabul; facilites include a bank, bar and restaurant.
Airport tax: Departure tax: Af200
Surface
Road: There are links to Iran and Pakistan via the Asia Highway and to the CIS via road and rail. Hostilities have periodically closed the Pakistan route; check before travelling.
In August 2007, a new road bridge spanning the River Pyanj in northern

Afghanistan opened, linking Tajikistan and Afghanistan. The bridge, costing US$37m, was paid for by the US.

The Regional Road Corridor Improvement Project, estimated at US$18 billion, to improve Central Asian roads, airports, railway lines and seaports and provide a vital transit route between Europe and Asia was agreed, on 3 November 2007. Six new transit corridors, between Afghanistan, Azerbaijan, China, Kazakhstan, Kyrgyzstan, Mongolia, Tajikistan and Uzbekistan, of mainly roads and rail links, will be constructed, or existing resources upgraded, by 2013. Half the costs with be provided by the Asian Development Bank and other multilateral organisations and the other half by participating countries.

Rail: Links exist between Kabul and the CIS.

Getting about

National transport

Air: Ariana Afghan Airlines flies a limited service to Herat and Mazar-e-sharif.

Road: Main centres are linked by paved roads but secondary roads vary in condition and by season. There are approximately 22,000km of roads.

Buses: Bus service are unreliable and dangerous for internal travel.

Water: There are 1,200km of navigable inland waterways, including the Amu Darya River.

City transport

Taxis: Taxis are available from Kabul airport to the city centre. Tipping is not usual. Fares are negotiable and can be high for foreigners.

Buses, trams & metro: A limited number of buses are operating.

Car hire

International driving licences are required for those hire cars available.

BUSINESS DIRECTORY

The addresses listed below are a selection only. While World of Information makes every endeavour to check these addresses, we cannot guarantee that changes have not been made, especially to telephone numbers and area codes. We would welcome any corrections.

Telephone area codes

The international dialling code (IDD) for Afghanistan is + 93, followed by the area code and subscriber's number. Landline telephones are still unreliable. Some of the numbers below are mobile/cell numbers.

Herat	40	Kandahar	30
Jalalabad	60	Marez-E-Sherif	50
Kabul	20	Mobil phones	70

Chambers of Commerce

Afghan Chamber of Commerce and Industry, Mohammed Jan Khan Watt, Kabul (tel/fax: 290-196).

Banking

Afghanistan International Bank, House no 1608 Behind Amani High School, Wazir Akhbar Khan, Kabul (tel: 792 03158; fax: 202 103567).

Agricultural Development Bank, Jaddeh-Maiwand, Kabul.

Export Promotion Bank, Jaddah-Temorshahi, Kabul.

First Micro-finance Bank of Afghanistan, Street West of Park Shahr-i-Naw, Charahi Ansari, Kabul (tel: 0790 95705).

Industrial Promotion Bank, Shahr-i-naw, Kabul.

Mortgage and Construction Bank, Shahri-i-naw, Kabul.

National Bank of Pakistan, House No 2, Street No 10, Wazir Akbar Khan, Kabul (tel: 20-230 1660; fax: 20-230 1659).

Pashtany Tejaraty Bank, Mohmmad Jan Khan Watt, Kabul.

Standard Chartered Bank, P.O. Box 16019, House No. 10, Street No. 10 B, Wazir Akhbar Khan, Kabul (tel: 790 88888, 790 20833).

Central bank

Da Afghanistan Bank, Ibni Sina Watt, Kabul (tel: 240-7579).

Travel information

Ariana Afghan Airlines, PO Box 76, Ansari Watt, Kabul (tel: +873-762-523-844; fax: +873-762-523-846; internet: flyariana.com).

Kabul Airport, PO Box 76, Anseri Watt, Kabul.

Ministries

Ministry of Communications (internet: www.af-com-ministry.org).

Ministry of Finance (internet: www.af/mof).

Ministry of Foreign Affairs: Malak Azghar Road, Kabul (tel: 210 0366; e-mail: contact@afghanistan-mfa.net).

Ministry of Information and Culture, Mohammad Jan Khan Watt, beside Spinzar Hotel, Kabul (internet: www.afghanistangov.org

Ministry of Rural Rehabilitation and Development (internet: www.af/mrrd).

Ministry of Irrigation, Water Resources and Environment, Darulman, Kabul

Other useful addresses

Afghan Islamic Press, House 208, Qafila Road, Tahkal Payan, Peshawar, Pakistan (tel: (+92- 91) 570-1100; fax: (+92- 91) 570-3355; e-mail: aip@pes.comsats.net.pk).

Afghanistan Embassy (USA), 2341 Wyoming Avenue, NW, Washington DC 20008 (tel: (+1-202) 234-3770; fax: (+1-202) 328-3516; e-mail: info@embassyofafghanistan.org; internet: www.embassyofafghanistan.org

Afghanistan Investment Support Agency, Opposite Ministry of Foreign Affairs, Kabul (tel/fax: 210-3404; internet: www.aisa.org.af).

Afghanistan Wireless Communication Corporation, Ministry of Communications Building, Mohammad Jan Khan Watt, Kabul (tel: 20-0000; fax: 20-0200; e-mail: info@afghan-wireless.com).

Arman FM (radio), PO Box 1045, Central Post Office, Kabul; House 3, St 12, Wazir Akbar Khan, Kabul (e-mail: info@arman.fm).

British Embassy, 15th Street, Roundabout Wazir Akbar, Khan, PO Box 334, Kabul (tel: 701-02000; fax: 701-02274; email: britishembassy.kabul@fco.gov.uk).

Fedex (Afghan Express), Karte 3, Khai Street, House 326, Kabul (tel: 25-00525; fax: 25-00524).

DHL Express, Street 10, Wazir Akbar Khan, House 310, Kabul (e-mail: kbl_hdesk@af.dhl.com).

TNT Express, Turabaz Khan Crossroads, Kabul.

National news agency: BNA (Bakhtar News Agency)

Other news agencies:
Pajhwok Afghan News: www.pajhwok.com

Afghan Islamic Press: www.afghanislamicpress.com

Internet sites

Afghanistan Embassy (Australia): www.afghanembassy.net

Afghanistan Online: www.afghan-web.com

Afghanistan government website: www.af

Guide to Travellers to Kabul: www.afghanembassy.net/n_travel.html

UN Development programme: www.undp.org.af/projects/lofta_july.html

UN Development Business on-line subscription service: www.devbusiness.com

World Bank: www.worldbank.org/afghanistan

Albania

Although Albania has made considerable advances since its transition from one of the world's most entrenched brands of communism, many of the country's successes have been tempered by the considerable challenges it continues to face. One quarter of the population live under, or close to, the poverty line. Ten per cent of Albania's population live on US$2.00 or less per day. Within Europe, only Moldova is poorer. Unemployment remains high, at 15 per cent; levels of unemployment in rural areas are considerably higher.

Prudence and productivity?

Economic stabilisation and structural reforms have created an environment favourable to economic growth over the past decade. Fiscal consolidation has reduced the government deficit from the 12.2 per cent of GDP levels recorded in 1999 to around a more tolerable 4 per cent by 2002. To their credit, successive governments have adhered to prudent monetary policies. Inflation has been stabilised, in turn creating higher confidence in the lek and bolstering foreign exchange reserves. Unlike the piecemeal measures adopted by many transitional economies, Albania lost no time in launching into what its governments regarded as essential economic steps. Trade was liberalised, the privatisation of small and medium enterprises completed. By 2003, the bulk of large state-owned companies in the heavy industry and mining sectors had been virtually completed.

Central to Albania's structural reforms was the re-allocation of resources from low productivity sectors such as agriculture to higher productivity areas such as construction and the services sector. The boldness of Albania's structural reforms meant that the rapid removal of the central controls typical to a command economy resulted in substantial disorganisation and chaos. Ironically, the chaos initially led to negative growth in productivity. Despite this uncertain start on the road to reform, during the decade 1993-2003 productivity growth – at around 6 per cent – contributed the bulk of growth which averaged 6.25 per cent for the period.

The diaspora's foreign remittances

Remittances from Albania's large and extensive diaspora (of an economically active population of around 1.8 million, some 700,000 work outside Albania) are estimated to exceed US$200 million per year. This makes foreign remittances Albania's largest source of foreign income, greater that the combined value of exports and foreign direct investment (FDI) combined. Although FDI has shown some growth, its levels are still depressingly low – at about 3 per cent of FDI levels in Romania for 2007. The export of goods and services represents less than 20 per cent of GDP – again unacceptably low.

According to the Bank of Albania, per capita income was US$2,883 in 2006. The official unemployment rate was 13.8 per cent, and 18.5 per cent of the population living below the poverty line according to the World Bank's 2005 Poverty Assessment. Almost 60 per cent of all workers are employed in the agricultural sector, although the construction and service industries have been expanding recently, the latter boosted significantly by ethnic Albanian tourists from throughout the Balkans. The GDP is comprised of

KEY FACTS

Official name: Republika ë Shqipërisë (Republic of Albania)

Head of State: President Bamir Topi (since 24 Jul 2007)

Head of government: Prime Minister Sali Berisha (elected 3 Jul 2005)

Ruling party: Coalition government, led by the Partia Demokratike ë Shqipërisë (PDS) (The Democratic Party of Albania (DP)), with the Partia Agrare Ambientaliste (AAP) (Agrarian Environmentalist Party (AAP)), the Partia Republikane e Shqipërisë (RP) (Republican Party), the Partia Demokrate e Re (PDR) (the New Democratic Party) and the Partia Bashkimi për të Drejtat e Njeriut (UHRP) (Union for Human Rights Party).

Area: 28,748 square km

Population: 3.20 million (2007)

Capital: Tirana

Official language: Since 1945, the official language has been based on Tosk Albanian. The Albanian language is divided into two dialects – Gheg, north of the river Shkumbinit, and Tosk in the south.

Currency: Lek (L) = 100 qindarka

Exchange rate: L76.99 per US$ (Jul 2008)

GDP per capita: US$3,702 (2007)*

GDP real growth: 6.00% (2007)*

Labour force: 1.62 million (2004)

Unemployment: 13.90% (2003)

Inflation: 2.90% (2007)*

Balance of trade: -US$1.87 billion (2006)

* estimated figure

agriculture (approximately 24 per cent), industry (approximately 13 per cent), service sector (approximately 39 per cent), transport and communication (12 per cent), construction (11 per cent), and remittances from Albanian workers abroad (approximately 12.8 per cent).– mostly in Greece and Italy.

Albania's trade imbalance is severe. In 2006, Albanian trade was US$3.1 billion in imports, and US$790 million in exports. Albania has concluded Free Trade Agreements (FTAs) with Macedonia, Croatia, UNMIK (Kosovo), Bulgaria, Romania, Bosnia and Moldova. In April 2006, these bilateral agreements were replaced by a multi-regional agreement which entered into force in May 2007, based on the Central European Free Trade Agreement (CEFTA) model. However, combined trade with all these countries constitutes a small percentage of Albania's trade, while trade with EU member states (mainly Greece and Italy) accounts for nearly 68 per cent. US two-way trade with Albania is very low.

Fiscal and monetary discipline has kept inflation relatively low, averaging roughly 2.5 per cent per year between 2004–06. Albania's public debt reached 57.5 per cent of GDP in 2006; the growing trade deficit was estimated at 25 per cent of GDP in 2006. Economic reform has also been hampered by Albania's very large informal economy, which the International Monetary Fund (IMF) estimates equals 50 per cent of GDP.

Since 1990 around 20 per cent of Albania's population has emigrated. There have also been large-scale population movements within Albania, from rural to urban areas with all the associated social problems that such movement creates. Estimates put the number of Albanians living in Greece and Italy alone at around 600,000, one sixth of Albania's total population. The Albanian government – with the encouragement of international agencies such as the European Bank for Reconstruction and Development (EBRD) and the World Bank – has recognised that however important, foreign remittances do not constitute a solid base for long term economic development. Albania's agricultural sector still employs over 40 per cent of the labour force. Continued urban migration will inevitably reduce this number. This re-allocation of labour resources goes alongside agriculture's declining contribution to GDP. It will also require vastly increased investment in education and vocational training to meet the needs of a changing labour market.

After initially encouraging signs in the period 1996–2002, Albanian standards of governance have since appeared to deteriorate. Government effectiveness – not helped by constant political in-fighting – has weakened, corruption has become widespread, often taking the form of bribery to obtain or release basic governmental resources, has worsened, adversely affecting both FDI and the growth of exports. Customs procedures, tax administration, land and construction permits are all singled out as either inadequate, inefficient or plain corrupt.

The EU ... and the USA

The Albanian government's long-stated foreign policy adjective is full membership of the European Union (EU). Albania's relationship with the EU is based on the latter's Stabilisation and Accession programme (SAP) which defines the framework for future membership. In Albania's case, no accession timetable has yet been drawn up, although the SAP does serve as an effective catalyst for reforms. Quite apart from EU concerns to see the more customary and obvious reforms introduced, in the case of Albania of exceptional concern is the apparently uncontrollable level of corruption and organised crime.

Albania's membership of the EU is certainly still some way off. Little headway has been made in addressing the much needed reforms to the judicial system and to public administration. Albania also endeavoured to join the North Atlantic Treaty Organisation (Nato) at the organisation's 2008 summit in Romania. Nato membership, while less onerous, would have been seen as a step towards EU membership. Nato membership would allow the government to claim to its electorate that some tangible progress had been made towards the ultimate goal of EU membership. It would also position Albania within the Western alliance. In the event, Albania, along with Ukraine and Bulgaria, was not admitted, although an accession protocol was later signed by Nato ambassadors in Brussels on 9 July 2008; Albania is expected to join in April 2009.

Albania's position within the western, pro-USA countries was symbolically strengthened in mid-2007 by President Bush's weekend visit. The visit will best be remembered for the apparent theft of his wristwatch while shaking hands with Albanians. In some embarrassment, US officials later claimed that the story was untrue and that the president did not lose his watch. Photographs later showed Mr Bush, surrounded by five bodyguards, putting his hands behind his back, enabling one of his bodyguards to remove his watch.

Education

Albania lags well behind its transitional neighbours in virtually every respect. Nowhere is this the case more than in education. In Albania the average total length of schooling is only 8.5 years. School enrolment rates dropped from 70 per cent under the command economy in 1990, to only 38.7 per cent in 2002, the lowest in the European region. More worryingly, expenditure on education declined from an already low figure of 5 per cent of GDP in

KEY INDICATORS — **Albania**

	Unit	2003	2004	2005	2006	2007
Population	m	3.16	3.16	3.13	*3.15	*3.17
Gross domestic product (GDP)	US$bn	6.18	7.59	8.38	9.11	*10.62
GDP per capita	US$	1,958	2,131	2,672	2,892	*3,210
GDP real growth	%	6.0	5.9	5.5	5.0	*6.0
Inflation	%	3.3	2.9	2.4	2.2	*3.4
Exports (fob) (goods)	US$m	426.0	552.4	656.3	750.0	–
Imports (cif) (goods)	US$m	1,800.0	2,076.0	-2,477.6	2,618.0	–
Balance of trade	US$m	-1,374.0	-1,523.6	-1,821.3	-1,868.0	–
Current account	US$m	-500.0	-380.0	-547.5	*-536.0	*-625.0
Total reserves minus gold	US$m	1,009.4	1,357.7	1,404.1	1,768.8	2,104.2
Foreign exchange	US$m	913.8	1,251.7	1,386.8	1,754.8	2,097.0
Exchange rate	per US$	120.17	98.50	96.73	96.73	83.21

* estimated figure

1991 to only 2.3 per cent in 2003. This was another European 'low' for Albania.

No power to the people

From being a net exporter of electricity until 1997, Albania has had to adapt to importing increasing amounts of power from its neighbours. To address the problem, in agreement with key international donors, the government was forced to introduce an emergency Action Plan. The crisis in energy supplies has had an inevitably negative effect on GDP growth and done little to encourage putative international donors. The fundamental cause has been a combination of climate change – Albania's reservoirs ran virtually dry in the early 2000s – resulting in the loss of hydropower, which has traditionally accounted for the bulk of Albania's electricity requirements with the surplus being exported. Under-investment, inadequate maintenance and a shortage of spare parts have also been held responsible for the electricity shortages. The crisis has resulted in the expensive purchase of costly generation equipment and has acted as a severe disincentive to FDI.

The energy crisis had peaked in 2000 when the hydro-dams which normally supplied 95 per cent of power, were dried out by drought. On top of this unavoidable disaster, some 50 per cent of the electricity generated by KESH, Albania's national power utility, was regularly lost to thieves who had become adept at illegally tapping into the power system. To make matters worse for KESH, many of its registered customers – including government departments according to the EBRD – regularly failed to pay their bills.

The Action Plan has, since 2002, brought about a 35 per cent increase in domestically generated electricity delivered to the national grid, and a 10 per cent drop in losses to the system. None the less, KESH's performance vis-á-vis other European power companies and utilities remains poor. A third of all power generated or imported is still lost to theft. Albania's long-standing reliance on hydropower has become a weakness rather than an asset.

Political – the voting goes on

When he assumed power in mid-2007, Albania's freshly-elected president, Banir Topi, was the country's first head of state not to have been a member of the communist party. President Topi's election was no simple matter, taking four rounds of voting for him to garner enough votes to ensure the 60 per cent majority he required.

Risk assessment

Economic stability	Fair
Politics	Fair
Regional stability	Fair

COUNTRY PROFILE

Historical profile

1920s Italy withdrew from Albania and agreed to recognise its independence. Tirana was declared the capital city. Political instability ensued. Prime Minister Ahmet Beg Zogu took the crown, proclaiming himself King Zog I.
1939 Italian troops under Benito Mussolini invaded Albania and King Zog fled.
1940 The Italians used Albania as their platform for the invasion of Greece.
1941 The Albanian Communist Party (ACP) was formed, with Enver Hoxha as its leader.
1943 German forces invaded and occupied Albania following surrender by the Italians.
1944 The Germans were forced out by Communist resistance fighters led by Enver Hoxha, who proclaimed the constitution of the Democratic Government of Albania as a provisional government and became first secretary of the politburo.
1945–46 Tribunals were held which condemned thousands of 'war criminals' and 'enemies of the people' to death or to prison.
Non-communists were purged from government positions.
1948 Albania broke its ties with Yugoslavia. The USSR began economic aid to Albania. The ACP was renamed the Party of Labour of Albania (PLA).
1955 Albania became a founding member of the Warsaw Pact.
1961 Relations with the USSR soured when Albania supported China in the Sino-Soviet ideology dispute. Albania withdrew from the Council for Mutual Economic Assistance (Comecon).
1967 The Communist government outlawed religion, making Albania the world's only atheist state.
1968 Albania withdrew from the Warsaw Pact over the Soviet-led invasion of Czechoslovakia.
1976 A new constitution was adopted. Albania declared itself the independent Peoples' Socialist Republic of Albania and reaffirmed its policy of self-reliance.
1985 Hoxha died and was replaced by Ramiz Alia as first secretary of the politburo.
1989 Communist rule in Eastern Europe collapsed. Freedom of religion was restored.
1990 The PLA was renamed the Partia Socialiste ë Shqipërisë (PSS) (Socialist Party of Albania) and pursued a more liberal democratic ideology. Albania legalised opposition parties. Albanians were granted the right to travel abroad; thousands of people tried to flee through Western embassies, and seized ships to sail illegally to Italy.
1991 After an interim constitution was approved, multiparty elections were won by the PSS. Ramiz Alia was elected by the People's Assembly to the new post of executive president. Fatos Nano was appointed head of government, but was forced to resign due to a deteriorating political and economic situation in the country. A caretaker government took power.
1992 The opposition Partia Demokratike ë Shqipërisë (PDS) (Democratic Party of Albania) won an overwhelming victory in parliamentary elections, ending five decades of communist rule. PDS leader, Sali Berisha, was elected president. Aleksander Meksi was appointed prime minister. Ramiz Alia, Fatos Nano and several others from the old Communist regime were arrested and charged with corruption.
1994 A national referendum rejected a new constitution which opponents said allowed the president too much power. Albania joined the NATO Partnership for Peace plan.
1995 Albania was admitted to the Council of Europe.
1996 The PDS won a landslide victory in parliamentary elections, which were tainted by accusations of fraud.
1997 After pyramid investment schemes collapsed, there were weeks of rioting. The government failed to convince the country that it had no part in the investment schemes. Rebels gained control of large sections of southern Albania and threatened the capital. Berisha dismissed the prime minister and the head of the army, closed down opposition newspapers and declared a state of emergency. Thousands of Albanians fled to Italy. An international force from eight European nations arrived to help restore order. Berisha was re-elected unopposed for a further five-year term by parliament which, boycotted by the opposition, was dominated by the PDS.
As a proposed solution to the profound political crisis, fresh parliamentary elections were held; these were won by the Socialists and President Berisha resigned. He was succeeded by Socialist Rexhep Kemal. The convictions of communist-era leaders were overturned; Fatos Nano was elected prime minister. King Zog I returned from South Africa.
1998 Refugees from unrest in Kosovo (Serbia) entered Albania. Nano resigned due to protests over the economy, and was succeeded by Pandeli Majko. Voters approved Albania's first post-Communist

constitution, which declared the country a parliamentary republic.

1999 There was a mass refugee exodus into Albania as thousands of Kosovans fled attacks by Serbian forces. Prime Minister Majko was succeeded by the Socialist, Ilir Meta.

2000 Albania joined the World Trade Organisation (WTO).

2001 Ilir Meta and the PSS won another term in office in the elections.

2002 Prime Minister Ilir Meta resigned after failing to resolve a party feud. Sali Berisha's opposition coalition announced that it would end its six-month boycott of Albania's parliament. The President asked Pandeli Majko to form a new cabinet. Alfred Moisiu was elected president by the People's Assembly. Pandeli Majko resigned and parliament approved a new government led by Prime Minister Fatos Nano. The royal family returned from exile.

2003 Albania and the EU began Stabilisation and Association Agreement (SAA) talks.

2004 In February, the opposition led a demonstration in Tirana protesting against the government's failure to improve living standards and demanding Prime Minister Nano's resignation.

2005 On 29 March, Albania signed a US$15 million deal with the US Occidental Petroleum Corporation for oil and natural gas drilling. The opposition, PDS, won the 10 July parliamentary elections, although the results were disputed by the ruling PSS. In September the PDS took office with Sali Berisha as prime minister.

2006 The first legal step towards EU accession was taken on 12 June when a Stabilisation and Association Agreement was signed.

2007 On the fourth attempt, Bamir Topi was elected president by parliament. Topi won 85 votes, one more that the minimum required. If the vote had failed it would have led automatically to a dissolution of parliament. Opposition parties had objected to his candidacy on the grounds that he was a representative of the ruling party. He was sworn into office on 25 July.

2008 An accession protocol was signed by Nato ambassadors in Brussels on 9 July. Albania will join in April 2009.

Political structure

Constitution

The constitution adopted on 28 December 1976 was declared invalid in April 1991, when the Socialist Republic of Albania was renamed the Republic of Albania under an interim constitution.

A new constitution was agreed by referendum and came into effect on 28 November 1998. It provides for multi-party elections and guarantees freedom of speech, religion, press, assembly, and organisation.

Form of state

Unicameral parliamentary democratic republic

The executive

The president is head of state and shares control of the armed forces with the prime minister. The president is elected by parliament to a five-year term and is limited to two terms. The president appoints the prime minister nominated by the party or coalition of parties that has a majority of seats in the Assembly. If the Assembly fails to approve the president's appointee three times, the president dissolves parliament. The prime minister and Council of Ministers are in charge of the country's economic, social and cultural affairs. The president and prime minister are jointly responsible for foreign relations and security affairs.

National legislature

The Kuvendi Popullor (People's Assembly) has 140 members, who serve a four-year term – 100 directly elected and 40 elected by proportional representation. The Assembly meets twice a year. In addition to passing legislation, the Assembly approves the president's appointment of the prime minister and the prime minister's choices for the Council of Ministers.

Legal system

The court system is headed by the Supreme Court. Its members are appointed by the president to nine-year terms with the consent of the Assembly. Judges in appeals and district courts are appointed by the president upon the recommendations of the Higher Judicial Council, which is headed by the president and includes the chair of the Supreme Court and the minister of justice. A separate constitutional court rules on constitutional matters and consists of nine members appointed by the president with the Assembly's consent.

Last elections

10 July 2005 (parliamentary); 20 July 2007 (presidential).

Results: Paliamentary: the opposition, Partia Demokratike ë Shqipërisë (PDS) (Democratic Party of Albania), won the elections. Fatos Nano refused to concede defeat, citing violations in 30 constituencies and his party (PSS) filed complaints with the Central Electoral Commission, delaying the official certification of the election results.

Presidential: Bamir Topi won 85 votes of the presidential vote in parliament.

Next elections

July 2012 (presidential); 2009 (parliamentary).

Political parties

Ruling party

Coalition government, led by the Partia Demokratike ë Shqipërisë (PDS) (The Democratic Party of Albania (DP)), with the Partia Agrare Ambientaliste (AAP) (Agrarian Environmentalist Party (AAP)), the Partia Republikane e Shqipërisë (RP) (Republican Party), the Partia Demokrate e Re (PDR) (the New Democratic Party) and the Partia Bashkimi për të Drejtat e Njeriut (UHRP) (Union for Human Rights Party).

Main opposition party

Partia Socialiste ë Shqipërisë (PSS) (Socialist Party of Albania)

Population

3.20 million (2007)

Last census: April 2001: 3,069,275 (provisional)

Population density: 120 inhabitants per square km. Urban population: 44 per cent (1996—2002).

Annual growth rate: 0.4 per cent (2005) (World Bank)

-0.2 per cent 1994–2004 (WHO 2006)

Ethnic make-up

Albanians make up 97 per cent of the population. The largest ethnic minority group is the Greeks, who account for around 2 per cent of the total. Other groups include Macedonian, Montenegrin, Vlach and Gypsy (Romany) groups.

Religions

Muslim (70 per cent), Christian Orthodox (20 per cent) and Roman Catholic (10 per cent).

Education

Despite its many failings, the communist regime virtually eliminated illiteracy. However, since 1991 the situation has deteriorated markedly, with equipment and buildings in a parlous state. Although high attendance rates in primary schools have been maintained, enrolment in pre-primary schooling and at the secondary or tertiary level has declined. In Albania, the government has closed down a third of public kindergartens and preschool attendance has dropped dramatically. Unqualified teachers in elementary schools account for 10 per cent of teaching staff, and in the secondary schools, 8 per cent.

The government has an ongoing programme to replace equipment and reconstruct buildings in urban areas and is also focussing on teacher training and enrolment rates. The current structure of the sector has resulted in a misalignment between the supply and demand of education. Consequently, the government is also engaged in a school construction programme to provide facilities for those areas where there are currently no school facilities.

The total expenditure on education is around 3 per cent of GDP.
Literacy rate: 99 per cent adult rate; 99 per cent youth rate (15–24) (Unesco 2005).
Enrolment rate: 100 per cent (primary); 71.5 per cent (secondary) (World Bank).
Pupils per teacher: 18 in primary schools.

Health

Per capita total expenditure on health (2003) US$366; of which per capita government spending was US$153, at the international dollar rate, (WHO 2006).
Although Albania's modest healthcare sector functioned adequately during the communist era, it suffered from substantial underfunding. The government recognises the problem and plans to strengthen managerial capacities and to decentralise health planning. It will take many years to create a system capable of providing even basic healthcare.

HIV/Aids

Albania had been screened from the initial impact of the Aids epidemic by the isolation imposed by the former communist state. However, the country opened its borders following the advent of democratic government in 1991 and the first HIV case of HIV was detected in 1993. By 2003, 177 cases had been reported of which 37 had died of Aids. Between 2001–03 the percentage of HIV positive females increased and their numbers now match male infection rates.
Life expectancy: 72 years, 2004 (WHO 2006)
Fertility rate/Maternal mortality rate: 2.2 births per woman, 2004 (WHO 2006)
Birth rate/Death rate: 18.2 per 1,000 crude birth rate; 6.5 per 1,000 crude death rate (USAID 2003).
Child (under 5 years) mortality rate (per 1,000): 18 per 1,000 live births in 2003; 14 per cent of children aged under five are malnourished (World Bank).
Head of population per physician: 1.31 physicians per 1,000 people, 2002 (WHO 2006)

Welfare

Albania's social infrastructure is in a poor state. Never well developed, social disintegration in 1997 led to further deterioration of virtually all services as funds dried up.
The collapse of central government authority in 1997 has led to already poor tax collection rates falling further. Neither the funds nor the infrastructure exist to provide adequate welfare coverage. It has been estimated that more than one million people are living below the poverty line. The Albanian Institute of Statistics reported in late-1999 that over one-third of families have only one income source averaging US$64 per month.
The government is attempting to remedy this by introducing community-based social services for vulnerable groups and is in the process of reorganising the state pension system based on the actuarial model. The aim is to increase coverage in rural areas in order to reduce poverty.

Main cities

Tirana (capital, estimated population 399,999 in 2008), Durrës (Durrazzo) (130,269), Elbasan (105,852), Shkoder (Scutari) (90,620), Vlore (93,812), Korca (57,758), Fier (65,244), Berat (48,068).

Languages spoken

Greek, Romanian, Bulgarian, Serbian, Tosk and Gheg are also spoken. English, Italian, German and French are also spoken in business circles.

Official language/s

Since 1945, the official language has been based on Tosk Albanian. The Albanian language is divided into two dialects – Gheg, north of the river Shkumbinit, and Tosk in the south.

Media

Press freedom in Albania has been declared partly free by the US-based media watchdog, Freedom House, and the government has used criminal and tax laws to target and intimidate media sources it wishes to stifle.
Due to the country's poor infrastructure, mountainous terrain and low economic development, access to media can be poor.
National news agency: Albanian Telegraphic Agency (ATA)

Press

The print media is not sophisticated and tends towards sensationalism. Many newspapers are published by political parties and interest groups.
Dailies: In Albanian, policital party publications include Rilindja Demokratike (http://pages.albaniaonline.net/rd), and Zeri i Popullit (www.zeripopullit.com). Private newspapers include Shekulli (www.shekulli.com.al) the largest daily, Gazeta Shqiptare (www.balkanweb.com/gazetav4), Koha Ditore (www.koha.net), Sot (www.sot.com.al), Korrieri (www.korrieri.com) Koha Jonë (www.kohajone.com), are tabloids. In English, Albanian Daily News (www.albaniannews.com). And Tirana Times (www.tiranatimes.com).
Weeklies: In Albanian, general interest magazines include Shqip (www.shqip.al), and Veriu Observer (www.gazetaveriu.netfirms.com). Sporti Shqiptar (www.sportishqiptar.com.al) is a sports publication.
Business: In Albanian, Biznesi (www.biznesi.com.al) is a newspaper, Monitor (www.monitor.al) is a magazine. The Albanian Chamber of Commerce publishes Probiznes News (www.cci.gov.al) magazine.

Broadcasting

Radio Televizioni Shqiptar (RTSH) (www.rtsh.al) is the state broadcaster, operating from Tirana.
Radio: In Albanian, RTSH (http://rtsh.sil.at) operates three national stations, including an international service. There are two commercial national broadcasters, Plus 2 Radio (www.plus2radio.com.al) and Top Albania Radio (www.topalbaniaradio.com). Other local commercial radio stations include Radio Saranda (www.radiosaranda.com), Radio Planet (www.planet93fm.com) and Radio IMR (www.radio-ime.com), which has talk and information programmes. There are foreign radio broadcasts received in foreign languages including, English, Italian, French and German.
Television: RTSH operates one national station; it also has a satellite service for expatriate communities in neighbouring countries. Funding is provided by government grants, subscription and commercial advertising. Programmes include news, current affairs and documentaries as well as popular shows. TV Arberia (www.telearberia.tv) is a private network.

Advertising

There is a total ban on cigarette advertising.

Economy

Albania ranks as the third poorest country in Europe with around a quarter of the population living below the poverty line. A socio-economic crisis in 1997, the Kosovo crisis in 1999 and political instability have hindered Albania's development. Low levels of productivity and capital investment combined with shortages of skilled labour have been major constraints on growth. GDP growth fell to 5.0 per cent in 2006 and was back at 6 per cent in 2007. However, GDP per capita remains low.
Agriculture is the largest, although declining, sector of the economy, contributing around 23 per cent of GDP in 2005. It has been an impetus to growth by attracting private-sector investment. The EU Common Agricultural Policy (CAP) subsidies on EU agricultural products makes it difficult for Albania to export its agricultural products.
There is a heavy reliance on remittances from Albanians working overseas, mainly in Greece and Italy. These contribute around 14 per cent of GDP.
The rebuilding of the technical and physical infrastructure, from

telecommunications to roads and railways, is a major priority. While the government encourages foreign investment in agriculture, agri-processing, manufacturing and export-oriented activities, poor basic services, such as electricity, discourage investor interest. Efforts to develop a larger tourist industry are also hindered by poor infrastructure and under-investment. Corruption and organised crime, which may account for up to 50 per cent of GDP, are a further deterrent to foreign investment confidence.

EU membership is still a distant prospect, but the EU continues to fund infrastructure improvements in anticipation of eventual membership and, in 2006, signed a Stabilisation and Association Agreement with Albania. International financial institutions, such as the World Bank and IMF, are also helping Albania's economic development.

External trade

Albania has a foreign trade imbalance of around 70 per cent, mostly with Greece, Italy and Germany. Its production and supply is hampered by a poor infrastructure and inadequate energy nationwide.

On 31 January 2007, Albania, Macedonia and Bulgaria signed a trilateral agreement to build a new Balkan oil pipeline (AMBO), from Burgas, on the Black Sea, to the port of Vlore, in southern Albania. Its estimated cost is US$1.2 billion and has a supply target of 750,000 barrels per day with construction due to begin in late 2008.

Imports

Principal imports include machinery, electrical and electronic goods, vehicles, minerals, fuels and oils.

Main sources: Italy (28.1 per cent of total, 2006), Greece (15.7 per cent), Turkey (7.6 per cent)

Exports

Principal exports are minerals, including hydrocarbons and hydroelectricity, chrome products, copper wire, ferro-nickel ore and bitumen. Major manufacturing plants include cement, textiles and footwear and food processing. Recent production has begun in engineering products, with chemicals and iron and steel.

Main destinations: Italy (72.6 per cent of 2006 total goods exports), Greece (9.6 per cent), Serbia and Montenegro (5.1 per cent)

Agriculture

Farming

Agriculture, formerly the largest sector in the economy, has declined to less than 25 per cent of GDP, but remains an important social as well as economic factor in Albanian life. The sector is dominated by small-scale subsistence farming, which is underdeveloped and poorly financed. There is minimal mechanisation and little use of fertilisers and pesticides. Despite government attempts to privatise farmland, outside financial assistance has been needed to develop farming.

Crop production in 2005 included: 515,900 tonnes (t) cereals in total, 260,000t wheat, 220,000t maize, 160,000t potatoes, 29,800t oats, 24,750t pulses, 4,600t citrus fruit, *80,000t grapes, *169,000t tomatoes, *40,000t sugar beet, *25,000t olives, *2,800t tobacco, *3,080t treenuts, 154,000t fruit in total, 677,400t vegetables in total. Livestock production included: 76,600t meat in total, *39,000t beef, *8,500t pig meat, *19,000t lamb and goat meat, 10,000t poultry, 31,000t eggs, 1,071,007t milk, *1,000t honey, *7,810t cattle hides, 3,400t sheepskins.

* Estimate

Fishing

Albania's fish catch declined sharply following the collapse of Communism and has not recovered. The sector is in generally poor shape. The fishing fleet comprises ageing and poorly equipped vessels and there is a shortage of fishermen. Development of the marine fisheries, including rehabilitation and construction of ports and other infrastructure, is a government priority.

There is some freshwater fishing in rivers, lakes and reservoirs. Fish farming of marine and freshwater species is increasingly important. Internal consumption of fish has increased in recent years, leaving about half of the approximately 4,000 tonnes of production for export, mainly to Greece and Italy.

In 2004 the total marine fish catch was 1,508 tonnes and the crustacean catch was 314 tonnes.

Forestry

Forests cover less than two-fifths of the land area, the equivalent of 991,000 hectares (ha).

The forest industry is small-scale and is based mainly on imported raw materials to meet domestic production needs. Forestry is of little importance to GDP, with most timber production being used for domestic fuel. Timber processing and associated activities have been transferred to the private sector, but forest management remains in state hands.

Industry and manufacturing

The industrialisation policy of the Communist era was aimed at making Albania completely self-sufficient. Although this meant that Albania was one of the few countries in the world without any foreign debt, it also meant that the industrial sector relied on outdated and inefficient machinery which produced poor quality goods unable to compete in international markets.

A side-effect of the search for higher productivity was a complete absence of environmental concerns, with industrial wastelands, oil slicks and abandoned equipment littering the country. Combined with thousands of broken concrete bunkers and derelict factories, Albania faces major, long-term environmental problems.

The industrial sector has experienced a disastrous decline in output since 1990. The sector is focused mainly on engineering, chemicals, metals, construction materials, food processing and other agro-allied industries. The sector employs around 10 per cent of the workforce and accounts for around 19 per cent of GDP. There is virtually no light industry.

Foreign investment is the key to reviving industrial output, and consequently the government has been attempting to portray Albania as a low-wage manufacturing base with extensive natural resources on Western Europe's doorstep. Foreign companies have become involved in rehabilitating and modernising Albania's chrome industry by taking over a number of steel plants and mines.

Tourism

Albania's post-communist efforts to create a tourism sector virtually from scratch have been tardy and haphazard. Infrastructure is inadequate and the country needs cleaning-up. There were around 41,000 arrivals in 2004, There is considerable potential for attracting the wider and more lucrative international market, especially to its unspoilt beaches. Tourism is expected to contribute 4.7 per cent to GDP in 2005.

Environment

Macedonia and Albania participate in the Lake Ohrid Conservation Project (LOCP) which is a bilateral project supported by the World Bank.

Mining

The mining sector contributes as much as 20 per cent to GDP and employs some 15 per cent of the workforce.

Albania used to be the world's third-largest producer and second-largest exporter of chromium. The industry is undergoing rehabilitation. As with all areas of the Albanian economy, the mining sector suffers from obsolete technology and techniques, the disruption of supply lines and lack of management skills.

There are extensive reserves of copper, iron, zinc and nickel. In addition, there are smaller reserves of uranium, titanium-magnetite, gold and silver. Most of these reserves are in remote and mountainous areas of northern Albania, which increases production costs.

Hydrocarbons

Albania has recoverable oil reserves of 165 million barrels. Oil is produced onshore and is the primary source of energy. Two small oil fields at Patos and Morinza account for the majority of the oil production. Around 6,000 barrels per day (bpd) are produced, but with consumption of 24,000bpd there is a reliance on imports.
Albania has natural gas reserves of 3.3 billion cubic metres. Production is around one billion cubic feet annually, which is sufficient to meet domestic requirements.
Albania has coal reserves estimated at around 700 billion tonnes. Sufficient coal (of generally low quality) is produced for domestic consumption. Production is carried out at 21 mines in four basins run by various state-owned stock companies.
Oil production, natural gas and coal output have all fallen since the collapse of communism, as outdated equipment and a lack of investment, technology and management skills have taken their toll.

Energy

Nearly all of Albania's electricity is generated by hydroelectric power stations. The infrastructure is in poor condition; about a quarter of electricity generated is lost during distribution because of damaged network. Theft of electricity and non-payment of bills are common. Power cuts are frequent, sometimes occasioned by drought hitting the hydroelectric sources. To meet growing demand, Albania imports up to five million kilowatts of power a year, mainly from Greece and Macedonia.
The discovery of a huge and untouched natural gas and oil field in northern Albania was announced in 2008. Unproven reserves were estimated at 2.98 billion barrels of oil and 225 billion cubic metres of natural gas, although if the field only has natural gas then it could hold up to 425 billion cubic metres. DMW Petroleum AG was given the rights to assist in exploration, development and production along with the government's Agency of Natural Resources.

Financial markets

Stock exchange

The Tirana Stock Exchange opened in mid-1996. Since the collapse of the pyramid schemes in 1997, it has been faced with the daunting task of rebuilding the confidence of potential investors.

Banking and insurance

The European Bank of Reconstruction and Development (EBRD) is involved in the development and privatisation of the banking system. An attempt to privatise the Savings Bank of Albania, the last state-owned bank, failed in June 2002 when two Italian banks pulled out of the tender.
Albania's central bank is the Banka e Shqipërisë (Bank of Albania). It has the power to authorise the creation of and supervise new banks, including those with foreign capital.

Central bank

Banka e Shqipërisë (Bank of Albania)

Time

GMT plus one hour (daylight saving, late March to late October, GMT plus two hours)

Geography

Albania's 28,748 square km are split into three main areas: a coastal plain, mountains and an inland plain. Albania shares a border with Montenegro and Serbia (Kosovo) to the north, the Former Yugoslav Republic of Macedonia (FYROM) to the north-west and Greece to the south. The Adriatic and Ionian Seas are to the west. The country's Albanian name, Shqipéria, which translates as 'land of the eagles', reflects its remote and mountainous nature; mountains cover over 70 per cent of the land area. The highest mountain entirely within Albania is Mt Jezerce (2,694 metres) in the north, although Mt Korab on the border with FYROM reaches 2,751 metres.
The longest river, the Drini (285km), drains into Lake Ohrid on the border with FYROM. To the north, the Drini joins the Buna river, the only navigable waterway in Albania. There are three natural freshwater lakes in Albania, all of which share borders with either Greece, Montenegro or the FYROM. Numerous artificial lakes have been created by hydroelectric power stations damming rivers, the largest of which are in the north around Kukes and Skhodra.

Hemisphere

Northern

Climate

Albania has a Mediterranean climate, with long, hot and dry summers and cool, cloudy and wet winters. Autumn has humid weather brought by the warm sirocco wind. The high inland mountains can become cold during the winter months. July is the hottest month; November, December and April are the wettest months. It is warmest in the south-west and coldest in the north-east.

Dress codes

During the summer, light clothing is recommended, with warmer clothes essential during the winter months, particularly in mountainous regions.

Entry requirements

Passports

Required by all.

Visa

Not required by most citizens of Europe, North America, Australasia and a few Asian countries for visits up to 90 days. A US$10 entry tax is levied. (For a full list of exemptions visit www.mfa.gov.al/english/info2.asp.) An entry-exit form is issued at the border: the entry portion is handed in at passport control and the exit portion should be kept until departure.

Currency advice/regulations

The import and export of local currency is not permitted.
The import of foreign currencies is allowed without limitation, although all amounts must be declared on arrival. Export of foreign currency is allowed within the limits of the declaration given, less the amounts exchanged or spent. Keep exchange receipts.
Travellers cheques are accepted by banks and large tourist hotels. ATMs are available in Tirana and other main towns.

Customs

Personal items may be taken into Albania without incurring duty.

Health (for visitors)

Medical facilities are limited and medicine is in short supply. Doctors and hospitals generally expect immediate cash payment for health services. Health care is free for citizens of countries with reciprocal health agreements. Full medical insurance is advisable.

Mandatory precautions

A vaccination certificate for yellow fever is required if travelling from an infected area.

Advisable precautions

It is advisable to have immunisations against hepatitis A and B, typhoid and tetanus. Polio immunisation is not recommended for adults who received childhood inoculations. There is a risk of rabies. Access to clean water in the country is variable, and it is not usual to drink tap water.

Hotels

Hotel provision of all standards, including international hotels, is improving. Increasing numbers of hotels can be contacted directly by telephone. Bookings can be arranged online through Albania Holidays Ltd (www.albania-hotel.com).

Credit cards

Major international hotels in Tirana accept American Express, Mastercard and Diners Club (but not Visa). Cases of credit card fraud have been reported.

Public holidays (national)

Fixed dates

1 Jan (New Year's Day), 28 Nov (Independence and Liberation Day), 25 Dec (Christmas Day).

Variable dates
Orthodox Easter Monday, Labour Day (first Mon in May), Eid al Adha, Islamic New Year, Birth of the Prophet, Eid al Fitr.
Islamic year – 1429 (10 Jan 2008–28 Dec 2008): The Islamic year contains 354 or 355 days, with the result that Muslim feasts advance by 10–12 days against the Gregorian calendar. Dates of feasts vary according to the sighting of the new moon, so cannot be forecast exactly.

Working hours
Banking
Mon–Fri: 0800–1600.
Business
Mon–Fri: 0800–1600.
Government
Mon–Fri: 0700–1500.
Shops
Mon–Sat: 0800–1200, 1500–1900.

Social customs/useful tips
It is customary to shake hands on meeting and taking leave. Business cards are exchanged. Albanian business meetings are reasonably relaxed. Delays to negotiations can be expected as bureaucratic tendencies still exist.
Albanians are a naturally friendly and curious people with a good sense of humour, and are keen to talk to and meet foreigners.
Small gifts are appreciated. Round up the bill slightly when in restaurants.
Local body language customs: nodding the head up and down indicates no, and side to side indicates yes.

Security
It is advisable to be extremely cautious in Albania. Security has improved in recent years, but crime is still a serious problem and armed criminal gangs operate in most areas. There are a large number of semi-automatic weapons in private hands. Travel to the north-eastern border areas between Albania and Kosovo is not recommended.
Avoid giving anything to women and children asking for money, as they target foreigners and will follow the compassionate whenever they see them again. Visitors should dress down and not display watches, cameras or other expensive items.

Getting there
Air
Albania is accessible by air from numerous European centres, including Athens, Bucharest, Budapest, Ioannina, Paris, Rome and Zurich.
National airline: Albanian Airlines.
International airport/s: Rinas Mother Teresa Airport (TIA), 25 km from Tirana.
Airport tax: US$10

Surface
Road: There are road links from all bordering countries, including Greece at Kakavia and Kristalopigi, and Kosovo (in Serbia) at Han-i-Hotit and Vrbnica, and Macedonia at Cafasan.
Rail: There are no passenger rail links between Albania and the rest of Europe and travel in some of the border regions is inadvisable.
Water: There are ferry services connecting Durrës and Vlora with Trieste, Ancona, Brindisi and Bari in Italy and Rijeka and Pula in Croatia. Others connect Durres to Kopa in Slovenia and Sarandra to Corfu.
Main port/s: Durrës, Vlora and Sarandra.

Getting about
National transport
Air: Ales Airlines (a private joint Italian-Albanian company licensed by the Albanian government) serves eight small airports across the country.
Road: Out of approximately 21,000km of roads, only 3,000km are paved. Road conditions can be unpredictable – narrow, unsurfaced and potholed, with the added risk of straying cattle or pedestrians. Mountain roads are often impassable. The roads are considered to be the worst in Europe.
Buses: Buses run frequently between Tirana and Durrës and other towns to the north and south. Tickets are sold on the bus.
Rail: The rail network is approximately 720km, single-track and unelectrified. Trains are diesel.
City transport
Taxis: The only city with a taxi service is Tirana. There are taxi transfers from Rinas airport to the city centre.
Buses, trams & metro: A flat-fare bus service operates in the main cities, including Tirana. Airport buses operate from the airport to the city centre every three hours. Journey duration is 30 minutes.
Car hire
Driving in Albania is only recommended for those with no other choice. An international driving permit or a national driving licence is required. It is advisable to hire a local car and driver through travel agencies. Traffic drives on the right.

BUSINESS DIRECTORY
The addresses listed below are a selection only. While World of Information makes every endeavour to check these addresses, we cannot guarantee that changes have not been made, especially to telephone numbers and area codes. We would welcome any corrections.

Telephone area codes
The international direct dialling code (IDD) for Albania is +355, followed by area code and subscriber's number:

Berat	32	Korca	82
Durrës	52	Shkoder	22
Elbasan	54	Tirana	4
Fier	34	Vlore	33

Useful telephone numbers
Police:	19
Fire:	18
Ambulance:	17

Chambers of Commerce
Albanian British Chamber of Commerce and Industry, PO Box 1547, Tirana (tel: 227-000; fax: 230-636; e-mail: info:abcci.com).

American Chamber of Commerce in Albania, Rruga Deshmoret e 4 Shkurtit, Tirana (tel: 259-779; fax: 235-350; e-mail: info@amcham.com.al).

Korça Chamber of Commerce and Industry, Bulevard Republika, Korça (tel/fax: 824-457; e-mail: albchamber1@albchamber.com).

Tirana Chamber of Commerce and Industry, Rruga e Kavajes 6, Tirana (tel: 230-284; fax: 227-997; e-mail: ccitr@abissnet.com.al).

Union of Chambers of Commerce and Industry of Albania, Rruga e Kavajes 6, Tirana (tel: 230-283; fax: 227-997; e-mail: root@ccitr.tirana.al).

Banking
Albanian State Agricultural Bank, Tirana (tel: 27-738).

Albanian State Bank for Foreign Relations, Tirana.

Alpha Credit Bank, Deshmoret e Kombit Blvd 47, Tirana (Internet site: http://www.alpha.gr).

Arab Albanian Islamic Bank, Deshmoret e Kombit, Tirana (tel: 23-873).

Bankandertregtare (Intercommercial Bank), Tirana Tower, Rruga e Kavajes 59, Tirana (tel: 58-755/60; fax: 58-752; e-mail: icbs1@albaniaonline.net).

Banko Italo Albanese (Banka Italo Shqiptare) (Italian-Albanian Bank), Rruga e Barrikadave, Tirana (tel: 33-966; fax: 35-701).

Fefad Bank, Tirana (tel: 3-496, 37-958; fax: 33-481).

National Bank of Greece, Blvd. Deshmoret e Kombit, VEVE Business Centre, Tirana (tel: 33-621, 35-542).

National Commercial Bank of Albania, Tirana (tel: 50-955; fax: 50-960; e-mail: bkt@albmail.com).

Savings Bank of Albania, Rr Deshmoret e 4 Shkurti, 6 Tirana (tel: 24-540/051; fax: 23-587/695).

Tirana Bank, Blvd. Deshmoret e Kombit, NR55/1, Tirana (tel: 33-441).

Central bank

Banka e Shqiperise (Bank of Albania), Sheshi Skënderbej 1, Tirana (tel: 222-152; fax: 223-558; e-mail: public@bankofalbania.org).

Travel information

Lufthansa Tirana Rinas Airport Office (tel: 42-350/54/58; fax: 42-350/60).

Ministry of tourism

Ministry of Tourism, Blvd Deshmoret e Kombit, Tirana (tel: 28-123); fax: 27-922).

Ministries

Albanian Assembly, Kurvendi, Blvd Dëdhmotët e Kombit, nr 4, Tirana (tel: 42-37-418, 42-47-354,43-62-003; fax: 42-27-949; email: head-directory@parlament.al; internet: www.parlament.al).

Committee of Environmental Protection, Ministry of Health and Environmental Protection, Bulevari Bajran Curri, Tirana (tel: 42-682; 35-229; fax: 35-229).

Department of Economic Development and Foreign Aid Co-ordination, Tirana (tel: 28-467; fax: 28-363).

Industrialeksport – 4 Shkurti Street 6, Tirana (tel: 4550).

Institute of Statistics, Tirana (tel: 22-411; fax: 28-300).

Makinaimport (State Trade Organisation for the Import of Machinery), 4 Shkurti Street 6, Tirana (tel: 25-220, 25-221).

Mineralimpex (State Organisation for Export of Minerals), 4 Shkurti Street 6, Tirana (tel: 25-832, 23-848).

Ministry of Agriculture and Food, Blvd Dëdhmotët e Kombit Tirana (tel: 28-318, 32-675; fax: 23-806, 27-924).

Ministry of Energy and Mineral Resources (tel: 32-833; fax: 34-052).

Ministry of Finance and Economy, Dëdhmotët e Kombit, Tirana (tel: 28-405; fax: 28-494).

Ministry of Health and Environment, Ministria e Shendetesise, Tirana (tel and fax: 34-615).

Ministry of Industry, Transport and Trade, Sheshi Skenderbey, Tirana (tel: 25-353, 32-289; fax: 27-773, 616-835).

Ministry of Transport and Telecommunications, Sheshi Skenderbey, Tirana (tel: 25-353; tel/fax: 27-773/616/835).

National Agency for Privatisation (tel/fax: 27-937).

National Committee of Energy, Dëdhmotët e Kombit, Tirana (tel/fax: 28-475).

President's Office, Tirana (tel: 28-491; fax: 33-761).

Prime Minister's Office, Tirana (tel: 34-816; fax: 34-818).

Small and Medium-Sized Enterprises (SME) Foundation, c/o Ministry of Industry and Trade, 3 Rruga Andon Zako Cajupi, Tirana (fax: 34-892); EU Expert (fax: 42-413, 34-609).

Transshqip (State Organisation for the Transport of Goods in Foreign Trade), 4 Shkurti Street 6, Tirana (tel: 23-076, 24-659).

Other useful addresses

Agroeksport – State Trade Organisation for the Export of Agricultural and Food Products, 4 Shkurti Street 6, Tirana (tel: 25-227, 25-229, 23-128).

Albanian Embassy (USA), 2100 S Street, NW, Washington DC (tel: (+1-202) 223-4942; fax: (+1-202) 628-7342).

Albanian Telecom, Myslim Shyri 42, Tirina (tel: 32-047; fax: 33-323).

Albkontrol (Organisation for Inspection of Exported and Imported Goods), Rruga Skënderbeu 15, Durrës (tel: 22-354; fax: 22-791).

Artimpex (State Organisation for Export), 4 Shkurti Street 6, Tirana.

British Embassy, Ruga Vaso Pasha 7/1, Tirana (tel: 34-973; fax: 34-975).

Bureau for the Registration of Patents & Trade Marks, Konferenca e Pezes Street 6, Tirana.

Business Economic Development Department, c/o Ministry of Industry and Trade, 3 Rruga Andon Zamo Cajupi, Tirana (tel: 34-673; fax: 34-658).

Foreign Investment Promotion Centre, Ekspozita Shqiperia Sot (Protokolli), Blvd Jeanne d'Arc, Tirana (tel: 27-626; fax: 28-439, 42-133).

Insig, Insurance Institute, Rruga e Dibres 91, Tirana (tel: 341-84, 341-69, 341-70; fax: 341-80, 238-38).

US Embassy, 103 Rruga Elbasanit, Tirana (tel: 424-7285; fax: 423-2222; e-mail: wm_tirana@pd.state.gov).

National news agency: Albanian Telegraphic Agency (ATA)

Internet sites

Albanian Daily News: www.albaniannews.com

Albanian parliament: www.parlament.al

Albanian Economic Development Agency: www.aeda.gov.al

Albanian Ministry of Foreign Affairs: www.mfa.gov.al

Albanian Telegraphic Agency: www.ata-al.net

Bank of Albania: www.bankofalbania.org

Algeria

KEY FACTS

Official name: Al Jumhuriya al Jazairiya ad Dimucratiya ash Shabiya (Democratic and Popular Republic of Algeria)

Head of State: President Abdelaziz Bouteflika (since 1999; re-elected Apr 2004)

Head of government: Prime Minister Ahmed Ouyahya (since 24 June 2008)

Ruling party: Coalition: Front de Libération Nationale (FLN) (National Liberation Front), Rassemblement National pour la Démocratie (RND) (National Rally for Democracy) and Mouvement de la Société pour la Paix (MSP) (Movement of the Society for Peace) (since 2002; re-elected 17 May 2007)

Area: 2,381,741 square km

Population: 34.40 million (2007)*

Capital: Algiers

Official language: Arabic

Currency: Algerian dinar (AD) = 100 centimes

Exchange rate: AD62.12 per US$ (Jul 2008)

GDP per capita: US$3,825 (2007)*

GDP real growth: 2.00% (2006)

Labour force: 10.50 million (2007)

Unemployment: 11.80% (2007)

Inflation: 4.60% (2007)

Oil production: 2.00 million bpd (2007)

Balance of trade: US$34.53 billion (2006)

Foreign debt: US$21.90 billion (2004)

* estimated figure

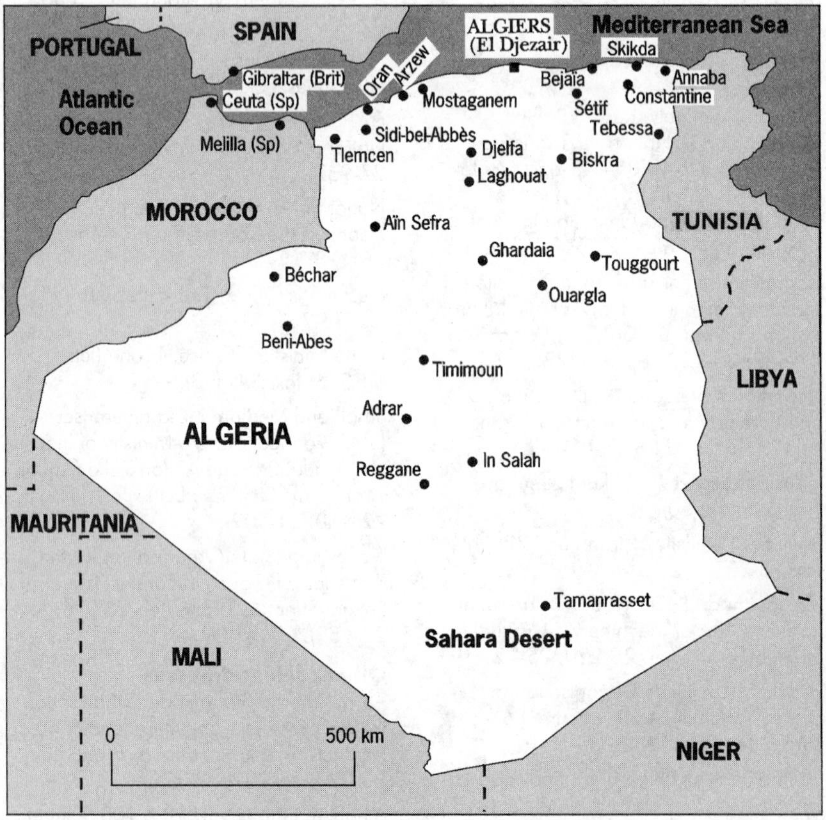

The April 2007 bombings in the canteen of the Algerian parliament that killed 33 people were the work of the so-called al Qaeda in the Islamic Mahgreb (AQIM), the Groupe Salafiste pova la Prédication et le Combat (GSPC) (Salafist Group for Call and Combat), before it re-branded itself as AQIM in September 2006.

The Algerian authorities have had some success in bringing to heel the bulk of the country's terrorist networks through an adroit combination of straightforward repression and offers of amnesty. Intelligence sources estimate that the GSPC/AQIM groupings represent no more than 500 militants. The al Qaeda re-branding exercise may well have given the terrorist movement greater access to funding, equipment, strategic and tactical training and advice. Intelligence sources believe that the grouping is operating training camps in northern Mali. US officials estimate that over 200 recruits, from as far afield as Nigeria and Libya, have received training in the camps.

Algeria's anti-Crusaders

Established by deserters from the Algerian army, the GSPC had owed some of its history and inspiration to Fidel Castro and his originally small band of Cuban revolutionaries in the Sierra Madre. For some time the GSPC operated from a base in the mountainous area of Kabylia, well known for being a rebellious region. Its attacks were focussed on military, rather than civilian targets. The government's amnesty strategy weakened and split the group into three factions, a division which appeared to end with its rapprochement with al Qaeda. Ayman Zawahiri, thought to be al Qaeda's second in command, has claimed that the new AQIM would become 'a bone in the throat of the American-French crusades'.

AQIM's threats to mount further attacks were soon realised. In December 2007 two car bombs were detonated in Algiers. One in a diplomatic quarter of the city which killed – inter alia – a number of UN employees. The other was detonated outside the Constitutional Council, managing to kill a number of students in a passing bus. The final death toll was 37.

Half-hearted elections

Algeria's May 2007 parliamentary elections could hardly be called a success. This was the third time Algerians had voted for a new parliament since 1992, when the election was annulled by the military following the apparent success of the Front Islamique du Salut (FIS) (Islamic Salvation Front). In 1992 the FIS has looked set to win an absolute majority of the seats in the National Popular Assembly, something that the country's military decided could not be allowed. In so doing, the military handed both FIS and others opposed to the government and to Algeria's establishment a propaganda gift, a state of affairs that ensuing governments have done little to try and rectify.

Since the annulled election, the gulf between the country's population and its government has inexorably widened. The lack of interest in the outcome of the 2007 election reflected its predictable result. Voters knew that the election was unlikely to change the government's policies, or its ability to see them through. All three of Algeria's principal (ie tolerated) political parties fell in behind the government of President Bouteflika.

Upon independence, Algeria was recognised as a model to be followed by the rest of the Arab world. Its economy was strong, with a powerful heavy industry sector. Since 1973 Algerians have enjoyed generous social benefits: free education and medical care, advanced workers' rights, and extensive (if unattractive) urban infrastructures. Thirty-five years later, with a population that has tripled, Algeria had fallen to a place among the lower orders of the Arab world in terms of income distribution, unemployment and productivity. Algeria has managed to combine impressive macro-economic development (largely based on increased oil and gas revenues) with something that now approaches macro-economic destitution. This widening economic gap has brought about a political indifference created by marginalisation.

Popular dissent in Algeria has expressed itself in sporadic rioting and occasionally violent protests of one kind or another. President Bouteflika's government has sought to attribute much of this social unrest to Islamist extremism; most observers accept that the real causes lie much deeper in what has been called the 'pauperisation' of Algerian society. The World Bank risks glossing over the reality of Algeria's situation in its description of the challenges that confront Algeria. The Bank refers to 'the weaknesses inherent to the education system, where the growing demand has simply not been met. Algeria continues to be plagued by inefficiencies in the allocation of resources, regional and gender inequalities in terms both of access and results. Poorly targeted public subsidies have also failed to deliver. While access to health services has improved, reforms are needed to improve the effectiveness, efficiency and quality of delivery of services.'

The World Bank concludes by observing that 'access to housing and water services and sanitation remains also critical, affecting mainly the middle class and the poor'. Not affecting, it needs to be noted, Algeria's political and business elite. The equation is as simple as it is obvious: poverty causes malnutrition, which in turn places a strain on health resources, while at the same time depriving Algeria's youth of educational opportunities. Many Algerians continue to face daily water shortages. An average of over seven people live in each dwelling or housing unit. The comparable figures for Morocco (5.7) and for Egypt (4.9) are bad enough, but better than Algeria's. Overall, the country is short of some 1.5 million housing units. Average annual housing construction in Algeria is little more than 60,000 for a growing population.

Bouteflika's policies.

Considerable speculation surrounds the health of President Bouteflika. He is known to be unwell, but his disappearances from the political scene (he appeared to be ill or out of the country at the time of the December 2007 bombings) do little to quell speculation. Nor is there an obvious successor to Bouteflika. His regime has been largely characterised by constant references to the market economy, economic reforms and trade liberalisation. To his credit, President Bouteflika has sought to take a stand against corruption and fraud. Reforms of the judicial system and of the state's outdated structures have also been undertaken.

Economic policy has focussed on the maintenance of financial and macroeconomic stability. The stated policy strategies are first to ensure the continuance of macro-economic stability, second – and this is where the government's intentions and results diverge – to address the social ills and discontent that increasingly threaten Algeria's precarious democracy. Under the Bouteflika scheme of things, the role of the private sector is to be

KEY INDICATORS — Algeria

	Unit	2003	2004	2005	2006	2007
Population	m	31.69	32.16	32.91	33.80	*34.40
Gross domestic product (GDP)	US$bn	60.13	84.65	102.38	114.83	*131.57
GDP per capita	US$	1,830	2,521	3,111	3,397	*3,825
GDP real growth	%	6.7	5.3	5.3	2.0	–
Inflation	%	2.6	3.6	1.6	2.5	4.6
Unemployment	%	28.4	25.4	15.4	12.3	11.8
Oil output	'000 bpd	1,520.0	1,933.0	2,015.0	2,005.0	2,000.0
Natural gas output	bn cum	82.8	82.0	87.8	84.5	83.0
Exports (fob) (goods)	US$m	19,500.0	32,160.0	44,390.0	59,839.0	*59,870.0
Imports (cif) (goods)	US$m	10,600.0	15,250.0	20,040.0	25,312.0	*25,160.0
Balance of trade	US$m	8,900.0	16,910.0	24,350.0	34,527.0	*34,710.0
Current account	US$m	8,840.0	10,800.0	21,183.0	25,211.0	*23,242.0
Total reserves minus gold	US$m	33,125.0	43,246.0	56,303.0	77,914.0	110,318.0
Foreign exchange	US$m	32,942.0	43,113.0	56,178.0	77,810.0	110,180.0
Exchange rate	per US$	75.73	71.80	71.71	69.83	67.21

* estimated figure

promoted and a favourable environment for investment to be created. The latter will involve the continuation of the government 's efforts to privatise the majority of Algeria's public enterprises. Trade liberalisation in the form of reduced trade protection in the domestic market is also proposed; some importance is attached to the French-inspired, and rather grandiose, Euro-Mediterranean Association Agreement with the European Union which envisages the creation of a Mediterranean free trade area. Central to this is Algeria's membership of the World Trade Association (WTO) (Algeria is one of the few remaining countries in the world still not to be admitted to membership).

President Bouteflika's economic strategy is characterised by repeated references to 'structural reforms', a catch-all description for the government's wish-list for a whole series of measures, not all of which have been introduced or achieved, and which to date have produced few benefits for an unsettled electorate.

Since taking office in 1999, President Bouteflika has focussed on national reconciliation and promised to restore national harmony and end years of bloodshed. He immediately released thousands of Muslim militants and won backing for a civil concord in 1999 which offered an amnesty to armed militants. Many accepted and the violence declined. He now supports a second amnesty for those remaining militants. The country backed his proposed 'charter for peace and reconciliation' in a 2005 referendum, one year after he was re-elected to a second term in a landslide victory. The military – traditionally a key player in Algerian politics – pledged neutrality during the poll.

Economic realities

In its annual report, the World Bank can hardly fail to note that Algeria has enjoyed something of an oil boom since 1999, during which time an unprecedented – and unexpected – amount of revenue has been generated. In the five year period 1999–2004, annual GDP growth averaged 4.1 per cent. In 2006, annual growth slowed dramatically to 1.8 per cent. From 1999–2005 Algeria's growth was lead by the hydrocarbon sector, but significant contributions were made by the non-hydrocarbon and non-agricultural sectors – notably construction and services. Things began to change in 2006 as the hydrocarbon sector registered a negative contribution to growth of -2.5 per cent. Agriculture registered a 4.9 per cent growth rate for 2006, construction 11.6 per cent and the services sector 5 per cent. In 2006 hydrocarbon exports rose by 17 per cent, to US$53.6 billion. The World Bank projection for growth in 2007 was 3.4 per cent, with non-hydrocarbon growth forecast at 6.5 per cent.

Inflation rose to 2.2 per cent in 2006, up from 1.16 per cent in 2005. Unemployment continued to edge down, from 15.3 per cent in 2005 to 12.3 per cent in 2006, no mean achievement given Algeria's population growth. Algeria's overall fiscal balance remained unchanged at 12 per cent of GDP, although that figure disguised a worsening non-hydrocarbon deficit, which was offset by general revenue increases. Over 60 per cent of Algeria's state revenues are derived from oil tax revenues. Hydrocarbons continue to make up over one third of GDP and a disproportionate 97 per cent of exports in value. For over thirty years, little has been achieved in terms of reducing this (over) dependence.

In June 2006, Algeria began a six month programme of repayments worth US$8 billion to the Paris Club of creditors. This move was aimed at improving the country's international credit ratings and generating future investment. The energy sector has been the top-performer though this sector is likely to be hit by large tax hikes which started in 2007, up to a maximum of 50 per cent tax. This is in an attempt to slow the drain on Algeria's oil reserves, eking out supplies and keeping the proceeds within the domestic economy. Contradicting the government's much vaunted liberalisation policy, the state owned energy company Sonatrach will be guaranteed a bigger role, up to 51 per cent, in new exploration deals. This is something of a triumph for economic nationalism and a decided U-turn in policy from 2005 when foreign companies were welcomed to invest in Algeria.

Economic outlook

Violence, in one form or another, risks becoming an economic as well as a social problem in Algeria. This manifestation shows itself not only in the al Qaeda attacks, but in widespread social discontent. The structural problems that confront President Bouteflika's government are colossal – small wonder that the President is suffering from ill-health. Algeria's 'real' unemployment rate is estimated to be nearer 30 per cent of the country's labour force – the highest in the Arab world after Iraq and Palestine. The bulk – around 50 per cent – of those unemployed are aged under thirty, and two thirds of this group have simply never worked.

Risk assessment

Politics	Poor
Economy	Fair
Regional stability	Fair

COUNTRY PROFILE

Historical profile

1830 Algeria was conquered by the French.

1848 It was made a département of France.

1954 The Front de Libération Nationale (FLN) (National Liberation Front) led the struggle for independence.

1962 Algeria gained independence and Ahmed ben Bella of the FLN was designated Algeria's first president.

1965 Ahmed ben Bella was ousted by Colonel Houari Boumédienne.

1976 Boumédienne won the presidential elections. He introduced a new constitution, which confirmed commitment to socialism, the FLN as the sole political party and Islam as the state religion. A programme of industrialisation was introduced.

1973–76 The Frente Popular para la Liberación de Saguia el Hamra y Río de Oro (Polisario) (Popular Front for the Liberation of Saguia el Hamra y Río de Oro) was formed with Algerian support, wanting self-determination for Spanish Sahara (later known as Western Sahara). Spain handed the territory over to Morocco and Mauritania, Polisario announced the formation of the Saharawi Arab Democratic Republic (SADR) and formed a government-in-exile.

1977–85 Fighting continued between Moroccan military and Polisario forces. Morocco left the African Unity in protest at the SADR's admission to the body.

1988 Full diplomatic relations with Morocco were resumed.

1978 President Boumédienne died and the FLN candidate, Colonel Chadli Benjedid, was elected president; he was re-elected in 1984 and 1989.

1986–91 Rising inflation and unemployment, exacerbated by the collapse of oil and gas prices, led to strikes and violent demonstrations. A UN-monitored cease-fire began in Western Sahara.

1989 The National People's Assembly revoked the ban on new political parties and the Front Islamique du Salut (FIS) (Islamic Salvation Front) was founded.

1991 The FIS won the first round of the parliamentary elections and the second round was cancelled when it seemed certain the FIS would gain an absolute majority in the next round.

1992 Outbreaks of violence followed the cancellation of the elections. The National People's Assembly was dissolved by presidential decree and President Chadli, apparently under pressure from the military leadership, resigned. A five-member Haut Conseil d'Etat (HCE) (High Council of State) was instituted. Violent clashes broke out between FIS supporters and security forces; after a state of emergency was declared, the FIS was banned. Mohammed Boudiaf, chairman of the HCE, was assassinated, allegedly by Islamists. The Armée Islamique du Salut (AIS) (Islamic Salvation Army), the military arm of the FIS, launched a campaign of guerrilla warfare, which killed an estimated 150,000 people.
1994 Liamine Zeroual became chairman of the HCE.
1995 Zeroual was elected president in the first multi-party democratic elections.
1997–98 The newly created Rassemblement Nationale Démocratique (RND) (National Democratic Rally) won the parliamentary elections.
1999 President Zeroual stood down (one year early) and Abdelaziz Bouteflika was elected president. A referendum approved Bouteflika's law on civil concord and thousands of members of the AIS and other armed groups were pardoned.
2000 Attacks continued by small groups of dissidents opposed to the civil accord.
2001 The Berber community were granted greater cultural and political recognition following months of unrest involving Berber youths in the Kabylie region.
2002 The Berber language, Tamazight, was officially recognised as a national language. Berber activists in Kabylie and several opposition parties elsewhere boycotted the parliamentary elections, which were won by the FLN.
2003 A major earthquake hit northern Algeria, the worst since 1980. The leader of the banned FIS and his deputy were freed from prison after serving 12-year sentences. Prime Minister Ali Benflis was dismissed by the President and Ahmed Ouyahia became prime minister.
2004 President Bouteflika was re-elected and re-appointed Prime Minister Ouyahia.
2005 Nourredine Boudiafi, the head of the AIS was arrested and his deputy killed. The government promised Berber leaders more investment in the Kabylie region and greater recognition for the Tamazight language. An official inquiry concluded that security forces abducted and killed over 6,000 citizens during the 1990s civil unrest. There was overwhelming agreement in a referendum, granting amnesty to many who were involved in the post-1992 killings.
2006 Ahmed Ouyahia resigned as prime minister and Abdelaziz Belkhadem was appointed in his place. Measures to increase Sonatrach's role in oil and gas exploration and refining were introduced.
2007 In parliamentary elections on 17 May, the FLN was returned with a reduced majority, losing seats on a low turnout to its coalition partners. Prime Minister Belkhadem resigned and was re-appointed by the president along with a new government, on 4 June.
2008 On 24 June President Bouteflika appointed Ahmed Ouyahia prime minister; he previously served as prime minister 1996–98 and 2003–06.

Political structure

Constitution
The 1976 constitution has been amended three times.
In 1997, the government banned religion-based parties and imposed a law restricting the formation of political parties. All political parties must hold a founding conference attended by 400–500 delegates elected by 25,000 supporters from 25 of the country's 48 provinces. This policy is intended to limit the number of political parties and place at severe disadvantage all parties that lack funding – particularly those, such as the FIS (Islamic Salvation Front), without access to state funds.

Form of state
Republic

The executive
The head of state is the president, elected by universal suffrage for five years. He appoints a prime minister, who in turn appoints a government.
The president has the power to dissolve the government and request elections.

National legislature
The parliament is composed of the 380-member Al Majlis al Sha'abi al Watani (Assemblée Populaire Nationale) (National People's Assembly) and the 144-member Al Majlis al Umma (Conseil de la Nation) (National Council). Members of the National People's Assembly, which holds legislative power, are elected for five years by universal suffrage. Members of the National Council (the lower house) are elected by communal councils and the president.

Legal system
The legal system is based on French and Islamic law.
The judicial system consists of 183 courts and 31 appeal courts organised on a regional basis.
There are three special criminal courts in Oran, Constantine and Algiers, which deal with economic crimes against the state (against which there is no appeal) – the Court of State Security which is composed of judges and army officers, the court of audit and the Supreme Court in Algiers, which is the ultimate judicial authority.
Algeria has not accepted International Court of Justice (ICJ) jurisdiction.

Last elections
17 May 2007 (parliamentary); 8 April 2004 (presidential).
Results: Presidential: Abdelaziz Bouteflika won 84.99 per cent of the vote; Ali Benflis won 6.42 per cent; and Abdallah Djaballah 5.02 per cent. Turnout was 58.07 per cent.
Parliamentary: FLN won 136 seats out of 389; RND 61; MSP 52; Parti du Travail (PT) (Workers' Party) 26; Rassemblement pour la Culture et la Démocratie (RCD) (Rally for Culture and Democracy) 19 seats; and independents 33. Turnout was 35.65 per cent. The ruling three-party coalition of FLN, RND and MSP retained their majority with 249 seats.

Next elections
2009 (presidential); 2012 (parliamentary).

Political parties

Ruling party
Coalition: Front de Libération Nationale (FLN) (National Liberation Front), Rassemblement National pour la Démocratie (RND) (National Rally for Democracy) and Mouvement de la Société pour la Paix (MSP) (Movement of the Society for Peace) (since 2002; re-elected 17 May 2007)

Main opposition party
Parti du Travail (PT) (Workers' Party).

Population
34.40 million (2007)*
Last census: June 1998: 29,100,867
Population density: 12 inhabitants per square km. Urban population: 58 per cent (1995—2001).
Annual growth rate: 2.8 per cent (2005) (World Bank)
1.6 per cent 1994–2004 (WHO 2006)

Internally Displaced Persons (IDP)
1.0 million (UNHCR 2004)

Ethnic make-up
The majority of Algerians are of Berber descent. The other significant ethnic group is Arab, although as a result of centuries of integration the two ethnic groups have become increasingly indistinguishable. The distinct Berber culture and language is best preserved in the north and eastern regions of Algeria.
The European population, most of whom are French, has declined from over one million before independence in 1962 to less than 50,000 in 2001.

Religions
Islam is the official religion. Approximately 99 per cent of the population is Sunni Muslim, while Christians make up about one per cent.

Education
Primary education lasts for six years. Secondary education, which begins at age 11, is divided into two courses of four years and three years. Approximately 13 per cent of students remain at tertiary level. Teaching is carried out in Arabic, although at higher levels French is widely used.
The government has encouraged girls to attend school to reduce the difference in literacy rates. A total of 86 per cent of girls are now educated to primary level, and 53 per cent to secondary level.
Total expenditure on education is 4–5 per cent of GDP.
Literacy rate: 69 per cent adult rate; 90 per cent youth rate (15–24) (Unesco 2005).
Compulsory years: 6 to 15.
Enrolment rate: 98 per cent gross primary enrolment of relevant age group (including repeaters); 63 per cent gross secondary enrolment (World Bank).
Pupils per teacher: 27 in primary schools.

Health
Per capita total expenditure on health (2003) was US$186; of which per capita government spending was US$150, at the international dollar rate, (WHO 2006).
All Algerians are entitled to free medical care. Medicines are sold through the state monopoly at subsidised prices, and are provided free to children and the elderly, though there have been some cutbacks.
Health indicators point to a deterioration in public health, with infant mortality ratios and infectious diseases increasing. Health care infrastructure and personnel show considerable urban-rural disparities.
Life expectancy: 71 years, 2004 (WHO 2006)
Fertility rate/Maternal mortality rate: 2.5 births per woman, 2004 (WHO 2006)
Child (under 5 years) mortality rate (per 1,000): 35 per 1,000 live births; 6 per cent of children aged under five are malnourished (World Bank).
Head of population per physician: 1.13 physicians per 1,000 people, 2002 (WHO 2006)

Welfare
During the 1990s, unemployment rates increased dramatically, poverty doubled and the purchasing power of the middle class experienced a huge drop.
Government expenditure on social protection is relatively high, but the welfare system is criticised as unsustainable and inefficient. The most serious challenge to the government is tackling unemployment.
The government continues to play a major role in providing housing and basic health services, particularly to urban populations. Substantial housing shortages have proven persistent, despite the deregulation efforts the government undertook to promote private sector construction.
Pensions

Main cities
Algiers (capital, estimated population 1.5 million in 2008), Oran (609,823), Constantine (462,187), Annaba (383,504), Batna (292,943).

Languages spoken
Arabic (modern standard), known as Fus'ha, is used in the courts, mosques, most of the media and in education.
About 80 per cent of Algerians speak the North African dialectal Arabic, Darja.
French is widely spoken, especially as a language of commerce.
In 2003, Tamazight (the Berber language) was categorised as a national language, but the Berbers want it to have equal status alongside Arabic as an official language. Tamazight belongs to the Afro-Asiatic family and is related to ancient Egyptian and Ethiopian. Berber groups and their dialects include: Kabyles (Taqbaylit), Kabylie region, Kabyle dialect; Chaouia (Ishawiyan), Eastern Algeria, Tashawit dialect; Mozabites (Imzabiyan), northern edge of Sahara, Tamzabit dialect; Tuaregs (Tamachaq), extreme south, Tuareg dialect.
Official language/s
Arabic

Media
Despite laws guaranteeing freedom of access to information and freedom of expression in accordance with the constitution journalists are regularly targeted by not only the authorities but also militant Islamists. There are libel laws with large fines and Sharia (Islamic moral principles) that can curb the media's ability to question and investigate; self-censorship is prevalent.
The law allows the formation of privately owned newspapers, but any new non-Arabic publication must first be approved by the independent Information Council.
National news agency: Algerian Press Service (APS)
Other news agencies: Agence Algérienne d'Information (AAI) (in French): www.aai-online.com
Press
Most newspapers are in private ownership.
Dailies: In Arabic, Ech Chaab (www.ech-chaab.com) is state-owned, Ech Chourouk (www.echoroukonline.com) and El Khabar are privately owned, with English editions. In French, El Moudjahid (www.elmoudjahid-dz.com) is state-owned, El Watan (www.elwatan.com), Liberte (www.liberte-algerie.com), La Tribune (www.latribune-online.com), and Le Soir d'Algeria (www.lesoirdalgerie.com) an evening newspaper, are all privately owned. Le jeune indépendant (www.jeune-independant.com) is a publication for the young.
Weeklies: In French, a privately owned, current affairs magazine is Algérie Actualité, while El Hakika is an Arab tabloid.
Business: In French, there are three publications, Le Maghreb (www.lemaghrebdz.com), is an influential daily along with Liberte Economie (www.liberte-economie.com), with wide ranging topics, Le Journal d'Affaires (www.lejournaldaffaires.com) is more informal.
Periodicals: In French and Arabic, El Manchar is a bi-monthly satirical magazine.
Broadcasting
All broadcasting is state controlled. National public broadcasting is provided by Radiodiffusion Télévision Algérienne (RTA).
Radio: Algerian Radio (www.algerian-radio.dz), operated by RTA, has 35 stations providing three radio networks with local and international services in Arabic, French and Tamazight. International services are also provided in Spanish and English.
Television: The state-run Enterprise Nationale de Télévision (ENTV) (www.entv.dz) provides services are in Arabic and French with online programmes. Satellite programming is provided by ENTV through Canal Algérie and Thalitha. ENTV also has collaborative links with French-based Berbère TV (www.brtv.fr).
News agencies
National news agency: Algerian Press Service (APS)
Other news agencies: Agence Algérienne d'Information (AAI) (in French): www.aai-online.com

Economy
Algeria has benefited from the sharp rise in global oil prices since 2005, tripling its record foreign exchange reserves between 2000–06. Oil and gas accounts for almost 30 per cent of GDP, 60 per cent of budget revenues and 95 per cent of export earnings. It has been able to pay back around 50 per cent of its outstanding debts to its Paris Club creditors, since the government introduced new hydrocarbon laws that opened up the market to redevelopment with deregulated oil and gas prices.
The IMF warned that the revenue from oil production could suppress growth

elsewhere in the economy and should be diversified and reinvested to expand the economy. The government embarked on a five-year US$55 billion spending programme in 2004 and the results have shown improvement in infrastructure and employment prospects. GDP growth was good in 2005 at 5.3 per cent, while unemployment fell from the high of 28.4 per cent (and as much as 50 per cent in the youth group) in 2003, to 13.4 per cent in 2006.

Algeria has huge potential, mainly due to its rich natural resources but also its strategic position close to the fast growing and fuel-hungry EU, to which Algeria has gas pipelines.

The government's policy of turning Algeria's command economy into a market economy is an unpopular one. Industrial action in protest at the sale of public enterprises has continued and the IMF is cautious about the balance between deregulating the market and the sharp rise in job losses this would cause, against the long term good of the market.

Government policy includes improving the investment climate in the tourist sector and the production of non-oil related goods. In reality, obstacles remain for non-oil trade, primarily due to the repatriation of revenues in foreign currencies. A climate of unrest and violence has resulted in a reluctance on the part of private investors to put money into Algeria. This may improve with the pending WTO membership and the EU trade association agreements, although the current ban on alcohol imports is undermining these trade agreements.

Algeria is taking tentative steps towards breaking the stranglehold oil and gas has on its economy, but it remains to be seen if it can diversify at a time when windfall revenue from high oil prices negates the value of any other industry or business.

External trade

The strict control of imports has begun to be relaxed, nevertheless the government still has a great influence in planning the economy, with hydrocarbon exports providing a huge trade surplus each year. Algeria has large gas and oil reserves and a ready market for its natural gas, with a major pipeline already connecting, through Spain, to the rest of Europe.

Algeria has moved closer to full membership of the WTO with changes to its foreign trade policy and the backing of the US, both of whom signed a free trade agreement in 2004. However, in a bid to become a member Algeria must revise legislation on the importation of alcohol that may prove unpopular.

Algeria has an Association Agreement, including free trade with the EU signed in 2005, which provides for the gradual removal of import duties on industrial products and the liberalisation of Algeria's agricultural export market by 2012.

Imports

Principal imports are capital goods electrical and electronic goods, semi-finished goods, food and tobacco, transport equipment and raw materials.

Main sources: France (22.1 per cent of total 2006), Italy (8.6 per cent), China (8.5 per cent).

Exports

Principal exports are hydrocarbons; chemical fertilizers, iron and steel, wine, tobacco and foodstuffs.

Main destinations: US (26.7 per cent of 2006 total goods exports), Italy (16.6 per cent), Spain (9.1 per cent).

Agriculture

Farming

The sector employs about 25 per cent of the labour force and contributes around 10.5 per cent of GDP. Just over 40,000,000 hectares (ha) are given over to agriculture, or around 16 per cent of total land available, of which over 8,250,000ha are under arable and permanent crops.

Climatic conditions and the availability of water for irrigation directly affect crop yields. Despite extensive irrigation programmes and the dividing of state holdings into smaller units, agricultural output has failed to keep pace with the rate of population growth. Imports typically represent around 25 per cent of import costs. Government policy had been to reduce reliance on imported food, now, however, an open market is developing as state owned agricultural land is returned to private hands.

Underlying constraints to growth include soil erosion, desert encroachment, inefficient management in the state sector, poor marketing, recurrent droughts and the inability of farmers to secure loan finance due to problems with land security. Government plans to reduce dependence on imports by a series of measures, included investing in new technology, financial incentives for state and private sector farms to buy equipment, encouraging foreign investment, less interference in the private sector and tree planting to arrest desertification.

There has been a large increase in the number of vineyards now operating in Algeria, providing a boost in export revenue. Although wine consumption is banned under Islamic law, production has been increasing; since the end of the 1990s it has doubled to around 500,000 hectolitres by 2005. It has provided a healthy income for farmers, in semi-arid regions, when other food crops have failed.

Main cash crops are grapes, oranges, olives, dates, tobacco, sugar beet and tomatoes. Hard and soft wheat and barley are grown for the home market, as are vegetables, and pulses.

Estimated crop production in 2005 included: 3,996,000 tonnes (t) cereals in total, 2,600,000t wheat, 1,314,000t barley, 1,800,000t potatoes, 560,090t citrus fruit, 170,000t olives, 880,000t tomatoes, 200,000t chillies & peppers, 33,000t treenuts, 40,000t garlic, 135,000t apples, 275,000t grapes, 63,000t figs, 470,000t dates 6,5000t tobacco, 1,892,890t fruit in total, 49,647t oilcrops, 52,580t pulses, 3,258,200t vegetables in total. Estimated livestock production included: 581,219t meat in total, 125,000t beef, 3,400t camel meat, 177,350t lamb and goat meat, 253,000t poultry, 165,000t eggs, 1,668,100t milk, 2,720t honey, 24,250t sheepskins, 20,000t greasy wool, 12,900t cattle hides.

Fishing

The fisheries sector largely consists of small-scale private sector operators, virtually all of whom do their fishing in the Mediterranean. Main catches include sardines, anchovies, sprats, tuna and shellfish.

The government plans to boost fisheries by modernising the Mediterranean ports, where most of the catch is landed. It has also set up a partnership with West African states for fishing in the Atlantic Ocean.

In 2004 the total marine fish catch was 135,929 tonnes and the crustacean catch was 2,631 tonnes.

Forestry

Less than 2 per cent of Algeria's total land area is covered with forest or wooded land and the country is one of the largest importers of wood in Africa.

Algeria's forest resources cover some 3.5 million hectares (ha), with the state monopoly processing some 272,000 cubic metres of wood annually. All of the forest and arable land is in a broad coastal strip, around 400km wide. As part of plans aimed at reducing desertification the government has established an extensive tract of plantation forests.

Algeria is among the world's largest producers of cork. Other forestry products include sawn timber, wood-based panels and paper based on non-wood fibres. Most domestic demand for forest products is met through imports.

Timber imports in 2004 amounted to US$273 million while exports amounted to US$2.8 million.

Production in 2004 included 7,663,603 cubic metres (cum) roundwood,

118,600cum industrial roundwood, 12,800cum sawnwood, 48,200cum wood-based panels, 7,545,003mcum woodfuel, 604,059t charcoal.

Industry and manufacturing

Industry represents 50 per cent of GDP and employs 23 per cent of the labour force. Algeria's industrial sector is dominated by large, inefficient state-owned companies that have largely survived only due to the credit extended them by the country's state-owned banks. Government attempts to privatise these industries have been frustrated by a lack of investor interest and the fear that the possible mass redundancies which may result will cause further social instability.

The largest company in Algeria is the state-owned hydrocarbons concern, Société Nationale pour la Recherche, la Production, le Transport, la Transformation et la Commercialisation des Hydrocarbures (Sonatrach).

Production is dominated by heavy industries such as steel, petrochemicals, fertilisers and cement, but the focus of development is changing to light industry. In November 2005 the first laptop computers produced in Algeria went on sale. The manufacturers, EEPAD, an Algerian Internet service provider, aim at producing one million units a year, enough to supply every home in Algeria, by 2010.

Traditional agri-allied industries are also important, particularly textiles, food processing and tobacco and cigarette production. However past lack of investment and inefficiencies in these industries resulted in generally low productivity. In an effort to modernise the government has allowed some entities to be expanded, charge competitive prices and invest profits. Industry is opening up to more foreign involvement, particularly in large-scale projects such as motor vehicle assembly.

Main constraints to development are shortages of vital inputs and skilled labour, high production and transport costs and maintenance problems. Industrial development is centralised in the northern coastal strip, but plans exist to extend industry to the high plateaux in the south.

Tourism

Algeria's tourism, which always lagged behind that of neighbouring Morocco and Tunisia, was wrecked by the civil war in the 1990s, from which it has not yet recovered. Now that the violence and insecurity is likely to be rare, the government is trying to revive the sector, with the focus on up-market rather than mass tourism. Capital investment in the sector is estimated at 5.9 per cent of the total. New hotels are being built along the Mediterranean coast and adventure holidays are planned for tourists to the south.

French tourists are the largest group visiting, followed by Tunisian and other Arab citizens. The tourist sector only contributes around 1 per cent of GDP, and less than 6 per cent of total employment, however the potential for growth is great. There are a good supply of airports and docks that could be utilised quickly, although the countrywide infrastructure still has to be redeveloped to cater for the 5.1 per cent per annum growth rate (2005–15) expected in travel and tourism.

Mining

The mining and hydrocarbons sector employs 4 per cent of the labour force and contributes 40 per cent to GDP.

Algeria is rich in minerals, including iron ore, uranium, zinc, phosphates, gold, antimony, bituminous coal, tungsten, manganese, lead, mercury and salt. The mining of iron ore and phosphate for feedstocks (for local steel and fertiliser production, respectively) and for export are the most important.

Also located near the Moroccan border are iron-ore reserves estimated at two billion tonnes. The remote location and the Western Sahara/Morocco conflict have so far prevented exploitation.

Hydrocarbons

In 2004, oil reserves stood at 11.8 billion barrels, although new oil discoveries, improved data on existing fields and a recent increase in exploration are likely to mean that Algeria's reserves will be revised upwards.

Natural gas reserves stood at 4.55 trillion cubic metres in 2004 with production of 82 billion cubic metres in 2004, a decrease of 1 per cent on 2003.

Coal represents approximately 1 per cent of total energy consumption. Algeria's total recoverable coal reserves are estimated at 40 million tonnes.

The state-run Sonatrach announced, in 2005, that the responsibility for the oil and gas sectors will be divided between exploration, Agence Nationale pour la Valorisation des Resources en Hydrocarbures (Alnaft) and control and regulation of activities, Autorité de Régulation des Hydrocarbures (ARH). Alnaft will deal with technical regulations and the ARH with investment and development.

Approximately 90 per cent of Algeria's crude oil exports go to Western Europe, with Italy as the main market followed by Germany and France. The Netherlands, Spain and Britain are other important European markets. Algeria's Saharan blend oil, 45 degrees API with negligible (0.05 per cent) sulphur content, is considered among the highest quality in the world.

Energy

Algerian energy demand has been increasing by 5 per cent per annum and is expected to continue to grow at this rate as the government housing programme unfolds.

The existing 6,600MW of generating capacity is produced by oil and natural gas. Three new generating stations are under construction to add an extra 2,525MW to the network. In September 2005 Sonelgaz subsidiary electricity supply company announced a US$7 billion investment in a new power grid, incorporating high voltage power lines.

Financial markets

Stock exchange

The Algiers stock exchange (Bourse d'Alger) was formally opened in 1999.

Banking and insurance

The Algerian banking sector is dominated by six state-owned banks. There is a total of 17 commercial banks and 10 financial institutions. The sector has been inefficient, with the large state banks acting mainly as depository institutions and financing loss-making public sector companies. In 2006 the government began financial sector reforms and by 2008 the 17 commercial banks had opened up to foreign investors and restructuring of the six public sector banks was underway. However, fallout from the subprime crisis in the United States led to the postponement in January 2008 of the sale of 51 per cent of Crédit Populaire d'Algérie. Algeria remains underbanked with some 26,000 people per branch and the government has confimed that it will continue with reforms.

Central bank

Banque d'Algérie.

Time

GMT plus one hour.

Geography

Algeria is the second largest country in Africa. With a total land area of 2.38 million square km, the country comprises three distinct regions: a narrow coastal plain, which has the most fertile soils and houses the majority of the country's population, agriculture and industry; the uplands of the Atlas mountain chain, which tend to be semi-arid steppe in the valleys; and the vast sandy desert to the south.

Algeria has borders with Morocco to the west, Tunisia and Libya to the east and Niger, Mali and Mauritania to the south.

Hemisphere

Northern

Climate

The coastal region has a temperate Mediterranean climate, averaging 13 degrees Celsius (C) to 24 degrees C throughout the year and rising to a daytime high of 32 degrees C during the summer (June to September). The rainy season is October to May, with rains especially heavy from November to February. The desert is constantly inhospitable, with temperatures rising to 45 degrees C during the day, falling to 10 degrees C at night, and with very little rainfall.

Dress codes
Western-style dress is acceptable, with lightweight or safari suits recommended in summer. Women should not wear revealing clothes.

Entry requirements
Passports
Required by all
Visa
Visas are required by most nationals: visit http://algeria.embassyhomepage.com/ for details and application form or contact your local Algerian embassy. Visas are usually valid for 90 days.
Business visas must be accompanied by an invitation from an Algerian company (in duplicate).
Prohibited entry
Nationals of Israel
Currency advice/regulations
The import of foreign currency is unlimited, but must be declared on arrival; export of foreign currency is permitted up to the amount declared on arrival. Local currency may be imported and exported.
Visitors are advised to change money through official sources only; it can sometimes be difficult to reconvert dinars to foreign currency. Declaration forms, issued on arrival, should be kept and used at each successive currency change to be surrendered on departure. Failure to comply with these regulations may mean visitors are liable to forfeit the currency.
Travellers cheques can only be used in very limited outlets; US dollars and Euros have most recognition.

Health (for visitors)
Mandatory precautions
A yellow fever and/or cholera vaccination certificate is required if arriving from infected or endemic areas.
Advisable precautions
Hepatitis A and B, diphtheria, TB, typhoid, tetanus and polio vaccinations are advisable. There is risk of malaria in some areas, therefore prophylaxis is recommended. There is also a rabies risk.
Water precautions should be taken throughout the country. Bottled water is often hard to find, particularly in southern parts of the country.

Hotels
There is a limited range of hotels on offer; hotels are either high-luxury or modest one- two-star hotels. It is advisable to book well in advance as accommodation in Algiers is difficult to obtain.
The service charge is usually 15 per cent.

Credit cards
The use of credit cards are restricted to urban areas.

Public holidays (national)
Fixed dates
1 Jan (New Year's Day), 1 May (Labour Day), 19 Jun (Revolutionary Readjustment), 5 Jul (Independence Day), 1 Nov (Anniversary of the Revolution).
Variable dates
Eid al Adha (two days), Eid al Fitr (two days), Islamic New Year, Ashura, Prophet's Birthday.
Islamic year – 1429 (10 Jan 2008–28 Dec 2008): The Islamic year contains 354 or 355 days, with the result that Muslim feasts advance by 10–12 days against the Gregorian calendar. Dates of feasts vary according to the sighting of the new moon, so cannot be forecast exactly.

Working hours
The Muslim weekend is Thursday afternoon and Friday, but many industries close all day Thursday.
Banking
Sun–Thur: 0900–1530.
Business
Sat–Tue: 0800–1200 and 1300–1700; Wed 0800–1200 and 1300–1600.
Government
Sat–Wed: 0800–1200 and 1400–1730; Thur 0800–1200.
Shops
Sat–Wed 0800–1230 and 1430–1800; Thu: 0800–1300.

Telecommunications
Mobile/cell phones
GSM 900/1800 services are available mostly in inhabited areas in the north and isolated towns in central and southern Algeria.

Electricity supply
Electricity supply varies from 127–220V; a compensator for use with electronic/computer equipement is advisable. A variety of plug fittings are used.

Social customs/useful tips
Business appointments should be made in advance. Business cards are exchanged after introductions. French-style courtesy should be adopted by visitors. Hospitality is regarded as very important, and visitors are usually entertained in restaurants and hotels. Wives seldom accompany their husbands to social engagements outside the home.
Care should taken to respect local customs, especially during the fasting month of Ramadan.

Security
Violence was endemic during the 1990s. Although there have been fewer violent incidents since 2000, visitors should still take precautions by avoiding travelling alone and avoid the provinces of Tamanrasset, Djanet and Illizi in the south-east, where tourists have been targetted for kidnapping. Incidents of assaults on foreigners have increased in some urban and rural areas and visitors should avoid carrying valuables and large sums of money.

Getting there
Air
National airline: Air Algérie
International airport/s: Algiers (Houari Boumédienne) (ALG), 20km from city. Facilities include duty-free shop, restaurant, bank, post office, shops, car hire.
Other airport/s: Annaba (Les Salines) (AAE), 12km from city; Constantine (Ain El-Bey) (CZL), 9km from city; Oran (Es Senia) (ORN), 10km from city.
Airport tax: None
Surface
Road: The border between Algeria and Morocco is closed and access is denied. Roads are good in the coastal and northern Sahara networks, while access to Mali, by the trans-Saharan highway, is unsealed and its use is subject to seasonal conditions.
Rail: A daily train service (the Trans-Maghreb) links Tunis with Algiers and Oran.
Water: Regular ferry services connect Algieria with France and Spain.
Main port/s: Algiers, Annaba, Arzew, Bejaia, Oran.

Getting about
National transport
Air: There are frequent services from Algiers to Annaba, Constantine and Oran provided by Air Algérie. Regular flights also link these towns with other principal centres. Fares are generally low for domestic flights but overbooking can occur, especially in summer.
Road: Main roads are in good condition generally, but desert routes are rarely maintained.
Buses: Long-distance coach services are operated by Société Nationale des Transports de Voyageurs (SNTV) and Altour. Bookings for long trips should be made well in advance.
Rail: The service is operated by Société Nationale des Transports Ferroviaires (SNTF). There are two classes; some services are air-conditioned and some have couchettes.
City transport
Taxis: Taxis are widely available in main centres; they are radio-controlled in Algiers. Taxis are identified by a local colour

code. They are supposed to be metered, but owing to demand, usually operate without a meter and use a minimum fare system instead. A surcharge is imposed after dark. Tips are usually 10 per cent of fare.

Buses, trams & metro: State-owned service operates in Algiers. Can be overcrowded during rush hours. Daily and longer duration tickets are available.

Car hire

Car hire is available in most main towns and at airports. An international driving licence and third-party insurance are required. The maximum speed limit is 50kph in towns and 100kph on main roads.

BUSINESS DIRECTORY

The addresses listed below are a selection only. While World of Information makes every endeavour to check these addresses, we cannot guarantee that changes have not been made, especially to telephone numbers and area codes. We would welcome any corrections.

Telephone area codes

The international dialling code (IDD) for Algeria is + 213 followed by the area code and subscriber's number:

Algiers	21	Ghardaia	29
Annaba	38	Oran	41
Béchar	49	Sétif	36
Boumerdes	24	Tiemcen	43
Constantine	31	Tindouf	49

Useful telephone numbers

Directory enquiries:	19
Telegrams:	13
Police:	17

Chambers of Commerce

Algerian Chambre de Commerce et d' Industrie, Palais Consulaire, 6 Boulevard Amilcar Cabral, Place des Martyrs, PO Box 100, 16003 Algiers (tel: 715-160; fax: 710-174; e-mail: caci@wissal.dz).

Constantine Chambre de Commerce et d' Industrie, 6 Rue de 24 Novembre 1954, PO Box 394, 25000 Constantine (tel: 935-923; fax: 937-807).

Dhara Chambre de Commerce et d' Industrie, 1 Avenue Benyahia Belcacem, PO Box 99, Mostaganem (tel: 216-709; fax: 216-578).

French Chambre de Commerce et Industrie en Algerie, Villa Clarac, 3 Rue des Cèdres, El Mouradia, Alger (tel: 606-496; fax: 609-509; e-mail: cfcia@cfcia.org).

Oran Chambre de Commerce et d' Industrie, 8 Boulevard de la Soummam, Oran (tel: 391-299; fax: 396-312).

Banking

Banque Al Baraka, Haï Bouteldja Houidif, Villa No 1 Rocade Sud, Ben Aknoun, Algiers (tel: 916-450; fax: 916-457; e-mail: info@albaraka-bank.com).

Banque de l'Agrulture et du Developpement Rural, 17 Boulevard Colonel Amirouche, Algiers (tel: 634-922; fax: 635-146).

Banque de Developpement Local, 5 Rue Gaci Amar, Staoueli, Algiers (tel: 393-755; fax: 393-757).

Banque Extérieure d'Algérie, 3 Rue du Docteur Lucien Reynaud, Algiers (tel: 239-330; fax: 239-099; e-mail: dircom@bea.dz).

Banque Nationale d'Algérie, 8 Boulevard Ernesto Che Guevara, Algiers (tel: 714-719; fax: 712-424; e-mail: nb@bna.com.dz).

Caisse d'Epargne et de Prevoyance, 42 Rue Khelifa Boukhalfa, Algiers (tel: 713-395; fax: 714-131).

Crédit Populaire d'Algérie, 2 Boulevard Colonel Amirouche, Algiers (tel: 740-528; fax: 642-383).

Central bank

Banque d'Algérie, Villa Jolie, 38 Avenue Franklin Roosevelt, 16000 Algiers (tel: 230-023; fax: 260-856; e-mail: ba@bank-of-algeria.dz).

Travel information

Air Algérie, 1 Place Maurice Audin, PO 483, 1600 Algiers (tel: 653-340; fax: 509-389; e-mail: contact@)airalgerie.dz).

Algiers-Houari Boumediene Airport, BP130 Dar El-Baida, 16100 Algiers (tel: 506-000; fax: 509-219; e-mail: hlamyl@hotmail.com).

Ministry of tourism

Ministry of Tourism and Handicraft, Rue des Frères Ziata, 16070 Algiers (tel: 792-301; fax: 792-632).

National tourist organisation offices

ONAT (Entreprise Nationale Algérienne du Tourisme), 126 bis Rue Didouche Mourad, Algiers (tel: 744-448; fax: 743-214; e-mail: onat@onat.dz.com).

Ministries

Prime Minister's Office, Rue Docteur Saadane, 16001 Algiers (tel: 732-300; fax: 717-927).

Ministry of Agriculture and Rural Development, 12 Boulevard Colonel Amirouche, 16001 Algiers (tel: 711-712; fax: 745-986).

Ministry of Commerce, Rue Docteur Saadane, 16001 Algiers (tel: 732-340; fax: 735-478).

Ministry of Communications and Culture, Palais de la Culture, El-Anassers, 16502 Algiers (tel: 679-420; fax: 684-459).

Ministry of Defence, Avenue Ali Khodja, Les Tagarins, 16030 Algiers (tel: 711-515).

Ministry of Education, 8 Avenue de Pékin, 16070 Algiers (tel: 605-560; fax: 606-757).

Ministry of Energy and Mines, 80 Avenue Ahmed Ghermoul, 16014 Algiers (tel: 673-300; fax: 650-997).

Ministry of Finance, Immeuble Mauretania, Place du Pérou, 16001 Algiers (tel: 711-366; fax: 736-450).

Ministry of Fisheries and Marine Resources, 4 Rue des Quatre Canons, 16001 Algiers (tel: 433-947; fax: 433-168).

Ministry of Foreign Affairs, Place Med Seddik Benyahia, 16070, Algiers (tel: 504-545; fax: 504-242).

Ministry of Health, Population and Hospital Reform, 125 Rue Abderrahmane Laala, 16075 Algiers (tel: 279-900; fax: 279-641).

Ministry of Higher Education and Scientific Research, 11 Rue Doudou Mokhtar, 16033 Algiers (tel: 912-323; fax: 912-113).

Ministry of Housing and Urbanism, 135 Rue Didouche Mourad, 16001 Algiers (tel: 740-722; fax: 747-664).

Ministry of Industry and Restructuring, Immeuble le Colisée, 4 Rue Ahmed Bey, 16030 Algiers (tel: 693-156; fax: 693-235; e-mail: info@mir-algeria.org).

Ministry of the Interior and Local Communities, Rue Docteur Saadane, 16001 Algiers (tel: 732-340; fax: 605-210).

Ministry of Justice, 8 Place Bir Hakem, 16030 Algiers (tel: 921-608; fax: 921-243).

Ministry of Labour and Social Protection, 44 Rue Med Belouizded, Belcourt, Algiers (tel: 683-366; fax: 745-306).

Ministry of Participation and Reforms Co-ordination (MPCR), Chemin Ibn Badis el Mouiz, 16030 Algiers (tel: 929-885; fax: 929-884).

Ministry of Post and Telecommunications, 4 Boulevard Krim Belkacem, 16027 Algiers (tel: 711-220; fax: 730-047).

Ministry of Public Works, 3 Rue du Caire, 16050 Algiers (tel: 689-500).

Ministry of Religious Affairs and Endowments, 4 Rue de Timgad, Algiers (tel: 608-555; fax: 600-936).

Ministry of Small and Medium Enterprises, Immeuble le Colisée, 4 Rue Ahmed Bey,

16030 Algiers (tel: 601-144; fax: 592-658).

Ministry of Transport, 119 rue Didouche Mourad, 16001 Algiers (tel: 740-699; fax: 646-637).

Ministry of Vocational Training and Professional Education, Route de Dély Ibrahim, 16033 Algiers (tel: 911-528; fax: 912-779).

Ministry of War Veterans, 9 Avenue Benarfa Mohamed, 16030 Algiers (tel: 922-355; fax: 922-739).

Ministry of Water Resources, 8 Place de Bir Hakem, 16030 Algiers (tel: 283-837; fax: 747-543).

Ministry of Youth and Sports, 3 Rue Mohamed Belouizdad, 16600 Algiers (tel: 683-350; fax: 657-778; e-mail: mjs@wissal.dz).

Other useful addresses

Algerian Embassy (USA), 2137 Wyoming Avenue, NW, Washington DC 20008 (tel: (+1-202) 265-2800; fax: (+1-202) 667-2174; e-mail: embalg.us@verizon.net).

APSI (investment promotion agency), Boulevard du 11 Décembre 1960, BP 336 El-Biar, 16030 Algiers (tel: 914-225; fax: 914-303; e-mail: apsi@wissal.dz).

British Embassy, 6 Avenue Souidani Boudiemaa, BP08 Alger-Gare, 16000, Algiers (tel: 230-068; fax: 230-067).

FINALEP (Algero-European Financial Participation Company), 11 Route Nationale, Staouéli, Algiers (tel: 393-494; fax: 392-020; e-mail: finalep@wissal.dz).

National Office of Statistics, 8/10 Rue des Moussebilines, BP 202 Ferhat Boussad, 16000 Algiers (tel: 744-100; fax: 743-839; e-mail: ons@onssiege.ons.dz).

SAFEX (Algerian fairs and exports company), Palais des Expositions, Pins Maritimes, BP 366 Alger Gare, Algiers (tel: 210-123; fax: 210-630; e-mail: safex@wissal.dz).

SNTF (national rail company), 21-23 Boulevard Mohamed V, Algiers (tel: 711-510; fax: 748-190).

Sonatrach (national oil and gas company), 10 Rue Djenane El-Malik, Hydra, 16035 Algiers (tel: 548-011; fax: 547-700; e-mail: sonatrach@sonatrach.dz).

US Embassy, 4 Chemin Cheikh Bachir El-Ibrahimi, BP 408 Alger-Gare, 16000, Algiers (tel: 691-255; fax: 693-979).

National news agency: Algerian Press Service (APS)

Address: Ave Des Frères Bouadou, Bir Mourad Rais, Algies (tel: 564-444; fax: 561-608; internet: www.aps.dz).

Internet sites

Africa Business Network: www.ifc.org/abn

Africa news outlet: allafrica.com

African Development Bank: www.afdb.org

Algeria Interface: www.algeria-interface.com

Algeria News Agency: www.aps.dz

Algeria On-Line: www.djazaironline.net

Mbendi AfroPaedia: www.mbendi.co.za

American Samoa

KEY FACTS

Official name: Territory of American Samoa

Head of State: President George W Bush

Head of government: Governor Togiola (Tala) Tulafono (since 2003; re-elected Nov 2004)

Area: 196 square km (five islands); Tutuila: 135 square km

Population: 64,869 (2006)*

Capital: Fagatogo (on Tutuila), usually known as Pago Pago

Official language: English and Samoan

Currency: US dollar (US$) = 100 cents

GDP per capita: US$9,041 (2005)

GDP real growth: 3.00%

Unemployment: 6.00% (2004)*

Inflation: 4.00% (2004)*

Balance of trade: -US$159.00 million (2004)

* estimated figure

COUNTRY PROFILE

Historical profile

1722 The Dutch navigator, Jacob Roggeveen, was the first European to sight the islands.
1831 The London Missionary Society arrived to convert native Samoans and established a British presence.
1872 The US gained exclusive use of the deep-water whaling port of Pago Pago.
1889 The Treaty of Berlin between Britain, the US and Germany promised an independent Samoan government.
1899 The Berlin Treaty was annulled by the Tripartite Treaty, which granted the US the right to all eastern islands of the Samoan group, giving Germany the remainder. In exchange, Britain gained control of Germany's rights in Tonga, Niue and the Solomon Islands (excluding Bougainville).
1900 American Samoa officially became a US territory. Traditional rights were protected in return for a military base and coaling station. Islanders became US nationals, but not citizens; they cannot vote in US elections.
1941 The US entered the Second World War and American Samoa became a strategic location, for the US Pacific Fleet.
1945 The US Marine Corps withdrew.
1951 The territory was transferred to the US Department of the Interior.
1956 The US appointed Peter Tali Coleman as the first Samoan governor; he went on to become the first popularly elected governor.
1960 A constitution was promulgated.
1967 A revised constitution was introduced, which guaranteed the rights of inhabitants in issues such as land ownership and civil rights.
2002 Following fears of overfishing in American Samoa's exclusive economic zone (EEZ) fishery, the Western Pacific Regional Fishery Management Council approved a decision to limit access of fleets to EEZ waters.
2003 Governor Tause Sunia died; deputy Togiola Tulafono was appointed acting governor.
2004 Cyclone Heta caused devastation and President Bush declared the islands a federal disaster area. Incumbent, Acting Governor Tulafono won the gubernatorial elections.
2005 Cyclone Heta's damage to the Manu'a islands was estimated at US$2 million. The government-owned KVZK-TV re-launched Channel 5, which had been off-air since 1991. Ttravellers from American Samoa were required to obtain entry permits to enter Samoa. The governor introduced legislation to ban human trafficking and involuntary servitude.
2006 Eni Faleomavaega was re-elected for a tenth term as Territorial Delegate in elections to the US House of Representatives.
2007 Samoa agreed to wave the US$30 entry permit fee for all nationals who could prove a Samoan ancestry.
2008 Hillary Clinton won the American Samoa Caucus vote on 5 February with 163 votes to Barack Obama's 121.

Political structure

Constitution

The 1960 constitution was revised in 1967.
American Samoa is represented in the US by a senator and a non-voting representative.
American Samoans are not US citizens; they are classified as US nationals and have freedom of entry into the continental US, but no voting rights.

Form of state

American Samoa is an unincorporated and unorganized territory of the US, administered by the Office of Insular Affairs, US Department of the Interior.

The executive

Local executive power rests with a popularly elected governor and lieutenant governor, who serve four-year terms.

National legislature

The Fono (Legislative Assembly) has two chambers. It consists of an 18-member Senate, elected according to Samoan custom by Matai (local chiefs), for a four-year term, and a 21-seat House of Representatives (20 of which are elected by popular vote, and one who is an appointed, non-voting delegate from Swains Island) elected for two years.

Legal system

High Court – the chief justice and associate justices are appointed by the US Secretary of the Interior.

Last elections

2/16 November 2004 (gubernatorial); 7 November 2006 (US House of Representatives)
Results: Gubernatorial (first round): incumbent Togiola Tulafono won 48.4 per

cent of the vote, Afoa Moega Lutu 39.4 per cent and Teo Fuavai 12.2 per cent.
Gubernatorial (second round): Togiola Tulafono defeated Afoa Moega Lutu 56 per cent to 44 per cent.
US House of Representatives: Eni Faleomavaega (Democrat) won 47.1 per cent of the vote; Aumua Amata Coleman (Republican) 40.7 per cent; and Muavaefaatasi Ae Ae (Independent) 12.2 per cent.

Next elections
November 2008 (gubernatorial)

Political situation
The relationship between American Samoa and the US has been exercising the country's leadership in 2007. Under the constitution American Samoa is an unorganised territory, so the people of American Samoa are US nationals but not citizens and they cannot migrate for work without visas to other US states and territories. In 2007 the US imposed a minimum wage, under federal laws that threatened the viability of the island's largest employers – two tuna canaries – raising wages from the local norm of US$2.63–4.09 per hour, depending on the industry, to US$7.25 by 2009. Added to which the US Congress, at the request of the American Samoan Congress representative, required three questions to be included in the 2008 political ballots, concerning whether American Samoans become US citizens, whether territorial senators should be elected by American Samoans and whether American Samoa should have it own federal district court and limited jurisdiction. Local politicians see these moves as a measure to sideline their influence.
Newly introduced, and some considered pre-emptive, measures to tighten immigration laws are also seen as another contentious issue that ignores the interests of local people.

Population
64,869 (2006)*
Last census: April 2000: 57,291
Population density: 320 inhabitants per square km.
Annual growth rate: 1.6 per cent (2003)

Ethnic make-up
Samoan (Polynesian) (89 per cent), Tongan (4 per cent), Caucasian (2 per cent), others (5 per cent).

Religions
Approximately half the population are Christian Congregational, but Roman Catholics, Latter Day Saints and Protestants are also represented.

Education
Extra federal funds were provided in 2006 for schools with students from deprived backgrounds, aimed at those at risk of dropping out of education. There were also schemes for early reading and English learning, and support for children with disabilities. Specific funding for American Samoa of US$29.5 million will be added to improve the island's education system.
Compulsory years: Six to 18

Health
Life expectancy: 75.8 years (2005 estimate)
Fertility rate/Maternal mortality rate: 3.25 births per woman (2005 estimate).
Birth rate/Death rate: 25.9 births and three deaths per 1,000 population (2005 estimate)
Child (under 5 years) mortality rate (per 1,000): 9.3 deaths per 1,000 live births (2005 estimate)

Main cities
Fagatogo, the capital, on Tutuila, is usually known as Pago Pago (estimated population 4,388 in 2008), Tafuna (13,552), Nu'uuli (5,828), Leone (4,289), Faleniu (4,556).

Languages spoken
English is used for business and commerce but Samoan, (closely related to Hawaiian), is in common use among the local population.

Official language/s
English and Samoan

Media
Other news agencies: ABC Pacific Beat: www.radioaustralia.net.au/pacbeat
Pacific Magazine:
www.pacificmagazine.net

Press
There are only two national, locally based daily newspapers, the Samoa News (www.samoanews.com) and the Samoa Observer (www.samoaobserver.ws).
A new, locally printed, five day publication began in February 2006, the American Samoa Tribune is bilingual and owned by the Samoa Observer Newspaper Group.

Broadcasting
Radio: There are two commercial radio stations operating, both using their call signs, KKHJ 93FM (www.khjradio.com) with music and general interest programming and KNWJ 104 FM (www.fm104.org) with religious programmes; both broadcast in English. Several radio station broadcasts can be picked up from Samoa.
Television: The government owned KVZK Television operates three channels, broadcasting for eight hours each day. KVZK is an affiliate of US broadcasters PBS, ABC and CBS. There are several privately owned cable TV stations including K34HI, a Fox affiliate, WVUV-LP an NBC affiliate, American Samoa Cablevision, a CNN affiliate and K11UU. K21GL broadcasts religious programmes. TV signals, by SBC TV1, neighbouring Samoa's public, commercial broadcaster, can be received.

Economy
The economy is reliant on agriculture, fishing, fish processing and aid from the US. The dependence on primary sectors means the economy is particularly vulnerable to adverse weather conditions and disease. Around half of the government's revenue is from US aid, making international support essential to the island's development.
Government efforts to attract investment to the territory have had limited success. Due to the islands natural beauty, tourism is a fast growing sector of the economy. The island is becoming an increasingly popular destination for the growing popularity in ecotourism. There are 10-year tax incentives for new businesses in the area, attempting to attract light manufacturing and service based industries.
The private sector continues to be dominated by the fish processing industry. However the canneries rely almost entirely on imported materials for production.
Changing global environments have made it clear the territory can no longer depend on fish production for its survival, meaning diversification is essential for future development. Tuna processing is an important source of government revenue as it contributes 93 per cent of the island's exports. A decline in production would severely damage the local economy and lead to mass unemployment.
In April 2004, the government was awarded over US$1.4 million in federal grants, and over US$7.5 million for improvements at Pago Pago, Fitiuta and Ofu Airports.
The Homeland Security Appropriations Act included US$5.03 million for American Samoa to use as funding for law enforcement training, terrorism prevention and port security. The 2005 appropriations bill included US$23.1 million for American Samoa's government operations and US$10 million for capital improvement projects.
US Army recruitment, which is a considerable source of income and employment has dropped in recent years. It is believed that the decrease is due to the war in Iraq, which has had negative publicity, arising from the death of a number of American Samoan servicemen. According to Governor Togiola, on a per capita basis, they have 'the highest death rate in the US military at present'.

External trade
American Samoa benefits from duty free entry into the customs territory of the US. Canned fish is considered a domestic product in US statistics and is not reflected

in export figures, nevertheless over 60 per cent of output from the two existing canneries goes to US markets.

Imports

Materials for the canneries, processed food, machinery and parts, timber and petroleum products.

Main sources: Australia (66.0 per cent of total 2005), Samoa (13.8 per cent), New Zealand (10.8 per cent)

Exports

Canned tuna (typically 93 per cent of total), small industrial products.

Main destinations: Indonesia (28.2 per cent of total 2005), India (22.3 per cent), Australia (15.3 per cent), Japan (11.2 per cent), New Zealand (7.1 per cent)

Canned fish to the US is not counted as an export.

Agriculture

Farming

The soil is volcanic. About 10 per cent of the land area is cultivable, half of which is under permanent cultivation.

The estimated smallholding crop production in 2005 included: 4,700 tonnes (t) coconuts, 1,500t taro, 1,620t roots and tubers, 100t yams, 1,195t fruit in total, 750t bananas, 490t vegetables in total and 611t oilcrops. Estimated meat production was 344t in total, including: 3t beef, 315t pig meat and 26t poultry meat; 30t eggs, and 16t milk.

Fishing

Tuna and deep-sea fishing is important to the economy. American Samoa is the main processing site for the US tuna fishing fleet in the Pacific. Typical fish catches up to 2000 had been less than 600t but in 2001 the catch jumped to 3,600t and concerns about overfishing prompted a decision in 2002 to limit fleet access to American Samoa's waters.

In 2004 the total marine fish catch was 4,043 tonnes.

Industry and manufacturing

The private sector is dominated by the fish processing industry, which employs one-third of the workforce. StarKist has the world's largest tuna cannery in American Samoa and has a 44 per cent US market share. The two other producers are BumbleBee and Chicken of the Sea (a Thai owned company). Between them they produce 80–90 per cent of American Samoa's principal export, the majority of which is directed to the US market. The tuna canneries export around US$470 million processed tuna annually. StarKist and Chicken of the Sea employ more than 5,150 people or 74 per cent of the private sector workforce. Sales from StarKist canneries are reported to have increased sharply in recent years. American Samoa is fighting to exclude tuna from the US/Thailand Free Trade Agreement in order to save around 3,000 jobs.

Ecuador and Columbia are a threat to the tuna canneries as they have the production capacity to supply the entire US market and wipe out the economy of American Samoa.

Other industries include textiles, meat canning, dairy produce, jewellery, handicrafts and tourism. There are also factories processing soap, liquor and perfume. The US government is trying to encourage joint ventures and other foreign investment for any product with a 30 per cent local content.

Tourism

Tourism plays an increasing role in the islands' economy. It is still relatively underdeveloped, but has potential and development is a government priority. Tourist arrival figures are small and have tended to fluctuate. The cruise ship business is being encouraged. Ecotourism is a growing attraction.

Mining

The only natural resources are pumice and pumicite.

Hydrocarbons

American Samoa does not produce gas, coal or oil. It relies entirely on imports of refined oil including gasoline, kerosene, distillate and jet fuel.

Energy

The monthly average generated is 8.4 million kW.

Banking and insurance

The Bank of Hawaii and the Amerika Samoa Bank provide 24-hour full banking services and correspond with banks in the US and the Pacific.

Time

GMT minus 11 hours

Geography

American Samoa comprises the seven islands of Tutuila, Ta'u, Olosega, Ofu, Aunu'u, Rose Atoll and Swains Island, lying in the southern central Pacific Ocean, about 3,700km (2,300 miles) south-west of Hawaii. Pago Pago has one of the best natural deepwater harbours in the region.

Hemisphere

Southern

Climate

Tropical with annual rainfall around three metres. There are two main seasons: rainy (November—April) and dry (May–October). Temperatures range from 20–32 degrees Celsius.

Entry requirements

Passports

Required by all except US citizens with proof of citizenship; (all US nationals require a passport for re-entry to the US from January 2007).

Passports must be valid for at least 60 days beyond the intended length of stay.

Visa

US entry requirements apply. Visas required by all, except US citizens with proof of identity and foreign nationals from countries covered by the 'Visa Waiver Program', who are in possession of machine readable passports. All other visitors and passport holders must apply for a visa.

Visas are valid for up to 90 days. A return/onward ticket is also required.

Further information can be found at http://travel.state.gov. More detailed information can be found at http://uscis.gov/graphics/services.

All visitors must have proof of adequate funds for up to 30 days and onward/return tickets. Entry to American Samoa does not give automatic entry to the US and visitors must apply separately through a US consulate.

Health (for visitors)

Mandatory precautions

Vaccination certificates required for yellow fever if travelling from infected area.

Advisable precautions

Vaccination for diphtheria, tuberculosis, hepatitis A and B, polio, tetanus and typhoid are advisable. There is a risk of rabies and dengue fever.

Public holidays (national)

Fixed dates

1 Jan (New Year's Day), 17 Apr (Flag Day), 4 Jul (Independence Day), 11 Nov (Veterans' Day), 25 Dec (Christmas Day).

Variable dates

Martin Luther King's Birthday (third Mon in Jan), Washington's Birthday (third Mon in Feb), Memorial Day (last Mon in May), Labour Day (first Mon in Sep), Columbus Day (second Mon in Oct), Thanksgiving Day (fourth Thu in Nov).

Working hours

Banking

Mon–Fri: 0900–1500; Sat: 0800–1200.

Business

Mon–Fri: 0730/0830–1730/1800; Sat: 0830–1200.

Government

Mon–Fri: 0730/0830–1730/1800; Sat: 0830–1200.

Shops

Mon–Fri: 0800–1700; Sat: 0800–1300.

Weights and measures

Imperial

Social customs/useful tips

Visitors should be sensitive to local conventions and respect local customs and practices. Care should be taken when dressed casually; bikinis and shorts are acceptable in hotels, but they are not considered appropriate when visiting urban and rural areas.

Getting there

Air

National airline: Hawaiian Airlines and Polynesian Airlines connect American Samoa to international air routes.

International airport/s: Pago Pago International (PPG), 11km from town; duty-free shop, restaurant and shops.

Airport tax: US$3, usually included in ticket price.

Surface

Main port/s: Pago Pago is an international port. It is served by a number of passenger cruise and cargo lines.

Getting about

National transport

Air: Samoa Air and Inter Island Air (a charter airline) serve the islands.

Road: There are approximately 150km of paved roads and 200km of unpaved or secondary roads, the majority of which are on Tutuila.

Buses: There is a local service operating between the airport and Pago Pago town centre. The 'aiga' bus service provides cheap travel between Pago Pago and outlying villages.

Water: A weekly service operates between Pago Pago and the Manu'a islands.

Car hire

An international driving licence or valid national driving licence is required. Minimum age of 21. Traffic drives on the right.

BUSINESS DIRECTORY

The addresses listed below are a selection only. While World of Information makes every endeavour to check these addresses, we cannot guarantee that changes have not been made, especially to telephone numbers and area codes. We would welcome any corrections.

Telephone area codes

The international direct dialling (IDD) code for American Samoa is +1 684, followed by subscriber's number.

Useful telephone numbers

Police, fire and ambulance911

Chambers of Commerce

American Samoa Chamber of Commerce, PO Box 2446, Pago Pago 96799 (tel: 699-6214; fax: 699-2219; e-mail: chamber@samoatelco.com).

Banking

Amerika Samoa Bank, PO Box 3790, Pago Pago 96799 (tel: 633-5053; fax: 633-5057).

Bank of Hawaii, PO Box 69, Pago Pago 96799 (tel: 633-4226; fax: 633-2918).

Central bank

Federal Reserve System, 20th Street and Constitution Avenue, NW, Washington DC 20551 (tel: (202) 452-3000; fax: (202) 452-3819).

Travel information

Flight information: (tel: 699-9101, 0800-2200).

Pago Pago International Airport, PO Box 1539, Pago Pago 96799 (tel: 699-9101/2/3; fax: 633-5281).

National tourist organisation offices

Office of Tourism, Convention Centre, Pago Pago, 96799 (tel: 633-1091/92/93; fax: 633-1094).

Ministries

Department of Commerce, Economic Development, American Samoa Government, Pago Page, American Samoa 96799 (tel: 84-633-5155; fax: 684-633-4195; email: Azodiacal@doc.asg.as

Other useful addresses

Office of Economic Development and Planning, Territorial Planning Commission, Pago Pago, 96799 (tel: 633-5156).

Office of the Governor, American Samoa Government, Pago Pago (tel: 633-4828; fax: 633-2269).

Other news agencies: ABC Pacific Beat: www.radioaustralia.net.au/pacbeat
Pacific Magazine:
www.pacificmagazine.net

Internet sites

Government website: www.asg-gov.net

Office of Tourism: www.amsamoa.com

Samoa News on-line:
www.samoanews.com

US Office of Insular Affairs:
www.doi.gov/oia

Andorra

KEY FACTS

Official name: Principat d'Andorra (Principality of Andorra)

Head of State: Co-Princes: Bishop of Seu d'Urgel (Spain), Joan Enric Vives i Sicília (from May 2003) and President Nicolas Sarkozy (France) (from 2007)

Head of government: Cap de Govern Albert Pintat Santolària (elected 2005)

Ruling party: Partit Liberal Andorra (PLA) (Liberal Party of Andorra) (since 2001; re-elected 2005)

Area: 468 square km

Population: 81,222 (2006)*

Capital: Andorra la Vella

Official language: Catalan

Currency: Euro (eur) = 100 cents

Exchange rate: eur0.63 per US$ (Jul 2008)

GDP per capita: US$38,800 (2005)

GDP real growth: 2.40% (2006)*

Labour force: 48,700 (2004)

Inflation: 3.20% (2005)

Balance of trade: -US$1.02 billion (2003)

* estimated figure

COUNTRY PROFILE

Historical profile

One of the world's smallest countries, Andorra is also one of the oldest nations in Europe, established by Charlemagne in 803 as a buffer state against a Muslim Spain.

803 Charlemagne captured the area from Spanish Muslims and his son, Louis the Pious, presented the area's inhabitants with a charter of liberties.

843 The Valls d'Andorra (Valleys of Andorra) were granted to Sunifred, Count of Urgell.

1278 Co-principality established between France (originally represented by a nominee of the king, then the emperor and latterly the president himself) and Spain (in the person of the Bishop of Seu d'Urgel).

1419 A parliament, the Consell de la Terra (Council of the Land), was established to represent the Andorran people.

1866 The Consell General de las Valls (Council of the Valleys) replaced the Council of the Land, during the year of the New Reform, which introduced democratisation to Andorra.

1933—34 The Council of the Valleys was temporarily dissolved by the courts. Elections were held and all men over 25 years were granted the right to vote.

1981 Constitutional reforms were enacted to move power away from the feudal co-princes and towards the parliament.

1983 Income tax was introduced following public spending needed for storm damage and a general recession.

1985 Universal suffrage was introduced.

1991 Andorra joined a customs union with the EU.

1993 Andorra introduced a new constitution, establishing the country as a sovereign parliamentary democracy, and a new 28-member parliament, the Consell General (General Council). The first elections were won by Agrupament Nacional Democratic (AND) (National Democratic Grouping).

1994 A coalition government was formed, led by Unió Liberal (UL), Marc Forné Molné of the Partit Liberal Andorra's (PLA) (Liberal Party of Andorra) was elected prime minister by the General Council.

2001 The PLA was elected.

2002 The Organisation for Economic Co-operation and Development (OECD) blacklisted Andorra as a tax haven with 'prejudicial' tax practices. The principality refused to agree to lift the secrecy surrounding the banking sector. Préfet Philippe Massoni was appointed representative of the President of France in Andorra.

2003 Joan Enric Vives Sicília succeeded Joan Martí Alanís as Bishop of Seu d'Urgel and ex officio co-prince of Andorra.

2004 An agreement on a Savings Tax Directive concerning tax withholding and savings between the EU and Andorra was reached.

2005 The ruling PLA was re-elected with 41.2 per cent of the vote (14 seats out of 28). Turnout was 80.4 per cent. Albert Pintat Santolària was elected head of government.

2006 Measures to reform the economy and improve the country's reputation as a financial centre were adopted

2007 On 16 May, Nicolas Sarkozy, as president of the French Republic, became co-prince.

Political structure

Constitution

The first written constitution was adopted 14 March 1993 after a referendum. The constitution allows Andorra to hold full sovereignty, to be able to form trade unions and political parties, and to have an independent judiciary. It can also decide its own foreign policy and join international organisations.

Form of state

Andorra is a co-principality under the joint sovereignty of the President of France and the Spanish Bishop of Seu d'Urgel, who are represented locally by officials called verguers.

The executive

The co-princes (the Bishop of Seu d'Urgel and President of France), are titular heads of state. The country is governed by an administration formed by the party or coalition with the largest number of seats in the legislature.

National legislature

Day-to-day government business is chaired by the Cap de Govern (head of government) and the 28-member Consell General (14 elected by a single national constituency and 14 to represent each of the seven parroquies, or parishes). Members serve for four years. The head of government is elected by the Consell General.

Legal system
Independent judiciary

Last elections
24 April 2005 (parliamentary)

Results: Parliamentary: the Partit Liberal Andorra (PLA) (Liberal Party of Andorra) won 41.2 per cent of the vote (14 seats out of 28), the Partit Socialdemòcrata (PSD) (Social-Democratic Party) 38.1 per cent (12 seats), the Partit Demòcrata (PD) (Democratic Party) 11 per cent (two seats), the Democratic Renovation party 6.2 per cent (no seats) and the Greens 3.5 per cent (no seats); turnout was 80.4 per cent.

Next elections
2009 (parliamentary)

Political parties

Ruling party
Partit Liberal Andorra (PLA) (Liberal Party of Andorra) (since 2001; re-elected 2005)

Main opposition party
Partit Socialdemòcrata (PSD) (Social-Democratic Party)

Population

81,222 (2006)*

Last census: July 2000: 66,089

Population density: 147 people per square km.

Annual growth rate: 0.7 per cent 1994–2004 (WHO 2006)

Ethnic make-up
Of Andorra's total population, only about 33 per cent are natives with the right to vote. The rest include Spaniards (43 per cent), Portuguese (11 per cent), French (7 per cent), English, Australians, Moroccans and others (6 per cent).

Religions
Roman Catholicism is predominant.

Education

A range of universal, free public French, Spanish and Andorran lay schools provide education up to secondary level. Although schools are built and maintained by Andorran authorities, teachers are paid for the most part by France or Spain. The government provides free nursery schools, although supply falls short of demand. About 50 per cent of Andorran children attend the French primary schools, and the rest attend Spanish or Andorran schools. In July 1997, the University of Andorra was established, which serves principally as a centre for virtual studies, connected to Spanish and French universities. The only two graduate schools in Andorra are the Nursing School and the School of Computer Science.

Compulsory years: Four to 16

Health

Per capita total expenditure on health (2003) was US$2,453; of which per capita government spending was US$1,683, at the international dollar rate, (WHO 2006).

Life expectancy: 80 years, 2004 (WHO 2006)

Fertility rate/Maternal mortality rate: 1.3 births per woman, 2004 (WHO 2006)

Birth rate/Death rate: 5.4 deaths to 10.29 births per 1,000 population (World Bank).

Child (under 5 years) mortality rate (per 1,000): 6 per 1,000 live births (World Bank)

Head of population per physician: 3.7 physicians per 1,000 people, 2003 (WHO 2006)

Welfare

Social security in Andorra is based on a points system with two distinct programmes covering health and old-age insurance.

Health insurance covers illness, pregnancy, accidents at work, disability and death. Social security payments cover nearly 75 per cent and 90 per cent of expenditure relating to illness and hospitalisation respectively. There is no discrimination against disabled persons in employment, education, or in the provision of other state services.

Unemployment benefit includes 50 per cent of the average salary calculated in the first month and 66 per cent calculated from the second month onwards.

Pensions
People pay contributions towards their old-age pension and on retirement receive a pension proportional to the number of points collected. All salaried workers pay contributions to the Andorran Social Security Fund (CASS). Old-age pension is paid to those covered from the age of 65.

Family support
Maternity care and childbirth are fully covered by social security, while disability benefits are calculated in each individual case.

Main cities

Andorra la Vella (capital, estimated population 25,204 in 2008), Les Escaldes (16,387), Encamp (14,861), Sant Julia de Loria (10,041).

Languages spoken

French and Castilian

Official language/s
Catalan

Media

The constitution guarantees the freedom of speech and of the press.

Press
In Catalan, there are several newspapers including the Diari d'Andorra (www.diariandorra.ad), Bondia (www.bondia.ad), and El Periodic d'Andorra (www.elperiodico.com).

Broadcasting
Radio Televisio d'Andorra (RTVA) (www.rtvasa.ad) is the national broadcaster; Spanish TV also broadcasts in Andorra (www.tvc.cat). All TV services are provided by digital technology.

Radio: Radio Nacional d'Andorra (RNA) is the only public station. Privately-owned commercial stations include Radio Valira, Andorra 1 (www.andorra1.ad) and Andorra 7 (www.andorra7radio.com). Radio signals from Spain and France can be picked up with ease.

Economy

With more than 10 million visitors a year, Andorra is heavily reliant on the tourist sector, which accounts for around 80 per cent of GDP. Financial services are an important magnet for foreign investment. Andorra is a tax haven with a banking system which is characterised by strict security and which contributes substantially to the economy. In 2003, Andorra was one of several countries named by the OECD as unco-operative tax havens; in June 2004, Andorra agreed to operate equivalent measures to those applied by EU member states regarding taxation of income from savings.

There is a very small-scale agriculture sector with only around 2 per cent of the land being usable for farming purposes. Consequently, there is a heavy reliance on food imports. Light industry in Andorra consists almost entirely of tobacco products and furniture, which are the primary exports.

The most important activities of the service sector are commerce and the hotel trade, which employ almost 40 per cent of the workforce. There are insufficient modern and dynamic services, such as specialised services for businesses, and a reliance on traditional sectors limits the economy's potential.

Andorra is a member of the EU customs union and is treated as an EU member with no tariffs on manufactured goods when trading with EU members.

Labour market and unemployment

Large immigrant workforce, mainly Spanish. Tourism and allied industries are major employers.

External trade

As a member of the European Union Customs Union with favourable excise duties Andorra is a major entrepôt for numerous European goods. However, Andorra is treated as a non-EU member and its agricultural products are subject to tariffs. Spain and France are Andorra's main export partners.

The nearly 3km long Envalira tunnel, between Andorra and France, runs under the highest mountain pass in Europe. It is one of the longest road tunnels in the world.

Imports
Three-quarters of Andorra's revenue is from import tariffs. Main imports are foodstuffs, electricity, raw materials, manufactures and consumer goods.
Main sources: Spain (51.5 per cent of total 2004), France (22.3 per cent), US (0.3 per cent)

Exports
The volume of exports is typically under 5 per cent of GDP, a figure far below that of most OECD countries, indicating the unusual nature of the economy, based on retail sales to tourists. Main exports include tobacco products and furniture.
Main destinations: EU members take 99.5 per cent of exports, including Spain (typically 58 per cent cent of total) and France (typically 34 per)

Agriculture
The agricultural sector is a small part of the economy and typically employs less than 1 per cent of the working population. Agricultural production is limited by a scarcity of arable land, and most food has to be imported. Milk is sourced domestically. Principal crops are tobacco and potatoes, rye, wheat, barley, oats. Some other vegetables are also grown.
The principal livestock activity is sheep husbandry.
Land use: 2 per cent permanent crops, 56 per cent forest and woodland, 20 per cent irrigated land.
Andorra imports fish from Spain for domestic needs. Trout are plentiful in streams.
Exports of forest materials in 2004 amounted to US$800,000, while imports amounted to US$6.3 million. Logs are transported to Spain. Most reforestation is in pines.

Industry and manufacturing
The industrial sector has fallen to around 20 per cent of economic activity. The small manufacturing sector primarily services tourism, but also includes cigarettes, cigars and furniture.

Tourism
Andorra depends heavily on its tourist industry, which accounts for as much as 80 per cent of GDP. There are typically 10 million tourist visits per annum, three-quarters of which are day-trips. Tourists and day-trippers, the majority of whom are Spanish and French, are drawn by the principality's duty-free status and its skiing resorts. There are 270 hotels and 400 restaurants.

Environment
Current issues are deforestation and overgrazing of mountain meadows contributing to soil erosion. Natural hazards include snowslides and avalanches.

Mining
Forges in Andorra were once famed. There are small amounts of iron ore and lead but access is a problem.

Hydrocarbons
Even though Andorra has good hydroelectric facilities, around three-quarters of energy consumed is by imported oil from France and Spain. It does not import coal or natural gas.

Energy
From 2003 until 2008, Endesa of Spain will supply 50 per cent of Andorra's electricity requirements. Electricity demand for Andorra in 2003 was estimated at 500GWh, of which around 290GWh was supplied by Endesa, 90GWh by the country's only hydroelectric plant and the remaining 120GWh by Electricité de France (EDF).

Banking and insurance
The banking sector with its tax haven status contributes substantially to the economy. Seven commercial banks operate some 34 branches. Strict secrecy laws are maintained.
Andorra's financial service sector is benefiting from the eurozone which provides greater stability and enhanced opportunities. After being denounced as an unco-operative tax haven by the OECD in 2003, Andorra conceded to EU standards regarding taxation of income from savings. From 2005 Andorra has imposed a withholding tax, up to 35 per cent, which is passed to the tax department of an EU citizen's country. Instead of informing the relevant EU country about the amount of money in savings accounts, the anonymity of the saver is preserved. Andorra refuses to back down from its commitment to banking secrecy, which is enshrined in the 1993 constitution.
Andorra has also agreed to supply information on tax fraud, for criminal or civil trials, and notify EU member states about additional malpractices.

Central bank
European Central Bank (ECB)

Time
GMT plus one hour (daylight saving, late March to late October, GMT plus two hours)

Geography
Andorra lies high in the eastern Pyrenees mountains in south-western Europe. The lowest elevation is 838 metres, reaching to nearly 3,000 metres at the peak of Coma Pedrosa. Andorra is landlocked, sharing borders with France and Spain.

Hemisphere
Northern

Climate
Warm summers and moderately cold winters; temperatures range from 0–30 degrees Celsius.

Entry requirements

Passports
Required by all except for nationals of France and Spain, who only require an identity card.

Visa
Not required, but the relevant regulations of Spain and France, depending on point of transit, should be followed. Stays of up to three months without a visa are allowed.

Currency advice/regulations
No currency restrictions.

Health (for visitors)

Mandatory precautions
None

Advisable precautions
Up-to-date tetanus, Measles-mumps-rubella, varicella and polio immunisations are recommended; also influenza if visiting Nov-Apr.

Hotels
Around 270 hotels, most with modern facilities.

Public holidays (national)

Fixed dates
1 Jan (New Year's Day), 6 Jan (Epiphany), 14 Mar (Constitution Day), 1 May (Labour Day), 24 Jun (St John's Day), 15 Aug (Assumption Day), 8 Sep (Mare de Déu de Meritxell, National Day), 1 Nov (All Saints Day), 4 Nov (St Charles Day), 8 Dec (Immaculate Conception), 24 Dec (Christmas Eve), 25–26 Dec (Christmas Holiday), 31 Dec (New Year's Eve).

Variable dates
Good Friday, Easter Monday, Ascension Day, Whit Monday.

Working hours

Banking
Mon–Fri: 0900–1300, 1500–1700; Sat: 0900–1200.

Business
Considerable variation in times, depending on whether following French or Spanish working practices.

Shops
Mon–Fri: 0900–2000; Sat: 0900–2100; Sun: 0900–1900.

Getting there

Air
International airport/s: The closest international airports are located in France (Toulouse-Blagnac, 180km) and Spain (Barcelona, 200km), connecting to inter-

and intra-continental destinations. Approximately three hours drive. Regular shuttle bus services connect both airports with Andorra.

Surface

Road: From Spain: Barcelona-Andorra via Cervera; Barcelona-Andorra via Calaf; Barcelona-Andorra via Solsonal. Madrid-Andorra via Zaragoza. Buses run regularly from Barcelona and Madrid. Other road connections to Lleida, Puigcerdà, Tarragona and Girona. Mountainous roads exist over the Envalira pass to Perpignan, Tarbes and Toulouse. From France: Paris-Andorra via Aix-les-Thermes; Marseilles-Andorra via Perpignan; Biarritz via St Gaudens. A road runs from the Spanish to the French frontiers through Saint Julia, Andorra la Vella, Escaldes-Engordonay, Encamp, Camnillo and Soldeu.

Rail: From Spain: Barcelona to Puigcerda, then by bus to La Seu d'Urgel and Andorra. Madrid to Lleida, then bus to La Seu d'Urgel and Andorra. From France: Paris to Aix-les-Thermes or L'Hospitalet, then bus to Andorra; Perpignan to La Tour de Carol, then bus to Andorra .

Getting about

National transport

Road: There are 269km of roads, of which 198km are paved. Roads can be blocked by snow in winter and congestion in summer.

Buses: Constant minibus services link all the villages.

BUSINESS DIRECTORY

The addresses listed below are a selection only. While World of Information makes every endeavour to check these addresses, we cannot guarantee that changes have not been made, especially to telephone numbers and area codes. We would welcome any corrections.

Telephone area codes

The international direct dialling (IDD) code for Andorra is +376, followed by customer's number.

Useful telephone numbers

Mountain rescue: 112
Police: 110
Fire: 118
Ambulance: 118

Chambers of Commerce

Andorra Chamber of Commerce, Industry and Services, C/Prat de la Creu 8, Edifice le Mans 204, Andorra La Vella (tel: 809-292; fax: 809-293; e-mail: ccis@andorra.ad).

Banking

Banc Agricol i Comercial d'Andorra, Mossen Cinto 6, Andorra la Vella (tel: 821-333).

Banca Cassany SA, Avinguda Meritxell 39-41, Andorra la Vella.

Banc Internacional, Avinguda Meritxell 32, Andorra la Vella (tel: 820-037).

Banca Mora SA, Placa Coprinceps 2, Les Escaldes (tel: 820-607).

Banca Reig, Avinguda Meritxell, Andorra la Vella (tel: 822-618).

Credit Andorra, Avinguda Princep Benlloch 19, Andorra la Vella (tel: 820-326).

La Caixa, Pl Rebés, Andorra la Vella (tel: 820-015).

Central bank

European Central Bank (ECB), Kaiserstrasse 29, D-60311 Frankfurt am Main, Germany (tel: +49(69) 13-440; fax: +49(69) 1344-6000).

Travel information

Caseta d'Informació i Turisme (tourism kiosk opposite Restaurant Martí), Andorra la Vella (tel: 827-117).

Sindicat d'Iniciativa Oficina de Turisme (national tourist office at the top of Carrer Doctor Vilanova between Plaça del Poble and Plaça Rebés), Andorra la Vella (tel: 820-214).

Ministries

Government of Andorra, C/ Prat de la Creu 62, Andorra La Vella (tel: 829-345; internet: www.govern.ad).

Ministry of Finance, Andorra la Vella (tel: 829-245).

Ministry of Commerce, Industry and Agriculture, Andorra la Vella.

Ministry of Tourism and Environment, C/Prat de la Creu, Andorra la Vella (tel: 875-7 02; fax: 860-184; e-mail: turisme@andorra.ad)

Other useful addresses

French Embassy, C/ Les Canals 38-40, Andorra La Vella (tel: 820-809).

French Post Office, C/Bonaventura Armengol, Andorra la Vella (tel: 820-408).

General Syndic's Office (tel: 821-234).

Pas de la Casa Customs Post (Andorran frontier with France) (tel: 855-120).

Police, Andorra la Vella (tel: 821-222).

Sant Julia de Loria Customs Post (Andorran frontier with Spain) (tel: 841-090).

Servei de Telecomunicacions d'Andorra STA, Avinguda Meritxell 110, Andorra la Vella (tel: 821-021).

Sindicat d'Iniciativa de les Valls d'Andorra, c/Dr Vilanova, Andorra la Vella (tel: 820-214).

Spanish Embassy, C/ Prat de la Creu 34, Andorra La Vella (tel: 820-013).

Spanish Post Office, c/o Joan Maragall, Andorra la Vella (tel: 820-257).

Internet sites

Only Andorra yellow pages: www.onlyandorra.com

Andorra information: www.andorra.ad/

KEY FACTS

Official name: Republica de Angola (Republic of Angola)

Head of State: President José Eduardo dos Santos (since 1979)

Head of government: Prime Minister Fernando da Piedade Dias dos Santos (from Dec 2002)

Ruling party: Government of Unity and National Reconciliation (GURN); dominated by Movimento Popular de Libertação de Angola (MPLA) (Popular Movement for the Liberation of Angola)

Area: 1,246,700 square km

Population: 16.33 million (2007)*

Capital: Luanda

Official language: Portuguese

Currency: Kwanza (Kz) = 100 Lwei

Exchange rate: Kz74.80 per US$ (Jul 2008)

GDP per capita: US$3,757 (2007)*

GDP real growth: 15.30% (2006)*

Labour force: 6.25 million (2004)

Unemployment: 13.90% (2005)*

Inflation: 21.00% (2007)*

Oil production: 1.72 million bpd (2007)

Balance of trade: US$7.64 billion (2005)

Foreign debt: US$10.45 billion (2004)

Annual FDI: -US$1.30 billion (2005)

* estimated figure

Angola

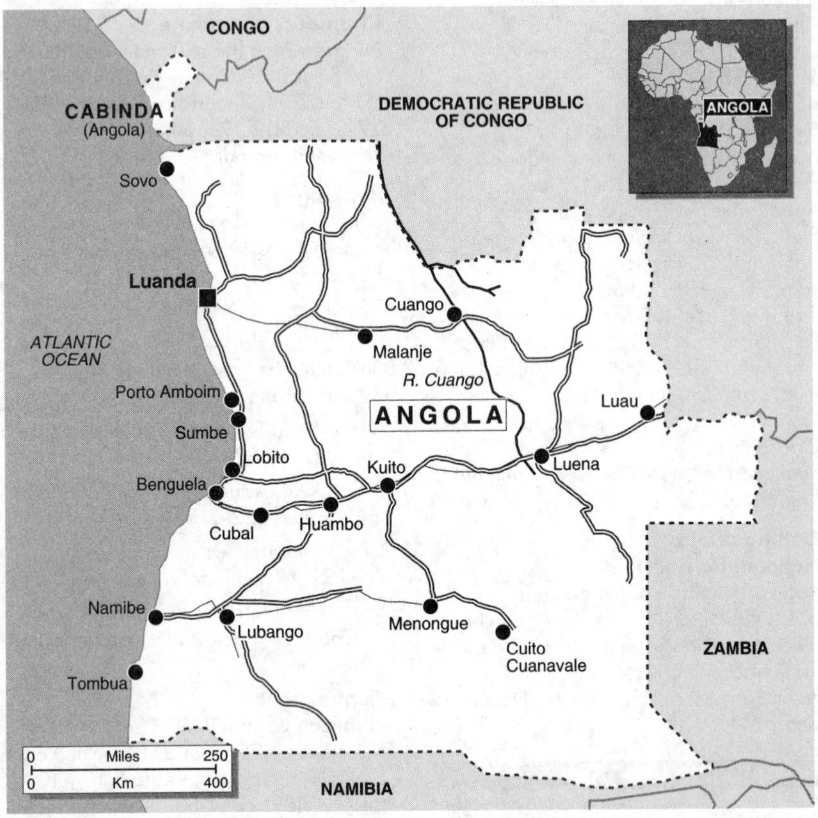

Angola in 2007–08 continued to distinguish itself in a number of ways. Established as Africa's second largest oil producer, Angola could also claim to have one of Africa's consistently fastest growing economies. It also held the more doubtful distinction of being one of Africa's more corrupt states. The *Futungo*, the coterie surrounding President dos Santos, Angola's autocratic ruler since 1979, is thought to have siphoned off billions of dollars in oil revenues and exploration payments.

Futungo-land

In a mind-boggling paper, *The End of Savimbiland? The Rise and Decline of UNITA's State-Within-a-State in Angola*, Canadian academic J Andrew Grant of Dalhousie University has analysed how, since independence, Angola has also become a shadow state, as oil and most other sources of revenue under the government's control run through the so-called *Futungo* – which although it sounds like a disease, in fact is the shortened name for the president's private residence, *Futungo* de Belas. Mr Grant goes on to describe how, as its name implies, the *Futungo* refers to Angolan president José Eduardo dos Santos and his entourage of political, military, and business elites. The national petroleum company Sociedade Nacional de Combustiveis de Angola (Sonangol), the Banco Nacional de Angola (BNA) (National Bank of Angola), and the *Futungo* represent an opaque financial Bermuda Triangle of actors which exploit sources of government income through secret and complex accounting procedures for personal gain. Elite members of this 'Bermuda Triangle' siphon off portions of oil revenues and signature bonuses (the bonuses paid upon the signature of exploration contracts) into private accounts, enjoy access to US dollars at the low official kwanza exchange rate (which in turn may be exchanged on the street at a much higher exchange rate), benefit from creative accounting procedures to reduce tax payments, and so on. Mr Grant also refers to a 1998 investigative media report published in the United Kingdom which intimates that President dos Santos holds a significant portion of his personal wealth invested in Brazil, making him the twentieth richest person in that country. Mr Grant states that graft and corruption abound in Angola's government institutions, as the patron-client linkages originating from the *Futungo* and the country's financial Bermuda Triangle are protected behind the façade of laws and government institutions.

Allegations of large-scale corruption have circulated in Angola for some years. The New York-based Human Rights Watch (HRW) has alleged that the Angolan government is unable to account for something like US$4 billion for the period 1997–2002 alone. The London-based Economist Intelligence Unit (EIU) estimates that there are some 20 Angolans worth US$100 million or more; six of the seven richest on the EIU's list were government officials, the seventh had recently taken retirement at the time of publication. The Angolan government has been at pains to counter the rumours, but to little effect. In January 2008 the London Financial Times described Angola as 'something of a honey-pot for oil companies'. Despite the continued, and hostile, scrutiny of organisations such as HRW, Angola appears to have done little to mend its ways. It has yet to join the petroleum industry's self-policing body the Extractive Industries Transparency Initiative (EITI). Berlin-based Transparency International has ranked Angola 142 in its Transparency Index of 163 countries. Surprisingly, the World Bank's 2007 Country Brief on Angola makes no reference at all to Angola's difficulty in achieving increased transparency.

Reforms

The civil war that ended in 2002 left Angola's political structure and institutions in a bad way. Despite the accusations of widespread corruption, some credit should be given to the governments that have exercised power since 2002, in that the challenges of Angola's infrastructural and socio-economic deficiencies appear to have begun to be addressed. The country's long-postponed parliamentary elections were re-scheduled for 2008; these and the presidential elections due in 2009 are hailed by the government's supporters as significant steps (if not landmarks) in the process of reform.

Key reforms include the transfer of Sonangol's functions as regulator and government concessionaire to other agencies; the establishment of a government oil revenue management unit; and more rigorous reconciliation and analysis of tax payments and profitable oil allocations by international oil companies and Sonangol. In a similar vein, the regulatory and licensing functions of Angola's diamond mining monopoly, Empresa Nacional de Diamantes de Angola (Endiama), could be separated from its commercial operations and diamond marketing liberalised further. While some controls on the marketing of diamonds have been eased, there is limited transparency concerning the supervision and taxation of the formal sector or of the granting of rights for diamond extraction.

Privatisation appears to have stalled and more fiscal stability would strengthen the private sector and improve the climate for private investment. Structural reform to improve competition is needed to develop the sector, which encompasses the great majority of the population. A World Bank report *The Cost of Doing Business* rated Angola as one of the least conducive business climates in the world.

Much credit for the success of Angola's structural and fiscal reforms as far as they go, is the work of the minister of finance Jose Pedro de Morais. In 2007 Mr de Morais was voted Africa's best finance minister by the UK-based Banker magazine. His reforms may have done well by readers of financial magazines, but Angola's social indicators continue to tell a different story. Approaching half Angola's children are still considered to be under-nourished. Many of its towns and villages still lack running water and electricity.

Mr de Morais has reportedly given priority to reducing corruption and tax evasion while continuing the implementation of market economy principles. He is recognised as the key figure in the post-war re-vitalisation of the economy.

IMF problems

Exceptionally for a developing country, Mr de Morais sought to distance Angola from the IMF rather than adopting its recommendations. A major cause of the coolness that arose between the IMF and the Angolan government in the years 2002–04 was the continued reluctance of the government to provide the IMF with the basic information it requested. According to the HRW this lack of fiscal transparency has particularly been the case with the exploration bonuses, the up front payments made to the government by oil companies for exploration rights. The size of the bonuses has customarily been determined by Angola's presidency in association with Sonangol executives. The funds in question would be placed outside the control of Angola's treasury. Long, and generally unaccountable delays

KEY INDICATORS — Angola

	Unit	2003	2004	2005	2006	2007
Population	m	13.64	15.94	14.41	*15.86	*16.33
Gross domestic product (GDP)	US$bn	12.10	19.81	30.63	45.17	*61.36
GDP per capita	US$	901	1,305	1,988	*2,847	*3,757
GDP real growth	%	4.5	11.2	20.6	*15.3	0.0
Inflation	%	115.0	43.6	23.0	18.6	*21.1
Industrial output	% change	–	10.6	23.4	20.0	–
Agricultural output	% change	–	14.1	17.0	8.9	–
Oil output	'000 bpd	885.0	991.0	1,242.0	1,409.0	1,723.0
Exports (fob) (goods)	US$m	9,515.0	12,760.0	13,475.0	31,862.0	–
Imports (cif) (goods)	US$m	5,480.0	4,896.0	5,831.8	9,586.0	–
Balance of trade	US$m	4,035.0	7,864.0	7,643.2	22,276.0	–
Current account	US$m	-720.0	1,260.0	4,137.0	10,538.0	*6,747.0
Total reserves minus gold	US$m	634.2	1,364.7	3,196.8	8,598.6	11,196.8
Foreign exchange	US$m	634.0	1,364.5	3,196.6	8,598.4	11,196.5
Exchange rate	per US$	68.85	82.38	80.28	80.28	75.10

* estimated figure

would then be recorded in their transfer to Angola's budgetary accounts. Discrepancies have also been discovered between the amounts reported as received by Sonangol and the amounts claimed to have been paid by foreign oil companies.

The economy

Angola's economy continued to boom in 2007, due in large measure to its strong oil sector and the consistently high price of crude. The non-oil sector also benefited from largely oil dependent activities in the construction and manufacturing sectors. Angola's GDP growth has averaged 17 per cent since 2005 and at the end of 2007 looked set to maintain similar rates.

At first glance, Angola looks to be a wealthy country; income per capita is US$1,340, higher than Nigeria (US$340) but still way down on that of the smaller African petroleum producing states such as Equatorial Guinea (US$3,300) and Gabon (US$4,100). Real growth in 2006 was 18.6 per cent according to the IMF. The IMF expects Angola's annual GDP growth to average 25 per cent in 2007–08, largely due to increased oil production, but also due to the continued expansion of sectors such as agriculture, manufacturing, construction and power generation. However, the World Bank expects annual GDP growth to drop to around 8 per cent in 2009–10, still largely driven by the oil sector.

The oil

According to the *Oil and Gas Journal* (OGJ) Angola had proven reserves of 8.0 billion barrels in January 2007, mostly located in offshore blocks. Angolan crude oil has a low sulphur content; crude oil production has quadrupled over the past 2.0 decades, and according to the US Energy Information Administration (EIA) is set to reach two million barrels per day (bpd). The World Bank has forecast Angolan oil production to peak at 2.6 million bpd, subsequently declining unless new oil discoveries are made. Angola's oil exports are principally to China (477,000bpd in 2006) and to the USA (473,000bpd in 2006). Angola is the USA's eighth largest supplier of crude oil. Other supplies are to Europe and Latin America.

On the first of January 2007 Angola became the twelfth member of the Organisation of Petroleum Exporting States (Opec). At the time, Angola was producing 1.5 million bpd and although not expected to be subject to an Opec production limit, its exclusion looked likely to become a contentious issue among Opec's fractious membership.

This turned out to be the case when, at its Abu Dhabi meeting at the beginning of 2008 Opec voted to impose a 1.9 million bpd quota on Angola. After the meeting the *Financial Times* reported that Angolan officials had expected a limit in the 2–2.4 million bpd range. The lower quota caused concern because although Angolan production had not reached the Opec ceiling, its very existence called into question the expectations of the foreign oil companies present in Angola, many of which had expressed reservations and puzzlement over the benefits of Angola's Opec membership in the first place. In the 2006 licensing round companies such as Eni (Italy), Total (France) and Petrobras (Brazil) paid a total of US$3 billion for offshore drilling licenses. In the period up to 2014 over US$50 billion is expected to be invested in Angola's oil sector.

Risk assessment

Politics	Fair
Economy	^Good
Regional stability	Fair

^ (but in need of reform)

COUNTRY PROFILE

Historical profile

1482 The Portuguese arrived in Angola, which became a staging post for trade with India and south-east Asia.
1575 The Portuguese founded Luanda. The country became a major source of slaves, who were transported to Brazil.
1836 The slave trade was abolished.
1885 The borders of Angola were set following the Berlin Conference of imperial powers who, with an eye on exploitable assets in Africa, agreed to formal boundaries. Angola provided Portugal with minerals and agricultural products.
1951 Angola's status changed from a colony to an overseas territory.
1956 The Movimento Popular de Libertação de Angola (MPLA) (Popular Movement for the Liberation of Angola) was founded as a guerrilla force fighting against Portuguese rule.
1961 An uprising in which 50,000 Angolans were massacred led to increased repression by colonial security forces.
1962 The Frente Nacional para a Libertacao de Angola (FNLA) (National Front for the Liberation of Angola) was formed by refugees of the uprising, living mainly in what is now the Democratic Republic of Congo.
1966 The União Nacional de Independencia Total de Angola (Unita) (National Union for the Total Independence of Angola) was formed.
1972 The FNLA and MPLA assumed joint leadership of the liberation struggle.
1975 Angola gained independence from Portugal. Scheduled elections failed to take place when the MPLA took power. Unita and the FNLA formed an alliance aimed at defeating the MPLA government.
1979 José dos Santos (MPLA) became president, backed the Soviet Union and Cuba. A civil war ensued, with Unita, supported by the US and South Africa.
1988 An agreement between South Africa, Angola and Cuba was signed, all foreign troops to be withdrawn by mid-1991.
1990 A UN mission, to verify Cuban troop withdrawals, was initiated.
1991 The MPLA introduced multi-party democracy and officially dropped its commitment to Marxism in favour of social democracy. Talks with Unita began and Cuban troops withdrew.
1992 The first multi-party elections resulted in a coalition government formed by the MPLA, and minor parties. The newly-legalised Unita lost the ballot and rejected the election results, ending the UN-brokered cease-fire.
1994 A cease-fire peace agreement, the Lusaka Protocol, was signed between the government and Unita.
1997 Unita joined the ruling MPLA in a power-sharing government of national unity, however, it did not disarm.
1998 Renewed hostilities between MPLA and Unita broke out.
2002 Jonas Savimbi, the leader of Unita, was killed by government forces. The Angolan government offered an amnesty for all Unita rebels who surrendered. A cease-fire was signed, ending the civil war. Fernando da Piedade Dias dos Santos became prime minister.
2003 The World Bank approved a US$125 million assistance programme.
2004 More than 3,000 people were arrested in a crackdown on illegal diamond mining and trafficking (around 11,000 were deported in four months).
2005 An outbreak of the deadly Marburg disease infected 360 people, mainly in the northern province of Rige, and killed 325 people before finally burning itself out.
2006 A cease-fire was signed between the government and the armed militia, Fórum Cabindês para o Diálogo (FCD) (Cabinda Forum for Dialogue), in Cabinda, the rebel Angolan enclave on 18 July, followed by the formal signing of a Memorandum for Peace and Reconciliation in Cabinda. Angola joined the Organisation of Petroleum Exporting Countries (OPEC) as a full member.

2007 In July the European Union banned the national air carrier TAAG from EU air space due to safety concerns.
2008 The first parliamentary elections since 1992 were announced by election organisers, to be held 5–6 September.

Political structure

Constitution
The Bicesse peace accords, signed in May 1991, led to the 1992 constitution. It recognises fundamental rights and duties, based on the principles of the major international treaties on human rights to which Angola is a signatory. It also established multi-party politics, enabling the first elections to be held in September 1992.
Form of state
Unitary republic
The executive
The president is the Head of State, elected by direct universal suffrage every five years.
Presidential elections have not been held since 1992.
National legislature
Unicameral legislature elected for a four-year term.
Legal system
The constitution defines the judiciary as an independent body that is nominated by the National Assembly on the decision of two-thirds of those casting their votes. The Judicial Proctorate is appointed for a four-year term of office and may be re-appointed for another four-year term.
Last elections
29/30 September 1992 (parliamentary and presidential).
Results: Parliamentary: the MPLA won 54 per cent of the votes.
Presidential: José Dos Santos received 49.6 per cent of the votes, making a run-off election necessary between him and second-place Jonas Savimbi; the run-off was not held and Savimbi's Unita disputed the results of the first election and led to a resumption of the civil war. Savimbi's death in 2002 resulted in a cease-fire and the end of the war.
Next elections
5–6 September 2008 (parliamentary); due by 2009 (presidential).

Political parties

Ruling party
Government of Unity and National Reconciliation (GURN); dominated by Movimento Popular de Libertação de Angola (MPLA) (Popular Movement for the Liberation of Angola)
Main opposition party
União Nacional de Independencia Total de Angola (Unita) (National Union for the Total Independence of Angola)

Population

16.33 million (2007)*
Last census: December 1970: 5,646,166
Population density: 10 inhabitants per square km. Urban population: 34 per cent (1994–2000).
Annual growth rate: 2.6 per cent 1994–2004 (WHO 2006)
Internally Displaced Persons (IDP)
450,000 (UNHCR 2004)
Ethnic make-up
37 per cent Ovimbundu, 25 per cent Mbundu, 13 per cent Bakongo, 2 per cent Mestico (mixed European and indigenous descent), 1 per cent European.
Religions
Traditional beliefs (47 per cent), Christianity (38 per cent), mainly Roman Catholic.

Education

Primary school enrolment has increased slowly, although the increase in male enrolment has been higher than for females. Education expenditure amounts to round 6 per cent of the national budget.
The government allocated US$40 million to hire the graduates of a Unesco scheme, which is set to train around 29,000 school teachers as part of a development programme.
Total expenditure on education is around 3 per cent of GDP.
Literacy rate: 66.8 per cent total; 53.8 per cent female; adult rates.
Compulsory years: 6 to 9
Enrolment rate: 74 per cent gross primary enrolment of relevant age group (including repeater) (World Bank)
Pupils per teacher: 29 in primary schools

Health

Per capita total expenditure on health (2003) was US$49; of which per capita government spending was US$41, (WHO 2006).
Public health has become a priority as Angola's human development indicators are poor, it is recognised to having a high rate of infant mortality and has to repair the damage done by 27 years of civil war. One in four children under aged five are likely to die of malaria, the single largest cause of child mortality.
Until the country can exploit its vast natural resources and raise the living standards of the population as a whole, it has to contend with inadequate numbers of doctors and antiquated medical equipment. Preventative care has been described as almost non-existent and primary care, outside former provincial capitals, limited to infrequent and inadequate drug supplies.
Most doctors, who work within the private sector, live in the capital, Luanda. The government has prepared a large package of incentives to encourage health workers to work in the provinces, however most measures are awaiting the financial resources to implement them.
There were cases of polio reported to the World Health Organisation – Global Polio Eradication Initiative in 2006; the country had previously been free of the disease and its re-emergence was due to infected travellers.
HIV/Aids
While the civil war wrought great destruction on the population, paradoxically it provided a buffer that stopped the disease from gaining a significant hold, as people were prevented from travelling. Now the citizens of Angola are free to travel and with a youthful population the government has taken measures to educate young people concerning the risks of HIV infection. A Unicef study presented in 2003 showed that almost 60 per cent of youths are sexually experienced by aged 15 years, and almost all by aged 18. A third of women had never heard of HIV/Aids and over half did not know that transmission could happen from mother to child. In October 2005 there had been 17,620 cases of HIV/Aids reported. While prevalence rates for countries in the region range between 25–40 per cent and the rate in Angola is only 3.9 per cent, UN agencies are still concerned the following years could determine whether Angola is engulfed by the pandemic, particularly if education and basic health provisions remain lacking.
HIV prevalence: 3.9 per cent aged 15–49 in 2003 (World Bank)
Life expectancy: 40 years, 2004 (WHO 2006)
Fertility rate/Maternal mortality rate: 6.7 births per woman, 2004 (WHO 2006); 1,700 maternal deaths per 100,000 live births (World Bank).
Child (under 5 years) mortality rate (per 1,000): 154 per 1,000 live births (2004); 42 per cent of all children are underweight for their age (World Bank).

Welfare

In 2005 plans to return 22,000 refugees living in Zambia got underway, however by November only 35,000 were able to make the return and the programme was extended into early 2006. The numbers of internally displaced persons (IDPs) total over 100,000 and are unable to return home due to poor access and mine infestation and lack of administrative capacity with basic services virtually non-existent. Mine clearance is ongoing as one in every 415 Angolans has been disabled by landmines, but it is estimated in 2005 that six million more remain to be destroyed.

Main cities

Luanda (capital, estimated population 2.5 million in 2008), Huambo (325,207),

Lobito (142,105), Benguela (128,084), Lubango (245,196), Malanje (152,675).

Languages spoken

Local languages: principally Ovimbundu, Kimbundu (the language of the Mbundu), Bakongo and Chokwe.

Official language/s

Portuguese

Media

While the constitution ensures freedom of expression the UNHCR considers Angola does not have press freedom as the government harasses private media outlets and uses anti-defamation laws to protect officials from reports deemed 'offensive'. There is also a special committee that has censorship authority over the media.

National news agency: Angola Press (Angop): www.angolapress-angop.ao

Other news agencies: AngoNoticias (www.angonoticias.com).

Press

There is only one national daily newspaper, operated by the government, in Portuguese Jornal de Angola (), referred to as JA. Private, independent newspapers are all weekly, including Angolense (www.jornalangolense.com), Semanário Angolense (www.semanarioangolense.net), Folha 8, A Capital, Actual, Cruzeiro do Sul and Agora; Diario de Luanda is government-owned.

Broadcasting

National media is state-controlled. Independent media is largely based in major cities, particularly Luanda.

Radio: With high levels of illiteracy radio services are important sources of news and information; most households have radios. The state-run Radio Nacional de Angola (RNA) (www.rna.ao) is the only national radio service, which has a network of five stations broadcasting in Portuguese and local languages, as well as some foreign languages. Other private stations include Luanda Antena Comercial (www.nexus.ao/lac) and Radio Ecclesia (www.recclesia.org), based in Luanda, run by the Roman Catholic Church. As a frequent critic of the government it was denied permission to extend its service into other areas of the country in 2005.

Television: There is a limited national service operated by Televisão Popular de Angola (TPA) (www.tpa.ao).

Pay-TV is available through JumpTV (www.jumptv.com) which carries Portuguese TV programmes from RTP Internacional (RTPi) (http://programas.rtp.pt). TV Cabo (http://www.tvcabo.pt) is a satellite TV network providing international programmes. These services are almost exclusively based in Luanda.

News agencies

National news agency: Angola Press (Angop): www.angolapress-angop.ao

Other news agencies: AngoNoticias (www.angonoticias.com).

Economy

A predicted annual growth rate of 23 per cent was largely attributed, by the IMF, to new deep-water oil fields, which came online in 2007 and added 13 per cent to the existing production rate.

Almost 30 years of civil war have left a trail of damage and destruction in both human and infrastructural terms. Poverty is widespread and human development indicators are low, but while rebuilding of the country and state institutions will take many years, Angola has the potential to provide a good level of income for its entire population. To achieve this, it must overcome corrupt practices, marshal its wealth and natural resources, invest wisely and develop an economy that is not wholly dependent on primary industries. Although the nation has vast natural resources, around three-quarters of the population live on less than US$1 per day. Much of the population relies on farming, despite the poor level of productivity. Land mines, although gradually being cleared, remain a danger.

Angola now has an oil driven economy, fuelled by international, especially Chinese, investment. GDP growth was strong in 2005 at 15.7 per cent, with inflation being brought gradually under control, falling to around 23 per cent (compared with 43.6 per cent in 2004 and 115 per cent in 2003). The positive growth rates are attributable to the high price of oil. Despite GDP of US$32.8 billion in 2005 (up from US$9.5 billion in 2001) most Angolans live in poverty as the oil bonanza has not yet filtered through to improve social indicators.

Structural reforms in the economy are underway, but the IMF maintains that the state still has to reduce the level of its influence in non-oil sectors and sustain macroeconomic management.

External trade

Angola is the second largest export of petroleum in Africa and oil, combined with diamonds, accounts for 99.7 per cent of all exports. Angola has been criticised and warned that the current accounting practices in the oil industry has led to widespread corruption with the loss of many millions of dollars each years. Oil revenue is mainly used to finance government spending. As tradable goods exports only account for 0.3 per cent Angola suffers from Dutch Disease with all non-oil local industries being stifled by the mono-industrial base.

Imports

Principal imports are oil and electrical equipment, vehicles and spare parts, machinery, foodstuffs, medicines, textiles, consumer goods and military goods.

Main sources: South Korea (17.3 per cent total 2006), US (14.3 per cent), Portugal (14.1 per cent).

Exports

Principal exports are crude oil, gas and derivatives (typically 92 per cent of total), diamonds (8 per cent), marble, coffee, sisal, fish and fish products, timber and cotton.

Main destinations: US (38.6 per cent of 2006 total goods exports), China (34.7 per cent), France (4.9 per cent).

Agriculture

Farming

Agriculture's share of GDP has slowly begun to rise as production has increased, as more displaced persons and ex-combatants have returned to their farms. Production was still severely hampered by a list of problems in 2005, including lack of seed and animals, as well as fertilisers, equipment and vehicles, landmines, lack of infrastructure, reduced capabilities of institutions and little access to investment. International donors and financial institutions have provided relief funds and personnel to improve the situation.

Even so, food insecurity is widespread and around 50 per cent of the population is undernourished.

Of the major crops, only coffee is produced in exportable volumes, while the cultivation of sisal and cotton has virtually ceased. Several overseas companies are reportedly interested in rehabilitating sugar cane, cotton and sisal estates.

Livestock farming has been disrupted by insecurity, the neglect of veterinary services and recurrent droughts have affected much of the south and centre of Angola.

Crop production in 2005 included: 8,606,210 tonnes (t) cassava, 870,789t cereals in total, 720,000t maize, 657,451t sweet potatoes, 307,296t potatoes, *360,000t sugar cane, *300,000t bananas, *280,000t oil palm fruit, 137,864t millet, *78,000t citrus fruit, *40,000t pineapples, 108,116t pulses, 92,927t oilcrops, *1,250t green coffee, 3,300t tobacco leaves, *450,000t fruit in total, *271,000t vegetables in total.

* Estimate

Estimated livestock production included: 138,610t meat in total, 85,000t beef, 27,885t pig meat, 10,485t lamb and goat meat, 7,740t poultry, 4,300t eggs, 195,000t milk, 23,000t honey, 10,956t cattle hides.

Fishing
The fishing sector represents less than 5 per cent of GDP. Government policy is aimed at increasing the amount of foreign fishing operations in territorial waters in order to increase foreign investment in the sector and increase licence revenue.
Angola's 1,600km coastline offers some of the richest fishing grounds in Africa, with the annual catch averaging 450,000 tonnes per year before independence. Production has shown a turnaround with an estimate of over 200,000 tonnes, largely due to increased government support for the sector.
In a meeting of African ministers in Namibia, held on 2 July, members discussed illegal and unregulated fishing, which is estimated to cost Africa US$1 billion per annum in lost revenue and the threat to stocks and local artisan fishing.
In 2004 the total marine fish catch was 224,192 tonnes and the total crustacean catch was 4,056 tonnes.

Forestry
Angola has around 18 per cent forest cover with an additional 43 per cent of other wooded land. Most forests are semi-deciduous and located in the north of the country. There are a large number of mangrove forests around Luanda, and in the south and west the forests give way to savannah forest. Around 6.6 per cent of the country's forests are protected, although Angola is the only African country which has not produced a forest law to bring forestry regulation up-to-date.
Angola has considerable timber resources. Valuable tree species, including rosewood, ebony, African sandalwood and mahogany, most of which can be found in the northern tropical forests that have not been commercially exploited since independence. Angola lost around 128,000 hectare of forest cover per year between 1990–2000, which is a modest 0.18 per cent per annum compared to the world average of 0.24 per cent and the African average of 0.78 per cent. In terms of wood products, Angola produces relatively small amounts of sawnwood, pulp and plywood panels. Most industrial roundwood is used for posts, poles and agricultural purposes. Averages annual charcoal production is under 240,000 tonnes and woodfuel just under 3.5 million cubic metres.

Industry and manufacturing
Industrial production is centred on food processing, brewing, sugar, textiles and tobacco products. Also important are light manufactures, such as electrical goods (eg radio production), construction materials, steel production, motor vehicles, detergents, bicycles and chemicals.
Manufacturing accounts for just 4 per cent of GDP.
Activity is concentrated in Luanda, Lobito and Huambo. Output is often sluggish due to shortages of foreign exchange, poor management and a low-paid labour force.
About 60 per cent of total production is accounted for by nationalised industries. The government has embarked upon a privatisation programme involving some 200 state-owned enterprises in a variety of industrial sectors. In early 2003, it passed laws to liberalise the sector and open it up to foreign investment.
The diamond industry has received a vital boom to the industry after De Beers agreed to a joint mining venture with Endiama. Angola is seeking to become one of the top three diamond producers in the world, increasing production to six million carrats between 2003–06.

Tourism
Much work still needs to be done to repair the war-damaged infrastructure, but visitor numbers continue to increase. The Ministry of Hotels and Tourism is attempting to attract foreign capital investment to rebuild the tourism sector. Hotels are in short supply and those that exist have a 99 per cent occupancy rate. The ministry estimates that 50 per cent of the hospitality sector's infrastructure needs renovating and coupled with the poor roads and internal air transport the sector has much to do but also much to gain. Travel and tourism demands are expected to grow by 13.5 per cent in 2005 and a steady 6.9 per cent between 2006–15. The sector contributes around 3 per cent of GDP but has the potential to rise sharply as more facilities become available.
Angola is in partnership with five of its southern African neighbours to establish a huge cross-border eco-tourism, game reserve and tourist resort. Angola has 13 national parks and reserves and has been underdeveloped since the 1960s so that once areas are designated free from landmines, tourism can expand into virtually untamed territories.

Mining
Before independence, Angola was a major producer of iron ore, gold and copper. However, the major disruptions to the country's infrastructure and economy throughout the war have meant that the country's considerable base metal and gold resources have been barely exploited.
Diamonds (mostly of gemstone quality) were the country's second-largest foreign exchange earner in 2004. Endiama is the state-owned diamond mining company dealing with all aspects of diamond exploitation.
Before the ban on Angolan 'conflict' diamonds in 2000, Angola was the fourth-largest diamond producer in the world, producing some US$600 million of rough diamonds per year. By 2003 US$1 billion rough diamonds were sold through the official trading company Sodiam, however the true figure can only be estimated as illegal mining and smuggling from the former Unita-held territories is still a major problem. Without punitive measures to deter this lucrative trade, the revenue from diamonds cannot be fully measured or used.
The government is introducing a register and to licence the many artisan prospectors and control the wholesale price of diamonds, and to establish an export certification scheme to identify legitimate production and sales.
Angola also has deposits of phosphates (Cabinda site, estimated 100 million tonnes; Kindonakasi, estimated 50 million tonnes), gold (at Cassinga and Lombige), copper, lead and zinc (in Tetelo and Alto Zambeze). There are deposits of marble and black granite in southern Angola. The production of ornamental stones was predominantly of black granite which was exported mainly to Spain and Portugal. Angostone Construction and Ornamental Rocks Ltd mines red granite from mines in Cunene province. With an initial investment of US$1.5 million, Angostone is producing 150 cubic metres of red granite per month.

Hydrocarbons
Angola's economic performance is largely determined by the internationally controlled price of oil, and by its level of oil production, which in 2005 accounted for 51.7 per cent of GNP, 92 per cent of exports and provided 90 per cent of government revenues. Production in 2005 was 1,242,000 barrels per day (bpd). There are proven oil reserves of 9.0 billion barrels.
In late 2005 both BP and ChevronTexaco, and the state-owned oil company, Sonangol, announced further oil discoveries in Angola's offshore fields. Added to the new discoveries of the Girassol oil field the level of reserves have substantially increased. Angola joined the Organisation of the Petroleum Exporting Countries (OPEC) in January 2006, at which time no quota was imposed, however it was warned, in March 2007, that plans to produce 2.0 million bpd would represent a limit of production acceptable to OPEC. The planned construction of a new refinery in Benguela will open new opportunities to increase production. International interest in Angolan oil and investment in offshore exploration will further raise potential production.

Proven gas reserves stood at 79.57 billion cubic metres (cum) in 2004, but undiscovered reserves could exceed 700 billion cum. In 2005, Sonangol with Chevron and other partners, began the construction of a liquefied natural gas (LNG) plant at Soyo, with an initial production capacity of five million tonnes of LNG. Until this plant is in production around 85 per cent of all natural gas production is flared. Angola does not produce or import coal.

Energy

The state-owned Empresa Nacional de Electricidade (ENE) is responsible for the generation and supply of electricity in Angola. The country's total electricity generating capacity is estimated at 596MW. Half of this is provided by thermal generation and half through hydroelectric dams. Only 15 per cent of the population has access to electricity. Much of the country's electricity generation and transmission infrastructure was damaged during the civil war. The government estimates it will need US$500 million to recover electricity capacity. Around US$200 million has already been allocated to Angola's six dams, only three of which are working. Rehabilitation of the Matala and Cambambe dams was completed in 2002. Electricity production was also scheduled to begin at the Capanda dam on the Kwanza river in October 2005. The project's second phase, to install two new turbines will be completed in 2007. The first phase will produce 130MW and the second phase 520MW.

A new hydroelectric dam, to be located at Baynes, on the Kunene River, was agreed by the governments of Angola and Namibia in October 2007.

Banking and insurance

The central bank is the Banco Nacional de Angola (BNA) (National Bank of Angola). It issues, and is responsible for, all foreign exchange transactions in conjunction with the ministries of planning, commerce and finance. The banking sector has long been undercapitalised and economically inept. However, the sector has seen some foreign interest, with Portuguese banks such as Banco Fomento Exterior and Banco Totta e Azores opening branches in Luanda.

In 2005 the Banco de Poupança e Crédito (Bank for Savings and Credit) and World Vision International, began a programme of micro-credit, by offering 1,900 families at least US$200 and 79 small farmers associations up to US$10,000 for agricultural purposes.

Central bank

Banco Nacional de Angola (BNA) started functioning in late-1996 as the central bank, ceasing its commercial activities, as part of the government's financial reforms.

Main financial centre

Luanda

Time

GMT plus one hour

Geography

Angola lies on the west coast of Africa, bordered by the Democratic Republic of Congo (DRC) to the north, Zambia to the east and Namibia to the south.The Cabinda district is separated from the rest of the country by the estuary of the River Congo and DRC, with the Republic of Congo lying to its north.

Hemisphere

Southern

Climate

In Luanda and northern regions, October–April is hot and humid with usual temperatures ranging from 28–32 degrees Celsius (C), with a maximum of 34 degrees C. April–September is hot but less humid with daytime temperatures ranging from 25–30 degrees C and cool evenings. Southern regions are more temperate and rainfall can be frequent and heavy, particularly in April.

Dress codes

Informal dress is suitable for most occasions. Lightweight suits are recommended for business meetings. Visitors to the central and southern plateaux will need warm clothes at night, as will visitors to the coastal region during May to September.

Entry requirements

Passport and visa requirements are liable to change at short notice. It is advisable to check with the local Angolan Embassy/consulate at the outset.

Passports

Required by all. Passport must be valid for at least six months and contain two blank pages for stamping. Return or onward ticket is also required.

Visa

Required by all (except transit passengers remaining within the airport). Must be obtained in advance of arrival. Valid for 90 days.

A business visitor must provide a letter of invitation from a local Angolan company or institution and an own company letter stating purpose of visit.

An exit permit, provided by the same office which issued the visa, is also required.

Currency advice/regulations

There are no restrictions on the amount of foreign currency that can be taken into Angola, but it must be declared on arrival. The export of foreign currency is limited to US$5,000; the export of Angolan currency is prohibited

Customs

Many goods may not be imported without government authorisation and licensing.

Health (for visitors)

Mandatory precautions

Yellow fever vaccination certificate is required on arrival and may be demanded by some airlines before departure.

Advisable precautions

Hepatitis A and B, typhoid, tetanus, meningococcus and polio vaccinations are recommended. Malaria prophylaxis is essential. There is a rabies and cholera risk.

Water precautions must be taken.

Travel insurance, including emergency medical evacuation, is essential. All medication, with prescriptions, should be carried by travellers.

Hotels

Hotel accommodation is in short supply, although much existing capacity has been upgraded. Bookings should be made at least one month in advance of travel. Bookings cannot be made by airline companies or at airports.

Credit cards

American Express accepted at Presidente and Tivoli hotels. Generally, credit cards are not accepted.

Public holidays (national)

Fixed dates

1 Jan (New Year's Day), 4 Jan (Martyrs of the Colonial Repression Day), 4 Feb (Anniversary of Start of Liberation War), 8 Mar (Women's Day), 4 Apr (Peace and Reconciliation Day), 1 May (Labour Day), 25 May (Africa Day), 1 Jun (International Children's Day), 1 Aug (Armed Forces Day), 17 Sep (Nation's Founder and National Heroes Day), 2 Nov (All Souls Day), 11 Nov (Independence Day), 25 Dec (Christmas Day).

Variable dates

Good Friday, Easter Monday.

Working hours

Banking

Mon–Fri: 0830–1130, 1400–1530.

Business

Mon–Fri: 0830–1230, 1430–1800; Sat 0830–1230.

Government

Mon–Fri: 0800–1200, 1400–1700.

Telecommunications

Telephone/fax

Telephone and mobile phone usage and infrastructure are expanding, but international connections are unreliable.

Electricity supply

220V AC, 50 cycles.

Social customs/useful tips

Travel permits may be required for travel outside Luanda province. Visitors are advised to carry spare passport photographs. Visitors should not attempt to photograph any public building, infrastructure or security forces or use binoculars in the vicinity.

Security
Travel by car in many parts of Luanda is relatively safe by day, but doors should be locked, windows closed and packages stored out of sight. Walking in Luanda after dark should be avoided.
There is the possibility of banditry and danger from landmines laid during the civil war. Frequent checkpoints and poor infrastructure contribute to unsafe travel on roads outside Luanda. Police and military personnel are heavily armed and can be unpredictable; their authority should not be challenged. No travel should be undertaken on roads outside the city after nightfall.
Throughout Angola, taking photographs or using binoculars near anything that could be perceived as being of military or security interest, including government buildings, could lead to problems with authorities and should be avoided at all costs.

Getting there
Air
National airline: TAAG (Linhas Aéreas de Angola). In July 2007 the European Union banned TAAG from EU air space, due to safety concerns.
International airport/s: Luanda-4 de Fevereiro (Code: LAD), 4km from city, restaurant. No taxis, public telephones or banking services.
Airport tax: None
Surface
Road: Road travel is not generally practicable, though access is now possible across the Namibian frontier to the south.
Rail: Rail travel to Angola is difficult due to regional conflict and war damage which has destroyed railways and bridges. The Benguela railway, which ran from the Zambian copperbelt to the port of Lobito, is being repaired.
Water: Angola has several ports along its Atlantic seaboard with the possibility of passenger traffic from other coastal African countries.
Main port/s: Cabinda, Lobito, Luanda, Namibe. Lobito and Luanda are being repaired.

Getting about
National transport
Air: Most of the country is only accessible by air. TAAG operates domestic flights connecting to main centres but these can be unreliable. There are separate helicopter services to the Cabinda enclave and some commercial companies, connected to the oil and diamond industries, who operate jet aircraft, may carry passengers. All passengers must carry authorisation to travel (guia de marcha), and business travellers should alert their embassy or representative of their travel plans.
Road: Angola's roads and bridges are gradually being restored. Landmines are a continuing danger, but traffic is now free to travel along the main roads between provincial capitals. The condition of roads ranges widely from reasonable to dire. Night travel is to be strictly avoided.
Buses: There are buses throughout the country but the service is poor and the buses are generally very crowded.
Taxis: Difficult to find and expensive. Travellers arriving by air will need to be met by their sponsors or by their hotel transport service.
Rail: The railway system is under repair, following the damage caused during the civil war. There are irregular passenger services on three routes from Luanda-Malanje, and Lobito-Dilolo, and Namibe-Menongue. Refreshements are available but no sleeping accommodation or air-conditioning is provided.
City transport
Taxis: Unregulated taxis should be avoided. No taxi service from airport to Luanda.
Buses, trams & metro: There are local city buses.

BUSINESS DIRECTORY

The addresses listed below are a selection only. While World of Information makes every endeavour to check these addresses, we cannot guarantee that changes have not been made, especially to telephone numbers and area codes. We would welcome any corrections.

Telephone area codes
Telephone direct dialling code for Angola is +244 followed by area code and subscriber's number.
Luanda 2

Chambers of Commerce
Angolan Chamber of Commerce and Industry, 14 Largo do Kinaxixi, PO Box 92, Luanda (tel: 344-506; fax: 344-629; e-mail: ccira@ebonet.net).

Banking
Banco de Comercio e Industria, 86 Avenida 4 de Fevereiro, Luanda (tel: 333-684; fax: 333-823; e-mail: secretariado@bci.ebonet.net).

Banco Comercial Angolano, 83A Avenida Comandante Valódia, PO Box 6900, Luanda (tel: 449-517; fax: 449-516; e-mail: bca@snet.co.ao).

Banco Africano de Investimentos, 34 Rua Major Kanhangulo, Luanda (tel: 337-369; fax: 335-486).

Banco de Poupança e Crédito, PO Box 1343, Luanda (tel: 233-9158).

Central bank
Banco Nacional de Angola, 151 Avenida 4 de Fevereiro, PO Box 1243, Luanda (tel: 332-633; fax: 390-579; e-mail: sec.gvb@bna.ao).

Travel information
Direcção de Emigração e Fronteiras de Angola (visa queries), Defa, Luanda (tel: 330-314, 330-019).

TAAG-Angola Airlines (Linhas Aéreas de Angola), Rua da Missão 123, CP 179, Luanda (tel: 332-485; fax: 393-548).

Ministry of tourism
Ministerio do Comercio e Turismo (Ministry of Commerce and Tourism), Largo 4 de Fevereiro 3, Luanda (tel: 338-741).

Ministries
Ministry of Agriculture and Rural Development, 2 Avenida Comandante Gika, CP 527 Luanda (tel: 322-694; fax: 323-217).

Ministry of Defence, Rua 17 de Setembro, Luanda (tel: 337-530; fax: 392-635).

Ministry of Education and Culture, Avenida Comandante Gika, CP 1281 Luanda (tel: 322-797; fax: 321-592).

Ministry of Energy and Water, 105 Avenida 4 de Fevereiro, CP 2229 Luanda (tel: 393-681; fax: 393-687).

Ministry of Ex-Servicemen and War Veterans, 2 Avenida Comandante Gika, CP 5466 Luanda (tel: 321-117; fax: 323-561).

Ministry of Family and Women's Advancement, Edifício Palácio de Vidro, Largo 4 de Fevereiro, 1242 Luanda (tel: 338-745; fax: 330-028).

Ministry of Finance, 127 Avenida 4 de Fevereiro, CP 592 Luanda (tel: 332-122; fax: 332-069).

Ministry of Fisheries and Environment, Edifício Atlantico, Avenida 4 de Fevereiro, CP 83 Luanda (tel: 390-690; fax: 333-814).

Ministry of Foreign Affairs, 8 Avenida Comandante Gika, CP 1500 Luanda (tel: 323-250; fax: 393-246).

Ministry of Geology and Mines, Avenida Comandante Gika, CP 1260 Luanda (tel: 326-724; fax: 321-655).

Ministry of Health, Rua 17 de Setembro, CP 1201 Luanda (tel: 322-797; fax: 321-592).

Ministry of Hotels and Tourism, Edifício Palácio de Vidro, Largo 4 de Fevereiro, CP 1242 Luanda (tel: 331-323; fax: 338-211).

Ministry of Industry, 25 Rua Cerqueira Lukoki, CP 594 Luanda (tel: 397-070; fax: 334-700).

Ministry of Information, 1 Avenida Comandante Valódia, CP 2608 Luanda (tel: 342-818; fax: 343-495).

Ministry of the Interior, 204 Avenida 4 de Fevereiro, CP 2723 Luanda (tel: 391-049; fax: 395-133).

Ministry of Justice, Rua 17 de Setembro, CP 2250 Luanda (tel: 330-327).

Ministry of Petroleum, Avenida 4 de Fevereiro, CP 1279 Luanda (tel: 337-440; fax: 372-373).

Ministry of Planning, Largo 17 de Setembro, Luanda (tel: 390-722; fax: 339-586).

Ministry of Posts and Telecommunications, 42 Avenida 4 de Fevereiro, CP 1459 Luanda (tel: 337-799; fax: 330-776).

Ministry of Public Administration, Employment and Social Security, 32 Rua 17 de Setembro, CP 1986 Luanda (tel: 338-654).

Ministry of Public Works and Town Planning, Rua Ed Mutamba, CP 1061 Luanda (tel: 336-717; fax: 333-814).

Ministry of Science and Technology, 25 Rua Cerqueira Lukoki, CP 1288 Luanda (tel: 338-987).

Ministry of Social Assistance and Reintegration, 117 Avenida dos Massacres, CP 102 Luanda (tel: 340-370; fax: 342-988).

Ministry of Territorial Administration, 8 Avenida Comandante Gika, Luanda (tel: 320-638; fax: 323-238).

Ministry of Trade, Edifício Palácio de Vidro, Largo 4 de Fevereiro, CP 1242 Luanda (tel: 338-737; fax: 370-804).

Ministry of Transport, 42 Avenida 4 de Fevereiro, Luanda (tel: 337-744; fax: 337-687).

Ministry of Youth and Sports, Avenida Comandante Gika, CP 5466 Luanda (tel: 321-117; fax: 323-561).

Other useful addresses

Angolan Embassy (USA), 2100 16th Street, NW, Washington DC 20009 (Tel: (+1-202) 785-1156; fax: (+1-202) 785-1258; e-mail: angola@angola.org).

ANGOP (news agency), CP 2181, Luanda (tel: 334-945).

Associação Comercial de Luanda, CP 1275, Edificio Palácio de Comércio, le Andar, Luanda (tel: 322-453).

DHL International Ltd, Avenida Che Guevara 52–52a, CP 1545 (tel: 390-326, 390-376, 392-082).

Direcção dos Servicos de Comércio, CP 1337, Largo Diogo Cão, Luanda.

Direcção dos Servicos de Estatistica (statistical agency), CP 1215, Luanda.

Direcção da Aviacao Civil (National Civil Aviation Directorate), Rua Frederich Engels, 92-6 andar, CP 569, Luanda (tel: 339-412, 338-196, 338-596).

Direcção dos Caminhos de Ferro (National Railways Directorate), Rua Major Kanhangulo, CP 1250, Luanda (tel: 370-061).

Direcção Nacional de Correios e Telecomunicacoes (National Posts and Telecommunications Directorate), Rua Frederich Engels, CP 1459, Luanda (tel: 339-750).

Direcção Nacional da Marinha Mercante e Portos (National Merchant Navy and Ports Directorate), Rua Rainha Ginga, 74-4 andar, Luanda (tel: 332-032, 339-847, 339-848).

Direcção Nacional dos Transportes Rodoviarios (National Road Transport Directorate), Rua Rainha Ginga, 74-1 andar, Luanda (tel: 339-390).

Empresa Nacional de Construcão de Obrtas Industrials (National construction Company for Industrial Projects), Bairro do Cazenga, 5 Avenida Zona Industrial, CP 18612, Luanda (tel: 390-087, 391-478).

Empresa Nacional de Diamantes de Angola (Endiama), Rua Major Kanhangulo 100, CP 1247, Luanda (tel: 333 018; fax: 337 216; www.endiama.co.ao).

Empresa Nacional de Electricidada (ENE - National Electricity Company), Edeficio de Geologia e Minas 7, CP 772, Luanda (tel: 323-382, 337-498, 323-568, 321-498, 321-499).

Importang (state import agency), Calçada do Município 10, CP 1003, Luanda (tel: 392-787).

Institute Foreign Investment, Rue Serqueira Lukoki 25 (tel: 334-700).

Instituto Nacional do Cafe de Angola (INCA – National Coffee Institute of Angola), Rua Dr Alves Maciel 17-1D, Luanda (tel: 370-386).

Instituto Nacional de Estradas de Angola (National Roads Institute), Rua Amilcar Cabral 35-4, Caixa Postal 5667, Luanda (tel: 332-828, 391-536; fax: 335-754).

Radio Nacional de Angola, CP 1389, Luanda.

Sociedade Nacional de Combustiveis (SONANGOL-Angola National Fuels Company), Rua I Congresso do MPLA, Caixa Postal 1316, Luanda (tel: 334-143/9; fax: 333-542/6, 391-782).

Televisão Popular de Angola (TPA), CP 2002, Luanda.

US Embassy, 32 Rua Houari Boumedienne, Luanda (tel: 445-481; fax: 446-924).

National news agency: Angola Press (Angop): www.angolapress-angop.ao

Internet sites

AllAfrica.com: www.allafrica.com

African Development Bank: www.afdb.org

Africa Online: www.africaonline.com

Angola News: www.angolanews.com

Jornal de Angola: www.jornaldeangola.com

Anguilla

KEY FACTS

Official name: Anguilla

Head of State: Queen Elizabeth II; represented by Governor Andrew George (from 10 Jul 2006)

Head of government: Chief Minister Osbourne Fleming (ANA) (since 2000; re-elected 2005)

Ruling party: Anguilla United Front (AUF) alliance, comprising the Anguilla National Alliance (ANA) and the Anguilla Democratic Party (ADP) (since 2000; re-elected 21 Feb 2005)

Area: 96 square km (Anguilla 91 square km, Sombrero 5 square km)

Population: 13,600 (2006)*

Capital: The Valley

Official language: English

Currency: East Caribbean dollar (EC$) = 100 cents

Exchange rate: EC$2.70 per US$ (fixed rate)

GDP per capita: US$9,711 (2006)*

GDP real growth: 12.00% (2007)*

Unemployment: 7.80% (rates for under aged 25 typically 29 per cent) (last published rate 2002)

Inflation: 2.40% (2007)

Balance of trade: -US$115.34 million (2004)

Foreign debt: US$11.00 million (2004)

Visitor numbers: 53,987 (2004)

* estimated figure

COUNTRY PROFILE

Historical profile

Anguilla was originally settled about 1,500BC by Arawak Indians, who called it Malliouhana, and later by Carib Indians.
1650 The British established a colony on Anguilla.
1745 and 1796 Anguilla repelled attacks by France.
1882 Anguilla became part of a larger colony governed from St Kitts.
1967 St Kitts-Nevis-Anguilla became a state, in association with the UK. (The status of an associated state allowed St Kitts-Nevis-Anguilla to become independent internally while the British government retained responsibility for external affairs and defence).
1969 Two brief Anguilla rebellions ended after British security forces were sent to to install a British commissioner.
1971 The Anguilla Act was passed by the British parliament. A major provision of the Act stated that, should St Kitts-Nevis-Anguilla initiate legislative steps to terminate the status of association, Anguilla could be separated formally from the other islands.
1980 Anguilla separated from St Kitts-Nevis and became a British Dependent Territory.
1982 A new constitution gave Anguilla greater control over its internal affairs.
1994 The Anguilla United Party (AUP) was elected and its leader, Hubert Hughes, became chief minister.
1999 Hughes was re-elected, but lost his parliamentary majority when Victor Banks, leader of his coalition partner, the Anguilla Democratic Party (ADP), resigned.
2000 Hughes called a general election – four years early – in order to break the constitutional deadlock. Hughes and the ANP lost the election, which was won by the Anguilla United Front (AUF), coalition led by the Anguilla National Alliance (ANA) and the ADP; Osbourne Fleming (ANA) was appointed chief minister.
2002 Under UK legislation all British Dependent Territories became British Overseas Territories.
2005 The AUF coalition was re-elected in the parliamentary elections. Andrew George was appointed governor.
2006 Wilhelm Bourne was appointed attorney general in succession to Ronald Scipio.
2007 A review of the constitution was begun in August.

Political structure

Constitution
Anguilla Constitutional Order 1 April 1982 (amended 1990), gave greater control over its internal affairs.

Form of state
A self-governing, British Overseas Territory; residents have British citizenship (and by extension access to the European Union). Foreign affairs and defence are administered from the UK

The executive
Executive power rests with an appointed British governor, assisted by an executive council (chief minister, two ex-officio members and not more than three other ministers).
The governor, appointed from the UK, is responsible for defence and external affairs, but is required to consult the chief minister on matters relating to internal security, the police and civil service.

National legislature
The House of Assembly has seven elected members, for five-year terms, plus two nominated members and two ex-officio members.

Legal system
The legal system is based on English common law. Anguilla is a member of the Eastern Caribbean Supreme Court, which is responsible for the high court and court of appeals. Final appeal rests with the Privy Council in the UK.

Last elections
21 February 2005 (parliamentary)
Results: Parliamentary: Anguilla United Front (AUF) coalition won 38.9 per cent of the vote (four seats out of seven), the ASA 19.2 per cent (two) and the AUM 19.4 per cent (one). Turnout was 74.6 per cent.

Next elections
2010 (parliamentary)

Political parties

Ruling party
Anguilla United Front (AUF) alliance, comprising the Anguilla National Alliance (ANA) and the Anguilla Democratic Party (ADP) (since 2000; re-elected 21 Feb 2005)

Main opposition party
Anguilla Strategic Alliance (ASA)
Political situation
The UK government began a new inquiry into the governance of British Overseas Territories in August 2007. The committee began taking submissions from interested parties with reference to UK appointed office holders, audit and accountability, procedures and amendments to constitutions, the application of international treaties and human rights and the interaction of Overseas Territories governments and the UK parliament. This is the first review for Anguilla since 1998 and is expected to modernise its constitution and take into account current awareness concerning immigration, development and full, internal self-government, where all executive power rests within Anguilla. An expanded role will also undertake regional treaties. The results of the inquiry may not be known until 2009.

Population
13,600 (2006)*
Last census: October 2001: 11,430
Population density: 104.5 inhabitants per sq km.
Annual growth rate: 3.3 per cent (2003)
Ethnic make-up
Mainly of African descent; some of Irish descent.
Religions
Anglican (40 per cent), Methodist (33 per cent), Seventh-Day Adventist (7 per cent), Baptist (5 per cent), Roman Catholic (3 per cent).

Health
Life expectancy: 77 years (estimate 2003)
Fertility rate/Maternal mortality rate: Two births per woman (2003).

Birth rate/Death rate: 15 births per 1,000 population; five deaths per 1,000 population (2003).
Child (under 5 years) mortality rate (per 1,000): 23 per 1,000 live births (2003)

Main cities
The Valley (capital, estimated population 1,680 in 2008), Stoney Ground (1,395), North Side (1,976).

Languages spoken
Official language/s
English

Media
Press
The only local newspaper, The Anguillan (www.anguillian.com), is published weekly.
Dailies: Chronicle and The Daily Herald are published in St Martin and cover Anguillan news.
Periodicals: What We Do in Anguilla is an annual magazine with tourist information.
Broadcasting
Radio: The government-owned national radio station, Radio Anguilla, operates Radio Axa (www.radioaxa.com) with news, music and talk shows. There are several private radio stations including some with religious programming such as New Beginning Radio, The Caribbean Beacon and Voice of Creation. General interest stations include Klass FM (www.klass929.com), Heart Beat Radio (http://hbr1075.com) and Kool FM (www.koolfm103.com).
Television: The Caribbean Cable Communications operates Anguilla Television with two channels offering local and international programmes.

Economy
There are very few natural resources in Anguilla, which has come to rely on financial services, tourism, export of lobsters, emigrants' remittances, grants-in-aid from the UK and EU, customs duties, bank licence fees and the sale of stamps. The UK, Canada, EU and the Caribbean Development Bank (CDB) are the leading sources of development aid. Anguilla is entirely reliant on imports of fuel and food.
In 2002 the banking sector was removed from an international list of countries obstructing the fight against money laundering. A zero-tax jurisdiction with no income, corporate or inheritance taxes attracts domestic and offshore business. The Anguilla Commercial Online Registration Network (ACORN), the world's first online instant company registration system, has been very successful.
In March 2004, the European Commission (EC) provided US$10 million under the Ninth European Development Fund (EDF) for the development of Anguilla's air transport sector. The balance of previous unspent EDF funds of US$350,000 also went towards this project.

External trade
Anguilla's international trade is largely confined to financial services and small-scale production of mechanical and engineering parts and marine crafts as well as livestock, food stuffs and agricultural products. It built-up a trade in photographic equipment from 2003, growing from US$100,000 to over US$1.6 million within two years of growth.
Imports
Principal imports include fuels, food products, chemicals, manufactures and textiles, vehicles.
Main sources: Typically US, Puerto Rico, UK
Exports
Principal exports include lobsters, fish and other seafood, livestock, salt, rum and concrete blocks.
Main destinations: Typically UK, US, Puerto Rico and other Caribbean islands.
Re-exports

Agriculture
The agriculture sector accounts for around 4 per cent of GDP. There is mainly small-scale farming of peas, corn, sweet potatoes, okra and tropical fruits. The average cultivated plot is less than 0.25ha. Traditional livestock raising (goats, sheep, poultry) is important, with some animals raised for export.
Fishing
Lobster fishing is a major employer and principal earner of foreign exchange; 70t are caught each year. The typical annual fish catch is 250t.

KEY INDICATORS — Anguilla

	Unit	2003	2004	2005	2006	2007
Population	m	0.01	0.01	0.01	0.01	*0.01
Gross domestic product (GDP)	US$bn	0.10	0.15	0.17	0.20	–
GDP per capita	US$	9,934	12,360	13,703	16,183	–
GDP real growth	%	2.6	21.6	8.8	0.1	12.0
Inflation	%	7.0	–	–	*5.3	–
Exports (goods and services)	US$m	73.0	85.0	97.0	109.0	–
Imports (goods and services)	US$m	111.0	137.0	166.0	202.0	–
Total reserves minus gold	US$m	33.3	34.3	39.7	41.8	44.9
Foreign exchange	US$m	33.3	34.3	39.7	41.8	44.9
Exchange rate	per US$	2.70	2.70	2.70	2.70	2.70

* estimated figure

Industry and manufacturing
The manufacturing sector is based primarily on boatbuilding, construction and fish processing and contributes less than 1 per cent to GDP.

Tourism
Tourism is a major source of income for Anguilla, accounting for some 30 per cent of GDP and 28.6 per cent of the labour force. The island caters to both stay-over visitors and excursionists. Like other Caribbean destinations, Anguilla experienced a decline in visitors in 2002, due to a variety of factors; recovery was under way by late 2003 and completed by 2004. The most important market for visitors to Anguilla continues to be the US. Tourists from the UK and Germany have also increased in numbers. A new luxury resort, Temenos Anguilla, with a world-class hotel and an 18-hole golf course, opened in 2006.

Banking and insurance
The island's banking sector is well-regulated and internationally competitive. With a neutral tax jurisdiction and no foreign exchange restrictions, Anguilla's financial services sector has attracted a lot of foreign interest over the years. Around 5,000 companies are registered in Anguilla, with most of them classified as International Business Companies (IBCs). The seven members of the Organisation of Eastern Caribbean States (OECS), Antigua and Barbuda, Dominica, Grenada, Montserrat, St Kitts and Nevis, St Lucia and St Vincent and the Grenadines, share a common currency and central bank. The British Virgin Islands and Anguilla are associate members.

As from July 2005 Anguilla has chosen to adhere to an EU tax directive and inform EU citizens' tax departments about the amount of money in savings accounts and allow tax to be levied from the home country, rather than imposing a withholding tax while retaining a saver's anonimity. Anguilla has also agreed to supply information on tax fraud, for criminal or civil trials, and notify EU member states about additional malpractices.

Central bank
Eastern Caribbean Central Bank, St Kitts and Nevis.

Offshore facilities
The offshore financial services sector in Anguilla is the responsibility of the governor, with day-to-day regulation carried out by the government's financial services department. There are strict laws to combat money laundering and only banks with a previous good record can be licensed as offshore banks. Companies can be incorporated through the Anguilla Commercial Online Registration Network (ACORN).

Time
GMT minus four hours

Geography
Anguilla, a coralline island of 91 square km, is the most northerly of the Leeward Islands. It lies to the north-west of St Kitts and Nevis and 8km (5 miles) to the north of St Maarten, Netherlands Antilles. The island of Sombrero (48km north of Anguilla) is also included in the territory, as are several other uninhabited small islands.

Hemisphere
Northern

Climate
Subtropical with a mean annual temperature of 27 degrees Celsius. It is hottest from July–October, coolest from December–February. Cooling trade winds blow throughout the year. Rain mainly falls September–December.

Entry requirements

Passports
Required by all, except US nationals (all US nationals require a passport for re-entry to the US). Passports must be valid for at least six months after date of entry.

Visa
Required by all, except nationals of US, Canada, EU, Japan and a number of other countries visiting for no longer than six months. All visitors require onward or return tickets and sufficient funds for their stay.

Currency advice/regulations
There are no restrictions on the import of local and foreign currency, but it must be declared. The export of local and foreign currency is limited to the amount imported and declared. Travellers are advised to take travellers cheques in US dollars to avoid additional exchange rate charges.

Health (for visitors)

Mandatory precautions
Vaccination certificate for yellow fever required if arriving from an infected area.

Advisable precautions
Hepatitis A vaccination recommended. Water and food precautions advisable.

Hotels
Several high-quality hotels and a wide selection of villas and apartments.
10–15 per cent service charge is usually included in the bill, plus 10 per cent room tax.

Public holidays (national)

Fixed dates
1 Jan (New Year's Day), 1 May (Labour Day), 25 Dec (Christmas Day), 26 Dec (Boxing Day).

Variable dates
Good Friday, Easter Monday, Anguilla Day (May), Whit Monday, Queen's Official Birthday (Jun), August Monday (first Mon in Aug), August Thursday (first Thu in Aug), Constitution Day (Aug), Separation Day (third Mon in Dec).

Working hours

Banking
Mon–Thu: 0800–1500; Fri: 0800–1700.

Business
Mon–Fri: 0800–1200, 1300–1600.

Government
Mon–Fri: 0800–1200, 1300–1600.

Electricity supply
110/220V AC, 50 cycles

Getting there

Air
National airline: Air Anguilla.
International airport/s: Wallblake (AXA), 3km from The Valley. Daily air service with St Maarten (Netherlands Antilles) and St Thomas (US Virgin Islands) and regular air services from Antigua, St Kitts and San Juan (Puerto Rico). Air taxi and charter services are available from Air Anguilla and Tyden Air.
Airport tax: Departure tax US$20.

Surface
Water: Tropical Shipping and Bernuth Lines sail from Miami to Anguilla. Frequent ferry services operate between Blowing Point and Marigot Bay, St Martin (French Antilles).
Main port/s: Road Bay, Sandy Ground; Blowing Point is a smaller port.

Getting about

National transport
Road: There is no public transport. Use taxis or car hire to travel. Anguilla has about 105km of roads, of which 65km are surfaced, but not to good standard. Public roads cover all parts of the island.

City transport
Taxis: Most generally used form of transport; readily available and inexpensive.

Car hire
Readily available. National licence needed to obtain temporary local licence. Drive on left.

BUSINESS DIRECTORY

The addresses listed below are a selection only. While World of Information makes every endeavour to check these addresses, we cannot guarantee that changes have not been made, especially to telephone numbers and area codes. We would welcome any corrections.

Telephone area codes
The international direct dialling code (IDD) for Anguilla is +1 264, followed by subscriber's number.

Useful telephone numbers
Police, ambulance, fire: 911

Chambers of Commerce
Anguilla Chamber of Commerce and Industry, PO Box 321, The Valley (tel/fax: 479-2839; e-mail: acoci@anguillanet.com).

Banking
Bank of Nova Scotia, PO Box 250, George Hill, The Valley (tel: 497-3333; fax: 497-3344).

Barclays Bank Plc (UK), PO Box 140, The Valley (tel: 497-2301/2304; fax: 497-2980).

Caribbean Commercial Bank (Anguilla) Ltd, PO Box 23, The Valley (tel: 497-2571/3; fax: 497-3570; e-mail: ccbaxa@anguillanet.com).

Caribbean Development Bank, PO Box 408, Wildey, st Michael, Barbados (1246) 431-1600; fax: (1246) 426-7269).

National Bank of Anguilla, PO Box 44, The Valley (tel: 497-2101/2104; fax: 497-3310).

Central bank
Eastern Caribbean Central Bank, Agency Office, PO Box 1385, Fairplay Commercial Complex, The Valley (tel: 497-5050; fax: 497-5150).

Travel information
Air Anguilla, PO Box 110, The Valley (tel: 497-2643; fax: 497-2982).

National tourist organisation offices
Anguilla Tourist Board, PO Box 1388, The Valley (tel: 497-2759; fax: 497-2710; e-mail: atbtour@anguillanet.com).

Ministries
Ministries: all located at The Secretariat, The Valley (tel: 497-2451).

Ministry of Finance, PO Box 60, The Secretariat, The Valley (tel: 497-5881/3881; fax: 497-5872; e-mail: anguillafsd@anguillanet.com).

Office of the Governor, Government House, PO Box 60, The Valley (tel: 497-2621/2, 497-3312/3; fax: 497-3314/3151; e-mail: govthouse@anguillanet.com).

Office of the Chief Minister, The Secretariat, The Valley (tel: 497-2518; fax: 497-3389).

Office of the Minister of Finance, Planning and Economic Development, The Secretariat, The Valley (tel: 497-2545/2451; fax: 497-3761).

Other useful addresses
Agriculture Department (tel: 497-2615).

All Island Cable TV, George Hill, PO Box 336 (tel: 497-3600; fax: 497-3602).

Anguilla Electricity Co Ltd, PO Box 400, The Valley (tel: 497-5200; fax: 497-5440).

Cable & Wireless (WI) Ltd, Telecoms House, PO Box 77, The Valley (tel: 497-3100; fax: 497-2501; internet site: www.anguillanet.com).

Caribbean Beacon Radio, PO Box 690, The Valley (tel: 497-4340).

Government of Anguilla Financial Services Department, The Secretariat, The Valley (tel: 497-5881; fax: 497-5872; e-mail: anguillafsd@anguillafsd.com; internet site: www.anguillaoffshore.com).

Immigration Office (tel: 497-2451, Ext 129).

Radio Anguilla, The Secretariat, The Valley (tel: 497-2218; fax: 497-2751).

Other news agencies: Caribbean Net News: www.caribbeannetnews.com

Internet sites
Anguilla Financial Services/ACORN: www.anguillafsc.com

Anguilla Guide: www.anguillaguide.com

The Anguillian newspaper: www.anguillian.com

Antigua and Barbuda

KEY FACTS

Official name: Antigua and Barbuda

Head of State: Queen Elizabeth II, represented by Governor General Louise Lake-Tack (from 17 Jul 2007)

Head of government: Prime Minister Winston Baldwin Spencer (UPP) (sworn in 24 Mar 2004)

Ruling party: United Progressive Party (UPP) (elected 23 Mar 2004)

Area: 280 square km (Antigua), 160 square km (Barbuda)

Population: 830,000 (2007)*

Capital: St John's (Antigua); Codrington (Barbuda)

Official language: English

Currency: Eastern Caribbean dollar (EC$) = 100 cents

Exchange rate: EC$2.70 per US$ (fixed)

GDP per capita: US$13,092 (2007)*

GDP real growth: 6.10% (2007)*

Labour force: 30,000 (2003)

Unemployment: 5.00% (2003)

Inflation: 1.50% (2007)*

Foreign debt: -US$543.00 million (2006)

Visitor numbers: 705,000 (2005)

* estimated figure

COUNTRY PROFILE

Historical profile

1493 Columbus sighted Antigua.
1632 Antigua and Barbuda was settled by the British.
1667 Control was passed to Great Britain after a brief period of French control.
1674 First sugar colony was set up in Antigua by Christopher Codrington.
1685 Codrington leased the island of Barbuda from the British crown and imported African slaves to help grow tobacco and sugar.
1834 The slaves of Antigua were freed.
1860 Barbuda reverted to the British crown.
1871–1956 Antigua and Barbuda were administered together as part of the Leeward Islands federation.
1946 Vere Bird formed the Antigua Labour Party (ALP).
1958–62 A member of the Federation of the West Indies.
1967 The island of Antigua and its two dependencies, Barbuda and the uninhabited islet of Redonda, entered into a free association with other British dependencies in the Windward and Leeward Islands.
1969 A Barbuda separatist movement was formed.
1972 The sugar industry was closed down.
1981 Antigua and Barbuda achieved full independence but retaining a monarchy. The ALP won the first post-independence elections with Bird becoming prime minister.
1990 Vere Bird Junior, son of the prime minister, was declared unfit for office by a judicial enquiry which uncovered links with money laundering.
1993 Prime Minister Vere Bird Senor resigned and was replaced by his son, Lester.
1994 The ALP, led by Lester Bird won the general elections.
1995 Riots erupted over the imposition of new taxes. Ivor Bird, brother of the prime minister was convicted of smuggling cocaine into the country. Hurricane Luis struck the islands and destroyed 75 per cent of all homes.
1998 Six Russian-owned banks were closed down by the government, which accused them of money laundering.
1999 The ALP won the elections. The US State Department warned that the country's democratic institutions were being undermined by money laundering and corruption. Hurricane José caused severe damage to the country's infrastructure.
2001 After an investigation by the UK and US into the islands' banking sector subsequent adoption of a series of recommendations resulted in the country being declared co-operative in the fight against international money laundering.
2002 The US$22 million Nevis Street pier was officially opened.
2004 The United Progressive Party (UPP) wonparliamentary elections, ousting the Antigua Labour Party (ALP), which had dominated the country's politics since the 1950s. Winston Baldwin Spencer was sworn in as prime minister.
2005 The development of a major tourist facility began with a land transfer to the US Federal Development LLC and Owens Development Group, in Hatton Bay, Antigua. The multi-million dollar development includes a resort hotel, convention centre, casino and entertainment venue.
2006 The Antigua and Barbuda finance minister chaired the 20th meeting of the Council for Trade and Economic Development (COTED), which opened in Guyana on 12 January. The dispute between Antigua and Barbuda and the US, involving the World Trade Organisation, over the US ban on internet gambling continued despite a WTO ruling in 2005 in favour of the islands. The newly constructed Parliament Building in St John's was dedicated on 30 October.
2007 On 17 July, Louise Lake-Tack was sworn in as the Governor General, after Sir James Carlisle resigned. The WTO ordered the US to pay Antigua compensation for loss of earnings during the dispute over online gambling.

Political structure

Form of state

Independent state; it is a member of the Commonwealth.

The executive

The British monarch is the head of state, represented by a governor general who acts on the advice of the prime minister and the cabinet.

National legislature

Legislative power rests with the bicameral parliament which consists of a 17-member House of Representatives (16 Antiguan seats and one representing Barbuda) elected every five years by universal

suffrage, and a 17-member Senate, appointed by the governor general, mainly on the advice of the prime minister.
The prime minister and the cabinet are responsible to the parliament.

Legal system
The legal system embodies the principles of English statutory and common law. Antigua is responsible for its own magistrate's courts. The regional Eastern Caribbean Supreme Court is responsible for the high court and the court of appeals. The final court of appeal is to the Privy Council in the UK.

Last elections
23 March 2004 (parliamentary)
Results: Parliamentary: the United Progressive Party (UPP) won 55.3 per cent of the vote (12 seats out of 17); the Antigua Labour Party (ALP) 41.8 per cent of the vote (four seats); and the Barbuda People's Movement (BPM) one per cent (one seat).

Next elections
2009 (parliamentary)

Political parties

Ruling party
United Progressive Party (UPP) (elected 23 Mar 2004)

Main opposition party
Antigua Labour Party (ALP)

Political situation
After a landslide victory in the general election in March 2004, Winston Baldwin Spencer and the UPP ended the Bird family's 50-year reign. The election was bitterly fought, with accusations of sleaze and corruption. Spencer promised to stamp out corruption, prosecute those responsible and introduce electoral reform to stop the fraud that had marred previous elections.

Population
830,000 (2007)*

Last census: October 2001: 77,426
Population density: 170 inhabitants per square km. Urban population: 37 per cent (2003).
Annual growth rate: 1.7 per cent 1994–2004 (WHO 2006)

Ethnic make-up
The majority of the population is of African descent; the remainder is of British, Portuguese, Lebanese and Syrian origin.

Religions
Anglican (90 per cent), Methodist, Moravian, Roman Catholic, Pentecostal, Baptist and Seventh Day Adventists.

Education
Literacy rate: 90 per cent (2003)
Enrolment rate: Primary education 6–11 years: 50 per cent; secondary education 33 per cent; tertiary education 20–24 years 6 per cent (2003).

Health
Per capita total expenditure on health (2003) was US$442; of which per capita government spending was US$304, at the international dollar rate, (WHO 2006).
Life expectancy: 72 years, 2004 (WHO 2006)
Fertility rate/Maternal mortality rate: 2.3 births per woman, 2004 (WHO 2006)
Birth rate/Death rate: 18 births per 1,000 population; six deaths per 1,000 population (2003).
Child (under 5 years) mortality rate (per 1,000): 11 per 1,000 live births, 2003 (World Bank)

Main cities
St John's (capital of Antigua, estimated population 22,077 in 2008); Codrington (capital of Barbuda, 150).

Languages spoken
English patois is widely spoken. French also spoken by a small number of people.

Official language/s
English

Media
Press
Dailies: There are two local newspapers including Antigua Sun (www.antiguasun.com), which also produces a Sunday edition, and The Daily Observer (www.antiguaobserver.com).

Broadcasting
The Antigua and Barbuda Broadcasting Service (ABS) (www.cmatt.com), provides radio and TV services.
Radio: There are several radio stations, including ABS Radio and private, commercial stations, Observer Radio (www.antiguaobserver.com), ZDK Liberty Radio (www.radiozdk.com) and VIBZFM (www.vibzfm.com). Crusader Radio (www.crusaderradio.com) is owned by the United Progressive political party and the Caribbean Radio Lighthouse (www.mannelli.com/lighthouse) is a Christian station.
Television: The government-owned ABS TV operates two channels and a cable service.

Economy
Tourism dominates the economy of Antigua and Barbuda, accounting for over half of GDP. The size of the tourist sector means the islands are vulnerable to international economic downturn, especially if this occurs in the nearby US. The necessary diversification in the economy is a difficult challange as labour is attracted to the higher wages of the service sectors and away from agriculture and manufacturing industries.
One area into which the islands have successfully diversified is the growing industry of internet gambling sites. This has resulted in a trade dispute with the US over restrictions on US citizens placing bets on these websites. A World Trade Organisation ruling in April 2005 allows the websites to operate in the US.

External trade
Antigua and Barbuda is a member of the Caribbean Community and Common Market (Caricom) which comprises a common market and customs union. It is also a member of the Eastern Caribbean Currency Union (ECCU) using the East Caribbean Dollar.
There is heavy dependence on imported food and energy. The large trading deficit is only partially offset by re-exports (mostly manufactured goods and fuel oil) and earnings from tourism and capital inflows.

Imports
Principal imports include chemicals, fuel and related materials, food and live

KEY INDICATORS — Antigua and Barbuda

	Unit	2003	2004	2005	2006	2007
Population	m	0.07	0.07	0.08	*0.82	*0.83
Gross domestic product (GDP)	US$bn	0.75	0.86	0.88	1.00	*1.03
GDP per capita	US$	11,000	11,270	10,748	*12,203	*13,092
GDP real growth	%	2.5	4.1	5.3	12.2	*6.1
Inflation	%	2.5	-1.3	2.1	1.8	*3.4
Exports (fob) (goods)	US$m	40.0	57.1	120.6	72.0	–
Imports (cif) (goods)	US$m	357.0	402.4	525.2	615.0	–
Balance of trade	US$m	-317.0	-345.2	-404.6	-543.0	–
Current account	US$m	-100.0	-110.0	-127.0	-162.0	*-160.0
Total reserves minus gold	US$m	113.8	120.0	127.3	142.6	143.8
Foreign exchange	US$m	113.8	120.1	127.3	142.6	143.8
Exchange rate	per US$	2.70	2.70	2.70	2.70	2.70

* estimated figure

animals, machinery and transport equipment, other manufactures.
Main sources: US (21.1 per cent total 2005), China (16.4 per cent), Germany (13.3 per cent), Singapore (12.7 per cent) Spain (6.5 per cent)

Exports
Principal exports include petroleum products while small-scale manufacturing enterprises produce bedding and handicrafts, and mechanical and electronic components for export.
Main destinations: Spain (34 per cent total in 2005), Germany (20.7 per cent), Italy (7.7 per cent), Singapore (5.8 per cent), UK (4.9 per cent)

Agriculture
Agriculture typically accounts for around 4 per cent of GDP. Farming is faced with several problems that could weaken its contribution to GDP still further. A limited water supply, soil depletion and drought cause hardship and workers are turning to more lucrative employment in tourism and construction.
The majority of food grown is consumed locally. Fruit and sea-island cotton are grown for export.
Government policy is to encourage self-sufficiency in food. To expand agricultural production capacity, the government, with assistance from the European Development Fund, is promoting livestock development.
An agreement with Cuba has seen Antigua and Barbuda provided with technical assistance in a range of agricultural sectors, including tobacco, fertilisers, pesticides and irrigation.
The estimated crop production in 2005 included: 70 tonnes (t) yams, 60t maize, 285t citrus, 200t sweet potatoes, 350t tomatoes, 220t bananas, 1,430t mangoes, 3,145t vegetables in total, 10,045t fruit in total, 95t seed cotton. Livestock production includes: 1,085t meat in total, 520t beef, 194t pig meat, 161t goat and lamb meat, 210t poultry, 250t eggs, 5,350t milk.

Fishing
Fishing is a growth area. There are shrimp and lobster farms in operation and the catch each year is over 300t. The typical annual fish catch is over 1,500t.
In 2004, the total marine fish catch was 1,728 tonnes and the total crustacean catch was 245 tonnes.

Industry and manufacturing
Activity is centred on food processing, galvanised sheet, paints and light industries (mainly assembly of household appliances, vehicles, garments, paper products). Industry contributes 19 per cent to GDP, of which the construction sector contributes about 13 per cent. Construction activity has been dominated by housing and infrastructure repair as a result of hurricanes.

Tourism
Tourism is the principal economic activity of Antigua and Barbuda, accounting for around 50 per cent of GDP, three-quarters of foreign exchange earnings and 35 per cent of the labour force. The sector was hurt by the depredations of several hurricanes in the 1990s, the global economic downturn and, to a lesser extent, the 11 September 2001 terrorist attacks in the US. The lucrative stay-over market is recovering, with most visitors coming from the US and the UK. Cruise tourism has been targetted for expansion by the government, including development of the St John's waterfront, which, in its first year of operation, resulted in an increase of 45 per cent of cruise-ship arrivals.

Mining
There are known deposits of high quality barytes, limestone and clay. Redonda island was once an important source of phosphates and guano.

Hydrocarbons
Anguilla does not produce any hydrocarbons, relying on imported refined oil, primarily gasoline, jet fuel and distillate.

Energy
The government-owned Antigua Public Utilities Authority (APUA) provides all electricity services to the islands.

Banking and insurance
The seven members of the Organisation of Eastern Caribbean States (OECS), Antigua and Barbuda, Dominica, Grenada, Montserrat, St Kitts and Nevis, St Lucia and St Vincent and the Grenadines, share a common currency and central bank. The British Virgin Islands and Anguilla are associate members.

Central bank
Eastern Caribbean Central Bank, St Kitts and Nevis.

Main financial centre
St John's

Offshore facilities
There is an offshore financial sector offering full tax haven facilities to international business companies, trusts, banks and insurance companies. A corporate income tax was introduced in 1999. The International Financial Sector Regulatory Authority has full oversight of the offshore sector. Service providers are required to report suspicious transactions to the authority under the money laundering legislation.

Time
GMT minus four hours

Geography
The country comprises three islands – Antigua, Barbuda and the uninhabited rocky islet of Redonda. They are situated along the outer edge of the Leeward Islands chain in the West Indies. Barbuda is the most northerly, 40km north of Antigua; Redonda is 40km south-west of Antigua. Guadeloupe lies to the south of the country, Montserrat to the south-west and St Kitts Nevis to the west.

Hemisphere
Northern

Climate
Tropical with temperature range from 21–32 degrees Celsius. Little variation throughout year, although driest from January–March.

Entry requirements
Passports
Required by all.

Visa
Not required for most countries. For a full list of those who may visit for business or tourism without a visa visit www.antigua-barbuda.com. Visits must not exceed six months and visitors must have onward/return tickets, confirmation of accommodation.

Currency advice/regulations
No restrictions on import or export of local or foreign currency, as long as amount is declared on arrival and not exceeded on departure.

Health (for visitors)
Mandatory precautions
Yellow fever vaccination certificate if arriving from an infected area.

Advisable precautions
Hepatitis A vaccination recommended. Water and food precautions advisable. Take medical kit.

Hotels
An 8.5 per cent room tax and 10 per cent service charge are added to hotel bills.

Public holidays (national)
Fixed dates
1 Jan (New Year's Day), 7 Oct (Merchant Holiday), 1 Nov (Independence Day), 9 Dec (VC Bird Day), 25 Dec (Christmas Day), 26 Dec (Boxing Day).

Variable dates
Good Friday, Easter Monday, Labour Day (first Mon in May), Whit Monday, Queen's Official Birthday (Jun), Caricom Day (Jul), Summer Carnival (first Mon and Tue in Aug).

Working hours
Banking
Mon–Thur: 0800–1300, 1500–1700; Fri: 0800–1200, 1500–1700.

Government
Mon–Fri: 0800–1200, 1300–1630. Offices close at 1500 on Fridays.

Shops
Mon–Sat: 0830–1200, 1300–1700. Many shops close Thur 1200.

Electricity supply
220/110V AC, 60Hz. American-style two-pin plugs. Some hotels also have outlets for 240V AC; in this case European-style two-pin plugs are used.

Getting there
Air
National airline: Antigua is a shareholder in LIAT, the regional Caribbean airline.
International airport/s: VC Bird International (ANU), 8km north-east of St John's; duty-free shop, restaurant, post office, car hire.
Airport tax: Departure tax: US$20.
Surface
Main port/s: St John's Deepwater Harbour, Falmouth Harbour, English Harbour.

Getting about
National transport
Air: Scheduled daily services between Antigua and Barbuda.
Road: A network connects all main centres. Over 1,000km of roads, mainly all-weather.
Buses: Restricted service.
City transport
Taxis: Fixed rate system. Taxis are not metered and it is advisable to negotiate fares in advance.
Car hire
National or international licence required to obtain visitor's driving permit. Driving is on the left.

BUSINESS DIRECTORY

The addresses listed below are a selection only. While World of Information makes every endeavour to check these addresses, we cannot guarantee that changes have not been made, especially to telephone numbers and area codes. We would welcome any corrections.

Telephone area codes
The international direct dialling code (IDD) for Antigua and Barbuda is +1 268, followed by subscriber's number.

Chambers of Commerce
Antigua and Barbuda Chamber of Commerce and Industry, North and Popeshead Street, PO Box 774, St John's (tel: 462-0743; fax: 462-4575; email: chamcom@candw.org).

Banking
Antigua and Barbuda Development Bank, 27 St Mary's St, Box 1279, St John's (tel: 462-0838; fax: 462-0839).

Antigua and Barbuda Investment Bank Ltd, High St, Box 1679, St John's (tel: 462-0067/1653; fax: 462-0804).

Antigua Commercial Bank, St Mary's and Thames Sts, PO Box 95, St John's (tel: 462-1217/9/2085/1860/4; fax: 462-1220).

Bank of Antigua, 1000 Airport Blvd, Box 315, St John's (tel: 462-4283; fax: 462-0040).

Bank of Nova Scotia, High St, Box 342, St John's (tel: 480-1500; fax: 480-1554).

Barclays Bank plc, High Street, Box 225, St John's (tel: 485-5000; fax: 462-4910).

Caribbean Banking Corporation Ltd, High Street, Box 1324, St John's (tel: 462-4217; fax: 462-5040).

CIBC Caribbean Ltd, High St and Corn Alley, Box 28, St John's (tel: 462-0836/7/0998/1278).

Royal Bank of Canada, High and Market Sts, Box 252, St John's (tel: 462-0325/6; fax: 462-1304).

Swiss American National Bank of Antigua, High St, Box 1302, St John's (tel: 462-4460; fax: 462-0274).

Central bank
Eastern Caribbean Central Bank, Agency Office, PO Box 741, Factory Road, St John's (tel: 462—2489; fax: 462-2490).

Travel information
Antigua Hotels and Tourist Association (AHTA), Lower Redcliffe St, PO Box 454, St John's (tel: 462-0374/3703; fax: 462-3702; e-mail: ahta@candw.ag).

LIAT (1974) Ltd, PO Box 819, VC Bird International Airport (tel: 462-0700; fax: 462-4765).

Ministry of tourism
Ministry of Tourism, Culture and the Environment, New Administration Building, Queen Elizabeth Highway, St John's (tel: 462-0787; fax: 462-2836).

National tourist organisation offices
Antigua and Barbuda Department of Tourism, PO Box 363, Long and Thames Streets, St John's (tel: 462-0480, 462-0029; fax: 462-2483).

Ministries
Minister of State in the Prime Minister's Office and Leader of Government Business in the Senate, Queen Elizabeth Highway, St John's (tel: 462-5933; fax: 462-3225).

Ministry of Agriculture, Lands, Fisheries, Planning and Co-operatives, Nevis and Temple Sts, St John's (tel: 462-1543/5571; fax: 462-6104).

Ministry of Education, Youth, Sports and Community Development, Church St, St John's (tel: 462-4959; fax: 462-4970).

Ministry of Finance and Social Security, High St, St John's (tel: 462-4301; fax: 462-1622/5093).

Ministry of Foreign Affairs, Queen Elizabeth Highway, St John's (tel: 462-4956; fax: 462-3225/9377).

Ministry of Health and Civil Service Affairs, Cross St, St John's (tel: 462-8783; fax: 462-9308/5003).

Ministry of Justice and Legal Affairs, Nevis St, St John's (tel: 462-8867; fax: 462-2465).

Ministry of Labour and Home Affairs, c/o State Insurance Building, Redcliffe St, St John's (tel: 462-0567; 462-1595).

Ministry of Public Utilities, Public Works and Energy, St John's St, St John's (tel: 462-3851/4772; fax: 462-4622).

Ministry of Trade, Industry and Commerce Affairs, Redcliffe Street, St John's (tel: 462-4951; fax: 462-5003).

Other useful addresses
Antigua and Barbuda Embassy (USA), 3216 New Mexico Avenue, NW, Washington DC 20016 (tel: (+1-202) 362-5122; fax: (+1-202) 362-5225).

Antigua Public Utility Authority (APUA), PO Box 416, St Mary's Street, St John's (tel: 462-4990; fax: 462-2516).

British High Commission, PO Box 483, 11 Old Parham Road, St John's (tel: 462-0008/9, 463-0010).

Cable and Wireless Telex Bureau, St Mary's Street, St John's (tel: 462-0840/2).

Directorate of Offshore Gaming, 2nd Floor, Mutual Finance Centre, 9 Factory Rd, Room 216, PO Box 588, St John's (tel: 481-3300; fax: 481-3305; e-mail: director@antiguagaming.com; internet site: http://antiguagaming.d2g.com).

Free Trade & Processing Zone, PO Box 817, St John's (tel: 460-5552; fax: 460-5553; e-mail: ftpzone@candw.ag; internet site: www.antiguafreezone.com).

Industrial Development Board, 34 Newgate Street, St John's (tel: 462-1038; fax: 462-2836).

Other news agencies: Caribbean Net News: www.caribbeannetnews.com

Internet sites
East Caribbean Central Bank: www.eccb-centralbank.org

Investment and general information: www.antigua-barbuda.com

Official travel guide: www.geographia.com/an

Argentina

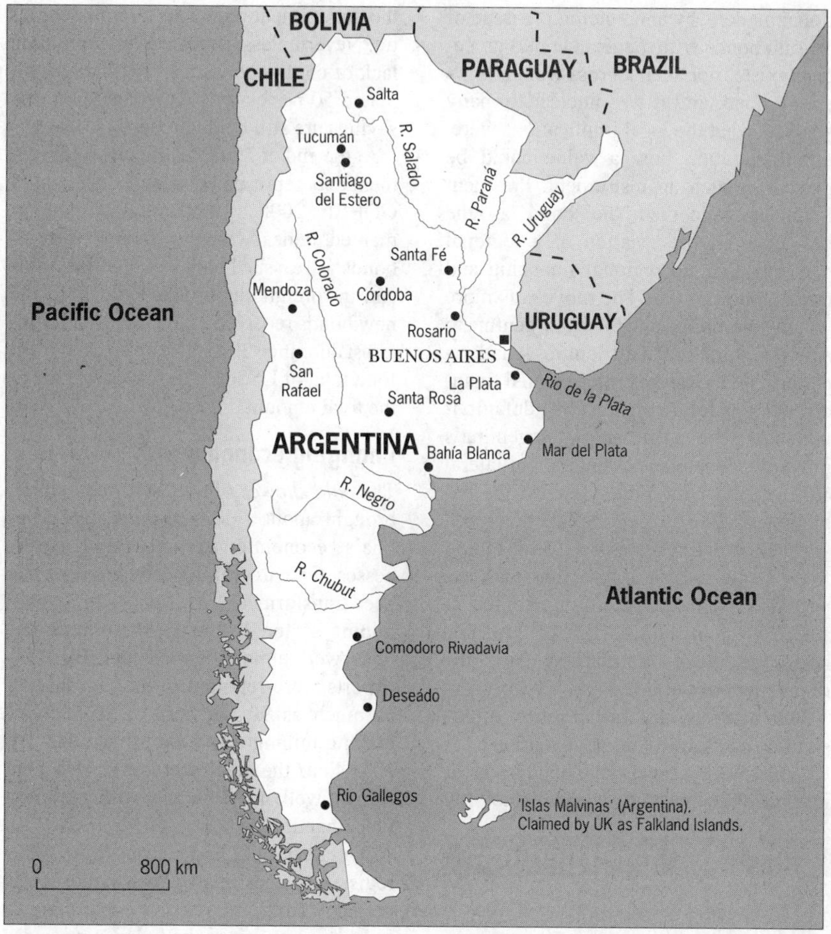

KEY FACTS

Official name: República Argentina (Argentine Republic)

Head of State: President Cristina Fernández de Kirchner (FPV) (from 10 Dec 2007)

Head of government: President Cristina Fernández de Kirchner

Ruling party: Frente para la Victoria (FPV) (Front for Victory)

Area: 2,766,889 square km

Population: 39.36 million (2007)*

Capital: Buenos Aires

Official language: Spanish

Currency: Peso (P) = 100 centavos

Exchange rate: P3.02 per US$ (Jul 2008)

GDP per capita: US$6,606 (2007)

GDP real growth: 7.50% (2007)

Labour force: 15.40 million (2004)

Unemployment: 10.60% (2006)

Inflation: 8.80% (2007)

Oil production: 698,000 bpd (2007)

Balance of trade: US$12.81 billion (2005)

Foreign debt: US$168.00 billion (2004)

Visitor numbers: 4.16 million (2006)*

Annual FDI: US$4.70 billion (2005)

* estimated figure

At first sight, in 2006 the Argentine economy appeared to be performing well. High prices for its raw materials and commodities, strong demand – especially from Asia – and a competitively valued currency had all conspired to create a deceptive 'never had it so good' impression, as current account surpluses continued to rack up. But Argentina's inexperienced president, Nestor Kirchner, was seen by many observers as an opportunistic small town politician rather than the visionary statesman that Argentina will need if it is ever going to get its economy on to a truly sound footing.

Mr Kirchner's popularity had overtones of the popularity that had surrounded many Argentine presidents in the past. A new stage production of the musical *Evita* in London served as an ironic reminder of the similarities between Mr Kirchner's populist policies and the failed, statist policies of many Argentine governments in the 1970s and 1980s. Somehow, Argentina's economic policies have never managed to develop in a linear fashion, preferring instead a short term fix generated by circular policies in which the same tired solutions seem to bring about the same weary problems. Mr Kirchner's worrying introduction of price ceilings, export duties and restrictions and the economic distortions they inevitably create were seen by most economists as the thin end of an interventionist wedge. The apparent affinity between President

Kirchner and Venezuela's maverick President Hugo Chavez smacked more of short term interests and expediency than of political wisdom and long term common sense.

Dissenting views

One serious dissenting view was expressed by former economics minister Roberto Lavagna, dismissed by President Kirchner in October 2005. Mr Lavagna is seen by many Argentines as the architect of their country's economic recovery following the 2001 debt default and ensuing crisis. Following his dismissal Mr Lavagna saw fit to register his concern over increased state controls and misdirected state investments, as well as over the increasingly close relationship with Venezuela, which Mr Lavagna saw as creating a climate for socialist economic policies. Argentina's next presidential elections are to be held in October 2007; Mr Kirchner's policies appear to have had the desired effect of increasing his popularity, rendering it unlikely that any alternative candidate would attract much popular support.

Debt and loans

In 2001 Argentina had made international financial history with the biggest sovereign debt default in history, followed by a less than orthodox – and certainly less than popular – restructuring programme. The aftermath of the restructuring continued into 2006 as bondholders attempted to enforce rulings against the Argentine government. By mid-2006 the figure for unresolved Argentine debt remained at around US$20 billion. In September 2006 the World Bank's International Court for the Settlement of Investment Disputes (ICSID) had registered 34 cases against the Argentine government, totalling US$16 billion. At about the same time, Argentina again surprised the international markets by announcing the issue of a 'joint bond' with Venezuela. No precedent existed for such a cross frontier sovereign bond, and it was unclear to many analysts what the legal implications were, not to mention how a value could be placed on such an instrument. President Kirchner welcomed the bond as the pre-cursor of the creation of a regional bank opening up regional financing and credit opportunities. The move was more widely interpreted as a bid by Argentina to side step some of the difficulties it had experienced in accessing international financial markets following the 2001 default. It was also seen as reflecting Argentina's growing dependency on its bi-lateral co-operation with Venezuela. At the beginning of 2006 Argentina had borrowed – at below market rates – US$3.2 billion from Venezuela, a figure that was expected to rise by US$2 billion with the issue of the joint bond. Most of the sums borrowed were earmarked for the re-payment of the IMF.

2006 also saw the formal return of Argentina to world money markets. A US$500 million seven-year bond issue for international investors was satisfactorily received internationally – over 80 per cent of demand coming from outside Argentina, attracted by the premium interest rates offered by the Argentina government to compensate for the continuing absence of an overall debt settlement. In 2005 Argentina began to benefit from World Bank loans. A combination of high raw material prices and domestic liquidity have helped the government reduce its overall debt ratio. Nevertheless, a measure of continuing lack of confidence is the fact that an estimated 50 per cent of Argentine domestic savings are still held abroad.

At the end of 2005, restructured government debt represented some 70 per cent of GDP. In 2005 a debt swap was implemented under which different types of bonds were issued both in Argentine pesos and in foreign currencies. Holders of the new bonds received cash payments for interest due since 2003. The swap accounted for a total of US$63 billion, 76 per cent of the total amount due.

Changing economy

The *cold shower* of the 2001 debt default brought about a deep re-think of Argentina's economic strengths and weaknesses. One area of the economy that has been transformed as a result is Argentina's mining sector. In the 1990s, mining exports were almost non-existent. By 2006 exports were reported to be contributing as much as 90 per cent of production, making mining a key export activity. By extension, the steel sector has also performed well on the back of strong domestic demand.

Overall growth had continued in 2005, registering an estimated growth rate of 9.2 per cent. Both imports and exports grew, leaving a surplus in the balance of trade. Estimates for 2006 suggested that this level of economic growth would continue, although doubts continued to surround the effect of the Kirchner government's controversial price controls and other interventionist measures.

The construction sector, both public and private, continued to register strong growth throughout 2005 and into 2006. Machinery and equipment investment and imports also flourished. In the agricultural sector output also showed strong growth, with record grain harvest figures and improved livestock exports. Industrial output grew at an annual rate of 7.5 per cent, held back by supply and labour restrictions. Over the full year of 2005, the employment rate increased by about one percentage point, causing the unemployment figure to drop to 11.6 per cent.

KEY INDICATORS — Argentina

	Unit	2003	2004	2005	2006	2007
Population	m	37.99	38.47	38.59	38.97	*39.36
Gross domestic product (GDP)	US$bn	129.60	153.00	181.55	212.71	260.00
GDP per capita	US$	3,222	3,912	4,704	5,458	6,606
GDP real growth	%	8.7	9.0	9.2	*8.5	7.5
Inflation	%	13.9	4.4	9.6	10.9	8.8
Unemployment	%	16.2	13.8	11.6	–	–
Oil output	'000 bpd	828.6	756.0	725.0	716.0	698.0
Natural gas output	bn cum	41.0	44.9	45.6	46.1	44.8
Exports (fob) (goods)	US$m	29,376.0	34,453.0	40,106.0	33,908.0	–
Imports (cif) (goods)	US$m	13,813.0	21,185.0	27,302.0	23,484.0	–
Balance of trade	US$m	15,563.0	13,267.0	12,805.0	10,424.0	–
Current account	US$m	7,390.0	3,060.0	3,495.0	5,156.0	*2,815.0
Total reserves minus gold	US$m	14,153.0	18,884.0	27,179.0	30,903.0	44,682.0
Foreign exchange	US$m	13,145.0	18,007.0	22,742.0	30,421.0	44,175.0
Exchange rate	per US$	3.14	2.94	3.08	3.07	3.14

* estimated figure

The estimated balance of payments surplus for 2005 was US$4.7 billion, representing around 2.5 per cent of GDP. After the repayment of loan to international agencies, Argentina's financial account still showed a surplus. Reserves rose to US$26 billion by late 2005. Exports rose across the board by an estimated 15 per cent, generating US$40 billion. Of significance was the 30 per cent increase in agricultural exports. The rise in exports was matched by a commensurate increase in imports.

Outlook

Argentina's short term economic prospects will be largely determined by the run up to the October 2007 presidential elections. President Kirchner has firmly hitched his colours to the populist mast, steadily increasing the role of the state in the economy – not always helpfully. In late 2006 it looked unlikely that a viable alternative candidate would emerge – even one with such sound credentials as Roberto Lavagna. Since being dismissed from the government, Mr Lavagna had distanced himself from Mr Kirchner, becoming overtly critical of the government's leftward leanings and rapprochement with Mr Chavez.

Like the curate's egg, Argentina's economy is only good in parts – inflation rates are probably understated, investment levels remain low, the stock market appears to be lifeless and a massive 50 per cent of domestic reserves continue to be held abroad. If re-elected, it looks unlikely that Mr Kirchner will have either the will or the vision to adopt less popular, but economically sounder, policies.

Risk assessment

Politics	Fair
Economy	Improving
Regional stability	Good

COUNTRY PROFILE

Historical profile

1916–22 and 1928–30 President Hipolito Yrigoyen was Argentina's first popularly elected president. He was ousted in his second term by the armed forces.
1939—1945 Argentina was neutral during the Second World War and initially refused to break diplomatic relations with Japan and Germany.
1943 A military government, with pro-fascist sympathies, assumed power.
1944 Argentina broke diplomatic relations with Japan and Germany and declared war on them.
1946 General Juan Domingo Perón, a leading figure in the military government, won a free presidential election. He and his wife, Evita, became increasingly popular as social services spending grew. However, foreign exchange reserves built up during the Second World War were squandered by nationalising the railways and other public utilities. President Perón became increasingly repressive towards his critics and the Catholic Church.
1949 A new constitution strengthened the power of the president and criticising the government became a criminal offence, leading to the jailing of Perón's opponents.
1951 Perón was re-elected with a large majority.
1952 Perón's popular wife, 'Evita', died of cancer. Consequently, his support began to wane.
1955 An attempted coup by the navy in June was crushed by the army. However, in September the armed forces seized power, sending Perón into exile. A series of unstable military and civilian governments in subsequent years saw the Perónists win the few elections held.
1973 Following a Perónist electoral victory, Hector Campora became president. He resigned, following widespread civil disturbances and was succeeded by Perón who had been allowed to return from exile.
1974 Perón died and was succeeded by his wife, María. The country sank into political and economic chaos.
1976 The armed forces overthrew the government and installed General Jorge Videla as president. The military junta suppressed left-wing opposition groups – between 6–15,000 people 'disappeared' in the 'dirty war' that followed the coup.
1981 General Roberto Viola succeeded Videla as president. After Viola, General Leopoldo Galtieri became president.
1982 The military government invaded the Falkland Islands/Islas Malvinas. Argentina's defeat by the UK, on top of a collapsing economy, was a major factor in the end of military government and a return to democracy.
1983 Raul Alfonsín of the Unión Cívica Radical (UCR) (Radical Civic Union) won the presidential elections.
1989 Perónist Carlos Ménem became president and began a programme of economic austerity in an effort to stabilise and restructure the ailing economy.
1990 Full diplomatic relations with the UK were restored, although Argentina continued to claim the Falklands.
1992 The peso was introduced as a new currency and was pegged to the US dollar at a one-to-one rate.
1995 Ménem was re-elected president.
1997 1997 International pressure was applied when a judge in Spain called for the arrest of senior military officers involved in human rights violations during the 'dirty war'. However an amnesty protected them.
1998 Argentine judges ordered arrests in connection with the abduction of hundreds of children of women arrested during the 'dirty war'. A protracted recession began.
1999 Fernando de la Rúa won the presidential election, but his centre-left Alianza failed to secure an absolute majority in the lower house of Congress.
2001 The amnesty laws allowing members of the armed forces to escape prosecution for human rights abuses was overturned. The economy, devastated by years of recession, was near to collapse, leading to public protests. The Perónists won the mid-term parliamentary elections and both houses of Congress came under opposition control. President Fernando de la Rúa resigned, Ramon Puerta took over briefly before Adolfo Rodríguez Saa became president. Saa's presidency only lasted until mass demonstrations against his austerity measures resulted in his resignation. Eduardo Camaño assumed the presidency for a 48-hour period.
2002 Presidential elections resulted in Perónist, Eduardo Duhalde, becoming the fifth president in two weeks. The peso was devalued breaking the link with the US dollar. The president was given the power to pass some laws, without congressional approval, for the following two years. The peso was floated.
2003 Carlos Saúl Menem withdrew from the presidential election leaving Néstor Kirchner to win by default. Nearly twice the annual average rainfall fell in two days in Santa Fe province in May, causing major flooding.
2004 In April, an international arrest warrant was issued for the former president, Carlos Menem, over allegations of fraud. Menem returned from exile in Chile in December, following the cancellation of two international warrants for his arrest. In July, the IMF accepted that its handling of Argentina's financial crisis in 2001 had aggravated the deepening recession and that it had continued to lend Argentina money when its debt burden had become unsustainable.
2005 In March, Argentina's US$100 billion debt restructuring offer was accepted. The country hosted a thirty-four nation Summit of the Americas in November; violent protests accompanied proceedings.
2006 Argentina cleared its debt to the IMF in January. Price controls were extended in October in a bid to counter inflationary tendencies.

2007 In presidential elections, held on 28 October; Cristina Fernández de Kirchner (FPV), the wife of the current president, won 44.95 per cent of the vote, Elisa Carrió (Confederación Coalición Cívica (CCC) (Civic Coalition Confederation)) the closest rival won 22.9 per cent. With more than a 10 per cent lead a second round was not required. Turnout was around 74.1 per cent. President Kirchner's inauguration took place on 10 December.
2008 Former president Fernando de la Rua was charged with 'aggravated bribery' by a federal court in February. He was accused of bribing senators during the 2001 Congress debate to vote in favour of labour reforms.

Political structure

Constitution

Under the 1853 constitution which was reinstated by the military government in 1955, power is separated into executive, legislative and judicial branches at federal and state level. Each of the 22 states has its own subordinated constitution, elects its own executive and legislature and establishes its own judiciary.

Form of state

Federal presidential democratic republic

The executive

Executive power is vested in the president, who is elected by popular vote every four years, with a limit of two terms in office.

National legislature

Legislative power is held by the bicameral Congress, consisting of the Chamber of Deputies with 257 members elected by universal suffrage for four years, with half of the chamber renewed every two years. The Senate has 72 members, directly elected for six years, with one-third renewed every two years.
The cabinet and chief of cabinet can be removed only by a majority vote in each congressional house.

Legal system

The judiciary is independent of the government and forms the third 'pillar' of the constitution. Since 1998, federal judges have been elected and dismissed by a body comprising lawyers and academics. The election of judges was intended to reduce the endemic political influence that had previously affected the Argentine legal system, especially at the local level, for many years. There is a Supreme Court system at national and provincial levels.

Last elections

23 October 2005 (parliamentary); 27 October 2007 (presidential).

Results: Presidential: Cristina Fernández de Kirchner (FPV) won 44.9 per cent of the vote, Elisa Carrio (Confederación Coalición Cívica (CCC) (Civic Coalition Confederation)) 22.9 per cent and Roberto Lavagna (UNA) 16.9 per cent; all other candidates won less than 10 per cent. Turnout was 74.14 per cent.
Parliamentary: Chamber of Deputies, the Frente para la Victoria (FPV) (Front for Victory) won 29.9 per cent of the vote (50 seats out of 127 contested), the Unión Cívica Radical (UCR) (Radical Civic Union) 8.9 per cent (10), the Alternativa por una República de Iguales (ARI) (Alternative for a Republic of Equals) 7.2 per cent (8), the Partido Justicialista (PJ) (Justicialist Party) 6.7 per cent (9), the Propuesta Republicana (PRO) (Republican Initiative Alliance) 6.2 per cent (9), and the Frente Justicialista (FJ) (Justicialist Front) 3.9 per cent (7); other minor parties won less than three seats each. Turnout is 70.9 per cent. Senate, the FPV won 45.1 per cent of the vote (14 seats out of 24 contested), the FJ 17.2 per cent (3), and the UCR 7.5 per cent (2). Turnout is 72.3 per cent.

Next elections

2011 (presidential and parliamentary)

Political parties

Ruling party

Frente para la Victoria (FPV) (Front for Victory)

Main opposition party

Unión Cívica Radical (UCR) (Radical Civic Union)

Political situation

Population

39.36 million (2007)*

Last census: November 2001: 36,260,130

Population density: 14 inhabitants per square km. Urban population: 88 per cent of total (1995–2001).

Annual growth rate: 1.1 per cent 1994–2004 (WHO 2006)

Ethnic make-up

White (97 per cent), principally descendants of Italian and Spanish immigrants. Minority groups include the Buenos Aires Jewish community and Anglo-Argentines throughout the country. The major indigenous nations are the Quechua of the north-west, the Mapuche of northern Patagonia and the Matacos, Tobas and others who inhabit the Chaco and north-eastern cities like Resistencia and Santa Fé.

Religions

Roman Catholic (92 per cent), Protestant (2 per cent), Jewish (2 per cent), others (4 per cent).

Education

Education is compulsory and free, so that Argentina has one of the highest literacy rates in Latin America. Secondary education consists of basic general education and polymodal education (multipurpose schools catering to ages between 15 and 18). In parallel to the polymodal cycle, there is a technical-,professional course, which leads after a further year's study to the title of Técnico. Higher education is provided by national and private universities, which are autonomous. There are 25 national universities. Technical institutes (Institutos de Formación Técnica) offer higher technical education, leading to the award of the Título menor. Professional courses are also available in a wide range of subjects.

Literacy rate: 97 per cent adult rate; 99 per cent youth rate (15–24) (Unesco 2005).

Compulsory years: 6 to 15

Enrolment rate: 120 per cent gross primary enrolment of relevant age group (including repeaters); 100 per cent gross secondary enrolment; 57 per cent in tertiary education (World Bank).

Pupils per teacher: 17 in primary schools

Health

Per capita total expenditure on health (2003) was US$1,067; of which per capita government spending was US$518, at the international dollar rate, (WHO 2006).
The healthcare sector was deregulated in 2001. In effect, this gives Argentinians the right to choose between the union-administered healthcare system, known as obras sociales, and private healthcare providers. The reorganisation meant that those who paid into, or were already members of, a private health scheme, would no longer have to pay 3 per cent of their salaries to the union-administered system.
Most children receive immunisations against childhood diseases.

HIV/Aids

HIV prevalence: 0.7 per cent aged 15–49 in 2003 (World Bank)

Life expectancy: 75 years, 2004 (WHO 2006)

Fertility rate/Maternal mortality rate: 2.3 births per woman, 2004 (WHO 2006); maternal deaths 38 per 100,000 live births (World Bank).

Child (under 5 years) mortality rate (per 1,000): 17 per 1,000 live births (2003); 5 per cent of children aged under five are malnourished (World Bank).

Welfare

The main portion of the Argentine social security system is borne by a pay-as-you-go system where employers' and employees' contributions fund payments. Workers must contribute 11 per cent of their pay regardless of whether workers participate in a private, or the public, social security system; employers must contribute the equivalent of 16 per cent of each workers' salary to the public system. Non-salaried workers must pay

the full amount of 27 per cent of their income.
The whole social security system is adversely affected when employers fail to pay or withhold their social security contributions. However, the percentage of non-registered employees in Argentina is very high. According to non-official records of the Argentine Ministry of Labour, 20 out of 100 employees are non-registered employees, thus depriving them of pensions. Measures have been taken by the Argentine Social Security Authority (SSA) to force employers to register employees and contribute to the social security fund.

Pensions

Argentina reformed its pension system in 1994 to a mixture of the old government-administered system and an individual retirement account programme administered by the Retirement and Pension Fund Administrators (AFJPs).
Argentina has retained the pay-as-you-go system. This system provides basic, universal old-age coverage (known as PBU) for all workers who reach retirement age and who have contributed for at least 30 years including a portion of the wealthiest Argentines' pensions. Payment of retirement benefits begin at age 65 for men and age 60 for women.

Main cities

Buenos Aires (capital, estimated population 12.1 million (m) in 2008), Córdoba (1.5m), Rosario (1.2m), La Plata (731,458), Tucumán (818,672), Mar del Plata (584,702), Mendoza (919,824), Salta (540,478), Santa Fé (500,365), Tucumán (818,672).

Languages spoken

Italian, German and French are still maintained within their respective communities. English is generally spoken in business circles. There are 17 native Indian languages, the most widely spoken of which is Quechua.

Official language/s

Spanish

Media

Argentina has a sophisticated media industry with over 150 daily newspapers, based in cities or regionally, hundreds of private commercial radio stations and dozens of televisions stations.

National news agency: Telam: www.telam.com.ar

Press

Dailies: In Spanish, La Nación (www.lanacion.com.ar) is a respected publication, Página 12 (www.pagina12.com.ar) has left-wing views, La Prensa (www.laprensa.com.ar), La Razón (www.larazon.com.ar) is a popular national broadsheet and Clarín (www.clarin.com). Regional newspapers includes La Mañana de Córdiba (www.lmcordoba.com.ar), La Capital (www.lacapital.com.ar) and El Tábano (www.eltabano.com).
In English, Buenos Aires Herald (www.buenosairesherald.com), has a business supplement and Buenos Aires Times (www.buenosairestimes.com).

Weeklies: In Spanish, 168 Horas (http://168horas.com.ar), Noticias (www.noticias.uolsinectis.com.ar) has features on business and current affairs, Foco (www.foco.uol.com.ar). In German, Argentinisches Tageblatt (www.tageblatt.com.ar).

Business: In Spanish, major newspapers include El Cronista (www.cronista.com), Negocio Nea (www.negocionea.com.ar), El Economista (www.eleconomista.com.ar) and Ambito Financiero (www.ambitoweb.com) with an online edition in English. Business magazines include Alzas y Bajas (www.alzasybajas.com.ar),Apertura (www.apertura.com), Bolsafe Valores (www.bolsafevalores.com),Edicion i (www.edicioni.com), El Grafico (www.elgrafico.uol.com.ar), Estrategas (www.revistaestrategas.com.ar), Fortuna (www.revista-fortuna.com.ar), Gestion (www.gestion.com.ar), Merdado (www.mercado.com.ar), Prensa Economica (www.prensaeconomica.com.ar) and Realidad Economica (www.iade.org.ar). Monthly magazines include Tiempo Empresario (www.tiempoempresario.com.ar) and Negocios Magazine.

Periodicals: There are numerous magazines available, covering all interests. Viva Sophia (www.vivisophia.com) is a monthly women's magazine.

Broadcasting

Radio: In Spanish, the national public radio is Radio Nacional (www.radionacional.gov.ar) with four channels. La Red (www.uol.com.ar) is a national, commercial network. Radio Intereconomía (www.intereconomia.com) has news and economic contents.
One of the most popular radio stations is based in Buenos Aires, Radio Rivadavia (www.rivadavia.com.ar) along with at least 40 other FM stations. All musical genres are broadcast, as well as news (Radio America, www.estoesamerica.com.ar), cultural (Radio Continental, www.continental.com.ar) and religious contents (Red Puerto Libre, www.redpuertolibre.com.ar).

Television: There are five national television networks operated through affiliates and many more local services. Canal 7 (www.canal7.com.ar) is the state-run national TV service specialising in cultural and educational programmes but with the lowest viewer numbers. Telefe (www.telefe.com) with the highest viewer figures produces local content programmes as well as showing internationally produced shows. Canal 13 (www.canaltrece.com.ar) is Telefe's rival, producing popular programmes as well as news and current affairs. America 2 (www.america2.com.ar) and Canal 9 (www.canal9.com.ar) are the remaining national networks.
Argentina has one of the world's highest take-up rate for cable television with over a dozen stations to choose from. Station contents can be specific to viewer interest such as sports, children's or lifestyle programming or general content.

Advertising

The Centro de Informaciones de Publicidad (www.cip.org.ar) has authority for advertising matters in Argentina.
Press advertising accounts for approximately 45 per cent of total advertising expenditure, with commercial television taking between 25 and 30 per cent. Outdoor sites for posters are usually controlled by a few major or local companies or local authorities.

Economy

Argentina's economy continued to expand in 2007 with GDP growth of 7.5 per cent, the fifth successive year of expansion. Coming as it does after its default on sovereign debt during the economic crisis of 2001–02, Argentina has outflanked international capital markets and performed an economic about face. In 2003 it began a loan restructuring process for its near US$100 billion sovereign debt, offering new bonds for old at US$0.35 per US$1 and told its creditors they could 'take it or leave it'. While it reduced its debt serving payments markedly, it took until the beginning of 2005 for all legal challenges to be overcome and for the plan to be fully implemented. The government paid back US$10 billion to the IMF and severed its links with the institution that it, in part, holds responsible for the economic crisis in the first place. Argentina has reached a position whereby its fiscal surplus allows it to pay back more to its creditors that it borrows from new loans or bond issues. For this, ironically, the ratings agency, Moody, upgraded Argentina's sovereign debt rating reflecting the value foreign investors put on the new bonds, which tripled in value in 2006. Inflation is the biggest hazard for an economy that rapidly expanded after the restructuring, almost doubling annually from 2003, reaching 9.6 per cent in 2005. Some analysts state that there is a gap between the measured and actual inflation rate of 3–5 percentage points.

Argentina's economy is underpinned by its vast natural resources and an export-oriented agricultural sector. The country is a major world producer of soya beans, beef and wheat. Financial services and tourism emerged as important sectors in Argentina's economic growth in the 1990s. Industry and manufacturing are also important and Argentina produces refined oil for export.

The Inter-American Development Bank estimated that in 2006 migrant workers sent some US$850 million to their families in Argentina.

Recent economic growth is largely attributable to the high commodity prices for soya bean in Asia, particularly from China. With China receiving around a third of Argentine soya exports and the industry growing by around 20 per cent every year, soya production is becoming a flourishing sector of the economy. China is also pursuing a policy of heavy investment in Latin America, with a planned US$20 billion being spent on Argentine infrastructure over the next 10 years.

Steady growth and political stability under President Kirchner is leading the country into recovery.

External trade

As a member of Mercosur, the world's fourth largest free-trade zone, Argentina (along with Brazil, Paraguay Uruguay and Venezuela), has access to a market of over 200 million consumers. The EU and Mercosur have been in negotiations to create a mutual free trade zone since 2004, with continued work including a technical summit and political dialogue between the parties.

In 2004, twelve South American countries signed an agreement to launch the South American Community of Nations (CSN), modelled on the European Union, to unite both politically and economically. The CSN seeks to integrate the Andean Union and Mercusur by 2007, with tariffs on non-sensitive products being abolished by 2014. However political tensions within the region have hampered the ongoing process.

Argentine plans to form a closer trading relationship with China have been in existence for some time due to the increasing trade in soya coupled with Chinese investment in Argentina.

Imports

Principal imports include metal manufactures, machinery and equipment, vehicles, chemicals and plastics.

Main sources: Brazil (36.1 per cent total 2006), US (14.9 per cent), China (6.3 per cent).

Exports

Mineral products, agricultural products, vehicles and parts, electrical machinery, live animals and related products, chemicals. Food processing particularly meat, flour and other canning are the largest manufacturing activities. Argentina is the primary source of tannin and linseed oil worldwide.

Main destinations: Brazil (16.8 per cent of 2006 total goods exports), Chile (8.8 per cent), US (8.4 per cent).

Agriculture

Farming

The agricultural sector as a whole contributes around 7 per cent to GDP and employs 11 per cent of the workforce, with the sector being composed predominantly of individual farmers and small companies. Arable land covers 12 per cent of Argentina's total land area. The country is an important producer of food, particularly soya beans, meat and wheat. Together, vegetable products and livestock account for nearly a quarter of total exports. Overall, the country is the fifth largest agricultural exporter in the world, with the sector accounting for 60 per cent of all Argentina's exports. It is the largest exporter of soy oil, soy flour oil and sunflower, the second largest exporter of corn after the United States, the third largest exporter of meat and the fifth largest flour producer.

Argentina's meat consumption is the highest in Latin America, at over 50kg per person per annum. Argentina is the world's third-largest organic meat producer, with 90 per cent of organic produce destined for export markets, particularly the EU. In previous years agricultural profitability has been hit by low international commodity prices, rising production costs, subsidiation of international competitors and an over-valued exchange rate which has diminished competitiveness. The weakness of the peso against the euro and the US dollar since the government ceased to peg the peso to the US dollar has provided a boost to sales volumes since 2002.

Crop production in 2005 included 40,998,000 tonnes (t) cereals in total, *16,000,000t wheat, 19,500,000t maize, 1,027,000t rice, 2,021,020 potatoes, 2,900,000t sorghum, 38,300,000t soya beans, *19,300,000t sugar cane, *1,262,444t apples, *2,690,000t citrus fruit, *2,365,000t grapes, 8,669,810t oilcrops, *180,000t bananas, *64,000t tea, 142,735t garlic, *118,000t tobacco, 676,000t tomatoes, *7,067t peppermint, 3,652,000t sunflower seed, *7,484,742t fruit in total, *3,184,982t vegetables in total. Livestock production included 4,174,873t meat in total, 3,024,000t beef, *150,200t pig meat, *61,270t lamb & goat meat, 828,153t poultry, *300,000t eggs, *8,100,000t milk, *80,000t honey, 432,000t cattle hides.

* Estimate

Fishing

Argentina has recently increased its fishing production and exports of surplus stock are becoming a valuable export earner, especially when processed into oil and fish meal. Because of the Argentines' preference for beef, the domestic demand for fish is relatively weak. Principal fishing ports are Mar del Plata and Bahía Blanca. The typical annual fish catch is around 925,000 tonnes, including 550,000 tonnes marine fish and 350,000 tonnes shellfish.

In 2004, the total marine fish catch was 761,447 tonnes and the total crustacean catch was 28,641 tonnes.

Forestry

About 12 per cent of Argentina's total land is covered by forest, equivalent to 34.6 million hectares, and a further 6 per cent of other wooded land.

Argentina is not self-sufficient in forestry goods, with most of the domestic harvest going towards lumber. Pine and cedar used for pulp are harvested in the north-west of the country. Significant quantities of sawn goods, wood-based panels and chemical pulps are produced from domestic hardwoods and softwoods. A large quantity of paper is imported, although Argentina's pulp and paper industry relies mainly on domestic pulp production.

Industry and manufacturing

Argentina's main industrial centres are Cordoba and to a lesser extent Buenos Aires. Industry as a whole contributes approximately 29 per cent to GDP and employs 24 per cent of the workforce. Major sectors of production include food, textiles, machinery and transport equipment, consumer durables, industrial chemicals, metal working, engineering, paper, iron and steel and electrical equipment. The beef industry has given rise to a number of associated industries, including hides, leather, meat extracts and processed meats. Sectors that have gained in prominence in recent years include software and petrochemicals.

The automobile sector represents an important growth sector for the economy. In recent years the sector has suffered from poor consumer demand and an uncompetitive exchange rate. Many car assembly plants have been closed and operations have been transferred to Brazil, where labour costs are lower and there is a more lucrative domestic market. With the exception of the automobile industry however, the manufacturing sector has been boosted by the acceleration of economic integration within Mercusor.

Tourism
Travel and tourism is a significant contributor to the economy. However, Argentina's tourism sector, which thrived during the 1990s (4,285,000 visitors in 1996), was badly affected by the country's political and economic problems, compounded by external events, such as the 11 September 2001 terrorist attacks in the US.
The World Travel and Tourism Council forecasts that the travel and tourism sector of Argentina will grow by more than 7 per cent in 2005, contributing some 2.6 per cent to GDP. The sector will generate over 1.3 million jobs (9.1 per cent of the total work force).
This recovery is on the back of Argentina's improving economic and political situation. Visitor numbers rose by 12 per cent in 2004, from 2.99 million to 3.35 million, with a rise in receipts of 28 per cent to US$2.56 billion.

Environment
Argentina's diverse environments have created a number of different ecological challenges from heavy pollution in Buenos Aires, deforestation in subtropical provinces to overgrazing in Patagonia.

Mining
The mining code was altered to create a more attractive investment environment in 1993, since when growth in the sector has picked up; mining exports in 2000 were estimated at US$1 billion and and had risen to US$2.3 billion by 2004. Altogether, there are over 70 companies with established projects in Argentina and some 40 companies actively seeking mining opportunities in the country.
Iron ore is the principal mineral extracted, mostly in Río Negro province, but output is only sufficient to supply about half of the requirements of the country's largest blast furnace complex, the remainder being made up from imports. Other minerals extracted include lead, zinc, tin, and uranium.
Argentina's largest mining project is the Alumbrera copper and gold mine in Catamarca province, thought to be the ninth largest copper mine in the world. Annual production of some 15 tonnes of gold is also expected until the end of its 20-year life in 2019. In addition, the Cerro Vanguardia silver and gold mine produces approximately five tonnes of gold per year. Now a significant gold producer Argentina – which occupies a top twenty world position – has recently seen considerable production activity in the north-west of the country, where the Veladero mine is situated. The Argentina-Chile border zone is particularly promising and output is predicted to rise in 2005 because of increased production in the area.

Hydrocarbons
Argentina has 2.7 billion barrels of proven oil reserves (as at year end 2004). It is the third-largest oil producer in Latin America, producing 756,000 barrels per day (bpd) and is the region's third-largest exporter. The oil sector is fully privatised.
Argentina is a net exporter of oil, consuming 393,000 bpd and exporting the remainder of its production.
At year end 2004, Argentina had 610 billion cubic metres (21.4 trillion cubic feet) of proven gas reserves, the third-largest in Latin America. It is the second-largest gas producer in Latin America after Mexico producing 44.9 billion cubic metres in 2004.
The gas sector is fully privatised and there are no restrictions on imports and exports. Chile is the largest consumer of Argentine gas exports and is supplied solely by the Neuquén gas fields . There are also pipelines to Argentina's second most important customer, Brazil.
Argentina has total coal reserves of 130 million tonnes. It produces 340,000 tonnes per year and consumes around 1.54 million tonnes per year.

Energy
The third largest power market in Latin America, Argentina relies predominantly on hydropower and natural gas to fuel its electricity generation. Argentina had 27 million KW of installed generation (as at end 2002), 49 per cent of which was fossil fuel based while 42 per cent was derived from hydroelectricity.
The Argentine electricity market for generation is highly competitive and is one of the most deregulated markets of its kind in the region. The liberated nature of the market combined with steadily rising demand through the 1990s ensured that the sector grew robustly. However, the economic crisis of 2001–02 led to a marked decrease in both production and consumption, though Argentina's relative stability in the last two years has allowed the sector to rebound.
Greater regulation in the distribution sector coupled with the domination of the market by three major organisations – Edenor, Edesur and Edelap – has resulted in a less competitive environment.
Compania Nacional de Transporte Energetica en Alta Tension, or Transener, controls the market in electricity transmission, having secured a 95 year licence with the Argentine government in 1993.
Hydroelectricity is of great importance to the energy sector, particular the Yacyreta hydroelectric dam, which helps power Argentina and neighbouring Paraguay. The Salto Grande dam is also co-owned by a bordering country, Uruguay, and as is the case with the Yacyreta, power generated from the project is shared equally between both nations.
Argentina relies on the Atucha I and Embalse nuclear power projects, both of which are operated by Nucleoelctrica Argentina SA. Construction of a further nuclear power station, Atucha II, was halted in 1994, though the national government formally announced in 2003 that it would invest US$300 million to complete construction by 2008.

Financial markets
Stock exchange
The growth of the pension fund market in Argentina has added considerable liquidity to the Argentine stock market since the late 1990s and increased the market capitalisation of the Buenos Aires stock exchange. However, the protracted recession has hit the stock exchange hard.

Banking and insurance
The country's economic crisis of 2001 severely undermined Argentina's banking system, when the freezing of deposit accounts and the conversion of deposits into pesos undermined liquidity in the financial system. The value of assets deteriorated throughout 2002 as the peso lost value and government bonds fell to a fraction of their purchase price. Banks were unable to meet claims on deposits, while savers filed law suits against institutions for failing to honour their deposits. As such, the entire banking system teetered on the edge of collapse in 2003. This led to the closure of many local subsidiaries of foreign banks. However, Argenina's recent economic recovery has enabled the sector to rehabilitate itself somewhat, with an increase in money supply demand and a significant recovery on bank deposits and loans. The acceptance of the national government's debt restructuring plan in early 2005 has led to a much needed increase in foreign capital inflow and greater stability in the sector. Despite this gradual upturn the banking sector remains very sensitive to macroeconomic conditions and though the level of credit is growing, it remains at a slow rate.
A new Bank of the South, with a headquarters in Venezuela, will be launched in 2008 to provide an alternative source of development funding for the participating countries. Assets of US$7 billion will underpin its operations.

Central bank
Banco Central de la República Argentina

Main financial centre
Buenos Aires

Time
GMT minus three hours

Geography
Argentina is situated in the south-east of South America, facing the Atlantic Ocean to the east. Argentina is bounded by Chile to the west, Bolivia and Paraguay to the north and Brazil and Uruguay to the north-east. There are four main geographic provinces: the Andes, the lowland north, the Pampas and Patagonia.
The Andes Mountains line Argentina's western edge, forming the boundary with Chile. The highest peak, Aconcagua, stands 6,960 metres (22,834 feet).
Gently rolling plains extend eastward from the base of the Andes and descend gradually to sea level. Open savannas alternate with almost impenetrable thorn forests in the western part of the region.
Vast, generally treeless plains of central Argentina gradually rise from the Atlantic coast to the Andes Mountains. These fertile plains are Argentina's breadbasket. They consist of the Humid Pampas along the coast and the Dry Pampas in the west and south.
Patagonia, south of the Pampas, is dry and desolate. The Patagonian steppes support flocks of sheep, the wool of which is exported to Europe.
The southernmost inhabited territory, Tierra del Fuego (Land of Fire), consists of various islands with the northern areas used for sheep farming, while the southern islands are mountainous and covered in glaciers and forests.
Hemisphere
Southern

Climate
Argentina's climate ranges from sub-tropical in the north to sub-antarctic in the south. The densely populated central zone (including Buenos Aires) is temperate. Summer, from December–March, is hot and humid with temperatures ranging from 26–35 degrees Celsius (C); autumn is April–May, with temperatures in the range 10–25 degrees C; winter is from June–August, with temperatures of 0–20 degrees C, when nights can be cold with temperatures below freezing; spring is from September–November, with temperatures of 12–25 degrees C.

Dress codes
Dress codes are fairly formal in Buenos Aires. Suits are worn for business appointments and, for men, jackets and ties are required for dining out and other social occasions. Casual clothing is often worn on the coast, but shorts and beachwear should be worn only at the beach or pool.

Entry requirements
Passports
Passports are required by all visitors except nationals of neighbouring countries with identity cards.
Visa
All business travellers are advised to contact an Argentine embassy for requirements, before departure.
Tourist visas are not required by most nationals of the Americas, Europe, Australasia and some Asian countries. Citizens of neighbouring countries of Argentina need only national identification cards. For further exemptions and details check with the appropriate embassy or consulate before departure.
Currency advice/regulations
There are no restrictions on the import and export of local or foreign currency.

Health (for visitors)
Mandatory precautions
None
Advisable precautions
Typhoid and hepatitis A vaccinations are recommended. Yellow fever vaccinations are advised for visitors to the north-eastern forest area. Malaria prophylaxis is advisable for visits to some lowland tropical areas. Water precautions should be taken outside main towns.
There is some risk of dengue fever and anthrax outside urban areas.
Medical insurance is necessary and doctors often expect immediate cash payment before treatment. Take medical kit.

Hotels
Wide range available, graded from one to five stars. There is a 21 per cent tax, which may be included in hotel tariff.

Public holidays (national)
Fixed dates
1 Jan (New Year's Day), 1 May (Labour Day), 25 May (Anniversary of the 1810 Revolution), 19 Jun (Flag Day), 9 Jul (Independence Day), 8 Dec (Immaculate Conception), 25 Dec (Christmas Day), 31 Dec (New Year's Eve).
Variable dates
Maundy Thursday, Good Friday, Malvinas Day (first Mon in Apr), Death of General José San Martin (third Mon in Aug), Columbus Day (second Mon in Oct).

Working hours
Banking
Mon–Fri: 09/1000–1500.
Business
Mon–Fri: 0900–1300, 1500–1800.
Government
Mon–Fri: 0800–1700.
Shops
Mon–Fri: 0900–2200, Sat: 0900–1300.

Telecommunications
Mobile/cell phones
GSM 850/1900 services are available in highly populated areas only.

Electricity supply
220V AC, 50 cycles

Social customs/useful tips
The normal form of greeting is a handshake. In general, European practices are followed. Standards on punctuality differ though and visitors may be kept waiting. Commercial quotations should be made in US dollars.
In their public behaviour, Argentines are very conscious of civilities. It is considered polite to first extend a greeting like buenos dias (good day) or buenas tardes (good afternoon) if you are approaching a stranger to ask for information.

Security
Although street crime is increasing in Argentina, personal security is a minor problem compared to other Latin American countries. Violent crime is rare in Buenos Aires. Travellers should take precautions against petty theft such as bag snatching, especially on trains.

Getting there
Air
National airline: Aerolíneas Argentinas.
International airport/s: Ministro Pistarini Ezeiza (EZE), 35km south-west of Buenos Aires; duty-free shop, restaurants, bank, car hire. A bus service operates to the city, every 30 minutes between 0500–2300, taking 45 minutes. Taxis are also available. A coach service also connects to Aeroparque Jorge Newbery airport for domestic flight connections.
Other airport/s: Aeroparque Jorge Newbery (AEP), 8km north-east of Buenos Aires, domestic terminal; duty-free shop, restaurant, bank, car hire.
Airport tax: International departures US$18; regional and to Uruguay US$8. International arrivals US$10. These levies are subject to inflation.
Surface
Road: There are well-maintained roads between all the neighbouring countries. Branches of the Pan-American Highway run from Buenos Aires to the borders of Bolivia, Brazil, Chile and Paraguay. Entry from Uruguay is possible via bridges over the Uruguay River at Puerto Colón, Puerto Unzué and the Salto Grande Dam. The long distances involved can make car journeys time-consuming: for example, the distance from Santiago in Chile to Buenos Aires is over 1,400 km.
Rail: The major direct route is north from Buenos Aires to Asunción in Paraguay. There are also direct rail links with Bolivia, Brazil and Chile. Services are often disrupted and delays can be expected.
Water: Ferry and hydrofoil services on the Río de la Plata link Colonia and Montevideo (Uruguay) with Buenos Aires. Ferries also operate from Paraguay on the Paraná River.
Main port/s: Buenos Aires, Ensenada (La Plata), Rosario and Bahía Blanca. There

are numerous smaller ports and some specialised terminals (for oil, cereals, raw materials, etc).

Getting about

National transport

Air: Given the great distances involved, air travel is the logical method for reaching domestic destinations. Internal flights for Buenos Aires land at Aeroparque Jorge Newbery, 10 minutes from city centre by taxi.

An extensive domestic service is offered to regional airports and demand for services is high, so it is advisable to book flights in advance.

Road: The network has been improved in recent years and links major centres. Tolls are collected on major roads, which are privately-owned.

Buses: Long-distance bus services are operated by a number of companies, mostly centred on Buenos Aires, and are extensive (e.g. routes to Mar del Plata, Córdoba, San Martín de Los Andes, Mendoza). The Buenos Aires bus terminal is next to Retiro, the central rail station.

Rail: Travelling by train is generally cheaper, but slower, than travelling by bus. A comprehensive rail system links main towns. Long-distance Pullman services, with air-conditioning, sleeping facilities and restaurants, are recommended. It is advisable to book well in advance.

Water: There are regular sailings to Rosario and Corrientes via the Paraná River. River transport company Flota Fluvial operates services on the Plate, Paraná, Paraguay and Uruguay Rivers. Patagonian ports are also served, but sailings are irregular.

City transport

Taxis: Taxis, of which there are some 32,000 in Buenos Aires, generally have yellow roofs. They can be hailed or found on ranks and are metered within cities. For trips in the Buenos Aires centre which are less than six blocks, it is usually faster to walk than to take a taxi. Tips are not necessary, though generally expected from tourists.

There is also a widely available and much-used system of cars called remises, which offer a safer and more comfortable service. Remises are also available for travel to and from the airports, where they can be booked at separate counters.

Journey time from Ezeiza airport to city centre is 40 minutes and 10 minutes from Aeroparque Jorge Newbery.

Buses, trams & metro: All major towns have good local services. In Buenos Aires there is a comprehensive public transport system with 'pay as you board' bus services, operating round the clock.

The Buenos Aires metro, known as Subte, has five lines and 80 stations; it operates from early morning to late at night. Tokens can be purchased at booking offices.

Ferry: The principal ferry connection in Buenos Aires is to Colonia in Uruguay and is frequented by tourists heading for the Uruguayan resort town of Punta del Este. River buses in the suburb of Tigre serve communities in the river delta and are a popular tourist attraction on weekends.

Car hire

Car hire is available in Buenos Aires and most main urban centres. An international driving licence, in addition to home licence, is advisable

BUSINESS DIRECTORY

The addresses listed below are a selection only. While World of Information makes every endeavour to check these addresses, we cannot guarantee that changes have not been made, especially to telephone numbers and area codes. We would welcome any corrections.

Telephone area codes

The international direct dialling code (IDD) for Argentina is +54, followed by area code and subscriber's number:

Bahía Blanca	291	Resistencia	3722
Balcarce	2266	Rio Cuarto	358
Buenos Aires	11	Rio Grande	2964
Catamarca	3833	Rosario	341
Córdoba	351	Salta	387
Formosa	3717	San Juan	264
Las Calera	351	San Lorenzo	3476
La Plata	221	San Miguel de Tucumen	381
Mar Del Plata	223	San Pedro	3329
Mendoza	261	San Rafael	2627
Neuquén	299	Santa Fé	342
Paraná	343	Santa Rosa	2954

Useful telephone numbers

Fire: 107
Police: 101
Ambulance: 101

Chambers of Commerce

American Chamber of Commerce in Argentina, 1133 Viamonte, 1053 Buenos Aires (tel: 4371-4500; fax: 4371-8400; e-mail: amcham@amcham.com.ar).

Argentine Chamber of Commerce, 36 Avenida Leandro N Alem, 1003 Buenos Aires (tel: 5300-5000; fax: 5300-9058; e-mail: centroservices@cac.com.ar).

British-Argentine Chamber of Commerce, 457 Avenida Corrientes, 1043 Buenos Aires, CF (tel: 4394-2762; fax: 4394-3860; e-mail: info@ccab.com.ar).

Rosario Chamber of Commerce, 1868 Córdoba, 2000 Rosario (tel: 425-7147; fax: 425-7486; e-mail: ccer@commerce.com.ar).

Banking

Asociación de Bancos Argentinos (ADEBA), San Martín 1229, Piso 10, 1004 Buenos Aires, CF (tel: 4394-1430; fax: 4394-6340).

Banco Crédito-Op Cooperativo Ltdo, Reconquista 484, Zona postal 1003, Buenos Aires, CF (tel: 4394-0105/0122; fax: 4325-9104).

Banco de Crédito Argentino, Reconquista 2, Zona postal 1092, Buenos Aires, CF (tel: 4334-1181/89; fax: 4334-5618).

Banco de Galicia y Buenos Aires, Tte Gral Juan D Perón 407, Zona postal 1038, Buenos Aires, CF (tel: 4329-6000; fax: 4329-6100).

Banco de la Ciudad de Buenos Aires, Florida 302, Zona postal 1313, Buenos Aires, CF (tel: 4325-5881/89).

Banco de la Nación Argentina (BNA), Bartolomé Mitre 326, Zona postal 1036, Buenos Aires, CF (tel: 4347-6000; fax: 4347-8078); international banking division (tel: 4347-8092; fax: 4347-8078); foreign trade promotion (tel: 4347-8763; fax: 4347-8764).

Banco de la Pampa, Reconquista 319, Zona postal 1003, Buenos Aires, CF (tel: 4325-3410; fax: 4325-8750).

Banco de la Provincia de Buenos Aires, San Martín 137, Zona postal 1004, Buenos Aires, CF (tel: 4331-2561/3584; fax: 4331-5154).

Banco del Buen Ayre, Cerrito 740, Zona postal 1309, Buenos Aires, CF (tel: 4350-020/054; fax: 4837-890).

Banco del Sud, Maipú 277, Zona postal 1084, Buenos Aires, CF (tel: 4326-3313, 4326-2965; fax: 4325-3177).

Banco Francés del Rio de la Plata, Reconquista 165, Zona postal 1003, Buenos Aires, CF (tel: 4331-7071; fax: 4954-8009).

Banco General de Negocios, Esmeralda 120, Zona postal 1035, Buenos Aires, CF (tel: 4394-3003, 4394-2879; fax: 4394-2698).

Banco Hipotecario Nacional, Balcarce 167, Zona postal 1064, Buenos Aires, CF (tel: 4342-9732; fax: 4331-0620).

Banco Holandés Unido, Florida 361, Zona postal 1005, Buenos Aires, CF (tel: 4394-4553; fax: 4322-0839).

Banco Medefín UNB, 25 de Mayo 489, Zona postal 1339, Buenos Aires, CF (tel: 4313-4125; fax: 4312-9450).

Banco Quilmes, Tte Gral Juan D Perón 564, Zona postal 1038, Buenos Aires, CF (tel: 4331-8111/9; fax: 4334-5235).

Banco República, Sarmiento 336, Zona postal 1041, Buenos Aires, CF (tel: 4331-8385/87; fax: 4331-2130).

Banco Río de la Plata, Bartolomé Mitre 480, Zona postal 1036, Buenos Aires, CF (tel: 4331-7551, 4331-8361; fax: 4331-7551; internet :/www.bancorio.com.ar).

Banco Roberts, 25 de Mayo 258, Zona postal 1002, Buenos Aires, CF (tel: 4334-1723, 4334-6682; fax: 4334-6679).

Banco Sudameris, Tte Gral Juan D Perón 500, Zona postal 1038, Buenos Aires, F (tel: 4331-4061/9; fax: 4331-2793).

Banco Supervielle Société Générale, Reconquista 330, Zona postal 1003, Buenos Aires, CF (tel: 4394-4051/9).

Banco Tornquist, Bartolomé Mitre 531, Zona postal 1036, Buenos Aires, CF (tel: 4343-784/49; fax: 4342-6090).

Banco Velox, San Martín 298, Zona postal 1004, Buenos Aires, CF (tel: 394-0115/0665; fax: 4394-8255).

Banesto Banco Shaw, Sarmiento 355, Zona postal 1041, Buenos Aires, CF (tel: 4325-6500; fax: 4312-4743).

Caja Nacional de Ahorro y Seguro, Hipólito Yrigoyen 1750, Zona postal 1308, Buenos Aires, CF (tel: 4476-4216; fax: 4111-568).

Deutsche Bank, Bartolomé Mitre 401, Zona postal 1036, Buenos Aires, CF (tel: 4343-2511/9; fax: 4343-3536).

The First National Bank of Boston, Florida 99, Zona postal 1005, Buenos Aires, CF (tel: 4342-3051/61; fax: 4343-7303).

Lloyds Bank, Reconquista 101, Zona postal 1003, Buenos Aires, CF (tel: 4331-3551/9; fax: 4342-7487).

Central bank

Banco Central de la República Argentina, Reconquista 266, 1003 Buenos Aires (tel: 4348-3500; fax: 4334-6489).

Travel information

Aerolíneas Argentinas, Paseo Colón 185, Zona postal 1063, Buenos Aires, CF (tel: 4320-2000; fax: 44317-3585; internet: www.austral.com.ar).

Austral Líneas Aéreas (ALA), Avda Corrientes 485, Piso 9, Zona postal 1398, Buenos Aires, CF (tel: 4340-7800, 4317-3605; fax: 4317-3992).

Ministry of tourism

Secretaría del Turismo, Presidencia de la Nación, Suípacha 1111, Piso 21, Zona potal 1360, Buenos Aires, CF (tel: 4312-5624, 4311-2089; fax: 4313-6834; internet: www.sectur.gov.ar/eng/menu.htm).

National tourist organisation offices

Asociación Argentina de Agencias de Viaje y Turismo (Travel Agents' Association), Viamonte 640, Piso 10, Zona postal 1053, Buenos Aires, CF (tel: 4322-2804).

Ministries

Ministry of Culture and Education, Pizzurno 935, Zona postal 1020, Buenos Aires, CF (tel: 424-1551/9, 445-666, 448-110).

Ministry of Defence, Av. Paseo Colón 255, Zona postal 1063, Buenos Aires, CF (tel: 343-1561).

Ministry of Economy, Public Works and Services, Hipólito Yrigoyen 250, Zona posal 1310, Buenos Aires, CF (tel: 342-6411, 342-6421/9, 349-8814, 349-8810/2; fax: 331-0292, 331-2619, 331-2090; internet: www.mecon.ar/default.htm).

Ministry of Foreign Affairs and International Trade, Reconquista 1088, Zona postal 1003, Buenos Aires, CF (tel: 331-0071, 312-1775, 312-3434; fax: 312-3593, 312-3423).

Ministry of the Interior, Balcarce 50, Zona postal 1064, Buenos Aires, CF (tel: 342-6081, 343-0880).

Ministry of Justice, Av Gral Gelly y Obes 2289, Piso 7, Zona postal 1425, Buenos Aires, CF (tel: 803-1051/3, 803-5453; fax: 803-3955).

Ministry of Labour and Social Security, Av L N Alem 650, Zona postal 1001, Buenos Aires, CF (tel: 311-3303, 311-2945).

Ministry of Public Health and Social Action, Av 9 de Julio 1925, Zona postal 1332, Buenos Aires, CF (tel: 381-8911, 381-8919).

Office of the President, Balcarce 50, Zona postal 1064, Buenos Aires, CF (tel: 331-5041, 303-608, 331-3183).

Other useful addresses

Administration of Agriculture and Agroindustrial Markets, Paseo Colón 922, Piso 1, Of 131, 1063 Buenos Aires (tel: 4349-2272/4; fax: 4349-2272).

Administration of Fish and Marine Resources, San Martín 459, Piso 2, 1004 Buenos Aires (tel: 4394-1869, 4394-5961).

Administration of Forestry Production, Av Paseo Colón 982, Piso 1, 1063 Buenos Aires (tel: 4349-2101, 4349-2103; fax: 4349-2108).

Administration of Geological and Mining Resources, Julio A Roca 651, Piso 8, 1322 Buenos Aires (tel: 4349-3131).

Administration of Livestock Markets, Paseo Colón 922, 1063 Buenos Aires (tel: 4349-2287, 4349-2294; fax: 4362-5144).

Administration of Markets of Non-Traditional Products, Paseo Colón 922, Buenos Aires (tel: 4362-1738, 4349-2280/2; fax: 4349-2280).

Administration of Mining Development, Av Julio A Roca 561, Piso 8, 1322 Buenos Aires (tel: 4349-3133).

Administration of Native Forestry Resources, San Martin 459, Piso 2, 1004 Buenos Aires (tel: 4394-1869).

Argentine Embassy (USA), 1600 New Hampshire Avenue, NW, Washington DC 20009 (tel: (+1-202) 238-6400; fax: (+1-202) 332-3171; e-mail: info@embajadaargentinaeeuu.org).

Argentine Industry Association, Av L N 1067, Piso 10, 1001 Buenos Aires (tel: 4313-2012, 4313-2512, 4313-2561; fax: 4313-2413).

Argentine Institute of Plant Sanitation and Quality, Av Paseo Colón 982, 1063 Buenos Aires (tel: 4313-8311).

Argentine Petrochemical Institute, Av Santa Fe 1480, Piso 5, Buenos Aires (tel: 4813-3436; fax: 4813-3436).

Argentine Petroleum Institute, Maipú 645, Piso 3, Primer Cuerpo, Buenos Aires (tel: 4322-3233, 4322-3652, 4322-3244; fax: 4322-3233).

Association of Importers and Exporters, Av Belgrano 124, Piso 1, 1092 Buenos Aires (tel: 4342-0010/9; fax: 4342-1312).

British Embassy, Dr Luis Agote 2412/52, Casilla de Correo 2050, 1425 Buenos Aires (tel: 4803-7070/1; fax: 4803-1731).

Bolsa de Comercio de Buenos Aires (Stock Exchange), Sarmiento 299, 1st Floor, AR 1353 Buenos Aires (tel: 4311-1174, 4311-5231, 4311-5235; fax: 4312-9332, 4312-6636).

Bureau of Export Promotion, Av Julio A Roca 651, Piso 6, 1322 Buenos Aires (tel: 4334-2975; fax: 4331-2266).

Centre for Business Promotion, Buenos Aires Stock Exchange, Sarmlento 299, Piso 1, 1353 Buenos Aires (tel: 4311-5231/4, 4313-4812, 4313-4544; fax: 4312-9332).

Customs Authority, Hipólito Yrigoyen 250 Of 606, 1310 Buenos Aires (tel: 4331-7330; fax: 4331-9839).

Department of Public Works and Transport, 250 Hipólito Yrigoyen Street, 11th Floor, Office 1141, PC 1310, Buenos Aires (tel/fax: 4349-7728; e-mail: arco@meyosp.mecon.ar).

Federal Board of Investment, San Martín 871, 1004 Buenos Aires (tel: 4313-5557; fax: 4313-1486).

Junta Nacional de Carnes (National Meat Board), San Martin 459, 104 Buenos Aires (tel: 4394-5161; fax: 4322-9357).

National Administration of Customs, Azopardo 350, 1328 Buenos Aires (tel: 4343-0661/9, 4343-0101/9).

National Administration of Fishing and Aquaculture, Av Paseo Colón 982, Anexo Jardin, Piso 1, 1063 Buenos Aires (tel: 4349-2330/1; fax: 4349-2332).

National Administration of Fuels, Av Paseo Colón 171, Piso 6, Of. 620, 1063 Buenos Aires (tel: 4319-8030/1).

National Commission of Telecommunications, Sarmiento 151, Piso 4, Of 435, 1041 Buenos Aires (tel: 4331-1203).

National Institute of Industrial Technology, Av L N Alem 1067, Piso 7, 1001 Buenos Aires (tel: 4313-3013).

National Institute of Mining Technology, Parque Tecnológico Migueletes, Casilla de Correo 327, 1650 San Martín (tel: 4754-5151, 4754-4141; fax: 4754-4070, 4754-8307).

National Institute of Statistics and Census, Dirección de Difusión Estadistics, Centro de Servicios Estadísticos, Av Julio A Roca 615, 1067 Buenos Aires (tel: 4349-9651).

National Viticulture Institute, Av Julio A Roca 651, Piso 5, Of 22, 1067 Buenos Aires (tel/fax: 4343-3816).

Public Works and Transport Department, 250 Hipólito Yrigoyen Street, 11th Floor, Office 1141, PC 1310, Buenos Aires (tel/fax: 4349-7728; e-mail: arco@meyosp.mecon.ar).

Secretariat of Agriculture, Livestock and Fisheries, Av Paseo Colón 982, 1063 Buenos Aires (tel: 4362-2365, 4362-5091, 4362-5946; fax: 4349-2504).

Secretariat of Energy, Av Paseo Colón 171, Piso 8 Of 803, 1063 Buenos Aires (tel: 4349-8003/5; fax: 4343-6404).

Secretariat of Finance, Hipólito Yrigoyen 250, 1310 Buenos Aires (tel: 4331-0731, 4342-2937, 4341-8900; fax: 4331-0292).

Secretariat of Industry, Av Junio A Roca 651, 1322 Buenos Aires (tel: 4334-5065, 4342-7822; fax: 4331-3218).

Secretariat of International Economic Relations, Reconquista 1088, 1003 Buenos Aires (tel: 4331-7281, 4331-1073; fax: 4312-0965).

Secretariat of Mining, Av Junio A Roca 561, Sector 9, 1322 Buenos Aires (tel: 4349-3212, 4349-3232; fax: 4343-3525).

Secretariat of Public Works and Communications, Sarmiento 151, 1041 Buenos Aires (tel: 4499-481; fax: 4312-1283).

Secretariat of Transportation, Av. 9 de Julio 1925, 1332 Buenos Aires (tel: 4381-1435, 4381-4007).

Secretariat of Trade and Investment, Hipólito Yrigoyen 250, 1310 Buenos Aires (tel: 4331-2208).

Sociedad Rural Argentina (one of the main associations of big landowners), Florida 460, 1005 Buenos Aires (tel: 4392-2030, 4322-2111).

Subsecretariat of Economic Planning, Hipólito Yrigoyen 250, Of 843, 1310 Buenos Aires (tel: 4349-5079; fax: 4349-5730).

Superintendencia de Seguros de la Nación (Insurance Superintendency), Av Julio A Roca 721, 1067 Buenos Aires (tel: 4306-653).

Telecom Argentina Stet-France Telecom SA, Maipú 1210, 9th Floor, Buenos Aires (tel: 4968-3604, 4968-3606).

Trade Information and Opportunities, Reconquista 1098, 1003 Buenos Aires (tel: 4315-1125; fax: 4311-1331).

Undersecretariat of Air, River and Maritime Transport, Hipólito Yrigoyen 250, 1310 Buenos Aires (tel: 4349-7205; fax: 4342-6365).

Undersecretariat of Interior Security, Balearce 50 Post box 1064, Buenos Aires (tel: 4342-9440 Ext 579; fax: 4331-7051).

Undersecretariat of Investments, Hipólito Yrigoyen 250, Piso 10 Of 1010, 1310 Buenos Aires (tel: 4349-8515/6, 4349-5037; fax: 4349-8522).

Undersecretariat of Medical and Sanitary Inspection, 9 de Julio 1925, Piso 10, Of 1003, 1332 Buenos Aires (tel: 4383-1811; fax: 4381-8912).

Unión Industrial Argentina (main private sector industrial association), Avenida Leandro N Alem 1067, 11 Piso, 1001 Buenos Aires (tel: 4313-2762).

US Embassy, Avenida Colombia 4300, 1425 Buenos Aires (tel: 5777-4533; fax: 5777-4240).

World Trade Centre Buenos Aires, Moreno 584, Piso 6, 1091 Buenos Aires (tel: 4331-3432, 4331-2604; fax: 4343-4270).

National news agency: Telam: www.telam.com.ar

Other news agencies: Agencia DIB (in Spanish): www.dib.com.ar
Agencia Nova (in Spanish): www.agencianova.com

Clave Noticias (in Spanish): www.clavenoticias.com.ar

Noticias Agrentinas (in Spanish): www.noticiasargentinas.com

Diarios y Noticias (DYN) (in Spanish): www.dyn.com.ar

Internet sites

Argentina: www.surdelsur.com

Automóvil Club Argentino: www.aca.org.artigua-barbuda

Buenos Aires: www.buenosaires.com

Fundacion Invertir Argentina: www.invertir.com

Tourism Secretariat: www.turismo.gov.ar

Armenia

KEY FACTS

Official name: Haikakan Hanrapetoutioun (Republic of Armenia)

Head of State: President Serge Sarkisian (since 1998; re-elected 9 Apr 2008)

Head of government: Prime Minister Tigran Sarkisian (no relation to the president) (appointed 9 Apr 2008)

Ruling party: Hayastani Hanrapetakan Kusaktsutyun (HHK) (Republican Party of Armenia) (from May 2007)

Area: 29,800 square km

Population: 3.47 million (2007)*

Capital: Yerevan

Official language: Armenian

Currency: Dram (D) = Luma 100

Exchange rate: D301.50 per US$ (Jul 2008)

GDP per capita: US$1,889 (2006)*

GDP real growth: 13.80% (2007)

Labour force: 1.64 million (2004)

Unemployment: 7.60% (2005)

Inflation: 4.40% (2007)

Balance of trade: -US$1.21 billion (2006)

Foreign debt: US$1.11 billion (2004)

* estimated figure

On paper, Armenia has a lot going for it. It has a well educated populace, internationally recognised not only for their business acumen, but also for their cultural creativity. Armenia, the first country in the world officially to adopt Christianity, also has a powerful, wealthy *diaspora*, notably in the USA and Europe, but also (albeit more thinly spread) in many Middle Eastern states. Armenia can claim greater ethnic homogeneity than any other former Soviet republic.

Faltering steps

Armenia's first ten years of independence, in economic terms, were largely wasted. As the cork was taken out of the Communist bottle, long standing obsessions, grudges and blood feuds took precedence over economic priorities. Armenia's military offensive for the integration of Nagorno Karabakh, the Armenian enclave within Azerbaijan, would have been fraught even if undertaken from a position of strength. But to embark on such a campaign with the economy in tatters was ill-advised. Inefficient and unproductive plants were being closed down causing unemployment and social unrest among the country's well educated work force. After almost a decade of conflict, whatever territorial gains had been achieved came at a cost: loss of life, the deterioration in standards of living, pervasive corruption and steady isolation from the international community.

Not that Armenia didnot have some justification for feeling that right was on its side. Armenian claims to sovereignty over Nagorno Karabakh go back as long ago as 1921 when the Bureau for Caucasian Affairs of the erstwhile USSR had voted to unite Nagorno Karabakh with Armenia, a decision that was overruled by Stalin himself. Armenian aspirations received a further setback in 1988 in the dying days of the USSR when the Supreme Soviet decided not to transfer Nagorno Karabakh to Armenia. This decision was a serious disappointment to Armenians who had expected the Gorbachev administration, with its lip-service to *perestroika*, to support Armenia's position. Not surprisingly, demand for unification has been strong within the enclave itself (Armenia's president Robert Kocharyan is a Karabakhian). The Nagorno Karabakh conflict also possesses religious overtones. For the most part Karabakhians are Christians, living in the Muslim republic of Azerbaijan. Almost the entire Azerbaijani population within Armenia (there is also an Azerbaijani enclave – Nakhichevan – within Armenia) has upped sticks in anticipation of ethnic tensions. The conflict has, *inter-alia*, – resulted in the economic blockade of Armenia not only by Azerbaijan, but also by Turkey.

A not so new President?

Armenia's February 2008 presidential elections went off tolerably well, considered by observers from the Organisation for Security and Co-operation in Europe (OSCE) to have been generally above board. Serge Sargsian, the current prime minister, was confirmed as the outright winner with 53 per cent of the vote at the first ballot. The 2008 contest was the fifth presidential election since independence from the USSR. The victorious Mr Sargsian is known to be more than just a close political ally of the high profile outgoing president, Robert Kochayan. Mr Kochayan was obliged to step down at the end of his term, having reached the constitutional limit on presidential terms in office.

Not that the supporters of the defeated candidate (and Armenia's first post soviet president) Levon Ter-Petrosian took the result lying down. Although Mr Ter-Petrosian only managed to poll a less than impressive 21 per cent, his supporters refused to accept the result. Thousands gathered in Yerevan's Freedom Square claiming that the vote had been rigged and vowing to have the result overturned. Speaking to the *New York Times* a spokesman for Mr Ter-Petrosian protested that the poll 'could hardly be called an election. There was an undeclared war against us.' The OSCE, however, maintained its position that the election had been fair. In the week after the election the protests did not degenerate into violence; in 1999, by contrast, the prime minister and speaker were both killed, along with six other officials, when nationalist gunmen stormed the Armenian parliament.

Strengthening economy

Following the parliamentary elections of June 2007, most of Armenia's ministerial portfolios had remained unchanged, as did the government's broader economic objectives. Central to government plans for the period 2008–12, are a framework of soundly-based macro-economic policies which are maintaining Armenia's impressive growth rate, improving standards of governance and reducing poverty.

Gross domestic product (GDP) continued to grow strongly in 2007, recording a 13.2 per cent growth rate for the period up to September. According to the International Monetary Fund (IMF), domestic demand was fuelled by remittance revenues from Armenia's vast *diaspora*. Inflation for the same period began to show a worrying upward trend, more than doubling from the annual rate of 2.6 per cent recorded in September to 5.7 per cent in October.

Armenia's fiscal policies have long demonstrated a high degree of prudence. In the first half of 2007, the IMF noted that the underspend on capital expenditure had combined with strong revenues to produce a lower than forecast deficit. Tax revenues were higher than the previous year as already predicted by the government's ambitious annual target, reflecting higher value added tax (VAT) and income tax collections. Budget provisions were amended four times during the course of 2007, raising both income and expenditure figures equally by 1.2 per cent of GDP, which had an overall neutral effect on the net deficit. The boost to exports represented by increased diamond exports was cancelled out by a steep rise in imports driven by Armenian's booming domestic demand. This resulted in an increased trade deficit in the first half of 2007. The resultant deterioration in the current account was alleviated by increased remittance inflows.

The IMF also noted that in 2007 most of its programme targets had been met, concluding that Armenia's short-term outlook was positive, despite the increase in inflationary risks, probably prompted by the increased food prices being increased globally. GDP growth for the full year 2007 was expected to fall back to 11 per cent, with full year inflation expected to reach 6 per cent. The target figure for Armenia's inflation had originally been within a 5 per cent band-width around 4 per cent. Had the government resorted to monetary tightening measures, the IMF considered that inflation might be reduced to around the 5 per cent mark. The government forecast for GDP growth in 2008 was 10 per cent. Looking ahead, GDP growth is expected to remain strong, albeit within the lower bandwidth of 6–8 per cent, with inflation dropping to around 4.5

KEY INDICATORS — Armenia

	Unit	2003	2004	2005	2006	2007
Population	m	3.33	3.00	3.32	*3.39	*3.47
Gross domestic product (GDP)	US$bn	2.33	3.55	4.90	6.41	7.97
GDP per capita	US$	700	1,093	1,478	*1,889	7,974
GDP real growth	%	7.0	10.1	14.0	13.4	13.8
Inflation	%	2.2	7.0	0.6	2.9	4.4
Unemployment	%	20.0	9.0	7.6	7.5	7.1
Industrial output	% change	–	7.2	18.8	18.5	18.5
Agricultural output	% change	–	14.2	11.2	0.4	0.4
Exports (fob) (goods)	US$m	525.0	730.4	1,004.9	985.0	985.0
Imports (cif) (goods)	US$m	991.0	1,195.4	1,592.8	2,192.0	–
Balance of trade	US$m	-466.0	-465.0	-587.9	-1,207.0	–
Current account	US$m	190.0	-200.0	-193.2	*-323.0	-518.0
Total reserves minus gold	US$m	510.2	575.9	669.5	1,071.9	1,659.1
Foreign exchange	US$m	491.4	563.9	659.3	1,058.0	1,649.5
Exchange rate	per US$	558.14	521.07	367.25	367.25	301.12

* estimated figure

per cent in 2009 and to 4 per cent in the medium term as more cautious monetary and fiscal policies are expected to hold sway and help contain what are regarded as inevitable rises in gas prices. The budget deficit is expected by the IMF to be capped at 1.8 per cent of GDP, substantially down on the recent level of 2.3 per cent. Armenia's 2008 budget contained provisions for a 60 per cent increase in pensions, requiring in turn a funding provision of 0.9 per cent of GDP. Other social provisions contained in the 2008 budget included targeted protection for the poor to mitigate the impact of the end of gas subsidies.

The IMF had queried the 0.8 per cent tax revenue increase anticipated by the 2008 budget. In riposte, the Armenian authorities had countered that the figure was reasonable given the continued scope for improvement in tax administration and the incoming government's strong commitment to countering tax evasion and avoidance. Armenia's business environment is considered by the IMF to have improved considerably in recent years, although tax administration, access to credit and domestic competition still leave room for improvement.

Election year

2007 was an election year for Armenia. The previous parliamentary elections – in 2003 – had been marred by widespread controversy; in 2003, the National Assembly's 131 seats had been divided between 75 proportional seats and a further 56 majoritarian seats, effectively one for each electoral constituency. Following the election, a number of the smaller parties found common cause in their opposition to President Robert Kocharyan, forming what they designated the Justice Alliance coalition. The Hayastani Zhoghordakan Kusaktsutyan (HZK) (Armenian People's Party) under the leadership of defeated presidential candidate Stepan Demirchyan constituted the largest party within this motley grouping.

Following the 2003 elections a coalition government headed by Andranik Margaryan of the Hayastani Hanrapetakan Kusaktsutyan (HHK) (Republican Party) had been formed. The leader of the Orinats Yerkir (Rule of Law) Artur Baghdasanjan was appointed Speaker of the National Assembly. The Orinats Yerkir party, a newcomer to the assembly with only 9 seats, was the junior member of the ruling coalition. The third member of the coalition was the Hay Hegapokhakan Dashnaktsutiun (Armenian Revolutionary Federation) (ARF) with 11 seats; the Republican Party had 39 seats. In May 2006 the Orinats Yerkir party had left the government coalition and gone into opposition. Mr Baghdasanjan had also resigned as speaker and a number of the Orinats Yerkir deputies subsequently defected to other factions, reflecting something of the volatility of Armenian politics. In March 2007, Armenia's prime minister and the leader of the HHK died, to be replaced by Serge Sargsian the same party.

A total of 24 parties contested the election, of which the centre-right HHK– which had held ten ministerial positions in the outgoing government – remained the dominant force, with almost 34 per cent of the vote and 64 seats, followed some way behind by the Bargavadj Hayastani Kusaktsutyan (BHH) (Prosperous Armenia). The performance of BHH was the surprise of the election; this newcomer party colleted over 15 per cent of the votes and 18 seats. The ARF polled 16 per cent if the vote (16 seats) under the leadership of Serge Sargsian. In the presidential elections, the outgoing president, Robert Kocharyan who did not proclaim any party allegiance, won 67.5 per cent of the vote, well ahead of his rival in the second round of voting, Stepan Demirchyan of the HZK, with 32.5 per cent. Mr Kocharyan appeared to have swept up the swing votes of the candidates fielded by the Azgayin Miabanutyun (National Unity) and Constitutional Rights Union parties, neither of which won any seats in the parliamentary elections. The turnout for the presidential elections was 61 per cent, slightly higher than for the parliamentary elections, where the turnout was 59 per cent.

Genocide

The debate surrounding the emotional subject of the treatment of Armenians by the old Turkish Ottoman empire continued to heat up in 2007 and into 2008. In October the US House of Representatives voted 27–21 in favour of a resolution according the massacres the status of genocide. The move was opposed by President Bush and the Pentagon, anxious to maintain cordial relations with Turkey, first to ensure the latter's support in the prolonged Iraq insurgency. Second, Muslim Turkey has become a key strategic ally of the US in demonstrating that Muslim states can be both democratic and allies of the USA.

The measure has strong support from Armenian Americans, calling as it does for the US to 'accurately characterise the systematic and deliberate annihilation of 1.5 million Armenians as genocide'. In 1915, the then US ambassador to Turkey, Henry Morgenthau Sr, had sent a telegram to Washington which read 'Persecution of Armenians assuming unprecedented proportions. Reports from widely scattered districts indicate systematic attempt to uproot peaceful Armenian population and through arbitrary arrests, terrible tortures, whole-sale expulsions and deportations from one end of the Empire to the other accompanied by frequent instances of rape, pillage and murder, turning into massacre to bring destruction and destitution on them.' In a later telegram, Morgenthau even referred to an 'effort to exterminate a race'. Turkey considers these descriptions to be an affront to its national pride, dismissing them as a distortion of history. It is even rumoured that lobbyists hired by the Turkish government have paid US congressmen to present their case.

Risk assessment

Politics	Fair
Economy	Good
Regional stability	Poor

COUNTRY PROFILE

Historical profile

At its height, the Armenian empire stretched from the Caspian Sea to the Mediterranean, before being incorporated into the Roman empire in AD301. In the eleventh century, Armenia was incorporated into the Turkish Seljuk empire.

1915 The Ottoman empire killed around 1.5 million Armenians in response to the independence movement.

1916 Armenia was conquered by Russia. It joined an alliance with Georgia and Azerbaijan.

1918–20 Armenia was an independent republic for two years.

1920 Turkey and Russia invaded Armenia. An agreement with Russia led to Armenia proclaiming itself a socialist republic.

1922 Armenia was incorporated into the Union of Soviet Socialist Republics (USSR).

1923 Stalin drew the current recognised borders that placed the mainly ethnic Armenian Nagorno-Karabakh in Azerbaijan.

1930s The country suffered under Stalin's purges, but Armenia also underwent industrial development.

1988–93 An earthquake in northern Armenia in 1988 killed 25,000. Nagorno-Karabakh demanded unification with Armenia, and conflict between Azerbaijan and Armenia began. It lasted intermittently for five years.

1990 The Pan-Armenian National Movement (PNM) won the parliamentary elections. A declaration of independence was made, but ignored by Moscow.
1991 The republic boycotted the Soviet referendum on the preservation of the USSR. In a referendum held shortly after the failed anti-Gorbachev coup in Moscow, 94 per cent voted for secession from the USSR. Levon Ter-Petrossian was elected president. Independence was formally proclaimed by the President. Armenia joined the Commonwealth of Independent States (CIS). The US recognised Armenia's independence.
1992 Armenia joined the UN. Conflict over Nagorno-Karabakh turned into full-scale war between Armenia and Azerbaijan.
1994 The war with Azerbaijan over Nagorno-Karabakh settled into an uneasy stalemate, with local Armenians backed by Armenian forces in control of the disputed enclave. A Russian-brokered cease-fire between Azerbaijan and Armenia has generally been honoured.
1995 The first post-independence parliamentary elections resulted in victory for the ruling party, PNM. A constitution was approved by referendum which gave the president substantial powers, including the right to pass decrees.
1996 Levon Ter-Petrosian was re-elected president. There were protests over alleged electoral fraud.
1998 President Levon Ter-Petrosian was forced out of office after stating his wish to open negotiations with Azerbaijan. Robert Kocharian was elected president. The domestic political scene experienced growing instability and politically motivated violence. Deputy minister of defence, Colonel Vagram Khorkhoruni, was murdered. Arkady Gukasian was elected president of Nagorno-Karabakh.
1999 Deputy minister of the interior, Artsun Markarian, was murdered. Prime Minister Vazgen Sargissian and other politicians were assassinated in the National Assembly. Aram Sargissian, the former prime minister's younger brother, was appointed to succeed him. The gunmen accused the government of leading Armenia into political and economic ruin.
2000 Prime Minister Andranik Markarian admitted that those affected by the 1988 earthquake were still living in a disaster zone. President Arkady Gukasian of Nagorno-Karabakh was seriously wounded in an assassination attempt.
2001 Armenia became a full member of the Council of Europe. There was no result in the US-brokered talks on Nagorno-Karabakh between the presidents of Azerbaijan and Armenia.
2002 The first meeting between the foreign ministers of Armenia, Azerbaijan and Turkey was held in Iceland to try to find a settlement for the Nagorno-Karabakh conflict.
2003 Incumbent Robert Kocharian won the second round of the presidential elections and the ruling Hayastani Hanrapetakan Kusaktsutyun (HHK) (Republican Party of Armenia), loyal to President Kocharian, won the parliamentary elections. There were criticisms of both elections. A referendum rejected constitutional amendments giving more power to the National Assembly. The death penalty was abolished.2005 A referendum, which endorsed constitutional change to strengthen parliament and limit presidential power, was held on 27 November.
2005 A referendum, endorsed constitutional changes to strengthen parliament and limit presidential power.
2006 The Orinats Erkir party withdrew from the coalition government. Armenia, together with Azerbaijan and Georgia, signed a European Neighbourhood Policy co-operation agreement with the EU in November.
2007 On 25 March, Prime Minister Andranik Margarian died of a heart attack. Serge Sarkisian was appointed prime minister on 4 April.
2008 In presidential elections, former prime minister Serge Sarkisian was elected with almost 53 per cent of the vote in an election that 'mostly met international standards', viewed by the Organisation for Security and Co-operation in Europe (OSCE). However opposition members claimed the vote was rigged and street protests began. Civil protests led to rioting in Yerevan on 1 March, which caused eight deaths and a declaration of a state of emergency with the deployment of the army on the streets of the capital. Police had started to clear a temporary encampment close to the parliamentary building, which had been passively protesting the result of the presidential elections, when protesters opposed the action and violence broke out. The state of emergency was lifted on 21 March. President Sarkisian was inaugurated on 9 April, when he appointed Tigran Sarkisian (no relation) as prime minister.

Political structure

Constitution

Although the country has had a directly elected president since 1991, a constitution was only approved by referendum in July 1995. It gave the president substantial powers, including the right to pass decrees.

In 2005 a referendum endorsed a number of constitutionals amendments, including reducing the power of the presidency, strengthening parliament and the judiciary, and enshrining in the constitution human rights provisions.

Form of state

Multi-party republic: divided into various marz (provincial divisions).

It is a member of the Commonwealth of Independent States (CIS).

The executive

The president has broad powers. He is elected by direct universal suffrage for a period of five years and has the right to pass decrees.

Under the 1995 constitution, the president is not the head of the executive power, but rather directs that power, by forming the government, appointing (and dismissing) the prime minister and on the proposal of the latter, the cabinet ministers.

The president is not a member of the government, but chairs the sittings and ratifies all government decisions. In consultation with the prime minister, the president has the power to dissolve the National Assembly. The president is commander of the armed forces, represents the country in international negotiations, signs agreements and treaties and appoints the chief prosecutor.

National legislature

The Azgayin Zhoghov (National Assembly) is the supreme legislative body and comprises 131 deputies; 41 seats are filled by direct election and 90 by proportional representation through party-lists. Parties must gain a 5 per cent threshold of electoral support for apportioned seats.

Legal system

The highest appellate court is the Court of Appeal, which ensures uniformity in how the country's laws are applied through its final review of cases. The Court of Appeal's members are nominated by the Council of Justice, an administrative body created to ensure independence of the courts, and then appointed by the president. Armenia also has a Constitutional Court, which is charged with ensuring that legislative decisions and presidential decrees are consistent with the constitution. Of the Constitutional Court's nine members, five are appointed by the president and four by the National Assembly. The president of Armenia heads the Council of Justice. The minister of justice and the prosecutor general serve as deputy heads of the council.

In January 1999, a new civil code came into effect which creates the legal framework for property rights and contract enforcement, as well as the legal and institutional framework necessary for commercial banking activities. Despite this, the enforcement of laws and contracts remains weak.

Last elections

12 May 2007 (parliamentary); 19 March 2008 (presidential).

Results: Presidential: Serge Sarkisian won 52.8 per cent of the vote, Levon Ter-Petrossian, 21.5 per cent and Artur Baghdasarian 17.7 per cent; all other candidates won less than 10 per cent. Parliamentary: HHK won 32.82 per cent of the vote (64 seats out of 131); Bargavadj Hayastani Kusaktsutyun (BHK) (Prosperous Armenia) won 14.68 per cent (24 seats); Hay Heghapokhakan Dashnaktsutyun (HHD) (Armenian Revolutionary Federation) 12.72 per cent (16); Orinants Erkir (OE) (Rule of Law) 6.84 per cent (nine); and Zharangutyun (Heritage) 5.81 per cent (six). Turnout was 59.9 per cent.

Next elections

February 2013 (presidential); May 2011 (parliamentary)

Political parties

Ruling party

Hayastani Hanrapetakan Kusaktsutyun (HHK) (Republican Party of Armenia) (from May 2007)

Main opposition party

Bargavadj Hayastani Kusaktsutyun (BHK) (Prosperous Armenia)

Population

3.47 million (2007)*

Last census: October 2001: 3,002,594

Population density: 137 inhabitants per square km. Urban population: 70 per cent (2000); projected at 1.03 per cent (2000–2005).

Annual growth rate: -0.8 per cent 1994–2004 (WHO 2006)

Internally Displaced Persons (IDP)

50,000 (UNHCR)

Ethnic make-up

Armenians (93 per cent), Azerbaijanis (3 per cent), Russians (2 per cent); Kurdish and Yezidi minorities.

Religions

Armenian Apostolic Church (90 per cent), Armenian Catholic and Protestant (9 per cent), Russian and Greek Orthodox and Jewish.

Education

Primary education is followed by seven years of secondary school which is divided into a four-year first cycle (ages 12 to 16) and a three-year second cycle (ages 16 to 19). In the second cycle, students can opt between general or technical education. Higher education is provided by the Université Marien-Ngouabi, which is largely state subsidised. It has a yearly enrolment of about 12,000 students.

Literacy rate: 99 per cent, adult rates (Unesco 2005).

Compulsory years: 6 to 11

Enrolment rate: 96 per cent gross primary enrolment, 87 per cent gross secondary enrolment, of relevant age groups, (including repeaters) World Bank.

Pupils per teacher: 19 in primary schools.

Health

Per capita total expenditure on health (2003) was US$302; of which per capita government spending was US$61, at the international dollar rate, (WHO 2006).

HIV/Aids

HIV prevalence: 0.1 per cent aged 15–49 in 2003 (World Bank)

Life expectancy: 68 years, 2004 (WHO 2006)

Fertility rate/Maternal mortality rate: 1.2 births per woman (2003); maternal deaths 35 per 100,000 live births (World Bank).

Birth rate/Death rate: 6 deaths to 12 births per 1,000 people (World Bank).

Child (under 5 years) mortality rate (per 1,000): 31 per 1,000 live births; 3 per cent of children aged under five are malnourished (World Bank).

Head of population per physician: 3.59 physicians per 1,000 people (2003) (WHO 2006)

Welfare

The poverty family allowance system is based on the principle of voluntary involvement and aims to target the most needy. Welfare issues concerning the elderly are crucial as almost 97 per cent of them need constant medication and 41 per cent need home care.

Pensions

In order to improve the state pension system, the government has increased the level of contributions for certain income groups. Under the state system, pensioners receive a uniform payment. There are no private pension funds.

Main cities

Yerevan (capital, estimated population 1.09 million in 2008), Vanadzor (116,929), Gyumri (168,918).

Languages spoken

Russian and Kurdish.

Official language/s

Armenian

Media

Despite censorship being prohibited in 2004 libel and defamation laws are often used to harass journalists, which has resulted in self-censorship particularly when reporting corruption and security matters particularly in Nagorno-Karabakh.

National news agency: Armenpress

Other news agencies: Arka: www.arka.am

Arminfo: www.arminfo.info

Noyan Tapan: www.nt.am

Mediamax: www.mediamax.am

Press

The National Press Club (NPC) of Armenia formed is a self-governing, apolitical, non-profit, independent public organisation that aims to support free and democratic press in Armenia.

There are around 30 newspapers available but circulations are low with the largest being only 10,000. Productions costs have been traditionally high but following international aid a printing plant was opened and since 2005 has provided an alternative and competition for the semi-state-owned printing house. A number of publications have since increased their days of publishing and increased their circulations. Newspapers are generally owned by wealthy individuals or political parties.

Dailies: Most newspapers are published in Armenian, with Russian and English languages editions, including Aravot (http://new.aravot.am), a privately owned daily. Parliamentary publications include Ayastani Anrapetutyun (www.hhpress.am) and Respublika Armenia (www.ra.am). Political party publications include Azg (www.azg.am), Yerkir (http://yerkir.am), and Aykakan Zhanamak (www.hzh.am). In Russian, Golos Armenii (www.golos.am).

Weeklies: In Armenian, Haykakan Zhamanak is a popular weekly newspaper; with a Russian edition Iravunk (www.iravunk.com); with English editions Eter (www.eter.tv), Lragir (www.lragir.am), Yerkir (www.yerkir.am), and 168 Jam (www.168.am). MFA Nagorno Karabakh (www.nkr.am) published in Stepanakert.

Broadcasting

Radio: The state-run Public Radio of Armenia (www.armradio.am) has two general interest stations, children's radio (http://lyunse.amradio.am) and (www.arevik.net) and an international service (http://int.armradio.am). There are a few private commercial radio stations including Hit FM (www.hit.am), Radio Van (www.radiovan.am) and City FM (www.cityfm.am).

Television: Television is the dominant media outlet. The state-run national service is provided by Public TV of Armenia (www.armtv.com) with local and imported shows most of which are translated into Armenian. Armenia TV (www.armeniatv.am) in the national commercial service. There are around 30 cable, digital and satellite TV stations broadcasting pay-to-view services.

Advertising

There is a complete ban on advertising of tobacco and alcohol. Advertising which targets children must only contain products suitable for them.

Economy

Armenia's government has made structural reform a priority. Efforts to make the economy a free market have resulted in steady GDP growth since 2001. In 2005,

domestic demand was boosted through public expenditure, remittances and investment, although agriculture, construction and the services remain the chief drivers of the 10.5 per cent GDP growth rate. Industry accounted for 44.3 per cent of GDP, of which manufacturing was 20.5 per cent and their combined average annual growth was 18.8 per cent. Construction reached 35.1 per cent of GDP, highlighting the investment in housing and industries. Agriculture accounted for 20.5 per cent of GDP and grew by 11.5 per cent in 2005.
Poverty reduction programmes were enhanced by overall growth; poverty was brought down from a 55 per cent of the population high in 1996 to 39 per cent in 2004. Likewise, extreme poverty was reduced from 27.7 per cent of the population to 7.2 per cent in the same period. Unemployment fell from 10.1 per cent in 2003 to 8.1 per cent in 2005, although unofficial unemployment is estimated at 30 per cent with the result that there is substantial migration.
Armenia has had to adapt its reliance on its old industries such as chemicals, electronic components, machinery, processed food, textiles and synthetic rubber, all of which were highly dependent on outside resources, and which were disrupted when the former Soviet Union broke up. New sectors now include processed precious stones and jewellery production, information and communication technology and a nascent tourism industry.

External trade
Armenia is a net energy exporter, supplying Georgia and the Nagorno-Karabakh region in Azerbaijan, although there has been external pressure applied to have its ageing nuclear power station closed down. Heavy industrial products have given way to light industrial products and agricultural produce for export. Imported pearls and precious gems combine with locally produced examples to form the full inventory of exports.

Imports
Imports of essential goods, including natural gas and petroleum, foodstuffs, tobacco products, equipment and diamonds.
Main sources: Russia (13.7 per cent total, 2006), Turkmenistan (7.7 per cent), Ukraine (7.5 per cent).

Exports
Principal exports include electricity, precious stones, (diamonds, pearls, lapis lazuli), precious metals, base metals, mineral products, transport equipment, electrical equipment.
Main destinations: Germany (14.6 per cent of 2006 total goods exports), The Netherlands (12.6 per cent), Russia (11.6 per cent).

Agriculture
Armenia is a major producer of grapes, vegetables, dairy products and some cotton and sheep breeding. Agriculture contributes around 25 per cent to GDP and employs over 45 per cent of the work force. Armenia was the first former Soviet republic to privatise agricultural land. There are around 335,000 family farms, which account for the bulk of agricultural output. Development has been inhibited by lack of private investment, an inadequate agricultural financing system and poor infrastructure.
Crop production in 2005 included: 384,200 tonnes (t) cereals in total, 253,000t wheat, 574,900t potatoes, 4,720t pulses, *80,000t grapes, 8,000t garlic, 245,000t tomatoes, 300t tobacco, 172,300t fruit in total, 776,300t vegetables in total. Livestock production included: 51,150t meat in total, 30,000t beef, 8,500t pig meat, *7,000t lamb, *5,000t poultry, 27,170t eggs, 571,900t milk, *1,000t honey, *5,320t cattle hides, *1,000t greasy wool.
* Estimate

Industry and manufacturing
The economy relies heavily on the industrial sector. Industry accounts for around 40 per cent of GDP and employs around 20 per cent of the workforce.
Industry is mainly based on the extraction and processing of natural resources, particularly ores and chemicals.
Other industries are mechanical engineering, electronic generators, textiles, synthetic rubber, wine and cognac, mineral water and food processing.

Tourism
Tourism is an increasingly important sector of the economy. Since 1997, much has had to be done to modernise and extend the infrastructure. Visitor numbers have increased by substantial annual percentages. Compared with 123,000 in 2001, there were 268,000 in 2004, with the trend continuing into 2005. A significant proportion of visitors are diaspora Armenians, but the numbers from other regions, including the EU and Asia, are growing. Tourism accounts for around five per cent of GDP.

Mining
Mining accounts for around 13 per cent of GDP and employs 3 per cent of the workforce.
There are large deposits of copper, zinc, aluminium and other metals, including gold. Copper accounts for 38 per cent of the reserve, iron and molybdenum 25 per cent each; gold 7.3 per cent, silver 1.6 per cent and lead and zinc 3.1 per cent.
Armenia is rich in varieties of building stone, such as marble, granite, tuffa, limestone and gypsum, and in semi-precious and ornamental stones, such as agates, jasper, amethyst and turquoise.
The major markets for Armenia's mining products are Belgium, Georgia, Iran, Liechtenstein, Switzerland and Germany.

Hydrocarbons
Armenia has no oil reserves and is completely dependent on imports of petroleum products, all of which are transported by rail or truck since there are no oil pipelines into Armenia.
Armenia has no natural gas reserves and is totally reliant on imports, mainly from Turkmenistan through the Georgian and Russian gas pipelines in the north. It imported 49.4 billion cubic feet in 2003. When the Nagorno-Karabakh conflict erupted, Azerbaijan ceased shipments of natural gas to the country. A 140km pipeline to deliver natural gas from Iran to Armenia began construction in July 2004. The natural gas pipeline, which will commence delivery of one billion cubic metres a year in 2007, should enable Armenia to diversify its supplies.

Energy
Installed electricity capacity is 3.2GW, generated by thermal, hydro and nuclear power. 40 per cent of the total is supplied by the Metsamor nuclear station, which was reopened in 1995 after being closed after the 1988 earthquake. Armenia has been under international pressure to close the plant. There are 32 hydroelectric plants, which account for 34 per cent of production. Thermal power plants supply the remaining 26 per cent. Armenia is linked to Iran's grid, permitting two-way exchange of electricity.
Armenia and Iran are co-operating on development of renewable energy sources. A wind power plant with a capacity of 10.4MW, supported by Iranian money, was inaugurated in December 2005 and will supply the electricity grid.

Financial markets
Non-banking financial institutions (such as leasing organisations, insurance companies and investment funds) are either non-existent or at an early stage of development.
A Securities and Exchange Commission was established in November 1998.

Stock exchange
The Yerevan Stock Exchange (YSE) was liquidated in early 2001. The only stock exchange operating in Armenia is the Armenian Stock Exchange Self-Regulatory Organisation (Armex), which was established in February 2001.

Banking and insurance
The banking system in Armenia is growing but still experiences difficulties in attracting deposits (representing less than 10 per cent of GDP). Most lending is available at short maturities only and at high interest rates. The range of facilities and services on offer to customers is increasing. HSBC Armenia was one of the most active banks.
There are over 30 commercial banks in the country.
Central bank
Central Bank of the Republic of Armenia

Financial markets
Non-banking financial institutions (such as leasing organisations, insurance companies and investment funds) are either non-existent or at an early stage of development.
A Securities and Exchange Commission was established in November 1998.

Time
GMT plus three hours

Geography
Armenia is a landlocked country of high mountains and fertile valleys situated in south-west Transcaucasia. Georgia lies to the north of Armenia, to the west is the border with Turkey. Azerbaijan is to the east of the country – the ethnic Armenian enclave, Nagorno-Karabakh, is wholly within Azerbaijan – and to the south Armenia has a short frontier with Iran. The autonomous republic of Nankhchivan, an Azerbaijani territory, is an enclave within southern Armenia. Lake Sevan is at an altitude of 1,924 metres and is surrounded by mountain ranges reaching 4,090 metres at Mount Aragats. Numerous rivers and streams flow from the mountains into the River Araks which marks the south-western border of the country, its basin forming a fertile lowland to the south of Yerevan – the Ararat Plain.
Hemisphere
Northern

Climate
Cool winters and hot summers characterise Armenia with the average January temperature in Yerevan at around 1 degree Celsius (C), while July averages 26 degrees C. Snow falls in early winter (November and December) and rain in April to June.
Annual rainfall in Yerevan averages 33cm but is much higher in mountain regions.

Entry requirements
Passports
Required by all. Must be valid at least four months after date of departure.
Visa
Required by all except nationals of CIS countries. An invitation is required for visits over 21 days.Visas can be obtained online: www.armeniaforeignministry.am/consular/visa.html.
Currency advice/regulations
There are no restrictions on import of local or foreign currency, but amounts over US$10,000 must be declared. Export of local or foreign currency unlimited, but cash restricted to US$10,000, amounts above which must be transferred through a bank.
Customs
Personal goods up to US$500 are duty-free. Advisable to declare valuables such as jewellery, cameras, computers and musical instruments.

Health (for visitors)
Mandatory precautions
None.
Advisable precautions
It is advisable to be in date for the following immunisations: tetanus (within 10 years), hepatitis A (moderate risk only); hepatitis B (if you need to spend more than six to eight weeks in the region); malaria precautions for western border areas only.
Any medicines required should be taken by the visitor. Take a medical kit including a disposable syringe. Food and water precautions should be observed.

Credit cards
Major credit cards and travellers cheques are accepted at the banks in Yerevan.

Public holidays (national)
Fixed dates
1–2 Jan (New Year), 6 Jan (Orthodox Christmas), 8 Mar (Women's Day), 7 Apr (Motherhood and Beauty Day), 24 Apr (Genocide Memorial Day), 9 May (Victory and Peace Day), 28 May (First Republic Day), 5 Jul (Constitution Day), 21 Sep (Independence Day), 7 Dec (Earthquake Memorial Day), 31 Dec (New Year's Eve).
Variable dates
Good Friday

Working hours
Banking
Mon–Fri: 0900–1800.
Business
Mon–Fri: 0900–1800.
Government
Mon–Fri: 0900–1730.
Shops
Mon–Fri: 0900–2000; Sat–Sun: 0900–1800.

Electricity supply
220V AC 50Hz

Weights and measures
Metric system

Social customs/useful tips
The Armenians are very hospitable and will invite strangers into their homes. Being unable to speak their language will not be a problem. Dress in rural areas should be modest.
Do not photograph military installations or equipment and seek permission to photograph religious buildings.

Security
Visitors should not travel to Nagorno-Karabakh in the west or the military occupied area surrounding it.

Getting there
Air
Armenia is increasingly accessible by air with flights from Europe, the Middle East and especially Moscow.
National airline: Armavia.
International airport/s: Zvartnots (EVN), 10km south-west of Yerevan; facilities include business and VIP halls plus duty-free shops, post office and cafés.
Airport tax: A departure tax of US$20, excluding transit passengers.
Surface
Road: Access is from Georgia to the north and Iran to the south. Routes from Turkey and Azerbaijan are closed.
Rail: There is a service running from Batumi on the Black Sea, via Tbilisi and the Georgian border, to Yerevan. There are also connections fromTbilisi to Gyumri and to Vanadzor. The gnatsk is a through train, running on alternate days.
Pre-booking is advised.

Getting about
National transport
Road: There are 7,705km (4,788 miles) of roads. The main roads are in reasonable condition, but local roads can be very poor.
Buses: Coaches operate between towns and city centres.
Rail: The railway system is aged and the service is unreliable.
City transport
Taxis: Taxis in Yerevan are unmetered. Expect to negotiate a fare to destination beforehand.
Buses, trams & metro: Vans (marshrutnis), charging a cheap flat fare, are the best way of travel in Yerevan. There is a short, single-line metro in Yerevan, which is cheap and efficient.
Car hire
Car rental services are available in Yerevan, but it is usual and advisable to hire a car and driver. Traffic drives on the right.

BUSINESS DIRECTORY

The addresses listed below are a selection only. While World of Information makes every endeavour to check these addresses, we cannot guarantee that changes have not been made, especially

to telephone numbers and area codes. We would welcome any corrections.

Telephone area codes

The international direct dialling (IDD) code for Armenia is +374, followed by area code and subscriber's number:

Abovyan	222	Vanadzor	322
Gyumri	312	Yerevan	10

Chambers of Commerce

American Chamber of Commerce in Armenia, Hotel Armenia, 1 Amiryan Street, Yerevan 375010 (tel: 599-187; fax: 599-151; e-mail: amcham@arminco.com).

European Union Chamber of Commerce in Armenia, 8/1 Khorenatsi Street, Yerevan 375010 (tel: 547-760; fax: 547-780; e-mail: info@eucca.am).

Chamber of Commerce and Industry of the Republic of Armenia, 11 Khanjyan Street, Yerevan 375010 (tel: 560-184; fax: 587-871; e-mail: armcci@arminco.com).

Kotayk Marz Chamber of Commerce and Industry, 11 Sevani Street, Abovyan 378510 (tel: 26-035; fax: 233-97; e-mail: ccikotayk@ccikotayk.am).

Yerevan Chamber of Commerce and Industry, 11 Khanjyan Street, Yerevan 375010 (tel: 560-184; fax: 587-871; e-mail: yercci@arminco.com).

Banking

Ardshinbank of the Republic of Armenia, 3 Deghatan Street, Yerevan (tel: 560-611; fax: 151-155, 584-761).

Arminpex Bank, 2 Nalbandian Street, 375010 Yerevan (tel: 589-927, 567-183, 565-873; fax: 151-786, 151-815).

HSBC Armenia Bank, 1 Vramshapouh Arka Street, Yerevan (tel: 151-717; fax: 151-886).

Armeconombank, 32 G.Nzdehi Street, Yerevan 375026 (tel: 562-705, 531-115; fax: 151-149).

Armagrobank, 7a Movses Khorenacu Street, Yerevan 375015 (tel: 534-342; fax: 390-712-6).

Mellat, 1 P.Byusandy, Yerevan (tel: 581-354; fax: 151-811).

Prometeus, 19 Kochari Street, Yerevan 375012 (tel: 273-000; fax: 274-818).

Haykap, 22 Sarian Street, Yerevan 375002 (tel: 532-080; fax: 390-703-3).

Erebuni, 13 Khagakh- Don Street, Yerevan 375087 (tel: 577-256).

Credit - Yerevan, 2/8 Vramshapouh Arkay Street, Yerevan 375010 (tel: 589-065; fax: 580-083).

Central bank

Central Bank of Armenia, Vazgen Sargsyan Street 6, 375010 Yerevan (tel: 583-841; fax: 523-852); e-mail: mcba@cba.am).

Travel information

Armavia Airline Co Ltd, 3 Amiryan Street, 50 Mashtotsi Avenue, 0010 Yerevan(tel: 593-316; fax: 582-604; e-mail: armavia@infocom.am).

Levon Travel Bureau, 10 Sayat Nova Avenue, 375001 Yerevan (tel: 525-210; fax: 561-483; e-mail: tourism@levontravel.am).

National tourist organisation offices

Armenia Tourism Development Agency, 3 Nalbandyan Street, 0010 Yerevan (tel: 542-303; fax: 544-792; e-mail: help@armeniainfo.am).

Ministries

Ministry of Agriculture and Food Supplies, 1 Government House, Republican Square, 375010 Yerevan (tel: 524-641; fax: 151-086, 151-583).

Ministry of Communications, 22 Sarian Street, 375002 Yerevan (tel: 526-632; fax: 151-446; 151-151); Union Bldg, Republic Square, Yerevan 375010.

Ministry of Culture, Youth and Sports, 5 Toumanian Street, 375010 Yerevan (tel: 528-869, 561-920; fax: 523-930, 523-922, 526-869).

Ministry of Defence, Proshian Settlement, 60 G. Shaush Road, Yerevan (tel: 357-822; fax: 526-560).

Ministry of Ecology and Natural Resources, 35 Moskovian Street, 375012 Yerevan (tel: 530-741; fax: 534-902).

Ministry of Economical Structural Reform, 1 Government House, Republic Square, Yerevan 375010 (tel: 151-069).

Ministry of Education and Science, 13 Movses Khorenatsi Street, 375010 Yerevan (tel: 526-602; fax: 151-150).

Ministry of Energy, 1 Government House, Republican Square, 375010 Yerevan (tel: 521-964; fax: 151-036).

Ministry of Finance and Economy, 1 Melik-Adamian Street, 375010 Yerevan (tel: 527-082; fax: 151-154).

Ministry of Foreign Affairs, 2 Government House, Republican Square, 375010 Yerevan (tel: 523-531; fax: 151-042).

Ministry of Health, 8 Tumanian Street, 375001 Yerevan (tel: 582-413; fax: 151-097).

Ministry of Industry and Trade, Division of Tourism, 5 Hanrapetutjan Street, 375010 Yerevan (tel: 560-274, 560-780, 589-472, 587-706; fax: 526-577).

Ministry of Internal Affairs and National Security, 2 Nalbandian, 375025 Yerevan (tel: 529-733).

Ministry of Justice, 8 Parliament Street, 375010 Yerevan (tel: 582-157; fax: 565-640).

Ministry of Local Government Affairs, 2 Government House, Yerevan (tel: 525-274).

Ministry of Operational Affairs, 1 Government House, Republican Square, Yerevan 375010 (tel: 151-036; fax: 520-321).

Ministry of Privatisation and Foreign Investment, 1 Government House, Republic Square, Yerevan 375010 (tel: 520-351; fax: 151-036).

Ministry of Social Security, 18 Issahakian Street, 375025 Yerevan (tel: 526-831; fax: 151-920).

Ministry of Statistics and Data, State Registrar, Republican Square, 375010 Yerevan (tel: 524-213).

Ministry of Transport, 10 Zakiyan Street, 375015 Yerevan (tel: 563-391; fax: 525-268).

Ministry of Urban Planning and Construction, 1 Government House, Republican Square, Yerevan (tel: 589-080; fax: 151-036).

Prime Minister's Office, 1 Government House, Republican Square, 375101 Yerevan (tel: 520-360; fax: 151-035).

Other useful addresses

Armenian Embassy (USA), 2225 R Street, NW, Washington DC 20008 (tel: (+1-202) 319-1976; fax: (+1-202) 319-2982).

Armenian Foreign Trade Organisation, V/O Armentorg, Dom Pravitelstva, Ploschad Lenina, 375010 Yerevan.

Armenian Foundation for SMEs, 19 Khandjian Street, 375010 Yerevan (tel: 578-231; fax: 151-690; e-mail: smeda@arminco.com).

Armenian State Foreign Economic and Trade Association, Str 25 Hr Kochar, 375012 Yerevan (tel: 224-310; fax: 220-034).

Azat Mamoul (Dashnak News Agency), Yerevan (tel: 563-493; fax: 565-728).

British Embassy, 28 Charents Street, Yerevan (tel: 151-842; fax: 151-807).

Business Communication Centres, 6 Baghramian Avenue 2, 375009 Yerevan (tel: 222-145; fax: 151-934; e-mail: ggv@bcc.arminco.com).

Committee of Privatisation and Management of State Property, Ul Budakhian 1, 375014 Yerevan (tel: 280-120).

Department of Emergency Situations, Government House, Republican Square,

Yerevan 375010 (tel: 531-612; fax: 151-036).

EC Energy Centre, Institute of Energy, Amaranotsayeen 127, Yerevan (tel/fax: 151-730).

Enterprise Development and Foreign Investment Promotion Armenian Agency (EDIPA), 23/1 Vramshapuh Arkah, Yerevan 375002 (tel: 538-929; fax: 151-149).

Secretariat of the Council of Ministers (tel: 520-360, 522-482; fax: 151-035, 141-036).

State Commission for Tax Inspection, Movses Khorenatsi, Yerevan 375010 (tel: 538-101, 538-073).

State Department for Statistics, State Register and Analysis of the Republic of Armenia, 3 Government House, Republic Square, Yerevan (tel: 524-213; fax: 521-921).

State TV and Radio, 5 Alex Manoogian, 375025 Yerevan (tel: 555-033).

TACIS (Technical Assistance to Commonwealth of Independent States), Ministry of Economy, 1 Government Building, Republic Square, Yerevan 10 (tel: 528-803; fax: 151-164).

US Embassy, 18 Baghramyan Avenue, Yerevan 375019 (tel: 520-791; fax: 520-800; e-mail: usinfo@arminco.com).

National news agency: Armenpress

Other news agencies: Arka: www.arka.am
Arminfo: www.arminfo.info

Noyan Tapan: www.nt.am

Mediamax: www.mediamax.am

Internet sites

Armenian Development Agency: www.businessarmenia.com

Armenian information: www.armgate.com

Armenian Stock Exchange: www.armex.am

Armenia Yellow Pages: www.armenian.com

Arminfo News Agency: www.arminfo.am

Aruba

COUNTRY PROFILE

Historical profile
1499 First European sighting of the islands of the Netherlands Antilles by Spanish mariners.
1636 Dutch took over; Spanish and Portuguese Jews escaping from persecution in Europe settled in the islands.
1800–02 British Protectorate.
1825 Gold discovered and mined until 1916.
1863 Slavery completely abolished.
1954 Internal autonomy was granted to Netherlands Antilles.
1986 Aruba seceded from Netherlands Antilles; both entities elected to remain part of the Kingdom of the Netherlands. Aruba has complete autonomy over its internal affairs; the Netherlands is constitutionally responsible for defence and external affairs.
2001 Movimiento Electoral di Pueblo (MEP) (People's Electoral Movement) won parliamentary elections and Nelson Oduber (MEP) became prime minister.
2003 A law was introduced in order to help fight money laundering more efficiently.
2004 Fredis Refunjol was sworn in as governor on 7 May.
2005 Negative publicity about the official investigation into the disappearance of a US teenager, Natalee Holloway, resulted in a drop in US visitor arrivals. In parliamentary elections, Prime Minister Nelson Oduber's MEP won 43 per cent of the vote (11 of 21 seats), the Aruban People's Party 33 per cent (8) and the Patriotic Movement of Aruba and the Real Democratic Party won 1 seat each. Turnout was 85 per cent.
2007 The chief prosecutor closed the official investigation into the disappearance of Natalee Holloway.

Political structure
Form of state
Parliamentary democracy
The executive
The Head of State is the monarch of The Netherlands, who is represented by a governor. The governor is appointed by the monarch, on the recommendation of the Aruban Council of Ministers.
Executive power is exercised by the governor and a prime minister who heads an eight-member council of ministers. The Council is accountable to the Staten (parliament).
National legislature
The Staten has 21 members, elected for a four-year term by proportional representation.
Legal system
Aruba's judicial system, which has mainly been derived from the Dutch system, operates independently of the legislature and the executive. Jurisdiction, including appeal, lies with the Common Court of Justice of Aruba and the Supreme Court of Justice in The Netherlands.
Last elections
23 September 2005 (parliamentary)
Results: MEP won 43 per cent of the votes (11 seats), the AVP 33 per cent, (eight seats). The PPA and OLA won one seat each. Turnout was 85 per cent.
Next elections
2009

Political parties
Ruling party
Movimiento Electoral di Pueblo (MEP) (People's Electoral Movement) (since 2001; re-elected 2005)
Main opposition party
Arubaanse Volks Partij (AVP) (Aruban People's Party)

Population
120,000 (2007)*
Last census: October 2000: 90,508
Population density: 516 inhabitants per square km. Urban population: 51 per cent (1995—2001).
Annual growth rate: 0.2 per cent (2003)
Ethnic make-up
Carib and Arawak Indian, European and African heritage.
Religions
Roman Catholic (82 per cent), Protestant (8 per cent), Hindu, Muslim, Confucian, Jewish.

Education
Literacy rate: 97 per cent

Health
Life expectancy: 78.8 years (estimate 2003)
Fertility rate/Maternal mortality rate: Two births per woman (2003)
Birth rate/Death rate: 12 births per 1,000 population; six deaths per 1,000 population (2003).

KEY FACTS

Official name: Aruba

Head of State: Queen Beatrix of the Netherlands; Governor Fredis Refunjol (from May 2004)

Head of government: Prime Minister Nelson Oduber (MEP) (since 2001, re-elected 2005)

Ruling party: Movimiento Electoral di Pueblo (MEP) (People's Electoral Movement) (since 2001; re-elected 2005)

Area: 193 square km

Population: 120,000 (2007)*

Capital: Oranjestad

Official language: Dutch

Currency: Aruban guilder (Af) = 100 cents (commonly called the florin)

Exchange rate: Af1.79 per US$ (Jul 2008)

GDP per capita: US$21,800 (2004)

GDP real growth: 2.50% (2005)

Labour force: 42 (2004)

Unemployment: 6.90% (2005)*

Inflation: 2.40% (2004)

Balance of trade: -US$795.00 million (2004)

Visitor numbers: 694,000 (2006)*

* estimated figure

Child (under 5 years) mortality rate (per 1,000): Six per 1,000 live births (2003)

Main cities
Oranjestad (capital, estimated population 32,748 in 2008), St Nicolas (18,126).

Languages spoken
Papiamento is the local language. Dutch, English and Spanish are widely spoken.
Official language/s
Dutch

Media
Press
In Papiamento, from Oranjestad, Diario (http://news.diario-aruba.com), Bon Dia (www.bondia.com), AWE Mainta (www.awemainta.com) and Solo di Pueblo (www.solodipueblo.com) published in Santa Cruz. In Dutch, with an English edition, Amigoe (www.amigoe.com). In English, Aruba Today (www.arubatoday.com).
Broadcasting
Radio: In Papiamento, Dutch and English, Radio Kelkboom (www.watapana-aruba.com) broadcasts news, talk and music. There are several other commercial music and religious programme stations including Hit FM (www.hit94fm.com), Magic 96.5 (www.magic965.com), Mega 88FM (www.mega88fm.com) and Cool FM (www.coolaruba.com).
Television: Tele-Aruba (www.telearuba.aw) provides a comprehensive service with locally produced news, current affairs, educational, cultural and sports as well as imported programmes. There are several cable and satellite TV stations, some of which are also US affiliates, including Cable TVAruba (CTA) (www.cta.aw), Venevisión, Flamingo TV, ATV and Caribbean Super Station.

Advertising
All newspapers accept advertising in English.

Economy
Tourism, oil refining, and financial services are Aruba's economic mainstays. Tourism contributes some 38 per cent of GDP and employs 35 per cent of the workforce. Future economic growth depends on increased capacity utilisation, moves to further upgrade the quality of tourism, and the diversification of the economy. To encourage financial services and manufacturing investment, the government has developed the offshore financial sector and free trade zones.
The IMF warns that the island's vulnerability to downturns in the tourist industry means that debt accumulation should be managed with more prudence.

External trade
There is an oil refinery and storage facility in operation with brings in important foreign exchange. There are free trade zones situated near the harbour of Oranjestad and Barcadera.
Imports
Crude oil is imported for refining. Other products include foodstuffs, machinery, electrical equipment and chemicals.
Main sources: US (55.9 per cent total, 2005), The Netherlands (12.9 per cent), UK (3.8 per cent)
Exports
Main exports include refined petroleum products, live animals, animal products, art and collectables, machinery and electronic equipment and vehicles.
Main destinations: The Netherlands Antilles (33.5 per cent total, 2004), Panama (16.7 per cent), Colombia (11.9 per cent), US (11.9 per cent), Venezuela (10.1 per cent), The Netherlands (9.0 per cent)

Re-exports
Crude oil is refined.

Industry and manufacturing
Oil processing is the dominant industry in Aruba, despite the expansion of the tourism sector.
The Lago refinery, originally owned by a subsidiary of Exxon, was closed in 1985, depriving the island of one-third of its revenue, and later sold to the Aruban government for a nominal amount. It was rehabilitated by Coastal Oil and Gas Corporation of Houston and reopened in 1990. US-based El Paso produced 169,000 barrels per day (bpd) of oil in the first quarter of 2003, around 50 per cent of capacity.
El Paso agreed to sell to Valero Energy Corporation of the US bought the refinery and related marine, bunkering and marketing affiliates for US$465 million in February 2004. The refinery has a throughput capacity of 315,000bpd.

Tourism
Tourism is the island's largest employer. Three-quarters of visitors to the island come from the US. South American countries and The Netherlands make up most of the rest. The government is seeking to attract more visitors from Europe. A national short-haul airline, connecting with the Netherlands Antilles, has been set up. The Reina Beatrix airport can handle 2.6 million travellers.

Hydrocarbons
Aruba does not import either coal or gas. Crude oil makes up 97.4 percent of all oil imported with 235.1 thousand barrels daily being imported with some consumed domestically but most is refined and exported.

Energy
The government-owned power plant has a capacity of 114MW and distributes electricity through Elmar NV.

Banking and insurance
The banking sector consists of six commercial banks, two of which are branches of banks established in The Netherlands and Curaçao, one is a subsidiary of a bank established in Curaçao and three have their head offices in Aruba.
Aruba is a signatory of a new EU tax agreement that was introduced in July 2005. It has agreed to pass on, to the tax department of an EU citizen's country, information concerning the amount of money in savings accounts, to allow tax to be levied from the account holder's home country.
Aruba has also agreed to supply information on tax fraud, for criminal or civil trials, and notify EU member states about additional malpractices.

KEY INDICATORS **Aruba**

	Unit	2003	2004	2005	2006	2007
Population	m	0.09	0.09	0.10	0.11	0.12
Gross domestic product (GDP)	US$bn	20.03	21.25	22.48	23.70	–
GDP per capita	US$	20,410	21,103	21,940	22,934	–
GDP real growth	%	1.5	3.5	2.3	2.4	–
Inflation	%	3.2	2.5	3.4	3.6	–
Exports (fob) (goods)	US$m	2,045.1	2,723.5	3,483.7	3,951.5	–
Imports (cif) (goods)	US$m	2,378.8	-2,997.7	-3,536.3	3,837.5	–
Balance of trade	US$m	-333.7	-274.1	-52.6	113.9	–
Current account	US$m	-155.4	-113.6	-258.8	213.4	–
Total reserves minus gold	US$m	295.2	295.4	273.5	337.8	372.1
Foreign exchange	US$m	295.2	295.4	273.5	337.8	372.1
Exchange rate	per US$	1.79	1.79	1.79	1.79	1.79

Central bank
Centrale Bank van Aruba
Offshore facilities
The offshore banking sector has great potential. The Central Bank has been better equipped to regulate the banking sector since the enactment of the State Ordinance on the Supervision of the Credit System, 1998. The minimum issued capital of an offshore bank is Af5 million (US$2.8 million). Aruba has pledged to phase out all 'harmful tax practices' identified by the OECD by 2006.

Time
GMT minus four hours

Geography
Located in the Caribbean Sea north of Venezuela, Aruba is a flat island with large white sandy beaches and sparse vegetation. The highest point is Mount Jamanota which is 188 metres above sea level.
Hemisphere
Northern

Climate
Aruba lies outside the Caribbean's hurricane zone. It has an almost constant temperature of 27 degrees Celsius with cooling trade winds and an absence of tropical storms and hurricanes. Low levels of humidity and rainfall.

Entry requirements
Passports
Required by all, except nationals of US and Canada, who only need proof of citizenship, and of EU countries with EU Travel Cards. (NB citizens of Canada and US require passports for re-entry to their countries).
Passports must be valid for at least three months after arrival. A return or onward ticket and adequate funds are required.
Visa
Not required, except by nationals of former Communist and some other countries. For details, visit www.visitaruba.com/travel/ toaruba/ customs.html or contact the nearest embassy.
Currency advice/regulations
Import/export of Aruban currency is forbidden. No restriction on import of foreign currencies, but a licence is required for export.
Customs
Besides articles for personal use, persons aged over 18 are allowed 2 litres of alcohol and 200 cigarettes, 50 cigars and 250 grammes of tobacco.

Health (for visitors)
Mandatory precautions
Yellow fever vaccination certificate required if arriving from an infected area.
Advisable precautions
hepatitis A and B and typhoid vaccinations.

Hotels
There are numerous tourist hotels. It is advisable to book in advance. There is a 17.66 per cent service and government tax on room prices and a 10–15 per cent charge on food and drinks.

Public holidays (national)
Fixed dates
1 Jan (New Year's Day), 25 Jan (G F Croe's Day),18 Mar (National Anthem and Flag Day), 30 Apr (Queen's Day), 1 May (Labour Day), 25 Dec (Christmas Day), 26 Dec (Boxing Day).
Variable dates
Good Friday, Easter Monday, Ascension Day.

Working hours
Banking
Mon–Fri: 0800–1600.
Business
Mon–Fri: 0800–1200, 1300–1700.
Government
Mon–Fri: 0800–1200, 1300–1700. Sat: 0800–1200.
Shops
Mon–Sat: 0800–1800. Some shops close 1200–1400 every working day. Malls and shopping centres open 9.30–1800.

Telecommunications
Mobile/cell phones
GSM 900/1800 services are available, with coverage throughout the island.

Electricity supply
110/120V 60 cycles

Getting there
Air
Regular flights from US, Venezuela, Colombia and The Netherlands.
International airport/s: Reina Beatrix (AUA), 2.5km from Oranjestad, duty-free shop, bar, restaurant, post office, car hire.
Airport tax: Except for transit passengers, US destinations US$36.75, all other international destinations US$33.50.
Surface
Main port/s: Oranjestad, Sint Nicolaas and Barcadera are deep-water harbours.

Getting about
National transport
Road: A well-developed road system connects all major towns.
Buses: Regular services in and around main centres. Also jitney services and sightseeing tours.
City transport
Taxis: Usually identified by 'TX' before the licence number. Taxis are not metered; fares are government-controlled according to destination.

Car hire
Prices are reasonable. An international licence is required. Driving is on the right.

BUSINESS DIRECTORY

The addresses listed below are a selection only. While World of Information makes every endeavour to check these addresses, we cannot guarantee that changes have not been made, especially to telephone numbers and area codes. We would welcome any corrections.

Telephone area codes
The international dialling code (IDD) for Aruba is +297, followed by subscriber's number.

Chambers of Commerce
Aruba Chamber of Commerce and Industry, 10 JE Irausquin Boulevard, PO Box 140, Oranjestad (tel: 582-1566; fax: 583-3962; businessinfo@arubachamber.com).

Banking
ABN-AMRO Bank NV, Caya GF Betico Croes 89, Oranjestad (tel: 821-515; fax: 821-856).

Aruba Bank NV, Caya GF Betico Croes 41, PO Box 192, Oranjestad (tel: 821-550; fax: 829-152).

Aruban Investment Bank NV, Middenweg 20, PO Box 1011, Oranjestad (tel: 827-327; fax: 827-461).

Banco di Caribe, Caya GF Croes 90, Oranjestad (tel: 832-168; fax: 832-422).

Caribbean Mercantile Bank NV, Caya GF Betico Croes 53, PO Box 28, Oranjestad (tel: 823-118; fax: 824-373).

First National Bank of Aruba NV, Caya GF Betico Croes 67, Oranjestad (tel: 833-221; fax: 821-756).

Interbank Aruba, Caya GF Betico Croes 38, Oranjestad (tel: 831-080; fax: 824-058).

Central bank
Centrale Bank van Aruba, JE Irausquin Boulevard 8, Oranjestad (tel: 525-2100; fax: 525-2101).

Travel information
National tourist organisation offices
Aruba Tourism Authority, L G Smith Boulevard 172, Eagle (tel: 821-019; fax: 834-702).

Aruba Tourism Authority P R, A Schutte Str 2, Oranjestad (tel: 823-778, 823-779, 837-254; fax: 830-075; internet site: http://www.arubatourism.com).

Ministries
Ministry of Economic Affairs and Tourism, Government of Aruba, L G Smith Boulevard 76, Oranjestad (tel: 826-977; fax: 835-084).

Ministry of Finance, Oranjestad (tel: 823-237; fax: 827-116).

Ministry of Foreign Affairs, J E Irausquinplein 2A, Oranjestad (tel: 583-4705; fax: 583-8108)

Ministry of Public Works and Public Health, L G Smith Boulevard, Oranjestad (tel: 824-900; fax: 826-826).

Ministry of Traffic, Communications and Utilities, Oranjestad (tel: 824-900; fax: 835-985).

Cabinet of the Minister Plenipotentiary of Aruba, R J Schimmelpennincklaan 1, 2517 JN The Hague, The Netherlands (tel: (+3170) 356-6200; fax: (+3170) 356-6210).

Other useful addresses

Aruba Foreign Investment Agency, 85 Caya G F Betico Croes, Oranjestad (tel: 826-070; fax: 822-745).

Aruba Trade & Industry Association, Pedro Gallegostraat 6, PO Box 562, Oranjestad (tel: 827-593).

Department of Economic Affairs, Commerce and Industry, L G Smith Boulevard 160, Sun Plaza Building, Oranjestad (tel: 821-181, 821-482; fax: 834-494).

Other news agencies: The Governor of Aruba: www.kabga.aw

Caribbean Net News: www.caribbeannetnews.com

Internet sites

Aruba government: www.aruba.com

Aruba online: www.arubatourism.com

Visit Aruba: www.visitaruba.com

Ascension Island

COUNTRY PROFILE

Historical profile

1501 Ascension Island was sighted by the Portuguese mariner Juan da Nova.
1815 The UK took possession (on Napoleon's exile to St Helena) and established a garrison.
1823 Responsibility for the island was taken over by the Admiralty Board until 1922, when it became a dependency of St Helena.
1922–64 The island was managed by the Eastern Telegraph Company (renamed Cable and Wireless in 1934).
1942 The US constructed a military airstrip by arrangement with the UK government and the island became an important transit point on the South African route between 1943–45.
1957 A US presence was re-established with the extension of the Eastern Test Range, and in 1967, a Nasa tracking station was built (since closed).
1964 In view of plans to establish BBC and Composite Signals Organisation (CSO) stations, an administrator was appointed.
1982 The island was re-garrisoned during the Falklands War and Ascension Island remains the intermediate stop for Royal Air Force (RAF) flights from the UK to the Falkland Islands.
1999 Geoffrey Fairhurst became the administrator.
2002 A referendum, in which 95 per cent of the islanders voted, agreed to the formation of an Island Council under the leadership of the administrator. Income tax and customs duties replaced the island's former tax-free status. Andrew Michael Kettlewell was appointed administrator. The first general election was held on 1 November.
2004 Michael Clancy became governor, resident in St Helena. Command of the renamed Ascension Island Base was transferred from Headquarters Strike Command, (RAF High Wycombe), to the Permanent Joint Headquarters (PJHQ), Northwood, London.
2005 Michael Thomas Hill was appointed as the new administrator. Elections for the second Ascension Island Council were held in November.
2007 HMS Nottingham, a destroyer class ship, became the South Atlantic patrol ship to maintain a British maritime presence in the South Atlantic around Ascension Island, St Helena, Tristan da Cunha, South Georgia, the South Sandwich Islands and the Falkland Islands. Six out of the seven island councillors resigned in March, in protest at a decision by the UK Foreign and Commonwealth Office (FCO) not to grant Right of Abode, Land Tenure, Fiscal Development and Social Development as previously announced when taxation and democratic representation was introduced. The FCO had said that it wanted to create a settled society but the projected costs for the plans proved prohibitive and were rejected by the UK government. The Ascension Island Council was dissolved on 2 April and was suspended for twelve months, with interim power reverting to the governor. The US-based Omni Air International began chartered operations to the Ascension Island in October.
2008 In February, the governor published a consultation document setting out a new framework for the new Island Council and offering a period of consultation.

Political structure

Constitution

The Ascension Island is a dependency of St Helena, which is a British Overseas Territory. The governor of St Helena appoints an administrator, who is responsible for the daily management of Ascension Island.

The executive

The Ascension Island government (AIG) is headed by the administrator, under the jurisdiction of the governor of St Helena who has overall control of defence, external affairs, internal security and the public service. Local services are managed by the AIG; the UK government has overall responsibility for good governance and island security.

National legislature

A directly elected seven-seat Island Council, plus two ex-officio appointees, (a director of financial services and attorney general) advise the administrator on matters of law and policy.

Last elections

16 November 2005

Results: The seven elected Councillors are independent members. Turn out for this, the second Ascension Island Council, was low at 39 per cent.

KEY FACTS

Official name: Ascension Island

Head of State: Queen Elizabeth II, represented by Governor and Commander-in-Chief, Andrew Gurr (since Nov 2007)

Head of government: Administrator of Ascension Island Michael Thomas Hill (from Sep 2005)

Area: 88 square km

Population: 1,000 (2006)

Capital: Georgetown

Official language: English

Currency: Pound sterling (£) = 100 pence

Exchange rate: £0.51 per US$ (Jan 2007)

Next elections
November 2008

Population
1,000 (2006)
Last census: March 1998: 712
Population density: 14 inhabitants per sq km.
Ethnic make-up
St Helenians, UK and US citizens.
Religions
Anglican and Roman Catholic

Main cities
There are no cities. Georgetown is the administrative capital and port (estimated population 560 in 2003). Two Boats village is a residential area; Traveller's Hill is the RAF garrison; Cat Hill is the US base.

Languages spoken
Official language/s
English

Media
Press
The only newspaper is The Islander (www.the-islander.org.ac), which is published weekly.
Broadcasting
The Ascension Island acts as a relay station for the BBC World Service (www.bbc.co.uk/worldservice) that broadcasts to Africa and provides radio programmes to the island along with the British Forces Broadcasting Service (BFBS) and the US military's Volcano Radio and TV services, which are also available to residents.

Economy
Ascension Island's main importance is as a military base and communications centre. The cost of government net of revenue is about £1.85 million (US$3.0 million). Public services, public works, healthcare facilities and the pier head are funded by the military and commercial organisations on the island. They each contribute an agreed sum annually.
Tax and customs duties were introduced in 2002.
A building project is under way to construct new homes to be owned by residents, with a view to increasing the population to 1,500 over the next few years.
The pier head facility is being developed and improved for both public and commercial use.
Cable and Wireless plc operates an international satellite telecommunications service and the Ariane Earth Station on behalf of the European Space Agency (ESA). The BBC operates its Atlantic relay station broadcasting to Africa and South America.

Agriculture
Fishing
There is a species of marteralia or flying squid that inhabit the waters around Ascension.

Tourism
The island is renowned for its wildlife.
The RMS St Helena operates twice a year from the UK (Portland) and monthly from Cape Town to Walvis Bay (Namibia), St Helena and Ascension Island. The ship is operated under contract by Passenger Services Department, Andrew Weir Shipping Ltd (see travel information addresses).

Environment
In 2002, the British government gave £500,000 to the Royal Society for the Protection of Birds (RSPB) to clear the Island of rats and feral cats that were destroying the seabird population. Ascension Island is also an important breeding colony for the green turtle.

Hydrocarbons
Ascension Island relies entirely on imports of hydrocarbons. It imports as much as its consumer requirement, which is around 200 barrels per day.

Banking and insurance
International banking facilities are available through the Bank of St Helena, including exchanging travellers' cheques and credit card facilities; foreign currency exchange is not offered.

Time
GMT

Geography
Ascension Island lies in the South Atlantic, north-west of St Helena. It is a rocky peak of volcanic origin with 44 craters. The last eruption took place about 600 years ago. The highest point is Green Mountain.
Hemisphere
Southern

Climate
The climate is sub-tropical. Showers occur throughout the year with slightly heavier rain in January–April.

Entry requirements
There is an £11 entry permit fee.
Visa
All visitors must have the Administrator's written permission to land, before beginning their visit. An Ascension Island Entry Permit form can be downloaded from www.ascension-island.gov.ac/visitors.htm and faxed for submission on (+247) 6152. Entry is only granted with evidence a full medical insurance policy, including medical evacuation.
Customs
Customs duties exist on alcohol, tobacco and petrol/diesel. Small amounts of personal goods are duty-free (see website above).

Hotels
A new consortium operates all public accommodation, including the Georgetown Obsidian Hotel (www.obsidian.co.ac, tel/fax: 6246, e-mail: accommodation@atlantis.co.ac).

Working hours
Banking
Mon–Fri: 0830–1500, except Thur: 0830–1230
Government
Mon–Fri: 0830–1230, 1330–1630.

Getting there
Air
There is a twice-weekly RAF Tristar flight (Mondays and Thursdays) that departs from RAF Brize Norton, Oxfordshire. Bookings can be made through Passenger Services Department, Andrew Weir Shipping Ltd (see travel information addresses).
Surface
Water: The RMS St Helena operates twice a year from the UK (Portland) and monthly from Cape Town to Walvis Bay (Namibia), St Helena and Ascension Island. The ship is operated under contract by Passenger Services Department, Andrew Weir Shipping Ltd (see travel information addresses).
Main port/s: Georgetown

Getting about
Car hire
Cars can be hired for £20 per day.

BUSINESS DIRECTORY

The addresses listed below are a selection only. While World of Information makes every endeavour to check these addresses, we cannot guarantee that changes have not been made, especially to telephone numbers and area codes. We would welcome any corrections.

Telephone area codes
The international dialling code (IDD) for Ascension Island is +247 followed by subscriber's number.

Travel information
Passenger Services Department, Andrew Weir Shipping Ltd, Dexter House, 2 Royal Mint Court, London EC N4XX, UK (tel: +44 (0)207-575-6480; fax: +44 (0)207-575-6200; internet: www.aws.co.uk; e-mail: reservations@aws.co.uk).

St Helena Line, Andrew Weir Shipping (SA) Pty Ltd, 3rd Floor, BP Centre, Thibault Square, Cape Town, South Africa (tel: +27-21-425-1165; fax: +27-21-421-7485; e-mail: sthelenaline@mweb.co.za).

Miss Kerry Yon, Solomon and Co Plc (agents for St Helena Line), Jamestown, St Helena, South Atlantic (tel: +290-2523; fax: +290-2423; e-mail: solco.shipping@helanta.sh).

Ministries

The AIG telephone number is 7000, which will take the caller to a pre-recorded menu, from which the caller can identify and dial the extension of the contact required.

Administrator's Office, Islander Building, Georgetown (tel: 6311; fax: 6152; e-mail: andrew.kettlewell@ascension.gov.ac; internet: www.ascension- island.gov.ac).

Chief Executive Officer, Ascension Island Works and Services Agency (AIWSA), Jamestown, St Helena (tel: 6346; fax: 6139; e-mail: chiefexecutive.aiwsa@atlantis.co.ac).

Other useful addresses

St Helena Government Representative, Suite 5, 30b Wimpole St, London W1G 8YB, UK (tel: +44 (0)207-224-5025; fax: +44 (0)207-224-5035).

St Helena Desk Officer, Foreign and Commonwealth Office, Room, King Charles Street, London SW1A 2AH, UK (tel: +44 (0)207-270-2695).

Miles Apart (books, maps, videos on South Atlantic Islands), 5 Harraton House, Exning, Newmarket, Suffolk CB8 7HF, UK (tel: +44 (0)1638-577-627: fax: +44 (0)1638-577-874); 5929 Avon Drive, Bethesda, Maryland 20814, USA (tel/fax: +1301-571-8942; e-mail: familycarter@msn.com).

The Islander, Fort Hayes, Georgetown (tel/fax: 6327; e-mail: the-islander@org.ac; internet site: www.the-islander.org.ac).

Internet sites

Andrew Weir Shipping: www.aws.co.uk

Ascension Island government: www.ascension-island.gov.ac

St Helena Bank: www.sainthelenabank.com/index.htm

St Helena web portal: www.sthelenaonline.com

Australia

KEY FACTS

Official name: Commonwealth of Australia

Head of State: Queen Elizabeth II (since 1952), represented by Governor General Major General Michael Jeffery (from 11 Aug 2003)

Head of government: Prime Minister Kevin Rudd (from 25 Nov 2007)

Ruling party: Australian Labor Party (ALP) (from 25 Nov 2007)

Area: 7,682,300 square km

Population: 20.98 million (2007)*

Capital: Canberra

Official language: English

Currency: Australian dollar (A$) = 100 cents

Exchange rate: A$1.03 per US$ (Jul 2008)

GDP per capita: US$43,312 (2007)*

GDP real growth: 3.90% (2007)

Labour force: 10.35 million (2004)

Unemployment: 4.30% (2007)*

Inflation: 2.30% (2007)

Oil production: 561,000 bpd (2007)

Balance of trade: -US$13.67 billion (2005)

Foreign debt: US$495.60 billion (2004)

Visitor numbers: 5.06 million (2006)*

* estimated figure

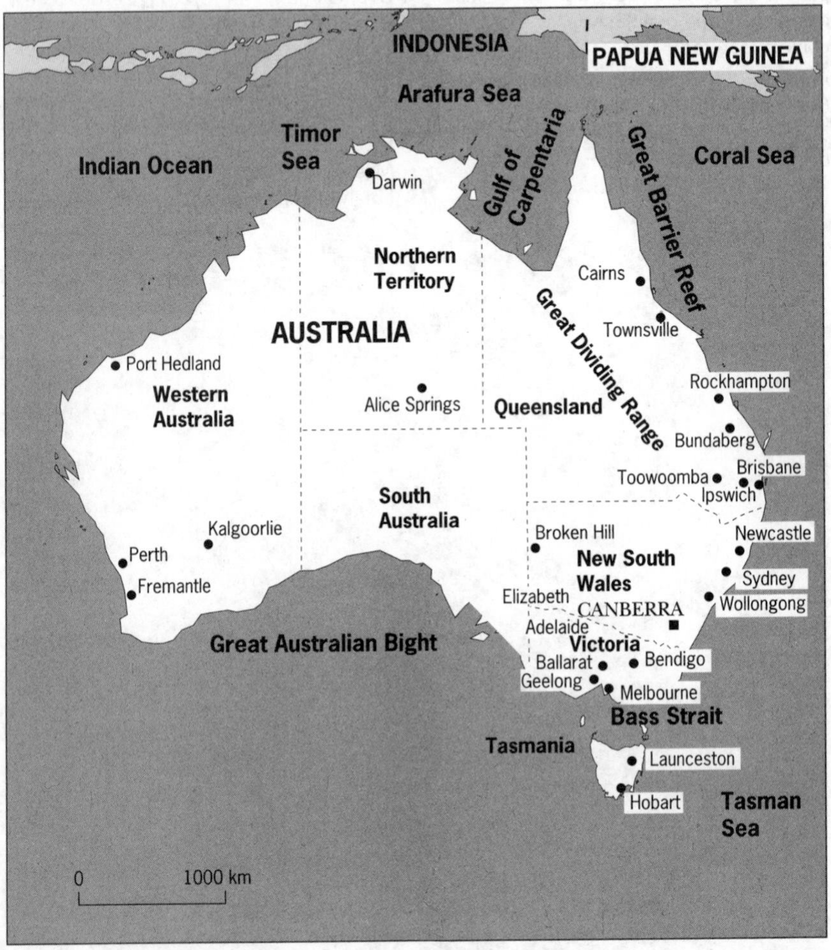

Contrary to the robust Crocodile Dundee image that Australia likes to project internationally, God's Own country has one of the most urban, or more accurately sub-urban populations in the world. More surprisingly, according to the World Health Organisation (WHO) Australia also has one of the world's highest rates for clinical depression. Immigration patterns have changed markedly since the immediate post-war years when the focus was one of attracting war weary Europeans to a land of sun and plenty. These were characterised in the UK as the ten pound immigrants, who only had to pay sterling £10 (US$20) for their sea ticket to Australia. Since the 1980s, immigrants from Asia have predominated, creating and developing extensive and vibrant Chinatowns in cities such as Sydney and Melbourne. A little known fact is that Australians are also great readers, second only to New Zealand in the world rankings for the number of books read per capita. Australia's primary and secondary education systems are acknowledged to be excellent. For some years, efforts have been made to improve university standards, but Australian universities have yet to make it into the world's top ten university rankings.

Howard's End

Political textbooks will long speculate on the reasons for the loss of power by Australia's Liberal (conservative) Party in the November 2007 elections.

Mr Howard's Liberal Party had governed in coalition with the largely rural

National Party for more than 11 years, during which time most Australians had seen not only their country's economy, but also their personal prosperity, transformed. Under Mr Howard, Australia saw far reaching tax reforms and an unprecedented liberalisation of the economy á la Thatcher. The election result was not only a setback for the Liberal Party, but also a personal rebuff for Mr Howard as he lost his Bennelong seat. He was only the second incumbent prime minister, and the third party leader, to lose in his own seat. parliamentary seat. Mr Howard also saw his deputy Peter Costello, long expected to succeed Mr Howard as prime minister, decline the party's leadership. After the resounding defeat, Mr Costello chose not to pick up the leadership baton. Instead it was the former defence minister Brendan Nelson who has the task of restoring the party's morale as leader of the opposition.

It's the economy, stupid

Perhaps ironically, the high profile issues that had dominated the Australian political debate since the Liberals' 2005 election victory. Notably Australia's – perhaps better defined as Mr Howard's – support for the US position in Iraq and on environmental issues such as the Kyoto Protocol, which Australia had refrained from ratifying, did not appear to count for much come the election night. Instead, it was Mr Howard's perceived abrasiveness and arrogance that assumed importance. The controversial proposed expansion of the unpopular Work Choices policy, details of which Mr Howard's administration had refused to release before the election, was seen as representing further reductions in employee rights in relation to wages and benefits that were enough to consolidate the swing to Labor. In many respects, Mr Howard and the Labor Party's leader, Mandarin speaking former diplomat Kevin Rudd, had both campaigned on largely parallel electoral platforms, albeit in rather different styles. Mr Rudd appeared to strike a more sympathetic stance. He was at pains to reassure Australia's electorate that the country's economic gains would not be frittered away by a Labor Party that in its previous spells in power had not been known for economic prudence or perhaps more significantly, an ability to cast off its historical allegiance to Australia's once dominant trades union movement. In this Mr Rudd had to strike a careful balance between the preservation of Australia's economic gains with support for workers' rights. Mr Rudd became the first Australian prime minister born after the end of World War II to hold office. The Liberal Party was left to lick its wounds and regroup. And among the electoral debris there was a lot of regrouping to do – the party had not only lost the election, but was also out of power in all of the Australian Commonwealth's states. Voting is compulsory in Australia; the official turnout was 94.76 per cent, with a swing of 5.75 to Labor which won 83 seats (a gain of 23 seats). The Liberal Party could only win 55 seats, a swing of 4.2 per cent against it (and a loss of 22 seats). In the final analysis, Labor's comfortable majority easily enabled it to form a government. Dubbed Tone's Clone for his policy similarities to Tony Blair, Mr Rudd is unlikely to rock too many boats. One high profile area of debate is likely to be the often fractious issue of whether the United Kingdom's Queen Elizabeth (or her successor) continues to be Australia's head of state. In the last referendum on the issue the Howard administration drafted a loaded question on the subject, with the effect that the vote gave a narrow victory to the monarchists. The question of Australia's continued, anachronistic, status as a constitutional monarchy ruled by a remote, octogenarian grandmother is certain to return to prominence before long.

Immigration issues

In what was interpreted by many observers as a major shift in Australia's international stance, the Rudd government announced in December 2007 that it was dismantling the so-called Pacific Solution on asylum seekers. This had seen the establishment of refugee camps in the Pacific, notably on the island of Nauru (which had always had a close and heavily dependent relationship with Australia) and on Papua New Guinea's Mann's Island (Papua New Guinea was once administered by Australia). Under the Pacific Solution, Australian naval vessels patrolling the Pacific diverted all boats carrying refugees to the island camps. Labour Immigration Minister Chris Evans announced that the policy was to be discontinued with the acceptance into Queensland of seven refugees from Myanmar. Plagued by often violent protests and hunger strikes, the camps had done little for Australia's international image.

A public apology

In what was described as Government business, Motion No 1 the first act of the Rudd administration after being sworn in in February 2008 was to make a formal and comprehensive apology for past errors in the treatment of Australia's aborigine population. In its 11 years in power, the Howard administration had refused to go as far as a formal apology. In parliament, Mr Rudd said that 'Parliament is today here assembled to deal with this unfinished business of the nation, to

KEY INDICATORS — **Australia**

	Unit	2003	2004	2005	2006	2007
Population	m	19.89	20.23	20.40	20.74	*20.98
Gross domestic product (GDP)	US$bn	518.40	522.40	712.44	755.95	908.83
GDP per capita	US$	25,100	30,445	34,932	36,442	*43,312
GDP real growth	%	3.3	3.2	2.8	3.3	3.9
Inflation	%	2.8	2.3	2.7	3.5	2.3
Unemployment	%	6.0	5.5	5.1	4.8	*4.3
Oil output	'000 bpd	731.0	541.0	554.0	544.0	561.0
Natural gas output	bn cum	33.2	35.2	37.1	38.9	40.0
Coal output	mtoe	188.7	199.4	202.4	203.1	53.1
Exports (fob) (goods)	US$m	70,358.0	87,063.0	106,505.0	124,913.0	142,133.0
Imports (cif) (goods)	US$m	88,618.0	105,278.0	120,177.0	134,509.0	160,047.0
Balance of trade	US$m	-18,260.0	-18,215.0	-13,672.0	9,596.0	17,914.0
Current account	US$m	-30,240.0	-39,390.0	-41,212.0	-41,690.0	-56,196.0
Total reserves minus gold	US$m	32,189.0	35,803.0	41,941.0	53,448.0	24,768.0
Foreign exchange	US$m	29,966.0	33,901.0	40,972.0	52,821.0	24,237.0
Exchange rate	per US$	1.55	1.36	1.28	1.27	1.16

* estimated figure

remove a great stain from the nation's soul, and in a true spirit of reconciliation to open a new chapter of this great land, Australia.'

A government sponsored that some of the actions of previous governments could be construed as genocide. For a long time misguided government policies focussed on educating aboriginal children. In a process which continued into the 1970s aborigine children, known as the Stolen generations, were in effect abducted from their families to be brought up in schools that resembled prisons as so accurately depicted in the 2002 Australian film *The Rabbit Proof Fence*. Mr Rudd's apology, which reportedly brought tears to the eyes of many parliamentarians, stated: 'To the Stolen generations I say the following. As prime minister of Australia, I am sorry. On behalf of the government of Australia, I am sorry. On behalf of the parliament of Australia, I am sorry. I offer you this apology without qualification.' The contrast with the hesitation and reluctance of the previous administration, which based its refusal on the fact that it was not responsible for the misdeeds of previous administrations, was sharp. However, Mr Rudd's speech failed to address, or even mention, the subject of compensation. There has been no mention of this, or even of a government body to handle the question. In 2007 a South Australia court awarded A$525,000 (US$?????????) to a 50 year old appellant in compensation for unlawful treatment and false imprisonment. The only practical proposal outlined in Mr Rudd's parliament speech was the provision of educational facilities for every aborigine child aged 4 or more. At present, it is estimated that less than 30 per cent of aborigine children of any age attend school.

The economy's resilience

Australia's economy ranks among the top twenty in the world, and can fairly be considered as one of the world's most resilient. Throughout 2006 and 2007, according to the Reserve Bank of Australia's (RBA) February 2008 report on domestic economic conditions, economic activity continued to grow. In the third quarter of 2007, GDP growth registered 4.3 per cent over 2006, a lower figure than originally forecast by the RBA. Although domestic demand remained buoyant, export growth had slowed somewhat, reflecting the effects of Australia's prolonged drought on rural production. The outlook for the rural sector appeared to be boosted in late 2007 by improved rainfall.

The RBA noted that Australia had remained largely unaffected by the turmoil in international capital markets. The strong position of Australia's household sector showed itself in an 8 per cent year on year increase in household disposable income. The income tax cuts introduced by the outgoing Howard administration, seen by many as an election gambit, turned out to have provided the economy with additional impetus in the fourth quarter. The household savings rate continued to rise to its highest rate for seven years, with apparently few households encountering repayment difficulties. The sustained rate of household savings also meant that house prices continued to rise at an annual rate of 12 per cent, with rises as high as 20 per cent in Adelaide, Brisbane and Melbourne. In Sydney and Perth house price growth evened out after three years of exceptionally strong growth. It would none the less be surprising, noted the RBA, if in the financial climate prevailing in late 2007 housing credits and loan approvals were not to register a fall in 2008.

Buoyant business climate

In what remained a generally favourable business climate throughout 2007, companies reliant on the agricultural sector, or exposed to foreign competition, fared less well than those benefiting from high commodity prices and business-related construction. The RBA also noted that at 31 per cent of GDP, private sector profits were at their highest levels for over three decades. Business investment, which increased by 10 per cent over the year, was characteristically focussed on construction and infrastructure projects. The overall buoyancy of the business sector was marred by the performance of the agricultural sector, which the Australian Bureau of Agricultural and Resource Economics (ABARE) expected to turn in an equally dismal performance for 2007–08 after the falls already experienced in 2006. Australia is the world's second largest wheat exporter after the USA. So even the good news that the 2007 wheat crop was estimated to be some 30 per cent greater than in 2006 had to be seen in the context of much lower than normal levels of previous years. The increased rainfalls experienced in the latter stages of 2007 were attributed to the *La Nina* weather system that had established itself in the Pacific. *La Nina* also accounted for the freak rain storms which had affected most parts of the country.

Exports rise

Overall export volumes were estimated to have risen by some 4 per cent in 2007, with raw material and commodity exports up by 6.5 per cent. Coal, oil and iron exports all performed well, much if not most of the demand emanating from China. Australia's

iron ore exports to China have been growing at an annual average rate of 25 per cent. According to the RBA, China now accounts for about half of all Australia's iron ore exports. Most Australian ore is sold at prices pre-negotiated once a year between, as it were, miner and smelter. At the beginning of 2007 this price hovered around the US$85 per ton mark. Over the year, the spot price for consignments negotiated outside these arrangements rose to around US$200 per ton mark (in part reflecting the weakness of the US dollar). By the end of 2007, the anticipated price rise for the year was 50 per cent. Australia's trade deficit was estimated to have increased to some 2.5 per cent of GDP by late 2007.

Unemployment contained

Unemployment remained unchanged over the second half of 2007, at 4.25 per cent of the working population. Many of Australia's fast-growth sectors such as iron-ore, petroleum and in, better years, agriculture, are capital, rather than labour intensive. Their fast growth rate is not necessarily reflected in improved employment rates. Overall employment rose by 2.7 per cent for the year, with full-time employment recording a 3.3 per cent growth for the year.

Risk assessment

Economic	Good
Political	Good
Regional stability	Good

COUNTRY PROFILE

Historical profile

The first Aborigines arrived from south-east Asia around 60,000BC and by 20,000BC had spread throughout the mainland and Tasmania. The Aborigines numbered a few hundred thousand when the British founded a penal settlement at Sydney in 1788, bringing over around 800 convicts. Free settlers arrived in increasing numbers, particularly after the discovery of gold in the mid-nineteenth century. Two centuries of discrimination and expropriation followed, and at one point the number of Aborigines fell as low as 60,000. Around 98.5 per cent of the

present Australian population are of European or Asian descent. Indigenous Australians suffer high rates of unemployment, imprisonment and drug abuse. Migration continues to shape Australia, although it remains a sensitive issue and the country has taken a tough stance on unauthorised arrivals.
Although the country has considered cutting its ties with the British monarchy, in 1999 Australians voted against plans for the country to become a republic.
1778 Captain James Cook reached Australia and sailed the entire length of the East Coast. He claimed the land for Britain.
1788 British Naval captain, Arthur Phillip, founded a penal colony at Sydney. He had arrived with a fleet of 11 vessels and nearly 800 convicts.
1829 The Colony of Western Australia was established at Perth by Captain James Stirling.
1837 South Australia was established with Adelaide as its capital city.
1851 The discovery of gold in New South Wales sparked a wave of migration to Australia, known as the 'gold rush'. Within 10 years of the gold find, the population was estimated to have grown from 500,000 to 1.5 million. The Aborigines were treated badly.
1856 Australia became the first country to introduce the secret ballot for elections (known as the 'Australian ballot').
1877 The first Test cricket match between Australia and England was played in Melbourne.
1901 The Commonwealth of Australia was created. The former British colonies became the six states of Australia: New South Wales, Victoria, Queensland, Western Australia, South Australia and Tasmania. There are two self-governing states – the Northern Territory and the Australian Capital Territory.
1911 Canberra was founded as the capital city.
1914–1918 Australia fought alongside Britain during the First World War. Australian troops bore the brunt of the fighting in some theatres of war and suffered heavy casualties during the ill-fated beach landing at Gallipoli in Turkey in 1915.
1929–31 Following the Wall Street Crash came the Great Depression, which hit the Australian economy badly. Recovery was slow and uneven. The Labor government was defeated in the elections.
1939–45 Australia fought alongside Britain and the US during the Second World War. In 1942, Japanese aircraft bombed Darwin (Northern Territory), the only direct foreign attack on Australia since its creation.
1948 Australia began to promote immigration from Europe and between the 1940–70s more than a million people arrived, a third of whom came from Britain.
1950 Australia participated in the Korean War.
1951 Australia, New Zealand and the US signed the Anzus Pact, a security pact for the South Pacific.
1956 Australia hosted the Olympic games in Melbourne.
1963 The 'White Australia' policy of immigration restrictions was ended.
1965 Australia fought alongside the US in Vietnam. At the height of Australia's involvement, the task force numbered 8,500 troops.
1967 A national referendum approved changes to the constitution: the section which excluded Aboriginal people from the official census was removed and another change enabled the federal government to pass laws on Aboriginal issues.
1975 Australia restricted the immigration of non-skilled workers. The governor general, Sir John Kerr, dismissed Gough Whitlam's government following its repeated failure to pass the budget in the upper house of parliament. A caretaker government under Malcolm Fraser was installed.
1985 The issue of Aboriginal land rights was first addressed.
1986 Australia's legislative links with the UK were severed by the Australia Act, which abolished the UK parliament's residual legislative, executive and judicial controls over Australian state law.
1990 Bob Hawke and his Australian Labor Party (ALP) government narrowly won the federal election – the first ALP administration to win three consecutive elections.
1991 Paul Keating (ALP) succeeded Bob Hawke as prime minister.
1992 The Citizenship Act was amended to remove the obligation to swear an allegiance to the British Crown. Keating's government pledged to make Australia a republic and develop links with the rest of Asia.
1993 The ALP won the general election with an increased majority. The Native Title Act granted the Aborigines compensation for the loss of land rights.
1996 The Liberal Party (LP)-National Party (NP) coalition won a landslide victory in elections and John Howard, leader of the LP, took over as prime minister.
1998 The LP-NP coalition was re-elected at the general elections, but with a reduced majority. Delegates to a constitutional convention voted to replace the Queen with a president elected by parliament.
1999 Fifty-five per cent of votes cast in a national referendum opposed Australia becoming a republic. After East Timor voted for independence from Indonesia, Australia led an intervention force to counter pro-Indonesia militia violence. Australia's relationship with Indonesia worsened.
2000 Australia hosted the Olympic Games in Sydney; they became known as the 'friendly games'.
2001 Peter Hollingworth was sworn in as governor general. Prime Minister Howard refused to apologise to the 'stolen generations' of Aborigines who were forcibly removed from their parents. Howard won a third term in the federal elections after gaining support for his 'Pacific Solution' – the policy of refusing entry to asylum seekers and directing them to other countries in Asia-Pacific.
2002 There were riots in the Woomera desert detention camp for asylum seekers. Eighty-eight Australian citizens were killed in a night club bombing in Bali, Indonesia.
2003 Australia sent 2,000 troops to the Iraq War. Governor General Peter Hollingworth stood down and Major General Michael Jeffery was appointed in his place. Bush fires raged across the country. The Senate passed a no-confidence motion in Prime Minister Howard over his handling of the Iraq crisis. Australia headed a peacekeeping force in the Solomon Islands.
2004 On 1 February, the first passenger train to cross Australia from south to north (the Ghan) made its journey from Adelaide to Darwin. In February, the inhabitants of a predominantly Aborigine Sydney suburb rioted in protest at the death of a young Aborigine as the result of a police car chase. In the same month, a parliamentary committee cleared the government of lying about the threat posed by weapons of mass destruction in Iraq. In September, there was a bomb attack outside the Australian embassy in Jakarta, Indonesia. John Howard won a fourth term as prime minister in the 9 October federal legislative elections. Mr Howard's Liberal-National coalition won with an increased majority. In November, the death of an Aboriginal man in police custody sparked more riots on Palm Island, off the north-east coast.
2005 In January, the worst bush fires for more than two decades killed nine people in South Australia. In December there were riots in the Cronulla suburb of Sydney, whether fuelled by racism, revenge or simply alcohol-induced aggression, the ferocity of the violence shocked the public.
2006 Australia experienced the worst drought on record. Troops were sent in April to aid the Timor-Leste government against rioting soldiers. In August, the government was forced by its own legislators to withdraw proposed legislation to process asylum seekers in offshore camps.

2007 In May, heavy rain began to fall in south-east Australia, breaking a six-year drought. However, the rains did not fall on the Murray-Darling river system of South Australia, the principal crop-growing region. John Howard called an election in an attempt to gain a fourth term in office. In parliamentary elections held on 25 November, the opposition Australian Labor Party (ALP) won 44.0 per cent of the vote (86 seats out of 150), the Liberal-National (LN) coalition won 41.8 per cent (62). Kevin Rudd became prime minister on 3 December and one of his first acts was to sign the Kyoto Agreement on greenhouse gas emissions targets, which Australia, under John Howard, had refused to sign.
2008 On 13 February the prime minister made a formal apology to indigenous Aboriginal peoples for former government policies which included the forcible removal of Aboriginal children – called the stolen generations – from their families, in a policy of assimilation.

Political structure

Constitution

The Commonwealth of Australia is a constitutional monarchy with a parliamentary democracy. It consists of a federation of six states (New South Wales, Victoria, Queensland, South Australia, Western Australia and Tasmania) and two territories (Australian Capital Territory (ACT), Northern Territory). Each state has its own constitution, government, administration and judiciary. There are some 900 local government bodies at city, town, municipal and shire levels.
The federal government is located in Canberra, ACT. Federal responsibilities tend to be those with an international and national focus while state governments deal with regional issues. However, the overlap of power is considerable and companies must be prepared to deal with both levels of government.
Any amendment to the constitution must be passed by an absolute majority in each House of Parliament and must be approved in a referendum by the majority of electors in a majority of states and territories. In the past, three states (Tasmania, Queensland and Western Australia) have consistently blocked any changes to the constitution.
There is compulsory universal adult suffrage for Australian citizens, with a voting age of 18. An automatic fine of A$50 (US$35) is issued by post to those who fail to cast a vote, although this is rarely imposed through legal proceedings.

Form of state

Federal commonwealth, with the British monarch as Head of State.

The executive

The governor general represents and is appointed by the British sovereign. The role of governor general is largely ceremonial, but he has the power to dissolve parliament or the government and call new elections. He is also the commander-in-chief of the armed forces. If the governor general is ill, dies, resigns or is out of the country, an administrator is appointed to undertake the governor general's duties.
Day-to-day executive responsibility is held by the national government, which is composed of a cabinet of senior ministers formed by the party with a majority in the House of Representatives.

National legislature

Legislative powers are divided between the bicameral Australian Federal Parliament, with a 150-member House of Representatives and a 76-member Senate.
The House of Representatives is directly elected by a preferential voting system for a three-year term.
The Senate is directly elected by proportional representation for a six-year term. One half of the Senate retires every three years, usually to coincide with elections for the House of Representatives. The Senate may not originate or amend money bills. In certain circumstances the governor general may dissolve the entire Senate.
The six state (or territory) parliaments also hold legislative powers. In five of the six states there is a bicameral legislature, in the other (Queensland) the legislature is unicameral.

Legal system

The legal system is based on the constitution of 1901. The governor general and state governors appoint judges on the advice of the cabinets of federal and state governments. Each state has state courts, federal courts, family courts and a supreme court. The High Court of Australia, which has seven judges, is the ultimate court of appeal. The High Court has jurisdiction to hear and determine appeals and judgments, decrees, orders and the sentences of most lower courts, but since 1984 cases have only been referred to it if there is a difference of opinion at lower levels. The High Court's main task is to interpret the Australian Constitution.

Last elections

25 November 2007 (federal legislative and 50 per cent of Senate)
Results: Parliamentary: Australian Labor Party (ALP) won 44.0 per cent of the vote (86 seats out of 150), the Liberal-National (LN) coalition won 41.8 per cent (62). Senate: LN coalition won 18 seats (total 37 seats), ALP won 18 seats (total 32), The Greens won three (total five).

Next elections

October 2010 (federal legislative)

Political parties

Ruling party

Australian Labor Party (ALP) (from 25 Nov 2007)

Main opposition party

Liberal-National (LN) coalition

Population

20.98 million (2007)*
Last census: August 2001: 18,972,350
Population density: Two inhabitants per square km (2000)
Annual growth rate: 1.2 per cent 1994–2004 (WHO 2006)

Ethnic make-up

The population is comprised mainly of immigrants and their descendants from over 120 countries, with Aboriginals and Torres Straits Islanders accounting for only 1.5 per cent of the population. The single largest immigrant group is from the British Isles, followed by Asians, New Zealanders, Italians, Croats, Serbs, Slovenes, Bosnians, Macedonians, Greeks, Germans, Vietnamese, Dutch, Poles and Lebanese. Over 20 per cent of the total population were born outside the country.

More than half the Aboriginal population lives in urban areas.

Religions

Predominantly Christian (Anglican and Roman Catholic), although many are non-practising. There are significant Eastern Orthodox, Jewish, Muslim, Hindu and Buddhist communities in many cities.

Education

In most states, children start primary school at the age of five when they enrol in a preparatory or kindergarten year, after which primary education continues for either six or seven years followed by secondary education, available for either five or six years and may be completed by tertiary education of a student's level and choice.
State and Territory governments and the Federal government provide major financial support for primary and secondary education, delivered in public and fee-paying schools run by governments and non-government providers.
Links between the education and training sectors have been strengthened, through the introduction of the Australian National Training Authority (ANTA) national system of vocational education and training in co-operation with all levels of governments and industry. Two national communications campaigns began in late 2000 based on extensive market research into the vocational education and training needs of Australian individuals and enterprises.

Total expenditure on education is 5.3 per cent of GDP. In 2001, government expenditure on higher education totalled US$5.8 billion.
Compulsory years: 6 to 15; Tasmania: 6 to 16.
Pupils per teacher: 18 in primary schools.

Health

Per capita total expenditure on health (2003) was US$2,874; of which per capita government spending was US$1,939, at the international dollar rate, (WHO 2006).
While health care funds direct assistance to hospitals and rebates individuals under the Medicare national health insurance system, consideration of private medical insurance is central to federal health budget funding.
Primary healthcare is provided by independent and privately owned medical practices, offering general and specialist treatment including minor surgary. Hospitals may be state, or privately run institutions.
HIV/Aids
HIV prevalence: 0.1 per cent aged 15–49 in 2003 (World Bank)
Life expectancy: 81 years, 2004 (WHO 2006)
Fertility rate/Maternal mortality rate: 1.7 births per woman, 2004 (WHO 2006)
Birth rate/Death rate: Seven deaths per 1,000 people (World Bank).
Child (under 5 years) mortality rate (per 1,000): 4.6 per 1,000 live births (World Bank).
Head of population per physician: 2.47 physicians per 1,000 people, 2001 (WHO 2006)

Welfare

Social security payments are intended as a 'safety net' to help low income groups and anti-fraud measures are increasingly tough. In recent years, payments have been the subject of intense scrutiny to ensure that they are only distributed to those in genuine need, this has resulted in cuts in some benefits while other categories, especially disability and service pensions, have increased. Other priority groups have been defined as low-income: families with children; the long-term unemployed; and single parents.
Pensions
Australia has a forced savings 'superannuation' scheme for employees, the total value of which is approaching A$1 trillion (US$620 billion). The scheme involves compulsory contributions by employees of 9 per cent of their income. The scheme does not cover the self-employed or low-income workers. It is estimated that 94 per cent of pension schemes operate through trusts. Employees often have no choice in becoming a member and are ill-informed as to who heads the trust.

Main cities

Canberra, (national capital, 329,200 in 2008); state capitals – Sydney (estimated population 3.7 million (m)); Melbourne (3.6m); Brisbane (1.9m); Perth (1.3m); Adelaide (1.0m); Hobart (126,841; Darwin (61,769).

Languages spoken

Aboriginal dialects are becoming scarce. Italian is spoken by 2.6 per cent of the population and Greek by 1.8 per cent. A wide variety of other languages are spoken, particularly from Asia, reflecting the diverse origins of Australia's population.
Official language/s
English

Media

Other news agencies: AAP (Australian Associated Press): http://aap.com.au
ABC News: www.abc.net.au/news
Press
In 2007 the government relaxed the laws on media cross-ownership of press and broadcasting and allowing greater levels of foreign ownership. Around 80 per cent of all print media is owned by four newspaper publishers, News Limited, Fairfax Media Publications, APN News and Media and West Australian Newspapers Holdings. All newspapers have a home market based on the major city and state in which they are published and very few are sold elsewhere.
Dailies: The only national daily is The Australian (www.theaustralian.news.com.au). Major regional publications include, in NSW The Sydney Morning Herald (www.smh.com.au), Sun Herald (www.sunherald.com.au) and The Daily Telegraph (www.news.com.au/dailytelegraph); in VIC The Age (www.theage.com.au) and Herald Sun (www.news.com.au/heraldsun) a tabloid with the biggest circulation; in The Canberra Times (http://canberra.yourguide.com.au); in QLD Courier Mail (www.news.com.au/couriermail), The Brisbane News (www.brisbanenews.net); in SA The Advertiser (www.news.com.au/adelaidenow); in WA The Western Australian (www.thewest.com.au); in NT Northern Territory News (www.ntnews.com.au); in Tasmania Mercury (www.news.com.au/mercury).
Weeklies: All major dailies produce weekend editions. The are a comprehensive range of magazine catering for all interests personal and professional. APC (www.acp.com.au) publishes many of the leading magazine titles including The Australian Womens Weekly, TV Week and Cleo (http://aww.ninemsn.com.au). Beat Magazine (www.beat.com.au) is an arts and entertainment magazine. The Chaser (www.chaser.com.au) and Brainsnap (http://brainsnap.com) are satirical publications.
Business: The only national daily is the Australian Financial Review (www.afr.com). All daily broadsheets have business sections. Weekly publications include Western Australian Business News (www.wabusinessnews.com.au), which has the largest circulation, Business Review Weekly (www.brw.com.au), with comprehensive articles on national matters, Lloyds List DCN (Daily Commercial News) (www.lloydslistdcn.com.au) dealing with transport matters and Stock & Land (http://sl.farmonline.com.au), reporting on agriculture. Monthly publications include Sydney Business Review,
There are numerous commercial and trade journals, including reports from the Australian Bureau of Agricultural and Resources Economics (Abare) (www.abareconomics.com).
Periodicals: For politics and culture Monthly (www.themonthly.com.au) and Quarterly Essay (www.quarterlyessay.com).
Broadcasting
The principal public broadcaster is the Australian Broadcasting Corporation (ABC), providing national, local and Pacific regional radio, TV and Internet services.
Radio: There are hundreds of commercial radio stations which in a combined number represent the largest audiences. They broadcast local interest shows and are affiliated to major, usually city stations, with personality presenters who command significant listenership numbers.
National radio services are provided by the public services ABC (www.abc.net.au) and SBS (www20.sbs.com.au) (with programmes broadcasts in many of the immigrant community languages), and commercial radio by Austereo (www.austereo.com.au), DMG Radio (www.dmgradio.com.au) and Southern Cross Broadcasting (www.southerncrossbroadcasting.com.au). Radio Australia (www.abc.net.au/ra) is the ABC's external service.
Television: National, public TV is provided by the ABC (www.abc.net.au) and the Special Broadcasting Service (SBS), which provides multicultural programmes in over 50 languages. Both broadcast additional digital channels aimed children and world news programmes respectively. There are three, free-to-air, commercial channels, Seven (http://au.tv.yahoo.com), Nine

(http://channelnine.ninemsn.com.au) and Ten (http://ten.com.au). Channels Seven and Nine regularly vie for top ratings, with domestically produced programmes and popular imports.

The conversion to digital services is expected to be completed by 2010. There are more than 250 privately owned regional TV stations that are affiliates to the metropolitan stations, the largest of which is WINTV (www.wintv.com.au).

Pay-to-view services have grown substantially since the 1990s, using terrestrial, cable and satellite platforms, including Foxtel (www.foxtel.com.au) and Optus (www.optus.com.au).

Advertising

Advertising is subject to the provisions of the Trade Practices Act, administered by the Australian Competition and Consumer Commission. Tobacco advertising is banned and alcohol has regulations for control. There is a voluntary code of conduct for advertising to children. The Advertising Standards Council interprets and applies all requirements and rules with punitive powers as necessary.

All forms of advertising are available, subject to privacy and consumer laws, including commercial press radio and TV, traditional outdoor advertising is available in many forms, along with direct mail facilities and house-to-house distribution of samples and literature. Modern advertising through personalised text-messaging and email adverts are all well established.

Economy

Australia has evolved from an agrarian and mining economy pre-1980s when raw materials, primarily sheep, wheat, coal and ore, were exported without added value, to one based overwhelmingly on services which by 2005 made up over 70 per cent of GDP. Agricultural and mining products are still significant to Australia's export revenue as combined they make up over 50 per cent of goods and services exports. Australia has a diverse ethnic population (offering a large multilingual workforce with good IT skills), transparent legal system, good governance and financial services, all of which have made it a prime regional hub for international companies. Tourism accounts for 5 per cent of GDP, roughly the same as all mining combined.

For over a decade Australia has enjoyed continued growth, low inflation and low unemployment. However the OECD considers the 5.1 per cent unemployment rate (a 30-year low) as too low for an advanced country. Australia suffers from labour shortages particularly in skilled and semi-skilled occupations, which prompted the government to establish 24 new technical colleges concentrating on trades, mainly various engineering skills. Before trained workers are available this lack of skilled workers, coupled with infrastructure bottlenecks in rail links and port facilities, will continue to threaten Australia's exports with stagnation.

The economy has been adversely effected by the nationwide persistent drought that began in 2002. Growth in 2005 was 2.7 per cent, however Australia has been avoiding the twin evils of recession and inflation with an independent central bank (released from government control in 1996) setting interest rates unfettered by political influence. To sustain the momentum however Australia has to overcome its labour shortage, infrastructure bottlenecks and lack of training.

In January 2005 Australia and the US began operating a Free Trade Agreement (AUSFTA) with planned cuts in entry tariffs. Australia is negotiating other FTAs with China, Singapore and Thailand and other Asean countries.

External trade

Australia is a member of the South Pacific Regional Trade and Economic Co-operation Agreement (Sparteca) along with 13 regional nations, which allows products duty free access by Pacific Island Forum members to Australian and New Zealand markets (subject to the country of origin restrictions).

Export marketing organisations established under government statutes supervise and promote the export of primary income-earning commodities, and the Export Market Development Grants scheme provides taxable cash grants for developing overseas markets. Australia has an industrial base that includes vehicle assembly, steel, aluminium and nickel smelting, textile and paper manufacturing and telecommunications and IT suppliers. There is a huge international trade in raw materials, minerals and agricultural produce supplying the Asia and Pacific region.

Imports

Principal imports are finished products such as vehicles and parts, industrial machinery, computers and office equipment, electrical goods, textiles and crude oil and petroleum products.

Main sources: US (13.9 per cent total, 2005), China (13.7 per cent), Japan (11.0 per cent), Singapore (5.6 per cent), Germany (5.6 per cent)

Exports

Principal exports are minerals: coal, gold, diamonds, alumina, iron ore, uranium; agricultural products: wheat, meat, wool and live animals; manufactures include vehicles, processed food, computers and telecommunications equipment.

Main destinations: Japan (20.3 per cent total, 2005), China (11.5 per cent), South Korea (7.9 per cent), US (6.7 per cent), New Zealand (6.5 per cent) India (5.0 per cent)

Agriculture

Farming

Agricultural output has doubled since the early 1960s, but the sector now only contributes 4 per cent of GDP, a reduction from 14 per cent, although agricultural production still accounts for 22 per cent of exports.

Larger, technologically-enhanced farms employing fewer workers are replacing many smaller operations; the number of farms has fallen by 25 per cent since the 1980s.

The long-running drought, which was only given a short-lived respite with rains in 2007, returned with greater force in 2008 with the driest June on record. Australia's principal food growing region, the Murray-Darling basin, which produces 40 per cent of the country's fruit, vegetables and grain, was particularly hard hit. Nationwide wheat production in 2006–07 was down by 59 per cent and was at its lowest since 1982–83. Severe cuts in water allocations also cut rice and cotton production by 90 per cent and 42 per cent respectively, with some farmers abandoning parts of their crops in the field and using the reduced water to irrigate smaller areas and maximise their returns. In July 2008, the government and land users agreed to water conservation plans with the commitment of A$3.7 billion (US$3.6 billion) in investment immediately and a further A$9.2 billion (US$9.5 billion) to restore the river system. It has been estimated that 10,000 farming families have been forced off the land since 2002 when the drought took hold, while those farmers that remain are adopting water efficient cropping methods.

Government involvement tends to be focussed on improving infrastructure as a means of facilitating investment.

Australia is the world's fourth-largest wheat producer, after the EU, the US and Canada. Since the 1980s, Australia has successfully diversified its wheat production, increasing the number of varieties grown and improving marketing. China's membership of the WTO has benefited Australian wheat growers, who have seen a rise in exports to Asia. As living standards improve in Asia, consumption of higher value commodities such as rice and noodles will increase.

Crop production in 2005 included 35,005,500 tonnes (t) cereals in total, 24,067,000t wheat, 6,640,000t barley, 1,125,000t rapeseed (canola), 1,748,000t sorghum, 38,246,000t sugar cane, 1,124,000t oats, 1,300,000t potatoes, 2,006,000t pulses, 1,834,000t grapes, 312,000t maize, 430,000t rice, 643,000t citrus fruit, 474,220t tomatoes, 250,000t bananas, 620,278t oilcrops, 1,178,000t seed cotton, 488,000t cotton lint, 3,508,539t fruit in total, 1,909,371t vegetables in total. Livestock production included 3,946,242t meat in total, 2,162,000t beef, 388,434t pig meat, 583,853t lamb, 16,750t goat meat, 773,925t poultry, 170,000t eggs, 10,150,000t milk, 16,000t honey, 255,000t cattle hides, 127,778t sheepskins, 508,791t greasy wool.

Fishing

Australia typically produces 220,000 tonnes of seafood and 13,000 tonnes of freshwater fish per annum. Around 80 per cent of annual fishing production is exported. Rock lobsters from Western Australia account for 30 per cent of exports by value. Other species include prawns, molluscs, carp and eels. The main destinations for fish exports are Japan, Hong Kong and Taiwan, while exports to the US and Europe have benefited from the weakness of the Australian dollar.
South Australia has the world's first tuna fish farm industry. The tuna is caught at sea and transferred to holding pens for fattening before being sold on. The industry exports A$261 million (US$180 million) worth of fish to Japan, where the fresh tuna, delivered within 72 hours, fetches ¥2,800 (US$24.30) per kilo.
In 2004, the total marine fish catch was 152,256 tonnes and the total crustacean catch was 50,968 tonnes.

Forestry

There is a substantial forestry industry in tropical Queensland, producing approximately 22 million cubic metres (cum) of timber annually, worth over A$1 billion (US$694 million). Japan has traditionally been the sector's biggest customer, with New Zealand the second largest export market. The sector employs around 75,000 people. There are projects for new plantations to increase production by 300 per cent. In 2004, exports of forest products totalled US$1.3 billion and imports amounted to US$1.8 billion.

Industry and manufacturing

Australia embarked on a basic reorientation of its economy in the 1980s, and has transformed itself from an inward-looking, import-substitution economy to an internationally competitive, export-oriented economy. In the early 1990s, the sector suffered from poor investment, despite boosts to exports provided by the low exchange rate. However, having shed labour, gained more effective investment and a sharper export focus, Australian industry has become more competitive internationally with manufacturers of wood and paper products, food, beverages and tobacco becoming dominant.
The Liberal Party (LP)-National Party (NP) coalition government, first elected in 1995, quickly made clear its aim of transforming a traditional commodity-based economy by value-added processing of domestic raw materials into high-value consumer products for the global market.
At the heart of industrial policy is a package to support innovation and improve access to venture capital for the commercial application of research and development. The government has also pledged to commit Australia to a free trade approach to the electronic market place – goods ordered and delivered electronically will remain duty free.

Tourism

Tourism is a major contributor to Australia's economy, accounting for around four per cent of GDP and employing 540,000 people. The country has become an increasingly popular destination for tourists from all around the world. While the largest market is New Zealand (exceeding a million visitors in 2004), significant numbers come from as far afield as the UK and other European countries, the US and east Asia. Arrivals increased annually for two decades until 2000, the year of the Sydney Olympics, encouraged by the relative weakness of the Australian currency. 4.9 million visitors were recorded in 2000 and the share of GDP was 4.6 per cent. Expectations of continuing growth to over five million visitors in 2001 were dashed, due to global conditions, including the 11 September terrorist attacks in the US, and a strengthening Australian dollar. As with many other countries, arrivals fell in 2001, but, against the general trend, the decline continued through 2002 and into 2003, when there were 4.75 million visitors. The sector recovered in 2004, when there were 5.2 million visitors, a trend which continued in 2005 .

Environment

A long-running drought, which began in 2002, was only given a short-lived respite with rains in 2007, returned with greater force in 2008 with the driest winter on record. In July 2008, the government and land users agreed to water conservation plans with the commitment of A$3.7 billion (US$3.6 billion) in investment immediately and a further A$9.2 billion (US$9.5 billion) to restore the river system. However the prime minister admitted that the plan would not produce swift results and the unique ecosystem in the lower reaches could be irreversibly damaged.
In 2004 the government announced plans including A$1.5 billion (US$2.14 billion) on fuel tax breaks and A$700 million (US$1 billion) funds for investment in technology that could reduce greenhouse gas emissions. Critics have said this still favours oil and coal and pollution is unlikely to be reduced significantly.
Australia is the second-largest producer of greenhouse gas emissions (after the US) among western nations. The government claims that the country only produces 1.6 per cent of the global total and cannot therefore make an individual difference overall.
Australia, Philippines, Indonesia, Papua New Guinea and Solomon Islands are the countries with the most coral reef fish species.

Mining

Mining contributed around 8.5 per cent of GDP in 2004 and employs 4 per cent of the workforce. Australia has major deposits of a variety of minerals, possessing the world's biggest economic reserves of lead, uranium, silver, zinc, tantalum, mineral sands and low-cost uranium. Australia is a significant producer of gold, iron ore, bauxite, nickel, diamonds, alumina, ilmenute, zircon and rutile. Australia is the largest exporter of gold and iron ore in the world.Total mining exploration expenditure had fallen dramatically by 2001, but the trend had reversed by 2005 to levels equalling those of 1997, when spending on exploration was US$676 million.

Hydrocarbons

Australia has proven oil reserves totalled 1.5 billion barrels and produces around 550,000 barrels per day (bpd). The main oil-fields are situated offshore in the Bass Strait and Carnarvon Basin. The rate of production has been in decline since 2000, partly due to depleting reserves. Domestic consumption is around 900,000bpd. Australia imports over a third of its crude oil requirements, a proportion which is forecast to rise to 50 per cent by 2010. At current levels of production, Australian reserves should last for another 15 years, but exploration is taking place.
Australia has proven natural gas reserves of 2.54 trillion cubic metres. At a production rate of 34.5 billion cubic metres per annum, reserves should last for 40 years. There are expected to be significant increases in gas consumption in the future. It is projected that natural gas will increase to 22 per cent of Australia's total energy consumption by 2005.
Proven coal reserves are 86.5 billion tonnes, representing 8.3 per cent of world reserves. Coal production is around 373 million tonnes and is growing by four per cent a year. Australia exports 60 per cent of production.

Energy
Australia has a total generating capacity of 47.1GW. Around 85 per cent is produced by coal-fired power stations, most of the rest by gas and hydropower. The sector represents 1.4 per cent of GDP. Each state has its own pattern of electric power development. The government plans to increase generating capacity to 50GW by 2010. Expansion costs are estimated at US$9 billion.

Financial markets
Stock exchange
The Australian Stock Exchange (ASX) is the eleventh largest in the world.

Banking and insurance
There are 15 national and regional domestic banks in Australia, with an annual turnover of approximately US$34 billion.
Central bank
Reserve Bank of Australia
Main financial centre
Sydney

Time
There are three time zones:
Queensland, New South Wales, ACT, Victoria, Tasmania (Eastern Standard Time (EST)) – GMT +10 hours.
South Australia and Northern Territory (Central Standard Time (CST)) – GMT + 9.30 hours.
Western Australia (Western Standard Time (WST)) – GMT + 8 hours
Daylight saving, plus one hour to GMT times in all states and territories except Western Australia and Queensland, (October to March).

Geography
Australia is an island continent with the Indian Ocean to the west, the Coral Sea to the east and the Tasman Sea and Pacific Ocean to the south. Australia is the flattest of the continents, the average elevation being less than 300 metres. It has three major landform features: the western plateau, the interior lowlands and the eastern uplands. Much of the land is desert.
Hemisphere
Southern

Climate
The climate ranges from tropical to temperate. About half of Queensland and Western Australia and 80 per cent of the Northern Territory are within the tropics. The remainder of the states and territories — New South Wales, Victoria, South Australia, Tasmania and the Australian Capital Territory — are in the temperate zone. Temperatures vary greatly from warm to very hot in summer (December—February) to cool and rainy in winter (June–August). In July, the temperature in Sydney averages 17 degrees Celsius (C) and in Melbourne 14 degrees C, but in the desert centre can reach 36 degrees. Average annual temperatures can vary from 25 degrees C in the far north to 13 degrees C in the far south. For most of Australia the hottest month is January.
Much of the country receives low rainfall, but some parts of Queensland, Tasmania, Victoria and New South Wales have annual rainfall of up to 4,200mm. Tropical cyclones develop over the seas to the north-west and the north-east in summer. An average of about three cyclones hit the Queensland coast every year. The Snowy Mountains in New South Wales, a famous ski resort, receives heavy snowfalls most years.
Some 70 per cent of the continent is arid, with extremes of daytime and night-time temperatures in the interior.

Dress codes
For business a suit and tie for men; suit, dress or skirt and blouse for women.

Entry requirements
Passports
Required by all.
Visa
Required by all and must be obtained in advance and from outside Australia.
Most citizens of EU and North America can apply for an Electronic Travel Authority (ETA) which can be issued by a travel agent or airline, or can be applied for online. See www.eta.immi.gov.au for details of those eligible, and follow links to the application site. ETA-eligible business visitors may stay for up to three months without additional documentation.
Those not eligible for an ETA must apply using form 456, through the nearest embassy or mission. Business visas will require a letter of invitation from a local company or organisation, a business letter from an employer stating purpose of trip and details of employee's function, proof of sufficient funds, and a full itinerary. Further details and application form can be obtained at www.immi.gov.au/business-services/index.htm.
Prohibited entry
Currency advice/regulations
This import and export of local and foreign currencies are unstricted but amounts over A$10,000 (or foreign equivalent) must be declared.
Travellers cheques are widely accepted.
Customs
Personal effects are exempt. Duty-free shops are open to international visitors on arrival in Australia.
Prohibited imports
Strict quarantine regulations make it inadvisable to carry food, fruit, vegetables, seeds, animals or plants without prior approval. Travellers are not permitted to carry fruit, vegetables or plants into the State of Victoria. Aircraft cabins are sprayed with insecticide before disembarkation.
Importation of certain items is prohibited, including narcotic and dangerous drugs, firearms and birds. Both import and export of protected wildlife or goods derived from (ie made from skins, feathers, shell, bone, etc) is strictly prohibited.

Health (for visitors)
Mandatory precautions
Vaccination certificates are required for yellow fever if travelling from an infected area.
Advisable precautions
UK nationals can obtain free hospital treatment through a reciprocal arrangement between the two governments, but they must pay for other medical treatment. Australia provides moderately expensive, good quality medical care.
Travellers should be wary of exposure to the sun and the use of sun screening creams is advised. Australia has a high incidence of skin cancer in peoples from northern Europe. The Northern Territory has occasional outbreaks of dengue fever; prevention measures include mosquito repellents, nets and clothing that fully cover the body at dawn and dusk.

Hotels
There is a full range of hotels in all cities, they should be booked well in advance, particularly during holiday seasons. A 10 per cent tip is optional.

Credit cards
Major international credit and debit cards are accepted by virtually everyone. Some taxis also accept credit card payments, check with the driver before the journey begins.

Public holidays (national)
In addition to official public holidays observed throughout Australia, extra statutory holidays are observed in individual states and the Australian Capital Territory (ACT).
Fixed dates
1 Jan (New Year's Day), 26 Jan (Australia Day), 25 Apr (Anzac Day), 27 Sep (Queen's Official Birthday, WA only), 25 Dec (Christmas Day), 26 Dec (Boxing Day).
If Christmas Day or New Year's Day falls on a Saturday, the next Monday is given as a holiday.
Variable dates
Good Friday, Easter Monday, Queen's Official Birthday (second Mon in Jun).

Working hours
Banking
Mon–Thu: 0930–1600; Fri: 0930–1700.
Business
Mon–Fri: 0900–1700.

Government
Mon–Fri: 0900–1700.
Shops
Mon–Fri: 0900–1700; Sat: 0900–1200. Late night shopping (to 2100) in Sydney, Perth and Darwin on Thursday, and in Melbourne, Brisbane, Hobart and Canberra on Friday.

Telecommunications
Mobile/cell phones
GSM 3G service is available in major cities only, 900/1800 services are available in the most populated areas.

Electricity supply
220–250V AC, with 3-pin plug fittings (not UK style) and bayonet-type light sockets. Leading hotels also supply 110V outlets for razors and small appliances.

Weights and measures
Metric system

Social customs/useful tips
Australians tend to be informal, first names are quickly adopted. A handshake is normal for greetings. Business, with traditional blunt, straight-to-the-point talk, is often conducted over lunch or dinner accompanied by local wines and beers.
Australians love outdoor life and business tends to come to a standstill on weekends and public holidays, when there is a steady exodus to country areas, particularly beaches or ski-slopes depending on the season.
Visitors often complain about bureaucracy and patience is required in dealing with government departments and large corporations. There are no short-cuts and although sometimes an approach to the top official of a department might help speed up matters, this must be done with extreme caution as Australians do not tolerate queue-jumping.
Australia has strict drink-driving laws, police conduct random roadside breath tests and penalties can be severe.

Security
Australian cities are relatively safe though care should be taken, particularly at night. Each capital city has separate emergency numbers on the inside cover of phone books. Otherwise dial 000 and the operator will direct you to the appropriate service.

Getting there
Air
National airline: Qantas Airways.
International airport/s: All states have international airports (with the exceptions of the capital territory, (which is served by NSW), and Tasmania) with connecting inter- and intra-state flights.
NSW: Kingsford Smith (SYD), 8km south of Sydney; Victoria: Tullamarine (MEL), 21km from Melbourne; Western Australia: Perth (PER), 10km from Perth, all of which have duty-free shop, bar, restaurant, bank, post office, shops; Queensland: Brisbane International (BNE), 11km north-east of city, with duty-free shop, bar, restaurant; South Australia: West Beach (ADL), 8km from Adelaide, with bar, restaurant, post office, shops; Northern Terrritory: Darwin (DRW), 8km from city with bar, money exchange and duty-free shops.
Other airport/s: Tasmania: Hobart (HBA), 17km north of city, with restaurant and bar. Queensland: Cairns (CNS), 4km north-west of Cairns, with duty-free shop, hotel reservations; Townsville (TSV), 5km from city. (More information on local airports is provided on: www.airportsaustralia.com).
Airport tax: None
Surface
Water: There are regular sea links with New Zealand. Cruiseliners call at major ports in Australia. International shipping lines that maintain contacts with Australia may provide passenger services on cargo ships.
Main port/s: There are more than 30 ports. The main ports are at Sydney, Brisbane, Melbourne, Adelaide and Fremantle. Sea transport is extensively used for internal and international freight shipment. Containerised cargo facilities are available.

Getting about
National transport
Air: Air transport is widely used and well developed. Regular services linking main centres and nearly 440 airfields are operated by Australian Airlines, East-West Airlines, Air Queensland and over 25 other operators. Charter aircraft are also available. Travellers holding international air tickets can obtain concessionary air, rail and bus fares within Australia.
Road: All cities have good arterial roads. Despite the vast distances, there are good highways and bus services between all major centres, but conditions in the interior are rugged, with road transport more limited. Seek advice from the appropriate local automobile association before travelling in remote areas, as roads may be affected by weather conditions.
Buses: Air-conditioned express coach services link main centres, including Tasmania via ferries. Buses provide good services on main town routes, but convenient cross-town transport is not always available.
Rail: Railways, mainly government-owned and operated, provide express inter-urban passenger services, electrified suburban services and long-distance freight services, using a 38,563km network of tracks. Long-distance passenger trains are air-conditioned, with dining and sleeping facilities, they are generally a slower option of transport than road or air. Advance booking is recommended.
The Ghan passenger train runs directly from Adelaide to Darwin through the centre of Australia, via Alice Springs. The refurbished, 47-hour, 2,979km transcontinental journey, began its regular services in 2004. Alice Springs is the closest base for access to the region around Uluru/Ayers Rock national park and Kings Canyon.
There are rail extensions to the Ghan from other state capital cities of Melbourne, Sydney and Perth.
Water: There is a regular passenger/vehicle ferry link between Melbourne and Hobart, Tasmania.
City transport
Taxis: Metered taxis operate in all main cities and towns from major hotels, shopping areas and signposted taxi ranks. Radio-controlled taxis are listed in local telephone directories. Tipping is not expected, but a tip of the balance of the fare rounded up to the nearest dollar is sometimes given.
Buses, trams & metro: Sydney (NSW): the rail service AirportLink connects Sydney international airport with the city centre; trains depart at 10 minute intervals, journey time 13 minutes. State Transit run extensive services of buses, trains and ferries around the city and suburbs.
Melbourne (Vic): VicTrip operate trams, buses and trains around the cityand suburbs. See www.victrip.com.au for a journey planner. Skybus links the airport to city centre; services run 24 hours, everyday with daytime departures every 15 minutes, journey time 20 minutes.
Brisbane (Qld): Buses and trains link the airport to the city centre, journey time 20 minutes, as well as to all other parts of the city and suburbs.
Ferry: In Sydney, ferries are an easy, regular and enjoyable mode of transport to the city centre and harbour suburbs. The main ferry terminal is at Circular Quay. In Brisbane there are over a dozen passenger stops along the city's river.
Car hire
Hire cars are widely available. Current overseas licences are recognised, but International Drivers Permits are recommended. The required third-party insurance is normally included in car hire charge. Use of seat belts is compulsory and speed limit in towns is generally 60km per hour. Driving is on the left. Trams have the right of way. Drink driving rules are vigorously enforced, with sizeable fines.

BUSINESS DIRECTORY

The addresses listed below are a selection only. While World of Information makes every endeavour to check these addresses, we cannot guarantee that changes have not been made, especially to telephone numbers and area codes. We would welcome any corrections.

Telephone area codes

The international direct dialling (IDD) code for Australia is +61, followed by area code and subscriber's number:

Adelaide	8	Hobart	3
Brisbane	7	Launceston	3
Cairns	7	Melbourne	3
Canberra	2	Newcastle	2
Darwin	8	Perth	8
Gold Coast	7	Sydney	2
Wollongong	2	Townsville	7

Useful telephone numbers

Emergency Services: 000.

Chambers of Commerce

ACT and Region Chamber of Commerce and Industry, 12a Thesiger Court, PO Box 192, 2600 Deakin West (tel: 6283-5200; fax: 6260-3369; e-mail: chamber@actchamber.com.au).

Australian Business Chamber, 140 Arthur Street, Locked Bag 938, North Sydney, NSW 2059 (tel: 9458-7500; fax: 9923-1166; e-mail: moreld@abol.net).

Australian Chamber of Commerce and Industry, 50 Burwood Road, PO Box E14, Kingston, ACT 2604 (tel: 6273-2311; fax: 6273-3196; e-mail: acci@acci.asn.au).

Commerce Queensland, 375 Wickham Terrace, Brisbane, QLD 4000 (tel: 3842-2244; 3832-3195; fax: 3832-3195; e-mail: qcci@qcci.com.au).

New South Wales State Chamber of Commerce, Level 12, 83 Clarence Street, GPO Box 4280, Sydney NSW 2000 (tel: 9350-8100; fax: 9350-8199; e-mail: worldtradecentre@thechamber.com.au).

Northern Territory Chamber of Commerce and Industry, 5/2 Shepherd Street, GPO Box 1825, Darwin, NT 0800 (tel: 8936-3100; fax: 8981-1405; e-mail: darwin@ntcci.com.au).

South Australian Employers Chamber of Commerce, 136 Greenhill Road, Unley, SA 5061 (tel: 8300-0000; fax: 8300-0001; e-mail: enquiries@business-sa.com).

Tasmanian Chamber of Commerce and Industry, 30 Burnett Street, PO Box 793, 7001 Hobart (tel: 6234-5933; fax: 6231-1278; e-mail: admin@tcci.org.au).

Victoria Employers Chamber of Commerce asnd Industry, 196 Flinders Street, Melbourne, VIC 3000/ PO Box 4352QQ, Melbourne, VIC 3001 (tel: 8662-5333; fax: 8662-5462; e-mail: webmaster@vecci.org.au).

Western Australia Chamber of Commerce and Industry, 180 Hay Street, East Perth, WA 6004/ PO Box, East Perth, WA 6892 (tel: 9365-7555; fax: 9365-7550; e-mail: info@cciwa.com).

Banking

Australia and New Zealand Banking Group, 100 Queen Street, Melbourne, Vic 3000 (tel: 9273-5555).

Australia & New Zealand Savings Bank Ltd, Collins Place, 55 Collins Street, Melbourne, Vic 3000 (tel: 9275-5555).

Barclays Bank Australia Ltd, Barclays House, PO Box 3357, 25 Bligh Street, Sydney, NSW 2001 (tel: 9233-6622; fax: 9221-3060).

Colonial State Bank of New South Wales, PO Box 41, Sydney, NSW 2001 (tel: 9226-8000).

Commonwealth Bank of Australia, Pitt Street and Martin Place, Sydney, NSW 2000 (tel: 9378-2000; fax: 9312-9905).

Commonwealth Savings Bank of Australia, GPO Box 2719, Pitt Street & Martin Place, Sydney, NSW 2001 (9227-7111; fax: 9232-6573, 9235-1653).

National Australia Bank, 500 Bourke Street, PO Box 84A, Melbourne, Vic 3001 (tel: 9605-3500).

Natwest Australia Bank Ltd, 41st Level, Qantas International Centre, International Square, George Street, Sydney, NSW 2000 (tel: 9250-8500; fax: 9251-2763).

Rural & Industries Bank of Western Australia, PO Box E237, 54-58 Barrack Street, Perth, WA 6001 (tel: 9320-6206; fax: 9320-6444).

State Bank of Victoria, PO Box 267D, 385 Bourke Street, Melbourne, Vic 3001 (tel: 9604-7000; fax: 9602-2150).

State Bank of New South Wales, PO Box 41, Sydney, NSW 2001 (tel: 9226-8000).

State Bank of South Australia, 97 King William Street, PO Box 399, Adelaide, SA 5001 (tel: 9210-4411; fax: 9210-4758, 9212-3056).

Westpac Banking Corporation, 60 Martin Place, PO Box 1, Sydney, NSW 2001 (tel: 9226-3311).

Australian branches

Bank of New Zealand, 333 George Street, PO Box 507, Sydney, NSW 2001 (tel: 9290-6666).

Banque Nationale de Paris, 12 Castlereagh Street, PO Box 269, Sydney, NSW 2001 (tel: 9232-8733).

Central bank

Reserve Bank of Australia, 65 Martin Place, PO Box 3947, Sydney, NSW 2001 (tel: 9551-8111; fax: 9551-8000; e-mail: rbainfo@rba.gov.au).

Travel information

Australian Capital Territory Tourist Bureau, Canberra Centre, Northbourne Avenue, Canberra City, ACT 2601 (tel: 6233-3666).

Automobile Association of the Northern Territory (AANT), 79-81 Smith Street, Darwin, NT 0800 (tel: 8981-3837).

Australian Tourist Commission, 80 William Street, PO Box 2721, Wooloomoloo, NSW 2011 (tel: 9360-1111; fax: 9361-1385; internet: www.atc.net.au).

Holiday WA Centre, 772 Hay Street, Perth, WA 6000 (tel: 9322-2999).

National Roads and Motorists Association (NRMA), 151 Clarence Street, Sydney, NSW 2000 (tel: 9260-9222).

NSW Government Travel Centre, 16 Spring Street, Sydney, NSW 2000 (tel: 9231-444).

Northern Territory Government Tourist Bureau, 31 Smith Street, Darwin NT 5750 (tel: 8981-6611/3).

Qantas Airways, Qantas Centre, QCA9, 203 Coward Street, Sydney, NSW 2020 (tel: 9691-3472; fax: 9691-4547; internet site: www.anzac.com/qantas/qantas.com).

Queensland Government Tourist Bureau, Corner Adelaide and Edward Streets, Brisbane, QLD 4001 (tel: 3312-211; internet: www.tq.com.au).

Royal Automobile Club of Queensland (RACQ), 300 St Paul's Tce, Brisbane, QLD 4006 (tel: 3253-4444).

Royal Automobile Association of South Australia, 41 Hindmarsh Square, Adelaide, SA 5000 (tel: 8223-4555).

Royal Automobile Club of Tasmania (RACT), Corner Patrick & Murray Streets, Hobart, Tas 7001 (tel: 6382-200).

Royal Automobile Club of Victoria (RACV), 123 Queen Street, Melbourne, Vic 3174 (tel: 9790-2211).

Royal Automobile Club of Western Australia Inc (RACWA), 228 Adelaide Terrace, Perth, WA 6000 (tel: 9421-4444).

South Australian Government Travel Centre, 18 King William Street, Adelaide, SA 5000 (tel: 8212-1644).

Tasmanian Government Tourist Bureau, 80 Elizabeth Street, Hobart, Tas 7000 (tel: 6300-211).

Victoria Tourism Commission, 230 Collins Street, Melbourne, Vic 3000 (tel: 9619-9444).

VicRail Information: 619-1111 (Melbourne).

Ministry of tourism
Department of Tourism, Burns Memorial Building, 28 National Circuit, Forrest, ACT 2603 (tel: 6279-7111; fax: 6248-0734).

National tourist organisation offices
Tourism Australia, PO Box 2721, Sydney NSW 1006 (tel: 9360-1111; fax: 9331-6469; internet: www.tourism.australia.com)

Ministries
Department of Administrative Services, GPO Box 1920, Canberra, ACT 2601 (tel: 6275-3000; fax: 6275-3819).

Department of Communications and the Arts, GPO Box 2154, Canberra, ACT 2601 (tel: 6279-1000; fax: 6279-1901; internet site: http//www.dcita.gov.au).

Department of Defence, Treasury Building, Newland Street, Parkes, ACT 2600 (tel: 6265-9111; fax: 6273-3021; internet site: http://www.defence.gov.au).

Department of Employment, Education and Training, GPO Box 9880, Canberra, ACT 2601 (tel: 6240-8111).

Department of Finance, Treasury Building, Newlands Street, Parkes, ACT 2600 (tel: 6263-2222; fax: 6273-3021; internet site: http://www.dofa.gov.au).

Department of Foreign Affairs and Trade, Administrative Building, Parkes Place, Parkes, ACT 2600 (tel: 6261-9111; fax: 6261-3111; internet site: http://www://dfat/gov.au).

Department of Housing and Regional Development, GPO Box 9834, Canberra, ACT 2601 (tel: 6289-2222).

Department of Human Services and Health, GPO Box 9848, Canberra, ACT 2601.

Department of Immigration and Ethnic Affairs, PO Box 25, Belconnen, ACT 2616 (tel: 6264-1111; internet site: http://www.immi.gov.au).

Department of Industrial Relations, GPO Box 9879, Canberra, ACT 2601 (tel: 6243-7333).

Department of Industry, Science and Technology, GPO Box 9839, Canberra, ACT 2601 (tel: 6276-1000; fax: 6276-1111; internet: www.industry.gov.au).

Department of National Development and Industry, Tasman House, Hobart Place, PO Box 5, Canberra, ACT 2600.

Department of Primary Industries and Energy, GPO Box 858, Canberra, ACT 2601 (tel: 6272-3933; fax: 6272-5161).

Department of the Prime Minister and Cabinet, Locked Bag 14, Queen Victoria Terrace, Parkes, ACT 2600 (tel: 6271-5111; fax: 6271-5414; internet site: www.dpmc.gov.au).

Department of Social Security, Box 7788, Canberra Mail Centre, ACT 2610 (tel: 6244-7788).

Department of Transport, GPO Box 594, Canberra, ACT 2601 (tel: 6274-7111; fax: 6257-2505; internet site: http://www.dot.gov.au).

Department of the Treasury, The Treasury, Parkes Place, Parkes, ACT 2600 (tel: 6263-2111; fax: 6273-2614; internet site: http://www.treasury.gov.au).

Department of Veterans' Affairs, PO Box 21, Woden, ACT 2606 (tel: 6289-1111; fax: 6281-3822; internet site: http://www.dva.gov.au).

Foreign Investment Review Board, Department of the Treasury, Parkes Place, Parkes, ACT 2600 (tel: 6263-3795; fax: 6263-2940).

Other useful addresses
ACT Department of Business, Arts, Sport and Tourism, Level 8, FAI House, 197 London Circuit, Canberra, ACT 2601 (tel: 6207-5111; fax: 6205-0577).

Attorney-General, Suite MF 21, Parliament House, Canberra, ACT 2600 (tel: 6277-7300; fax: 6273-4102; internet site: www.law.gov.au).

Australian Bureau of Agriculture and Resource Economics, MacArthur House, Lyneham, ACT 2601 (tel: 6246-9111).

Australian Bureau of Statistics, Cameron Office, Chandler Street, Belconan, ACT 2617 (tel: 6252-7911).

Australian Dairy Corporation, Dairy Industry House, St Kilda Road, Melbourne, VIC 3004 (tel: 9819-4000).

Australian Embassy (USA), 1601 Massachusetts Avenue, NW, Washington DC 20036-2273 (tel: (+1-202) 797-3000; fax (+1-202) 797-3331; e-mail: library.washington@dfat.gov.au).

Australian Industrial Development Corporation (AIDC), 212 Northbourne Avenue; PO Box 3024, Canberra, ACT 2600 (tel: 6230-1300).

Australian Mining Industry Council, 216 Northbourne Avenue, Braddon, ACT 2601 (tel: 6249-8955).

Australian Securities Commission, Corporate Affairs Commission, National Mutual Centre, 15 London Court, Canberra City, ACT 2601 (tel: 6247-5011; internet site: www.asc.gov.au).

Australian Stock Exchange Ltd, Stock Exchange Center, 530 Collins Street, PO Box 1784 Q, AU Melbourne, VIC 3001 (tel: 9617-8611; fax: 9614-0303; internet site: www.asx.com.au).

Australia Trade Commission, Austrade Centre Cnr Bary Drive and Northbourne Ave, Canberra City, ACT 2601 (tel: 6276-5111; fax: 6276-5105).

Australian Trade Development Council, Department of Trade and Resources, Canberra, ACT 2600.

Australian Wheat Board, Ceres House, Lonsdale Street, Melbourne, VIC 3000 (tel: 9605-1555).

Australian Wool Corporation, Wool House, Royal Parade, Parkville, VIC 3000 (tel: 9341-9111).

British High Commission, Commonwealth Avenue, Yarralumia, Canberra City, ACT 2600 (tel: 6270-6666; fax: 6273-3236).

Business Council of Australia, Ethos House, 28 Ainslie Avenue, Canberra City, ACT 2601 (tel: 6247-8208).

Business Victoria, Level 13, 55 Collins Street, Melbourne, VIC 3000 (tel: 9651-9999; fax: 9651-9962).

BZW Australia Ltd, Level 22, 255 George Street, Sydney 2000 (tel: 9259-5913; fax: 9259-5477); Airports Team, GPO Box 4675, Sydney 1042 (fax: 9259-5477).

Confederation of Australian Industry, 12a The Siger Court, Deakin, ACT 2600 (tel: 282-2199); PO Box E14, Queen Victoria Terrace, Canberra, ACT 2600 (tel: 6732-311; fax: 6733-196).

International Trade Department Centre, Edgecliff Centre, 203 New South Head Road, Edgecliff, NSW 2027 (tel: 9329-297).

Major Projects Tasmania, 10/fl, 22 Elizabeth Street, Hobart, TAS 7000 (tel: 6233-5869; fax: 6233-5755).

New South Wales Department of State, Level 44, Grosvenor Place, 225 George Street, Sydney, NSW 2000 (tel: 9242-6963; fax: 9242-6970).

New South Wales Government Department of Industrial Development and Decentralisation, GPO Box 4169, Sydney, NSW 2001 (tel: 9927-2741).

Northern Department of Asian Relations, Trade and Industry, 1/fl Development House, 76 The Esplande, Darwin, NT 0800 (tel: 8999-5210; fax: 8999-5106).

Northern Territory Development Corporation, GPO Box 2245, Darwin, NT 5794 (tel: 8989-4211).

Queensland Department of Economic Development & Trade, Executive Building, 100 George Street, Brisbane QLD 4000 (tel: 3224-5970; fax: 3225-8914).

South Australia Department of Trade and Industry, Terrace towers, 178 North Towers, Adelaide SA 5000 (tel: 8303-2400; fax: 9303-2410).

Telecom Australia, 199 William Street, Melbourne, VIC 3000 (tel: 9606-5511).

US Embassy, Moonah Place, Yarralumla, ACT 2600 (tel: 6214-5600; fax: 6214-5970).

Western Australia Department of Industry and Trade, 170 St Georges Terrace, Perth, WA 6000 (tel: 9327-5666; fax: 9322-3361).

Western Australian Development Corporation, 28th Floor, City Mutual Tower, 197 St George's Terrace, Perth, WA 6000 (tel: 9322-7933).

World Trade Promotions (trade fairs and exhibitions), 291 Sussex Street, Sydney, NSW 2000 (tel: 9267-5122).

Other news agencies: AAP (Australian Associated Press): http://aap.com.au
ABC News: www.abc.net.au/news

Internet sites

Austrade (information for overseas business people): www.austrade.gov.au/index.asp

Australian Broadcasting Corporation (ABC): www.abc.net.au

Australian Capital Territory government: www.act.gov.au

British Chamber of Commerce: www.whoswhere.com.au/abcc

Customs service: www.customs.gov.au

Department of Agriculture, Fisheries and Forestry: www.daff.gov.au

Department of the Environment and Heritage: www.environment.gov.au

Department of Health and Aged Care: www.health.gov.au

Foreign Affairs & Trade Dept: www.dfat.gov.au

Farmwide information on weather reports, commodity prices, etc: www.farmwide.com.au

Federal Government: www.fed.gov.au

Federal Parliament (Canberra): www.aph.gov.au/

General Information: www.about-australia.com

Immigration Department: www immi.gov.au

Invest Australia: www.investaustralia.gov.au

New South Wales state government: www.nsw.gov.au

Northern Territory state government: www.nt.gov.au/

Qantas: www.qantas.com.au

Queensland state government: www.qld.gov.au/

Reserve bank: www.rba.gov.au

South Australia: www.sa.gov.au

Stock Exchange: www.asx.com.au

Statistics: www.abs.gov.au

Tasmania state government: www.tas.gov.au

Taxation office: www.ato.gov.au

Tourism: www.australia.com

Tourism: www.tourism.australia.com

Victoria state government: www.vic.gov.au

Western Australia state government: www.wa.gov.au/

White pages: www.whitepages.com.au

Yellow pages: www.Yellowpages.com.au

Austria

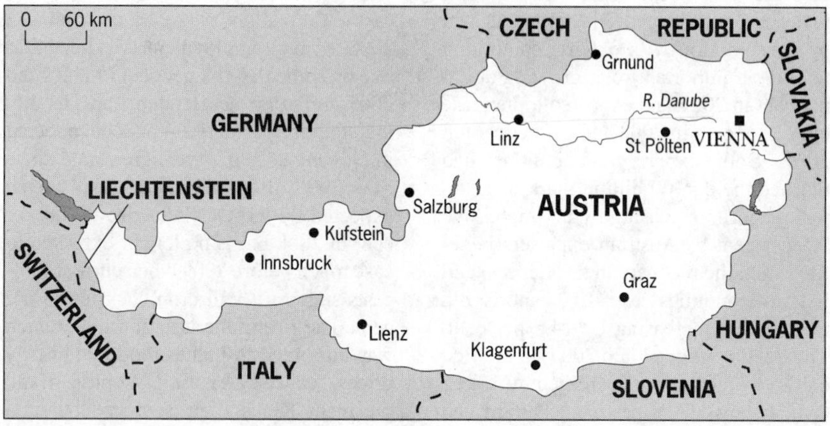

Austria, that for three centuries played a pivotal role in European affairs, has endeavoured to maintain its neutrality into the twenty-first century while at the same time being a fully paid up member of the European Union (EU) (but not of NATO). In terms of GDP per capita Austria has a lot to be proud of, ranking fourth in the EU and tenth in the world. Described in the London *Financial Times* as the country of 'either or', a description that can be interpreted favourably or otherwise, of late Austria has certainly benefited economically from its position at the Eastern end of the 'old' EU. But that same proximity has caused many Austrians to express concern at possible waves of immigration and the perceived prospect of large numbers of immigrants placing further strains on the country's educational and health resources as well as its social services in general.

Schuessel departs...

Austria certainly boasts one of the EU's strongest economies, supported by levels of infrastructure and public services that are second to none. All of which would lead most observers to infer that the country's citizens were a contented lot. But as the country's former and high profile chancellor, Wolfgang Schuessel found out to his cost in the 2006 election, for some time the general disposition of Austria's electorate has been one of gloom rather than glee. Austrians appear to be reluctant rather than enthusiastic members of the EU, often verging on the xenophobic when it comes to matters of immigration, social policy and their view of the Brussels bureaucracy.

On becoming a member of the EU in 1995, Austria began an ambitious programme of structural change in key sectors of what had traditionally been a less than dynamic economy. The telecommunications, banking and energy sectors were both liberalised and privatised. The eastern enlargement of the EU in 2004 acted as a further catalyst for the Austrian economy, particularly in the energy (electricity and natural gas) and financial services sectors. Austria's banks had always seen Eastern Europe as their natural backyard. However far successive administrations have gone in reforming the economy, there is still much to be done. This is particularly the case in respect of labour legislation; Austria still lags behind the EU's leading reformists in labour flexibility and greater labour participation by its ageing population.

...and Gusenbauer does his best

Austria's Chancellor Alfred Gusenbuaer can hardly be described as an internationally known figure. Leader of the Social Democratic (SPO) party, he also heads up the country's fractious ruling coalition alongside the conservative People's party (OPV). Somewhat improbably, the 48 year old Gusenbauer manages to combine being Austria's Chancellor with also being its minister for sport – Austria is

KEY FACTS

Official name: Republik Österreich (Republic of Austria)

Head of State: Federal President Heinz Fischer (SPÖ) (sworn in 8 Jul 2004)

Head of government: Chancellor Alfred Gusenbauer (SPÖ) (from 11 Jan 2007)

Ruling party: Coalition: Österreichische Volkspartei (ÖVP) (Austrian People's Party) and Sozialdemokratische Partei Österreichs (SPÖ) (Social Democratic Party of Austria) (from 11 Jan 2007)

Area: 83,855 square km

Population: 8.28 million (2007)*

Capital: Vienna

Official language: German

Currency: Euro (eur) = 100 cents (from 1 Jan 2002; previous currency schilling, locked at S13.76 per euro)

Exchange rate: eur0.63 per US$ (Jul 2008)

GDP per capita: US$45,181 (2007)*

GDP real growth: 3.40% (2007)

Labour force: 3.45 million (2004)

Unemployment: 4.40% (2005)

Inflation: 2.20% (2007)

Balance of trade: US$3.43 billion (2005)

Foreign debt: US$492.70 billion (2004)

Visitor numbers: 20.30 million (2006)*

Annual FDI: US$43.80 billion (cumulative, 1995–2004, OECD); US$4.90 billion (OECD, 2004)*

* estimated figure

co-host with Switzerland of the 2008 European Football Championship.

In early 2008 Mr Gusenbauer came under criticism in the Austrian press for accepting free upgrades to business on a Christmas family holiday to Vietnam from Austrian Airlines, the national carrier. Polls indicated that most Austrians regarded the upgrade affair as a storm in a teacup, many preferring their Chancellor to arrive on holiday in a less than crumpled suit! Austria's daily press is largely supportive of the OPV and, like most Austrians, had been taken by surprise by Mr Gusenbauer's narrow election victory. Following the election Mr Gusenbauer saw himself obliged to hand over the finance and foreign affairs portfolios to the OPV. After taking over from Mr Schuessel as Chancellor in January 2007, Mr Gusenbauer has struggled to strike a chord with the Austrian electorate.

Just look at the figures

Austrian GDP has grown at an impressive rate for some years, averaging more than three per cent annually for the period 2005–07.This is well above the average growth rate for the eurozone (countries that have adopted the euro) and also that of all the EU's 25 members. The budget deficit is a manageable one per cent of GDP. The target date for balancing the budget has been put back from 2008 to 2009–10.Unemployment in 2007 was 4.3 per cent, approximately half that of France or Germany, Austria's principal trading partner.

Impressive exports...

The Oesterreichische Nationalbank (OeNB) in its economic outlook for 2007 estimated Austria's real GDP to have risen by 3.3 per cent. As is the case with all European economies, the OeNB forecast lower growth for 2008 and 2009, at 2.5 per cent and 2.3 per cent respectively. Growth in the eurozone is seen to be largely driven by consumption with exports continuing to play an important role, growing at 6.4 per cent in 2007 and expected to increase by 6.1 per cent in 2008 and 6.7 per cent in 2009. Both exports and imports had reached the eur100 billion mark in 2006, with exports increasing by an impressive 9.5 per cent as Austrian exporters benefited from the recovery in the German and Italian economies. Non-EU exports did even better, increasing by 14.5 per cent. The trend continued into 2007, in the first half of which exports increased by 10 per cent, imports by 8 per cent. Diminished global demand will depress export growth to a forecast 6.5 per cent in 2008. Austria's dynamic export growth has lead to healthy trade surpluses and a current account surplus of 2.8 per cent in 2007, a figure which is expected to reach 4.6 per cent by 2009.

Austria's private household consumption has lagged behind real disposable income, producing a sustained increase in the rate of savings since 2002. This has meant that consumer demand has developed at much lower rates than the economy as a whole, registering only 1.6 per cent in 2007 and dropping to 1.5 per cent in 2008 before returning to 1.5 per cent again in 2009. Diminished business confidence (Austria's industrial confidence indicator dropped to -4 in February 2008 down from +7 in mid-2007).

...inflation worries

Austria's unemployment rate remained virtually unchanged at 4.3 pr cent throughout 2007. Unemployment is forecast to drop slightly – to 4.2 per cent – in 2008 as total employment is expected to rise by some 0.7–0.8 per cent in 2008 and 2009. Inflation accelerated considerably in late-2007, rising to 3.4 per cent per cent in November 2007, the highest rate since May 2006. Inflation had originally been expected by the OeNB to rise to 2.4 per cent in 2008 but is no longer expected to ease much before 2009 when current forecasts suggest it will drop back to 1.8 per cent. The rise in the inflation rate, which was attributed to higher food and energy prices, caused Austria's Central Bank president Klaus Liebscher to label it a 'worrying development' as he appealed to industry, unions and the government to keep prices under control. Wage moderation has in fact been a characteristic of the Austrian economy, with wages only increasing modestly despite labour demand.

Short term interest rates are set at 4.5 per cent and expected to drop to 4.3 per cent for 2008 and 2009. Long-term interest rates differ little, based as they are on market expectations for ten-year bonds. The unknown factor in the Bank's economic forecasts (and those of many others) is the price of crude oil. For 2007 a market price of US$72.6 per barrel had been adopted, which turned out to be too low, as did the forecasts for 2008 (US$88.6) and 2009 (US$83.7). The rise in the price of oil was partially mitigated by the drop in the value of the US dollar. The OeNB noted that in real terms, taking into account the strength of the euro and the weakness of the dollar, the oil price pertaining at the end of 2007 still remained below the price levels seen between 1981 and 1985.

Market turmoil

In early 2008 the OeNB noted that it was difficult to quantify the turmoil in international capital markets. The bank expressed concern that the financial market crisis could spread to what it described as the 'real economy'. The crisis could obviously affect both private households and businesses, resulting in lower levels of business investment and business consumption. A combination of lower investment and domestic consumption would inevitably depress GDP growth. Austrian

KEY INDICATORS — Austria

	Unit	2003	2004	2005	2006	2007
Population	m	8.07	8.08	8.23	8.26	*8.28
Gross domestic product (GDP)	US$bn	251.50	290.11	305.34	323.83	373.94
GDP per capita	US$	30,250	35,809	37,086	39,190	*45,181
GDP real growth	%	0.8	2.0	2.0	3.2	3.4
Inflation	%	1.3	2.0	2.1	1.7	2.2
Unemployment	%	4.3	4.5	5.2	4.8	4.4
Exports (fob) (goods)	US$m	70,000.0	111,134.0	117,233.0	133,844.0	162,147.0
Imports (cif) (goods)	US$m	74,000.0	106,929.0	113,806.0	133,419.0	160,302.0
Balance of trade	US$m	-4,000.0	4,205.0	3,427.0	425.0	1,845.0
Current account	US$m	-2,310.0	-1,980.0	3,753.0	7,927.0	10,037.0
Total reserves minus gold	US$m	8,470.0	7,858.0	6,839.0	7,010.0	10,689.0
Foreign exchange	US$m	7,144.0	6,763.0	6,298.0	6,573.0	10,261.0
Exchange rate	per US$	0.88	0.80	0.77	0.75	0.69

* estimated figure

banks felt the effect through generally more difficult re-financing conditions in the long-term bond and money markets. But at the end of 2007, Austrian banks had yet to see any real effect on their lending policies; credit guidelines in the corporate sector were tightened, but conversely were actually loosened for retail customers, especially in cases of retail construction. For some years now, Austrian banks have actively expanded into central and eastern Europe, with the beneficial effect of reducing their exposure to the indirect consequences of the problems of the US sub-prime mortgage market.

Austria's ageing population will for some time present future governments with a demanding challenge. Austria is not alone in experiencing a lower birth rate caused by decreased fertility and birth rates and increased life expectancy. Ageing populations place inevitable strains on pension, health and care expenditure. In Austria's case, some of this additional expenditure is mitigated by reduced expenditure on education and youth benefits (although increased levels of immigration may negate this). Austria's relatively generous state pension provisions are forecast to double their demands on the exchequer (from 3 to 6 per cent of GDP) by 2050. Anticipating this, the government introduced far-reaching pension reforms in 2003.

Big names...

The driving force in the Austrian economy remains its industrial sector, where engineering (both electro-chemical and metallurgical) is predominant. In many respects Austria resembles Germany, in that it is its large number of smaller enterprises – the mittelstand – that provides the solid industrial base. Despite the smaller scale of much Austrian industry, Austrian companies achieve productivity rates that are well above the European average, enabling a number of them to be global leaders. The energy conglomerate OMV, which is Austria's largest listed company, is the leading oil and gas company in eastern and central Europe. Drinks company Red Bull has developed a global brand, as has the crystal and costume jewellery group Swarovski. Austria's national airline (Austrian Airlines) has positioned itself as the regional carrier throughout eastern and central Europe and central Asia, turning Vienna's once rather sleepy airport into a vibrant regional and international hub. Notwithstanding the credible performance of its manufacturing and engineering sector, it is the services sector that generates the bulk of Austria's GDP, employing over 20 per cent of the national work force. Tourism, both in winter and summer, is one of Austria's most important economic sectors, accounting for over 16 per cent of GDP.

...small farms

The productivity gains seen in Austria's industry have yet to be seen in the agricultural sector, where small scale and inefficient farm units still prevail. Agriculture contributes a modest 2 per cent to GDP, employing around 6 per cent of the population and supplying 80 per cent of Austria's food requirements.

Risk assessment

Politics	Good
Economy	Good
Regional stability	Good

COUNTRY PROFILE

Historical profile

For centuries the Austrian (later Austro-Hungarian) Empire covered most of central Europe.

1918 After the Austro-Hungarian Empire was defeated in the First World War, the first Austrian Republic was declared; three-quarters of the Empire's territory was ceded to neighbouring states.

1933 Pro-fascist Engelbert Dollfuss (elected federal chancellor in 1932) gained dictatorial powers and banned all political opposition to his Vaterländische Front (VF) (Fatherland Front). Dollfuss forged a strong relationship with fascist Italy in an attempt to preserve Austria's independence.

1934 The government put down an uprising by Socialists in February. Dollfuss was assassinated in July by Austrian Nazis, who had been conspiring to oust the government and integrate Austria with Nazi Germany.

1938 The new chancellor, Kurt Von Schuschnigg, met with Adolf Hitler in an attempt to preserve Austria's independence. After refusing to meet Hitler's demands for concessions for the banned Austrian Nazi Party, Von Schuschnigg resigned as chancellor and was replaced by Arthur Seyss-Inquart (leader of the Austrian Nazi Party). In March, Austria was integrated with Nazi Germany. Austria was renamed Ostmark.

1945 After Nazi Germany was defeated in the Second World War; Austria re-emerged as an independent state but was divided into four zones of occupation by the US, UK, France and USSR. The conservative Österreichische Volkspartei (ÖVP) (Austrian People's Party) and the Sozialdemokratische Partei Österreichs (SPÖ) (Social Democratic Party of Austria) formed a coalition government.

1955 The 1955 State Treaty confirmed Austria's independence and banned re-integration with Germany. Austria joined the UN, declared its neutrality and the occupation forces withdrew.

1960 Austria joined the European Free Trade Area (EFTA).

1966 The ÖVP came to power after 20 years of a coalition.

1970–87 The SPÖ was in power until 1983, when it formed a coalition government with the Freiheitliche Partei Österreichs (FPÖ) (Freedom Party of Austria).

1986 The presidential election was won by Kurt Waldheim (independent but with ÖVP's backing). Controversy surrounded allegations of his implication in Nazi atrocities in the Balkans (1942–45), culminating in his listing as an undesirable alien by the US Department of Justice.

1987 Following an inconclusive election, the SPÖ and the ÖVP formed a coalition.

1992 Waldheim stepped down and was replaced by Thomas Klestil.

1995 Austria joined the EU. The one-year-old governing coalition collapsed over the 1996 budget.

1997 Franz Vranitsky led the government as chancellor from 1995 until his resignation in 1997, when he was replaced by Viktor Klima.

1998 Federal President Klestil was re-elected for a second term of office.

1999 After indecisive election results, the ÖVP-SPÖ coalition collapsed, leading to a coalition between the ÖVP and the FPÖ.

2000 The ÖVP's Wolfgang Schüssel became chancellor. The inclusion of the FPÖ in the government led to EU diplomatic sanctions against Austria, which were formally lifted in September.

2002 Euro currency replaced the Austrian schilling. After three FPÖ ministers resigned, Schüssel announced that ÖVP was withdrawing from the coalition government. The ÖVP won the snap election.

2003 Chancellor Schüssel's coalition government was sworn in: the ÖVP and the right-wing populist FPÖ, with more power to the ÖVP than in the previous coalition.

2004 Heinz Fischer (SPÖ) won the 25 April presidential elections. On 6 July, President Klestil died, he had been critically ill for some time; Heinz Fischer was sworn in as president on 8 July.

2005 The EU constitution was endorsed by parliament. The FPÖ split in April and a breakaway faction, the Bündis Zukunft Österreich (BZÖ) (Alliance for Austria's Future), joined the government coalition. In December, Austria began making payouts to those whose property was looted during the Holocaust. Most of the victims are elderly, and most are resident in the US.

2006 Austria assumed the presidency of the EU for the first six months of the year. On 1 October, in general elections, the ruling coalition lost to the SPÖ which won 35.3 per cent of the vote. Chancellor Schüssel, whose party, the ÖVP, won 34.3 per cent, resigned on 3 October. Alfred Gusenbauer (SPÖ) was invited to form a new coalition on 11 October.

2007 After two months of negotiations, the SPÖ and ÖVP formed a coalition government on 11 January; Alfred Gusenbauer was confirmed as Chancellor. Former president and secretary-general of the United Nations, Kurt Waldheim died on 14 June.

2008 The ruling coalition government collapsed on 7 July when the ÖVP withdrew, following disagreement over policy issues. New elections will be held in September, but Chancellor Gusenbauer decided not to stand for re-election.

Political structure

Constitution

The 1920 constitution was amended in 1929.

The state is a federal republic consisting of nine Länder (states), each with its own state Ländtag (legislature) and government. The nine states are Burgenland, Carinthia, Lower Austria, Upper Austria, Salzburg, Styria, Tyrol, Vorarlberg and Vienna. A considerable amount of political power is devolved to the state assemblies, although all matters of national interest are decided in Vienna. Each state parliament appoints its own state governor.

For some functions (for example, appointing the new president) the Nationalrat (National Council) and the Bundesrat (Federal Council) of the federal Bundesversammlung (parliament) meet in joint session, as the Nationalversammlung (National Assembly). Certain issues may be put to the popular vote in a national referendum and the people may also force a direct vote in the Nationalrat if any petition gathers more than 200,000 signatures.

Traditionally, the government has been required to work according to the principles of the sozialpartner (social contract). This informal organisation, comprising the Chamber of Economy, Chamber of Agriculture, Chamber of Labour and trade unions, is at the heart of the policy-making process. Such a system has served Austria well in the past as it both guarantees and feeds on national consensus and unity. However, it is becoming unworkable in a fully globalised world economy.

Form of state

Federal parliamentary democratic republic

The executive

Executive power rests with the head of the federal government, who is the chancellor appointed by the president, and usually the leader of the largest party in the Nationalrat.

The president is elected by popular vote every six years for a maximum of two terms. He has no executive powers in peace time. He has special emergency powers, as well as overseeing elections and swearing in new chancellors and governments, but in practice, he acts in accordance with the decisions of the government.

National legislature

The bicameral parliament consists of the lower house, the Nationalrat, and the upper house, the Bundesrat.

The 183 constituent members of the Nationalrat are elected every four years by proportional representation. The seats are distributed first among 43 constituencies then among the nine states, and the remainder at federal level.

The 64 members of the Bundesrat are elected for various terms by the nine state legislatures and are chosen to reflect the party political strengths in their respective state parliaments. The chairmanship of the Bundesrat rotates on a six-monthly basis between the states.

Legal system

The legal system is divided between legislative, administrative and judicial power. There are three supreme courts Verfassungsgerichtshof (Constitutional Court), Verwaltungsgerichtshof (Administrative Court) and Oberster Gerichtshof (Judicial Court). There are around 200 local judicial courts (Bezirksgerichte), 17 provincial and district courts (Landes-und Kreisgerichte) and four higher provincial courts (Oberlandesgerichte) in Vienna, Graz, Innsbruck and Linz.

Last elections

25 April 2004 (presidential); 2 October 2006 (parliamentary).

Results: Presidential: Heinz Fischer (Sozialdemokratische Partei Österreichs (SPÖ) (Social Democratic Party)) won 52.4 per cent of the vote and Foreign Minister Benita Ferrero-Waldner (Österreichische Volkspartei (ÖVP) (Austrian People's Party)) 47.6 per cent; turnout was 70.8 per cent.

Parliamentary: the SPÖ won 35.7 per cent of the vote (68 out of 183 seats), the ÖVP won 34.2 per cent (66), Freiheitliche Partei Österreichs (FPÖ) (Liberal Party of Austria) 11.2 per cent (21) and Die Grünen (Grüne) (Greens) 10.5 per cent (20). Turnout was 74.2 per cent.

Next elections

2010 (presidential asnd parliamentary).

Political parties

Ruling party

Coalition: Österreichische Volkspartei (ÖVP) (Austrian People's Party) and Sozialdemokratische Partei Österreichs (SPÖ) (Social Democratic Party of Austria) (from 11 Jan 2007)

Main opposition party

Die Grünen (Grüne) (Greens); Freiheitliche Partei Österreichs (FPÖ) (Liberal Party of Austria)

Population

8.28 million (2007)*

Last census: May 2001: 8,032,926

Population density: Urban population: 65 per cent (1994–2000).

Annual growth rate: 0.2 per cent 1994–2004 (WHO 2006)

Ethnic make-up

Around 93 per cent are of German-Austrian origin. Minorities include Slovenes, Croats, Hungarians and Czechs and are mostly concentrated in the south-east. There are ethnic communities from Africa, the Middle East and Asia.

Religions

Roman Catholic (89 per cent); Protestant (6 per cent).

Education

Primary schooling lasts for four years. There are two main forms of secondary education; one academic and one geared more to technical and vocational education. The former, Allgemeinbildende, school may be attended for eight years or the latter, Hauptschule, attended for four years followed by a school offering specialised training of a technical or vocational nature. Tertiary education takes place in universities or specialist colleges including technology, music and art higher education institutions.

Compulsory years: 6 to 15

Enrolment rate: 103 per cent total primary enrolment, 99 per cent total secondary enrolment, 57 per cent tertiary enrolment; of relevant age groups (including repetition rates) World Bank.

Pupils per teacher: 12 in primary schools

Health

All Austrians have access to healthcare. Per capita total expenditure on health (2003) was US$2,306; of which per capita government spending was US$1,560, at the international dollar rate, (WHO 2006).

HIV/Aids

HIV prevalence: 0.3 per cent aged 15–49 in 2003 (World Bank)

Life expectancy: 79 years, 2004 (WHO 2006)

Fertility rate/Maternal mortality rate: 1.4 births per woman, 2004 (WHO 2006)

Child (under 5 years) mortality rate (per 1,000): 4.5 per 1,000 live births (World Bank)
Head of population per physician: 3.38 physicians per 1,000 people, 2003 (WHO 2006)

Welfare

Austrian social insurance is compulsory and covers health insurance, pension insurance, accident insurance and unemployment insurance. Contributions are shared by employers and employees.

Pensions

Reforms adopted in 2003, extend the years required for employee contributions from 40 to 45, before a worker can retire on a full pension with all benefits; the statutory retirement age was set at 65 for all; 10 disparate pension systems for various categories of workers were harmonised. This is expected to reverse the trend for early retirement. In 2003 the average age of retirement was 57.5, with less than 30 per cent of workers being in the 55–64 age range. With an ageing population the pension scheme will become progressively more expensive; it is expected that the new reforms wll limit spending by between 1.5–1.75 per cent of GDP a year. The government is proposing to stagger the rise in the official retirement age, while reducing state pensions by up to 30 per cent, in some cases.

Main cities

Vienna (capital, estimated population 1.6 million in 2005), Graz (223,297), Salzburg (143,259), Innsbruck (112,693), Klagenfurt (90,666), Linz (180,684), Villach (58,412), Wels (57,552), St Pölten (48,889), Dornbirn (43,005).

Languages spoken

About 94 per cent of Austrian nationals speak German, although a heavy dialect is in daily use. There are linguistic minorities of Slovenes, Croats, Hungarians, Slovaks and Czechs.

Official language/s

German

Media

Other news agencies: APA (Austria Presse Agentur): www.apa.at
Presstext Austria (in German): www.pressetext.at

Press

Almost all ownership of the print media is held by two Germany-based publishing houses, the Bertelsmann Media owns most magazine titles and Westdeutsche Allgemaine Zeitung (WAZ), through Mediaprint Group, controls most newspapers.

Dailies: In German, national newspapers include Der Standard (http://derstandard.at), Die Presse (http://diepresse.com), Der Kurier (www.kurier.at) a mass-circulation and Neue Kronenzeitung (www.krone.at), which has regional editions. Major regional newspapers include Der Grazer (www.grazer.at) from Graz, Salzburger Fenster (www.salzburger-fenster.at) from Salzburg and Österreich (www.oe24.at/zeitung), published in Vienna.

Weeklies: In German, Profil (www.news.at/profil), Österreich Journal (www.oe-journal.at), and News Magazin (www.news.at/magazin), for news and analysis, Die Bezirksblätter (www.noe-anzeiger.at), for regional and local news, Wienerin (www.wienerin.at), for women and Wiener Zeitung (www.wienerzeitung.at) a semi-official publication from Vienna.

Most daily newspapers have weekend editions, which tend to be bigger and contain a large amount of advertising.

Business: In German, Wirtschafts Blatt (www.wirtschaftsblatt.at) is a daily, Industrie Magazin (www.industriemagazin.at), and Trend (www.news.at/trend), are weekly magazines.

Broadcasting

Österreichischer Rundfunk (ÖRF) (Austrian Broadcasting Corporation) (www.orf.at) is the national, public broadcasting network.

Radio: ÖRF broadcasts four national radio networks (including Ö1 Hit Radio and FM4), 10 regional stations and two international channels (Radio Österreich 1 International and Radio 1476). Private, commercial radio stations includes Krone Hit (www.kronehit.at) a national network and local locally Energy 104.2 (http://energy.t-online.at) and Radio Anabella (www.radioarabella.at), from Vienna, Radio Osttirol (http://radio.osttirol.net) from Lienz, and Radio Fabrik (www.radiofabrik.at) from Saltburg.

Television: ÖRF (http://tv.orf.at) has two public channels ÖRF1 and ÖRF2, broadcasting domestically produced and imported programmes. Private networks include ATV (http://atv.at) and OKTO TV (http://okto.tv) is a non-profit community TV station. There are several cable and satellite TV networks including Pulse TV (www.puls4.com), Premiere Austria (www.premiere.at) and Austria 9 TV (www.austria9.tv). There are a number of German TV affiliates throughout Austria.

Advertising

The Österreichischer Werberat (ÖWR) (Austrian Advertising Council) (www.werberat.at) is the self-regulating body that applies the code and rules for the advertising industry.

Advertising and sponsorship on television is allowed in both public and private schedules; public programmes may only broadcast advertising between programmes. There are also three advert-free days each year including 24 December, Good Friday and 21 November. Adverts may only represent 5 per cent of the length of programmes and not more than 20 per cent of the day's schedule. Radio advertising is permitted on both private and public programmes.

Austria has an opt-in condition for commercial e-mails and telephony advertisements whereby customers must agree to their delivery.

Newspapers (especially weekend editions) and magazines are a popular location for adverts. Poster sites are available through municipal authorities. Advertising in cinemas and by direct mail is also widely used.

Economy

There has been a gradual shift away from agriculture towards heavy industry and services since the 1950s, leading to higher living standards and lower unemployment. The industrial sector has been largely restructured, but the process of divesting state holding company shares in large enterprises, which began in 1987, has not been entirely consistent. In May 2005, the government's 49 per cent stake in the postal service, valued at US$833 million, was sold off to investors.

Austria joined the EU in 1995 and became a member of the euro-zone in January 2002, when euro notes and coins replaced the schilling as Austria's national currency. The country is well-placed to benefit from the euro as its trade is well integrated with other EU partners.

There is broad consensus among trades unions, business and government on commitment towards full employment and sustained economic growth. Austria has the third highest labour costs in the EU, but also one of the lowest levels of strikes. To ease the burden of an ageing population and to improve the economy, older citizens are being encouraged to enter the labour force by eliminating the pension system's incentives for early retirement.

Strong exports pushed GDP growth to an estimated 3.3 per cent in 2006. The government needs to improve public-sector efficiency – public sector debt is high at 65 per cent of GDP – in order to balance the budget by 2008. The OECD said in its 2005 survey that Austria should improve its economic competitiveness and while a great deal is spent on higher education, graduation rates are among the lowest among the OECD countries, and better investment in education would spur growth.

External trade

As a member of the European Union, Austria operates within a communitywide free trade union, with tariffs sets as a whole. Internationally, the EU has free trade agreements with a number of nations and trading blocs worldwide.

Foreign trade is a vital component of the Austrian economy and accounts for over 95 per cent of GDP of which 90 per cent is attributed to the motor vehicle sector, in particular engine and transmissions production. The EU accounts for more than 70 per cent of both imports and exports while Germany is Austria's major trading partner accounting for 40 per cent of trade. Exports to the US has increased, while Austria has invested heavily in Eastern Europe particularly in banking and industrial sectors.

Imports

Major imports are oil and oil products, chemicals, vehicles, machinery, foodstuffs and consumer durables.

Main sources: Germany (42.1 per cent total, 2006), Italy (6.6 per cent), France (3.7 per cent).

Exports

Major exports include machinery, vehicles and parts, paper and paperboard, chemicals (chiefly plastics and pharmaceuticals) and manufactured goods, electronic components, metal goods in ferrous and steel, textiles, foodstuffs.

Main destinations: Germany (31.1 per cent of 2006 total goods exports), Italy (8.1 per cent), US (5.7 per cent).

Agriculture

Farming

The agricultural sector contributes 2.2 per cent to GDP and employs 6.9 per cent of the labour force. The sector is dominated by small scale farming (50 per cent of farms cover less than 10 hectares), although the trend is towards larger, more mechanised units leading to increased productivity. Labour input is falling while workers' earnings are rising: by 2.5 per cent in real terms during 2004.

About 18.2 per cent of land is crop land, 24.1 per cent permanent pasture land and 39 per cent forests and woodland.

Farming is concentrated in Upper Austria, the northern part of Lower Austria, Burgenland and Styria.

Principal products are milk, beef, veal, pork, sugar beet, maize, barley, wheat and wine, but government is encouraging diversification to oilseeds, herbs, spices, hops and fast-growing timber. Quality wine, improved since a 1985 wine scandal, has become a major export product. Although output fluctuates, the country remains almost 90 per cent self-sufficient.

Fundamental reform to the Common Agricultural Policy (CAP) was introduced on 1 January 2005 in Austria. The subsidies paid on farm output, which tended to benefit large farms and encourage overproduction, were replaced by single farm payments not conditional on production. This is expected to reward farms that provide and maintain a healthy environment, food safety and animal welfare standards. The changes are also intended to encourage market conscious production and cut the cost of CAP to the EU taxpayer.

The growing of ornamental flowers and plants takes up much of Austria's horticultural land.

Crop production in 2005 included: 4,469,571 tonnes (t) cereals in total, 1,453,072t wheat, 1,604,818t maize, 879,628t barley, 2,988,921t sugar beets, 707,911t potatoes, 97,079t rapeseed (canola), 111,500t pulses, *351,000t grapes, 95,883t oilcrops, 17,735t treenuts, 52,521t apples, 986,222t fruit in total, 520,229t vegetables in total.

Livestock production included: 990,550t meat in total, 210,000t beef, *654,000t pig meat, *7,600t lamb and goat meat, *12,365t poultry, *88,700t eggs, 3,621,000t milk, 11,000t honey, *23,100t cattle hides.

* Estimate

Fishing

The fisheries industry in Austria is based on professional lake fishing, which entails traditional breeding of trout, carp and other freshwater species. Austria promotes the EU's Common Fisheries Policy (CFP) as it benefits from the EU's structural funds for the development of aquaculture and the processing and marketing of products. Typically Austria's fishing haul is about 350 tonnes, amounting to 0.01 per cent of the EU total. Family firms run most businesses in both aquaculture and lake fishing. Despite its tradition of fish farming the sector suffers a lack of technical support.

Forestry

Forest and other wooded land occupy nearly a half of the total land area, with forest cover estimated at 3.8 million hectares (ha) in 2000. Forest cover increased an annual average of 0.20 per cent, the equivalent of 8,000ha between 1990–2000, as a result of afforestation in protected areas and natural extension onto agricultural land. Most of the forest is available for wood supply.

Forestry remains a major source of income within agriculture. Austria produces large quantities of paper and sawn wood, and is the fifth-largest exporter of sawnwood in the world with Germany, Italy and France the main export markets. The wood processing industry places an emphasis on value-added production including skis and solid wood panel manufacturing. A large proportion of raw materials including roundwood, pulp and recovered paper are imported.

Industry and manufacturing

The industrial sector contributes 31 per cent to GDP and employs 34 per cent of the labour force.

Tourism

With the relaxation of border restrictions to Eastern Europe, overnight stays by visitors from neighbouring eastern countries are increasing. Overall arrivals in 2004 numbered 19 210 800, up on the previous year.

The tourism industry in Austria comprised an estimated 6.1 per cent of GDP in 2005 and accounted for 6.9 per cent of total employment. Tourism was forecast to stimulate eur59.0 billion (US$78.7 billion) in 2005, with an increase in demand of 4.4 per cent.

Mining

The mining sector accounts for approximately 11 per cent of annual GDP and employs 1 per cent of the workforce.

There are deposits of various minerals, notably magnesite (of which Austria is the world's largest producer), iron, lead and zinc ores, salt, graphite, coal and gypsum. Commercial exploitation is restricted by the very small number of viable deposits and geological difficulties.

Hydrocarbons

With extraction relatively expensive, estimated reserves of 86 million barrels (2003) are under-exploited and will last for little more than a decade. The main oil and gas company is Österreichische Mineralölverwaltung (ÖMV), the country's largest industrial concern. The government is the largest shareholder in ÖMV, with a 35 per cent stake.

Some 80 per cent of natural gas is imported, in particular from countries of the former Soviet bloc. Austrian gas reserves are projected to last until around 2015.

Compliance with the first stage of the EU directive for liberalisation of the gas market in 2000 freed up half the market, which was largely controlled by ÖMV.

Austria produces over a million tonnes of coal per year, supplying approximately 20 per cent of domestic demand. Much of this production is low quality brown coal. The remainder of Austria's coal supplies are imported, particularly from Germany and the Czech Republic. At current production levels, Austrian coal reserves will last several decades.

Energy

Despite a successful energy conservation programme and an increase in local oil and gas production, there is still a heavy dependence on energy imports, especially gas from the former Soviet Union.

The country is more than self-sufficient in electricity, with hydroelectric power accounting for 70 per cent of total

production. The Freudenau hydroelectric power plant on the Danube, which cost US$1.2 billion to build, has been operating since 1997 and is one of the world's most advanced hydroelectric power generating facilities.
Austria is one of the leading European nations in terms of solar energy utilisation.

Financial markets
Stock exchange
The Wiener Börse (Vienna Stock Exchange) is one of the smallest in Europe.

Banking and insurance
Consolidation of the Austrian banking sector began in 1997 when Bank Austria, the largest bank, took over Creditanstalt and Erste Bank took over Giro Credit. In 1998, Bank Austria merged with Germany's HypoVereinsbank. Bank Austria officially merged with Creditanstalt in May 2002. During the first half of 2005 Bank Austria Creditanstalt's (BA-CA) profits rose 59 per cent, up to eur453 million.
There are around 1,000 national and local banks in Austria. Many are active in Central and Eastern Europe. Austria remains overbanked. In order to remain competitive in the new European market, significant consolidation is required.
Central bank
Österreichische Nationalbank (ÖeNB) (Austrian National Bank); European Central Bank (ECB).

Time
GMT plus one hour (daylight saving, late March to late October, GMT plus two hours)

Geography
Austria's land surface area is 83,855 square km. Austria is famous for its Alpine terrain, but the bulk of the country's economic activity and all of its major population centres are based on the low-lying areas around Vienna and Linz, in the north and east, and around Salzburg, on the German border.
Hemisphere
Northern

Climate
Climatic conditions vary widely across the country, with deep winter snows in the north and west, which are an essential element in the country's very important tourist economy. Seasonal variations are particularly marked: in Vienna, temperatures range from an average minus 1 degree Celsius (C) in January to 21 degrees C in July and August. Summers are often wet, with July and August recording averages of 84mm and 71mm of rainfall respectively.

Dress codes
Formality in dress is generally expected in business and for social events such as theatre and concerts. Warm clothing is essential for the winter months.

Entry requirements
Passports
Required by all, except nationals of countries which are signatories of the Schengen Accords, which includes most EU/EEA member states, who may visit on national IDs.
Visa
Visas are not required by nationals of EU and EEA countries; nationals of the US, Japan, Australia and a number of other countries do not need visas for visits of less than three months. For further exceptions contact the nearest embassy. A Schengen visa application (offered in several languages) can be downloaded from http://europa.eu/abc/travel/ see 'documents you will need'.
Currency advice/regulations
There are no restrictions on import or export of local or foreign currencies, although a permit is needed for export of over eur7,000.
Customs
Personal items are duty-free. There are no duties levied on alcohol and tobacco between EU member states, providing amounts imported are for personal consumption.
Prohibited imports

Health (for visitors)
Nationals of the European Economic Area (EEA) countries and Switzerland can access reduced cost and sometimes free medical treatment using a European Health Insurance Card (EHIC) while visiting the EEA. Exceptions include nationals of the 10 countries which joined the EU in 2004 whose EHIC is not valid in Switzerland. Applications for the EHIC should be made before travelling.
Mandatory precautions
None
Advisable precautions
Vaccination for tick-borne encephalitis is recommended if visiting rural or forest regions.

Hotels
Generally of a high standard with a large selection available in most cities. Classified from five stars to one star. Rates vary according to category but are generally cheaper outside the capital.

Credit cards
Eurocard, Mastercard, Visa and, less widely, American Express and Diners Club are accepted.

Public holidays (national)
Fixed dates
1 Jan (New Year's Day), 6 Jan (Epiphany), 1 May (Labour Day), 15 Aug (Assumption Day), 26 Oct (National Day), 1 Nov (All Saints' Day), 8 Dec (Immaculate Conception), 25 Dec (Christmas Day), 26 Dec (St Stephen's Day).
Variable dates
Good Friday, Easter Monday, Ascension Day, Whit Monday, Corpus Christi.

Working hours
Banking
Mon–Wed and Fri: 0800–1500; Thu: 0800–1730.
Business
Mon–Fri: 0900–1800. Many offices do not work Friday afternoon.
Government
Mon–Fri: 0800–1230, 1300–1730. Many offices do not work Friday afternoon.
Shops
Mon–Fri: 0900–1800 (many shops close for two hours at midday); Sat: 0900–1300 or 1700. Longer opening hours exist in tourist areas.

Telecommunications
Mobile/cell phones
GSM G3 service operates in major cities only; 900 and 1800 services are available throughout the country

Electricity supply
220V AC

Social customs/useful tips
Appointments must be made in advance and punctuality is important; the usual form of address is Herr or Frau, followed by family or surname. People with an academic of professional title, eg Doktor, are addressed as Herr or Frau Doktor. Handshaking is universal in business and private meetings, both when arriving and leaving. Business is usually conducted in German. For restaurant meetings, dress formally, as for business meetings. Exchange pleasantries for a few minutes before getting down to business. When visiting private homes, it is usual to take flowers or confectionery for the host or hostess.

Security
There are no special problems and normal precautions apply. Vienna is possibly one of the safest cities in Europe.

Getting there
Air
National airline: Austrian Airlines
International airport/s: Vienna International (VIE), 18km south-east of city; facilities include duty-free shops, banks, bureaux de change, post office, restaurants, left luggage, conference facilities, medical facilities, tourist information, car hire.
Other airport/s: Graz (GRZ), 12km from city; Salzburg (SZG), 4km from city; Innsbruck (INN), 5km from city; Klagenfurt

(KLU), 4km from city; Linz (LNZ), 15km from city.
Airport tax: None
Surface
Road: There are good road links with all surrounding countries. Motorists should check advisability of routes, especially in winter, with ÖAMTC or ARBÖ (Austrian automobile clubs).
Rail: Austria participates in European rail pass schemes.
Water: Ships provide regular passenger services and cruises on the Danube, starting at Passau or Regensburg in Germany, to Vienna. There are also links with the Rhine and Main rivers and the Black Sea.

Getting about

National transport
Air: Austrian Arrows operate regular flights between main cities.
Road: There is a good road network. A toll must be paid to travel on motorways and highways – stickers (vignettes) to display on windscreens can be purchased from petrol stations, tobacconists and offices of Austrian automobile associations. There are additional charges for certain major routes.
Buses: Services are provided by federal and local authorities, in addition to private companies. There are more than 1,800 services in operation.
Rail: State-owned network of almost 6,000km, most of which is electrified. Also about 20 private railways covering a total 660km. There are frequent intercity services from Vienna to Salzburg, Innsbruck, Graz and Klagenfurt.
Water: There is a passenger ferry service between Vienna and the Black Sea and on upper Danube in mid-May to mid-September. Austrian Federal Railways operate passenger services on all the larger lakes.
City transport
Taxis: Widely available from stands or via radio/telephone services. The taxi journey time to the city centre from the airport is 25–30 minutes. Fares are metered but expensive, and in some areas zone charges or set charges for standard trips apply; a 10 per cent tip is usual.
Buses, trams & metro: Vienna has a very efficient, integrated system which avoids the crowded city traffic. Public transport operates between 0500 and 2400 and tickets, for all services, can be bought for 24 hour/3 day and set periods. An airport bus operates 24 hours every 20 minutes, and takes approximately 30 minutes to get to the city centre.
Trains: The OBB train service S7 operates between 0511—2216 every hour, and takes 25 minutes from the airport to the city centre.
Car hire
Self-drive and chauffeur-driven services are available at railway stations, airports and in major cities. Rates per day vary with size of car, plus additional charge per kilometre. A 'green card' (third party motor insurance) is compulsory. The speed limit is 100kph on most roads and 130kph on motorways, in built-up areas it is 50kph, unless otherwise stipulated.
EU issued driving licences are required, permitting the holders to drive in Austria for one year. Minimum driving age is 18.

BUSINESS DIRECTORY

The addresses listed below are a selection only. While World of Information makes every endeavour to check these addresses, we cannot guarantee that changes have not been made, especially to telephone numbers and area codes. We would welcome any corrections.

Telephone area codes

The international direct dialling code (IDD) for Austria is +43, followed by area code and subscriber's number:

Baden bei Wein	2252
Gmunden	7612
Graz	316
Innsbruck	512
Kitzbühel	5356
Klagenfurt	463
Krems an der Donau	2732
Linz	732
St Pölten	2742
Salzburg	662
Steyr	7252
Vienna	1
Villach	4242
Wels	7242
Wien	2252
Wiener Neustadt	2622

Chambers of Commerce

American Chamber of Commerce in Austria, 35 Porzellangasse, A-1090 Vienna (tel: 319-5751; fax: 319-5151; e-mail: office@amcham.or.at).

Austrian Economic Chamber, 63 Wiedner Hauptstrasse, A-1045 Vienna (tel/fax: 059-0900; e-mail: wkoe@wko.at).

Burgenland Economic Chamber, 1 Robert-Graf-Platz, A-7000 Eisenstadt (tel/fax: 059-0907; e-mail: wkgbld@wkbgld.at).

Kärnten Economic Chamber, 1 Europaplatz, A-9021 Klagenfurt (tel/fax: 059-0904; e-mail: wirtschaftskammer@wkk.or.at).

Lower Austria Economic Chamber, 10 Herrengasse, A-1014 Vienna (tel/fax: 015-3466; e-mail: wknoe@wknoe.at).

Salzburg Economic Chamber, 1 Julius-Raab-Platz, A-5027 (tel/fax: 0662-8888; e-mail: wirtschaftskammer@sbg.wk.or.at).

Steiermark Economic Chamber, 111 Körblergasse, A-8021 Graz (tel/fax: 031-6601; e-mail: office@wkstmk.at).

Tirol Economic Chamber, 14 Meinhardstrasse, A-6020 Innsbruck (te/fax: 059-0905; e-mail: office@wktirol.at).

Upper Austria Economic Chamber, 3 Hessenplatz, A-4010 Linz (tel/fax: 059-0909; e-mail: wirtschaftskammer@wkooe.at).

Vienna Economic Chamber, 8 Stubenring, A-1010 Vienna (tel/fax: 514-50; e-mail: postbox@wkw.at).

Vorarlberg Economic Chamber, 9 Wichnergasse, A-6800 Feldkirch (te/fax: 0552-2305; e-mail: praesidium@wkv.at).

Banking

Bank Austria Creditanstalt AG, Am Hof 2, A-1010 Vienna (tel: 531-240; fax: 5312-4155).

Bank für Arbeit und Wirtshaft AG (BAWAG), Seitzergasse 2 - 4, A-1010 Vienna (tel: 534-530; fax: 5345-32930).

Erste Bank, Graben 21, A1010 Vienna (tel: 531-000; fax: 5310-0625); also at Schubertring 5-7, A-1010 Vienna (tel: 711-940; fax: 713-7032).

Österreichische Postsparkasse, Georg Coch-Platz 2, A1020 Vienna (tel: 514-000; fax: 5140-01700).

Österreichische Volksbanken AG, Peregringasse 3, A-1090 Vienna (tel: 313-400; fax: 3134-03683).

Raiffeisen Zentralbank Österreich AG, Am Stadtpark 9, A-1030 Vienna (tel: 717-070).

Central bank

Österreichische Nationalbank, Otto Wagner-Platz 3, PO Box 61, A-1011 Vienna (tel: 404-20-2398; fax: 404-20-666; e-mail: oenb.info@oenb.co.at).

European Central Bank (ECB), Kaiserstrasse 29, D-60311 Frankfurt am Main, Germany (tel: (+49-69) 13-440; fax: (+49-69) 1344-6000; e-mail: info@ecb.int).

Travel information

ARBÖ (Auto-, Motor- und Radfahrerbund Österreichs), A-1150 Vienna, Mariahilfer Strasse 180 (tel: 891-217; fax: 891-236).

Austrian Airlines (Österreichische Luftverkehrs), PO Box 50, Fontanastrasse 1, Vienna A-1010 (tel: 683-5110; fax: 685-505).

ÖAMTC (Österreichischer Automobil-Motorrad und Touring Club), A-1010 Vienna, Schubertring 1-3 (tel: 711-990).

National tourist organisation offices

Österreich Werbung (Austrian National Tourist Office), 1 Margarethenstrasse, 1040 Vienna, (tel: 587-2000; fax: 588-6620).

Ministries

Federal Chancellor's Office, Ballhausplatz 2, 1014 Vienna (tel: 531-150; fax: 535-0338).

Federal Ministry of Agriculture & Forestry, Environment and Water Resources, Stubenring 1, 1010 Vienna (tel: 711-000; fax: 715-9651).

Federal Ministry of Defence, Dampfschiffstr. 2, 1033 Vienna (tel: 515-950; fax: 515-9521).

Federal Ministry of Economic Affairs and Labour, Stubenring 1, 1010 Vienna (tel: 711-000; fax: 713-7995).

Federal Ministry of Education, Science and Culture, Minoritenplatz 5, 1014 Vienna (tel: 531-200; fax: 533-7797).

Federal Ministry of Finance, Himmelpfortgasse 8, 1015 Vienna (tel: 514-330; fax: 512-7869).

Federal Ministry of Foreign Affairs, Ballhausplatz 2, 1014 Vienna (tel: 531-150; fax: 533-2547).

Federal Ministry of the Interior, Herrengasse 7, 1010 Vienna (tel: 531-260; 531-263910).

Federal Ministry of Justice, Museumstrasse 7, 1070 Vienna (tel: 521-520; fax: 521-52727).

Federal Ministry of Public Affairs and Sport, Minoritenplatz 3, 1014 Vienna (tel: 531-150).

Federal Ministry of Social Security and Generations, Stubenring 1, 1010 Vienna (tel: 711-000; fax: 713-9311).

Federal Ministry of Transport, Innovation and Technology, Radetskystrasse 2, 1030 Vienna (tel: 711-620).

Other useful addresses

Austrian Business Agency, Opernring 3, A-1010 Vienna (tel: 202-588-5820; fax: 202-586-8659; e-mail: austrian.business@telecom.at; internet: www.aba.qv.at).

Austria Presse-Agentur (APA) (Co-operative Agency of the Austrian Newspapers and Broadcasting Co), A-1199 Vienna, Gunoldstrasse 14 (tel: 36-050).

Austrian Telecommunications Regulatory Authority, Ministry of Science and Transport, Sektion IV, Kelsenstrasse 7, Vienna A-1030 (tel: 79731-4100; fax: 79731-4109; e-mail: Christian.Singer@bmv.gv.at).

Interpreters' Institute of Vienna University (tel: 347-649 ext. 298).

Österreichisches Statistisches Zentralamt (Central Statistical Office), Hintere Zollamtstrasse 2b, A-1030 Vienna (tel: 711-280; fax: 7112-87728).

Post und Telekom Austria AG, Postgasse 8, 1010 Vienna (tel: 515-510; fax: 512-8414).

US Embassy, Boltzmangasse 16, A-1090 Vienna (tel: 313-390; fax: 310-0682; e-mail: embassy@usembassy.at).

Vereinigung Österreichischer Industrieller (Association of Austrian Industrialists), A-1030 Vienna, Schwarzenbergplatz 4 (tel: 711-350).

Wiener Börse (Vienna Stock Exchange), A-1011 Vienna, Wipplingerstrasse 34 (tel: 53-499).

Other news agencies: APA (Austria Presse Agentur): www.apa.at
Presstext Austria (in German): www.pressetext.at

Internet sites

Austrian Business Agency: www.aba.gv.at

Austrian National Tourist Office: www.austria.info

Statistics Austria: www.statistik.at/index_englisch.shtml

Azerbaijan

KEY FACTS

Official name: Azarbaijchan Respublikasy (Republic of Azerbaijan)

Head of State: President Ilham Aliyev (YAP) (elected Oct 2003)

Head of government: Prime Minister Artur Rasizade (YAP) (appointed Nov 2003)

Ruling party: Yeni Azerbaycan Partiyasi (YAP) (New Azerbaijan Party) (re-elected Nov 2005)

Area: 86,600 square km

Population: 8.55 million (2007)*

Capital: Baku

Official language: Azeri (Turkic)

Currency: new manat (M) = 100 gopik (new currency introduced 1 Jan 2006)

Exchange rate: M0.80 per US$ (Jul 2008)

GDP per capita: US$3,663 (2007)*

GDP real growth: 23.30% (2007)

Labour force: 3.98 million (2004)

Unemployment: 17.50% (unofficial, 2005); 1.20% (official, 2005)

Inflation: 16.60% (2007)

Oil production: 868,000 bpd (2007)

Balance of trade: US$1.52 billion (2006)

Foreign debt: US$1.60 billion (2004)

Annual FDI: US$1.70 billion (2005)

* estimated figure

The soubriquet of 'the fastest growing economy in the world' sits uncomfortably alongside the World Bank's estimate that one third of Azerbaijan's population live in poverty and a further eight per cent in extreme poverty. The IMF presents an even gloomier picture, estimating that as much as 45 per cent of the population live in poverty. Azerbaijan demonstrates the classic characteristics of an underdeveloped – but mineral rich – economy.

The dispute with Armenia continues

Political geography has not been kind to Azerbaijan. Not only has the Nagorno Karabakh struggle with neighbouring Armenia been a major distraction, but the dispute is compounded by Azerbaijani concerns about its own enclave of Nakhichevan within Armenia. Azerbaijan's Armenian (and Christian) population are largely located in the enclave of Nagorno (meaning mountainous) Karabakh. Armenia had sought to annex the enclave, which it has considered part of Armenian territory since the nineteenth century, by establishing an ethnically 'cleansed' corridor between the enclave and its eastern border.

Former President Aliyev had met with his Armenian counterpart, Robert Kocharian, twice in 2005 (in May and August), and their respective foreign ministers also held several meetings. The OSCE Minsk Group, formed in 1992 to settle the dispute also insisted that momentum was gathering for a breakthrough, the last such occasion being in 2001.Against these positive developments must be weighed other, less encouraging events. Dozens of Azeri and Armenian servicemen continued to be engaged along the cease-fire line in small-scale clashes. President Aliyev had announced in 2005 that he was nearly doubling defence spending (to US$300 million) and would double it again in 2006. The Armenians duly promised to try and match these rises. Also in June, Nagorno-Karabakh's hard-line separatist administration was re-elected in a landslide. Following the Armenian presidential campaign and disputed result in February 2008, violent protests in Yerevan spilled over to the border with Armenia, resulting in the worst violence between the two countries for a decade, with casualties on both sides.

In 1995 Azerbaijan's president Heydar Aliyev, father of the present incumbent Ilham Aliyev, created a State Oil Fund of the Republic of Azerbaijan (SOFAZ) expressly designed to exploit the funds generated by oil related foreign investment to improve education, reduce poverty and raise rural living standards. At the end of 2006 the fund had assets of US$2 billion, expected to rise to a whopping US$36 billion by 2010. The IMF has warned Azerbaijan that institutional reform and economic liberalisation are essential if Azerbaijan is to sustain its oil revenues.

The Aliyev clan

The Aliyev clan has dominated Azeri politics since 1969. To all intents and purposes, the Aliyevs behave in the manner of a royal family. The 2005 elections were very much a stage managed affair. Both the OSCE and the Council of Europe declared that the elections 'did not meet international standards despite some improvements' and opposition parties rejected the results out of hand. Although the ruling Yeni Azerbaycan Partiyasi (YAP) (New Azerbaijan Party) lost its legislative majority, the result revealed that the main opposition parties had won only ten seats. The election of scores of pro-government independent MPs ensured that YAP would not be denied a majority on most issues. Illuminatingly, both President Aliyev's wife and uncle won seats in parliament. Having dominated Azeri politics since 1969, these victories did little to dispel the notion that the Aliyev clan maintained their controlling interest in Azeri affairs.

The lop-sided economy

Azerbaijan's apparently impressive GDP growth moderated slightly in 2007, to an estimated 23.3 per cent, down from the 30.6 per cent of 2006. Non-oil GDP grew at 11.3 per cent virtually unchanged from the 11.8 per cent of 2006. According to the National Bank of the Republic of Azerbaijan (NBRA) the growth rate for capital investments also dropped slightly in 2007, to 17.8 per cent (2006 was 14.8 per cent). Overall GDP growth is forecast to drop again in 2008, to 17 per cent. In this Texas of the East according to the Asian Development Bank (ADB), oil and gas revenues are expected to continue to outstrip non-oil growth for some time.

According to the World Bank, in 2006 Azerbaijan's non-oil economy, including the agricultural sector, began to recover. In a number of respects Azerbaijan has set the pace within the CIS in farm privatisation and the registration of arable land. However, construction and services (much of which is directly or indirectly related to the oil industry) have led the non-oil sector's growth. In theory, Azerbaijan's location at the crossroads between Europe and Asia ought to stimulate the growth not only of trade, but also of transit facilities. However, Azerbaijan is not the only country to try to take advantage of its location in this way. Unless greater attention is given to continuing the reforms that have, to a degree already been set in motion by both the IMF and the World Bank, many of these initial reforms will have been in vain. Standards of transparency, productivity and efficiency need to be improved, as does the strength of both the legislative and judicial branches of the government.

These priorities are reflected in the IMF/World Bank Programme for Poverty Reduction and Sustainable Development for the period 2006–15, aimed at 'improving the transparency and quality of public sector governance, supporting sustainable and balanced growth in the non-oil economy, increasing the quality of, and access to, social services and improving environmental management'.

Production soars

The hydrocarbons' share of GDP growth is expected to continue to rise in the short term. However, in the absence of new oil discoveries, greater importance will be assumed by the foreign direct investment (FDI) that has revitalised Azerbaijan's oil sector. The US Energy Information Administration (EIA) in its latest report on Azerbaijan notes that although production from the fields operated by the State Oil Company of Azerbaijan's (SOCAR) Soviet era fields is in decline, the development of large scale new projects and the refurbishment of existing facilities have provided a welcome boost.

According to the EIA, oil production rose to 860,000 barrels per day (bpd) in 2007, largely due to growth in extraction from the Azeri Chirag Guneshli (ACG) field (formerly known in Soviet days as the 28th of April Field). Azerbaijan was the largest contributor to non-OPEC (Azerbaijan is not a member) supply growth in both 2006 and 2007. Oil sector revenues in 2007 were US$5,272 million, virtually double the US$2,921 of 2006, which in turn was double the 2005 figure. Net oil exports in 2007 were estimated at 700,000bpd, destined for the most part to Russia, Italy, Turkey and Germany. The ACG field produces 65 per cent of Azerbaijan's oil, a figure which is expected to rise as ACG oil production grows. The increase in ACG oil production increased the production capacity of the operator, the Azerbaijan International

KEY INDICATORS **Azerbaijan**

	Unit	2003	2004	2005	2006	2007
Population	m	8.25	8.32	8.41	8.48	*8.55
Gross domestic product (GDP)	US$bn	6.18	8.72	12.56	20.95	31.32
GDP per capita	US$	750	1,024	1,493	2,469	*3,663
GDP real growth	%	9.5	10.1	24.3	30.6	23.3
Inflation	%	3.0	8.1	9.7	8.4	16.6
Unemployment	%	10.0	14.0	*17.5	–	–
Oil output	'000 bpd	313.0	318.0	452.0	654.0	868.0
Natural gas output	bn cum	4.8	4.6	5.3	6.3	10.3
Exports (fob) (goods)	US$m	2,625.0	3,743.0	7,649.0	7,649.0	21,269.3
Imports (cif) (goods)	US$m	2,723.0	3,581.7	4,349.9	5,269.3	6,045.0
Balance of trade	US$m	-98.0	161.3	3,299.1	7,745.3	15,224.3
Current account	US$m	-2,021.0	-2,330.0	167.3	3,708.0	9,018.9
Total reserves minus gold	US$m	820.9	1,089.6	1,177.7	2,500.4	4,273.1
Foreign exchange	US$m	802.8	1,075.0	1,163.8	2,484.9	4,262.9
Foreign direct investment (FDI)	US$bn	3.2	4.4	1.7	–	–
Exchange rate	per US$	4,912.00	4,920.10	1,293.11	^87.00	0.85

* estimated figure

^ New currency introduced 1 Jan 2006,

Oil Consortium (AIOC) from 140,000bpd in 2005 to an average 650,000bpd in the first nine months of 2007.

Reserves and revenues

Estimating Azerbaijan's oil reserves has not been an exact science, with Western oil companies using figures ranging from 7 to 13 billion barrels. SOCAR continues to use a somewhat antiquated classification system which it is suspected includes reserves that are not viable or are yet to be proven. SOCAR's figure of 17.5 billion barrels therefore needs to be treated with some caution. Most of Azerbaijan's current production is from offshore fields in the Caspian Sea. By far the biggest change in the make-up of Azerbaijan's oil production has been the replacement of SOCAR as the main producer by the AIOC, which in 2007 accounted for 80 per cent of total production. According to the EIA, SOCAR's oil production has been declining by around one per cent annually. AIOC's participants include BP (the consortium's leader), Chevron, Exxonmobil and Norway's Statoil. SOCAR is also a minority participant. In 2005 SOCAR revised its assessment of the ACG field's recoverable reserves upwards, from 5.4 billion barrels to 6.9 billion.

According to the ADB, about one third of Azerbaijan's budget revenues come from SOCAR, and a further 17 per cent comes from the SOFAZ. The fund's income is mainly generated by oil sales, but is supplemented by revenues from oil transport, bonuses paid by foreign oil companies, the excess between market and projected oil prices and income from financial investments. The spectacular rises in oil prices since 2006 have substantially boosted SOFAZ's current revenues as well as its forecast income.

Estimated oil exports in 2007 were 730,000bpd. In the summer of 2006 the opening of the Baku-Tiblisi-Ceyhan (BTC) pipeline marked a transformation of Azerbaijan's oil export potential as well as providing Azerbaijan with the strategic advantage of by-passing Russia. The pipeline runs some 1,600km from Baku to the Mediterranean port of Ceyhan in Turkey.

The gas flows

According to the *Oil and Gas Journal* (OJG), Azerbaijan has natural gas reserves of some 30 trillion cubic feet (Tcf). British Petroleum's estimates put the country's reserves somewhat higher, at around 48Tcf. For the most part, Azerbaijan's natural gas is produced from offshore fields. Output from the major Bakhar field has been in decline, leading SOCAR to examine the potential of other fields. Production from the Guneshli field is expected to enable SOCAR's natural gas production to reach 330 billion cubic feet (Bcf) by 2010. Despite increases in production, in 2007 Azerbaijan was a net importer of natural gas. In July 2007 the first natural gas began to flow from the Shah Deniz field to Turkey via the South Caucasus Pipeline (SCP), also known as the Baku-Tiblisi-Erzurum pipeline, which for most of its route runs parallel to the BTC pipeline.

In an innovative swap arrangement, Azerbaijan's isolated Nakhchivan enclave within Armenia is supplied with gas via Iran using the Baku-Astara pipeline; Iran borders both Azerbaijan and the enclave.

Treading gently with Iran

In some respects, Azerbaijan can be described as only half a country. The 1821 Turkmenchay Treaty between Russia and Persia (now Iran) divided Azerbaijan into two parts. Northern Azerbaijan became part of the Russian empire and later (in 1920) part of the USSR, while southern Azerbaijan joined Iran. As a result of this, Iran has long had a sizeable Azeri population, estimated at between 16 and 30 million, far larger than Azerbaijan's population of 8.5 million. Iranian research suggests that most Iranian Azeris are reluctant to re-join their erstwhile mother country. According to Iranian pollsters, this response is attributable to the high levels of poverty and corruption still pertaining in Azerbaijan proper. Despite this divergence, Azerbaijan's ethnic identity still remains closely associated with Islam.

The major investments and presence of European and US oil companies in Azerbaijan has led to an extensive network of both commercial and governmental contacts between the two. Thus it is hardly surprising that Azerbaijan has been largely supportive of the US driven war on terror. None the less, Azerbaijan has to tread carefully; its proximity to Iran marks it out as an easy target in any proliferation of the tensions between Iran and the West. In a balancing manoeuvre Azerbaijan also has developed its co-operation with Iran. Outwardly, President Aliyev has been less supportive of the US position on Iran.

Generally, relations have improved markedly with Iran, although complicated by the presence of the Azeri minority in north-western Iran – greater than the population of Azerbaijan-proper (8.5 million). President Aliyev had visited Tehran in 2006 to reach agreement on the provision of gas to the Nakhichevan enclave. Azerbaijan has also cultivated relations with Kazakhstan. At stake is control of the export route to Europe for Kazakh natural gas. Azerbaijan and its backers, including the US, favour south Caucasus routes such as the SCP, while Russia has lobbied for transit across its own territory. In 2007, the presidents of Azerbaijan and Kazakhstan signed agreements deepening trade relations between the two countries.

Risk assessment

Economic	Fair
Political	Good/imbalanced
Regional stability	Poor

COUNTRY PROFILE

Historical profile

Azerbaijan has at various times been part of the Persian, Muslim Arab, Turkish Seljuk, Mongol, Ottoman and Russian empires. The modern Republic was formed from territory ceded to Russia by Iran following the second of the two Russian-Persian wars.

1916 Azerbaijan joined an alliance with Armenia and Georgia.

1918–20 Azerbaijan existed as an independent republic until April 1920, when it became part of the Soviet Union.

1936 Assumed the status of a full Soviet member as the Azerbaijan Soviet Socialist Republic.

1988–94 War broke out with Nagorno-Karabakh, an ethnic Armenian enclave that lies wholly inside Azerbaijan territory, when Armenians in Nagorno-Karabakh voted to break away from Azerbaijan and join neighbouring Armenia. With the assistance of Armenian troops, separatists in Nagorno-Karabakh managed to expel Azeri forces by 1994 and have since maintained de facto independence from Azerbaijan. The self-proclaimed break-away Nagorno-Karabakh Republic (Artsakh in Armenian) occupies approximately 4,400 square kilomtres, to which the separatists have added through military conquest some 7,700 square kilomtres of Azerbaijan proper. The six-year war threw Azerbaijan into political turmoil.

1989 Azerbaijan became the first Soviet Republic outside the Baltics to declare its national sovereignty.

1991 Formal independence was declared.

1992 Violent demonstrations over repeated failures in the Nagorno-Karabakh war forced the Communist regime, under the leadership of Ayaz Mutalibov, to flee. After presidential elections the Popular Front came to power, under the leadership of Abulfaz Elchibey.

1993 Suret Huseinov, a military commander, took advantage of Elchibey's military failures to organise a military insurrection, forcing Elchibey to abandon the presidency. Heidar Aliyev, a veteran politician, came out of retirement and won 70 per cent of the vote in the presidential referendum.
1994 A cease-fire agreement came into force. The conflict between Azerbaijan and Armenia over the predominantly Armenian region in western Azerbaijan resulted in an estimated 35,000 deaths and created 850,000 internally displaced persons, mainly Azeris, between 1988–94.
1995 A new constitution was adopted.
1996 The National Assembly election produced large majorities for the Aliyev-backed Yeni Azerbaycan Partiyasi (YAP) (New Azerbaijan Party). Artur Rasizade became prime minister.
1998 Aliyev returned to power.
2000 The ruling YAP won the general election, which was denounced as unfair by foreign observers, and leaders of five major opposition parties initiated a mass protest, calling for new elections.
2001 The government ordered that the local Azeri language should be written with a Latin, rather than Cyrillic, alphabet. Azerbaijan became a full member of the Council of Europe. There was no result in the US-brokered talks on Nagorno-Karabakh between the the presidents of Azerbaijan and Armenia.
2002 US sanctions, imposed in 1992 following the outbreak of war with Armenia over the Nagorno-Karabakh enclave, were lifted after Azerbaijan agreed to participate in the US-led war on terrorism. President Aliyev announced he would run for a third five-year term. Arkady Gukasyan was re-elected president of Nagorno-Karabakh. A referendum on amendments to the constitution was said to have received strong support from voters, but critics cited voting irregularities. In Baku, thousands of people held a protest against poor living conditions; they also demanded the resignation of Aliyev and the annulment of the referendum on constitutional change.
2003 France's TotalFinaElf revealed plans to invest about US$150 million in oil projects in Azerbaijan. Aliyev collapsed during a televised speech and was taken to Turkey for hospital treatment. The President's son, Ilham Aliyev, was elected prime minister by parliament so that he could stand in the presidential elections, in which he won a landslide victory. After President Ilham Aliyev's resignation as prime minister, Artur Rasizade's candidacy for the post was endorsed by parliament. Former president Heidar Aliyev died.
2005 The Baku-Tbilisi-Ceyhan (BTC) oil pipeline, carrying one million barrels per day of Caspian oil to Western markets, was opened. In parliamentary elections in Nagorno-Karabakh, the Artsakhi Demokratakan Kusaktsutyun (ADK) (Democratic Party of Artsakh) won 31.1 per cent of the vote (12 seats), the Azat Hayrenik (Free Motherland) 26.7 per cent (10 seats), an alliance of Hai Heghapokhakan Dashnaktsutyun) (ARF) (Pan-Armenian social democratic party) and Movement 88 won 24.4 per cent (3 seats), independent candidates won 8 seats. Turnout was 73.6 per cent. In parliamentary elections in Azerbaijan, the ruling YAP and its allies won more than half the available 125 seats. Turnout was around 47 per cent. The Organisation for Security and Co-operation in Europe (OSCE) and Council of Europe observers declared that the election fell short of democratic norms. Around 15,000 people responded to opposition calls for election results to be anulled by marching in Baku. A new natural gas pipeline between Iran and Azerbaijan was inaugurated.
2006 A new manat was introduced on 1 January, which was valued at one manat per 5,000 old manat. The old currency remained in circulation until the end of the year. New parliamentary elections were held in ten constituencies, where ballots in the 2005 elections had been annulled. Azerbaijan, together with Armenia and Georgia, signed a European Neighborhood Policy co-operation agreement with the EU in November.
2007 Bako Sahakian replaced Arkadiy Gukasian as president of Nagorno-Karabakh.
2008 Fierce fighting in Nagorno-Karabakh broke out in March; Azerbaijan accused Armenia of incitement.

Political structure

Constitution

A constitution was adopted by national referendum in November 1995, and was amended following a referendum in August 2002, which made changes to the parliamentary system. The changes included replacing proportional representation in the National Assembly with the majority system (first-past-the-post), and changing the election of the president from a two-thirds to a 50 per cent majority of the votes cast.
The Republic of Azerbaijan is officially a democratic, secular and unitary state, with power separated among three branches: executive, legislative and judicial.
Administratively, the country is divided into 65 districts, the autonomous republic of Nakhichevan (which is separated from the main part of the country by southern Armenia), and the region of Nagorno-Karabakh (which has been occupied by Armenian forces since 1992).
Under the constitution, the autonomous republic of Nakhichevan is an autonomous state within the Republic of Azerbaijan. Executive power in Nakhichevan is implemented by the Cabinet of Ministers of Nakhichevan, which is appointed by the Nakhichevan prime minister on approval of the Milli Mejlis (National Assembly). However, presidential decrees have authority in Nakhichevan.

Form of state

Presidential republic, where despite democratic structures, there is no fair chance for the opposition.

The executive

The president is head of state. The president must be over 35-years-old and have been living permanently in the territory of Azerbaijan for over 10 years, having no previous convictions.
The president appoints a prime minister and Council of Ministers.
The president is also the supreme commander-in-chief of the armed forces and has powers to declare martial law and states of emergency.
Presidential elections are held every five years. The president is elected by a majority of half of all votes cast. If the presidential candidates fail to win a majority, a second round of elections is held between the two leading contestants. The candidate who wins the most votes in the second round is elected president.
According to the constitution, the president can only be removed from the post in cases of 'grave crimes'. In these cases the Supreme Court submits an application for removal to the Milli Mejlis (National Assembly), who must pass the application by a majority of 95 votes (over two-thirds majority).

National legislature

There is a one-chamber, 125-member Milli Mejlis (National Assembly). Its members are elected by majority vote (first-past-the-post). The National Assembly's term of authority is five years, with elections to take place every fifth year on the first Sunday in November.
Legislative power in the autonomous republic of Nakhichevan is held by a 45-member Ali Mejlis (Assembly) of Nakhichevan. The Ali Mejlis independently settles questions which according to the constitution fall under its competence: taxes, budget, economic development, social policy, environmental protection, tourism, health, science and culture. It also has powers to appoint and dismiss the prime minister and Cabinet of Ministers of Nakhichevan. However, the Ali Mejlis lacks power to 'contradict' the constitution and laws of the Republic of Azerbaijan.

Legal system

The highest judicial body is the Supreme Court, which is divided into criminal and

civil sections. There is also a Constitutional Court, Economic Court, ordinary and specialised courts.
Judges of the Supreme Court are appointed by the Milli Mejlis on the recommendation of the president. It is the highest judicial body in civil, criminal, administrative and other cases directed to general and specialised courts.
The Constitutional Court consists of nine judges appointed in the same way as in the Supreme Court. It is constitutionally bound to inquire into the activities of the president, Milli Mejlis, Cabinet of Ministers, Supreme Court and Milli Mejlis of the autonomous republic of Nakhichevan. In 2002, the constitutional changes included the remit of the Constitutional Court to hear cases brought by individuals. The Economic Court is the highest court on matters of economic dispute (as envisaged by legislation) and oversees activities in the relevant specialised courts.
Judicial power in the autonomous republic of Nakhichevan is exercised by the courts of Nakhichevan, although the Republic of Azerbaijan's laws apply in most cases.

Last elections
15 October 2003 (presidential); 6 November 2005 (parliamentary).
Results: Presidential: fomer president Heidar Aliyev's son, Prime Minister Ilham Aliyev (YAP), won a landslide victory with 79.5 per cent of the vote; his nearest rival, Musavat Party leader, Isa Gambar, had 12.1 per cent; turnout was 71.6 per cent. Opposition leaders alleged electoral fraud.
Parliamentary: the ruling YAP, headed by Aliyev, won comfortably. Turnout was 47 per cent. Opposition leaders alleged electoral fraud.

Next elections
2008 (presidential); 2010 (parliamentary).

Political parties

Ruling party
Yeni Azerbaycan Partiyasi (YAP) (New Azerbaijan Party) (re-elected Nov 2005)

Main opposition party
Azadliq (Freedom), an electoral alliance formed for the 6 November 2005 election and consisting of Müsavat Partiyasi (Equality Party), Azerbaycan Khalq Cabhasi Partiyasi (AXCP) (Popular Front of Azerbaijan), and the Azerbaycan Demokrat Partiyasi (ADP) (Azerbaijan Democratic Party) won 8 seats.

Population

8.55 million (2007)*
Last census: January 1999: 7,953,438
Population density: 97 inhabitants per square km; urban population, 51.6 per cent (ADB 2006).
Annual growth rate: 0.8 per cent 1994–2004 (WHO 2006)
Internally Displaced Persons (IDP)
570,000 (UNHCR 2004)

Ethnic make-up
The majority are Azeri (90 per cent). Minority groups include Dagestani (3.2 per cent), Russians (2.5 per cent) and Armenian (2.3 per cent). Almost all Armenians live in the separatist Nagorno-Karabakh region.

Religions
The main religious affiliation is Shi'ite Muslim (93.4 per cent). Others include Russian Orthodox (2.5 per cent) and Armenian Orthodox (2.3 per cent).

Education

Compulsory schooling lasts for eight years, the last two of which can be undertaken in either general secondary schools, technical schools or vocational schools. Education is free, except for higher education for which there are student grants. There are approximately 4,500 schools, including 960 primary eight-year schools, more than 2,300 secondary schools, 20 higher schools, 74 colleges and 162 technical-vocational schools. In urban areas educational services are better than in rural areas.
Literacy rate: 97 per cent of the adult population
Compulsory years: Eight to 16
Pupils per teacher: 20 in primary schools

Health

Per capita total expenditure on health (2003) was US$140; of which per capita government spending was US$33, at the international dollar rate, (WHO 2006).
In conjunction with the IMF, a new health policy has been developed. The focus of government expenditure will be shifted away from input-based allocations (for example, based on the number of beds) to capital transfers based on the number and structure of local populations. Local autonomy will be increased in healthcare and the elements of a basic package are being developed, which the government will provide free of charge in all public health facilities.
Healthcare is universal and virtually free of charge but there is a chronic shortage of basic medicines and despite pay increases doctors' morale remains low. Over 60 per cent of health expenses goes to hospitals with acute care facilities and staffed by specialised doctors rather than to preventive and basic health care. Fifty per cent of the population are severely iodine deficient.

HIV/Aids
HIV prevalence: 0.1 per cent aged 15–49 in 2003 (World Bank)
Life expectancy: 65 years, 2004 (WHO 2006)
Fertility rate/Maternal mortality rate: 1.8 births per woman, 2004 (WHO 2006); maternal deaths 43 deaths per 100,000 live births (World Bank).
Child (under 5 years) mortality rate (per 1,000): 75 per 1,000 live births; 10 per cent of children aged under five were malnourished (World Bank).
Head of population per physician: 3.55 physicians per 1,000 people, 2003 (WHO 2006)

Welfare

Although it has an abundance of natural resources, Azerbaijan is classified as the poorest country in Europe with 60 per cent of the population living in poverty. The former Soviet Union developed an extensive welfare system but price liberalisation and soaring inflation have rendered pensions, unemployment benefit and money paid to single parent families virtually worthless. The government intends to initiate a participatory poverty reduction strategy, as existing social safety nets are not enough to keep the unemployed out of poverty.

Main cities

Baku (capital, estimated population 2.1 million in 2005), Gyandzha (306,217, Sumgayit (268,522), Mingechaur (95,426), Ali Bayramli (70,626), Sheki (61,476).

Languages spoken

Azeri is spoken by 95 per cent of the population. Russian (3 per cent as first language) and Armenian (2 per cent) are also spoken. English language lessons are being introduced in schools and colleges. Some Azeris speak Russian as a second language although the use of Russian is being phased out.

Official language/s
Azeri (Turkic)

Media

Freedom of speech is guaranteed under the constitution however media outlets and journalist have been in subject to sporadic harassment by the government.
National news agency: Azar Tac www.azertag.com
Other news agencies: Turan: www.turaninfo.com
Trend: http://news.trendaz.com

Press
The circulation of all newspapers is very small. Newspapers dropped Cyrillic script in favour of Latin in 2001.
Dailies: In Azerbaijani, national newspapers, some with online editions in Russian and English, include 525 Ci (www.525ci.com), (Tues–Sat), Yeni Azerbaycan (www.yeniazerbaycan.com) a broadsheet, Echo (www.echo-az.com), Azadliq (www.azadliq.az), Uc Noqta (www.ucnoqta.com) and Zerkalo

(www.zerkalo.az). In Russian, Bakinskiy Rabockiy (www.br.az), Yeni Musavat (www.musavat.com), Nash Vek (www.nashvek.com) and Nedelya (www.nedelya.az). In English, The Azeri Times (www.theazeritimes.com), Baku Sun (www.bakusun.az:8101), and Azer News (www.azernews.net).

Weeklies: In Azerbaijani, Ayna-Zerkalo (Azeri language) is a tabloid issued 156 days per year. In English Our Century (http://ourcentury.media-az.com),

Business: In Azerbaijani, CBN Extra (www.cbnextra.com) is a tabloid with a business section,

Broadcasting

Radio: Azerbaijan Radio (www.aztv.az), the national public radio is government-operated with two domestic stations (AzR 1 and 2) and one international channel. The independent, Public Television and Radio Broadcasting Company (www.itv.az) broadcasts in Azerbaijani, Russian and English. Private radio stations include Burc FM (www.burc.fm), Lider Jazz FM (www.lider.fm) and Antenn FM (www.antenn.az).

Television: AzTV () is the government-controlled, national public television service. The independent, Public Television and Radio Broadcasting Company (www.itv.az). Private TV stations include Space TV (www.spacetv.az), Lider TV (www.lidertv.com) and Azad TV.

Russian and Turkish TV channels are also available.

Advertising

There is a complete ban on tobacco advertising in all mediums. Advertising is allowed on national TV, radio, newspapers and bill posting.

Economy

Azerbaijan may have been one of the poorest countries in Europe and Central Asia, but its vast resources of oil and natural gas, which are already being tapped, are increasing its wealth and raising its population's living standards. In 2002, just under half the population lived below the poverty line with access to services such as healthcare and education limited, particularly in rural areas. However, per capita income rose from US$555 in 2001, to an estimated US$7,300 by 2006, a level higher than Russia and Turkey and one comparable with Poland.

Economic growth has been strong in recent years, albeit from a low base. GDP growth reached 24.3 per cent in 2005 and it is estimate to have reached 32.5 per cent in 2006, largely due to the sharp rise in global oil prices since the beginning of 2005. This however has triggered inflation, which was 9.4 per cent in 2005 and estimated at 8.0 per cent in 2006.

The economy is, nevertheless, stable with the nation's debt under control (in 2006 government revenues were US$6 billion and expenditures US$5.8 billion). Public debt is 10.4 per cent of GDP.

Oil companies represent most foreign direct investment (FDI); foreign interest has not extended to other areas of the Azeri economy. FDI inflows into the oil sector rose from US$821 million in 2001 to US$1.7 billion in 2003. By early 2007, Azerbaijan had concluded 21 production sharing agreements with foreign oil companies. If diversification does not take place, the country faces the prospect of once more becoming a supplier of raw materials, but this time to the West rather than Russia. Consequently, it is essential that the government concentrates on its privatisation programme in conjunction with investment incentives.

The opening of the Baku-Tbilisi-Ceyhan (BTC) pipeline in 2005 gave the oil industry a large boost. The pipeline transports Azerbaijan oil from the Caspian Sea to the Mediterranean and began pumping one million barrels per day, sea-to-sea shipment, in January 2006. It is estimated that this project will double Azerbaijan's 2006 GDP by 2010. The South Caucasus Pipeline (SCP), runs parallel with the BTC, transporting Azerbaijan gas from the Caspian to Turkey, from December 2006.

International companies that produce from the Caspian Sea resources contributed around an annual US$200 million to government finances. It is estimated that revenues from oil and natural gas resources may reach US$7 billion in the near future.

The State Oil Company of the Republic of Azerbaijan (SOCAR), established a generation fund (State Oil Fund (SOFAZ)) that will hold a proportion of the country's oil wealth in trust for future development; in 2006 it stood at US$1.3 billion.

The government has begun a process of opening up the economy: privatisation of agricultural land and small- to medium-sized enterprises has been largely completed but the inefficient public administration hampers and reduces the ability of commerce to perform efficiently.

There are still a number of problems to be addressed, such as import and trading restrictions which inhibit inward investment (while propping up old state monopolies), a poor legal system, an inefficient tax system and corruption.

The conflict with Armenia over the Nagorno-Karabakh region has the potential to destabilise the country's economic progress. Although a cease-fire was signed in 1994, no final agreement has been reached.

External trade

International trade is vital to the economy, however 90 percent of all exports is oil, which indicates a disproportionate influence oil production has on the economy. The second largest sector in the economy is shipbuilding; in April 2007 a memorandum of understanding was signed with South Korea's shipyard manufacturer STX Corporation and Azerbaijan investment interests to construct a modern port with new facilities at the new Baku Port. Other export commodities include primary production and oil industry by-products.

Imports

Imports include machinery equipment, oil products, foodstuffs, metals and chemicals.

Main sources: Russia (17.0 per cent total, 2005), UK (9.1 per cent), Singapore (9.1 per cent), Turkey (7.4 per cent), Germany (6.1 per cent), Turkmenistan (5.8 per cent), Ukraine (5.4 per cent), China (4.1 per cent)

Exports

Exports and re-exports include oil and gas (90 per cent of total exports), plastics, chemical fertilizers, cotton fibre, machinery, foodstuffs and marine crafts.

Main destinations: Italy (30.3 per cent total, 2005), France (4.9 per cent), Russia (6.6 per cent), Turkey (6.3 per cent), Turkmenistan (6.3 per cent), Georgia (4.8 per cent), Israel (4.5 per cent), Croatia (4.1 per cent)

Agriculture

Farming

Agriculture has declined by more than 50 per cent since independence, but it continues to employ 30 per cent of the labour force and contributes about 17 per cent to GDP. It is the second-largest export sector with large potential markets in the Middle East, Europe and the former Soviet Union.

Around 2 million hectares (ha) out of a total land area of 8.7 million ha is classified as arable. Some 70 per cent of the 77 per cent of land used for agricultural purposes is irrigated through an extensive canal system. Most farming takes place in the fertile lowlands surrounding the Kura and Araz rivers, in central Azerbaijan.

The whole country is well endowed with fertile land, although adversely affected by periodic drought. A wide range of crops is grown, notably cotton, tobacco, nuts, grapes, grain, tea, vegetables and citrus fruits. Cattle, sheep, pigs and poultry are reared.

Grain is the leading agricultural product, followed by raw cotton (the country's largest cash crop).

Livestock, dairy products and alcoholic beverages are also important products.

There is potential for agricultural development, greatly enhanced by the country's rich soils, wide agricultural plains and varied climatic conditions. There is scope for the cultivation of vegetables, fruits, cotton, tobacco, subtropical cultures, silkworm and sheep breeding.

However, agriculture comprises mainly smallholder farming, and is generally subsistence oriented. Despite the fact that 45 per cent of the country's population depend largely on agricultural income, the sector remains largely underdeveloped.

Crop production in 2005 included 2,107,241 tonnes (t) cereals in total, 1,566,000t wheat, 151,366t maize, 1,082,500t potatoes, 377,200t barley, 12,183t rice, 29,000t citrus fruit, 76,000t grapes, 435,595t tomatoes, 30,495t oilcrops, 7,200t tobacco leaves, 52,600t sugar beets, 670t tea, 158,000t apples, 193,000t seed cotton, 55,005t cotton lint, 58,400t treenuts, 625,100t fruit in total, 1,490,627t vegetables in total. Livestock production included: 147,331t meat in total, 70,868t beef, 1,678t pig meat, 41,700t lamb, 33,085t poultry, 47,990t eggs, 1,232,280t milk, 570t honey, *100t cocoons, silk, 11,856t cattle hides, *5,220t sheepskins, 13,000t greasy wool.

* Estimate

Fishing

Salyan on the Kura River is the main centre for processing and canning fish.

Azerbaijan once produced 10 per cent of the world's supply of caviar. The division of the Caspian Sea, which accounts for 90 per cent of world caviar production, has caused disputes between Azerbaijan and Russia. There is little effective policing of the Caspian, with smuggling and illegal fishing widespread. The Caspian is also being overfished, and combined with the threat of pollution, production levels are set to fall. International regulation of the trade in caviar was tightened in January 2006 and is expected to further restrict, for the forseeable future, Azerbaijan's caviar industry.

Forestry

Forest and other wooded land, mostly concentrated in the mountainous north, account for little more than one-tenth of its total land area.

Forests in the flood plain areas remain in poor condition and are prone to overgrazing and pollution. There is no large-scale forest industry, with most wood products imported from the Russian Federation. Commercial exploitation is limited, and production is used mostly for domestic purposes. Most forest is classified as either 'protected' or 'preserved' and is public owned.

Industry and manufacturing

The oil industry dominates the Azeri economy, providing the driving force for all other sectors.

The emphasis on heavy industry, combined with substantial primary resources, enabled the development of a major oil equipment manufacturing sector in the Soviet era. However, the disintegration of the Soviet Union meant that supplies and markets dried up, leading to the virtual collapse of most industries.

It is hoped that the development of Azerbaijan's oil and gas industry will benefit all sectors of the economy, with widespread infrastructure improvements and developments essential. The construction industry has expanded particularly rapidly on the back of Azerbaijan's oil and gas boom (by 42 per cent in 2004).

In order to stimulate growth the government has developed a medium- and long-term strategy to restructure the economy in consultation with the IMF.

Tourism

During Soviet rule, there was considerable investment in tourist infrastructure such as hotels and Azerbaijan has inherited these assets. Little has been done to develop Azerbaijan's tourist potential since independence, despite the existence of many historical sites and sites of natural beauty.

Environment

Pollution comes from four main sources – agriculture, industrial plants, oil exploitation and domestic waste. It will take time and investment to clean up Azerbaijan's environment.

Mining

The mining sector accounts for 1 per cent of GDP and since independence has suffered from a lack of infrastructure investment.

The republic has abundant mineral resources, including iron, lead, zinc and copper ores, cobalt, bauxite, matrium sulphate, marl, limestone, marble, lake and rock salts, and some small amounts of gold and silver. The largest iron ore field in the Caucasus region lies within Azerbaijan.

Copper reserves are attracting foreign investors. Azerbaijan has several deposits of pure copper, the largest of which is the Karadag, in western Azerbaijan, with reserves of about 320,000 tonnes.

Hydrocarbons

Oil from the Caspian basin has dominated the economic history of Azerbaijan since the late 19th Century. In 1891, half of the world's crude oil was extracted from Azerbaijan.

The Caspian is still the centre of oil exploration for Azerbaijan. Production averaged 319,000 bpd in 2004. Azerbaijan has two refineries, Azneftyag and Azneftyanajag, with a total refining capacity of 399,000bpd (2005 estimate).

The situation in the Caspian is complicated by a dispute between Iran, Russia and Azerbaijan over the division of the oil rich area. The government is placing huge store by the development of an oil-driven economic boom. While this may have negative implications for other industries, the estimated oil wealth that exists in the country could generate huge earnings and inward investment for years. As the Azeris lack the necessary financial resources and expertise to develop the fields on their own, foreign petrochemical corporations have been encouraged to invest. In order to keep control of the industry, however, the resulting exploration and production projects have usually been joint ventures between Socar and foreign companies.

Azerbaijan's main project is the Baku-Tbilisi-Ceyhan (BTC) oil pipeline, which will transport 50 million tonnes of oil per annum from the Sangachai Terminal in central Azerbaijan to Ceyhan in Turkey via Georgia. Construction of the 1,768km pipeline began in mid-2002 and it opened on 25 May 2005.

In June 2004, the government said that US$3.4 billion would be invested by 2006 in the first phase of development of the Azeri-Chirag-Guneshli (ACG) oil field.

Several exploratory wells for oil have yielded natural gas instead, but this is economically less viable to produce given the current state of Azerbaijan's transportation infrastructure.

Azerbaijan's proven gas reserves total 850 billion cubic metres, although actual reserves are likely to be far higher. Natural gas production stood at 4.8 billion cubic metres in 2003.

The Bakhar gas field is the country's most important source of natural gas production, accounting for over 40 per cent of total production. However, future development is likely to concentrate on the Nakhichevan, Gunashli and Shah Deniz fields. The South Caucasus Pipeline (SPC), financed in large part by the consortium behind the BTC, is being built to transport Azerbaijani gas from the Shah Deniz field to Erzurum in Turkey through Georgia. In late 2005 the pipeline was 95 per cent complete and was projected to be fully operational by September 2006.

Energy

Azerbaijan is one of the region's largest power generators, with installed capacity of 5,200MW. Actual production is, however, limited to around 4,300MW due to ageing facilities. Thermal power plants produce 80 per cent of total electricity, the balance coming from hydroelectric sources. Azerbaijan also imports electricity from Iran for the autonomous Nakhichevan area.

Financial markets
Stock exchange
The Baku Stock Exchange, set up in August 1999, is regulated by the State Securities Committee.

Banking and insurance
Azerbaijan's banking sector is underdeveloped and dominated by four Soviet-era state-owned banks. The majority of Azerbaijani banks are undercapitalised and illiquid and during the course of 2005 several had their commercial licences revoked. In May 2005 there were 46 banks operating in Azerbaijan. Banking law states that foreign ownership of any bank in Azerbaijan cannot exceed 30 per cent.

Central bank
National Bank of Azerbaijan (NBA)

Main financial centre
Baku

Time
GMT plus four hours (daylight saving, late March to late October, GMT plus five hours)

Geography
Azerbaijan is situated in eastern Transcaucasia bordering Armenia, Georgia, the Russian Federation (Daghestan Autonomous Republic), Iran and the Caspian Sea. It is the largest of the three Transcaucasian republics, covering 87,000 square km. Azerbaijan is split in two, with the Nakhichevan Autonomous Republic separated from Azerbaijan proper by southern Armenia. Approximately 20 per cent of Azeri territory is occupied by Armenia. The ethnic Armenian enclave of Nagorno-Karabakh is an area of 4,000 square km situated in the south-west of the country.

The greater part of the republic includes the lowlands of the River Kura and the lower reaches of its tributary, the Araks. The oil-rich Apsheron Peninsula, on which the capital city, Baku, is located, juts out into the Caspian Sea.

The level of the Caspian Sea, the largest salt water lake in the world, is subject to continuous change. In 1929 its surface area was larger than the Black Sea at 422,000 square km, before it started to decline reaching a record low point in 1951. Since then it has risen to about 436,000 square km. Higher water levels are causing problems along the Azeri coast.

Hemisphere
Northern.

Climate
Azerbaijan is considered to contain nine of the world's 13 climatic zones, from Alpine meadows to the subtropics. In Baku the climate is dry and Mediterranean. Due to its diversity, there are extremes of temperature in many areas – harsh winters and hot summers. Baku and other places on the Caspian Sea have mild winters. Temperatures in Baku are 0–5 degrees Celsius (C) in winter and 25–35 degrees C in summer.

Dress codes
Business dress should include a jacket and tie for men, and smart 'business-like' clothes for women.

Entry requirements
Passports
Required by all. Must be valid for at least three months after departure date.

Visa
Required by all with the exception of CIS citizens other than Armenia and Turkestan.

Application must be accompanied by an invitation from an Azerbaijani body or citizen, submitted through the Consular Department of the Ministry of Foreign Affairs of Azerbaijan in Baku. Contact the local embassy for further explanation.

Currency advice/regulations
Import/export of local currency by non-residents is prohibited.

There are no restrictions on the import of foreign currency by non-residents, although declaration on arrival is required. There are no limitations on the export of foreign currency, up to the amount declared on arrival.

US dollars, pounds sterling and euros are the preferred currencies and can be exchanged at the airport, bureaux de change, hotels, some restaurants and major banks. Hotels, exchange bureaux and restaurants will not accept US dollar bills dated before 1992 or those which are torn or in any way disfigured. Travellers are advised to take banknotes in small denominations and change small amounts of money as required. Rates offered by banks and bureaux de change are unlikely to vary significantly.

Travellers'cheques are accepted only by the International Bank of Azerbaijan.

Customs
On arrival foreign currency and personal and valuable items must be declared.

Prohibited imports
Weapons, drugs, animals, anti-Azerbaijan literature and pictures, fruit and vegetables are prohibited.

Health (for visitors)
Only emergency medical treatment is available free to visitors, with small payments for medicines or hospital treatment. The level of care is limited. Private chemists in Baku stock a range of the more basic medicines. Travellers are advised to take out an insurance policy which includes emergency repatriation in case of serious illness or accident.

Mandatory precautions
None

Advisable precautions
It is advisable to be in date for the following immunisations: tetanus (within 10 years), typhoid, hepatitis A and B, tuberculosis. Anti-malarial prophylaxis are advisable. There may be some risk of meningitis, tick-borne encephalitis and leishmaniasis (cutaneous and visceral). Rabies is present.

It is advisable to take a supply of those medicines that are likely to be required (but check first that they may be legally imported). A travel kit including a disposable syringe is a reasonable precaution. Water precautions are recommended.

Hotels
Hotel space in Baku is very limited. Payment for the full stay is required in advance upon arrival at the hotel in cash (in US dollar bills which should be in good condition). VAT and service charges are included in all bills; tipping the waiters is appreciated but not compulsory.

Credit cards
Accepted in the major hotels, some restaurants and all banks in Baku. Credit cards can be used to purchase tickets at the airport.

Public holidays (national)
Fixed dates
1 Jan (New Year), 20 Jan (Day of the Martyrs), 8 Mar (Women's Day), 21 Mar (Novruz Bayramy), 9 May (Victory Day), 28 May (Republic Day), 15 Jun (Day of National Salvation), 26 June (Army and Navy Day), 18 Oct (Independence Day), 12 Nov (Constitution Day), 17 Nov (National Revival Day), 31 Dec (Solidarity Day).

Variable dates
Ramazam Bayram, Kurban Bayram.

Islamic year – 1429 (10 Jan 2008–28 Dec 2008): The Islamic year contains 354 or 355 days, with the result that Muslim feasts advance by 10–12 days against the Gregorian calendar. Dates of feasts vary according to the sighting of the new moon, so cannot be forecast exactly.

Working hours
Banking
Mon–Fri: 0900–1700.

Business
Mon–Fri: 0900–1800.

Government
Mon–Fri: 0900–1300; 1400–1800.

Shops
Mon–Fri: 0900–1900.

Telecommunications
Mobile/cell phones
There are two GSM mobile phone companies, Azercell and Bakcell.

Electricity supply
Voltage is usually 220V, 50 Hz.

Weights and measures
Metric system

Social customs/useful tips
Azeri culture blends Soviet-style courtesy with Middle Eastern informality.

The approach to business is not very well developed by Western standards, although technical knowledge and education standards are high.

Although Azeris are Muslim, they are probably the most secular of all the Muslim people of the former Soviet Union, with many considering themselves Eastern European rather than Asian. Consequently, Azerbaijan bears little relation to the Middle East with the exception of its oil and gas reserves. Business and negotiation habits are more akin to those in the rest of the former Soviet Union than with Middle Eastern practices.

The business environment has been reported to suffer from a number of ills, including very low wages for civil servants which act as an encouragement to corruption, a lack of transparency in the legal system and the inability to make decisions at lower governmental levels.

Bribery and 'gifts' were part and parcel of everyday business life in the former Soviet Union, and little has changed since 1991. However, moderate gifts and souvenirs discreetly given are usually more suitable than offers of foreign trips and shopping sprees.

Security
Crimes against foreigners are in general rare, but since late 2005 there has been an increase in violent muggings at night in the city centre (sometimes with the collusion of taxi drivers). It is advisable to arrange in advance to be transported to and from your hotel and to be vigilant in moving around on foot. Travellers should carry their passports with them at all times and ensure they travel with photocopies of their passports in case of theft.

Avoid all travel to Nagorno-Karabakh.

Getting there
Air

National airline: Azerbaijan Hava Yollari (Azal) (Azerbaijan Airlines)

International airport/s: Heydar Aliyev International (GYD), is located 25km east of Baku. Facilities include car hire, bank/bureau de change and VIP lounge.

Airport tax: None

Surface

Road: Inter-city bus routes link Baku with Tbilisi (Georgia), Derben (Dagestan) and Istanbul (Turkey).

The Regional Road Corridor Improvement Project, estimated at US$18 billion, to improve Central Asian roads, airports, railway lines and seaports and provide a vital transit route between Europe and Asia was agreed, on 3 November 2007. Six new transit corridors, between Afghanistan, Azerbaijan, China, Kazakhstan, Kyrgyzstan, Mongolia, Tajikistan and Uzbekistan, of mainly roads and rail links, will be constructed, or existing resources upgraded, by 2013. Half the costs with be provided by the Asian Development Bank and other multilateral organisations and the other half by participating countries.

Rail: There are rail connections to Tbilisi (Georgia), Derben (Dagestan) and various cities in the Russian Federation, including Moscow.

Water: Passenger ferries on the Caspian Sea link Azerbaijan with the Russian Federation, Central Asia and Iran. Ferries sail regularly to Baku from Turkmenbashy in Turkmenistan and from Bandar Anzali and Bandar Nowshar in Iran. Winter storms may disrupt services.

Main port/s: Baku.

Getting about
Travel within some regions of the country is restricted and visitors must obtain special permission from the Ministry of Interior.

National transport

Road: Azerbaijan has more than 57,770km of roads, of which over 31,000km are paved. Roads are generally in poor condition. Buses connect Baku and the main cities. The main motorway runs from Baku to Russia via the Caspian Coast.

Rail: Azerbaijan has a rail network of approximately 2,100km (1,300km electrified). The rail network is the most important form of transport, handling an estimated 75 per cent of total traffic.

City transport

Taxis: Taxis can be distinguished by a sign on top. Agree a price beforehand. Taxis are cheap, but drivers are unlikely to speak English. As the cost of a trip can vary widely, it is better to use hotel taxis or pre-arrange a car with driver.

Buses, trams & metro: Buses tend to be overcrowded. More expensive but more comfortable are marshruts (privately–operated minibuses), which follow the same routes. There is a metro in Baku with a total length of 28km.

Car hire

Car hire is available in Baku. An international driving licence is needed. Traffic drives on the right.

BUSINESS DIRECTORY
The addresses listed below are a selection only. While World of Information makes every endeavour to check these addresses, we cannot guarantee that changes have not been made, especially to telephone numbers and area codes. We would welcome any corrections.

Telephone area codes
The international direct dialling code (IDD) for Azerbaijan is +994, followed by area code and subscriber's number:

Baku	12	Neftechala	153
Dashkasan	216	Sumgayit	164
Nakhichevan	136		

Useful telephone numbers
Fire	01
Police	02
Ambulance	03

Chambers of Commerce
American Chamber of Commerce in Azerbaijan, ISR Plaza, 340 Nizami Street, Baku 370000 tel: 971-333; fax: 971-091; e-mail: info@amchamaz.org).

Azerbaijan Chamber of Commerce and Industry, 31/33 Istiglaliyyat Street, Baku 370001 (tel: 928-912; fax: 971-997; e-mail: expo@chamber.baku.az).

Banking
Azakbank (private), 25 Xagani Street, 370070 Baku (tel: 983-109, 932-491; fax: 932-085).

Azcombank, 1 Inshaatchilar Avenue, 370073 Baku (tel: 388-323, 387-206).

AzEkoBank (joint stock bank), 11/39 Mustafa Subhi Street, Baku 370001 (tel: 929-433; fax: 980-406; e-mail: ecob@ecob.crack.azerbaijan.su; internet site: http://www.azekobank.com).

Azerbaijan Agricultural Industrial Bank, 125 Qadirli Street, Baku 370006 (tel: 389-293; fax: 389-115).

Azerbaijan Commercial Savings Bank, 71 Fizuli Street, Baku 370010 (tel: 930-561; fax: 939-489).

Azerbaijan Industrial Investment Bank, 71 Fizuli Street, 370010 Baku (tel: 931-701; fax: 931-266).

Azerbaijan National Bank, 19 Bulbul Ave, Baku 370070 (tel: 935-058; fax: 937-374).

Azerdemiryolbank, 31 Qarabagh Street, Baku 370008 (tel: 972-380, 675-321; fax: 987-936).

Azerigazbank, 37 Tbilisi Avenue, 370065 Baku (tel: 385-021; fax: 390-243).

Azerturkbank, 5 Islam Safarli Street, 370005 Baku (tel: 948-090; fax: 983-702).

Bakobank (private), 35 Yusif Safarov Street, 370025 Baku (tel: 666-549; fax: 981-927).

British Bank of the Middle East, 1 Bakihanov Street, Baku (tel: 981-234; fax: 980-817).

International Bank of Azerbaijan (IBA), 67 Nizami Street, Baku 370005 (tel:

930-091; fax: 934-091; e-mail: ibar@bar.az; internet site: http://www.ibar.az).

Most-Bank, 70 Nizami Street, Baku (tel: 971-070; fax: 972-094).

Promtekhbank (joint stock commercial bank), 69 Fizuli Street, Baku 370014 (tel: 957-874; fax: 958-360; e-mail: bank@devi.baku.az).

Rabitabank, 1 Buniat Sardarov Street, Baku 370001 (tel: 926-099; fax: 926-157).

Tajbank (commercial investment bank), 185 Azadlyg Ave, Baku 370087 (tel: 691-464; fax: 691-474).

Central bank
National Bank of Azerbaijan, 32 R. Behbudov Street, Baku (tel: 931-122; fax: 935-541; e-mail: mail@nba.az).

Travel information
Azal (Azerbaijan Hava Yollari) (Azerbaijan Airlines), Prospect Azadlig 11, Baku 370000 (tel: 934-434; fax: 985-237, 651-120).

Azerbaijani Railways, Dilara Aliyeva Str 230, 370010 Baku (tel: 984-467; fax: 984-280).

Azertur Travel Agency of the State Council for Foreign Tourism (tours, hotel reservations, translation and interpreting services), 1 Azadlyg Ave, Baku 370000 (tel: 933-481; fax: 933-481).

Eur Tourism, 82 Topchubashev Str, Baku (tel: 973-444; fax: 986-810; e-mail: eurotourbaku@azeri.com).

Improtex (travel tours and conferences), 115 Azi Aslanov Str, Baku 370000 (tel: 930-896, 933-941; fax: 651-238; e-mail: toor@impro.Azerbaijan.su).

Ministries
Ministry of Agriculture and Food, 4 Shihali Kurbanov Street, Baku 370079 (tel: 935-355; fax: 943-952).

Ministry of Communications, 33 Azerbaijan Ave, Baku 370139 (tel: 930-004; fax: 984-285).

Ministry of Culture, Government House, Azadlyg Square, Baku 370016 (tel: 934-398; fax: 935-605).

Ministry of Defence, 3 Azerbaijan Ave, Azizbekov Baku 370601 (tel: 394-362; fax: 382-296).

Ministry of Economics, Government House, Azadlyg Square, Baku 370016 (tel: 936-920; fax: 932-025).

Ministry of Education, Government House, 1 Azadlyg Square, Baku 370016 (tel: 937-266; fax: 984-207).

Ministry of Finance, Sameda Vurguna Ul 6, Baku 370000 (tel: 933-012; fax: 987-969).

Ministry of Foreign Affairs, Gandjlar Meydani 3, Baku 370004 (tel: 923-401; fax: 629-756).

Ministry of Foreign Economic Relations, Lermontov Street 69, Baku 370601 (tel: 929-492; fax: 980-011).

Ministry of Grain Products, 13 Yusifzade Street, Baku 370033 (tel: 667-451; fax: 939-023).

Ministry of Health, Malaya Morskaya Street 4, Baku 370014 (tel: 932-977; fax: 988-559).

Ministry of Information and Press, 12 Ahmad Javad Street, Baku 370001 (tel: 926-357; fax: 926-747).

Ministry of Internal Affairs, 7 Gusi Hajiyev Street, Baku 370005 (tel: 986-396; fax: 923-471).

Ministry of Justice, 13 Kirov Avenue, Baku 370601 (tel: 939-785; fax: 938-367).

Ministry of Labour and Social Protection, Azadlyg Square, Baku 370016 (tel: 930-542; fax: 939-472).

Ministry of Material Resources, 83-23 Alaskar Alakbarov Street, Baku 370141 (tel: 394-296; fax: 399-176).

Ministry of National Security, 1 Azadlyg Square 1, Baku 370016 (tel: 931-000; fax: 936-296).

Ministry of Trade, Government House, Azadlyg Square 1, Baku 370016 (tel: 985-074; fax: 987-431).

Ministry of Youth and Sports, 98a Fatali Han Khoyski Avenue, Baku 370072 (tel: 981-426; fax: 643-650).

Office of the President of the Azerbaijan Republic, 19 Istiglaliyyat Street, Baku 370066 (tel: 983-113).

Other useful addresses
Azerbaijan News Service, Block 504, 1128 Street, Baku 370073 (building of the Institute of Zoology) (tel: 929-221/3; fax: 989-498).

Azerbintorg Foreign Trade Association, 14 Boyuk Gala Str, 370004 Baku (tel: 920-481, 926-492, 924-545; fax: 983-292).

Azerigaz, 23 Yusif Safarov Street, Baku 370025 (tel: 677-447; fax: 674-255).

Azerkimia, 86 Samed Vurgun Street, Baku 373200 (tel: 937-620).

Azertaj State Information Agency, Bulbul Avenue 18, 370000 Baku (tel: 935-445; fax: 938-138).

Baku General Customs Board, 62 Neftchilar Ave, Baku 370601 (tel: 939-588).

Baku Statistics Office, 10 Tabriz Street, Baku 370008 (tel: 669-327, 672-265).

Baku Telegraph Office, 41 Azerbaijan Avenue, Baku 370000 (tel: 936-142).

Baku Television, M. Husein St 1, Baku.

Board of Azerbaijan Railways, 230 Dilara Aliyeva Street, Baku 370010 (tel: 984-467).

British Embassy, 2 Izmir Street, 370065 Baku (tel: 924-813; fax: 985-558).

Caspian Shipping Company, 5 Rasulzade Street, Baku 370005 (tel: 922-058; fax: 935-339).

Central Post Office, 36 Uzeyir Hajibeyov Street, Baku 370000 (tel: 985-251).

EU Co-ordinating Unit in Azerbaijan, Government House, 8th Floor, Room 851, Baku 370016 (tel: 936-018; fax: 937-638).

Radio Baku, M Husein St 1, 370011 Baku.

Scientific Research and Test Constructive Institute of Oil Machinery of Azerbaijan Republic (Azinmash), Aras Street 4, Baku 370029 (tel: 670-888; fax: 672-888).

SME Development Agency 83, Mr Vagif G. Alikperov, S Vurguna, Azneftiechimprom Bld. 5th Floor, PO Box 114, 37000 Baku (tel: 957832; fax: 957832; e-mail: quirin@smeda.baku.az).

State Committee for Statistics, 24 Inshaatchylar Ave, Baku-136 370136 (tel: 381-171; fax: 380-577).

State Customs Committee, 2 Inshaatchilar Ave, Baku 370073 (tel: 927-545).

State Oil Company of the Azerbaijan Republic (SOCAR), 73 Neftchilar Ave, Baku 370004 (tel: 924-480, 920-745, 920-685; fax: 936-492, 923-204).

Statoil Caspian Region, 96 Nizami Street, 370010 Baku (tel: 977-340; fax: 977-944).

US Embassy, 83 Azadliq Avenue, Baku 370007 (tel: 980-335; fax: 983-755; e-mail: webbaku@pd.state.gov).

National news agency: Azar Tac
www.azertag.com

Other news agencies: Turan:
www.turaninfo.com
Trend: http://news.trendaz.com

Internet sites
Heydar Aliyev International Airport: www.airport–baku.com

President of Azerbaijan: www.president.az

KEY FACTS

Official name: Commonwealth of The Bahamas

Head of State: Queen Elizabeth II, represented by Governor General Arthur Dion Hanna (took office 1 Feb 2006)

Head of government: Prime Minister Hubert Ingraham (FNM) (elected 2 May 2007)

Ruling party: Free National Movement (FNM) (elected May 2007)

Area: 13,935 square km

Population: 333,000 (2007)*

Capital: Nassau

Official language: English

Currency: Bahamian dollar (B$) = 100 cents

Exchange rate: B$1.00 per US$ (fixed)

GDP per capita: US$19,781 (2007)*

GDP real growth: 3.10% (2007)*

Labour force: 167,000 (2004)

Unemployment: 10.20% (2004)

Inflation: 2.40% (2007)

Balance of trade: -US$1.21 billion (2004)

Visitor numbers: 1.60 million (2006)*

* estimated figure

Bahamas

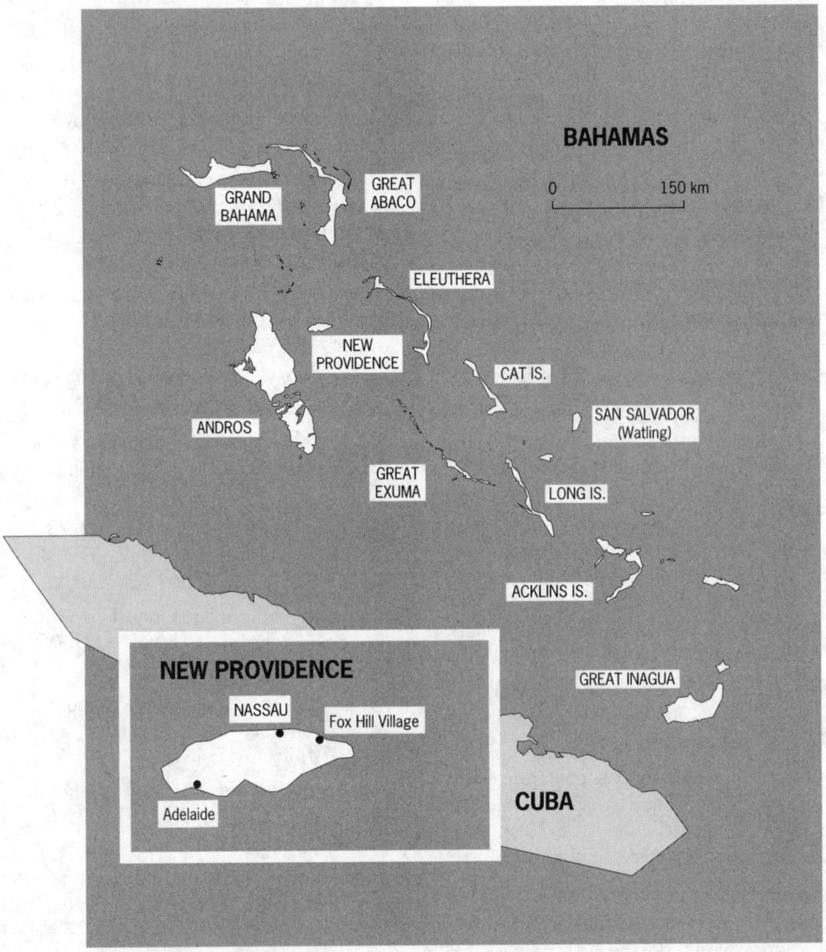

The Bahamas (from the Spanish *Baja Mar* – meaning low tide) originally inhabited by Arawak Indians were occupied by British settlers in 1647, only becoming recognised as a colony over a hundred years later in 1783. Gaining independence in 1973 the islands' legitimate economy has been largely based on tourism and offshore banking. The size of the Bahamas considerable illegitimate economy, using the Bahamas' strategic location as a base for smuggling drugs between South America and the USA, is difficult to estimate.

Election fever

The 2007 general election was certainly conducted in a febrile climate. Allegations of vote-buying and uncharacteristic violence (which included the use of flame throwers and bullets) were features of the election campaigning as the incumbent Progressive Liberal Party (PLP) endeavoured to obtain re-election for a second term in office, while erstwhile (1992–2002) prime minister Hubert Ingraham's Free National Movement (FNM) fought to regain the power it had lost in 2002. The PLP has been perceived as the party of the black majority, while the FNM had to face allegations of allegiance to the so-called Bay Street Boys who, prior to independence from Britain in 1973 had dominated Bahamian politics. The FNM was also seen as the party of the white colonial class.

In what was expected to be a close-run thing, Ingraham had claimed that the US$20 billion of tourist related investment projects begun and developed during the PLP's period in office represented the sale of the islanders' birth right. The voters seemed to agree with the FNM, voting it to power in 23 seats as against the PLP's 18. The voting figures represented a narrower majority, giving the FNM, with 68,500 votes 49.86 of the vote, and the PLP, with 64,600, 47.02 per cent. This was the first time that the ruling party had been voted out of power after only one term in office.

Laing's optimism

In a newspaper interview in January 2008, finance minister Zhivargo (sic) Laing forecast that the country would weather the sub-prime storm as long as the expected downturn didn't last too long. Mr Laing observed that in the first instance the foreign direct investment (FDI) projects in the Bahamas that were already under way would probably not be affected because they were already well advanced. Major developments such as Kerzner Phase Four, the expansion at the Freeport Container Port and the Ritz Carlton Rose Island were expected to continue to create employment and generate income. Mr Laing pointed out that the International Monetary Fund (IMF) forecast for the Bahamian economy in the order of 3.5–4 per cent GDP growth took into account the problems affecting the US economy. Mr Laing also said that he was 'hardly one to share the view' that the US economic policymakers would allow a recession – were it to happen – to last for longer than two to three years.

Tourism stalls

As 2007 ended data produced by the Central Bank of the Bahamas suggested that economic activity was slowing as both the tourism and construction sectors began to show weakness. This offset whatever growth there had been in consumer demand. Total visitor arrivals fell by 3.8 per cent to 4.14 million for the first eleven months of 2007, having improved in the quarter up to the end of June 2007 with an increase for the period of 1.7 per cent.

Consumer price inflation for 2007 also moved in the wrong direction, up to an annual rate of 2.5 per cent, compared to 1.8 per cent in 2006. In the same quarter (to end June 2007) the government's fiscal position had deteriorated, recording a deficit of US$50.7 million in contrast to a deficit of 1.2 per cent of GDP for the same period in 2006. Total government revenues dropped by 10.2 per cent to US$293.6 million. This was down on receipts for the previous financial year when government revenue was boosted by extraordinary tax receipts. Total government revenue for the period rose to US$344.4 million, largely due to higher salaries and interest payments. Capital expenditure, largely on infrastructure projects, rose by 1.5 per cent, to US$30.5 million.

Growth falters

According to the Economic Commission for Latin America and the Caribbean (ECLAC), the Bahamas' annual economic growth in 2006 of 3.4 per cent had been the highest for seven years, driven by continued tourism buoyancy. At the end of 2006 everything still looked pretty rosy – demand for real estate from non-residents was strong, continued investment in hotel complexes also boosted the construction sector, which grew by an impressive 25 per cent in the year. The estimated growth figure for 2007 was 2.8 per cent. In December 2007 the Bahamas' excess reserves contracted by US$17 million, in contrast to a contraction of US$28.7 million in December 2006. Excess liquid assets decreased by US$24.8 million, after falling by US$42.8 million in 2006. The overall gain in external reserves increased to US$7.5 million, up from US$3.3 million in 2006. This enabled the Central Bank to increase its net purchases of foreign currency in 2007 to US$5.5million, again up on the 2006 figure of US$2.1 million. The Bahamas liquidity conditions throughout 2007 were relatively buoyant, as the Central Bank's excess reserves increased by US$105.5 million, a welcome turnaround from the US$59.2 drop of 2006. The Central Bank adopted a positive view of prospects for 2008, despite persistently high oil prices and the inevitably negative effect on tourism and real estate markets of the recessionary trends in the USA.

The lifeblood of tourism

Like many, if not all, Caribbean island nations, in late 2007 the Bahamas began to notice the effects of the sub-prime downturn in the US economy. Before this shift, tourism growth rates in the Caribbean had already lagged behind world tourism growth rates, which in 2007 had averaged 7 per cent, well above the Caribbean's more leisurely 2.5 per cent. What is unquestionable is that tourism remains the lifeblood of the Bahamian economy, with two jobs out of three dependant on it. The World Tourism Council ranks the Bahamas seventh in the world in terms of the relative contribution of tourism to the national economy.

The importance of tourism infrastructure development projects to the Bahamian economy was illuminated in late 2007 and early 2008 by the controversy surrounding the decision of Harrah's Entertainment, one of the largest gambling industry companies in the world, to pull out of the US$2.6 million Baha Mar project. Harrah's decision to pull out of the project was on the grounds that it 'had lost confidence' as there were a number of conditions that 'had not been met'. In the Bahamas' capital, Nassau, it was rumoured that comments made by ministers in the House of Assembly had caused Harrah to withdraw. Upon

KEY INDICATORS — Bahamas

	Unit	2003	2004	2005	2006	2007
Population	m	0.32	0.33	0.33	*0.33	*0.33
Gross domestic product (GDP)	US$bn	5.26	5.60	5.87	6.24	*6.59
GDP per capita	US$	17,000	17,486	18,062	19,917	*19,895
GDP real growth	%	0.9	3.3	2.7	4.0	*4.5
Inflation	%	1.7	1.5	2.2	1.9	1.9
Exports (fob) (goods)	US$m	636.0	424.7	549.2	692.1	–
Imports (cif) (goods)	US$m	1,630.0	1,630.2	2,401.2	2,626.0	–
Balance of trade	US$m	-994.0	-1,205.6	-1,852.0	-1,933.9	–
Current account	US$m	-420.0	-480.0	-818.6	-1,578.0	*-888.0
Total reserves minus gold	US$m	491.1	674.4	586.3	461.3	464.5
Foreign exchange	US$m	481.8	664.7	577.3	451.9	454.5
Exchange rate	per US$	1.00	1.00	1.00	1.00	1.00

* estimated figure

its completion in 2011 the Baha Mar project is ambitiously scheduled to employ 10,000 Bahamians, with 2,000 jobs created during the three year period of construction. Harrah had committed to an injection of some US$400 million into the project by March 2009.

The Bahamas' Prime Minister Hubert Ingraham suggested that the government would proceed with the approvals process for the project, despite Harrah's withdrawal. The government has until March 2009 to find a joint venture partner, the appointment of which would enable it to meet the conditions precedent for funding the project. The government attributed Harrah's withdrawal to 'the prevailing financial climate'. However, one of Harrah's allegations appeared to relate to delays caused by opposition resistance to the transfer of land to the project.

Risk assessment

Politics	Fair
Economy	Fair
Regional stability	Good

COUNTRY PROFILE

Historical profile

1729 A parliamentary system of government was introduced.
1834 Britain emancipated its slaves.
1964 Internal self-government was granted.
1967 In the first elections under full universal adult suffrage, the Progressive Liberal Party (PLP), led by Lynden (later Sir Lynden) Pindling won with the support of the United Bahamian Party (UBP).
1972 The PLP won a landslide victory and began independence talks with the UK.
1973 The Bahamas gained full independence as a member of the Commonwealth.
1992 Sir Lynden Pindling and the PLP lost power to the Free National Movement (FNM).
1997 The FNM were re-elected.
2000 Sir Lynden Pindling died. The Bahamas was placed on the Financial Action Task Force (FATF) list of Non-Co-operative Countries and Territories (NCCT) for a financial system that did not comply with international banking regulation on money laundering and terrorist financing.
2001 The US awarded the Bahamas certification as being one of 20 countries fully co-operating with anti-drug efforts. Dame Ivy Dumont became the first female governor general.
2002 The PLP won the parliamentary elections. Perry Christie became prime minister.
2004 The FATF reported it remained concerned about the ability of the authorities to respond to foreign judicial and regulatory requests and would continue to monitor the situation. Hurricane Frances caused widespread damage.
2005 Dame Ivy Dumont retired; Paul Adderley, became Acting Governor General. The Bahamas banking system was removed from the FATF list of NCCT.
2006 Arthur Dion Hanna was inaugurated as governor general.
2007 In parliamentary elections on 2 May, the FNM won 23 out of 41 seats, defeating the incumbent PLP, which won 18 seats. The FNM leader, Hubert Ingraham, was sworn in as prime minister on 4 May.

Political structure

Constitution

The 1973 constitution was enacted to validate independence. Rights of citizenship and freedom of the individual were guaranteed. The composition of parliament, with a senate and house of assembly, was mandated and the function and authority of the executive were set forth.
Voting eligibility is for citizens of the Bahamas who are 18 years or older.

Form of state

Constitutional multi-party parliamentary democracy; it is a member of the Commonwealth.

The executive

The British monarch is the nominal head of state, represented by the governor general. Executive power is exercised by the prime minister and cabinet, which advises the governor general on appointments and ratifies laws.

National legislature

The bicameral legislature consists of a House of Assembly with 40 members elected for five-year terms, in single-seat constituencies. The Senate has 16 members appointed by the governor general; nine members are appointed on the recommendation of the prime minister, four members are appointed on the recommendation of the leader of the opposition and three members are appointed on the recommendation of the prime minister and leader of the opposition together. The senate always reflects the political make-up of the House of Assembly.

Legal system

The Bahamian legal system is based on British common law with elements of former colonial legislation. Much of the business legislation enacted since independence is based on the US system. The Privy Council in London is the highest court of appeal.

Last elections

2 May 2007 (parliamentary)

Results: Parliamentary: the Free National Movement (FNM) won 56 per cent of the vote (23 of 41seats); the Progressive Liberal Party (PLP) won 44 per cent (18 seats). Turnout was 90 per cent.

Next elections

2012 (parliamentary)

Political parties

Ruling party

Free National Movement (FNM) (elected May 2007)

Main opposition party

Progressive Liberal Party (PLP)

Political situation

The Caribbean Forum (Cariforum), the organisation appointed to negotiate with the European Union on the Economic Partnership Agreement (EPA), signed the agreement in December 2007. As the EU is one of the world's largest trading bloc countries in the Caribbean cannot take a lone stand and attempt to negotiate their own terms but likewise maximum benefit will be predicated on each Caribbean country taking full advantage of the trade agreement. While the expectation that the agreement will foster greater foreign direct investment, development and guaranteed markets these will have to be fought for and The Bahamas is one of many small islands that may be outstripped by bigger or more motivated regional economies in Cariforum.

Population

333,000 (2007)*

Last census: May 2000: 303,611

Population density: 30 inhabitants per square km. Urban population: 89 per cent (1995–2001).

Annual growth rate: 1.5 per cent 1994–2004 (WHO 2006)

Ethnic make-up

African (85 per cent), European and mixed race (12 per cent), other (3 per cent).

Religions

Baptist (32 per cent), Anglican (20 per cent), Roman Catholic (19 per cent), Evangelical Protestant (12 per cent), Methodist (6 per cent), Church of God (6 per cent).

Education

There is an extensive primary and secondary school system, and education is free. There are numerous options for tertiary education, including the College of the Bahamas, which is affiliated with the University of the West Indies (UWI). Local post-secondary vocational and technical training is available in mechanical, electrical and automotive engineering, television and radio, technology, computer science, electronics, construction, carpentry, secretarial services, bookkeeping, printing, photography, straw craft and dressmaking. A scholarship programme provides university training abroad in medicine, agriculture, engineering, science, education and other subjects considered necessary for national development but not available locally.

Literacy rate: 96 per cent of adults (2003)
Compulsory years: Five to 16
Enrolment rate: 98 per cent, gross primary enrolment (World Bank).

Health

Per capita total expenditure on health (2003) was US$1,220; of which per capita government spending was US$579, at the international dollar rate, (WHO 2006).
There are three main hospitals in the Bahamas: Princess Margaret in Nassau and Rand Memorial in Freeport, both government owned, and the privately owned Doctors Hospital in Nassau. Lyford Cay Hospital is a smaller private establishment offering specialised treatment.

HIV/Aids
Deaths by Aids, once a leading cause, had by 2005 been halved due to the use of anti-retroviral (ARV) drugs – 1,600 patients received the treatment, up from 470 in 2002. Deaths from Aids dropped from 250 to 140 per annum between 2002–04.
Over 2,000 HIV positive patients are cared for by a speciality clinic in Nassau and it was reported that no new cases of infants born to HIV positive mothers were infected while patients. HIV-positive pregnant women's rate dropped from 2.7 per cent in 2001 to 1.6 per cent in 2004, nevertheless, child mortality was 25.21 per 1,000 live births in 2004.
HIV prevalence: 3.0 per cent aged 15–49 in 2003 (World Bank)
Life expectancy: 73 years, 2004 (WHO 2006)
Fertility rate/Maternal mortality rate: 2.3 births per woman, 2004 (WHO 2006)
Child (under 5 years) mortality rate (per 1,000): 11 per 1,000 live births (World Bank)

Welfare

Welfare conditions in the Bahamas are among the best in the Caribbean and the government is working towards ensuring that economic growth is accompanied by improvements in the social sector.
The National Insurance Act of 1972 set out the law governing social security. It provides for contributions from employers and employees to be paid to the National Insurance Fund. Anyone who is employed or self-employed is insured under the act, including non-Bahamians with work permits. Benefits include sickness and maternity payments, retirement and widows' pensions and social assistance payments.

Main cities

Nassau (capital and seat of government, on New Providence Island, estimated population 233,832 in 2005) and Freeport (on Grand Bahama Island, 27,270).

Languages spoken

English, Creole (among Haitian immigrants).

Official language/s
English

Media

Press
Dailies: Newspapers include the Nassau Guardian (www.thenassauguardian.com), The Tribune and the intellectual Bahama Journal (www.jonesbahamas.com);Freeport News (http://freeport.nassauguardian.net) is published on Grand Bahama.
Weeklies: Tabloid newspapers include Punch published twice weekly and has the largest circulation of all newspapers; The Abaconian is published once fortnightly, on Abaco.
Business: A quarterly magazine The Bahamas Financial Digest (www.bfsb-bahamas.com) is a government publication that reports on financial services and investments.

Broadcasting
The national public broadcaster is ZNS (www.znsbahamas.com), (the name is derived from its call sign: Zephyr Nassau Sunshine).
Radio: ZNS operates three commercial radio station; ZNS 1 and 2 from Nassau and ZNS3 from Freeport. There are around a dozen private stations include Splash FM (www.splash899fm.com), Radio Abaco (www.radioabaco.com) and 100 Jamz (www.100jamz.com).
Television: ZNS operates the only domestic TV station on the islands. Cable TV is available to around 96 per cent of the population offering a wide choice of imported TV programmes, sporting events and films.

Economy

Tourism and offshore financial banking are the mainstays of the Bahamian economy. This small open plan economy is becoming less dependent on the tourist sector, although it still contributes 18–19 per cent of GDP. The Bahamas ranks number seven in the world for the largest amount of tourism-GDP produced.
Visitor spending stands at US$2 billion or 11.4 per cent of overall economic growth. Cruise ship visitors typically account for over 50 per cent of all visitors to the Bahamas and growth in this sector has averaged 9 per cent over the past decade.
The USA accounts for the majority of visitors, a dependency which weakens the economy, as downturns in the US economy feed through to the islands. The introduction of new US passport requirements is expected to have adverse effects on the sector from 2007.
The government is attempting to increase investment in the financial centre. New financial service laws were passed in 2004 to increase the Bahamas' competitiveness in this sector.
The tax-neutral environment, with no direct taxation, makes the Bahamas banks attractive to international businesses. The financial centre accounts for around 20 per cent of the country's GDP and annual expenditures in the banking sector amount to US$400 million. The government has concentrated on improving the integrity of the banks and as a result of tighter controls the Bahamas has been removed from the OECD list of countries with dubious banking sectors.
The high incidence of hurricanes in the Bahamas affects the economy, although due to the islands' general preparedness, the economic impact is kept to a minimum. Hurricanes in 2004 affected 9 per cent of the population; it is estimated that they reduced GDP by around 1 per cent, principally due to the adverse impact on tourism.
Debt servicing is a budgetary priority. Total debt levels are estimated at around 35 per cent of GDP.

External trade

Although the Bahamas was a founder member of the Caribbean Community (Caricom), it did not adopt the single market and economy (CSME), which was ratified by 12 other member states on 1 January 2006. The large trade deficit is traditionally offset by invisible earnings from offshore financial business, tourism and shipping.

Imports
Principal imports include crude oil for refinement, fuel oil, machinery and transport equipment, manufactured goods, livestock and foodstuffs, and chemicals.
Main sources: US (20.9 per cent total, 2006), South Korea (17.9 per cent), Brazil (16.8 per cent).

Exports
Exports include chemicals, pharmaceuticals, rum, crawfish, agricultural products, salt, aragonite, sponges, cosmetics and perfume.
Main destinations: Spain (23.5 per cent of 2006 total goods exports), US (20.9 per cent), Poland (14.2 per cent).

Re-exports
Petroleum products

Agriculture

Farming
The agricultural and fisheries sector contributes approximately 3 per cent to annual GDP and employs about 5 per cent of the labour force.

Although only about 1 per cent of land area is cultivated, near self-sufficiency has been achieved in poultry, pork, eggs, fruit and vegetables. The expansion of export crops such as limes, pineapples, papayas, avocados, cucumbers and mangoes is being promoted.

The government has provided marketing facilities through the Product Exchange in Nassau for small-scale producers, and also supplies seed and fertilisers. There are special incentives to foreign investors in food production and processing.

The chicken industry accounts for 40 per cent of agricultural production.

Estimated crop production in 2005 included: 355 tonnes (t) maize, 55,500t sugar cane, 700t potatoes, 880t sweet potatoes, 240t taro, 3,500t bananas, 21,700t citrus fruit, 5,000t tomatoes, 155t cassava, 125t pulses, 29,000t fruit in total, 25,709t vegetables in total. Livestock production included: 8,379t meat in total, 28t beef, 205t pig meat, 96t lamb and goat meat, 8,050t poultry, 900t eggs, 1,750t milk.

Fishing

The commercial fishing sector was originally reserved for Bahamians until 2002, when the authorities began opening up the sector to foreign participation. The sector employs around 9,000 Bahamians.

The commercial harvesting of pearls and shells has seen a dramatic rise from the typical 8,400 units in 1997 to the high of 40,000 units in 2000; the annual harvest is now typically 13,000 units. The harvest of sponges averages 70,000 per annum.

Forestry

Total forest cover is estimated at 842,000 hectares, equivalent of 15 per cent of the total land area. Most forests are concentrated on the four islands of the north-western Bahamas including Ahaco, Andros, Grand Bahamas and New Providence.

Industry and manufacturing

The industrial sector is small-scale, contributing around 10 per cent to annual GDP and employing 10 per cent of the labour force.

The largest contributor to the industrial sector is the crude oil transshipment terminal operated by Burmah Oil. Re-exports of crude and refined oil (mainly to the US) are estimated to account for around 16 per cent of GDP.

Other activity is centred on the production of rum, chemicals and pharmaceuticals for export. The companies manufacturing these products are largely foreign-owned and located in the Freeport trade area on Grand Bahama.

Other light industries include rum production, food processing, confectionery, garments, small boat building and furniture making.

The Bahamas Agricultural and Industrial Corporation (BAIC) is encouraging light manufacturing, furniture, toiletries, cosmetics, jewellery, linens, beachwear and the assembly of air conditioners and refrigerators.

The construction industry is also important, fuelled by the tourist trade and financial institutions requiring offices.

Tourism

Tourism is one of the Bahamas' primary economic activities and accounts for around 19 per cent of GDP, with another 20 per cent in tourist related construction. Tourism, and visitor numbers in 2004 were damaged by hurricanes, which closed a major resort on Grand Bahama causing a drop in the number of cruise ships visiting. Overall, only 2,369,000 visitors arrived in 2004 compared to the 4,594,000 visitors who arrived in 2003. In mid-2005 the sector was showing a 5.32 per cent decline. Gross receipts for tourism in 2004 were US$2.06 billion. Employment in the tourist industry is forecast to be some 43,000, or 25.7 per cent of the total labour force, in 2005.

Mining

Mining contributes approximately 1 per cent to annual GDP and employs around 1 per cent of the labour force.

Crude salt is produced by solar evaporation in Great Inagua and Long Island and aragonite deposits are found near Bimini Island.

Hydrocarbons

The Bahamas does not have any significant oil reserves, but the country is an important re-exporter of oil and transshipment earns the islands a significant amount of foreign exchange. The state-owned Bahamas Oil Refining Company (Borco) is the principal domestic player on the petroleum market and has been involved in several joint ventures with larger international oil companies.

The Bahamas is poised to increase its hydrocarbons re-export sector with the construction of new liguidified natural gas (LNG) re-gasification terminals in Ocean Cay connected by pipeline to nearby Florida in the US. Two companies – AES Ocean LNG, and Tractebel – have invested over US$1 billion for the new gas terminals in their bid to corner the Florida gas market. However, the Bahamian government had not, by mid-2005, approved the deal. The US Federal Energy Regulatory Commission and the Bahamas Environmental Impact Assessment have given approval to the bids despite local environmental concerns. The proposed US$144 million Calypso pipeline would convey about 23.5 million cubic metres of natural gas per day to Broward County, Florida, from a LNG terminal in Freeport.

Energy

The Bahamas imports all of its energy needs, mainly oil. It imports around 25,000 barrels per day (bpd).

Installed electrical capacity is estimated at 410MW.

Financial markets

Stock exchange

The Bahamas International Stock Exchange (BISX) began trading in 2000 as a virtual stock exchange – all transactions by brokers are carried out online – which acts as a listing of convenience for mutual funds administered from all over the world. The BISX was set up with technical and financial support from the Inter-American Development Bank (IADB).

Banking and insurance

Central bank

Central Bank of the Bahamas

Main financial centre

Nassau

Offshore facilities

The Bahamas is one of the largest offshore financial centres in the world. It was taken off the OECD's blacklist of countries that did not meet international requirements on taxation and transparency after it enacted new legislation which eliminated banking operations that did not have a physical presence in the Bahamas, and allowed for the exchange of tax information and the establishment of a comprehensive anti-money laundering regime. It resulted in the number of banks and trust companies licenced in the offshore sector declining.

Time

GMT minus five hours (daylight saving, April–October, minus four hours)

Geography

The Bahamas archipelago, which consists of 700 islands and nearly 2,500 small islets or cays sprawled across roughly 259,000 square km, stretches south-east from the southern coast of Florida (US). Virtually all the islands are surrounded by coral reefs and sandbanks, and nearly all are low lying.

Hemisphere

Northern.

Climate

The Bahamas is said to have one of the finest climates in the world. There are two seasons: winter (November–April), which is cool and dry, and summer (May–October), which is warm and wet. The climate is semi-tropical with temperatures ranging from 20 degrees Celsius (C) in winter to 30 degrees C in summer. Hurricanes can occur between June–November.

Dress codes
Business dress is more formal in the Bahamas than elsewhere in the Caribbean or in Florida; a business suit and tie is recommended for men and conservative business dress for women.
Visitors should bring lightweight or tropical clothing and, during the wet season, rainwear.
If invited to a Bahamian's home for dinner, dress should be business attire for men and conservative evening wear for women.

Entry requirements
Passports
Required by all, except nationals of the US and Canada with evidence of citizenship (all US and Canadian nationals require a passport for re-entry to their country). All passports must be valid for at least six months from the date of arrival and visitors must show proof of a return/onward ticket and sufficient funds to provide for maintenance during their stay.
Visa
Required, but nationals of various countries are exempt for periods ranging from two weeks to eight months. For details contact nearest consulate or embassy or consult www.bahamas.com.
Currency advice/regulations
Permission is required from the Central Bank of the Bahamas to import local currency, which may be exported up to a maximum of B$70. The import and export of foreign currency is unlimited.
US dollars are accepted as legal tender. To avoid additional exchange rate charges, travellers are advised to take travellers cheques in US dollars.
Prohibited imports
Illegal drugs, firearms and other offensive weapons, animals.

Health (for visitors)
Medical facilities are on a par with the US, but can be costly and therefore medical insurance is recommended.
Mandatory precautions
A yellow fever vaccination certificate is required if arriving from an infected area.
Advisable precautions
Recommended immunisations are typhoid, diphtheria, hepatitis A and B, and tetanus. Malaria prophylaxis is recommended for Great Exuma. Tap water is safe to drink, although it can often be salty in taste. Food precautions should be observed.

Hotels
Wide variety available. Bills usually include a service charge and a hotel room tax.

Public holidays (national)
Fixed dates
1 Jan (New Year's Day), 10 Jul (Independence Day), 25 Dec (Christmas Day), 26 Dec (Boxing Day).
Holidays which fall on a Saturday or Sunday are observed on the following Monday.
Variable dates
Good Friday, Easter Monday, Whit Monday, Labour Day (first Mon in Jun), Emancipation Day (first Mon in Aug), National Heroes Day (second Mon in Oct).

Working hours
Banking
Mon–Thu: 0930–1500; Friday: 0930–1700.
Business
Mon–Fri: 0900–1700.
Government
Mon–Fri: 0900–1730.
Shops
Mon–Sat: 0900–1700. Sunday closing laws are generally strictly observed, except for some grocers open for a few hours, as well as the tourist shops on Bay Street in Nassau if cruise ships are docked.

Telecommunications
Mobile/cell phones
A GSM 1900 service is available.

Electricity supply
120V AC, 60 cycles

Social customs/useful tips
Bahamians shake hands upon meeting and business cards may be exchanged. Address first-time business acquaintances by their last names – conversations generally move to a first-name basis more slowly than in most Western countries. Appointments for business meetings should be made in advance.
Business lunches are often held. If invited to dinner at home, it is customary to take a small gift for the hostess and send a thank-you card afterwards.

Security
Visits to the Bahamas are generally trouble-free. Crime exists in the main cities of Nassau and Freeport, including incidents of murder and armed robbery. Much of this is within the local community, but tourists are often perceived as wealthy and have been the victims of robbery, particularly when alone or in isolated locations. Passports are a particular target for theft.
Visitors should take sensible precautions and be vigilant at all times. It is advisable not to carry large amounts of cash or jewellery. Do not offer resistance in the event of an attempted robbery as the assailant may be armed.
The outlying Family Islands are relatively free of crime, but sensible precautions should still be taken.
Penalties for possession or trafficking of drugs are severe. Pack all luggage yourself and do not carry anything through customs for anyone else unless you are aware of the contents.

Getting there
Air
National airline: Bahamasair
International airport/s: Nassau International (NAS), 16km west of city, shop, restaurant, bank, post office, car hire; Grand Bahama International (FPO), 5km north of Freeport, shop, bar, restaurant, buffet, shops, car hire.
Other airport/s: Paradise Island (PID), 5km from Nassau; George Town (GGT), 6km from city.
Airport tax: US$18.
Surface
Water: All the major cruise lines operating out of Florida and liners from New York and Florida make calls in the Bahamas, either in Nassau or Freeport.
Main port/s: Freeport Container Port on Grand Bahama, Nassau on New Providence and Matthew Town on Inagua.
There are modern berthing facilities for cruise ships at Potters Cay on New Providence, Governor's Harbour on Eleuthera, Morgan's Bluff on North Andros and George Town on Exuma.

Getting about
National transport
Air: An extensive air charter network covers the islands, serving over 50 landing sites. Local enquiries should be made for particular requirements.
Road: The main centres are well served by 1,535km of surfaced roads.
Buses: There are few conventional buses, which serve only in the main towns.
Mini-buses (jitneys) operate in the Nassau and Freeport areas.
Water: Ferry and mail-boat services are operated between the various islands in the archipelago, but for business travellers the length and frequency of journeys may prove a major drawback.
City transport
Taxis: Taxis are often metered and use a fixed-rate system, but the rate should be agreed before setting off. A 15 per cent tip is usual.
Car hire
A national or international licence valid for three months is required. Rates vary according to the season. Traffic drives on the left.

BUSINESS DIRECTORY

Telephone area codes
The international direct dialling code (IDD) for Bahamas is +1 242, followed by subscriber's number

Chambers of Commerce

Bahamas Chamber of Commerce, Shirley Street and Collins Avenue, PO Box N-665, Nassau (tel: 322-2145; fax: 322-4649; e-mail: bahamaschamber@coralwave.com).

Grand Bahama Chamber of Commerce, The Mall and Pioneer Way, PO Box F-40808, Freeport (tel: 352-8329; fax: 352-3280; e-mail: info@thegrandbahamachamberof commerce.com).

Banking

Bahamas Development Bank, West Bay Street, PO Box N-3034, Nassau (tel: 327-5780; fax: 322-6457).

Bank of the Bahamas Ltd, PO Box N-7118, Nassau (tel: 326-2560).

Bank of Nova Scotia, PO Box N-7518, Nassau (tel: 356-1400).

Banque Privée Edmond de Rothschild Ltd, 51 Frederick Street, PO Box N-1136, Nassau (tel: 328-8121; fax: 328-8115).

Barclays Bank, PO Box N-8350, Nassau (tel: 322-4921).

British-American Bank, PO Box N-7502, Nassau (tel: 327-5170).

Canadian Imperial Bank of Commerce (CIBC), PO Box N-7125, Nassau (tel: 322-8455).

Citibank, PO Box N-8158, Nassau (tel: 322-4240).

Commonwealth Bank, PO Box SS-6263, Nassau (tel: 328-1854).

Finance Corporation of Bahamas Ltd, PO Box N-3038, Nassau (tel: 322-4822).

Handelsfinanz-CCF Bank International ltd, Maritime House, Frederick Street, PO Box N-10441, Nassau (tel: 328-8644, 328-1737; fax: 328-8600).

Inter-American Development Bank, PO Box N-3743, Nassau (tel: 393-7159).

Royal Bank of Canada, PO Box N-7537, Nassau (tel: 322-8700).

Central bank

Central Bank of the Bahamas, Frederick Street, PO Box N-4868, Nassau (tel: 322-2193; fax: 356–4307; e-mail: queries@centralbankbahamas.com).

Travel information

Bahamasair, Windsor Field, PO Box N-4881, Nassau (tel: 327-8451; fax: 327-7409).

Bahamas Hotel Association, Dele West Bay Street, sub Dean's Lane, PO Box N-7799, Nassau (tel: 322-8381; fax: 326-5346).

Nassau/Cable Beach/Paradise Island Promotion Board, Dean's Lane, Fort Charlotte, PO Box N-7799, Nassau (tel: 322-8381; fax: 326-5346).

Ministry of tourism

Ministry of Tourism, PO Box N-3701, Nassau (tel: 302–2000; fax: 302–2098; e-mail: tourism@bahamas.com).

Ministries

Ministry of Agriculture and Industry, Levy Building, East Bay Street, Nassau (tel: 325-7502; fax: 322-1767).

Ministry of Economic Development, Manx Building, West Bay Street, Nassau.

Ministry of Education, Youth and Sports, Shirley Street, Nassau (tel: 322-5495; fax: 322-3267).

Ministry of Financial Services and Investment, Sir Cecil V Wallace Whitfield Centre, Cable Beach, PO Bx N-10980, Nassau (tel: 327-5826; fax: 327-5006).

Ministry of Foreign Affairs, Post Office Building, East Hill Street, Nassau (tel: 322-7624; fax: 328-8212).

Ministry of Health, Ministry of Health Building, Royal Victoria Gardens, Nassau (tel: 322-7425; fax: 322-7788).

Ministry of Housing and Social Development, Frederick House, Frederick Street, Nassau (tel: 356-0765; fax: 323-3883).

Ministry of Justice, Post Office Building, East Hill Street, Nassau.

Ministry of Labour and Immigration, Post Office Building, East Hill Street, Nassau (tel: 323-7240; fax: 326-7344).

Ministry of Public Works, John F Kennedy Drive, Nassau (tel: 323-7814; fax: 325-2016).

Ministry of Tourism, PO Box N-3701, Bolam House, George Street, Nassau (tel: 302–2000; fax: 302–2098; e-mail: tourism@bahamas.com).

Ministry of Transport, Aviation and Local Government, Pilot House Complex, Nassau (tel: 394-0451; fax: 394-5023).

Office of the Deputy Prime Minister, Churchill Building, Bay Street, Nassau (tel: 356-6792; fax: 356-6087).

Office of the Prime Minister, Cecil V Wallace Whitfield Centre, West Bay Street, Nassau (tel: 322-2805; fax: 328-8294).

Other useful addresses

Bahamas Agricultural and Industrial Corporation, PO Box N-4940, Levy Building, East Bay Street, Nassau (tel: 322-3740; fax: 322-2133).

Bahamas Economic Development Corporation, Bahamas Development Bank, Adderley Building, Bay Street/Rawson Square, PO Box N-3034, Nassau (tel: 327-5780; fax: 327-5907).

Bahamas Electricity Corporation, Big Pond and Tucker Road, PO Box N-7509, Nassau (tel: 328-7700).

Bahamas Employers' Confederation, PO Box N-166, Nassau (tel: 328-1757, 326-6644; fax: 328-1346).

Bahamas Financial Services Board, PO Box N–1764, West Bay Street, Goodman's Bay Corporate Centre, Nassau (tel: 326-7001; fax: 326–7007; e-mail: info@bfsb-bahamas.com).

Bahamas Information Services, Nassau Court, PO Box N-8172 (tel: 325-6028).

Bahamas Investment Authority, Cecil Wallace Whitfield Centre, PO Box CB-10980, Nassau (tel: 327-5970/4; fax: 327-5907; e-mail: investbahama@batelnet.bs; internet site: http://www.opm.gov.bs).

Bahamas Telecommunications Corporation, J F Kennedy Drive, PO Box N-3048, Nassau (tel: 323-4911).

Bahamas Water and Sewerage Corporation, J F Kennedy Drive, PO Box N-3905, Nassau (tel: 323-3944).

British High Commission, Bitco Building, 3rd Floor, East Street, PO Box N-7516, Nassau (tel: 325-7471/2/3; fax: 323-3871).

Cabinet Office, Churchill Bldg, Rawson Square, PO Box N-7147, Nassau (tel: 322-2805; fax: 328-8294).

Central Post Office, Post Office Building, PO Box N-8302, Nassau (tel: 322-3344).

The Comptroller of Customs, Seaban Building, Oakes Field, PO Box N-155, Nassau (tel: 326-4401).

Gaming Board of the Bahamas, West Bay Street, PO Box N-4565, Nassau (tel: 327-7478).

Government Publications Office (import regulations), East Bay Street, PO Box N-7147, Nassau (tel: 322-2410).

Port Department, East Hill Street, PO Box N-8173 Nassau (tel: 326-7354).

Securities Commission of the Bahamas, PO Box N-8347, Nassau (tel: 356-6271/2; fax: 356-7530; e-mail: secbd@batelnet.bs).

Other news agencies: Caribbean Net News: www.caribbeannetnews.com

Internet sites

Bahamas Guide On-line: bahamas–guide.info

Bahamas International Securities Exchange: www.bisxbahamas.com

Bahrain

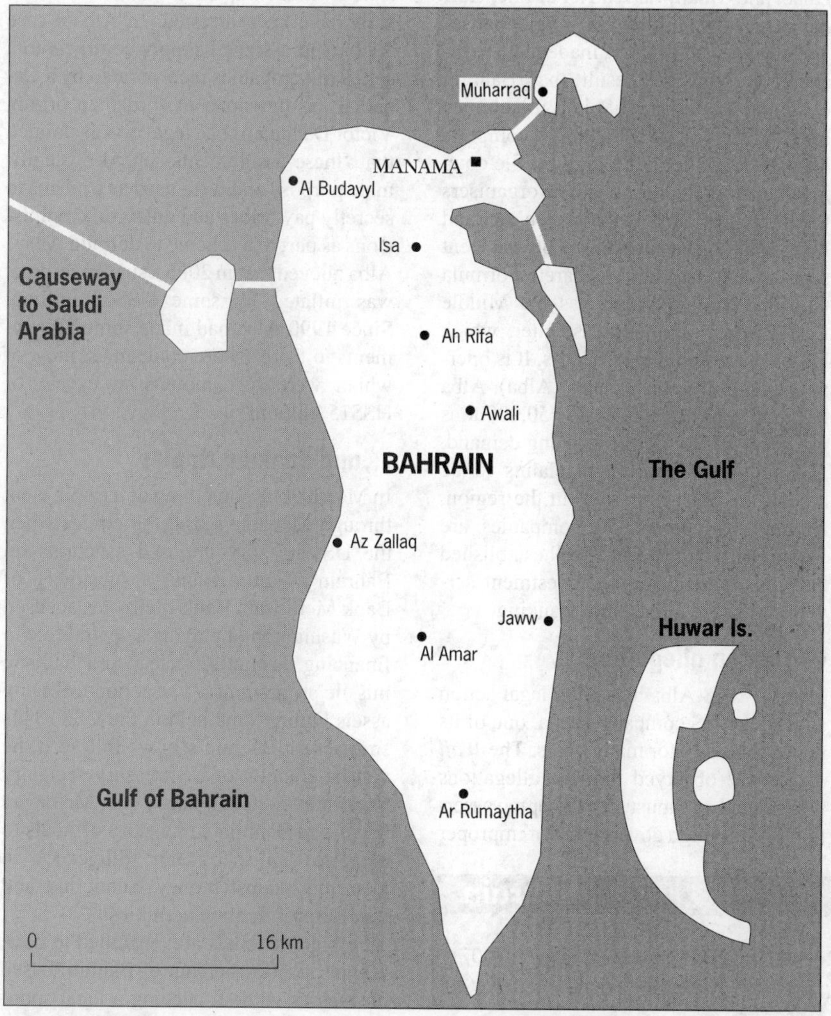

February 2008 saw further developments in Bahrain's gentle reform process, started some twenty years earlier by the island state's Crown Prince, Sheikh Salman bin Hamad al Khalifa. The changes have sought to increase efficiency and end corruption, while creating a functioning national parliament.

Continued reforms

The moves to modernise, spearheaded by the Crown Prince, have not always been welcomed by the more conservative rearguard of Bahrain's extensive ruling family, a well entrenched bureaucracy and even elements of the island's business community. The mix is further complicated by the fact that Bahrain's ruling family and the higher echelons of society are Sunni Arabs, while 65 per cent of the population are Shi'a. What has all the makings of a potentially explosive mix has in fact worked well, as an enlightened royal family has exercised a measured and well thought-out balance in its rule.

As Gulf rulers go – and he has in time become recognised as Bahrain's *de-facto* ruler – the Cambridge educated Crown Prince is, at 39, still a young man. He has grouped much of Bahrain's decision

KEY FACTS

Official name: Al Mamlakah al Bahrayn (Kingdom of Bahrain)

Head of State: King Hamad bin Isa al Khalifa (ruler since Mar 1999; King since 14 Feb 2002)

Head of government: Prime Minister Sheikh Khalifa bin Sulman al Khalifa

Area: 676 square km (35 islands)

Population: 764,000 (2007)*

Capital: Manama

Official language: Arabic

Currency: Bahraini dinar (BD) = 1,000 fils

Exchange rate: BD0.38 per US$ (fixed)

GDP per capita: US$25,731 (2007)*

GDP real growth: 6.60% (2007)*

Labour force: 349,000 (2004)

Inflation: 3.40% (2007)*

Balance of trade: US$3.79 billion (2005)*

Foreign debt: US$6.21 billion (2004)

Visitor numbers: 4.52 million (2006)*

* estimated figure

making machinery within the Economic Development Board (EDB), headed up Sheikh Mohammed bin Essa al Khalifa. In theory, the EDB's steadily increasing powers represent the erosion of parliament's already limited powers. But the gradual strengthening of the EDB appears to have been welcomed, rather than opposed, by parliament.

Bahrain's parliament was reactivated in 1999, and there have since been two elections to the lower house. What protests there have been over parliament's lack of power have come from disaffected, rather than specifically motivated, Shi'a. Sunnia-Shi'a community tensions in Iraq have not helped, but the particular complaints of the more marginalised elements of the Shi'a population focus on exclusion from senior government jobs and other more petty forms of discrimination. The apparent loser in a January 2008 government re-shuffle was Bahrain's prime minister Sheikh Khalifa bin Sulman al Khalifa, who was on holiday at the time.

Economic diversification

In a number of respects, Bahrain has been left at the post in the Gulf's economic development stakes. In the 1970s, along with Kuwait, it boasted the area's most developed infrastructure, enjoying a close relationship with the southerly emirate of Abu Dhabi (with which it shared its currency for a period) and the UK. The only thing that Bahrain really lacked was oil; its meagre resources were totally out-gunned, not only by the vastness of Saudi Arabia's oilfields, but also by those of Kuwait, Abu Dhabi and Oman. Before too long, it would also be overtaken by Qatar's natural gas reserves. The refining capacity that had enabled Bahrain to keep up with its neighbours was also quickly overtaken.

In response, Bahrain sought to diversify into less certain areas of economic activity, not always successfully. Its dry-dock project was soon eclipsed by that of Dubai and its partially owned (along with Abu Dhabi and Oman) flag carrier airline, Gulf Air – once the Gulf region's major carrier – succumbed to years of inadequate management, with the result that Bahrain ceased to be the regional hub it had once been. The state holding company Muntakalat pulled off a high profile coup in persuading the Formula One organisers to choose Bahrain for the region's Grand Prix. Muntakalat also has a 30 per cent shareholding in the McClaren Formula One operation. Bahrain has the Middle East's largest aluminium smelter, which has been a commercial success. It is operated by Aluminium Bahrain (Alba). Alba has increased its capacity to 750,000 tons per year (TPA) to meet growing demand. Bahrain's stock exchange claims to be among the most important in the region, although only some 50 companies are listed. Bahrain also has a well established banking sector covering investment services, offshore and Islamic banking.

Corruption allegations...

In early 2008 Alba brought a legal action against the US company Alcoa, one of its major suppliers for many years. The *Wall St Journal* observed that the allegations represented an 'unusually sweeping assertion' by a foreign government of improper behaviour by a US corporation. According to Alba Alcoa had steered payments to a group of small companies abroad in order to pay kickbacks to a Bahraini 'senior government official' following overcharging to Alba. Under a contract signed in 2007, the US investigation company Kroll Associates Bahrain has uncovered a number of cases of corruption in state-owned companies. As a result, officials have been arrested. In Alba's case Alcoa had assigned supply contracts to a series of companies incorporated by a Canadian businessman of Jordanian origin, Victor Dahdaleh. The legal action claimed that 'these assignments served no legitimate purpose and were used as a means to secretly pay bribes and unlawful commissions as part of a scheme to defraud Alba'. Alba alleged that in 2005 a supply contract was inflated by some US$65 million. Since 1990 Alba had made some 80 payments to the offshore companies, most of which were for amounts in excess of US$15 million.

...and banking ripples

In March 2008 something of a ripple went through Manama's banking circles when the US Treasury imposed sanctions on Bahrain's Future Bank, a subsidiary of Bank Melli Iran. Bank Melli was accused by Washington of playing a central role in financing Tehran's nuclear and ballistic missile programmes. The action froze any assets Future Bank held in the USA. This shot across Bahrain's bows followed the visit to Bahrain of US treasury secretary Stuart Levey in February 2008. Mr Levey had urged Bahrain's monetary officials to exercise 'enhanced due diligence' in guarding against money laundering and nuclear proliferation activities.

Foreign nationals are permitted to have 100 per cent ownership of Bahrain based businesses without needing a local sponsor. The attractiveness of setting up shop in Bahrain has generated strong flows of foreign direct investment (FDI), making Bahrain Gulf leader in this respect. Nevertheless, Bahrain's economy has to come to terms with three long term problems. First, the depletion of its oil reserves. Second, unacceptably high levels of youth unemployment. Bahrain is one of the first Gulf states to introduce unemployment benefits. Third, like its neighbours, Bahrain cannot afford to ignore the threat of regional instability, which risks having lasting effects on Bahrain's economic prospects. Average forecasts for the period 2008–11 which suggest an annual GDP growth rate of around 4.8 per cent

KEY INDICATORS — Bahrain

	Unit	2003	2004	2005	2006	2007
Population	m	0.68	0.70	0.73	*0.75	*0.76
Gross domestic product (GDP)	US$bn	9.61	11.00	13.38	15.82	*19.66
GDP per capita	US$	10,096	13,848	18,216	21,123	*25,731
GDP real growth	%	4.0	5.5	7.8	6.5	*6.6
Inflation	%	0.4	4.9	2.6	2.2	*3.4
Natural gas output	bn cum	9.6	9.8	9.9	11.1	11.5
Exports (fob) (goods)	US$m	6,592.0	7,620.7	11,170.0	11,702.6	–
Imports (cif) (goods)	US$m	5,357.0	6,135.4	7,380.0	8,565.2	–
Balance of trade	US$m	1,055.0	1,485.3	3,790.0	3,137.4	–
Current account	US$m	-50.0	870.0	1,600.0	2,112.0	3,913.0
Total reserves minus gold	US$m	1,778.4	1,940.5	1,820.0	2,910.0	*3,000.0
Foreign exchange	US$m	1,673.8	1,829.6	–	–	–
Exchange rate	per US$	0.38	0.38	0.38	0.37	0.37

* estimated figure

are based on continued macroeconomic stability. Understated government forecasts for oil prices may enable fiscal equilibrium to be maintained.

In the medium term, it looks as though the high oil prices will continue to boost Bahrain's economy. This manifests itself principally in increased government expenditure, but any increased activity will inevitable boost the financial sector. Government efforts to address unemployment and housing shortages should also show through positively.

Social tensions

As is the case with most Gulf States, despite high levels of unemployment among the Shi'a, Bahrain has long been dependent on imported labour. Most of this comes from the Indian sub-continent. This over-dependence sits uncomfortably alongside the absence of many human and political rights for the immigrant community. In a January 2008 interview with the pan-Arab newspaper *Asharq al-Aswat*, Bahrain's labour minister Majid al Alawi touched a raw nerve when he claimed that the Gulf was facing an Asian Tsunami because Gulf nationals are 'lazy' and 'spoilt'. The minister went further in his interview, expressing what many considered to be the alarmist view that the estimated 17 million foreign nationals working in the Gulf represented 'a danger worse than the atomic bomb or an Israeli attack'. His remarks were endorsed and expanded upon by Mansour al Jamri, the newspaper's Bahraini editor, who stated that foreign labour should not be classified as temporary, since for the most part they had become virtually permanent members of the community. Mr al Jamri further expanded on his theme, suggesting that the political influence of a renascent India could well end up making the Gulf states part of a 'Commonwealth of India' as its former citizens assume greater confidence and responsibility in both private and public sectors.

The oil still counts

Bahrain is the Gulf's smallest oil producer. None the less, oil still accounts for about 75 per cent of total government revenues. Bahrain's total energy consumption is mostly provided by natural gas. According to the *Oil and Gas Journal* (OGJ) and as reported by the US Energy Information Administration (EIA), Bahrain's proven oil reserves in January 2007 were a modest 125 million barrels, located entirely in the Awali Field. Bahrain shares with Saudi Arabia on a 50/50 basis the 300,000 barrels per day (bpd) of the offshore Abu Saafa field. The state-owned Bahrain Petroleum Company (Bapco) is responsible for all exploration and production for both domestic and international markets. As part of wider government reorganisation, the National Oil and Gas Authority (NOGA) replaced the oil ministry in 2005 to become the national regulatory authority.

Although Bahrain is one of the Gulf's oldest oil-producing states, its estimated oil production in 2007 of 35,000bpd was less than half the production levels of the 1970s. Between 2007 and 2015 Bapco expects to drill a further 700 new wells in the Awali Field, in the expectation of producing an additional 12,000bpd. This is forecast to offset any further declines in production. NOGA has also opened a new licensing round for offshore exploration and production projects. Bahrain's notional refining capacity of 250,000bpd at Bapco's Sitra refinery was surpassed in 2006, when the refinery ran at an annual rate of 263,000bpd. The OGJ reports that in January 2007 Bahrain's natural gas reserves were 3.25 trillion cubic feet (Tcf). The last recorded figures (for 2004) suggest that domestic natural gas consumption and production, at an annual rate of 344 Bcf, were in equilibrium.

Risk assessment

Economy	Good
Politics	Fair
Regional stability	Fair

COUNTRY PROFILE

Historical profile

Around 3000BC, the archipelago was the seat of the Dilmun trading empire linking Mesopotamia (southern Iraq) with the Indus Valley (India and Pakistan). Because of Dilmun's lush greenery in the midst of regions rapidly becoming arid, some scholars have suggested that it may have been the site of the biblical Garden of Eden. As well as a trading centre, it was also famous for pearl fishing. After being occupied by several other countries, the land subsequently became part of the Ottoman Empire. Later, it was administered by Britain until full independence. Since his accession to the throne in 1999, King Hamad bin Isa al Khalifa has instituted a process of political liberalisation. However, the process has been tightly controlled to ensure that the ruling Khalifa family and its close associates maintain control of both political and economic power.

1816 Bahrain's first treaty with Britain was signed

1861 The second treaty made it a British protectorate.

1869 Sheikh Isa bin Ali al Khalifa was named ruler.

1913 A treaty between Britain and Turkey recognised Bahrain as an independent state, but the country remained under British administration.

1923 After more than half a century of peace and stability, Sheikh Isa bin Ali al Khalifa abdicated in favour of his son, Sheikh Hamad.

1928 Iran claimed ownership of Bahrain; the dispute was not resolved until 1970 when Iran accepted a UN report stating that the vast majority of Bahrainis wanted their complete independence.

1932 Bahrain became the first country in the Gulf to strike oil.

1942–61 Sheikh Hamad died in 1942 and his son, Sheikh Sulman bin Hamad al Khalifa ruled Bahrain until his death in 1961, when he was succeeded by Sheikh Isa bin Sulman al Khalifa.

1968 Britain announced its intention to withdraw from the Gulf by 1971. The British plan was to form a single state consisting of Bahrain, Qatar and the Trucial States, but this idea did not find favour with the states concerned.

1971 Bahrain and Qatar became independent states.

1973–74 Bahrain's constitution was promulgated; it limited the Sheikh's powers and established an elected 30-member National Assembly.

1975 The National Assembly refused to ratify a bill to arrest and detain people for up to three years without trial, and was dissolved by the ruler, Sheikh Isa. The government subsequently ruled by decree.

1981 Bahrain was one of the six founder members of the Gulf Co-operation Council (GCC).

1986 The opening of the King Fahd Causeway between Bahrain and Saudi Arabia gave a boost to business and tourism.

1991 Bahrain actively supported the allied forces against Iraq in the Gulf military conflict.

1994 The majority Shi'ites staged demonstrations demanding better living conditions and the return of an elected parliament. The Sunnis, although in a minority, are dominant in both politics and business.

1999 Sheikh Isa bin Sulman al Khalifa, who had ruled since 1961, died and was succeeded by his son, Sheikh Hamad bin Isa al Khalifa.

2000 For the first time, non-Muslims and women were appointed to the Consultative Council.

2001 A referendum on political reform was approved, under which Bahrain would become a constitutional monarchy

with an elected lower chamber of parliament and an independent judiciary.
2002 Hamad bin Isa al Khalifa was declared king on 14 February, and the state became a constitutional monarchy. As part of the reform process, legislation was approved to allow women to vote in elections and run for national office. In legislative elections (the first since 1973), parliament became a mix of secular and Islamic candidates. The Shi'ite opposition boycotted the election resulting in a Sunni dominated parliament.
2004 In April, the first woman to be appointed head of a government ministry, Nada Haffadh, was made health minister. In September a free trade agreement was signed with the US.
2005 In March, King Hamad called for increasing global co-operation to combat international terrorism. Between March and June thousands protested in favour of a fully elected parliament.
2006 Legislative elections were held in November and December, in which Sunni representatives won 22 seats (out of 40) and Shi'ites won 18.
2007 There were several days of rioting in majority Shia areas towards the end of December. The protesters were demanding compensation for human rights violations between 1980–90.
2008 On 1 January, a common market was created by Bahrain, Kuwait, Oman, Qatar, Saudi Arabia and UAE, the six wealthiest Gulf states. Citizens of these countries are now allowed to travel between and live in any of the six states, where they may find employment, buy properties and businesses and use the educational and health facilities freely.

Political structure

Constitution
The 1973 constitution was suspended in 1975 and reinstated by royal decree, with significant amendments, in February 2002.
By a charter, agreed through a referendum, Bahrain was declared a constitutional monarchy with a bicameral parliament and independent judiciary. Women were given suffrage and although political parties remained illegal, eleven new political societies were licensed, in 2001.
The King is the symbol of the country and is inviolate.

Form of state
Constitutional monarchy

The executive
Executive power rests with the King, who is Head of State, he appoints a prime minister and members of the Consultative Council, which is an advisory body that, since 2002, is empowered to make laws. The King may dissolve or extend the term of the Consultative Council. The King has the right to initiate, ratify and promulgate laws.
The King is the head of the armed forces and head of the Judiciary.

National legislature
A bicameral national assembly; the Chamber of Deputies is a 40-member, popularly elected lower house legislature. The upper Consultative Council is a 40-member appointed chamber. Membership of both houses is four years. The King may renew membership of the Council and dissolve the Chamber of Deputies by decree. Terms of both houses may be extended by the King for up to two extra years.
The King and prime minister present bills to the Chamber of Deputies for consideration, before they are passed to the Consultative Council.

Legal system
The judiciary is a constitutionally independent body, whose function and organisation is regulated by law. It is a mixture, based on English common law and Sunni and Shi'a Sharia (Islamic law) traditions, where Sharia is the principal source of law.
The Supreme court is the final court of appeal for all civil, commercial and criminal matters.

Last elections
25 November/2 December 2006 (parliamentary)
Results: Parliamentary: al Wefaq (Islamic National Accord Association) won 17 seats out of 40; al Menbar (Islamic National Tribune Association) won seven seats; al Asala (Islamic Purity Association) six; and al Wa'ad (National Democratic Action Association) one; and independents nine.

Next elections
2010 (parliamentary)

Political parties
Political parties are not permitted; MPs are members of 'political societies'.

Ruling party

Population
764,000 (2007)*
Last census: April 2001: 650,604
Population density: 966 inhabitants per square km, one of the highest in the world. Bahrain's population is highly urbanised (92 per cent).
Annual growth rate: 2.4 per cent 1994–2004 (WHO 2006)

Ethnic make-up
Bahrain's inhabitants are mostly Arab, with a sizeable minority of Iranian descent.
Approximately 38 per cent of the population are foreign residents, mostly from South Asia and other Arab countries,

Religions
According to the constitution, Islam is the state religion. Approximately 98 per cent of the indigenous population are Muslim – two-thirds Shi'as and the remainder belonging to the Sunni branch of Islam. The remaining 2 per cent are Jewish and Christian.
About half of the foreign population are non-Muslim, including Christians, Jews, Hindus, Baha'is, Buddhists and Sikhs.

Education
Primary schooling lasts for six years between the ages of six and 12. Secondary education lasts for three years and offers students a choice of three main branches: the general, the technical or the commercial.
The government is seeking to establish Bahrain as a regional centre for human resource development. In addition to several universities, there are a number of training centres, such as the Bahrain Training Institute (BTI) and the Bahrain Institute of Training and Finance (BITF) that are designed to prepare local graduates for the modern, technology driven workforce.
There are 188 government-owned and 42 private schools.
Literacy rate: 91 per cent and 82.6 per cent for males and females respectively (World Bank).
Compulsory years: 6 to 15
Enrolment rate: 105 per cent boys, 106 per cent girls total primary school enrolment of the relevant age group (including repetition rates) (World Bank).

Health
Per capita total expenditure on health (2003) was US$813; of which per capita government spending was US$562, at the international dollar rate, (WHO 2006).
Health services in Bahrain are of a high quality and all Bahrainis receive free health care from the state. There are a mixture of government and private hospitals, with additional government health centres and maternity hospitals.

HIV/Aids
HIV prevalence: 0.2 per cent aged 15–49 in 2003 (World Bank)
Life expectancy: 74 years, 2004 (WHO 2006)
Fertility rate/Maternal mortality rate: 2.4 births per woman, 2004 (WHO 2006)
Child (under 5 years) mortality rate (per 1,000): 12 per 1,000 live births (World Bank)
Head of population per physician: 1.9 physician per 1,000 people, 2004 (WHO 2006)

Welfare
The government provides direct financial assistance to those considered needy in addition to assistance provided by religious organisations and local charitable societies. There are seven social centres operated by the ministry of labour and social affairs (MoLSA) that provide training and assistance, especially to needy women. Public and private facilities for the elderly, handicapped and orphaned provide first class care, using the latest professional methods, approaches, and equipment. The number of needy families on government assistance lists has been growing for the past decade at double the rate of the population growth.
Family support
The social assistance programme provides approximately BD30 (US$80) per month to every family being assisted.

Main cities
Manama (capital, estimated population 140,616 in 2005), Rifa (97,194) Muharraq (58,254) Madinat Isa (40,665), Hammad (66,846), Jid Hafs (11,883).

Languages spoken
English is widely spoken. Persian (Farsi), Hindi and Urdu are also frequently used.
Official language/s
Arabic

Media
While press laws guarantee the independence of journalists, criminal penalties may be imposed for infringements, such as insulting the King and as such self-censorship is widespread.
Bahrain is striving to achieve a status as the primary media centre for the Middle East in competition with Dubai in United Arab Emirates.
National news agency: Bahrain News Agency
Press
Dailies: In Arabic, Akhbar al Khaleej (www.akhbar-alkhaleej.com), al Wasat (www.alwasatnews.com), al Ayam (www.alayam.com), al Meethaq (www.almeethaq.net) and al Waqt (www.alwaqt.com). In English the Bahrain Tribune (www.bahraintribune.com) and Gulf Daily News (www.gulf-daily-news.com). Bahrain Voice and Middle Xpress.
Weeklies: In Arabic, Layalina (www.layalinamag.com) and Sada al-Usbu'. In English, Gulf Weekly (www.gulfweekly.com), has general news and information.
Business: In Arabic, Akhbar al Khaleej (www.akhbar-alkhaleej.com) has a business section. In English, the online website Trade Arabia (www.tradearabia.com), has a comprehensive range of business information topics and a hard copy Gulf Industry in English and Arabic, concerning the petroleum industry.
Periodicals: In Arabic, Huna al Bahrain, published by the Ministry of Information. In English, Bahrain This Month (www.bahrainthismonth.com).
Broadcasting
The state-owned Bahrain Radio and Television Corporation (BRTC) (www.bahraintv.com) operates the national public broadcasting networks.
Radio: BRTC operates Radio Bahrain (www.radiobahrain.fm) over three wave lengths, in the English language, offering news and current affairs, popular music and classical music. The Radio Bahrain Second Programme broadcasts general and cultural programmes including sports events and the Qur'an in Arabic. There are other private radio stations including Voice FM (www.voicefmbahrain.com), and, via satellite, Radio Sawa Gulf (www.radiosawa.com) and Monte Carlo Doualiya (www.rmc-mo.com) broadcasting in Arabic and French.
Television: BRTC operates five channels. The private and independent Orbit Satellite Television and Radio Network (www.orbit.net) operates 48 channels in Arabic and English, by subscription. Residents also have access to hundreds of regional channels broadcasting via foreign satellite or cable TV companies.

Economy
Bahrain is the least wealthy of the six Gulf states. It has only a small hydrocarbon reserve, with production limited to 40,000 barrels per day. However Bahrain also has an oil refining industry and receives 50 per cent of the net output and revenue of Saudi Arabia's Abu Sa'afa offshore oilfield. GDP growth was 6.9 per cent in 2005, rising from 5.5 per cent in 2004. While oil revenue accounts for around 11 per cent of GDP, the banking and the financial sector accounts for almost 28 per cent.
The government has been active in ensuring that the economy has diversified away from being oil revenue driven, to a varied multi-industry economy. Bahrain is now a major Middle Eastern banking centre, with some 370 offshore banking units and is the leading Islamic financial centre, with the largest concentration of Islamic commercial, investment and leasing banks, as well as Islamic insurance (Takaful) companies. One of the world's largest aluminium smelting plants, with annual production of 843,000 tonnes was expanded in 2005 and now includes related factories and a rolling mill.
Large-scale tourist resorts and projects have become a significant source of revenue, with further development designed to attract greater regional tourism.
Infrastructure development has included a new port and expanded airport, strengthening Bahrain's position as a regional hub. The Economic Development Board (EDB) has been active in attracting foreign investment. Electricity and water production are being privatised.
Bahrain is a member of the WTO. To meet the demands of international competition the government has increased its spending on education and training for its young work force, a move also intended to bring down its relatively high unemployment rate of 15 per cent in 2005.
Bahrain is one of six members of the Gulf Co-operation Council (GCC), which aims at improving relations between members both economically and politically. The Unified Economic Agreement encourages the establishment of joint projects in agriculture, services and industry. There are moves to establish a customs union which will result in free trade between the members. The GCC is also committed to issuing a common currency by 2010, which may have the effect of changing the medium of oil transactions from the dollar to the new currency.

External trade
In 2005 the Greater Arab Free Trade Area (Gafta) was ratified by 17 members, including Bahrain, creating an Arab economic bloc. A customs union was established whereby tariffs within Gafta will be reduced by a percentage each year, until none remain.
The export of goods and services accounts for around 80 per cent of GDP. In the face of falling oil reserves the government switched its investment into processed aluminium which has become a major export commodity, while supporting many domestic downstream industries.
Imports
Main imports are crude oil, machinery, chemicals and foodstuffs.
Main sources: Japan (5.4 per cent total, 2006), Saudi Arabia (5.3 per cent).
Exports
Main exports are petroleum and related goods, aluminium and textiles.
Main destinations: Saudi Arabia (4.7 per cent of 2006 total goods exports), US (1.9 per cent), India (1.4 per cent).

Agriculture
Farming
The agricultural sector typically accounts for less than 1 per cent of GDP and employs 5 per cent of the workforce.
Apart from being a small island, development of agriculture is limited by labour shortages, lack of water and salinity of the soil. The major crop is alfalfa for animal fodder, although farmers produce modest amounts of crops including dates, watermelons, pomegranates, bananas,

potatoes, eggplants and tomatoes for the local market.
Government agricultural plans emphasise drainage to reduce salinity, improvement of the soil and new irrigation and cultivation techniques; experiments with hydroponics are also under way.
The land tenure system, under which over 60 per cent of cultivable land is held on three-year leases, discourages the stability needed for development.
The lack of grazing inhibits livestock production. One large dairy has annual milk production of 500,000 litres. Small dairy farmers, responsible for 15 per cent of production, have established a co-operative and constructed a milk pasteurising plant.
The estimated crop production for 2005 included: 40 tonnes (t) potatoes, 16,508mt dates, 730t bananas, 12t pulses, 950t citrus fruit, 130t grapes, 15,000t dates, 2,100t tomatoes, 350t treenuts, 22,010t fruit in total, 112t chillies & peppers, 1,149t onions 7,826t vegetables in total. The estimated livestock production included: 13,495t meat in total, 875t beef and veal, 83t camel meat, 1,557t lamb, 5,700t goat meat, 5,280t poultry, 4,950t eggs, 10,924t milk, 950t goatskins.

Fishing

The waters surrounding Bahrain have traditionally been rich, with more than 200 varieties of fish, many of which constitute a staple of the local diet. The discovery of oil in 1935 led to a steady decline in the fishing industry, which has been unable to meet domestic demand, noticeably since the 1970s. Moreover, pollution in the Gulf, since the 1980s, has increasingly threatened fish production and the shrimp industry.
Fish catches have dropped amid claims of illigal fishing, habitat destruction from land reclamation and environmental pollution that threatens overall fish stocks.
In 2004, the total marine fish catch was 7,851 tonnes and the total crustacean catch was 5,866 tonnes.

Industry and manufacturing

The industrial sector contributed 39.6 per cent of GDP in 2004, of which manufacturing was 10.8 per cent. The sector typically employs 34 per cent of the labour force.
Bahrain's most prominent non-oil industry is the Aluminium Bahrain (Alba) plant, which supplies various downstream manufacturing plants as well as the Gulf Aluminium Rolling Mill Company (Garmco). Aluminium exports are one of Bahrain's biggest earners as a result of increased world prices. Alba dominates the manufacturing sector with a production capacity of 500,000 tonnes per year. Alba commissioned its 450,000 tonnes per annum coke calcining plant and 41,000 cubic metres per day seawater desalination plant. This was the first plant of its kind in the Middle East. More than 50 per cent of the aluminium produced at Alba is sold on the local and regional market, while the remainder goes mainly to the Far East.
Export-oriented small- and medium-sized industries have been attracted to free industrial zones established at Mina Sulman, Ma'amir, Abu Gazal and North Sitra, which enjoy tax and duty incentives. Industries located in these areas include plastics, paper, steel-wool and wire-mesh producers, marine service industries, aluminium, asphalt, cable manufacturing, prefabricated building and furniture.
Iron and steel production is increasing. The Bahrain Ispat Company, under the control of the Indian Ispat Group (based in London), operates a plant with a capacity of 1.2 million tpy of iron briquettes produced from iron pellets.
Growth in industrial production fell to -0.2 per cent in 2004; whereas growth in 2003 was 2.9 per cent.

Tourism

Tourism is a major element of Bahrain's economic strategy of diversification to replace its depleted oil reserves. Bahrain is second only to Egypt in the number of arrivals, receiving over four million visitors each year. Around three-quarters of these come from neighbouring states, mainly Saudi Arabia and Kuwait, on short-term visits. The aim is to attract more visitors from the region, as well as from other markets. In addition to the existing causeway link with Saudi Arabia, a causeway to Qatar is scheduled to open in 2006. Bahrain is well-served with accommodation, leisure and conference facilities and continues to pursue an expansive infrastructure programme, involving private investment.
The sector is estimated to have accounted for 7.6 per cent of GDP in 2005 and provided 23.4 per cent of total employment. The revenues were estimated at US$2.1 billion or 19.5 per cent of export revenue in 2005, so its share of total capital investments at 4.2 per cent or US$54.2 million appears to be less than the government had planned.

Hydrocarbons

Oil accounts for more than 60 per cent of exports and around 65 per cent of government revenue; the government is attempting to diversify but the economy is heavily dependent on oil.
The Bahrain Petroleum Company has responsibility for all aspects of the oil industry including exploration, production, refining and distribution in both domestic and international markets.
Bahrain has 90 billion cubic metres (cum) of natural gas and produced 9.8 billion cum in 2004 – an increase of 1.4 per cent on 2003. With the imminent loss of all hydrocarbon reserves, Qatar has signed an agreement to supply Bahrain with natural gas in the future.
Bahrain does not produce or import coal.

Energy

Peak domestic demand for electricity rose to 1,600MW in 2005. The government has restricted the price, to users, at a rate set in 1992. Responding to the rise in demand, capacity was increased by 675MW from a combined cycle gas turbine generating station at al Hidd. There are three other power stations at Rifa, with a capacity of 700MW, Manama with 167MW and Sitra with 125MW.

Financial markets

Stock exchange

In 2005 Bahrain won the Financial Centre of the Future Award, in the Middle East and Africa Category. It has a solid reputation as an international financial hub.
Bahrain remains attractive as a result of a combination of factors, including its relative political stability, open and tax-free business climate, central geographical position, low costs, excellent communications and an accommodating government. The financial sector is one of the most diverse in the region and has the largest volume of transactions in the Middle East. The International Islamic Financial Market (IIFM) has attracted a number of major financial institutions to deal specifically in Sharia compliant deals.

Banking and insurance

There are more than 200 financial instiutions in Bahrain. The Bahrain Monetary Agency (BMA) has full regulations for its Islamic banking community.

Central bank

Bahrain Monetary Agency (BMA) is an independent judicial organisation and the central monetary institution.

Main financial centre

Manama

Time

GMT plus three hours

Geography

Bahrain is an archipelago of 33 islands. Only three of the islands are inhabited. The main island of Bahrain contains most of the population and is linked by a causeway to the island of Muharraq. Another causeway links Bahrain to Saudi Arabia.

Hemisphere

Northern

Climate

Summer temperatures are hot and humid, reaching 49 degrees Celsius (C) in the shade, while January, the coldest winter month, has temperatures ranging from 3 degrees C to 28 degrees C. Humidity, particularly on the coast, can be extreme. Between December and the end of March the climate is temperate, with temperatures ranging between 19–25 degrees C.

Dress codes

A lightweight suit or lightweight jacket and trousers are advised. A long-sleeved shirt with a tie should be worn at business and official meetings but a jacket need not be worn. Women should dress modestly. However, bikinis may be worn on certain beaches and at international hotel swimming pools. The dress code for women is less severe than in Saudi Arabia or some other Islamic countries.

Entry requirements

Passports

Passports are required by all.

Visa

Visas are required by all except nationals of Kuwait, Oman, Qatar, Saudi Arabia and the United Arab Emirates (UAE).

For details of requirements for business and tourist visas visit: www.bahrainembassy.org/visareq.html.

Tourist visas can be obtained on arrival at Bahrain airport, business visas must be applied for in advance. Journalists must make prior arrangements with the Ministry of Information.

Women arriving in Bahrain alone and without a visa could be refused entry. Lone female travellers are advised to obtain a visa before departure.

Prohibited entry

Israeli nationals or anyone holding a passport with an Israeli visa/stamp may be denied entry.

Currency advice/regulations

Any currency, including Bahraini, may be freely imported and exported.

Customs

Personal effects are duty free. The duty free allowance is 400 cigarettes or 50 cigars and two bottles of alcoholic beverages, for non-Muslim passengers only, and 227ml of perfume for personal use. Jewellery, drugs, firearms and ammunition are subject to import permits.

Prohibited imports

Pornographic and obscene literature and pictures, cultured or undrilled pearls, and goods of Israeli origin are prohibited.

Health (for visitors)

Medical services in Bahrain are of high quality with a good general hospital in Manama and modern health centres in smaller communities. Medical insurance is advised. Consultations are offered at the American Mission Hospital, 133 Isa Al-Kabeer Avenue, Manama (tel: 17-253-447; internet: www.amh.org.bh).

Mandatory precautions

Yellow fever certificate, for visitors arriving from infected areas.

Advisable precautions

Recommended immunisations are hepatitis A and B, polio, tetanus and typhoid. There is a risk of rabies.

Hotels

There are plenty of first class hotels. A 12 per cent service charge is usual. Major hotels and most restaurants are licensed.

Credit cards

All major credit cards are accepted.

Public holidays (national)

Fixed dates

1 Jan (New Year's Day), 16–17 Dec (National Day).

Variable dates

Eid al Adha (three days), Eid al Fitr (three days), Islamic New Year, Ashura, Prophet's Birthday.

Islamic year – 1429 (10 Jan 2008–28 Dec 2008): The Islamic year has 354 or 355 days, with the result that Muslim feasts advance by 10–12 days against the Gregorian calendar each year. Dates of the Muslim feasts vary according to sightings of the new moon, so cannot be forecast exactly.

Working hours

Thursday and Friday are weekly holidays. Regular hours are subject to change during the month of Ramadan. Some banks and businesses close on Saturday.

Banking

Sat–Wed: 0730–1200; Thu: 0730–1100; some branches are open three days weekly in the afternoon; some offshore banking units close on Sunday; 1000–1330 during Ramadan.

Business

Sat–Thu: 0800–1530 or 0800–1300, 1500–1730.

Government

Sat–Tue: 0700–1415; Wed: 0700–1400. During Ramadan government offices open 0930–1430.

Shops

Sat–Thu: 0830–1230, 1530–1830; large superstores are open Sat–Thu: 0800–1900; late opening Wed and Thu: 0800–1200, 1530–2130; some are open for a few hours on Fri in the Souk.

Telecommunications

Mobile/cell phones

GSM 900/1800 services are available throughout the country.

Electricity supply

230V 50 cycles AC everywhere except Awali, which has 120V 60 cycles; various types of plug fitting, normally three-pin flat.

Weights and measures

Metric system (local measures are also used).

Social customs/useful tips

Traditionally much time is spent in exchanging small talk at business meetings; embarking on business matters before the atmosphere is favourable may cause offence. Decisions are often taken by consensus, according to the Arabian tradition, rather than exclusively on the advantages and disadvantages of the case submitted. In business, it is essential to create a mood of trust and to be persistent even when the case is apparently lost. Always shake hands on meeting and leaving. You may find the handshake lasts longer than in the West, but this is a sign of friendship. If you have made a good impression, the handshake on departure will be longer than that on arrival.

Muslims pray five times a day although shops and offices do not close during prayer. Although alcohol is not forbidden by law, like pork, it is forbidden by Islam and should be consumed with discretion. It is polite to avoid eating, drinking or smoking in the presence of Muslims during daylight hours in the month of Ramadan (it is illegal to do so in public). Unless addressing members of the royal family normal Western forms of address and greeting are usual.

Everyone, including the visitor, is subject to sharia (Islamic law) although it is less rigorously applied than in some other Islamic countries.

Security

Visitors to Bahrain should keep in touch with developments in the Middle East as any increase in regional tension might affect travel advice.

It is advisable to avoid village areas, especially after dark. Local security precautions, religious and social sensitivities should be observed and respected.

Getting there

Air

National airline: Gulf Air (owned jointly with Oman).

International airport/s: Bahrain International, Muharraq (BAH), 6.5km north-east of city, with bar, restaurant, buffet, bank, shops, hotel reservations.

Airport tax: International departures BD3; not applicable for transit passengers.

Surface

Road: The Saudi-Bahrain Causeway links Bahrain, Saudi Arabia and Qatar.

Water: There are passenger ferries running between Iran and Bahrain; the trip takes about 16 hours each way. There is a port tax of BD3.

Main port/s: Mina Sulman, Mina Manama and Mina Muharraq.

Getting about

National transport

Road: Bahrain's road network is fairly good. There are good tarmac roads between centres, and six-lane highways form a ring road by-pass system for Manama and Muharraq.

Buses: A national bus company provides public transport throughout the populated areas of the country.

Rail: There are no railways in Bahrain.

Water: Dhow trips are arranged most weekends to sand bars and nearby islands from the old wharf (Mina Manama) on King Faisal Road. Boat trips to neighbouring islands are frequently arranged on Friday and publicised in the local press.

City transport

It is easy to cover both Manama and Muharraq on foot, though renting a car will make it easier to get to farther-flung locations.

Taxis: Taxis (with orange side wings and black-on-yellow number plates) are plentiful and fares are regulated. Fares are by meter and only vary when coming from the airport or when travelling by night. Taxis are readily available for the 6.5km journey from Bahrain International airport to Manama, for which there is a charge in addition to the meter reading. Recommended fares from the airport are displayed outside the arrivals terminal. Shared taxis or 'pick-ups' can be hailed from any bus stop. They do not use meters. Fares vary depending on the destination, but are lower than standard taxi fares. However, they can be very cramped and uncomfortable. The 'pick-ups' have white and orange number plates, and a yellow circle with the licence number in black painted on the driver's door.

Car hire

Insurance is compulsory and international driving licences must be validated at the Ministry of Interior Traffic Headquarters before use in Bahrain. Car hire firms are listed in the local telephone directory, and it is generally recommended to compare prices. Driving is on the right. Seatbelts are compulsory for both the driver and front seat passenger, and young children must be seated in the back. Road signs are in English and Arabic. The maximum speed limit on highways is 100kph, and on inner city roads it is generally between 50–80kph. If an accident occurs, the vehicle must not be moved until traffic police get to the scene.

BUSINESS DIRECTORY

The addresses listed below are a selection only. While World of Information makes every endeavour to check these addresses, we cannot guarantee that changes have not been made, especially to telephone numbers and area codes. We would welcome any corrections.

Telephone area codes

The international direct dialling code (IDD) for Bahrain is +973 followed by subscriber's number.

Useful telephone numbers

Emergency service: 999
Directory enquiries: 181
International enquiries: 191
International bookings: 151
Operator: 100
Time in Arabic: 141
Time in English: 140
Telephone faults: 121

Chambers of Commerce

Bahrain Chamber of Commerce and Industry, Bld 122, Road 1605, Block 216, PO Box 248, Manama (tel: 17-229-555; fax 17-224-985; email: bastaki @ bahrainchamber.org.bh; internet: www.bahrainchamber.org.bh/english/index.htm)

Banking

Ahli United Bank Bahrain, 126 Government Avenue, PO Box 5941, Manama (tel: 17-221-700; fax: 17-224-322; e-mail: info@ahliunited.com).

Al Baraka Islamic Bank, PO Box 1882, Manama (tel: 17-535-300; fax: 17-533-993; e-mail: baraka@batelco.com.bh).

Arab Banking Corporation, ABC Tower, Diplomatic Area, PO Box 5698, Manama (tel: 17-543-000; fax: 17-533-163; e-mail: webmaster@arabbanking.com; internet: www.arabbanking.com).

Bahrain Development Bank, PO Box 20501, Manama (tel: 17-537-007; fax: 17-534-005).

Bahrain Islamic Bank, Al Salam Tower, Diplomatic Area, PO Box 5240, Manama (tel: 17-535-888; fax: 17-535-707; e-mail: bahisi@batelco.com.bh).

Bahraini Saudi Bank, PO Box 1159, Manama (tel: 17-211-010; fax: 17-210-989; e-mail: helpdesk@bahrainisaudibank.com).

Bank of Bahrain & Kuwait, 43 Government Avenue, PO Box 597, Manama (tel: 17-223-388; fax: 17-229-822; e-mail: bbkonline@batelco.com.bh).

First Islamic Investment Bank EC, PO Box 1406, Manama (tel: 17-218-333; fax: 17-217-555).

Gulf International Bank, PO Box 1017, Al-Dowali Building, 3 Palace Avenue, Manama (tel: 17-534-000; fax: 17-522-633; e-mail: info@gibbah.com; internet site: http://www.gibonline.com).

National Bank of Bahrain , PO Box 106, Manama (tel: 17-228-800; fax: 17-228-998; e-mail: nbb@nbbonline.com).

TAIB Bank, Sehl Centre, Diplomatic Area, PO Box 20485, Manama (tel: 17-533-334; fax: 17-533-174; e-mail: taib@taib.com).

Central bank

Bahrain Monetary Agency, PO Box 27, Manama (tel: 17-535-535; fax: 17-533-342; e-mail: bmalbr@batelco.com.bh).

Travel information

Bahrain International Airport, PO Box 586, Manama (tel: 17-321-151; fax: 17-324-096).

Bahrain Tourism Company, PO Box 5831, Manama (tel: 17-534-321; fax: 17-531-353; e-mail: btc@alseyaha.com).

Gulf Air, PO Box 138, Manama (tel: 17-228-820; fax: 17-224-452).

Ministry of tourism

Tourism Affairs, Ministry of Information, PO Box 26613, Manama (tel: 17-201-203; fax: 17-211-717; e-mail: btour@bahraintourism.com).

Ministries

Ministry of Cabinet Affairs, PO Box 26141, Manama (tel: 17-731-544; fax: 17-731-863).

Ministry of Commerce and Industry, PO Box 5479, Manana (tel: 17-531-531; fax: 17-530-455; email: drmansoor@commerce.gov.bh; internet: www.commerce.gov.bh).

Ministry of Defence, PO Box 245, Manama (tel: 17-653-333; fax: 17-663-923).

Ministry of Education, PO Box 43, Manama (tel: 17-680-105; fax: 17-687-866).

Ministry of Electricity and Water, PO Box 2, Manama (tel: 17-546-666; fax: 17-533-035).

Ministry of Foreign Affairs, PO Box 547, Manama (tel: 17-227-555; fax: 17-212-603).

Ministry of Health, PO Box 12, Manama (tel: 17-255-555; fax: 17-252-569).

Ministry of Housing and Public Works, PO Box 5802, Manama (tel: 17-533-000; fax: 17-536-431).

Ministry of Information, PO Box 253, Manama (tel: 17-781-888; fax: 17-682-777).

Ministry of the Interior, PO Box 13, Manama (tel: 17-272-111; fax: 17-262-169).

Ministry of Justice and Islamic Affairs, PO Box 450, Manama (tel: 17-531-333; fax: 17-531-284).

Ministry of Labour and Social Affairs, PO Box 32333. Manama (tel: 17-687-800; fax: 17-686-954).

Ministry of Municipalities and Agriculture, PO Box 53, Manama (tel: 17-226-060; fax: 17-229-666).

Ministry of Oil, PO Box 1435, Manama (tel: 17-291-511; fax: 17-293-007).

Ministry of Transport, PO Box 10325, Manama (tel: 17-534-534; fax: 17-534-041).

Prime Minister's Office, PO Box 1000, Manama (tel: 17-200-000; fax: 17-532-839).

Other useful addresses

Aluminium Bahrain (Alba), PO Box 570, Manama (tel: 17-830-000; fax: 17-830-083; e-mail: alba@alba.com.bh).

Arabian Exhibition Management, PO Box 20200, Manama (tel: 17-550-033; fax: 17-553-288; aeminfo@batelco.com.bh).

Bahrain International Exhibition Centre, PO Box 11644, Manama (tel: 17-550-111; fax: 17-553-447; e-mail: biec@batelco.com.bh).

Bahrain National Gas Company (Banagas), PO Box 29099, Manama (tel: 17-756-222; fax: 17-756-991; e-mail: bng@banagas.com.bh).

Bahrain Petroleum Company (Bapco), PO Box 25555, Awali (tel: 17-704-040; fax: 17-704-070; e-mail: info@bapco.net).

Bahrain Stock Exchange, PO Box 3203, Manama (tel: 17-261-260; fax: 17-256-362; e-mail: info@bahrainstock.com).

Central Municipal Council, PO Box 53, Manama (tel: 17-276-060; fax: 17-263-666).

Consultative Council (Majlis al-Shura), PO Box 2991 Manama (tel: 17-714-422; fax: 17-715-715).

Customs Directorate, PO Box 15, Manama (tel: 17-725-333; fax: 17-725-534).

Ports Directorate, PO Box 453, Manama (tel: 17-725-555; fax: 17-725-534).

National news agency: Bahrain News Agency

Internet sites

Arab Net: www.arab.net

Arabia OnLine: www.arabia.com

Bahrain Economic Development Board: www.bahrainedb.com

Bahrain Financial Harbour: www.bfharbour.com/html.index.html

Bahrain Institute of Banking and Finance: www.bibf.com

Bahrain Ministry of Finance and National Economy: www.mofne.gov.bh

Bahrain Promotions and Marketing Board: www.bpmb.com

Gulf business explorer: www.igulf.com/main.htm

Bangladesh

KEY FACTS

Official name: Gana Prajatantri Bangladesh (People's Republic of Bangladesh)

Head of State: President Iajuddin Ahmed (sworn in 6 Sep 2002)

Head of government: Chief Adviser (acting) Fazlul Haque (from 11 Jan 2007)

Ruling party: There is no ruling party until elections are held later in 2007

Area: 143,998 square km

Population: 159.01 million (2007)*

Capital: Dhaka

Official language: Bengali (Bangla)

Currency: Taka (Tk) = 100 poisha

Exchange rate: Tk68.51 per US$ (Jul 2008)

GDP per capita: US$455 (2007)*

GDP real growth: 5.60% (2007)*

Labour force: 72.39 million (2004)

Unemployment: 40.00% (2004) (includes underemployment)

Inflation: 8.40% (2007)*

Balance of trade: -US$2.89 billion (2006)

Foreign debt: US$19.97 billion (2004)

Annual FDI: US$800.00 million (2005)

* estimated figure

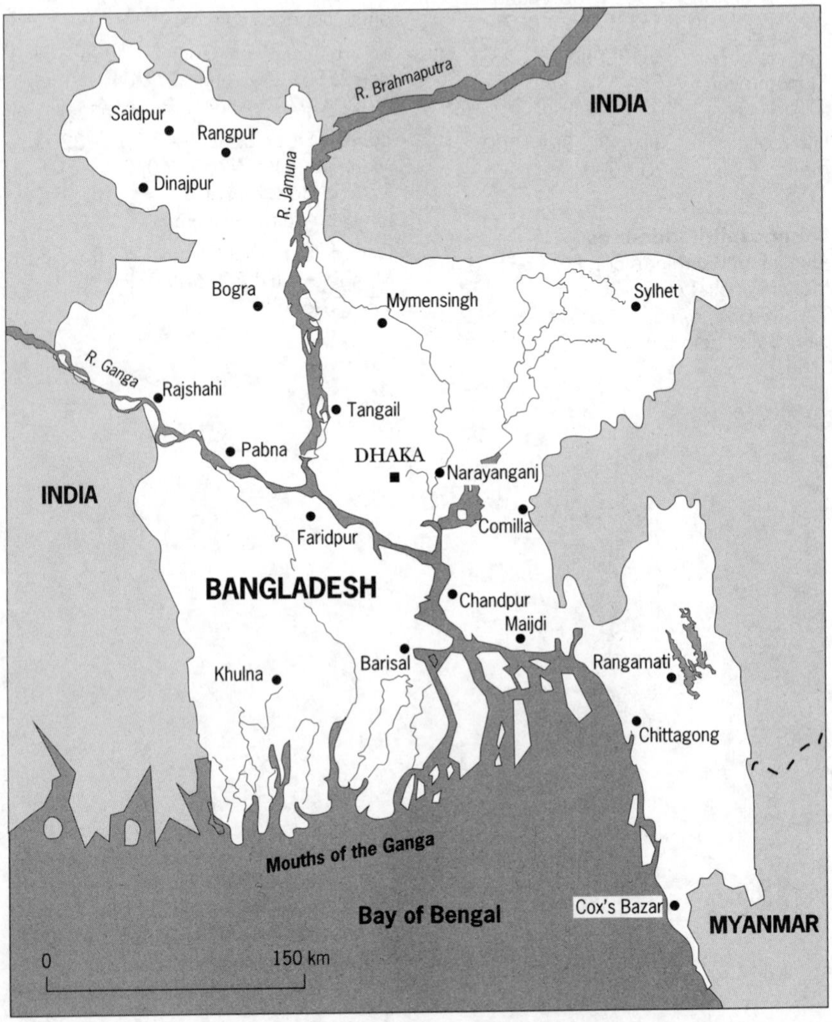

Bangladesh's vulnerability to cyclones and floods once again became apparent in late 2007, when cyclonic winds ripped in to the southern coastline. Thousands of people were killed by the storms, and several million found their homes destroyed, if not by the cyclone itself, by the flooding that followed. The International Red Cross (IRC) estimated the total death toll to be as high as 10,000. The effects would have been worse had it not been for Bangladesh's cyclone warning system and the cyclone shelters which gave refuge to some 1.5 million people.

GDP growth dips

Estimated annual GDP growth for the fiscal year (FY) 2008, which closes at the end of March 2008, is forecast to have dropped below the 6 per cent mark, inevitably affected by the cyclone and flooding. For the four years to 2006, Bangladesh's annual GDP growth had averaged more than 6 per cent, boosted by more market-oriented policies, the continued strength of the garment industry and buoyant overseas workers' remittances.

To achieve GDP growth of 6 per cent in the 2008 financial year as originally forecast by the Asian Development Bank (ADB) would have entailed something of a turnaround. The floods and cyclone damage, combined with the political uncertainty surrounding the army backed interim government all contributed to a climate of low business confidence. At the beginning of calendar year 2008 the government faced the daunting challenge of boosting business confidence while at the same time restoring flood and cyclone affected infrastructure and livelihoods.

Agricultural growth is obviously the biggest casualty of the flood damage. The ADB expected this to drop from 3.2 per cent in FY2007 to 2.4 per cent in 2008. Rice production in FY2008 is, however, expected to be close to the figure for 2007. The cyclonic flooding and resultant collateral damage caused substantial losses in the aman crop (a variety of rice grown July–December), estimated to have dropped to 9.6 million tons compared to 10.8 million tons for the year before. The extent of the losses incurred will depend to a significant degree on the size of the boro crop (another variety of rice grown under irrigation in the dry season from December–July). Traditionally the largest crop of the year, boro planting began in December 2007. To mitigate sharply rising international fertilizer prices, the government has introduced large subsidies to supply farmers at lower prices.

The fertilizer subsidies were part of wide ranging measures adopted by the government to assist and accelerate the recovery by ensuring supplies not only of fertilizer but of other key support items such as credit, diesel fuel and seeds. Overall credit increased to Tk45 billion (US$???) in the third quarter of FY2008, well up from the Tk28 million (US$???) for the same period of the preceding year. The general erosion of business confidence came at the same time as a slowdown in export demand for the garment industry. This caused manufacturing growth in medium and large scale industries to slow to 3.5 per cent in the first 5 months of FY2008. Small scale manufacturing, aimed principally at the domestic market, was less affected and grew at an annual rate of 8.1 per cent in the period April–June 2007. In the same period, growth in the power (electricity generation etc) sector was at an annual rate of 5.5 per cent. Loans to the industrial sector as a whole continued their strong growth, increasing by 42.3 per cent in the April–June 2007 period over the same period in 2006. Post cyclone and flooding re-generation should boost the construction sector, as will the Bangladesh Bank's lower rate for its housing re-financing scheme.

Competitive exports?

According to the ADB, Bangladesh's key competitive advantage in the vitally important garment industry has long been its cost advantage. This advantage, however, is being steadily eroded by other non-price items such as delivery times, quality and design. The expiry of the EU quota restriction on China also represents a major challenge; as does the introduction in 2007 of the US New Partnership Development Act (NPDA). In theory, the provisions of the NPDA legislation could provide a major export boost to Bangladesh, which currently sends 33 per cent of its exports to the US. The Act's removal of an average 15 per cent tariff on Bangladeshi garments could – according to one study – result in Bangladesh's exports to the US increasing by as much as US$500–1,000 million annually. However, to qualify for NPDA status, Bangladesh will have to meet a number of eligibility criteria with, inter alia, labour rights, conditions of work and health and safety measures featuring prominently on a long list. Achieving eligibility will mean investment in infrastructure, policy reforms and institutional changes.

Investor uncertainty

While laudable in their intention, the caretaker government's anti-corruption efforts have created some concern and uncertainty among investors. Investor uncertainty has focussed on whether the proposed reforms – which have resulted in the arrest of senior politicians from both major parties – would prove sustainable. The uncertainty resulted in lower levels of foreign direct investment (FDI), which in turn contributed to the dip in annual GDP growth in the first half of FY2008. Government economic policy also risked distortion as energy, in Bangladesh's case oil, prices rose inexorably throughout 2007 and into early 2008. By the end of 2007 government subsidies for diesel and kerosene products had risen to an estimated US$1.2 billion, representing 1.6 per cent of GDP. Continued subsidies at this level risked affecting the government's external and domestic balances, thereby reducing the funds available for social and infrastructure expenditure.

The fiscal deficit for fiscal year 2008 looked likely to rise to 4.7 per cent of GDP, well up on the 3.2 per cent of 2007. Improved tax collection and other reform measures have helped contain the figure, but energy and fertilizer subsidies continued to represent substantial challenges. None the less, in the period July 2007 to January 2008 revenue collection as a whole increased by some 25 per cent. Income tax collection went up by a massive 41.6 per cent for the period. Total exports in the third quarter of FY 2008 (October–December 2007) rose by 15.4 per cent, outpaced by imports which grew at an annual rate of 17.5 per cent. The rise in imports contributed to an increased trade

KEY INDICATORS — Bangladesh

	Unit	2003	2004	2005	2006	2007
Population	m	144.36	146.39	141.82	156.12	*159.01
Gross domestic product (GDP)	US$bn	51.90	56.84	61.28	64.85	*72.42
GDP per capita	US$	358	376	432	451	*455
GDP real growth	%	5.3	5.4	6.3	6.4	*5.6
Inflation	%	6.0	6.1	7.0	6.5	*8.4
Industrial output	% change	–	7.6	8.3	9.7	–
Agricultural output	% change	–	4.1	2.2	4.9	–
Natural gas output	bn cum	12.2	13.2	14.2	15.2	16.3
Exports (fob) (goods)	US$m	6,549.0	7,478.0	9,186.2	11,553.7	12,449.1
Imports (cif) (goods)	US$m	8,707.0	10,030.0	12,291.7	14,443.4	16,665.3
Balance of trade	US$m	-2,158.0	-2,552.0	-3,105.5	-2,889.7	-4,216.2
Current account	US$m	50.0	-670.0	-158.0	762.0	*334.0
Total reserves minus gold	US$m	2,577.9	3,172.4	2,767.2	3,805.6	5,183.4
Foreign exchange	US$m	2,574.4	3,170.9	2,766.0	3,803.9	5,182.2
Exchange rate	per US$	58.39	59.28	70.23	70.23	68.59

* estimated figure

deficit of US$2.1 billion for the period July–November 2007, up from US$1.2 billion for the same period in 2006. The cushion provided by workers' remittances, aid and other external assistance produced a modest overall surplus of US$368 million for the same period. Higher food prices and reduced domestic production both drove up inflation, to an annual 11.6 per cent in December 2007. The figure in July had been 10.1 per cent.

Interim government – for how long?

Bangladesh's army-backed interim government had assumed power in January 2007 following a period of extreme political confusion and deadlock. The outgoing Bangladesh National Party's government mandate had expired at the end of October 2006. The failure of the two main parties, the Bangladesh National Party (BNP) and the Awami League, to agree on the appointment of an election commissioner to take charge of government during the run-up to the elections originally scheduled for January 2007. Although a date – 21 January – had been set for the election, the former opposition party the Awami League and its allies had rejected the schedule, claiming that it had been announced without any of the promised electoral reforms being carried out. So complex and prone to dispute is the whole electoral process in Bangladesh that even the choice of a an election date is fraught with political danger. The 2007 election date had coincided with a time of general uncertainty in Bangladeshi politics. President Iajuddinn Amed had taken charge in October 2006 as chief adviser to the coalition government when the major political parties could not agree on anyone else to do the job. Under Bangladesh's constitution in the pre election period the president was supposed to be running a neutral administration. However, the Awami League and its allies claimed that the president was biased towards the BNP view. The first choice for election commissioner was forced out of office on similar charges.

The outgoing BNP government, lead by Begum Khaleda Zia, had to hand over power to a bi-partisan administration 90 days before the election. The former government's mandate had expired at the end of October 2006. Such were the tensions surrounding the political in-fighting that at least 6 people were reported killed and more than 2,000 wounded in riots in Dhaka.

War crimes

For the most part the caretaker government had maintained the outgoing BNP's established economic policies, and even accelerated some scheduled structural and sector reforms. However it was its anti-corruption drive that attracted most attention and was seen by many as a precursor to free and fair elections. As part of this process, the caretaker government has been under some pressure to prosecute those allegedly responsible for war crimes during Bangladesh's war of independence in 1971. This bitter conflict lasted only nine months, during which the Bengali speaking population of what was then called East Pakistan rose up against the Punjabi rulers of West Pakistan. West Pakistan and its appeal to Islamic unity received considerable support from East Pakistan's fundamentalist Islamic parties, notably the Jamaat e Islami, whose student wing was believed to be responsible for many atrocities. Jamaat e Islami later became Bangladesh's third largest political party (behind the BNP and the Awami League) and its leader Motiur Rahman Nizami is thought by many to be linked to war crime atrocities. Over 35 years after the war ended, in late 2007 there seemed to emerge a consensus between the army and Bangladesh's two major parties of the need for war crimes to be prosecuted. This is also thought to be motivated on the part of both the army and more moderate politicians on a desire to curb the activities of some of Bangladesh's more extremist religious parties.

The question remained whether it was down to the government or private individuals to initiate the appropriate legal action. Given the scale of some of the crimes, and the need to act quickly (given the age of some witnesses) some initiative began to appear likely. Jamaat e Islami is considered by many Bangladeshis to be an enemy of the state that had opposed the creation of Bangladesh as a nation in the first place and then continued to collaborate with its enemies.

Freedoms curtailed

Although many Bangladeshis at first welcomed the army controlled interim government, it soon became apparent that much was being sacrificed to the altar of stability. Elections were further postponed until late 2008 as – under emergency rules – the temporary government suspended parts of the country's constitution, making any criticism of the government a punishable offence. Political activities were radically curtailed, as was press freedom. Measures taken in the name of reform and anti-corruption have allegedly been unnecessarily extreme. The Directorate General of Forces Intelligence – known by its acronym of DGFI – has reportedly carried out both overt and covert actions against opposition parties and members of the media. The balance between the need to address rampant corruption and political paralysis while maintaining basic freedoms has not always been correctly observed by the authorities in what has become – if not a police state – then at least an army fiefdom.

Risk assessment

Economy	Fair
Politics	Poor
Regional stability	Fair

COUNTRY PROFILE

Historical profile

1200 The start of five-and-a-half centuries of Muslim rule over the region began with the Sultanate era.

1757 The region gradually came under the influence of British rule after the battle of Plassey.

1947 Named East Pakistan, Bangladesh became a province of Pakistan following the partition of India.

1949 The Awami League (AL) was established to campaign for East Pakistan's autonomy from West Pakistan.

1970 The AL, under Sheikh Mujibur Rahman, won the elections in East Pakistan, but West Pakistan refused to accept the result, resulting in civil unrest.

1971 The People's Republic of Bangladesh was unilaterally declared; a de facto secession from Pakistan followed the nine-month Indo-Pakistan war. Around 10 million Bangladeshis fled to India during the conflict.

1972 Sheikh Mujibur became prime minister and, in an attempt to improve living standards, began a programme of industrial nationalisation.

1974 Severe flooding destroyed much of the grain harvest. A state of a emergency was declared as political unrest grew. A famine killed 100,000 people as wealthy farmers hoarded food that the poor could not afford to buy.

1975 Sheikh Mujibur became president, but was assassinated in a military coup. Martial law was imposed following the coup.

1976 Elections were postponed indefinitely. General Zia ur Rahman took over the post of Chief Martial Law Administrator from President Sayem.

1977 General Zia assumed the presidency, amending the constitution, making Islam, instead of secularism, its first basic principle.

1978 General Zia won the first direct presidential election.

1979 Parliamentary elections were won by Zia's Bangladesh Jatiyatabadi Dal (Bangladesh Nationalist Party) (BNP). Martial law was repealed and the state of emergency revoked.
1981 General Zia was assassinated.
1982 General Ershad seized power in a bloodless coup. The country was placed under martial law as the constitution and political parties were suspended.
1983–86 The country remained unstable, with opposition groups demanding the resignation of Ershad and his government. Ershad imposed Islam on the education system and forced teachers to teach in Arabic. This led to social unrest, particularly among the non-Muslim minority.
1986 Martial law ended and constitutional government was revived. Ershad was elected to a five-year term.
1987 A state of emergency was imposed during a wave of strikes and opposition demonstrations.
1988 Islam became the state religion. Floods covered around 75 per cent of the land and millions of people were made homeless.
1990 Ershad resigned following mass protests which made the country ungovernable.
1991 Elections resulted in a victory for the BNP, led by Begum Khaleda Zia, the widow of General Zia; she became prime minister. Ershad was jailed for corruption and the illegal possession of weapons. The position of president was made ceremonial and executive power was given to the office of prime minister.
1996 After two decades of military and authoritarian rule, the AL, led by Sheikh Hasina (Sheikh Mujibur's daughter), won the election .
1998 Floods covered two-thirds of the country, causing many deaths. Fifteen former army officers were sentenced to death for their involvement in the assassination of President Mujibur.
2000 Sheikh Hasina spoke out against military regimes and the government expelled a Pakistani diplomat for denying that three million Bangladeshis were murdered by Pakistani forces in 1971. Diplomatic relations broke down between Bangladesh and Pakistan.
2001 There were violent clashes, strikes and a growth in Islamic fundamentalism in the build-up to parliamentary elections. The alliance led by Zia's BNP won a landslide victory. AQM Badruddoza Chowdhury was sworn in as president.
2002 Chowdhury resigned and Iajuddin Ahmed was elected as president by parliament in September.
2004 The AL called 21 general strikes in a campaign to force early elections, accusing the government of being corrupt. The constitution was amended to reserve 45 parliamentary seats for women. Floods in July covered two-thirds of the country, killing over 800 people. Sheikh Hasina survived a grenade attack that killed 22 people at a party rally.
2005 In January a senior AL politician, Shah AMS Kibria, was killed in a grenade attack. In February a ferry capsized near Dhaka and killed over 140 people. Bangladesh signed the South Asia Free Trade Agreement (Safta), due to come into effect on 1 January 2006. Bombings around the country in August and November blamed on Islamic militants.
2006 In February, the AL ended a year-long boycott of parliament. General strikes, called by the AL, brought the country to a standstill in April and June. Tension and violence continued in the lead-up to the end, in accordance with the constitution, of the government's five-year term of office in October; the choice of the head the non-party body, which assumed caretaker responsibilities until the January 2007 elections, was a major bone of contention. President Ahmed's solution was to take on the role as chief adviser himself.
2007 President Iajuddin Ahmed resigned as chief adviser and Fazlul Haque became acting chief adviser on 11 January after general elections due on 22 January were suspended and a state of emergency was imposed, as rioting broke out in protest. The suspended elections violate a constitutional requirement that elections be held within 90 days of the resignation of a government. The president announced that new voter lists were required to ensure elections were 'free, fair and credible'. In August severe monsoon flooding caused death and destruction and left an estimated one million people in urgent need of international aid.
2008 The first passenger train since 1965 began operations between Dhaka and Kolkata (India) on 14 April. The Electoral Commission announced on 22 July that it had completed the registration of voters, necessary for the general election to be held in the third week of December. Over 80 million people were recorded and 13 million names were removed from the previous, discredited list.

Political structure

Constitution

The constitution was enacted in 1972. It was suspended following the coup of 1982, restored in 1986, and has been amended several times.

In 1977, the constitution was amended making Islam, instead of secularism, its first basic principle.

The country has six political divisions: Dhaka, Chittagong, Rajshahi, Barisal, Sylhet and Khulna. These are further subdivided into districts, thanas (parish-level government) and villages.

Form of state

Parliamentary republic

The executive

The president, who is elected by the legislature for a five-year term, performs ceremonial functions. The president is also commander-in-chief of the armed forces. The cabinet is led by the prime minister, who is usually the leader of the ruling party. The elections are preceded by a 'caretaker' government which is supposed to have no political affiliation, in order to allow elections to be fought on an equal and fair basis.

Bangladesh's judiciary is separate from the executive – judges and magistrates are appointed by the Supreme Court.

National legislature

Legislative authority is vested in the Jatiya Sangsad (parliament), a unicameral legislature; 300 members are elected by popular vote from single territorial constituencies every five years.

Over and above the 300 directly elected members, the May 2004 constitutional amendment includes reservation of 45 seats for women (formerly 30 seats were reserved), on a proportional representation basis for the next 10 years.

Legal system

The judiciary is a civil court system based on the British model. The highest court of appeal is the appellate division of the Supreme Court.

Last elections

1 October 2001 (parliamentary); 5 September 2002 (presidential)

Results: Parliamentary: the four-party alliance led by Begum Khaleda Zia's Bangladesh Jatiyatabadi Dal (Bangladesh Nationalist Party) (BNP) won a landslide victory.

Presidential: Iajuddin Ahmed was elected by parliament.

Next elections

September 2007 (presidential); Third week of December 2008 (parliamentary).

Political parties

Ruling party

There is no ruling party until elections are held later in 2007

Main opposition party

Awami League (AL) (People's League)

Population

159.01 million (2007)*

Last census: January 2001: 123,151,246 (provisional)

Population density: 928 inhabitants per square km (ADB 2006). Urban population: 25 per cent of total (1995–2001).

Annual growth rate: 2.0 per cent 1994–2004 (WHO 2006)

Ethnic make-up
Bengalis (98 per cent) and Biharis. There are about one million tribal people, the majority of whom live in the Chittagong Hill Tracts in the east of the country. The tribes have distinct cultures of their own.
Religions
Islam (88 per cent), Hinduism (10 per cent), Buddhism and Christianity. Although Islam is the state religion, freedom of worship is guaranteed under the constitution.

Education
The investment in education amounts to 2.2 per cent of GDP.
In November 2003, the Asian Development Bank (ADB) announced it was leading the jointly financed Second Primary Education Development Program (PEDP-II), designed to reorganise primary education in Bangladesh, with a US$1.815 billion package, including US$654 million external financing, provided by, among others, 11 international donors. The programme will run over the six-year period 2004–09. The package includes a 32-year, US$100 million, loan. The objectives of PEDP-II are to raise standards in school governance, and teacher training, improve the quality of school buildings and enhance the accessibility of schooling for students, particularly those from poor families.
By 2004 nearly 18 million students were enrolled in over 78,000 primary level schools, in the world's largest primary education system. Bangladesh has gender parity and has strived to expand access to the very poor and disadvantaged, including those with special needs. Enrolment rates suggest that about four million primary school-aged children are absent from school and about one-third of children drop out before completing primary school; children in remote rural and tribal regions still have significantly less access to schooling. Despite Bangladesh's official policy of gender parity, gender differences in learning persist.
Micro level strategies for basic education in rural areas are being developed through concerted co-operation between local communities, NGOs, government, and international donors. The Bangladesh Rural Advancement Committee (Brac) has developed strategies for intense community participation, operating 35,000 schools, providing education to 1.2 million children with a strong emphasis on the recruitment of local female teachers. Schools operated by Brac have improved outcomes to state-run schools, with better life skills and higher transition to secondary schools. Satellite village schools linked with larger schools in the area bring education services to children living in remote parts of the country. International support in basic education helps combat the problem of child labour by giving incentives to educate children employed in industries.
Government programmes include free education for girls up to class 10 and stipends for female students; food-for-education; and the total literacy movement.
Madrasas (schools offering an Islamic education to Muslim boys and girls) have increased in number from 1,500 in 1970 to 8,000 in 2004. Hindus and Buddhists also receive religious education at institutes called Tol and Chatuspathi.
Literacy rate: 41 per cent adult rate; 50 per cent youth rate (15–24) (Unesco 2005).
Compulsory years: Six to 10
Enrolment rate: 98 per cent in primary education (2003) (ADB). Bangladesh aims to achieve universal primary school enrolment by 2015.
Pupils per teacher: 55 overall, and 67 in state schools (ADB 2003)

Health
Per capita total expenditure on health (2003) was US$68; of which per capita government spending was US$21, (WHO 2006).
In June 2003, the World Bank approved a US$300 million loan to implement the Poverty Reduction Strategy (PRS) and is taking a leading role in helping Bangladesh implement an integrated Health and Population Sector Programme. The focus is on nutrition, HIV/Aids and maternal and infant health.
In the past decade, the infant mortality rate has been reduced by half – a faster reduction than any other country. With the highest incidence of malnutrition in the world, Bangladesh has made great efforts to improve the nutritional status of women and children.
Primary health care facilities have been expanded throughout the country and are provided though government sponsored Union and Thana Health Complexes; secondary health care facilities are provided by District level hospitals, and tertiary health-care facilities through Medical College Hospitals, Post-graduate Institutes and specialised hospitals at divisional and national levels.
It is estimated that at least 1.2 million people are exposed to poisoning by naturally occurring arsenic in groundwater, and about 40 million of Bangladesh's 144 million people are considered at risk. Since 1993, experts have found that tube wells in more than half of Bangladesh's 64 districts (mainly in the south-western, middle and north-eastern parts of the country) are likely to be contaminated with arsenic. The effects may take as long a 14 years to become visible but treatment can be successful before levels of poison reaches a certain level.
A cheap filter, costing around US$4, was launched in 2002, which can process 25–30 litres of drinking water a day, enough for a family of five.
There were cases of polio reported to the World Health Organisation – Global Polio Eradication Initiative in 2006; the country had previously been free of the disease and its re-emergence was due to infected travellers.
HIV/Aids
The HIV prevalence rate among adults between is relatively low; the rates among high-risk groups are greater – sex workers 0.5 per cent and unregistered injecting drug uses 1.7 per cent (World Bank).
HIV prevalence: 0.03 per cent ages of 15-49
Life expectancy: 62 years, 2004 (WHO 2006)
Fertility rate/Maternal mortality rate: 3.2 births per woman, 2004 (WHO 2006); maternal deaths 440 per 100,000 live births (World Bank).
Birth rate/Death rate: 28 births and 8 deaths per 1,000 (World Bank)
Child (under 5 years) mortality rate (per 1,000): 46 per 1,000 live births (World Bank)
Head of population per physician: 0.26 physicians per 1,000 people, 2004 (WHO 2006)

Welfare
Over 67 million people live below the poverty line, and Bangladesh still has the highest incidence of poverty in South Asia; only India and China have higher numbers of poor. Added to which, Bangladesh has one of the highest density populations (roughly 800 people per square kilometre), however it has achieved near self sufficiency in food production and made good progress in improving natural disaster management and social safety nets. In the 2002/03 budget, an allowance of Tk125 each was given to 900,000 people, (up from a previous 600,000), deemed disadvantaged: orphans, retarded, very-old, widows, and deserted women.
The World Bank suggests that while economic development and lasting poverty reduction is being hampered by the absence of reliable power (an estimated 10 million rural households lack access to electricity), even poor households are eager to join community-based saving projects such as Safe Save, and the Social Investment Program Project designed to give the poor in remote areas access to decision-making processes through small-scale infrastructure and social assistance projects. Communities will be

expected to provide participation by contributing at least 15 per cent of the expenditure needed and donors the remaining 85 per cent.

Main cities

Dhaka (capital, estimated population 11.7 million (m) 2005), Chittagong (3.7m), Khulna (872,087), Rajshahi (712,400), Mymensingh (447,974), Narayanganj (522,321), Comilla (297,352), Rajshahi (647,545), Rangpur (318,014), Bogra (211,969), Nawabganj (225,991).

Languages spoken

Bengali (Bangla) is spoken by 95 per cent of the population. The remaining 5 per cent speak various tribal dialects.
English is widely spoken and understood within the business community.

Official language/s

Bengali (Bangla)

Media

The constitution guarantees freedom of the press but pressure by politicians and the police is often exerted on journalists, who are also targeted but Islamist and Maoist groups. The government influences media outlets through awarding or witholding official advertising revenue.

National news agency: Bangladesh Sangbad Sangstha (BSS)

Other news agencies: BDNEWS24: www.bdnews24.com

Press

Dailies: Most newspapers are privately-owned, diverse and can be outspoken, with a strong tradition of owner-editorship. Newspapers that are published in English target the educated urban readership.

In Bengali The Daily Ittefaq (www.ittefaq.com), Jugantor Daily News (http://jugantor.com), Prothom Alo (www.prothom-alo.com), Bhorer Kagoj (http://bhorerkagoj.net) and The Daily Inqilab (www.dailyinqilab.com). In English, The Bangladesh Today (www.thebangladeshtoday.com), The Daily Star (www.thedailystar.net), The Independent (theindependent-bd.com), Dhaka (www.dhaka.com), New Age (www.newagebd.com), New Nation (www.nation-online.com), The News Today (www.newstoday-bd.com).

Weeklies: In Bengali, Shaptahik2000 (www.shaptahik2000.com), Anannya (www.my-anannya.com), is a women's weekly, Jai Jai Din (www.jaijaidin.com), Unmad (www.homeviewbangladesh.com/unmad) is a satirical magazine and Weekly Amod (www.weeklyamod.com) comes from Chittagong. In English Dhaka Courier (www.dhakacourier.net) and Holiday (www.weeklyholiday.net) are news publications and Blitz (www.weeklyblitz.net) is a tabloid, Weekly Evidence (www.evidence-int.com) covers international news and comment.

Business: In English, The Financial Express (www.thefinancialexpress-bd.com), the Independent Bangladesh (www.independent-bangladesh.com) is in collaboration with The Daily Commercial Times from Chittagong.

Periodicals: In Bengali At Tahreek is an Islamic monthly publication. In English, Business info Bangladesh (www.bizbangladesh.com) is an annual trade and business directory.

Broadcasting

Radio: The state-owned broadcaster is Bangladesh Betar (www.betar.org.bd) with three national networks, A, B and C, as well as local stations, providing news, information, educational and cultural programmes as well as an external service in English, Hindi, Arabic, Urdu and Nepalese.

Private, commercial stations includes Radio Metrowave (www.metrowave-bd.com) Radio Foorti (www.proshikanet.com/radiofoorti), Radio Today (www.radiotodaybd.fm) and Capital FM (www.drivetimedhaka.com).

Television: The only terrestrial broadcaster is the national state-owned Bangladesh Television (BTV) (www.btv.com.bd). Other cable and satellite TV networks include Channel i (www.channel-i-tv.com), NTV (www.ntvbd.com), ATN Bangla (www.atnbangla.tv), RTV and Ekushey TV. ENB News (www.enbnewsbd.com) is a 24-hour news network.

Advertising

With illiteracy at around 50 per cent, radio, television and cinema advertising are primary sources of news and information. Newspapers accept advertising and some direct mail services are available. There are outdoor advertising sites in major towns.

Economy

The government is dedicated to reforms aimed at liberalising and stabilising the state-dominated economy to transform it into a market economy. Annual GDP growth was 5.8 per cent in 2005 and was expected to grow by 6.5 per cent in 2006. Inflation remains in single figures, rose by 7.0 per cent in 2005.

As part of macroeconomic reforms, tax administration and revenue collection have been targetted as necessary improvements. State-bank corporatisation has yet to be achieved although divestment will begin with the sale of government shares in the Rupali Bank. A reform in the foreign exchange regime has underpinned sustained growth in exports and remittances.

The economy is made up of a 52 per cent service sector, 20 per cent agriculture and 28 per cent industry, of which manufacturing provides 17 per cent of GDP. International trade was 38 per cent of GDP in 2006, when manufacturing was growing by over 10 per cent. Raw jute and leather are also significant export items.

One of Bangladesh's great resources is its huge workforce and rich farmland. The infrastructure, however, is vulnerable to typhoons and productive land is subject to recurring annual monsoon flooding. The high population density is a brake on development. Poverty rates are in decline, with improvements in healthcare and education triggering social improvement.

Government revenues rely on foreign aid, which contributes 40 per cent to total revenue figures. International financial institutions continue to urge the government to tackle obstacles to development but the main problem in attracting FDI is the crumbling infrastructure with little, if any, investment in ports, customs and trade-supporting utilities.

External trade

Bangladesh has regional trade agreements with all of its neighbours offering preferential conditions for trade. The textile and garment industry has remained a major export sector, with annual sales increased to the US by 22 per cent and by 34 per cent to the EU, in 2006. Bangladesh produces around 50 per cent of the world's supply of jute.

Imports

Main imports are manufactured goods, machinery and transport equipment, petroleum and petroleum products, chemicals and pharmaceuticals, cement, raw cotton, food, vegetable oil, fats and cereal crops.

Main sources: China (17.9 per cent total, 2006), India (12.6 per cent), Kuwait (8.0 per cent).

Exports

Main exports typically include jute manufactures and raw jute (over 20 per cent of total), garments, frozen fish and seafood, leather, ceramics and tea. There is a ban on the export of natural gas. /07/07

Main destinations: US (25.1 per cent of 2006 total goods exports), Germany (12.7 per cent), UK (9.9 per cent).

Agriculture

Farming

Agriculture dominates the economy and contributes around 20 per cent to GDP. It employs 66 per cent of the labour force and determines incomes and consumption for the vast majority of Bangladeshis.
Bangladesh is largely self-sufficient in food grains, although a food deficit may occur when weather conditions are adverse.

Rice is the principal crop, accounting for about 70 per cent of cropped land. Improvements in rice production have been achieved through research, which has produced high-yielding rice varieties, improved farming methods, greater use of fertiliser and more widespread irrigation. Agricultural employment increased with the use of high-yield rice, which is between 20 and 50 per cent more labour-intensive than traditional varieties. Other crops are pulses, wheat, jute, oil seeds, sugar cane, tea, spices, vegetables and fruit. The livestock sector contributes about 3 per cent to GDP.

The amount of cultivable land under irrigation has increased to about 35 per cent. Much of the land is broken into tiny plots. Farms of less than one acre account for about 40 per cent, while about 5 per cent of farm households own and operate more than 25 per cent of agricultural land. The government leases farm machinery to groups of farmers forming co-operatives and increasing farm sizes.

Bangladesh is the world's largest exporter of raw jute and jute goods, amounting to around half of the world shipments. The jute industry has been restructured and modernised with aid from the World Bank.

About 2 per cent of the world's tea is grown in Bangladesh on some 150 plantations in the north-east region of Sylhet. After meeting domestic demand, a significant amount is exported to other Asian countries and Europe.

The estimated crop production in 2005 included 40,054,000 tonnes rice, 4,000,000t cassava, 1,200,000t wheat, 3,908,000t potatoes, 6,500,000t sugar cane, 320,000t sweet potatoes, 800,000t jute, 700,000t bananas, 225,000t rapeseed (canola), 243,000t mangoes, 138,000t allspice, 48,000t ginger, 122,000t lentils, 352,000t pulses, 103,000t tomatoes, 55,627t tea, 39,000t tobacco, 49,000t citrus fruit, 146,170t oilcrops, 45,000t seed cotton, 1,684,100t fruit in total, 2,097,000t vegetables in total. Estimated livestock production included 448,600t meat in total, 180,000t beef, 3,600t buffalo meat, 137,000t goat meat, 116,000t poultry, 160,500t eggs, 2,263,930t milk, 41,800t goatskins, 30,600t cattle hides

Fishing

Fishing has been identified by the government as a rapidly growing sector with increased production, which could generate revenue and foreign earnings while improving local nutrition. The sector has grown by 8 per cent per year since 1996 and contributes 3.3 per cent to GDP and directly employs around 1.3 million people. The typical annual catch is over 1.7 million tonnes.

Development by government, NGOs and private initiatives include: new hatcheries, extensive marine fisheries in the Bay of Bengal, south of the country, supporting infrastructure and training programmes. In 2004, the total marine fish catch was 233,881 tonnes and the total crustacean catch was 36,488 tonnes.

Forestry

Bangladesh's total forest cover is estimated at 1.3 million hectares. The forestry sector typically contributes about 2.5 per cent to GDP, providing raw materials for the construction industry.

Bangladesh is one of the world's most densely populated countries and, as a consequence, its forests are subject to heavy demand pressures, both in wood production and competing land uses. An estimated 80 per cent of wood production is used for fuel; most of the remainder is converted to sawnwood. Coastal forests comprise mangroves, which account for nearly half of total forest cover, and bamboo. Inland valley forests comprise sal, gamari, chaplish, telsu, jarui, teak, garjan, chandon and sundari.

Industry and manufacturing

The industrial sector accounts for around 26 per cent of GDP and employs 10 per cent of the workforce. Some 40 per cent of industrial capacity is publicly-owned, mostly in jute and textile milling, steel and chemical production. Around one-third of fixed assets in manufacturing enterprises are held by the public sector, but account for less than 10 per cent of output. The main activities are jute processing, contributing around 15 per cent to gross manufacturing output, and cotton spinning and weaving.

The garment industry, which is the principal exporter, grew rapidly during the 1990s, helped by economic liberalisation, fiscal incentives and a relatively disciplined workforce. It is the largest industrial employer, with about 1.5 million workers. Other industries include leather goods, newsprint, cement, refined sugar, beverages, pharmaceuticals, electronic components and fertilisers. The US$510 million fertiliser plant in Chittagong exports 500 tonnes of ammonia and 1,725 tonnes of urea a day, mainly to India and China; earnings are estimated at US$100 million a year.

Bangladesh has established export processing zones in Chittagong, Dhaka, and Gazipur. Improving the efficiency and flexibility of labour and the financial markets and public enterprise reform will be critical for the performance of the industrial sector.

Long-term financing is virtually impossible to obtain and few companies have access to overseas financing, resulting in only modest growth in the industrial sector, the garments industry aside. Low wage rates, labour and an entrepreneurial society make the country an ideal manufacturing base, although poor infrastructure, high tariffs, corruption and bad governance still need to be addressed. Power constraints are also cited as a reason for low investment, although the government has opened the energy sector to private and foreign investment.

Tourism

Tourism is undeveloped in Bangladesh. The government recognised the potential of the sector in the early 1990s, but promotion has been minimal. Bangladesh's proneness to natural disasters, especially flooding, is a disadvantage. The 11 September 2001 terrorist attacks in the US, the ensuing Afghan war and the Sars scare in 2003 adversely affected the sector. Of around 200,000 visitors, only a fifth are holiday-makers.

Environment

A ban exists on the production and use of polythene bags which have caused serious problems blocking the drainage system.

Mining

The 550km of coastline hold large resources of beachsands with rare mineral deposits spread over 17 areas containing monazite, ilmenite, zircon, rutile and magnetite. There are large limestone deposits, which are used to produce cement. The Jaipurhat Limestone Mining and Cement Works extracts one million tonnes per year of limestone to operate the plant. Other mineral resources include peat, white clay and mineral-bearing sands. The general trend of government incentives to foreign investors, including share holding and private investment in exploration activities, is likely to develop the mining sector.

Hydrocarbons

Bangladesh has oil reserves of 57 million barrels and produces around 6,200 barrels per day (bpd) of oil. The breakdown of the monopoly of the state oil and gas company, Petrobangla, sparked foreign interest and has in recent years resulted in the arrival of several foreign oil companies.

Bangladesh has proven natural gas reserves of 374.7 billion cubic metres (cum)and produces around 11 billion cum per year.

The large gas reserves and Bangladesh's proximity to the potentially huge energy market in India has resulted in a wave of energy companies. Bangladesh could also become a major natural gas transit corridor, linking India's easternmost states with West Bengal.

An adequate regulatory framework is required. Bangladesh has been ill-equipped to cope with even the bidding round for the remaining gas and oil blocs. This deficiency would need to be addressed to ensure increased certainty in investments. Bangladesh's coal reserves remained unexploited until recently. The Barapukuria coal mine in north-west Bangladesh, the first major coal mine was opened in April 2003. The mine has a production capacity of one million tonnes per annum, which will be mainly used for electricity generation.

Energy

Bangladesh has an electricity generation capacity of 3.8GW, 87 per cent of which is generated by natural gas and the remainder by oil and hydro-power.

The electricity generation and distribution sectors have deteriorated while demand has grown. Plant efficiency is low, power supply is erratic and electricity theft is widespread. Blackouts are common, putting a severe strain on industry. The sector is faced with a severe shortage of funds and investment needed to maintain and improve the electricity sector's infrastructure. The government's Power System Master Plan (PSMP) projects a required doubling of electric generating capacity between 2000 and 2010 to keep up with demand. The government aims for universal electrification by 2020.

Financial markets

Stock exchange

There has been an equity market in Bangladesh since colonial times. There are small, long-established, stock exchanges in Dhaka and Chittagong. However, their size and lack of liquidity means that foreign interest is minimal. Total market capitalisation is less than 1 per cent of GDP. The market is also too small to appear in the Morgan Stanley indices and this further restricts interest from investors. Eleven private commercial banks and six leasing companies are due to go public in 2004. This should broaden the market's capital base and boost investor interest in equities.

Banking and insurance

The banking system dominates the financial sector, accounting for about 97 per cent of the market in terms of assets.

There are four nationalised commercial banks, six development banks, 27 private banks and 19 non-bank financial institutions. The four nationalised commercial banks have consistently accounted for over 60 per cent of assets since the mid-1990s, while private domestic banks account for about 32 per cent, and foreign banks for the remaining 6–7 per cent.

Successive Bangladeshi governments have failed to address the inefficiencies and mis-allocation of funds by the state-owned banks. The government's emphasis on private sector led growth, if implemented, requires the development of a more efficient, transparent financial sector. Development of a properly regulated banking system is one priority in this regard, the equity market is another.

Central bank

Bangladesh Bank

Main financial centre

Dhaka

Time

GMT plus six hours

Geography

Bangladesh is bordered mostly by India except for a short border with Myanmar to the south-east. The Bay of Bengal washes the southern edge of the country. The Ganges (Padma) and Brahmaputra (Jamuna) rivers flow from the Himalayas into the Bay of Bengal and each river has a massive and ever-changing delta system where they meet the sea. The silt deposits from these rivers have created a vast alluvial plain where the soils are among the most agriculturally rich in the world. Apart from some hills around Aylhet in the north-east and the Chittagong Hills in the south-east, the country is flat and low-lying, and is criss-crossed by numerous waterways.

Hemisphere

Northern

Climate

Bangladesh has a sub-tropical monsoon climate and is dominated by the seasonally-reversing monsoons. There are three main seasons: winter (November–February) with an average temperature of 19 degrees Celsius (C); summer (March–May) when the average temperature is 29 degrees C and the climate is remarkably equable; and monsoon (June–October) which is humid and warm and accounts for 80 per cent of the country's annual rainfall of 1,200–3,500mm. It is normal for monsoon floods to cover around one-third of the country each year.

Dress codes

Lightweight cottons and linens are suitable during all seasons except winter when warm clothing is required.

Most Bangladeshis wear traditional dress: lungi (sarong) and kurta (loose shirt) for men and sari for women. However, urban and professional men prefer Western clothes: trousers, suits and ties; very few women wear skirts.There is no recognised national dress, but at official functions, Bengali men are expected to wear a closed collar jacket and trousers; for less formal occasions, safari suits are popular.

Visiting businessmen should wear a lightweight or tropical suit and tie, and women should dress modestly.

Entry requirements

Passports

Required for nationals of all countries. Passports must be valid three months beyond the intended length of stay. A return ticket is required.

Visa

Required by nationals of most countries, with the exception of a number of Commonwealth countries and several others (for a list of exemptions, see www.bangladeshhighcommission.org.uk). Applications for business and tourist visas must be accompanied by a letter of invitation or other specified documentation (see www.bangladeshhighcommission.org.uk).

Prohibited entry

Nationals of Israel

Currency advice/regulations

The import and export of local currency is limited to Tk500. The import of foreign currency is allowed but amounts greater than US$3,000 must be declared on arrival. The export of foreign currency is limited to US$3,000 or the amount declared on arrival.

All foreign currency exchanged must be entered on a currency declaration form. Travellers cheques can be exchanged on arrival at Dhaka Airport. To avoid additional exchange rate charges, it is advisable to take travellers cheques in US dollars or UK pounds sterling.

Customs

Personal effects duty-free provided they are declared on entry.

Prohibited imports

Firearms and some animals.

Health (for visitors)

Health regulations may change and it is advisable to make detailed enquiries before travelling.

Mandatory precautions

A vaccination certificate is required for yellow fever if travelling from an infected area.

Advisable precautions

Immunisations are recommended for tetanus, typhoid, polio and hepatitis A. In some circumstances, immunisations for hepatitis B and Japanese B encephalitis are advisable – seek medical advice. Malaria prophylaxis is recommended for areas outside Dhaka. There is a rabies risk. Water and food precautioons should be observed.

Hotels

Hotel bills must be paid in a major convertible currency or with travellers cheques.

Provincial towns have government rest-houses with fairly Spartan accommodation, for which booking well in advance is advisable.

Credit cards
Credit cards are accepted. There is limited acceptance of Mastercard, Diners Club and American Express outside Dhaka.

Public holidays (national)
Fixed dates
1 Jan (New Year's Day), 21 Feb (Shaheed Day), 26 Mar (National Day), 14 Apr (Bengali New Year), 1 May (Labour Day), 7 Nov (National Revolution Day), 16 Dec (Victory Day), 25 Dec (Christmas Day), 26 Dec (Boxing Day), 31 Dec (New Year's Eve).
Variable dates
Eid al Adha, Islamic New Year, Birth of the Prophet, July Bank Holiday (first Mon in Jul), Ascent of the Prophet, Shab e-Qadr, Eid al Fitr.
Islamic year – 1429 (10 Jan 2008–28 Dec 2008): The Islamic year contains 354 or 355 days, with the result that Muslim feasts advance by 10–12 days against the Gregorian calendar. Dates of feasts vary according to the sighting of the new moon, so cannot be forecast exactly.

Working hours
Banking
Sun—Wed: 0900–1500; Thur: 0900–1300.
Business
Sunday–Thursday: 0900–1700.
Government
Sunday–Thursday: 0900–1700.
Shops
Saturday–Thursday: 0900–2000; Friday 0900–1230; 1400—2000.

Telecommunications
Mobile/cell phones
The use of mobile phones is extremely limited.

Electricity supply
220V AC, 50 Hz with British-type 2 or 3 round pin plug fittings.

Weights and measures
Metric system

Social customs/useful tips
Normal Muslim customs predominate. Food and drink should be proffered with the right hand only. It is offensive to drink, eat or smoke in public or in the presence of Muslims during the month of Ramadan. Pork is considered unclean. However, alcohol is not prohibited and is available. Muslim women should not be photographed unless it is certain that no objection will be made. Females are expected to dress soberly and act discreetly. If travelling without a man, women sit together at the front of the bus.

People are usually warm and informal and do not hesitate to invite foreigners to their homes.
Gratuities in restaurants are around 10 per cent and 5 per cent for taxis.

Security
Thieving, armed robbery and kidnapping are a threat. Caution should be exercised when moving around, including in choice of transport. Ostentatious displays of wealth such as money, watches and cameras should be avoided.

Getting there
Air
National airline: Biman Bangladesh Airlines
International airport/s: Zia International (DAC), 20km north of Dhaka, with VIP lounge, duty-free shop, bank, post office, restaurant and car hire; Patenga (CGP), 22km from Chittagong.
Other airport/s: Sylhet (ZYL), in the north-east of the country catering for visitors to the highlands of Sylhet.
Airport tax: Tk300 for all passengers, excluding those under two-years-old and immediate transit passengers.
Surface
Road: It is possible to travel by road from a number of points in India, including West Bengal, Assam and Tripura. Travel may be difficult during monsoon seasons.
Main port/s: Chittagong, Chalna.

Getting about
National transport
Transport links in Bangladesh are often slow and prone to disruption by bad weather. Allow time for delays.
Air: There are regular daily flights between main centres operated by Air Parabat. Biman Bangladesh also serves main centres.
There are regional airports at Barisal, Jessore, Saidpur, Sylhet, Cox's Bazar, Thakurgaon and Rajshahi. Local storms can disrupt schedules.
Road: Bangladesh has an extensive road system, but does not have the capacity to deal with the amount of traffic. An estimated 7 per cent of roads are paved, and around half are metalled. Travel on roads during the monsoon season is difficult. The 4.8km long road/rail bridge across the Jamuna River links the eastern and western parts of the country. Numerous ferry crossings sometimes make journey times unpredictable.
Buses: There are express buses and local ones which stop en route. The latter charge around 25 per cent less, but are slow. In remote areas local buses are often the only means of transport.
Rail: About one-third of Bangladesh is serviced by railways. Inter City (IC) trains are frequent, clean and reasonably punctual, especially in the eastern zone, although they may be relatively slow. Six classes of rail travel are available: 'first' and 'express' are recommended for air-conditioned coaches that also provide more room.
Water: The river is the traditional means of transport. There are 8,000km of navigable waterways, although flooding in the monsoon season, silting in the dry season, and fogs may make routes inaccessible. The main routes are covered by the Bangladesh Inland Waterway Transport Corporation (BIWTC), but there are many private companies operating on shorter routes. Passage should be booked well in advance.
City transport
Taxis: Taxis, generally identifiable by their black body and yellow top, are few and far between in Dhaka; they are available at main hotels and airports. Negotiate fares before travelling. A 10 per cent service charge is usual.
It is probably best to organise a car from the hotel for the 20km trip from Dhaka Zia International Airport; journey time is 30 minutes.
Rickshaws and autorickshaws are available, but are not recommended for use at night. Autorickshaws should be metered, but often are not. Negotiate fares in advance.
Buses, trams & metro: Buses are generally overcrowded and unreliable.
Car hire
There are a number of private car hire companies in Dhaka and other cities. The Bangladesh Parjatan Corporation (BPC), the government tourism organisation, has a fleet of air-conditioned and non air-conditioned cars, microbuses and jeeps for hire. The BPC also offers a transfer service for tourists between Dhaka airport and the city centre and main hotels. Driving is on the left. A national licence or international driving permit is required.

BUSINESS DIRECTORY

The addresses listed below are a selection only. While World of Information makes every endeavour to check these addresses, we cannot guarantee that changes have not been made, especially to telephone numbers and area codes. We would welcome any corrections.

Telephone area codes
The international direct dialling code (IDD) for Bangladesh is + 880, followed by area code and subscriber's number:

Bagerhat	401	Khulna	41
Barisal	431	Kushtia	71
Bogra	51	Moulvi Bazar	861
Chittagong	31	Mymensingh	91
Comilla	81	Narayanganj	671
Dhaka	2	Patvakhali	441

Dinajpur	531	Rajshashi	721
Jamalpur	981	Sylhet	821

Useful telephone numbers
Police: 866-551/3.
Fire: 9-555-5555.
Ambulance: 112.

Chambers of Commerce

American Chamber of Commerce in Bangladesh, Dhaka Sheraton Hotel, 1 Minto Road, Dhaka 1000 (tel: 861-3391; fax: 831-2915; e-mail: amcham@bangla.net).

Chittagong Chamber of Commerce and Industry, Agrabad Commercial Area, Chittagong (tel: 711-355; fax: 710-183; e-mail: ccci@globalctg.net).

Dhaka Chamber of Commerce and Industry, 65 Motijheel Commercial Area, Dhaka 1000 (tel: 955-2562; fax: 956-0830; e-mail: dcci@bangla.net).

Federation of Bangladesh Chambers of Commerce and Industry, 60 Motijheel Commercial Area, Dhaka 1000 (tel: 956-0102; fax: 861-3213; e-mail: fbcci@bol-online.com).

Foreign Investors Chamber of Commerce and Industry, 35-1 Purana Paltan Line, Inner Circular Road, Dhaka 1000 (tel: 831-9448; fax: 831-9449; e-mail: ficci@bangla.net).

Khulna Chamber of Commerce and Industry, 5 KDA Commercial Area, Khan-A-Sabur Road, Khulna (tel: 721-695; fax: 731-213).

Metropolitan Chamber of Commerce and Industry, 122 Motijheel Commercial Area, Dhaka 1000 (tel: 956-5208; fax: 956-5212; e-mail: sg@citechco.net).

Banking

Agrani Bank, Agrani Bank Building, 9D Motijheel Commercial Area, Dhaka 1000 (tel: 956-6160; fax: 956-2346).

Arab Bangladesh Bank, BCIC Bhaban, 30-31 Dilkusha Commercial Area, Dhaka 1000 (tel: 956-0312; fax 956-4122).

Bangladesh Krishi Bank (Agricultural Bank), 83-85 Motijheel Commercial Area, Dhaka 100 (tel: 956-0021; fax: 867-102).

Bangladesh Shilpa Bank (Industrial Bank), PO Box 975, 8 Rajuk Avenue, Dhaka (tel: 955-8326; fax: 956-2061).

Banque Indosuez, 47 Motijheel Commercial Area, Dhaka 1000 (tel: 956-6566; fax: 956-5707).

Citibank N A, Chamber Building, 122-124 Motijheel Commercial Area, Dhaka 1000 (tel: 955-0061; fax: 956-2236).

Dutch-Bangla Bank Limited, Sena Kalyan Bhaban, 195 Motijheel Commercial Area, Dhaka 1000 (tel: 956-8537, 956-8542-44; fax: 956-1889; e-mail: dbbl@bdmail.net).

Grameen Bank, Grameen Bank Bhaban, Mirpur, Section-2, Dhaka-1216, Bangladesh (tel: 900-5256; e-mail: grameen.bank@grameen.net).

Hongkong & Shanghai Banking Corporation, Anchor Tower, 1.1-B Sonargaon Road, Dhaka 1205 (tel: 966-0536; fax: 966-0554).

International Finance Investment and Commercial Bank, BSB Building, 8 Rajuk Avenue, Dhaka 1000.

Islam Bank Bangladesh, PO Box 233, Islami Bank Tower, 40 Dilkusha Commercial Area, Dhaka 1000 (tel: 956-3182; fax: 956-4532).

Janata Bank, Janata Bhadan, 110 Motijheel Commercial Area, PO Box 468, Dhaka 1000 (tel: 956-000; fax: 956-4644).

National Bank Limited, 18 Dilkusha Commercial Area, Dhaka 1000 (tel: 956-3081/5; fax: 956-3953; e-mail: nblho@citechco.net).

Pubali Bank Ltd, 26 Dikusha Commercial Area, Dhaka 1000 (tel: 956-9050; fax: 956-4009).

Rupali Bank Ltd, 34 Dilkusha Commercial Area, Dhaka 1000 (tel: 955-1624; fax: 956-4148).

Sonali Bank, Motijheel Commercial Area, PO Box 147, Dhaka 1000 (tel: 955-0426; fax: 956-1410).

Standard Chartered Bank, 18-20 Motijheel Commercial Area, Dhaka 1000 (tel: 956-1465; fax: 956-1758).

United Commercial Bank, 60 Motijheel Commercial Area, Dhaka 1000.

Uttara Bank, 90 Motijheel Commercial Area, Dhakar 1000 (tel: 955-1162; fax: 863-539).

Central bank

Bangladesh Bank, Motijheel Commercial Area, PO Box 325, Dhaka 1000 (tel: 956-6203; fax: 956-6212; e-mail: banglabank@bangla.net).

Travel information

Automobile Association of Bangladesh, 3/B Outer Circular Road, Dhaka 17 (tel: 402-241).

Biman Bangladesh Airlines, Biman Bhaban, 100 Motijheel Commercial Area, Dhaka 1000 (tel: 240-151/90; fax: 863-005); airport (tel: 894-771/79); flight enquiries (tel: 894-350, 894-870).

Railway enquiries (tel: 409-686).

National tourist organisation offices

Bangladesh Parjatan Corporation, 233 Airport Road, Tejgaon, Dhaka 1215 (tel: 811-7855; fax: 812-6501; e-mail: bpcho@bangla.net).

Ministries

Ministry of Agriculture, Bangladesh Secretariat, Dhaka 1000 (tel: 869-277; fax: 867-040).

Ministry of Civil Aviation and Tourism, Bangladesh Secretariat, Dhaka 1000 (tel: 867-244; fax: 869-206).

Ministry of Commerce, Bangladesh Secretariat, Dhaka 1000 (tel: 869-679; fax: 865-741).

Ministry of Communications, Bangladesh Secretariat, Dhaka 1000 (tel: 864-977; fax: 866-636).

Ministry of Cultural Affairs, Bangladesh Secretariat, Dhaka 1000 (tel: 868-977; fax: 860-290).

Ministry of Defence, Ganabhaban Complex, Sher-e-Bangla Nagar, Dhaka 1207 (tel: 816-955; fax: 817-945).

Ministry of Disaster Management & Relief, Bangladesh Secretariat, Dhaka 1000 (tel: 868-744; fax: 869-623).

Ministry of Education, Bangladesh Secretariat, Dhaka 1000 (tel: 868-711; fax: 867-577).

Ministry of Energy and Mineral Resources, Bangladesh Secretariat, Dhaka 1000 (tel: 866-188; fax: 861-110).

Ministry of Environment & Forest, Bangladesh Secretariat, Dhaka 1000 (tel: 860-587; fax: 869-210).

Ministry of Finance, Finance Division, Bangladesh Secretariat, Dhaka 1000 (tel: 860-406; fax: 865-581).

Ministry of Fisheries and Livestock, Bangladesh Secretariat, Dhaka 1000 (tel: 864-700).

Ministry of Food, Bangladesh Secretariat, Dhaka 1000 (tel: 862-240; fax: 860-762).

Ministry of Foreign Affairs, Foreign Affairs Building, Segunbagicha, Dhaka 1000 (tel: 955-6020; fax: 956-2557).

Ministry of Health & Family Welfare, Bangladesh Secretariat, Dhaka 1000 (tel: 866-975; fax: 869-077).

Ministry of Home Affairs, Bangladesh Secretariat, Dhaka 1000 (tel: 864-611; fax: 869-667).

Ministry of Industries, Shilpa Bhaban, 91 Motijheel Commercial Area, Dhaka 1000 (tel: 956-3549; fax: 956-3553).

Ministry of Information, Bangladesh Secretariate, Dhaka 1000 (tel: 868-555; fax: 862-211).

Ministry of Jute, Bangladesh Secretariat, Dhaka 1000 (tel: 862-250; fax: 868-766).

Ministry of Labour and Manpower, Bangladesh Secretariat, Dhaka 1000 (tel: 862-141; fax: 868-660).

Ministry of Land, Bangladesh Secretariat, Dhaka 1000 (tel: 869-644; fax: 862-989).

Ministry of Law, Justice and Parliamentary Affairs, Bangladesh Secretariat, Dhaka 1000 (tel: 860-560; fax: 868-557).

Ministry of Local Government and Rural Development, Bangladesh Secretariat, Dhaka 1000 (tel: 869-176; fax: 864-374).

Ministry of Planning, Sher-e-Bangla Nagar, Dhaka 1207 (tel: 815-175; fax: 814-638).

Ministry of Post and Telecommunications, Bangladesh Secretariat, Dhaka 1000 (tel: 864-800; fax: 865-775).

Ministry of Primary and Mass Education, Bangladesh Secretariat, Dhaka 1000 (tel: 862-484; fax: 868-871).

Ministry of Religious Affairs, Bangladesh Secretariat, Dhaka 1000 (tel: 860-682; fax: 865-040).

Ministry of Science & Technology, Bangladesh Secretariat, Dhaka 1000 (tel: 866-144; fax: 869-606).

Ministry of Shipping, Bangladesh Secretariat, Dhaka 1000 (tel: 868-155; fax: 862-219).

Ministry of Social Welfare, Bangladesh Secretariat, Dhaka 1000 (tel: 860-452; fax: 868-969).

Ministry of Textiles, Bangladesh Secretariat, Dhaka 1000 (tel: 864-388; fax: 860-600).

Ministry of Water Resources, Bangladesh Secretariat, Dhaka 1000 (tel: 868-688; fax: 862-400).

Ministry of Women and Children Affairs, Bangladesh Secretariat, Dhaka 1000 (tel: 861-012; fax: 867-550).

Ministry of Youth and Sports, Bangladesh Secretariat, Dhaka 1000 (tel: 867-053; fax: 862-344).

President's Office, Bangabhaban, Dhaka 1000 (tel: 966-8041; fax: 946-6242).

Prime Minister's Office, Old Sangsad Bhaban, Tejgaon, Dhaka (tel: 888-160; fax: 813-244).

Other useful addresses

Asian Development Bank, Bangladesh Resident Mission, BSL Office Complex, Sheraton Hotel Annex, 1 Minto Road, Ramna, Dhaka 1000 (tel: 933-4017; fax: 933-4012; e-mail: abddrm@mail.asiandevbank.org).

Bangladesh Agricultural University, Mymensingh (tel: 4333, 4191/93).

Bangladesh Export Processing Zones Authority, 222 New Eskaton Road, Dhaka (tel: 832-553; fax: 834-963).

Bangladesh Jute Mills Corporation, Adanjee Court, Motijheel Commercial Area, Dhaka (tel: 238-182/6, 238-192/6; fax: 883-329, 883-985).

Bangladesh Small and Cottage Industries Corporation, 137-138 Motijheel Commercial Area, Dhaka (tel: 865-161).

Bangladesh Telegraph and Telephone Board, 36/1 Mymensingh Road, Dhaka (tel: 831-500; fax: 832-477).

Board of Investment, Shilpa Bhaban, 91 Motijheel Commercial Area, Dhaka (tel: 955-9378; fax: 956-2312).

Bangladesh University of Engineering & Technology, Ramna, Dhaka 2 (tel: 505-171-5).

British High Commission, United Nations Road, PO Box 6079, Baridhara, Dhaka 12 (tel: 882-705/9; fax: 883-437).

Chittagong Port Authority, Port Road, Chittagong (tel: 712-504; fax: 710-593).

Chittagong Stock Exchange, 1/F Kashfia Plaza, 923/A Sheikh Mujib Road, Chittagong (tel: 714-100; fax: 714-101).

Department of Environment, Poribesh Bhaban, Plot £16 Agargaon, Sher-e-Bangla Nagar, Dhaka (tel: 812-416).

Department of Fisheries, Matsa Bhaban Segunbagicha, Dhaka (tel: 956-9320).

Department of Immigration and Passports, 17 Segunbagicha, Dhaka (tel: 834-320; fax: 956-2787).

Department of Shipping, 8/F, 141-143, Motijheel Commercial Area, Dhaka (tel: 955-5128).

Department of Textiles, Bastra Bhaban, Kazi Nazrul Islam Avenue, Dhaka (911-6385).

Dhaka Electric Supply Authority, 1 Abdul Gani Road, Dhaka (tel: 956-3520).

Dhaka Stock Exchange, 9F Motijheel Commercial Area, Dhaka 1000 (tel: 955-1935; fax: 867-552).

Export Promotion Bureau, Chamber Building, 122-124 Motijheel Commercial Area, Dhaka 1000 (tel: 955-2245/9; fax: 956-8000; e-mail: epb.tic@pradeshta.net).

Infrastructure Development Co Ltd, c/o Economic Relations Division, Block 16, Room 3, Sher-e-Bangla Nagar, Dhaka (tel: 811-971; fax: 811-660).

Mongla Port Authority, Mongla, Bagerhat (tel: 416-2331; fax: 403-1224).

National Board of Revenue, Segunbagicha, Dhaka (tel: 838-120; fax: 836-143).

Planning Commission, G.O. Hostel, Sher-e-Bangla Nagar, Dhaka.

Power Development Board, WAPDA Building, Motijheel Commercial Area, Dhaka (tel: 956-2154; fax: 956-4765).

Privatisation Board, 14/F Joban Bima Tower, 10 Dilkusha Commercial Area, Dhaka (tel: 956-3763; fax: 956-3723).

Registrar of Joint Stock Companies and Firms, 24-25 Dilkusha Commercial Area, Dhaka (tel: 956-4005).

Securities and Exchange Commission, Jiban bima Tower, 10 Dilkusha Commercial Area, Dhaka (tel: 956-8101; fax: 956-3721).

US Embassy, Madani Avenue, Baridhara, Dhaka 1212 (tel: 882-4700; fax: 882-3744; e-mail: dhaka@pd.state.gov).

Water Sewerage Authority, 98 Kazi Nazrul Islam Avenue, Dhaka (tel: 816-792; fax: 812-109).

National news agency: Bangladesh Sangbad Sangstha (BSS)
Other news agencies: BDNEWS24: www.bdnews24.com

Internet sites

Bangladesh Parjatan Corporation (National tourist organisation): www.bangladeshtourism.gov.bd

Bangladesh News: www.bangladeshnews.net

Virtual Bangladesh: www.virtualbangladesh.com

Barbados

In common with most of its neighbours, Barbados suffered a sharp recession on the 1990s. By 2004 the economy appeared to have got back on track. In 2007, modest growth in tourism, and a 5.2 per cent increase in both wholesale, retail and construction sectors meant that the economy as a whole grew by 4.5 per cent for the first half of the year, well up on the 3.7 per cent recorded for the same period in 2006.

Cricket's boost

Accelerated business activity related to the preparations for, and subsequent staging of, the Cricket World Cup (CWC) which compensated for the sluggish growth recorded by both the manufacturing sector and lower than expected levels of agricultural – notably sugar – production. Lower house prices and transport costs accounted for a drop in the inflation rate to 5.5 per cent annually, 1.7 per cent lower than the rate recorded at the end of 2006. Barbados' overall inflation rate was driven by increased prices for many food items, alcohol, tobacco and household items. Unemployment was also lower in the first half of 2007. The government failed to publish the end 2007 unemployment figure, which was estimated at 6.7 per cent.

The government incurred a deficit for the first half of 2007 of B$100.1 million (US$50.05 million), a disappointing contrast with the surplus of B$3.9 million (US$1.95 million), for the same period in 2006. The shift in the government's finances was attributed to lower tax revenues and a continued expansion in current expenditure.

Tourism grows – just

The influx of visitors for the CWC in the second quarter of 2007 resulted in a 13.6 per cent increase in total tourist arrivals, mainly from non-traditional markets. In the first half of 2007, arrivals from Barbados' traditional markets of the UK, Canada and the US rose by 5.6 per cent, 3.9 per cent and 2.3 per cent respectively. The CWC caused a 14.6 per cent increase in tourists from the UK in the second quarter. Visitor arrivals from the rest of the world for the period more than doubled in comparison to 2006. These increases went some way in compensating for a 32 per cent drop in tourists from non-cricket loving Germany (in fact the drop was attributed to increased transport costs) and a surprising 20.9 per cent drop in Caribbean Community (Caricom) visitors. In contrast, the number of cruise ship passengers grew by 13.7 per cent in the first half of 2007, reversing the 17 per cent decline seen for the same period in 2006.

Bees out, Dems in

The defeat of the long-ruling Barbados Labour Party (BLP) which had governed for 14 years, was a result that many Barbadians would not have thought possible. Even six months before the election, the victorious new prime minister, David Thompson, of the Democratic Labour Party (DLP) was considered to be the under-dog, in charge of an ineffective and weak party. As things turned out, the DLP won twice as many seats (20) as the BLP, which ended up with only ten.

Politics in Barbados have long been based on the electorate's perception that it is time for a change. This was the DLP's simple electoral message. The issues which swung the election in favour of the DLP could not all be blamed on the outgoing government. Inflation was at the top of the list of grievances, although this had actually begun to fall during the run-up to the election. The inflationary pressures that Barbados was having to cope with were common to all the Caribbean economies, reflecting the higher prices of imported food and fuel. None the less, there existed within the electorate that perceived corruption was linked to the price rises, where illegal distribution monopolies were blamed. The outgoing BLP government was blamed for failing to address the perceived problem.

After the cost of living, crime came second on the list of grievances, although crime levels on Barbados are much less than elsewhere in the Caribbean. Largely unfounded rumours that government ministers had illegally amassed fortunes did little to help the BLP's electoral prospects.

KEY FACTS

Official name: Barbados

Head of State: Queen Elizabeth II, represented by Governor General Sir Clifford Straughn Husbands (since 1996)

Head of government: Prime Minister David Thompson (DLP) (since 16 Jan 2008)

Ruling party: Democratic Labour Party (DLP) (since 15 Jan 2008)

Area: 430 square km

Population: 275,000 (2007)*

Capital: Bridgetown

Official language: English

Currency: Barbados dollar (BD$) = 100 cents

Exchange rate: BD$2.00 per US$ (Jul 2008)

GDP per capita: US$13,605 (2007)*

GDP real growth: 4.20% (2007)*

Labour force: 152,000 (2004)

Unemployment: 9.80% (2004)

Inflation: 5.50% (2007)

Balance of trade: -US$1.39 billion (2005)

Foreign debt: US$643.50 million (2004)

Visitor numbers: 1.11 million (2005)

* estimated figure

Risk assessment

Politics	Good
Economy	Good
Regional stability	Good

COUNTRY PROFILE

Historical profile

Barbados was formerly a British colony and is now an independent sovereign state.

1951 Universal adult suffrage was introduced. The Barbados Labour Party (BLP) won the general election, and held office until 1961.

1961 Barbados achieved full internal self-government. The Democratic Labour Party (DLP) won the elections.

1966 Barbados gained independence.

1994 The BLP won the election. Owen Arthur became prime minister.

2002 Barbados was removed from the Organisation for Economic Co-operation and Development (OECD's) blacklist of non-co-operative countries in OECD efforts to combat money laundering.

2003 The ruling BLP won the general elections.

2006 The opposition leader, Clyde Mascoll, resigned from the DLP and joined the ruling BLP.

2008 In parliamentary elections held on 15 January the opposition DLP won 52.5 per cent, (20 seats out of 30), the BLP 47.3 per cent, (10); turnout was 56.6 per cent. David Thompson (DLP) was sworn in as prime minister on 16 January. The Barbados Defence Force received military aid of B$840,000 (US$1.68 million) provided by the Chinese Army. The donation included computers, power generators and other equipment and military training.

Political structure

Constitution

Promulgated on 30 November 1966.

Form of state

Parliamentary democracy, within a constitutional monarchy.

The executive

Executive power is vested in the British monarch, represented by a governor general, who is appointed by the monarch, and exercised by the prime minister and cabinet.

National legislature

Legislative power is exercised through the bicameral National Assembly, comprising a 30-member House of Assembly, popularly elected in single seat constituencies, for terms of five years and a 21-member Senate of appointed members for five-year terms.

Following National Assembly elections, the leader of the majority party, or majority coalition, assumes the post of prime minister, to be confirmed by the governor general. The cabinet is selected by the prime minister and confirmed by the governor general.

Legal system

The legal system is based on English common law. Judges are appointed by the service commissions for the judicial and legal service. There is no judicial review of legislative acts.

Last elections

15 January 2008 (parliamentary)

Results: Parliamentary: the DLP won 52.5 per cent, (20 seats out of 30), the BLP 47.3 per cent, (10); turnout was 56.6 per cent.

Next elections

2013 (parliamentary)

Political parties

Ruling party

Democratic Labour Party (DLP) (since 15 Jan 2008)

Main opposition party

Barbados Labour Party (BLP)

Population

275,000 (2007)*

Last census: May 2000: 250,010

Population density: 620 inhabitants per square km. Urban population: 51 per cent (1995–2001).

Annual growth rate: 0.3 per cent 1994–2004 (WHO 2006)

Ethnic make-up

African (90 per cent), mixed race (6 per cent), European (4 per cent).

Religions

Mainly Christian, with an Anglican majority and dozens of smaller sects, plus small Jewish, Hindu and Muslim communities.

Anglican (40 per cent), Pentecostal (8 per cent), Methodist (7 per cent), Roman Catholic (4 per cent).

Education

Educational spending is around US$150 million per year. Expenditure on primary education typically fluctuates between 25–29 per cent of total public expenditure on education. The government provides assistance to all private secondary schools.

Public education at primary and secondary levels is free, although parents can opt to send their children to private schools. Primary education begins at aged five and lasts for six years.

The secondary school programme begins at aged 11 years and last until aged 16, when students choose between academic higher education or applied further education.

The Samuel Jackman Prescod Polytechnic (SJPP), the Barbados Community College (BCC), Erdiston College and the University of the West Indies cater for higher education. Eligible students also pursue their studies in North American colleges and universities.

Compulsory years: 5 to 16

Enrolment rate: 94.7 per cent to 100 per cent, primary school enrolment of the relevant age group.

Pupils per teacher: 18 in primary schools

Health

Per capita total expenditure on health (2003) was US$1,050; of which per capita government spending was US$729, at the international dollar rate, (WHO 2006).

With 16 per cent of the population aged 60 years and over, Barbados has the highest percentage of elderly population in the English speaking Caribbean.

KEY INDICATORS — Barbados

	Unit	2003	2004	2005	2006	2007
Population	m	0.27	0.27	0.28	0.27	*0.28
Gross domestic product (GDP)	US$bn	*2.63	2.80	3.06	3.43	*3.74
GDP per capita	US$	10,000	10,334	11,099	12,523	*13,605
GDP real growth	%	1.6	3.0	4.1	3.9	*4.2
Inflation	%	1.5	1.5	6.0	7.2	5.5
Exports (fob) (goods)	US$m	227.0	312.4	211.0	–	–
Imports (cif) (goods)	US$m	987.0	1,277.9	1,604.0	–	–
Balance of trade	US$m	-760.0	-945.5	-1,393.0	–	–
Current account	US$m	-210.0	-280.0	-386.0	-278.0	*-254.0
Total reserves minus gold	US$m	737.9	579.9	603.5	636.1	839.3
Foreign exchange	US$m	730.5	571.8	595.9	627.9	830.3
Exchange rate	per US$	2.00	2.00	2.00	2.00	2.00

* estimated figure

Barbados provides high quality primary and secondary care with free treatment for young children. The Queen Elizabeth Hospital benefits from government aid.
There is universal access to improved water and sanitation facilities.

HIV/Aids

HIV prevalence: 1.5 per cent aged 15–49 in 2003 (World Bank)
Life expectancy: 75 years, 2004 (WHO 2006)
Fertility rate/Maternal mortality rate: 1.5 births per woman, 2004 (WHO 2006)
Birth rate/Death rate: 13 births per 1,000 population; nine deaths per 1,000 population (2003).
Child (under 5 years) mortality rate (per 1,000): 13 per 1,000 live births (2003)

Welfare

The government provides an extensive welfare programme for the poor and the elderly. Assistance for the elderly comprises housing, transportation, home care and free utilities (water and utilities), assistance in kind, and food vouchers.
Financial assistance is provided to parents of underprivileged children as well as subsidies for school expenses.
Low rent housing is available to all residents; some housing is available to be purchased by low income earners.

Pensions

There is universal pension coverage from a non-contributory pension.

Main cities

Bridgetown (capital, estimated population 98,900 in 2003), Speightstown (3,600), Oistins, Holetown.

Languages spoken

A local Bajan dialect is spoken.

Official language/s

English

Media

National news agency: Caribbean News Agency (Cana)

Press

Dailies: There are two, The Daily Nation (www.nationnews.com) and the Barbados Advocate (www.barbadosadvocate.com).
Weeklies: Daily newspapers publish weekend editions. Others include Eastern Caribbean News, Weekend Investigator and Caribbean Week (published fortnightly).
Business: The Broad Street Journal (www.broadstreetnews.com) and Business Monday (www.barbadosadvocate.com), are business publications while most daily newspapers have business sections.
Periodicals: The Government Information Service (BGIS) (www.barbados.gov.bb) publishes data and research articles.

Broadcasting

The Caribbean Broadcast Corporation (CBC) (www.cbc.bb) is the nation public broadcaster.
Radio: CBC (www.cbc.bb) has three networks which cover news, cultural and sports events and all genre of music.
There are several private, commercial and religious radio stations operating including Voice of Barbados (VOB) (www.vob929.com), which competes with CBC for content, Hott FM (www.hott953.com), Mix 96.9 (www.mix969fm.com) and Gospel 97.5 (www.gospel975.com); the Barbados Broadcasting Service operates BBS 90.7 and Faith FM (www.barbadosadvocate.com).
Television: CBC (www.cbc.bb) is the only terrestrial TV network in operation, showing domestic news and current affairs, art and cultural programmes as well as imported shows. Programmes are also provided by Jump TV (www.jumptv.com), via the internet. It is the largest provider worldwide of internet programming.

Economy

For some time Barbados has compared favourably with other Caribbean countries on most social and economic indicators. Its economy continues to be heavily dependent on the tourism and financial sectors.
In 2006, the Barbadian economy recorded an annual growth rate of 3.8 per cent, down from the 4.2 per cent recorded in 2005. According to the United Nations Economic Commission for Latin America and the Caribbean (ECLAC/CEPAL) government economic policy was aimed at improving the island nation's balance-of payments position and containing inflation which had passed the 5 per cent mark in mid-2005.
The tourism sector continued to look relatively buoyant, with higher revenues expected in 2007 reflecting increased visitor levels from the Cricket World Cup. Tourism revenues rose by 1.9 per cent, contrasting satisfactorily with a 3.1 fall in 2005. Stay-over tourists' arrivals – which generate the most revenue – rose by 4.0 per cent; cruise ship arrivals also showed significant increases. Construction was boosted by infrastructure spending in readiness for the Cricket World Cup.
Government expenditure rose by a manageable 4.7 per cent in the first nine months of 2006, well down on the 11.1 per cent recorded for the same period of 2005. As a temporary fiscal measure the government increased the tax paid on extra-regional imports, known as the 'cess'. The move was designed to protect domestic manufacturers and to raise funds to finance the creation of a new export promotion agency. The unfortunately named cess was expected to be removed entirely by April 2007. The Barbadian fiscal situation improved, with a surplus on the current account contrasting with the deficit recorded in 2005. The tight monetary policy put into effect in 2005 was maintained in 2006. Inflation remained a concern as prices rose by 7.7 per cent in the 12 months to July 2006, although this figure was expected to drop reflecting falls in energy prices. Unemployment was also on a downward trend, dropping from the 9.9 per cent recorded for the first three months of 2005 to a still high 8.1 per cent.

External trade

Even though the government sees the high trade deficit as excessive it is reliant on imports of basic goods such as foodstuffs. Barbados was the first single-crop agrarian economy to switch to the service sector provision of back office operations and its financial sector, combined with the tourist sector, provides the greater proportion of GDP. The offshore financial centre utilises the highly educated, English-speaking workforce with its proximity to the US and Canada, as well as traditional links with the UK.
As a member of the Caribbean Community and Common Market (Caricom), Barbados operates within the single market (Caribbean Single Market and Economy (CSME)), which became operational on 1 January 2006.

Imports

Principal imports are machinery (typically 17 per cent of total), food and beverages (15 per cent), fuels (5 per cent), vehicles (3 per cent), and other include consumer goods, construction materials, electrical components and marine crafts.
Main sources: US (37.6 per cent total, 2006), Trinidad and Tobago (22.5 per cent), US (5.8 per cent).

Exports

Principal exports are sugar and molasses (typically 30 per cent of total), electrical and electronic components (25 per cent), clothing (12 per cent), chemicals (11per cent), others include rum, foods and beverages.
Main destinations: US (20.1 per cent of 2006 total goods exports), Trinidad and Tobago (11.0 per cent), UK (7.5 per cent).

Agriculture

Farming

The agricultural sector contributes around 7 per cent to GDP and employs around 5 per cent of the labour force.
Around 76 per cent of the total land area is under cultivation.
Emphasis has been placed on diversifying production away from sugar and towards

the farming of sea island cotton, green vegetables and market garden produce. The EU quota of just under 50,000 tonnes per year and its guaranteed price mechanism came to an end in 2007. The pressure is on Barbados to make the sugar sector profitable, although it seems unlikely that the island will be able to compete with low-cost producers and the heavily subsidised sugar beet farmers in North America and the EU. As well as trade liberalisation, the Barbados sugar sector has had to cope with environmental degradation and the rising price of land.
Crop production in 2005 included: 260 tonnes (t) maize, 2,000t sweet potatoes, 430,000t sugar cane, 1,950t coconuts, 1,150t yams, 260t taro, 1,100t tomatoes, 1,250t chillies & peppers, 1,230t pulses, 660t bananas, 265t oilcrops, 375t cassava, 3,540t fruit in total, 14,520t vegetables in total. Livestock production included: 16,137t meat in total, 300t beef, 2,096t pig meat, 126t lamb and goat meat, 13,615t poultry, 1,950t eggs, 6,785t milk.

Fishing

There are complaints that the small fishing industry has not been supported by the government. The government issued fish importing licences permitting processors to import fish, when the domestic catch could have provided for domestic processing needs.
In 2004, the total marine fish catch was 2,500 tonnes.

Industry and manufacturing

Manufacturing employs around 9 per cent of the workforce and construction and quarrying, 11 per cent.
Production is centred on light manufacturing and assembly of electrical and electronic goods, food processing, clothing, sugar refining, petrochemicals and beverages.
Most new foreign-owned export-oriented industries are based on the island's nine purpose-built industrial estates, which are largely managed by the Barbados Industrial Development Corporation.
Emphasis is placed on expanding the number of value-added joint venture assembly industries.

Tourism

Tourism accounts for around 11 per cent of GDP, employing 21 per cent of the workforce, generating 70 per cent of foreign exchange earnings. Visitor numbers grew by 10 per cent and cruise ship passengers by 32 per cent, in 2004.

Hydrocarbons

As Barbados has no refining capacity, its oil is refined in Trinidad and returned to Barbados for domestic consumption. Most oil produced is used domestically.

Energy

Barbados relies on imported oil for most of its energy requirements. Under the San José pact, Mexico and Venezuela supply crude oil and refined products on concessionary terms.
There are plans to expand solar and wind energy programmes.

Banking and insurance

The financial sector continues to expand.

Central bank

Central Bank of Barbados

Main financial centre

Bridgetown

Offshore facilities

Barbados is a major international business centre. It has several tax treaties in place with developed countries including Canada.

Time

GMT minus four hours

Geography

Barbados is the most easterly of the Caribbean islands, lying about 320km (200 miles) north-east of Trinidad. It is relatively flat and is one of the few coral-capped islands in the region.

Hemisphere

Northern

Climate

Generally warm but cooled by trade winds with temperature around 26–30 degrees Celsius (C) in the day and 15–18 degrees C at night. Rainy season, includes tropical storms: July–November. Humidity rises in the rainy season.

Dress codes

Business suits may be worn with jackets removed. Generally, smart casual wear is suitable in restaurants, although some restaurants may require suits and ties for men. Lightweight cottons are advised.

Entry requirements

Passports

Required by all.

Visa

Visas are not required by most European, American, Australasian and some Asian citizens. For a list of those that do, see http://www.barbados.org/docs.htm. All visitors must have return/onward passage.

Currency advice/regulations

No restrictions on import of local currency, but it may not be exported. Unlimited foreign currency may be imported and exported, limited to the amount declared on arrival.

Health (for visitors)

Mandatory precautions

Yellow fever vaccination certificate if arriving from an infected area.

Advisable precautions

Typhoid/polio vaccination.

Hotels

There is wide range of first-class hotels available. A 5 per cent government tax and 10 per cent service charge are generally applied.

Public holidays (national)

Fixed dates

1 Jan (New Year's Day), 21 Jan (Errol Barrow Day), 28 Apr (National Heroes' Day), 1 May (Labour Day), 30 Nov (Independence Day), 25 Dec (Christmas Day), 26 Dec (Boxing Day).

Variable dates

Good Friday, Easter Monday, Whit Monday, Emancipation/Kadooment Day (first Mon in Aug).

Working hours

Banking

Mon–Thu: 0800–1500; Fri: 0800–1700.

Business

Mon–Fri: 0800–1600/1630; Sat: 0800–1200.

Government

Mon–Fri: 0800–1600/1630.

Telecommunications

Mobile/cell phones

GSM 900/1900, 900/1800 services are available throughout most of the island.

Internet/e-mail

Electricity supply

110V AC, 50Hz. American-style two-pin plugs are in use.

Social customs/useful tips

Make and confirm appointments before travelling. Many hotels do not start check-in procedures until 1500 so advise the hotel if arriving earlier. Most hotels have a business centre, although facilities vary.

Getting there

Air

International airport/s: Grantley Adams International (BGI), 13km east of Bridgetown; duty-free shops, restaurant, bank, hotel reservations, car hire.

Airport tax: Departure tax BD$25; not applicable to transit passengers.

Surface

Water: Cruise-ship passengers may conclude their journey and depart by air, normal immigration and visa control standards would apply.

Main port/s: Bridgetown Harbour.

Getting about

National transport

Road: There are over 2,000km of surfaced road. Main roads radiate from Bridgetown.

Buses: Frequent and efficient standard fare services operate throughout the island.

City transport

Taxis: Taxis are easily available. They can be hailed, ordered by telephone or found

on ranks. The Tourism Board publishes a list of standard fares.
Some hotels run pick-up services.

Car hire
A local driver's permit must be obtained; they are available at police stations and the licensing authority or through car rental agencies on presentation of a national driving licence or an international driving permit. A registration fee of B$10 will be due.
Traffic drives on the left and is often heavy during the rush hours. Strict speed limits of 20mph in Bridgetown and Speightstown and 30mph elsewhere.

BUSINESS DIRECTORY

The addresses listed below are a selection only. While World of Information makes every endeavour to check these addresses, we cannot guarantee that changes have not been made, especially to telephone numbers and area codes. We would welcome any corrections.

Telephone area codes
The international direct dialling code (IDD) for Barbados is +1 246, followed by subscriber's number.

Chambers of Commerce
Barbados Chamber of Commerce and Industry, Nemwil House, Collymore Rock, St Michael (tel: 426-2056; fax: 429-2907; e-mail: bdscham@caribsurf.com).

Banking
Bank of Nova Scotia, PO Box 202, Broad St, Bridgetown (tel: 431-3000; fax: 426-0969).

Barbados Agency for Microenterprise Development Ltd (Fund Access), 30 Tudor Street, Bridgetown (tel: 228-1366; fax: 228-1343).

Barbados National Bank, PO Box 1002, Broad St, Bridgetown (tel: 431-5700; fax: 426-0969).

Barclays Bank PLC, PO Box 301, Broad St, Bridgetown (tel: 431-5151; fax: 436-7957).

Caldon Finance Merchant Bank Ltd, Hilton Hotel, 7 Shopping Arcade, St Michael (tel: 437-7550; fax: 436-4999).

Caribbean Commercial Bank, PO Box 1007C, Broad St, Bridgetown (tel: 431-2500; fax: 431-2530).

Caribbean Development Bank, PO Box 408 Wildey, St Michael, Barbados (tel: 431-1600; fax: 426-7269).

Intel Overseas Bank Inc, Suite No 7, Goding House, Spry St, Bridgetown (tel: 436-8826).

Mutual Bank of the Caribbean Inc, Triden House, Lower Broad St, Bridgetown (tel: 436-8335; fax: 429-5734).

Royal Bank of Canada, PO Box 68, Broad Street, Bridgetown (tel: 431-6700; fax: 427-8393).

Central bank
Central Bank of Barbados, Spry Street, PO Box 1016, Bridgetown (tel: 436-6870; fax: 427-3334; e-mail: cbb.libr@caribsurf.com).

Travel information
Caribbean Airways, Terminal 1, Grantley Adams International Airport, Christ Church (tel: 428-1950; fax: 428-1652; e-mail: info@caribairways.com; internet site: www.caribairways.com).

Ministry of tourism
Ministry of Foreign Affairs, Tourism and International Transport, Tourism Division, Sherbourne Conference Centre, Two Mile Hill, St Michael (tel: 436-4830; fax: 436-4828).

National tourist organisation offices
Barbados Tourism Authority, Harbour Road, PO Box 242, Bridgetown (tel: 427-2623/4; fax: 426-4080; email: btainfo@barbados.org; internet: www.barbados.org).

Ministries
Ministry of Agriculture and Rural Development, Graeme Hall, Christ Church (tel: 428-4061; fax: 420-8444).

Ministry of Education, Youth Affairs and Culture, Jemmotts Ln, St Michael (tel: 426-5416; fax: 436-2411).

Ministry of Finance and Economic Affairs, Civil Service, Government Headquarters, Bay St, St Michael (tel: 426-3179; fax: 436-9280).

Ministry of Health and the Environment, Jemmotts Ln, St Michael (tel: 426-4669; fax: 426-5570).

Ministry of Home Affairs, Sir Frank Walcott Bldg, Culloden Rd, St Michael (tel: 431-7750; fax: 437-3794).

Ministry of Industry, Commerce and Business Development, Reef Rd, Fontabelle, St Michael (tel: 426-4452; fax: 431-0056).

Ministry of International Trade and Business, 1 Culloden Rd, St Michael (tel: 427-0427; fax: 429-6652).

Ministry of Labour, Community Development and Sports, National Insurance Bldg, Fairchild St, Bridgetown, St Michael (tel: 427-2326; fax: 426-8959).

Ministry of Public Works, Transport and Housing, The Pine, St Michael (tel: 429-3495; fax: 437-8133).

Ministry of Trade, Industry and Commerce, Savannah Lodge, Garrison, St Michael (tel: 427-270).

Prime Minister's Office, Government Headquarters, Bay St, St Michael (tel: 426-3179; fax: 436-9280).

Other useful addresses
Barbados External Telecommunications, Wildey, St Michael (tel: 427-5200; fax: 427-5808).

Barbados Investment and Development Corporation, Pelican House, Princess Alice Highway, St Michael (tel: 427-5350; fax: 426-7802; internet site: http://www.bidc.com/index.htm).

Barbados Manufacturers' Association, Prescod Blvd, Harbour Road, Bridgetown (tel: 426-4474, 427-9898; fax: 436-5182).

Barbados National Trust, 10th Avenue Relleville, St Michael (tel: 436-9033);

Barbados Tourism Investment Inc, 2nd Floor, Nemwil House, Collymore Rock, St. Michael (tel: 426-7085; fax: 426-7086; e-mail: btii@tourisminvest.com.bb; internet site: http://barbadostourisminvestment.com).

British High Commission, PO Box 676, Lower Collymore Rock, St Michael (tel: 436-6694; fax: 436-5398, 426-7916).

Caribbean Broadcasting Corporation, PO Box 900, Bridgetown (tel: 429-2041).

The Future Centre Trust, Edgehill Street, St Thomas (fax: 425-0075).

US Embassy, PO Box 302, Canadian Imperial Bank of Commerce Building, Broad Street, Bridgetown (tel: 436-4950; fax: 429-5246).

National news agency: Caribbean News Agency (Cana)
Other news agencies: Caribbean Net News: www.caribbeannetnews.com

Internet sites
Barbados Cruise Tourism: www.cruisebarbados.com

Government information service: www.bgis.gov.bb

Barbados government portal: www.gov.bb

Barbados Nation (newspaper): http://nationnews.com

Travel and Tourism Encyclopedia: www.barbados.org

KEY FACTS

Official name: Respublika Belarus (Republic of Belarus)

Head of State: President Aleksandr Lukashenko (since 1994; re-elected 19 Mar 2006; inaugurated 8 Apr 2006)

Head of government: Prime Minister Sergei Sidorski (since 2003)

Ruling party: Coalition of Kommunisticheskaya Partuya Belarusi (KPB) (Communist Party of Belarus) and Agrarnaya Partiya Belarusi (APB) (Agrarian Party of Belarus) (since 1995)

Area: 208,000 square km

Population: 9.65 million (2007)*

Capital: Minsk

Official language: Belarusian since 1990 and Russian since 1995 referendum.

Currency: Rouble (R)

Exchange rate: R2,119.00 per US$ (Jul 2008)

GDP per capita: US$4,641 (2007)*

GDP real growth: 8.20% (2007)*

Labour force: 5.37 million (2004)

Unemployment: 2.00% (official, 2004) (additional large number of underemployed)

Inflation: 8.40% (2007)

Balance of trade: -US$2.58 billion (2006)

Foreign debt: US$600.00 million (2004)

Annual FDI: US$300.00 million (2005)

* estimated figure

Belarus

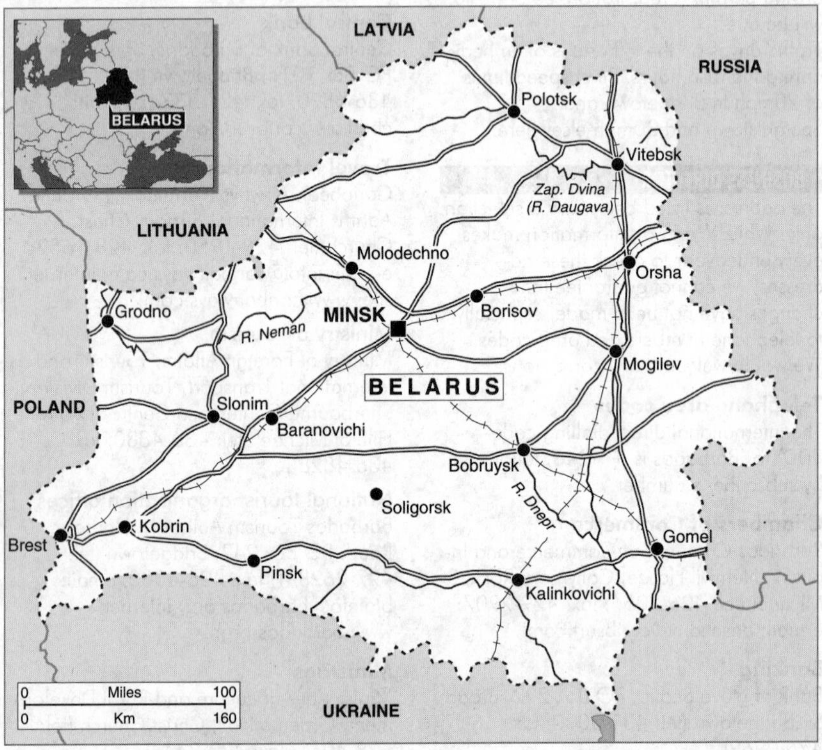

In terms of business and trade freedoms, Belarus does not rank very highly. In its 2008 *Index of Economic Freedom*, the US-based Heritage Foundation ranked it last of the 41 countries of the European region. What the Index describes as a 'persistently low score' is attributed to the failure of Belarus' post-Soviet reforms. Belarus' economic institutions are cited as creating 'major barriers' to development. A notoriously corrupt government dominates Belarus' financial system and either owns or controls all but one of the country's 31 banks. The Index also states that Belarus' still state controlled economy and international isolation have discouraged foreign investment and the continued development of a once flourishing high-tech sector.

The importance of not being Russia

Post-Soviet Belarus went through two stages of development. Between 1990 and 2000 the focus was very much on the rebuilding and developing a pattern of the country's Soviet style trade relationships. Belarus' imports and exports were for the most part traded with Russia. Fuelled, quite literally, by cheap Russian energy, Belarus' state-owned companies were able to maintain an apparently competitive market position. From 2001 onwards, things changed, not least because Russian consumers began to enjoy choice and to have the money to exercise that choice – to choose between an outdated Lada or a state of the art Mercedes. What had been a healthily positive trade balance with Russia soon turned into a deficit. During the same period, export revenues from the West began to increase, driven higher by increased oil and gas prices. In the space of ten years, the Belarus economy changed from labour intensive to capital intensive. But little was done by the government to make the changes and reforms necessary to reflect this shift. Privatisation was only apparent on the edges of the economy, in more easily manageable small- to medium-size service enterprises.

The economy shifts Westwards

Gradually, Belarusian products had become more expensive to produce and less competitive to sell. The fall in export revenues from Russia was to a degree compensated for by an increase in oil and gas prices from the West, which had nothing at all to do with any economic reforms or privatisation. What it did have to do with was the fact that about half of Russia's oil exports and some 20 per cent of its gas exports had to pass through Belarus, a simple reality which continues to give Belarus a very strong bargaining position. This will continue to be the case until Russia is able to develop alternative pipeline routes.

The shift in Belarus' trade patterns has produced an essentially unprofitable and ultimately uncomfortable position for Belarus. The trade deficit that has resulted from the drop in exports corresponds to some 5 per cent of GDP; this figure would be an estimated four times higher if Belarus was already paying international prices for its energy, which it will eventually have to. However, the revenue that Belarus derives from its oil and gas exports and transit fees is simply not enough to support what has become a largely unproductive work force. If the Belarus economy is to become competitive, far-reaching and politically unattractive reforms are needed. In the first instance, these will have to address the inherent structures of the economy, where not only the populace in general, but also inefficient state-owned enterprises have got used to low energy prices.

Economic cloud cuckoo land

Belarus' energy consumption, in relation to GDP, is roughly double that of other European countries. Under Lukachenko privatisation has been avoided because, particularly in the case of the larger enterprises, it represents a loss of political control. To put off the evil day when its outdated economic model can no longer foot the bill, Belarus under Lukachenko has resorted to the simple remedy of borrowing. As long as his country's credit rating – probably based on misleading data – remains acceptable, the government can continue to borrow on the international markets. For the time being, this option enables Lukachenko and his team to continue living in an economic cloud cuckoo land until the game is over. When the loans can no longer be serviced and the international financial community obliges the adoption of economic reforms and restructuring on a massive scale, reality will have to be faced.

Doubts over official data were expressed when the The National Bank of the Republic of Belarus (NBRB) (the central bank) announced that inflation for the period January–September 2007 was only 5.4 per cent, a monthly rate for the period of 0.6 per cent. Conservative, if more empirical estimates for the same period put the rise in the cost of milk and meat at around 40 per cent (a figure apparently acknowledged by Belarus' prime minister, Sergei Sidorski). Electricity tariffs were unofficially calculated to have risen by 23 per cent for the period, as had gas. On the same basis of calculation, butter was estimated to have risen by 80 per cent, vegetable oil by a staggering 100 per cent. The ministry of statistics inflation calculations appeared to be based on the inclusion in the price basket items deemed to be 'socially significant' – a few, generally subsidised, goods. Belarussian economist Leonid Zlotnika quoted in the *Belarussian Review* in November 2007 observed that the inaccurate calculation applied not only to inflation, but also to other government indexes – such as GDP. The official calculation of Belarussian GDP figures, according to Mr Zlotnika, does not apply the methodology of the market economy. Instead, the Belarussian authorities appear to apply what they term the 'productive method' whereby goods and items that are produced, rather than consumed, form the basis of the calculation.

Indicators of impending economic shock abound in Belarus. The fuel (oil and gas) sector of the economy is no longer its most profitable, as an increasing number of fuel-related companies began to report losses in 2007. Imported energy prices for 2008 will cost the economy an estimated US$6 billion, at the same time denting the profitability of the important automotive sector. In the meantime, Lukachenko has been cosying up to the world's anti-Washington club; state visits by Hugo Chávez of Venezuela and Iran's President Mahmoud Ahmadinejad gave a clue to the likely source of Belarus' beleaguered administration's salvation. President Lukachenko was trying to negotiate more attractive energy supply contracts with his country's few supporters; oil for arms deals were struck in 2006 and 2007 with Venezuela and Iran. Also on Lukachenko's shopping list were Kazakhstan and the Ukraine. North Korea next?

Cuts, and more cuts

Belarus' international economic standing was under severe pressure in 2007. On 1 August, Russia's giant gas monopoly, Gazprom, announced that it proposed to cut supplies to Belarus by a whopping 45 per cent by August 3, just two days later. The proposed August 2007 cuts were in many respects a continuation of what became known as the 'Gas War' at the end of 2006. The Russian monopoly certainly knew where Belarus' raw nerve lay exposed. Any loss of cheap energy had serious implications for Lukachenko's regime

KEY INDICATORS — Belarus

	Unit	2003	2004	2005	2006	2007
Population	m	9.90	9.88	9.76	9.70	*9.65
Gross domestic product (GDP)	US$bn	17.50	23.10	30.13	36.94	*44.77
GDP per capita	US$	1,430	2,641	3,089	3,808	*4,641
GDP real growth	%	4.8	11.0	9.3	9.9	*8.2
Inflation	%	29.0	18.1	10.3	7.0	8.4
Unemployment	%	3.1	2.5	1.7	1.4	1.1
Industrial output	% change	–	18.6	14.5	*9.9	–
Agricultural output	% change	–	13.3	1.7	*9.9	–
Exports (fob) (goods)	US$m	10,092.0	13,916.8	16,095.3	19,739.0	24,380.4
Imports (cif) (goods)	US$m	11,326.0	15,982.5	16,622.6	22,323.0	28,346.8
Balance of trade	US$m	-1,264.0	-2,065.7	-527.3	-2,584.0	-3,984.4
Current account	US$m	-500.0	-680.0	469.1	-1,515.0	-2,944.0
Total reserves minus gold	US$m	594.8	749.4	1,136.6	1,068.6	3,952.1
Foreign exchange	US$m	594.8	749.3	1,136.6	1,068.5	3,952.1
Exchange rate	per US$	2,046.00	2,178.50	2,142.00	2,142.00	2,156.50

* estimated figure

and the 'economic miracle' it still endeavoured to present to a sceptical international audience. At issue was the small matter of US$500 million in unpaid gas delivery bills relating to deliveries in the first half of 2007. Some observers felt that the Belarus government's negotiating position was in fact stronger than it wished to be known. In 2007, the proceeds from the sale of gas-pipeline operator Beltranshaz (to the Russians) had provided it with a substantial windfall, certainly more than enough to pay the gas bill. A common theory was that the Lukachenko government was using the dispute to leverage a long-term loan agreement with the Russians.

Control...

Underlying the government's stance in the dispute and in all its discussions with international banks and other financial organisations was an imbedded reluctance to make any 'non-essential' changes. The status quo enabled the Lukachenko government to extend its political control to the control of all of Belarus' major companies. These included important (inasmuch as they have large payrolls) companies such as the Minsk Tractor Works, Minsk Automobile, the Belaz Heavy Truck Works and the Azot chemical company. Employing hundreds of thousands, these largely inefficient companies account for an estimated 80 per cent of Belarus' GDP.

...and isolation

To add to Belarus' general paranoia, the European Union's (EU) Generalised System of Preferences (GSU) benefits for Belarus were suspended in June 2007 as a punishment for the Lukachenko administration's failure to implement the International Labour Office (ILO) recommendations regarding the country's trades' unions. The GSU system is intended to benefit developing countries by lowering tariffs. The EU, perhaps protesting too much, was at pains to point out that the move had been taken to apply pressure on Belarus to grant workers' rights rather than to isolate it further. None the less, the step (which in cash terms probably amounted to little more than a penalty of between US$20 million and US$50 million) did little to give Belarus a warm feeling about its international standing at a time when relations with Russia continued to be strained and those with the US were also at something of a low.

The low was reached in February 2008 when the US ambassador to Minsk, Karen Stewart, left the country. The ambassador's departure followed two requests for her to leave as Minsk diplomats responded to US sanctions imposed following unheeded requests from the US that Belarus release its political prisoners. Minsk had already withdrawn its ambassador from Washington. A US statement bluntly stated that 'Following the unconditional release of all political prisoners, the United States stands ready to improve our bilateral relations'.

One such high profile prisoner was opposition leader Aleksandr Kazulin, who had threatened to starve himself if not released to attend his wife's funeral. In what represented something of a parable for Belarus' condition, the decision not to release Mr Kazulin was overturned following protests from both the US and the EU.

During the 12 years of Lukachenko rule, a network of *silovki* (law enforcement structures) has enabled the administration to silence dissent in any form. Belarussians deemed 'unreliable' not only find it impossible to obtain government employment, but are also prevented from opening small businesses. Not only are new businesses the preserve of regime servers; the corollary is that existing, but 'unreliable' businesses are systematically undermined.

Risk assessment

Economy	Poor
Politics	Poor
Regional stability	Fair

COUNTRY PROFILE

Historical profile

During the thirteenth and fourteenth centuries, Belarus was part of the Grand Duchy of Lithuania.
1500s The Grand Duchy was united with Poland.
1800s The dismemberment of Poland led to Belarus becoming a part of the Russian empire.
1918 Belarus became part of the Soviet Union, following the Russo-German treaty of Brest Litovsk.
1941–44 Belarus was occupied by Nazi Germany.
After the war, Belarus was returned to its status as a Soviet republic, although, uniquely, it was granted membership of the UN in its own right.
1988 The Narodni Front Belarusi (NFB) (Belarusian Popular Front) was formed.
1991 Independence was declared. Following the disintegration of the Soviet Union, the Kommunisticheskaya Partuya Belarusi (KPB) (Communist Party of Belarus) quickly established itself as the main political force. Stanislau Shushkevich (NFB), a moderate reformer, was chosen as head of the Supreme Soviet, a body dominated by old-guard communists.
1994 Shushkevich was dismissed after a vote of no-confidence. The constitution was settled. Belarus was influential in the creation of the Commonwealth of Independent States (CIS). The first free presidential elections were won by Aleksandr Lukashenko.
1996 A constitutional referendum changed the structure of government and gave the president sweeping powers. It also extended President Lukashenko's term of office until 2001.
1997 Belarus and Russia ratified the treaty establishing a Union of Russia and Belarus.
1998 Belarus and Russia agreed to begin steps to merge their currencies and taxation systems.
2000 The Belarus rouble exchange rate was re-denominated on 1 January. Prime Minister Sergei Ling was dismissed at the president's request; he had been prime minister since November 1996. The parliamentary elections were boycotted by the opposition. The presidents of Belarus, Kazakhstan, Kyrgyzstan, Russia and Tajikistan (formerly the Customs Five) established the Eurasion Economic Community (EEC).
2001 The Russian Federation Council approved the introduction of a single currency (the Russian rouble) for Russia and Belarus as of 1 January 2005. President Lukashenko was returned to power and began a second five-year term amid controversy over the fairness of the election. The president appointed Henadz Navitski as prime minister.
2002 The IMF refused financial assistance stating that Belarus had not made sufficient reforms.
2003 Nearly 73 per cent of voters took part in Belarus's local elections. President Lukashenko dismissed Prime Minister Navitski; Sergei Sidorski became prime minister. Russia, Ukraine, Kazakhstan and Belarus signed an economic union treaty.
2004 Parliamentary elections and a referendum were held. Of the 110 seats in the House of Representatives, 107 were won by government supporters; an approval for a change to the constitution enabled Lukashenko to stand for a third term as president in 2006.
2006 President Lukashenko was re-elected with 82.6 per cent of the vote. The EU and US considered the election seriously flawed.
2007 On 17 October, the second amendment to the constitution was adopted. Presidential terms in office will no longer be limited to two.
2008 In March international relations with US soured when Belarus expelled the US

ambassador and then 10 US diplomats, on May 11, in a row over US-imposed sanctions. In June, Belarus launched an international tender for the construction of a nuclear power plant.

Political structure

Constitution

The 1994 constitution vested legislative power in a 260-member Sejm (Supreme Council).

The first free presidential elections were held in 1994, after which differences emerged over the distribution of power between the president and the Supreme Council.

The constitutional referendum held in late 1996 and the subsequent introduction of a new constitution allowed an expansion of presidential powers and introduced a new two-chamber National Assembly, replacing the Sejm.

On 17 October 2007, the second amendment to the constitution was adopted. Presidential terms in office will no longer be limited to two.

Form of state

Authoritarian presidential republic, where political life is dominated by the president and no real opposition is allowed.

The executive

The president is directly elected for a maximum of two five-year terms and also serves as commander-in-chief of the armed forces, appoints the cabinet and prime minister and has the power to declare a state of emergency, but not to dissolve parliament.

National legislature

The Natsionalnoye Sobranie (National Assembly has two chambers.

The Soviet Respubliki (Council of the Republic) is the upper house. Eight of the 64 members are appointed directly by the president and form the Council of Ministers, and the 56 are indirectly elected by members of the local soviets in the six Belarusian regions and Minsk (eight each). The list of candidates is subject to the final approval by President Lukashenko.

The 110-member Palata Predstavitely (House of Representatives) is the the lower house. Members are elected for four-year terms.

Legal system

Judicial power in the Republic of Belarus is vested in courts. The Constitutional Court adjudicates on whether law is constitutional. The prosecutor general is responsible for ensuring that all laws and presidential decrees are executed properly and uniformly across all state bodies and local Soviets.

Last elections

17 October 2004 (parliamentary); 19 Mar 2006 (presidential).

Results: Parliamentary: 107 of 110 deputies were elected, all supporters of the government, with 12 of them representing political parties. The remaining three seats are to be decided in a second round. Presidential: Aleksandr Lukashenko was re-elected with 82.6 per cent of the vote.

Next elections

2008 (parliamentary); 2011 (presidential).

Political parties

Ruling party

Coalition of Kommunisticheskaya Partuya Belarusi (KPB) (Communist Party of Belarus) and Agrarnaya Partiya Belarusi (APB) (Agrarian Party of Belarus) (since 1995)

Main opposition party

Population

9.65 million (2007)*

Last census: March 1999: 10,045,237

Population density: Approximately 48 per square km. Urban population: 71 per cent.

Annual growth rate: -0.5 per cent 1994–2004 (WHO 2006)

Ethnic make-up

Belorussian (78 per cent), Russian (13 per cent), Polish (4 per cent), Ukranian (3 per cent), other (2 per cent).

Religions

Eastern Orthodox (80 per cent), Roman Catholic, Protestant, Jewish and Islam (20 per cent).

Education

School education is divided into three stages: primary from aged four; basic from aged nine; then secondary schooling, from aged 11. Secondary schooling may be taught through gymnasiums, lyceums or colleges, as well as specialised or technical schools. Gymnasiums provide secondary education at a higher level, while lyceums provide vocational education. The certificate of lyceum education gives right of admission to any higher education institution.

Specialised secondary education lasts for two to four years. Colleges are a new type of institution in Belarus and provide advanced specialist training.

Public expenditure on education is estimated at some 6 per cent of annual gross national income.

Literacy rate: 100 per cent adult rate; 100 per cent youth rate (15–24) (Unesco 2005).

Compulsory years: 4 to 9.

Enrolment rate: 94.2 per cent net primary enrolment; 77.5 per cent net secondary enrolment, of the relevant age groups (including repetition rates), in 2002 (World Bank).

Pupils per teacher: 19 in primary schools.

Health

Per capita total expenditure on health (2003) was US$570; of which per capita government spending was US$406, at the international dollar rate, (WHO 2006).

The population declined by 0.5 per cent per annum between 1994—2000 and is projected to decline at the same rate between 1999—2015. The Ministry of Statistics and Analysis reported that the cause of the decrease is due to the number of deaths exceeding the number of births.

The dramatic fall in life expectancy since the early 1990s is caused by environmental degradation, economic distress and the ever-present radiation from Chernobyl fall-out which continues to affect health, particularly among children.

Medical care in Belarus is limited. There is a severe shortage of basic medical supplies, including anaesthetics, vaccines and antibiotics.

Life expectancy: 68 years, 2004 (WHO 2006)

Fertility rate/Maternal mortality rate: 1.2 births per woman, 2004 (WHO 2006); maternal deaths 28 per 100,000 live births (World Bank).

Birth rate/Death rate: 14 deaths to 9 births per 1,000 people (World Bank).

Child (under 5 years) mortality rate (per 1,000): 13 per 1,000 live births in 2003 (World Bank).

Head of population per physician: 4.55 physicians per 1,000 people, 2003 (WHO 2006)

Welfare

For some years now both economic and political standards have deteriorated under President Lukashenko. As long ago as 1998, a poll by the Ministry of Economy reported that almost 80 per cent of families believed their material well-being had worsened since the collapse of the Soviet Union. Although the state exercises control and mobilises funds for social care and protection, Belarus, along with other Eastern European countries, is planning to privatise its social security systems. Foreign citizens and people permanently living in Belarus have equal rights to social services.

Since independence, the number of local non-governmental organisations (NGOs) has increased dramatically in Belarus. To strengthen the NGO sector, USAID has created the Counterpart Alliance Program (CAP), which provides seed grants to social service organisations in Belarus.

There is a two tiered system of social security coverage: general employed workers and special employees (such as aviators, civil servants and certain medical personnel). Contributions are acquired from three sources: workers, 1 per cent of earnings; employer, 4.7–35 per cent of

the payroll, dependent on industry or enterprise; government revenue covers the cost of social pensions and subsidies as needed.
Social security payments are made to the unemployed and those without pension rights through a general social insurance.

Pensions

Pensions are provided for old age (beginning for men at age 60 and women at age 55, with 25 or 20 years contributions, respectively), disabilities and survivors, including payments for sickness and maternity benefits.

Main cities

Minsk (capital, estimated population 1.9 million in 2005), Homel (Gomel) (548,770), Brèst (354,732), Hrodna (Grodno) (356,334), Mahileu (Mogilev) (401,261), Vitsebsk (Vitebsk) (378,186). Names in brackets are the Russian placenames.
Minsk is the headquarters for the Commonwealth of Independent States (CIS) organisation.

Languages spoken

Ukrainian, Polish and Yiddish.

Official language/s

Belarusian since 1990 and Russian since 1995 referendum.

Media

Press freedom is severely curtailed by presidential policy, with libel laws being both civil and criminal offences, resulting in either heavy fines or imprisonment. The government denies access by the opposition to the state-owned media and can close any independent publication house without judicial review. It appoints senior editors to state-run media outlets and decides on news content, even banning musicians performing pro-opposition music from radio airtime. The state-run press distribution monopoly has refused to deliver independent newspapers around the country and internet news websites are monitored by the State Centre on Information Security. In 2006, the US Media watchdog Freedom House ranked Belarus' freedom of the press as 185 out of 194 in the world and 'not free'.
A new media law was passed in parliament that independent journalists say will restrict online reporting and private media funding ahead of the 2008 parliamentary elections.
National news agency: Belta (Belarusian Telegraph Agency)
Other news agencies: Belapan: http://en.belapan.com
Nashe Mneniye: www.nmnby.org

Press

All state-owned newspapers are heavily subsidised. Newspapers in the Russian language have the major share of the Belarusian market.
Dailies: In Russian, Sovetskaya Belorussia (www.sb.by), is the main government organ, Respublika (www.respublika.info), is a Council of Ministers newspaper, other government publications include 7 Dney (http://7days.belta.by). Private newspapers include Beloruskaya Gazeta (http://www.belgazeta.by) and Narodnaya Volya. In Belarusion Zvyazda (www.zvyazda.minsk.by). In English Belarus Today (www.belarustoday.info).
Weeklies: In Russian, Studenckaja Dumka (http://studumka.iatp.by) is a youth magazine. In English The Minsk Times (www.sb.by/minsktimes), Belarus (www.belarus-magazine.by) are general news and interest magazines.
Business: In Russian, BDG Delovaya Gazeta (www.bdg.by), Belorussky i Rynok (www.br.minsk.by) and Ekonomicheskaya Gazeta (www.neg.by). Delo (East+West) (www.delobelarus.com) and Entrepreneurship in Belarus (www.nbrb.by/bv) are monthly magazines.

Broadcasting

The national, state-run broadcaster is Teleradiocompany (TVR) (www.tvr.by).
Radio: Belarus Radio operates a network of two national stations and three local, with internet broadcasting (www.tvr.by). Programming includes of news, music, cultural and sports events. External services are broadcast in English, German, Polish and Russian. Other radio stations include Radio Roks (www.roks.com), Unistar (http://unistar.by), Alfa Radio (http://alpha.by), and Pilot FM (in Russian).
Television: TVR operates TV-First (www.tvr.by), the only national public service, it also operates the satellite service Belarus TV. The majority state-owned Nationwide TV (ONT) (www.ont.by) is operated by Russia's Channel One. Stolichnoye Televideniye (STV) (http://ctv.by) is a local Minsk broadcaster.

Advertising

The advertising market has been developing very slowly. Advertisers use radio, television, newspapers (rarely used by foreign advertisers) and posters.

Economy

During the Soviet era, the Belarus economy was geared towards industrial production of chemicals, metals and machinery, resulting in serious environmental problems. The break-up of the Soviet Union in 1991 had a strongly negative impact on the economy. Despite this, Belarus entered on a period of privatisation and preliminary reform supported by several international organisations. Continuing dependency on Russia for trade and aid undermined Belarus, particularly following the Asian financial crisis of 1997/98, which threw Russia and consequently Belarus into turmoil.
Since being swept to power in 1994 in the wake of public disillusionment with the negative effects of liberalisation, President Lukashenko has gradually reversed the economic reforms and returned to Soviet-style centralised planning. Price controls were reintroduced, exchange regulations reimposed, privatisation halted and the government has prevented output collapse through subsidised credits to enterprises and farms. More than 95 per cent of the economy is in state control.
There has been a strong growth in the economy with GDP increasing by 11 per cent in 2004 and 9.2 per cent in 2005, compared with 4.8 per cent in 2003. The economy is diverse, with a high level of industrialisation, producing machinery, vehicles, construction materials and chemicals. Most industry, however, relies on imports of raw materials and energy, principally from Russia. The labour force is highly skilled with a large number of engineers and scientists. The policy of centralisation means that there is a severe lack of foreign investment in industry and the infrastructure.

External trade

The US condemned the presidential election as anti-democratic and fraudulent and imposed sanctions on the Belarus leadership in 2004.
Principal trading partners are Russia and CIS countries. Trading relations with Russia which had been strained for several years came to a head in January 2007 when Russia cut oil supplies to Belarus, accusing it of siphoning off supplies destined for the EU. Belarus claimed the oil was seized as outstanding transit payment. Belarus is the third largest exporter of tractors worldwide.

Imports

Principal imports include mineral products, machinery and equipment, metals, gas and energy, chemicals, foodstuffs, electrical and electronic equipment.
Main sources: Russia (58.6 per cent total, 2006), Germany (7.5 per cent), Ukraine (5.5 per cent).

Exports

Principal exports include machinery, vehicles and parts, mineral products, chemicals, foodstuffs, iron and steel.
Main destinations: Russia (34.7 per cent of 2006 total goods exports), The Netherlands (17.7 per cent), UK (7.5 per cent).

Agriculture

Farming

About 60 per cent of arable land is used for livestock (cattle and pigs), the rest

being used for cultivation of potatoes, grain, sugar beet and flax. Although agricultural lands occupy 9.4 million hectares (45.2 per cent of the total area), more than 30 per cent of the land is still contaminated as a consequence of the Chernobyl nuclear plant explosion in Ukraine in 1986. Particularly badly hit was the area around Gomel, where high levels of contamination are still recorded.
The sector receives heavy state support in the form of tax reductions, consumer goods, fertilisers and fuels and remains collectivised, although there are huge unpaid wage arrears on collective farms.
The climate in Belarus means that production is concentrated on hardier crops, including grains, flax, sugar beet and potatoes, of which Belarus is a leading producer.
Belarus meets its own food needs except for feed grains, sugar and vegetable oils, which the government has targetted for increased production. Agriculture is oriented towards meeting domestic market demands for food products with a trend towards animal production.
There has been a steady growth in the amount of agricultural land under private ownership, although the process is slow and obstructed by political and bureaucratic problems.
Crop production in 2005 included: 6,071,000 tonnes (t) cereals in total, 1,000,000t wheat, 1,900,000t barley, 1,250,000t rye, 3,070,000t sugar beets, 8,185,000t potatoes, 150,000t apples, 40,000t maize, 350,000t pulses, 15,300t treenuts, 30,050t oilcrops, 1,500t tobacco, 60,000t flax, 279,000t fruit in total, 2,014,000t vegetables in total.
Livestock production included: 698,800t meat in total, 247,000t beef, 345,000t pig meat, 2,400t lamb, 100,000t poultry, 179,630t eggs, 5,600,000t milk, 3,000t honey, 27,550t cattle hides, 96,000t sheepskins lamb.

Fishing

All fishing in Belarus is derived from rivers, lakes and reservoirs, mainly with drag nets by small teams moving from location to location. There is some fish farming, owned by the state or joint stock companies with government shareholdings.
Belarus has the capacity to process up to 20,000 tonnes per year of mainly smoked and salted fish, with a total of around 300 organisations involved in the fishery industry. The main traditional products include cold smoked fish, salted, preserved and canned fish. Government programmes include increasing the level of catches, the volume and efficiency of fish processing activity by introducing new technologies.
Belarus has had an agreement with Russia since 2002, under which Belarus receives fish quotas in the Russian exclusive economic zone for 10 years, Russian-Belarussian joint ventures base their fleets in Russian ports and both countries co-ordinate their fisheries policies.

Forestry

Forest and other wooded land accounts for over two-fifths of the land area, with forest cover of 9.4 million hectares. About three-quarters of the forest is available for wood supply. Timber includes spruce and birch, which are generally of high quality.
The state owns all forest and other wooded land. The Belavezhskaja Pusha Nature Reserve (north of Brest on the Polish border) is Europe's largest remaining area of primeval forest, totalling 1,300 square km in size.
The forest sector in Belarus makes an important contribution to the economy. The government has attempted to turn back the sector's deterioration in recent years by increasing exports of wood, wood processing and pulp products. It has also investigated environmentally sustainable forestry and has launched a programme of information collation, using satellite technology, to assess the best use of forestry resources.
There is abundant roundwood production, which is mainly used for sawnwood in both large state-owned and small private enterprises. A significant proportion of roundwood and nearly half of pulpwood production is exported. There is very little domestic consumption of production of sawnwood and panels, but pulp and paper production do not meet domestic demand.

Industry and manufacturing

The industrial sector accounts for 25.5 per cent of GDP and employs 40 per cent of the workforce. It has benefited from Soviet-era industrialisation, which transformed Belarus from an agricultural economy into the region's industrial hub.
The sector is diverse and comprises heavy machine production, micro-electronics, computers, chemical and mineral processing, synthetic fibre production, textiles, consumer durables and food processing. Raw materials have to be imported and manufacturing is reliant on energy imports, mainly from Russia.
One of the prime industrial sub-sectors is the automative industry. Belarus is the world's third largest producer of tractors and also produces a large number of lorries, motorbikes and other vehicles, which are exported mainly to Europe. The Minsk Tractor Works (MTZ) produces up to 8 per cent of the world's tractors, which are exported to more than 100 countries.
Belarus' electronics sector is highly developed, due to its role in supplying the Soviet military machine. It manufactures radios, televisions and electronic devices used in engineering, as well as supplying consumer goods, including refrigerators and freezers, to countries inside and outside the former Soviet Union.
Production of chemicals is concentrated in Soligorsk, Gomel and Grodno. The chemical sector produces potassium and nitrate fertilisers, aminophosphate, medicines, polymers and plastics, chemical and synthetic fibres, pesticides, rubber goods and building materials.

Tourism

Tourist facilities are inadequate with poor quality hotels and bureaucratic obstacles hindering visitors; visas cost more than those charged by neighbouring states, border crossings are tedious and costly, while levies on hotel rooms for tourists put them out of the reach of most visitors. Investment in upgrading facilities and conserving historic tourist attractions is in short supply. Tourism is expected to contribute 1.9 per cent to GDP in 2005.

Environment

One-third of the nation's agricultural land has been unusable since it was contaminated by fall-out from the 1986 Chernobyl nuclear accident.

Mining

Belarus is not rich in natural resources, except for deposits of peat, used in power stations and for the manufacture of chemicals. There are significant deposits of potassium, which is a major export, and rock salt. Other resources include clay, sand, iron ore, cobalt, phosphate, silver and gold. Many known mineral deposits await development, while a full survey of the country's resources has yet to be carried out.

Hydrocarbons

Belarus has proven oil reserves of 198 million barrels. The country typically produces over 35,000 barrels per day (bpd), but imports 75 per cent of its oil needs, all of which come from Russia. Refining capacity is over 300,000bpd, higher than both domestic production and consumption. There are two refineries in the regions of Novopolotsk Vitebsk and Gomel.
Natural gas reserves stand at 2.83 billion cubic metres (cum). Belarus produces around 210 million cum of natural gas, but with consumption amounting to 19.6 billion cum, the country is heavily reliant on Russian gas imports.
There are deposits of brown coal of little value. Coal is not produced, but is imported from Russia.

Energy

Belarus has a total electricity generating capacity of 7.5GW. Net electricity imports amount to 20 per cent of annual electricity demand. Gas accounts for approximately 71 per cent of electricity generation and oil for the rest. Fears of accelerating inflation have slowed the implementation of tariff reform and price rises have been consistently outstripped by inflation.

Banking and insurance

The National Bank of the Republic of Belarus (NBRB) (central bank) and the Commercial Bank for Foreign Economic Activity (CBFEA) were established in 1991. All enterprises were instructed to transfer hard currency funds from the Russian Vnesheconombank to the CBFEA. The banking system has seen an increase in state participation since President Lukashenko was first elected in 1994. Priorbank is the largest private bank and holds 8 per cent of the total assets of the banking system, making it the fifth largest in Belarus. Foreign capital participation is present in 19 banks, including two which are wholly foreign owned. Credit to the private sector amounts to 9 per cent of GDP. In January 2003, Austria's Raiffeisen Bank bought a 50 per cent stake in Priorbank for US$30.5 million, injecting competition into the sector.

Central bank

The National Bank of the Republic of Belarus

Time

GMT plus two hours, (daylight saving, late March to late October, GMT plus three hours)

Geography

Belarus is situated in north-eastern Europe. It has frontiers with Poland, in the west, Lithuania in the north-west and Latvia in the north. It has long frontiers with Russia from the north to the east, and with the Ukraine from the east to the south. The land is a plain with numerous lakes, swamps and marshes. There is a region of low lying hills north of Minsk. The highest point, Mount Dzyarzhynskaya, is only 346 metres above sea-level. The southern part of the country is an extensive flat marshland. Forests cover some 30 per cent of the territory. The main rivers are the Dnepr which flows south to the Black Sea, and the Pripyat which flows eastwards to the Dnepr through the Pripyat Marshes.

Hemisphere

Northern

Climate

Temperature ranges from minus 6 degrees Celsius (C) in January, to a high of 18 degrees C in August. The average annual rainfall is 550mm to 700mm.

Dress codes

With grey, freezing winters and wet summers, fashion takes second place to practicality in Belarus. Smart dress is required for business.

Entry requirements

Passports

Valid passport required by all and must be valid for six months after departure.
All foreign nationals must register their passports at the local police station within three days of their arrival; if staying at a hotel, reception will do this automatically.

Visa

Visas are required by almost all and must be obtained by anyone travelling through Belarus by train, including international routes Warsaw-Moscow and St Petersburg-Kiev.
Some visa exceptions include nationals of the CIS, travelling as tourists. For further details of those exempt and full requirements for visas see www.mfa.gov.by/eng/consul/3.
Business visas allow stays for up to 90 days. Applications must include an invitation, (may be originally supplied as fax) on official letterhead and should have a signature of the head of a company as well as a corporate seal. It should also indicate the expected period of stay and a pledge by the host company to provide the invited person full support during their stay in Belarus including all possible medical expenses.
Visitors must register their stay with Belarus authorities for visits of over three days. Exit permits are required by foreigners intending to leave the country with expired visas.

Currency advice/regulations

Import and export of local currency is not permitted and all remaining money must be reconverted before departure. Import of foreign currency is unlimited; however, export of same is possible only to the amount declared on arrival. Currency exchange receipts should be retained and all transactions must be recorded on a currency declaration form, issued on arrival and surrendered on departure. The US dollar and euro currencies offer the best options for conversion. Many public services can only be paid for in hard currencies.
Traveller' cheques, in US dollars or euros, may be exchanged in large banks only, other currencies may be more problematic.

Customs

Small amounts of personal goods are duty-free. Valuable items such as jewellery, cameras, computers and musical instruments should be declared.

Health (for visitors)

Medical insurance is required by all foreign citizens visiting Belarus.

Mandatory precautions

None

Advisable precautions

Water precautions are recommended (water purification tablets may be useful).
Dairy products, mushrooms and fruits of the forest (all of which may still be contaminated by radiation from the Chernobyl disaster) should be avoided.
Some immunisations may be advantageous: polio, typhoid, diphtheria and tetanus, and hepatitis A for longer term visitors.
It is wise to carry adequate supplies of prescribed medicines, and have precautionary antibiotics if going outside major urban centres. A travel kit including a disposable syringe is a reasonable precaution.

Hotels

Minsk and Vitebsk boast two-, three- and four-star hotels; other cities have two and three-star hotels. There are no five-star Western-standard hotels in Belarus (as of 2006).

Credit cards

Large hotel, restaurants and at foreign currency shops accept major credit cards. There are a few ATMs in Minsk.

Public holidays (national)

Fixed dates

1 Jan (New Year), 7 Jan (Orthodox Christmas Day), 8 Mar (Women's Day), 15 Mar (Constitution Day), 1 May (Labour Day), 9 May (Victory Day), 3 Jul (Independence Day), 2 Nov (Dzyady/Remembrance Day), 7 Nov (Day of the October Revolution), 25 Dec (Christmas Day).

Variable dates

Good Friday, Orthodox Good Friday, Easter Monday, Orthodox Easter Monday.

Working hours

Banking

Mon–Fri: 0900–1700, including Priorbank, Minsk 2 airport.
Foreign exchange outlets are open all day until late, and some open 24 hours.

Business

Mon–Fri: 0900–1800 (appointments best between 0900–1000).

Government

Mon–Fri: 0900–1300, 1400–1800.

Shops

Most food stores are now open Mon–Sat: 0900–1400 and 1500–2000. Sat: 0900–1800.
General stores open Mon to Fri: 1000–1400 and 1500–1900. Sat: 1000–1800.
There are some 24-hour food stores.

Telecommunications

Mobile/cell phones

GSM 900/1800 services are available throughout most of the country.

Electricity supply
220V AC 50Hz. European-style round two-pin plugs are in use.

Social customs/useful tips
Business is conducted formally and appointments are essential. A firm handshake is important as is negotiating an agenda at the beginning of the meeting. Smoking in meetings is very common. Ask permission before lighting a cigarette and offer cigarettes generously.
Written communications are particularly important with large bureaucracies. Address the recipient formally and keep a copy of everything. It is customary to take a small gift on a business or social visit. Offering basic food is considered insulting; offer little luxuries. It is impolite to accompany guests who are not invited to a social function. Gratuities are not obligatory but are becoming more widespread. Vodka is the national drink.

Security
Crime is still negligible and visitors should avoid political demonstrations.
It is advisable to keep away from military establishments.

Getting there
Air
National airline: Belavia
International airport/s: Minsk 2 (MSQ), 43km east of the city, facilities include banks and bureaux de change, bars, car hire, duty-free shops, post office and restaurants.
Airport tax: None
Surface
Road: Good road connections exist with Ukraine, the Baltic States, Poland and Russia. Visitors arriving by car are advised to insure their vehicle with a Belarusian insurer (eg Belingosstrakh); offices can be found at crossing sites. Note that petrol is limited and only 4-star and diesel are available. Most petrol stations only accept cash.
A fee for drivers of foreign vehicles is collected at border checkpoints and varies according to the length of stay.
Rail: There are train connections with all neighbouring countries, with express trains from most European capitals.

Getting about
National transport
Road: There is road network of over 55,000km, the majority of which is hard surfaced. Petrol is limited; only 4-star and diesel are available; and most petrol stations only accept cash. Motorways connect many of the major cities.
Rail: Total railtrack is about 5,523km broad gauge, of which approximately 875km is electrified. Train tickets and reservations can be purchased at Francyska Skaryny Prospekt No 18, Minsk.
Water: Belarus is landlocked, but there is an extensive network of inland waterways (3,800km) which mainly convey cargo goods. The Mukhavets and Pripyat rivers in south Belarus are connected by the strategic Dnepr-Buh Canal, which in turn gives access to the Baltic and Black Seas.
City transport
Taxis: Taxis are plentiful; they can be found waiting in front of hotels, at the airport, railway station and bus station. Journey time from the airport to city centre is about 40 minutes.
Buses, trams & metro: The city of Minsk has a metro that covers the central district, with two lines and 23 stations. Trains run between 0600-0100; entry to the underground is by tokens which are obtainable from stations.
There are buses from the international airport to city centre, journey time about 60 minutes.
Urban buses, trams and trolleybuses run between 0535-0055; tickets for these can be purchased at news-stands or kiosks and must be punched when boarding.
Car hire
Cars can be rented, with or without a driver. An international driving licence with international permit is required. There are numerous restrictions that apply to driving. It is illegal to drive after consuming any amount of alcohol, no matter how little. Driving is on the right. International traffic signs and regulations are in use. Speed limits are 60kph (37mph) in towns and cities and 90kph (55mph) on country lanes and speed traps are widespread.

BUSINESS DIRECTORY

The addresses listed below are a selection only. While World of Information makes every endeavour to check these addresses, we cannot guarantee that changes have not been made, especially to telephone numbers and area codes. We would welcome any corrections.

Telephone area codes
The international direct dialling (IDD) code for Belarus is +375, followed by area code and subscriber's number:

Brest	16	Minsk	17
Gomel	23	Mogilev	22
Grodno	15	Vitebsk	21

Chambers of Commerce
Belarussian Chamber of Commerce and Industry, Communisticheskaya Street, 220029 Minsk (tel: 290–7249; fax: 290–7248; e-mail: mbox@cci.by).

Brest Chamber of Commerce and Industry, 14 Kubysheva Street, 224016 Brest (tel: 223-2400; fax: 223-4854; e-mail: bo@tppbrs.belpak.brest.by).

Grodno Chamber of Commerce and Indutry, Sovetskaya Street, 20023 Grodno (tel: 224-9070; e-mail: anat@grocci.belpark.grodno.by).

Minsk Chamber of Commerce and Industry, 65 Ya Kolas Street, 220113 Minsk (tel: 266-0473; fax: 266-2604; e-mail: secret@mdbcci.belpak.minsk.by).

Vitebsk Chamber of Commerce and Industry, Kosmonavtov Street, 210001 Vitebsk (tel: 236-3052; fax: 236-4674; e-mail: vitebsk@cci.by).

Banking
Belagroprom Bank, 44 Kropotkina Street, Minsk 220002 (tel: 503-958).

Bel Vnesh Econom Bank (Belarus Bank for Foreign Economic Affairs), 10 Zaslavskaya Street, Minsk 220004 (tel: 269-757, 267-022; fax: 269-759).

Commercial Bank for Reconstruction and Development (Belbusinessbank), 6a Partizansky Ave, 220033 Minsk (tel: 298-147, 768-942; fax: 298-147, 768-504).

Central bank
The National Bank of the Republic of Belarus, 20 F Skorina Avenue, 220008 Minsk (tel: 219-2303; fax: 227-4879; e-mail: email@nbrb.by).

Travel information
Belavia (Belarusian Airlines), 14 Nemiga Street, Minsk 220004 (tel: 210-4100; fax: 220-2383; email: info@belavia.by; internet: www.belavia.by/index_en.htm).

National tourist organisation offices
Belintourist, 19 Masherov Avenue, 220004 Minsk (tel: 226-9840; fax: 223-1143: email: office@belintourist.by; internet: www.belintourist.by).

Ministries
Department of Foreign Economic Co-operation (tel: 269-169).

Department of International Relations (tel: 269-187; fax: 269-936).

Ministry of Agriculture, Dom Pravitelstva, Minsk (tel: 271-377, 271-352, 205-492).

Ministry of Finance, Dom Pravitelstva, 220010 Minsk (tel: 296-949).

Ministry of Foreign Affairs, ul. K. Mark 16, 220050 Minsk (tel: 272-011; fax: 293-383).

Ministry of Information, Prospekt Mashirova 11, Minsk (tel: 237-574).

Ministry of Statistics and Analysis of the Republic of Belarus, 12 Partizan Avenue, Minsk 220658 (tel: 491-261, 495-200; fax: 492-204).

Ministry of Trade, Kirov St. Building, Minsk 220084 (tel: 276-121).

State Committee for Foreign Economic Relations, House of Government, Minsk 220010 (tel: 296-345).

State Committee for Economic Planning, Dom Pravitelstva, Minsk (tel: 296-944).

Other useful addresses

Belarusintorg, Foreign Trade Organisation, Ulitsa Kollektornaya 10, 220048 Minsk (tel: 207-812, 209-756, 208-188; fax: 209-470, 204-763).

British Embassy, 37 Karl Marx Street, Minsk 220016 (tel: 292-303/4/5, 172105920; fax: 292-306, 172292306); Visa and Consulate Section (tel: 292-310; fax: 292-311).

Minsk Expo Exhibition Company, pr. Masherova 14, Minsk 220035 (tel: 226-9193/9890; fax: 226-9192/9936; e-mail: minskexpo@brm.minsk.by; internet: www.minskexpo.com.by).

National Centre for Marketing and Price Study, 7-1117 Masherov Avenue, Minsk, PO 220004 (to reach the National Centre call for voice connection and/or fax: 266-758).

News Agency, Minsk (tel: 293-040).

Union of Enterpreneurs, 13 Internatsional'naya St, Minsk 220050 (tel: 172-587; fax: 271-596).

US Embassy, 46 Starovilenskaya Street, Minsk 220002 (tel: 210-1283; fax: 234-7853).

National news agency: Belta (Belarusian Telegraph Agency)

Other news agencies: Belapan: http://en.belapan.com
Nashe Mneniye: www.nmnby.org

Internet sites

Belarus portal: http://www.e-belarus.org

Belarusian web links: www.belarusian.com/links

Belarusian web sites: www.ac.by/country/belwww.html

General information: www.belarus.net

Investment: www.ib.by

Chamber of Commerce: www.cci.by

Business information: www.delobelarus.com

General information: www.open.by

Belgium

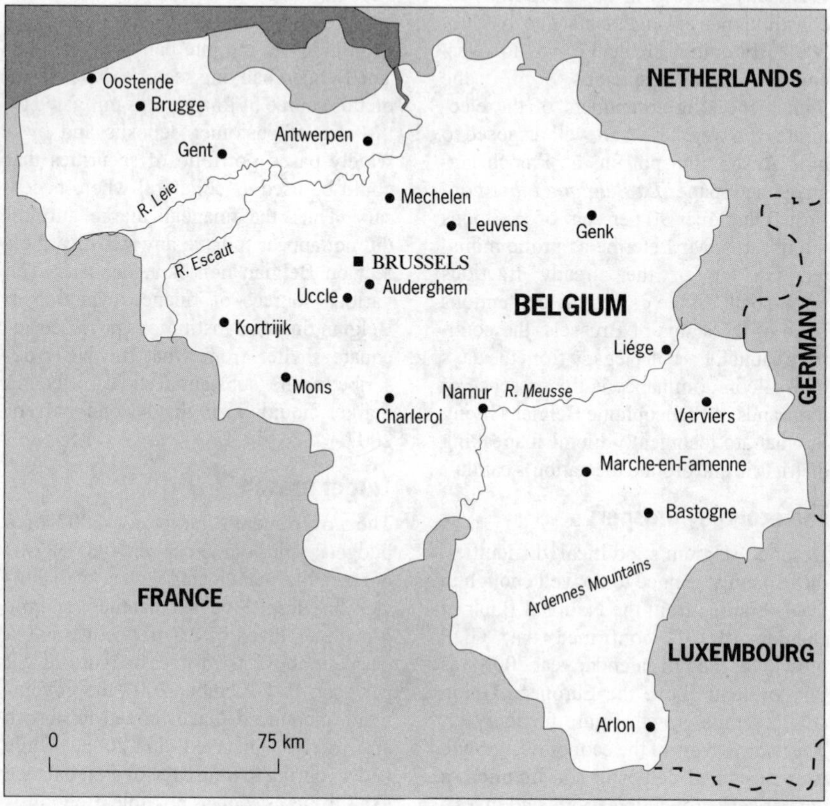

Belgium can hardly be classed a 'happy' country. The ethnic and linguistic divisions do little for national harmony. In the late 1990s and the first few years of the twenty-first century, recurrent national paedophilia scandals apparently implicating senior police and political figures have done little for national morale. Belgium is also a young country, younger than the USA and many Latin American republics. In the Belgian context, the word 'country' is perhaps a misnomer.

Concept or country?

Belgium is more of a concept than a country. Few Belgians can provide a rational explanation for the creation and the continued existence of their country. What has held Belgium together has been its negatives rather than its positives. A profound mutual dislike between Flemings and Walloons has combined with an equally deep reluctance to live under French or Dutch hegemony.

In an attempt to overcome these differences and dislikes, a process of devolution in the Belgian constitution was begun as far back as 1968, leading to the establishment of separate Flemish and French speaking regions (Flanders and Wallonia) in 1983, and a separate Brussels area in 1988. These moves were seen by many as a phase in a gradual move towards total autonomy for the regions. For a nine month period from mid-2007 it looked more than likely that as a body politic Belgium would divide irreparably along linguistic lines. The tensions and divisions that had prevailed following the stalemate of the 2007 general election were papered over rather than resolved by the formation of a five-party coalition government in March 2008. Most observers felt that their country's first permanent administration since 2007 was stillborn, or at best simply

KEY FACTS

Official name: Royaume de Belgique (French), Koninkrijk België (Dutch), Königreich Belgien (German) (Kingdom of Belgium)

Head of State: King Albert II (since 1993)

Head of government: Prime Minister Yves Leterme (CDV) (from 20 Mar 2008)

Ruling party: Coalition Open Vlaamse Liberalen en Democraten (Open VLD) led by Christen-Democratisch en Vlaams (CDV) (Christian Democratic and Flemish), with Mouvement Réformateur (MR) (Reform Movement), Parti Socialiste (PS) (Socialist Party) and Centre Démocrate Humaniste (CDH) (French Christian Democrats) (since 20 Mar 2008)

Area: 30,518 square km

Population: 10.66 million (2007)

Capital: Brussels

Official language: Dutch (Flemish), French and German

Currency: Euro (eur) = 100 cents (from 1 Jan 2002; previous currency Belgian franc, locked at Bf40.34 per euro)

Exchange rate: eur0.63 per US$ (Jul 2008)

GDP per capita: US$42,557 (2007)

GDP real growth: 2.70% (2007)

Unemployment: 7.50% (2007)

Inflation: 1.80% (2007)

Balance of trade: US$5.24 billion (2005)

Foreign debt: US$949.47 billion (2004)

Visitor numbers: 7.00 million (2006)*

Annual FDI: US$34.40 billion (OECD, 2004)*

* estimated figure

too weak to survive. A poll conducted shortly after the government's formation, suggested that over 60 per cent of the electorate expected the government – lead by Flemish Christian Democrat Yves Leterme – to fall within three years.

The odd couple

The acrimonious interregnum that followed the June 2007 general election failed to produce anything resembling a government. During this period it often looked as though Belgium as a recognisable entity was going to disappear, to be replaced by a relatively prosperous Flemish (Dutch) speaking Flanders to the north, and a relatively impoverished, Francophile, Wallonia to the south. Most of the argument surrounding the process of devolution has always focussed on the contributions (or lack of them) by the respective regions to the collective wealth of the nation. For some time Wallonia has depended on government subsidies, estimated at US$9 billion annually in late 2007. The three million Walloon population only represent some 30 per cent of the total population. The subsidies they receive represented about US$3,000 per head in 2007. The political deadlock is nothing new to Belgium, representing as it does the shift in Belgium's economic make up. Wallonia's coal and steel industries once gave it prosperity and preponderance at a time when Flanders' economy was largely agricultural. Belgium's politics, along with its economy, was largely shaped by its French-speaking élite. Times have changed, however; as is the case with many European countries, Belgium's north now looks upon its south as lazy and lacking in enterprise. Flanders' economy is driven by its ports and its chemical industries, working alongside a more aggressive *mittelstand* of small and medium-sized enterprises that dominate the services and light industrial sectors.

Pragmatism tends to prevail in Belgian politics; Mr Leterme's government may eventually succeed in thrashing out new constitutional arrangements due by July 2008. His initial challenge was to overcome the suspicions of the French-speaking component of the electorate who were less than well disposed to him. An opinion poll in the French language newspaper *La Belgique Libre* confirmed that over 90 per cent of Walloons did not trust Mr Leterme as prime minister. On top of the already fractious north-south divide comes the contentious issue of the status of Brussels, the country's capital. Part of a legacy from the days of Walloon dominance is the presence of thousands of Francophone Belgians living in what are technically Flemish speaking districts in and around the nation's capital.

The economy prospers

Despite Belgium's political difficulties, the economy seemed to do well enough in 2007. Figures from the National Bank of Belgium (NBB) confirmed that GDP growth for the full calendar year 2007 was 2.7 per cent, above the European Union (EU) average growth figure for the year. The main drivers of the economy's growth were sustained domestic consumption, a 4.6 per cent growth in exports and investment growth of over 5 per cent for the year. Inflation appeared to be contained below the EU average at 1.5 per cent and unemployment continued its downward trend to reach 7.5 per cent. As was the case with most European economies, growth was expected to dip in 2008 – in Belgium's case to 1.9 per cent.

Banking constraints

As reported by the NBB, in the third quarter of 2007 Belgium's credit institutions experienced a relatively sudden tightening of liquidity in the interbank loan market. The Belgian banking sector's dependence on this source of finance was mitigated by the size of customer deposits and by a widely based portfolio of securities that could be used as collateral where necessary. Thus, the financial market turmoil did not appear to have any significant effect on Belgian non-bank deposits. The various sources of finance available to Belgian financial institutions provided adequate shelter from what the NBB described as the 'substantial shock' affecting market liquidity in the second half of 2007.

Target missed

The government's target for 2007 of a budget surplus of 0.3 per cent of GDP was not met, the year closing with a small deficit. This, despite the fact that the economic growth achieved of 2.7 per cent was 0.5 per cent above the forecast figure of 2.2 per cent. In December 2007 the government announced that it aimed to absorb any deficit incurred in 2008, while endeavouring to return the overall balance to a surplus as soon as possible. Belgium's continuing high level of public debt and an ageing population make returning to a surplus essential to ensure sustainable public finances.

Of particular note for Belgium's longer term economic prospects was a report by the government's newly-created *Study Committee on Ageing* concerning the budgetary impact of demographic developments. The report suggested that public spending on pensions and health care will increase by some 8 percentage points of GDP between 2006 and 2050. Coincidental factors – principally lower unemployment benefits and reduced family allowances – will mean that in real terms the net increase in public expenditure will only amount to some 6 percentage points of GDP. The same report anticipated the budget surplus increasing by an annual 0.2 per cent, to reach 1.3 per cent by 2012.

The Belgian economy is a high tax economy. Overall employment taxes are put at around 6.5 per cent higher than the average for the eurozone (countries using the

KEY INDICATORS — Belgium

	Unit	2003	2004	2005	2006	2007
Population	m	10.37	10.41	10.51	10.59	10.66
Gross domestic product (GDP)	US$bn	296.44	349.83	372.73	398.14	453.64
GDP per capita	US$	28,700	34,244	35,461	37,613	42,557
GDP real growth	%	1.3	2.7	1.5	3.0	2.7
Inflation	%	1.5	1.9	2.5	2.3	1.8
Unemployment	%	8.2	7.8	8.4	8.3	7.5
Exports (fob) (goods)	US$m	255,300.0	244,552.0	268,180.0	281,135.0	322,805.0
Imports (cif) (goods)	US$m	235,500.0	235,590.0	262,944.0	277,778.0	322,241.0
Balance of trade	US$m	19,800.0	8,962.0	5,236.0	3,357.0	564.0
Current account	US$m	13,340.0	14,910.0	9,221.0	10,558.0	14,635.0
Total reserves minus gold	US$m	10,989.0	10,361.0	4,241.0	8,783.0	10,384.0
Foreign exchange	US$m	7,651.0	7,715.0	6,815.0	7,619.0	9,298.0
Exchange rate	per US$	0.88	0.80	0.77	0.75	0.69

euro). Although the Belgian tax rate is roughly comparable to those of three other high-tax economies – Finland, France and Italy – it is well above all the others. Income tax is principally responsible for any differential. In 2007, the effective individual tax rate on earned income in Belgium was 42 per cent.

The 2.7 per cent increase in GDP for 2007 reflected robust export demand from the economies of Eastern Europe, Asia and the world's commodity producing economies. Domestic consumption and investment also continued to rise, giving Belgium two uninterrupted years of rising economic activity. Although events in international financial markets created some background uncertainty, in the fourth quarter of 2007 consumer confidence only appeared to be endangered by higher levels of inflation. Although annual GDP growth had decelerated slightly to 2.3 per cent by the end of the year, this was not totally unexpected. The process of deceleration had in fact started before the financial markets were gripped by uncertainty, and after a period of two years' growth, it was not a surprise for the markets. In contrast to the sharp falls of earlier years, the decline in late 2007 was moderate. Business confidence was certainly lower at the end of 2007, reflecting lower levels of demand; but employment prospects remained strong and the appreciation of the euro against the US dollar appeared to have little detrimental effect on exports. Belgium's industrial activity grew at an annual rate of 3.2 per cent in the first three quarters of 2007, roughly comparable to the rate registered in 2006. It was the services sector, which represents some 75 per cent of value-added trade in Belgium, which recorded the lowest growth rate of the economy as a whole. Despite its relative economic success, Belgium can hardly be classed a 'happy' country. Its ethnic and linguistic divisions do little for national harmony. And recurrent national paedophilia scandals implicating senior police and political figures have done little for national morale.

Risk assessment

Economy	Good
Politics	Fair
Regional stability	Good

COUNTRY PROFILE

Historical profile

In the eighth and ninth centuries, the area which is now Belgium was part of the Charlemagne empire. It achieved independence by the tenth century. Flemish towns, with their large textile industries, enjoyed great financial and political power.

1322 The area fell under French control again.

1419 The accession of Philip of Burgundy ended a period of instability.

1477 The Low Countries (Belgium and the Netherlands) passed to the Habsburgs of Spain on the death of Philip's son, Charles the Bold.

1500–55 Under the reign of Emperor Charles V, Antwerp was a leading commercial centre and financial centre.

1555–98 Reign of Philip II, King of Spain. The Belgians and the Dutch reacted against the tyranny of Philip II. There was trouble between the protestants and the catholics.

1580s The northern Netherlands managed to secede. King Philip reconquered the south, where catholicism was imposed. The leading traders and intellectuals migrated to the north.

1598–1621 Under Archduke Albert and Archduchess Isabella (daughter of Philip II), the southern Netherlands (Belgium excluding Liège) became semi-autonomous.

1648 The Peace of Westphalia confirmed this position.

1700–13 The War of the Spanish Succession resulted in the southern Netherlands passing to the Austrian Habsburgs. Liège remained independent within the Holy Roman Empire.

1790 The United States of Belgium was established after a local revolution inspired by the French revolution.

1792 French troops conquered the southern Netherlands and Liège.

1793 The Austrians reoccupied the territory.

1794 The southern Netherlands and Liège were invaded by the French and the newly integrated territories were annexed to France. When Napoleon came to power, Belgium became part of the French empire.

1814–15 After the defeat of Napoleon, the allies met at the Congress of Vienna and decided to unite the northern and southern Netherlands and the princedom of Liège under the rule of King William I. The catholic church refused to accept a protestant King. William tried to impose Dutch in Flanders. The young Walloon and Flemish upper classes, which spoke French, were afraid that their careers would be affected.

1828 The Catholics and young Liberals formed an association called Unionism and drew up a programme of demands.

1830 Revolution erupted in Brussels and the south broke away from the north and formed an independent Belgian state.

1831–65 Leopold I of Saxe-Coburg became the first King of Belgian.

1865–1909 His son Leopold II succeeded him. He backed expeditions to Africa. In 1908, Congo was transferred to the Belgian state.

1909–34 King Albert I reigned.

1914 Following the outbreak of the First World War, Germany invaded Belgium and the country became a battlefield until the end of the war in 1918.

1918–39 Inter-war years saw rapid industrialisation, developing colonial wealth in Africa and the forging of regional links, leading to the Belgium-Luxembourg Economic Union (BLEU).

1940–45 Belgium was invaded and occupied by Nazi Germany.

1947 Belgium formed a customs union with Luxembourg and the Netherlands, known as Benelux.

1951 King Leopold III, who had been on the throne since 1934, abdicated in favour of his son, Baudouin (Boudewijn) I.

1958 Belgium was a founder member of the forerunner of the EU, the European Economic Community (EEC), with Brussels becoming the favoured location for the organisation.

1960 Belgium withdrew rapidly from the Belgian Congo.

1970s There was a succession of unstable coalition governments.

1979–92 Christian Democrat Wilfried Martens was appointed prime minister twice during this period, with Mark Eyskens serving for some months in 1981.

1992 Jean-Luc Dehaene was appointed prime minister.

1993 King Baudouin I died and was succeeded by his brother, Albert II. Belgium became a federal state.

1999 Belgium was one of the first 11 countries to adopt the euro. Guy Verhofstadt was appointed prime minister.

2001 A government reform package was approved, which provided more money for schools in the French-speaking communities of the south and more political influence for the Dutch-speaking Flemish around Brussels even though they are a minority.

2002 Euro currency replaced the Belgian franc.

2003 The May parliamentary elections were won by the Vlaamse Liberalen en Demokraten (VLD) (Flemish Liberal and Democrats), led by Guy Verhofstadt, who formed a coalition government in July, which included the Socialistische Partij Anders-Spirit (SPA-Spirit) (Socialist Party-Spirit), Parti Socialiste (PS) (Socialist Party) and Mouvement Réformateur (MR) (Reform Movement).

2004 Following conviction for racial incitement in November, the Vlaams Blok (VB) (Flemish Bloc) party reconstituted itself as Vlaams Belang (VB) (Flemish Interest)

2005 After failing to resolve a dispute between French and Dutch speakers over the re-drawing of the country's biggest electoral district, the government comfortably won a parliamentary vote of confidence on 13 May.
2006 An investigation into the activities of right-wing extremists in the military resulted in raids on barracks and arrests in September. In local elections in October, the VB made appreciable gains.
2007 In elections for the Chamber of Representatives held on 10 June, the CDV-NVA won 30 out of 150 seats, MR won 23, VB won 17, VLD won 18, PS won 20, SPA-Spirit won 18, the Centre Démocrate Humaniste (CDH) (French Christian Democrats) won 10; all other parties won less than ten seats. Turnout was 91.1 per cent. The VLD, SPA-Spirit, PS and MR coalition of liberals and socialist lost too many votes to retain power jointly. Prime Minister Guy Verhofstadt resigned on 11 June, however he was re-appointed as a caretaker prime minister. By 1 December Verhofstadt's second attempt at forming a coalition had failed due to wrangling between political parties representing Flemish and French speakers, each advocating more rights for their constituents. To break the political impasse, on 17 December the King asked Verhofstadt to form an interim government.
2008 After nine months of political stalemate, Yves Camille Désiré Leterme (Christen-Democratisch en Vlaams (CDV) (Christian Democratic and Flemish)) was sworn in as prime minister and his coalition government was endorsed by the lower house of parliament on 20 March. Prime Minister Leterme tended his resignation on 14 July, having failed to achieve legislation to devolve more power to the country's regions. However the King rejected Leterme's resignation and charged three other ministers to resolve the problem.

Political structure

Constitution

A new constitution was introduced in 1994, re-defining the federal structure and introducing devolution on both a regional and language-speaking level. In 2001, a constitutional amendment allowed greater autonomy in taxation, spending, agricultural and trade policy.
The federal state is responsible for economic, domestic, foreign, defence, legal, welfare and health policy.
The are three Régions/Gewests (Regions) of Flemish, Wallonia and Brussels. Each has its own executive and assembly, responsible for regional policies (such as transport and housing).
Overlapping the Regions are three Communautés/Gemeenschaps (Communities), representing Belgium's Flemish, French and German-speakers. They are responsible for policy on language and cultural affairs. The French and German Communities operate separate parliaments. The Flemish Region and Community (which represent the same geographical area) operate a joint assembly. Language and cultural affairs in the Brussels Region are divided between the Flemish and French Communities.
In May 2003 electoral reforms allowed changes to electoral districts for the House of Representatives, which now match the borders of the provinces, a new system of distribution of seats, an electoral threshold and Belgians abroad allowed to vote.

Form of state

Federal parliamentary democratic monarchy

The executive

Executive responsibilities reside with the federal prime minister and Council of Ministers (cabinet) and with the regional prime ministers and cabinets. The monarch has a largely ceremonial role.
The Council of Ministers is appointed by the monarch and approved by parliament. Following legislative elections, the leader of the majority party or the leader of the majority coalition is usually appointed prime minister by the monarch and then approved by parliament.

National legislature

Legislative power is vested in a bicameral parliament, consisting of the Senate (71 seats; 40 members are directly elected by popular vote, 31 are indirectly elected; members serve four-year terms) and the Chamber of Representatives (150 seats; members are directly elected by popular vote on the basis of proportional representation to serve four-year terms). Both chambers can propose and veto legislation.

Legal system

The Code Napoléon, became the basis of civil law in Belgium.
The constitution guarantees the independence of the judiciary from the executive and legislative branches. Court hearings are public and trials of a serious nature are heard before a jury of civilians.
The highest court is the Cour de Cassation (Supreme Court), composed of judges appointed by the Crown. A Cour d'Arbitration rules on conflicts of authority between the many layers of federal and national government and their legal instruments.
A Consultation Committee, made up of regional and national representatives including the prime minister, is the final recourse for conflicts of interest arising from devolution. Formed with equal numbers of French and Dutch/Flemish speakers, it makes its decisions by consensus.

Last elections

10 June 2007 (Chamber of Representatives and Senate).
Results: Parliamentary: (Chamber of Representatives) Christen Democratisch en Vlaams-Nieuw Vlaamse Alliantie (CDV-NVA) (Christian Democratic and Flemish-New Flemish Alliance) won 18.5 per cent of the vote (30 out of 150 seats); Mouvement Réformateur (MR) (French Liberals) 12.5 per cent (23); Vlaams Blok (VB) (Flemish Bloc) 12 per cent (17); Vlaamse Liberalen en Demokraten (VLD) (Flemish Liberals and Democrats) 11.8 per cent (18); Parti Socialiste (PS) (French Socialists) 10.9 per cent (20); Socialistische Partij Anders-Spirit (SPA-Spirit) (Socialist Party-Spirit) (Flemish Socialists) 11.8 per cent (18); Centre Démocrate Humaniste (CDH) (French Christian Democrats) 6.1 per cent (10); Ecologistes Confédéres (Ecolo) (French Greens) 5.1 per cent (8); 4 per cent (5), Lijst Dedecker (LD) List Dedecker 3.4 per cent (1); Front National (FN) (National Front) 2.3 per cent (1).
Senate: the CDV-NVA won 19.4 per cent of the vote (nine out of 40 seats); Open VLD 12.4 per cent (5); MR 12.3 per cent (6); VB 11.9 per cent (5); PS 10.2 per cent (4); Socialistische Partij Anders-Spirit (SPA-Spirit) (Socialist Party- Spirit) 10 per cent (4); CDH 5.9 per cent (2); Ecolo 5.8 per cent (2); Groen! (Greens!) 3.6 per cent (1); LD 3.4 per cent (1) and FN 2.3 per cent (1). Turnout was 91.1 per cent.

Next elections

May 2011 (parliamentary)

Political parties

Ruling party

Coalition Open Vlaamse Liberalen en Democraten (Open VLD) led by Christen-Democratisch en Vlaams (CDV) (Christian Democratic and Flemish), with Mouvement Réformateur (MR) (Reform Movement), Parti Socialiste (PS) (Socialist Party) and Centre Démocrate Humaniste (CDH) (French Christian Democrats) (since 20 Mar 2008)

Main opposition party

Vlaams Blok (VB) (Flemish Bloc) and Socialistische Partij Anders-Spirit (SPA-Spirit) (Socialist Party-Spirit) (Flemish Socialists).

Population

10.66 million (2007)
Last census: October 2001: 10,296,350
Population density: Urban population: 97 per cent (1994–2000).
Annual growth rate: 0.3 per cent 1994–2004 (WHO 2006)

Ethnic make-up

Around 57 per cent of the population live in Dutch-speaking Flanders, 32 per cent in French-speaking Wallonia, 10 per cent in bilingual Brussels and 1 per cent in the German-speaking border region. There are also some 860,000 foreign expatriates and immigrants. The largest expatriate communities are Italian, French, Moroccan, Dutch, Turkish and Spanish. Foreigners comprise about 27 per cent of the population of Brussels.

Religions

Predominantly Roman Catholic (75 per cent). Also Protestant, Jewish and Muslim.

Education

Education budgets are set by the French, Dutch/Flemish and German language communities.

Most schools are state-run and free. Catholic and international schools are fee-paying. The Belgian education system is widely recognised as being of a very high standard. Government expenditure on education typically accounts for 3 per cent of GDP.

The teaching language is determined by the linguishic region in which a school is based: Dutch, French or German.

Brussels is a bilingual region of its own, and here separate schools use the language appropriate to their pupils, drawn from the surrounding community. International schools (concentrated in Brussels and Antwerp), may teach in foreign languages and follow foreign curricula.

Belgian French and Flemish schools follow the same school cycles. However exams are particular to each language.

Primary schooling lasts from age six to 12 when students undertake exams to determine progression to one of four different schools and programmes: general, technical, artistic or vocational.

Universities and colleges offer a full range of subjects and qualifications.

Compulsory years: 6 to 18.

Enrolment rate: 103 per cent, gross primary enrolment; 146 per cent, gross secondary enrolment; of the relevant age group (including repeaters and training for the unemployed); 56 per cent teriary enrolment (World Bank).

Pupils per teacher: 12 in primary schools.

Health

Per capita total expenditure on health (2003) was US$2,828; of which per capita government spending was US$1,902, at the international dollar rate, (WHO 2006).

Adequate healthcare is provided for all citizens. The patient pays for treatment, but the fee is reimbursed by his or her health insurance company. The reimbursement may cover almost all of the cost or very little, depending on the patient's choice of doctor. The mutuelles (health insurance companies) also have their own clinics where basic healthcare, optometry and dentistry can be obtained for a token fee.

HIV/Aids

HIV prevalence: 0.2 per cent aged 15–49 in 2003 (World Bank)

Life expectancy: 78 years, 2004 (WHO 2006)

Fertility rate/Maternal mortality rate: 1.7 births per woman, 2004 (WHO 2006); maternal deaths 8 per 100,000 (World Bank)

Child (under 5 years) mortality rate (per 1,000): 4 per 1,000 live births (World Bank)

Head of population per physician: 4.49 physicians per 1,000 people, 2002 (WHO 2006)

Welfare

A social insurance scheme covers welfare payments. Contributions are taken from all workers at 7.5 per cent of earnings and pensioners 0.5–2 per cent of pensions or pre-pensions; employers pay 8.86 per cent of the payroll and the government provides annual subsidies.

Old age pensions, disability, sickness, maternity benefits, survivors pensions are dependent on contributions to worker's insurance funds.

Workers' contributions cover around 70 per cent of social security costs. Unemployment benefits are administered by three regional offices, the Vlaamse Dienst Arbeidsbemiddeling Beroepsopleiding (VDBA) in Flanders, the Organisme de Formation et d'Emploi de la Wallonie (FOREM) in Wallonia and the Office Régional Bruxellois d'Emploi-Brusselse Gewestelijke Dienst voor Arbeidsbemiddeling (ORBEM-BGDA) in Brussels.

Pensions

The statutory age of retirement is 65 and 62 for men and women respectively; in 2009 it will be set at 65 for all.

Main cities

Brussels (Bruxelles, Brussel, Brüssel , Bruessel) (capital, estimated population 981,200 in 2003), Antwerp (Anvers, Antwerpen) (450,000), Gent (Ghent) (226,900), Charleroi (201,200), Liège (Luik, Lüttich, Liege, Luettich, Luttich) (185,700), Brugge (Bruges)(117,200), Namur (105,700), Mons (91,200).

Languages spoken

The northern part of Belgium, Flanders, is Dutch-speaking and the southern part, Wallonia, is French-speaking. Brussels is officially bilingual, but over 80 per cent of its population are French-speakers. There is also a small German-speaking area in eastern Wallonia, which became part of Belgium after the First World War.

English, Luxembourgish, Italian, Spanish, Greek, Arabic and Turkish are also spoken.

Official language/s

Dutch (Flemish), French and German

Media

The linguistic division of Belgium society circumscribes its media.

Other news agencies: Belga News Agency: www.belga.be

Flandersnews (VRT news): www.deredactie.be

Press

Dailies: Nation newspapers include, in Dutch, The Nieuwsblad (www.nieuwsblad.be),Het Laatste Nieuws (www.hln.be) is a tabloid and De Morgen (www.demorgen.be), Belgisch Staatsblad (www.ejustice.just.fgov.be) is a government gazette; in French, La Libre Belgique (www.lalibre.be) and Le Soir (www.lesoir.be); in German, Grenz-Echo (www.grenzecho.be).

Several regional newspapers are published by SudPress (www.lacapitale.be) including La Capitale, La Meuse, La Gazette and Nord Eclair; others include Le Courrier Mouscron (www.actu24.be), Metro (www.metrotime.be), and Gazet van Antwerpen (www.gva.be).

Weeklies: Les Nouvelles du Dimanche Matin is a Sunday newspaper. Le 7e Soir is a national weekly. Other weekly publications include Knack and Le Vif/L'Express.

Business: The principal daily financial newspaper is owned and published by Mediafin and in French called L'Echo (www.lecho.be) and in Dutch De Tijd (www.tijd.be). In French and Dutch, other weeklies include Imediair (www.imediair.be) and Trends (www.trends.be). Forward (www.vbo-feb.be) is the monthly publication of the Chamber of Commerce. In Dutch, Impuls (http://intersight.org/impuls) is an annual business directory.

Periodicals: Some daily newspapers publish weekend editions. In French and Dutch, Flair (www.flair.be), Jet Magazine (www.jetmagazine.be), and Loving You (www.lovingyou.be) are women's magazines. In English New Europe (www.neurope.eu), gives analysis of EU issues.In French and Dutch, monthly magazines include Test Aankoop (www.test-aankoop.be), a consumer magazine and Meervoud (www.meervoud.org) advocates Flemish sovereignty and MM (www.mm.be) is a magazine on marketing,

Broadcasting

National, public broadcasting is provided by Radio-Télévision Belge de la Communauté Française (RTBF) for the

French-speaking community and Vlaamse Radio en Televisie (VRT) for the Dutch-speaking community.
Radio: There are two public and one commercial national networks, RTBF (www.rtbf.be/radio) has five stations and an international programme, VRT (www.vrt.be) has five stations and Belgischer Rundfunk (www.brf.be) transmitting programmes in German, has two stations. All broadcasters offer full internet access.
There are many independent, private, regional radio stations including C Dance Network (www.c-dance.be) and Topradio (www.topradio.be/); local stations include Crooze FM (www.crooze.fm) and Geel FM (www.geelfm.be) from Antwerp, Ciel Radio (www.cielradio.be) and Q Music (www.q-music.be) from Brussels and Zone 80 (www.zone80.be) from Liège.
Television: All terrestrial TV will be broadcast via digital technology by 2011.
VRT is Belgium's leading broadcaster, which uses external production houses to provide domestic programmes. It has two TV channels, één (one) (www.een.be), which has a full range of programmes, Ketnet (www.ketnet.be) is for children and Canvas (www.canvas.be) is an in-depth news, alternative arts and entertainment channel. Ketnet shares its channel (0700–2000) with Canvas (2000–0100).
RTBF (www.rtbf.be) operates two terrestrial, TV channels (La Une and La Deux) and a satellite network (www.rtbfsat.be).
Vlaamse Televisie Maatschappij (VTM) (www.vtm.be) is the leading commercial TV network in the Dutch-speaking area, with three channels, VTM, Kanaal Twee (for children) and JIMtv.
There are many pay-to-view services provided via satellite or cable. TV Vlaanderen Digitaal (www.tvvlaanderen.be) and Liberty TV (www.libertytv.com) are satellite stations. Plug TV (www.plugtv.be) and AB3 (www.ab3.be) are cable TV services.
Belgian TV viewers can also tune into a great number of channels from Germany, France, Luxembourg, The Netherlands, Spain, Italy and the UK.

Advertising

There are different authorities responsible for advertising in French and Flemish speaking communities.
There is a total ban on tobacco advertising and food adverts aimed at children are controlled by a self-regulatory code.
Besides advertising carried by commercial television and radio channels (over 40 per cent of total advertising by expenditure), other popular forms of advertising include telemarketing, catalogues, direct mail, the internet and personalised mobile/cell phone texting.

Economy

Belgium has used its geographic situation at the heart of the EU to develop a sophisticated transport system of roads, rail, canals and ports. With this network in place, and although it has few natural resources and has to import almost all its raw materials, Belgium nevertheless has a diversified industrial sector, generally in the north (Flanders) and based on a highly skilled, productive and multi-lingual work force. Per capita exports from Belgium are five times as great as Japan's, and twice as great as Germany's. Industry accounts for some 24 per cent of GDP, the services sector 74 per cent and agriculture 2 per cent. It has one of the world's most open economies measured by the value of exports and imports relative to GDP, largely thanks to its highly integrated economic interdependence with its three main neighbours – France, Germany and the Netherlands. Around 75 per cent of all trade is contracted with EU countries.
The government has run an economy that was close to balance in 2005 with only a slight risk of a deficit. Unemployment is relatively high at over 8 per cent, a figure which masks considerable differences between the prosperous Flanders in the north and Wallonia in the south, which has double Flander's unemployment rate. GDP growth slowed from 2.7 per cent in 2004 to 1.4 per cent in 2005.

External trade

As a member of the European Union, Belgium operates within a communitywide free trade union, with tariffs sets as a whole. Internationally, the EU has free trade agreements with a number of nations and trading blocs worldwide.
It has a complex and open market economy; national and multinational companies have operations that import raw materials and semi-finished items that are readied and re-exported. While 75 per cent of all exports go to other EU states, international trade has been hampered by the high value of the euro.

Imports

Imports consist of fuels, diamonds, machinery and equipment, metal products, pharmaceuticals, foodstuffs, vehicles and products, chemicals and oil products
Main sources: The Netherlands (18.4 per cent total, 2006), Germany (17.5 per cent), France (11.3 per cent).

Exports

Many companies export more than 80 per cent of their production. Principal exports include machinery and equipment, diamonds, steel, glass, pharmaceuticals and organic chemicals, motor vehicles, foodstuffs and carpets. A new biotechnology sector has developed.
Main destinations: Germany (19.9 per cent of 2006 total goods exports), France (17.0 per cent), The Netherlands (12.0 per cent).

Agriculture

Farming

The agriculture sector accounts for around 1.4 per cent of GDP and employs 2.5 per cent of the workforce. Although small-scale, cultivation is intensive, especially in Flanders, which has better soils for arable farming. Here one quarter of the organically managed land is used for arable crops. Belgium is self-sufficient in sugar, eggs, butter and meat, and is an exporter of vegetables and horticultural produce. The amount of land under cultivation (approximately 25 per cent of total land area) is falling.
Reform to the EU Common Agricultural Policy (CAP) was introduced on 1 January 2005 in Belgium, whereby subsidies paid on farm output, which tended to benefit large farms and encourage overproduction, were replaced by single farm payments not conditional on production. This is expected to reward farms that provide and maintain a healthy environment, food safety and animal welfare standards. The changes are also intended to encourage market conscious production and cut the cost of CAP to the EU taxpayer.
The crop production in 2005 included: 2,713,082 tonnes (t) cereals in total, 1,768,410t wheat, 553,775t maize, 2,653,949t potatoes, 306,215t barley, 30,617t oats, 395t hops, 100t vanilla, 230,000t tomatoes, 15,036t oilcrops, 900t tobacco, 5,606,025t sugar beets, 350,000t apples, 633,350t fruit in total, 1,872,000t vegetables in total. Livestock production included: 1,865,245t meat in total, 280,000t beef, 1,000,000t pig meat, 3,500t lamb, 4,600t horsemeat, 476,800t poultry, 210,000t eggs, 3,120,000t milk, 2,150t honey.

Fishing

Fishing is a smaller and less important industry in Belgium than in neighbouring countries, largely because of its short coastline. The mussel- and oyster-bearing waters of the Scheldt estuary are bordered on both sides by the Netherlands. Belgium has a flotilla of small offshore trawlers, but no major deep sea fleet.

Forestry

Forest and other wooded land cover around 22 per cent of the land area – one of the lowest ratios in Europe. The majority of timber materials imported come from Germany and France.

Industry and manufacturing

The large-scale, export-based industrial sector accounts for 22 per cent of GDP and employs approximately 28 per cent of the labour force.

Belgium's industrial sector is strongly regional. Flanders, which accounts for some 60 per cent of GDP, has a modern industrial base. It is also more integrated into international markets than other regions, with around 85 per cent of its output going abroad and accounting for some 70 per cent of total Belgian exports. The region of Wallonia, on the other hand, accounts for 25 per cent of GDP and is burdened with declining heavy industry. The government has made considerable efforts to restructure the industrial base in Wallonia, with substantial investment incentives available.

The government's policy is aimed at facilitating the renewal and restructuring of industry so that it can adapt to new technologies and maintain its competitive position internationally. This includes encouraging domestic and foreign investment in industry with tax incentives, particularly in advanced technology fields.

Tourism

Tourism is expected to account for 3.6 per cent of GDP in 2005. Belgium's historic towns and rich cultural heritage are particularly attractive to short-stay visitors, mainly from neighbouring countries.

Mining

The mining sector accounts for approximately 0.3 per cent of GDP and employs 0.4 per cent of the workforce. There is no longer a mining industry. Only clay and sand are mined on any scale.

Hydrocarbons

Belgium has no oil or gas reserves. Belgium imports 16 billion cubic metres of gas annually and one million barrels per day (bpd) of oil, of which 436,000bpd is re-exported. Belgian refineries have a total capacity of 805,000bpd. Belgium's coal-mining industry having been closed down, only a negligible quantity of coal is produced by tip-washing; coal has to be imported to meet domestic demand.

Energy

Belgium has the highest energy consumption per capita in the EU. Electricity capacity is 16GW. Nuclear power is the primary source of energy, accounting for around 60 per cent of electricity output; most of the rest comes from thermal sources, fired by gas, coal and oil. There are seven nuclear stations. Legislation adopted in 2002 provides for nuclear energy to be phased out by 2025, but Belgium's environmental obligations are leading to second thoughts.

Financial markets

Stock exchange

The Brussels Stock Exchange is part of Euronext, an integrated cross-border single currency stock, derivatives and commodities market composed of the Brussels, Paris and Amsterdam exchanges. This arrangement gives the relatively small Belgian stock exchange important external visibility.

Banking and insurance

The banking sector is divided into three main groups – commercial banks, public credit institutions and private savings banks.

Belgium's efforts to meet the conditions for European Economic and Monetary Union (Emu) involved major restructuring of the financial sector.

Central bank

Banque Nationale de Belgique; European Central Bank (ECB)

Time

GMT plus one hour (daylight saving, late March to late October, GMT plus two hours)

Geography

Belgium is a small European state bordered to the north by the North Sea and The Netherlands, to the east by The Netherlands, Germany and Luxembourg, and to the south and west by France. It is flat near the coast, but hillier in the Ardennes region in the south-east.

Hemisphere

Northern

Climate

The country has a temperate climate; the proximity of the sea reduces the harshness of winter, but makes summers relatively cool.

Temperatures overall do not show great variations. The average for the hottest month, July, is 17 degrees Celsius (C) and for the coldest, January, 3 degrees C. Temperatures tend to be slightly higher along the coast and cooler in the Ardennes.

There is regular but moderate rainfall with average annual precipitation of 800mm.

Dress codes

Belgian dress codes are in general the same as those in other industrialised nations. Suit and tie for men are usual for business and formal occasions, but often a jacket and trousers are sufficient. For women, a suit, dress or skirt and blouse are suitable for most business and social occasions.

Entry requirements

Passports

Passport are required by all visitors, except EU citizens of Schengen Accord states, who require ID cards.

Visa

Required by all, except nationals of EU and Schengen area signatory countries, North America, Australasia and Japan. For further exceptions contact the nearest embassy. A Schengen visa application (offered in several languages) can be downloaded from http://europa.eu/abc/travel/ see 'documents you will need'.

Currency advice/regulations

No restrictions on foreign or local currency movements.

Customs

Personal items are duty-free. There are no duties levied on alcohol and tobacco between EU member states, providing amounts imported are for personal consumption.

Health (for visitors)

Nationals of the European Economic Area (EEA) countries and Switzerland can access reduced cost and sometimes free medical treatment using a European Health Insurance Card (EHIC) while visiting the EEA. Exceptions include nationals of the 10 countries which joined the EU in 2004 whose EHIC is not valid in Switzerland. Applications for the EHIC should be made before travelling.

Mandatory precautions

There are no mandatory health precautions.

Advisable precautions

No exceptional precautions are necessary; any necessary medication should be kept with its original packaging.

Hotels

It is advisable to book hotel or pension in advance either directly or through Belgium Tourist Reservations. By law, all tariffs must be displayed. Service charges are usually included. Tipping is roughly 10 per cent. Major credit cards are accepted.

Public holidays (national)

Fixed dates

1 Jan (New Year's Day), 1 May (Labour Day), 21 Jul (Independence Day), 15 Aug (Assumption Day), 1 Nov (All Saints' Day), 2 Nov (All Souls' Day), 11 Nov (Armistice Day), 15 Nov (Dynasty Day), 25 Dec (Christmas Day), 26 Dec (St Stephen's Day). Also community public holidays: 11 Jul.(Flemish community); 27 Sep (French-speaking community).

Fixed-date holidays that fall on a Sunday are observed on the following day.

Variable dates

Easter Monday, Ascension Day, Whit Monday.

Working hours

Banking

Mon–Fri: 0900–1600. Banks are open most days, although a few small banks close at lunch-time.

Business

Mon–Fri: 0830–1730; Sat: 0900–1200.

Government

Mon–Fri: 0900–1700.

Shops
Mon–Sat: 0900/1000–1800/1900. In large cities, convenience stores (magasins de nuit/avondwinkels) stay open either all night or until around 2200 every day, including Sundays.

Telecommunications
Mobile/cell phones
There are G3 and 900/1800 GSM services available throughout the country.

Electricity supply
220V AC

Social customs/useful tips
It can be considered impolite to use French in Dutch-speaking Flanders or Dutch in Wallonia due to historical friction between the two language groups. English is quite widely understood and has made headway as a lingua franca, in Brussels in particular.
In Flanders, the names of Walloon cities are generally in Flemish and vice versa in Wallonia. There are also different names for German place names in both Belgium and Germany.
Business relations require some degree of formality and the use of the formal pronoun in French and Dutch (vous/U). It is customary to shake hands at the beginning and end of a meeting. Punctuality is valued.
Belgium has one of the highest ratios of police to population of any western European country and officers are permitted to undertake random identity checks. It is compulsory to have a passport or identity card with you at all times.
Alcohol is sold freely at any time of day or night. Smoking is banned in public places (including stations and airports).
Traffic coming from the right has priority in most situations (if the driver who has priority slows down or hesitates, he/she still has priority; a driver who has priority only loses this after having stopped and started moving again). Therefore, foreign drivers should be aware that vehicles could suddenly emerge from side-streets to their right.

Security
There is very little street crime or violence in Belgium, though the inner cities have isolated problem areas.

Getting there
Air
National airline: SN Brussels Airlines is an independent, Belgium airline.
International airport/s: Brussels Zaventem (BRU), 13km north-east of the city centre; amenities include, banks, restaurant, duty-free shops (arriving and departing), medical facilities and business centre. Antwerp International (ANR), 3km east of Antwerp; Brussels-South Charleroi (CRL), 55km south-east of Brussels; Ostend International (OST), 6km from city; Liège (LGG) 5km from the city centre.
Airport tax: Departure tax: Brussels Zaventem eur20.93; Brussels-South Charleroi: eur13.49; Antwerp and Ostend eur10; Liège eur7.

Surface
Rail: Express trains (TEE) ensure rapid connection with all French, Dutch and German cities.
Water: There are daily crossings by ferry or jetfoil to Ostend or Zeebrugge from the UK and Norway.
Main port/s: Antwerp, Ghent, Zeebrugge, Ostend, Brussels, Liège.

Getting about
National transport
Road: There is an extensive road network. Toll-free motorways serve all main towns with the exception of those in the Ardennes.
Buses: Extensive coach services operate throughout the country, particularly to rural areas, run by Société Nationale des Chemins de Fer Belges (SNCB) and Société Nationale des Chemins de Fer Vicinaux (SNCV).
Rail: First- and second-class services run between all main towns. Combined tickets allowing stop-overs in main towns offer best value. Over half the railway network is electrified.
Water: There are over 1,500km of inland waterways. Services are operated by Administration des Voies Hydrauliques. Inland canals connect with major French, Dutch and German ports.

City transport
Taxis: Readily available throughout the country. The standardised, metered fare system includes a tip in the final price. Taxis booked to call for a pick-up include a surcharge in their fare. Chauffeur-driven cars are cheaper on long journeys.
Buses, trams & metro: Flat fares are charged on tram and bus service. There are metro services in Brussels and Antwerp.
Trains: Special airport shuttle service operates from Brussels Central Station and North Station, departing every hour.

Car hire
Available at aiports and in most main towns. The minimum age of a hire car driver is 23 years. A full driving licence, valid for at least one year remaining is required. All vehicles must carry a fire extinguisher and first aid kit
Speed limit: urban roads 60kph, main roads 90kph. Maximum speed on dual carrageways and motorways 120kph, minimum speed 70kph. Drive on the right. The wearing of seat belts throughout the vehicle is compulsory. Trams have right of way on any road.

BUSINESS DIRECTORY

Telephone area codes
The international direct dialling code (IDD) for Belgium is +32, followed by area code and subscriber's number:

Antwerp	3	Ypres	57
Arlon	63	Liège	41
Bastogne	61	La Louvière	64
Brugge	50	Libramont	61
Brussels	2	Mechelen	15
Charleroi	71	Mons	65
Chimay	60	Ostende	59
Dendermonde	52	Verviers	87
Ghent	9	Zeebrugge	50

Chambers of Commerce
American Chamber of Commerce, 50 Avenue des Arts, 1000 Brussels (tel: 513-6770; fax: 513-3590; e-mail: gch@postl.amcham.be).

Antwerp Chamber of Commerce,12 Markgravestraat, 2000 Antwerp (tel: 232-2219; fax: 233-6442; e-mail: eic@kkna.be).

British Chamber of Commerce, Egmont House, 15 Rue d'Egmont, 1000 Brussels (tel: 540-9030; fax: 512-8363; e-mail: brit.cham@britcham.be).

Bruges Chamber of Commerce and Industry, 25 Ezelstraat, 8000 Bruges (tel: 333-696; fax: 342-297; e-mail: brugge@ccibkw.be).

Brussels Chamber of Commerce and Industry, 500 Avenue Louise, 1050 Brussels (tel: 648-5002; fax: 640-9328; e-mail: inscription@ccib.irisnet.be).

Charleroi Chamber of Commerce and Industry, 1a Avenue Général Michel, 6000 Charleroi (tel: 321-160; fax: 334-218; e-mail: info@ccic.be).

Federation of Chambers of Commerce and Industry of Belgium, 1-2 Avenue des Arts, 1210 Brussels (tel: 209-1550; fax: 209-0568; e-mail: fedcci@cci.be).

Ghent Chamber of Commerce and Industry, 41 Martelaarslaan, 9000 Ghent (tel: 266-1440; fax: 266-1441; e-mail: kkngent@cci.be).

Liège Chamber of Commerce and Industry, Palais des Congrès de Liège, 2 Esplanade de l'Europe, 4020 Liège (tel: 343-9292; fax: 343-9267; e-mail: info@ccilg.be).

Banking
AXA Bank Belgium, 214 Grotesteenweg, 2600 Antwerp (tel: 286-2211; fax: 286-2407; e-mail:contact@axa.be).

Dexia, Boulevard Pachéco 44, 1000 Brussels (tel: 222-1111; fax: 222-1122; e-mail: info@dexia.be).

Fortis Banque, 20 Rue Royale, 1000 Brussels (tel: 510-5211; fax: 510-5626 e-mail: info@fortis.com).

ING Belgium., 24 Avenue Marnix, 1000 Brussels (tel: 547-2111; fax: 547-3844; e-mail: info@ing.be).

KBC Bank and Insurance, Havenlaan 2, 1080 Brussels (tel: 429-1111; fax: 429-8123; e-mail: kbc.bank@kbc.be).

Central bank

Banque Nationale de Belgique, Boulevard de Berlaimont 14, BE-1000 Brussels (tel: 221-2111; fax: 221-3100; email: info@nbb.be).

European Central Bank (ECB), Kaiserstrasse 29, D-60311, Postfach 16 03 19, Frankfurt am Main, Germany (tel: (+49-69) 13-440; fax: (+49-69) 1344-6000; email: info@ecb.int; internet: www.ecb.int).

Travel information

Brussels International Airport Company (BIAC), Brussels Airport, B-1930 Zaventem, (tel: 2753-4200; email: info@biac.be).

Brussels International Tourism and Congress, Hôtel de Ville, Grand Place, 1000 Brussels (tel: 513-8940; fax: 513-8320; e-mail: info@brusselstourism.be).

SN Brussels Airlines, The Corporate Village, Da Vincilaan 9, 1935 Zaventem (customer service tel: 070 351-111; internet: www.flysn.be).

National tourist organisation offices

Belgian Tourist Office (Brussels and Ardennes), 61 Rue du Marché aux Herbes, 1000 Brussels (tel: 504-0390; fax: 504-0270; e-mail: info@opt.be).
Belgian Tourist Office (Tourism Flanders), 63 Rue du Marché aux Herbes, 1000 Brussels (tel: 504-0390; fax: 504-0270; e-mail: info@toerismevlaanderen.be).

Ministries

Ministry of Agriculture and Small and Medium-Sized Enterprises, 1 Rue Marie-Thérèse, 1000 Brussels (tel: 211-0611; fax: 219-6130).

Ministry of the Budget, 180 Rue Royale, 1000 Brussels (tel: 219-1911; fax: 217-3328).

Ministry for the Civil Service, Résidence Palace, 51 Rue de la Loi, 1040 Brussels (tel: 790-5800; fax: 790-5790).

Ministry of Consumer Affairs, Public Health and Environment, 7 Avenue des Arts, 1210 Brussels (tel: 220-2011; fax: 220-2067; e-mail: environment@health.fgov.be).

Ministry of Defence, 8 Rue Lambermont , 1000 Brussels (tel: 550-2811; fax: 550-2919).

Ministry of Economic Affairs and Scientific Research, 23 Square de Meeûs, 1000 Brussels (tel: 506-5111; fax: 514-4683).

Ministry of Employment, 51 Rue Belliard, 1040 Brussels (tel: 233-5111; fax: 230-1067; e-mail: info@cabmeta.fgov.be).

Ministry of Finance, 12 Rue de la Loi, 1000 Brussels (tel: 238-8111; fax: 233-8003; e-mail: contact@ckfin.minfin.be).

Ministry of Foreign Affairs, 15 Rue des Petits Carmes, 1000 Brussels (tel: 501-8211; fax: 511-6385; internet site: http://www.diplobel.fgov.be/default_em.htm).

Ministry of Interior Affairs, 60 Rue Royale, 1000 Brussels (tel: 504-8511; fax: 504-8500; e-mail: info@mibz.fgov.be).

Ministry of Justice, 115 Boulevard de Waterloo, 1000 Brussels (tel: 542-7911; fax: 538-0767; info@just.fgov.be).

Ministry of Mobility and Transport, 65 Rue de la Loi, 1040 Brussels (tel: 237-6711; fax: 230-1824).

Ministry of Social Affairs and Pensions, 62 Rue de la Loi, 1040 Brussels (tel: 238-2811; fax: 230-3895).

Ministry of Telecommunications, Public Enterprises and Participations, 7 Queteletplein, 1030 Brussels (tel: 250-0303; fax: 219-0914; e-mail: info@telcobel.be).

Prime Minister's Office, 16 Rue de la Loi, 1000 Brussels (tel: 501-0211; fax: 512-6953).

Other useful addresses

Belgian Association of International Trading Houses (ABNEI), 7 Israëlietenstraat, 2000 Antwerp (tel: 226-0712; fax: 231-9969; e-mail: tradechem@cmc.be).

Belgian Embassy (USA), 3330 Garfield Street, NW, Washington DC 20008 (tel: 202-333-6900; fax: 202-333-3079).

Belgian Foreign Trade Board, World Trade Centre, Tower 1, 30/36 Boulevard du Roi Albert II, 1000 Brussels (tel: 206-3511; fax: 203-1812; e-mail: info@obcebdbh.be).

Belgian Institute of Standardisation, 29 Avenue de la Brabançonne, 1000 Brussels (tel: 738-0111; fax: 733-4264; e-mail: info@ibn.be).

British Embassy, 85 Rue d'Arlon, 1040 Brussels (tel: 287-6211; fax: 287-6360; e-mail: info@britain.be).

Brussels Regional Development Agency, 6 Rue Gabrielle Petit, 1080 Brussels (tel: 422-5111; fax: 422-5112; info@sdrb.irisnet.be).

Ducroire/Delcredere (export credit agency), 40 Square de Meêus, 1000 Brussels (tel: 509-4211; fax: 513-5059; e-mail: ducroire@ondd.be).

Euler-Cobac (credit insurance), 15 Rue Montoyer, 1000 Brussels (tel: 289-311; fax: 289-329).

Euronext Brussels (stock exchange), Palais de la Bourse, Place de la Bourse, 1000 Brussels (tel: 509.1211; fax: 509-1212; e-mail: info@euronext.be).

Federation of Belgian Companies (VBO-FEB), 4 Rue Ravenstein, 1000 Brussels (tel: 515-0811; fax: 515-0999; e-mail: info@vbo-feb.be).

Flemish Economic Alliance (VEV), 5 Brouwersvliet, 2000 Antwerp (tel: 202-4400; fax: 233-7660; e-mail: vev@vev.be).

Flemish Foreign Trade Board, 40 Boulevard du Régent, 1000 Brussels (tel: 504-8711; fax: 504-8899; e-mail: info@export.vlaanderen.be).

Investment Company for Flanders (GIMV), 37 Karel Oomsstraat, 2018 Antwerp (tel:290-2100; fax: 290-2105; e-mail: receptie@gimv.be).

National Institute of Statistics, 44/46 Rue de Louvain, 1000 Brussels (tel: 548-6365; fax: 548-6367; e-mail: info@statbel.mineco.fgov.be).

US Embassy, 27 Boulevard du Régent, 1000 Brussels (tel: 508-2111; fax: 511-2725; e-mail: ic@usinfo.be).

Walloon Business Union (UWE), 1-3 Chemin du Stockoy, 1300 Wavre (tel: 471-940; fax: 453-343; e-mail: info@uwe.be).

Walloon Export Agency (AWEX), 2 Place Sainctelette, 1080 Brussels (tel: 421-8211; fax: 421-8787; e-mail: mail@awex.wallonie.be).

Other news agencies: Belga News Agency: www.belga.be
Flandersnews (VRT news): www.deredactie.be

Internet sites

Belgium companies: www.belgium.com/business/tradecontact.php

Belgium Federal Information Service: www.belgium.fgov.be/

Belgium Foreign Trade Board: www.obcebdbh.be

Belgium White Pages: www.infobel.be

Export services: http://exportservices.be

Travel information: www.visitbelgium.com

Railway information: www.b-rail.be

Statistics: www.statbel.fgov.be

Le Soir (newspaper): www.lesoir.be

La Poste (newspaper) www.brusselspost.com

Government of Flanders: www.flanders.be

Government of Wallonia: www.wallonie.com

Belize

KEY FACTS

Official name: Belize

Head of State: Queen Elizabeth II (since 1952); Governor General Sir Colville Norbert Young (since 1993)

Head of government: Dean Barrow (UDP) (from 8 February 2008)

Ruling party: United Democratic Party (UDP) (from 7 February 2008)

Area: 22,965 square km

Population: 311,000 (2007)*

Capital: Belmopan

Official language: English

Currency: Belize dollar (Bz$) = 100 cents

Exchange rate: Bz$1.95 per US$ (Jul 2008)

GDP per capita: US$4,098 (2007)*

GDP real growth: 2.20% (2007)*

Labour force: 101,000 (2004)

Unemployment: 11.00% (2005)

Inflation: 3.00% (2007)*

Balance of trade: -US$287.00 million (2005)

Foreign debt: US$950.90 million (2004)

Annual FDI: US$126.00 million (2005)

* estimated figure

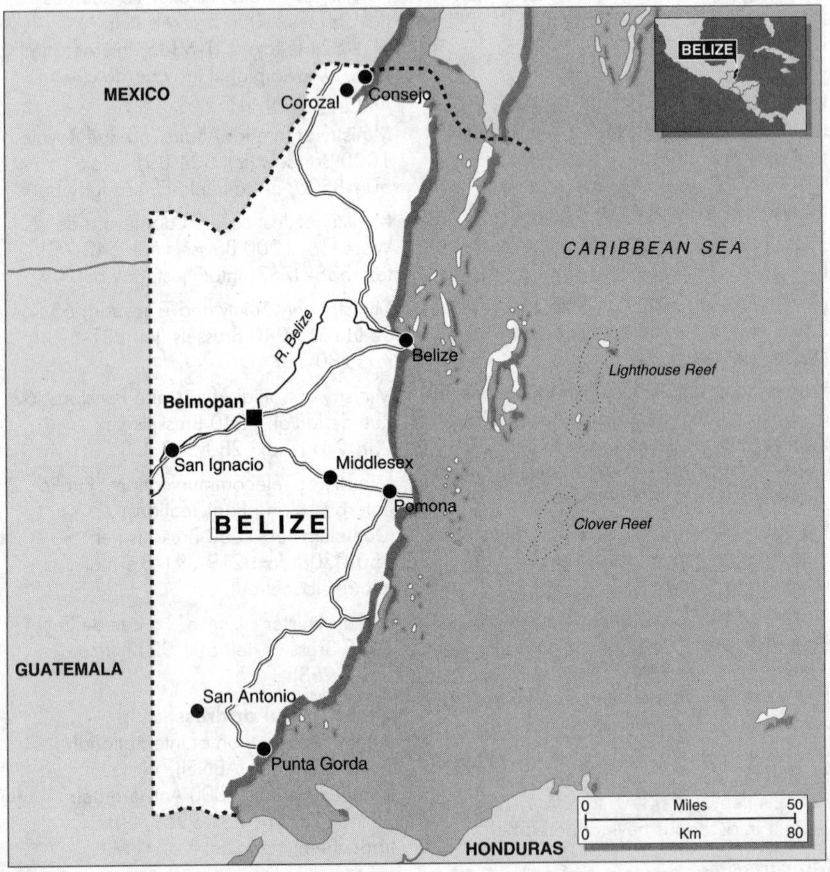

Throughout 2007 scandals involving the misuse of social security funds and the management of the country's discredited Development Finance Corporation (DFC) had severely weakened prime minister Said Musa's People's United Party (PUP) administration. This weakness had already become public in 2006 when the ruling party suffered a resounding defeat in municipal elections. The half hearted measures taken by the Musa government to improve standards of governance ultimately proved both too little and too late to restore the government's credibility.

Election reversal

A strong two-party system operates in Belize with the PUP and the United Democratic Party (UDP) operating something of an electoral duopoly in the country. In the 2003 elections the PUP claimed 22 seats out of a total of 29 in the House of Representatives, while the UDP, despite achieving a 45.6 per cent share of the vote, won just 7 seats. The PUP is a Christian democratic organisation, while the UDP presents itself as the party of the progressive left. The parties' positions were neatly reversed when, in February 2008, Belize's first black prime minister, Dean Oliver Barrow, scored a landslide victory in the general election. Promising an open and honest government, Mr Barrow was sworn in as Belize's fourth prime minister since independence in 1981. The election majority of 25 seats for the UDP over the PUP's 6 seats left few illusions that the Belizean electorate were not looking for a change from Said Musa's two term rule. In an interview with the British Broadcasting Corporation Mr Barrow listed the first of his priorities as the lowering, or even total elimination, of the recently introduced general sales tax (GST).

Resilient economy

The IMF reports that in 2007 Belize's economic growth continued to be boosted by the oil discoveries of 2006, alongside the strong exports underpinned by favourable external conditions. Tighter macroeconomic conditions also helped keep inflation under control. In its annual report on Belize, the United Nations Economic Commission for Latin America and the Caribbean (ECLAC) attributed much of the economy's deceleration to the devastating effects of Hurricane Dean. The hurricane's effect was particularly felt by Belize's agricultural, fisheries and tourism sectors.

In early 2007 Belize underwent what ECLAC described as a successful debt-restructuring which, at least in theory, was designed to give the government some latitude in fiscal management. The commercial debt-restructuring which was completed in February 2007 extended Belize's debt maturities and lowered debt servicing costs while preserving principal. As is often the case with national economic management policies (not only in the Caribbean) 'Events' can easily intervene. In Belize's case the events were part foreseeable: first, election spending in the run up to the February 2008 vote-casting went well over budget. Second, the effects of Hurricane Dean caused capital spending to increase by an estimated 30 per cent. This expenditure was largely on social development projects, rehabilitation and reconstruction after the hurricane, which was the most intense Atlantic hurricane since Hurricane Wilma of 2005.

Oil begins to flow

The government's overall budget deficit in 2007 increased from 1.8 per cent to 2.1 per cent of GDP, despite the substantial revenue boost from both the introduction of the GST first introduced in 2006 and from new oil production. Inflation in 2007 dropped to 3.5 per cent, one per cent lower than the rate recorded in 2006. The inflationary effect of the hurricane was principally produced through food shortages. By contrast, the price of clothing, transport and medical care all decreased. Unemployment also fell, from 9.4 per cent in 2006 to 8.5 per cent in 2007. The 2006 GDP growth rate of 5.8 per cent was exceptionally high, so it came as no surprise that the 2007 rate fell back somewhat. The aftermath of the hurricane pushed the eventual rate down below 3 per cent. One of the main drivers of Belize's growth in 2006 was the beginning of oil production, which rose dramatically as Belize Natural Energy's (BNE) Spanish Lookout came on stream at 1,000 barrels per day (bpd), later rising to 2,600bpd. Belize has no oil refining capacity; crude oil is exported to neighbouring countries for processing, mostly to the USA. In 2007, following Hurricane Dean, agricultural output fell by 13 per cent.

Tourism and hurricanes

Tourism growth was sluggish, with an estimated US$9.4 million shortfall over 2006. Over recent years the tourism industry has expanded considerably and is now of importance to the country's economic wellbeing. The longest barrier reef in the Western Hemisphere is in Belizean waters, together with several small islands and superb fishing opportunities. These attractions, together with the country's Maya ruins and raw jungle regions ensure that Belize's travel and tourism industry continues to grow. The World Travel and Tourism Council estimates that 20 per cent of Belize's total GDP is generated from tourism activity and almost the same figure (19.7 per cent) is employed in the industry. Crucially, capital investment in the sector has increased markedly and now stands at almost one quarter (24.5 per cent) of total capital investment in the economy. The continued wellbeing of the nascent tourism industry is dependent on favourable weather conditions, particularly during the hurricane season. Before the extensive damage inflicted by Hurricane Dean in 2007, the sector's infrastructure was seriously damaged by Hurricane Keith (2000) and Hurricane Iris (2001), but had managed to recover well.

As was to be expected, Belize's balance of payments deteriorated in 2007, contracting from 4.1 per cent of GDP in 2006 to 0.6 per cent in 2007. This caused the current account deficit to widen from the 2 per cent recorded in 2006 to an estimated 3.7 per cent of GDP in 2007. Foreign direct investment (FDI) remained buoyant at US$69 million for the year, a figure expected to rise in 2008 as further oil exploration takes place. The 2006 debt-restructuring exercise provided the government with some degree of latitude; however, if this breathing space is not to be dissipated, the government will need to maintain fiscal discipline – something that the run-up to the 2008 election had already showed to be vulnerable.

Long term prospects

In its 2008 report on the longer term Belizean economy, the International Monetary Fund (IMF) Baseline Scenario forecasts an average annual growth rate of 2.5 per cent up to 2020, with the government's budget surplus averaging 1.5 per cent. The IMF's more positive Active Scenario has GDP growth gradually rising to 3.75 per cent and the budget surplus increasing to 4.75 per cent of GDP by 2011. In its 2007 report on Belize, the World Bank highlights the fact that although progress has been achieved with a number of social indicators, the alleviation of poverty continues to be a major challenge for Belize's government. Although the government looks set to meet the Millennium Development Goals relating to education,

KEY INDICATORS **Belize**

	Unit	2003	2004	2005	2006	2007
Population	m	0.26	0.27	0.29	0.30	*0.31
Gross domestic product (GDP)	US$bn	1.28	1.00	1.11	1.21	*1.27
GDP per capita	US$	4,900	3,977	3,807	4,028	*4,098
GDP real growth	%	4.9	3.0	3.5	5.6	*2.2
Inflation	%	1.5	2.7	3.7	4.3	*3.0
Exports (fob) (goods)	US$m	290.0	401.4	*3,349.9	427.0	428.5
Imports (cif) (goods)	US$m	430.0	579.9	*3,636.9	611.9	642.0
Balance of trade	US$m	-140.0	-178.5	*-287.0	-184.8	-213.5
Current account	US$m	-190.0	-150.0	-159.0	-27.0	*-51.0
Total reserves minus gold	US$m	84.7	48.3	71.4	113.7	108.5
Foreign exchange	US$m	76.1	39.1	62.8	104.4	98.4
Exchange rate	per US$	1.97	1.98	1.97	1.97	1.97

* estimated figure

access to clean water, child and maternal mortality, it is still failing to reduce overall poverty levels. Belize's Human Development Index rating dropped from 58 in 1998 (when Said Musa was first elected) to a more lowly 95 by 2006.

Risk assessment

Politics	Fair
Economy	Fair
Regional stability	Good

COUNTRY PROFILE

Historical profile

1802 Spain recognised British sovereignty of what became known as British Honduras, but after gaining their independence from Spain, both Mexico and Guatemala laid claim to the territory.
1970 Belmopan became the captial after Belize City was devastated by a hurricane.
1973 The territory was renamed Belize.
1981 Belize attained independence from the UK.
1984 After 30 years in power, the People's United Party (PUP) was defeated by the United Democratic Party (UDP). Manuel Esquivel became prime minister.
1989 The PUP narrowly won the general election.
1993 The UDP won the general election; Esquivel became prime minister again.
1998 In elections, the PUP defeated the UDP.
2000 The government began reforming the offshore banking sector following international criticism of the country's reputation as a tax haven for the rich. Hurricane Keith caused extensive damage.
2001 Hurricane Iris devastated the southern part of Belize. The UK government suspended its plan to grant Belize US$14 million of debt relief due to the government's failure to reform the financial services sector and abolish tax breaks.
2002 The Supreme Court advised holding a public hearing of the environmental lawsuit against Fortis Inc, a Newfoundland-based power company, regarding the proposed Chalillo hydro project.
2003 The ruling PUP won the 5 March general elections.
2004 In January Britain's Privy Council dismissed an appeal by environmental protestors against the proposed construction of the Chalillo dam. On 16 August, the Prime Minister accepted the resignations of seven members of the cabinet.
2005 Workers in the private and public sectors struck in January citing tax increases and low salaries. In April anti-government riots broke out in the capital Belmopan. In August oil was discovered by Belize Natural Energy Ltd .
2006 Belize began producing and exporting oil.
2008 A new political party, the National Reform Party (NRP), was formed in January to fight the February parliamentary elections. Eleven candidates stood for the NRP, led by Cornelius Dueck, a businessman from the Mennonite community in western Belize. In parliamentary elections held on 7 February, the opposition won a landslide victory with 25 seats (out of 31), the ruling PUP won 6. Dean Barrow (UDP) became prime minister on 8 February.

Political structure

Constitution
The governor general is advised by the cabinet (led by the prime minister) which holds executive power.

Form of state
Independent state with the British monarch as head of state, represented by the governor general.

The executive
The cabinet, led by the prime minister, holds executive power.

National legislature
The legislature is the bicameral National Assembly consisting of the Senate (nine members, appointed for a five-year term), and the House of Representatives (29 members elected by universal adult suffrage for a five-year term in single-seat constituencies).

Last elections
7 February 2008 (parliamentary)
Results: Parliamentary: the PUP won 6 seats (out of 31), the UDP won 25 seats.

Next elections
March 2013 (parliamentary)

Political parties

Ruling party
United Democratic Party (UDP) (from 7 February 2008)

Main opposition party
People's United Party (PUP)

Population

311,000 (2007)*
Last census: May 2000: 240,204
Population density: 11 inhabitants per square km. Urban population: 48 per cent (1995–2001).
Annual growth rate: 2.4 per cent 1994–2004 (WHO 2006)

Ethnic make-up
Mestizos (44 per cent), Creoles (30 per cent), Mayans (15 per cent), Garifunas (7 per cent), Mennonites (3 per cent). Other races: Spanish, British, Lebanese, Chinese and Eastern Indian.

Religions
Roman Catholic (62 per cent), Anglican (12 per cent), Methodist (6 per cent), Mennonite (4 per cent), Seventh-Day Adventist (3 per cent).

Education

About 22.35 per cent of the budget expenditure in 2002/03 was allocated to the education sector, of which a total of Bz$61 million (US$31 million) and Bz$16 million (US$8.1 million) were budgeted for salaries and education grants respectively. Since 1998, dozens of new school buildings have been constructed, with more than 700 new classrooms catering for additional 3,000 students. The government contributes some Bz$20 million (US$10.1 million) towards higher education student loans for the University of Belize.
Literacy rate: 77 per cent adult rate; 84 per cent youth rate (15–24) (Unesco 2005).
Enrolment rate: 123 per cent for boys, 119 per cent for girls; total primary school enrolment of the relevant age group (including repetition rates) (World Bank).

Health

Per capita total expenditure on health (2003) was US$309; of which per capita government spending was US$152, at the international dollar rate, (WHO 2006).
The ministry of health plans to implement the National Health Insurance as part of its overall health sector reform programme, with Bz$4 million (US$2 million) from the Social Security Fund.

HIV/Aids
HIV prevalence: 2.5 per cent aged 15–49 in 2003 (World Bank)
Life expectancy: 68 years, 2004 (WHO 2006)
Fertility rate/Maternal mortality rate: 3.1 births per woman, 2004 (WHO 2006)
Child (under 5 years) mortality rate (per 1,000): 33 per 1,000 live births (World Bank)

Welfare

As part of its poverty alleviation strategy, the Social Investment Fund (SIF) has sought assistance from the World Bank to spend some Bz$10.5 million (US$5.2 million) in water supply, sanitation, health, education and social services projects.
Seven per cent of a worker's weekly earning is paid into the social security fund; a ratio is determined and divided between the employer and employee. Benefits include maternity, sickness, injury and dependant's grants.

Pensions
Old age pensions are paid to those aged between 60 and 65 who have made at least 130 contributions.

Main cities

Belmopan (capital, estimated population 10,277 in 2005), Belize City (51,535), Cayo (16,246), Orange Walk (14,964), San Ignacio (16,246), Dangriga (9,497).

Languages spoken
Spanish, Creole, Garifuna and Mayan dialects are widely spoken throughout the country.
Official language/s
English

Media
Press
Weeklies: There are no daily newspaper, the most widely read weeklies include Amandala (www.amandala.com.bz), and The Reporter (www.reporter.bz), The San Pedro Sun (www.sanpedrosun.net) is a community newspaper published on the island of Ambergris Caye. The Belize Times (www.belizetimes.bz) is the newspaper that speaks for the political party People's United Party and The Guardian (www.guardian.bz) for the United Democratic Party.
Broadcasting
Radio: There are around 10 radio stations, all of which are private and commercial. Most broadcast either music, religious or news contents, including People's Radio, (www.belizeweb.com), see news & entertainment, also includes Integrity Radio and Positive Vibes Radio. Others stations are Love FM, (www.lovefm.com) Krem FM (www.krembz.com) and Wave Radio (http://waveradiobelize.org).
Television: All TV stations are commercial. The privately-owned, Channel 5 (www.channel5belize.com) is the leading TV channel and, along with Channel 7 (www.7newsbelize.com) and Channel 9, is a terrestrial broadcaster. Centaur Cable Network, called CTV3 (www.ctv3belizenews.com) provides a subscriber cable services, with over 60 channels, to the region of Orange Walk in the north of the country.

Economy
The economy of Belize has more in common with the nearby Caribbean region than its Central American neighbours. A small enterprise economy, in the past it has been dominated by the agricultural sector, on which the country's well being was dependent. Although Belize is still dependent on agricultural exports, tourism is the fastest growing sector in the economy, accounting for around 20 per cent of GDP and a fifth of total employment. The growth in tourism is predominantly attributable to the rapidly expanding cruise sector. The services sector contributes around 60 per cent to GDP and is based on a number of privately-owned monopoly utilities, such as Belize Telecommunications Limited (BTL).
Belize is in the top ten of the most heavily indebted emerging-economy governments. The public debt increased from 41 per cent of GDP in 1998 to 93 per cent by 2004. Faced with the prospect of default, the government initiated a partial restructuring of its debts in 2006, which was successfully completed in February 2007.
The Inter-American Development Bank estimated that in 2006 migrant workers sent some US$93 million to their families in Belize.

External trade
As a member of the Caribbean Community and Common Market (Caricom), Belize operates within the single market (Caribbean Single Market and Economy (CSME)), which became operational on 1 January 2006. Goods, services, businesses and money are free to move within CSME without barriers and tariffs.
Belize relies on imports to fuel economic activity, which are largely centred on tourism, clothing manufacture and food processing. Imports have a value of over 65 per cent of total GDP while exports account for around 35 per cent.
Imports
Main imports are machinery and transport equipment, food, beverages, tobacco, manufactured goods, fuels, chemicals and pharmaceuticals.
Main sources: US (38.8 per cent total, 2006), Netherlands Antilles (10.7 per cent), Panama (9.6 per cent).
Exports
Principal exports are sugar, bananas, citrus, garments, fish and cultured shrimp, molasses and timber.
Main destinations: US (42.0 per cent of 2006 total goods exports), UK (16.1 per cent), Costa Rica (7.8 per cent).

Agriculture
Farming
The agricultural sector forms the mainstay of the economy contributing approximately 20 per cent of total GDP and employing 25 per cent of the workforce. The sector accounts for about 65 per cent of foreign exchange earnings and the banana industry is the country's largest employer. Approximately 65 per cent of the country's land mass is considered to have arable potential but only 2 per cent is used for farming; 45 per cent of the total land mass is forest, much of which is commercially exploitable.
Sugar is the main cash crop though Belize has diversified into exporting other crops, particularly banana and citrus production (mainly oranges), and fisheries. Winter vegetables, papayas, mangoes and cocoa are also grown for export, while rice, maize, roots, beans and vegetables are produced for livestock consumption.
Hurricane Dean, which struck in August 2007, destroyed the entire export crop of papaya, valued at over US$20 million and caused around US$1.2 million in damages to the sugar crop.
Crop production in 2005 included: 1,149,475 tonnes (t) sugar cane, 49,364t cereals in total, 30,538t maize, 10,680t rice, 726t potatoes, 8,146t sorghum, 36,900t plantains, 79,419t bananas, 269,393t citrus fruit, 27,727t papayas, 563t mangoes, 1,191t cassava, 591t tomatoes, 1,430t teenuts, 231t green coffee, 223t oilcrops, 6,697t pulses, 419,512t fruit in total, 9,342t vegetables in total. Livestock production included: 17,074t meat in total, 2,400t beef, 501t pig meat, 20t lamb, 14,152t poultry, 2,851t eggs, 3,618t milk, 38t honey, 182t cattle hides.
Fishing
Fishing, mainly for lobsters, conch and shrimp, contributes significantly to the economy.
In 2004, the total marine fish catch was 44 tonnes and the total crustacean catch was 715 tonnes.
Forestry
Forestry has played an integral role in the economy of Belize but the rise of the tourism industry has reduced its importance. Over half of the country's land mass is covered by forests, though the majority of this area has now been logged. Of the timber cut, the majority is sold in local markets including that of mahogany, soft pine, cedar, santa maria and yemeri. In recent years there have also been an increased harvesting of chicle (a latex gum of the sapodilla tree), throughout the country.

Industry and manufacturing
Centered on agricultural processing such as sugar-milling, citrus-processing and the processing of domestic foodstuffs, the industrial sector is small-scale. Garment manufacturing previously played a prominent role in the economy of Belize but has decreased in significance since the 1990s. In all, manufacturing contributes approximately one fifth of GDP (including a manufacturing contribution of 12.6 per cent). Manufacturing employs about 10 per cent of the workforce and construction employs 6 per cent.

Tourism
Tourism is Belize's principal economic activity, contributing up to 23 per cent of GDP and accounting for a quarter of jobs and foreign earnings. Diving, sailing and fishing on the coral reef and among the islands, archaeology and wildlife tours inland are the main attractions. The annual increase in the number of arrivals was stalled by the economic downturn in the United States and the effects of the 11 September 2001 terrorist attacks. Americans account for over 50 per cent of visitors and the number of Canadian tourists

visiting the country also increased significantly by 23 per cent. Some 357 cruise ships arrived at Belize's ports, bringing with them 747, 746 passengers. One in every five jobs in the country is in the tourism industry and travel and tourism constitute an estimated 20 per cent of total GDP in 2005.

Environment

Scientists warned that the proposed Chalillo hydro project, which involves building a 50-metre high dam in the rainforest, would destroy rare habitat for jaguar, tapir and a sub-species of scarlet macaw. The Belize Supreme Court halted construction in 2002. However the Privy Council in London, ruled that work on the controversial Chalillo Dam could proceed in 2004.

Mining

Belize has insignificant mineral deposits. During the 1980s extensive drilling was undertaken in the country in a vain attempt to discover oil. Nowadays, mining mainly involves surface removal of gravel for use in the construction industry. Approximately 0.4 per cent of the workforce is employed in the mining and quarrying sector.

Hydrocarbons

Despite an extensive oil exploration programme, commercial quantities have not so far been found. Consequently Belize still relies on the import of refined oil for its energy needs. Imports come primarily from Venezuela and Mexico under the San Jose Pact, signed in 1988, which obligues both countries to offer concessions of up to 25 per cent on the market price of their oil. In 1991 the terms of the San Jose agreement were revised, increasingly the amount of oil available at a discounted price to each of the signatories.

Energy

With no reserves of its own, Belize imports oil from Mexico and Venezuela under the auspices of the San Jose Pact and the Caracas Energy Accord. Belize purchases around 50 per cent of electricity from Mexico, 30 per cent is generated from the Mollejon dam and the remaining 20 per cent is derived from thermal plants. The government has outlined plans to develop a 7MW Chalillo dam on the Macal river.

Banking and insurance

Belize's banking sector is small, but contains both an offshore and onshore sector. The offshore sector is undergoing continued expansion owing to generous tax schemes and there are now eight banks, one insurance house and more than 22,000 international business companies. The International Financial Services Commission acts as the regulator of the offshore sector.

The onshore sector is composed of five domestic commercial banks, seven international banks and three quasi-governmental institutions, with credit unions also being prominent. Belize Banking Ltd retains a dominant market position with 45 per cent of domestic banks' assets. The Central Bank of Belize supervises banking activity and the Register of Co-operatives is the Credit union regulator.

The country's insurance sector is also small with 17 firms competing in the market; six insurance houses, nine general companies and three composites. At present there are no reinsurance firms in Belize.

Central bank

Central Bank of Belize

Main financial centre

Belize City

Offshore facilities

Belize has an important offshore banking sector. In April 2002, Belize was taken off the Organisation for Economic Co-operation and Development's (OECD) blacklist of 'un-co-operative tax havens' after the government made a commitment to greater transparency of its tax and regulatory systems and agreed to exchange information on tax matters with OECD countries from end-2005.

Time

GMT minus six hours

Geography

Belize lies on the Caribbean coast of Central America, with Mexico to the north-east and Guatemala to the south-west.

In the north the coastal area is low with fresh and sea water lagoons as well as swamps and mangroves. In the south, east and west the Maya mountain range, the Cockscomb range and the Mountain Pine Ridge, respectively, occupy around 40 per cent of the land and are dense rain forests. Close to the Guatemala border the land is relatively open. Belize possesses many small islands (Cayes) that straddle a coral reef which is the world's second largest, after the Great Barrier Reef in Australia.

Hemisphere

Northern

Climate

Sub-tropical with temperatures ranging from 10–30 degrees Celsius. Hottest months between March–September and rainy season June–October.

Entry requirements

Passports

Required by all and validity must be for at least six months longer than the intended period of stay.

Visa

Required by all, except north American, most European and Australasian citizens. For further exemptions contact the local embassy.

For a copy of the visa application visit www.un.int/belize/visappli.pdf.

All visitors should show that they have sufficient funds for the purpose and period of their stay and must be in possession of a valid return or onward ticket. Evidence in support of both funds and travel arrangements must be presented with applications for visas. Visitors are permitted to stay in Belize for up to 30 days.

Currency advice/regulations

A currency declaration form must be completed on arrival. Visitors are advised to keep a copy of the declaration form because travellers are not permitted to export more than this amount of currency.

Health (for visitors)

Mandatory precautions

Yellow fever vaccination certificate if travelling from infected area.

Advisable precautions

Typhoid, polio and rabies vaccinations. Malaria prophylaxis advisable. Water precautions should be taken.

Hotels

There are a good range of hotels. There are three charges likely to be levied locally: 8 per cent sales tax, 9 per cent hotel tax and a service charge of up to 10 per cent.

Public holidays (national)

Fixed dates

1 Jan (New Year's Day), 9 Mar (Baron Bliss Day), 1 May (Labour Day), 24 May (Commonwealth Day), 10 Sep (St George's Caye Day), 21 Sep (Independence Day), 12 Oct (Columbus Day), 19 Nov (Garifuna Settlement Day), 25–26 Dec (Christmas Holiday).

Variable dates

Good Friday, Easter Monday

Working hours

Banking

Mon–Thu: 0800–1300; Fri: 0800–1300 and 1500–1800.

Business

Mon–Fri: 0800–1200, 1300–1700.

Some businesses are open on Saturday.

Government

Mon–Fri: 0800–1200, 1300–1700; closes 1630 on Fridays.

Telecommunications

Mobile/cell phones

A GSM 1900 service operates around the capital, and north and south along the coastline.

Electricity supply

110/220/V AC, 60Hz, with US style two-pin plugs.

Getting there

Air

Intercontinental flights usually arrive via the US, other international flights are regional.

International airport/s: PSW Goldson International (BZE), 16km west of Belize City; duty-free shops, bar. Taxis to the city

Airport tax: Departure tax US$36.25, payable in cash or travellers cheques only – credit cards are not accepted.

Surface

Road: Main routes are from Melchor de Mencos (Guatemala) and Chetumal (Mexico).

Main port/s: Belize City.

Getting about

National transport

Air: Maya Airways and Tropic Air operate domestic services to main centres. The charter flight company AeroBelize flies to minor airfields.

Road: Over 1,500km of surfaced road linking the eight major towns and cities, the network in the north is in better repair than south of Belize city. Occasionally during torrential downpours all-weather roads may be flooded, especially close to ferry crossings.

A new all-weather road to Charcoal, the largest and most important archaeological site in Belize, was completed in 2004 at a cost of around US$2.5 million.

Buses: Services operate within Belize City; long-distance coach services link major centres.

Water: Regular ferry services and small boats ply to offshore cayes.

City transport

Taxis: Taxis are available in towns and resort areas, and at the airport. They are easily recognised by their green licence plates.

Fixed rates apply within Belize City (higher at night). With no meters it is advisable to agree the fare beforehand. Tipping is discretionary.

Car hire

Foreign or international licences are acceptable for 30 days. Driver must be over 18 years old. Driving on the right.

BUSINESS DIRECTORY

The addresses listed below are a selection only. While World of Information makes every endeavour to check these addresses, we cannot guarantee that changes have not been made, especially to telephone numbers and area codes. We would welcome any corrections.

Telephone area codes

The international dialling code (IDD) for Belize is +501 followed by the area code and subscriber's number:

Belize City	2	Dangriga	5
Belmopan	8	Independence	6
Corozal	4	San Ignacio	92

Useful telephone numbers

Directory enquiries: 113.

Local and regional operator-assisted calls: 114.

International operator-assisted calls: 115.

Fire and ambulance: 90.

Police: 911.

Chambers of Commerce

Belize Chamber of Commerce and Industry, 63 Regent Street, PO Box 291, Belize City (tel: 227-3148; fax: 227-4984; e-mail: bcci@btl.net).

Banking

Alliance Bank of Belize Ltd, PO Box 1988, 18 Cnr New Road & Hydes Lane, Belize City (tel: 236-783, 236-784; fax: 236-785).

Atlantic Bank Ltd, PO Box 481, Cnr Cleghorn & Freetown Road, Belize City (tel: 234-123, 277-124; fax: 233-907, 234-150).

Atlantic International Bank Ltd, PO Box 481, Cnr Freetown Road & Cleghorn Streets, Belize City (tel: 230-681; fax: 230-677).

Banca Serfin of Mexico, PO Box 1636, Cnr Eyre & Hudson Streets, Belize City (tel: 027-8179, 027-8225; fax: 027-8970).

Bank of Nova Scotia, PO Box 708, Albert Street, Belize City (tel: 027-7027/030/415/416; fax: 027-7416).

Barclays Bank PLC, PO Box 363, Albert Street, Belize City (tel: 027-7211; fax: 027-8572).

Belize Bank Ltd, PO Box 364, 60 Market Square, Belize City (tel: 277-132, 272-390; fax: 272-712, 274-519).

Development Finance Corporation, PO Box 40, Bliss Parade, Belmopan, Cayo District (tel: 082-2360, 082-2350; fax: 082-3096).

National Development Foundation of Belize, PO Box 1210, 109 Cemetery Road, Belize City (tel: 027-2139, 027-2874; fax: 027-8437).

Provident Bank & Trust of Belize Limited, PO Box 1867, 1st Floor, 35 Barrack Road, Belize City (tel: 235-698; fax: 230-368).

Central bank

Central Bank of Belize, Gabourel Lane, PO Box 852, Belize City (tel: 223-6194; fax: 223-6226; e-mail: info@centralbank.org.bz).

Travel information

AeroBelize (air charter), PSW Goldson International Airport, Ladyville (tel: 252-535).

Belize Airport Authority, PSW Goldson International Airport, Ladyville (tel: 252-045; fax: 252-439).

Belize Port Authority, Caesar Ridge Road, Belize City (tel: 272-439; fax: 273-571).

Belize Tourism Industry Association (BTIA), 99 Albert Street, PO Box 62, Belize City (tel: 275-717; fax: 271-144; e-mail: btia@btl.net).

Maya Airways (administrative office), 6 Fort St, PO Box 458, Belize City (tel: 272-312; fax: 30-585); PSW Goldson International Airport, Ladyville (tel: 252-336).

Ministry of tourism

Ministry of Tourism, 14 Constitution Drive, Belmopan (tel: 223-394; fax: 222-862).

National tourist organisation offices

Belize Tourism Board, Lower Flat, New Horizon Investment Bld, 3 1–32 Miles Northern Highway, P.O. Box 325, Belize City (tel: 223-1913; fax: 223-1943; email: info@travelbelize.org; internet: www.travelbelize.org).

Ministries

Ministry of Agriculture and Fisheries, West Block, Belmopan (tel: 222-332, 222-241; fax: 222-409).

Ministry of Budget Management, Investment and Trade, Central Bank of Belize Building, Gaol Lane, Belize City (tel: 232-128, 236-194; fax: 235-097; e-mail: chalilio@bti.net).

Ministry of Economic Development, PO Box 42, Belmopan (tel: 222-526, 222-527, 222-023, 222-672; fax: 223-111, 223-673).

Ministry of Education and Public Service, West Block, Belmopan (tel: 222-329, 222-798, 222-067; fax: 223-389, 222-206).

Ministry of Energy, Science, Technology and Transportation, Belmopan (tel: 222-435; fax: 223-317).

Ministry of Finance, Belmopan (tel: 222-169; fax: 2222-886).

Ministry of Foreign Affairs, PO Box 174, Belmopan (tel: 222-322; fax: 222-854).

Ministry of Health and Sports, Belmopan (tel: 222-325; fax: 222-942).

Ministry of Home Affairs and Labour, Belmopan (tel: 222-281; fax: 222-016).

Ministry of Housing, Urban Development and Co-operatives, Belmopan (tel: 223-339; fax: 223-298).

Ministry of Human Resources, Community and Youth Development, Culture and Women's Affairs, Belmopan (tel: 222-161; fax: 223-175).

Ministry of National Security, Belmopan (tel: 222-225; fax: 222-615).

Ministry of Natural Resources, Belmopan (tel: 222-331, 222-249; fax: 222-333).

Ministry of Statistics, Central Statistical Office, Belmopan (tel: 222-207; fax: 223-206).

Ministry of Tourism and The Environment, Belmopan (tel: 223-394; fax: 222-862).

Ministry of Trade and Industry, Belmopan (tel: 222-199; fax: 222-329).

Ministry of Works, Belmopan (tel: 222-139; fax: 223-282).

Other useful addresses

Association of National Development Agencies (ANDA), Princess Margaret Drive, Belize City (tel: 35-115; fax: 32-362).

Attorney General's Ministry, Belmopan (tel: 222-504; fax: 223-390).

Belize Electricity Board, 115 Barrack Road, Belize City (tel: 277-141; fax: 231-905).

Belize Embassy (USA), 2535 Massachusetts Avenue, NW, Washington DC 20008 (tel: 202-332-9636; fax: 202-332-6888).

Belize Export and Investment Promotion Unit (BEIPU), PO Box 291, 63 Regent Street, Belize City (tel: 273-148, 274-394, 275-108/9; fax: 274-984).

Belize Information Service, P.O. Box 60, Belmopan (tel: 222-019; fax: 223-242).

Belize Marketing Board, 117 North Front Street, PO Box 479, Belize City (tel: 272-439; fax: 273-571).

Belize Port Authority (tel: 272-439; fax: 273-571; e-mail: portbze@btl.net).

Belize Offshore Centre (tel: 234-351; fax: 233-501; e-mail: cititrust@btl.net).

Belize Telecommunications Ltd. St Thomas Street, PO Box 603, Belize City (tel: 232-868; fax: 277-600; internet site: www.btl.net).

Belize Trade and Investment Development Services (BELTRAIDE) (tel: 223-737; fax: 220-595; e-mail: beltraide@belize.gov.bz).

British High Commission, PO Box 91, Belmopan (tel: 222-146; fax: 222-717).

Central Statistical Office (CSO), Ministry of Finance, Belmopan (tel: 222-207; fax: 222-206).

Citrus Control Board, 87 Commerce Bight, Melinder Road, Dangriga Town (tel: 222-145, 222-447; fax: 222-686).

Customs & Excise, PO Box 146, Fort Street, Belize City (tel: 277-405; fax: 277-091).

Export Processing Zone, Ministry of Trade and Industry, Belmopan (tel: 222-199, 222-153; fax: 222-923).

Fisheries Department, Princess Margaret Drive, Belize City (tel: 244-552, 232-623; fax: 232-983; e-mail: species@btl.net).

Forest Department, Forestry Drive, Belmopan (tel: 223-629; fax: 222-083).

Geology and Petroleum Office, Unity Boulevard, Belmopan (tel: 222-178, 222-651; fax: 223-538).

National Development Foundation of Belize, 2882 Coney Drive Coral Grove, Belize City (tel: 231-207, 231-132; fax: 231-195).

Society for the Promotion of Education & Research (SPEAR), Corner Pickstock and New Road, PO Box 1766, Belize City (tel: 231-668; fax: 232-367).

Water and Sewerage Authority, Central American Boulevard, Belize City (tel: 224-757; fax: 224-759).

Other news agencies: Caribbean Net News: www.caribbeannetnews.com

Internet sites

Belize hotels website: www.belizehotels.com/

Belize yellow pages: www.ipl.com.gt/cgi-bin/busca-beling

Inter-American Development Bank: www.iadb.org

Latin American Network Information Center: www.lanic.utexas.edu

Benin

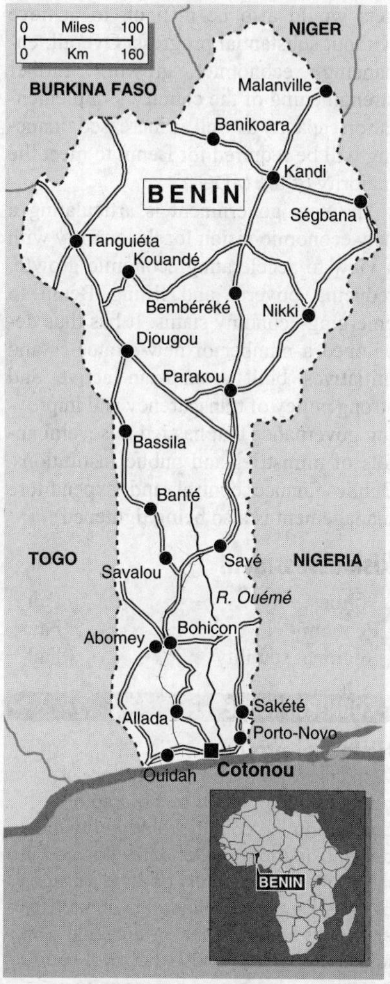

April 2006 saw Benin embark upon a new political era, when President Thomas Yayi Boni was sworn in. President Yayi Boni's qualifications for his new job were somewhat limited – he had been manager of the Banque Ouest Africaine de Développement (BOAD), a regional development bank established by the French west African countries (Benin, Burkina Faso, Côte d'Ivoire, Guinea Bissau, Mauritania and Togo).

Kérékou's political successes…

President Boni had inherited a depressing economic legacy from the years of rule by former president Kérékou. Not that Kérékou's reign will be necessarily remembered as completely negative. For better or worse, he will be remembered by most of his fellow citizens as the man who not only shaped the unity of the nation, but also enabled that unity to be maintained. As was the case with many former colonies in Africa, political instability characterised Benin's first years of independence from France in 1960. The former colony was known as Dahomey until the army coup of 1972, engineered by a Captain Assogba, who, immediately after taking power, handed it to his hierarchical chief, Colonel Mathieu Kérékou. Whatever changes in government took place subsequently, it was Kérékou who continued to call the shots for the best part of the next 30 years, whether officially in power or not. Kérékou was none the less a complex personality, who did not quite fit the stereotype of an insensitive African dictator. In 1990, when his power was threatened by the Conférence Nationale movement, he declined to use troops to suppress the opposition, instead accepting the decision taken by the Conférence to reduce his power by appointing a prime minister, Mr. Nicéphore Dieudonnee Soglo – who led a short-lived interim government till March 1991.

Kérékou lost 1991's presidential election against Soglo, accepting Soglo as president for a 5 year term. Kérékou ran again against Soglo in1996 and 2001 winning on each occasion in what were generally deemed to be free and fair elections. He appeared to respect the institutions put in place to protect democracy in the country. Kérékou was the acknowledged leader of Benin's post-independence Marxist-regime. He appeared to respect the idea of a free press and free speech, and endeavoured to maintain peace through balanced political and regional appointments. Kérékou's Achilles heel was the apparent blind-eye he turned towards the widespread corruption that gradually became rooted in Benin, which lead to speculation and accusations of his possible involvement.

Since independence, Benin's politics have tended to divide on a fairly clear north-south axis. Northerners and Southerners have traditionally voted for

KEY FACTS

Official name: République du Bénin (Republic of Benin)

Head of State: President Yayi Boni (elected 19 March 2006, sworn in 6 April)

Head of government: President Yayi Boni (sworn in 6 April 2006)

Ruling party: Forces Cauri pour un Bénin Emergent (FCBE) (Cauri Forces for an Emerging Benin) (elected Mar 2007)

Area: 112,622 square km

Population: 7.86 million (2007)*

Capital: Cotonou (seat of government); Porto-Novo (administrative)

Official language: French

Currency: CFA franc (CFAf) = 100 centimes (Communauté Financière Africaine (African Financial Community) franc).

Exchange rate: CFAf413.80 per US$ (Jul 2008)

GDP per capita: US$962 (2007)*

GDP real growth: 4.20% (2007)*

Labour force: 3.14 million (2004)

Inflation: 1.90% (2007)*

Balance of trade: -US$573.00 million (2005)

* estimated figure

candidates originating from their own regions. President Boni, who hails from the country's north-east, made some progress in breaking this tradition. He obtained votes from beyond his homeland that were critical in gaining a majority in the 2006 election. In March 2007, President Boni was able to strengthen his position following the legislative elections in which his coalition, Force Cauris pour un Bénin Emergent (FCBE) won 35 out of the 83 seats. This enabled a pro-government majority to be negotiated in the Parliament with seven minor parties and coalitions joining the FCBE. The government's hopes were that its majority would ensure the implementation of its ambitious reform programme. Boni also carried out a cabinet reshuffle, with 17 new ministers joining the government. The government dutifully set about implementing the President's reform programme, which included economic renewal and the fight against corruption. Municipal elections were scheduled for April 2008.

...and economic failures

Benin's economic development, hardly compares with its political successes. It is one of the poorest countries of the World, ranked 162 out of 177 by the World Bank. Kérékou's successive governments simply failed to live up to the job. Worse, the last years of his reign had been tainted by heavy corruption and financial scandals. Overall, the economy of Benin is underdeveloped although there are small oil deposits, as well as limestone, marble and timber. It remains dependent on subsistence agriculture, cotton production and regional trade. There are allegations that the country is a trans-shipment point for illicit drugs associated with Nigerian trafficking organisations and most commonly destined for Western Europe and the US; and that it is vulnerable to money laundering due to a poorly regulated financial infrastructure.

In its 2008 briefing, the World Bank observed that Benin's macroeconomic management has remained sound, despite a difficult global and regional environment. Macroeconomic performance under the three-year Poverty Reduction and Growth Facility arrangement approved by the IMF Board in August 2005 has been satisfactory with strong fiscal performance, containment of inflation, and satisfactory, albeit lower than expected, growth. Macroeconomic performance picked up slightly in 2006–07 with real GDP growth recovering to 4.6 per cent in 2007 from 2.9 per cent in 2005 following a rebound in the cotton and services sectors. Inflation has been broadly contained under the West African Economic and Monetary Union (WAEMU) convergence criterion of 3.0 per cent in 2006–07, despite unrelenting increases in the international prices of oil and foods. The external current account deficit remained broadly in line with the IMF-supported programme targets at 6.7 per cent of GDP in 2007 as compared with 7.9 per cent of GDP in 2004, and the overall budget deficit (on a payment order basis and excluding grants) narrowed from 4.6 per cent of GDP in 2005 to 3.7 per cent of GDP in 2007. Finally, debt cancellation has helped to steadily reduce the country's total public external debt from 58.3 per cent in 2000 to around 13.6 per cent of GDP at end-2007.

Despite these achievements on the macroeconomic front, available data suggest that Benin would not be able to reach all the United Nations Millennium Development Goals (MDG) targets by 2015. In particular, Benin is unlikely to meet the health MDGs without enhanced targeted measures and a sharp acceleration of current trends. The gender-related MDG targets would also be difficult to achieve without substantial progress. Overall, enhancing economic growth, further strengthening of the country's implementation capacity as well as increased financing will be required for Benin to meet the majority of the MDGs.

The new government is articulating a new economic vision for the country with a view to accelerating economic growth, reducing poverty and lifting Benin to emerging-economy status. It has thus developed a number of new strategies and initiatives built around an active and strong policy of transparency and improving governance that has led to several audits of ministries and public institutions. Public finance control and expenditure management is also being tightened.

Risk assessment

Politics	Fair
Economy	Fair
Regional stability	Fair

KEY INDICATORS — Benin

	Unit	2003	2004	2005	2006	2007
Population	m	65.85	6.94	7.39	*7.61	*7.86
Gross domestic product (GDP)	US$bn	2.63	4.08	4.41	4.76	*5.43
GDP per capita	US$	400	565	596	*625	*692
GDP real growth	%	3.9	3.1	2.9	3.7	*4.2
Inflation	%	1.5	2.6	5.4	3.8	*3.0
Exports (fob) (goods)	US$m	207.0	720.9	627.0	–	–
Imports (cif) (goods)	US$m	479.0	934.5	1,183.0	–	–
Balance of trade	US$m	-272.0	-213.6	-573.0	–	–
Current account	US$m	-300.0	-350.0	-273.0	-304.0	*-324.0
Total reserves minus gold	US$m	509.8	442.9	656.8	912.2	1,209.2
Foreign exchange	US$m	506.3	439.5	653.5	908.9	1,205.6
Exchange rate	per US$	574.89	496.63	507.22	496.60	454.40

* estimated figure

COUNTRY PROFILE

Historical profile

With little known about the history of northern Benin, much of the area now comprising the country belonged to the ancient kingdom of Dahomey (located in the south of the country and the strongest of three kingdoms founded by three brothers). At its height, in the seventeenth century, the kingdom boasted a royal court complex as large as a European town, with palaces and buildings decorated with carvings and copper castings and housing bronze and ivory treasures. The wealth of the kingdoms was built on slave trading, a lucrative business that sold over 10,000 prisoners a year up to the nineteenth century. In 1879 the royal court of the Oba King was destroyed and its treasures looted; most pieces ended up in the British Museum. France, with a strategy of denying other European powers expansion into the region, overthrew King Behanzin and declared Dahomey a protectorate in 1893. In 1904 it was later absorbed into French West Africa, and gained autonomous status in 1946. Following independence from France in 1960 until 1972 the Republic of Dahomey endured a period of chronic

instability enduring five coups, nine changes in government and five different constitutions.
1960 Gained independence from France as the Republic of Dahomey. Hubert Maga, was elected president.
1963 Maga was overthrown by General Christophe Soglo leading a military coup d'état.
1965 Soglo declared himself head of state.
1967 A military coup deposed Soglo.
1969 Lt Col Paul-Émile de Souza became president.
1970 Election were scheduled but failed to take place due to irreconcilable differences between politicians of the north and south. Instead, a three-man presidential council was formed; with a two-year rotating precedency for each.
1972 Maga, the first president, was replaced, without incident in May, by Justin Ahomadegbé. In October, the military staged another coup and installed an 11-man government headed by Major Mathieu Kérékou who declared Benin a Marxist-Leninist state.
1975 The Republic of Dahomey was renamed The People's Republic of Benin.
1990 With the country bankrupt and on the brink of social collapse, President Kérékou handed power to a national conference. The government abandoned Marxism-Leninism and committed itself to political reform.
1991 Nicéphore Soglo became president and introduced sweeping austerity measures.
1995 Parties opposed to the president won a majority in the National Assembly in the legislative elections.
1996 Kérékou became president and Adrien Houngbédji, leader of the Parti du Renouveau Démocratique (PRD) (Party of Democratic Renewal), assumed the role of prime minister.
1998 Houngbédji resigned, a new government was formed without a post of prime minister.
1999 After National Assembly elections, the Parti de la Renaissance du Benin (PRB) (Benin Renaissance Party), led by former president Soglo's wife, Rosine, emerged as the largest single opposition party. Adrien Houngbédji (PRD) was elected president of the new Assembly.
2001 President Kérékou was re-elected for his last five-year term.
2002 The first municipal elections were held.
2003 A large coalition of parties backing President Mathieu Kérékou won the National Assembly elections.
2004 An International Development Association (IDA) credit of US$45 million was approved to assist Benin in expanding electrification and restructuring its power sector. Benin and Nigeria agreed to redefine their mutual border.
2005 The International Court of Justice awarded Niger most of the river islands that had been disputed along the Niger/Benin border.
2006 The first round of the presidential election was won by Boni Yayi with 33.56 per cent of the vote. A second round run-off between Boni Yayi and Adrien Houngbedji (who had won 22.72 per cent of the first vote), was won by Boni Yayi with almost 75 per cent of the vote. He was sworn in as president after long-term ruler, Mathieu Kérékou, left office at midnight on 5 April.
2007 In February, Benin assumed control of nine islands in the river Niger in accordance with the 2005 International Court of Justice ruling, settling the border dispute with Niger, which received the large island of Lete and several others. In parliamentary elections on 31 March, President Boni's coalition, Forces Cauri pour un Bénin Emergent (FCBE) (Cauri Forces for an Emerging Benin), won 35 out of 83 seats; Alliance pour une Dynamique Démocratique (ADD) (Alliance for a Dynamic Democracy) won 20 seats.
2008 Local elections in March were temporarily postponed when voter lists were found to be faulty. Four million voters had registered to vote but many found their names had been omitted. In June at the Community of the Sahelian-Saharan States (CEN-SAD) Executive Council meeting in Cotonou, an investment guarantee agency was agreed to provide funds for infrastructure projects.

Political structure

Constitution
The 1990 constitution provides for multi-party politics and a president to be directly elected by popular vote. Presidential candidates cannot be aged over 70. No provision is made for a prime minister; the president is head of government.

Form of state
Republic

The executive
The president is directly elected by popular vote for a five-year term and has ultimate power and control.

National legislature
Benin has a directly elected legislature, the 83-member Assemblée Nationale (National Assembly), with a maximum life of four years.

Legal system
The legal system is based on French civil law and customary law.

Last elections
31 March 2007 (parliamentary); 5/19 March 2006 (presidential).

Results: Presidential: Yayi Boni (independent) won 74.5 per cent of the vote and Adrien Houngbédji (Democratic Renewal Party) 25.5 per cent. Turnout was 69.5 per cent.
Parliamentary: President Boni's coalition, Forces Cauri pour un Bénin Emergent (FCBE) (Cauri Forces for an Emerging Benin), won 35 out of 83 seats; Alliance pour une Dynamique Démocratique (ADD) (Alliance for a Dynamic Democracy) won 20 seats.

Next elections
2011 (presidential and parliamentary).

Political parties

There are over 100 registered parties in Benin, but only a handful are represented in parliament.

Ruling party
Forces Cauri pour un Bénin Emergent (FCBE) (Cauri Forces for an Emerging Benin) (elected Mar 2007)

Main opposition party
Alliance pour une Dynamique Démocratique (ADD) (Alliance for a Dynamic Democracy) ; Parti du Renouveau Démocratique (PRD) (Party of Democratic Renewal).

Population

7.86 million (2007)*
Last census: February 2002: 6,769,914
Population density: 51 inhabitants per square km. Urban population: 43 per cent (1995–2001).
Annual growth rate: 3.2 per cent 1994–2004 (WHO 2006)

Ethnic make-up
African (99 per cent) (42 ethnic groups, most important being Fon, Adja, Yoruba, Bariba), European (1 per cent).

Religions
Animists (70 per cent), Christians (15 per cent) and Muslims (15 per cent).

Education

Annual expenditure on education is 3–3.5 per cent of GDP of which over 55 per cent is spent on primare education.
Literacy rate: 40 per cent adult rate; 56 per cent youth rate (15–24) (Unesco 2005).
Enrolment rate: 99 per cent gross primary enrolment, of relevant age group (including repeaters); 20 per cent net secondary enrolment (UN HDR)
Pupils per teacher: 52 in primary schools.

Health

Per capita total expenditure on health (2003) was US$36; of which per capita government spending was US$16, at the international dollar rate, (WHO 2006).

HIV/Aids
70,000 people, 3,000 of whom are aged under 15 (World Bank). Half of sex workers have tested positive, so a pandemic could cause future problems if issues of contraceptive use are not addressed.

HIV prevalence: 1.9 per cent aged 15–49 in 2003 (World Bank)
Life expectancy: 53 years, 2004 (WHO 2006)
Fertility rate/Maternal mortality rate: 5.7 births per woman, 2004 (WHO 2006)
Child (under 5 years) mortality rate (per 1,000): 91 per 1,000 live births; 23 per cent of children aged under five were malnourished (World Bank).
Head of population per physician: 0.04 physician per 1,000 people, 2004 (WHO 2006)

Welfare

The National Social Security fund provides for general workers and farmers who have made contributions. The fund is supervised by the Ministry of Labour although its assets are autonomous and administered by trustees. Every employer must provide a contribution for each worker to cover disability and family allowances. Old age pension benefits are accrued by workers contributions to the fund.
Pensions

Main cities

Cotonou (seat of government, estimated population 898,790 in 2003), Porto-Novo (administrative capital, 240,744), Parakou (175,792), Abomey (115,283), Natitingou (243,414).

Languages spoken

French; African languages (Yoruba, Bariba and Fon) are widely used in everyday life.
Official language/s
French

Media

Benin is considered one of the most liberal media markets in Africa.
National news agency: Agence Benin-Presse (ABP)
Press
Dailies: In French, Fraternite (www.fraternite-info.com), Le Matinal En Ligne (www.actubenin.com) and Le Nation (www.gouv.bj/presse/lanation), is a government publication.
Weeklies: In French La Gazette du Golfe with political debate.
Business: The Le Magazine de l'Entreprise (www.creationdentreprise.org), is a magazine of regional business affairs.
Periodicals: In French, a fortnightly publication includes the government information bureau's Journal Officiel de la République du Benin.
Broadcasting
The state-owned Office des Radiodiffusion et Télévision du Bénin (ORTB) broadcasts radio and television services.
Radio: Radio is the prime medium for public news and information and phone-in programme are popular. The ORTB broadcasts Radio Benin (www.ortb.net, site under construction), in French, English and 18 local languages. Commercial stations include Golfe FM (www.eit.to), the pan-African Radio Africa No 1 (www.africa1.com) and Radio Planete (www.planetefm.com); Radio Maranatha (www.eit.to) and Radio Immaculee Conception (www.immacolata.com/fibenafr) are religious stations.
Television: Fewer residents watch TV than listen to radio. ORTB operated Television Nationale. Internet TV is provided Espace Informatique et Telecommunications (EIT) including Canal Sat Horizons (www.eit.to), LBC (www.lbcgroup.tv) and Future Television (www.future.com.lb). Television LC2 International (www.lc2international.tv) is a satellite station.
News agencies
National news agency: Agence Benin-Presse (ABP)

Economy

Benin was forced to restructure its economy in the early 1990s following the devaluation of the CFA franc. This resulted in sustained growth for almost a decade. However, the IMF, in a 2007 review, observed that Benin's macroeconomic situation was fragile as it had experienced a steady decline in real GDP growth: from 5.2 per in cent 2001 to 3.59 per cent in 2005.
The economy is reliant on primary industries with agriculture providing 36.9 per cent of GDP, of which cotton accounts for over 65 per cent of exports. Benin is one of Africa's largest cotton producers. Just under 30 per cent of its labour force depend on cotton production for their livelihood. A decline in cotton production along with restrictions on exports to Nigeria and the continuation of cotton subsidies in developed countries resulted in a fall in exports in 2004/05. Most other agricultural products grown are sold on local markets or are subsistence crops.
Despite the progress made, poverty and social indicators have not improved significantly over the past decade. Benin remains one of the poorest countries in the world, with 29 per cent of the population living below the national poverty line; it was rated at 163 out of 177 in 2006, by the UN Human Development Report.
The IMF advised that structural economy reforms should be implemented to improve Benin's export competitiveness through privatisation of national entities, tightened controls on revenue collection and administration. It also warned that public expenditure management with enhanced transparency and governance of public finances was vital.
The government's policy is focused on attempting to increase the level of foreign direct investment. This is hoped to be achieved by attracting investment into the growing tourist industry and communication sectors. Approval of a natural gas pipeline from Nigeria will help the nation's poor energy situation, this in turn should create jobs and an enhanced business climate.
The World Bank and IMF agreed in 2005 to approve a three-year arrangement of US$9.1 million, with a first tranche of US$1.3 million. This follows on from the 2003 final disbursement of US$460 million that successfully completed the debt relief programme under the enhanced Heavily Indebted Poor Countries (HIPC) initiative, after Benin fulfilled several conditions. These included implementing a poverty reduction strategy, maintenance of a macroeconomic framework, and introducing structural and social reforms to improve poverty reduction, school enrolment and governance in other areas. Donors also pressed for further action to reduce the civil service and privatise state enterprises. However only limited success was achieved on the latter as state control of the cotton sector has yet to be relinquished, although the government has plans for reforms due after the 2006 national elections.
Corruption and the informal sector also dog government control of the economy. Smuggling, including of people, between Benin and Nigeria, is rife and it has been estimated that the informal sector accounts for over 45 per cent of gross national income.

External trade

Benin, along with Burkina Faso, Mali and Chad, lodged a complaint with the WTO calling for the removal of cotton subsidies in developed countries and particularly in the US.
Benin acts as a transit country for goods from Nigeria to Togo and its landlocked neighbours Niger, Burkina Faso and Mali.
Imports
Principal imports are refined oil and petroleum products, foodstuffs, tobacco and capital goods.
Main sources: France (21.8 per cent total, 2004), Ghana (7.1 per cent), Côte d'Ivoire (7.0 per cent), China (6.7 per cent), UK (5.2 per cent), Belgium (4.9 per cent), Togo (4.5 per cent), Thailand (4.2 per cent), Nigeria (4.0 per cent)
Exports
Principal exports are palm oil, cotton, coffee and cocoa.
Main destinations: China (31.3 of total, 2005), Indonesia (8.1 per cent), India (7.4 per cent), Niger (4.5 per cent), Togo

(4.8 per cent), Niger (4.5 per cent), Thailand (6.0 per cent), Nigeria (4.6 per cent)

Agriculture

Farming

The agricultural sector is the most important economic sector. It accounted for 36.9 per cent of GDP in 2004 and employs over 55 per cent of the workforce.

Cotton is the principal cash crop and foreign exchange earner, farmed mainly on large industrial plantations. It is also important to the rural economy as it supports almost half of rural households.

Other cash crops include palm oil, coffee, sugar, cocoa, karité nuts and tobacco.

Subsistence farming (mainly collectivised) shows low productivity but the country is virtually self-sufficient in food. Livestock farming is particularly important in the north. The principal food crops are yams, cassava, sorghum, beans, millet, maize and rice.

Crop production in 2005 included: 1,109,465 tonnes (t) cereals in total, 3,100,000t cassava, 2,257,254t yams, 842,626t maize, 244,000t oil palm fruit, 163,831t sorghum, *130,000t groundnuts in shell, 144,234t tomatoes, 64,699t rice, 50,018t sweet potatoes, 36,817t millet, 116,839t oilcrops, *425,000t seed cotton, *150,000t cotton lint, *70,000t sugar cane, 119,376t pulses, 33,563t chillies & peppers, *1,000t tobacco leaves, *12,000t citrus fruit, *249,000t fruit in total, 376,797t vegetables in total.

Livestock production included: 54,627t meat in total, 21,780t beef, 4,060t pig meat, 7,587t lamb & goat meat, *15,200t poultry, *9,360t eggs, 35,325t milk, 3,564t cattle hides, 514t sheepskins.

* estimate

Fishing

Fishing is confined mainly to inland waters and augments local food supplies.

In 2004, the total marine fish catch was 14,187 tonnes and the total crustacean catch was 6,752 tonnes.

Industry and manufacturing

The industrial sector is small-scale, contributing 8.4 per cent to GDP and employing 6 per cent of the workforce.

Manufacturing activity is centred on processing primary products (palm oil, fats, sugar, beverages, cotton) for export, and the manufacture of consumer goods and construction materials for home consumption.

Cement production and oil refining are the main heavy industries.

The government has encouraged foreign investment in canning, paper processing, glass manufacturing, salt processing, agribusiness, pharmaceuticals, clothing, palm oil, building materials and chemicals.

The cottonseed oil plant at Bohicon was extended and modernised, raising capacity to 12,000 tonnes of oil, and a sugar producing enterprise was reopened.

Tourism

Tourism in Benin is at a formative stage of development. The government recognises its potential value to the economy and is encouraging promotion of the country's under-exploited attractions and the expansion of infrastructure.

Mining

The mining sector accounts for 5.5 per cent of GDP and employs 3 per cent of the workforce.

Activity is confined to extraction of limestone for the local cement industry, and marble. There is a limestone quarry at Onigbolo. There are known reserves of phosphate, chromite, uranium, low grade iron ore, marble and gold. The government has awarded a number of gold exploration licences to foreign investors.

Under Beninese law, all mineral resources belong to the state, which grants exclusive rights for exploration, development and mining activities.

Hydrocarbons

Proven reserves of oil have fallen below eight million barrels and ongoing exploration has been unsuccessful. Oil production is on a very small scale, with the downstream oil industry dependent on refined petroleum products imported from neighbouring Nigeria. An oil terminal with a capacity of 55,000 cubic metres (cum) of crude is based at Cotonou.

Proven gas reserves totalled 1.2 billion cubic metres. When it is complete, the US$260 million West African Gas Pipeline (WAGP) will supply natural gas from Nigeria's Escravos field to Benin, Togo and Ghana. The WAGP consortium will invest about US$500 million to pipe Nigerian natural gas across the region. The 1,000km pipeline is to be managed by Chevron Texaco and was expected to come into operation in 2005. However, protracted debate on the environmental impact of the pipeline has delayed construction. Nigeria has said it will use gas that at the moment is being flared off, but has so far (early 2006) refused to name the wells. Benin is expected to consume only 5 per cent of the piped gas until a market for it is fully established.

Energy

Benin produces about 25 million kilowatt-hours of electricity each year. Traditional fuels account for over 70 per cent of total energy consumption. The rest is mainly hydroelectric power.

Electricity is imported from the hydroelectric Akosombo Dam in Ghana. The Akosombo and Nkong hydroelectric dams generate about 1,072MW annually.

A joint hydroelectric power project with Togo on the river Mono has been in full operation since the building of the Nangbeto Dam.

Transmission Company of Nigeria (TCN) said it was due to complete the 70 kilometre power transmission line to Benin in February 2007. The project is part of the West African Power Pool action plan and cost US$25 million.

Banking and insurance

Central bank

Banque Centrale des États de l'Afrique de l'Ouest

Main financial centre

Cotonou and Parakou

Time

GMT plus one hour

Geography

Benin is a narrow stretch of territory 700km long running north/south. The country has an Atlantic coastline of about 100km, flanked by Nigeria to the east and Togo to the west. In the north it is bordered by Burkina Faso and Niger.

Hemisphere

Northern

Climate

Equatorial in the south with average daytime temperatures reaching 30–38 degrees Celsius (C). Main dry season from January–March. Rainy seasons from May–July and from September–December. Very humid in coastal areas. The north is tropical with more extreme temperatures, and single dry and rainy seasons. Length of rainy seasons varies with location but it is generally very wet from July–October.

Entry requirements

Passports

Required by all except nationals of certain African countries who have identification documents.

Visa

Required by all, except for nationals of Economic Community of West African States (Ecowas) countries. For the latest requirements and to apply, contact the local embassy or representative.

Currency advice/regulations

There are no restrictions on import of local or foreign currency, but amounts of foreign currency must be declared on arrival.

Foreign currency exports are allowed up to the equivalent of CFAf500.

Health (for visitors)

Mandatory precautions

Yellow fever and cholera vaccination certificates required.

Advisable precautions

Inoculations and boosters should be current for cholera, tetanus, polio, hepatitis A, diphtheria, typhoid and yellow fever.

There may be a need for vaccinations for tuberculosis, hepatitis B and meningitis. Malaria prophylaxis, which also provides protection for hepatitis B and yellow fever, include mosquito repellents, nets and clothing that cover the body after dark. There is a risk of rabies.

Other diseases that require preventative measures, such as condoms, are HIV/Aids and hepatitis B; to avoid bilharzia, avoid exposure to fresh water and use only well-maintained, chlorinated swimming pools. Use only bottled or boiled water for drinks, washing teeth and making ice. Eat only well cooked meals, preferably served hot; vegetables should be cooked and fruit peeled. Dairy products are unpasteurised and should be avoided. There is a shortage of routine medications, including sun-screens, and visitors should take all necessary medicines with them. A first aid kit that includes disposable syringes, is a reasonable precaution. Healthcare is not to Western standards and medical insurance, including emergency evacuation, is necessary.

Hotels

Available in all main towns. Better class accommodation is found only in and around Cotonou. Advance booking is advisable. Service charge usually included in bill, otherwise 10 per cent tip.

Credit cards

Access, Mastercard, Visa accepted on limited basis. Some banks may advance cash on Visa cards, check with card company.

Public holidays (national)

Fixed dates

1 Jan (New Year's Day), 10 Jan (Traditional Day), 1 May (Labour Day), 1 Aug (Independence Day), 15 Aug (Assumption Day), 26 Oct (Armed Forces Day), 1 Nov (All Saints' Day), 30 Nov (National Day), 25 Dec (Christmas Day).

Variable dates

Good Friday, Easter Monday, Ascension Day, Whit Monday, Eid al Adha, Eid al Fitr, Birth of the Prophet.

Islamic year – 1429 (10 Jan 2008–28 Dec 2008): The Islamic year contains 354 or 355 days, with the result that Muslim feasts advance by 10–12 days against the Gregorian calendar. Dates of feasts vary according to the sighting of the new moon, so cannot be forecast exactly.

Working hours

Banking

Mon–Fri: 0800–1100, 1500–1700.

Business

Mon–Fri: 0800–1230, 1530–1900. (Sat) 0900–1300.

Government

Mon–Fri: 0800–1230, 1500–1830.

Shops

Mon–Sat: 0830–1300, 1600–1930; (Sun) 0800–1200. Shops that open Sun mainly close Mon am.

Electricity supply

Electricity supply 220V AC 50 cycles.

Getting there

Air

International airport/s: Cotonou-Cadjehoun (COO), 6km west of city; taxi and limousine service (15–20 minutes to city centre), restaurant, business centre, 24 hours medical facility.

Airport tax: None

Surface

Road: There are routes from Burkina Faso, Togo, Nigeria and Niger.

Rail: A line linking Niger to Benin is under construction.

Water: Shipping lines from Marseille (France) and Lagos (Nigeria).

Main port/s: Porto Novo, Cotonou

Getting about

National transport

Air: Regular services between Cotonou, Parakou, Natitingou, Kandi and Djougou.

Road: Good main roads in south connecting towns to Cotonou and Porto Novo.

Mainly laterite, but the main coast road, which connects Lagos with Accra, is surfaced, and the road north from Cotonou is surfaced to Savalou.

In northern areas some roads are only passable in dry season.

Buses: Bus services link towns on these main routes.

Rail: There is only one operation railway line going north from Cotonou to Bohicon, Savé and Parakou. Facilities are limited.

City transport

Taxis: Fixed charge within towns, but advisable to negotiate fares in advance. Tipping is optional.

Car hire

Available in Cotonou. Chauffeur-driven services are recommended. Insurance/liability position should be checked. International driving licence required.

BUSINESS DIRECTORY

The addresses listed below are a selection only. While World of Information makes every endeavour to check these addresses, we cannot guarantee that changes have not been made, especially to telephone numbers and area codes. We would welcome any corrections.

Telephone area codes

The international direct dialling code (IDD) for Benin is +229, followed by subscriber's number.

Chambers of Commerce

Benin Chamber of Commerce and Industry, Avenue Général de Gaulle, PO Box 31, Cotonou (tel: 312-081; fax: 313-299; e-mail: ccib@bow.intnet.bj).

Banking

Bank of Africa Bénin (BOA), BP 08-0879, Ave Pape Jean Paul II, Cotonou (tel: 313-228; fax: 313-117).

Banque Centrale des Etats de l'Afrique de l'Ouest, BP 325, Ave Jean Paul II, Cotonou (tel: 312-466/7; fax: 312-465).

Banque Internationale du Bénin (BIBE) BP 03-2098, Carrefour des 3 Banques, Cotonou (tel: 315-549; fax: 312-365).

Continental Bank Bénin, 01 BP, Avenue Pope Jean Paul II, 2020 Cotonou (tel: 312-424, 313-393; fax: 315177).

Ecobank Bénin, BP 1280, Rue du Gouverneur Bayol, 01 Cotonou (tel: 314-023, 313-069; fax: 313-385, 313-718).

Financial Bank Bénin (FBB), BP 2700, Rue du Commandant Decoeur, Cotonou (tel: 313-100, 313-103, 313-104; fax: 313-102).

Central bank

Banque Centrale des États de l'Afrique de l'Ouest, PO Box 325, Avenue Jean Paul II, Cotonou (tel: 312-466; fax: 312-465; e-mail: webmaster@bceao.int).

Travel information

Transports Aériens du Bénin (tel: 314-797).

National tourist organisation offices

Office National du Tourisme et de l'Hôtellerie (ONATHO), BP 89, Contonou (tel: 315-402).

Ministries

Ministry of Public Service, Labour and Administrative Reform (tel: 313-112).

Ministry of Public Works and Transport, PO Box 16, Cotonou, Benin (tel: 313-380).

State Ministry of Government Co-ordination, Planning, Development and Employment Promotion (tel: 301-553).

Other useful addresses

Agence Bénin-Presse, BP 120, Cotonou.

Benin Embassy (USA), 2737 Cathedral Avenue, NW, Washington DC 20008 (tel: 232-6656; fax: 265-1996).

Import/Export Alimentation de Bénin, BP 53, Cotonou.

Institut National de la Statistique et de L'Analyse Economique, BP 323, Cotonou (tel: 314-101/103).

Mission de Co-opération et d'Action Culturelle, BP 476, Cotonou (tel: 300-824).

Mission Permanente d'Aide et de Co-opération, BP 476, Cotonou (administers aid from France).

Organisation Commune Benin-Niger des Chemins de fer et des Transports (OCBN) (Benin Railways), PO Box 16, Cotonou, Benin (tel: 313-380).

Société Nationale d'Equipement, BP 2042, Cotonou (deals with capital goods).

Société Nationale de Commercialisation et d'Exportation du Bénin (Sonaceb), BP 933, Cotonou (tel: 312-822).

Société Nationale de Commercialisation des Produits Pétroliers (Sonacop), BP 245, Cotonou (tel: 312-290).

Société Nationale d'Importation du Bénin, BP 2042, Cotonou.

Syndicat National des Commerçants et Industriels Africains du Bénin, BP 367, Cotonou.

National news agency: Agence Benin-Presse (ABP)
Address: 01 BP 72 Cotonou (tel: 2131-2655; fax: 2131-1326; internet: www.gouv.bj/presse/abp).

Internet sites
Africa Business Network: www.ifc.org/abn

AllAfrica.com: www.allafrica.com

African Development Bank: www.afdb.org

Africa Online: www.africaonline.com

Benin: www.guide-benin.

Embassy in Paris: www.ambassade-benin.org

General tourist information: www.africaguide.com/

Mbendi AfroPaedia (information on companies, countries, industries and stock exchanges in Africa): http://mbendi.co.za

Mission to the UN: www.un.int/benin

Bermuda

KEY FACTS

Official name: Bermuda

Head of State: Queen Elizabeth II; represented by Governor Sir Richard Gazney (from 12 Dec 2007)

Head of government: Prime Minister Ewart Brown (PLP) (sworn in 30 Oct 2006)

Ruling party: Progressive Labour Party (PLP) (since 1998; re-elected 12 Dec 2007)

Area: 55 square km

Population: 65,000 (2007)*

Capital: Hamilton

Official language: English

Currency: Bermudan dollar (BD$) = 100 cents

Exchange rate: BD$1.00 per US$ (fixed)

GDP per capita: US$80,676 (2006)

GDP real growth: 2.50% (2005)

Labour force: 38,360 (2004)

Unemployment: 2.10% (2004)

Inflation: 3.10% (2005)

Balance of trade: US$487.00 million (2004)

Visitor numbers: 635,272 (2006)

* estimated figure

COUNTRY PROFILE

Historical profile

1503 A Spaniard, Juan de Bermudez, sighted the islands.
1609 Settled by the British.
1612 A charter was given by James I to the Virginia Company to include Bermuda in the dominion. The first permanent settlers arrived shortly afterwards.
1684 The islands were sold to the City of London and became the property of the Crown.
1620 Bermuda was granted limited self-government when the House of Assembly was formed.
1700s Bermuda developed links with the American colonies.
1815 Hamilton was named the capital city.
1834 Slavery was abolished.
1940 An agreement between the US and Britain granted about 10 per cent of Bermuda's land to the US for military use.
1963 The first political party was formed.
1968 Bermuda was granted internal self-government. The first elections held under universal adult suffrage were won by the United Bermuda Party (UBP).
1998 The UBP lost power for the first time since 1968 when the Progressive Labour Party (PLP) won the general election under Jennifer Smith. She was the first female party leader.
2001 Regulation of the insurance sector was moved from the ministry of finance to the Monetary Authority, in order to increase the transparency of the sector.
2002 The Bermuda Companies Amendment Act simplifying the procedure for forming companies was passed.
2003 The ruling PLP won parliamentary elections. Following an internal revolt in the PLP, Prime Minister Jennifer Smith resigned and Alex Scott became premier. Hurricane Fabian, the most powerful storm since the 1950s, hit the islands and caused widespread destruction. A Constitutional amendment introduced 36 single seat constituencies within the islands (from the previous 20 dual seat constituencies).
2004 The PLP published plans for independence from the UK.
2005 Bermuda entered into a tax sharing agreement with Australia, only the second agreement signed after the US; it allows requests and information on specific tax matters under investigation or audit to be passed between states. The OECD welcomed the agreement as a measure to 'counter abuse of the financial system'.
2006 On 30 October, Ewart Brown was sworn in as prime minister, having replaced Alex Scott as leader of the PLP.
2007 Sir John Vereker retired and Sir Richard Hugh Turton Gazney became governor, on 12 December.

Political structure

Bermuda has had a broad measure of internal self-government since 1968. Queen Elizabeth II is represented by a UK-appointed governor who is responsible for defence, external affairs and internal security. The governor is guided on most internal matters by a cabinet appointed from the bicameral legislature.

Form of state
Representative democracy; crown colony of the UK.

The executive
The prime minister is chosen from the majority party and heads a cabinet of no more than 14 members of the legislature.

National legislature
The legislature is bicameral. The upper house, the Senate, consists of 11 members, five appointed by the governor on the advice of the prime minister, three on the advice of the leader of the opposition and three by the governor. The lower house, the 36-member House of Assembly, is directly elected for a maximum term of five years.

Legal system
The legal system and Bermudian law are based on the British model. The ultimate court of appeal is the Judicial Committee of the Privy Council in the UK.

Last elections
12 December 2007 (parliamentary)

Results: Parliamentary: the ruling PLP won 52.5 per cent of the vote, 22 seats (out of 36) and the UBP 47.3 per cent, 14 seats.

Next elections
2012 (parliamentary)

Political parties

Ruling party
Progressive Labour Party (PLP) (since 1998; re-elected 12 Dec 2007)

Main opposition party
United Bermuda Party (UBP)

Political situation
Since 2004, when plans for an independent Bermuda were published by the PLP,

the government has remained impassive and refused to include a discussion of independence in the December 2007 election campaign. However, in April 2008 the newly elected PLP scrapped the public holiday on the Queen's official birthday in June, to be replaced by a National Heroes' Day in October. The decision was not popular with everyone and prompted an online petition to retain the holiday, claiming that the change was 'a blatant insult to Her Majesty'.

The image of tax havens, such as Bermuda, suffered in 2008 as evidence of tax evasion schemes came to light, coupled with the downturn in the global economy in 2008 and the collapse of some hedge funds have forced Bermuda to work harder for its share of the US$2 trillion worldwide hedge fund business, and offshore banking and insurance. Some headquarters have been moved to other less questionable destinations to bolster company images, prompting Bermuda to introduce new laws to provide greater transparency and good governance.

Population
64,174 (2005)
Last census: May 2000: 62,059
Population density: 1,280 inhabitants per square km. Urban population: 100 per cent.
Annual growth rate: 0.8 per cent (2003)

Ethnic make-up
African (58 per cent), European (36 per cent). Approximately 73 per cent of the population is Bermuda-born.

Religions
Non-Anglican Protestant (39 per cent), Anglican (27 per cent), Roman Catholic (15 per cent), African Methodist Episcopal (10 per cent), Methodist (6 per cent), Seventh-Day Adventist (3 per cent).

Health
Life expectancy: 77 years (estimate 2003)
Fertility rate/Maternal mortality rate: Two births per woman (2003)
Birth rate/Death rate: 12 births per 1,000 population; eight deaths per 1,000 population (2003).
Child (under 5 years) mortality rate (per 1,000): Nine per 1,000 live births (2003)

Welfare
An insurance scheme takes contributions from the employer and employee to benefit workers during sickness or disability, for maternity leave or survivors of deceased workers, funded by contributions of a set amount, paid by both the employer and employee, each paying 50 per cent of the sum per week.

Pensions
There is an old age pension scheme funded by contributions of a set amount, paid by both the employer and employee, each paying 50 per cent of the sum per week.

Main cities
Hamilton (capital city, estimated population 97,000 in 2003), St George's (St George's Island) (1,800).

Languages spoken
English and Portuguese.

Official language/s
English

Media
Press
Dailies: The only newspaper is The Royal Gazette (www.royalgazette.com).
Weeklies: Magazines include the Bermuda Sun (www.bermudasun.bm) and the Mid-Ocean News published by The Royal Gazette. Worker's Voice is published by the Industrial Union.
Periodicals: Monthly magazines include Bermudian and Bermudian Business. Preview Bermuda (www.previewbermuda.com) is a free publication for visitors. Bottom Line covers business matters and is published six times annually and issued free with The Royal Gazette.
Broadcasting
Radio: All stations are private and commercial. The Bermuda Broadcasting Company (BBC) operates four of the most listened to stations, providing a mix of programmes including news, music and local contents, however, the top ranking station is HOTT 107.5 (www.hott1075.com). VSB operates four channels including news, religious, music and tourist information. Radio Bermuda (www.marops.bm) gives shipping weather forecasts.
Television: There are two main networks, both commercial and free-to-air. The Bermuda Broadcasting Company (BBC) and DeFontes Broadcasting (Television) Ltd) (www.vsb-bm). There is ready access to satellite and cable TV services.
Advertising
Available in all forms of media from traditional newspaper ads to targeted mobile/cell texts and sponsorship.

Economy
Despite its small size and negligible resource base, Bermuda has one of the highest per capita incomes in the world. The economy is based upon tourism and international business transactions, which take advantage of Bermuda's offshore banking status.

Inflation has been kept low through the policy of fixing the Bermudan dollar at parity with the US dollar. Bermuda has low levels of public debt and although borrowing has risen due to an increase in capital spending, debt remains well below the government's ceiling of 10 per cent of GDP.

External trade
The large trade deficit is offset by net invisible earnings from tourism and international business, especially insurance and shipping registration. High import duties on all items are the government's main source of income.

Imports
Main sources: Principal imports include foodstuffs, tobacco, clothing, fuels, chemicals, machinery, transport equipment, and live animals.

Exports
Principal imports include foodstuffs, tobacco, clothing, fuels, chemicals, machinery, transport equipment, and live animals, pharmaceuticals and petroleum
Main destinations: France (65.6 per cent total, 2005), Spain (11.7 per cent), UK (4.5 per cent)

Re-exports
Pharmaceuticals and petroleum, machinery and transport equipment.

KEY INDICATORS **Bermuda**

	Unit	2003	2004	2005	2006	2007
Population	m	0.06	0.06	0.06	0.06	0.07
Gross domestic product (GDP)	US$bn	4.29	4.50	4.86	5.19	–
GDP per capita	US$	67,324	70,452	63,731	80,676	–
GDP real growth	%	4.4	1.6	2.5	3.5	–
Inflation	%	2.3	3.6	3.1	–	–
Exports (fob) (goods)	US$m	51.0	35.0	25.0	–	–
Imports (cif) (goods)	US$m	719.0	965.0	964.0	–	–
Balance of trade	US$m	-668.0	-930.0	-939.0	–	–
Tourist numbers	'000	482.7	477.8	517.2	–	–
Exchange rate	per US$	1.00	1.00	1.00	1.00	1.00

Agriculture
Agriculture contributes about 1 per cent to GDP annually. Less than 6 per cent of total area is cultivated arable land, most of which is used by tenant farmers for growing fruit, vegetables and flowers. Although self-sufficient in eggs and milk, around 80 per cent of food requirements need to be imported. There is a small fishing industry. Estimated crop production in 2005 included: 820 tonnes (t) potatoes, 90t sweet potatoes, 115t tomatoes, 330t bananas, 330t fruit in total, 2,855t vegetables in total. Estimated livestock production included: 25t beef, 2t goat meat, 50t pig meat, 101t poultry, 280t eggs, 1,350t milk.
The typical annual fish catch is over 350t, plus 25t per annum other seafood.
In 2004, the total marine fish catch was 349 tonnes and the total crustacean catch was 30 tonnes.

Industry and manufacturing
Manufacturing and construction combined contribute around 10 per cent to GDP and employ less than 5 per cent of the workforce. Major activities include ship repair, small boat building and manufacture of paints, perfumes, pharmaceuticals, mineral water extracts and handicraft souvenirs. The emphasis is on encouraging light industry in the Freeport area on Ireland Island North. Bermuda has large marine engineering interests, and operates one of the world's largest flag of convenience shipping fleets.

Tourism
Tourism, formerly the mainstay of the economy, is now second to the financial sector as a source of foreign exchange. Due in part to the high cost of visiting the island, a decline in visitor numbers had already set-in even before the terrorist events of 11 September 2001, which affected the all-important US market.
From arrival numbers below 500,000 in 2001 there has been a steady increase despite the set-back caused by the destruction wrought by Hurricane Fabian in 2003 – the most powerful storm to hit the island in 50 years.
Visitors arriving by air in 2006 numbered 298,973, an increase of 10.9 per cent, however cruise ship numbers were greater at 336,299 with the majority of visitors (227,725) arriving from the US.
The total estimated tourist expenditure for 2006 was US$464 million. Expenditure on shopping, entertainment and transport was US$2.7 million, an annual increase of 17.8 per cent, and spending on accommodation and food was US$62.9 million, an increase of 17.1 per cent.

Hydrocarbons
Bermuda relies on imported refined oil products and does not produce oil, natural gas or coal. Only ExxonMobil and Shell Oil Company are allowed to sell petroleum products on the market. Refined oils are imported to run electricity generators.
Gas is used mainly for domestic appliances and some commercial machines. It is imported by Shell from Argentina and is supplied by three commercial gas companies. There is no national grid; gas is supplied in cylinders and pumped into appliances.

Financial markets
Stock exchange
The Bermuda Stock Exchange (BSX) is rapidly becoming one of the world's leading offshore electronic securities markets. The BSX launched a securities depository in 2001.

Banking and insurance
Central bank
Bermuda Monetary Authority
Main financial centre
Hamilton
Offshore facilities
Bermuda is a signatory of a commitment to the Organisation for Economic Co-operation and Development (OECD) agreeing to exchange information with overseas authorities in criminal tax matters.
Following the 11 September 2001 terrorist attacks on the US, a number of new re-insurance companies located on the island.

Time
GMT minus four hours (GMT minus three hours from April to October).

Geography
The Bermudas or Somers Islands are an isolated archipelago, comprising about 150 islands in the Atlantic Ocean about 917km (570 miles) off the coast of South Carolina, USA. Ten of the islands are linked by bridges and causeways to form the principal mainland.
Hemisphere
Northern

Climate
Semi-tropical with temperatures usually ranging between 16—28 degrees Celsius, from winter (Nov–Mar) to summer (Apr–Oct), with no marked rainy season. Bermuda is located more than 1,600km north of the Caribbean and is subjected to occasional hurricane-force winds between June and September.

Dress codes
There is no occasion on the island when shorts cannot be worn. For the office, tailored shorts of one colour may be worn, with long socks to the knees with at least an inch to turn over.

Entry requirements
Passports
Required by all visitors except UK, US and Canadian nationals with other documentary proof of identification. All US and Canadian nationals have required a passport for re-entry to their country since January 2007.
A return/onward ticket is required by all visitors.
Visa
Visas are not required by transit passengers and most citizens of the Americas, Europe, Australasia and some Asian countries, provided their stay does not exceed six months. For further details visit www.immigration.gov.bm, or contact a UK diplomatic or consular mission locally. All visitors must have return/onward passage. Those wishing to travel to the US must have entry clearance for the country to be visited after leaving the US.
Currency advice/regulations
There is no limit to the import of local or foreign currency, provided it is declared on arrival. The export of local currency is limited to BD$250. The export of foreign currency is limited to the amount imported and declared.

Health (for visitors)
Mandatory precautions
Yellow fever vaccination certificate if travelling from an infected area.
Advisable precautions
Hepatitis, typhoid, tetanus and polio vaccinations.

Hotels
Generally expensive. Reduced rates are available in the November–March period. There is a 7.25 per cent occupancy tax payable at check-out in addition to room rates, and a 10–15 per cent tip is added unless a service charge has already been included in bill.

Credit cards
Credit cards are accepted at most hotels, restaurants and shops.

Public holidays (national)
Fixed dates
1 Jan (New Year's Day), 24 May (Bermuda Day), 11 Nov (Remembrance Day), 25–26 Dec (Christmas).
Variable dates
Good Friday, Cup Match and Somers' Day (first Thu and Fri of Aug), Labour Day (first Mon in Sep), Heroes' Day (Oct).

Working hours
Banking
Mon–Fri: 0900–1500; also 1630–1730 Fridays only.
Business
Mon–Fri: 0900–1700.

Government
Mon–Fri: 0900–1700.
Shops
Mon–Sat: 0900–1700. During summer many stores stay open until 2100.

Telecommunications
Mobile/cell phones
GSM 1900 coverage is available throughout the islands

Electricity supply
115–230V AC, 80 cycles

Getting there
Air
International airport/s: Bermuda International Airport (BDA), 16km from Hamilton; bar, restaurant, bank, shops, hotel reservations.
Airport tax: A departure tax of BD$25 is included in air tickets.
Surface
Main port/s: Hamilton, St George's. Weekly cruises link Bermuda with several east coast US ports during the summer months.

Getting about
National transport
Road: There are around 250km of well-surfaced roads.
Buses: Regularly scheduled buses operate at frequent intervals to most destinations throughout Bermuda. Passengers must have the exact fare, tokens or transport passes which provide unlimited travel by bus or ferry which can be purchased at the Central Terminal in Hamilton.
Water: Ferries to and from Hamilton, Paget, Warwick, Somerset and Dockyard.
City transport
Taxis: Metered taxis with 25 per cent surcharge between midnight and 0600; tariffs are fixed by law. Taxis displaying a small blue flag are approved by the Department of Tourism for sightseeing purposes.
Car hire
Foreign visitors are not permitted to drive cars. Motor-assisted cycles (mopeds and scooters) may be hired throughout the island and through hotel and guest-houses. Safety helmets must be worn and insurance is compulsory, although a driver's licence is not.

BUSINESS DIRECTORY

The addresses listed below are a selection only. While World of Information makes every endeavour to check these addresses, we cannot guarantee that changes have not been made, especially to telephone numbers and area codes. We would welcome any corrections.

Telephone area codes
The international direct dialling (IDD) code for +1441, followed by subscriber's number.

Chambers of Commerce
Bermuda Chamber of Commerce, 1 Point Pleasant Road, PO Box HM 655, Hamilton HM CX (tel: 295-4201; fax: 292-5779; e-mail: info@bermudacommerce.com).

Banking
Bank of Bermuda, 6 Front Street, Hamilton HM DX (tel: 295-4000, 299-5005; fax: 299-6501, 295-1386).

The Bank of N T Butterfield & Son Ltd, PO Box HM 195, 65 Front Street, Hamilton HM AX (tel: 295-1111; fax: 295-0658).

Bermuda Commercial Bank Ltd, 44 Church Street, Hamilton HM 12 (tel: 295-5678; fax: 295-8091).

Central bank
Bermuda Monetary Authority, Burnaby House, 26 Burnaby Street, Hamilton HM 11 (tel: 295-5278; fax: 292-7471; e-mail: Info@bma.bm).

Travel information
National tourist organisation offices
Department of Tourism, Global House, 43 Church Street, Hamilton HM 12 (tel: 292-0023; fax: 292-7537; internet site: http://www.bermudatourism.org).

Ministries
Ministry of Finance, Government Administration Building, 30 Parliament Street, Hamilton HM 12 (tel: 295-5151; fax: 295-5727).

Office of The Governor, Government House, 11 Langton Hill, Pembroke, Hamilton HM 13 (tel: 292-3600; fax: 292-6831; e-mail: governor@gov.bm).

Other useful addresses
Bermuda Broadcasting Company, PO Box HM 452, Hamilton HM BX (tel: 295-2828; fax: 295-4282).

Bermuda Hotel Association, 102 Reid Street, Hamilton HM 19 (tel: 295-2127; fax: 292-6671; internet site: http://www.bermudahotels.com).

Bermuda International Business Association (BIBA), Suite 203, 48 Par-la-Ville Road, Hamilton HM 11 (tel: 292-0632; fax: 292-1797).

Bermuda Insurance Management Association (BIMA), PO Box HM 1752, Hamilton HM GX (tel: 295-4864; fax: 292-7375).

Bermuda Small Business Development Corp, PO Box HM 637, Hamilton HM CX (tel: 292-5570; fax: 295-1600).

Bermuda Stock Exchange, PO Box HM 1369, 3 F Washington Mall, Church Street, Hamilton HM FX (tel: 292-7212; fax: 292-7619; e-mail: info@bsx.com; internet site: http://www.bsx.com).

Department of Civil Aviation, Bermuda International Air Terminal, 2 Kindley Field Rd, St George's GE CX (tel: 293-1640; fax: 293-2417).

Government Information Services, Global House, 43 Church Street, Hamilton HM 12 (tel: 292-6384; fax: 292-5267).

Government Statistical Department, 43 Church Street, Hamilton HM 12 (PO Box HM 3015, Hamilton HM MX) (tel: 297-7761; fax: 295-8390).

Insurance Information Office, PO Box HM 2911, Hamilton HM LX (tel: 292-9829; fax: 295-3532).

The Registrar of Companies, Government Administration Building, 30 Parliament Street, Hamilton HM 12 (tel: 295-5151; fax: 292-6640; internet site: www.roc.bdagov.bm).

Other news agencies: Caribbean Net News: www.caribbeannetnews.com

Internet sites
Bermuda Sun: www.bermudasun.bm/

Bermuda Yellow Pages: www.bermudayp.com/

Bermuda online: www.bermuda-online.org

Bhutan

KEY FACTS

Official name: Druk-yul (The Kingdom of Bhutan)

Head of State: Druk Gyalpo (Dragon King) Jigme Kesar Namgyal Wangchuk (since 14 Dec 2006).

Head of government: Prime Minister Jigme Y Thinley (DPT) (from 9 Apr 2008)

Ruling party: Druk Phuensum Tshogpa (DPT) (Bhutan Peace and Prosperity Party) (from 23 Mar 2008)

Area: 47,000 square km

Population: 2.33 million (2007)*

Capital: Thimphu

Official language: Dzongkha

Currency: Ngultrum (Nu) = 100 chetrums

Exchange rate: Nu42.76 per US$ (Jul 2008) (pegged to Indian rupee)

GDP per capita: US$2,012 (2007)*

GDP real growth: 22.40% (2007)*

Labour force: 448,695 (2005)

Unemployment: 3.10% (2005)

Inflation: 4.90% (2007)*

Balance of trade: -US$225.00 million (2005)

* estimated figure

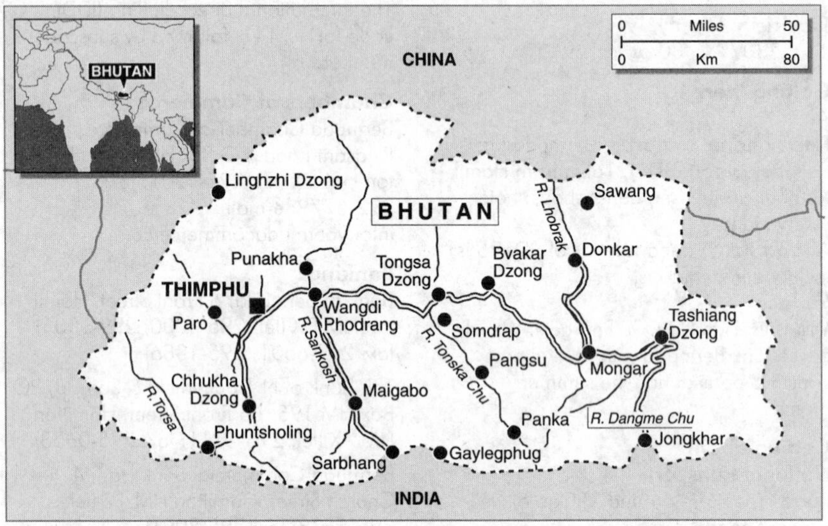

The people of the Himalayan kingdom of Bhutan surprised even themselves in March 2008, when they managed to vote for stability and experience in their first ever parliamentary polls while overwhelmingly rejecting the political party led by the King's uncle. This was not generally interpreted as a vote against the much-loved King of Bhutan, or a century of royal rule. Voters simply felt reluctant wholeheartedly to embrace democracy; to complicate matters further, the winner of the elections, the improbably named Jigmi Thinley, was himself a staunch royalist.

Contradictory messages

Critics had claimed that King Wangchuk was merely putting on a show for foreign observers and that democracy would not be fully permitted. It was also claimed that the country's new constitutional developments were a smokescreen for the still messy refugee situation. Bhutan's ethnic Nepalese were re-defined as illegal immigrants after a census in 1988: at the time the King sought to protect the nation's Buddhist culture against foreign influence. The effect was that Hindu Nepalese have been marginalised and persecuted by the government and their language banned from schools. This antagonism has led to violent disturbances and the expression of pro-democracy, anti-government sentiment in 1990.

But the scale of the victory, in which Jigmi Thinley's Druk Phuensum Tshogpa (DPT) (Bhutan Peace and Prosperity Party) won 44 of the 47 seats on offer according to the provisional results announced by the election commission, as one local observer commented, sent out subtle messages which echoed around the deeply traditional and conservative land. 'It is truly amazing', said Palden Tshering, spokesman for Thinley's DPT. 'The people really have made the decision.' The King's uncle, Sangay Ngedup did not manage even to win a seat in his own constituency. 'By all means let the King stand aside', the people of Bhutan seemed to be saying, 'but we are not sure we want his relatives by marriage to take over'.

Mopai miracles?

At the claimed centre of this investment success is the *Mopai* an ancient 250 page goatskin volume which provides a revered number of human calculators, who are called *tsips*, with intricate mathematical and astronomical formulas to compute a client's fate and fortune before birth, during life and in the afterlife. There are some 40 calculators. In 2007 an estimated 300 American and European bankers and businessmen made the gruelling journey to Bhutan – a country smaller than Switzerland, with 180 broadband subscribers, five elevators and less than 700,000 inhabitants – to meet those responsible for the country's impressive economic success. Bhutan is certainly the only country in the world where the roles of financial analyst and Bhuddist monk are combined. The Bhutanese do, after all, have the highest per capita income in South Asia. This, despite the King's refreshing policy of maximising 'Gross National Happiness' rather than gross domestic product. Using the *Mopai* as a financial forecast tool may be purely coincidental – or not.

In preparation for its planned transition from a monarchy to a two-party democratic system in 2008, Bhutan's government has established the institutions it considers necessary to ensure high standards of governance and transparency. An autonomous Anticorruption Commission has been established, and autonomous status is envisaged for the existing Auditor General's Office. The National Assembly has set up a public accounts committee, and a fiscal responsibility bill is in the pipeline. The actual transformation and workings of a two-party democracy may lead to some initial uncertainty, but the transition is unlikely to result in any significant economic policy changes.

It's all about Tala

According to the Asian Development Bank (ADB) with the start of commercial operations, the massive Tala hydroelectric project will be the main driver of economic expansion over the next 2 years, with growth expected to have accelerated further to 18 per cent in 2007 and then moderate to 10 per cent in 2008. The ADB has expressed reservations that the Tala project – which is forecast by the Bank to double electricity exports – will make Bhutan even more reliant on exporting the single commodity of electricity to India. Growth in other sectors together is expected to average 6–8 per cent, while inflation should stay around 5 per cent. As the ngultrum (Nu) is pegged to the Indian rupee, monetary developments have limited impact on prices within Bhutan – inflation is much more influenced by price developments in India.

In broad terms the Tala project is expected to generate Nu40 million (approximately US$1 million) in daily revenues, and raise hydropower's share of total government revenues from 45 per cent to about 60 per cent. Export income from the additional power sales is expected to turn the trade balance to a surplus, and with current transfers likely maintained at about the present level, the current account balance is also projected to switch to a surplus, of 3 per cent of GDP.

The ADB anticipates that further growth in the medium term will benefit from continued international co-operation in the hydropower sector. Memorandums of understanding have been signed between Bhutan and India for preparing detailed project reports on the 1,095MW Punatsangchu I, the 992MW Punatsangchu II, and the 670MW Mangdechu hydropower projects. The full feasibility report of the Punatsangchu I project is complete and India has agreed to finance it with 60 per cent loan and 40 per cent grant components.

Bhutan's budget for the 2007 fiscal year anticipated a further reduction of the deficit to Nu1.5 billion (3.3 per cent of estimated GDP), largely on account of much stronger domestic revenues (up 42 per cent) associated with Tala. With grants estimated at a similar large amount as in the previous fiscal year, total receipts are projected to increase by 21 per cent. Expenditures – both current and capital – are budgeted to increase by about 11 per cent, due to a higher salaries and wages bill, preparations for the introduction of a constitution in 2008, construction of a Supreme Court building, road projects, hospital construction, and pre-construction work for Punatsangchu I and Dagachhu hydropower projects.

In its *Development Outlook*, the ADB concludes that the main challenge for Bhutan's government is that hydropower employment elasticity is low. With more people entering the labour market each year, Bhutan's government must stimulate greater private sector activity and diversify the economy to boost employment, in line with the government's poverty reduction strategy. The government might aim to do this by improving transportation and communications infrastructure for better integration of the national economy, strengthening the private sector enabling environment (particularly for tourism and high-value agriculture), and enhancing the efficiency of the financial sector.

Risk assessment

Regional stability	Fair
Politics	Fair
Economy	Good

COUNTRY PROFILE

Historical profile

1907 The first hereditary king was enthroned.

1910 The Anglo-Bhutanese Treaty was signed, granting the government of British India full control of Bhutan's foreign relations.

1949 India became independent and the 1910 treaty was re-negotiated. Bhutan became free to pursue its own foreign policy, although it agreed to seek India's advice.

1952 King Jigme Dorji Wangchuk was enthroned and established the Tsogdu (National Assembly) in 1953.

1958 The Lhotshampa population of the southern districts of Bhutan was granted Bhutanese citizenship and tenure of lands.

1965 The Lodoi Tsokde (Royal Advisory Council) was established.

1972 King Jigme Singye Wangchuk was enthroned.

1979 Bhutan supported China in preference to India at the UN, beginning a

KEY INDICATORS — Bhutan

	Unit	2003	2004	2005	2006	2007
Population	m	2.17	2.22	2.25	*2.28	*2.33
Gross domestic product (GDP)	US$bn	0.61	0.73	0.83	*0.98	*1.31
GDP per capita	US$	287	817	1,079	*1,437	*2,012
GDP real growth	%	6.5	7.0	6.5	*11.0	*22.4
Inflation	%	2.0	4.5	5.3	4.9	*4.9
Exports (fob) (goods)	US$m	154.0	*8,292.9	186.0	*15,857.5	–
Imports (cif) (goods)	US$m	196.0	*18,625.1	411.0	*14,498.2	–
Balance of trade	US$m	-42.0	*-10,332.2	-225.0	*1,359.3	–
Current account	US$m	-10.0	-53.0	-28.0	*-29.0	116.0
Total reserves minus gold	US$m	366.6	398.6	467.4	545.3	0.0
Foreign exchange	US$m	364.7	396.6	465.6	543.3	–
Exchange rate	per US$	46.81	44.46	44.43	44.43	39.34

* estimated figure

gradual reorientation of foreign policy away from India.
1987 Bhutan's Sixth Five Year Plan included a policy of 'one nation, one people'. A code of traditional Drukpa dress and etiquette (Driglam Namzhag) was introduced. This led to discontent in the 1990s.
1990 The teaching of Nepali in schools was halted. Mass public demonstrations in southern Bhutan were held.
1998 King Wangchuk handed over full executive power to a Lhengye Zhungtshog (Council of Ministers).
1999 The King granted the Tsogdu the right to dismiss a reigning monarch. The WTO Working Party on Accession for the Kingdom of Bhutan was established.
2001 A draft constitution included proposals for a democratic system of government.
2002 The Ninth Five-Year Plan was drawn up to continue Bhutan's decentralisation process and promote 'Gross National Happiness'.
2003 The representative of the Kingdom of Bhutan to the WTO delivered Memorandum on the Foreign Trade Regime, describing all aspects of Bhutan's economy and legal system and its compliance with WTO norms and requirements. A new government was installed with Jigme Yozer Thinley as prime minister.
2004 Indian insurgents entered Nepal and were reported to be working with Nepalese Maoists with a view to attacking Bhutan's royal palace.
2005 A draft constitution was unveiled that aimed to transform the country's absolute monarchy into a two-party democracy. Sangey Ngedup took office as prime minister. The King announced he would abdicate in 2008, in favour of his son, Crown Prince Jigme Khesar Namgyel Wangchuk, when parliamentary elections are held. In the meantime responsibilities held by the king would be delegated to the crown prince, so that he could gain experience.
2006 The king appointed a chief elections commissioner and other officers to prepare for the first national elections in 2008. A mock election, to be followed by others, was held to train officials for the 2008 elections. Khandu Wangchuk took office as prime minister. King Jigme Singye Wangchuk abdicated in favour of his son, Crown Prince Jigme Kesar Namgyal.
2007 Bhutan and India signed a treaty allowing Bhutan more control of foreign policy and military purchases. India was asked to provide increased security in border regions to prevent Assam Ulfa insurgents carrying out attacks in Bhutan. On 26 July, Lyonpo Khandu Wangchuk resigned as prime minister. In July, Lyonpo Kinzang Dorji took office as the acting prime minister between in early August and December, before the formation of the interim government and the first parliamentary general elections in March 2008. On 31 December elections for the National Council of Bhutan (the upper house), were held for the first time since the King dissolved his absolute monarchy. Of the 25 members, 20 independent candidates were directly elected and five appointed by the King. Elections in five constituencies were postponed for one month as the minimum two candidates per district was not achieved.
2008 On 24 March in the first parliamentary elections ever held in Bhutan, the Druk Phuensum Tshogpa (DPT) (Bhutan Peace and Prosperity Party) won 67.04 per cent of the vote (winning 45 seats out of 47), the People's Democratic Party (PDP) won 32.96 per cent (two seats); turnout was 79.4 per cent. Jigme Y Thinley (DPT) became prime minister on 9 April. King Jigme Wandchuck will be crowned on 6 November, following the declaration, by three astrologers, that this was the most propitious date.

Political structure

Constitution

A draft constitution aiming to transform the country's absolute monarchy into a two-party democracy was drawn up in April 2005. It was approved by the people in a referendum during 2007.

Form of state

Hereditary monarchy

The executive

On 20 July 1998, King Jigme Singye Wangchuk handed over full executive power to the six-member Lhengye Zhungtshog (Council of Ministers).
The King is Head of State, assisted by the 10-member Lodoi Tsokde (Royal Advisory Council), the Tsogdu (National Assembly) and the monastic head of the kingdom's Buddhist priesthood.

National legislature

The bicameral parliament consists of the National Assembly (lower house) with between 47–55 directly elected members (dependent on the proportion of the population in each district) who serve five-year terms. The Nation Council (upper house) consists of 25 members (20 directly elected and five appointed by the monarch), all of which must be unaligned, members serve five-year terms. The Druk Gyalpo (Dragon King) is also a member of the National Assembly.

Last elections

24 March 2008 (parliamentary)
Results: National Assembly: Druk Phuensum Tshogpa (DPT) Bhutan Peace and Prosperity Party won 67.04 per cent (45 seats out of 47), the People's Democratic Party (PDP) won 32.96 per cent (two seats); turnout was 79.4 per cent.

Political parties

Ruling party
Druk Phuensum Tshogpa (DPT) (Bhutan Peace and Prosperity Party) (from 23 Mar 2008)
Main opposition party
People's Democratic Party (PDP)

Population

2.33 million (2007)*
Last census: November 1969: 1,034,774
Population density: 20 inhabitants per square km; urban population: 21 per cent (ADB 2006).
Annual growth rate: 2.2 per cent 1994–2004 (WHO 2006)

Ethnic make-up

There are many ethnic groups: the Sharchhop in the east (the largest group), the Ngalong in the west, the Lhotsampas, who speak Nepali, in the south and the Bumtaps, Khengpas, Layaps, Doyas and other nomadic groups.

Religions

Mahayana Buddhism is the state religion; Hinduism. Christianity is banned.

Education

The United Nations Children's Fund (Unicef) reported that in four decades, the government established 343 primary schools and a college that offers undergraduate degrees in arts and commerce. Since education remains a national priority in the country's development process, more than 150 community schools are available from which every school-age child may choose. However, classrooms are in short supply and most schools lack basic sanitation facilities. Each teacher may have an average of 37 students but in some schools, class sizes can reach 70 pupils.
Literacy rate: 61.1 per cent and 33.6 per cent for men and women respectively; adult rates (World Bank 2002).
Enrolment rate: 45 per cent enrolment for girls in primary schools.
Pupils per teacher: 37 in primary schools.

Health

Per capita total expenditure on health (2003) was US$59; of which per capita government spending was US$49, at the international dollar rate, (WHO 2006).
Although improvement in the primary healthcare system has reduced the maternal mortality rate the figure is still one of the highest in south and east Asia. The United Nations Children's Fund (Unicef) reports that about four out of five women still deliver at home, without professional help.

Bhutan conducts national and regional immunisation days annually to achieve 90 per cent coverage. Unicef estimates that 22.2 per cent of households do not have safe drinking water.
Out-reach clinics spread across rural Bhutan provide low cost health care. A network of 145 basic health units supports the clinics, with each unit serving communities of 2,000 to 5,000 people. There are 28 hospitals, which provide more advanced and referral treatment.
The Asian Development Bank (ADB) provided the government with a loan of about US$10 million covering the five years 2001–2005 to improvement of the health sector.
Unicef initiated model villages established in almost all the 202 sub-district blocks in the country have adopted a variety of health and education programmes. Its initial success has prompted Unicef to expand the model village experience into a more general community development programme.
Life expectancy: 63 years, 2004 (WHO 2006)
Fertility rate/Maternal mortality rate: 4.2 births per woman, 2004 (WHO 2006)
Child (under 5 years) mortality rate (per 1,000): 70 per 1,000 live births; around 19 per cent of children aged under five are malnourished (World Bank).
Head of population per physician: 0.05 physician per 1,000 people, 2004 (WHO 2006)

Welfare

In October 2001, the Bhutan government and the Asian Development Bank (ADB) signed a partnership agreement aimed at poverty reduction by 2012 through income and employment generation led by the private sector. Emphasis will be put on lifting monthly average rural incomes to about Nu3,000 (about US$65) per head. In March 2002, the ADB agreed to provide a US$700,000 grant to prepare a rural electrification and network expansion project.
There is a national pension plan and provident fund plan that currently provides for government employees and members of the armed forces. Between 16 per cent and 24 per cent of monthly earnings are paid into the funds, to provide for workers and their dependents. The amounts paid are split evenly between the employer and employee. These schemes are expected to be offered to other salaried workers over the next few years.
Pensions

Main cities

Thimphu (capital, estimated population 101,622 in 2003), Phuntsholing (113,262), Somdrup Jongkhar (15,091), Gaylegphug (15,091).

Languages spoken

There are 19 dialects and languages in Bhutan. Dzongkha bears similarities to Tibetan. English (the working language), Bumthangkha, Sharchop, Nepali and other dialects also spoken.
Official language/s
Dzongkha

Media

The government regulates the freedom of the media, excluding most private broadcasters.
Press
Weeklies: Weekly newspapers include, in Dzongkha Kuensel (www.kuenselonline.com); in English Bhutan Observer (www.bhutanobserver.com) and Bhutan Times (www.bhutantimes.bt) is published on Sunday.
Broadcasting
The government-operated Bhutan Broadcasting Service (BBS) (www.bbs.com.bt) is the only terrestrial television broadcaster.
Radio: The only independent radio station is Kuzoo FM (www.kuzoo.net), broadcasting in Dzongkha and English.
Television: The majority of programmes on the BBS are broadcast in Dzongkha (the national language and English (the working language).While the BBS is the only broadcaster, there is cable TV with many channels on offer.

Economy

This small landlocked country has achieved good economic growth and considerable improvement in its social indicators since the mid-1990s. Even so, around 36 per cent of the population live below the upper poverty line, with the majority of these living in remote rural areas. India and international organisations support the government's development plans. Government policy is directed towards conservative economic modernisation. Work has been carried out on tariff reform, liberalising foreign exchange and foreign direct investment (FDI) regulations, and deregulating interest rates. Poverty alleviation is being pursued through improvement of infrastructures such as healthcare and education. These projects receive substantial international aid.
The wellbeing of the population relies on agriculture and forestry. Bhutan is almost entirely self-sufficient in the production of food. The agricultural sector employs around 90 per cent of the labour force and accounts for 26 per cent of total GDP.
Tourism has strong potential for growth, although travellers are restricted to pre-packaged holidays and arranged tours.
The growing strength of the economy is due to the hydroelectric power sector. New power projects have led to significant growth in the construction and transport sectors. Export of electricity, mainly to India, provides 60 per cent of government revenue. The Tala hydroelectric power project, which came on line in 2006 and which alone generates some US$1 million per day, has doubled power exports. This will lead to a spike in GDP growth to 10 per cent in 2006 and 12 per cent in 2007.
Growth of foreign investment continues to be restrained by problematic policies in finance, labour and trade. Difficulties in industrial licensing stem from the government's policy towards environmental protection. The current five-year plan is to encouraging growth in communication technology, energy and tourism with clearer legal and regulatory systems to enable this. Bhutan's application to join the WTO, if successful, could spur foreign investment.

External trade

In 2007, Bhutan was in ongoing negotiations to join the World Trade Organisation. Trade is limited to small scale agricultural production and cottage industry manufacturing, as modern industrial production is limited. Bhutan's economy is closely linked to India, which provides financial and technical aid and manpower.
Imports
Principal imports are fuel and petroleum products, rice, machinery parts, vehicles and textiles.
Main sources: India (83.2 per cent total, 2006), Japan (4.2 per cent), Singapore (2.9 per cent).
Exports
Main exports include electricity (to India), cardamom, gypsum, timber, handicrafts, cement, fruit, precious stones and spices
Main destinations: India (87.6 per cent of 2006 total goods exports), Hong Kong (6.0 per cent), Bangladesh (4.9 per cent).

Agriculture

Agriculture annually contributes around 26 per cent to GDP and employs 90 per cent of the workforce.
Approximately 15 per cent of the land area is fertile lowland arable and 72.5 per cent is forested. No trees can be cut down without a special permit.
Main crops are rice, maize, potatoes, citrus fruits, wheat, buckwheat, barley, millet, vegetables, mustard, apples and cardamom. Vegetable production is hindered by the cold climate.
Cattle, yaks, sheep, goats and pigs are raised.
Estimated crop production in 2005 included 127,350 tonnes (t) cereals, 4,800t wheat, 45,000t rice, 70,000t maize,

40,000t potatoes, 36,000t citrus fruit, 12,800t sugar cane, 5,800t nutmeg, 3,100t ginger, 1,318t oilcrops, 1,600t pulses, 2,800t chillies and peppers, 350t jute, 43,500t fruit in total, 4,600t vegetables in total. Estimated livestock production included 6,717t meat in total, 5,100t beef, 1,101t pig meat, 90t lamb, 135t goat meat, 259t poultry, 240t eggs, 41,440t milk, 1,080t cattle hides.

Industry and manufacturing
The industrial sector contributes around 43 per cent to GDP annually. Manufacturing accounts for around 7.5 per cent of GDP, with cement as the principal product.
Small-scale local industries produce woodwork, fruit processing, weaving, textiles, soap, metals, handicrafts, carpets, matches and plywood manufacture. Most manufacturing industries are owned by the government.
Industrial growth has risen mainly because of increased value of electricity exports to India (from the Chukha hydroelectric plant). The Tala project will further enhance growth when it comes on stream in 2006–07. There has also been significant hydropower investment in industry.

Tourism
The annual number of visitors is kept deliberately low by the government. The object of this policy is to protect the country's environmental and cultural integrity from the adverse effects of mass tourism. Visitor numbers are regulated by measures such as a high tariff (US$200 each per day) and restriction of travel arrangements to authorised Bhutanese operators. In addition, visits may only be made to designated regions and holy sites. Government policy is to increase visitor numbers gradually to 20,000 by 2012. Arrivals peaked in 2000 at 7,559, but fell sharply in the following years due to external events. By 2004, the sector had recovered its momentum, registering 9,249 arrivals.

Mining
Mining contributes about 1 per cent to GDP and employs 1 per cent of the workforce.
Deposits of many minerals exist, but quarrying is restricted to limestone, dolomite, gypsum and slate due to difficulties of access. Talcum powder is the major mineral export.

Hydrocarbons
Bhutan has no known oil or gas reserves. Around 1,000 barrels per day of oil are imported.
Bhutan has coal reserves of 1.3 million tonnes and produces only 1,000 tonnes of coal per annum, which are used for domestic consumption. Some exploration is being carried out in the southern borders and the New Policy is encouraging private sector investment into exploration and production.

Energy
Hydropower is Bhutan's most important economic asset and supplies 97 per cent of total installed generating capacity of 457MW. Domestic consumption is around 112MW. The surplus is exported to India and is the largest component of Bhutan's total exports, contributing around 45 per cent of total revenues. The main hydroelectric facility is the Chukha plant, which generates around 336MW of electricity and is connected to the Indian electricity grid. A hydroelectric plant with a capacity of 1.02 GW, due to be commissioned in 2006, is being built at Tala. It is expected eventually to increase total revenues to 60 per cent.
More than 90 per cent of Bhutan's domestic energy requirements are provided by biomass, such as firewood, due to low levels of rural electrification. Over 70 per cent of domestic energy consumption is accounted for by the household sector.

Financial markets
Stock exchange
In 1993, a Royal Securities Exchange was established, supervised by the Royal Monetary Authority (RMA) and capitalised by the four financial institutions – the Bank of Bhutan, the Royal Insurance Corporation of Bhutan, Unit Trust of Bhutan and the Bhutan Development Finance Corporation. In 1996, auctions of government securities were introduced and the Unit Trust of Bhutan was converted into the country's second commercial bank, the Bhutan National Bank.

Banking and insurance
Central bank
Royal Monetary Authority (RMA)
Main financial centre
Phuntsholing

Time
GMT plus six hours

Geography
Bhutan is a landlocked country that lies in the Himalayan range of mountains, with Tibet (the People's Republic of China) to the north and India to the south.
Bhutan has three distinct regions. The high Himalayas is mountainous with little population. The tallest peak, at 7,554 metres is Kulha Gangri; there are 20 other peaks over 7,000m high.
The inner Himalayas is mostly rugged terrain, cut through with gorges and fast flowing snow-fed rivers. Mountain spurs that turn south divide the country and produce fertile, forest-lined valleys and terraced farming basins.
The southern foothills, including the Duar Plain, is only 20km wide; it is fertile flatland and home to some exotic wildlife: tigers, leopards, elephants and rhinoceros. Snow leopards, the world's rarest big cat, live at higher altitudes.
Hemisphere
Northern
Climate
There are three distinct climatic regions: the lowlands, along the border with India, are tropical with an annual monsoon, the middle band is temperate and the north is high frozen, glacial mountains. The capital Thimphu lies in the temperate zone with temperature variation ranging from: winter 12– minus 3 degrees Celsius (C) (day–night); summer 24–15 degrees C. The hottest region, in the south and Duar Plain, can range from: winter 20–11 degrees C (day–night); summer 31–23 degrees C. The monsoon usually arrives from mid-June to the end of August, with up to 4.5–5.0 metres of rain falling, although a high of 7.5 metres has been recorded.

Entry requirements
Passports
Required by all, except Indian nationals.
Visa
All visitors, except Indian nationals, require visas and these must be arranged prior to arrival.
Independent travel is not permitted, even for business purposes. Businessmen and tourists are admitted only in groups by pre-arrangement through registered tour operators in Bhutan. This can be done directly or through a travel agent abroad. A minimum daily tariff is regulated and fixed by the government. The rate includes all accommodation, meals, transport, and services.
Overseas Bhutanese embassies do not issue visas; they are issued from Thimphu. Visa applications should be made at least three months in advance. Add an extra three weeks for business visas, when a letter of introduction from a Bhutan company and an employer's guarantee, plus an itinerary should accompany applications.
The only airline servicing Bhutan is Druk-Air, which will only board travellers with visa clearance from the tourism authority. Entry is via India, Bangladesh, Nepal or Thailand.
At the point of entry, visas are stamped and a payment of US$20 is required, along with two passport photographs. The visa is required for exit from Bhutan.
If travelling overland from India a transit pass from the Indian authorities is required to permit passage through prohibited areas of the India-Bhutan border. For this, apply to the Indian Ministry of

External Affairs in Delhi some months before travelling.
Enquiries can be made to the Bhutan Tourism Corporation (see travel information directory, below).
Although Bhutan has no formal diplomatic representation in Europe or the US, it has a Permanent Mission to the UN at 2 United Nations Plaza, 27th Floor, New York, NY 10017 (tel: (+1) (212) 826-1919), which has consular jurisdiction in the US. Informal contact is maintained between the Bhutanese and US Embassy in New Delhi (India).

Customs
All visitors will complete a customs declaration on arrival, when all videos, computer and personal electronic equipment must be declared,
Export of antiques and religious antiquities, plants and animal products is prohibited.

Health (for visitors)
Mandatory precautions
A vaccination certificate for yellow fever is required if arriving from an infected area.
Advisable precautions
Anti-malarial precautions are advisable. Bhutanese hospitals only provide basic care. Comprehensive medical insurance should therefore be obtained.

Hotels
All hotel bookings are made through the Bhutan Tourism Corporation. Private hotels are open only to Bhutan nationals, some Indian nationals and certain business contacts; state hotels are of adequate standard.

Credit cards
Of limited use, they may be accepted in a few shops; travellers cheques are accepted in many more places.

Public holidays (national)
Fixed dates
2 May (Third King's Birthday), 2 Jun (Coronation Day), 8 Aug (Independence Day), 11 Nov (three days, Birthday of HM Jigme Singye Wangchuck), 17 Dec (National Day).
Variable dates
Winter Solstice (Jan), Offerings Day (Jan), Losay (Lunar New Year) (two days Feb), Shabdrung Kuchoe (Apr/May), Buddha Parinirvana (May/Jun), Buddha's First Sermon (Jul/Aug), Third King's Death (Jul), Guru Rinpoche's Birthday (Jul), Blessed Rainy Day (Sep), Dashaim (Oct), Buddha Descension Day (Oct/Nov).
Bhutan uses a lunisolar calendar that follows, essentially, the Tibetan lunar calendar. There are 12 or 13 months in a year, each beginning and ending with a new moon (approximately 28 days), in a three year cycle. An extra month is added in the third year so that, on average, the calendar matches the solar year (365.25 days). Months do not have names and are referred to by their numbers. The new year begins in February and is called Losay. Buddhist festivals are declared according to local astronomical observations.

Working hours
Banking
Bank of Bhutan: 0630–0930 and 1200–1600. Other banks, Mon—Fri: 0900–1700; 0900–1300 (cash transactions); Sat: 0900–1100.
Business
Mon–Fri: 0900–1700.
Shops
Mon—Sun: 0900–2000. Closed Tuesday.

Telecommunications
Mobile/cell phones
GSM 900 service is available in major cities and towns.

Electricity supply
220 Volts, 50Hz.

Weights and measures
Metric system

Social customs/useful tips
Prior permission is required to visit some of the religious and administrative buildings (Dzongs) and special permits are required to visit certain areas.

Security
Most visits are trouble-free and the country is generally peaceful.

Getting there
Air
Air transport into Bhutan is by Druk-Air, which flies from India (New Delhi and Kolkata), Nepal (Kathmandu), Bangladesh and Thailand. Druk-Air bookings can only be arranged after a visa has been issued and must also be obtained from a Bhutanese tour operator.
National airline: Druk-Air (Royal Bhutan Airlines).
International airport/s: Paro (PBH), 8km south of Paro, 68km from Thimpu.
Airport tax: International departures Nu300
Surface
Road: There are two overland access routes, both from India. A new crossing between Assam and Samdrup Jongkhar in eastern Bhutan allows tours to travel on a single-lane road to the capital. The older crossing, from the Indian frontier (Jaigaon) to Phuntsholing, has the added problem for travellers of crossing the Indian state of West Bengal before reaching Bhutan. Whichever route is taken the journey is arduous.

Getting about
National transport
Air: No services exist.
Road: The road network comprises some 3,000km, largely surfaced. The mountain roads are hazardous and subject to landslides in the monsoon season. No roads exist in the northern high Himalaya regions.
Buses: Bus services are available between main centres, although local enquiries are recommended.
City transport
Taxis: The airport journey to Thimphu is 90 minutes.
Buses, trams & metro: There is a bus service to the airport from Thimphu, journey time 90 minutes.
Car hire
Certain services are available, and local enquiries are recommended. An international driving licence is needed.
Traffic drives on the left and 40kph is the average speed.

BUSINESS DIRECTORY
The addresses listed below are a selection only. While World of Information makes every endeavour to check these addresses, we cannot guarantee that changes have not been made, especially to telephone numbers and area codes. We would welcome any corrections.

Telephone area codes
The international dialling code (IDD) for Bhutan is +975, followed by area code and subscriber's number:

Jakar	3	Thimphu	2

Chambers of Commerce
Bhutan Chamber of Commerce and Industry, PO Box 147, Doybum Lam, Thimphu (tel: 322-742; fax: 323-936; e-mail: bsdbcci@druknet.net.bt).

Banking
Bank of Bhutan, (tel: 322-621, 322-266; fax: 323-433).

Bhutan National Bank, PO Box 439, Thimphu (tel: 322-767, 323-602; fax: 323-601; e-mail: mdbnb@druknet.net.bt).

Central bank
Royal Monetary Authority of Bhutan, PO Box 154, Thimphu (tel: 323-111; fax: 322-847; e-mail: rma@rma.org.bt).

Travel information
Association of Bhutanese Tour Operators (ABTO), PO Box 938, Thimphu (tel: 322-862, 327-715; fax: 325-286; email: abto@druknet.net.bt).

Bhutan Yodsel Tours and Treks, PO Box 574, Thimphu (tel: 323-912; fax: 323-589; e-mail: dawa@druknet.net.bt).

Department of Tourism PO Box 126, Thimphu, Bhutan (tel: 232-3251, 232-3252; fax: 232-3695; email: dot@tourism.gov.bt).

SITA Travels, SITA House, Presidential Business Park, C-9, Vasant Kunj, New Delhi 110070, India (tel: (+9111) 2612-1110; fax: (9111) 2612-1125; email: info@sitaindia.com and lokeshb@sitaindia.com; internet: www.sitaspecialtours.com).

Ministry of tourism
Bhutan Tourism Corporation Ltd (BTCL), PO Box 159, Thimphu (tel: 322-045, 322-854, 322-647; fax: 323-392, 322-479; e-mail: btcl@druknet.net.bt; ynorbu@druknet.net.bt; internet site: www.kingdomofbhutan.com).

National tourist organisation offices
Tourism Authority of Bhutan (supplies lists of operators and trekking agencies), PO Box 126, Thimphu (tel: 323-251/2, 325-121/2; fax: 323-695; e-mail: tab@druknet.net.bt).

Ministries
Ministry of Agriculture, PO Box: 252, Thimphu (tel: 232-3765; fax: 232-3153; internet: www.moa.gov.bt).

Ministry of Education PO Box 112, Thimphu (tel: 232-5325; fax: 232-5183; internet: www.education.gov.bt).

Ministry of Finance, PO Box: 117, Thimphu (tel: 232-2223; fax: 232-3154; internet: www.mof.gov.bt).

Ministry of Health, PO Box: 108, Kawangsa, Thimphu (tel: 232-2602, 232-2961; fax: 232-3113, 232-4649; internet: www.health.gov.bt).

Ministry of Home and Cultural Affairs Tashichodzong, Thimphu (tel: 232-6015; fax: 232-4320).

Ministry of Information and Communications, PO Box: 278, Thimphu (tel: 232-2144, 232-4439; fax: 232-1055; internet: www.moic.gov.bt).

Ministry of Labour and Human Resources, PO Box: 1036, Thongsel Lam, Lower Motithang, Thimphu (tel: 232-6732, 232-1482; fax: 232-6731; internet: www.employment.gov.bt).

Ministry of Trade and Industry, PO Box 126 Thimphu (tel: 23-251; fax: 23-695; internet: www.mti.gov.bt).

Ministry of Works and Human Settlement, PO Box: 791, Thimphu (tel: 232-7998, 232-2182; fax: 232-270; internet: www.mowhs.gov.bt).

Other useful addresses
Bhutanese Embassy, India, Chandragupta Marg, Chanakyapuri, New Delhi, 110 021 India (tel: (+91-11) 2688-9230/9806/7).

Bhutanese Permanent Mission to the UN, 2 United Nations Plaza, 27th Floor, New York, NY 10017 (tel: (+1-212) 826-1919; fax: (+1-212) 826-2998).

State Trading Corp of Bhutan, 52 Trivoli Court, Ballygange Circular Road, Calcutta, 700019, India.

United Nations Development Programme, United Nations Building, Dremton Lam, GPO Box 162, Thimphu (tel: 322 424; fax: 322-657; e-mail: fo.btn@undp.org).

Internet sites
Bhutan Expeditions: www.bhutan-expeditions.com

Bhutan government portal: www.bhutan.gov.bt

Bhutan News Online: www.bhutannewsonline.com

Bolivia

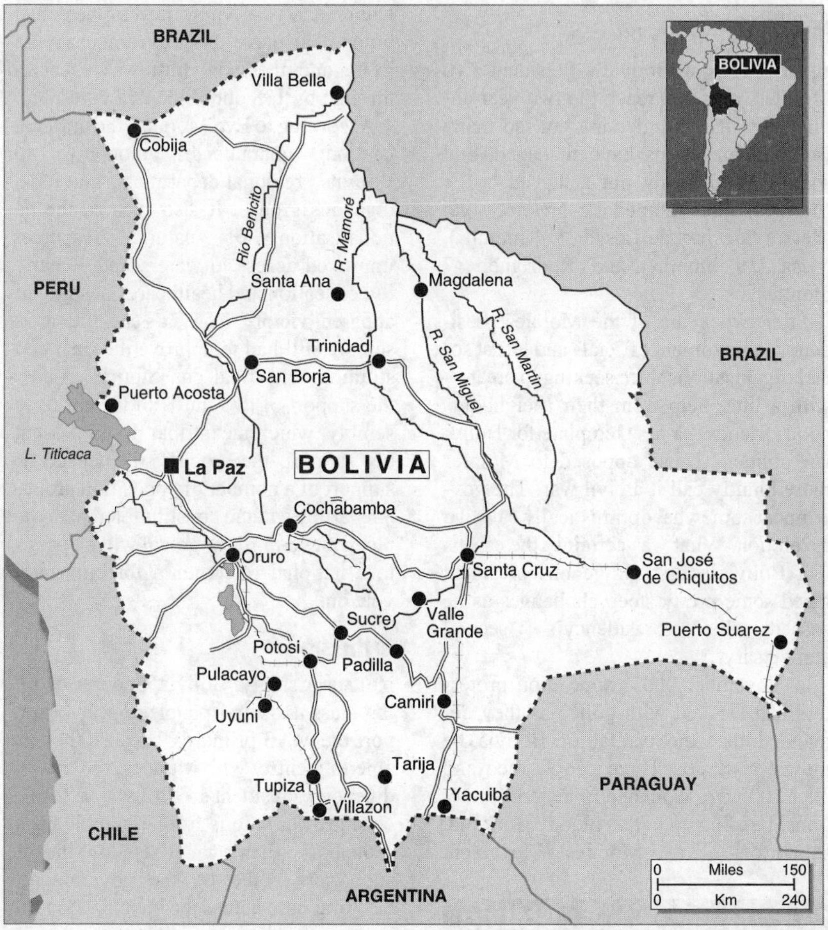

Bolivia, despite its abundant natural resources, has shown very modest economic growth. According to the World Bank over the 50 years up to 2006, Bolivia's income per capita fell by one per cent. In the same period, it rose by 350 per cent in Brazil, 200 per cent in Chile and even by 75 per cent in Argentina, a country not known for economic management. In 2002 it was estimated by the World Bank that 65 per cent of Bolivia's population lived in poverty, 40 per cent of them in extreme poverty. Malnutrition and infant and maternal mortality are the highest in the South American region.

Drought and floods ruin everything

According to the United Nations Commission for Latin America and the Caribbean (ECLAC/CEPAL), in 2007 Bolivia's GDP growth was an estimated 3.8 per cent, slightly down on the 2006 figure. Flooding caused the production of many agricultural crops to drop. The flood damage, which was mostly in the east of Bolivia, was estimated by ECLAC at US$443 million. Tin production was adversely affected by social unrest at the Huanuni mine; although this situation was expected to improve in early 2008 as the Huanuni mine recovered its production levels and the San Cristobal mine was due to start exporting. Inflation continued to outstrip GDP growth in 2007, with an estimated figure of 12 per cent for the year. The increase over the 4.95 per cent recorded in 2006 was attributed to increased meat and wheat flour prices. Two weather

KEY FACTS

Official name: República de Bolivia (Republic of Bolivia)

Head of State: President Juan Evo Morales Ayma (since 22 Jan 2006)

Head of government: President Juan Evo Morales Ayma

Ruling party: Movimiento al Socialismo (MAS) (Movement toward Socialism) (from Dec 2005)

Area: 1,098,581 square km

Population: 9.83 million (2007)*

Capital: La Paz (administrative); Sucre (legislative and judicial)

Official language: Spanish

Currency: Boliviano (B) = 100 centavos

Exchange rate: B7.12 per US$ (Jul 2008)

GDP per capita: US$1,342 (2007)*

GDP real growth: 4.20% (2007)*

Labour force: 3.75 million (2004)

Unemployment: 11.70% (2004) (additional widespread underemployment)

Inflation: 8.70% (2007)*

Balance of trade: US$1.31 billion (2006)

Foreign debt: US$5.44 billion (mid-2004)

* estimated figure

patterns caused the problems: the *El Nino* phenomenom brought flooding to the east of the country, while the associated *La Nina* brought drought to the high Andean plateau. To mitigate the effects both of flooding and of drought, the government suspended import tariffs on meat and wheat in the second half of 2007. The situation was not helped, however, by rising food prices in global markets. To contain a dangerously volatile inflationary situation, the central bank also took steps to increase liquidity. The central bank also orchestrated a 3 per cent appreciation of the Bolivian peso between September 2006 and September 2007.

Public investment grows

Government expenditure has continued to focus on the social sector. Hospitals and schools accounted for a 34 per cent rise in social spending between 2005 and 2006, and the figure for 2006–07 was expected to be similar. The rise in public expenditure in the social sector contrasted sharply with the still stagnant levels of investment – both private and public – in the productive sectors of the economy. This lack of investment expenditure has been identified as a problem for many years, to the extent that the Morales administration has adopted measures to stimulate investment and promote greater public sector investment. Capital investment for 2007 was forecast to have increased by over 60 per cent in nominal terms. The external surplus for 2007 was forecast to be some US$1,300 billion, over 11.00 per cent of GDP. By the end of 2007 Bolivia's international reserves were expected to be over US$5 billion, corresponding to 18 months' imports. The central bank anticipates agricultural activity, hydrocarbons and mining production at the San Cristobal and San Bartolome projects to be the main drivers of the economy. ECLAC anticipates GDP growth rate of 4.00 per cent to be achievable in 2008, subject to diminished political instability.

Morales soldiers on

April 2008 saw Bolivia's President Evo Morales' mandate reach the two year anniversary mark, something not too many Bolivian presidents have managed, and something certainly not achieved by Sr Morales' three immediate predecessors: Messrs Sánchez de Losada (14 months), Mesa (19 months) and Rodriguez (7 months).

After two years of the Morales presidency, government officials and leftist social organisations were seeking to create – with a little help from their (neighbourhood) friends – a new template for Bolivian politics. Those opposed to Morales more bluntly call it a civil war. The government somewhat optimistically calls it a revolution. What was certainly the case is that Bolivia's first indigenous president faced some pretty steep challenges as he passed his presidency's second anniversary.

In November 2007, opposition protestors had clashed with police as they demanded that the capital of Bolivia be moved to Sucre. Three people died and over 100 were wounded in the confrontations. Leading up to this bloody weekend, supporters of the Morales' Movement Toward Socialism (MAS), had been attacked by opposition groups advocating the new location for the capital and expressing their opposition to the MAS and the new constitution. The MAS moved the assembly to a nearby military college for security, whereupon the opposition boycotted the assembly. In the absence of the opposition, the MAS and allied parties gathered to pass a new draft of the constitution. This gave the government its majority and the new draft was squeezed through by 138 out of the 255 votes.

According to Evo Morales, the draft legislation guaranteed autonomy for Bolivia's regional departments and its indigenous groups. It also secured the nationalisation of natural resources, improved access to water, land, electricity, education and healthcare. Despite this apparent victory, Bolivia's constituent assembly still had to approve the final constitution. The final constitution required the support of two thirds of the entire assembly, which meant that despite assembly support, the articles still needed the support of a number of opposition groups. Any articles in the constitution that do not receive two thirds approval will be passed to a national referendum for citizens to vote on.

Criticism

Not surprisingly, Bolivia's poorer, working class and rural people appear to support the MAS primarily because they are able to identify with Morales, the first indigenous president of Bolivia, a former coca grower who is from a humble background like their own. These low-income supporters make up the government's electoral base across the country. Populist measures such as the nationalisation of the gas distribution network, the redistribution of agricultural land, improved access to basic services and the work of the constituent assembly (in spite of its problems) are the more obvious, superficially ideological reasons for their support.

Morales' supporters' populist enthusiasm also extends to the expropriation of more private land and the further nationalisation of the gas industry. The more extreme would claim that the MAS is continuing to depend on the old, almost post-colonial structure of a corrupt state, rather than seeking to transform the current state. Criticisms of the regime are growing, particularly after the violence and problems encountered at the November constituent assembly. However, although the policy's more extreme supporters may weaken support for the

KEY INDICATORS **Bolivia**

	Unit	2003	2004	2005	2006	2007
Population	m	8.79	8.88	9.43	*9.63	*9.83
Gross domestic product (GDP)	US$bn	8.00	8.77	9.36	11.23	*13.19
GDP per capita	US$	853	1,125	993	1,125	*1,342
GDP real growth	%	2.6	3.8	4.1	4.6	*4.2
Inflation	%	3.3	4.4	5.4	4.3	*8.7
Natural gas output	bn cum	5.2	8.5	10.4	11.2	13.5
Exports (fob) (goods)	US$m	1,479.0	1,986.0	2,670.8	3,863.0	4,490.4
Imports (cif) (goods)	US$m	1,675.0	1,595.0	2,189.8	2,809.0	3,249.2
Balance of trade	US$m	-196.0	391.0	481.0	1,312.0	1,241.2
Current account	US$m	40.0	250.0	618.0	1,317.5	1,758.0
Total reserves minus gold	US$m	716.8	872.4	1,327.6	2,614.8	4,554.0
Foreign exchange	US$m	663.3	817.3	1,276.7	2,561.2	4,497.7
Exchange rate	per US$	7.65	7.95	7.99	7.99	7.64

* estimated figure

government, they appear to lack a coherent political strategy or any affiliation to a major party outside the MAS.

The government's alleged lack of expertise, management and technical skills also attracts criticism. Opponents argue that instead of picking people with technical and political competence, since being elected the MAS has chosen to appoint close political allies, and indigenous people with union organiing experience. It is claimed that these appointments have contributed to poor management within the government.

There are also those who are against the indigenous president for little more than racist reasons; others oppose the government for ideological reasons, advocating continued, if largely discredited, neo-liberal policies. What is certain is that for decades, the issues of a constituent assembly and gas nationalisation have not been far from the political agenda. It is certain that a considerable amount of political influence continues to reach Bolivia from Cuba, and both money and influence from Venezuela.

Middle class opposition

Bolivia's middle class and bourgeoisie continue to provide substantial, and vocal, opposition to the Morales administration. This opposition is organised primarily through right of centre political parties and civic organisations in the eastern parts of the country. These groups have led the charge against the MAS in the assembly, the media and the streets. A late 2007 strike was called by prefects in the six departments considered to be opposed to Morales. The strike represented the cohesion of the right, and the regional division in the country. Though the MAS won the presidency, it did not win a number of prefectoral and mayoral positions. The local government and right wing leaders have united against the MAS, creating an opposition grouping which poses the biggest challenge to the MAS government. Some political observers already detect a drop in the excitement and enthusiasm engendered in the first year of the Morales administration. The bold plans of 2006 had largely fallen apart in 2007.

The oil...

Bolivia, perhaps more than any other country in the region, demonstrates that a country's wealth and prosperity cannot be measured in simple terms. With such a large proportion of its population living in poverty, it is difficult to appreciate that Bolivia has the second-largest natural gas reserves in South America, passed only by Venezuela. The *Oil and Gas Journal* (OGJ) reports that Bolivia had proven oil reserves of 440 million barrels (mb) in 2007. This figure is well up on the years before the privatisation of the 1990's. Improved exploration resources and production techniques lead to estimated proven reserves increasing from 132mb in 1999 to 397mb in 2000. According to the US Energy Information Administration (EIA) estimates, Bolivia produced some 61 thousand barrels per day (bpd) in 2006. In 2006, Brazilian Petrobras was the largest producer in Bolivia followed by Repsol-YPF of Spain. Bolivia's consumption of 53 thousand bpd in 2006 provided an exportable surplus of 12 thousand bpd of crude oil.

Controversially, the private company Transredes controls most of the oil and gas transportation system in Bolivia. The Morales government has plans for the former state monopoly, Yacimientos Petrolíferos Fiscales Bolivianos (YPFB) to take a majority position in all hydrocarbon transportation projects in Bolivia. The 430-mile Northern System transports crude oil and condensates from Carrasco to the cities of Santa Cruz and Cochabamba. The 610-mile Southern System connects Yacuiba to Santa Cruz, carrying both crude oil and liquefied petroleum gas. The 310-mile Central System links Santa Cruz with Cochabamba. Transredes also operates an 18 thousand bpd crude oil pipeline between Cochabamba and Arica.

...and the gas

According to the OGJ, Bolivia had natural gas reserves of 24.0 trillion cubic feet (Tcf) in 2007. The Tarija department has over 85 per cent of the country's total reserves, followed some way behind, by Santa Cruz department (10.6 per cent) and Cochabamba (2.5 per cent). In the mid-1990's, the privatisation of Bolivia's natural gas sector, lead to a dramatic rise in foreign investment. The subsequent increase in exploration led to a 600 per cent increase in proven natural gas reserves from 1997–2005. There have been several important discoveries in recent years, many containing reserves (proven, probable and possible) in excess of 10Tcf. The most important of these finds include Margarita (13.4Tcf), Ipati (12.0Tcf), San Alberto (11.8Tcf) and Sabalo (10.8Tcf). Since 2003, probable and proven reserves have declined, as exploration has failed to keep pace with production.

Bolivia's history has often tended to catch up with itself. This is particularly the case with its less than cordial relations with neighbouring Chile following Bolivia's loss of its coastline in the Guerra del Pacífico which ended in 1884 (and still warrants more than one dedicated website). Thus the exploitation of Bolivia's natural gas reserves has become a controversial issue. There are countless questions surrounding the proposed export routes for liquefied natural gas (LNG), since Bolivia is landlocked. In 2001, Repsol-YPF led a consortium to develop the Pacific LNG project, which included a natural gas pipeline connecting an LNG export terminal to a port in

Chile. The plan presented political problems due to the unresolved land dispute between Bolivia and Chile In 2003, the Bolivian government boldly decided to proceed with the Pacific LNG project. This gave rise to widespread protests ultimately leading to the resignation of President Losada Sánchez.

Chavez lurks

Any re-nationalisation of Bolivia's natural gas resources will affect the way in which the energy sector in the Southern Cone develops. An already complex geo-political situation is not helped by the increasing presence of Venezuela on the scene. Venezuela has developed cordial relations not only with Bolivia, but also with Argentina, a major player in this particular arena. According to the EIA Bolivia's ability to expand its natural gas exports will depend upon its ability to harness its reserves before competing gas sources in Brazil and Argentina (not to mention pipelines from Venezuela) entrench themselves in the region. In 2006, Bolivia formally joined a regional pipeline project intended to join South America from Venezuela to Argentina. The viability of the project is still in question.

Risk assessment

Politics	Fair
Economy	Good
Regional stability	Good

COUNTRY PROFILE

Historical profile

Bolivia was inhabited by the ancient Aymará peoples, who were conquered by the Incas.
1538 The Incas were conquered by the Spanish.
1825 There were many revolts against Spanish rule; independence was finally gained under the leadership of Simón Bolívar.
1826 Bolivia's first constitution was established.

1879–83 War of the Pacific between Bolivia, Peru and Chile over disputed territory along the Pacific coast. Bolivia and Peru suffered a humiliating defeat against Chile's armed forces. A new elite, with mining interests, combined with the traditional ruling oligarchy, supported by external capitalist interests, gained power and polarised civil society into conservative and liberal factions.
1890s The successful exploitation of tin brought a degree of prosperity and peace after years of turbulent and unstable government. A new constitution established centralised political control and the separation of powers between the legislature, executive and judiciary. The indigenous population was excluded from political life when property and literacy were made a prerequisite.
1933–35 Defeat during the Chaco Wars with Paraguay led to a large part of the Chaco region, much of it arid and infertile, being annexed by Paraguay. The defeat discredited the ruling elite and formed the basis for a realignment of Bolivian politics with the middle-class joining the working-class and campesinos (peasant farmers) to form a broad revolutionary movement.
1941 Formation of the Movimiento Nacionalista Revolucionario (MNR) (Nationalist Revolutionary Movement), a broad multi-class coalition to resist the power of the traditional oligarchy and what was seen as US imperialism.
1951 A military Junta prevented the newly elected president, Victor Paz Estenssoro (MNR) from taking office. With the help of a militia, recruited from the national police, miners and peasants, a rebellion succeeded in installing a revolutionary council. It nationalised tin holdings and instigated land reform. Universal suffrage was extended to the indigenous population. A state-capitalist development programme was initiated, backed by the IMF and later by the US programme 'Alliance for Progress'.
1964 Vice President René Barrientos Ortuño led a coup d'état. The military continued to implement similar policies to the MNR's state-capitalist model.
1969 Barrientos died in a mysterious helicopter crash that many suspected was an assassination. A brief period of military populism was followed by the succession of the Bolivian left, the expulsion of the US Peace Corps and the creation of a Soviet-style People's Assembly.
1971 A violent coup led by Colonel Hugo Bánzer Suárez led to the repression of labour leaders and left-wing politicians in a period of a Junta known as the Banzerato.
1978 Strains within the ruling elite and pressure from US President Jimmy Carter forced Bánzer to call elections.
1978–1982 A period of political turbulence: seven military and two civilian governments held office for an average of six months each. Meanwhile, political parties split into different factions, resulting in 70 different parties – the MNR alone split into thirty parties – resulting in a weak civil society.
1979 The Acción Democrática Nacionalista (ADN) (Democratic Nationalist Action) was formed by Bánzer.
1982 Siles Zuazo was elected president, his rule was ineffective as he struggled to appease both the IMF and growing militant elements within the civilian population. Meanwhile, the Bolivian economy collapsed from hyperinflation and high levels of foreign debt.
1985 Elections followed Siles' resignation. President Paz Estenssoro (MNR) implemented austere fiscal policies and brought about economic liberalisation. He also signed a Pact for Democracy with the ADN to resolve the impasse between the executive and legislature.
1989 The new president, Paz Zamora (MIR), offered tax incentives for direct foreign investment in the mining industry.
1993 Gonzalo Sánchez de Lozada (MNR) won the presidential election.
1998 Hugo Bánzer was elected president following popular discontent with economic liberalisation measures initiated by the MNR. Bánzer's rule intensified efforts to restructure the economy prescribed by the IMF, while implementing a coca-eradication programme demanded by the US.
2001 Bánzer resigned due to ill health and was replaced by Vice President Jorge Quiroga.
2002 Hugo Bánzer died. Congress appointed Lozada (known universally by his nickname 'Goni') Gonzalo Sánchez de as president.
2003 Civil unrest throughout the year led to the resignation of President Lozada. Vice President Carlos Mesa was sworn in as president.
2004 President Mesa signed a natural gas export deal with Argentina. Opponents criticised the deal as a pre-emption of the following referendum on gas exports.
2005 President Mesa offered his resignation to Congress after 17 months in office, as a new wave of anti-government protests spread throughout Bolivia; it was unanimously rejected. He resigned again in an effort to resolve the crisis over how to divide up the country's natural gas wealth, and it was accepted. Eduardo Rodríguez was appointed president, after both presidents of the Congress and Chamber of Deputies declined the post. The leftist candidate Evo Morales won the presidential election, beating former president Jorge Quiroga.
2006 Evo Morales was inaugurated as president. The oil and gas industry was nationalised. A constituent assembly, opened proceedings to draft a new constitution, giving greater rights to the indigenous population.
2007 Bolivia, Brazil and Chile agreed to build a South American highway to link the Atlantic and Pacific coasts, running from Santos in Brazil, through Bolivia, to Arica and Iquique in Chile, at an estimated cost of US$600 million.
2008 An unofficial referendum was held on 4 May in the resource-rich Santa Cruz region. Voting was in favour of autonomy, including land and taxes with more local decision-making. President Morales rejected the vote as illegal. In June three other, (Tarija, Pando and Beni), opposition-led states also voted for autonomy.

Political structure

Constitution

The first constitution was promulgated in 1826. The 1947 constitution was revised in 1967, and again in 1994.
Bolivia is divided into nine departments, each of which elects three Senators. The prefect of each department is appointed by the president. There is obligatory universal adult suffrage.

Form of state

Presidential democratic republic

The executive

Executive power is vested in the president and his appointed cabinet.
The president is directly elected for a five-year term, but is chosen by Congress if no candidate gains a majority of the vote.
An incumbent president cannot seek immediate re-election and candidates for president and vice president must be at least 35 years old. In the event of the president's death or failure to assume office, the next in line would be the vice president followed by the president of the Senate.

National legislature

Legislative power is held by the bicameral Congress, comprising a Senate (27 members) and a Chamber of Deputies (130 members). Senators must be over the age of 35. The Deputies must be over 25 years. Both Senators and Deputies hold office for five years. Half the Deputies are elected under party lists; the rest – although identified with political parties – must run for the representation of a particular district.

Legal system

There are five levels of jurisdiction headed by the Supreme Court.
From 1 June 2001, a criminal code was introduced which allows for public jury trials and a prosecution service independent of the police.

Last elections

18 July 2004 (referendum on oil and gas industries); 18 December 2005 (presidential and parliamentary); 2 July 2006 (constituent assembly elections and

referendum on greater regional autonomy)
Results: Oil and gas referendum: approval of the five questions proposed by the government in order to define Bolivia's new energy policy; endorsement of an increased role for the state in the natural gas sector.
Presidential: Evo Morales (MAS) won about 54 per cent of the vote, former president Jorge Quiroga (Podemos) about 29 per cent, Samuel Doria Medina (FUN) about 8 per cent and Michiaki Nagatani (MNR) about 6 per cent. Turnout was around 85 per cent.
Parliamentary: (Chamber of Deputies) MAS won 72 out of 130 seats, Podemos won 43 seats, FUN won 8 seats and MNR won 7 seats. (Senate) Podemos won 13 out of 27 seats, MAS 12 seats, FUN and MNR 1 seat each.
Constituent assembly elections and regional autonomy referendum: The government won 51 per cent of the vote, giving it 134 out of 255 seats in the constituent assembly; another 10 seats won by allies failed to secure the majority needed to control the drafting of the new constitution. In the accompanying referendum, 57 per cent of the electorate voted against regional autonomy, although four out of the nine departments voted in favour.

Next elections
2010 (presidential and parliamentary)

Political parties

Ruling party
Movimiento al Socialismo (MAS) (Movement toward Socialism) (from Dec 2005)

Main opposition party
Poder Democrático y Social (Podemos) (Democratic and Social Power)

Population

9.83 million (2007)*
Last census: September 2001: 8,280,184
Population density: Seven inhabitants per square km. Urban population: 64 per cent (1995—2001).
Annual growth rate: 2.1 per cent 1994–2004 (WHO 2006)

Ethnic make-up
Official figures estimate that approximately 4.2 million Bolivians (50.6 per cent of the population) are indigenous, comprising 37 different indigenous and aboriginal peoples. Of these, most live in the Andean highlands.

Religions
In 1961, the church was separated from the state and there is complete freedom of worship. The majority of the population is Roman Catholic, although Protestant denominations are expanding. Many indigenous groups mix Christian symbolism with pre-Columbian worship.

Education

Education is free of charge. Nevertheless, the average schooling completed is less than seven years.
The need to integrate education policy into broader anti-poverty strategies is exemplified by a high rate of primary school drop out among poor children. In Bolivia the wealth gap contributes to more than 90 per cent of the shortfall in primary-school completion. Education deprivation and poverty intersects with gender disparities, particularly in the case of Bolivia's indigenous population. More than half of indigenous males and two-thirds of indigenous females do not complete primary education.
Public expenditure on education is equivalent to approximately 5 per cent of annual GDP and includes subsidies to private education at the primary, secondary and tertiary levels. Bolivia has one of the lowest levels of provision in the developing world.
Literacy rate: 87 per cent adult rate; 97 per cent youth rate (15–24) (Unesco 2005).
Compulsory years: Six to 14
Enrolment rate: 114 per cent gross primary enrolment of relevant age group (including repeaters); 84 per cent gross secondary enrolment; 39 per cent gross tertiary enrolment (World Bank).

Health

Per capita total expenditure on health (2003) was US$176; of which per capita government spending was US$113, at the international dollar rate, (WHO 2006).
Some companies provided private medical care for their employees.
International funding has been donated to provide increased family planning and community based healthcare.
Yellow fever continues to be an important public health problem in the Americas. In 2000, Bolivia introduced the yellow fever vaccine in their child vaccination schedule, as well as the vaccination of all age groups in enzootic areas.

HIV/Aids
HIV prevalence: 0.5 per cent aged 15–49 in 2003 (World Bank)
Life expectancy: 65 years, 2004 (WHO 2006)
Fertility rate/Maternal mortality rate: 3.8 births per woman, 2004 (WHO 2006)
Child (under 5 years) mortality rate (per 1,000): 53 per 1,000 live births (in 2003); 10 per cent of children aged under five tend to be malnourished (World Bank).
Head of population per physician: 1.3 physicians per 1,000 people 2001 (WHO 2006)

Welfare

The social security scheme is a defined contribution system based on individual capitalisation accounts and managed by the private sector. To avoid high marketing costs, Bolivia has two private consortia to administer its private pension system: The Spanish BBVA, y AFP Futuro de Bolivia S.A. and Zurich Financial Services Group with roughly equal shares of the market.
Employers and employees contribute 13 per cent of employee salary to the AFPs, of which 10 per cent is put aside for a capitalisation fund, 2 per cent to a disability fund and 1 per cent for a workers compensation fund. Proceeds from the capitalisation programme (in 1997, when the previous pension scheme was reformed) were used to pay an annuity to all Bolivians 65 and older. The collection system is streamlined so that non-payment, one of the major difficulties with the previous pay-as-you-go system, can be more readily identified.

Pensions

Main cities

La Paz (administrative capital, estimated population 812,986 in 2005), Sucre (legislative and judicial capital, 226,668), Santa Cruz (1.4 million), Cochabamba (592,594), El Alto (775,836), Oruro (214,058), Tarija (161,677), Potosi (143,281), Sacaba (136,746).

Languages spoken

Approximately half the population speak Spanish as their first language. The campesinos (peasant farmers) often speak only Aymará or Quechua, but these languages are seldom written and are of limited commercial importance. Aymará is mainly spoken in the departments of Oruro, La Paz and Potosí. Quechua (often mixed with Spanish) is spoken in the departments of Cochabamba, Potosí and Sucre.

Official language/s
Spanish

Media

Freedom of the press is generally expressed, although journalist do not have a reputation for reporting on sensitive topics such as corruption and drug trafficking.
National news agency: Agencia Boliviana de Informacion (ABI)

Press
Dailies: In Spanish, La Prenza (www.laprensa.com.bo), La Razon (www.la-razon.com) and El Diario (www.eldiario.net) are published in La Paz; El Deber (www.eldeber.com.bo), El Mundo (www.elmundo.com.bo) are from Santa Cruz; Los Tiempos (www.lostiempos.com) from Cochabamba

and Correo del Sur (http://correodelsur.com) is from Sucre.
Weeklies: In Spanish Pulso (www.pulsobolivia.com), reports on current affairs, as does Samanario (www.semanario.8m.net) based in Tarija.
Business: The weekly Nueva Economía (www.elmundo.es/nuevaeconomia) and Periódico Jornada (www.jornadanet.com) report on economics.

Broadcasting

The government-controlled broadcasting authority is the Dirección General de Telecomunicaciones.
Radio: Low literacy levels make radio listenership, particularly in rural areas, high and important for news and information broadcasting in not only Spanish but also the Aymará and Ouechua languages.
There are over 100 mostly private owned radio stations La Paz has around 40 radio stations alone. National networks include the government owned Radio Illimani (http://abi.bo) and the Catholic-run Radio Fides (www.radiofides.com), the independent Radio Panamericana (www.panamericana.bo), commercial stations include FM La Pas (www.fmlapaz.com), Melodia FM (www.melodiafm.com) and Radio WKM (www.wkmradio.com).
Television: There are several TV networks, all of which are commercial, including the government-run Television Boliviana (Canal 7) privates network include Bolivision (Canal 4) (www.redbolivision.tv), Unitel (Canal 9) (www.unitel.tv) both from Santa Cruz and ATB Red Nacional (Canal 9) (www.atb.com.bo), Red Uno from (Canal 11) (www.reduno.com.bo) and Red PAT (Canal 13) (www.red-pat.com) from La Paz. The university television service, Televisión Universitaria (www.umsa.bo), provides educational programmes.

Economy

Political and social upheaval has hindered economic development in Bolivia over the years, although the economy has continued to record positive, albeit slow, growth in recent times, sustained largely by the hydrocarbons industry. GDP grew by 3.9 per cent in 2005.
Despite recent continued growth and a wealth of hydrocarbon resources, Bolivia remains South America's poorest nation. An estimated 70 per cent of the population lives below the poverty line, the majority in rural areas. While recent economic reforms have stabilised the economy, they have also forced thousands of people into the informal economy and concentrated wealth in the hands of the small upper class.
There have been efforts to develop manufacturing and improve public services. However, these policies have been met with hostility, as many in Bolivia believe liberalisation and diversification of the economy will lead to greater problems. The previous government, backed by international financial institutions, cut fiscal expenditure in response to a rising budget deficit, privatised some of the public sector and attempted to eradicate coca production. These measures were highly unpopular and contributed to the fast declining political stability.
Since January 2006, under the Morales government, there has been greater emphasis on state participation in the economy. In 2006, the all-important hydrocarbons industry was nationalised and the multinational companies required to renegotiate their contracts. This is a popular policy as many wish to ensure that profits from the industry benefit ordinary Bolivians and help address income inequality throughout the country. Nationalisation of the industry, however, could have an adverse effect on foreign investment in other areas of the economy, as business confidence has already declined.
Mining is an important industry, though Bolivian tin mines have in recent years faced growing competition from South East Asia. This has resulted in the closure of several mines throughout the country. However, increased demand led to a 13.5 per cent increase in production in 2006.
Agriculture is another key component of the economy, especially the growing of coffee, soybeans, wheat, rice and potatoes.
Bolivia is the third largest coca cultivator in the world. The presence of such a large illegal trade in the country has harmed Bolivian development as a sizeable proportion of the labour force is engaged in coca production. In a move that has angered international observers, particularly the United States, President Morales has pledged to resist efforts to eradicate coca production.
The Inter-American Development Bank estimated that in 2006 migrant workers sent some US$1,030 million to their families in Bolivia.

External trade

Bolivia is a full member of the World Trade Organisation (WTO), it is an associate member of Mercosur (the South American Common Market), which allows 80 per cent of it trade to pass freely to the other nations within Mercosur. The country is also a beneficiary of the US's Andean Trade Preference Act. Free trade agreements have been signed with Brazil in addition to a preferential trade deal signed with Chile. Bolivia also has Generalised System of Preferences (GSP) status with the United States, the European Union and Japan.
International trade is largely based on primary industrial and agricultural production. Bolivia is a major producer of coca leaves used in the production of illegal cocaine. A UN report of January 2007 estimated that 94 tonnes of cocaine was produced and smuggled abroad, mainly to North America and Europe

Imports

Manufactured goods, petroleum products, plastics, paper, aircraft and aircraft parts, machinery and vehicles, chemical products and foodstuffs.
Main sources: Brazil (20.4 per cent total, 2006), Argentina (15.8 per cent), US (12.1 per cent).

Exports

Principal exports are natural gas, soya beans and soya products, zinc and tin.
Main destinations: Brazil (37.7 per cent of 2006 total goods exports), US (9.8 per cent), Argentina (9.3 per cent).

Agriculture

Farming

Although agricultural produce remains Bolivia's main export, agriculture's share of GDP has fallen from 30 per cent in the early 1960s to around 15 per cent by the end of the century. Yet it is still economically important, employing nearly half the country's labour force. Most agricultural activities in rural areas are performed in small family units with low levels of productivity and income.
The cultivation of commercial crops is central to the advancement of Bolivia's 'agricultural frontier' and an intrinsic element of Bolivia's export-oriented development programme. This development drive is backed by a major road-building programme and changes in land tenure laws.
Since the 1990s, the Bolivian government has fought a US-backed war against the production of coca leaves – the raw source of cocaine. By 2002, the government had eliminated a total of 40,000 hectares of the crop, representing the eradication of 95 per cent of the country's coca fields since the programme began. Before the initiation of the eradication programme, coca production represented nearly 10 per cent of the country's GDP, so efforts are being made to replace coca production with alternative economic activities, such as commercial crops and textile manufacturing.
Unlike the Colombian drug fiefdoms, coca production in Bolivia was largely associated with indigenous peasants who have grown the crops as a traditional medicine since pre-Colombian times and, latterly, as a cash crop to alleviate their

enduring poverty. Unsurprisingly, the government's efforts to destroy coca crops damaged the rural economy and inflamed social and racial tensions. Protests by coca farmers, who rely on the crop for their income, have culminated in mass unrest.

Significantly, President Evo Morales has underlined his opposition to the previous government's crackdown on coca production. In a hugely populist move he has pledged to reverse the policy.

Estimated crop production in 2005 included 1,340,700 tonnes (t) cereals in total, 1,670,000 soya beans, 4,800,000t sugar cane, 107,870t wheat, 686,110t maize, 304,530t rice, 827,690t potatoes, 151,080t sorghum, 62,100t barley, 646,310t bananas, 380,971t oilcrops, 186,500t plantains, 258,730t citrus fruit, 40,810t pulses, 130,110t tomatoes, 1,372,670t roots and tubers, 4,330t cocoa beans, 24,670t green coffee, 434,040t cassava, 72,840t treenuts, 29,850t grapes, 25,600t cotton lint, 3,640t tea, 11,670t natural rubber, 1,290,800t fruit in total, 571,940t vegetables in total. Livestock production included 445,6285t meat in total, 172,000t beef, 107,750t pig meat, 23,786t lamb and goat meat, 133,703t poultry, 38,680t eggs, 274,590t milk, 20,840t cattle hides, 5,643t sheep skins, 8,550t greasy wool.

Fishing

Bolivia produces approximately 6,000 tons of fresh water fish per year, almost entirely for the domestic market. Bolivia's lakes, among them Lake Titicaca the world's highest navigable lake, provide the basis for this yield. However, the fishing industry does suffer from limited access to external markets, which is exacerbated by poor road transport infrastructure owing to the extreme altitude of the lakes. In addition to the domestic catch, about 7,000 tons of marine fish are imported per year.

Forestry

With a total land mass of 1.1 million sq km (424,164 sq miles), 53 per cent of which is covered by forests and woodlands, Bolivia has the potential to be one of the world's most significant forestry nations.

Sawnwood accounts for more than 90 per cent of Bolivia's total export of forest products. Brazil nuts, palm hearts and rubber are also important sources of income and are mainly derived from the Amazon forests. The export of more value- added products, such as material for doors, window frames and furniture, has increased rapidly in recent years, surpassing the levels of sawn wood, Bolivia's traditional forest export. This diversification of forest products and improvement in production processes has increased the commercial viability of Bolivian forestry.

There continue to be significant problems with the forestry sector however. Legal efforts to promote diversification and sustainability are limited and deforestation continues to out-pace forest regeneration. Though productivity has improved with the introduction of more sophisticated technology in the sawing and drying processes, there are still comparatively few sawmills for a country of Bolivia's forestry capacity and the industry suffers from poor transport infrastructure. The majority of the sawmills are located in the eastern region around Santa Cruz, where the standard of roads is particularly poor. Small- and medium-sized forestry companies that use old technology and outmoded production methods continue to operate with inefficient capacity and no method of producing value-added products. Valuable tree species such as mahogany, oak and cedar are dwindling in numbers. As well as contributing to the overall decline of biodiversity in the Amazon, these precious woods are now below commercial volumes. Efforts to control logging are limited as illegal colonisation of the forests and 'slash and burn' techniques continue.

Industry and manufacturing

Although it constitutes approximately 18 per cent to the total GDP of Bolivia, the industrial sector is considerably underdeveloped. Manufacturing in Bolivia is also capital intensive, employing just 14 per cent of the total work force.

Production is centred on the processing of minerals (mainly tin, lead and zinc smelting) and agricultural products. Oil refining and cement production are also important activities. There is a large workshop and artisan sector of small-scale domestic industries producing textiles, clothing and food. Bolivia is a producer of natural textile fibres: cotton, alpaca wool, llama wool, merino lambswool and rabbit fur. There is no heavy industry or electronics industry. Bolivian industry is under pressure to become more competitive. Traditionally, unprocessed or semi-processed materials have dominated Bolivian exports. The government has created new and more decentralised industries, to stimulate the development of competitive industries, particularly agro-based industries.

Tourism

The Bolivian tourism industry is undergoing expansion. The country's wealth of diversity and cultural and natural attractions has made it a destination for eco-tourists and backpackers. Most of the country's hotels are located in the capital La Paz, but there has been an expansion of hotel accommodation in other cultural centres. The travel and tourism industry generated 9.2 per cent of total GDP in 2005 and visitor levels continued to rise. The continued expansion of the Bolivian tourism industry will depend significantly on the relative level of civil unrest in future years.

Mining

Mining has long been a mainstay of the Bolivian economy and its importance to the country continues today. The mining sector contributes up to one fifth of GDP and employs 10 per cent of the labour force. Mining accounts for approximately 45 per cent of the country's total export earnings and the country's unexploited mineral potential is significant.

The industry has continued to show an improved performance especially, the mining of tin, silver and gold. Total tin reserves are estimated at 1.6 million tonnes and are mainly composed of low quality ore and accounts for approximately 17 per cent of total mining production. Bolivia is the world's fifth-largest tin producer and one of the world's leading producers of antimony and tungsten. Other minerals extracted include zinc, silver, gold, lead, copper and limestone, while large reserves of iron ore, lithium and potassium are as yet unexploited.

Zinc accounts for 27 per cent of total mining production. Gold production is significant, totalling some 14 tonnes per year. Privately owned mining enterprises account for the majority of output. Most mining operations are small and inefficient, with many of the more promising deposits occupied by co-operatives, with little exploration being carried out.

Hydrocarbons

With 441 million barrels of proven oil (as at end 2003) reserves, Bolivia has considerable oil supplies. With a consumption rate of 53,000 barrels per day (bpd) and production of 40,700 bpd Bolivia is relatively self-sufficient in oil. Despite its significant proven reserves however, Bolivia does suffer from poor transport infrastructure and a challenging topography which render the transportation of oil extremely difficult, as many of the country's oil fields are located in remote areas.

Bolivia's natural gas reserves are second only to Venezuela in South America; the country's potential gas reserves are estimated at approximately 1.32 trillion cubic metres. Due to the extensive exploration in recent years, there have been several large discoveries of oil fields holding over 10 million cubic metres of natural gas. There is particular interest in exporting to the large markets of the US and Mexico and there are plans to link the gas reserves to Paraguay via a new pipeline. The domestic gas market is small but there are plans to install 230,000

residential gas connections by 2007 and so the market is set to grow.
Bolivia's reserves are greater in size than those of Canada – 52.3 trillion cubic feet.

Energy

Bolivia's capacity to generate electricity has improved markedly over the decade to 2005. This increase is predominantly attributable to an increase in thermoelectric power plants, with around two thirds of the country's electricity output now being generated by such plants. Hydroelectric power and other sources of renewable energy have contributed to the growth in recent years of electricity generation.
Bolivia's consumption of energy has also grown considerably, with an increase of 70 per cent throughout the 1990s. The annual growth rate in 2004 was approximately 5.5 per cent in terms of energy consumption.
The Bolivian electricity market is dominated by four electricity companies, all of which are controlled by foreign (mostly US) investors.

Financial markets

Stock exchange

The Bolsa Boliviana de Valores (Bolivian Stock Exchange) was granted official status in 1989. Trading in securities is thin.

Banking and insurance

Bolivia's banking system has been undergoing extensive reform since the mid-1990s. The last decade has seen the full-scale privatisation of formerly state-owned banks and significant regulatory upheaval. A high level of dollarisation has meant that approximately 90 per cent of Bolivian deposits are denominated in US dollars and the holding of deposits is highly concentrated in the country's wealthy elite. This means that the banking system is highly dependent on the financial fortunes of a select number of wealthy Bolivians. Concern has been expressed in various quarters that President Evo Morales will seek to redistribute income to the poor. Thus the banking system may feel the effects of diminished holdings by wealthy clients in future years.
Bolivia's banking system has remained largely immune from the contagious effects of financial sector turmoil that inflicted the region in the early part of the decade. This fact owes to Bolivia's comparatively low exposure to international capital markets; the majority of Bolivia's debt is with foreign states and multilateral institutions, which have worked to change the structure of the country's debt portfolio and maintain vital foreign currency reserves.
A new Bank of the South, with a headquarters in Venezuela, will be launched in 2008 to provide an alternative source of development funding for the participating countries. Assets of US$7 billion will underpin its operations.

Central bank

Banco Central de Bolivia

Main financial centre

La Paz

Time

GMT minus four hours

Geography

Bolivia straddles the Andes and is made up of mountainous areas with cold desolate plateaux and semi-tropical and fertile lowlands. It is landlocked with Chile and Peru to the west, Brazil to the north and east and Argentina to the south. The Andean range is at its widest in Bolivia, some 650km.
The Western Cordillera separating Bolivia and Chile has peaks of between 6,000 metres and 6,500 metres above sea level and a number of volcanoes along its crest. Passes across the Cordillera are at 4,000 metres. To the east of the range lies the bleak treeless Altiplano also at around 4,000 metres. The Altiplano makes up about 10 per cent of the country and is divided into basins by spurs of mountains. Around 70 per cent of the population lives on the Altiplano, particularly the northern part where most of the larger cities are located. In the south, the parched desert landscape is mostly unpopulated.
Lake Titicaca, the highest navigable lake in the world, is situated at the northern end of the Altiplano. It is 171km in length, 64km in breadth and 280 metres at its deepest point. The immense depth of water keeps the lake at an even temperature of 10 degrees Celsius and modifies extremes of winter and night temperatures on the surrounding land, thereby making the basin favourable for farming.
The Eastern Cordillera rises sharply from the Altiplano in the east and four of its peaks rise to above 6,000 metres. These north-eastern slopes are heavily forested and are indented by fertile valleys in an area known as the Yungas.
In the north and east, the Oriente has dense tropical forest and in the centre there are plains covered with rough pasture, swamp and scrub.

Hemisphere

Southern

Climate

The climate varies with the area. It is tropical in the lowlands (eastern region) with an average temperature of 25 degrees Celsius (C); temperate in the highland valley regions (middle of the country), average temperature 15 degrees C, and cooler in the Altiplano (highland) areas (western region), average temperature 10 degrees C.
La Paz is in the Altiplano where temperatures vary between three degrees C in June and 25 degrees C in November and December. In the highlands the rainy season begins in December and ends in late March.

Dress codes

For business meetings men should wear a suit and tie, women a two-piece suit, or equivalent. Warm clothing is required in the high plateau region. Lightweight clothing is needed during the day and warmer clothing for the evenings in the valleys, and very lightweight clothing for both day and night in the tropical valleys.

Entry requirements

Travellers who arrive without the correct documentation will be fined.

Passports

Passports are required by all (valid for one year beyond departure date), except holders of Cedula de Identidad issued to nationals of Argentina, Paraguay, Peru and Uruguay.

Visa

A visa is not required for tourist visits up to 90 days, by nationals of most of the Americas, Western Europe, Australasia and some Asian countries. (For further details contact the local embassy or see www.embassyofbolivia.co.uk/visas.html#2.)
The 'specific purpose visa' for non-tourist visitors requires a letter of introduction, including an itinerary and letters of guarantee by employer and host company. (See www.embassyofbolivia.co.uk/visaformfiles/specificvisaform.html for application form.).

Currency advice/regulations

There are no restrictions on the import and export of local or foreign currency; currency must be declared.
US dollar travellers' cheques are the best form of currency to take. UK sterling cheques can sometimes be exchanged, but only with difficulty.

Customs

Visitors are not required to declare valuable personal effects such as cameras and radios. Business samples are duty-free as long as they are re-exported within 90 days.

Health (for visitors)

Mandatory precautions

A yellow fever vaccination certificate is required for visitors arriving from infected areas, and for those travelling to high risk areas such as the Departments of Beni, Cochabamba, Santa Cruz and the subtropical area of La Paz Department.

Advisable precautions

Typhoid, paratyphoid, hepatitis A, tetanus and polio vaccinations. Malaria risk exists in rural areas – prophylaxis recommended. Owing to the altitude of La Paz and other places in the Altiplano region, sufferers from heart or lung complaints should seek medical advice before leaving for Bolivia. Water precautions should be taken.

Hotels
There is a wide range available. Service charge and local tax are added to the bill. Tipping 5–10 per cent.

Credit cards
Mastercard, Diners Club, Visa and American Express have limited acceptance.

Public holidays (national)
Fixed dates
1 Jan (New Year's Day), 1 May (Labour Day), 6 Aug (Independence Day), 1 Nov (All Saints' Day), 25 Dec (Christmas Day). There are other additional holidays celebrated in individual provinces and towns.
Variable dates
Carnival (Feb, seven days), Good Friday, Easter Sunday, Corpus Christi (May/Jun).

Working hours
Banking
Mon–Fri: 0830–1200, 1430–1800; Sat: 0830–1200.
Business
Mon–Fri: 0830–1200, 1430–1830.
Government
Mon–Fri: 0800–1200, 1430–1830.
Shops
Mon–Fri: 0930–1230, 1500–1930; Sat: 1000–1500.

Telecommunications
Mobile/cell phones
GSM 1900 service available.

Electricity supply
110V and 200V in La Paz and 220V in Cochabamba and most other towns; US-type flat-prong plugs.

Weights and measures
The metric system is standard, although the Imperial is sometimes used.

Social customs/useful tips
In business circles, local customs are similar to those in Europe or North America. While English is widely used in commercial and business circles, a knowledge of Spanish is a valuable asset to the visitor. Correspondence in Spanish is almost essential. On business visits, cards are presented and it is normal to shake hands when arriving or leaving. It is advisable to arrange appointments before visiting. Bolivians are informal about observing prescribed times and will often arrive 30–45 minutes late.
It is customary to address persons by their professional title, eg, doctor, engineer and licenciado for social science graduates. Holders of law degrees are addressed as doctor.
It is offensive to refer to rural Indians as indios; they are referred to as campesinos (peasants).
It is customary to give gratuities in a hotel or restaurant of around 5–10 per cent even if a service charge has been added to the bill. The minimum drinking age is 21 years.

Security
Since the civil disruption in 2003, road blockades can happen on all main roads at any time. Visitors should not attempt to breach road blockades and should stay away from demonstrations.

Getting there
Air
National airline: Lloyd Aéreo Boliviano (LAB).
International airport/s: La Paz-El Alto (LPB), 14km from city, duty-free shop, bar, restaurant, bank, post office, hotel reservations.
Other airport/s: Cochabamba-J Wilstermann (CBB), 4km from city..
Airport tax: US$25 for all adults, excluding 12-hour transit passengers. An additional exit tax (US$25) is levied for all visitors staying over 90 days.
Surface
Road: Road access is possible from Peru, Argentina and Chile.
Travellers who use overland routes are generally advised to check border post opening hours.
Rail: Rail services connect La Paz with Chile (Arica and Calama) and Argentina (Buenos Aires). The Expreso del Sur is a special train service from La Paz to Buenos Aires.
Water: It is possible to take the steamer on Lake Titicaca from Puno (Peru) to Guaqui.
Main port/s: Although Bolivia is landlocked, access to the sea (and in certain cases free port facilities) has been granted by Paraguay (via River Paraguay), Brazil (Belem, Santos, Corumbá, Port Velho) and Argentina (Buenos Aires, Rosario).

Getting about
National transport
Air: Air transport is the best method of travelling around the country. Lloyd Aéreo Boliviano (LAB), Aerosur, TAM (army airline) and Aero Xpress (AX) operate domestic services to main centres.
Road: Around 50,000km of road exists, but only 5.5 per cent is paved and only 20 per cent can be classed as all-weather roads. The main centres are connected by highways of reasonable standard. A toll permit system is in operation; garage and petrol services are sparse outside main centres.
Buses: Flotas are long-distance buses, they mostly leave in the evening and travel overnight, except on the major routes where there are some daytime departures. It is advisable to book in advance and take warm clothing.
Rail: A north-south line runs from La Paz to Oruro and Uyuni, with spurs to Cochabamba, Uncia, Potosi, Sucre and Villazón at the Argentine border. The eastern system runs from Santa Cruz to Yacuiba and to Corumbá at the Brazilian border. Sleeper and first-class services are available; advance booking is essential.
Water: Half of Bolivia's territory lies in the Amazon Basin. Transport is by cargo boats, which carry passengers, vehicles and livestock. The tributaries of the Amazon are the Ichilo, Mamoré, Beni, Madre de Dios and Guaporé rivers.
City transport
Taxis: There are remise (yellow cabs) which have fixed rates applicable per passenger – the cabs are frequently shared. Within La Paz, trufis (cabs with green flags) ply along fixed routes. Tips are not expected.
Car hire
An international driving permit is required. This may be issued in Bolivia by the Federación Interamericana de Touring y Automovil Clubes (www.fitac.org) on presentation of a national licence, but it is advisable to procure one before travelling. At the frontier, drivers must also obtain a hoja de ruta, a form which notes the driver's itinerary.
Traffic drives on the right.

BUSINESS DIRECTORY

Telephone area codes
The international direct dialling code (IDD) for Bolivia is + 591, followed by area code and subscriber's number:

Beni	3465	Potosi	262
Buena Vista	3932	Saavedra	3924
Cochabamba	441	Santa Cruz	33
La Belgica	3923	Sucre	4691
La Paz	22	Tarija	466
Montero	3922	Trinidad	346
Oruro	252	Villamontes	4672
Portachuelo	3924		

Useful telephone numbers
Police: 110
Fire: 119
Ambulance (La Paz): 118

Chambers of Commerce
American Chamber of Commerce of Bolivia, Avenida 6 de Agosto, Edificio Hilda, PO Box 8268, La Paz (tel: 244-3939; fax: 244-3972; e-mail: amgalin@caoba.entelnet.bo).

Cochabamba Chamber of Commerce, 336 Calle Sucre, Cochabamba (tel:

425-7715; fax: 425-7717; e-mail: sistema@cadeco.org).

Chuquisaca Chamber of Industry and Commerce, 64 Calle España, Sucre (tel: 645-1194; fax: 645-1850; e-mail: info@cicch.com).

National Chamber of Commerce, 1392 Avenida Mariscal Santa Cruz, La Paz (tel: 237-8606; fax: 239-1004; e-mail: cnc@boliviocomercio.org.bo).

Santa Cruz Chamber of Industry, Commerce and Services, 7 Avenida Las Américas esquina Saavedra, Santa Cruz (tel: 333-4555; fax: 334-2353; e-mail: cainco@cainco.org.bo).

Banking

Banco Bisa, Avenida 16 de Julio 1628, La Paz (tel: 359-471; fax: 316-597; e-mail: bancbisa@caoba.entelnet.bo).

Banco de Crédito de Bolivia, Calle Colón esquina Mercado 1308, La Paz (tel: 360-025; fax: 391-044).

Banco de la Nación Argentina, Avenida 16 de Julio 1486, La Paz (tel: 359-218; fax: 391-392; e-mail: bancnalp@caoba.entelnet.bo).

Banco Económico, Calle Ayacucho 166, Santa Cruz (tel: 361-177; fax: 361-184; e-mail: baneco@roble.scz.entelnet.bo).

Banco Ganadero, Calle 24 de Septiembre 110, Santa Cruz (tel: 361-616; fax: 361-617; e-mail: bangan@roble.scz.entelnet.bo).

Banco Mercantil, Calle Ayacucho esquina Mercado, La Paz (tel: 315-131; fax: 391-442; e-mail: bercant@caoba.entelnet.bo).

Banco Nacional de Bolivia, Avenida Camacho esquina Colón 1312, La Paz (tel: 318-732; fax: 359-146; e-mail: info@bnb.com.bo).

Banco Real, Avenida 16 de Julio 1642, La Paz (tel: 334-477; fax: 335-588; e-mail: real@caob.entelnet.bo).

Banco Santa Cruz, Calle Junín 154, Santa Cruz (tel: 369-911; fax: 350-114; e-mail: bancruz@mail.bsc.com.bo).

Banco Sollidario, Calle Nicolás Acosta 289, La Paz (tel: 484-242; fax: 486-468; e-mail: info@bancosol.com.bo).

Banco Unión, CalleLibertad 165, Santa Cruz (tel: 366-869; fax: 340-684; e-mail: info@bancounion.com.bo).

Interbanco, Calle Mercado No 1046, PO Box 14758, La Paz (tel: 317-707; fax: 316-787).

Central bank

Banco Central de Bolivia, PO Box 3118, Calle Mercado esquina Ayacucho, La Paz (tel: 409-090; fax: 406-598; e-mail: bancocentraldebolivia@bcb.gov.bo).

Travel information

Automovil Club Boliviano, Avenida 6 de Agusto 2993, La Paz (tel: 431-132; fax: 431-139; e-mail: acblapaz@acelerate.com).

AeroSur, Calle Colón esquina Avenida Irala, Santa Cruz (tel: 364-446; fax: 365-246; e-mail: mail@aerosur.com).

Lloyd Aéreo Boliviano, Aeropuerto Jorge Wilstermann, Cochabamba (tel: 25-903; fax: 50-744; email: gergen@labairlines.com).

Ministry of tourism

Viceministerio de Turismo, Avenida Mariscal Santa Cruz, Edificio Palacio de Comunicacióónes, Piso 16, La Paz (tel: 236 7463/4; fax: 237 4630; e-mail: vturismo@mcei.gov.bo; internet:www.mcei.gov.bo).

National tourist organisation offices

Secretaría Nacional de Turismo, Calle Mercado 1328, Edificio Ballivián, La Paz (tel: 367-441; fax: 374-630).

Ministries

Ministry of Agriculture and Rural Development, Avenida Camacho 1471, La Paz (tel: 367-968; fax: 313-601).

Ministry of Defence, Avenida 20 de Octubre esquina Pedro Salazar, La Paz (tel: 431-364; fax: 433-159).

Ministry of Economic Development, Palacio de Comunicaciones, Avenida Mariscal Santa Cruz, La Paz (tel: 375-000, fax: 360-534; e-mail: contactos@desarrollo.gov.bo).

Ministry of Education, Culture and Sport, Avenida Arce 2147, La Paz (tel: 440-160; fax: 440-376).

Ministry of Finance, Palacio de Comunicaciones, Avenida Mariscal Santa Cruz, La Paz (tel: 392-220; fax: 359-955).

Ministry of Foreign Affairs, Calle Ingavi esquina Junín, La Paz (tel: 336-200; fax: 333-521; email: mreuno@rree.gov.bo).

Ministry of Foreign Trade and Investment, Palacio de Comunicaciones, Avenida Mariscal Santa Cruz, La Paz (tel: 343-519; fax: 377-451; internet site: http://www.mcei-bolivia.com).

Ministry of Government, Avenida Arce 2409 esquina Belisario Salinas, La Paz (tel: 440-114; fax: 442-589).

Ministry of Health and Social Security, Plaza del Estudiante, La Paz (tel: 371-373; fax: 391-590; e-mail: minsalud@ceibo.entelnet.bo).

Ministry of Housing, Avenida 20 de Octubre 2230, La Paz (tel: 372-241; fax: 371-335; e-mail: minviv@ceibo.entelnet.bo).

Ministry of Information, Edificio La Urbana, Avenida Camacho 1485, La Paz (339-027; fax: 391-607).

Ministry of Justice and Human Rights, Avenida 16 de Julio 1769, La Paz (tel: 361-083; fax: 392-982).

Ministry of Labour and Micro-enterprises, Yanacocha esquina Mercado, La Paz (tel: 407-740; fax: 406-867).

Ministry of Presidency, Palacio de Gobierno, Plaza Murillo, La Paz (tel: 371-082; fax: 371-388).

Ministry of Sustainable Development and Planning, Avenida Mariscal Santa Cruz 1092, La Paz (tel: 330-074; fax: 330-540).

Other useful addresses

Bolivian Embassy (USA), 3014 Massachusetts Avenue, NW, Washington DC 20008 (tel: 202-483-4410; fax: 202-3712; e-mail: embassy@bolivia-usa.org).

Bolsa Boliviana de Valores, Calle Montevideo 142, La Paz (tel: 443-232; fax: 442-308; e-mail: info@bolsa-valores-bolivia.com).

British Embassy, Avenida Arce 2732, La Paz (tel: 357-424; fax: 431-073).

Confederación de Empresarios Privados de Boliva, Avenida Mariscal Santa Cruz 1392, Edificio Camara Nacional de Comercio, La Paz (tel: 315-562: fax: 379-970; e-mail: cepbol@ceibo.entelnet.bo).

Empresa Nacional de Electricidad (ENDE), Calle Colombia 655, Cochabamba (tel: 59-500; fax: 59-509).

Eurocentro de Cooperación Empresarial de Bolivia, Calle Suárez de Figueroa 127, Santa Cruz (tel: 334-555; fax: 365-108; e-mail: eurocentro@cainco.org.bo).

National news agency: Agencia Boliviana de Informacion (ABI)

Other news agencies: Agencia de Noticias Fides (Catholic news agency): www.noticiasfides.com

Bolpress: www.bolpress.com

Internet sites

Bolsa Boliviana de Valores SA (Bolivian Chamber of Commerce): www.bolsa-valores-bolivia.com

Bolivia Business Online: www.boliviabiz.com

Bolivia Government website: boliviaweb.com/gov.htm

Bolivian Times: www.boliviantimes.com

Bosnia and Hercegovina Republic

By its own recognition, Bosnia-Herzegovina (BiH) has perhaps the most complex, not to say contradictory, political structure of any country in the world, imposed upon it under the terms of the 1995 Dayton Accords. The Accords formally reaffirmed the country's sovereignty and independence. At the same time, however, they ratified the involvement within its borders of hostile neighbours (Serbia and Croatia), provided for its virtual occupation by Nato troops, entrenched the continued existence on its territory of two (if not three) domestic armies, and endowed it with extremely weak central state powers. Not a promising scenario for a country trying to forget the effects of a horrendous civil war.

The Dayton Accords formally evoked the right of refugees and displaced persons to return to their homes. Perversely, however, they left in power in Republika Srpska (RS) and Herzeg-Bosna the very forces who had driven them out. The Accords endorsed the fledgling republic's aspirations to democracy, human rights and multi-ethnicity. At the same time, however, they seemed to legitimise ethnic antagonisms in the very definition of the two entities into which BiH was divided, and in every aspect of the labyrinthine constitutional order with which they left the poor old Bosnians saddled.

The complexity of Bosnia's internal politics became acutely apparent in March 2008 when a dispute over the command structure of Bosnia's police force threatened to jeopardise its movement towards European Union (EU) membership. The original plan had been for the unification of Bosnia's two police forces, those of the Muslim-Croat federation and of the RS. Serb opposition to the loss of what it perceived to be a cornerstone of its autonomy meant that the proposed merger became

KEY FACTS

Official name: Republika Bosne i Hercegovine (BiH) (Republic of Bosnia and Hercegovina). BiH consists of two distinct entities: Federacija Bosne i Hercegovine (FBiH) (Federation of Bosnia and Hercegovina) and Republika Srpska (RS) (Serb Republic)

Head of State: Three-member rotating collective presidency: Nebojsa Radmanovic (Serb); Zeljko Komsic (Croat); Haris Silajdzic (Muslim) (elected Oct 2006)

Head of government: Prime Minister Nikola Spiric (SNSD) (from Jan 2007; re-elected 28 Dec 2007)

Ruling party: Seven-party coalition government (formed 9 Jan 2007)

Area: 51,129 square km

Population: 3.98 million (2007)*

Capital: Sarajevo (BiH)

Official language: Bosanski (Bosnian)

Currency: Konvertibilna marka (KM) = 100 fennings

Exchange rate: KM1.23 per US$ (Jul 2008)

GDP per capita: US$3,712 (2007)*

GDP real growth: 5.80% (2007)*

Labour force: 1.95 million (2007)

Unemployment: 29.00% (2007)

Inflation: 1.30% (2007)

Balance of trade: -US$5.05 billion (2007)

Foreign debt: US$3.00 billion (2004)

* estimated figure

KEY FACTS

Official name: Republika Srpska (RS) (Serb Republic)

Head of State: President Rajko Kuzmanovic (SNSD) (elected 9 Dec 2007)

Head of government: Prime Minister Milorad Dodik (appointed 5 Feb 2006)

Ruling party: Stranka Nezavisnih Socijaldemokrata (SNSD) (Alliance of Independent Social Democrats) (re-elected 1 Oct 2006)

Area: 25,053 square km

Population: 1.49 million *

Capital: Sarajevo (de jure); Banja Luka (de facto)

Currency: Konvertibilna marka (KM) pegged to the euro at KM1 per eur0.51 (since 2001); the KM is the only legal tender

Exchange rate: KM1.51 per US$ (Jan 2007)

Labour force: 0

Unemployment: 40.10% (2001)*

Inflation: 1.80% (2005)*

* estimated figure

largely cosmetic. In a classic compromise, under the plan as it finally emerged, state bodies will control and co-ordinate the work of state security and intelligence agencies, as well as of the state border police, but will not interfere with the work of regional police forces. The last minute compromise agreement was designed to enable Bosnia to start the process of joining the EU. The EU had laid down a number of deadlines for police reforms to be completed, thereby enabling the signature of the Stabilisation and Association Agreement (SAA), the first step towards the eventual membership of the bloc. Bosnia's prime minister, Nikola Spiric had threatened to resign if parliament could not agree on the reforms. As frequently happens in Bosnian politics, disagreement between ethnic groups had threatened to put at risk the police reforms as it had many others. Bosnia, along with neighbour Serbia and the newly independent Kosovo, are the only Balkan states without any formal contract with the EU. Kosovo's independence was greeted with protests in the RS, some of which turned violent.

One ray of political hope shone on the long-suffering Bosnian electorate in April 2008 when Bosnia's Oscar-winning film director Danis Tanovic launched a new political party in a bid to rise above the ethnic divisions that continue to beset the country. Mr Tanovic whose *No Man's Land* film about the absurdity of war won an Oscar for the best foreign language film in 2001, said he hoped his Nasa Stranka (Our Party) would appeal to the many disillusioned people who have not bothered to vote in recent elections. Mr Tanovic sought to break the Bosnian political deadlock, claiming to offer a fresh choice to Bosnians who have long complained about their country's paucity of political choice. Political commentators have ventured that Tanovic's stature within Bosnia could translate into ballot box success. Mr Tanovic had expressed the hope that Nasa Stranka will appeal to younger voters, those who see their future lying within Europe. Mr Tanovic, a Bosnian Muslim, will co-chair the Nasa Stranka party alongside a Bosnian Croat and a Serb.

Economy strengthens ...

In May 2005 the World Bank had stated that Bosnia had been successful in achieving macroeconomic stability. Anchored in a currency board arrangement, the local currency konvertibilna marka (KM) remains stable. Bosnia has adopted the most liberal foreign trade regime in South East Europe. The World Bank has ranked Bosnia and Herzegovina as a lower middle-income country with a gross national income per capita of A$1,941. According to the World Bank approximately 53 per cent of GDP is created in the services sector, 32 per cent in industry, and 15 per cent in agriculture. Since 1995, the year in which its civil war ended, GDP has tripled, merchandise exports are up tenfold, and price stability has been maintained with inflation rates below 1 per cent in the past two years. Nonetheless, the absence of a single, integrated market still hampers economic development and deters foreign investment. Bosnia's economy currently stands at only 70 per cent of its pre-war level. Poverty levels are still high at 20 per cent, and a further 30 per cent of all citizens live just above the poverty line.

Bosnia's GDP per capita is one of the lowest of the region. Between 1996 and 1999 real GDP growth, fuelled by high levels of foreign reconstruction aid, artificially averaged above 30 per cent. However, GDP growth has since slowed, resulting from inadequate growth in domestic sources, particularly in private sector activity. In 2006, GDP growth was 5.5 per cent helped by an improvement in exports. However, methodological issues concerning the reliability of official figures and sizeable black economies operating in both the Federation and Republika Srpska mean that Bosnia's economic data should be interpreted cautiously.

Estimates of unemployment also vary considerably, ranging from the mid-20s to as high as 44 per cent. Most employment in the Federation is within the government sector, international organisations present in the country and other services sectors. GDP per capita rose to US$6,450 in 2006. Bosnia has one of the lowest rates of foreign investment in the region. Faster progress is still needed on key structural reforms, such as privatisation of large state enterprises and improvements in the business climate. Foreign direct investment (FDI) has reached close to 5 per cent of GDP. The most significant FDI has come from Croatia, Lithuania, Austria, Slovenia, Germany and Kuwait. Over half the FDI went to industry, 15.1 in banking sector, 4.6 per cent in trade and 4.2 per cent in services. Bosnia's lone success story is the banking sector, which has been successfully privatised.

Bosnia's GDP has tripled since 1995, the year in which its civil war ended, although around 40 per cent of GDP is reckoned to be made up by the grey economy. The steady decline in international aid is also expected to raise pressure on Bosnia to increase its domestic savings. US financial assistance to Bosnia was US$51.0 million in 2005 while the EU contributed US$121.4 million. Worryingly, unemployment also proved to be an intractable problem, reaching 47.7 per cent in 2005. Bosnia's stubbornly high unemployment, falling levels of international aid, corporate malaise and economic growth of around 5 per cent, doesn't exactly add up to a glowing picture.

Azra Hadziahmetovic, a former Bosnian foreign trade minister, has stated that Bosnia will probably struggle to reach its pre-war GDP level before 2015. However, the 2006 tax reforms are expected to improve revenue collection. The European Bank for Reconstruction and Development (EBRD) has observed that Bosnia's GDP growth remained steady during 2006 but public spending continued to be high and Bosnia's current account deficit remains one of the largest in the region. Long-term sustainability depends on further restructuring, an improved business environment and increased integration into both the regional and world economy. After growing 5.8 per cent in 2005, the economy was seen to be on course for a similar increase in 2006. Estimates from the Central Bank for 2006 showed strong industrial output growth in the Republika Srpska, with more modest increases in the Federation. Exports continued to grow sharply, reflecting increasing access by Bosnian producers to regional and EU markets.

Bosnia has managed to depend less and less on aid, and growth rates have held up well. The outlook is for continued growth in the region of 5-6 per cent a year, allied to low inflation, but with significant downside risks. The European Union is expected to provide a strong anchor for reform, particularly after the Office of the High Representative (OHR) is closed in mid-2008. The main risks to this generally positive outlook lie in the small appetite of public officials for serious reform and the understandable difficulties and sensitivities concerning the constitution established by the Dayton Accord; this constitution needs to evolve in order to modernise Bosnia and Herzegovina and ensure the country's rapid progress towards EU membership. In 2007 the EU announced cuts to its peacekeeping force in Bosnia (Eufor). The force was to drop from 6,500 to 2,500. At the same time as the cuts were made, it was announced that the mandate of the OHR was to be prolonged until the end of June 2008.

Risk assessment

Politics	Fair
Economy	Improving
Regional stability	Fair

COUNTRY PROFILE

Historical profile

1463 Bosnia and Hercegovina (BiH) became a province of the Ottoman empire. Many of BiH's Christian Slavic population (principally Serb and Croat) were converted to Islam.

1877–78 The Congress of Berlin assigned BiH to the Austro-Hungarian Empire following the end of the Russo-Turkish War.

1914 Gavrilo Princip, a Serbian nationalist, assassinated Austrian Archduke Ferdinand in Sarajevo (capital of BiH), precipitating the First World War.

1918 The defeat of the Austro-Hungarian empire during the First World War saw the creation of the Kingdom of the Serbs, Croats and Slovenes, encompassing BiH, Croatia, parts of Dalmatia and Macedonia, Montenegro, Serbia, Slavonia and Slovenia.

1929 The Kingdom was renamed Yugoslavia.

1941 Parts of Yugoslavia were occupied by the Germans, Italians, Hungarians and Bulgarians. Most of BiH was incorporated into Croatia, which was granted independence by the Axis powers and ruled by the country's fascist Ustasha movement. Two opposition movements, the communist Partisans led by Josip Broz Tito and the royalist Chetniks led by Draza Mihailovic and backed by the Allied powers, formed to resist Nazi rule.

1944–45 After hostilities broke out between the Chetniks and Partisans, the Allies withdrew support for the Chetniks and backed the Partisans. The Partisans then defeated the occupying forces, the Ustasha, and the Chetniks.

1945 BiH became a constituent republic of a new Yugoslav federation. Tito assumed power and a Soviet-style constitution was adopted. The rest of the Yugoslav federation comprised Croatia, Macedonia, Slovenia, Montenegro, Serbia and the two autonomous regions of Vojvodina and Kosovo. In an attempt to create a Yugoslav unity, Tito imposed restrictions on religious worship while socialism was encouraged as the country's national ideology.

1953 Constitutions adopted in 1953, 1963 and 1974 increased the autonomy of the constituent republics.

1989 Following the death of Tito in 1980 and the fall of communism elsewhere in Eastern Europe, friction between the wealthier republics, Slovenia and Croatia, and the different ethnic groupings intensified.

KEY FACTS

Official name: Federacija Bosne i Hercegovine (FBiH) (Federation of Bosnia-Hercegovina)

Head of State: President Borjana Krišto (appointed 21 Feb 2007)

Head of government: Prime Minister Nedzad Brankovic (from 22 Mar 2007)

Ruling party: Coalition government with 16 members chosen from the quota of nationalies. There are eight Bosniak, five Croat and three Serb cabinet ministers.

Capital: Sarajevo

Currency: Konvertibilna marka (KM) (The Croatian kuna also circulate widely)

Exchange rate: KM1.51 per US$ (Jul 2004) (pegged at KM1.96 per euro)

GDP per capita: US$2,129 *

GDP real growth: 5.20% (2001)*

Labour force: 722,000 (2007)

Unemployment: 31.00% (2007)

Inflation: 0.80% (2001); 2.0% (2002)*

* estimated figure

1990 Multi-party elections in BiH brought to power a government which supported outright independence.
1992 After independence from Yugoslavia, civil war engulfed the whole of BiH.
1993 The Yugoslav dinar was replaced by the new dinar as the national currency.
1995 Hostilities were brought to an end by the Dayton Peace Agreement in late 1995. BiH was divided almost equally into two distinctive entities, based along ethnic lines: the Federacija Bosne i Hercegovine (FBiH) (Federation of Bosnia and Hercegovina) (comprising the Croat and Muslim population, 51 per cent of BiH) and the RS (comprising the Serb population, 49 per cent of BiH). The disputed region of Brcko in the north-west of the country became a self-governing district within BiH. A multi-national Nato military force was deployed in BiH to enforce the military aspects of Dayton.
1996 A democratic government was elected comprising the main nationalist parties of the three ethnic communities: the Muslim Stranka Demokratski Akije (SDA) (Democratic Action Party), Hrvatska Demokratska Zajednica Bosne i Hercegovine (HDZ BiH) (Croatian Democratic Union of Bosnia and Hercegovina) and the Srpska Demokratska Stranka (SDS) (Serb Democratic Party). Alija Izetbegovic, Ante Jelavic and Zivko Radisic were elected to the three-member collective presidency.
1999 The new dinar was replaced by the Konvertibilna marka as the national currency.
2000 Nationalists did well in the general election and international hopes of multi-ethnic political co-operation declined. The Organisation for Security and Co-operation in Europe (OSCE) reported that several political parties abused the regulations during the elections.
2001 Ante Jelavic was dismissed from the BiH presidency by the then UN High Representative, Wolfgang Petritsch, after he threatened to form his own government in Croat-dominated parts of the FBiH. He was replaced by Jozo Krizanovic. The BiH parliament elected Zlatko Lagumdzija as prime minister to replace Bozidar Matic, who had resigned.
2002 Dragan Covic (Croat), Mirko Sarovic (Serb) and Sulejman Tihic (Muslim) were elected to the BiH presidency in the presidential elections. The SDA won the BiH parliamentary elections.
2003 Borislav Paravac replaced Mirko Sarovic who resigned from the BiH presidency in April after accusations of being involved with illegal arms sales to Iraq. In June, Dragan Covic became the chairman of the presidency.
2004 Sulejman Tihic became chairman of the presidency in February. On 29 June, the High Representative, Paddy Ashdown, dismissed 60 top officials in the RS, including the interior minister, Zoran Djeric, for failing to implement measures to catch Radovan Karadzic, the Bosnian Serb leader, and his military commander, General Ratko Mladic, both of whom are indicted on war-crimes charges. In December, the EU force (EUFOR) took over NATO's peacekeeping mission in Bosnia. On 17 December, the prime minister of the RS, Dragan Mikerevic, resigned.
2005 On 15 February, the RS parliament elected Pero Bukejlovic as prime minister. Dragan Covic was dismissed by the High Representative on 29 March. On 4 May, Ivo Miro Jovic was appointed as the Croat member of the presidency. In November the EU agreed to stabilisation and association agreement talks as pre-entry measures for BiH to join the EU.
2006 Christian Schwarz-Schilling took office as UN High Representative on 31 January, following the retirement of Lord Ashdown. Political reforms necessary for the High Representative (the UN and European envoy), holding de facto power, to transfer control to local politicians hit an obstacle when elections that could have shown Bosnia had moved towards a pluralistic society, a decade after the internecine Bosnian war, was still dominated by ethnic matters. Elections were held on 1 October for the three-member presidency and the Zastupnicki dom (House of Representatives), in which the Stranka Demokratske Akcije (SDA) (Democratic Action Party) won nine seats (out of 42); Stranka za Bosnu i Hercegovinu (SBiH) (Assemby of Bosnia and Hercegovina) won eight; Savez Nezavisnih Socijaldemokrata (SNSD) (Alliance of Independent Social Democrats) won seven; Socijaldemokratska Partija BiH (Socijaldemokrati) (Social Democratic Party of BiH) (Social Democrats) won five; HDZ BiH and SDS each won three seats and six political parties shared the remaining seven seats. On 6 November, Nebojsa Radmanovic, a Serb, was inaugurated president, a post he will hold until July 2007 when the next scheduled rotation occurs.
2007 Nikola Spiric became prime minister on 11 January. His government was approved by parliament in February. In July Miroslav Lajcák (of Slovakia) became the top EU official in Office of the High Representative. Igor Radojicic (SNSD) was appointed acting-President of Republika Srpska, following the death of President Milan Jelic, of a heart attack, in September. Radojicic will stay in office until presidential elections are held in December. Nikola Spiric resigned as prime minister on 1 November in protest at measures introduced by High Representative Lajcák to speed up decision making in the central parliament. Serb leaders were concerned that the measures would reduce their influence in the central government and result in Muslim domination. Bosnia initialled an agreement on 4 December that began the process towards EU pre-membership when internationally sponsored parliamentary reforms were backed by representatives from all ethnic backgrounds. The reforms should strengthen the central government, as

KEY INDICATORS — Bosnia and Hercegovina Republic

	Unit	2003	2004	2005	2006	2007
Population	m	4.14	4.36	3.92	3.95	*3.98
Gross domestic product (GDP)	US$bn	7.00	8.62	10.06	12.23	*14.78
GDP per capita	US$	1,544	2,129	2,566	3,105	*3,712
GDP real growth	%	3.3	5.2	5.0	6.2	*5.8
Inflation	%	1.1	0.8	1.9	7.5	1.3
Unemployment	%	40.0	44.0	48.0	–	–
Industrial output	% change	–	2.5	7.7	5.3	–
Agricultural output	% change	–	15.8	3.7	1.9	–
Exports (fob) (goods)	US$m	1,272.0	2,086.7	2,580.0	3,539.0	4,243.3
Imports (cif) (goods)	US$m	3,890.0	6,656.2	7,534.3	8,587.0	9,947.2
Balance of trade	US$m	-2,618.0	-4,569.5	-4,954.3	-5,048.0	-5,703.9
Current account	US$m	-1,250.0	-1,430.0	-2,183.0	-1,025.0	*-1,920.0
Total reserves minus gold	US$m	1,796.0	2,408.0	2,531.0	3,372.0	4,525.0
Foreign exchange	US$m	1,792.0	2,407.0	2,531.0	3,371.0	4,525.0
Exchange rate	per US$	1.72	1.49	1.51	1.51	1.35

* estimated figure

regional legislatures will no long be able to block and boycott a vote. On 9 December, in presidential elections for Republika Srpska, Rajko Kuzmanovic (SNSD) won with 41.8 per cent of the vote; his closest rival, Ognjen Tadic (SDP), had 35.2 per cent. Turnout was 37.1 per cent. On 28 December, the parliament re-appointed Nikola Spiric as prime minister of BiH.

2008 On 6 March Haris Silajdzic became president of the BiH, in accordance with the rotating presidency. On 16 June BiH took the first step in joining the European Union when it signed the Stabilisation and Association Agreement. It is estimated that full membership may not be achieved until 2018. The agreement is seen as a measure to bolster democratic values and counter ethnic tensions. On 21 July former Bosnian Serb leader Radovan Karadzic was arrested in Belgrade. Seven Bosnian Serbs were convicted of genocide by aiding the systematic killing of over 1,000 Bosnian Muslim men and boys in one day during the siege of Srebrenica in 1995 in which 8,000 Bosniaks were killed. All defendants had been members of either the police or army and were given jail terms of 38–42 years.

Political structure

Constitution

The effective founding constitution of modern Republika Bosne i Hercegovine (BiH) (Republic of Bosnia and Hercegovina) is the 1995 Dayton Peace Agreement. This set out the federal state, divided between the Federacija Bosne i Hercegovine (FBiH) (Federation of Bosnia and Hercegovina) and the Republika Srpska (RS) (Serb Republic). The two republics are then subdivided into cantons based on the Swiss model. A European Union pre-membership agreement in December 2007 produced parliamentary reforms to strengthen the BiH central government, whereby FBiH and RS legislatures will no long be able to block and boycott a BiH vote.

The disputed region of Brcko in the north-west of the country was placed under international arbitration in 1995. In March 1998, the Brcko Tribunal declared the Brcko municipality a separate self-governing neutral district under the sovereignty of BiH.

In 2002, the FBiH and RS governments signed an agreement to make constitutional amendments designed to give equal status to all ethnic Muslims, Croats and Serbs in BiH.

Under the terms of the Dayton Agreement, the BiH is responsible for foreign affairs, foreign trade, monetary policy and law enforcement. The FBiH and RS are primarily responsible for fiscal policy, defence and law.

Constitutional government is not yet in full operation. The UN's Office of the High Representative (OHR) is responsible for overseeing and implementing the civilian aspects of the Dayton Agreement.

Universal suffrage at 18 years of age (16 years if employed). The 2001 election law only allows voters to cast ballots for members of their own ethnic group in elections for the collective three-member presidency. Voters may only vote in constituencies where they lived prior to the 1992–95 civil war.

Form of state

Confederated parliamentary democratic republic, separated into two constituent states – Bosnia-Hercegovina Federation and Bosnia Serb Republic (RS).

The executive

BiH has a three-member collective presidency, one representative from each of the three main ethnic groups. Although this is nominally the executive for the whole country, in practice, the RS appointed its own president and has frequently disregarded the authority of the three-man presidency. In 2002, the collective presidency was elected for a four-year mandate.

The government is formed from a Council of Ministers drawn from the Zastupnicki dom, which are nominated by the president and confirmed by the Zastupnicki dom. The council appoints a chairman (prime minister) as head of government; in December 2005, the post of prime minister was enhanced, with the power to appoint and dismiss ministers.

National legislature

BiH has two state parliaments (FBiH and NSRS – see below) and one central legislature.

The Federacija Bosne i Hercegovina (FBiH) (Bosniak/Croat Federation of Bosnia and Hercegovina) has a bicameral parliament with a House of Representatives (98 seats – members elected by popular vote for four-year terms); and a House of Peoples (30 Bosniak and 30 Croat seats).

The Narodna Skuptstina Republika Srpska (NSRS) (Serb Republic National Parliament) is unicameral, with 83 members elected for a four-year term by proportional representation.

The central legislature is the Parlementarna Skupstina BiH (National Parliament of BiH), with representatives from both of the state parliaments, occupying seats in two chambers. The Zastupnicki dom (House of Representatives) (lower house) has 42 members elected by party-list proportional representation, for a four-year term – 28 members from the FBiH (14 Bosniaks and 14 Croatians) and 14 from the RS. The Dom Naroda (House of the Peoples) (upper house) has 15 members appointed from the lower house and elected by the Zastupnicki dom, with equal representation of the three ethnic groups, five Bosniaks, five Croats and five Serbs.

The Brcko Distrikt (Brcko district), in north-east BiH, is under internationally administered supervision.

Legal system

Civil law system of former Yugoslavia. Legal infrastructure has been in disarray since the war.

Last elections

1 October 2006 (national and state presidential and state parliaments)

Results: Republic of Bosnia and Hercegovina. Presidential (three-member rotating presidency): Nebojsa Radmanovic (SNSD) won 53.3 per cent of the vote for the Serb seat; Zeljko Komsic (Social Democrats) won 39.6 per cent for the Croat seat; and Haris Silajdzic (SBiH) won 62.8 per cent for the Bosniak (Muslim) seat.

Federation of Bosnia-Hercegovina. Parliamentary: Stranka Demokratske Akcije (SDA) (Democratic Action Party) won nine seats (out of 42); Stranka za Bosnu i Hercegovinu (SBiH) (Assembly of Bosnia and Hercegovina) won eight; Savez Nezavisnih Socijaldemokrata (SNSD) (Alliance of Independent Social Democrats) won seven; Socijaldemokratska Partija BiH (Socijaldemokrati) (Social Democratic Party of BiH) (Social Democrats) won five; Hrvatska Demokratska Zajednica BiH (HDZ BiH) (Croatian Democratic Community of BiH) and Srpska Demokratska Stranka (SDS) (Serb Democratic Party) each won three seats; and six political parties shared the remaining seven seats.

Republika Srpska. Presidential: Rajko Kuzmanovic (SNSD) won 41.8 per cent of the vote, Ognjen Tadic (SDS) won 35.2 per cent, Mladen Ivanic Partija Demokratskog Progresa (PDP) (Party of Democratic Progress) 17.1 per cent. Turnout was 37.1 per cent. Parliamentary: the Savez Nezavisnih Socijaldemokrata (SNSD) (Alliance of Independent Social Democrats) won 43.3 per cent of the vote (41 of 82 seats), the Srpska Demokratska Stranka (SDS) (Serbian Democratic Party) 18.3 per cent (17), and PDP 6.9 per cent (8). Turnout is 54.8 per cent.

Next elections

2010 (parliamentary and presidential)

Political parties

Ruling party

Seven-party coalition government (formed 9 Jan 2007)

Main opposition party

Socijaldemokratska Partija (SPD) (Social Democratic Party)

Population
3.98 million (2007)*
Last census: March 1991: 4,377,033
Population density: 76 inhabitants per square km. Urban population: 43 per cent (1994–2000).
Annual growth rate: 1.0 per cent 1994–2004 (WHO 2006)
Internally Displaced Persons (IDP)
330,000 (UNHCR 2004)
Ethnic make-up
Muslims (44 per cent), Serbs (31 per cent) and Croats (17 per cent). The RS is a mostly Serb enclave, while Muslims (also known as 'Bosniaks') and Croats control and inhabit the FBiH.
Religions
Islam (Muslims), Serbian Eastern Orthodoxy (Serbs), Roman Catholicism (Croats).

Education
The education system in BiH was largely destroyed by the civil war and is now influenced by politics. International aid and tax revenues are being used by the entity governments to re-build and fund the education system. In the FBiH, each canton has responsibility for education. The RS has responsibility for its own education system. Despite the FBiH and RS signing the Declaration and Agreement on Education in BiH in 2000 to introduce much-needed reforms to the post-war education system, educational curriculums in each of the entities follow ethnic and religious lines. Segregation of students along ethnic lines is not uncommon.
BiH has universities at Banja Luka, Mostar, Sarajevo and Tuzla. Higher education is also poorly financed and most international aid has come from non-governmental organisations (NGOs).
Literacy rate: 95 per cent adult rate; 100 per cent youth rate (15–24) (Unesco 2005).

Health
Per capita total expenditure on health (2003) was US$327; of which per capita government spending was US$166, at the international dollar rate, (WHO 2006).
The health system in BiH is poor and receives little funding from the central government, having handed down the funding responsibilities to cantonal and local government. The health system is largely dependent on aid but is also financed through employee insurance schemes.
HIV/Aids
HIV prevalence: 0.5 per cent aged 15–49 in 2003 (World Bank)
Life expectancy: 73 years, 2004 (WHO 2006)
Fertility rate/Maternal mortality rate:
1.3 births per woman, 2004 (WHO 2006)
Child (under 5 years) mortality rate (per 1,000): 14 per 1,000 live births (World Bank)
Head of population per physician:
1.34 physicians per 1,000 people, 2003 (WHO 2006)

Welfare
Higher spending on specific areas of the welfare system compared to other areas of the economy has become a major impediment to achieving economic growth in BiH. The welfare system is highly geared to supporting military veterans, war widows and their families, thus only benefiting around 230,000 people – about six per cent of the population. According to the IMF, benefits and spending for military invalids and war widows in the FBiH and the RS account for 10–12 per cent of the country's government revenues. These payments also accounted for over 80 per cent of the annual pension fund.
The unemployment benefit system in BiH is of limited assistance to the claimant. Unemployment benefits – 30 per cent of the state average wage – in the FBiH are only available for six months – although these are available longer for those who had been in continuous employment for more than five years. Claimants need to have paid through an insurance scheme to gain unemployment benefits, while military invalids and war widows are funded by the state. As a result of the system, few register as unemployed, confusing official statistics of the unemployed in BiH (estimated at 40 per cent in 2003). About 5 per cent of those registered as unemployed actually receive state benefits.

Main cities
Sarajevo (capital, estimated population 383,604 in 2005), Banja Luka (capital of RS) (173,748), Zenica (85,649), Tuzla (88,521), Prijedor (29,876), Mostar (the main town in Hercegovina province) (64,301), Bihac (39,195).

Languages spoken
Bosanski (Bosnian) is one of the southern Slavonic languages and is most closely related to Serbian, Croatian and Slovene. Croatian and Serbian are also spoken. Bosnian is written in Latin script but can also be seen written in the Cyrillic alphabet.
German is a useful language for the business traveller.
English is not widely spoken, but is becoming more common as a language for business.
Official language/s
Bosanski (Bosnian)

Media
The civil war of the 1990s resulted in a highly polarised media, which the Dayton Agreement addressed by developing a media to bridge inter-communal groupings. The media is partially free although state bodies and political parties have endeavoured to bring pressure on journalists and media outlets.
National news agency: FENA (Federal News Agency)
Other news agencies: SRNA (Bosnian Serb): www.srna.co.yu
Onasa (independent):
www.onasa.com.ba
Press
Dailies: From Sarajevo in Bosnian, Dnevni Avaz (www.avaz.ba), and the independent Oslobodjenje (www.oslobodjenje.ba). From Banja Luka, in Serbian, Nezavisne Novine (www.nezavisne.com) and the Bosnian Serb government Glas Srpske (www.glassrpske.com). From Mostar, in Croatian, Dnevni List (www.dnevni-list.ba).
Weeklies: From Sarajevo in Bosnian, Dani (www.bhdani.com), Slobodna Bosna (www.slobodna-bosna.ba), and from Banja Luka Reporter an independent bi-weekly.
Broadcasting
National, public broadcasting is provided by Radio Televizija Bosne i Hercegovine (BHRT) (www.bhrt.ba), by Radio Televizija BiH in the Bosniak-Croat region (RTBiH) (www.rtvfbih.ba) and in the Serb region by Radio Televizija Republik Srpske (RTRS) (www.rtrs.tv).
Radio: Public radio has the highest listening figures. There are over 200 commercial radio stations; however the number has been restricted due to the inadequate advertising market.
The BHRT (www4.bhrt.ba) broadcasts two national networks and one international. Popular commercial stations include Bosanska Radio Mreza (Boram) (www.boram.ba), BM Radio (www.bmradio.com), Radio Stari Grad (http://rsg.software.ba), Radio M (www.radiom.net), Radio Tuzla (www.radiotuzla.com) and Big Radio 2 (www.bigradiobl.com).
Television: BHRT, RTVBiH and RTRS provide public services in all local languages. There are over 40 channels to choose from, the majority are provided by foreign cable or satellite networks. Domestic commercial channels include Balkanmedia 7 (www.balkanmedia.com), BN TV Bijelina (www.rtvbn.com) and Mreza Plus (www.mrezaplus.ba).

Economy
Since the Dayton peace accord in 1995, the country has achieved substantial success in post-war reconstruction efforts and social stabilisation. This has been achieved through a high level of international support, with a total of US$1.9

billion being committed to the nation's development from 60 donors. As a result, GDP has more than tripled since 1995. Despite impressive growth, there are still significant challenges ahead for Bosnia and Hercegovina (BiH) as poverty affects a fifth of the population and 30 per cent of the population could easily descend below the poverty line.

A strong regional export market has supported GDP growth of around five per cent per annum. Inflation has remained low, although it increased in 2005 to 2.8 per cent (compared with 0.8 per cent in 2004). Unemployment, however, is high at 40 per cent and over.

Compensation for land and property seizures by the former Yugoslavia could have a significant impact on BiH's economy over the medium-term. The IMF has warned that it could destabilise fiscal planning unless restitution payments are postponed 'until the burden of domestic debts' is clarified.

The government is committed to increasing foreign direct investment through privatisation programmes. In August 2004, the sale of the Zenica steelworks to the LNM Group gave a boost of 12.4 per cent in industrial production and to the resurgent metals sector.

In 2004, BiH's World Bank status changed from a post-conflict economy to a transition economy, reflecting the improvements made in GDP growth. BiH has taken the first step towards eventual EU accession, following agreement in November 2005 to commence talks on a Stabilisation and Association Agreement. To be eligible for EU membership, BiH will have to encourage the development of the private sector along with increasing competitiveness within the country. BiH joined NATO's Partnership for Peace programme in December 2006 and is negotiating accession to the World Trade Organisation.

Since the civil war ended in 1995, international peace-keeping operations have been needed to maintain BiH's fragile stability. Divisions within civil society run deep, although politically the three rival groups have come together and agreed to strengthen central government. This should enhance the chances of improving the economy for all the regions.

Labour market and unemployment

Labour force: 2 million (1999). Annual growth rate: 0.6 per cent (1980–99). Projected growth rate: 0.9 per cent per annum (1999–2010).

The unemployment rate in Bosnia is close to 40 per cent; however, the official statistics do not reflect the real level of unemployment in the country. Many citizens do not register with the country's unemployment agencies because of the benefit system which only allows for financial assistance for six months (longer if the claimant has worked continuously for more than five years) and only if the claimant has paid insurance while employed – in the RS, for example, this system provided benefits to only 2.8 per cent of the 146,247 registered unemployed in 1999. Furthermore, many of Bosnia's unregistered unemployed are engaged in activities in the country's 'grey' economy.

External trade

In 2008, BiH was still working towards WTO membership. It became a member of the Central European Free Trade Agreement in 2006. A Stabilisation and Association Agreement (SAA) with the EU was initiated in 2005 with the prospect of enhanced trading links.

Industrial productions include heavy industries such as steel and mining, with vehicle and aircraft assembly and oil refining. Lighter industries include furniture and domestic appliances manufacture.

Imports

Imports consist of fuels, foodstuffs, chemicals, machinery and equipment.

Main sources: Croatia (17.1 per cent total, 2006), Germany (12.4 per cent), Serbia (9.8 per cent).

Exports

Exports consist of mainly steel, minerals, clothing and timber products.

Main destinations: Croatia (18.7 per cent of 2006 total goods exports), Italy (13.8 per cent), Serbia (13.2 per cent).

Agriculture

Farming

The legacy of war in the region has implications for BiH's agricultural policy. There is considerable uncertainty over land rights, with fragmented and small-sized farm units hindering any large-scale investment opportunities.

The varying climatic conditions in BiH offer wide possibilities both in terms of crop choice and cultivation of land farming, fruit-growing, vine-growing, vegetable-growing, forage crops and livestock production.

Agricultural activities in the RS extend over different farming systems including mixed farming enterprises (crops and cattle) on lower flat lands that alternate with more extensive sheep grazing systems in mountainous areas.

Most of the FBiH is mountainous, with farms in the south and south-east growing vegetables, fruits and rearing livestock.

The issue of land mines in rural areas complicates policies related to post-war agricultural development.

The estimated crop production in 2005 included 1,231,500 tonnes (t) cereals in total, 250,000t wheat, 850,000t maize, 447,000t potatoes, 62,500t barley, 30,000t pimento, 24,764t pulses, 73,000t plums, 40,000t tomatoes, 1,834t oilcrops, 4,246t tobacco, 3,000t walnuts, 35,000t apples, 48,200t chillies and peppers, 157,700t fruit in total, 784,400t vegetables in total. Estimated livestock production included 36,750t meat in total, 14,000t beef, 8,400t pig meat, 2,700t lamb, 11,650t poultry, 16,000t eggs, 596,500t milk, 2,500t honey, 3,520t cattle hides.

Fishing

Fishing is of little importance to BiH's agricultural sector as a whole with the fish catch totalling some 2,500 tonnes per year.

Forestry

Over half of BiH's land area is forested, covering over 2.2 million hectares (ha). Three-fifths of woodland are used for wood supply, mostly for export. Most of the woodland is state-owned. The country has a small forest sector, which produces mainly sawnwood and wood-based panels from domestic resources.

Industry and manufacturing

The industrial sector typically accounts for around 25 per cent of GDP, of which manufacturing is 10 per cent.

Since the end of the civil war, the construction industry has been the main engine of industrial growth, and since the Zenica steelworks was sold to LNM Group steel production has boosted state industrial production based on the resurgent metals sector, as well as the civil engineering projects and Balkan regeneration. State-owned telecommunication entities are due to be one of the first organisations offered up for privatisation.

Tourism

Travel and tourism is expected to have contributed US$118.3 million or 1.3 per cent of GDP in 2005 and has a hard road to travel before tourist numbers match those of its neighbour, Croatia. There was little tourist infrastructure before 2004 and by 2006 its market is centred on adventure holidays to its unspoilt mountains and lakes. An estimated US$138 million or 7.8 per cent of total capital investment was spent on travel and tourism, in 2005. Direct flights from the UK to Sarajevo have helped to provide access, with the re-opening of the bridge at Mostar, the national symbol of reconciliation, being used as a tourist attraction.

Mining

BiH has deposits of iron ores and good reserves of bauxite, as it used to be a major source of minerals for former Yugoslavia.

Hydrocarbons
BiH imports all of its oil and gas supplies from Russia. Oil imports total over 20,000 barrels per day (bpd). Consumption of gas, at around 311 million cubic metres per year, is covered by imports from Russia via the Bratsvo gas pipeline through Hungary and Serbia and Montenegro.
BiH has deposits of coal and produces enough for its own consumption. The Visca mines, near Tuzla, in the north, produce 1,000 tonnes of coal a day. The coal industry is one of the big loss-makers in the state sector.

Energy
BiH's electricity network has been returned to about 80 per cent of its pre-war capacity with international loans to re-build and develop the energy sector.
Elektroprivreda RS, a state-owned power company, exports electricity to Serbia.

Financial markets
Stock exchange
The Sarajevo Stock Exchange (SASE) and Banja Luka Stock Exchange both have official markets (for blue chip companies only) and free markets.

Banking and insurance
BiH's banking system has undergone reform since 1995. Although heavily indebted and close to bankruptcy, a number of banks underwent privatisation in the late 1990s. Foreign companies that have already invested in BiH banking have streamlined and modernised major banks. Croatia's Zagrebacka Banka has taken a major share in the banking sector, acquiring stakes in four banks. Three RS banks were granted licences from the Federation Banking Agency (FBA) and opened branches in the FBiH, assisted by the introduction of a harmonised banking code between the entities.
The central bank has responsibility as the monetary authority and currency board.
Central bank
The Centralna Banka Bosne i Hercegovine (CBBH) (Central Bank of Bosnia and Hercegovina)

Time
GMT plus one hour (daylight saving, late March to late October, GMT plus two hours)

Geography
BiH is a mountainous territory with only about 20km of coastline. Croatia forms its western border (running from north-west to south-east, along the Dinaric Alps) and its northern border. Serbia lies to the east and Montenegro to the south-east.
The ancient province of BiH lies between the Sava, Drina and Una rivers. There are fertile lowlands along the River Sava which forms the northern border.
Hemisphere
Northern
Climate
The climate in BiH is continental with warm summers and cold winters. The temperature averages one degree Celsius (C) in January and 21 degrees C in July. As the country is dominated by mountainous and hilly terrain, with central and southern BiH dominated by the Dinaric Alps, the weather can be unpredictable in valley areas in the spring and winter months.

Dress codes
During the summer, light clothing is recommended, with warmer clothes essential during the winter months.

Entry requirements
Passports
Required by all except nationals of Austria, Belgium, Finland, France, Germany, Greece, Italy, Luxembourg, The Netherlands, Norway, Portugal, Spain and Sweden, who only need a national identity card.
Visa
Not required by citizens of Europe, North America, Australasia, Kuwait, Qatar, South Korea, Malaysia and Brunei.
Currency advice/regulations
BiH has a cash economy. The Konvertibilna marka (KM) is the local currency. The dollar and euro, but not sterling, are the most acceptable foreign currencies, but it is likely that change will be supplied in KM. Credit card facilities are limited, although hotels, restaurants and shops in the major centres are beginning to accept them. Travellers cheques can be changed at only a few banks in major cities and are not recommended.
Import and export of local currency are permitted to a limit of KM200,000. There are no restrictions on import and export of foreign currencies.
Customs
A unified customs territory has been established in BiH. 200 cigarettes, 20 cigars or 200g of tobacco; one litre of wine or spirits; one bottle of perfume; and gifts up to eur76.70 are admitted duty-free.

Health (for visitors)
Medical services are not comprehensive. Visitors should carry a sufficient supply of medicines or prescription drugs.
Ensure that personal travel and health insurance covers all eventualities, including accident and evacuation.
Mandatory precautions
None.
Advisable precautions
Typhoid, tetanus and hepatitis A and B vaccinations are recommended.
Water and food precautions advisable.

Credit cards
Credit cards can be used in some shops, hotels and travel agencies (Croatia Airlines, Air Bosna) in Sarajevo and is accepted by the Privredna Banka Sarajevo for cash withdrawals.

Public holidays (national)
Fixed dates
1 Jan (New Year's Day), 7 Jan (Orthodox Christmas Day), 14 Jan (Orthodox New Year), 1 Mar (Independence Day), 1 May (Labour Day), 15 Aug (Assumption Day), 28 Aug (Orthodox Assumption Day), 8 Sep (Nativity of the Virgin Mary), 21 Sep (Orthodox Nativity of the Virgin Mary), 1 Nov (All Saints' Day), 2 Nov (All Souls' Day), 25 Nov (National Statehood Day), 25 Dec (Christmas Day).
Variable dates
Easter, Orthodox Easter, Eid al Adha, Birth of the Prophet, Eid al Fitr.
Islamic year – 1429 (10 Jan 2008–28 Dec 2008): The Islamic year contains 354 or 355 days, with the result that Muslim feasts advance by 10–12 days against the Gregorian calendar. Dates of feasts vary according to the sighting of the new moon, so cannot be forecast exactly.

Working hours
Banking
Mon–Fri: 0800–1900.
Business
Mon–Fri: 0800–1700.
Government
Mon–Fri: 0730–1530, except Wed, 0730–1730.
Shops
Mon–Fri: 0800–1200 and 1700–2000, Sat: 0800–1500, but many shops open throughout day.

Telecommunications
Mobile/cell phones
GSM 900 facilities are available throughout most of the country.

Electricity supply
220V AC

Social customs/useful tips
Punctuality depends on the region: it is important in some, more casual in others. It is customary to shake hands on meeting and taking leave.

Security
Unexploded mines are still a danger away from main centres and routes and travellers should keep to roads or paved areas. There is a threat from terrorism. Visitors are advised to keep clear of demonstrations or crowds. Beware of pickpockets in Sarajevo and tourist areas.

Getting there
Air
National airline: B&H Airlines

International airport/s: Sarajevo International Airport (SJJ), 12km south of the city centre.
Other airport/s: Mostar (OMO) and Banja Luka(BNX).
Airport tax: US$12. Transit passengers remaining in airport transport area are exempt.

Surface

BiH is included in the Pan-European Corridor 5 scheme. The project has some 3,270km of railways, linking Kiev in the Ukraine with western Europe via Italy, and 2,850 of new and upgraded roads.
Road: From Zagreb (Croatia) the border can be crossed at Zupanja/Orasje, Stara Gradiska/Bosanska Gradiska, Maljevac/Velika Kladusa and Licko Petrovo Selo/Izacic.
From Split (Croatia): Kamensko/Livno and Metkovic/Capljina.
Water: Bosnia has 20km of coastline on the Adriatic, but no ports.

Getting about

National transport

Air: The BiH national airline is B&H Airlines. Air Srpska operates from the RS.
Road: Night travel by road is not advised and travellers on back roads risk landmines left over from the war. Drivers should also be aware of the local population's disregard for the country's traffic laws. Speeding, particularly on dangerous valley roadways, is commonplace. Horse transport is used by substantial numbers of the local population.
Buses: Buses run between Split and Zagreb to Sarajevo. Journey times from Split vary between five hours during the summer to six in the winter. Journey times from Zagreb take eight hours in the summer and 11 in the winter.
Rail: The country's two railway services are BiH's Zeljeznice Bosne i Hercegovina (ZBH) and RS's Zeljeznice Republike Srpska (ZRS).

City transport

Taxis: Inexpensive taxi services operate in all the main cities. All taxis are metered, but there is no basic charge. A 10 per cent tip is usual.
Buses, trams & metro: Most city centres are served by trams, while buses serve the suburbs. The service is generally cheap and regular. Bus transfers operate out of Sarajevo airport.

Car hire

Avis and Hertz and other international car hire companies operate in neighbouring Croatia. Although the majority of hire cars have Croatian licence plates and are normally insured for travelling within BiH, it is advisable to check before booking.
Car rental firms mainly operate from Sarajevo airport.
Because the international Green Card is not applicable in BiH, car insurance is restricted to Third Party only. Travellers are likely to be asked for either a large deposit or to leave an open credit card voucher with the hire company.
Should travellers have an accident in BiH which is reported to the police, the hire company will impose an automatic charge fine, over and above any other hire costs; check all agreements carefully.
Drivers should be 21 years with a minimum of two years' driving experience.
It is recommended that visitors who rent a car also hire a driver, especially if they intend to travel outside Sarajevo.

BUSINESS DIRECTORY

The addresses listed below are a selection only. While World of Information makes every endeavour to check these addresses, we cannot guarantee that changes have not been made, especially to telephone numbers and area codes. We would welcome any corrections.

Telephone area codes

The international direct dialling (IDD) code for BiH is +387 followed by area code and subscriber's number.

Banja Luka	51	Sarajevo	33
Mostar	36	Tuzla	35
Pale	57	Zenica	72

Useful telephone numbers

Vehicle assistance: 1282
Fire and rescue: 123/124
Police: 122
Ambulance: 124
Emergency hospital, Koldovorska Street, Sarajevo (English spoken): 611-111

Chambers of Commerce

American Chamber of Commerce in Bosnia and Hercogovina, 4 Zmaja Od Bosne, 71000 Sarajevo (tel: 269-230; fax: 269-232; e-mail: amcham@lsinter.net).

Bosnia-Hercegovina Chamber of Foreign Trade, 10 Branislava Durdeva, 71000 Sarajevo (tel: 663-631; fax: 663-632; e-mail: cis@komorabih.com).

Federation of Bosnia-Hercegovina Chamber of Economy, 10 Branislava Durdeva, 71000 Sarajevo (tel: 217-782; fax: 217-783; e-mail: info@kfbih.com).

Sarajevo Canton Chamber of Economy, 8 La Benevolencije, 71000 Sarajevo (tel: 250-100; fax: 250-137).

Banking

Aurobanka, Mostar (tel: 444-444/5, 444-456; fax: 444-400; internet site: www.aurobanka.com; e-mail: aurobanka.com).

Gospodarska Banka, International Division, Ferhadija 11/III, 71000 Sarajevo (tel: 208-907, 667-688; fax: 444-605).

Hercegovacka banka, Kneza Domagoja Street, Sarajevo (tel: 320-555; fax: 324-771; internet: www.hercegovacka-banka.com; e-mail: herbank@hercegovacka-banka.com).

Hrvatska Banka, Kardinala Stepinca bb, 88000 Mostar (tel: 312-112; fax: 312-121).

Hrvatska Postanska Banka, Kneza Domagoja, Mostar (tel/fax: 316-020; e-mail: hpb-hb@int.tel.hr).

Investment Bank of the Federation of Bosnia and Hercegovina, Igmanska 1, 71000 Sarajevo (tel: 277-900; fax: 668-952; e-mail: info@ibf-bih.com).

Komercijalna Banka, Dzafer mahala 65/67, 75000 Tuzla (tel/fax: 259-000, 252-630; internet site: www.kombanka.com.ba; e-mail: kombanka@kombanka.com.ba).

Privredna Banka Sarajevo, Obala Vojvode Stepe 19, 71000 Sarajevo (tel: 213-144).

Universal Banka, Branilaca sarajeva 20/V, 71000 Sarajevo (tel: 664-139; fax: 668-239; internet: www.universalbanka.ba; e-mail: uniba@bih.net.ba).

Central bank

Central Bank of Bosnia and Hercegovina, Maršala Tita 25, 71000 Sarajevo (tel: 278-100; fax: 278-299; e-mail: contact@cbbh.ba).

Travel information

B&H Airlines, Kurta Schorka 36, Sarajevo(tel: 767-725; fax: 767-726; e-mail: opc@airbosna.ba).

Air Commerce, Sarajevo (tel: 663-396; fax: 663-395).

Avio Express, Sarajevo (tel/fax: 653-179).

Air Srpska, Veselina Maslese 28, 78000 Banja Luka (tel: 212-806; fax: 211-348).

Ministries

Ministry of External Trade and International Communication, 9 Musala, 71000 Sarajevo (tel: 664-831; fax: 655-060).

Ministry of Foreign Affairs of BiH, Musala 2, Sarajevo (tel: 281-100; internet site: http://www.mvp.gov.ba/Index_eng.htm).

RS Ministry of Foreign Economic Affairs, Vuka Karadzica 4, 51000 Banja Luka (tel: 331-430; fax: 331-436).

RS Ministry of Trade and Tourism, Vuka Karadzica 4, 51000 Banja Luka (tel: 331-523; fax: (331-499).

Other useful addresses

Agency for Privatisation in Federation of Bosnia and Hercegovina, Alipasina 41,

Sarajevo (tel: 218-550; fax: 218-552; e-mail: apftbiro@bih.net.ba).

US Embassy of Bosnia and Hercegovina, 2109 E Street, NW, Washington DC 20037 (tel: 337-1500; fax: 337-1502; e-mail: info@bosnianembassy.org).

British Embassy, BFPO 543, 8 Tina Ujevica, Sarajevo (tel: 444-429; fax: 666-131; e-mail: britemba@bih.net.ba).

British Embassy Commercial Department, Petrakijina 22, Sarajevo (tel: 204-781, 204-782, 679-635; fax: 204-780).

Communications and Regulatory agency (CRA), Vilsonovo Setaliste 10, 71000 Sarajevo.

Directorate for Reconstruction and Development, Saravejo (tel: 650-563).

RS Directorate for Privatisation, Mladena Stojanovica 4, Banja Luka (tel: 308-311; fax: 311-245; e-mail: dip@inecco.net).

Elektrodistribucija (Power Distribution Company), Sarajevo (tel: 472-462).

Elektroprivreda BiH, Vilsonovo setaliste 20, 71000 Sarajevo (tel: 651-722; fax: 653-004).

Gras (Public Transport Company), Sarajevo (tel: 664-624).

Institute for City Development Planning, Saravejo (tel: 664-638).

Institute for City Construction, Saravejo (tel: 663-901).

Institute for Information and Statistics, Saravejo (tel: 664-450).

Office of the High Representative, Emerika Bluma 1, 71 000 Sarajevo (tel: 283-500; fax: 283-501).

Public Information Office HQ SFOR, Butmir Camp, 71 000 Sarajevo (tel: 495-149).

PTT (Post/Telegraph/Telephone), Sarajevo (tel: 664-813).

Sarajevo City Council, Reisa Dz Causevica Street No 3, Sarajevo (tel: 664-773; fax: 648-016).

Sarajevogas (Gas Company), Sarajevo (tel: 467-713).

Sarajevostan (Housing Company), Saravejo (tel: 663-522).

Sarajevski Sajam (trade fairs), Terezije bb, 71 000 Sarajevo (tel: 664-163, 201-208, 445-156; fax: 201-178, 201-208).

Telekom Srpske (e-mail: tskabinet@telekom-rs.com).

World Bank Resident Mission, Bosnia and Hercegovina, Hamdije Kresevljakovica 19, 71000 Sarajevo (tel: 440-293; fax: 440-108).

National news agency: FENA (Federal News Agency)

Other news agencies: SRNA (Bosnian Serb): www.srna.co.yu
Onasa (independent): www.onasa.com.ba

Internet sites

RS Directorate for Privatisation: www.rsprivatizacija.com

Republika Srpska Government: www.vladars.net

United States BiH Embassy: www.bosnianembassy.org

World Bank Resident Mission: www.worldbank.org.ba

UN Office of the High Representative: www.ohr.int

Botswana

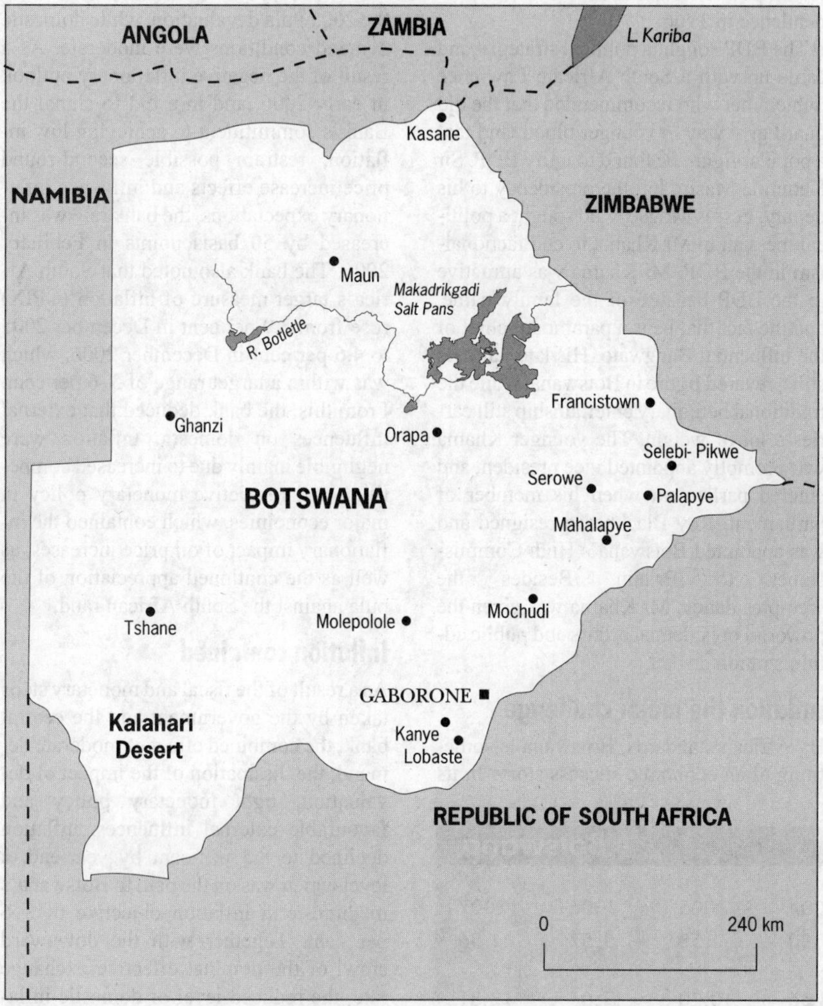

KEY FACTS

Official name: Republic of Botswana

Head of State: President Seretse Ian Khama (since 1 Apr 2008)

Head of government: President Seretse Ian Khama (since 1 Apr 2008)

Ruling party: Botswana Democratic Party (BDP) (since 1965; re-elected Oct 2004)

Area: 582,000 square km

Population: 1.56 million (2007)*

Capital: Gaborone

Official language: English (official); Setswana (national).

Currency: Pula (P) = 100 thebe

Exchange rate: P6.43 per US$ (Jul 2008)

GDP per capita: US$7,888 (2007)*

GDP real growth: 5.40% (2007)*

Labour force: 759,000 (2004)

Unemployment: 28.00% (2005)

Inflation: 7.10% (2007)*

Balance of trade: US$1.96 billion (2006)

Foreign debt: US$531.00 million (2004)

Annual FDI: US$279.00 million (2005)

* estimated figure

Botswana's fortunes have always been closely linked with those of the region as a whole. The majority Tswana people settled in the area during the great Bantu migration. Under threat of incorporation into the Boer settlements of Inner Africa, faced by economic and social destruction through white adventurers, cattle raiders, profiteers and other forerunners of European 'civilisation', the leading Tswana chiefs called for Imperial British protection and rule in 1884. A crown colony was created in the southern parts in 1885, while a protectorate was established in the north. The colony was then integrated into existing white-ruled colonies in South Africa which, (in 1910) were combined in the Union of South Africa. The protectorate remained an Imperial backwater, surviving a number of take-over attempts by its powerful neighbour. In the end Tswana resistance prevented only political integration. What was to become known until its independence as the Bechuanaland protectorate, was little more than a supplier of migrant labour. Cattle farming continued on a subsistence basis.

Khama comes

The improbably named Ian Khama took over as Botswana's fourth president on 1

April 2008. Following his appointment, most of Botswana's citizens had precious little idea about what sort of a man their new president was. Although Mr Khama has been in public life since 1977, when he became Botswana's youngest brigadier at the age of 24, he is something of a mystery. His people find it hard to relate to him for the simple reason that he rarely talks or responds to his critics. Botswana's new president is the son of the country's respected founding president, Sir Seretse Khama. Aged 55, he is a bachelor and a teetotaller. Details of his education are sketchy, but it would seem that its most important feature has been his military training at Britain's Sandhurst military academy (he insists on being addressed as Lt-General). When he became deputy commander of Botswana's fledgling army in 1977, his superior was Lt-General Mompati Merafhe, a policeman-turned-soldier (and now turned politician). Mr Merafhe, who has been Botswana's long-serving foreign minister, was appointed vice president by Mr Khama on his appointment. The future President had tken over command of the Botswana Defence Force (BDF) in 1989 when Mr Merafhe stepped aside to enter politics.

In 1998, Mr Khama was moved from the military by his political mentor and predecessor, Festus Mogae, and appointed Botswana's vice president. At the time, Mr Khama was seen as the messiah who would save the Botswana Democratic Party (BDP) from incessant infighting and an imminent rout at the 1999 general elections. In the 1994 elections, the perennially poorly-performing main opposition party, the Botswana National Front (BNF), had caused a major shock by winning 13 of the 40 elective seats. As the 1999 general elections approached, a divided BDP was facing the possibility of losing power for the first time since independence in 1966.

The BDP sought a political strategist and came up with a South African, Lawrence Schlemmer who recommended that the old guard give way to younger blood, and that a popular figure be found to unify BDP. Sir Ketumile Masire left the presidency to his deputy, Festus Mogae, who sought a political messiah in Mr Khama to end factionalism in the BDP. Mr Khama was attractive to the BDP because of the family name, and the fact that he is a paramount chief of the influential Bangwato. His late father is still a revered figure in Botswana, while the traditional hereditary chieftainship still carries a lot of weight. The younger Khama was promptly appointed vice president and entered parliament when his member of parliament, Roy Blackbeard resigned and was appointed Botswana's High Commissioner to Britain. Besides the vice-presidency, Mr Khama was given the powerful presidential affairs and public administration docket.

Inflation the major challenge

By African standards, Botswana is something of an economic success story. In its report on Botswana's economic condition in 2006, the Bank of Botswana (the central bank) noted that the rise in inflation during 2006 was a major policy challenge to the Bank's monetary policy stance. Inflation accelerated at the beginning of the year, from 11.4 per cent in December 2005 to a peak of 14.2 per cent in April 2006 due to domestic supply shocks and the effects of the 2005 Pula devaluation, while domestic demand conditions were moderate. As a result of the negative inflationary outlook in early 2006, and in a bid to signal the Bank's commitment to achieving low inflation, restrain possible second-round price increase effects and influence inflationary expectations, the bank rate was increased by 50 basis points in February 2006. The bank also noted that South Africa's target measure of inflation (CPIX) rose from 3.9 per cent in December 2005 to 4.6 per cent in December 2006, which was within a target range of 3–6 per cent. From this, the bank deduced that external influences on domestic inflation were negligible mainly due to increased competition and restrictive monetary policy in major economies, which contained the inflationary impact of oil price increases, as well as the continued appreciation of the pula against the South African rand.

Inflation contained

As a result of the fiscal and monetary steps taken by the government and the central bank, the combined effect of moderate demand, the dissipation of the impact of devaluation, tight monetary policy and favourable external influences, inflation declined to 8.5 per cent by year-end, a level which was on the path to Botswana's medium-term inflation objective of 3–6 per cent. Together with the downward crawl of the nominal effective exchange rate, the reduced level of domestic inflation and external inflationary trends, the real effective exchange rate stabilised during the year, and this contributed to the ongoing efforts to improve export competitiveness and the resultant economic diversification.

According to the World Bank, Botswana's significant development gains of the past decades are evidenced by improved social and economic infrastructure throughout the country and relatively high international rankings on governance (16 out of 212 by The Worldwide Governance Indicators), doing business (51) and economic freedom indicators (38 out of 141 by Economic Freedom of the World Index). Botswana has achieved two Millennium Development Goals (MDG's)

KEY INDICATORS **Botswana**

	Unit	2003	2004	2005	2006	2007
Population	m	1.75	1.80	1.58	1.57	*1.56
Gross domestic product (GDP)	US$bn	7.40	8.66	10.20	11.05	*12.31
GDP per capita	US$	4,554	5,740	6,438	7,021	*7,888
GDP real growth	%	5.4	5.2	6.2	3.6	*5.4
Inflation	%	10.1	6.3	8.6	11.3	*7.1
Unemployment	%	40.0	23.8	28.0	–	–
Industrial output	% change	–	7.6	3.8	0.6	–
Agricultural output	% change	–	3.1	3.8	-0.7	–
Exports (fob) (goods)	US$m	3,038.0	2,940.0	3,772.0	4,567.0	–
Imports (cif) (goods)	US$m	2,039.0	2,255.0	2,488.0	2,603.0	–
Balance of trade	US$m	999.0	685.0	1,284.0	1,964.0	–
Current account	US$m	500.0	580.0	1,565.0	1,947.0	*2,074.0
Total reserves minus gold	US$m	5,339.8	5,661.4	6,309.1	7,992.4	9,789.7
Foreign exchange	US$m	5,244.9	5,576.1	6,247.6	7,927.5	9,722.0
Exchange rate	per US$	4.92	4.40	6.18	6.18	6.50

* estimated figure

(universal access to basic education and reduced gender disparity in access to and control of productive resources) and has a strong supportive environment to achieve several more. Nevertheless, the country continues to face significant development challenges, including high social inequality (put by some indexes) at the third lowest in the world, high unemployment at around 20 per cent and growing particularly among the youth; a need for economic diversification away from diamonds; and the world's second most severe HIV/AIDS pandemic. Botswana's social indicators are weaker than those of other economies in similar income levels. In 2006 Botswana ranked 131 out of 177 countries on the Human Development Index (HDI) as the HIV/AIDS pandemic risks jeopardizing the social gains of recent decades with many key health indicators on decline. The pandemic weighs heavily on society and on the economy. There are already over 120,000 AIDS orphans in Botswana. Life expectancy has quickly fallen from 60 to a disturbing 35 years. Infant mortality is up from 45 (per 1,000 births) in 1990 to 85 in 2005. Tuberculosis is up from 236.2 (per 100,000) in 1990 to 670.2 in 2005.

Diamonds are (not) for ever

Currently industry accounts for 53 per cent of GDP (of which the diamond industry accounts for 38 per cent), followed by services (44 per cent), construction (7 per cent), manufacturing (4 per cent) and agriculture (2 per cent). While Botswana has witnessed tremendous economic growth since independence, the trend has been gradually declining. Over the past six years, GDP growth has averaged around 5 per cent and this trend is expected to continue in the medium-term. Botswana's major challenge is to diversify its economy and look for other engines of growth as the diamond led growth begins to taper off. Despite the government's effort to promote diversification, growth in the non-mineral sector has been slow lagging behind the target set in the National Development Plan 9 (2003/04–2008/09) of 5 + per cent per year.

Botswana has a gross national product (GNP) per capita estimated in mid-2007 at US$5,900. A key objective of government's fiscal policy has been to support macroeconomic stability by ensuring prudent levels of deficits and debt consistent with debt sustainability. To this end, recurrent spending, excluding health and education, has been limited by the use of non-mineral revenue sources. In recent years, government revenue has averaged around 35 per cent of GDP, with the bulk of revenue coming from minerals and the South African Customs Union (SACU). Government expenditure accounts of around 37 per cent of GDP (one-quarter of it spent on development and the rest on recurrent expenditure). While the authorities have been prudent with their policy of budget balance, there have been increases in more recent years which may not be sustainable over the long term given the anticipated decline of mining revenue over the next 15 years. The current account position is healthy, averaging a surplus of around 8 per cent over the past 6 years, on the back of strong diamond exports. Inflation, which had been on a downward trend, rose recently on the back of the devaluation of the pula and high oil prices, but the outlook remains favourable. Public debt, comprising mainly domestic debt issued to develop a domestic bond market and multilateral debt, remains low at 10 per cent of GDP, and strong years of large current account surpluses have enabled the accumulation of significant reserves, providing almost 25 months of imports at end-2006.

High unemployment persists

Botswana is a mining country and mining is never for ever. It is also a capital-intensive industry, which does not help create employment. Botswana's unemployment problem is growing, with 28 per cent official unemployment in ??????????. Even discounting a growing informal sector; there are an estimated 40 per cent of a 600,000 workforce looking for jobs. The solution has been the attempted diversification of the economy with more labour intensive manufacturing industries. The campaigns still continue, but competition from South Africa – just four driving hours down the road – inhibits success. A new approach has been to generate increased revenues from the country's diamond mines through international marketing in co-operation with, instead of by, the De Beers Diamond Trading Company (DTC). De Beers is a 50 per cent shareholder in Botswana's diamond industry. And because diamonds are not for ever, the government has encouraged an exploration and exploitation boom: copper; gold – for which a mine has opened; coal – a new power station is proposed; and methane – the energy hungry US is supporting a methane project. A new lease of life for the existing copper-nickel mines is also envisaged – new technology will eliminate the need for smelting. But there are still few new job-creating industries. There are tax packages, factory shells and a reliable supply of competent, but increasing numbers of unemployed workers up to graduate level. DIAMOND CUTTING IND?

Risk assessment

Economy	Fair
Politics	Fair
Regional stability	Fair

COUNTRY PROFILE

Historical profile

The majority Tswana people settled in the area during the great Bantu migration. Under threat of incorporation into the Boer settlements of Inner Africa and faced by economic and social destruction through white adventurers, cattle raiders, profiteers and other forerunners of European civilisation, the Tswana chiefs called for Imperial British protection and rule in 1884. A crown colony was created in the southern parts in 1885, while a protectorate was established in the north. The colony was then integrated into existing white-ruled colonies in South Africa which (in 1910) were combined in the Union of South Africa.

The protectorate, however, survived as the Bechuanaland Protectorate as a political entity separate from South Africa. Economically, the protectorate was very dependent on its larger neighbour, a fact recognised by the protectorate's inclusion in the Southern Africa Customs Union. The role assigned to the Bechuanaland Protectorate was that of supplier of migrant labour. During most of the British colonial period Bechuanaland was never given any positive social, cultural or political development. When, at a relatively late stage of de-colonisation in Africa, British rule ended, the newly created Republic of Botswana was generally regarded as an economic hostage to South Africa. Two things changed that perception: first the discovery of mineral wealth – diamonds now account for more than a third of GDP and 80 per cent of total exports – and post independence governments' determination to pursue a policy of independence from at the time white-ruled South Africa.

1885 Britain declared the country a protectorate and called it Bechuanaland, defining its modern borders.

1966 Independence for Botswana came a year after the territory's first election, which was won by Seretse Khama and his Botswana Democratic Party (BDP).

1980 On his death, Khama was succeeded by his vice president, Quett Ketumile Masire.

1984 and 1989 The ruling BDP easily won elections but was tainted by allegations of corruption.
1994 In the elections, the opposition party, Botswana National Front (BNF), took 13 seats and unseated three ministers.
1998 President Sir Quett Ketumile Masire retired from the presidency.
1999 The legislative elections were won by the BDP. The National Assembly chose Festus Mogae as president.
2001–02 The government's policy towards the San people (formerly called the Bushmen) in the Central Kalahari Game Reserve has been criticised internationally for its refusal to recognise the ownership rights of the Bushmen over the land they have lived on for at least 20,000 years. The Reserve was originally created in 1961 to constitute a refuge for the marginalised San people. However, the potential for tourism and diamonds increased the value of these marginal lands, leading the government to relocate the original inhabitants.
2003 A partnership between the government, a pharmaceutical giant and the Bill and Melinda Gates Foundation began providing free anti-retroviral drugs to the country's HIV-infected population.
2004 The pula was devalued by 7.5 per cent on 5 February. Festus Mogae won a landslide victory in October when he was elected for a second (and final) five-year term.
2008 On 1 April President Mogae resigned and Seretse Ian Khama took office. Khama is the son of the independence leader and former president, Sir Seretse Khama, and paramount chief of the Bamangwato tribe of Botswana.

Political structure

Constitution

The constitution came into effect on 30 September 1966. It enshrines a code of human rights.

The approval of a 15-member House of Chiefs is needed for some measures, but it cannot veto legislation.

Form of state

Multi-party democratic republic

The executive

The National Assembly elects a president who has executive power for a maximumu of two five-year terms. He appoints a vice president and the cabinet, over which he presides. The president is an ex-officio member of the Assembly.

National legislature

The legislature is the National Assembly, which comprises 63 members, 57 of whom are elected for five years by universal adult suffrage and four are elected by the elected assembly members. The membership is expanded every 10 years following the census.

A 15-member House of Chiefs advises on tribal and customary matters.

Legal system

Roman-Dutch law. Rural areas have customary courts.

Last elections

30 October 2004 (presidential and parliamentary)

Results: Parliamentary: the ruling Botswana Democratic Party (BDP) won with 51.7 per cent of the vote (44 seats out of 57 contested), Botswana National Front (BNF) 26.1 per cent (12 seats) and Botswana Congress Party (BCP) 16.6 per cent (one seat).

Presidential: Festus Mogae was elected in a landslide victory for a second (and final) five-year term.

Next elections

2009 (presidential and parliamentary)

Political parties

Ruling party

Botswana Democratic Party (BDP) (since 1965; re-elected Oct 2004)

Main opposition party

Coalition of Botswana National Front (BNF), Botswana Congress Party (BCP) and Botswana Alliance Movement (BAM).

Population

1.56 million (2007)*

Last census: September 2001: 1,680,863 (provisional)

Population density: Three inhabitants per square km. Urban population: 49 per cent (1995–2001).

Annual growth rate: 1.1 per cent 1994–2004 (WHO 2006)

Ethnic make-up

The Batswana, of which the largest group is the Bamangwato, comprise 79 per cent of the total population. The Kalanga 11 per cent, Basarwa (the Bushmen) 3 per cent, Kgalagadi and the rest 7 per cent.

Religions

Most of the population are Christians (about 49 per cent); other religions include various traditional beliefs, including animism, mostly in rural areas (50 per cent), and a small Muslim population.

Education

Primary education is free but with a high drop-out rate. In 2001, the gender gap in primary enrolment was 25 per cent, with net enrolment among girls remaining at only 50 per cent.

Secondary schooling starts from the age of 12 and lasts till the age of 18.

The National Policy on Education (1977) and the Revised National Policy on Education (1994) have provided the policy framework for the education system in Botswana.

The United Nations International Children's Emergency Fund's (Unicef) Girls' Education Programme has focussed on the prevention of HIV/Aids, particularly among children aged 6–15. Unicef in association with the government has been formulating primary school curricula and developing four 'model' community-based pre-schools.

Literacy rate: 79 per cent adult rate; 89 per cent youth rate (15–24) (Unesco 2005).

Compulsory years: 6 to 11 years.

Enrolment rate: 84 per cent, primary school enrolment; 10 per cent for girls and 24 per cent for boys gross enrolment for secondary schools.

Pupils per teacher: 28 in primary schools.

Health

Per capita total expenditure on health (2003) was US$375; of which per capita government spending was US$218, at the international dollar rate, (WHO 2006).

An outbreak of a polio related disease in 2006 prompted an international alert and increased vigilance in Botswana's northern border region with Namibia, Zimbabwe and Angola. Acute Flaccid Paralysis (AFP) is classed as a symptom which may lead to polio and can attack adults as well as children.

HIV/Aids

Projections by UNAids show that the impact of HIV on firms could equal 4.9 per cent of their total wage bill between 1996–2004. It also reported that Botswana was the first country to begin providing antiretroviral drugs through its public health system, courtesy of a bigger health budget and drug price reductions negotiated with pharmaceutical companies.

UNAids said in September 2003 'rampant epidemics are under way in southern Africa' including Botswana, with a national adult HIV prevalence rising higher than thought possible.

Testing for HIV has been considered by most NGOs as best done voluntarily. In Botswana the testing has been changed to routine, any test that requires a blood sample will be checked for HIV/Aids, unless the donor expressly forbids it. This change in policy was initiated in January 2004 to overcome the reluctance of people to know their status regarding the disease. The head of the Botswana Aids Treatment Programme, Dr Darkoh, points out that without knowing their status patients cannot be treated in time or effectively. He also changed the method of testing with patients attending open, rather than separate, clinics. Testing for HIV/Aids has increased from 20 per cent to 95 per cent.

The change from voluntary to regular testing has not been welcomed by all, some rights activists fear the discrimination of patients if their results become public.
HIV prevalence: 37.3 per cent aged 15–49 in 2003 (World Bank). One of the highest in the world.
Life expectancy: 40 years, 2004 (WHO 2006)
Fertility rate/Maternal mortality rate: 3.1 births per woman, 2004 (WHO 2006)
Child (under 5 years) mortality rate (per 1,000): 82 per 1,000 live births; 17 per cent of children under aged five are malnourished (World Bank).
Head of population per physician: 0.4 physician per 1,000 people, 2004 (WHO 2006)

Welfare

Botswana provides a non-contributory social pension for about 80,000 elderly citizens of 65 years and older, a flat-rate 151 Pula each month. This income has become an important source of revenue for families and communities and has had a significant impact on poverty reduction, as it alleviates the needs of more than just the elderly. Studies have shown that multi-generational households derive a 'safety-net' against economic hardship and these pensions support families where grandparents are fostering children of HIV/Aids parents. Pensioners are economically independent and valuable family members, this contradicts any perception that they may be a financial burden on their offspring.
Pensions

Main cities

Gaborone (capital, estimated population 225,656 in 2005), Francistown (98,104), Molepolole (64,327), Selebi-Phikwe (54,472), Maun (52,488), Mogoditshane (48,936), Serowe (46,839), Mahalapye (44,330)

Languages spoken

Official language/s
English (official); Setswana (national).

Media

The constitution guarantees the freedom of the press. However, since 2006 the government has been moving to enact the Mass Media Communications (MMC) bill, which journalists claim with inhibit reporting as the government-appointed press council will adjudicate complaints and recommend disciplinary sanctions where necessary.
National news agency: Bopa (Botswana Press Agency)
Press
Low circulations limit newspapers to mainly urban areas.
Dailies: There are few daily newspaper, including Daily News (www.mcst.gov.bw/dailynews) is government-owned and the private Mmegi (www.mmegi.bw).
Weeklies: Most newspapers are published weekly, including the Botswana Guardian, Botswana Gazette (www.gazette.bw), The Midweek Sun, Sunday Standard (www.sundaystandard.info) and The Voice (www.thevoicebw.com), for news and entertainment.
Business: The government-owned Daily Business is an imprint of the Daily News.
Broadcasting
Radio: Radio is the primary medium for public news and information. In English and Setswana, the national, state-run station is Radio Botswana (www.dib.gov.bw), which also operates the commercial Botswana 2 (RB2). Commercial stations include Yarona FM (www.yaronafm.co.bw), Gabz FM (www.gabzfm.com) and Duma FM.
Television: The government-owned national, public broadcaster is Botswana TV (www.btv.gov.bw). The pay-to-view, Kenyan satellite station, Prime (www.gtv.tv) provides around a dozen channels.
News agencies
National news agency: Bopa (Botswana Press Agency)

Economy

Botswana continues to live off its large diamond reserves although the IMF as warned that long-term growth is dependent on structural reforms to the economy to move it away from diamonds into other sectors such as tourism and agriculture. The main strategy should be to diversify export markets. It also highlighted, in its February 2006 report, that HIV/Aids, at levels estimated at 35 per cent of the population, had to be combated as it was undermining past achievements. In 2005, GDP growth was 3.8 per cent, a fall from the average 8.0 per cent achieved for over a decade.
Despite attempts to increase foreign involvement in non-mining sectors, through privatisation and other measures, diamonds are still a motor for the economy providing one-third of GDP, 75 per cent of export earnings and 45 per cent of government spending. In 2004 Botswana exported over 31 million carats with an estimated valued of US$2.7 billion. A further 10 per cent is provided by nickel and copper production. In recent years, the government has invested heavily in communications and water technology.
Botswana is basically an open desert about the size of France. There is little room for agricultural diversification beyond livestock rearing and the country does not have a population or domestic market that is large enough to warrant a significantly large industrial sector. There is a small but growing tourist industry, consisting mainly of affluent big game hunters. While the government is attempting to grow the tourist industry, its main attraction, lions, are fast declining.
Although Botswana's infrastructure is highly developed and therefore attractive to foreign investors, the possibility that it can compete with South Africa within the Southern African Development Community (SADC) in manufactured goods is remote, particularly given the cost of start-up and the generally higher wage rates.
A high level of unemployment, at an average 20 per cent, remains a stubborn problem, exacerbated by the rise in orphans of HIV/Aids victims. The government has led a concerted and largely successful Aids campaign, increasing the availability of antiretroviral drugs and giving financial aid to orphans.

External trade

As a member of the Southern African Customs Union (SACU) Botswana trades freely with the other members (Lesotho, Namibia, South Africa and Swaziland) and operates a common customs border with them; SACU presents a united negotiating entity to foreign traders and importers.
In June 2006, the Convention of International Trade in Endangered Species (Cites) approved the sale and export of 30 tonnes of ivory by the government of Botswana.
Imports
Principal imports are vehicles machinery, electrical and transport equipment, food products and consumer goods, chemical and rubber products, textiles and tobacco.
Main sources: (SACU (over 70 per cent), EFTA (over 15 per cent), Zimbabwe (around 5 per cent)
Exports
Principal exports are diamonds (typically 70–80 per cent of total) and copper-nickel ore, soda-ash, textiles, meat and meat products
Main destinations: European Free Trade Association (EFTA) (typically over 80 per cent,), Southern African Customs Union (SACU) (around 10 per cent), Zimbabwe (around 5 per cent)

Agriculture

Farming
The agricultural sector contributes around 3.5 per cent to GDP and employs 60 per cent of the workforce.
Production is divided between small, traditional farms and around 360 large-scale commercial units (including Barolong Farms, Pandamantenga and Tuli Block).

The climate and poor soil are suitable for extensive ranching, with the result that livestock produce accounts for about 80 per cent of marketed output. In the past, rearing of livestock has been hampered by frequent outbreaks of foot-and-mouth disease – now largely controlled – and more recently by drought. However, the livestock sector has predominated due to a lack of cultivatable land – only 5 per cent of the land is suitable for arable production – in a country which is mostly arid and contributes around 80 per cent of agriculture's share of GDP. Beef is one of the country's main exports and the Botswana Meat Commission (BMC) operates three abattoirs with a combined capacity of up to 2,000 head of cattle and smaller stock every day.

Government aims for self-sufficiency in basic foodstuffs, such as maize, millet, beans and sorghum, are far from being realised. There is potential for investment in adding value to primary products through increasing processing capacity. There is also a growing market in farm machinery, irrigation and water pumps.

Estimated crop production in 2005 included 45,250 tonnes (t) cereals in total, 32,000t sorghum, 10,000t maize, 550t wheat, 17,500t pulses, 93,000t roots and tubers, 1,100t millet, 600t citrus fruit, 3,306t oilcrops, 770t cotton lint, 10,600t fruit in total, 16,400t vegetables in total.

Estimated livestock production included 54,095t meat in total, 28,000t beef, 375t pig meat, 8,160t lamb and goat meat, 11,000t game meat, 5,360t poultry, 3,000t eggs, 105,350t milk, 3,500t cattle hides, 330t sheepskins.

Fishing

Botswana has a small freshwater fishing industry with annual average catches amounting to 2,000 tonnes.

Forestry

About 25 per cent of the total land area has forest cover. Another 20 per cent of its terrain is classified as wooded land. There are several large game reserves in the west, including the Central Kalahari Game Reserve, the largest protected area in Africa. There are no large-scale forest industries in the country. Some varieties of woods are used for fuel consumption and for the manufacture of wooden handicrafts.

Industry and manufacturing

The industrial sector as a whole contributes around 5 per cent to GDP and employs 10 per cent of the workforce.

The manufacturing sector is underdeveloped. There is a wide range of consumer products manufactured by a relatively small number of enterprises. There is also a large number of village industries, mainly producing handicrafts. The main industrial base depends on the livestock sector. Beverages, chemicals, paper, plastics and electrical goods are also produced.

The small domestic market has hampered attempts to stimulate production. Emphasis is on expansion of the export market for traditional products, such as textiles, leather goods, processed meat and import substitution.

The government is pushing for increased value-added on the country's primary goods production. The soda ash industry has helped develop the local manufacture of detergents, potash and fertilisers. The country also produces electrical components, which utilise copper and nickel production.

The government has set up the Botswana Development Corporation (BDC) in an effort to promote industrial development, particularly in sugar refining, furniture, clothing, milling, brewing, packaging and handicrafts.

Tourism

Botswana's tourism sector is being actively developed as part of a strategy to diversify the economy away from dependence on diamond mining. The sector accounts for around 5 per cent of GDP. The main attractions are the country's rich variety of wildlife and its wilderness areas. Around 40 per cent of the land is dedicated to national parks, game reserves and wildlife management areas. Long-term sustainability is a key element of development policy. Botswana has tended to cater to up-market tourists, but in order to expand the market and the variety of the attractions, eco-tourism, in which private investors collaborate with local communities, is being fostered.

Mining

Exploitation of rich mineral reserves, notably diamonds, provided the key to Botswana's rapid economic growth, with the mining sector accounting for up to 50 per cent of GDP and employing 7 per cent of the workforce. Botswana's diamond reserves are expected to last until 2030 at current production rates.

Diamonds, together with copper and nickel production, are the main focus of prospecting activities and account for most of the country's export revenue. Botswana is the largest producer of diamonds, and second-largest producer of gem diamonds, in the world, after Russia. All diamond mining is carried out by De Beers Botswana Mining Company (Debswana), a company jointly owned by the government and UK-based De Beers of South Africa. De Beers produces 60 per cent of the world's diamond output, a significant proportion of which comes from Botswana.

In November 2005 President Mogae proposed that diamonds mined in southern Africa should be sent to Botswana for processing. This would return more of the profits to the producers in the scheme, after value-added cutting and polishing had been included.

Hydrocarbons

Botswana has the largest known coal reserves in Africa: proven reserves are 17 billion tonnes, total reserves are estimated at about 50 billion tonnes, although of low quality. Coal output from the Morupule coal mine, which is mainly used in domestic power stations, has increased to around 900,000 tonnes.

There are no known domestic oil reserves; all refined petroleum products are sourced via South Africa.

Energy

Total installed electricity generating capacity (all thermal) is 220MW. Consumption per capita is estimated at 874kWh; only 22 per cent of the population have access to electricity. Electricity prices are the highest in Southern Africa and consequently demand is falling. There is potential for hydroelectric generation and solar power. Half of total primary energy requirements is met by fuelwood.

Financial markets

Stock exchange

Botswana Stock Exchange (BSE) was launched in 1989 and became a fully-fledged stock market in 1995. The Contributory Funded Pension Scheme was launched in 2000. The BSE is dominated by Barclays and Standard Chartered and is widely seen as a small but vibrant market.

In 2006 the African-owned, Pan African commodities and derivatives exchange (PACDEX Africa) was given the go-ahead by the African Union, the UN Conference on Trade and Development, the Pan African Commodities Platform and Botswana's finance ministry and services.

Banking and insurance

Of the established commercial banks, the largest is Barclays Bank of Botswana, which was launched in 1950 and has approximately 42 branches and agencies. It has 19.6 per cent local equity with the rest held by the UK's Barclays Bank. Standard Chartered Bank of Botswana has been operating in the country since 1897 and has 14 branches and four agences.

Central bank

Bank of Botswana

Main financial centre

Gaborone

Time

GMT plus two hours

Geography
Botswana is a landlocked country in southern Africa, with South Africa to the south and east, Zimbabwe to the north-east and Namibia to the west and north. A short section of the northern frontier adjoins Zambia.
Botswana is a flat, arid country, 84 per cent of which is occupied by the Kalahari sandveld. The desert occupies most of the northern, central and western regions.
There are some shallow valleys and low hills, notably the Tsodilo Hills, rising to 410m, located in the north-west. Other parts of the landscape, mainly along the south-eastern borders and the far north-west, are dotted with outcrops of rock and low hills.
There is little surface water outside the Okavango delta and the Chobe river areas in the north. The Okavango river rises in Angola and forms a 15,000km system of water channels, swamps, lagoons and islands, the largest inland delta in the world.
The majority of the population live in the south-eastern hardveld, which has a slightly higher elevation than the rest of the country. The rainfall is more reliable, but the agricultural potential remains low.
The highest point in Botswana, Otse Mountain, which reaches 1,491m, is near Lobatse. 38 per cent of the country is given over to wildlife areas and national parks, including two-thirds of the Okavango delta.

Hemisphere
Southern

Climate
Sub-tropical, with hot summers and dry winters. Temperatures range from about 5–23 degrees Celsius (C) in July to 18–31 degrees C in January.

Entry requirements
Passports
Required by all. Passports should be valid for at least 12 months.

Visa
Required by all except citizens of North America, Western Europe, Australasia and Japan, plus transit passengers. All other visitors should confirm requirements from consular sections of local embassy before travelling.
Business visas should be accompanied by letters of invitation.

Currency advice/regulations
Import and export of foreign currency is unlimited, provided it is declared on arrival.
Import of local currency is unlimited but export is restricted to P50.

Customs
Member of Southern African Customs Union, therefore virtually no restrictions on movement of goods from South Africa, Namibia, Lesotho and Swaziland.

Health (for visitors)
Mandatory precautions
Yellow fever vaccination certificate required for visitors arriving from infected areas.

Advisable precautions
hepatitis A and B, tetanus, polio and typhoid immunisations are advisable.
Anti-malarial prophylaxis is recommended for visitors to northern regions. Insect repellant is a necessary precaution. A medical examination is advisable within 10 days if bitten by insects while visiting game reserves, in case of sleeping sickness.
AIDS infection rates are high throughout the country but particularly in Francistown and Gaborone.
Food, water, swimming and bathing precautions should be observed.
Medical insurance is essential.

Hotels
First-class hotels available in all main towns. Generally advisable to book in advance – essential at weekends and during public holidays.

Credit cards
American Express, Access/MasterCard, Barclaycard/Visa, Diners.

Public holidays (national)
Fixed dates
1–3 Jan (New Year), 1 Jul (Sir Seretse Khama Day), 18–19 Jul (President's Day), 30 Sep–1 Oct (Botswana Day), 25–27 Dec (Christmas Holiday).

Variable dates
Good Friday, Easter Monday, Ascension Day, President's Day (third Tue and Wed in Jul).

Working hours
Banking
Mon–Fri: 0900–1530; Sat: 0815–1045.

Business
Mon–Fri, Apr–Oct: 0800–1300, 1400–1700; Mon–Fri, Oct–Apr: 0730–1630.

Government
Mon–Fri: 0730–1230, 1345–1630.

Shops
Mon–Fri: 0830–1300, 1400–1700; Sat: 0830–1300.

Telecommunications
Telephone/fax
Land lines connect the 12 main towns by microwave links. Botswana is directly connected to South Africa, Zimbabwe, Zambia and Namibia.

Mobile/cell phones
Mascom and Vista Cellular provide CSM 900 network, though coverage is limited to main towns.

Social customs/useful tips
A lightweight or tropical suit should be worn for meetings, casual clothes are acceptable at other times.
Most people rise early in the morning and nightlife is limited.
The noun for the people of Botswana is: singular, Motswana; plural, Batswana.

Getting there
Air
National airline: Air Botswana
International airport/s: The Sir Seretse Khama international airport (GBE) is 15km from Gabarone. Facilities include left luggage, bank, bar, restaurant, post office, shops and car hire.
There are no regular bus services to and from the airport but several hotels run minibuses
Taxis are available to the city centre.
Other airport/s: Francistown (FRW), 6km from city; Maun (MUB), Kasane (BBK) and Selebi-Phikwe (PKW).
Airport tax: US$20.

Surface
Road: Bitumised roads link Botswana with South Africa in the south, and Zambia and Zimbabwe in the north.
The Trans-Kalahari highway provides a shorter all-tarred road link between Namibia and South Africa's Gauteng province, crossing south-west Botswana, via Kanye and Ghanzi.
Botswanan border posts are at Ngoma Bridge and Shakawe. The road from Namibia, via Shakawe border post, is paved all the way to Maun.
Rail: There are good connections between South Africa and Zimbabwe with Botswana. Passengers are advised to take their own refreshments as the alternatives are limited. There are three classes, and sleeping compartments are available. First-class cars have comfortable reclining seats.
Plans to extend the network include the extension of the line into Namibia, following the construction of the Limpopo line from Zimbabwe to Mozambique.
Water: A car ferry operates across the Zambezi River to Zambia.

Getting about
National transport
Air: Air travel is the best way to get around Botswana.
Regular flights operated by Air Botswana connect Gaborone, Francistown, Maun and Kasane. Air Botswana and other operators provide direct charter flights to airstrips throughout the country.
Road: There are around 20,000km of well-developed roads, of which some 5,000km are tarred, the rest being gravelled or sand tracks.
Most major towns are connected by good roads. Travellers to Okavango should

note that the road to Maun is tarred, but it is impossible to travel further without use of an overland vehicle.

Buses: Bus services remain underdeveloped. Services run between Gaborone and Francistown, going on to Nata and Maun.

Rail: Botswana's railway system consists of 641km of main line plus three branch lines – between Morupule and Palapye, Selebi-Pikwe and Serule, and between Sua Pan and Francistown.

The main Cape Town (South Africa)-Bulawayo (Zimbabwe) railway runs for over 700km through Botswana, linking several towns. This section is operated by Botswana Railways, along with freight-only lines to Selebi-Pikwe and Sua Pan.

Botswana Railways has lost a great deal of freight business to road transporters. It has established the Gaborone Container Terminal (Gabcon), a dry port facility acting as a container terminal, specifically for locally based importers and exporters.

City transport

Taxis: Taxis are available in the capital. Tips are not common; if offered, 10 per cent would be acceptable.

Car hire

National driving licence (in English) or international driving licence, valid for six months, is required. Speed limits: 120kph on main roads, 60kph in built-up areas. Seat-belts must be worn. Facilities are available to hire Avis car in South Africa and deposit it in Botswana, or vice versa. Hire cars are only available for driving from Botswana to Zimbabwe or Zambia by special prior arrangement.

BUSINESS DIRECTORY

The addresses listed below are a selection only. While World of Information makes every endeavour to check these addresses, we cannot guarantee that changes have not been made, especially to telephone numbers and area codes. We would welcome any corrections.

Telephone area codes

The international direct dialling (IDD) code for Botswana is +267, followed by subscriber's number:

Francistown	24
Gaborone	31,35,36,39
Jwaneng	58
Kasane	62
Lobatse	53
Maun	68
Selebe-Pikwe	26

Chambers of Commerce

Botswana Chamber of Commerce and Industry, PO Box 00290, Gaborone (tel: 359-292; fax: 372-467).

Botswana Confederation of Commerce, Industry and Manpower, Boccim House, Old Lobatse Road , PO Box 432, Gaborone (tel: 353-459; fax: 373-142; e-mail: boccim@info.bw).

Francistown Chamber of Commerce and Industry, PO Box 196, Francistown (tel: 241-2149; fax: 241-2175; e-mail: boccim@info.bw).

Banking

Barclays Bank of Botswana, PO Box 478, Barclays House, Plot 8842 Khama Crescent, Gaborone (tel: 352-041; fax: 313-672).

National Development Bank, PO Box 225, Development House, Plot 1123, The Mall, Gaborone (tel: 352-801; fax: 374-446).

Standard Chartered Bank Botswana Ltd, PO Box 496, 5th Floor, Standard House, The Mall, Gaborone (tel: 360-1500, 353-111; fax: 372-933, 353-446).

Central bank

Bank of Botswana, Private Bag 154, Khama Crescent, Gaborone (tel: 360-6000; fax: 391-6000; e-mail: webmaster@bob.bw).

Travel information

Air Botswana, Sir Seretse Khama Airport, PO Box 92, Gaborone (tel: 395-2812; fax: 397-4802; commercial@airbotswana.co.bw).

Ministry of tourism

Department of Tourism, Ministry of Environment, Wildlife and Tourism, Private Bag 0047, Gaborone (tel: 395-3024; fax: 390-8675; e-mail: botswanatourism@gov.bw).

Ministries

Ministry of Agriculture, Private Bag 003, Gaborone (tel: 350-500; fax: 356-027).

Ministry of Commerce and Industry, Private Bag 004, Gaborone (tel: 360-1200; fax: 371-539).

Ministry of External Affairs, Private Bag 00368, Gaborone (tel: 360-0700; fax: 313-366).

Ministry of Finance and Development Planning, Private Bag 008, Gaborone (tel: 350-100, 355-272; fax: 356-086).

Ministry of Mineral Resources and Water Affairs, Private Bag 0018, Gaborone (tel; 352-452; fax: 372-733).

Ministry of Works, Transport and Communications, Private Bag 007, Gaborone (tel: 358-500, 355-563, 355-303; fax: 358-500, 313-303).

Office of the President, Private Bag 001, Gaborone (tel: 350-800).

Other useful addresses

Botswana Development Corporation Ltd, Private Bag 160, Gaborone (tel: 351-790; fax: 305-375).

Botswana Diamond Company (Pty) Ltd, Debswana House, The Mall, Gaborone (tel: 351-131; fax; 356-110).

Botswana Enterprise Development Unit (promotes industrial & rural development), PO Box 0014, Gaborone.

Botswana Meat Commission, Private Bag 4, Lobatse (tel: 330-321; fax: 330-530).

Botswana Power Corporation, Motlakase House, Macheng Way, PO Box 48, Gaborone (tel: 360-300; fax: 373-563).

Botswana Telecommunications Corporation, PO Box 700, Gaborone (tel: 358-000).

Botswanan Embassy (USA), Suite 7M, 3400 International Drive, NW, Washington DC 20008 (tel: 202-244-4990; fax: 202-244-4164)

Debswana Diamond Company, Gaborone (tel: 351-131; fax: 356-110).

Department of Geological Survey, Private Bag 14, Lobatse (tel: 330-0327; fax: 332-013).

Department of Information and Broadcasting, Private Bag 0060, Gaborone (tel: 365-8000, 365-3081; fax: 357-138, 301-675; e-mail: ib.publicity@info.bw).

Department of Mines, Private Bag 0049, Gaborone (tel: 352-641; fax: 352-141).

Department of Trade and Investment Promotion (TIPA), Private Bag 004, Gaborone (tel: 351-790; fax: 305-375).

Stockbrokers Botswana Ltd, Ground Floor, Barclays House, Khama Crescent, Post Bag 00417, Gaborone (tel: 357-900; fax: 357-901).

Water Utilities Corporation, Private Bag 00276, Gaborone (tel: 352-521).

National news agency: Bopa (Botswana Press Agency)

Address: (email: dailynews@gov.bw; internet: www.gov.bw/cgi-bin/news).

Internet sites

Africa Business Network: www.ifc.org/abn

AllAfrica.com: www.allafrica.com

African Development Bank: www.afdb.org

Africa Online: www.africaonline.com

Mbendi AfroPaedia (information on companies, countries, industries and stock exchanges in Africa): mbendi.co.za

Brazil

It is worth looking up the overview of the Brazilian economy published in the 1987 edition of the *Latin America and Caribbean Review* (later to become the *Americas Review*) simply to measure just how far Brazil has progressed in a 20 year period. Following a short-lived spell of optimism about the country's prospects, in 1988 all appeared to be doom and gloom. Patrick Knight, the Brazil correspondent of the two London based publications, the *Economist* and the *Times*, wrote that: 'Brazil's second complete year of democracy was marked by an intensifying political and economic crisis which even the most optimistic felt would not begin to be resolved until at least the end of 1988.' How times have changed. In 1988, Mr Knight observed that 'rumblings were being heard from the military, concerned with the failure of the civilian government to resolve the economic and political mess.' Mr Knight's article is peppered with references to what were at the time accepted as almost stereotyped Brazilian problems: 'record inflation' (which had reached an annual 225.00 per cent in 1986), 'trade deficits', 'devaluation', 'recession' and so on.

What a difference two decades make

By 2007, however, no less an authority than the World Bank was reporting that Brazil was the world's ninth economic power in terms of its GDP measured by purchasing power parity. The World Bank also noted that with the largest population in Latin America and the Caribbean, by 2006 Brazil had made important economic, social and environmental advances. Most important among these was a degree of macroeconomic stability combined with reductions in poverty and income inequality. Brazil is gradually

KEY FACTS

Official name: Republica Federativa do Brasil (Federative Republic of Brazil)

Head of State: President Luiz Inácio da Silva ('Lula') (PT) (elected 2002; re-elected 2006)

Head of government: President Luiz Inácio da Silva (since 2003)

Ruling party: Coalition government led by the Partido dos Trabalhadores (PT) (Workers' Party) (since 2002; re-elected 2006)

Area: 8,511,965 square km

Population: 189.34 million (2007)*

Capital: Brasília

Official language: Portuguese

Currency: Real (R$) (plural reais)

Exchange rate: R$1.59 per US$ (Jul 2008)

GDP per capita: US$6,938 (2007)*

GDP real growth: 5.40% (2007)

Labour force: 83.34 million (2004)

Unemployment: 11.50% (2004)

Inflation: 3.60% (2007)

Oil production: 1.83 million bpd (2007)

Balance of trade: US$44.76 billion (2005)

Foreign debt: US$219.80 billion (2004)

Visitor numbers: 5.02 million (2006)*

Annual FDI: US$15.16 billion (2005)

* estimated figure

increasing its participation in the international community, to the extent of taking a leadership role in areas such as climate change, bio-fuels and biodiversity.

Lula

President Lula da Silva's popularity is due in large measure to vastly improved conditions for Brazil's poor. The social programmes that have brought about this turn-around were initiated by the previous government, but Mr da Silva had the political nouse not only to adopt them, but to expand upon them. Wages rose in 2006 by 7.2 per cent, the biggest increase in the last decade. Having won a second term in 2006, Mr da Silva's popularity rapidly nosedived following a series of high-profile corruption cases involving members of Lula's Workers Party. Three former ministers and most of the party's leadership were charged in September 2007. Lula's current term of office ends in 2010, and he is barred by the constitution from running for a third consecutive term. Such has been Lula's success and manifest popularity, the question of who will succeed him, and whether he will make a bid for the 2014 presidency were already talking points half way through his second term.

On the international stage, Lula is acknowledged to have performed well. He is, after all, one of the few world leaders who is on equally good terms with George W Bush and president Hugo Chávez of Venezuela. That is probably because Brazil just cannot be ignored. It is the world's largest exporter of coffee, beef, sugar and orange juice. Not to mention fast expanding exports of both chicken (US$4.2 billion worth in 2007), soya. and iron ore. In his book *Forgotten Continent* author Michael Reid writes: 'If China is becoming the world's workshop, and India its back office, Brazil is its farm – and potentially its centre of environmental services.'

Growth and stability?

In sharp contrast to the hesitant economic progress of 1987, in 2007 for the first time in a generation, Brazilians enjoyed something approaching the stable economic growth and low inflation it had long sought. The World Bank notes that the economy achieved moderate growth in 2004 and 2005 which accelerated in 2006 and in 2007 largely driven, it should be added, by highly favourable external conditions. With annual inflation at around 4 per cent, Brazil's balance of payments is beginning to rack up record surpluses, creating much larger foreign exchange reserves.

However, of critical importance to Brazil is the opportunity not only to create jobs for its rapidly growing population, but also to provide the education that will enable its youth to carry out the jobs that are created. Since the nineties, according to the World Bank, Brazil has practically achieved universal basic education, with 97 per cent enrolment of children of 7 to 14 years. The Bank also reports that there has been an impressive reduction in poverty which has reached lower than ever figures. Extreme poverty, defined as income of less that a dollar a day (in purchasing power parity), has halved from 8.8 per cent to 4.2 per cent. Infant mortality declined from around 50 per 1,000 live births in 1990 to 21.1 per 1000 in 2005.

Government can't keep up

The United Nations Commission for Latin America and the Caribbean (ECLAC) goes into more detail on the Brazilian economy in its 2007 report .It opens by pointing out that Brazil's strong performance was boosted by events in the world economy, with high international and domestic demand for commodities and abundant liquidity in both private and public sectors. Lower domestic interest rates helped, too; they enabled the growth of credit in the domestic capital market. ECLAC draws attention to the constraints on economic development in the infrastructure and energy

supply sectors. ECLAC also holds the government to account for Brazil's growing tax burden and the inflexibility of public expenditure. The latter have revived the debate on the need for tax reform and the role of public investment. It is noteworthy that in the past two years, the contribution of investment to growth has been almost 10 per cent per year, although its level has not exceeded 17 per cent of GDP. Encouraged by the Programa de Aceleração do Crescimento (PAC) (Growth Acceleration Programme), the public sector once again boosted its investments, especially in the transport and energy sectors.

Again in contrast to the situation in 1987, according to ECLAC, the Brazilian economy has reduced its vulnerability to unfavourable changes in the world economy. The trade surplus and the balance of payments surpluses of recent years and the sizeable inflows of foreign capital (both in foreign direct investment (FDI) and financial flows) have led to a record level of international reserves. According to ECLAC these amount to US$176 billion, close to Brazil's reported total external debt of US$194.6 billion. Lastly, the growth of the country's economy has been focused on the domestic market,

KEY INDICATORS — **Brazil**

	Unit	2003	2004	2005	2006	2007
Population	m	177.82	181.20	184.18	*186.77	*189.34
Gross domestic product (GDP)	US$bn	492.30	604.86	882.04	1,072.36	1,313.59
GDP per capita	US$	2,774	3,417	4,789	5,742	*6,938
GDP real growth	%	0.5	5.2	2.9	3.7	5.4
Inflation	%	11.0	6.6	6.9	4.2	3.6
Unemployment	%	12.3	11.5	10.6	8.4	9.3
Industrial output	% change	–	6.2	2.7	2.7	–
Agricultural output	% change	–	5.3	2.7	4.1	–
Oil output	'000 bpd	1,552.0	1,542.0	1,718.0	1,809.0	1,833.0
Natural gas output	bn cum	10.1	11.1	11.4	11.5	11.3
Coal output	mtoe	1.9	1.6	2.4	2.4	2.2
Exports (fob) (goods)	US$m	73,084.0	96,475.0	118,308.0	127,305.0	160,649.0
Imports (cif) (goods)	US$m	48,260.0	62,782.0	73,551.0	96,835.0	120,621.0
Balance of trade	US$m	24,824.0	33,693.0	44,757.0	30,470.0	40,028.0
Current account	US$m	4,180.0	11,670.0	14,193.0	13,621.0	3,555.0
Total reserves minus gold	US$m	49,111.0	52,740.0	53,574.0	85,156.0	179,433.0
Foreign exchange	US$m	49,108.0	52,736.0	53,545.0	85,148.0	179,431.0
Exchange rate	per US$	3.18	2.92	2.14	2.15	1.78

* estimated figure

especially the expansion of industrial production and construction, as well as formal job creation. In June 2007 both Standard & Poor's and the credit rating agency Fitch upgraded Brazil to B+ from BB. The new rating brought Brazil one step closer to achieving the coveted investment grade rating.

Uncertainties over developments in the world economy and a greater increase of demand in relation to domestic supply have encouraged the Banco Central do Brasil (central bank) to take a moderate approach to monetary policy. Following a gradual decline in interest rates since September 2005 (when the Sistema Especial de Liquidação e Custodia (Selic) (Special System of Clearance and Custody) rate stood at 19.5 per cent), the central bank decided in October 2007 to stabilise the rate at 11.25 per cent. That measure cut the real yearly interest rate to about 8 per cent, which is the lowest since 2002, although high in relation to international rates. Pushed up by volatile prices for energy and some foodstuffs, the inflation rate exceeded forecasts for the second quarter. In August, the wholesale price index posted a worrying monthly variation of 1.96 per cent. This volatility partly reflected trends in the exchange rate: in early August 2007 this exceeded 2.00 reais to the dollar but by November 2007, the nominal exchange rate had fallen to almost 1.73 reais to the dollar, the lowest since March 2000 and almost 19 per cent below its level in late 2006. Consumer price inflation remained below the annual target of 4.5 per cent for 2007 showing cumulative increases of 3.3 per cent for the year and 4.1 per cent for the 12 months to October. ECLAC notes that projections for 2008 suggest that the level of inflation of around 4.1 per cent will continue, and that the nominal exchange rate will stabilise at around 1.80 reais to the dollar. Federal government spending rose by 12.4 per cent between January and October 2007. The Brazilian finance ministry lowered its forecast for the interest rate to 9.5 per cent for 2010 from a previous forecast of 10 per cent.

Benevolent economic climate

Encouragingly, higher government spending did not endanger the budget surplus target of 3.8 per cent of GDP for 2007, thanks to the financial results of sub-national governments and state-owned corporations. Thanks, too, to a generally benevolent economic climate which saw total federal government revenue in the first 10 months of 2007 rise by 15.4 per cent. Burgeoning economic activity (production and imports), unprecedented profits in banking and other businesses, and rising salaries and financial-sector gains all boosted revenue from taxes of all kinds. Revenue from social security contributions reflected the expansion of the payroll (11.5 per cent in real terms). The strong growth of receipts increased the tax burden to a new maximum of 35 per cent of GDP, calculated by Brazil's new methodology for national accounts; as a result, in the 12 months to October the primary fiscal surplus remained at 4.2 per cent of GDP and the nominal overall fiscal deficit stood at 2.2 per cent of GDP. Mining, which had performed strongly in the previous two years, is expected to post a growth rate close to 5 per cent. Civil construction achieved a growth rate of over 5.5 per cent, higher than the 2006 figure (4.6 per cent); the figure for manufacturing industry is expected to be 5.3 per cent, significantly higher than the 1.6 per cent of 2006. ECLAC reports that the investment mood is optimistic in the petroleum and mining sectors, encouraged by very favourable world prices and the availability of natural resources, as well as the recent discovery of a large oil and gas deposit. There are signs that this favourable trend may be spreading throughout the private sector.

The balance of payments was also improved by considerable inflows of foreign exchange. In the first 10 months of 2007, the overall balance of payments surplus more than tripled relative to the same period in 2006 (from US$23.1 billion to US$78 billion) and the current account surplus rose to US$6 billion (0.5 per cent of GDP), on the basis of a trade surplus of US$34.4 billion and a US$32.2 billion deficit in the services and income balance (US$30 billion in 2006). This result is much less striking than that of the first 10 months in 2006, when the surplus reached 1.3 per cent of GDP. Imports rose to US$98 billion. The capital and financial account posted a surplus (US$77.5 billion) larger than that of 2006 (US$11.8 billion), reflecting net FDI inflows (US$31.1 billion in the first nine months of 2007 compared with US$4.1 billion during the same period in 2006).

In the environmental area, the co-ordination of governmental efforts, together with favourable economic conditions, has caused Brazilian programmes against Amazon deforestation to achieve considerable success. Deforestation rates declined from approximately 25,000 square kilometres in 2002/03 to 14,000 in 2005/06, a 52 per cent reduction.

The oil's on the up...

Given the size and scale of the Brazilian economy, it is easy to overlook the fact that Brazil is one of the world's major oil producers. This is probably because oil is only a part of the vast economic machine that is Brazil, rather than its whole. According to the *Oil and Gas Journal* (OGJ), Brazil had 11.7 billion barrels of proven oil reserves in 2007, the second-largest in South America after Venezuela. The offshore Campos and Santos Basins, located on the country's south-east coast, contain the vast majority of Brazil's proven reserves. In 2006, Brazil produced 2.2 million barrels per day (bpd) of oil, of which 77 per cent was crude oil. Brazil's oil production has risen steadily in recent years, with the country's oil production in 2006 about 6 per cent (or 130,000 bpd) higher than 2005. The US Energy Information Administration (EIA) estimates that Brazil's oil consumption in 2006 averaged 2.3 million bpd. Based on its August 2007 *Short Term Energy Outlook*, the EIA forecasts Brazilian oil production to have been 2.32 million bpd in 2007 and will be 2.64 million bpd in 2008. As a result of this rising oil production, the EIA estimates that Brazil was a net oil exporter by the end of 2007. State controlled Petrobras controls over 95 per cent of the crude oil production in Brazil. This figure will be increased dramatically when the newly discovered Tupi field comes on-stream. This offshore field contains between five and eight billion barrels of oil. The announcement of its discovery caused Petrobras' shares to leap 14 per cent on the New York Stock Exchange. British gas is Petrobras' partner in the Tupi project, with a 25 per cent share. The largest oil-production region of the country is Rio de Janeiro state, which contains about 80 per cent of Brazil's total production. Most of Brazil's crude oil production is offshore in very deep water and mostly consists of heavy grades. The discovery of the Tupi field represents some 40 per cent of all the oil ever discovered in Brazil. Petrobras has expanded production in recent years and plans to spend at least a further US$39 billion on exploration and production projects in Brazil up to the year 2011. Brazil has 1.9 million bpd of crude oil refining capacity spread among 13 refineries, 11 of which are operated by Petrobras.

Brazil is also one of the largest producers of ethanol in the world, as well as its largest exporter. In 2006, Brazil produced 308,000bpd of ethanol. The EIA forecasts that Brazil's ethanol production will reach

329,000bpd in 2007 and 365,000bpd in 2008. Over half of all cars in the country are of the flex-fuel variety, meaning that they can run on 100 per cent ethanol or an ethanol-gasoline mixture. Eight in ten new cars sold in Brazil are flex-fuel vehicles. All gasoline in Brazil contains ethanol, with blending levels varying from 20–25 per cent. Ethanol in Brazil comes from sugar cane.

The OGJ reports that Brazil had 10.8 trillion cubic feet (Tcf) of proven natural gas reserves in 2007. In 2005, Brazil produced 345 billion cubic feet (Bcf) of natural gas, up 1 per cent from 2004 levels. Natural gas consumption is a small part of the country's overall energy mix, constituting only 7 per cent of total energy consumption in 2004. However, natural gas demand is rising. In 2005, Brazil consumed 660Bcf of natural gas, up 8 per cent from 2004. High oil prices have helped spur natural gas demand in Brazil: natural gas is mostly used as a substitute for fuel oil in industrial and power-generating applications, and domestic prices for natural gas are much lower than international fuel oil prices. Further, the introduction of natural gas imports has lead to a rapid growth in domestic consumption.

World Bank reservations

In surprising contrast to the generally optimistic note taken in the body of its 2007 report on Brazil, the World Bank adopts a rather more pessimistic note in covering the challenges that continue to confront Brazil. Unsurprisingly, the Bank states that 'Sustained growth is the major challenge for the Brazilian economy'. Brazil may be becoming an economic giant but, says the Bank, 'average growth has remained close to half of the global and Latin American averages'. According to the Bank, 'activity by the private sector remains stifled by various barriers and regulations that prevent the country from achieving its growth potential'. The Bank identifies economic and regulatory bottlenecks such as inadequate infrastructure, poor business climate, high tax rates, high cost of credit and still rigid labour markets. Government expenditure still accounts for about 40 per cent of GDP.

The Bank stresses that Brazil's poverty and inequality remain at high levels. Despite vastly improved educational levels there is still a long way to go: there is still a large gap in access to pre-school and secondary education (especially among the poor). Although education indicators show that enrolments in basic education are nearing 100 per cent, the frequency in pre-primary and secondary education remains low, if compared to other middle income countries. Despite apparent improvements, the educational system still suffers from poor quality at the basic and secondary levels. Brazil also experiences extreme regional differences, especially regarding health, infant mortality and nutrition.

Outlook

In early 2008 the outlook for Brazil's economy remained stable, although the continuation of prudent macroeconomic policies remains essential. Longer term economic growth is forecast at somewhere between the 2–3 per cent range, but Brazil's vast potential for economic development remains largely dependent first on the stability of the political system and second on the government to improve the regulatory climate. If investors are able to view Brazil as a stable country with a minimum of political unrest and corruption scandals then they will continue to place faith in this emerging economic power of the South.

Risk assessment

Politics	Improving
Economy	Good
Regional stability	Good

COUNTRY PROFILE

Historical profile

1500 First sighted by Portuguese mariner, Pedro Alvares Cabral. The area was claimed by the Portuguese crown.
Sugar cane plantations were started by the Portuguese, with Indian slave labour. The Indians were decimated by disease and the survivors fled to the interior. The Portuguese turned to Africa as another source of slaves.
1807 Portuguese imperial court moved to Brazil after the invasion of Portugal by Napoleon's armies and Brazil became a kingdom within the Portuguese empire.
Following Napoleon's retreat, Prince Pedro, the son of João VI, became regent of Brazil.
1822 Brazil gained independence from Portugal and Emperor Pedro became Brazil's first monarch. The immediate post-independence period was marked by minor civil wars, slave rebellions and attempts at secession, with many in the south favouring a republican form of government.
1831 Pedro I abdicated following a period of political turmoil. He was succeeded by his five-year-old son, Pedro II, under a regency.
1840 Emperor Pedro II was granted full powers as monarch at the age of 14, ending the regency period. Although his reign was characterised by stability and a move towards political liberalism, wealth was concentrated in the hands of a small feudal elite while the rest of the population remained illiterate and poor.
1850 Pedro II abolished the slave trade.
1864–70 Brazil, Argentina and Uruguay were at war with Paraguay, ending with Paraguay's defeat and ruination.
1888 Pedro II abolished slavery, leading to a revolt by the country's landed gentry.
1889 The monarchy was overthrown by a revolution led by Manuel Deodoro da Fonseca and the king was sent into exile. A federal republic was established, although ruled in the interest of coffee plantation owners.
1929 Turmoil caused by the Wall Street crash led to a military coup which installed a civilian politician, Gertulio Vargas, as president in 1930.
1937 Vargas assumed dictatorial powers and began a revolution in welfare provision and reformed laws governing industry.
1939–45 Brazil remained neutral in the Second World War, but received a large number of exiled Nazis after the defeat of Germany.
1945 Vargas was ousted in a military coup. Elections were held under a new caretaker government and a new constitution was promulgated.
1951 Vargas was narrowly elected president.
1954 Vargas committed suicide after the military gave him the option of resigning or being overthrown.
1956 Juscelino Kubitschek, a strong democrat, came to power after fresh elections. Construction of the new capital, Brasília, began.
1960 Brasília was declared the country's new capital city.
1964 João Goulart was elected president, but after months of hyperinflation leading to the country's virtual bankruptcy he was overthrown by the military. General Humberto Castello Branco was installed as president, overseeing a period of political repression and economic growth based on state-owned industries.
1974 General Ernesto Geisel became president and introduced reforms which allowed limited political activity and elections.
1982 Brazil defaulted on its foreign debt repayments, which were among the world's biggest.
1985 Tancredo Neves was elected president, but died before his inauguration. His vice-president, José Sarney, was declared president, taking over a country wracked by hyperinflation.
1986 Sarney introduced the Cruzado Plan which froze prices and wages in an effort

to control inflation. However, growing public opposition led to the abandonment of the controls thereby maintaining hyperinflation.
1988 A new constitution was promulgated, reducing presidential powers.
1989 Fernando Collor de Mello was elected president. He introduced a radical economic reform, which involved trade liberalisation, privatisation and a controversial freeze on savings and bank accounts. However, this failed to meet expectations, inflation remained high and the country defaulted on its debt repayments.
1992 Earth Summit in Rio. Collor resigned after being accused of corruption, of which he was later cleared. He was replaced by Vice President Itamar Franco.
1994 Fernando Henrique Cardoso won the presidential election. A constitutional amendment limited presidential terms to four years.
1997 The constitution was changed to allow presidents to run for a second term in office.
1998 President Cardoso was re-elected.
2000 Brazil's 500th anniversary celebrations were disrupted by protests by indigenous peoples on the issue of land reform and against the legacy of European colonialism, including genocide and the destruction of their cultures.
2001 Corruption scandals rocked the political establishment and a number of senior figures in government and Congress resigned.
2002 Luiz Inácio da Silva (known as Lula), leader of the Partido dos Trabalhadores (PT) (Workers' Party), was elected president.
2003 Lula was sworn in as president, heading a broad coalition government, led by the PT. The centrist Partido do Movimento Democratico Brasileiro (PMDB) (Democratic Movement Party) joined the coalition, ensuring a congressional majority to pass social security and tax reforms.
2004 The Moviemento dos Trabalhadores Rurais Sem Terra (MST) (Landless Workers' Movement) launched its biggest wave of farm occupations to force speedier expropriation and redistribution of unused farmland. The campaign was known as Red April. Brazil applied for a permanent seat on the UN Security Council. The country launched its first rocket into space.
2005 Allegations of corruption were made against the ruling Workers' party (PT). President Lula later made a televised apology to the nation, while denying any personal responsibility for illegal actions. A referendum was held on a proposal to ban the sale of firearms and was defeated.
2006 Elections took place for federal president, vice president and legislators (deputies and one-third of the senate) and state governors, lieutenant governors and members of state unicameral legislatures. In the first round of presidential elections the incumbent, Lula da Silva won 48.61 per cent and his nearest rival, Geraldo Alckmin, won 41.64 per cent; a successful candidate must reach 50 per cent for outright victory. In the runoff, da Silva won a second term in office with over 60 per cent of the vote.
2007 Over 1,000 people were freed from sugar cane plantations in the Amazon by Brazil's ministry of labour's anti-slavery teams. The world's largest iron ore mine in the Carajas region, operated by Compañhía Vale do Rio Doce (CVRD), reached a record 1 billion tons (972 million tonnes) of ore processed. Bolivia, Brazil and Chile agreed to build a South American highway to link the Atlantic and Pacific coasts, running from Santos in Brazil, through Bolivia, to Arica and Iquique in Chile, at an estimated cost of US$600 million.
2008 In May, a previously unknown aboriginal tribe was found in the border region of Brazil and Peru.

Political structure

Constitution

The 1988 constitution is the country's seventh charter since independence from Portugal in 1822. The federal republic consists of 26 states and one federal district (Brasília). Congress passed a constitutional amendment in 1997 allowing Fernando Henrique Cardoso to become the first president to stand for re-election.

Form of state

Federal presidential democratic republic

The executive

Executive power is exercised by the president, aided by ministers of state who are appointed by the president. The president is elected for a four-year term.
The president is also assisted by the Council of the Republic, an advisory body consisting of the vice president of the republic, the presidents of the Chamber of Deputies and the Senate, the leaders of the majority and minority in each house, the minister of justice, and six other members (two appointed by the president of the republic, two elected by the Chamber of Deputies and two elected by the Senate). These six members have a three-year term of office. The national defence council is the president's advisory body on defence matters. It consists of the vice president of the republic, the presidents of the Chamber of Deputies and the Senate, the minister of justice, ministers of the army, navy and air force, and the ministers of foreign affairs and planning.

National legislature

The Congresso Nacional consists of the Senado Federal, (federal senate) (upper house) and Câmara dos Deputados (chamber of deputies) (lower house).
The federal senate has 81 members, of which two-thirds are directly elected and one-third indirectly elected. Members are elected in rotation for eight years. The chamber of deputies has 513 members directly elected on a constituency basis for a period of four years.
All decrees must be submitted to congress. As well as fiscal and budgetary control, congress must be consulted on matters concerning payments of external debt. Congressional committees have powers of oversight on nominations to important posts proposed by the executive. The senate must approve issues of treasury bills. Constitutional amendments must be approved by a three-fifths majority of both the chambers of the Congresso Nacional.

Legal system

An 11-member Supreme Federal Tribunal is Brazil's highest judicial body. Judges are appointed by the president of the republic and approved by the Senate. It gives decisions in cases involving the president, vice president, ministers of state, members of Congress, its own members and judges of other courts. It interprets the constitution, judges disputes between the federal and state authorities, between different state authorities, between federal and state authorities and foreign governments, between different levels of the judicial system, and cases involving extradition, habeas corpus and habeas data.
The Higher Tribunal of Justice is composed of at least 33 members and gives decisions in cases involving state governors. Its members are appointed by the president and approved by the Senate. Regional federal tribunals have at least seven members, who are appointed by the president. The Higher Labour Tribunal is composed of 27 members appointed by the president and approved by the Senate. The Higher Electoral Tribunal includes at least seven judges, three from the Supreme Federal Tribunal, two elected by secret ballot from the Higher Tribunal of Justice and two appointed by the president. The labour and electoral tribunals each have regional counterparts. The Higher Military Tribunal is composed of 15 judges appointed by the president and approved by the Senate for life. Four of its judges are selected from the army, three from the navy and three from the air force. The remaining five are civilians. There is a federal court of appeal. The Federal Audit Court provides for the

administrative review of national and state accounts.

Last elections

1 October 2006 (parliamentary); 1/29 October 2006 (presidential, first and second round).

Results: Presidential: (first round) Luis Inácio (Lula) da Silva won 48.61 per cent of vote, Geraldo Alckmin won 41.64, Heloísa Helena won 6.85 per cent. Second round da Silva won 60.83 per cent, Alckmin won 39.17 per cent; turnout was 83.2 per cent.

National congress (Chamber of Deputies): the PT won 15 per cent of votes (83 seats out of 513), the PSDB won 14.6 per cent (89), the PMDB won 13.6 per cent (65), the Partido da Frente Liberal (PFL) (Liberal Front Party) won 10.9 per cent (65), the Partido Progressista (PP) won 7.1 per cent (27); all other parties won less than 7 per cent of the vote.

Federal Senate (one-third (27 seats) up for re-election): The PT won 19.2 per cent, won six seats (giving 11 seats in total, out of 81), the PSDB won 12 per cent (15), the PMDB won 12.5 (5), the PFL won 25.7 (18); all other parties won less than 6 per cent of the vote. Turnout was 83.3 per cent.

Next elections

2010 (presidential and parliamentary)

Political parties

Ruling party

Coalition government led by the Partido dos Trabalhadores (PT) (Workers' Party) (since 2002; re-elected 2006)

Main opposition party

Partido da Social Democracia Brasileira (PSDB) (Party of Brazilian Social Democracy)

Population

189.34 million (2007)*

Last census: August 2000: 169,799,170

Population density: 20 per square km.

Urban population: 82 per cent of the total population.

Annual growth rate: 1.5 per cent 1994–2004 (WHO 2006)

Ethnic make-up

European (54 per cent), mixed race (39 per cent), black (6 per cent) and Japanese (1 per cent). The major cities in the centre-south area of the country contain substantial communities of Portuguese, Italian, Lebanese and German immigrants. There are an estimated 210 indigenous groups in Amazonia, making up only 0.2 per cent of the total population of Brazil.

Religions

Catholic (90 per cent); Protestant (5 per cent). Brazil is the largest Catholic country in the world. There is freedom of worship and many other religions are represented.

Education

The investment in education amounts to 4.2 per cent of GDP.

State education is free from pre-primary level. Primary education begins at the age of seven and lasts for eight years. Secondary education, which is not compulsory, begins at the age of 15 and lasts for four years.

Primary and secondary education suffer from scarce resources. Although the initial enrolment rate is similar between the rich and the poor, the inequality is evident at later stages. Only 15 per cent of poor children compared to 80 per cent of children from the richest households complete primary school. Inequalities in budget affect enrolment patterns between those prosperous regions and the north-east where over half of rural children receive less than four years of schooling, and one-quarter of the population has had no schooling at all.

Brazil has doubled the number of students reaching their final year in secondary school but has only places for 11 per cent of them. If the country is to compete internationally it will have to increase this amount to at least 40 per cent, to match even its neighbour Argentina.

To combat the problem of lack of opportunity for poorer students in higher education, the president introduced tax concessions, in July 2004, for private universities who reserve at least 20 per cent of their places to black or native Indian students. It is expected that these tax breaks will provided places for up to 100,000 underprivileged students.

Literacy rate: 86 per cent adult rate; 94 per cent youth rate (15–24) (Unesco 2005).

Compulsory years: 7 to 14.

Pupils per teacher: 24 in primary schools.

Health

Per capita total expenditure on health (2003) was US$597; of which per capita government spending was US$270, at the international dollar rate, (WHO 2006).

In theory, medical, pharmaceutical and dental treatment is free. However, in practice the social health system is underfunded and cannot meet the growing needs of the population. Private health insurance and healthcare facilities are widely available for those who can afford them. The National Social Security and Assistance Institute for Medical Care (INAMPS) is responsible for healthcare.

HIV/Aids

The UNAID/WHO reported that an estimated 105,000 Brazilians were receiving antiretroviral drugs, through the public health system.

HIV prevalence: 0.7 per cent aged 15–49 in 2003 (World Bank)

Life expectancy: 70 years, 2004 (WHO 2006)

Fertility rate/Maternal mortality rate: 2.3 births per woman, 2004 (WHO 2006); maternal mortality 160 per 100,000 live births (World Bank).

Birth rate/Death rate: 7 deaths to 20 births per 1,000 people respectively.

Child (under 5 years) mortality rate (per 1,000): 33.0 per 1,000 live births; 6 per cent of children aged under five are malnourished (World Bank).

Welfare

Employers pay 20 per cent of the payroll into the Social Insurance Scheme to cover payments for social benefits: pensions, invalidity pensions, sickness pay, family allowances, funeral grants, maternity grants, prisoners' family pensions, widows' pensions and special pensions for workers in dangerous jobs. The state sets aside taxes to cover the costs of collection and administration. Brazil shows a highly unequal distribution of income among households and individuals in both rural and urban economies. Pensions can vary from matching the minimum wage of R$130 to the maximum of R$1,200, dependant of contributions.

The Instituto Nacional de Providencia Social (INPS) (National Social Security Institute), administers the scheme for all workers except military personnel, civil servants and agricultural workers, who are covered by a separate system.

Pensions

The retirement ages for those in urban areas are 70 and 65 for men and women respectively, with 35 years contributions; in rural areas 60 and 55 for men and women respectively, with 30 years contributions.

Main cities

Brasília, (capital, estimated population 2.1 million (m) in 2005), São Paulo (10.1m), Rio de Janeiro (6.0m), Salvador (2.6m), Belo Horizonte (2.3m), Fortaleza (2.3m), Curitiba (1.7m), Manaus (1.6m), Recife (1.5m), Belém (1.4m), Porto Alegre (1.4m), Goiânia (1.1m), Guarulhos (1.2m), Campinas (1.0m), Nova Iguaçu (1.0m).

Languages spoken

Many business people and officials speak English. Spanish, Italian, French and German are also widely spoken, especially in tourist areas. There are nearly 200 indigenous languages.

Official language/s

Portuguese

Media

The constitution guarantees freedom of the press.

Brazil is the largest media market in South America and its media is dominated by a few domestically owned conglomerates of broadcasters and publishers.

National news agency: Agencia Brazil (in Portuguese): www.agenciabrasil.gov.br

Press

There are many publications for most interest groups.

Dailies: There are around 280 daily newspapers but the difficulty of distribution has limited readership to regional centres. Nevertheless, major media conglomerates supplies news and views through privately owned news agencies to local outlets.

In Portuguese, major city newspapers include Correio Braziliense (www.correioweb.com.br/cbonline) and Tribuna do Brasil (www.tribunadobrasil.com.br) from Brazíllia, O Dia (http://odia.terra.com.br) and O Globo (http://oglobo.globo.com) from Rio de Janeiro, Folha de Sao Paulo (www.folha.uol.com.br) and O Estado de Sao Paulo (www.estado.com.br) from Sao Paulo, Correio da Bahai (www.correiodabahia.com.br) from Salvador, Super Notícia (www.supernoticia.com.br) from Belo Horizonte and O Povo (www.opovo.com.br) from Fortaleza.

Weeklies: In Portuguese, Istoé (www.terra.com.br/istoe), Veja (http://veja.abril.uol.com.br) and Época (http://revistaepoca.globo.com), are general news magazines.

In English, Brazzil Magazine (www.brazzil.com) covers general news.

Business: In Portuguese, Panorama Brazil (www.panoramabrasil.com), Prima Pagina (www.primapagina.com.br), Valor Economico (www.valoronline.com.br) and Gazeta Mercantil (www.gazetamercantil.com.br) offer a wide range of news and information. Magazines include the weekly Carta Capital (www.cartacapital.com.br) and the monthly Amanhã (www.amanha.com.br) and Banco Hoje (www.bancohoje.com.br) for banking news.

Periodicals: In Portuguese, monthly magazine include Claudia (http://claudia.abril.com.br) for women Continente Multicultural (www.continentemulticultural.com.br) for the Latin culture and (),

Popular magazines published in Portuguese include Epoca, Isto E and Veja. Brazzil is an English-language magazine covering the Brazilian economy, politics and culture.

Broadcasting

The responsiblity for radio and television broadcasting is overseen by the state body Empresa Brasileira de Radiodifusão (Radiobrás) (www.radiobras.gov.br).

Radio: There are over 2,000 radio stations, with an estimated 80 per cent of homes with access to a radio receiver. The state-run public radio network Radiobrás (www.radiobras.gov.br) operates four radio stations over AM/FM. The largest commercial network is Globo Radio (http://globoradio.globo.com), others include Radio Eldorado (www.radioeldorado.com.br), Radio Bandeirantes (http://band.com.br), Radio Cultura (www.radiocultura.com.br) is a public cultural station.

Television: The conversion to digital TV began in São Paulo in 2007 and should be completed nationwide by 2016.

The state-run public TV network Radiobrás (www.radiobras.gov.br) operates four channels including news, documentaries and indigenous and cultural programmes. Large commercial TV networks include Rede Globo (http://redeglobo.globo.com), Sistema Brasileiro de Televisao (SBT) (www.sbt.com.br), TV Record (www.rederecord.com.br) and TV Band (http://band.com.br).

There are many cable TV providers, although most are foreign-owned, domestic networks include Televisão Abril (www.tva.com.br) and Rede TV (www.redetv.com.br).

Economy

Brazil has a diverse economy, which is rated the ninth-largest in the world. The industrial base is broad, including the production of aircraft, motor vehicles, armaments and oil refining, while the agricultural sector produces a significant quantity of exports, notably coffee and soya. Poverty remains a serious problem with large income inequalities and almost a third of the country living below the poverty line. Social reform, although occurring, is taking a back seat to the priority of stabilising the macroeconomy and lowering the budget deficit.

Since the mid-1990s, Brazil has moved from a policy of import-substituting industrialisation and protectionism to one of free markets and liberalisation in a programme known as the 'Plano Real'. This was in response to a number of structural problems in the economy, namely persistent hyperinflation, high levels of external debt, low growth and an inability to adapt to adverse external situations. The government was forced to shift policy again as a result of the 1997/98 Asian financial crisis, when the government was unable to maintain the overvalued exchange rate, which had become a central part of its efforts to encourage capital inflows and reduce the current account deficit. Since 1998, the government has attempted to stabilise the economy and institute policies to initiate recovery, under the auspices of the IMF. In an effort to reduce the debt burden, the government resorted to cuts in expenditure with a reduction in social spending, freezing of public sector wages and a dramatic decrease in infrastructural investment. Such austere measures allowed the government to reduce the debt burden. In December 2005, President da Silva announced the early repayment of the outstanding US$15.5 billion of an original US$33.7 billion IMF loan. The interest rate gap between Brazilian and US Treasury bonds fell to its lowest level in eight years on the back of news of the early repayment. Having controlled inflation relatively well in recent years the central bank cut its target interest rate in October 2005 by half a percentage point, to 19 per cent a year. Brazil was voted the most investor-friendly emerging-market country in December 2005 by the Institute for International Finance. The current account deficit has been transformed in recent years on the back of an export boom, the result of China-led global growth.

The Inter-American Development Bank estimated that in 2006 migrant workers sent some US$7,373 million to their families in Brazil.

External trade

During the third summit, Heads of States of all signatory countries inaugurated the political creation of the Unión de Naciones Suramericanas (in Spanish), União das Nações Sul-Americanas (in Portuguese) (Unasur/Unasul) (Union of South American Nations). It is working to gradually unite the Mercusur trade group and the Andean Community to produce a large trading bloc. The grouping is modelled on the European Union, with a projected central bank and single currency.

Brazil is the world's largest producer of coffee, sugarcane and oranges and has the largest commercial cattle herd. With forest covering 50 per cent of the land, timber products form a large constituency of exports. Many international car manufactures have assembly plants in Brazil.

Imports

Principal imports include mineral fuels and oil products, machinery and electrical equipment.

Main sources: US (16.3 per cent total, 2006), Argentina (8.8 per cent), China (8.7 per cent).

Exports

Principal exports include vehicles and machinery, iron and steel, coffee, beef and other agricultural products, footwear and textiles.

Main destinations: US (18.0 per cent of 2006 total goods exported), Argentina (8.5 per cent), China (6.1 per cent).

Agriculture

Farming

Brazil's agricultural sector accounts for 8.8 per cent of total GDP. This figure is no higher than that in comparable countries, but the significance of Brazil's agriculture sector lies in the fact that it has not declined as a percentage of GDP as development has gathered pace. Approximately 60 million hectares of the total land mass is used for agricultural purposes with another 90 million hectares available for cultivation. Large-scale farming is concentrated in the south and south-east of Brazil.

Brazil has shown remarkable progress in agribusiness development, which includes not just farming production but also increased investment in the sale of farm machinery and processing activities.

Brazil's agribusiness offers a diversified range of products from several regions and supplies cost-effective high quality food products. It accounts for over 40 per cent of the country's total exports.

Irrigated fruit growing in the São Francisco River and the Açu River Valleys, both located in north-eastern part of Brazil has contributed to its prosperous agribusiness sector.

Major agricultural exports include coffee (the world's largest producer and exporter), sugar cane (world's largest producer) and soya beans (world's second-largest producer after US). Orange juice (supplies 85 per cent of world market for orange juice concentrates), tobacco, cocoa, cotton, butter, maize and cattle (around 10 per cent of total world trade) are also significant.

Though agriculture has performed well in recent years, the sector's growth potential continues to be held back by poor transport infrastructure. Only 10 per cent of Brazil's roads are paved.

Crop production in 2005 included 55,722,261 tonnes (t) cereals in total, 34,859,600t maize, 13,140,900t rice, 26,644,700t cassava, 2,950,990t potatoes, 5,200,840t wheat, 2,529,600t sorghum, 10,119,300t oilcrops, 6,702,760t bananas, 420,120,992t sugar cane, 3,303,530t tomatoes, 3,033,830t coconuts, 20,142,100t citrus fruit, 2,179,270t green coffee, 1,208,685t grapes, 50,195,000t soya beans, 1,418,420t pineapples, 878,651t tobacco, 213,774t cocoa beans, 3,087,010t pulses, 251,268t cashew nuts, 28,500t Brazil nuts, 97,000 natural rubber, 3,726,930t seed cotton, 1,195,500t cotton lint, 213,082t sisal, 35,423,429t fruit in total, 7,502,961t vegetables in total. Estimated livestock production included 19,919,135t meat in total, 7,774,000t beef, 3,110,000t pig meat, 116,500t lamb and goat meat, 8,895,410t poultry, 1,619,500t eggs, 23,455,000t milk, 24,500t honey, 11,000t cocoons, silk, 792,000t cattle hides.

Fishing

Brazil has a coastline of 8,500km, 12 per cent of the world's freshwater reserves and two million hectares of flooded land. The country is yet to fulfill its vast potential for marine and freshwater fishing despite efforts by the national government to promote fish as an export commodity. Brazil's annual catch is typically in the range of 980,000 metric tonnes (mt) including 505,957mt marine fish and 117,863mt shellfish.

Forestry

Brazil has vast forest areas; some 543.9 million hectares with the humid tropical areas of the Amazon forests in the north-west of the country accounting for 95 per cent of the total forested area. There are approximately five million hectares of forest plantations, the majority of which are pine and eucalyptus. However, vast areas of protected woodland land exist; 30 million hectares inclusive of state parks and national reserves.

* Estimate

Industry and manufacturing

Brazil's industrial sector is one of the most well developed in Latin America. Manufacturing contributes over 23 per cent to annual GDP and industrial goods account for up to 60 per cent of exports. Industry as a whole accounts for approximately 29 per cent of GDP and employs 20 per cent of the labour force.

Industry has relied primarily on imports of capital and intermediary goods, which are either higher quality or cheaper than domestically produced goods. This has caused balance of payments problems and depressed some sectors of industry, such as machine tools. In a drive to replace imports with domestically produced goods, the government has encouraged multinational investment in key sectors of industry. Problems arose in the pharmaceutical, biotechnology and computer industries when the government's desire for self-sufficiency caused it to ignore foreign patent rights and the payment of royalties.

Tourism

The Brazilian travel and tourism industry has developed massively in recent years and is expected to contribute US$55.1 billion of economic activity in 2005. The tourism industry accounts for 7 per cent of total employment and 7.2 per cent of the country's total GDP.

The September 2001 terrorist attacks in the US and domestic uncertainties at the beginning of the decade had severe consequences on the industry, visitor arrivals falling from a record 5,313,463 in 2000 to 3,783,400 in 2002. The government began a shake-up of the sector's administration in 2003. The tourism authority, Embratur, was redefined as an agency to market Brazil abroad and the Ministry of Tourism was established.

Investment in infrastructure and services, particularly in the north-eastern coastal area, is being pursued through the government's Tourism Development Programme (PRODETUR). Cultural and eco-tourism are being developed. Brazil has long been a destination for the world's backpackers and continues to be immensely popular at the budget end of the market.

The Brazilian airline industry underwent upheaval in 2004, with the Department of Civil Aviation (DAC) introducing a new policy of fare control, whereby the government banned the sale of airfares it considered to be too low. Despite the new DAC regulations Brazil's first budget airline GOL, established in 2001, had a very profitable year.

Embratur, the Brazilian Institute of Tourism, has launched its largest ever promotional programme, which aims to make Brazil one of the top twenty most-visited destinations by 2007. Embratur has targeted the US, EU countries and China in a bid to attract greater numbers of visitors in the future.

Environment

Around 20 per cent of the Amazon rain forest was felled between mid-1960s and 2007. The land cleared was given over to cattle and soya bean production. Illegal logging accounted for a proportion of this deforestation and in January 2008 a presidential decree made it unlawful to trade in beef and soya produced on deforested properties.

Mining

Brazil is a major mining nation, ranking twelve in the world gold production league (second in Latin America) with an annual output of 55 million tonnes. Forty tonnes is accounted for by formal mines and the remainder is generated by alluvial operations which are worked by prospectors.

The mineral potential of Brazil has not been fully assessed. Less than one-third of the country has been thoroughly prospected. The authorities are keen to exploit the country's raw material wealth and a comprehensive aerial survey has been completed by the government's National Mineral Resources Company (CPRM).

The centre of the mining industry is the state of Minas Gerais, named after the large number of gold and precious stone mines discovered in colonial times. Minas Gerais is also Brazil's main producer of mica, beryl, talc, marble, dolomite, graphite, zirconium, bauxite and nickel.

There are also large known reserves of minerals scattered throughout the country with concentrations in the state of Rio Grande do Sul (copper, lead, zinc and wolfram), Bahia (lead, barite, quartz crystal and magnesite), Amapa (manganese) and São Paulo (lead, wolfram and zinc). Brazil ranks as the world leader in production and reserves of niobium/colombium and as the world's top producer of tantalite (28 per cent of total world output). It is the second largest producer of iron ore, third largest producer of bauxite and fourth largest producer of tin. The Carajas mineral deposit contains most of these reserves.

Brazil has vast iron ore reserves, reportedly the world's sixth largest in volume, and is one of the world's leading iron ore exporters. Iron ore is produced from the Quadrilateral area of Minas Gerais in the south-east and the Carajas region in Southern Para. The privatised Companhia Vale do Rio Doce (CVRD), which operates the Carajas deposit with 67 per cent iron metal content, is one of the world's top iron ore exporters.

Brazil is also an important gold producer. Gold production has been decentralised and the market has become more accessible. Minas Gerais is Brazil's main gold producing area, accounting for 45 per cent of the sector's total exports.

Copper has been mined from two sources, the state-owned Caraiba Metals in Bahia and a small mine in Rio Grande do Sul. Production at these two sites is uneconomic. CVRD expects to initiate production from Salobo in the Carajas complex.

Hydrocarbons

Brazil is the third-largest oil producer in Latin America. Due to intensified oil exploration and development, particularly in the offshore Campos basin, and falling domestic consumption, the government is working to become self-sufficient in oil by 2006. Total proven oil reserves were 11.2 billion (as at end 2004), total oil reserves and production totalled 1.5 million barrels per day (bpd). However, with consumption estimated at 1.8 million bpd in the same year, Brazil is a net importer of oil. Much of this is crude, imported from Venezuela and Argentina. Brazil's oil refining capacity, with 13 refineries, was estimated at 1.94 million bpd in 2004. On 8 November 2007, Petrobras announced that it a new offshore oil field, Tupi, could hold between 5–8 billion barrels of recoverable light oil and reserves of natural gas. Tupi alone could represent 40 per cent of the oil reserves that Brazil has ever discovered.

Natural gas reserves totalled 330 billion cubic metres (cum), (2004). The country's largest gas fields are located in the Campos and Santos basins with Petrobrás dominating the natural gas market. Gas production was 11.1cum (2004), which satisfies about 95 per cent of Brazil's annual consumption. However as demand for natural gas is growing there is an increasing need for new pipelines.

There are two international pipelines running into Brazil from Bolivia and Argentina. Other pipelines are planned, mainly from Argentina, including the extension of the Cruz del Sur, which runs from Argentina to Uruguay. There are strong possibilities that new pipelines will be built connecting newly discovered gas fields in Bolivia. There is also a likelihood of pipelines from Venezuelan gas fields as well as Liquefied Natural Gas (LNG) imports from Trinidad and Tobago.

At 10.1 billion tonnes (2004), Brazil has the largest coal reserves in Latin America. However production was 1.6 million tonnes of oil equivalent (toe) and consumption of coal is 11.4 million toe in 2004. This means Brazil relies on imports to meet domestic demand.

Energy

Brazil has installed electric capacity of 82.5GW. Approximately 90 per cent of electricity is generated by hydropower. Brazil and Paraguay jointly run the world's largest hydroelectric complex, Itaipu on the Paraná river, which has a capacity of 12.6GW. Other electricity generation comes from coal and natural gas. The majority of the electricity imported by Brazil comes from Argentina.

Rapid growth in the demand for electricity in the 1990s was not met by similar increases in generating capacity and the country's heavy reliance on hydroelectricity became a liability.

Many blame the government's privatisation programme for the problems of underdevelopment in the energy sector. The sale of plants and transmission lines piecemeal in smaller constituent parts has arguably undermined the ability of the electricity sector to attract sufficient investment. Efforts to reduce the country's debt through expenditure cuts under the auspices of the IMF have also discouraged public investment in the electricity infrastructure. Large profits from the state-owned electricity company, Eletrobrás, have not been ploughed back into capital investment, but instead have gone towards maintaining the government's fiscal accounts in order to satisfy IMF demands. The oil and gas corporation, Petrobrás, was also prevented from investing its profits in the electricity sector, which could have bolstered gas-fired generation and helped Brazil off dependency on hydroelectricity.

Conventional thermal plants generate only 7.4 per cent of Brazil's total electricity. President Lula has expressed his administration's desire to expand hydroelectric power plants and thus the future of conventional thermal generation is unclear

Brazil has two nuclear power plants, both of which are operated by a subsidiary of Electrobras, Electronuclear. The construction of the country's third nuclear facility, Angra-3 has been slowed by political disagreements and a shortfall of funds. A final decision on the completion of the plant is expected from the Brazilian government in early 2006.

Financial markets

Stock exchange

Brazil has major stock exchanges in São Paulo and Rio de Janeiro and smaller bourses in seven other cities. The Bolsa de Valores de São Paulo (Bovespa) has usually accounted for about 60 per cent of all transactions. Together, the two major exchanges account for 90 per cent of total transactions. They both have computerised operations.

Banking and insurance

The government of President Lula da Silva, signalled its more cautious approach to bank privatisation, with the cancellation of the sale of a 17.8 per cent stake in Banco do Brasil, Latin America's largest retail bank. Less than a quarter of the banking industry in Brazil is owed by foreign institutions. The major market operators are domestic finance houses.

A new Bank of the South, with a headquarters in Venezuela, will be launched in 2008 to provide an alternative source of development funding for the participating countries. Assets of US$7 billion will underpin its operations.

Central bank

Banco Central do Brasil

Main financial centre

Rio de Janeiro and São Paulo

Time

GMT minus three hours (daylight saving GMT minus two hours): most eastern cities, São Paulo, Rio de Janeiro and Brasília

GMT minus two hours (no daylight saving): Fernando de Noronha Archipelago

GMT minus four hours (no daylight saving): Amazonas State

GMT minus five hours (no daylight saving): Acre State

Daylight saving time is determined and set locally.

Geography

Brazil borders all South American countries except Chile and Ecuador. The distance from north to south is 5,320km, and from east to west 4,328km. Brazil has

a land frontier of 15,719km and an Atlantic coastline of 7,408km.
Although Brazil's topography varies greatly, it can be divided roughly into five zones: the Amazon basin, the River Plate basin, the Guiana highlands, the Brazilian highlands and the coastal strip.
The densely forested Amazon basin covers some 40 per cent of Brazil's territory but has only one inhabitant per square km. It receives heavy rainfall and floods annually.
The River Plate basin in southern Brazil is less heavily forested. The land is higher and the climate cooler. The Guiana highlands, north of the Amazon, are part forest and part scrubland. The Brazilian highlands, lying between the Amazon and the River Plate basin, form a tableland from 300 metres to 900 metres high. There are a few mountain ranges, mostly in south-eastern Brazil.

Hemisphere
Southern

Climate
The average annual temperature increases from south to north. On the equator in the Amazon basin, average temperatures are 27 degrees Celsius (C) with no seasonal variation. From the latitude of the port of Recife to the border with Uruguay, the average temperature range is 17–19 degrees C. The two winter months in the south are June and July. Humidity is relatively high in Brazil, particularly in the Amazon basin and on the coast. The rainy seasons are January–April in the north, April–July in the north-east and November–March in the southern coastal area.

Dress codes
Suits are normally worn to business meetings, particularly in Brasília. They are also worn for formal social events and in exclusive restaurants and clubs. For other occasions smart casual clothes are suitable. Lightweight clothing is advisable for all seasons in the north and for all but the two winter months in the south, when warmer clothing is necessary. Rainproof clothing or umbrellas are necessary during the rainy seasons.

Entry requirements
Passports
Required by all, except nationals of Argentina, Chile, Paraguay and Uruguay. Must be valid for at least six months from date of entry.
Visa
Required by all, except nationals of most EU member states, South America, Israel and some other countries. It is advisable to check online or with the nearest embassy or consulate for latest details.

Currency advice/regulations
There is no restriction on the import and export of local currency. Foreign currency import is unlimited but amounts must be declared; export of foreign currency is allowed up to US$4,000. Regulations may change at short notice. International credit cards are widely used, though cash advances are only paid in local currency.

Health (for visitors)
Mandatory precautions
A yellow fever certificate is required from travellers arriving from an infected country and any of the following countries: Angola, Bolivia, Cameroon, Colombia, Democratic Republic of Congo, Ecuador, Gabon, Gambia, Ghana, Guinea Republic, Liberia, Mali, Nigeria, Peru, Sierra Leone and Sudan.
Advisable precautions
Yellow fever vaccinations are essential for visits to infected areas within Brazil; these include Mato Grosso, Rondônia and states surrounding the Amazon.
Typhoid, tetanus and hepatitis A and B vaccinations are recommended. Malaria prophylaxis is advisable for visits to Amazon regions. There is a high risk of catching dengue fever. Rabies is also a risk. Water precautions should be taken.

Hotels
Graded from one- to five-stars. Wide range available in main towns but sometimes heavily booked (especially during Carnival) and advance booking advisable. Listings available from local tourist offices. Only five-star hotels are not price controlled.
A service charge is usually included in bill; if not, a 10 per cent tip is usual.

Credit cards
Amex, Diners, Mastercard and Visa widely accepted for purchases other than fuel.

Public holidays (national)
Fixed dates
1 Jan (New Year's Day), 21 Apr (Tiradentes Day), 1 May (Labour Day), 7 Sep (Independence Day), 12 Oct (Our Lady Aparecida, Patroness of Brazil), 2 Nov (All Souls' Day), 15 Nov (Proclamation of the Republic), 25 Dec (Christmas Day).
Variable dates
Carnival (five days, Feb), Good Friday, Easter Sunday, Corpus Christi (May/Jun).

Working hours
In Rio de Janeiro and São Paulo there is no siesta break; in Brasília there is a three-hour siesta from 1200–1500.
Banking
Mon–Fri: 1000–1600.
Business
Mon–Fri: 0900–1200; 1400–1800.
Government
Mon–Fri: 0930–1800.
Shops
Mon–Fri: 0900–1830/1900, Sat: 0900–1300. Shopping centres Mon–Sat: 0900–2200.

Telecommunications
Mobile/cell phones
GSM 900 and 1800 services available in most regions of the country.

Electricity supply
127V AC (Bahia (Salvador) and Manaus); 220V AC, 60Hz (Brasília and Recife); 110/220V AC, 60Hz (Rio de Janeiro and São Paulo).
Most hotels provide 100V and 220V outlets, transformers and adaptors.

Social customs/useful tips
There is generally a relaxed attitude towards timekeeping in Rio de Janeiro and the north-east, but people are much more punctual in São Paulo and Brasília. It is the usual practice to shake hands in greeting and on departure. When invited to someone's home for a meal, a gift of flowers for the hostess is customary.

Security
The Brazilian authorities insist on extensive personal documentation. This should be carried at all times.
Brazil's big coastal cities, particularly Rio de Janeiro and those situated in the north-east, have serious crime problems. Street robberies are common and press estimates put the number of armed assaults on bus passengers in Rio alone at about 20 per day.
First-time visitors to Rio are advised to be extremely cautious in allowing strangers to engage them in conversation, especially in areas such as the Avenida Atlantica (the Copacabana sea-front) and the western suburbs. It is inadvisable to visit the Baixada Fluminense, where a murder rate of 20 deaths per day makes the district one of the most violent areas in the world.

Getting there
Air
National airline: Varig (Viação Aérea Rio Grandense, privatised in July 2006).
International airport/s: Brasilia-International (BSB), 11km from city, with duty-free shop, bar, restaurant, buffet, bank, post office, shops, hotel reservations, car hire; Rio de Janeiro Galeão-International (GIG), 15km north of city, bank, hotel, taxi, duty-free shop, restaurant; São Paulo-Cumbica (GRU) 25km north-east of city; Recife (REC).
Other airport/s: Fortaleza (FOR), Salvador-Dois de Julho (SSA), Belem-Val de Cans (BEL), Belo Horizonte-Pampulha (BHZ).

Airport tax: US$36, but should be included in ticket price.

Surface

Road: It is possible to reach Brazil by road from Argentina, Bolivia, Paraguay and Uruguay.

Rail: There are rail connections to Argentina and Uruguay.

Water: There are boats sailing along the Rio Paraguay between Asunción in Paraguay and Corumba. There are also boat services to Peru along the Amazon.

Getting about

When travelling between cities on public transport, visitors must carry passports as proof of identity is required.

National transport

Air: Regular domestic and charter flights to all main cities. Air is the main form of long-distance travel. Air taxis are available at most domestic airports. Advance booking is not necessary for shuttle flights between Rio de Janeiro and São Paulo (about one hour). Domestic flights are expensive, although safety and quality of service are good.

Road: All main centres are connected by surfaced highways, with particularly good roads in the north. Many of the local roads are in need of urgent repair. In total, around 1.6 million km of roads are supervised by the Departmento Nacional de Estradas de Rodagem (DNER).

Buses: Buses are the most popular means of transport with frequent inter-city bus services between main centres. Standards are variable although many routes are now served by modern high quality coaches. Sleeping berths (leito) are available on some routes.

Rail: State- and privately-owned railways operate limited services to most main centres throughout the country. Service is generally slower than bus and long distance travelling can be uncomfortable. Good sleeper services with restaurant cars operate between São Paulo, Rio de Janeiro and Belo Horizonte.

Water: Services on São Francisco River between Juazeiro and Pirapora and up the Amazon to Manaus. Hydrofoil service between Rio de Janeiro and Niteroi.

City transport

Taxis: Metered taxis, identified by their roof lights, are available almost everywhere in urban areas. They are inexpensive and often rudimentary. The fare is regularly adjusted according to a table posted on the inside of a rear window. In Rio de Janeiro, there are several types; these include so-called 'common' taxis (yellow with checkered stripe) and the more expensive radio taxi (white, with a red and yellow stripe). A 40 per cent surcharge operates between 2300–0600, on Sundays and public holidays. Tipping is optional.

Travellers arriving by plane are advised to use the main taxi companies which operate desks at major airports and run on a fixed-charge basis. Their cars are big and air-conditioned and although rates are more expensive than those officially charged by standard taxis, it is advisable to use them to avoid frequent exploitation of unwary travellers by individual operators.

Buses, trams & metro: Extensive services operate in all main centres. Efficient though crowded. Two types – regular and special (fresces).

Metro: Two-line service in Rio de Janeiro. Line one goes from Botafogo Station to Saenz Peña Station (Tijuca): Mon–Sat: 0600–2300. Line two cuts across the city's centre, from Estácio Station to the Maria de Graca Station: Mon–Sat: 0600–2000.

There is also a two-line network in São Paulo.

Integrated bus/metro tickets available.

Car hire

Car hire is expensive.

An international driving licence is advisable. Traffic is often congested in main cities. Petrol is of poor quality and expensive.

Service stations are rare on some roads and often close on Sundays.

BUSINESS DIRECTORY

The addresses listed below are a selection only. While World of Information makes every endeavour to check these addresses, we cannot guarantee that changes have not been made, especially to telephone numbers and area codes. We would welcome any corrections.

Telephone area codes

The international dialling code (IDD) for Brazil is +55 followed by the area code:

Belem	91	Porto Alegre	51
Belo Horizonte	31	Recife	81
Brasilia	61	Rio de Janeiro	21
Campinas	19	Salvador	71
Curitiba	41	Santos	132
Fortaleza	81	São Paulo	11
Manaus	92		

Chambers of Commerce

American Chamber of Commerce in Brazil (Rio de Janeiro), Praça Pio X 15, 20040-020 Rio de Janeiro (tel: 2203-2477; fax: 2223-0438; e-mail: achambr@amchamrio.com.br).

American Chamber of Commerce in Brazil (São Paulo), Rua da Paz 1431, Chácara Santo Antônio, 04713-001 São Paulo (tel: 5180-3804; fax: 5180-3777; e-mail: amhost@amcham.com.br).

Brazilian International Chamber of Commerce, 1.200 Rua Timbiras, 30140-060 Belo Horizonte (tel/fax: 3273-7021; e-mail: camint@camint.com.br).

British Chamber of Commerce in Brazil (Rio de Janeiro), Avenida Graça Aranha 1, Centro, 20030-002, Rio de Janeiro (tel: 2262-5926; fax: 2240-1058; e-mail: rio@britcham.com.br).

British Chamber of Commerce in Brazil (São Paulo), Rua Ferreira de Araújo 741, Pinheiros, 05428-002 São Paulo (tel: 3819-0265; fax: 3819-7908; e-mail: britcham@britcham.com.br).

Rio de Janeiro Chamber of Commerce and Industry, Rua da Assembléia 93, Centro, 20011-001 Rio de Janeiro (tel: 2532-0089; fax: 2532-1918; e-mail: chamber@ccirj.com).

São Paulo Associação Comercial, 51 Rua Boa Vista, Centro, 01014-911 São Paulo (tel: 3244-3322; fax: 3244-3355; e-mail: infocem@acsp.com.br).

Banking

Banco America do Sul, Alameda Ribeirão Preto 87, 7 andar, Zona postal 01331, PO Box 8075, São Paulo (tel: 287-7955; fax: 287-2762).

Banco Bandeirantes, Rua Boa Vista 162, 7 andar, Zona postal 01014-902, São Paulo (tel: 823-1122; fax: 239-5959).

Banco Boavista, Familia Paula Machado, Zona postal 20091-040, PO Box 1560, Rio de Janeiro (tel: 211-1711; fax: 253-9036).

Banco Bozano Simonsen, Av Rio Branco 138, Zona postal 20057, PO Box 3074, Rio de Janeiro (tel: 271-8232; fax: 271-8160).

Banco Brasileiro Iraquiano, Praça Pio X 54 Centro, Zona postal 20091, Rio de Janeiro (tel: 253-2020/ 2255; fax: 253-3498).

Banco Chase Manhattan, Rua Alvares Penteado 131, Zona postal 01012, São Paulo (tel: 345-751; fax: 239-0594).

Banco de Credito Nacional, Rua Boa Vista 208, Zona postal 01014-030, PO Box 4222, São Paulo (tel: 235-1079, 235-1118; fax: 356-892).

Banco de la Nación Argentina, Av Paulista 2319, Sobreloja, Zona postal 01311, PO Box 22-25, São Paulo (tel: 280-2674; fax: 881-4630).

Banco de la Provincia de Buenos Aires, Rua L Badaró 425, 26 andar, Zona postal 01009, São Paulo (tel: 258-8798; fax: 257-4557).

Banco de la República Oriental del Uruguay, Av Paulista 1776, 9 andar, Zona postal 01310, São Paulo (tel: 251-2699/ 2454; fax: 289-8245).

Banco de Montreal, Trav do Ouvidor 4, Zona postal 20149, Rio de Janeiro (tel: 270-209/ 0210; fax: 221-2706).

Banco do Estado de São Paulo, Praça Antonio Prado 06, 6 andar, Zona postal 01062-900, PO Box 35565, São Paulo (tel: 259-6622, 259-7722; fax: 348-523).

Banco Exterior de España, Av Paulista 1963, 1 andar, Zona postal 01311, PO Box 51623, São Paulo (tel: 251-4344; fax: 288-8015).

Banco Francés e Brasileiro, Av Paulista 1294, 12 andar, zona postal 01310-915, PO Box 8017, São Paulo (tel: 252-7163/64; fax: 283-0794).

Banco Geral do Comercio, Rua Funchai 160, 5 andar, Zona postal 04551-060, São Paulo (tel: 828-7322; fax: 828-7208).

Banco Mercantil de São Paulo, Av Paulista 1450, 9 andar, Zona postal 01310-917, PO Box 4077, São Paulo (tel: 252-2121/2228; fax: 284-3312).

Banco Mitsubishi Brasileiro, Rua Libero Badaró 6633/641, Zona postal 01009-904, PO Box 8449, São Paulo (tel: 239-5244; fax: 362-128, 362-060).

Banco Noroeste, Rua Alvares Penteado 216, 3 andar, Zona postal 010102, PO Box 8119, São Paulo (tel: 239-0844, 378-401; fax: 354-858).

Banco Real, Av Paulista 1347, 3 andar, Zona postal 01310-916, PO Box 5766, São Paulo (tel: 285-5645, 251-9796; fax: 251-9222).

Banco Region de Desenvolvimento do Extremo Sul, Rua Uruguai 155, Porto Alegre (tel: 228-9200; fax: 228-8283).

Banco Safra, Av Paulista 2100, Bela Vista, Zona postal 01310, PO Box 9139, São Paulo (tel: 251-7575; fax: 251-7211).

Banco Sogeral, Av Paulista 1355, 12 andar, Zona postal 01311-924, São Paulo (tel: 251-5533; fax: 283-1449).

Banco Sudameris Brasil, Av Paulista 1000, 14 andar, Zona postal 01310-100, PO Box 3481, São Paulo (tel: 283-9251/9260; fax: 283-9269).

Unibanco-União de Bancos Brasileiros, Av Euzébio Matoso 891, 4 andar, Zona postal 05423-901, PO Box 8185, São Paulo (tel: 817-4322; fax: 815-5084).

Central bank

Banco Central do Brasil, Setor Bancário Sul, Quadra 03, Bloco B, Edificio Sede, PO Box 08670, 70074-900 Brasília DF (tel: 3414-2401; fax: 3321-9453; e-mail: cap.secre@bcb.gov.br).

Travel information

Car Club do Brasil, Rúa Mexico 11, Rio de Janeiro 20006-900 (tel: 2533-1129; fax: 2220-2400; e-mail: viasat@carclubdobrasil.com.br).

EMBRATUR (Empresa Brasileira de Turismo), Rua Mariz e Barros 13, Rio de Janeiro 20270 (tel: 273-2212).

VARIG SA, Edif Varig, Avenida Almirante Silvio Noronha 365, 20021 Rio de Janeiro (tel: 272-5000; fax: 272-5700).

Ministry of tourism

Conselho Nacional de Turismo (CNTUR), Ministry of Infrastructure, Rua Mariz e Barros 13, 5 andar, 20270 Rio de Janeiro (tel: 273-0691).

National tourist organisation offices

Centro Brasileiro de Informação Turística (CEBITUR) (Brazilian Tourist Office), Rua Mariz e Barros 13, 6 andar, Praça da Bandeira, 20270-000 Rio de Janeiro (tel: 293-1313; fax: 273-9290).

Ministries

Ministry of Administration, Esplanada dos Ministérios, Bloco C, CEP 70046-900 Brasília-DF (tel: 224-2682; fax: 225-8927).

Ministry of Agrarian Policy, SBN Ed Palácio do Desenvolvimento, CEP 70057-900 Brasilia-DF (tel: 223-8852; fax: 226-8727).

Ministry of Agriculture, Esplanada dos Ministerios, Bloco D, 8 andar, CEO 70043-900 Brasília DF (tel: 226-5161, 226-5380; fax: 225-9046).

Ministry of the Air Force, Esplanada dos Ministérios, Bloco M, CEP 70045-900 Brasília-DF (tel: 321-5303; fax: 223-2592).

Ministry of the Armed Forces, Esplanada dos Ministérios, Bloco Q, CEP 70049-900 Brasília-DF (tel: 223-5356; fax: 321-2477).

Ministry of the Army, QG/EX, Bloco A, SMU, CEP 70630-900 Brasília-DF (tel: 315-5200, 224-2844; fax: 223-1145).

Ministry of Communications, Esplanada dos Ministerios, Bloco R, 80 andar, CEP 70040-900 Brasília DF (tel: 225-9381, 224-9723; fax: 226-3980).

Ministry of Culture, Esplanada dos Ministérios, Bloco B, CEP 70068-900 Brasília-DF (tel: 224-6064; fax: 225-9162).

Ministry of Education, Esplanada dos Ministérios, Bloco L, CEP 70047-900 Brasília-DF (tel: 321-1076; fax: 224-3618).

Ministry of Environment, Water Resources and Amazonia, Esplanada dos Ministérios, Bloco B, CEP 70068-900 Brasília-DF (tel: 322-7819; fax: 226-7101).

Ministry of External Relations, Esplanada dos Ministérios, Palácio do Itamaraty, CEP 70170-900 Brasília-DF (tel: 211-6100; fax: 223-7362).

Ministry of Finance, Esplanada dos Ministérios, Bloco P, CEP 70048-900 Brasília-DF (tel: 314-4805; fax: 322-5009).

Ministry of Health, Esplanada dos Ministérios, Bloco G, CEP 70058-900 Brasília-DF (tel: 224-5269).

Ministry of Industry, Trade and Tourism, Esplanad dos Ministerios, Bloco J, CEP 70056-900 Brasília DF (tel: 325-2001; fax: 325-2209).

Ministry of Institutional Reform, Palácio do Planalto, Praca dos Tres Poderes, CEP 70150-900 Brasília-DF (tel: 322-9619; fax: 211-1192).

Ministry of Justice, Esplanada dos Ministérios, Bloco T, Ed Sede, CEP 70064-900 Brasília-DF (tel: 226-2296; fax: 322-6817).

Ministry of Labour, Esplanada dos Ministérios, Bloco F, CEP 70056-900 Brasília-DF (tel: 226-6137; fax: 226-3577).

Ministry of Mines and Energy, Esplanada dos Ministerios, Bloco U, 70 andar, CEP 70065-900 Brasília DF (tel: 218-5447, 223-9059; fax: 225-5407).

Ministry of the Navy, Esplanada dos Ministerios, Bloco N, 20 andar, CEP 70055-900 Brasília DF (tel: 223-6858, 312-1000; fax: 312-1202).

Ministry of Planning and Budget, Esplanada dos Ministérios, Bloco K, CEP 70048-900 Brasília-DF (tel: 224-0679; fax: 225-4032).

Ministry of Science and Technology, Esplanada dos Ministérios, Bloco E, CEP 70067-900 Brasília-DF (tel: 224-4364; fax: 225-1141).

Ministry of Social Security, Esplanada dos Ministérios, Bloco F, CEP 70059-900 Brasília DF (tel: 224-5914; fax: 223-2293).

Ministry of Sport, Esplanada dos Ministérios, Bloco A, CEP 70054-900 Brasília-DF (tel: 224-5285; fax: 224-3618).

Ministry of Transport, Esplanada dos Ministerios, Bloco R, CEP 70040-900 Brasília DF (tel: 224-0185, 224-0995; fax: 226-4864).

President's Office, Palácio do Planalto, 40 andar, CEP 70150-900 Brasília-DF (tel: 211-1303, 211-1034; fax: 226-2078, 321-5804).

Other useful addresses

Associação do Comercio Exterior do Brasil (Exporters' Association), Avenida General Justo 335, Rio de Janeiro (tel: 240-5048).

Bolsa de Valores de Rio de Janeiro (Rio de Janeiro Stock Exchange), Praça 15 de Novembro 20, 2010 Rio de Janeiro (tel: 271-1001; fax: 221-2151).

Bolsa de Valores de São Paulo (São Paulo Stock Exchange), Alvares Peuteado 151, São Paulo (tel: 233-2147; fax: 233-2226).

Brazilian Embassy (USA), 3006 Massachusetts Avenue, NW, Washington DC 20008 (tel: 202-238-2700; fax 202-238-2827; e-mail: webmaster@brasilemb.org).

British Consulate-General, Praia do Flamengo 284, 22210-030 Rio de Janeiro (tel: 553-3223; fax: 553-6850).

British Embassy, Setor de Embaixadas Sul, Quadra 801, Loto 8, Conjunto K, 70408-900 Brasília DF (tel: 225-2710, 223-5357; fax: 225-1777).

Companhia Vale do Rio Doce (CVRD – State Mining Company), Avenida Graca Aranha 26, Bairro Castelo, 20005 Rio de Janeiro (tel: 272-4477).

Confederação Nacional de Agricultura (CNA – National Agriculture Federation), Brasília DF (tel: 225-3150).

Confederação Nacional da Industria (CNI – National Confederation of Industry, comprising the 21 state industry federations), Edificio Roberto Simonsen, 16 andar, 70040 Brasília DF (tel: 224-1328).

Council of the State's Reform Programme, Av Borges de Medeiros, No 1501, 7 Andar, CEP 90119-900, Porte Alegre, Rio Grande do Sul (tel: 228-2708, 334-5275; fax: 226-5893, 382-4607).

Departamento Nacional de Telecomunicaes (Dentel), Via N2, Anexo do Ministerio das Comunicações, Esplanada dos Ministerios, Bloco R, 70044 Brasília DC (tel: 223-3229).

Divisão de Feiras e Turismo-Departamento de Promocão Comercial (Organisers of Trade Fairs and Tourism), Ministerio das Relacões Exteriores, Esplanada dos Ministerios, 2 andar, 70170 Brasília (tel: 211-6644).

Fundacão Instituto Brasileiro de Geografia e Estatistica (IBGE – Brazil Institute of Geography and Statistics), Avenida Franklin Roosevelt 166, Castelo, 20021 Rio de Janeiro (tel: 220-6671).

National Department of Foreign Trade, Avenida Presidente Vargas 328, 11 andar, 20091 Rio de Janeiro (tel: 271-7504).

Petrolo Brasileiro-Petrobras Segen/Gasbol (State Oil Company), Rua General Canabarro 500, CEP 20271-201, Maracana, Rio de Janeiro (tel: 566-3733; fax: 566-5723/5299).

Rede Ferroviaria Federal (SA – Federal Railway Corporation), Praça Procopio Ferreira 86, 2221 Rio de Janeiro (tel: 223-5795).

Secretaria Especial de Desenvolvimento Industrial (Industrial Development Council), Ministerio de Desenvolvimento da Industria e Comercio, Lotes 2/5-2/8, Bloco G, 8 andar, 70070 Brasília DF (tel: 225-7556).

Superintendencia da Zona Franca de Manaus (Manaus Free Zone Authority), Rua Ministro João Gonçalves de Souza, Cidade Universitaria, Distrito Industrial, 69000 Manaus (tel: 237-3288).

US Embassy, Avenida das Naçoes, Lote 3, 70403-900 Brasília DF (tel: 321-7272; fax: 225-9136).

World Trade Centre (WTC), Av das Naçoes Unidas, 12-551, Sao Paulo (tel: 893-7113; fax: 893-7101).

National news agency: Agencia Brazil (in Portuguese): www.agenciabrasil.gov.br

Other news agencies: Agencia Estado: www.ae.com.br/institucional

Agencia Globo: www.agenciaoglobo.com.br

Folha Press (business news): www.folhapress.com.br

PR Newswire (business news): www.prnewswire.com.br

Safras e Mercado (business news): www.safras.com.br

Internet sites

Banco do Brasil: www.bancobrasil.com.br

Banco Itaú: www.itau.com.br

Brazilian Embassy in London: www.brazil.org.uk

Brazilinfo: www.brazilinfo.net

Brazil American Chamber of Commerce: www.amcham.com.br/

Brazil Statistics: www.ibge.gov.br

Brazzil (English-language magazine): www.brazzil.com

National Industry Confederation (markets and industry information): www.cni.org.br

British Virgin Islands

KEY FACTS

Official name: British Virgin Islands

Head of State: Queen Elizabeth II; represented by Governor David Pearey (sworn in 18 Apr 2006)

Head of government: Premier Ralph O'Neal (sworn in 23 Aug 2007)

Ruling party: Virgin Islands Party (VIP) (elected 20 Aug 2007)

Area: 153 square km

Population: 23,000 (2007)*

Capital: Road Town

Official language: English

Currency: US dollar (US$) = 100 cents

GDP per capita: US$16,000 (2004) (US$15,600 (2007) (BVI stats))

GDP real growth: 7.20% (2006)*

Labour force: 12,770 (2004)

Inflation: 1.90% (2005)

Visitor numbers: 784,000 (2005)

* estimated figure

COUNTRY PROFILE

Historical profile

Historical profile
1493 The islands were sighted by Columbus.
1595 Sir Francis Drake visited the channel which runs through the islands and which now bears his name.
1648 The islands were settled by the Dutch.
1666 English settlers arrived.
1672 Tortola was taken over by the English.
1872 The islands became part of the UK colony of the Leeward Islands. The British Virgin Islands (BVI) continued to come under the authority of the governor of the Leeward Islands until 1960.
1960 An appointed administrator (renamed governor in 1971) assumed responsibility for the islands.
1967 Lavity Stoutt of the Virgin Islands Party (VIP) became the first chief minister as the islands were granted internal self-government.
1995 The VIP won the elections.
1997 The National Democratic Party (NDP) was formed.
1999 The VIP was re-elected.
2002 Islanders became British citizens under the British Overseas Territories Act.
2003 The NDP won the 16 June parliamentary elections and Orlando Smith became chief minister.
2004 A review of the constitution, by the BVI Constitutional Review Commission, began.
2005 The BVI began imposing a withholding tax on EU citizens' savings. The tax is passed to the relevant EU country, although without the savers' names. The BVI government purchased the Virgin Gorda Airport for US$2.9 million. The airport will be upgraded and fully licensed to maintain the tourist interests of the territory's second most populated island.
2006 David Pearey was sworn in as governor in April.
2007 In March, a new constitution was promulgated. On 20 August, in parliamentary elections, the opposition Virgin Islands Party (VIP) won 10 seats out of 13, defeating the National Democratic Party (NDP) with two, and one independent; turnout was 62.3 per cent. Premier Ralph O'Neal was sworn in on 23 August.
2008 On 1 April, Premier O'Neal became the first locally elected leader to chair a meeting of the cabinet.

Political structure

Constitution

BVI is a British Overseas Territory with a large degree of internal self-government, based on a new constitution which was promulgated in March 2007. A ministerial system of government is enshrined. It increases the authority of the BVI government, particularly with new powers for international affairs and internal security and direct local control of police matters. Fundamental human rights for individuals were included. The prime minister has greater influence for setting cabinet agenda and a new role of cabinet secretary has been created.
The post of premier replaced the former role of chief minister.
The British monarch appoints a governor as a representative.

Form of state

British Caribbean dependency

The executive

Executive power is exercised by the governor, appointed by the British monarch, the premier and four other ministers elected by members of the house of assembly.

National legislature

The House of Assembly comprises 13 members, plus an ex-officio attorney general and a speaker of parliament. Nine members are elected to represent each district with the remaining four representing a territory-wide vote.

Legal system

The legal system is based on the English common law system with local variations. Justice is administered by the Eastern Caribbean Supreme Court. A resident puisne judge presides over the High Court, Admiralty and associated courts. There is a Court of Appeal. Final appeals go to the Privy Council in the UK.

Last elections

20 August 2007 (parliamentary)

Results: Parliamentary: Virgin Islands Party (VIP) won 10 seats (out of 13), the National Democratic Party (NDP) won two, and one independent; turnout was 62.3 per cent.

Next elections

2011 (parliamentary)

Political parties
Ruling party
Virgin Islands Party (VIP) (elected 20 Aug 2007)
Main opposition party
National Democratic Party (NDP)
Political situation

Population
27,000 (2006)*
Last census: May 2001: 20,647 (provisional)
Population density: 121 inhabitants per square km.
Annual growth rate: 3.2 per cent (2003)
Ethnic make-up
African (83 per cent), white, Indian, Asian and mixed race.
Religions
Methodist (45 per cent), Anglican (21 per cent), Church of God (7 per cent), Seventh-Day Adventist (5 per cent), Baptist (4 per cent).

Education
The education sector will receive US$46.7 million from the 2004 Budget.

Health
A national health insurance scheme is being planned. In the 2004 budget, US$37.3 million was allocated to the health and welfare sector.
Life expectancy: 76 years (estimate 2003)
Fertility rate/Maternal mortality rate: Two births per woman (2003)
Birth rate/Death rate: 15 births per 1,000 population; five deaths per 1,000 population (2003).
Child (under 5 years) mortality rate (per 1,000): 19 per 1,000 live births (2003)

Welfare
A social security scheme exists for workers between the ages of 16 and 65. The scheme covers old age pensions, disability and a survivors fund. Contributions are shared between the employer and employee, each providing 3.25 per cent of salary. Self-employed workers pay the full 6.5 per cent.

Main cities
Road Town, on Tortola island (capital, estimated population 9,100 in 2003), East End-Long Look (5,200).

Languages spoken
Official language/s
English

Media
Press
There are three local weekly newspapers including Island Sun (http://islandsun.com), BVI Beacon (www.bvibeacon.com) and the BVI Stand Point (www.vistandpoint.com).
Broadcasting
All broadcasting is private and commercial and listeners benefit from easy access to US Virgin Island media outlets.
Radio: There are four stations located on the islands and named after their call signs. Radio ZBVI (www.zbviradio.com), Isle 95, WJKC (www.isle95.com), and ZVCR (www.zvcr1069fm.com) playing island music; Zking Radio (www.zkingradio.com) is a religious broadcaster.
Television: The Virgin Islands Television Network (VITV) is privately-owned. Orbit Satellite TV (www.orbit.net) and Innovative (www.iccvi.com) cable TV, provide many channels.

Economy
The economy is dependent on tourism and the financial services sector, which is based on the large offshore banking business which contributes approximately 75 per cent to annual GDP.
Economic growth in 2005/06 was adversely effected by the sharp rise in global oil prices and the downturn in the US economy, which limited growth in tourism. Nevertheless, in 2006, GDP was estimated at 7.2 per cent, up from 5.7 per cent in 2005 and tourist numbers and company registrations remained high, stimulating the economy and allowing for an increase in public investment. Government revenues for 2006 were expected to be US$233.1 million, compared to US$254.02 million collected in 2005.
A government and private sector delegation visited the Gulf region, specifically the United Arab Emirates for the first time in April 2008. Discusions included the mutual experiences of offshore financial centres. High-level talks between representatives of BVI International Finance Centre and the BVI International Affairs Secretariat of the Office of the Premier and key figures in Dubai's financial community culminated in a private seminar. BVI officials were intent on learning about UAE's infrastructure development and education system and how BVI could benefit from its experience of growth.

External trade
The visible trade deficit is offset by tourist spending, capital inflows and by workers' remittances from overseas. BVI is an associate member of Caricom and the Organisation of Eastern Caribbean States (OECS).
Imports
Principal imports are machinery and equipment, building materials, vehicles, foodstuffs and fuel.
Main sources: US Virgin Islands, Puerto Rico, US
Exports
Principal exports are fruit, vegetables, live animals, fish, rum, gravel and sand.
Main destinations: US Virgin Islands, Puerto Rico, US

Agriculture
Farming
The agricultural sector contributes approximately 15 per cent to annual GDP. About 60 per cent of the total land area is agricultural.
Production is centred on livestock farming, fishing (langoustine, prawns), food crops (mainly fruit and vegetables) and sugar cane for rum production.
Main areas of activity are Tortola, Virgin Gorda and Jost Van Dyke.
The expansion of the tourist industry has increased the dependence on imported foodstuffs, mainly from the US.
Estimated crop production in 2005 included: 340 tonnes (t) bananas, 420t fruit in total, 25t coconuts, 3t oilcrops. Livestock production included: 266t meat in total, 139t beef, 36t goat meat, 71t lamb, 20t pig meat.

Industry and manufacturing
The industrial sector typically contributes around 10 per cent to annual GDP. Industries include construction, concrete and rum production.

Tourism
Tourism is the mainstay of the economy. The British Virgin Islands (BVI) are marketed as a quality tourist destination offering such activities as diving, yachting and boat chartering, eschewing mass-market attractions such as casinos. The infrastructure is proving inadequate to meet the demands of increasing cruise tourism.

Hydrocarbons
The British Virgin Islands do not produce coal, oil or gas. They import refined oil products, but not coal or gas.

Banking and insurance
The business and financial services sector is the largest contributor to government income, accounting for around 60 per cent of the total. There are over 500,000 International Business Corporations (IBC) incorporated in the British Virgin Islands, regulated by the Financial Services Commission (FSC). The FSC operates as an independent regulator and is responsible for domestic and offshore finance.
The seven members of the Organisation of Eastern Caribbean States (OECS), Antigua and Barbuda, Dominica, Grenada, Montserrat, St Kitts and Nevis, St Lucia and St Vincent and the Grenadines, share a common currency and central bank. The British Virgin Islands and Anguilla are associate members.

Under a new EU tax directive, introduced in July 2005 in a number of associate and dependent EU countries, the BVI imposed a withholding tax for EU citizens. The tax will be passed to the relevant EU tax department while retaining the anonymity of the saver. Withholding taxes began at 15 per cent and will rise to 35 per cent by 2011.

BVI has also agreed to supply information on tax fraud, for criminal or civil trials, and notify EU member states about additional malpractices.

Central bank

There is no central bank.

Main financial centre

Tortola

Offshore facilities

The British Virgin Islands Financial Services Commission licenses and regulates all service providers operating within the offshore sector.

Time

GMT minus four hours

Geography

At the northern end of the Leeward Islands, in the eastern Caribbean, the British Virgin Islands consist of more than 60 islands and cays, of which only 16 are inhabited. Most of the islands are mountainous and of volcanic origin; the coralline island of Anegada is the only exception of any size. They lie about 100km to the east of Puerto Rico and adjoin the US Virgin Islands.

Hemisphere

Northern

Climate

The climate is sub-tropical, with no marked seasonal variation in temperature – generally 24–30 degrees Celsius (C) during the day and 10 degrees C cooler at night. Rainfall is generally low, although the hurricane season, occuring between July–November, can produce violent, torrential downpours.

Entry requirements

Passports

Required by all

Visa

Not required by most tourists for visits up to one month, with return/onwards tickets, pre-arranged accommodation and sufficient funds for stay. Longer stays require premission from the immigration department.

Some visitors will, and business visitors may, require a visa; see www.bvitourism.com/immigration for more details.

Currency advice/regulations

No restriction on import of foreign currency but amounts should be declared. Exports limited to the amounts declared on arrival.

Health (for visitors)

Mandatory precautions

None.

Advisable precautions

Typhoid vaccinations. Dengue fever is a viral disease transmitted by mosquitoes, which are most likely to bite two hours after sunrise and two hours before sunset. Use an effective insect repellent on all exposed skin. Take water precautions.

Hotels

Expensive, but wide range available. There is a 7 per cent government tax and hotels may impose a 10 per cent service charge usually added to the bill.

Public holidays (national)

Fixed dates

1 Jan (New Year's Day), 1 Jul (Territory Day), 21 Oct (St Ursula's Day), 25–26 Dec (Christmas).

If a holiday falls at the weekend the following Monday is taken in lieu.

Variable dates

H Lavity Stoutt's birthday (first Mon in Mar), Commonwealth Day (second Mon in Mar), Good Friday, Easter Monday, Whit Monday, Queen's Official Birthday (Jun), August Festival Day (first Wed in Aug).

Working hours

Banking

Mon–Fri: 0900–1500; also Fri: 1600–1700.

Business

Mon–Fri: 0800/0900–1600/1700. Sat 0800–1200

Government

Mon–Fri: 1230–2030.

Shops

Open for longer than offices and bank and are open all day Saturday.

Telecommunications

Mobile/cell phones

GSM 900/1900 coverage throughout the islands.

Electricity supply

110 volts AC, 60Hz, using US two-pin plugs.

Getting there

Air

There are no direct North American or intercontinental flights to the islands, all major air-carriers arrive via regional hubs. There are around six air charter-hire companies operating in BVI that fly to surrounding Caribbean islands.

National airline: There is no national airline.

International airport/s: Terrance B Lettsome International Airport (EIS) on Beef Island, 15km from Road Town on Tortola. Only inter-island and intra-Caribbean flights arrive at this airport, including regular flights from Puerto Rico, US Virgin Islands and Antigua.

Airport tax: Departures tax US$20, not applicable to transit passengers.

Surface

Water: There are regular, daylignt running, ferries to and from St Thomas and St John on the US Virgin Islands.

There is a US$5 departure tax when leaving by boat and US$7 for cruise passenger leaving the islands.

Main port/s: Tortola: West End, Beef Island, Road Town; Virgin Gorda: Spanish Town, Yacht Harbour.

Getting about

National transport

Air: There are around 10 domestic air charter companies that fly between the islands.

Road: The main highway from Beef Island through Road Town to West End is surfaced. There is a bridge connecting Beef Island with Tortola. There is also a surfaced road on the northern ridge from east to west. Roads on Virgin Gorda are in variable condition.

Taxis: On Tortola taxis may be chartered by agreement.

Water: Various types of boats ply between islands. Regular ferry services operate between Road Town and West End (Tortola).

City transport

Taxis: Widely available with published fixed fares. The taxi rank in Road Town is opposite the central post office, and the Taxi Association on Wickhams Cay.

Tipping is optional. Taxis can be hired on an hourly or daily basis.

Car hire

Vehicles can be hired on Tortola and Virgin Gorda. Drivers must be aged at least 25 years and hold their own valid, national driving licence. A BVI driving permit must be obtained, for a fee – the rental company can issue this.

Driving is on the left and roads can be steep and unpaved.

BUSINESS DIRECTORY

The addresses listed below are a selection only. While World of Information makes every endeavour to check these addresses, we cannot guarantee that changes have not been made, especially to telephone numbers and area codes. We would welcome any corrections.

Telephone area codes

The international direct dialling (IDD) code for the British Virgin Islands is +1284, followed by subscriber's number.

Chambers of Commerce

BVI Chamber of Commerce and Hotel Association, James Frett Building, PO Box

376, Road Town, Tortola (tel: 494-3514; fax 494-6179; e-mail: bviccha@surfbvi.com).

Banking

Banco Popular de Puerto Rico, PO Box 67, Road Town, Tortola (tel: 494-2117; fax: 494-5294).

Bank of Nova Scotia, PO Box 434, Road Town, Tortola (tel: 494-2526; fax: 494-4657).

Barclays Bank International, PO Box 70, Road Town, Tortola (tel: 494-2171; fax: 494-4315).

Chase Manhattan Bank, PO Box 435, Road Town, Tortola (tel: 494-2662; fax: 494-3863).

CITCO Ban (BVI) Ltd, PO Box 662, Road Town, Tortola (tel: 494-2217; fax: 494-3917).

Crorebridge Bank, PO Box 71, Road Town, Tortola (tel: 494-2233; fax: 494-3547).

Disa Bank BVI, PO Box 985, Road Town, Tortola (tel: 494-4977; fax: 494-4980).

Guyerzeller Bank, PO Box 3162, Road Town, Tortola (tel: 494-5414; fax: 494-5417).

London International Bank and Trust Company, PO Box 3151, Road Town, Tortola (tel: 494-3045; fax: 494-3050).

Rathbone Bank, PO Box 986, Road Town, Tortola (tel: 494-6544; fax: 494-6532).

The Bank of East Asia, PO Box 901, Road Town, Tortola (tel: 495-5588; fax: 494-4513).

United Chinese Bank, PO Box 901, Road Town, Tortola (tel: 494-6775; fax: 494-8180).

VP Bank, PO Box 3463, Road Town, Tortola (tel: 494-1100; fax: 494-1199).

Travel information

Air Sunshine Inc (tel: 495-8900; email: EMail@AirSunshine.com).

Caribbean Wings (tel: 495-6000; email: carwings@yahoo.com).

Fly BVI Ltd, PO Box 3347, Roadtown (tel: 495-1747; fax: 495-1973; email: info@fly-bvi.com).

Island Birds, PO Box 993 Road Town, Tortola; Beef Island Airport (tel: 495-2002; email: info@islandbirds.com).

Island Helicopters International Ltd, PO Box 2900, East End; Beef Island Airport, Tortola (tel: 495-2538; (emergency medical transfers, tel: 499-2663); internet: info@helicoptersbvi.com; internet: www.helicoptersbvi.com).

National tourist organisation offices

BVI Tourist Board, Joshua Smith Building, PO Box 134, Road Town, Tortola (tel: 43-134; fax: 43-866; internet: www.bvitourism.com).

Ministries

Governor's Office, Government House, PO Box 702, Road Town, Tortola (tel: 494-2345, 494-2370, 494-3520; fax: 468-4490).

Other useful addresses

BVI Hotel and Commerce Association, PO Box 376, Wickhams Cay, Road Town, Tortola (tel: 43-514, 42-947; fax: 46-179).

BVI Financial Services Commission, Pasea Estate, Road Town, Tortola (tel: 494-4190; fax: 494-9399; e-mail: commissioner@bvifsc.vg; internet site: http://www.bvi.org).

BVI Offshore Financial Centre, Financial Services Department, Ministry of Finance, Pasea Estate, Road Town, Tortola (tel: 494-6430; fax: 494-5016; internet site: http://www.bvi.org).

Cable and Wireless (West Indies), PO Box 440, Road Town, Tortola (tel: 44-444; fax: 42-506).

Immigration Department, Road Town, Tortola (tel: 494-3701, 494-3471; fax: 494-4399).

Trade and Investment Promotion, Trade Department, Central Administration Complex, Road Town, Tortola (tel: 494-3701; fax: 494-5676).

VITV (Virgin Islands Television) Network, Butu Mountain, PO Box 118, Road Town, Tortola (tel: 494-8488/2257; fax: 494-5323).

ZBVI Radio, PO Box 78, Road Town, Tortola (tel: 494-2250; fax: 494-1139).

ZRODFM (radio station), PO Box 992, Road Town, Tortola (tel: 494-1037/5832; fax: 494-4564).

Other news agencies: Caribbean Net News: www.caribbeannetnews.com

Internet sites

BVI homepage: www.britishvirginislands.com

Caribbean Wings - BVI Airlines: www.bvi-airlines.com

Islands on-line: www.islandsonline.com

The Island Sun: www.islandsun.com

Brunei

KEY FACTS

Official name: Negara Brunei Darussalam (The Sultanate of Brunei)

Head of State: Sultan Haji Hassanal Bolkiah Mu'izzaddin Waddaulah, the Sultan and Yang Di-Pertuan of Brunei Darussalam (crowned Aug 1967)

Head of government: Sultan Haji Hassanal Bolkiah Mu'izzaddin Waddaulah, the Sultan and Yang Di-Pertuan of Brunei Darussalam

Ruling party: There is no ruling party.

Area: 5,765 square km

Population: 385,000 (2007)*

Capital: Bandar Seri Begawan

Official language: Behasa Melayu

Currency: Brunei dollar (B$) = 100 cents

Exchange rate: B$1.35 per US$ (Jul 2008) (the Brunei dollar is set at parity with the Singapore dollar.)

GDP per capita: US$32,167 (2007)*

GDP real growth: 0.40% (2007)*

Labour force: 169,000 (2004)

Unemployment: 4.80% (2004)

Inflation: 0.40% (2007)*

Oil production: 194,000 bpd (2007)

Balance of trade: US$2.87 billion (2004)

* estimated figure

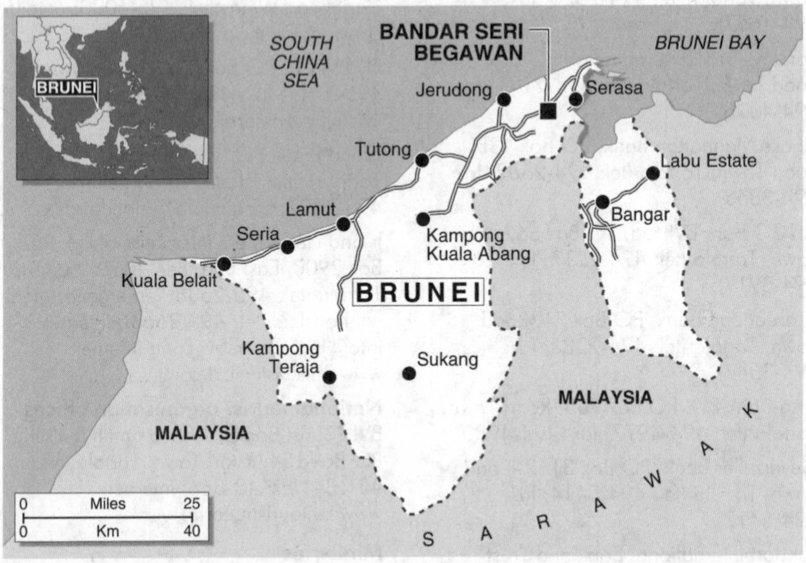

The miniscule state of Brunei comprises two territorial enclaves on the northern coast of the island of Borneo, linked only by the sea and surrounded on the landward sides by the Malaysian state of Sarawak. Brunei's recorded history dates back to Magellan's visit on his return from the Philippines in 1521. Brunei was then the centre of a powerful empire stretching and retaining influence from Sarawak as far north as Manila. Brunei's sea power dominated the southern part of the South China Sea. That power began to decline, however, and during the nineteenth century the much reduced territory controlled by the state was further eroded by the so-called White Rajahs of Sarawak and the British North Borneo Company in what is now the Malaysian state of Sabah. Having enjoyed treaty links with Britain since 1847, at the end of the nineteenth century Brunei became a British protectorate.

Don't mention the rebellion

In 1962 a rebellion came very close to unseating the Sultan, Sir Omar Ali Saifuddin. The uprising was put down by British troops flown in from Singapore. Partly as a result of the rebellion, Brunei did not join the Federation of Malaysia when it was created in 1963. Sultan Omar Ali abdicated in favour of his eldest son, Sultan Haji Hassanal Bolkiah Mu'izzaddin Waddaulah. Brunei eventually gained full independence from Britain in 1984. Brunei's government was restructured into a formal ministerial system with the Sultan at its head as prime minister. The Sultan also serves as minister of defence and minister of finance. He is advised by and presides over four policy councils: the religious council, the privy council, the council of cabinet ministers and the legislative council. Sultan Hassanal Bolkiah reconvened the Brunei Legislative Council on 25 September 2004 with 30 appointed members, including the Sultan and cabinet ministers. In 2004 amendments to the constitution provide for an expanded council of up to forty five members, with the long-term possibility of fifteen elected members from Brunei's four districts. In May 2005, the Sultan announced a major cabinet reshuffle as well as the creation of a new ministry, the ministry of energy. The Crown Prince, Prince Haji Al-Muhtadee Billah, now holds the position of senior minister at the prime minister's office. The eleven other ministers in the cabinet are from outside the royal family. There are several political parties in Brunei, the most visible of which is the Parti Pembangunan

Bangsap (NDP) (National Development Party).

Modest growth

The International Monetary Fund (IMF) estimates that Brunei's annual GDP grew by 3.7 per cent in 2006 to US$11.4 billion. GDP was estimated to have grown by 2.6 per cent, to US$12.03 billion in 2007. The IMF expected GDP to reach US$12.5 billion in 2008. GDP per capita was estimated to be US$30,415 in 2006, the highest in south-east Asia. Goods exports accounted for 65.6 per cent of GDP in 2005. None the less, growth has been largely driven by consistently high global oil prices and the strong demand from neighbouring Asian economies. In 2006, the rate of unemployment was 4 per cent and the annual rate of inflation was a lowly 0.5 per cent. Brunei's economy enjoyed moderate growth in the mid-2000s, again primarily due to rising world oil and gas prices. At 3.7 per cent GDP growth in 2006, Brunei had the lowest annual growth rate of any Association of South East Asian Nations (Asean) member nation. Weak oil prices, the East Asian financial crisis, and the collapse of the Amedeo Development Corporation had all contributed to very low growth rates in the late 1990s and early 2000s. Small scale manufacturers (mainly textiles and furniture) and primary production (including agriculture, forestry and fisheries) constitute the rest of Brunei's merchandise economy. Brunei imports nearly all of its major manufactured products and approximately 80 per cent of its total food requirements. There is a low tariff regime and no capital gains or personal income tax, although private businesses pay company tax. Brunei operates a currency board system and has no central bank, with the Brunei dollar (B$) being tied at parity with the Singapore dollar. Both currencies are legal tender in Brunei and Singapore.

For some years the government has been seeking to diversify the economy away from oil and gas as the primary source of revenue and economic activity by promoting private sector development in other industry sectors. The creation of the Brunei Economic Development Board (BEDB) in November 2001 was to stimulate the growth, expansion and development of the economy by promoting Brunei as an investment destination. Brunei is also one of four participants in the Brunei, Indonesia, Malaysia, Philippines – East Asean Growth Area (BIMP-EAGA). The objective of BIMP-EAGA is to secure enhanced growth and development in this sub-region of Asean. On 25 November 2004 the Northern Territory's observer status in BIMP-EAGA was upgraded to that of Development Partner.

Brunei's economy is inevitably vulnerable to the movements in global oil prices. These make it difficult to predict long-term prospects. The government has sought in the past decade to diversify the economy, with limited success. Oil and gas and government spending still account for most of Brunei's economic activity. Brunei's non-petroleum industries include agriculture, forestry, fishing, aquaculture, and banking. The garment-for-export industry has been shrinking since the US eliminated its garment quota system (the Multi-Fibre Agreement) at the end of 2004. The BEBD announced plans in 2003 to use proven gas reserves to establish downstream industrial projects. In 2006, the Brunei Methanol Company, a joint venture between Petroleum Brunei, Mitsubishi, and Itochu, was established. Initial construction on a US$400 million methanol plant, fed by natural gas, was started in 2007 and the plant is expected to come on line in 2010. The government plans to build a power plant in the Sungai Liang region to power a proposed aluminium smelting plant that will depend on foreign investors. A second major project depending on foreign investment is in the planning stage: a giant container hub at the Muara Port facilities.

The government regulates strictly the immigration of foreign labour out of concern it might disrupt Brunei's society. Work permits for foreigners are issued only for short periods and must be continually renewed. Despite these restrictions, the estimated 100,000 foreign temporary residents of Brunei make up a significant portion of the work force. The government reported a total work force of 180,400 in 2006, with a derived unemployment rate of 4.0 per cent.

Brunei's massive foreign reserves are managed by the Brunei Investment Agency (BIA), which is an arm of the ministry of finance. The BIA's guiding principle is to increase the real value of Brunei's foreign reserves while pursuing a diverse investment strategy, with holdings in the United States, Japan, Western Europe and the Asean countries.

The Brunei government seeks to encourage foreign investment. New enterprises that meet certain criteria are given pioneer status, exempting profits from income tax for up to five years, depending on the amount of capital invested. The normal rate of corporate income tax is 30 per cent.

The oil is declining...

Oil is the mainspring of the economy. Although small, Brunei is still the fourth-largest oil producer in south-east Asia, averaging an estimated 219,000 barrels per day (bpd) in 2006. Significantly, Brunei is also the world's ninth-largest exporter of liquefied natural gas (LNG). Like many oil producing countries, Brunei's economy has followed the swings of the world oil market. Economic growth averaged around 2.8 per cent in the

KEY INDICATORS — Brunei

	Unit	2003	2004	2005	2006	2007
Population	m	0.37	0.37	0.37	0.38	*0.39
Gross domestic product (GDP)	US$bn	4.50	5.20	9.53	11.56	*12.39
GDP per capita	US$	12,335	15,612	25,754	30,626	32,167
GDP real growth	%	3.0	1.1	0.4	5.1	*0.4
Inflation	%	1.0	0.9	1.1	0.2	*0.4
Oil output	'000 bpd	214.0	211.0	206.0	221.0	194.0
Natural gas output	bn cum	12.4	12.1	12.0	12.3	12.3
Exports (fob) (goods)	US$m	4,505.0	4,514.0	6,247.0	7,627.0	–
Imports (cif) (goods)	US$m	1,540.0	1,641.0	1,412.9	1,585.9	–
Balance of trade	US$m	2,965.0	2,873.0	4,834.1	6,041.1	–
Current account	US$m	3,810.0	4,240.0	5,339.0	6,462.0	*7,101.0
Total reserves minus gold	US$m	481.5	505.1	494.2	523.3	683.5
Foreign exchange	US$m	0.0	400.9	433.6	469.5	461.4
Exchange rate	per US$	1.72	1.66	1.54	1.54	1.45

* estimated figure

2000s, heavily dependent on oil and gas production. Oil production averaged around 200,000 barrels a day during the early 2000s, while LNG output has been slightly under or over 1,000 trillion btu per day over the same period. Brunei's oil reserves are expected to last 25 years, and its natural gas reserves to last 40 years.

According to the US *Oil & Gas Journal* (OGJ), Brunei's oil reserves are declining and stood at 1.1 billion barrels of proven oil reserves as of January 2007. To prolong the life of Brunei's hydrocarbon reserves, the government controls oil production levels. During 2006, Brunei produced an estimated 220,000bpd of oil, of which 198,000bpd was crude oil and the remainder was natural gas liquids. Crude oil production had peaked at about 240,000bpd in 1979, but the government's conservation efforts have subsequently kept output below 200,000bpd. In 2006, Brunei consumed an estimated 13,000bpd of oil, with most of the country's crude oil production exported to other countries in the region. Despite its status as a net exporter of oil, Brunei imports about half the refined petroleum products that it consumes, due to its limited domestic refining capacity.

Brunei Shell Petroleum (BSP), a joint venture between Shell (UK/Netherlands) and the government of Brunei, dominates the country's oil industry. Until 1999, BSP had a monopoly on all upstream and downstream activities in Brunei's oil sector. Since then, the government has awarded some exploration blocks to other companies, most notably Total. In 2002, the government established the country's first national oil company (NOC), Brunei National Petroleum Corporation (BNPC, also known as PetroleumBRUNEI). PetroleumBRUNEI lacks significant industry experience and

controls a relatively small portion of the country's exploration acreage. As a result, the NOC has chosen to award private companies the exploration rights for the blocks that it controls rather than develop the blocks itself. Despite some efforts to introduce competition, BSP will continue to be the country's dominant oil producer by virtue of its control over all of Brunei's major oil and natural gas fields. The principal agency charged with regulating Brunei's oil sector is the petroleum unit, which reports directly to the office of the prime minister. The petroleum unit sets overall energy policy, regulates company activities, sets fuel prices, and acts as the point of contact for all foreign companies operating in the country. BSP controls all of Brunei's most productive oil fields, including the Southwest Ampa field, which is the country's oldest and largest, accounting for about 60 per cent of total oil and natural gas output. BSP also operates the Champion, Iron Duke, Magpie, Gennett, and Farley fields. BSP

and the few companies that hold exploration licences in Brunei have actively conducted exploration activities in an effort to replace depleting oil reserves. In 2004 and 2005, BSP logged new oil finds that the company estimated to hold 100 million barrels of recoverable reserves.

...the gas holds up

Brunei exports most of its natural gas production. According to the OGJ, Brunei had 13.8 trillion cubic feet (Tcf) of proven natural gas reserves in January 2007. Most of Brunei's natural gas reserves are from associated fields, occurring alongside the country's crude oil deposits. In 2004, Brunei produced 406 billion cubic feet (Bcf) of natural gas while consuming 71Bcf. During 2004, Brunei exported 357Bcf of LNG, of which 88 per cent went to Japan and the remainder to South Korea. Brunei became the first Asian exporter of LNG in 1972. It is an important regional producer of LNG, with 2005 exports totalling 333Bcf, or 6.8 million metric tons (MMt). In 2005, 92 per cent of Brunei's LNG exports were sent to Japan, with the rest going to South Korea. BLNG operates the country's sole natural gas liquefaction plant and LNG export terminal, located at Lumut. The facility has a total capacity of 7.2MMt/y (350Bcf/y), and BLNG has announced plans to add a

new production train with 4.0MMt/y (195Bcf/y) of additional capacity. While the planned expansion has been discussed at length, there are no firm agreements in place that guarantee the production train will be built.

Risk assessment

Economy	Good
Politics	Fair
Regional stability	Good

COUNTRY PROFILE

Historical profile

1839 When an English explorer, James Brooke, arrived on the island of Borneo, he helped the Sultan to suppress an uprising against the rule of the Brunei Sultanate. As a reward for the role he played in quelling the rebellion, in 1841, the Pengiran Mahkota of Brunei made Brooke the Rajah of Sarawak on the north-west coast of Borneo (Sarawak is now the largest state in Malaysia). The British North Borneo Company was expanding its influence on the island.

1888 Brunei became a British protectorate, keeping the Sultanate out of the Malaysian confederacy. Brunei's monarch retained control over internal matters while the British took charge of external affairs.

1906 A treaty with Britain assured Brunei's status as a protectorate and the succession of the ruling dynasty. Executive power, including the right to advise the Sultan on all affairs except religion, was transferred to the British.

1929 Oil was discovered in the Seria field, ensuring the country's future prosperity.

1941–45 Brunei was occupied by the Japanese.

1959 An agreement was drawn up to allow Brunei internal self-government.

1962 In the run-up to Brunei's proposed amalgamation with Malaysia, the British pressured Sultan Omar Saifuddin (the current Sultan's father) into holding elections. The opposition Partai Rakyat Brunei (PRB) (Brunei People's Party) won a convincing victory, campaigning against unification, for complete independence from the UK and the creation of a constitutional monarchy. The Sultan's rejection of the result and his plans to unite with Malaysia led to an armed uprising which was quickly crushed (with British backing). The Sultan decided against union with Malaysia.

1979 Brunei concluded a treaty of friendship with the UK.

1984 Brunei became independent from the UK, under Sultan Haji Hassanal Bolkiah Mu'izzaddin Waddaulah, who had ruled since the abdication of his father in 1967.

1991 The sale of alcohol was forbidden. Nationals were required to wear muslim garments.

1998 Prince al Muhtadee Billah, the Sultan's eldest son, was inaugurated as crown prince.

2000 Legal action was initiated against Prince Jefri Bolkiah, younger brother and former favourite of the Sultan, for misusing US$15 billion while head of the state investment agency.

2001 The Association of Southeast Asian Nations (Asean) summit was held in Brunei and agreed to step up co-operation to combat terrorism in the region.

2002 Licences were awarded to two foreign consortiums, Royal Dutch/Shell and TotalFinaElf, to explore for oil deposits in Brunei's 200-mile Exclusive Economic Zone (EEZ) in the South China Sea.

2003 A battalion of the British Brigade of Gurkhas is to continue to be stationed in Brunei until 2008.

2004 Parliament was reconvened for first time since 1984.
2005 The Sultan sacked four members of his cabinet, replacing them with younger, more progressive candidates, and introduced reform measures. The constitution was changed so that the Sultan is infallible under the law.
2007 In November Prince Jefri Bolkiah, former finance minister and brother of the Sultan, lost an appeal to the supreme court over the embezzlement of an estimated US$6 billion in public funds and was required to pay back the sum.
2008 On the 12 June a warrant for the arrest of Prince Jefri Bolkiah, was issued by a UK high court after he failed to attend a court summons to determine ownership of his exclusive, luxury London home.

Political structure

Constitution

The Sultanate of Brunei (Negara Brunei Darussalam) became a fully independent sovereign state on 1 January 1984, when a ministerial system of government was established. Previously it had been a protectorate of Britain.
The Sultan rules partly by decree, and a state of emergency has been in force since a large-scale revolt in December 1962 which resulted in the suspension of sections of the constitution.
In lieu of democracy and to act as conduits of two-way communication between government and populace, there is a system of village and rural-district consultative councils.
In addition to the cabinet or council of ministers, three other councils advise the Sultan on the running of the country.
These are:
- the Religious Council, which advises on all Islamic matters. The council also gives advice on legal matters; the Islamic court falls under its jurisdiction.
- the Privy Council, which is concerned with constitutional matters such as the exercising of royal prerogative and the awarding of honorary titles.
- the Council of Succession, which is empowered to determine the succession to the throne should the need arise.

In September 2004 the Sultan signed a new constitution that will allow limited elections of up to 15 members to an expanded 45-seat legislative council; 30 council members will be appointed by the Sultan. No timetable for the elections has been announced although a new parliament building is planned.

Form of state

Autocratic sultanate

The executive

The Sultan and Yang Di-Pertuan (paramount ruler) is the sovereign head of state and prime minister, retaining supreme executive authority. He is also head of the Islamic faith in Brunei and minister for defence.
A ministerial system of government was introduced following independence in 1984. The cabinet, presided over by the Sultan in his position as prime minister, consists mostly of members of the Sultan's family. Ministers are appointed to hold office at the Sultan's pleasure.

National legislature

The Legislative Council of 20 appointees was abolished at independence in 1984, ending a purely consultative role.
A General Assembly of 1,000 village chiefs from 150 villages and 35 mukim (village groups) took place in 1996, described as an expression of a 'grassroots political system' by the government.
Chiefs were chosen by secret ballot of villagers but government appointed the Assembly's advisers.

Legal system

Syariah (Islamic) courts were established in 1996 to handle family and criminal law. Their emphasis on publicly shaming offenders is designed to prevent anti-social and anti-Islamic activities.
Brunei has an independent legal system. It is a distinctive, separate branch of government, based on the English common law system. Apart from the Syariah courts, the legal system includes:

- the High Court, which hears appeals in criminal and civil matters from subordinate courts. It is presided over by the chief justice and various commissioners.
- the Court of Appeal, which hears appeals against High Court decisions. It consists of a president and two commissioners.
- subordinate courts, which have limited jurisdiction in civil and criminal cases, and are presided over by a chief magistrate.
- the Courts of Kathis, which deal with certain religious (Islamic) matters. These are marriage, divorce, inheritance and sexual crimes. The Courts of Kathis have jurisdiction over Muslims and supercede the civil law only in these matters.

Last elections

There have been no elections since 1962.

Political parties

There are three legally registered parties: Parti Perpaduan Kebangsaan Brunei (PPKB) (Brunei National Solidarity Party), Parti Kesedaran Rakyat Brunei (PAKAR) (Brunei People's Awareness Party) and Parti Pembangunan Bangsap (NDP) (National Development Party). As members of parliament, which was re-opened in 2004, are appointed, the parties have no representation at present. The constitution has been amended to allow election of a proportion of the parliament

Ruling party

There is no ruling party.

Main opposition party

The absence of any recognisable opposition movement is explained by a number of factors, not least the state of emergency, press censorship and the growing influence of Melaya Islam Berjaya (MIB) (Malay Islam Monarchy) policy (which emphasises obedience and deters the questioning of authority).

Population

385,000 (2007)*

Last census: August 2001: 332,844 (provisional)

Population density: 61 inhabitants per square km. Urban population: 73 per cent.

Annual growth rate: 2.4 per cent 1994–2004 (WHO 2006)

Ethnic make-up

Indigenous (predominantly Malay) (69 per cent), Chinese (18 per cent), Indian (3 per cent), other (10 per cent). There are severe obstacles to further Chinese naturalisation and their emigration to China has been encouraged. The 50,000 Chinese living in Brunei play a negligible role in the country's political life, although they are vital to its economic success. Around a third of the Chinese population is naturalised. The same is true of the non-Malay indigenous population, which remains on the fringe of society but forms a crucial part of the workforce.

Religions

Sunni Islam (official faith and religion of all Malays). Members of the Chinese community are either Buddhist, Confucianist, Taoist or Christian. There are also ancient native religions.

Education

Primary schooling includes one year of compulsory pre-school education. Secondary education is divided into junior schools, lasting for three years between the ages of 12 and 15, and upper secondary schools, for another two years.
Pre-university further education lasts for up to two years.
In 1985, the government established the University of Brunei Darussalam. In addition, there are two state-run teacher training colleges and six technical schools. If a university course is not available in Brunei, the government will pay for its students to study at a foreign university.
Education for expatriate children is provided by missionary schools, the International School and Chinese schools. All are fee paying and education at the International School follows a UK curriculum, but only caters for children up to the age of 12.

Literacy rate: 91 per cent, adult rates (World Bank)
Compulsory years: Five to 12

Health

Per capita total expenditure on health (2003) was US$681; of which per capita government spending was US$545, at the international dollar rate, (WHO 2006).
The government has used its revenues from oil to provide one of the best healthcare systems in Asia. Health services are free for Brunei citizens, although there is a nominal fee for hospital and dentist treatment.
The healthcare system is based on health clinics, which provide primary care and include mobile clinics to reach the most isolated regions, health centres and district hospitals. The central hospital in Bandar Seri Begawan (Raja Isteri Pengiran Anak Saleha) has 550 beds and provides diagnostic and therapeutic facilities for the whole country. There are also government-operated hospitals in Tutong, Temburong and Kuala Belait. A Flying Medical Service reaches areas inaccessible by road. British Shell Petroleum (BSP) has its own private facilities in Seria.
The government is committed to increase its expenditure towards health care and building more clinics. Brunei continues to rely on expatriate doctors to run its health system. Government health surveys have shown that local doctors have made up only 10 per cent, and local dentists 32 per cent, of the medical workforce in the country.

HIV/Aids

HIV prevalence: 0.1 per cent aged 15–49 in 2003 (World Bank)
Life expectancy: 77 years, 2004 (WHO 2006)
Fertility rate/Maternal mortality rate: 2.4 births per woman, 2004 (WHO 2006)
Child (under 5 years) mortality rate (per 1,000): 5.0 per 1,000 live births (World Bank)

Welfare

The Employees Trust Fund or Tabung Amanah Pekerja (Tap) provides membership to a providence fund that is open to all government workers and private sector employees. The scheme requires compulsory contributions from both the employer and the employee at a contribution rate of 5 per cent each. Universal old age pensions are granted those who have been residents for 30 years.
The ministry of culture, youth and sport oversees the distribution of pensions to citizens not holding contributory pensions and also provides welfare provisions for needy families and the handicapped. The government subsidises housing and food. Under the National Housing Scheme (NHS), the state grants housing to those who have lived under Temporary Occupation Licences (TOL). The Housing Scheme for Landless Citizens also gives land title deeds to those who have been occupying land under TOL.

Main cities

Bandar Seri Begawan (capital, estimated population 78,000 in 2003), Kuala Belait (27,800), Seria (oil field) (23,400).

Languages spoken

The national education system is formally bilingual for all, in Malay and English. Chinese is spoken; English is the principal commercial language.

Official language/s

Behasa Melayu

Media

With media ownership in the hands of, or controlled by, the royal family or if privately owned where self-censorship for political or religious reasons is widespread press freedom is severely curtailed. Legal sanctions against journalist can be up to three years imprisonment for 'false' reporting. The US-based media watchdog, Freedom House, rated Brunei as not free, with virtual no criticism of the government allowed.
Other news agencies: BruDirect (in English): www.brudirect.com
Brunei News (in English): www.bruneinews.net

Press

Publications that provide a variety of views and information beyond anything the newspapers controlled by the Sultan's family are able to achieve are either The Straits Times or Chinese publications produced in Sarawak and Singapore.
Dailies: In Malay, Media Permata (www.brunei-online.com/mp), in English, Borneo Bulletin (www.brunei-online.com/bb), and the independent The Brunei Times (www.bt.com.bn), which reports on international news.
Weeklies: In Malay, the official government newspaper Pelita Brunei is published every Wednesday, and in English, the Brunei Darussalam Newsletter (www.information.gov.bn/bdnewsletter) is a fortnightly publication and is also produced by the government.

Broadcasting

The only broadcasting organisation is Radio Televisyen Brunei (RTB) (www.rtb.gov.bn), which is government operated, under the control of the Department of Broadcasting and Information.
Radio: RTB (www.rtb.gov.bn) operates five radio stations, including an international service. There are several private stations broadcasting in Brunei but only Kristal FM (www.dst-group.com) is a domestic station; all others originate in Malaysia.
Television: RTB (www.rtb.gov.bn) operates channels 5 and 8 as well as an RBT International, broadcast via a satellite service. Foreign cable and satellite networks provide the only alternatives to the state-run broadcaster. Viewers with access to the internet may access foreign TV.

Advertising

Apart from traditional forms of advertising, new media has opened up opportunities for personalised advertising through emails and mobile/cell SMS texts.

Economy

Brunei is the richest, in terms of GDP per capita, and the smallest, Asean member, with an economy based on the extraction of natural gas and oil, which account for over half of GDP and over 90 per cent of export earnings.
Brunei enjoys a high standard of living, with medical services, education and pensions provided free. Half of Brunei's income comes from its international investment portfolio, managed by the Brunei Investment Agency (BIA). The exact value of these assets is secret.
Economic diversification and an increase in foreign investment by US$4.5 billion by 2008, in order to maintain growth and long-term viability, are central issues. Key to this policy is the transformation of Brunei into an offshore financial centre and tourist destination. Brunei's ambition is to become a service hub for trade and tourism (SHuTT) to take advantage of regional economic integration. Economic development has concentrated on infrastructure, roads, schools and numerous government buildings. In addition to promoting tourism, Brunei intends to increase the financial sector and energy-intensive industries, especially petrochemicals.
Major obstacles to growth include labour shortages, as many local unemployed workers are unwilling to do manual work. Complex bureaucracy and high wages are seen as deterrents to foreign investment.

External trade

As the Association of Southeast Asian Nations (Asean) moves towards the creation of a free trade area, Brunei is likely to benefit from increased transit trade and the rapidly developing economies of its neighbours, particularly within the East Asean Growth Area (EAGA). Brunei also belongs to the Asia Pacific Economic Co-operation (Apec) organisation

Imports

Brunei's limited industrial and agricultural base requires a range of principal imports including machinery, transport equipment, manufactured goods, food and chemicals.

Most items can be imported under an open general licence. There are some restricted goods which require special licences, including used vehicles, certain listed drugs, livestock, some foodstuffs and gambling equipment (eg fruit machines).
Main sources: Malaysia (21.6 per cent total, 2006), Singapore (17.4 per cent), Japan (12.8 per cent).

Exports

Crude oil (typically 50 per cent of the total exports) and liquefied natural gas (around 40 per cent) and refined products dominate the export schedule.
The government is encouraging exports from the non-hydrocarbons sector, which includes small-scale manufacturing in textile, furniture and food processing. Primary production includes timber, marine and agricultural produce. Some items are heavily subsidised by the government and their export is consequently restricted. Such goods include rice, petrol, kerosene and diesel fuels as well as cigarettes.
Main destinations: Japan (30.6 per cent of 2006 total goods exports), Indonesia (19.8 per cent), South Korea (15.1 per cent).

Agriculture

Farming

The agricultural sector plays only a minor role in Brunei's economy, typically accounting for less than 3 per cent of GDP and employing 2 per cent of the workforce. Brunei has to import 80 per cent of its food needs. Only around 15 per cent of the total land area is cultivated or under grazing.
Brunei's agricultural base consists mainly of small farms growing rice and vegetables. Farming is primarily a part-time occupation. The main crops are rice, vegetables, arable crops and fruits. A wide range of tropical fruit varieties are produced, but in low volumes. Vegetable production is intensive and concentrated in the fertile alluvial plain close to the urban centres. With smallholding rice production declining, the government has initiated a pilot large-scale rice mechanisation project aimed at increasing output; it is hoped that once fully mechanised, 30 per cent of Brunei's rice needs will be met by domestic production.
Government attempts to increase the importance of the sector and moves towards self-sufficiency are hampered by the population's lack of interest in outdoor, manual work. Another disincentive is that farming is perceived as less lucrative than other areas of the economy, so reducing further the likelihood of significant small-scale development. High wage costs mean that the expansion of larger-scale production depends very much on increased mechanisation rather than labour-intensive techniques, unless large scale immigrant labour can be guaranteed.
Estimated crop production in 2005 included: 620 tonnes (t) rice, 1,800t cassava, 990 pineapples, 215t natural rubber, 220t sweet potatoes, 680t bananas, 28t pepper spice, 395t citrus fruit, 5,565t fruit in total, 10,500t vegetables in total. Livestock production included: 19,795t meat in total, 2,775t beef, 568t buffalo, 81t pig meat, 79t lamb and goat meat, 16,392t poultry, 6,000t eggs, 120t milk, 468t cattle hides.

Fishing

Since 1990, the government has attempted to expand the fishing industry. The ministry of industry and primary resources granted more fishing licences to match the extension of the country's fishing boundary to 200 miles offshore. Several other sites were located for aquaculture projects. The government also improved the distribution system to ensure that the local catch reaches more remote areas of the country. The trawling industry has also been developed. The important trawling areas are Pulau Tambisan and north of Sandakan (Marchesa and Labuk Bay).
Typical annual fish production is over 1,600 tonnes and other seafood over 400 tonnes.

Forestry

About 70 per cent of Brunei is covered by primary and secondary rain forest; 37 per cent of the country is designated as a national Forest Reserve. There is growing concern locally about the conservation of the forests and the environment, and exports of timber and logs are now strictly limited. Consequently timber production of logs and sawnwood is for domestic consumption only. Some natural rubber is produced. The government hopes to develop the forestry sector as part of its diversification strategy, but investment opportunities are limited by legal restrictions. Private companies wishing to become involved in the sector must have local business participation of 51 per cent.

Industry and manufacturing

The industrial sector, including hydrocarbons, accounts for approximately 44 per cent of GDP and employs almost a quarter of the workforce. The industrial structure, long dependent on export of oil and gas, consists mainly of small-scale enterprises. Apart from the energy and construction sectors, Brunei's industrial base is limited. The small domestic market, high wage costs, bureaucracy and poor co-ordination between government departments has deterred both local and foreign investment.
Despite the government's emphasis on diversification, the industrial sector remains underdeveloped. The manufacturing sector is small and consists mainly of the production of materials for the construction sector, petroleum refining, food-processing and garment manufacture. There are also factories producing canned food, mineral water and dairy products.
Areas the government wants to develop include the manufacture of furniture, pottery, tiles, cement, chemicals, plywood and glass. As part of the industrial development programme a number of industrial estates have been established. These include a 40 hectare site near Bandar Seri Begawan and the Beribi Light Industrial Complex, which consists of four blocks including textiles, food and electrical manufacturers.
The government is eager to promote the development of a financial centre and of export-oriented, value-added industries. Investment policy is open and flexible and welcomes investors, both local and foreign, in any productive industrial activity which furthers diversification.

Tourism

Tourism is relatively undeveloped, although the government is actively trying to promote the sector. Efforts have been made to attract visitors to such attractions as the 20ha Sungai Basong National Park at Bukit Bendera and the Jerudong Park Playground.
Brunei is marketing itself as a service hub for trade and tourism (ShuTT), using the country as a stop-off point for international travellers.
Despite areas of extensive natural beauty that could be visited by tourists, expansion of the sector is hampered by strict rules affecting clothing and alcohol and the difficulties associated with travelling caused by the relative scarcity of taxi drivers.
Tourism is expected to contribute 3.3 per cent to GDP in 2005.

Environment

Brunei is prone to occasional typhoons, earthquakes and flooding. Environmental management is overseen by the ministry of development, ministry of health and the ministry of industry and primary resources. Brunei is party to major international environmental agreements that include endangered species, ozone layer protection, ship pollution and whaling.

Mining

Brunei possesses only limited raw materials. Its principal resources are clay and silica in the form of 20 million tonnes of high quality beach sands at Tutong.

Hydrocarbons

Brunei's international status depends upon its oil and gas. Revenues from hydrocarbons make up over 50 per cent of GDP and 90 per cent of Brunei's exports.

Brunei has proven crude oil reserves of 1.3 billion barrels, with a production rate of 214,000 barrels per day (bpd). Brunei has plans to diversify the oil-based economy, which should lead to a greater emphasis on natural gas in the future.

Brunei has seven offshore fields of which the largest, Champion, contains about 40 per cent of total reserves and accounts for 50,000bpd in output. There are believed to be significant undeveloped oil reserves in the existing fields and these will be tapped by advanced technology and modern drilling methods.

Brunei has natural gas reserves of 350 billion cubic metres and produces around 12.2 billion cubic metres per year. Brunei is south-east Asia's third-largest gas producer (after Indonesia and Malaysia), and the world's fourth-largest producer of liquefied natural gas (LNG). Brunei LNG operates the LNG plant at Lumut, which ranks as one of the largest in the world, processing almost all of Brunei's LNG, the majority of which is exported to Japan. Brunei does not produce or import coal.

Energy

Electricity generation capacity is around 500MW. All Brunei's electricity is produced by gas-fired power plants. Electricity demand is expanding by 7—10 per cent annually, making long-term electricity development a priority. A programme of electricity expansion includes the construction of a 400MW power plant in Tutong, which will feature new, more efficient combine cycle turbines.

Banking and insurance

The regulatory system is based on the 1906 British Banking Act, although various modifications have been made to bring it up-to-date with modern banking requirements.

The fourth pillar of the Brunei International Financial Centre (BIFC), the International Insurance and Takaful Order, was set up, designed to provide for foreign investors in the banking scene. This will enable Brunei to have a fully operational foreign offshore banking sector. The Royal Bank of Canada (RBC) became the first foreign bank to operate in the BIFC. RBC is focussing its activities on private bank services for the rich and assisting the management of Islamic funds.

Three local banks dominate the domestic banking sector – the Islamic Bank of Brunei (IBB), Baiduri Bank (BB) and the Development Bank of Brunei. Thw IBB conducts its savings and loans operations in accordance with Islamic law. The Sultan and his family own 80 per cent of IBB's paid up capital, Japan's Daiichi Kangyo Bank holds the other 20 per cent.

The three largest foreign banks in Brunei are Citibank, the Hong Kong and Shanghai Banking Corporation (HSBC) and Standard Chartered Bank. Other foreign banks include the Overseas Union Bank, Malayan Banking and the United Malayan Banking Corporation.

Central bank

Brunei has no central bank; the main duties are carried out by the ministry of finance.

Main financial centre

Bandar Seri Begawan

Time

GMT plus eight hours

Geography

Brunei lies 442km north of the equator on the northern coast of the island of Borneo. It consists of two wedges of land, within the Malaysian province of Sarawak and with the South China sea in the north.

The country is divided into separate administrative districts: Brunei/Muara, Tutong and Seria/Belait in the western section, and Temburong, which makes up the entire eastern section of the country. Although there is a mountainous region in the eastern half of the country, Brunei mostly consists of a low-lying coastal plain. The highest peak is Bukit Pagon (1,841 metres). Brunei has four main rivers – the Belait, Tutong, Brunei and Temburong. Approximately 75 per cent of the total land area is covered by tropical rain forest.

Hemisphere

Northern

Climate

The climate is typically equatorial. Humidity averages 82 per cent, and daily temperatures range between 24 and 31 degrees Celsius (C). The rainy season lasts from September to January, although rainfall can be expected throughout the year. It can reach up to 7,500mm in the interior, but on the coast it tends to average around 2,500mm. The driest months are from January to April.

Dress codes

Lightweight clothing is suitable. In deference to the Islamic culture, Western business women should dress modestly at all times.

Entry requirements

Passports

Required by all. Must be valid for six months.

Visa

Required by all. Exceptions are granted for short stays of up to 14 or 30 days to nationals of certain countries and 90 days for US citizens (see www.mfa.gov.bn for details). Business visas require a sponsorship letter from a local company or government entity (for details see www.immigration.gov.bn/visiting.htm).

Prohibited entry

Holders of Israeli passports.

Currency advice/regulations

There are no restritions on the import of foreign and local currency, with the exception of the Singapore dollar, which is limited to B$1,000 equivalent, and Indian and Indonesian banknotes, which are prohibited. Export of local currency is restricted to B$1,000, while the export of foreign currency is limited to the amount imported. The Brunei dollar is at par with the Singapore dollar and the currencies are interchangeable in both countries.

Customs

Two litres of alcohol and 12 cans of beer; 200 cigarettes and 250g tobacco; 60ml perfume and 250ml eau de toilette allopwed duty free.

Prohibited imports

Trafficking and illegal importation of controlled drugs are very serious offences carrying the death penalty.

Health (for visitors)

Health services are not free for visitors, as it is for Brunei citizens, but there is only a very nominal charge for permanent residents and expatriate government officials and their dependants. Malaria has been eradicated in Brunei. Certificates of vaccination for both cholera and yellow fever are advisable. Normal precautions should be taken for food and drink. The authorities are becoming concerned over the growing amount of drug abuse.

Mandatory precautions

Vaccination certificates for yellow fever are required for travellers over one year of age travelling from an infected area.

Advisable precautions

Chest X-ray and blood film examination for malaria are required for the issue and renewal of labour permits as Brunei is malaria-free. Immunisations are recommended for hepatitis A, polio, tetanus, typhoid, and also advice should be sought regarding diphtheria, hepatitis A, Japanese encephalitis and TB. There is a risk of rabies.

Hotels

Rooms in major hotels have air-conditioning, telephones, TV, bathrooms and showers. A 10 per cent service charge is usual.

Credit cards

Major credit cards are accepted at some hotels and at some shops.

Public holidays (national)

Friday and Sunday are non-working days, if a holiday falls on these, then Saturday or Monday are substituted. Banks close on 30 June and 30 December.

Fixed dates

1 Jan (New Year's Day), 23 Feb (National Day), 31 May (Armed Forces Day), 15 Jul (Sultan's Birthday), 25 Dec (Christmas Day).

Variable dates

Chinese New Year (Jan–Feb), Hari Raya Aidiladha, Hari Raya Aidilfitra, Islamic New Year, Birth of the Prophet, Ascension of the Prophet, First day of Ramadan, Revelation of the Quran Anniversary.

Islamic year – 1429 (10 Jan 2008–28 Dec 2008): The Islamic year contains 354 or 355 days, with the result that Muslim feasts advance by 10–12 days against the Gregorian calendar. Dates of feasts vary according to the sighting of the new moon, so cannot be forecast exactly.

Working hours

Banking

Mon–Fri: 0900–1500; Sat: 0900–1100. Many banks close during lunch hour.

Business

Mon–Thur: 0745–1215, 1330–1630; Sat: 0800–1200.

Government

Mon–Thu, Sat: 0745–1215, 1330–1630. Fasting month (Ramadan) 0800–1400.

Shops

Mon–Sat: 0800–1900/2100, 1000–2200 (most shopping centres). Post offices: Mon–Thu, Sat: 0730–1600; Fri: 0830–0930.

Telecommunications

Mobile/cell phones

There is a 900 GSM service available along with a G3 (2100) service.

Electricity supply

230V AC, with 3-pin round or 3-pin square plug fittings.

Weights and measures

Metric system.

Social customs/useful tips

The public sale and consumption of alcohol is prohibited by law. Muslims do not eat pork or drink alcohol. The right hand should be used for offering or receiving anything, from food to money. Refusal of offered refreshment is discourteous.

To point with the index finger is also considered discourteous; the thumb of the right hand should be used instead with the four fingers folded beneath it. To call a taxi or attract someone's attention, wave the whole hand with the palm facing downwards. Do not smack the fist of your right hand into your left palm; it has a different meaning in Brunei to that of Western countries. It is not customary to shake hands with members of the opposite sex. When visiting a mosque, shoes should first be removed. Do not pass in front of a person at prayer, or touch the Qur'an. Women should cover their heads, and not have their knees or arms exposed.

Security

There is no major problem with petty crime in Brunei.

Getting there

Air

National airline: Royal Brunei Airlines (RBA)

International airport/s: Brunei International Airport (BWN), 10km north of Bandar Seri Begawan, with car hire and taxi service.

Airport tax: Departures to Singapore and Malaysia B$5. All other international departures B$12.

Surface

Road: Road connections between Brunei and Sarawak (Malaysia) are good. There is a bitumen road between Miri and Kuala Belait.

Water: Most sea traffic is handled by the deep-water port at Muara, while the smaller port at Kuala Belait handles shallow-draught vessels.

Main port/s: Muara (27km from Bandar Seri Begawan), Kuala Belait, Lumut.

Getting about

National transport

Road: The total road network is around 2,500km. Brunei has 1,500km of main roads, 500km of district roads and 500km of unpaved road surface. There is no road connecting the Temburong district but a water taxi service is available. A main highway links Bandar Seri Begawan with Kuala Belait and Seria, with a road linking Muara and Tutong providing access to western districts.

Buses: There are six bus lines in Bandar Seri Begawan. Services operate betwen Bandar Seri Begawan and Kuala Belait and Seria, and also serve rural areas. Buses run from 0630–1800.

Water: The Brunei, Belait and Tutong rivers are the main inland waterways and are principally used for passenger traffic. River-going vessels use the old port at Bandar Seri Begawan. Large river taxis operate to the Temburong district; service starts at 0745 and ends at 1600.

River taxi and boat services are also available to Limbang in Sarawak and Labuan in Sabah.

City transport

The City Transport Service (CTS) is the easiest way to travel in the city. Fixed fare within the CTS zone.

Taxis: From the airport to the city centre, metered taxis are in operation 0700–0030. Metered taxis are also available from hotels and shopping centres near the capital to all parts of Brunei, but are otherwise scarce. Tipping is not usual.

Buses, trams & metro: From the airport to the city centre, buses operate 0630—1800, every 15—20 minutes.

Car hire

Self-drive and chauffeur-driven cars are available from major hotels and the airport. An international driving licence is required.

BUSINESS DIRECTORY

The addresses listed below are a selection only. While World of Information makes every endeavour to check these addresses, we cannot guarantee that changes have not been made, especially to telephone numbers and area codes. We would welcome any corrections.

Telephone area codes

The international direct dialling (IDD) code for Brunei is +673, followed by subscriber's number.

Useful telephone numbers

Police: 993

Fire: 995

Ambulance: 991

Flight information: 331-747

Directory enquiries: 0213

International calls: 000

Chambers of Commerce

Brunei Darussalam International Chamber of Commerce and Industry, PO Box 2246, Bandar Seri Bagawan 1922 (tel: 2 228382; fax: 2 228389).

Brunei Malay Chamber of Commerce, PO Box 1099, Bandar Seri Begawan 8672 (tel: 2 422752; fax: 2 422753).

Chinese Chamber of Commerce, 72 Jalan Roberts, PO Box 281, Bandar Seri Begawan 8670 (tel: 2 235494; fax: 2 235492).

National Chamber of Commerce and Industry, 144 2nd Floor Jalan Pemancha, Bandar Seri Begawan BS8711 (tel: 2 243321; fax: 2 228737).

Banking

Baiduri Bank Berhad (BB), 145 Jalan Pemancha, PO Box 2220, Bandar Seri Begawan 1922 (tel: 233-233; fax: 235-722).

Citibank, 12-15 Bangunan Darussalam, Bandar Seri Begawan (tel: 243-983; fax: 225-704).

Development Bank of Brunei Bhd, 1st Floor RBA Plaza, Jalan Sultan Bandar Seri Begawan 2085 (tel: 233-430; fax: 233-429).

Hongkong & Shanghai Banking Corporation, cnr Jalan Sultan and Jalan Pemancha, PO Box 59, Jalan Sultan, Bandar Seri Begawan (tel: 242-305/10, 242-204; fax: 241-316).

Islamic Bank of Brunei Berhad (IBB), lot 159, Jalan Pemancha, Bandar Seri Begawan (tel: 235-686/7; fax: 235-722).

Malayan Banking Berhad, 148 Jalan Pemancha, Bandar Seri Begawan 2085 (tel: 242-494).

Overseas Union Bank (OUB), Unit G5, RBA Plaza, Jalan Sultan, Bandar Seri Begawan 2089 (tel: 225-477; fax: 240-792).

Sime Bank Berhad, Unit G 02, Kompleks Yayasan Sultan Haji Hassanal Bolkiah, Bandar Seri Begawan (tel: 222-516; fax: 237-487).

Standard Chartered Bank, 51-55 Jalan Sultan, Bandar Seri Begawan (tel: 242-386; fax: 242-390).

Central bank

Brunei Currency and Monetray Board, Simpang 295, Jalan Kebangsaan, PO Box 660, Bandar Seri Begawan BS 8670 (tel: 238-3999; fax: 238-2232; e-mail: bcb@brunet.bn).

Travel information

Brunei Travel Service, Sdn Bhd, Bandar Seri Begawan (tel: 225-664).

Department of Civil Aviation, Ministry of Communications, Brunei International Airport, 2015 (tel: 330-483, 330-142/3; fax: 331-7066).

Royal Brunei Airlines, PO Box 737, Bandar Seri Begawan 1907 (tel: 240-500, 242-222; fax: 244-737).

Tourist information (on arrival level at airport) (tel: 331-747).

Ministries

Ministry of Communications, Old Airport, Berakas, Bandar Seri Begawan 1150 (tel: 383-838; fax: 380-127).

Ministry of Culture, Youth and Sports, Jalan Residency, Bandar Seri Begawan 1200 (tel: 240-585; fax: 241-620).

Ministry of Defence, Bolkiah Garrison, Bandar Seri Begawan 1110 (tel: 230-130; fax: 230-110).

Ministry of Development, Old Airport, Berakas, Bandar Seri Begawan 1190 (tel: 241-911; fax: 240-271).

Ministry of Education, Old Airport, Berakas, Bandar Seri Begawan 1170 (tel: 244-233; fax: 240-250).

Ministry of Finance, Bandar Seri Begawan 1130 (tel: 242-405; fax: 241-829).

Ministry of Foreign Affairs, Jalan Subok, Bandar Seri Begawan 1120 (tel: 241-177; fax: 224-709).

Ministry of Health, Old Airport, Berakas, Bandar Seri Begawan 1210 (tel: 226-640; fax: 240-980).

Ministry of Home Affairs, Bandar Seri Begawan 1140 (tel: 223-225).

Ministry of Industry and Primary Resources, Old Airport, Berakas, Bandar Seri Begawan 1220 (tel: 224-822; fax: 244-811).

Ministry of Law, Jalan Tutong, Bandar Seri Begawan 1160 (tel: 244-872; fax: 223-100).

Ministry of Religious Affairs, Bandar Seri Begawan 1180 (tel: 242-565).

Other useful addresses

Asean Investment Promotion Agency, Ministry of Industry and Primary Resources, Bandar Seri Begawan 1220 (tel: 238-119; fax: 238-811).

British High Commission, 2.01, 2nd Floor, Block D, Kompleks Bangunan Yayasan Sultan Haji Hassanal Bolkiah, Jalan Pretty, PO Box 2197, Bandar Seri Begawan 8711 (tel: 222-2231; fax: 223-4315).

Brunei Darussalam Embassy (USA), 3520 International Court, NW, Washington DC 20008 (tel: (+1-202) 237-1838; fax: (+1-202) 885-0560; e-mail: info@bruneiembassy.org).

Brunei Industrial Development Authority (BINA), Km 8, Jalan Gadong, BE 1118 (tel: 444100; fax: 423300; e-mail: bruneibina@brunet.bn).

Controller of Customs and Excise, Jabatan Customs and Excise Di-Raja, Bandar Seri Begawan (tel: 222-342).

Economic Development Board, Ministry of Finance, 2nd Floor, RBA Plaza, Jalan Sultan, Bandar Seri Begawan 2085 (postal address: Locked Bag 15, Bandar Seri Begawan 1999) (tel: 229-269; fax: 241-417).

University of Brunei Darussalam, Gadong, Bandar Seri Begawan (tel: 227-001).

US Embassy, 3rd Floor, Teck Guan Plaza, cnr Jalan Sultan and Jalan MacArthur, Bandar Seri Begawan (tel: 229-670; fax: 225-293).

Other news agencies: BruDirect (in English): www.brudirect.com

Brunei News (in English): www.bruneinews.net

Internet sites

Brunei Darussalam homepage: www.brunet.bn

Government of Brunei: www.brunei.gov.bn

Bulgaria

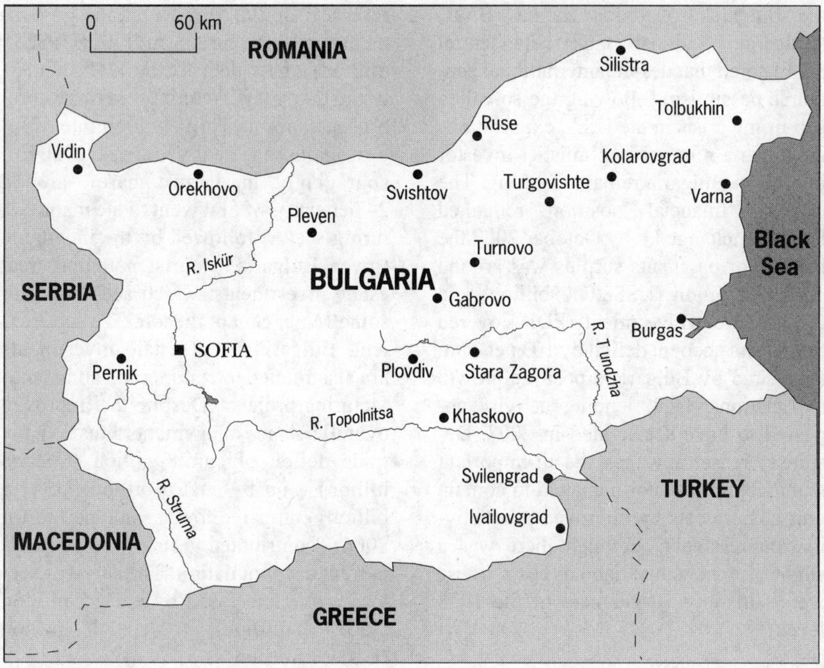

Bulgaria was significantly affected by the economic embargo placed on former Yugoslavia in the 1990s, suffering billions of dollars in GDP losses due to disrupted trade, transport and investment. Bulgaria joined the North Atlantic Treaty Organisation (Nato) in March 2004 and also aspired to membership of the European Union (EU). The World Bank notes that strong support from all political parties for EU accession has effectively governed Bulgaria's macroeconomic policies and structural reforms for some time. Bulgaria successfully completed its EU negotiations in June 2004. In April 2005, the accession treaty to the EU was signed and on 1 January 2007 Bulgaria joined up.

Unsteady politics

In Bulgaria's June 2005 parliamentary elections, the Bulgarska Socialistièska Partija (BSP) (Bulgarian Socialist Party) emerged as the leading party with 82 seats, but struggled to form a workable coalition. Eventually, in August, the BSP formed a coalition with (former King) Simeon's Nacionale Dvisenie Simeon Vtori (NDST) (National Movement Simeon II) and the ethnic Turk-based Dvisenie za Pravata i Svobodie (DPS) (Movement for Rights and Freedoms). BSP leader, Sergey Stanishev became prime minister. Mr Stanishev announced that his government's perhaps predictable priorities were to join the EU in 2007 and to tackle corruption and organised crime. The parliamentary elections were also significant for the emergence of the Obedinenie Ataka (Ataka) (Union Attack Coalition), an extreme nationalist party headed by Volen Siderov (a former television host), which won 22 seats.

Presidential elections were held in October 2006, and went to a second round run-off between Georgi Purvanov, the incumbent, and extremist candidate Volen Siderov (Ataka). Purvanov received 76 per cent of the vote, and Volen Siderov 24 per cent, making Purvanov the first Bulgarian president to retain office via popular mandate since the changes of 1989. As with the 2005 parliamentary elections, turnout was low, with around 42 per cent of the electorate voting in each of the rounds.

The European Parliamentary elections held in May 2007 saw the recently (December

KEY FACTS

Official name: Republika Bulgaria (Republic of Bulgaria)

Head of State: President Georgi Parvanov (since 2002; re-elected 29 Oct 2006)

Head of government: Prime Minister Sergey Stanishev (BSP) (took office 17 Aug 2005)

Ruling party: Koalicija za Bulgaria (KzB) (Coalition for Bulgaria): led by the Bulgarska Socialistièska Partija (BSP) (Bulgarian Socialist Party), with Nacionalno Dvizenie za Stabilnost i Vazhod (National Movement for Stability and Progress) (NMSP) and the Dvisenie za Pravata i Svobodie (DPS) (Movement for Rights and Freedoms) (MRF) (formed 15 Aug 2005).

Area: 110,994 square km

Population: 7.64 million (2007)*

Capital: Sofia

Official language: Bulgarian

Currency: Lev (Lev) = 100 stotinki

Exchange rate: Lev1.23 per US$ (Jul 2008)

GDP per capita: US$5,186 (2007)

GDP real growth: 6.20% (2007)

Labour force: 4.05 million (2004)

Unemployment: 12.00% (2004); 10.73% (Dec 2005)

Inflation: 7.50% (2007)

Balance of trade: -US$5.40 billion (2005)

Foreign debt: US$16.10 billion (2004)

Visitor numbers: 5.16 million (2006)*

Annual FDI: US$2.61 billion (2004)

* estimated figure

2006) formed populist Grazhdani za Evropeysko Razvitie na Balgariya (GERB) (Citizens for the European Development of Bulgaria) party win the largest proportion of the vote (5 seats), followed by the BSP (also 5 seats) and the Dvizhenie za Prava i Svobodi (Movement for Rights and Freedom) (MRF) (4 seats). The extreme nationalist Ataka Party increased their representation in the European Parliament to three seats, consolidating the position of the far right Identity, Tradition, Sovereignty grouping. Turnout was low, with only 28.6 per cent of the electorate voting.

In a dramatic move, a total of 13 Bulgarian deputy ministers and 24 deputy district governors were dismissed from their positions at the end of April 2008. Gone were the deputy minister of emergency situations Valeri Nikolov (whose title suggested that he was well equipped to deal with the situation) as well as his colleagues Ekaterina Vitkova from the education ministry, Milena Paunova and Savin Kovachev from the regional development ministry, Yordan Dimov and Lachezar Borissov from the economy ministry, Georgi Petarneychev from the transport ministry, Baki Hyuseinov from the social policy ministry and Atanas Dodov from the health ministry. To add to the confusion, three out of five deputy defence ministers have also been dismissed. The interior ministry's deputy head Kamen Penkov, had also recently resigned before the further dismissals. The Socialist and the centrist NMSP parties removed six officials each; Yordan Dardov from the environment ministry was the only representative of the Turkish ethnic party to lose his position. All the ministerial changes were made as part of a far-reaching cabinet re-shuffle.

Continued optimism...

In its December 2007 economic report, the Bulgarska Narodna Banka (BNB) (Bulgarian National Bank) (the central bank) noted that despite international economic pessimism following the so-called sub-prime crisis in the USA, expectations in Bulgaria remained optimistic. Investor interest in Bulgaria remained strong. The external financial position remained largely unchanged – by October 2007 the balance of payments surplus was around eur8,000 billion (US$8,000 billion) and foreign direct investment (FDI) covered the current account deficit by 103 per cent. Reassured by Bulgaria's positive growth expectations, bank lending activity appeared to have accelerated in 2007. Despite increases in wages, the all-important manufacturing sector managed to contain unit labour costs by improved productivity. Impressively, although there was a slight rise in actual labour costs, these were still only 70 per cent of the 1998 level.

...means continued cash

The BNB records that in 2007 the Bulgarian economy continued to attract a large volume of foreign capital, despite the increased uncertainty prevailing in the international financial markets. Between January and October 2007, Bulgarian FDI reached eur4.6 billion (US$4.6 billion). Alongside this, the overall balance of payments ended the year in surplus to the tune of eur3.1 billion (US$3.1 billion), resulting in a eur2.8 billion (US$2.8 billion) increase in central bank reserves. In 2007 the Bulgarian government paid off eur255 million (US$255 million) of its debt to the IMF. Underlying this rosy picture were investors' prospects for a relatively high rate of return against an equally low risk level. Encouragingly, the largest share – around 24 per cent – of FDI went to the manufacturing sector, followed by the inevitable (given Bulgaria's tourist potential) real estate investments, which accounted for some 16 per cent of the total. To some extent, Bulgaria's real estate investments are also related to commercial and manufacturing projects. Despite the improved overall balance of payments situation, the trade deficit of eur5.8 billion (US$5.8 billion) – up by eur1.6 billion (US$1.6 billion) compared to the same period for 2006 – contributed to the increase in the current account deficit. The services sector surplus increased by eur135 million US$135 million), to eur1.1 million (US$1.1 million).

It's all about robust growth...

In the second quarter of 2007, Bulgaria's annual GDP growth increased to 6.6 per cent. Household consumption growth, which reached 9.0 per cent in the first quarter of 2007, dropped to 6.4 per cent in the second quarter. Industrial sales, bolstered by high export levels, maintained their high growth rates, In general the high growth rates reached in 2007 were expected to be maintained well into 2008, possibly moderated by the continued downward trend in household consumption growth. Bulgaria's consumer confidence indicator decreased in November 2007 reflecting growing pessimism in consumer assessment of the general economic situation. These assessments were negatively affected by the increased inflation rate; this was particularly the case in the continued, and expected, loss in purchasing power as basic food and fuel costs continued to rise globally.

None the less, the strong domestic demand seen in the third quarter of 2007 generated substantial increases in indirect tax growth. Direct tax revenue also increased, reflecting favourable trends in both employment and income levels. Tax

KEY INDICATORS — Bulgaria

	Unit	2003	2004	2005	2006	2007
Population	m	7.94	7.91	7.72	7.69	7.64
Gross domestic product (GDP)	US$bn	19.90	24.13	26.72	31.69	39.61
GDP per capita	US$	2,591	3,074	3,462	4,120	5,186
GDP real growth	%	4.5	5.7	5.5	6.2	6.2
Inflation	%	2.4	6.1	5.0	7.4	7.5
Unemployment	%	14.8	12.7	10.1	9.0	6.9
Industrial output	% change	–	5.8	7.3	8.3	–
Agricultural output	% change	–	3.0	-8.6	-1.9	–
Coal output	mtoe	4.5	4.4	4.4	4.6	8.1
Exports (fob) (goods)	US$m	7,445.0	9,858.6	11,739.7	15,101.0	18,523.5
Imports (cif) (goods)	US$m	9,923.0	13,211.5	17,138.5	23,179.0	28,664.9
Balance of trade	US$m	-1,778.0	-3,352.9	-5,398.7	-8,078.0	-10,141.4
Current account	US$m	-1,850.0	-1,770.0	-3,021.0	-4,940.0	-8,464.0
Total reserves minus gold	US$m	6,291.0	8,776.3	8,040.5	10,943.0	16,477.9
Foreign exchange	US$m	6,174.6	8,171.2	7,992.4	10,892.1	16,424.2
Exchange rate	per US$	1.71	1.57	1.51	1.48	1.35

revenue growth was expected to continue into 2008.

...and conservative policies

The draft 2008 budget suggested a conservative fiscal policy aimed at preserving the macroeconomic stability, maintaining a budget surplus over the 3 per cent mark and reducing overall budget expenditure to 40 per cent of GDP. Bulgaria has the tightest fiscal stance of any EU country, with a 3.8 per cent budget surplus in 2007. Principal innovation components of the 2008 budget were the introduction of a 10 per cent flat rate individual income tax and an increase in the maximum monthly 'insurance income' to lev2,000 in 2008. Excise increases on cigarettes, fuels, coals and industrial electricity were due to be increased.

For what is still very much a transitional economy, Bulgaria's unemployment rate for 2007 of 6.6 per cent was acceptably low. The employment rate had risen in 2006 to almost exactly half of the population. The positive trend in both employment and unemployment rate was expected to continue in 2008, due in some measure to the low

values of the existing ratios and increased motivation for labour market participation in general. The improved competitiveness of the economy as a whole bodes well for continued strength in export markets; export orders at the end of 2007 remained high. Between January and September 2007 exports increased by 9 per cent on an annual basis. Imports have also been strong, growing by 17.8 per cent between January and September 2007. Uncertain consumer demand and levels of domestic investment – particularly of machines and electrical equipment – will affect import levels in 2008.

Depending on the basis of calculation, official figures for inflation between January and November 2007 suggested a high of 10.4 per cent or a lower figure of 7.2 per cent. Food prices rose by 12.6 per cent for the same period. Food inflation is expected to remain high. The BNB expects inflation to remain high. In late 2007 the popular feeling was that inflation was a lot higher than the official figures might suggest. Most popular estimates put the figure at around 13 per cent. In Bulgaria the problem has been exacerbated by a drought. Prices for food have risen to such an extent that many Bulgarians have begun to travel to Greece or neighbouring Turkey to shop for food. Some Greek businessmen have even built supermarkets close to the border to cater for Bulgarian shoppers. Food inflation has particularly hit Bulgaria's poor. Bulgaria's average monthly wage is around eur250 (US$250), the lowest in the EU.

The problem of progress

Summing up the economic situation, the World Bank also notes that Bulgaria has made impressive progress towards long-term stability and sustained growth. The Bank attributes this to 'sound macroeconomic policies and deep structural reforms'; according to the Bank, Bulgaria's average annual GDP growth exceeded 6 per cent in the period 2004–07. Growth is led by the private sector, which now accounts for more than three quarters of the economy, very much in line with the average for the eight Central European and Baltic countries that joined the European Union (EU) on 1 May 2004.

The country's living standards improved thanks to increasing economic integration, rising FDI flows, and improved investor confidence. Per capita income increased by an average 6 per cent per year since 1998 (at purchasing power parity in real terms). Unemployment has been reduced substantially from close to 20 per cent in 2000 to below 7 per cent in 2007. Stability, growth and Bulgaria's extensive social protection system helped reduce poverty.

Never-the-less, and despite an overall positive performance, Bulgaria continues to be one of the poorest countries in the EU. The country's per capita income in 2006 at purchasing power standards was just 37 per cent of the average level of eur27. The large income differences reflect significant gaps in investment and productivity, in the level and quality of human and physical capital stock, in the functioning of products and factor markets, and, despite many recent improvements, more generally in the quality of the Bulgarian policy and institutional frameworks. Improving the efficiency of the economy, and closing these gaps, are the central challenges of convergence towards EU averages and sustained improvements in living standards.

If only we had oil

In February 2005, Bulgaria announced that its energy sector was 66 per cent privatised in accordance with EU directives. According to the US *Oil and Gas Journal* (OGJ) Bulgaria had 15 million barrels of proven oil reserves in 2006, producing 3,000 barrels per day (bpd) and consuming 180,000bpd in 2005. The US Energy Information Administration (EIA) notes that Bulgaria's geographic location on the Black Sea gives it the ability to serve as a transit route for Caspian Sea oil exports headed to European refineries, as well as a transit point for Russian natural gas exports to Turkey. Oil is imported through Bulgaria's main port at Burgas, where both the oil terminal and refinery are connected by pipeline to several Bulgarian cities.

In early 2008 outgoing Russian President Vladimir Putin won Bulgaria's support for Russia's South Stream gas pipeline project. The project, a joint venture between Russia's Gazprom and Eni of Italy, plans to carry 30bn cubic metres of gas a year, and will make Bulgaria the gateway for Russian natural gas deliveries to southern Europe. South Stream is also designed to counter EU backed moves to supply gas from Central Europe to Europe in an attempt to reduce the EU's dependence on Russia. South Stream also allows Russia to by-pass the Ukraine for its gas exports to the EU. To obtain Bulgaria's agreement Russia pulled out all the stops, sending both Mr Putin and Mr Medvedev, his successor as president and, coincidentally the chairman of Gazprom, to clinch the deal. Moscow rejected Bulgaria's ambitious request for an 80 per cent share in the project; the compromise solution adopted was a 50 per cent equal share in the project's equity. Mr Putin's visit to Sofia also saw agreement reached on a pipeline to carry Russian crude from the Black Sea port of Burgas in Bulgaria to Alexandroupolis on the Aegean. The second deal signed during Mr Putin's visit was for the construction of two nuclear reactors at Belene on the Danube. The Russian projects have stirred fears among some Bulgarians over what is perceived by many as Bulgaria's increased energy dependence on Russsia.

Bulgarian oil and natural gas exploration occurs predominately in the northern part of the country and the Black Sea. In January 2005, the Bulgarian government offered the offshore Shabla block in the northern Black Sea shelf under a three-year exploration licence. Potential reserves are expected at 200 million barrels. In 2006, the Bulgarian government extended the permit of the Pleven-based Oil and Gas Exploration and Production Company by two years to explore for oil and gas in the Pleven region of northern Bulgaria. Melrose Resources (Melrose) began its latest offshore Bulgarian oil and gas search in September 2004. In 2006, Melrose received an extension of its permit for the offshore block Emine, and also signed a 25-year concession agreement to develop the Galata offshore field, which has estimated reserves of 53 billion cubic feet (Bcf).

Bulgaria's biggest oil refiner, Lukoil's Neftochim, has a nameplate capacity of 140,000bpd. The facility processed roughly 129,000bpd of crude in 2005, up 13.7 per cent from 2004. The company invested US$62 million in reconstructing and upgrading its assets and in the construction of new facilities in 2005, in addition to US$45 million invested the previous year. Lukoil Neftochim recently began producing fuels under the European emission standards Euro 3 and plans to upgrade its facilities to the more difficult Euro 4 standards. Lukoil has stated that it will invest around US$1.0 billion in the development of its oil refinery and retail network in Bulgaria until 2011.

Risk assessment

Economy	Good
Politics	Fair
Regional stability	Good

COUNTRY PROFILE

Historical profile

The Bulgars were a Finno-Ugrian people, whose ancestors crossed the River Danube in the seventh century and merged with the Slavonic population. Bulgaria is the oldest surviving state in Europe to have retained its original name.

681 The state of Bulgaria was founded.

811–927 After defeating the Byzantine Empire, Bulgaria expanded into the Balkans.

1014–18 The Byzantines regained control of lost territory and took over much of Bulgaria.

1185–97 The Bulgarians revolted against Byzantine rule. Bulgaria re-emerged as a state and major Balkan empire.

1396 Bulgaria was conquered by Ottoman Turkey and became its European stronghold for the next 500 years.

1800s The Ottoman Empire began to fall apart as many Balkan states launched uprisings.

1878 Russia defeated Turkey and Bulgaria came into existence again as a sovereign state.

1908 German Ferdinand Saxe-Coburg-Gotha proclaimed himself Tsar of Bulgaria.

1912 The Balkan powers of Bulgaria, Greece and Montenegro defeated the remnants of the Ottoman Empire.

1913 In the Second Balkan War, Bulgaria tried to take Macedonia from Serbia, but was defeated. Balkan states ended the war by signing the Treaty of Bucharest, which also reduced the territorial size of Bulgaria.

1915 Bulgaria invaded Serbia and Macedonia, after joining on the side of the Central Powers (Germany and Austro-Hungary).

1918 The Entente powers (Great Britain, France and Russia) defeated Bulgaria and an armistice was signed in September. The Bulgarian defeat led to the abdication of Tsar Ferdinand I and his son, Boris, was crowned.

1923 As internal divisions intensified between the peasants, ethnic Macedonians and communists, the army overthrew the government, which was dominated by agrarian parties. Prime Minister Alexander Stambolisky was assassinated. Alexander Tsankov formed a new pro-democracy government.

1924–25 Violence from communist militants and Macedonian nationalists prevented the Tsankov government from bringing political stability to Bulgaria.

1926 An ethnic Macedonian, Andrei Liapchev, replaced Tsankov as prime minister.

1929–31 The Great Depression devastated the Bulgarian economy. Thousands of jobs were lost and a wave of strikes hit the country. In the 1931 parliamentary election, the Liapchev government was defeated by the centre-left Naroden Blok (NB) (People's Bloc), led by Alexander Malinov.

1934 A coalition of political parties, led by Zveno's Kimon Georgiev and Colonel Damyan Velchev of the Voenni Sayuz (VZ) (Military Union), overthrew Malinov's government. The new government introduced one-party rule and turned Bulgaria into an authoritarian state.

1935 Disillusioned by the government's authoritarianism, Tsar Boris III began a personal dictatorship of Bulgaria.

1939—1941 Having remained neutral at the start of the Second World War, Bulgaria joined the Axis powers (Germany, Italy and Japan) in 1941. Bulgaria ruled German-captured Macedonia and Western Thrace in Greece.

1943 Boris III died of a heart attack. The heir to the Bulgarian throne, Simeon II, was too young to rule. A three-man regency was established to rule on Tsar Simeon II's behalf and Prime Minister Bogdan Filov became the de facto head of state.

1944 The Soviet Union invaded Bulgaria. The Fatherland Front, a left-wing alliance dominated by the Soviet-backed Bulgarska Komunistieska Partija (BKP) (Bulgarian Communist Party), gained power.

1946 A referendum abolished the monarchy, which had ruled Bulgaria periodically since the ninth century.

1947 All opposition parties were abolished. Political trials and executions on the Stalinist model were carried out under Vulko Chervenkov until 1953 when Todor Zhivkov became the general secretary of the BKP.

1962–88 Zhivkov cemented his position as leader of Bulgaria and the country moved politically and economically closer to the Soviet Union.

1989 Petur Mladenov was appointed Zhivkov's successor.

1990 The BCK changed its name to the Bulgarska Socialistièska Partija (BSP) (Bulgarian Socialist Party). The BSP won the first multi-party elections in Bulgaria since the inter-war period. However, growing political infighting and nationwide strikes led to its fall. An interim government was confirmed, under the leadership of Dimitur Popov.

1991 The BSP lost power in the parliamentary elections. The Sajuz na Demokratienite Sili (SDS) (Union of Democratic Forces) formed a government.

1992 The SDS's Zhelyu Zhelev became Bulgaria's first directly-elected president.

1994 The BSP returned to government in the parliamentary elections.

1996 Amid a severe economic and political crisis, Petar Stoyanov won the presidential elections.

1997 An early general election was held, resulting in a win for the SDS-led centre-right coalition, the Obedineni Demokratièni Sili (ODS) (United Democratic Forces).

2001 The Nacionale Dvisenie Simeon Tvori (NDST) (National Movement for Simeon II) won the general election. The NDST's leader and former king, Simeon II, accepted the nomination to be prime minister and formed a coalition government. The BSP's Georgi Parvanov won the run-off presidential elections.

2003 The IMF approved of Bulgaria's efforts to improve its macroeconomic situation with a loan tranche of US$36 million.

2004 In April, Bulgaria was admitted to NATO.

2005 The Koalicija za Balgarija (KzB) (Coalition for Bulgaria) (led by the BSP) won the 25 June parliamentary elections, defeating the ruling NDST. On 27 July parliament approved Sergey Stanishev as prime minister.

2006 The EU officially agreed to Bulgaria's membership from 1 January 2007. Curbs on organised crime and corruption and the use of EU funds were among the conditions imposed and were stronger than those placed on previous accession countries. In presidential elections in October, incumbent Georgi Parvanov (BSP) won 65 per cent of the vote; however turnout was less than the 50 per cent required for a first round

result, so a runoff election was required. Volen Siderov (Ataka (Attack) party), the closest rival candidate, won 20 per cent. On 29 October, in the second round election, Parvanov won a landslide victory with 77.3 per cent of the vote; Siderov 22.7 per cent. Turnout was 41.2 per cent, in what was seen as voter apathy due to long-term political ineffectiveness in fighting organised crime and implementing social justice and reforms.
2007 On 1 January Bulgaria and Romania joined the European Union, bringing the total number of member-countries to 27. After eight years in prison and two death sentences, commuted to life, six Bulgarians (five nurses and a Palestinian born doctor) were released by Libya on 24 July. They had been held responsible for the deliberate infection of Libyan children with HIV/Aids. In June the NDST became the Nacionalno Dvizenie za Stabilnost i Vazhod (National Movement for Stability and Progress) (NMSP).
2008 The EU has judged that Bulgaria has not sufficiently tackled corruption and organised crime, as required by its EU entry agreement. The EU suspended millions of euros in aid to upgrade roads and agriculture. Bulgaria risks further loss of not only US$1 billion in EU funds but also joining the Schengen area of passport-free travel and trade.

Political structure

Constitution
A democratic constitution was passed in July 1991, defining Bulgaria as a republic with a parliamentary form of government.
Form of state
Parliamentary democratic republic
The executive
The Council of Ministers is the supreme executive body of the government and usually consists of elected members of the National Assembly. The right to initiate new legislation is vested in the deputies and the Council of Ministers.
The head of state is the president of the Republic, elected by a direct popular vote every five years, and assisted by a vice president. The president is not allowed to initiate or veto new laws, but can bring a law back to parliament for further consideration.
National legislature
Legislative functions are carried out by the Narodno Sabranie (National Assembly) consisting of 240 deputies elected for a four-year term by universal adult suffrage.
Legal system
The legal system is based on the 1991 constitution.
The judiciary is the third component within the political system. It is an autonomous power with an independent budget. The Supreme Legal Council has 45 members. The Constitutional Court is the supreme arbiter.
Last elections
25 June 2005 (parliamentary); 22/29 October 2006 (presidential).
Results: Parliamentary: the KzB coalition led by the BSP won 31.1 per cent of the vote (82 seats out of 240), the ruling NDST 19.9 per cent (53), the DPS 12.7 per cent (34), the Ataka 8.2 per cent (21), ODS 7.7 per cent (20), DSB 6.5 per cent (17) and the BNS 5.2 per cent (13).
Presidential: Georgi Parvanov (BSP) won 77.3 per cent; Volen Siderov (Attack party) 22.7 per cent. Turnout was 41.2 per cent.
Next elections
2009 (parliamentary); 2011 (presidential).

Political parties

Ruling party
Koalicija za Bulgaria (KzB) (Coalition for Bulgaria): led by the Bulgarska Socialistièska Partija (BSP) (Bulgarian Socialist Party), with Nacionalno Dvizenie za Stabilnost i Vazhod (National Movement for Stability and Progress) (NMSP) and the Dvisenie za Pravata i Svobodie (DPS) (Movement for Rights and Freedoms) (MRF) (formed 15 Aug 2005).
Main opposition party
Nacionalno Obedinenie Ataka (Ataka) (National Union Attack)

Population

7.64 million (2007)*
Last census: March 2001: 7,928,901
Population density: 74 inhabitants per square km.
Annual growth rate: -0.7 per cent 1994–2004 (WHO 2006)
Ethnic make-up
Turks, Gypsies (around one million in 2002), Russians, Armenians, Jews and Greeks.
Religions
Eastern Orthodoxy is the main religion, but Catholic, Protestant, Jewish and Muslim communities also exist.

Education

Primary education comprises basic education and pre-secondary education. Secondary school education lasts for four or five years and is provided in three types of schools – comprehensive (general secondary) schools, profile-oriented schools and vocational (technical and vocational-technical) schools. Universities, institutes and academies provide higher education. Some universities are private.
Public expenditure on education is typically equivalent to 3.2 per cent of annual gross national income.
Literacy rate: 99 per cent adult rate; 100 per cent youth rate (15–24) (Unesco 2005).
Compulsory years: 7 to 18.
Enrolment rate: 100 per cent boys and 98 per cent girls, total primary school enrolment of the relevant age group, (World Bank).
Pupils per teacher: 17 in primary schools.

Health

Per capita total expenditure on health (2003) was US$573; of which per capita government spending was US$312, at the international dollar rate, (WHO 2006).
Health care reform was initiated in 2000 with the introduction of outpatient care reform, with future plans for transforming the hospitals into commercial enterprises. The IMF and the World Bank agreed to extend a loan of over US$60 million towards the health fund reform.
The National Health Insurance Fund (NHIF) is responsible for the development of the compulsory health insurance scheme in Bulgaria. Health insurance financing by the NHIF will replace funding through taxes for nearly 90 per cent of hospitals.
HIV/Aids
HIV prevalence: 0.1 per cent aged 15–49 in 2003 (World Bank)
Life expectancy: 72 years, 2004 (WHO 2006)
Fertility rate/Maternal mortality rate: 1.2 births per woman, 2004 (WHO 2006); maternal mortality 1.5 per 1,000 live births (World Bank).
Child (under 5 years) mortality rate (per 1,000): 12.3 per 1,000 live births (World Bank)
Head of population per physician: 3.56 physicians per 1,000 people, 2003 (WHO 2006)

Welfare

The Bulgarian social security system consists of a public pay-as-you-go system, a mandatory state-funded system of privately managed savings accounts and an additional voluntary private contribution.
The National Social Security Institute (NSSI) administers mandatory insurance programmes for maternity, sickness, disability and old age benefits including those related to work injuries and occupational diseases. It is also responsible for the collection, control and information services for all obligatory contributions.
The current system of funding benefits was instigated in 2002. A mandatory social insurance scheme provides universal coverage for all members; contributions by individuals to a private insurance fund provide for old age pensions. These schemes are open to all employees, farmers, and artists who pay 21.75 per cent of earning for the social insurance and 0.5 per cent for the private insurance. Employers pay 8.25 per cent of payroll as a whole into these funds. The self-employed

pay 31 per cent in total to the funds. The retirement is at aged 61.5 years (men) and 56.5 years (women), however the age is being increased every year until 2009 when retirement will be at age 63 (men) and 60 (women).

Main cities
Sofia (capital, estimated population 1.0 million in 2005), Plovdiv (340,050), Varna (317,570), Burgas (196,378), Ruse (156,564), Stara Zagora (142,337).

Languages spoken
Turkish (permitted since 1992), Macedonian, Romani, Gagauz, Tartar and Albanian.

Official language/s
Bulgarian

Media
The constitution guarantees freedom of the press.
National news agency: Bulgarian News Agency (BTA)
Other news agencies: BGnes: www.bgnes.com
Focus: www.focus.bg
Mediapool: www.mediapool.bg
Novinite (in English): www.novinite.com
SEEnews (in English): www.seenews.com

Press
There are no laws regulating the print media, with publishing entirely liberated since the end of Communist control in 1989. Hybrid tabloids, which integrates elements of good journalism from the quality press with sensational stories, dominate the market.
In 2006 there were over 900 print media outlets, of which 15 were national and 10 regional, daily newspapers. All dailies have suffered from a steady drop is circulation figures and a sustainable market is dissipating.
Dailies: In Bulgarian, but with English online editions, include Dnevnik (http://news.dnevnik.bg), the leading quality newspaper and Standart (http://standartnews.com); others include 24 Chasa (www.24chasa.bg), Trud (www.trud.bg), Novinar (www.novinar.org), and the Monitor (www.monitor.bg). The only English-language newspaper is The Sofia Echo (www.sofiaecho.com).
Weeklies: There are a variety of magazines for all interest groups. In Bulgarian, Tema (www.temanews.com) is a leading magazine for politics and current affairs, others include 7 din Sport (www.7sport.net), Novo Vreme (www.novovreme.com) and Kultura (www.online.bg/kultura), which is published by the government.
Business: In Bulgarian, Pari (www.pari.bg) is a daily, with an English online edition; Capital (www.capital.bg) and the Banker (www.banker.bg), are both weeklies.

Broadcasting
Radio: The Bulgarian National Radio (BNR) (www.bnr.bg) has the largest market share with two national, public stations and regional services as well as an international service. There are over 100 private commercial stations, with over 30 in Sophia alone. Darik Radio (http://dariknews.bg), is a private national network. Regional stations include Radio Info (www.inforadio.bg), with news and information, from Sophia, Jazz FM (www.jazzfmbg.com) from Blagoevgrad and Radio Mixx (www.radiomixx.net), from Burgas.
Television: There are three national, commercial networks broadcasting for 24 hours. They include the public, Bulgarian National Television (www.bnt.bg) operates Kanal 1 and a satellite channel, the private bTV (www.btv.bg) with the largest audience and Nova Televisia (www.ntv.bg). There are over 180 registered cable TV operates throughout the country with digital TV services due to be fully implemented by 2015.

Economy
Bulgaria's is a mixed economy with services providing 60 per cent of GDP, industry 30 per cent (of which manufacturing is 19 per cent) and agriculture 9 per cent.
Much of the improved economic performance, achieved by Bulgaria since the economic crisis in Eastern Europe in 1996, was gained through restrictive fiscal and monetary policies and economic reforms, such as privatisation. So much so that by 2002 Bulgaria had a 'functioning market economy' according to a European Commissioner. Bulgaria has averaged 5.1 per cent GDP growth since 2000 and by 2006 its steady progress in structural reform and improved business environment gave it the necessary economic progress for a successful entry to the European Union (EU) on 1 January 2007.
In 2006, Bulgaria attracted the highest level of foreign direct investment (FDI) of any east European country at US$5.06 billion (or 16.6 per cent of GDP), due largely to low corporate tax. GDP growth is expected to be 6.2 per cent in 2006, with falling inflation and wages growing in line with productivity. Unemployment has fallen steadily since 2000 when it was 17.9 per cent; it was estimated to be 9.6 per cent in 2006, down from 10.7 per cent in 2005.
While Bulgaria has shown itself capable of taking measures to reform its economy, with all the concomitant social consequences that implies, the concern of international analysts is now focused on the government's efforts to curb corruption and organised crime.

Labour market and unemployment
The unemployment rate is very high. Unemployment is highest in the Targovishte area in north-central Bulgaria) and lowest in the Sofia area. Real wages and labour productivity have increased steadily.
The workforce totals around four million. It is well-educated and highly skilled and employment costs are very low. About 48 per cent of the labour force is female.
In March 2001, amendments to the labour code were approved, making it easier for companies to adjust their workforce to changes in the economy.

External trade
As a member of the European Union, Austria Belgium Cyprus operates within a communitywide free trade union, with tariffs sets as a whole. Internationally, the EU has free trade agreements with a number of nations and trading blocs worldwide. When Bulgaria joined the EU it was with the proviso that its progress in maintaining an open market economy would determine EU benefits.

Imports
Principal imports include energy, mining, metallurgical and petroleum equipment, raw materials, perfumes and cosmetics, vehicles, chemicals and plastics.
Main sources: Germany (12.4 per cent total, 2006), Italy (8.8 per cent), Turkey (6.0 per cent).

Exports
Significant exports include footwear and clothing, iron and steel, copper, machinery and equipment and fuels.
Main destinations: Turkey (11.6 per cent of 2006 total goods exports), Italy (10.1 per cent), Germany (9.7 per cent).

Agriculture
Farming
Agriculture accounts for around 11 per cent of GDP. About 16 per cent of Bulgaria's workforce is employed in farming. Land for agricultural use covers 6.16 million hectares (ha). Principal crops are wheat, maize, barley, sugar beet; other crops include sunflowers, grapes and tobacco.
In February 2001, the Bulgarian government approved proposals to establish market-based institutions, including the revival of its land market, and make the farming sector more competitive. The government supported funding to promote economic diversification, particularly in the rural areas.
Official policy towards land reform has mainly focused on restoring property rights, which included over 99.58 per cent

of agricultural land and 90 per cent for wooded areas.

With the exception of cereals, farm prices and trade have been liberalised. The outlook for wheat producers has brightened since the reduction of a 15 per cent tax on wheat export earnings to 10 per cent.

There is a sizeable wine industry, which accounts for around a third of agricultural exports. Bulgaria exports 80 per cent of its wine output, amounting to about 220,000 litres, of which 25 prer cent are exported to the UK, still the biggest market for Bulgarian wine.

Long-term development of agriculture is based on further concentration and specialisation, mechanisation, improved irrigation, increased grain production and expansion of the dairy sector. The government offers subsidised credits to farmers owning more than 10 cows.

Crop production in 2005 included: 5,852,127 million tonnes (t) cereals in total, 3,478,070t wheat, 1,585,700t maize, 420,000t potatoes, 50,138t oats, 657,863t barley, 20,163t rice, 934,855t sunflower seeds, 21,200t pulses, 6,767t treenuts, 380,000t grapes, 400,000t tomatoes, 397,914t oilcrops, 62,000t tobacco, 800t cotton lint, 160,000t chillies & peppers, 540,400t fruit in total, 1,179,400t vegetables in total. Livestock production included: 411,060t meat in total, 24,885t beef, 189t buffalo meat, 250,000t pig meat, 36,500t lamb, 6,386t goat meat, 88,000t poultry, 92,000t eggs, 1,590,560t milk, 6,000t honey, 10,560t cattle hides, 15,000t sheepskins, 6,500t greasy wool, 50t cocoons, silk, 5,542t cattle hides.

Fishing

Bulgaria's implementation of EU fisheries legislation is yet to be completed. Since progress in the compilation of standardised market data has been slow, privatisation of the processing and marketing sectors has been largely affected.

Bulgaria is collaborating on a draft convention on fishing and conservation of resources in the Black Sea, which provides an abundance of fish for domestic and external markets, although it is under-utilised. The main species caught include sprats, mussels and turbot.

Forestry

Forest and other wooded land accounts for over a third of the total land area, with 3.6 million hectares of forest cover. The proportion of forest cover has been increasing as a result of afforestation intended chiefly for soil protection, rather than wood production. Plantations account for more than a quarter of the forest area.

Most of the forest and wooded land is available for wood supply with the main species being beech and oak. Coniferous species include Norwegian spruce and Austrian pine.

Local demand for sawn wood, panels, pulp and paper is generally met by using domestic wood. Large amounts of sawlogs are also exported.

Industry and manufacturing

The industrial sector accounts for around 30 per cent of GDP and employs 38 per cent of the workforce.

The machine building sector includes over 400 enterprises specialising in various areas including casting, machine tools, wood processing machines, machines for the mining industry, machines for the textile industry, machines for the food processing industry, agricultural machines, shipbuilding, vehicle manufacture, fine mechanics, metal constructions and household instruments.

The key markets are the EU (particularly Germany and the Netherlands), Russia and North America.

Tourism

Bulgaria has become a major tourist destination, despite limited infrastructure. The sector is expected to contribute around 4.6 per cent to GDP in 2005.

Winter ski-ing and Black Sea summer resorts are the main attractions for an increasing flow of tourists. Investment is urgently needed in the existing, increasingly inadequate infrastructure, which is in danger of being overwhelmed, and in new development. The sector is short of up-market facilities. The authorities are seeking to diversify away from package tourism and to spread the benefits of tourism throughout the country, by encouraging cultural, rural and eco-tourism. A Ministry of Culture and Tourism was created in 2005.

The majority of visitors come from south-eastern Europe, especially Greece, followed by Germany, the UK and Russia.

Mining

The mining sector accounts for 2 per cent of GDP and employs 2 per cent of the workforce.

Bulgaria has some deposits of iron, manganese and chromium, and large reserves of zinc, lead and copper.

Apart from zinc, lead and copper, the non-ferrous ores contain some gold, silver and other precious metals. The Chala gold deposit in the area of Haskovski Mineralni Bani is one of Bulgaria's richest. The average gold content is higher than that in Madjarovo where it exceeds three grams per tonne.

Large deposits of copper ore have been discovered in the Sredna Gora mountains.

There are deposits of marl, limestone, granite, sandstone and clay, and plenty of stone which can be used in the building industry.

Hydrocarbons

Bulgaria has oil reserves of around 15 million barrels; known oil and natural gas deposits are of small amounts and at considerable depth. Exploration for oil and gas is concentrated in the north of the country and in the Black Sea.

Bulgaria is a net importer of oil, with most of the supply coming from Russia. In December 2004, Bulgaria, Macedonia and Albania agreed to construct a 900km oil pipeline linking the Bulgarian Black Sea port of Burgas with Vlore on the Adriatic coast of Albania. On the 15 March 2007, Russia, Bulgaria and Greece signed a US$1.2 billion pipeline deal. The pipeline will run inland, from Burgas to the northern Greek town of Alexandroupolis, on the Aegean Sea, to carry 750,000 barrels per day. Russian oil will be transported via the 285km pipeline to the huge EU market, avoiding the busy Bosphorus, where oil tankers can wait for days for access to open waters. A Russian consortium will hold a 51 per cent stake in the deal to build and operate the pipeline and a joint Greek/Bulgarian consortium 24.5 per cent each. The project is expected to be completed in 2010.

Natural gas reserves total 210 billion cubic feet. Production is negligible and Bulgaria is dependent on Russia for the 6.5 billion cubic metres of natural gas it consumes annually. In 2003 Russia and Bulgaria agreed 10–15 year extension of an agreement guaranteeing gas supplies.

Bulgaria also transits Russian gas to other countries in the Balkans and Eastern Europe that do not have access to the pipelines.

Deposits of coal are estimated at around three billion tonnes, mostly of a low calorific value. Around 25 million tonnes of coal is produced annually.

Energy

Bulgaria's installed electricity capacity is approximately 12.5GW, composed of 5.8GW of coal-powered thermal power, 3.8GW of nuclear power and 2.9MW of hydroelectric power.

The coal-fired Maritsa Iztok complex accounts for 60 per cent of the power generated by coal-fired plants. A new thermal plant, agreed in December 2005, is to be constructed at Maritsa Iztok to replace capacity lost by the closure of two nuclear reactors at the Kozloduy power plant after the EU had raised safety concerns. In early 2003, the supreme administrative court blocked Bulgaria's 2002 agreement with the EU to close another two Kuzloduy reactors by 2006. In June 2004, the government announced that it will build a new nuclear power plant on the river

Danube, to take over when the remaining plants go off-line. The new plant is expected to keep Bulgaria the leading exporter of electricity in Europe's south-east.

Financial markets

Stock exchange

Trading volumes are low despite the number of large companies that are quoted. Most trading on the Bulgarian Stock Exchange (BSE) is concentrated in the free markets, where privatised stakes under the government's privatisation programme are placed.

Commodity exchange

Sofia Commodity Exchange

Banking and insurance

There is a two-tier system in which an independent central bank supervises and regulates commercial banks and has exclusive rights over the issue of currency. There are approximately 33 commercial banks, with total bank credit to the private sector accounting for 14 per cent of GDP, one of the lowest rates of former Soviet countries.

Central bank

Bulgarska Narodna Banka (BNB) (Bulgarian National Bank)

Time

GMT plus two hours (daylight saving, late March to late October, GMT plus three hours)

Geography

Bulgaria lies in south-eastern Europe, on the east of the Balkan Peninsula. It is situated on the western shores of the Black Sea and shares borders with Romania to the north, Turkey to the south-east, Greece to the south, Macedonia (FYROM) to the south-west and Serbia to the north-west. The lower River Danube forms most of the border with Romania. The Balkan Mountains dominate central Bulgaria, running from west to east and separating the Danubian plains in the north from the Thracian plains of Eastern Rumelia in the south-east. The Rhodope Mountains occupy south-west Bulgaria and separate it from Greece and Macedonia.

The Sofia depression in the west of the country is hill country which separates the Balkan Mountains from the southern mountains. It is the main centre of population and communications.

The fertile Bulgarian plateau, between the Danubian border and the Balkan Mountains, averages some 100km in width and contains several tributaries of the Danube, the major one being the Iskur. The main rivers south of the Balkan watershed are the Struma and the Maritza which run into the Aegean Sea. The broad Maritza Valley, which leads on to the Thracian plains, is one of the principal agricultural areas.

Hemisphere

Northern

Climate

Summer is hot and dry, April–September average temperature 23 degrees Celsius (C). Cold winters, average temperature minus 1 degree C, with heavy snow.

Dress codes

Dress for business is usually quite conservative but not overly formal.

Entry requirements

Passports

Passports are required by all visitors.

As from 1 January 2006, all visitors staying for longer than 24 hours must be registered with the authorities; hotels will automatically undertake this task.

Visa

Not required by citizens of Europe, North America, Australasia and some Asian countries for either 90 or 30 days. Full details and information can be found at www.bulgariatravel.org and see 'getting to Bulgaria'.

Businessmen from visa-free states may visit without a visa for up to 30 days. All other businessmen must apply for visas and include a letter of invitation from a company registered in Bulgaria endorsed by the Bulgarian Chamber of Commerce.

All visitors, tourist and business, must have travel and medical insurance to cover emergency medical expenses, repatriation, transport of mortal remains, funeral and hospitalisation. A copy of the policy, with legible policy number, company name, duration of validity and sum of coverage or a letter from the insurance company including such data, should be submitted with the application.

Currency advice/regulations

The import and export of local currency up to Lev5,000 is allowed without restrictions. Between Lev5,000–20,000 import and export is permitted if the amount was declared on arrival. The import and export of over Lev20,000 is allowed only with written permission from the central bank.

Foreign currency may be import in unlimited amounts, but must be declared on arrival; export of foreign cannot exceed the amount imported and declared.

A bordereaux is issued to all visitors on arrival, to record all money exchanges and must be returned to the authorities when departing. Local currency can only be exchanged on departure with the bordereaux. Visitors are advised to exchange money in banks and hotels.

ATMs are widespread; check with the card provider concerning terms and conditions. Travellers cheques are accepted in major hotels and establishments; US dollars and pound sterling attract less additional rate charges.

Customs

Small quantities of spirits, wines and beverages are allowed in duty-free. Valuable personal effects should be declared verbally to Customs on entry. There are no restrictions on goods bought for foreign exchange in duty free shops at ports of entry.

Health (for visitors)

Foreign travellers must present valid evidence of health insurance to the Bulgarian border authorities in order to be admitted into the country.

Mandatory precautions

None

Advisable precautions

Recommended immunisations: hepatitis A, polio, tetanus and typhoid.

Hotels

Deluxe, first- and second-class ratings system. Hotels have been upgraded to attract business people. Radisson, Sheraton and Hilton groups have hotels in Sofia.

Credit cards

Main international credit cards are accepted in larger hotels and stores in larger cities, and in some restaurants in Sofia.

Public holidays (national)

Fixed dates

1 Jan (New Year's Day), 3 Mar (National Day), 1 May (Labour Day), 6 May (St George's Day), 24 May (St Cyril and Methodius Day/Culture Day), 6 Sep (Unification Day), 22 Sep (Independence Day), 24–26 Dec (Christmas).

Variable dates

Orthodox Good Friday, Orthodox Easter Monday.

Working hours

Banking

Mon–Fri: 0800–1230, 1330–1530; Sat: 0830–1130.

Business

Mon–Fri: 0800 (0900)–1730 (1800).

Government

Mon–Fri: 0800 (0900)–1730 (1800).

Shops

Mon–Fri: 1000–2000; Sat: 0800–1400.

Telecommunications

Mobile/cell phones

There is good GSM coverage of 3G, with nationwide coverage of GSM 900 and 1800.

Electricity supply

220–240V AC/50 HZ

Social customs/useful tips

A nod of the head means 'No', a shake of the head means 'Yes'. Shaking hands is the traditional form of greeting. It is usual to invite your host to a good restaurant.

Security
By Western standards, the streets of Sofia and other towns and cities are generally safe. Street crime is slowly rising and the usual precautions should be taken.

Getting there

Air

National airline: Bulgaria Air
Hemus Air connects Sofia to some European and Middle Eastern destinations.
International airport/s: Sofia (SOF) airport, 10km east of the city centre. Facilities include banks, post office, duty-free shops, restaurant and car hire.
By day, buses run every 10 minutes to the city, at night they run every 20 minutes between 2100–0030. Taxis are available, if the metre is not in use, a fare may have to be negotiated before travelling.
Other airport/s: Varna (VAR), 9km from city; Burgas (BOJ), 13km from city.
Airport tax: None, except US nationals who are charged US$20.

Surface

Road: The pan-European corridor, which is being built or existing roads upgraded, links Bulgaria to the European motorway network. Border crossings exist from all surrounding countries; new roads and border controls are planned with Turkey, Greece and Serbia. The Trans-European Motorway (TEM), includes routes connecting Budapest with Athens via Sofia and with Istanbul via eastern Bulgaria. In July 2006 the proposal for a north-south road tunnel under Shipka Mountain estimated at US$120 million, was still under consideration.
Rail: There are no direct rail services between Bulgaria and Western Europe. Links exist to Serbia, Turkey, Romania and Greece.
Water: Ships provide regular passenger service and cruises on the Danube, starting at Passau in Germany, to Vienna, passing through Slovakia, Hungary and Serbia. There are also links with the Rhine, Black Sea and Main.
Main port/s: Burgas, Varna.

Getting about

National transport

Air: Bulgaria Air operates a domestic flight from Sofia to Varna. Hemus Air connects Sofia to the Black Sea cities of Varna and Bourgas.
Road: The overall quality of the 13,000km of roads linking the major cities is good but some roads are in poor repair and full of potholes. International road signs are used and traffic drives on the right.
Rail: Approximately 6,500km of track connect all main towns. First-class travel is recommended. It is necessary to make reservations.

City transport

Taxis: Taxis are plentiful and cheap. Official taxis have meters, although some privately operated ones may not. A 5–10 per cent tip in local currency is usual.
Taxis to Sofia airport have a journey time of 15 minutes. Fares should be agreed before departure.
Buses, trams & metro: Efficient and cheap tram and bus services operate in Sofia. Flat rate fares are charged.
Trolleybus services are available in Plovdiv and Varna.
Buses to the city centre from the airport run every 10 minutes during the day and every 20 minutes between 2100–0030, and take 25 minutes.

Car hire

An international driving permit is required. A green card (international car insurance) is compulsory. Most car hire accounts are transacted in hard currency. Drivers are normally given special petrol coupons, which can be used throughout the country. Speed limits: out of town 90kph and 120kph on motorways, in town 50kph. Drinking and driving is strictly prohibited. There are tolls on motorways and other major roads.

BUSINESS DIRECTORY

The addresses listed below are a selection only. While World of Information makes every endeavour to check these addresses, we cannot guarantee that changes have not been made, especially to telephone numbers and area codes. We would welcome any corrections.

Telephone area codes

The international direct dialling (IDD) code for Bulgaria is +359, followed by area code and subscriber's number:

Blagoevgrad	73	Rousse	82
Burgas	56	Smoliyan	301
Dobritch	58	Sofia	2
Gabrovo	66	Stara Zagora	42
Lovech	68	Varna	52
Plovdiv	32	Veliko Tûrnovo	62

Useful telephone numbers

Ambulance: 150
Fire brigade: 160
Police: 166
Operator: (inland) 121
(international) 123
Directory enquiries: (business) 144
(domestic lines) 145
Traffic police: 165
Road service: 91-146

Chambers of Commerce

American Chamber of Commerce in Bulgaria, Building 2, Mladost 4 Area, Business Park Sofia, 1715 Sofia (tel: 976-9565; fax: 976-9569; e-mail: amcham@amcham.bg).

British Bulgarian Chamber of Commerce, 8 Charles Darwin Street, 1113 Sofia (tel: 971-4756; fax: 738-331; e-mail: info@bbcc.bg).

Bulgarian Chamber of Commerce and Industry, 42 Parchevich Street, 1058 Sofia (tel: 987-2631; fax: 987-3209; e-mail: bcci@bcci.bg).

Burgas Chamber of Commerce and Industry, 12B L Karavelov Street, PO Box 644, 8000 Sofia (tel: 812-007; fax: 810-130; e-mail: bscci@bcci.bg).

Dobritch Chamber of Commerce and Industry, 14 Nezavisimost Street, PO Box 182, 9300 Dobritch (tel: 601-433; fax:601-434; e-mail: dbcci@bcci.bg).

Gabrovo Chamber of Commerce and Industry, 1Vazrazhdane Square, PO Box 217, 5300 Gabrovo (tel: 288-39; fax: 341-83; e-mail: gbcci@mbox.eda.bg).

Plovdiv Chamber of Commerce and Industry, 7 Samara Street, 4003 Plovdiv (tel: 652-645; fax: 652-647; e-mail: pcci@plovdiv-chamber.org).

Sousse Chamber of Commerce and Industry, 3 A Ferdinand Boulevard, PO Box 484, 7000 Rousse (tel: 825-884; fax: 825-873; e-mail: info@chamber.rousse.bg).

Stara Zagora Chamber of Commerce and Industry, 66 GS Rakovski Street, 6000 Stara Zagora (tel: 461-94; fax: 260-33; e-mail: office@chambersz.com).

Varna Chamber of Commerce and Industry, 135 Primorsky Boulevard, 9000 Varna (tel: 615-140; fax: 612-146; e-mail: office@vcci.bg).

Banking

Biochim Bank, 1 Ivan Vazov Street, 1040 Sofia (tel: 926-9210; fax: 981-9151; e-mail: info@biochim.com).

BulBank Ltd, 7 Sveta Nedelya Square, 1000 Sofia (tel: 984-1111; fax: 988-4636, 988-5370; e-mail: infor@sof.bulbank.bg).

Bulgarian Post Bank, 1 Bulgaria Square, 1414 Sofia (tel: 963-2104/5; e-mail: iap@postbank.bg).

DSK Bank, 19 Moskovska Street, 1040 Sofia (tel: 939-1220; fax: 980-6477).

Central bank

Bulgarska Narodna Banka, 1 Alexander Battenberg Square, 1000 Sofia (tel: 91-459 fax: 980-2425).

Financial markets

Bulgarian Stock Exchange, 10 Tri ushi Street, 1303 Sofia (tel: 937 09 34; fax: 937 09 46; e-mail: bse@bse-sofia.bg; www.bse-sofia.bg).

Sofia Commodity Exchange, Sofia (tel: 952 6212; fax: 952 6232; e-mail: sce@sce-bg.com; www.sce-bg.com).

Travel information

Bulgaria Air, 1 Brussels blvd, Sofia Airport Sofia 1540 (tel: 402-0306; fax: 937-3254; email: office@air.bg; internet: www.air.bg/en/).

Balkantourist, 2 Enos Street, 1408 Sofia (tel: 981-9806; fax: 988-4177; email: sofia.agency@balkantourist.bg; internet: www.balkantourist.bg).

Central Railway Station, Maria Luisa Boulevard, Sofia (tel: 31-111; internet: www.sofia.com/transport).

Hemos Air, Airport Sofia, 1 Brussels Blvd, Sofia 1540 (tel: 942-0202; fax: 945-9147; email: office@hemusair.bg; internet: www.hemusair.bg).

Sofia Airport (email: public@sofia-airport.bg; internet: www.sofia-airport.bg/En).

National tourist organisation offices

Bulgarian Tourism Authority, 1 Sveta Nedelia Square, 1000 Sofia (tel: 987-9778; fax: 989-6939; email: webmaster@bulgariatravel.org; internet: www.bulgariatravel.org).

Ministries

Ministry of Agriculture and Forests, 55 Hristo Botev Boulevard, 1000 Sofia (tel: 981-1546; fax: 885-557).

Ministry of Culture, 17 Alexander Stamboliiski Boulevard., 1000 Sofia (tel: 980-5384; fax: 981-8145).

Ministry of Defence, 3 Vassil Levsky Street, 1000 Sofia (tel: 862-4135; fax: 873-626).

Ministry of Economy, 12 Kniaz Alexander Batenberg Street, 1000 Sofia (tel: 981-9965, 987-9778; fax: 981-2515, 981-5039).

Ministry of Education and Science, 2a Doundukov Boulevard, 1000 Sofia (tel: 84-81; fax: 987-1289).

Ministry of Environment and Waters, 67 Gladstone Street, 1000 Sofia (tel: 814-269; fax: 521-634).

Ministry of Finance, 102 Georgi Rakovski Street, 1000 Sofia (tel: 869-1870; fax: 980-6863); external department (tel: 869-223; fax: 876-008).

Ministry of Foreign Affairs, 2 Alexander Jendov Street, 1000 Sofia (tel: 714-3507; fax: 736-069).

Ministry of Health, 5 Sveta Nedelya Square, 1000 Sofia (tel: 86-31; fax: 875-040).

Ministry of the Interior, 23 Gurko Street, 1000 Sofia (tel: 877-511; fax: 824-047).

Ministry of Justice, 1 Slavianska Street, 1000 Sofia (tel: 86-01; fax: 876-3226).

Ministry of Labour and Social Policy, 2 Triaditza Street, 1000 Sofia (tel: 981-1717; fax: 800-609).

Ministry of Regional and Urban Development, 17 Kiril & Methodius Street, 1000 Sofia (tel: 83-841; fax: 872-517).

Ministry of Transport, 9 Levski Street, 1000 Sofia (tel: 872-862; fax: 885-094).

Council of Ministers, 1 Dondoukov Blvd., 1000 Sofia (tel: 8501; fax: 884-252).

Other useful addresses

Agency for Economic Co-ordination and Development, 1 Vassil Levsky Street, 1000 Sofia (tel: 543-386; fax: 833-323).

Agency for Privatisation, 29 Aksakov St, 1000 Sofia (tel: 873-188; fax: 882-938, 885-395).

Amex Representative Office, BICD, Rila Hotel, 6 Kalojan Street, Sofia 1000 (tel: 871-516).

Board of Customs Houses at the Ministry of Finance, 1 Aksakov Street, Sofia 1000 (tel: 869-528; fax: 884-909).

British Embassy, 38 Boulevard Vassil, Levski, Sofia 1000 (tel: 980-1220; fax: 988-5367).

Bulgarian Academy of Sciences, 1 7-mi Noemvri Street, 1000 Sofia (tel: 841-41; fax: 803-023).

Bulgarian Embassy (USA), 1621 22nd Street, NW, Washington DC 20008 (tel: (+1-202) 387-0174; fax: (+1-202) 234-7973; e-mail: office@bulgaria-embassy.org).

Bulgarian Foreign Investment Agency, 3 Sveta Sofia Street, 1000 Sofia (tel: 980-0918; fax: 980-1320; e-mail: fia@geobiz.com; internet site: www.bfia.org).

Bulgarian Industrial Association (BISA), 14 Alabin Street, 1000 Sofia (tel: 879-611, 872-960; fax: 872-604).

Bulgarian National Television, 29 San Stefano Str, 1504 Sofia (tel: 446-329; fax: 662-388).

Bulgarian News Agency (BTA), 49 Tzarigradsko Chaussee Blvd, 1024 Sofia (tel: 877-363, 877-739; fax: 802-488).

Bulgarian Telecommunication Company (BTC), 8 Totleben Blvd (tel: 870-143; fax: 875-885).

Bulgarian Telegraph Agency, Trakija Boulevard 49, Sofia (tel: 8461).

Bulgarian Translators' Union, 16 Graf Ignatiev Street, 1000 Sofia (tel: 661-602, 662-564; fax: 510-845, 661-233).

Bulgarreklama (trade show agency), 147 Tsarigradsko Chaussee Blvd, 1784 Sofia 1784 (tel: 965-5220; fax: 965-5230; email: bul-reklama@bulgarreklama.com; internet: www.bulgarreklama.com).

Central Co-operative Union, 99 Rakovski Street, 1000 Sofia (tel: 84-41; fax: 878-157).

Central Post Office, 4 Gurko Street, Sofia.

Committee for Energy, 8 Triaditsa Street, 1000 Sofia (tel: 861-91; fax: 876-279).

Committee for Forests, 17 Antim I Street, 1000 Sofia (tel: 861-71; fax: 873-235).

Committee for Geology and Mineral Resources, 22 Maria Louisa Blvd, 1000 Sofia (tel: 832-767; fax: 833-976).

Committee for Posts and Telecommunications, 6 Gourko Street, 1000 Sofia (tel: 889-646, 871-837; fax: 814-512, 800-044).

Committee for Television, 29 San Stefano Street, 1504 Sofia (tel: 43-481).

Committee for Standardisation and Metrology, 21 6-ti Septemvri Street, 1000 Sofia (tel: 85-91; fax: 801-402).

EU Energy Centre (Thermie), 51 James Boucher Blvd, 1407 Sofia (tel: 681-461, 683-542; fax: 681-461).

Euro Information Centre, Network/Correspondence Centre, 54 Dr GM Dimitrov Blv, 1125 Sofia (tel: 738-448; fax: 730-435).

First Bulgarian Stock Exchange, 1 Macedonia Square, 1040 Sofia (tel: 815-711; fax: 875-566; internet site: www.bse-sofia.bg).

Foreign Aid Agency, 1 Vrabcha Street, 1000 Sofia (tel: 881-951; fax: 885-039).

Intercommerce (import, export, re-export and transit operations, compensation deals and foreign trade transactions), 21 Aksakov Str, 1000 Sofia (tel: 879-364; fax: 873-753).

International Fair – Plovdiv, G. Dimitrov Boulevard 37 (tel: 553-191, 553-146, 26-129, 26-139).

International Road Transport (SO MAT), Gorublyane, 1738 Sofia (tel: 712-121, 758-015; fax: 758-015).

Interpred World Trade Centre (representation of foreign companies), 36 Dragan Tzankov Boulevard, 1040 Sofia (tel: 7146-4646; fax: 700-006, 706-401).

Law Offices for Foreign Legal Matters (tel: 877-782).

Medical Industry Association, Bademova Gora Street 20-a, Sofia 1404 (tel: 592-111).

Scientific Institute for International Co-operation and Foreign Economic Activities, 3A 165 Street, Zh K Izgreva, 1113 Sofia (tel: 708-336; fax: 705-154, 700-131).

Small and Medium-Sized Enterprises (SME) Development Programme, Agency for Privatisation, 29 Aksakov Str, 1046 Sofia (tel: 871-913; fax: 871-912).

Sofia Press Agency, 113 Tsarigradsko Shosse Blvd. (tel: 878-428; fax: 883-455).

Sofia Customs Office, 1 Aksakov Street, 1000 Sofia (tel: 800-402; fax: 884-909).

State Insurance Institute, 3 Benkovski Street, 1000 Sofia (tel: 879-341; fax: 871-429).

Union for Private Economic Enterprise, 2a Suborna Street, 1000 Sofia (tel: 659-371; fax: 659-411).

National news agency: Bulgarian News Agency (BTA)
Other news agencies: BGnes: www.bgnes.com
Focus: www.focus.bg

Mediapool: www.mediapool.bg

Novinite (in English): www.novinite.com

SEEnews (in English): www.seenews.com

Internet sites
Background information on the government and useful links: www.vii.org/afgrbulg.htm

Bulgaria business catalogue and useful links: www.bulgaria.com

Bulgarian Economic Forum: www.biforum.org

Bulgaria financial and business newspaper: www.pari.bg

Bulgarian International Business Association: www.biba.bg

Bulgarian News Agency: www.bta.bg/site/en/indexe.shtml

SG Expressbank AD: www.sgexpressbank.bg

Full list of air carriers at Sofia airport: www.sofia-airport.bg/flights/image/airlines_en.htm

Burkina Faso

KEY FACTS

Official name: République Démocratique Populaire de Burkina Faso (Popular Democratic Republic of Burkina Faso)

Head of State: President Captain Blaise Compaoré (since 1987, re-elected 2005)

Head of government: Prime Minister Tertius Zongo (since 4 Jun 2007)

Ruling party: Coalition led by Congrès pour la Démocratie et le Progrès (CDP) (Congress for Democracy and Progress) (since 1997; re-elected 6 May 2007)

Area: 274,000 square km

Population: 13.31 million (2007 government census)

Capital: Ouagadougou

Official language: French

Currency: CFA franc (CFAf) = 100 centimes (Communauté Financière Africaine (African Financial Community) franc). New notes have been issued; old notes cease to be legal tender from Jan 2005.

Exchange rate: CFAf413.08 per US$ (Jul 2008) CFAf655.95 per euro (pegged from Jan 1999)

GDP per capita: US$508 (2007)*

GDP real growth: 4.20% (2007)*

Labour force: 5.77 million (2004)

Inflation: -0.20% (2007)*

Balance of trade: -US$334.00 million (2006)

* estimated figure

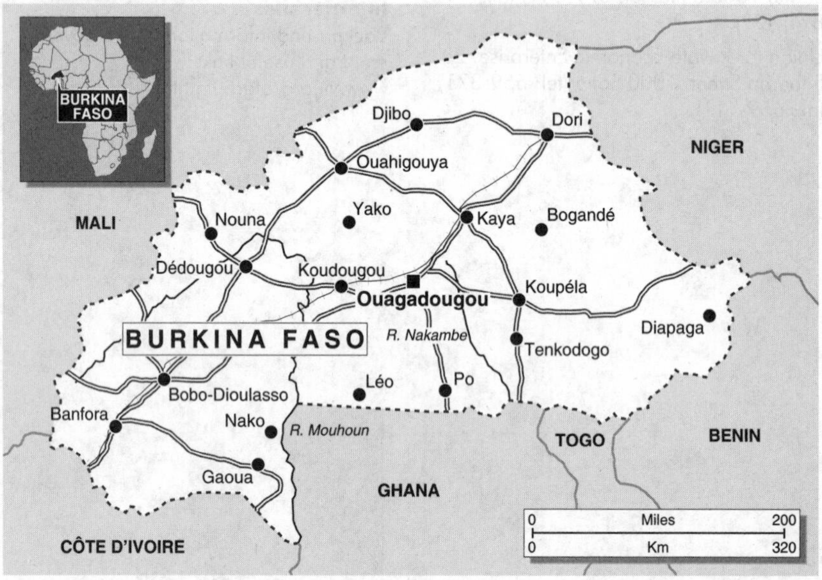

Traditionally, agriculture is Burkina Faso's most important economic activity: 10 million Burkinabe ultimately depend on it, 60 per cent of the rural population are employed in the agricultural sector. Despite efforts to develop and expand agricultural productivity, Burkina Faso has not been able to generate true self-sufficiency, importing on average 12,000 tons of cereals annually. With the elusive objective of self sufficiency still in view, most agricultural cultivation is devoted to cereal cultivation of one kind or another. The choice of crop largely depends on the fertility and the moisture content of the soil.

Cotton socks

However, it is not in cereal production that Burkina Faso has notched up its major agricultural success. Cotton production has increased spectacularly. In the 1970s total national cotton production was little more than 32,000 tons annually. The targeted crop total for 2006–07 was 800,000 tons, most of which is slated for export to Europe and the Far East. The increase has been achieved by greater soil fertility and improved methods of crop treatment. All cotton treatment is channelled through three companies, SOFITEX (which until 2004 had held a monopoly position) SOGOMA in the east of the country, and Faso Coton (a company with Swiss investment) in the south. The ending of the monopoly, and the introduction of new companies, has played a significant role in the expansion of production.

According to the International Monetary Fund (IMF), in a paper *Burkina Faso: Weathering its Cotton Crisis* published in the March 2008 IMF Survey Burkina Faso's cotton production has grown by some 19 per cent a year in the ten years up to 2007, providing a welcome boost to gross domestic product (GDP) growth. But at the same time the cotton sector has been hurt by lower world prices and the appreciation of the euro (to which the region's CFA franc is pegged) against the US dollar. To make matters worse, an inflexible pricing mechanism prevented lower world cotton prices being passed on to producers. Burkina Faso's cotton processing companies, the creation of which had done so much to re-invigorate the sector, obliged to sell at world prices, ended up with sizeable losses. Initiatives to address the problem have begun, but more needs to be done to make the sector more competitive. The sector's viability in Burkina Faso, as well as in other West

African countries, is under pressure from distortions in global cotton trade caused by producer subsidies and the surge in low cost output from other developing countries. Perhaps more important, however, are the low efficiency of ginning companies, low yields, and generally slow productivity growth. According to the IMF, the financial difficulties of Burkina Faso's cotton sector are affecting the general economy.

Cotton crisis

This is because cotton's success has made it a major pillar of Burkina Faso's economy. Although it represents only 5–8 per cent of GDP, it accounts for around 50–60 per cent of export earnings and is the main source of foreign exchange. Burkina Faso's share of world cotton exports has tripled over the past 10 years – unprecedented for an African agricultural product. What makes it more remarkable is that this occurred despite a slump in world prices. The sale of cotton seed is the main or only source of cash revenue for farmers and is critical in the fight against poverty. Cotton provides about 700,000 jobs to about 17 per cent of the population. In cotton-growing zones, poverty has been reduced by a quarter.

The IMF believes that steps have been taken to address the crisis. The government re-capitalised SOFITEX, Burkina Faso's largest ginning company in 2007, at a cost of more than one per cent of GDP, increasing its shareholding from 35 per cent to more than 60 per cent. Perhaps perversely, it is now seeking to reduce its role in the sector.

One step toward insuring the sector's viability has been the adoption of a market-based producer price setting mechanism, implemented for the 2007/08 harvest.

Again according to the IMF, the new mechanism aligns domestic producer prices with world market prices and thus makes producers share the risk. Following the introduction of the new pricing mechanism, if current world prices prevail the ginning companies should break even for the fiscal year, and farmers might even make a small profit. However, cotton output for 2007/08 is expected to fall by more than 25 per cent because of bad weather, but it is expected to recover in 2008/09.

Painful consequences

According to the IMF, Burkina Faso's macroeconomic performance in 2006 was better than projected despite the difficult external environment. Annual GDP growth was estimated at 5.5 per cent, and inflation fell to a respectable 3 per cent as food prices fell. The cotton crisis of declining world prices meant that Burkina Faso's producers had to be sheltered in some degree, with painful consequences for national ginning plants. GDP growth was expected to drop to 4.5 per cent in 2007. The current account deficit looked likely to widen in 2007 and into 2008. The rise in value of the euro has also been a negative factor, particularly affecting Burkina Faso's exports. Rising oil prices will also have a negative effect on growth and macroeconomic stability. The tax reform measures planned for 2008 were also expected to improve revenue raising. But Burkina Faso has a long way to go, ranked a very lowly 176 out of 177 countries in the 2007 Human Development Index (HDI), published by the United Nations Development Programme.

Predictable elections

Legislative elections took place in May 2007. In the last presidential elections in November 2005, President Blaise Compaoré won a third, five-year term. Municipal elections took place on 23 April 2006, resulting in the first-ever elections of local governments for 302 newly established rural communes.

In early 2008, several protests erupted in Ouagadougou and other towns against the high cost of living. In early marches there was some violence and property destruction, and many demonstrators were arrested. A peaceful protest in Ouagadougou on 15 March 15 drew large numbers of people. The government took measures to temporarily suspend import taxes on a set of basic commodities in response to the rising cost of living. Despite the unrest, the May 2007 National Assembly Elections did little more than endorse the predominance of the ruling Congrès pour la Démocratie et le Progrès (CDP) (Congress for Democracy and Progress). The CDP won 73 seats out of 111, way ahead of the second strongest party, Alliance pour la Démocratie et la Féderation-Rassemblement Démocratique Africain (ADF-RDA) (Alliance for Democracy and Federation-African Democratic Rally), which managed to win 14 seats.

The importance of Compaoré

Burkina Faso has spent many of its post-independence years under military rule. The last but one coup was in 1983, led by Thomas Sankara who adopted a policy of nonalignment. His rule was cut short after only four years, when in the final coup to date he was overthrown by his minister of state, Blaise Compaoré, and subsequently executed.

In 1991 Burkina Faso had adopted a constitution which provided for direct multi-party elections. Blaise Compaoré was returned as president in elections the following year and continues to dominate the politics of Burkina Faso. Compaoré, having successfully managed the multi-party coalition democracy he subsequently created is now in his nineteenth year of presidency. Not until the 2002 elections was the grip of his CDP party on the national assembly broken. The main opposition parties, which had boycotted previous elections in 1992 and 1998, succeeded in reducing the CDP's representation in the 111-seat assembly from 103 seats to 57. This democracy in action did

KEY INDICATORS — Burkina Faso

	Unit	2003	2004	2005	2006	2007
Population	m	12.31	12.44	13.11	*13.22	13.31
Gross domestic product (GDP)	US$bn	2.68	4.82	5.62	*6.12	*6.98
GDP per capita	US$	218	412	429	*456	*508
GDP real growth	%	6.5	4.8	7.1	*5.4	*4.2
Inflation	%	1.7	-0.4	6.4	2.4	-0.2
Exports (fob) (goods)	US$m	250.0	418.6	395.0	563.0	–
Imports (cif) (goods)	US$m	525.0	866.3	992.0	897.0	–
Balance of trade	US$m	-275.0	-447.7	-597.0	-334.0	–
Current account	US$m	-300.0	-440.0	-661.0	*-585.0	*-688.0
Total reserves minus gold	US$m	434.8	430.6	438.4	554.9	1,029.2
Foreign exchange	US$m	423.6	419.1	427.7	543.7	1,017.4
Exchange rate	per US$	574.89	496.63	507.22	496.60	454.40

* estimated figure

not please Compaoré and tension between the two sides continues.

Compaoré won his third straight term as president in November 2005 by a landslide, beating 11 other contenders and taking 80 per cent of the vote. Born in 1950 and trained as a soldier, he has disarmed local militias and, despite his reputed left-wing leanings, embarked on a programme of privatisation and austerity measures urged upon him by the IMF.

Burkina Faso has faced international censure over its record of human rights and, more recently, allegations that it was involved in the smuggling of blood diamonds from Sierra Leone to world markets. This was tacit support for rebels opposing the Sierra Leone government and using money from the sale of the gems to fund their campaign. Similarly, there is tension with Côte d'Ivoire, which has accused Burkina Faso of backing rebels who hold the north of that country.

Outlook

The cotton crisis and its consequences combined with high oil and food prices are expected to, at least for a year or so, take the shine off Burkina Faso's IMF-lauded sound macroeconomic policies and structural reforms. Structural reforms continue to be necessary to establish the conditions for a resumption of robust economic growth.

Risk assessment

Politics	Fair
Economy	Fair
Regional stability	Poor

COUNTRY PROFILE

Historical profile

Formerly an ancient African kingdom, the area was taken over by France in the nineteenth century, who did little to develop it preferring to provide local workers for neighbouring Côte d'Ivoire.

Translated into English as the 'land of honest men', Burkina Faso (known as Upper Volta until 1938) was created as an administrative unit, by the French, as late as 1947. It became politically independent in 1960, ruled by a civilian government under Maurice Yameogo. He was ousted by the army in 1966 following mass opposition to austerity measures. To its credit, the army had been reluctant to assume power and set about organising the introduction of a new civilian government, drawing up the 1970 constitution which provided for semi-civilan rule for the next four years. Fractional struggles within the civilian political parties came to a head in 1974 and the army again formally took over government. Later all political parties were banned. A wave of strikes in 1976 finally forced the complete demilitarisation of politics. Instability – in the form of coups d'état and even assassinations – remained the determining feature of Burkinabe politics until the early 1990s.

1958 The country was given self-government.

1960 Granted full independence from France as Upper Volta. Maurice Yameogo became first president.

1966 Yameogo was ousted in a military coup by Colonel Sangoule Lamizama.

1970 A new constitution was agreed by a referendum, it detailed the introduction of an elected president and civilian administration by 1975.

1974 Lamizama suspended the constitution and assumed the presidency.

1978 Multiparty elections for president and National Assembly were held. Lamizama and his followers won and he retained the presidency.

1980 Yameogo, was overthrown in a coup by Colonel Saye Zerbo.

1982 Major Jean-Baptiste Ouédraogo overthrew Zerbo.

1983 Captain Thomas Sankara led a coup and took over as president.

1984 Upper Volta's name was changed.

1987 Sankara was assassinated. Captain Blaise Compaoré seized power backed by the Organisation pour la Démocratie Populaire-Mouvement du Travail (ODP-MT) (Organization for People's Democracy-Workers' Movement).

1991 Compaoré was elected president, following the withdrawal of opposition candidates.

1992 The ODP-MT won a convincing victory in the national legislature elections.

1996 The ODP-MT merged with the Parti pour la Démocratie et le Progrès (Party for Democracy and Progress) to become the Congrès pour la Démocratie et le Progrès (CDP) (Congress for Democracy and Progress).

1998 Compaoré won the presidential election, which was boycotted by opposition parties.

1999 Prime Minister Ouédraogo and his cabinet resigned, but he and his cabinet were reinstated by presidential decree.

2000 A UN report accused the president of not only allowing Burkina Faso to be involved in sanctions busting of UN embargoes to Angola but also of being in personal receipt of payments for diamond smuggling activities undertaken through his country by Unita rebels.

2001 International donors agreed to fund a US$85 million programme to combat the HIV/Aids epidemic.

2002 The CDP retained its majority in parliamentary election.

2004 Burkina Faso was included on the US African Growth and Opportunity Act (AGOA) list of countries allowed preferential trading with the US.

2005 Blaise Compaoré was re-elected president 13 November with 80.3 per cent of the votes, while Bénéwendé Stanislas Sankara won 4.9 per cent. Turnout was 57.5 per cent.

2007 In the general elections on 6 May, the ruling CDP won 73 seats (out of 111) the opposition ADF-RDA won 14, eleven other parties won less than six seats each. Turnout was 56.4 per cent. On 4 June, Tertius Zongo became prime minister following Paramanga Ernest Yonli's resignation.

2008 Workers from both the public and private sectors held a two day strike in April to protest at the high cost of living, and to demand pay rises.

Political structure

Constitution

Constitutional changes were adopted in January 1997. These included the abolition of the limit of two seven-year terms for the president, and an increase in the number of seats in the legislature from 107 to 111.

Form of state

Unitary and secular state

The executive

Executive power is vested in the head of state (the president), who is elected by universal suffrage for a seven-year term. The president may serve unlimited terms. The Council of Ministers is appointed by the president on the recommendation of the prime minister who is also appointed by the president, with the consent of the legislature.

National legislature

The parliament comprises two chambers, the Assemblée des Députés Populaires (ADP) (National Assembly) and the Chambre Des Représentants (House of Representatives).

The multi-party ADP has 111 members, who are elected for a four-year term. The House of Representatives, which acts only as a consultative chamber, has 120 members, who are elected for a three-year term.

Last elections

13 November 2005 (presidential); 6 May 2007 (parliamentary).

Results: Parliamentary: the ruling CDP won 73 seats (out of 111) the opposition ADF-RDA won 14, eleven other parties won less than six seats each. Turnout was 56.4 per cent.

Presidential: Blaise Compaore was re-elected with 87.5 per cent of the vote.

Next elections

24 May 2007 (parliamentary); 2010 (presidential),

Political parties

Ruling party

Coalition led by Congrès pour la Démocratie et le Progrès (CDP) (Congress for Democracy and Progress) (since 1997; re-elected 6 May 2007)

Main opposition party

Alliance pour la Démocratie et la Féderation-Rassemblement Démocratique Africain (ADF-RDA) (Alliance for Democracy and Federation-African Democratic Rally)

Population

13.31 million (2007 government census)

Last census: 2007, 13.31 million.

Population density: 39 inhabitants per square km. Urban population: 17 per cent (1995–2001).

Annual growth rate: 2.95 per cent according to 2007 government census.

Ethnic make-up

There are a number of ethnic groups, the most numerous of whom are the Mossi in the north (49 per cent), the Gourma in the east and the Bobo in the south-west. Other sizeable groups include the Fulani, the Hausa, the nomadic Tuareg with their Bella domestic serfs in the north-west and the Lobi in the south.

Religions

Animist (55 per cent), Muslim (40 per cent), Catholic (5 per cent).

Education

Only two in five children are able to attend school, due to the chronic lack of places.

Burkina Faso secured financial aid from the international donor community in 2002, in the form of a three-year package aimed at building capacity in education. The agreement encompassed the Education For All Fast Track Initiative (EFA-FTI) with the goal of providing every child with primary school education by 2015. The first phase of financing is aimed at the 1.2 million children currently unable to attend primary school. The initial financing will also be used to train new teachers, pay teachers' salaries, build new schools, help education systems, respond to HIV/Aids, and put in place other steps to ensure a quality primary education for all children.

French is the language used in schools, although most children will not have heard any spoken at home. School fees are charged although payment can be deferred until after harvest. About 10 per cent of schools are run outside the state system.

Literacy rate: 13 per cent adult rate; 19 per cent youth rate (15–24) (Unesco 2005).

Pupils per teacher: 47 in primary schools.

Health

Per capita total expenditure on health (2003) was US$68; of which per capita government spending was US$32, at the international dollar rate, (WHO 2006).

A CFA6 billion, 10 year (2006–15) plan to make contraceptives available throughout the country is supported by the USAID and the UN Population Fund. The government believes that increasing the use of contraception will help reduce the maternal mortality rate, which at 484 per 100,000 births is one of the highest in West Africa.

HIV/Aids

Burkina Faso has the second highest infection rate in West Africa, next to Côte d'Ivoire. In February 2003, the UN Development Programme (UNDP) announced the provision of US$9.5 million in funding for the fight against HIV/Aids, poverty reduction and other activities in Burkina Faso. It is expected that half of the funding will be concentrated on the HIV/Aids programme, including prevention of HIV transmission, improved co-ordination and monitoring, and care for infected and affected persons.

A programme to provide anti-retroviral drugs was scaled down in December 2004, instead of the 27,000 patients WHO said should receive treatment, it is expected in 2005 that only 15,000 patients will be targetted. Lack of political commitment, poor infrastructure – with a lack of medical personnel – and a centralised distribution network are sited as major contributing factors in the programme's shortcomings.

HIV prevalence: 4.2 per cent aged 15–49 in 2003 (World Bank)

Life expectancy: 48 years, 2004 (WHO 2006)

Fertility rate/Maternal mortality rate: 6.6 births per woman, 2004 (WHO 2006)

Child (under 5 years) mortality rate (per 1,000): 107 per 1,000 live births; 34 per cent of children aged under five are malnourished (World Bank).

Head of population per physician: 0.06 physician per 1,000 people, 2004 (WHO 2006)

Welfare

The Social Insurance Scheme provides benefits for old age pensions, disability and a surviviorʼs fund. The fund is open to workers who contribute 4.5 per cent of the wages and this is matched by their employer.

Main cities

Ouagadougou (capital, estimated population 1.0 million in 2005), Bobo Dioulasso (386,678), Koudougou (87,841).

Languages spoken

African languages include More, Dioula, Gourmantche and Peul. French is the universal medium for documentation.

Official language/s

French

Media

The government regulates the media through the Ministry of Communications and Culture.

National news agency: Agence d'Information du Burkina

Press

Dailies: In French, Sidwaya (www.sidwaya.bf), is the official government newspaper, other private publications include Le Pays (www.lepays.bf) and L'Observateur Paalga (www.lobservateur.bf).

Weeklies: In French, magazines or weekend editions of daily newspapers include L'Observateur Dimanche (www.lobservateur.bf), Bendré (www.journalbendre.net), Indépendent (www.independant.bf), L'Opinion (www.zedcom.bf), Journal du Jeudi (www.journaldujeudi.com), is a satirical magazine. L'Evénement (www.evenement-bf.net), is published fortnightly.

Broadcasting

The national, public broadcaster is Radio Télévision du Burkina (RTB) (www.tnb.bf).

Radio: For most of the population radio is the primary means of accessing news and information. There are many private and community stations in operation.

Radio Burkina (RTB) (www.radio.bf) has a national network with regional services, broadcasting in French and 13 local languages. Private stations include Savane FM (www.savanefm.bf), Africa No 1 (www.africa1.com), Radios Gambidi, Pulsar and Horizon FM and Radio Maria Burkina Faso (www.radiomaria.org) run by the Catholic Church.

Television: The public TV service is La Télévision du Burkina (RTB) (www.tnb.bf), which transmits programmes in French and local languages. Alternatively Canal 3 (www.tvcanal3.com), is a private, commercial TV station. There is satellite TV, primarily from French sources but with other international services available.

News agencies

National news agency: Agence d'Information du Burkina

Economy

Burkina Faso is one of the poorest countries in Africa, with 45 per cent of the population, mainly in the countryside, living below the poverty line. More than 80 per cent of the population are engaged in subsistence agriculture and nomadic livestock rearing. Agriculture accounts for around 30 per cent of GDP.

Reforms since 1991, supported by the IMF and the World Bank, have contributed to growth in GDP, stabilisation of inflation and some reduction in the poverty rate, but Burkino Faso continues to be dependent on foreign aid. The economy, despite positive developments, remains fragile and vulnerable to weather conditions and world commodity prices. The growing strength of the economy is encouraging foreign support for poverty reduction and reform.

The civil war and ensuing instability in neighbouring Côte d'Ivoire since 2003 has added to Burkino Faso's woes. Resources have had to be diverted for humanitarian assistance and extra security measures, and the export of cotton via rail through Côte d'Ivoire to the coast has been curtailed.

Cotton is the main source of foreign currency, accounting for around 60 per cent of export earnings. Competition from subsidised cotton growers in the US and other OECD countries is a continuing problem, contributing to a decline in world prices since 2003. Although, as a consequence of low prices, farmers in Burkina Faso are being tempted to move out of cotton growing, favourable weather conditions in recent years have resulted in bumper crops. Burkino Faso has been encouraged by the World Bank and the IMF to diversify as a means of strengthening the economy against external shocks.

External trade

As a member of the Economic Community of West African States (Ecowas), Burkina Faso is also a member of the West African Economic and Monetary Union using the common currency, the CFA franc. Remittances from seasonal workers adds to the balance of trade. Industries include processed food and cotton, brewing and bottling.

Imports

Main imports are machinery, foodstuffs, fuel and energy, and capital goods.

Main sources: France (24.2 per cent total, 2005), Côte d'Ivoire (23.7 per cent), Togo (6.8 per cent)

Exports

Main exports include cotton, gold, live animals, hides and skins.

Main destinations: China (38.3 per cent total, 2005), Singapore (12.6 per cent), Thailand (5.7 per cent), Ghana (5.2 per cent), Taiwan (4.4 per cent)

Agriculture

Farming

The agricultural sector accounts for around a third of GDP and employs three-quarters of the workforce. It accounts for around 65 per cent of export earnings. Over 80 per cent of the population is engaged in subsistence farming and nomadic stock raising.

Burkina Faso is prone to drought and has poor soil. Only 10 per cent of the total land area is cultivated. There are plans to mechanise farming and open up new areas for development.

Principal food crops are sorghum, millet, yams, maize, rice and beans.

Cotton is the main cash crop and is the country's principal foreign exchange earner; others are sheanuts, sesame and sugar cane.

Livestock production is concentrated in the north, mainly for export to Côte d'Ivoire (which has severely restricted its Burkinabè beef imports in recent years) and Ghana.

Crop production in 2005 included: 2,901,973 tonnes (t) cereals in total, 1,399,302t sorghum, 937,630t millet, 481,474t maize, 95,501t rice, 40,3864t sweet potatoes, 89,695t yams, 450,000t sugar cane, 245,307t groundnuts (in shells), 188,682t pulses, 65,500t roots and tubers, 147,009t oilcrops, 535,367t seed cotton, 210,000t cotton lint, 78,110t fruit in total, 232,000t vegetables in total. Livestock production included: 221,572t meat in total, 105,514t beef, 32,885t pig meat, 16,385t lamb, 27,750t goat meat, 30,882t poultry, 45,045t eggs, 229,352t milk, 17,266t cattle hides, 4,005t sheepskins.

Industry and manufacturing

The industrial sector as a whole contributes around 20 per cent to GDP and employs 10 per cent of the workforce; manufacturing contributes 13.5 per cent.

Production is centred on the processing of agricultural commodities (flour milling, sugar refining, manufacture of cotton yarn and textiles) and production of consumer goods, including moped/bicycle assembly, footwear and soap manufacture.

Foreign investment is minimal and development remains handicapped by the chronic shortages of raw materials and spares.

Tourism

Tourism is at an early stage of development. While hotel accommodation is expanding, most of it is confined to Ouagadougou and Bobo Diaoulasso, and access to some tourist sites is difficult. The sector is expected to contribute 2.1 per cent to GDP in 2005. Europe is the main source of visitors, especially France, followed by Africa. The country comprises four tourist regions. Ouagadougou is an artistic and business centre, while the west specialises in indigenous culture, the Sahel in adventure holidays, and the east, which is home to two national parks, in safaris and hunting. The economic importance of the sector is recognised, with rural and eco-tourism being the focus of further development.

Mining

The sector contributes around 7 per cent to GDP and employs 2 per cent of the workforce.

Activity is confined to extraction of gold-bearing quartz at Poura (reserves estimated at 30 tonnes), marble and antimony.

There are viable deposits of zinc and silver at Perkoa, and some 15 million tonnes of manganese deposits at Tambao, as well as known reserves of limestone, bauxite, nickel, phosphates and lead.

Exploitation of resources is hindered by weak infrastructure.

Burkina Faso has a geological structure similar to that of the world's richest gold producing areas.

Hydrocarbons

There are no known reserves of oil or gas. Burina Faso relies entirely on imports of refined oil, mainly gasoline and distillate. Nigeria has made trade deals of oil with Burkina Faso as a way of improving relations.

Energy

The rural population relies on wood as a fuel for cooking, which is leading to deforestation and desertification in some areas.

Electricity supply is overseen by the Societé Nationale Burkinabe d'Electricité (Sonabel). Installed generation capacity is estimated at around 90MW. Only 14 per cent of the country, mainly the urban areas, has access to electricity and there is no national electricity grid. 85 per cent of electricity is supplied by thermal power. Some electricity is imported from Côte d'Ivoire.

Electricity is regarded as crucial to the country's development and the government is keen to extend transmission lines and improve supply to meet growing demand.

Financial markets

Burkina Faso has no stock exchange.

Banking and insurance

The banking sector has undergone liberalisation in recent years, with the government restricting its involvement to around a quarter of the sector.

Central bank

Banque Centrale des Etats de l'Afrique de l'Ouest (central banking authority for the members of the West African Monetary Union)

Main financial centre

Ouagadougou

Time

GMT

Geography
Burkina Faso is a landlocked country in West Africa, bordered by Mali to the west and north, by Niger to the east, and by Benin, Togo, Ghana and Côte d'Ivoire to the south.
Burkina Faso is a generally flat country. The north lies in the Sahel region, the semi-arid fringes of the Sahara desert. To the south-west there are hills. The highest point in the country, Ténakourou, which rises to 749m, is in this region. Rainfall is negligible in the Sahel area, but is heavier to south, supporting areas of wooded savannah, rice-growing and large plantations.
The main rivers, which flow southwards into Lake Volta in Ghana, are the Mahoun, Nakambé and Nazinon (formerly known as the Black, White and Red Volta rivers respectively). Other rivers include tributaries of the Niger. Only the Mahoun flows throughout the year, the rest being seasonal. There are many lakes.
Hemisphere
Northern

Climate
The climate is tropical. The dry season runs from November–March, when the Harmattan wind blows, keeping the humidity low. Temperatures in Ouagadougou range from 14 degrees Celsius (C) at night to over 35 degrees C during the day. The main rainy season is from June–October. The highest rainfall is in the south, lowest in the far north where an arid desert climate prevails.

Entry requirements
Passports
Required by all, except holders of national identity cards issued to nationals of Ecowas countries.
Passports must have at least six months validity.
Visa
Required by all, except nationals of Ecowas countries and transit travellers.
Applications for tourist and business visas should include itineraries and vaccination certificates against yellow fever. Business visas require a company letter of introduction.
An onward or return ticket is also required.
Currency advice/regulations
There are no restrictions on the import/export of foreign currency or local currency.

Health (for visitors)
Mandatory precautions
Yellow fever vaccination certificate.
Advisable precautions
Typhoid, tetanus, hepatitis A and polio vaccinations are recommended. Malaria prophylaxis should be taken as risk exists throughout the country. Water precautions are also advisable. There is a risk of rabies. Visitors should seek advice with regard to vaccinations for diphtheria, hepatitis B, meningitis and tuberculosis.
Hotels
Hotels are available in Ouagadougou and Bobo Dioulasso with limited availability elsewhere. It is advisable to book in advance. Service is included in bills and gratuities are customary for taxis and porters.

Public holidays (national)
Fixed dates
1 Jan (New Year's Day), 3 Jan (Anniversary of the 1966 Coup d'État), 8 Mar (Women's Day), 1 May (Labour Day), 4 Aug (Revolution Day), 5 Aug (Independence Day), 15 Aug (Assumption Day), 15 Oct (Anniversary of the 1987 Coup d'État), 1 Nov (All Saints' Day), 11 Dec (Proclamation of the Republic), 25 Dec (Christmas Day).
Variable dates
Easter Monday, Ascension Day, Eid al Adha, Eid al Fitr, Islamic New Year, Birth of the Prophet.
Islamic year – 1429 (10 Jan 2008–28 Dec 2008): The Islamic year contains 354 or 355 days, with the result that Muslim feasts advance by 10–12 days against the Gregorian calendar. Dates of feasts vary according to the sighting of the new moon, so cannot be forecast accurately.

Working hours
Banking
Mon–Thur: 0730–1130 and 1500–1600; Fri: open to 1700.
Business
Mon–Fri: 0730–1230 and 1500–1730.
Government
Mon–Fri: 0730–1230 and 1500–1730.
Shops
(Mon–Sat) 0800–1300 and 1500–1900; (Sun) 0800–1200.

Electricity supply
220/380 V AC, 50 cycles.

Getting there
Air
National airline: Air Burkina
International airport/s: Ouagadougou (OUA), 8km from city, banks, shops, post office, restaurants, car hire.
Other airport/s: Bobo Dioulasso (BOY), 16km from city.
Surface
Road: Most practical during dry seasons – from Mali (Bamako), Côte d'Ivoire (Abidjan) and Niger (Niamey), when buses operate on these routes. Land journeys are also possible from Ghana, Benin and Togo. Skirmishing between rival political factions makes it advisable to check conditions locally before departure.
Rail: Ouagadougou is linked to Abidjan (Côte d'Ivoire) by an express service, which operates up to three times a week. Sleeping and dining cars.

Getting about
National transport
Air: Air Burkina serves Ouagadougou, Bobo Dioulasso and other main centres. Bobo Dioulasso is the main domestic airport.
Road: Conditions vary; some roads are only passable in dry season, although international roads are all-weather.
Buses: Services between Ouagadougou and main towns. Advance booking advisable.
Rail: Daily service runs Ouagadougou-Bobo Dioulasso and on to Côte d'Ivoire; two classes; some trains have restaurant cars, sleeping accommodation and air-conditioning. Service can become overcrowded.
City transport
Taxis: Unmetered and available in main centres. A 10 per cent tip is usually given.
Buses, trams & metro: Frequent in Ouagadougou and Bobo Dioulasso.
Car hire
National licence plus permit or international driving licence required. Use of chauffeur-driven cars advised.

BUSINESS DIRECTORY
The addresses listed below are a selection only. While World of Information makes every endeavour to check these addresses, we cannot guarantee that changes have not been made, especially to telephone numbers and area codes. We would welcome any corrections.

Telephone area codes
The international direct dialling code (IDD) for Burkina Faso is +226, followed by subscriber's number.

Useful telephone numbers
Police: 17
Fire: 18
Ambulance: 3066-43/44/45

Chambers of Commerce
Burkina Faso Chamber of Commerce, Industry and Handicrafts , 118/220 Rue 3.119, 01 PO Box 502, Ouagadougou (tel: 306-114; fax: 306-116; e-mail: ccia-bf@ccia.bf).

Banking
Banque Internationale du Burkina, BP 1336, Av Nelson Mandela 800, Ouagadougou 01 (tel: 307-888, 307-878; fax: 310628).

Banque Internationale du Burkina SA, BP 362, Rue de la Chance, Ouagadougou 01 (tel: 306-170, 306-171; fax: 300-171, 310-094).

Banque Internationale pour le Commerce, l'Industrie et l'Agriculture du Burkina SA, BP 8, Avenue Dr Kwamé N'Krumah 479, Ouagadougou 01 (tel: 306-226/8, 306-227; fax: 311-955).

Caisse Nationale de Crédit Agricole du Burkina (CNCAB), BP 1644, Avenue Gamal Abdel Naser 2, Ouagadougou 01 (tel: 333-333).

Ecobank-Burkina, BP 145, Rue Maurice Bishop 633, Espace Fadima, Ouagadougou 01 (tel: 318-975, 318-980; fax: 318-981, 318-982).

Société Générale de Banque au Burkina (SGBB), BP 585, Rue du Marché 4, Ouagadougou 01 (tel: 323-232; fax: 310-561).

Central bank

Banque Centrale des Etats de l'Afrique de l'Ouest, Avenue Gamal Abdel Nasser, PO Box 356, Ouagadougou (tel: 306-015; fax: 310-122).

Travel information

Air Burkina, Avenue de la Nation, BP 1459, Ouagadougou 016 (tel: 5030-7676; fax: 5031-4517).

Direction du Tourisme et de l'Hôtellerie, BP 624, Ouagadougou 01(tel: 306-399; fax: 311-904).

Ministry of tourism

Ministry of Culture, Arts and Tourism, 03 BP 7007, Ouagadougou 03 (tel: 5033-0963; fax: 5033-0964; e-mail:webmestre–mcat@mcc.gov.bp).

National tourist organisation offices

Office Nationale du Tourisme Burkinabè, BP 1311, Avenue Frobénius, Ouagadougou 01 (tel: 311-959; fax: 314-434).

Ministries

Ministry of Agriculture, 03 BP 7005, Ouagadougou 03 (tel: 324-114).

Ministry of Administration, 03 BP 7034, Ouagadougou 03 (tel: 324-833).

Ministry of Commerce and Industry, 01 BP 365 Ouagadougou 01 (tel: 324-786).

Ministry of Communications, 03 BP 7045, Ouagadougou 03 (tel: 324-833).

Ministry of Defence, 01 BP 496, Ouagadougou 01 (tel: 307-214).

Ministry of Education, 03 BP 7032, Ouagadougou 03 (tel: 324-870).

Ministry of Employment and Social Security, 03 BP 7016, Ouga 03 (tel: 310-960).

Ministry of Energy and Mines, 01 BP 3922 Ouagadougou 01 (tel: 324-786).

Ministry of the Environment and Water, 03 BP 7044 Ouagadougou 01 (tel: 324-074).

Ministry of the Family, 01 BP 515, Ouagadougou 01 (tel: 310-960).

Ministry of Finance and Economy, 03 BP 7012, Ouagadougou 03 (tel: 306-995).

Ministry of Foreign Affairs, 03 BP 7038, Ouagadougou 03 (tel: 324-733; fax: 308-792; internet: www.mae.gov.bf/).

Ministry of Health, 03 P 7009 Ouagadougou (tel: 324-158).

Ministry of Higher Education and Scientific Research, 03 BP 7047, Ouagadougou 03 (tel: 324-567).

Ministry of Integration and African Affairs, 01 BP 6943, Ouagadougou 01 (tel: 324-833).

Ministry of the Interior, 03 BP 7011, Ouagadougou 03 (tel: 324-905).

Ministry of Justice, 01 BP 526, Ouagadougou 01 (tel: 324-833).

Ministry of Public Relations and Modernisation of Administration, 03 BP 7006, Ouagadougou 03 (tel: 306-995).

Ministry of Youth and Sports, 03 BP 7035, Ouagadougou 03 (tel: 324-786).

Other useful addresses

Burkina Faso Embassy (USA), 2340 Massachusetts Avenue, NW, Washington DC 20008 (tel: 202-332-5577; fax: 202-667-1882; e-mail: ambawdc@rcn.com).

Groupement des Petits Commerçants, BP 952, Ouagadougou.

Institut de la Statistique et de la Démographie, BP 374, Ouagadougou (tel: 335-537).

Office National de Commerce Extérieur, BP 389, Ouagadougou (tel: 336-225).

Société de Commercialisation, BP 531, Ouagadougou (tel: 333-007); BP 375, Bobo-Dioulasso (tel: 390-423).

Syndicat des Entrepreneurs et Industriels, BP 446, Ouagadougou.

Télévision Nationale du Burkina, BP 7029, Ouagadougou (tel: 336-801).

West African Economic Community, BP 643, Ouagadougou.

National news agency: Agence d'Information du Burkina
Address: 01 BP 2507 Ouagadougou 01 (tel: 50 324-640; fax: 50 337-316; email: infos@aib.bf; internet: www.aib.bf).

Internet sites

Africa Business Network: www.ifc.org/abn

Air Burnina : www.air-burkina.com

AllAfrica.com: www.allafrica.com

African Development Bank: www.afdb.org

Africa Online: www.africaonline.com

Mbendi AfroPaedia (information on companies, countries, industries and stock exchanges in Africa): mbendi.co.za

Burundi

The fragility of Burundi's peace became apparent in 2007 when the Supreme Court in Burundi sentenced the former Chairman of President Pierre Nkurunziza's ruling Forces pour la Défense de la Démocratie (FDD), (Forces for the Defence of Democracy) to 13 years behind bars. Mr Hussein Radjabu had been found guilty of attempting to 'recruit former rebels with the aim of destabilising the state and insulting President Nkurunziza, referring to him as an 'empty bottle'. The party's ascension to power after winning a 2004 election ended Burundi's 12-year civil conflict, which killed more than 300,000 people. A rift between President Nkurunziza and Mr Radjabu had resulted in the replacement of the latter as the party chairman in February 2007. This was followed by the arrest of Mr Radjabu in April 2007 and replacement of ministers loyal to him from holding key positions. As a key political figure, Mr Radjabu had the support of two thirds of Burundian lawmakers and of the minority Muslim community. Many people believed the sentence to be part of a political vendetta. The 1993 assassination of Burundi's first Hutu president, Melchior Ndadaye, plunged the country into a civil war. A 2001 power-sharing deal, brokered by South Africa, probably saved the country.

Macroeconomic stability?

Annual inflation was held to the single digits but economic growth, at 3.6 per cent in 2007, will be lower than targeted because of a very poor coffee harvest and exports, and delays in implementing structural reform, owing primarily to the political difficulties. Monetary policy was strengthened and continued to be prudent. Gross international reserves declined to about 2.8 months of imports by September 2007 owing to delays in external budget support. The real effective exchange rate depreciated by 11.4 per cent through August 2007. On 1 July 2007, Burundi became a member of the East African Community (EAC).

Scandal

Unbudgeted payments totalling 1.6 per cent of GDP were made to the largest domestic petroleum distribution firm, Interpetrol. The inspector general's office found these payments to be fraudulent and implicated the former minister of finance and the former Banque de la République du Burundi (BRB) (central bank) governor. The governance incident was a serious blow to fiscal policy, especially after another governance shock in 2006. Fiscal performance was further affected by a cut in petroleum taxation in July from 20 to 10 per cent in the face of the large increase in world market price (0.3 per cent of GDP), delays in demobilisation, promises of a large increase in civil service allowances, and a budget estimate error on excises and anticipated dividend receipts (about 1.0 per cent of GDP).

The government has made efforts to recover funds, launch legal proceedings against those allegedly responsible and launch an external audit of petroleum sector cross–arrears with the budget. Revenue measures were introduced, proposed expenditure increases were postponed, and expenditure commitments in non-priority areas were cut by about 1.5 per cent of GDP. Disbursement of the bulk of donor budget support was expected in late 2007. The monetary impact of additional interim budget financing was to be

KEY FACTS

Official name: Republika y'Uburundi (Republic of Burundi)

Head of State: President Pierre Nkurunziza (Hutu) (elected 19 Aug 2005)

Head of government: President Pierre Nkurunziza

Ruling party: Conseil National pour la Défense de la Démocratie-Forces pour la Défense de la Démocratie (CNDD-FDD), (National Council for Defence of Democracy-Forces for the Defence of Democracy)

Area: 27,834 square km

Population: 7.79 million (2007)*

Capital: Bujumbura (plans to build a new capital nearer to the centre of the country were announced in March 2007).

Official language: Kirundi and French

Currency: Burundi franc (Buf) = 100 centimes

Exchange rate: Buf1,188.69 per US$ (Jul 2008)

GDP per capita: US$128 (2007)

GDP real growth: 3.60% (2007)

Labour force: 3.92 million (2004)

Inflation: 8.40% (2007)

Balance of trade: -US$182.80 million (2005)

Foreign debt: US$1.39 billion (2004)

* estimated figure

largely offset by a run-down in external reserves.

Political difficulties

Political tensions during most of 2007 handicapped the passage of key economic legislation. The November announcement of an agreement to bring the major opposition parties into the government was a promising development. None the less, social indicators in the education sector have improved markedly, especially since free primary education was declared in 2005. Coffee washing stations were not sold in the second half of 2007, as expected, because of continuing delays in elaborating a privatisation strategy and in drafting a new legal and regulatory framework. Managing public expectations of a peace dividend will be critical to macroeconomic stability, as will be reinvigorating structural reform, particularly privatisation, which is critical to raising investment and growth.

The IMF expects the economy to strengthen in 2008. Growth is projected to rise to about 6 per cent as cyclical coffee output rebounds. Prudent monetary policy and a budget that avoids domestic financing are expected to keep inflation in the single digits. The monetary programme provides room for credit to the economy to rise strongly in real terms. Fiscal policy for the rest of 2007 seeks to recover from the impact of the governance incident and for 2008 will continue shifting expenditure from security to social and infrastructure needs while financing the deficit entirely with external grants and highly concessional loans. The revenue effort is being buttressed with revenue measures equivalent to 1.3 per cent of GDP in 2008. The 2008 budget contains expenditure contingencies of about 1 per cent of GDP linked to possible additional financing requirements. All being well, the primary deficit is expected to improve and the overall deficit is expected be kept to one per cent of GDP, without recourse to domestic financing. Spending on the social sectors will rise further to 10.1 per cent of GDP in 2008.

Revenue administration is being gradually reinforced and tax policy reform is being introduced to remove distortions and improve economic efficiency. The intent is to prepare for the introduction a value added tax (VAT) in 2009 – something especially needed following Burundi's entry into the EAC – and modernise the country's outdated tax code. Burundi's inflated wage bill will be better managed; it is among the highest in sub-Saharan Africa. The wage bill will be held at 10.5 per cent of GDP as improved management and a further round of demobilisation compensate for the hiring of new school teachers, predictable benefits increases for civil servants and the inevitable salary increases for high-ranking officials.

Since 2000, according to the World Bank, Burundi's government has implemented a programme of financial and structural reforms aiming to stabilise the economy and revive economic activity. Between 2001 and 2006, gross domestic product (GDP) grew by a somewhat disappointing 2.7 per cent per annum, while inflation was contained in single digits. The World Bank reported that GDP growth was about 5 per cent in 2006, despite supply and oil shocks that were offset, in part, by recovery in coffee production and in the services sector, as well as reconstruction activities. With the exception of 2003 and 2005 – during which bad weather in the north severely affected agriculture production – the past few years have seen annual growth rates between 2 and 6 per cent. Reforms and political progress have resulted in increased agricultural production and construction, as private confidence has returned and donors have re-engaged. However, the poor rains of 2003 and 2005 which hit the agriculture sector hard (GDP growth was -1.3 per cent and 0.9 per cent, respectively) highlighted the need to develop a more diversified economy and sources of growth.

Bleak house

With half the population living below the poverty line, the social situation in Burundi remains pretty bleak. According to the World Bank, poverty is widespread in both rural and urban areas. There has been a sharp deterioration in all social indicators which are now among the worst in Africa. The odds of Burundi reaching the Millennium Development Goals (MDGs) by 2015 are slim. The poverty index is now 67 per cent (compared to the 2015 MDG target of 30 per cent). The spread of HIV/AIDS is taking a heavy toll on communities, with an overall rate of infection rate of 11.2 per cent, leaving many households vulnerable. Infant mortality rates are as high as 114 (2004) per 1,000 (compared to the African average of 103.1 per 1,000, and to the MDG target of 36 per 1,000), and maternal mortality rates average 990 (2000) per 100,000 (compared to African averages of 916.8 per 100,000, and to the MDG target of 202 per 100,000 by 2015). Major causes of morbidity and mortality include malaria, acute respiratory infections, diarrhoea, tuberculosis, and malnutrition.

Less than half of Burundi's population is literate. Primary school enrolments are now restored to the pre-crisis long-term trend level, with a net primary enrolment ratio of 57 per cent in 2002 (compared to the MDG target of 100 per cent by 2015). However, only an estimated 37 per cent of the official primary school age cohort (7–12 year olds) is in school. At the secondary level, the gross enrolment ratio of 12 per cent (2004) is below the average for sub-Saharan Africa. In the non-formal education system, approximately 300,000 people are enrolled for basic literacy and numeracy instruction. However, the quality of this type of education is very low.

KEY INDICATORS — **Burundi**

	Unit	2003	2004	2005	2006	2007
Population	m	7.22	7.80	7.49	7.64	*7.79
Gross domestic product (GDP)	US$bn	0.69	0.66	0.80	0.91	1.00
GDP per capita	US$	95	91	107	*120	*128
GDP real growth	%	-0.5	5.5	0.9	5.1	*3.6
Inflation	%	11.0	7.9	13.4	2.8	8.4
Exports (fob) (goods)	US$m	26.0	31.8	56.9	58.7	–
Imports (cif) (goods)	US$m	135.0	138.2	240.7	249.4	–
Balance of trade	US$m	-109.0	-106.4	-183.8	-190.7	–
Current account	US$m	-40.0	-160.0	-83.0	-132.0	-124.0
Total reserves minus gold	US$m	67.0	65.8	100.1	130.5	176.3
Foreign exchange	US$m	66.3	64.8	99.3	129.7	175.4
Exchange rate	per US$	1,065.00	1,060.00	1,000.15	1,000.15	1,139.23

* estimated figure

Risk assessment

Economy	Poor
Politics	Fair
Regional stability	Fair

COUNTRY PROFILE

Historical profile

Virtually unheard of until its first round of massacres in 1972–73, in which a quarter of a million people died, Burundi is a small, poor and overpopulated African republic. For years, Burundi's politics were unhappily preoccupied with the maintenance of Tutsi supremacy over the majority Hutu people.

Although the origins of Burundi's second major civil war, which broke out in 1993, were ethnic, the conflict degenerated into a bewildering free-for-all in which an estimated 300,000 people died. At issue was a struggle for control of one of Africa's poorest countries, with a GDP of less than US$1 billion.

1899 Burundi and its neighbour, Rwanda, were incorporated into German East Africa.

1916 Belgium occupied the area.

1923 Re-named Ruanda-Urundi, Belgium continued its administration.

1959 Many Tutsi refugees from Rwanda sought shelter from ethnic violence.

1962 On July 1, the Kingdom of Burundi became independent from Belgium under a Tutsi King, Mwambutsa IV.

1963 Many Hutus fled into Rwanda due to ethnic violence.

1965 Hutu candidates won a majority in parliamentary elections. However, Mwambutsa refused to appoint a Hutu prime minister. A Hutu coup led by Michel Micombero failed and the Hutu elite were massacred in retaliation.

1966 Mwambutsa was deposed by his son Ntare V. Micombero led a successful coup d'état overthrowing the monarchy.

1972 Ntare was killed, supposedly by Hutus, sparking violence that led to the killing of 150,000 Hutus.

1976–87 Micombero was deposed by Tutsi Colonel Jean-Baptiste Bagaza. Bagaza's dictatorship was notorious for its violations of human rights.

1987 Bagaza was overthrown by Tutsi Major Pierre Buyoya.

1988 Thousands of Hutu were killed and many more fled into Rwanda

1992 A new constitution endorsed multi-party elections.

1993 Melchior Ndadaye, who was committed to reforming the Tutsi-dominated army, won the elections and became the first Hutu president. Ndadaye was assassinated by pro-Bagazza paratroopers. More massacres followed.

1994 Cyprien Ntaryamira, a Hutu, was appointed president by the National Assembly. He and the Hutu president of Rwanda were killed in a plane crash. Sylvestre Ntibantuganya, a Hutu, became president.

1995 A coalition government was formed under Antoine Nduwayu, a Tutsi. Ethnic violence continued.

1996 Major Pierre Buyoya seized power and suspended the constitution.

1998 Buyoya came to an agreement with parliament under a transitional constitution and was formally sworn in as president.

1999 Tutsi and Hutu factions agreed to talks brokered by former Tanzanian president Julius Nyerere.

2000 President Buyoya and 13 political parties signed the Arusha peace accord but two important Hutu groups refused to sign.

2001 In talks chaired by former South Africa president Nelson Mandela, it was agreed that Buyoya, a Tutsi, should remain president for 18 months of a new three-year transitional government, when a Hutu vice president would become president.

2002 The Burundi franc was devalued by 20 per cent to the US dollar. Violence between government forces and Hutu rebel groups continued.

2003 Vice President Domitien Ndayizeye was sworn in as president in accordance with the power-sharing agreement. The president and Pierre Nkurunziza, the leader of the main rebel group the Conseil National de Défense de la Démocratie-Forces de Défense de la Démocratie (CNDD-FDD) Forces for Defence of Democracy, signed an agreement to end the of civil war.

2004 A South African-style truth and reconciliation commission was set up. A new constitution was deferred until the transitional government was replaced with a fully elected Assembly.

2005 A referendum approved a new power-sharing constitution. The main former rebel Hutu group, CNDD-FDD, won the parliamentary elections. Pierre Nkurunziza was sworn in as president. Martin Nduwimana (Tutsi) and Alice Nzomukunda (Hutu) were appointed vice presidents.

2006 The 34-year old midnight-to-dawn curfew was lifted. A cease-fire between the government and the longest-established Hutu rebel group, the Forces Nationales de Libération (FNL) (National Liberation Forces), the armed wing of the Parti Pour la Liberation du Peuple Hutu (Palipe Hutu), was agreed. Burundi was admitted to membership of the East African Community (EAC).

2007 In April the Communaute Economique des Pays des Grands Lacs (CEPGL) (Great Lakes Countries Economic Community) was re-launched by Burundi, Democratic Republic of Congo and Rwanda. CEPGL is intended to promote regional economic co-operation and integration. Fighting between rival FNL factions resulted in 100 deaths; 40,000 civilians fled the fighting. Burundi joined the African Union (AU) peacekeeping force in Somalia. On 14 November, a new government was sworn in.

2008 The UN assessment mission to implement the peace agreement was postponed due to fighting between government forces and the FNL.

Political structure

Constitution

The constitution endorses multi-party elections by universal suffrage.

The February 2005 referendum approved a new power-sharing constitution, under which Burundi's president has a deputy from each of the ethnic groups while 60 per cent of the cabinet is Hutu and 40 per cent Tutsi.

Representation in the National Assembly is apportioned on a 60/40 basis between the Hutu and Tutsi with three seats reserved for the Twa ethnic group. In the Senate (upper house) two members are elected from each of Burundi's 17 provinces (one Hutu and one Tutsi), plus three from the Twa ethnic group. Women must account for at least 30 per cent. Four former presidents were also co-opted as senators in July 2005.

The army and the police service are staffed equally along ethnic lines.

Form of state

Republic

The executive

Executive power is vested directly in the elected president, with one each Hutu and Tutsi vice presidents.

National legislature

Legislative power is vested in the Assemblée Nationale (National Assembly) and Senate. The National Assembly is elected for a five-year term by universal suffrage. Senators are appointed by the President.

Legal system

Burundi law is based on Belgian and German law. The legal system is composed of a Supreme Court, Constitutional Court and a Courts of Appeal.

Last elections

4 July 2005 (parliamentary); 19 August 2005 (presidential)

Results: National Assembly: CNDD-FDD won 59 per cent of the vote (59 seats, out of 100), Frodebu 22 per cent (25) and Uprona 7 per cent (10), National Council for the Defence of Democracy (CNDD) 4

per cent (4), Movement for the Rehabilitation of Citizens-Rurenzangemero (MRC-Rurenzangemero) 2 per cent (2). In order to comply with the 60/40 Hutu/Tutsi split, and the 30 per cent quota for women, a further 18 members were co-opted after the elections. Of these, 5 each were allocated to the CNDD-FDD, Frodebu and Uprona, and three to the ethnic Twa, making a total in the National Assembly of 118.
Senate: CNDD-FDD won 30 seats, plus 2 co-opted members (out of 34 seats plus 15 co-opted and other members), Frodebu won 3 seats (plus 2 co-opted), CNDD 1 seat (plus 2 co-opted), Uprona (2 co-opted), ethnic Twa (3 co-opted), ex-presidents 4
Presidential: Pierre Nkurunziza (CNDD-FDD) was elected president by parliament by 151 votes out of 162 votes.

Next elections
2010 (parliamentary).

Political parties

Ruling party
Conseil National pour la Défense de la Démocratie-Forces pour la Défense de la Démocratie (CNDD-FDD), (National Council for Defence of Democracy-Forces for the Defence of Democracy)

Main opposition party
Front pour la Démocratie au Burundi (Frodebu) (Front for Democracy in Burundi)

Population

7.79 million (2007)*
Last census: September 1990: 5,139,073
Population density: 250 inhabitants per square km. Urban population: 9 per cent (1995–2001).
Annual growth rate: 1.8 per cent 1994–2004 (WHO 2006)
Internally Displaced Persons (IDP)
381,000 (UNHCR 2004)
Ethnic make-up
The Hutu people are believed to comprise 85 per cent of the population, the Tutsi 14 per cent and the Twa 1 per cent, but there have never been any census statistics on ethnic groups.
Religions
Christianity (over 60 per cent), 32 per cent traditional beliefs.

Education

Burundi typically spends around 3 per cent of its public expenditure on education, however this will increase following an announcement by the president that primary education will be free. Primary education will be boosted by a US$4 million Unicef grant aimed at doubling enrolment by March 2006. Classrooms are due to be refurbished and upgraded and 3,000 qualified teachers will be recruited, as well as training for less skilled teachers.
Secondary education is divided into two: academic and technical. Academic secondary education is available for four years between ages 12 and 16, then a national test determines access to higher education. Technical secondary education lasts from ages 12–19.
Kirundi is the language of instruction in primary schools and French in secondary schools.
Higher education is mainly provided by the Université du Burundi, which is largely financed by the government.
Literacy rate: 50 per cent adult rate; 66 per cent youth rate (15–24) (Unesco 2005).
Compulsory years: Six to 12.
Enrolment rate: 55 per cent boys and 46 per cent girls, total primary school enrolment for the relevant age groups (including repetition rates) (World Bank).
Pupils per teacher: 42 in primary schools.

Health

Per capita total expenditure on health (2003) was US$15; of which per capita government spending was US$4, at the international dollar rate, (WHO 2006).
Burundi's infant mortality rate is relatively high compared to the other African countries. Although women have a higher life expectancy, it is still less than the other East African countries. Immunisation campaigns have resulted in high levels of vaccinations against measles, TB, polio and other childhood deseases.

HIV/Aids
There were 220,000 adults living with HIV/Aids, of which 130,000 were women, as well as another 27,000 children diagnosed as HIV positive in 2003. The number of HIV/Aids cases has risen dramatically, particularly in rural areas. It is estimated that 20 per cent of the urban population, and six per cent of the rural population, are HIV positive. Infection rates in girls aged 15–19 are four times greater than boys of the same age and there are over 200,000 children orphaned by Aids.
HIV prevalence: 6.0 per cent aged 15–49 in 2003 (World Bank)
Life expectancy: 45 years, 2004 (WHO 2006)
Fertility rate/Maternal mortality rate: 6.8 births per woman, 2004 (WHO 2006)
Child (under 5 years) mortality rate (per 1,000): 114 per 1,000 live births (World Bank)
Head of population per physician: 0.03 physicians per 1,000 people, 2004 (WHO 2006)

Welfare

Burundi has 800,000 internally displaced people, while another 250,000 refugees fled to Tanzania.
The National Social Security Institute administers the old age, disability and survivor's pension insurance fund. It is a scheme funded by workers who contribute 2.6 per cent of their wages (3.8 per cent if working an arduous job), and employers contribute 3.9 per cent of the payroll (5.7 for arduous occupations). Old age pensions are paid at aged 60 (45 for arduous work).

Main cities

Bujumbura (capital, estimated population 384,461 in 2005), Gitega (25,412).

Languages spoken

French is the administrative language; KiSwahili is used commercially. English is a compulsory subject in secondary academic education.
Official language/s
Kirundi and French

Media

National news agency: Agence Burundaise de Presse: www.cbinf.com
Other news agencies: Burundi Information (in French): www.burundi-info.com
Burundi Quotidien (in French): www.burundi-quotidien.com
Iteka (in French and English): www.ligue-iteka.africa-web.org
Net press (L'Agence Burundaise d'Information): www.netpress.bi

Press
There is a low readership for newspapers.
Dailies: In French, Le Renouveau du Burundi is a government-run newspaper that has had Unesco investment to allow it to publish every day and increase readership.
Weeklies: In French, Arc-en-Ciel and in Kirundi (local language) Ubumwe is government-run and the fortnightly Ndongosi is a Catholic publication and Intahe published by the Tutsi dominated political party, Union pour le Progrès national (Uprona) (National Progress Union).

Broadcasting
The government-controlled, Radiodiffusion et Télévision Nationale du Burundi is the national public broadcaster.
Radio: With low levels of literacy radio is the primary source of news and information. Radio Burundi (RTNB) broadcasts in Kirundi and Swahili as well as French and English. It also broadcasts an educational network. Radio Culture is funded partly by the health ministry. Private radio stations include Radio Isanganiro (www.isanganiro.org) and Radio CCIB+ is operated by the Chamber of Commerce. Bonesha FM

(www.boneshafm.org) and Studio Ijambo (www.studioijambo.org) are funded by international organisations.

Television: The only TV station operating is the state-owned RTNB.

News agencies

National news agency: Agence Burundaise de Presse: www.cbinf.com

Other news agencies: Burundi Information (in French): www.burundi-info.com

Burundi Quotidien (in French): www.burundi-quotidien.com

Iteka (in French and English): www.ligue-iteka.africa-web.org

Net press (L'Agence Burundaise d'Information): www.netpress.bi

Economy

The government, democratically elected in 2005, has been attempting to manage a post-conflict economy, which has deteriorated significantly since the 1990s. Per capita income in 2005 was just US$100, and GDP growth dragged along at 0.9 per cent. It picked up sharply in 2006 with an estimated growth of 3.8 per cent, as business confidence grew. The IMF has backed efforts to revitalise the economy through financial support on highly preferential terms from the international community, providing substantial debt relief under the enhanced Heavily Indebted Poor Countries (HIPC) initiative. In August 2005 the IMF and World Bank agreed to bring forward US$826 million in debt relief under the HIPC programme and reduced Burundi's debt schedule from 110 per cent of exports in 2004 to 34 per cent in 2005.

Structural economic reforms, required under the agreement, were initiated to provide good governance and develop social services, while providing broad macroeconomic improvements. A major sign of the commitment to a market economy will come when the coffee-sector is privatised.

Inflation rose as food prices increased when a poor coffee harvest and an intensifying drought in the north nulled expected growth rate. Burundi recorded its worst ever trade deficit after coffee exports collapsed. In January 2006, heavy rains following the drought flooded much agricultural land and international food aid was necessary along with development aid.

External trade

As a founding member of the Common Market of Eastern and Southern Africa (Comesa), and the Economic Community of Central African States (ECCAS). Burundi operates a free trade zone to 13 of the 19 Comesa member states.

Imports

Principal imports are capital goods, machinery and equipment, petroleum products, foodstuffs.

Main sources: Kenya (18.9 per cent total, 2006), Italy (15.1 per cent), Tanzania (11.1 per cent).

Exports

Principal exports are coffee (normally 75 per cent of total), manufactures, tea, sugar, cotton and hides.

Main destinations: Germany (18.3 per cent of 2006 total goods exports), Switzerland (8.7 per cent), Belgium (5.6 per cent).

Agriculture

Farming

The agriculture sector is the mainstay of the economy, although there was a sharp drop in agricultural output due to disruptions caused by the civil war. The sector has to contend with a damaged infrastructure, broken market networks and poor productivity. Internally displaced persons (IDP) caught up in the civil war were made to over-exploit land causing ecological damage. Although Burundi is potentially self-sufficient in food, large numbers of IDP rely on humanitarian assistance. Food products account for around 13 per cent of all imports.

The main cash crop is coffee, which accounts for up to three-quarters of the country's exports. More than 90 per cent of coffee production is arabica, which is being encouraged for its higher producer prices. The Burundian brand of coffee has won international best quality prizes.

Other cash crops include tea, cotton, palm oil and tobacco.

Agriculture traditionally employs around 90 per cent of the population and contributes around 50 per cent of GDP. Most land under cultivation is devoted to subsistence crops – mainly cassava, bananas, sweet potatoes, pulses, maize and sorghum

Cattle rearing is also an important source of food, as is fishing on Lake Tanganyika.

Estimated crop production in 2005 included: 280,095 tonnes (t) cereals in total, 64,532t rice, 7,493t wheat, 123,199t maize, 709,574t cassava, 834,394t sweet potatoes, 26,091t potatoes, 74,171t sorghum, 1,600,000t bananas, 255,518t pulses, 61,703t taro, 6,000t green coffee, 180,000t sugar cane, 1,300t cotton lint, 6,600t tea, 1,685,000t fruit in total, 250,000t vegetables in total.

Estimated livestock production included: 23,393t meat in total, 9,100t beef, 4,160t pig meat, 1,020t lamb, 2,850t goat meat, 6,065t poultry, 3,002t eggs, 28,300t milk, 240t honey, 1,750 cattle hides, 238t sheepskins.

Lake Tanganyika is a rich source of fish.

Forestry

Almost 4 per cent of the land area, around 95,000 hectares, is forest. Around 8.7 million cubic metres of wood is felled each year, of which 8 million cubic metres is used for firewood.

Industry and manufacturing

The industrial sector, which is centred almost entirely in Bujumbura, is based on import substitution and typically accounts for around 20 per cent of GDP. Production includes beer, soft drinks, cigarettes, glass, textiles, insecticides, cement, oxygen and coffee processing.

The civil war discouraged foreign investment and high import costs hampered development of industrial capital, with strengthening peace these trends are reversing.

Tourism

The sector has only had two years since the civil conflict precluded tourists from visiting Burundi and therefore the US$22.6 million or 2.7 per cent of GDP expected in 2005 is remarkable. Capital investment in tourism is expected to reach 8.7 per cent of total investment in 2005, while one in every 26 jobs is in travel and tourism,.

Mining

Gold and tungsten are mined.

Substantial nickel reserves (up to 5 per cent of world total) have been found, but low world prices and an inadequate infrastructure mean extraction is not economically viable. Deposits of vanadium and uranium are being surveyed.

Phosphates and limestone are used for cement production.

Hydrocarbons

Burundi is reliant on imported petroleum. Petroleum reserves have been located under the Ruzizi Plain and under Lake Tanganyika.

Plans, put forward in 2000, for an extension to be added to a proposed oil pipeline between Kenya and Uganda, supplying Burundi, Rwanda, north-western Tanzania and eastern DRC have not progressed due to lack of investment.

Energy

Biomass, including wood, charcoal and peat, provides around 85 per cent of all energy consumption.

Burundi has three power stations and around 90 per cent of electricity services are consumed in the capital, by about 1.5–2 per cent of the country's population.

Burundi is hoping to secure finance for the development of the electricity sector, which has been fully liberalised, including the first phase of the Mpanda power station. This will involve the construction of a 10.4MW hydroelectric power station.

Rwanda and Burundi are also looking at joint plans to construct a hydroelectric dam on the Ruzizi river.

Banking and insurance

Central bank

Banque de la République du Burundi

Main financial centre

Bujumbura

Time

GMT plus two hours

Geography

Burundi is a landlocked country lying on the eastern shore of Lake Tanganyika, in central Africa, just south of the Equator. It borders Rwanda to the north, Tanzania to the south and east, and the Democratic Republic of Congo to the west.

Plains rise from Lake Tanganyika in the west to a central sloping plateau; hills and valleys have cultivated fields and pastures. In the east the region in mostly savanna. The southern tributary of the Nile begins its 6,650km journey to the Mediterranean in the south. The highest peak is Karonje at 2,760 metre.

Hemisphere

Southern

Climate

Around Lake Tanganyika (including Bujumbura), equatorial with hot, humid temperatures 23–33 degrees Celsius (C), and frequent winds. Elsewhere is temperate with average temperatures of 20 degrees C. The rainy season is from October–May (except brief dry period December–January); the long dry season is from June–September.

Entry requirements

Passports

Required by all, with at least six months validity remaining at time of departure.

Visa

Required by all. Applications for tourist and business visas should include itineraries and vaccination certificates against yellow fever and cholera. Business visas require a company letter of introduction from the employer and a local host company.

Currency advice/regulations

Import and export of the local currency is limited to Buf2,000.

Import and export of foreign currency is unlimited but subject to declaration on entry. All currency exchanges must be made through the main banks in Bujumbura or Gitega.

Travellers cheques have a limited market and commissions can be high; to avoid extra exchange rate charges cheques are best in US dollars or euros.

Health (for visitors)

Mandatory precautions

Cholera vaccination certificates are required by all visitors. Visitors arriving from countries where yellow fever is endemic are required to have meningitis and yellow fever vaccination certificates.

Advisable precautions

Yellow fever and cholera vaccinations are considered essential. Occasionally a certificate for meningococcal meningitis is required when arriving. Vaccinations for hepatitis A, polio, tetanus and typhoid are recommended. Malaria prophylaxis should be taken as risk exists throughout the country. Hepatitis B is endemic; visitors should seek advice on diphtheria, dysentery and tuberculosis vaccinations. There is a rabies risk.

To avoid the risk of Bilharzia use only well-maintained swimming pools.

Drinking water precautions are essential and water must first be boiled or otherwise sterilised for drinking, brushing teeth or making ice. Eat only well-cooked meat and fish, preferably served hot; vegetables should be cooked and fruit peeled. Pork, salad and mayonnaise and most dairy products, made from unboiled milk, may carry an inherent risk. Avoid food from street vendors.

HIV/Aids is widespread, with 15 per cent HIV positive among adults in Bujumbura. A travel kit including a disposable syringe is a reasonable precaution; all personal medications should be carried, along with their original packaging. Medical insurance, including repatriation is essential.

Hotels

Advisable to book in advance. Very little accommodation available outside Bujumbura. A 10 per cent tip is usual.

Public holidays (national)

Fixed dates

1 Jan (New Year's Day), 5 Feb (Unity Day), 12 Mar (Labour Day), 1 Jul (Independence Day), 15 Aug (Assumption), 13 Oct (Anniversary of Rwagasore's Assassination), 21 Oct (Anniversary President Ndadaye's Assassination), 1 Nov (All Saints' Day), 25 Dec (Christmas Day).

Variable dates

Easter (Mar/Apr), Ascension (May), Eid al Fitr.

Working hours

Banking

Mon–Fri: 0800–1130; 1500–1600.

Business

Mon–Fri: 0730–1200, 1400–1730.

Government

Mon–Fri: 0730–1200, 1400–1730.

Shops

Mon–Fri: 0830–1200, 1500–1800. Sat: 0830–1230.

Telecommunications

Mobile/cell phones

Several GSM 900 services operate in major areas of population in the north, west and south of the country.

Electricity supply

220V AC

Security

It is not recommended driving to and from Rwanda, unless travelling as part of a UN convoy; militia from rival political factions are likely to ambushed lone travellers.

Getting there

Air

The only direct intercontinental flights are from Europe.

National airline: Air Burundi (not approved by IATA)

International airport/s: Bujumbura (code: BJM), 11km north of city; café, currency exchange and post office.

Airport tax: Departure tax: US$20.

Surface

Road: All border crossings can be closed at very short notice depending on prevailing political conditions. There are reasonably passable roads from the Democratic Republic of Congo, either north or south, however the roads from Tanzania are generally in poor condition. The road from Kigali in Rwanda may be passable.

Water: There are connections across Lake Tanganyika, with ferries operating from Kigoma, (Tanzania), Kalenjie (DCR) and Mpulungu (Zambia).

Dar es Salam (Tanzania) is the closest sea port.

Main port/s: Bujumbura, Nyanza-Lac

Getting about

National transport

Air: There are no scheduled internal flights operating.

Road: Most of the roads leading to provincial towns are surfaced. Unsurfaced roads elsewhere can be difficult in the rainy season. Surfaced routes are being extended and local advice should be sought. Major roads are often closed after 1600 for security reasons. Driving outside the cities can be dangerous, particularly in border areas.

Buses: Very little public transport is available and buses are not recommended.

Water: Local boats are available on Lake Tanganyika, they can be slow depending on their cargo.

City transport

Taxis: Available in Bujumbura.

Car hire

Local firms only. International driving licence is required.

BUSINESS DIRECTORY

The addresses listed below are a selection only. While World of Information makes every endeavour to check these addresses, we cannot guarantee that changes have not been made, especially to telephone numbers and area codes. We would welcome any corrections.

Telephone area codes
The international direct dialling (IDD) code for Burundi is +257, followed by area code and subscriber's number:

Bubanza	42	Gitega	40
Bujumbura	2	Muramvya	43
Bururi	50	Ngozi	30
Cibitoke	41		

Useful telephone numbers
Police: 18, 19.

Chambers of Commerce
Burundi Chamber of Commerce, Industry, Agriculture and Handicrafts, Avenue du 18 Septembre, PO Box 313, Bujumbura (tel: 222-280; fax: 227-895; e-mail: ccib@cbinf.com).

Banking
Banque Commerciale du Burundi, PO Box 990, Libere Ndabakwaje; 84 Chaussee Prince Louise Rwagasore, Bujumbura (tel: 222-317; fax: 221-018).

Banque de Crédit de Bujumbura, PO Box 300, Avenue Patrice Emery Lumumba, Bujumbura (tel: 222-091; fax: 223-007; email: bcb@bi-network.com).

Interbank Burundi SA, PO Box 2970; 15 Rue de l'Industrie, Bujumbura (tel: 220-629; fax: 220-461; email: interb@cbinf.com).

Central bank
Banque de la République du Burundi, PO Box 705, Avenue du Gouvernement, Bujumbura, Burundi (tel: 225-142 fax: 223-128).

Travel information
Air Burundi, BP 2460, Avenue du Commerce, Bujumbura (tel: 223-460; fax: 223-452).

Bujumbura International Airport, PO Box 694, Bujumbura (tel: 223-707; 223-797; fax: 223-428).

Tourist office (for accommodation) 7 place de L'Indépendence, Bujumbura, BP 1402, (tel: 222-321, 220-704; email: nitra@cbinf.com).

National tourist organisation offices
Office National du Tourisme, 2 Avenue des Euphorbes, BP 902, Bujumbura (tel: 222-202/023; fax: 222-390; email: ontbur@cbinf.com); internet (in French): www.burundi.gov.bi).

Ministries
Ministry of Agriculture, Bujumbura (tel: 210-342; fax: 222-873).

Ministry of Commerce, Industry and Tourism, Bujumbura (tel: 217-775; fax: 225-595).

Ministry of Communication with the Government, Bujumbura (tel: 212-601; fax: 216-318).

Ministry of Community Development, Bujumbura (tel: 213-098; fax: 224-678).

Ministry of Defence, Bujumbura (tel: 219-994; fax: 225-686).

Ministry of Education, Bujumbura (tel: 217-776; fax: 226-839).

Ministry of Energy and Mines, Bujumbura (tel: 218-586; fax: 223-337).

Ministry of the Environment, Bujumbura (tel: 221-649; fax: 228-902).

Ministry of Finance, Bujumbura (tel: 217-918; fax: 223-827).

Ministry of Foreign Affairs and Co-operation, Bujumbura (tel: 217-595; fax: 226-313).

Ministry of Health, Bujumbura (tel: 218-200; fax: 229-916).

Ministry of Human Rights, Law Reforms and Relations with the National Assembly, Bujumbura (tel: 217-365; fax: 213-847).

Ministry of the Interior, Bujumbura (tel: 212-480; fax: 223-904).

Ministry of Justice, Bujumbura (tel: 210-595; fax: 222-148).

Ministry of Labour, Public Office and Professional Education, Bujumbura (tel: 217-928; fax: 224-079).

Ministry of Peace Process, Bujumbura (tel: 219-457; fax: 219-459).

Ministry of Planning, Development and Reconstruction, Bujumbura (tel: 219-079; fax: 224-193).

Ministry of Public Works and Equipment, Bujumbura (tel: 219-646; fax: 226-840).

Ministry of Repatriation of Displaced Persons, Bujumbura (tel: 218-184; fax: 218-201).

Ministry of Social Action and Promotion of Women, Bujumbura (tel: 210-376; fax: 216-102).

Ministry of Transport, Post and Telecommunications, Bujumbura (tel: 210-462; fax: 226-900).

Ministry of Youth Sport and Culture, Bujumbura (tel: 216-729; fax: 226-231).

Office of the President, Bujumbura (tel: 217-806; fax: 226-424).

Other useful addresses
APEE (export promotion) BP 3535, Bujumbura (tel: 225-997; fax: 222-767).

BCC (Burundi Coffee Co) BP 780, Bujumbura.

Burundi Embassy (USA), Suite 212, 2233 Wisconsin Avenue, NW, Washington DC 20007 (tel: (+1-202) 342-2574; fax: (+1-202) 342-2578).

Burundi Mining Co. BP468 Bujumbura (tel: 223-229).

CIGERCO (Cotton growers), BP 2571, Bujumbura (tel: 222-208).

National news agency: Agence Burundaise de Presse: www.cbinf.com

Internet sites
Africa Business Network: www.ifc.org/abn

AllAfrica.com: www.allafrica.com

African Development Bank: www.afdb.org

Africa Online: www.africaonline.com

Mbendi AfroPaedia (information on companies, countries, industries and stock exchanges in Africa): http://mbendi.co.za

Cambodia

KEY FACTS

Official name: Preah Réachéanachâkr Kâmpuchéa (The Kingdom of Cambodia)

Head of State: King Norodom Sihamoni (crowned 14 Oct 2004)

Head of government: Prime Minister Hun Sen (KPK) (since 1985)

Ruling party: Coalition government: Kanakpak Pracheachon Kâmpuchéa (KPK) (Cambodian People's Party) and United National Front for an Independent, Neutral, Peaceful and Co-operative Cambodia (Funcinpec) (from 2004; re-elected 27 Jul 2008)

Area: 181,035 square km

Population: 14.34 million (2007)*

Capital: Phnom Penh

Official language: Khmer

Currency: Riel (R) = 100 sen

Exchange rate: R4,147.50 per US$ (Jul 2008)

GDP per capita: US$600 (2007)

GDP real growth: 9.60% (2007)*

Labour force: 6.81 million (2004)

Unemployment: 3.10% (2004)

Inflation: 5.90% (2007)

Balance of trade: -US$1.06 billion (2006)

Foreign debt: US$3.38 billion (2004)

Visitor numbers: 1.70 million (2006)*

Annual FDI: US$943.13 million (2004)

* estimated figure

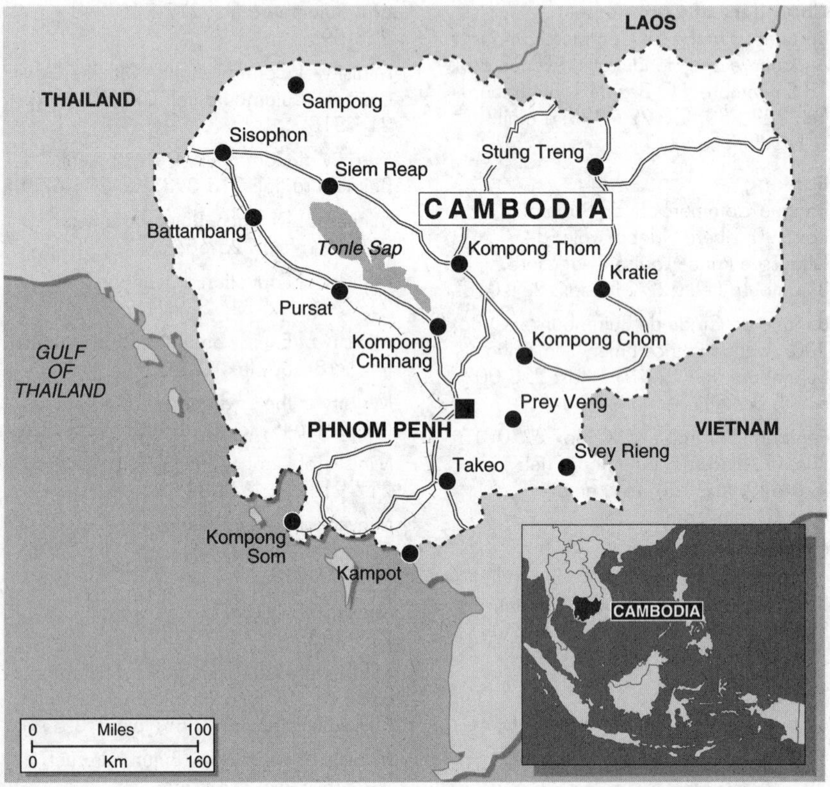

Cambodia was originally the most pleasant of all the Indo-Chinese states. Phnom Penh was once a city of broad tree lined boulevards. The sense of history and civilisation with the great Angkor Wat complex not far away was always close. Cambodia always appeared to have more economic potential than shabby land-locked Laos. And for decades in Cambodia there seemed to be a better social balance than was the case in Vietnam, where relations between north and south remained uneasy. In the 1970s Cambodia was a surplus rice producer and had considerable agricultural potential. With only 7.5 million inhabitants in 1975, population was not a problem. By 1979 some estimates put the population as low as 4 million; Cambodia, or Kampuchea as it became known for a few unfortunate years, was to become well known for all the wrong reasons.

From Colony to Khmers

But the reality behind this rosy picture of the mid-1970s left a lot to be desired. French colonial rule had not helped. The French plantations belonged to a colonial model that belonged in the nineteenth century, designed quite simply to bleed money from the country. Industry had hardly been developed, consisting of textiles, a few latex plants and a handful of factories for processing agricultural and forest products. China had helped to build a glass plant, and the then Czechoslovakia had provided tractor assembly and motor tyre factories as well as a sugar refinery. To prevent an expansionist Vietnam from strangling the Mekong lifeline, the French had built a port on the Gulf of Thailand, Kompong-Som (Sihanoukville). The US had helped with road construction, France and Germany together contributed a railway line linking the new port with the capital.

Cambodia was never really allowed to develop, or even given the chance to develop. Under Sihanouk widespread corruption was the order of the day among the small elite that occupied positions of any power or influence. Most of Sihanouk's time in power was spent trying to perform a balancing act between the great powers of the day, trying to avoid little Cambodia being sucked into the Indo-China conflict. But Sihanouk had got it wrong: in March 1970, General Lon Nol deposed Prince Sihanouk and assumed power. In October of the same year, the Cambodian monarchy was simply abolished, and Cambodia renamed the Khmer Republic. The scene was set for the bloody accession of the infamous Khmers Rouge under their leader, Pol Pot. Pol Pot's regime claimed that it was not seeking to create just a peasant society: 'Our people do not seek to produce only rice, but also to produce goods for industrial use, cotton, rubber, textile fibres.' Agriculture was collectivised, and what was left of the industrial base was abandoned or placed under state control. Cambodia had neither a currency nor a banking system. Before long, the once gracious and bustling city that had been Phnom Penh became what one observer described as a 'Pompeii without the ashes'. The buildings remained, apart from the French built cathedral which had been removed completely. There were, it was said, more chickens than people in the ghostly city. All the influences regarded in the West as civilising: books, religion, culture, were banished. Families were separated for long periods and subjected to the authority of the commune, which usually numbered some 1,000 families. Estimates of the dead range from 1.7 million to 3 million, out of a 1975 population estimated at 7.5 million.

The devastation – human, social, material – wrought by the Khmers eventually brought Cambodia into conflict with its former ally and more powerful neighbour to the north, Vietnam. By late 1977 Vietnam had decided that it could no longer tolerate the Khmer presence under Pol Pot in Phnom Penh any longer.

In December 1978 Vietnam – or more accurately Hanoi – lined up 14 divisions along the borders of Laos and Vietnam itself. Tanks, MiG aircraft and heavy artillery all went in to action as the map of Cambodia was rolled up in classic style by the Vietnamese invaders. This was a blitzkrieg in the best traditions, assuring Vietnam's Army Chief of staff Van Tien Dung of a place in military history books.

No easy ride

Despite their military defeat, the Khmers Rouges did not go quietly. For years Cambodia's internal politics assumed a sadly Ruritanian aspect. As late as 2005, thirty years after the event, Cambodia was still taking steps to confront its past and redress some of the terrible wrongs of the Khmer Rouge regime. The funds for a tribunal to investigate the remaining accused commanders were finally raised, fuelling expectation that judicial proceedings would eventually begin. Despite this progression, human rights groups have complained of ongoing abuses such as unlawful imprisonment of government critics.

Violence and intimidation

Following a period of relative stability for Cambodia in the ten years between 1993 and 2003, marred only by occasional violence, the 1998 National Assembly elections saw the Kanakpak Pracheachon Kâmpuchéa (KPK) (Cambodian People's Party) win 41 per cent of the vote, Funcinpec 32 per cent, and the improbably named Sam Rainsy Party (SRP) 13 per cent. Violence and intimidation characterised the elections to the extent that many international observers judged the elections to have been seriously flawed. The KPK and Funcinpec formed another coalition government, with KPK the senior partner. Cambodia's first commune elections were held in 2002. These elections were also marred by political violence and once again judged not to be acceptable by international standards. National Assembly elections in July 2003 again failed to give any one party the two-thirds majority of seats necessary under the constitution to form a government. The KPK secured 73 seats, Funcinpec 26 seats, and the SRP 24 seats. The incumbent KPK-led government continued in power in a caretaker role pending the formation of a coalition with the required number of National Assembly seats to form a government.

While the politicians were behaving as only politicians can, in 2004 King Sihanouk abdicated the throne due to illness. In October 2004, the Cambodian Throne Council selected Prince Norodom Sihamoni to succeed Sihanouk as King. King Norodom Sihamoni officially ascended the throne in a coronation ceremony in the same month. Subsequently, Cambodian politics began to acquire the characteristics of musical comedy, combined with musical chairs. In 2004, the National Assembly approved a controversial addendum to the constitution to end the nearly year-long political stalemate. In July 2004 the National Assembly approved a new coalition government comprised of the KPK and Funcinpec, with Hun Sen as prime minister and Prince Norodom Ranariddh as President of the National Assembly. The SRP and representatives of civil society non-governmental organisations continued to assert that the new addendum was unconstitutional. In early 2005, the National Assembly voted to lift the parliamentary immunity of three opposition parliamentarians, including the SRP leader Sam

KEY INDICATORS — Cambodia

	Unit	2003	2004	2005	2006	2007
Population	m	13.65	13.81	13.86	14.16	*14.34
Gross domestic product (GDP)	US$bn	3.82	4.60	6.23	7.26	*8.60
GDP per capita	US$	280	314	450	512	*600
GDP real growth	%	5.2	4.3	13.4	10.7	*9.6
Inflation	%	3.5	2.0	5.8	4.8	*5.9
Industrial output	% change	0.0	-0.2	12.7	18.5	–
Agricultural output	% change	0.0	4.4	15.7	5.5	–
Exports (fob) (goods)	US$m	1,380.0	2,311.0	2,910.3	3,693.0	4,089.0
Imports (cif) (goods)	US$m	1,730.0	3,129.0	3,927.8	4,749.0	5,423.6
Balance of trade	US$m	-350.0	-818.0	-1,017.5	-1,056.0	-1,334.6
Current account	US$m	-140.0	-100.0	-268.0	-146.0	-77.0
Total reserves minus gold	US$m	815.5	943.2	953.0	1,157.3	1,806.9
Foreign exchange	US$m	815.3	0.0	952.7	1,157.1	1,806.7
Exchange rate	per US$	3,912.50	3,918.00	4,025.00	4,025.00	3,950.00

* estimated figure

Rainsy, following lawsuits filed against them by members of the ruling parties. One of the MPs, Cheam Channy, was arrested and tried, while a sulking Sam Rainsy went into self-imposed exile. In October 2005, the government arrested critics of Cambodia's border treaties with Vietnam and detained four human rights activists. In January 2006, the political climate took a turn for the better following the prime minister's decision to release all political detainees and allow Sam Rainsy to return to Cambodia. But the tantrums weren't over: following public criticism by Hun Sen, Prince Ranariddh resigned as President of the National Assembly in March 2006. Some degree of normality was regained when Cambodia's second commune elections were held in April 2007; this time there was little in the way of the pre-election violence that characterised the 2002 and 2003 elections. The KPK won 61 per cent of the seats, the SRP won 25.5 per cent and Funcinpec and Prince Ranariddh's new party combined won some to 6 per cent. National elections are scheduled for 27 July 2008.

Good prospects

The Asian Development Bank (ADB) estimated annual gross domestic product (GDP) growth in 2007 to be 9.6 per cent, a little below the annual average of around 11 per cent for the three previous years. The drop in growth was put down to a sharp slowdown in garment exports and a slower rate of agricultural expansion. Cambodia's garment industry is the country's main industry and its leading export revenue earner. In 2006, exports totalled US$2.5 billion and the sector employed 330,000 mostly poorer rural women, who in turn support extended families. In total, an estimated 1.7 million people depend on the garment industry directly or indirectly. According to the Economic Institute of Cambodia, in June 2007 garment industry workers earned an average of US$73 per month, 29 per cent of which comes from overtime work.

Representing almost 80 per cent of Cambodia's total exports, the sector is crucial to Cambodia's economy. However, increasing global competition makes the industry vulnerable, and so a variety of approaches are needed to help the industry sustain itself. Garment exports were estimated to have fallen by 8 per cent in 2007.

The decline in export meant that 2007 GDP growth was largely driven by consumption and investment. Foreign direct investment (FDI) reached US$600 million in 2007, some 7 per cent of GDP. Domestic investment, largely generated by the private sector, accounted for around 23 per cent of GDP. Economic prospects for 2008 remain strong, despite the drop in export revenues. The projected GDP growth rate for 2008 of 7.5 per cent reflects a combination of a growth in services – mainly tourism – and construction. Although exports of cash crops have grown in recent years, the drop in garment exports is difficult to overcome. The slower exports have resulted in an enlarged trade deficit; Cambodia's current account deficit is expected to widen from 6.8 per cent in 2007 to 7.3 per cent of GDP in 2008. None the less, Cambodia has continued to accumulate international reserves, with a 47 per cent increase in 2007 to US$1.6 billion. The projected reserve figure by the end of 2008 is US$2 billion, corresponding to 2.8 months of imports of goods and services.

By the end of 2007, annual inflation had reached 10.8 per cent, a nine-year high. Behind the increased inflation rate were sharply increased global food prices (20 per cent) and fuel costs (12 per cent). The depreciation of the US dollar also contributed to Cambodia's inflation. Cambodia is a country of – for the most part – net food consumers. The poorer segments of the population, who spend some 70 per cent of their total household income on food, will inevitably be adversely affected. Despite the worsening international situation, Cambodia's finances are in good shape. The overall fiscal deficit has declined from 2.8 per cent of GDP in 2006 to 0.4 per cent of GDP in 2007 although government estimates put the figure much higher at 3.2 per cent, discounting the debt forgiveness granted by the International Monetary Fund (IMF). Fiscal performance has been improving on a number of fronts, notably revenue mobilisation, higher tax revenues and lower capital spending. The government has embarked upon a mid-term review of the five-year National Strategic Development Plan (NSDP 2006-2010). Overall, the ADB projects a generally good outlook for both 2008 and 2009, provided that macroeconomic stability is maintained and the structural reforms set out in the NSDP are eventually implemented. Cambodia's highly dollarised economy means that fiscal policy is the main macroeconomic instrument available to the government.

Risk assessment

Economy	Good
Politics	Fair
Regional stability	Good

COUNTRY PROFILE

Historical profile

1863 Cambodia was made a French Protectorate.
1941 Prince Norodom Sihanouk became King. Cambodia was occupied by the Japanese during the Second World War.
1945 Japanese occupation ended.
1946 France re-imposed its protectorate. A new constitution permitted Cambodians to form political parties. Communist guerrillas began an insurgency against French rule.
1953 Cambodia became independent with King Sihanouk as head of state.
1955 Sihanouk abdicated to pursue a political career as prime minister. His father, Norodom Suramarit, became King.
1960 King Suramarit died and Sihanouk became head of state.
1965 Sihanouk cut off relations with the US and gave support to North Vietnamese guerrillas fighting the US-backed regime in South Vietnam.
1969 The US began bombing Cambodia.
1970 Sihanouk was overthrown in a US-backed coup. General Lon Nol became president, proclaimed the Khmer Republic and began fighting the North Vietnamese in Cambodia. Sihanouk formed a guerrilla movement, known as the Khmer Rouge, while in exile in China.
1970–75 Civil war and intensive American bombing caused widespread destruction.
1975 Lon Nol was overthrown by the Khmer Rouge, led by Pol Pot. Sihanouk briefly served as head of state.
1975–79 Under the Khmer Rouge regime, around 1.7 million people were killed and towns and industry destroyed. The cities were emptied and people were forced into the countryside to become agricultural workers.
1976 Sihanouk was replaced by Khieu Samphan as head of state and Pol Pot as prime minister.
1979 The Khmer Rouge was ejected by a Vietnamese invasion and the regime's policies were reversed.
1981 The pro-Vietnamese Kampuchean People's Revolutionary Party (KPRP) won the elections to the National Assembly, but the international community, led by the US, refused to recognise the new government. Instead, Cambodia was represented in the UN by the Khmer Rouge.
1985 Hun Sen became prime minister.
1989 Vietnam claimed to have withdrawn its remaining troops from the country. Hun Sen abandoned his socialist programme in an effort to appease the US and gain international recognition.
1991 The signing of a peace agreement brought to an end 13 years of civil war. A UN transitional authority was established

to share power between the country's varius factions. Sihanouk became head of state.
1993 The UN organised elections. The Cambodian National Unity Party (Khmer Rouge) guerrilla group boycotted the poll. The two main parties, United National Front for an Independent, Neutral, Peaceful and Co-operative Cambodia (Funcinpec) and Kanakpak Pracheachon Kâmpuchéa (KPK) (Cambodian People's Party), agreed on a joint government under which they would share power. A constitutional monarchy was established and, in May, the country was renamed the Kingdom of Cambodia. The government-in-exile lost its seat in the UN.
1994 Thousands of Khmer Rouge fighters surrendered after the government called an amnesty.
1997 Second Prime Minister Hun Sen (KPK) seized power, removing First Prime Minister Prince Norodom Ranariddh (Funcinpec) from office, in a move condemned by the international community.
1998 The Khmer Rouge founder, Pol Pot, died. The KPK won the elections, but the opposition parties objected saying the election was fraudulent. A coalition government was formed with Funcinpec. Hun Sen became prime minister and Ranariddh became president of the National Assembly.
1999 Two Khmer Rouge leaders were arrested and charged with genocide.
2001 Parliament approved a law to create a special tribunal to bring genocide charges against Khmer Rouge leaders.
2002 The KPK scored an overwhelming victory in the country's first multi-party local elections, giving it control of over 98 per cent of the country's communes.
2003 Anti-Thai riots were set off by claims that Angkor Wat really belonged to Thailand and not to Cambodia. The KPK was re-elected in parliamentary elections, but failed to secure the two-thirds majority required under the constitution to govern alone.
2004 The two main political parties, KPK and Funcinpec, agreed to form a coalition government with Hun Sen remaining as prime minister, ending a government crisis that had crippled the kingdom for almost a year. Cambodia became a member of the WTO. The Council of the Throne chose Prince Norodom Sihamoni as the new King.
2005 The UN agreed to the funding of a tribunal to try the leaders of the Khmer Rouge for genocide. Cambodia concluded a border agreement with Vietnam. The opposition leader, Sam Rainsy, was convicted in absentia for defaming prime minister Hun Sen.
2006 In senate elections the ruling KPK won a majority. Sam Rainsy was given a royal pardon and returned from exile. One of the top Khmer Rouge leaders, Ta Mok, died aged 80. The royalist political party, Funcinpec, dismissed Prince Norodom Ranariddh as leader.
2007 In March Prince Ranariddh was sentenced in absentia to 18 months in prison, for selling the headquarters of Funcinpec, for an alleged US$3.6 million. In September, the most senior, surviving member of the Khmer Rouge, Nuon Chea (Brother Number Two) was arrested and charged with crimes against humanity. The Khmer Rouge genocide tribunal held its first public hearing in November.
2008 The registration of the Preah Vihear Hindu temple as a Unesco World Heritage site reignited tension in the disputed border territory between Thailand and Cambodia. The temple had been awarded to Cambodia by the UN in 1962 but ownership of the surrounding area is still contentious. On 15 July, three Thai nationalist protesters were arrested by Cambodian troops and Thai troops crossed the border in support. A rapid military deployment, by both sides, laid siege to the temple; by 24 July both sides agreed to talks to resolve the matter. In parliamentary elections held on 27 July the ruling KPK claimed victory. Despite the European Union monitors stating that the running of the elections had been 'technically good' it also said it had fallen short of international standards, with the ruling party dominating access to the media and that tens of thousands of voters had been disenfranchised.

Political structure

Constitution

The 1993 constitution provides for a pluralistic, liberal democratic political system and for a limited monarchy.
To govern alone, a political party is required to have a two-thirds majority.

Form of state

Multiparty liberal democracy under a constitutional monarchy established in 1993.

The executive

Executive power is vested in the Council of Ministers led by the prime minister. The King appoints the prime minister from the representatives of the largest party in parliament on the recommendation of the president of the National Assembly.

National legislature

Under the constitution, the National Assembly has at least 120 members who are all elected by universal suffrage. Only those who were Cambodian citizens at birth and who are aged over 25 years are entitled to stand for election. The National Assembly is elected every five years.

Legal system

The judiciary is granted independence under the constitution. The Supreme Council of the Magistracy, chaired by the King, has the right to discipline any judge who breaks the law, but judges cannot be dismissed. The King has sole authority to appoint judges on the advice of the Supreme Council of the Magistracy.

Last elections

27 July 2003 (National Assembly); 22 January 2006 (Senate).
Results: Parliamentary: The ruling coalition was re-elected — the Kanakpak Pracheachon Kâmpuchéa (KPK) (Cambodian People's Party) won 73 seats out of 123; the United National Front for an Independent, Neutral, Peaceful and Co-operative Cambodia (Funcinpec) party 26 seats and the Sam Rainsy Party (SRP) 24.
Senate: The KPK increased their seats in the Senate winning 43 of the 57 seats. They had previously held 35.

Next elections

2008 (National Assembly); 2011 (Senate)

Political parties

Ruling party

Coalition government: Kanakpak Pracheachon Kâmpuchéa (KPK) (Cambodian People's Party) and United National Front for an Independent, Neutral, Peaceful and Co-operative Cambodia (Funcinpec) (from 2004; re-elected 27 Jul 2008)

Main opposition party

Sam Rainsy Party (SRP)

Population

14.34 million (2007)*
Last census: March 1998: 11,437,656
Population density: 78 inhabitants per square km; urban population: 18 per cent (ADB 2006).
Annual growth rate: 2.2 per cent 1994–2004 (WHO 2006)

Religions

Theravada Buddhism, Christianity (Roman Catholicism).

Education

Primary school lasts between the ages of six and 12.
Secondary education is divided into lower secondary and upper secondary lasting for three years each. All students follow the same curriculum through the six years. Nearly 40 per cent of total expenditure in primary schools is paid through household contributions. Public expenditure on education typically amounts to around 3 per cent of annual gross national income.
Literacy rate: 69 per cent adult rate; 80 per cent youth rate (15–24) (Unesco 2005).
Enrolment rate: 123 per cent and 104 per cent for boys and girls respectively, total primary school enrolment of the relevant age group (including repetition rates) (World Bank).

Pupils per teacher: 44 in primary schools.

Health

Per capita total expenditure on health (2003) was US$188; of which per capita government spending was US$36, at the international dollar rate, (WHO 2006).

HIV/Aids

HIV prevalence: 2.6 per cent aged 15–49 in 2003 (World Bank)

Life expectancy: 54 years, 2004 (WHO 2006)

Fertility rate/Maternal mortality rate: 4.0 births per woman, 2004 (WHO 2006); maternal mortality ratio 470 deaths per 100,000 live births (World Bank).

Child (under 5 years) mortality rate (per 1,000): 97 per 1,000 live births; 47 per cent of children under aged five are malnourished (World Bank).

Welfare

Five Cambodian government ministries and their departments directly or indirectly offer social welfare support for the general population, including people with disabilities. There is provision for pensions of disabled veterans. There are no universal social security benefit entitlements in Cambodia.

Main cities

Phnom Penh (capital, estimated population 1.2 million in 2004), Bat Dâmbâng (158,124), Kâmpóng Saôm (175,891), Siem Réab (158,884), Sisophon (111,673).

Languages spoken

French is spoken. English is becoming the most commonly used business language, superseding French.

Official language/s

Khmer

Media

Press freedom, while not guaranteed, is practiced with the support of Prime Minister Hun Sen.

National news agency: AKP (Agence Kampuchea Presse)

Press

Dailies: In Khmer, Kaoh Santepheap (www.kohsantepheapdaily.com.kh), Reaksmei Kampuchea and Rasmei Angkor. In Chinese, Jian Hua Daily Cambodic and Con Rhuong Pao. In English, Cambodian Daily (www.cambodiadaily.com).

Weeklies: In Khmer, the pro-communist Trung Lap and Pracheachon (Communist Party) published twice weekly. In English, The Cambodian Magazine (www.cambodianscene.com) and Phnom Penh Post (www.phnompenhpost.com) is published every Friday.

Business: In Chinese The Commercial News (www.thecommercialnews.com), has various news and economy articles.

Broadcasting

The unregulated ownership of satellite dishes allows full access to domestic and foreign broadcasts.

Radio: The National Radio of Cambodia (NRC) operates three stations, relayed nationwide and NRC International in English, French, Thai, Lao and Vietnamese. There are several other private commercial stations, including Radio 103 FM, Radio 97 FM, Radio 95 FM, Beehive 105 FM (www.sbk.com.kh), Bayon Radio is part of the Bayon TV network.

Television: The National Television of Cambodia (TVK) (www.tvk.gov.kh) is the state broadcaster. Other, private and commercial stations include TV3 (based in Phnom Penh), TV5 (www.ch5cambodia.com), CTN (www.ctncambodia.com), CTV9 (www.tv9.com.kh), Bayon TV (www.bayontv.com.kh) and Apsara TV. All TV stations provide satellite coverage, to which three other foreign channels are available.

Economy

Cambodia is, for the most part a rural, developing country which, despite extensive reforms and massive donor support, has an economic basis that remains weak. It is one of the least developed countries in the world, per capita income was US$430 in 2005 with 36 per cent of the population living below the poverty line, 80 per cent of whom live in rural areas. Agriculture accounts for around 33 per cent of GDP and is mostly subsistence farming.

Sustainable development is not possible without greater private sector commitment coupled with social programmes. The government is in the process of applying power to its trade policy machinery in expectation of improving the prospects of its nascent market economy. Economic growth has been driven by increases in garment production (around 80 per cent of export revenue is contributed by manufacturing), tourism (over one million people visited Angkor Wat, Cambodia's main tourist attraction in 2005), agriculture and construction activity. Nevertheless, Cambodia continues to rely on foreign assistance – around 50 per cent of the government's budget is provided by donors, the principal amount supplied by Japan.

The economy grew by 7.0 per cent in 2005 and has much to achieve after decades of serious underinvestment and waste. The major economic challenge for Cambodia over the next decade will be to encourage a private sector that can create enough jobs for its young population, while improving the living standards of the population as a whole.

External trade

Cambodia is one of the world's least developed countries, its export market was dominated by the textile industry, the loss of preferential trading arrangements with the US and EU has not caused as much disruption to production as anticipated in 2005. Cambodia is a member of Asean and is negotiating free trade arrangements with the other regional members.

Imports

Main imports are petroleum products, vehicles and machinery, construction materials, pharmaceutical products, cigarettes, gold, artificial textiles and cotton yarns and textiles.

Main sources: Hong Kong (18.1 per cent total, 2006), China (17.5 per cent), Thailand (13.9 per cent).

Exports

Major exports are clothing and footwear, timber and rubber, precious gems, rice, fish and tobacco.

Main destinations: US (53.3 per cent of 2006 total goods exports), China (15.2 per cent), Germany (6.6 per cent).

Agriculture

Agriculture accounts for 33 per cent of GDP and employs around 75 per cent of the workforce. Agriculture is hampered by poor soil fertility and irrigation and unclear land-ownership rights.

The principal crop is rice (both hill and lowland types), which is grown on 70 per cent of the cultivated land. Rice output accounts for around 17 per cent of GDP. Only 16 per cent of rice lands are irrigated and there have been no large-scale projects since the 1960s.

Other crops include rubber (a major export), maize, cassava and fruit and vegetables. The smuggling of rubber to neighbouring countries, to get a better price, is a problem. Cambodia also produces jute and sawn timber products. Cattle stocks are improving, but fish represents the only animal protein for most people.

Estimated crop production in 2005 included 4,458,000 tonnes (t) cereals in total, 4,200,000t rice, 258,000t maize, 550,000t sorghum, 365,000t cassava, 135,000t potatoes, 36,000t sweet potatoes, 148,000t bananas, 29,000t pulses, 71,000t coconuts, 68,200t citrus fruit, 37,283t oilcrops, 310t green coffee, 35,000t mangoes, 27,000t natural rubber, 2,500t pepper spice, 135,000t sugar cane, 650t jute, 83,000t soya beans, 2,479t tobacco leaves, 324,700t fruit in total, 481,250t vegetables in total. Livestock production included 225,850t meat in total, 60,000t beef, 13,600t buffalo

meat, 127,500t pig meat, 24,750t poultry, 17,050t eggs, 20,400t milk, 300t cocoons, silk, 15,000t cattle hides.
Tonle Sap (Great Lake), floods during the monsoon and is the breeding ground for many fish. It is one of the world's most productive inland fisheries; it provides around 75 per cent of the annual inland fish catch and 60 per cent of Cambodia's protein intake.

Forestry

Between 2000–2005 it is estimated that logging of forests amounted to 140,500 hectares (ha) per year or 1.9 per cent annual deforestation. Primary forest cover fell from 766,000ha in 1999 to 322,000ha in 2005. Illegal logging, within the country and along Cambodia's borders, threatens not only the forests but also the communities that depend on these local resources.

Industry and manufacturing

The industrial sector accounts for 29 per cent of GDP and employs around 20 per cent of the workforce.
Most of what little industry Cambodia possessed was wrecked during the 1970s under the Khmer Rouge, particularly by the virtual closure of the towns in the drive to force people back to the land. Development has been hampered by the absence of adequate transport and other infrastructure. The manufacturing sector is beset by shortages of power and raw materials and by poor quality products. A number of state factories have been leased to the private sector since 1990 and joint ventures established in enterprises such as hotels, rattan, mineral water, wood processing, a tannery, plywood, tyres and textiles.
Industrial expansion has been led by the growth in the garment-manufacturing sector, but the level of growth might be affected by the ending of garment quotas by the WTO in 2005. In order to offset this, the government will need to create a more investor-friendly environment.

Tourism

The government has a target of three million tourists per annum by 2010. Particular focus is geared towards the cultural attractions such as the ancient city of Angkor Wat. Tourism, which has had to overcome the effects of years of upheaval, has led growth in the services sector. After a disappointing year in 2003, occasioned by external events, the sector recovered in 2004, receiving just over a million visitors, rising to over 1.4 million in 2005. The main market is South Korea, followed by Japan, USA and the UK. Tourism is expected to contribute 7.3 per cent to GDP in 2005.

Environment

The UN designated Tonle Sap (Great Lake) as an ecological hotspot and designated it a Unesco biosphere.

Mining

The mining sector typically contributes 9 per cent to GDP and employs 1 per cent of the workforce.
There are deposits of iron ore, copper, manganese, gold and bauxite, but exploitation is hindered by the absence of transport facilities. Phosphates are the only economically viable mineral and are mined for use in the local fertiliser industries. Gemstones are also mined.

Hydrocarbons

Cambodia has no oil or natural gas reserves. Cambodia is dependent on imports of refined oil, mainly from Thailand. Exploration is being undertaken particularly in offshore areas, where indications of oil and gas have been detected.
There are indications of small coal reserves.

Energy

Cambodia has an electricity generating capacity of around 150MW nationally, a level insufficient to sustain rapid economic growth. About 15 per cent of the population have access to electricity, but only in Phnom Penh and provincial towns. Generation is small-scale and inefficient, mostly oil-fired with some hydropower. There is no national power grid and rural consumers as well as industries frequently use costly generators to ensure an uninterrupted supply. The cost of electricity is the highest and consumption the lowest in the region.

Banking and insurance

The banking system is underdeveloped. The economy is highly dollarised, with foreign currency making up 70 per cent of the total money supply. This hinders the central bank's ability to implement an effective monetary policy.
Since 2000, Cambodia has been reforming the banking sector, introducing a minimum capitalisation requirement of US$11 million. This led to the closure of 11 banks by 2002.

Central bank

National Bank of Cambodia

Time

GMT plus seven hours

Geography

Cambodia occupies part of the Indochinese peninsula in south-east Asia. It is bordered by Thailand and Laos to the north, by Vietnam to the east and by the Gulf of Thailand to the south.
Around 60 per cent of Cambodia is rain forest, of which 3 per cent is primary forest with extensive bio-diversity. The Tonle Sap (Great Lake) is the largest freshwater lake in south-east Asia, at 2,700 square km but only about one metre deep for most of the year. During the monsoon the lake grows by another 16,000 square km and its depth increases by nine metres. The lake flows out into the Mekong River. The highlands are located in the north-east and there are numerous islands along the south-west coast.

Hemisphere

Northern

Climate

Generally hot and very humid, with a rainy season from June to October/November. Likely temperatures in Phnom Penh are 22–30 degrees Celsius (C) from November–December and 24–34 degrees C in April.

Entry requirements

Passports

Required by all. Must be valid for six months from departure date.

Visa

Visas are required by all, with a few exceptions; to find a list and download a tourist one-month e-visa, see http://evisa.mfaic.gov.kh. An e-visa can only be used at Pochentong (Phnom Penh) and Siem Reap airports. Tourists can also get a visa on arrival at the Pochentong and Siem Reap airports, as well as the Poi Pet international checkpoint, overland from Thailand. If planning to arrive by boat from Vietnam, or overland at checkpoints other than Poi Pet, a visa must be obtained prior to arrival; the place of entry must be specified.
A business visa should be applied for before departure, contact the closest Cambodian consulate for further details.

Currency advice/regulations

Import and export of local currency is prohibited. Import of foreign currency must be declared on arrival; export of foreign currency can only be up to amount declared.

Health (for visitors)

Mandatory precautions

Vaccination certificates for yellow fever if travelling from an infected area.

Advisable precautions

Vaccinations recommended for diphtheria, tuberculosis, hepatitis A and B, Japanese B encephalitis. Anti-malarial precautions should be taken. There is risk of rabies.

Credit cards

Credit cards are only accepted in large hotels and shops.

Public holidays (national)

Fixed dates

1 Jan (New Year's Day), 7 Jan (Victory Day), 8 Mar (Women's Day), 14–16 Apr

(Traditional Cambodia New Year), 1 May (Labour Day), 13–15 May (King's Birthday), 16 May (Royal Ploughing day), 18 Jun (Queen's Birthday), 24 Sep (Constitution Day), 29 Oct (Coronation Day), 31 Oct (last King's Birthday), 9 Nov (Independence Day), 10 Dec (International Human Rights Day).

Variable dates

Birth of Buddha Day (Visaka Buja Day) (May); Royal Ploughing Ceremony (Visakha Bochea Day) (May); three-day spirit festival (Pchum Ben festival) (Sep/Oct); three day Water Festival (Bonn Om Touk) (Nov).

The religious festivals are determined by the Buddhist lunar calendar.

Any public holiday that falls at the weekend is carried over to the next working day.

Working hours

Banking

Mon–Fri: 0800–1500.

Business

Mon–Fri: 0800–1200 and 1400–1700.

Government

Mon–Fri: 0800–1200 and 1400–1700.

Shops

0700–1800.

Telecommunications

Mobile/cell phones

There are 900 and 1800 GSM services available around main towns and cities only.

Social customs/useful tips

Business cards are essential and are usually exchanged during introductions; offering and receiving business cards with both hands is considered particularly polite.

Punctuality is important and visitors should allow plenty of time for travelling. It is acceptable to shake hands with both men and women.

In conversation speak clearly using a moderate pace and complete sentences. Always give time for your host to answer and maintain courtesies.

Even during difficult negotiations remain calm as anger will give a poor impression.

Criticism of the Royal Family and Buddhism should be avoided.

Learning some Cambodian greetings will both surprise and impress your host.

Photography is permitted although it is polite to ask permission before photographing Cambodian people, particularly monks.

Gratuities are welcome in restaurants and hotels.

The minimum drinking age is 18 years.

Security

The government has taken action to reduce crime but visitors are still advised not to walk alone at night in many areas of the city. Most hotels can arrange cars with drivers.

When visiting the temples at Angkor Wat, travel by air to Siem Reap airport, remain within the main temple complex and do not attempt to travel to Banteay Srei or to other outlying temples.

Getting there

Air

National airline: Only foreign carriers provide international services and usually only from neighbouring countries.

International airport/s: Pochentong International (PNH), 8km from Phnom Penh.

Airport tax: International departures from Pochentong and Siem Reap airports US$25; from all other airports US$20.

Surface

Not all crossings are open to foreign visitors, check with local authorities before travelling. Some crossings will issue visas, but to avoid disappointment organise all visas before arriving at a crossing.

Road: Overland access is via Thailand, Vietnam and Laos.

Rail: The government is rehabilitating the railways to build links to Thailand by the Phnom Penh–Poipet line, and constructing a new line linking Phnom Penh and Ho Chi Minh City. These projects are part of the Asian Development Bank's (ADB) Greater Mekong sub-regional co-operation scheme. The Phnom Penh–Ho Chi Minh City link is part of the Trans-Asia railway aimed at linking Singapore to Kunming in Yunnan province of China.

Water: There are ferry services, via the Mekong River, from Vietnam and Laos. A sea-ferry runs from Thailand.

Main port/s: The Mekong river port of Phnom Penh, the seaport of Sihanoukville.

Getting about

National transport

Air: Domestic flights connect all major cities.

Road: There are 13,500km of roads. Only 12 per cent of national highways are paved, meaning that many communities are cut off during the rainy season.

The Phnom Penh–Ho Chi Minh City (HCMC) Highway refurbishment project is expected to be completed by 2012.

Buses: Some bus or passenger truck services are available.

Rail: There are 612km of track. Rail services operate between Phnom Penh–Aranyaprathet, and Phnom Penh–Kompong Som. There is a critical need to improve infrastructure over the medium-term.

Water: Ferries operate along the Mekong River.

City transport

The most convenient way to travel around the capital is by cyclo (tricycle) or motodops (motorcycles).

Taxis: There are ranks of cars with taxi signs at the airport and can be hired in all the main cities, but cruising taxis are not the norm.

Buses, trams & metro: Buses link all of Phnom Penh's suburbs.

Car hire

It is advisable to hire a car with driver as local conditions can overwhelm foreign visitors; most hotels can arrange the services of a car and driver.

BUSINESS DIRECTORY

The addresses listed below are a selection only. While World of Information makes every endeavour to check these addresses, we cannot guarantee that changes have not been made, especially to telephone numbers and area codes. We would welcome any corrections.

Telephone area codes

The international direct dialling (IDD) code for Cambodia is +855, followed by area code and subscriber's number.

Battambang	53	Pusat	52
Kampong Som	62	Stung Treng	74
Phnom Penh	23	Siem Riep	63

Useful telephone numbers

Police: 722-353

Fire: 723-555

Ambulance: 723-173

Local directory assistance: 1213

Chambers of Commerce

Phnom Penh Chamber of Commerce, 7B Street 81 corner Street 109, Sangkat Beung Raing, Daun Penh District, Phnom Penh (tel: 212-265; fax: 212-270; e-mail: ppcc@camnet.com.kh).

Banking

Cambodia Mekong Bank Public Ltd, 1 Kramuon Sar Street, Khan Daun Penh, Phnom Penh (tel: 217-112; fax: 217-122).

Cambodian Commercial Bank Limited, 26 Monivong Road, Sangkat Phsar Thmei 2, Khan Daun Penh, Phnom Penh (tel: 426-145, 426-639, 213-601, 213-602, 426-638; fax: 426-116).

Cambodian Public Bank Ltd, Villa No. 23, Street 114, Vithei Kramounsar, Phnom Penh (tel: 426-067; fax:426-068).

Canada Bank Ltd, 265-269 Prash Ang Doung Street, Sangkath Wattphnom, Khan Daun Penh, Phnom Penh (tel:-266-046, 725-548).

Crédit Agricole Indosuez, 70 Blvd Norodom, Phnom Penh (tel: 427-233).

First Commercial Bank, 263 Ang Duong St, Phnom Penh (tel: 210-026; fax: 210-029).

Foreign Trade Bank of Cambodia, 24/26 Preah Norodom Boulevard, Phnom Penh (tel: 724-466, 723-866, 722-466, 723-466).

National Bank of Cambodia, PO Box 25, 22-24 Preah Norodom Blvd, Phnom Penh (tel: 428-105, 722-563; fax: 426-117).

Singapore Banking Corporation Ltd, 68 Samdech Pan Street (St. 214), Sangkat Beung Raing, Khan Daun Penh, Phnom Penh (tel: 217-771).

Singapore Commercial Bank Ltd, 316 Preah Monivong Boulevard, Sangkat Chak To Mok, Khan Daun Penh, Phnom Penh (tel: 427-471).

Union Commercial Bank Plc, UCB Bldg, No. 61, 130 Road, Psa Chas Quater, Khan Daun Penh, Phnom Penh (tel: 724-831, fax: 427-997).

Central bank
National Bank of Cambodia, 22-24 Preah Boulevard Norodom, Phnom Penh (tel/fax: 426-117).

Travel information
Canby Publications, PO Box 2349, Phnom Penh 3; House #23A, Street 55, Sangkat Chaktomuk, Khan Duan Penh, Phnom Penh (tel: 16-779-900; fax: 23-216-754; email: cambodia@canbypublications.com; internet: www.canbypublications.com).

Ministry of tourism
Ministry of Tourism, 3 Monivong Bld, Phnom Penh 12258 (tel: 211-593, 222-409; internet: www.mot.gov.kh).

National tourist organisation offices
Tourism of Cambodia, 262 Monivong Blvd, Khan Daun Penh, Phnom Penh (tel: 216-666; fax: 213-331; e-mail: info@tourismcambodia.com; internet: www.tourismcambodia.com).

Ministries
Ministry of Agriculture, 200 Norodom Blvd, Phnom Penh (tel: 723-689, 722-127).

Ministry of Commerce, Norodom Blvd, Phnom Penh (tel: 723-263; fax: 426-396).

Ministry of Culture, Monivong Blvd, Red Cross Street, Phnom Penh (tel: 724-769).

Ministry of Defence, Pochentong Blvd, Phnom Penh (tel: 725-697).

Ministry of Education, Youth and Sport, 80 Blvd Norodom, Phnom Penh (tel: 362-338; fax: 426-791).

Ministry of Finance, 60 St 92, Phnom Penh (tel: 426-841).

Ministry of Foreign Affairs and International Co-operation, Sisowath Quay, St 240, Phnom Penh (tel: 426-146, 724-441; fax: 26-144).

Ministry of Health, 153-153 Blvd Kampuchea Krom, Phnom Penh (tel: 725-833, 724-573).

Ministry of Industry, 45 Norodom Bld, St 45, Phnom Penh (tel: 723-477; fax: 427-840).

Ministry of Information, 62 Monivong Bld, Phnom Penh (tel: 723-369, 722-869).

Ministry of the Interior, 275 Norodom Blvd, Phnom Penh (tel: 426-494).

Ministry of Justice, Sothearos Blvd, Phnom Penh (tel: 724-543, 360-329).

Ministry of Planning, 386 Monivong Blvd, Phnom Penh (tel: 725-143, 724-543).

Ministry of Posts and Telecommunications, Street 13, Street 102, Phnom Penh (tel: 723-911, 426-817; fax: 426-786).

Ministry of Public Works and Transport, Norodom Blvd, Mahaksatriyani St, Phnom Penh (tel: 427-862; fax: 427-862).

Ministry of Religious Affairs, Sothearos Blvd, St 240, Phnom Penh (tel: 725-699).

Ministry of Rural Development, Pochentong Blvd, Phnom Penh (tel: 426-814).

Ministry of Social Welfare, 68 Norodom Blvd, Phnom Penh (tel: 725-191, 427-322).

Prime Minister's Office, 22 Street 214, Phnom Penh (tel:426-053 and 426-025).

Other useful addresses
ASEAN Investment Promotion Agency, Cambodian Investment Board, Government Palace, Sisowath Quay, Wat Phnom, Phnom Penh (tel: 50-428; fax: 61-616, 60-606).

ASEAN Secretariat, 70 A J1 Sisingamangaraja, Jakarta 12110, Indonesia (tel: 62(21)726-2991, 724-3372; fax: 724-3504, 739-8234).

Asian Development Bank, Cambodia Resident Mission, 93 Preah Norodom Boulevard, Phnom Penh (tel: 725-805; fax: 725-807).

British Embassy, 27-29 Street 75, Phnom Penh (tel: 427-124; fax: 427-124/5).

Cambodian Development Council (CDC), Phnom Penh.

Cambodian Embassy (USA), 4530 16th Street, NW, Washington DC 20011 (tel: (+1-202)- 726-7742; fax: (+1-202)-726-8381; e-mail: cambodia@embassy.org).

Cambodia Mine Action Centre, 22 Street 122, Phnom Penh (tel: 913-506).

Chemins de Fer du Cambodge, Moha Vithei Pracheathippatay, Phnom Penh (tel: 25-156).

Department of Civil Aviation, 62 Boulevard Norodom, Phnom Penh (tel: 427-141; fax: 26-169).

Global, Business Centre, 378 EO Sivutha Street, Group 1, Sangkat Olympic, Khan Chamcarmon, Phnom Penh (tel: 27-124; fax: 27-125).

Phnom Penh Port Authority (tel: 23-369).

National news agency: AKP (Agence Kampuchea Presse)

Internet sites
Asian Development Bank: www.adb.org/carm

Cambodia web sites: http://mekong.net/cambodia/links.htm

Cambodian web directory: www.kampuchea.com/

Cameroon

KEY FACTS

Official name: République du Cameroun (Republic of Cameroon)

Head of State: President Paul Biya (since 1982; re-elected Oct 2004)

Head of government: Prime Minister Ephraïm Inoni (appointed Dec 2004)

Ruling party: Coalition led by Rassemblement Démocratique du Peuple Camerounais (RDPC) (Cameroon People's Democratic Rally) with Union Nationale pour la Démocratie et le Progrès (UNDP) (National Union for Democracy and Progress) and Union des Populations du Cameroun (UPC) (Union of the Peoples of Cameroon) (since 1992; re-elected July 2007)

Area: 475,442 square km

Population: 18.86 million (2007)*

Capital: Yaoundé

Official language: French, English

Currency: CFA franc (CFAf) = 100 centimes (Communauté Financière Africaine (African Financial Community) franc)

Exchange rate: CFAf413.80 per US$ (Jul 2008); CFAf655.95 per euro (pegged from Jan 1999)

GDP per capita: US$1,095 (2007)*

GDP real growth: 3.30% (2007)*

Labour force: 6.83 million (2004)

Inflation: 0.90% (2007)

Oil production: 62,000 bpd (2007)

Balance of trade: US$580.00 million (2006)

Foreign debt: US$8.46 billion (2004)

* estimated figure

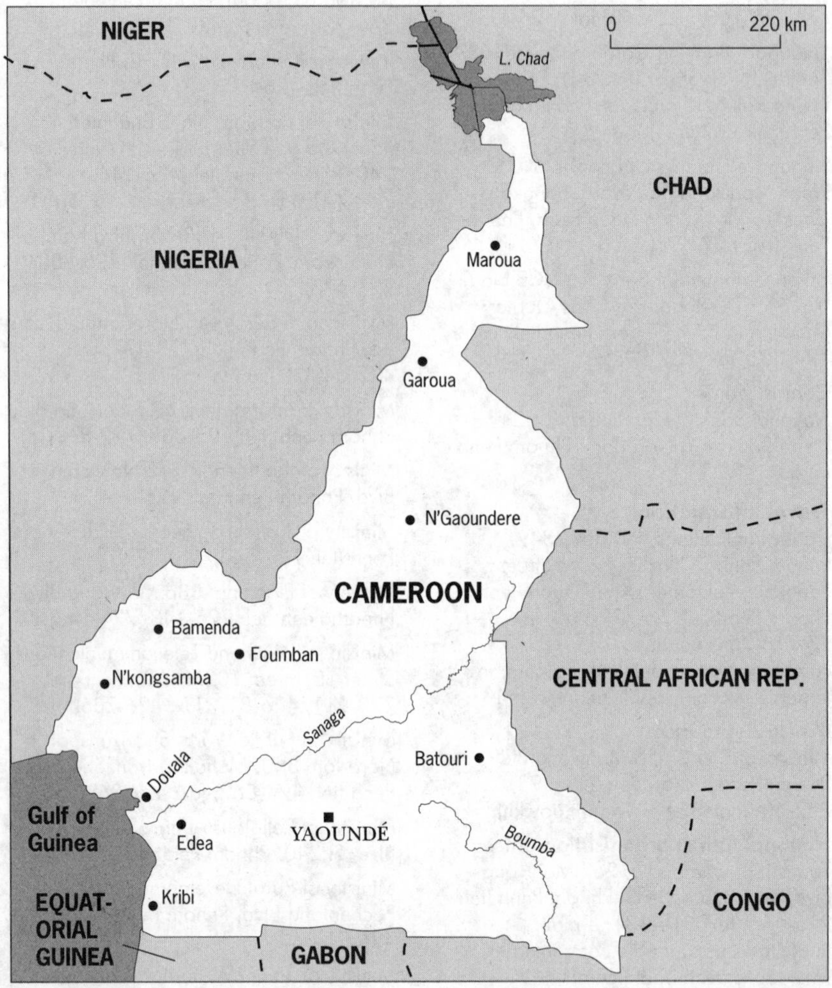

In Africa, it would seem that the old saying 'no news is good news' is – for most countries – particularly appropriate. It means in some ways that there is a lack of what most journalists and the reading public seem to regard as 'newsworthy' by that many states would hope to avoid: coups, invasions, arrests, trials, crop failures and so on. In its day, Cameroon has probably had its fair share of 'news'; stories of the quarrels between parties and leaders, between Anglophones and Francophones, the subversive activities launched in different parts of the country, not to mention an insidious civil war. In the twenty-first century relatively little seems to be happening in Cameroon – cabinet re-shuffles, the fall of a politician and the rise of a newcomer, even the announcement of an IMF loan or, sadly, the incidence levels of HIV/Aids seem to be about it. Cameroon has one of the best-endowed primary commodity economies in sub-Saharan Africa, with its oil resources and favourable agricultural conditions.

Word Bank

The World Bank reported in its 2007 survey of Cameroon that the country's stable macroeconomic framework and far-reaching structural and institutional reforms had enabled it to sustain real GDP growth at around 4.7 per cent per annum during 1995–2000, with inflation at around 3.1 per cent. With the renewed growth, the incidence of poverty fell by an estimated 13 percentage points to about 40 per cent of households, between 1996 and 2001.

According to the World Bank, overall economic growth dropped to about 3.8 per cent per annum during 2001–05, due mainly to a rapid decline in oil production. In addition, the completion of the construction of the Chad-Cameroon oil pipeline, and the lower electricity supply that adversely affected industrial activities also contributed to weakening economic growth in 2004 and 2005 .

However, the Bank reported that a slight economic rebound was observed in 2006 with the GDP growth rate reported at 3.9 per cent as a result of higher agriculture production and recovery in oil production following the discovery of new fields. Inflation has remained stable at around 1.9 per cent per annum in 2001–05, but was higher in 2006 (5.1 per cent) mainly because of higher oil prices.

The IMF approves

In October 2005, after a year of negotiations, Cameroon realised an ambitious International Monetary Fund (IMF)-backed arrangement to bring its economy into line. Over three years, the IMF is making available US$35 million to support the government's programme of economic reform and poverty reduction. Targets include annual real growth up to 4.5 per cent from 2.8 per cent, with non-oil growth of 5.1 per cent from 3.7 per cent. This will be in the face of declining oil output – down to 74,000 barrels per day (bpd) from 82,000bpd, and at three dollars a barrel less. Growth in exports of the non-oil sector will reach 5.4 per cent (negative 3.7 per cent in 2005), while growth in oil exports will have slowed to 3.2 per cent.

Total government revenue is set to remain reasonably constant at 17 per cent of GDP, while expenditure will jump to 17 per cent from 15 per cent. Debt servicing after debt relief will be cut to 4.2 per cent of GDP from 6.7 per cent. The current account balance will worsen from a negative 2.4 per cent to 4.8 per cent.

Monitoring of the programme so far (over 2005) has seen 'broadly satisfactory' performance. The policies have contributed to solid growth, low inflation and a narrowing of the current account deficit. But progress in structural reforms needs to be strengthened, particularly with respect to improving governance and the business climate, privatisation and fuel price adjustments. There is also considerable room for improvement in the transparency of government operations.

In recent years, the business climate has also been adversely affected by the government's failure to pay salaries and slow progress in restructuring loss-making public enterprises. The targets doggedly, and probably optimistically, assume an end to this and although oil production is expected to decline over the medium term, growth in the non-oil economy is expected to strengthen as the business climate improves.

Cameroon's economy is mainly agricultural. The principal commercial crops are cocoa, coffee, tobacco, cotton, and bananas. Petroleum products make up more than half of all exports. Timber is also a major export. Potential for development includes bauxite, iron ore, timber and hydropower. Underlying economic and policy weaknesses were exposed in 1985, when sharp declines in coffee, cocoa and oil prices had led to a 60 per cent degeneration in the external terms of trade. In late 1996, Cameroon changed course and committed itself to correcting the years of economic mismanagement. The success of government reforms (forestry, transportation, banking system, and privatisation of public utilities) supported by the IMF and the World Bank translated into better economic performance, but impetus flagged because of a top-heavy civil service and a generally unfavourable climate for business enterprise.

Politics

Cameroon has generally enjoyed stability, but despite movement toward democratic reform, political power remains firmly in the hands of an ethnic oligarchy. The Anglophone community has felt for some time that it is discriminated against by a remote Yaoundé-based government and has long campaigned for greater autonomy, seeing itself as increasingly marginalised in the Francophone-dominated country. Most in the Anglophone community favour the reintroduction of a federal system.

Cameroon has the advantage of one of the best literacy rates in Africa. Almost all members of the indigenous population over 15 years of age can read and write. However, the country's continued development is hampered by a level of corruption that is among the highest in the world. Ratings agency Standard and Poor's in January 2006 reaffirmed Cameroon's CCC long term and C short term ratings, saying they reflected the country's weak public finances.

Veteran Cameroon leader Paul Biya won his third term in presidential elections in October 2004, with more than 70 per cent of the vote. Commonwealth observers accepted the result, but noted that the poll lacked credibility in key areas. Opposition parties alleged widespread fraud. Biya has been in power since 1982. Born in 1933, he was educated in Cameroon and France, where he studied law at the Sorbonne. Before becoming president, he spent his entire political career in the service of previous president Ahmadou Ahidjo, becoming his prime minister in 1975. When Ahidjo resigned in 1982 he assumed the leadership and set about replacing his predecessor's northern allies

KEY INDICATORS — Cameroon

	Unit	2003	2004	2005	2006	2007
Population	m	16.14	16.79	17.84	*18.34	*18.86
Gross domestic product (GDP)	US$bn	12.40	14.73	16.88	17.96	*20.65
GDP per capita	US$	841	831	946	*979	*1,095
GDP real growth	%	4.2	4.3	2.0	3.5	*3.3
Inflation	%	0.6	0.3	2.0	5.3	0.9
Oil output	'000 bpd	68.0	62.0	58.0	63.0	82.0
Exports (fob) (goods)	US$m	2,078.0	2,445.0	3,026.0	3,490.0	–
Imports (cif) (goods)	US$m	1,962.0	1,979.0	2,785.0	2,910.0	–
Balance of trade	US$m	116.0	466.0	241.0	580.0	–
Current account	US$m	-300.0	-240.0	-569.0	118.0	*85.0
Total reserves minus gold	US$m	639.6	829.3	949.4	1,716.2	2,906.8
Foreign exchange	US$m	637.2	827.6	946.3	1,710.5	2,900.7
Exchange rate	per US$	574.89	528.29	507.22	496.60	454.40

* estimated figure

with his own fellow southerners. In 1983 he accused Ahidjo of organising a coup against him, forcing the former president to flee the country. His current prime minister is Ephraïm Inoni.

Risk assessment

Economic	Fair
Political	Fair
Regional stability	Fair

COUNTRY PROFILE

Historical profile

1470s Portuguese mariners arrived and gave Cameroon its name. Having found what they thought to be shrimps (camaroes) in the main river, they named it Rio dos Camaroes.
1884 Germany established the protectorate of Kamerun.
1916 The German administration was ousted by Allied forces in the First World War.
The post-war League of Nations gave mandates for four-fifths of the territory to France, and the remainder to Britain.
1960 French East Cameroon gained its independence.
1961 British West Cameroon gained its independence.
1972 A unified state was formed, with the Union Nationale Camerounaise (UNC) (Cameroonian National Union) dominating both the executive and legislative branches.
1982 Prime Minister Paul Biya became president after the resignation of President Ahidjo.
1985 Biya renamed the ruling party the Rassemblement Démocratique du Peuple Camerounais (RDPC) (Cameroon People's Democratic Rally), and introduced a number of political reforms which were largely viewed as cosmetic.
1990 A multi-party political system was legalised. Although this change marked the gradual opening of the Cameroonian political system, subsequent elections were marred by irregularities and accusations of electoral fraud.
1997 President Paul Biya was re-elected. The elections were boycotted by the three main opposition parties after their complaints about the handling of voter registration were ignored. Biya won 92 per cent of the vote.
1999 English-speaking secessionists, led by the Southern Cameroon National Council (SCNC), announced a breakaway Federal Republic of Southern Cameroon.
2001 Demonstrations calling for decentralisation of power were banned and several southern Cameroon separatists were killed.
2002 The ruling RDPC increased its number of seats in the legislative elections. The International Court of Justice gave Cameroon sovereignty of the potentially oil-rich Bakassi Peninsula, claimed by Cameroon and Nigeria.
2003 The communications minister ordered the closure of an English-speaking private radio station, Magic FM, for running programmes critical of the government.
2004 Presidential Biya was re-elected. Ephraïm Inoni was appointed prime minister. Nigeria failed to withdraw troops from the Bakassi Peninsula.
2005 Presidents Obasanjo and Biya and UN Secretary Annan failed to resolve the dispute concerning Bakassi Peninsula, thought to hold about 10 per cent of the world's oil and gas reserves.
2006 Nigeria ceded the Bakassi peninsula to Cameroon in accordance with a 2002 International Court of Justice ruling.
2007 In the general elections, held on 22 July, the ruling RDPC won 152 seats (out of 180) and the opposition SDF won 21.
2008 In April, parliament voted to amend the constitution and scrap a limited number of presidential terms, allowing incumbent Paul Biya to run again in the 2011 presidential elections. Nigeria finally surrended sovereignty of the oil-rich territory on 11 June.

Political structure

Constitution
The constitution was promulgated in 1972 and revised in 1975 and 1996. The main provisions of the 1996 revision were for a more decentralised government, the creation of a unicameral national assembly (Assemblée Nationale), and the extension of the president's term of office from five years to seven, at the same time allowing a fourth consecutive term.

Form of state
Unitary republic

The executive
Executive power is vested in the president, who appoints a cabinet. The president serves a seven-year term. A prime minister, who acts as head of government, is appointed by the president. The president names and dismisses cabinet members and judges, ratifies treaties, heads the armed forces, controls legislation and can rule by decree.

National legislature
Legislative power is held by the 180-member unicameral Assemblée Nationale (National Assembly), elected for a five-year term.

Legal system
Cameroon's legal system is based on French civil law with common law influences. The country has a Supreme Court, the judges of which are appointed by the president. Provisions in the 1996 constitution for judicial independence have not been put into force. Cameroon does not accept the compulsory jurisdiction of the International Court of Justice, but does belong to the International Court of Arbitration of the International Chamber of Commerce.

Last elections
11 October 2004 (presidential); 22 July 2007 (parliamentary).
Results: Presidential: Paul Biya was re-elected with 70.9 per cent of the vote against 17.4 per cent for John Fru Ndi, 4.5 per cent for Adamou Ndam Njoya and 3.7 per cent for Garga Haman Adji. Turnout was 82.8 per cent.
Parliamentary: The ruling RDPC won 152 seats (out of 180); SDF 15; Union Démocratique du Cameroun (UDC) (Democratic Union of Cameroon) 4; Union Nationale pour la Démocratie et le Progrès (UNDP) (National Union for Democracy and Progress) 4; Mouvement Progressiste (MP) (Progressive Movement) 1; undecided 4. Turnout was over 60 per cent.

Next elections
June 2007 (parliamentary); 2011 (presidential).

Political parties

Ruling party
Coalition led by Rassemblement Démocratique du Peuple Camerounais (RDPC) (Cameroon People's Democratic Rally) with Union Nationale pour la Démocratie et le Progrès (UNDP) (National Union for Democracy and Progress) and Union des Populations du Cameroun (UPC) (Union of the Peoples of Cameroon) (since 1992; re-elected July 2007)

Main opposition party
Front Social-Démocratique (SDF) (Social Democratic Front)

Population

18.86 million (2007)*
Last census: April 1987: 10,493,655
Population density: 29 inhabitants per square km. Urban population: 50 per cent (1995–2001).
Annual growth rate: 2.1 per cent 1994–2004 (WHO 2006)

Ethnic make-up
Cameroon has a highly diversified population comprising some 200 ethnic groups, including Cameroon Highlanders (31 per cent), Equatorial Bantu (19 per cent) and Kirdi (11 per cent). There are about 200,000 Europeans in the country, mainly French speakers.

Religions
Indigenous beliefs are practiced by 40 per cent of the population, another 40 per cent are Christian, and 20 per cent are Muslim.

Education
Literacy rate: 68 per cent adult rate (Unesco 2005)
Enrolment rate: 107 per cent gross primary enrolment, 33 per cent gross secondary enrolment; of relevant age groups (including repeaters) (World Bank).
Pupils per teacher: 44 in primary schools.

Health
Per capita total expenditure on health (2003) was US$64; of which per capita government spending was US$19, at the international dollar rate, (WHO 2006).
HIV/Aids
HIV prevalence: 5.5 per cent aged 15–49 in 2004 (World Bank)
Life expectancy: 50 years, 2004 (WHO 2006)
Fertility rate/Maternal mortality rate: 4.5 births per woman, 2004 (WHO 2006)
Birth rate/Death rate: 34.7 births and 15.4 deaths per 1,000 population (2005)
Child (under 5 years) mortality rate (per 1,000): 95 per 1,000 live births; 22 per cent of children aged under five are malnourished (World Bank).
Head of population per physician: 0.19 physician per 1,000 people, 2004 (WHO 2006)

Welfare
Cameroon's social insurance system provides cover for old-age pension, disability pension, sickness and maternity benefits, work injuries and family allowances.

Main cities
Douala (commercial centre, estimated population 1.9 million in 2004), Yaoundé (capital, 1.9 million), Garoua (287,586), Kousséri (176,241), Bamenda (229,109), Maroua (205,635), Bafoussam (185,635).

Languages spoken
24 major African language groups including Bamileke, Ewondo, Bassa and Bamoun are spoken. Around 80 per cent of the population speak French as a second language (francophone Cameroon) and 20 per cent speak English as a second language (anglophone – formerly British West Cameroon).
Official language/s
French, English

Media
The government maintains a tight control of media outlets with official restrictions and stringent libel laws that have regularly imprisoned journalists and led to self-censorship.
Other news agencies: Africa News Agency: www.africanewsagency.co.uk
APA: www.apanews.net
Panapress: www.panapress.com

Press
Dailies: In French, the Cameroon Tribune is the official state-owned newspaper, with an English edition, published twice weekly, La Nouvelle Expression (www.lanouvelleexpression.net), is published three-times weekly. In English, The Post (www.postnewsline.com).
Weeklies: In French, private publications include Le Messager (www.lemessager.net), and in English Postwatch (www.postwatchmagazine.com).
Business: In French, La Dépeche économique is a bi-weekly publication.
Periodicals: In French, monthly publications include La Voix du paysan a farmer's magazine, Dikalo (http://www.dikalo.biz) and Le Météo an independent magazine.
Broadcasting
The national broadcaster is Cameroon Radio and Television (CRTV).
Radio: CRTV (www.crtv.cm) operates one national and several provincial services in French, English and local languages. Other commercial stations include Nostalgie (www.cameroun-plus.com), Sky One (www.skyonecameroun.com) and the pan-African Radio Africa No 1 (www.africa1.com).
English-speaking separatists in the south of the country have used pirate-radio for propaganda.
Television: CRTV (www.crtv.cm) is the national public TV station. There are two private stations Canal 2 and STV (www.stvgroup.com) with two channels, which broadcast via satellite.
News agencies
Other news agencies: Africa News Agency: www.africanewsagency.co.uk
APA: www.apanews.net
Panapress: www.panapress.com

Economy
Cameroon has, for a number of years, been working in close co-operation with the IMF to improve its economic policies. It has introduced structural reforms with adjustments to emphasise non-oil revenue, to improve public finance management and reporting. Although there has been some improvement in recent years, real growth slowed from 4.3 per cent in 2004 to 2.6 per cent in 2005, while inflation grew from 0.3 per cent to 2 per cent in the same period. Public finances have deteriorated, poverty is still widespread and public investment remains low. Nevertheless, the government has been advised that it should remain firm on improving governance, enterprise restructuring, privatisation and removal of fuel price subsidies. The IMF has stated that reform priorities should include increasing public investment in infrastructure and removing obstacles to private sector activities.
In 2005 the IMF announced that Cameroon had been awarded a three-year arrangement of US$26.8 million under the Poverty Reduction and Growth facility. This followed the additional amount of US$8.2 million offered under the Heavily Indebted Poor Countries Initiative, which will be released from late 2005 through to 2006. In 2006, 27 per cent of the national debt was written off by creditors, including the World Bank and the IMF. Also in 2006, France announced a five-year package of aid amounting to US$627 million
Oil and cocoa prices have a great impact on the economy. Both commodities rose in price in 2004 bringing an unexpected surge in revenue, which the IMF advised should be used for poverty reduction programmes and debt reduction.
Cameroon has the possibility of becoming a major net exporter of oil and gas following the cession by Nigeria in 2006 of the Bakassi Peninsula in the Gulf of Guinea, which is estimated to hold about 10 per cent of the world's oil and gas reserves.

External trade
As a member of the Customs and Economic Union of Central Africa (Ceuca) and the Economic Community of Central African States (ECCAS) and the Bank of Central African States, using the CFA franc, Cameroon has a customs union and free trade zone with other member states.
Imports
Imports consist mainly of semi-processed products and industrial outputs, machinery and food products. Imports consist principally of vehicles, machines and electrical equipment, fuel and food. Import volume has been constrained because of the strong growth of domestic industries (especially in food processing) which are offering cheaper alternatives to expensive imported goods. Light crude oil for refining and re-export.
Main sources: Nigeria (23.3 cent total, 2006), France (17.2 per cent), China (6.3 per cent).
Exports
Principal exports include crude oil and petroleum products, timber, coffee, cotton cocoa beans and tobacco.
Main destinations: Spain (25.9 per cent of 2006 total goods exports), Italy (23.1 per cent), France (10.6 per cent).

Agriculture
Farming
In order to broaden the country's economic base and increase the value added to domestic production, the government is encouraging development of its full agricultural potential. Agricultural production as a percentage of GDP has been steadily increasing since the early 1980s, reaching

43.9 per cent of national output in 2004. Some 70 per cent of Cameroon's labour force is employed in the agricultural sector, although only 2 per cent of Cameroon's land area is used for permanent crops. Principal crops include cocoa, coffee, bananas, cotton and oil palms. Virtually all food requirements are met by local production. Most agricultural production is in the hands of smallholders, with the exception of rubber and palm, which are run under the plantation system.

Mayuka, located in the northern region of Cameroon, is the centre of the cocoa industry, where business made sweeping profits as prices soared following the political crisis in Côte d'Ivoire. As demand for cocoa rises, so the government aims to double the amount of production.

Crop production in 2005 included: 1,660,400 million tonnes (t) cereals in total, 1,200,000t cassava, 1,100,000t taro, 280,000t yams, 1,450,000t sugar cane, 1,300,000t oil palm fruit, 950,000t maize, 1,300,000t plantains, 60,000t millet, 140,000t potatoes, 190,000t sweet potatoes, 600,000t sorghum, 170,000t seed cotton, 124,000t cotton lint, 50,000t rice, 225,000t groundnuts in shells, 790,000t bananas, 289,230t oilcrops, 296,600t pulses, 400,000t tomatoes, 48,000t pineapples, 4,500t tobacco, 180,000t cocoa beans, 60,000t green coffee, 45,892t natural rubber, 2,305,927t fruit in total, 1,331,870t vegetables in total. Livestock production included: 218,649t meat in total, 90,000t beef, 16,200t pig meat, 16,380t lamb, 15,700t goat meat, 50,000t game meat, 30,000t poultry, 13,400t eggs, 189,300t milk, 3,000t honey,12,400t cattle hides, 2,730t sheepskins.

Fishing

As a consequence of its short coastline and the intrusion on its territorial waters of Bioko Island, which belongs to Equatorial Guinea, Cameroon's fishing industry is underdeveloped. Offshore waters are not well stocked, as the currents which provide richer fishing grounds off Nigeria and other parts of West Africa do not flow close to Cameroon's coastline. Nevertheless, catches of both freshwater and marine fish have been steadily increasing in recent years.

Fisheries legislation in Cameroon contains specific clauses dealing with the aquaculture sector, covering issues related to registration and licensing, and the export/import of fish species. It aims to improve artisanal fishing methods, preservation and processing of fishery products.

Forestry

While the country is well-forested, with more than 40 per cent forest cover and an additional 30 per cent of other wooded land, unsustainable deforestation has resulted in the loss of over 222,000 hectares. Nevertheless Cameroon is the second-largest area of tropical rainforest in Africa after the Democratic Republic of Congo (DRC). It is one of Africa's leading producers and exporters of tropical logs and sawn timber; smaller quantities of veneer and plywood are also exported. Important non-wood forest products include medicinal plants, nuts, wild fruits, rattan and bushmeat.

Three-quarters of Cameroon's forestry exports consist of industrial roundwood, with sawnwood accounting for another 18 per cent. Forestry imports to Cameroon are composed almost exclusively of paper and paperboard, totalling 96.5 per cent of forestry imports.

Industry and manufacturing

The industrial sector has been contracting and accounts for less than 20 per cent of GDP, while services accounted for 40.5 per cent. However, the agri-industrial sub-sector has been growing, gradually substituting imports with domestically produced goods. The sector employs around 10 per cent of the workforce. Industrial output accounts for 25 per cent of Cameroon's exports.

The government has been a major participant in the industrial sector, mainly through the Société Nationale d'Investissement (SNI) (National Investment Agency), however economic imperatives have required that public entities become market driven and private enterprise has yet to become competitive. The Technical Commission for the Rehabilitation of Public Enterprises oversees privatisation and restructuring of all state-owned companies.

Tourism

There is considerable potential for tourism in Cameroon although development has been slow due to expensive air fares, the high cost of tourist visas, limited tourist infrastructure and the relatively high prices of hotels. A Tourist Development Plan is being undertaken in co-operation with the World Tourism Organisation (WTO). The government has devised a special investment code to encourage private investors. The deregulation of air traffic should help reduce air fares.

Environment

Cameroon's tropical forest is the largest in-tact rainforest in the world but it is being exploited at a faster rate than is sustainable threatening the habitat of numerous species and the long-term existence of elephants and gorillas.

As the forests have become more accessible, poachers are shooting antelope, chimpanzees and gorillas, for commercial purposes. In 2006, as part of its commitment to debt relief, the French government agreed to invest in the conservation of Cameroon's natural resources, to include better management of protected areas, wildlife and forest production.

In 2005 a UN inspection team warned that a natural dam in the north-west province was in imminent danger of collapsing and flooding the Nyos Valley. The cost to repair the dam is estimated at US$15 million.

Mining

The mining sector accounts for around 10 per cent of GDP and employs 2 per cent of the workforce. Bauxite deposits of some 1,100 million tonnes at Adamaoua Province have been identified but remain unexploited, although an upturn in world aluminium prices encouraged Société des Bauxitese de Cameroun (SBC) to begin mining operations. There are deposits of iron ore at Kribi (reserves estimated at 197 million tonnes), and potential reserves of gold, diamonds, uranium, rutile, industrial clays and low-grade nickel and cobalt. Tin is mined on a very small scale. Investment by large mining companies is needed to exploit underground riches.

Hydrocarbons

Cameroon used to be sub-Saharan Africa's fifth-largest oil producer but by 2005 had dropped to seventh place as Equatorial Guinea and Chad have developed their oil reserves.

The country also had natural gas reserves of over 110 billion cubic metres. The industry is still in early stages of development, but would take off dramatically if the territorial dispute with Nigeria over the Bakassi Peninsula were to be resolved in Cameroon's favour. The Bakassi Peninsula is reckoned by some to hold some 10 per cent of the world oil and gas reserves. The government also believes there is considerable potential in two largely unexplored areas – the Logone Birni and Douala basins – and is also hoping for the discovery of big offshore finds. However, the coastline is limited and the country's maritime area is small.

Energy

Total electricity generation capacity is estimated at 850MW, nearly 90 per cent of which is hydroelectric. Although Cameroon has the greatest hydroelectric power potential in Africa after the Democratic Republic of Congo (DRC), its plants are old, having been mainly built in the 1950s, and operate well below capacity. Therefore, gas will be especially important as an alternative source of power in the dry season. Cameroon expects its demand for power to double in the course of the next decade. Production from the Edéa Dam complex, Lagdo near Garoua and Song-Loulou generate enough to meet 85 per cent of needs. All electricity is produced by the Société Nationale d'Electricité du Cameroun (AES-Sonel), which is 51 per cent owned by the US's AES Sirocco.

The government decided to go ahead with plans for the Lom-Pangar hydroelectric project, which includes a 50 metre high barrage flooding an area of 610 square km and a hydroelectric plant of approximately 50MW. An environmental impact study is to be the initial step and construction of the project was not expected to start before 2008.

It is estimated that only 2 per cent of the population has access to electricity supplies and only 9 per cent of the capital's potential consumers use electricity; most of the country relies on wood fuel.

To comply with a World Bank loan to develop the electricity sector emphasis on sustainable energy has increased

Banking and insurance

Cameroon's banking sector has become significantly stronger as the result of IMF-led restructuring, but is still poorly developed. The last state-owned bank in Cameroon was bought by a French banking company in 1999. Cameroon's largest bank is the Société Générale de Banques au Cameroun (SGBC). The commercial banking sector is made up of nine commercial banks with 60 branches, but suffers from a lack of available capital, an unwillingness to take risks and outdated products.

Central bank

Banque des Etats de l'Afrique Centrale

Main financial centre

Douala

Time

GMT plus one hour

Geography

Cameroon lies on the Gulf of Guinea. Nigeria is to the west, Chad and the Central African Republic to the north-east and east, and the Republic of Congo, Gabon and Equatorial Guinea to the south.

The country can be divided into four main regions. The coastal plain is tropical but tempered by the effects of the sea. The tropical plateau in the south is heavily forested and cut through by a number of rivers flowing west into the Bight of Biafra or south-east to join the River Congo. The Adamawa and Bamenda highlands rise to 2,500 metres and are drier and cooler than the forest areas. The highlands are volcanic in origin, and include Mount Cameroon (4,070 metres). The savannah grasslands to the north lie between Nigeria and Chad, and stretch northwards to Lake Chad.

Hemisphere

Northern

Climate

In the north the single wet season is between April and September, and there is a dry season during the rest of the year.

It is tropical in the south with fairly constant average temperatures throughout the year, ranging between 18 degrees Celsius (C) at night and 30–32 degrees C during the day. In the south rainfall is distributed throughout the year with two wet seasons and two dry seasons.

Dress codes

Tropical clothes are advised, with warmer clothes required for the higher altitudes. Lightweight raincoats are recommended for the rainy season.

Entry requirements

Passports

Passports are required by all and should be valid for at least six months from date of arrival.

Visa

Required by all, except nationals of Central African Republic, Chad, Mali and Nigeria. Nationals of countries without Cameroonian diplomatic representation may be issued with a visa on arrival. A business visa requires a letter from applicant's company outlining purpose of visit and a letter from business partners in Cameroon (endorsed by the local police), plus a full itinerary.

An onward/return ticket and proof of sufficient funds are required.

Currency advice/regulations

There are no restrictions on the import or export of foreign currency.

Local currency import is limited to CFAf20,000 (approximately US$35) and export is limited to CFAf20,000 for tourists and CFAf45,000 (approximately US$80) for business purposes. Travellers cheques are accepted, but cash is advised.

Prohibited imports

Pornographic materials, illegal drugs, weapons and ammunitions may not be brought into Cameroon. Alcohol and other spirits (maximum 30 bottles) should be sent separately.

An invoice must accompany all furniture and electrical appliances to prove that they are more than six months old. Newer items are subject to customs duties and taxes. Home computers do not qualify as personal effects, and are subject to customs duties and taxes.

Health (for visitors)

Mandatory precautions

An international certificate of vaccination against yellow fever.

Advisable precautions

The principal health hazards are cholera, malaria and HIV. Vaccination against tetanus, typhoid, polio, meningitis, and hepatitis A and B are all advisable. Rabies and bilharzia also occur, and necessary precautions should be taken. Avoid swimming in fresh water; well-chlorinated swimming pools should be safe. Bottled water is readily available. Milk is unpasteurised and should be boiled; meat and vegetables should be cooked and fruit peeled.

Medical care is adequate, but can be expensive.

Hotels

Good hotel accommodation is available in main centres. Service charges usually added to bill.

Credit cards

There is limited acceptance of the major credit cards only.

Public holidays (national)

Fixed dates

1 Jan (New Year's Day), 11 Feb (Youth Day), 1 May (Labour Day), 20 May (National Day), 21 May (Sheep Festival), 15 Aug (Assumption Day), 1 Oct (Unification Day), 25 Dec (Christmas Day).

Variable dates

Good Friday, Easter Monday, Ascension Day, Eid al Adha, Eid al Fitr, Birth of the Prophet.

Islamic year – 1429 (10 Jan 2008–28 Dec 2008): The Islamic year contains 354 or 355 days, with the result that Muslim feasts advance by 10–12 days against the Gregorian calendar. Dates of feasts vary according to the sighting of the new moon, so cannot be forecast exactly.

Working hours

Different hours are kept in the French-speaking (including Yaoundé and Douala) and English-speaking areas (south-west and north-west frontier areas) of Cameroon.

Banking

French-speaking areas: Mon—Fri: 0800—1200 and 1515—1630.

English-speaking areas: Mon—Fri: 0800—1330.

Business

French-speaking areas: Mon—Fri: 0730—1200 and 1430—1800.

English-speaking areas: Mon—Fri: 0730—1500; Sat: 0730—1200.

Government

French-speaking areas: Mon—Fri: 0730—1200 and 1430—1800.

English-speaking areas: Mon—Fri: 0730—1500; Sat: 0730—1200.

Shops

French-speaking areas: Mon—Sat: 0700/0800—1230 and 1430/1500—1830/1900.

English-speaking areas: Mon—Sat: 0700/0800—1200 and 1430/1530—1830—1900.
Post offices:
French-speaking areas: Mon—Fri: 0800—1200 and 1400—1700; Sat: 0800—1200
English-speaking areas: Mon—Fri: 0800—1200 and 1430—1700.

Telecommunications

Mobile/cell phones

Cellular telephones services are available.

Electricity supply

220V AC, 50 cycles; plugs are of the two-pin round type.

Social customs/useful tips

Handshaking is the customary form of greeting. Business is conducted primarily in English or French.
Care should be taken to respect Islamic and other local religious practices and conventions, and visitors should be aware of restrictions on food and drink in Muslim areas, particularly during the Islamic fasting period of Ramadan.
Visitors should take care when photographing. It is considered polite to ask permission to photograph traditional dances, and it is advisable not to take pictures of official buildings or military installations.
If there is no service charge included in a bill, gratuities in hotels and restaurants are up to 10 per cent.

Security

Muggings and petty crime have increased in recent years, mainly in the large cities. It is unwise to carry valuables or large amounts of cash in the street and thieves should not be resisted. Armed bandit attacks are a serious problem throughout the country. Journeys should be carefully planned and travelling in convoy is recommended. At the international airports, to avoid luggage being stolen, care should be taken to employ only the official porters.

Getting there

Air

National airline: Cameroon Airlines
International airport/s: Douala International (DLA), 10km from the city; duty-free shop, bars, restaurants, bank, post office and shops.
Other airport/s: Yaoundé-Nsimalen (YAO), 20km from the city; Garoua International (GOU), 6km from the city, also accept international flights.
Airport tax: Approximately US$18.

Surface

Road: Road access is possible from Nigeria, Chad, Gabon, Equatorial Guinea and the Central African Republic. These routes are rough and may become impassable during rainy seasons. Bush taxis and minibuses are available. Armed banditry is a problem in the area bordering the Central African Republic and in other parts of Cameroon.
Rail: Rail access is available from N'Gaoundal and Belabo in the Central African Republic.
Water: There are two boats a day from Calabar (Nigeria) across the Cross River to Oron, and from Ikang (Nigeria) there are speedboats to Ekondo Titi.
Douala offers more freight links with Europe than other Central African ports. Cameroon Shipping Lines (Camshiplines) maintains an office in Paris.
Main port/s: Douala. Other ports are at Limbe, Kribi and Garoua (on the River Bénoué), which handle river trade during the dry season.

Getting about

National transport

Air: Cameroon Airlines operates domestic services between the main cities, including several daily flights between Yaoundé and Douala. Early arrival at the airport terminal is advisable, as overbookings are common. However, air services are generally efficient and certainly the fastest means of travelling within Cameroon.
Road: Cameroon's road network totals 31,800km of roads. Surfaced roads run between main centres although there are no tarmac road links between Yaoundé and Ngaoundéré. Major routes are from Douala to Limbé, Buea, Bafoussam, Sangmelima, Bamenda and Yaoundé (all-weather road). Most other roads are unsurfaced and are often impassable during rainy season.
Buses: There are coach services between the main centres. Connections to rural areas are unreliable, dangerous and subject to suspension in the rainy season.
Rail: The track network extends 1,168km. Cameroon Railways (Camrail) links Kumba, Douala, Yaoundé and Ngaoundéré. An overnight service runs from Yaoundé to Ngaoundéré (12 hours). Second-class travel is cheap but uncomfortable. Sleeping facilities are available on some trains. There is an express three-hour service between Yaoundé and Douala with good facilities.

City transport

Taxis: Taxis are not metered but have a minimum fare and fixed prices. Long journeys and daily hire should be negotiated. A 10 per cent tip is optional. There are taxis from the airport to Douala city centre.

Car hire

Chauffeur- or self-driven cars are available in Yaoundé and Douala, but can be expensive. An international driving licence is required.

BUSINESS DIRECTORY

The addresses listed below are a selection only. While World of Information makes every endeavour to check these addresses, we cannot guarantee that changes have not been made, especially to telephone numbers and area codes. We would welcome any corrections.

Telephone area codes

The international direct dialling code (IDD) for Cameroon is +237 followed by the subscriber's number.

Useful telephone numbers

Police:	17
Fire:	18
Ambulance:	23-40-20

Chambers of Commerce

Cameroon Chamber of Commerce, Industry and Mines, Rue de Chambre de Commerce, PO Box 4011, Douala (tel:342-6855; fax: 342-5596; e-mail: cride-g77@camnet.cm).

Banking

Amity Bank Cameroon, PO Box 2705, Douala (tel: 432-055; fax: 432-046).

Banque Internationale pour le Commerce et l'Industrie du Cameroun (BICIC), PO Box 1925, Avenue du Général-de-Gaulle, Douala (tel: 428-431, 420-001; fax: 424-184, 424-116).

Commercial Bank of Cameroon, PO Box 4004, Douala (tel: 420-202; fax: 433-802).

First Investment Bank; PO Box 13276, Douala (tel: 431-304; fax: 428-423).

International Bank of Africa-Cameroon, PO Box 3300, Douala (tel: 428-422; fax: 428-423).

Société Générale de Banques au Cameroun, PO Box 4042, 78 Rue Joss, Douala (tel: 427-010, 427-004; fax: 430-353) .

Standard Chartered Bank Cameroon, PO Box 1784, Boulevard de la Liberté, Douala (tel: 424-191; fax: 422-789).

Central bank

Banque des États de l'Afrique Centrale, Direction Nationale, PO Box 83, Yaoundé (tel: 223-0511; fax: 223-3380; e-mail: beacyde@beac.int).

Travel information

Cameroon Airlines, Littoral BP 4092, 3 Avenue General de Gaulle, Douala (tel: 422-525, 424-949; fax: 422-487, 423-459).

Douala International Airport, BP 3131, Douala (tel: 423-630, 423-577; fax: 423-758).

Ministry of tourism

Ministry of Tourism, Yaoundé (tel: 223-353, 235-258; fax: 221-295).

National tourist organisation offices

Société Camerounaise de Tourisme (Socatour), BP 7138, Yaoundé (tel: 233-219).

Ministries

Ministry of Agriculture, Yaoundé (tel: 234-085, 225-166, 231-190).

Ministry of Communications, Yaoundé (tel: 234-075; 223-155, 233-974).

Ministry of External relations, Yaoundé (tel: 220-133).

Ministry of Economy and Finance, BP 18, Yaoundé (tel: 234-000, 232-299).

Ministry of Environment and Forestry, BP 14276, Yaoundé (tel: 229-483, 221-225).

Ministry of Industrial and Commercial Development, Yaoundé (tel: 234-040, 225-085).

Ministry of Culture, Yaoundé (tel: 223-155, 233-974).

Ministry of Livestock, Fisheries and Animal Industries, Yaoundé (tel: 223-311, 220-443).

Ministry of Mines, Water and Energy, Yaoundé (tel: 233-404).

Ministry of Post and Telecommunications, Yaoundé (tel: 234-016; fax: 223-497).

Ministry of Public Works and Transport, Yaoundé (tel: 232-236).

Other useful addresses

British Embassy, Avenue Winston Churchill, BP 547, Yaoundé (tel: 220-545, 220-796; fax: 220-148).

Cameroon Development Corporation (CDC), BP 28, Bota, Limbe (tel: 332-251).

Cameroon Embassy (USA), 2349 Massachusetts Avenue, NW, Washington DC 20008 (tel: 202-265-8790; fax: 202-387-3826; e-mail: info@ambacam-usa.org).

Cameroon Press and Publishing Co, BP 1218, Yaoundé (tel: 234-012).

Cameroon Telecommunications, BP 1571, Yaoundé (tel: 234-065; fax: 230-303).

Commission Technique de la Mission de Réhabilitation des Entreprises due Secteur Public et Parapublic, SNI Building, 9th Floor, Yaoundé (tel: 239-750; fax: 235-108).

Centre National d'Assistance aux Petites et Moyennes Entreprises, BP 1377, Douala (tel: 425-858).

Centre National du Commerce Exterieur (CNCE), BP 2461, Douala (tel: 421-685).

Department of Statistics, BP 25, Yaoundé (tel: 220-788).

EU Delegate, BP 847, Yaoundé (tel: 221-387, 222-149).

FEICOM (Special Equipment and Intercommunity Intervention Fund), BP 718 Yaoundé (tel/fax: 231-759).

National Tenders Board, Mballa II, 4th Floor, PO Box 6604, Yaoundé (tel: 201-803; fax: 206-042; e-mail: DGTC@GCNET.CM).

Office National du Café et du Cacao (ONCC), BP 378, Douala (tel: 426-776, 425-088) – sole marketing agency for cocoa, coffee, cotton, groundnuts, palm kernels.

Office de Radiodiffusion-Télévision Camerounaise (CRTV), BP 1634, Yaoundé (tel: 234-088).

Regifercam, BP 304, Douala (tel: 407-159; fax: 423-205).

Société Camerounaise des Depots Petroliers, Siège Social BP 2271, Douala (tel: 405-445; fax: 404-796).

Société de Développement du Cacao SODECAO), BP 1651, Yaoundé (tel: 220-991).

Société de Développement du Coton, Headquarters, BP 302, Garoua (tel: 271-556; fax: 272-068).

Société Nationale des Eaux du Cameroun, BP 157 Douala (tel: 433-066, 430-067; fax: 422-945).

Société Nationale de Raffinage, Cape Limboh, PO Box 365, Limbe (tel: 423-815, 423-817; fax: 423-444, 424-199).

Société Nationale d'Investissement, BP 423, Place de la Poste, Yaoundé (tel: 224-499, 224-422).

Société de Recouvrement des Créances du Cameroun, BP 11991, Yaoundé (tel: 223-739, 220-911, 230-067; fax: 233-833).

Sydicate of Wood Producers and Exporters (SPEBC), BP 2064, Douala (tel/fax: 428-617).

Syndicat des Commerçants, Importateurs et Exportateurs du Cameroun (SCIEC), BP 562, Douala (tel: 420-304).

Syndicat des Industriels du Cameroun, BP 1516, Yaoundé (tel: 222-468; BP 673, Douala (tel: 423-058).

Technical Committee for Privatisation and Liquidations, SNI Building, 9th Floor, Yaoundé (tel: 239-750; fax: 235-108).

US Embassy, rue Nachtigal, BP 817, Yaoundé (tel: 234-014).

Internet sites

Africa Business Network: www.ifc.org/abn

AllAfrica.com: allafrica.com

African Development Bank: www.afdb.org

Africa Online: www.africaonline.com

Mbendi AfroPaedia (information on companies, countries, industries and stock exchanges in Africa): mbendi.co.za

Canada

KEY FACTS

Official name: Canada

Head of State: Queen Elizabeth II (since 1952), represented by Governor General Michaëlle Jean (since 27 Sep 2005)

Head of government: Prime Minister Stephen Harper (from 6 Feb 2006)

Ruling party: Conservative Party of Canada (CPC) (elected 23 January 2006)

Area: 9,976,139 square km

Population: 32.93 million (2007)

Capital: Ottawa

Official language: English, French

Currency: Canadian dollar (C$) = 100 cents

Exchange rate: C$1.00 per US$ (Jul 2008)

GDP per capita: US$43,485 (2007)

GDP real growth: 2.60% (2007)

Labour force: 17.18 million (2004)

Unemployment: 6.00% (OECD, 2004)

Inflation: 2.10% (2007)

Oil production: 3.31 million bpd (2007)

Balance of trade: US$53.79 billion (2005)

Foreign debt: US$608.11 billion (2004)

Visitor numbers: 18.27 million (2006)*

Annual FDI: US$206.60 billion (cumulative, 1995–2004, OECD); US$6.30 billion (OECD, 2004)*

* estimated figure

By early 2008, the economic growth to which Canadians had become accustomed had begun to moderate. In its Monetary Policy Report the Bank of Canada (central bank) noted that buoyant growth in domestic demand, supported by high employment levels and improved terms of trade had been substantially offset by a fall in net exports. By the end of the first quarter of 2008, both total and core consumer price index (CPI) inflation were running at an annual rate of 1.5 per cent. However, the Bank of Canada judged the underlying trend of inflation to be nearer an annual 2 per cent, a level consistent with an economy running above its production capacity.

It's the US, of course

In the same report the Bank of Canada also judged that the deterioration in economic and financial conditions in the US would inevitably have direct consequences for the Canadian economy. In the first instance, Canadian exports were predicted to decline with a resultant negative impact on growth in 2008. Growth was also likely to be diminished by the continued turbulence in global financial markets, which was certain to affect the cost and availability of credit. In response to these uncertainties, the Bank of Canada had used the standard mechanisms at its disposal to keep money markets liquid and maintain the overnight interest rate. The increased demand for liquidity had caused the rate on collateralised loans to move well above the target rate. In response, the Bank entered special purchase and resale arrangements, providing overnight funds to primary dealers in exchange for government of Canada securities. These operations had proved generally effective in supporting Canadian capital markets. None the less, business and consumer confidence were also expected to soften.

In sharp contrast to Canada's neighbour to the south, domestic demand also looked likely to remain strong, supported by firm commodity prices, high employment levels and Canada's successful monetary policy.

Monetary policy works

The Bank of Canada projected that the Canadian economy would grow by 1.4 per cent in 2008, 2.4 per cent in 2009 and by 3.3 per cent in 2010. The benign presence of excess supply capacity in the economy was expected to keep inflation below 2 per cent until the end of 2009.

In 2007, Canada's stable monetary policy had been challenged by a number of factors, not least high energy prices combined with a steady rise in the value of the Canadian dollar against its US counterpart. Despite what were perceived to be adverse factors, Canada's monetary policy remained successful in keeping the average rate of CPI inflation within the 1–3 per cent control range and generally close to the bank's 2 per cent target. In the first half of the year, both economic growth and inflation had been stronger than expected. As underlying inflation hovered around the 2.2–2.5 per cent mark, the CPI was in fact slightly above the Bank's target rate at between 2.0 and 2.3 per cent. It is to be noted that the CPI rate had been effectively lowered by 0.5 per cent by the 2006 reduction in the general sales tax (GST) and other beneficial changes in indirect taxes. In July 2007, in response to rising capacity pressures within the economy, the Bank had raised the interest rate to 4.5 per cent from the 4.25 per cent rate that had prevailed since May 2006. The largest single inflationary component was stronger than anticipated domestic demand; this was to some degree balanced by the rapid appreciation of the Canadian dollar, accentuated by the weakness of the US dollar and the prospect of a deeper and more prolonged contraction in the US housing sector.

In the second half of 2007, the financial urbulence that had characterised global capital markets began to exert some pressure on the Canadian economy. The Bank of Canada had identified this likelihood earlier in the year; however, household demand in Canada was much stronger and less volatile than in the US, which seemed to account for the continued appreciation of the US dollar against its US counterpart. The target interest rate was left unchanged in September and October; however in December 2007 the Bank recorded that there had 'been a shift to the downside in the balance of risks around its (earlier) October projection', One effect was that both total CPI inflation and core inflation expectations were now lower. International credit conditions had also tightened markedly in the period. Although significant upside risks were considered to persist, the overall shift in the economic climate caused the Bank to lower its target interest rate back to 4.25 per cent. By March 2008, things had moved on apace, as the bank continued to respond to the international situation with further cuts, reducing its overnight lending rate to 3.5 per cent, the two cuts since December 2007 lowering it by a full percentage point and significantly narrowing the gap with the US Federal Reserve rate of 3.0 per cent. The 2008 reductions were the first interest rate decisions by the Bank's new governor, Mark Carney, and suggested that he was more troubled by the effects of the US sub-prime problems than had been the case with his predecessor, David Dodge. Mr Carney was obviously mindful, inter alia, of the fact that Canada sells three quarters of its exports to the US.

It's the research that counts...

Possibly reflecting the canny Presbyterian influences that had originally characterised Canadian banking institutions, research has long been central to the Bank of Canada's decision making process. In 2007 a report was commissioned from five external economists to evaluate the Bank's research in all its functions. With immaculate timing, this ad-hoc committee was due to report its findings in early 2008.

...and the soaring loonie

In 2007 the Bank also decided to improve its monitoring of the Chinese economy, with a view to assessing the impact of China – and more broadly of emerging Asia – on global prices. It is worth noting that Canada has close trading and investment links with China. Western Canada, notably British Columbia and more particularly Vancouver, is host to a large and prosperous Chinese community. The committee's preliminary studies supported the view that the Chinese connection had resulted in inflation being reduced by between 0.1 and 0.4 percentage points in resent years. Bank research on the relationship between commodity prices and the Canadian dollar also suggested that the dollar had become more sensitive to commodity prices. This became apparent throughout 2007 as the Canadian dollar appreciated from about US$0.86 at the beginning of the year to just above par by the end of 2007. In the volatile period between September and November 2007 at one point the Canadian dollar – affectionately known as the 'loonie' by Canadians after the acquatic bird that appears on the Canadian one-dollar coin – reached a high of just over US$1.10. The appreciation of the Canadian dollar was not, however, matched by lower retail prices in Canada's stores. Economists at the Bank of Montreal calculated that prices on a Canadian basket were an average of 24 per cent higher than in the US.

High employment – lower productivity

Throughout 2007 the Canadian economy was operating above its production

KEY INDICATORS — Canada

	Unit	2003	2004	2005	2006	2007
Population	m	31.58	31.75	32.26	32.60	32.93
Gross domestic product (GDP)	US$bn	834.40	979.76	1,132.44	1,269.10	1,432.14
GDP per capita	US$	27,199	31,209	35,105	39,115	43,485
GDP real growth	%	2.0	2.8	2.9	2.7	2.6
Inflation	%	2.8	1.8	2.2	2.0	2.1
Unemployment	%	7.8	7.2	6.8	6.3	6.0
Oil output	'000 bpd	2,800.0	3,085.0	3,047.0	3,147.0	3,309.0
Natural gas output	bn cum	180.5	182.8	185.5	187.0	183.7
Coal output	mtoe	33.3	34.9	34.4	32.3	30.4
Exports (fob) (goods)	US$m	272,054.0	331,070.0	374,308.0	401,786.0	434,049.0
Imports (cif) (goods)	US$m	245,618.0	279,337.0	320,517.0	356,641.0	388,211.0
Balance of trade	US$m	26,436.0	51,734.0	53,791.0	45,146.0	45,838.0
Current account	US$m	17,050.0	26,040.0	26,261.0	20,792.0	13,263.0
Total reserves minus gold	US$m	36,222.0	34,430.0	32,962.0	34,994.0	40,991.0
Foreign exchange	US$m	31,537.0	30,167.0	30,664.0	33,198.0	39,314.0
Exchange rate	per US$	1.43	1.30	1.17	1.15	1.02

capacity level. The employment to population ratio reached a historic high of 63.8 per cent, as unemployment fell to a 33-year low of 5.8 per cent. One area identified by the central bank for special attention has been growth in productivity. Since 2000, growth in Canadian labour productivity has been weak, growing at little more than one per cent per annum, well below the Bank's original projection of 1.5 per cent. There is some uncertainty over the extent to which this low figure reflects some of the changes that are taking place in the Canadian economy.

At the beginning of March 2008, Statistics Canada announced that economic growth had 'slowed considerably' in the fourth quarter of 2007, to the unexpectedly low rate of 0.2 per cent for the quarter, Canada's slowest rate of growth since August 2003. In the third quarter of 2007, the economy had grown by 0.7 per cent. Economic growth patterns are by no means equal across Canada. Alberta, British Columbia, Ontario and Saskatchewan have become known as the 'have' provinces, no longer qualifying for the budget handouts known as 'equalisation payments' from the federal treasurer.

Election murmurings

Speculation that Canada's minority conservative government was preparing for an election early in 2008 was fuelled by the administration's success not only in posting a record surplus of C$13.8 billion (US$16.1 billion) in 2007, but also in reducing Canada's debt ratio to its lowest level for 25 years. This opened up the prospect of tax cuts. It is to the credit of successive Canadian administrations' fiscal policies, and to the success of the Bank of Canada's monetary policy, that Canada has run a budget surplus every year since 1998. Canada's debonair Prime Minister Stephen Harper had promised to use all the interest savings on the reduced debt to lower personal income tax. In his throne speech, Mr Harper announced that the fiscal savings would result in tax cuts of C$750m (US$746m). Despite what added up to a lot of good news for the Canadian electorate, Canada's finance minister Jim Flaherty saw fit to add a word of caution that Canada could not afford to be complacent when faced both with intensified competition from China, Brazil and India, as well as the effects of Canada's appreciating dollar. The two principal opposition parties, the Liberal Party of Canada and the Bloc Québécois (BQ), suffering from by-election defeats, had set out policy demands that the minority conservative government would find hard to accommodate. Mr Harper managed to manoeuvre the opposition parties into having no option but to call an election if they choose to vote down any of the legislation stemming from the 2008 throne speech.

Tar sands

Canada's energy reserves are substantial. Estimates indicate that there is enough bitumen in Alberta alone to produce 1.7 trillion barrels of synthetic crude. Even assuming that only 10 per cent of this amount is recoverable, it still represents the second largest oil reserve in the world, second only to Saudi Arabia. Putting it another way, Canada's reserves hold more oil than those of Kuwait, Norway and Russia combined. Significantly (in view of the state of relations between the US and Venezuela) Canada has become the US's main source of imported oil, supplying more than all of the Arabian Gulf states combined. By 2010 the tar sands yield is expected to double, and by 2015 to triple. Not that tars sands' oil production is necessarily simple, or inexpensive. By 2010 tar sands operations are expected to consume some two billion cubic feet of natural gas a day. In context, this would be enough to heat all the homes in Canada – and Canada is a cold country. Tar sands oil production, while hugely beneficial to the Canadian economy, also has an environmental downside. Stéphan Dion the leader of the opposition Liberal Party has said: 'There is no environmental minister on earth who can stop the oil from coming out of the sand, because the money is too big'.

Canada has considerable natural resources; according to US Energy Information Administration (EIA) estimates in 2004 producing 18.6 quadrillion British Thermal Units (Btu) of total energy, the fifth-largest amount in the world. Since 1980, Canada's total energy production has increased by 81 per cent, while its total energy consumption has increased only by 40 per cent; by comparison, total world energy production increased by 54 per cent during 1980-2004. Canada is also the largest source of US natural gas and electricity imports. According to the EIA in 2006, Canada exported to the United States 2.3 million barrels per day (bpd) of oil and petroleum products, 11 per cent of total US supply, 3.6 trillion cubic feet of natural gas (16 per cent), and 41.2 billion kilowatt hours of electricity (1 per cent).

Over 1984–04, the share of oil in total energy consumption has remained mostly constant, whereas natural gas has increased from 21 per cent to 25 per cent.

According to the US *Oil and Gas Journal* (OGJ), Canada had an estimated 179.2 billion barrels of proven oil reserves as of January 2007, second only to Saudi Arabia. Over 95 per cent of oil reserves are the tar sands deposits in Alberta. Canada's total oil production (including all liquids) was 3.3 million bpd in 2006. Tar sands production has increased from 445,000 bpd to 1.2 million bpd.

Oil production comes mainly from three sources: the Western Canada Sedimentary Basin (WCSB); the tar sands deposits of northern Alberta; and the offshore fields in the Atlantic Ocean. Alberta contains the largest share of Canada's oil production, as it holds the majority of oil sands deposits and the bulk of the WCSB: according to Canada's National Energy Board, Alberta represented 69 per cent of Canada's national oil production in 2006. The Athabasca tar sands deposit, in northern Alberta, is one of largest tar sands deposits in the world. There are other tar sands deposits on Melville Island in the Canadian Arctic, and two smaller deposits in northern Alberta near Cold Lake and Peace River. Analysts predict that the production of synthetic crude from tar sands is only economically viable with crude prices in the US$30–40 per barrel range. While further advances in tar sands technology could reduce production costs, it is likely that synthetic oil production will continue to be dependent on the high crude oil prices seen in 2007. Any increase in natural gas prices or sharp reduction in natural gas supply would have critical repercussions for the tar sands industry. Newer technologies may reduce the need for natural gas.

There have been reports that the tar sands boom is creating a labour shortage in Alberta's oil industry, especially in Fort McMurray. This has led to an escalation in labour costs and construction delays due to a lack of available workers. According to the EIA most forecasts of world oil markets estimate that Canadian tar sands will become an increasingly important component of world oil supply.

The gas

The OGJ reports that Canada had 57.9 trillion cubic feet (Tcf) of proven natural gas reserves in January 2007. Canada produced 6.5Tcf of natural gas in 2004, making it the second largest producer of natural gas in the Western Hemisphere, after the United States. In 2006, Canada exported 3.6Tcf of natural gas to the United States, representing 86 per cent of total US natural gas imports that year.

Canadian natural gas production and exports are expected to decline, with net exports to the United States forecast to reach 1.2Tcf in 2030, or 22 per cent of net US natural gas imports.

Canada's natural gas production is also concentrated in the WCSB, particularly in Alberta.

According to the EIA Canada holds an estimated 7.3 billion short tons of recoverable coal reserves. Coal production has declined steadily in recent years. Canada produced 68.5 million short tons (Mmst) in 2003, down from a peak of 86.7Mmst in 1997. Coal production is concentrated in the western part of the country, with Alberta containing about half of total coal production. Canada exports over half its coal production, mostly to Asia, with the rest going chiefly to Europe and Latin America. These exports are overwhelmingly coking coal. On the other hand, Canada imports some thermal and coking coal, mostly from the United States. Canada is also the world's largest producer of hydroelectricity, generating over 334Bkwh from the source in 2004.

Risk assessment

Politics	Good
Economy	Good
Regional stability	Good

COUNTRY PROFILE

Historical profile

1497 John Cabot claimed Newfoundland for Henry VII of England.
1534 Jacques Cartier explored Newfoundland and charted the Gulf of St Lawrence as far as what is now Québec city and Montréal. He claimed this land for France.
1600 King Henry IV of France granted fur trading rights in the Gulf of St Lawrence to a group of French merchants.
1608 Founding of Québec as France's first colony by Samuel Champlain.
1629 Québec city was captured by the English fleet.
1632 Québec was returned to France by the treaty of St Germain-en-Laye.
1642 Founding of Ville Marie, which later became Montréal.
1660 The English Navigation Act prohibited foreigners from trading with English colonies.
1663 Louis XIV assumed personal control of the French settlements that included Québec, Montréal, Nova Scotia, New Brunswick and the area around the Gulf of St Lawrence and called this Nouvelle France (New France). Québec became a royal province.
1665 Jean Talon came from France to administer colonial affairs and brought about a significant expansion of the colony, encouraging agriculture, arts and business that stimulated immigration. By this time, the English, fighting for territorial dominance, controlled 10 colonies on the Atlantic coast and exceeded New France in terms of population and self-sufficiency.
1670 In competition with the French, the English established the Hudson Bay Company, giving themselves a monopoly on the fur trade in the Hudson Bay area.
1702 Queen Anne's War broke out between the English and the French. This led to the capture of Port Royal by the English.
1713 Peace was established under the Treaty of Utrecht. This required France to surrender the Hudson Bay Area, Newfoundland and Acadia to Britain. France was permitted to keep Cape Breton island and her inland colonies.
1754 The French and Indian War began in North America; it became the Seven Years War when fighting spread to Europe.
1755–56 The British attacked Québec, the nerve-centre of the French empire. Québec came under British rule.
1759 Montréal, cut off from reinforcements and supplies from France, fell to the British.
1774 Britain passed the Québec Act, that officially recognised French civil law and granted religious freedom to Roman Catholics. Britain assumed full control of the North Atlantic provinces: Canada, Nova Scotia, New Brunswick, Prince Edward Island and Newfoundland.
1858 British Columbia became a Crown Colony.
1862 The British withdrew troops from Canada.
1867 Ontario, Québec, Nova Scotia and New Brunswick joined together under the terms of the British North America Act to become the Dominion of Canada. These four territories became provinces with their own governments, law making bodies and lieutenant governors.
1870 Manitoba joined the Dominion, followed by British Columbia and Prince Edward Island. Hudson Bay became part of Canada and was renamed the Northwest Territories.
1898 The territory of Yukon was carved out of the Northwest Territories and entered the Dominion. The Territories, unlike the provinces that existed within their own right, were subject to federal legislative power. The federal government had the right to intrude in administrative and social affairs.
1905 Alberta and Saskatchewan became provinces of Canada.
1914—18 Canada joined the allies in the First World War.
1931 The Statute of Westminster was passed by the British parliament, granting dominion parliaments the right to reject the laws of British parliament and allowing British dominions, including Canada, complete autonomy. Canada became a free associate of the British Commonwealth of Nations, but had to swear allegiance to the British Crown.
1939–45 Canada joined the allies against Nazi Germany, Italy and Japan in the Second World War.
1949 Newfoundland became Canada's tenth province.
1969 Canada recognised English and French as its two official languages.
1977 Following an amendment to the Citizenship Act, Canadians ceased to be British subjects.
1980 A referendum to make Québec a separate country was rejected by the people of Québec.
1982 The Constitution Act stated that Canada no longer required British approval for new laws.
1995 The Canadian parliament passed a resolution recognising Québec as a distinct society within Canada. A referendum in Québec produced another 'no' vote for independence.
1999 Nunavut, created out of part of the Northwest Territories, became Canada's third territory.
2000 Jean Chrétien called snap elections, in which the Liberal Party of Canada (LPC) took 40.8 per cent of the vote, winning 172 seats.
2001 Québec's premier, Lucien Bouchard, resigned. Bernard Landry took over the post. Canada became the first country to legalise cannabis for people suffering from chronic medical conditions and terminal illnesses.
2002 Jean Chrétien announced he would resign in 2004.
2003 Toronto was seriously hit by an outbreak of the flu-like Sars virus. A power blackout – the biggest in North American history – hit Toronto, Ottawa and other parts of Ontario, as well as cities in the north-eastern US. Paul Martin took over as prime minister after Jean Chrétien's retirement.
2004 The ruling LPC won the parliamentary elections, but lost its majority.
2005 Haitian-born Michaëlle Jean was appointed as Governor General. The government lost a no-confidence vote.
2006 In general elections the Conservative Party of Canada (CPC) won but without an overall majority. Parliament approved a government motion recognising Quebec as a nation within a united Canada.
2007 Due to the increase of melting ice in Arctic waters the Northwest Passage between the Pacific and Atlantic Oceans

became navigatable during summer months. Canada asserted its territorial rights to manage the waterway ahead of any international recognition of its control, and plans to build a military site in the area.

2008 An independent report published in January recommended that Canadian troops should stay in Afghanistan for the foreseeable future, but only if NATO deployed 1,000 more troops to support the 2,500 Canadian (along side US, UK and Dutch) troops, stationed in Kandahar. The prime minister warned US President Bush that Canada would remove its troops by February 2009 without greater support from NATO. The Canadian military presence in Afghanistan was extended to December 2011, on the proviso that NATO supplied more reinforcements and equipment.

Political structure

Constitution

Although Canada is formally a constitutional monarchy with the British monarch as the nominal head of state, for all practical purposes the country is a sovereign state. The governor general is the Queen's representative in Canada.

The Canadian government has a federal structure, with 10 provincial governments plus the three northern territories of the Northwest Territories, Yukon and Nunavut on the lower tier and a national government on the upper tier.

The constitution is contained in the Constitution Act of 1982, although the province of Québec did not agree to this legislation. The division of power between the national and provincial governments is set out in the constitution which also contains a Charter of Rights and Freedoms. The federal government has authority over areas of national interest, while provincial governments have specific authority over local matters, including education, hospitals and public lands (including natural resources). The provinces exercise considerable autonomy over their affairs. Each province has an elected legislature together with an executive led by a provincial premier.

All Canadian citizens aged 18 years and over have the right to vote.

Form of state

Constitutional monarchy

The executive

The executive comprises the prime minister, appointed by the governor general, and his cabinet. The prime minister is the leader of the majority party in the House of Commons; the cabinet is also drawn from the ruling party's ranks.

National legislature

The bicameral federal parliament, based in Ottawa, is styled on the British model. The House of Commons (lower house) has 301 seats, for which constituency elections must be held at least once every five years. The upper house, the Senate, has very little influence, although it may delay legislation. It has a total membership of 105 senators who are appointed on a regional basis, by the prime minister, and who may serve until their 75th birthday.

Legal system

Based on English common law, except in Québec, where a French civil law system prevails.

The prime minister, through the governor general, appoints all judges to the federal courts, but not those to the provincial courts. Apart from this, the judiciary is independent of the executive. The Supreme Court of Canada is the highest court of appeal in both civil and criminal cases. Each province has its own court structure, headed by a provincial Supreme Court.

Last elections

23 January 2006 (parliamentary)

Results: Parliamentary: the Conservative Party of Canada (CPC) won 36.25 per cent of the vote (124 seats out of 308), the Liberal Party of Canada (LPC) 30.2 per cent (1039), the New Democratic Party/Nouveau Parti Démocratique (NDP) 17.5 per cent (29), the Bloc Québécois (BQ) 10.5 per cent (51), and independents 0.1 per cent (1).

Next elections

2011 (parliamentary)

Political parties

Ruling party

Conservative Party of Canada (CPC) (elected 23 January 2006)

Main opposition party

The Liberal Party of Canada (LPC).

Population

32.93 million (2007)

Last census: May 2001: 30,007,095

Population density: Three inhabitants per square km. Urban population: 77 per cent.

Annual growth rate: 1.0 per cent 1994–2004 (WHO 2006)

Ethnic make-up

British and Irish origin (28 per cent), French origin (23 per cent), other European origin (15 per cent), indigenous (2 per cent), other (including Asian, African, Arab) (6 per cent), mixed background (26 per cent).

In 2002, about 52 per cent of immigrants settled in Toronto, 15 per cent in Vancouver and 11 per cent in Montréal; the populations of many rural areas are declining.

Religions

Christianity is the prevailing religion in Canada. Approximately 45 per cent of the population belong to the Roman Catholic Church. The leading Protestant churches are the Anglican Church of Canada and the United Church of Canada. Orthodox Churches are also represented. Jews make up 1.2 per cent of the population and Muslims just under 1 per cent.

Education

Public investment in education amounts to 5.5 per cent of GDP. Universal primary education and gender parity, at this level and in secondary schools, have been achieved. Although methods of funding higher education vary from province to province, the federal and provincial governments fund approximately 85 per cent of the expenditure. Canada has strong initiatives to monitor and detect inequities in schooling across the provinces. There is stiff entrance exams for teaching courses and extensive in-service training for qualified teachers, which affords them high status in the community.

Each province is responsible for its own education system. In general, education is provided free of charge to the end of the secondary level. The number of private schools is small, except in the province of Québec. Levels of educational attainment continue to rise, with record numbers attending university. However, enrolments at elementary and secondary schools have steadily declined since the late 1960s, reflecting the decline in both the birth rate and the number of new immigrants.

The proportion of young people attending full-time university and college courses continues to expand, while part-time higher education courses for mature students are becoming increasingly popular. Canada has over 80 universities and 160 community and technical colleges, as well as 35 colleges of religious study.

Education services for indigenous students are an area of responsibility that is not clearly defined between provincial, territorial and federal government, who along with various local authorities have come up with different plans. There has been a rapid development of non-formal educational programmes, provided by non-governmental organisations. Citizenship education is a subject of renewed interest in the education curriculum.

Enrolment rate: 100 per cent total gross primary enrolment; 107 per cent boys, 106 per cent girls, gross secondary enrolment of relevant age groups (including repeaters) (Unesco).

Pupils per teacher: 16 in primary schools.

Health

Per capita total expenditure on health (2003) was US$2,989; of which per capita government spending was US$2,090, at the international dollar rate, (WHO 2006).

Private expenditure averages 29 per cent of GDP, 39 per cent of which is funded by prepaid health plans and 52 per cent in out-of-pockets expenses.
Nationwide state-sponsored health insurance is achieved through a series of interlocking provincial plans, with the federal government providing substantial financial support through national Hospital Insurance and Medical Care Programmes. The insurance programmes are designed to ensure that all residents have access to medical services as needed. Most hospitals are run by non-profit, non-governmental, corporations.

HIV/Aids

HIV prevalence: 0.3 per cent aged 15–49 in 2003 (World Bank)
Life expectancy: 80 years, 2004 (WHO 2006)
Fertility rate/Maternal mortality rate: 1.5 births per woman, 2004 (WHO 2006)
Child (under 5 years) mortality rate (per 1,000): 5 per 1,000 live births (World Bank)
Head of population per physician: 2.14 physicians per 1,000 people, 2003 (WHO 2006)

Welfare

Canada has a comprehensive welfare system, which is administered at both federal and provincial levels of government. The system provides for social assistance, old age pensions, family allowances and unemployment insurance. Family allowances are credited for dependent children up to the age of 18.
Social assistance or welfare is the income programme of last resort in Canada. It helps people in need who are not eligible for other benefits. Benefit payments help pay for food, shelter and other health services.
The federal government provides monthly payments to parents or guardians on behalf of children under the age of 18, through a programme called the Child Tax Benefit. The amount is different according to family income, number of children and their ages. Successive federal governments have moved to target their financial support to families at the lower end of the income spectrum.

Pensions

Old age pensions become payable at the age of 65 and are indexed to inflation. There are essentially two social security programmes aimed at providing income for the elderly in Canada.
The Old Age Security (OAS) pension is given to people aged 65 and over, who meet residence requirements. Those who have little or no other income are eligible for the Guaranteed Income Supplement (GIS). People who have lived in Canada for less than 40 years receive a reduced pension.
The Canada and Québec Pension Plans are a form of insurance into which people must contribute during their working years to receive monthly payments starting at age 65. These plans also include survivor's pensions for the spouses of deceased pensioners, disability pensions and children's and death benefits.

Main cities

Ottawa (capital, estimated population 1.1 million (m) in 2005), Toronto (5.0m), Montréal (3.3m), Vancouver (2.1m), Calgary (1.0m), Edmonton (975,723), Québec City (696,886), Winnipeg (675,187), Hamilton (686,926).

Languages spoken

English is spoken by 61 per cent of the population, French by 26 per cent and both languages by 13 per cent. French predominates in the province of Québec (Montréal is the second largest French-speaking city in the world). A wide variety of other languages are spoken, reflecting the diverse origins of Canada's population.

Official language/s

English, French

Media

Press

Nearly all cities have at least one daily newspaper, and there is likely to be a tabloid if there is more than one on offer. The bilingual cities of Montreal and Ottawa offer newspapers in both English and French.
Dailies: The only national newspapers are the National Post (www.nationalpost.com) and Globe and Mail (www.theglobeandmail.com). The newspapers with the highest circulation include Toronto Star (www.thestar.com), The Toronto Sun (www.torontosun.com) a tabloid, Vancouver Sun (www.canada.com) and The Gazette (www.canada.com) from Montreal, and in French Le Journal de Montréal (www.canoe.com), and La Presse (www.cyberpresse.ca).
Weeklies: There are numerous local and community newspapers with dailies publishing weekend editions.
Business: National publications include Canadian Business (www.canadianbusiness.com), The Northern Miner (www.northernminer.com), Black Press has over 100 publications. Regional publications include Business in Calgary (www.businessincalgary.com) and Business Edge (www.businessedge.ca), from Alberta, Business Examiner (from Black Press), Toronto Business Times (www.torontobusinesstimes.com) and Ottawa Business Journal (www.ottawabusinessjournal.com) from Ontario and, in French, Business (www.hebdosquebecor.com) and Regard Économique (http://www.linfonet.com) from Quebec.
Periodicals: There are a range of magazines published by central and regional government, including Government Executive (www.networkedgovernment.ca), Municipal World (www.municipalworld.com), and The Hill Times (www.thehilltimes.ca). News and current affairs are covered by Inroads (www.inroadsjournal.ca) published in November and May, L'Actualité (www.lactualite.com), published 20-times a year and This Magazine (www.thismagazine.ca) a bi-monthly with alternative political views. Monthly magazines include women's titles Chatelaine (http://en.chatelaine.com) in English and French and Flare (www.flare.com), others include Our Times (www.ourtimes.ca), and Yourthink Magazine (www.youthink.ca) for the young.

Broadcasting

The Canadian Broadcasting Corporation (CBC) is the national, public broadcaster with programmes in English and French that can be accessed by internet.
Radio: There are over 2,000 private, commercial radio stations providing entertainment, news and information for most tastes. CBC (www.cbc.ca/radio) operates four networks, including Radio One, Two, Radio Canada International and a radio station for indigenous communities with broadcasting news, cultural and speech-based programmes. Newcap (www.ncc.ca) has a network of 76 radio stations, and Rogers Broadcasting Limited (www.rogers.com) operates a pay-to-listen network, throughout the country. Local radio stations are found in all urban and many rural areas.
Television: Analogue TV is due to be replaced by digital TV by 31 August 2011. Until then all pay-to-view cable TV companies must supply a proportion of their output in analogue form until it has a digital subscription rate of 85 per cent.
CBC Television has three channels, CBCtelevision, CBCnews and CountryCanada with some domestic programmes broadcast in English and French.
CTV (www.ctv.ca) is the largest, English-language, privately-owned network, broadcasting mainly high rating US shows, as well as its own productions. The Global Television Network (Global TV) (www.globaltv.com) is the second English-language, privately-owned network, which relies on foreign programmes for its contents.
There are several French-language TV stations mainly based in Province of

Quebec, including Télé-Québec (www.telequebec.tv) and CJNT-TV (www.cjntmontreal.ca) from Montreal. The national, Aboriginal People's Television Network (www.aptn.ca) is based in Winnepeg.
There are many cable and satellite channels in English and French, available throughout the country offering all varieties of entertainments, news and educational programmes.

Advertising

Advertising Standards Canada is an independent, industry led agency created to ensure the integrity and viability of advertising. It regulates the Canadian Code of Advertising Standards through an Advertising Clearance Division, which preview adverts in five industries, specifically alcohol, children's advertising, cosmetics, consumer medications and food and soft drinks.
There is a full range of traditional and modern advertising media. Television accounts for the greatest part of net revenue, followed by magazines and newspapers.
Although the majority of Canadians speak English as their first language, the Francophone market, which is concentrated in Québec, is served extensively by its own French-language press, radio and television.

Economy

The Canadian economy performed well in 2005, due in large part to the high commodity prices for its natural resources. Oil and natural gas prices rose, and although the US dollar weakened energy exports to the US remained high, while other sectors in manufacturing, services and trade were affected with a lower than expected growth. Nevertheless, the Canadian economy overall remained buoyant, with real GDP growth at 3.9 per cent.
The rate of inflation remained low at 1.6 per cent in 2005, while unemployment fell from the plus-7 per cent trend since 2001 to 6.8 per cent. Nevertheless, the government is attempting to reduce a skills shortage which is having an adverse affect on productivity growth.
Canada's economy is reliant on, and can be adversely affected by, its main trading partner the US. The fall in exports to the US from 81 per cent of total exports in 2005 to 79 per cent in 2006, was due mainly to a reduction in forestry and automotive exports as the US dollar weakened. The US had a US$763.6 billion trade deficit with Canada in 2006.
Canada is a member of the North American Free Trade Association (Nafta) with the US and Mexico. Approximately 80 per cent of Canada's exports and 70 per cent of imports are with the US. It is a major exporter of agricultural products, marine fish, timber and minerals, particularly oil and gas, as well as gold and other minerals.

External trade

Canada's largest trading partner by far is the US and the country is now the leading export market for 35 separate US states. The North American Free Trade Agreement (Nafta) has been in operation since 1994, under which Canada has tri-lateral trade agreements with Mexico and the US. Canada's other top trading partners are China and Japan.
Canada is the world's largest source of nickel, zinc and uranium and has large reserves of hydrocarbons, exported main to the US.

Imports

Main imports are machinery and equipment, vehicles and parts, industrial materials, crude oil, consumer goods, foodstuffs, durable consumer goods and construction materials.
Main sources: US (54.9 per cent total, 2006), China (8.7 per cent), Mexico (4.0 per cent).

Exports

Major exports include primary industry products including, wheat and agricultural products, fish, timber and minerals including gold and silver, as well as processed and manufactured such as vehicles and parts, industrial machinery, aircraft, telecommunications equipment; chemicals, plastics, fertilisers; wood pulp and aluminium.
Main destinations: US (81.6 per cent of 2006 total goods exports), UK (2.3 per cent), Japan (2.1 per cent).

Agriculture

Farming

The agricultural industry is of considerable importance to the country's economy. Canada has somewhere in the region of 280,000 farms and is the world's second-largest wheat exporter, with its high-quality spring wheat commanding a premium price on world markets. The country is also a sizeable producer of other grains, notably barley, rapeseed (canola) and oats. Livestock rearing is as important a source of income as field crops.
Despite the relative importance of agriculture in the Canadian economy compared with other industrialised nations, the federal government tends to argue that it cannot afford to match the plentiful subsidies and other aid offered to farmers in the EU and US. However, delays in co-ordinated elimination of the world's farm subsidies through the WTO are focussing the government's attention on support programmes for Canadian farmers.
Cattle exports to US markets were due to resume in early 2005, following a ban placed on imports in 2003, after one case of bovine spongiform encephalopathy (BSE) was detected. However another two cases were identified and prompted the US to reinstate its ban in 2005. About two million head of young cattle were due to be exported in 2005. The number of cattle on farms in 2005 reached a record high of 15.1 million head.
During the embargo of live cattle, plans were advanced to expand slaughtering facilities and increase the amount of Canadian processed beef, and open new export markets. The latest ban increased the enthusiasm for the plans, and has had added impetus since a US Senate decision in 2005 not to designate Canada as an area of 'minimal risk' from BSE, and a US cattle association won a temporary injunction blocking any US government move to reopen the border to live cattle imports.
In 2005 the government announced a US$820 billion support package for its farmers to offset the drop in sales due to the strong Canadian dollar and low prices for some produce on international markets. Beef producers are eligible for US$24.6 billion from the package with the rest distributed between grain and oilcrop growers.
Crop production in 2005 included: 50,362,600 tonnes (t) cereal in total, 25,546,900t wheat, 8,392,000t maize, 4,850,000t potatoes, 12,132,500t barley, 3,333,800t oats, 2,998,800t soya beans, 4,753,200t pulses, 8,446,600t rapeseed (canola), 4,225,796t oilcrops, 720,000t sugar beets, 861,750t tomatoes, 369,500t apples, 81,900t blueberries, 43,000 tobacco leaves, 692,060t fruit in total, 2,619,630t vegetables in total. Livestock production included: 4,680,100t meat in total, 1,530,000t beef, 1,960,000t pig meat, 17,000t lamb, 1,154,300t poultry, 376,560t eggs, 8,100,000t milk, 33,000t honey, 2,723t sheepskins, 115,000t cattle hides.

Fishing

Canada remains the largest exporter of fish in the world. Approximately half of the country's sizeable annual fish catch is processed for export. Aggressive fishing depleted Canada's stocks causing the closure of Canada's Atlantic fisheries in 1992, which led to a bitter salmon war with the US when wild salmon stocks dipped to perilously low levels. Such were the tensions, annually renewed during the salmon spawning season, that Canada encouraged the capture of fish bound for rivers in Washington and Oregon, in retaliation for rising US catches of Canadian-origin salmon. A deal agreed in 1999 will be effective for 10 years along the coast and for 12 years along the

Fraser River run, which should enable flexible reductions in catches through a managed scheme, replacing the more rigid quota system formerly in effect. Despite past tension between the national governments on this issue the US remains the largest market for Canadian fish exports.

Criticism has been raised that Canada has not protected its wild salmon population of fish. Three of the world's largest salmon farming companies operate in British Columbia and overall there are 17 companies managing 105 salmon farms. The fear is that Canada is raising non-native species of salmon and feeding them fish protein that creates risks for other species of wild fish. The resulting intermingling of populations risks the spread of disease, a competition for habitat and the alteration of the wild salmon gene pool. A salmon enhancement programme has been set up to enable the annual catch to reach 150,000 tonnes instead of the current average 70,000 tonnes.

Canada has imposed a moratorium on commercial cod fishing and has a 320km exclusion zone off its eastern coast, patrolled by an increased number of coast guard vessels.

Limited cod fishing in the northern and southern Gulf of St Lawrence resumed in the 2004–05 season, with maximum removals of up to 3,500 tonnes in the northern, and 3,000 tonnes in the southern, gulf.

Forestry

Over 70 per cent of Canada's total landmass is covered with forests and woodland. The country accounts for approximately 10 per cent of the world's forests and the forestry industry accounts for more than US$24 billion annually.

Canada is the largest exporter of newsprint, softwood timber and wood pulp worldwide. There is enormous variation in forest types across this vast country, including temperate softwood rainforests in coastal British Columbia, mixed boreal shield forests in central Canada, the maritime forests of New Brunswick and Nova Scotia on the Atlantic seaboard, and the sparse and slow-growing forests found at the Arctic tree line.

Québec, Ontario and British Columbia have the largest forest resources. Most forest and other wooded land is publicly owned, with 71 per cent under provincial jurisdiction and a further 23 per cent under the wing of the federal and territorial governments. Just 6 per cent is privately owned, and is generally located in the more productive regions. Large areas of forest land are under legislative protection, including the almost 8 per cent protected from harvesting.

Canada is the world's largest exporter of market pulp (almost 30 per cent of world total) and newsprint (near 40 per cent), with most production located in British Columbia, Ontario and Québec.

Non-wood forest products in Canada include maple syrup, berries, mushrooms, medicinal plants and game.

Industry and manufacturing

In a typical year for the Canadian economy the industrial sector contributes approximately 27 per cent to total GDP. The sector also accounts for around 18 per cent of the country's workforce.

Canada's traditional manufacturing sectors include petroleum refining, pulp and paper mills, motor vehicles, steel, sawmills and planing mills, the dairy products industry, motor vehicle spare parts and accessories, metal stamping and pressing, smelting and refining, industrial chemicals, food processing, commercial printing, communications equipment, feed industries, plastics fabricating industries and aircraft and aircraft parts. Notable new sectors are in advanced telecommunications and network technology.

Production of primary metals and transport equipment has grown in recent years, reflecting exceptional growth in the automotive industry. The vast majority of automobile production is exported to the US.

Tourism

Canada's travel and tourism industry has expanded in recent years and contributes 11.8 per cent of total GDP. Employment in the sector accounts for 12.8 per cent of the country's total workforce and capital investment in the industry has also increased, representing 8.1 per cent of total capital investment in the Canadian economy.

Environment

The Northwest Passage between the Pacific and Atlantic Oceans opened up in 2007 as a result of record ice melting in the Arctic. The ice shelf had retreated further than at any time in recorded history.

Mining

Canada remains a significant producer of gold. Other base metal and metal stocks have declined, but Canada remains a major producer of nickel, copper, zinc, lead, iron ore and diamonds.

Most of Canada's exploration is focused on diamonds, mainly in Northwest Territories, Alberta, Québec and Saskatchewan. The country's first diamond mine opened in 1998.

Hydrocarbons

Canada has considerable natural resources; with production of 18.6 quadrillion British Thermal Units (Btu) of total energy, the fifth-largest amount in the world. Since 1980, Canada's total energy production has increased by 81 per cent (total world energy production increased by 54 per cent during), while its total energy consumption has increased only by 40 per cent. Canada is also the largest source of US-imported natural gas and electricity. According to the EIA in 2006, Canada exported to the United States 2.3 million barrels per day (bpd) of oil and petroleum products, 11 per cent of total US supply, 3.6 trillion cubic feet of natural gas (16 per cent), and 41.2 billion kilowatt hours of electricity (1 per cent).

According to the US Oil and Gas Journal (OGJ), Canada had an estimated 179.2 billion barrels of proven oil reserves as of January 2007, second only to Saudi Arabia. Over 95 per cent of oil reserves are the tar sands deposits in Alberta. Canada's total oil production (including all liquids) was 3.3 million bpd in 2006. Tar sands production has increased from 445,000 bpd to 1.2 million bpd.

Oil production comes mainly from three sources: the Western Canada Sedimentary Basin (WCSB); the tar sands deposits of northern Alberta; and the offshore fields in the Atlantic Ocean. Alberta contains the largest share of Canada's oil production, as it holds the majority of oil sands deposits and the bulk of the WCSB: according to Canada's National Energy Board, Alberta represented 69 per cent of Canada's national oil production in 2006. The Athabasca tar sands deposit, in northern Alberta, is one of largest tar sands deposits in the world. There are other tar sands deposits on Melville Island in the Canadian Arctic, and two smaller deposits in northern Alberta near Cold Lake and Peace River. Analysts predict that the production of synthetic crude from tar sands is only economically viable with crude prices in the US$30–40 per barrel range. While further advances in tar sands technology could reduce production costs, it is likely that synthetic oil production will continue to be dependent on the high crude oil prices seen in 2007. Any increase in natural gas prices or sharp reduction in natural gas supply would have critical repercussions for the tar sands industry. Newer technologies may reduce the need for natural gas.

There have been reports that the tar sands boom is creating a labour shortage in Alberta's oil industry, especially in Fort McMurray. This has led to an escalation in labour costs and construction delays due to a lack of available workers. According to the EIA most forecasts of world oil markets estimate that Canadian tar sands will become an increasingly important component of world oil supply.

Canada had proven reserves of over 178 billion barrels of oil (including 174.4 billion barrels from Alberta's oilsands), with oil production averaging 3.1 million barrels per day (bpd) and consumption at 2.2 million bpd. Most oil is extracted from the west of the country, particularly Alberta which typically produces 55 per cent of Canada's total oil production. While oil production is steadily declining in the west, it is rising in the east, where production costs are higher and reserves are smaller. The US is the largest supplier of refined oil products to Canada. Bitumen production from Canada's oilsands is due to expand over the next decade with several large investment projects being developed. Currently this form of production is reliant on natural gas, however due to the high prices of natural gas this industry is seeking alternative methods of production. Until it becomes economically viable the development of this industry could be slow.

There are two major pipeline networks. The Enbridge Pipelines cover 14,000km, delivering oil from Edmonton, Alberta, to Montréal, Québec, eastern Canada and refineries in the US Great Lakes region. The Trans-Mountain Pipeline (TMPL) delivers oil from Alberta to Vancouver and British Columbia as well as the US state of Washington.

Canada had 1.6 trillion cubic metres (cum) of natural gas reserves and produced 183 billion cum per year, making it the world's third-largest gas producer after Russia and the US and the second-largest gas exporter after Russia. Canada's gas exports are exclusively destined for the US. Domestic gas consumption is rising due to an increase in demand from the electricity generating sector.

The 3,000km Alliance Pipeline, carries 36.8 million cum of gas per day from western Canada to the Chicago area in the US. The Millennium Pipeline is planned to connect Canadian gas fields to New York and Pennsylvania in the US.

Canada's coal reserves amounted to around 6.6 billion tonnes. The typical coal production is over 34 million tonnes oil equivalent (Mtoe). Canadian coal consumption of around 20.5 mtoe is primarily used for electricity generation with the remainder used for steel production.

Energy

Canada currently has one of the world's most diversified electricity generation bases. The country retains hydroelectricity, natural gas, oil, coal and nuclear power sources, which are used to produce electricity.

By the end of the 1990s, Canada's electricity generating capacity was 109.8GW, of which 60 per cent was hydroelectric, 26 per cent was thermal, 12 per cent was nuclear and 1 per cent was produced from geothermal and other sources. The use of gas in electricity generation is on the rise, with a 300 per cent increase in gas-fired electricity capacity by 2010.

There are 22 nuclear reactors, of which 5 are inoperative until refurbishments have been completed. Canada exports its reactor technology with projects in Argentina, China, Romania and South Korea with the most being built in India.

Under the Canadian constitution, electricity production is the responsibility of the provincial administrations. Most electricity generation, transmission and distribution facilities are owned by the provinces. Alberta and Ontario hace a fully deregulated market.

In 2003 a massive power failure left most of Ontario and the US Midwest and Northeast without power. Initial recriminations swung across the border as each authority, under heavy public criticism, sort to shift blame for the outage away from themselves. The final report concluded that the blackout was caused by procedural failures such as inadequate backup facilities; operations not kept within secure limits; ineffective training; poor judgement about the nature of the critical conditions, and poor communications within neighbouring systems; and the lack of a guiding overview. The power was cut when vegetation, that should have been cut-back, short-circuited powerlines and no one was available to stop the cascade of disruption this caused. Regulatory bodies have introduced mandatory systems to provide management and regulatory procedures, and compliance to standards, in both Canada and the US.

Financial markets

Stock exchange

The principal Canadian stock market is the Toronto Stock Exchange (TSE), which is the fourth most active stock exchange in North America after the NYSE, Nasdaq and Chicago.

Banking and insurance

Toronto Dominion Bank is Canada's largest banking and financial services institution, in terms of both its retail network and overall personal deposits and lending, having merged with Canada Trust in 2000.

Financial legislation, (Bill C–8) allows foreign and local banks to increase stakes in Canadian banks and to encourage global competitiveness and economic growth. The legislation allows a single shareholder to hold up to 20 per cent of the voting shares of a big Canadian bank, and opened the way to strategic alliances with foreign banks.

Central bank

Bank of Canada

Main financial centre

Toronto

Time

Canada has six time zones:
Newfoundland – GMT minus 3.5 hours;
Atlantic standard time (Maritimes and Labrador) – GMT minus four hours;
Eastern zone (Québec and most of Ontario) – GMT minus five hours;
Central zone (Manitoba, north-west Ontario and eastern Saskatchewan) – GMT minus six hours;
Mountain zone (west Saskatchewan, Alberta and north-east Columbia) – GMT minus seven hours;
Pacific zone (Yukon and the bulk of British Columbia) – GMT minus eight hours;
Daylight saving operates, in all states except Saskatchewan, from early March to late October – local time plus one hour.

Geography

Canada is the second-largest country in the world (Russia is the largest) and it stretches from the Atlantic Ocean to the Pacific. Apart from the border with Alaska in the north-west, Canada's frontier with the US follows the upper St Lawrence Seaway and the Great Lakes, extending westwards along latitude 49 degrees N.

There are six principal geographical regions. The south-east corner is the most densely populated part of the country and comprises the Atlantic Provinces and the lowland area to the north of the Great Lakes and the St Lawrence Seaway. To the north and west of this region lies the Canadian Shield, which is covered by forests, bare rock and lakes. Further to the west are the Interior Plains which are largely prairies, while the coastal area along the Pacific is dominated by the Rocky Mountains. The Northwest Territories extend into the Arctic with a barren landscape and sparse population density.

Hemisphere

Northern

Climate

The climate is extreme, especially inland. Winter temperatures drop well below freezing, but summers are usually warm. There are often heavy snowfalls in winter, making travel difficult.

Dress codes

Canadians are generally casual about dress. It is best to ask about dress codes if you are unsure.

Entry requirements

Passports

Required by all, except permanently resident US citizens with photo-ID; (all US nationals require a passport for re-entry to the US from January 2007).

Visa

Are required by all, except citizens of EU, the Commonwealth and US. For further information see www.cic.gc.ca/english/index.html and choose 'to visit'.

Business travellers should seek further information from a Canadian consulate or see http://canadainternational.gc.ca/dbc/Business-travel-entering-canada-en.aspx. Business visitors from exempted countries do not need to fulfil extra entry criteria, as long as their permanent employment is typically outside Canada, however work may not be undertaken beyond that allowed.

Prohibited entry

Currency advice/regulations

There are no restrictions on the import and export of currency.

Customs

Personal effects are allowed duty-free. Certain items, such as plants, meat, cereals, dairy products and live animals are subject to import licensing.

Prohibited imports

Include illegal drugs, marijuana, firearms, mace, pepper spray, switchblades (flick-knives) and fireworks. Vegetable matter including, apples, pears, stoned fruit, potatoes, fresh corn and firewood.

Health (for visitors)

Advisable precautions

No vaccinations or certificates are required. Comprehensive travel and medical insurance is essential though, as medical treatment can be very expensive.

Hotels

Many international hotel chains operate in most cities. However, it is advisable to book rooms in advance.

A goods and services tax of 7 per cent applies to all hotel bills, although visitors may be able to apply for a refund (for details and procedure see: www.nationaltaxrefund.com/eng/demarch.htm). Some states and provinces apply their own taxes.

Most large hotels have facilities for small displays or exhibitions, and smaller rooms may be rented as sample rooms. Most hotels impose a substantial surcharge on telephone calls.

For visitors travelling by car, good quality motels are available around all major towns and cities where rates are considerably less than those charged by city-centre hotels.

Credit cards

Credit cards are widely used.

Public holidays (national)

Fixed dates

1 Jan (New Year's Day), 1 Jul (Canada Day), 11 Nov (Remembrance Day), 25–26 Dec (Christmas).

When Canada Day falls on a Sunday, the next day is considered a holiday.

When Christmas Day or Boxing Day fall at a weekend, an extra day is given in lieu.

Additional holidays are observed by individual provinces and territories.

Variable dates

Good Friday, Easter Monday, Victoria Day (Mon preceding 24 May), Labour Day (first Mon in Sep), Thanksgiving Day (second Mon in Oct).

Working hours

Working hours vary throughout the country and government departments may work variable or flexible hours, especially during the summer months.

Banking

Mon–Wed: 1000–1500; Thu: 1000–2000; Fri: 1000–1600. Opening hours depend on the region and institution.

Business

Mon–Fri: 0830–1700.

Government

Mon–Fri: 0830–1700. Post offices Mon–Fri 0800–1745.

Shops

There is a five-day working week, but most retail stores in cities open on Saturday and a few on Sunday as well. Late shopping (to 2100) on Thursday or Friday is common in large cities; in suburban shopping centres, supermarkets often stay open until 2100 or 2200 Mon–Fri. Some convenience stores and supermarkets remain open 24 hours, especially in heavily populated areas.

Telecommunications

Mobile/cell phones

GSM 850/1900 services available in highly populated areas.

Electricity supply

120–240V (mostly 120V) 60 cycles AC, with two-pin flat-prong plug fittings (or three-pin with one round and two flat prongs) and screw-type lamp sockets. Adapters and transformers are available for appliances using other voltages.

Weights and measures

Metric system (Imperial and US systems also still in use).

Social customs/useful tips

When making introductions, the hand shake is considered rather formal unless you are meeting someone for the first time. To Canadians, eye contact is very important in conversation as it shows that you are paying attention.

It is best to avoid touching people unless you know someone fairly well. Touching someone of the opposite sex may well be considered harassment but touching the arm of your conversation partner is acceptable.

Tipping is expected and tends to be more generous in Canada than in other countries. 10 or 12 per cent would be considered frugal.

Getting there

Air

National airline: Air Canada

International airport/s: Ottawa (YOW) (www.ottawa-airport.ca), 13km south of the capital city. All major airports have full banking and catering facilities, duty-free shops and car hire. Airport-to-city bus and taxi services and, in some cases, rail links, are available.

Toronto Pearson International (YYZ) (www.gtaa.com), 27km north-west of Toronto, is Canada's busiest airport. It has three terminals catering for domestic and international flights; the latest was opened in April 2004 and handles Air Canada's domestic and international passengers.

Other airport/s: Calgary (YYC) (www.calgaryairport.com), 8km north of city. Edmonton (YEG) (www.edmontonairports.com), 28km south of city. Montréal Dorval (YUL) (www.admtl.com), 25km west of Montréal. Vancouver (YVR) (www.yvr.ca), 15km south-west of city. Winnipeg (YWG), 10km north-west of city.

Airport tax: There are two taxes that may or may not be included in the price of the ticket.

Both levies vary depending on destination, the Airport Improvement Fee (AIF) is C$5 for intrastate, C$10 interstate and US, and C$15 for all other international flights; the Air Travellers Security Charge is C$12 for intrastate and C$24 for interstate and all international flights. Travel agents and airport information can provide last minute details.

Surface

Road: Numerous border crossings from the US link directly with the Canadian highway system. Avoid crossings during peak times at weekends during the summer months when there are long delays.

Rail: Via Rail Canada Inc provides links with the US. Routes include: Montréal-New York; Toronto-New York; Toronto-Chicago; Toronto-Cleveland/Detroit.

Water: Ferries connect the east coast of the US with Canada across the great lakes. Hudson Bay ports are subject to closure during winter months.

Main port/s: On the Atlantic Ocean: Halifax (Nova Scotia), St John (New Brunswick) and St John's (Newfoundland). Montréal and Québec have ports on the St Lawrence Seaway (linking the Atlantic with the Great Lakes). Toronto's port is on the north-western shore of Lake Ontario. Montréal is the only port for passenger liners from Europe.

On the Pacific Ocean: Vancouver (British Columbia).

Getting about

National transport

Air: There are frequent and extensive air services connecting all towns and cities of importance with 68 major airports and over 700 smaller ones lacking control tower facilities. Privatised Air Canada serves the main routes, and several regional carriers operate as well. Air travel is the most widely recommended form of travel between major cities, except between Toronto, Montréal and Ottawa, where train service is comfortable, reasonably priced and usually punctual.

Road: There are about 392,000km of roads, about 84 per cent surfaced. Motorways connect some large industrial centres and most large cities have a motorway network. The trans-Canada highway at 7,821km is the longest national highway worldwide. It runs from Victoria in British Colombia in the west to St Johns in Newfoundland in the east. The speed limit on motorways is 100kmph, 80kmph on rural highways and 50kmph on urban roads. Seatbelts are compulsory for all passengers.

Buses: Long-distance coach services link all major centres. They are very well air-conditioned, and it is often recommended that travellers keep a sweater handy.

Rail: There is an extensive rail network that comprises around 100,000km of track. The Canadian National Railway (CN) and Canadian Pacific Rail are the two main railway services, but passenger services are operated by Via Rail Canada (Canrail), a government agency. Air-conditioning, refreshment facilities and sleeping accommodation are available on long-distance passenger services. The Transcontinental, runs a northern route through Saskatoon, Edmonton and Jasper, three times a week. It is advisable to book seats/sleepers as early as possible. Canrail passes give unlimited travel for certain areas and routes.

The southern route through Regina, Calgary and Banff was cut when government subsidies were stopped.

Water: The St Lawrence Seaway provides deep-water passage from the Atlantic to the Great Lakes; there are 3,017km of canals, mainly used for leisure.

City transport

Taxis: Good taxi services operate in all major cities; rates vary between cities.

Buses, trams & metro: Toronto, Montréal, Vancouver and Edmonton have efficient, safe and clean underground systems. Most cities have reliable and extensive bus services.

Car hire

Car hire is widely available. Overseas driving licences may be used for the first three months of a visitor's stay (six months in British Columbia). Driving is on the right-hand side of the road.

BUSINESS DIRECTORY

The addresses listed below are a selection only. While World of Information makes every endeavour to check these addresses, we cannot guarantee that changes have not been made, especially to telephone numbers and area codes. We would welcome any corrections.

Telephone area codes

The international direct dialling (IDD) code for Canada is +1, followed by area code and subscriber's number:

Calgary	403	Québec	514
Edmonton	780	Saskatoon	306
Fredericton	506	St John	506
Halifax	902	St John's	709
Kingston	613	Toronto	416
London	519	Vancouver	604
Montréal	514	Windsor	519
Niagara Falls	905	Winnipeg	204
Ottawa	613		

Chambers of Commerce

American Chamber of Commerce in Canada, 260 Adelaide Street, PO Box 160, Toronto, Ontario, M5A 1N1 (tel: 777-8512; fax: 738-7714; e-mail: info@amchamcanada.ca).

British Canadian Chamber of Trade and Commerce, PO Box 1358, Station 'K', Toronto, Ontario, M4P 3J4 (tel: 502-0847; fax: 502-9319; e-mail: central@bcctc.ca).

Canadian Chamber of Commerce, Delta Office Towers, 350 Sparks Street, Ottawa, Ontario, K1R 7S8 (tel: 238-4000; fax: 238-7643; e-mail: info@chamber.ca).

British Columbia Chamber of Commerce, 750 West Pender Street, Vancouver, British Columbia, V6C 2T8 (tel: 683-0700; fax: 683-0416; e-mail: bccc@bcchamber.org).

Halifax Chamber of Commerce, 7 Spectacle Lake Drive, Dartmouth, Nova Scotia (tel: 468-7111; fax: 468-7333;e-mail: info@halifaxchamber.com).

Kingston Chamber of Commerce, 67 Brock Street, Kingston, Ontario, K7K 1R7 (tel: 5448-4453; fax: 548-4743; e-mail: info@kingstonchamber.on.ca).

Manitoba Chamber of Commerce, 227 Portage Avenue, Winnipeg, Manitoba, R3B 2A6 (tel: 948-0100; fax: 948-0110; e-mail: mbchamber@mbchamber.mb.ca).

Montréal Board of Trade, 380 St Antoine Street West, Montréal, Québec, H2Y 3X7 (tel: 871-4000; fax: 871-1255; e-mail: info@ccmm.qc.ca).

North Vancouver Chamber of Commerce, 124 West 1st Street, North Vancouver, British Columbia, V7M 3N3 (tel: 987-4488; fax: 987-8272; e-mail: info@nvchamber.bc.ca).

Ontario Chamber of Commerce, 180 Dundas Street West, Toronto, Ontario M5G 1Z8 (tel: 482-5222; fax: 482-5879; e-mail: info@occ.on.ca).

Ottowa Chamber of Commerce, 1701 Woodward Drive, Ottowa, Ontario, K2C 0R4 (tel: 236-3630; fax: 236-7498; info@greaterottowachamber.com).

Québec Federation of Chambers of Commerce, 500 Place d'Armes, Montréal, Québec, H2Y 2W2 (tel: 844-9571; fax: 844-0226; e-mail: info@ccq.ca).

Toronto Board of Trade, 1 First Canadian Place, PO Box 60, Toronto, Ontario, M5X 1C1 (tel: 366-6811; fax: 366-8406; e-mail: info@bot.com).

Vancouver Board of Trade, World Trade Centre, 999 Canada Place, Vancouver, British Columbia, V6C 3E1 (tel: 681-2111; fax: 681-0437; e-mail: contactus@boardoftrade.com).

Winnipeg Chamber of Commerce, 259 Portage Avenue, Winnipeg, Manitoba, R3B 2A9 (tel: 944-8484; fax: 944-8492; e-mail: info@winnipeg-chamber.com).

Banking

Bank of Montréal, First Canadian Place, Concourse Level, PO Box 3, Toronto, Ontario M5X 1A1 (tel: 867-7662).

Bank of Nova Scotia, 44 King Street West, Toronto, Ontario M5H 1H1 (tel: 866-6161).

Business Development Bank of Canada, 3rd Floor, 5 Place Ville Marie, Montréal, Québec H4Z 1L4 (tel: 283-5904; fax: 496-8036).

Canadian Imperial Bank of Commerce (CIBC), Commerce Court, Toronto, Ontario M5L 1G9 (tel: 980-2211).

National Bank of Canada, 50 O'Connor Street, Suite 1224, Ottawa, Ontario K1P 6C2 (tel: 238-8383).

Royal Bank of Canada, 200 Bay Street, Royal Bank Plaza, Toronto, Ontario M5J 2J5 (tel: 974-5151; internet site: www.royalbank.com).

Toronto Dominion Bank, PO Box 1, Toronto Dominion Centre, 55 King Street, Toronto, Ontario M5K 1A2 (tel: 982-7730).

Central bank

Bank of Canada, 234 Wellington Street, Ottawa, Ontario, K1A 0G9 (tel: 782-8111; fax: 782-7713; e-mail: paffairs@bankofcanada.ca).

Travel information

Tourism Industry Association of Canada, 130 Albert Street, Suite 1016, Ottawa K1P 5G4 (tel: 238-3883).

Air Transport Association of Canada, 99 Bank St, Suite 747, Ottawa, ON, K1P 6B9 (tel: 233-7727; fax: 230-8648).

Ministry of tourism

Tourism Canada, Federal Department of Industry, Science and Technology, 235 Queen Street, 4th Floor East, Ottawa K1A 0H6 (tel: 954-3851).

Ministries

Ministry of Agriculture and Agri-Food, Sir John Carling Building, 930 Carling Avenue, Ottawa, Ontario, K1A OC5 (tel: 995-8963).

Ministry of Foreign Affairs and International Trade, Lester B Pearson Building, 125 Sussex Drive, Ottawa, Ontario, K1A OG2 (tel: 996-9134; fax: 952-3904).

Ministry of Industry, CD Howe Building, 235 Queen Street, Ottawa, Ontario, K1A OH5 (tel: 952-4782).

Ministry of Natural Resources, 580 Booth Street, Ottawa, Ontario, K1A OE4 (tel: 995-0947; fax: 992-6424/5230).

Ministry of Public Works and Government Services, Sir Charles Tupper Building, Confederation Heights, Ottawa, Ontario, K1A OM2 (tel: 736-2027; fax: 736-23440).

Other useful addresses

Advertising Standards Canada, 350 Bloor Street, Suite 402, Toronto ON M4W 1H5 (tel: 961-6311; fax: 961-7904; email: info@adstandards.com; internet: www.adstandards.com).

Alberta Stock Exchange, 10th Floor, 300 Fifth Avenue SW, Calgary T2P 3C4 (tel: 974-7400; fax: 237-0450).

Bourse de Montréal (Stock Exchange), Tour de la Bourse, CP 61, 800 Square Victoria, Montréal H4Z 1A9 (tel: 871-2424; fax: 871-3553; e-mail: info@me.org).

British High Commission, 80 Elgin Street, Ottawa, Ontario, K1P 5K7 (tel: 237-1530; fax: 237-7980).

Canadian Broadcasting Corporation, 1500 Bronson Avenue, PO Box 8478, Ottawa, Ontario K1G 3J5 (tel: 724-1200; fax: 738-6843).

Canadian Embassy (USA), 501 Pennsylvania Avenue, NW, Washington DC 20001 (tel: 202-682-1740; fax: 202-682-7701; e-mail: webmaster@canadianembassy.org).

Canadian Importers' Association, 210 Dundas St West, Suite 700, Toronto, Ontario, M5G 2E8 (tel: 595-5333; fax: 595-8226).

Canadian Manufacturers' Association, One Yonge St, Toronto, Ontario, M5E 1J9 (tel: 363-7261; fax: 363-3779).

CTV Television Network, 42 Charles St East, Toronto, Ontario, M4Y 1T5 (tel: 928-6000; fax: 928-0907).

Department of Energy, Mines and Resources, 580 Booth St, Ottawa, Ontario, K1A 0E4 (tel: 995-3065; fax: 996-9094).

Department of Finance, 140 O'Connor St, Ottawa, Ontario, K1A 0G5 (tel: 992-1575; fax: 996-2690).

Department of Labour, Labour Canada, Ottawa, Ontario, K1A 0J2 (tel: 997-2617; fax: 953-0176).

Department of Regional Industrial Expansion, 235 Queen St, Ottawa, Ontario, K1A 0H5 (tel: 995-9001).

Economic Council of Canada, PO Box 527, Ottawa, Ontario, K1P 5V6 (tel: 993-1253; fax: 991-4904).

Investment Canada, PO Box 2800, Station 'D', Ottawa, Ontario, K1P 6A5 (tel: 996-2515; fax: 995-0465).

Ontario International Trade Corporation, 5th Floor, Hearst Block, 900 Bay Street, Toronto, Ontario, M7A 2E1 (tel: 325-6514; fax: 325-6509).

Retail Council of Canada, 210 Dundas St West, Suite 600, Toronto, Ontario, M5G 2E8 (tel: 598-4684; fax: 598-3707).

Statistics Canada, Statistical Reference Centre, Ottawa, Ontario, K1A OT6 (tel: 951-8116; internet site: www.statcan.ca/start.html).

Toronto Stock Exchange, The Exchange Tower, 2 First Canadian Place, Toronto, Ontario, M5X 1J2 (tel: 947-4700, 947-9301; fax: 947-4662).

Vancouver Stock Exchange, Stock Exchange Tower, 609 Granville Street, PO Box 10333, Vancouver, BC V7Y 1H1 (tel: 689-3334; fax: 688-6051).

Winnipeg Stock Exchange, 620 One Lombard Place, Winnipeg, Manitoba R3B 0X3 (tel: 987-7070; fax: 987-7079).

Other news agencies: CBCNews: www.cbc.ca/news

CNW Group (in English and French): www.newswire.ca

The Canadian Press: www.thecanadianpress.com

Internet sites

Asia-Pacific Economic Co-operation (APEC): www.apecsec.org.sg

Air Canada: www.aircanada.ca

Canada Online: strategis.ic.gc.ca

Canada Yellow Pages: www.canadayellowpages.com

Canadian Airlines: www.cdnair.ca

Canadian Automobile Association: www.caa.ca

Canadian Energy: www.centreforenergy.com

Canadian International Development Agency (CIDA): www.acdi-cida.gc.ca

Canadian Parliament: www.parl.gc.ca

Canadian Statistics: www.statcan.ca

Government of Canada (all dept): www.canada.gc.ca

Government of Alberta: www.gov.ab.ca

Government of Ontario: www.gov.on.ca

Government of Québec: www.gouv.qc.ca

Inuit and Artic news: www.nunatsiaq.com

North American Free Trade Agreement: www.nafta-sec-alena.org

Strategis (business and consumer site): strategis.ic.ca

Thomas Register: www2.thomasregister.com

Trans-Canadian highway: www.transcanadahighway.com

Cape Verde

KEY FACTS

Official name: República de Cabo Verde (Republic of Cape Verde)

Head of State: President Pedro Verona Rodrigues Pires (PAICV) (since 2001; re-elected 12 February 2006)

Head of government: Prime Minister José María Neves (PAICV) (since 2001; re-elected 22 January 2006)

Ruling party: Partido Africano da Independência de Cabo Verde (PAICV) (African Party of Independence of Cape Verde) (since 2001; re-elected January 2006)

Area: 4,033 square km (nine islands and 10 islets)

Population: 494,000 (2007)*

Capital: Praia

Official language: Portuguese and Creole (national language)

Currency: Cape Verde escudo (CVEsc) = 100 centavos

Exchange rate: CVEsc71.50 per US$ (Jul 2008); (pegged CVEsc110.27 per euro)

GDP per capita: US$2,891 (2007)

GDP real growth: 6.90% (2007)*

Labour force: 204,000 (2004)

Inflation: 4.40% (2007)*

Balance of trade: -US$387.00 million (2006)

Foreign debt: US$517.00 million (2004)

Visitor numbers: 242,000 (2006)*

* estimated figure

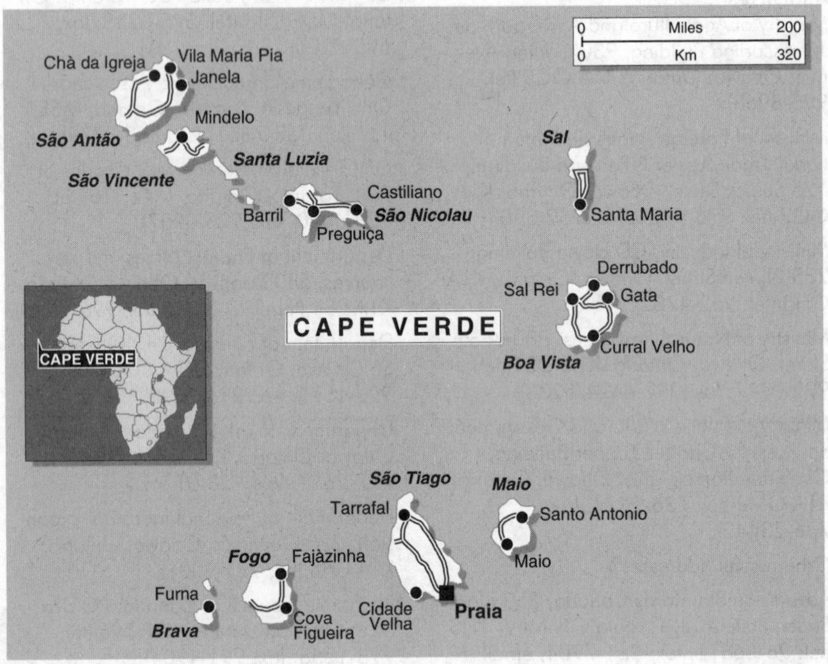

The three month period of November and December 2007 and January 2008 was a successful time for Cape Verde. First, it was accepted as a special partner of the European Union (EU) in November, was invited to join the World Trade Organisation in December and then in January Cape Verde lost its United Nations least-developed country (LDC) status. According to the International Monetary Fund (IMF), Cape Verde has achieved a major economic transformation compared with other small economies in the sub-Saharan region of Africa. Gross domestic product (GDP) growth has averaged around 6.5 per cent since 2003, reaching 10.8 per cent in 2006, while unemployment dropped more than 10 percentage points between 2001 and 2006. The IMF also reckons that the country will achieve most of its Millennium Development Goals by 2015, including halving its 1990 poverty level.

As a country with hardly and natural resources, the economy is service-oriented, with commerce, transport, tourism, and public services accounting for 72 per cent of gross domestic product. Although almost 70 per cent of the population live in rural areas, the share of agriculture in GDP is around 12 per cent. The fishing potential, mostly lobster and tuna, is not fully exploited.

Cape Verde annually runs a high trade deficit, financed by foreign aid and remittances from emigrants which supplement GDP by more than 20 per cent. Several state-owned enterprises have been privatised, including Empresa Nacional de Administracao dos Portos (ENAPOR), the port authority, and TACV, the national airline. In mid-2008 the market capitalisation of the Cape Verde Stock Exchange was 25 per cent of GDP, having been zero in 2005. These and other structural reforms have improved competition and the private sector's role in the economy.

Political openness

Since the adoption of a multi-party system in 1991, there have been four national elections and two orderly changes in government. A free press further supports the building of an open society. The last legislative and presidential elections were held in January and February 2006, respectively, and the Partido Africano da Independência de Cabo Verde (PAICV) (Africa Party of Independence of Cape Verde) won both elections. President Pedro Pires was re-elected with 49.43 per cent of the vote against 49.42 per cent for Carlos Viega (Movimento para a Democracia (MDP) (Movement for Democracy)) for a five-year term. The PAICV won the parliamentary elections with 52.34 per cent of the votes (41 seats), against 43.93 per cent (29 seats) for the MPD. The re-elected prime minister, José María Neves, and his appointed Council of Ministers, took office in March 2006.

Social issues

According to the World Bank, Cape Verde's growth performance since the late 1980s has raised it to the ranks of lower middle income countries, with a GDP per capita of US$2,891in 2007. Thanks to growth of 10.8 per cent in 2006 and 6.9 per cent in 2007, poverty has declined by one-fourth over the last decade, while the human development index increased from 0.59 in 1990 to 0.67 in 2003. Adult literacy rates are high (approximately 76 per cent in 2002), and life expectancy at birth (69) is the third highest in Africa. Notwithstanding the country's economic successes, its small size and geography make it vulnerable to exogenous shocks and the country is highly dependent on foreign aid and remittances.

During the twentieth century severe droughts caused the deaths of 200,000 people, prompting heavy emigration, with the result that more people with origins in Cape Verde live outside the country than inside it. The money that they send home brings in much-needed foreign currency. Nonetheless, the country enjoys a per capita income that is higher than that of many continental African nations (US$1,971 in 2005). Tourism is growing in importance, but there are concerns that it poses a threat to Cape Verde's rich marine life. It is an important nesting site for loggerhead turtles and humpback whales feed in the island waters.

Outlook

Cape Verde continues to exhibit one of Africa's most stable democratic governments. Cape Verde's expatriate population is greater than its domestic one and will continue to underpin the economy. One worrying development is the allegations that Cape Verde is a transshipment point for illicit drugs moving from Latin America and Asia destined for Western Europe and that it is only the lack of a well- developed financial system that limits the country's utility as a money-laundering centre.

Risk assessment

Economic	Good
Political	Good
Regional stability	Fair

COUNTRY PROFILE

Historical profile

The uninhabited islands that now are Cape Verde were colonised by the Portuguese in the 15th century; Cape Verde subsequently became a trading center for African slaves and later an important coaling and re-supply stop for whaling and transatlantic shipping. Following independence in 1975 a one-party system was established and maintained until multi-party elections were held in 1990. After independence, Cape Verde planned to unit with Guinea-Bissau, but the plan was ditched after a coup in Guinea-Bissau in 1980 strained relations.

Following Cape Verde's independence from Portugal in 1975, the country was ruled by the Guinea-Bissau based Partido Africano da Independência da Guiné e Cabo Verde (PAIGC) (African Party for the Independence of Guinea and Cape Verde). The PAIGC had been founded in 1956 by Dr Amilcar Cabral, as a left-wing nationalist movement which led an 11-year guerrilla struggle in mainland Guinea-Bissau from 1963 to 1974 for independence from Portuguese rule. The PAIGC was prevented by Portuguese repression from establishing an effective organisation in the Cape Verde islands. In 1974, following the April coup in Lisbon, Portugal's new military leaders agreed to give the islands their independence, although there was more hesitation in the case of Cape Verde in view of the island republic's strategic mid-Atlantic importance. Cape Verde was actually granted independence 10 months later than Guinea-Bissau. The historical ties between the two countries are strong – the majority of Cape Verdians are descended from slaves transported from the African mainland – principally from what are now Guinea-Bissau and Senegal.

1462 The previously uninhabited islands were colonised by the Portuguese and became one of the most important slaving stations in West Africa.

1961 The movement for independence gathered strength, adopting guerrilla tactics against the Portuguese.

1975 Cape Verde gained independence after the fall of the dictatorship in Portugal.

1975–80 Moves to unite Cape Verde and Guinea-Bissau were made, but came to nothing following the overthrow of President Luiz Cabral in Guinea-Bissau.

1980 The constitution was adopted.

1981 A revision to the constitution was passed.

1990 A multi-party system was introduced.

1991 Cape Verde's first free multi-party elections were won by the Movimento para a Democracia (MPD) (Movement for Democracy) and a government under Carlos Veiga was formed.

1992 A new constitution was adopted.

1995 The MPD secured an absolute majority in the elections to the National Assembly.

1996 President Antonio Mascarenhas Monteiro (MPD) was re-elected; no other parties put up candidates.

1999 Amendment to constitution.

KEY INDICATORS — Cape Verde

	Unit	2003	2004	2005	2006	2007
Population	m	0.46	0.48	0.48	0.48	*0.49
Gross domestic product (GDP)	US$bn	0.65	0.95	1.00	*1.18	*1.43
GDP per capita	US$	1,400	2,097	2,099	*2,424	*2,891
GDP real growth	%	5.0	4.0	5.8	*10.8	*6.9
Inflation	%	1.2	-1.9	0.4	5.4	*4.4
Exports (fob) (goods)	US$m	30.0	61.1	100.0	111.0	76.5
Imports (cif) (goods)	US$m	220.0	387.3	452.0	498.0	743.6
Balance of trade	US$m	-190.0	-326.2	-352.0	-387.0	-667.1
Current account	US$m	-80.0	-80.0	-34.0	-6,000.0	-144.0
Total reserves minus gold	US$m	93.6	139.5	174.0	254.5	–
Foreign exchange	US$m	93.6	139.5	173.9	254.4	–
Exchange rate	per US$	108.95	95.05	85.50	85.50	75.50

* estimated figure

2001 Pedro Pires was elected president.
2003 The IMF approved a three-year programme for US$11.5 million under the Poverty Reduction and Growth Facility (PRGF).
2004 Poor rainfall and locust damage resulted in reduced harvests and a larger than usual food deficit.
2006 Elections to the national assembly were won by the PAICV with 52.34 per cent of the vote against the 43.93 per cent won by the MPD. PAICV have 41 seats, the MPD 29 seats. Pedro Pires was re-elected in the presidential election.
2007 Cape Verde withdrew its support for Polisario, the separatist movement in Western Sahara, and allied itself to Morocco. In December the WTO approved Cape Verde's membership.
2008 In May, The Netherlands granted a three-year aid programme of US$14.2 million for education and vocational training. In July, Cape Verde announced its backing of the Moroccan Sahara autonomy plan which allows Morocco and Polisario to discuss the future of Western Sahara without pre-conditions.

Political structure
Cape Verde has a mixed presidential/parliamentary form of government.
Constitution
A new constitution was adopted in 1992 and amended in 1999. There are 17 municipios (administrative districts).
Form of state
Unitary republic
The executive
Executive power rests with the prime minister and the Council of Ministers, proposed by the prime minister and appointed by the president. The prime minister is appointed by the president, in consultation with the National Assembly. The president is elected by universal suffrage by electors registered in the electoral census in the national territory and abroad, for a five-year term. The presidential candidate must be a Capeverdean citizen by origin, thirty-five or more years of age on the date of his candidature, and, in the three years immediately preceding that date, have had permanent residence in the national territory.
National legislature
The legislative unicameral parliament, the Assembléia Nacional (National Assembly), serves a five-year term. It has 66 deputies elected in Cape Verde by universal suffrage, under a system of proportional representation, and six deputies elected by Cape Verdeans living abroad (two each for Africa, the Americas and the rest of the world).
Legal system
The legal system is derived from that of Portugal.
Last elections
22 January 2006 (parliamentary); 12 February 2006 (presidential)
Results: Presidential: Pedro Pires (PAICV) won 49.43 per cent of the votes; Carlos Veiga (MPD) 49.42 per cent.
Parliamentary: the PAICV won 52.34 per cent of the votes (41 seats), the MPD 43.93 per cent, (29 seats).
Next elections
2011 (presidential and parliamentary)

Political parties
There are six registered political parties.
Ruling party
Partido Africano da Independência de Cabo Verde (PAICV) (African Party of Independence of Cape Verde) (since 2001; re-elected January 2006)
Main opposition party
Movimento para a Democracia (MPD) (Movement for Democracy)

Population
494,000 (2007)*
Last census: June 2000: 436,863
Population density: 237 inhabitants per square km. Urban population: 63 per cent 1995—2001).
Annual growth rate: 2.4 per cent 1994–2004 (WHO 2006)
Ethnic make-up
Creole (71 per cent), African (28 per cent), European (1 per cent).
Religions
Constitutional separation of church and state allows for freedom of religion. Christian (97 per cent Roman Catholic).

Education
The National Development Plan of 2002–06 aims to increase vocational training and job creation and reduce illiteracy in an effort to generate foreign investment and therefore increase employment.
Literacy rate: 74 per cent adult population.
Enrolment rate: 100 per cent of children age six to 11 will enrol for school in 2015, Oxfam estimate.

Health
Per capita total expenditure on health (2003) was US$185; of which per capita government spending was US$135, at the international dollar rate, (WHO 2006).
HIV/Aids
The government had a National Aids programme in place for the period 2001–04, financed by the World Bank.
Life expectancy: 70 years, 2004 (WHO 2006)
Fertility rate/Maternal mortality rate: 3.6 births per woman, 2004 (WHO 2006)
Child (under 5 years) mortality rate (per 1,000): 26 per 1,000 births (World Bank).
Head of population per physician: 0.49 physicians per 1,000 people, 2004 (WHO 2006)
Welfare
Around a third of the population live under the poverty line with around 14 per cent living in absolute poverty. Unemployment is estimated at 25 per cent, while underemployment is far higher. Poverty is worse in rural areas where employment opportunities are poor and incomes are declining. As a result, there is a steady migration to urban areas, creating pockets of extreme poverty within cities and towns.

Main cities
Praia, on Santiago Island (capital, estimated population 125,464 in 2005); Mindelo, on São Vicente (commercial centre, 67,452).

Languages spoken
Official language/s
Portuguese and Creole (national language)
Media
National news agency: Inforpress (Agência de Notícias de Cabo Verde)
Other news agencies: Voz di Povo: www.vozdipovo-online.com
APA: www.apanews.net
Panapress: www.panapress.com
Press
The only daily is the government-run Jornal Horizonte, the only other local publications are Expresso das Ilhas (www.expressodasilhas.cv) and A Semana (www.asemana.cv). Terra Nova is a weekly based on São Vicente. Government publications include Novo Jornal Cabo Verde published twice a week and the periodical Boletim Informativo.
Broadcasting
The state-run broadcaster is Radio e televisão de Cabo Verde (RTC).
Radio: The state-run radio RTC (www.rtc.cv) has one station that has programmes relayed throughout the islands on a variety of frequencies. Private commercial stations include Praia FM (www.praiafm.biz), Mosteiros FM (www.mosteiros.com), Rádio Nova (www.radionovaonline.com) and Crioula FM (www.crioulafm.cv). Several foreign broadcasts, from Portugal and France, are readily available.
Television: RTC (www.rtc.cv) operates the country's only television station.
News agencies
National news agency: Inforpress (Agência de Notícias de Cabo Verde)
Other news agencies: Voz di Povo: www.vozdipovo-online.com
APA: www.apanews.net
Panapress: www.panapress.com

Economy
Cape Verde has limited natural resources. Only 20 per cent of the total land area can be used for agriculture, because of the rugged volcanic nature of the landscape, erosion and persistent periods of severe drought. Although nearly three-quarters of the population live in rural areas, agriculture accounts for only 11 per cent of GDP. Most essentials, including food and fuel, have to be imported.
Cape Verde is reliant on external donor assistance and food aid. Around half of the country's development expenses are funded by foreign aid with basic products (cereals, cooking oil, milk) making up 20 per cent of public development aid. Much aid is aimed at transforming the country into a self-sustainable economy.
Tourism is being developed as the main generator of economic growth. In 2005, the sector accounted for 10 per cent of GDP. The number of visitors has steadily risen year-on-year, despite restricted facilities, increasing by over 26 per cent in 2005. Major expansion of infrastructure is underway.
Mass emigration following serious droughts in the twentieth century has benefited the economy by the inflow of remittances, which account for around 20 per cent of GDP.
There is a high rate of unskilled workers – 30–40 per cent of the population – and foreign investors are able take advantage of low wage rates.

External trade
Cape Verde is a member of the Economic Community of West African States (Ecowas) and has indicated that it was interested in joining the West African Monetary Zone (WAMZ) with a common currency to be introduced in 2009. In 2007 Cape Verde was still in negotiation to join the WTO.
The trade deficit is partly offset by income from services, including ship repairs, intermediary goods, workers' remittances and substantial foreign aid.

Imports
Principal imports are foodstuffs such as foodstuffs: rice, wheat and maize, cooking oil and milk; and consumer goods, industrial products, transport equipment, fuels, machinery and textiles.
Main sources: Portugal (41.5 per cent total, 2005), Italy (8.0 per cent), The Netherlands (7.3 per cent), Spain (5.5 per cent), France (4.8 per cent), Belgium (4.7 per cent), Brazil (4.3 per cent),

Exports
Principal exports are fuel, shoes and garments, fish, hides, salt and entrepôt trade.
Main destinations: Spain (38.2 per cent total, 2005), Portugal (33.2 per cent), US (9.2 per cent), Morocco (5.4 per cent)

Agriculture
The agricultural sector forms the backbone of the economy, even though only 20 per cent of total area is cultivable, with 48 per cent of the population engaged in subsistence farming. Agriculture accounts for around 13 per cent of GDP. Most arable land is on the island of São Tiago.
Recurrent drought, interrupted by torrential rains and floods, soil erosion, disease and a weak infrastructure have reduced agricultural production considerably, but there are schemes for water conservation and irrigation.
Beans and maize are the staple foodstuffs. Maize covers 25–80 per cent of cultivated land according to rainfall. Only 10 per cent of food is produced locally.
Other crops include bananas, sweet potatoes, yams, manioc, pumpkins, sugar cane, coffee and groundnuts. About 90 per cent of food requirements are met by imports, largely in the form of food aid.
The estimated crop production for 2005 included: 4,042 tonnes (t) maize, 3,000t cassava, 3,500t potatoes, 6,000t bananas, 4,000t sweet potatoes, 5,000t pulses, 6,000t coconuts, 4,500t tomatoes, 1,000t pimento, 792t oilcrops, 14,000t sugar cane, 15,000t fruit in total, 15,665t vegetables in total. Estimated livestock production included: 8,586t meat in total, 470t beef, 7,200t pig meat, 38t lamb and 474t goat meat, 405t poultry, 1,770t eggs, 11,000t milk, 86t cattle hides.

Fishing
Although fishing (lobster and tuna) has been of growing importance, supporting some 20,000 people and accounting for over 60 per cent of export revenues and 4 per cent of GDP, it is under-exploited. Construction of a fishing port in Mindelo on São Vicente was completed in 2001.

Industry and manufacturing
The industrial sector accounts for around 19 per cent of GDP and employs 15 per cent of the workforce.
Industries include ship repair and fuelling, construction, fish processing and canning, flour milling, soft drinks, cigar manufacture and garment making. Construction and civil engineering contribute about 10 per cent of GDP and are primarily related to the development of the tourism sector.
Two zones have been set up with industrial parks: Lazareto on São Vicente and Achada Grande Tras in Praia.

Tourism
Tourism is a primary contributor to the economy and is being vigorously developed as an engine of economic growth. The increase in 2005 was expected to be around 2 per cent. Most tourist activity is centred on Sal, whose airport has been the only one catering to charter flights from Europe. Most visitors come from Portugal and Italy. In 2005, a new international airport was inaugurated on Santiago near the capital, Praia, which will open up Santiago and other islands to tourism. Other infrastructure works are in progress, including the Santiago Golf Club, a huge resort near Praia. Tourism was expected to contribute around 11 per cent to GDP in 2005.

Environment
Cape Verde faces serious environmental problems, particularly concerning water management. Serious drought caused by global warming and the country's geographical location has undermined agriculture as well as plant cover. The government has drawn upon the Global Environment Facility (GEF) to help protect biodiversity and is supported by the UN's Food and Agriculture Organisation (FAO) in a forestry action plan.

Mining
The mining sector employs about 1 per cent of the workforce.
Activity is largely confined to exploitation of pozzolana (volcanic derivative) at São Antão, gypsum at Maio and production of salt on Sal and in Mindelo by evaporation method.

Hydrocarbons
Cape Verde has no oil or gas reserves. Oil requirements are imported mainly from Portugal and West African countries. Imported refined oil products supply 96 per cent of the country's energy needs.
Current consumption of oil products is around 20,000 tonnes per annum. The downstream industry is regulated by Direcão Geral da Energia and distribution is by Shell Capo Verde and Enacol.

Energy
Cape Verde is dependent on oil imports for electricity generation. Around 96 per cent of energy needs come from oil-derived products.

Banking and insurance
Central bank
Banco de Cabo Verde
Main financial centre
Praia

Time
GMT minus one hour

Geography
Cape Verde is an archipelago of 10 islands and five islets in the North Atlantic Ocean, about 500km (300 miles) west of Dakar, Senegal.
Hemisphere
Northern

Climate
Hot with very little rainfall. Temperatures range from around 20 degrees Celsius

(C) at night to 32 degrees C during the day. Hottest months are July, August and September and rain most likely from August–September.

Entry requirements

Passports

Required by all. Passport must be valid for six months.

Visa

Required by all, except nationals of Ecowas countries, former Cape Verde nationals (with proof of origin) and transit passengers.

Currency advice/regulations

Import and export of local currency prohibited. No restriction on import of foreign currency, but amounts must be declared on arrival. Export of foreign currency is limited to equivalent of CVEsc1,000,000 or the amount declared on arrival if higher.

Health (for visitors)

Mandatory precautions

Yellow fever certificates if arriving from countries having notified cases in the last six years.

Advisable precautions

Typhoid, tetanus, hepatitis A and polio vaccinations. Malaria limited risk exists September to November in São Tiago Island. Water precautions should be taken. There is a rabies risk. There is a slight risk of cholera. Milk is unpasteurised and should be boiled. Dairy products should be avoided.

Hotels

Accommodation is available in all islands but the best establishments are situated in Fogo, Sal, Santiago, São Vicente.

Credit cards

Credit cards are only accepted in the bigger hotels.

Public holidays (national)

Fixed dates

1 Jan (New Year's Day), 20 Jan (Heroes' Day), 1 May (Labour Day), 5 Jul (Independence Day), 15 Aug (Assumption Day), 12 Sep (National Day), 1 Nov (All Saints' Day), 25 Dec (Christmas).

Variable dates

Carnival (Feb), Ash Wednesday, Good Friday.

Working hours

Banking

Mon–Fri: 0800–1400.

Business

Mon–Fri: 0800–1230, 1430–1800.

Shops

Mon–Fri: 0800–2000; Sat: 0900–1700.

Electricity supply

220V AC, 50Hz

Weights and measures

Metric system

Getting there

Air

TAAG of Angola flies weekly from São Tomé and Príncipe. South African Airlines, TAP Air Portugal and Tower Airlines also service Cape Verde.

National airline: Transportes Aéreos de Cabo Verde (TACV) guarantees daily inter-island flights and weekly flights.

International airport/s: Amilcar Cabral International (SID), 2km south of Espargos on Sal island; Praia International (RAI) on Santiago island.

Airport tax: None.

Getting about

National transport

Air: Transportes Aéreos de Cabo Verde (TACV) flies daily to all islands except Brava and Santo Antâo. Discounted trips among the islands are available with the Cape Verde Airpass, which can be purchased when booking international flights with TACV. A charter service is provided by Cape Verde Express.

Buses: Buses available on main islands.

Water: Boats ply between the islands.

City transport

Taxis: Available on main islands. Taxis are available from Amilcar Cabral International Airport to city centre.

BUSINESS DIRECTORY

The addresses listed below are a selection only. While World of Information makes every endeavour to check these addresses, we cannot guarantee that changes have not been made, especially to telephone numbers and area codes. We would welcome any corrections.

Telephone area codes

The international dialling code (IDD) for Cape Verde is +238 followed by subscriber's number.

NB From 3 July 2004, standard and cellular numbers have seven digits: add '2' to the beginning of the existing standard number; add '9' to the beginning of the existing cellular number.

Useful telephone numbers

Praia, Santiago

Airport docks: 2615-821, 2615-646
Electricity Board: 2611-909
Fire brigade: 2612-727
Ambulance: 2612-462
Police: 2613-637

Chambers of Commerce

Barlavento Câmara de Comércio, Indústria, Agricultura e Serviços, Rua de Luz 31, PO Box 728, Mindelo, São Vicente (tel: 2328-495; fax: 2328-496; e-mail: camera.com @mail.cvtelecom.cv).

Sotavento Câmara de Comércio, Indústria e Serviços, Rua Andrade Corvo, PO Box 105, Praia, Santiago (tel: 2617-234; fax: 2617-235; e-mail: cciss@mail,cvtelecom.cv).

Banking

Banco Insular (IFI), PO Box 556, Conjunto Residencial Comunidades, Lote Oito- Bloco D Fracção Oitava, Achada Santo Antonio-Praia (e-mail: bancoinsular@mail.cvtelecom.cv).

Banco Comercial do Atlantico, PO Box 474, Avenida Amílcar Cabral, Praia (tel: 2614-953; fax: 2613-235).

Banco Interatlântico, Avenida Cidade de Lisboa 131-A, Praia (tel: 2614-008, 2613-829, 2614-425; fax: 2614-712, 2614-752).

Caixa Económica de Cabo Verde SARL, PO Box 199, Avenida Cidade de Lisboa, Praia (tel: 2615-561; fax: 2615-560).

Central bank

Banco de Cabo Verde, Avenida Amilcar Cabral, PO Box 101, Praia (tel: 2615-526; fax: 2611-914; e-mail: drs@bcv.cv).

Travel information

Agencia Cabetur, Viagens e Turismo, Rua Guerra Mendes 4, Praia (tel: 2615-551; fax: 2615-553).

Intertur SARL, Av Cidade de Lisboa, 2 Esq Fazenda, Praia (tel: 614-643; fax: 614-644); Rua 5 de Julho Espargos, Sal (tel: 2411-580/590).

Orbitur, Rua Roberto Duarte Silva, CP 161, Praia (tel: 2615-737; fax: 2613-888).

Praiatur, 100 Av Amilcar Cabral, CP 470, Praia (tel: 2615-746/7; fax: 2614-500).

Sal Amilcar Cabral International Airport, ASA-Empresa Nacional de Aeroportos E Seguranca Aerea-EP, PB 50, Ilha do Sal (tel: 2411-135, 2411-394, 2411-468; fax: 2411-570, 2411-323; e-mail: asacv@milton.cvtelecom.cv).

Transportes Aéreos de Cabo Verde (TACV), Av Amilcar Cabral, CP 1, Praia (tel: 2615-813; fax: 2615-905).

Ministries

Ministry of Agriculture, Alimentation and Environment, Praia (tel: 2615-716; fax: 2614-717).

Ministry of Defence, Praia (tel: 2610-372; fax: 2611-286).

Ministry of Economic Co-ordination, Avenue Amilcar Cabral, Praia (tel: 2613-210; fax: 2611-922).

Ministry of Education, Science and Culture, Praia (tel: 2610-507; fax: 2612-764).

Ministry of Foreign Affairs, Praia (tel: 2614-773; fax: 2611-960).

Ministry of Health and Social Promotion, Praia (tel: 2615-721; fax: 2613-991).

Ministry of Justice and Internal Administration, Praia (tel: 2615-687; fax: 2611-396).

Ministry of Sea, Praia (tel: 2616-662; fax: 2611-770).

Ministry of Transport and Infrastructure, Praia (tel: 2615-709; fax: 2614-822).

Prime Minister's Office, Palacio do Governo, Praia (tel: 2610-513; fax: 2612-288).

Other useful addresses

Associação Commercial e Agricola de Sotavento de Cabo Verde, CP 78, Praia (tel: 2612-991).

Associação Comercial Barlavento, CP 62, Mindelo, S Vicente (tel: 2313-281).

Cabo Verde Motors, CP 51-B, Praia (tel: 2612-345; fax: 2612-612).

Ceris, Sociedade Caboverdiana de Cerveja e Refrigerantes (beer and refrigeration), CP 320, Praia (tel: 2615-575; fax: 2614-488).

Direcção-Geral das Alfandegas (customs body), CP 98, Praia (tel: 2613-835, 2613-026).

Direcção-Geral do Comércio (trade body), CP 105, Praia (tel: 2614-159).

Direcção-Geral de Estatistica (Statistics Department of the Ministry of Economic Co-ordination), Avenida Amilcar Cabral, Praia (fax: 2611-922).

Direcção-Geral das Pescas (national fisheries authority), Praia (tel: 2612-976).

Direcção-Geral do Plano (Planning Department of the Ministry of Economic Co-ordination), Avenida Amilcar Cabral, Praia (fax: 2611-922).

Embassy of Portugal, Achada de S António, Praia (tel: 2615-602).

Empresa Nacional de Aeroportos e Segurança Aérea, Aeroporto Amilcar Cabral, Ilha do Sal (tel: 2411-394).

Empresa Nacional de Combustivels (national combustibles corporation), CP 1, Mindelo, S Vicente (tel: 2313-659).

Garantia (insurance company) (tel: 2615-661, 2615-662; fax: 2313-221, 2313-470).

Promex (Centro de Promoção Turística, do Investimento e das Exportações), CP89c, Praia (tel: 2622-736; fax: 2622-657; e-mail: promex@cvtelecom.cv).

Radio Nacional de Cabo Verde, CP 26, Praia (tel: 2613-729).

Shell Cabo Verde, CP 4, S Vicente (tel: 2314-470; fax: 2314-755).

US Embassy, R Abilio Macedo, Praia (tel: 2615-616).

National news agency: Inforpress (Agência de Notícias de Cabo Verde)
Address: A Largo de Marconi, Achada de Santo António, Cabo Verde CP 40 (tel/fax: 262-2554; email: inforpress@mail.cvtelecom.cv; internet: www.inforpress.cv).

Internet sites

Africa Business Network: www.ifc.org/abn

African Development Bank: www.afdb.org

Africa Online: www.africaonline.com

Allafrica.com: http://allafrica.com

Mbendi AfroPaedia (information on companies, countries, industries and stock exchanges in Africa): http://mbendi.co.za

Cayman Islands

KEY FACTS

Official name: Cayman Islands

Head of State: Queen Elizabeth II; represented by Governor Stuart Jack (from 23 Nov 2005)

Head of government: Leader of Government Business: Kurt Tibbetts (PPM) (since 2005)

Ruling party: People's Progressive Movement (PPM) (since 2005)

Area: 259 square km

Population: 53,252 (2006)*

Capital: George Town (Grand Cayman)

Official language: English

Currency: Cayman Islands dollar (CI$) = 100 cents

Exchange rate: CI$0.82 per US$ (Jul 2008)

GDP per capita: US$46,500 (2006)*

GDP real growth: 6.50% (2006)*

Unemployment: 3.50% (2005)

Inflation: 7.00% (2005)

Balance of trade: -US$841.70 million (2004)

Visitor numbers: 1.97 million (2005)

* estimated figure

COUNTRY PROFILE

Historical profile

1503 Little Cayman and Cayman Brac were sighted by Christopher Columbus during his fourth and final voyage to the New World. The islands were first named Las Tortugas (turtles); the name was later changed to Lagartos (alligator or large lizard).

1540 The name Caymanas was given to the islands, derived from the Carib word for marine crocodile.

1585–86 Sir Frances Drake visited the islands.

During the sixteenth, seventeenth and eighteenth centuries, Dutch, English, Spanish and French ships used the islands for watering and provisioning.

1655 The islands came under British control when Jamaica was captured from the Spanish.

1670 In the Treaty of Madrid, Spain recognised UK sovereignty over Jamaica and the Cayman Islands. The early settlers were ex-soldiers from Oliver Cromwell's army, and other settlers transplanted from Jamaica, together with shipwrecked or marooned sailors.

1773 Grand Cayman's population reached 400.

1831 It was agreed that representatives should be appointed for the five different districts of Grand Cayman for the purpose of forming local laws for better government. After elections in the five districts, the legislative assembly met in George Town.

1833 Cayman Brac and Little Cayman were settled permanently.

1835 The proclamation was read declaring the emancipation of all slaves throughout the colonies.

1962 When Jamaica became independent, Caymanians retained direct links with the Crown and the Cayman Islands became a separate British Crown Colony.

1971 The first governor was appointed.

1972 A new constitution was adopted giving great autonomy and making the islands a British Overseas Territory.

1994 A constitutional amendment introduced a ministerial form of government.

2000 Only independents candidates were elected to parliamentary.

2001 The United Democratic Party (UDP) was formed. Its leader, W McKeeva Bush, became the leader of government business.

2002 The People's Progressive Movement (PPM) was formed. A new constitution, which would have created an office of chief minister and a fully ministerial government failed due to the lack of agreement between the leader of government business, the opposition leader and the UK government concerning a bill of rights.

2003 The previously informal title for the government's chief minister, the leader of government business, was formally recognised by the UK government.

2004 The worst hurricane for structural damage since 1918, Hurricane Ivan, struck the islands, causing severe flooding and infrastructure damage.

2005 The PPM won the 11 May parliamentary elections; Kurt Tibbetts became leader of government business.

2007 Phase one of the Constitutional Modernisation Initiative, with public discussion of a proposed new constitution, began.

Political structure

Constitution

The constitution of 1972, revised in 1994, created ministers and ministries and provided for a system of government headed by a governor, an Executive Council (ExCo) and Legislative Assembly. Unlike other Caribbean Overseas Territories, there is no chief minister, but a leader of government business. The appointed governor retains responsibility for the civil service, defence, external affairs and internal security.

Phase one of the Constitutional Modernisation Initiative, with public discussion of a proposed new constitution, began in 2007.

Form of state

Self-governing British Crown Colony

The executive

The British monarch is Head of State and is represented by the governor. Government is exercised by the Executive Council (ExCo) presided over by the governor, consisting of three official members appointed by the governor and five members drawn from the elected members of the Legislative Assembly. As ministers, the five elected members of the ExCo have direct responsibility for government portfolios.

National legislature
The Legislative Assembly has 18 members, 15 elected members (MLAs) for a four-year term in two-seat constituencies, and three ex-officio members.

Legal system
The legal system is based on English common law with local changes. Courts: Juvenile Court, Summary Court Grand Court and the Cayman Islands Court of Appeal. Final appeals go to the Privy Council in the UK.

Last elections
11 May 2005 (parliamentary)

Results: Parliamentary: the People's Progressive Movement (PPM) won nine seats out of 15; the United Democratic Party (UDP) won five seats; one independent candidate was returned.

Next elections
2009 (parliamentary)

Political parties

Ruling party
People's Progressive Movement (PPM) (since 2005)

Main opposition party
United Democratic Party (UDP)

Political situation
With a weird statistic that shows there are more companies register on the Cayman Islands than there are people living on them, business leaders were pleased when the Cayman Islands maintained its international ranking of sixth, in 2007, in total banking assets. Nevertheless, the Cayman Islands have come in for a battering from several sources. Bermuda set out to take a major share of the US$2 trillion hedge funds business from both the Cayman Islands and the British Virgin Islands and the 2007–08 crisis in US banking, has taken its toll on the Cayman Islands' reputation, as hedge funds have failed and tax evasion schemes have come to light. Officials from the UK and US treasury have begun investigations into offshore tax havens, with accusations of tax dodges and money laundering. Almost as soon as scrutiny began the Basis Capital Funds Management was declared bankrupt and in January 2008 Bear Stearns had two hedge funds falter.
The Cayman Islands has the highest standard of living of any other Caribbean country and it relies heavily on its offshore banking to maintain this and must judge the balance between offering a discrete, and no-questions-asked, banking service against the potential retaliatory action of foreign governments keen to stem the flow of revenue from their coffers.

Population
53,252 (2006)*

Last census: October 1999: 39,410

Population density: 150 inhabitants per square km.
Annual growth rate: 4.4 per cent (2003)

Ethnic make-up
Mixed race (40 per cent), white (20 per cent), black (20 per cent). Thirty-four per cent of the population are foreign residents, of whom 10 per cent are British or American.

Religions
Mainly Presbyterian with Anglican, Roman Catholic, Seventh-Day Adventists, Pilgrims, Pilgrim Holiness Church of God, Jehovah's Witnesses and Baha'i minorities on Grand Cayman. Baptists on Cayman Brac.

Health
The Cayman Islands have a variety of modern medical facilities. There are government-operated hospitals on Grand Cayman and Cayman Brac. The George Town Hospital on Grand Cayman is affiliated with the Baptist Hospital of Miami, USA, for patient referrals involving advanced care or treatment.
Life expectancy: 80 years (estimate 2003)

Fertility rate/Maternal mortality rate: Two births per woman (2003)

Birth rate/Death rate: 13 births per 1,000 population; five deaths per 1,000 population (2003).

Child (under 5 years) mortality rate (per 1,000): Nine per 1,000 live births (2003)

Main cities
George Town, on Grand Cayman (capital, estimated population 26,798 in 2005); West Bay (10,006), Bodden Town (8,084).

Languages spoken
Spoken English has a distinctive 'brogue'. The Jamaican patois and a stronger accent is also common. Spanish, particularly regional dialects of Central America and Cuba, is also spoken.

Official language/s
English

Media

Press
The private publisher Cayman Free Press (CFP) (www.caymanfreepress.com) has a variety of publications.

Dailies: There are two newspapers, The Caymanian Compass (www.caycompass.com) published by CFP and Cayman Net News (www.caymannetnews.com).

Weeklies: The New Caymanian newspaper is published on Friday. There are two TV guide publications.

Business: The Cayman Observer (www.caymanobserver.com) is a weekly publication. The Cayman Islands Yearbook and Business Directory is published yearly.

Periodicals: A free-issue tourist magazine Key to Cayman is a quarterly, Inside Out is a bi-annual home and lifestyle magazine, The Journal is a monthly general interest broadsheet; these are published by CFP. Newstar is a tourist publication.

Broadcasting

Radio: The public broadcaster is Radio Cayman (www.radiocayman.gov.ky), which has two networks, One (for news, information and music) and Two (for popular music). Private, commercial radio stations include Vibe FM (www.vibefm-cayman.com), Z99FM (www.z99.ky), Hot 106.1 (www.hot1041fm.ky), Kiss FM (www.kiss1061fm.ky) and X107.1 (www.x1071.ky).

Television: There are four commercial, free-to-air TV stations, Cayman International Television Network (CITN), called Channel 27 (www.cayman27.com.ky), transmits local, Caribbean and International news and entertainment, Cayman Television Service (CTS) with Island 24, which has evolved into a tourism information channel. There are two religious channels, CCTV and CATN.
There are four pay-to-view platforms. Digital cable providers include WestTel (www.weststartv.com) with 120 channels and CITN with 35-channels showing imported programmes. Satellite stations include Dish Direct TV with over 200 channels and Island TV.

KEY INDICATORS — Cayman Islands

	Unit	2003	2004	2005	2006	2007
Population	m	0.04	0.05	0.05	0.05	0.05
Gross domestic product (GDP)	US$bn	1.42	1.39	–	–	–
GDP per capita	US$	44,125	45,808	47,761	46,000	–
GDP real growth	%	2.0	0.9	6.5	6.5	–
Inflation	%	0.6	4.4	7.0	–	*2.8
Unemployment	%	3.6	4.3	3.5	–	–
Tourist numbers	'000	2,112.5	1,953.2	1,966.8	–	–
Exchange rate	per US$	0.82	0.82	0.85	0.85	0.85

* estimated figure

Economy

The economy is dominated by the offshore financial services sector and tourism, which are virtually the sole sources of export earnings. The Cayman Islands is dependent on imports for the bulk of its consumption and investment requirements. This level of openness renders the economy vulnerable to external pressures, such as a downturn in the US economy, while at the same time it must prepare for the devastation that frequent hurricanes typically inflict.

Nevertheless the Cayman Islands has a stable economy due to its leading place as the largest offshore banking centre in the world and second largest insurance base, after Bermuda, with assets, in 2006, worth US$20 billion. It has over 300 registered offshore banks with deposits of more than US$1 trillion, and over 73,000 registered companies.

The first Islamic compliant bond (Sukuk) issuance programme to be listed on the London Stock Exchange in January 2007, was issued by the Cayman Islands, valued at US$5 billion. The Cayman Islands has a growing reputation as a leader in Islamic finance

GDP growth in 2006 was again 6.5 per cent. In 2005 GDP had jumped to 6.5 per cent after the devestation caused by Hurrican Ivan in 2004; inflation was 7.0 per cent. The trend of unemployment has declined from a high of 7.5 per cent in 2001 to 3.5 per cent in 2005, at a time when tourist arrivals also increased.

Over 50 per cent of the workforce are expatriates and most are working in the financial industry. The Cayman Islands keeps abreast of international compliance measures for money laundering and retains its reputation for business acumen its prospects appear to be healthy.

External trade

The economy is heavily dependant on the financial services sector and tourism. A substantial deficit is traditionally run on the merchandise trade account, which is usually covered by invisible earnings and capital inflows from tourism and financial services .Trade is limited to small scale agricultural and marine production and manufactured consumer goods.

Imports

Principal imports are foodstuffs, petroleum and derivatives, machinery and transport equipment, tourist-related goods.

Main sources: US, UK, The Netherlands Antilles, Japan

Exports

Principal exports are aquaculture products including turtles and crustacean livestock and manufactured consumer goods.

Main destinations: US, Canada and other Caribbean islands.

Agriculture

Farming

Poor soil conditions and scarcity of land make agriculture uneconomic. Only about 8 per cent of the total land area is farmed. The Cayman Islands do not produce enough food to meet local demand and are reliant on imports. A National Tree Crop Husbandry Programme has increased the output of mangoes, citrus fruit and bananas. Government policies focus on sustainable development and using new technologies.

Estimated crop production in 2005 included 32 tonnes (t) yams, 33t plantains, 36t mangoes, 206t bananas, 56t citrus, 27t tomatoes, 18t cassava, 10t coconuts, 344t fruit in total, 118t vegetables in total. Livestock production included: 5t eggs, 9t honey.

Fishing

The typical annual fish catch is 125t. All spawning areas for groupers were closed for fishing for a period of eight years from 2003, in a move aimed at preserving stocks for future generations. Groupers take eight years to mature.

Industry and manufacturing

The industrial sector makes only a very small contribution to the economy; diversification is hampered by factors such as high labour costs and a shortage of labour. Activity is centred on building materials (concrete blocks and tiles) and tourist-related industries such as jewellery, printing and food processing.

Tourism

Tourism is the most important sector of the economy, accounting for around 10 per cent of GDP and employing over 13 per cent of the labour force. The majority of visitors come from the US. Most arrivals are by cruise ship. The growth in cruise ship arrivals was encouraged by government measures to relax the restriction on the number of passengers allowed to disembark and the number of ships allowed to dock. The sector was badly hit in September 2004 when Hurricane Ivan devastated the islands.

Hydrocarbons

The Cayman Islands do not produce any hydrocarbons. To supply the only public electrical utility, refined oil products, primarily diesel, are imported. Over 2,000 barrels are imported daily from refineries in the Carribean and the Gulf of Mexico. No coal or gas is imported.

Financial markets

Stock exchange

The Cayman Islands Stock Exchange (CSX) started operations in 1997 as an offshore investment market.

Banking and insurance

Under an EU tax directive introduced in 2005 in dependent EU countries, the Cayman Islands now informs all EU citizens' tax departments about the amount of money in savings accounts to allow tax to be levied from the home country while retaining a saver's anonyimity.

The Cayman Islands has also agreed to supply information on tax fraud, for criminal or civil trials, and notify EU member states about additional malpractices.

Central bank

The Cayman Islands Monetary Authority (CIMA) was established in 1997.

Main financial centre

George Town, Grand Cayman

Offshore facilities

Time

GMT minus five hours

Geography

The Cayman Islands are located in the western Caribbean, south of Cuba and north-west of Jamaica.

The three islands of Grand Cayman, Cayman Brac and Little Cayman are limestone outcroppings, the tops of a submarine mountain range called the Cayman Ridge, which extends west-south-west from the Sierra Maestra range of the south-east part of Cuba to the Misteriosa Bank near Belize. There are no rivers or streams because of the porous nature of the limestone rock. All three islands are surrounded by healthy coral reefs.

Hemisphere

Northern

Climate

Prevailing north-east trade winds; moderate, otherwise hot climate. Average temperatures 24–29 degrees Celsius. The rainy season is May–Oct, but annual rainfall is low.

Dress codes

Neat, casual, tropical attire is appropriate. Public nudity and topless bathing are strictly prohibited by law.

Entry requirements

Passports

Required by all except citizens of the UK, US and Canada with proof of citizenship (authenticated birth certificate and photographic identity document) and a return ticket (all US and Canadian nationals require a passport for re-entry to their country from January 2007).

The pink immigration slip given upon arrival should be kept with travel documents and presented when departing.

Visa

Not required by transit passengers or nationals of the EU, North America, Australasia or Japan, provided their stay does not exceed 30 days. For further

exceptions see http://cayman.com.ky/visiting/reqs.htm.
Salespeople planning to solicit business and take orders require a temporary work permit, applications should be obtained in advance from the Department of Immigration.

Currency advice/regulations
There is no restriction on import of foreign or local currency, apart from import of Jamaican dollars, which are restricted to J$20.

Customs
It is advised not to export products made from wild green sea turtles as they are illegal in most countries; farmed sea turtles may be allowed by a visitor's home country, however, the US prohibits its transshipment and will confiscate any such material.

Prohibited imports
Illegal drugs, including marijuana. Permits are necessary for firearms of any kind, including spearguns (or pole spears or Hawaiian slings), live plants and plant cuttings, raw meat and raw fruits and vegetables.

Health (for visitors)
Modern medical facilities are available, particularly on Grand Cayman and Cayman Brac. The George Town Hospital is well equipped for any diving accidents.

Mandatory precautions
None

Advisable precautions
Immunisation against typhoid, and less so TB, diphtheria and hepatitis B and C. Outbreaks of dengue fever and dengue haemorrhagic fever can occur. Hepatitis A has been reported in the northern Caribbean generally.
Tap water is safe to drink.

Hotels
There is a wide choice of hotels throughout the islands, mainly on the beach. There is a government room tax of 10 per cent and an automatic gratuity of 10 per cent of the room rate. Restaurants often add a 15 per cent gratuity to their bills.

Credit cards
Major credit cards are widely accepted.

Public holidays (national)
Fixed dates
1–2 Jan (New Year's holiday), 23 Jan (Heroes' Day), 15 May (Discovery Day), 12 Jun (Queen's Birthday), 3 Jul (Constitution Day), 31 Nov (Remembrance Day), 25–26 Dec (Christmas).
Some bank, legal and public holidays that fall on days other than Monday are moved to the following Monday. The above dates take this into account.

Variable dates
Feb/Mar (Ash Wednesday), Mar/Apr (Easter, three days).

Working hours
Banking
Mon–Thu: 0900–1600; Fri: 0900–1630.

Business
Mon–Fri: 0830–1700.

Government
Mon–Fri: 0800–1700
Post offices: Mon–Fri 0830–1530; Sat 0830–1200.

Shops
Mon–Sat: 0900–1700.

Telecommunications
Mobile/cell phones
There are 850/1900 and 900/1800 GSM services available throughout the islands.

Electricity supply
110V AC, 60Hz. American-style (flat) two-pin plugs are standard.

Getting there
Air
National airline: Cayman Airways.
International airport/s: Owen Roberts International (GCM), 3km from the centre of George Town, duty-free shop, bar, restaurant, buffet, money exchange, shops.
Other airport/s: Gerrard Smith (CYB) on Cayman Brac. Little Cayman is served by inter-island flights arriving at the Edward Bodden Airstrip.
Airport tax: Departure tax US$25

Getting about
National transport
Air: Cayman Airways operates a service from Grand Cayman to Cayman Brac. Island Air offers a four-times-a-day service between Grand Cayman and both Cayman Brac and Little Cayman.
Road: There are over 175km of road, mostly surfaced. Speed limits of 50, 40, 30, 25mph are strictly enforced. Most hotels have bicycles available for complimentary guest use.
Buses: Daily bus services start at 0600. There are regular bus services between West Bay and George Town, and between the latter and Bodden Town and East End. Mini-buses are operated by licensed operators.

City transport
Taxis: Taxis are readily available at hotels and airport. Fares are based on a fixed place-to-place tariff. Tipping optional.

Car hire
An international licence is recommended. A local permit is obtainable on production of a national licence. Traffic drives on the left. Wearing seat belts is mandatory.

BUSINESS DIRECTORY
The addresses listed below are a selection only. While World of Information makes every endeavour to check these addresses, we cannot guarantee that changes have not been made, especially to telephone numbers and area codes. We would welcome any corrections.

Telephone area codes
The international direct dialling code (IDD) for the Cayman Islands is + 1 345, followed by subscriber's number.

Useful telephone numbers
Emergency service (island-wide): 911.

Chambers of Commerce
Cayman Islands Chamber of Commerce, Harbour Centre, PO Box 1000, George Town, Grand Cayman (tel: 949-8090; fax: 949-0220; e-mail: info@caymanchamber.ky).

Banking
The Bank of Nova Scotia, PO Box 689, Grand Cayman (tel: 949-7666; fax: 949-0020).

Bank of Butterfield International (Cayman) Ltd, PO Box 705 G, Grand Cayman (tel: 949-7055; fax: 949-7761).

Barclays Bank International, PO Box 68 G, Grand Cayman (tel: 949-7300; fax: 949-7179).

Canadian Imperial Bank of Commerce and Trust Co (Cayman), PO Box 694 G, Grand Cayman (tel: 949-8666; fax: 949-7904).

The Cayman Islands Bankers' Association, PO Box 1321, Grand Cayman (tel: 949-0330).

Cayman National Bank and Trust Co, PO Box 1097, Grand Cayman (tel: 949-4655; fax: 949-7506); Galleria Branch, PO Box 1097, Grand Cayman (tel: 949-7137; fax: 949-7506).

First Home Banking, PO Box 914, Grand Cayman (tel: 949-7822; fax: 949-6064).

The Royal Bank of Canada, PO Box 245 G, Grand Cayman (tel: 949-4600; fax: 949-7396).

Swiss Bank and Trust Corporation Ltd, PO Box 852 G, Grand Cayman (tel: 949-7344; fax: 949-7308).

Central bank
Cayman Islands Monetary Authority, PO Box 10052 APO, Elizabethan Square, 80e Shedden Road, Grand Cayman (tel: 949-7089; fax: 949-2532; e-mail: cima@cimoney.com.ky).

Travel information
Cayman Airways, PO Box 1101, George Town, Grand Cayman (tel: 949-2311/8272; fax: 949-7607).

Ministry of tourism
Ministry of Tourism, Aviation and Commerce, Government Administration Building, Grand Cayman (tel: 949-7900; fax: 949-1746).

National tourist organisation offices
Cayman Islands Department of Tourism, PO Box 67, The Pavilion, Cricket Square, George Town, Grand Cayman (tel: 949-0623; fax: 949-4053; fax: 949-4053; internet sites: http://www.caymanislands.ky; http://www.divecayman.ky).

Ministries
Governor's Office, 4th Floor, Government Administration Building, Elgin Avenue, George Town, Grand Cayman (tel: 949-7900; fax: 945-4131).

Ministry of Agriculture, Environment, Communications and Works, Government Administration Building, Grand Cayman (tel: 949-7900; fax: 949-2922).

Ministry of Community Development, Sports, Women's and Youth Affairs, Government Administration Building, Grand Cayman (tel: 949-7900; fax: 949-0726).

Ministry of Education and Planning, Government Administration Building, Grand Cayman (tel: 949-7900; fax: 949-9343).

Ministry of Health, Drug Abuse, Prevention and Rehabilitation, Government Administration Building, Grand Cayman (tel: 949-7900; fax: 949-7544).

Ministry of Internal and External Affairs, Government Administration Building, Grand Cayman (tel: 949-7900; fax: 949-7544).

Ministry of Finance and Development, Government Administration Building, Grand Cayman (tel: 949-7900; fax: 949-9838).

Ministry of Legal Affairs, Government Administration Building, Grand Cayman (tel: 949-7900; fax: 949-1746).

Sports Office, Ministry of Community Development, Sports, Women's and Youth Affairs, Third Floor, Tower Building, Grand Cayman (tel: 914-3480; fax: 949-8487).

Other useful addresses
Cable and Wireless (West Indies) Ltd, PO Box 293, George Town (tel: 949-7800; fax: 949-5472).

Cayman Islands Port Authority, PO Box 1358, Georgetown, Grand Cayman (tel: 949-2055; fax: 949-5820; e-mail: info@caymanport.com).

Cayman Islands Stock Exchange, Fourth Floor, Elizabethan Square, P.O Box 2408GT, Grand Cayman (tel: 945-6060; fax: 945-6061; e-mail: csx@csx.com.ky; internet site: www.csx.com.ky).

Civil Aviation Authority, PO Box 278, George Town, Grand Cayman (tel: 949-7811).

Customs Department, PO Box 898GT, Grand Cayman (tel: 949-2473; fax: 945-1573).

Government Information Services, Broadcasting House, Grand Cayman (tel: 949-8092; fax: 949-5936).

Immigration Department (tel: 949-8344; fax: 949-8486).

Radio Cayman, PO Box 1110, George Town, Grand Cayman (tel: 949-7799).

Registrar of Companies, Ground Floor, Tower Building, Grand Cayman (tel: 949-7999; fax: 949-0969).

Other news agencies: Caribbean Net News: www.caribbeannetnews.com

Internet sites
Cayman Islands information: http://www.cayman.com.ky/cayman.htm

Cayman Net News: http://www.caymannetnews.com

Central African Republic

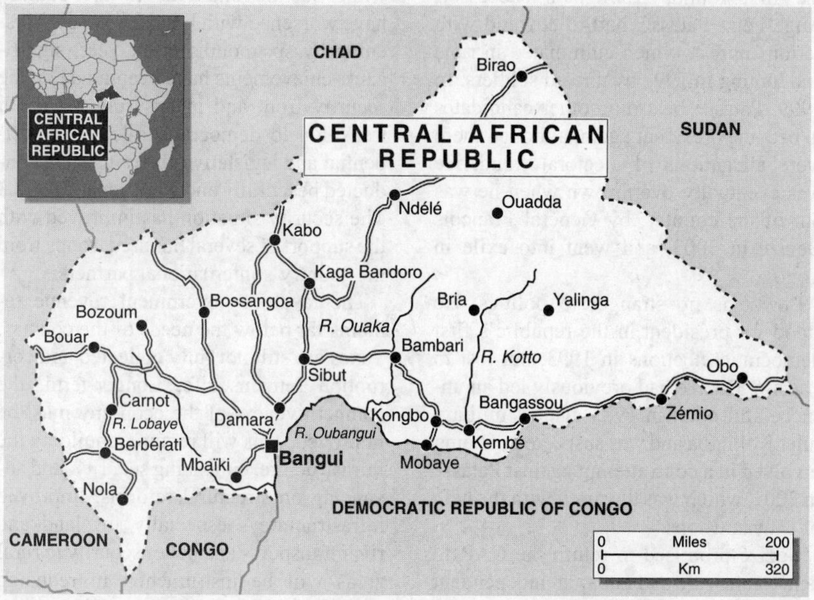

According to the 2007 assessment of the US based Heritage Foundation, the CAR is the world's 137th freest economy, ranked 32nd out of 40 countries in the sub-Saharan Africa region, with a lower than average overall score. CAR scores well in freedom from government and monetary freedom. Government expenditures are low, and state-owned businesses do not account for an exceptionally large amount of revenue. Tax revenue is not high as a percentage of GDP, but tax rates are high. Inflation is low, but the government interferes extensively with market prices. Business freedom, trade freedom, financial freedom, property rights, and freedom from corruption are weak. Regulatory procedures are burdensome, and business operations tend to be significantly hampered by the government. Labour laws are restrictive, imposing exceptionally high costs on employers. The banking system is subject to political pressure, as is the rule of law. Property rights cannot be guaranteed, and corruption is rampant. Starting a business in the CAR takes an average of 14 days, compared to the world average of 48 days. Obtaining a business licence is difficult, and even closing a business can be very difficult.

In July 2008, an International Monetary Fund (IMF) report stated that the CAR, after several years of armed conflict and deterioration in living standards, had begun a period of economic recovery and re-engagement with the international community. A two month strike of civil servants over payment of salary arrears led to the resignation of Élie Doté as prime minister on January 18. As a result a new government under Prime Minister Faustin-Archange Touadéra was appointed on 22 January. Never-the-less, the security situation was still tense in mid-2008 while the issue of salaries remained unresolved.

The presidential and legislative elections in May 2005 had brought to an end a two-year transition period in the CAR. During the transition period, slightly longer than the original two-year agreement, a new constitution was ratified (passed by referendum in December 2004), and two rounds of presidential and legislative elections were held. Most observers judged the election process to be satisfactory.

Economic performance

Real gross domestic product (GDP) growth was estimated at 4.2 per cent in 2007, slightly up from the 4.0 per cent in

KEY FACTS

Official name: République Centrafricaine (Central African Republic)

Head of State: President François Bozizé (since 2003; re-elected 8 May 2005)

Head of government: Prime Minister Faustin-Archange Touadéra (appointed 22 Jan 2008)

Ruling party: Coalition government led by the Convergence Nationale-Kwa Na Kwa (CN-KNK) (National Convergence-Kwa Na Kwa) (since 2005)

Area: 622,984 square km

Population: 4.27 million (2007)*

Capital: Bangui

Official language: French

Currency: CFA franc (CFAf) = 100 centimes (Communauté Financière Africaine (African Financial Community) franc)

Exchange rate: CFAf413.80 per US$ (Jul 2008); CFAf655.95 per euro (pegged from Jan 1999)

GDP per capita: US$402 (2007)

GDP real growth: 4.20% (2007)*

Labour force: 1.85 million (2004)

Inflation: 0.90% (2007)*

Balance of trade: US$32.00 million (2004)

Foreign debt: US$1.08 billion (2004)

* estimated figure

2006. Economic activity benefited from a recovery in diamond and timber exports. Agriculture, the largest sector of the economy, also recovered with higher yields moderating food prices and bringing inflation down to below 1 per cent in 2007.

Even so, the country remains poor despite the economic potential of it's natural resources (diamonds, gold, uranium, and timber) and favourable farming conditions. In fact, the CAR's considerable agricultural potential means that in an ideal world it would be capable of feeding itself. The majority of the population still lives off the land on subsistence plots. Vast areas of land, however, are covered by forest (a rich resource in itself) which probably deters organised, industrial scale agriculture.

Subsistence agriculture and forestry are the traditional backbone of the economy of the CAR. Timber accounts for about 16 per cent of export earnings and the diamond industry for 54 per cent, yet the agricultural sector as a whole generates half of the country's gross domestic product. There is understandable caution on the part of investors as they add to the mix the country's landlocked position, a poor transportation system, a largely unskilled work force, and a legacy of misdirected macroeconomic policies.

Political stability still to come

The CAR has been unstable since independence from France in 1960. During an internationally notorious period, self-declared emperor, Jean-Bedel Bokassa, presided over a brutal regime and pursued an extravagant lifestyle. The Bokassa era ended in 1979, when he was overthrown in a coup led by David Dacko, backed by French commandos based in the country. After just two years in office Dacko was toppled by André Kolingba, who eventually allowed multi-party presidential elections - and was duly rejected in the first round. Kolingba's successor, Ange-Félix Patassé, had to contend with serious unrest, which culminated in riots and looting in 1997 by unpaid soldiers. In 1999, Patassé beat nine other candidates to become president again, although there were allegations of electoral fraud. He was eventually overthrown when he was out of the country, by General Francois Bozizé in 2003, and went into exile in Togo.

Bozizé is no stranger to politics. He stood for president in the republic's first democratic elections in 1993, but lost to Patassé. Bozizé had previously led an unsuccessful coup in 1983 against military ruler Kolingba and was suspected of being involved in a coup attempt against Patassé in 2001, which was thwarted with the help of Libyan troops.

Bozizé promised to return the CAR to democratic rule and ran as an independent in the 2005 poll when he took more than 64 per cent of the vote in the second round of the presidential elections in May 2005, ending two years of military rule. The newly elected president called for national unity. He had pledged in his campaign to bring security to the coup-prone country.

Bozizé and his Convergence Nationale (Kwa Na Kwa) (KNK) (National Convergence) coalition now have the support of civil society groups and the main political factions, and control of a country politically and economically destroyed by three tumultuous decades of misrule - mostly by military governments - which will take years to re-establish.

However, it must be acknowledged that while social conditions in the country have worsened with life expectancy worsening by six months every year, significant achievements have been made on the security front and in ensuring a smooth transition to democratic rule. The presidential and legislative elections were conducted peacefully and were generally free. The security situation has improved with the support of several hundred troops from the country's international partners.

The level of government revenue remains far below the needs of the country. Taxes are still not fully collected and corruption remains rife. Longer-term, the competitiveness of the economy must be improved. This will require rebuilding the infrastructure, enhancing security, and advancing on structural reforms. Improved infrastructure - especially for land and river transport - and better security in rural areas will be instrumental in reducing costs faced by agricultural producers and exporters. Steps to strengthen the judiciary and improve property rights and contract enforcement should also contribute to reducing the cost of doing business in the CAR, and thereby enhancing competitiveness.

KEY INDICATORS — Central African Republic

	Unit	2003	2004	2005	2006	2007
Population	m	3.97	4.09	4,104.00	*4.19	*4.27
Gross domestic product (GDP)	US$bn	1.17	1.33	1.38	1.48	*1.71
GDP per capita	US$	306	331	335	*355	*402
GDP real growth	%	-5.8	0.9	2.2	*4.0	*4.2
Inflation	%	4.2	-2.2	2.9	6.6	*0.9
Industrial output	% change	–	2.4	2.6	–	–
Agricultural output	% change	–	-0.5	2.6	3.2	–
Exports (fob) (goods)	US$m	134.0	–	101.0	–	–
Imports (cif) (goods)	US$m	102.0	–	111.0	–	–
Balance of trade	US$m	32.0	32.0	-10.0	–	–
Current account	US$m	-60.0	-60.0	-39.0	*-49.0	-77.0
Total reserves minus gold	US$m	132.4	148.3	139.2	125.3	82.6
Foreign exchange	US$m	132.2	145.6	138.9	124.4	81.6
Exchange rate	per US$	574.89	496.63	507.22	496.60	454.40

* estimated figure

Risk assessment

Economic	Improving
Political	Improving
Regional stability	Poor

COUNTRY PROFILE

Historical profile

1889 The French established themselves at Bangui.

1907 The colony of Oubangi-Shari (named after two main rivers) was founded.

1958 The country was proclaimed a republic.

1960 David Dacko became the president of the independent and newly named country

1966 Dacko's cousin, Jean-Bedel Bokassa, an army commander, seized power, declaring himself life-president in 1972.

1977 Bokassa crowned himself emperor – the coronation consumed about one quarter of the country's annual income.

1979 Bokassa's repressive regime was forced from office when French troops reinstated David Dacko.
1981 Dacko was ousted by the army chief of staff, General André Kolingba.
1986 Kolingba established a one-party state.
1990 Opposition groups united and forced the government to adopt a multi-party system.
1992 Elections were held but the results were nullified after several groups boycotted the poll.
1993 Ange-Félix Patassé became president in the first multi-party elections.
1995 A democratic constitution was adopted.
1996 Three episodes of army mutiny erupted, the last, in November, degenerated into ethnic violence and was suppressed by French troops in January 1997.
1997 Patassé appointed Michel Gbezera-Bira at the head of an 11-party coalition government.
1998 Parliamentary elections were indecisive.
1999 Some deputies defected to Patassé's Mouvement de Libération du Peuple Centrafricain (MLPC) (Movement for the Liberation of the Central African People) and it then had a slight majority. Presidential elections confirmed support for Patassé. France withdrew its troops.
2001 Libya sent troops to protect the Patassé from military overthrow.
2002 Rebels seized part of Bangui; they were fought off by the army, aided by Libyan warplanes.
2003 General François Bozizé led a military coup that captured Bangui while President Patassé was abroad. Bozizé proclaimed himself president, suspended the constitution and dissolved the National Assembly.
2004 The National Transitional Council created an independent commission to oversee elections. A new constitution was approved in December.
2005 The Convergence Nationale (Kwa Na Kwa) (KNK) (National Convergence) coalition won the May parliamentary elections and incumbent François Bozizé was elected president. Elie Doté was named as prime minister in June
2006 For three months the president ruled by decree to address administrative problems. Rebel activity continued throughout the year, causing the president to seek French military assistance and to cut short a visit to China in November.
2007 An agreement was signed between Sudan, Chad and the Central African Republic in February whereby no shelter will be given to rebel movements from another country.
2008 On 18 January, Prime Minister Élie Doté resigned. The president appointed Faustin-Archange Touadéra as prime minister on 22 January. Jean-Pierre Bemba was arrested (in Belgium) and will face the International Criminal Court (ICC) on charges that his troops allegedly committed atrocities in the Central African Republic in 2002.

Political structure

Constitution
A new constitution was approved in December 2004.
Form of state
Republic
The executive
Under the new constitution, approved in December 2004, the presidential term has been reduced from six to five years. Presidents can only serve a maximum of two terms in office.
National legislature
The National Assembly has a five-year mandate.
Last elections
13 March/8 May 2005 (presidential and parliamentary)
Results: Presidential: incumbent François Bozizé won 64.7 per cent of the vote and Martin Ziguélé 35.3 per cent; turnout was 64.6 per cent.
Parliamentary: the Convergence Nationale 'Kwa Na Kwa') (KNK) (National Convergence 'Kwa Na Kwa') coalition won 42 seats out of 105 (including the Party for National Unity with three seats and the Movement for Democracy and Development with two), the Liberation Movement of the Central African People won 11, the Central African Democratic Rally eight, the Social Democratic Party four, the Patriotic Front for Progress two, the Alliance for Democracy two, the Londo Association one and independents 34.
Next elections
2010 (presidential and parliamentary)

Political parties

Ruling party
Coalition government led by the Convergence Nationale-Kwa Na Kwa (CN-KNK) (National Convergence-Kwa Na Kwa) (since 2005)
Main opposition party
Mouvement de Libération du Peuple Centrafricain (MLPC) (Movement for the Liberation of the Central African People)

Population
4.27 million (2007)*
Last census: December 2003: 3,151,072
Population density: Five inhabitants per square km. Urban population: 42 per cent (1995–2001).
Annual growth rate: 1.8 per cent 1994–2004 (WHO 2006)
Ethnic make-up
Bayas (34 per cent), Bandas (27 per cent), Manzas (21 per cent), Saras (10 per cent), Mbums (4 per cent), Mbakas (4 per cent)
Religions
About 24 per cent of the population hold traditional beliefs; 25 per cent Protestants; 25 per cent Catholics; 15 per cent Muslims.

Education
Only 60 per cent of eligible children receive education. Basic education lasts for 10 years divided into six years' basic first stage and four years' basic second stage. General secondary school lasts for three years, which gives access to higher education. Only 10 per cent of secondary school-aged children are enrolled due to limited resources. Technical education at the secondary level is offered at two levels. School instruction is primarily in French, but the government has sought to promote Sango literacy and encourages its use in schools.
Higher education is offered at the Université de Bangui, which also has a teacher training college.
Literacy rate: 49 per cent adult rate; 59 per cent youth rate (15–24) (Unesco 2005).
Compulsory years: Six to 14

Health
Per capita total expenditure on health (2003) was US$47; of which per capita government spending was US$18, at the international dollar rate, (WHO 2006).
Modern healthcare facilities exist only in Bangui (with one major hospital) and a few other towns.
In 2004, CAR launched a 10-year programme to reduce maternal deaths and infant mortality rates.
HIV/Aids
HIV prevalence: 13.5 per cent aged 15–49 in 2003 (World Bank)
Life expectancy: 41 years, 2004 (WHO 2006)
Fertility rate/Maternal mortality rate: 4.9 births per woman, 2004 (WHO 2006); maternal mortality 1,100 per 100,000 live births (World Bank).
Child (under 5 years) mortality rate (per 1,000): 115 per 1,000 live births; 23 per cent of children under aged five are malnourished (World Bank).
Head of population per physician: 0.08 physicians per 1,000 people, 2004 (WHO 2006)

Welfare
The country is in deep poverty, with two out of three people earning less than US$1 a day. All social security

programmes are administered by the Central African Social Security Office.

Main cities
Bangui (capital, estimated population 731,548 in 2005), Berbérati (62,319), Bouar (52,300), Carnot (66,346), Bambari (47,207).

Languages spoken
Sango, Banda, Baye and Zanda are widely spoken.
Official language/s
French

Media
Despite the repeal of press laws the resulted in criminal prosecution, journalist are still subject to harassment and imprisonment by government ministers.
National news agency: Centrafrique Presse
Other news agencies: Africa News Agency: www.africanewsagency.co.uk
APA: www.apanews.net
Panapress: www.panapress.com
Press
The press does not have a great influence due to the relatively costliness of newspapers and high levels of illiteracy.
Dailies: In the Sango-language E Le Songo is state-owned. In French, Le Confident (www.leconfident.net), is a private publication as are Le Citoyen, L'Hirondelle Le Démocrate and L'Evenementiel.
Weeklies: In French, Centrafrique Presse (www.centrafrique-presse.com) is a published newsletter, twice a week. There are several private newspapers including, Les Collines de l'Oubangui, Temps Nouveaux, and Le Centrafricain,
Periodicals: In French, Journal Officiel de la République Centrafricaine is a government publication.
Broadcasting
Radio: The state-owned Radio Centrafrique (www.radiocentrafrique.org) does not provide independent news, alternatively, Radio Ndeke Luka (www.radiondekeluka.org), a UN-sponsored station provides a balanced output and international rebroadcasts from France, UK and US.
Other radio stations and signals are provided by international organisations, including the pan-African, Radio Africa No 1 (www.africa1.com), the French Radio Nostalgie and the Roman Catholic Radio Notre Dame.
Television: Television Centrafricaine is state-run and the private, Tropic RTV, is the only other broadcaster.
News agencies
National news agency: Centrafrique Presse
Other news agencies: Africa News Agency: www.africanewsagency.co.uk
APA: www.apanews.net
Panapress: www.panapress.com

Economy
The economy is dominated by subsistence agriculture and is vulnerable to drought and domestic and regional political strife. The Central African Republic's (CAR) landlocked position and relative isolation cause considerable problems in exploiting the country's economic potential. Foreign technical and financial assistance will remain necessary for some time. Poverty is hindering development. It is estimated that two-thirds of the population live on less than US$1 a day and CAR has one of the highest rates of urban poverty in Africa. The workforce is largely unskilled and only half of the population over 15 years of age is literate. The wealth of natural resources are largely unexploited with the exception of diamonds, which account for over half of export earnings.
Serious reform is necessary to attract foreign investment. The economy would be enhanced by improved transport facilities and domestic reforms by the government. Under pressure from the World Bank and the IMF, CAR has privatised state-owned enterprises and introduced other measures to encourage investment and combat corruption.
The Communauté Economiquedes Etats de l'Afrique Centrale (CEEAC) (Economic Community of Central African States (ECCAS)), of which CAR is a member, is hoping to set up a free trade area in 2007, which should increase incentives to foreign investors as there will be immediate access to the 100 million consumers in the CEEAC trade agreement.

External trade
The Central African Republic is a member of the Economic Community of Central African States (ECCAS) and Equatorial Customs Union; import taxes and capital among member states flow freely, import duties, levied on third parties, are pooled and shared between members.
International trade is largely based on the export of diamonds (around 50 per cent of export earnings). There is a potential for a great deal more in mineral exports but a poor investment record and weak infrastructure hampers progress.
Imports
Principal imports are food, textiles, chemicals and pharmaceuticals, petroleum products, machinery, vehicles and electrical equipment.
Main sources: France (16.7 per cent total, 2005), The Netherlands (10.4 per cent), Cameroon (9.8 per cent), US (7.4 per cent)
Exports
Principal exports are diamonds and gold, coffee, timber and natural rubber, tobacco, cotton and leather.
Main destinations: Belgium (34.1 per cent total, 2005), France (9.5 per cent), Spain (8.5 per cent), Italy (7.9 per cent), China (6.9 per cent), Indonesia (6.2 per cent), Democratic Republic of Congo (4.6 per cent), US (4.4 per cent), Turkey (4.4 per cent)

Agriculture
Agriculture and forestry are the mainstays of the economy. Agriculture accounts for around 55 per cent of GDP and employs 66 per cent of the workforce. Around 12 per cent of the total land is arable; much of the rest is savannah.
The sector consists mainly of subsistence farming and animal husbandry. The main crops are maize, cassava, sorghum, groundnuts, sesame and rice. Cotton and tobacco are also cultivated. The main export crop is coffee.
Production is hampered by soil erosion, widespread drought and underdeveloped marketing and infrastructure, as well as poor internal security and mass migration.
The estimated crop production for 2005 included: 192,180 tonnes (t) cereals in total, 140,000t groundnuts (in shell), 110,000t maize, 350,000t yams, 100,000t taro, 563,000t cassava, 42,480t sorghum, 29,700t rice, 110,000t bananas, 80,000t plantains, 42,800t sesame seeds, 28,000t oil palm fruit, 27,000t pulses, 26,100t citrus fruit, 75,382t oilcrops, 90,000t sugar cane, 475t tobacco, 243,800t t fruit in total, 4,500t green coffee, 63,900t vegetables in total. Estimated livestock production included: 127,300t meat in total, 74,000t beef, 13,500t pig meat, 11,500t goat meat, 1,500t lamb, 14,000t game meat, 4,000t poultry, 1,476t eggs, 65,000t milk, 13,000t honey, 9,460t cattle hides, 1,240t goatskins.
Forestry
Forest covers 50 per cent of the country. There is significant forestry potential, including over 60 species of commercially viable trees, but it is under-exploited because of poor transport infrastructure.

Industry and manufacturing
The industrial sector typically accounts for around 18 per cent of GDP and employs 9 per cent of the workforce. Manufacturing accounts for around 9 per cent of GDP.
Manufacturing is relatively small-scale and is concentrated in the brewing, tanning, food processing, soap manufacture and textile sectors. There are also import substitution industries such as motor cycle and bicycle assembly.

The main industrial centre is the Bangui district.

Tourism

The tourist sector is under-developed, although with a wealth of natural resources, the potential, especially for eco-tourism, is considerable. Tourism is expected to contribute 3.0 per cent to the economy in 2005 and provide employment to 2.4 per cent of the workforce.

Mining

The mining sector officially accounts for around 4 per cent of GDP, employs 3 per cent of the workforce and generates 40 per cent of the country's export earnings. Smuggling is endemic and production and trade is likely to be far higher than official estimates.

Around 80,000 autonomous artisanal miners are engaged in mining production, mostly of diamonds and gold. Diamond output is around 500,000 carats per year, over half of which are gem quality. Other mineral deposits include uranium, limestone, iron ore, copper and manganese.

The Bozizé government withdrew mining licences and seized mines belonging to foreigners and figures associated with the government of former president Patassé. The measures were taken as part of an anti-corruption campaign which targetted divested interests associated with vital revenue-generating sectors.

Hydrocarbons

There are no known oil or gas fields in the Central African Republic, but exploration is being undertaken in the expectation of locating deposits. The downstream oil industry relies on imports from neighbouring African countries. Petroleum products provide around 90 per cent of the country's energy demands and the revenue from taxes on refined oil products provides over 50 per cent of the total revenue from indirect taxes.

Energy

There is a strong dependence on imported fuels.

Around 80 per cent of electricity production is generated at the country's two hydro-stations: Boali and M'Bali, a joint project with the Democratic Republic of Congo.

Banking and insurance

Central bank

Banque des Etats de l'Afrique Centrale

Main financial centre

Bangui

Time

GMT plus one hour

Geography

The Central African Republic is a land-locked country in the heart of equatorial Africa. It is bounded by Chad to the north, and Sudan to the east, by the Republic of Congo and the Democratic Republic of Congo to the south and Cameroon to the west.

Most of the land is rolling or flat plateau, apart from the rising land in the west. Around 36 per cent of the country is covered in tropical forest particularly in the south-west. Desertification in the north-east has resulted in scrubland. The Chari River runs through the centre from the east.

Hemisphere

Northern

Climate

Hot all year with temperatures up to 36 degrees Celsius. The dry season runs from November–February with cooler nights. The rainy season runs from May–October.

Entry requirements

Passports

Required by all

Visa

Visas are required by all except citizens of surrounding countries, Israel and Switzerland. Visas can be issued in neighbouring countries, generally within 24 hours but are expensive. Visas can be obtained in advance from the Central African Republic Embassy in Paris, 30 rue des Perchamps, 75116 Paris.

A business letter and itinerary must accompany the application for a business visa.

Proof of onward/return passage is required.

Currency advice/regulations

No restrictions on import of foreign currency, but amounts must be declared; export up to declared amount allowed. Unlimited import of local currency; export limited to CFAf75,000.

Health (for visitors)

Mandatory precautions

Yellow fever vaccination certificate required by all.

Advisable precautions

Typhoid, tetanus, hepatitis A and polio vaccinations are recommended. Malaria prophylaxis should be taken as risk exists throughout country. There is a rabies risk. Water precautions are necessary – bilharzia risk in some areas. AIDS risk.

Hotels

Good standard hotels are available in Bangui – limited accommodation elsewhere. Where service charge is not included in bill a 10 per cent tip is usual.

Public holidays (national)

Fixed dates

1 Jan (New Year's Day), 29 Mar (President Boganda's Remembrance Day), 1 May (Labour Day), 30 Jun (Prayer Day), 13 Aug (Independence Day), 15 Aug (Assumption Day), 1 Nov (All Saints' Day), 1 Dec (National Day), 25 Dec (Christmas Day).

Variable dates

Easter Monday

Working hours

Banking

Mon–Fri: 0730–1230.

Business

Mon–Fri: 0730–1530.

Government

Mon–Fri: 0700–1200, 1430–1700; Sat: 0700–1200.

Shops

(Mon–Sat) 0800–1200; 1600–1900.

Telecommunications

Mobile/cell phones

A GSM 900 service is available in limited areas.

Electricity supply

220/380V AC, 50 cycles

Weights and measures

Metric system

Security

Full civil control following the 2003 coup has yet to be restored. Visitors are recommended not to travel to the Central African Republic unless it is absolutely necessary. When travelling outside the capital extra precautions should be taken and advice sort from local authorities and diplomatic missions.

Getting there

Air

National airline: Air France and Sudan Airways serve CAR.

International airport/s: Bangui-M'Poko (Code: BGF), 4km from city, restaurant, post office, shops, car hire.

Getting about

National transport

Air: Small light aircraft can be chartered.

Road: Eight main roads run from Bangui to the main towns and those that are surfaced are toll roads. The Trans-African Lagos-Mombasa highway passes through the Central African Republic. Most other roads can become impassable during rainy season. NB Spare parts and petrol stations tend to be rare outside Bangui.

Buses: Limited coach service operates between Bangui and Bangassou.

Water: Large volume of freight is carried on rivers. The principal trading route is on the Oubangui River south of the capital Bangui which runs into the River Congo, connecting Bangui to the Democratic Republic of Congo and the Congo Republic (including Brazzaville, from where railway runs to Pointe-Noire). Also services from Salo on the Sangha River.

City transport
Taxis: Available in Bangui; fares by negotiation.
Car hire
Self- or chauffeur-driven cars available. International driving licence required.

BUSINESS DIRECTORY

The addresses listed below are a selection only. While World of Information makes every endeavour to check these addresses, we cannot guarantee that changes have not been made, especially to telephone numbers and area codes. We would welcome any corrections.

Telephone area codes
Dialling code for Central African Republic: IDD access code +236 followed by subscriber's number.

Chambers of Commerce
Chambre de Commerce, d'Industrie, des Mines et d'Artisinat de Centrafrique, PO Box 252/ 813, Bangui (tel: 611.668; fax: 613-561; e-mail: ccima@intnet.cf).

Chambre de d'Agriculture, d'Elevage, des Eaux, Forêts, Chasses, Pêches et du Tourisme, PO Box 850, Bangui (tel:/fax: 619-052; e-mail: denissio@intnet.cf).

Banking
Banque de Crédit Agricole et de Développement, BP 801, Place de la République, Bangui (tel: 613-200).

Banque Internationale pour le Centrafrique, BP 910, Place de la République, Bangui (tel: 610-042; fax: 616-136, 613-438).

Banque Populaire Maroco-Centrafricaine, BP 844, Rue Guerlliot, Bangui (tel: 613-190, 611-290; fax: 616-230).

Caisse Nationale d'Epargne, BP 839, Siège social, Bangui (tel: 612-296).

Commercial Bank Centrafrique SA, BP 839, Rue de Brazza, Bangui (tel: 612-990; fax: 613-454).

Central bank
Banque des États de l'Afrique Centrale, Direction Nationale, PO Box 851, Bangui (tel: 612-405; fax: 611-995; e-mail: beacbgf@beac.int).

Travel information
Inter-RCA, BP 1413, Bangui.

Ministry of Water, Forests, Wildlife, Fisheries and Tourism, Bangui.

Office Centrafricain de Tourisme (OCATOUR), BP 655, Bangui (tel: 614-566).

Ministries
Ministry of Economy and Finance, Planning and International Co-operation, Bangui (tel: 610-811).

Ministry of Energy, Mines, Geology and Water Resources, Bangui.

Ministry of Posts and Telecommunications, Bangui (tel: 612-946).

Ministry of Rural Development, Bangui (tel: 612-800).

Ministry of Trade, Industry and Small- and Medium-scale Enterprises, Bangui (tel: 614-488).

Ministry of Transport and Civil Aviation, Bangui (tel: 612-307).

Other useful addresses
Central African Republic Embassy (USA), 1618 22nd Street, NW, Washington DC 20008 (tel: 202-483-7800; fax: 202-332-9893).

European Development Fund, BP 1298, Bangui (tel: 613-053, 610-113).

Office of the President, Palais de la Renaissance, Bangui (tel: 610-323).

Société Centrafricaine de Développement Agricole (SOCADA), ave David Dacko, BP 997, Bangui (tel: 613-033).

National news agency: Centrafrique Presse
Address: (email: info@centrafrique-presse.com; internet: www.centrafrique-presse.com).

Internet sites
Africa Business Network: www.ifc.org/abn

AllAfrica.com: http://allafrica.com

African Development Bank: www.afdb.org

Africa Online: www.africaonline.com

Mbendi AfroPaedia (information on companies, countries, industries and stock exchanges in Africa): http://mbendi.co.za

Chad

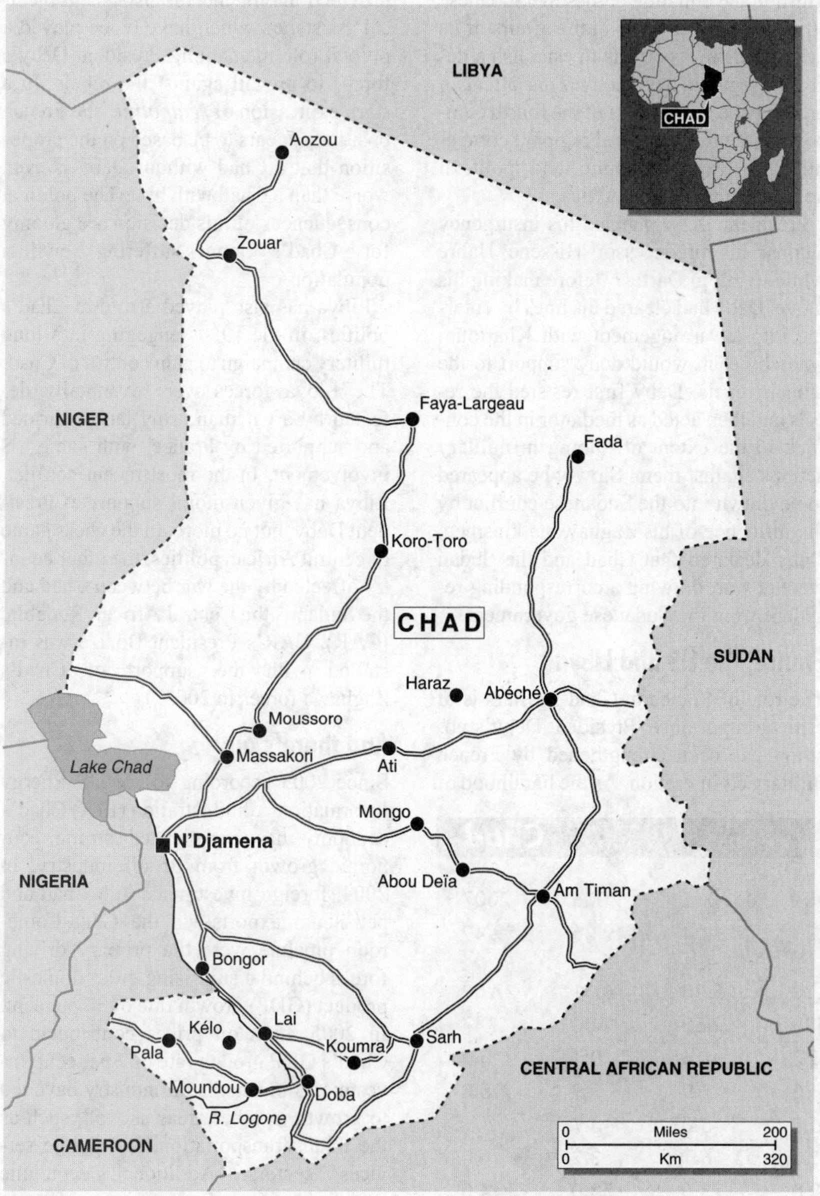

Chad can certainly claim to be one of the most unstable countries in Africa. Early 2008 saw a beleaguered President Idriss Déby fighting to defend his position as Sudanese supported rebels reached the capital city N'Djamena. Entirely land-locked, the people of Chad have never known which way to face. In the northern two thirds of the country, the wealth of the tribes traditionally came from plundering and exploiting the trans-Saharan caravans on their way to and from the Mediterranean coast. Those tribes looked north, and only used the south as a reservoir of slaves. When the French came, they concentrated on the agriculturally richer south. This ambivalence is at the heart of the perceived

KEY FACTS

Official name: République du Tchad (Republic of Chad)

Head of State: President Colonel Idriss Déby (MPS) (first elected 1996; re-elected May 2006)

Head of government: Prime Minister Youssouf Saleh Abbas (from 16 Apr 2008)

Ruling party: Mouvement Patriotique du Salut (MPS) (Patriotic Movement for Salvation) (since 1997; re-elected 2002)

Area: 1,284,000 square km

Population: 9.49 million (2007)*

Capital: N'Djamena

Official language: French and Arabic

Currency: CFA franc (CFAf) = 100 centimes (Communauté Financière Africaine (African Financial Community) franc)

Exchange rate: CFAf413.80 per US$ (Jul 2008); CFAf655.95 per euro (pegged from Jan 1999)

GDP per capita: US$747 (2007)*

GDP real growth: 0.60% (2007)*

Labour force: 4.02 million (2004)

Inflation: -8.80% (2007)*

Oil production: 144,000 bpd (2007)

Balance of trade: US$2.76 billion (2006)

Foreign debt: US$1.70 billion (2004)

* estimated figure

division of Chad into two factions, a Muslim north and an animist or Christian south. This is, of course, a simplification. Chad's divisions, be they economic, religious or political, are more numerous and more complex.

The Darfur connection

These complexities came to a head in February 2008 as the Chadian army found itself engaged in fierce fighting against rebels intent on taking N'Djamena. The rebels' stated objective was to force Chad's President Déby to step down or share power. Déby has family connections that spread across the region including with the Zaghawa ethnic group which spans Chad, Sudan and Kibya. The three armed groups at the centre of the rebellion were seeking to put into effect the Sudanese desire to cut off the support that Déby has been giving to Darfur rebels, especially the inappropriately named Justice and Equality movement. Chad's civil war has been described as a consequence of the Darfur conflict in Sudan. In reality, the opposite is more the case, as Darfur's conflict began as a spillover from Chad in the 1980s. Many of the Arab militia fighting in Darfur are of Chadian origin.

A beleaguered Déby

There are four components to the war in Chad. First, is a simple conflict for power and land inside Chad. Second, is the potential Chadian civil war that has been simmering for some time as President Déby has gathered more power around him at the expense of the civil opposition within Chad. There is some irony of this situation since, after taking power and broadening his political base in the late 1990s, President Déby subsequently reverted to one-man military rule. Like so many African rulers, M Déby treats state funds as his own and relies on a tight-knit circle of kinsmen to carry out his orders. Third in the equation comes the Sudanese strategy for interfering in the affairs of its neighbours in its efforts to establish a degree of regional hegemony. This latter can probably be seen as part of the fourth component, the more general regional competition to gain economic and political dominance in Central Africa.

President Déby planned his insurgency against his predecessor Hissène Habré while living in Darfur. Before making his move, Déby had cleared his lines by entering into an arrangement with Khartoum whereby each would deny support to the other's rebels. Déby first resisted the rebels and then acted as mediator in the conflict, to the extent of joining in military actions against them. Slowly he appeared to be drawn into the Sudanese conflict by the influence of his Zaghawana kinsmen. Déby declared that Chad and the Sudan were at war, drawing a corresponding response from the Sudanese government.

France, the US and Libya

The role of France in Chad's affairs is of critical importance. President Déby's position has been strengthened by French military co-operation. As the likelihood of the rebels achieving their objective increased, France, the former colonial power announced that it was strengthening the 1,100 strong troop force it has long had based in Chad. French involvement pre-dates Déby's arrival as president, going back to 1986 when France sent troops to Chad to provide support in the war against Libya. Since then the French have provided intelligence, logistics and medical assistance which have twice played a pivotal role in enabling President Déby's forces to prevail against the rebels. In a stark expression of *realpolitik*, the French position appears to be based on the proposition that a Chad without Déby is even worse than a Chad with him. The political consequences of this decision are gloomy for Chad's long suffering civilian population.

Libya has also played a role in Chad's politics, in the 1980s engaging in a long military campaign to gain control of Chad. The Libya forces were eventually defeated by a Chadian army largely armed and supported by France, with some US involvement. In the most recent conflict, Libya has given moral support to President Déby, but no more. In the chess game of central African politics, the other country affected by the war between Chad and the Sudan is the Central African Republic (CAR). CAR's President Bozizé was installed with the support of Chad's Zaghawa forces in 2003.

And there's oil

Since 2003 according to the US Energy Information Administration (EIA) Chad's economy has experienced strong economic growth from its oil industry. In 2004, foreign investments into Chad and petroleum exports via the Chad-Cameroon pipeline were the primary driving forces behind a surprising gross domestic product (GDP) growth rate of 30 per cent. In 2005, high oil prices contributed to Chad's GDP growth rate of 7 per cent. Investments in Chad's oil industry have led to growth in other areas as well, such as the trade, transportation, and public services sectors. Additional economic growth is expected to come from foreign investment in the new oil exploration licences that were awarded in 2007. A large question mark hangs over the future of Chad's oil industry, however, as the country risks descending into an all out civil war.

Chad only became a petroleum exporter following the inauguration of the Chad-Cameroon pipeline as recently as 2003. The industry still considers Chad to

KEY INDICATORS — Chad

	Unit	2003	2004	2005	2006	2007
Population	m	8.16	8.21	9.04	*9.26	*9.49
Gross domestic product (GDP)	US$bn	1.76	4.30	5.90	6.31	*7.09
GDP per capita	US$	216	523	653	*680	*747
GDP real growth	%	11.8	30.5	8.6	0.1	*0.6
Inflation	%	2.8	-4.8	7.9	7.9	*-8.8
Industrial output	% change	–	126.5	5.0	-3.7	–
Agricultural output	% change	–	-5.3	6.1	3.2	–
Oil output	'000 bpd	24.0	168.0	173.0	153.0	144.0
Exports (fob) (goods)	US$m	197.0	1,191.0	2,955.0	3,479.0	–
Imports (cif) (goods)	US$m	570.0	1,881.0	719.0	721.0	–
Balance of trade	US$m	-373.0	-690.0	2,236.0	2,759.0	–
Current account	US$m	-1,040.0	-760.0	176.0	485.0	*-302.0
Total reserves minus gold	US$m	187.1	221.7	225.6	625.1	955.1
Foreign exchange	US$m	186.7	221.2	225.1	624.6	954.5
Exchange rate	per US$	574.89	496.63	507.22	496.60	454.40

* estimated figure

be under-explored, and future oil discoveries could increase petroleum exports. Chad lacks refining infrastructure and relies on Cameroon and Nigeria for refined product imports. Delivery problems often leave Chad faced with refined product shortages. Chad has no known natural gas reserves.

World Bank woes

Originally seen as the answer to a maiden's prayer, in 2006 Chad's oil revenues had become something of a political hot potato following the World Bank's decision in January 2006 to withhold new loans and grants and suspend the disbursement of US$124 million International Development Association funds. Somewhat dramatically the World Bank froze Chad's account at Citibank, London, into which revenues from the transfer of oil through a pipeline to Cameroon were paid. At the heart of the spat was Chad's decision to amend its Petroleum Revenue Management Law, a decision which, said the Bank, would substantially weaken programmes intended to improve the lives of Chad's poor. The Petroleum Revenue Management Law formed the framework for an agreement, under which the Bank alleged, oil revenues intended to alleviate poverty would be diverted to address the pressing financial difficulties of the government. The Bank had previously offered to assist the government of Chad to address those difficulties by analysing the relevant financial issues and determining how public finances should be managed. The Bank had also proposed a review of how the law would be implemented.

The law had been, in the Bank's analysis, the deciding factor in its support for the Chad-Cameroon oil pipeline project, which enabled Chad to use its oil revenues to finance poverty reduction. The government had specifically undertaken not to amend or waive any provisions of the law in ways that would 'materially and adversely and affect' the direction of revenue to the agreed priority sectors such as health, education and rural development. Additionally, a Future Generations Fund ensured there would be some benefits to the population once the oil reserves were exhausted.

Faced with the demands of fighting an increasingly menacing war, the government had unilaterally added more priority sectors – essentially territorial administration and security – and simply eliminated the Future Generations Fund, allowing the transfer of more than US$36 million already accumulated there to the general budget. It also gave itself the power to add more priority sectors by decree and doubled the share of royalties and dividends that could be allocated to non-priority sectors. The Chad government drew up a medium term expenditure framework for the period 2007–09. In 2007, 70 per cent of all budgetary resources were allocated to the priority sectors. The government planned to revise the national poverty reduction strategy prepared in the early 2000s and approved by the Chadian authorities in 2003.

Risk assessment

Politics	Poor
Economy	Poor
Regional stability	Poor

COUNTRY PROFILE

Historical profile

Once described as a land of lost opportunities, this huge land-locked state with its reserves of gold, uranium and oil remains one of the world's poorest countries. Chad's post-independence governments have failed to give the country the unified platform it requires for serious economic development. Instead, Chad has been plagued with innumerable variations on the themes of civil war, human rights violations, regional conflicts, economic mismanagement and rampant corruption.

1900s France defeated the local ruler, Rabeh Zubeit, at a battle in Kousseri in 1916, and the territory of Chad was formed.

1929 A northern, Saharan, segment was added.

1946 Chad was granted status as a French overseas territory and gained its own regional assembly.

1960 Chad was granted independence. A one-party regime was imposed under President Francois Tombalbaye. A series of rebellions against Tombalbaye's rule were repressed.

1975 Tombalbaye was killed in a coup and replaced by Colonel Félix Malloum. Malloum agreed to share power with a rebel leader, Hissène Habré.

1979 Habré forced Malloum out of N'Djamena after a violent power struggle.

1980 A new alliance was formed between Habré and Goukouni Oueddei, which lasted until 1980 when Libya sided with Goukouni and Habré fled. Libyan troops and Chadian factions defeated Habré, at which point France intervened and the invading force was driven back from N'Djamena, leaving Habré in nominal control of the country.

1987 After several years of stalemate, an effort was made to resolve the conflict by President Mitterand of France and Colonel al Qadafi of Libya, who both agreed to withdraw their forces from Chad. The French troops withdrew but those of Libya did not. The French returned and pushed Libya back across the Chad-Libya border.

1989–90 A rebellion was launched by Idriss Déby, an army commander. Habré fled to Senegal and Déby proclaimed himself president.

1996 In Chad's first multi-party presidential elections, Idriss Déby was elected to remain as Chad's president.

1997 Legislative elections were won by the Mouvement Patriotique du Salut (MPS) (Patriotic Movement for Salvation).

2001 President Déby was re-elected. A peace agreement was signed in Libya between the Chadian government and the northern rebel movement, Mouvement pour la Démocratie et la Justice au Tchad (MDJT) (Movement for Democracy and Justice in Chad).

2002 The ruling MPS won the parliamentary elections. Haroun Kabadi was appointed prime minister by the president after the resignation of Nagoum Yamassoum.

2003 In January, Chad and the Central African Republic began peace talks. Moussa Faki became prime minister. Chad became an oil exporter, with the opening of a pipeline from its oil fields to Cameroon.

2004 Thousands of Sudanese refugees fleeing the unrest in the Darfur region of western Sudan arrived. Fighting between Chadian troops and pro-Sudanese government militias (Janjaweed) spilled across the border.

2005 Prime Minister Moussa Faki resigned and was replaced by Pascal Yoadimnadji.

2006 The World Bank suspended all loans to Chad due to the government intentions of steering oil revenue, originally destined for healthcare and education, to the military. Chad broke-off diplomatic relations with Sudan, following attacks on Chadian towns by Chad rebels based in the Darfur region of Sudan. An agreement was reached with the World Bank to resume loans and release oil revenue from an escrow account in return for an amount of petroleum profits being set aside for programmes for the poor. The presidential election, which were boycotted by the main opposition parties, was won by the incumbant Idriss Deby, giving him his third five-year term in office; Kassiré Coumakoye (RNDP) was runner-up.

2007 An agreement was signed between Sudan, Chad and the Central African Republic, in February, whereby no shelter will be given to rebel movements from each others countries. In February Prime

Minister Pascal Yoadimnadji died; Adoum Younousmi became interim prime minister.
2008 A state of emergency was declared on 14 February after a coup attempt on 2 February. The rebels were defeated after two days and driven back towards the border with Sudan. France admitted to helping transport weapons to the government forces under a military co-operation agreement. President Deby accused the Sudanese government of complicity, although this was denied. The president dismissed Koumakoye and appointed Youssouf Saleh Abbas as prime minister on 16 April. Former president, Hissen Habre living in exile in neighbouring Senegal, was sentenced to death in absentia, on 15 August, convicted for planning to overthrow the government.

Political structure

Constitution

A referendum in March 1996 passed (with 61.46 per cent of votes) a constitution based on the French model, providing for a unitary state.

Form of state

Republic

The executive

The executive branch consists of the president who is head of state, and the prime minister and cabinet. The president is elected by popular vote to serve a five-year term; the prime minister is appointed by the president.

National legislature

The legislature consists of a National Assembly (155 seats; members elected by popular vote to serve four-year terms).

Legal system

Based on the French civil law system and customary law.

Last elections

21 April 2002 (parliamentary); 3 May 2006 (presidential).
Results: Presidential: incumbant Idriss Deby (MPS) won his third five-year term with 64.67 of the vote, Kassiré Coumakoye (RNDP) was runner-up with 15.13 per cent. Turnout was 53.08 per cent.
Parliamentary: the ruling MPS won 113 seats out of 155; the RDP 10 seats; FAR 10 seats; Rassemblement National pour le Développement et le Progrès (RNDP) (National Development and Progress Party) five seats; Union Nationale pour la Démocratie et le Rénouveau (UNDR) (National Union for Democracy and Renewal) five seats; Union pour le Rénouveau et la Démocratie (URD) (Union for Renewal and Democracy) three seats. All other parties won one seat each; turnout was 52.4 per cent.

Next elections

2007 (parliamentary); 2011 (presidential)

Political parties

Ruling party

Mouvement Patriotique du Salut (MPS) (Patriotic Movement for Salvation) (since 1997; re-elected 2002)

Main opposition party

Rassemblement pour la Démocratie et le Progrès (RDP) (Party for Democracy and Progress) and Front des Forces d'Action pour la République (FAR) (Action Forces for the Republic Front) have equal numbers of national assembly members.

Population

9.49 million (2007)*
Last census: April 1993: 6,279,931
Population density: Six inhabitants per square km. Urban population: 24 per cent (1995–2001).
Annual growth rate: 3.3 per cent 1994–2004 (WHO 2006)

Ethnic make-up

There are 200 distinct groups of Chadeans. In the north and centre: Arabs, Gorane (Toubou, Daza, Kreda), Zaghawa, Kanembou, Ouaddai, Baguirmi, Hadjerai, Fulbe, Kotoko, Hausa, Boulala, and Maba, most of whom are Muslim; in the south: Sara (Ngambaye, Mbaye, Goulaye), Moundang, Moussei, Massa, most of whom are Christian or animist. About 1,000 French citizens live in Chad. Of the population, 48 per cent of over 15s can read and write.

Religions

Muslim (44 per cent), traditional beliefs, Christians (33 per cent).

Education

As reform in the education sector has been slow following from the period of disturbances, local communities continue to play a greater role in financing and operating their schools. To rebuild the education system, the government of Chad developed an Education-Training-Employment strategy for 1990—2000 with the help of the International Labour Organisation, and other UN development agencies.
Five national programmes were developed including basic, secondary, higher education and research, vocational training and literacy. Estimates show that the programme has trained some 2,400 teachers and 1,000 classrooms have been built.
French is the primary language of instruction in most higher education institutions. The University of N'Djamena is the country's main university, with three faculties.
Literacy rate: 46 per cent adult rate; 70 per cent youth rate (15–24) (Unesco 2005).
Enrolment rate: 73 per cent gross primary enrolment, 12 per cent gross secondary enrolments; of relevant age groups, inlcuding repeaters (World Bank).
Pupils per teacher: 67 in primary schools.

Health

Per capita total expenditure on health (2003) was US$51; of which per capita government spending was US$20, at the international dollar rate, (WHO 2006).
As one of the poorest countries in the world, Chad has the largest proportion of external resources committed to health at 62.9 per cent of all spending on healthcare.
Unicef and the Public Health Ministry began a campaign to inoculate nearly 90,000 children – half of them Sudanese refugees – against measles in the most remote areas, in 2004; their target was children aged between six months and 15 years. As well as the inoculations, staff distributed Vitamin A to children to reinforce their immune systems and protect them from blindness.

HIV/Aids

HIV prevalence: 4.8 per cent aged 15–49 in 2003 (World Bank)
Life expectancy: 46 years, 2004 (WHO 2006)
Fertility rate/Maternal mortality rate: 6.7 births per woman, 2004 (WHO 2006)
Child (under 5 years) mortality rate (per 1,000): 117 per 1,000 live births (World Bank)
Head of population per physician: 0.04 physicians per 1,000 people, 2004 (WHO 2006)

Welfare

An old age pension is paid at age 55 to workers with full contributions who pay 2 per cent of their wages. An employer pays 10 per cent of a worker's wage overall, for old age, disability and survivors' pensions. The government does not pay social security benefits. Roughly half the workforce has no jobs.
While Chad remains a traditional society, the role of women is expected to remain unchanged. Female Genital Mutilation (FGM) is practiced on 60 per cent of females, prior to puberty; and girls as young as 11 may be forced into an arranged marriage. Wives are subservient to their husbands and domestic violence is not uncommon. In 2003 a law was passed prohibiting FGM.

Main cities

N'Djamena (capital – formerly Fort Lamy – estimated population 751,288 in 2005), Moundou (140,830), Sarh (106,823), Abéché (77,296), Koumra (37,782).

Languages spoken
The language group in Chad is Afro-Asiatic; Arabic is spoken by most of the population and there are more than 50 African dialects.
Official language/s
French and Arabic

Media

Other news agencies: Afrik (French based): www.afrik.com/tchad
Africa News Agency: www.africanewsagency.co.uk
APA: www.apanews.net
Panapress: www.panapress.com
Press
Newspapers are generally considered to be independent; however they have small circulations and are not distributed much beyond urban areas.
In French, daily newspapers include Le Progres and Tchadien (www.tchadien.com), other, weekly, private newspapers includes N'Djamena Hebdo (http://www.chez.com/ndjamenahebdo), and Le Temps, Le Contact is a bi-weekly.
Broadcasting
Radio: With high levels of illiteracy, radio services are the main medium of mass communication and sources of news and information.
The government-owned, Radiodiffusion Nationale Tchadienne, operates a national and three regional stations. Private radio stations include FM Liberté, owned by international human rights groups, Dja FM and Al Nassr are privately owned and La Voix du Paysan and Radio Arc-en-ciel are Roman Catholic stations.
Television: In Arabic and French, the only television station is the state-owned Téléchad, which favours the government.
News agencies
Other news agencies: Afrik (French based): www.afrik.com/tchad
Africa News Agency: www.africanewsagency.co.uk
APA: www.apanews.net
Panapress: www.panapress.com

Economy

Chad is one of the poorest countries in the world, it is landlocked with a low population density in a largely desert terrain. It has suffered civil war and long-term economic instability and slow development since independence in 1960. Development investment, in one of Africa's smallest oil fields began in 2001 and production began in 2003, with the completion of the Doba oil pipeline (allowing Chad to export its oil production via Cameroon). Despite production predicted to peak at 225,000 barrels per day (bpd), the country will remain dependent on imports of refined petroleum products as there are no refineries.
Most of the population still depends on agricultural production for a living and is therefore vulnerable to external shocks: cotton prices, the principal export, fluctuate while there have been droughts in 2004 and 2006 which decimated the national cattle herd. The agricultural sector, which until 2003 accounted for the bulk of GDP, employment and export earnings, was hit by adverse weather conditions in 2002–03, leading to a down turn in cotton output. Then in 2004 a plague of locusts destroyed large areas of maize, millet and sorghum.
In 2005, GDP growth was 5.6 per cent with an estimated rate of 7.0 per cent for 2006; inflation was 7.9 per cent in 2005 and an estimated 4.0 per cent in 2006. Oil production was 173,000bpd in 2005, providing around 50 per cent of GDP.
The economy has been undergoing a programme of liberalisation under the auspices of the IMF's Poverty Reduction and Growth Facility (PRGF). This has been coupled with debt service relief under an enhanced Heavily Indebted Poor Countries (HIPC) initiative. The government has privatised public enterprises, aimed at securing macroeconomic stability and strengthening its fiscal position. Chad in 2005 was one of the fastest growing economies in the world, albeit from a very low base; per capita income, at around US$200, was one of the lowest in the world during 2000–01, but had increased to US$603 by 2005.

External trade

Chad is a member of the Economic and Monetary Union of Central Africa (Cemac) which has free borders to all members and imposes common external tariffs from third parties. As a member of Cemac it has a common currency with other members.
Imports
Principal imports are machinery and transport equipment, industrial goods, petroleum products, foodstuffs and textiles.
Main sources: France (21.1 per cent total, 2005), Cameroon (15.5 per cent), US (12.1 per cent), Belgium (6.8 per cent), Portugal (4.6 per cent), Saudi Arabia (4.3 per cent), The Netherlands (4.1 per cent)
Exports
Principal exports are oil, raw cotton, fish, meat and cattle, hides, sodium carbonate, ground nuts, gum arabic and resins.
Main destinations: US (78.1 per cent total, 2005), China (9.9 per cent), Taiwan (4.1 per cent)

Agriculture

Farming
The agricultural sector forms the mainstay of the economy, accounting for around 40 per cent of GDP and 60 per cent of employment. Around 20 per cent of land is arable and most of this is the southern flood plains of the Logone and Chari rivers.
Rice is produced on the irrigated land along the banks of the Oubangi river north of Lake Chad. Subsistence farming and livestock predominate in the north. The country's main food crops are sorghum, millet, dry beans, sesame, potatoes, rice and maize. Cash crops include oil seeds (groundnuts and sesame), sugar cane and tobacco. Cotton is the most important agricultural product.
Cattle farming involves nearly 40 per cent of the population. It contributes 39 per cent to total agricultural production and 20 per cent to Chad's GDP. About 90 per cent of beef production is exported to Nigeria.
In 2004 the worst locust plague for 15 years attacked crops across much of west Africa and the Sahel region of southern Sahara. The UN organised a nine-country response group with Morocco and Algeria sending aid of vehicles and pesticide but, a year after the warning was first given, it was estimated that only 3 per cent of the 4.3 million hectares that required spraying were treated. Mauritania is the hatching ground for the largest swarms, although the insects are breeding elsewhere in the region.
Estimated crop production for 2005 included 1,212,000 tonnes (t) cereals in total, 450,000t groundnuts in shell, 325,000t cassava, 297,529t millet, 107,422t maize, 230,000t yams, 449,427t sorghum, 91,083t rice, 121,000t pulses, 684,000t roots and tubers, 176,530t oilcrops, 366,000t sugar cane, 64,000t sweet potatoes, 233,000t seed cotton, 81,500t cotton lint, 113,000t fruit in total, 95,000t vegetables in total. Estimated livestock production included 127,293t meat in total, 80,600t beef, 481t pig meat, 13,564t lamb, 21,876t goat meat, 3,200t game meat, 1,395t camel meat, 4,900t poultry, 4,680t eggs, 238,309t milk, 960t honey, 14,690t cattle hides, 2,286t sheepskins.

Industry and manufacturing

The industrial sector contributes around 15 per cent of GDP and employs 10 per cent of the workforce.
The sector is small-scale and underdeveloped. Activity is centred in N'Djamena, Moundou and Sarh and is based on agriculture, particularly food processing, textiles, brewing, tobacco processing, leather and construction materials.

Tourism

Tourist arrivals increased by 10.26 per cent in 2003, compared to 2002. The World Travel and Tourism Council forecast in 2004 that tourism will grow at an annualised rate of 7.70 per cent over the period 2005–14.

Mining
Mining contributes less than 3 per cent to GDP. The only minerals extracted in any quantities are soda and rock salt (which are exported mainly to Nigeria) and natron from Lake Chad (used in preservation of meat and in tanning).
Known deposits of chromium, tungsten, titanium, iron, wolfram, gold, uranium and tin remain unexploited.
Other mineral deposits are thought to lie in the disputed Aouzou Strip along the Libyan border.

Hydrocarbons
West Africa is one of the world's fastest growing oil regions. It is projected that 25 per cent of US oil imports will be from this region by 2010. The development of Chad's oil industry is the subject of intense debate, although it could hold the key to the country's development. Chad has proven oil reserves of one billion barrels, most of which is located in the Doba basin.
In 1996, a consortium (Exxon Mobil (40 per cent), Royal Dutch/Shell (40 per cent), Elf Aquitaine (20 per cent)) signed a memorandum of understanding (MOU) with the government to develop the Doba fields and construct a 1,070km pipeline to offshore facilities in Cameroon. Chevron and Petronas replaced TotalFinaElf and Royal Dutch/Shell in the consortium. Both the development of the oil fields and the construction of the pipeline have been the subject of political wrangling. While politicians squabble over oil revenues, organisations involved in environmental protection and human rights have criticised the Chad-Cameroon pipeline. The World Bank (which provided US$200 million for the US$3.70 billion project) initially hailed the project as a model of poverty alleviation in Africa. According to its critics, however, the Doba development increased regional problems, particularly in relation to conflict and corruption. Oil production is typically 40,000 barrels per day (bpd). Chad started exporting oil with the opening of the pipeline connecting its oil fields with Cameroon.
Chad's upstream oil industry is entirely reliant on imports of refined oil products from Nigeria and Cameroon. All energy requirements are fuelled by petroleum, athough currently Chad has no refinery. There are plans to build a small refinery in N'Djamena to process the oil from Sedigi in the Lake Chad Basin. The upfield oil industry is regulated by the Ministry of Mines, Energy and Oil.
Chad is not known to have either natural gas or coal reserves.

Energy
Chad has an installed electricity generation capacity of 29MW with electricity generation of 90 million kWh. Only 2 per cent of the population have access to electricity. The electricity supply is provided by two power stations in N'Djamena and plants in Moundou, Sarh and Abéché. Imports from Nigeria and Cameroon provide most of Chad's power requirements.
The Société Tchadienne d'Eau et d'Électricité (STEE) is the company responsible for electricity generation and supply in Chad. STEE is scheduled for privatisation under the terms of the country's IMF structural adjustment programme.

Banking and insurance
The banking sector was fully privatised in 1999. The two main banks in Chad are the Banque Internationale de l'Afrique au Tchad (BIAT) and the Société Générale de Banque Tchadienne (SGBT).
Central bank
Banque des Etats de l'Afrique Centrale.
Main financial centre
N'Djamena

Time
GMT plus one hour

Geography
Chad is a landlocked country in north and central Africa, bordered in the north by Libya, the east by Sudan, the south by the Central African Republic, the south-west by Cameroon, to the west by Nigeria and the north-west by Niger.
Lake Chad is a large body of freshwater that forms part of the border in the south-west and is fed largely by the Chari River.
There are tropical forests in the south and the Sahara desert stretches across the north, which includes Ennedi and Tibesti volcanic mountain ranges.
Hemisphere
Northern

Climate
Hot and arid in northern desert regions, and wet and tropical in the south. Southern rainy season from May to October, central rainy season from June to September with temperatures ranging from 20 degrees Celsius (C) at night to as high as 40 degrees C during the day. Dry season throughout the rest of the year, lower evening temperatures.

Entry requirements
Passports
Required by all except nationals of certain African countries. Passports must be valid for six months after date of visit.
Visa
Required by all, except a number of nationals of West and Central Africa.
Ordinary visas are issued for both business and tourist purposes, valid for one month. Apply at either a Chadian consulate or a French consulate.
All visitors must register with authorities on arrival. Exit permits must also be obtained if leaving via Niger or Sudan.
Currency advice/regulations
The import and export of CFA francs from outside the African Financial Community is limited to CFAf10,000; import of CFA francs from inside the community is unlimited. There is unlimited import of foreign currency but it must be declared on arrival; export of foreign currency is limited to declared amount.
To avoid extra exchange fees US dollars or euros are preferred.

Health (for visitors)
Mandatory precautions
Yellow fever vaccination certificate required if arriving from an infected area.
Advisable precautions
Hepatitis A, tetanus, typhoid and polio vaccinations. Malaria prophylaxis recommended as risk exists throughout the country. There is a rabies risk. Water precautions necessary outside the capital.

Hotels
Reservations should be made well in advance of visit. If service charge is not included in bill a 10 per cent tip is usual. Limited availability outside of N'Djamena.

Public holidays (national)
Fixed dates
1 Jan (New Year's Day), 13 Apr (National Day), 1 May (Labour Day), 25 May (Africa Day), 11 Aug (Independence Day), 1 Nov (All Saints' Day), 28 Nov (Proclamation of the Republic), 1 Dec (Day of Liberty and Democracy), 25 Dec (Christmas Day).
Variable dates
Easter Monday, Eid al Adha, Eid al Fitr.
Islamic year – 1429 (10 Jan 2008–28 Dec 2008): The Islamic year contains 354 or 355 days, with the result that Muslim feasts advance by 10–12 days against the Gregorian calendar. Dates of feasts vary according to the sighting of the new moon, so cannot be forecast exactly.

Working hours
Banking
Mon–Thu and Sat: 0700–1300; Fri: 0700–1030.
Business
Mon–Sat: 0900–1230, 1600–1930.
Government
Mon–Thu and Sat: 0700–1400; Fri: 0700–1200. Specific times vary within this period.
Shops
Tue–Sat: 0900–1200; 1600–1930.

Telecommunications

Mobile/cell phones

GSM 900 services are available in populated areas only.

Electricity supply

220V AC, 50 cycles

Getting there

Air

National airline: Government owned Air Tchad provides only domestic flights. International flights are best provided by Air France.

International airport/s: N'Djamena (NDJ), 4km from city. Facilities include a post office, refreshments, bar, duty-free and car hire.

Airport tax: CFAf5,000 (tourist tax) and CFAf3,000 (security tax), except transit passengers continuing their journey within 24 hours.

Surface

Road: Access is possible via Sarh (Central African Republic), Bongor and Maroua (Cameroon). There is a paved road through the province of Kanem to Ngiugmi in Niger – the road runs to the Nigerian border.

Road conditions are variable and access can be very difficult, especially in the rainy season; driving is best undertaken between November and May.

It is dangerous to drive in the border region of Chad and Sudan, due to the situation in Darfur, Sudan.

Water: The main overland points of entry by ferry are via the Logone River (Cameroon) and Lake Chad (Nigeria).

Getting about

National transport

Air: Restricted domestic service operated by Air Tchad. Scheduled services occasionally commandeered by armed forces.

Road: Permits and four-wheel drive vehicles are required for all travel outside N'Djamena. Conditions are arduous, there are no emergency services; rest houses and petrol stations are not widely available. The government restricts travel in the central and northern territories. It is advisable to travel in convoy.

There are surfaced roads around N'Djamena; most other roads are not in good condition and are often impassable during rainy season (Jun–Oct).

City transport

Taxis: Available in N'Djamena and the principal towns – Sarh and Moundou; set-fare system in operation; 10 per cent tip is usual; can be hired on a time basis or by the day.

Car hire

Availablity is limited to N'Djaména only. French or international driving licence is required as well as a autorisation de circuler.

BUSINESS DIRECTORY

The addresses listed below are a selection only. While World of Information makes every endeavour to check these addresses, we cannot guarantee that changes have not been made, especially to telephone numbers and area codes. We would welcome any corrections.

Telephone area codes

The international dialling code (IDD) for Chad is + 235 followed by subscriber's number.

Chambers of Commerce

Chad Chamber of Commerce, Industry, Agriculture, Mines and Handicrafts, PO Box 458, N'Djamena (tel: 525-264; fax: 521-452; e-mail: cciamat@hotmail.com).

Banking

Banque Agricole du Soudan au Tchad, BP 1727, 1727 N'Djamena (tel: 519-041, 519-042; fax: 519-040).

Banque Commerciale du Chari Tchad, BP 757, N'Djamena (tel: 515-958, 515-231; fax: 516-249).

Banque de Développement du Tchad, BP 19, N'Djamena (tel: 522-829, 523-284; fax: 523-318).

Banque Internationale pour l'Afrique au Tchad, BP 87, Ave Charles de Gaulle, N'Djamena (tel: 525-684, 524-321; fax: 523-053, 522-345).

Banque Tchadienne de Crédit et de Dépôts, BP 461, N'Djamena (tel: 524-203, 522-801, 524-195; fax: 523-713).

Financial Bank, BP 804, N'Djamena (tel: 523-389, 522-660; fax: 522-905).

Central bank

Banque des États de l'Afrique Centrale, Direction Nationale, PO Box 50, N'Djamena (tel: 525-014; fax: 524-487; e-mail: beacndj@beac.int).

Banque des États de l'Afrique Centrale, (headquarters), 736 Ave Monseigneur Vogt, 1917 Yaoundé, Cameroon (tel: +237 223-4030/4060; fax: (+237) 223-3329/3350; email: beac@beac.int

Travel information

Air Tchad, 27 Avenue du Président Tombalbaye, BP 168, N'Djamena (tel: 515-090, 513-581, 514-564).

Direction du Tourisme, BP 86, N'Djamena (tel: 515-032, 512-303, 512-305).

Ethiopian Airlines, BP 989, N'Djamena (tel: 513-027, 513-143).

Sudan Airways, BP 167, N'Djamena (tel: 515-148).

National tourist organisation offices

Direction du Tourisme, BP 86, N'Dajmena (tel: 524-416; fax: 524 419).

Other useful addresses

Chad Embassy (USA), 2002 R Street, NW, Washington DC 20009 (tel: 202-462-4009; fax: 202-265-1937; e-mail: info@chadembassy.org; internet: www.chadembassy.org).

Chambre Consulaire du Tchad, BP 458, N'Djamena (tel: 515-264).

Commission for Trade and Industry, BP 453, N'Djamena (tel: 515-656).

European Development Fund, BP 532, N'Djamena (tel: 515-977, 512-276).

Office National des Céréales (ONC), BP 21, N'Djamena (tel: 513-731, 574-014).

Internet sites

Africa Business Network: www.ifc.org/abn

AllAfrica.com: http://allafrica.com

African Development Bank: www.afdb.org

Africa Online: www.africaonline.com

Chad: www.tchadrepertoire.com

Mbendi AfroPaedia (information on companies, countries, industries and stock exchanges in Africa): http://mbendi.co.za

Chile

KEY FACTS

Official name: República de Chile (Republic of Chile)

Head of State: President Verónica Michelle Bachelet Jeria (took office 11 Mar 2006)

Head of government: President Verónica Michelle Bachelet Jeria (since 11 Mar 2006)

Ruling party: Concertación de Partidos por la Democracia (Concertación) (Coalition of Pro-Democracy Parties) (centre-left coalition, comprising the Partido Demócrata Christiano (PDC) (Christian Democratic Party), Partido por la Democracia (PPD) (Party for Democracy), Partido Socialista (PS) (Socialist Party), Partido Radical Social Demócrata (PRSD) (Social Democratic Radical Party) and independents (since 1989; re-elected Dec 2005)

Area: 756,626 square km

Population: 16.58 million (2007)*

Capital: Santiago

Official language: Spanish

Currency: Chilean peso (CH$) = 100 centavos

Exchange rate: CH$493.47 per US$ (Jul 2008)

GDP per capita: US$8,903 (2006)

GDP real growth: 5.00% (2007)*

Labour force: 6.76 million (2004)

Unemployment: 8.50% (2004)

Inflation: 3.10% (2005)

Balance of trade: US$10.18 billion (2005)

Foreign debt: US$44.60 billion (2004)

Visitor numbers: 2.28 million (2006)*

Annual FDI: US$7.60 billion (2004)

* estimated figure

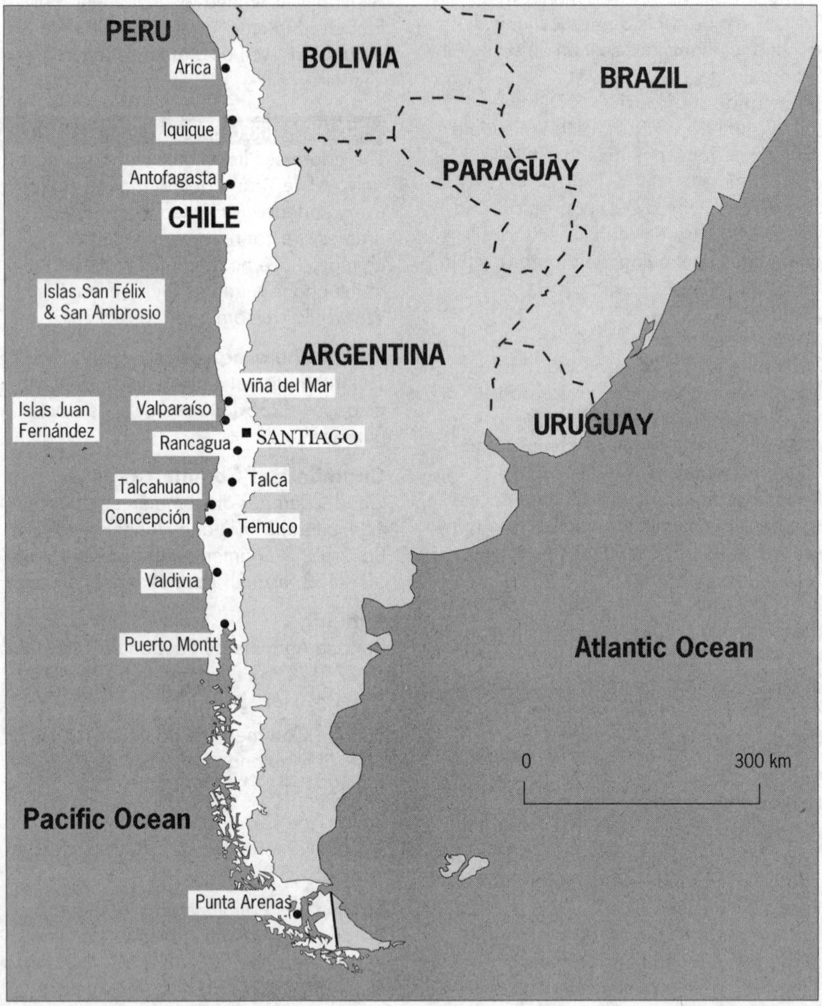

With its abundance of natural resources and variety of climates, Chile has a lot going for it: it possesses about a quarter of the world's known copper reserves, not to mention iron ore, nitrates, lithium, molybdenum, silver and gold. Its 4,000km coastline is rich in fish and all kinds of seafood. The snow-capped Andes provide abundant supplies of water and have a large hydro-electric potential. Chile's south is covered by rich forests and the dry central region is ideal for tropical fruits as well as more traditional crops and livestock-raising. Non-traditional exports such as citrus fruits, vegetables and wine now form a major part of Chile's exports. Economically, Chile in 2008 could hardly be more different from the lame-duck republic of the early 1970s.

Lots of pain…

Until 1973, the main characteristic of the Chilean economy was its inward-looking growth, based on an import substitution programme proposed by the economists of the United Nations Economic Commission for Latin America and the Caribbean (ECLAC). Chile had been devoted to industrialisation at any cost, protected by high tariff barriers that either eliminated or barred any foreign competition. This brand of protectionism helped build a local industry, but also built high levels of inefficiency and distorted resource allocation. Pricing became an area of conflict between businessmen and officials. The liberalisation of the economy and the cuts in public expenditure introduced by the military government led to high levels of inflation and sharp drops in levels of personal income.

...and the beginnings of gain

The recession that followed coincided with one of the earlier international oil crises, driving local industry to seek foreign markets and increase its productivity. The outcome, as expected by some, but discounted by many, was a growth of exports, particularly of non traditional products. Export earnings doubled in little more than five years as Chile began its retreat from the planned economy and allowed market forces to prevail in a way that not even the UK's Mrs Thatcher could have thought possible. Steadily the country's industrial and economic structure changed. While some branches of the economy such as agriculture, viticulture and horticulture expanded rapidly, others simply vanished.

Bumbling Bachelet

As countries go, the Chilean presidency would seem to be a lot less challenging a position than most. On taking office as Chile's first female president, Verónica Michelle Bachelet looked like being be a new breed of Latin American politician, ready to lead a 'citizens' democracy'. Her first cabinet had only two ministers with previous experience. In a rather contrived arrangement, half of the cabinet were women. Some reshuffles later, in January 2007, President Bachelet unveiled her latest team, one full of party hacks. That is not to denigrate Bachelet's achievements, such as her agreement on education reform, new child-care centres and wider health care. But she has somehow struck a mediocre note, and like so many presidents (not just in Latin America it might be added) is much less popular than she was. Chile's economy no longer outperforms its neighbours, despite the record copper prices of 2007 and 2008. Bachelet has been blamed for the inadequacies of a new transport scheme in Santiago, designed under her predecessor, that has been a disaster. But, á la Sarkozy, she has interfered too often, and has preferred the advice of a small kitchen cabinet to that of her ministers.

Looking for a fresh start, Ms Bachelet had finally opted for a ministerial re-shuffle when her hand was forced by the resignation of the interior minister. The replacement, Edmundo Pérez Yoma, does not mince his words and as defence minister in the 1990s oversaw the contentious departure as army commander of Chile's former president General Augusto Pinochet. Pérez Yoma is expected to act as a *de facto* prime minister – if the president lets him. The changes have weakened the position of Andrés Velasco, Chile's finance minister. Sr Pérez Yoma has often criticised him. Following the re-shuffle, the ruling Concertación coalition lost its majority in Congress. Municipal elections are due in October 2008, effectively marking the beginning of the run up to the next parliamentary elections in December 2009.

Prosperity's people

By the beginnings of the 21st century, Chile's population had become economically mature, with bus drivers telephoning their brokers on mobile telephones and housewives ordering clothes on-line. Poverty has fallen further, faster, in Chile than anywhere else in Latin America. Sustained economic growth and job creation since the mid-1980s are the main explanations, though it helps that poorer Chileans are having fewer children than in the past. In recent years public policies, such as *Chile Solidario*, have played a bigger role. In the 1990s poverty dropped by half a percentage point for each point of economic growth, but now it falls by one-and-a-half points, according to Clarisa Hardy, the planning minister.

An August 2007 article in the London based *Economist* magazine suggested that Chile has a real chance of eliminating poverty. According to the article, some Chileans argue that the national poverty line, of US$90 a month, is set too low. Income distribution in Chile is becoming slightly less unequal. The richest tenth of the population still take 38.6 per cent of national income, slightly less than they take in the United States. Using the relative yardstick favoured in many European countries, 27 per cent of Chileans would be poor, according to Juan Carlos Feres of ECLAC. The fact that alternative ways of measuring poverty are now being discussed is a sign of how far Chile has come in the past two decades. It is also an indication of the tasks that still lie ahead in creating a middle-class society.

Chileans have certainly become politically mature, having followed the transition to democracy well aware of its limitations: the constraints of the constitution, the unmissable presence of a competent and ambitious – if no longer sabre rattling – military, less than impartial judges and a lingering fear that the political parties still sympathetic to the military might continue to gain favour. Despite these concerns, it is hard to see any massive demand for change or confrontation. Much of the credit for this benign political horizon goes to the political canniness of Chile's presidents and their advisors. Today, the objective conditions for a military coup have simply disappeared. Chile is now a very different country.

KEY INDICATORS — Chile

	Unit	2003	2004	2005	2006	2007
Population	m	15.34	15.48	16.18	16.38	*16.58
Gross domestic product (GDP)	US$bn	72.40	94.91	118.99	145.21	*163.79
GDP per capita	US$	4,408	5,856	7,351	8,903	–
GDP real growth	%	3.3	6.0	5.7	4.0	*5.0
Inflation	%	3.4	1.1	3.1	*3.4	4.4
Industrial output	% change	–	15.6	18.2	2.7	–
Agricultural output	% change	–	9.6	3.8	3.5	–
Exports (fob) (goods)	US$m	19,898.0	32,025.0	40,574.0	58,485.0	67,644.0
Imports (cif) (goods)	US$m	18,009.0	23,006.0	30,394.0	35,899.0	43,991.0
Balance of trade	US$m	1,889.0	9,019.0	10,180.0	22,587.0	23,653.0
Current account	US$m	-1,130.0	1,390.0	703.0	5,256.0	6,050.0
Total reserves minus gold	US$m	15,839.6	15,993.8	16,929.2	19,392.0	16,386.8
Foreign exchange	US$m	15,211.0	15,495.4	16,689.1	19,224.9	16,695.3
Exchange rate	per US$	652.95	609.36	539.90	527.68	498.75

* estimated figure

Pokemones, Punks and Ponceando

And how! In 2008, the economic maturity of Chilean's electorate had begun to express itself through the behaviour of its children. If there was any national debate, it was no longer about the behaviour of General Pinochet and his entourage, and certainly not about the economic theories of the 'Chicago Boys' that had characterised the 1970s and 1980s. The subject of national debate in 2008 was what many Chileans saw as the affront to their traditional values constituted by the behaviour of the Pokemones, Chile's apparently amoral, androgynous teenagers. The Pokemon phenomenon, at least in this particular form and expression, appears to be uniquely Chilean. Chile's still conservative Catholic society found it hard to take these radical teenagers in their stride. A *Newsweek* article suggested that (possibly akin to their 'punk' predecessors, what united the Pokemones was not politics or religion, but simply the anger and opposition their wildly liberal behaviour generated among their parents. The Pokemones were described in *Newsweek* as the 'darlings of a booming neo-liberal economy, which has provided them with all the material accoutrements necessary to be Pokemones'. The *Newsweek* journalist claimed that these hedonistic teenagers' sexual rebellion was not their only defining characteristic; these-high fashion, gadget-conscious rebels without a cause were also defined by their consumerism, a characteristic which 'neatly conforms to Chile's free-market ideals'.

Weathering the sub-prime storm

As turmoil continued to engulf the world's financial markets in early 2008, those free market ideals seemed to stand Chile in good stead, as its money and fixed income markets appeared to be less affected than most by the 'sub-prime' crisis. Whatever volatility that there was in Chilean markets was largely attributable to domestic rather than external factors. The Chilean stock market may have been an exception, showing some degree of increased volatility. The Chilean peso, however, continued to appreciate against the US dollar, in line with what had become a worldwide trend of depreciation.

Although growth in household consumer loans decelerated substantially in early 2008, this was mainly in bank consumer credits. Retailer credits, in contrast, increased, offsetting the overall reduction in bank credits. The Banco Central de Chile (central bank) (Bank of Chile) in its Monetary Policy Report on the first quarter of 2008 said that Chile's macroeconomic policy framework, combined with the Chilean banks' capital position and the generally healthy levels of external solvency and liquidity of the Chilean economy would enable the more restrictive global financial conditions to be accommodated.

According to the Bank of Chile, the level of annual consumer price inflation (CPI) continued to rise in the first quarter of 2008, although at a slower rate than had been expected at the beginning of the year. In fact, Chile's inflation began to decline in April 2008, a process that was expected to continue over the rest of the year. Controlling inflation is the principal focus and the major contribution of the Bank of Chile to the economy, with the policy objective of driving annual inflation below an annual 3 per cent within two years. How realistic this objective is remains to be seen; annual inflation reached 8.3 per cent in April 2008, well above the target level. This largely reflected further increases in food prices; fuel price increases were to some degree mitigated by the application of tax rebates. Encouragingly, the so called 'propagation' of specifically high inflation rates to other prices in the economy in the first quarter turned out to be less than forecast at the beginning of the year. None the less, many household incomes had suffered from food and energy price increases, as had major energy users and the electricity generation sector. The overall increase in energy costs also affected productivity levels. Inflation continues to be a raw nerve in Chile's make-up. Quite apart from macro-economic considerations, an essential element of Chile's inflation target regime is that of maintaining public confidence in the country's commitment to low inflation as an objective.

Growth falters

The Bank of Chile's report considered that the most likely scenario for 2008 included a diminished rate of growth for the economy. The continued negative effects of increased energy costs were expected to depress manufacturing output. As global growth prospects deteriorated, the risks inherent in the external sector increased proportionately, causing the Bank of Chile to undertake a programme of intervention in the foreign exchange markets to bolster Chile's international liquidity. In practical terms, these measures were designed to increase Chile's reserves by US$8 billion over a period of eight months, prudently providing a cushion against any further deterioration in the world economy.

Forecasts put Chile's annual gross domestic product (GDP) growth for 2008 at between 4 and 5 per cent, with a modest improvement expected in 2009. In 2007 GDP growth was estimated at 5.3 per cent, well up on the 4 per cent recorded in 2006. Investment rose by an impressive 12 per cent; this was complemented by strong export growth due to high international demand for Chile's main exports. Private consumption also increased, and public consumption was up by 8.5 per cent. The external price index (EPI) in US$ dollars relevant to the Chilean economy increased from an annualised rate of 8 per cent in 2007 to over 15 per cent in the first quarter of 2008. The forecast for EPI for the whole of 2008 is 12 per cent, well up on the 7 per cent originally forecast in January 2007. Commodity prices continued to rise in 2008; the price of copper was expected to average US$3.5 per pound for the year, probably dropping to US$3 per pound in 2009. Forecasts for oil prices inevitable looked seriously low by the end of the first quarter.

Chile's fiscal policy continued to target a structural surplus set at one per cent of GDP for 2007, but lowered to 0.5 per cent in 2008. The third quarter of 2007 saw the lowest unemployment rates for a decade; unemployment was expected to average 7 per cent in 2007, down on the 7.5 per cent recorded in 2006. For the first six months of 2007, exports showed an annual growth rate of 13.6 per cent, outdone by a 17.5 per cent increase in imports, mostly due to imports of capital goods. The state-owned copper production corporation Corporación Nacional del Cobre de Chile (Codelco) is the world's largest copper producing company, as well as the largest company in Chile. Copper and other minerals are the mainstay of Chile's international trade; this is not to discount the importance of the non-traditional exports, which has become increasingly significant since the economic *choque* of the early 1980s. Chile is an associate member of the Common Market of the Southern Cone (Mercosur) and full member of the Asia-Pacific Economic Co-operation (Apec) organisation. Chile is a member of a number of free trade agreements (FTAs) with various countries, such as Canada, Mexico, South Korea, the United States and the European Union. The FTA with the United States entered into force in January 2004 and is planned to lead to full trade liberalisation within 12 years.

The gas is turned off

Unlike many of its neighbours, Chile has limited domestic energy resources. As a result, the country is heavily dependent on energy imports. This dependence was underlined in July 2007 when restrictions were placed on the supply of natural gas from Argentina. The problems surrounding gas supplies from Argentina dated back to 2004, when Argentina began restricting natural gas exports to Chile, with cuts reaching nearly 50 per cent of contracted volumes on some days. Chile, in turn, began to reconsider its energy policy, which, prior to the import restrictions, had assumed an increased use of natural gas and power imports from Argentina. Most importantly, Chile has begun to pursue other sources of natural gas, such as liquefied natural gas (LNG) or piped gas from other countries. The cuts did not materially affect levels of electricity power generation, as many of Chile's power stations are also able to run on diesel fuel. However, the production and export of methanol, which depends on natural gas, was adversely affected. According to the US Oil and Gas Journal (OGJ), Chile had 150 million barrels of proven crude oil reserves at the beginning of 2006. Oil production is limited, reaching 15,100 barrels per day (bpd) during the first eight months of 2006. In contrast, Chile consumed an estimated 238,000bpd of oil during the same period. The country's main source of oil imports is Argentina, followed by Brazil, Angola and Nigeria. OGJ reported that Chile had 3.5 trillion cubic feet (Tcf) of proven natural gas reserves in January 2006. The country has little domestic production, totalling 38.5 billion cubic feet (Bcf) in 2004. Empresa Nacional del Petróleo (ENAP) controls all natural gas production in Chile, which occurs mostly in the Magallanes basin. Chile has vigorously explored the country for natural gas reserves, but has so far not met with any significant success.

According to the US Energy Information Administration (EIA), one project is a pipeline linking Peru's Camisea natural gas project with northern Chile, featuring a pipeline system between Pisco, Peru and Tocopilla, Chile, with installed capacity of 810Mmcf/d. The pipeline would also connect to the GasAtacama and NorAndio, possibly – and ironically – allowing potential exports to Argentina. This pipeline would be part of the natural gas 'ring' proposed by Peru, Chile, Argentina, Uruguay, and Brazil. The ring would utilise new and existing pipelines to link natural gas reserves in those countries, facilitating greater energy integration in the Southern Cone. In its efforts to diversify its natural gas supply away from Argentina, Chile awarded a US$400 million contract to BG Group (BG) of the UK in February 2006 for the construction of an LNG re-gasification terminal near Quinteros in central Chile. BG hopes to bring the plant on stream by 2009. The facility will have an estimated capacity of 330 Mmcf/d.

Risk assessment

Politics	Good
Economics	Good
Regional stability	Good

COUNTRY PROFILE

Historical profile

Inca rule barely touched Chile, with Aymara and Atacameno farmers and herders pre-dating the Incas. Chango Indians fished along the coastal areas while Diaguitas farmed the interior of Coquimbo. Beyond the central valley, Araucanian or Mapuche Indians resisted Inca aggression.

1535 Indigenous Araucanian people successfully resisted the first Spanish invasion of Chile.

1540 Santiago was founded by Pedro de Valdivia, who began the Spanish conquest of Chile.

1553 Araucanians captured and executed Valdivia.

1553–58 Indigenous people staged an uprising against Spanish colonialism, however most of the country was eventually subdued, although the Mapuche managed to hold onto their remaining territory for almost three centuries.

1578 Sir Francis Drake, an English adventurer, led a raid on the port of Valparaíso, which was repulsed by the Spanish armies.

1700 For most of the eighteenth century it was ruled by a small oligarchy of landowners.

1759 Chile began reforms under the auspices of the Bourbon monarchs, who succeeded the Habsburg dynasty in Spain.

1788 Irish-born Ambrosio O'Higgins y Ballenary began his tenure as governor of Chile. He outlawed slavery and forced labour, strengthened production and administration and bolstered the power of the military. Chile was granted more autonomy than most other Latin American colonies.

1807 Napoleon Bonaparte's invasion of Spain fuelled the independence movement in Chile.

1810 Independence leader Bernardo O'Higgins Riquelme, son of Ambrosio O'Higgins, led a revolt against José Miguel Carrera Verdugo, the Chilean leader who had brought more autonomy to the country.

1814 Spanish troops reconquered Chile.

1818 Bernado O'Higgins joined forces with José de San Martín in Argentina and led successful battles against the Spanish that resulted in Chile's independence from Spain. Bernado O'Higgins became Chile's first post-independence leader.

1823 O'Higgins was forced to resign. Civil war between liberal federalists and conservative centralists ensued, lasting for seven years.

1830 The Conservatives won the civil war.

1851–61 President Manuel Montt liberalised the constitution, reducing the power of landowners and the Roman Catholic Church.

1879–84 Chile's victory in the War of the Pacific against Peru and Bolivia increased its territory by one-third.

1880s–90s The pacification of the Araucanians led to increased European immigration. Mining of nitrates and copper began.

1891 A civil war over a constitutional dispute between the president and congress led to a congressional victory, with the role of the president reduced to a figurehead.

1925 A new constitution saw the disestablishment of the church.

1927 General Carlos Ibañez del Campo seized power in a military coup and established a dictatorship.

1938–46 A Popular Front coalition was formed by communists, socialists and radicals.

1948–58 The Communist Party was banned.

1952 Carlos Ibañez was elected president, promising to strengthen law and order.

1964 Eduardo Frei Montalva was elected president, pledging to introduce limited social reform.

1970 Salvador Allende Gossens was elected president and imposed an extensive programme of nationalisation.

1973 The government failed to win a congressional majority in the elections as opposition to its policies mounted and the country faced ever increasing economic problems. Food shortages followed high inflation and fighting broke out between pro- and anti-government activists. Backed by the CIA, the armed forces intervened. President Allende died during the military takeover.

1974 General Augusto Pinochet Ugarte became president, remaining in power for 16 years.

1988 Chilean voters rejected Pinochet's bid to extend his power until 1997.

1989 The Concertación de Partidos por la Democracia (CPD) (Coalition of Parties for Democracy) was formed to contest the general elections. Patricio Aylwin (CPD) defeated both Pinochet's protégé and a right-wing independent candidate in the presidential election.
1990 The CPD won the general elections with 49.3 per cent of the vote in the Chamber of Deputies and 50.5 per cent in the Senate.
1993 Eduardo Frei Ruíz-Tagle won the presidential election. He began reducing the military's influence in government.
1998 Pinochet retired from the army and was made senator-for-life. He was arrested in the UK on a warrant issued by a Spanish magistrate on murder charges related to his 'caravan of death' in the 1970s.
2000 Ricardo Lagos Escobar (CPD) won the elections and became Chile's first socialist president since 1973. The UK government declared Pinochet unfit for extradition to Spain and the former dictator was returned to Chile. A Chilean judge subsequently charged Pinochet with kidnap.
2001 Chile's appeal court ruled that General Augusto Pinochet was mentally unfit to stand trial on human rights violation charges. The ruling centre-left CPD held on to its majority in Congress in the legislative elections.
2002 All charges against Pinochet were dropped after the Supreme Court upheld a verdict finding him mentally unfit to stand trial for human rights crimes. Pinochet resigned from his post as a lifelong senator.
2004 President Lagos signed a new law giving Chileans the right to divorce, despite continued opposition from the Roman Catholic Church. Chile's court lifted Pinochet's immunity from prosecution, opening the way to possible trials of the octogenarian general on charges of human rights abuses during his 17 year rule.
2005 In elections, for the chamber of deputies, the CPD was re-elected with 47.9 per cent of the vote (65 out of 120 seats), the Alliance won 38.6 per cent (54 seats). In the senate, following partial elections, coupled with those elected in 2001, the CPD hold 20 seats and the Alliance 17 seats.
2006 Michelle Bachelet took office as Chile's first female president, after she won 53.5 per cent in the presidential election runoff; Sebastián Piñera, a moderate conservative, won 46.5 per cent of the votes. Augusto Pinochet, former Head of State (1973-90), died. The controversy surrounding his rule denied him a state funeral.
2007 Former president of Peru, Alberto Fujimori was extradited from Chile after two years in exile. Bolivia, Brazil and Chile agreed to build a South American highway to link the Atlantic and Pacific coasts, running from Santos in Brazil, through Bolivia, to Arica and Iquique in Chile, at an estimated cost of US$600 million. The cruise ship M/S Explorer sank in the Antarctic Ocean and passengers and crew had to be rescued and many flown to Chile.
2008 Chile called home its ambassador to Peru on 17 January, after Peru had asked the International Court of Justice (ICJ) to make a ruling over the disputed maritime border between them. The sea is a rich fishing ground and source of commercial income. On 3 May the Chaiten volcano in Patagonia erupted after laying dormant for 9,000 years; thousands of people from the immediate area were evacuated.

Political structure

Constitution

The constitution dates from 1980, when it was accepted by two-thirds of voters in a plebiscite organised by the military government. Following a further plebiscite in 1989, 54 reforms passed into law. They included increasing the number of directly elected members in the Senate, abolishing Article 8 (which outlawed Marxist groups) and balancing the number of civilian and military representatives on the powerful Council of National Security. Further changes to the constitution require a two-thirds majority in both houses of the Congreso Nacional (National Congress).

Form of state

Presidential democratic republic

The executive

Executive power is held by the president and cabinet. The president is head of state and commander-in-chief of the armed forces. Elected for a fixed term of six years, the president cannot be re-elected for the following period.
The relationship between the executive and the armed forces is enshrined in the constitution. The president should take note of discussions within the Council of National Security. This consists of eight members, four military and four civilian. The four military members are the heads of the army, navy, air force and police. The four civilian members are the president of the republic, president of the Senate, president of the Supreme Court and the comptroller general of the republic. According to the constitution, the Council of National Security provides a forum within which it is possible to present, at the highest level, the military's opinion. The armed forces see the council as having the function of letting civilian governments know of potential conflicts between military and civilian interests, thereby acting to prevent future military intervention in government.

National legislature

The bicameral Congreso Nacional (national congress), together with the president of the republic, co-legislate within a multi-party legislature. The 38 elected and 10 appointed senators of the Senado (senate), serve for eight years; an alternate half their number are re-elected every four years. Five of the appointed senators are chosen by the council of national security, three by the supreme court and two by the president. Ex-presidents who have served for six uninterrupted years are also given a seat. The 120 Camara de Diputados (chamber of deputies) are elected for four-year terms. Laws can originate in either of the chambers or be proposed by the president.

Legal system

The main tribunals of the independent judiciary system are the Supreme Court, 16 regional courts of appeal and the lower courts. The Supreme Court consists of 16 members appointed for life by the president from a list of five names proposed by the Supreme Court as vacancies arise. Members of the courts of appeal are appointed in the same way as those of the Supreme Court. Judges in lower courts are appointed in a similar manner, but from lists submitted by the court of appeal of the district in which the vacancies arise.

Last elections

11 December 2005 (Senate half the number;); 11 December 2005/15 January 2006 (presidential – first round and runoff).

Results: Presidential: Runoff, Michelle Bachelet Jeria won 53.5 per cent of the vote, while Sebastián Piñera, won 46.5 per cent. Turnout was 87.12 per cent. First round Michelle Bachelet Jeria won 45.96 per cent of the vote, Sebastián Piñera Echenique won 25.41 per cent, Joaquín Lavín Infante won 23.33 per cent and Tomás Hirsch Goldschmidt won 5.4 per cent. Turnout was 87.67 per cent. Parliamentary: (chamber of deputies) the Concertación won with 47.9 per cent of the vote (65 out of 120 seats), the Alliance won 38.6 per cent (54 seats). (Senate) Following partial elections, coupled with those elected in 2001, Concertación hold 20 seats and the Alliance 17 seats.

Next elections

2009 (senate half the members, chamber of deputies all members); 2012 (presidential).

Political parties

Ruling party

Concertación de Partidos por la Democracia (Concertación) (Coalition of Pro-Democracy Parties) (centre-left coalition, comprising the Partido Demócrata

Christiano (PDC) (Christian Democratic Party), Partido por la Democracia (PPD) (Party for Democracy), Partido Socialista (PS) (Socialist Party), Partido Radical Social Demócrata (PRSD) (Social Democratic Radical Party) and independents (since 1989; re-elected Dec 2005)

Main opposition party

Alianza por Chile (Alliance for Chile coalition), comprising the Unión Demócrata Independiente (UDI) (Independent Democratic Union), the Renovación Nacional (RN) (National Renewal) and independents.

Population

16.58 million (2007)*

Last census: April 2002: 15,116,435

Population density: 20 inhabitants per square km. Urban population: 86 per cent.

Annual growth rate: 1.3 per cent 1994–2004 (WHO 2006)

Ethnic make-up

Mixed European and indigenous peoples (mestizos) account for approximately 75 per cent of the population, with a further 23 per cent of European descent and 2 per cent Indians, mainly Mapuches, in the south.

Religions

Approximately 85 per cent Roman Catholic, 10 per cent Protestant, with small minorities of Jews, Muslims and other religions.

Education

The investment in education amounts to 4.0 per cent of GDP. This figure has doubled since the early 1990s. Chile has achieved gender parity in both primary and secondary education and has extended the school year by around 15 per cent.

Education is free and compulsory for the first eight years, beginning at the age of five or six.

All other education institutions charge fees, either partly or in full. The subsidies system applies equally to municipal and private education but has been directed mostly to basic education. The role of the ministry of education is now limited to licensing private education and carrying out school inspections.

Over 80 per cent of children complete secondary education, which begins at the age of 13 or 14 years and is divided into a humanities/science programme or a technical/vocational programme. Higher education consists of universities, professional and technical institutes.

Literacy rate: 96 per cent adult rate; 99 per cent youth rate (15–24) (Unesco 2005).

Compulsory years: Five or six to 13 or 14 (eight years in total)

Enrolment rate: 103 per cent boys, 100 per cent girls, total primary school enrolment of the relevant age group (including repetition rates), (World Bank).

Pupils per teacher: 30 in primary schools

Health

Per capita total expenditure on health (2003) was US$707; of which per capita government spending was US$345, at the international dollar rate, (WHO 2006).

Healthcare is distributed between the ministry of health and social security institutions as well as private funds and the public sector. Health and social security have increasingly come into the hands of pension fund administration companies (AFPs). Since 1999, over a quarter of Chileans had taken out private health insurance. The state is responsible for the financing of health promotion, protection and prevention through the National Health Fund. The decentralised national health service is able to provide healthcare at different levels. The most basic care is in the hands of regional health authorities, responsible for preventive medical services which are part of the health promotion and protection programmes.

Care for pregnant women, children under six and members of indigent and low income families is free. More specialised medical consultation and care is given at hospitals and maternity units. For patients who voluntarily choose the state system, a contribution of 25 to 30 per cent of the cost is required (depending on income). People under any social security scheme are entitled to preventive medical services (periodical health examinations) and in the case of illness, are granted full-paid sick leave. Occupational accidents or disease are covered by a special fund.

Life expectancy: 77 years, 2004 (WHO 2006)

Fertility rate/Maternal mortality rate: 2.0 births per woman, 2004 (WHO 2006)

Child (under 5 years) mortality rate (per 1,000): 8.0 deaths per 1,000 live births; 1 per cent of children aged under five are malnourished (World Bank).

Head of population per physician: 1.09 physicians per 1,000 people, 2003 (WHO 2006)

Welfare

The statutory age of retirement is 65 years for men and 60 years for women. The system requires 13 per cent of a worker's wage to be deducted and accumulated in one of seven independently managed mutual-fund companies selected by the worker, with a small part of the contribution going towards disability insurance. Neither employers nor the government contribute to the individual accounts. The contributions remain under the workers' control, if they change jobs, and are deferred from any tax.

However, critics of the Chilean pension model argue that given the country's poverty rate, some workers would never be able to save enough toward retirement. Besides, 42 per cent of the workforce, in the informal economy, are not covered by any pension system, according to government statistics. Although they can make voluntary contributions to the system, most workers' incomes are very low. Hence, the government guarantees a minimum pension to anyone who has worked as a regular employee for 20 years.

Monetary subsidies apply to those outside any social security scheme include a special family allowance for both pregnant women and children under 15, in extreme poverty, and a special pension allowance for people over 65, or the handicapped without economic resources.

The system allows up to 20 per cent foreign investment in pension funds and it is likely to push that limit to 35 per cent with new legislation.

Main cities

Santiago (capital, estimated population 4.8 million in 2005), Puente Alto (602,586), Viña del Mar (326,790), Antofagasta (313,054), Valparaíso (267,367), Talcahuano (252,800), San Bernardo (261,454), Temuco (285,766), Iquique (224,970), Concepción (390,639).

Languages spoken

English is the main second language.

Official language/s

Spanish

Media

National news agency: Agencia Chile Noticias

Press

Dailies: In Spanish, national newspapers include the state-owned La Nación (www.lanacion.cl) and privately owned El Mercurio (http://diario.elmercurio.com) a long established publication La Tercera (www.latercera.cl) is it rival. Tabloids include Las Ultimas Noticias (www.lun.com) and La Cuarta (www.lacuarta.cl), which is written in Chilean vernacular. La Segunda (www.lasegunda.com) is an evening newspaper.

In Spanish, regional newspapers include from Santiago La Hora (www.lahora.cl) and Publimetro (www.publimetro.cl), which are free newspapers. From Los Angeles La Tribuna (www.diariolatribuna.cl), from Punta Arenas La Prensa Austral (www.laprensaaustral.cl), and from Antofagasta La Estrella del Norte (www.estrellanorte.cl). Prensa Al Día (www.prensaaldia.cl) carries a compilation of daily reported news. In English, the Santiago Times (www.tcgnews.com/santiagotimes) provides news and general information about Chile and Santiago.

Weeklies: Some daily newspapers have weekend edition and there are many magazines for all tastes and ages. Fortnightly publications include, in Spanish, La Firme (www.lafirme.cl), a analytical political magazine, The Clinic (www.theclinic.cl), a satirical magazine and Ercilla (www.ercilla.cl) for general information. Women's magazines include Cosas (http://www.cosas.cl) and Vanidades (www.vanidades.cl); Conozca Más (www.conozcamas.cl) for men and Condorito (www.condorito.com) is a humourus publication.

In German Condor (http://www.condor.cl), is a general news weekly.

Business: In Spanish, dailies include Estrategia (www.estrategia.cl) and Diario Financiero (www.diariofinanciero.cl), is an influential newspaper. Monthlies include América Economia (www.americaeconomia.com), was the first business magazine published, Datos Sue (www.datossur.cl) and Estrategia (www.capital.cl). Punto Final (www.puntofinal.cl) for fortnightly general business news. For Latin American news, Business News Americas (www.bnamericas.com) with an English daily on-line digest.

Broadcasting

The Ministerio de Transportes y Telecommunicaciones (www.mtt.cl) has overall authority for broadcasting.

The geography of Chile has resulted in more nationwide coverage of radio than TV signals.

Radio: There are over 300 radio stations, most of which are private, local and commercial. Several national networks include the private, Radio Cooperativa (www.cooperativa.cl) with news based programmes, Radio Agricultura (www.radioagricultura.cl), Bío Bío La Radio (www.radiobiobio.cl) and Radio Infinita (www.infinita.cl). Local stations in Santiago include Radio Tiempo (http://fmtiempo.cl), Radio Oasis (www.radiooasis.cl) and Radio Integral (www.radiointegral.cl).

Television: The national public, commercial broadcaster is Televisión Nacional de Chile (TVN) (www.tvn.cl). There are several other private TV networks, including Chilevision (www.chilevision.cl), Megavision (www.megavision.cl), Red TV (www.redtv.cl) and Canal 13 (www.canal13.cl).

There are many foreign and domestic channels available via satellite or cable.

Advertising

Advertising spending is dominated by TV (over 50 per cent), newspapers (over 10 per cent) and magazines (around 5 per cent).

Economy

Chile remains one of Latin America's most robust and stable economies. Successful exploitation of the country's natural resource base and diversification into non-traditional sectors continue to fuel growth. The boom in international copper prices since 2004 has maintained the economy's key strength. Chile's export sector is relatively strong and diversified, with copper typically accounting for around 60 per cent of exports.

Chile's reputation for sound economic management has created a level of international confidence without equal in Latin America. At the heart of these policies lies the government's concentration on sound monetary, fiscal and exchange rate policies. Interest rates have traditionally been high, but were progressively eased from 2002 as the authorities sought to counter the effects of falling consumer demand and rapidly rising unemployment. The economy has been liberalised through an extensive privatisation policy, tax revenue increases and allowing the peso to float freely, enabling the country to maintain its competitiveness. Key to the government's economic policy has been investment, with foreign direct investment (FDI) flowing into the mining, construction and telecommunications sectors in particular.

Points of major concern include high unemployment and the influence of copper prices on the exchange rate and their tendency to distort the wider economy. Although interest rates are low, domestic demand remains sluggish and the growth of the export sector has barely impacted on domestic consumption and investment. Despite lacklustre domestic demand, the rebound of the world's economy in recent years and the increased Chinese demand for copper have boosted prices and increased Chilean copper exports. As a result, GDP grew by six per cent in 2004, a trend which continued in 2005. However, adverse factors – industrial unrest and accidents in the copper-mining industry and higher international oil and gas costs – slowed growth to under five per cent in 2006.

External trade

Chile is an associate member of Mercusur, a member of the Organisation of American States (OAS) and has a free trade agreement with the European Union (EU) as well as other individual countries in Asia. Plans are afoot to create a free trade bloc modelled on the EU, under the auspices of the South American Community of Nations (SACN). The SACN seeks to merge two existing free trade zones in the region, the Andean Community and Mercusur but in July 2007 Chile had still not joined its neighbours to become a single trading union. Chile is the world's largest source of copper.

Imports

Main imports include petroleum and petroleum products, natural gas, chemicals, electrical and telecommunications equipment, industrial machinery and vehicles.

Main sources: US (16.0 per cent total, 2006), Argentina (13.0 per cent), Brazil (12.2 per cent).

Exports

Major exports include copper, fruit and processed foods including wine and fish products, timber, paper and pulp.

Main destinations: US (16.0 per cent total, 2006), Japan (10.8 per cent), China (8.8 per cent).

Agriculture

Farming

The contribution of the agricultural sector to the Chilean economy is significant, employing 15 per cent of the total workforce and generating 6 per cent of GDP. Approximately 8 per cent of the total land mass is cultivated. The country's soil is fertile and well irrigated, particularly in the central area and main river valleys.

Dependence on imported foodstuffs has been reduced by improved wheat, sugar and vegetable oil production. Other important crops are oats, barley, rice, beans, lentils, maize and chickpeas. Important cash/export crops are maize, beans, asparagus, onions and garlic.

The production and export of a variety of fruit have all recorded impressive figures, given Chile's favourable growing conditions and good soil, relatively cost-effective labour and protection from disease. Table grapes, citrus fruits, avocados, pears, nectarines, peaches, kiwis, plums and nuts have done well. Chilean wine is growing in importance as a value-added agricultural product and a highly important export.

Livestock farming is concentrated in the south of the country.

Crop production in 2005 included 3,936,457 million tonnes (t) cereals, 1,851,940t wheat, 1,507,766t maize, 1,115,736t potatoes, 2,800,000t sugar beets, 309,000t citrus fruit, 2,250,000t grapes, 1,230,000t tomatoes, 1,124,736t roots and tubers, 116,832t rice, 24,290t oilcrops, 357,352t oats, 27,000t olives, 112,875t pulses, 64,000t chillies & peppers, 1,350,000t apples, 9,850t tobacco leaves, 22,035t treenuts, 5,107,300t fruit in total, 2,793,000t vegetables in total. Livestock production included 1,191,030t meat in total, 222,000t beef, 399,000t pig meat, 8,920t lamb, 5,310t goat meat, 11,000t horsemeat, 544,800t poultry, 132,500t eggs, 2,374,900t milk, 9,000t honey, 31,500t cattle hides, 2,460t sheepskins, 14,000t greasy wool.

Fishing

The Fishing industry in Chile is one of the economy's most important export industries. Chile is second only to Norway as a producer of fresh, frozen and prepared salmon, with annual exports totalling more than US$800 million. The productivity of the fishing industry is largely attributable to the large number of salmon farms in the south of the country.

Fishing and fish processing have become a diversified industry. Pilchards have traditionally been the main species of fish landed (75 per cent), with jack mackerel second. Abalone is exported to Japan, algae to Taiwan, hake to Spain, fresh salmon to the US and canned pilchards to the UK. Such diversification has been fuelled by substantial and continued increases in investment.

The typical annual fish catch is 4.3million tonnes, including 3.6 million tonnes marine fish and 164,477 tonnes shellfish.

Forestry

Chile has a significant amount of forested land, approximately 15.5 million hectares (ha), equating to 23 per cent of the total land area. In the period 1990–2000, deforestation accounted for a decrease of forest cover by an average of 0.13 per cent per annum or 20,000ha. Forestry is an important sector suitable for commercial exploitation.

Chile has abundant softwood plantations used for the manufacture of forest products. The forestry industry is primarily located in the south, stretching from the Seventh to the Tenth region, with the main concentration in the Eighth Region around Concepción. The three ports of the area (San Vicente, Lirquén and Talcahuano) handle up to 95 per cent of all forestry exports.

The sawn wood sector is characterised by a wide variety of producers, ranging from small portable sawmills to large highly automated mills. The larger sawmills tend to specialise in pinus radiata. Sawnwood production is largely a seasonal industry, with the highest activity occurring between spring and autumn (September to April). In the global market, Chile is the third-largest exporter of woodchips while nearly 50 per cent of its sawn timber, panels and softwood pulp production are exported.

Japan is the single most important purchaser of Chilean wood cellulose. Paper production has a large domestic market. The government has promoted private sector investment in forestry with land tax exemptions, rebates and subsidies.

Industry and manufacturing

Chile's manufacturing sector employs approximately one quarter of the country's total workforce. The sector also contributes around a third of Chilean GDP. Financial conglomerates control a substantial section of denationalised industries, although small firms with less than 10 employees still dominate.

Export-based industries include petrochemicals, pulp and paper, base metals, plastics, rubber and food processing (particularly fish and malted barley). Domestic market industries include textiles, footwear, cement, food processing, beverages and machinery.

Tourism

Chile's tourism industry continues to grow, with the country's variety of natural environments and climates attracting an increasing number of visitors. In line with the expansion of the industry Chile's infrastructure is being expanded to cater for the growth of the sector. In 2005 travel and tourism accounted for 6.5 per cent of total GDP and 6.8 per cent of total employment, a rise of 11.8 per cent on 2004 in the latter. The largest market is Argentina, but many tourists come from further afield, including a considerable number from the US and Europe. Capital investment in the industry rose by 9.4 per cent on the figure for 2004 and now represents 8.7 per cent of total capital investment in the country.

Environment

Santiago suffers from a serious smog problem, which is at its worst May–September and is aggravated when the winter weather is interrupted by spells of milder temperatures.

Mining

The mining sector is of great importance to the Chilean economy, contributing 9 per cent to GDP and providing employment for 6 per cent of the workforce. It is the main export earner and a major focus of foreign investment in the country.

Activity is concentrated in copper, of which Chile is the world's leading producer and holds around 30 per cent of the world's proven reserves. The state-owned copper enterprise, Corporación Nacional del Cobre de Chile (Codelco), holds 70 per cent of national reserves and administers the four largest mines: Chuquicamata, El Teniente, Andina and El Salvador. Copper is also extracted from the Escondida mine, the biggest proven deposit in the world.

The sector was hit by falling copper prices until 2003 when demand for copper was fuelled by Chinese expansion in particular and prices rose. Copper continued to rise at a rapid rate in 2005, in line with increased demand in the international market.

Mining of silver, gold (the El Indio mine ranks among the highest grade mines in the world), iron ore, manganese and lead is also undertaken. Other mining sub-sectors include natural nitrates, mercury, marble, coal, sulphur and limestone Proven and probable reserves at the Fachinal mine in southern Chile (Coeur d'Alene Mines Corporation) are estimated at 317,915 ounces of gold and 14.6 million ounces of silver.

Hydrocarbons

The country is a net importer of energy and is heavily reliant on imports of crude oil. Chile's domestic oil production, which is extracted mainly from offshore fields at the Straits of Magellan and onshore at Tierra del Fuego and the southern mainland, provides only 6 per cent of domestic consumption. Chile's oil reserves totalled only 150 million barrels in 2005. There were plans to privatise Empresa Nacional de Petróleo (ENAP), the state oil company, but these were shelved by President Lagos in 2003. The country's oil sector is controlled by ENAP including the three primary refineries which between them produce 226,800bpd.

Investments by ENAP in exploration outside Chile have not been successful.

Chile had 100 billion cubic metres of proven natural gas reserves in 2005. Production is limited, and is geared to the urban markets of central Chile, particularly Santiago. However since 1997 gas consumption has risen by an average 21.7 per cent per year, and most of this growth is satisfied through increased imports of natural gas.

Liquid natural gas (LNG) production is being increased; ENAP called for international tenders, in July 2005, for the construction of a LNG terminal. The government held talks with various international LNG suppliers, while ENAP concluded agreements with domestic energy companies to supply the LNG.

Chile's coal resources come mainly from Lota/Coronel and the extreme south of Tierra del Fuego. All domestic coal production goes to power generation. Chile has total recoverable coal reserves of 1.3 million tonnes and typically produces around 500,000 tonnes a year.

Energy

Generation, transmission and distribution are undertaken by private companies. The sector is jointly regulated by the Ministerio de Economía y Energía (MEE) (ministry of economy and energy) and Comisión Nacional de Energía (CNE) (national energy commission).

Chile generates a total capacity of 10.5GW electricity. Some 43 per cent of the country's electricity is generated by thermal power sources and 41 per cent by hydroelectricity. Renewable energy sources account for the remainder.
Around 90 per cent of the country is served by the Central Grid, while the rest is supplied by the Northern Grid and the Aisén and Magallanes systems which supply the south. Empresa Nacional de Electricidad (Endesa), part of the Enersis Group owned by Spain's Endesa, is the country's largest electricity producer with 50 per cent of output. US-owned Gener is the second largest producer, generating 20 per cent of national power.

Banking and insurance

Chile's banking and insurance sector was once an exclusive enclave of the economy where only the rich were able to access financial services. However, the 1990s saw an expansion of the banking sector throughout the country. Today Chile has one of Latin America's most developed and sophisticated banking sectors and Chilean banks have shown relative strength in a weak economic environment.
The authorities do not allow new banks to enter the Chilean market, except via the purchase of an existing bank. Restrictions remain on the range of activities a bank can undertake, with pension fund management reserved for private pension fund companies.
Competitive pressures have increased with domestic banks facing increased competition from Spanish banks. Following Banco Santander Central Hispano's (BSCH) takeover of Banco Santiago and Santander Chile – two of Chile's largest banks – BSCH has a market share of just under 30 per cent.

Central bank

Banco Central de Chile

Main financial centre

Santiago

Time

GMT minus four hours (daylight saving, mid-October to mid-March, GMT minus three hours)

Geography

Chile occupies a thin strip of land, rarely more than 200km wide, which stretches 4,640km down the west coast of Latin America from north of the tropic of Capricorn to Cape Horn. Geography and climate range from hot deserts in the north to icy Andean peaks at almost 7,000 metres high in the east and thousands of rainswept islets in the south. Chile is bordered by the Pacific to the west, by Argentina to the east, by Bolivia in the north-east and Peru to the north. Several Pacific islands, including the Juan Fernandez archipelago and Easter Island, are Chilean.
There are three main geographical belts running from north to south – the Andes, the central valley, and the narrow coastal range. The Andes are characterised not only by their great height but also by being a broad mass, generally over 80km wide, and making a superb natural border with Argentina. West of the Andes, the central valley has a varied form. In the north, it is a high desert basin, characterised by inward drainage and near complete aridity. Further south it disappears, until re-emerging near Santiago. From Santiago to Puerto Montt, it constitutes the agricultural heart of Chile, until it disappears under the sea at Puerto Montt. The coastal range, significantly lower than the Andes and generally under 3,000 metres, forms a barrier between the populated central valley and the coast, except for certain gaps made by powerful rivers, as at Concepción in the south. Of the mainland area, 2.2 per cent is suitable for crops, 17.1 per cent for livestock and 10.8 per cent for forestry. The remaining 69.9 per cent is considered unproductive and is mostly covered by deserts or mountains.

Hemisphere

Southern

Climate

Generally hot and dry in north, Mediterranean in central region (cool nights) and wet and cold in the south. Temperatures in Santiago range from 10–33 degrees Celsius (C) in summer (December–March) and 2–20 degrees C in winter (June–September). The rainy season in the Santiago area is from May to September.

Dress codes

Relatively formal. A suit or a jacket and tie for men and skirts for women are usual for business.

Entry requirements

Passports

Required by all, with the exception of tourists travelling direct to Chile from Argentina, Brazil, Colombia, Paraguay and Uruguay, for whom national identity cards are sufficient. Entry will be permitted only with proof of return/onward passage and sufficient funds for stay.

Visa

Visas are not required by citizens of neighbouring countries or most EU states. For further details contact the local embassy.
Business visas are not required by those citizens who do not need a tourist visa, all others, including those who do not normally require them but who are visiting on short-term contracts or receive fees from a local company, do need a visa.
On arrival a 'tourist card' is issued and must be returned when leaving.

Currency advice/regulations

No restrictions on import and export of foreign or domestic currency. International credit cards are widely accepted. Receipts for money changed on entry should be retained. Travellers cheques are readily acceptable in cities only.

Health (for visitors)

Mandatory precautions

None

Advisable precautions

Typhoid, polio, hepatitis A and tetanus vaccinations are useful.
Water precautions should be taken (avoid tap water) and eating unpeeled fruit or uncooked vegetables is not advised. Foreigners may get free primary health care from the state-run health service's hospitals, but for more serious cases they are required to pay the costs. Travel health insurance is advised if not already covered by one's own national health insurance.

Hotels

Numerous luxury and first-class hotels as well as good hotels in lower price range. The Stars Classification System is used. Bookings may be made at the Sernatur information office at Pudahuel Airport. An 19 per cent hotel tax is added to bill, unless paid for with foreign currency. Service charge is usually included, but an extra 5–10 per cent tip is usual.

Public holidays (national)

Fixed dates

1 Jan (New Year's Day), 1 May (Labour Day), 21 May (Navy Day), 26 Jun (St Peter and St Paul Day), 15 Aug (Assumption Day), 18 Sep (Independence Day), 19 Sep (Army Day), 12 Oct (Columbus Day), 1 Nov (All Saints' Day), 8 Dec (Immaculate Conception), 25–26 Dec (Christmas).

Variable dates

Mar/Apr (Good Friday, Holy Saturday), May/Jun (Corpus Christi), first Mon in Sep (Reconciliation Day).

Working hours

Banking

Mon–Fri: 0900–1400.

Business

Mon–Fri: 0900–1800.
Business visits are best made outside the summer month of February when the great majority of people are on holiday.

Government

Mon–Fri: 0830–1730.

Shops

Mon–Sat: 0900–2000. Supermarkets and many shopping centres are open continuously until 2100, including Sundays and public holidays.

Telecommunications

Mobile/cell phones

GSM 1900 services exist throughout most of the country.

Electricity supply

220V AC, with two-pin plugs.

Social customs/useful tips

People are expected to be punctual for business appointments. However, for social appointments, being 30 or 40 minutes late is quite usual. Chileans are very hospitable and do not necessarily expect reciprocity. Entertaining at home is common practice and a small gift of thanks is acceptable.

In Latin American Spanish it is acceptable to address others in a familiar form tu, or in a polite form usted. The latter is more appropriate for business although the familiar form is often rapidly adopted. Chileans are quite easy about smoking habits, but it is banned in cinemas, theatres, churches and public transport.

It is necessary to carry car documents when driving.

Security

Santiago is generally regarded as a safe city with low incidences of assault and mugging compared with other Latin American capitals. However, pickpocketing is common in the city centre and on buses.

Getting there

Air

National airline: LAN-Chile (Línea Aérea Nacional de Chile).

International airport/s: Santiago-Comodoro Arturo Merino Benítez (often known as 'Pudahuel') (SCL), 21km west of city; bar, restaurant, bank, post office, shops, tourist office, car hire. A bus service to the city runs 24 hours.

Other airport/s: Arica-Chacalluta (ARI), 18km from city; bar, restaurant, buffet, shops, car hire.

Airport tax: Departure tax: US$18

Surface

Road: The road system is dominated by the 3,455km Pan-American Highway, which links the Peruvian frontier to Puerto Montt in the south. Between Santiago and Puerto Montt, the Pan-American follows the course of the central valley. A trans-Andean highway links Valparaíso with the Argentine city of Mendoza. This is frequently closed during winter due to snow, when more southerly and lower passes have to be used.

Rail: Five lines to neighbouring Argentina, Bolivia and Peru are operated by the government-owned Ferrocarriles del Estado.

Water: Empremar (Valparaíso) is the principal port with developed passenger routes mainly to Argentina. Chile has around 60 ports.

Getting about

National transport

Air: Línea Aérea del Cobre (Ladeco) provides most domestic services. Lanexpress operates frequent flights to major centres only. Air taxi services also operate. The south of the country relies heavily on air links and seats must be booked well in advance.

Road: There are 80,000km of good roads including the Pan-American Highway running north-south and qualified as first-class. It is only possible to reach Punta Arenas by land from Rio Gallengos (Argentina).

Buses: Express coaches link main centres and are generally recommended (eg Santiago-Arica, typically one departure daily; Santiago-Valparaíso, approx hourly service).

Rail: A fast diesel-electric train service is available. The main line runs from Santiago to Puerto Montt (includes sleeper service, restaurant cars, air-conditioning, typical total journey time around 18 hours); Japanese-built train links between Santiago and Concepción (first-class service and a journey time around nine hours including bus service from Chillián to Concepción).

City transport

Taxis: From Santiago's Arturo Merino Benitez airport, there are metered taxis into town.

Taxis are cheap and widely available in main towns. An initial charge (Bajada de Bandera) is displayed on front windscreen. Large blue taxis do not have meters. Tipping is not customary. Radio taxis charge higher fares.

Within Santiago and Chile's main towns black and yellow taxis can be hailed but are scarce at rush hour. These taxis are mostly metered but for long journeys fares should be negotiated in advance. There are extra charges at night and on holidays.

Taxis operating from the airport require a special permit, and it is advised that visitors check a taxi's authenticity before boarding. The journey to central Santiago takes about 30 minutes. However, any taxi can go to the airport and the fare is often cheaper than from the airport.

Buses, trams & metro: Frequent inner city bus service. Shuttle service – mini-buses for several passengers – from airport to city centre.

Fast, frequent, clean and safe metro system in Santiago consisting of two main lines: line 1 San Pablo-Escuela Militar line; line 2 Lo Ovalle-Cal y Canto line which has 13 stations. Trains run 0700–2245.

Car hire

A national or international licence is accepted. Car hire can be arranged at the airport and in most major towns. A large deposit may be required. All car drivers require a 'Carnet de Passages et Douanes' issued by the Automobile Club. Traffic drives on the right.

BUSINESS DIRECTORY

The addresses listed below are a selection only. While World of Information makes every endeavour to check these addresses, we cannot guarantee that changes have not been made, especially to telephone numbers and area codes. We would welcome any corrections.

Telephone area codes

The international dialling code (IDD) for Chile is +56, followed by area code and subscriber's number:

Antofagasta	55	Linares	73
Arica	58	Punta Arenas	61
Chillán	42	Santiago	2
Concepción	41	Temuco	45
Coquimbo	51	Valparaíso	32
Iquique	57	Vina del Mar	32
La Serena	51		

Chambers of Commerce

American Chamber of Commerce in Chile, Avenida Kennedy 5735, Las Condes, Santiago (tel: 290-9700; fax: 212-0515; e-mail: amcham@amchamchile.cl).

British-Chilean Chamber of Commerce, Avenida Suecia 155-C, Providencia, Santiago (tel: 231-4366; fax: 231-8211; e-mail: cambrit@entelchile.net).

Antofagasta Cámara de Comercio, Servicios y Turismo, Latorre 2580, Antofagasta (tel: 225-175; fax: 55-222-053; e-mail: info@comercioantofagusta.cl).

Arica Cámara de Comercio, Industria, Servicios y Turismo, Rafael Sotomayor 252, Arica (tel: 224-643; fax: 253-718; e-mail: comercio@camaracomercioarica.cl).

Iquique Cámara de Comercio, Industria, Servicios y Turismo, San Martín 225, Iquique (tel: 412-942; fax: 414-090; e-mail: info@iquiquenegocios.cl).

Talca Cámara de Comercio, Servicios y Turismo, 2 Sur 1061, Talca (tel/fax: 233-569; e-mail: contact@camaradecomerciotalca.cl).

Temuco Cámara de Comercio, Servicios y Turismo, Vicuña Mackenna 396, Temuco (tel: 210-556; fax: 237-047; e-mail: camcotem@entelchile.cl).

Valparaiso Cámara Regional del Comercio y la Produccion, Pasaje Ross 149, Valparaiso (tel: 253-065; fax: 212-770).

Banking
Banco de A Edwards, Huérfanos 740, Santiago (tel: 388-3000; fax: 388-4100; e-mail: marketing@baenet.cl).

Banco de Chile, Ahumada 251, Santiago (tel: 637-1111; fax: 637-3434)

Banco de Crédito e Inversiones, Huérfanos 1134, Santiago (tel: 692-7000; fax: 699-0729; e-mail: consulta@bcl.cl).

Banco del Estado de Chile, Avenida Libertador Bernardo O'Higgins 1111, Santiago (tel: 670-7000; fax: 670-5478; e-mail: msoto9@bech.cl).

Central bank
Banco Central de Chile, PO Box 967, 1180 Agustinas, Santiago 8340454 (Tel: 670-2000; fax: 670-2099; e-mail: bcch@bcentral.cl).

Travel information
LADECO (Línea Aérea del Cobre), Avenida Américo Vespucio 901, Santiago (tel: 661-3131; fax: 639-5757; e-mail: josecotd@cmbchile.cl).

LAN-Chile (Línea Aérea Nacional de Chile), Avenida Américo Vespucio 901, Santiago (tel: 687-2525; fax: 687-2483; e-mail:sdelpino@lanchile.cl; internet: www.lan.com).

National tourist organisation offices
Servicio Nacional de Turismo (SERNATUR), (National Tourist Service) Avenida Providencia 1550, Santiago (tel: 236-1416; fax: 251-8469; internet: www.visit-chile.org; e-mail: sernatur@ctc-mundo.net or info@sernatur.cl).

Ministries
Ministry of Agriculture, Teatinos 40, Santiago (tel: 393-5000; fax:672-5654; e-mail: xbarrera@minagri.gob.cl).

Ministry of Defence, Edificio Diego Portales, Villavicencio 364, Santiago (tel: 222-1202; fax: 634-5339; e-mail: dn@defensa.cl).

Ministry of Economy, Mining and Energy, Teatinos 120, Santiago (tel: 672-5522; fax: 672-6040; e-mail: conomia@minecon.cl).

Ministry of Education, Avenida Libertado Bernardo O'Higgins 1371, Santiago (tel: 390-4000; fax: 380-0317; e-mail: ineduc@chilnet.cl).

Ministry of the Government, Palacio de la Moneda, Santiago (tel: 671-4103; fax: 699-1657).

Ministry of Housing, Avenida Libertado Bernardo O'Higgins 924, Santiago (tel: 638-0801; fax: 633-3892; e-mail: martinez@minvu.cl).

Ministry of the Interior, Palacio de la Moneda, Santiago (tel: 690-4000; fax: 699-2165; e-mail: alopez@interior.gov.cl).

Ministry of Justice, Morandé 107, Santiago (tel: 696-8151; fax: 696-6952).

Ministry of Labour and Social Security, Huérfanos 1273, Santiago (tel: 695-5133; fax: 671-6539).

Ministry of Mining, Teatinos 120, Santiago (tel: 671-4373; fax: 698-9262; e-mail: chileminero@mixmail.com).

Ministry of National Properties, Pdte. Juan Antonio Rios 6, Santiago (tel: 633-9305; fax: 633-6521; e-mail: aleonp@mbienes).

Ministry of Planning and Co-operation, Ahumada 48, Santiago (tel: 675-1400; fax: 672-1879; e-mail: misoto@mideplan.cl).

Ministry of the Presidency, Palacio de la Moneda, Santiago (tel: 690-4000; fax: 698-4656).

Ministry of Public Health, Enrique Mac-Iver 541, Santiago (tel: 639-4001; fax: 633-5875; e-mail: info@minsal.cl).

Ministry of Public Works, Morandé 59, Santiago (tel/fax: 361-2700; e-mail: mop.doh@chilnet.cl).

Ministry of Transport and Telecommunications, Amunategui 139 Santiago (tel: 672-6503; fax: 699-5138).

Ministry of Women's Affairs, Teatinos 950, Santiago (tel: 549-6100; fax: 549-6247; e-mail:sernam@entelchile.net).

Other useful addresses
Asociación de Exportadores de Manufacturas (ASEXMA Chile), Nueva Tajamar, Santiago (tel: 203-6699; fax: 203-6730; e-mail: asexma@asexmachile.cl).

Bolsa de Comercio de Santiago, La Bolsa 64, Santiago (Tel: 698-2001; fax: 697-2236; e-mail: fledermann@comercio.bolsantiago.cl).

British Embassy, Avenida el Bosque Norte 125, Piso 3, Las Condes, Santiago (tel: 231-3737; fax: 231-9771; e-mail: embsan@portal.cl).

Chilean Embassy (USA), 1732 Massachusetts Avenue, NW, Washington DC 20036 (tel: 202-785-1746; fax: 202-887-557; e-mail: embassy@embassyofchile.org).

Comisión Chilena del Cobre (Cochilco), Agustinas 1161, Santiago (tel: 382-8100; fax: 382-8300; e-mail: cochilco@cochilco.cl).

Comisión Económica para America Latina y el Caribe (CEPAL) (Economic Commission for Latin America – ECLAC), United Nations Building, Avenida Dag Hammarskjold s/n, Santiago (tel: 210-2000; fax: 208-0252).

Comité de Inversiones Extranjeras, Teatinos 120, Santiago (tel: 698-4254; fax: 698-9476; e-mail: investment@cinver.cl).

Corporación de Fomento de la Producción (CORFO) (Development Corporation), Moneda 921, Santiago (tel: 631-8692; fax: 631-8686; e-mail: drmetro@corfo.cl).

Corporación Nacional de Cobre (CODELCO), Huérfanos 1270, Santiago (tel: 690-3000; fax: 690-3059; e-mail: comunica@stgo.codelco.cl).

Empresa Nacional de Minería (ENAMI), MacIver 459, Santiago (tel: 664-7244; fax: 637-5436;e-mail: ghormaza@enami.cl).

Empresa Nacional de Petróleo (ENAP), Vitacura 2736, Santiago (tel: 280-3000; fax: 280-3199).

Instituto de Promoción de Exportaciones (ProChile), Avenida Libertador Bernardo O'Higgins 1315, Santiago (tel: 565-9000; fax: 696-0639; e-mail: info@prochile.cl).

Instituto Nacional de Estadísticas (INE), Avenida Presidente Bulnes 418, Santiago (tel: 366-7777; fax: 671-2169; e-mail: inecedoc@terra.cl).

Sociedad de Formento Fabril (SOFOFA)(Chilean Federation of Industry), Avenida Andrés Bello 2777, Santiago (tel: 391-3100; fax: 391-3200; e-mail: sofofa@sofofa.cl).

US Embassy, Avenida Andrés Bello 2800, Santiago (tel: 232-2600; fax: 330-3710).

National news agency: Agencia Chile Noticias

Internet sites
Chile Business Directory: http://www.chilnet.cl/

Chile Trade Commission: http://www.prochile.cl

Government of Chile: http://www.gobiernodechile.cl

Latin Trade Online: http://www.latintrade.com

Latin World: http://www.latinworld.com

Organisation of American States: http://www.oas.org

China

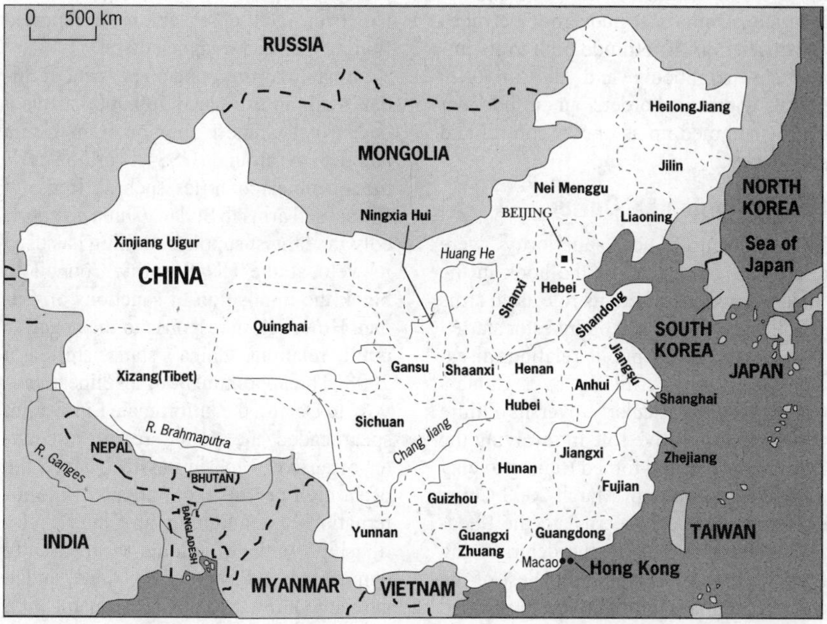

China's economic growth has created a new Chinese society and a new set of challenges for the government on how to handle a range of problems from the more banal of land seizure for redevelopment projects to more demanding environmental issues and the almost intractable reform of China's inefficient and often corrupt state enterprise system. The general opening up of the economy and greater individual economic freedom has led to an improved legal framework. None the less, the development of the country's legal system and its legal professionals still lags far behind China's economic progress. In this respect, looking at China's international competitive status, it still lags behind India where the colonial legacy included a well developed legal system.

The Year of the Pig, which ended in early 2008, not only saw China reach record breaking growth figures. Prices on the Shanghai stock-exchange index reached a record level of 6,000, having risen six-fold in two years. China's foreign exchange reserves were more than US$1.4 trillion. On top of all this, Petro-China passed Micro-Soft to become the most valuable company on earth, one of five Chinese companies in the world's top ten.

Image problems – Tibet

Globalisation has begun to make China's government and its leaders more mindful of their image, a process accentuated by the advent of the 2008 Summer Olympic Games and the need to present the image of a harmonious society. However, as the year progressed, China's public relations efforts seemed to be thwarted at every turn. First the Tibet question, which the government had hoped to mollify with PR coups such as the new railway link between Beijing and Lhasa. Talks on future policies between Tibet's Dalai Lama and the Chinese government had been taking place since 2002. These had ground to a halt, however, with China lamely, but implacably, insisting that the Tibetan side gave up all claims to independence. Since the Dalai Lama had said all along that no claims to independence had actually been expressed in the negotiations, a stalemate appeared to have been reached. The protests that burst out in early 2008 were fuelled by long simmering frustration;

KEY FACTS

Official name: Zhonghua Renmin Gongheguo (Zhongguo) (People's Republic of China)

Head of State: President Hu Jintao (from 2003; re-elected 2008)

Head of government: Premier of the State Council Wen Jiabao (from 2003; re-elected 2008)

Ruling party: Zhongguo Gongchangdang (Chinese Communist Party) (CCP)

Area: 9,596,961 square km

Population: 1.32 billion (2007)*

Capital: Beijing (Peking)

Official language: Putonghua (Mandarin Chinese – Beijing dialect).

Currency: Renminbi yuan (Rmb) = 100 fen

Exchange rate: Rmb6.81 per US$ (Jul 2008); (In 2005, the currency peg with the US$ ended and there was a 2.1 per cent revaluation of the renminbi)

GDP per capita: US$2,461 (2007)*

GDP real growth: 11.40% (2007)*

Labour force: 752.00 million (2004)

Unemployment: 4.20% (2004, urban areas); 20.00% (2004, urban and rural areas)

Inflation: 4.70% (2007)*

Oil production: 3.74 million bpd (2007)

Balance of trade: US$177.46 billion (2006)

Foreign debt: US$233.30 billion (2004)

Visitor numbers: 49.60 million (2006)*

Annual FDI: US$82.70 billion (2007)

* estimated figure

caught by surprise, the Chinese responded harshly, drafting military reinforcements to Tibet as the death toll in the protests mounted. Foreign press were denied access to Tibet with the fortuitous exception of a British Broadcasting Corporation (BBC) China correspondent who had been granted a visa beforehand for what was planned to be a routine visit to Tibet.

Tibetan protests have been routinely suppressed harshly, with estimates of as many as a million lives lost. In 1989 the then provincial leader and now President Hu Jintao reportedly authorised the military to kill street protestors. What China describes as 'autonomous regions' such as Tibet is in fact a misnomer. If anything these regions are more closely controlled than others. Certainly the sympathetic governmental response seen after the Sichuan earthquake was totally lacking in the case of Tibet. Blamed by China on the Dalai Lama's machinations, Tibetan feelings ran deep, evincing popular dissatisfaction over increased religious restrictions, environmental policies and the generally harder line coming from Beijing in the year of the Olympics. A further factor was the ethnic engineering represented by continued Han Chinese immigration into Tibet.

The Tibetan independence movement certainly gained momentum internationally by skilful linkage of its protests to the imminent Olympic Games. The process of the Olympic torch from Athens to Beijing was constantly interrupted by Tibetan protestors and supporters, despite the best efforts of China's heavy-handed security forces. Quite apart from the public relations disaster of the Olympic torch affair, China was concerned that the protests might spread elsewhere, to other autonomous provinces such as Xinjiang. Fundamentally, China's attitude to Tibet does not differ from its attitude both to its immediate neighbours and the minority groups within its borders, an attitude that can be summed up as one of control and superiority.

Image Problems – Darfur

Neither control nor superiority were enough to get China off the hook in the Sudan, however, where its role as an arms supplier and the largest oil investor started to look like another public relations disaster. International criticism over China's position, and particularly over its failure to take a more active role in resolving the Darfur conflict, had forced Beijing to play a more active role. In March 2008 China expressed 'grave concerns' to the Sudanese government about the deteriorating Darfur situation in the South West of the country. China's initial failure to respond to widespread criticism of its Sudanese involvement came to an end in February 2008 when film director Stephen Spielberg announced his withdrawal from his position as artistic advisor for the Beijing Olympics. Mr Spielberg issued a statement saying that 'China's economic, military and diplomatic ties with the government of Sudan continue to provide it with the opportunity to press for change'. China has claimed that it is abiding by United Nations (UN) embargoes on supplying weapons to the Darfur militia. However, UN observers have reported finding Chinese weapons there.

China imports around 60 per cent of Sudan's oil, an estimated 500,000 barrels a day. Total Chinese imports from China add up to around US$4.1 billion. Although other countries such as Iran and Russia sell arms to Sudan, China is reportedly the largest supplier. Beijing has used its veto at the UN Security Council to block the imposition of sanctions on Sudan. However, in response to the negative public relations, China's stance shifted in 2008. The appointment of a Chinese 'envoy' to Darfur, the unfortunate Liu Guijin, spearheaded the public relations counter-offensive. Mr Liu has to balance the often high profile expectations of the international community with China's relationship with Khartoum's apparently cynical views. Prompted by China, Sudan agreed to allow a joint UN African Union peace-keeping force into Darfur. Having initially said that China had no plans to send troops to Sudan, Mr Liu later back-tracked and announced that 135 Chinese troops would join the UN force. However, whether the Sudanese population welcome them or not (and the word on the street inclines to the latter) following the visit of President Hu Jintao to Khartoum in 2007, China appears to have signed an extensive co-operation agreement with Sudan, the details of which are mostly secret.

Sichuan

In contrast, the May 2008 Sichuan earthquake, which caused some 70,000 deaths, looked at cynically became something of a public relations success for the government. The earthquake was China's worst natural disaster for three decades. Apart from the horrifying death toll, in Tangjiashan the earthquake left over a million people at risk from earthquake formed lakes; and many more survived but were left homeless as aftershocks caused houses to collapse. In south-western Sichuan over 30,000 were left without any water supply.

The government response was as rapid as it was impressive. In less than two hours Prime Minister Wen Jiabao was on a

KEY INDICATORS — China

	Unit	2003	2004	2005	2006	2007
Population	m	1,308.37	1,335.84	1,307.56	1,314.10	*1,321.05
Gross domestic product (GDP)	US$bn	1,378.00	1,939.33	2,243.69	2,644.64	*3,250.83
GDP per capita	US$	1,060	1,269	1,716	2,011	*2,461
GDP real growth	%	8.5	10.1	10.4	10.7	*11.4
Inflation	%	0.6	3.9	1.8	1.5	*4.7
Industrial output	% change	–	11.1	10.8	12.5	–
Agricultural output	% change	–	6.3	5.0	5.0	–
Oil output	'000 bpd	3,396.0	3,490.0	3,627.0	3,684.0	3,743.0
Natural gas output	bn cum	34.1	40.8	50.0	58.6	69.3
Coal output	mtoe	842.6	989.8	1,107.7	1,212.3	1,311.4
Exports (fob) (goods)	US$m	413,600.0	583,100.0	762,484.0	969,073.0	–
Imports (cif) (goods)	US$m	384,900.0	552,400.0	628,295.0	791,614.0	–
Balance of trade	US$m	44,652.0	30,700.0	134,189.0	177,459.0	–
Current account	US$m	45,880.0	70,000.0	160,818.0	249,866.0	*360,705.0
Total reserves minus gold	US$m	408,151	614,500	821,514	1,068,493	1,530,282
Foreign exchange	US$m	403,251	609,932	818,872	1,066,344	1,528,249
Exchange rate	per US$	8.28	8.28	7.80	7.82	7.37

* estimated figure

flight to Sichuan. Since becoming Prime Minister Mr Wen – whose sympathetic role as the figurehead of government rescue and recovery efforts was to earn him the nickname of Grandpa Wen – had endeavoured to cultivate the image of a man of the people. His media-conscious role quickly made him the face of the nation's grief. Following the public relations disaster of the Tibet protests, in the year of the Beijing Olympic Games Granpa Wen and his more aloof boss, President Hu Jintao, managed to project a more human and responsive image backed up by the realities of a massive rescue effort, free access to the disaster zone for Chinese and foreign (after a few hiccoughs) press and for foreign aid. Quoted in the Paris based *International Herald Tribune*, Cheng Li of the Washington Brookings Institute observed that: 'a lot of Chinese have been overwhelmed by Wen and his sincerity, honesty and humanity'.

As the scale of the earthquake disaster became apparent, official co-operation with NGOs and civil society provided the government with positive political fallout, raising nationalistic sentiment to almost worrying levels, even among those hardest hit by the disaster. China appeared to have regained its national self confidence, with some reservations. Chinese disaster funds quickly reached over US$500 million, but there was little prospect of the country turning its back on the attractions of consumerism and materialism. Journalist Nicholas Kristof labelled China's emerging society as 'Market-Leninist'.

The authorities lost no time in preparing reconstruction plans for the stricken Sichuan province – this time ensuring that construction companies adhered to the anti-earthquake specifications that many of them had previously ignored in building schools and hospitals. Initial estimates put Sichuan's direct economic losses at US$9.25 billion. The most heavily damaged areas were in Sichuan's mountainous regions. In the reconstruction plans cities of 100,000 inhabitants were to be rebuilt within 12 months. The overall effect of the disaster on China's economy was not expected to be significant. The effect on China's politics was uncertain; greater national confidence had combined with shades of nationalism and populism, But the swift and overtly sympathetic government response had gone a long way to restoring China's international standing.

Political succession

Uncertainty continued to surround the future direction of China's ruling Communist Party. The uncertainty fuelled a tense political climate in Beijing where debate on economic reform and the Taiwan question was already well under way before irritants such as Tibet and the energy situation came along. The fundamental question confronting the party leadership was that of who should succeed Hu Jintao as president in 2012. China's political 'system' is anything but 'systematic'. The immediate challenge is the appointment of a cadre of senior officials who will serve under Hu Jintao until he steps down. But observers suspect that the President and his influential predecessor, Jiang Zemin do not see eye to eye on the succession. The horse trading over the succession dominated China's political scene in 2007.

Growth and more growth

The Chinese government began taking steps to rein in its burgeoning economy in 2007. According to the Asian Development Bank (ADB) China's gross domestic product (GDP) growth rate reached 11.4 per cent in 2007, a 13 year high and the fifth year of double-digit growth. Doubts have long been expressed about the accuracy of China's official statistics: in an article entitled *An Aberrant Abacus* the London *Economist* magazine reported that, if anything, China's growth figures had been understated. In April 2008 the National Bureau of Statistics (NBS) revised the GDP growth figure upwards by half a percentage point for both 2006 and 2007, to 11.6 per cent and 11.9 per cent respectively, well above the ADB's more cautious figure. The reason given by the NBS was increased growth in the services sector, although according to *The Economist* even the revised figures were probably on the cautious side. Economists at the Standard and Chartered Bank estimated that the combined output of China's provinces was some 10 per cent higher than the figure recorded by Beijing. In its efforts to cool an overheating economy, Beijing may well be understating the true figure; the reported growth in annual GDP figures may well be an attempt to correct previously understated figures. The long and short of it, however, is that China's growth is well into the lower teens.

However, not all China's statistical errors were understatements. It also appeared that prices in China were much higher than had originally been thought. This meant that as Chinese incomes and earnings had been more accurately estimated, the total income figure for 2005 of 18.4 trillion yuan (US$2.2 trillion at then market prices) could buy some 40 per cent less than had originally been estimated. By extension, this meant that in total the Chinese economy was some 40 per cent smaller than had originally been thought. In the year that the Chinese government was anxiously looking for statistics with which to impress the world, the fact that some 130 million more Chinese had suddenly fallen below the World Bank's poverty threshold was not something to be proudly broadcast. The average Chinese has an annual economic output worth US$1,721, corresponding to an income of US$4,000 in an industrialised economy. On balance, China could still be proud of its record in eliminating poverty. Between 1990 and 2004 the number of poor had dropped by some 470 million.

Continued export growth combined with strong domestic demand to push growth from 11.1 per cent in the first quarter of 2007 to 11.9 per cent in the second quarter. Attempting to cool the overheated economy, the government raised interest rates and also increased the banks' reserve requirements. Export tax rebates on designated products were abolished and tariffs imposed on some exports. These moves appeared to work, as GDP growth decelerated gently from 11.5 per cent in the third quarter to11.2 per cent in the fourth. Even taking in to account the braking effect on the contribution to GDP growth made by net exports, the modest drop in the apparently understated figures hardly represented a major cooling of the economy. Industry continued to be the mainspring, contributing 7.5 per cent to total growth, with services a further 3.5 per cent, although it was the calculation of this latter figure that appeared to be the less reliable. Agriculture's contribution to economic growth was minimal, as reflected in the population's continued urban drift. Twelve million new jobs were created in urban areas in 2007, comfortably above the government's target of nine million. However, according to the National Development and Reform Commission, a total of 24 million new jobs were needed just to absorb the newcomers to the labour market. Around 80 per cent of new jobs were created by the private sector, particularly by small and medium size (SME) enterprises, although in 2007 these only accounted for 16 per cent of total employment.

Inflation pressures – and expectations

Inflation rose sharply in 2007, due in large measure to increased food and fuel prices. According to the ADB inflation had reached 6.9 per cent by November 2007, the highest level since 1996, Food prices lead the way, rising at 12.3 per cent. Housing prices also rocketed, driven by rising demand. In terms of value, sales of new houses rose by 42.1 per cent in 2007. Wage cost pressure was also more evident in 2007, but did not spill over into the general economy. Although price pressures in general are likely to weaken in 2008, in tune with the global economy, Chinese inflation looks unlikely to drop much.

The World Bank has stressed the need for China to contain economic expectations through the continued imposition of tight monetary conditions and exchange rate policies. One key monetary measure has been the appreciation of the yuan against the US dollar. Other measures have focussed on softening price rises with a view to keeping staple items affordable and managing popular expectations. The snowstorms of January and February were certain to create extraordinary rises in the rate of inflation; in the first quarter of 2008 the People's Bank of China (PCB) (central bank) estimated that the Consumer price index (CPI) had risen by an annualised 8 per cent.

At the beginning of 2008 it was reasonable to expect China's monetary conditions to tighten further. The ADB had forecast Chinese interest rates to continue to edge up further; the PCB was also expected to increase Chinese banks' reserve requirements and strengthen its efforts to reduce lending to already overheated industries. The reserve requirement had been almost doubled from 9.5 per cent to 14.5 per cent in 2007, a 20-year high. The reserve requirement was raised by a further percentage point, to 15.5 per cent, in the first quarter of 2008.

China's economic policy for the period 2006–10 is enshrined in the 11th Five Year Plan. Investment is expected to continue underpinning GDP growth for 2008 and into 2009. Despite the uncertainties confronting the Chinese economy such as rising fuel and grain prices, the economy's basic drivers remain the low cost of borrowing for state-owned companies and buoyant profit levels; these two factors enable Chinese companies to continue their investment and expansion, contributing to strong domestic demand. This, in turn, is supported by government spending on social and rural development. The 2008 Beijing Summer Olympics were expected to impact positively on domestic expenditure, although their overall benefits were expected to be limited to the greater Beijing area.

Imbalances and inequalities

The ADB has expressed fears that the imbalances within China's economic model risk making it unsustainable. These imbalances are most evident in the gap between external and internal demand; China's ever increasing trade and current account imbalances have inevitably aggravated relations with its major trade partners, notably the EU and the USA. Some effort has been made by the government to restore equilibrium by restructuring the economy through the promotion of consumption, but the share of net exports and capital formation has continued to increase while the proportion of domestic consumption within the GDP has shrunk rather than expanded.

The PCB in its quarterly Monetary Policy Report (MPR) noted in May 2008 that 'general price levels remain high'; numerous factors constrain agricultural production and an income increase for farmers. In the ADB's continued assessment, the second economic imbalance arises from China's energy and environmental strains. China uses between 1.5 and twice as much energy to produce the same result as more developed countries, thereby generating a disproportionately high level of fuel consumption and oil imports. China still relies on coal for 70 per cent of its total energy consumption. Air pollution is unacceptably high, as are emissions. In the May MPR the PCB also notes that 'energy saving and pollution reduction endeavours remain arduous tasks'. The third imbalance as identified by the ADB is increasing inequality. There are a number of different dimensions to this: urban/rural, coastal/inland, east/west . In east and central China, the lives of the majority of the inhabitants have little or nothing in common with those of Shenzen or Shanghai. What is certain is that China's social – or more precisely economic – inequality is worsening.

As recessionary trends in the US and the EU took a firmer grip in the first quarter of 2008, China appeared better prepared to deal with them than most countries. The London *Financial Times* (FT) noted that a recession in China could well deflate the dangerous bubbles present in the real estate and stock markets, as well as releasing the pressure on natural resources and the environment. The FT also thought that an export slowdown would help limit the Chinese trade surplus, no bad thing in a US election year when critics of China's trade policies would be at their most vociferous. China, it was considered by the FT, was fortunately not too dependent on the US market, but quite advantageously positioned in the world's economic middle ground.

Financial reforms

In mid-2007 China began to ease restrictions on foreign security firms, allowing foreign banks to issue domestic credit and debit cards, foreign insurance companies to establish local subsidiaries and increasing the investment limit for qualified institutional investors from US$10 billion to US$30 billion. While easing restrictions on foreign investors, China tightened the screws on domestic investors as part of its strategy to cool the economy. A new government agency, the State Management Company was formed to manage China's US$1.4 trillion in foreign exchange reserves.

Coal is king…

According to the US Energy Information Administration (EIA) China is both the largest consumer and producer of coal in the world. China has an estimated 126.2 billion short tons of coal reserves, the third-largest in the world after the United States and Russia. Northern China, especially Shanxi Province, contains most of China's easily accessible coal and virtually all of the large state-owned mines. Coal from southern mines tends to be higher in sulphur and ash. In 2004, China consumed 2.1 billion short tons of coal, representing more than one third of the world total and a 46 per cent increase since 2002. Coal consumption, providing 70 per cent of total energy requirements, has grown dramatically over the last five years, reversing the decline seen from 1997 to 2000.

China's coal industry has traditionally been spread out among large state-owned coal mines, local state-owned coal mines, and thousands of town and village coal mines. In February 2006, plans were revealed to restructure China's coal sector and reduce the fragmentation in the industry, with the aim of establishing five to six giant conglomerates in China's main coal-producing provinces and closing down all small coal mines by 2015.China is opening up to foreign investment in the coal sector, in an effort to modernise existing large-scale mines and introduce new technologies into China's coal industry. The China National Coal Import and Export Corporation is the primary Chinese partner for foreign investors in the coal sector.

According to the US *Oil & Gas Journal* (OGJ), China had 18.3 billion barrels of proven oil reserves as of January 2006, flat from the previous year. The EIA estimated that China produced 3.8 million barrels per day (mbpd) of oil in 2006, slightly higher than the previous year. Of this, 96 per cent was expected to be crude oil. The EIA also estimated that China would consume 7.4mbpd of oil in 2006, representing nearly a half million barrels per day increase from 2005. For 2007, EIA data estimated that China's increase in oil demand would represent 38 per cent of the world total increase in demand.

...and oil gets expensive

In 1998, the Chinese government reorganised most state owned oil and gas assets into two vertically integrated firms: the China National Petroleum Corporation (CNPC) and the China Petroleum and Chemical Corporation (Sinopec). Each of these companies operates a range of local subsidiaries. The other major state sector firm is the China National Offshore Oil Corporation (CNOOC), which handles offshore exploration and production and accounts for roughly 15 per cent of China's domestic crude oil production. CNPC, Sinopec, and CNOOC all carried out initial public offerings (IPOs) of stock between 2000 and 2002. However, the government maintains a majority stake in each through state-owned holding companies bearing the same name. In general, CNPC and its affiliates tend to dominate in the north and west, Sinopec companies in the south, and CNOOC in offshore regions.

The EIA reports that many foreign companies have been contracted to undertake oil exploration and production activities in China. According to Chinese law, however, China's national oil companies are entitled to take a majority (51 per cent) stake in any commercial discovery, although they can choose to take a minority stake if they wish. Recently, offshore oil exploration in China has been the greater focus of the oil majors. CNOOC has initiated several Production Sharing Contracts (PSCs) with international oil companies for exploration and development in the Bohai Bay region. With China's expectation of growing future dependence on oil imports, the country has been acquiring interests in exploration and production abroad. CNPC has acquired exploration and production interests in 21 countries in four continents. During 2005, CNPC announced its intentions to invest a further US$18 billion in foreign oil and gas assets between 2005 and 2020. In Sudan, CNPC has invested more than US$8 billion in the country's oil sector, including investments in a 900 mile pipeline to the Red Sea. China's position in the Sudan, and its initial failure to address the Darfur situation has caused a negative international public relations response.

Historically, natural gas has not been a major fuel in China, but its share in the country's energy mix is increasing. The OGJ estimates that China's domestic proven reserves of natural gas stood at 53.3 trillion cubic feet (Tcf) as of January 2006. Other sources have put reserves much higher. Cedigaz estimates that China held 83 Tcf of proved natural gas reserves as of January 2006. EIA figures show that China consumed 1.3 Tcf of natural gas in 2004, almost doubling the level of natural gas consumption from five years earlier. In 2004, natural gas accounted for only around 3 per cent of total energy consumption in China, although this figure is expected to rise in the coming years. Until recently, natural gas was used primarily as a feedstock in chemical fertilizer production and an energy source at oil and gas fields.

Telecommunications

Anyone who has visited China recently cannot fail to have noticed the national addiction to mobile telephony. The scale of the industry is simply mind-boggling – there are some 600 million mobile subscribers (as countries go, only India has more inhabitants) almost double the number of fixed line subscribers (360 million). The industry as a whole had been allowed to grow 'like Topsy', with six companies happily sharing annual revenues of some US$250 billion, a figure well in excess of the total GDP of most of the world's countries.

In an attempt to rationalise this Sorceror's Apprentice scenario, in May 2008 the government announced a complex restructuring of the industry whereby the six companies would be reduced to three, each with a share of both mobile, fixed line and internet subscribers. Under this arrangement, China Mobile – by far the world's largest operator in terms of subscriber numbers – would merge with China Tietong, a much smaller fixed line company. China Telecom, China's largest fixed line company would acquire one of the mobile networks operated by a company called China Unicom. The latter would then merge its other mobile networks with China Netcom, a fixed line operator. In case this wasn't complicated enough, a sixth telecommunications company, China Satcom would be taken over by China Telecom. The principal loser in all this appeared to be Chian Mobile, a view seemingly shared by investors as the company's shares dropped in value by US$31 billion (ten per cent of the company's stock market valuation).

On the agenda for this reorganisation was the long awaited introduction of third generation (3G) mobile telephony into China. China has developed its own 3G technology; under the reorganisation arrangement China Mobile will be obliged to adopt this technology, known as TD SCDMA. The other two companies will have the more nimble, and tested alternative of foreign developed technologies.

Risk

While China's domestic demand looked set to continue growing in 2008, net exports looked likely to suffer from weaker external demand. Merchandise exports' annual growth was expected to slow to 19 per cent in 2008 and 18 per cent in 2009, well down on the 26 per cent growth recorded in 2007. Import growth, however was expected to remain at around 20 per cent, reflecting to some degree the government's pro-import policies. The negative effects on growth of the Sichuan earthquake and the bad weather of early 2008 were expected to become apparent as the year progressed. Both of these natural disasters were also expected to fuel inflation. The inflation figure for the first two months of 2008 was 7.9 per cent. Overall inflation for 2008 was forecast at an average 5.5 per cent, dropping to 5.0 per cent in 2009. In early 2008 the government froze prices for a number of goods and services, with a view to controlling inflation further and, just as importantly, public expectations of inflation.

The ADB saw the major risks confronting the Chinese economy in 2008 to be a possible – or more severe than expected – deterioration in global trading conditions weakening Chinese exports. The second risk is a stock market or property market crash, either bringing with it increased unemployment. This, in turn, would cause the banks to further tighten credit conditions. Finally, any unforeseen increase in inflation from its already high level would also result in an unwelcome tightening of credit. The ADB calculated that were these three risk factors to coincide, annual GDP growth could fall to as low as 7 per cent, requiring the government to relax its monetary programmes and raise spending on welfare and urban redevelopment programmes. To strengthen the central government's ability to handle the economy, in March 2008 five new 'super' ministries were created: for industry and information, human resources and social security, environmental protection, housing and urban/rural construction, and transport. A National Energy Commission was also created.

Risk assessment

Economy	Good
Politics	Fair
Redional stability	Good

COUNTRY PROFILE

Historical profile

From the nineteenth century onwards, the ruling Qing Dynasty (1644–1911) came under increasing pressures from internal demographic and economic imbalances, and incursions from Western powers. Following defeat at the hands of the Japanese (1895) and escalating concessions to Western powers after the Boxer Uprising (1901), the centuries-old system of promotion to the civil service via examinations ended in 1905 and dynastic rule collapsed in 1911. Yuan Shikai failed to become emperor and a chaotic period of rule by 'warlords', regional power-brokers with military resources, ensued.

1920s The Zhongguo Gongchangdang (CCP) (Chinese Communist Party) was formed and declared the southern province of Jiangxi an autonomous 'soviet' in 1927. The Communists were brutally suppressed by the rival Kuomintang (Nationalist Party).

1935 Mao Zedong took control of the CCP during the 'Long March', begun in October 1934, in which thousands of Communist fighters fled Jiangxi for the northern Shanxi province.

1937–45 The Japanese occupied increasingly large areas of China. The government of Chiang Kai-shek and the Kuomintang retreated to Sichuan province in the west of China.

1949 The People's Republic of China was established in October following the victory of Communist guerrilla forces led by Mao Zedong over the Kuomintang government, which fled to the island province of Formosa (now Taiwan).

1950 Tibet (Xizang), an independent region of western China, was occupied by the Chinese People's Liberation Army (PLA).

1958–60 In Mao's Great Leap Forward to collectivise agriculture and bring about a socialist economic system, some 40 million people died from hunger.

1965 Tibet became an autonomous region of China, but has not enjoyed any real political or cultural autonomy.

1966 To prevent the establishment of a ruling class and to destroy his enemies within the CCP, Chairman Mao launched the Great Proletarian Cultural Revolution. Some 800,000 died in the cities, but the wider effects of enforced rural re-education were widespread psychological trauma and the breakdown of industry and educational institutions.

1980–97 During this period, the CCP with over 40 million members and political control, was dominated by China's elder statesman, Deng Xiaoping, who initiated gradualist economic reform designed to create a socialist market economy.

1986 The CCP Central Committee adopted a resolution redefining the general ideology of the CCP to provide a theoretical basis for the programme of modernisation and the open door policy of economic reform. An anti-corruption campaign was launched and there was significant liberalisation in the field of culture and the arts. However, student demonstrations in major cities were regarded by China's leaders as excessive 'bourgeois liberalisation'.

1987 In the ensuing clampdown, in January, Hu Yaobang unexpectedly resigned as CCP general secretary, accused of 'mistakes on major issues of political principles'. The 'reformist' faction within the Chinese leadership emphasised the need for further reform and the extension of an open door policy. Li Peng became premier of the state council.

1989 The death of Hu Yaobang in Beijing served as a catalyst for the most serious student demonstrations ever seen in the People's Republic of China. The protests were against alleged corruption and nepotism within the government and sought a limited degree of Soviet-style glasnost in public life. A state of martial law was declared in Beijing. With the government fearing for its security, the army attacked protesters in and around Tiananmen Square. All over China, similar demonstrations were put down using force. The reformist Zhao Ziyang, CCP general secretary, was confined under house arrest. Deng brought in Jiang Zemin as general secretary to replace him. Jiang was also made chairman of the Central Military Commission (CMC), (head of the PLA).

1990 Martial law was lifted.

1992 China's economy is ranked third in the world after the US and Japan, by the World Bank.

1993 Deng retired from his civilian offices, but continued to exert influence over the 'third generation' of leaders, including Jiang, who was elected state president.

1997 China re-established sovereignty over Hong Kong, which had been under British control under a treaty signed during the Qing dynasty.

1998 The Quanguo Renmin Daibiao Dahui (National People's Congress) (NPC) re-elected Jiang as president and chairman of the CMC. Li Peng stepped down as premier, but was named chairman of the NPC and retained his number two ranking in the party hierarchy, officially outranking the new premier Zhu Rongji. The NPC also approved major changes in the leadership, bringing in a new cabinet of younger technocrats.

2000 China signed bilateral trade deals with the EU and the US in preparation for its eventual accession to the World Trade Organisation (WTO) and consequent deeper integration within the global trading system.

2001 Tajikistan, China, Russia, Kazakhstan, Kyrgyzstan and Uzbekistan formed the Shanghai Co-operation Organisation (SCO). Beijing won its bid to host the 2008 Olympic Games. President Jiang Zemin offered China's support to the US for military action against terrorist activities following the 11 September attacks in the US. China was formally admitted to the WTO.

2002 Vice President Hu Jintao was formally appointed General Secretary of the CCP.

2003 The NPC elected Hu as state president and Zeng Qinghong as vice president; Wen Jiabao was appointed premier. China and Egypt joined a WTO agreement removing all tariff barriers to information technology products. China became the third country to put a man in space.

2004 Legislators ruled out direct elections for a Hong Kong leader in 2007. Instead of waiting until 2007, Jiang Zemin resigned as chairman of the CMC and President Hu assumed supreme authority as chairman of the CMC, general secretary of the CCP and president of China. A landmark free-trade agreement was signed with 10 south-east Asian countries; the trading zone could eventually contain 25 per cent of the world's population.

2005 The NPC passed an anti-secession law, enshrining Beijing's claim of sovereignty and its threat of military force in the event of Taiwan's formal independence. Lien Chan, the first Taiwanese leader to visit China since 1949, arrived in Beijing. Later, China led the opposition to the proposal that Japan should become a permanent member of the UN Security Council citing Japan's failure to acknowledge its aggression during the 1930–40s. China scrapped its decade-old currency peg with the US dollar and sanctioned a 2.1 per cent revaluation of the renminbi against the dollar. A blast at a chemical factory in Jilin, north-east China, resulted

in a spillage of highly toxic benzene and nitrobenzene into the Songhua river, which is the main water source for the city of Harbin and its surrounds (total population nine million). The Songhua is a tributory of the Amur river which runs through south-east Russia where cities which draw their water supplies from the Amur prepared for the slick. Yao Wenyuan, last of the 'Gang of Four' died.
2006 The government issued China's Africa Policy a document setting out its objectives in relations with Africa, which promised investment and technical aid in return for African natural resources. The Three Gorges Dam, the world's largest hydroelectric project, was completed. The project got underway in 1993 and created a lake almost 600 kilometres long and submerged dozens of sites of cultural and historic heritage. The first tourist passenger train ran between Quinghai and Tibet. The new, 1,142km, railway line is the highest in the world, reaching altitudes of over 5,000 metres above sea-level, with 11 railway stations and 18 unmanned halts. The project, begun in 2001, cost US$4.2 billion and provides for passenger and freight trains. An extension was announced which will add another 270km of line to the Tibetan-Indian border. A China-Africa summit began when 41 African heads of state and 48 heads of government visited Beijing and met hundreds of Chinese trade negotiators and business people. The global annual trade surplus reached a record US$177 billion, an increase of 74 per cent.
2007 January trade figures showed a surplus of US$15.9 billion, a monthly increase of 67 per cent. Critics claim the renminbi (yuan) has been kept deliberately undervalued to keep exports cheap. Vice Premier Huang Ju died in early June. The Dalai Lama, the Tibetan spiritual leader, announced that he was considering breaking a long tradition and naming his own successor in an attempt to reduce the influence of Communist China on his succession. The Panchen Lama has an exclusive responsibility, among senior Buddhist officials, of choosing the Dalai Lama, but China took into custody the chosen Panchen Lama, Gedhun Choekyi Nyima, in 1995 and replaced him with its own, Gyancain Norbu, considered loyal to the communist party. Tibetan Buddhists fear that China will subvert their religion and culture by appointing its own Dalai Lama after the death of the reigning Dalai Lama.
2008 Hu Jintao and Wen Jiabao were both re-elected president and prime minister respectively by the National People's Congress on 15 March. A devastating earthquake of 7.9 magnitude struck the south-west province of Sichuan on 12 May. Buildings collapsed in the regional capital Chengdu, killing thousands and trapping many hundreds. The relief effort, including 50,000 troops and aid to the mountainous area, was hampered by landslides that closed roads and poor weather that grounded helicopters. A recorded 55,239 people were killed, 24,949 people missing and 281,006 injured by the earthquake by 22 May. Over 5.46 million buildings collapsed and the authorities asked for 3.3 million tents from international aid to help house the 5.47 million people who were left homeless. One million small, temporary houses were commissioned to help survivors. An agreement was signed with Taiwan on 13 June to allow 36 direct flights (18 each) a week. A further agreement will allow 3,000 tourists per day into each country from 18 July. The first regular, direct flights between China and Taiwan, since 1949, were inaugurated on 4 July. In July China was given permission by CITES to import ivory; it may particpate in the one-off auction of 108 tons of government-owned ivory being sold by Botswana, Namibia, South Africa and Zimbabwe.

Political structure

Constitution

The current constitution came into effect in 1982 and mandates complete CCP rule of the country. China's constitution emphasises strict ideological homogeneity and forbids acts that endanger the state security. It states that the Chinese people must adhere to Marxism-Leninism and Mao Zedong Thought.
The People's Republic of China, a unitary state consisting of 22 provinces, four special municipalities under central government control and five autonomous regions, was established in October 1949. The provinces, special municipalities and autonomous regions elect local people's congresses and are administered by people's governments.

Form of state

People's republic

The executive

The executive is the 15-member State Council which is elected by the National People's Congress (NPC). State Council members, including the premier of the State Council, who is appointed by the president, may not serve more than two consecutive five-year terms. The NPC also elects the 155 members of the Standing Committee which convenes annually when the NPC is not in session.
Effective political control is in the hands of the CCP which has over 40 million members. All ministers are party members. The party's central committee of 175 full members meets irregularly for plenary sessions. A National Congress is usually held every five years when a new central committee is elected.
The political bureau (politburo) of the CCP sets policy and controls all administrative, legal and executive appointments; the nine-man politburo standing committee is the focus of power.
CCP committees are the key decision-making bodies in the provinces, cities and regions into which China is divided.
The president, who plays no formal role in administration, and vice president, are elected for a maximum of two consecutive five-year terms by the NPC.

National legislature

Legislative authority is vested in the unicameral NPC, the 2,979 members of which are elected for five years by provinces, municipalities, autonomous regions and the armed forces.

Legal system

The Chinese legal system is an opaque mix of custom and statute. The judiciary and the government are closely connected. Much of the legal system remains at a partial stage of development.
The hierarchy of people's courts, ranging from Local People's Courts through Intermediate and then Higher People's Courts to the Supreme People's Court, is headed by the Ministry of Justice. The ministry was re-established in 1979 (it had been abolished in 1959 during Mao's 'Great Leap Forward'). Before 1979, arrests and sentences had to be approved by Communist Party committees. Although this practice was abolished in 1979, criminal law is still largely applied by the government as a form of public education, with periodic campaigns of mass arrests and executions used to frighten law-breakers.
People's courts, at all levels, deal with criminal, civic and economic matters in separate tribunals. Local people's mediation committees supplement the work of the courts by dealing with minor criminal offences and civil disputes, as well as helping implement government policy (such as the one-child per couple policy) at street level.
There is a similar hierarchy of people's procurates, re-established in 1978 after their abolition in the cultural revolution, extending from the localities to the Supreme People's Procurate. These monitor the work of state officials in the courts and the public security organs to ensure that they are observing the constitution and the law.
Supreme People's Court judges are appointed by the National People's Congress (NPC).

Last elections

15 March 2008 (NPC; presidential and State Council).

Results: Parliamentary: the CCP and the eight 'democratic' parties – all members of the China People's Political Consultative Conference – are allowed to stand in elections. The CCP forms the government.
Next elections
By March 2013 (NPC; presidential and State Council).

Political parties
Ruling party
Zhongguo Gongchangdang (Chinese Communist Party) (CCP)
Main opposition party
Opposition parties are strictly controlled and do not offer alternative policies. There are no multi-party democratic elections.

Population
1.32 billion (2007)*
Last census: November 2000: 1,242,612,226
Population density: 136 inhabitants per square km; urban population: 43 per cent (ADB 2006).
Annual growth rate: 0.8 per cent 1994–2004 (WHO 2006)
Ethnic make-up
The largest ethnic group is the Han, constituting 93.3 per cent of the population, which is largely concentrated around the basins of the main rivers (the Yellow River, the Yangtse and the Pearl River) and along the coast. Of the 55 other ethnic groups, 15 number over a million people each, including the Zhuang (Guangxi province), Hui (Muslims), Uygurs (in Xinjiang), Manchus, Tibetans, Mongolians and Koreans. The rest vary in size from several hundred thousand down to a few hundred.
Religions
China is officially atheist, but religion is tolerated to the extent that it does not challenge the state. Buddhism, Taoism, Islam, Catholicism and Protestantism all have followings. The formerly dominant belief system, Confucianism, continues to influence habits throughout society. Old temples, mosques and churches are being reopened and new ones built, but numbers are still far short of pre-revolutionary days. The Falun Gong religious movement is one of the religions considered to be subversive and its members have been arrested and imprisoned.

Education
The Ministry of Education in China estimates that 99 per cent of school-age children enter primary education, the length of which is six years. The retention rate in primary education for the whole country is 93 per cent.
Secondary education extends over six years, divided into general secondary education and vocational/technical secondary education. Both include two stages, junior secondary and senior secondary, of three years each. There are specialised schools and skilled workers' schools which cater for vocational training. The Ministry of Education estimated that 94 per cent of pupils finishing primary education enter secondary schools. It also says that half of pupils finishing junior secondary schools enter senior high education.
The Ministry of Education has encouraged the establishment of community colleges in major cities across China. Public expenditure on education was equivalent to less than 3 per cent of annual GDP in 2001 and included subsidies to private education at the primary, secondary and tertiary levels.
Literacy rate: 91 per cent adult rate; 99 per cent youth rate (15–24) (Unesco 2005).
Compulsory years: 7 to 16.
Pupils per teacher: 24 in primary schools.

Health
Per capita total expenditure on health (2003) was US$278; of which per capita government spending was US$101, at the international dollar rate, (WHO 2006).
Employers pay for the medical care of most Chinese city-dwellers, while the rural population is in theory covered by local insurance schemes, village collectives or rural factories. The state and collective entities, such as factories or villages, run all large hospitals. There are a large number of private practitioners and privately run clinics.
It is estimated that more than one in five Chinese will be 60 years or older by 2030, which is likely to increase state expenses towards old age health care.
World Bank estimates show that 68 per cent and 24 per cent respectively in urban and rural areas have access to improved sanitation. Safe water facilities are available to 94 per cent of the urban population and 66 per cent of the rural population. Around 90 per cent of women use contraceptives, mainly due to the government's drive to keep down the birth rate.
Chinese consumption of tobacco products is popular and estimates say two-thirds of men smoke by the age of 25, with the vast majority maintaining the habit for many years. It is estimated that one third of Chinese men will die from smoking-related diseases, with the annual death toll reaching three million by 2050.
Hospitals rely on drug sales for 70 per cent of their budgets; in May 2004 the Chinese government ordered price cuts for antibiotics, which account for 35 per cent of the Rmb49.6 billion (US$6 billion) pharmaceutical market. This measure is expected to have repercussions as it decreases hospital sales. Analysts say antibiotics are prescribed unnecessarily and the government is concerned about incentives, legal and illegal, that have resulted in hospital doctors prescribing them to about 80 per cent of in-patients.
In January 2008, it was announced that a basic healthcare programme would be introduced for every citizen of China. Healthy China 2020 will provide universal health services to replace the patchy service that disadvantaged poorer patients, particularly the rural poor. The service will also monitor disease control and evaluate public health hazards.
HIV/Aids
The virus is now present in 31 regions and has exploited distinct risk groups. The prevalence of HIV infection among injecting drug users ranges from 35–80 per cent in Xinjiang, and 20 per cent of the population in Guangdong. Some rural communities in Anhui, Henan and Shandong have been hit by infection levels of 10–20 per cent, and as much as 60 per cent in the worst hit areas, where locals sold their blood plasma to supplement their poor incomes. Death rates in these areas are high, although not yet significant enough to affect national statistics.
HIV prevalence: 0.1 per cent aged 15–49 in 2003 (World Bank).
Life expectancy: 72 years, 2004 (WHO 2006)
Fertility rate/Maternal mortality rate: 1.7 births per woman, 2004 (WHO 2006); maternal mortality 55 per 100,000 live births (World Bank).
Birth rate/Death rate: 7 deaths and 16 births per 1,000 people
Child (under 5 years) mortality rate (per 1,000): 30 deaths per 1,000 live births (World Bank)
Head of population per physician: 1.6 physicians per 1,000 people, 2001 (WHO 2006)

Welfare
China's economic development is uneven, with a wide gap between cities and the countryside and between regions. China's social security expenses are typically equivalent to around 10 per cent of GDP. The social insurance system includes provision for old age pensions, unemployment, medical care and industrial injury. Social insurance is implemented in accordance with state laws. The current focus of reform is on old age pension and unemployment insurance systems for urban enterprises. Social security entitlements have been allocated on a geographical footing with the working population being divided into urban and rural residents with the

latter receiving far less in terms of benefits. Moreover, the urban population has been further split up into various layers depending on the size and importance of the employing enterprise or work unit.
Therefore, a key state-owned enterprise (SOE) would offer better pension rights, wages and medical benefits than a smaller SOE or a township collective enterprise (COE).
The government increased the availability of the social security fund to more beneficiaries in 2003. The pension system is available to 150 million people, up from 130 million; the unemployment insurance system benefits approximately 110 million up from 100 million; and the medicare insurance system treats 100 million, an increase of 10 million people.
Another safety net beneath these systems is the minimum livelihood guarantee (MLG), which is administered by the Ministry of Civil Affairs (MCA). There are unemployment insurance schemes and some regions have started reforms of the basic medical insurance system.

Pensions

There is a partially funded pension scheme, which was launched in 1997, with two mandatory elements, a pay-as-you-go state pension administered by provinces, and individual pension accounts. There are also voluntary company pensions and for those most disadvantaged a social security fund. The pay-as-you-go system is based on contributions from employers and employees with the funds being pooled into a general account. In case of any shortfall, it is the responsibility of the local government to ensure funds are available to pay basic pension allowances. Government statistics indicate that SOEs contribute the majority of cash to pension funds.
In general, the contribution of the employer does not exceed 20 per cent of the overall wage bill of an enterprise. Employee contributions are between 4 and 8 per cent with employees in more developed areas paying the higher rate. The lower tier pension, known as the basic pension, is calculated at 20 per cent of the average wage of employees in the town or city.
As yet, China does not have a national policy for pension provision. Nevertheless the government is aware that with an ageing population and falling fertility rate China's dependency ratio – the numbers in work supporting the numbers in retirement – is projected to drop from 9:1 to 2.6:1 by 2045.
In 2005 the government awarded operating licenses to 15 investment managers to operate China's new corporate pension scheme. Of the 15, four are foreign financial services ING, Fortis, Deutsche Bank and Bank of Montreal which are required to be in joint Chinese partnership. The new scheme will hold pension contributions in a legally distinct fund governed by trust law.

Main cities

Beijing (capital, estimated population 7.7 million (m) in 2004), Shanghai (10.8m), Tianjin (5.0m), Wuhan (5.1m), Shenyang (4.1m), Guangzhou (Canton, 5.0m), Nanjing (3.3m) Harbin (2.7m), Chongqing (2.4m), Jinan (2.1m), Changchun (2.4m), Chendu (2.5m), Taiyuan (2.0m), Jinan (2.1m), Dalian (1.7m), Qingdao (2.0m), Fushun (1.5m), Lanzhou (1.6m), Xi'an (2.9m), Zhengzhou (1.9m), Hangzhou (2.6m).

Languages spoken

There are seven main Chinese dialects, but the written language is the same for all dialects. Other languages include Tibetan, Uygur (a Turkic language) and Mongolian.
English is not widely spoken, especially outside the main cities, although there will usually be someone who can speak a little in hotels, restaurants and taxi stations.

Official language/s

Putonghua (Mandarin Chinese – Beijing dialect).

Media

All forms of media are tightly controlled by the authorities and recent labialisation has only been extended to distributions and advertising and not to editorial content.
The growth of the internet has resulted in 'the most extensive and effective legal and technological systems for internet censorship and surveillance in the world' according to an academic report of 2005.
China regularly blocks websites for groups it considers dissenting. Internet service providers and news organisations have agreed to Chinese censorship as part of their business contracts with China, which then allows access to its vast market.

National news agency: Xinhua (New China News Agency)

Press

Dailies: The primary government-owned, Communist party, national newspaper, published in seven languages is Renmin Ri Bao (People's Daily) (www.people.com.cn), which has ten other separate newspapers. All cities have their own newspaper, typically published by the Communist party and therefore lacking much criticism of it. Corruption and inefficiency is reported but only after approval by Communist party officials. News outlets that have flouted this convention are subject to censure or swift closure.
In Chinese, Zhongguo Qingnian Bao (China Youth Daily) (www.cyol.net) aimed at Communist Young League, Jie Fang Ri Bao (JF Daily) (www.jfdaily.com) from Shanghai, Dongnan Kuai Bao (Southeast Express) (www.dnkb.com.cn), from Fujian, and Guangzhou Metro Daily (http://ycdtb.dayoo.com).
From Shanghai, in English, Shanghai Daily (www.shanghaidaily.com), East Day (http://english.eastday.com), includes business news, The Shanghai News (www.theshanghainews.net), Shanghalist (http://shanghaiist.com).
From Lassa, in Tibetan, Bod Kyi Dus Bob (Tibet Times) (www.tibettimes.net), in Chinese Lasa Wan Bao and online China Tibet News (www.chinatibetnews.com).

Weeklies: In Chinese, Sanlian Shenghuo Zhoukan (Life Week) (www.lifeweek.com.cn) a weekly of general interest, Feng Hua Yuan (Chinese News & Culture Magazine) (www.fhy.net), Hau Xia Wen Zhai (www.cnd.org) are bi-weeklies news magazines. Trends (www.trendsmag.com.cn) for women. In English, Beijing Review (www.bjreview.com.cn), is a national weekly news magazine and Beijing Scene (www.beijingscene.com), is a popular lifestyle magazine.

Business: There are several daily business newspapers, printed in Chinese, and some with English online editions, including Jingii Ri Bao (Economic Daily) (http://paper.ce.cn), Jingii Guancha Bao (The Economic Observer) (www.eeo.com.cn), Guo Ji Shang Bao (http://ibdaily.mofcom.gov.cn), Qihuo Ri Bao (www.qhrb.com.cn), Zhongguo Gongshang Bao (China Industry & Commerce News) (www.cicn.com.cn), Zhongguo Jingji Shibao (China Economic Times) (www.jjxww.com) and Zhongguo Jinggii Bao (China Business), which specifically focusses on steel (www.chinaccm.com/0n). Other, major, regional cities have their own editions of the Economic Daily.
Magazines include a bi-weekly Caijing (Business and Financial Review) (www.caijing.com.cn).

Periodicals: In English, Beijing This Month is a semi-tourist magazine.

Broadcasting

All broadcasting is overseen by the Ministry of Radio, Film and Television.
Broadcast media, for most people, is limited to government-run organs, as foreign short wave radio signals are regularly jammed and the use of satellite receivers restricted. There are more than one billion television views and TV is a popular source of news and information.
Pay-to-view TV is a growing market and is expected to have around 130 million customers by 2010.

Radio: The government-run China National Radio has four national networks, plus China Radio International (CRI) (www.cri.cn) with services in 45 languages and a service devoted to Taiwan. Domestic radio services broadcast in the country's major languages and dialects. There are over 500 government-owned local radios stations, including the Beijing People's Broadcasting Station (BPBS), which has several services including a Special Educational Service, and Economic, Traffic and Literary stations.

The first foreign language radio station, in Beijing, Radio 774 (http://am774.bjradio.com.cn), was set up in 2004 by the Chinese government, specifically for foreign residents.

Television: The national state-run, China Central Television (CCTV) (http://english.cctv.com), has over 2,000 channels available for its viewers through a network of regional and municipal stations. Non-domestic programmes are limited, with a few foreign TV companies providing services via either cable or satellite dishes.

Advertising

The Advertising Law of 1995 regulates all aspects of advertising under the auspices of the State Administration for Industry and Commerce. Certain products require additional approval before advertising such as tobacco, alcohol, pharmaceuticals and medical products and services.

As China's middle class has grown so has its consumerism, so that the advertising market in Asia is second only to Japan. It is worth over US$20 billion annually and has had a growth rate of over 10 per cent since 2004. Multinational corporations dominate the advertising industry with either products or techniques, but domestic enterprises are growing in importance and provision of services. Multinationals are as intent on protecting their brands as they are in promoting them throughout the country.

Economy

The Chinese economy has shown an average annual GDP growth rate of 9.5 per cent in real terms since the mid-1980s. This remarkable growth has been achieved as the ruling Chinese Communist Party (CCP) veered from its ideological path, characterised by a Marxist, central government planning and inflexible economic activity, into a pragmatic one of a decentralised, liberal market economy with entrepreneurial activity and individual reward. It now follows a strategy of 'Socialism with Chinese characteristics' with mixed forms of private and public ownership competing within a market environment (espoused by former president, Deng Xiaping, 2006). In so doing , China has benefited from the largest reduction in poverty, with the fastest growth in incomes it has ever experienced. The stratergy was began in the mid-1980s when an emphasis was placed on light industrial development, both for exports and to provide consumer goods for domestic consumption. As the government switched production from labour-intensive to higher technology industries, officials and industrial managers were increasingly marked by their technocratic, rather than ideological background. A World Bank report published in December 2007 stated that almost 50 per cent of the World's total GDP was produced between the US, China, Japan, Germany and India. The slowdown in the US economy began having an adverse effect on China's trade surplus, which fell from US$23.7 billion in February 2007 to US$8.6 billion in February 2008. Factory gate prices also rose by 6.6 per cent per annum and reflected the rise in consumer inflation.

Since 1996 China has contributed one quarter of the global growth in output and international trade. The drawback to this situation is that China's need for raw materials has measurably increased world prices. A huge rise in global oil prices in 2003 was sparked by China's need to import oil, around 50 per cent more than its 2002 level of 4.9 million barrels per day (bpd), and rising further to 6.4 million bpd in 2004. The US energy agency estimated that by 2006 China's consumption would have increased by 500,000 barrels per day, or 38 per cent of total growth in world oil demand, making it the world's third-largest net importer of oil (after the US and Japan).

President Hu Jintao embarked on a worldwide trade tour in 2006 and secured many deals, primarily based on its rapacious energy needs being met by trade, investment and loans to producers. China now has exploration and production interests in 21 countries and intends to invest US$18 billion in foreign oil and gas between 2005–20. China is also scouring the globe in search of primary products: bauxite from Vietnam and Guinea, uranium, iron ore and copper from Australia, diamonds from Namibia and chrome from Zimbabwe. It is buying soya from Brazil, medical supplies from Sweden and airplanes from the US and all paid for by its US2.26 trillion economy (in 2005) and its US$1.0 trillion global trading surplus (1 October 2006).

The central bank de-linked the renminbi from the US dollar in 2005, and has kept it within a 3 per cent margin of the US dollar. China's foreign trade remained stable despite the resultant 2.1 per cent revaluation.

In 2005, GDP growth was 9.9 per cent, and an estimated 10.7 per cent in 2006. Foreign direct investment (FDI) was US$86.1 billion, a record and around twice the FDI level of 2001.

China's economy does not seem to be tiring and it will take an enormous shock to deflect it from its given path. In the meantime the government has to juggle the requirements of a free market economy with some worrying developments in social disaffection, environmental damage and corruption caused by a government regulatory system that is weak, naïve or still under construction.

The state-owned oil company PetroChina became the world's largest company on 5 November 2007, the first day of its trading on the Shanghai stock exchange, with a market value of US$1 trillion – more that twice the value of the world's next largest company, Exxon Mobil. Nevertheless, PetroChina's profits do not approach the world's top 50 companies and analysts have warned the valuation may be vastly overrated.

Official figures showed China's economy grew by 11.4 per cent in 2007, a 13-year high. Exports and a booming construction industry were leaders in the expanding economy. Inflation became a tangible and persistent problem in 2007, which corresponded with an impressive growth in GDP. Global demand, primarily from China and India, pushed up world prices for fuel and other commodities and, with China's widening trade surplus – US$262.2 billion in 2007, up 48 per cent on the previous year – resulted in excessive liquidity as monetary pressures forced a rise in domestic prices. Consumer inflation, particularly because of the steady rise in food prices, which reach an 11-year high of 6.9 per cent in November 2007. Some food prices soared such as pork which doubled in price. Low income families can spend up to 50 per cent of their income on basic foodstuffs and the government, in a move to avert potential civil unrest, introduced a series of heavy fines for any retailer or producer who increased prices for basic necessities.

Foreign direct investment grew by 13.8 per cent, to US$82.7 billion in 2007, which excludes investment in the financial sector. By December 2007 foreign exchange reserves reached US$1.53 trillion, an annual increase of 40 per cent, the world's largest reserve.

In its first case of a defeat before the WTO it was determined that China had restrictions on the import of foreign cars. The EU, Canada and US brought the case accusing China of protectionist policies whereby either 60 per cent of all vehicle components must be Chinese-made or foreign manufactures must pay higher import duties.

The monthly record trade surplus fell in May by 10 per cent to US$20.2 billion, following a surge in the cost of imported raw materials, particularly oil, which grew by 25 per cent in May compared with a year earlier.

External trade

After becoming a member of the WTO in 2001, trade has grown so much that by 2007 China had become the third leading trading nation in the world, after the US and Germany.

Its agricultural, manufacturing and industrial sectors exports a huge range of items from seeds to hi-tech electronic equipment, from mass produced garments to custom built oil tankers; its service sector is not as well developed. The trade surplus for the first half of 2007 was US$113 billion.

In February 2007 President Hu visited eight African countries when he signed over 50 co-operation agreements and provided over US$5 billion in preferential loans and export credit guarantees and a further US$5 billion to encourage Chinese firms to invest in Africa.

In June 2007 some Chinese exports were banned in a few countries around the world, when pharmaceuticals and food products were found to be contaminated and resulted in the death and injury of consumers. New national standards for food production were introduced in October 2007, to improve China's reputation following international concern for poor processing and adulterated and dangerous foods and medicines.

Imports

Main categories are light industrial and metal products, machinery and equipment, plastics, optical and medical equipment, organic chemicals, iron and steel.

Main sources: Japan (14.6 per cent total, 2006), South Korea (11.3 per cent), Taiwan (11.0 per cent).

Exports

Principal exports include machinery and equipment, plastics, clothing, optical and medical equipment, iron and steel.

Main destinations: US (21.0 per cent total, 2006), Hong Kong (16.0 per cent), Japan (9.5 per cent).

Agriculture

Farming

China's economy has traditionally been based on agriculture, but since collectivisation and the Mao-era requirement for self-sufficiency in food was replaced with co-operatives in 1976, farming has experienced the progressively hard realities of the market place with large unprofitable state farms closing down and workers made redundant. Agriculture remains an important sector, employing 50 per cent of the labour force, while contributing around 15 per cent of GDP. Since China joined the WTO in 2001 its domestic farmers have been in competition from foreign imports and in 2005, for the first time in decades, China was a net importer of food. There has also been a shift from land-intensive farming of grains to labour intensive crops such as fruit and vegetable to relieve the pressure on farmland and to soak up the abundance of workers.

With a burgeoning industrial base, China is experiencing rapid urbanisation and rural workers, looking for better wages and a share of China's increasing standard of living, have joined the factory line. A land reform law enabled farm collectives and members to sell their land; the government's ultimate aim is land privatisation. About 5 per cent of farmland, or 6.7 million hectares (ha), have been lost to mainly industrial development since 1997 and pressure on resources, such as water, is, in some areas, becoming critical. Land use and erosion have resulted in pollution and flooding, which prompted the government to modify the new reforms, including delisting 70 per cent of development zones, thus saving over 24,000 square kilometres of farmland. Although all land is officially owned by the state, land ownership comes in the form of 'land use rights', which give the title-owner rights for between 30–70 years. Forty million farmers have lost the rights to their land since 1984 and rural communities are protesting at the manner of the purchase and sale of farmland.

Re-designated land use has also been initiated by the government with 5.4 million ha of arable land given over to forestry, while cotton growing has dropped by over 7 per cent. Both of these measures, and the reinforced embankment of the middle and lower reaches of the Yangtze and Yellow rivers, are measures designed to stem the disastrous flooding seen increasingly since the early 1990s.

Government policy, incorporating the changes that entry to the WTO has imposed, is mostly concerned with food security. The government's traditional agricultural policy has been to encourage farmers to increase production to meet the needs of the cities, while keeping prices low. This has involved guaranteeing farmers a price for a proportion of their crop and offering it at a subsidised price in the towns. Grain imports prompted government funding for rural regional development with rice procurement prices increased by 20 per cent in 2004.

The government is attempting to increase farm incomes – which are markedly below those in the cities – in the hope that the sector can provide the impetus for growth of consumer products. The government is considering changing agricultural policy to focus more on grain quality rather than quantity in order to cope with external competition. There is likely to be increased rural poverty and unemployment in the medium-term as cheaper imports bite. The conundrum remains of how to increase rural incomes and provide food for a huge population without significant state intervention and, by extension, state distortion of the market.

From 2005, a policy that limits foreign producers of genetically modified (GM) seed crops from accessing the Chinese market runs concurrently with the country's own research and development to produce its GM crops in cotton and rice (US$121 million in 2004). The government's problematic position is hampered by its appreciation of the sales potential for unmodified crops in overseas markets that are reluctant to take GM crops, against the need for higher domestic yields and the possibility for sales of Chinese patented GM seed crops abroad.

According to the Centre for Chinese Agricultural Policy, China will need to produce more than 1.5 times the 1999 level of grain output to feed a population of 1.6 billion by 2030. The demand for livestock and aquatic products is forecast to double in the same period.

Crop production in 2005 included 426,613,448 tonnes (t) cereal in total, 185,454,000t rice, 132,645,000t maize, 107,176,100t sweet potatoes, 4,215,700t cassava, 16,900,300t soya beans, 1,638,500t taro, 96,340,250t wheat, 73,036,500t potatoes, 14,408,500t groundnuts in shell, 13,050,010t rapeseed (canola), 17,100,000t seed cotton, 6,581,100t fibre crops, 7,910,000t sugar beets, 2,592,800t sorghum, 16,411,995t oilcrops, 16,019,500t citrus fruit, 2,685,500t tobacco, 88,730,000t sugar cane, 31,644,040t tomatoes, 12,531,000t chillies and peppers, 11,093,500t garlic, 27,000t green coffee, 6,390,000t bananas, 25,006,500t apples, 5,698,000t grapes, 1,363,400t treenuts, 5,908,500t pulses, 87,055,600t fruit in total, 435,024,075t vegetables in total, 940,500t tea, 625,000t natural rubber. Livestock production included 77,564,060t meat in total, 6,800,200t beef, 50,094,700t pig meat, 2,420,000t lamb, 1,926,914t goat meat, 14,675,345t poultry, 28,674,390t eggs, 28,670,480t milk, 305,000t honey, 1,711,521t cattle hides, 290,003t cocoons, silk.

Fishing

With its extensive river network and long coastline, China produces a substantial quantity of fish and exports much of it to its regional neighbours. The total marine

fishing ground area is about 818,000 square nautical miles and China has a total of 150 commercially exploitable marine species in its waters. The main species are silver carp, bighead carp, grass carp and tilapia.
China's marine fishing production is made up of small-scale fisheries and the state-owned enterprises (SOEs). The small scale fisheries produce an estimated 90 per cent of the total seafood supply. The reform of SOEs has improved productivity in large-scale fishing operations. In common with other fishing grounds, stocks in the South and East China Seas are becoming depleted. Inland fishing is showing an increase, following a period of decline caused by the depletion of inland freshwater habitats due to dam-building, industrial pollution and land reclamation for agriculture.

Forestry

China has around 14 per cent forest cover, almost evenly divided between coniferous and broadleaved forests. Southern forests are mainly lowland rain forests and monsoon forests. In the north, the majority of forests are mixed coniferous.
The government has embarked on a policy of reforestation. Deforestation was partially blamed for the disastrous extent of the 1998–99 floods which killed thousands and swamped cities, agricultural land and industrial enterprises. Huge coniferous forests have been planted and it is hoped that slower-growing deciduous trees will augment them in the reforested areas.
The State Forestry Administration, has set ambitious targets for China to raise afforestation by 26 per cent by 2050.
China is one of the world's five largest wood-producing countries, although the majority of production is burned as fuel. It is a net exporter of wood products and also produces a large amount of non-wood forest products such as resins, tung oil, essential oils, bamboo poles and bamboo shoots, nuts, mushrooms, honey and medicinal plants.

Industry and manufacturing

China's industrial base is highly diversified and ranges from the production of metals and oil refining to light industry such as textiles and computer hardware. The manufacturing sector accounts for around 37 per cent of GDP. The major industries are mechanics, electronics, metallurgy, chemicals, building materials, furniture, woodwork, textiles, clothing, food, petroleum and coal processing. The government has been focussing on restructuring the industrial sector and introducing advanced technology. The government hopes to phase out small scale production and encourage foreign participation, particularly in the chemicals industry. The development of effective, low-cost chemicals for agricultural use is a top priority.
China has become a production centre for a multitude of labour-intensive assembly industries. China produces around 75 per cent of the global supply of textiles. There is considerable foreign investment coming from Hong Kong (which accounts for most of new funding in the Shenzhen Special Economic Zone), Japan and the US. China has the ability to exploit vertical economic linkages from its impressive natural resources to heavy industy and the manufacturing of white goods, which has shown impressive growth since the early 1990s.
China is a net exporter of aluminium and stands to become one of the world's largest aluminium producers. It is also a major exporter of magnesium, although competitors have complained that China has driven down global magnesium prices through price dumping on commodity markets. China is the world's largest steel producer. Steel exports more than doubled in 2004 and the growth continued into 2005, making China the third leading exporter of steel after Japan and Russia. At the same time, imports of steel have fallen.
Vehicle production is an important growth sector. On the basis of growth levels sustained since the late 1990s, China stands to become one of the world's largest car exporters by 2010.
China's attraction as a foreign investment destination has increased since it became a WTO member, since low production costs and cheap labour have encouraged many foreign businesses to transfer their operations to the mainland. The main concern is that increased competition will have a devastating effect on state-owned industries. More joint-venture companies are likely to evolve over time, leading to mixed-ownership control in the industrial sector.
Chinese industry is faced with an increasing domestic oversupply problem. At the same time, domestic demand has fallen as state-owned enterprises lay off workers as part of the government's restructuring programme. This has increased competition within Chinese industry, causing deflation and putting pressure on factory gate prices. The problems facing the industrial sector have led to concerns that Chinese companies, stimulated by the government's fiscal pump-priming of the economy, have been investing too much in increasing capacity.
Problems facing China's industrial sector are the lack of workable bankruptcy laws and the corruption of local officials, who are keeping failing industries afloat. State-owned banks are forced to carry the burden of the industrial sector's debt, a burden that is unsustainable. An eventual clamp-down on non-performing loans within the banking sector will affect the industrial sector. The government is encouraging investment in privately-owned industrial firms, with the possibility of opening up the sector to further foreign investment.

Tourism

China is one of the world's most visited destinations. In 2004, China displaced Italy as the world's fourth most popular desination. The tourism sector is being vigorously developed and promoted. Infrastructure has been being expanded and received extra impetus from the preparations for the 2008 Olympic Games in Beijing. However, in the run up to the Olympics the government issued visa rules restricting the issue of business visas until after the games. The move was said to be an attempt to keep out potential terrorists and political activists. Despite the expected rise in visitors over the Olympics, hotels were said to be down on occupancy levels and in July 2008 anounced a cut in the cost of room rates to try and encourage late bookers. Prices had initially risen to take advantange of the anticipated rise in visitor numbers.
Visitor numbers to Tibet increased by 64 per cent in 2007 to just over 4 million. The increase was put down to better marketing and the new high-speed rail service to China.
On 13 June 2008 an agreement was signed with Taiwan to allow 3,000 tourists per day into each country from 18 July.

Environment

China is a land of contrast. While a project of land reclamation has been in operation since 2001 in the north- western Ningxia Hui autonomous region, where willows and grass are helping to beat back the desert, for many regions around China the prospects are not so good. The Yellow River typically runs dry before it reaches the sea due to the overuse of water for irrigation. Desertification is accelerating and threatens one-third of the country and 400 million people. The national policy of self-sufficiency in food in the past resulted in the cultivation of unsuitable grain crops in desert areas and, coupled with logging and over-exploitation exacerbated by a natural lack of water and rainfall, has led to rapid soil erosion. The beginnings of a forest have been planted in Yanchi in an effort to avert the spring sandstorms that sweep through Beijing each spring.
In contrast, the central and southern regions are hit every summer by severe floods. The worst affected areas are the middle and upper reaches of the Yangtze

River, where the Three Gorges Dam is expected to bring some relief when it is completed. As it neared its completion, the risk to the environmental and ecology, wich included landslides and loss of drinking water, prompted officials to plan to relocate over four million people to the city of Chongqing from the immediate vicinity of the Three Gorges Dam between 2007–22.

In 2005 an explosion in a state-run chemical plant caused an 80km toxic benzene slick that flowed down the Songhua River endangering over nine million inhabitants who depend on the river for their supply. Many residents of the city of Harbin joined an exodus to avoid the danger when authorities halted river-water supplies and handed out thousands of bottles of water while the slick passed.

In April 2008, China was reported to be the biggest carbon polluter in the world. The figures in the report came from provincial-level data from China's own Environmental Protection Agency.

Nevertheless, the US per capita emission is still 5–6 times higher than China and any pressure to cap emissions in either country will require overcoming their no-harm-to-economic-growth stance.

Mining

China's mining industry ranks as one of the largest in the world, although production statistics are sketchy. Most of China's mineral production is consumed locally by state-owned enterprises (SOEs). There are around 80,000 SOEs and 200,000 collectively-owned mines. China is an important producer of copper, tungsten, antimony, lithium and molybdenum, and also produces significant quantities of zinc, lead, manganese, tin, mercury and rare earths. China ranks among the top five countries for its reserves of antimony, barite, graphite, magnesite, fluorite, molybdenum, tin and tungsten. China imports alumina, chromite, cobalt, copper, iron ore, manganese and other platinum-group metals. China is an extremely important market for the global minerals industry and is one of the largest mineral exporters, importers and producers in the world.

China is becoming increasingly important in the molybdenum market and has substantially more deposits of rare earth elements than the rest of the world, 97 per cent of them in the Bayan Obo iron ore mined in Inner Mongolia.

A Chinese-owned mining company won a tender to develop one of the world's largest copper mines sited in Logar Province in Afghanistan. It is estimated that the site has 13 million tonnes of copper. Australia, Canada, China and Russia all contested the tender, ultimately won by Metallurgical Group with an investment of US$3 billion.

Hydrocarbons

China had proven oil reserves of 17.1 billion barrels in 2004 and produced around 3.5 million bpd. Ninety per cent of Chinese oil production is located onshore, with Daqing in north-eastern China accounting for nearly a third of total production. Offshore exploration is concentrated on the Bohai Sea, which is believed to have 1.5 billion barrels of reserves. The Pearl River Delta is also a major area of exploration. Oil production is currently dominated by several large state-owned firms and the government is in the process of restucturing state sector oil companies. The state-owned oil company PetroChina became the world's largest company on 5 November 2007, the first day of its trading on the Shanghai stock exchange, with a market value of US$1 trillion – more that twice the value of the world's next largest company, Exxon Mobile. Nevertheless, PetroChina's profits do not approach the world's top 50 companies and analysts have warned the valuation may be vastly overrated.

China is one of the largest oil consumers in the world, overtaking Japan to be second to the US. China, whose oil requirements are increasing year by year to feed the burgeoning economic expansion, is a net importer of oil and is active in securing supplies around the world.

China has natural gas reserves of 2.23 trillion cubic metres (cum), mainly located in Xinjiang Uyghur Autonomous region and Inner Mongolia. A 4,000km pipeline, bringing gas to the urban coastal areas, opened in 2005. China plans to replace coal with gas as the main source of power generation in homes in the main urban areas and this pipeline could eventually be extended to tap the large gas reserves of Central Asia.

China has coal reserves of 114.5 billion tonnes and produced 989.8 million tonnes oil equivalent (mtoe). Consumption was 956.9 mtoe and is expected to increase. The main export destinations for Chinese coal are South Korea and Japan. China is becoming more open to foreign investment in its coal industry.

Energy

China's total installed generating capacity stood at 508GW in 2005 but figures released in January 2007 showed that it had added another 102GW as it expands to meet the demands of its rapid economic growth. The figures surprised all industry experts, which included the State Grid Corporation, the authority that controls 80 per cent of China's power transmission, who had underestimated the annual increase by 25 per cent.

Around 70 per cent is supplied by coal, reserves of which China has in abundance. Although more coal will be used for generation in the future and a large number of new coal-fired power stations are projected, the proportion of natural gas use is rising. Electric consumption by sector is: heavy industry – 60 per cent, light industry – 15 per cent, residential – 10 per cent, government – 7 per cent, agriculture – 6 per cent, transport and telecommunications – 2 per cent.

The use of hydropower for generation is being expanded with new stations being constructed. On completion in 2009, the giant Three Gorges dam will have a capacity of 18.2GW produced by 26 separate 700MW generators. Another large hydroelectric project will involve a series of dams on the Yellow River, with 25 generating stations with a combined installed capacity of 15.8GW.

The government is also expanding nuclear power generating capacity, with the construction of a number of plants in joint ventures with Russian, French and Canadian firms.

The government hopes eventually to unify electricity distribution into one national power grid with power generators selling their electricity at rates determined by a free market.

Financial markets

Stock exchange

In 1986, the stock market in Shanghai, the largest in East Asia before 1949, reopened to trade shares and bonds. China has since opened securities exchanges in 44 cities, including the capital Beijing, but trading so far has been thin. Shanghai and the Shenzhen Stock Exchange (formally opened in 1991) remain the two major markets for both domestic and foreign investors. Both markets list 'A' shares (for domestic investors) and 'B' shares (for foreign investors) as well as bonds and warrants. As a result of further planned privatisation, Shanghai's total market capitalisation is expected to increase from US$600 billion in 2002 to US$2 trillion by 2010, although there are uncertainties surrounding the government's commitment to the privatisation programme. The market, driven by millions of retail investors, is thought to be overvalued and subject to illegal manipulations.

Banking and insurance

China's accession to the WTO in 2001 means that reform in the country's banking sector became essential for China's domestic banks to compete with foreign-owned banks in the future. This meant eliminating corruption at the highest levels of management. Under the WTO agreement, foreign banks were allowed to offer renminbi banking services

to Chinese corporations from 2004, and will be allowed to offer services to Chinese individuals from 2007.
In 2003, the country was dominated by four large banks, the Bank of China, the Agricultural Bank of China, China Construction Bank and Industrial and Commercial Bank of China, which between them controlled 80 per cent of banking services. WTO membership gives foreign banks the right to compete with domestic ones and all restrictions on the setting up, operation and licensing of foreign banks were eliminated by 2005. In addition, state-owned banks are to provide foreign currency services. In 2001, HSBC became the first foreign bank to obtain equity in mainland China when it acquired 8 per cent in the Bank of Shanghai.

Central bank

People's Bank of China. The central bank became an autonomous financial institution in 1995.

Time

GMT plus eight hours
Despite its size, China works to one time zone only.

Geography

China is the third-largest country in the world after Russia and Canada. Its 28,000km land boundary touches North Korea, Russia, Mongolia, Afghanistan, Pakistan, India, Nepal, Bhutan, Myanmar, Laos and Vietnam.
China is bounded by the Yellow and East China Seas to the east and by the South China Sea to the south.
Deserts and semi-arid grasslands make up much of the western and northern parts of the country. Central and eastern China are the most heavily populated parts of the country. The plains of north and north-east China are flat and fertile, but frequently suffer from prolonged drought. Mountain ranges occupy 33 per cent of China's area. Most of China's main rivers run west to east. The longest is the Yangtze River, followed by the Yellow River. The Yangtze River is known as Chiangjiang (long river) in China.
Much of China was once covered by forest, but due to dense settlement and intensive agriculture, most forests have disappeared.

Hemisphere

Northern

Climate

China, with its extensive land mass, has a diverse climate with five temperature zones: cold-temperate, mid-temperate and warm-temperate, subtropical and tropical zone, as well as a plateau climate zone in Tibet.
Weather patterns for most of China are influenced by the monsoon periods that strike in different parts from April to October. Not only is there a series of monsoons drawn from the Pacific Ocean that dominate in turn, the south-east, eastern then northern regions but also one that is drawn from the Indian Ocean that strikes southern mainland China.
The average temperature in summer in Beijing is 28 degrees Celsius (C); Shanghai 16 degrees C and Guangzhou 32 degrees C.

Dress codes

Foreign businessmen generally wear suits and ties to negotiating sessions with Chinese counterparts, who have abandoned the Mao suit for Western dress. Less formal attire is acceptable outside the main cities.
Fashion-consciousness is growing among younger urban Chinese.

Entry requirements

Passports

All visitors need to hold a passport with validity of a minimum of six months. Passports should have at least a few blank pages for visas and entry and exit stamps.

Visa

Required by all, except transit passengers. Business visits can only be made with an invitation fom a Chinese organisation such as a ministry or commercial institution. Foreign firms may request such invitations from a trading corporation. An invitation in the form of a fax is usually sufficient for the visa application which should also include a business letter and itinerary. For up-to-date information concerning visas contact the nearest consulate.
It is possible for individuals to organise their own itinerary and when this has been confirmed by the authorities, the visitor must finance the cost of accommodation and the tour by depositing the amount, through a home bank, with China International Travel Service.
If arriving from Mongolia, airlines in Ulaanbaatar require holders of foreign passports to have a Chinese visa in order to board the aircraft for flights to Beijing. This requirement applies regardless of the length of time in transit at Beijing.

Currency advice/regulations

Unlimited import of foreign currency is allowed, provided it is declared on arrival. Export and import of local currency is limited to Rmb20,000; export of foreign currency up to the amount imported and declared is permitted.
Travellers cheques, perferably in US dollars, are accepted in major cities.

Customs

Certain items produced in China before 1949, such as embroidery, silks, porcelain, scrolls and objets d'art, may be subject to export restrictions. When arriving, listing electonic equipment and camera gear etc is compulsory on customs forms; if these items are not with the traveller on departure, the traveller is liable to pay duty on them. Receipts for any major purchases, especially paintings and antiques, should be kept.

Prohibited imports

Printed material, films, tapes that are viewed to be adverse to China's politics, economy, culture and ethics.

Health (for visitors)

Mandatory precautions

Vaccination certificates are required for yellow fever if travelling from an infected area.

Advisable precautions

Take precautions against HIV/Aids and malaria (generally confined to the southern part of China near the border with Myanmar and Vietnam, although in the summer months the Yangtze River basin is also affected). Rabies is endemic and bilharzia is present in southern and eastern parts of the country. Vaccinations should be taken against hepatitis A and B, diphtheria, tuberculosis, Japanese A encephalitis, polio, tetanus and typhoid. Drink only bottled water, avoid unpeeled fruit and salads and try to ensure all food has been thoroughly cooked. It is advisable to have emergency medical insurance; in Beijing two companies – Asia Emergency Assistance (AEA) and International SOS Assistance – offer evacuation services.

Hotels

There is no shortage of accommodation in peak seasons. The main hotels in major cities are of a reasonable standard, but many hotels are frugal, often with fixed-time, fixed-menu meals and even cold water only during certain hours in the evening and morning. There are new hotels built, with foreign assistance, in Nanjing, Guangzhou, Beijing and Zhjanjiang and international-standard joint-venture hotels in Tianjin, Hainan, Xiamen, Fujian, Hangzhou and Shenzen. Charges for government guest houses, which are used to accommodate hotel overflows, are high.
Reservations for business visitors are made by their host organisations. Joint venture hotels are able to accept bookings from outside China. Hotel reservations for over 70 Chinese cities are being computerised. Tipping is officially forbidden in China, although small tips are occasionally 'expected' by porters in larger hotels. The custom is uneven, and tips will often be refused.

Credit cards

Credit cards are accepted at tourist hotels and tourist shops in major cities. Use of cash or traveller's cheques is more usual.

Cash withdrawals from banks are possible with major cards, but are not encouraged and frequently entail long delays.

Public holidays (national)
Fixed dates
1–2 Jan (New Year's Holiday), 1–3 May (May Day), 1–3 Oct (National Day).
Variable dates
Chinese New Year (Jan/Feb)

Working hours
Banking
Mon–Fri: 0900–1200, 1400–1700.
Business
Mon–Fri: 0800–1130, 1300–1700.
Government
Mon–Fri: 0800–1200, 1300–1700.
Shops
Mon–Sun: 0900–1900.

Telecommunications
Mobile/cell phones
GSM 900 service available in eastern provinces.

Electricity supply
220/240V AC, 50Hz. Two-pin sockets and some three-pin sockets used. Mostly flat plug fittings, with two-pin round as well in some hotels, and generally, screw-type light bulb fittings.

Weights and measures
Metric system (with Chinese units in use).

Social customs/useful tips
Although tipping is officially discouraged, it is now more common in places such as the Special Economic Zones (SEZs), although even there it is still optional. However, it is courteous to thank hotel and restaurant staff for their services. It is customary to present a business card. The full title of the People's Republic of China should be used for formal communications.
Doing business needs patience; punctuality is vital, being especially valued on the part of the visitor.
Unofficial contact between foreigners and local Chinese was effectively banned until reforms gathered momentum in the 1980s and 1990s. The borderline of what is permissible remains unclear, and contact by Chinese with some categories of foreigners such as journalists may still attract adverse attention.
Taiwan (Formosa) is considered a province of China, and should not be referred to as a country. It is quite acceptable nowadays to discuss Taiwan, though the visitor may have to ask questions with considerable art as the Chinese do not volunteer much information.
Bureaucratic procedures are many and the frustrations of grappling with the Chinese bureaucracy are considerable. The visitor should assume that virtually all negotiations are going to take far longer than expected.
It is advisable to have a destination written in Chinese characters.
Eating can be a tricky business but there are a few important things to remember to save embarrassment on the part of the foreigner. When dining with the Chinese, and certainly with professionals, you should wait until your seat is 'allocated' by a nod or a subtle indication by the host. The Chinese have great respect for authority and title and this determines where a person will be seated at a table. One should not begin eating until indicated to do so. Take care not to 'upset' the presentation of the food as this is considered very offensive. When eating with chopsticks do not position them upright in your ricebowl. The gesture is symbolic of death and should be avoided.
When being served tea, it is customary to tap the table with your forefingers as a gesture of thanks.
The Chinese are highly 'face' conscious and try to avoid self-embarrassment at all costs. It is important that foreigners endeavour not to mock, satirise or embarrass their Chinese counterparts in any way as this will definitely ruin any developing relationship.

Security
China's cities probably rate among the world's safest after dark, although some, such as Shenzhen and Wuhan have a worse reputation. Thefts are relatively rare, perhaps because the authorities investigate and punish crimes against foreigners with special vigour. The usual precautions should be taken with valuables.
Organised gangs, some of them Hong Kong-based, are reported to operate in the southern city of Guangzhou (formerly Canton). Their methods include drugging and robbing businessmen.
Chinese criminal law is much harsher than in most Western countries, and Chinese society is still very puritanical in sexual matters.

Getting there
Air
An agreement was signed with Taiwan on 13 June 2008 to allow 36 direct flights (18 each) a week to start on 4 July. A further agreement will allow 3,000 tourists per day into each country from 18 July.
National airline: Air China.
International airport/s: Capital, Beijing (PEK), 26km north of the city, with duty-free shop.
Hongqiao (SHA), 12km from Shanghai, with restaurant, shops; Pudong International, 30km from Shanghai, 60 minutes by car. There are special buses; services to and from the city run from 0600–1900. Facilities include internet cafés and short-stay hotel rooms for passengers.
Baiyun International (CAN) 12km north of Guangzhou.
All airports have duty-free shops, banks, restaurants, post offices and business facilities.
Other airport/s: Include: Chengdu; Guilin; Haikou; Kunming and Tianjin.
Airport tax: Departure tax: domestic Rmb50; international Rmb90, to be paid in local currency only, excluding 24-hour transit passengers.
Surface
Road: Motorways have been built between Guangzhou and Shenzhen and Guangzhou and Zhuhai. These roads link the cities of Dongguan, Zhongshan, Foshan, Jiangmen, Huizhou and Shunde to Hong Kong and Macau. Motorway links to major cities from neighbouring countries are few, partly reflecting the fact that most of China's neighbours, including Laos and North Korea, are poorer than China itself.
The Regional Road Corridor Improvement Project, estimated at US$18 billion, to improve Central Asian roads, airports, railway lines and seaports and provide a vital transit route between Europe and Asia was agreed, in November 2007. Six new transit corridors, between Afghanistan, Azerbaijan, China, Kazakhstan, Kyrgyzstan, Mongolia, Tajikistan and Uzbekistan, of mainly roads and rail links, will be constructed, or existing resources upgraded, by 2013. Half the costs with be provided by the Asian Development Bank and other multilateral organisations and the other half by participating countries.
Rail: The Kowloon-Canton Railway Corporation (KCRC) has express trains serving Kowloon-Guangzhou and an indirect Kowloon-Lowu service.
The Trans-Siberian Express operates two weekly services between Beijing and Moscow, one via Ulaanbaatar in Mongolia and a second via Harbin in northern China.
Nanning, in Guangxi province, is linked by rail to Hanoi, Vietnam. A second cross-border track runs from Kunming, the capital of China's south-western province of Yunnan, via Lao Cai, to Hanoi.
Water: Ferry services operate between Weihai and Inchon in South Korea, and between Shanghai and Osaka in Japan.

Getting about
National transport
Air: Air travel is the quickest way of getting around the country. There are several airlines including China Eastern, China Northern, China Southern and Yunnan Airlines. These provide regular services between the major cities, with first-class service on some routes. Flights are

frequently overbooked and seats should be confirmed as a matter of course. Independent regional airlines also operate. Tickets not booked through an official guide/travel service should be booked and collected well in advance. Allow plenty of time for inevitable and often prolonged delays in services. Airport announcements are not multilingual.

Road: There are over 1.18 million km of internal roads, around 250,000km are paved, but most are narrow and poorly surfaced making long-distance travel time-consuming. A superhighway links Beijing and Tianjin, and a 138km four-lane toll highway links Hangzhou and the port of Ningbo in Zhejiang Province. These are linked into a network of 12 major highways across the country.

Buses: Extensive, long distance services are available, it is advisable to book seats in advance.

Rail: The rail network has over 64,900km of track, with 10,400km electrified, although most locomotives are steam-powered. Beijing is the hub of the rail network with lines radiating throughout the country. There are two major railway stations, the Beijing Railway Station and Beijing West Railway Station, which between them run various services to Guangdong, Shanghai, Heilongjiang, Shanxi, Hebei and Kowloon.

On 1 July 2006 the 1,930km passenger service between Quighai and Tibet, at elevations of 4,000–4,800 metres, began operating.

Rail services operate between main cities. Deluxe rail services, with opulent German-made sleeping cars and private dining coaches, are available. Generally, rail travel is comfortable and safe, but time-consuming because of the long distances involved.

The 2007/08 budget has set aside US$175bn for railway investment. The China Railway Construction floated on the Shanghai Stock Exchange in February 2008, raising Rmb22.25bn (US$3.1bn). The China Railway Group had previously raised US$5.5bn in December 2007.

Water: Hydrofoil and ferry services operate between Hong Kong and Guangzhou, and also serve Shekou, Shenzhen and Zhuhai. Inland waterways and coastal shipping services are an important form of transport.

City transport

Taxis: Taxi service is available in all major cities, from railway stations, hotels and shopping districts. Not all taxis are metered, but a standard rate per kilometre is regulation check before starting a journey. Taxis may be hailed in the street. Destinations may need to be written down in Chinese characters, as not many drivers speak a foreign language. It may be best to retain a taxi until returning to the hotel and paying the driver a small waiting fee during appointments or meals. Tipping is not practised.

Buses, trams & metro: Beijing has a serious transport problem with heavy congestion during the day and the risk of grid-lock during rush-hours. It has a metro system, with over 60 stations, with an upgrade and new lines, including the Olympic branch line, under construction, most of which are expected to be completed for the 2008 Olympic Games. However for the size of the city and population it is a small operation. The yikatong transport card is the only ticket that allows travel on most lines; individual lines have their own, non-transferable tickets. There are also buses, trams and trolleybuses but these are unsuitable for visitors without a working knowledge of Chinese.

There are metro systems in Chongqing, Guangzhou, Nanjing, Shanghai, Shenzhen, Tianjin and Wuhan.

There are extensive local bus services in all main cities, generally inexpensive but crowded and without timetables.

Trains: There are six main, metropolitan railway station that handle traffic from surrounding suburbs and districts.

Car hire

Most rental companies require the driver's passport as deposit, making car rental impractical. Cars with a driver can be hired for a day or week.

Bicycle hire is available in some towns, but it is advisable to carry proof of identity when riding.

BUSINESS DIRECTORY

The addresses listed below are a selection only. While World of Information makes every endeavour to check these addresses, we cannot guarantee that changes have not been made, especially to telephone numbers and area codes. We would welcome any corrections.

Telephone area codes

The International direct dialling (IDD) code for China is +86, followed by the area code:

Beijing	10	Qingdao	532
Chengdu	28	Shanghai	21
Dalian	411	Shenyang	24
Fuzhou	591	Shenzen	755
Guangzhou	20	Tianjin	22
Harbin	451	Wenzhou	577
Jinan	531	Wuhan	27
Lhasa	891	Xi'an	29
Nanjing	25		

Useful telephone numbers

Beijing
Police: 110
International calls, English-language: 337-431, 553-536
Local, long-distance enquiries: 116
Cable and telex information: 664-900
Taxis: 557-671
Airport-flight enquiries: 552-515, 555-531, ext 382

Shanghai
Ambulance: 120
Police: 110
Fire: 119
Taxis for disabled: 6215-5555

Chambers of Commerce

American Chamber of Commerce PRC, 1903 China Resources Building, 8 Jianguomenbai Dajie, Beijing 100005 (tel: 8519-1920; fax: 8519-1910; e-mail: amcham@amcham-china.org.cn).

British Chamber of Commerce in China, China Life Tower, 16 Chaoyangmenwai Avenue, Beijing 100020 (tel: 8525-1111; fax: 8525-1100; email: director@pek.britcham.org).

Banking

Agricultural Bank of China, Jia 23 Fu Xing Road, Beijing 100036 (tel: 6847-5321; fax: 6829-7160).

Bank of China, 410 Fuchengmen Nei Dajie, Beijing 100818 (tel: 6601-6688; fax: 6601-6869).

Beijing City Commercial Bank Corp Ltd, 2nd Floor, Tower B Beijing International Financial Building, 156 Fuxingmennei Street, Beijing 100031 (tel: 6642-6928; fax: 6642-6691/9).

Bank of Communications, 18 Xianxia Lu, Shanghai 200335 (tel: 6275-1234; fax: 6275-6784).

China Construction Bank, No 25 Finance Street, Beijing 100032 (tel: 6759-8050; fax: 6759-7353).

China Minsheng Banking Corporation Ltd, 4 Zheng Yi Lu, Dong Cheng District, Beijing 100006 (tel: 6526-9578).

Hua Xia Bank, Xidan International Mansion, No. 111 Xidan North Avenue, Xicheng District, Beijing 100032 (tel: 6615-1199, 6612-9139; fax: 6618-8484).

Central bank

People's Bank of China, 32 Chengfang Street, Xi Cheng District, Beijing 100800 (tel: 6619-4114; fax: 6601-5346; e-mail: webbox@pbc.gov.cn; internet: www.pbc.gov.cn/english).

Travel information

Air China, Beijing Capital Airport, Beijing 100621 (tel: 6456-3201; fax: 6456-3831; e-mail: webmaster@airchina.com.cn).

Beijing Capital Airport, Beijing 100621(tel: 6456-4247; fax: 6457-0487).

China Eastern Airlines, 2550 Hingqiaolu, Shanghai 200335 (tel: 6268-6268; fax:

6268-6116; e-mail: webmaster@ce-air.com).

China International Travel Service (CITS), 103 Fuxingmennei Dajie, Beijing 100800 (tel: 6601-1122; fax: 6601-2021; e-mail: webmaster@cits.net).

China Southern Airlines, Baiyun International Airport, Guangzhou 510405 (tel: 8612-4738; fax: 8665-9040; e-mail: webmaster@cs-air.com).

Shanghai Hongqiao Airport, Shanghai 200335 (tel: 6269-0029; fax: 6269-0027).

Ministry of tourism

National tourist organisation offices

National Tourism Administration of the People's Republic of China (CNTA), 9A Jianguomennei Avenue, Beijing 100740 (tel: 6520-1114; fax: 6512-2096; internet site: www.cnta.gov.cn/lyen/index.asp).

Ministries

Ministry of Agriculture, 11 Nonzhanguan Nanli, Beijing 100026 (tel: 6419-1114; fax: 64192468).

Ministry of Civil Affairs, 147 Beiheyan Dajie, Beijing 100721 (tel: 6523-5511; fax: 6513-5332).

Ministry of Communications, 11 Jianguomennei Dajie, Beijing 100736 (tel: 6529-2114; fax: 6529-2345).

Ministry of Construction, Baiwanzhuang, Haidian District, Beijing 100835 (tel: 6839-3970; fax: 6839-3333).

Ministry of Culture, A83 Dong'anmen Beijie, Beijing 100722 (tel: 6401-2255; fax: 6403: 1266).

Ministry of Defence, 20 Jinshanquianjie, Beijing 100009 (tel: 6673-0000).

Ministry of Education, 37 Damucang Hutong, Xidian, Beijing 100820 (tel: 6609-6114; fax: 6601-1049).

Ministry of Foreign Affairs, 2 Chaonei Dajie, Dongcheng Districti, Beijing 100701 (tel: 8596-1114).

Ministry of Health, 44 Beiheyan, Xicheng District, Beijing 100725 (tel: 6403-4433; fax: 6401-2369).

Ministry of Information Industry, 13 Xichang'anjie, Beijing 10084 (tel: 6601-4249; fax: 6201-6362).

Ministry of Justice, 10 Chaoyangmen Nandajie, Beijing 100020 (tel: 6520-5254).

Ministry of Labour and Social Security, 12 Hepingli Zhongjie, Dongcheng District, Beijing 100716 (tel: 6421-3240).

Ministry of Land and Natural Resources, 64 Funeidajie, Xicheng District, Beijing 100812 (tel: 6616-5566; e-mail: master@mail.mlr.gov.cn).

Ministry of Personnel, 12 Hepingli Zongjie, Beijing 100716 (tel: 6421-3240).

Ministry of Public Security, 14 Dongchang'anjie, Beijing 100741 (tel: 6512-1967).

Ministry of Railways, 10 Fuxinglu, Haidian District, Beijing 100844 (tel: 6324-0114; fax: 6324-2150).

Ministry of Science and Technology, 15 Fuxinglu, Haidian District, Beijing 100038 (tel: 6851-5544; fax: 6851-5004).

Ministry of State Security, 14 Dongchang'anjie, Beijing 100741 (tel: 6524-4702).

Ministry of Supervision, 4 Zaojunmiao, Haidian District, Beijing 100081 (tel: 6225-4129).

Ministry of Water Resources, 2 Ertiao, Baiguanglu, Xuanwu District, Beijing 100053 (tel: 6320-2114; fax: 6320-2650).

Other useful addresses

China International Trust and Investment Corporation (Citic), Capital Mansion, 6 Xinuan Nanlu, Beijing (tel: 6466-0088; fax: 6466-1186; e-mail: g-office@citic.com.cn).

China National Chemicals Import & Export Corporation (Sinochem), A2 Fuxingmenwai Dajie, Beijing 100046 (tel: 6856-8888; fax: 6856-8890).

China National Instruments Import & Export Corporation, Erligou, Xijiao, Beijing 100044 (tel: 6831-7393; fax: 6831-59251).

China National Light Industrial Products Import & Export Corporation (Chinalight), 910 Jinsongjiu Qu, Beijing 100747 (tel: 6776-6688; fax: 6774-7245).

China National Machinery Import & Export Corporation, PO Box 49, Erligou, Xijiao, Beijing (tel: 6849-4851; fax: 6831-4143).

China National Metals & Minerals Import & Export Corporation, Building 15, Block 4, Anhui Li, Chaoyang District, Beijing 100101 (tel: 6491-6666; fax: 6491-7031).

China National Offshore Oil Corporation, PO Box 4705, 6 Dongzhimenwai Xioajie, Beijing 100027 (tel: 8452-1010; fax: 8452-1044; e-mail: webmaster@cnooc.com.cn).

China National Petroleum Corporation, 6 Liupukang Jie, Xicheng District, Beijing 100724 (tel: 6422-2946; fax: 6426-6302; e-mail: webmaster@hq.cnpc.com.cn).

China National Technical Import and Export Corporation (CNTIC), Jiuling Building, 21 Xisanhuan Bei Lu, Beijing 100081 (tel: 6840-4106; fax: 6841-4877).

China Ocean Shipping Agency (PENAVICO), Tower Crest Plaza, 3 Maizidian Road West, Chaoyang District, Beijing (tel: 6461-1188; fax: 6467-3118; e-mail: general@penavico.com.cn).

Chinese Embassy (US), 2300 Connecticut Avenue, NW, Washington DC 20008 (tel: (+1-202) 238-5000; fax: (+1-202) 588-0032; e-mail: chinaembassy_us@fmprc.gov.cn).

Chinese Export Commodities Fair, 117 Liuhua Road, Guangzhou (tel: 8666-1664; fax: 8333-5880; e-mail: info@cecf-info.com).

General Administration of Customs, 6 Jiannei Dajie, Beijing 100730 (tel: 6519-4114; fax: 6519-4004).

Shanghai Advertising Corporation, 117 Xianggang Road, Shanghai 200002 (tel: 6321-7599; 6329-0068).

State Administration for Industry and Commerce, 8 Sanlihe Donglu, Xicheng District, Beijing 100820 (tel: 6803-2233; fax: 6857-0848).

State Administration of Entry-Exit Inspection and Quarantine, A10 Chaowai Dajie, Chaoyang District, Beijing 100020 (tel: 6599-4600; fax: 6599-4306).

National news agency: Xinhua (New China News Agency)

Internet sites

Archive of Chinese news digest, also contains links to other Chinese sites: www.cnd.org.

China Business Pages: www.chinapages.com.

China Web (investment data, Shanghai city information, stock prices, travel arrangements and a searchable directory of key figures in commerce, industry and government): www.comnex.com

China Window information on country, government and business activities: http://china-window.com

Shanghai business: www.sh.com

Colombia

KEY FACTS

Official name: República de Colombia (Republic of Colombia)

Head of State: President Álvaro Uribe Vélez (since 2002; re-elected May 2006)

Head of government: President Álvaro Uribe Vélez

Ruling party: A coalition led by Partido Social de Unidad Nacional (PSUN) (Social National Unity Party) with Cambio Radical (CR) (Radical Change), the Partido Social Conservador (PSC) (Social Conservative Party) and other smaller parties (elected 12 Mar 2006). All parties are supporters of the president.

Area: 1,138,914 square km

Population: 47.52 million (2007)*

Capital: Santa Fé de Bogotá

Official language: Spanish

Currency: Colombian peso (Col$) = 100 centavos

Exchange rate: Col$1,779.10 per US$ (Jul 2008)

GDP per capita: US$3,611 (2007)*

GDP real growth: 7.00% (2007)*

Labour force: 20.22 million (2004)

Unemployment: 13.60% (2004)

Inflation: 5.50% (2007)

Oil production: 561,000 bpd (2007)

Balance of trade: US$1.45 billion (2006)

Foreign debt: US$38.70 billion (2004)

Visitor numbers: 1.05 million (2006)*

Annual FDI: US$2.35 billion (2004)

* estimated figure

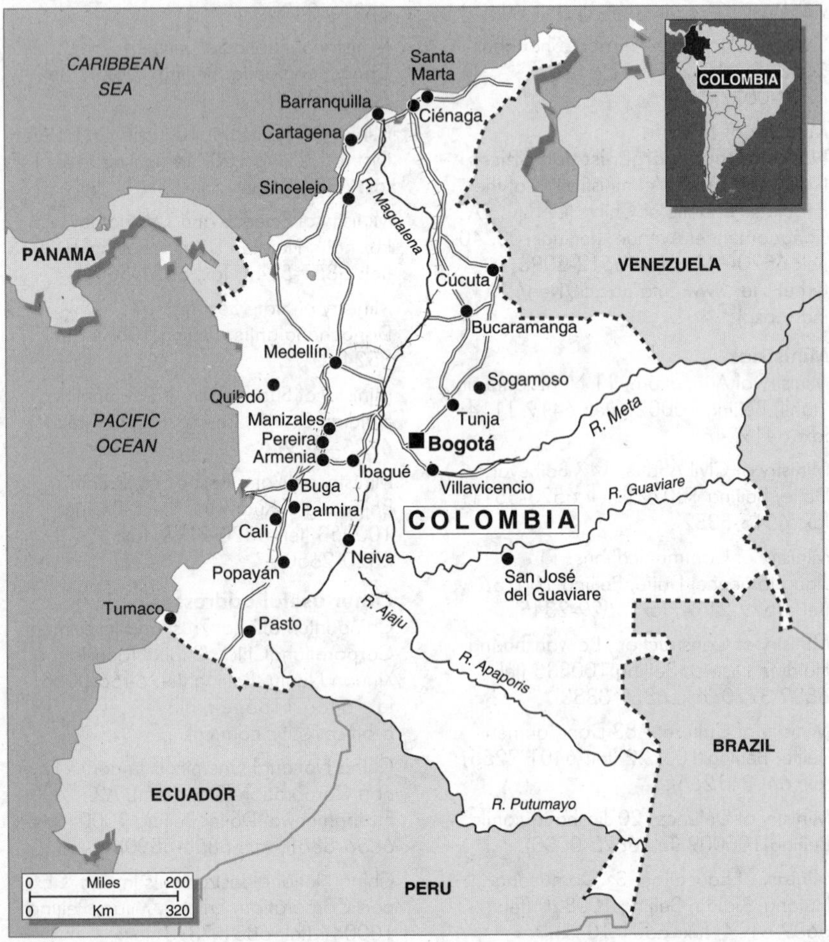

In July 2007 hundreds of thousands of Colombians joined street demonstrations to protest at the killing of eleven hostages who had been held by guerrillas of the Fuerzas Armadas Revolucionarias de Colombia-Ejército del Pueblo (Farc) (Revolutionary Armed Forces of Colombia-Peoples' Army). Quite how the hostages died was a matter of conjecture, with each side – government and guerrillas – blaming the other. The hostages were local councillors captured in a 2002 Farc raid on a government building in Cali. The killing of the hostages (whose bodies were later exhumed from shallow graves by the Red Cross following directions supplied by the Farc) place Colombia's hard line President Alvaro Uribe on the defensive, Altogether the Farc were believed to be holding some 60 'political' hostages, including three American contractors and the one time presidential aspirant Ingrid Betancourt who holds both French and Colombian passports. In the world's kidnap centre, hundreds of other hostages are simply being held to ransom.

The hostage killings placed Mr Uribe in a tight spot. While the feelings behind the street demonstrations gave some legitimacy to whatever measures he decided to take against the Farc, the same measures inevitably risked invoking criticism from human rights lobbies and politicians in the USA and Europe. In June 2007 the US Democrats who had recently regained control of the House of Representatives had declared their opposition to the ratification of a free trade agreement with Colombia until 'concrete evidence of sustained results' in the reduction of violence and the bringing to justice of corrupt politicians and rogue vigilantes. Not that Colombia had exactly been starved of US support: since 1999 the country had received some US$5 billion in US aid, mostly military.

Rebels without a cause

In June 2007, President Uribe had begun to release some 200 Farc rebels from prison, in the hope of encouraging the Farc to reciprocate. The Farc dismissed the offer as a 'farce'. Venezuelan President Hugo Chávez's efforts to mediate with the Farc to broker the release of 45 high-profile hostages ended in disarray, as President Uribe called a halt to the initiative accusing Mr Chávez of attempting to legitimise the Farc. Perhaps predictably President Chávez responded by branding President Uribe a 'liar and a cynic' and vowing to put relations with Colombia 'in the freezer'. In a somewhat disappointing gesture, the Farc responded to Chávez's efforts by releasing former vice-presidential candidate Clara Rojas and former congresswoman Consuelo González in January 2008.

Mr Uribe's tight spot did not last long. The whole complexion of the government's campaign against the Farc, and its international ramifications changed dramatically in March 2008 with the killing of Farc commander Raúl Reyes in a cross border raid by Colombian commandos into Ecuador. The success of the raid brought with it a predictable response, first from Ecuador's President Rafael Correa, who deployed troops to the area and withdrew Ecuador's ambassador from Bogotá. The Colombian government had long complained that Farc rebels were given safe haven in both Ecuador and Venezuela.

Venezuela's initial response to the raid was one of rhetoric and bluster. President Hugo Chávez called the raid – in which a total of 18 Farc rebels were killed – an attack by a 'terrorist state'. Describing President Uribe as 'a criminal', in his exaggerated response, President Chávez reportedly ordered the mobilisation of the Venezuelan air force and closed the Venezuelan embassy n Bogotá. The tension did not last long; at a regional conference in the Dominican Republic all became sweetness and light as the three heads of state – Chávez, Correa and Uribe – all shook hands; Uribe apologised to Correa and undertook to withdraw a complaint Colombia had lodged with the International Court of Justice that Venezuela had financed the Farc. Mr Uribe may later have had cause to regret and reconsider this move.

In early 2008 Mr Chávez had claimed the credit for brokering two deals that released six Farc hostages. Four of those released were members of Congress. The highest profile hostage, Ingrid Betancourt a one time presidential aspirant with dual French nationality remained a prisoner. The Colombian government, and more particularly President Uribe, expressed reservations over Chávez' involvement; these were against the backdrop of uneasy relations between the countries and an international awareness that President Chávez' popularity in his own country was beginning to wane.

Any final resolution of the guerrilla question is likely to prove difficult, as neither party is likely to accept the inevitable compromises involved. Mr Uribe's position is not helped by the hard line he adopted towards the right-wing paramilitaries in forcing them into a peace deal. The Farc's substantial involvement in drug trafficking and other apparently documented activities means that they will be seeking some form of amnesty, something Mr Uribe will certainly be reluctant to grant.

Uribe the tough guy

President Uribe, had won the 2002 presidential elections on a conservative independent campaign platform. His victory altered the balance of the three main political parties, the centre left Partido Liberal (PL) (Liberal Party), the Polo Democrático Alternativo (PDA) (Alternative Democratic Pole) and the conservative Partido Social Conservador (PSC) (Social Conservative Party). Uribe stood as an independent for his first term, with the support of a number of smaller parties and many of his former PL colleagues. In the 2006 congressional elections Mr Uribe's party gained a clear majority in both the Congress and Senate. Mr Uribe was re-elected to the Presidency in the first round of the 2006 elections. His term runs until 2010. He is expected to maintain the macroeconomic policies initiated during his first term aimed at improving public finances, reducing inflation and boosting growth. The election also gave him a strong public mandate for his tough policies on security and drugs. He had been re-elected on the basis of his strong leadership, improvements in public security, and economic recovery.

The commercial worth of the illicit narcotics trade is difficult to gauge, but is thought to be approximately 5-10 per cent of GDP. Significant in value, the trade has negatively affected the economy, with

KEY INDICATORS Colombia

	Unit	2003	2004	2005	2006	2007
Population	m	44.59	45.30	46.04	46.77	*47.52
Gross domestic product (GDP)	US$bn	77.59	97.38	123.08	135.07	*171.61
GDP per capita	US$	1,740	2,099	2,673	2,910	*3,611
GDP real growth	%	3.4	4.0	5.3	6.8	*7.0
Inflation	%	6.1	5.9	5.0	4.3	5.5
Industrial output	% change	–	6.4	5.3	4.3	–
Agricultural output	% change	–	4.2	2.1	2.4	–
Oil output	'000 bpd	564.0	551.0	549.0	558.0	561.0
Natural gas output	bn cum	6.1	6.4	6.8	7.3	7.7
Coal output	mtoe	32.1	35.8	38.4	42.7	2.6
Exports (fob) (goods)	US$m	12,900.0	17,011.0	21,729.0	23,941.0	30,579.0
Imports (cif) (goods)	US$m	12,500.0	15,878.0	20,130.0	22,492.0	31,173.0
Balance of trade	US$m	400.0	1,134.0	1,595.0	1,449.0	-594.0
Current account	US$m	-1,190.0	-1,010.0	-1,981.0	-2,909.0	-5,851.0
Total reserves minus gold	US$m	10,784.0	13,394.0	14,787.0	15,296.0	20,767.0
Foreign exchange	US$m	10,188.0	12,769.0	14,206.0	14,673.0	20,096.0
Exchange rate	per US$	2,811.75	2,627.33	2,218.60	2,261.80	1,998.60

* estimated figure

money laundering and contraband goods reducing the effectiveness of macroeconomic controls and distorting the consumer market. In addition, the current drug cartels have sought to exclude the government from large regions of the country in order to secure areas for growing coca and poppy and for trafficking routes to North American and European markets, although the Uribe government has had success in extending its authority in regions previously under the control of the Farc and smaller ELN (National Liberation Army). The uncontrolled use of fragile tropical and jungle ecosystems to grow coca has caused considerable environmental harm, as has the indiscriminate use of chemicals and fertilisers.

Colombia's economy was boosted in 2007 by the continued strength of domestic demand. The United Nations Economic Commission for Latin America and the Caribbean (ECLAC) forecast the growth figure to drop to 5 per cent in 2008, reflecting global trends and the measures taken by the government to avoid overheating and to contain inflationary pressures. Global developments apart, ECLAC warned that inflationary pressures were inevitable following the effects of the *El Nino* southern oscillation phenomenon at the beginning of 2007 and the sluggish response to the Banco de la República's (central bank) dampening measures.

Often adopting an unassuming profile in regional economic assessments, Colombia has in fact long been something of an economic success story. In 2007 this largely positive trend had continued; benign economic conditions resulted in increased tax collections, reducing the public sector deficit from 0.8 to 0.7 per cent. The central government deficit also continued to fall, down from 4.2 per cent in 2006 to 3.3 per cent in 2007. Expenditure forecasts for 2008 were reduced following the adoption of an austerity budget which projected a public sector deficit of 1.4 per cent of GDP. The figure would be lower if it were not for pension liabilities and the prudent need to transfer funds to the government's Fondo de Ahorro para la Estabilización Petrolera (FAEP) (Petroleum Saving and Stabilisation Fund). Conversely, Colombia's economy benefits from the black economy surrounding its drug industries. The figure is high enough to have a significant impact on Colombia's overall economic figures, but is virtually impossible to quantify. Colombia's central bank raised interest rates 12 times between April 2006 and August 2007 when the annual rate reached 9.25 per cent. Although inflation showed signs of beginning to retreat in mid-year, the central bank saw fit increase the interest rate to 9.5 per cent, anticipating the effects of continued strength in domestic demand.

The peso continued to appreciate against the dollar, buoyed up by strong private consumption and investment. The improved security situation also boosted economic confidence. By the end of 2007, ECLAC reported that inflation estimates for 2008 stood at 5.5 per cent, a full percentage point higher than the Banco de la República's target figure. The bank forecast that 2008 inflation would drop to between an annual 3.5 to 4.5 per cent, adopting a target figure of 4.00 per cent, unchanged from 2007. It needs to be noted that the bank's figures, and expectations, date from a period before oil prices topped US$120 per barrel. The central bank's end year inflation target for 2009 was between 3.0 and 3.5 per cent.

Unemployment dropped to 11.6 per cent in 2007, down from 13.0 per cent in 2006. According to the World Bank, the national employment rate grew from 50.31 per cent in the last quarter of 2006 to 53.24 per cent for the same period in 2007, an increase of 2.44 per cent. Much of the drop in unemployment was due to generally higher levels of employment. Reflecting this, export levels increased by some 15 per cent in 2007; non-traditional exports lead the way with growth of 20 per cent. Imports also increased, by 25 per cent, reflecting the demand for capital, rather than consumer goods. The World Bank has noted that the Uribe government's public order objectives are generally shared by the population at large. More than 40,000 combatants have been 'de-mobilised' on Mr Uribe's watch. According to the World Bank, if Colombia had been at peace for the last 20 years, Colombia's average per capita income would today be 50 per cent higher. It is also estimated that some 2.5 million children would no longer be living below the poverty line.

Coal is the goal

As oil prices continued to surge throughout 2007 and 2008, Colombia's energy balance looked more and more positive thanks to its substantial reserves of high quality coal. According to the World Energy Council (WEC) Colombia had 6,959 million tonnes (mt) of high quality coal reserves in 2007. These are the second-largest coal reserves in South America, behind Brazil, with an average sulphur content of less than one per cent. According to Colombian government estimates, coal production could reach 102mt by 2010, up from 46.6mt in 2007.

Colombia's largest coal producer is the Carbones del Cerrejón consortium, composed of Anglo-American, BHP Billiton, and Glencore. The consortium operates the Cerrejón Zona Norte (CZN) project, the largest coal mine in Latin America and the largest open-cast coal mine in the world. Most Colombia coal exports go to Europe, North America and Latin America. There has been discussion that a planned expansion of the Panama Canal would allow Colombia to export coal to new markets in Asia. Some of the non-integrated coal mines in Colombia export their production via the Venezuelan ports of La Cieba and Maracaibo. In order to sustain the rise in coal exports, Colombia will need to invest in transportation infrastructure to remove potential production bottlenecks. In May 2006, President Uribe announced plans to build a US$300 million export terminal near Santa Marta. The facility will have special measures to reduce the spreading of coal dust in the nearby area, a popular tourist destination.

The US Energy Information Administration (EIA) reports that (according to the US *Oil and Gas Journal* (OGJ)), Colombia had 1.45 billion barrels of proven crude oil reserves in 2007. These were the fifth-largest in South America. producing 561,000 barrels per day (bpd) in 2007, up from 559,000bpd in 2006. Despite the small rise in production, Colombia's oil production has declined since 1999, when it reached 838,000bpd. Colombia's oil consumption reached 228,000bpd in 2007. Half Colombia's oil production goes to the United States. For the most part Colombia's crude oil is lighter and sweeter than that of other Latin American oil producers.

Colombia's government has endeavoured to make investment in the oil industry attractive to international oil companies. Measures include allowing foreign oil companies to own 100 per cent stakes in oil ventures, the establishment of a lower, sliding-scale royalty rate on oil projects; longer exploration licences; and forcing state-owned Ecopetrol to compete with private operators. The reforms have created a revived interest in Colombia's oil exploration industry. The improved security situation as guerrillas have been forced into remote southern regions has also helped to create what the EIA describes as 'one of the most attractive oil investment regimes in the world'. Despite higher levels of foreign investment, the EIA forecasts that Colombian oil production will decline at around 4 per cent annually in the short term, dropping to 510,000bpd in 2008.

The OGJ estimated that Colombia had proven natural gas reserves of 4.0 trillion cubic feet (Tcf) in 2007. Colombia has natural gas reserves spread across 18 basins, seven of which have active production. The bulk of Colombia's natural gas reserves are located in the Llanos basin, although the Guajira basin accounts for most of current production. Chevron is the largest natural gas producer in Colombia. Initially, the pipeline will carry natural gas from Colombia to Venezuela, but the EIA reports that there has also been talk of eventually reversing the flow of the pipeline to allow Venezuelan natural gas exports instead. Construction on the project began in July 2006, and was inaugurated by the two presidents in October 2007.

Risk assessment

Regional stability	Good
Politics	Fair
Economy	Good

COUNTRY PROFILE

Historical profile

1820 Colombia became independent from Spain.
1800s Outbreaks of fighting erupted sporadically throughout the nineteenth century, often between anti-clerical Liberals and pro-church Conservatives.
1899–1903 The (Civil) War of 1,000 Days in which some 100,000 people were killed. Panama separated from Colombia during the war and became an independent state.
1930 A Liberal president was elected, leading to social reform.
1948–57 The two major parties, the Partido Social Conservador (PSC) (Social Conservative Party) and the Partido Liberal (PL) (Liberal Party) became more extreme – the Conservatives veering towards fascism and the Liberals towards left-wing populism. Civil war broke out, resulting in up to 300,000 deaths.
1957 The civil war ended when the PSC and PL agreed on a power-sharing pact with the presidency going alternately to a PL then PSC member, with seats in cabinet and Congress to be split equally.
1965 The Ejército de Liberación Nacional (ELN) (National Liberation Army) and the Maoist People's Liberation Army were founded.
1966 Another and largest rebel group, the Fuerzas Armadas Revolucionarias de Colombia-Ejército del Pueblo (Farc) (Revolutionary Armed Forces of Colombia-Peoples' Army), was formed.
1971 After disputed elections, elements of the defeated Alianza Nacional Popular (Anapo) formed an armed movement (M-19) to fight the PSC government. They were joined by dissident members of the Farc.
1970s Guerrilla violence increased, at the same time as an increase in cocaine production.
1982 President Belisario Betancur granted guerrillas an amnesty and freed political prisoners.
1984 The assassination of the justice minister led to a step-up in the government war on drugs traffickers.
1985 M-19 guerrillas stormed the Palace of Justice, killing 11 judges and 90 other people. The Andean volcano, Nevado del Ruiz, erupted and killed around 23,000 people in four surrounding towns.
1986 Virgolio Barco Vargas (PL) won an overwhelming victory in the presidental election. Violence becomes endemic as right-wing paramilitaries target PL politicians, left-wing groups carry out insurgency actions and death squads are controlled and sent out by drug cartels.
1989 A peace agreement between the government and M-19 allows it to become a legal political party; other guerrilla groups remained active. PL and Unión Patriótica (UP) Patriotic Union (founded by Farc) presidential candidates were killed on the hustings, allegedly by drug cartels.
1991 A new constitution was adopted which legalised divorce and gave indigenous people democratic rights, although it fell short of addressing their territorial claims.
1993 The infamous Medellin drugs lord, Pablo Escobar, was shot dead while trying to evade a police arrest.
1994 Ernesto Samper won the presidential election.
1998 Andrés Pastrana Arango won the presidential election, bringing the Partido Conservador Colombiano (PCC) (Colombian Conservative Party) to power and ending 12 years of rule by the PL. In a move to allow peace talks to continue uninterrupted, the government agreed on a demilitarised area where military action against rebel groups would be suspended.
1999 President Pastrana began formal peace talks with the Farc in an attempt to end the region's longest-running civil war; after only two weeks the talks stalled. The two rebel movements, the Farc and the ELN, were estimated to control 40 per cent of Colombia. The president's Plan Colombia won US$1 billion in US support of the anti-drug trafficking and insurgency plan. The peace talks breakdown with recrimination on both sides.
2000 President Pastrana issued 11 emergency decrees to increase the armed forces from 10,000 to 42,000 by the end of the year, with further increases to 52,000 by end-2001. The demilitarised area were disbanded.
2001 Pastrana agrees to extend the life of the demilitarised areas for a further eight months; Farc releases 359 police and military an exchanges of 14 rebel prisoners. An agreement to negotiate a cease-fire was signed.
2002 After three years of complex peace talks Pastrana broke of negotiations with Farc and ordered rebels out of the demilitarised area and stepped up a government crackdown. Threats from Farc and the Autodefensas Unidas de Colombia (AUC) (United Self-Defence Forces of Colombia) hindered electoral campaigning in rural areas, despite a security operation involving 150,000 troops and police; only 48 per cent of the population voted. Presidential candidate Ingrid Betancourt was kidnapped by Farc during campaigning. The PCC and the PL remained the largest groups in the legislature. Álvaro Uribe Vélez won the presidential election.
2003 Confidence grew following Uribe's congressional approval of legislation raising tax revenues and boosting funding for the state pension system. Certain regional factions of the AUC disarmed.
2004 Farc guerrilla leader Ricardo Palmera was sentenced to 35 years imprisonment. The right wing AUC movement and the government began peace talks.
2005 An international confrontation erupted when a leading Farc guerrilla commander was captured in Venezuela. In February the Presidents of both countries held a summit to resolve the matter. The national government passed new legislation in June, reducing jail terms for members of paramilitary groups who surrendered and disarmed. In Cuba in December, tentative peace talks began with ELN, the second-largest rebel group.
2006 A disarmament agreement with right-wing paramilitaries led to a reported 20,000 fighters surrendering their weapons to government forces. In exchange for their co-operation, most fighters were expected to be pardoned and retrained for civilian life. Colombia and the US signed a free-trade agreement. In parliamentary elections for the chamber of representatives the PL won 38 seats, the Partido Social de Unidad Nacional (PSUN) (Social National Unity Party) 30 seats, the PCC 29 seats, the Cambio Radical (CR) (Radical Change) 20 seats and the Polo Democrático Alternativo (PDA) (Alternative Democratic Pole) 9 seats. In the senate the PL won 17 seats, the PSUN 20, the PCC 18 seats, the CR 15 seats and the

PDA 11 seats. Of the 20 registered political parties these five won 72 per cent of the total votes cast and over three-quarters of the all allotted seats. Incumbent Álvaro Uribe Vélez won the presidential election with 62.2 per cent of the vote. Turnout was 45.1 per cent.
2008 Colombia took pre-emptive strikes against terrorists of Farc hiding out in Ecuador and Venezuela, killing over a dozen including the senior Farc leader Raul Reyes. On 3 March, following the incursion, Ecuador cut diplomatic relations with Colombia and Venezuela expelled Colombian diplomats. The founder and leader of Farc, Manuel Marulanda, died on 26 March. Ingrid Betancourt was freed by government troops, along with 14 other hostages, on 3 July.

Political structure

Constitution

The current constitution dates from 6 July 1991. Colombia has a representative democracy composed of an executive, legislative and a judicial branch.
Administratively, the country is divided into 32 departments ruled by governors, representing the executive branch, and a Departmental Assembly representing the legislative branch. Cities are governed by a mayor and a municipal council. All are elected by democratic vote.
Colombian citizens aged 18 and over are eligible to vote.

Form of state

Presidential democratic republic

The executive

Executive power is vested in the president, elected by universal adult suffrage for four years but not for consecutive terms. The president appoints a cabinet.

National legislature

The legislature is the bicameral Congreso (Congress), which comprises the 167-member Cámara de Representantes (chamber of representatives) and the 102-member Senado de la República (senate of the Republic). Members of Congress are elected for four-year terms by universal suffrage.

Legal system

The judicial system maintains formal independence but has experienced problems operating normally in circumstances that have extended to massed attacks using heavy firepower on major court institutions.

Last elections

28 May 2006 (presidential); 12 March 2006 (congressional).
Results: Presidential: incumbent Álvaro Uribe Vélez won the presidential election with 62.2 per cent of the vote, Carlos Gaviria Díaz won 22 per cent and Horacio Serpa Uribe won 11.8 per cent. Turnout was 45.1 per cent.
Parliamentary: in the chamber of representatives the PL won 38 seats, the PSUN 30 seats, the PCC 29 seats, the CR 20 seats and the Polo Democrático Alternativo (PDA) (Alternative Democratic Pole) 9 seats. In the senate the PL won 17 seats, the PSUN 20, the PCC 18 seats, the CR 15 seats and the PDA 11 seats. Turnout was 39.8 per cent.

Next elections

2010 (presidential and congressional)

Political parties

Ruling party

A coalition led by Partido Social de Unidad Nacional (PSUN) (Social National Unity Party) with Cambio Radical (CR) (Radical Change), the Partido Social Conservador (PSC) (Social Conservative Party) and other smaller parties (elected 12 Mar 2006). All parties are supporters of the president.

Main opposition party

Colombiano Partido Liberal (PL) (Liberal Party)

Population

47.52 million (2007)*
Last census: October 1993: 33,109,840
Population density: 39 inhabitants per square km. Urban population: 79.1 per cent (2002).
Annual growth rate: 1.7 per cent 1994–2004 (WHO 2006)

Ethnic make-up

Mestizo 57 per cent, white 20 per cent, mulatto 14 per cent, Indian 1 per cent, and others 8 per cent.

Religions

Roman Catholicism is the official religion and the vast majority of Colombians consider themselves Catholic. There is freedom of worship.

Education

Financing for the education sector is decentralised and municipalities are required to use 30 per cent of the resources transferred to them from central government for education purposes.
Although the illiteracy rate averages 8 per cent among adults over 15 years of age, drop-out rates are increasing on an annual basis; Oxfam estimates that one in every four children drops out before completing primary education and girls' enrolment rates, estimated at 65 per cent, are at least 30 per cent lower than boys' enrolment rates. Primary education has also suffered due to cuts in government budget, while per capita spending is 12 times higher in the tertiary sector.
The New School Programme, known as the Escuela Nueva, was begun in the mid-1970s and governs the principles of the Colombian education system. It emphasises flexible school schedules and an appropriate curriculum catering to the needs of the poor rural areas.
Literacy rate: 92 per cent adult rate; 97 per cent youth rate (15–24) (Unesco 2005).
Compulsory years: Nine years in urban areas
Five years in rural areas
Enrolment rate: 113 per cent in primary; 67 per cent in secondary, of relevant age groups (including repitition rates) (World Bank).
Pupils per teacher: 25 in primary schools

Health

Per capita total expenditure on health (2003) was US$522; of which per capita government spending was US$439, at the international dollar rate, (WHO 2006).

HIV/Aids

HIV prevalence: 0.7 per cent aged 15–49 in 2003 (World Bank)
Life expectancy: 73 years, 2004 (WHO 2006)
Fertility rate/Maternal mortality rate: 2.6 births per woman, 2004 (WHO 2006); maternal mortality 80 per 100,000 live births (World Bank).
Child (under 5 years) mortality rate (per 1,000): 18 per 1,000 live births; 7 per cent of children aged under five were malnourished (World Bank).
Head of population per physician: 1.35 physicians per 1,000 people, 2002 (WHO 2006)

Welfare

UN agency World Food Programme (WPF) stated that in 2003 there were two million internally displaced persons (IDP) who had fled their homes due to conflict and violence; 80 per cent of the two million lacked access to food production. Food aid is being provided for over 300,000 people, particularly in the northern states. International medical aid provides primary care, prenatal treatment and vaccinations for victims of the internal conflict, and the rural and urban disadvantaged.

Pensions

Colombia undertook major reforms in its pension system in the 1990s by shifting its priorities from government-run pay-as-you-go systems to multi-tier systems characterised by a privately run and fully-funded scheme. New workers have the choice of a pay-as-you-go defined-benefit as the primary system, if they prefer. An individual can only be a member of one scheme. In addition, there is a redistributive scheme for the elderly poor who are not entitled to a social insurance pension. Estimates show that only 30 per cent of individuals above the age of 60, or 2 per cent of the population, receive a pension. Consequently, compared to other industrial countries, the average pension remains very high and is estimated at about twice the GDP per capita.

Main cities

Bogotá (capital, estimated population 7.0 million in 2004, 2,640 metres above sea-level), Cali (2.3 million), Medellín (2.0 million), Barranquilla (1.4 million), Cartagena (853,900), Cucuta (657,100), Bucaramanga (542,400), Pereira (419,600), Ibagué (411,700), Santa Marta (404,800). More than 30 cities have populations of over 100,000.

Languages spoken

Some 200 Indian dialects are spoken. English is spoken in the business community.

Official language/s

Spanish

Media

Colombia is one of the most dangerous countries in the world for journalists to work in, with intimidation coming from drug runners, guerrillas, paramilitary groups and corrupt politicians.

Press

Dailies: There are many newspapers, in Spanish, including El Espectador (www.elespectador.com), El Tiempo (www.eltiempo.com) and El Nuevo Siglo (www.elnuevosiglo.com.co) are owned by political parties, Vanguardia Liberal (www.vanguardia.com) and El Espacia (www.elespacio.com.co) is an evening edition. Other provincial dailies include El Colombiano (www.elcolombiano.com) and El Mundo (www.elmundo.com) from Medellín, Diario Occidente (www.diariooccidente.com.co), from Cali and El Heraldo (www.elheraldo.com.co) from Barranquilla.

Weeklies: In Spanish, Semana (www.semana.com) is a news magazine with several specialist imprints. Reviste Gatopardo (www.gatopardo.com) and Revista Diner (www.revistadiners.com.co).

Business: In Spanish, dailies include La Republica (www.la-republica.com.co) is an authoritative newspaper, Portafolio (www.portafolio.com.co), La Nota Económica (www.lanota.com), also publishes special supplements. Deporte y Negocios (Sports & Business) (www.deporteynegocios.com) is a monthly magazine.

Broadcasting

The Comisión de Regulación de Telecommunicaciones is responsible for all broadcasting regulations. The national broadcaster is the Radio Televisíon Nacional de Colombia (RTVC) (www.rtvc.gov.co).

Broadcasting is closely controlled by the government although most programmes are produced by commercial companies.

Radio: RTCV operates Radio Nacional de Colombia (www.radionacionaldecolombia.gov.co) with music and cultural programmes for news. Radio Continental de Noticias (RCN) (www.rcn.com.co) operates a national network of 27 stations across the frequencies offering programmes of news, music and culture, for all audiences including the young and international listeners.

There are many local and regional commercial stations including La Z (www.laz92.com), Radio Activa (www.radioactiva.com.co) and Caracol Cadena Basica (www.caracol.com.co) with news programmes, from Bogata and Tropicana Estereo (www.tropicanafm.com) from Cartagena.

Television: There are over 30 TV stations broadcasting a wide variety of channels and programmes via cable and satellite facilities providing local, regional and national services. Most people gather their news from television.

RTCV operates Señal Colombia (www.senalcolombia.tv) with cultural and information programmes. Other national networks include Caracol TV (www.canalcaracol.com) and RCN Television (www.rcntv.com), showing domestically produced news, cultural, entertainment and sports programmes

Advertising

Advertising expenditure is equivalent to 2.1 per cent of GDP.

Economy

The economy of Colombia grew by 4 per cent in 2005 and 5.1 per cent in 2006. The country's rate of growth is steady but not spectacular, as the Colombian economy is still struggling to recover from the economic crisis of 1998/99. With political unrest destabilising investor confidence and the two major export commodities – oil and coffee – facing a degree of uncertainty, the Colombian economy is in need of considerable reform.

President Álvaro Uribe emphasised fiscal and structural reform as a government priority when he took office in August 2002. A series of economic reforms were passed in January 2003, which placed emphasis on changing the tax, pension, labour, public administration and banking systems, with the aim of sparking growth and increasing investor confidence. However, there are still major problems of debts, high unemployment and oil production slowdown.

Economic recovery is gaining momentum with inflation falling to 5.1 per cent in 2005 (compared with 11.2 per cent in 1999) and unemployment to 13.6 per cent in 2004 and 2005 (compared with 19.5 per cent in 1999). GDP, at US$122.3 billion in 2005, returned to and exceeded levels not seen since 1997. Discussions on free trade agreements with the US and between Andean Group members have had a beneficial effect on confidence levels.

The Inter-American Development Bank estimated that in 2006 migrant workers sent some US$4,200 million to their families in Colombia.

External trade

Colombia belongs to the Andean Community which is in the process of being incorporated into the South American Community of Nations (SACN) (along with Mercosor – the Southern Common Market) in the creation of an economic and legislative union.

Coffee and petroleum, both commodities that react to world prices, are the main export products and Colombia is the world's second largest exporter of cut flowers (after The Netherlands).

Colombia is the world's largest exporter of illegal cocaine. A UN report of January 2007 estimated that 610 tonnes of cocaine was produced and smuggled abroad, mainly to North America and Europe. Economist, Francisco Thoumi, claimed the drug industry 'depressed the growth of the formal sector of the economy' and limited the amount of legitimate investment, even though a 10 per cent rise in cocaine production increases GDP by 2 per cent. Drug trafficking accounts for around 25 per cent of foreign earnings.

Imports

Principal imports include industrial equipment, vehicles and equipment, consumer goods, chemicals, paper products, fuels and electricity, plastics and natural rubber products.

Main sources: US (26.6 per cent total, 2006), Mexico (8.8 per cent), China (8.5 per cent).

Exports

Principal exports are crude oil and derivatives, coffee, coal, clothing, bananas and cut flowers.

Main destinations: US (40.8 per cent total, 2006), Venezuela (11.1 per cent), Ecuador (5.1 per cent).

Agriculture

Farming

The agricultural sector has traditionally played a prominent role in the Colombian economy and it continues to contribute a sizable amount to total GDP. A wide variety of crops are grown throughout Colombia, depending on the altitude in a given region, but coffee is by far the most lucrative crop farmed.

Agricultural exports, primarily coffee, earn US$2 billion or more annually, and when prices have been high, have generated over half of the country's US dollar income. Colombia is the world's second largest producer of coffee after Brazil. Other important cash-export crops include bananas, exotic fruits, cut flowers, tobacco, cotton, sugar cane and cocoa.

The price of coffee on the international markets fell dramatically in 2001, partly caused by a surge in coffee production in Vietnam which led to high levels of oversupply. This damaged production prospects for Colombian coffee producers and there were fears after the 2002 season that coffee growers would shift to growing cocaine. However, coffee prices had recovered by the end of 2004.

The illegal export of cocaine, and to a lesser extent marijuana, has been estimated to earn the country between US$500 million and US$1 billion per year.

The government has been successful in promoting the diversification of agricultural export crops and lessening the economy's dependence on coffee revenues. Projects included drainage and irrigation schemes to bring more land under cultivation, cheaper credit for farmers, the improvement of road networks and taking electricity to isolated areas. Basic food subsidies in favour of urban consumers were revised to increase incentives for farmers.

Colombia's flower industry began in 1970 and the country is now the world's second-largest exporter of cut flowers after The Netherlands. The US is the main destination for this product. Climatic conditions are ideal, with no special heating or cooling conditions required. Colombia produces over 3.5 billion flowers a year, mostly on the plains near Bogotá. Shipments of fresh and processed tropical fruit are also increasing.

Meat production was hit by guerrilla violence in ranching zones. The government has launched emergency development programmes in low-income farming districts as part of its plans to boost agricultural output and to passify politically turbulent regions.

Crop production in 2005 included 4,314,425 tonnes (t) cereals in total, 2,662,300t rice, 1,441,501t maize, 2,623,194t potatoes, 2,125,163t cassava, 39,849,240t sugar cane, 3,300,000t oil palm fruit, 3,450,000t plantains, 1,600,000t bananas, 333,532t yams, 537,320t citrus fruit, 132,347t pulses, 374,684t tomatoes, 33,967t chillies & peppers, 5,157,889t roots & tubers, 770,276t oilcrops, 55,298t cocoa beans, 682,580t green coffee, 35,760t tobacco leaves, 7,840,222t fruit in total, 1,768,168t vegetables in total. Livestock production included: 1,567,008t meat in total, 750,000t beef meat, 108,500t pig meat, 6,960t lamb, 6,673t goat meat, 5,750t horsemeat, 685,000t poultry, 470,000t eggs, 6,770,000t milk, 2,600t honey, 1,200t sheepskins, 2,835t greasy wool, 80,300t cattle hides.

Fishing

Despite a substantial coastline of 2,880km and recent modest successes in developing the shrimp and shellfish industries, the fishing industry as a whole remains underdeveloped. As a member state of the Andean Community Colombia has benefitted form special duty-free status and is increasing its shipments of canned tuna to the EU. Exports of artificially reared shrimps are rising as the sector gathers strength.

The typical annual catch is 190,000mt, inclusive of 91,420mt marine fish and 20,580mt shellfish.

Forestry

Approximately half of Colombia's total landmass is forested. There are 49.6 million hectares (ha) of forests in the country. Most of the forests are located in the south-east of the country and form part of the Amazon jungle. Around 20 per cent of forested land is protected, with 40 national parks and reserves.

Despite its extensive forest resources, Colombia has a very modest production of industrial round timber. Sawn timber and panels have a large domestic market. Import of paper meets nearly one-third of the country's demand.

Industry and manufacturing

Manufacturing accounts for 14.3 per cent of Colombia's total GDP. Products include textiles and garments, chemicals, metal products, cement, cardboard containers, plastic resins and manufactures, beverages, wood products, pharmaceuticals, machinery and electrical equipment.

The industrial sector typically contributes a quarter of GDP, including the manufacturing sector which contributes 13 per cent, and employs 46 per cent of the workforce.

Food processing, beverages and textiles are the largest industries, followed by chemicals, leather goods, shoes and clothing, capital goods industries and motor vehicles. Metals, tobacco, cement, electrical engineering and paper are also important.

Tourism

Colombia's tourism industry is concentrated on the coastal region and the cities, especially Cartagena. Over the years Colombia's travel and tourism industry has suffered greatly from the ongoing civil conflict in the country. The industry has been severely damaged since its heyday in the 1990s, suffering from an image problem which was exacerbated by a reputation as the 'kidnap capital' of the world.

The travel and tourism industry is now beginning to make a moderate recovery. The industry now employs 5.9 per cent of the total workforce, a growth of 3.5 per cent year on year. The GDP contribution of the sector is 6.6 per cent of the country's total in 2005.

Mining

Mining in Colombia is concentrated on gold and other precious metals, iron ore, nickel and coal. In a typical year the mining industry contributes 4 per cent to the country's total GDP and employs 5 per cent of the total workforce. The industry is Colombia's main legal source of foreign exchange.

In recent years foreign investors have become fully aware of Colombia's potential for coal mining. With 20,000 tonnes of proven and inferred reserves the country's coal resource base is extensive and the quality of Colombian coal is high. Colombia is the second largest exporter of coal to Europe and the largest exporter to the US.

Colombia is one of the largest gold producers in the world, the fifth largest in Latin America after Peru, Brazil, Chile and Argentina. About 70 per cent of Colombian gold originates from the mines of Buritaca in Antioquia, using small-scale and primitive methods. Other precious minerals include silver and platinum (fourth largest producer of platinum), which are found in Choco Province along the Pacific coast.

Colombia is the world's top producer of high-grade emeralds, accounting for over 90 per cent of world output. The Muzo mine in the Eastern Andes near Bogotá is the world's largest emerald mine. Estimates put total emerald exports at US$250 million, of which a little more than 15 per cent is exported legally, for the most part (90 per cent) to Japan. Worker supervision in many of the emerald mines is minimal, fuelling the problems of smuggling.

Reserves of 100 million tonnes of iron ore assure Colombia of self-sufficiency until 2050. The known reserves are owned by Colombia's only steel company, Acerías Paz del Rio. The reserves are on the whole deep, expensive to extract and of low quality with a high sulphur content. A large part of the industry is located north-east of Bogotá, including the fully integrated steel works of Acerías Paz del Río.

Colombia has a high output of nickel supplying around 12 per cent of world demand. The country also mines copper, lime, sulphur, manganese, phosphates and salt.

Hydrocarbons

Colombia has the fifth largest proven crude oil reserves in South America, at 1.5 billion barrels. The country's oil production level has declined steadily since 1999. This fact together with the recent revised estimate of proven reserves and the toll taken on the industry by the country's long standing civil conflict, demonstrates how the oil industry has suffered. Colombian officials recently warned that unless considerable new oil supplies are discovered, the country will become a net importer of petroleum in the near future. Crude oil remains Colombia's largest export earner, a key source of foreign exchange earnings and is a major contributor to the fiscal revenues.

Natural gas production stands at 6.1 billion cubic metres, just exceeding consumption at 6 billion cubic metres. Reserves are estimated to stand at 110 billion cubic metres. However demand is set to increase due to the government's Plan de Masificacion de Gas Natural programme, which is aiming to increase natural gas use.

Colombia has high-quality proven coal reserves of around 7.3 billion tonnes (as at end 2004) and is the largest producer in Latin America. Much of the coal production goes to power plants both at home and abroad. Sixty per cent of Colombia's coal reserves lie in the interior around Bogotá, where the giant El Cerrejón Norte mine is located. New development is centred on this open-cast mine in Guajira. Coal is Colombia's third most important export after oil and coffee. With government investment in the promotion of the coal industry it is estimated that output will double between 2000 and 2010.

Although the privatisation of Carbocol (the state coal mining company and 50 per cent partner in El Cerrejón Norte) in 2001 added impetus to the improvement of the sector's infrastructure network and port facilities, many are worried about future security problems. Several incidents, including the destruction of railway lines by the guerrillas, have worried observers about the feasibility of the project to expand the sector.

Energy

With a generating capacity of 13.1GW Colombia has been self sufficient in energy since 1984. Approximately 44.9 billion kilowatthours (kwh) of electricity is generated each year and 41.1 kwh is consumed.

Seventy-seven per cent of total electricity generated is hydroelectric with conventional thermal and renewable sources constituting the remainder.

The electricity sector has been plagued by rebel attacks that damaged infrastructure. Grid connections have been blown up, leaving the country divided into small grids. A plan to connect Colombia's Atlantic coast and the capital city Bogotá was put on hold in 2002 due to increased guerrilla attacks.

The energy sector was deregulated in the 1990s and is now composed of a mixture of private and publicly owned operators. Colombia actively trades electricity with neighbouring countries, particularly Ecuador. Plans to increase electricity trade with Venezuela and other Andean Community nations have also been promoted.

Financial markets

Stock exchange

To improve stock market efficiency, the three stock markets: Bolsa de Valores de Bogotá, Bolsa de Valores de Medellín in Antioquia and Bolsa de Valores de Occidente in Cali merged in July 2001 to provide a combined capitalisation of Col$13 billion (US$5.8 million), with 42 member brokers.

Banking and insurance

Both Bancolombia and BBVA Colombia, two of the country's largest banking houses, have enjoyed significant profitability in recent years. Bancolombia, one of the oldest banks in Latin America, recorded pre tax profits of US$339 million in 2004, an increase of 53 per cent on the previous year's total. BBVA Colombia reported an earnings increase of 80 per cent in 2004. Both banks have indicated the likelihood of continued robust growth in 2005.

Following several years of a difficult economic and financial environment in the Colombia, the country's banking sector is now considered to be one of the leading markets in Latin America.

Central bank

Banco de la República

Main financial centre

Bogotá

Time

GMT minus five hours

Geography

Colombia, covering 1.14 million square km, is split between a coastal plain, high Andean peaks rising to more than 5,000 metres and a tropical Amazonian lowland. The only nation in South America with both Pacific and Caribbean coastlines, Colombia is bordered by Venezuela and Brazil to the east, Peru and Ecuador to the south and Panama to the north. Colombia owns the Isla de Malpelo in the Pacific and several Caribbean islands – including the San Andrés y Providencia islands. Its territorial waters border those of nations as distant as Honduras and Haiti.

Around 80 per cent of the population is concentrated in the Andean region, which covers around a quarter of the country's area. The Andes fan out northwards from the Ecuadorian border into three high cordilleras (parallel ranges) separated by deep valleys. Many of the peaks are volcanic. Colombia's highest mountain, the Pico Cristobal Colón, reaches 5,800 metres; it is 50km from the Caribbean coast in the Sierra de Santa Marta, which is isolated from the three main cordilleras.

Just over half of the country lies east of the Andes. Known as Los Llanos, most of this region is virtually unexplored and sparsely populated jungle. A low plain fringes most of the coast in the west and the north. About a fifth of the population lives in this area, which is also about a fifth of the total land area.

Hemisphere

Northern

Climate

The equator runs across the south of Colombia. The low coastal plain and the jungle regions east of the Andes have a tropical climate, with frequent rains and temperatures between 24–28 degrees Celsius (C). Temperatures fall with the higher altitudes. In Bogotá, at 2,650 metres, temperatures average around 14 degrees C.

Dress codes

Dress codes in Colombia are partly determined by formality but mostly by climate. In the capital, Bogotá, at 2,650 metres, suits for men and skirts for women are usual for business. Residents recommend a light coat for the evenings. In low-lying cities such as Cali in the south or Cartagena on the Caribbean coast, informal lightweight clothing is common.

Entry requirements

Passports

Required by all with few exceptions (eg certain nationals of Ecuador and certain tourist visitors from Trinidad and Tobago).

Visa

Required for all business visits and must be obtained before arrival. A letter, issued by the traveller's company, giving name and position of applicant, a detailed summary of intended purpose of trip, an itinerary, and the acceptance of full responsibility for any expenses incurred during the term of stay must be submitted with the application, (an original and copy, to be translated into Spanish), which will be notarised by the Colombian embassy.

Tourist visas are not required by citizens of North America, most EU and West European and most South American countries for stays up to 90 days. For further details and confirmation, contact the nearest embassy.

Currency advice/regulations
There are no limitations on the import of foreign and local currency. The export of foreign currency is limited to US$25,000. Travellers' cheques are recommended. Banks are generally the only reliable location for changing travellers' cheques or cash.

Prohibited imports
Illegal drugs, food products, vegetables and plant material are prohibited. Permits are required for the import of firearms and ammunition.

Health (for visitors)

Mandatory precautions
None, although vaccination against yellow fever is essential for visitors travelling to certain parts of the country, notably the central valley of the Magdalena River, the inland border areas (with Ecuador, Peru, Brazil and Venezuela), Uraba district, the south-eastern part of the Sierra Nevada de Santa Marta and the forest area along the Guaviare River. A certificate of inoculation may be required by immigration officials.

Advisable precautions
Precautions should be taken against cholera, malaria, hepatitis; typhoid immunisation should be current. There are risks of dengue fever, TB, measles and rabies. Tap water is not considered safe to drink, boiled or bottled water should be used at all times. Milk is unpasteurised and should therefore be boiled or avoided. Meat and fish should be thoroughly cooked and preferably eaten hot. It is advised to avoid uncooked vegetables and dairy products made from local milk. Fruit should be peeled. Visitors to Bogotá should take it easy for a few days to get used to the altitude, which may induce drowsiness, dizziness or altitude sickness.
Health insurance including medical evacuation is strongly recommended.

Hotels

Hotels are graded from one- to five-star by the Colombian Hotel Organisation. There are two seasonal tourist tariffs, low season is May–Nov and high season is Dec–Apr. A 5 per cent tax is imposed on all hotel bills. It is advisable to book well in advance. Service charge is normally added to bill, otherwise a 10 per cent tip is expected.

Credit cards

American Express, Diners, Visa and Master Card are widely used.

Public holidays (national)

Fixed dates
1 Jan (New Year's Day), ^6 Jan (Epiphany), ^19 Mar (St Joseph's Day), 1 May (Labour Day), ^17 Jun (Corpus Christi/Thanksgiving Day), ^29 Jun (St Peter and St Paul Day), 20 Jul (Independence Day), 7 Aug (Battle of Boyacá), ^21 Aug (Assumption Day), ^16 Oct (Columbus Day), ^6 Nov (All Saints' Day), 8 Dec (Immaculate Conception), 25 Dec (Christmas Day).

Variable dates
Maundy Thursday, Good Friday, ^Ascension Day, ^Corpus Christi (May/Jun).
^ Holidays that do not fall on Monday are taken on the following Monday.

Working hours

Banking
In Bogotá: Mon–Fri: 0900–1500.
Other cities: 0800–1130 and 1400–1630.
On the last working day of the month, banks open up to 1200 only.

Business
Mon–Fri: 0800–1230, 1400–1800.

Shops
Mon–Fri: 0900–1900 or 2000.

Telecommunications

Mobile/cell phones
Some GSM 850 and 1900 services available in limited areas.

Electricity supply

110V AC 60 cycles; two-pin flat blade plugs.

Social customs/useful tips

It is customary to tip porters but not maids or clerks in hotels.

Security

With a virtual war being fought between the government, drug barons and Farc insurgents, realistic security measures must be carried out as kidnapping, armed robbery and bomb explosions are frequent hazards. Visitors should exert due care and vigilance at all times. It is advisable that embassy officials be informed of their national's presence in Colombia and itinerary, particularly if travelling to the north of the country.
Colombia has the highest murder rate in the Americas and one of the worst reputations, in South America, for street crime, which is common during daylight hours in main cities. Visitors are advised not to display jewellery and to carry as little cash and documentation as possible; watches and briefcases are prime targets. It is advisable to keep a copy of all documents in an hotel safe in case of mishap. Much crime is drug-related and visitors should be wary of any unwarranted attention from strangers.

Getting there

Air

National airline: Avianca (Aerovías Nacionales de Colombia).

International airport/s: Bogotá-El Dorado (BOG), 12km from city, duty-free shop, restaurant, post office, bank, shops, hotel reservations, car hire.

Other airport/s: Regional international flights also arrive at Barranquilla-Ernesto Cortissos (BAQ), 10km from city, car hire; Cali-Palmaseca (CLO), 19km from city, restaurant; Cartagena-Crespo (CTG), 2km north-east of city; Medellín-Rionegro (MDE), 15 minutes' flight by scheduled and frequent helicopter service to city, (36km south-east of Medellín).

Airport tax: International departures US$25–29 in cash, not applicable to transit passengers. An exit tax of US$19 is charged to travellers whose stay exceeds two months.

Surface

Road: Access is possible by road from Ecuador via Tulean to Ipiales and Venezuela from Christóbal to Cucuta.

Water: The rivers Meta, between Venezuela, Putumayo and a section of the upper Amazon in Peru, and the Orinoco between Brazil and Colombia, all act as borders. They are used by small boats.

Main port/s: Caribbean: Santa Marta, Barranquilla, and Cartagena. Pacific: Buenaventura and Tumaco. Upper Amazon: Leticia.

Getting about

National transport

Air: Domestic air travel is the most practical way of getting around the country. There are frequent and cheap air services between Bogotá and all main centres. Major international air carriers operate internal flights as well as smaller companies that operate domestic services.

Road: Travelling by road can be arduous and potenially dangerous. There are paramilitary groups in rural areas.
Fifty per cent of the main roads wind through steep cordilleras, with bridges and tunnels in constant need of repair. Only 4,600km of the country's 120,000km road network are considered to be in good condition and less than 13,000km are paved.
There are highway links for Bogotá-Cali; for other journeys local enquiries are advisable.

Buses: There are many bus companies providing services between coastal towns and cities. Bogotá-Medellín inter-city service is fairly reliable and comfortable.

Rail: There is no longer an intercity passenger rail service.

Water: Cargo boats that travel along the Magdalena, Guaviare, Caqueta, and Meta river systems offer passage to passengers; the is a slow means of travel. There are 10,000km of navigable rivers between the three main Andean ranges.

City transport

Taxis: Within Bogotá, taxis are usually metered with minimum charge and extra at night, holidays, Sundays and for out-of-town journeys. Tourist taxis (green and cream) are likely to have drivers able to speak English and can be hired by the hour/day from major hotels. Typical taxis can be hailed in the street and tipping is not usual. For unmetered, taxis fares should be agreed in advance of journey. Shared taxis, colectivos, operate within cit-ies and suburbs.

Buses, trams & metro: Bogotá has a trolleybus system, buses and minibuses with flat rate fares.

Car hire

It is not recommended for foreign drivers as local conditions are so poor. Nevertheless, major car hire companies exist. Urban speed limits are 45–60kph while the rural speed limit is 80kph. An international driving licence (in Spanish) is required. Traffic drives on the right and during the working day is heavily congested in main towns.

BUSINESS DIRECTORY

The addresses listed below are a selection only. While World of Information makes every endeavour to check these addresses, we cannot guarantee that changes have not been made, especially to telephone numbers and area codes. We would welcome any corrections.

Telephone area codes

The international dialling code (IDD) for Colombia is +57 followed by the area code:

Armenia	67	Cartagena	5
Baranquilla	5	Cucuta	70
Bogotá	1	Manizales	69
Bucaramanga	73	Medellín	4
Cali	2		

Chambers of Commerce

American-Colombian Chamber of Commerce, 22-64 Calle 98, Bogotá (tel: 623-7088; fax: 621-6838; e-mail: info@amchamcolombia.com.co).

Barranquilla Chamber of Commerce, 36-135 Via 40, Barranquilla (tel: 330-3701; fax: 330-3750;e-mail: info@camarabaq.org.co).

Bogotá Chamber of Commerce, 16-21 Carrera 9, Bogotá (tel: 2381-0270; fax: 284-7735; e-mail: ccbcentro@ccb.org.co).

British-Colombian Chamber of Commerce, 77A-52 Carrera 12A, Bogotá (tel: 321-7077; fax: 321-7964; e-mail: britanica@cable.net.co).

Bucaramanga Chamber of Commerce, 36-20 Carrera 19, Bucaramanga (tel: 652-7000; fax: 633-4062).

Cali Chamber of Commerce, 3-14 Calle 8, Cali (tel: 886-1300; fax: 886-1399; e-mail: contacto@ccc.org.co).

Cartagena Chamber of Commerce, 32-41 Calle Santa Teresa, Cartagena (tel: 660-0795; fax: 660-0802; e-mail: camaradecomercio@cccartagena.org.co).

Colombian Confederation of Chambers of Commerce, 27-47 Carrera 13, Oficina 502, Bogotá (tel: 346-7055; fax: 346-7026; e-mail: confecamaras@confecamaras.org.co).

Cucuta Chamber of Commerce, 4-38 Calle 10, Cucuta (tel: 571-5922; fax: 571-2502; e-mail: cccuc02@col1.telecom.com.co).

Manizales Chamber of Commerce, 26-60 Carrera 23, Manizales (tel: 884-1840; fax: 884-0919; e-mail: ccm@ccm.org.co).

Medellín Chamber of Commerce, 52-82 Avenida Oriental, Medellín (tel: 511-6111; fax: 513-7757; e-mail: subcontramed@camaramed.org.co).

Pereira Chamber of Commerce, 23-09 Carrera 8, Local 10, Risaralda, Pereira (tel: 252-587; fax: 250-957; e-mail: camarap@pereira.multi.net.co).

Banking

Banco Andino, Carrera 7a No 14-23, Piso 3, Apdo Postal 6826, Bogotá (tel: 284-8800; fax: 286-7919).

Banco Anglo Colombiano (associated to Lloyds Bank plc), Cra 8 No 15-46/60, Zonal postal 1, Bogotá (tel: 334-5088; fax: 286-1383).

Banco Cafetero, Calle 28 No 13 A-15, Apdo Postal 240332, Bogotá (tel: 282-7742; fax: 284-5430).

Banco Caldas, Calle 72 No 7-64, Apdo Postal 240332, Bogotá (tel: 282-7742; fax: 284-5430).

Banco Central Hipotecario, Carrera 6a No 15-32, Zona Postal 1, Bogotá (tel: 283-7100; fax: 283-2802).

Banco Colombo Americano, Carrera 7a No 16-36, Piso 10, Apdo Postal 12327, Bogotá (tel: 334-5530; fax: 283-2939).

Banco Colpatria, Calle 13, No 7-90, Piso 2, Apdo Postal 30241, Bogotá (tel: 283-1567; fax: 286-3914).

Banco Co-operativo de Colombia (Bancoop), Calle 98 No 14-41, Apdo Postal 12242, Bogotá (tel: 257-7411; fax: 218-1601).

Banco de Antioquia (Bancoquia), Calle 12 No 746, Bogotá (tel: 334-9040).

Banco de Bogotá, PO Box 3436, Calle 36 No 7-47, Bogotá (tel: 332-0032 fax: 338-3302).

Banco de Colombia, Calle 30A No 6-38, Zona Postal 1, Apdo Postal 6836, Bogotá (tel: 285-6767; fax: 287-0595).

Banco de Cio Exterior de Colombia (Bancoldex) (Foreign Trade Bank of Colombia), Calle 28 No 13A-15, Apdo Postal 240-092, Bogotá (tel: 341-0677; fax: 282-5071).

Banco de Crédito, Calle 27 No 6-48, Zona Postal 1, Bogotá (tel: 286-8400; fax: 282-7256).

Banco del Occidente, Carrera 5a No 12-42, Apdo Postal 7607, Cali, Valle (tel: 824-081; fax: 822-705).

Banco del Estado, Carrera 10 No 18-15, Apdo Postal 8711, Bogotá (tel: 282-8471; fax: 284-9775).

Banco Extebandes de Colombia, Calle 74 No 6-65, Zona postal 2, Bogotá (tel: 217-7200; fax: 212-5786).

Banco Ganadero, Carrera 9A No 72-21, Apdo Postal 53851/9, Bogotá (tel: 217-0100; fax: 255-2457).

Banco Industrial Colombiano, Carrera 52 No 50-20, Apdo Postal 768, Medellín, Antioquia (tel: 251-5216; fax: 251-4716).

Banco Latino de Colombia, Calle 72 No 10-07, Apdo Postal 056397, Bogotá (tel: 210-999; fax: 284-0056).

Banco Mercantil Colombia, Carrera 9A No 99-02, Zona Postal 8, Bogotá (tel: 618-2249; fax: 618-2111).

Banco Popular, Calle 17 No 7-35, Zona Postal 1, Bogotá (tel: 334-9640; fax: 282-4246).

Banco Real de Colombia, Carrera 7a No 33-80, Apdo Postal 034262, Bogotá (tel: 269-8523; fax: 287-0507).

Banco Sudameris Colombia, Carrera 8a No 15-42, Zona Postal 1, Bogotá (tel: 283-8700; fax: 281-6191).

Banco Superior, Carrera 10a No 64-28, Bogotá (tel: 217-3888; fax: 235-4352).

Banco Tequendama, Diagonal 27 No 6-70, Apdo Postal 29799, Bogotá (tel: 285-9900; fax: 287-7020).

Banco Uconal, Calle 72 No 8-56, Bogotá (tel: 310-5155; fax: 212-2094).

Banco Unión Colombiano, Piso 2, Carrera 7 N°71-52, Bogotá (tel: 3120411 fax: 3120843).

Caja de Crédito Agrario Industrial y Minero, Carrera 8a No 15-43, Zona Postal 1, Bogotá (tel: 334-9066; fax: 286-5824).

Caja Social, Calle 72 No 10-71, Apdo Postal 58175, Bogotá (tel: 310-0099; fax: 211-6036).

Citibank, Carrera 9a No 99-02, Bogotá (tel: 618-4455; fax: 618-2515).

Central bank

Banco de la República, Carrera 7, No 14-78, Bogotá (tel: 342-1111; fax: 286-1686; e-mail: wbanco@banrep.gov.co).

Travel information

American Express, TMA, Cra.10 No 27-91, Offices 1-26, Bogotá (tel: 283-2955).

Avianca (Aerovías Nacionales de Colombia), Avenida, Eldorado 93-30, Piso 4, Bloque 1, Bogotá (tel: 413-9511; fax: 413-8325).

Colombian Hotel Organisation, Carrera 7, No 60–92 Bogotá (tel: 130-3640; internet: www.cotelco.org).

Fondo de Promoción Turistica de Colombia, Carrera 16A No 78-55 Of. 604, Bogotá (tel: 611-4330, 611-4185; fax: 236-3640; e-mail: turismocolombia@andinet.com; internet site: http://www.turismocolombia.com).

National tourist organisation offices

National Tourist Office, Calle 28 No. 13A-15 P 17 Y 18, Bogotá (tel: 283-9466; fax: 283-8945).

Ministries

Ministry of Agriculture and Rural Development, Avenida Jiménez No. 7-65, Santafé de Bogotá (tel: 334-1199; fax: 284-1775).

Ministry of Communications, Edificio Murillo Toro, Carrera 7 y 8 Calle 12 y 13, Santafé de Bogotá (tel: 286-6911; fax: 286-1185).

Ministry of Culture, Calle 8 No 6-67, Santafé de Bogotá (tel: 282-0854; fax: 282-0666).

Ministry of Economic Development, Carrera 13 No. 28-01, Apartado Aéreo 99412, Santafé de Bogotá (tel: 320-0077; fax: 287-6025).

Ministry of the Environment, Calle 38 No 8-61, Santafé de Bogotá (tel:288-6010; fax: 243-3004).

Ministry of Finance and Public Credit, Carrera 7a No. 6-45, Santafé de Bogotá (tel: 284-5400; fax: 284-5396).

Ministry for Foreign Affairs, Palacio de San Carlos, Calle 10 No. 5-51, Santafé de Bogotá (tel: 282-7811, 287-6800; fax: 341-6777).

Ministry of Foreign Trade, Calle 28 No. 13A-15 P 5,6,7,9, Santafé de Bogotá (tel: 286-9111; fax: 284-9537, 334-9908).

Ministry of Health, Carrera 13 No. 32-76, Santafé de Bogotá (tel: 336-5066; fax: 336-0116, 336-0296).

Ministry of the Interior, Palacio Echeverry, Carrera 8a No. 8-09, Santafé de Bogotá (tel: 283-0676, 283-6853; fax: 281-5884, 286-8025).

Ministry of Justice and Law, Avenida Jiménez No. 8-89, Santafé de Bogotá (tel: 286-0211, 286-5888, 286-9711; fax: 281-6384, 283-2761).

Ministry of Labour and Social Security, Carrera 7a No. 34-50, Santafé de Bogotá (tel: 287-3434/5045, 285-7092/7098, 285-8362/7361; fax: 285-7091, 287-3861/8342).

Ministry of Mines and Energy CAN, Santafé de Bogotá (tel: 222-4555, 2068, 222-0179; fax: 222-3651).

Ministry of National Defence, Avenida El Dorado Cra 52 CAN, Santafé de Bogatá (tel: 220-4999; fax: 222-1874).

Ministry of National Education, CAN, Santafé de Bogotá (tel: 222-2800; fax: 222-0324).

Ministry of Transport, CAN, Santafé de Bogotá (tel: 222-4411, 222-7577, 7966; fax: 222-1647, 222-1121).

Other useful addresses

Asociación Nacional de Industriales (ANDI), Carrera 13 No 26-45, Bogotá (tel: 334-6673, 281-0600).

Bolsa de Bogotá (Stock Exchange), Carrera 8a, No 13-82, Apartado Aéreo 3584, Bogotá (tel: 243-6501, 243-8471; fax: 281-3170).

Bolsa de Medellín S.A. (Stock Exchange), Carrera 50 No 50-48 Piso 2, Medellín (tel: 260-3000; fax: 251-1981).

British Embassy, Apartado Aéreo 4508, Torre Propaganda Sancho, Calle 98, No 9-03, Piso 4, Bogotá (tel: 218-5111; fax: 218-2330, 218-2460).

Caja de Crédito Agrario Industrial y Minero, Carrera 8 No 15-43, Bogotá (tel: 284-4600).

Carbones de Colombia (CARBOCOL), Carrera 7, No 31-10, Pisos 5-18, Bogotá (tel: 287-3100).

Colombian Embassy (USA), 2118 Leroy Place, NW, Washington DC 20008 (tel: 202-387-8338; fax: 202-232-8643; e-mail: emwash@colombiaemb.org).

Colombian Government Trade Bureau (Proexport Colombia) Calle 28 No. 13 A - 15 Piso 35, Santafé de Bogotá, (tel: 341-2066; fax: 282-8130, 282-8230).

Departamento Administrativo de Aeronáutica Civil (DAAC), Aeropuerto Internacional El Dorado, Bogotá (tel: 266-2237).

Departamento Administrativo Nacional de Estadísticas (DANE), Oficina 222, CAN-Avenida Eldorado, Bogotá.

Departamento Nacional de Planeación, Calle 26 No 13-19, Bogotá (tel: 282-4055; fax: 281-3348).

Empresa Colombiana de Mina (ECOMINAS), Calle 32, No 13-07, Apartado Aéreo 17878, Bogotá (tel: 287-7136; fax: 287-4606).

Empresa Colombiana de Petróleos (ECOPETROL), Carrera 13 No 36-24, Bogotá (tel: 285-6400).

Empresa Nacional de Telecomunicaciones (TELECOM), Calle 23 No 13-49, Bogotá (tel: 286-0077, 282-8280).

Federación Nacional de Cafeteros de Colombia, Calle 73 No 8-13, Apartado Aéreo 57534, Bogotá DE (tel: 217-0600).

Instituto Colombiana de Comercio Exterior (INCOMEX), Edifico Centro Comercio Internacional, Calle 28 No 13A-15, Bogotá (tel: 281-2200).

Instituto de Fomento Industrial (IFI), Calle 16, No 6-66, Pisos 7-15, Bogotá (tel: 282-2055).

Instituto Nacional de Investigaciones Geológico-Mineras (INGEOMINAS), Diagonal 53, No 34-53, Apartado Aéreo 4865, Bogotá (tel: 222-1811; fax: 222-3597).

Instituto Nacional de Radio y Televisión, Via del Aeropuerto Eldorado, Bogotá (tel: 222-0700; fax: 222-0080).

Invertir Corporation of Colombia (COINVERTIR), Cra 7 no 71-52 Torre A, Oficina 702, Bogotá (tel: 312-0312; fax: 312-0318).

US Embassy, Calle 38, No 8-61, Bogotá (tel: 285-1300; fax: 288-5687).

Other news agencies: Prensa Latina: www.plenglish.com

Internet sites

Business News, Latin Trade online: www.latintrade.com

Organisation of American States: www.oas.org

President of the Republic (in Spanish): www.presidencia.gov.co/webpresi/

Colombia Trade: www.coltrade.org/

Comoros

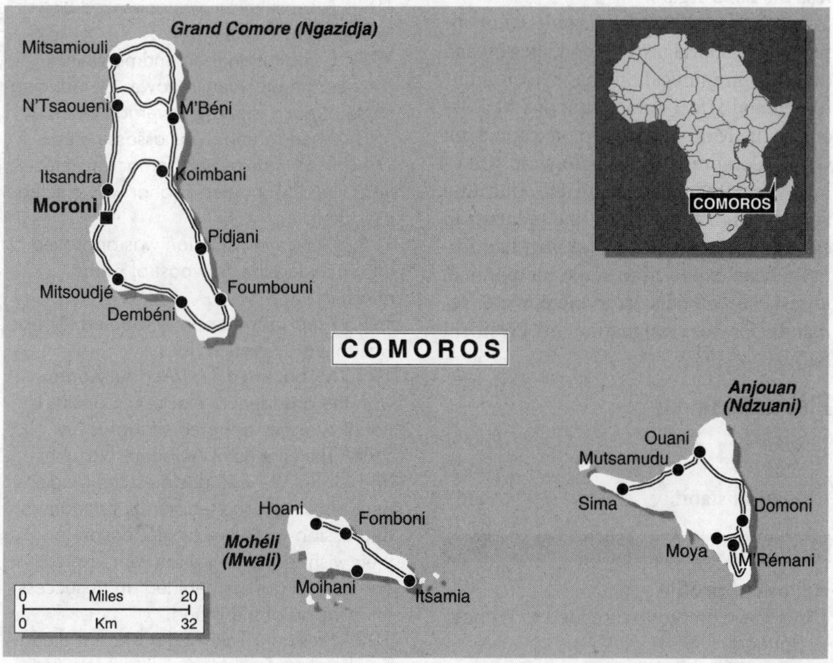

Potentially a holiday paradise, the Comoros islands have tried since independence from France in 1975 to consolidate political stability amid tensions between semi-autonomous islands and the central government. A history of political violence has left the islands desperately poor. At times, the country has teetered on the brink of disintegration. The three Indian Ocean islands have experienced more than 20 coups or attempted coups in just over 30 years, beginning just weeks after independence when President Ahmed Abdallah was toppled in a coup assisted by French mercenary Colonel Bob Denard. To add to the country's troubles, the islands of Anjouan and Moheli declared unilateral independence in a violent conflict in 1997. In an effort to bring them back into the fold, Moheli, Anjouan and the largest island, Grande Comore, were in 2001 granted their own presidents and greater autonomy. The renamed L'Union des Comores (The Union of Comoros) retained control of security and financial matters. The Comoros lay claim to French-administered Mayotte Island, which has one of only two ports in the archipelago.

The allocation of power and resources has been a contentious issue, and the whole fragile system has been criticised as being expensive. Ahmed Abdallah Mohamed Sambi was named president of the Union after elections in May 2006. The presidents of the three semi-autonomous islands – Anjouan, Moheli and Grande Comore – became vice presidents of the Union of Comoros, including Mohamed Bacar as president of Anjouan.

The latest trouble arose in April 2007 when President Bacar refused to step down ahead of elections scheduled for June, to be conducted under the auspices of the African Union (AU). Elections on Anjouan were suspended, but went ahead on the other islands. Bacar printed his own ballot papers and held elections that were not recognised by the Union government. After extensive, but unsuccessful, mediation talks held by the AU, Union troops, supported by a coalition force of AU troops from Tanzania, Sudan and Senegal, retook the island in March 2008. Bacar and about 20 of his aides escaped to the French island of Mayotte (Mayotte had been part of the Autonomous State of

KEY FACTS

Official name: Udzima wa Komori (L'Union des Comores) (The Union of the Comoros) (from Jan 2002)

Head of State: President Ahmed Abdallah Mohamed Sambi (since 26 May 2006)

Head of government: President Ahmed Abdallah Mohamed Sambi (since May 2006)

Ruling party: Camp des Îles Autonomes (CIA) (Autonomous Islands Party); (since 2004)

Area: 2,171 square km

Population: 639,000 (2007)*

Capital: Moroni

Official language: Arabic and French

Currency: Comoros franc (Cf) = 100 centimes

Exchange rate: Cf310.35 per US$ (Jul 2008); (pegged Cf491.97 per euro)

GDP per capita: US$691 (2007)*

GDP real growth: -0.10% (2007)*

Labour force: 290,000 (2004)

Inflation: 3.00% (2007)*

Balance of trade: -US$84.00 million (2006)

Foreign debt: US$306.00 million (2004)

* estimated figure

Comoros until 1974 when they were the only island in the archipelago that voted to retain its link with France and forgo independence). They were arrested for illegally entering French territory and held in custody on the French island of Réunion. France has refused to extradite the group to Comoros, although it has also refused to grant asylum to Bacar.

Meanwhile, the people of the Comoros remain among the poorest in Africa and are heavily dependent on foreign aid. The islands' chief exports – vanilla, cloves and perfume essence – are prone to price fluctuations. Money sent home by Comorans living abroad is an important source of foreign exchange. The descendants of Arab traders, Malay immigrants and African peoples contribute to the islands' complex ethnic mix.

The islands have inadequate transportation links and a young and rapidly increasing population. The low educational level of the labour force contributes to a subsistence level of economic activity, high unemployment, and a heavy dependence on foreign grants and technical assistance. Agriculture, including fishing, hunting, and forestry, contributes 40 per cent to GDP, employs 80 per cent of the labour force, and provides most of the exports. The country is not self-sufficient in food production; rice, the main staple, accounts for the bulk of food imports. The government has been struggling to upgrade education and technical training, privatise commercial and industrial enterprises, improve health services, diversify exports, promote tourism, and reduce the high population growth rate. Increased foreign support is essential if annual growth targets are to be met. GDP growth in 2006 was a disappointing 1.2 per cent, down on the 2.0 per cent recorded in 2005. Inflation fell to 3.8 per cent (from 4.9 per cent in 2005) and annual GDP per capita hovered around the US$630 mark, again more or less the 2005 figure.

By August 2008 the islands were affected by shortages of food, petrol and diesel. Communications have been interrupted and street demonstrations had occurred in Moroni, the Union capital on Grand Comore island. There were strikes in key sectors such as health and education and although the military intervention to end the insurrection on Anjouan had initially been expected to settle the political unrest, six months later there were demands for the resignation of President Sambi.

Risk assessment

Politics	Poor
Economy	Poor
Regional stability	Fair

KEY INDICATORS — Comoros

	Unit	2003	2004	2005	2006	2007
Population	m	0.76	0.77	0.61	0.63	*0.64
Gross domestic product (GDP)	US$bn	0.32	0.37	0.39	0.40	*0.44
GDP per capita	US$	417	582	633	645	*691
GDP real growth	%	2.1	1.9	4.2	1.2	*-0.1
Inflation	%	4.5	4.3	3.0	3.4	*3.0
Industrial output	% change	–	2.5	2.5	8.8	–
Agricultural output	% change	–	2.7	3.0	-10.3	–
Exports (fob) (goods)	US$m	16.3	18.0	–	16.0	–
Imports (cif) (goods)	US$m	39.8	92.0	–	100.0	–
Balance of trade	US$m	-23.5	-74.0	–	-84.0	–
Current account	US$m	-20.0	-9.0	-13.0	-21.0	*8.0
Total reserves minus gold	US$m	94.3	103.7	85.8	93.5	117.2
Foreign exchange	US$m	93.5	102.9	85.0	92.7	116.3
Exchange rate	per US$	462.34	408.14	380.41	380.41	340.80

* estimated figure

COUNTRY PROFILE

Historical profile

1843 The Comoros was ceded to France by Portugal.
1947 The Comoros became a separate French Overseas Territory, detached from administration by Madagascar.
1961 It achieved internal self government.
1972 Elections produced a large majority for parties advocating independence and Ahmed Abdallah Abderrahman became president of the government council.
1973 Abderrahman was restyled president of the government.
1975 The Federal Islamic Republic of the Comoros gained independence from France, Mayotte was the only island in the archipelago that voted to retain links with France.
1978 A constitution was approved by referendum.
1982 Constitutional amendments increased the president's power by reducing those of each island's governor.
1989 Abderrahman was assassinated.
1990 In Comoros' first democratic elections, Said Mohamed Djohar was elected president.
1992 A new constitution was approved that included the new post of prime minister.
1995 An abortive coup to toppled Djohar was foiled by French troops.
1996 Mohammed Taki Abdoul-Karim won the presidential election. Constitutional changes adopted sharia as law.
1997 The islands of Anjouan (Ndzuani) and Mohéli (Mwali) declared their independence from the Comoros. Economic depression was sited as the reason for their wish for reintegration with France. The central government led an unsuccessful invasion of the island.
1998 President Taki Abdoul-Karim died. Tajidine ben Said Massonde became president.
1999 Colonel Azali Assoumani seized power in a bloodless coup and became president. In legislative elections on Anjouan, hardline secessionists won every seat.
2001 A military, unionist force on Anjouan took control in August. Attempts to wrest control from it failed and in December the Comoran government, with amendment to the constitution, implemented a change to unify the country in a loose federation as a decentralised Comoran Union of three autonomous islands: Anjouan, Mohéli and Grand Comoros.
2002 The country's name was changed to L'Union des Comores (The Union of the Comoros). In May, Assoumani was declared president of The Union. Mohamed Bacar was elected president of Anjouan. Mohamed Said Fazul was elected president in Mohéli, and Abdou Soule Elbak was elected president of Grande Comore.
2003 Power-sharing agreements were signed to allow national elections to take place and the presidency to rotate between the islands.
2004 In April, parliamentary elections for the Union were held in which the opposition candidates to the Union president (Assoumani) formed an alliance: Camp

des Îles Autonomes (CIA) (Autonomous Islands Party) and won 27 seats against six seats for the president's party. The first federal government was sworn in on 14 July.
2005 Mount Karthala, a volcano on Gran Comore, erupted in April and again in November, causing population flights and public health concerns.
2006 Presidential elections for the Union took place on 16 April and 14 May. In the first round, held on Anjouan, 10 of the 13 candidates were eliminated. In the nationwide, second round Ahmed Abdallah Mohamed Sambi won 58.02 of the vote, Ibrahim Halidi Djaanffari 28.32 per cent and Mohamed Djaanfari 13.65 per cent. President Sambi took office on 26 May.
2007 President Becar (of Anjouan) refused to give up his office in April, as constitionally he is required to do, before the scheduled June elections. His forces clashed with the national army sent to inforce the constitution; the African Union sent troops to support the constitution. On 11 May, Dhoihirou Halidi was appointed interim president of Anjouan. On 18 May, the constitutional court dismissed the president of Mohéli; Mohamed Ali Said was sworn in a president of Mohéli on 1 July.
2008 Forces of the African Union overthrew the renegade president of Anjouan, Mohamed Bacar, on 25 March. Ikililou Dhoinine, a federal vice president, was appointed as provisional administrator. Moussa Toybou took office as president of Anjouan on 7 July.

Political structure

Constitution
The new national constitution was ratified by referendum in December 2001; it created a federation – The Union of the Comoros – with greater autonomy for each of the three islands.
Each island has its own president (who also becomes a federal vice president), with a federal president assuming overall authority. The federal presidency rotates every four years between the three islands. Each island has its own legislature, constitution and budget. Foreign relations, defence and currency are the responsibility of the Union.

Form of state
Federal republic

The executive
The presidency of the Union of the Comoros rotates between the islands of Grand Comore, Anjouan, and Moheli every four years according to the 2001 power-sharing constitution.
First round presidential elections are held on the island that will hold the next presidency; the top three candidates become the only candidates that the whole union votes on in the second round.

National legislature
The 33-member Assemblée de l'Union (federal parliament) has 15 members appointed by the three island legislatures (five each) and 18 elected through direct universal suffrage. Each island has its own assembly.

Legal system
French Nepolean Code and Sharia (Islamic) law in a new consolidated code.

Last elections
16 April/14 May 2006 (federal presidency); 18/25 April 2004 (parliamentary); 17/ 21 March 2004 (autonomous islands' assemblies).
Results: Second round parliamentary: the islands' candidates won 12 seats, the supporters of The Union, six. Turnout in the election for those 18 seats was over 65 per cent. The remaining 15 seats in the 33-seat assembly will be nominated by the island parliaments.
Autonomous islands' assemblies:
Grande Comore: supporters of the island president won 13 seats out of 20 and supporters of the Union president (Assoumani), seven.
Anjouan: supporters of the island president won 23 seats out of 25 and supporters of the Union president (Assoumani), two.
Mohéli: supporters of the island president won nine seats out of 10 and supporters of the Union president (Assoumani), one.
The opposition candidates to the Union president (Assoumani) formed an alliance: Camp des Îles Autonomes (CIA) (Autonomous Islands Party).
Presidential: first round (held on Anjouan) Ahmed Abdallah Mohamed Sambi won 23.7 per cent of votes, Mohamed Djaanffari 13.1 per cent and Abderemane Ibrahim Halidi 10.37 per cent. Second round (Union) Sambi won 58.02 per cent, Djaanffari 13.65 per cent and Halidi 28.32 per cent. Turnout was 54.9 and 57.3 per cent respectively.

Next elections
2009 (parliamentary); 2010 (federal presidency (on Moheli))

Political parties

Ruling party
Camp des Îles Autonomes (CIA) (Autonomous Islands Party); (since 2004)

Main opposition party
Convention pour le Renouveau des Comores (CRC) (Convention for the Renewal of Comoros)

Population

639,000 (2007)*
Last census: September 2003: 575,660
Population density: 244 per square km.
Urban population: 34 per cent (1995–2001).
Annual growth rate: 2.8 per cent 1994–2004 (WHO 2006)

Ethnic make-up
Antalote, Cafre, Makao, Oimatsaha, Sakalava.
The descendants of Arab traders, Malay immigrants and African peoples contribute to the islands' complex ethnic mix.

Religions
Sunni Muslim 86 per cent (official religion), Roman Catholic 14 per cent.

Education

Unicef concluded that school enrolment dropped due to insufficient classrooms and qualified teachers, among other infrastructural inadequacies. Education also suffers from poor performance and quality. A Unicef-sponsored humanitarian action plan in 2002 provided US$122,000 towards basic education.
Literacy rate: 59 per cent; adult rates (World Bank 2002).
Enrolment rate: 60 per cent (Unicef).

Health

Per capita total expenditure on health (2003) was US$25; of which per capita government spending was US$14, at the international dollar rate, (WHO 2006).
The World Health Organisation (WHO), in 2003, funded health projects aimed at reducing mortality from common diseases and encouraging better use of existing health facilities, while improving the quality of healthcare overall. It also organised mosquito control activities to reduce the incidence of malaria.

HIV/Aids
Although prostitution is relatively rare, over 60 per cent of sex workers in Moroni tested HIV positive.
HIV prevalence: 0.12 per cent aged 15–49 in 2000
Life expectancy: 64 years, 2004 (WHO 2006)
Fertility rate/Maternal mortality rate: 4.7 births per woman, 2004 (WHO 2006); maternal mortality five per 1,000 live births (World Bank).
Child (under 5 years) mortality rate (per 1,000): 54 per 1,000 live births; 26 per cent of children aged under five years are malnourished (World Bank).
Head of population per physician: 0.15 physicians per 1,000 people, 2004 (WHO 2006)

Welfare

There is no minimum wage, there are no laws prohibiting bonded or forced labour and no protection for anti-union practices by employers. The labour code allows for one day off per week and one month of paid leave per year, although the government generally does not enforce the law due to a lack of provision.
The World Bank reported, in October 2003, that 47 per cent of households were living in poverty and 42 per cent of

the population were malnourished. It stated that the government were poor in implementing, even in partnership, basic social infrastructure, and health and educational services tended to be of low quality and poorly utilised. Local communities were found to be keen to undertake projects in partnership with a World Bank poverty reduction plan, the 'Social Fund Project,' to creat small, income-generating activities. In future, proposed projects will rely mainly on village committees, community groups, NGOs and private firms.

Main cities

Moroni (on Grand Comore (Ngazidja) (capital, estimated population 60,200 in 2003), Mutsamudu (on Anjouan (Ndzuani), (30,900), Mutsamudu (30,900), Mitsamiouli (21,400), Domoni (19,100), Fomboni (on Mohéli (Mwali) (13,300).

Languages spoken

Shikomor and numerous African languages are spoken. English is rarely spoken.

Official language/s

Arabic and French

Media

The government maintains tight control of the media, with newspapers and radio stations suspended and journalists risk arrest following items deemed disrespectful to its interests. Consequently self-censorship is prevalent.

Other news agencies: APA (African Press Agency): www.apanews.net
The Comoran Press: www.comores-online.com
Panapress: www.panapress.com

Press

There are few commercial publications due to a small advertising market and a poor distribution network

In French, weeklies include Al Watwan (www.alwatwan.net) and La Gazette de Comores are official publications. Independent newspapers include KashKazi (www.kashkazi.com) (weekly), and L'Archipel (monthly).

Broadcasting

The national, state broadcaster is Office Radio et Télévision des Comores (ORTC) (www.radiocomores.km).

Radio: With high levels of illiteracy and poverty the radio is the principal medium for news and information.

ORTC operates Radio Comoros which broadcasts in Arabic, French, Comoran and Swahili. Two regional governments run their own stations, including Radio Television Anjouanaise (RTA) (www.rtanjouan.org) on Anjouan, and Radio Ngazidja on Grand Comore. Other stations include Radio Ocean Indien (www.radioceanindien.km) and Radio Dziyalandze (www.radiodziyalandze.com). Radio France International (RFI) (www.rfi.fr) has news programmes in French.

Television: ORTC operates the national, Television Nationale Comorienne (TNC). Other TV stations include RTA (www.rtanjouan.org) on Anjouan, TV Ulezi is a private provider while Mtsangani Television (MTV) broadcasts educational and cultural programmes. There are satellite services from Arabnet.

TV and radio services can be received from Mayotte.

News agencies

Other news agencies: APA (African Press Agency): www.apanews.net
The Comoran Press: www.comores-online.com
Panapress: www.panapress.com

Economy

The Comoros economy is based on local services, agriculture and industry. Economic activity is largely based on subsistence farming, while exports consist principally of agricultural plantation products, including cloves, essence of ylang-ylang (a major component of perfume) and vanilla, of which Comoros is a leading world producer. Comoros has inherent disadvantages such as its small local market, high transport costs and a poor investment climate. As such, economic growth between 2001–05 was only 2.75 per cent, well below the regional average.

The trade in vanilla was hit by a slump in world prices to just US$50 per kilo in 2005, down from the high of US$600 in 2003. The earlier high prices encouraged foreign growers in Uganda, India and Indonesia to cultivate the crop and international buyers to turn to synthetic vanilla. Exports are typically 60–80 tonnes.

In 2005 GDP growth was 2.0 per cent, up from 1.9 in 2004. Expatriate remittances are important to the economy, representing around 12 per cent of GDP.

The distribution of wealth between the islands is a problem, given the lack of constitutional clarity over revenue collection, but an agreement to transfer shared revenues to a special account at the Central Bank to secure fiscal policy was agreed in 2005. Harmonisation of customs tariffs was expected to increase revenue but pre-election public finances deteriorated significantly as fiscal policy was disrupted and expenditure was higher than expected. Since the 2006 presidential elections the government has attempted to reverse the trend and encourage international donors to back its 2006–09 strategy for investment, particularly in tourism, with aid worth eur250–300 million (US$330–396 million).

External trade

Comoros is a member of the Common Market for Eastern and Southern Africa (Comesa), and operates within a free trade zone with 13 of the 19 member states. The country runs annual deficits on its trade account, largely because of a limited export base.

Imports

Principal imports are rice and other foodstuffs, consumer goods; petroleum products, cement and transport equipment.

Main sources: France (25.0 per cent total, 2006), UAE (9.9 per cent), South Africa (6.5 per cent).

Exports

Principal exports are vanilla, ylang-ylang, cloves, perfume oil, copra.

Main destinations: The Netherlands (35.8 per cent total, 2006), France (18.3 per cent), Italy (12.7 per cent).

Agriculture

Farming

The agriculture sector is the principal source of export earnings. It contributes around 40 per cent to GDP and employs 65 per cent of the workforce.

Although as much as 50 per cent of the total land area is cultivated, the agricultural sector remains underdeveloped (due to poor soil, adverse weather conditions and inadequate facilities) and over 50 per cent of the country's food requirements (notably rice) have to be imported.

Major food crops grown are cassava, sweet potatoes, rice and bananas; yams and coconuts are also produced, while main cash crops are cocoa, ylang-ylang (perfumes), vanilla and cloves.

Comoros produces around 1,700 tonnes of vanilla a year but its cultivation has suffered a drop in value due to overseas competition from new plantations and synthetic vanilla. Processed vanilla beans earned US$600 per kilo in 2003–04, while in 2006 the price had dropped to US$20–30.

Estimated crop production in 2005 included 21,000 tonnes (t) cereals in total, 17,000t rice, 4,000t maize, 58,000t cassava, 5,500t sweet potatoes, 9,200t taro, 4,000t yams, 65,000t bananas, 14,320t pulses, 77,200t roots and tubers, 77,000t coconuts, 10,271t oilcrops, 27t cocoa beans, 100t green coffee, 140t vanilla, 3,000t cloves, 68,600t fruit in total, 3,715t vegetables in total. Estimated livestock production included: 2,095t meat in total, 1,100t beef, 350t goat meat, 560t poultry, 776t eggs, 4,550t milk.

Fishing

Fishing is underexploited, with tuna being the main catch. The fishing sector has

received considerable aid from Japan and the EU.
In 2004, the total marine fish catch was 14,916 tonnes and the total crustacean catch was 20 tonnes.

Forestry
Deforestation, caused by clearing for the cultivation of the ylang-ylang crop, is an increasing ecological problem.

Industry and manufacturing
The industrial sector contributes around 13 per cent to GDP and employs 5 per cent of the workforce; manufacturing contributes 5.4 per cent. The sector is underdeveloped, with activity confined to distillation of essences and perfumes (particularly from ylang-ylang), vanilla processing, soft drinks, plastics and woodwork.

Tourism
The tourism sector has potential, but remains under-developed. Tourists have been deterred by political instability and social turmoil, although there are no reports of attacks on foreigners. Tourism contributes around 4 per cent to GDP.

Mining
There is no mining activity.

Hydrocarbons
There are no known oil or gas reserves and the country relies on imports of refined oil for its energy needs. However, consumption is low, around 670 barrels per day. There is only one oil company in Comoros, the Société Comorienne des Hydrocarbures (SCH), which owns two storage depots.

Energy
There is heavy dependence on imports for all fuel requirements. The electricity generating infrastructure is poor and there are frequent blackouts, partly due to generator breakdowns and partly due to a lack of fuel. Electricity is provided by the parastatal utility Electricite et Eaux des Comores (EEDC).

Banking and insurance
The Banking sector is composed of the Banque Centrale des Comores (BCC), the central bank, the Banque de Développement des Comores (BDC), which focusses on development lending, and the Banque pour l'Industrie et le Commerce des Comores (BIC). The BDC stopped lending in 1997 due to liquidity problems, but still exists and is scheduled for restructuring some time in the future. The BIC is linked to France's BNP-Paribas and provides full international trade finance as well as local personal and business banking services.

Central bank
Banque Centrale des Comores (BCC)

Main financial centre
Moroni

Time
GMT plus three hours

Geography
The Comoros is an archipelago in the Mozambique Channel, between the island of Madagascar and the east coast of the African mainland. The group comprises four main islands (Grand Comore, Anjouan, Mohéli and Mayotte), and numerous islets and coral reefs. Mayotte, although geographically part of the Comoros group of islands, elected to remain as a French overseas territory, in 1975, and is politically separate from the Comoros.

Hemisphere
Southern

Climate
Tropical. Dry season May to October with average temperature 24 degrees Celsius (C). Rainy season from November to April with temperature 27–35 degrees C. Very hot and humid on coasts, cooler on inner highlands.

Entry requirements

Passports
Required by all.

Visa
Required by all.
Tourist visas obtained at the port of entry, are valid for 14 days. Visas valid for up to 90 days can be obtained in advance of travelling. Proof of return/onward passage is needed.
For business visas, information can be obtained from the Comoran Embassy 20 Rue Marbeau, 75116 Paris France (tel: (+33) 140-679-054; fax: (+33) 140-677-296).

Currency advice/regulations
There are no restrictions on the import of domestic or foreign currencies.
There are limited banking facilities for foreign travellers, credit cards are not universally accepted and travellers cheques can only be cashed in the Banque Internationale des Comores, in the capital. To avoid additional fees travellers cheques should be in euros. Foreign currency is exchanged in city and provincial banks.

Prohibited imports
Firearms, ammunition and radio transmission equipment, plants and soil.

Health (for visitors)

Mandatory precautions
Yellow fever vaccination certificates requested from visitors arriving from infected areas.

Advisable precautions
Typhoid, hepatitis A, tetanus and polio vaccinations recommended. Malaria prophylaxis advisable as risk exists throughout the country. Water precautions should be taken. There is a rabies risk. Seek further advice with regard to vaccinations for diphtheria, hepatitis B, meningitis and tuberculosis.

Hotels
Advisable to book in advance. Limited first-class accommodation available on Grande Comore, Anjouan and Mayotte (Maore), but several high-quality resort hotels have been built.

Public holidays (national)

Fixed dates
18 Mar (Death of Said Mohamed Cheikh Day), 25 May (Africa Day), 29 May (Death of President Ali Soilih Day), 6 Jul (Independence Day), 26 Nov (Death of President Ahmed Abdallah Day), 25 Dec (Christmas Day).

Variable dates
Eid al Adha, El am Hejir (Islamic New Year), Ashura, Eid al Fitr.

Islamic year – 1429 (10 Jan 2008–28 Dec 2008): The Islamic year contains 354 or 355 days, with the result that Muslim feasts advance by 10–12 days against the Gregorian calendar. Dates of feasts vary according to the sighting of the new moon, so cannot be forecast exactly.

Working hours

Banking
Mon–Thu: 0730–1300; Fri: 0730–1100.

Business
Mon–Thu: 0730–1430; Fri: 0730–1130, Sat: 0730–1200.

Government
Mon–Thu: 0730–1200 and 1500–1730, Fri: 0730–1100, Sat: 0730–1200.

Shops
Closed daily between 1200–1500.

Telecommunications

Mobile/cell phones
A GSM 900 service is in operation.

Internet/e-mail

Electricity supply
220V AC

Social customs/useful tips
Few people speak English, business is usually conducted in French or Arabic.

Getting there

Air
Regional flights from Africa are supplemented by scheduled flights from Paris, France and Dubai.
National airline: Air Comores International
International airport/s: Moroni International Prince Said Ibrahim (Code: HAH), 25km north of Moroni, on Ngazidja. Facilities include refreshments and a post office. There are no money changing

facilities. Taxis, with fixed prices are available.
Airport tax: None
Surface
Water: Cargo ships that carry passengers provide an irregular service from East Africa, Réunion, Madagascar and Mauritius.
Main port/s: Moroni (Grand Comore) and Fomboni (Anjouan): both have offshore anchorage for larger vessels.

Getting about
National transport
Air: Each island is served by Air Comores. There are regular flights between the islands.
Road: Surfaced roads on Grande Comore and Anjouan; other islands' roads can be difficult in rainy season. Mohéli has only very basic tracks.
Water: Small boats, which can be hired, ply between the islands.
City transport
Taxis: Service is provided by taxi-brousse (bush taxis) on each island. The journey from the International Airport to the city centre takes 30 minutes.
Car hire
International driving licence required.

BUSINESS DIRECTORY
The addresses listed below are a selection only. While World of Information makes every endeavour to check these addresses, we cannot guarantee that changes have not been made, especially to telephone numbers and area codes. We would welcome any corrections.

Telephone area codes
The international direct dialling code (IDD) for Comoros is +269, followed by the area code and subscriber's number:

Anjouan	71	Moroni	73
Mohali	72		

Useful telephone numbers
Emergency services: 744-890

Chambers of Commerce
Chambre de Commerce, d'Industries et d'Agriculture, PO Box 763, Moroni (tel: 730-958;fax: 731-983; e-mail: pride@snpt.km).

Banking
Banque de Development des Comores, Place de France, BP-298 Moroni (tel: 730-154, 730-818; fax: 730-397, e-mail: bdc@snpt.km).

Banque pour l'Industrie et le Commerce - Comores, BP 175, Place de France, Moroni (tel: 730-243, 730-225, 730-289; fax: 731-229).

Central bank
Banque Centrale des Comores, BP 405, Place de France, Moroni (tel: 73-1002/1814; fax: 73-0349).

Travel information
Comorian Association of Tourism (ACT) (tel: 732-847, 731-942; fax: 732-846).

Société Comorienne de Tourisme et d'Hotellerie (COMOTEL), Itsandra Hotel, Ngazidja (tel: 732-365).

International Prince Said Ibrahim Airport, BP 1003, Moroni (tel: 731-593, 732-452, 732-135; fax: 731-468).

Ministry of tourism
Ministry of Transport, Tourism, Post and Telecommunications, BP 97 Moroni (tel: 744-242; fax: 744-241).

Ministries
Ministry of Culture, Youth and Sports, Moroni (tel: 744-044).

Ministry of the Economy, Commerce, Handicrafts and Investment, BP 474 Moroni (tel: 744-232; fax: 730-144).

Ministry of Education, Professional Formation and Human Rights, BP 73 Moroni (tel: 744-185; 744-180).

Ministry of Equipment, Energy and Urbanism, Moroni (tel: 744-500).

Ministry of Finance, Budget and Privatisation, BP 324 Moroni (tel: 744-141; fax: 744-140).

Ministry of Foreign Affairs and Co-operation, BP 428 Moroni (tel: 744-100; fax: 744-111).

Ministry of Health, Population and Women's Affairs, Moroni (tel: 744-070).

Ministry of the Interior and Decentralisation, BP 686 Moroni (tel: 744-666; fax: 744-688).

Ministry of Justice and Islamic Affairs, Moroni (tel: 744-200).

Ministry of Production and the Environment, BP41 Moroni (tel: 744-630; fax: 744-632).

Ministry of Public Service, Employment and Labour, Moroni (tel: 744-540).

Other useful addresses
British Honorary Consulate, BP 986, Moroni (tel/fax: 733-182).

Comoros Embassy (France) 20 Rue Marbeau, 75016 Paris, France (tel: (+33) 1-4067-9054; fax: (+33) 1-4845-1365).

Comoros Mission to UN (US), 866 United Nations Plaza, Suite 418, New York, NY 10017 (tel: (+1-212) 750-1637; e-mail: comun@undp.org; internet: www.un.int/comoros).

Société Internationale des Comores, BP 175, Moroni (tel: 730-243).

Internet sites
Africa Business Network: http://www.ifc.org/abn

AllAfrica.com: http://allafrica.com

African Development Bank: http://www.afdb.org

Africa Online: http://www.africaonline.com

Mbendi AfroPaedia (information on companies, countries, industries and stock exchanges in Africa): http://mbendi.co.za

Congo

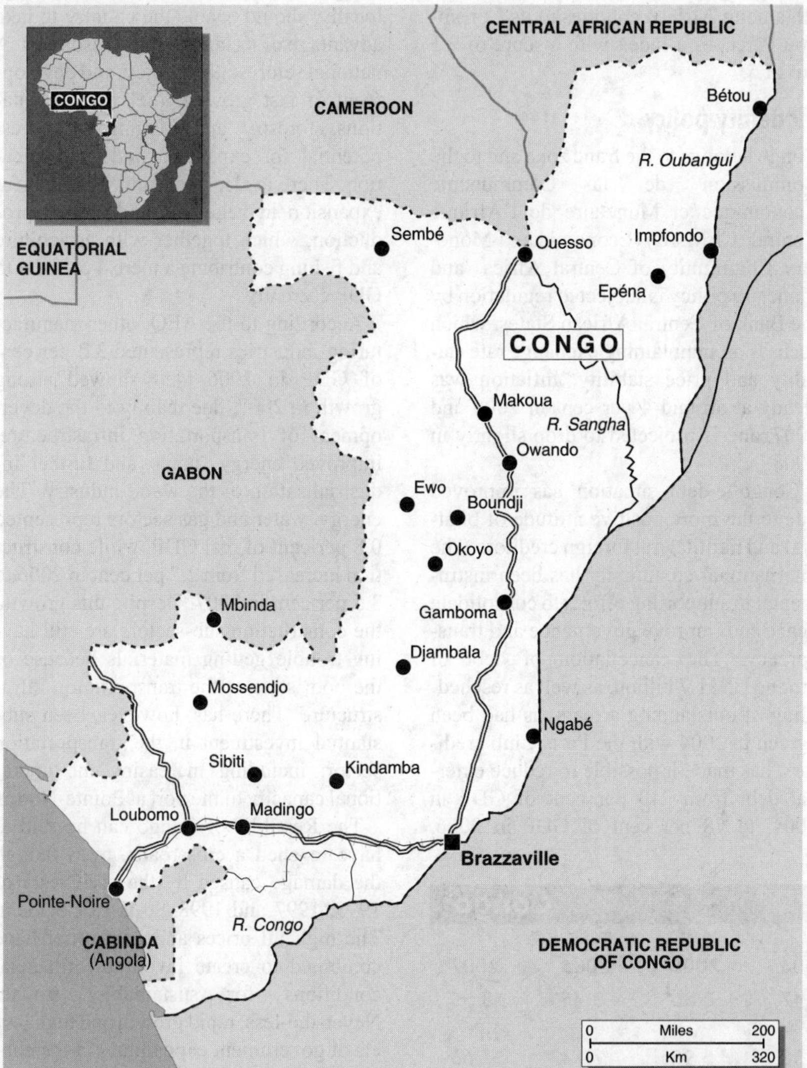

The Congo Republic (Congo-Brazzaville, to distinguish it from its larger neighbour to the south, the Democratic Republic of Congo) had Africa's seventh largest reserves of oil at the end of 2007. Yet the results of a survey conducted in 2005 showed over half of the population were considered to be in poverty and there was a lack of health care, sanitation services and a high prevalence of HIV/Aids. There was also a severe shortage of teachers, with class numbers as high as 100 pupils in state schools. With a population of just some 3.5 million, this suggests that the government has failed to distribute revenues in an equitable manner.

Oil dominates the economy of Congo-Brazzaville, accounting for 70.4 per cent of GDP in 2006. Production in 2007 was 222,000 barrels per day (bpd), down from 262,000bpd in 2006, after a fire at the Nkossa field interrupted pumping. Although a number of fields have reached maturity, and production has fallen as a result, the Moho-Bilondo

KEY FACTS

Official name: République du Congo (Republic of Congo)

Head of State: President Denis Sassou-Nguesso (PCT) (since 1997; re-elected Mar 2002)

Head of government: Prime Minister Isidore Mvouba (appointed Jan 2005)

Ruling party: Coalition of Parti Congolais du Travail (PCT) (Congolese Labour Party), and its allies (since 2002; re-elected Aug 2007)

Area: 342,000 square km

Population: 3.55 million (2007)*

Capital: Brazzaville (political); Pointe-Noire (economic)

Official language: French

Currency: CFA franc (CFAf) = 100 centimes (Communauté Financière Africaine (African Financial Community) franc)

Exchange rate: CFAf413.80 per US$ (Jul 2008); CFAf655.95 per euro (pegged from Jan 1999)

GDP per capita: US$2,158 (2007)*

GDP real growth: -1.60% (2007)*

Labour force: 1.56 million (2004)

Inflation: 2.60% (2007)

Oil production: 222,000 bpd (2007)

Balance of trade: US$4.85 billion (2006)

Foreign debt: US$5.83 billion (2004)

* estimated figure

off-shore field, with estimated reserves of 1 billion barrels, is expected to come on-stream in 2009.

Elections, but still no change

According to the *African Economic Outlook* (AEO), published by the African Development Bank Group and the Organisation for Economic Co-operation and Development, non-budgeted expenditures observed in 2007 were mostly associated with the June and August parliamentary elections. The expenditures included border security and additional costs of infrastructure and urban road works in regions where independence celebrations were to take place. These investments raised the most questions in terms of transparency and effectiveness of government spending.

The elections resulted in the ruling Parti Congolais du Travail (PCT) (Congolese Labour Party) and its allies winning 88 seats out of the 137 available (the PCT itself won 46 seats). The opposition Union Panafricaine pour la Démocratie Sociale (UPDS) (Pan-African Union for Social Development) won 11 seats, the Union pour la Démocratie et la République- Mwinda (UDR-Mwinda) (Union for Democracy and Republic-Mwinda) 1 seat and there were 37 independents. The elections were considered to be neither fair nor transparent. Although they had been expected to consolidate efforts to stabilise the political climate, turn out was low at only 40–50 per cent. The opposition parties had in large part boycotted the elections, accusing the government of serious failures.

In late-2007 a national anti-corruption committee was set up, including representatives of both government and civil society. An anti-corruption surveillance body is also to be established. Transparency International, the Berlin based global civil society organisation, ranks Congo as fortieth among African counties in its Corruption Perception Index with a score of 2.1 out of 5.

Monetary policy

Congo belongs to the franc zone and to the Commission de la Communaute Economique et Monetaire de l'Afrique Central (CEMAC) (Economic and Monetary Community of Central Africa) and monetary policy is subject to regulation by the Bank of Central African States, which focuses on maintaining exchange rate stability and price stability. Inflation was steady at around 4 per cent in 2006 and 2007, and is projected to drop slightly in 2008.

Congo's debt situation has improved due to the more positive attitude of bilateral and multilateral foreign creditors. The international community has been instrumental in supporting efforts to consolidate peace and improve governance and transparency. The cancellation of debt of around US$1.7 billion, as well as rescheduling of outstanding arrears, as had been agreed in 2004 with the Paris Club creditors, has made it possible to reduce external debt from 213 per cent of GDP in 2004, to 78 per cent of GDP in 2006. Outstanding payments due to private creditors have also dropped, from US$174.5 million at the end of 2005, to US$66.2 million by September 2007.

The International Monetary Fund (IMF) would like to see the economy diversify away from dependence on the oil sector. A forestry code passed in 2002, requiring companies to process 85 per cent of logs locally, should enable the country to take advantage of its large natural resources. A national reforestation policy, and development of fast growing fuel wood plantations, forestry and logging offer real potential for expansion and diversification. There is also enormous potential for expansion in vegetable and animal production, which together with agriculture and fishing contribute a mere 4 per cent to GDP currently.

According to the AEO, other manufacturing industries represented 3.2 per cent of GDP in 2006, and showed strong growth in 2007, due mainly to the development of transportation infrastructure, improved energy supply and further industrialisation of the wood industry. The energy, water and gas sectors represented 0.8 per cent of real GDP, while construction increased from 2.7 per cent in 2006 to 3.5 per cent in 2007. Despite this growth, the construction sub-sectors are still having trouble getting materials because of the poor state of the transportation infrastructure. There has, however, been substantial investment in the transportation sector, including increasing the operational capacity of the port at Pointe-Noire.

The Republic of Congo can be said to have reached a crossroads, even though the damage caused by the civil wars of 1993, 1997 and 1998–99 is still evident. The high oil prices and debt relief have combined to create favourable financial conditions for sustainable growth. Never-the-less, rapid growth and high levels of government expenditure in the context of low absorptive and administrative capacity risk compromising macroeconomic stability, the sustainability of public finances and foreign competitiveness.

KEY INDICATORS — Congo

	Unit	2003	2004	2005	2006	2007
Population	m	3.23	3.47	3.35	3.45	*3.55
Gross domestic product (GDP)	US$bn	2.91	4.38	5.98	7.74	*7.66
GDP per capita	US$	900	1,427	1,786	2,245	*2,158
GDP real growth	%	1.2	4.0	7.7	6.4	*-1.6
Inflation	%	2.0	2.0	2.5	4.7	*2.6
Oil output	'000 bpd	243.0	240.0	253.0	262.0	222.0
Exports (fob) (goods)	US$m	2,400.0	2,224.0	4,729.8	6,387.0	–
Imports (cif) (goods)	US$m	730.0	749.3	1,356.1	1,533.0	–
Balance of trade	US$m	1,670.0	1,474.7	3,373.7	4,854.0	–
Current account	US$m	–	330.0	653.0	125.0	-1,490.0
Total reserves minus gold	US$m	34.8	119.6	731.8	1,840.9	2,174.3
Foreign exchange	US$m	33.4	111.5	728.6	1,839.9	2,173.2
Exchange rate	per US$	574.89	528.29	507.22	496.60	454.40

* estimated figure

Risk assessment

Economy	Improving
Politics	Fair
Regional stability	Fair

COUNTRY PROFILE

Historical profile

From the fifteenth century, the Bakongo, Bateke and Sanga began settling what is now the Republic of Congo.

1482 Portuguese explorer Diogo Cao mapped the coastline.
1880s The colonisation of what is now Congo began in the late nineteenth century after the French explorer Pierre Savorgnan de Brazza signed a treaty with the Chief of the Batekes to establish a French protectorate over the north bank of the Congo river.
1910 Middle Congo, as the country was then known, became a colony of French Equatorial Africa.
1928 Africans revolted over forced labour which was used to build the Congo railway. More than 17,000 Africans died in the revolt.
1946 Congo was granted a territorial assembly by the French and representation in the French parliament.
1960 Congo became independent with a catholic priest, Abbé Fulbert Youlou, as president.
1963 Alfonse Massamba-Debat became president and Pascal Lissouba became prime minister. The country became a one-party socialist state.
1969 Captain Marien Ngouabi led a coup against Massamba-Debat and became president. The Parti Congolais du Travail (PCT) (Congolese Workers' Party) was declared the only legal political party.
1970 Ngouabi proclaimed Congo a Marxist state.
1977 Ngouabi was assassinated by forces loyal to Massamba-Debat, who in turn was executed for treason. Joachim Yhombi-Opango of the Comité Militaire du Parti (CMP) (Party of the Military Committee) became president.
1979 Colonel Denis Sassou-Nguesso took over the PCT, and remained in power under one-party PCT rule until 1992.
1990 The PCT abandoned Marxism.
1992 A new constitution was approved by referendum. Multi-party legislative elections were won by the Union Panafricaine pour la Démocratie Sociale (UPADS) (Pan-African Union for Social Development), led by Pascal Lissouba. Lissouba was elected president, defeating Sassou-Nguesso.
1993 Political unrest forced new elections, which were won by UPADS. Civil war broke out over disputes over the elections.
1994 A peace agreement saw members of the opposition join the government. The currency was devalued.
1997 Civil war broke out after the government attempted to disarm rebels militia loyal to Sassou-Nguesso. Thousands of people were killed and tens of thousands forced to flee their homes. After several months of fighting the Angolan Army invaded and sided with Sassou-Nguesso who succeeded in overthrowing the government of Pascal Lissouba. Sassou-Nguesso assumed the presidency at the head of the Conseil National de Transition (CNT) (National Transitional Council).
1999 The warring factions signed a peace accord with the government. However, armed conflict continued.
2001 A peace conference proposed a new constitution and 15,000 militia were demobilised through financial incentives. In December, Lissouba was convicted in absentia of treason and corruption and sentenced to 30 years' hard labour. Congo signed a treaty establishing the Gulf of Guinea Commisssion.
2002 The new constitution was endorsed by 80 per cent of the electorate, which strengthen the power of the president. Sassou-Nguesso was elected presiden with almost 90 per cent of the vote after his rivals were either banned from running or withdrew. The legislative election for the new bicameral parliament led to the creation of a pro-Sessou-Nguesso coalition consisting of the PCT, the Forces Démocratiques Unies (FDU) (United Democratic Forces) and a number of independents. Electoral disputes led to intense fighting, which reached Brazzaville, between government forces and the rebels in the south, loyal to former prime minister Bernard Kolelas. An agreement on power-sharing was reached between the government and two main rebel groups, but fighting continued in the east.
2003 All parties signed a peace agreement ending the civil war. A new constitution was adopted paving the way for elections.
2004 The Congo, which was held responsible for large-scale diamond smuggling from the Democratic Republic of Congo, was expelled from the Kimberley Process Certification Scheme, when it was unable to explain why its exports outstripped its production, which severely limited the Congo's exports of diamonds.
2005 The president appointed his close ally, Isidore Mvouba, as prime minister and caused a wave of criticism, as the constitution does not allow for presidential appointees. Floods and mudslides, caused by heavy rains in December, left thousands of people without shelter in the capital, Brazzaville. Bernard Kolelas was given an amnesty and allowed to return home after eight years in exile.
2006 Congo was chosen as the year's leader of the African Union, after Sudan withdrew its candidacy amid diplomatic concern about its human rights record. In November, after weeks of soaking rains at least 5,000 Brazzaville residents were homeless through landslides and flood damage or buildings that had been swept away.
2007 Former Ninja rebels, who had been led by Pastor (Frederic) Ntoumi, symbolically burned their weapons to demonstrate their commitment to peace. Around 40 political parties boycotted parliamentary elections held on 24 June and 5 August. The ruling PCT won 88 seats (out of 137). A group of private sector creditors (the London Club) cancelled 80 per cent of Congo's debt in November.
2008 In June, a satellite-monitoring project was announced that would map tree-felling in the Congo basin, the world's second-largest tropical forest (after the Amazon). The government programme to demobilise, disarm and re-integrate ex-combatants of Paster Ntoumi, was launched on 9 June.

Political structure

Constitution
A new constitution was endorsed by referendum in 2002 and as a result the power of the president was increased.

Form of state
Republic

The executive
Executive authority is vested in the directly elected president, who serves a seven-year term.

National legislature
Parliament consists of the Assemblée Nationale (national assembly) with 137 members and Sénat (senate) with 66 members, both elected by popular vote. Parliament does not have the power to impeach the president.

Legal system
Based on the French civil, and traditional customary law

Last elections
10 March 2002 (presidential); 24 June/5 August 2007 (parliamentary).

Results: Presidential: Denis Sassou-Nguesso was elected with 89.4 per cent of the vote, Joseph Kignoumbi Kia Mboungou 2.7 per cent.
Parliamentary: (national assembly, first and second round) the PCT and its allies won a total 88 seats (out of 137) the coalition includes Mouvement Congolais pour la Démocratie et la Développement Integral (MCDDI) (Congolese Movement for Democracy and Integral Development) 11. The Union Panafricaine pour la Démocratie Sociale (UPDS) (Pan-African Union for Social Development) 11 seats; Union pour la Démocratie et la République-Mwinda (UDR-Mwinda) (Union for Democracy and Republic-Mwinda) 1; Independents 37. Turnout was between 40–50 per cent.

Next elections
2009 (presidential).

Political parties
Ruling party
Coalition of Parti Congolais du Travail (PCT) (Congolese Labour Party), and its allies (since 2002; re-elected Aug 2007)
Main opposition party
The Union Panafricaine pour la Démocratie Sociale (UPDS) (Pan-African Union for Social Development)

Population
3.55 million (2007)*
Last census: June 1996: 2,600,000 (provisional)
Population density: 7.6 inhabitants per square km. Urban population: 73 per cent (1995–2001) – the highest urbanisation rate in Africa.
Annual growth rate: 3.2 per cent 1994–2004 (WHO 2006)
Internally Displaced Persons (IDP) 100,000 (UNHCR 2004)
Ethnic make-up
Kongo (48 per cent), Sangha (17 per cent), Teke (17 per cent).
Religions
Traditional beliefs (over 50 per cent), Christianity (about 40 per cent, mainly Roman Catholic, some Protestant).

Education
Primary education is followed by seven years of secondary school which is divided into a four-year first cycle (ages 12 to 16) and a three-year second cycle (ages 16 to 19). In the second cycle, students can opt between general or technical education.
Higher education is provided by the Université Marien-Ngouabi, which is largely state subsidised. It has a yearly enrolment of about 12,000 students.
Public expenditure on education typically amounts to 6 per cent of annual gross national income.
Literacy rate: 83 per cent adult rate; 98 per cent youth rate (15–24) (Unesco 2005).
Compulsory years: Six to 12
Enrolment rate: 120 per cent for boys, 109 per cent for girls, total primary school enrolment of the relevant age group (including repetition rates) (World Bank)
Pupils per teacher: 70 in primary schools.

Health
Per capita total expenditure on health (2003) was US$23; of which per capita government spending was US$15, at the international dollar rate, (WHO 2006).
In February 2004 a measles epidemics broke out in remote regions of northern Congo due to 'weak vaccination coverage' in earlier programmes and it was expected that, without a thorough immunisation campaign, measles would continue to return in two- to three-year cycles.
Pneumonic plague broke out in February 2005 in the north-east killing over 60 people and prompted control teams to be sent by international medical agencies to treat the victims. Many locals had fled the area and raised the fear of the infection spreading.
HIV/Aids
HIV prevalence: 4.9 per cent aged 15–49 in 2003 (World Bank)
Life expectancy: 54 years, 2004 (WHO 2006)
Fertility rate/Maternal mortality rate: 6.3 births per woman, 2004 (WHO 2006)
Child (under 5 years) mortality rate (per 1,000): 81 per 1,000 live births; 16 per cent of children aged under five were malnourished (World Bank).
Head of population per physician: 0.2 physicians per 1,000 people, 2004 (WHO 2006)

Welfare
The World Food Programme (WFP) in 2004 appealed for US$1.5 million, warning that without the necessary funding, food aid to vulnerable people would have to be reduced or entirely cut.
In moves to encourage full cessation following the peace agreement of 2003, international donors have contributed over US$900,000 to projects set up to reintegrate demobilised soldiers into society. These projects were a second phase, the first built on credit offered by the World Bank of US$5 million.

Main cities
Brazzaville (political capital, estimated population 1.1 million in 2005), Pointe-Noire (economic capital, 630,883), Loubomo (114,869), Jacob (56,175).

Languages spoken
French is used for all business documentation. Numerous African languages are also spoken, including Lingala and Kikongo.
Official language/s
French

Media
Despite the repeal of repressive press laws in 2000 the international human rights watchdog, Freedom House, described the Republic of Congo in 2006 as only partially free, as the government monopolised the broadcast media, which has a much larger share of the potential media audience.
National news agency: Les Dépêches de Brazzaville
Other news agencies: APA (African Press Agency): www.apanews.net
Congopage (in French): www.congopage.com
Mwinda Press (in French): www.mwinda.org
Panapress: www.panapress.com
Press
While there are many, small, independent newspapers published in Brazzaville few have a sustainable market outside the capital.
In French, the principal newspapers include the government-owned Les Dépêches de Brazzaville (www.brazzaville-adiac.com), the independent Le Choc (www.lechoc.info), and the Catholic publication Semaine Africaine (www.lasemaineafricaine.com).
Broadcasting
Radiodiffusion-Télévision Nationale Congolaise (RTN) is the state-run broadcaster.
Radio: RTN operates Radio Congo which broadcasts programmes in French, Lingala and Kikongo. The capital's own station, Radio Brazzaville, is also state-run and canal FM is a community station for the city. Radio Liberte is a private station. Foreign radio stations include Reveil FM, from Kinshasa (Democratic Republic Congo) and Radio France International (RFI) (www.rfi.fr) with news programmes in French.
Television: RTN operates the only locally broadcasting TV station, while satellite reception is available.
News agencies
National news agency: Les Dépêches de Brazzaville
Other news agencies: APA (African Press Agency): www.apanews.net
Congopage (in French): www.congopage.com
Mwinda Press (in French): www.mwinda.org
Panapress: www.panapress.com

Economy
The civil war in Congo left a legacy of widespread damage to essential infrastructure and living standards. The peace deal signed in 2001 gave the economy a much needed break from the devastation and encouraged international financial institutions, led by the IMF, to aid recovery through economic means.
Congo is attempting to strengthen its medium-term macroeconomic and financial framework in order to achieve steady growth and reduce its levels of poverty. The government's main fiscal policy is to increase revenue to pay for the post-war reconstruction and meet IMF targets. On-going plans aim to increase the amount of foreign investment. World Bank donors have pledged up to US$3.9 billion, with around three-quarters of this sum being invested in the transportation system. Improvements to the roads and mass transit could further encourage

foreign investment. The government will have to broaden the tax base and improve revenue collection.
The oil industry is the powerhouse of the economy, generating around 50 per cent of GDP. Congo has benefited from the rise in world oil prices in recent years. Oil revenue accounts for around 90 per cent of export earnings. Oil production, which had fallen sharply in 2003, began to recover in 2005 in response to the higher prices and is expected to continue to rise as new fields are developed.
The agricultural sector, including forestry, is the country's largest employer. Subsistence farming does not produce enough food to feed the population. About half the area of forest is exploitable for commercial logging, while only 5 per cent remains protected from development
Although Congo's economic performance has improved steadily since the end of the civil war, it has been unable to alleviate problems of poverty and underdevelopment. The IMF has advised that any windfalls from high oil prices should be spent on poverty-related problems (such as basic health and education) and domestic and international debt repayment.
GDP growth more than doubled in 2005 to 9.2 per cent and should continue to improve under President Sassou-Nguesso's Nouvelle Espérance (New Hope) economic programme, which is scheduled to run from 2003–10.

External trade

As a member of the Central African Economic and Monetary Community (Cemac) and the Economic Community of Central African States (ECCAS) the Republic of Congo operates within a common financial, regulatory, and legal structure, and maintains a common external tariff on imports from non-Cemac countries. While free movement of capital had been achieved, full implementation of free trade within the grouping in 2007 had not been achieved.
There is a regular large trade surplus from oil export earnings, but invisibles and debt payments keep the current account in deficit.

Imports

Principal imports manufacturing equipment, construction materials and foodstuffs.
Main sources: France (25.6 per cent total, 2005) , China (11.3 per cent), US (8.1 per cent), India (8.0 per cent), Italy (7.5 per cent), Belgium (5.1 per cent), The Netherlands (4.2 per cent)

Exports

Principal exports are petroleum, timber, plywood, sugar, cocoa, coffee and diamonds.
Main destinations: China (38.9 per cent total, 2005), US (29.0 per cent), Taiwan (11.8 per cent), South Korea (7.2 per cent)

Agriculture

The agricultural sector contributes around 25 per cent of GDP and employs a third of the workforce. Agriculture has been overshadowed by development of the petroleum industry.
Approximately a third of the total land area is given over to agriculture, of that almost all is pasture land. Only an estimated 2 per cent of the total land area is under cultivation (mainly in the alluvial Niari Valley). Farming is small-scale with output concentrated on subsistence crops such as plantains, cassava, yams, groundnuts, manioc, potatoes, wheat, maize, beans and paddy rice. Despite some growth in food production, Congo relies heavily on food imports.
The main cash crops are coffee, cocoa, tobacco and sugar. Attempts to expand production of other cash crops include the rehabilitation of oil palm estates and a major new cocoa project.
Estimated crop production in 2005 included 880,800 tonnes (t) cassava, 7,200t maize, 4,800t potatoes, 6,000t sweet potatoes, 12,000t yams, 90,000t oil palm fruit, 1,500t rice, 88,000t bananas, 73,000t plantains, 9,300t pulses, 940,800t roots and tubers, 90,000t oil palm fruit, 6,200t avocados, 10,700t citrus fruit, 25,000t mangoes, 3,200t tomatoes, 3,300t pineapples, 26,919t oilcrops, 100t tobacco, 1,260t cocoa beans, 1,700t green coffee, 4,000t coconuts, 460,000t sugar cane, 1,350t natural rubber, 229,200t fruit in total, 41,555t vegetables in total. Livestock production included: 30,423t meat in total, 20,000t game meat, 2,028t beef, 2,072t pig meat, 340t lamb, 783t goat meat, 5,200t poultry, 1,185t eggs, 1,100t milk.

Fishing

Fishing is underdeveloped but is practised commercially on a small scale.

Forestry

The main agricultural export is timber, mostly Okoumé logs (of which Congo is a major world supplier). About half the total timber output is used for wood processing. Approximately 60 per cent of the country is covered by woodlands and forests, much of it unsuitable for commercial exploitation. There are large eucalyptus (fast growing) plantations near Pointe-Noire.

Industry and manufacturing

The industrial sector contributes over 10 per cent to GDP and employs a fifth of the workforce. The manufacturing sector is largely underdeveloped, contributing less than 5 per cent to GDP. Construction contributes a further 5 per cent, although this figure could grow rapidly, particularly in the repair of the damaged infrastructure, if political stability remains calm and reconstruction efforts are sustained.
Most manufacturing enterprises operate in the Brazzaville and Pointe-Noire districts and in the Niari Valley. Activity is centred on agri-food and timber processing, textiles and oil refining.
There are also a few small-scale import substitution industries (footwear, soft drinks, metal working, chemicals) and a cement plant.
Structure and ownership of parastatals is being reformed and the privatisation programme is expected to be renewed after years of delay. Emphasis is on joint-venture enterprises, particularly in pulp/paper and light manufacturing.

Tourism

The tourist industry had great potential for eco-tourism, but until peace can by assured foreign governments continue to advise strongly that their citizens do not visit Congo unless absolutely necessary.

Mining

Congo has significant deposits of magnesium, gold, diamonds, cement, potash and salt. Commercial exploitation of these deposits was either damaged by the civil war or have yet to be developed.
In 2004, Congo was expelled from the Kimberley Process, set up to curb the trade in 'conflict diamonds', when the Congo could not account for the discrepancy between reported production and its exports of rough diamonds. As these diamonds are mined mostly by artisans the government claimed it was unable to confirm production, or curb smuggling along its uncontrolled borders. The ban on Congo diamonds effectively suspended legal exports of diamonds.
Gold production from the Yangadou Mine experienced technical problems and production has only amounted to 4kg per month since it opened in 2003, instead of the 1,500kg as expected.
A major magnesium processing plant at Kouilou could have a significant role in the economy when it is up and running. The plan, by Canada's MagIndustries Corporation (MagMetals), is to construct a 72,000 tonnes per annum (tpa) smelter of the local magnesium salt deposits and produce 60,000tpa of magnesium alloy. However, by the beginning of 2005 the project was still awaiting financial backing.
As a by-product of the magnesium mining MagMetals also proposes to exploit the potash and salt deposits found in the locale, with a 300,000tpa potash fertiliser plant and 400,000tpa salt plant.

Hydrocarbons
Congo is sub-Saharan Africa's fifth largest oil producer with proven reserves of 1.5 billion barrels. Oil production had exceeded the 2005 production of 93 million barrels by 8.5 per cent by August 2006. New fields – Libondo, Tchibeli, Litanzi and Yanga-Sud – have boosted output since 2004. Western Europe and North America are Congo's predominant markets although there is hope of future expansion into Asian Markets.
France's TotalFina has the dominant role in oil production in the Congo, although it has lost its monopoly status as other foreign companies, especially Italy's Agip have begun investing in the country's petroleum industry.
The Congo has, as yet, no refining capacity and limited port facilities, which will hamper future growth in the short- to medium-term.
In 2004, natural gas reserves stood at around 90.4 billion cubic metres, most of which is oil-associated. A lack of infrastructure and investment means that most gas is vented or flared. The new 25MW gas plant in Djeno utilises gas for electricity production for supply to the Pointe Noire area.
Congo does not produce or import coal.

Energy
Installed generating capacity is 89MW, although generating potential is estimated at 3,000MW. Most electricity is produced by the 74MW Bouenza and the 15MW Djoué hydroelectric plants. Around a quarter of the country's electricity requirements are imported from the Democratic Republic of Congo (DRC). The development of the postponed US$925 million Sounda Gorge hydroelectric project could increase capacity by 1,000MW and turn the country into a net electricity exporter. Consumption is low as most rural inhabitants rely on wood fuel as a primary source of power.
The power infrastructure is in need of repairs and upgrading. The Congo and two Chinese companies signed a US$220 million contract to build a 120MW hydroelectric power plant on the Congo River and when completed in 2006, it is expected to double Congo's power generating capacity.
Construction of a 300 megawatts gas-fired power plant began in May 2008, at the coastal site of Mateve, 15km south of Pointe-Noire.

Banking and insurance
In 2004 the banking system was considered fragile by the IMF, with credit growth limited by the lack of viable projects and a reluctance by banks to make loans as loan recovery is problematic. Of the four domestic banks two have been classified as in good condition and two in either a fragile or critical condition and in need of restructuring.
Central bank
Banque des Etats de l'Afrique Centrale
Main financial centre
Brazzaville

Time
GMT plus one hour

Geography
The Republic of Congo is an equatorial country on the west coast of Africa. A flat, treeless plane stretches down from the highlands to the coast. The coastline stretches about 170km along the Atlantic Ocean. The rain-forested highlands extends northward to Cameroon and the Central African Republic. Congo is bordered by Gabon in the west, and with the Democratic Republic of Congo to the east. In the south there is a short frontier with the Cabinda enclave of Angola.
Hemisphere
Straddles the equator.

Climate
Equatorial or sub-equatorial. Main dry season from June–September with average temperatures ranging from 15 degrees Celsius (C) at night to 32 degrees C during the day. Rainy season from October–May with higher average temperatures and high humidity. Generally hotter and more humid in Congo Basin, drier and cooler in highlands.

Entry requirements
Passports
Required by all, valid for at least six months.
Visa
Required by all. Tourists must provide evidence of accommodation arrangements in Congo and of sufficient funds. If on business, a letter, issued by the traveller's company, giving a detailed summary of intended purpose of trip, a full itinerary including intended contacts with host company, and the acceptance of full responsibility for any expenses incurred during the term of stay, and repatriation expenses in case of emergency, must be submitted with the application to the local embassy.
Currency advice/regulations
There is no limit to the amount of foreign currency which can be imported, but amounts above US$335 must be declared; export of foreign currency is limited to the amount declared on arrival. The import and export of local currency is prohibited, except between countries in the CFAf zone.

Health (for visitors)
Medical and dental facilities are inadequate.
Mandatory precautions
A yellow fever vaccination certificate is required by all.
Advisable precautions
Typhoid, hepatitis A and B, polio and tetanus vaccinations are recommended. Malaria prophylaxis should be taken, as a risk exists throughout the country. Water precautions should be taken. Visitors should avoid uncooked fruit and vegetables. There is an Aids risk and a risk of rabies.

Hotels
Good hotels are available in Brazzaville, Pointe-Noire and Loubomo; there are few elsewhere. It is advisable to book well in advance. A 10 per cent tip is usual.

Credit cards
Two hotels in Brazzaville and several in Pointe Noire accept major credit cards.

Public holidays (national)
Fixed dates
1 Jan (New Year's Day), 5 Feb (President's Day), 8 Mar (Women's Day), 18 Mar (Marien Ngouabi Day), 1 May (Labour Day), 22 Jun (Army Day), 31 Jul (Revolution Day), 13–15 Aug (Independence celebrations), 25 Dec (Christmas Day), 31 Dec (Republic Day).
Variable dates
Easter Monday; Ascension Day.

Working hours
Banking
Mon–Fri: 0630–1300. Counters close at 1130.
Business
Mon–Fri: 0800–1200 and 1430–1730, Sat: 0800–1200.
Government
Mon–Fri: 0700–1400, Sat: 0700–1200.
Shops
Mon–Fri: 0800–1200 and 1530–1800. Sat: 0800–1200 and 1530–1800/1900. Some shops close on Mon afternoons; a few open Sun mornings.

Telecommunications
Telephone/fax
Telephone services are inadequate. Major hotel may provide fax and Internet services.
Mobile/cell phones
There there are two GSM 900 networks operating: CelTel Congo, and Libertis Telecom; however, coverage is generally restricted to Brazzaville and Pointe Noire.

Electricity supply
220V AC 50 cycles; the voltage varies erratically.

Weights and measures
The metric system is used.

Getting there
Air
National airline: Lina Congo

International airport/s: Brazzaville-Maya Maya Airport (BZV), 4km from city; restaurant.
Other airport/s: Pointe-Noire Airport (PNR), 6km from city.
Airport tax: CFAf500.
Surface
Road: There is a road from Lambaréné, in Gabon, to Loubomo and Brazzaville; this is not surfaced all the way. Entry from Cameroon is only practicable in the dry season. There is a surfaced road from the Cabinda enclave of Angola.
Water: A ferry service across the River Congo is operational daily from 0800–1200 and 1400–1700 between Kinshasa (Democratic Republic of Congo) and Brazzaville. Cars can be carried. The ferry takes about half an hour. There is also a vedette service for passengers only, which takes 15 minutes. Both services are liable to short-notice cancellation or delay.
Main port/s: Pointe-Noire. Brazzaville is the inland river port.

Getting about
National transport
Air: Internal air service operated by Lina Congo from Brazzaville to Pointe-Noire and the main provincial towns.
Road: There are 1200km of tarred roads; other routes are mainly tracks which can be impassable in wet weather.
There are very few metalled roads outside Brazzaville and Pointe-Noire, while the roads within the towns are generally poor. The main route from Pointe-Noire, through Brazzaville to Ouesso, is not uniform in quality; the section from Loubomo to Pointe-Noire is liable to become impassable in the rainy season.
Rail: The Congo-Océan railway runs from Pointe-Noire to Brazzaville, a distance of around 500km. The service has been improved, but the journey is slow. The only other line is the 280km Comilog railway from Mbinda on the Congo/Gabon border which links to the Congo-Océan railway and is used mainly for the carriage of manganese ore produced by Comilog. The railways suffer from lack of maintenance and general upkeep.
Water: The ferries on the rivers Congo and Oubangui are a principal form of transport.
City transport
Taxis: Freely available in Brazzaville and Pointe-Noire; tipping is not usual. Can be hired by the hour or day. Fares should be negotiated in advance of journey.
Car hire
Available from main hotels in Brazzaville and Pointe-Noire. International or national driving licence accepted. Traffic drives on the right.

BUSINESS DIRECTORY

The addresses listed below are a selection only. While World of Information makes every endeavour to check these addresses, we cannot guarantee that changes have not been made, especially to telephone numbers and area codes. We would welcome any corrections.

Telephone area codes
The international direct dialling code (IDD) for Congo is + 242, followed by subscriber's number.

Useful telephone numbers
Fire: 18.
Police: 17.
Ambulance: 822-365/368.

Chambers of Commerce
Congo National Chamber of Commerce, Industry and Agriculture, PO Box 1119, Brazzaville (tel: 832-956).

Brazzaville Chamber of Commerce, Industry, Agriculture and Crafts, Avenue Amilcar Cabral, PO Box 92, Brazzaville (tel/fax: 811-608; e-mail: cciam_brazza@hotmail.com).

Dolisie Regional Chamber of Commerce, Industry and Agriculture, PO Box 78, Dolisie (Tel: 910-017).

La Sangha Regional Chamber of Commerce, Industrie and Agriculture, PO Box 122, Ouessa (tel: 983-200).

Pointe-Noire Chamber of Commerce, Agriculture, Industry and Crafts, PO Box 665, Pointe-Noire (tel: 941-280; fax: 943-467; e-mail: cciampnr@cg.celtelplus.com).

Banking
Banque de Développement des Etats de l'Afrique Centrale, PO Box 1177, Brazzaville (tel: 811-885, 811-761; fax: 811-880).

Banque des États de l'Afrique Centrale, PO Box 126, Brazzaville (tel: 832-814/5, 833-626, 833-362; fax: 836-342).

Banque Internationale du Congo, PO Box 33, Avenue Amilcar Cabral, Brazzaville (tel: 830-308, 831-411; fax: 815-092, 835-382).

Crédit pour l'Agriculture, l'Industrie et le Commerce (CAIC), PO Box 2889, Brazzaville (tel: 810-978, 814-050; fax: 810-977, 835-352).

Mutuelle Congolaise d'Epargne et de Crédit, PO Box 13237, Brazzaville (tel: 837-001; fax: 837-930).

Union Congolaise de Banques; PO Box 147, Avenue Amilcar Cabral, Brazzaville (tel: 833-000; fax: 836-845).

Central bank
Banque des États de l'Afrique Centrale, Direction Nationale, PO Box 126, Brazzaville (tel: 813-684; fax: 811-094; e-mail: beacbzv@beac.int).

Travel information
Direction Générale du Tourisme et de Hotellerie, BP 2480, Brazzaville (tel: 814-030; fax: 815-549; e-mail:mcatcongo@yahoo.fr).

Ministries
Ministry of Construction and Urban Development, BP 1218, Brazzaville.

Ministry of Decentralisation and Regional Development, BP 630, Brazzaville.

Ministry of Defence, BP 1219, Brazzaville.

Ministry of the Economy, BP 2120, Brazzaville.

Ministry of Finance and the Budget, BP 64, Brazzaville (tel: 411-266; fax: 814-145).

Ministry of Foreign Affairs, BP 2070, Brazzaville.

Ministry of Industry, Fisheries and Crafts, Palais du Peuple, Brazzaville (tel: 835-130).

Ministry of the Interior and of Security, BP 64, Brazzaville.

Ministry of Trade and Small- and Medium-sized Enterprises, Brazzaville (tel: 831-827).

Ministry of Transport and Civil Aviation, BP 2146, Brazzaville.

Other useful addresses
Agence Congolaise d'Information (ACI), BP 2144, Brazzaville

Bureau pour le Développement de la Production Agricole, BP 2222, Brazzaville.

Direction de la Statistique, BP 2031, Brazzaville (tel: 834-324).

Institut de Développement Economique de la République Populaire du Congo, c/o The Presidency, Brazzaville.

Office du Café et du Cacao (OCC), BP 2488, Brazzaville (tel: 831-902).

Office Congolais des Bois (OCB), BP 1229, Pointe-Noire (tel: 948-248).

Office Congolais de l'Entretien Routier (OCER), BP 2073, Brazzaville.

Office National du Commerce (ONC), BP 2305, Brazzaville (tel: 834-399).

Republic of Congo Embassy (USA), 4891 Colorado Avenue, NW, Washington DC 20011 (tel: 726-5500; fax: 726-1860; e-mail: info@embassyofcongo.org).

Société Nationale de Recherche et d'Exploitation Pétrolières (Hydro Congo), BP 2008, Brazzaville (tel: 833-560).

Syndicat des Commerçants, Importateurs et Exportateurs de l'Afrique Equatoriale (Sycomimpex), BP 84, Brazzaville.

National news agency: Les Dépêches de Brazzaville
Les Manguiers, 76 Ave Paul Doumer, Brazzaville (tel: 532-0109; fax: 532-0110; email: belie@congonet.cg; internet: www.brazzaville-adiac.com).

Internet sites
Africa Business Network: www.ifc.org/abn

AllAfrica.com: http://allafrica.com

African Development Bank: www.afdb.org

Africa Online: www.africaonline.com

Congo-Brazzaville (French only, Actualité dossier): www.solcongolais.net/

Mbendi AfroPaedia (information on companies, countries, industries and stock exchanges in Africa): http://mbendi.co.za

Democratic Republic of Congo

The Democratic Republic of Congo (DRC, or Congo-Kinshasa to distinguish it from its northern neighbour) boasts some of the richest natural resources in the continent, yet its people are among the poorest and suffer from some of the worst and continuous acts of violence. The history of the DRC has been one of civil war and corruption. After independence in 1960, the country immediately faced an army mutiny and an attempt at secession by its mineral-rich province of Katanga. A year later, its prime minister, Patrice Lumumba, was seized and killed by troops loyal to army chief Joseph Mobutu. In 1965 Mobutu seized power, later renaming the country Zaïre and himself Mobutu Sese Seko. He turned Zaïre into a springboard for operations against Soviet-backed Angola and thereby ensured US backing. But he also made Zaïre synonymous with corruption. However, when the Cold War ended, so did US interest in Zaïre. In 1997 anti-Mobutu rebels quickly captured the capital, Kinshasa, installed Laurent Kabila as president and renamed the country. A rift between Kabila and his former allies backed by Rwanda and Uganda sparked a new rebellion. Angola, Namibia and Zimbabwe took Kabila's side and the country became a vast battleground. The United Nations sent in peacekeepers in 1999, but to little effect. Rebel fighters criss-cross borders between Uganda, Burundi and Rwanda at will, terrorising villages on both sides. Militias, rebel and other armed groups remain active in the illegal exploitation of minerals, especially in the east. The Kinshasa government has no control over large parts of the country and tension remains high in the east. The Crisis Group, a Brussels-based think-tank, said in 2005 that 1,000 people were dying every day from war-related causes, including disease, hunger and violence.

KEY FACTS

Official name: République Démocratique du Congo (Democratic Republic of Congo) (DRC)

Head of State: President Joseph Kabila (elected 29 Oct 2006)

Head of government: Prime Minister Antoine Gizenga (Parti Lumumbiste Unifié (Palu) (Unified Lumumbist Party)), (appointed by the president 30 Dec 2006)

Ruling party: Parti du Peuple pour la Reconstruction et la Démocratie (PPRD) (People's Party of Reconstruction and Democracy) (elected 30 Jul 2006)

Area: 2,345,409 square km

Population: 61.05 million (2007)*

Capital: Kinshasa

Official language: French

Currency: Congolese franc (Cf)

Exchange rate: Cf551.50 per US$ (Jul 2008)

GDP per capita: US$166 (2007)*

GDP real growth: 6.30% (2007)*

Labour force: 22.08 million (2004)

Inflation: 16.70% (2007)

Balance of trade: -US$423.00 million (2005)

Foreign debt: US$11.84 billion (2004)

* estimated figure

No riches for the people

Since 2001, the DRC has experienced a significant turnaround under difficult circumstances, but the figures do not tell the full story. In some instances, overall economic objectives have been met, but the composition of expenditure did not improve as envisaged. Low levels of spending on public investment and social sectors are offset by overspending by security and political institutions. In 2006, according to the World Bank, the DRC's economic performance continued to improve, although levels of poverty remained unacceptable. Gross domestic product (GDP) growth remained strong at 6.5 per cent, the same figure as 2005. There was a large fiscal overrun (2 per cent of GDP) in 2005, in particular on wages, military, the presidency, vice presidencies and parliament, which was only partially offset by the higher than expected revenues, helped by high petroleum prices. Despite this, the 12-month inflation fell from 21 per cent in December 2005 to an almost manageable 10.0 per cent in 2006, in part due to the 15 per cent appreciation of the Congo franc over that period (a reflection of an increased use of foreign revenues financing government spending, while controlling base money expansion). The International Monetary Fund's (IMF) Poverty Reduction and Growth Facility (PRGF) was allowed to expire at the end of March 2006; the IMF anticipated negotiating a new PRGF with the new government to be appointed following the 2006 elections.

According to the World Bank, external debt represented a heavy burden for DRC recovery prospects: the DRC is one of the world's most debt-laden countries, with an estimated total stock of external debt of US$12 billion (about 225 per cent of GDP and 1,280 per cent of exports). DRC was granted access to the Highly Indebted Poor Countries (HIPC) initiative in July 2003. In 2006 the DRC's annual GDP per capita figure was US$134, one of the lowest in the world.

The long-term challenge for the DRC is to create an environment that is conducive to private sector-led growth and capitalises on the country's large resource endowment and potential. The macroeconomic framework for 2005–08 envisages average real growth of 7 per cent, implying an average increase in per capita gross domestic product of 4 per cent, a decline in inflation to 5 per cent (better than most economies in Africa), and a gradual build-up in gross international reserves to about nine weeks of non-aid-related imports.

Much needs to be done to strengthen budget execution, contain current expenditure, observe spending priorities, and improve capacity to implement poverty-reducing projects and fight corruption. There were, of course, no attempts to digest bitter pills of enhanced tax collection before the mid-2006 elections. However, progress in key areas is essential to attract private investment and maintain the momentum for growth. Particular effort should be made to address delays in reforming the mining sector and public enterprises and to ensure that the pace of reforms in the social sectors is sustained.

Corruption remains a major obstacle to any economic improvements, but the most important risks to progress are insecurity and social tensions. Although legislation has been adopted to intensify the fight against corruption, renewed impetus is needed to rebuild institutions, strengthen budget procedures and reporting, improve transparency in tax administration, and pursue the auditing and restructuring of public enterprises. There needs to be co-ordinated efforts to simultaneously tackle political, economic and security challenges. The more active involvement of UN peacekeepers in the east has succeeded in containing the activities of militias although widespread human rights violations continue.

KEY INDICATORS — Democratic Republic of Congo

	Unit	2003	2004	2005	2006	2007
Population	m	56.39	58.78	57.55	*59.27	*61.05
Gross domestic product (GDP)	US$bn	5.70	6.57	7.10	8.54	*10.14
GDP per capita	US$	90	112	123	146	*166
GDP real growth	%	5.0	6.8	6.5	5.6	*6.3
Inflation	%	12.8	3.9	21.4	13.2	*16.7
Industrial output	% change	–	13.3	10.5	9.8	–
Agricultural output	% change	–	0.6	3.1	2.5	–
Exports (fob) (goods)	US$m	1,128.0	1,813.0	2,042.0	2,044.0	–
Imports (cif) (goods)	US$m	1,351.0	2,056.0	2,465.0	2,607.0	–
Balance of trade	US$m	-223.0	-243.0	-710.0	-563.0	–
Current account	US$m	-80.0	-160.0	-451.0	-212.0	*-402.0
Total reserves minus gold	US$m	97.8	236.2	131.2	154.5	182.9
Foreign exchange	US$m	89.8	230.7	129.8	154.2	179.6
Exchange rate	per US$	369.00	409.25	530.00	530.00	556.50

* estimated figure

China to the rescue?

In May 2008 China and the DRC announced a US$9.25 billion agreement involving copper and cobalt for a resource-needy Chinese industry. In return China will assist with the construction of some 3,000 kilometres each of rail and road, as well as hydroelectric dams, schools and hospitals. The agreement has been eyed with some concern by international lenders who have been in negotiations to write-off some US$8 billion in debt. The Chinese won't find this an easy agreement to fulfil – Congo-Kinshasa has an unenviable reputation for being ungovernable and with high levels of corruption and violence.

In its 2008 edition of *African Economic Outlook* (AEO) the African Development Bank noted that the economy had grown by 6.2 per cent, under the target of 6.5 per cent, but up on 2006 (5.1 per cent). Raised expectations in 2007 had not necessarily been satisfied. Institutions had been established, but conflicts persisted in the east of the country and although the new government installed in February had pledged rigorous management of public finances, macroeconomic stability did not materialise. Continuing reforms have not made sufficient progress to address the problems weighing on the Congolese economy.

Outlook

Growth prospects still fall short of the country's potential, reported the AEO, largely because of problems related to the institutional framework and business environment. The 2007 *Doing Business* report ranked the DRC as the world's most difficult place to do business, while

Berlin-based Transparency International ranked DRC as 168th out of 180 countries, based on the level of corruption in the world of business. To expand the business sector, it will be necessary to further clean up business practices, fight corruption and instill good corporate governance, as well as restrain the numerous rebel factions still as war with the central government.

Risk assessment

Economic	Poor
Political	Poor
Regional stability	Poor

COUNTRY PROFILE

Historical profile

During the sixteenth and seventeenth centuries, the British, Dutch, Portuguese and French bought slaves from the Kongo empire and began a slow drain of manpower in the region.

1870 King Leopold II of Belgium set up a private venture to exploit the riches of the Kongo empire.

1879–87 British explorer, Henry Stanley was commissioned to established Belgian authority over the Congo basin.

1884–85 European governments recognised Leopold's claim to the Congo basin.

1885 Leopold established the Congo Free State, which he headed.

1891–92 Belgium conquered Katanga.

1892–94 Belgium conquered eastern Congo, which was controlled by Arab and east African merchants.

1908 The Belgian state annexed Congo following atrocities carried out by Leopold's officials.

1959 A nationalist uprising based in Leopoldville (now Kinshasa) began the disintegration of Belgian colonial authority.

1960 Congo gained independence. Joseph Kasavuba became president. The Belgian community fled and too few professionals were left to run the government. Chaos ensued as the diamond and copper mining province of Katanga attempted to secede under the leadership of Joseph Tshombe.

1961 Prime Minister Patrice Lumumba was deposed and murdered, allegedly by Katangan separatists. Marshal Joseph Mobutu was appointed prime minister. UN soldiers began disarming the Katangese soldiers on behalf of the Kasavuba government.

1963 Tshombe agreed to end the Katangan separatist war.

1964 President Kasavuba dismissed Mobutu and appointed Tshombe as prime minister.

1965 Mobutu seized power after a coup.

1971 Congo was renamed Zaïre. Mobutu renamed himself Mobutu Sese Seko.

1973–74 Mobutu nationalised foreign firms and forced foreign investors out of the country.

1977 French, Belgian and Moroccan troops fought an attack on Katanga by Angolan-based rebels.

1989 Zaïre defaulted on its debt servicing to Belgium; the economy began to deteriorate as development programmes were suspended.

1990 Mobutu appointed a transitional government and lifted the ban on mulit-party politics.

1991 A series of short-lived coalition governments were presided over by President Mobutu, who retained control of security and key ministries.

1993 Rival pro- and anti-Mobutu governments were formed

1996 Tutsi rebels, of eastern Zaire, captured much of the eastern border area

1997 Mobutu fled to Togo when the Alliance des Forces Démocratiques pour la Libération (AFDL) (Alliance of Democratic Forces for Liberation), led by Laurent-Désiré Kabila, seized Kinshasa, after a seven-month campaign. Kabila was backed by Tutsi rebels and the Rwandan government. Zaïre was renamed the Democratic Republic of Congo (DRC). Kabila became president. All government institutions were dissolved and a new constitution drafted. Mobutu Sese Seko died in Morocco.

1998 The Rassemblement Congolais pour la Démocratie-Goma (RCD-Goma) (Congolese Democratic Coalition) was formed, supported by Rwanda, Burundi and Uganda, and aimed at overthrowing Kabila, who was backed by Zimbabwe, Namibia and Angola. A full-scale civil war broke out. Peace talks began in Zambia but were ultimately unsuccessful.

1999 A split developed between the Mouvement pour la Libération Congolaise (MLC) (Movement for Congolese Liberation) backed by Uganda and the RCD-Goma supported by Rwanda. The six countries involved in the war signed a cease-fire, and the RCD-Goma and MLC signed later.

2000 A 5,500-strong UN force to monitor the supposed cease-fire: fighting continued between government and rebel forces and Rwandan and Ugandan forces.

2001 President Kabila was assassinated. His son, Major General Joseph Kabila became president. The currency was floated on 28 May. A peace agreement between DCR, Uganda and Rwanda allowed foreign troops to withdraw. An estimated 2.5 million people had died in the conflict and the UN declared the warring parties continued the fighting to mask plundering DCR's rich mineral assets.

2002 Goma was devastated by the eruption of Mount Nyiragongo. Rwanda and the DRC signed a peace deal whereby Rwanda withdrew troops and DRC disarmed and arrested Rwandan Hutu militia held responsible for the genocide in Rwanda in 1994. The DRC government signed a peace deal with the two main rebel groups. UN sponsored power-sharing talks were undertaken in South Africa.

2003 A transitional constitution sanctioned an interim government pending democratic elections to be held within two years. Leaders of the principal former rebel groups were sworn in as vice presidents.

2004 The massacre of 160 mostly Tutsi DRC refugees in Burundi prompted renewed warnings of war, and the Tutsi-led RCD-Goma, the former main rebel group during the DRC's civil war, suspended its participation in the power-sharing government.

2005 Nine UN peacekeepers were killed in the north-east; UN troops retaliated, killing over 50 militia members. The national assembly adopted a draft constitution, which had been agreed by former rebel groups. A referendum on the new constitution, the result of which was a resounding approval for the changes with 84.31 per cent voting 'yes'. The result paved the way for presidential and parliamentary elections.

2006 Etienne Tshisekedi, leader of the opposition Union pour la Démocratie et le Progrès Social (UDPS) (Union for Democracy and Social Progress) withdrew his call for a boycott of the general elections. In the first free democratic elections since the 1960s began, over 9,700 candidates contested 500 seats in the national assembly. In the first round presidential election, incumbent Joseph Kabila won 44.81 per cent of the vote and Vice President Jean-Pierre Bemba won 20.03 per cent, followed by Antoine Gizenga with 13.06 per cent. Turnout was over 70 per cent. The constitution required at least a 51 per cent majority or a run-off vote in which Kabila won 58.05 per cent of the vote and Bemba 41.95 per cent. Following an accusation of election irregularities by Bemba, the Supreme Court confirmed Kabila's victory and dismissed the complaint. Bemba did not attend the president's inauguration ceremony. Antoine Gizenga – Parti Lumumbiste Unifié (Palu) (United Lumumbist Party) – was appointed prime minister.

2007 Senate elections held on 19 January were won by Kabila's Alliance pour la Majorité Présidentielle (AMP) (Alliance for a presidential majority) with 58 seats (out of 108). The Union pour la Nation (UN) (Union of the Nation) coalition won 21 (including a seat for Jean Pierre Bemba, its leader). In April the Communaute Economique des Pays des Grands Lacs (CEPGL) (Great Lakes Countries Economic Community) was re-launched by Burundi, Democratic Republic of Congo and Rwanda. CEPGL is intended to promote regional economic co-operation and integration. General Laurent Nkunda, leader of rebel forces in the eastern provinces of North and South Kivu, declared in October that the ceasefire with government forces was at an end. Fighting displaced over 300,000 people from the area to UNHCR camps near the city of Goma, while many more fled into rebel held territory and out of reach of international aid. Renegade leader Kasereka Kabamba was forced to surrender by government forces in North Kivu province on 26 October.

2008 Jean-Pierre Bemba was arrested (in Belgium) and will face the International Criminal Court (ICC) on charges that his troops allegedly committed atrocities in the Central African Republic in 2002. Bemba has been in exile since he was accused of high treason for refusing to disarm his militia, following his defeat in 2006 presidential elections.

Political structure

Constitution

A draft of a new constitution was approved by the national assembly in May 2005, and by a majority (84.31 per cent) of the people in a referendum held in December. It was officially adopted on 18 February 2006. The new constitution increases the number of provinces from 10 to 26, allows greater autonomy for some of the mineral-rich regions and lowers the minimum age for presidents from 35 to 33, thereby allowing 33-year-old Joseph Kabila, who has been president since the death of Laurent Kabila (his father) in 2001, to stand for the presidency in the 2006 elections. The president, who is limited to two five-year terms, names the prime minister from the largest party.

The flag is blue, to symbolise peace, crossed by a red line (the blood of the four million people who died in the civil war) and hedged by two yellow lines (the vast mining deposits of the country).

Form of state

Presidential republic

The executive

Under an accord signed in 2002 by the government, rebel groups and the civilian opposition, President Joseph Kabila was expected to remain in office until election in 2004, however elections have been postponed to 2006. The president is assisted by four vice presidents, each representing the government, two armed rebel groups and the civilian opposition.

National legislature

The legislature consists of a 500-member Assemblée Nationale (national assembly) and a 120-member Senat (senate).

Legal system

The civil code is based on the Belgian system, including the structure of the Supreme Court. Legal issues at the local level are usually dealt with according to tribal law.

Last elections

30 July 2006/29 October 2006 (presidential); 30 July 2006 (national assembly); 19 January 2007 (senate)

Results: Presidential: (first round) Joseph Kabila won 44.81 per cent, Jean-Pierre Bemba won 20.03 per cent and Antoine Gizenga won 13.06 per cent. (Run-off) Kabila won 58.05 per cent of the vote and Bemba 41.95 per cent.

National assembly: over 9,700 candidates contested 500 seats in the national assembly. Kabila's Parti du Peuple pour la Reconstruction et la Démocratie (PPRD) (People's Party of Reconstruction and Democracy) won 22.2 per cent of the vote (111 seats), Bemba's Mouvement Libération Congolaise (MLC) (Movement for Congolese Liberation) won 12.9 per cent, (64); Parti Lumumbiste Unifié (PLU) (United Lumumbist Party) 6.8 per cent, (34); Mouvement Social pour le Renouveau (MSR) (Social Movement for Renewal) 5.4 per cent, (27); Forces du Renouveau (FR) (Forces of Renewal) 5.2 per cent, (26); Rassemblement Congolais pour la Démocratie (RCD) (Congolese Rally for Democracy) 3.0 per cent, (15); Coalition des Démocrates Congolais (CODECO) (Coalition of Congolese Democrats) 2.0 per cent, (10); Convention des Démocrates Chrétiens (CDC) (Convention of Christian Democrats) 2.0 per cent, (10). Forty seats were won by parties wining less than 10 seats and 94 seats were won by independents or parties wining only one seat.

Senate: the Alliance pour la Majorité Présidentielle (AMP) (Alliance for a presidential majority) won 58 seats (out of 108, of with PPRD won 22), the Union pour la Nation (UN) coalition won 21 (of which MLC won 14, including a seat for Jean Pierre Bemba, its leader).

Next elections

2011 (presidential and parliamentry).

Political parties

Ruling party

Parti du Peuple pour la Reconstruction et la Démocratie (PPRD) (People's Party of Reconstruction and Democracy) (elected 30 Jul 2006)

Main opposition party

Mouvement Populaire de la Revolution (MPR) (Popular Movement of the Revolution)

Population

61.05 million (2007)*

Last census: July 1984: 29,916,800

Population density: 20 inhabitants per square km. Urban population: 30 per cent.

Annual growth rate: 2.5 per cent 1994–2004 (WHO 2006)

Internally Displaced Persons (IDP)

3.4 million (UNHCR 2004)

Ethnic make-up

There are over 200 ethnic groups in DRC. The largest is the Kongo, which predominates in Bandundu province. The Mongo are mainly found in the heavily forested north and north-west. The Luba predominate in the two Kasai provinces and the Shabans and Bemba live mainly in Katanga (formerly Shaba) province. Other large ethnic groups include the Zande, the Bwaka, the Lulua and the Songe. There are a large number of people of Nilotic origin, mainly concentrated in the eastern North Kivu province.

Religions

Some 50 per cent of the population adhere to animist beliefs. The remainder are mostly Christian, of which a majority are Roman Catholic. Muslims make up some 10 per cent of the population, residing mainly in North Kivu province.

Education

Estimates by major non-government organisations show that at least four out of every 10 children of primary school age are denied the basic right to education in the DRC. Several obstacles towards accessing basic education include the inability of parents to pay school fees, massive displacement of population and destruction of school buildings during the civil war. Between 1997 and 2003, millions of children had no access to schools, leading to an increase in the dropout rate from 49 per cent to 75 per cent during the period.

The UN Children's Fund (UNICEF) has helped in the rehabilitation of seven schools and four health centres in Kisangani (damaged in 2000), which cater for 20,000 children. Unicef will also provide financial assistance towards training teachers and for various educational materials.

Literacy rate: 72 per cent men and 49 per cent women, adult rates (World Bank).

Compulsory years: Six to 12.

Pupils per teacher: 45 in primary schools.

Health

Per capita total expenditure on health (2003) was US$14; of which per capita government spending was US$3, (WHO 2006).

The Mobutu government had placed a low priority on standards of health and welfare, and continuing civil war inhibited improvement. From this low base, expenditure has slowly risen from the 1.5 per cent in 2000.

Only one-third of the population, mostly those in the larger cities, have access to local healthcare. There are more than 900 hospitals with a total capacity of over 75,000 beds, but many of these are not operating due to a lack of resources and loss of unpaid staff. There are an estimated 1,900 physicians working in the DRC, for a population of 58 million.

Tuberculosis incidence is about 260 per 100,000 population.

Unicef in association with the DRC government started a major measles immunisation campaign in October 2002, targetting some 15 million children initially.

Forty five per cent of the population have access to an improved water sources.

There were cases of polio reported to the World Health Organisation – Global Polio Eradication Initiative in 2006; the country had previously been free of the disease and its re-emergence was due to infected travellers.

HIV/Aids

One million people were HIV positive in 2003, of which 570,000 were women, plus there were 110,000 children infected and 770,000 orphans (aged 0–17) created. Deaths from Aids amounted to 100,000 in 2003.

An HIV infection rate of 12 per cent has been characteristic for women who were caught up in civil war atrocities, or attacked by exiled Hutu Militia, and been raped. Such militia erroneously believe that raping a woman will be protection from HIV infection.

HIV prevalence: 4.2 per cent aged 15–49 in 2003 (World Bank)

Life expectancy: 44 years, 2004 (WHO 2006)

Fertility rate/Maternal mortality rate: 6.7 births per woman, 2004 (WHO 2006); maternal mortality 9.4 per 1,000 (World Bank)

Birth rate/Death rate: 15 deaths to 45 births per 1,000 people (World Bank 2001).

Child (under 5 years) mortality rate (per 1,000): 129 per 1,000 live births; 34 per cent of children aged under five were malnourished (World Bank 2004).

Head of population per physician: 0.11 physicians per 1,000 people, 2004 (WHO 2006)

Welfare

While several UN agencies and non-governmental organisations, through a diverse range of activities, manage the welfare situation in the DRC, there have been setbacks when humanitarian teams were withdrawn for safety reasons. The western provinces of the country have remained stable, but the eastern provinces, featuring unrivalled poverty and insecurity, are gripped by a humanitarian emergency. Over 3.3 million people are estimated to have been killed or died as a result of the war, to overthrow the DRC government, which started in 1998.

The UN estimates that there are 3.4 million internally displaced persons (IDPs), and the UN World Food Programme (WFP) estimates that 16 million people (including refugees from Angola), are in need of emergency food aid, or have been cut off from traditional means of subsistence. In early 2004, two million people benefited from WFP's programmes, at a total cost of US$196 million.

The UN reported that during 2002–03, there were 'unprecedented levels of violence by armed factions in eastern DRC, including cannibalism, systematic killings, rape and lootings,' despite some political stability following the installation of a government of transition in mid-2003. While there are no precise rape figures, records show over 40,000 cases were reported since the civil war of 1998 began, and exiled Hutu militia (from Rwanda) began attacking villagers in eastern DRC.

Main cities

Kinshasa (capital, estimated population 6.8 million in 2004), Lubumbashi (1.1 million), Mbuji-Mayi (938,000), Kolwezi (832,400), Kananga (557,800), Kinsangani (523,000).

Languages spoken

Among the many African languages spoken, Lingala, KiSwahili, Tshiluba and Kikongo are the most prominent in DRC.

Official language/s

French

Media

National news agency: ACP (Agence Congolaise de Presse)

Press

Dailies: There are several dailies, all published in French, the majority of which are located in Kinshasa, including La Potentiel (www.lepotentiel.com), the independent, La Référence Plus (http://groupelareference.afrikart.net), L'Avenir (www.groupelavenir.net), L'Observateur (www.lobservateur.cd), La Conscience (www.laconscience.com), La Phare (www.lepharerdc.com), La Prospérité (www.laprosperiteonline.net), and La République (www.la-republique.com).

Weeklies: In French, Le Soft (www.lesoftonline.net), covers political matters.

Periodicals: In French, Observatoire de l'Afrique Centrale (www.obsac.com), a quarterly magazine with reviews of the news in Central Africa and the bi-monthly C Retro Actuel (http://c-retro-actuel.net), covering current affairs, politics, the economy and culture.

Broadcasting

The national, public broadcaster is Radio Télévision Nationale Congolaise (RTNC).

Radio: Radio services are the main medium of mass communication and sources of news and information.

RTNC operates La Voix du Congo (The Voice of Congo), which broadcasts programmes in French, Swahili, Lingala, Tshiluba and Kikongo. Private radio stations include the UN-backed Radio Okapi (www.radiookapi.net), Top Congo FM (www.topcongo.com) and Mangembo FM (www.mangembo-fm.com). There are also several stations broadcasting religious content. International transmissions from Radio France International (RFI) (www.rfi.fr) and the BBC World Service (www.bbc.co.uk/worldservice) (92.7 FM) are available through satellite and internet or relayed via local radio stations. There are many more private radio stations broadcasting in small localities throughout the country.

Television: Television coverage is almost nationwide, with four channels available including the government-owned RTNC. Commercial stations include RTGA (www.groupelavenir.net), Canal Tropical TV and Raga TV. There are many more private TV stations broadcasting in small localities throughout the country.

News agencies

National news agency: ACP (Agence Congolaise de Presse)

Economy

The Democratic Republic of Congo (DRC) has a long, hard road to travel to gain all the benefits that its huge mineral wealth of cobalt, copper, gold, diamonds and uranium, its rivers with abundant hydroelectric potential, its fertile land and its virgin forests could bestow on it. Now that a democratically elected regime is in power it may begin to reap the rewards of widespread redevelopment and growth.

Improved relations with the IMF came about after the government cleared its arrears and in 2005 DRC received the fifth tranche of US$39.2 million from the IMF's Poverty Reduction and Growth Facility (PRGF) arrangement. In total, the DRC will have received US$813.2 million from the PRGF by March 2006. The IMF supports the government in implementing reforms necessary to restore macroeconomic stability. To begin with, the IMF offered measures for improving public resource management and strengthening central bank operations. Fiscal measures were split into two, the first concerned with revenue collection. It included proposals that the customs office be the sole tax collector, people were to be given an individual tax number (to mitigate tax fraud) and more tax centres to be opened. In addition, tax breaks will no longer be offered to mining and logging companies and the tax on oil exports will reflect the global price of oil. The second was concerned with expenditure measures, which included a limit on public sector wages, an enforced ceiling on ministry spending, of which budgets must be justified, double-entry accounting for transparency and with a scheduled, professional audit.

After a decade or more of economic contraction, growth, which began in 2002, reached 6.5 per cent by 2005 and was estimated to be 7.1 per cent in 2006. Inflation was 357 per cent in 2001 but has been steadily reduced to 21.4 per cent by 2005 and is expected to be less than 10 per cent in 2006, helped by a 15 per cent appreciation in the Congolese franc in the second half of 2005.

Corruption is a major problem, especially in dealings in natural resources. With a country so large (the third largest in Africa, behind Sudan and Algeria) and a world market willing to accept a dubious provenance the authorities in DRC have a hard task securing its assets and borders. Diplomatic tension and militia fighting in the border region with Burundi has isolated the area from total government control and the smuggling of gold, diamonds and other minerals is rife.

The country is still poor with weak infrastructure and fragile peace but with foreign investment and a reasonable return on its assets it could be a powerhouse for Africa, supplying raw materials and surplus energy.

External trade

The DRC is a member of the Common Market for Eastern and Southern Africa (Comesa), however in 2007 it was still not a member of the free trade zone, as operated by 13 other member states, nor are there plans to join the customs union proposed to begin in December 2007. It is also a member of the Economic Community of Central African States (ECCAS) and the Southern African Development Community (SADC), which in July 2007 was still negotiating an Economic Partnership Agreement with the EU, through the East and Southern African (ESA) countries as part of the African, Caribbean and Pacific (ACP) grouping.

DRC was a world leading producer of industrial diamonds, before its civil war, and they still remain dominant in the economy, accounting for around 50 per cent of exports.

The narrow export base is concentrated mainly on minerals, with some agricultural cash crops; this has made the DRC's balance of trade susceptible to the vagaries of world commodity markets. Under-investment and regular strikes have further weakened the mining industry.

Imports

Principal imports are foodstuffs, mining and other machinery, transport equipment and fuels.

Main sources: South Africa (19.2 per cent total, 2006), Belgium (11.8 per cent), France (9.3 per cent).

Exports

Principal exports are diamonds, copper, palm oil, cobalt, crude oil, rubber, cotton and coffee.

Main destinations: Belgium (34.0 per cent total, 2006), China (24.4 per cent), Chile (9.0 per cent).

Agriculture

Farming

Agriculture contributes around 50 per cent of GDP, around half of which is derived from subsistence farming, even though it provides the livelihood of 57 per cent of the population. There are almost 23 million hectares (ha) of agricultural land available, of which 7.8 million ha is given over to permanent arable and 15 million ha to pasture.

Despite enormous agricultural potential, the sector has been handicapped by transport problems, occasional drought, smuggling and inflexible pricing policies. Farmers in the eastern provinces have also had to contend with lethal Hutu militia, exiled from Rwanda, who target isolated farms and villages for supplies while often committing atrocities.

The government is developing the forestry sector with multilateral financial assistance.

Main food crops are cassava, maize, rice and plantain. Production is insufficient to meet demand, and poor transport restricts supplies to the urban areas. Main cash and export crops are plantation-grown coffee, cocoa, oil palm, rubber, tea, cotton, sugar and tobacco.

Crop production in 2005 included: 1,572,930 tonnes (t) cereals in total, 1,155,260t maize, 14,974,470t cassava, 93,200t potatoes, 229,760t sweet potatoes, 84,900t yams, 315,480t rice, 65,690t taro, 36,690t millet, 1,193,024t plantains, 313,970t bananas, 185,910t pulses, 342,669t oilcrops, 15,518,130t roots and tubers, 62,630t avocados, 197,300t citrus fruit, 203,270t mangoes, 195,210t pineapples, *3,700t tobacco, 5,630t cocoa beans, 31,990t green coffee, 368,110t groundnuts in shell, *1,800,000t sugar cane, *7,000t natural rubber, *30,000t seed cotton, *8,000t cotton lint, 2,435,404t fruit in total, 453,425t vegetables in total. Livestock production included: 211,908t meat in total, 12,400t beef, 88,735t game meat, 23,860t pig meat, 2,778t lamb, 18,499t goat meat, 10,636t poultry, *6,000t eggs.

* estimate

Fishing

Although the DRC has only a narrow coastline, the fisheries sector is evenly based between inland and coastal resources. Around 150,000 artisanal fisherman operate in the DRC, providing 90 per cent of the total national catch. Excluding subsistence production, inland fishing in the many rivers and lakes produces around 150,000 tonnes, comparable with the 160,000 for seafood production. The country is a substantial net importer of seafood and freshwater fish.

In 2004, the total marine fish catch was 5,000 tonnes.

Forestry

DRC has 135.2 million hectares (ha) of tropical forest, roughly half the timber resources of the African continent. The first industrial exploitation started in 1930 at Mayumbe. The sector is vastly under-exploited and holds out much potential, particularly in terms of export revenue. From 1970 onwards, the focus of activity shifted from Mayumbe to the Cuvette region. The DRC produces large quantities of sawnwood, as well as plywood and veneer and tropical hardwood logs and sawnwood are the principal exports. However the principal use of timber is as domestic firewood.

In 2004, the export of forest products amounted to US$52,4 billion while imports totalled US$7.9 billion.

An estimated US$12 million per annum is being lost through tax avoidance by international logging companies, according to Greenpeace in July 2008.

Estimated production in 2004 included 73,430,400 cubic metres (cum) roundwood, 3,653,000cum industrial roundwood, 40,000cum sawnwood, 170,000cum sawlogs and veneers, 69,777,400cum woodfuel, 1,645,773t charcoal.

Industry and manufacturing

The industrial sector contributes around 17 per cent to GDP and employs around 10 per cent of the workforce. Approximately three-quarters of production is centred around Kinshasa or in Katanga province, owing to the availability of electricity and adequate transport facilities in these areas.

In an environment of political instability, endemic corruption and poor regulation, few manufacturing industries have developed. The few that remain have also been hindered by a lack of technical and management expertise, the comparatively poor transport infrastructure and a chronic decline in domestic purchasing power eroded by inflation and lack of foreign exchange to purchase essential manufacturing inputs.

Output is geared towards the domestic market and is mainly concentrated on brewing, food processing, textiles, consumer goods, construction industry inputs and transport equipment.

Mismanagement and shortages of spare parts and materials have led to cut-backs in production with most firms operating at below half capacity. The government is attempting to increase production by encouraging foreign investment and offering substantial tax incentives.

Tourism

Tourism was never an important economic activity, but with its immense rainforests and rich bio-diversity, a peaceful DRC would provide a rich abundance of eco-tourist destinations for the adventurous traveller. The infrastructure deteriorated as a result of warfare and this will have to be improved if there is to be any major growth in the sector.

Capital investment in the tourist industry was a modest US$74.6 million in 2004, which accounted for 5.1 per cent of total capital investment; the government invested US$20.4 million, which was 2.5 per cent of total government spending, on tourism in 2004. The country earned US$58.7 million, or 1.2 per cent of GDP from the sector and it employed 8,300 people, or 1.1 per cent of total employment while achieving a 0.3 per cent growth in 2004.

With the necessary investment and a return to civilian government the projected annualised growth in travel and tourism is 5.5 per cent (2006–15).

In February 2008 the governments of DRC, Rwanda and Uganda agreed to joint measures to protect the mountain gorillas found within their shared border regions. Tourists visiting the area to view the endangered great apes raise a combined US$5 million for the countries concerned.

Environment

In February 2008 the governments of DRC, Rwanda and Uganda agreed to joint measures to protect the mountain gorillas found within their shared border regions. Tourists visiting the area to view the endangered great apes raise a combined US$5 million for the countries concerned. However, poaching and civil strife have dropped the numbers of gorillas to critically endangered levels, so that a 10-year conservation project which focuses of security and encouraging local people to preserve the animals and habitat is seen as the only hope for the gorilla's survival.

Mining

The country is rich in mineral resources and is potentially one of Africa's richest countries. DRC's copper reserves are estimated at 75 million tonnes with iron at one billion tonnes, 240 million carats of diamonds and over 600 tonnes of gold.

In the past, mining contributed around a third of GDP and employed 5 per cent of the workforce. With around half of DRC's foreign exchange earnings gained from diamond exports (US$700 million in 2007), the industry watchdog called for stricter application of existing laws to reduce smuggling and exploitative practices that lead to less revenue for DRC than was possible.

Moves towards peace should lead to a resumption of investment in the mining sector, backed by planned new mining and investment codes. Mining is likely to be the driving force of the economy over the medium-term.

Diamonds are mined on a commercial scale by the Société Minière de Bakwanga (Miba) at Bakwanga in Kasai Oriental, but artisanal diggers account for almost three-quarters of total output.

Gold production has been erratic and has fallen to record lows during the years of war. However, renewed investor interest will increase production.

There is tin mining and small-scale mining of cadmium, cassiterite and wolframite. Activity is concentrated in the copper-rich Katanga (formerly Shaba) province.

Twangiza gold deposits are estimated at 4.1 million tonnes of ore. With the exception of diamonds, these minerals have been hit by weak world demand.

Katanga Province is part of the Central African Copperbelt, which extends from Angola through the DRC into Zambia. The state-run Gécamines has holdings containing the biggest concentrations of copper and cobalt in the world. Gécamines' troubles are rooted in long-term problems of corruption and mismanagement. Its misfortune is exacerbated by the civil war, which has led to foreign partners scaling down or pulling out of joint ventures.

In October 2002, Australia's Anvil Mining began production at the Dikulushi copper and silver mine.

Hydrocarbons

Proven oil reserves totalled 187 million barrels in 2005, most of which are located off the Atlantic coastline and in the River Congo estuary. Oil production totalled 21,100 barrels per day (bpd) in 2004, however all oil has to be exported as DRC does not have a refinery.

Total natural gas reserves stood at 990 million cubic metres in 2005, most of which is located beneath Lake Kivu, however the cost of exploiting this reserve has made production non-viable.

In 2005 coal reserves stood at 88 million tonnes, with production running at 9.9 million tonnes per annum. Mines are located at Luena and Kalemie.

Energy

The DRC has the potential to produce 100,000MW of electricity, twice the power necessary to supply the entire southern African region, if it were able to harness the power of its rivers. The civil war has left the country without the infrastructure and investors needed to exploit the natural resources and in the meantime actual electricity production in 2005 was estimated at no more than 650–750MW.

Hydroelectric power, produced by the Inga Dam near the port of Matadi at the mouth of the Congo River, supplies around 30 per cent of the electricity consumed in Brazzaville, the capital of the Republic of Congo. The dam also supplies the copper mines in Katanga, and produces two-thirds of the rest of DRC's consumption.

Energy in rural areas is mainly derived from charcoal and wood.

The DRC imports most of its oil requirements, due to the inability to refine its own crude oil.

Banking and insurance

The banking system is virtually non-existent as persistent hyperinflation has led to the collapse of all the country's banks.

Central bank

Banque du Congo

Main financial centre

Kinshasa

Time

Kinshasa and the western provinces – GMT plus one hour

Elsewhere – GMT plus two hours

Geography

The country is bordered by the Republic of Congo in the west, by the Central African Republic in the north, by Sudan in the north-east, by Uganda, Rwanda and Burundi in the northeast to east, by Tanzania in the east to south-east, Zambia in the south and Angola in the south to south-west. Lake Tanganiyka forms most of the border with Tanzania.

DRC is the second largest country in Africa (after Sudan), it is over two million square kilometres in area, encompassing a huge central basin of tropical rain forest, with mountains that rise in the east and the continent's second longest river (after the Nile) running through its northern and western regions. It has a tiny 37km coastline where the River Congo drains into the eastern South Atlantic seaboard. In its eastern range of mountains live the endangered mountain gorilla whose habitat is under threat from illegal logging and deforestation. Pic Marguerite on Mont Ngaliema (Mount Stanley) at 5,110 metres is the tallest peak. Close to the city of Goma are Africa's two most active volcanoes, Nyamuragira and Nyiragongo – which has the world's fastest flowing lava. The southern part of the country is savannah grassland.

Most of the population is concentrated in areas with the best communications, near Kinshasa in the far west, along the Congo River and other main rivers, and in the southern and eastern border regions.

Hemisphere

Straddles the equator, although most of the country is situated in the southern hemisphere.

Climate

The climate varies widely owing to the size of the country. The lowlands in the western region are hot and humid, including Kinshasa, where rain is concentrated in the period from November to March and temperatures reach 32 degrees Celsius (C) in the hottest month, January, with 26 degrees C in the coolest month, June. On the central plateau, the likely temperature range is 18–20 degrees C. In the south and the eastern province of Kivu the climate is a Mediterranean type and is slightly cooler, particularly in the winter months.

Dress codes

Business clothes may be casual and lightweight clothing is essential, especially if visiting during the rainy season.

Entry requirements

Visitors are advised to contact embassy representatives in advance to ascertain current entry requirements. Visitors are also advised to register their presence in DRC with their local embassy representative.

Passports

Required by all. All passports must be valid for six months from the date of departure. Proof of return/onward passage is also necessary.

Visa

Required by all.

Applications for a business visa requires a letter from a tour company stating the trip has been paid in full, or from an employer accepting responsibility for any expenses incurred; proof of status and a letter of finance giving proof of sufficient funds and a full itinerary. An official letter of invitation endorsed by the DRC authorities must also accompany the application.

Travel regulations should be studied carefully before a visit as restrictions apply.

Prohibited entry

Those with visas/entry/exit stamps for Rwanda, Burundi or Uganda are likely to be refused entry.

Currency advice/regulations

The import or export of local currency is prohibited. Foreign currency import is limited to US$10,000 and must be declared. Currency declaration forms must be kept and all currency exchanges should be recorded.

Customs

Visitors are advised not to take in any equipment which may arouse suspicion, such as cameras, binoculars, maps or any kind of tools or military equipment.

Health (for visitors)

Mandatory precautions

Yellow fever vaccination certificate is required if arriving from an infected area.

Advisable precautions

Visitors should take precautions against all tropical diseases. Vaccinations for diphtheria, tetanus, hepatitis A, polio and typhoid are recommended. Other vaccinations that may be recommended are cholera, tuberculosis, hepatitis B and meningitis. There is a risk of rabies.

Anti-malaria tablets are essential, and HIV/Aids is widespread among both men and women. Dysentery, typhoid and typhus are prevalent, especially outside Kinshasa. Bubonic plague exists in the Bunia region.

Tap water must be treated as unsafe unless boiled and filtered (bottled water is available in the main cities). Outside Kinshasa and Lubumbashi, eat only hot, cooked food and avoid raw salad, fruit, vegetables and ice cubes. Dairy products are unpasteurised and should be avoided.

A first aid kit that includes disposable syringes, is a reasonable precaution. Medical insurance is essential, including emergency evacuation, and an adequate supply of personal medicines is necessary.

Hotels

Several major hotels in Kinshasa and other cities. Most tend to be expensive and are often heavily booked. A service charge is usually added to bill and further tipping is optional.

Public holidays (national)

Fixed dates

1 Jan (New Year's Day), 4 Jan (Commemoration of the Martyrs of Independence), 17 Jan (National Heroes' Day), 1 May (Labour Day), 17 May (National Liberation Day), 30 Jun (Independence Day), 1 Aug (Parents' Day), 17 Nov (Army Day), 25 Dec (Christmas Day).

Working hours

Banking

Mon–Fri: 0800–1130.

Business

Mon–Fri: 0730–1200, 1430–1700; Sat: 0730–1200.

Government

Mon–Fri: 0730–1500; Sat: 0730–1200.

It is normal practice for ministers and senior officials to work Mon–Fri: 0830–1300 and from 1600–2000.

Shops

Mon–Fri: 0800–1200, 1500–1700; Sat: 0800–1200.

Telecommunications

Mobile/cell phones

There are 900 and 1800 GSM services operating in highly populated areas.

Electricity supply

220V AC

Social customs/useful tips

With its vast range of ethnic groups and huge land area, there are many different traditions, according to the locality.

As in most French-speaking African countries, business etiquette when visiting government and (to a lesser degree) private commercial offices is more formal than in English-speaking Africa.

Do not openly criticise the government or attempt to photograph public buildings. Military installations are also best avoided if possible.

Security

The insecurity and lawlessness in eastern and northern DRC makes travelling to these areas dangerous. Visitors should consider whether their journey is vital before travelling in the rest of DRC.

Street crime is rife, especially in Kinshasa. Visitors are advised not to wear expensive jewellery or watches or to carry cameras conspicuously. To achieve anything expect to pay katamulomo tips, especially to soldiers (both genuine and fake), who are seldom paid and who man the roadblocks. Visitors should beware of unofficial 'porters' at N'djili airport. Those visiting for the first time should try to arrange for a local business associate or friend to meet them at the airport. Visitors are advised to stay in their hotels after dark. They should avoid public transport altogether and use hire cars rather than taxis whenever possible.

The DRC is undergoing profound political change which means that any official efforts which may be made to protect foreign visitors are unlikely to be effective outside Kinshasa. The best advice is to contact embassy representatives in advance in order to check the safety of the region to which you wish to travel.

Getting there

Air

National airline: Hewa Bora Airways

International airport/s: Kinshasa-N'djili International airport (FIH) is 25km from central Kinshasa. As N'djili is located a long way from the city, it is advisable to pre-arrange transport either with a hotel or local car hire firm such as Hertz (office within the shopping gallery at the Inter-Continental Hotel) or to arrange for a business or social contact to meet first-time visitors to the country at the airport.

Other airport/s: There are almost 60 airports and airfields around DRC.

Airport tax: Departure tax: Cf500

Surface

Road: There are 2,400km of poorly maintained asphalted roads leading to neighbouring countries. However, most borders are closed and the roads leading to them are considered very dangerous.

Rail: The three main lines into DRC are the Voie Nationale running from Matadi port to Kinshasa (366km); the eastern route entering from Tanzania at Kalemie and the northern route entering from the Sudan at Mungbere. There are also links to southern African states via Zambia.

An end to Angola's civil war would allow reconstruction of the Benguela line from Shaba to Lobito port in Angola, but this could take several years.

Water: From Kinshasa there is a regular ferry service to Brazzaville, although it is subject to distruption.

Main port/s: The main port is Matadi, about 150km inland on the Congo River. Kinshasa is the main inland river port and the ferry crossing point from Brazzaville.

Getting about

National transport

Air: There are connections from Kinshasa-N'djili to over 40 local destinations. Charter facilities are available.

Road: There are indefinite restrictions on travel throughout the country. A permit from the interior ministry is required for travel outside Kinshasa.

The 240,000km road network is in poor condition outside main population centres and some parts have become impassable through lack of maintenance. Bridges should be checked before crossing and banditry is common.

Buses: Very irregular, crowded and infrequent service.

Rail: A network of over 5,000km is operated by Société Nationale des Chemins de Fer Zaïroise (SNCZ), but some parts are inoperable while others subject to disruption. Of the four classes – 'deluxe' and first-class are advisable.

Water: Inland navigation is important, particularly for freight on the Congo River between Kinshasa and Kisangani and the Kasai River from Ilebo to the Congo River north of Kinshasa. However, all routes around Kisangani have been disrupted by the civil war. When available, passenger services run on all major rivers and lakes. It is advisable to travel luxury or first class.

City transport

Shared taxis provide the best form of transport and are widely available. There is little or no public transport outside Kinshasa.

Taxis: Volatile inflation rates and political instability mean it is virtually impossible to keep track of taxi fares in local currency. If resorting to a local taxi, it is absolutely essential to negotiate a fixed fare before starting the journey.

Car hire

Self-drive cars are available in Kinshasa and at the airport. A deposit is required unless an acceptable credit card can be produced. International driving licence required. Traffic drives on the right.

BUSINESS DIRECTORY

The addresses listed below are a selection only. While World of Information makes every endeavour to check these addresses, we cannot guarantee that changes have not been made, especially to telephone numbers and area codes. We would welcome any corrections.

Telephone area codes

The international direct dialling (IDD) code for DRC is +243, followed by the area code and subscriber's number. In late 2006 the landline telephone system was not functioning. To call a mobile number (beginning with 8 or 9) dial +243 and then the number.

Kinshasa	12	Lubumbashi	2
Cellular network	8		

Chambers of Commerce

Fédération des Entreprises du Congo, 10 Avenue des Aviateurs, PO Box 7247, Kinshasa (tel: 880-7297; fax: 780-0660; e-mail: feccongo@hotmail.com).

Franco-Congolaise Chambre de Commerce et d'Industrie, 407 Avenue Roi Baudouin, PO Box 8.211, Kinshasa 1 (tel: 780-5871; fax: 880-7158).

Banking

Banque Commerciale du Congo SARL, BP 2798, Boulevard du 30 Juin, Kinshasa-Gombe (tel: 217-73, 217-76; fax: 221-770).

Banque Continentale Africaine (Zaire) SARL, 4 Avenue de la Justice, Kinshasa-Gombe (tel: 28-006, 28-537; fax: 25-243).

Banque Internationale de Credit SARL, 191 Ave de l'Equateur, Kinshasa-Gombe (tel: 882-0404, 884-1940/5631, 884-3159/3790, 880-1487; fax: 880-1125, 377-97900/34).

Citibank NA Congo, BP 9999, Citibank Building, Coin des Avenues Colonel Lukusa et Ngongo Lutete, Kinshasa-Gombe 1 (tel: 20555/57; fax: 40015).

Fransabank (Congo) SARL, BP 9497, Avenue du Port, 14/16 Immeuble Zaïre-Shell, Kin. 1, Kinshasa-Gombe (tel: 20121/2/3/4; fax: 12-27864).

Nouvelle Banque de Kinshasa, 1 Place du Marché, Kinshasa-Gombe 1 (tel: 12-20562-5, 12-0459-60, 12-3461-63; fax: 12-581-4961 80043).

Stanbic Bank Congo SARL, 12 Avenue de la Mongala, Kinshasa-Gombe (tel: 88-48445, 88-41984, 88-43453, 88-43419, 88- 04512; fax: 88-46216).

Union de Banques SARL, BP 197, Coin des Avenues de la Nation et des Aviateurs, Kinshasa-Gombe (tel: 88-4133, 88-43620, 88-44887; fax: 88-46628).

Central bank

Banque Centrale du Congo, 563 Boulevard Colonel Tshashi, PO Box 2697, Kinshasa-Gombe (tel: 20-704; fax: 880-5152; e-mail: cabgouv@bcc.cd).

Travel information

Air Zaïre, BP 10120, Airport de N'Djili, Kinshasa (tel: 20-939; fax: 20-940).

N'Djili International Airport, BP 10124, Kinshasa 24 (tel: 23-570).

SNCZ Railways, BP 597, Kinshasa.

Ministry of tourism

Ministry of Tourism, BP12.348, 15 Avenue Papa Ileo (ex des Cliniques), Kinshasa 1 (tel: 34-390, 88-02-394; fax: 88-44-987).

National tourist organisation offices

Office National du Tourisme de la République Démocratique du Congo, BP 9502, Kinshasa-Gombe 1 (tel: 89-32-2238, 815-091-627, 99-31-939; fax: 33-781; e-mail: ont-rdc@raga.net).

Ministries

Civil Service Ministry, Avenue des Ambassadeurs, BP 3, Kinshasa-Gombe.

Ministry of Agriculture, Boulevard du 30 Juin, Building Sozacom, 3e Etage, BP 8722 KIN I, Kinshasa-Gombe.

Ministry of Economy, Industry and Commerce, Boulevard du 30 Juin, Building Onatra, BP 8500 KIN I, Kinshasa-Gombe.

Ministry of Energy, 239 Avenue de la Justice, Building SNEL, BP 5137 KIN I, Kinshasa-Gombe.

Ministry of Environment and Tourism, 15 Avenue des Cliniques, BP 12348 KIN I, Kinshasa-Gombe.

Ministry of Finance, Boulevard du 30 Juin, BP 12998 KIN I, Kinshasa-Gombe.

Ministry of Foreign Affairs and International Co-operation, Place de l'Indépendance, BP 7100, Kinshasa-Gombe 14 (tel: 32-450, 30-248, 32-239, 30-996, 32-735, 33-325; fax: 88-02-368; internet site: www.minaffeci-rdcongo.net/).

Ministry of Health, Boulevard du 30 Juin, BP 3088 KIN I, Kinshasa-Gombe.

Ministry of Home Affairs, Kinshasa-Gombe.

Ministry of Information and Cultural Affairs, Avenue du 24 Novembre, BP 3171 KIN I, Kinshasa-Kabinda.

Ministry of International Co-Operation, Avenue de la Justice, Enceinte SNEL, Kinshasa-Gombe.

Ministry of Justice, 228 Avenue des 3 Z, Kinshasa-Gombe.

Ministry of Mines, 239 Avenue de la Justice, Building SNEL, BP 5137 KIN I, Kinshasa-Gombe.

Ministry of National Education, Enceinte de l'Institut de la Gombe, BP 3163, Kinshasa-Gombe.

Ministry of Planning and Development, 4155 Avenue des Coteaux, BP 9378 KIN I, Kinshasa-Gombe.

Ministry of Post and Telecommunications, 4484 Avenue des Huiles, Building Kilou, BP 800 KIN I, Kinshasa-Gombe.

Ministry of Public Works, Building Travaux Publics, Kinshasa-Gombe.

Ministry of Reconstruction, Boulevard Colonel Tshatshi, Building Travaux Publics, BP 26, Kinshasa-Gombe.

Ministry of Transport, Boulevard du 30 Juin, Building Onatra, BP 3304, Kinshasa-Gombe.

Ministry of Youth and Sports, 77 Avenue de la Justice, BP 8541 KIN I, Kinshasa-Gombe.

Other useful addresses

Democratic Republic of Congo Embassy (USA), 1800 New Hampshire Avenue, NW, Washington DC 20009 (tel: (+1-202) 234-7690; fax: (+1-202) 237-0748).

Democratic Republic of Congo Permanent mission the UN, 866 United Nations Plaza, Suite 511, New York (tel: (+1-212) 319-8061; fax: (+1-212) 319-8232; email: drcongo@un.int).

National news agency: ACP (Agence Congolaise de Presse)

44-48 Avenue Tombalbaye, BP 1595, Kinshasa (internet: www.un.int/drcongo).

Internet sites

Africa Business Network: www.ifc.org/abn

AllAfrica.com: http://allafrica.com

African Development Bank: www.afdb.org

Africa Online: www.africaonline.com

Democratic Republic of Congo (French only): www.congonline.com

Mbendi AfroPaedia (information on companies, countries, industries and stock exchanges in Africa): http://mbendi.co.za

Cook Islands

COUNTRY PROFILE

Historical profile

1200 The islands were believed to have been settled by neighbouring Tahitians.
1596 The Spaniard, Alvaro de Mendana, was thought to be the first European to sight the islands.
1733 The islands were named in honour of Captain James Cook.
1789 Rarotonga, the main island, was sighted by the Bounty mutineers.
1888 The islands became a British protectorate.
1901 New Zealand became colonial administrators of the Cook Islands.
1965 The islands became self-governing, as a New Zealand dependency. Albert Henry of the Cook Islands Party (CIP) became prime minister.
1978 The Democratic Party (DP) won the election and Tom Davis became prime minister.
1994 The CIP won the general elections with 20 seats in the 25-seat parliament – the greatest margin of victory in 30 years and Geoffrey Henry became prime minister.
1997 The DP experienced internal conflict and a majority of party members broke away to become the Democratic Alliance Party (DAP). A faction of the DP became the New Alliance (NA) Party, led by Norman George.
1999 The CIP lost the general election and Terepai Maoate of the DAP formed a government with the NA.
2001 The Cook Islands was placed on the international money laundering blacklist.
2002 Maoate was ousted as prime minister in a vote of no-confidence. Robert Woonton (DAP) formed an all-party coalition.
2003 The DAP and the NA merged and reverted to the original name, Democratic Party (DP). Cook Islands Mäori became an official language.
2004 In parliamentary elections there was even balance between the two groupings with Prime Minister Robert Woonton having the deciding vote. Woonton lost his seat when it was found, in a recount that his constituency votes had tied; in the re-vote he lost. Jim Marurai, leader of DP was elected prime minister.
2005 In a dispute with his party, Marurai, remained prime minister with the support of the CIP. The Cook Islands was removed from the OECD international money laundering blacklist. Marurai's alliance with the CIP broke down and he returned to the DP for support, but not the party leadership.
2006 A by-election tipped the balance of power in parliament. Prime Minister Marurai, called a snap election which the DP won with 15 out of 24 seats, the CIP won seven, independents one and one tied. The leader and deputy leader of the CIP were beaten and lost their seats. A by-election, was won by the CIP. A census was held on 1 December at which 19,569 people were recorded, including tourists.
2008 Brian Donnelly become high commissioner on 21 February.

Political structure

Constitution

Under the 1965 constitution, New Zealand has responsibility for defence and foreign affairs and the Cook Islands is self-governing with full responsibility for internal affairs. Local affairs are handled by island councils and village committees in the outer islands.

Form of state

Self-governing state in free association with New Zealand.

The executive

Executive power is excised by the prime minister and cabinet, through the High Commissioner (Queen's Representative).

National legislature

The unicameral parliament comprises 25 members (10 representing the main island of Rarotonga, 14 representing constituencies on other islands, and one representing expatriate Cook Islanders), elected by universal suffrage for a four-year term. Parliament chooses a prime minister from among its members, who then appoints a cabinet.
The House of Ariki is a 15-member chamber of hereditary chiefs, which advises on matters of land and issues of tradition.

Last elections

26 September 2006 (parliamentary)
Results: Parliamentary: the DP won 51.9 per cent of the vote (15 of 24 seats), the CIP 45.5 per cent (7), and independents 2.7 per cent (1); one seat was undecided. Turnout was 86.7 per cent. The CIP won the by-election for the seat declared undecided after the general election.

KEY FACTS

Official name: Cook Islands

Head of State: Queen Elizabeth II; represented by High Commissioner Brian Donnelly (from 21 Feb 2008)

Head of government: Prime Minister Jim Marurai (elected 2005, re-elected 2006)

Ruling party: Demo Tumu (DT) (elected 2006)

Area: 234 square km (15 islands); Rarotonga (67 square km)

Population: 21,750 (2007)*

Capital: Avarua, on the island of Rarotonga

Official language: English and Cook Islands Mäori

Currency: New Zealand dollar (NZ$) = 100 cents; Cook Islands' own currency is defunct

Exchange rate: NZ$1.45 per US$ (Jan 2007)

GDP per capita: US$10,137 (2006)

GDP real growth: 2.50% (2007)

Labour force: 6,820 (2001)

Inflation: 2.10% (2005)

Balance of trade: -US$78.84 million (2005)

Visitor numbers: 92,082 (2006)

* estimated figure

Next elections
2009 (parliamentary)

Political parties
Ruling party
Demo Tumu (DT) (elected 2006)
Main opposition party
Cook Islands Party
Political situation
At a time when the Cook Islands were looking outward for investment good news came in December 2007 when the US credit rating service Standard and Poors' (S&P) raised its foreign and local currency rating from BB- to BB, based on the improvement in the Cook Islands' fiscal position and reduction in debt. The outlook for the country fell though, from positive to stable and days later the Asian Development Bank (ADB) re-classified the Cook Islands' borrowing rating to C. The government were understandably dismayed as from 2008 the Cook Islands will no longer by eligible for soft ADB loans at 2 per cent per annum and must pay the commercial rate of 12 per cent. The finance minister urged a reconsideration, claiming that the strengthening GDP is not reflected throughout the islands and much of the infrastructure and development plans are predicated on low loans. S&P had warned that infrastructure shortcomings would limit growth and raise the cost of investment. However, the B rating for short-term ratings for the Cook Islands remained the same.

Population
21,750 (2007)*
Last census: November/December 2006: 19,569
Population density: According to the 2006 census, some 14,148 people live on Rarotonga, 4,031 on the rest of the Southern Group and just 1,389 on the six Northern Group islands.
Annual growth rate: 8.6 per cent 2001–06 (2006 census)
Ethnic make-up
Polynesian (81 per cent), Polynesian and European mixed (8 per cent), Polynesian and non-European mixed (8 per cent), European 2 per cent.
Religions
The majority are Cook Islands Christian Church (70 per cent), although Roman Catholics, Latter Day Saints, Seventh-Day Adventists and Assembly of God are also represented.

Health
Per capita total expenditure on health (2003) was US$425; of which per capita government spending was US$373, at the international dollar rate, (WHO 2006).
Life expectancy: 72 years, 2004 (WHO 2006)
Fertility rate/Maternal mortality rate: 2.6 births per woman, 2004 (WHO 2006)
Child (under 5 years) mortality rate (per 1,000): 21 per 1,000 live births
Head of population per physician: 0.78 physicians per 1,000 people, 2001 (WHO 2006)

Main cities
Avarua, on the island of Rarotonga (capital, estimated population 10,500 in 2003).

Languages spoken
Rarotongan is spoken on Rarotonga; Pukapuka and Nassau both have their own quite different languages, while other islands have differing versions of Cook Islands Mäori. Most of the islanders also speak English.
Official language/s
English and Cook Islands Mäori

Media
Elijah Communications (EC) owns and operates radio and television stations and publishes a newspaper.
Other news agencies: ABC Pacific Beat: www.radioaustralia.net.au/pacbeat
Pacific Magazine:
www.pacificmagazine.net
Press
Dailies: EC publishes the Herald (www.ciherald.co.ck), while the News (www.cookislandsnews.com) is another independent newspaper and both are weeklies.
Broadcasting
Radio: There are two radio stations with services that are broadcast in English and Mäori. The EC-owned Radio Cook Islands has a network that includes AM, FM and Internet streaming for coverage throughout the islands. It also operates HITZ 101.1 aimed at a young audience. Radio Ikurangi is also a private station.
Television: The EC-owned Cook Islands Television broadcasts for up to 18 hours per day. Services are provided via satellite and include not only domestic programmes but also some broadcast from New Zealand.

Economy
The economy is based mainly on tourism, although subsistence agriculture and fishing continue to be important activities. Remittances from migrant workers, aid from New Zealand and Australia, sales of postage stamps and export of agricultural produce also have significant roles in the economy. The pearl industry based on the islands of Manihiki and Penrhyn is growing in importance. There has been a shift to paid labour and small businesses on the southern atolls, although many still work their own plantations. A significant offshore banking business has developed; regulations have been revised and a Financial Supervisory Commission established, allowing for further improvements to be implemented. The sale of fishing licences to foreign fleets is a key revenue earner.
Major projects include expansion of the electricity system, solarisation in the Northern Group Islands, and improvements to telecommunications and the harbour and shipping services.
The government has problems in maintaining basic health and education services on the outer islands, due to continued migration of skilled workers to New Zealand.

Labour market and unemployment
The government has been the main source of paid work. The Public Service Association has the largest membership of worker associations and is influential. Other unions are relatively small (Cook Islands Industrial Union of Waterside Workers and the Airport Workers' Union). During 2004/05, poor job opportunities and the high cost of living continued to push young Cook Islanders out of the country. While foreign workers entered to take up promised employment, overall the local population declined in number, primarily due to lack of employment.

External trade
The Cook Islands is a member of the South Pacific Regional Trade and Economic Co-operation Agreement (Sparteca) along with 12 other regional nations, which allows products duty free access by Pacific Island Forum (PIF) (which includes the Cook Islands) members to Australian and New Zealand markets (subject to the country of origin restrictions).
In March 2006, the PIF published a strategy for trade promotion among member states under the Economic Partnership Agreement (EPA).
The Cook Islands suffer from an adverse balance of trade, particularly with New Zealand, with which it maintains a free trade agreement and free movement of workers.
Imports
Principal imports are manufactured goods, foodstuffs, textiles, fuels, timber, capital goods and live animals.
Main sources: New Zealand (68.7 per cent total, 2006), Fiji (16.7 per cent), Australia (5.2 per cent).
Exports
Principal exports are predominantly black pearls, copra, papayas, fresh and canned citrus fruit, fish, and pearl shells and clothing manufacture.
Main destinations: Japan (34.7 per cent total, 2006), New Zealand (29.3 per cent), Australia.

Agriculture

Farming

The rich volcanic soil on the southern islands helps subsistence farming cater for local consumption.

Crop production in 2005 included: 1,250 tonnes (t) cassava, 650t papayas, 250t mangoes, 550t sweet potatoes, 240t oilcrops, 86t citrus fruit, 250t tomatoes, 50t bananas, 1,850t coconuts, 1,466t fruit in total and 1,301t vegetables in total. Estimated livestock production included 569t meat in total, with 2t beef, 2t goat meat, 550t pig meat, 14t poultry meat and 25t eggs and 1t honey.

Fishing

Long-line fishing of tuna and billfish catches are most often exported to either American Samoa or Japan. The problems of the Cook Islands' huge fishery exclusive economic zone includes the continued attraction of illegal operators, too little data on migratory fish stock and the high cost of its operation. In order to develop the domestic fishing industry, the government introduced exemption on levies for fuel, bait and equipment, but labour shortages are a constant constraint. Since 2000 the number of licences issued for fishing has dropped from 60 to less than 20 boats and New Zealand has been approached for assistance.

Pearl farming used to be the second-largest income earner, after tourism. In 2000 the black pearl fishing industry was hit hard by disease, due to overcrowding in the main producing lagoon, and the growth in good quality cultivated pearls for China. Commercial fishing now generates three times as much export income as pearl production. The bases for pearl fishing are the northern group atolls Manihiki, Penrhyn and Rakahanga.

Industry and manufacturing

The Cook Islands economy earns around US$4.5 million per annum from its pearl industry. The other main secondary industries include agricultural exports, clothing manufacture, fruit canning/processing, electronic component assembly and handicrafts.

Tourism

Tourism is the main source of income, accounting for around 40 per cent of GDP in 2005 and providing a third of local jobs. The sector has not been helped by poor marketing and a general lack of resources and funds. However, future arrivals are expected to increase yearly by four per cent.

The sector continues to be the main element in economic growth, with the Islands receiving more visitors pre capita than any other South Pacific destination. However the government is interested in re-developing the industry away from 'sun and sand' holidays to value added geotourism, 'that sustains or enhances the geographical character of a place – its environment, culture, aesthetics, heritage, and well-being of its residents'.

The islands have quintessential tropical beaches with soft white-sand, fringed with coconut palms and beautifully clear waters.

The largest number of visitors are from New Zealand, with around 45 per cent share followed by Europe with 25 per cent and Australia with 14 per cent.

Virgin Blue, a subsidiary of UK based Virgin Airlines, allow passengers to join their low-cost flights en route to and from Christchurch, New Zealand. Routes from Australia to Rarotonga are also available.

Mining

The Japanese government's Metal Mining Agency has discovered significant reserves of manganese in nodules on the seabed in Cook Islands territorial waters. New techniques are being developed to exploit this resource.

Hydrocarbons

There are no oil, gas or coal reserves. The Islands rely entirely on the import of refined oil, importing 390 barrels per day of jet fuel, distillate and gasoline.

Banking and insurance

Legislation to enable Cook Islands' development as an offshore financial centre and tax haven was enacted in 1981/82. Since 2001, when the Cook Islands was among nine countries listed by the OECD as havens for money laundering, offshore banking regulations have been revised and the Financial Supervisory Commission established in 2003 to license and regulate all trustee companies both domestic and international.

In February 2005, the Cook Islands came off the list of non-co-operative countries and territories of the OECD Financial Action Task Force (FATF).

There have been limited attempts to consolidate the banking sector, with 16 licensed banks in operation.

Main financial centre

Avarua (on Rarotonga).

Offshore facilities

The offshore financial industry provides 8 per cent of GDP.

Time

GMT minus ten hours.

Geography

The Cook Islands comprise 13 inhabited and two uninhabited islands located in the southern Pacific Ocean, between American Samoa to the west and French Polynesia to the east. The islands are spread over about two million square km (more than 750,000 square miles) of ocean, and form two groups – the Northern Group of the six atolls of Nassau, Pukapuka, Rakahanga, Penrhyn, Suwarrow and Manihiki, and the more populous Southern Group which includes Rarotonga, Aitutaki, Mangaia, Palmerston, and Takutea, all volcanic islands.

Rising sea levels as a result of global climate change are a potential threat to the low-lying islands.

Hemisphere

Southern

Climate

Damp and tropical, mild from Apr–Nov but Dec–Mar hot and humid, with likelihood of hurricanes. The mean temperature is 24 degrees Celsius, with average yearly rainfall over 2,000mm; heaviest on the forested volcanic slopes of the southern islands.

Entry requirements

Passports

Required by all, valid for six months beyond initial visa-free 31 days.

Proof of onward passage, adequate funds and suitable booked accommodation are also required.

Visa

For tourist purposes, visas are not required for stays of up to 31 days. Monthly extensions can be arranged up to a maximum of five months.

Currency advice/regulations

No restrictions on import of local and foreign currency. Export of local currency is limited to NZ$250 and of foreign currency to amount declared on arrival. .

Customs

Incoming passengers are permitted to bring in a maximum of 200 cigarettes, 1kg of tobacco or 50 cigars and two litres of wine or spirits or 4.5 litres of beer.

Health (for visitors)

Mandatory precautions

None.

Advisable precautions

Vaccinations for diphtheria, tuberculosis, hepatitis A and B, polio, tetanus and typhoid are recommended.

The World Health Organisation has warned of a high risk of catching dengue fever.

Hotels

A 10 per cent Government Turnover Tax applies. Tipping is not customary.

Credit cards

Visa and Mastercard are accepted.

Public holidays (national)

Fixed dates

1 Jan (New Year's Day), 25 Apr (Anzac Day), 25 Jul (Gospel Day, Rarotonga), 4 Aug (Constitution Day), 27 Oct (Gospel

Day), 25 Dec (Christmas Day), 26 Dec (Boxing Day).

Variable dates

Good Friday, Easter Monday, Queen's Official Birthday (first Mon in Jun).

Working hours

Banking

Mon–Thur: 0900–1500; Fri: 0900–1100.

Business

Mon–Fri: 0800–1600.

Government

Mon–Fri: 0800–1600.

Shops

Mon–Fri: 0900–1600; Sat: 0900–1200.

Telecommunications

Telephone/fax

There are automatic telephone exchanges in Rarotonga and Aitutaki. International telecommunications are via Cable and Wireless and Peacesat satellite links.

Electricity supply

240V DC/50 cycle.

Social customs/useful tips

Bargaining is discouraged. Gratuities are not customary, as tradition requires that something is then given in return.

Dress: Brief attire (eg bikinis) should not be worn in towns or villages. Nude or topless sunbathing will cause offence.

Getting there

Air

There are limited services from Hawaii via American Samoa and Auckland, plus a weekly flight from Christchurch, New Zealand.

International airport/s: Rarotonga (RAR), three kilometres west of Avarua. Restaurants, duty-free shop, shops, car rental. Hotel coaches meet each flight and taxis and buses are also available.

Airport tax: Adults NZ$30; children three-12 years old NZ$15.

Surface

Water: Inter-island shipping services are provided by major passenger carrying cargo lines, operators include Express Cook Islands Line Shipping Ltd and Hawaii-Pacific Maritime Ltd.

Main port/s: Avatiu (on Rarotonga), and Aitutaki. Penrhyn Island (northern Cook Islands) is also a Port of Entry.

Getting about

National transport

Air: Air Rarotonga operates inter-island services. Airstrips for small planes on Aitutaki, Penryhn, Rakahanga, Mitiaro, Atiu, Mauke, Mangala and Manitiki. Services do not operate on Sunday.

Road: The Ara Tapu surfaced road runs 32km around Rarotonga coast. There is also an older inland road, which winds cross-country.

Buses: The Island Bus (yellow buses) – a round-the-island service in both directions (Mon–Fri 0700–1600; Sat 0800–1300).

Taxis: Taxi service is available on Rarotonga.

Water: There are harbours on Aitutaki, Atiu, Penrhyn and Suwarrow.

Car hire

Car, scooter and bicycle hire are available on Rarotonga and Aitutaki. Driving is on the left.

A local licence is required; they can be obtained from the police station on Avarua, on presentation of an international or Commonwealth national driving licence.

BUSINESS DIRECTORY

The addresses listed below are a selection only. While World of Information makes every endeavour to check these addresses, we cannot guarantee that changes have not been made, especially to telephone numbers and area codes. We would welcome any corrections.

Telephone area codes

The international direct dialling (IDD) for Cook Islands is +682 followed by subscriber's number.

Useful telephone numbers

Police: 999

Fire: 996

Ambulance: 998

Chambers of Commerce

Cook Islands Chamber of Commerce PO Box 242, Avarua, Rarotonga (tel: 20-925; fax: 20-969).

Banking

Bank of the Cook Islands, PO Box 113, Rarotonga (tel: 29-341; fax: 29-343).

Wall Street Banking Corporation Ltd, PO Box 3012, CITC House, Avarua (tel: 23-445; fax: 23-446; e-mail: info@wallbank.co.ck).

Westpac Banking Corporation, PO Box 42, Rarotonga (tel: 22-014; fax: 20-014).

Travel information

Air Rarotonga (tel: 22-888; e-mail: bookings@airraro.co.ck; internet site: http://www.airraro.com).

Flight information (24 hours) (tel: 25-890).

Government Information Office, PO Box 106 (tel: 29-304; fax: 20-856).

Principal Immigration Officer, Ministry of Foreign Affairs and Immigration, PO Box 105, Rarotonga (tel: 29-347; fax: 21-247).

Rarotonga International Airport, PO Box 90, Rarotonga (tel: 25-890; fax: 21-890; e-mail: aaci@airport.gov.ck).

National tourist organisation offices

Cook Islands Tourism Corporation, PO Box 14, Avarua, Rarotonga (tel: 29-435; fax: 21-435; e-mail: headoffice@cook-islands.com).

Other useful addresses

Asian Development Bank (ADB), South Pacific Regional Mission, La Casa di Andrea, Fr. Dr. W. H. Lini Highway; PO Box 127, Port Vila (tel: +678 2 23-300; fax: +678 2 23-183; email: adbsprm@adb.org; internet: http://www.adb.org/SPRM).

Cook Islands Development Investment Board, Rarotonga (tel: 24-296; fax: 24-298; e-mail: cidib@oyster.net.ck; internet site: http://www.cookislands-invest.com).

Cook Islands Investment Corporation, Rarotonga (tel: 29-391; fax: 29-381; e-mail: ciic@oyster.net.ck).

Cook Islands News, PO Box 15, Rarotonga (tel: 22-999; fax: 25-303; e-mail: editor@cookislandsnews.com; internet site: http:/www.cinews.co.ck).

Other news agencies: ABC Pacific Beat: www.radioaustralia.net.au/pacbeat

Pacific Magazine: www.pacificmagazine.net

Internet sites

Yellow pages: www.yellowpages.co.ck

Cook Islands government: www.cook-islands.gov.ck

Cook Islands News: www.cinews.co.ck

Cook Islands shipping movements: www.ck/shipping.htm

Cook Islands website: www.ck

Tourism Council of the South Pacific: www.tcsp.com

Costa Rica

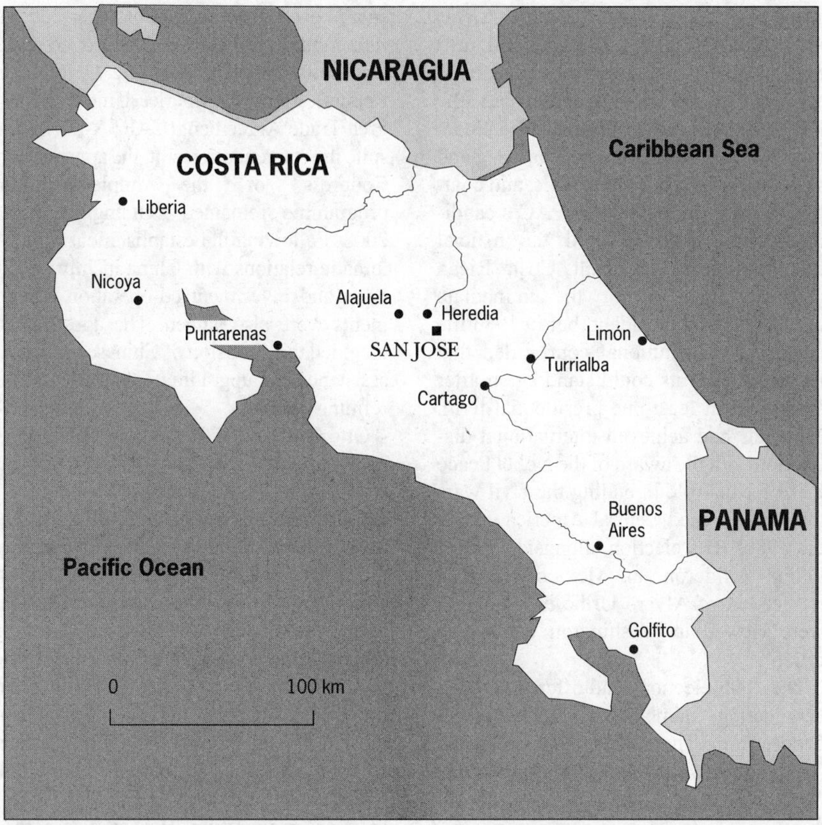

KEY FACTS

Official name: República de Costa Rica (Republic of Costa Rica)

Head of State: President Óscar Arias Sánchez (PLN) (since 8 May 2006)

Head of government: President Arias (from 8 May 2006)

Ruling party: Partido Liberación Nacional (PLN) (National Liberation Party) (from May 2006)

Area: 51,060 square km

Population: 4.44 million (2007)

Capital: San José

Official language: Spanish

Currency: Colón (CC) = 100 céntimos

Exchange rate: CC550.60 per US$ (Jul 2008)

GDP per capita: US$5,905 (2007)*

GDP real growth: 6.80% (2007)

Labour force: 1.67 million (2004)

Unemployment: 6.60% (2005)

Inflation: 9.40% (2007)

Balance of trade: -US$3.31 billion (2006)

Foreign debt: US$5.96 billion (2004)

Visitor numbers: 1.73 million (2006)*

* estimated figure

Costa Rica's economic policies are generally considered to be sound. The International Monetary Fund (IMF), World Bank and the United Nations Economic Commission for Latin America and the Caribbean (ECLAC) broadly concur that strong business and consumer confidence, falling interest rates and rapid growth in the construction sector have contributed to something of a domestic boom which has risked overheating the economy. Gross domestic product (GDP) growth slowed from 8.2 per cent in 2006 to 7.0 per cent in 2007, above expectations for the third consecutive year. The IMF notes that rising real incomes and 'well targeted social transfers' led to a fall in poverty in 2007.

Steady as she goes

ECLAC forecasts GDP growth of 6 per cent for 2008. ECLAC appears to have revised its forecast for 2008 inflation upwards from 7 per cent to 10 per cent, the figure it was edging towards by the end of the year, in view of rising oil prices and excess demand 'especially in the private sector'. This inflation figure is very much in line with the 9.4 per cent registered for both 2006 and 2007. It was expected that the continued inflationary pressures would result in interest rate rises. Investment and private consumption have accelerated, with the IMF recording consumer goods imports growing at an annual rate of 26 per cent by October 2007. Unemployment in 2007 dropped to 4.6 per cent, its lowest level since 1994.

Despite the dramatic rise in oil prices, Costa Rica's export growth resulted in the trade deficit narrowing in 2007. Foreign direct investment (FDI) grew by 7 per cent in 2007, boosted by continued investment in real estate and in the tourism sector. Tax revenues have also registered growth of 24 per cent in 2006 and 2007, allowing the central government deficit to drop to its lowest level for over a decade. Public debt dropped from 56 per cent of GDP in 2005 to an estimated 45 per cent of GDP at the end of 2007.

Political panorama

In recent decades Costa Rica has emerged as a fully developed democratic polity with a healthy respect for human rights. In sharp contrast to many of its Central American neighbours the country – which has no national army – has fostered strong democratic institutions and devised an orderly constitutional process for governmental succession. Historically, the political scene has been dominated by the governing Partido Unidad Social Cristiana (PUSC) (Social Christian Unity Party) and the Partido Liberación Nacional (PLN) (National Liberation Party), both broadly of the centre-right.

However, just fourteen months after its founding, a new party, the Partido Acción Ciudadana (PAC) (Citizen's Action Party) ruffled the feathers of the political establishment when it's economist candidate, Ottón Solnís, ran a strong campaign for president in 2002. Other parties include the Partido Movimiento Libertario (ML) (Libertarian Movement Party) and smaller political organisations such as the Partido Renovación Costarricense (PRC) and Fuerza Democrática (FD). The Partido Unión para el Cambio (PUC) (Union for Change Party) along with other minor parties, contested the February 2006 presidential elections for the first time.

Arias and the also rans

In a close run result, 65 year old Oscar Arias who had served as president from 1986 to 1990 won the February 2006 presidential election, some 20 years after last holding the same office. The outcome had been forecast by Costa Rica's opinion polls, but the winning margin of just over 18,000 votes of the 1.6 million cast was lower than anticipated. The electoral turnout was 64 per cent, high by North American and European standards, but the lowest in Costa Rican history. The closeness of the result meant that a hand re-count had to take place. This, and challenges from the opposition PAC's candidate Ottón Solís delayed the official confirmation of the result. Costa Rican law does not permit the immediate re-election of a president, but in 1983 the country's constitutional court ruled that former presidents could stand again after sitting out at least one presidential term. Mr Arias had achieved international distinction with the award of the Nobel Peace Prize for his role in ending the civil wars that had plagued Central America during the 1980s. His election, alongside that of Felipe Calderón in Mexico and the re-election of Álvaro Uribe in Colombia were viewed in Washington with some relief.

The 2006 elections had offered voters a bewildering number of candidates to choose from, The PAC's Ottón Solís, had ran strongly as the third party candidate in 2002, had contested the presidency again. He was expected to garner some support for his anti-Central American Free Trade Agreement (Cafta) stance, having stated his belief that the proposed free trade agreement would be disadvantageous for Costa Rica: 'I never imagined Cafta was going to be so one sided... the law of the jungle benefits the big beast. We are a very small beast'. However, in October 2007 a referendum was held which approved what was now snappily called the Dominican Republic-Central America-United States Free Trade Agreement (CAFTA-DR). Despite the referendum result, the approval by Congress of the implementation programme remained pending in June 2008. Following the establishment of diplomatic relations with China in July 2007, trade and investment co-operation agreements were also signed. The agreements included the provision of Chinese technical assistance for upgrading Costa Rica's oil refining facilities.

Otto Guevara Guth of ML, a libertarian, had advocated a slashing of government expenditure. Throughout 2005 he had also emphasised his belief that Costa Rica should play a more active role in making the case for political liberty in the Central American and Caribbean region. He had long been a vehement critic of Castro's authoritarian rule in Cuba and had attacked other Latin American politicians for not vocally opposing authoritarianism throughout the region. Antonio Álvarez was the confirmed candidate of the UPC and had adopted a hard line on illegal Nicaraguan immigration. He had also advocated harsher penalties for employers of illegal immigrants, suggesting that many Nicaraguans were being unfairly exploited for cheap labour by Costa Rican landowners.

Ricardo Toledo, a close personal friend of President Pacheco, was nominated by the PUSC. He is an experienced politician having held many prominent positions within his party. President Arías was known for his role in securing the Esquipulas Peace Agreement during the 1980s, for which he received the Nobel Peace Prize. After receiving the prestigious award in 1987 he established a human rights advocacy group which has worked toward resolving conflicts throughout the Americas.

Outlook

Costa Rica has one of the most stable democracies in Latin America with a fully competitive party system. The country's political elite continues to be a leading

KEY INDICATORS — Costa Rica

	Unit	2003	2004	2005	2006	2007
Population	m	4.13	4.27	4.33	4.35	4.44
Gross domestic product (GDP)	US$bn	16.54	18.59	19.94	22.52	26.24
GDP per capita	US$	4,002	4,361	4,609	5,173	5,905
GDP real growth	%	3.0	4.2	5.9	8.8	6.8
Inflation	%	9.7	12.3	13.8	11.5	9.4
Unemployment	%	6.7	6.6	6.6	*6.6	*4.6
Industrial output	% change	–	3.0	3.0	11.0	–
Agricultural output	% change	–	0.8	2.5	10.8	–
Exports (fob) (goods)	US$m	6,029.0	6,184.0	7,099.6	8,238.0	9,267.8
Imports (cif) (goods)	US$m	7,700.0	7,842.0	9,230.3	11,547.0	12,255.4
Balance of trade	US$m	-1,671.0	-1,658.0	2,130.7	-3,309.0	-2,987.6
Current account	US$m	-930.0	-890.0	-957.0	-1,108.0	-1,519.0
Total reserves minus gold	US$m	1,836.3	1,917.9	2,312.7	3,114.6	4,113.6
Foreign exchange	US$m	1,806.5	1,886.7	2,284.0	3,084.4	4,081.9
Exchange rate	per US$	398.67	439.08	517.94	517.94	498.86

* estimated figure

advocate for human rights throughout the Central American and Caribbean region. With the economy under-performing, the first task for the country's new president has been a reduction in the rate of inflation, followed by the continued implementation of market reforms. Although no longer a young man, President Arías brings a wealth of administrative experience to the post, although through 2007 his determination to rid the economy of chronic inflationary pressures and other inbuilt imbalance continued to come up against parliamentary opposition.

Risk assessment

Economy	Good
Politics	Good
Regional stability	Good

COUNTRY PROFILE

Historical profile

1502 Christopher Columbus visited the region, naming it Costa Rica (Rich Coast).
1561 Colonisation of Costa Rica began. The country became a dependency of Nicaragua within the kingdom of Guatemala in the vice-royalty of Mexico, then known as Nuevo España (New Spain).
1808 Coffee was introduced into Costa Rica and became the country's main crop.
1821 The Central American provinces (Costa Rica, Guatemala, Honduras, Nicaragua and El Salvador) declared independence from Spain.
1822 Central American confederation annexed itself to the Mexican Empire, under General Agustín de Iturbde, later Emperor Agustín I.
1823 Agustín I was overthrown and Mexico became a republic. The Central American states formed the United Provinces of Central America.
1825 Costa Rica, Guatemala, Honduras, Nicaragua and El Salvador formed the Central American Federation (CAF).
1838 The CAF was dissolved and Costa Rica became a fully independent republic.
1849 Under the leadership of Juan Rafael Mora, Costa Rica helped organise Central American resistance against William Walker, the US bucaneer who took over Nicaragua.
1859 A coup d'état saw Mora lose power.
1870 Costa Rican leader, Tomás Guardía, began a process of development, encouraging foreign investment in the rail system.
1874 The United Fruit Company began operations in Costa Rica.
1889 The country embraced democracy and Bernardo Soto was elected as the country's first president.
1940 President Rafael Angel Calderón Guardía, founder of the Partido Unidad Social Christiana (PUSC) (Social Christian Unity Party), introduced social reforms, including labour rights and a minimum wage.
1948 The result of the presidential election was annulled after the government's candidate, Rafael Calderón, who came second, refused to accept defeat. An opposition leader, José Figueres Ferrer, led a revolt in favour of the winning candidate, Otilio Ulate. An interim regime was set up, the constitution was changed, the army was abolished and Otilio Ulate became president.
1953 José Figueres Ferrer, a democratic socialist and leader of the Partido Liberación Nacional (PLN) (National Liberation Party), won the election. He began to effect social reforms with the help of the reformist bishop of San José and a communist union leader, remaining president until 1958.
1982 Luis Alberto Monge (PLN) was elected president. He introduced a programme of austerity measures designed to stabilise the deteriorating economy.
1986 Oscar Arías Sánchez (PLN) was elected president and began brokering a peace plan with the leaders of Nicaragua, El Salvador, Guatemala and Honduras to end regional political turbulence and civil war.
1987 Arías won the Nobel Peace Prize for securing a regional peace deal.
1990 Rafael Angel Calderón Fournier of the PUSC was elected president and enacted a series of austerity measures.
1994 José María Figueres (PLN) won the presidential election.
1998 Miguel Angel Rodríguez of the PUSC was elected president.
2000 Costa Rica and Nicaragua reached an agreement to end a dispute over navigation along the San Juan river, which serves as the border between the two countries.
2001 Privatisation of Costa Rica's Pacific ports commenced.
2002 The PUSC defeated the PLN in the parliamentary elections. Abel Pacheco de la Espriella (PUSC) won the run-off election and became president.
2003 Strikes were held by energy and telecommunications workers over President Pacheco's privatisation plans for the sector and by primary and secondary school teachers over problems in paying their salaries. The strikes led to the resignations of three ministers.
2004 Three former presidents – José María Figueres, Miguel Angel Rodríguez and Rafael Angel Calderón – were investigated over allegations of corruption.
2005 A national state of emergency was declared after days of heavy rainfall resulted in severe flooding along the Caribbean coast.
2006 In presidential and parliamentary elections, Oscar Arías Sánchez (PLN) narrowly won, while the PLN comfortably won 25 of the 57 seats in the parliamentary elections.
2007 Costa Rica broke diplomatic ties with Taiwan in June; President Arias said his country needed to attract more investment from China. In a referendum on 7 October, voters narrowly approved the Central American Free Trade Agreement (Cafta) with the US.
2008 The central bank's dollar reserves fell by US$706 million between April–July leaving US$4.23 billion; the bank's base saving rate was raised by 50 points from 6.5–7 per cent over the same period.

Political structure

Constitution

Under the November 1949 constitution, government consists of three branches: legislative, executive and judicial.
In April 2003, the constitutional court annulled a constitutional reform enacted by the Legislative Assembly in 1969, barring presidents from running for re-election; the law reverts to the 1949 constitution, which states that presidents may run for re-election after being out of office for two presidential terms – eight years.
Voting: compulsory over 18 years.

Form of state

Presidential democratic republic

The executive

Executive power is held by the president, elected by popular vote for one four-year term — if a 40 per cent vote for any candidate is not obtained, a second ballot is held. The president is also head of government. The president appoints and is assisted by a 15-member cabinet.

National legislature

The unicameral 57-member Asamblea Legislativa (Legislative Assembly) is elected every four years.

Legal system

The legal system is based on the Spanish civil law system. There are judicial reviews of legislative acts in the Supreme Court. Justices are elected for renewable eight-year terms by the Legislative Assembly. Costa Rica has not accepted compulsory International Court of Justice (ICJ) jurisdiction.

Last elections

5 February 2006 (presidential); February 2006 (parliamentary)
Results: Presidential: Oscar Arías Sánchez won 40.5 per cent of the vote, narrowly beating Ottón Solís with 40.3 per cent. Turnout 65.4 per cent.

Parliamentary: the PLN won 36.4 per cent of the votes (25 seats out of 57); PAC 25.8 per cent of the vote (17); Partido Movimiento Libetario (PML) (Libertarian Movement Party) won 9.1 per cent (6), Partido Unidad Social Cristiana (PUSC) (Social Christian Unity Party) won 7.6 per cent (5); other parties won one seat each. Turnout was 65.1 per cent.

Next elections
February 2010 (presidential and parliamentary)

Political parties

Ruling party
Partido Liberación Nacional (PLN) (National Liberation Party) (from May 2006)

Main opposition party
Partido Acción Ciudadana (PAC) (Citizens' Action Party)

Population

4.44 million (2007)

Last census: June 2000: 3,810,179

Population density: 70 inhabitants per square km. Urban population: 60 per cent of total (1995—2001).

Annual growth rate: 2.3 per cent 1994–2004 (WHO 2006)

Ethnic make-up
The majority of the population, 98 per cent, is white or racially mixed, except in Limón province on the Caribbean coast, where an estimated 70,000 blacks and 5,000 Indians live. The Northern Guanacaste province also has a sizeable Indian population.

Religions
Roman Catholic (approximately 2.33 million followers); Methodist (estimated 6,000 followers); Baptist and Episcopalian.

Education

Education is compulsory at the elementary level, between the ages of six and 13, and is free at both elementary and secondary level. State-owned and private primary and secondary schools are of a high standard and the country has one of the highest literacy rates in Latin America. The adult illiteracy rate is estimated at 4.4 per cent and 4.3 per cent for men and women respectively. World Bank estimates show that the total primary school enrolment of the relevant age group typically stood at 104 per cent for boys and 103 per cent for girls (including repetition rates) between 1994 and 2000.

Costa Ricans are very proud of their education system, with about 12,000 university graduates joining the workforce each year. Costa Rica has 250,000 graduates from higher education per annum and 630,000 graduates from secondary academic schools and around 50,000 graduates of vocational schools.

Public expenditure on education typically amounts to 5–6 per cent of annual gross national income according to UN surveys.

Literacy rate: 96 per cent adult rate; 98 per cent youth rate (15–24) (Unesco 2005).

Pupils per teacher: 29 in primary schools.

Health

Per capita total expenditure on health (2003) was US$616; of which per capita government spending was US$486, at the international dollar rate, (WHO 2006).

It is estimated that 10 per cent of all deaths are caused by prenatal or infectious diseases. Immunisation programmes against measles, diphtheria, polio and tetanus are very successful with between 85 and 95 per cent of all relevant ages being immunised.

Improved water sources and sanitation facilities are available to 98 per cent and 96 per cent of the population, respectively.

The Ministry of Health units operate a preventive health programme in all parts of the country. Most of Costa Rica's health services are supplied by the Caja Costarricense del Seguro Social (CCSS) (Costa Rican Social Security Agency), an independent state institution which operates a national insurance fund.

HIV/Aids

HIV prevalence: 0.6 per cent aged 15–49 in 2003 (World Bank)

Life expectancy: 77 years, 2004 (WHO 2006)

Fertility rate/Maternal mortality rate: 2.2 births per woman, 2004 (WHO 2006); maternal mortality 29 per 100,000 live births (World Bank).

Child (under 5 years) mortality rate (per 1,000): 8 per 1,000 live births; 5 per cent of children aged under five are malnourished (World Bank).

Welfare

The state-owned National Insurance Institute (INS) administers all social security insurance. Wage-earners and their dependants enjoy disability and retirement pensions, workers' compensation and family assistance. A pay-as-you-go system operates alongside voluntary individual accounts which provide second-tier benefits. The pay-as-you-go benefit, financed by employee, employer, and government contributions, is equal to a proportion of adjusted average monthly earnings.

Main cities

San José (capital, estimated population 1.5 million in 2004), Alajuela (791,900), Cartago (475,100), Puntarenas (397,700), Heredia (390,400), Limón (380,200).

Languages spoken
Business is conducted in Spanish, but many executives speak English. French, German and Italian are also spoken.

Official language/s
Spanish

Media

Press
Granma is the official publication of the central committee of the Communist Party of Cuba.

Dailies: In Spanish, major newspapers include La Nación (www.nacion.com), La República (www.larepublica.net), Al Día (www.aldia.co.cr), Diario La Extra (www.diarioextra.com) and La Prensa Libre (www.prensalibre.co.cr), which is an evening publication.

Weeklies: In English, Tico Times is an independent publication.

Business: In Spanish, El Financiero (www.elfinancierocr.com) is a daily, while Actualidad Economica (www.actualidad-e.com) and EKA (www.ekaenlinea.com), with an online version in English, are monthly magazines.

Broadcasting
Radio: There are over 100 commercial radio stations. Radio Nacional (www.sinart.go.cr) is the state broadcaster with cultural, news, information and music programmes. Other national networks include Radio Reloj (www.radioreloj.co.cr) and Radio Colombia (www.columbia.co.cr).

Television: Canal 13 (www.sinart.go.cr) is the national, public TV network. There are another seven national private TV stations offering a wide range of domestic and foreign programmes, including Repretel (www.repretel.com) with channels 4, 6 and 11 and Teletica (www.teletica.com) with channel 7. There has been a strong growth in cable and satellite TV with over a dozen companies offering international programming.

Economy

The economy grew by 5.9 per cent in 2005 and an estimated 8.0 per cent in 2006, making Costa Rica one of the strongest performers in the region, according to the IMF. As the economy was growing steadily over the years since 2003, inflation fell below 10 per cent keeping the current account deficit broadly unchanged as the public sector deficit declined. The last 15 years have seen a marked reduction in the level of poverty – halved since 1990 – as the standard of living has improved and purchasing power parity (PPP) per capita has risen to an estimated US$10,500 in 2006. Although poverty has been reduced, distribution of income has remained unequal.

The Costa Rican economy relies predominantly on a combination of tourism, with services accounting for 62.8 per cent, industry 28.8 per cent, of which manufacturing such as electronic components is 21.1 per cent and agriculture at 8.4 per cent of the economy. There was an average growth rate of 3.0 per cent in all these sectors in 2005.

Foreign investment led the industrial development, initially from the free trade zone operating in Costa Rica since the 1990s, where companies invested in plant and people within the zone to take advantage of favourable tax rates. The country has a well educated population and is situated within easy reach of eastern Atlantic and western Pacific ports of the US. It has attracted investment by top US companies operating manufacturing plants, administrative centres and warehousing facilities. The opening of an Intel Corporation plant was a major boost to the economy, and electrical components soon overtook both bananas and coffee as the country's largest export product.

The tourist industry accounts for around 13 per cent of total GDP and is Costa Rica's largest sector. Eco-tourism is set to rise as visitors experience Costa Rica's well-preserved rain forests, 25 per cent of land is dedicated national parks and reserves. The country received 1,645,470 tourists and a further 315,187 excursionists (visits for less than a day, from cruise ships and neighbouring countries) in 2006, which added US$1.7 billion to the economy.

Costa Rica plans to become a net exporter of electricity as further hydroelectric plants are added to its current dozen that keep the country largely self-sufficient in power.

The Inter-American Development Bank estimated that in 2006 migrant workers sent some US$520 million to their families in Costa Rica.

External trade

Costa Rica has free trade agreements with most countries of Central and North America and has a customs union with members of Mercado Común Centroamericano (MCCA), the common market of Central America.

The diversification of the Costa Rican economy into hi-tech electronic products and healthcare products, which also includes call centres. Agricultural products maintain their importance in trade, with pineapples replacing coffee as the principal export commodity.

Imports

Main imports are industrial raw materials (typically 40 per cent of total), consumer goods, manufacturing equipment and fuel.

Main sources: US (38.3 per cent total, 2006), Mexico (5.2 per cent), Venezuela (5.2 per cent).

Exports

Main exports are pineapples, coffee, bananas, sugar, textiles, electronic components and medical equipment.

Main destinations: US (35.9 per cent total, 2006), The Netherlands (5.1 per cent), Hong Kong (4.7 per cent).

Agriculture

Farming

Costa Rica's agricultural sector is an important contributor to the country's GDP. The sector represents approximately17 per cent of total GDP and employs a fifth of the workforce.

The most important cash crops are coffee, bananas and sugar. A considerable amount of meat, mostly beef, is also exported. The share of traditional agricultural exports declined from 95 per cent of total exports in 1990 to less than 30 per cent by 2004. Bananas account for just over a fifth of Costa Rica's exports. Costa Rica is the world's second-largest banana exporter, representing 12 per cent of the world's banana trade.

Around 10 per cent of the total land is cultivated arable land and 25 per cent is pasture.

Production of cash crops has risen in recent years, but increased exports have tended to be offset by falling prices.

Staple food crops including rice, maize and beans are grown, although Costa Rica is not self-sufficient in these.

Non-traditional products include tropical fruits, ornamental plants and cut flowers.

Estimated crop production in 2005 included 234,342 tonnes (t) cereals in total, 3,945,000 sugar cane, 2,220,000t bananas, 1,110,000t oil palm fruit, 435,000t roots and tubers, 12,200t maize, 222,142t rice, 80,000t potatoes, 725,224t pineapples, 400,920t citrus fruit, 50,000t tomatoes, 126,000t green coffee, 216,590t oilcrops, 708t cocoa beans, 36,000t mangoes, 26,458t papayas, 25,000t avocados, 1,070t chillies and peppers, 300,000t cassava, 3,712,762t fruit in total, 431,939t vegetables in total. Livestock production included: 190,372t meat in total, 68,799t beef, 38,395t pig meat, 83,158t poultry, 50,412t eggs, 790,000t milk, 1,270t honey, 10,450t cattle hides.

Fishing

industry has the potential for positive growth. However, the industry has suffered from a lack of organisation and infrastructure over the years.

The majority of the fishing industry is concentrated on the Pacific coastline. Shrimp fishing has decreased due to overfishing, but the potential for tuna, shark and sardine fishing has remained largely untapped due to a lack of investment in modern canning factories.

In a typical year the annual fish catch is 35,003mt, including 19,838mt marine fish and 6,341mt shellfish.

Forestry

Approximately 25 per cent of Costa Rica's total landmass is forested. Significant variations in elevation and topography have led to the development of a wide array of vegetative zones ranging from coastal mangroves to sub-alpine paramó. The predominant forests of Costa Rica can be broadly classified according to elevation and precipitation. The most extensive are lowland humid tropical forests in the south-east of the country and on the Peninsula de Osa. Common species are guacimo colorado (Luehea seemanii) and laurel (Cordia alliodora). Dry tropical forests are characteristic of the Guanacaste province in the north-west. The most extensive montane forests occur in the Cordillera de Talamanca mountain range in the south. Quercus are the most common trees at higher elevations. Costa Rica has an extensive network of protected areas with more than 25 per cent of the country´s land area protected as forest reserves, national parks, and reservations for indigenous peoples.

Costa Rica produces a moderate amount of roundwood, three-quarters of which is used as fuel. The majority of industrial roundwood is used for sawn timber, but Costa Rica also has small wood-based panels and paper industries. Most pulp and paper is imported.

Industry and manufacturing

The Costa Rican industrial sector contributes approximately 23 per cent to the country's total GDP. The sector is also responsible for 24 per cent of Costa Rica's total level of employment.

The manufacturing sector alone contributes 18 per cent to GDP and is concentrated on export-oriented processing of agricultural products and electronic components. Costa Rica's manufacturing sector is divided into small- and medium-sized companies producing among other things shoes, packing materials, glass and leather goods, and larger companies involved in producing beer, cement, paper, textiles and palm oil.

There is also a growing number of companies involved in the processing of fish, fruit and meat. Other important industries are petroleum refining and pulp/paper processing.

There are industrial free zones (Zonas Francas), where incentives apply, at Puerto Limón, Puntarenas and Cartago.

The government's promotion of the manufacturing sector, with investment

incentives and tax holidays, has largely been curtailed in the name of fiscal discipline.
Costa Rica has one of the lowest unit costs among developing countries for the creation of new jobs.

Tourism
Travel and tourism is one of Costa Rica's most significant economic sectors and now accounts for 13.7 per cent of total GDP. Employment is predicted to rise by 8.3 per cent in 2005 and now constitutes 13.3 per cent of total employment in Costa Rica.
Eco-tourism and resorts, coupled with the country's stability, are the main attractions. The sector doubled in size during the nineties, passing the million visitors mark by 1999, and is projected to double again by 2012. In 2001, despite the 11 September terrorist attacks in the US, tourist arrivals numbered a record 1,132,000, but the effects were felt the following year when the number fell to 1,113,000. The US, together with Canada, is the main market, followed by Europe.

Environment
Since the 1960s and 1970s, the Costa Rican authorities have been increasingly anxious to protect the environment.
By 2001, over a quarter of the total land area was protected. There has also been a great deal of success in protecting valuable natural resources in a sustainable way, while at the same time promoting a growing eco-tourism sector.

Mining
The mining sector in Costa Rica is not a substantial contributor to total GDP. However, Costa Rica does have substantial deposits of various precious metals and the industry is notable for the activity of Canadian firms in the country. In October 2005 two of the largest Canadian corporations operating in Costa Rica announced positive news. Glencairn announced that the Bellavista mine, which it operates, was nearing completion, while Vannessa Ventures Ltd announced the go-ahead of its Las Crucitas Project.
Gold and silver are mined in the western part of Costa Rica. Deposits of manganese, nickel, mercury and sulphur are largely unused. Petroleum deposits are found in the south, but not exploited. Salt is produced from seawater. Large gold deposits in Costa Rica are found near the border with Nicaragua, although estimates vary wildly on the level of reserves. The government is reluctant to explore other reserves found in national parks in the Peninsula de Osa region, due to the environmental impact.
Deposits of manganese, bauxite, aluminium, zinc, copper and sulphur exist in Costa Rica, although their quantity and potential for commercial mining is unknown. Discovery of a valuable bauxite deposit in Boruca area prompted large-scale investment in an aluminium smelting plant. Commercial deposits of iron ore may also be present.

Hydrocarbons
Costa Rica is thought to possess considerable oil reserves. However, exploration and exploitation of these potential reserves has so far proved illusive as the process has proved too costly. Foreigners are permitted to undertake exploration exercises but have been met by environmental protesters on several occasions.
Costa Rica imports its oil from Venezuela and Mexico and the state-run oil monopoly Refinadora Costarricense de Petróleo (Recope) refines it at Moin on the Caribbean coast.
Costa Rica produces neither natural gas nor coal. The country imports approximately 54,000 tonnes of coal each year.

Energy
The majority of Costa Ricans, approximately 80 per cent, have access to electricity. Hydroelectricity is responsible for 90 per cent of total electricity generated and Costa Rica is considered to have huge potential for further hydroelectric generation. Other energy sources include geothermal power and wind generation.
The government estimates that the electricity sector requires over US$10 billion in investment between 2001—2011 in order to satisfy demand, which is forecast to grow by 6 per cent annually up to 2020.
The government hopes to build 29 hydroelectric power plants by 2020.
Following the establishment of diplomatic relations with China in July 2007, trade and investment co-operation agreements were also signed. The agreements included the provision of Chinese technical assistance for upgrading Costa Rica's oil refining facilities.
Instituto Costarricense de Electricidad (ICE), the state power monopoly, is undergoing restructuring to make it profitable, although privatisation remains highly unpopular.

Financial markets
Stock exchange
The main stock exchange in Costa Rica, the Bolsa Nacional de Valores (BNV), was established in 1976. Most transactions are in finance ministry debt and central bank monetary stabilisation bonds. The stock market index is the ALDESA and all shares are traded electronically. There is another exchange, the Bolsa Electrónica de Valores de Costa Rica (BEVCR), which trades in the same amount of paper and shares. There is an agricultural commodities exchange, set up in 1990 and trading in coffee, maize, potatoes and timber.

Banking and insurance
Costa Rica's financial services sector is composed of the Central Bank, three state-owned commercial banking houses, nineteen private commercial banks (including one jointly owned state bank), one workers' bank, one state-owned mortgage bank and four mutual house-building companies. There are also 15 private finance companies, 27 savings and loans co-operatives and 30 investment and retirement funds/trusts.
Both local and international companies have looked to raise capital abroad because of the poor service and high costs offered by the state banks in Costa Rica. Some of the larger private banks have capitalised on this by offering a wide range of international services and financing in dollars through offshore banks affiliated to them. However, reforms introduced under the administration of Manuel Angel Rodríguez (1998–2002) introduced regulations for the interbank market and for offshore banking operations and made the banking sector more flexible.
By opening up the financial sector to both domestic and foreign investors, Costa Rica is going down the same path as other Latin American countries which have secured economic stability by having a foreign presence in the financial sector.
The last few years have seen a number of joint ventures and takeovers by both domestic and foreign banking groups. The banks with the most presence in Costa Rica's banking system include Citibank, Banco de la Industria, Bancrecén, Banco de San José, Banco del Pacifíco, Banca Promérica and Scotiabank.
There is also a sizable offshore banking service with the financial services sector.
In recent years the Costa Rican authorities have co-operated with international agencies in order to guard against money laundering.

Central bank
Banco Central de Costa Rica

Main financial centre
San José

Time
GMT minus six hours

Geography
Costa Rica is the second smallest country in Central America after El Salvador. The country lies between Nicaragua and Panama and has coastlines on the Caribbean Sea and the Pacific Ocean. A low, thin line of hills between Lake Nicaragua and the Pacific extends into northern Costa Rica, broadening and rising into high and

rugged mountains in the centre and south. The capital city, San José, lies in the Meseta central basin set in these highlands.
Both coasts have lowland areas. The sparsely inhabited east coast has a narrow swamp strip and tropical forests as the terrain rises inland. The Pacific coast has two peninsulas: the mountainous Nicoya peninsula in the north and the lowland Osa peninsula in the south. A rich lowland savannah patched by deciduous forests stretches along the Pacific coast between the two peninsulas.

Hemisphere
Northern

Climate
Costa Rica's weather is influenced by altitude. The Pacific coast is drier while the Caribbean coast has the most rainfall – about 300 days a year. It is hot and humid in lowland coastal areas; temperate and warm in central highlands. The dry season is December–May; the rainy season runs from June–November. The temperature in San José ranges from a high of 24–27 degrees Celsius (C) to a low of 14–16 degrees C. The hottest months are March and April.

Dress codes
Formal dress is required for business engagements. Shorts, especially for women, are for the beach and should not be worn in restaurants or at parties. Women can wear trousers. Strapless dresses are only acceptable for evening events.

Entry requirements
Passports
Passports are required by all, and must be carried at all times. Passports must be valid for at least six months.
Visa
Required by all, except nationals of the Americas, Europe, Australasia and some Asian countries visiting either as tourists or for business purposes, for up to 30 or 90 days. For confirmation and further details contact the nearest consulate or email: miginfor@racsa.co.cr. Business visitors should carry a company letter stating that they represent a foreign company on legitimate business.
Those staying up to 90 days must obtain an exit visa from the Immigration Department in San José at least three days before leaving. Those whose stay is less than 30 days need only their disembarkation card (issued on arrival).
Prohibited entry
Entry is refused to persons of unkempt appearance or without sufficient funds (minimum US$200), who will be deported immediately.

Currency advice/regulations
No restrictions on import of foreign or local currency. Foreign currency should be changed only at banks and authorised bureaux. Street-corner foreign exchange transactions are illegal. Visitors may change excess local currency back to US dollars, but only at main offices of state commercial banks and on production of an onward airline ticket and passport.
Customs
It is prohibited to import arms and drugs. Import tariffs range from 1 to 20 per cent except for vehicles, textiles, shoes, clothing (which are higher). Food products and medicines require registration.

Health (for visitors)
Mandatory precautions
There are no compulsory vaccinations.
Advisable precautions
Typhoid, tetanus and hepatitis A vaccinations are advised.
There is a malaria risk in some low-lying areas – prophylaxis is advisable if visiting the provinces of Limón, Guanacaste, Alajuela and Heredia. Dengue fever mosquitoes are present throughout the country.
Water precautions should be taken outside of San José. There is a risk of rabies.

Hotels
It is advisable to book well in advance. A 3 per cent tourism tax, 10 per cent sales tax and 10 per cent service charge will be added to the bill. Gratuities of around 5–10 per cent are also expected.

Public holidays (national)
Fixed dates
1 Jan (New Year's Day), 19 Mar (Feast of San José (San José only)), 11 Apr (Anniversary of the Battle of Rivas), 1 May (Labour Day), 29 Jun (St Peter and St Paul Day), 25 Jul (Guanacaste Annexation), 2 Aug (Our Lady of the Angels), 15 Aug (Assumption/Mothers' Day), 15 Sep (Independence Day), 12 Oct (Columbus Day), 8 Dec (Immaculate Conception), 24 Dec (Christmas Eve), 25 Dec (Christmas Day), 31 Dec (New Year's Eve).
Most businesses close for Holy Week and between Christmas and New Year.
Variable dates
Maundy Thursday, Good Friday, Corpus Christi (Mon/Jun).

Working hours
Banking
Mon–Fri: 0900–1500.
Business
Mon–Fri: 0800–1200; 1400–1600.
Government
Mon–Fri: 0800–1600.
Shops
Mon–Sat: 0900–1800/1900.

Telecommunications
Mobile/cell phones
GSM 1800 service available.

Electricity supply
110/220V AC, 60Hz. Two-pin plugs are standard.

Social customs/useful tips
Appointments should be made in advance. It is customary to shake hands on meeting and taking leave. The usual form of address is Don for a man, and Doña for a woman, followed by the first name. Business cards to indicate academic/professional titles are exchanged after introduction.
Costa Ricans are not very punctual for social activities, except for football matches, the cinema and weddings, but are more formal with their business appointments. Mothers are regarded as the leading family figures; grandparents and elders are highly respected.
The national pastimes are football and politics. The people have a strong sense of democracy.
Costa Ricans are called Ticos for short.
Although a service charge is added to restaurant and hotel bills, gratuities of 5–10 per cent are also expected.

Security
Petty crime is frequent. Thefts, especially in urban areas, and car break-ins are common. Thefts take place on the street and from cars. The loss or theft of a passport should be reported immediately to the local police and the relevant embassy. Some remote trails in national parks have been closed because of the low number of visitors and reported robberies of hikers in the area. Tourists should check with forest rangers for current park conditions. There are pickpockets in downtown San José. Beware of mugging in the national parks at night and of theft at beaches and ports.

Getting there
Air
National airline: Taca International Airlines
International airport/s: Juan Santamaría International (SJO), 22km from San José; duty-free shop, bar, restaurant, buffet, bank, post office, shops, car hire.
Airport tax: US$26; also payable in local currency or combination of both currencies.
Surface
Road: It is possible to travel overland from North or Central America. The nearest US town is Brownsville, Texas, on the Mexican border. From there it is about 4,000km by road on the Inter-American Highway to San José, crossing Mexico and going through Guatemala,

Honduras, Nicaragua and into Costa Rica. There is one major crossing point between Nicaragua and Costa Rica at Peñas Blancas, which is not a town, so there is nowhere to stay. There are two border crossings between Panama and Costa Rica.

Rail: There is no rail link with neighbouring countries.

Water: Cruise ships stop at Limón, Punterenas and Caldera. Freighters may accept a small number of passengers and private yachts cruise down the Pacific coast from North America.

Main port/s: Limón (Caribbean coast), Puntarenas and Caldera (Pacific coast).

Getting about

National transport

Air: SANSA is the main domestic carrier and operates cheap regular flights from San José to provincial towns. Travelair also provides domestic services. It is advisable to book in advance. A number of smaller airlines provide internal flights. There are over 200 small airfields throughout the country.

Road: Total network of some 30,000km of all-weather roads. Main routes are the Pan-American Highway; San José-Caldera; San José-Guapiles; and San José-Puerto Limón. Tolls are paid on all four-lane highways entering San José. Taxis are a form of public transport outside urban areas and can be hired by the hour, half-day or the day. Arrange the fare beforehand.

Buses: There are bus services around the country, but both the quality of services and prices vary considerably. Major tourist areas are better provided with short-distance bus services.

Rail: There is a short commuter train which links San José with Heredia and one which links Puerto Limón with the Río Estrella area. There is also a 'banana train' which travels on a section of track in the banana plantations around Guápiles.

Water: There are passenger and car ferries in operation.

City transport

Taxis: Taxis are red, except those serving Juan Santamaría International airport which are orange. Taxis are usually metered, but where there are no meters, it is advisable to agree a price before setting off. Taxis connecting to the airport or distant destinations charge a flat, official rate, but negotiation is possible.

Car hire

A temporary permit must be obtained from local traffic authorities on production of a national licence. Always carry a driving licence. There are tough drink-drive laws – the penalty includes having your driving licence impounded for a minimum of three years.

BUSINESS DIRECTORY

The addresses listed below are a selection only. While World of Information makes every endeavour to check these addresses, we cannot guarantee that changes have not been made, especially to telephone numbers and area codes. We would welcome any corrections.

Telephone area codes

The international direct dialling (IDD) code for Costa Rica is +506 followed by the subscriber's number.

Useful telephone numbers

Emergencies: 911
Ambulance: 128
Fire: 118
Police: 222-1365, 221-5337
Highway police: 222-9330, 222-8245

Chambers of Commerce

American-Costa Rican Chamber of Commerce, PO Box 4946-1000, San José (tel: 220-2200; fax: 220-2300; e-Mail: chamber@amcham.co.cr).

Costa Rican Cámara de Comercio, PO Box 1114-1000, San José (tel: 221-0005; fax: 233-7091; e-mail: servicos@camara-comercio.com).

Costa Rica Cámara de Industrias, PO Box 10003-1000, San José (tel: 281-0006; fax: 234-6163; e-mail: cicr@cicr.com).

Franco-Costa Rican Chambre de Commerce et d'Industrie, PO Box 912-1007 Centro Colon, San José (tel: 257-1138; fax: 257-1345; e-mail: cfcci@camarafranco-cr.org).

German-Costa Rican Cámara de Comercio, PO Box 2139-1000, San José (tel: 222-4789; fax: 221-1219; e-mail: cacoral@racsa.co.cr).

Unión Costarricense de Cámaras y Asociaciones de la Empresa Privada, PO Box 539-1002 Paseo de los Estudiantes, San José (tel: 290-5594; fax: 290-5596; e-mail: uccaep@uccaep.or.cr).

Banking

Banco Banex, Apdo 7983, 1000 San José (tel: 233-4855; fax: 223-7192).

Banco BCT, Apdo 7698, 1000 San José (tel: 233-6611; fax: 233-6833).

Banco Continental, Apdo 7969, 1000 San José (tel: 257-1155; fax: 255-3983).

Banco Co-operativo Costarricense, Apdo 8593, 1000 San José (tel: 233-5044; fax: 233-9661).

Banco Crédito Agrícola de Cartago, Apdo 5572, 1000 San José (tel: 251-3011; fax: 252-0364).

Banco de Costa Rica, Apdo 10035, 1000 San José (tel: 255-1100; fax: 255-0911).

Banco del Comercio SA, Apdo 1106, 1000 San José (tel: 233-6011; fax: 222-3706).

Banco de Fomento Agrícola, Apdo 6531, 1000 San José (tel: 231-4444; fax: 232-7476).

Banco de la Construcción, Apdo 5099, 1000 San José (tel: 221-5811; fax: 222-6567).

Banco de la Industria, Apdo 4254, 1000 San José (tel: 221-3355; fax: 233-8383).

Banco de San José, Apdo 5445, 1000 San José (tel: 221-9911; fax: 222-8208).

Banco Federado de Co-operativas de Ahorro y Crédito, Apdo 4748, 1000 San José (tel: 222-3323; fax: 257-1724).

Banco Fincomer, Apdo 57, Cartago (tel: 251-1351, 233-7822; fax: 222-0405).

Banco Germano Centroamericano, Apartado 2559, 1000 San José (tel: 233-8022; fax: 222-2648).

Banco Interfín, Apdo 6899, 1000 San José (tel: 221-8022; fax: 233-4823).

Banco Internacional de Costa Rica, Apdo 6116, 1000 San José (tel: 223-6522; fax: 233-6572).

Banco Lyon, Apdo 10184, 1000 San José (tel: 221-2611; fax: 221-6795).

Banco Mercantil de Costa Rica, Apdo 32101, 1000 San José (tel: 231-0724, 255-3636; fax: 255-3076).

Banco Metropolitano, Apdo 3932, 1000 San José (tel: 233-8111; fax: 222-8840).

Banco Nacional de Costa Rica, Apdo 10015, 1000 San José (tel: 223-2166; fax: 255-2436).

Corporación Costarricense de Financiamiento Industrial, Apdo 10507, 1000 San José (tel & fax: 221-2212).

Central bank

Banco Central de Costa Rica, Avenida Central y Primera, Calles 2 y 4, Apdo 10058, San José (tel: 243-3333; fax: 243-3011).

Travel information

American Airlines, Calle 26 & 28, Paseo Colón, San José (tel: 257-1266; fax: 222-5213).

British Airways, Calle 32, paseo Colón and Avenida 2, San José (tel: 223-5648; fax: 223-4863).

SANSA (Servicios Aéreos Nacionales), Apdo 999-1007, Centro Colón, San José (tel: 233-2714, 233-1673; fax: 255-2176).

Tourist Information Office, Plaza de la Cultura, Calle 5, Avenida 0-2, San José (tel: 223-1733 Ext 277; fax: 222-1090).

Ministry of tourism
National tourist organisation offices
Instituto Costarricense de Turismo (ICT), Edificio Genaro Valverde, Calles 5 y 7, Avenida 4, PO Box 777, 1000 San José (tel: 223-8423; fax: 223-5452).

Ministries
Ministry of Agriculture and Livestock, Science and Technology, Apdo 10094, 1000 San José (tel: 232-4496; fax: 232-2103).

Ministry of Culture, Apdo 10227, 1000 San José (tel: 223-1658; fax: 233-7066).

Ministry of Economy, Industry and Commerce, Foreign Commerce, Apdo 10216-1000, San José (tel: 222-1016; fax: 222-2305).

Ministry of Environment and Energy, Apdo 10104 1000 San José (tel: 257-1417; fax: 257-0697).

Ministry of Finance, Apdo 5016, San José (tel: 222-2481; fax: 255-4874).

Ministry of Foreign Affairs, Apdo 10027-1000, San José (tel: 223-7555; fax: 223-9328).

Ministry of Foreign Trade, Apdo 96-2050 Mtes de Oca, San José (tel: 222-5910; fax: 233-5090).

Ministry of Health, Apdo 10123, 1000 San José (tel: 233-0683; fax: 255-4997).

Ministry of Housing, Apdo 222-1002 Paseo de Los Estudiantes, San José (tel: 233-3665; fax: 255-1976).

Ministry of Information, PO Box 520-2010, Zapote (tel: 225-9936/9797; fax: 253-6984).

Ministry of the Interior, Police and Public Security, Apdo 10006, 1000 San José (tel: 223-8354; fax: 222-7726).

Ministry of Justice, Apdo 5685, 1000 San José (tel: 223-9739; fax: 223-3879).

Ministry of Labour and Social Security, Apdo 10133, 1000 San José (tel: 221-0238; fax: 222-8085).

Ministry of the Presidency and Planning, Apdo 520 Zapote, San José (tel: 224-4092; fax: 253-6984).

Ministry of Public Education, Apdo 10087, 1000 San José (tel: 222-0229; fax: 255-2868).

Ministry of Public Security, Apdo 55-4874, San José (tel: 226-0093; fax: 226-6581).

Ministry of Public Works and Transport, Apdo 10176, 1000 San José (tel: 226-7311; fax: 227-1434).

Ministry of Science And Technology, Apdo 5589-1000, San José (tel: 253-7446; fax: 224-8295).

Other useful addresses
Bolsa Nacional De Valores S.A. (Stock Exchange), Central Street, 1st Avenue, PO Box 1736-1000, San José (tel: 221-8011; fax: 255-0131).

British Embassy, Apdo 815, 11th Floor, Edificio Centro Colón, 1007 San José (tel: 221-5566, 255-2937; fax: 233-9938).

Centro de Promoción de Exportaciones e Inversiones (CENPRO) (Costa Rican Export & Investment Promotion Centre), PO Box 5418 San José (tel: 221-7166; fax: 223-5722).

Costa Rican Electricity Institute (ICE), PO Box 10032, 10 San José (tel: 220-7720; fax: 220-1555).

Costa Rican Embassy (USA), 2114 S Street, NW, Washington DC 20008 (tel: (+1-202)-234-2945; fax: (+1-202)-265-4795; e-mail: embassy@costarica-embassy.com).

Costa Rican Institute of Pacific Ports (INCOP), Calle 36, Avenida 3, San José (tel: 223-7111).

Costa Rican Investment and Development Corporation (CINDE), P.O. Box 7170-100 San José (tel: 220-0366, 220-4755; fax: 220-4750, 220-4754).

Costa Rican Investment Promotion Programme (CINDE-EUROPE), Eisenhowerlaan 128, 22517 KM Den Haag, The Netherlands (tel: (31-70)512-1212, 515-010).

Costa Rican Oil Refinery (RECOPE), Apdo 43351, 1000 San José (tel: 223-9611; fax: 255-2049).

Costa Rican Stock Exchange (BNVSA), Apartado 1736-1000, San José (tel: 222-8011; fax: 255-0131).

Ferias Internacionales SA (FERCORI), Apartado 1843, 1000 San Jose (tel: 233-6990; fax: 233-5791).

Free Zones Export Corporation, Apdo 96, 2020 Montes de Oca (tel: 222-5855).

Grupo Centro, PO Box 6133, 1000 San José (tel: 235-4509; fax: 240-7591).

National Association for Economic Development (ANFE), Apartado 3577-1000, San José (tel: 253-4497).

Red Nacional de Televisión, PO Box 7-1980, 1000 San José (tel: 231-333; fax: 231-6604).

Sistema Nacional de Radio y Televisión Cultural (SINART), PO Box 27941, Administración Central, 1000 San Jose (tel: 231-6474; fax: 231-6604).

Televisora de Costa Rica, PO Box 3786, 1000 San Jose (tel: 232-2222; fax: 231-7545).

TNT Correos de Costa Rica, Calle 34-36, Avenida 1RA, San Jose (tel: 233-4993; fax: 221-5046).

Union Pack de Costa Rica (UPS), Aveida 3, Calle 30 & 32, San Jose (tel: 257-7447; fax: 257-5343).

US Embassy, Pavas Frente Centre Comercial, Apdo 920-1200, San José (tel: 220-3939; fax: 220-2305).

Internet sites
Information about the country, investment and the Stock Exchange: http://incostarica.net/

Bolsa Nacional de Valores (stock market): www.bnv.co.cr/

Central Bank: www.bccr.fi.cr/

Côte d'Ivoire

KEY FACTS

Official name: République de Côte d'Ivoire (Republic of Côte d'Ivoire)

Head of State: President Laurent Gbagbo (FPI) (since 2000)

Head of government: Prime Minister Guillaume Soro (FN) (from 4 Apr 2007)

Ruling party: Coalition: Front Populaire Ivorienne (FPI) (Ivorian Popular Front); Forces Nouvelles (FN) (New Forces); Rassemblement des Républicains (RDR) (Rally of Republicans); Parti démocratique de la Côte d'Ivoire (PDCI) (Democratic Party of Côte d'Ivoire); Mouvement des Forces d'Avenir (MFA) (Movement of the Forces of the Future); Parti Ivoirien des Travailleurs (PIT) (Ivorian Workers Party); Union Démocratique et Citoyenne de Côte d'Ivoire (UDCY) (Citizens Democratic Union of Côte d'Ivoire) and Union pour la Démocratie et la Paix en Côte d'Ivoire (UDPCI) (Union for Democracy and Peace in Côte d'Ivoire) (formed 7 Apr 2007)

Area: 322,630 square km

Population: 18.75 million (2007)

Capital: Yamoussoukro (administrative capital); Abidjan (economic and diplomatic centre)

Official language: French

Currency: CFA franc (CFAf) = 100 centimes (Communauté Financière Africaine (African Financial Community) franc). New notes have been issued; old notes cease to be legal tender from Jan 2005.

Exchange rate: CFAf413.80 per US$ (Jul 2008); CFAf655.96 per euro (pegged Jan 1999)

GDP per capita: US$1,045 (2007)

GDP real growth: 1.60% (2005)

Labour force: 7.08 million (2004)

Inflation: 2.10% (2007)

Balance of trade: US$2.08 billion (2006)

Foreign debt: US$11.81 billion (2004)

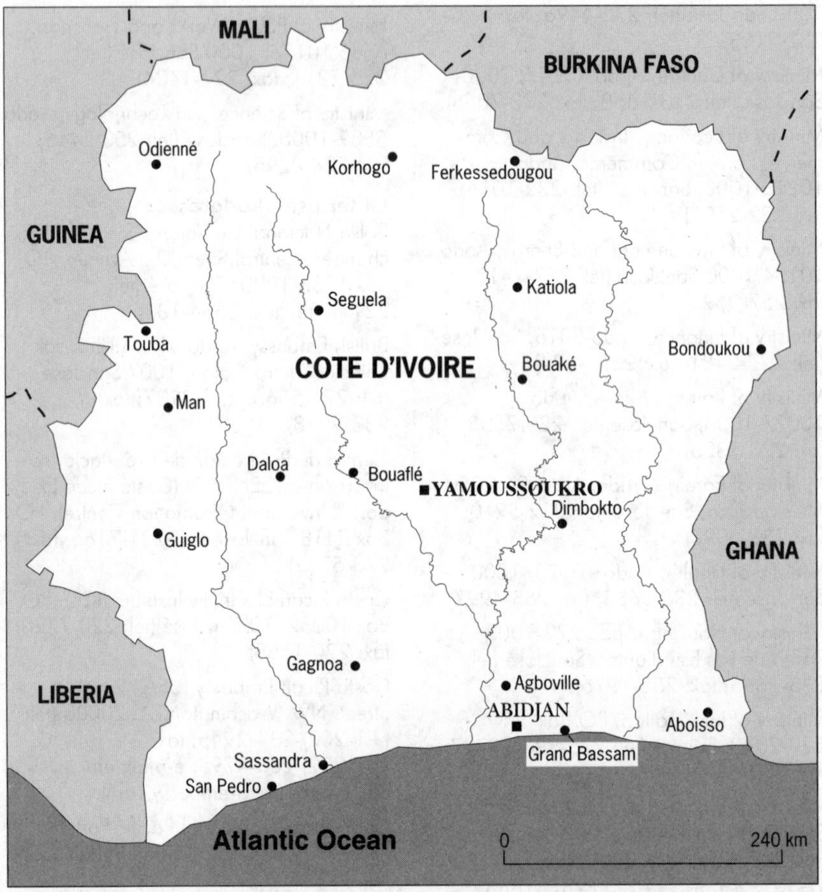

For more than three decades after independence, under the leadership of its first president, Felix Houphouet-Boigny, Côte d'Ivoire was conspicuous for its religious and ethnic harmony. Its economy was among the most developed on the continent. Once the jewel in the crown of French African territories, all this ended in when the late Robert Gueï led a coup which toppled Houphouet-Boigny's successor, Henri Bédié, in 1999. This in turn led to a civil war which began in 2002, leaving the country divided between the rebel-held north and army-controlled south, and beginning five years of economic and political turmoil.

Côte d'Ivoire is still suffering the consequences of this on-going political crisis. The economic infrastructure has been destroyed, government administration, once the pride of French Africa, has broken down, nearly 2 million people have fled the country and there has been a drastic fall in output, a substantial drop in employment and worsening security conditions.

After five years of mediation, on-off agreements and postponed elections, on 4 March 2007 the latest agreement, the Ouagadougou Agreement, was signed. This agreement is based on United Nations Security Council Resolution 1712, which was implemented through the formation of a new government made up of representatives of the main political parties involved. Guillaume Soro, secretary general of the northern Force Nouvelle (FN) (New Force), became prime minister. Laurent Gbagbo, of the Front Populaire Ivorienne (FPI), continued as president. Dismantling of the 'Trust Zone' under international control, which had separated north from south, began on 16 April and a seminar was held in May to formulate an action plan for implementing a post-conflict programme. Presidential elections were scheduled for June 2008, but then postponed until November. This was generally welcomed by all parties, mainly because the <I>audiences foraines<W0> (mobile public identity hearings for those who have no birth certificates) which are necessary to provide identity documents as a first step towards an electoral list for the presidential elections, were taking longer than planned.

Economy

Côte d'Ivoire is rich in petroleum, natural gas, diamonds, manganese, iron ore, cobalt, bauxite, copper, gold, nickel, tantalum, silica sand, clay, cocoa beans, coffee, palm oil and hydropower. It should be economically sound but for the civil conflict. Fortunately the oil industry, which is primarily located offshore, has been relatively unaffected by the civil strife. In addition, new fields are coming online, which are helping to bolster economic growth in the country.

In 2006, Côte d'Ivoire's gross domestic product (GDP) fell by 0.3 per cent but rose by 1.6 per cent in 2007. In 2006, the country's inflation was 4.9 per cent, falling to 2.1 per cent in 2007. In its 2008 edition of <I>African Economic Outlook<W0> (AEO), the African Development Bank (AfDB) said that the country's economy was recovering, but remained fragile, as the political situation returned to normal. The Ouagadougou Agreement led to the signing of an economic reform programme supported by emergency post-conflict assistance from the International Monetary Fund (IMF), and to plans to clear the country's debt arrears to the World Bank and AfDB.

The country is among the world's largest producers and exporters of coffee, cocoa beans and palm oil. Consequently, the economy is highly sensitive to fluctuations in international prices for these products and weather conditions. Despite government attempts to diversify the economy, it is still heavily dependent on agriculture and related activities, which engage 66 per cent of the population and contribute 70 per cent of export revenues. According to the AEO, output of cocoa dropped by 20.1 per cent in 2007, cotton by 16.3 per cent and pineapples by 17.7 per cent. Other export agricultural sectors performed well, under the combined effect or higher producer prices and the expansion of the area planted with coffee, rubber and cashew nuts. Rubber and cashew were estimated to have increased by 7.5 per cent and 16.4 per cent respectively. This was also considered to be due to the gradual normalisation of the social and political situation, which made it easier to market produce from the centre and north-west of the country.

Despite this improvement in the agriculture sector, foreign investment has shrivelled, businessmen have fled, travel within the country has fallen and criminal elements that traffic in weapons and diamonds have gained ground. The government will have to prove itself to both the international community as well as Ivorians on both sides if the civil conflict. The first political test of this will come with the elections currently scheduled for November 2008.

Risk assessment

Politics	Improving
Economy	Improving
Regional stability	Fair

COUNTRY PROFILE

Historical profile

When Côte d'Ivoire became independent from France in 1960, it had only just acquired a secondary school, the colonial practice of forced labour had only been abolished a couple of years earlier and industrial development was virtually nil, whether in the dense tropical forests of the coast and west, or the central savannah and dry north. A few thousand French settlers eked out a desultory trading or farming existence and a few thousand more Ivorian followed them into cocoa and coffee farming. Economically Côte d'Ivoire ranked among the world's poorest, with little prospect of hauling itself up the development ladder. No mineral wealth seemed readily exploitable, the internal market of five millions (today the population numbers around 19 million) was not tempting for large-scale industrial foreign investment, the commodities on which the country depended for foreign exchange were fluctuating wildly on world markets: cocoa, coffee and timber seemed a highly unstable base.

However, by the late twentieth century Côte d'Ivoire become an example of a certain style of African enterprise and capitalism. Airlines linked Abidjan with dozens of capitals and it was an established port of call for the world's businessmen. For Paris, it was the most thriving of its former West African colonies.

1960 Côte d'Ivoire gained independence from France. Felix Houphouet-Boigny, selected by French colonial rulers as the most promising successor to their rule, established a benevolent authoritarian regime which tended towards paternalism. Politics were based around oligarchs who gained power through government position, ran state-owned companies or gained positions in the ruling party, the Parti Démocratique de la Côte d'Ivoire (PDCI) (Democratic Party of Côte d'Ivoire.

1970s–1980s Economic decline increased the pressure for political reform. Laurent Gbagbo, a lecturer and long-term dissident, emerged as the main opposition leader. He went into exile in 1982.

1988 Gbagbo returned from exile and founded the Front Populaire d'Ivoirie (FPI)

KEY INDICATORS — Côte d'Ivoire

	Unit	2003	2004	2005	2006	2007
Population	m	17.97	18.95	18.20	18.47	18.75
Gross domestic product (GDP)	US$bn	12.76	15.59	16.37	17.34	19.60
GDP per capita	US$	710	852	900	939	1,045
GDP real growth	%	-2.2	-0.9	1.5	-0.3	1.6
Inflation	%	3.4	1.5	3.9	4.9	2.1
Industrial output	% change	–	3.8	-0.5	-3.6	–
Agricultural output	% change	–	4.0	-1.5	1.5	–
Exports (fob) (goods)	US$m	4,400.0	6,707.0	7,376.0	8,144.0	8,475.9
Imports (cif) (goods)	US$m	2,500.0	4,853.0	5,266.0	6,067.0	5,931.6
Balance of trade	US$m	1,900.0	1,854.0	2,110.0	2,077.0	2,544.2
Current account	US$m	550.0	500.0	-11.0	529.0	265.0
Total reserves minus gold	US$m	2,230.5	2,422.1	1,321.5	1,797.7	2,519.0
Foreign exchange	US$m	2,229.3	2,420.9	1,320.0	1,795.7	2,517.3
Exchange rate	per US$	574.89	528.29	507.22	496.60	454.40

(Ivorian Popular Front) to campaign for multi-party democracy.

1990 Houphouet-Boigny was forced to call elections, which were won by the PDCI. Houphouet-Boigny was elected president; Alassane Dramane Ouattara became prime minister.

1993 President Felix Houphouet-Boigny died after 30 years in power. Henri Konan-Bédié became president.

1995 Legislative and presidential elections were convincingly won by Konan-Bédié and the PDCI party.

1999 President Bédié was toppled in a military coup and General Robert Gueï seized the presidency. Gueï continued the incitement instigated by Bédié to highten inter-communal tension, between the Muslim north and Christian south, by banning Alassane Ouattara the northern Muslim leader from standing in the forthcoming presidential election.

2000 Laurent Gbagbo declared himself president following controversial elections, as Gueï fled the country and supporters of Ouattara were killed after he called for new elections.

2002 An uprising split the country, the rebel Force Nouvelle (FN) (New Force), took control of the north and about 60 per cent of the country. Alassane Ouattara, leader of the political party, Rassemblement des Républicains (RdR) (Republican Party) and head of FN, was granted citizenship resolving his status in future elections. A cease-fire was negotiated and a French-manned buffer zone imposed between north and south. In September, former president Gueï was shot dead in Abidjan.

2003 10,000 UN and French troops separated the warring sides.

2004 Rebels appointed ministers to join a coalition government. On 4 March, PDCI pulled out of the power-sharing government amid ongoing violence. Abidjan came under bombardment from rebel forces. When the Ivorian airforce targetted Bouake, the northern stronghold of the FN, it killed nine French soldiers in the air raid. The French airforce retaliated by destroying the Ivorian airforce.

Pro-government demonstrators erupted onto the capital's streets, looting and threatening foreign, particularly French, targets.

2005 A UN report accused both rebel and government forces of atrocities including torture, systematic rape and mass execution. In April, the government, FN and opposition leaders signed a deal to end the civil war which had started in 2002; the deal was brokered by South Africa's President Thabo Mbeki. A previous Government of National Reconciliation was revived to take over until elections were held. However, the October presidential elections were cancelled. On 4 October Presidents Obasanjo and Mbeki of Nigeria and South Africa respectively named Charles Konan Banny as interim prime minister. Banny was given powers to run an interim government (planned to end in October 2006) and organise presidential elections; for this all militias must be disarmed and voter registration undertaken.

2006 Banny faced his first test in January when international mediators called for the dissolution of parliament, which backed President Gbagbo. As a result, the ruling FPI briefly withdrew from the transitional government, accusing the mediators of a 'constitutional coup d'etat'. In February in the first meeting since 2000, the four main Ivorian leaders, Gbagbo (FPI), Bedie (PDCI), Ouattara (RdR) and Guillaume Soro, Mouvement Patriotique de Côte d'Ivoire (MPCI) (Patriotic Movement of Côte d'Ivoire), attended a meeting with the prime minister to discuss the plans for future elections and government. In June, militia loyal to Gbagbo failed to disarm as scheduled. Public identity hearings began in July, to determine who could claim Ivorian citizenship and vote in the next elections. (The rebellion in the north was predicated on the loss by citizens of this status.) The hearings were suspended following violent clashes between supporters of the president and vice president. In September negotiators failed to agree terms for disarmament and voter registration. Presidential elections that were due in October were postponed until 2007. On 1 November the UN Security Council voted to extend President Gbagbo and Prime Minister Konan Banny's mandate for another year.

2007 A peace agreement was reached on 4 March, between President Gbagbo and Guillaume Soro (FN). A plan to integrate some members of rebel militias with the regular army, while others are to be disbanded, was mandated by president decree. Soro became prime minister on 4 April. President Gbagbo visited the former rebel-held north on 30 July and watched as weapons were destroyed at a peace party attended by five other African Heads of State, plus ministers and diplomats. On 7 August the president declared that the, twice postponed, general elections could be held by December. The introduction of identity papers for all citizens in September sparked fears that large numbers would be given to foreigners fraudulently. A strike by cocoa processors halted exports of the country's primary crop in December, the busiest time of the year for cocoa production. At a ceremony held on 3 May, former rebels of the north began disarming; they will either be absorbed into the regular army or given training and a three-month stipend as they return to civilian life.

2008 Presidential elections that were due to be held in June were postponed until the end of November. The decision was welcomed by all political groupings. In July a public sector strike was ended when ministers cut their own wages by 50 per cent to help cover the cost of reintroducing subsidised fuel. The subsidy had been scrapped by the government on 6 July, leading to the strike.

Political structure

Constitution

A multi-party system is enshrined in the constitution, but in practice no party other than Parti Démocratique de la Côte d'Ivoire (PDCI) (Democratic Party of Côte d'Ivoire) was allowed to operate until May 1990 when the government legalised party political activity.

A 1990 constitutional amendment allowed for the appointment of a prime minister, with the speaker of the National Assembly empowered to assume the office of president of the republic prior to a presidential election in the event of a sudden presidential vacancy.

The constitution was suspended following a military takeover in December 1999. In 2000, the constitution was revised, stipulating that presidential candidates must be of Ivorian origin, born of parents who are not naturalised Ivorians, should not have dual nationality and must have lived in Côte d'Ivoire for a minimum and uninterrupted period of five years. Those with at least 21 years of Ivorian citizenship are eligible to vote.

Form of state

Republic

The executive

Executive power rests with the president (elected by universal suffrage for a five-year term) who appoints the cabinet. The president can veto legislation, but his veto can in theory be overridden by a two-thirds vote of the National Assembly.

National legislature

The 175-member National Assembly was dissolved in December 1999 and replaced by an appointed National Council for Public Salvation formed by the military junta. This was dissolved following elections to a new 225-seat assembly in December 2000 and January 2001. From time to time, the president also summons an informal grass-roots body known as the National Council for Consultations on Controversial Issues.

Legal system

All civil, criminal, commercial and administrative cases come under the jurisdiction of the tribunaux de première instance (magistrates' courts), the assize courts and the court of appeal.

Last elections
22 October 2000 (presidential); 10 December 2000 (parliamentary).
Results: Parliamentary: FPI won 96 seats, PDCI 94.
Presidential: Laurent Gbagbo won 59.4 per cent of the vote, Robert Guei 32.7 per cent, Francis Wodie 5.7 per cent.
Next elections
Late November 2008 (presidential)

Political parties
Ruling party
Coalition: Front Populaire Ivorienne (FPI) (Ivorian Popular Front); Forces Nouvelles (FN) (New Forces); Rassemblement des Républicains (RDR) (Rally of Republicans); Parti démocratique de la Côte d'Ivoire (PDCI) (Democratic Party of Côte d'Ivoire); Mouvement des Forces d'Avenir (MFA) (Movement of the Forces of the Future); Parti Ivoirien des Travailleurs (PIT) (Ivorian Workers Party); Union Démocratique et Citoyenne de Côte d'Ivoire (UDCY) (Citizens Democratic Union of Côte d'Ivoire) and Union pour la Démocratie et la Paix en Côte d'Ivoire (UDPCI) (Union for Democracy and Peace in Côte d'Ivoire) (formed 7 Apr 2007)

Population
18.75 million (2007)
Last census: November 1998:15,366,672
Population density: 44 inhabitants per square km. Urban population: 43 per cent (1995–2001).
Annual growth rate: 2.2 per cent 1994–2004 (WHO 2006)
Internally Displaced Persons (IDP)
500,000–800,000 (UNHCR 2004)
Ethnic make-up
Akan (the Baoule subgroup accounts for 23 per cent of the population), Kru (the Bete subgroup accounts for 18 per cent), Senoufo 15 per cent, Malinke 11 per cent, Agni, Mande. There are nearly 3 million foreign Africans (mainly from Burkina Faso and Mali) and an estimated 130,000–330,000 non-Africans (French 30,000 and Lebanese 100,000–300,000).
Religions
Islam (60 per cent), Christianity (mainly Roman Catholic) (22 per cent), traditional animist beliefs (18 per cent) (some of these are also numbered among the Christians and Muslims).

Education
Education is provided free of charge. Primary education lasts for six years from the age of six. Secondary education lasts for up to seven years from the age of 13. There are universities at Abidjan and Yamoussoukro, but many students attend French universities.
Only 50 per cent of girls attend primary school.
Literacy rate: 60 per cent, youth rate (15–24) (Unesco 2005)
Pupils per teacher: 41 in primary schools.

Health
Per capita total expenditure on health (2003) was US$57; of which per capita government spending was US$16, at the international dollar rate, (WHO 2006).
HIV/Aids
Aids-related costs typically absorb 11 per cent of the total public health budget.
HIV prevalence: 7.0 per cent aged 15–49 in 2003 (World Bank)
Life expectancy: 44 years, 2004 (WHO 2006)
Fertility rate/Maternal mortality rate: 4.9 births per woman, 2004 (WHO 2006); maternal mortality six per 1,000 live births (World Bank).
Child (under 5 years) mortality rate (per 1,000): 117 per 1,000 live births; 24 per cent of children under aged five are malnourished (World Bank).
Head of population per physician: 0.12 physicians per 1,000 people, 2004 (WHO 2006)

Welfare
An employer must declare each worker employed to the Caisse National de Prevoyance Sociale (CNPS), the national social security fund, and is responsible for deducting social security contributions paid by the worker. Large firms are also expected to provide in-house medical care.
Social security is divided into three areas: family allowances, retirement pensions, medical care and compensation payments in case of accident at work. There are no payments for illness unconnected to work. Contributions are paid every quarter by firms employing fewer than 20, and each month for those employing over 20, people. The CNPS funds are ring-fenced from the government's main budget.
The social security system does not cover unemployment, which is paid monthly through labour exchanges and financed by a national solidarity contribution of 1 per cent of salary, which is levied on each employee's wages.
Child labour is used in domestic service, farming, mining and factory work as well as casual labour in street markets. Law restricting the age of employment is enforced in large enterprises but is more lax in small industries and the informal sector. Local opinion concerning child labour is equivocal; while rural children are needed for subsistence farming, and urban street children can avoid destitution through work, the need for change would seem to be moot.

Main cities
Abidjan (economic and diplomatic centre, estimated population 4.9 million in 2005), Yamoussoukro (political capital since 1983, 454,929), Bouaké (549,800), Daloa (309,363), Gagnoa (215,664), Korhogo (349,953), San Pédro (202,714), Soubré (254,247).

Languages spoken
Approximately 60 local African languages are spoken, including Dioula, Baoule, Akan, Kru and Bete.
Official language/s
French

Media
According to the France-based media watchdog Reporters Without Borders, Côte d'Ivoire is one of the Africa's most dangerous places for journalists to carry out their work.
National news agency: AIP (Agence Ivoirienne de Presse)
Other news agencies: APA (African Press Agency): www.apanews.net
Panapress: www.panapress.com
Press
Dailies: In French, national newspapers includes the government-owned, Fraternité Matin (www.fratmat.info) and Notre Voie (www.notrevoie.com) and Le Partriote (www.lepatriote.net), which are owned by the political parties PCT and UDR-Mwinda respectively. Other, national, private newspapers include Le Nouveau Reveil,24 Heures (www.24heuresci.com), Le Front and Soir Info (www.soirinfo.com). Newspapers with the same internet address (http://news.abidjan.net), include L'Inter and Le Jour and Fraternité Matin. Newspapers published in Abidjan include Le Courrier d'Abidjan (www.lecourrierdabidjan.info), Le Matin d'Abidjan (www.lematindabidjan.com) and Nord-Sud (www.nordsudmedia.info).
Broadcasting
For most of the population, radio is the principal medium for news and information. Radiodiffusion Télévision Ivoirienne (RTI) (www.rti.ci) is the national, public broadcaster funded through a license fee, advertising revenue and grants.
Radio: There are many private radio stations with a limited area of broadcasting around cities and other urban regions. RTI relays its two channels, RTI Frequence 2 (www.frequence2.ci) and La Nationale (www.lanationale.ci), with entertainment, news, education, information and cultural programmes, through a network of numerous, local stations. Other private stations include Nostalgie (www.nostalgie.ci) from Abidjan and Radio Jam (www.radiojam.ci), from Yamoussoukro. Religious stations include the Catholic Radio Paix Sanwi (www.radiopaixsanwi.net)

and the Islamic Radio al Bayane (http://radio-albayane.com).
Television: The government controls the only terrestrial TV station although private, pay-to-view cable and satellite services are available through the French-owned Canal Satellite Horizons (www.canalhorizons.com).
RTI (www.rti.ci) operates La Premiere, a national channel and TV2, which for viewers of terrestrial TV can only be received within a radius of 150km of Abidjan. RTI also have dedicated sports and music channels. RTI services can be received throughout the country and also into some neighbouring countries via satellite services.

News agencies

National news agency: AIP (Agence Ivoirienne de Presse)
Other news agencies: APA (African Press Agency): www.apanews.net
Panapress: www.panapress.com

Economy

Although classified by the World Bank as a low income economy, Côte d'Ivoire in good times has been sub-Saharan Africa's second most developed economy, after South Africa, even though it depends on a limited range of traditional exports. However, since the civil war of 2000–03 and the stalemate in political intergration that followed, the economy has suffered with stagnation for the last few years. With the country split between rebel and government-held areas and rail and road links between the two halves of the country closed down, the movement of goods has ground to a halt. People fled the economically important cocoa-growing areas, leaving crops to rot and starving the economy of its most important source of foreign exchange. Food prices rose sharply, as agricultural output, particularly meat supplies from the north, fell. The decline in food output and problems with supply led to hunger in the north of the country. Continuing instability during 2005 and 2006 impeded any prospects of a return to growth. The country's debt arrears led to the cessation of World Bank and IMF projects. The tax base has been eroded by the poor economic conditions, GDP growth in 2005 was -0.3 per cent, a figure that could have been worse if it had not been for the revenue from oil exploration concessions, enough to keep the government afloat. Cocoa production fell in 2005 by 2.4 per cent and farmers went on strike in 2006 and refused to sell their cocoa until they received a higher price it at the farm gate from traders. Côte d'Ivoire produces around 40 per cent of world global output.

External trade

As a member of the Economic Community of West African States (Ecowas), Côte d'Ivoire is also a member of the West African Economic and Monetary Union (WAEMU) with a common external tariff and using the common currency, the CFA franc.
The country was divided following the civil war and has been under unification since a political agreement was achieved in 2007. The northern rebel-held region was a primary area for growing cocoa, the country's major export commodity, while the principal port for international trade was held in the government-controlled south. Export of cocoa and other agricultural products were either curtailed or redirected to neighbouring countries for onward shipments. The country is a hub for international trade in West Africa and transhipment is an important element of the economy.
The UN banned the export of rough diamonds after it was found they were used in the purchase of weapons during the civil war.

Imports

Principal imports include fuel, capital equipment and foodstuffs.
Main sources: France (27.7 per cent total, 2004), Nigeria (24.5 per cent), Singapore (6.6 per cent)

Exports

Principal exports include cocoa (typically 40 per cent of total), coffee, timber, fuel, cotton, bananas, pineapples, palm oil, fish and diamonds (currently banned).
Main destinations: France (18.3 per cent total, 2005), US (14.1 per cent), The Netherlands (11.0 per cent), Nigeria (8.0 per cent), Panama (4.4 per cent)

Agriculture

Farming

The agricultural sector is the mainstay of the economy. It accounts for around 30 per cent of GDP, earns over 60 per cent of export revenues and employs some 54 per cent of the workforce. The climate in some parts of the north is suitable for the production of wheat to support an estimated local consumption of about 200,000 tonnes a year.
The principal cash crops are cocoa and coffee. Côte d'Ivoire accounts for around 40 per cent of total world cocoa production. The cocoa and coffee sectors have undergone liberalisation and institutional reform since 1995. This has included transferring some responsibility for price stabilisation to the private sector, making operations more transparent, and reducing customs duties on cocoa and abolishing them for coffee. Price liberalisation was achieved for coffee in 1998 and cocoa in 1999, when Caistab, the price stabilisation fund, was disbanded and replaced by a private-sector operation. Privatisation of the coffee and cocoa sectors was highly controversial among farmer.
In 2002, the government set up a new cocoa and coffee marketing institution, the Fonds de Regulation et de Controle (FRC), which took over the financial aspects of marketing from the Bourse du Café et Cacao (BCC), which had been two-thirds owned by farmers and one-third by exporters. The FRC is owned by farmers (45 per cent), banks (20 per cent), insurance companies (20 per cent) and the government (15 per cent). It determines minimum guaranteed farm-gate prices and bears the cost of implementing the price stabilisation mechanism, which cushions farmers' exposure to volatile international markets. Nevertheless, in 1006 farmers blocked the supply of cocoa to the docks for export – an action that had happened twice before, in 1999 and 2004 – amid complaints that prices to farmers were too low.
Coffee and cocoa production is regulated by the Autorité de Regulation du Café et Cacao (ARCC), which determines export quotas. Since internal conflict began in 2002 these developments have become more or less irrelevant and exports have fallen.
In 2005–06 production was hit by the spread of swollen shoot virus, a disease that de-foliates and eventually kills cocoa trees. Nevertheless cocoa production for 2006–07 is expected to be 1,000,000 tonnes.
Estimated crop production for 2005 included 2,205,000 tonnes (t) cereals in total, 1,500,000t cassava, 370,000t taro, 3,000,000t yams, 1,100,000t sugar cane, 1,400,000t oil palm fruit, 1,330,000t cocoa beans, 1,150,000t rice, 910,000t maize, 253,000t bananas, 1,350,000t plantains, 4,918,000t roots and tubers, 240,000t coconuts, 61,250t citrus fruit, 170,000t tomatoes, 300,000t seed cotton, 152,000t cotton lint, 150,000t groundnuts in shell, 180,000t pineapples, 424,972t oilcrops, 10,200t tobacco, 160,000t green coffee, 99,630t treenuts, 135,000t natural rubber, 22,500t chillies and peppers, 1,885,400t fruit in total, 633,200t vegetables in total.
Estimated livestock production included 170,126t meat in total, 51,786t beef, 13,000t game meat, 11,760t pig meat, 9,280t lamb and goat meat, 69,300t poultry, 31,214t eggs, 25,912t milk, 6,804t cattle hides, 1,245t sheepskins.

Fishing

Côte d'Ivoire is the second largest exporter of canned tuna in the world. The port of Abidjan handles more than 400,000 tonnes of fish a year. The government has launched a series of initiatives to modernise local fishing and assist local fishermen to benefit from the country's 150,000 hectares of lagoon and 350,000 hectares of lakes and rivers. The EU and Côte d'Ivoire run a fisheries agreement which provides EU fishermen with fishing rights in Côte d'Ivoire waters in return for the funding of research and training programmes.

Forestry

Côte d'Ivoire has 17 per cent forest cover and an additional 25 per cent of other wooded land. Ten per cent of forests are inside protected reserves, including the Parc National de Tai which has the largest tract of primary rainforest in West Africa. The southern half of the country, which was once covered by tropical forest, has suffered extensive deforestation for logging and agriculture. The northern half contains savannah woodland. Forestry is important and Côte d'Ivoire has been Africa's leading exporter of sawn timber. Wood is also an important source of domestic fuel.

Industry and manufacturing

The industrial sector contributes around 20 per cent to GDP, but output has fallen due to instability since 2002.

The industrial and manufacturing sectors expanded rapidly following independence in 1960, but suffered some setbacks in the late 1980s as a result of increased foreign competition and a decline in consumer purchasing power. In addition, the industrial plant is ageing and has often not been renewed on account of the low level of private investment.

During the 1990s, privatisation reduced the state's role in industry and manufacturing. Policy has focussed upon encouraging private sector involvement in the hydrocarbons sector which it is hoped will encourage the expansion of the industrial and manufacturing sectors.

Mining

The mining sector holds considerable potential and could become the second mainstay of the economy. It contributes around 3.7 per cent to GDP annually and employs 1 per cent of the workforce. A state company, Société pour le Développement Minier Ivorien (Sodemi) carries out exploration and production, in some cases in joint ventures with foreign companies. Gold is found in three main reserves: Issia, Lobo and Ity.

Diamonds have traditionally been mined by small independent prospectors, but the incidence of diamond smuggling and consequent loss of revenue prompted the Ministry of Mines to introduce licences for prospectors and diamond purchasing offices in 2000. Diamonds are produced at Séguéla and Tortiya. Reserves at Séguéla are estimated at 150,000 carats, and at Tortiya 450,000 carats.

Grand-Lehou produces 90,000 to 100,000 tonnes of manganese per year. A deposit, estimated at 1.2 million tonnes (47 per cent manganese), was discovered at Ziemougoula, near Odienne.

A large iron ore deposit at Monogaga-Victory has estimated reserves of 140 million tonnes. Further reserves, estimated at three billion tonnes, are located on the border with Guinea at Mount Nyumba and Mount Kalayo.

Hydrocarbons

Côte d'Ivoire is self-sufficient in oil and natural gas. Proven oil reserves in 2005 were 100 million barrels (bpd) and natural gas reserves 1 trillion cubic feet. Most of the oil and gas wells are located offshore in the shallow waters Espoir field and, since 2005, the deep-water Baobab field. Oil production is around 33,000 barrels per day, but set to increase as new fields come on-stream.

Côte d'Ivoire's oil refinery has a capacity of 65,200bpd, sufficient to supply domestic requirements as well as some export volumes for neighbouring countries. The refinery is connected to the Lion and Panther fields and receives crude oil from Nigeria for processing.

Consumption of natural gas is expected to increase by 50 per cent. Côte d'Ivoire is in line to become a regional exporter of natural gas. In 1999 Côte d'Ivoire signed agreements with Ghana for a feasability study in building a pipeline running from Abidjan to Takoradi in Ghana. There is also a possibility that this gas pipeline would be eventualy linked to the West Africa Gas Pipeline.

Côte d'Ivoire does not produce or import coal.

Energy

Installed electricity generating capacity is 911 megawatts. More than 50 per cent of annual production is generated by gas-powered plants, with a declining contribution from hydroelectric sources. Côte d'Ivoire is an exporter of electricity, supplying Ghana, Benin, Togo, Mali and Burkina Faso.

Access to electricity is concentrated mainly in the cities and towns. Electricity reaches less than 15 per cent of the rural population, a shortcoming which the government is seeking to remedy by progressive connection of rural communities to the distribution system.

Financial markets

Stock exchange

The Abidjan bourse is a regional stock exchange serving eight West African Economic and Monetary Union countries – Côte d'Ivoire, Benin, Burkina Faso, Mali, Niger, Senegal, Togo and Guinea-Bissau.

Banking and insurance

Abidjan is traditionally a major regional banking centre. There is no clear distinction between commercial, merchant and development banks since they may all accept deposits and engage in long- and short-term financing. Local banks generally handle retail banking and export-crop financing as well as funding small- and medium-sized businesses and housing. Some specialise in development of industry, agriculture and small businesses.

Côte d'Ivoire has a liberal policy towards foreign banks, but entry has become more difficult in recent years because of the large number of banks already present. A minimum capital is required for a new bank to start operating, but Ivorian participation is not obligatory.

Political instability has undermined the Ivorian banking sector, with the African Development Bank (AfDB) tranferring its head-quarters from Côte d'Ivoire to Tunisia in early 2003.

Central bank

Banque Centrale des Etats de l'Afrique de l'Ouest

Main financial centre

Abidjan

Time

GMT

Geography

Côte d'Ivoire is in West Africa on the Atlantic coast, bordered by Liberia and Guinea to the west, Mali and Burkina Faso to the north, and Ghana to the east. To the south is a 470 kilometre coastline on the Gulf of Guinea, the eastern part of which is inset with lagoons.

The terrain rises from the coastal plains to a plateau, 300 metres high for most of its length, rising to 1,200 metres near the country's western border.

The three main geographical areas are the equatorial zone along the coast, the tropical rain forests of the south and the drier savannah belt in the north.

There are four main rivers, the Bandama, Comoe, Sassandra and Cavally, but they are not navigable for long distances due to rapids.

Hemisphere

Northern

Climate

There are four distinct seasons in the centre and south of the country. Here the climate is tropical, with a long dry season running from December–April, followed by the rainy season from May–July. From August–September a dry spell is followed in October–November by a short rainy spell.

Average temperatures on the southern coastal plains are 21–34 degrees Celsius (C). Humidity is 80–90 per cent. Annual rainfall can be as heavy as 2.5 metres spread over about 140 days. In the central region temperature ranges are 14–39 degrees C. Annual rainfall varies from 1–2.5 metres.

In the northern savannah the climate is more extreme, but less humid with temperatures between 21–40 degrees C. Rainfall averages 1.4 metres a year. There are two seasons, rains from July–November and the dry season from December–June.

Dress codes

When calling on senior personnel, businessmen should wear suits, even though this may be uncomfortable in Abidjan's hot and humid climate. The capital, Yamoussoukro, is less humid and at an altitude of 220 metres is cooler. In general loose-fitting, tropical lightweight clothing is advisable.

Women may wear sleeveless cotton dresses or lightweight skirts and blouses, and this mode of dress is adequate for business calls.

Entry requirements

Passports

Required by all except particular document holders of certain African countries.

Visa

Required by all except citizens of other Ecowas countries, and nationals of Andorra, Chad, Monaco, Morocco, Seychelles, Tunisia and Vatican City, for stays of up to three months. Applications for business visas require a letter from the visitor's company accepting responsibility for any expenses incurred, and a letter of invitation (can be faxed copy) from host company in Côte d'Ivoire.

Currency advice/regulations

The import of CFA francs is unlimited; export is limited to CFAf10,000. The import of euros is unlimited, all other currencies must be declared. Export of all foreign currencies is limited to CFAf25,000, or the amount declared on arrival.

Travellers cheques are accepted in banks and hotels.

Health (for visitors)

Mandatory precautions

Yellow fever vaccination certificate.

Advisable precautions

Cholera, hepatitis A and E and typhoid vaccinations are strongly recommended and polio immunisation is a benefit. Malaria prophylaxis should be taken as risk exists throughout the country all year. Avoid tap water and drink only bottled beverages (including water) or beverages made with boiled water; cooked food is advisable and all fruit should be peeled. Bilharzia is present, use only well chlorinated swimming pools. Rabies and sleeping sickness are a risk. It is advisable to pack a sterilised syringe kit.

Hotels

Abidjan and Yamoussoukro have several five-star hotels. There are a wide range of other hotels in the other main centres. Tipping usually 10–15 per cent.

Credit cards

American Express and Mastercard are widely accepted; charge cards are of limited use.

Public holidays (national)

Fixed dates

1 Jan (New Year's Day), 1 May (Labour Day), 7 Aug (Independence Day), 15 Aug (Assumption Day), 1 Nov (All Saints' Day), 9 Nov (Day of Mourning), 15 Nov (Peace Day), 7 Dec (Félix Houphouët-Boigny Remembrance Day), 25 Dec (Christmas Day).

Variable dates

Easter Monday, Ascension Day, Whit Monday, Eid al Adha, Eid al Fitr, Birth of the Prophet, Ascent of the Prophet.

Some companies allow an informal one-day holiday before or after a Sunday holiday

Islamic year – 1429 (10 Jan 2008–28 Dec 2008): The Islamic year contains 354 or 355 days, with the result that Muslim feast advance by 10–12 dars against the Gregorain calendar. Dates of feasts vary according to the sighting of the new moon, so cannot be forecast exactly.

Working hours

Banking

Mon–Fri: 0800–1130 and 1430–1630.

Business

Mon–Fri: 0800–1200 and 1430–1700.

Government

Mon–Fri: 0730/0800–1200 and 1430–1730.

Shops

Mon–Fri: 0800–1200 and 1530–1830/1900, Sat: 0800–1200 and 1430–1730.

Telecommunications

Mobile/cell phones

There are several 900 and a 1800 GSM services operating in main urban areas.

Electricity supply

220V AC, 50 cycles

Social customs/useful tips

Ivorians like to shake hands and exchange greetings and other pleasantries before getting down to business.

It is considered polite to arrive punctually to social occasions when kissing on the cheek and hugging are reserved only for old friends.

Security

There are ongoing security problems in the country in general and increased trouble in the west – visitors are advised not to travel to the area. Foreign visitors should register their presence with their diplomatic missions on arrival, although many suspended their representation in 2005. Visitors must take added precaution for their own safety and take note of local warnings.

Getting there

Air

National airline: Air Ivoire: flies to France, South Africa and Dubai.

International airport/s: Abidjan-Félix Houphouet-Boigny (ABJ), is the country's airport hub accepting all intercontinental flights. It is 16km from city; duty-free shop, restaurant, bank, post office, pharmacy, car hire.

Yamoussoukro (ASK) accepts regional flights .

Airport tax: Departure tax: continental, CFAf3,000; intercontinental: CFAf5,000.

Surface

Road: There are good links from Ghana, Burkina Faso, Guinea and Liberia.

Rail: Travellers should check information concerning regular services from Burkina Faso, connecting Ouagadougou with Abidjan. Sleeping and restaurant facilities are available for these long journeys.

Getting about

National transport

Air: Air Ivoire no longer operates internal flights. Contact local airports for information on charter flights.

Departure tax: CFAf800.

Road: Extensive network of roads stretching from south to north with transverse roads interconnecting.

Buses: The once extensive service has been curtailed by the civil war. Contact local operators concerning services.

Taxis: Bush taxis run to all parts of the country.

Rail: A 1,145km network from Abidjan to Ouagadougou passes through Agboville, Dimbokra, Bouaké, Katiola and Ferkessedougou.

City transport

Taxis: In Abidjan, red taxis with meters can be hailed or ordered by telephone in main centres. Two tariffs operate: one from 0600–2400, the other 2400–0600. The early morning tariff is double that for the day and evening. Do not hesitate to haggle over the fare, especially if the meter is not running, or if arriving at the airport.

Buses, trams & metro: Buses usually run from 0600–2100 or 2200, operated in Abidjan by state-run Sotra.

Most hotels have their own airport buses. Check at hotel booths near the terminal exit.

Car hire

Self-drive and chauffeur-driven cars can be hired in Abidjan, Bouaké, Daloa, Gagnoa, Man and Sassandra.

An international driving licence is required (not less than 12 months old). Drivers must be at least 21-years-old. Seat-belts must be worn in front seats. Traffic drives on the right.

BUSINESS DIRECTORY

The addresses listed below are a selection only. While World of Information makes every endeavour to check these addresses, we cannot guarantee that changes have not been made, especially to telephone numbers and area codes. We would welcome any corrections.

Telephone area codes

The international direct dialling (IDD) code for Côte d'Ivoire is +225, followed by subscriber's number.

Useful telephone numbers

Ambulance (SAMU): 185, 2044-3445, 2044-5353.

Police (emergency): 111, 170.

International telephone enquiries: 160.

National telephone enquiries: 120.

Chambers of Commerce

American Chamber of Commerce, 01 PO Box 3394, Abidjan 01 (tel: 2021-4616; fax: 2022-2437; email: amcham@AfricaOnline.co.ci).

Côte d'Ivoire Chambre de Commerce et Industrie, 6 Avenue Joseph Anoma, PO Box 1399, Abidjan 01 (tel: 2033-1600; fax: 2032-3942; email: mail@ccici.org).

French Chambre de Commerce et d'Industrie, 141 Boulevard de Marseille, Immeuble Jean Lefebvre, 01 PO Box 189, Abidjan 18 (tel: 2025-8206; fax: 2024-1000; email: ccifci@ccif.ci).

Banking

Bank of Africa Côte d'Ivoire, BP 4132, 11 Ave Joseph Anoma, Abidjan 01 (tel: 2033-1536; fax: 2033-2398, 2032-8993).

Banque Atlantique (Côte d'Ivoire SA); BP 04, Immeuble Atlantique, Avenue Nogues, 1036 Abidjan 04 (tel: 2031-5950; fax: 2021-6852).

Banque de l'Habitat de Côte d'Ivoire, BP 2325, 22 Ave Joseph Anoma, Abidjan 01 (tel: 2022-6000; fax: 2022-5818).

Banque Internationale pour le Commerce et l'Industrie de la Côte d'Ivoire SA; Avenue Franchet d'Espérey, 01 BP 1298 Abidjan 01 (tel: 2020-1600, 2020-1700; fax: 2020-1700) .

Banque Paribas Côte d'Ivoire; BP 09, 17 Avenue Terrasson de Fougères, Abidjan 17 (tel: 2021-8686, 2021-3032; fax: 2021-8823).

BIAO-Côte d'Ivoire; BP 1274, 8/10 Avenue Joseph Anoma, Abidjan 01 (tel: 2020-0720, 2020-0722; fax: 2020-0700).

Caisse Autonome d'Amortissement Société d'Etat, BP 670, Immeuble SCIAM, Ave Marchant, Abidjan 01 (tel: 2021-0611, 2032-8575; fax: 2021-3578).

Cofipa Investment Bank Côte d'Ivoire, BP 411, Rue Botreau Roussel/ Ave Delafosse, Abidjan 04 (tel: 2021-8452; fax: 2021-8599).

Compagnie Bancaire de l'Atlantique en Côte d'Ivoire, 01 BP, Immeuble Atlantique, Avenue Nogues, 522 Abidjan 01 (tel: 2021-2804, 2030-1520; fax: 2021-0798).

Compagnie Financière de la Côte d'Ivoire; BP 1566, Tour BICICI 01, Rue Gourgas 15e étage, Abidjan 01 (tel: 2021-2732; fax: 2021-2643, 2020-1700).

Ecobank Côte d'Ivoire SA, BP 4107, Immeuble Alliance, 1 Av Terrasson de Fougères, Abidjan 01 (tel: 2031-9200, 2021-1041; fax: 2021-8816).

Société Générale de Banques en Côte d'Ivoire SA; BP 1355, 5 & 7 Avenue Joseph Anoma, Abidjan 01 (tel: 2020-1234, 2020-1111; fax: 2020-1482, 2020-1486).

Société Générale de Financement et de Participation en Côte d'Ivoire (SOGEFINANCE); BP 3904, 5-7 Avenue Joseph Anoma, Abidjan 01 (tel: 2022-5530, 2022-1234; fax: 2032-6760, 2020-1492).

Société Ivoirienne de Banque, BP 1300, Immeuble Alpha 2000, 34 Boulevard de la Republique, Abidjan 01 (tel: 2020-0000; fax: 2021-9741).

Central bank

Banque Centrale des Etats de l'Afrique de l'Ouest, Direction National, Angle Boulevard Botreau-Roussel et Avenue Delafosse, PO Box 1769, Abidjan (tel: 208-500; fax: 222-852).

Travel information

Air Ivoire, 2 Avenue du Général de Gaulle, PO Box 7782, Abidjan 01 (tel: 2021-3429; internt: www.airivoire.com).

Félix Houphouet-Boigny International Airport (tel: 2027-7322, 2023-4000).

Wagonlits (Railway Information), Boulevard de Marseille, Abidjan (tel: 2021-2066, 2021-3910).

Ministry of tourism

Ministry of Tourism, BP V184, Abidjan (tel: 2044-5500, 2044-5129, 2044-6953; fax: 2044-5580).

National tourist organisation offices

Office Ivoirien du Tourisme et de l'Hôtellerie (OITH), Place de la République, BP 8538, Abidjan 01 (tel: 2020-2516; fax: 2020-3388; email: oith@tourismeci.org; internet: www.tourismeci.org).

Ministries

Ministry of Agriculture and Animal Resources, Immeuble de la Caisse de Stabilisation, BP V84, Abidjan (tel: 2021-3858; fax: 2021-4618; e-mail: minagra@cimail.net).

Ministry of Communication and Information Technology, Tour C, Tours Administratives, BP V138, Abidjan (tel: 2021-1116; fax: 2021-8495).

Ministry of Construction and Urbanism, Tour D, Tours Administratives, 20 BP 650, Abidjan (tel: 2021-8235; fax: 2021-3568).

Ministry of Defence and Civil Protection, Immeuble EECI, BP V 241, Abidjan (tel: 2021-2682; fax: 2022-4175).

Ministry of Economic Infrastructures, Immeuble Postel 2001, 18 BP 2203, Abidjan (tel: 2034-4273; fax: 2034-7322).

Ministry of Economy and Finance, Immeuble SCIAM, BP V163, Abidjan (tel: 2020-0842; fax: 2021-3208).

Ministry of Education, Tour D, Tours Administratives, BP V 120, Abidjan (tel: 2022-7406; fax: 2022-9322).

Ministry of Family, Women and Children, Tour E, Tours Administratives, BP 200, Abidjan (tel: 2021-7626; fax: 2021-4461).

Ministry of Foreign Affairs, Bloc Ministériel, Boulevard Angoulvand, BP V109, Abidjan (tel: 2022-7150; fax: 2033-2308).

Ministry of Health, Tour C, Tours Administratives, 01 BP V 04, Abidjan (tel: 2021-0871; fax: 2021-5240).

Ministry of Higher Education and Scientific Research, Tour C, Tours Administratives, BP V 151, Abidjan (tel: 2021-3316; fax: 2021-2225).

Ministry of the Interior and Decentralisation, Bloc Ministériel, Boulevard Angoulvand, BP V 121, Abidjan (tel: 2022-3816; fax: 2022-3648).

Ministry of Justice and Public Freedom, Bloc Ministériel, Boulevard Angoulvand, BP V 107, Abidjan (tel: 2021-1727; fax: 2033-1259).

Ministry of Labour, Civil Service and Administrative Reform, Immeuble Fonction Publique, Boulevard Angoulvand, BP V 93, Abidjan (tel: 2021-4290; fax: 2021-1286).

Ministry of Mines and Energy, Immeuble Postel 2001, BP V 40, Abidjan (tel: 2034-4851; fax: 2021-3730).

Ministry of Trade, Immeuble CCIA, Rue Jean-Paul II, BP V65, Abidjan (tel: 2021-6473; fax: 2021-6474).

Ministry of Transport, Immeuble Postel 2001, BP V 06, Abidjan (tel: 2034-7315; fax: 2021-3730).

Other useful addresses

Agence des Télécommunications de Côte d'Ivoire (ATCI), BP 2203, Immeuble Postel 2001, Rue le Coeur, Abidjan 18 (tel: 2034-4255; fax: 2034-4254).

Association of Businessmen and Industry of Côte d'Ivoire, Imm Lefébre, Bd de Marseille, 01 BP 464, Abidjan 01.

Association of Exporters of Coffee-Cocoa, Imm CCIA, 01 BP 1399, Abidjan 01 (tel: 2022-5446/5).

Association of Fishing Industry, Port de Pêche, 01 BP 14, Abidjan 01 (tel: 2025-7998; fax: 2025-2065).

Association of Import and Export Traders, Imm Résidence du Front Lagunaire 2 étage, 01 BP 3792, Abidjan 01 (tel: 2032-5427; fax: 2032-5652).

Association of West African Home Grown Product Dealers, Imm CCIA 7 étage, O & BP 5407, Abidjan 01 (tel: 2022-5795).

Bourse des Valeurs Abidjan, Ave Marchand 10, BP 1878, 01 Abidjan (tel: 2021-5783, 215742; fax: 2022-1657).

British Embassy, 3rd Floor, Immeuble Les Harmonies, Angle Boulevard Carde et Avenue Dr Jamot, BP 2581, Plateau, 01 Abidjan (tel: 2022-6850/2, 2032-8209; fax: 2022-3221).

Bureau National d'Etudes Techniques et de Dévéloppement (BNETD) (National Office for Technical and Development Studies), BP 945, 04 Abidjan (tel: 2044-2805, 2044-5877; fax: 2044-5666; email: nzoro@bnetd.sita.net; internet site: http://www.bnetd.sita.net.).

Caisse de Stabilisation (CAISTAB), BP V132, Abidjan (tel: 2020-2700; fax: 2021-8994).

Centre de Commerce Internationale d'Abidjan (conference bookings), Abidjan (tel: 2022-4070).

Centre de Promotion des Investissements en Côte d'Ivoire (CEPICI), CCIA-WTR 5th Floor, BP V152, Abidjan 01 (tel: 2021-4070; fax: 2021-4071).

Committee of Insurers, Imm Les Arcades, 01 BP 3873, Abidjan 01 (tel: 2022-5437; fax: 2021-1835).

Committee of Privatisation, 6 Boulevard de l'Indénié, Abidjan-Plateau, BP 1141, Abidjan 01 (tel: 2022-2231/2232/2236; fax: 2022-2235).

Compagnie Ivoirienne pour le Développement des Textiles, BP 622, Bouaké (tel: 2063-3113, 2063-3013; fax: 2063-4167).

Conseil Economique et Social, 04 BP 301, Abidjan (tel: 2021-2060).

Côte d'Ivoire Embassy (USA), 3421 Massachusetts Avenue, NW, Washington DC 20007 (tel: (+1-202) 797-0300; fax: 20(+1-202) 265-2454).

The Customs Department, Boulevard de la République, BP V 25, Abidjan (tel: 2021-5223).

Direction et Controle des Grands Travaux, Département Industrie et Energie, Boulevard de la Corniche, Cocody, 04 BP 945, Abidjan 04 (tel: 2044-2118; fax: 2044-5866).

Energie Electrique de la Côte d'Ivoire, BP 1345, 1 place de la République, Abidjan (tel: 2020-6000; fax: 2032-7477).

French Embassy; BP 175, Rue Lecoueur 17, Abidjan 17 (tel: 2020-0404; fax: 2020-0447).

General Surveillance Co (Responsible for Import Controls), PO Box 795, Abidjan (tel: 2021-1290).

Ivorian Investment Promotion in Côte d'Ivoire (CEPECI), PO Box V 152, Abidjan 01 (tel: 2021-4070; fax: 2021-4071; internet site: http://www.cepici.go.ci).

National Enterprise Assistance and Promotion Centre (CAPEN), Immeuble La Pyramide, 9th floor, 08 BP 868, Abidjan 08 (tel: 2032-0145).

Organisation Centrale pour la Commercialisation de l'Ananas et la Banane (OCAB), Imm Corniche, 16 BP 1908, Abidjan 16 (tel: 2032-5882; fax: 2032-1060).

Port Autonome d'Abidjan, BP V85, Abidjan (tel: 2024-0866, 2024-2640; fax: 2024-2328).

Professional Association of the Oil Industry, 13 Impasse Paris Village, 01 BP 1777, Abidjan 01 (tel: 2021-7320; fax: 2022-2858).

Société des Mines d'Ity, BP 872, Abidjan 08 (tel: 2044-6363; fax: 2044-4100).

Société Ivoirienne de la Poste et de L'Epargne, BP 105, Abidjan 17 (tel: 2034-7004; fax: 2034-7107).

Société Ivoirienne de Raffinage (SIR), Boulevard de Petit-Bassam, BP 1269, Abidjan 01 (tel: 2027-0427, 2027-0160; fax: 2027-1798, 2027-3217).

Société Nationale d'Opérations Petroliéres de la Côte d'Ivoire, BP V194, Abidjan (tel: 2021-4058).

Société pour le Développement Minier de la Côte d'Ivoire, BP 2816, Abidjan (tel: 2021-2994).

SODEMI (State Company for Mineral Development), BP 2816, 31 Boulevard Latrille, Abidjan Cocody-Nord, Abidjan 01 (tel: 2044-0994; fax: 2044-0821).

US Embassy, 5 rue Jesse Owens, 01 BP 171, Abidjan 01 (tel: 2021-0979).

World Trade Centre, PO Box V 68, Abidjan (tel: 2021-6189, 2022-4072/3; fax: 2022-7112).

National news agency: AIP (Agence Ivoirienne de Presse)

Address: 04 Avenue Chardy, BP 312, Adidjan 04 (tel: 20-22-64-13; fax: 20-21-57-12; internet: www.aip.ci).

Internet sites

Africa Business Network: www.ifc.org/abn

AllAfrica.com: allafrica.com

African Development Bank: www.afdb.org

Africa Online: www.africaonline.com

Mbendi AfroPaedia (information on companies, countries, industries and stock exchanges in Africa): mbendi.co.za

Croatia

Following parliamentary elections in November 2007, the largest party in the government, the centre-right Croatian Democratic Union (HDZ), formed a coalition with two smaller parties and seven independents. The coalition held a small parliamentary majority.

The HDZ, obtained a narrow lead in the general election. The electoral commission announced that the HDZ would have 61 MPs – five more than the opposition Social Democrat Party (SDP). Immediately after the election both parties said they had begun talks with potential coalition partners to secure the parliamentary majority of 77 seats necessary to govern. Both parties were committed to completing Croatia's entry into the European Union (EU), which they hoped to achieve by 2010, although the EU has warned them to do more to tackle corruption.

The Croatian State Election Commission said the HDZ had won 34.78 per cent of the vote. The SDP trailed with 32.46 per cent, followed by the Croatian People's Party, and the coalition between the Croatian Peasant Party (HSS) and Croatian Social Liberal Party (HSLS). The results left the HDZ with 61 seats in the 153-seat parliament, the SDP with 56 seats, the HSS-HSLS coalition with eight and the HNS with seven. Analysts say the 400,000-strong Croatian *diaspora*, based mainly in neighbouring Bosnia, swung the result in favour of the HDZ. Prime minister and HDZ leader, Ivo Sanader, claimed his party's victory was 'certain', and that 'Croatian voters have shown that they trust the HDZ and the policies we've been implementing in the last four years'. The main campaign issues in the election were corruption, the economy, and reforms needed to take Croatia into the EU.

KEY FACTS

Official name: Republika Hrvatska (Republic of Croatia)

Head of State: President Stjepan (Stipe) Mesic (HNS) (since 2000; re-elected 16 Jan 2005)

Head of government: Prime Minister Ivo Sanader (HDZ) (since 2003)

Ruling party: Coalition led by the Hrvatska Demokratska Zajednica (HDZ) (Croatian Democratic Union) with the Hrvatska Seljacka Stranka-Hrvatska Socijalno Liberalna Stranka (HSS-HSLS) (Croatian Peasant's Party)-(Croatian Social Liberal Party) (from 2003; re-elected 3 Dec 2007)

Area: 56,538 square km

Population: 4.44 million (2007)

Capital: Zagreb

Official language: Croatian

Currency: Kuna (K) = 100 lipas

Exchange rate: K4.55 per US$ (Jul 2008)

GDP per capita: US$11,576 (2007)

GDP real growth: 5.80% (2007)

Labour force: 2.12 million (2004)

Unemployment: 18.00% (2005)

Inflation: 2.90% (2005)

Balance of trade: -US$10.51 billion (2006)

Foreign debt: US$26.40 billion (2004)

Visitor numbers: 8.66 million (2006)*

* estimated figure

EU accession

A European Commission Progress Report, published on 6 November, 2007, confirmed that Croatia's accession negotiations were advancing well and entering a decisive phase. The report also emphasised that Croatia could serve as a positive example for the region as a whole. On the other hand, further progress particularly in relation to judicial and public administration reform, minority rights, refugee return, as well as in pursuing stronger internal market policies, in particular those related to the state aid and restructuring of the steel and shipbuilding industries, still needed to be made. The original date set for Croatia's EU membership was 2009, but by mid-2008, this was beginning to look somewhat optimistic.

Growth, but slow growth

Croatia's economy continued to record strong growth in 2007. Gross domestic product (GDP) growth had accelerated in 2006 to 4.8 per cent and surged further to 6.8 per cent in the first half of 2007, an increase of two percentage points compared to the same period in 2006. Croatia's GDP per capita at PPS (purchasing power standards) is at 54 per cent of the average for the EU's 27 member countries. However impressive, Croatia's annual GDP growth rate lagged behind the growth of almost all the new EU member states. The growth has been underpinned primarily by personal consumption and gross fixed capital formation; these accelerated by 6.8 and 8.3 per cent in 2007, respectively. Government consumption also increased, by 2.7 per cent. The main drivers of growth are industrial production, retail trade, construction and tourism.

Exports and debt

Positive fiscal developments also continued in the first half of 2007, driven by Croatia's success in revenue generation. In July 2007, Croatia's parliament adopted the 2007 budget revision, which envisaged a reduction of the accrual based government deficit to 2.6 per cent of GDP, down from 3.0 per cent of GDP in 2006. Total public debt dropped further to 47.1 per cent of GDP in August 2007 and the government's share of external debt decreased to 20 per cent. Croatia's gross external debt represented 85.3 per cent of GDP in December 2006, up from 82.4 per cent at the end of 2005, following strong capital inflows to domestic banks. Slower growth in export volumes, together with higher prices for imported energy and increased earnings accruing to foreign investors, widened the current account deficit to 7.6 per cent of GDP in 2006 up from 6.6 per cent in 2005. Net direct foreign investment (FDI) was exceptionally high in the first half of 2007, surging to eur2 billion. FDI looked set to grow further in the second half of 2007 due to the sale of the government's stake in Croatian Telecom. The government expected the widening of the current account deficit to above 8 per cent of GDP in 2007, a level which was recognised to be unsustainable in the long run.

Croatia's monetary policy tightened further in 2007 to limit the credit expansion and accompanying rise in indebtedness. In addition to its efforts towards keeping low inflation and a stable exchange rate, the Croatian National Bank had also focused in 2006 on measures aimed at reducing external debt growth and halting any worsening of the current account deficit. As a result, the central bank pursued a more restrictive monetary policy with the aim of slowing down rapid growth of monetary aggregates. Further tightening occurred in July 2007, when the CNB tightened the credit growth ceiling for the second half of the year to 3 per cent. The credit growth rate to the private sector in the first eight months of 2007 was 9.9 per cent, lower than the same period last year (14.3 per cent). Credit growth was mainly spurred by household loans, especially housing loans.

KEY INDICATORS — Croatia

	Unit	2003	2004	2005	2006	2007
Population	m	4.38	4.38	4.44	4.44	4.44
Gross domestic product (GDP)	US$bn	27.34	35.20	38.51	42.46	51.36
GDP per capita	US$	6,240	7,378	8,670	9,558	11,576
GDP real growth	%	3.7	3.8	4.3	4.6	5.8
Inflation	%	2.0	2.1	3.3	3.2	2.9
Unemployment	%	21.9	13.8	18.0	17.2	*11.8
Industrial output	% change	–	4.3	4.8	5.4	–
Agricultural output	% change	–	4.2	0.1	2.5	–
Exports (fob) (goods)	US$m	6,300.0	8,208.2	8,991.6	10,606.0	12,622.7
Imports (cif) (goods)	US$m	14,200.0	16,554.5	18,282.5	21,117.0	25,556.1
Balance of trade	US$m	-7,900.0	-8,346.3	-9,290.9	-10,511.0	-12,933.4
Current account	US$m	-1,770.0	-1,790.0	-2,482.2	-3,377.0	-4,412.1
Total reserves minus gold	US$m	8,190.5	8,758.2	8,800.3	11,487.8	13,674.5
Foreign exchange	US$m	8,190.2	8,757.9	8,799.8	11,487.4	13,674.0
Exchange rate	per US$	6.64	5.82	5.70	5.56	5.06

* estimated figure

Risk assessment

Politics	Good
Economy	Improving
Regional stability	Fair

COUNTRY PROFILE

Historical profile

The Croats formed an independent kingdom during the tenth century.

1089 Inner Croatia came under the control of Hungary and then the Habsburg empire, remaining that way for eight centuries.

1529 After Hungary's defeat by the Ottoman Turks, a militarised border was formed between Croatia and Bosnia-Hercegovina.

1918 The defeat of the Austro-Hungarian empire during the First World War saw the creation of the Kingdom of the Serbs, Croats and Slovenes, encompassing Bosnia and Hercegovina (BiH), Croatia, parts of Dalmatia and Macedonia, Montenegro, Serbia, Slavonia and Slovenia.

1921 Prince Alexander, Regent of Serbia, became King.

1929 Following disputes between Serbs and Croats, King Alexander assumed dictatorial powers and the country was renamed Yugoslavia.

1934 King Alexander of Yugoslavia was assassinated in France by Croatian extremists. Power passed to Prince Paul, acting as Regent to 11-year-old King Peter II. He ruled with the support of the armed forces.

1939 Croatia was granted internal autonomy.

1941 A coup by air force officers replaced Prince Paul and the pro-Nazi Germany government with the 17-year-old King Peter II and established a pro-Allied government. In response, German and Italian forces invaded Yugoslavia, forcing the royal family and government into exile. The fascist Ustasha movement, led by Ante Pavelic, created the Nezavisna Drzava Hrvatska (NDH) (Independent State of Croatia).
1943 Civil war ensued between two rival groups, the communist partisans, led by General Tito, and the Royalist Chetniks. The partisans proclaimed their own government in liberated areas.
1944 King Peter II was deposed.
1945 The Federal People's Republic of Yugoslavia was proclaimed, with Josip Broz Tito as prime minister – a Croat opposed to expressions of Croat (or any other) nationalism. Croatia became a constituent republic of the federation. The other republics were: BiH, Macedonia, Slovenia, Montenegro, Serbia and the two autonomous regions of Vojvodina and Kosovo.
1953 Constitutions were adopted and Tito became president of Yugoslavia. Increased autonomy for the constituent republics was extended in 1963 and 1974.
1971 A mass movement in favour of Croatian nationalist revival was crushed by Tito.
1980 Tito died. A system of a collective (rotating) presidency was adopted.
1989 Differences and friction between the wealthier republics, Slovenia and Croatia, and the different ethnic groups intensified.
1980 Tito died. A system of a collective (rotating) presidency was adopted.
1989 Differences and friction between the wealthier republics, Slovenia and Croatia, and the different ethnic groups intensified.
1990 Following Slovenia's secession from Yugoslavia, Croatia held its own free elections which were won by the nationalist Hrvatska Demokratska Zajednica (HDZ) (Croatian Democratic Community). Franjo Tudjman became the first president of the Republic of Croatia. In August, Croatian Serbs held their own referendum, which favoured maintaining their cultural autonomy. Rebel Serbs took control of the Krajina and two other regions in Croatia – Eastern and Western Slavonia. The secession of Croatia, Slovenia and BiH led to invasions of these republics by the Jugoslovenska Narodna Armija (JNA) (Yugoslav National Army).
1991 Independence from Yugoslavia was unilaterally declared.
1992–94 Croatia was recognised as an independent state by the then European Community (EC) on 15 January and became a member of the UN. Franjo Tudjman was re-elected president. The declaration of independence was followed by several months of war, first against the JNAand then against local rebel ethnic Serbs. JNA units had been incorporated into the ethnic Serb armies in the Krajina region. The Croatian government began to finance and support Bosnian Croat attempts to separate from BiH. This exacerbated the civil war in BiH between the Muslim and Bosnian Croats, until a cease-fire was achieved and the Muslim-Croat Federation was established in 1994.
1995 After nearly four years of Serb control, western Slavonia and Krajina were recaptured by the Croatian army. Tudjman's ruling nationalist HDZ won the parliamentary elections and Zlatko Matesa became prime minister. President Tudjman of Croatia, along with President Slobodan Milosevic of Yugoslavia and President Alija Izetbegovic of BiH, agreed to end the Bosnian civil war.
1996 Yugoslavia (consisting of Serbia and Montenegro and the two autonomous regions of Kosovo and Vojvodina) and Croatia signed an agreement on mutual recognition, formally ending five years of hostility.
1997 The HDZ won a majority in the upper house of the Sabor and President Franjo Tudjman was re-elected.
1998 Eastern Slavonia (some 5 per cent of Croatia's total territory) was handed back to Croatia by the UN Transition Authority for Eastern Slavonia (UNTAES).
1999 Due to Tudjman's deteriorating health, the president of the House of Representatives, Vlatko Pavletic, took over as acting Croatian president in November. Franjo Tudjman died on 10 December.
2000 The Socialdemokratska Partija (SDP) (Social Democratic Party) won the general election. A centre-left coalition government was formed, led by the SDP, with Ivica Racan (SDP) as prime minister. Stipe Mesic of the Hrvatska Narodna Stranka (HNS) (Croatian People's Party) and regarded as an ally of the SDP, was sworn in as president.
2001 A constitutional amendment abolished of the upper house of parliament, the Zupanijski dom (House of Counties). Croatia agreed to extradite several suspected war criminals to the International Criminal Tribunal for former Yugoslavia (ICTY) at The Hague in The Netherlands. War veteran groups protested strongly at the government's co-operation.
2002 Ivica Racan resigned as prime minister, but was re-appointed and formed a new centre-left coalition government, comprising the SDP, HNS, Hrvatska Seljacka Stranka (HSS) (Croatian Peasant Party), Liberalna Stranka (LS) (Liberal Party) and Libra.
2003 Croatia submitted its formal application for EU membership. The HDZ – Croatian nationalists – defeated the pro-Western parties in parliamentary elections. President Mesic appointed Ivo Sanader (HDZ) as prime minister and a coalition government was formed by the HDZ and the Hrvatska Socialna Liberalna Stranka, Demokratski Centar (HSLS, DC) (Croatian Social Liberal Party, Democratic Centre).
2004 Milan Babic, a Croatian Serb, was jailed for 13 years by the ICTY Tribunal in The Hague for war crimes during his leadership, in the early 1990s, of the self-proclaimed Krajina Serb republic.
2005 In the run-off presidential elections incumbent Stjepan Mesic won 66 per cent of the vote, defeating Jadranka Kosor with 34 per cent. The EU began accession talks with Croatia; they had been stalled because Croatia was deemed unco-operative in handing over suspected war criminals. The fugitive, General Ante Gotovina was arrested in the Canary Islands and sent to the war crimes tribunal in The Hague.
2006 Croatia membership talks with the EU was caught up in internal discord about enlargement when the EU decided to wait until at least 2010 before offering Croatia membership. However in June, talks with Croatia continued with the EU separately from Turkey, which had applied for membership at the same time.
2007 In November parliamentary elections the ruling HDZ retained its 66 seats, the opposition SPH increased its number of seats to 56. A coalition between the HDZ and the Hrvatska Seljacka Stranka-Hrvatska Socijalno Liberalna Stranka (HSS-HSLS) (Croatian Peasant's Party)-(Croatian Social Liberal Party) coalition formed the government on 3 December.
2008 An accession protocol was signed by Nato ambassadors in Brussels on 9 July. Croatia will join in April 2009.

Political structure

Constitution

The written constitution was first adopted in December 1990, with amendments in 2000 and 2001 that cut back presidential powers and abolish the upper house of parliament.
Under the constitution there is a principle of the separation of power into legislative, executive and judicial branches, which are limited by the right to local and regional self-government.
The laws of Croatia must conform to the constitution
The electoral law gives the vote to all Croatians over the age of 18, including those living abroad. Ethnic minorities are equal with ethnic Croats according to the

constitution. However, in recent years the international community has raised strong objections to laws that de facto discriminate against other groups – specifically returning Serb refugees. Until these problems are solved, Croatia is unlikely to be recognised as a fully democratic state. The administration of Croatia is divided into 21 zupanije (counties). There are also two kotari, or special districts, at Glina and Knin, which are under direct Serb control.

Form of state

Unitary, democratic republic

The executive

Executive power is vested in the president who is Head of State and supreme commander of the armed forces and is directly elected for five years and a maximum of two terms.

The president appoints the prime minister and, by recommendation of the prime minister, other members of the government. These appointments are subject to confirmation by the House of Representatives.

National legislature

In 2001, a constitutional amendment abolished Croatia's bicameral legislature and the upper house, the Zupanijski dom (House of Counties). The remaining chamber, Zastupnici dom (House of Representatives), is composed of 152 members, each elected for a four-year term in multi-member constituencies.

Following the 2001 amendment, the House of Representatives has been referred to more commonly as the Sabor (parliament).

Legal system

All civil and criminal cases are dealt with by basic and higher courts. The Supreme Court is the highest authority for civil and criminal law, charged with ensuring uniform application of laws and equality of citizens. All judges and other judicial officials are appointed by the Judicial Council, an elected body that is answerable to the parliament. The Judicial Council also acts as the Constitutional Court to determine the conformity of national legislation with the Constitution.

All prosecutions are the responsibility of the Office of the Public Prosecutor. There is also a Public Attorney. The Justice Ministry is the administrative authority of the Croatian judiciary. Its major instrument is the Croatian police, which falls under the jurisdiction of the interior minister.

Last elections

2/16 January 2005 (presidential); 25 November 2007 (parliamentary).

Results: Presidential: Stipe Mesic won 66 per cent of the vote; Jadranka Kosor won 34 per cent. Turnout was 51 per cent. Parliamentary: the HDZ Union won 66 seats (out of 152); the SPH won 56; the Hrvatska Seljacka Stranka (HSS) (Croatian Peasant's Party) won seven; Hrvatska Narodna Stranka-Liberalni Demokrati (HNS-LD) (Croatian People's Party- Liberal Democrats) won seven; Istarski Demokratski Sabor/Dieta Democratica Istriana (IDS/DDI) (Istrian Democratic Assembly) won three; Hrvatski Demokratski Sabor Slavonije i Baranje (HDSSB) (Croatian Democratic Assembly of Slovonija and Banranja) won three; the Hrvatska Socijalno Liberalna Stranka (HSLS) (Croatian Social Liberal Party) won two; all other parties won one seat only or were ethnic minority seats.

Next elections

2011 (parliamentary); 2009 (presidential).

Political parties

Ruling party

Coalition led by Hrvatska Demokratska Zajednica (HDZ) (Croatian Democratic Community) with Hrvatska Socialna Liberalna Stranka-Demokratski Centar (HSLS-DC) (Croatian Social Liberal Party-Democratic Centre) (since 2003)

Main opposition party

Socijaldemokratska Partija Hrvatske (SPH) (Social Democratic Party of Croatia)

Population

4.44 million (2007)

Last census: March 2001: 4,437,460

Population density: 79.8 inhabitants per square km. Urban population: 58 per cent (1995–2001).

Annual growth rate: -0.3 per cent 1994–2004 (WHO 2006)

Internally Displaced Persons (IDP)

11,000 (UNHCR 2004)

Ethnic make-up

Croats (90 per cent of the population), plus Serbs, Hungarians and Gypsies. The April 2001 census, the first since the 1991—95 war, indicated that Serbs made up 4.5 per cent of the population (the figure was 12 per cent in the early 1990s).

Religions

Predominantly Roman Catholic, with Christian Orthodox, Muslim and Jewish minorities, living mostly in Zagreb.

Education

Primary education is compulsory and free of charge. Secondary education is between the ages of 14–18. Vocational schools offer courses lasting for three or four years, including a period of practical instruction. There are four universities offering courses in science, engineering and medicine that meet international standards.

Public expenditure on education typically amounts to 5 per cent of annual gross national income.

Literacy rate: 98 per cent adult rate; 100 per cent youth rate (15–24) (Unesco 2005).

Compulsory years: Six to 14

Enrolment rate: 99 per cent; gross primary enrolment, of the relevant age group (including repetition rates), (World Bank).

Pupils per teacher: 19 in primary schools

Health

Per capita total expenditure on health (2003) was US$838; of which per capita government spending was US$701, at the international dollar rate, (WHO 2006).

The healthcare system has recovered since the internal conflict ended in 1995, but national coverage remains patchy, notably in the Krajina and Eastern Slavonia regions.

HIV/Aids

HIV prevalence: 0.1 per cent aged 15–49 in 2003 (World Bank)

Life expectancy: 75 years, 2004 (WHO 2006)

Fertility rate/Maternal mortality rate: 1.3 births per woman, 2004 (WHO 2006); maternal mortality 6 per 100,000 live births (World Bank).

Child (under 5 years) mortality rate (per 1,000): 6 per 1,000 live births; 1 per cent of children under five years are malnourished (World Bank).

Head of population per physician: 2.44 physicians per 1,000 people, 2003 (WHO 2006)

Welfare

The government faces a huge fiscal burden with an ageing population and a legacy of insufficient funds to pay retirees, particularly those who retired early following reforms of the late 90s. In 2002 the government introduced a dual social insurance and mandatory, privately managed, compulsory pension schemes, for all workers, with contributions that vary depending on the class of old age pension. Regular pensions require contributions of 10.75 per cent and 8.75 per cent (of payroll), from employee and employer respectively. Basic pensions require contributions of 8.75 per cent and 5.75 per cent (of payroll), from employee and employer respectively. Insurance contributions cover among other benefits, medical, disability and survivor's pensions. By 2020 projected pension fund assets should reach 25–30 per cent of GDP.

Main cities

Zagreb (capital, estimated population 699,164 in 2003), Split (192,589), Rijeka (141,063), Osijek (87,955), Zadar (71,457), Slavonski Brod (60,990), Pula (59,080), Sesvete (53,397), Sibenik (37,088), Sisak (35,664), Karlovac (48,057), Dubrovnik (29,916), Varazdin (41,801), Velika Gorica (35,238), Vinkovci (33,289), Vukovar (29,569).

Languages spoken
Croatian is written using the Latin alphabet. German and English are commonly used as second languages and business people are fluent in English. Bosnian and Serbian are also spoken and, near the Adriatic coast, Italian is spoken.
Official language/s
Croatian

Media

The constitution guarantees press freedom and bans censorship.
Other news agencies: HIC (Croatian Information Centre): www.hic.hr
Hina (Croatian News Agency): http://websrv2.hina.hr
Press
Dailies: Most popular newspapers have a tabloid format with commercialised stories.
In Croatian, national newspapers include Jutarnji List (www.jutarnji.hr), Vecernji List (www.vecernji.hr), and Vjesnik (www.vjesnik.com). Regional newspapers include Slobodna Dalmacija (www.slobodnadalmacija.hr) from Split, Novi List (www.novilist.hr) from Rijeka, 24 Sata (www.24sata.hr) from Zagreb and Glas Istre (www.glasistre.hr) from Pula.
Weeklies: In Croatian, the most influential news magazine Globus (www.globus.com.hr) has reported on corruption and organised crime that have been avoided by more mainstream publications. Another independent political magazine is Nacional (www.nacional.hr). Gloria (www.gloria.com.hr) is the most popular women's magazine and Nogometni Magazin (www.nogometni-magazin.com) is a sports publication.
Business: In Croatian, Business.hr (http://business.hr) and Privredni Vjesnik (www.privredni-vjesnik.hr with an English online edition) are both weekly newspapers.
Broadcasting
Television is the medium of choice for news and information for most people. Hrvatska Radiotelevizija (HRT) (www.hrt.hr) is the national, public broadcaster, which is funded through license fees and advertising revenue.
Radio: RTH operates three stations RTH1, 2 and 3, with a network provides by regional linking stations. There are numerous private stations centred on cities and regional centres, including Radio Samobor (www.radiosamobor.hr) with news and music, from Zagreb, Radio Mre nica (www.radio-mreznica.hr) from the Central region, Radio Laus (www.radio-laus.hr) from Dubrovnik, Radio Istra (www.radioistra.hr) from Istria and Gradski Radio (www.eter.hr) from Slavonia.
Television: There are three national, commercial, networks including the government-owned HRT (www.hrt.hr) TV, which has two channels providing domestically produced news and entertainment programmes and foreign imports. The private TV channels include RTL Televizija (www.rtl.hr) and Nova TV (http://dnevnik.hr). The Croatian media company OIV (www.oiv.hr) provides a comprehensive cable TV service, with 21 channels, to Croatia and neighbouring countries.
The conversion of terrestrial signals to digital is scheduled to be completed by 2010 and will provide the opportunity for transmission of many more channels.

Economy

Croatia has made significant attempts to rebuild and liberalise its economy since it seceded from Yugoslavia in 1991, and repair the damage caused by the conflict that ensued. It achieved an average annual GDP growth of 4.75 per cent over the period 2001–06. In 2005, GDP growth was 4.1 per cent and is estimated to be 4.6 per cent in 2006. The economy has been driven primarily by tourism – the sector accounts for almost 20 per cent of GDP. By 2005, services represented 62.2 per cent of the economy, over twice the size of the next largest sector, industry at 30.8 per cent, of which manufacturing represents 17 per cent. Agriculture represents only 7 per cent of GDP.
Government measures have successfully kept inflationary pressures in check with inflation at 3.3 per cent in 2005; it has remained stable at between 2–4 per cent since 2001. Despite improved employment rates, unemployment remains high at 13.8 per cent.
The IMF gave a positive analysis of Croatia in a February 2007 report, but warned that the economy was vulnerable, due to a widening current account deficit estimated at around 8.0 per cent of GDP in 2006, and rapid credit growth. It urged a reduction in the size of government while speeding up structural reforms, required to help business become more competitive.

External trade

In 2007, Croatia was a candidate member of the European Union and was still in negotiation with the EU to become a full member by about 2009.
International trade plays an important role in the economy, although combined only provide secondary foreign earnings to tourism. Timber production, textiles, ship building, steel, aluminium and food processing are the major industries and minerals, boats, garments, electrical goods and machinery are major export products.

Imports
Principal imports are transport, machinery and electrical equipment, chemicals, fuels and lubricants and foodstuffs.
Main sources: Italy (16.8 per cent total, 2006), Germany (14.5 per cent), Russia (10.1 per cent).
Exports
Principal exports are transport equipment, textiles, chemicals, foodstuffs and fuels.
Main destinations: Italy (23.1 per cent total, 2006), Bosnia and Hercegovina (12.6 per cent), Germany (10.4 per cent).

Agriculture

Farming
Almost half of the population lives in rural areas where agriculture continues to be the traditional source of income. The government has prepared a Rural Development Plan 2005–06 with four principal measures: farm investment, processing and marketing of agricultural and fish products, improved rural infrastructure and technical assistance. This programme is intended to align agriculture with conditions necessary for accession to the EU.
Of a total of 3.2 million hectares (ha) of arable land, 63 per cent is cultivated and the rest is pastureland. Only 68 per cent of agricultural land is privately owned. Agriculture contributed 8.2 per cent to GDP, and recorded growth of 4.2 per cent in 2004; it employed 16.2 per cent of the workforce.
Family farms with an average holding of 2.8ha per farm, contribute to the overall animal and horticultural production. Crop production is especially well developed, covering the needs for cereals, while cattle breeding accounts for almost 50 per cent of agriculture-generated GDP. The warm weather and mild winters suit grape-growing.
The government is committed to initiating agricultural market reform and promoting private farming. Reform in the agrarian production sector is accompanied by rising food imports, mostly from the EU. Agriculture within the country meets the domestic demand for wine, wheat, corn, eggs and poultry. Croatia's oil and sugar processing facilities are big enough to provide exports. However, with high production costs and a series of free trade agreements farm products cannot compete internationally.
Estimated crop production in 2005 included: 3,177,855 tonnes (t) cereals in total, 2,100,000t maize, 850,000t wheat, 180,000t barley, 340,000t potatoes, 14,400t citrus fruit, 350,000t grapes, 71,400t tomatoes, 65,890t oilcrops, 10,200t tobacco leaves, 1,000,000t sugar beets, 58,000t apples, 35,000t chillies and peppers, 110,000t soya beans, 492,550t fruit in total, 440,823t

vegetables in total. Livestock production included 120,536t meat in total, 25,000t beef, 48,500t pig meat, 2,750t lamb, 40,970t poultry, 45,700t eggs, 737,000t milk, 1,800t honey, 2,340t cattle hides, 595t sheepskins.

Fishing

There are rich marine resources concentrated on the Dalmatian Adriatic coast.

Forestry

Of a total of 1.7 million hectares (ha) of forest cover, nearly four-fifths of the forest is owned by the state, and the rest is in private hands.

Croatia has a well-developed wood processing industry. Although a large amount of wood is reserved for domestic fuel consumption, the country manages to export industrial roundwood and sawnwood mainly to Slovenia and Italy respectively. Small volumes of wood pulp and panels are also exported, but paper is largely imported.

Industry and manufacturing

State owned enterprises (SOE) are due to be restructured, in preparation for the expected competition within the EU.

Privatisation of SOE has begun, although progress is slow. In 2005 government commitment to fiscal constraints, necessary for staff cuts, is still needed as SOE incur significant losses, particularly in the shipbuilding industry and the railway system.

Investment in road infrastructure has resulted in an increased motorway network from 100km to 700km (1995–05).

Tourism

Tourism is one of the most important elements in Croatia's economy. It is the most important in foreign exchange earners, typically accounting for 20 per cent of GDP.

It is expected to contribute US$3.3 billion in 2005, or 9.0 per cent of GDP and employ 22.9 per cent of the workforce.

The state still has a dominant position in tourism and the sector will have to be restructured in preparation for accession to the EU. It is expected that the travel and tourist sector will attract US$1 billion or 10.2 per cent of total capital investment in 2005.

There are approximately 190,000 beds in hotels and apartments, with an equal number of beds in private accommodation. The majority of visitors come from Germany, Italy, Slovenia, Czech Republic and Austria.

Hydrocarbons

Croatia was the former Yugoslavia's biggest oil producing region, however with around 50 per cent of total energy being thermal, consumption is correspondingly high; new energy efficiency initiatives are expected to reduce demand.

Oil fields are located in Slavonia and offshore, near the Dalmatia coast.

The 400,000bpd capacity Croatian Adriatic Oil (Adria) Pipeline, run by Jadranski Naftovod (JANAF) of Croatia takes oil that arrives by tanker at the Croatian Adriatic port of Omisalj into the interior of Croatia. There are currently negotiations between Transneft and Croatia to increase the capacity of the Adria pipeline.

Croatia has two refineries and two lubrication production plants.

Croatia has extensive coal reserves but production runs at less than 100,000 tonnes per annum, mostly for domestic power plant consumption.

Energy

Hydroelectric power is the largest source of domestic energy, accounting for approximately 35 per cent of local production and around 20 per cent of total energy consumption. Hydroelectric plants are mainly located along the Adriatic coastline (Obrovac, Senj, Zakucac).

Imports of electricity account for around 10 per cent of total energy consumption.

An important source of energy is the Krsko nuclear plant in Slovenia in which Croatia has a 50 per cent stake. Demand for electricity is increasing by around 5 per cent per year, creating an urgent need to increase generating capacity in Croatia.

Croatia's first wind farm began generating electricity in January 2005. The cost of the installation was put at US$8.4 million and it is expected to generate 15 million kilowatts per year. Another wind farm is under construction close to Sibenik and two others are planned for the island of Vis, in the south, and the town of Obrovac.

Financial markets

Stock exchange

The Zagreb Stock Exchange (ZSE) began trading in 1994.

Banking and insurance

The central bank has general supervisory powers, endorsed by law, of the banking system. Legislation, since 2001, permits foreign investment in banks and since 2004 foreign banks may open branches in Croatia, although the EU is unimpressed about some of the restrictive stipulation necessary for this. Foreign exchange laws permit individuals opening foreign exchange accounts abroad and local banks offering foreign currency denominated loans.

There will be an amount of merging of supervisory authorities of the insurance, securities, investment funds and pensions into a financial services authority in line with EU requirements, before accession.

Central bank

Hrvatska Narodna Banka (HNB) (Croatian National Bank)

Main financial centre

Zagreb

Time

GMT plus one hour (daylight saving, late March to late October, GMT plus two hours)

Geography

Croatia is bounded by Slovenia to the north-west, Hungary to the north-east and the Serbian province of Vojvodina to the east. Bosnia and Hercegovina (BiH) takes a bite out of Croatia causing a rough horse shoe shape in the middle of the country from the east to the south-west. There is a very short border with Montenegro at the southern tip of the narrowing stretch of Croatia, near Dubrovnik. In the Adriatic Sea, Croatia also has maritime boundaries with Slovenia, Italy and Montenegro. There are 1,185 islands and islets along the 1,778km Croatian coast. At 56,538km square, the country consists of two principal parts: the Slavonian or Danubian plains of the north and east, through which the River Sava flows, and the extended Mediterranean coastal region of the Istrian peninsula and Dalmatia to the south-west and south-east. The hinterlands of this coastal region are the Dinaric Alps, which also extend into BiH. To the south-west of Zagreb, a narrow neck of territory connects the two elongated parts of the country.

Hemisphere

Northern

Climate

In northern Croatia, the climate is continental, on the Adriatic it is Mediterranean, while in the mountainous regions, it is alpine. The coastal hinterlands have a colder climate with heavy snow in winter, but they can be very hot in summer. Temperatures inland average around 10 degrees Celsius (C), while average temperatures on the coastal areas are around 15 degrees C. During the summer months, temperatures along the coast are often in excess of 30 degrees C. Precipitation is fairly constant country-wide throughout the year. The summer is the wettest season in the north, where the average annual rainfall in Zagreb is 890 millimetres. During the winter months, violent wind storms, known locally as the Bora, are common along the coast. A subsidiary sea of the Mediterranean, the Adriatic exercises a major influence on Croatia's climate, moderating the excesses of the continental climates of the north and east.

Dress codes
Business dress is formal, particularly in Zagreb.

Entry requirements
Passports
Required by all, except citizens of the EU, Switzerland, Norway and BiH who only need valid, official photographic identification.
Visa
Required by all, except nationals travelling as tourists from North America, Europe, Australasia, and some Asian countries, for stays of up to 90 days. Visitors are issued border passes on arrival, these must be kept until departure. For further details and exemptions see www.mfa.hr – visa requirements overview.
Nationals who do not require a tourist visa may visit for business purposes without a visa. All others business persons must apply for a business visa. Business visas require an official letter of invitation from a registered Croatian company or entity, on a formal declaration form that can be downloaded from www.hgk.hr. For further information contact the Croatian Chamber of Commerce e-mail: hgk@hgk.hr.
Prohibited entry
Currency advice/regulations
The import and export of local currency is limited to K15,000 in total, of which K500 is the maximum in banknotes. The import and export of foreign currency is unlimited. Amounts over K40,000 equivalent should be declared. Foreign currency can be exchanged in banks, by authorised dealers and post offices. Automated teller machines (ATMs) are common.
Travellers cheques in US dollars, pounds sterling or euros avoid extra exchange fees.
Customs
Goods for personal use up to the value of K300 can be imported free of duty.
Export of objects historic, cultural or scientific value must have a licence from the appropriate authorities.
A foreign national can be exempt from paying customs duties on equipment imported on the basis of a foreign investment contract. Appeals for exemption from duty should be submitted to the Ministry of Finance.
Prohibited imports
Illegal drugs. Firearms and ammunition must have the relevant Croatian permits.

Health (for visitors)
Nationals of the European Economic Area (EEA) countries and Switzerland can access reduced cost and sometimes free medical treatment using a European Health Insurance Card (EHIC) while visiting the EEA. Exceptions include nationals of the 10 countries which joined the EU in 2005 whose EHIC is not valid in Switzerland. Applications for the EHIC should be made before travelling.
Mandatory precautions
None

Credit cards
American Express, Diners' Club, Mastercard and Visa are accepted.

Public holidays (national)
Fixed dates
1 Jan (New Year's Day), 6 Jan (Epiphany), 1 May (Labour Day), 22 Jun (Anti-Fascism Day), ^25 Jun (National Day), 5 Aug (Thanksgiving Day), 15 Aug (Assumption Day), ^2 Oct (Independence Day), 1 Nov (All Saints' Day), 25–26 Dec (Christmas).
^ Some companies allow an informal one-day holiday before or after a Sunday holiday.
Variable dates
Mar/Apr Easter Monday, Jun Corpus Cristi

Working hours
Banking
Mon–Fri: 0700–1900; Sat: 0700–1300.
Business
Mon–Fri: 0800–1600.
Government
Mon–Fri: 0830–1630.
Shops
Food shops: Mon–Fri: 0700–2000, Sat: 0700–1500.
Non-food shops: Mon–Fri: 0800–1200, 1700–2000; Sat: 0800–1500.

Telecommunications
Mobile/cell phones
There are GSM roaming facilities available in the 900 band width, the 1800 is planned. Coverage is virtually throughout the country.

Electricity supply
220V AC, 50 Hz

Weights and measures
Metric system

Social customs/useful tips
Although Croats are a rather gregarious people, there is a growing tendency to reserved formality in business contexts. The formality extends to the exchange of business cards that state professional and acedemic status.
On balance, foreigners should avoid informality with their business and other hosts and should observe western business standards. Foreigners are advised to avoid discussions of a political nature in Croatia.
Trade fairs are part of the regular business life in Croatia and are a useful way to meet potential partners and gain entry to the market. The principal venue is Zagreb, although Rijeka, Split and Osijek also host fairs.

Security
There is some street crime in Zagreb and other major cities.

Getting there
Air
National airline: Croatia Airlines
International airport/s: Zagreb-Pleso International Airport (ZAG), 17km from the capital; business centre, bank, post office, restaurants, bars, duty-free shopping and car hire. Buses to the city run between 0700–2000. Taxis are available; travelling time 25 minutes.
Other airport/s: Dubrovnik International (DBV), 18km south-east of the city. Flights are inter-Euopean only. Facilites include money-changing offices, duty-free shopping, post office and car hire.
Airport tax: None
Surface
Croatia is included in the Pan-European Corridor 5 scheme. The project has some 3,270km of railways, linking Kiev in the Ukraine with western Europe via Italy, and 2,850 of new and upgraded roads.
Road: International buses connect Croatia with Austria, Italy, Hungary, France, Germany, Slovak Republic, Bosnia and Hercegovina.
Rail: There are international rail routes to Zagreb from Munich, Vienna, Venice, Budapest and Graz.
Water: Ferry services connect Rijeka and Pula with Durres and Vlora (Albania).

Getting about
National transport
Air: There are regular routes from Zagreb-Rijeka, Zagreb-Split and Zagreb-Ljubljana (Slovenia).
The main domestic airports are Rijeka (RJK), 25km from Rijeka and Split (SPU), 24km from Split.
Road: The government plans construction of 700km of new roads by 2011, making a total of 1,220km of highways and superhighways. The last 33km of the 380km Dalmatian Motorway, joining Zagreb and Split was opened on 26 June 2005.
Buses: Intercity bus services are available across the country.
Rail: Major rail links run from Zagreb to Rijeka and Varazdin.
Water: Split and Rijeka are connected by a daily sea-ferry service, but domestic sea connections with Dubrovnik are less frequent.
City transport
Taxis: Good taxi services operate in all main cities. All taxis are metered with a basic charge. A 10 per cent tip is usual.
Buses, trams & metro: Trams in Zagreb and Osijek only; buses in other cities and

towns. Services are generally cheap and regular.

Car hire

A national driving licence is usually acceptable, although there have been instances where hire companies also requested an international driver's licence. Traffic drives on the right. Speed limits are 130kph (81mph) on motorways, 100kph (62mph) on dual carriageways, 50kph (31mph) in built-up areas and 80kph (50mph) outside built-up areas. Right turns on red lights are strictly forbidden unless an additional green light (in the shape of an arrow) allows it. Right of way is always to the vehicle entering from the right.

Drink-driving is banned and subject to heavy penalties. The police also crack down on speeding and other road traffic offences. Croatia has a poor road safety record.

BUSINESS DIRECTORY

The addresses listed below are a selection only. While World of Information makes every endeavour to check these addresses, we cannot guarantee that changes have not been made, especially to telephone numbers and area codes. We would welcome any corrections.

Telephone area codes

The international direct dialling code (IDD) for Croatia is +385, followed by area code and subscriber's number:

Zagreb	1	Split	21
Dubrovnik	20	Rijeka	51

Useful telephone numbers

Emergency road help and information (Croatian Automobile Association (HAK), English speakers):	987
Police:	92
Ambulance:	94

Chambers of Commerce

American Chamber of Commerce in Croatia, 1 Krsnjavoga, 10000 Zagreb (tel: 483-6777; fax: 483-6776; e-mail: info@amcham.hr).

Croatian Chamber of Economy, 2 Rooseveltov trg, PO Box 630, 10000 Zagreb (tel: 456-1555; fax: 482-8380; e-mail: hgk@hgk.hr).

Dubrovnik County Chamber, 6 Pera Cingrije, 20000 Dubrovnik (tel: 411-376; fax: 412-044; e-mail: hgkdu@hgk.hr).

Rijeka County Chamber, 23 Bulevar Oslobodjenja, 51000 Rijeka (tel: 209-111; fax: 216-033; e-mail: hgkri@hgk.hr).

Split County Chamber, 4 Obala A Trumbica, 21000 Split (tel: 321-100; fax: 346-956; e-mail: hgkst@hgk.hr).

Zagreb County Chamber, 45 Draskoviceva, 10000 Zagreb (tel: 460-6777; fax: 460-6803; e-mail: hgkzg@hgk.hr).

Banking

Croatian Bank for Reconstruction and Development, Trg J J Strossmayera 9, 10 000 Zagreb (tel: 459-1620; fax: 459-1721).

Privredna Banka Zagreb, Corporate Finance Division, Capital Markets, Rackoga 6, Zagreb (tel: 472-3124; e-mail: capital.markets@pbz.hr; internet site: http://www.pbz.hr).

Central bank

Hrvatska Narodna Banka (Croatian National Bank), PO Box 603, Trg hrvatskih velikana 3, Zagreb 10002 (tel: 456-4555; fax: 461-0551; e-mail: info@hnb.hr).

Travel information

Croatian Chamber of the Economy, Director of Tourism, Rosseveltov Trg 2, 10000 Zagreb (tel: 456-1570; fax: 448-618).

Croatia Airlines, Savska 4A, 41000 Zagreb (tel: 616-0066; fax: 530-475).

Croatian Railways (HZ-Hrvatske Zeljeznice), Mihanoviceva 12, Zagreb (fax: 457-7597).

Tourist Community of Zagreb, Kaptol 5, 41000 Zagreb (tel: 426-411; fax: 272-628).

Tourist Information Centre, Trg bana Jelacicá 11, 41000 Zagreb (tel: 278-855; fax: 274-083).

Ministry of tourism

Ministry of Tourism, International Relations Department, Ulica grada Vukovara 78, 10000 Zagreb (tel: 610-6300; fax: 610-9300).

National tourist organisation offices

Hrvatska Turisticka Zajednica (Croatian Tourist Board), Gunduliceva 3, 41000 Zagreb (tel: 424-637, 431-015; fax: 428-674).

Ministries

Government of the Republic of Croatia, Trg Svetog Marka 2, 10000 Zagreb (tel: 456—9222; fax: 630-3023).

Ministry of Administration, Republike Austrije 16, Zagreb 10000 (tel: 378-2111; fax: 378-2192).

Ministry of Agriculture and Forestry, Ulica grada Vukovara 78, 10000 Zagreb (tel: 610-6111; fax: 610-9200).

Ministry of Culture, Trg Burze 6, 1 000 Zagreb (tel: 461-0477, 456-9022; fax: 461-0489).

Ministry of Defence, Trg Kralja Petra Kresimira 4 br 1, 10000 Zagreb (tel: 456-7111; fax: 455-1105).

Ministry of Development and Reconstruction, Nazorova 61, 10000 Zagreb (tel: 378-4500; fax: 378-4551).

Ministry of Economic Affairs, Ulica grada Vukovara 78, 10000 Zagreb (tel: 610-6111; fax: 610-9120).

Ministry of Education and Sports, Trg Burze 6, 10000 Zagreb (tel: 456-9000; fax: 456-9087).

Ministry of Environmental Protection and Zoning, Ul Republike Austrije 20, 10000 Zagreb (tel: 378-2444; fax: 377-2822).

Ministry of European Integration, Ul grada Vukovara 62, 10000 Zagreb (tel: 456-9335, 456-9336; fax: 469-8310).

Ministry of Finance, Kataneiaeva 5, 10000 Zagreb (tel: 459-1333; fax: 492-2583).

Ministry of Foreign Affairs, Trg Nikole Subica Zrinskog 7–8, 10000 Zagreb (tel: 456-9964; fax: 456-9988, 455-1795; internet: www.mfa.hr).

Ministry of Health, Ulica baruna Trenka 6, 10000 Zagreb (tel: 459-1333, 460-7555; fax: 467-7076).

Ministry of Homeland War Veterans, Park Stara Tresnjevka 4, 10000 Zagreb (tel: 365-7888; fax: 365-7852).

Ministry of Immigration, Savska cesta 41/12, 10000 Zagreb (tel: 617-6011; fax: 617-6161).

Ministry of Internal Affairs, Savska 39, 10000 Zagreb (tel: 612-2111; fax: 612-2036, 612-2452).

Ministry of Justice, Administration and Local Self-Government, Ul Republike Austrije 14, 10000 Zagreb (tel: 371-0666; fax: 371-0772).

Ministry of Labour and Social Care, Prisavlje 14, 10000 Zagreb (tel: 616-9111; fax: 616-9200).

Ministry of Maritime Affairs, Transportation and Communication, Prisavlje 14, 10000 Zagreb (tel: 616-9111; fax: 615-6292, 619-6473).

Ministry of Physical Planning, Building Construction and Housing, Ulica Republike Austrije 20, Zagreb (tel: 378-2444; fax: 377-2555).

Ministry of Privatisation and Property Management, Gajeva 30a, 10 000 Zagreb (tel: 456-9103; fax: 456-9133).

Ministry of Public Works, Reconstruction and Construction, Ul Vladimira Nazora 61, 10000 Zagreb (tel: 378-4500; fax: 378-4598).

Ministry of Science and Technology, Trg J J Strossmayera 4, 10000 Zagreb (tel: 459-4444; fax: 459-4469; e-mail: office@science.hr; internet site: www.mzt.hr).

Ministry of Trades and Small and Medium Businesses, Ksaver 200, 10000 Zagreb (tel: 469-8300; fax: 469-8310).

Parliament of the Republic of Croatia, Trg Sv Marka 6 i 7, 10000 Zagreb (tel: 456-9222; fax: 492-0384).

Other useful addresses

Association of Croatian Hoteliers, Hotel Kvarner, Park 1 maja 4, 51410 Opatija (tel: 711-415; fax: 711-415).

British Embassy, Commercial Section, Vlaska 121 (3rd Floor), PO Box 454, 10000 Zagreb (tel: 455-5310; fax: 455-1685; email: commercial.section@zg.htnet.hr).

Croatian Parliament, Trg SV, Marka 6, 10000 Zagreb (tel: 456-9222, 630-3222; fax: 630-3018; email: sabor@sabor.hr).

Croatian Embassy (USA), 2343 Massachusetts Avenue, NW, Washington DC 20008 (tel: (+1-202) 588-5899; fax: (+1-202) 588-8936; e-mail: webmaster@croatiaemb.org).

Croatian Guarantee Agency, Ilica 49, 10000 Zagreb (tel: 484-6622; fax: 484-6612).

Croatian Investment Promotion agency, World Trade Centre Building, Avenija Dubrovnik 15, 10000 Zagreb (tel: 655-4558; fax; 655-4563).

Croatian Privatisation Fund, Lueiaeeva 6, 10000 Zagreb (tel: 456-9119, 459-6377; fax: 456-9140, 611-5568; e-mail: croatia.eoi@hfp.hr; internet site: www.hfp.hr).

Croatian Securities Exchange Commission, Bogovieeva 3, 10000 Zagreb (tel: 481-1407; fax: 481-1507).

Croatian Shipbuilding Co Ltd (Hrvatska brodogradnja-Jadranbrod), Av V Holjevca 20, 10020 Zagreb (fax: 652-8420).

Economic Development Corporations – see Ministry of Development and Reconstruction.

Information Department, Ilica 1a, 10000 Zagreb (tel: 455-6455; fax: 455-7827; internet site: www.hic.hr/english/index.htm).

Luka Ploce (second largest Croatian Port), Trg Kralja Tomislava 21, 20340 Ploce (tel: 067-9601; fax: 067-9836; email: luka-ploce@du.tel.hr).

State Agency for Deposit Insurance and Bank Rehabilitation, Jurisiceva 1, 10000 Zagreb (fax: 481-3222: fax: 481-1907; e-mail: dragbank@zg.tel.hr).

State Bureau of Standards and Measures, Ul grada Vukovara 78, 10000 Zagreb (tel: 610-6111; 610-9324; e-mail: pisarnica@dznm.hr).

State Bureau of Statistics, Ilica 3, 10000 Zagreb (tel: 480-6111; fax: 481-7666; e-mail: ured@agram.dzs.hr).

Zagrebacki Velesajem (Zagreb fairs, exhibitions and conferences), Dubrovacka Avenija 2, Zagreb (fax: 520-6430).

Zagreb Stock Exchange, Ksaver 208, 41000 Zagreb (tel: 455-1866; fax: 455-1118; internet site: www.zse.hr).

Other news agencies: HIC (Croatian Information Centre): www.hic.hr
Hina (Croatian News Agency): http://websrv2.hina.hr

Internet sites

Croatia homepage: www.hr/english

Croatian Business Pages: www.hrvatska.com

Croatian Government: www.vlada.hr/english/contents.html

HINA, Croatian News Agency: www.hina.hr/nws-bin/ehot.cgi

Croatian Heritage Foundation: www.matis.hr/english/index.php

Hrvatska Radio Televizija: www.hrt.hr

Hrvatski Telekom: www.ht.hr

Cuba

KEY FACTS

Official name: República de Cuba (Republic of Cuba)

Head of State: President of the Council of State Raul Castro Ruz (since 24 February 2008)

Head of government: President of the Council of State Raul Castro Ruz (since 24 February 2008)

Ruling party: Partido Comunista de Cuba (PCC) (Cuban Communist Party)

Area: 110,860 square km

Population: 11.35 million (2005)

Capital: Havana

Official language: Spanish

Currency: Cuban Convertible peso and Cuban peso (Cu$) (CUC) both = 100 centavos (NB From 2004, the US dollar was only to be used to convert to CUC)

Exchange rate: CUC0.82 per US$ (Jul 2008); (a government 10% surcharge is imposed on all US$ transactions converting to CUC, which was revalued by 8% in April 2005). Cu$ cannot be used for local payments, nor exchanged for any other currency.

GDP per capita: US$4,650 (2006)

GDP real growth: 6.50% (2007)

Labour force: 5.72 million (2004)

Unemployment: 1.90% (2005)

Inflation: 7.00% (2005)

Oil production: 27,000 (2005)

Balance of trade: -US$4.53 billion (2005)

Foreign debt: US$12.09 billion (2004)

Visitor numbers: 2.15 million (2006)*

* estimated figure

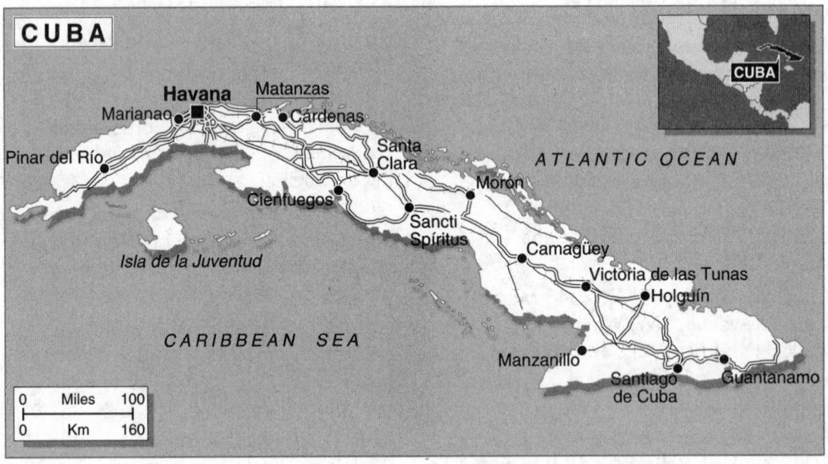

In February 2008 the average monthly wage in Cuba was the equivalent of US$17. The monthly ration available to each Cuban included 283g of fish, 226g of chicken, ten eggs and 1.8kg of potatoes. Rationing in Cuba dates back to the imposition of the US economic embargo on the island in 1962, when Cuba put itself on a war footing. An ill-thought out central planning system preoccupied itself with quotas rather than with necessities. Rationing wasn't limited to food: under the rationing system every Cuban was entitled each year to two shirts, a pair of trousers, a pair of shoes and two pairs of underpants. The country's *apparatchicks* appeared to fare better. In 2007 the Cuban government purchased a number of Series 3 and 5 BMWs for its ambassadors and a series 5 BMW for its then *de facto* leader, Raúl Castro. It is not known how many pairs of underpants were allocated to Raúl and his brother Fidel.

Social and economic conditions in Cuba have given new meaning to the expression 'long-suffering'. As if things weren't hard enough for the average Cuban, after the collapse of the USSR in 1991 Fidel Castro (by then an expert in the field) decreed a Special Period of hardship, which paradoxically enabled the embryonic development of a limited free market in a desperate attempt to obtain dollars. Almost as quickly, Fidel Castro's protégé Hugo Chávez, the president of Venezuela, and his subsidised oil for Cuba enabled these tentative openings to be reversed as state control was tightened again and the centrally planned economy re-asserted its control.

Fidel Fades

In February 2008 Fidel Castro was still recovering from a series of abdominal operations which had left him as a gaunt, frail rather Quixotic figure. In 2006 Fidel had temporarily handed over power to his brother Raúl when he underwent the first of these operations; he has not made a public appearance since. On 19 February 2008 however, Fidel finally relinquished power announcing that he was stepping down from the presidency. The announcement was not made as part of the five hour speeches of old, but in a letter published in the official newspaper *Granma* (named after the boat that brought Castro and his band of brothers back to Cuba from Mexico to re-launch the revolution). In unemotional language, the letter stated simply that he, Fidel, would not be accepting a new presidential term when the National Assembly met a few days later. The letter went on to say that 'this is not my farewell to you. My only wish is to fight as a soldier in the battle of ideas'. Undeniably, Fidel castro had already claimed a place among the world's greatest political survivors. When he and his unkempt soldiers marched into Havana in 1959, Dwight

Eisenhower was president of the USA; Fidel Castro survived to deal with (but not to talk to) a further nine US presidents. Against all predictions, Fidel Castro remained in power for two decades after the fall of the Soviet Union. And despite the obsessive but unsuccessful machinations of the CIA he was able to ensure an orderly, even subdued, transfer of power to his 'younger' brother, the 76 year old Raúl.

In early 2008 the future direction of the Cuban government looked uncertain even though stability seemed to be the order of the day. Since taking over daily control of the government in 2006, Raúl Castro hadsdone little to rock the Cuban boat or even change its course significantly. Raúl, who has always been known as something of a political hardliner may (as was generally considered to be the case) have disagreed with his brother on a number of doctrinal issues. On assuming power Raúl was the world's longest serving defence minister, and it was thought by many observers that following the transition, Cuba was in reality ruled by both brothers with Raúl presenting the public face and Fidel lurking in the wings.

In his new guise as the nation's grandfather rather than its ruler, despite almost half a century of austerity and hardship Fidel appeared to retain substantial popularity. Critics of Cuba's political system have always had to differentiate their criticism of the system from any criticism of Fidel himself. And within Cuba great care had to be exercised in criticising the system. Unlike its East European counterparts, Cuba's communism was not imposed upon the Caribbean island, but arose from within with popular support in response to the perception that until 1959 the island (and its manifestly corrupt rulers) was little more than a United States' playground and sugar plantation. When Castro handed over power in 2008, for most Cubans he was the only ruler they had known.

As Fidel Castro's letter of resignation was read out on radio and television most Cubans seemed to take the news in their stride. Reactions were muted, possibly expressing resignation and acceptance rather than any expectations of political change or that decades of 'hardship' and meaningless sacrifice were coming to an end. The reforms that Cubans most sought were those which were likely to provide them with enough to eat. Who provided it, or how, seemed to be of little importance.

Raúl's reforms

On taking over effective rule from his brother in mid-2006, Raúl Castro had clearly concentrated on trying to improve the impoverished nation's living standards. He was clearly under no illusions; a mid-2007 poll conducted by the National Statistics Office reportedly confirmed that in 75 per cent of families, the combined salaries failed to cover basic needs. The state ration book which was calculated to provide a month's food barely covered two weeks. The poll also suggested that average wages just about purchased one week's shopping – and that was still at a time when global food prices had not begun to escalate wildly. Public discontent and potential unrest was also vocal over Cuba's inadequate public transport system, which remained stuck at 1964 levels. The cost of bus transport between the capital city Havana and Cuba's second city, Santiago, had risen by 150 per cent in the same period. Another social tinderbox is the run-down state of some 3 million Cuban living dwellings, many of which are in overcrowded tenement buildings. Despite Venezuela's subsidised oil, energy inflation was also running riot. The pay-rises made across the board in 2005 were promptly wiped out by the 400 per cent rises in electricity costs between 2005 and 2008.

To address food shortages, Raúl Castro reverted to basics, paying off debts due to the farmers responsible for over 60 per cent of Cuba's food production and raising by 250 per cent the prices paid to farmers for milk and meat production. In many other areas Raúl Castro has been able to nibble at the edges: palliative measures such as allowing anyone with a car to operate as a taxi did little to address the deep-seated economic problems that confront Cuba. Raúl Castro appeared caught between the hard place of his brother's failed policies and the rock of structural reform. Labour Minister Alfredo Morales made references to a 'revision of productivity', and the dramatically mis-titled Information Technology Minister Ramiro Valdés managed to state the obvious at some length when he announced that 'the only way to make the revolution and socialism irreversible is to improve economic efficiency and raise living standards'. When it comes to meaningless pronouncements or exhortations Cuba's ministers take some beating. Sr Morales took the biscuit by alluding to the need for a 'revision of productivity' and the establishment of 'salary policies that guarantee wages are the main incentive.' Beneath the veneer of improving (but often questionable) economic statistics though, lurks a growing problem of bureaucratic paper trails and thick red tape induced by increasing centralisation, which has resulted in economic activity being held back. Consequently, crucial services such as medical care, pension provision and public transport have all suffered.

Sea change?

The two ministries that most appeared to have their feet still on the ground were the ministry of foreign investment (MINVEC) and the ministry of the armed forces (MINFAR) which in late 2007 had been informally inviting tenders for a number of tourist related projects – golf courses, hotels etc. As tourism to Cuba has dropped off dramatically since a peak of 2.5 million visitors in 2005, questions began to be asked if the ministries were anticipating a Barack Obama inspired embargo policy change. The number of tourists to Cuba fell by 7 per cent in 2006 and by a further 13 per cent in 2007, despite the opening of new tourist facilities. The effects on European visitors of the financial crises of late 2007 and early 2008 were

KEY INDICATORS — Cuba

	Unit	2003	2004	2005	2006	2007
Population	m	11.24	11.29	11.35	11.37	*11.40
Gross domestic product (GDP)	US$bn	26.58	34.55	36.20	–	*45.50
GDP per capita	US$	2,300	2,900	3,500	–	4,051
GDP real growth	%	2.6	3.0	8.0	–	6.5
Inflation	%	7.1	3.0	7.0	–	*2.8
Exports (fob) (goods)	US$m	1,800.0	2,104.0	2,388.0	–	–
Imports (cif) (goods)	US$m	4,800.0	5,296.0	6,916.0	–	–
Balance of trade	US$m	-3,000.0	-3,192.0	-4,528.0	–	–
Exchange rate	per US$	1.00	1.00	0.82	0.82	0.82

* estimated figure

expected to be equally depressing. Overall hotel occupancy dropped to only 50 per cent in 2006, a drop blamed by the tourism industry on the poor quality of Cuba's tourist services. In response to what was seen as a management failure, Fidel Castro had ordered that the responsibility for tourism be moved away from Raúl and, strangely, be entrusted to the armed forces. At its peak in 2005 the tourist industry brought in some US$1.8 billion and directly employed 300,000 Cubans. The policy reversal that obliged foreign visitors to convert their dollars into pesos at disadvantageous rates resulted in Cuba's prices becoming less competitive than competing Caribbean destinations. The backtracking on earlier market reforms was interpreted by some as a government effort to reduce the growing importance of the tourist industry, seen by the more hardline Cuban politicians as 'ideologically contaminating'.

One mould breaking investment project was the mooted US$250 million investment whereby Dubai Ports World of Dubai (denied access to the USA for 'strategic' reasons) would invest in the conversion of the Port of Mariel into an international container facility. As with MINFAR's interest in developing further tourist projects, the Mariel project prompted some to scent a wind of change. The Florida coastline is only 90 miles (150km) away. The refurbished port is expected to be open for business by 2012 by which time much may have changed in the complexion of US politics.

Cuba's antagonistic relations with the US continue to dominate its foreign policy. Since the end of the Cold War, Cuban foreign policy has largely been directed at gaining international support for the lifting of the embargo, which the US maintains under the terms of the Cuban Liberty and Democratic Solidarity (Libertad) Act of 1996 (also known as the Helms-Burton Act). The US military base which has operated at Guantanamo Bay since 1903, continues to be an issue. US policy towards Cuba has focused on the lack of political and economic freedom and on the outstanding claims for compensation for property expropriated from US citizens and Cuban Americans in the 1960's. President Bush's Initiative for a New Cuba challenges the Castro government to undertake political and economic reforms and to maintain multilateral and international momentum on human rights issues generally, through institutions such as the UN Human Rights Commission. Cuba's relations with the EU and Canada have cooled since the 2003 arrests of large numbers of dissidents in Cuba.

Risk assessment

Regional stability	Good
Politics	Poor
Economy	Poor

COUNTRY PROFILE

Historical profile

1492 Christopher Columbus landed in Cuba and claimed the island for Spain.
1511 Diego Columbus, son of Christopher, settled the island. Spanish settlers established sugar plantations and exploited slaves from West Africa.
1514 The city of Havana was founded.
1607 Havana was named the capital of Cuba.
1762–64 Havana was captured by the British but was returned to Spain under the Treaty of Paris.
1868–78 The first war of independence ended in a truce after Spain promised reforms and greater autonomy – which were never fulfilled.
1886 Slavery was abolished.
1895–98 José Marti led a second war of independence; the US declared war on Spain.
1898 Spain was defeated and gave up all claims to Cuba, ceding it to the US.
1901 The constitution of the Republic of Cuba, modelled on the US constitution, was adopted.
1902 Cuba was officially granted independence from the US. Tomas Estrada Palma became its first president. However the US retained the right to intervene in Cuban domestic affairs.
1925 The Partido Comunista de Cuba (PCC) (Cuban Communist Party) was founded.
1933 Fulgencio Batista took power in a coup détat.
1934 The US abandoned its right to intervene in Cuban internal affairs.
1940 A new constitution was promulgated.
1944 Batista retired from office.
1952 Batista seized power again, backed by the US government. His regime was oppressive and corrupt.
1956 Fidel Castro began a guerrilla war against Batista's dictatorship.
1958 US backing for Batista was withdrawn.
1959 The Cuban revolution concluded when Castro's revolutionaries defeated the Cuban army and assumed power, founding a socialist state.
1960 All US owned businesses in Cuba were nationalised without compensation; the US broke off diplomatic.
1961 The US sponsored an unsuccessful military invasion, by Cuban exiles, at the Bay of Pigs. Cuba was declared a Communist state and Castro allied it to the USSR.
1962 Castro's fear of US aggression resulted in the Cuban missile crisis when he agreed to deploy USSR nuclear missiles on Cuba. The US blockaded Cuba, published evidence of the missiles and US President Kennedy gave an ultimatum that they be removed or the US would bomb Cuba. The crisis was resolved when the USSR agreed and withdrew the missiles, and in return the US closed its missile sites in Turkey. The US imposed a full trade embargo on Cuba.
1976 A new constitution created a National Assembly, which held its first session and elected Fidel Castro Ruz as president.
1989 The USSR began to breakdown and the trade in Cuban sugar for subsidised oil collapsed.
1991 Soviet troops left Cuba. The economy fell into depression.
1993 To ameliorate the economy some market reforms were adopted and the US dollar was made an official currency alongside the Cuban peso.
1998 US restrictions on remittances are eased.
2000 US approves the sale of food and medicines to Cuba.
2001 The first shipment in 40 years of US exported food arrived.
2002 The UN criticised Cuba for its poor civil rights. It was announced that at least 71 of Cuba's 156 sugar refineries were to be scrapped.
2003 A crackdown on dissidents resulted in international condemnation as 75 people were imprisoned. The EU broke off diplomatic contacts.
2004 The official exchange rate of Cu$1 per US$ replaced the convertible rate of Cu$21 per US$. The US tightened restrictions on visits and money remittances to Cuba; the US dollar ceased to be legal tender and a 10 per cent commission for converting dollars to pesos was imposed.
2005 EU diplomatic relations with Cuba were re-established. President Hugo Chávez of Venezuela and Fidel Castro signed a co-operation agreement; Cuba will supply doctors and medical treatment to Venezuela in exchange for crude oil at a preferential price.
2006 President Castro underwent emergency stomach surgery and his brother, Raul, the defence minister, became acting president. The Non-Aligned Movement held its 14th meeting in Havana under Cuban chairmanship in September. Fidel Castro, amid rumours and speculation about his condition, did not attend delayed celebrations of his 80th birthday in

November or the 50th anniversary parade of his return to Cuba
2007 Revolution Day is celebrated without President Castro's presence, it was the first time he had been absent since the revolution. In December a letter by Castro was read out on national TV saying he would not hold on to power indefinitely.
2008 Parliamentary elections were held on 20 January. There were 609 candidates, including Fidel Castro, contesting 609 seats. Turnout was 95 per cent. The new legislative voted on candidates for the executive and cabinet. On 19 February Fidel Castro, temporarily on leave from office due to ill health, announced that he would not return to the presidency. Raul Castro Ruz was voted in unopposed as president, by the national assembly, on 24 February. The Marxist ideologically driven system of equal pay for all was abandoned in June. The EU lifted sanctions imposed in 2003.

Political structure

Constitution
The 1979 constitution gives all legislative power to the Asamblea Nacional de Poder Popular (National Assembly of People's Power) which runs local and central government. An amendment in 2002 made the Partido Comunista de Cuba (PCC) (Cuban Communist Party) the permanent party of government.

Form of state
Socialist republic.

The executive
The president and the Consejo de Estado (Council of State) and council of ministers are appointed by the national assembly and drawn from the state (communist) party.
The council of state is the highest-ranking executive institution and is made up of a president, first vice president, and five vice presidents and 30 members. It has legislative powers when the national assembly is in recess. The council runs foreign trade and foreign relations, draws up the draft budget and is responsible for the general organisation of the revolutionary armed forces.

National legislature
The national assembly has 609 members elected for a five-year term from a closed list of PCC members. Its chief role is to approve laws put forward by the council of state.
According to the constitution the national assembly is the 'supreme organ of state power and represents and expresses the sovereign will of all the working people'. Its role includes approving laws, discussing and approving the state budget and supervising other official bodies.

Legal system
While the constitution provides for independent courts it explicitly subordinates the courts to state control. The national assembly chooses all judges. The People's Supreme Court is the highest judicial body; it oversees a system of regional tribunals and is accountable to the national assembly.

Last elections
February 2008 (presidential election by National Assembly); 20 January 2008 (parliamentary).
Results: Parliamentary: 609 pro-government candidates stood for exactly the same number of seats in the National Assembly and were elected unopposed. Turnout was 95 per cent

Next elections
January 2013 (parliamentary and presidential election by National Assembly).

Political parties

Ruling party
Partido Comunista de Cuba (PCC) (Cuban Communist Party)

Main opposition party
There is no opposition party.

Population
11.35 million (2005)
Last census: September 2002: 11,177,743
Population density: Population density: 102 inhabitants per square km.
Annual growth rate: 0.4 per cent 1994–2004 (WHO 2006)

Ethnic make-up
The Cuban population is a product of the mix of four cultural groups: the indigenous people, Spaniards, Africans and Asians.
Mulatto (51 per cent), white (37 per cent), black (11 per cent), Chinese (1 per cent).

Religions
Many Cubans are agnostic or atheist, while unofficial estimates are of 75,000–100,000 practising Catholics. There is a smaller Protestant community. Practices based on African religions are reported to be increasing in popularity.

Education
Public expenditure on education amounts to 8.7 per cent of GDP. There is sustained investment in education with incentive rewards for excellence in pupils, teachers and schools. The education system promotes inclusively for learning outcomes and curriculum development between teachers and students.
Education is free at all levels. It is based on the Communist principle of combining learning with manual labour. Day nurseries and pre-school centres are available to all children after just six weeks. Primary schools are compulsory for six years until aged 12. Secondary schools are for 13- to 18-year-olds. State subsidies are available for workers returning to education to complete university courses.
Literacy rate: 97 per cent adult rate; 100 per cent youth rate (15–24) (Unesco 2005).
Compulsory years: 6 to 12.
Enrolment rate: 106 per cent gross primary enrolment, of the relevant age group (including re-enrolment); 81 per cent gross secondary enrolment, of the relevant age group (World Bank).
Pupils per teacher: 12 in primary schools.

Health
Per capita total expenditure on health (2003) was US$251; of which per capita government spending was US$218, at the international dollar rate, (WHO 2006).
There are approximately 260 hospitals and over 400 clinics that provide full and free medical services in all regions of the country. However, current US economic embargoes limit access to internationally purchased branded medical supplies.
In 2005 US$100 million was allocated to invest in the pharmaceutical industry. Generic medicines have become a major export item.

HIV/Aids
HIV prevalence: 0.1 per cent aged 15–49 in 2003 (World Bank)
Life expectancy: 77.6 years, 2004 (MEDICC 2007)
Fertility rate/Maternal mortality rate: 1.4 births per woman; maternal mortality 52.2 per 100,000 live births (MEDICC 2007).
Birth rate/Death rate: 10.7 births per 1,000 population; seven deaths per 1,000 population (2003).
Child (under 5 years) mortality rate (per 1,000): 8 per 1,000 live births (World Bank)
Head of population per physician: 6.2 physicians per 1,000 people (MEDICC 2007)

Welfare
In a 2005 economist reported to Castro that the minimum monthly income to survive in Cuba was Cu$300 (US$14.4). The minimum monthly wage was increased to Cu$225 (US$10.8), and monthly pension payments to CU$150 (US$7.2) benefiting 54 per cent of state employees. Wages in other sectors grew in line with these increases. Pensions and social assistance were also increased by 50 pesos a month.
The 1976 constitution guarantees all Cubans the right and duty to have a job, while the state provides basic support for the aged, the disabled and others unable to work. Although the principle of full employment stands unchanged, the government has admitted that unemployment does indeed exist.

Main cities
Havana (estimated population 2.8 million in 2004), Santiago de Cuba (554,400), Camagüey (354,400), Holguín (319,300), Guantánamo (274,300), Santa Clara (251,800), Bayamo (191,100), Pinar del Río (180,400), Cienfuegos (171,500).

Languages spoken
The Spanish in use in Cuba is more Latin American than Castillian and many words are quite different from the Spanish used in Spain. Quite often the endings of words are dropped, shortened nouns are used and slang is prevalent. The further south in Cuba, the more pronounced the accent.
English is quite widely spoken, as it is the main foreign language taught in schools.
Official language/s
Spanish

Media
The constitution prohibits private ownership of electronic media and there are punitive laws which suppress journalists in a country where the media is tightly controlled and independent media and journalists are targeted for intimidation. The government strictly regulates Internet access so that only 2 per cent of the population has access to the Internet.
The Cuban Communist party sees the media as an important tool for reinforcing socialist ideals within the scope of entertainment and education.
National news agency: Agencia de Información Nacional (Cuban News Agency)
Press
There are several news agencies publishing newspapers in six major languages.
Dailies: In Spanish, regional and local newspapers include Cubahora (www.cubahora.co.cu), Periódic 26 (www.periodico26.cu) from Las Tunas, Guerrillero (www.guerrillero.co.cu) form Pinar del Rio, Venceremos (www.venceremos.co.cu) from Gauntanamo, with an English online edition, Sierra Maestra (www.sierramaestra.cu) from Santiago de Cuba, and Vanguardia (www.vanguardia.co.cu) from Villa Santa.
Weeklies: In Spanish, national publications include the government-run Trabajadores (www.trabajadores.cubaweb.cu), and Communist party-run Granma (www.granma.co.cu), Cinco de Septiembre (www.5septiembre.cu) from Cienfuegos, with an English online edition. Alternative magazines include Bohemia (www.bohemia.cubaweb.cu) an illustrated and Dedete (www.dedete.cubaweb.cu) is a humorous publication.
Business: In Spanish, El Economista de Cuba (www.eleconomista.cubaweb.cu), Opiones (www.opciones.cu), a weekly publication by the tourist industry and Negocios en Cuba (www.prensa-latina.cu) published by Prensa Latina.
Broadcasting
Services controlled by the Ministerio de la Informática y las Comunicaciones (Ministry of Information and Communications).
Radio: There are over 40 radio stations throughout Cuba, most local and catering for their captive audiences. National transmissions run parallel to international services provided via satellite and the Internet. Radio Cubana (www.radiocubana.cu) (with access to local radio streaming), Radio Havana Cuba (www.radiohc.cu) and Radio Rebelde (www.radiorebelde.com.cu) are the principal organs of state for news and propaganda.
Television: The national, state-run Cubavision (Sistema Informativo de la Televisión Cubana), (www.cubavision.cubaweb.cu) shows domestic programmes ranging from soap operas to university education and a wide range of imported material. There is also an international channel, Cubavision Internacional via satellite.
Cuba also joined Venezuela, Argentina and Uruguay – and later Bolivia, Ecuador and Nicaragua – to form a pan-American public news channel, Telsur (www.telesurtv.net) to broadcast programmes to offset what they saw as the overwhelming influence of popular, privately-run channels such as the US-run CNN en Español.
The only officially approved domestic satellite TV service is available to resident foreigners, tourist and approved Communist party officials. Illegal satellite provisions, using the US-based, anti-Castro TV Marti, have resulted in criminal convictions.
Advertising
Advertising facilities are limited and state-controlled and generally not available to foreign companies.

Economy
Cuba began opening up its state-run economy to external investment after the collapse of the Soviet Union in 1991. Shortages of supplies, such as fuel, spare parts, fertilisers and herbicides, crippled Cuba's sugar production and the industrial sector, and caused a significant drop in GDP growth. The US trade embargo (in place since 1962), and politically inspired bureaucracy, have prevented sufficient foreign direct investment (FDI) for the economy to develop to its full potential. There was some liberalisation of the early 1990s, when a few market-orientated reforms were introduced. Tourism become of the country's largest sectors and one of the chief foreign exchange earners. Tourist numbers have risen steadily; 2.32 million visitors were recorded in 2005. However, since 2004, the government has been reasserting its control over the economy; it suspended licences to self-employed workers and limited foreign involvement and investment in local business. Greater trade is being undertaken with China and Venezuela. China is investing in Cuba's infrasture in exchange for nickel ore. Venezuela is trading oil for medical personnel and services.
The importance of the sugar industry collapsed as production fell. In 2002, around 50 per cent of the country's sugar mills were closed and over 100,000 workers made redundant. Sugar production has steadily declined with only 1.2 million tonnes harvested in 2005 (compared to 7.2 million tonnes in 1989). Remittances from Cuban exiles (mainly in Miami), which were estimated to bring the island over US$1 billion a year, were curtailed by US law in 2004. Cuban Americans are now forbidden to visit Cuba more than once every three years, and can carry a maximum of US$300. This has serious implications for Cuba's cash flow and economy, as it attempts to find other sources of foreign revenue.
Government figures recorded GDP growth at 12 per cent in 2006, up on the 8.0 per cent in 2005. Cuba's biggest export was nickel ore which benefited from a record world price increase of 157 per cent in 2006. Production remained relatively constant at 68,000 tonnes between 2005–06
There are two currencies in Cuba: all local people use the Cuban peso (Cu$) while a convertible peso (CUC) is used for international trade and by foreign visitors. In March 2005 the convertible peso was re-valued by 8 per cent against foreign currencies and broke parity with the US dollar. The government maintains the price of certain basics for its citizens but all products outside this system must be paid for in CUC, which has led to a flourishing black market, estimated to be as much as 40 per cent of the economy.
The Marxist ideologically driven system of equal pay for all was abandoned in June 2008 when the government announced that workers and managers would begin to earn performance bonuses. The government expects that wage differentiation will increase production and improve services. Workers will earn a minimum 5 per cent if targets are met and managers can earn up to 30 per cent when increased production can be demonstrated.
The EU lifted sanctions, which had been imposed in 2003, in June. Human rights

conditions would continue to be monitored.

External trade

The balance of payments is reliant on foreign currency earnings from tourism, remittances, nickel and cobalt. Sugar was the leading export commodity but declining harvests since the 1990s and falling world prices have left the industry a spent force. Production of nickel and cobalt has expanded to take advantage of increasing world prices.

The US trade embargo continues to have a negative effect on trade, although Venezuela has been supporting Cuba with preferential oil imports in exchange for Cuban goods and services. China and Russia have both entered agreements for investment in Cuba.

Cuba has a trade co-operation protocol with the 15-member Caribbean Community and Common Market (Caricom).

Imports

Domestic companies require a licence to import certain goods, and the withdrawal of these licences is a way for the government to control imports and its trade deficit, although the mechanism is regarded as heavy-handed.

Imports comprise petroleum, machinery and equipment, food, chemicals.

Main sources: China (14.9 per cent total, 2005), Spain (13.9 per cent), Canada (8.6 per cent), US (8.5 per cent), Germany (7.4 per cent), Italy (5.7 per cent), Mexico (5.2 per cent), Japan (4.1 per cent)

Exports

Principal exports are included, nickel, cobalt, sugar tobacco, fish, bio-technical medical products, citrus and coffee.

Main destinations: The Netherlands (25.4 per cent total, 2005), Canada (20.7 per cent), China (9.8 per cent), Spain (6.8 per cent)

Agriculture

Farming

The agricultural sector contributes approximately 7 per cent to GDP. Approximately 28 per cent of the total land area is cultivated. The economy was affected by a severe drought that lasted from 2003–05 and cost the country an estimated US$1.2 billion. The drought caused the sugar harvest to drop by about a third from an average 34.8 million tonnes to 22.9 million tonnes. A recovery in 2004 was slow with a harvest of 24 million tonnes. In 2005 it was announced that the growing season would be shorter than usual and that the expected harvest would be smaller than 2004.

Sugar is Cuba's most important export crop, however since its collapse as a top cash crop, there has been a concerted effort to diversify. The sugar industry has undergone restructuring to make the production more efficient and identify new markets. Over 70 of the 156 sugar refineries in Cuba have been decommissioned with some 100,000 workers laid off. Half of Cuba's 3.5 million hectares (ha) of sugar cane fields have been re-utilised to produce other crops, particularly foodstuffs for domestic consumption and reduce the need for imports.

Two new cocoa processing plants with a capacity of 45,000 tonnes are planned to provide exports of high quality cocoa butter.

Approximately 95 per cent of Cuba's coffee plantations are the highly prized arabica bean. Coffee exports should be enhanced by the refurbishment of seven processing mills.

Cuba has begun developing organic farming, and there are over 100,000 small-to medium-sized organic farms reflecting the government's commitment to the 'greening of Cuba'.

Crop production in 2005 included: 12,500,000 tonnes (t) sugar cane, 1,050,195t cereals in total, 650,000t rice, 400,000t maize, 585,000t cassava, 330,000t potatoes, 490,000t sweet potatoes, 460,000t bananas, 770,000t plantains, 168,000t yams, 135,000t pulses, 120,000t coconuts, 13,500t green coffee, 1,650t cocoa beans, 844,000t citrus fruit, 800,000t tomatoes, 230,000t mangoes, 60,000t garlic, 18,600t oilcrops, 34,500t tobacco, 92,000t chillies and peppers, 120,000t papayas, 2,905,000t fruit in total, 4,234,000t vegetables in total. Livestock production included: 205,328t meat in total, 63,000t beef, 95,000t pig meat, 7,150t lamb, 3,050t goat meat, 36,036t poultry, 79,000t eggs, 610,000t milk, 6,500t honey.

Fishing

Catches have fallen since the mid-1980s. The contraction of fin fish catches by the deep sea fleet, partly as a result of changes in fishing agreements, has been largely responsible. Cuba is investing considerable resources in shrimp farming, but production has not been commercially significant.

Forestry

Forests cover around 2.3 million hectares (ha), around 15 per cent of the total land area. Since 1990 forest cover has increased by an average of 1.27 per cent per annum or 28,000ha.

Industry and manufacturing

The industrial sector contributes approximately 37 per cent to GDP.

Cuba's free trade zones, especially those of Wajay and Mariel have attracted a number of foreign companies. Mariel, located 48.2km west of Havana, is likely to play an important role in the future, especially if trade opens with the US.

The Hola processing plant in Havana toasts and grinds coffee beans for export to the UK, Ukraine, Bulgaria, the Bahamas and Spain.

The cigar industry is significant, with production increasing substantially in the late-1990s and generating annual revenues of an estimated US$150 million.

Tourism

Cuba has turned to tourism as a source of much-needed foreign earnings. Despite the US embargo, the sector, which had been neglected since 1959, has shown a steady growth since the early 1990s. Government figures show the annual growth in 2004 was 8 per cent and bookings for 2005 are expected to reach 2,300,000. The majority of tourists come from Canada and the EU.

Four new hotels began operation in 2005, adding 1,921 more rooms to the international tourist sector.

The US dollar was adopted as a legal currency, for tourists only, in 1993 and all visitors were expected to pay for goods and services in dollars, or a peso that was linked to the dollar. However international condemnation of Cuba's action in imprisoning dissidents led to increasingly strained relations with the US and the dollar was dropped as legal tender in 2004. A Cuban Convertible peso (CUC), for use in international trade, was introduced instead of the dollar. Bank notes are printed locally and have to be used by visitors after exchanging at the official rate. Any dollar/peso conversation attracts a 10 per cent tax. The euro has been accepted in major tourist resorts since 2002, although the exchange rate is set by the US dollar.

Tourist assets are state-owned. Some competitiveness and joint ventures with foreign companies have been allowed, however these have not proved palatable to the regime and such schemes have been scaled back. The government reinforced control over the sector, ostensibly to curb corruption, and structural reforms have been introduced.

Environment

Incessant rain, following tropical storm Noel, falling from 11 October to 5 November 2007, caused the worst floods in forty years, destroying tens of thousands of homes, leaving roads impassable and damaging crops of sugar and coffee.

Mining

Mining contributes around 6 per cent to GDP. The island's extensive nickel and cobalt ore reserves, among the largest in the world, offer attractive large-scale mining opportunities. Cuba's rich mineral

resources are open to foreign exploration and development.
Exploration for gold, silver and base metals is carried out by more than a dozen foreign firms in concession areas covering nearly a third of Cuba's national territory. Cuba has updated its mining legislation, bringing it into line with most other Latin American countries.
Nickel production has been boosted by the injection of Canadian capital and technology. Government figures for 2004–05 showed nickel production reached 35,000 tonnes and overtook sugar as Cuba's biggest merchandise export, earning US$545 million. Since 2000 Cuba has supplied over half the nickel China uses in the production of stainless steel, and to maintain supplies China agreed to invest US$500 million in the nickel industry.
Cuba intends to modernise its processing plants and continue exploration for other base and precious metals. More than half the production comes from the Comandante Pedro Sotto Alba processing plant at Moa Bay, jointly operated by Sherritt (Canada) and a Cuban company, Compania General de Niquel (General Nickel Company). Cuba's two other operating nickel plants are being modernised with the help of export-linked revolving credits from Dutch, German and other foreign banks and trade houses.

Hydrocarbons
Proven oil reserves are modest the island imports over half of its oil needs, mainly from Mexico and Venezuela. In an agreement made in 2005 Venezuela provides Cuba with 90,000 barrels of crude oil a day under favourable terms, in exchange for Venezuelan access to Cuban healthcare opportunities.
Domestic oil production accounts for 80 per cent of the country's electricity needs. Most of Cuba's production is from oil fields on land, however following the first offshore rig, financed jointly by Cuba and Spain, more rigs are planned. The government plans to become self sufficient in energy produced by domestic oil.
Cuba has an estimated 70 billion cubic metres of natural gas reserves.
Cuba does not produce or import coal.

Energy
Cuba has installed hydropower capacity of some 57.3MW in 176 power stations, with an estimated 400MW of total potential capacity.
Electricity supplies have been erratic, with power failures experienced intermittently throughout the island, as a result of equipment failure. In 2005 the government announced the investment of US$100 million in a programme of maintenance and US$282 million to be invested in new equipment and materials. A refurbished electricity plant, converted to utilise natural gas and new generators are expected to provide an extra one million kilowatts of electricity.
There is an emphasis on energy conservation, with an increased use of bagasse (residue of sugar cane, burned to produce energy) as an oil substitute, expansion of electricity capacity and re-use of old windmills.

Banking and insurance
The Cuban banking sector has been transformed from a closed and highly centralised Soviet-style model to a diversified two-tier banking system.
In a bilateral agreement signed in 2005 Cuba opened a subsidiary of the Foreign Bank of Cuba in Caracas, Venezuela, while a subsidiary of the Industrial Bank of Venezuela has been approved to open in Cuba.
Central bank
Banco Central de Cuba (BCC)

Time
GMT minus four hours in summer, GMT minus five hours in winter (October – March).

Geography
Cuba is the largest island in the Caribbean, lying 150km south of Florida. Together with offshore islands and an archipelago of about 1,600 coral cays surrounding the main island, the country has an area of 110,860 square km. The largest offshore island is the Isla de la Juventud, formerly known as the Isla de Piños, which covers 2,200 square km.
Most of the long, thin main island consists of plains and low ranges of hills. The highest mountains are in the Sierra Maestra in the extreme south-east, where the Pico Real de Turquina rises to 1,974 metres.
Hemisphere
Northern.

Climate
Subtropical, with an annual mean temperature of 26 degrees Celsius (C) the average summer shade temperatures can rise to 30 degrees C and higher. November–April is the cooler, dry season with maximum temperatures peaking at around 26 degrees C. Trade winds and sea breezes cool the air; there are sudden, short showers in summer. The months of June, September and October–November usually bring hurricanes. The north is wetter than the south and the south, in particularly Santiago Province, is much hotter than the north.
There is rainfall of up to 250mm a year in the mountains.
It can be humid between May and October with some heavy rain. Humidity averages 62 per cent. However, during September and October, humidity can reach 95 per cent.

Dress codes
Dress since the 1959 revolution has been casual. Cubans wear lightweight and loose-fitting clothes, and formal dress, such as a tie, is an extremely rare sight.

Entry requirements
Passports
Required by all. Passports of nationals of countries without diplomatic relations with Cuba must be valid for two months beyond date of arrival.
Visa
Required by all, except nationals of countries who have reciprocal visa-free agreements.
Business visas, valid for 90 days from issue, are only obtained through sponsorship by an appropriate Cuban government organisation. For sponsorship contact the relevant State Trading Organisation or the commercial office of a Cuban embassy. Without a sponsor a visa will not be issued and a tourist card does not provide local firms with the opportunity to trade with business visitors.
Tourist cards are provided by airlines and tour operators who are registered with Cubatur. Exit visas are required for visitors staying more than 90 days.
Currency advice/regulations
The import and export of local currency is forbidden. There are no restrictions on the import of foreign currency, subject to declaration of amounts over US$5,000. Currency can be exchanged at the airport or hotel for 'convertible pesos'. When departing, they can be converted back again.
Hard currency is generally required from visitors for most transactions, although the US dollar is no longer legal tender. Visitors arriving with US currency must change it into 'convertible pesos', for which a 10 per cent commission is charged.

Health (for visitors)
Mandatory precautions
A yellow fever vaccination certificate is required if arriving from an infected area.
Advisable precautions
Vaccinations are recommended for typhoid, hepatitis A, tetanus and polio, as well as malaria prophylaxis – mosquitoes are a problem outside Havana.
The water supply in most upmarket hotels is excellent but elsewhere water precautions should be taken. Bottled water is readily available.
Medical services are good and free to visitors in an emergency. Insurance is advisable in case repatriation is required.
Resorts and major cities have international

clinics for tourists but the US embargo often means branded medicines may not be available. An adequate supply of regularly administered medication should be carried.
A visitor admitted to hospital is likely to be tested for HIV/Aids and will be deported if found to be a carrier.

Hotels
The best hotels can be found in Havana and Varadero beach. Foreign currencies should be exchanged at official Cadeca outlets.
The practice of tipping is growing – restaurants 5–10 per cent.

Credit cards
Only credit cards which are not issued in the US (Visa, Eurocard, MasterCard, Access) are accepted, generally only at tourist sites.

Public holidays (national)
Fixed dates
1 Jan (Liberation Day), 1 May (Labour Day), 25 Jul (Rebellion anniversary, three days), 10 Oct (Anniversary of the War of Independence), 25 Dec (Christmas Day).
Variable dates
Carnival: Havana (Feb); Varadero (late Jan/Feb); Trinidad and Santiago de Cuba (Jun).

Working hours
Banking
Mon–Fri: 0830–1200, 1330–1500; Sat: 0830–1030.
Banks in resorts tend to stay open longer. Banks and post offices do not accept Eurocheques or American Express travellers cheques.
Business
Mon–Fri: 0830–1230 and 1330–1630; some offices open alternate Saturdays between 0800–1700.
Government
Mon–Fri: 0830–1230, 1330–1730.
Shops
Mon-Fri: 0900-1700; Sat: 0900-1200. Shops are normally closed on Sunday, except those in tourist areas. Resort shops and supermarkets often open seven days a week and their hours vary according to demand.
Pharmacies are open daily 0800–2000; those with turno permanente signs are open 24 hours.

Telecommunications
Postal services
Cuba has very few official mail collection boxes, so visitors are advised to post mail in a hotel, or at the airport.
Mobile/cell phones
GSM 900 service available in main tourist areas and cities only.
In March 2008 reforms were announced which gave Cubans unlimited access to mobile phones. Until then Cubans could only own them through a third party, which meant that mobile phone usage in Cuba was one of the lowest in Latin America. However, payment has to be made in foreign currency.

Electricity supply
110V AC, 60 cycles
Most plugs in hotels are two-pin, flat-pin type, although some are the two-pin, round-pin variety.
Some electric shaver points can be 220/240V.
Lighting is usually of the screw in, rather than bayonet, type.

Social customs/useful tips
Foreign residents say there are few restrictions on foreign visitors, however, they advise against vociferous public criticism of the government.
Cuba has placed great emphasis on sports; baseball, originally imported from the US, is the national sport with boxing vying as the most popular spectator sport.
Cubans address each other, and often foreign visitors, as compañero or compañera, and the informal tu form is often used when speaking Spanish.
Photographing airports and sensitive sites is forbidden and permission should be sought before photographing public or religious buildings.

Security
Although Cuba is considered to be a generally safe country, the usual precautions should be followed.
Keep to the main busy areas in the cities. Keep valuables and money belt out of sight. Avoid going out alone if possible, especially at night.

Getting there
Air
National airline: Cubana de Aviación.
International airport/s: Havana-José Marti International (HAV), 25km from city, with duty-free shops, bank, tourist information, hotel reservation and car hire; Varadero-Juan Gómez International (VRA), 12km from Cuba's main beach resort.
Other airport/s: Santiago-Antonio Macea (SCU).
Airport tax: 25 convertible Cuban pesos, except transit passengers.
Surface
Water: There is no scheduled passenger traffic due to the US blockade. Some cruise vessels and private yachts visit Cuba.
Main port/s: Antilla, Cienfuegos, Guayabal, Havana, Mariel, Matanzas, Nuevitas, Santiago de Cuba.

Getting about
National transport
Air: Cubana operates limited domestic services to main centres. Internal flights by visitors are generally arranged through Cubatur.
Road: The Central Highway (Autopista Nacional) runs for over 1,100km, virtually from end to end of the island and gives access to a network of local roads. Total road system exceeds 30,000km, at least 40 per cent surfaced although some roads/tracks may not be passable in wet weather.
Buses: Cross-country buses are cheap and fairly reliable, but can be overcrowded. Coaches link main centres. An air-conditioned service operated by Viazul offers more comfortable travel around the island; payment in convertible pesos is required.
Rail: Cuba's rail capacity is not as extensive as it once was, due to natural disasters and lack of investment. There was 4,226km of public service track in 2003, an increase on the previous year. The main line connects Havana and Santiago de Cuba; some services on this route offer refreshments and air-conditioning. Other lines include between Havana-Cienfuegos and Cardenas-Jaguey. Railway stations in Cuba are immaculately clean, but timetables are often unreliable.
Water: Hydrofoils run twice daily from the southern port of Surgidero de Batananó to the Isla de la Juventud. There are also slower boats sailing three times a week, but a day trip is not possible using these.
City transport
Taxis: There are state and private taxi services, usually ordered through a hotel. Official taxis are metered and less expensive and more comfortable than private taxis, with which prior agreement on the fare is advisable. Turistaxis, the official taxi service for tourists, has stands at tourist centres and can also be flagged down in the street. Taxis can also be hired for the day; for travel outside Havana, taxis or cars with drivers are cheap but scarce.
Buses, trams & metro: Services in towns are generally considered erratic, inexpensive but invariably crowded. Cubanacan buses are available for tours of cities.
Car hire
Car hire is the most reliable form of transport for covering larger distances. Modern cars are available and can be booked in advance via the Internet through Cubatur (www.cubatur.cu). Hired locally, the price may rise sharply outside airport, city or tourist areas. Chauffeur-driven vehicles are also available.
A valid driver's licence is necessary. Traffic drives on the right; seat belts are not compulsory and the blood alcohol limit is 80mg/100ml.

Speed limits: autopista 100kph; paved roads 90kph; dirt roads 60kph; urban roads 50kph (40kph near schools).
Petrol is relatively easy to obtain and comes in two grades: especial and regular. Both are leaded and as a rule only the dearer especial is available to tourists. It is sold at 24-hour Servi-Cupet and Oro Negro petrol stations.

BUSINESS DIRECTORY

The addresses listed below are a selection only. While World of Information makes every endeavour to check these addresses, we cannot guarantee that changes have not been made, especially to telephone numbers and area codes. We would welcome any corrections.

Telephone area codes

The international direct dialling code (IDD) for Cuba is +53, followed by the area code and subscriber's number:

Camaguey	32	Manzanillo	23
Ciego de Avila	33	Matanzas	45
Cienfuegos	43	Pinar del Rio	82
Florencia	33	Santiago de Cuba	226
Havana	7	Villa Clara	42

Useful telephone numbers

There is an efficient, almost omnipresent, police service, but officers are unlikely to speak English.
Police: 116 can be dialled from any call box.
Havanautos (24-hour breakdown service): 338176 or 338177.

Chambers of Commerce

Cámara de Comercio de la República de Cuba, Calle 21, esq. A No 661, Vedado, Havana (tel: 551-321; fax: 333-042; e-mail: bic@camara.com.cu).

Banking

Banco de Inversiones SA, 5ta Ave No 6802 e/ 68 y 70, Miramar, Havana (tel: 243-374/5; fax: 243-373; e-mail: bdi@bdi.colombus.cu).

Banco Exterior de España, Línea esq a 2, El Vedado, Havana (tel: 334-560; fax: 334-559).

Banco Financiero Internacional SA, Línea No 1, Vedado, PO Box 4068, Havana 4 (tel: 333-003, 333-148; fax: 333-006).

Banco Internacional de Comercio SA, 20 de Mayo y Ayestarán, Apartado 6113, Plaza de la Revolución, Havana 6 (tel: 335-482/5484; fax: 335-112; e-mail: bicsa@bicsa.columbus.cu).

Banco Metropolitano SA, (successor of the international branch of the Banco Nacional de Cuba), Línea No 63 esq a M, Vedado, Plaza, Havana (tel: 553-116/7; fax: 334-241; e-mail: banmet@nbbm.columbus.cu).

Casas de Cambio SA (CADECA), Calle Aguiar No 411, e/ Obrapia y Lamparilla, Habana Vieja, Havana (tel: 335-673; fax: 335-673; e-mail: cadeca@cadeca.columbus.cu).

Grupo Nueva Banca SA (NB), Calle 1ra, No 1406 e/ 14 y 16, Miramar, Havana (tel: 247-564/67; fax: 245-674; e-mail: nbanca@nbanca.columbus.cu).

The Netherlands Caribbean Banking, 5ta Avenida No 6407 esq a 76, Miramar, Havana (tel: 240-419/21; fax: 240-472).

Central bank

Banco Central de Cuba, PO Box 746, Cuba 402, Habana Vieja, Havana (tel: 866-8003; fax: 866-6601; e-mail: webmaster@bc.gov.cu).

Travel information

Cubamar, Paseo 306 esq a 15, Vedado, Havana (tel: 662-523.4; fax: 333-111; e-mail: cubamar@cubamar.mit.cma.net).

Cubana, Calle 23, No 64 esq Infanta, Vedado, Havana (tel: 334-949/50; fax: 333-323; e-mail: eca@iacc.3.get.cma.net).

Havanatur/Infotur, Calle Obispo 358, (e/ Habana y Compostella), Old Havana (tel: 614-881); Plaza de Martí, Santiago de Cuba (tel: 23-302).

Ministry of tourism

Ministerio de Turismo Calle 19, No 710, Entre Paseo y A, Vedado, Havana (tel: 334 087; 334 318/9; fax: 334 086: Internet: www.cubatravel.cu; www.cubaweb.cu; www.ceniai.inf.cu).

National tourist organisation offices

Cubatur (Empresa de Turismo Nacional e Internacional), Calle F No 157 el Calzada y Novena, Vedado, Havana (tel: 835-4155; fax: 836-3170; e-mail: casamatriz@cubatur.cu).

Ministries

Ministry of Agriculture, Avenida Independencia, entre Cornill y Sta Ana, Havana (tel: 845-770; fax: 335-086).

Ministry of Basic Industries, Avenida Salvador Allende 666, Havana (tel: 707-711; fax: 333-845).

Ministry of Communications, Plaza De la Revolucion 'José Martí', CP 10600, Havana (tel: 817-654).

Ministry of Construction, Avenida Carlos M de Cespedes y Calle 35, Havana (tel: 818-385; fax: 335-585).

Ministry of Construction Materials Industry, Calle 17, esq 0, Vevado, Havana (tel: 322-541; fax: 333-176).

Ministry of Culture, Calle 2, No 258, entre 11y 13, Vedado, Havana (tel: 399-945).

Ministry of Economy and Planning, 20 de Mayo y Ayestaran, Plaza de la Revolucion, Havana (tel: 816-444).

Ministry of Education, Obispo 160, Havana (tel: 614-888).

Ministry of Finance and Prices, Obispo 211, esq Cuba, Havana (tel: 604-111; fax: 620-252).

Ministry of the Fishing Industry, Avenida 5 y 248 Jaimenitas, Santa Fé, Havana (tel: 297-034).

Ministry of the Food Industry, Calle 41, No 4455, Playa, Havana (tel: 726-801).

Ministry of Foreign Affairs, Calzada 360, Vedado, Havana (tel: 324-074).

Ministry of Foreign Investment and Economic Co-operation, Calle 1, No 201, Vedado, Havana (tel: 736-661).

Ministry of Foreign Trade, Infanta 16, Vedado, Havana (tel: 786-230; fax: 786-234).

Ministry of Health, Calle 23, No 301, Vedado, Havana (tel: 322-561).

Ministry of Higher Education, Calle 23, No 565, esq aF, Vedado, Havana (tel: 552-314).

Ministry of the Interior, Plaza de la Revolucion, Havana (fax: 733-5261).

Ministry of Internal Trade, Calle Habana 258, Havana (tel: 625-790).

Ministry of Iron and Steel, Metallurgical and Electronic Industries, Avenida Rancho Boyeros y Calle 100, Havana (tel: 204-861).

Ministry of Justice, Calle 0, No 216, entre 23 y Humboldt, Vedado, Havana (tel: 326-319).

Ministry of Labour and Social Security, Calle 23, esq Calle P, Vedado, Havana (tel: 704-571).

Ministry of Light Industry, Empedrado 302, Havana (tel: 624-041).

Ministry of the Revolutionary Armed Forces, Plaza de la Revolución, Havana.

Ministry of Sugar, Calle 23, No 117, Vedado, Havana (tel: 305-061).

Ministry of Transport, Avenida Independencia y Tulipán, Havana (tel: 812-076).

Other useful addresses

British Embassy, Calle 34, No 702/4, Miramar, Havana (tel: 24-1049; fax: 24-9214).

CariFin (financial services Cuba), 311 and 313 22nd Street, Between 3rd and 5th Avanues, Mirimar, Havana (tel: 244-468/70; fax: 244-140; e-mail: havana@cdc.com.cu).

Compañía Fiduciaria SA (investments), Calle 36A No 121 apto, 2 e/ 1ra y 3ra,

Miramar Playa, Havana (tel: 247-434/5; fax: 249-745; e-mail: nbfid@nbfid.columbus.cu).

Cuban Investment Company, PO Box 30003, North Vancouver, B.C. Canada V7H 2Y8 (tel: 00(1-604)929-9694; fax: 00(1-604)929-3694; e-mail: cubaninvestments@idmail.com).

Etecsa (Empresa de Telecomunicaciones de Cuba SA), Havana (tel: 452-221, 451-221; fax: 578-036).

Financiera Nacional SA (FINSA) (non-banking activities), Calle G No 301, esq a 13, Vedado, Havana (tel: 553-177, 338-863; fax: 662-232; e-mail: finsa@finsa.columbus.cu).

TIPS (Technological and Commercial Information Promotion System), National Office, No 302, Calle 30, Miramar, Havana (tel: 331-797/798; fax: 331-799).

National news agency: Agencia de Información Nacional (Cuban News Agency)
Other news agencies: Prensa Latina: www.plenglish.com.mx

Internet sites
Cubana de Aviación airline: www.cubana.cu

Granma International (daily update in English, French, Spanish and Portuguese, with a summary in German): www.granma.cu

Viazul Bus Transportation: www.viazul.com

Cyprus

KEY FACTS

Official name: Kypriaki Dimokratia-Kibris Cumhuriyeti (Republic of Cyprus)

Head of State: President Demetris Christofias (Akel party) (from 28 Feb 2008)

Head of government: President Demetris Christofias (from 28 Feb 2008)

Ruling party: Coalition led by Anorthotikon Komma Ergazemenou Laou (AKEL) (Progressive Party of the Working People) with Dimokratikon Komma (DIKO) (Democratic Party) and Kinima Sosialdimokraton (KISOS) (Social Democrats Movement) (since 2003; re-elected May 2006)

Area: 9,251 square km (including the north)

Population: 780,000 (2007)*

Capital: Lefkosia (Nicosia); Greek spellings in use since 1995

Official language: Greek and Turkish

Currency: Cyprus pound (C£) = 100 cents

Exchange rate: C£0.63 per US$ (Jul 2008)

GDP per capita: US$27,326 (2007)*

GDP real growth: 4.40% (2007)

Labour force: 386,000 (2004)

Unemployment: 3.90% (2007)

Inflation: 2.10% (2007)

Balance of trade: -US$1.12 billion (2007)

Foreign debt: US$7.33 billion (2004)

* estimated figure

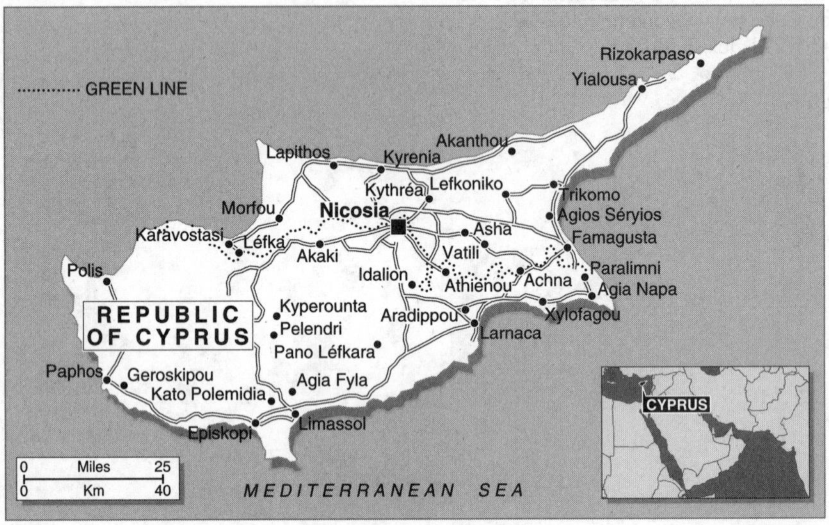

April 2008 saw a symbolic shift in relations between the Greek Cypriots and their northern, Turkish neighbours. Since 1974 the Mediterranean island has not only been divided, the division has been virtually absolute, with no contact between the two communities. Turkish Cyprus has only ever been recognised as a body politic by Turkey. The Greek Republic of Cyprus has achieved normal international recognition. In 2008, Ledra Street, in Lefkosia (previously known as Nicosia), the focal point of the island's division was re-opened as a crossing point between north and south.

Back to back

In 1974 Turkish troops secured northern Cyprus in response to moves inspired by the then military junta in Athens to join Cyprus with Greece. The result was a stand-off between the two sides and their mentors, which for over 40 years has needed to be policed by the United Nations (UN). The island had come close to resolving its differences in 2004, but days before the Republic of Cyprus was set to join the European Union (EU) Greek Cypriots under their hard line leader Tassos Papadopoulos, voted against adopting a UN brokered peace agreement. Ironically, this was in contrast with the largely ostracised Turkish Cypriots, who voted in favour of the UN agreement. The breaking point for the Greek community under Mr Papadopoulos was the failure of the agreement to require property restitution for the Greeks who were forced to abandon their homes in the north when they fled south. The southern Greeks also baulked at the failure of the agreement to insist on an almost complete reduction of the Turkish 30,000 troop presence in the north.

Tassos goes, Christofias comes

In February 2008, Demetrias Christofias easily won Cyprus' general election, gaining over 53 per cent of the vote as against the 47 per cent won by his opponent Yiannakis Kassoulides, a former foreign minister. Mr Christofias is the leader of the Cypriot Communist Akel party, which won the election in an unusual coalition with Cyprus' nationalist party. Mr Christofias' election meant that Cyprus had leaders in both north and south who genuinely wanted to see an end to the island's division. Politically, Northern Cyprus' leader, Mehmet Ali Talat, has something in common with Mr Christofias – both were left wingers and their respective political parties had maintained contact for some time.

The economy stays sound

In its 2007 annual assessment of Cyprus' economic prospects and challenges, the

International Monetary Fund (IMF) pointed out that as the easternmost country in the EU, Cyprus was well placed to emerge as a gateway to the east and a hub of business operations in the region. The IMF sees the thriving Cypriot economy as testimony to the government's implementation of reforms and pursuit of prudent policies. According to the IMF, the goal of adopting the euro appears to have galvanised the collective Cypriot will to place the island republic's fiscal accounts on a strong footing and reform the economy. However, the IMF goes on to note that success in the euro area will require the safeguarding of external competitiveness and the confronting of medium-term challenges.

According to the Central Bank of Cyprus, during the period 2000–06, Cyprus' real gross domestic product (GDP) grew by an average of 3.6 per cent per annum, which compares favourably with the EU average. This was accomplished in an environment of full employment conditions, low inflation and a stable and strong currency. In 2006 Cyprus's per capita GDP had reached about 93.7 per cent of the EU-27 average. In addition, structural reforms within the context of the EU's Lisbon Strategy were in progress to modernise and liberalise an already market-oriented economy, with a view to enhancing its international competitiveness and EU compatibility. It was hoped that these structural reforms, combined with macroeconomic stability, would provide a strong foundation for the participation of Cyprus in the euro area.

In 2007, Cyprus' economic policy continued to be governed by efforts to reach equal standing with the other EU members and with the longer term so-called Lisbon Agenda to improve the island Republic's competitiveness. The Republic joined the eurozone on 1 January 2008. GDP growth for 2007 was an annual 3.8 per cent. Inflation was low, staying at 2 per cent for the year. The government's austerity programme has kept the fiscal deficit under the 3.0 per cent Maastricht limit, notwithstanding the pressures for increased social welfare expenditure in the run-up to the 2008 presidential election.

Turkish Republic

The isolated Turkish Republic of Northern Cyprus (TRNC) functions on a unique and uneasily balanced presidential/parliamentary system, with political power shared between its president and prime minister. The president is elected for a five-year term and has the power to propose legislation or return it to the 50 seat National Assembly.

For all of its 44 year existence, the TRNC's sole foreign policy objective has been to obtain some sort of international recognition as a sovereign state, and to consolidate ties with Turkey, which in any event is the only state to recognise it formally. Under President Talat, the regime has voted in a referendum for conditional reunification and the resolution of the Cyprus problem, subject to the political equality and separation of the two major communities. Meanwhile, the TRNC has embarked on an active campaign to develop ties with the outside world, and has established representative trade and/or tourism offices in a number of countries, including Brussels, London and New York. It has observer status at the Organisation of the Islamic Conference (OIC) and sends two observers to meetings of the Parliamentary Assembly meetings of the Council of Europe (PACE).

The TRNC economy is much smaller and more narrowly based than its southern counterpart. The GDP growth rate is estimated at around 8.0 per cent. The New Turkish lira (YTL) is the currency used in the north, where the inflation rate has been estimated at over 9 per cent. In general, per capita incomes in the north are estimated to be 50 per cent lower than those in the south.

The TRNC is inevitably dependent on Turkey for credits, grants and trade although it has received modest grants in aid from the European Union. Reliance on the Turkish lira has meant that there is no effective local control over monetary policy. The economy has therefore been exposed to currency shocks from Turkey. Exports are very low, and likely to remain so even if direct trade with the EU and other markets is developed. As well as fiscal transfers from Turkey, the economy is sustained by a real estate and construction boom, tertiary education services tourism, gambling and related services. The local authorities see tourism development as a major hope, but the lack of direct air links to potential markets is a major constraint. One positive development was the EU's release in June 2007 of eur259 billion for economic assistance to the Turkish Cypriot community over a five-year period.

Risk assessment

Economy	Good
Politics	Good
Regional stability	Good

Risk assessment (KKTC)

Politics	Fair
North	Fair
Economy	Poor

COUNTRY PROFILE

Historical profile

Cyprus, traditionally the birthplace of the ancient goddess of love Aphrodite, has, in contrast, been the scene of political unrest for some 50 years. The tensions arise from the polarisation of the inhabitants into two political groups with diametrically opposed aspirations: the Greek Cypriots constituting 80 per cent of the population and the Turkish Cypriot minority. During the British colonial period, both communities had a common enemy – then upon

KEY INDICATORS — Cyprus

	Unit	2003	2004	2005	2006	2007
Population	m	0.86	0.96	0.76	0.77	*0.78
Gross domestic product (GDP)	US$bn	15.84	15.42	16.96	18.37	21.30
GDP per capita	US$	18,326	19,202	22,378	23,779	*27,326
GDP real growth	%	1.9	3.7	3.9	4.0	4.4
Inflation	%	4.2	2.3	2.6	2.2	2.1
Unemployment	%	4.4	5.6	5.3	4.5	3.9
Exports (fob) (goods)	US$m	1,030.0	1,175.0	1,454.0	1,416.6	1,495.1
Imports (cif) (goods)	US$m	3,900.0	5,217.8	5,745.7	6,439.5	7,839.8
Balance of trade	US$m	-2,870.0	-4,042.8	-4,291.8	-5,022.9	-6,344.7
Current account	US$m	-450.0	-640.0	-950.0	-1,090.6	-2,144.1
Total reserves minus gold	US$m	3,256.7	3,910.0	4,191.1	5,646.8	6,118.6
Foreign exchange	US$m	3,154.5	3,832.7	4,155.9	5,621.5	6,100.1
Exchange rate	per US$	0.51	0.47	0.45	0.44	0.40

* estimated figure

independence seemingly intractable enmities surfaced. Over the years, the situation was further aggravated by the periodic, tacit intervention of both Turkey and Greece in Cyprus' affairs. As a colonial hangover, the UK retains two sovereign military bases on Cyprus; Turkey has around 30,000 troops in the north.

1878 After three centuries of rule, a weakening Ottoman Empire ceded the island to the British in return for security guarantees against possible Russian expansion in the area. The origins of future problems lay in the composition of Cyprus' population – approximately 80 per cent Greek-speaking Christians, 18 per cent Turkish-speaking Muslims and 2 per cent others (Armenian, Latin and Maronite).

1925 Cyprus became a British crown colony.

1955 The Greek Cypriots of the Ethniki Organosis Kipriakou Agonos (Eoka) (National Organisation of Cypriot Combatants) launched a guerrilla war against the British. The Eoka wanted Cyprus to unify with mainland Greece.

1960 Cyprus was granted independence under President Makarios. Independence followed a compromise agreement between Greek and Turkish Cypriots, with Britain retaining sovereignty over two military bases.

1961 Cyprus joined the IMF and World Bank.

1963 Makarios upset the Turkish Cypriots when he proposed constitutional change which would abrogate power-sharing arrangements. Inter-communal fighting erupted and the Turkish Cypriot community withdrew from the central government.

1964 A UN peace-keeping force was sent to the island.

1968–74 Talks on constitutional reform were inconclusive, as Turkish Cypriots sought separate municipalities in the five main towns.

1974 A brief Greek junta-sponsored coup by supporters of a union with Greece toppled President Makarios, who escaped. Turkey invaded northern Cyprus and Greek Cypriots fled their homes in the north; 37 per cent of the island came under Turkish control, enforcing partition between north and south. The border between the two became known as the Green Line.

The coup failed and Glafcos Clerides took over as the Greek Cypriot president, until Makarios returned at the end of the year.

1975 Northern Cyprus declared the formation of the 'Turkish Federated State of Cyprus' with Rauf Denktash as president and with the aim of eventually gaining independence.

1977 President Makarios died and was succeeded by Spyros Kyprianou.

1980 UN-sponsored peace talks resumed.

1983 Rauf Denktash suspended talks and northern Cyprus officially declared its independence as the Kuzey Kýbrýs Türk Cumhuriyeti (KKTC) (Turkish Republic of Northern Cyprus) and introduced its own government and legal system. The international community rejected the independence move and only Turkey recognised it as a state.

1985 There was no agreement between Denktash and Kyprianou.

1988 Georgios Vassiliou was elected Greek Cypriot president.

1989 Talks between the two presidents were abandoned.

1992–93 Additional UN-sponsored talks with Rauf Denktash failed when the UN Security Council rejected Turkish demands for the recognition of separate sovereignty for the KKTC, including a right to secession.

1993 Glafcos Clerides defeated George Vassiliou in the presidential election.

1994 The European Court of Justice ruled that all direct trade between northern Cyprus and the EU was illegal.

1994–95 Talks continued between north and south with little progress. The Greek Cypriots and the UN pushed for a federal system, but this was rejected by the KKTC.

1996 Tension between the two sides increased and there was violence along the Green Line.

1997 UN-mediated talks between Clerides and Denktash failed.

1998 Clerides was narrowly re-elected for a second term. The EU listed Cyprus as a potential member.

1999 Further peace talks in the US failed to find a solution to Cyprus' division.

2000 Rauf Denktash was elected for a fourth five-year term as the KKTC president.

2001 The leaders of the two Cypriot communities held their first direct talks in four years and agreed to restart peace talks to pave the way for EU membership.

2002 A UN-sponsored plan for reunification as a federation with a rotating presidency was rejected by the KKTC, which insisted on international recognition. The EU invited Cyprus to join in 2004, however if the two estranged communities could not agree to reunification then only the Greek Cypriot part of the island would gain membership.

2003 Tassos Papadopoulos, Dimokratikon Komma (DIKO) (Democratic Party) won the presidential elections. A coalition led by the leftist, Anorthotikon Komma Ergazemenou Laou (AKEL) (Progressive Party of the Working People) with KISOS (Social Democrats) won parliamentary elections. The UN deadline for agreement on reunification passed without agreement. Crossing points between the two zones were temporarily opened and the government lifted 20-year-old trade sanctions against the KKTC, thus allowing farmers in the north to sell produce in the south and export to the EU, and permitting Turkish Cypriots to work in the south.

2004 Twin referenda on the UN reunification plan and united EU entry, resulted in Greek Cypriots voted against unification with the north by 76 per cent, while in the north, 65 per cent voted in favour of the proposal. Internationally recognised Cyprus joined the EU on 1 May. Turkey agreed that it would recognise Cyprus as an EU member.

2005 In KKTC parliamentary elections Cumhuriyetçi Türk Partisi (CTP) (Turkish Republican Party) won a majority of seats. Turkey agreed to extend a free trade accord with the EU, to include Cyprus and other new EU members that joined 2004. In the KKTC presidential election, Mehmet Ali Talat won with 55 per cent of the vote, compared to 23 per cent for runner-up Dervis Eroglu. In Cyprus' worst ever air accident, 121 people on board a Cypriot plane were killed in a crash as it approached Athens' airport.

2006 The ruling coalition won the parliamentary elections with a combined vote of 49 per cent. The result was a victory for the president's plan of maintaining opposition to the UN's strategy on reunification with KKTC.

2007 In July EU officials formally invited Cyprus to join the third stage of the European Monetary Union (EMU). In July, the ruling coalition was dissolved as AKEL nominated its own candidate for the 2008 presidential election. Ministerial posts were filled by technocrats. On 20 December Cyprus became a member of the European Union Schengen area wereby all travellers may cross borders without a passport or visa.

2008 On 1 January 2008, Cyprus adopted the euro as its official currency. After two rounds of presidential elections, Demetris Christofias, of the communist Akel party, won 53.36 per cent of the vote on a platform of Cyprus reunification; incumbent president, Ioannis Kasoulides won 46.64 per cent. Ledra Street, which runs through the UN buffer zone in Lefkosia, was reopened on 3 April; it had been closed since 1964.

Political structure

The government of southern Cyprus is internationally recognised as the sole administration of the Republic of Cyprus. Occupied by Turkish troops since 1974, northern Cyprus has its own government and calls itself the Kuzey Kýbrýs Türk

Cumhuriyeti (KKTC) (Turkish Republic of Northern Cyprus). It is only recognised by Turkey.

Constitution

The constitution was promulgated in 1960. For the first time, at the 1998 presidential election, suffrage was extended to include all citizens above the age of 18.
Northern Cyprus introduced its own consitution after declaring unilateral independence in 1983.

Form of state

Presidential republic

The executive

Executive power is held by the president who is directly elected for a five-year term by universal suffrage. A council of ministers is appointed by the president, who convenes and presides over its meetings. Ministers may not sit in the house of representatives, but may introduce bills.

National legislature

Legislative power is vested in an 80-member unicameral Vouli Antiprosópon (house of representatives). Members are elected for a five-year term – 56 members of the house are Greek Cypriots, elected by the Greek Cypriot community; 24 seats are reserved for Turkish Cypriots, elected by the Turkish Cypriot community. The Turkish Cypriots seats have not been filled since 1963.
In 1983, northern Cyprus introduced its own parliament, the 50-member Temsilciler Meclisi (House of Representatives).

Legal system

The Republic of Cyprus' legal system is embodied in the 1960 constitution and is based on British common law. The legal system in northern Cyprus is based on Turkish law.

Last elections

21 May 2006 (parliamentary); 17 and 24 February 2008 (presidential, first and second round); 20 February 2005 (Kuzey Kýbrýs Türk Cumhuriyeti (KKTC) (Turkish Republic of Northern Cyprus) (parliamentary).

Results: Parliamentary: Akel won 31.2 per cent of the vote (18 out of 59 seats); Disi 30.3 per cent (18); Diko 17.9 per cent (11); Socialistiko Komma Kyprou (Edek) (Socialist Party of Cyprus) 8.9 per cent (five); and the European Party (Evroko) 5.7 per cent (three). Turnout was 89 per cent.
Presidential: (first round), Ioannis Kasoulides won 33.5 per cent, Dimitris Christofias 33.3 per cent and Tassos Papadopoulos won 31.8 per cent; turnout was 89.6 per cent. Second round: Demetris Christofias won 53.36 per cent of the vote, Ioannis Kasoulides won 46.64 per cent.
KKTC parliamentary: Cumhuriyetçi Türk Partisi (CTP) (Turkish Republican Party) won 44.5 per cent of the vote (24 seats out of 50), National Unity Party 31.7 per cent (19), Demokrat Parti (DP) (Democrat Party) 13.5 per cent (six), Baris ve Demokrasi Hareketi (BDH) (Peace and Democracy Movement) 5.8 per cent (one); turnout was 80.8 per cent.

Next elections

February 2013 (presidential); 2011 (parliamentary).

Political parties

Ruling party

Coalition led by Anorthotikon Komma Ergazemenou Laou (AKEL) (Progressive Party of the Working People) with Dimokratikon Komma (DIKO) (Democratic Party) and Kinima Sosialdimokraton (KISOS) (Social Democrats Movement) (since 2003; re-elected May 2006)

Main opposition party

Dimokratikos Sinagermos (Disi) (Democratic Coalition)

Population

780,000 (2007)*

Last census: October 2001: 689,565 (excluding Northern Cyprus)

Population density: 82 inhabitants per square km. Urban population: 57 per cent (1994–2000).

Annual growth rate: 1.4 per cent 1994–2004 (WHO 2006)

Ethnic make-up

Greeks (84.1 per cent), Turks (11.8 per cent), Maronites (0.6 per cent), Armenians (0.3 per cent), Latins (0.1per cent), foreign residents (mainly British and Greek) (3.1 per cent).

Religions

Christian Orthodox (77 per cent), Muslim (18 per cent).

Education

Primary schooling lasts for six years between the ages of six and 12. Public general secondary education extends over six years. Almost 20,000 students, mostly from Turkey, Eastern Europe and the Middle East, attend six private universities in northern Cyprus.

Literacy rate: 97 per cent, adult rate (World Bank)

Compulsory years: Six to 15.

Enrolment rate: 100 per cent gross primary enrolment, of the relevant age group, (including repeaters), (World Bank)

Health

Per capita total expenditure on health (2003) was US$1,143; of which per capita government spending was US$561, at the international dollar rate, (WHO 2006).
The government is looking for ways to persuade Greek-Cypriot medical specialists to return from overseas and offer high-quality healthcare services at a considerably lower cost than in Western Europe.

Life expectancy: 79 years, 2004 (WHO 2006)

Fertility rate/Maternal mortality rate: 1.6 births per woman, 2004 (WHO 2006)

Birth rate/Death rate: 8 deaths and 17 births per 1,000 people (World Bank)

Child (under 5 years) mortality rate (per 1,000): 4 per 1,000 live births (World Bank)

Head of population per physician: 2.34 physicians per 1,000 people, 2002 (WHO 2006)

Welfare

Cyprus offers a statutory social insurance scheme securing decent pensions and allows pensioners to continue working without affecting their pensions. The Social Insurance Scheme provides insurance for all employees who contribute 16.6 per cent on the insured income. The employer deducts 6.3 per cent of the employees' income and contributes 6.3 per cent, while the remaining 4 per cent is paid by the state. There is provision for a non-contributory social pension for elderly people who are not entitled to a pension from any other source. There is also a complementary public assistance scheme for people whose resources are not sufficient to meet their basic and special needs. There is provision for unemployment and disability benefits. The National Social Security System allows women a paid 16-week maternity leave and a substantial birth allowance. Cyprus also offers crime victims a financial compensation programme.

Main cities

Nicosia municipal council voted to change the capital city's name to Lefkosia, Nicosia's Greek name, in 1995. The change was the result of a campaign to standardise place names according to their Greek pronunciation, although Nicosia is still the name in common use.
Lefkosia (capital, estimated population 197,600 in 2003), Lemesos (Limassol) (149,100), Larnaka (Larnaca) (48,200), Pafos (Paphos) (32,700).
Northern Cyprus, cities include Lefkosa (the part under Turkish control – 45,800), Gazimagusa (35,700), Girne (19,000).

Languages spoken

Armenian and Arabic; English is widely spoken in tourist regions.

Official language/s

Greek and Turkish

Media

Media services are fractured along the island's divided territories with outlets in each zone operating under their own regulations.

National news agency: Cyprus News Agency (CNA)

Other news agencies: TAK (Arca Haber Ajansi) (in Turkish): www.arcaajans.com

Press

Dailies: In Greek, the most popular newspapers are all independents, including Phileleftheros (www.philenews.com), Simerini (Today) (www.simerini.com.cy), Politis (Citizen) (www.politis-news.com) and Haravgi (www.haravgi.com.cy). In Turkish important newspapers include Kibris Gazetesi (www.kibrisgazetesi.com) and Halkin Sesi (Voice of the People) (www.halkinsesi.org), both independents and Yeni Kibris (www.ykp.org.cy) published by the unification, YKP (New Cyprus Party), with Greek and English online versions. In English, The Cyprus Mail, (www.cyprus-mail.com).

Weeklies: In Greek, the SSP Media Group publishes several titles for women, men and lifestyle magazines (www.sppmedia.com). To Periodiko (www.toperiodiko.com) for current affairs, The Cyprus Government Gazette (www.cygazette.com) is a comprehensive weekly publication. In English, The Cyprus Weekly (www.cyprusweekly.com.cy) has the largest circulation, followed by the Cyprus Observer (www.observercyprus.com).

Business: Two publications that are closely linked are the Financial Mirror (www.financialmirror.com), published in English, with a Greek version Xpress Economiki.

In Greek, Euro Kerdos (Euro Profit) (www.eurokerdos.com) a financial and Chrimatistiriaki a stock exchange, monthly magazines.

Periodicals: Monthlies include, in Greek, Flash (www.flashcy.com) for young people, as is, in English, Scoop (www.scoop-magazine.com) and Sports in the City (www.sportsinthecitynews.com), In Touch (www.intouchcyprus.com) for lifestyle articles.

Broadcasting

Cyprus Broadcasting Corporation (CyBC) (www.cybc.com.cy) is state broadcaster for the Republic of Cyprus.

Bayrak Radio and Television Corporation (BRT) (www.brtk.cc) operates in Northern Cyprus.

Radio: CyBC operates three radio stations the First Program, International program, Third Progam and Fourth program, offering a range of news, talk, education, entertainment and music programmes, also in English, Armenian and Turkish.

BRT (www.brtk.cc) has five stations including Bayrak Radio, Bayrak FM, Baryrak International, Bayrak Classic FM and Bayrak Turkish Music, all broadcasting from Famagusta.

Private commercial radio stations include Radio Astra (www.astra.com.cy) Radio 91.4 FM (www.91.4coastfm.com) and Mix FM (www.mixfmradio.com).

Television: (CyBC) (www.cybc.com.cy) is the national public TV station, which operates two terrestrial channels, Pik 1, with news and factual programmes and Pik 2, with entertainment programmes and one satellite television channel (Pik TV).

BRT (www.brtk.cc) operates two TV channels Bayrak TV 1 and 2.

There are several other, satellite and pay-to-view TV stations including Sigma (www.sigma.com.cy), Music Box TV (www.musicbox.com.cy) and Lumiere TV (www.lumieretv.com).

Economy

By 2006 GDP growth had risen to 3.7 per cent. The growth was spurred by private consumption and investment, as tourist numbers and revenue increased. The government had been successful in cutting its fiscal deficit to below 2.5 per cent of GDP in 2005 and an estimated 1.9 per cent in 2006 and inflation remained relatively low.

Cyprus formally joined the EMU on 1 January 2008.

The economy is export-oriented with exports of goods comprising mainly manufactured products and, to a lesser extent, agricultural products. The labour force is well-educated with a good level of English speakers. Tourism and other private services are the main factors in GDP growth with over 2.4 million visitors annually.

The growing importance of the services industry, and in particular the offshore financial sector, is reflected in its typical contribution to GDP of around 70 per cent, of which financial services account for 6 per cent. Annual net, direct foreign investment (FDI) was estimated at US$789 million in 2006.

Northern Cyprus, which uses the Turkish lira, suffers from high inflation. Financial aid from Turkey and remittances from the 200,000 Turkish Cypriots living abroad are vital sources of revenue.

External trade

As a member of the European Union, Cyprus operates within a communitywide free trade union, with tariffs sets as a whole. Internationally, the EU has free trade agreements with a number of nations and trading blocs worldwide.

In 2007 Cyprus licensed oil exploration in its territorial waters. This angered Turkish administered Northern Cyprus which agued that such exploration should be a joint venture and result in the benefit of both communities.

Imports

Cyprus has a large trade deficit as most goods must be imported, including cigarettes, crude oil, raw materials and machinery for manufacturing, and all transport vehicles.

Main sources: Greece (17.3 per cent total, 2006), Italy (11.4 per cent), UK (8.9 per cent).

Exports

Export of manufactured goods, including electric and electronic equipment, processed food, chemicals, paper, textiles and refined oil represent the largest portion of foreign earnings; important agricultural exports include potatoes, grapes and citrus. Minerals exported include copper, pyrites, chrome, asbestos, and gypsum.

Main destinations: UK (14.6 per cent total, 2006), Greece (13.2 per cent), France (7.4 per cent.

Re-exports

Refined oil, accounts for a significant share of total annual exports.

Agriculture

Farming

The agriculture sector contributes 5 per cent annually to GDP. Major crops are potatoes, grapes, citrus fruits and barley. Cattle, sheep and goats, swine and poultry are raised. Fresh pork, poultry meat and eggs satisfy local demand. Local production of beef, veal, mutton and lamb is supplemented by imports. Agriculture typically contributes 3.5 per cent to GDP and employs 7 per cent of the workforce.

The implentation of modern irrigation technologies has helped to address the sector's water shortage. A large-scale water development programme culminated in the Southern Conveyor Project that carries surplus water from the south-western part of the island to the central and eastern areas in an effort to broaden and boost agricultural production and alleviate water shortages.

Now a member of the EU, Cyprus is only eligible for full EU agricultural subsidies and rural development aid through the Common Agricultural Policy (CAP) by 2013.

During its transitional entry stage Cyprus has decided to implement the reform of the CAP on 1 January 2009. The reform was introduced throughout most of the EU on 1 January 2005, when subsidies on farm output, which tended to benefit large farms and encourage overproduction, were replaced by single farm payments not conditional on production. The change is expected to reward farms that provide and maintain a healthy environment, food safety and animal welfare standards. The changes are also intended to encourage market conscious production and cut the cost of CAP to the EU taxpayer.

Estimated crop production in 2005 included: 107,450 tonnes (t) cereals in total, 13,000t wheat, 116,000t potatoes, 10,500t bananas, 886t pulses, 3,900t figs, 132,000t citrus fruit, 80,860t grapes, 38,200t tomatoes, 6,575t oilcrops, 360t tobacco, 2,255t treenuts, 27,500t olives, 259,020t fruit in total, 151,190t vegetables in total. Estimated livestock production included: 109,448t meat in total, 4,300t beef, 54,000t pig meat, 4,900t lamb, 8,200t goat meat, 36,718t poultry, 12,300t eggs, 202,000t milk, 1,000t honey.

Fishing

The fishing industry largely consists of in-shore and trawl fishing, as well as aquaculture. Annual fish production typically totals 4,000 tonnes.

Forestry

Forest and other wooded land accounts for less than a third of the land area. Industrial wood and paper products are largely imported.

Industry and manufacturing

The industrial sector contributes around 12 per cent to GDP and accounts for 16 per cent of the workforce.

Major growth industries, which are mainly export-based, include cement, food and drink, footwear and clothing. Chemical and pharmaceutical products, plastics and publishing are also expanding areas.

Foreign investment is encouraged. Industrial activity in northern Cyprus is limited to food and textiles.

Industrial production was projected to climb 3.8 per cent in 2005.

Tourism

Tourism provides 54,000 jobs (15 per cent of the workforce) and contributes to approximately 20 per cent of GDP.

The UK is the principal market, accounting for 60 per cent of visitors, or 1.3 million annual visits. The majority of other arrivals come from other European countries. A Strategic Plan to improve the quality of tourism and increase visitor numbers by 2010 began in 2003. Competition from Turkish-occupied northern Cyprus has been limited in the past, as a result of the lack of direct air connections to that part of the island and restricted access from the south. However, visitor numbers to the north are increasing and have reached around 500,000. Most visitors come from Turkey. Restrictions on south-to-north visits have been reluctantly relaxed since EU accession, but only for daytrips. In summer 2005 an airliner flew from the Turkish Cypriot north to Baku, the capital of Azerbaijan. This was the first time a direct flight from the region has flown anywhere but Turkey.

Environment

The problems of water shortages, sewage disposal, industrial and agricultural pollution and waste disposal are acute. The government has introduced a programme of legislation incorporating the principle that the polluter pays. By July 2008, Cyprus had had no substantial winter rainfall since 2004 and water reservoirs were at their lowest since 1908 so that potable water had to be imported from the Greek mainland; contamination fears condemned a shipment of 40,000 cubic metres of water, which had to be discarded and pumped into the ground. Cyprus will import eight million cubic metres of water, costing US$70 million, by November 2008.

Northern Cyprus is particularly badly affected by water shortages, a problem accentuated by the Turkish soldiers stationed on the island. Shortages have caused many to stop cultivating the land as low rainfalls mean water reserves are used faster than they are replenished. The Turkish government has proposed building a water pipeline to northern Cyprus, capable of carrying 70–100 million cubic metres a year to the island. Since the 1990s, giant plastic 'sacks' of water have been pulled across the Mediterranean from Turkey to northern Cyprus; there is a concern about a long-term shortage of water.

Mining

Cyprus was once famous for its enormous copper reserves. It has a 3,000 year tradition of copper mining, which was the biggest source of the nation's revenue. However after the 1974 Turkish invasion copper mining stopped. In 2005 East Mediterranean Resources obtained prospecting licences allowing access to 370 sq km. Test drillings were planned for late 2005.

Continued expansion in the construction industry has led to a boom in quarrying of construction materials and non-metallic minerals. Other quarried materials include marble, bentonite, umber, sienna, ochra and limonite.

Hydrocarbons

Cyprus has de-limited its continental shelf to ward off encroachment by other countries. Egypt pledged to assist Cyprus in locating and exploiting its oil and gas reserves thought to be located off the southern and eastern edges of the country.

Cyprus does not produce or import natural gas, although it does import coal, typically 45,000 tonnes per annum. In 2007 Egypt and Lebanon began undertaking oil and gas exploration in 60,000 square klometers of Cyprus' territorial waters.

Energy

Cyprus is almost completely dependent on imported petroleum. The Vassiliko electric power station was established in 2000. Four additional gas boilers will be installed by 2008, increasing the capacity from around 300MW to 778MW.

Cyprus is well suited to solar power with over 300 days of sunshine per annum. The government subsidies the implementation of solar technology to a maximum 55 per cent of the cost, and has now started to subsidise wind power.

Financial markets

Stock exchange

The Cyprus Stock Exchange (CSE) was transformed in 1996 from an over-the-counter market to an official stock exchange. The CSE became a fully computerised trading system in 1999. The overall supervision of the stock exchange is assigned to the minister of finance and is exercised by the minister through the Securities and Exchange Commission.

Banking and insurance

The Bank of Cyprus, which was founded in 1899, leads the Cypriot banking sector. The Central Bank of Cyprus (CBC) oversees monetary policy. There are nine commercial banks. The abolition of the interest rate ceiling was part of a drive to reform banking practices in line with those of the EU.

Central bank

Central Bank of Cyprus

Time

GMT plus two hours (daylight saving, late March to late October, GMT plus three hours)

Geography

Cyprus is an island in the eastern Mediterranean Sea, about 100km south of Turkey. The landscape varies between rugged coastlines, sandy beaches, rocky hills and forest-covered mountains. The Troodos Mountains in the centre of the island rise to almost 1,950 metres.

Hemisphere

Northern

Climate

Mediterranean. Summers are long and dry. Winters are changeable with occasional rain. Temperatures range from 0–27 degrees Celsius (C) (in the mountains), 5–40 degrees C (inland) and 9–35 degrees C (on the coast). Hottest months are July and August; coldest are January and February. Average annual rainfall is 500mm.

Entry requirements

Passports

Required by all except citizens of EU, Switzerland, Iceland and Norway travelling with official national ID cards. Passports must have at least three months validity from the date of departure from Cyprus.

Visa

Required by all except citizens of most European, American and Japan. Contact the local embassy or High Commission for a full list of exceptions and application, see consular and protocol information in: www02.mfa.gov.cy. A Schengen visa application (offered in several languages) can be downloaded from http://europa.eu/abc/travel/ see 'documents you will need'. For a business visa, applications should include an introductory letter from the employer, which gives details and the nature of business to be conducted.

Prohibited entry
Passport holders of the Turkish Republic of Northern Cyprus; Citizens of the Former Yugoslavia Republic of Macedonia travelling on passports with a renewal stamp of Macedonia.
Cypriot authorities do not recognise any ports of entry other than those in the Republic of Cyprus. Visitors with passports stamped in the Turkish Republic of Northern Cyprus must have their passports visa stamps cancelled by the Republic of Cyprus immigration authorities.

Currency advice/regulations
Local currency may be imported without restriction but must be declared; foreign currency over US$1,000 (or the equivalent) must be declared. The export of foreign and local currency is limited to the amount declared on arrival. Export of local currency withdrawn from Cypriot banks is permitted, provided a holding certificate is obtained.
To avoid extra exchange fees travellers cheques in UK pounds sterling or Cyprus pounds are advised.

Customs
Personal items are duty-free. There are no duties levied on alcohol and tobacco between EU member states, providing amounts imported are for personal consumption.
Unauthorised export of antiquities is prohibited; permission of the Cyprus Museum is required.

Health (for visitors)
Nationals of the European Economic Area (EEA) countries and Switzerland can access reduced cost and sometimes free medical treatment using a European Health Insurance Card (EHIC) while visiting the EEA. Exceptions include nationals of the 10 countries which joined the EU in 2004 whose EHIC is not valid in Switzerland. Applications for the EHIC should be made before travelling.

Mandatory precautions
None

Advisable precautions
Recommended immunisations include tetanus and polio, while long-term visitors are advised to consider a hepatitis A immunisation.
Tap water is safe to drink, but fruit, especially soft fruit, should be washed.

Hotels
There are over 500 hotels (from deluxe to one star). Visitors should book well in advance, especially during the peak holiday season (April–October). Cyprus Tourism Organisation (CTO) operates a rating system, both for hotels and any other licensed tourist accommodation. Tipping is not obligatory. A 15 per cent valued added tax (VAT) is charge on all bills.

Credit cards
Most leading cards are accepted in the main hotels, restaurants and shops.

Public holidays (national)
Fixed dates
1 Jan (New Year's Day), 6 Jan (Epiphany), 25 Mar (Greek National Day), 1 Apr (Greek Cypriot National Day), 1 May (Labour Day), 15 Aug (Assumption Day), 1 Oct (Cyprus Independence Day), 28 Oct (Greek National Day/Ochi Day), 24–26 Dec (Christmas Holiday).

Variable dates
Green Monday (Feb/Mar), Greek Orthodox Easter (Mar/Apr, four days Thu–Mon); Pentecost (Festival of the Flood (Jun)).

Working hours
Banking
Mon–Fri: 0815–1230; Mon (only) 1515–1645, (year around).
In summer (Jun–Aug), in central districts, some banks have extended hours Tue–Fri: 1515–1645.

Business
Mon–Fri: 0800–1300 and 1500–1800 (winter), 0730–1300 and 1600–1830 (summer); Wed and Sat half-day (year round).

Government
Mon–Fri: 0730–1430; in winter Sept–June, Thu: 1500–1800.

Shops
Mon–Fri: 0800–1300 and 1430–1800 (winter), 0730–1300 and 1600–1830 (summer); Wed and Sat half-day 0800–1400.

Telecommunications
Telephone/fax
GSM 900/1800 and G3 services are available in Greek Cypriot areas

Electricity supply
240V AC. Sockets are the UK flat three-pin style.

Weights and measures
The metric system is used.

Social customs/useful tips
It is considered impolite to refuse drinks offered at a first meeting. Cypriots customarily offer fruit preserves to guests. Between 1300–1600 hours is siesta time in the summer (May–September).

There are restrictions on photographing military installations in both south and north Cyprus.

Getting there
Air
National airline: Cyprus Airways
International airport/s: Larnaka International (LCA), 8km from Larnaka (49km from Lefkosia); Pafos International (PFO), 10km east of Pafos (146km from Lefkosia). Both airports offer tourist information, foreign exchange, hotel reservations and duty free shops.
Other airport/s: Northern Cyprus has an airport at Ercan with flights to and from Turkey. Flights are provided by a number of Turkish airlines and the northern Cypriot airline, Kibris Türk Hava Yollari (KYHY) (Cyprus Turkish Airlines). Visitors planning to arrive via Turkey are not allowed into southern Cyprus.
Airport tax: None

Surface
Water: Access by ship from Greece, Syria, Israel, Italy, Lebanon and Egypt.
Main port/s: Lemesos (Limassol)

Getting about
National transport
Buses: An efficient intra-cud (inter-town) bus service is available. All buses run from the central bus depots, connecting towns and villages. A rural bus operation is limited to once or twice a day, usually to the local market.

City transport
Taxis: An efficient service is operated throughout the island by metered taxis. The transurban service-taxis are shared taxis connecting all main towns. Prices are regulated. Between 2300–0600 an additional 15 per cent is charged. Tipping is standard practice.
Buses, trams & metro: Urban buses operate frequently during the day. In certain tourist areas during the summer, buses extend their operations until midnight.

Car hire
Car hire is available in all parts of the island, particularly from airports and commercial centres. Rates vary depending on the size of the car and are also subject to seasonal variations. For a higher price, a prestige service is also available. Cheap rates are available for hire periods of more than one week. Visitors should book cars well in advance during the period June–September. A national or international driving licence is required. Driving is on the left. Road signs are in both Greek and English.

BUSINESS DIRECTORY
The addresses listed below are a selection only. While World of Information makes every endeavour to check these addresses, we cannot guarantee that

changes have not been made, especially to telephone numbers and area codes. We would welcome any corrections.

Telephone area codes

The international direct dialling codes (IDD) for Cyprus is +357, followed by area code and subscriber's number:

Larnaka	24	Lemasos	25
Lefkosia	22	Pafos	26

North Cyprus numbers are preceded by +90-392, in place of +357. Area code for Famagusta 366, Kyrenia 815.

Useful telephone numbers

Emergencies 112

Chambers of Commerce

Cyprus Chamber of Commerce and Industry, Chamber Building, 38 Grivas Dighenis Ave and 3 Deligiorgis Street, PO Box 21455, 1509 Lefkosia (tel: 889-600; fax: 667-433).

Famagusta Chamber of Commerce and Industry, 339 Ayiou Andreou Street, Andrea Chamber Bldg, PO Box 3124, Limassol (tel: 370-165, 370-167; fax: 370-291).

Larnaka Chamber of Commerce and Industry, 12 12 Gregoriou Afxentiou Str, Skourou Bldg, 4th Floor, PO Box 287, Larnaka (tel: 655-051; fax: 628-281).

Lefkosia Chamber of Commerce and Industry, 38 Grivas Dighenis Ave and 3 Deligioris Str, Chamber Building, PO Box 1455, Lefkosia (tel: 449-500; fax: 367-433).

Limassol Chamber of Commerce and Industry, PO Box 347, 25 Spyrou Araouzou Street, Verengaria Building, PO Box 347, Limassol (tel: 362-556; fax: 371-655).

Pafos Chamber of Commerce and Industry, 32 Grivas Dighenis Avenue, Demetra Court, 2nd Floor, Flat 22, Pafos (tel:235-115; fax: 244-602).

Banking

Alpha Bank Ltd, Yiorkion Bldg, 1 Prodromou Street, 1095 Lefkosia (tel: 77-3799, 88-8888; fax: 77-3744).

Bank of Cyprus Ltd, Box 1472, 86-90 Phaneromeni Street, Lefkosia (tel: 46-4064; fax: 46-4340).

Cyprus Development Bank, PO Box 1415, Alpha House, 50 Archbishop Makarios III Avenue, Lefkosia (tel: 45-7575; fax: 46-4322).

Cyprus Investment and Securities Corporation, 60 Digenis Akritas Avenue, PO Box 597, Lefkosia (tel: 45-1535; fax: 44-5481).

Cyprus Popular Bank Ltd, PO Box 2032, 39 Archbishop Makarios III Avenue, Lefkosia (tel: 45-0000; fax: 44-9169).

Federal Bank of the Middle East Ltd, J & P Building, 90 Archbishop Makarios III Avenue, 1077 Lefkosia (tel: 88-8444; fax: 88-8555).

Hellenic Bank Ltd, Corner 92 Dhigenis Akritas Ave & Cretes Str, 1061 Lefkosia (tel: 86-0000; fax: 76-507).

Sociéte Générale Cyprus Ltd, PO Box 25400, 7-9 Grivas Dighenis Ave, 1309 Lefkosia (tel: 81-7777; fax: 76-4471).

Central bank

Central Bank of Cyprus, 80 Kennedy Avenue, PO Box 25529, 1395 Lefkosia (tel: 714-100; fax: 378-153; internet: www.centralbank.gov.cy).

Travel information

Cyprus Airways, PO Box 1903, 21 Alkeou Street, Lefkosia (tel: 44-3054, 2246-1800; fax: 44-3167, 2236-0075; e-mail: marketing@cyprusair.com.cy; internet site: www.cyprusairways.com.cy).

Cyprus Hotel Association, PO Box 24772, Lefkosia (tel: 37-4251; fax: 36-5460).

Ministry of tourism

Ministry of Commerce, Industry and Tourism, 1421 Lefkosia (fax: 375-120).

National tourist organisation offices

Cyprus Tourism Organisation (main office, for postal enquiries only), 19 Limassol Ave, PO Box 4535, Lefkosia (tel: 315-715; fax: 313-022); (for personal and telephone enquiries only, open every morning except Sun, and on Mon and Thurs afternoons) Laiki Yitonia, East of Eleftheria Sq, Lefkosia (tel: 444-264); (24-hour service) Larnaka International Airport (tel: 654-389).

Ministries

Ministry of Agriculture, Natural Resources and Environment, Loukis Akritas Avenue, Lefkosia (tel: 30-0807; fax: 78-1156).

Ministry of Commerce, Industry and Tourism, 2 A Araouzos Street, Lefkosia (fax: 35-7120).

Ministry of Communication and Works, 28 Acheon Street, Lefkosia CY-1101 (tel: 30-2830; fax: 77-6272, 46-5462, 36-0578).

Ministry of Defence, 4 Emmanuel Roides Street, Lefkosia (tel: 80-7528; fax: 36-6225).

Ministry of Education and Culture, Gr Afxentiou Street, Lefkosia (tel: 30-5188; fax: 42-7559).

Ministry of Finance, Ex Secretariat Compound, Lefkosia (tel: 80-3530; fax: 36-6080).

Ministry of Foreign Affairs, Dem Severis Avenue, Government House No. 18-19, Lefkosia (tel: 30-0600; fax: 45-1881).

Ministry of Health, Ex Secretarial Offices, Lefkosia (tel: 30-9526; fax: 36-8883).

Ministry of Interior, Dem Severis Avenue, Ex Secretariat Offices, Lefkosia (tel: 51-0222; fax: 45-3465, 36-6709).

Ministry of Justice and Public Order, 12 Helioupoleos, Lefkosia (tel: 30-2355; fax: 76-1427).

Ministry of Labour and Social Insurance, Byron Avenue, Lefkosia (tel: 30-3481; fax: 45-0993).

Presidential Palace, Lefkosia (tel: 45-1333; fax: 44-5016).

Other useful addresses

British High Commission, Alexander Pallis St, PO Box 1978, Lefkosia (tel: 47-3131/7; fax: 36-7198).

Central Post Office, Eleftheria Square, Lefkosia (tel: 30-3219).

Cyprus Broadcasting Corporation, PO Box 4824, Lefkosia (tel: 42-2231; fax: 31-4050).

Cyprus Employers' and Industrialists' Federation, 30 Grivas Dhigenis Avenue, PO Box 1657, Lefkosia (tel: 44-5102; fax: 45-9459).

Cyprus News Agency, 7 Kastorias St, PO Box 3947, Lefkosia (tel: 31-9009; fax: 31-9006).

Cyprus Petroleum Refinery Ltd, PO Box 40275, 6302 Larnaka (fax: 2464-1401; e-mail: lambroug@cprl.com.cy).

Cyprus Telecommunications Authority, PO Box 4929, Lefkosia (tel: 31-3111).

Department of Customs & Excise, Customs Headquarters, 29 Katsonis Street, Ay Omoloyitae, Lefkosia (tel: 30-5404, 30-5737; fax: 35-5050).

Department of Statistics and Research, Ministry of Finance, 13 Andreas Araouzos Street, 1444 Lefkosia (tel: 30-9305, 30-3208; fax: 37-4830, 45-6712).

Embassy of the United States of America, Therissos St & Dositheos St, Lefkosia (fax: 45-9571).

Press and Information Office, Apellis Street, Ay Omoloyitae, 1456 Lefkosia (tel: 80-1155/1164/1177; fax: 36-6123; email: communications@pio.moi.gov.cy).

National news agency: Cyprus News Agency (CNA)

Other news agencies: TAK (Arca Haber Ajansi) (in Turkish): www.arcaajans.com

Internet sites

Cyprus News: www.cyprusnews.com

Cyprus Telecommunications Authority: www.cytanet.com.cy

Cyprus Tourism Organisation: www.cyprustourism.org

Official Cyprus homepage: www.pio.gov.cy

Czech Republic

KEY FACTS

Official name: Ceská Republika (Czech Republic)

Head of State: President Václav Klaus (since 2003; re-elected 15 Feb 2008)

Head of government: Prime Minister Mirek Topolánek (since 16 Aug 2006)

Ruling party: Coalition: Obcanská Demokratická Strana (ODS) (Civic Democratic Party); Krestanská a Demokratická Unie-Ceskoslovenská Strana Lidova (KDU-CSL) (Christian and Democratic Union-Czechoslovak People's Party); and Strana Zelených (Green Party)

Area: 78,864 square km

Population: 10.27 million (2007)*

Capital: Prague

Official language: Czech

Currency: Czech koruna (Kc) = 100 hellers

Exchange rate: Kc14.53 per US$ (Jul 2008)

GDP per capita: US$17,070 (2007)*

GDP real growth: 6.50% (2007)

Labour force: 5.10 million (2004)

Unemployment: 8.30% (OECD, 2004)

Inflation: 2.80% (2007)

Balance of trade: -US$1.74 billion (2005)

Foreign debt: US$45.30 billion (2004)

Visitor numbers: 6.43 million (2006)*

Annual FDI: US$4.45 billion (2004)*

* estimated figure

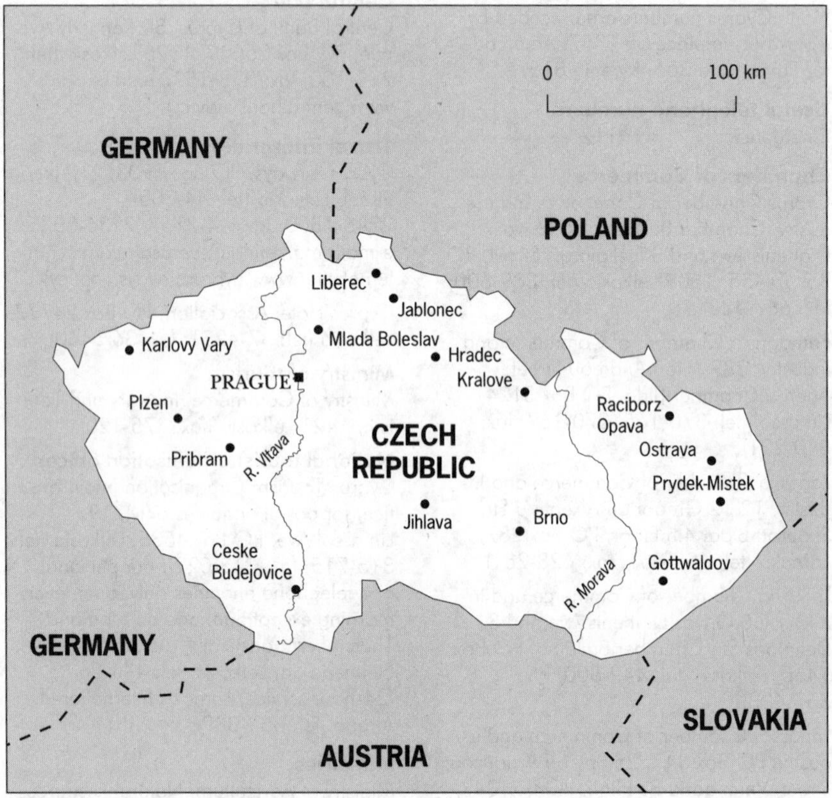

With strong economic indicators, in 2007 the Czech Republic continued on course to fulfil the minimum criteria for entering the eurozone. However, widespread scepticism about the euro and about the proposed Lisbon constitution were expressed in a series of public opinion polls. A senior banker from the Ceska Národnì Banka (CNB) (Czech National Bank) publicly questioned the value of adopting the euro, pointing out that economic growth in the eurozone was far less than that in the Czech Republic. This view found support with Czech president, Václav Klaus, a hard-line eurosceptic long at odds with the relatively pro-EU integration policies of the government. President Klaus hails from the right-wing Obcanská Demokratická Strana (ODS) (Civic Democratic Party). Previously, in April, President Klaus had called for a referendum on the EU constitution, at a time when opinion polls were showing that the constitution would be rejected.

Roma rejection

The curious bystander does not need to go far from Prague's prosperous and booming centre to come across quite a different world, where one of the country's major social problems is all too apparent. The run-down inner city areas hosting Prague's Roma communities are less than 2 kilometres from Wenceslaus Square. For generations Roma and Sinti people – often simply referred to as Gypsies – have been excluded from Prague's mainstream, 'white' schools. In 2007 the European Court of Human Rights ruled that this was discrimination against the continent's largest ethnic minority. Without doubt, the simmering discontent of the Czech Republic's 150,000 Roma inhabitants represents one of the republic's major social problems, and one that governments have done little to address.

But the responsibility is not only that of the government. Increasingly, members of the Roma community accept that parents also need to take more responsibility for how their children get on at school. Foremost among these is Radek Bhanga, a Roma rapper who draws large, mixed-race audiences – mixing hip-hop with traditional gypsy sounds. Mr Bhanga has become notorious for challenging what he has called the 'victim mentality' of Czech Roma. He notes, depressingly, that Czech people are racist and xenophobic. But points out that many Gypsies are worse, failing to send their children to school because they don't want them to be 'white'. Some observers have likened the Czech Republic's Roma problem to that of France's Muslim community, describing both sets of tensions as 'simmering beneath the surface'.

The economy's strong fundamentals

Over the past few years, growing international trade and continued foreign direct investment (FDI), and the benign effects of the regional cyclical economic surge, have underpinned the Czech Republic's export-led boom, accompanied by low inflation and an improving external balance. Reassured by these strong fundamentals, market sentiment has remained positive, allowing the economy to overcome protracted political gridlock and the global financial market turmoil with low levels of volatility.

Sustaining this growth momentum and maintaining external stability still requires the key challenge of fiscal consolidation to be addressed. This is also a prerequisite to ensuring smooth euro entry. With one of the highest primary fiscal deficits in the region and large demographic shifts underway, structural fiscal and pension reform remains a key priority to restore longer run debt sustainability and improve incentives to work. Labour market reforms to reduce structural unemployment, and increase flexibility and participation could make a substantial contribution to reducing the fiscal gap and enhancing income convergence.

IMF approval

In 2007 the IMF expected the Czech Republic's GDP growth to be close to 6 per cent for the third year in a row, driven by domestic demand. Export growth has remained robust, led by the automobile sector, while strong corporate profitability has fuelled fixed investment. Consumption has remained strong, reflecting rising disposable earnings from strong wage gains, higher social transfers and rapid credit expansion. However, this rapid growth has begun to stretch capacity limits. The unemployment rate has declined to the lowest level this decade, marked by a decline in both short and long term unemployment. With labour shortages emerging despite a steady rise in immigration, wage gains are rapidly catching up with strong productivity growth, squeezing profitability margins. Capacity utilisation rates in industry also stand at record high levels. Estimates of output gap measures also point to a positive gap in 2007.

The current account deficit has widened, but remains largely financed by inflows of direct investment. Although the saving rate remains relatively high, the pickup in investment led to a rise in the current account deficit to around 3.5 per cent of GDP in 2007 from about 3 per cent in 2006. Trade and services balance surpluses continued to improve on account of strong exports of the automobile and electronic sectors. However, with record profits, these were offset by a sharp rise in repatriation of dividends by foreign investors.

The IMF reports that underlying inflation has picked up from the low levels of recent years. Core inflation, which had remained subdued at around one per cent, has risen steadily since late 2006, fuelled by higher domestic demand amid tightening labour markets, strong credit expansion, and rising food and regulated prices. The depreciation of the koruna during the first half of 2007 has added to inflation. Strong demand and rising food and oil prices pushed headline inflation to 5 per cent in the year to November 2007, well above the upper margin of the CNB's tolerance band of 1 per cent around the target of 3 per cent.

Consistent with the inflation targeting framework, monetary policy was tightened in the first half of 2008 to counter rising inflation pressures. The rapid appreciation of the koruna in recent months – about 5 per cent since October 2007 – has contributed to tightening monetary conditions. Fiscal policy in 2007 was expansionary even though strong growth resulted in a considerably more favourable out-turn than budgeted. Spurred by the strength in household incomes, consumption and corporate profits, buoyant tax revenues are likely to keep the general government deficit below 3 per cent of GDP, fortuitously offsetting the large increase in social benefits stemming from pre-election commitments. With a widening positive output gap, the fiscal stance for 2007 was nevertheless estimated to be expansionary, albeit modestly.

Economic growth is expected to slow in 2008 but should remain solid on the back of continued strong domestic demand. The IMF projects growth to decline to about 4.5 per cent, in line with the consensus, as recent fiscal measures to raise VAT and reduce social benefits weigh on private consumption, and growth in the euro area weakens. The planned tightening of the fiscal stance will also contribute to a dampening of domestic demand. On the

KEY INDICATORS — Czech Republic

	Unit	2003	2004	2005	2006	2007
Population	m	10.29	10.29	10.23	10.27	*10.27
Gross domestic product (GDP)	US$bn	81.82	108.05	123.98	143.02	175.31
GDP per capita	US$	7,951	10,480	12,120	13,933	*17,070
GDP real growth	%	3.6	4.0	6.1	6.4	6.5
Inflation	%	0.7	2.8	1.8	2.5	2.8
Unemployment	%	7.5	9.9	8.9	7.2	*6.6
Coal output	mtoe	70.8	23.5	23.5	23.7	18.9
Exports (fob) (goods)	US$m	40,800.0	66,510.0	78,243.0	95,119.0	–
Imports (cif) (goods)	US$m	43,200.0	68,190.0	76,507.0	92,139.0	–
Balance of trade	US$m	-2,400.0	-1,680.0	1,735.0	2,979.0	–
Current account	US$m	-5,570.0	-5,570.0	-3,217.0	-4,462.0	-4,384.0
Total reserves minus gold	US$m	26,771.0	28,259.0	28,259.0	31,182.0	34,550.0
Foreign exchange	US$m	26,294.0	27,844.0	27,844.0	31,054.0	34,445.0
Exchange rate	per US$	27.90	25.68	21.50	21.02	18.28

* estimated figure

other hand, fixed investment is projected to rise supported by strong corporate profits, tax cuts and the need for capacity expansion. Over the medium term, output is expected to be boosted by the coming on stream of a large export-oriented project in the automobile sector, boosting integration with domestic supplier chains. Output is thus likely to remain above its potential level, and unemployment low.

Risk assessment

Economy	Good
Politics	Fair
Regional stability	Good

COUNTRY PROFILE

Historical profile

1918 Czechoslovakia's independence was established. Before this, Moravia and Bohemia had been ruled by Austria, while Slovakia had been governed by Hungary.
1938 Czechoslovakia ceded its German-speaking areas of Sudetenland to Germany.
1939–45 The country fell under German control until the end of the Second World War.
1946 The Czechoslovak Communist Party (CPCz) formed a power-sharing government following national elections.
1948 After mass protests and strikes orchestrated by the Communists, a government crisis left the CPCz with a majority in government. Czechoslovakia became a People's Republic, adopting a Soviet-style system.
1949–67 Stalinist-style rule, complete with party purges.
1968 Alexander Dubcek, the CPCz leader, introduced the policy of socialism with a human face – a period known as the 'Prague Spring' – which ended with the crushing of the reformist movement by the Soviet army.
1969–88 There were on-going protests at occupation by the Soviet troops. Václav Havel and a group of dissidents called for the restoration of civil and political rights. Mass demonstrations in 1988 marked the anniversary of the 1968 invasion.
1989 The new spirit of glasnost was met with scepticism as the government initially resisted political and economic change. However, large public demonstrations in the major cities, the 'Velvet Revolution', led to the resignation of the Communist Party leadership. Václav Havel was elected president and a pluralistic political system and market economy were introduced.
1990 The country was renamed the Czech and Slovak Federative Republic. The first free elections since 1946 resulted in a coalition government involving all major parties, with the exception of the CPCz, and Havel was re-elected president.
1991 The Soviet forces completed their withdrawal.
1992 In elections, the Czech voters backed the centre-right, while the Slovaks supported Slovak separatists and left-wing parties. Vladimir Meciar (a supporter of Slovak separatism) became Slovak prime minister. He opposed the rapid privatisation of the public sector proposed by the Czech prime minister, Václav Klaus. Neither was prepared to compromise and agreed to the separation of Slovakia, despite President Havel's objections.
1993 Czechoslovakia divided into two independent countries, the Czech Republic (comprising the regions of Bohemia, Moravia and Silesia) and the Slovak Republic (Slovakia). Václav Havel was elected president of the Czech Republic and Václav Klaus continued as prime minister.
1996 Klaus was reappointed prime minister in a minority coalition government, following the Czech Republic's first parliamentary election.
1997 The Klaus government resigned following the collapse of the coalition over disagreements on the economic reform programme and allegations of financial corruption.
1998 Milos Zeman, leader of the Ceská Strana Sociálne Demokratická (CSSD) (Czech Social Democratic Party), became prime minister and Václav Havel was re-elected president.
1999 The Czech Republic joined NATO.
2000 In elections, a coalition of four small liberal parties, the '4Koalice', became the strongest force in the upper house.
2002 Areas of Prague were flooded when the river Vltava rose to its highest level since 1890. The CSSD won parliamentary elections. President Václav Havel appointed Vladimír Spidla as prime minister.
2003 Parliament elected Václav Klaus as president. In a referendum to join the EU 77.3 per cent voted in favour; turnout was 55 per cent.
2004 The Czech Republic entered the EU. The government resigned and the President asked Stanislav Gross to form a government.
2005 Despite surviving a no-confidence vote Gross resigned and Jirí Paroubek became prime minister; the new cabinet, unchanged in the key posts, was endorsed on the same day.
2006 Parliamentary elections resulted in a stalemate with both CSSD and Obcanská Demokratická Strana (ODS) (Civic Democratic Party) coalitions winning 100 seats each in the lower house. The president appointed Mirek Topolánek as prime minister, but parliament rejected his government and he resigned. Nevertheless the president re-appointed Mr Topolánek, who went on to form a government.
2007 On 20 December the Czech Rep became a member of the European Union Schengen area whereby all travellers may cross borders without a passport or visa.
2008 After two sets of three-rounds of presidential voting in parliament, the final vote was for incumbent President Václav Klaus on 15 February; he won with 141 votes in both houses against the 111 votes of Jan Svejnar . An agreement for visa-free visits of citizens to the US was signed in February.

Political structure

Constitution

The constitution came into force on 1 January 1993. A majority of three-fifths of the members of parliament is required to change the constitution.
All citizens over the age of 18 are eligible to vote.

Form of state

Parliamentary democratic republic

The executive

The highest organ of executive power is the Council of Ministers, composed of the prime minister, the deputy prime ministers and ministers. It is answerable to the Chamber of Representatives.
The two legislative bodies together elect the president of the republic for not more than two five-year terms. The president's post is largely ceremonial but the president is the commander-in-chief of the armed forces. The president appoints the prime minister, and on the prime minister's recommendation, appoints the remaining members of the Council of Ministers.

National legislature

The Parlament (Parliament) is composed of two legislative bodies: the 200-member Poslanecká Snìmovna (Chamber of Deputies) (lower house), elected by proportional representation for a four-year term, and the 81-member Senát (Senate) (upper house), which is elected under a two-round majority system in 81 single-member constituencies. The Senate is partially renewed every two years, with one-third of the seats coming up for election. Senators serve a six-year term.

Legal system

The civil law system is based on Austro-Hungarian codes. Judicial power is exercised by independent courts.

Last elections

2–3 June 2006 (Chamber of Deputies); 27–28 October 2006 (Senate).
Results: Parliamentary: Chamber of Deputies – Obcanská Demokratická Strana (ODS) (Civic Democratic Party) won 35.4

per cent (81 seats out of 200); Ceská Strana Sociálne Demokratická (CSSD) (Czech Social Democratic Party) won 32.3 per cent (74 seats); Komunistická Strana Cech a Morava (KSCM) (Communist Party of Bohemia and Moravia) 12.8 per cent (26 seats); Krestanská a Demokratická Unie-Ceskoslovenská Strana Lidova (KDU-CSL) (Christian Democratic Union-Czechoslovak People's Party) 7.2 per cent (13 seats); Strana Zelených (Green Party) 6.3 per cent (6 seats). Turnout was 64.5 per cent. Senate: ODS won 14 of the 27 seats contested (out of overall 81 seats), CSSD 6, KDU-CSL 4; three seats unknown.

Next elections

January 2008 (presidential); 2010 (parliamentary).

Political parties

Ruling party

Coalition: Obcanská Demokratická Strana (ODS) (Civic Democratic Party); Krestanská a Demokratická Unie-Ceskoslovenská Strana Lidova (KDU-CSL) (Christian and Democratic Union-Czechoslovak People's Party); and Strana Zelených (Green Party)

Main opposition party

Ceská Strana Sociálne Demokratická (CSSD) (Czech Social Democratic Party)

Population

10.27 million (2007)*

Last census: March 2001: 10,230,060

Population density: 133 inhabitants per sq km (2000). Urban population: 75 per cent (1995–2001).

Annual growth rate: -0.1 per cent 1994–2004 (WHO 2006)

Ethnic make-up

The chief minorities are Slovaks (3 per cent of the population), Poles (0.6 per cent), Germans (0.5 per cent) and Silesians, Roma, Hungarians and Ukrainians.

Religions

Christianity is the principal religion, although 40 per cent of the population define themselves as atheist. Roman Catholicism is the main denomination (39 per cent of the population), followed by Protestant (5 per cent), Orthodox (3 per cent). There is a very small Jewish community, mainly in Prague.

The state and the church are linked, but there is growing pressure for their separation and the state no longer exercises control over church affairs.

Education

Compulsory education is free. Basic schooling is divided into two cycles with primary lasting for five years from aged six to 11; the second cycle lasts for four years until aged 15. Secondary schooling is offered in one of three designated institutions, a secondary general, technical or vocational school. Technical school programmes last up to six years, vocational courses last between three and four years and general secondary education last for four years and leads to higher education.

There are three universities, Prague's Charles' University (the oldest in Central Europe, founded in 1348), Masarykova University in Brno and Palacky University in Olomouc.

Public expenditure on education typically amounts to 5.1 per cent of annual gross national income.

Literacy rate: Virtually universal.

Compulsory years: Six to 15

Enrolment rate: 104 per cent gross primary school enrolment; 95 per cent gross secondary enrolment, of the relevant age group (including repetition rates) (World Bank).

Pupils per teacher: 18 in primary schools.

Health

Per capita total expenditure on health (2003) was US$1,302; of which per capita government spending was US$1,172, at the international dollar rate, (WHO 2006).

Since a market economy replaced the previously planned centralised economy healthcare has become more reative to local requirements, there are more clinics, many operated by foreign medical companies. Recently instituted heath insurance companies took in US$5.3 billion in 2004. The Czech constitution guarantees free health care for all citizens and sponsors health insurance through the General Health Insurance Company. Pure supplementary health care insurance is scarce and simply covers those items outside the mandatory state insurance. Some private companies cover four supplementary areas such as surgery, hospitalisation in the event of illness or accident, permanent disability and accidental death.

HIV/Aids

HIV prevalence: 0.1 per cent aged 15–49 in 2003 (World Bank)

Life expectancy: 76 years, 2004 (WHO 2006)

Fertility rate/Maternal mortality rate: 1.2 births per woman, 2004 (WHO 2006); maternal mortality 9 per 100,000 live births (World Bank).

Child (under 5 years) mortality rate (per 1,000): 3.9 per 1,000 live births (World Bank)

Head of population per physician: 3.51 physicians per 1,000 people, 2003 (WHO 2006)

Welfare

The social security scheme provides old age pension insurance, sickness insurance, state social support benefits, and social care. Those registered in contracted employment, as self-employed (including farming personnel), and informal employment (employed for household duties), pay insurance premiums.

Pensions

In 1999, the Czech government encouraged domestic savings through gradual reforms and development of a supplemental pension insurance programme. The amended law assured both employers and employees of significant tax relief. An employer who assists his employees to pay for supplementary pension insurance saves money both on tax payments for social and health insurance (to which supplementary pension insurance is not subject) and income taxes.

A contribution not exceeding 3 per cent of the gross pay is regarded as a tax-deductible expense. The pension scheme significantly altered the conditions for retirement savings. The minimum retirement age for both men and women gradually increases to 63 years by 2012 and the government is proposing stricter criteria for early retirement.

The Czech Republic has a challenge ahead. The current pay-as-you-go system, where employees pay the pensions of those already retired, is poorly suited to cope with a negative population growth. It has been estimated that the system, by 2020, will have debts amounting to Kc1.5 trillion (US$50 billion), with insufficient assets or income to fund pensions.

Proposals for private pension funds that rely on market equities to pay pensions also have their critics; market growth and volatility could fluctuate and disadvantage many. However, economic growth would be strengthened, and the government would only need to fund retirement for the poorest citizens.

Main cities

Prague (capital, estimated population 1.1 million in 2005); Brno (main city of Moravia) (365,182), Ostrava (Moravia) (310,652), Plzen (Pilsen) (161,910).

Languages spoken

The Czech and Slovak languages are mutually comprehensible. A large proportion of the population, particularly those engaged in industry and foreign trade, speak German. Hungarian, Romani and Polish are also spoken.

Official language/s

Czech

Media

National news agency: CTK (Czech News Agency)

Press

Dailies: In Czech, by popularity Mladá fronta Dnes (www.mfdnes.cz), (known as

MF Dnes), Právo (http://pravo.novinky.cz) and Lidové Noviny (www.lidovky.cz). Other national newspapers include the tabloid, Blesk (www.blesk.cz), ZN Zemské Noviny, Hospodárské Noviny and Haló Noviny (www.halonoviny.cz) which publishes political news.

Weeklies: Regional publications include weekly newsmagazine and special interest publications. One of the largest regional media groups, Vktava-Labe-Press (VLP) (www.vlp.cz) publishes daily newspapers in all major cities and regions under the Deník (daily) (www.denik.cz) suffix, such as Brunenský Deník (http://brnensky.denik.cz) from Brno. In Czech, Respekt (www.respekt.cz), reports on political and economic issues, Týden (www.tyden.cz) is a newsmagazine Mladý Svet, takes a humorous view of the news. Some of the dailies publish weekend or supplementary weekly magazines. Spy (www.ispy.cz) is a tabloid

Business: In Czech, the daily Hospodárske Noviny (www.ihned.cz) is an authoritative newspaper. Magazines include Ekonom (http://ekonom.ihned.cz) and Profit (www.profit.cz). In English, Czech Business Weekly (www.cbw.cz) and the The Prague Tribune (www.prague-tribune.cz) have comprehensive coverage of news and the markets. The magazine Finance New Europe (www.financeneweurope.com) that began publication in 2006, was the first to focus on business matter within the new EU members; it is published every two months.

Periodicals: In Czech, Sedmá Generace (www.sedmagenerace.cz), is an environmentalist publication. The monthly Awrot (The Return) (www.zwrot.cz) is the largest Polish circulation.

Broadcasting

Radio: The national pubic radio station is Ceský Rozhlas (www.rozhlas.cz) operated several national services including Radio 1, Radiozurnal for news and information, Radio 2, Praha (www.radio.cz), for family audiences, Radio 3 Vltava, for culture, Radio 6 is a magazine style programme and Radio 7 (through Praha) is an international, multilingual service. There are also 12 regional stations.

There are numerous private stations broadcasting on FM and AM frequencies, including Evropa 2 (www.evropa2.cz) and Radio City (www.radiocity.cz), both from Prague, Kiss Hády (www.kisshady.cz) and Radio Petrov (www.radiopetrov.com) from Brno, and Radio Cas (www.casradio.cz) from Ostrava. Radio Blanik (www.radioblanik.cz) broadcasts in the western regions.

Television: All analogue TV is scheduled to be replaced by digital signals in 2012 as the TV services market share provided via satellite and cable grows.

Ceská Televize (CT) (www.ceskatelevize.cz), is the national, public broadcaster, operating channels CT1 and CT2, CT24 (www.ct24.cz), the 24-hour news channel and CTSport.

Other private TV stations include TV Nova (www.nova.cz) and Prima (www.iprima.cz).

Advertising

The advertising sector is well-developed with television typically gaining 50 per cent of the annual adspend. Magazines and newspapers each have around a 20 per cent market share. Most media expenditure is spent on advertising of food and drink. Tobacco is banned from advertising and alcohol and pharmaceuticals advertising are restricted.

Economy

The economy has sustained steady annual improvements since 1999, with an average GDP growth of 3.3 per cent; it achieved a growth of 6.0 per cent in both 2005 and 2006. International observers consider the economy to be stable and approve of successive government actions, intended to keep it steady while undertaking structural reforms.

Monetary policies have been introduced gradually, alleviating the impact of a market economy on a defunct socialist centrally planned economy of the early 1990s. Social welfare and pension reforms have been undertaken, as advised by the IMF, but the current account deficit is funded by foreign direct investment effectively. Productivity in industrial manufacturing and a strong currency has kept inflation well below the targetted 3.0 per cent, at 1.8 per cent in 2005.

The structure of the economy is composed of services at 59.8 per cent, a strong industrial base of 37.2 per cent, of which manufacturing is 25.2 per cent, and a minor role for agriculture at 2.9 per cent, of GDP. All of these sectors experienced growth in 2005, with manufacturing growing by an impressive 13.8 per cent.

In 2006, the newly elected government suspended plans to join the European Monetary Union (EMU), planned for in 2010, claiming the budget deficit could not be brought down in time, while tax cuts and fiscal reforms were more of a priority.

The Czech Republic's main industries are vehicle assembly, iron and steel production, chemicals and pharmaceuticals, glass, china and ceramics, small goods manufacturing and electronics, transport equipment, textiles and brewing. Cars and electrical appliances are manufactured by foreign-owned companies and target the export market.

External trade

As a member of the European Union (EU), the Czech Republic operates within a communitywide free trade union, with tariffs sets as a whole. Internationally, the EU has free trade agreements with a number of nations and trading blocs worldwide.

The industrial sector is still being restructured as it meets the challenge of competition within the EU and as the Czech Republic adopts the regulations that shape its business environment. There are several foreign owned car assembly plants in the Czech Republic, output of which contributes significantly to export earnings.

Imports

The main classes of imports are machinery and transport equipment, typically around 45 per cent, raw materials and fuels, chemicals.

Main sources: Germany (28.5 per cent total, 2006), China (6.1 per cent), Russia (6.0 per cent).

Exports

The modernisation of production facilities, resulting in the improved quality of exports have helped to promote export growth. Principal exports are vehicles and machinery (52 per cent), chemicals, raw materials and fuel.

Main destinations: Germany (31.9 per cent total, 2006), Slovakia (8.4 per cent), Poland (5.7 per cent).

Agriculture

Farming

The agricultural sector accounts for around three per cent of GDP and 4.2 per cent of employment. Approximately 41 per cent of the country is arable land, 11 per cent permanent pasture and 2 per cent permanent crops. The most important crops are sugar beet, wheat, potatoes, maize, barley, rye and hops. The livestock industry is well developed with cattle, pigs, chickens and dairy products supplying the food processing industry.

Agriculture was collectivised during the communist period. Although production increased with the creation of large farms, soil erosion and the heavy use of machinery and chemicals have had a long-term detrimental effect on the landscape and environment. In 1991, parliament passed a law on land restitution, under which all land taken by the state after February 1948 was returned to its original owner or, if such a return was not possible, provided for the owner to be compensated.

Large-scale operations still dominate the sector, with many of the same problems experienced during the communist era. Agriculture remains labour intensive, relying on inefficient techniques, outdated technology and a poor distribution system. EU membership should eventually help the sector to modernise and redevelop.

The crop production in 2005 included: 8,079,008 tonnes (t) cereals in total, 4,536,040t wheat, 2,280,820t barley, 775,252t rapeseed (canola), 28,000t poppy seed, 101,500t sunflower seed, 575,051t maize, 195,434t oats, *1,000,000t potatoes, 74,551t pulses, *78,000t grapes, 363,601t oilcrops, 17,830t flax fibre, *6,800t hops, 4,976t treenuts, 3,189,740t sugar beet, *240,000t apples, 447,050t fruit in total, 289,800t vegetables in total. Livestock production included: 715,232t meat in total, 87,000t beef, 351,500t pig meat, 970t lamb, *38,500t rabbit, 236,147t poultry, 105.747t eggs, 2,672,450t milk, *7,000t honey, 10,500t cattle hides.

* estimate

Fishing

The Czech Republic has a long tradition in freshwater fishing and aquaculture, owing to the thousands of man-made fish ponds dating from the middle ages. The principal catch is the common carp. The Czech Republic produces around 25,000 tonnes of freshwater fish per annum, of which around 13,000 tonnes are exported. Being landlocked, the country also imports over 200,000 tonnes of seafood per year. There are 12 processing plants.

Forestry

Forests cover around 2.6 million hectares (ha), about one-third of the total land area, with the growing stock volume per hectare considered among the highest in Europe. Coniferous species make up more than four-fifths of the stock volume. There is no other wooded land.

Three-quarters of forest land is publicly-controlled, mainly at national level; the remainder is privately-owned. Forest output is moderate and the industry depends largely on processing of domestic raw materials. Austria and Germany are important export markets for roundwood and sawn wood respectively.

The domestic wood industry satisfies the majority of industrial needs for newsprint, plywood, furniture and traditional woodworking.

Industry and manufacturing

The industrial sector was among the most advanced in the world before the Second World War, with national GDP per capita the seventh highest in the world in 1938. The Communist takeover in 1948 led to the nationalisation of all enterprises and a concentration on heavy industry. Under communism there was insufficient capital investment, while a lack of management, marketing and financial skills handicapped the development of the sector. In common with its counterparts in other communist countries, Czech industry became characterised by outdated and inefficient technology, over-staffing and poor quality.

Engineering is beginning to dominate the industrial sector. Automotive engineering accounts for around 20 per cent of manufacturing exports.

Tourism

Tourism is a burgeonong sector, which has become a key contributor to the economy.The Czech Republic is one of the most popular tourist destinations in the world and Prague is one of Europe's favourite destinations. Annual visitor numbers typically exceed seven million people. A programme of renovation and moderisation has enhanced tourist facilities. Historic and cultural sites are the usual destinations for most visitors, but the health spas are increasingly popular. Tourism is expected to contribute 2.5 per cent to GDP in 2005.

Environment

One of the most lasting legacies of the communist era is pollution, with the Czech Republic one of the most despoiled corners of Europe. Not only is air pollution a major problem, water supplies have become infected and raw sewage has reportedly been dumped in waterways by individuals as well as factories. Although environmental awareness has grown since 1989, the government and the majority of the population have focussed on economic transformation and improving living standards rather than on the environment.

Hydrocarbons

The Czech Republic has proven oil reserves of only 17.3 million barrels, producing around 7,400 barrels per day. However oil companies are still interested in the region and currently the Western Carpathians are being explored for potential reserves. The Czech Republic currently imports oil from both Russia and Germany. There are three oil refineries with the Ceská Rafinérská being the largest. Natural gas reserves are around 3.1 billion cubic metres. Natural gas consumption increased by 35 per cent between 1993 and 2001 and is continuing to grow. The Czech Republic is reliant on imports to meet domestic demand with most of the natural gas coming from Russia and Norway.

The mining and hydrocarbons sector accounts for less than 5 per cent of GNP and employs a slightly smaller proportion of the workforce.

Energy

Electrical capacity is predominantly from thermal sources, with the remainder from hydroelectric and nuclear stations. The Czech Republic is a net exporter of electricity to Germany, Austria, Poland and Slovakia.

Strong emphasis is placed on the commissioning of new nuclear power stations and the upgrading of Chernobyl-style reactors to western safety standards. The country has two nuclear power plants, at Dukovany and Temelin.

Construction of the controversial Temelin nuclear power station began in the 1980s. The first reactor became operational in 2000, but was shut down several times due to technical problems. A second reactor became operational in 2003, allowing Temelin to generate an extra 2,000MW of power. The power station will have to conform to EU safety standards by 2009.

Financial markets

Stock exchange

The Burza Cennych Papíru Praha (BCPP) (Prague Stock Exchange) was opened in 1993.

Banking and insurance

The country is suffering from high levels of public debt, approximately 18.8 per cent of GDP. Most of this debt can be attributed to government bail-outs in the banking sector. The IMF has estimated that continued bank restructuring will take up a large percentage of the Czech Republic's GDP.

Much of the bank restructuring has been as a result of the government attempting to ensure that there is compatibility between Czech and EU laws, following EU membership in 2004. This also includes continued privatisation, not least in the banking sector, where state-owned stakes in banks will gradually be eliminated.

The Foreign Exchange Act introduced partial liberalisation for capital account and full convertibility for current account transactions in Czech koruna. It also cleared the way for Czech membership of the Organisation for Economic Co-operation and Development (OECD), enabled companies to accept credit from non-resident banks and eased restrictions on direct investment.

The accumulation of bad domestic and international debt and non-performing loans, particularly to Russia, has reduced the attraction of Czech banking corporations to foreign investors. However, with the introduction of more stringent financial regulations and an improvement in accounting standards, bank privatisation will likely gain momentum.

Central bank

Ceska Národnì Banka (CNB) (Czech National Bank).

Time

GMT plus one hour (daylight saving, late March to late October, GMT plus two hours)

Geography
The Czech Republic is a landlocked country in central Europe, bordering Germany to the west, Poland to the north, Slovakia to the east, and Austria to the south. The landscape varies greatly from lowlands to Alpine-type mountains. It has numerous rivers (the Elbe (Labe), and its largest tributary, the Vltava, provide important links to sea ports).
With a total area of 78,864km square the Czech Republic is slightly smaller than Austria and one-third the size of the UK. The country is split into two principal regions, Bohemia in the west and Moravia to the east. Surrounded by low mountains Bohemia is a plateau forming a basin drained by the Elbe and the Vltava – on which Prague is situated. The lowlands of Moravia are drained by the Morava River which flows into the Danube and by the Oder (Odra) eventually flows into the Baltic Sea.
Hemisphere
Northern
Climate
The climate is continental with warm, showery summers and cold, snowy winters. June is the hottest month and January the coldest. February and March are the driest months and June, July and August the wettest. The average temperature in winter is minus 5 degrees Celsius (C) and in the summer around 20 degrees C.
Dress codes
Most people wear standard casual clothes. They do, however, dress up when eating out or going to the theatre or a concert. Some more exclusive restaurants do not admit people in casual wear and it is useful to enquire beforehand. For business, a suit and tie is advisable for men and a suit or dress for women.

Entry requirements
Passports
Passport required by all, except nationals of EU/EEA and Switzerland, with valid national ID cards.
Visa
Required by all, except nationals of EU and Schengen area signatory countries, North America, Australasia and Japan. For further exceptions contact the nearest embassy. A Schengen visa application (offered in several languages) can be downloaded from http://europa.eu/abc/travel/ see 'documents you will need'.
See http://czech.embassyhomepage.com for a full list of exceptions to visa controls. Business visas for nationals requiring visas require evidence of invitation from a local company and business letter of intention from employer.

Currency advice/regulations
The import and export of local currency is limited to Kc200,000, while there are no restrictions on the import of export of foreign currency.
Travellers cheques are readily accepted but euros, US dollars, or UK pounds avoid extra exchange fees. ATMs are found in most banks.
Customs
Personal items are duty-free. There are no duties levied on alcohol and tobacco between EU member states, providing amounts imported are for personal consumption.

Health (for visitors)
Nationals of the European Economic Area (EEA) countries and Switzerland can access reduced cost and sometimes free medical treatment using a European Health Insurance Card (EHIC) while visiting the EEA. Exceptions include nationals of the 10 countries which joined the EU in 2004 whose EHIC is not valid in Switzerland. Applications for the EHIC should be made before travelling.
Mandatory precautions
None
Advisable precautions
Immunisation for hepatitis A and B may be useful.
Hotels
Prague has a wide range of hotels. Business travellers are advised to book rooms well in advance.

Credit cards
All major credit and charge cards are accepted.

Public holidays (national)
Fixed dates
1 Jan (New Year's Day), 1 May (Labour Day), 8 May (Liberation Day), 5 Jul (St Cyril and St Methodius Day), 6 Jul (Jan Hus Day), 28 Sep (Czech Statehood Day), 28 Oct (National Day), 17 Nov (Freedom and Democracy Day), 24–26 Dec (Christmas).
Variable dates
Easter Monday

Working hours
Banking
Mon–Fri: 0800–1800; some banks close early on Fri.
Bureau de Change in main city centres operate seven days a week until 1900.
Business
Mon–Fri: 0800–1700.
Government
Mon–Fri: usually 0800–1600, but may vary.
Shops
Mon–Fri: 0800–1800; Sat: 0900–1200; some shops remain open late on Thursday evening.

Telecommunications
Mobile/cell phones
GSM 900/1800 services are available throughout the country.

Electricity supply
Domestic: 220V, 50 cycles AC is almost universal, with two-pin continental plugs.
Weights and measures
The metric system is in use. In addition, the following measures are used: quintal or metric hundredweight = 100kg. Food is usually purchased by the decagram and kilogram.

Social customs/useful tips
A handshake is a traditional accompaniment to a greeting. Using a person's title is customary. Managing directors should be addressed as reditel and the chairman as predseda.
When visiting private homes it is customary to take flowers for the hosts. Visitors also generally leave their shoes in the hallway, partly as a mark of respect and partly because of pollution in the streets.
The difference between a Slovak and a Czech may be difficult to spot; however mistaking one for the other can cause offence.
Tipping is appreciated in any restaurant, usually 5 to 10 per cent.
Drinking and driving is strictly forbidden. Illegally parked cars tend to be towed away by the police and it is advisable to park at attended car parks where the cost is relatively low.

Security
Street crime, especially in the centre of Prague, has increased since the 1989 revolution, as the police tend to keep a low profile. It is advisable to carry as little as possible in the way of valuables and cash. Car vandalism and theft have also increased.
Report any robberies in central Prague to the Central Police Office, Jungmannova 9, Prague 1 (tel: 6145-1760), where interpreters are available.

Getting there
Air
National airline: CSA Czech Airlines
International airport/s: Prague-Ruzyne Airport (PRG), 20km north-west of the city. Facilities include duty free shopping, post office, money exhange, restaurants and car hire. An airport bus service runs every 30 minutes between 0600–2100, with a journey time of 30 minutes to the city centre. Taxis are available 24 hours.
Airport tax: Departure tax, from Prague only: Kc700
Surface
Road: Entry is possible from Germany, Poland, Slovak Republic and Austria.

Rail: As part of the European intercity network there are convenient routes to the Czech Republic from Western Europe including the cities of Berlin, Frankfurt, Munich, Zurich and Vienna. The most famous and fastest trains include the Kafka, Goethe and the Einstein, which are operated by the formerly state-owned Ceské Dráhy (CD) (Czech Railways).

The Vindobona Express operates daily from Vienna to Prague and on to Berlin. For more rail information call (tel: 2422-4200).

Water: There are ferries along the Vltava River from Germany.

Getting about

National transport

Air: CSA Czech Airlines operates extensive low-cost domestic network.

There are regular daily flights from Prague to Brno, Ostrava, Presov, Holesov, Kosice, Piestany, Bystrica, Karlovy Vary and Poprad.

The approximate travel time from Prague to Brno is 45 minutes, one hour to Karlovy and 30 minutes to Karlovy Vary.

Road: There are several major highways linking Prague with the main towns (usually marked with an E). Motorways run from Prague to Plzen and Podebrady to Bratislava (Slovak Republic) via Brno. Users of the Czech motorways are required to purchase a vignette (season ticket) for each year.

Buses: The services of the national bus company, CAD, are faster and more comfortable than the train for many routes. Tickets can be bought in advance from larger stations.

Rail: The rail service is efficient and coverage is comprehensive, composed of approximately 9,365km of track. It is advisable to book seats in advance on the main routes. Fares are low, although supplements may be charged for travel on express trains.

Water: There are many navigable waterways in the Czech Republic. The main river ports are located at Prague, Usti nad Labem and Decin.

City transport

Taxis: Taxis travelling to and from the airport are allowed to charge higher rates. Within the city, it is advisable to either negotiate a price before travelling or agree the use of the meter. Higher charges are usually levied for night services.

Buses, trams & metro: The bus network is extensive, covering many areas not visited by rail. In addition to a flat-fare service, the buses are reliable and comfortable.

In Prague, tickets can be bought in advance from tabak shops and other shops displaying the sign Predprodej Jizdenek. On boarding the buses, insert your ticket into the top of the machines attached to the poles, then pull the handle towards you. Passes do not need to be punched. City buses operate predominantly on the outskirts of towns. City bus 119 leaves daily every five to seven minutes (peak times) or every 15 minutes (off-peak) for round trips from Dejvicka metro station to the airport. From the metro, follow the exit signs for Ruzyne Airport. An ordinary city transport ticket or pass is required before boarding. The CSA Czech Airline bus service operates every 30 minutes from its terminal, off Revolucni near the river, to the airport. It also stops at Dejvicka metro station. Look for the sign that says Ruzyne. For more city transport information see: www.dp-praha.cz/en/index.htm

Trams cover all the major streets and intersect with metro lines. There are tram services in Prague, Brno, Ostrava, Plzen and several other towns. Services usually operate between 0430–2400. After midnight, night trams run approximately every 40 minutes. Blue badges on tram and bus stops denote an all night service. Tram 91, the 'historic tram', stops at most of the city's top sights, except for the castle. These trams run Saturdays, Sundays and during holidays, making hourly stops during the summer. Tickets should be punched in the appropriate machine on entering the tram. Note that a separate ticket is required when changing tram routes.

Car hire

Many of the international car hire companies, including Avis, Eurodollar and Hertz, operate in the Czech Republic. Speed limits are 60kph in towns and villages, 90kph on the main roads and 110kph on motorways. The speed limit is reduced to 80kph on motorways in built-up areas. It is advisable to avoid driving in the city centre as illegal parking will result in the use of car clamps.

Traffic drives on the right. Seat belts are compulsory and drink driving is strictly prohibited. An emergency road rescue service is available by calling 154. A valid national driving licence is required.

BUSINESS DIRECTORY

The addresses listed below are a selection only. While World of Information makes every endeavour to check these addresses, we cannot guarantee that changes have not been made, especially to telephone numbers and area codes. We would welcome any corrections.

Telephone area codes

The international dialling code (IDD) for the Czech Republic is + 420, followed by area code and subscriber's number:

Breclav	51	Ostrava	59
Brno	54	Plzen	37
Havirov	6994	Prague	2

Useful telephone numbers

Emergency calls:	158
Ambulance service:	112/155
Police:	158 2121-1111
Traffic accidents:	154 2121-3747
Emergency Medical Aid	298-341
(24-hours: doctors speak English and German):	290-65
Fire:	150
Directory enquiries: (Prague only):	120
International enquiries:	0135
Breakdown assistance:	154, 123 777-521
Car repair service (24-hours):	733-351/3
Lost property office:	235-8887

Chambers of Commerce

American Chamber of Commerce, 10 Dusni, 11000 Prague 1 (tel: 2232-9430; fax: 2232-9433; email: amcham@amcham.cz).

Breclav Chamber of Commerce, 10 namisti TG Masaryka, 69002 Breclav (tel: 932-6116; fax: 937-4126; email: ohk@breclav.net).

British Chamber of Commerce, 3 Pobrezni, 18600 Prague 8 (tel: 2483-5161; fax: 2483-5162; email: britcham@britcham.cz).

Czech Chamber of Commerce, Freyova 27, 19000 Prague 9, (tel: 9664-6111; email: office@komora; internet: www.komora.cz).

Ostrava Regional Economic Chamber, 2224/8 Vystavni, 70900 Ostrava-Marianske Hory (tel: 747-9328; fax: 747-9324; email: info@rhko.cz).

Banking

ABN AMRO Bank NV, Amsterdam, Revolucni 1, 110 15 Prague 1 (tel: 2481-5141; fax: 2481-5100, 22481-5139).

Agrobanka Praha A S (largest private bank), Hybernska 18, 110 00 Prague 1 (tel: 2444-1111; fax: 2444-6199, 22444-1500).

Bankovni Asociace (Banking Association), Vodickova ulice 30, 110 00 Prague 1 (tel: 2422-5926; fax: 2422-5957).

BNP - Dresdner Bank, Vitezna 1, 150 000 Prague 5 (tel: 5700-6111).

Ceska Sporitelna A S (Czech Savings Bank), Na Prikope 29, 113 98 Prague 1 (tel: 2422-9268; fax: 2421-3455).

Ceskomoravska Stavebni, Ruzova 15, 110 00 Prague 1 (tel: 2407-2024; fax: 2407-2225).

Ceskomoravska Zarucni a Rozvojova Banks A S, Jeruzalemska 4, 115 20 Prague 1 (tel: 2423-0734).

Ceskoslovenska Obchodni Banka A S (CSOB), Na Prikope 14, 115 20 Prague 1 (tel: 2411-1111; internet: www.csob.cz).

Chase Manhattan, Karlova 27, 110 01 Prague 1 (tel: 2423-4313).

Citibank A S, Evropska 178, 166 40 Prague 6 (tel: 2430-4243).

Commerzbank AG Frankfurt/Main, Pobocka Praha, Masarykovo Nabrezi 30, 110 00 Prague 1 (tel: 2491-5077, 22491-5329; fax: 2491-5850).

Credit Lyonnais Bank Praha, Ovocny trh 8-Myslbek Building, Prague 1 (tel: 2433-3543).

Creditanstalt A S Praha, Siroka 5, 110 01 Prague 1 (tel: 2110-2111; fax: 2481-2185).

Deutsche Bank AG, Pobocka Praha, Jungmannova 34, 110 00 Prague 1 (tel: 2421-2857; fax: 2422-5727).

Evropabanka A S, Strosmayerovo nam 1, 170 01 Prague 7 (tel: 6671-2134).

GiroCredit Banka Praha A S, Vaclavske nam 56, PO Box 749, 111 21 Prague 1 (tel: 2403-3333).

HVB Czech Republic, Prague (tel: 2111-2111; internet: www.hvb.cz).

Interbanka A S Praha, Vaclavske nam. 40, 110 00 Prague 1 (tel: 2440-6111).

Komercni Banka A S, Na Prikop 33, 114 07 Prague 1 (tel: 2402-1111; fax: 2424-3020).

Podnikatelska banka A S, Rohacova 79, 130 79 Prague 3 (tel: 6121-6089; fax: 6121-6085).

Raiffeisenbank A S Praha, Vodickova 38, 110 00 Prague 1 (tel: 2423-1270; fax: 2423-1278).

Realitbanka A S, Antala Staska 32, 146 20 Prague 4 (tel: 6104-5439).

Royal banka CS A S, Krocinova 1, 110 00 Prague 1 (tel: 2422-8582; fax: 2422-4833).

Wustenrot - Stavebni Sporitelna A S, Jugoslavska 29, 120 00 Prague 2 (tel: 2400-7200; fax: 2400-7204).

Zivnostenka Banka A S, Na Prikope 20, 113 80 Prague 1 (tel: 2412-1111; fax: 2412-5555).

Central bank

Czech National Bank, Na Prikope 28, 110 03 Prague 1 (tel: 2441-1111; fax: 2441-2404; e-mail: info@cnb.cz).

Travel information

Cedok (travel and hotel corporation), Na Prikope 18, 111 35 Prague 1-Nove Mesto (tel: 2419-7642; internet www.cedok.com).

Ceske Drahy (CD), Nábrezi Ludvíka Svobody 1222/12 110 15 Praha 1 (tel: 97-224-1881 reservations for inter-city trains only; internet: www.cd.cz/static/eng/).

Cestovni Kancelar, (national rail travel agency), V Celnici 6 110 00 Praha 1 (tel: 2423-9464; email: CKPHApob692@dop.pha.cd.cz; internet: www.czech-travel-guide.com).

CSA Czech Airlines, Airport Praha, Ruzyne 16008 (tel: 2480-6111; fax: 2481-5183; internet: www.czechairlines.com/en/; City Service Centre, V Ceinici 5, 110 00 Prague 1 (underground line B, station Namesti Republiky) (tel: 2010-4111); sales and ticket reservations (tel: 2010-4310).

National tourist organisation offices

Czech Tourism, PO Box 46, Vinohradska 12041 Praha 2 (tel: 2158-0111; fax: 2424-7516; internet: www.czechtourism.com); tourist information (tel: 2011-3229, between 0800 and 2000 hours; 2011-4512, 24 hours a day).

Ministries

Ministry of Agriculture, Tisnov 17, 117 05 Prague 1 (tel: 2181-2111; fax: 2481-0478).

Ministry of Culture, Milady Horakove 220, 160 41 Prague 6 (tel: 5708-5111; fax: 2431-8156; email: minkult@mkcr.cz).

Ministry of Defence, Tychonova 1, 160 01 Prague 6 (tel: 2021-0255; fax: 2021-0257; email: otevrenalinka@army.cz).

Ministry of Education, Youth and Sport, Karmelitska 8, 118 12 Prague 1 (tel: 5719-3111; fax: 5719-3790).

Ministry of the Environment, Vrsovicka 65, 100 10 Prague 10 (tel: 6712-1111; fax: 6731-0308: internet: www.env.cz).

Ministry of Foreign Affairs, Loretanske Namisti 5, 125 10 Prague 1 (tel: 2418-1111; fax: 2431-0017; email: info@mzv.cz; internet: www.czech.cz/).

Ministry of Health, Palackeho nam 4, 128 01 Prague 2 (tel: 2497-1111; fax: 2497 2111; email: mzcr@mzcr.cz).

Ministry of the Interior, Nad Stolou 3, 170 34 Prague 7 (tel: 6142-1115; email: dotazy@mvcr.cz; internet: www.mvcr.cz).

Ministry of Justice, Vysehradska 16, 128 10 Prague 2 (tel: 2199-7111; fax: 2491-9927; email: msp@msp.justice.cz: internet: www.justice.cz).

Ministry of Labour and Social Affairs, Na Poøienim Pravu 1, 128 01Prague 2 (tel: 2491-8391; fax: 2192-2664).

Ministry of Regional Development, Staromestske Namisti 6, 110 15 Prague 1 (tel: 2486-1111; fax: 2486-1333).

Ministry of Transport and Communications, Nabøei Ludvika Svobody 12, 110 15 Prague 1 (tel: 5143-1111; fax: 2481-0596; email: utv0001@mdcr.cz).

Office of the Prime Minister, Nabøei Eduarda Benese 4, 118 01 Prague 1 (tel: 2400-2111; fax: 2481-0231).

Office of the President, Prague Castle, 119 08 Prague 1 (tel: 2437-1111; fax: 2437-3300).

Other useful addresses

Asociace Investicnich Fondu (Association of Investment Companies and Funds), Tynska 21, 110 00 Prague 1 (tel: 2481-0063; fax: 2481-0063).

Asociace Obchodnich Spolecnosti a Podnikatelu CR (Association of Trading Companies and Businessmen), Skretova 6, 120 59 Prague 2 (tel: 2421-5371/81; fax: 2423-0570).

Association of Czech Entrepreneurs, Skretova 6, 12059 Prague 2 (tel and fax: 2423-0580).

BBC (Radio), Na Porící 12, Prague 1 CZ-110 00 (tel: 2487-2545; fax: 2487-2546).

Board of Legislation and Public Administration, Vladislavova 4, PO Box 596, 117 15 Prague 1 (tel: 2419-1111; fax: 2421-5060).

British Embassy, Commercial Section, Palac Myslbek Na Prikope 21, 11719 Prague 1 (tel: 2224-0021/22/33; fax: 2224-3625).

Centrum Vnejsich Ekonomickych Vztahu (Centre For Foreign Economic Relation), Politickych Veznu 20, PO Box 791, 111 21 Prague 1 (tel: 2422-1586, 22406-2421; fax: 2422-1575).

Cesky Statisticky Urad (Czech Statistical Office), Sokolovska 142, 180 00 Prague 8 (tel: 6604-2414).

Confederation of Industry of the Czech Republic, Mikulandska 7, 11361 Prague 7 (tel: 2499-5679).

CzechInvest (Czech Agency for Foreign Investment), Stepanska 15, 120 00 Prague 2 (tel: 9634-2500; fax: 9634-2502; e-mail: marketing@czechinvest.org; internet site: http://www.czechinvest.org).

Czech Republic Embassy (USA), 3900 Spring of Freedom Street, NW, Washington DC 20008 (tel: (+1-202) 274-9100; fax: (+1-202) 966-8540; e-mail: amb_pol_washington@embassy.mzv.cz).

Czech Television (CTV) - Public Corporation, Kavcí Hory, Prague 4 CZ-140 70 (tel: 6113-1111).

Euro Information Centre, Network/Correspondence Centre, NIS Havelkova 22, 130 00 Prague 3 (fax: 2423-1114).

Fond Narodniho Majetku (National Property Fund), Rasinovo Nabrezi 42, 120 00 Prague 2 (tel: 2491-1111; fax: 206-618).

Nejvyssi Soud CR (Czech Supreme Court), Buresova 20, 657 37 Brno (tel: 4132-1237; fax: 4121-3493).

NIS (National Information Centre of the Czech Republic), Havelkova 22, 130 00 Prague 3 (tel: 2421-5808–15, 2422-2026–9; fax: 322-1484, 2422-3177).

Prazska Informacni Sluzba (Prague Information Service), Senovazne Namesti 23, 110 00 Prague 1 (tel: 544-444; fax: 421-1989).

Sdruzeni Soukromych Zemedelcu Cech, Moravy a Slezska (Association of Private Farmers of Bohemia, Moravia and Silesia), Tesnov 17, 117 05 Prague 1 (tel: 491-3606; fax: 491-0162).

Svaz Prumyslu a Dopravy CR (Confederation of Industry of the Czech Republic), Mikulandska 7, 113 61 Prague 1 (tel: 2491-5253).

UNIDO (Federation of Czech Industries), Mikulandska 7, 113 61 Prague 1 (tel: 2491-5679; fax: 2491-5253).

Ustavni Soud CR (Czech Constitutional Court), Jostova 8, 660 83 Brno 2 (tel: 4216-1111).

National news agency: CTK (Czech News Agency)

Internet sites

Atlas (the national coach company) http://jizdnirady.atlas.cz/

Brno Trade Fairs and Exhibitions Co Ltd (press information): www.bvv.cz/bvv

Ceské Dráhy, (national rail information) www.cd.cz/static/eng/

Czech business directory: www.muselik.com/czech/cbd.html

Czech directory: www.inform.cz/def.asp

Czech Embassy in Washington DC: www.mzv.cz/washington

Czech Ministry of Finance: www.mfcr.cz

Czech Ministry of Industry and Trade: www.mpo.cz

Czech Office for Protection of Competition: http://compet.cz

Czech Republic (provides links to information about the country): www.muselik.com/czech/toc.html

Czech Telecommunications Office: www.ctu.cz

Czech Trade Promotion Agency: www.czechtrade.cz/

Czech Trade Promotion Agency (in English): www.czechtradeoffices.com/Global

Hotels and history: www.abaka.com/Czech/

IPB (Investicni A Postovni banka as): www.ipb.cz

Office of Czech Republic: http://vlada.cz

Prague city transport www.dp-praha.cz/en/index.htm

Denmark

KEY FACTS

Official name: Kongeriget Danmark (The Kingdom of Denmark)

Head of State: Queen Margrethe II (since 1972)

Head of government: Prime Minister Anders Fogh Rasmussen (V) (since 2001, re-elected 13 Nov 2007)

Ruling party: Right-wing coalition government comprising the Venstre (Liberal Party) and the Konservative Folkeparti (KF) (Conservative People's Party), supported by the Dansk Folkeparti (DF) (Danish People's Party) (coalition re-elected 8 Feb 2005)

Area: 43,080 square km

Population: 5.45 million (2007)*

Capital: Copenhagen

Official language: Danish

Currency: Danish krone (Kr) = 100 ore

Exchange rate: Kr4.70 per US$ (Jul 2008); (pegged through the original European Exchange Rate Mechanism; trades around Kr7.43 per euro)

GDP per capita: US$57,261 (2007)

GDP real growth: 1.80% (2007)

Labour force: 2.85 million (2004)

Unemployment: 2.80% (2007)*

Inflation: 1.70% (2007)*

Oil production: 312,000 bpd (2007)

Balance of trade: US$10.26 billion (2005)

Foreign debt: US$348.96 billion (2004)

* estimated figure

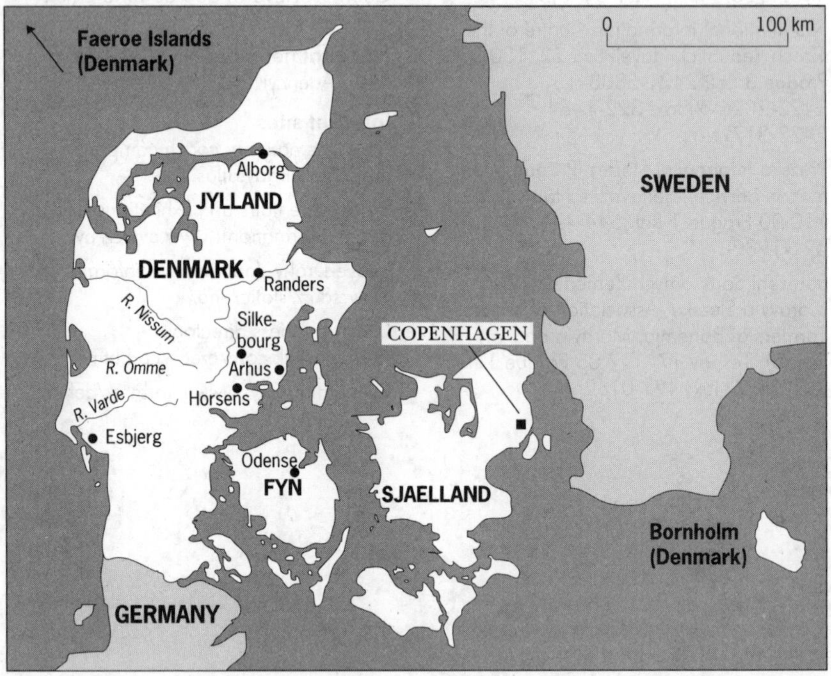

In its quarterly economic report for June 2008, the Danmarks Nationalbank (Danish Central Bank) reported that (in common with most European countries) Denmark was seeing a slowdown in growth, a trend that the bank considered would continue in the following years. Employment remained high and there was a shortage of labour. Wage increases were significantly higher than those of Denmark's principal trading partners, and output was high in relation to the capacity of the Danish economy. Lower growth and higher unemployment were seen as essential for sustainable development in wages and prices in the longer term. Weaker export-market growth was also seen as a useful contribution to this sustainable development. Rising food and energy prices had caused consumer prices to soar, creating expectations of continued high inflation, which could trigger a wage and price spiral to the detriment of already strained wage competitiveness. The strong pressure on the labour market also made it imperative not to ignore the risk of rising inflation expectations. The bank saw it as important that fiscal policy in 2009 avoided stimulating demand.

Economy slows

Growth in the Danish economy declined to 1.8 per cent in 2007 after a strong increase in the preceding years. In mid-2008 no official figures were available for the development of GDP in 2008, but on the basis of the available data releases, the slowdown was estimated to have continued in 2008. The Danish economy remained close to its capacity limit, with labour and capital shortages constraining the scope for further growth.

Stable krone.

The Danish krone has been stable at around its central rate in ERM II. The krone weakened a little from the middle of January and was slightly weaker than the central rate against the euro at the end of April and the beginning of May. The weakening can be attributed to the narrowing of the short-term yield spread to the euro area in the light of the turbulence in the money markets. Since the international financial turmoil spilled over into the money market of the euro area, the bank's demand for liquidity in the

European Central Bank's (ECB) weekly tenders has grown. As a result, the ECB's marginal rate has normally been somewhat higher than the minimum bid rate. The spread between Danmarks Nationalbank's lending rate and the ECB's marginal rate narrowed by 0.15–0.2 percentage points from August 2007 until mid-May 2008, and was thus virtually non-existent. It was even negative for short periods. The Danmarks Nationalbank intervened in the foreign-exchange market to purchase krone against foreign exchange.

Wage increases ...

The pressure on the labour market contributed to high wage demands from the employee side in the 2008 spring collective bargaining for the public sector. Bargaining has been concluded for central government, but dragged on for some employees in local and regional government. The general framework for the collective agreements concluded was around 13 per cent over three years, including the expected outcome of the regulation scheme that is designed to ensure parallel wage development between the private and public sectors. However, several elements of the new collective agreements were kept out of the regulation scheme, which risked boosting wage growth in the public sector, over the term of the collective agreement. The agreed wage increases were strongest in 2008; the annual wage increases in the public sector were expected to reach 5–6 per cent towards the end of the year. In the private sector, labour shortages had pushed up wage increases to a high level. In the first quarter, the overall rate of wage increase for the area covered by the Confederation of Danish Employers was 4.6 per cent, year-on-year. The pace of wage increases had thus reached a level that was unsustainable in the longer term. For several years, the rate of wage increases had been higher in Denmark than abroad. Wage competitiveness was also squeezed by the strong depreciation of the dollar, which had brought the krone to its highest level for 25 years.

...means inflation.

In April 2008, the Harmonised Index of Consumer Prices, (HICP), had risen by 3.4 per cent year-on-year. Price inflation had been rising since the third quarter of 2007 and had now reached its highest level for over 11 years. Higher consumer price inflation was primarily driven by strong increases in energy and food prices. Price inflation for the other goods and services in HICP – core inflation – was moderate at 1.5 per cent year-on-year in April 2008. The increases in energy and food prices were reflected in wholesale commodity prices, including notably fuel and raw materials for agriculture. Wholesale prices had accelerated since September 2007, and the year-on-year increase had reached 7.7 per cent by April 2008. Domestic market-determined inflation (IMI) is an indicator of the price pressures from payroll costs and profits. It had shown a declining trend since mid-2007. In the calculation of the IMI, a number of elements are excluded from the consumer price index: such as food prices since they are affected by special factors such as harvest and weather. The IMI thus failed to reflect the later increases in food prices, which had pushed consumer prices upwards overall. Despite significantly higher commodity prices, the increase in consumer prices for food was partly attributable to higher domestic payroll costs and profit margins, including those of Danish farmers. Despite the slowdown in economic growth, the strong pressure on the Danish economy and especially the labour market looked set to continue. Against this background, it remained important that fiscal policy in 2009 did not stimulate demand.

Rasmussen's victory

Denmark's prime minister, Anders Fogh Rasmussen took politics to the wire in mid-November 2007 when he called a snap election in an attempt to win a third term with a stronger mandate. In 2001 Mr Rasmussen had ended the Social Democrat domination with his election victory. Clinging to a one seat majority, Mr Rasmussen was the first leader of his Venstre party to win a third term, a victory attributed to Denmark's continued strong economic growth , a popular tax freeze and a hard line on immigration. Mr Rasmussen's governing 'Blue Bloc' coalition won a total of 89 seats in the November election, losing five of the seats it had won in 2005 to the New Alliance Party. The official opposition coalition lead by the Social Democrats under the glamorous Helle Thorning-Schmidt won 81 seats, unchanged from 2005.

Mr Rasmussen needed to seek agreement with the centre-right New Alliance party if he was to increase his majority and continue to dominate Danish politics. The broader electoral support was also seen as essential if Mr Rasmussen was to continue his reforming agenda of tax cuts and wage control. Following his election victory, Mr Rasmussen also announced that Denmark would hold a new referendum on whether or not to adopt the euro as the national currency and whether the country should continue to adhere to its other opt-outs on European defence co-operation and judicial affairs. Mr Rasmussen's government has seen itself as constrained by the opt-outs, which it considers as limiting its scope for proper European co-operation. The Danish government has long followed a *de facto* policy of adhering to the same interest rate policy

KEY INDICATORS — Denmark

	Unit	2003	2004	2005	2006	2007
Population	m	5.39	5.41	5.41	5.43	*5.45
Gross domestic product (GDP)	US$bn	212.76	243.04	259.22	276.28	311.90
GDP per capita	US$	39,453	44,929	47,906	50,904	*57,261
GDP real growth	%	0.5	2.3	3.1	3.9	1.8
Inflation	%	2.0	1.2	1.8	1.9	*1.7
Unemployment	%	5.5	5.4	5.7	4.0	*2.8
Oil output	'000 bpd	368.0	394.0	377.0	342.0	312.0
Natural gas output	bn cum	7.9	9.4	10.4	10.4	9.2
Exports (fob) (goods)	US$m	67,887.0	73,060.0	84,950.0	90,557.0	101,235.0
Imports (cif) (goods)	US$m	58,749.0	63,450.0	74,690.0	87,778.0	101,985.0
Balance of trade	US$m	9,138.0	9,610.0	10,260.0	2,779.0	-751.0
Current account	US$m	6,340.0	3,460.0	9,278.0	8,118.0	4,279.0
Total reserves minus gold	US$m	37,105.0	39,084.0	32,930.0	29,724.0	32,534.0
Foreign exchange	US$m	36,004.0	38,196.0	32,510.0	29,160.0	32,029.0
Exchange rate	per US$	6.52	5.99	5.76	5.64	5.17

* estimated figure

decisions as those adopted by the ECB; joining the euro would present few practical problems. A decision on the date of a possible referendum was delayed pending the increasingly doubtful ratification of the EU constitutional reform treaty. The astute Mr Rasmussen had in any event hedged his bets, when he announced that any referendum would be held 'within four years'.

Risk assessment

Regional stability	Good
Economy	Good
Politics	Good

COUNTRY PROFILE

Historical profile

Denmark is an ancient kingdom situated on an archipelago, which has historically served as a bridge between continental Europe and the Scandinavian peninsula. During the Napoleonic era, the Danes sided with the French and, as a result of their defeat, lost their dominance in Scandinavia.

1397 The Union of Kalmar united Denmark, Sweden and Norway under a single monarch.

1523 Denmark recognised Swedish independence.

1729 Greenland became a Danish province.

1814 Denmark ceded Norway to Sweden.

1849 Denmark became a constitutional monarchy with a bicameral parliament.

1903 Iceland was granted home rule from Denmark.

1918 Iceland became a sovereign state in union with Denmark.

1914–18 Denmark was neutral during the First World War.

1918 Denmark's transition to parliamentary government with universal suffrage was fully established after the First World War and has been suspended only during the Nazi occupation of the Second World War.

1939 Denmark signed a non-aggression pact with Nazi Germany.

1940 Germany invaded Denmark.

1945 The German occupation ended. Denmark recognised the independence of Iceland.

1948 The Faroe Islands were granted self-government within the Kingdom.

1949 Denmark was one of the founder members of NATO.

1953 A revision of the constitution allowed for female succession to the throne, abolition of the upper house of parliament and the introduction of proportional representation. Greenland became an integral part of Denmark.

1959 Denmark joined the European Free Trade Association (EFTA).

1972 Queen Margrethe ascended the throne.

1973 Denmark joined the European Economic Community (EEC).

1979 Greenland was granted home rule; Denmark retained control over Greenland's foreign affairs and defence.

1985 Parliament passed legislation to ban the construction of nuclear power plants.

1992 In a referendum, voters rejected the Maastricht Treaty on further European integration.

1993 Poul Schlüter, prime minister since 1982, resigned after a judicial enquiry criticised him for misleading parliament in 1989 over the Tamil visa scandal. A four-party coalition government was formed by Poul Nyrup Rasmussen. Denmark voted in favour of a revised Maastricht treaty.

1994 Rasmussen was returned to power after a general election.

1998 Danish voters endorsed the EU's Amsterdam treaty, which prepared the way for former eastern bloc countries to join the EU.

2000 In a referendum, Denmark voted against joining Europe's single currency.

2001 The Venstre (Liberal Party), led by Anders Fogh Rasmussen, won a slim majority in the parliamentary elections, he was only able to form a minority administration, in coalition with the Konservative Folkeparti (KF) (Conservative People's Party), relying on support from the far right-wing Dansk Folkeparti (DF) (Danish People's Party) in order to command a majority in parliament.

2002 New immigration rules sparked controversy. The EU-Russia summit was moved from Copenhagen to Brussels, when Russian President Putin threatened to boycott the summit if it was held in Copenhagen. A conference of Chechen exiles was also due to begin in Copenhagen at the same time.

2004 In May, Crown Prince Frederik married Australian-born Mary Donaldson, (their first son was born on 15 October 2005). Denmark and US agreed a deal to modernise the US Thule airbase in Greenland, over the objections of many local people.

2005 In the 8 February parliamentary elections, the ruling coalition retained power. The DF gained two more seats. A dispute with Canada over the ownership of Hans Islands, halfway between Greenland and Canada, erupted in July. In September the dispute was settled with a draft protocol to manage their dealings concerning the island.

2006 In January and February, cartoons of Mohammed which had appeared in Jyllands Posten newspaper in Septermber 2005 provoked protests and boycotts of Danish exports in Middle Eastern countries.

2007 Danish troops were withdrawn from Iraq in August. In late October Prime Minister Rasmussen called a snap parliamentary election for 13 November, 15 months earlier than was necessary. On 13 November in parliamentary elections, the ruling Venstre won 26.3 per cent of the votes (46 seats out of 175) and with their coalition parties secured another term in office. Prime Minister Rasmussen retained his office. Rasmussen announced on 11 December that he had decided against holding a referendum on the EU Reform Treaty.

2008 According to the US National Science Foundation, World Values Survey, Denmark was the found to be the country with the happiest people in the world.

Political structure

Constitution

Denmark has a written constitution – The Constitution Act – adopted on 5 June 1953. It sets out the rights and requirements of the monarchy, state church, government, judiciary and the individual. The monarchy is governed by the Succession to the Throne Act, adopted 27 March 1953, whereby royal power is inherited. The Faroe Islands are a Danish external territory, electing two members to the Danish parliament, which maintains responsibility for constitutional, foreign and defence matters. A High Commissioner represents the Danish government and advises on joint affairs.

Greenland is a special cultural community in the Kingdom of Denmark. Only foreign policy, defence, police and monetary policy are Danish state affairs. Greenland elects two members to the Danish parliament.

Form of state

Constitutional monarchy

The executive

Executive power is vested in the monarch, and legislative power vested jointly in the monarch and parliament. The King appoints the prime minister and cabinet, who form the Council of State; they are responsible to the Folketing (parliament). All legislation is subject to the constitution.

National legislature

Since 1953, the Folketing has been a unicameral parliament of 179 members (175 members are elected for a four-year term, 135 of them by proportional representation in 17 districts and 40 others allotted in proportion to their total vote, plus two representatives each from the Faroe Islands and Greenland). Voting is not compulsory, and is open to all men and women over 18 years.

Legal system
Denmark's highest court is the Supreme Court in Copenhagen, made up of 15 judges. It hears appeals from two superior courts in Copenhagen and Viborg. These courts deal with appeals from the 84 tribunals, or lowest courts of justice, around the country. They can also deal initially with cases of greater consequence.
Last elections
13 November 2007 (parliamentary).
Results: Parliament: the Venstre won 26.3 per cent of the vote (46 seats out of 175), the SD 25.5 per cent (45), the Dansk Folkeparti (Danish People's Party) 13.8 per cent (25), the Socialistisk Folkeparti (SF) (Socialist People's Party) 13 per cent (23), the Det Konservative Folkeparti (Conservative People's Party) 10.4 per cent (18), the Det Radikale Venstre (Social Liberal Party) 5.1 per cent (9), the Ny Alliance (New Alliance) 2.8 per cent (5), and the Enhedslisten-de-rød-grønne (Unity List) 2.2 per cent (4). Turnout was 86.6 per cent.
Next elections
2011

Political parties
Ruling party
Right-wing coalition government comprising the Venstre (Liberal Party) and the Konservative Folkeparti (KF) (Conservative People's Party), supported by the Dansk Folkeparti (DF) (Danish People's Party) (coalition re-elected 8 Feb 2005)
Main opposition party
Socialdemokratiet i Danmark (SD) (Social Democracy in Denmark), Det Radikale Venstre (Radical Left (social liberal party)); Socialistisk Folkeparti (SF) (Socialist People's Party); De Grønne (The Greens).

Population
5.45 million (2007)*
Last census: January 2001: 5,349,212
Population density: 120 inhabitants per square km. Urban population: 85 per cent (1995–2001).
Annual growth rate: 0.4 per cent 1994–2004 (WHO 2006)
Ethnic make-up
Danes make up the majority of the population, along with some 9,000 Greenlanders and around 12,000 Faroese. The largest immigrant groups from outside the kingdom are Turkish, British and Norwegian. There is a small German minority in southern Jutland.
Religions
The majority of the population (90 per cent) belong to the Lutheran Church although there are small groups of other Christian denominations.

Education
There are 10 years of compulsory schooling, although the average student attends school for 15 years.
The participation rate at primary and secondary levels is close to 100 per cent of the relevant age groups. Forty-six per cent of the relevant age group attend education at a tertiary level. The cost of university or post-high school further education is financed by a system of student grants supplemented by bank loans carrying a state guarantee.
Compulsory years: Seven to 16.
Pupils per teacher: 10 in primary schools.

Health
Per capita total expenditure on health (2003) was US$2,762; of which per capita government spending was US$2,292, at the international dollar rate, (WHO 2006).
Hospitalisation and treatment by general practitioners is free of charge, but there are part-charges for medicine prescribed by GPs. Treatment by dentists and opticians is subsidised but not free. Since 1988, several small private hospitals have opened, the fees for which can be covered by insurance schemes.
HIV/Aids
HIV prevalence: 0.2 per cent aged 15–49 in 2003 (World Bank).
Life expectancy: 78 years, 2004 (WHO 2006)
Fertility rate/Maternal mortality rate: 1.8 births per woman, 2004 (WHO 2006); maternal mortality 0.1 per 1,000 live births: (World Bank)
Child (under 5 years) mortality rate (per 1,000): 4.4 per 1,000 live births (World Bank)
Head of population per physician: 2.93 physicians per 1,000 people, 2002 (WHO 2006)

Welfare
There is an extensive cradle-to-the-grave social security system, however the size of the welfare system has gradually been reduced since the 1990s. In 2005, the system came under close scrutiny and a government commissioned appraisal recommended that the pension aged should be raised and early retirement phased out, and charges set for some healthcare and educational services.
Currently welfare benefits include unemployment benefits, supplementary benefits and rent and heating grants.
Social security and welfare spending as a share of GDP is approximately 5.8 per cent.
Pensions
Denmark was the first country to introduce old age pensions in 1895, funded by two general taxes. To sustain the current pensions, there is a three pillar approach to provision. Pillar one is a basic, mandatory, publically administered scheme, maintained to provide for the poor in old age and may be supplemented by other allowances. Pillar two are mandatory, privately administered schemes and workplace pensions, which are devised to attract contributions as high as 16 per cent of wages. Pillar three are privately administered schemes with individual and voluntary contributions. Other schemes exist and fall within the rules of the three pillars.

Main cities
Copenhagen (capital, estimated population 1.1 million in 2004), Aarhus (220,700), Odense (144,600), Aalborg (120,600), Esbjerg (72,700).

Languages spoken
English and German are widely spoken in business and administration.
Official language/s
Danish

Media
Press freedom is guaranteed by law, as demonstrated in 2006 by the international furores following the publication of images of the Prophet Mohammad by a Danish newspaper, which was un-censured.
Press
Most publications are privately owned and tend to have fairly strong political leanings.
Dailies: There are around 50 daily newspapers, with Sunday readership particularly high. The leading newspapers are Morgenavisen Jyllands Posten (http://jp.dk) Ekstra Bladet (http://ekstrabladet.dk) a tabloid, BT (www.bt.dk), Politiken (http://politiken.dk) and Berlingske Tidende (www.berlingske.dk).
Weeklies: Most daily newspapers publish weekend editions. In Danish, a variety of political magazines include LO (www.lo.dk), Solidaritet (www.solidaritet.dk), and Danske Regioner (www.regioner.dk). For general news Weekend Avisen (www.weekendavisen.dk), and Grønland (www.groenlandselskab.dk) for news from Greenland. In English, The Copenhagen Post (www.cphpost.dk).
In Danish, women's magazines include Ingelise (www.ingelise.dk), and Alt for Damerne (www.altfordamerne.dk); Euroman (www.euroman.dk) is for men. Udfordringen (Showtime) (www.udfordringen.dk) covers music and performing arts.
Business: In Danish, national dailies include Net Posten (www.netposten.dk) and Scandinavia Now (www.scandinavianow.com), national magazines include Berlingske Nyhedsmagasin (www.business.dk) and Pengte & Privatøkonomi (www.penge.dk).

Regional newspapers from Copenhagen include Børsen (http://borsen.dk), Erhvervs Bladet (www.erhvervsbladet.dk), and Okonomisk Ugebrev (www.ugebrev.dk). Ase Nyt is a commercial quarterly.

Periodicals: Periodicals on general interest, life-style, consumer and commercial interest include Blender, En Skør Skør Verden and Social Demokraten.

Broadcasting

The national public broadcaster is DR (www.dr.dk).

Radio: DR (www.dr.dk/drdkradio) operates two national stations (P1 and P2), plus a regional station (P3) and a DAB, digital radio (P4), providing a comprehensive mix of all music genre, talk radio and information. A DR station also broadcasts in Nyheder (an Indonesian and Malaysian language).

There are many privately operated commercial radio stations and most located within relatively small areas or population centres. Regional and national networks include The Voice (www.thevoice.dk), Radio Mojn (www.mojn.dk) and Hit FM (www.hitfm.nu).

Television: Analogue transmissions will begin to be closed down by late 2009, with High Definition TV transmissions begun in January 2008.

DR (www.dr.dk) operates two national channels DR1 and DR2.

Other commercial TV services are provided by either cable or satellite, of which TV 2 (http://tv2.dk) the government-owned network is a multi-channel service. Foreign-owned services, include the Swedish, MTG (www.mtg.se), SBS (www.sbsbroadcasting.com) and US Disney Channel, which provide a wide variety of programmes.

Advertising

Press and cinemas advertising is the most popular form of medium, while direct mail is limited to a customer requesting material. There is limited advertising on radio, and poster sites are heavily regulated. On television and radio, there are advertising restrictions, with bans of tobacco and alcohol and a limit on pharmaceutical products and items for children. Only 12 minutes per hour is given over to advertising with a maximum of 15 per cent of total daily output.

Economy

Denmark has a balanced economy with a well-developed, export-based manufacturing sector, and an important agricultural sector. However, exports suffered a downturn in 2006 due to the international furore following the publication of cartoons portraying the Prophet Mohammed in a Danish newspaper in September 2005. Islamic countries, particularly in the Middle East, imposed a boycott. In February 2006, exports of dairy products were reduced by 85 per cent, down to Kr130 million (US$21 million); in February 2005, exports had been Kr840 million (US$134 million). Danish exports to Arabic countries are typically worth Kr3 billion (US$500 million), or 2 per cent of total exports, and while Europe-wide discussion of freedom of the press was debated, Danish companies and the government acted to reduce the anger and violence by apologising and encouraging improved ties with the Islamic world.

Denmark's GDP, after several years of slow growth, picked up in 2004 and by 2005 GDP growth was estimated to be 3.2 per cent, one of the highest in the EU. Based on increased disposable income from tax reductions in 2004, low interest rates and rising house prices, moderate unemployment at 4.5 per cent and low inflation at 1.8 per cent, GDP growth was expected to be 2.75 per cent in 2006.

Denmark is one of the wealthier EU countries on a per capita basis, benefiting from offshore oil and gas reserves, developed since the 1970s. The government has maintained a stable currency and successive foreign debt reductions. The economy is heavily oriented towards export markets and it had a healthy US$10 billion balance of trade surplus in 2005.

In 2006, the government agreed to reform the comprehensive welfare system with an increase in the retirement age and revised unemployment benefit. These measures should address the drain on the public purse of an ageing population and the problems of unproductive citizens.

External trade

As a member of the European Union (EU), Denmark operates within a communitywide free trade union, with tariffs sets as a whole. Internationally, the EU has free trade agreements with a number of nations and trading blocs worldwide.

Denmark's heavy industrial base is limited by a lack of natural resources however it has a sophisticated hi-tech pharmaceutical and biotechnical industry and over 80 per cent of its GDP is provided by foreign trade.

Denmark is the world's largest exporter of pork and manufactured wind turbines.

Imports

Principal imports are machinery and equipment, raw materials and semi-manufactures for industry, chemicals, grain and foodstuffs and consumer goods.

Main sources: Germany (21.5 per cent total, 2006), Sweden (14.3 per cent), The Netherlands (6.2 per cent).

Exports

Principal export commodities include machinery and instruments, pork and meat products, dairy products, fish, chemicals and pharmaceuticals, furniture, ships.

Main destinations: Germany (15.5 per cent total, 2006), Sweden (13.8 per cent), UK (8.4 per cent).

Agriculture

Farming

The agricultural sector typically contributes around 3 per cent of GDP and employs 4 per cent of the labour force. The sector is organised into local co-operatives which are united in national federations.

Agriculture benefits from the Common Agricultural Policy (CAP), which imposes import duties on products entering the EU from other countries in order to equalise the price of imported commodities with those produced within the union. Efforts to reform the CAP could have a significant impact on future production.

The government primarily acts as a regulator in the agricultural sector. It sets veterinary standards and lays down the rules for farm mergers and ownership. The government does not set production or export and import targets, and as a member of the EU, agriculture is subject to the EU agricultural production quota regime.

Intensive farming is concentrated on livestock production, mainly pig-meat, beef, veal, poultry and dairy produce.

Denmark has large world market shares in products such as pig-meat, dairy products, seeds, mink pelts and fish products.

Crop production for 2005 included: 9,212,703 tonnes (t) cereals in total, 4,826,013t wheat, 3,730,110t barley, *1,600,000t potatoes, 358,400t rapeseed (canola), 325,380t oats, 129,600t rye, 66,600t pulses, 136,211t oilcrops, *2,800,000t sugar beets, 65,510t fruit in total, 259,000t vegetables in total. Livestock production included: 2,148,176t meat in total, *150,000t beef, *1,800,000t pig meat, *1,690t lamb, 192,586t poultry, *82,000t eggs, *4,600,000t milk, 18,150t cattle hides.

* estimate

Fishing

Typical seafood catches total around 1.7 million tonnes per annum (tpy), yielding over 140,000 tpy of fish oils.

Denmark ranks fourth among the world's leading seafood exporters. It continues to export significant quantities of processed seafood, fish oil and meal mainly processed from imported raw material. Decreased Danish cod catches are putting pressure on prices and import substitutes. Cod and other fish imports from other countries have considerably increased.

Forestry
Forest and other wooded land accounts for only one-eighth of the land area, with forest cover estimated at 455,000 hectares (ha). Plantations constitute about 75 per cent of the forest area, with the remainder classed as semi-natural. Less than 25 per cent of the forest is under public ownership, with the rest shared between individuals and private institutions. Demand for forest products is high and is mostly met by imports. Most of the softwood logs are processed locally while high quality hardwood logs are increasingly imported. The furniture industry depends on imported raw materials and exports most of its production.

Industry and manufacturing
Denmark has a highly developed and diversified industrial sector, which is almost wholly under private ownership. The industrial sector contributes around 25 per cent of GDP and employs a quarter of the labour force.
As a country with a market economy and free external trade, government industrial policy plays a relatively minor role, especially as there is no significant state ownership in the industrial sector. The World Bank ranked Denmark in its at 8 for ease of doing business, and 15 for starting a business, out of 155 in 2005.
Government support for industry is largely confined to export credit arrangements and funds for research and development. The engineering, food processing and wood-paper industries are the economy's three biggest production areas.

Tourism
Tourism plays an important role in Denmark's economic life. It is a modern, highly developed country with extensive infrastructure and can cater for millions of tourist each year. As tourism is a combination of elements such as attractions, amenities, infrastructure and accompanying services, they are unlikely to be controlled by a single authority and the industry has an organic nature with growth dependent on local or individual stimulation. The industry is considering the impact of tourisim on the environment and society, with schemes proposed that will manage its influence, both beneficial and harmful.
It is expected that travel and tourism in 2005 will generate US$11 billion, adding 3.5 per cent or US$10 billion to GDP. Around 9 per cent of the population is employed in the sector, which is expected to attract US$5.5 billion or 10 per cent of all capital investment in 2005.

Mining
The mining sector contributes under 1 per cent to Denmark's GDP. Denmark has no exploitable raw materials other than sand and gravel for construction.
In Greenland, there are substantial deposits of coal, iron ore, uranium, gold and diamonds, none of which are currently being exploited.

Hydrocarbons
Denmark is Western Europe's third-biggest oil and gas producer (after Norway and the UK).
In 2004 proven oil reserves amounted to 1.3 billion barrels of oil and production was 394,000 barrels per day (bpd).
Proven reserves of natural gas were 90 billion cubic metres in 2004, and gas production was 9.4 billion cubic metres, 37 per cent of which is exported. Denmark has gas pipelines connecting its gas fields to its port of Kaergard in Jutland.
Oil and gas production comes from 20 fields in the North Sea. Mærsk Olie and Gas is the operator of 16 of these fields, while DONG E&P is an operator of three and Amerada Hess ApS operates one.
Denmark does not produce coal but imported 4.4 million tonnes oil equivalent (toe) in 2004, making it the second largest coal importer in Europe. Coal accounts for around a third of total primary energy supply. Primarily importing from South Africa, Columbia, Poland, the US and Australia, Denmark is hoping to replace coal energy with renewable sources.

Energy
Total electricity capacity amounts to around 1.3 million GW, most of which is from thermal power stations. Emphasis is on energy conservation and conversion of power stations from imported coal to locally produced gas. There is increased emphasis on developing renewable sources, such as wind, sun and biomass. Wind power has expanded rapidly, Denmark has the largest wind farm in the EU, producing 166MW of electricity, in Nysted; it went into operation in 2003. The target is to reach 50 per cent of capacity by 2030.

Financial markets
Stock exchange
The Københavns Fondsbørs (Copenhagen Stock Exchange) trades in the equity market, investment fund market, bond market and derivatives market.

Banking and insurance
Denmark has a healthy banking sector which is open to foreign competition. There are around 100 commercial banks in operation, although the two largest account for 60 per cent of total bank assets.
Central bank
Danmarks Nationalbank
Main financial centre
Copenhagen

Time
GMT plus one hour (daylight saving, late March to late October, GMT plus two hours)

Geography
Denmark is a low-lying country in northern Europe. Its only land frontier is with Germany and totals 67.7km, while the coastline exceeds 7,300km. Nowhere is more than 52km from the sea. Norway lies to the north of Denmark, across the Skagerrak – a gulf in the North Sea. Sweden lies to the north-east, its most southerly region being separated from Zealand by a narrow strait.
Outlying territories of Denmark are Greenland and the Faroe Islands in the North Atlantic Ocean.
The mainland consists of the peninsula of Jutland, the islands of Zealand, Funen, Lolland, Falster and Bornholm and 401 smaller islands. The average elevation of land above sea level is 30 metres and its highest point is only 173 metres above sea level. Denmark lies between the North Sea to the west and the Baltic Sea to the east.

Hemisphere
Northern

Climate
Predominantly western winds bring warm, moist air from the West Atlantic, tempering the climatic influences from the east. In winter these can take the form of long periods of frost with ice-bound waters and, in summer, occasional high temperatures and drought. The average temperature in Denmark is 7.5 degrees Celsius (C); the temperature varies from minus 0.1 degrees C in the coldest months to 16 degrees C in July. The average rainfall amounts to 664mm and is distributed fairly evenly over the year, with August normally being the wettest.

Dress codes
Danes are generally informal about clothing. Businessmen usually wear jackets and ties at meetings and only adopt a dinner jacket (or long dresses for women) on very formal occasions.

Entry requirements
Passports
Required by all, except EU visitors travelling on national ID cards.
Visa
Required by all except nationals of EU, North America, Australasia or Japan. For further exceptions contact the nearest consulate. Denmark is a member of the Schengen visa accord and all visitors that require a visa must apply to a Danish consulate; when a visa has been issued a visitor may travel to any other Schengen zone without further visas.

Business trips can be undertaken on a Schengen visa, nevertheless, an original invitation from a business contact in Denmark is necessary when applying. A Schengen visa application (offered in several languages) can be downloaded from http://europa.eu/abc/travel/ see 'documents you will need'.

Currency advice/regulations
There are no restrictions on import and export of local or foreign currency, however sums over eur15,000 should be declared on arrival. Some banks refuse to change large denomination foreign notes. ATMs are plentiful. Travellers cheques in US dollars, pound sterling and euros save additional exchange fees.

Customs
Personal items are duty-free. There are no duties levied on alcohol and tobacco between EU member states, providing amounts imported are for personal consumption.

Health (for visitors)
Nationals of the European Economic Area (EEA) countries and Switzerland can access reduced cost and sometimes free medical treatment using a European Health Insurance Card (EHIC) while visiting the EEA. Exceptions include nationals of the 10 countries which joined the EU in 2004 whose EHIC is not valid in Switzerland. Applications for the EHIC should be made before travelling.

Mandatory precautions
None.

Advisable precautions

Hotels
There is no official rating system. Tarrifs include 15 per cent service charge. It is advisable to book accommodation in Copenhagen in advance, especially during summer.

Credit cards
All the usual credit and charge cards are accepted.

Public holidays (national)

Fixed dates
1 Jan (New Year's Day), 5 Jun (Constitution Day), 24–26 Dec (Christmas).

Variable dates
Maundy Thursday, Good Friday and Easter Monday, Great Prayer Day, Ascension Day, Whit Monday.
Public holidays that fall on the weekend are not carried over to a weekday.

Working hours

Banking
Mon–Fri: 0930–1600; Thu: 0930–1800.

Business
Mon–Fri: 0800/0900–1600/1700; offices frequently close early before the weekend or on the eve of public holidays.

Government
Mon–Fri: generally 0900–1700.

Shops
Mon–Thu: 0900–1730; Fri: 0900–1900/2000; Sat: 0900–1300/1400. First Saturday in each month most shops open: 0900–1600/1700.

Telecommunications

Mobile/cell phones
The GSM 1800 and 900 networks operate throughout the country.

Electricity supply
220/380V AC.

Social customs/useful tips
Shaking hands is the acceptable way to greet and depart from both business contacts and friends. Punctuality is expected on all occasions.
Service is normally included on bills and further tipping is not necessary in hotels, restaurants or taxis.

Security
Apart from the occasional pickpocket, the streets of Copenhagen are generally safe.

Getting there

Air
National airline: Scandinavian Airline System (SAS) – jointly owned with Sweden and Norway.
International airport/s: Copenhagen (CPH) at Kastrup, 8km south-east of capital. Business/conference centre, Internet access, duty-free shops, bars, restaurants, bank, post office, transfer hotel (maximum stay 18hrs), shower and sauna facilities. Car hire available. A new rail link between the airport and main railway station in Copenhagen takes 12 minutes. There are also regular bus services from the airport departing every 10–20 minutes taking 20 minutes.
Other airport/s: Aalborg (AAL), 6km north-west of city; Aarhus (Tirstrup) (AAR), 44km north-east of city; Billund (BLL), 2km east of city, Esbjerg (EBJ), 8km from city.
Airport tax: None

Surface
Road: The 18km Great Belt bridge and tunnel, linking Copenhagen to the island of Funen (Fyn), provides the first seamless surface connection from mainland Europe to Copenhagen. It includes a 6.5km long suspension bridge, the world's second longest. A second bridge and tunnel, the Øresund connection, links Copenhagen with Malmø in Sweden consisting of an 8km bridge and an 8km tunnel connected by an artificial island. Tolls are applicable on both bridges.
Rail: High-speed Intercity trains via Copenhagan airport connect to Funen (1 hour) and Jutland (2 hours) with additional connections to Malmø (Sweden) on a 30-minute journey via the Øresund link. Access from other European countries is via Germany.
Water: Regular ferry services from UK, Norway, Sweden, Poland, Iceland, the Faroe Islands and Germany.

Getting about

National transport
Air: The network of scheduled services radiates from Copenhagen. Domestic airports are generally situated between two or more cities which are within easy reach of each other. Domestic flights are usually of no more than 30 minutes duration.
Road: About 70,000km of roads including 593km of motorway. The road system in the Danish archipelago makes frequent use of ferries. Motorways are not subject to toll duty.
Buses: There are few private long-distance coaches.
Rail: Approximately 2,500km of railways are operated by Danish State Railway (DSB) and a few private companies, providing a very efficient service linked to the ferry services. Country bus network operates where there are no railways.
Water: Ferry services connect the islands of Zealand, Funen and Lolland and Jutland peninsula, operated by DSB.

City transport
Taxis: There is a good service in all major towns. Taxis can be hailed in the street when they display their green 'Fri' sign, or by telephone or at ranks. Fare includes a tip.
Buses, trams & metro: Good bus service in Copenhagen, including night buses until 0230. Frequent, efficient services in other main towns. Flat-rate fares are usual.

Car hire
Hire cars are available throughout the country at main DSB stations and all airports. They can be booked in advance through stations, international car hire firms and travel agents. A valid driving licence is required, which must be carried when driving. Most firms stipulate a minimum age between 20–25. The speed limits are 130kmph on motorways, 80kmph on highways, and 50kmph in urban areas; speed traps are commonplace. Even for minor speed limit offences, drivers are liable to pay heavy on-the-spot fines; if payment cannot be made, the car may be detained. Avoid drinking and driving, as the laws of misuse are tough. Seatbelts, throughout a vehicle, are compulsory.

BUSINESS DIRECTORY

The addresses listed below are a selection only. While World of Information makes every endeavour to check these addresses, we cannot guarantee that changes have not been made, especially

to telephone numbers and area codes. We would welcome any corrections.

Telephone area codes

The international direct dialling code (IDD) for Denmark is +45, followed by subscriber's number.

Useful telephone numbers

Fire, police, ambulance	112
Emergency dental treatment	3138-0251
24-hour chemist	3314-8266

Chambers of Commerce

American Chamber of Commerce in Denmark, 28 Christians Brygge, 1559 Copenhagen V (tel: 3393-2932; fax: 3313-0507; e-mail: mail@amcham.dk).

Danish Chamber of Commerce, Børsen, 1217 Copenhagen K (tel: 7013-1200; fax: 7013-1201; e-mail: hts@hts.dk).

Banking

BG Bank, 68 Nørre Voldgard, 1390 Copenhagen K (tel: 7011-9999; fax: 3914-4899; internet: www.bgbank.dk).

Den Danske Bank AS (commercial bank), Holmens Kanal 2-12, DK-1092 Copenhagen K (tel: 3344-0000; fax: 3118-5873; internet: www.danskebank.com).

Finansrådet (bankers' association), Bankernes Hus, Amaliegade 7, DK-1256 Copenhagen (tel: 3312-0200; fax: 3393-0260; internet: www.finansraadet.dk).

Jyske Bank (Bank of Jutland, private bank), Vestergade 8-16, DK-8600 Silkeborg (tel: 8922-2222; fax: 8922-2499; internet: www.jbpb.com).

Spar Nord Bank AS, 15 Skelagervij, PO Box 162, 9100 Aalborg (tel: 9634-4000; email: ine@sparnord.dk; internet: www.sparnordbank.com).

Sydbank, PO Box 169, 4 Peberlyk, DK-6200 Aabenraa (tel: 7463-1111; fax: 7463-1320; email: info@sydbank.dk; internet: www.sydbank.dk).

Nordea Bank AS, PO Box 850, Christiansbro Strandgade 3, DK-0900 Copenhagen C (tel: 3333-3333; email: hotline@nordea.dk; internet: www.nordea.dk).

Central bank

Danmarks Nationalbank, Havnegade 5, DK-1093 Copenhagen (tel: 3363-6363; fax: 3363-7103; e-mail: info@nationalbanken.dk).

Travel information

Copenhagen Airport, PO Box 74, Lufthavnsboulevarden 6 DK-2770, Kastrup (tel: 3231-3231; fax: 3231-3132; email: cphweb@cph.dk; internet: www.cph.dk).

Copenhagen Airtaxi, Copenhagen Airport Roskilde, DK-4000 Roskilde (tel: 391-114).

DSB (Danish State Railways), 1349 Sølgade 40, 1349 Copenhagen (tel: 3314-0400).

Forenede Danske Motorejere (FDM) (the Danish motoring organisation), Blegdamsvej 124, DK-2100 Copenhagen Ø (tel: 7013-3040; fax: 4527-0993).

Scandinavian Airlines System (SAS), Frosundaviks Alle 1, Stockholm S-16187, Sweden (tel: (+46-8) 7970-000; fax: (+46-8) 858-741).

National tourist organisation offices

Danmarks Turistrad (tourist board), Vesterbrogade 6 D, 1620 Cogenhagen V (tel: 3311-1415; fax: 3393-1416).

Ministries

Ministry of Agriculture, Fisheries and Food, Holbergsgade 2, 1057 Copenhagen K (tel: 3392-3301; fax: 3314-5042; e-mail: fvm@fvm.dk).

Ministry of Business and Industry, Slotsholmsgade 10-12, 1216 Copenhagen K (tel: 3392-3350; fax: 3312-3778; e-mail: em@em.dk).

Ministry of Business and Industry, Invest in Denmark, Slotsholmsgade 10-12, Copenhagen K, DK-1216 (tel: 3392-3350; fax: 3312-3778; e-mail: Investdk@em.dk; internet site: www.investindk.com).

Ministry of Culture, Nybrogade 2, 1203 Copenhagen K (tel: 3392-3370; fax: 3391-3388; e-mail: kum@kum.dk).

Ministry of Defence, Holmens Kanal 42, 1060 Copenhagen K (tel: 3392-3320; fax: 3332-0655; e-mail: fmn@fmn.dk).

Ministry of Economic Affairs, Ved Stranden 8, 1061 Copenhagen K (tel: 3392-3222; fax: 3393-6020; e-mail: oem@oem.dk).

Ministry of Education, Fredriksholms Kanal 21-25, 1220 Copenhagen K (tel: 3392-5000; fax: 3392-5547; e-mail: uvm@uvm.dk).

Ministry of Employment, Holmens Kanal 20, 1060 Copenhagen K (tel: 3392-5900; fax: 3312-1378; e-mail: am@am.dk).

Ministry of the Environment and Energy, Hojbro Plads 4, 1200 Copenhagen K (tel: 3392-7600; fax: 3332-2227; e-mail: mem@mem.dk).

Ministry of Finance, Christiansborg Slotsplads 1, 1218 Copenhagen K (tel: 3392-3333; fax: 3332-8030; e-mail: fm@fm.dk).

Ministry of Foreign Affairs, 2 Asiatisk Plads, 1448 Copenhagen K (tel: 3392-0000; fax: 3254-0533; e-mail: um@um.dk; internet site: www.um.dk/english).

Ministry of Health, Holbergsgade 6, 1057 Copenhagen K (tel: 3392-3360; fax: 3393-1563; e-mail: sum@sum.dk).

Ministry of Housing and Urban Affairs, Slotsholmgade 1, 3, 1216 Copenhagen K (tel: 3392-6100; fax: 3392-6104; e-mail: bm@bm.dk).

Ministry of the Interior, Christiansborg Slotsplads 1, 1218 Copenhagen K (tel: 3392-3380; fax: 3311-1239; e-mail: inm@inm.dk).

Ministry of Justice, Slotsholmsgade 10, 1216 Copenhagen K (tel: 3392-3340; fax: 3393-3510; e-mail: jm@jm.dk).

Ministry of Research, Bredgade 43, 1260 Copenhagen K (tel: 3392-9700; fax: 3332-3501; e-mail: fsk@fsk.dk).

Ministry of Social Affairs, Holmens Kanal 22, 1060 Copenhagen K (tel: 3392-9300; fax: 3393-2518; e-mail: sm@sm.dk).

Ministry of Taxation, Slotsholmsgade 12, 1216 Copenhagen K (tel: 3392-3392; fax: 3314-9105; e-mail: skm@skm.dk).

Ministry of Transport, Fredriksholms Kanal 27, 1220 Copenhagen K (tel: 3392-3355; fax 3312-3893; e-mail: trm@trm.dk).

Parliament, Christiansborg, 1240 Copenhagen K (tel: 3337-5500; fax: 3332-8536).

Prime Minister's Office, Christiansborg, Prins Jorgens Gard 11, 1218 Copenhagen K (tel: 3392-3300; fax: 3311-1665; e-mail: stm@stm.dk).

Other useful addresses

American Embassy, Dag Hammarskjolds Alle 24, DK-2100 Copenhagen Ø (tel: 423-144; fax: 430-223).

British Embassy, Kastelsvej 36, DK-2100 Copenhagen Ø (tel: 264-600; fax: 381-012, 431-400).

Central Telegraph Office, Købmagergade 37, DK-1150 Copenhagen K (tel: 3312-0903).

Copenhagen Stock Exchange, Nikolaj Plads 6, DK-1067 Copenhagen K (tel: 3393-3366).

Danish Convention Bureau, 27 Skindergade, 1159 Copenhagen K (tel: 3332-8601; fax: 3332-8803).

Danmarks Agentforening (association of commercial agents of Denmark), Børsen, DK-1217 Copenhagen K (tel: 3314-4941).

Danmarks Statistik, Sejrøgade 11, DK-2100 Copenhagen Ø (tel: 3917-3917; fax: 3118-4801).

Dansk Arbejdsgiverforening (employers' confederation), Vester Voldgade 113,

DK-1503 Copenhagen V (tel: 3393-4000; fax: 3312-2976).

Det Okonomiske Rad (economic council), Kampmannsgade, DK-1604 Copenhagen V (tel: 3313-5128).

Grosserer Societetet, Børsen (royal exchange), DK-1217 Copenhagen (tel: 3391-2323).

Industriraadet (Confederation of Danish Industries), H C Andersen's Boulevard 18, DK-1790 Copenhagen V (tel: 3377-3377; fax: 3377-3410).

IPC (International Press Centre), Snaregade 14, DK-1205 Copenhagen K (tel: 131-615; fax: 911-613).

Regional Development Organisation (Copenhagen Capacity), Kongens Nytorv 6, 4, sal DK-1050 Copenhagen K (tel: 3333-0300; fax: 3333-7333).

Ritzaus Bureau 1/S (news agency), Mikkel Bryggersgade 3, DK-1460 Copenhagen K.

Royal Danish Embassy (USA), 3200 Whitehaven Street, NW, Washington DC 20008 (tel: (+1-202) 234-4300; fax: (+1-202) 238-1470; e-mail: wasamb@um.dk).

Teknisk Forlag AS (technical press-publishing house), Skelbaekgade 4, DK-1717 Copenhagen V.

Thomson Communications (Scandinavia) AS, Hestemøllestrede 6, Postboks 2181, DK-1017 Copenhagen K.

Internet sites

Danish web index: www.web-index.dk

Interactive travel site: www.visitdenmark.com

Statistical Office: www.dst.dk

Trade directory for Denmark: http://uhk.dk

White pages: http://infobel.com/denmark/default.asp

Yellow pages: www.yellowpages.dk

Djibouti

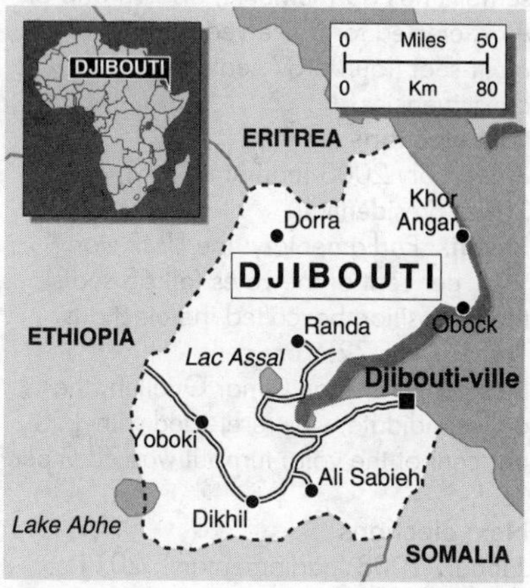

Djibouti was once picturesquely known as the 'Territory of the Afars and the Issas' (and long claimed by Somalia), has traditionally been dependent upon port trade, the rail link to Addis Ababa and the consumption of a once substantial French community. Traditionally, but no longer, Djibouti was dependent on its two neighbours and their relations with the country's two main ethnic groups, the Issas linked to the Somalis and the Afars, more inclined towards the Ethiopians. Roughly 60 per cent of the population are Issas. However, in the years before independence, the French systematically bolstered the position of the minority Afars.

Economy

In a report made in March 2008 the International Monetary Fund (IMF) stated that the macroeconomic environment of Djibouti had improved significantly over the last few years. Annual real GDP growth accelerated from an annual average of 3 per cent in 2001–05 to 4.8 per cent in 2006 and further to an estimated 5.3 per cent in 2007, mainly driven by large foreign direct investments (FDI) in the port, tourism, and construction sectors. Investment as share of GDP doubled within two years, rising from 23 per cent in 2005 to over 40 per cent in 2007. However, inflation accelerated to 8.1 per cent in 2007, compared with 3.5 per cent in 2006, mainly on account of the higher international food and oil prices. After remaining stagnant for several years, credit to the private sector increased by 23 per cent in 2007, owing in part to a real estate and construction boom. The recent arrival of new foreign banks has fostered competition.

Fiscal policy remained expansionary, with an estimated overall deficit of 2.6 per cent of GDP in 2007, above the revised budget target of 1 per cent. Nonetheless, the increase in external financing allowed repaying domestic arrears for an estimated amount equivalent to 0.7 per cent of GDP.

The surge in FDI-related imports led to the strengthening of the external position, despite a deterioration of the trade and current account balances. Based on preliminary data, the current account deficit is estimated to have increased from 14.7 per cent in 2006 to 24.1 per cent in 2007. This was more than offset by the large capital and financial account surplus, resulting in an increase in gross official reserves to US$130 million at end-2007 (equivalent to 2.1 months of imports of goods and services, and a currency board cover of 116 per cent).

Progress has been made in implementing structural reforms. The new Labour Code adopted in December 2005 has been implemented, increasing labour market flexibility. Preparations for the introduction of a value added tax in 2009 are well under way. A new Commerce Code has been drafted and is expected to be sent to the National Assembly during 2008. Fiscal transparency has improved with the publication of the accounts of key public enterprises.

Risk assessment

Economy	Improving
Politics	Fair
Regional stability	Fair

COUNTRY PROFILE

Historical profile

1862 France reached agreements with local leaders which gave the French the right to settle in Djibouti. They also acquired the port of Obock. The country was called French Somaliland.

1888 Construction of Djibouti-ville began on the southern shore of Tadjoura Bay. At the end of the century, France signed an

KEY FACTS

Official name: République de Djibouti/Jumhouriyya Djibouti (Republic of Djibouti)

Head of State: President Ismail Omar Guelleh (since 1999; re-elected 8 Apr 2005)

Head of government: Prime Minister Dileita Mohamed Dileita (since 2001; re-appointed 21 May 2005)

Ruling party: Four-party Union pour la Majorité Présidentielle (UMP) (Union for a Presidential Majority) coalition, led by the Rassemblement Populaire pour le Progrès (RPP) (Popular Rally for Progress) (since 2005; re-elected 8 Feb 2008)

Area: 23,200 square km

Population: 765,000 (2007)*

Capital: Djibouti-ville

Official language: French/Arabic (Somali/Afar are the national languages)

Currency: Djibouti franc (Df) = 100 centimes

Exchange rate: Df176.01 per US$ (Jul 2008)

GDP per capita: US$1,099 (2007)*

GDP real growth: 5.20% (2007)

Unemployment: 50.00% (2004)

Inflation: 5.00% (2007)*

Balance of trade: -US$263.00 million (2005)

Foreign debt: US$429.00 million (2004)

* estimated figure

agreement with the Emperor of Ethiopia designating French Somaliland as the 'official outlet of Ethiopian commerce'. The agreement led to the construction of the vital Addis Ababa-Djibouti railway.
1892 Djibouti-ville became the capital of French Somaliland.
1917 The Addis Ababa-Djibouti railway was completed.
1946 French Somaliland was made an overseas territory, with its own parliament and representation in the French parliament.
1967 A referendum favoured continued French rule. French Somaliland was renamed the French Territory of the Afars and the Issas.
1977 The re-named Republic of Djibouti was granted independence by France after several years of growing protests and demonstrations. Hassan Gouled Aptidon of the Rassemblement Populaire pour le Progrès (RPP) (Popular Rally for Progress) was elected president.
1981 Djibouti became a one-party state, with the RPP as the only legal political party.
1991 The Front pour la Restauration de l'Unité et de la Démocratie (FRUD) (Front for the Restoration of Unity and Democracy) launched a civil war in northern Djibouti. The ethnic Afar organisation demanded multi-party elections.
1992 Following several months of fighting, Aptidon agreed to a referendum, which led to a limited, multi-party constitution. In the elections to the Chamber of Deputies only four parties are allowed to take part; the RPP won 72 per cent of the vote while a newly formed alliance led by the Parti du Renouveau Démocratique (PRD) (Party of Democratic Renewal) won the remainder.
1993 President Aptidon was re-elected for a fourth term.
1994 Despite the new constitution, FRUD did not end its armed struggle until December, when the government and FRUD signed a peace accord confirming the constitutional and electoral reforms of 1992.
1997 President Aptidon was re-elected for a fifth term. FRUD joined RPP in a coalition government.
1999 The 83-year-old president resigned after 22 consecutive years in power. Ismael Omar Guelleh was elected president.
2001 Dileita Mohamed Dileita replaced Barkat Gourad Hamadou as prime minister.
2002 The law limiting four parties to contest elections, passed in 1992, expired. US led coalition troops arrived, in preparation for military action in Afghanistan and against al Qaeda targets in the region.
2003 The first fully multi-party elections held since independence were won by parties supporting President Guelleh. Large numbers of illegal immigrants – estimated at 15 per cent of the population – were deported.
2005 In the presidential elections, Ismail Omar Guelleh, the only candidate, was re-elected with 100 per cent of the vote.
2008 In parliamentary elections held on 8 February the ruling UMP won all 65 seats, as the opposition boycotted the elections. Border clashes in June in the Mount Gabla area – also known as Ras Doumeira – that killed nine Djibouti troops and injured many more was blamed, by the US, on 'military aggression' by Eritrea. The US and France called for a cease fire and troop withdrawals on both sides and for negotiations to begin.

KEY INDICATORS — Djibouti

	Unit	2003	2004	2005	2006	2007
Population	m	0.71	0.77	0.73	0.75	*0.77
Gross domestic product (GDP)	US$bn	0.67	0.66	0.71	*0.77	*0.84
GDP per capita	US$	938	793	973	1,030	*1,099
GDP real growth	%	3.0	3.0	3.2	*4.8	*5.2
Inflation	%	-2.2	3.0	3.1	3.5	*5.0
Exports (fob) (goods)	US$m	70.0	38.0	40.0	55.2	–
Imports (cif) (goods)	US$m	255.0	303.0	303.0	335.7	–
Balance of trade	US$m	-185.0	-263.0	-263.0	-280.5	–
Current account	US$m	-60.0	-70.0	8.0	-99.1	*-212.0
Total reserves minus gold	US$m	100.1	93.9	89.3	120.3	–
Foreign exchange	US$m	98.4	91.2	87.7	117.8	–
Exchange rate	per US$	175.00	175.43	174.70	174.70	175.47

* estimated figure

Political structure
The executive
Executive power is vested in the Council of Ministers, headed by a prime minister, and responsible to the president, who is directly elected by absolute majority vote for a six-year term.
National legislature
The Assemblée Nationale (National Assembly) has 65 members, 33 Issa and 32 Afar, elected for a five-year term in multi-seat (four to 37 seats) constituencies.
Last elections
8 February 2008 (parliamentary); 8 April 2005 (presidential).
Results: Parliamentary: the UMP won 94.1 per cent of the votes (all 65 seats); the opposition boycotted the elections. Turnout was 72.6 per cent.
Presidential: Ismail Omar Guelleh, the only candidate, was re-elected with 100 per cent of the vote; turnout was 78.9 per cent.
Next elections
January 2008 (parliamentary); 2011 (presidential).

Political parties
Ruling party
Four-party Union pour la Majorité Présidentielle (UMP) (Union for a Presidential Majority) coalition, led by the Rassemblement Populaire pour le Progrès (RPP) (Popular Rally for Progress) (since 2005; re-elected 8 Feb 2008)
Main opposition party
Union pour l'Alternance Démocratique (UAD) (Union for Democratic Change)

Population
765,000 (2007)*
Last census: December 1960 81,200
Population density: 28 inhabitants per square km. Urban population: 84 per cent (1995–2001).
Annual growth rate: 2.7 per cent 1994–2004 (WHO 2006)
Ethnic make-up
About 60 per cent of the national total are Issas, of Somali origin and about 35 per cent are Afars who have links with Ethiopia; there are about 5 per cent European residents.
The population also includes refugees from the Ogaden and Eritrean wars in Somalia and Ethiopia.
The nomadic population (principally Afars) totals around 100,000.
Religions
Islam (94 per cent), Christianity (6 per cent)

Education
Literacy rate: 75.6 per cent men, 54.4 per cent women; adult rates (World Bank).
Enrolment rate: 45 per cent boys, 33 per cent girls, total primary school

enrolment of the relevant age group (including repetition rates) (World Bank).

Health

Per capita total expenditure on health (2003) was US$72; of which per capita government spending was US$48, at the international dollar rate, (WHO 2006). The results of this spending appear limited, due mainly to poor management and the high costs of foreign staff and medicines.

HIV/Aids

This percentage is high enough to pose a significant threat to the country's future prosperity. Under a funding agreement in June 2004, US$12 million from the Global Fund to fight Aids, tuberculosis (TB) and malaria, will be spent on antiretroviral drugs to be supplied to Aids suffers until 2007. From an initial 200 patients it is expected that 4,000 patients will be treated, however the estimate of HIV positive cases in Djibouti is 9,000, with only 1,000 people registered – gaining them access to free treatment – though there has been an improvement in the numbers of people being tested.

HIV prevalence: 2.9 per cent aged 15–49 in 2003 (World Bank)

Life expectancy: 56 years, 2004 (WHO 2006)

Fertility rate/Maternal mortality rate: 4.9 births per woman, 2004 (WHO 2006)

Child (under 5 years) mortality rate (per 1,000): 97 per 1,000 live births; 18 per cent of children aged under five are malnourished (World Bank).

Head of population per physician: 0.18 physicians per 1,000 people, 2004 (WHO 2006)

Welfare

The average unemployment rate in the country is about 45 per cent. Although poverty is more acute in the rural areas, 72 per cent of those defined as living in absolute poverty reside in urban areas. Djibouti has been severely affected by the large influx of refugees from Ethiopia, Somalia and Eritrea, putting great strain on its financial resources. In August 2003 thousands of refugees and illegal immigrants were given an ultimatum to leave the country. Most had fled the wars in Somalia and Ethiopia and their numbers were as high as 100,000, or 15 per cent of the Djibouti population. The reason given by the government for their expulsion was security. By February 2004, 3,361 had been repatriated to Somaliland, by the UN High Commission for Refugees (UNHCR), who provided food and other provisions for each person, to last for the first nine months. Other refugees ended up in camps in Ethiopia as internally displaced persons.

Main cities

Djibouti-ville (capital, estimated population 547,100 in 2003).

Languages spoken

English is understood by the larger trading houses. Cushitic languages, as well as Somali and Saho-Afar are widely spoken.

Official language/s

French/Arabic (Somali/Afar are the national languages)

Media

Although the constitution provides for a free press, in practice the government maintains tight control of media outlets and circulation of information is highly restricted. Journalists generally have to avoid sensitive issues covering human rights, the army, and the government, relations with Ethiopia and foreign financial aid. A law prohibits the dissemination of false information and regulates the publication of newspapers, which has led to journalists exercising self-censorship. Journalists are largely untrained and poorly paid.

National news agency: ADI (Agence Djiboutienne d'Information)
(internet: (in French): www.adi.dj).

Other news agencies: Presidential Press Office: www.spp.dj

Press

In French, the main locally published newspaper La Nation (www.lanation.dj) is government owned. Political parties, Parti National Démocratique publishes La Republique, and Union pour l'Alternance Démocratique publishes Le Renouveau.

Broadcasting

The government owns the only radio and television stations allowed within the country with news programmes uncritical of the government or government policy. External services are available.

Radio: Radio Télévision Djibouti (RTD) (www.rtd.dj) provides a national network for news, information, religious and musical programmes. External services via AM and local FM relays provide foreign broadcasts.

Television: RTD (www.rtd.dj) has a monopoly in broadcasting, providing a few hours TV per day.

News agencies

National news agency: ADI (Agence Djiboutienne d'Information)
(internet: (in French): www.adi.dj).

Other news agencies: Presidential Press Office: www.spp.dj

Economy

Djibouti's economy is reliant on services. The agricultural sector is small and there is very little manufacturing. Economic activity centres on the port, the railway and other services, although the presence of foreign military directly and indirectly accounts for over half the country's income. The French military base, which once contributed around a quarter of Djibouti's GDP, has declined in importance since the French government decided to scale down its military presence in Africa. However, since the 11 September 2001 terrorist attacks in the US, American and German forces have used Djibouti as a military base from which to carry out the war on terrorism.

Around half the population live below the poverty line and the number is growing; rising unemployment is a significant problem with around 50 per cent of the population living without a job.

However, Djibouti's location on the Horn of Africa is the main economic asset of a country that is mostly barren. It is strategically located at the mouth of the Red Sea, close to the world's busiest shipping lanes and the Arabian oilfields; it is the terminus of rail traffic into Ethiopia. It serves as an important transshipment location for goods entering and leaving the east African highlands. Its transport infrastructure enables several landlocked African countries to fly in their goods for re-export. This earns Djibouti much-needed transit taxes and harbour fees. There are plans for a port at Doraleh and a new free trade zone.

The present leadership still favours close ties with France, which maintains a military presence in the country, but it has also developed increasingly stronger ties with the United States in recent years, which has been allowed to set-up what is the only US military base in sub-Saharan Africa. This has made Djibouti a front-line state in the US' global war on terrorism. It is a centre for US intelligence gathering.

External trade

Djibouti is a member of the Common Market for Eastern and Southern Africa (Comesa), and operates within a free trade zone with 13 of the 19 member states. The country has few assets with an unskilled labour force, limited natural resources and little scope for agriculture with poor, unproductive soil. The majoring of foreign earnings comes from its strategic function as a trans-shipment corridor for goods transported to and from the Port of Djibouti and Ethiopia.

There is a free trade zone near the port of Djibouti.

Imports

Principal imports are fresh fruits and vegetables (from Ethiopia), foods, beverages, transport equipment, chemicals and petroleum products.

Main sources: Saudi Arabia (21.4 per cent total, 2006), India (17.9 per cent), China (11.0 per cent).

Exports
Principal exports transiting Djibouti are live animals, cotton, sugar, cereals, salt, skins, leather and coffee.
Main destinations: Somalia (66.3 per cent total, 2006), Ethiopia (21.5 per cent), Yemen (3.4 per cent).

Agriculture
Farming
The underdeveloped agricultural sector contributes only 3 per cent to GDP.
Due to poor terrain (mostly desert), most agricultural producers are nomads engaged in herding goats, sheep and camels. Drought has severly affected the livelihoods of the herd owners. Around 95 per cent of food requirements are imported.
Projects under consideration include increasing the amount of arable land by irrigation schemes and rehabilitation of water dams and wells.
The estimated crop production for 2005 included: nine tonnes (t) maize, 1,805t citrus fruit, 1,283 tomatoes, 1,500t pulses, 450t mangoes, 317t allspice, 3,234t fruit in total, 25,680t vegetables in total. Estimated livestock production included: 11,244t meat in total, 6,050t beef, 4,534t lamb and goat meat, 660t camel meat, 13,950t milk, 1,100t cattle hides, 420t sheepskins.
In 2004, the total marine fish catch was 260 tonnes.

Industry and manufacturing
The industrial sector is limited to construction and small-scale concerns such as mineral water bottling, tanning, dairy and animal food plants. New industries set up in Djibouti include cement, tiles, paints and meat processing. Foreign investment is being encouraged and should be aided by renewed political stability in the region.

Tourism
Tourism is undeveloped, although its potential contribution to economic regeneration is acknowledged. Around 20,000 visitors were recorded in 2000, the majority from France.

Mining
Surveys have indicated the presence of minerals such as copper, gypsum and sulphur. No minerals are mined commercially. Salt is extracted and exported.

Hydrocarbons
Reported discoveries of gas reserves could make the country self-sufficient in gas and provide a surplus for export, although the exact amount is unknown. Chevron is engaging in oil exploration although so far there has been little success. The downstream industry serves as a supply centre for the export of petroleum products, mostly for Ethiopia. The Dubai Ports Authority hopes the new Doraleh terminal, which began construction in 2003, will double Djbouti's handling capacity, making it the largest transshipment point on the African continent, attracting inward investment. Djbouti relies entirely on refined oil product imports for its domestic demands.
Djibouti does not produce or import either natural gas or coal.

Energy
There is a geothermal power station; supply and distribution is overseen by the state-owned Electricité du Djibouti.

Banking and insurance
Central bank
National Bank of Djibouti
Main financial centre
Djiboutiville

Time
GMT plus three hours

Geography
Djibouti is in the Horn of Africa, at the southern entrance to the Red Sea. It is bounded on the north, west and south-west by Ethiopia, and on the south-east by Somalia. The land is volcanic desert.
Hemisphere
Northern

Climate
Very hot and arid from April–August; average temperature 32 degrees Celsius (C) and can reach 45 degrees C. Slightly cooler from October–March, with occasional light rain.

Dress codes
Djibouti has a large Muslim population so visitors should dress modestly, especially in the city. However, it is far less strict than other Islamic countries.

Entry requirements
Passports
Required by all. Must be valid for six months beyond date of departure.
Visa
Required by all, except French nationals. For business visits, a letter of invitation from a company in Djibouti is necessary.
Currency advice/regulations
No restrictions on import/export of local or foreign currency.

Health (for visitors)
Mandatory precautions
Yellow fever vaccination certificate if arriving from an infected area.
Advisable precautions
Yellow fever, typhoid, tetanus, hepatitis A and polio vaccinations. Malaria prophylaxis recommended as risk exists throughout the country. There is a rabies risk. Water precautions should be taken. Eat only well cooked meals, preferably served hot. Pork, salad and mayonnaise may carry increased risk. Vegetables should be cooked and fruit peeled.

Hotels
Available in Djibouti-ville – limited elsewhere. Service charge is normally included. Tipping is not usual.

Credit cards
Generally not accepted, except by airlines and Sheraton Hotel.

Public holidays (national)
Fixed dates
1 Jan (New Year's Day), 1 May (Labour Day), 27 Jun (Independence Day), 25 Dec (Christmas Day).
Variable dates
Eid al Adha, Eid al Fitr, Islamic New Year, Birth of the Prophet.
Islamic year – 1429 (10 Jan 2008–28 Dec 2008): The Islamic year contains 354 or 355 days, with the result that Muslim feasts advance by 10-12 days against the Gregorian calender. Dates of feasts vary according to the sighting of the new moon, so cannot be forecast exactly.

Working hours
Banking
Sat–Thu: 0715–1145.
Business
Sat–Thu: 0630–1300.
Government
Sat–Thu: 0630–1300.
Shops
0730–1200, 1600–1900; closed Fri.

Telecommunications
Telephone/fax
A 100 per cent automatic service; outside Djibouti-ville there are very few telephones.

Electricity supply
220V AC, 50 cycles.

Getting there
Air
International airport/s: Djibouti-Ambouli (JIB), 5km south of city; restaraunts, duty free shops, bureau de change, car hire.
Airport tax: US$20
Surface
Road: There is a surfaced road from Addis Ababa (Ethiopia). Local advice should be taken as to when to travel by road as it can be difficult, with problems caused by the political situation.
Rail: There is a rail link with Ethiopia with a daily service, but it is not reliable or safe.
Main port/s: Djibouti-ville.

Getting about
National transport
Air: Djibouti Airlines operates a daily domestic service to Obock and Tadjoura

from Djibouti. Dikhil and Ali-Sabieh can be reached by chartered aircraft.
Road: There are surfaced roads to the Ethiopian border and to Arta, and from Djibouti-ville to Tadjoura; most roads are in need of repair. Take local advice when planning to travel by road.
Rail: Some towns are served on the Djibouti– Addis Ababa railway.
Water: Ferry service links Djibouti-ville with Tadjoura and Obock.

City transport

Taxis: They are available in main towns. Tipping is not usual as fares include gratuities; there is an official tariff, but it is usual for visitors to be charged 50 per cent more; there is a similar increase at night.
The journey from the airport to the centre of Djibouti-ville takes 10 minutes.

Car hire

Available in Djibouti-ville and at the airport. Valid international driving licence recommended. A temporary licence can be obtained on presentation of national licence. Traffic drives on right.

BUSINESS DIRECTORY

The addresses listed below are a selection only. While World of Information makes every endeavour to check these addresses, we cannot guarantee that changes have not been made, especially to telephone numbers and area codes. We would welcome any corrections.

Telephone area codes

The international dialling code (IDD) for Djibouti is + 253 followed by subscriber's number.

Useful telephone numbers

Police: 17
Fire: 18

Chambers of Commerce

Djibouti International Chamber of Commerce et Industry, Place de LaGuarde, PO Box 84, Djibouti (tel: 351-070; fax: 350-096; e-mail: cicid@intnet.dj).

Banking

Banque de Développement de Djibouti; PO Box 520, Angle Ave Georges Clémenceau et rue Pierre Curie, Djibouti-ville (tel: 353-391; fax: 355-022).

Banque Indosuez Mer Rouge; PO Box 88, 10 Place Lagarde, Djibouti-ville (tel: 353-016; fax: 351-638).

Banque pour le Commerce et l'Industrie-Mer Rouge; PO Box 2122, Place Lagarde, Djibouti-ville (tel: 350-857; fax: 354-260).

Central bank

Banque Centrale de Djibouti, Avenue Saint Laurent du Var, PO Box 2118, Djibouti-ville (tel: 352-751 fax: 356-288; e-mail: bndj@intnet.dj).

Travel information

Daallo Airlines (Airline of Horn of Africa), PO Box 1954, Djibouti-ville (tel: 353-401, 356-660; fax: 351-765).

Djibouti Airlines, Place Lagarde, PO Box 2240, Djibouti-ville (tel: 351-006; fax: 352-429).

Djibouti Airport, BP 204, Djibouti-ville (tel: 340-101 ext 300, 382-322; fax: 340-723).

Puntavia Airline de Djibouti, CP 2240, Djibouti-ville (tel: 351-036, 351-006; fax: 353-429, 356-660).

National tourist organisation offices

Office National du Tourisme de Djibouti, BP 1938, place du 27 Juin, Djibouti-ville (tel: 353-790; fax: 356-322; e-mail: onta@intnet.dj).

Ministries

Ministry of Agriculture and Rural Development, BP 453, Djibouti-ville (tel: 351-297).

Ministry of Commerce, Transport and Tourism, BP 121, Djibouti-ville (tel: 352-540).

Ministry of Foreign Affairs and Co-operation, BP 1863, Djibouti-ville (tel: 353-342).

Ministry of Industry and Industrial Development, BP 175, Djibouti-ville (tel: 350-340).

Other useful addresses

British Consulate, BP 81, Gellatly Hankey et Cie, Djibouti-ville (tel: 355-718; fax: 353-294); c/o Inchcape Shipping Office, Djibouti-ville (tel: 353-836/844).

Central Post Office, boulevard de la République, Djibouti-ville (tel: 350-669).

Compagnie du Chemin de Fer Djibouti-Ethiopien, BP 2116, Djibouti-ville (tel: 350-353).

Djibouti Embassy (USA), 1156 15th Street, NW, Washington DC 20005 (tel: (+1-202)-331-0270; fax (+1-202)-331-0302).

Office National d'Approvisionnement et de Commercialisation (ONAC), BP 75, Djibouti-ville (tel: 350-327).

Office of the Prime Minister, BP 2086, Djibouti-ville (tel: 351-494; fax: 355-049).

Radiodiffusion Télévision de Djibouti (RTD), BP 97, Djibouti-ville (tel: 352-294).

Service de Statistique et de Documentation, BP 1846, Djibouti-ville (tel: 353-331).

US Embassy, BP 185, Villa Plateau du Serpent, Boulevard Maréchal Joffré, Djibouti-ville (tel: 353-995).

National news agency: ADI (Agence Djiboutienne d'Information)

(internet: (in French): www.adi.dj).

Internet sites

Africa Business Network: http://www.ifc.org/abn

AllAfrica.com: http://allafrica.com

African Development Bank: http://www.afdb.org

Africa Online: http://www.africaonline.com

Information on Horn of Africa: http://www.djibouti.com

Local online newspaper: http://www.djiboutipost.com

Mbendi AfroPaedia (information on companies, countries, industries and stock exchanges in Africa): http://www.mbendi.co.za

Dominica

KEY FACTS

Official name: The Commonwealth of Dominica

Head of State: President Nicholas Liverpool (from Oct 2003)

Head of government: Prime Minister Roosevelt Skerrit (DLP) (sworn in 8 Jan 2004; re-elected 5 May 2005)

Ruling party: Dominica Labour Party (DLP) (since Feb 2000; re-elected 5 May 2005)

Area: 750 square km

Population: 72,000 (2007)*

Capital: Roseau

Official language: English

Currency: East Caribbean dollar (EC$) = 100 cents

Exchange rate: EC$2.70 per US$ (fixed)

GDP per capita: US$4,300 (2005)

GDP real growth: 1.50% (2007)

Unemployment: 16.00% (2006)*

Inflation: 5.50% (2007)

Balance of trade: -US$82.00 million (2005)

* estimated figure

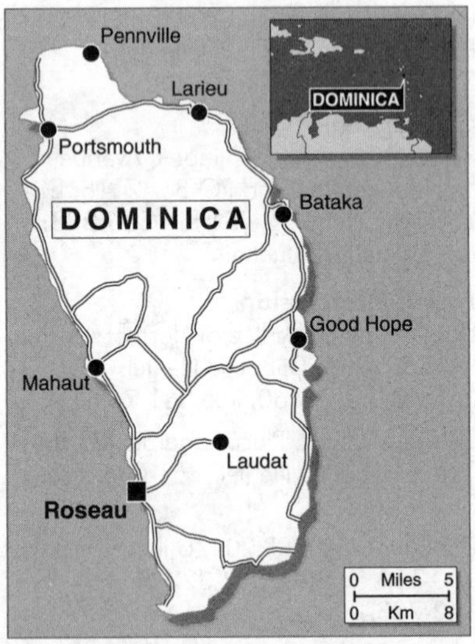

COUNTRY PROFILE

Historical profile

1940 The administration of Dominica was transferred to the Windward Islands.
1951 Universal adult suffrage was established.
1958 Dominica became part of the UK-sponsored West Indies Federation.
1960 Dominica was granted self-government by the UK.
1967 Full autonomy of its internal affairs was gained.
1978 Dominica became an independence republic within the Commonwealth.
1981 Two attempted coups failed and the Dominican Defence Force was disbanded.
1995 The United Workers' Party (UWP), led by Edison James, won the general election, defeating the ruling Dominica Freedom Party (DFP).
2000 The UWP lost the election to a coalition composed of the Dominica Labour Party (DLP) and the DFP. Prime Minister Roosevelt Douglas died suddenly and Pierre Charles was appointed as his successor. Under legislation, the National Commercial Bank was permitted to engage in offshore financial services.
2002 Dominica ended the sale of passports under its economic citizenship programme.
2003 Dr Nicholas Liverpool became president, elected by parliament despite an opposition boycott of the sitting.
2004 Prime Minister Pierre Charles died; Roosevelt Skerrit was sworn in as his successor. Diplomatic relations with Taiwan was cut in favour of China, which agreed to provide aid of US$100 million over five years. An earthquake damaged building in the north of the island and cost millions of dollars in repairs.
2005 Roosevelt Skerrit's DLP won the parliamentary elections; the DFP, the junior partner in the former coalition government, lost both of its seats – the first time in 35 years that the DFP did not win a seat.
2006 A section of the fibre optic cable, which when completed will traverse the entire Eastern Caribbean (around 1900km in lenth), was landed in Dominica.
2007 In August, Hurricane Dean ruined around 99 per cent of the banana crop, severely damaging the country's principal industry. However, the tourist infrastructure remained largely untouched.

Political structure

The executive

Executive power rests with the prime minister who acts on the advice of the cabinet.
The role of the president, as Head of State, is largely ceremonial. The president is nominated by the prime minister, in consultation with the leader of the opposition, and is then elected by the House of Assembly for five years, renewable once.

National legislature

The House of Assembly has 30 members, consisting of 21 directly elected members, nine senator appointed by either the president or other members of the assembly. Parliamentary terms run for five years.
The assembly appoints the president, who is a ceremonial head of state. The prime minister is the leader of the majority in the House of Assembly and the leader of the opposition is appointed by the president as leader of the main grouping outside the government.

Legal system

The legal system is based on English common law. There are three local levels of judiciary courts. The Eastern Caribbean Supreme Court, located in St Lucia, hears appeals. The Privy Council in the UK is the highest court of appeal.

Last elections
5 May 2005 (parliamentary); 16 May (presidential).
Results: Parliamentary: The DLP won 12 seats out of 21, the UWP eight and independents one.
Next elections
2010 (parliamentary)

Political parties
Ruling party
Dominica Labour Party (DLP) (since Feb 2000; re-elected 5 May 2005)
Main opposition party
United Workers' Party (UWP)
Political situation
Following the devastating hurricane, Ivan, in 2004 that crippled the economies of so many Caribbean countries, governments, Caricom and the Caribbean Development bank agreed to set up the Caribbean Catastrophic Risk Insurance Facility (CCRIF), which provides remuneration following natural disasters.
Although the hurricane that destroy so much of the banana plantations in the northern of the island in August 2007 did not benefited from a CCRIF payout, Dominica did receive over US$279,000 for damage caused during an earthquake in 2004. Nevertheless, international aid was forthcoming from the IMF, the EU, China and Venezuela.
An IMF report in May 2008 stated that economic recovery, following the hurricane, was well underway and growth that was 1.5 per cent in 2007 was running at 2.5–3.0 per cent in 2008.

Population
72,000 (2007)*
Last census: May 2002: 69,625
Population density: 97 inhabitants per square km. Urban population: 71 per cent (1995—2001).
Annual growth rate: 0.5 per cent 1994–2004 (WHO 2006)
Ethnic make-up
Black, mixed black and European, European, Syrian, Carib.
Religions
Roman Catholic (77 per cent), Methodist (5 per cent), Pentecostal (3 per cent), Seventh-Day Adventist (3 per cent), Baptist (2 per cent).

Education
Literacy rate: 94 per cent, adult rate (2003)
Compulsory years: Five to 16

Health
Per capita total expenditure on health (2003) was US$320; of which per capita government spending was US$228, at the international dollar rate, (WHO 2006).
The country has experienced notable improvements with a decline in infant and maternal mortality and communicable diseases and an increase in life expectancy; chronic and other non-communicable diseases are now the leading causes of death and ill-health, even as new problems such as HIV/Aids present themselves.
Life expectancy: 74 years, 2004 (WHO 2006)
Fertility rate/Maternal mortality rate: 2.0 births per woman, 2004 (WHO 2006)
Birth rate/Death rate: 17 births per 1,000 population; seven deaths per 1,000 population (2003).
Child (under 5 years) mortality rate (per 1,000): 12 per 1,000 live births (2003)

Welfare
Dominica has a national insurance system in which employee contributions are 3 per cent of salary and employer contributions are 7 per cent.

Main cities
Roseau (capital, estimated population 20,000 in 2003), Berekua (3,900), Portsmouth (3,600).

Languages spoken
English and French-Creole.
Official language/s
English

Media
Press
There are no daily newspapers. Weekly publications include The Chronicle (www.dachronicle.com) The Times, The Sun and The Tropical Star.
Online news is carried by Dominica News (www.dominicanewsonline.com), Dominican Weekly (www.dominica-weekly.com) News-Dominica (www.newsdominica.com) and Cakafete (www.sakafete.com).

Broadcasting
Radio: DBS (Dominica Broadcasting Services) (www.dbcradio.net) is the government-operated radio service. Commercial stations include Q95 FM (www.wiceqfm.com), Kairi FM (http://kairifmonline.com) and Voice of Life Radio (www.voiceoflife.com) plays religious programmes
Television: There is no national TV service although a Marpin Telecoms (www.marpin.dm) provides a cable service with 52 channels.

Economy
The IMF has been supportive of Dominica's progress over the last few years, as its macroeconomic performance has significantly expanded in all sectors. Domestic demand has been buoyant, while private sector confidence has grown. Services typically dominate the economy, accounting for over 50 per cent.
Construction and the tourist industry both expanded in 2005/06 while in agriculture, banana production increased by 7 per cent. Manufacturing did not perform as well as other sectors of the economy but it did not, nor did high oil prices, unduly spoil the economic trend. GDP growth in 2006 was estimated to be 4 per cent, up from the 2.4 per cent in 2005, while inflation remained low at 1.6 per cent in 2005, and was estimated at 1.5 per cent in 2006.
The government has successfully implemented programmes that have reformed revenue collection, including a reform of the customs department and the introduction of value added tax (VAT). It has also restructured around 79 per cent of the country's eligible debt and hopes to increase the percentage further. A list of reforms to improve the investment climate

KEY INDICATORS — Dominica

	Unit	2003	2004	2005	2006	2007
Population	m	0.07	0.07	0.07	*0.07	*0.07
Gross domestic product (GDP)	US$bn	0.38	0.27	0.28	0.30	*0.31
GDP per capita	US$	5,400	3,643	3,979	4,203	*4,333
GDP real growth	%	-1.0	1.0	3.4	4.0	*0.9
Inflation	%	0.5	2.3	1.6	2.6	*2.7
Exports (fob) (goods)	US$m	50.0	42.0	43.3	–	–
Imports (cif) (goods)	US$m	135.0	119.0	145.5	–	–
Balance of trade	US$m	-85.0	-77.0	-102.2	–	–
Current account	US$m	-50.0	-47.0	-78.0	-58.0	*-72.0
Total reserves minus gold	US$m	47.7	42.3	49.2	63.0	60.5
Foreign exchange	US$m	47.7	42.3	49.1	63.0	60.5
Exchange rate	per US$	2.70	2.70	2.70	2.70	2.70

* estimated figure

included reorganising the process for investment approvals, reducing the cost of doing business, establishing a smaller, streamlined public sector and improving the social and physical infrastructure.
Although unemployment was estimated at 16 per cent in 2006 and poverty is high, both the government and IMF are confident that the economic measures undertaken can improve the prospects of the community by economic growth and job creation.

External trade
Dominica is a member of the Caribbean Community and Common Market (Caricom) and operates within the single market (Caribbean Single Market and Economy (CSME)), which became operational on 1 January 2006. As a member of the Eastern Caribbean Currency Union (ECCU) Dominica uses the common Eastern Caribbean Dollar, among eight member countries.
As the EU has begun reducing trade preference for Dominica's banana imports, diversification is underway with emphasis on light manufacturing.

Imports
Principal imports include manufactured goods, machinery and equipment, food and chemicals.
Main sources: US (36.1 per cent total, 2006), Trinidad and Tobago (22.1 per cent), UK (5.7 per cent).

Exports
The principal exports include bananas (around 40 per cent), soap, bay oil, vegetables and citrus fruit.
Main destinations: UK (18.5 per cent total, 2006), Jamaica (15.1 per cent), Antigua and Barbuda (12.9 per cent).

Agriculture
The agriculture sector is the mainstay of the economy, accounting for around 18 per cent of GDP and employing 40 per cent of the labour force. About 25 per cent of the total land area is agricultural. Bananas are the main crop, with exports destined mainly for the UK. Banana exports are controlled through the Dominican Banana Marketing Board (DBMB), a government agency. Dominica's climate makes the banana crop highly vulnerable. Hurricanes occur periodically and in the past have wiped out as much as 95 per cent of the crop.
The government is trying to promote new crops as part of its diversification plan, for when the market is fully liberalised in 2006; these include coffee, mangos, and aloe vera.
Estimated crop production in 2005 included: 180 tonnes (t) cereals in total, 25,220t citrus fruit, 120t potatoes, 1,850t potatoes, 1,000t cassavas, 4,550t yautia, 11,200t taro, 8,000t yams, 4,400t sugar cane, 11,500t coconuts, 29,000 bananas, 5,700t plantains, 1,900t mangoes, 380t green coffee, 220t cocoa beans, 188t assorted spices, 63,490t fruit in total, 1,495t oilcrops, 6,630t vegetable. Estimated livestock production included: 1,364t meat in total, 540t beef, 420t pig meat, 64t lamb and goat meat, 340t poultry, 225t eggs, 6,100t milk.

Fishing
The typical annual fish catch is over 1,100t, plus 4t of other seafood.
In 2004, the total marine fish catch was 1,020 tonnes.
Forestry potential is not exploited.

Industry and manufacturing
Industry accounts for 24 per cent of GDP. The manufacturing sector is small-scale and centred on soap production, construction, agricultural processing (mainly coconut oil and copra), canned fruit juices, cigarettes, cigars and rum. Water bottling for export is also important.

Tourism
Tourism is an increasingly important sector of Dominica's economy, despite the lack of such attractions as white sand beaches. Tracts of rainforest cover a large area and the island is being developed as an eco-tourist destination. Boiling Lake, for instance, is among the top 25 nature experiences in the Caribbean. Cruise ship visitors are the largest and fastest-growing tourist group, followed by stay-overs and excursionists. The main markets are the Caribbean area and French West Indies, North America and UK. The sector is projected to contribute 9.6 per cent to GDP in 2005. It provides some 8,500 jobs, over 20 per cent of the total work force.

Hydrocarbons
Dominica does not produce oil, gas or coal. It relies on importing refined oil to meet domestic demand. The country needs fossil fuels to meet around half its energy consumption needs. Imports are mainly from other Caribbean islands and the US.
Trinidad and Tobago is planning to build a 600 mile undersea pipeline connecting islands on the way to Guadaloupe, which would give Dominica access to natural gas.

Energy
Around 80 per cent of Dominica's electricity needs are met by hydropower, of which there are plentiful resources.
Dominica, St Lucia and St Kitts and Nevis are investigating the commercial development of geothermally-fueled electric power plants.

Banking and insurance
The seven members of the Organisation of Eastern Caribbean States (OECS), Antigua and Barbuda, Dominica, Grenada, Montserrat, St Kitts and Nevis, St Lucia and St Vincent and the Grenadines, share a common currency and central bank. The British Virgin Islands and Anguilla are associate members.

Central bank
Eastern Caribbean Central Bank, St Kitts and Nevis.

Offshore facilities
The offshore financial sector makes a significant contribution to Dominican GDP and it is an area that the government would like to see progress. The government introduced anti-money laundering legislation and in 2003 Dominica was removed from the OECD blacklist of non-compliant countries.

Time
GMT minus four hours

Geography
Dominica is situated in the Windward Islands group of the West Indies, lying between Guadeloupe to the north and Martinique to the south.
The island has a rugged mountainous interior. It has volcanic activity, with the second largest boiling lake in the world (after Rotorua, New Zealand), where a waterfall feeds water onto a crater that is thought to have a magma chamber below. Morne Diablatins is the highest peak at 1,447 metres.
Much of the island is virgin rain forest with steep rivers flowing down to the shore of either black volcanic or golden sands.

Hemisphere
Northern

Climate
Sub-tropical with year-round tradewinds moderating the heat. Daytime temperatures range from 24–32 degrees Celsius; coolest from December–March. It is driest from January–May. The hurricane season, when storms can be very violent, is from June–October; rainfall is much higher in mountain areas. Annual rainfall in Roseau is 125–200cm and much higher inland.

Dress codes
Formal business attire.

Entry requirements
Passports
Required by all except, Canadian citizens travelling with proof of citizenship with photo ID and French nationals using their national Carte identite. Proof of onward/return passage is also required.
Canadian nationals require a passport for re-entry to their country from January 2007).

Visa
Tourist visas up to 21 days are valid for all visitors who can show proof of a return/onward ticket and sufficient funds for

the duration of the stay. Longer visa-free stays are only granted to designated nationals of the Americas, Europe and Australasia. Business visas will be issued to visitors who represent foreign companies, who must present proof of employment.
Contact the nearest High Commission or embassy for further information and application form.

Currency advice/regulations
The import of local and foreign currency is unlimited but must be declared, export is limited to the amount imported. Travellers cheques are accepted but to avoid extra exchange fees US dollar denominations are recommended. ATMs are available.

Health (for visitors)
Mandatory precautions
Yellow fever vaccination certificate required if arriving from infected area.
Advisable precautions
Immunisation for hepititis A is useful. Other lesser risks include typhoid, bacillary and amoebic dysentery and occasional outbreaks of dengue fever as well as haemorrhagic dengue fever. Water precautions should be taken in rural areas. As visitors are required to pay up-front for treatment, it is strongly recommended to take out full medical insurance.

Hotels
Most hotels are family-run and situated around the capital. Hotel bills include a 10 per cent service charge.

Credit cards
All major cards are accepted.

Public holidays (national)
Fixed dates
1 Jan (New Year's Day), 3 Nov (Independence Day), 4 Nov (Community Service Day), 25–26 Dec (Christmas).
Variable dates
Carnival (Feb), Good Friday, Easter Monday (Mar/April), May Day (first Mon in May), Whit Monday (last Mon in May), August Monday (first Mon in Aug).

Working hours
Banking
Mon–Thu: 0800–1500; Fri: 0800–1700.
Business
Mon–Fri: 0800–1600. Sat: 0800–1300.
Government
Mon: 0800–1300, 1400–1700; Tue–Fri: 0800–1300, 1400–1600.

Telecommunications
In December 2006, a section of the fibre optic cable, which when completed will traverse the entire Eastern Caribbean (around 1900km in length), was landed in Dominica. The cable begins in Puerto Rico and will end in Trinidad, connecting 12 islands. The cable will allow delivery of internet and telephony services.
Telephone/fax
Mobile/cell phones
GSM 850 and 900/1900 services available throughout most of the islands.

Electricity supply
220/240V AC, 50 cycles, with European three pin plugs.

Social customs/useful tips
Dominica's national dish is made from a large land frog, the crapaud or mountain chicken. In 2004, a ban was placed on hunting the amphibians, which are facing extinction.

Getting there
Air
National airline: None
International airport/s: Melville Hall (DOM), 64km north-east of Roseau; Canefield (DCF), 5km north of Roseau. Both of these airports are too small for international jets; access by air is via Antigua, Barbados, Costa Rica, Martinique or Guadeloupe.
Airport tax: Departure tax: EC$55, for a stay of more than 24 hours.
Surface
Water: There are ferries to surrounding islands.
Main port/s: Roseau (Woodbridge Bay) and Portsmouth (Prince Rupert's Bay).

Getting about
National transport
Air: Regional airline Carib Express based in Barbados.
Road: The network is over 750km, most of which is classified as first class.
City transport
Taxis: Available at airports and through hotels. Fixed rate system.
Car hire
A temporary local driver's permit is required, priced EC$30, and can be obtained on production of an national driving licence. Drivers must be aged between 25–65 years with at least two years experience.
The speed limit is generally 20mph.

BUSINESS DIRECTORY

The addresses listed below are a selection only. While World of Information makes every endeavour to check these addresses, we cannot guarantee that changes have not been made, especially to telephone numbers and area codes. We would welcome any corrections.

Telephone area codes
The international direct dialling code (IDD) for Dominica is +1 767, followed by subscriber's number.

Chambers of Commerce
Dominica Association of Industry and Commerce, 6 Cross Street, PO Box 85, Roseau (tel:448-2874; fax: 448-6868; e-mail: daic@marpin.dm).

Banking
Agricultural, Industrial & Development Bank (AID Bank), Charles Avenue, Goodwill (tel: 448-2853).

Bank of Nova Scotia, 28 Hillsborough Street, PO Box 520, Roseau (tel: 448-8580).

Banque Française Commerciale Antilles Guiyane, Queen Mary Street, PO Box 166, Roseau (tel: 448-4040).

Barclays Bank, 2 Old Street, PO Box 4, Roseau (tel: 448-2571).

Dominica Co-operative Credit Union, Great Marlborough Street, Roseau (tel: 82-191).

National Commercial Bank of Dominica, 64 Hillsborough Street, PO Box 271, Roseau (tel: 448-4401).

Royal Bank of Canada, Bay Front, PO Box 19, Roseau (tel: 448-2771).

Central bank
Eastern Caribbean Central Bank, Agency Office, PO Box 23, Dorsett House, Corner Old Street and Hodges Lane, Roseau (tel: 448-8001; fax: 448-8002).

Travel information
Cardinal Airlines, 26 King George V Street, PO Box 661, Roseau (tel: 449-8922; fax: 449-8923).

Ministry of tourism
Ministry of Tourism, Port and Employment, Government Headquarters, Kennedy Avenue, Roseau (tel: 82-401).

National tourist organisation offices
Dominica Tourist Board, National Development Corporation, PO Box 293, Roseau (tel: 82-045; fax: 85-840).

Division of Tourism (National Development Corporation), PO Box 73, Valley Road, Roseau (tel: 82-186, 82-351; fax: 85-840).

Ministries
Ministry of Agriculture and the Environment, Government Headquarters, Kenedy Avenue, Roseau (tel: 82-401; fax: 87-999).

Ministry of Communications, Works and Housing, Government Headquarters, Kennedy Avenue, Roseau (tel: 82-401; fax: 84-807).

Ministry of Community Development and Women's Affairs, Kennedy Avenue, Roseau (tel: 82-401; fax: 98-220).

Ministry of Education, Sports and Youth Affairs, Government Headquarters,

Kennedy Avenue, Roseau (tel: 82-401; fax: 80-080).

Ministry of External Affairs, Legal Affairs and Labour, Government Headquarters, Kennedy Avenue, Roseau (tel: 82-401; fax: 85-200).

Ministry of Finance, Industry and Planning (The Economic Development Unit), Government Headquarters, Kennedy Avenue, Roseau (tel: 82-401; fax: 80-054).

Ministry of Health and Social Security, Government Headquarters, Kennedy Avenue, Roseau (tel: 82-401; fax: 86-086).

Ministry of Privatisation and Foreign Investment (National Development Corporation), PO Box 293, Valley Road, Roseau (tel: 82-045).

Ministry of Trade and Marketing, Government Headquarters, Kennedy Avenue, Roseau (tel: 82-401; fax: 86-103).

Office of the Prime Minister, Government Headquarters, Kennedy Ave, Roseau (tel: 82-406).

Other useful addresses

Co-operative Citrus Growers' Association, 21 Hanover St, Roseau (tel: 82-062).

Dominica Banana Marketing Corp (DBMC), Corner of Queen Mary St and Turkey Lane, Roseau (82-671).

Dominica Broadcasting Corporation, Victoria Street, Roseau (tel: 83-283; fax: 82-918).

Dominica Embassy in US, 3216 New Mexico Ave, NW Washington DC 20016 (tel: (+1-202) 364-6781).

Dominica Export-Import Agency (Dexia), PO Box 173, Roseau (tel: 82-780; fax: 86-308).

Dominica Hotel Association, PO Box 270, Roseau (tel: 84-436).

Dominica National Development Corporation (NDC), PO Box 293, Valley Road, Bath Estate, Roseau (tel: 82-045; fax: 85-840; internet site: http://ndcdominica.dm/index.htm).

International Business Unit, Ministry of Finance, Government Headquarters, Kennedy Avenue, Roseau (tel: 82-401; fax: 80-406; e-mail: ibu@cwdom.dm).

Other news agencies: Caribbean Net News: www.caribbeannetnews.com

Internet sites

Tourist website: www.avirtualdominica.com

Dominican Republic

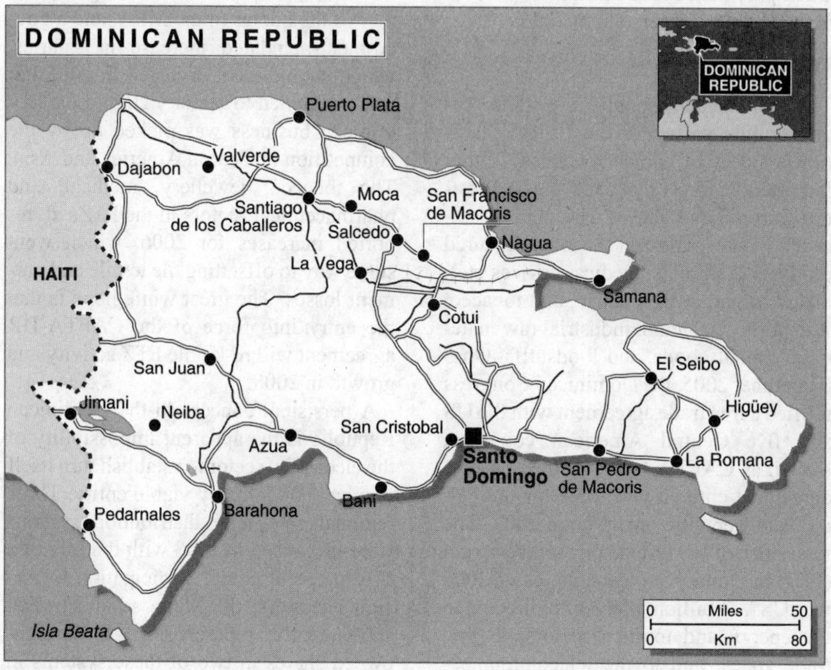

The end of the infamous Trujillo dictatorship, in 1962, was not all good news for the Dominican Republic. Juan Bosch was elected as president, but not for long – he was deposed in a military coup in 1963. The coup prompted a controversial United States led intervention into the Dominican Republic in 1965, amidst a civil war sparked by an uprising to restore Bosch. Since 1996 however, the Dominican electoral process has been seen as generally free and fair. In June 1996, Leonel Fernández Reyna of the Dominican Liberation Party (PLD) was elected to a 4-year term as president. Fernández's political agenda was one of economic and judicial reform. He helped enhance Dominican participation in hemispheric affairs, such as the OAS and the follow up to the Miami Summit. In May 2000, Hipólito Mejía, the PRD candidate, was elected president in another free and fair election, soundly defeating PLD candidate Danilo Medina and former president Balaguer. Mejía championed the cause of free trade and Central American and Caribbean economic integration. The Dominican Republic signed a free trade agreement (CAFTA-DR) with the United States and five Central American countries in August 2004, in the last weeks of the Mejía administration. It implemented the agreement in March. During the Mejía administration, the government sponsored and obtained anti-trafficking and anti-money-laundering legislation, sent troops to Iraq for Operation Iraqi Freedom, and ratified the Article 98 agreement it had signed in 2002. Mejía faced mounting domestic problems as an economy in decline – caused in large part by the government's measures to deal with massive bank fraud – and constant power shortages plagued the latter part of his administration.

Fiscal austerity and growth

During the Mejía administration, the Constitution had been amended to permit an incumbent president to seek a second successive term, and Mejía ran for re-election. However, in the May 2004 elections , Leonel Fernández was elected president, winning 20 per cent more votes than Mejía and taking office in August 2004. The principal platforms of the Fernandez campaign were fiscal austerity,

KEY FACTS

Official name: República Dominicana (Dominican Republic)

Head of State: President Leonel Fernández Reyana (PLD) (since 2004; re-elected 16 May 2008)

Head of government: President Leonel Fernández Reyana

Ruling party: Partido Revolucionario Dominicano (PRD) (Dominican Revolutionary Party) (since 2002; re-elected May 2006)

Area: 48,400 square km

Population: 8.78 million (2007)

Capital: Santo Domingo de Guzmán

Official language: Spanish

Currency: Dominican Republic peso (RD$) = 100 centavos

Exchange rate: RD$34.30 per US$ (Jul 2008)

GDP per capita: US$4,147 (2007)*

GDP real growth: 8.50% (2007)*

Labour force: 3.96 million (2004)

Unemployment: 17.00% (2004)

Inflation: 6.10% (2007)*

Balance of trade: -US$4.75 billion (2006)

Foreign debt: US$7.75 billion (2004)

Visitor numbers: 3.96 million (2006)*

* estimated figure

clamping down on corruption and social advancement. In the 2006 parliamentary elections, Fernández' PLD won 60 per cent of seats in the House of Representatives and 22 of 32 Senate seats, as well as a majority of mayoral seats. In May 2008, President Fernández was re-elected President with 53.8 per cent of the vote. His new term runs until 2012

Since his first term election in 2006 some of President Fernández's objectives have been achieved, not least economic growth, which reached 9.3 per cent in 2005, 10.7 per cent in 2006, and was estimated by the United Nations Economic Commission for Latin America and the Caribbean (ECLAC) to be 7.5 per cent in 2007 which, although down on the 2006 rate, was still higher than the original target of 6 per cent set out in the government's monetary programme. According to ECLAC, unlike 2006, GDP growth in 2007 was largely driven by private consumption. The sectors of greatest growth in 2006 had been communications (which showed 26 per cent growth over 2005), construction (23 per cent), financial mediation services (22 per cent) and trade (12 per cent). Nonetheless, the Free Zone sector continues incurring significant losses: in 2005 production fell by 9 per cent and in 2006 there was an additional contraction of 8.3 per cent. These slowdowns in production are explained, in part, by the end of quotas under the Multi-Fibre Agreement (MFA) and the entry of China into market competition.

While financial and business services performed well in 2007, in the tourism and communications sectors growth appeared to slow. Manufacturing and agricultural output also grew more slowly than the economy as a whole. Inflation reached an annual 7 per cent in 2007, largely determined by the persistent increase in oil prices which accounted for 45 per cent of the rise in the consumer price index (CPI). Unemployment edged down to 15 per cent in 2007, from 16 per cent in 2006.

Free trade

The Dominican Republic's most important trading partner is the United States (75 per cent of export revenues). Other important markets include Canada, Western Europe, and Japan. The country exports free-trade-zone manufactured products (garments, medical devices etc), nickel, sugar, coffee, cacao, and tobacco. It imports petroleum, industrial raw materials, capital goods, and foodstuffs. On 5 September 2005, the Dominican Congress ratified a free trade agreement with the US and five Central American countries, known as CAFTA-DR. The CAFTA-DR agreement entered into force for the Dominican Republic on 1 March 2007. The total stock of US foreign direct investment (FDI) in Dominican Republic as of 2006 was US$3.3 billion, much of it directed to the energy and tourism sectors, to free trade zones, and to the telecommunications sector. Remittances were close to US$2.7 billion in 2006.

An important aspect of the Dominican economy is the Free Trade Zone industry (FTZ), which made up US$4.55 billion in Dominican exports for 2006 (70 per cent of the total). The FTZs shed approximately 60,000 jobs between 2005 and 2007 and suffered a 4 per cent decrease in total exports in 2006. The textiles sector experienced an approximate 17 per cent drop in exports due in part to the appreciation of the Dominican peso against the dollar, but also due to Asian – particularly Chinese –competition following the expiry of the quotas of the MFA, and a government-mandated increase in salaries, which should have occurred in 2005 but was postponed to January 2006. Lost Dominican business was picked up by the competition in Central America and Asia. The tobacco, jewellery, medical, and pharmaceutical sectors in the FTZs all reported increases for 2006, which went some way to offsetting the textile and garment losses. The great white hope is that the entry into force of the CAFTA-DR agreement will re-kindle FTZ activity and growth in 2008.

A persistent concern in the Dominican Republic is the apparent impossibility of the electricity sector to establish turn itself into an economically viable entity. Three regional electricity distribution systems were privatised in 1998 with the sale of a fifty per cent equity participation to foreign operators; the Mejía administration subsequently repurchased all foreign-owned shares in two of these systems in late 2003. The third, serving the eastern provinces, is operated by US concerns and is 50 per cent US-owned. The World Bank has reported that electricity distribution losses for 2005 totalled some 38.2 per cent of total revenues, a rate of losses exceeded in only three other countries, of which Nigeria leads the way. Due to low collection rates, theft, infrastructure problems, and corruption, distribution losses remain high. Annual subsidies to the electricity sector amount to hundreds of millions of dollars.

The Dominican Republic is already a signatory of the Caracas Energy Accords, which facilitates the purchase of Venezuelan oil at reduced prices and also allows for extended credit in order to purchase energy supplies. As a means to ease the still growing problem of a high energy import bill, the government has initiated negotiations with other governments in the Latin American and Caribbean region. A delegation representing the Dominican government has visited Venezuela to conclude the Petrocaribe agreement. Petrocaribe is an initiative promoted by Venezuelan President Hugo Chávez designed at supplying oil at preferential rates to 13 countries in the Latin American and Caribbean region.

KEY INDICATORS — Dominican Republic

	Unit	2003	2004	2005	2006	2007
Population	m	8.71	8.79	8.53	*8.65	*8.78
Gross domestic product (GDP)	US$bn	18.56	18.67	29.09	31.72	*36.40
GDP per capita	US$	2,400	2,190	3,411	*3,667	*4,147
GDP real growth	%	-0.4	2.0	9.3	10.7	*8.5
Inflation	%	42.5	51.5	4.2	7.6	*6.1
Industrial output	% change	–	0.2	1.0	13.1	–
Agricultural output	% change	–	3.5	3.5	9.9	–
Exports (fob) (goods)	US$m	5,300.0	5,446.0	6,132.5	6,441.0	7,237.2
Imports (cif) (goods)	US$m	8,700.0	8,093.0	9,613.9	11,190.0	13,817.1
Balance of trade	US$m	-3,400.0	-2,647.0	-3,481.4	-4,749.0	-6,579.9
Current account	US$m	1,010.0	1,130.0	-422.0	-1,122.0	2,230.2
Total reserves minus gold	US$m	253.1	798.3	1,843.2	2,115.6	2,546.4
Foreign exchange	US$m	253.0	796.7	1,842.6	2,091.2	2,447.8
Exchange rate	per US$	28.85	35.15	33.75	33.75	33.37

* estimated figure

The Dominican Republic made substantial progress in overcoming its long history of political instability which has predictably given rise to the 'banana republic' epithet. The last political revolution took place in April 1965, since when governments have been systematically elected every four years, and the political climate has calmed down. None the less, Dominican Republic politics are inevitably parochial. Family and extended family networks, patronage systems, old friendships, ethnic considerations and other personal connections are exaggeratedly important; often as much as political parties, and other organisations. To comprehend Dominican politics, an understanding of these complex alliances is essential.

Risk assessment

Politics	Fair
Economy	Good
Regional stability	Good

COUNTRY PROFILE

Historical profile

The island was inhabited by a group of Arauaco Indians known as Tainos.
1492 Land was sighted by Christopher Columbus. His brother Bartolomeo founded Santo Domingo and his son Diego was the first governor of the Spanish colony, who named the island Hispaniola.
1797 Ceded to France.
1808 Regained by Spain.
1821 Gained independence.
1822–44 Ruled by Haiti.
1844 Became independent as Dominican Republic.
1916–24 US armed forces invaded and occupied the island.
1930–1961 Rafael Trujillo ruled Dominican Republic directly as dictator between 1930–47 and indirectly until 1961 – through his brother and then close colleagues.
1962 Democratic election of Juan Bosch in the first free election for 38 years.
1963 Juan Bosch was deposed in a military coup.
1965 Civil revolt caused another intervention of the US armed forces.
1966 The presidential election was won by Joaquín Balaguer (a president during the Trujillo era) of the Partido Reformista Social Cristiana (PRSC) (Social Christian Reform Party). Balaguer was re-elected in 1970 and 1974, during which period he survived several coup attempts.
1978 Silvestre Antonio Guzmán of the Partido Revolucionario Dominicano (PRD) (Dominican Revolutionary Party) defeated Balaguer in the presidential election – the first time an elected president yielded power to an elected successor.
1994 The consitution was established, setting out the duties and powers of the president.
1996 Leonel Fernández Reyana of the Partido de la Liberación Dominicana (PLD) (Dominican Liberation Party) narrowly won the presidential election.
1998 The PRD won the majority of seats in both houses. In order to pass legislation, President Leonel Fernández had to reach agreement with the PRD.
2000 Rafael Hipólito Mejía Domínguez (PRD) won the presidential elections.
2002 The PRD won legislative elections.
2004 In January eight people died during a two-day general strike held to protest at the economic policies that included the peso's sharp devaluation, soaring inflation and persistent power cuts. The Dominican Republic acceded to the Central American Parliament in February. Leonel Fernández Reyana (PLD) won the 16 May presidential elections, and during his inaugural speech, in August, said he would promote fiscal austerity, fight corruption and support social concerns. Around 2,000 people died or were lost during severe flooding in May.
2005 On 6 September the Chamber of Deputies approved joining the Central American Free Trade Agreement (Cafta).
2008 In presidential elections, held on 16 May, the incumbent Leonel Fernández (PLD) won with 53 per cent of the vote, Miguel Vargas (PRD) 41 per cent, and Amable Aristy (PRSC) less than 5 per cent. His third term in office will begin on 16 August. In presidential elections, the incumbent, Leonel Fernández (DLP) won 53.8 per cent of the vote, Miguel Vargas (DRP) 40.5 per cent and Amable Aristy (Social Christian Reformist Party) 4.6 per cent.

Political structure

In addition to their unicameral national parliaments, El Salvador, Guatemala, Honduras, Nicaragua, Panama and Dominican Republic also return directly-elected deputies to the supranational Central American Parliament.

Constitution
The 1994 Constitution prevents the re-election of an individual as president for consecutive periods.

The executive
Executive power rests with the president, who is also head of government and commander-in-chief of the armed forces. The president is directly elected for a one-off four-year term. The cabinet is appointed and presided over by the president. The president, by constitutional decree, names the provincial governors, who are his representatives in each province.

National legislature
The legislature is the bicameral Congress. The 32-member Senate is elected for a four-year term, one member for each province plus one for the Distrito Nacional. The Senate elects the members of the judiciary.
The Chamber of Deputies (150 members) is elected under a system of proportional representation with members chosen on a provincial basis.

Last elections
16 May 2008 (presidential); 16 May 2008 (parliamentary).
Results: Presidential: Leonel Fernández (DLP) won 53.8 per cent of the vote, Miguel Vargas (DRP) 40.5 per cent, and Amable Aristy (Social Christian Reformist Party) 4.6 per cent.
Parliamentary: PRD won 41.9 per cent of the vote, 73 deputies, 29 senators; PLD 29.1 per cent, 41and two; PRSC 24.3 per cent, 36 and one.

Next elections
2012 (presidential and parliamentary)

Political parties

Ruling party
Partido Revolucionario Dominicano (PRD) (Dominican Revolutionary Party) (since 2002; re-elected May 2006)

Main opposition party
Partido de la Liberación Dominicana (PLD) (Dominican Liberation Party)

Population

8.78 million (2007)
Last census: October 2002: 8,562,541
Population density: 168 inhabitants per square km. Urban population: 66 per cent (1995—2001).
Annual growth rate: 1.5 per cent 1994–2004 (WHO 2006)

Ethnic make-up
Mixed race (73 per cent), white (16 per cent), black (11 per cent).

Religions
Roman Catholic (95 per cent). There is also a small Protestant community.

Education

Primary education lasts for six years and is free of charge. There are two systems of secondary education in operation, the traditional has six years of study divided into two-year then four-year cycles. The reform system has two cycles of three years. The emphasis of the former is academic and the latter scientific/technical. Both systems allow for specialised studies.
Secondary schooling is subsidised in private schools.
Literacy rate: 84 per cent adult rate; 92 per cent youth rate (15–24) (Unesco 2005).
Compulsory years: Seven to 17
Pupils per teacher: 28 in primary schools.

Health
Per capita total expenditure on health (2003) was US$335; of which per capita government spending was US$111, at the international dollar rate, (WHO 2006).
Seventy-nine per cent of the population have access to an improved water source.
HIV/Aids
The HIV/Aids infection rates is one of the largest in the Caribbean.
HIV prevalence: 1.7 per cent aged 15–49 in 2003 (World Bank)
Life expectancy: 67 years, 2004 (WHO 2006)
Fertility rate/Maternal mortality rate: 2.7 births per woman, 2004 (WHO 2006)
Birth rate/Death rate: 24 births per 1,000 population; seven deaths per 1,000 population (2003).
Child (under 5 years) mortality rate (per 1,000): 29 per 1,000 live births (World Bank)

Main cities
Santo Domingo de Guzmán (capital, estimated population 2.2 million in 2004), Santiago de los Caballeros (501,800), La Romana (198,0000), San Pedro de Macoris (167,100), Puerto Plata (133,400), San Francisco de Macoris (131,300), San Cristobal (121,800).

Languages spoken
English is widely spoken.
Official language/s
Spanish

Media
Press freedom is guaranteed by law although some contentious matters are generally avoided, such as the army and Roman Catholic Church.
Press
Dailies: In Spanish, there are several national and regional newspapers including El Caribe (www.elcaribecdn.com), Hoy (www.hoy.com.do), Listín Diario (www.listin.com.do), Diario Libre (www3.diariolibre.com) La Información (www.lainformacionrd.net), El Día (www.eldia.com.do), Nuevo elDiario (www.elnuevodiario.com.do) and El Observador Cibaeño (www.observador.tk) from Santiago de los Caballeros. An evening newspaper is El Nacional (www.elnacional.com.do).
In English, from the northern coast, Dominican Today (www.dominicantoday.com), Gringo News (www.gringo-times.com) is a humours publication and The Adscene (www.theadscene.com) is also in Spanish and German.
Weeklies: In Spanish (A)Hora (www.ahora.com.do), covers general interest news.
Periodicals: In English the monthly The Puerto Plata Report (www.popreport.com), is a regional magazine from the northern coast.
Broadcasting
The national government-owned broadcaster is Corporación Estatal de Radio y Televisión (CERTV).
Commercial broadcasting companies are generally owned by a few either economically or politically powerful entities.
Radio: There are over 200 FM radio stations. CERTV (www.certvdominicana.com) operates three stations, Dominicana FM, Quisqueya FM and 620 AM. Commercial stations include LA91 FM (www.la91fm.com), Super Mix (CDN) (www.elcaribecdn.com.do), La Nueva 106.9 FM (www.lanueva106fm.com) and Radio Moca (http://cima100fm.com).
Television: The national public broadcaster is CERTV (www.certvdominicana.com), which operates Canal 4. There are many cable and satellite services including the government-run, commercial Antena Latina (http://antenalatina.antena-sin.com) Canal 7. Private stations include Hola Gente (www.holagente.com.do), Color Vision (www.colorvision.com.do), Telemicro (www.telemicro.com.do), Cadena de Noticias (CDN) (www.elcaribecdn.com) news TV, Aster TV (www.aster.com.do) for children, Telesistema (www.telesistema11.tv) and Teleantilles (www.tele-antillas.tv).
Advertising
All forms of media accept advertising, which is widely distributed.

Economy
The economic situation had deteriorated badly in 2003 with the collapse of Banco Intercontinental (Baninter) and two smaller banks, leading to a currency devaluation, along with a rapid increase in public debt and inflation. The Central Bank guaranteed 100 per cent of deposits in the three failed banks, which tripled the national debt from around 18 per cent of GDP to over 50 per cent; short-term, high-interest loans were taken out to cover the cost. A nationwide energy crisis, due to a surge in demand and non-payment of bills, resulted in periodic blackouts, adding to the crisis. An IMF restructuring package was agreed and austerity measures implemented. As a result, the economy has bounced back, with GDP in 2005 growing by 9 per cent. Growing domestic consumption and an expanding export sector contributed to the revival.
In July 2005, the Dominican Republic signed the Central American Free Trade Accord (DR-Cafta), under which tariffs and barriers to trade with other members will be removed over a 20-year period. The Dominican Republic is keen to supply goods to the US market, although in return the US will have unlimited access to Dominican markets for goods and services.
Remittances from expatriate workers make an essential contribution to the economy, accounting for around 10 per cent of GDP. One and a half million Dominicans live abroad, mostly in the US but increasingly in Europe. The Inter-American Development Bank estimated that in 2006 migrant workers sent some US$2,900 million to their families in the Dominican Republic.
The administration has addressed the fallout but with rising oil prices and the poor peso exchange rate the problems can still be exacerbated. It has been estimated that the 2005 oil bill was around US$2.4 billion.

External trade
The Dominican Republic is the only Caribbean member of the Central America Free Trade Agreement (DR-Cafta), which includes Costa Rica, El Salvador, Guatemala, Honduras and the US; it is working to remove all tariffs and barriers between members by 2024.
The Dominican Republic also has an FTA with the 15-member Caribbean Community Common Market (Caricom).
There are a number of free trade zones (FTZ) which manufacture clothes and footwear, leather goods and jewellery, electronic and medical products, pharmaceuticals and tobacco for export.
Textile and garment manufacturing exports have fallen since the loss of quotas under the Multi-Fibre Arrangement with the US, required by a ruling of the WTO in 2006. However, as a member of the DR-Cafta a rise in exports of other FTZ products are expected to offset the loss.
Imports
Foodstuffs, petroleum, industrial raw materials, cotton and fabrics, chemicals and pharmaceuticals, consumer goods and foodstuffs.
Main sources: US (50.2 per cent total, 2005), Colombia (6.2 per cent), Mexico (5.8 per cent)
Exports
Ferro-nickel, sugar, gold, silver, coffee, cocoa, tobacco, meats and consumer goods.
Main destinations: US (79.0 per cent total, 2005), The Netherlands (2.8 per cent), Mexico (1.9 per cent)

Agriculture
Farming
The agricultural sector employs 50 per cent of the workforce, produces two-thirds of all exports and contributes 25 per cent of GDP.

The principal commercial crop is sugar cane, production of which has fluctuated due to vagaries of weather, falling export demand and labour shortages.
The main agricultural exports – sugar, coffee, cocoa and tobacco – account for just under a half of the country's export earnings. Rice, vegetables and citrus fruits are grown for home consumption.
Cattle-raising has expanded considerably and commercial fishing is being developed.
Estimates of cultivated arable land vary between 18–25 per cent; pasture 17–30 per cent; woodland/forest 25–40 per cent. Soil is generally fertile and rainfall/water availability is adequate.
Agriculture is becoming more commercialised. The country benefits from agreements that provide it with duty free access to the US markets. These include the Generalised System of Preferences, the US Caribbean Basin Initiative.
Estimated crop production in 2005 included: 4,950,000 tonnes (t) sugar cane, 607,500t cereals in total, 566,000t rice, 175,000t tomatoes, 140,000t avocados, 28,000t sweet potatoes, 18,000t yams, 500,000t bananas, 195,000t plantains, 95,000t cassava, 40,000t potatoes, 32,000t chillies and peppers, 86,000t citrus fruit, 32,000t cocoa beans, 180,000t coconuts, 170,000t mangoes, 60,000t green coffee, 12,000t tobacco leaves, 55,520t oilcrops, 165,000t oil palm fruit, 1,500t ginger, 1,251,160t fruit in total, 390,720t vegetables in total. Livestock production included: 330,080t meat in total, 78,000t beef, 66,000t pig meat, 1,080t lamb and goat meat, 185,000t poultry, 61,700t eggs, 690,000t milk, 2,000t honey.

Industry and manufacturing

The industrial sector contributes around a third of GDP and employs up to a quarter of the workforce.
Activity is centred on sugar refining (which is the dominant industry), cement production, the processing of foodstuffs, tobacco, beverages and textiles. The country is the largest exporter in the Caribbean region of apparel to the US. Some of the best known labels are manufactured in the Dominican Republic. The Caribbean Basin Initiative allows the country's textiles duty-free entry to the US market. However, with China now a member of the WTO this trade is threatened.
Other light industries include plastics, rubber, chemicals and paper.
The emphasis is on encouraging joint ventures that utilise a high percentage of local materials, expanding facilities at the main industrial free zones (La Ramona, San Pedro de Macoris, Santiago) and overcoming the serious supply/energy problems. The free trade zone programme is the country's leading earner of foreign exchange.

Tourism

Tourism is the second-largest source of foreign exchange earnings, providing over 22.9 per cent of GDP and employing about 696,000. Government spending has included the refurbishment of tourist facilities.

Mining

The mining sector as a whole typically accounts for 2 per cent of GDP and employs 3 per cent of the workforce.
Gold, silver and ferro-nickel are all mined in significant quantities. Gypsum, limestone and marble are mined for the domestic market. Deposits of copper, iron, titanium and platinum also exist.
In March 2003, Canada-based Placer Dome was given ownership of the Pueblo Viejo gold mine for 25 years, following a vote in the Senate. The mine, which has reserves of 15–30 million troy ounces, is set to see around US$350 million of investment between 2003–08.
The country's largest mining facility is operated by Falconbridge, a Canadian company, which exports 33,000 tonnes of nickel per year.
Some industry analysts believe that large deposits of nickel, copper and gold have yet to be discovered.

Hydrocarbons

Small deposits of oil are located at Charco Largo. However the Dominican Republic is heavily reliant on the import of petroleum products. Under the San José pact refined and unrefined oil from Mexico and Venezuela are imported under favourable terms. There are two oil refineries with a capacity of 48,300 barrels per day. Crude oil imports fill this capacity.
The Dominican Republic does not produce natural gas but imports liquefied natural gas from Trinidad and Tobago for power generation.
No coal is produced.

Energy

There is a heavy dependence on imported oil, most of which is used to generate electricity. Although power blackouts had become less common since the privatisation of the electricity sector in 1999, in 2003/04, the country's financial troubles led to many blackouts, sometimes lasting 20 hours. It was determined that price controls, high incidences of electricity theft and low collection rates contributed to the widespread distruption. Businesses have said that the high cost and poor provision of electricity has increased costs and lowered international competitiveness.

Financial markets

Stock exchange

The Bolsa de Valores de Santo Domingo (BVSD), the Dominican Republic's stock exchange, dates from 1991.

Banking and insurance

The foreign investment law of 1997 permits overseas banks to operate banks in the Dominican Republic.
The banking sector hit a crisis in 2003 when the Banco Intercontinental (Baninter) collapsed as a result of massive fraud.
The Women's Development bank (Banmujer) began operations in 2001, lending small loans of around US$1,000 to women for entrepreneurial ventures.

Central bank

Banco Central de la República Dominicana.

Main financial centre

Santo Domingo.

Time

GMT minus four hours

Geography

The Caribbean island of Hispaniola is divided north/south into the Dominican Republic in the east, occupying around 65 per cent of the land, and Haiti in the west.
The closest other islands are Jamaica in the south-west, Cuba in the west, the Turks and Caicos in the north and Puerto Rico in the east.
In the centre of the island the Cordillera Central is the tallest mountain range with peaks over 3,000 metres. Lake Enriquillo, the largest lake and lowest spot, is located in the south-west.

Hemisphere

Northern

Climate

Tropical with temperatures ranging from 27 degrees Celsius (C) during the dry season (November–April) to 37 degrees C from June–October when humidity is highest.

Entry requirements

Passports

Required by all. The exception is nationals of US and Canada, who may travel with proof of citizenship including photo ID, birth certificate or driving licence and after purchasing a tourist card (US$10). All US and Canadian nationals require a passport for re-entry to their country from January 2007.
All passports must have twice as much time left of validity as the length of stay in the Dominican Republic.

Visa

Required by all. Some exceptions can be found at www.dr1.com/travel/prepare/documentation.shtml; a list of nationals that may enter with a tourist card is also given.

Business visitors and visitors from countries that may not use a tourist card should contact the nearest Dominican Republic consulate.

Currency advice/regulations

The import and export of local currency is prohibited. Only a limited number of foreign currencies may be exchanged in the Dominican Republic. While the accepted currencies include the euro, the Canadian dollar, and pound sterling, the US offers the maximum exchange rate. On departure up to 30 per cent of exchanged currency can be reconverted, in US dollars only, on presentation of official exchange reciepts.

Import of foreign currency must be declared and export cannot exceed the imported amount. Travellers cheques, in US dollars, are accepted in most locations. ATMs, dispensing the Dominican Republic peso only, are found in city and tourist centres.

Customs

Prohibited imports

Illegal drugs, weapons, plants and vegetables and pornographic material.

Health (for visitors)

Mandatory precautions

Yellow fever certificate if travelling from an infected area.

Advisable precautions

Vaccinations for meningitis, typhoid, diphtheria polio and TB; other lesser risks include hepatitis A and B and dengue fever. Bilharzia is endemic; use only well chlorinated and maintained swimming pools. Malaria precautions are recommended. Rabies is a risk.

Water precautions are essential; use only bottled or boiled water. Eat only well cooked meals, preferably served hot. Pork, salad and mayonnaise may carry increased risk. Vegetables should be cooked and fruit peeled.

Health insurance (to include emergency medical repatriation) is strongly recommended, as medical care is limited and variable in quality. All personal medication should be carried, with their prescription.

Hotels

Following intensive tourist development, there are a full range of hotels available. Tourist locations charge more than city hotels and in general hotels are considerably more expensive during the winter. Bills usually include 12 per cent government tax and 10 per cent service charge.

Public holidays (national)

Fixed dates

1 Jan (New Year's Day), 6 Jan (Epiphany), 21 Jan (Our Lady of Altagracia), 26 Jan (Duarte's Birthday), 27 Feb (Independence Day), 1 May (Labour Day), 16 Jul (Restoration Day), ^24 Sep (Our Lady of las Mercedes), 6 Nov (Constitution Day), 25 Dec (Christmas Day).

^ Businesses may take Mondays in lieu.

Variable dates

Good Friday (Mar/Apr), Corpus Christi (May/Jun).

Working hours

Banking

Mon–Fri: 0830–1700.

Business

Mon–Fri: 0800–1200, 1400–1800.

Government

Mon–Fri: 0800–1500.

Telecommunications

Mobile/cell phones

There are 1800/1900 GSM services available in most urban areas.

Electricity supply

110–120V AC, 60 cycles.

Weights and measures

The metric system has been adopted. However, certain other units are still in use, eg ounces and pounds are used in weighing solids, petrol and motor oils are measured in imperial gallons, cooking oil is retailed in pounds and fabrics are measured by the yard. Land surfaces in rural areas are generally measured by tarea – equal to 624 square metres.

Getting there

Air

International airport/s: Santo Domingo-Las Américas (SDQ), 30km east of city, duty-free shop, bar, restaurant, bank, post office, shops, hotel reservations, car hire; Gregorio Luperon International Puerto Plata (POP), 18km from city, bank, duty-free shop, restaurant, bar, car hire.

Airport tax: International departures US$10, excluding transit passengers.

Surface

Road: The main route runs from Haiti via Elias Pina.

Main port/s: There are 14 ports, including Santo Domingo (the largest) and Haina.

Getting about

National transport

Air: There are flights between Santo Domingo, Santiago, Samana, Punta Cana and Puerto Plata. These are provided by Bavaro Sun Flight, Aerolineas Santo Domingo and Dorado Air.

Road: There are about 17,120km of roads. Highways link Santo Domingo-Hinguey, Montecristo, Dajabon, San Juan, Elias Pina. There is a direct route from Santo Domingo to Port-au-Prince in Haiti.

Buses: There are bus stations in all towns. Fairly numerous services from Santo Domingo to Puerto Plata, La Romana – journey times vary. Also to Barahona and Samana.

Rail: There are a number of freight-only railways.

City transport

Taxis: In Santo Domingo taxis are freely available in the main business districts. These are not metered and it is advisable to agree the price with the driver before setting out. Taxis which travel off these routes may be difficult to find, especially at night. No tip is expected.

Buses, trams & metro: Buses in Santo Domingo are cheap, though crowded.

Car hire

National or international licence required. Chauffeur-driven cars can be negotiated with taxi drivers outside main hotels. Car hire facilities are good, but fairly expensive.

BUSINESS DIRECTORY

The addresses listed below are a selection only. While World of Information makes every endeavour to check these addresses, we cannot guarantee that changes have not been made, especially to telephone numbers and area codes. We would welcome any corrections.

Telephone area codes

This international direct dialling code (IDD) for the Dominican Republic is +1 809 followed by subscriber's number.

Useful telephone numbers

Santo Domingo

Emergency (Ambulance, Police):	911
Police:	682-3151
Police (radio patrol):	533-1074
Centro Médico Nacional (hospital):	682-0171
Fire Department:	682-2000
Red Cross:	682-4545

Chambers of Commerce

American Chamber of Commerce of the Dominican Republic, Avenida Sarasota 20, Torre Empresarial, PO Box 95-2, Santo Domingo (Tel: 381-0777; fax: 381-0286; e-mail: amcham@codetel.net.do).

British Chamber of Commerce of the Dominican Republic, Avenida San Martin 253, Edificio Santanita, PO Box 718-2, Santo Domingo (tel: 616-2335; fax: 616-2336; e-mail: britcham@tricom.net).

Santiago Cámara de Comercio y Producción, Avenida Las Carreras 7, Edificio Empresarial, Santiago (tel: 582-2856; fax: 241-4546; e-mail: csantiago@camarasantiago.com).

Santo Domingo Cámara de Comercio y Producción, Calle Arzobispo Nouel 206, PO Box 815, Santo Domingo (tel: 682-2688; fax: 685-2228; e-mail: camara.sto.dgo@codetel.net.do).

Banking

Banco BHD, Ave 27 de Febrero esq, Winston Churchill, Santo Domingo DN (tel: 243-3232; fax: 541-4949).

Banco del Exterior Dominicano, Ave Abraham Lincoln No. 756, Piantini, Santo Domingo (tel: 565-5540; fax: 565-5547).

Banco de los Trabajadores De La República Dominicana, Av México Esq Calle Altagracia, Santo Domingo (tel: 682-0171; fax: 685-6536).

Banco de Reservas de la República Dominica, Isabel La Catolica No. 72, Santo Domingo (tel: 688-2241; fax: 685-0602).

Banco Dominicano del Progreso, Ave John F Kennedy No. 3, Miraflores, Santo Domingo (tel: 563-3233; fax: 563-2451).

Banco Gerencial y Fiduciario Dominicano, Ave 27 de Febrero No 50, El Vergel, Santo Domingo (tel: 541-9400; fax: 567-6747).

Banco Latinoamericano, Gustavo Mejía Ricart Esq Agustín Lara, Ens Piantini, Santo Domingo (tel: 562-2662; fax: 562-1915).

Banco Mercantil, Ave Bolivar No. 308 Esq Jose Joaquín Pérez Gazcue, Santo Domingo (tel: 221-7151; 688-0608).

Banco Metropolitano, Ave Lope de Vega Esq Gustavo Mejía Ricart, Edif. Goico Castro, Ens Naco, Santo Domingo (tel: 562-4242; fax: 540-1566).

Banco Nacional de Crédito, John F Kennedy Esq Tiradentes, Ens Naco, Santo Domingo (tel: 540-4441; fax: 567-4698).

Banco Popular Dominicano, Av. John F Kennedy No 20 Esq Máximo Gómez, Torre Popular, 11 Avo. Piso, Santo Domingo (tel: 544-5900; fax: 544-5999).

Bank of Nova Scotia, Ave. John F Kennedy Esq Lope de Vega, Ens Naco, Santo Domingo (tel: 544-1700; fax: 542-6302).

Citibank, Ave John F Kennedy No 1 Esq San Martín, Santo Domingo (tel: 566-5611; fax: 567-2255).

Central bank

Banco Central de la República Dominicana, PO Box: 1347, Calle Pedro Henríquez Ureña, Esq Leopoldo Navarro, Santo Domingo (tel: 221-9111; fax: 686-7488; e-mail: info@bancentral.gov.do).

Travel information

Aerolíneas Argo, Avenida 27 de Febrero 409, Santo Domingo (tel: 566-1844).

Dominicana de Aviación, Leopoldo Navarre, Edificio San Rafael, PO Box 1415, Santo Domingo (tel: 687-7111).

Santo Domingo-Las Américas International Airport, Santo Domingo (tel: 549-0450/0480).

Ministry of tourism

Secretaría de Estado de Turismo, PO Apdo 497, Avenida México esp, 30 de Marzo, Ofiinas Gubernanentales Bloque B, Santo Domingo (tel: 221-4660; e-mail: dominicantourism@globalserve.net).

Other useful addresses

Asociación Dominicana de Empresas de Inversión Extranjera (ASIEX), Av Independencia Santo Domingo, RD (tel: 535-6165; fax: 535-1744).

Asociación Dominicana de Exportadores (ADOEXPO), Av W Churchill 5, Santo Domingo (tel: 532-6779; fax: 533-9734).

Asociación Dominicana de Zonas Francas (ADOZONA), Gustavo Mejía Ricart 72, Santo Domingo, RD (tel: 566-0230, 566-0437).

British Embassy, Floor 7, Edificio Corominas Pepín, Avenida 27 de Febrero No. 233, Santo Domingo (tel: 472-7111; fax: 427-7574).

Centro Dominicano de Promoción de Exportaciones (CEDOPEX), Av 27 de Febrero, Plaza de la Independencia, Santo Domingo, RD (tel: 530-5549; fax: 530-8208).

Consejo Nacional de Zonas Francas de Exportación, Leopoldo Navarro 61, Edif San Rafael 5ta Planta, Santo Domingo (tel: 686-8077; fax: 686-8079).

Corporación de Fomento Industrial, Av 27 de Febrero, Plaza de la Independencia, Santo Domingo, RD (tel: 530-1686; fax: 530-1303).

ITT-America Cables and Radio Inc, Julio Verne 21, Santo Domingo (tel: 682-3115).

Public Enterprise Reform Committee, Gustavo Mejía Ricart No 73, Santo Domingo (tel: 683-3591; fax: 683-3964).

RCA Global Communications Inc, Edificio Diez, Calle Conde 203, Santo Domingo (tel: 682-3722).

Secretariat of State for Finance, Avda México, Santo Domingo, DN.

Secretariat of State for Industry and Commerce, Edif. de Oficinas Gubernamentales 7, Avda México, Santo Domingo, DN (tel: 685-171).

Other news agencies: Caribbean Net News: www.caribbeannetnews.com
Prensa Latina: www.prensalatina.com.mx

Internet sites

Dominican Republic One: www.dr1.com/

Export promotion (in Spanish): www.cedopex.gov.do/

Easter Island

KEY FACTS

Official name: Isla de Pascua (Easter Island) (Rapa Nui)

Head of State: President of Chile: Verónica Michelle Bachelet Jeria; represented by Intendenta Melania Carolina Hotu Hey (from 2006)

Head of government: Mayor Pedro Pablo Edmunds Paoa (since 1996)

Area: 180 square km

Population: 3,800 (2007)

Capital: Hanga Roa (only inhabited township)

Official language: Spanish

Currency: Chilean peso (CH$) = 100 centavos

Exchange rate: CH$539.90 per US$ (Jan 2007)

Visitor numbers: 15,000 (annually)*

* estimated figure

COUNTRY PROFILE

Historical profile

1680 Work on the moai ceased due to tribal wars induced by overpopulation and famine.
1722 The Dutch navigator, Jacob Roggeveen, came to the Island on Easter Sunday, hence its name.
1770 Spaniards came from Peru and named the island San Carlos.
1774 Captain Cook visited the island.
1862–63 More than 1,000 islanders were kidnapped and despatched to Peru to work on the guano islands and plantations. Only 15 survived to be repatriated, but some were carrying infectious diseases which quickly decimated the population.
1866 Catholic missionaries converted the remaining population to Christianity.
1871 Conflict between the missionaries and a French settler, who had established a sheep farm, forced the missionaries to leave with around 100 followers. Around 110 natives remained on the island.
1888 The island was annexed by Chile.
1966 The international airport opened and Chile declared the island a province.
1986 The airport runway was extended for use as an emergency landing strip for the US Nasa space shuttle.
1996 Easter Island was declared a World Heritage Site by Unesco.
2002 The first outbreak of dengue fever in Chile occurred on Easter Island.
2003 Unesco awarded a German company a contract for US$11.5 million to restore the stone moai. Work was completed in 2005.
2008 Forest fires in January were contained in time to prevent damage to homes, the airport and the island's satellite antenna. A Finnish visitor was arrested for damaging an ancient monument when he chipped off a piece of a moai, while wishing to find how hard the stone was. He was later made to make a public apology, pay a fine of US$17,000 and was banned from the island until 2011.

Political structure

Easter Island is administered as a province of Chile (part of the Valparaíso region), with a governor and locally elected council.

Elections are held every four years for six councillors, who then elect the mayor.

A Council of Elders was formed in 1983 to represent the interests of the native Rapa Nuis (Easter Islanders).

Form of state

Province of Chile

Political parties

Island politicians belong to a number of national political parties including Partido Demócrata Cristiano (PDC) (Christian Democratic Party), Partido Humanista (PH) (Humanist Party), Unión Demócrata Independiente (UDI) (Independent Democratic Union) and the Partido por la Democracia (PLD) (Democratic Party)

Political situation

There is a budding independence movement. Objections from locals concerning the immigration of Chileans has grown. The mayor, Pedro Pablo Edmunds Paoa threatened the central government saying that the island would declare unilateral independence after a plan to launch a casino on the island was proposed but without reference to the islanders. He has also claimed that Easter Island should be its own province to allow for investment and a better administration of the island and its culture but the legislation to grant this has been stalled in the upper house of the Chilean parliament since 2007.

Population

3,800 (2007)

Last census: 2002: 3,791

Annual growth rate: 0.0 per cent (2003)

Religions

Christianity

Main cities

Hanga Roa is the only inhabited township.

Languages spoken

Rapa Nui, an Eastern Polynesian language, is spoken. English is not used.

Official language/s

Spanish

Media

Press

News publications are pamphlets and internet connections, such as Te Rapa Nui (www.rapanui.co.cl). Newspapers from the mainland have to be flown in and may be days old. The bi-annual (May and October) Rapa Nui Journal (www.islandheritage.org) is an academic publication.

Broadcasting
Radio: There are several radio stations, broadcasting in Spanish, including the (Chilean) government-run Radio Cooperativa (www.cooperativa.cl), the private Radio Activa (www.radioactiva.cl) from Santiago, ADN Radio (www.adnradio.cl) and Armada de Chile broadcasts to military personnel. Radio Manukena is a community radio station broadcasting in the local language.
Television: Satellite television is broadcast from Chile (TV Chile: www.tvchile.cl) with reception available on the island.

Economy
Tourism is the principal industry. There are a number of hotels and guesthouses catering for visitors interested in archaeological and activity pursuits. The Rapa Nui National Park and open museum encompasses almost the entire island and is run by the inhabitants. Flights link the island with Santiago, Chile, and French Polynesia.
Fishing and commerce also provide income.

External trade
As a province of Chile, all international trade agreements are negotiated by the government in Santiago.
Imports
Main imports are food, fuel, construction materials and machinery from Chile.
Exports
Main exports are tuna, avocados and pineapples to Chile.

Agriculture
Traditional subsistence farming is carried out.
Although the island is predominantly grassland, pine, eucalyptus and fruit trees have been planted.
The island's main crops are bananas, pineapples, sweet potatoes, yams, sugar cane, maize, potatoes, tomatoes, castor beans, melons, grapes and avocados.
Sheep farming has declined rapidly since the mid-twentieth century due to soil erosion. There are wild horses in addition to those used as draught animals and for riding. Poultry bred on the island includes pigeons, quail and ducks.
Lobster, tuna and king fish are an important local source of protein.

Industry and manufacturing
There is a small manufacturing sector, based on the production of local handicrafts.

Tourism
Famous for its giant stone moai (statues), Easter Island is visited by around 40,000 tourists each year. Nearly a thousand of these ancient statues are strewn along its beautiful coastline and extinct volcano. There are also opportunities for hiking, horse-riding, cycling and swimming.

Banking and insurance
Central bank
Banco del Estado de Chile

Time
GMT minus six hours

Geography
Easter Island is a small volcanic rock, measuring 166 sq km, in the southern Pacific Ocean. It lies about 3,500km off the coast of Chile, the closest land mass. The nearest inhabited island (Pitcairn) is about 1,600km to the west. The island is roughly triangular in shape, with a rugged coastline and few beaches. Inland are low rolling hills and grasslands. There is no flowing water; volcanic craters round the edge of the island hold standing water.
Hemisphere
Southern

Climate
Subtropical, cooled by constant winds. Average rainfall is 1,250mm falling mainly in June–July; average temperature ranges from 16–27 degrees Celsius.

Entry requirements
Passports
Required by all, with the exception of tourists travelling from Argentina, Brazil, Colombia, Paraguay and Uruguay, for whom national identity cards are sufficient. Entry will be permitted only with proof of return/onward passage and sufficient funds for stay.
Visa
As a province of Chile, the requirements are the same. Citizens of neighbouring countries or most EU states do not need visas. For further details contact the local embassy. Business visas are not required by those citizens who do not need a tourist visa; all others, including those who do not normally require them but who are visiting on short-term contracts or receive fees from a local company, do need a visa.
On arrival a 'tourist card' is issued and must be returned when leaving. Onward/return passage is necessary.

Health (for visitors)
Mandatory precautions
Vaccination certificates are required for yellow fever if travelling from an infected area.
Advisable precautions
Vaccinations for diphtheria, tuberculosis, hepatitis A and B, polio, tetanus and typhoid are recommended. There is a risk of rabies.

Telecommunications
Telephone/fax
There is a limited telephone service available. There is no direct international dialling, although satellite links enable calls to be made through the international operator in Chile.
Internet/e-mail
There are internet bars in Hanga Roa.

Getting there
Air
National airline: Lan-Chile
International airport/s: Mataveri International (IPC), 1.6km south of Hanga Roa.
Surface
Main port/s: Hanga Roa.

Getting about
National transport
There are few surfaced roads. Four-wheel drive vehicles, motor cycles and horses are the main means of transportation. Minibuses are used by tourists.
Car hire
Make local enquiries regarding availability of car hire.

BUSINESS DIRECTORY
The addresses listed below are a selection only. While World of Information makes every endeavour to check these addresses, we cannot guarantee that changes have not been made, especially to telephone numbers and area codes. We would welcome any corrections.

Telephone area codes
The international direct dialling (IDD) code for Easter Island is +56 (Chile) followed area code 32 and Easter Island number 100 + subscriber's number.

Other useful addresses
Gobernación Provincial, Isla de Pascua (tel: 100-254)

Internet sites
Easter Island Foundation:
www.netaxs.com/~trance/rapanui.html

Ecuador

KEY FACTS

Official name: República del Ecuador (Republic of Ecuador)

Head of State: President Rafael Vicente Correa Delgado (sworn in 15 Jan 2007)

Head of government: President Rafael Correa

Ruling party: Alianza PAIS (Patria Altiva i Soberana) (Alliance Proud and Sovereign Fatherland)

Area: 270,670 square km

Population: 13.34 million (2007)*

Capital: Quito

Official language: Spanish

Currency: US dollar (US$) = 100 cents

Exchange rate: US$25,000.00 per US$ (Jul 2008)

GDP per capita: US$3,218 (2007)*

GDP real growth: 1.90% (2007)*

Labour force: 5.40 million (2004)

Unemployment: 13.70% (2007)*

Inflation: 2.20% (2005)

Oil production: 520,000 bpd (2007)

Balance of trade: US$614.00 million (2006)

Foreign debt: US$16.87 billion (2004)

Visitor numbers: 841,000 (2006)*

* estimated figure

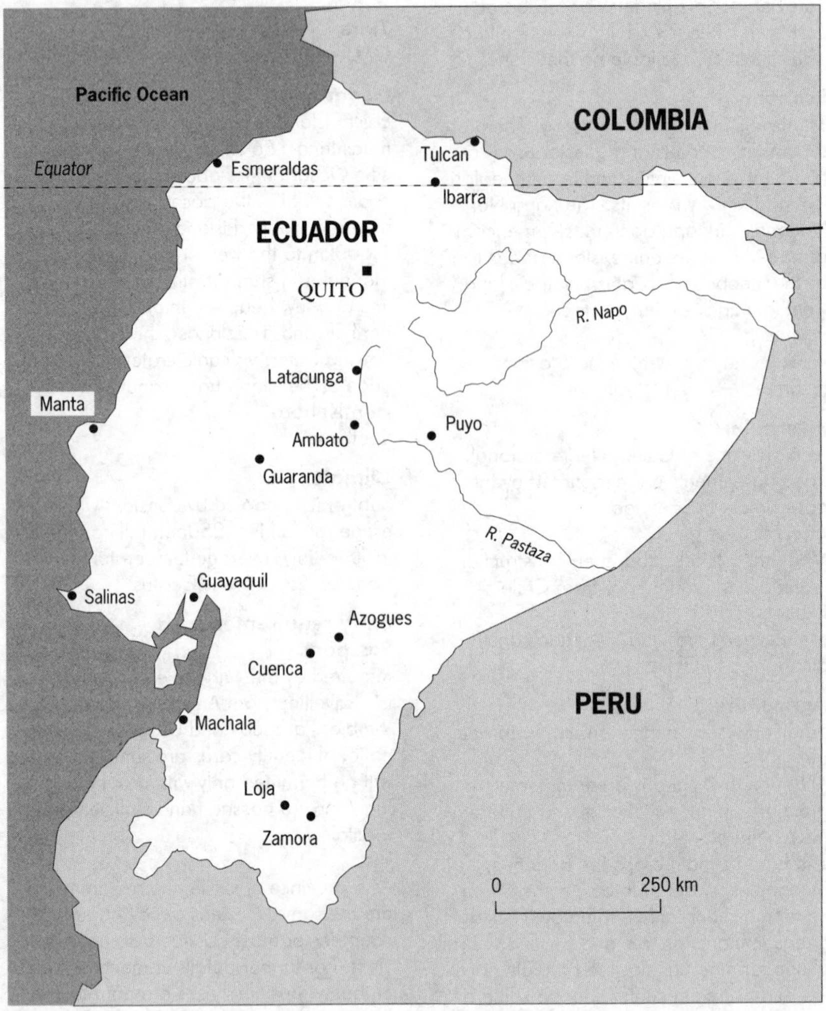

In October 2007 Ecuador's electorate gave President Rafael Correa something of a sweeping victory in the Constituent Assembly, giving a boost to his plan to rewrite Ecuador's constitution. Mr Correa's Alianza País party took around 80 of the 130 seats as Ecuador's once pivotal traditional parties were marginalised. Ultimately Mr Correa's objective was to allow the constituent assembly to replace Congress, although achieving this would involve Congress dissolving itself to give way to the constituent assembly.

Out with the old...

Since taking office in January 2007, the photogenic Rafael Correa has made the constituent assembly the focal point of his drive against the ensconced traditional parties. Held responsible for much of Ecuador's instability and corruption, Ecuador's unpopular congress has been targeted by Mr Correa. But foes vow to stop a leader they say threatens democracy by seeking to amass power. His victory in the elections to the constituent assembly also enabled Mr Correa to strengthen his political control over the Banco Central del Ecuador (central bank). The November election victory appeared to grant Mr Correa a popular mandate to bypass congress and rewrite the constitution. Concern has been expressed in both political and business circles over Mr Correa's attacks on free-market policies and apparent intention to renegotiate Ecuador's debt. Once elected, the assembly, will have to draft the proposed constitutional reforms. The final version will be approved in a popular referendum. Mr Correa's enthusiasm for the assembly has been tempered by clashes with congress as opposition politicians sought to thwart his proposals.

Claiming that his supporters had achieved 'a historic victory' Mr Correa announced that 'We accept this triumph with great humility and total responsibility. We know we cannot fail', he said. Mr Correa's opponents have accused him of seeking to concentrate power and note he proposes letting presidents serve two consecutive four-year terms instead of the one previously allowed. Mr Correa has denied that he plans to maintain himself in power indefinitely. He has however claimed that the assembly will pave the way for socialism. Whatever Mr Correa's enthusiasm, opposition leader Gilmar Gutierrez, however, initially refused to accept defeat, saying he was waiting for the official results. The assembly has six months in which to prepare a final draft of the new constitution and present it to voters in a referendum.

...but keep the economy strong

In the first half of 2007, according to the United Nations Economic Commission for Latin America and the Caribbean (ECLAC), Ecuador's GDP increased by 1.3 per cent, and was projected to reach 2.7 per cent for the whole year. This was well down on the 3.9 per cent recorded in 2006.

The economy's slowdown was attributed to a decline in the mining and quarrying sector, which dropped 5.3 per cent in the first half of the year linked to a decrease in oil production and to a weakness in the construction sector which also saw a 4.2 per cent drop in activity. Domestic production fared better, especially the manufacturing and services sectors. In contrast to 2006, exports also slowed down, by 1.0 per cent. This caused the balance of payments surplus to drop from US$1.04 billion for the first half of 2006 to US$101.7 million for the same period of 2007. Non-oil exports' growth slowed down, but remained strong

Often flying in the face of expectations, Ecuador's overall macroeconomic performance has been strong, supported by favourable global conditions. According to the International Monetary Fund (IMF) the drop in growth levels registered in 2007 was largely attributed to a decline in oil output from long-standing underinvestment and a fall in non-oil growth. By regional standards, Ecuador's inflation remained low at an annual rate of 2.4 per cent for 2007.

The higher global oil prices enabled Ecuador's external and fiscal positions to remain healthy. The IMF noted that the 2007 external current account surplus was estimated to have been unchanged from the previous year. In the financial sector, banking system soundness indicators remained generally positive. Deposits and credit to the private sector continued to grow but at a slower pace than in 2006. After spiking at the beginning of the year on concerns over the authorities' debt service policies, Ecuador's sovereign spread (EMBI) declined significantly, but still remained the highest in the region.

Oil

The US Energy Information Administration (EIA) reported that in 2007 Ecuador re-joined the Organisation of the Petroleum Exporting Countries (OPEC), after leaving the organisation at the end of 1992. Ecuador is the smallest oil producer in OPEC, with an assigned production quota of 520,000 barrels per day (bpd) (April 2008). Since Ecuador is currently producing below its quota level, it is unclear what effect OPEC membership will have on its oil production levels.

Although a smaller producer, Ecuador is one of Latin America's largest crude oil exporters, with net oil exports estimated at 350,000bpd in 2006. The oil sector dominates the Ecuadorian economy, accounting for almost half of total export earnings and one-third of all tax revenues. Despite its large oil exports, Ecuador still needs to import refined petroleum products due to a lack of refining capacity. This means that Ecuador does not always enjoy the full benefits of high world oil prices: while these high prices bring Ecuador greater export revenues, they also increase the country's refined product import bill.

Reserves

According to the *US Oil and Gas Journal* (OGJ) as reported by the EIA, Ecuador held proven oil reserves of 4.5 billion barrels in January 2008, the third largest in South America. Ecuador is the fifth-largest producer of oil in South America, producing 512,000bpd of oil in 2007 (almost all of which was crude oil), down from 538,000bpd in 2006.

Crude oil production has increased sizably since the opening of the Oelducto de Crudos Pesados (OCP) in September 2003. The EIA reports that in 2006, Ecuador consumed 152,000 bpd of oil, leaving

KEY INDICATORS — Ecuador

	Unit	2003	2004	2005	2006	2007
Population	m	13.08	13.18	13.22	*13.54	13.34
Gross domestic product (GDP)	US$bn	27.20	30.28	36.49	41.45	*44.18
GDP per capita	US$	2,160	2,145	2,761	*3,057	*3,218
GDP real growth	%	2.0	6.6	4.7	4.2	*1.9
Inflation	%	6.6	2.7	2.1	3.3	2.2
Unemployment	%	11.7	11.1	10.7	10.1	8.8
Industrial output	% change	–	13.8	4.0	2.0	–
Agricultural output	% change	–	0.6	2.5	4.1	–
Oil output	'000 bpd	427.0	535.0	541.0	545.0	520.0
Exports (fob) (goods)	US$m	6,038.0	7,560.0	9,824.0	12,728.0	*13,852.4
Imports (cif) (goods)	US$m	6,534.0	7,650.0	9,286.0	12,114.0	*12,591.4
Balance of trade	US$m	-496.0	-90.0	462.0	614.0	*1,261.0
Current account	US$m	-460.0	-150.0	618.0	1,503.0	*1,464.0
Total reserves minus gold	US$m	812.6	1,069.6	1,714.2	1,489.5	2,816.4
Foreign exchange	US$m	786.1	986.9	1,667.9	1,456.1	2,764.9
Exchange rate	per US$	1.00	1.00	1.00	1.00	1.00

* estimated figure

2006 net exports of 350,000 bpd. Ecuador sends over 50 per cent of its oil exports to the US, the remainder split between Latin America and Asia; in 2007, Ecuador exported 203,000 bpd of crude oil and refined products to the United States, about two per cent of US oil imports. Ecuador is the second-largest source of US crude oil imports from South America after Venezuela. Other important destinations of Ecuador's crude oil exports include Peru, Chile and Central America.

The tax structure changes

From 2001 to 2005, Petroecuador's share of national crude oil output declined from 56 per cent to 37 per cent. However, Petroecuador's share of national production jumped to 46 per cent in 2006, following the company's controversial takeover of the former production assets of Occidental Petroleum

Possibly inspired by President Chávez's moves against the oil multinationals in Venezuela, in October 2007, President Correa signed a decree establishing a 99 per cent windfall tax on oil company profits, up from the 50 per cent rate already established in 2006. This tax takes effect whenever Ecuador's oil export basket exceeds US$24 per barrel; while Ecuador's export basket trades at a substantial discount to world benchmark crude prices like WTI, it was well higher than this threshold level in 2007 and expected to remain so in the short-term. The decree offered an alternative to the higher tax levels: oil companies could agree to change their projects to service agreements, where they would produce oil on behalf of the government for a fee. However, under these deals, the companies would transfer existing investments to the government and would no longer be able to reflect (for accounting purposes) oil reserves on their balance sheets. According to media reports, oil companies were still continuing to negotiate the terms of the new policies with the Ecuadorian government in early 2008.

Gas

According to the OGJ, Ecuador had 345 billion cubic feet (bcf) of natural gas reserves in January 2006. The negligible domestic demand or support infrastructure for natural gas renders it an under-utilised resource. The only large-scale natural gas project in Ecuador is the Amistad field, located in the Gulf of Guayaquil, which produced an estimated 30 million cubic feet per day (mcf/d) during the first half of 2007. All of Amistad's natural gas production flows to Noble's Machala facility, a 130 megawatt (MW), onshore, gas-fired power plant that supplies electricity to the Guayaquil region.

Ecuador's oil industry also produces a significant amount of natural gas as part of their operations: oil operators produced 118mcf/d of natural gas during the first half of 2007. However, most of that natural gas is flared, due to a lack of infrastructure to capture it. Ecuador's lack of infrastructure to develop natural gas reserves or capture associated gas production is a contributing factor to the imbalance in its refined product trade.

Farc problems

Ecuador's already cool relations with Colombia took a turn for the worse when, in March 2008, Colombian troops crossed into Ecuador in pursuit of Fuerzas Armadas Revolucionarias de Colombia (Farc) (Revolutionary Armed Forces of Colombia) (Colombia's revolutionary Marxist *guerilleros*) leaders. The Colombian mission was successful in that it resulted in the deaths of three guerrilla leaders and the capture of valuable anti-FARC intelligence. President Correa saw this as rather more – an indefensible breach of Ecuador's territorial integrity. Apparently in collusion with President Chavez, Correa mobilised troops and broke off diplomatic relations. A hastily arranged summit meeting in the Dominican Republic enabled President Uribe of Colombia to make his peace with President Correa.

Risk assessment

Regional stability	Fair/good
Economy	Good
Politics	Poor

COUNTRY PROFILE

Historical profile

1530 Ecuador formed part of the Inca Empire until its conquest by the Spaniards.
1822 Antonio José de Sucre Alcalá defeated the monarchist forces of Spain at the battle of Pichincha. Ecuador gained its independence as part of the federation of Gran Colombia.
1930 Ecuador seceded from Gran Colombia and became an independent republic.
1941 Peru invaded the mineral-rich province of El Oro.
1942 Ecuador lost about 200,000 square kilometres of the disputed land to Peru.
1960s and 1970s A series of elected and appointed presidents (usually by the armed forces) ruled Ecuador. Few saw out their full terms of office.
1972 Ecuador became a significant oil producer.
1978 A new constitution was approved, which provided for presidential elections.
1979 Jaime Roldós became president. Democratisation was encouraged and supported by US policy.
1981 Roldós was killed. Oswaldo Hurtado became president.
1984 President Febres Cordero introduced free-market economy measures. An earthquake destroyed a long length of Ecuador's only oil pipeline.
1992 Sixto Durán Ballén became president. Ecuador resigned its membership of the Organisation of Petroleum Exporting Countries (Opec) to increase production.
1997 President Abdala Bucarem was removed from office; he was accused of corruption and mental incompetence. Fabian Alarcón, became interim president. Popular protests called for a national assembly and new constitution.
1998 A new constitution was inaugurated. Jamil Mahuad Witt became president.
2000 The economy was in recession and inflation ran at almost 60 per cent. Mahuad was ousted during widespread protests. Vice President Gustavo Noboa assumed the presidency. The US dollar was formally adopted as Ecuador's currency.
2002 Colonel Lucio Gutiérrez became president. Indigenous peoples protested against the oil companies bringing production to a halt, demanding that more revenue be spent on their communities.
2003 Former president Noboa escaped to Dominican Republic to avoid corruption charges.
2004 Hundreds of people were held hostage in several prisons around the country as prisoners demanded better conditions and the release of prisoners whose remission was overdue. The Congress dismissed and replaced most members of the Supreme Court. Gutiérrez accused the former court of bias in favour of the opposition.
2005 Congress voted (60–2) to remove President Gutiérrez; Vice President Alfredo Palacio was sworn in as interim president. A state of emergency was declared in two provinces after protestors brought oil production to a halt. Former president Lucio Gutierrez was arrested on conspiracy charges following his return from exile in Colombia.
2006 The parliamentary elections were won by the Partido Renovador Institucional de Acción Nacional (PRIAN) (Institutional Renewal Party of National Action) with 28 of the 100 seats in the national congress. In the first round of the presidential election, Álvaro Noboa (PRIAN) won 26.8 per cent of the vote, Rafael Correa (PAIS Alianza) 22.8 per

cent, Gilmar Gutiérrez 17.5 per cent, León Roldós Aguilera 14.8 per cent and Cynthia Viteri 9.6 per cent. The run-off took place on 26 November; Correa won 57 per cent of the vote against Noboa with 43 per cent.

2007 Rafael Correa was sworn in as president on 15 January. After his inauguration he called for a Constituent Assembly to reform Congress, which he considered was corrupt and unrepresentative of the people. The Congress agreed to a referendum, although most members boycotted the vote. Later, however, Congress withdrew its support, claiming the president had changed the text of the referendum after it had been agreed. An electoral tribunal was empowered to conduct the referendum, but members were threatened with impeachment by congress. The supreme electoral court dismissed 57 Congress members on 7 March for attempting to obstruct the referendum. On 20 March, 21 substitute Congress members were sworn in, achieving the 50-plus necessary for a quorum. However, the dismissed members could also form a quorum and threatened to set up a rival congress, which could have provoked a constitutional crisis. In the referendum, held on 15 April, 81.72 per cent of the voters supported the proposition to re-write the constitution and form a Constituent Assembly (turnout was 71 per cent). Elections to the new Constituent Assembly, held on 30 September, were won by the president's political party PAIS Alianza, which will not only amend the constitution but will also present the president with a mandate to close the National Congress. The Constituent Assembly's first undertaking was to dissolve the National Congress on 29 November, although as the Congress had risen for the Christmas break, overt conflict was avoided. The Constituent Assembly was given a mandate to draft a new constitution by 26 July 2008, to replace the congress.

2008 Colombia took pre-emptive strikes against its terrorists, Fuerzas Armadas Revolucionarias de Colombia-Ejército del Pueblo (Farc) (Revolutionary Armed Forces of Colombia-Peoples' Army) hiding out in Ecuador and Venezuela, killing over a dozen including the senior Farc leader Raul Reyes. On 3 March, following the incursion, Ecuador cut diplomatic relations with Colombia, and Venezuela expelled Colombian diplomats. Diplomatic relations with Colombia were renewed in June. On 23 June, Alberto Acosta, president of the Constituent Assembly, resigned in protest at the denial for an increase in the deadline for completion of the new constitution. Acosta was replaced by Fernando Cordero on 24 June. The new draft constitution was agreed by a majority of the Constituent Assembly on 25 July. A national referendum for its ratification will be held on 28 September.

Political structure

Constitution

The deadline for a new constitution was 26 July 2008; details have yet to be published.

The 1979 constitution was amended in 1998 to strengthen the executive branch of government and abolish mid-term congressional elections and restrict the power of congress to dismiss cabinet ministers.

Ecuador comprises 24 provinces, including the Galapagos Islands, each is administered by an appointed governor.

Form of state

Presidential democratic republic

The executive

Executive power rests with the president, elected by direct vote for a four-year term. The president cannot be re-elected. The president appoints and presides over a cabinet.

National legislature

The unicameral Congreso Nacional (National Congress) consists of 100 members elected from party-lists by proportional representation, for four-year terms. Each of the country's 24 provinces returns a minimum of two deputies, plus an additional member for every 200,000 inhabitants. The 130-member Asamblea Constituyente (Constituent Assembly) dissolve the National Congress on 29 November, although as the Congress had risen for the Christmas break, overt conflict was avoided.

Legal system

The Supreme Court heads the judiciary. Its judges are appointed by Congress for four-year, renewable terms.

Last elections

15 October 2006 (National Congress and first round presidential); 26 November 2006 (presidential run-off).

30 September 2007 Asamblea Constituyente (Constituent Assembly)

Results: Parliamentary: Partido Renovador Institucional de Acción Nacional (PRIAN) (Institutional Renewal Party of National Action) won 27.7 per cent of the vote (28 of 100 seats), the Partido Sociedad Patriótica 21 de Enero (PSP) (January 21 Patriotic Society Party) 18.6 per cent (23), the Partido Social Cristiano (PSC) (Social Christian Party) 15.2 per cent (13), the Partido Izquierda Democrática (ID) Democratic Left Party-Red Etica y Democracia (Ethics and Democracy Network) (ID-RED) 10.7 per cent (13), and the Partido Roldosista Ecuatoriano (PRE) (Ecuadorian Roldosist Party) 7.6 per cent (6).

Presidential (first round): Noboa (PRIAN) won 26.8 per cent of the vote, Correa (Alianza Patria Altiva y Soberana (Alianza PAIS) (Proud and Sovereign Fatherland Alliance)) 22.8 per cent, Gilmar Gutiérrez (PSP) 17.5 per cent, León Roldós Aguilera (ID-RED) 14.8 per cent and Cynthia Viteri (PSC) 9.6 per cent. Turnout 72.2 per cent.

Presidential (run-off): Rafael Correa won 56.7 per cent of the vote, Álvaro Noboa won 43.3 per cent. Turnout was 76 per cent.

(Constituent Assembly): PAIS Alliance won 74 seats (out of 130).

Next elections

2010 (presidential)

Political parties

Ruling party

Alianza PAIS (Patria Altiva i Soberana) (Alliance Proud and Sovereign Fatherland)

Main opposition party

Partido Renovador Institucional de Acción Nacional (PRIAN) (Institutional Renewal Party of National Action)

Political situation

In the 15 October 2006 parliamentary elections the Partido Renovador Institucional de Acción Nacional (PRIAN) (Institutional Renewal Party of National Action) won 28 of the 100 seats in the national congress, the Partido Sociedad Patriótica 21 de Enero (PSP) (January 21 Patriotic Society Party) won 23, the Partido Social Cristiano (PSC) (Social Christian Party) won 13, and the Partido Roldosista Ecuatoriano (PRE) (Ecuadorian Roldosist Party) won six. No candidates stood for the Alianza Patria Altiva y Soberana (PAIS Alianza) (Proud and Sovereign Fatherland Alliance)). In the first round of the presidential election, Álvaro Noboa (PRIAN) won 26.8 per cent of the vote, Rafael Correa (PAIS Alianza) 22.8 per cent, Gilmar Gutiérrez 17.5 per cent, León Roldós Aguilera 14.8 per cent and Cynthia Viteri 9.6 per cent. The run-off took place on 26 November; Correa won 57 per cent of the vote against Noboa with 43 per cent. Noboa called for a recount, claiming vote rigging by his opponent; the electoral commission confirmed the result on 28 November.

In the 30 September 2007 Asamblea Constituyente (Constituent Assembly) the PAIS Alliance won 74 seats (out of 130).

Population

13.34 million (2007)*

Last census: November 2001: 12,156,608

Population density: 42 inhabitants per square km. Urban population: 63 per cent (1995—2001).

Annual growth rate: 1.5 per cent 1994–2004 (WHO 2006)

Ethnic make-up

Mestizo (mixed Indian and white) (65 per cent), Indian (25 per cent), white and others (7 per cent), black (3 per cent). The indigenous Indian population is composed of eight main groups, five in the Oriente and three on the coast, each with their own language. One of the Oriente groups, the Quechua, also live in the highlands (sierra).

Religions

Over 95 per cent of the population is nominally Roman Catholic, although Protestant churches have made inroads in recent years. There is freedom of worship.

Education

The education sector in Ecuador needs increased funding and technology.

Enrolment in primary schools has been increasing at an annual rate of 4.4 per cent per year, although many children drop out before the age of 15.

Public universities have an open admissions policy. The number of people entering university, however, has increased and this is putting a strain on resources, contributing to a decline in academic standards.

Literacy rate: 91 per cent adult rate; 96 per cent youth rate (15–24) (Unesco 2005).

Compulsory years: Six to 15

Enrolment rate: 117 per cent gross primary enrolment (including repeaters); 59 per cent gross secondary enrolment (World Bank).

Pupils per teacher: 25 in primary schools

Health

Per capita total expenditure on health (2003) was US$220; of which per capita government spending was US$85, at the international dollar rate, (WHO 2006).

Improved water sources and sanitation facilities are available to 71 per cent and 59 per cent of the population, respectively.

HIV/Aids

HIV prevalence: 0.3 per cent aged 15–49 in 2003 (World Bank)

Life expectancy: 72 years, 2004 (WHO 2006)

Fertility rate/Maternal mortality rate: 2.7 births per woman, 2004 (WHO 2006); maternal mortality 160 per 100,000 live births (World Bank).

Child (under 5 years) mortality rate (per 1,000): 24 per 1,000 live births; 14 per cent of children, aged under five, are malnourished (World Bank).

Welfare

The Ecuadorian Social Security Institute operates under the ministry of social welfare and offers old-age benefits, sickness and maternity coverage, work, injury and unemployment benefits. The system covers only around 30 per cent of the working population. Coverage is particularly poor in rural areas.

Main cities

Quito (capital, estimated population 1.5 million (m) in 2005), Guayaquil (2.2m), Cuenca (305,772), Santo Domingo (238,325), Alfaro (212,924), Machala (228,351), Manta (201,700), Portoviejo (187,369).

Languages spoken

Quechua and Jarvo are spoken. There is pressure from indigenous groups for Quechua to be made an official language.

English, taught to all schoolchildren, is also widely spoken.

Official language/s

Spanish

Media

Freedom of the press is guaranteed but foreign investment in the media is prohibited. Journalists operate a form of self-censorship particularly concerning perceived sensitive issues and defamation is a criminal offence and liable to up to three years in prison.

Press

Dailies: In Spanish, national newspapers include El Comercio (www2.elcomercio.com) and El Universo (www.eluniverso.com). Regional publications include El Telégrafo (www.telegrafo.com.ec) and Expreso (www.expreso.ec) from Guayaquil, La Hora (www.lahora.com.ec) and Hoy (www.hoy.com.ec) from Quito, Correo (www.diariocorreo.com.ec) from Machala and La Prensa (www.laprensa.com.ec) from Chimborazo.

Business: In Spanish, El Financiero (www.elfinanciero.com) is published weekly.

Broadcasting

The government seized TC Television in Quito and Guayaquil and Gamavision in Quito in July 2008, in a dispute lnked to the collapse of banks in the late 1990s. The Deposit Guarantee Agency (AGD) seeks to recover funds from banks that closed or went bankrupt in the financial crisis.

Radio: Radio is the most popular medium for entertainment, news and information and there are hundreds of stations, some in rural areas broadcasting in indigenous languages. Private, national commercial radio stations include Radio Sucre (www.radiosucre.com.ec), JC Radio (www.jcradio.com.ec) and Radio Caravana (http://radiocaravana.com); from Quito Radio Megaestacion (www.radiomegaestacion.com) and Radio i99 (www.i99.com.ec); from Guayaquil Radio America (www.americaestereo.com) and Radio Latina (www.radiolatina.com.ec). There are several religious radio stations.

Television: There are several national, commercial broadcasters, programming mostly consists of Latin American soap opera shows and US imports, but domestic productions are growing. News, sports and music are also featured. Ecuavisa (www.ecuavisa.com), ETV Telerama (www.etvtelerama.com), Teleamazonas (www.teleamazonas.com), Telesistema (www.rts.com.ec) and Gamavision (www.gamavision.com).

The satellite TV station RTU (www.rtu.com.ec), which began transmitting in 2005, offers news and current affairs programmes.

Economy

The economy suffered greatly in the late 1990s and early 2000s, due to a combination of hazardous weather conditions and political unrest. The economy has only just managed to maintain itself, largely as a result of the remittances sent from Ecuadorians living and working abroad and the rise in world oil prices. The Inter-American Development Bank estimated that in 2006 migrant workers sent some US$2,900 million to their families in Ecuador.

The Ecuadorian authorities have been criticised by the IMF for poor fiscal management and large increases in the public wage bill. In September 2002, congress passed a Fiscal Responsibility and Transparency Law, which sets medium-term fiscal rules. The law was praised by the IMF, which urged the new government, appointed in January 2003, to continue efforts to lower the public debt in order to prevent crowding out of non-oil investment. The IMF also lauded the new government's commitment to a controversial public sector wage freeze, which should help maintain real exchange rate stability and generate investor confidence.

Ecuador is heavily dependent on the oil industry, which accounts for 25 per cent of GDP and 40 per cent of export revenues, making the economy vulnerable to world price fluctuations. Domestic politics also affected the sector in 2006: nationalisation of Occidental-owned assets has resulted in declining output, while a 50 per cent tax on 'extraordinary profits' by other foreign companies has deterred new investment. A consequence of the dispossession of Occident was the suspension by the US of free trade negotiations, which were in any case unpopular in Ecuador.

Agriculture is the next most important activity, employing a third of the workforce. Ecuador is the world's largest exporter of bananas and the fourth largest of flowers.

Inflation has been brought under control and relatively strong GDP growth of 6.6 per cent was recorded in 2004, although slowing to 3.3 per cent in 2005.

External trade
Ecuador belongs to the South American Community of Nations (SACN) (which combines the Andean Community of Nations and Southern Common Market) in the creation of an economic and legislative union.
Talks to establish a free trade agreement between Ecuador and the US broke down in 2006 and political differences have stalled further negotiations.
Imports
Principal imports are vehicles, pharmaceuticals and medical products, telecommunications equipment and electricity.
Main sources: US (22.6 per cent total, 2006), Colombia (12.8 per cent), Brazil (7.3 per cent).
Exports
Principal exports are petroleum, bananas, cut flowers and shrimp.
Main destinations: US (53.6 per cent total, 2006), Peru (8.2 per cent), Colombia (5.6 per cent).

Agriculture
Farming
Prior to the rise in significance of the oil industry and other related economic activities, the agricultural sector was Ecuador's most prominent economic activity. In recent years output from the sector has fluctuated due to the adverse effects of the El Niño weather phenomena in the 1990s and shifts in world cocoa and banana prices.
Virtually the whole of the country is suitable for some form of agricultural exploitation. However, the sector has suffered from low levels of mechanisation and irrigation, and lack of financial incentives.
In coastal regions the main crops are bananas, cocoa, coffee, oil palms, sugar cane, cotton, rice and maize, while the sierra produces legumes, maize, wheat, potatoes, rye and barley. Ecuador is the world's largest producer of bananas.
Cattle are mainly reared in the highlands. There is small-scale poultry farming in Manabi province.
Rose growing and cut-flower production started in the early 1980s and the country has a number of rose growing enterprises. The potential for rose exports from Ecuador is enormous since all-year-round production is possible with no heating or cooling costs.
Temperate crops include blackberries, tamarillos (tree tomatoes), lemons, limes and avocados. In warmer regions, mangoes, pineapple, passion fruit, papaya, pepper, heart-of-palm and orito (kind of banana) thrive. In colder and temperate areas, broccoli, strawberry, asparagus, artichoke and peppers are grown. In addition, cucumbers, okra and melons are cultivated. The majority of the annual pineapple harvest is sold to the US and to Europe.
Crop production in 2005 included: 2,182,048 tonnes (t) cereals in total, 1,375,502t rice, 1,929,919t oil palm fruit, 5,877,830t bananas, 1,012,720t plantains, 5,656,608t sugar cane, 750,727t maize, 118,883t cassava, 417,542t potatoes, 342,538t oilcrops, 95,873t tomatoes, 306,020t citrus fruit, 102,923t green coffee, 137,178t cocoa beans, 1,855t tea, 118,619t soya beans, 66,309t pineapples, 154,174t mangoes, 33,772t fibre crops, 7,685t tobacco, 13,500t natural rubber, 7,753,423t fruit in total, 550,518t vegetables in total.
Livestock production included: 601,489t meat in total, 206,532t beef, 164,628t pig meat, 11,394t lamb, 1,243t goat meat, 208,870t poultry, 75,014t eggs, 2,545,990t milk, 31,722t cattle hides, 900t honey, 1,689t greasy wool.
Fishing
Over recent years the fishing industry has increased in importance. Both sea and shrimp fishing have become more economically significant, with shrimp now being the second most important foreign exchange earner in the agricultural sector, after bananas.
Government policy has concentrated on the development of sea food, including tuna, fish oil and fishmeal for export.
The fisheries union in Ecuador has pressed for immediate reforms within the sector, asking for modernised management. The country's fishing legislation lacks organisation with poorly defined fishing rights.
In a typical year the annual fish catch is over 654,500mt, including 5,645mt freshwater fish and 64,200mt shellfish.
In 2004, the total marine fish catch was 333,154 tonnes and the total crustacean catch was 2,062 tonnes.
Forestry
Over 40 per cent of Ecuador's total land mass is forested; approximately 10.5 million hectares (ha). Timber imports in 2004 were US$199.9 million, while exports amounted to US$84.1 million.
Forests are mostly concentrated in the eastern Amazonian region characterised by lowland humid tropical rainforests. Forest plantations are mainly eucalyptus.
Large quantities of sawn timber and wood based panels are produced, although exports remain limited. Production of hardwoods and balsa wood is dependent on the Andean market. Most of the paper and pulp demand is met by imports.
According to some critics, there will be no forests left in Ecuador by 2030 and the government has been supporting a project which aimed to re-forest 500,000 hectares by the end of 2005, both for commercial and ecological reasons, with an emphasis on profitable exotic species.
Timber production in 2004 included 6,638,159 cubic metres (cum) roundwood, 1,211,000cum industrial roundwood, 755,000cum sawnwood, 298,000cum sawlogs & veneer logs, 261,400cum wood-based panels, 5,427,159cum wood fuel, 98,800 tonnes (t) charcoal, 100,000t paper and paperboard, including 2,000t newsprint,

Industry and manufacturing
Approximately 20 per cent of Ecuador's total GDP is generated by activity in the industrial sector, which is geographically concentrated in Quito and Guayaquil.
The sector accounts for 15 per cent of the entire labour force in a typical year.
A free trade zone (FTZ), offering incentives for the manufacture of export products, was established at Esmeraldas.

Tourism
The tourism sector is playing an increasingly important role in the economy of Ecuador. The sector is the country's third most important economic activity, after petroleum and bananas. Travel and tourism employs 7.4 per cent of Ecuador's total labour force and constitutes 8.6 per cent of total GDP.
The mixture of environmental systems, including rain-forest and mountains, and especially the Galapagos Islands, favours eco-tourists as well as attracting trekkers, climbers, divers and backpackers. Ecuador converted to the US dollar in 2000, making it a more expensive country to visit than neighbouring countries. Visitor numbers have been rising steadily over recent years and the country hopes to attract one million visitors by 2007.

Mining
Mining concessions can be found over approximately 5.6 million hectares of Ecuador's total land mass. Approximately 36,000 miners make their living in the informal sector, which represents about 1 per cent of the country's labour force.
Despite a growing foreign presence, Ecuador's mining industry is very much in its infancy, although it could become one of the economy's most dynamic sectors. The government is keen to make mining a high priority in view of its enormous production potential and the opportunity it offers to diversify the country's export base as an alternative to oil.
The most important mineral is gold, which is mined on a small-scale basis, although a number of foreign and local companies are negotiating with miners to take over their operations and introduce more technical expertise. Interest has been shown in gold, with a joint government and private mining venture in the Nambija region.

There are also major deposits of limestone, clay, plaster, barytine, feldspar, silica, phosphate, bentonite and pumice stone (Ecuador has one of the biggest reserves of pumice stone in the world). Kaolin, marble, puzzolan and gypsum are mined.

Hydrocarbons

Ecuador has significant proven oil reserves of 4.6 billion barrels and the country is the fifth largest crude oil producer in Latin America. The petroleum sector plays a driving role in the Ecuadorian economy, representing approximately 11 per cent of total GDP, some 52 per cent of export earnings and generating 35 per cent of total government revenues.

Oil production was 534,800 barrels per day (bpd) in 2004, with exports totalling 226,000bpd. Emphasis is on developing exploration and expanding refining capacity to increase the production of lighter products. However oil transportation has been a serious constraint for company investment until the construction of the Oleducto de Crudos Pesados (OCP) pipeline in 2003.

Ecuador's natural gas reserves are relatively small, at approximately 12.18 billion cubic metres (cum) of natural gas reserves, located in Oriente and the Gulf of Guayaquil. However, a lack of infrastructure has inhibited the capacity to utilise these resources. Annual gas production is approximately 112 million cum. The long-awaited natural gas project in the Amistad Field in the Gulf of Guayaquil has had drilling operations since 2000.

Ecuador is neither a producer nor consumer of coal. Although, there are small reserves of recoverable coal (lignite and sub-bituminous) estimated at 23.5 million tonnes, these remain unexploited.

Energy

Ecuador's installed electricity capacity stands at over 3,000MW. Hydroelectricity plays an important role in generation, as approximately two-thirds of electricity is generated from hydroelectric plants. The massive Paute hydro-plant generates more than 60 per cent of the country's electricity.

There are shortfalls in supply typically during the October–March dry season; two new hydroelectric dams and power plants, expected to be completed by 2007, should make up any shortfalls. Mazur is sited upstream of, and will also act as a reservoir for, the Paute power station; the San Francisco project is downstream from the existing Agoyan plant on the Pastaza river.

Ecuador has few reserves of natural gas or the infrastructure to exploit what does exist. There is a natural gas-fired power plant near Machala, which, with a new pipeline linking it to a gas field, Amistad, in the Gulf of Guayaquil and an import deal with Peru agreed in late 2004, is forcast to have an energy capacity of 240MW.

The former state-owned electricity conglomerate (INECEL) has been broken up into single operating companies for either transmission or distribution. The reorganisation did not lead to any significant increase in efficiency or expansion. The government has been prevented from rationalising the industry by partisan interests and a lack of private investment.

Financial markets

Stock exchange

There are two stock exchanges in Ecuador: the Bolsa de Valores de Quito (BVQ) (the largest) and the Bolsa de Valores de Guayaquil.

Banking and insurance

A new Bank of the South, with a headquarters in Venezuela, will be launched in 2008 to provide an alternative source of development funding for the participating countries. Assets of US$7 billion will underpin its operations.

Central bank

Banco Central del Ecuador

Main financial centre

Guayaquil and Quito

Time

Mainland Ecuador: GMT minus five hours
Galapagos Islands: GMT minus six hours

Geography

Ecuador has three main regions – a low coastal strip, a high Andean cordillera with peaks rising to more than 6,000 metres, and a tropical lowland in the Amazon basin. The Andes, which here comprise two parallel ranges running north to south, form a barrier between 100 and 120km wide.

Chimborazo, an extinct volcano, is the highest mountain, at 6,310 metres, and there are several active volcanoes. Quito itself, which lies at 2,850 metres above sea level, is the second highest capital in South America, and visitors are advised to take things easy for a few days after arrival to avoid altitude sickness.

To the north, Ecuador is bordered by Colombia and to the east and south by Peru. To the west lies the Pacific Ocean. Of the Spanish-speaking nations of South America, only Uruguay is smaller in area.

Hemisphere

Straddles the Equator

Climate

Although the equator crosses the north of the country (and gives it its name), only the eastern lowlands (the Oriente) and the northern coastal region have a typically tropical climate, with abundant rains, high humidity and little seasonal change in temperature, which averages around 25 degrees Celsius (C). The port city of Guayaquil is in the tropical zone and has most rain between January and April. In the Andes, the climate varies from the cold of the high glaciers to the temperate zone of the central valley around Quito, where the mean annual temperature is between 13 degrees C and 19 degrees C. Days are warm and nights are cool all year round. The rainy season in the valley lasts from November–May.

Dress codes

In government offices and private businesses in Quito, dress is relatively formal. Women usually wear skirts, while the men wear suits or jacket and tie. Dress is generally less formal in Guayaquil, the largest city and Ecuador's major port.

Entry requirements

Passports

Passports are required by all. Passports must be valid for six months.

Visa

Nationals of most countries do not need a visa for stays up to three months, but travellers should contact the local embassy for confirmation.

Currency advice/regulations

No restrictions on import or export of foreign or local currency.

International credit cards are generally accepted in Quito and Guayaquil. Travellers cheques can be difficult to exchange outside main towns. US dollar travellers cheques are the most easily negotiable.

Prohibited imports

Firearms, ammunition, illegal drugs, fresh or dry meat and meat products, plants and vegetables are prohibited/restricted unless prior permission is obtained.

Health (for visitors)

Mandatory precautions

A yellow fever certificate is required if arriving from infected areas and for those intending to visit Pastaza province in the east.

Advisable precautions

Typhoid, tetanus and hepatitis A and B vaccinations are recommended. Malaria prophylaxis is advisable; the malaria risk is high and widespread all the year. Yellow fever vaccinations are recommended for most areas east of the Andes. There is a rabies risk.

Tap water is not safe to drink. Bottled mineral water is widely available.

Hotels

Wide range available in Quito and Guayaquil. A government tax of 5 per cent and a service charge of 10 per cent payable on all rates.

Credit cards
Major credit cards are generally accepted.

Public holidays (national)
Fixed dates
1 Jan (New Year's Day), 1 May (Labour Day), 24 May (Battle of Pichincha Day), 10 Aug (Independence Day), 12 Oct (Columbus Day), 2 Nov (All Souls' Day), 25 Dec (Christmas Day), 31 Dec (New Year's Eve).
If New Year's Day falls on a Sunday, 2 Jan becomes a holiday instead. Holidays falling on a Tuesday are observed on the preceding Monday, while those falling on Wednesday and Thursday are moved to Friday. The exceptions to the latter rule are 1 Jan, 1 May, 2 Nov and 25 Dec.
Variable dates
Carnival (two days), Maundy Thursday, Good Friday.
Carnival is celebrated on Shrove Tuesday and Ash Wednesday (six weeks before Good Friday).

Working hours
Banking
Mon–Fri: 0900–1330, 1430—1030; Sat: 0900–1800.
Business
Mon–Fri: 0800–1630.
Government
Mon–Fri: 0830–1630.
Shops
Mon–Fri: 0900–1300, 1500–1900. Sat: 1000–2000. (Shopping centres, Mon–Sat: 1030–2030; Sun: 1030–1830.)

Telecommunications
Mobile/cell phones
GSM 850 service available in cities and large towns.

Electricity supply
110/120V AC, 60 cycles

Weights and measures
The metric system is in use.

Social customs/useful tips
Speak Spanish; if not, ensure that promotional material is in Spanish or has Spanish inserts.
Ecuadoreans prefer to deal with people they have spent time getting to know; lunches/business meetings can last from 1330 to 1800, dinners from 2000 onwards. Meetings often start late.
Ecuadoreans are polite and formal. Do not be discouraged by lack of enthusiasm; they like to be convinced. The use of the title Doctor, Engineer or Economist is common.

Security
Guayaquil has a serious street crime problem. Crime in Quito is on the increase, especially in the colonial centre of town, and police advise visitors to be wary of thieves and pickpockets and to watch luggage at all times.

Getting there
Air
National airline: TAME (Línea Aérea del Ecuador); Lan Ecuador.
International airport/s: Quito-Mariscal Sucre (UIO), 8km from city centre, duty-free shop, bar, restaurant, buffet, bank, post office, shops, car hire, tourist information. Guayaquil-Simón Bolivar (GYE), 5km north of city centre, duty-free shop, restaurant, buffet, currency exchange, post office, shops, car hire, tourist information;
Airport tax: US$25.
Surface
Access is possible from Colombia and Peru, although the quality of roads and railway services may vary.
Road: Buses run between Colombia and Ecuador via Tulcán, and between Peru and Ecuador via either Huaquillas or Macará.
Main port/s: Guayaquil, Manta and Esmeraldas.

Getting about
Passport checks are frequently made by the police, especially near the borders.
National transport
Air: Air transport is the usual mode of travel between cities. TAME, the commercial wing of the Ecuadorian Air Force, and several other airlines operate domestic services to main centres. Air-taxi and charter services are available from Guayaquil and Quito.
With the exception of flying to the Galapagos Islands, internal flights are cheap.
Road: Most parts of the country are accessible by surfaced or all-weather roads. Major routes run north-south in the coastal lowlands and the sierra. The Pan-American Highway runs from Tulcan via Ibarra, Quito, Riobamaba, Cuenca, Loja to Macara. Good roads link the sierra to the coastal ports.
Buses: Bus services link main towns, including Quito-Esmeraldas, Quito-Manta, Guayaquil-Manta and Quito-Guayaquil. Most towns have a terminal terrestre (central bus terminal). Reservations in advance should be made for long-distance services. Timetables are changed frequently and not always adhered to.
Rail: Routes include Quito-Riobamba, Guayaquil-Bucay, Alausi-Huigra, Sibambe-Cuenca and Ibarra-San Lorenzo. Rail travel is generally uncomfortable and unreliable.
Water: Boats are a frequent mode of travel, particularly in the Oriente region, and on the north-west coast.

City transport
Taxis: Taxis are cheap. They can be hailed or found on ranks. It is best to ask the fare beforehand. At weekends and at night, fares are 25–50 per cent higher. Journey time from airport to city centre 20—30 minutes. Tips are not expected.
Car hire
Major companies operate from Quito and Guayaquil. An international permit is required. Traffic drives on the right. Police checks are common.

BUSINESS DIRECTORY

The addresses listed below are a selection only. While World of Information makes every endeavour to check these addresses, we cannot guarantee that changes have not been made, especially to telephone numbers and area codes. We would welcome any corrections.

Telephone area codes
The international direct dialling code for Ecuador is +593, followed by area code:

Ambato	3	Machala	7
Cuenca	7	Manta	4
Esmeraldas	6	Portoviejo	4
Guayaquil	4	Quito	2

Useful telephone numbers

Police:	101
Fire:	102
Ambulance (Quito):	131

Chambers of Commerce
American-Ecuadorian Chamber of Commerce, Avenida 6 de Diciembre y La Niña, Edificio Multicentro, Quito (tel: 250-7450; fax: 250-4571; e-mail: info@ecamcham.com).

British-Ecuadorean Chamber of Industry and Commerce, Avenida El Tiempo 464 y El Telegrafo, Quito (tel: 244-9239; fax: 225-7433; e-mail: info@egbcc.org).

Guayaquil Cámara de Comercio, Avenida Francisco de Orellana y Miguel H Alcivar, Centro Empresarial Las Cámaras, Guayaquil (tel: 268-2771; fax: 268-2725; e-mail: info@lacamara.org).

Quito Cámara de Comercio, Avenida Amazonas y República, Edificio Las Cámaras, Quito (tel: 244-3787; fax: 243-5862; e-mail: ccq@ccq.org.ec).

Banking
Banco Bolivariano, Junín 200 y Panamá, Guayaquil (tel: 562-777; fax: 565-025).

Banco de Guayaquil, Pichincha 105 y P Icaza, Guayaquil (tel: 514-209; fax: 512-427; e-mail: glasso@bankguay.com).

Banco del Pacifico, P Icaza 200 y Pedro Carbo, Guayaquil (tel: 566-010; fax: 564-636; e-mail: webadmin@bp.fin.ec).

Banco del Pichincha, Avenida Amazonas 4560 y Pereira, Quito (tel: 980-980; fax: 981-280).

Banco la Previsora, Avenida 9 de Octubre 100, Guayaquil (tel: 561-656; fax: 566-665; e-mail: blp@bprevisora.fin.ec).

BancoUnion, Cordova 916 y VM Rendon, Guayaquil (tel: 566-555; fax: 313-295; e-mail: info@banunion.com).

Filanbanco, Avenida 9 de Octubre 203 y Pichincha, Guayaquil (tel: 322-780; fax: 326-916).

Superintendencia de Bancos (Banking Supervisory Agency), Avenida 12 de Octubre 24-185, Quito (tel: 554-422).

Central bank

Banco Central del Ecuador, Avenida 10 de Agosto y Briceño, Plaza Bolivar, Quito (tel: 519-384, 571-807).

Travel information

Ecuatoriana Airlines, Reina Victoria y Colón, Edificio Torres de Almagro, Quito (tel: 563-003; fax: 563-920).

SAETA Airlines, Avenida Carlos Julio Arosemena Km 2.5, Guayaquil (fax: 201-153; e-mail: ehbuzon@saeta.com.ec).

TAME Airlines, Avenida Amazonas 13-54 y Colón, Quito (tel: 509-392; fax: 509-594).

Ministry of tourism

Ministry of Tourism, Av Eloy Alfaro N32-300 y Carlos Tobar, Quito (tel: 228-303, 507-560; fax: 507-564, 229-330; e-mail: mtur1@ec_gov.net).

National tourist organisation offices

Asociación Ecuatoriana de Agencias de Viajes y Turismo (ASECUT), Avenida Amazonas 2468, Quito (tel: 552-617; fax: 552-916).

Corporación Ecuatoriana de Turismo (CETUR), Reina Victoria 514 y Roca, Quito (tel: 527-002; fax: 568-198).

Ministries

Ministry of Agriculture, Avenida Amazonas y Eloy Alfaro, Quito (tel: 504-433; fax: 504-922).

Ministry of Defence, Exposición 208, Quito (tel: 512-803; fax: 569-386).

Ministry of Education, San Gregorio y Juan Murillo, Quito (tel: 583-337; fax: 580-116).

Ministry of Energy and Mines, Santa Prisca 223, Quito (tel: 552-533; fax: 502-092).

Ministry of the Environment, Avenida Eloy Alfaro y Amazonas, Quito (tel: 540-920; fax: 255-172).

Ministry of Finance and Public Credit, Avenida 10 de Agosto 1661 y Jorge Washington, Quito (tel: 503-328; fax: 500-702).

Ministry of Foreign Affairs, Avenida 10 de Agosto y Carrión, Quito (tel: 503-093; fax: 227-025; e-mail: dgproeco@mmrree.gov.ec).

Ministry of Foreign Trade, Avenida Amazonas y Eloy Alfaro, Quito (tel: 529-076; fax: 507-549).

Ministry of Government, Espejo y Benalcázar, Quito (tel: 584-919; fax: 580-067).

Ministry of Housing and Urban Development, Avenida 10 de Agosto 2270 y Cordero, Quito (tel: 238-060; fax: 566-785).

Ministry of Labour, Luis Felipe Borja y C Ponce, Quito (tel: 566-148; fax: 503-122).

Ministry of Public Health, Juan Larrea 445, Quito (tel: 529-163; fax: 569-092).

Ministry of Public Works, Avenida Orellana y Juan León Mera, Quito (tel: 222-749; fax: 223-077).

Ministry of Social Welfare, Robles 850 y Páez, Quito (tel: 227-975; fax: 563-469).

Other useful addresses

Bolsa de Valores de Quito (Stock Exchange), Avenida Amazonas 540 y Carrión, Quito (tel: 526-805; fax: 500-942; e-mail: informacion@ccbvq.com).

Bolsa de Valores de Guayaquil, 9 de Octubre 110 y Pichincha, Guayaquil (tel: 561-519; fax: 561-871; e-mail: earosemena@bvg.fin.ec).

British Embassy, Avenida Naciones Unidas y República de El Salvador, Quito (tel: 970-800/1; fax: 970-809).

Corporación Financiera Nacional, Juan León Mera 130 y Patria, Quito (tel: 564-900; fax: 223-823).

Ecuadorian Embassy (USA), 2535 15th Street, NW, Washington DC 20009 (tel: (202) 234-7200; fax: (202) 667-3482; e-mail: embassy@ecuador.org).

Empresa Estatel de Telecomunicaciones (EMETEL), Avenida 6 de Diciembre y Colón, Edificio Partenon, Quito (tel: 200-700; fax: 568-000).

Instituto Nacional de Estadística y Censos, Juan Larrea 534 y Riofrio, Quito (tel: 529-858; fax: 509-836).

National Bureau of Mines (DINAMI), Baquedano E7-13 y Reina Victoria, Edificio Araucaria, Quito (tel: 554-110; fax: 554-110; e-mail: dinami@accessinter.net).

National Council for the Modernisation of the State (CONAM), Edificio Corporación Financiera, Avenida Juan León Mera 130 y Patria, Quito (tel: 509-432; fax: 509-437).

Petroecuador, Avenida 6 de Diciembre y Paul Rivet, Edificio El Pinar, Quito (tel: 561-250; fax: 524-766).

Secretary General of the Administration, García Moreno 1043, Quito (tel: 580-750; fax: 580-751).

Superintendencia de Compañías del Ecuador (Companies Supervisory Authority), Roca 660 y Avenida Amazonas, Quito (tel: 529-960; fax: 565-685).

US Embassy, Avenida 12 de Octubre y Patria, Quito (tel: 562-890; fax: 502-052).

Other news agencies: Prensa Latina: www.prensalatina.com.mx

Internet sites

Economic Commission for Latin America (gateway site): www.eclac.cl/index1.html

Inter-American Development Bank: www.iadb.org

Latin Trade Online: www.latintrade.com

Latin World (directory of Internet resources): wwwlatinworld.com

Organisation of American States: www.oas.org

Egypt

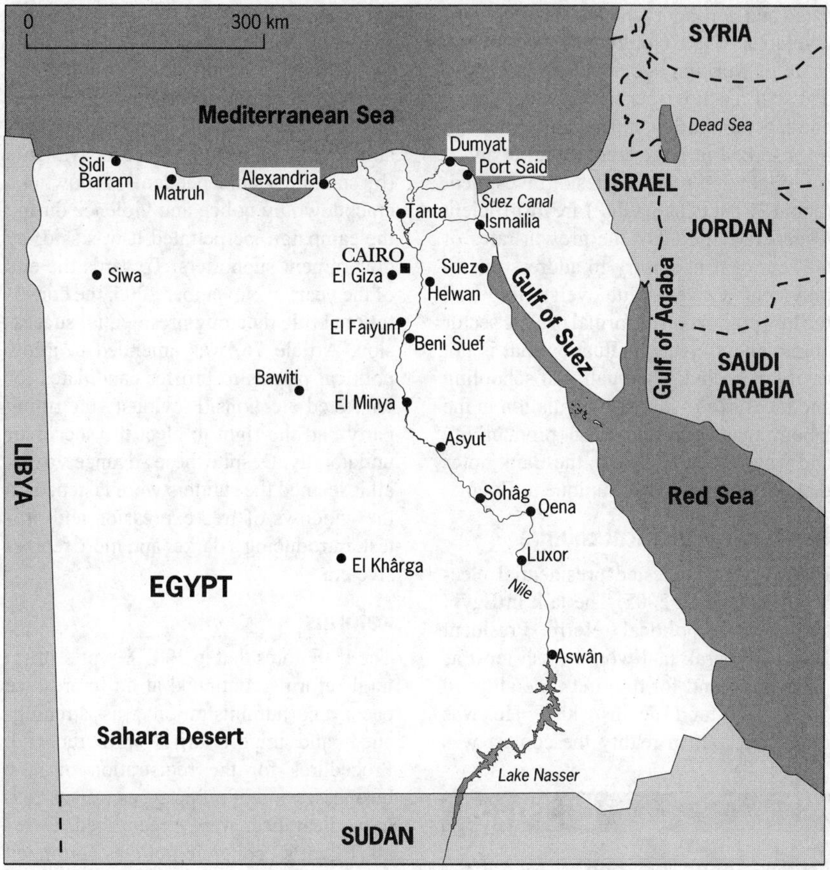

In February 2008 the International Monetary Fund (IMF) published a survey on Egypt entitled *Reforms Trigger Economic Growth*. On 1 May, in an apparent rejection of IMF advice, President Hosni Mubarak increased government salaries by an annual 30 per cent. This could hardly be termed a counter-inflationary move.

IMF approval

According to the IMF in its December 2007 report on the economy, in 2007 Egypt had had 'another year of impressive performance supported by sustained reforms, prudent macroeconomic management, and a favourable external environment'. In 2007 the economy grew at 7 per cent a year. Non-hydrocarbon growth surged from 5.8 per cent in 2005/06 to 7.1 per cent in 2006/07, broadening to labour-intensive agriculture, manufacturing, services, and construction. The rise in inflation was largely the result of one-off factors, but demand pressures and imported inflation also played a role. The growth spurt had created about 2.5 million jobs between end-2004 and March 2007, reducing Egyptian unemployment from 11.8 per cent to 9 per cent. Skill mismatches remained a hindrance to job growth, and formal sector employment was hindered by high non-wage labour costs and expensive firing rules.

Egypt's economic growth was undoubtedly strong, and by the end of 2007 had become more broad-based, creating record numbers of jobs. Egypt's inflation

KEY FACTS

Official name: Jumhuriyat Misr al Arabiya (Arab Republic of Egypt)

Head of State: President Hosni Mubarak (since 1981; re-elected 6 Sep 2005)

Head of government: Prime Minister Ahmed Nazif (appointed Jul 2004)

Ruling party: Al Hizb al Watani al Dimuqrati (National Democratic Party) (NDP) (since 1996; re-elected 9 Dec 2005)

Area: 1,001,499 square km

Population: 73.57 million (2007)*

Capital: Cairo

Official language: Arabic

Currency: Egyptian pound (LE) = 100 piastres

Exchange rate: LE5.31 per US$ (Jul 2008)

GDP per capita: US$1,739 (2007)*

GDP real growth: 7.10% (2007)

Labour force: 27.49 million (2004)

Unemployment: 9.50% (2005)

Inflation: 10.90% (2007)

Oil production: 710,000 bpd (2007)

Balance of trade: -US$9.10 billion (2005)

Foreign debt: US$33.80 billion (2004)

Visitor numbers: 8.65 million (2006)*

* estimated figure

had returned to single digits after a temporary surge triggered by supply shocks and administered price adjustments. There had been a surge in inflation between March 2006 and March 2007 before it began to moderate after March 2007, with the Consumer Price Index (CPI) falling steadily to 8 per cent by July 2007. The CPI rose

again to 8.5 per cent in August largely because of increases in food prices. The surge in world prices for several commodities (the global food price index increased by 10 per cent in 2006) also contributed to inflation. Some imported food items such as wheat, oils, and sugar are heavily subsidised by the government, but these constitute only some 3–4 per cent of the CPI basket by weight compared to 40 per cent for all food items. Prices of domestic agricultural produce have also risen because of higher prices for imported fertiliser and seeds. Inflationary pressures from strong domestic demand and rising world food prices have persisted into 2008. This is not all good news as the overall demand in Egypt, boosted by high growth, rising employment, and wealth effects, has caused signs of demand pressures to emerge.

Social pressures

The World Bank notes that in Egypt social indicators for health and education continued to improve. According to the Bank, between the early 1970s and 2005, life expectancy at birth increased from 53 to 70 years, the number of children dying in the first year of life declined from 110 to 26 (per 1,000 live births), and primary school enrolment increased from 63 per cent to 101 per cent. During the same period, Egypt's population increased from 36 million to 76 million. Yet, poverty remains an issue with 17 per cent of the population (mainly in Upper Egypt and rural areas) living on less than US$1 per day.

According to the World Bank, Egypt's unemployed are mostly the young, educated and non-poor who await better entry level jobs. While employment is growing, share of working age population is rising and will reach 67 per cent in 2020. New entrants (about 600,000 annually) need to be absorbed into the labour market and it is thought that present rates of investment (about 20 per cent of GDP) are insufficient to generate the GDP the growth rates of 6–7 per cent necessary to address unemployment. Government overstaffing and the low proportion of formal private sector employment create a situation that is not easily remedied. The quality of schooling and measures to increase regulation in the labour market would raise productivity and wages. In conclusion, the Bank notes that this situation is not unique to Egypt.

Pressure for political change

Egypt's first contested presidential election was held in 2005. The talk in Egypt had been of political reform. President Hosni Mubarak had won a fresh term as president – and for the first time allowed others to stand against him. He was re-elected, but in reality the contest was one-sided, with a weak opposition unable to mount a strong campaign. Nevertheless, the police allowed demonstrations to go ahead, which were remarkably outspoken, by Egyptian standards. It seemed that one of the most important countries of the Middle East was responding to pressure for change coming from the grass roots – and from the Bush administration in Washington, which was sometimes blunt in telling its Egyptian ally that reform had to be genuine and lasting.

The only grouping strong enough to worry the president, the Jama'at al Ikhwan al Muslimun (Muslim Brotherhood) was able to win 88 of the 444 seats available (by standing as independents) following a crackdown by police and violence during the campaign, perpetrated it was said, by government supporters. Towards the end of the year, in November 2005, the constitutional rule dictating presidential succession, Article 76, was amended to allow political parties to proffer candidates for contested elections. Previously the ruling party had the right to elect the successor unilaterally. Despite these advances, overall it seemed the shutters were fastened on the windows of free expression and protest, introducing a darker and more repressive era.

Reforms

The IMF notes that in 2007 Egypt's structural reforms continued at an impressive pace: tax administration was strengthened, and import tariffs were reduced. Procedures for the registration of new businesses and of property, as well as customs clearance, were streamlined. Overall, Egypt's economic policies continued to be geared toward sustaining high growth and creating jobs for a rapidly growing labour force. Reforms were introduced to enhance investment incentives by further improving the business environment, while raising national savings and ensuring domestic and external stability through continued fiscal adjustment. This required a reduction in energy subsidies, containment of the wage bill, overhaul of the sales and property tax regimes, and continued reform of the tax administration. Improvements in public spending efficiency, including on social safety nets, were equally critical to sustain growth and strengthen the needed consensus for reforms, especially given the disaffection of many groups with the delays in the trickling down of the benefits of reform. Egypt's move toward greater exchange rate flexibility needed to continue in order to provide better support for the conduct

KEY INDICATORS — Egypt

	Unit	2003	2004	2005	2006	2007
Population	m	68.00	70.83	70.72	72.13	*73.57
Gross domestic product (GDP)	US$bn	82.40	75.15	89.79	107.38	127.93
GDP per capita	US$	956	1,111	1,270	1,489	*1,739
GDP real growth	%	3.1	4.1	4.5	6.8	7.1
Inflation	%	4.2	8.1	8.8	4.2	10.9
Unemployment	%	10.7	10.9	9.5	11.0	10.7
Oil output	'000 bpd	750.0	708.0	696.0	678.0	710.0
Natural gas output	bn cum	25.0	26.8	34.7	44.8	46.5
Exports (fob) (goods)	US$m	8,205.0	11,000.0	16,073.0	19,036.0	–
Imports (cif) (goods)	US$m	14,821.0	10,210.0	23,818.0	30,653.0	–
Balance of trade	US$m	-6,616.0	-8,210.0	-7,745.0	-11,617.0	–
Current account	US$m	1,940.0	3,420.0	2,910.0	2,635.0	1,862.0
Total reserves minus gold	US$m	13,589.0	14,273.0	20,609.0	24,462.0	30,188.0
Foreign exchange	US$m	13,400.0	14,108.0	20,508.0	24,341.0	30,054.0
Exchange rate	per US$	5.40	6.21	5.71	5.71	5.54

* estimated figure

of a monetary policy aimed at fighting inflation and achieving short term stabilisation, in line with the Egyptian authorities' choice of a managed float regime.

The government planned to gradually reduce the budget deficit to 3 per cent of GDP by 2010/11 to put public debt on a clearly declining path. According to preliminary data, the general government deficit improved from over 9 per cent of GDP in 2005/06 to 7.75 per cent in 2006/07, while the central government deficit improved from 8.2 per cent to 7.5 per cent. The underlying central government balance, that is, excluding one-off factors, improved by about 2 percentage points of GDP, largely from wage restraint and savings on subsidies, transfers, and interest payments due to cash and debt management reforms. A significant increase in domestic fuel prices helped contain the fuel subsidy bill. Structural reforms advanced significantly in promoting what in Egypt had become a private sector driven economy. The fourth largest state bank (Bank of Alexandria) and a large department store chain, along with smaller firms and unused public land, were sold to foreign investors for the equivalent of about 1.3 per cent of GDP. Following the sale of the Bank of Alexandria to Italy's Gruppo Sanpaoli IMI, it was hoped that the remaining two banks still in state hands would proceed. The sale of a majority stake in the Banque du Caire had attracted widespread interest.

Natural gas

According to the US Energy Information Administration (EIA), following major recent discoveries, natural gas is likely to be the primary growth engine of Egypt's energy sector for the foreseeable future. Egypt's natural gas sector is expanding rapidly with production having increased over 30 per cent between 1999 and 2007. In 2006, Egypt produced roughly 1.9 trillion cubic feet (Tcf) and consumed 1.3Tcf of natural gas. According to the US based *Oil and Gas Journal* (OGJ), Egypt's estimated proven gas reserves stand at 58.5Tcf, or roughly 1 per cent of world reserves. With the continued expansion of the Arab Gas pipeline, which increased its exports to roughly 68 billion cubic feet (bcf) during fiscal 2006 from 8bcf in 2003, the EIA considers Egypt to be on its way to becoming a leading supplier of natural gas throughout the Mediterranean region. According to Egyptian government reports, the country's electricity sector has the largest share of natural gas consumption at 58 per cent, followed by the industrial sector with 26 per cent. The government is encouraging households, commercial premises and industries to consider natural gas as a substitute for costlier and more polluting fuels. In January 2008, the World Bank approved loans for the Natural Gas Connections Project, which serves to switch consumption of liquefied petroleum gas (LPG) to natural gas through investment in new connections and further expand natural gas use in densely populated low income areas.

According to the OGJ in January 2008, Egypt's proven oil reserves stood at 3.7 billion barrels. In 2007, Egypt's oil production averaged 664,000 barrels per day (bpd), less than 1 per cent of world production. Despite discoveries and enhanced oil recovery techniques at mature fields, production is declining annually. The Saqqara field, discovered in 2003 and estimated by the UK's BP to contain reserves of 80 million barrels, represents the last major find since 1989.

Risk assessment

Economy	Good
Politics	Fair
Regional stability	Fair

COUNTRY PROFILE

Historical profile

1811 Governor Mohammed Ali exterminated the Mamluks, the former ruling oligarchy, in the Citadel massacre. Mohammed Ali was permitted hereditary rights to rule, providing Egypt remained a part of the Ottoman Empire.
1859–69 The Suez Canal was built.
1882 Britain occupied Egypt and although it still remained under Ottoman suzerainty, it became de facto a British colony.
1914 Britain eliminated the Ottoman suzerainty and the country became a British protectorate – the Egyptian Sultanate.
1922 Egypt was renamed Kingdom of Egypt and was officially independent, although Britain supervised until 1946.
1936 Signing of the Anglo-Egyptian Treaty, which restricted British military presence to the Suez Canal Zone.
1947–49 Egypt contributed to a pan-Arab military force that failed to occupy the newly-created state of Israel.
1952 The 23 July Revolution, led by the army, ousted King Fu'ad, who had just succeeded his father, King Faruq.
1953–56 Egypt was declared a republic in 1953, under President Mohammed Neguib. Neguib relinquished power in 1954 to Colonel Gamal Abdel Nasser, who was officially elected in 1956.
1956 Nasser nationalised the Suez Canal to fund the construction of the Aswan High Dam to regulate the annual flooding of the Nile River. After Egypt blockaded the Israeli Red Sea port of Eilat, Israeli forces attacked and occupied the Sinai peninsula, later being joined by Britain and France, which sought to regain control of the Canal Zone. In the face of strong international opposition, particularly from the US, all three withdrew their forces.
1967 Egypt again blockaded Eilat; Israel launched and won the Six Day War against Egypt, Jordan and Syria, taking control of the Sinai peninsular and the Gaza Strip, which had been Egyptian territory. Crucially, they also took control of the Golan Heights, overlooking Syria.
1968–70 The War of Attrition was a limited war fought between Egypt and Israel, initiated by Egypt as a way to recapture the Sinai peninsular from Israel; the war ended with frontiers at the same place as when the war started.
1970–73 Anwar al Sadat was elected president following the death of Nasser. He renamed the country the Arab Republic of Egypt and ruled it as a one-party state. The Aswan High Dam was inaugurated by the President. In the 6 October War (also known as the Yom Kippur War), Egypt and Syria invaded Israel to reclaim some of the land lost in the Six Day War, but despite early successful strategic gains for Egypt and Syria, Israel counter-attacked and repelled the invasion, re-conquering the Golan Heights from Syria.
1975 The Suez Canal reopened, having been closed since the 1967 war.
1978–84 Sadat visited Jerusalem, which led to the Camp David Peace Accords, the signing of the Egyptian-Israeli Peace Treaty and the eventual Israeli withdrawal from the Sinai peninsular in 1982. Egypt was expelled from the Arab League. Sadat was assassinated by Islamic extremists in 1981. A national referendum approved Hosni Mubarak as president and political opposition parties were allowed for the first time.
1989 Egypt rejoined the Arab League.
1991–94 Egypt contributed to the US-led military campaign against Iraq. The outcome of the Gulf War established the political and economic framework for an Arab-Israeli peace process. Egypt was a party to peace agreements between Israel and the Palestinians, which began negotiations on the status of the former Egyptian territory of Gaza.
1996–2000 The National Democratic Party (NDP) was re-elected in the 1996 and 2000 elections. Mubarak was re-elected president for a fourth term.
2003 Emergency powers established when Sadat was assassinated in 1981 were extended for another three years.

2004 Ahmed Nazif became prime minister. In November, the funeral of Palestinian leader, Yasser Arafat, was held in Cairo.
2005 Egypt hosted the Sharm El Sheik summit, at which Palestinian President Abbas and Israli Prime Minister Sharon signed a truce; Isreal was to withdraw from Gaza and the Palestinian authorities curb the violence of militant groups opposed to Israel. Egypt resumed diplomatic ties with Israel. A constitutional amendment allowed multiple candidates in the presidential elections, which was won by incumbant Mubarak, for a fifth consecutive term. Three-stage parliamentary elections took place. The ruling NDP won 311 of the 442 elective seats; the outlawed Muslim Brotherhood contested the elections as independents and won 88 seats, more than the other opposition parties and independents combined.
2006 Emergency laws, which gave broad powers of arrest and detention to the security forces, were extended by two years.
2007 In March, a referendum to amend 34 articles in the constitution, which among other items aimed at banning political activities and the establishment of political parties based on race, religion and ethnicity; to increase the power of the president and the adoption of anti-terrorism law to replace emergency laws was undertaken. A majority of voters passed the referendum.
2008 On 22 January sections of the Gaza border wall that blocked access by Palestinians into Egypt was blown-up by Hamas militants. The breach allowed thousands of people to cross into Egyptian territory, many to stock up on food and necessities. Israel demanded that the border be closed to prevent the restocking of militant's armouries. Egypt rejected the demand allowing access for humanitarian reasons. On 25 February the border was closed at 1500, but other openings elsewhere were made and hundreds more Palestinians continued to cross into Egypt. International negotiations to provide a permanent solution failed, while Hamas and Egyptian officials reached their own agreement. On 3 February Egyptian forces closed the last breach using razor-wire and metal barricades.

Political structure

Constitution

Under the 1971 constitution, amended in 1980, Egypt is an Arab Republic with a democratic socialist system. The constitution states that there should be no discrimination on the grounds of race or religion. The country is divided into 26 governorates, with governors appointed by the president. There is universal suffrage with a voting age of 18.

Form of state

Democratic socialist republic

The executive

Executive power rests with the president, who is elected by universal suffrage for a six-year term (and may be re-elected), having been nominated by at least one-third of the People's Assembly and approved by at least two-thirds. The president may choose one or more vice presidents, and appoints, and may dismiss, the prime minister and cabinet.
The president may take emergency measures, but these must be approved by a referendum within 60 days; he may also dissolve the People's Assembly (the legislative body) prematurely, but a referendum and elections must be held within 60 days.
The president is supreme commander of the armed forces and head of the police.

National legislature

The legislative body is the Majlis al Shaab (People's Assembly). Most members (444 out of the total 454) are elected every five years by universal suffrage. The remaining 10 representatives are appointed by the president.
A second 264-member chamber, the Majlis al Shura (Advisory Council), has no legislative powers and acts only as a consultative body. Elections are held every three years when one-third of members are elected for six-year terms. Two-thirds of the members are elected by direct universal suffrage, with the provision that half are manual workers, including small farmers, and the remaining one-third is appointed by the president.

Legal system

The legal system is based on the constitution of 1971. Officially, Egyptian law is based on Sharia (Islamic law), although in practice it is based on English common law and the French Napoleonic code. Christians and Jews are subject to their own jurisprudence in personal status affairs. The Court of Cassation, consisting of five judges, is the highest court of appeal. Courts of appeal (three judges) sit in Cairo and four other cities. Assize courts (three judges) deal with serious crimes. Central tribunals (three judges) handle ordinary civil and commercial cases. Summary tribunals (one judge) deal with both civil and criminal cases and have the power to impose fines and decree three-year prison terms.

Last elections

7 November–9 December 2005 (parliamentary, lower house); 6 September 2005 (presidential); 11–15 June 2007 (parliamentary, upper house).
Results: Parliamentary: (lower house) the ruling National Democratic Party (NDP) won 311 of 444 elective seats, independents 112 seats (including 88 affiliates of the Muslim Brotherhood), New Wafd Party six seats, the Tagammu Party two seats and the al Ghad Party one seat. 12 seats were unallocated due to irregularities. The president appoints 10 members out of a total membership of 454. Turnout was 26.6 per cent.
Presidential: The incumbent, Hosni Mubarak (NDP), won 88.6 per cent of the vote; Ayman Nour (al Ghad) 7.3 per cent. Turnout was low at 23 per cent of the electorate.
Parliamentary: (upper house, 88 seats available) the ruling NDP won 84 seats, independents three, Tagammu Party (Progressive National Unionist Party) one. Turnout was 31 per cent.

Next elections

2010 (parliamentary); 2011 (presidential).

Political parties

Ruling party

Al Hizb al Watani al Dimuqrati (National Democratic Party) (NDP) (since 1996; re-elected 9 Dec 2005)

Main opposition party

New Wafd Party (NWP).

Population

73.57 million (2007)*
Last census: November 1996: 59,312,914
Population density: 63 inhabitants per square km. Urban population: 43 per cent of the total (1995–2001).
Annual growth rate: 1.9 per cent 1994–2004 (WHO 2006)

Ethnic make-up

Eastern Hamitic (99 per cent); the remaining 1 per cent comprises minorities including Armenian, Italian and Greek.

Religions

Muslim (mostly Sunni, but including between six and seven million Sufis) (92 per cent); Coptic Christian and others (8 per cent).

Education

Primary education is compulsory and free; followed by three years of intermediate school and two years of secondary school, which are also free, but not compulsory. University graduates have long been guaranteed employment by the state, and this has contributed to the growth of a bloated and overstaffed state bureaucracy. The desire by graduates for office-based professional employment has led to a shortage of skilled technical labour. The government is encouraging more students to go into technical education.
Literacy rate: 56 per cent adult rate; 73 per cent youth rate (15–24) (Unesco 2005).
Compulsory years: 6 to 12
Enrolment rate: 101 per cent, total primary school enrolment of the relevant age

group (including repetition rates); 78 per cent, total enrolment of the relevant age group, in intermediate and secondary schools, (World Bank).
Pupils per teacher: 23 in primary schools

Health

Per capita total expenditure on health (2003) was US$235; of which per capita government spending was US$100, at the international dollar rate, (WHO 2006).
Healthcare in the private sector has become increasingly popular in recent years, especially in Cairo, with the construction of a number of private hospitals that provide an alternative to the severely over-stretched public health service. However the general decline in living standards has placed many private sector healthcare institutions in financial difficulties.
Family planning is widely available and officially encouraged, although many religious leaders continue to preach that it is against Islam. The population continues to grow and the government expects it to double to 110 million over the next 30 years, even if the target of halving the average family size is achieved.
Improved water sources and sanitation facilities are available to 95 per cent and 94 per cent of the population, respectively.
HIV/Aids
HIV prevalence: 0.1 per cent aged 15–49 in 2003 (World Bank)
Life expectancy: 68 years, 2004 (WHO 2006)
Fertility rate/Maternal mortality rate: 3.2 births per woman, 2004 (WHO 2006); maternal mortality 170 per 100,000 live births (World Bank).
Child (under 5 years) mortality rate (per 1,000): 33 per 1,000 live births; 4 per cent of children aged under five were malnourished (World Bank).
Head of population per physician: 0.54 physicians per 1,000 people, 2003 (WHO 2006)

Welfare

Social security provisions include sickness benefits, pensions, health insurance, training and subsidies on basic goods, including pharmaceuticals. The government places particular stress on the improvement of rural living standards and has established rural social units to provide health, education and agricultural services. Social services include care for mothers and children, the aged, the handicapped and prisoners, family planning, cultural education and literacy courses.
The government, employers and employees contribute to a national insurance scheme that covers pensions and sickness benefit. A social development fund provides retraining, unemployment insurance and assistance to people who lose their jobs as a result of reforms and the privatisation of public enterprises.

Main cities

Cairo (capital, estimated population 8.1 million in 2004); Greater Cairo, 10.6 million, is the largest city in Africa.
Other cities include Alexandria (4.0 million), Giza (2.7 million), Shubra al Khaymah (1.0 million), Port Said (548,900), Suez (488,200), Luxor (421,500), Asyut (401,600), El Faiyum (305,100), Ismailia (297,500), Aswan (256,100), El Minya (235,400).

Languages spoken

French and English are widely spoken, especially in business circles.
Official language/s
Arabic

Media

Egypt is the centre for pan-Arab electronic broadcasting having been the first with its own satellite (Nilesat 101) (www.nilesat.com.eg), it has the largest production facilities for Arabic films and TV shows and is the most influential news broadcasting and publishing centre in the Middle East.
While libelling the president, state institution and foreign heads of state may carry a penality of imprisonment, criticism of the regime in unexceptional.
National news agency: MENA (Middle East News Agency)
Press
Dailies: In Arabic, Al Ahram (www.ahram.org.eg) the oldest Arabic newspaper anywhere and the government-owned Al Jumhuriyah (www.algomhuria.net.eg), and the semi-state owned Al Akhbar (www.elakhbar.org.eg). Party political newspapers include and Al Messa (www.almessa.net.eg), Almasry Alyoum (www.almasry-alyoum.com), and Al Ahali (www.al-ahaly.com). Other private newspapers include Al Wafd (www.alwafd.org), El Akhbar (www.elakhbar.org.eg) and El Fagr (www.elfagr.org).
In English, the state-owned The Egyptian Gazette (www.algomhuria.net.eg/gazette) and Daily News Egypt (www.dailystaregypt.com).
In French, in government-owned Al-Ahram Hebdo (http://hebdo.ahram.org.eg) and Le Progrès Egyptien (www.progres.net.eg).
Weeklies: Some daily newspapers have weekend editions. In Arabic, the political magazine Al Watan al Arabi (www.alwatanalarabi.alqanat.com) covers regional news, Akidaty for general interest and Horreyati (www.horreyati.net.eg) for entertainment. Women's magazines include Nisf el Dunia with social and women's issues, Hawwa covers home and family issues and Kolenas is distributed internationally.
In English, the Middle East Times (www.metimes.com) provides general interest and commercial and financial news, Watani (www.wataninet.com), and Al-Ahram (http://weekly.ahram.org.eg).
Business: Most daily newspapers have sections on business matters. The only dedicated newspaper is the Business Today Egypt (www.businesstodayegypt.com), in English, which has a section called In the Black specifically covering commercial and corporate news.
In Arabic the weekly Al Ahram Iktisadi covers analysis of Egyptian business.
Periodicals: Monthly publications in Arabic includes the influential Sabah el Kheir (www.rosaonline.net/sabah) which covers general interest features. The quarterly Al Siassa al Dawlya covers domestin and international politics.
IBA Media is Egypt's leading English-language publisher with Egypt Today (www.egypttoday.com), published six times per year.
Broadcasting
The national, public broadcaster is the Egypt Radio Television Union (ERTU) (www.ertu.org).
Radio: ERTU provides cultural, news, entertainment, youth and sports programmes through a network of eight national radio stations with two external services. Private, commerical stations include El Gouna Radio (www.romolo.com) and Nile FM (http://nilefmonline.com), both playing western music.
Television: ERTU operates two national and local channels. There are numerous satellite TV stations available, led by the ERTU Nile Channel, (www.nilesat.com.eg), Dream TV and Al Mihwar (www.elmehwar.tv) are privately owned.
Egyptian broadcasters transmit over 80 channels throughout the Middle East and the Mediterranean region.
News agencies
National news agency: MENA (Middle East News Agency)

Economy

The government has been introducing essential structural reforms in taxes, trade and subsidies since 2004. It has also restructured the financial system, modernised fiscal accounts and strengthened monetary policy, while speeding up the sale of state entities. Customs procedures have been overhauled and import tariffs reduced. Egypt also moved to a system of unified, flexible exchange rates in December 2004, which has operated well since its inception. The economy has responded promisingly to the reforms and is in the early stages of recovery. GDP grew by around seven per cent in 2006 (compared with five per cent in 2005).

The economy is sustained traditionally by hydrocarbons, agriculture, tourism, Suez Canal tolls and remittances from expatriate workers. The oil and natural gas industry is the mainstay of the economy, accounting for around 30 per cent of GDP and 40 per cent of exports; refinery capacity is one of the largest in Africa. Agriculture contributes 14 per cent to GDP; cotton is the most important agricultural product in terms of output, employment and export revenues. The financial sector is growing in importance. Foreign direct investment (FDI) has risen from US$2 billion in 2003 to over US$6 billion in 2006, an increasing proportion of which is going towards non-hydrocarbons activities.

Labour market and unemployment

Unemployment is a major problem, particularly in the cities. The World Bank estimates that 70 per cent of registered unemployed are under 20 years of age. Independent estimates place the number of Egyptian expatriates working in Gulf and other Arab countries at up to four million. Before the 1990 Iraqi invasion of Kuwait, nearly two million Egyptians worked in Iraq.

External trade

Egypt, as a member of the Common Market for Eastern and Southern Africa (Comesa), and operates within a free trade zone (FTZ) with 13 of the 19 member states. It also signed the Agadir Agreement which proposes to set up a FTZ between Egypt, Jordan, Tunisia and Morocco. In 2005 the Greater Arab Free Trade Area (Gafta) was ratified by 17 members, including Egypt, creating an Arab economic bloc. A customs union was established whereby tariffs within Gafta will be reduced by a percentage each year, until none remain. It is also a signatory of the Euro-Mediterranean Partnership agreement, which provides for the introduction of free trade between the EU and 10 Mediterranean countries, by 2012.

Imports

Principal imports are machinery and equipment, foodstuffs, chemicals, wood products and fuels.

Main sources: US (7.8 per cent total, 2006), Saudi Arabia (6.9 per cent), China (5.8 per cent).

Exports

Principal exports are crude oil and petroleum products, cotton, textiles, metal products and chemicals. Other exports include refined sugar cane, raw cotton, potatoes, rice and oranges.

Main destinations: India (10.1 per cent total, 2006), Italy (9.2 per cent), US (8.7 per cent).

Agriculture

Farming

The agriculture sector contributed 15.5 per cent to GDP in 2004 and employed around 30 per cent of the workforce. Its importance is declining in relation both to industry and to population growth.

Irrigation is supplied by the River Nile and the government is looking at ways to improve the efficiency of water use through the construction of lined canals and pipes. Problems surrounding the ecological effects of the Aswan High Dam persist.

Fertile land is found in the Nile Valley and Delta – the cultivable area accounts for only 2.4 per cent of the total land area at around 3.1 million hectares.

The construction of the Aswan High Dam in the 1970s initially improved crop yields by providing a constant source of water for irrigation. However, the dam had a damaging long-term effect on agriculture. It has permanently raised the water table, causing serious drainage problems and high salinity as well as depriving the Nile valley of annual silt, a natural fertiliser, previously brought down by the river during the flood season. The silt has had to be replaced by costly chemical fertilisers.

Virtually all water in Egypt comes from the River Nile, from which Egypt is allowed to take 55.5 billion cubic metres of water a year, under its agreement with nine other Nile basin countries. This imposes strict limitations on the expansion of agriculture.

A number of major irrigation schemes are under way. These are along the coast north-west of Alexandria, the Nile border with Sudan, East Oweinat in the desert and the largest project of them all, the Southern Valley Scheme. The cost of the Southern Valley Scheme is projected to reach US$85 billion by 2017. Saudi investment will build the largest farm in the world (six times bigger than Singapore) which will reach full production in 2010 and will employ 25,000 people permanently, as well as additional seasonal labour.

Agricultural production in Egypt is highly labour-intensive. Output suffers from crop infestation, price controls, fragmented land tenure, increased soil salinity and consumer preference for imported foods.

Major subsistence crops include maize, sorghum, rice, wheat, beans and vegetables. Egypt's wheat consumption far outstrips local production, with Egyptian wheat crops supplying just 40 per cent of annual domestic demand. Some 65 per cent of food requirements are imported, making Egypt's annual food import bill around US$5.5 billion.

Cotton is a major export crop; however, WTO agreements, which came into force on 1 January 2005, removed tariffs and trade and will put enormous pressure on the industry as it attempts to compete with Asia that has lower production costs and lower prices. Egypt produces high-quality long staple cotton that has been traditionally exported to Europe, the US and Japan, and it may have to lose many jobs as it carves out a niche market in quality cotton rather than competing for the mass market.

Crop production in 2005 included: 22,283,961 million tonnes (t) 8,140,961t wheat, 6,800,000t maize, 6,200,000t rice, *2,500,000t potatoes, *6,600,000t tomatoes, *1,300,000t grapes, 1,170,000t dates, 2,797,600t citrus fruit, *16,335,000t sugar cane, 3,429,535t sugar beets, *310,000t olives, *820,000t seed cotton, *294,000t cotton lint, 242,210t oilcrops, 484,040t pulses, *950,000t sorghum, 33,700t treenuts, 8,195,635t fruit in total, 16,140,402t vegetables in total. Livestock production included: 1,435,923tt meat in total, *320,000t beef, 270,000t buffalo, *69,840t rabbit, *40,000t camel meat, 60,500t lamb and goat meat, *664,240t poultry, *240,000t eggs, 4,708,100t milk, *8,000t honey, *117t cocoons, silk, 5,100t sheepskins, 32,480t cattle hides, 7,550t greasy wool.

* estimate

Fishing

There are active fishing industries in the Mediterranean and the Red Sea, as well as more limited freshwater fishing on the Nile and Lake Nasser. Egypt typically produces over 300,000 tonnes of seafood and 190,000 tonnes of freshwater fish per annum. Virtually all of this is used for domestic consumption. Eleven lakes used to provide an annual 173,000 tonnes of fish but this rate has declined in recent years due to overfishing, lack of investment and pollution.

Forestry

Forests covers less than 1 per cent of Egypt's land area.

Industry and manufacturing

The government places emphasis on: industrial diversification and import substitution, the development of downstream chemicals, and of heavy industry such as the Helwan Iron and Steel Company, the Nag Hammadi aluminium plant and El Dikheila integrated steel works. Industry and manufacturing has been dominated by state-owned companies however there is a renewed interest by the government to sell off enterprises, including

metallurgical, food, wood pulp, and chemical processing, and various smelting works.
A number of cotton concerns are also on the privatisation list, although these companies are at risk, not from the shift in economic rationalisation, by rather global trading dynamics. World Trade Organisation (WTO) rulings that came into practice on 1 January 2005 removed all global tariffs and subsidies on processed cotton. Egypt, as a major manufacture of cotton thread and cloths, could lose thousands of jobs and millions of dollars in export sales. However, a niche market is being formed, supplying cotton apparel to the US under the Qualified Industrial Zones (QIZ) protocol, whereby manufactured goods from nominated QIZ, which must contain 11.7 per cent Israeli input, will be given free access to US markets.
The petrochemical sector is a leading contributor to GDP and has a predicted 6 per cent annual growth.
Egypt has a growing automotive industry, supplying both vehicles and components. There are 18 vehicle manufacturers operating under joint trade agreements with foreign companies. BMW invested US$35 million in a new factory, providing jobs for 500 workers, which opened in May 2004. There are plans to invest a further US$25 million in more facilities. Nissan will open a new assembly plant, geared to produce 3,800 cars a year, which is scheduled to be operational by 2007.

Tourism

Tourism has become the single greatest foreign exchange earner and represents a significant component of Egypt's GDP at 15.4 per cent, contributing US$13 billion in 2005. The industry employed 13 per cent of all workers and earned US$7 billion from tourists alone, with a further US$2.6 billion in capital investment. Annual growth is predicted to increase by 5.4 per cent for 2006–15.
The industry has been able to weather a sequence of damaging events such as the bombings of the tourist resort at Sharm al Sheikh in July 2005, and those in the Red Sea resorts of the Sinai Peninsula in October 2004. This has been achieved by providing cheaper holidays, which has the drawback of impacting on the quality of the tourist base and level of spending.
Archaeological attractions are the primary visitor attractions, although Egypt has increasingly enhanced its facilities by the development of resort tourism, especially on the Red Sea coast. More than 50 per cent of visitors are from Europe, nevertheless, in 2004 Gulf Arabs arrived in Cairo (by up to 32 per cent) in much larger numbers than before. They were particularly welcome as they are high-spending and longer visiting holidaymakers. These were tourists that had been deterred from visiting US and European destinations due to extra security and suspicion of middle-eastern travellers.

Mining

Government policy aims to encourage foreign and local companies to explore for and exploit raw materials. Agreements have been reached for exploration and production of sulphur, phosphate and gold. The government is keen to extend franchises for other minerals, especially titanium and silver. Among non-oil raw materials, only iron ore, phosphate rock and limestone is produced on a significant scale. Other minerals produced include baryte, clay, feldspar, fluorspar, gypsum, kaolin, quartz, salt, silica sand and talc. Manganese and chrome deposits have also been exploited, while commercial deposits of zinc, tin, lead and copper have been discovered in Sinai.
A contract to mine sulphur in Sinai is held by Freeport Egyptian Sulphur Company, a wholly owned subsidiary of US firm Freeport McMoran. The annual production capacity is thought to be around 250,000 tonnes per year (tpy). Egypt also has deposits of uranium.
Although Egypt has no bauxite, it has developed a significant aluminium industry based on electric power from the Aswan High Dam. Production was initially used for basic consumer goods but Egypt now exports a wide range of basic aluminium products.

Hydrocarbons

The upstream oil and gas industry generates around 10 per cent of GDP and represents an important source of foreign currency, with oil accounting for about 40 per cent of total export revenues.
Egypt's production in 2004 was 350,000 barrels per day (bpd), with proven oil reserves of 3.6 billion barrels. Increasing industrialisation and the rise in domestic oil consumption, has encouraged the government into continue with partnership deals for oil exploration. Egypt signed exploration deals with two prospecting firms, one from Tunisia and the other the US. In total, 14 wells will be drilled up to 2011. BP's Saqqara oil field is expected to produce 40,000–50,000bpd annually from 2005. Other petroleum deposits have been discovered in the Qaran area of Egypt's Western Desert by the US-based Apache Corporation.
Coal reserves at Maghara in Sinai total about 27 million tonnes, however, there is no commercial production.

Energy

Electricity is generated at thermal power stations throughout the country, and about a quarter of the total is supplied by the hydroelectric plant at the Aswan High Dam in Upper Egypt.
Around 98 per cent of all electricity needs is provided by the electricity sector but domestic demand is growing fast and to keep up with it Egypt has embarked on a major programme of capital investment. Not only are some current power stations being upgraded to produce more electricity but a number of new generating plants with the total capacity of 33,000MW are under construction. The OECD agreed a loan of US$20 million to fund the North Cairo Electricity Network, which should be operational by 2007, adding 750MW to the system.
There are a number of wind and solar power plants either newly opened or under construction with an expected total capacity of 297MW when they all become operational; the first began generating 93MW in 2004, in Za'farana.

Financial markets

Stock exchange

Egypt's stock market is considered the best of the emerging markets. After seven years of stagnation caused by a series of knocks starting with the Asian financial crisis, then the 2000 Palestinian intifada, followed by the terrorist attack on the US in 2001and the devaluation of the Egyptian pound in 2003, the market has boomed on the back of rising oil prices, increased tourism and Arab money returning from the West.

Banking and insurance

The banking sector is dominated by four public-sector commercial banks – Banque Misr, Bank of Alexandria, Banque du Caire and the National Bank of Egypt – which hold about 60 per cent of deposits, 70 per cent of assets and 65 per cent of loans, and are the main conduit for public-sector trade, savings and financing.
The Central Bank of Egypt (CBE) strengthened the monetary policy framework which should aid it as it manages and limits inflationary pressures while stimulating market driven interest rates. The IMF in a 2005 report stressed that the CBE independence from political interference should be maintained.
As a whole, strong current account trading enabled banks to strengthen their net foreign assets and the CBE also took advantage of market conditions to build up its reserves.
As part of the privatisation programme under way by the government two state banks are in the process of being sold off to the commercial sector. In 2006, bids for the Bank of Alexandria valued the bank at US$1.6 billion – a figure over five times greater than the government's own valuation. Proceeds of the sale will go to

re-capitalising other state-owned banks and a reduction in Egypt's public debt.

Central bank
Central Bank of Egypt

Main financial centre
Cairo

Time
GMT plus two hours (GMT plus three hours from May to September).

Geography
Most of Egypt is located in the north-east corner of Africa between the Mediterranean Sea, the Red Sea, Sudan and Libya. The Sinai peninsula, separated from the African continent by the Suez Canal and the Red Sea, borders Israel. The peninsula also faces Jordan and Saudi Arabia across the Gulf of Aqaba.

The world's longest river, the Nile, flows through deep gorges from mountains in the south, before ending its journey in the Nile delta on Egypt's northern coast, with outlets into the Mediterranean Sea. Its influence on Egypt has been profound as over thousands of years the river has been the lifeblood of the country, its flood plains have provided fertile agricultural land and the necessary freshwater for life in an arid landscape. About 95 per cent of Egypt is uninhabitable desert and over 90 per cent of the population lives within 20km of the Nile.

The Awan Dam, completed in 1970, created Lake Nasser, the world's third largest reservoir. Its hydroelectric power station produces about half of Egypt's electricity and maintains a steady flow of water downstream.

Hemisphere
Northern

Climate
The climate is dry with very little rainfall, hot in summer and cool in winter. Temperatures in Cairo in the north vary from 43 degrees Celsius (C) maximum in summer to 18 degrees C maximum in winter. Sandstorms (the khamsin or simoon winds) can disrupt air traffic between March and May.

Rainfall is largely confined to the Mediterranean coast, with around 200 millimetres a year in Alexandria. Egypt is dependent on the Nile for nearly all its water needs. The government is pressing ahead with desert reclamation schemes, but these are also dependent on limited Nile waters as reserves of water under the desert have so far proved relatively insignificant.

Dress codes
Lightweight clothing is necessary for the hot summer months (May to September). Business dress is formal – suits are worn for all occasions. Men should not wear shorts, except at the beach and women should wear modest clothing in public, covering their arms and legs.

Entry requirements
Passports
Required by all. Some exceptions are allowed for a few nationals of the Middle East. Contact the nearest Egyptian Consulate for more information.

Passports must be valid for six months beyond the intended length of stay.

Visa
Required by all, except citizens of some adjacent countries, for full list of exceptions contact the local embassy or visit http://egypt.embassyhomepage.com.

Business and tourist visas, valid for three months, available for most Europeans and North Americans, can be obtained at the point of entry.

All visitors, except those Europeans and US nationals on tourist visas, must register at the Office of Foreigners and Nationality within seven days of arrival. Hotels will normally undertake this on the visitor's behalf.

Currency advice/regulations
The Import of local currency is unlimited, however its export is prohibited. The import and export of foreign currency is unrestricted.

Customs
It is permitted to import one bottle of alcohol and 200 cigarettes. Camera, video equipment and computers should be declared at customs.

Prohibited imports
Illegal drugs, firearms and cotton.

Export of any antiquity older than 100 years must have a clearance from the Ministry of Cultural Affairs.

Health (for visitors)
Mandatory precautions
A vaccination certificate against yellow fever is required if travelling from an infected area.

Advisable precautions
Typhoid, hepatitis A, tetanus vaccinations are recommended. Malaria exists from June–October in the El Faiyum area.

There is also a rabies risk. Polio was eradicated in 2005.

Avoid drinking tap water and use bottled water instead; water used for brushing teeth or making ice should be boiled first or otherwise sterilised. All fruit should be peeled and only well-cooked meat, vegetables and fish, served hot, should be eaten. Salad and mayonnaise may carry increased risk, except in top-class restaurants. Avoid food sold on the streets.

Hotels
There is a wide range available. Bills are quoted in US dollars and may be settled in Egyptian currency. A 20 per cent tax and service charge should be added to all prices.

Credit cards
Most credit cards are widely accepted. Excepting airline tickets, the free market exchange rate is used in calculating credit card transactions.

Public holidays (national)
Fixed dates
^ 7 Jan (Coptic Christmas Day), 25 Apr (Sinai Liberation Day), 1 May (Labour Day), 23 Jul (Revolution Day), 6 Oct (Armed Forces' Day), 24 Oct (Suez Victory Day).

Variable dates
^ Coptic Easter Monday, Eid al Adha, Eid al Fitr, Islamic New Year, Birth of the Prophet.

^ Followers of the Coptic faith observe this holiday.

Islamic year – 1429 (10 Jan 2008–28 Dec 2008): The Islamic year contains 354 or 355 days, with the result that Muslim feasts advance by 10–12 days against the Gregorian calendar. Dates of feasts vary according to the sightings of the new moon, so cannot be forecast exactly.

Working hours
As a Muslim country the official weekend begins on Friday. Embassies and the offices of some foreign companies also close on Saturday and Sunday. Some companies treat Thursday as a half day. Hours may also vary between winter and summer.

Banking
Sun–Thu: 0830–1400. Money exchanges in city centres also 1700–1900 or 1800–2000.

Business
Sat–Thu: 0900–1700.

Government
Sun–Thur: 0900–1500.

Shops
Sat–Thur: 0900—1300 and 1600—2000 (summer); 1000—1800 (winter). During Ramadan Sat–Thur: 0930—1530 and 2000—2200.

Department stores offer extended hours and local shops may vary their hours to suit.

Telecommunications
Mobile/cell phones
There are GSM 900 services operating in all popluated areas.

Electricity supply
220–440V AC in most areas; in some rural districts 110–380V AC is still found.

Weights and measures
Metric system (local units also in use).

Social customs/useful tips
Hospitality is considered a prime virtue and it would be rude for visitors not to

accept a token drink or other invitation. Many hosts will not allow a guest to pay for anything during his or her stay. Guests should therefore not squabble over paying at a restaurant, for example. In address, use the first name with the appropriate title (for instance Mr, Madame, Doctor, Engineer). Business cards in Arabic are appreciated.

Security

Violent crime against foreigners is rare. However, thieves operate in busy tourist areas such as Giza and Luxor. In these areas it is best to avoid wearing flashy or expensive jewellery.

Given its strategic position in the Middle East, Egypt is particularly sensitive regarding national security. Photographing bridges, railway stations and military installations is forbidden. Carrying a video camera can cause problems with the Egyptian authorities.

Getting there

Air

National airline: Egyptair

International airport/s: Cairo International (CAI), 24km from city, facilities include incoming/outgoing duty-free shops, banks, post office, restaurants and car hire. Borg el Arab-Alexandria International (HBE), 60km from city, including business centre, bank, post office, restaurant, shops, pharmacy and car hire. Luxor Airport (LXR) 5.5km from the city.

Taxis and bus services run to all.

Airport tax: None

Surface

Road: There are road links from Libya and Israel.

A new road from Aswan to Port Sudan was under construction in 2003 but has yet to be completed. Until then no roads to Sudan are recommended.

Water: There are ferry services to Port Said and Alexandria from many destinations across the Mediterranean, run by Menatours. There are ferries between Aqaba in Jordan and Nuweiba on the Sinai peninsular and to Suez from Jeddah in Saudi Arabia. There are steamer services across Lake Nasser from Sudan, although these are suspended during periods of instability in Sudan.

Main port/s: Alexandria, Al Ghardaqah, Aswan, Bur Safajah, Damietta, Marsa Matruh, Port Said and Suez.

Getting about

National transport

Air: Egyptair operates domestic services from Cairo to Luxor, Aswan, Hurghada, Abu Simbel and Alexandria. Air Sinai operates services to North and South Sinai. If planning to fly south, book well in advance. Travel to certain areas of the Nile Delta is restricted.

Road: There is a 31,000km surfaced network which includes good roads linking Cairo-Alexandria, Cairo-Port Said, Ismailia-Suez-Sinai, Cairo-El Faiyum-Luxor-Aswan.

Buses: There are four intercity bus companies: luxury service Superjet, West Delta Bus Company, East Delta Bus Company, and Upper Egypt Bus Company. There are fast and comfortable services between most towns and cities, although they tend to be crowded, and tickets should be booked in advance where possible.

Rail: There are train services to all main cities and towns in Egypt, including express and through trains from Cairo to Alexandria, Luxor and Aswan. Four classes available; certain routes have air-conditioned sleeping cars and buffet service. Tickets must be reserved, sometimes up to two days in advance.

Water: Traditional sailboats (felucca) offer rides along the Nile river.

City transport

Taxis: Metered and unmetered taxis are readily available, but meters where fitted are often not used. Fares should be agreed in advance.

Air-conditioned limousines are available at airports and main hotels. Chauffeured taxis from Cairo airport to the city centre are recommended. Hotels have their own shuttle services. Hotel taxis or chauffeured hire cars are more efficient and can be hired by the day, subject to negotiation. Fares are usually listed in the major hotels.

City centre taxis are cheap, although often uncomfortable and never have air-conditioning. If you are travelling beyond the city centre, it is a good idea to carry a map to guide the taxi driver. The journey time from Cairo International Airport to the city is about 40–60 minutes. Tipping is usually 10 per cent.

Buses, trams & metro: Local buses are numerous, cheap and crowded, as are the few trams still in existence. The Cairo metro is fast, inexpensive and not too crowded, it has 43 stations, five of which run through central Cairo.

Ferry: Several routes run north and south of the city plied by waterbuses.

Car hire

An international driving licence and third-party insurance are needed. Hire charges should be negotiated in advance. The maximum speed limit on main roads is 90kph, rising to 100kph on the Cairo-Alexandria desert road; fines for speeding are substantial. Traffic in Cairo is heavily congested.

BUSINESS DIRECTORY

The addresses listed below are a selection only. While World of Information makes every endeavour to check these addresses, we cannot guarantee that changes have not been made, especially to telephone numbers and area codes. We would welcome any corrections.

Telephone area codes

The international direct dialling code (IDD) for Egypt is +20, followed by area code and subscriber's number:

Alexandria	3	Ismailiya	64
Ashara Ramadan	15	Kafr El Sheik	47
Aswan	97	Luxor	95
Asyut	88	Maeria	3
Benha	13	Mahalla	43
Beni Suef	82	Mansoura	50
Cairo	2	Marsa Matruh	3
Damanhur	45	Port Said	66
Damietta	57	Pyramids	2
El Arish	68	Sacheia	16
El Minya	86	Sohag	93
Fayoum	84	Suez	62
Giza	2	Tanta	40
Heliopolis	2	Zagazig	55

Useful telephone numbers

Cairo
Police: 122
Fire: 125
Ambulance: 123

Aswan
Police: 22147

Alexandria
Police: 960-151-122

Suez
Police: 23-929

Chambers of Commerce

Alexandria Chamber of Commerce, 31 El-Ghorfa El-Togaria Street, Alexandria (tel: 809-339; fax: 808-993).

American Chamber of Commerce in Egypt, 33 Soliman Abaza Street, Doki-Giza, Cairo (tel: 338 1050; fax: 338-1060; e-mail: info@amcham.org.eg).

Aswan Chamber of Commerce, Abtal El-Tahreer Street, Aswan (tel: 323-084).

Cairo Chamber of Commerce, 4 Midan El-Falaki, Cairo (tel: 354-2943; fax: 355-7940).

Damietta Chamber of Commerce, Saad Zaghloul Street, Damietta (tel: 322-799; fax: 320-632).

Egyptian-British Chamber of Commerce, PO Box 4EG, 299 Oxford Street, London W1A 4EG (tel: 020-7499-3100; fax: 020-7499-1070; e-mail: info@theebcc.com).

Fayoum Chamber of Commerce, El-Nadi El-Reyadi Street, El Fayoum (tel: 322-148).

Federation of Egyptian Chambers of Commerce, 4 Midan El-Falaky, Cairo (tel: 795-1136; fax: 795-1164; e-mail: fedcoc@menanet.net).

Ismailia Chamber of Commerce, 163 Saad Zaghloul Street, Ismailia (tel: 221-663; fax: 322-515).

Port Said Chamber of Commerce, Benayet Souk El Goumla, Port Said (tel: 222-733; fax: 236-141).

Red Sea Chamber of Commerce, Old City Council Building, Hurghada (tel: 440-761).

Suez and South Sinai Chamber of Commerce, 47 Salah Eldin Elayoubi Street, Suez (tel: 227-783).

Banking

Alexandria Commercial and Maritime Bank, PO Box 2376, 85 El Horreya Avenue, 21519 Alexandria (tel: 392-1237, 392-1556, 392-9203; fax: 391-3706).

Arab African International Bank, 5 Midan Al-Saray Al Koubra, Garden City, Cairo (tel: 794-5094/5/6; fax: 795-8493).

Arab International Bank, 35 Abdel Khalek Sarwat Street, Cairo (tel: 391-8794, 391-6391; fax: 391-6233).

Bank of Alexandria, 49 Kasr El Nil Street, Cairo (tel: 393-6262, 391-1203; fax: 391-0481, 391-980).

Bank of Commerce & Development, 'Al Tegaryoon', PO Box 1373, 13 26th July Street, Sphinx Square, Mohandessin, Cairo (tel: 302-8156, 302-1623; fax: 302-3963).

Cairo Barclays Bank, PO Box 110, Maglis El Shaab, 12 Midan El Sheikh Youssef, Garden City, Cairo (tel: 366-2600; fax: 366-2810/11).

Cairo Far East Bank, PO Box 757, 104 El Nil Street, Dokki, Cairo (tel: 336-2516/18; fax: 348-3818).

Crédit International d'Egypte, 46 El Batal Ahmed Abdel Aziz Street, Mohandessin, Cairo (tel: 336-1897, 336-1898; fax: 360-8673).

Delta International Bank, PO Box 1159, 1113 Corniche El Nil Street, Cairo (tel: 575-3492; fax: 574-3403).

Egyptian American Bank, PO Box 1825, 4 & 6 Hassan Sabri Street, Zamalek, Cairo (tel: 738-0126, 738-0136, 738-2661; fax: 738-0609, 738-0450).

Misr Exterior Bank; Cairo Plaza Building, Cornish El Nil, Boulaque, Cairo (tel: 778-701, 778-619, 766-381, 766-360; fax: 762-806, 578-0238).

Misr International Bank, PO Box 218, Embaba, 54 El Batal Ahmed Abdel Aziz Street, Mohandessin, Cairo (tel: 749-4424, 749-7091; fax: 700-928).

National Bank for Development (NBD), PO Box 647, 5(A) El Borsa El Gedida Street, 11511 Cairo (tel: 392-3245; fax: 390-5681).

National Bank of Egypt, PO Box 11611, National Bank of Egypt Tower, 1187 Corniche El Nil, Cairo (tel: 574-9101; fax: 576-2672).

Nile Bank, PO Box 2741, 35 Ramses Street, Abdel Moneim Riyad Sq, Cairo (tel: 574-1417, 574-3502, 575-1105; fax: 575-6296, 575-3640).

Suez Canal Bank, PO Box 2620, 11 Mohamed Sabri Abu Alam St, Cairo (tel: 393-1066, 393-1048, 393-1215; fax: 391-3522).

Central bank

Central Bank of Egypt, 31 Kasr el Nil Street, Cairo (tel: 392-6211; fax: 391-7168; email: info@cbe.org.eg).

Travel information

Cairo Airport, Airport Road, Heliopolis, 11776 Cairo (tel: 265-4611; fax: 263-7132; internet: www.cairo-airport.com).

Egyptair, New Administrative Complex, Airport Road, Cairo (tel: 267-4700–4709; fax: 418-3715; internet: www.egyptair.com).

Ministry of tourism

Ministry of Tourism, Misr Tourist Tower, Abbassiya Square, Abbassiya (tel: 284-1707; fax: 285-9551; email: mot@idsc.gov.eg).

National tourist organisation offices

Egyptian Tourist Authority, Misr Travel Tower, Abbassia Square, Cairo (tel: 286-4509, 284-1970; fax: 285-4363; internet: www.touregypt.net).

Ministries

Ministry of Agriculture, Animal and Fish Wealth and Land Reclamation, Nadi El Seid Street, Dokki, Giza (tel: 702-677; fax: 703-889; email: capi@idsc.gov.eg)..

Ministry of Cabinet Affairs and Administrative Development, 1 Magles El Shaab Street, Cairo (tel: 354-1722; fax: 355-6306; email: cabinet1@idsc.gov.eg).

Ministry of Culture, 2 Shagaret El Dor St, Zamalek Cairo 03 (tel: 341-5568; fax: 340-6449; email: mculture@idsc.gov.eg).

Ministry of Defence and Military Production, 5 Ismail Abaza Street, Cairo (tel: 355-3063; fax: 354-8739; email: mod@idsc.gov.eg).

Ministry of Economy and International Co-operation, 8 Adly St, Cairo (tel: 390-6796; fax: 390-3029; email: mineco@idscl.gov.eg; internet site: www.sis.gov.eg).

Ministry of Education, 4 Ibrahim Naguib St, Garden City, Cairo (tel: 355-7952; fax: 356-2952; Email: moe@idsc.gov.eg).

Ministry of Electricity and Energy, Ramses Street, Abbassia, Nasr City Cairo (tel: 261-6514; fax: 261-6302; email: mee@idsc.gov.eg).

Ministry of Finance, Lazoughly Square, Justice and Finance Building, Cairo (tel: 354-1055; fax: 354-5433; email: mofinance@idsc1.gov.eg).

Ministry of Foreign Affairs, Maspero, Cairo (tel: 574-9820; fax: 574-9533).

Ministry of Information Maspero, Corniche El Nil, Cairo 02 (tel: 574-8986; fax: 574-8781; email: minexter@idsc1.gov.eg; internet: www.mfa.gov.eg).

Ministry of Health and Population, Magles El Shaab St, Cairo (tel: 354-1076; fax: 355-3966; email: moh@idsc.gov.eg).

Ministry of Higher Education, 4 Ibrahim Naguib Street, Garden City, Cairo (tel: 355-7952; fax: 356-2952; email: mheducat@idsc1.gov.eg, info@sti.sci.eg).

Ministry of Housing, Reconstruction and New Urban Communities, 1 Ismail Abaza St, Cairo (tel: 355-3320; fax: 355-7836; email: mhuuc@idsc1.gov.eg).

Ministry of Industry and Mineral Wealth, 2 Latin America Street, Garden City (tel: 355-7034; fax: 354-8362; email: moimw@idsc.gov.eg).

Ministry of Information, Maspero, Corniche El Nil, Cairo (tel: 747-193; fax: 757-144; email: rtu2@idsc.gov.eg).

Ministry of Insurance & Social Affairs, El Sheikh Rihan Street, Bab El-Louq, Cairo (tel: 337-0039; fax: 337-5390; email: msi@idsc.gov.eg).

Ministry of Interior, El Sheikh Rihan St, Cairo (tel: 355-7500; fax: 355-7792; email: moi1@idsc.gov.eg).

Ministry of Justice, Justice and Finance Building, Lazoughli Sq, Cairo 15 (tel: 355-1176; fax: 355-8103; email: mojeb@idsc1.gov.eg).

Ministry of Land Reclamation, Nadi El Seid St, Cairo 10 (tel: 703-011).

Ministry of Local Administration, Kasr El Aini St, Cairo 04 (tel: 355-3566).

Ministry of Manpower and Immmigration, 3 Youssef Abbas St, Nasr City, Cai (tel: 260-9363; fax: 260-9891; email: mwlabor@idsc1.gov.eg).

Ministry of Petroleum, 16 El Mokhayyam El Da'em Street, Nasr City (tel: 262-2268; fax: 263-6060; email: mopm@idsc1.gov.eg).

Ministry of Planning, Salah Salem Road, Nasr City (tel: 602-935; fax: 263-4747).

Ministry of Public Enterprises, Magles El Shaab Street, Cairo (tel: 355-8026; fax: 355-3606); PEO, 2 Latin America Street,

Garden City, Cairo (tel: 794-3484; fax: 795-9233).

Ministry of Public Works and Water Resources, El Nil St, Embaba, Cairo 04 (tel: 354-5884; fax: 355-8008; email: mpwwr@idsc.gov.eg).

Ministry of Rural Development, 4 Shooting Club Street, Dokki, Cairo (tel: 349-7470; fax: 349-7785).

Ministry of Shipping, 7 Abdel Khalek Sarwat St, Cairo, 01 (tel: 764-343).

Ministry of Social Affairs and Insurance, El Sheikh Rihan St, Bab El Louk, Cairo 06 (tel: 354-2900; fax: 917-799).

Ministry of State for Administrative Development and Environment and Ministry of the Public Enterprise, 1 Magles El Shaab Street, Lazoughli Square, CAI 06 (tel: 355-8026; fax: 355-5882; email: mops3@idsc.gov.eg).

Ministry of State for the Affairs of the People's Assembly and the Shoura Council, Magles El Shaab St, Cairo 04 (tel: 355-7750; fax: 355-7681; email: parli@idsc.gov.eg).

Ministry of State for Environmental Affairs, Helwan Road, Cairo (tel: 375-7306; fax: 378-4285; email: eeaa@idsc.gov.eg).

Ministry of State for Military Production, 23 Kobri Al Kubba St, Cairo 36 (tel: 257-8697/2915).

Ministry of State for Planning and International Co-operation, Salah Salem Street, Nasr City (tel: 401-4615; fax: 401-4733; email: miceu@idsx.gov.eg).

Ministry of State for Scientific Research Affairs, 101 Kasr El Aini St, Cairo 04 (tel: 355-7952).

Ministry of Trade and Supply, 99 Kasr El Aini St, Cairo 04 (tel: 355-0360; fax: 354-4973; email: msit@idsx.gov.eg).

Ministry of Transport, Communications and Civil Aviation, 105 Kasr El Aini Street, Cairo (tel: 354-3623; fax: 355-5564; email: garb@idsc.gov.eg).

Ministry of Waqfs, 5 Sabry Abou Alam Street, Bab El-Louq, Cairo (tel: 392-6163; fax: 392-6305; email: mawkaf@idsc1.gov.eg)

Prime Minister's Office, 1 Magles El Shaab St, Lazoughli Square, Cairo 04 (tel: 354-7376; fax: 355-8048).

President's Office, Abdin palace, CAI 06 (tel: 391-0130).

Other useful addresses

Arab League, The Arab League Building, Corniche El Nil, Cairo (tel: 393-4499; fax: 775-626).

Arab Organisation for Industrialisation, 2D Abassiya Square, PO Box 770 (tel: 823-377; fax: 826-010).

Arab Republic of Egypt National Telecommunications Organisation (ARENTO), 26 Ramses Street (tel: 760-333; fax: 771-306).

British Embassy, 7 Ahmed Ragheb St, Garden City, Cairo (tel: 354-0852; fax: 354-0859).

Cabinet Office, 1 Maglis El Shaab Street, Lazoughli Square, CAI 04 (tel: 354-7376; fax: 355-8048).

Cairo Regional Center for International Commercial Arbitration, 3 Aboul Feda Street, Zamalek, Cairo (tel: 340-1330; fax: 340-1336).

Cairo Stock Exchange, 4 Sharia esh-Sherifein, Cairo (tel: 392-1402; fax: 392-8526).

Capital Market Authority, 20 Emad El Din Street, Sixth Floor, Downtown (tel: 777-774; fax: 755-339).

Central Agency for Public Mobilisation and Statistics (CAPMAS), Saleh Salem Street, Nasr City, Cairo (tel: 603-717; fax: 604-099).

Central Post Office, Ataba Square, Cairo.

Commercial International Investment Company (CIIC), 66-68 Mohie El-Din Abou El-Ezz St, Dokki, Cairo (tel: 335-8035, 335-7093, 337-6251; fax: 335-7095).

Commercial Representation Office, 96 Ahmed Orabi Street, Mohandiseen (tel: 347-1892; fax: 345-1840).

Commission of the European Communities Delegation in Egypt, 6 Ibn Zenki Street, Zamalek, Cairo (tel: 340-8388; fax: 340-0385).

Customs Information Centre, 4 El Tayaran Street, Nasr City (tel: 260-5711; fax: 261-2672).

Egyptian Electricity Authority, Abassia, Cairo (tel: 261-6537; fax: 261-6512, 401-1630).

Egyptian Embassy (USA), 3521 International Court, NW, Washington DC 20008 (tel: (+1-202) 895-5400; fax: (+1-202) 244-5131).

Egyptian General Petroleum Corporation (EGPCC), 4 Palestine Street, Fourth Sector, new Maadi (tel: 353-1438; fax: 353-1457).

Egyptian Radio and Television Corporation (ERTC), Radio and TV Building, Sharia Maspiro, Corniche el Nil, PO Box 504, Cairo (tel: 749-508; fax: 746-989).

Faud Nemah (Interpreter Service), 40 Kasr El Nil Street, Cairo (tel: 746-394).

General Authority for Control of Imports and Exports, Atlas Building El Sheikh Maarouf and Ramses Streets (tel: 574-2830; fax: 766-971).

General Authority for Investment and Free Zones, 8 Sharia Adly, PO Box 1007, Cairo (tel: 390-6804).

General Organisation for Industrialisation (GOFI) 6 Khali Agha Street, Garden City (tel: 355-7005; fax: 354-4984).

General Organisation for International Exhibitions and Fairs (GOIEF), Exhibition Ground, Nasr City, Cairo (tel: 260-7811; fax: 260-7845, 260-7848).

International Finance Corp (IFC), 5 El Fallah Street, Mohandessin, Cairo (tel: 347-8081; fax: 347-3738).

Internatinal Monetary Fund (IMF), 31 Kasr El Nil Street, Central Bank, Cairo (tel: 392-4257; fax: 351-7137).

Kamel Bros Ltd (interpreter service), 20 Hassan Sabri Street, Cairo (tel: 817-575).

Local Governorates, El-Islah El-Zerai Building, 10th Floor, 4 Nadi El-Seid Street, Dokki (tel: 349-4770; fax: 349-7788).

Sales Tax Authority, 4 El Tayaran Street, Nasr City (tel: 260-7500; fax: 260-7501).

Social Fund for Development (SFD), Hussein Hegazy and El Aini Streets, Cairo (tel: 354-8339; fax: 355-0628).

Taxation Authority, 5 Hussein Hegazi Street (tel: 355-7784; fax: 355-5438).

US Embassy, 5 Sharia Latin America, Garden City, Cairo (tel: 355-7371).

National news agency: MENA (Middle East News Agency)
Address: MENA Head Office, PO Box 1165, 17 Hoda Sharawi Street, Cairo (tel: 393-3000; internet: www.mena.org.eg).

Internet sites

Africa Business Network: www.ifc.org/abn

Africa Online: www.africaonline.com

AllAfrica.com: http://allafrica.com

American Chamber of Commerce in Egypt: www.amcham.org.eg

Arab Bank: www.arabbank.com

Egypt Business Directory: www.telefax.com.eg/default.htm

Egypt corporate information: www.corporateinformation.com/egcorp.html

Egypt economic indicators: www.economic.idsc.gov.eg/

Egypt www index: http://ce.eng.usf.edu/pharos/

El Salvador

KEY FACTS

Official name: República de El Salvador (Republic of El Salvador)

Head of State: President Elias Antonio Saca (Arena) (since 2004)

Head of government: President Elias Antonio Saca

Ruling party: Coalition government led by Alianza Republicana Nacionalista (Arena) (Nationalist Republican Alliance)

Area: 21,400 square km

Population: 7.13 million (2007)*

Capital: San Salvador

Official language: Spanish

Currency: US dollar (US$) (from 1 Jan 2001; previous currency colón locked at C8.75 per US dollar)

Exchange rate: US$1.00 per US$ (fixed)

GDP per capita: US$2,857 (2007)*

GDP real growth: 4.60% (2007)*

Labour force: 2.88 million (2007)

Unemployment: 6.50% (2005)* (additional underemployment)

Inflation: 3.80% (2007)

Balance of trade: -US$4.06 billion (2006)

Foreign debt: US$7.25 billion (2004)

Visitor numbers: 1.14 million (2006)*

* estimated figure

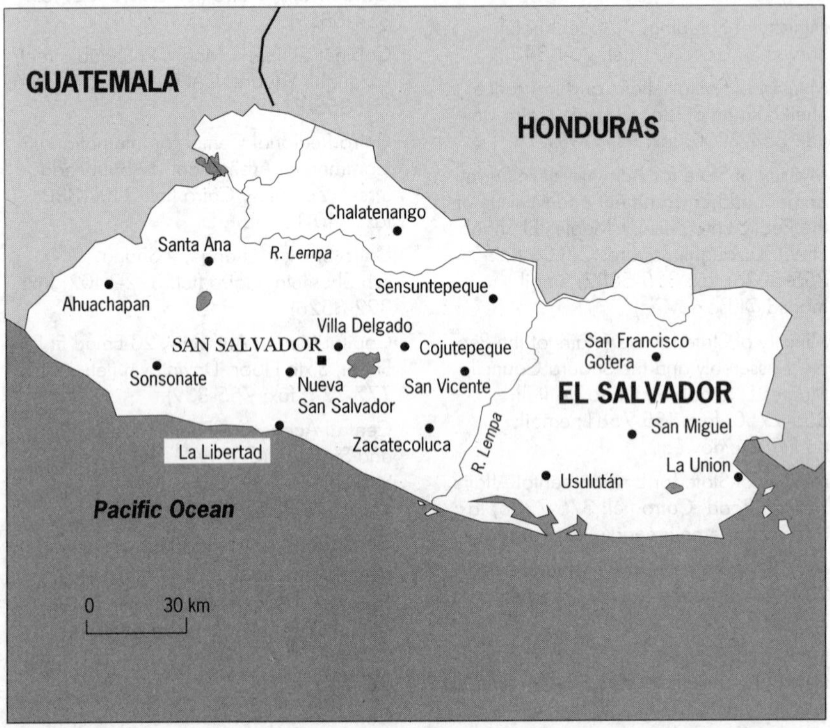

In its briefing on El Salvador, the World Bank defines El Salvador's major challenge as that of improving its economic growth rates, which have been relatively low since the late 1990s. GDP growth slowed during 2000–04 averaging a bit less than 2 per cent, compared to about 4 per cent in the 1990s. This situation has recently begun to improve as the economic growth rate reached 4 per cent in 2006 and maintained the same level in 2007.

Improving growth

In 2007 the Salvadoran economy continued to grow at its fastest pace in a decade. The International Monetary Fund (IMF) in its country report on El Salvador, noted that after several years of sluggish activity in the early 2000s, growth started improving in 2005, and has sustained an annual rate of between 4 and 4.25 per cent since the first quarter of 2006, despite slower growth in the United States since mid-2006. According to the United Nations Commission for Latin America and the Caribbean (ECLAC), the GDP growth rate of 4.5 per cent in 2007 was half a percentage point higher than the previous year and the best level in 12 years. The recovery in growth was generated mainly by family remittances (accounting for almost 20 per cent of GDP), consumption and investment. On the supply side, non-traditional agriculture, tourism, and other services were the most dynamic sectors.

Inflation peaked at 5.5 per cent in January 2007, due to a rise in food prices, but moderated over the rest of the year.

El Salvador's current account deficit was stable in 2006, at about 5 per cent of GDP. It widened in the first half of 2007, reflecting robust domestic demand. During

the latter period, imports of consumer, intermediate, and capital goods grew at annual rates slightly exceeding 10 per cent. Export growth lagged behind that of imports, as buoyant non-traditional exports, rising at a 16 per cent annual rate, were offset by stagnant exports of the *maquila* sector. Remittances remain the most important source of external financing; they have kept growing so far in 2008, albeit more slowly than in previous years. The other main sources of external financing in 2007 were foreign direct investment (FDI), partly related to domestic bank acquisitions, and grants to the public sector.

The real effective exchange rate remained broadly stable in 2007, as was the case during the previous decade. Modest real appreciation against the US dollar was compensated by the weakness of the dollar against third-country currencies. Based upon the current real effective exchange rate level and the baseline scenario (reflecting current policies for 2007–08 and a forecast improvement in the fiscal balance of 0.5 per cent of GDP in 2009, medium-term projections show a sustainable current account position: the current account deficit should fall to 3.5–4 per cent of GDP toward the end of the five-year projection period, and external debt decline steadily from 50 per cent of GDP to below 40 per cent of GDP by 2012.

Robust non traditional export growth, particularly to Central American countries, suggests that the export sector remains competitive. There are also signs that the restructuring of the *maquila* sector is yielding tangible results. Government revenue had risen by about 0.75 per cent of GDP in 2006, reflecting in part tax administrative measures and cyclically higher economic activity (each accounting for about 0.25 per cent of GDP). Higher capital outlays related to tropical storm Stan and rising subsidies on petroleum products (0.25 per cent of GDP) kept the fiscal deficit close to the budgeted figure of 3 per cent of GDP. Continued strong tax revenue performance during the first half of 2007, coupled with under execution of some programmes, resulted in a lower-than-forecast deficit. Seasonal acceleration in the implementation of the public sector investment programme should bring the deficit close to the budgeted 2.3 per cent of GDP for the year as a whole. The 2007 fiscal deficit will be financed primarily by domestic resources.

It is frequently heard in San Salvador that foreign critics tend to overlook the difficulties posed by social and economic development, ignoring the changes that have taken place in recent years. These observations do not take into account the fact that despite the changes, El Salvador's economy is still heavily dependent on coffee and cotton growing.

Military reined in

With a total land area of 21,400 square km coupled with a population of 6.7 million, El Salvador is the most densely populated of all the countries on the American mainland. The country has a history of political divisions, but in recent years political and social conflict has been minimised, though some tensions, naturally, still exist. One of the key reasons for the relatively placid atmosphere in El Salvador today is the successful reduction in the power of the military. El Salvador's constitution now prevents the military from intervening in matters of internal security. Furthermore, the military's manpower has also been reduced. At their peak during the civil war the armed forces numbered 63,000 men.

El Salvador is now a democratic republic, governed by the president as head of state. Both the office of the president (single five year term only) and each of the 84 deputies who make up the Legislative Assembly are elected by means of universal suffrage. Current President Elías Antonio Saca González, popularly known as 'Tony', was elected on 21 March 2004, by a clear margin of 22 per cent over leftist candidate Schafik Jorge Handal of the Frente Farabundo Martí para la Liberación Nacional (FMLN) (Farabundo Martí National Liberation Front). Saca was inaugurated as president on 1 June 2004, succeeding fellow Alianza Republicana Nacionalista (Arena) (National Republican Alliance) member and former president Francisco Flores. A Salvadorean national of Palestinian descent, Saca, prior to taking office, was a renowned businessman and radio sports commentator.

El Salvador is now one of the more stable economies in Central America and increased integration with the US economy looks set to continue. The country's trade deficit is large; one of the major sources of foreign income originates in the US, where Salvadoreans working legally and illegally, send money back to family members in El Salvador.

Dollarisation

Since dollarisation became an official reality in Salvadorean life on 1 January 2001, it is generally acknowledged that prices have risen in the country. As so often happens when a new currency is injected into the economy a rounding up of prices occurs – witness the effect of the introduction of the euro in many European Union member countries in the late 1990s/early 2000s. Both currencies, the US dollar and the Salvadorean colón, circulated for three years, before the latter was abolished and the US dollar was officially adopted in 2004. Despite the displeasure felt by many Salvadoreans at the loss of their currency and the consequent rise in prices, it is now generally acknowledged throughout the country, that a return to the former currency would be catastrophic for the economy as a whole.

Furthermore, the adoption of the dollar in 2001 resulted in lower interest rates, thus facilitating increased opportunities for gaining short and long-term credit for

KEY INDICATORS **El Salvador**

	Unit	2003	2004	2005	2006	2007
Population	m	6.65	6.70	6.88	7.01	*7.13
Gross domestic product (GDP)	US$bn	14.85	15.82	16.97	18.65	*20.37
GDP per capita	US$	2,234	2,335	2,468	*2,661	*2,857
GDP real growth	%	1.8	1.5	2.8	4.2	*4.6
Inflation	%	2.1	4.5	3.7	4.0	3.8
Unemployment	%	6.8	6.3	6.5	6.0	6.2
Industrial output	% change	–	-1.3	1.4	3.5	–
Agricultural output	% change	–	3.0	5.7	7.5	–
Exports (fob) (goods)	US$m	1,357.0	3,329.6	3,383.0	3,567.0	–
Imports (cif) (goods)	US$m	3,926.0	5,948.8	6,766.0	7,628.0	–
Balance of trade	US$m	-2,569.0	-2,619.1	-3,383.0	-4,061.0	–
Current account	US$m	-640.0	-700.0	-786.0	-854.9	*-985.0
Total reserves minus gold	US$m	1,942.9	1,927.2	1,722.8	1,814.9	2,110.0
Foreign exchange	US$m	1,905.8	1,888.4	1,687.1	1,777.3	2,070.5
Exchange rate	per US$	1.00	1.00	1.00	1.00	1.00

* estimated figure

Salvadorean citizens. The increase in liquidity in the economy brought about by more personal spending power and greater levels of disposable income led to an increase in consumer sales, as more Salvadoreans purchased sizeable assets such as motor cars and residential property. Dissatisfaction with dollarisation often returns to the surface of public debate at the time of elections though. This was certainly the case in 2004, when the left made great play of Arena's alleged servitude to Washington.

The incumbent Arena administration has outlined its intention to pass fresh legislation designed to improve labour mobility, so as to allow workers in unproductive sectors to transfer more easily to lucrative industries. The Saca government argues that by passing such legislation, El Salvador will be better placed to take advantage of Cafta membership. In addition to Cafta, El Salvador also enjoys free trading relationships with Mexico, the Dominican Republic, Chile and Panama.

Poverty prevails

According to the World Bank, poverty levels declined significantly between 1991 and 2002 (close to 27 percentage points), extreme poverty was halved in the same period, and impressive progress was also made in social areas – including basic education enrolment, infant and maternal mortality, access to reproductive health services and access to safe water. However, despite the generally improving economy, progress in the fight against poverty slowed after 2002 – mostly due to the coffee crisis, the 2001 earthquakes, and the slow down in the global economy. The proportion of the population below the nationally defined poverty line still stands at 31 per cent of households or 35 per cent of total population. Income inequality, already high by international standards, has increased since the mid-1990s.

The persistently high levels of crime and violence have negatively affected the image of the country and the investment climate (55 homicides per 100,000 persons in 2006). Crime and violence in El Salvador also undermines social capital and erodes the assets and incomes of the poor, for example by devaluing property values in insecure neighbourhoods, impeding safe access to education (when gangs take over schools) and reducing employment opportunities, particularly at night because of the dangers of public transportation. A broad national, consensus is needed on how to tackle the complex social, economic and political nature of violence and crime, while preserving human rights and civil liberties.

Risk assessment

Political	Improving
Economy	Improving
Regional stability	Improving

COUNTRY PROFILE

Historical profile

1821 The Central American provinces (Costa Rica, Guatemala, Honduras, Nicaragua and El Salvador) declared independence from Spain.
1825 Costa Rica, Guatemala, Honduras, Nicaragua and El Salvador formed the Central American Federation (CAF).
1838 The CAF was dissolved and El Salvador became an independent republic. By the twentieth century, the majority of the indigenous population was reduced to poverty and discontent, having been pushed off their land, and the land turned over to crops for export. Most of El Salvador's income came from coffee exports.
1929 Coffee prices plummeted following the US stock market crash.
1932 During the uprising of peasants and Indians and estimated 30,000 people were killed by the military, referred to as La Matanza (the massacre).
1961 The right-wing Partido de Conciliación Nacional (PCN) (National Reconciliation Party) came to power following a military coup.
1969 Honduras and El Salvador fought what became known as the 'soccer war', which was prompted by land disputes and El Salvador's win in the World Cup play-offs between the two countries; over 3,000 people died.
1970s There were demonstrations, civil disobedience and strikes. The esquadrones de muerte (death squads) were formed. Thousands of Salvadorians were kidnapped, tortured and murdered.
1977 General Carlos Romero was elected president.
1979 Romero was ousted by reformist military officers, although this failed to stem the number of deaths at the hands of military-backed death squads.
1980 Napoleón Duarte became El Salvador's first civilian president since 1931.
1980s Civil war between the US-backed right-wing government and a leftist guerrilla group, Frente Farabundo Martí para la Liberación Nacional (FMLN) (Front for National Liberation), was based largely in the countryside. Right-wing groups carried out indiscriminate street killings of 'subversives'. Some rural communities were targeted by the security forces for eradication.
1982 The far-right Alianza Republicana Nacionalista (Arena) (Nationalist Republican Alliance) came to power following violent parliamentary elections.
1984 Duarte won the presidential election and began to negotiate a settlement with the FMLN.
1989 Arena's Alfredo Cristiani was elected president.
1992 A formal cease-fire, under UN auspices, came into effect. An estimated 75,000 people had been killed in the 12-year civil war.
1994 Political killings and threats continued right up to the elections. Arena's Armando Calderón Sol was elected president.
1997 Arena won the Assembly elections.
1999 Francisco Flores (Arena) won the presidential election.
2000 The FMLN become the largest party in the National Assembly. Arena formed a coalition government with the PCN, giving the right-wing block a majority in the Assembly.
2001 The US dollar was adopted as the official currency. Around 1,500 people were killed in the worst earthquakes for more than a decade and 1.5 million were made homeless.
2003 A free trade agreement (FTA) with Panama came into effect.
2004 Antonio Saca (Arena) won the presidential elections. El Salvador along with Dominican Republic, Costa Rica, Guatemala, Honduras and Nicaragua agreed to a proposed Central American Free Trade Agreement (Cafta) with the US.
2005 The OAS human rights court voted to re-open an investigation into the El Mozote massacre in 1981. Thousands of people fled the area surrounding the Ilamatepec volcano after it erupted and a tropical storm caused many deaths and damaged the surrounding area.
2006 Arena won 34 seats in the national assembly elections; the FMLN won 32 seats. The newly defined border between Honduras and El Salvador was inaugurated.
2007 Three members of Arena were murdered in Guatemala. In October after eight years of conflict, the International Court of Justice (ICJ) ruled on a new maritime boundary between Honduras and Nicaragua. The result gives both countries equal access to the rich fishing grounds and oil and gas exploration waters in the area.
2008 In January over 400 judges protested against allegations of corruption against four of their colleagues.

Political structure

In addition to their unicameral national parliaments, El Salvador, Guatemala, Honduras, Nicaragua, Panama and

Dominican Republic also return directly-elected deputies to the supranational Central American Parliament.

Constitution

The constitution came into effect in December 1983. It delineated the three arms of government – legislative, executive and judicial – granting them official autonomy. Executive power is held by the president who serves a non-renewable five-year term of office. Legislative power, formed of members elected on three-year terms is held by the unicameral National Assembly – which also holds the power to appoint a president if no candidate gains an absolute majority in the elections. In 1991 constitutional reforms strengthened the judicial and electoral systems. There are 14 departamentos (administrative divisions) which each have a governor and an elected local council headed by a mayor.

Form of state

Presidential democratic republic

The executive

Executive power is vested in the president (who is elected every five years in March), assisted by the vice president and council of ministers. A second round of elections must be held within 30 days of the declaration of the result of the first round if no candidate secures an absolute majority (51 per cent) at the first attempt.

The presidential term begins on 1 June. The president is both the head of state and head of government.

National legislature

Legislative power is held by the unicameral Asamblea Legislativa (Legislative Assembly), which has 84 members elected for three years by proportional representation; 20 deputies serve in the Central American Parliament Parlacen. The term of office begins on 1 May.

Legal system

Since 1993, El Salvador has undergone a full-scale review of its judicial structure. In order to achieve a basic level of judicial independence, judicial appointments are the responsibility of the Legislative Assembly, and funding for the courts has been ensured. In 1998, the Legislative Assembly replaced the 1860 criminal code and code of criminal procedure with more efficient procedures. With a US$22.2 million loan from the Inter-American Development Bank (IDB), approved in 1996, El Salvador began a programme of judicial training, the renovation and expansion of efforts to educate juvenile offenders, and projects to strengthen administration and planning. The process of reform is continuing and is more autonomous and professional than at any time in El Salvador's history.

Last elections

21 March 2004 (presidential); 12 March 2006 (parliamentary).

Results: Presidential: Antonio Saca (Arena) won 57.7 per cent of the vote against 35.6 per cent for Schafik Hándal (FMLN); Héctor Silva (CDU) 3.9 per cent. Parliamentary: the Alianza Republicana Nacionalista (Arena) (Nationalist Republican Alliance) 39.4 per cent of the vote, 34 seats; Frente Farabundo Martí para la Liberación Nacional (FMLN) (Front for National Liberation) 39.7 per cent, 32 seats; Partido de Conciliación Nacional (PCN) (National Conciliation Party) 11 per cent, 10 seats; Partido Demócrata Cristiano (PDC) (Christian Democratic Party) 6.8 per cent, six seats. Cambio Democrático (Democratic Change) 3.1 per cent, two seats. Turnout was 41.4 per cent.

Next elections

2009 (presidential and parliamentary)

Political parties

Ruling party

Coalition government led by Alianza Republicana Nacionalista (Arena) (Nationalist Republican Alliance)

Main opposition party

Frente Farabundo Martí para la Liberación Nacional (FMLN) (Farabundo Martí Front for National Liberation)

Population

7.13 million (2007)*

Last census: September 1992: 5,118,599

Population density: Is high, with around 280 inhabitants per square km.

Annual growth rate: 2.0 per cent 1994–2004 (WHO 2006)

Ethnic make-up

Approximately 94 per cent of the population are mestizo, 5 per cent Amerindian and 1 per cent white.

Religions

Predominantly Roman Catholic (75 per cent); most of the remaining 25 per cent belong to a number of Protestant churches.

Education

Low levels of literacy and educational skills are regarded by the government as a major impediment to foreign investment.

Literacy rate: 80 per cent adult rate; 89 per cent youth rate (15–24) (Unesco 2005).

Enrolment rate: 112 per cent gross primary enrolment of relevant age group, including repeaters; 56 per cent gross secondary enrolment; 17 per cent gross tertiary enrolment (World Bank).

Pupils per teacher: 33 in primary schools

Health

Per capita total expenditure on health (2003) was US$378; of which per capita government spending was US$174, at the international dollar rate, (WHO 2006).

Approximately 55 per cent of the population has access to safe water.

HIV/Aids

HIV prevalence: 0.7 per cent aged 15–49 in 2003 (World Bank)

Life expectancy: 71 years, 2004 (WHO 2006)

Fertility rate/Maternal mortality rate: 2.8 births per woman, 2004 (WHO 2006): maternal mortality 1.2 per 1,000 live births (World Bank).

Child (under 5 years) mortality rate (per 1,000): 32 per 1,000 live births; 11 per cent of children aged under five are malnourished (World Bank).

Head of population per physician: 1.24 physicians per 1,000 people, 2002 (WHO 2006)

Welfare

El Salvador operates a mandatory private insurance system, introduced into law in 1996 and implemented in 1998 as part of the government's privatisation strategy. The law ensured state provision for those aged over 36-years in 1996 but was closed to new entrants. The new private system is funded through a mixture of contributions made by workers and employers.

The state also operates a welfare system for benefits covering sickness, maternity and work injury. These are based on contributions by the employer and worker and subsidised by the state, but exclude casual workers and those involved in domestic work. Agricultural workers are denied sickness and maternity pay and teachers are excluded from work injury benefits.

Pensions

Old-age pensions are available to men aged over 60 and women over 55 with 25 years of contributions. There is no minimum age requirement for those with more than 30 years' contributions. The 1996 pension reform created five private pensions funds, but in 2000 three of these were merged into a new fund – AFP Crecer, run by Spanish bank BBVA – which in 2002 controlled around 60 per cent of the country's pensions market.

Main cities

San Salvador (capital, estimated population 521,366 in 2005), Soyapango (300,388), Santa Ana (181,131), Mejicanos (201,517), San Miguel (181,819).

Languages spoken

Nahua is spoken by some Amerindians. English is widely spoken in business circles.

Official language/s

Spanish

Media

Press freedom is guaranteed by constitution.

Press

Dailies: In Spanish, Most newspapers include sections on business and economic matters.

National newspapers include El Diario de Hoy (www.elsalvador.com) and La Prensa Gráfica (ultra-conservative) (www.laprensagrafica.com) and El Mundo (www.elmundo.com.sv), an evening newspaper. Local newspapers include Diario Co Latino (www.diariocolatino.com) from San Salvador and El Pais (www.elpais.com.sv) from Santa Ana. El Faro (www.elfaro.com.sv) is a weekly publication.

Broadcasting

Radio: There are over 80 commercial radio stations. Radio El Salvador (www.radioelsalvador.com.sv) is the state-run network with local stations providing nationwide coverage. Most stations provide services for a localised area and the majority are located around San Salvador.

Television: There are 17 TV channels provided by around five networks. One of the largest private, commercial network is Telecorporacion Salvadorena (TCS), with ESMI TV (www.esmitv.com), which has five channels, covering news, sport, music and drama and entertainment. Agape TV (www.agapetv8.com) has both commercial and religious programmes. Iglesia del Camino (www.delcamino.org.sv) is run by the Catholic Church. The government runs a cultural and educational channel (canal 10).

There are many pay-to-view digital, cable and satellite services available.

Advertising

All advertising methods are available through the press, cinemas, commercial TV and radio, periodicals and posters. Modern venues such as website and individual mobile/cell phone advertising are available to a lesser extent.

Economy

El Salvador has a poor economy, suffering from a weak tax collection system, factory closures, social inequality and fluctuating world coffee prices. Dependency on the export of coffee and the marginal position of poor farmers remain a stumbling block to the development of El Salvador. Unlike other Latin American countries, El Salvador's problem of economic dependence has been less a question of neglect and mismanagement of its assets by foreigners than one of battling unpredictable cycles of export commodities. For much of the post-colonial period, the economy remained relatively stagnant due to its lack of mineral wealth and the failure to break through the barriers of European protectionism to market its agricultural goods.

High levels of unemployment and under-employment persist and remain a government priority. Although official unemployment was 6.5 per cent in 2005, under-employment was over 30 per cent. The ability to earn foreign exchange is hampered by El Salvador's comparative disadvantage in terms of productivity due to low levels of capital. However, world prices for coffee, the main agro-export, have risen sharply since 2004.

Remittances from Salvadoreans living abroad are one of the main pillars of the economy, helping to ease the balance of payments deficit. Annual transfers of US$2.8 billion in 2005 accounted for 17 per cent of GDP while the Inter-American Development Bank estimated that in 2006 the figure had risen to some US$3.3 billion. Over 22 per cent of families are dependent on remittances.

The government's emphasis on the development of the export-processing sector through the creation of a favourable investment climate and free zones has led to the growth of the textile and financial sectors.

The economy has experienced sluggish growth in recent years, but there was an improvement in 2005 when. GDP grew by 2.8 per cent (compared with 1.5 per cent in 2004). Membership of Cafta, since March 2006, should spur growth by increasing investor interest and diversifying the economy. The Inter-American Development Bank estimated that in 2006 migrant workers sent some US$3.316 million to their families inEl Salvador.

External trade

El Salvador is a member of the Central American Free Trade Agreement (Cafta) along with the US, Costa Rica, Guatemala, Honduras and Dominica Republic. The maquiladora sector dominates trade with manufactured goods (in particular garments) exported, typically, to the US. There has been an increase in non-traditional exports such as shrimps, sesame seeds, nuts, fruits and honey.

Imports

Principal imports include raw materials, consumer goods, capital goods, fuels, foodstuffs, petroleum and electricity.

Main sources: US (30.7 per cent total, 2006), Guatemala (8.9 per cent), Mexico (7.1 per cent).

Exports

Principal exports include offshore assembly exports, coffee, sugar, shrimp, textiles, handcrafts, chemicals and electricity.

Main destinations: US (49.6 per cent total, 2006), Guatemala (14.4 per cent), Honduras (8.8 per cent).

Agriculture

Farming

The agricultural sector of El Salvador's economy employs approximately a third of the country's total workforce. The sector contributes about 12 per cent to total GDP. Approximately 34 per cent of total land is arable; 30 per cent permanent pastures.

Coffee is the most important crop. Other major crops are cotton, sugar cane, maize, beans and rice. There has been some diversification within the sector, with non-traditional exports such as sesame seeds, nuts, vegetables, fruits, honey and, above all, shrimps, taking an increasing share.

Estimated crop production in 2005 included 822,195t tonnes cereals in total, 5,280,400t sugar cane, 648,045t maize, 65,000t bananas, 75,709t plantains, 26,519t rice, 18,136t cassava, 13,000t potatoes, 147,631t sorghum, 10,814t chillies and peppers, 17,075t oilcrops, 25,416t tomatoes, 98,600t citrus fruit, 78,510t green coffee, 84,300t pulses, 83,686t roots and tubers, 284,948t fruit in total, 141,907t vegetables in total. Estimated livestock production included: 127,042t meat in total, 26,500t beef, 8,313t pig meat, 92,111t poultry, 63,649t eggs, 412,602t milk, 2,362t honey, 6,665t cattle hides.

Fishing

The Gulf of Fonseca is regarded as one of Central America's greatest natural resources with rich fisheries and diverse marine life, which is shared by Honduras, Nicaragua and El Salvador. Typically, the annual catch is over 18,000mt per year.

Industry and manufacturing

Contributing approximately 28 per cent to total GDP and employing around a fifth of the total workforce, the industrial sector is a significant part of El Salvador's economy.

The national government has made efforts to shift the industrial sector towards manufacturing for export through the development of the maquila (in-bond manufacturing) sector and the creation of free zones. Maquila exports have accounted for the bulk of growth in the export sector since 1992. Investment incentives in the free zones include a 10-year income tax exemption, import duty exemptions or reduced exposure to taxes on equity or assets for 10 years.

Tourism

Tourism has traditionally played an insignificant role in El Salvador's economy. However, the travel and tourism sector is continuing to expand and now accounts around 10 per cent of total GDP. The industry employs over 7 per cent of the total labour force.

Mining
Mining has been a stable sector of the El Salvadorian economy for several years. Gold, silver, sea salt and limestone are mined or quarried and there are deposits of copper, iron ore, sulphur, mercury, lead, zinc and perlite. There are two gold mines, one at San Cristobal and the other near San Salvador which also mines silver. However, the mining sector is small and underdeveloped, contributing only 0.1 per cent to GDP. There are two cement works, the 240,000 tonnes per year (tpy) Cemento Mayan at Canton Tecomapa and the 684,000tpy Cemento de El Salvador at El Ronco.

Hydrocarbons
El Salvador has no proven reserves of oil, gas or coal. The country is totally reliant on imported petroleum products. Mexico and Venezuela are El Salvador's main suppliers; both nations offer preferential rates on their oil exports under the terms of the San José Pact.
Guatemala and Mexico signed a deal to create a 347mile, US$450 million, natural gas pipeline. There is a 17,000 barrel per day oil refinery operating at Acajutla.

Energy
El Salvador is the largest producer of hydroelectricity in Central America. Electric energy is produced by four hydroelectric installations (Guajoyo, Cerrán Grande, 5 de Novembre and 15 de Septembre) and one geothermal plant (Ahuachapan in the west of the country, with generating capacity of 95MW). Total installed capacity is about 650MW.

Financial markets
Stock exchange
The Bolsa de El Salvador was founded in 1964 and is situated in San Salvador.

Banking and insurance
The banking system of El Salvador remained under state ownership until 1991. Thereafter the government implemented market reforms that handed control to private investors. Interest rates are determined by the market.
Central bank
Banco Central de Reserva de El Salvador

Time
GMT minus six hours

Geography
El Salvador lies on the Pacific coast of Central America. Guatemala is to the west and Honduras to the north and east. The basins in the centre of the country rise to little more than 600 metres at San Salvador. Across this upland and surmounting it, run two more or less parallel rows of volcanoes, 14 of which are over 900 metres. Lowlands lie to the north and south of the high backbone. The ash and lava from the volcanoes have produced an ideal soil in which to grow coffee.
Hemisphere
Northern.

Climate
The climate is semi-tropical. The dry season is from November–April; temperatures range from 15–23 degrees Celsius (C); the rainy season runs from May–October, when the average temperature is 28 degrees C. Generally, the temperature depends on the altitude; coastal areas are hotter and more humid than upland areas.
The driest month is February with just 5mm average rainfall. The wettest month is June with 328mm. The coldest month is December when the average daily temperature varies between 16 and 32 degrees C. In May, the hottest month, the variation is only slightly different, ranging between 19 and 33 degrees C.

Dress codes
Light cotton suits and ties are the generally accepted form of dress for businessmen, although some Salvadoreans will dress less formally in guyaberas (styled cotton shirts worn outside the trousers), particularly in the warmest months. Businesswomen should wear a light suit or equivalent. Dress as for business if invited to a social occasion unless suggested otherwise.
A sweater or light jacket will be required for evenings and for the highlands.

Entry requirements
Passports
Required by all. Passports must be valid for six months from date of departure.
Visa
Required by all, except citizens of most Central American, EU and some Asian countries (for a full list visit www.elsalvador.org or contact the local embassy). Business visas require, in Spanish, a letter of invitation from an El Salvadorian company and a letter from the foreign company being represented.
Currency advice/regulations
There are no restrictions on the import or export of local or foreign currencies. In the case of foreign currencies, the quantity being imported, especially if sizeable, should be declared, as there is a restriction on export of larger amounts to the level imported.
Prohibited imports
Fruit, vegetables, plants and animals.

Health (for visitors)
Mandatory precautions
A yellow fever vaccination certificate is required if arriving from an infected area.
Advisable precautions
Typhoid, polio, hepatitis A and tetanus vaccinations. Dengue fever cases have risen, visitors should avoid exposing their skin during early morning and evening when the risk of being bitten by mosquitoes is highest. Malaria is not a virulent strain but prophylaxis should be taken as there is some risk in the Santa Anna province and rural locations. There is a high rabies risk. Water precautions are essential and only well-cooked food should be eaten. Milk is unpasteurised and should be boiled.

Hotels
The best hotels can be found in the capital. A 10 per cent tip is usual.

Public holidays (national)
Fixed dates
1 Jan (New Year's Day), 1 May (Labour Day), 4 Aug (Transfiguration Bank Holiday), 15 Sep (Independence Day), 12 Oct (Columbus Day), 2 Nov (All Souls' Day), 24 Dec (Christmas Eve), 25 Dec (Christmas Day), 31 Dec (New Year's Eve).
Variable dates
Holy Wednesday, Maundy Thursday, Good Friday.

Working hours
Banking
Mon–Fri: 0900–1700. Sat: 0900–1300.
Business
Mon–Fri: 0900–1800.
Government
Mon–Fri: 0800–1730.
Shops
Mon–Sat: 0900–1200, 1400–1800. Supermarkets Mon–Sat: 0800–2200. The main shopping centres are open on Sunday.

Electricity supply
110V AC, 60Hz

Social customs/useful tips
Appointments should be made in advance. Salvadorans have a distinctly Latin sense of time and can be among the least punctual people in Central America, although many businessmen and bankers, particularly those with export experience, keep horas inglesas (punctual time).
Business relationships and meetings tend to be formal in early stages. Use proper titles such as Licenciado (college graduate), Ingeniero (engineering graduate) and Doctor (physicians and lawyers), followed by the person's surname. Handshaking before and after meetings is important.
First names should not be used until a business relationship has been consolidated. Upon introduction it is important to exchange cards; a supply of Spanish-printed cards is advisable.
Business is conducted in Spanish although some executives speak English. Some knowledge of spoken Spanish is much better than none.

Meetings over meals, including breakfast, are becoming common. Working lunches and dinners can be lengthy. Gratuities in restaurants and hotels are around 10 per cent.

Security

El Salvador has a poor personal security environment, with a homicide rate twice that of Los Angeles. Kidnappings, carjackings, and robbery are common and can occur anywhere. There is a risk of murder for those robbed, even if they do not resist. Downtown San Salvador should be avoided at all times, as should roads outside the city after dark. Reports indicate the border with Guatemala has been a site for attacks on vehicles. Jewellery or large amounts of cash should not be carried.

Business travellers should arrange to be met at the airport and be accompanied by a local representative, as this has been shown to reduce problems.

Getting there

Air

National airline: TACA Airlines.

International airport/s: El Salvador International (SAL), 35km south of San Salvador; bank, car hire, restaurants, shops. The airport and the highway that runs to it are the most modern and developed in the region. It is expanding its services in order to become an international cargo warehousing and distribution centre.

Airport tax: US$27.15.

Surface

Road: Roads run from Guatemala and Honduras. Duty is paid at the border when entering or leaving the country by land. It is advisable to carry small denomination notes to pay the border duties.

Rail: Lines run through El Salvador from Guatemala to Honduras.

Main port/s: Acajutla, La Unión/Cutuco, La Libertad (fishing only). Major ports on the Pacific are Puerto Barrios and Santo Tomás de Castilla.

Getting about

National transport

Air: Scheduled internal services from San Salvador to San Miguel, La Unión and Usulután. Charter flights are available.

Road: There is a network of 9,800km of paved roads. The Pan-American Highway (over 300km) runs through the country linking San Salvador with Santa Ana in the west and San Miguel in the east; Carretera Litoral runs south of the Pan-American Highway linking the capital with Sonsonate, Zacatecoluca and Usulatan. Many roads have fallen into considerable disrepair as a result of the war and cuts in government spending.

Buses: The bus system is excellent, with services between major towns. The buses are often crowded and run frequently.

Rail: There are 602km of railway, including 429km of line from Guatemala to Honduras. A narrow gauge line links the western town of Ahuachpan and the port of Acajutla with San Salvador, which is in turn connected to La Union in the east. The railway is used largely for freight traffic.

City transport

Taxis: Taxis are bright yellow. The regular taxi line is Taxi Acacya. Taxis can be hailed or ordered by telephone. The fixed rate system is not rigidly followed – check before proceeding. No taxis have meters. Tipping is unusual but 10 per cent of fare is appreciated. Taxi from airport to city centre journey time is 25 minutes.

Car hire

A national or international permit valid for 30 days is required. Traffic drives on the right.

BUSINESS DIRECTORY

The addresses listed below are a selection only. While World of Information makes every endeavour to check these addresses, we cannot guarantee that changes have not been made, especially to telephone numbers and area codes. We would welcome any corrections.

Telephone area codes

Dialling code for El Salvador: IDD access code +503 followed by subscriber's number.

Useful telephone numbers

Emergency:	121
Information:	114
International operator:	119, 120
For collect calls (US only):	190
Migration Office:	222-7328
Foreign Office:	222-6611

Chambers of Commerce

American Chamber of Commerce of El Salvador, Paseo General Escalón 5432, San Salvador (tel: 264-7609; fax: 263-3237; e-mail: contact@amchamsal.com).

El Salvador Cámara de Comercio e Industria, 9a Avenida Norte y 5a Calle Poniente, PO Box 1640, 1118 San Salvador (tel: 244-2000; fax: 271-4461; e-mail: camara@camarasal.com).

Banking

Ahorromet Scotiabank, Avenida Olímpica 129, Edificio Torre Ahorromet Scotiabank, San Salvador (tel: 245-1211; fax: 245-2884).

BANCASA (Banco de Construcción y Ahorro), 75 Avenida Sur 709, Colonia Escalon, San Salvador (tel: 263-5508; fax: 263-5506).

Banco Agrícola Comercial, Paseo General Escalón 3635, Colonia Escalón, San Salvador (tel: 224-0283; fax: 224-3948).

Banco de Comercio de El Salvador, 25 Avenida Norte y 23 Calle Poniente, San Salvador (tel: 226-4577; fax: 225-7767; e-mail: webmaster@banco.com.sv).

Banco Creditomatic, 55 Avenida Sur y Alameda Roosevelt, Centro Roosevelt, San Salvador (tel: 298-1855; fax: 224-4138).

Banco Cuscatlan, Km 10 Carretera a Santa Tecla, Edificio Pirámide Cuscatlán La Libertad (tel: 228-7777; fax: 228-9999).

Banco Hipotecario, Pje. Senda Florida Sur, Paseo General Escalón, San Salvador (tel: 223-3753; fax: 298-0447).

Banco Salvadoreño, Alameda Dr Manuel Enrique Araujo 3550, San Salvador (tel: 298-4444; fax 298-0102).

Grupo Capital, Alameda Dr Manuel Enrique Araujo, Edificio Century Plaza, San Salvador (tel: 245-6000; fax: 224-3303).

Unibanco, Alameda Roosevelt 2511, San Salvador (tel: 245-0651; fax: 298-5261).

Central bank

Banco Central de Reserva, Alameda Juan Pablo, entre 15 y 17 Avenida Norte, PO Box 106, San Salvador (tel: 281-8000; fax: 281-8013; e-mail: comunicaciones@bcr.gob.sv).

Travel information

Corporación Salvadoreña de Turismo (CORSATUR), Boulevard del Hipódromo 508, San Benito, San Salvador (tel: 243-7835; fax: 243-0427).

TACA International Airlines, Edificio Caribe, San Salvador (tel: 298-5055; fax:279-4345).

National tourist organisation offices

Instituto Salvadoreño de Turismo (ISTU) (El Salvador Tourist Board), Calle Rubén Darío 619, San Salvador (tel: 228-000, 222-8699, 222-8144, 222-9366; fax: 221-208).

Ministries

Ministry of Agriculture and Livestock, Final 1a Avenida Norte 13 Calle Oriente y Avenida Manuel Gallardo 704, San Salvador (tel: 279-1579; fax: 224-2944).

Ministry of Defence, Alameda Manuel Enrique Araujo, Carretera a Santa Tecla, San Salvador (tel: 223-0233; fax: 298-2005).

Ministry of Economy, Alameda Juan Pablo II Calle Guadalupe, Centro de Gobierno, San Salvador (tel: 281-7134; fax: 221-2797).

Ministry of Education, Alameda Juan Pablo II Calle Guadalupe, Centro de

Gobierno, San Salvador (tel: 281-0256; fax: 281-0257).

Ministry of Environment, Alameda Roosevelt y 55 Avenida Norte, Torre El Salvador, San Salvador (tel: 260-8876; fax: 260-3092).

Ministry of Finance, Edificio Las Tres Torres, Avenida Alvarado, San Salvador (tel: 225-6500; fax: 225-7491).

Ministry of Foreign Affairs, Alameda Manuel Enrique Araujo 5500, San Salvador (tel: 243-3805; fax: 243-3710).

Ministry of Health, Calle Arce 827, San Salvador (tel: 271-0008; fax: 221-0985).

Ministry of Interior, Centro de Gobierno, San Salvador (tel: 221-8582; fax: 281-5959).

Ministry of Justice and Public Security, 6a Calle Oriente 42, Antiguo Local Policia Nacional, San Salvador (tel: 271-2655; fax: 245-2650).

Ministry of Labour, Paseo General Escalón 4122, San Salvador (tel: 263-5423; fax: 263-5272).

Ministry of Public Works, 1a Avenida Sur 603, San Salvador (tel: 293-6603; fax: 271-0163).

Other useful addresses

Asociación Nacional de la Empresa Privada (ANEP), 1a Calle Poniente y 71a Avenida Norte 204, Colonia Escalón, San Salvador (tel: 224-1236; fax: 223-8932; e-mail: anep@telesal.net).

Asociación Salvadoreña de Industriales (ASI), Calles Roma y Liverpool, Colonia Roma, San Salvador (tel: 279-2488; fax: 279-2070; e-mail: unatias@sv.cciglobal.net).

Bolsa de Valores de El Salvador, Alameda Roosevelt 3107, Edificio La Centroamericana, San Salvador (tel: 298-4244; fax: 223-2898; e-mail: webmaster@bves.com.sv).

British Embassy, Paseo General Escalón 4828, Edificio Inter-Inversiones, San Salvador (tel: 263-6527; fax: 263-6516; e-mail: britemb@sal.gbm.net).

Corporación de Exportadores de El Salvador (COEXPORT), Condominios del Mediterráneo A-23, Colonia Jardínes de Guadalupe, San Salvador (tel: 243-3110; fax: 243-3159; e-mail: service@coexport.com).

El Salvador Embassy (USA), 2308 California Street, NW, Washington DC 20008 (tel: (202) 2265-9671; fax: (202) 234-3834; e-mail: correo@elsalvador.org).

Fundación Salvadoreña para el Desarrollo Económica y Social (FUSADES), Urbanización y Boulevard Santa Elena, Edificio FUSADES, Antiguo Cuscatlán, La Libertad (tel: 278-3366; fax: 278-3369; e-mail: fusades@fusades.com.sv).

Superintendencia del Sistema Financiero, 7a Avenida Norte 240, San Salvador (tel: 281-24444).

Unión de Dirigentes de Empresas Salvadoreñas (UDES), Condominios del Mediterráneo C-22, Colonia Jardines de Guadalupe, San Salvador (tel: 243-2746; fax: 243-3145).

US Embassy, Boulevard Santa Elena Final, Antiguo Cuscatlán, La Libertad (tel: 278-4444; fax: 278-6011).

Other news agencies: Prensa Latina: www.prensalatina.com.mx

Internet sites

Bolsa de El Salvador (Stock Exchange) (Spanish): www.bolsavalores.com.sv/

El Salvador trade and investment: www.elsalvadortrade.com.sv/

Fundación Salvadoreña para el Desarrollo Económico e Social (Salvadorean Foundation for Social and Economic Development) (Spanish): www.fusades.com.sv/

Equatorial Guinea

KEY FACTS

Official name: República de Guinea Ecuatorial (Republic of Equatorial Guinea)

Head of State: President Teodoro Obiang Nguema Mbasogo (PDGE) (since 1979; re-elected 2002)

Head of government: Prime Minister Ignacio Milam Tang (from 8 Jul 2008)

Ruling party: Partido Democrático de Guinea Ecuatorial (PDGE) (Democratic Party of Equatorial Guinea) (from 1993; re-elected 4 May 2008)

Area: 28,051 square km

Population: 1.21 million (2007)

Capital: Malabo

Official language: Spanish and French

Currency: CFA franc (CFAf) = 100 centimes (Communauté Financière Africaine (African Financial Community) franc)

Exchange rate: CFAf413.80 per US$ (Jul 2008); CFAf655.95 per euro (pegged from Jan 1999)

GDP per capita: US$8,702 (2007)*

GDP real growth: 12.40% (2007)*

Labour force: 2.90 million (2004)

Inflation: 4.50% (2007)

Oil production: 363,000 bpd (2007)

Balance of trade: US$3.80 billion (2006)

* estimated figure

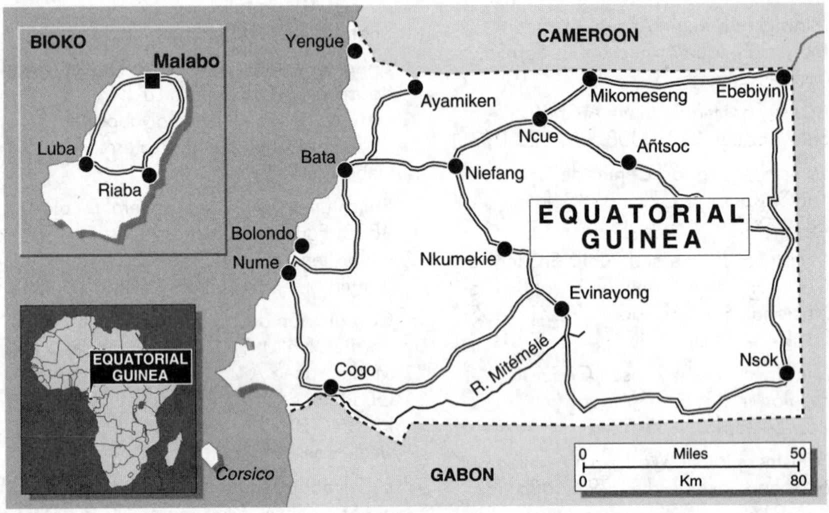

Equatorial Guinea once again hit the headlines for unnecessary reasons in 2008 when Simon Mann, supposed leader of a coup attempt back in 2004, was extradited from Zimbabwe, put on trial, convicted and sentenced to 34 years in jail. The prosecution accused him of attempting to overthrow President Teodoro Obiang Nguema on behalf of Severo Moto, leader of the opposition Progress Party. Moto, who is resident in Spain and has formed a 'government in exile' denies the charges.

Rapig growth

Since 1995, average annual growth in Equatorial Guinea has been a staggering 31 per cent, as oil exports (currently 97 per cent of total export earnings) have created boom conditions. In 2006, the country's real gross domestic product (GDP) grew by 5.6 per cent, and was estimated to have grown 9.8 per cent in 2007. Despite the earlier rapid growth in real GDP, allegations abound over how the government has misappropriated its oil revenues. While the government has made some infrastructure improvements to bolster the oil industry, the average inhabitant has yet to experience a higher standard of living from the oil revenues. The government has attempted to privatise the state-run businesses and continues to promote foreign investment.

The third-largest oil producer in Africa (after Nigeria and Libya) Equatorial Guinea had total proven oil reserves of 1.8 billion barrels at the end of 2007. The majority of these reserves are located in the oil-rich Gulf of Guinea. Since the 1995 discovery of the Zafiro field, Equatorial Guinea's oil production has increased more than tenfold. In 1995, average oil production was 5,000 barrels per day (bpd), which increased to an average oil production of 363,000bpd in 2007.

Equatorial Guinea also had 1.3 trillion cubic feet of proven natural gas reserves as of 1 January 2006. The majority of the reserves are located offshore Bioko Island, primarily in the Alba and Zafiro associated natural gas fields. From 2001–02, natural gas production increased rapidly as new projects came online; in 2003, natural gas production was 45 billion cubic feet and natural gas consumption was the same.

Oil and gas deposits were first discovered off the island of Bioko, which also houses the capital Malabo, in the mid-1990s. Their exploitation will dominate economic development and continue to be the engine of growth for the foreseeable future, although revenues are now set to level out.

The African Development Bank in its annual publication *African Economic Outlook* (AEO) said that Equatorial

Guinea's continued growth was confirmed in 2007 with real gross domestic product (GDP) of 9.8 per cent. The boost is due mainly to improved oil and gas production and the buoyancy of the public infrastructure construction works. This was accompanied by continuous improvement in the performance of the construction sector, banking services, telecommunications, tourism and wood processing.

Poor little rich country

The sustained economic growth and the increase in oil revenue, however, have had very little effect on poverty reduction in the country and on improving the general standard of living of the population. The poverty rate remains extremely high and is reflected in a high infant mortality rate (123 per 1,000 live births), high maternal mortality rate (680 per 100,000 live births) and low life expectancy (50.4 years at birth).

The United Nations Development Programme (UNDP) publication *Human Development Report (2007–2008)* ranked the country 127th out of 177 countries surveyed. Of the total population, 67 per cent were living in extreme poverty (income of less than US$1.00 per day); this figure rises to 70 per cent in rural areas. According to a household survey for poverty evaluation (EEH) conducted in 2006, 76.8 per cent of the population is poor, which translates into a head-of-household poverty ratio of 66.4 per cent. Yet average GDP per capita is nearly US$9,000.

Forestry, farming and fishing are components of gross domestic product, where subsistence farming predominates. Pre-independence Equatorial Guinea counted on cocoa production for hard currency earnings, but the neglect of the rural economy has diminished potential for agriculture-led growth. Equatorial Guinea is now better positioned to target these and other sectors while safeguarding macroeconomic stability, and to address the large social and development needs of its population. Undeveloped natural resources include titanium, iron ore, manganese, uranium, and alluvial gold. There are considerable inflows of foreign direct investment (FDI) but it is all into the hydrocarbon sector.

Foreign aid cuts

No longer eligible for concessionary financing because of its large oil revenues, the government has now asked the IMF to put in place a 'shadow' poverty reduction programme. It has had to publicly recognise that the objectives of poverty reduction under its last National Development Plan (1997–2001) were not achieved.

The IMF has come up with what is very much a standard answer in such a situation: manage the oil money. Make oil revenues sustainable over a longer term, use the surplus money to fund sustainable secondary development that will create jobs and reduce poverty, budget conservatively, target spending. There was concern that over 2004 alone, a substantial increase in public spending had more than offset improved revenues. The World Bank has been asked to undertake a review of public expenditure in Equatorial Guinea.

What goes around...

President Obiang Nguema originally came to power by overthrowing his uncle Macias Nguema in 1979. The two have been described by a variety of human rights organisations as being among the worst abusers of human rights in Africa. The country became notorious under the widespread human rights abuses of Macias who caused a third of the population to flee. Obiang had his uncle tried and then executed him. Obiang when he came to power proclaimed an amnesty for refugees and released some 5,000 political prisoners, but kept the absolute control he had inherited. Officials said Nguema kept the presidency in the 2002 elections by winning more than 97 per cent of the vote. Opposition candidates had withdrawn from the poll, citing fraud and irregularities.

In parliamentary elections on 4 May 2008, the ruling PDGE, allied to the Front of Democratic Opposition (FOD), won 99 seats out of 100 (one more than in 2002), the Convergencia para la Democracia Social (CPDS) (Convergence for Social Democracy) won one seat. The government of Prime Minister Nfubea resigned on 4 July and Ignacio Milam Tang was appointed as his replacement on 8 July.

Risk assessment

Politics	Poor
Economy	Fair
Regional stability	Fair

COUNTRY PROFILE

Historical profile

1470 The island of Anobon was first visited by the Portuguese, who subsequently settled it and the other islands in the Gulf of Guinea, including Bioko.
1477 Portugal ceded Bioko to Spain. Bioko became an important slave-trading base for several European nations up to the nineteenth century.
1844 Spanish began settling the mainland region of Río Muni.
1904 Río Muni and Bioko became the West African Territories, later named Spanish Guinea.
1968 Spanish Guinea was granted independence from Spain and renamed Equatorial Guinea. Macias Nguema became president.
1972 Nguema's presidency had degenerated into a tyranny as democratic institutions and practices were dismissed. The regime used terror to maintain power and up to one third of the population fled the country as the economy collapsed.

KEY INDICATORS — Equatorial Guinea

	Unit	2003	2004	2005	2006	2007
Population	m	0.48	0.49	1.14	1.17	*1.21
Gross domestic product (GDP)	US$bn	2.20	3.23	7.48	8.56	*10.48
GDP per capita	US$	2,700	4,120	6,571	*7,315	*8,702
GDP real growth	%	15.5	10.0	6.5	5.6	*9.8
Inflation	%	6.0	8.0	5.7	4.4	*4.5
Oil output	'000 bpd	249.0	350.0	355.0	358.0	363.0
Exports (fob) (goods)	US$m	2,500.0	2,771.0	7,125.0	8,096.0	0.0
Imports (cif) (goods)	US$m	562.0	1,167.0	2,035.7	4,295.0	0.0
Balance of trade	US$m	1,938.0	1,604.0	5,089.3	3,802.0	0.0
Current account	US$m	-740.0	-650.0	-898.0	385.0	*188.0
Total reserves minus gold	US$m	237.7	945.0	2,101.5	3,066.7	3,845.9
Foreign exchange	US$m	237.7	944.3	2,101.9	3,066.1	3,845.2
Exchange rate	per US$	574.89	496.63	507.22	496.60	454.40

* estimated figure

1979 Teodoro Obiang Nguema Mbasogo (the president's nephew) seized power in a coup d'état. Nguema was executed. Even though a ruling Supreme Military Council was established Obiang retained all effective power.
1984 and 1989 President Obiang was re-elected unopposed.
1993 The first multi-party elections were won by the president's Partido Democrático de Guinea Ecuatorial (PDGE) (Democratic Party of Equatorial Guinea); the main opposition parties boycotted the election.
1995 Zafiro, the country's largest oil field was discovered off Bioko Island.
1996 President Obiang won the presidential elections, which were described as 'a farce' by international observers.
1999 PDGE won 75 seats in the first fully contested parliamentary elections. Opposition parties alleged fraud and boycotted parliament.
2000 Equatorial Guinea and Nigeria signed a treaty agreeing to the demarcation of their maritime border.
2002 Opposition members accused the government of mass human rights abuse. President Obiang was re-elected.
2004 The ruling and allied parties won the 25 April parliamentary elections; foreign observers criticised both the poll and the results. Perpetrators of an alleged coup were arrested in Harare, Zimbabwe, when their plane landed for refueling. Nineteen mercenaries accused of the planned overthrow were convicted, including opposition leader, Severo Moto, who was sentenced to 63 years in prison
2005 Sir Mark Thatcher, son of the former UK prime minister, Margaret Thatcher, was arrested in South Africa and pleaded guilty to financing the helicopter to be used in the 2004 attempted coup; he was fined US$500,000 and given a suspended gaol sentence. Spain overturned the asylum status of opposition leader, Severo Moto, after receiving evidence he had been involved in a number of coup attempts.
2006 The government resigned in August following accusations by the president of corruption and incompetence.
2008 Opposition leader, Severo Moto, was arrested in Spain in March and charged with trafficking weapons into Equatorial Guinea. He had been given political asylum by Spain in 1986; it had been revoked in 2005 after he was accused of attempting to promote a coup d'etat in Equatorial Guinea from Spain and was re-instated in 2008. In parliamentary elections on 4 May, the ruling PDGE, allied to the Front of Democratic Opposition (FOD), won 99 seats out of 100, the Convergencia para la Democracia Social (CPDS) (Convergence for Social Democracy) won one seat. The government of Prime Minister Nfubea resigned on 4 July; Ignacio Milam Tang was appointed as his replacement on 8 July. On 6 July Simon Mann was sentenced to more than 34 years in jail over a 2004 coup plot in Equatorial Guinea. He had been deported from Zimbabwe earlier in the year after serving a four year prison sentence for purchasing arms in Zimbabwe to use in the coup attempt.

Political structure

Constitution

A new constitution designed to usher in multi-party politics was adopted on 16 November 1991. It provided for the separation of powers between the president and prime minister and gave the president protection from impeachment, prosecution and subpoena before, during and after his term of office.

Form of state

Republic

The executive

The president is elected for a seven-year term by universal suffrage. The prime minister is appointed by the president.

National legislature

There is a 100-seat Cámara de Representantes del Pueblo (legislative assembly) elected for five years.

Legal system

Judges are appointed, transferred and dismissed for political reasons, even though the constitution provides for judicial independence. The judicial system does not appear to operate independently, thus undermining basic rights.

Last elections

4 May 2008 (parliamentary); 15 December 2002 (presidential)

Results: Parliamentary: Partido Democrático de Guinea Ecuatorial (PDGE) (Democratic Party of Equatorial Guinea), allied to the Front of Democratic Opposition (FOD), won 99 seats out of 100, the Convergencia para la Democracia Social (CPDS) (Convergence for Social Democracy) won one.
Presidential: President Teodoro Obiang Nguema Mbasogo (PDGE) was re-elected with 97.1 per cent of the vote against 2.2 per cent for Celestino Bonifacio Bacalé. Opposition parties withdrew their candidates about two hours after voting started, citing irregularities.

Next elections

2009 (presidential); 2013 (parliamentary)

Political parties

Ruling party

Partido Democrático de Guinea Ecuatorial (PDGE) (Democratic Party of Equatorial Guinea) (from 1993; re-elected 4 May 2008)

Main opposition party

Convergencia para la Democracia Social (CPDS) (Convergence for Social Democracy).

Population

1.21 million (2007)

Last census: February 2002: 1,014,999

Population density: 16 inhabitants per square km. Urban population 49 per cent (1995–2001).

Annual growth rate: 2.4 per cent 1994–2004 (WHO 2006)

Ethnic make-up

The mainland region of Rio Muni is occupied by 75 per cent of the population, 90 per cent of whom belong to the Fang ethnic group. The island province of Bioko consists of Bubis, Fangs and Creoles.

Religions

Christianity (98 per cent, mostly Roman Catholic), traditional beliefs (2 per cent).

Education

Public expenditure on education typically amounted to 2.3 per cent of annual gross national income between 1994–1997 according to World Bank estimates.

Literacy rate: 83.2 per cent adult rate; 92.5 per cent male rate (Unesco).

Enrolment rate: 126 per cent gross primary enrolment of relevant age group (including repeaters); 115 per cent gross secondary enrolment.

Pupils per teacher: 41 in primary schools.

Health

Per capita total expenditure on health (2003) was US$179; of which per capita government spending was US$121, at the international dollar rate, (WHO 2006). Approximately 43 per cent of the total population is under 15 years. World Bank surveys show that 43 per cent of the population have access to improved water sources.

HIV/Aids

The government has failed in its commitments to eradicate the continuing epidemics of malaria and yellow fever, while allowing HIV prevalence to increase. There are an estimated 1,100 people living with HIV/Aids – most sufferers are over the age of 15.

Life expectancy: 43 years, 2004 (WHO 2006)

Fertility rate/Maternal mortality rate: 5.9 births per woman, 2004 (WHO 2006)

Child (under 5 years) mortality rate (per 1,000): 97 per 1,000 live births (World Bank)

Head of population per physician: 0.3 physicians per 1,000 people, 2004 (WHO 2006)

Welfare

Welfare conditions in the country are virtually non-existent, with limited access to primary healthcare, education and job opportunities.

In 2003 the Government introduced a two-tier system that created a separate wage system for private sector workers inside and outside of the oil sector. The minimum monthly wage for all private sector workers was set at CFAf77,000 (approximately US$154), and an additional differential payment is made dependent on a worker's skills.

However the minimum wage law does not apply to public sector workers who are generally paid much less than their counterparts in the private sector.

Under-age youths perform both family farm work and street vending. The government does not enforce the legal minimum age for child employment.

Equatorial Guinea is also a destination and transit point for the trafficking in children (as unpaid workers) and women (for prostitution).

Human rights conditions in the country are considered, by Amnesty International, as 'alarming' as the security forces continue to harass civilians and political dissidents; imprisonment, torture and extrajudicial killings have been cited in all parts of the country.

Main cities

Malabo (capital, on island of Bioko, estimated population 100,677 in 2005), Bata (Rio Muni) (71,901).

Languages spoken

Fang, Bubi Ibo and Creole (pidgin English) are spoken.

Official language/s

Spanish and French

Media

In 2006 Equatorial Guinea was ranked 137 out of 168 for press freedom by the French-based, Reporters without Borders. Despite a constitutional guarantee of freedom of the press, rights to freedom of opinion, expression, the sharing and publication of information are severely restricted, with the government using military courts, repressive laws and arbitrary arrests and prosecutions to restrict political freedom and civil rights.

Other news agencies: AFP (Agence France-Presse): www.afp.com
AllAfrica: www.allafrica.com
APA (African Press Agency): www.apanews.net
Panapress: www.panapress.com

Press

There are few newspapers available. In Spanish, Ebano is state-owned and La Nacion and La Opinion (a weekly), are privately owned. La Gaceta (de Guinea Ecuatorial) (www.lagacetadeguinea.com) is published monthly.

Periodicals: In Spanish, La Diaspora (Spanish) is published overseas every other month.

Broadcasting

Radio: There are two radio stations broadcasting in Spanish and local African languages Radio Nacional de Guinea Ecuatorial is state-run and the commercial, Radio Asonga, is run by Teodorino Obiang Nguema (the president's son). The French-based RF1 and several foreign Christian radio stations broadcast into the country.

Television: There is a limited service provided by the state-run Television Nacional.

News agencies

Other news agencies: AFP (Agence France-Presse): www.afp.com
AllAfrica: www.allafrica.com
APA (African Press Agency): www.apanews.net
Panapress: www.panapress.com

Economy

Government officials believe the oil industry has the capacity to transform Equatorial Guinea into an African Kuwait. However, according to an IMF report of April 2006, a rapid rise in GDP per capita income has not improved the standard of living for the majority of the population. It recommends that measures must be undertaken to provide well-designed development strategies to channel oil and gas revenue into poverty reduction.

The Equatorial Guinea economy has grown by an average 37 per cent since the early 1990s. The hydrocarbon sector is dominant and provided more that 80 per cent of GDP in 2005, while the non-oil sector, also buoyant, recorded a growth rate of 10.5 per cent. Although inflation, at 6.8 per cent, was higher than the 3 per cent criterion for convergence, as set for members of the Economic and Monetary Community of Central Africa (CEMAC), it is expected to be below 4 per cent in 2006.

Equatorial Guinea is the third largest oil exporter in sub-Saharan Africa (after Nigeria and Angola) and foreign oil companies – particularly ExxonMobil and TotalFinaElf – have open access to one of the world's largest oil reserves. It received the largest foreign direct investment (FDI) of all the oil producing CEMAC countries between 1999–2005 (except 2002, when Chad's FDI was greater). Production was around 400,000 barrels per day in 2005 and due to the sharp rise in global oil prices, in 2004–05, Equatorial Guinea has built up huge trade surplus. Nevertheless, it had a current account deficit of 13.3 per cent of GDP in 2005, down from 24.2 per cent in 2004, and if the trend is continued, it is expected to move into surplus in 2008.

Other than the oil sector, the economy is underdeveloped. Equatorial Guinea is rich in timber, fishing and agricultural land and there is significant room for expansion in all these areas. President Obiang has curtailed the fishing industry for fear that fishing boats might allow people to flee his regime. There are also undeveloped mineral resources of titanium, iron ore, manganese, uranium, and alluvial gold. The cocoa industry has suffered from falling world prices, a higher foreign exchange rate than competitor countries and stagnation due to a loss of immigrant farm labourers and farmers leaving the land to seek higher wages in the oil and related sectors.

High unemployment rates, of around 30 per cent, indicates a segmented employment pattern with the majority of the population dependent on primary industries and too few employed in valued-added secondary or tertiary industries.

External trade

Equatorial Guinea is a member of the Economic and Monetary Community of Central Africa (Cemac), the Economic Community of Central African States (ECCAS) and the Bank of Central African States, using the CFA franc.

As a primary producer over 90 per cent of exports are unprocessed petroleum, timber, coffee and cocoa.

Imports

Principal imports are petroleum sector equipment, other general equipment.

Main sources: US (24.6 per cent total, 2005), Italy (20.7 per cent), France (12.1 per cent), Spain (10.8 per cent), Côte d'Ivoire (8.7 per cent), UK (7.0 per cent)

Exports

Principal exports are petroleum, methanol, timber and cocoa.

Main destinations: US (25.8 per cent total, 2005), China (22.9 per cent), Spain (11.4 per cent), Canada (7.7 per cent), Taiwan (7.5 per cent), Portugal (5.7 per cent), The Netherlands (5.5 per cent), France (4.2 per cent)

Agriculture

Farming

Agriculture typically accounts for around 5 per cent of GDP, but employs 70 per cent of the workforce. The main cash crop, cocoa is grown on Bioko and Rio Muni, which also produces timber and coffee for export. Main food crops are cassava, sweet potatoes, bananas, palm oil and kernels.

The estimated crop production for 2005 included: 45,000 tonnes (t) cassava, 36,000t sweet potatoes, 20,000t bananas, 31,000t plantains, 105,000t roots and tubers, 6,000t coconuts, 35,000t oil palm fruit, 6,430t oilcrops, 3,000t cocoa beans, 3,500t green coffee, 51,000t fruit in total. Estimated livestock production included: 551t meat in total, 46t beef, 142t pig meat, 139t lamb and goat meat, 224t poultry, 190t eggs, 26t sheepskins.

Fishing

The fishing sector is a developing, and potentially lucrative, sector of the economy. The industry has been partially restored, since the 1970s when former President Nguema had banned fishing and destroyed the entire fishing fleet. Nevertheless, the industry is held back by low levels of investment and President Obiang's reluctance to permit a potential conduit that might allow access into the country by those opposed to his regime.

The government is developing the 314,000 square kilometre exclusive maritime economic zone surrounding the island of Anobon, off the mainland territory coastline, which is one of the Atlantic's richest fishing fields.

An EU-Equatorial Guinea fisheries agreement, signed in 2001, gives EU trawlers the right to capture 5,500 tonnes of fish per year. Under the deal, the EU pays Equatorial Guinea eur412,500 (US$458,000) per year, much of which goes into expanding and improving local fishing production.

In 2004, the total marine fish catch was 2,429 tonnes and the total crustacean catch was 50 tonnes.

Forestry

Equatorial Guinea has 63 per cent forest cover and logging is an important economic sector. In 2004, the export of forest products amounted to US$110.57 million.

Estimated production in 2004 included 811,000 cubic metres (cum) roundwood, 364,000cum industrial roundwood, 364,000cum sawlogs and veneers, 447,000cum woodfuel.

Industry and manufacturing

The industrial sector used to contribute around 90 per cent of GDP but since the boom in oil exports industry and manufacturing have been reduced to minor elements in the economy. Most production is related to the oil sector although as of 2005 there is no refining capacity. The manufacturing sector is very small, contributing less than 2 per cent of GDP. The non-oil industrial sector is underdeveloped, with activity centred on very small-scale food and timber processing. The traditional industries of cocoa and coffee suffer from a lack of investment. Industrial production remains around 30 per cent.

Mining

Industrial production in mining is underdeveloped, activity is limited to artisan exploitation of alluvial gold. There are reserves of copper, iron ore, uranium, tantalum and manganese.

Hydrocarbons

The hydrocarbons sector accounts for around 60 per cent of GDP and 90 per cent of exports. Oil is the country's most important foreign exchange earner and Equatorial Guinea has become one of the largest oil producers in the Gulf of Guinea. Proven oil reserves were conservatively put at 1.28 billion barrels in 2004, with oil production capped at 350,000 barrels per day (bpd). With political stability, a liberal investment framework, few regulations and favourable Production Sharing Contracts (PSCs) (in which the government has a 25 per cent stake), oil companies are flocking to the small west African state.

There have been various disputes between Equatorial Guinea and its neighbours over the demarcation of maritime borders, however President Obiang adopted an equidistant line defining maritime boundaries and Nigeria, Cameroon and São Tomé and Principé have accepted this solution. Gabon and Equatorial Guinea agreed to joint exploration of sites of mutual interest until mediation finds a solution to their disagreement concerning ownership of three islands. The main oil and gas fields are found offshore in the Alba and Aafiro fields.

In 2004, proven gas reserves stood at 36.8 billion cubic metres (cum) and estimated reserves at 124.5 billion cum. Gas consumption has increased and a new state gas company Société Nationale de Gaz (Songaz) was launched in January 2005 to manage gas assets. The company will also have responsibility for developing the industrial and residential gas market, as well as the exploitation, treatment, marketing, and distribution of natural gas.

Equatorial Guinea does not produce or import coal.

Energy

Equatorial Guinea's estimated installed electricity generating capacity is 131MW, but this is well below the potential of 11,000MW that could be produced through hydropower alone. Electricity is produced on Bioko Island by a combination of thermal and hydroelectric plants. Ageing equipment and past under investment in the system has left potential private investors reluctant to buy it from state control.

A new gas-fired power station with increased capacity is in operation but is constrained by its original supply lines. Increased capacity, of an expected 4–6MW, is due with the construction of another plant under construction in 2005.

Banking and insurance

Central bank

Banque des Etats de l'Afrique Centrale

Main financial centre

Malabo

Time

GMT plus one hour

Geography

Equatorial Guinea is situated on the west coast of Africa. The country comprises the island of Bioko (formerly Fernando Po), 40km off the coast of Cameroon; the mainland territory of Río Muni, 250km south of Bioko; and the islands of Annobón, Corisco, Great Elobey and Small Elobey. The Río Muni enclave is bounded to the north by Cameroon and to the east and south by Gabon.

The islands, in the Gulf of Guinea, are volcanic and mountainous with beaches. Malabo, the capital, is located on Bioko, which covers 2,000 square km. Annobón (17 square km), together with the other smaller islands, are close to the mainland and are all part of Río Muni region.

The mainland is heavily forested with some mountains. There is a coastal plain, which supports plantations. The south of the region is fairly inaccessible.

Hemisphere

Northern

Climate

Equatorial with heavy rainfall for most of the year except for slightly drier period from December–February. The mainland Rio Muni is drier and cooler than Bioko. Average temperature is 26 degrees Celsius throughout the year, and generally very humid.

Entry requirements

Passports

Required by all, valid for six months beyond date of departure.

Visa

Required by all, except US nationals. Business visas require a letter of invitation from a local company and proof of visitor's status and a letter of finance giving proof of sufficient funds for length of stay and a full itinerary.

Currency advice/regulations

Import of local and foreign currencies is unrestricted, provided that amounts in excess of CFAf50,000 (approximately US$90) are declared on arrival. Export of currencies is limited to the amount declared. Failure to declare excess currency risks forfeiture of any amount over the CFAf50,000 limit when departing.

Equatorial Guinea is a cash economy and CFA francs is the only form of payment accepted. Foreign currency should be exchanged at banks, which are few in number.

Health (for visitors)
Mandatory precautions
A yellow fever vaccination certificate is required if arriving from an infected area.
Advisable precautions
Vaccinations against hepatitis A and B, tetanus, diphtheria, polio, typhoid and meningitis are strongly recommended. Malaria prophylaxis is advisable as risk exists throughout the country. There is a rabies risk. Water precautions should be taken.
Medical facilities are limited so it is advisable to pack any personal medications required.

Hotels
Accommodation is very limited but there are hotels in Malabo and Bata. It is essential to book a hotel before travelling, preferably through local business contacts.
Food is rarely available at the Bata Hotel and, in Malabo, air-conditioning is available only in some rooms in the Apartotel Impala.
When there is no service charge, gratuities are around 10 to 15 per cent.

Public holidays (national)
Fixed dates
1 Jan (New Year), 8 Mar (Women's Day), 1 May (Labour Day), 25 May (Africa Day), 5 Jun (President's Day), 3 Aug (Armed Forces Day), 15 Aug (Constitution Day), 12 October (Independence Day), 10 Dec (Human Rights' Day), 25 Dec (Christmas Day).
Variable dates
Good Friday, Corpus Christi (May/Jun), Human Rights Day (Dec).

Working hours
Banking
Mon–Sat: 0800–1200.
Business
Mon–Fri: 0800–1500.
Government
Mon–Fri: 0830–1500; Sat: 0830–1200, (alternate Sat) 1000–1200.
Shops
(Mon–Sat) 0800–1300 and 1600–1900.

Telecommunications
Telephone/fax
Electricity supply
220 V AC, 50 cycles

Social customs/useful tips
Corruption is endemic. Special permits from the Ministry of Information and Tourism are required for most photography, including the presidential palace and its environs, military installations, government buildings, airports, harbours and other areas.

Getting there
Air
Several European airlines link Malabo with Madrid, London, Paris, Amsterdam and Zurich.
International airport/s: Malabo Airport (SSG), 7km from the capital city on the island of Malabo.
Bata Airport (FGBT), 6km from city, on the mainland of Equatorial Guinea.
Surface
Road: There is access by semi-surfaced road from Gabon to Mbini and Bata, although this route is not generally recommended.
Main port/s: Malabo, Bata, Luba, Mbini and Kogo.

Getting about
National transport
Air: There are a number of small airlines serving domestic routes, especially Ecuato Guineana, which operates between Bata and Malabo. They do not meet international standards and most of them have been grounded.
Road: On Bioko a surfaced road links major towns in the north. On mainland Río Muni a surfaced road links Bata with Mbini and a partly surfaced road links Bata with Ebebiyin (near Gabon border). Other roads are unsurfaced and can be difficult.
Water: There is a boat service between Malabo and Bata.

BUSINESS DIRECTORY

The addresses listed below are a selection only. While World of Information makes every endeavour to check these addresses, we cannot guarantee that changes have not been made, especially to telephone numbers and area codes. We would welcome any corrections.

Telephone area codes
The international direct dialling code (IDD) for Equatorial Guinea is +240 followed by area code and subscriber's number:

Bata	8	Malabo	9

Chambers of Commerce
Camara Oficiel de Comercio, Agricola y Forestal, 43 Avenida de la Indepencia, PO Box 51, Malabo (tel: 923-43; fax: 932-66).

Banking
Banco de Crédito y Desarrollo (credit and development bank), 1 Avenida de la Libertad, PO Box 39, Malabo (tel: 2146).

Banco Exterior de Guinea Ecuatorial, Carretera de Aeropuerto, Malabo (tel: 2001).

Banque Internationale pour l'Afrique Occidentale, Calle de Argelia No 6, PO Box 686, Malabo (tel: 2367, 2887).

Caisse Commune d'Epargne et d'Investissement en Guinée Equatoriale (CCEI-GE); PO Box 428, Malabo (tel: 2003, 2910; fax: 3311).

Société Générale de Banque GE; PO Box 686, Calle Argelia, Malabo (tel: 3337; fax: 2743).

Central bank
Banque des Etats de l'Afrique Centrale, Direction Nationale, PO Box 501, Malabo (tel: 20-10; fax: 20-06; e-mail: beacmal@beac.int).

Other useful addresses
Comite Sindical de Cacao (cocoa growers' organisation), Bioko.

Dirección General de Correos y Telecomunicaciones, Malabo.

Empresa Estatal de Comercio Interior y Exterior, Malabo.

Empresa General de Industria y Comercio (EGISCA), Malabo.

Empresa Guineano-Española de Petróleos (Gepsa), Malabo.

Internet sites
Equatorial Guinea oil: http://www.equatorialoil.com/

Africa Business Network: http://www.ifc.org/abn

AllAfrica.com: http://allafrica.com

African Development Bank: http://www.afdb.org

Africa Online: http://www.africaonline.com

Mbendi AfroPaedia (information on companies, countries, industries and stock exchanges in Africa): http://mbendi.co.za

Official site (in Spanish): http://www.guineaecuatorial.net/ms/main.asp

Eritrea

KEY FACTS

Official name: Hagere Ertra (State of Eritrea)

Head of State: President Issaias Afwerki (since 1991; elected president 8 Jun 1993)

Head of government: President Issaias Afwerki

Ruling party: People's Front for Democracy and Justice (PFDJ) (formerly the Eritrean People's Liberation Front (EPLF))

Area: 125,000 square km

Population: 4.68 million (2007)*

Capital: Asmara

Official language: There is no official language but the working languages are Tigrinya, Arabic and English.

Currency: Nakfa (Nk) = 100 cents

Exchange rate: Nk15.00 per US$ (Jul 2008); (From 26 Jan 2005, all transactions are to be conducted in the national currency, the nakfa)

GDP per capita: US$281 (2007)*

GDP real growth: 1.30% (2007)*

Labour force: 2.25 million (2004)

Inflation: 9.30% (2007)*

Balance of trade: -US$501.00 million (2006)

* estimated figure

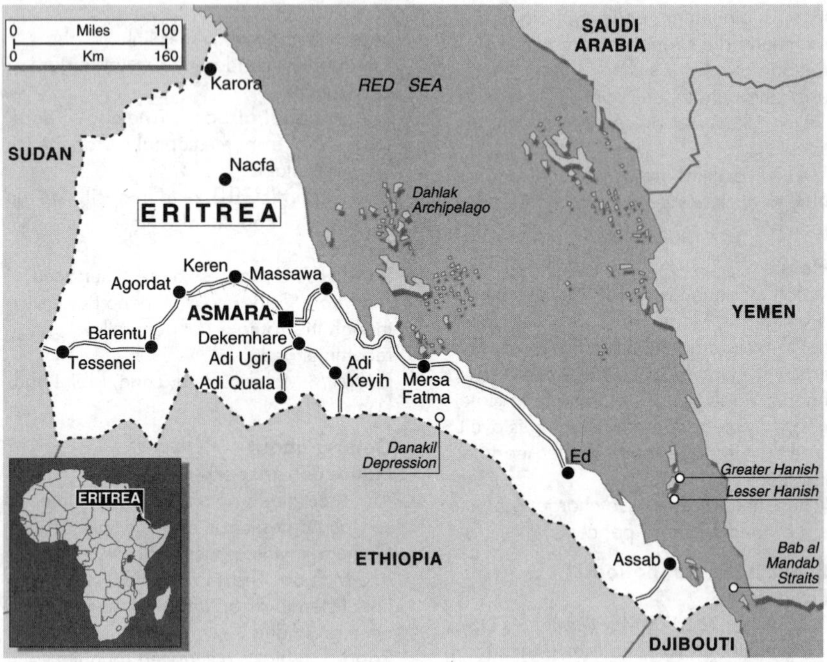

Eritrea's separation from Ethiopia in 1991, and its formal incorporation as an independent state in 1993 seemed to many to be distant dreams by the beginning of 2008. Eritrea had been independent under the rule of the Eritrean People's Liberation Front (EPLF) until the referendum of 1993 endorsed its independence with over 1.1 million votes in favour, and only 1,800 against. Such was the cordial climate between Ethiopia and Eritrea that agreement was rapidly reached on Eritrea's continued use of Massawa and Assab ports. Full freedom of movement between the two countries was also agreed.

But then the two countries fought a bloody war over their 1,000km border in 1998–2000. The peace accord signed in Algiers in 2000 set up an independent commission to defuse tensions issued a ruling in 2002 placing the symbolic town of Badme in Eritrea. However, physical demarcation of the border never actually took place. As tensions rose, the UN Security Council announced the creation of the UN Mission in Ethiopia and Eritrea (UNMEE) to patrol the border. UNMEE's mandate was renewed by the Security Council every six months until July 2008 when it was terminated after relations between Eritrea and UNMEE deteriorated.

Analysts thought it unlikely that tensions between the two countries were unlikely to escalate immediately following the withdrawal of UNMEE; representatives of both countries agreed. But a mechanism should be found as soon as possible to engage them in dialogue. The International Crisis Group (ICG) warned in June 2008 that the border impasse carried serious risks of as new war and was a major source of instability in the Horn of Africa, most critically Somalia. ICG said that 'both regimes have used it as an excuse to enhance their domestic power at the expense of democracy and economic growth, thus reducing the attractiveness to them of diplomatic compromise'. In a further complication, Ethiopia has sent troops (since 2006) to intervene on behalf of the transitional government (TG) in Somalia, while Eritrea was accused of arming the Islamist opponents of the TG. In June 2008 clashes on the Eritrea/Djibouti border in the Mount Gabla area – also known as Ras Doumeira – killed nine Djibouti troops and injured many more; the US blamed the clashes on 'military aggression' by Eritrea.

A dollar a day

Eritrea is one of the poorest countries in the world and its people live under a regime of political and religious repression. For its religious intolerance it has been blacklisted by the United States. It is a one party state, with the People's Front for Democracy and Justice (PFDJ) the only party allowed to operate. There are two opposition groups, which have united and run the risk of being jailed for their efforts to promote a national dialogue with President Issaias Afwerki.

More than half of the population lives on less than US$1 per day and about one third lives in extreme poverty – consuming less than 2,000 calories per day. The authorities have produced a poverty and national food security strategy, which together set out plans aimed at increasing rural incomes and raising productivity.

Economy

Since independence from Ethiopia on 24 May 1993 Eritrea has faced the economic problems of a small, desperately poor country. Like the economies of many African nations, the economy is largely based on subsistence agriculture, with 80 per cent of the population involved in farming and herding. Growth of the economy was badly hindered by the war with Ethiopia. Eritrea's real GDP growth in the two years prior to the conflict had averaged an impressive 7.4 per cent. Since then GDP growth fell to 4.0 per cent in 1998, 0.0 per cent in 1999 and -13.1 per cent in 2000. With the official cessation of hostilities, real GDP growth of 3.0 per cent was achieved in 2001, dropping back to 1.6 per cent in 2002. Growth was 5.0 per cent in 2003, 1.8 per cent in 2004 and 4.8 per cent in 2005. Growth in 2006 was -0.9 per cent but had risen again by 2007 to 1.3 per cent. Inflation was 15.0 per cent in 2006, but had recovered to 9.3 per cent by 2007.

Since the war ended, the government has maintained a firm grip on the economy, expanding the use of the military and party-owned businesses to complete Eritrea's development agenda.

The unresolved border issue compounds other pressing problems. These include Eritrea's simple inability to provide enough food for its people; over two thirds of the population receive food aid. Moreover, economic progress is hampered by the proportion of Eritreans who are in the army rather than the workforce.

On top of everything, Eritrea is also having to cope with the effects of four consecutive years of drought. Malnutrition has increased in many parts of the country. Macroeconomic imbalances have grown and overall performance has been weak. Eritrean monetary policy continues to be subservient to the government's financing requirements and budgeting is irregular.

Surprisingly, the commercial banks remain profitable, owing to income from their foreign exchange activities, and they appear to be in compliance with prudential regulations. However, they continue to hold a high proportion of non-performing loans, largely on account of the effects of the border war, and their core lending activities do not generate enough income to cover operational costs.

Although paying lip-service to market-based policies, the authorities have increasingly resorted to an administrative-controlled approach to economic management.

Politics

Issaias Afwerki was elected president of independent Eritrea by the country's national assembly in 1994. He had been the *de facto* leader before independence. Presidential elections, planned for 1997, never materialised. Eritrea remains a one-party state. Afwerki has been criticised for failing to implement democratic reforms. His government has clamped down on its critics and has closed the private press.

Born in 1946 in Asmara, he joined the Eritrean Liberation Front (ELF) in 1966. He received military training in China the same year, and then went on to be deputy divisional commander of the ELF. In 1970 he co-founded the Eritrean People's Liberation Front (EPLF) and in 1987 he was elected secretary general of the organisation. EPLF is now the People's Front for Democracy and Justice.

Risk assessment

Economic	Poor
Political	Poor
Regional stability	Poor

COUNTRY PROFILE

Historical profile

Since gaining independence from Ethiopia in 1993, Eritrea has had to weather constant political, economic and social upheaval. A two-year war with Ethiopia in 1998–99 left the economy in tatters with a peace agreement that left both sides disgruntled and unwilling to restore constructive relations. The optimism that surrounded independence has become disillusion, as the government has sidelined the democratic process and conducted widespread repression of any form of political or even religious dissidence.

1889–1941 Under Italian rule. Eritrea first emerged as a political entity following the Italian occupation of the Red Sea port of Massawa and other coastal enclaves in the 1880s. In 1889, Italy signed the Treaty of Ucciali with the Ethiopian Emperor, Menelik, and in 1890, named the country Eritrea.

1941 The UK defeated Italy during the Second World War and Eritrea became a British protectorate.

1952 UN-sanctioned federation with Ethiopia.

1962 Eritrea was annexed to Ethiopia as a province under Emperor Haile Selassie.

KEY INDICATORS — Eritrea

	Unit	2003	2004	2005	2006	2007
Population	m	4.23	4.27	4.63	4.54	*4.68
Gross domestic product (GDP)	US$bn	0.63	0.93	0.96	1.21	*1.32
GDP per capita	US$	150	138	207	267	281
GDP real growth	%	5.0	1.8	4.8	-0.9	*1.3
Inflation	%	18.8	21.4	12.5	15.0	*9.3
Exports (fob) (goods)	US$m	20.0	64.4	64.0	64.0	0.0
Imports (cif) (goods)	US$m	500.0	622.0	572.0	564.0	0.0
Balance of trade	US$m	-480.0	-557.6	-508.0	-501.0	0.0
Current account	US$m	-90.0	-105.0	40.0	-41.0	-62.0
Total reserves minus gold	US$m	24.7	34.7	27.9	25.4	0.0
Foreign exchange	US$m	24.7	34.7	27.9	25.3	0.0
Exchange rate	per US$	8.43	8.58	13.50	13.50	13.24

* estimated figure

1991 The Eritrean People's Liberation Front (EPLF) overthrew Ethiopian Colonel Mengistu's forces and liberated the territory; Issaias Afwerki assumed power.
1993 A vote resulted in a virtually 100 per cent acceptance of independence.
1994 Eritrea achieved nationhood and Afwerki was elected president by the National Assembly.
1998 Eritrea and Ethiopia resumed border warfare. The Permanent Court of Arbitration in the Hague ruled that Yemen should have the Red Sea island of Greater Hanish, fought over in 1995 by Eritrea and Yemen, and it was announced that Eritrea would return it to Yemen. The nakfa was introduced as Eritrea's national currency, to be used alongside the Ethiopian birr.
2000 UN peacekeepers opened a 1,000km cease-fire land corridor between Ethiopia and Eritrea and the two countries signed a peace deal in Algiers, ending the two-year war.
2001 The UN established a buffer zone along the border of Ethiopia and Eritrea.
2002 Eritrea and Ethiopia accepted a ruling on the border dispute, made by the Boundary Commission at the Permanent Court of Arbitration of The Hague. A new 1,000km boundary was established between the two countries.
2003 The UN Mission in Ethiopia and Eritrea (UNMEE) mandate was extended.
2004 Eritrea suffered from a harsh drought in June, resulting in severe drinking-water problems both for humans and animals. Implementation of the peace process that was to resolve the border conflict between Ethiopia and Eritrea remained stalled.
2005 New Bank of Eritrea regulations required all transactions to be conducted in the national currency, the nakfa. Eritrea restricted the movement of UN peacekeepers along the Eritrea/Ethiopia border, leading to fears that the war would flare up again. The independent commission at the Permanent Court of Arbitration in The Hague, set up as part of the peace deal signed in Algiers in 2000 between Eritrea and Ethiopia, ruled that Eritrea had launched unlawful attacks against Ethiopia in 1998, thereby triggering the border war between the two countries.
2006 Tensions continued in the border dispute with Ethiopia. Eritrea rebuffed international attempts to mediate. Eritrea was accused of arming Islamist opponents of the Somali transitional government, which was supported by Ethiopia.
2007 In December, talks, set by the Ethiopia-Eritrea Border Commission, to confirm the demarcation between Ethiopia and Eritrea, failed to reach an agreement on time. The Commission considers the border it drew in 2006 to be binding in the face of the impasse. While Ethiopia and Eritrea accepted the ruling neither attempted to implement its recommendation and 1,700 UN peace-keeping troops remained in the area in a notional demilitarised zone.
2008 In February, United Nation's troops along the disputed border began what was described as a 'temporary relocation' out of Eritrea, after the government cut off fuel supplies. Border clashes in June in the Mount Gabla area – also known as Ras Doumeira – that killed nine Djibouti troops and injured many more was blamed, by the US, on 'military aggression' by Eritrea. The US and France called for a cease fire and troop withdrawals on both sides and for negotiations to begin. The Security Council terminated the UNMEE on 31 July.

Political structure
A transitional national assembly was constituted in 1997 pending elections, which, although scheduled to be held in 2001, have been postponed indefinitely.

Constitution
A new constitution was adopted in May 1997.
A 150-member National Transitional Council was set up, with 75 seats allocated to the People's Front for Democracy and Justice (PFDJ), 60 to the Constitutional Assembly and 15 to overseas Eritreans.
The president governs with the help of his 24-member Consultative Council. The Consultative Council is composed of ministers and regional governors.
There are six administrative regions, each with regional, sub-regional (55) and village administrations (651). The regions enjoy a degree of autonomy.

Last elections
24 May 1993 (presidential)
Results: Presidential: Issaias Afwerki was elected by the National Assembly with 95 per cent of the vote.

Next elections

Political parties
Ruling party
People's Front for Democracy and Justice (PFDJ) (formerly the Eritrean People's Liberation Front (EPLF))

Main opposition party
Opposition parties are not allowed.

Population
4.68 million (2007)*
Last census: May 1984: 2,748,304
Population density: 32 inhabitants per square km. Urban population: 19 per cent (1995–2001).
Annual growth rate: 3.3 per cent 1994–2004 (WHO 2006)
Internally Displaced Persons (IDP)
59,000 (UNHCR 2004)

Ethnic make-up
There are nine ethno-linguistic groups.

Religions
Tigrigna-speaking Christians (mainly Orthodox), are the traditional inhabitants of the highlands, with some Protestant and Roman Catholic communities (49 per cent); Muslim communities of the western lowlands, northern highlands and east coast are 49 per cent. A small number of the population adhere to traditional beliefs.

Education
There are approximately 260 primary schools and over 50 secondary schools. It has been estimated by Oxfam that 93 per cent of children age 6–11 will enrol for school in 2015.
Literacy rate: 67 per cent men, 36 per cent woman; adult rates (World Bank 2002).
Enrolment rate: 53 per cent gross enrolment, of relevant age group, in primary education (World Bank 2001).
Pupils per teacher: 44 in primary schools.

Health
Per capita total expenditure on health (2003) was US$50; of which per capita government spending was US$23, at the international dollar rate, (WHO 2006).
Access to an improved water source is available to 46 per cent of the population.

HIV/Aids
A survey published in 2001 revealed that 4.6 per cent of soldiers were HIV-positive and 22.8 per cent of female bar workers were affected as well. By 2002, more than 13,000 people had been registered as infected with HIV/Aids. The main incidences are in Asmara, the capital, and Assab, the sea port, where prostitution is rife. Up to 30 per cent of prostitutes are HIV positive.
HIV prevalence: 2.7 per cent aged 15–49 in 2003 (World Bank)
Life expectancy: 60 years, 2004 (WHO 2006)
Fertility rate/Maternal mortality rate: 5.4 births per woman, 2004 (WHO 2006); maternal mortality 10 per 1,000 per live births (World Bank).
Child (under 5 years) mortality rate (per 1,000): 45 per 1,000 live births (2003); 44 per cent of children aged under five were malnourished (World Bank).
Head of population per physician: 0.05 physicians per 1,000 people, 2004 (WHO 2006).

Welfare
A post-war rehabilitation project, implemented by the UN Development Programme (UNDP), has put metal roofs, doors and windows back on houses that were deserted and ransacked during the

border war with Ethiopia. An estimated 60,000 children were left crippled by the war, and another 45,000 orphaned. A large proportion of the population is dependent on food aid. UNICEF appeals in 2002 for refugee welfare raised a total of US$10.3 million, a large part of which was spent on establishing and rehabilitating water supplies in settlement areas, as well as setting up basic health and sanitation facilities.

Main cities

Asmara (capital, estimated population 543,707 in 2005), Keren (86,483), Dek'emhare (30,180), Massawa (Mitsiwa) (24,419).

Languages spoken

The principal language group in Eritrea is Afro-Asiatic; Arabic, Afar, Bilen, Hedareb, Kunama, Nara, Saho, Tigray and Tigrinya are spoken. English is rapidly becoming the language of business and is the medium of instruction at secondary schools and at university.

Official language/s

There is no official language but the working languages are Tigrinya, Arabic and English.

Media

In 2006 Eritrea was ranked 166 out of 168 and one of the three worst press freedom violators (after North Korea and Turkmenistan) worldwide. Journalists have been imprisoned and media outlets were closed down in 2001, so that, in 2008, government organs have a monopoly.

Other news agencies: Erina (Eritrean News Agency): www.dehai.org/erina

Press

There are no daily newspapers, all publications are government-owned, including in Tigrinya and Arabic Hadas Eritrea (New Eritrea), Tirigta (owned by the PFDJ political party) and Geled for a youth readership and in English Eritrea Profile.

Broadcasting

Radio: Two radio stations exist, Radio Zara and Dimtsi Hafash Radio (Voice of the Broad Masses of Eritrea) operates two networks that broadcast in Arabic and local languages. Services can also be received via Arabsat satellite.

Television: The government-owned ERI-TV broadcasts in Arabic, and local languages although transmissions are limited to Asmara and surrounding areas.

News agencies

Other news agencies: Erina (Eritrean News Agency): www.dehai.org/erina

Economy

The main problems affecting the Eritrean economy are an inadequate and war-ravaged infrastructure, a lack of hard currency to pay for imports, a weak tax collection system and the predominance of unproductive subsistence agriculture. Eritrea is still reeling from the 1998–2000 border war, which cost the economy up to US$800 million. A long period of tension on the borders has not helped attract investment or promote macroeconomic stability. A series of droughts in recent years has exacerbated Eritrea's problems.

The government wants to diversify the economy (70 per cent of Eritreans are employed in agriculture), so that it can afford to buy abroad what it cannot grow itself. Some 70 per cent of the population depends on foreign aid for all or part of its food supply.

The country's economic future depends on its ability to eradicate major social and economic problems. These include widespread illiteracy, unemployment and poor levels of foreign investment. The border between Ethiopia and Eritrea, implemented after the Boundary Commission ruling in 2002, ought to have encouraged stability and allowed Eritrea to focus on these problems, but relations between the two countries remain heated and continuing tensions are likely to deter investment until accord is reached.

In the long term, Eritrea may benefit from the development of offshore oil, fishing and tourism industries.

External trade

Eritrea is a member of the Common Market of Eastern and Southern Africa (Comesa), however in May 2007 it did not have plans to join the customs union and free trade area as agreed by other member states.

Imports

Principal non-petroleum imports include machinery, food and manufactured goods.

Main sources: Germany (22.2 per cent total, 2005), Italy (20.3 per cent), France (15.9 per cent), US (12.8 per cent), Ireland (8.2 per cent)

Exports

Principal exports include livestock, sorghum, textiles, food and small manufactures.

Main destinations: Italy (39.3 per cent total, 2005), US (14.9 per cent), Belarus (7.3 per cent), Germany (5.8 per cent), UK (4.9 per cent)

Agriculture

Farming

Crop production in 2005 included: 151,672 tonnes (t) cereals in total, 672t wheat, 2,472t maize, 17,399t millet, 17,488t potatoes, 114,292t sorghum, 9,263t barley, 35,213t pulses, 14,117t oilcrops, *2,000t fruit in total, *23,000t vegetables in total. Livestock production included: 30,907t meat in total, 16,650t beef, *732t camel meat, 5,600t lamb, 5,800t goat meat, 2,125t poultry, *1,978t eggs, *56,725t milk, 3,213t cattle hides, 560t sheepskins, 785t greasy wool.

* estimate

Fishing

Fishing for sardines, anchovies, tuna, shark and mackerel is practised in the Red Sea on a very small scale. There are over 1,000 different species of fish off Eritrea's shores, with the stocks virtually untouched since the 1950s. The government believes there is potential for exporting 80,000 tonnes of fish annually. The sector has been badly affected by the closure of its market in Yemen as a result of a territorial dispute.

In 2004, the total marine fish catch was 6,964 tonnes and the total crustacean catch was 413 tonnes.

The majority of timber harvested is used for domestic purposes. Timber imports in 2004 were US$2.9 million, while exports amounted to US$334,000.

Estimated timber production in 2004 included: 2,407,576 cubic metre (cum) roundwood, 1,924cum industrial roundwood, 2,405,652 cum wood fuel, 156,660t charcoal.

Industry and manufacturing

The industrial sector contributes around 27 per cent of GDP and employs 10 per cent of the workforce.

The industrial base is traditionally centred on the production of glass, cement, footwear and canned goods, but most industrial enterprises have been badly damaged by war. All state-owned distribution and import/export enterprises established by the former government have been dissolved.

Major problems include outdated machinery and techniques, supply of energy, and the need for imports throughout the sector. With a lack of foreign currency and investment, industry is suffering from outdated machinery and intermediary goods which need to be imported.

Tourism

The tourism sector was badly affected by the war with Ethiopa. Around 165,000 tourists a year visited the country before hostilities broke out. Since the resumption of peace in 2000, arrivals have continued to increase year-on-year, rising from 40,000 in 2001 to over 100,000 by 2005. The continuing tensions between Eritrea and Ethiopia, as well as the need for improved infrastructure, may have held back faster growth. The government, with the support of UN agencies, is pursuing a 20-year development strategy, emphasising nature and heritage tourism and aiming for between 600,000 and 1 million visitors a year by 2020. The main markets are Italy and Germany.

Mining

Fighting along the border regions disrupted mining activities, although exploration continued elsewhere in Eritrea. The Phelps Dodge Exploration Corporation conducted exploration on the Debarwa copper-zinc deposits and identified up to four million tonnes of reserves, including at least two million tonnes of mineable high-grade copper and a large amount of gold.

Gold-bearing seams exist in highland areas. There are over 15 gold mines and a large number of prospects close to Asmara. The potential for new discoveries in the area is good. Substantial gold reserves have also been identified at Adi Nefas by LaSource Development SAS.

Artisanal mining production is estimated to produce around 550kg per year.

Despite Eritrea's mining potential, salt and marble remain the country's main exported minerals.

Hydrocarbons

Large offshore oil reserves beneath the Red Sea and substantial natural gas reserves in the Danakil depression have yet to be effectively exploited. Several oil companies have negotiated oil exploration contracts for the shallow waters off Eritrea's coast. Eritrea had a refining capacity of 18,000 barrels per day until the refinery in Assab was closed down in 1997 due to high maintenance costs, rendering Eritrea dependent on imports.

Eritrea's economic plight and shortage of foreign currency has led to the suspension of petrol sales since October 2004 and a ban on private imports of oil since February 2005.

Energy

Electricity supply is available mainly to urban areas, leaving the majority of the population without access. Existing 66MW generating capacity was supplemented in 2003 by the completion of an 88MW plant funded by Saudi Arabia and the United Arab Emirates.

In July 2004, the World Bank approved an International Development Association (IDA) credit of US$29 million and an IDA grant of US$21 million in support of power distribution and rural electrification in Eritrea.

Some villages provide themselves with electricity from community diesel generators, while photovoltaic power is used to a limited extent for health centres, schools and water pumps.

Banking and insurance

Central bank

Bank of Eritrea

Time

GMT plus three hours

Geography

Eritrea extends inland from the Red Sea coast of eastern Africa. To the south, the country has a long frontier with Ethiopia, and a short frontier with Djibouti. Sudan lies to the north and west.

The coastal area is a desert plain, around 50km wide in the south, and one of the driest places in the world. Inland, the terrain becomes hillier, rising to 2,000m, in the north-west, while further south it turns to rolling plains.The highlands are cool and receive up to 60cm of rainfall annually; fertile valleys support agricultural activity.

Hemisphere

Northern

Climate

Coastal and lowland regions very hot and dry throughout the year. On the plateau, which includes Asmara, the dry season runs from October–May with temperatures ranging from as low as 6 degrees Celsius (C) in December to 26 degrees C in March (light rain from February–April). Temperatures can fall sharply at night during the dry season.

The rainy season runs from June–September with average temperature 21 degrees C. Rainfall is less than 500mm per year in lowland areas, increasing to 1,000mm in the highlands. The temperature gradient is similarly steep: average annual temperatures range from 17 degrees C in the highlands to 30 degrees C in Massawa. The Danakil depression in the south-east, which is more than 130 metres below sea-level in places, experiences some of the highest temperatures recorded, frequently exceeding 50 degrees C.

Entry requirements

Passports

Required by all, valid for three months beyond intended length of stay.

Visa

Required by all except nationals of Kenya and Uganda. Business visas are valid for one month, but can be extended on application to the Eritrean Foreign Ministry. A business letter giving proof of sufficient funds for length of stay, a full itinerary and copy of return/onward ticket, should accompany application.

Currency advice/regulations

There are no restrictions on import or export of local and foreign currency. From January 2005, all transactions have been conducted in the national currency, the nakfa.

Health (for visitors)

Mandatory precautions

A yellow fever vaccination certificate is required if travelling from or via an infected area.

Advisable precautions

Inoculations and booster should be current for diphtheria, polio, tetanus, hepatitis A, and typhoid. There may be a need for vaccinations for, tuberculosis, hepatitis B and meningitis. Use malaria prophylaxis if travelling in areas below 2000 metres. Malaria and hepatitis B are caused by mosquitoes, precautions including mosquito repellents, nets and clothing covering the body after dark should be used. There is a risk of rabies in rural areas.

There is a shortage of routine medications and visitors should take all necessary medicines with them. A first aid kit that includes disposable syringes, is a reasonable precaution. Use only bottled or boiled water for drinks, washing teeth and making ice. Eat only well cooked meals, preferably served hot; vegetables should be cooked and fruit peeled. Dairy products are unpasteurised and should be avoided, unless cooked.

Healthcare is not to Western standards and medical insurance, including emergency evacuation, is necessary.

Hotels

Both Asmara and Massawa suffer from a severe shortage of hotel space; booking is advisable. Standards are low but are being improved. Service charge of 10 per cent and a small tip is usual in addition to service charge. Visitors are expected to pay bills at government-run hotels in US dollars or denominated traveller's cheques.

Credit cards

Credit cards are only accepted at a few outlets in Asmara.

Public holidays (national)

Fixed dates

1 Jan (New Year's Day), 8 Mar (Women's Day), 24 May (Independence Day), 20 Jun (Martyrs' Day), 1 Sep (Start of the Armed Struggle), 25 Dec (Christmas Day).

Variable dates

Eid al-Fitr, Eid al-Adha, Prophet's Anniversary, Easter.

Islamic year – 1429 (10 Jan 2008–28 Dec 2008): The Islamic year contains 354 or 355 days, with the result that Muslim feasts advance by 10–12 days against the Gregorian calendar. Dates of feasts vary according to the sighting of the new moon, so cannot be forecast exactly.

Working hours

Banking

(Mon–Fri) 0800–1200, 1400–1700; (Sat) 0800–1200.

Business

Mon–Thu: 0700–1200, 1400–1800; Fri: 0700–1130, 1400–1800.

Shops

Mon–Fri: 0830–1300, 1430–2030.

Electricity supply
220V AC, 50 cycles.

Weights and measures
The metric system is in force.

Security
Street crime such as theft and robbery is rare in most cities. However, it is advisable not to walk around alone late at night in any town, particularly Asmara and Massawa. Valuables, especially cameras and including passports, should be kept out of sight.

Getting there
Air
National airline: Eritrean Airlines
International airport/s: Asmara (ASM), 6km from city, restaurant, currency exchange, post office, duty-free.
Airport tax: International departures: US$20; domestic departures Nk15.
Surface
Road: There are no roads considered safe to enter the country. The 300km road from Kassala in Sudan, to Tessenai, is largely unsurfaced.
Main port/s: Massawa and Assab.
Assab's cargo levels are very low. The port had previously relied on Ethiopia for 90 per cent of its trade.

Getting about
National transport
Road: The extensive road network is undergoing major rehabilitation with US$27m allocated by the government to road reconstruction.
There are 622km of asphalt roads. The Massawa-Asmara main route (107km) is open. Other main routes (largely unsurfaced) are Asmara-Keren to Afabet-Nacfa in the north, and Asmara-Tessenai to the west.
In many parts of the country, roads are difficult or impassable during the rainy season. There are extensive mine fields in Eritrea, especially near the border with Ethiopia. Travelling on main roads outside of the border areas is generally safe, but it is advisable not to drive off-road or travel after dark in rural areas.
Buses: Some bus services available, including one service to Addis Ababa.
Taxis: Taxis are available for trips outside the city, but the fares are higher.
Rail: The link from Asmara to the coast is functioning.
City transport
Taxis: The journey time by taxi from the Asmara International Airport to the city is 15 minutes. Taxi drivers do not expect a tip.

BUSINESS DIRECTORY
The addresses listed below are a selection only. While World of Information makes every endeavour to check these addresses, we cannot guarantee that changes have not been made, especially to telephone numbers and area codes. We would welcome any corrections.

Telephone area codes
The international dialling code (IDD) for Eritrea is +291 followed by 1 and subscriber's number.

Chambers of Commerce
Eritrean National Chamber of Commerce, 46 Aboit Avenue, PO Box 856, Asmara (tel: 121-589; fax: 120-138; e-mail: encc@eol.com.er).

Banking
Commercial Bank of Eritrea; PO Box 291, 212 Liberty Avenue, Asmara (tel: 116-005, 121-844/48; fax: 124-887l, 121-849).

Eritrean Development & Investment Bank; PO Box 1266, 29 Atse Yohannes Street, Asmara (tel: 123-787, 114-520, 126-777).

Housing & Commerce Bank of Eritrea; PO Box 235, Bahti Meskerem Square, Asmara (tel: 120-350; fax: 120-401).

Central bank
National Bank of Eritrea, Zeraai Derres Square, PO Box 849, Asmara (tel: 123-033; fax: 122-091; e-mail: tekieb@eol.com.er).

Travel information
Ministry of tourism
Ministry of Tourism, PO Box 1010, Asmara (tel: 126-997).

Ministries
Ministry of Agriculture, PO Box 124, Asmara (tel: 181-499; fax: 181-415).

Ministry of Defence, PO Box 629, Asmara (tel: 113-349; fax: 114-920).

Ministry of Education, PO Box 5610, Asmara (tel: 113-044; fax: 113-866).

Ministry of Energy and Mines, PO Box 5285, Asmara (tel: 116-872; fax: 127-652); Department of Energy (fax: 112-339); Department of Mines (fax: 112-994).

Ministry of Finance and Development, PO Box 896, Asmara (tel: 113-633; fax: 117-947).

Ministry of Fisheries, PO Box 923, Asmara (tel: 114-271; fax: 112-185).

Ministry of Foreign Affairs, PO Box 190, Asmara (tel: 113-811; fax: 123-788).

Ministry of Health, PO Box 212, Asmara (tel: 112-877; fax: 112-899).

Ministry of Information, PO Box 242, Asmara (tel: 115-171; fax: 119-847).

Ministry of Justice, PO Box 241, Asmara (tel: 111-822).

Ministry of Local Government, PO Box 225, Asmara (tel: 113-006).

Ministry of Public Works, PO Box 841, Asmara (tel: 119-077).

Ministry of Trade and Industry, PO Box 1844, Asmara (tel: 118-386, 113-910; fax: 120-586).

Ministry of Transport and Communications, PO Box 204, Asmara (tel: 110-444; fax: 127-048).

Other useful addresses
African Minerals Inc (AMI), PO Box 3508, Asmara (tel: 120-280, 120-030; fax: 120-332).

British Consulate, 27 Lorenzo Tazaz Street, PO Box 997, Asmara (tel: 123-415; fax: 127-230).

Communications and Postal Authority, PO Box 234, Asmara (tel: 112-900; fax: 110-938).

Eritrean Association in London, UK (tel: (0)181-748-0547).

Eritrean Business Licence Office, PO Box 3045, Asmara (tel: 114-809, 114-752; fax: 126-694).

Eritrean Shipping Lines, PO Box 1110, Asmara (tel: 120-308/359/257; fax: 120-331).

Grain Board of Eritrea, PO Box 1234, Asmara (tel: 115-624; fax: 120-586).

Investment Promotion Centre, Asmara (tel: 118-822, 118-124; fax: 124-293).

Prima Eritrea Oil Company, Asmara (tel: 120-050; fax: 120-099).

Red Sea Trading Corporation (import/export services operated by the PFDJ), 29/31 Ras Alula Street, PO Box 332, Asmara (tel: 127-846; fax: 124-353).

US Embassy, PO Box 211, Asmara (tel: 120-004, 120-009; fax: 127-584).

Voice of the Broad Masses of Eritrea (Dimtsi Hafash), Ministry of Information, Radio Division, PO Box 872, Asmara.

Internet sites
Eritrean news: http://www.messelna.com

Africa Business Network: http://www.ifc.org/abn

AllAfrica.com: http://www.allafrica.com

African Development Bank: http://www.afdb.org

Africa Online: http://www.africaonline.com

Mbendi AfroPaedia (information on companies, countries, industries and stock exchanges in Africa): http://mbendi.co.za

Estonia

KEY FACTS

Official name: Eesti Vabariik (The Republic of Estonia)

Head of State: President Toomas Hendrik Ilves (since 9 Oct 2006)

Head of government: Prime Minister Andrus Ansip (RE) (elected 2005; re-elected 4 Feb 2007)

Ruling party: Three-party coalition led by Reformierakond (RE) (Reform Party); Eestimaa Rahvaliit (Rahvaliit) (ER) (Estonian People's Union); Eesti Keskerakond (Keskerakond) (Estonian Centre Party) (since 2005; re-elected 4 Feb 2007)

Area: 45,227 square km

Population: 1.34 million (2007)

Capital: Tallinn

Official language: Estonian

Currency: Kroon (plural krooni) (EEK) = 100 senti

Exchange rate: EEK9.87 per US$ (Jul 2008); (pegged at EEK15.65 per euro)

GDP per capita: US$15,851 (2007)

GDP real growth: 7.10% (2007)

Labour force: 659,000 (2004)

Unemployment: 1.60% (2007)

Inflation: 6.60% (2007)

Balance of trade: -US$1.84 billion (2005)

Foreign debt: US$8.40 billion (2004)

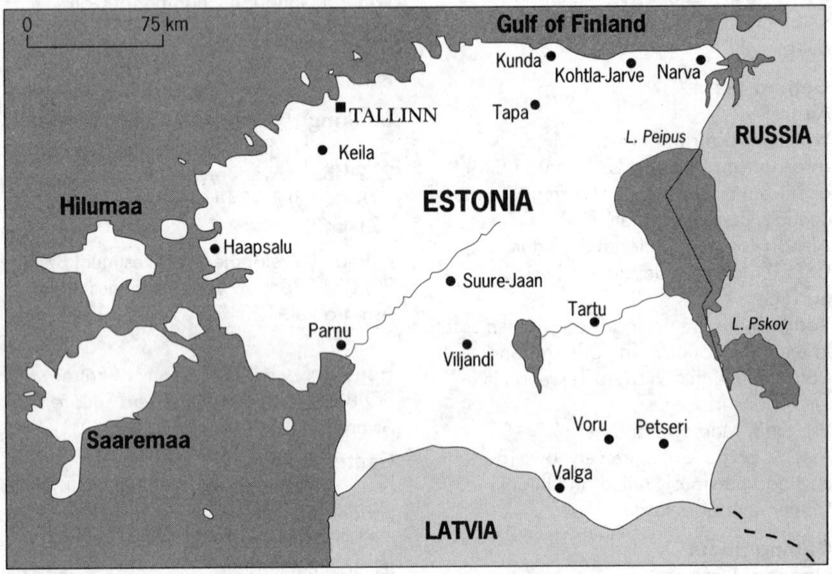

While a new border treaty appeared to signal a thaw in Estonian-Russian relations, this was all to change by the end of June 2007. Then President Rüütel, like his Lithuanian counterpart, Valdas Adamkus, refused an invitation to attend celebrations in Moscow to mark the end of the Second World War in Europe. According to a local newspaper poll, 61 per cent of Estonians supported the refusal. Most Estonians still recall that Stalin's defeat of Hitler also brought with it nearly fifty years of annexation, deportation and Russification. If Russia were in any doubt that Estonians still felt strongly about deprivations suffered during the Soviet era, these were swept away in June. The Estonian parliament ratified the border treaty but only after inserting clauses referring to the Russian occupations of 1940–41 and 1945–91. In a fit of pique, an increasingly bullying Russia responded by stating that the treaty was null and void.

Russian irritation at the loss of its former empire, or sphere of influence has grown as it looses the power and military might it once had – as the Soviet Union. In May 2007 officials in Estonia relocated the Bronze Soldier, a Soviet-era war memorial commemorating an unknown Russian who died fighting the Nazis. The move incited rioting by ethnic Russians and the blockading of the Estonian embassy in Moscow. The event also marked the beginning of a large and sustained distributed denial-of-service attack on several Estonian national web sites, effectively immobilising computer systems, including those of government ministries and the prime minister's Reform Party. The Estonia attacks certainly were overwhelming and crippled many of the Estonian websites. But it was the clearly political nature of the attacks that was novel, in comparison to other 'denial-of-service' attacks.

No extortion was involved. The objective was clear enough: one of menace, a simple political statement. The attacks were eventually traced to Russian sources.

Small countries try harder

A small country of about 1.34 million people, Estonia has few natural resources and is heavily reliant on trade, with telecommunications being one of its main exports. Its GDP has grown at an average of over 8.5 per cent since 2002, making it and the other Baltic countries among the fastest growing economies in Europe during the period. Estonia joined the North Atlantic

Treaty Organisation (NATO) and acceded to the European Union (EU) in the spring of 2004. Estonia's strong economic growth has translated into higher living standards. Life expectancy (at birth) for Estonian citizens is 73 years and the infant mortality rate is 4.4 per thousand live births – indicators substantially better than the averages for the Europe and Central Asia Region.

In its 2008 consultation document on Estonia, the International Monetary Fund (IMF) noted that the Estonian economy was undergoing its first significant slowdown in nearly ten years. This was principally caused, as was the case in neighbouring Baltic countries, by what the IMF described as a 'reversal' of credit conditions as cheap global credit gave way to cautious lending at higher interest rates. Domestic demand slowed and the external current account deficit narrowed sharply. The slowdown was seen as a necessary adjustment – it had been preceded by two years of unsustainable high growth and wide imbalances but had none the less begun to proceed faster than expected. Estimates of first quarter 2008 gross domestic product (GDP) suggested that growth for the year as a whole might turn out to be negative. In mid-2008, the labour market and inflation had still to respond. There had been layoffs in some sectors –notably construction – but overall employment continued to rise in the first quarter of 2008 and wage growth was still close to the peak attained in 2007. A still tight labour market, combined with soaring food and energy prices and increases in excise taxes, had driven inflation above 10 per cent.

The IMF considered that any Estonian recovery of growth would depend in large part on the competitiveness of the economy. Consumption was likely to remain subdued because households were saving to build financial buffers in the light of increased economic uncertainties. A revival of exports or investment would be needed to prime the pump for a recovery. For investment growth to resume, and exporters to be competitive in relatively sluggish global markets, wage growth would have to be consistent with productivity gains – not higher, as had been the case in the two previous years. The uncertain economic outlook and reduced profitability created conditions for wage growth to slow. In the opinion of the IMF, and assuming no further external price shocks, inflation was expected to moderate in 2009. The currency board arrangement will continue to provide the key anchor to prices and price expectations. In addition, the impact of the 2008 increases in administrative prices and excises will recede, while the economic slowdown should dampen demand-related pressures.

In the IMF's view, Estonia's fiscal policy needed to strike a balance between reversing past slippages in the fiscal position and supporting demand during the economic downturn. The strong fiscal outcomes of the previous two years disguised large increases in current expenditure (40 per cent over the past two years) that were covered by exceptionally high revenues related to the economic boom. Further increases in 2007 resulted in an expansionary budget and, with the economy slowing, the fiscal outcome risked heading for negative territory. The Estonian authorities' proposals for 2008 appeared to strike a balance between the two objectives, continuing to adhere to their commitment to prudent fiscal management.

Risk assessment

Politics	Good
Economics	Good
Regional stability	Good

COUNTRY PROFILE

Historical profile

Around 3,000 BC the Finno-Ugric peoples began to migrate from Eastern Europe to the north-east coast of the Baltic Sea.

1219 Valdemar II of Denmark and the German Sword Brethren, a crusading order, conquered Estonia.

1346 The Danes sold their share of Estonian territory to the Livonian Order of Teutonic Knights (an alliance of the Sword Brethren and the German Order of Teutonic Knights).

1524–39 The State of Teutonic Knights, including Estonia, renounced religious allegiance to Rome and converted to Lutheranism.

1561 In the secularisation and partition of the State of Teutonic Knights, Estonia (now northern Estonia) became part of Sweden and Livonia (now Latvia and southern Estonia) and placed under Polish rule.

1721–1917 Estonia became a Baltic province of Russia.

1918–40 Independent republic.

1940–88 Constituent republic of USSR.

1988 Estonia declared its sovereignty.

1989 Economic autonomy was granted.

1990 Independence from the USSR was declared. The break-up of the Soviet Union led to a sharp decline in output.

1991 Independence was reaffirmed.

1992 Following the country's first free elections since independence, a coalition of various right-wing conservative parties, operating under the name Isamaa Pro Patria, was the heart of the government coalition, headed by Mart Laar as prime minister. Lennart Meri became president. A new constitution was adopted based on the 1938 model that provided the legal continuity to the Republic of Estonia prior to the Soviet occupation. Inflation soared to nearly 1,000 per cent as the Soviet energy and food supply system crumbled and hard currency was required for imports. A new currency, the kroon, was introduced and pegged to the Deutsche mark under a currency board system at a ratio of eight to one.

1994 GDP growth was registered for the first time since independence. Estonia

KEY INDICATORS — Estonia

	Unit	2003	2004	2005	2006	2007
Population	m	1.39	1.24	1.35	1.35	1.34
Gross domestic product (GDP)	US$bn	8.42	10.81	13.75	16.61	21.28
GDP per capita	US$	6,060	8,287	10,206	12,353	15,851
GDP real growth	%	5.2	6.2	10.5	11.1	7.1
Inflation	%	1.5	3.0	4.1	4.4	6.6
Unemployment	%	4.6	3.9	3.2	1.8	1.6
Exports (fob) (goods)	US$m	4,181.0	5,970.3	7,783.0	9,635.1	11,087.1
Imports (cif) (goods)	US$m	5,867.0	7,936.3	9,627.8	12,373.6	14,697.8
Balance of trade	US$m	-1,686.0	-1,966.1	-1,844.8	-2,738.5	-3,610.7
Current account	US$m	-1,200.0	-1,540.0	-1,444.9	-2,575.0	-3,684.0
Total reserves minus gold	US$m	1,373.4	1,788.2	1,943.2	2,781.2	3,262.7
Foreign exchange	US$m	1,373.3	1,788.1	1,943.1	2,781.1	3,262.6
Exchange rate	per US$	13.72	11.85	12.10	12.10	10.83

joined the NATO Partnership for Peace programme (PfP). Laar lost a vote of no-confidence and Andres Tarand became caretaker prime minister until elections.
1995 The governing coalition parties lost ground in the parliamentary elections. A centre-left government was formed under Tiit Vähi as prime minister. Estonia applied to join the EU. The government collapsed when the Eesti Keskerakond (EK) (Estonian Centre Party) left.
1996–97 The re-formed coalition collapsed when six ministers resigned and the resulting minority government also collapsed after Vähi's resignation. The ECP leader, Mart Siimann, became prime minister and formed a minority government with the Estonian Rural Union (EM) and independents.
1999 The EK became the largest party in parliament; Mart Laar remained in office as prime minister. Estonia joined the World Trade Organisation (WTO).
2000 The economy recovered from the 1998 Russian crisis and foreign investment picked up.
2001 Arnold Rüütel was elected president by the electoral college.
2003 Juhan Parts formed a coalition government comprising Uhendus Vabariigi Eest-Res Publica (ResP) (Union for the Republic-Res Publica), the Reformierakond (RE) (Reform Party) and Eestimaa Rahvaliit (ER) (Estonian People's Union). Estonians voted to join the EU.
2004 Estonia acceded to NATO and joined the EU.
2005 The government fell in a parliamentary vote of no confidence (54/47), following the mishandling of a controversial anti-corruption plan. Andrus Ansip (RE) was appointed prime minister of a new, three-party coalition government of RE, EK and ER.
2006 Toomas Hendrik Ilves defeated the incumbent president, Arnold Rüütel.
2007 In parliamentary elections, held in February, the ruling coalition won with an increased majority of 66 seats (out of 101). On 20 December Estonia became a member of the European Union Schengen area whereby all travellers may cross borders without a passport or visa.
2008 An agreement for visa-free visits of citizens to the US was signed on 12 March.

Political structure

Constitution

The constitution was adopted on 28 June 1992. It is based on the 1938 model, that provides legal continuity to the Republic of Estonia prior to Soviet occupation.
The constitution defines the areas of responsibility of the government as: to implement domestic and foreign policies; to direct and co-ordinate the work of government institutions; to organise and implement legislation, the resolutions of the Riigikogu (parliament) and edicts of the president; to submit draft laws and foreign treaties to the parliament; to prepare drafts of the state budget and to implement and report on the budget and to organise relations with foreign states.
Only Estonian citizens are allowed to vote, leaving the 38 per cent non-Estonian population largely disenfranchised. The constitution can only be amended by referendum and two successful passages through the Riigikogu.
Estonia is divided into 15 counties and six towns (the other 27 towns form part of the counties). The counties are divided into 193 parishes.
There is universal suffrage – for Estonian citizens only – from age 18.

Form of state

Democratic republic

The executive

Executive power is vested in the president who is directly elected for a five-year term by an electoral college consisting of 101 parliamentary deputies and 266 local government representatives. The winning candidate has to secure a majority within two rounds of voting otherwise the election returns to parliament.
The president nominates the prime minister who then forms a government. In case of the failure of the president's candidate(s) to form a government (the constitution permits the president two nominations), the parliament will name a prime minister to form a government. The prime minister alone nominates the ministers of his cabinet, who are formally appointed by the president and swear an oath before the parliament. Members of the government need not have any political party affiliation nor be members of the parliament.

National legislature

The Riigikogu (parliament) is a unicameral legislature, composed of 101 representatives elected by proportional representation for a four-year term. Its prime constitutional function is legislation, but it also has constitutional duties to review the activities of the executive and directly represent voters.

Legal system

Estonia's legal system is similar to that of continental Europe. The Civil Code underwent large-scale reforms in 2002, the most notable being the implementation of the Law of Obligations Act, which overhauled old contract laws that dated back to the Soviet era.
The Supreme Court has seventeen justices, of which the chief justice is appointed by the parliament after nomination by the president; the rest are appointed by the parliament after nomination by the chief justice. Justices are appointed for life. The Supreme Court can hear appeals, either in full session, or by means of a special ad hoc panel.
There are town and county courts where cases are heard by a judge and assistant judges, elected by popular vote.

Last elections

4 March 2007 (parliamentary); 23 September 2006 (presidential).
Results: Parliamentary: the RE won 27.8 per cent of the vote (31 seats out of 101), Keskerakond 26.1 per cent (29), the IRL 17.9 per cent (19), Sotsiaaldemokraatlik Erakond (SDE) (Social Democratic Party) 10.6 per cent (10), Erakond Eestimaa Rohelised (Estonian Green Party) 7.1 per cent (6), ER 7.1 per cent (6); turnout was 61 per cent.
Presidential: Toomas Hendrik Ilves won 174 votes in the 354-member electoral college; President Arnold Rüütel won 162 votes.

Next elections

2007 (parliamentary); 2011 (presidential).

Political parties

Ruling party

Three-party coalition led by Reformierakond (RE) (Reform Party); Eestimaa Rahvaliit (Rahvaliit) (ER) (Estonian People's Union); Eesti Keskerakond (Keskerakond) (Estonian Centre Party) (since 2005; re-elected 4 Feb 2007)

Main opposition party

Isamaa ja Res Publica Liit (IRL) (Union of Pro Patria and Res Publica)

Population

1.34 million (2007)
Last census: March 2000: 1,370,052
Population density: 33.2 inhabitants per square km. Urban population: 69 per cent (1995–2001).
Annual growth rate: -1.0 per cent 1994–2004 (WHO 2006)

Ethnic make-up

Estonians make up the majority of the population (62 per cent), followed by Russians (30 per cent), Ukrainians (3 per cent) and Belarussians (2 per cent). Russians are in the majority in many towns.

Religions

The main religious denominations are Lutheran, Russian Orthodox and Baptist, with Lutherans in the majority.

Education

Schools may be private, municipal or state run. The backbone of the education system is general comprehensive schooling, which caters for children of all ages and abilities. Pre-school attendance is high but is not a prerequisite for primary schooling. This is part of basic school education, lasting for nine years, starting from the age of seven.

On completion of basic education (aged around 16 – a student may choose to extend or abbreviate their study), a student may continue in an upper secondary or vocational school. The majority of schools offer a general curriculum. Some specialise in a branch of the humanities or sciences.

The oldest university is Tartu University, founded in 1632. Since 1999, some selected post-secondary vocational schools have been given the right to offer vocational higher education. There are six public universities, nine private universities and seven state vocational education institutions. The usual duration of studies is three to four years.

Literacy rate: 100 per cent adult rate; 100 per cent youth rate (15–24) (Unesco 2005).

Compulsory years: 7 to 17

Enrolment rate: 95 per cent boys, 93 per cent girls, total primary school enrolment of the relevant age group (including repetition rates) (World Bank).

Pupils per teacher: 17 in primary schools.

Health

Per capita total expenditure on health (2003) was US$682; of which per capita government spending was US$526, at the international dollar rate, (WHO 2006).

Private healthcare provision is negligible. Overall indices show an improvement in health in the general population. Life expectancy has increased by a half a year since 2000 and there has been 10–15 per cent more births registered in the first three months of 2004, stimulated perhaps by a large increase in maternity and paternity allowances, agreed in 2003. Infant mortality has seen a marked improvement down from 12 death per 1,000 live births to eight per 1,000 in 2003.

HIV/Aids

HIV prevalence: 1.1 per cent aged 15–49 in 2003 (World Bank)

Life expectancy: 72 years, 2004 (WHO 2006)

Fertility rate/Maternal mortality rate: 1.4 births per woman, 2004 (WHO 2006); maternal mortality 50 per 100,000 live births (World Bank).

Child (under 5 years) mortality rate (per 1,000): 8 per 1,000 live births (World Bank)

Welfare

The guiding principle behind the government's social welfare development policy is the complete dismantling of the state-centred Soviet system. Government priorities include the establishment of an adequate social security system, funded by contributions from employers and employees.

Estonia is moving away from the pay-as-you-go pension system to a three-tier partially state-funded pension scheme. The first tier is financed by a 33 per cent social tax, 20 per cent of which is kept for pensions. The fully funded second pillar came into effect in 2002. The scheme offers additional pension coverage and it is suggested it be mandatory only for people currently under the age of 18. The third tier consists of voluntary contributions administered by private pension funds and insurance companies.

In 2002, the retirement age was 63 years for men and 58 years for women, which is likely to increase gradually to 63 years by 2016.

Main cities

Tallinn (capital, estimated population 392,555 in 2005), Tartu (100,672), Narva (67,288), Kohtla-Järve (41,311), Pärnu (43,758).

Languages spoken

Estonian belongs to the Baltic-Finnic group of the Finno-Ugric languages, which also includes Hungarian and Finnish. The Latin alphabet is used. Various other languages spoken include Latvian, Lithuanian, Ukrainian, Belarusian, Russian, Finnish, Yiddish and German. English has replaced Russian as the primary business language.

By law, all transactions, contracts and company returns have to be in Estonian. Notarised transactions in English often accompany these.

Official language/s

Estonian

Media

Other news agencies: BNS (Baltic News Service): www.bns.ee

Delfi (in Estonian): www.delfi.ee

Press

Dailies: There are 11 daily newspapers, of which six are distributed nationally. In Estonian the highest circulating newspapers are Postimees (www.postimees.ee), Eesti Päevaleht (www.epl.ee), Maaleht (www.maaleht.ee), SL Õhtuleht (www.sloleht.ee) is an evening tabloid. In Russian, Vesti Dnya (www.vesti.ee) Sillamyaesky Vestnik (www.vestnik.ee) and Narva (www.narvaleht.ee).

Weeklies: In Estonian Kesknädal (www.kesknadal.ee), for general interest, Eesti Loodus (www.eestinaine.ee) for cultural items, Kroonika (www.kroonika.ee) is a tabloid and Sirp (www.sirp.ee) another popular publication. In English, the Baltic Independent and Baltic Times (www.baltictimes.com).

Business: In Estonian, Aripäev (www.ap3.ee) is published daily, with online English and Russia editions.

Broadcasting

Eesti Rahvusringhääling (ERR) (Estonian Public Broadcasting) (www.err.ee) replaced Eesti Televisioon (Estonian Television) and incorporated Eesti Raadio (Radio Estonia), as the combined national, public broadcasting service, in June 2007.

Radio: Eesti Raadio (Radio Estonia) (www.er.ee) operates five stations catering for all domestic demographics and foreign listeners. The private, national, commercial radio network, U-Pop (www.u-pop.ee) has five stations including Radio Elmar (Estonia music), Radio Uuno and Radio Kuku. There are many local commercial radio stations broadcasting throughout Estonia.

Television: ERR has one TV channel. There are several private TV stations, some of which are foreign and broadcast through cable or satellite channels. Domestic TV includes Kanal 2 (www.kanal2.ee) and TV3 (www.tv3.ee), showing foreign imports, Seitse (www.seitse.tv) and Alo TV, based in Tartu.

Advertising

Adspend is typically over US$70 million, the majority of which is spend in newspapers (around 45 per cent) television (30 per cent) and magazines (10 per cent). Tobacco advertising is banned as well as any that promotes the consumption of alcohol. It is forbidden to use newscasters or political commentators in advertising.

Economy

Estonia has restructured and stabilised its economy in a remarkably short period of time, achieving substantial progress in creating a market economy. It has one of the most liberal trading environments in Central and Eastern Europe (CEE). The World Bank ranked Estonia in its Doing Business Economy Ranking 16 for ease of doing business, and 43 for starting a business, out of 155, in 2005. In 2005 Estonia registered GDP growth of 9.8 per cent. These figures came on top of an already impressive 6.2 per cent in 2004. Robust domestic demand has been the main driving force of the economy, sucking in imports and causing the current account deficit to balloon. In 2005, IMF officials warned that this deficit could increase Estonia's external vulnerabilities. The painful macroeconomic reforms of the post-Soviet years have led to large productivity gains and suggest that the economy is capable of sustaining high levels of economic growth for a number of years. Inflation has increased since 2003, from 1.5 per cent to 4.6 per cent by 2006. The unemployment rate has continued to fall, down to 5.9 per cent in 2006. The overall signs are of the beginnings of an economy overheating as output is close to capacity and labour shortages are appearing in the construction industry.

Given the small size of the economy, the Estonian authorities regard early membership of the euro-zone as a priority, and as a means of protecting the economy – and the country in general – from global economic turbulence. Estonia joined the EU Exchange Rate Mechanism (ERM) – a centralised exchange rate that sets a margin within which a currency must remain – in June 2004 and unilaterally maintains its currency pegged to the euro.

The government has set its sights on the huge EU market and membership of the European Monetary Union (EMU) to sustain Estonia's growth, exports of goods and services and the inflow of foreign and EU investment. The IMF has called for fiscal restraint and careful supervision of credit, while maintaining competitiveness, a call that seems to echo the government's strategy.

External trade

As a member of the European Union, Estonia operates within a communitywide free trade union, with tariffs sets as a whole. Internationally, the EU has free trade agreements with a number of nations and trading blocs worldwide.

Imports

Principal imports are machinery and equipment (33.5 per cent), chemical products, textiles, foodstuffs and vehicle equipment.

Main sources: Russia (13.5 per cent total, 2006), Germany (13.2 per cent), Finland (12.7 per cent).

Exports

Main exports include electrical and electronic equipment (33 per cent), wood, charcoal and paper, textiles, food products, furniture, metals, chemical products and vehicles.

Main destinations: Finland (18.2 per cent total, 2006), Sweden (12.3 per cent), Latvia (8.8 per cent).

Agriculture

Farming

The agricultural sector experienced a severe decline following independence until 2004 when it jumped by 2.5 per cent, from -1.5 per cent in 2003. The agriculture sector accounts for around 4.4 per cent of GDP – a fall from 9.9 per cent in 1994 – and employs 29 per cent of the workforce.

The agricultural reform programme has produced mixed results. Most large state-run farms have been dismantled but some co-operatives and state-owned farms persist.

Government agricultural policy is designed to provide affordable food for Estonians while balancing farm income and guaranteeing farm workers equivalent earnings to industrial workers.

Estonia is eligible for EU subsidies and rural development funds through the Common Agricultural Policy (CAP). However, like the other new EU member countries, it will only get the full amount by 2013. The EU decided to introduce CAP support funds gradually over a 10-year period. During its transitional entry stage Estonia has decided to implement the reform of the CAP on 1 January 2009. The reform was introduced throughout most of the EU on 1 January 2005, when subsidies on farm output, which tended to benefit large farms and encourage overproduction, were replaced by single farm payments, not conditional on production. The change is expected to reward farms that provide and maintain a healthy environment, food safety and animal welfare standards. The changes are also intended to encourage market conscious production and cut the cost of CAP to the EU taxpayer.

Crop production in 2005 included: 758,200 tonnes (t) cereals in total, 267,900t wheat, 224,800t potatoes, 366,100t barley, 73,000t oats, 3,600t pulses, 4,000t tomatoes, 29,105t oilcrops, 2,200t apples, 8,100t fruit in total, 53,300t vegetables in total. Livestock production included: 65,640t meat in total, *14,000t beef, 37,700t pig meat, *300t lamb, 13,600t poultry, 12,251t eggs, 670,400t milk, *600t honey, 1,653t cattle hides.

* estimate

Fishing

Some 130,000 tonnes of fish are caught per annum. The total catch has fallen dramatically as disputes with Latvia over territorial waters and falling investment have contributed to lower catches. Estonia has been a net fish importer since independence, although the value of exports has increased.

In 2004, the total marine fish catch was 70,337 tonnes and the total crustacean catch was 13,586 tonnes.

Forestry

Forest makes up 40 per cent of available land in Estonia. As with all sectors the forestry industry suffers from outdated machinery, equipment and a lack of finance and investment, yet despite this, total timber production has increased.

The government has established special credits for the forestry industry to develop technology. Traditionally most Estonian timber exports were of logs and for paper. A further increase in the overall value of timber exports is anticipated as paper related exports decline and the export of finished timber products increases.

The timber-processing industry has developed quickly, and the export potential for Estonian timber products is good, principally in Scandinavia, but also in Russia and Ukraine.

Estonia's only pulp mill at Kehra is owned by Horizon Pulp and Paper, part of the Singapore-based Tolaram group. In 2006, Estonian Cell, which is owned by Norway's Larvik Cell, will begin constructing a pulp mill at Kunda in northern Estonia. The mill, which will cost around US$184 million, will be partly financed by the European Bank for Reconstruction and Development (EBRD).

Timber imports in 2004 were US$304.5 million, while exports amounted to US$549.3 million.

Timber production in 2004 included 10,300,000 cubic metres (cum) roundwood, 8,100,000cum industrial roundwood, 2,000,000cum sawnwood, 2,800,000cum pulpwood, 4,200,000cum sawlogs & veneer logs, 387,825cum wood-based panels, 2,200,000cum wood fuel, 3,381t charcoal.

Industry and manufacturing

Industry contributed 29.3 per cent to GDP, of which 18.2 per cent was supplied by the manufacturing sector in 2004; both registered a 5 per cent growth rate.

During the Soviet era, the Estonian industrial sector was characterised by a high degree of concentration (20 per cent of enterprises produced two-thirds of industrial output), dependence on imports from the Soviet Union (80 per cent of all imports) and a reliance on the markets of the Soviet Union (90 per cent of exports).

Since independence in 1990 industry has undergone much restructuring, with long-term investment following privatisation. Traditional industries such a furniture making are still thriving accounting for 9 per cent of exports in 2004, to modern advanced biomedical research and production with an emphasis on gene research and technologies. Electronics factories provide high-tech components for international corporations such as Nokia and Philips.

Estonia's relatively cheap labour, energy and raw materials are the main reasons for the country's industrial competitiveness, coupled with tax incentives for businesses and a well-educated and motivated workforce.

Tourism

Tourism is an important sector of the economy that is expected to contribute US$574 million or 4.9 per cent of GDP. In line with the lack of direct foreign investment, travel and tourism is expected to attract US$706 million, however this represents 21.3 per cent of total capital

investment. The sector should generate US$1.5 billion in total exports and employ 17.7 per cent of the workforce.
Travel links, especially by air, and infrastructure continue to improve. The visitor attractions are mainly heritage-related, with Tallinn being the main destination, but other sectors, including rural and adventure tourism, are being developed. Visitor numbers in 2004 were 1.7 million; Finland continues to be the principal market, accounting for over 50 per cent of visitors.

Mining
Estonia has a limited range of mineral resources, principally for use in the construction industry. Mining and quarrying activities contribute less than 1 per cent of GDP.

Hydrocarbons
Estonia has no proven crude oil reserves, however there is a substantial amount of oil shale in the north-east. Estonian oil shale is produced by the state owned company Eesti Polevkivi (Estonian Oil Shale). Some 75 per cent of the country's energy needs are provided from oil shale. However due to the heavily polluting nature of oil shale the industry is under pressure from the EU to slow down and meet regulations. No new mines are scheduled to be built and it is predicted that in the next few years production targets will be lowered. Estonia remains important for the oil industry as Russian exports travel through the Estonian ports to be exported into the EU.
Estonia imports around 90 per cent of its oil needs. All Estonia's natural gas consumption is imported primarily through a 250-mile pipeline from Russia. The country produces no coal and relies entirely on imports, however coal consumption is expected to taper off as EU environmental regulations take effect.

Energy
Up to 75 per cent of Estonia's energy supply is derived from oil shale, but this is due to change by 2006 when the adoption of EU environmental regulations should have taken effect. The Narva Power Plants, which transform oil shale, supply some 90 per cent of the country's electricity. Natural gas, petroleum and by-products are all imported, mainly from Russia.

Financial markets
Stock exchange
The Tallinn Stock Exchange (TSE) is run by OMX Exchanges, a company that owns and operates the largest integrated and regulated Nordic and Baltic securities market in Northern Europe.

Banking and insurance
The commercial banking sector is licensed by the central bank. Foreign-owned banks are permitted to operate and bank shares are freely traded.
Central bank
Eesti Pank (Bank of Estonia)
Main financial centre
Tallinn

Time
GMT plus two hours (daylight saving, late March to late October, GMT plus three hours)

Geography
Estonia is situated in north-east Europe, the northernmost of the three Baltic States, bordering the Russian Federation to the east and Latvia to the south. Its northern coastline is on the Gulf of Finland and its western coastline in the Gulf of Riga and the Baltic Sea. From north to south the country measures 240km, from east to west 360km. With a total land area of 45,227 square km, Estonia is the smallest of the Baltic states and about the same size as Denmark.
The terrain is flat and heavily wooded; there are numerous lakes, rivers and bogs. Offshore, there are around 1,500 islands.
Hemisphere
Northern

Climate
The mildest areas are along the Baltic coast. Summer is short, with sunshine lasting up to nine hours a day, and an average temperature of 15 degrees Celsius (C). Winters are cold, with slush, ice and repeated light coverings of snow (average minus 4 degrees C). Spring and autumn are very short.

Dress codes
Warm clothes are required during winter, with a raincoat and umbrella necessary during the summer. Business dress is conservative but relatively informal, with a jacket and tie expected for meetings.

Entry requirements
Passports
Required by all, except nationals of EU/EEA countries and Switzerland
Visa
Required by all, except nationals of EU and Schengen area signatory countries, North America, Australasia and Japan. For further exceptions contact the nearest embassy or see full list can be found at www.vm.ee. A Schengen visa application (offered in several languages) can be downloaded from http://europa.eu/abc/travel/ see 'documents you will need'.

Currency advice/regulations
There are no restrictions on the import and export of local or foreign currency.
Customs
Personal items are duty-free. There are no duties levied on alcohol and tobacco between EU member states, providing amounts imported are for personal consumption.

Health (for visitors)
Nationals of the European Economic Area (EEA) countries and Switzerland can access reduced cost and sometimes free medical treatment using a European Health Insurance Card (EHIC) while visiting the EEA. Exceptions include nationals of the 10 countries which joined the EU in 2004 whose EHIC is not valid in Switzerland. Applications for the EHIC should be made before travelling.
Mandatory precautions
No specific requirements.
Advisable precautions
Vaccinations may be advised for hepatitis A and diphtheria.
Take mosquito lotion if travelling outside the towns. There is a risk of rabies.

Hotels
There are numerous good quality western style hotels in Tallinn. It is advisable to book a hotel before travelling.
For the peak period of June and July, the Estonian Tourist Board suggests the traveller books in January.
Bills must be paid in Estonian kroons if credit cards are not accepted.

Credit cards
Most major hotels and restaurants and a few shops accept American Express, Visa, Eurocard and Diners' Club.

Public holidays (national)
Fixed dates
1 Jan (New Year's Day), 24 Feb (Independence Day), 1 May (Spring Day), 23 Jun (Victory Day), 25 Jun (St John's Day, Midsummer), 20 Aug (Restoration of Independence Day), 24 Dec (Christmas Eve), 25 Dec (Christmas Day), 26 Dec (St Stephen's Day).
Variable dates
Good Friday.

Working hours
Banking
Mon–Fri: 0900–1600.
Business
Mon–Fri: 0830–1830. Lunch around 1300. Some offices stop work at 1630.
Government
Mon–Fri: 0900–1700.
Shops
Mon–Fri: 0930–1900, Sat: 0930–1600.

Telecommunications
Mobile/cell phones
Estonia has three mobile service providers, operating on a GSM system.

Social customs/useful tips
Estonians can be quite reserved and are not particularly talkative. Shaking hands is the normal form of greeting. Flowers are generally acceptable as a gift.
There is a service charge of 10 to 15 per cent, but a small tip in addition is appreciated.
Saunas are popular in Estonia, usually followed by a substantial meal washed down with liberal quantities of beer and vodka.
Until you are sure of the ethnic background of your host avoid talking about Russians and the communist past. Many Estonians have relatives who were sent to Siberia, which has left strong feelings when it comes to Russia. Also avoid asking what your host did during the Soviet occupation – it may sound as if you are asking if they were a member of the Communist Party or even if they were sent to Siberia.
There is a strong sense of national pride and identity among Estonians and they do not appreciate being lumped together with Latvia and Lithuania as 'the Baltic states', or even being described as part of eastern Europe.

Security
Estonia is a safe place to visit compared to some of the other former Soviet republics, although muggings do occur in urban areas, especially at night. Car theft is also a problem.

Getting there
Air
National airline: Estonian Air
International airport/s: Tallinn (TLL) airport, 5km north-west of city. Includes a business centre, bank, post office, restaurant, bar, shops and car rental. Conference facilities also available. Bus no 2 runs between the city and the airport, taking 15 minutes. A shuttle bus to the main hotels and the city centre meets all flights.
Airport tax: There is no airport tax.
Surface
Road: Foreign cars are flagged down at borders to examine the documents in an attempt to block the flow of stolen foreign cars. Check insurance before travelling and do not buy cheap insurance at the frontier. There are direct routes along the Baltic coast connecting Latvia and Lithuania and also the Russian Federation.
Rail: International lines run from surrounding countries, although rail travel between Estonia, Latvia and Lithuania is time-consuming.
Water: Ferry services run between Stockholm and Tallinn, Helsinki and Tallinn and Rostock (Germany) and Tallinn via Helsinki.
Main port/s: Muuga is Tallinn's port and is the most modern in the country.

Getting about
National transport
Air: There is limited domestic air travel with Baltic Aeroservis, which serves the islands of Kuressaare and Kärdla. Charter flights to other destinations can also be booked.
Road: Estonia has a high density of roads although there are few major highways. Signs are not illuminated and fairly small, so driving at night is best avoided. In winter roads can be icy and ungritted.
The high level of car crime in the Baltic States means that border crossings can be very lengthy processes and insurance can be difficult to find.
Buses: Estonia has a very extensive bus network linking every area of the country. Tickets should be booked in advance.
Rail: The majority of major cities are covered. Tallinn and Tartu are connected by an express service.
City transport
Taxis: Taxis in Tallinn are relatively cheap. There is a good taxi service from Tallinn International Airport to the city centre, with a journey time of 10 minutes.
Private services should display the name of the company and its number on the roof. Fares should be agreed upon beforehand. There are also minibuses called Marshrut-taxis, which operate on set routes, stopping at fixed destinations and seating up to 10 people.
Buses, trams & metro: All parts of the city can also be reached by bus, trolley-bus and tram. Tickets can be bought from stalls in the main shopping areas.
Car hire
Car hire can be arranged at the airport. Never drink and drive – no level of alcohol is permitted. Speed limit is 50km per hour in built-up areas, 90km per hour in the country and 110km per hour on motorways. In towns there are parking permits, fines and wheel clamps. Driving is on the right. EU nationals should be in possession of a national driving licence. The international car hire firms Avis, Hertz and Europcar all have bureaux in Estonia. Roads, although deteriorating, are of a reasonably good standard but can be dangerous in winter due to ice.

BUSINESS DIRECTORY
The addresses listed below are a selection only. While World of Information makes every endeavour to check these addresses, we cannot guarantee that changes have not been made, especially to telephone numbers and area codes. We would welcome any corrections.

Telephone area codes
The international direct dialling code (IDD) for Estonia is +372, followed by area code and subscriber's number:

Haapsalu	47	Rapla	48
Jögeva	77	Tallinn	none
Narva	35	Valga	76
Pärnu	44	Viljandi	43
Polva	79	Voru	78

Useful telephone numbers
Fire brigade: 01
Police: 02
Ambulance: 03
Gas: 04
NB Numbers 01–04 cannot be dialled from mobile telephones; 112 should be dialled instead.

Chambers of Commerce
American Chamber of Commerce Estonia, Tallinn Business Centre, 6 Harju, 10130 Tallinn (tel: 631-0522; fax: 631-0521; e-mail: acce@acce.ee).

British-Estonian Chamber of Commerce, 21 Suur-Karja, 10148 Tallinn (tel: 640-5872; fax: 640-5873; e-mail: info@becc.ec).

Estonian Chamber of Commerce and Industry, 17 Toom-Kooli, 10130 Tallinn (tel: 646-0244; fax: 646-0245; e-mail: koda@koda.ee).

Banking
Eesti Forekspank (Estonian Forexbank), Narva mnt 9a, Tallinn (tel: 630-2100; fax: 630-2200; e-mail: bank@forex.ee); international settlements (tel: 640-6400).

Eesti Hoiupank (Estonian Savings Bank), Kinga 1, Tallinn (tel: 630-2600; fax: 630-2602; e-mail: mailbob@esb.ee).

Eesti Investeerimispank (Estonian Investment Bank), PO Box 26, Narva mnt 7, Tallinn (tel: 620-0800; fax: 620-0812/0801; e-mail: info@estib.ee); international settlements (tel: 620-0828).

Eesti Krediidipank (Estonian Credit Bank), Narva mnt 4, Tallinn (tel: 640-5000; fax: 631-3533; e-mail: krediidipank@ekp.ee).

Eesti Maapank (Land Bank of Estonia), Tallinna 12, Rakvere (tel: 43-821; fax: 43-617); in Tallinn (tel: 646-6295; fax: 646-6649/6313-720); international settlements (tel: 640-8321).

Eesti Pangaliit (Estonian Association of Banks), Pärnu mnt 19, Tallinn (tel: 245-5400; fax: 245-5401; e-mail: panagaliit@teleport.ee).

Eesti Uhispank (Union Bank of Estonia), Tartu mnt 13, Tallinn (tel: 610-4300, 631-2728; fax: 610-4302); international settlements (tel: 640-3516, 640-3519).

Hansapank, Liivalaia 8, EE0001 Tallinn (tel: 631-0311/310; fax: 631-0410; e-mail: webmaster@hansa.ee).

Merita Bank Ltd (foreign bank's branch), Harju 6, Tallinn (tel: 631-4040; fax: 631-4153; e-mail: merita@estpak.ee).

Tallinna Aripanga Aktsiaselts (Tallinn Business Bank), Estonia pst 3/5, Tallinn (tel: 245-5349; fax: 242-3322; e-mail: tbb@torn.ee).

Tallinna Pank, Parnu mnt 10, Tallinn (tel: 631-0100/0102, 640-5880; fax: 631-0111; e-mail: info@tp.ee); international settlements (tel: 640-5829).

Central bank

Eesti Pank (Bank of Estonia), Estonia Boulevard 13, Tallinn 15095 (tel: 668-0719; fax: 668-0836; e-mail: info@epbe.ee).

Travel information

Estonian Air, Vabaduse, Valjak 10, Tallinn (tel: 244-6383, 244-0295; fax: 631-2740).

Estonian Association of Travel Agents, Pikk 71, Tallinn (tel: 260-1705; fax: 242-5594).

Estonian Railways, 36 Pikk Str, Tallinn (tel: 240-1610; fax: 240-1710).

National tourist organisation offices

Estonian Tourist Board, Liivalaia 13/15, Tallinn (tel: 627-9770; fax: 627-9777; e-mail: tourism@eas.ee).

Ministries

Ministry of Agriculture, Lai 39/41, Tallinn (tel: 244-1166; fax: 244-0601).

Ministry of Citizenship and Immigration, Ministry of the Interior, Pikk 61, Tallinn (tel: 244-5080; fax: 260-2785).

Ministry of Culture and Education, Suur Karja 23, Tallinn (tel: 244-5077; fax: 244-0963).

Ministry of Defence, Pikk 57, Tallinn (tel: 239-9160/50; fax: 239-9165).

Ministry of Economic Affairs, Harju 11, Tallinn (tel: 244-0577; fax: 244-6860).

Ministry of Energy, Ministry of Economy, Kiriku 6, Tallinn (tel: 244-3941; fax: 244-8091).

Ministry of Environment, Toompuiestee 24, Tallinn (tel: 245-2507; fax: 245-3310).

Ministry of Finance, Suur Ameerika 1, Tallinn (tel: 268-3445; fax: 268-2097).

Ministry of Finance (Foreign Affairs Dept), Kohtu 8, Tallinn (fax: 245-2992).

Ministry of Foreign Affairs, Ravala 9, Tallinn (tel: 231-7091; fax: 277-1677, 231-7099; internet site: http://www.vm.ee).

Ministry of Industry and Energy, Gonsiori Str 29, Tallinn (tel: 242-3550; fax: 242-1133); Foreign Relations Dept (fax: 242-5468).

Ministry of the Interior, Pikk 61, Tallinn (tel: 266-3611; fax: 260-2785, 244-1112).

Ministry of Justice, Suur Karja 19, Tallinn (tel: 244-5120; fax: 224-6235).

Ministry of Reform, State Chancellery, Lossi Plats 1a, Tallinn (tel: 231-6730; fax: 244-0372).

Ministry of Social Affairs, Gonsiori 29, Tallinn (tel: 242-3434; fax: 242-1862).

Ministry of Trade and Commerce, Kiriku Tn 6, Tallinn (tel: 244-3941, 244-5921); Foreign Relations Dept (fax: 244-8091).

Ministry of Transport and Communication, Viru 9, Tallinn (tel: 239-7613; fax: 239-7606); Foreign Relations Department (fax: 244-9206).

Prime Minister's Office, Losi Plats 1a, Tallinn (tel: 231-6701; fax: 244-0372).

Other useful addresses

A/S Seesam Insurance, Kreutzwali 2/Narva mnt 24, Tallinn (tel: 243-3518; fax: 242-4886).

Association of Construction Materials Producers of Estonia, Jaama 1A, Tallinn (tel: 251-2230; fax: 650-6178).

Baltic Insurance Co, Olevimagi 12, Tallinn (tel: 260-1384; fax: 260-1790).

Baltic Trade Company (commercial service organising exhibitions, seminars, joint ventures), Ravala Str 27, Tallinn (tel: 245-5089; fax: 244-5768).

Baltlink, Tartu mnt 13, Tallinn (tel: 242-1003; fax: 245-0893).

Confederation of Estonian Industry, Gonsiori 29, Tallinn (tel: 242-2235; fax: 242-4962).

Department for Foreign Economic Relations, Suur Ameerika 1, Tallinn (tel: 268-3559; fax: 268-3622).

Department of Statistics, Endla 15, Tallinn (tel: 245-3889; fax: 245-3923; internet site: http://stat.vil.ee/K.E.S-ENGL.htm).

Estonian Association of Construction Entrepreneurs, Ravala 8, Tallinn (tel/fax: 243-3213).

Estonian Business Advisory Services, Tallinn BAS Centre, Lai 0, Tallinn (tel: 260-9795; fax: 631-3523).

Estonian Embassy (USA), 1730 M Street, NW, Washington DC 20036 (tel: 202-588-0101; fax: 202-588-0108; e-mail: info@estemb.org).

Estonian Export Council, Kiriku 2/4, Tallinn (tel: 244-4703; fax: 244-3615).

Estonian Foreign Trade Association, Uus 32/34, Tallinn (tel: 260-1462; fax: 260-2184).

Estonian Institute for Market Research, Vaike-Karja 1, Tallinn (tel: 244-8605; fax: 244-1378, 277-1675).

Estonian Institute (information service), PO Box 3469, Tonismagi 8, Tallinn (tel: 244-0513; fax: 268-2057; e-mail: einst@einst.ee; internet site: http://www.einst.ee).

Estonian Investment Agency (EIA), Ravala Str 6 (room 602B), Tallinn (tel: 641-0166; fax: 641-0312).

Estonian Maritime Industry, Sadama 17, Tallinn (tel: 260-1723; fax: 244-4808).

Estonian State Energy Department, 29 Gonsiori Str, Tallinn (tel: 242-1579; fax: 242-5468, 242-1908); external department (tel: 242-1480).

Estonian Trade Council, Kiriku Str 2/4, Tallinn (tel: 244-4703; fax: 244-4615).

Loksa Shipyard, Tallinn (tel: 257-5241; fax: 263-91230).

Municipality of Tallinn, Vabaduse Valjak 7, Tallinn (tel: 266-6146; fax: 244-1230).

National Customs Board, Ravala pst 9, Tallinn (tel: 231-7722; fax: 231-7727).

Port of Tallinn Authority, Sadama 25, Tallinn (tel: 242-7009; fax: 242-2950).

Radio Estonia – Foreign Service, Gonsiori 21, Tallinn (tel: 243-4282; fax: 243-4139).

Reklaam/Television Ltd, Tonismagi 2, Tallinn (tel: 243-4606; fax: 231-1077).

Ookean State Stock Corporation (Estonian Fishing Company), Paljassaare Str 28, Tallinn (tel: 247-1421, 249-7212; fax: 249-8190).

State Department of Foreign Trade, Komsomoli 1, Tallinn (tel: 268-3559; fax: 268-3097).

State Chancellery, Lossi Plats 1a, Tallinn (tel: 231-6730; fax: 244-0372).

Tallink, PO Box 3495, Tallinn (tel: 244-0770; fax: 244-5224).

Tallinn New Port, Maardu tee 57, Tallinn (tel: 223-6500, 223-4313; fax: 223-8805).

Tallinn Stock Exchange, Tallinn (tel: 244-1920; fax: 244-9382).

Other news agencies: BNS (Baltic News Service): www.bns.ee
Delfi (in Estonian): www.delfi.ee

Internet sites

Estonia Business:
http://www.ee/www/Business/welcome.html

Estonia Country Guide:
http://www.ciesin.ee/estcg/

Estonia Investment:
http://www.investinestonia.co

Ethiopia

KEY FACTS

Official name: Ityopia (Federal Democratic Republic of Ethiopia)

Head of State: President Girma Wolde Giorgise (elected by parliament 2001; re-elected 9 Oct 2007)

Head of government: Prime Minister Meles Zenawi (EPRDF) (since 1995; re-elected 9 May 2005)

Ruling party: Ethiopian People's Revolutionary Democratic Front (EPRDF), an alliance led by the Tigray People's Liberation Front (TPLF)

Area: 1,251,282 square km

Population: 77.17 million (2007)*

Capital: Addis Ababa

Official language: Amharic

Currency: Birr (Birr) = 100 cents

Exchange rate: Birr9.67 per US$ (Jul 2008)

GDP per capita: US$252 (2007)*

GDP real growth: 11.40% (2007)

Labour force: 30.68 million (2004)

Inflation: 17.00% (2007)

Balance of trade: -US$3.59 billion (2006)

Foreign debt: US$6.57 billion (2004)

* estimated figure

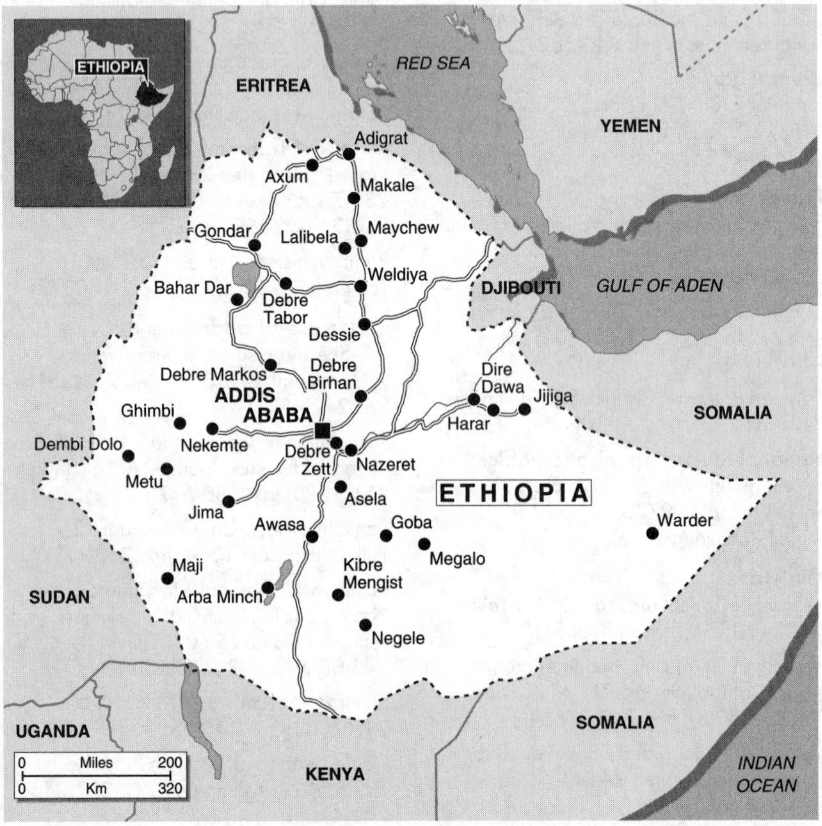

Once again, in 2008, Ethiopia was struggling to feed its people. The rains that had been on time for the last four years, came too late. By September 2008 the United Nations estimated that there were 4.6 million people needing emergency food aid, and a further 5.7 million in drought-affected areas in need of other handouts. This time the food shortages have generated debate about whether the government's support for small scale farming rather than larger commercial farms is right. Bigger farms would create opportunities for land consolidation and mechanisation.

Ethiopia is the second most populous country in sub-Saharan Africa. One of the world's oldest continuous civilisations, it is also one of the world's poorest – the per capita GDP of US$252 (2007) is well below the sub-Saharan average although even this comparison is distorted by the more developed countries in the region, such as South Africa. Ethiopia's poverty-stricken economy is based on agriculture, which accounts for half of GDP, 60 per cent of exports and 80 per cent of total employment. The agricultural sector suffers from frequent drought and poor cultivation practices. Coffee is critical to the Ethiopian economy, but historically low prices have seen many farmers switching to qat (a mildly narcotic leaf) to supplement their income.

Economy strengthens

Ethiopia's GDP growth in the four years since 2004 has been impressive, averaging over 11 per cent. However, inflation almost doubled, from the 6.8 per cent recorded in 2005 to a worrying 12.3 per cent in 2006, and even more worrying level of 17.0 per cent in 2007. Although donor support remains essential to Ethiopia's economic reform, both the IMF and the World Bank had suspended new lending to Ethiopia during its border war with Eritrea. Although the suspension was lifted after the peace accord was signed in December 2000, the threat of further suspensions remained and in December 2005 donors put on hold a loan of US$275 of budget support. In 2005, Ethiopia received a US$4.9 million grant from the Global Environmental Facility (GEF) to provide solar photovoltaic (PV) systems and micro-hydro capacity.

Social development

According to the World Bank to clean water has risen from 34.1 per cent in 2002/03 to 42.2 per cent in 2004/05. By European or North American standards, this is still a worryingly low figure. A new five-year strategy, the snappily named Plan for Accelerated and Sustained Development to End Poverty (PASDEP), has been completed by the government and was endorsed by the House of Peoples' Representatives in May 2006. This ambitious plan focuses on the commercialisation of agriculture and promoting much more rapid non-farm private sector growth, geographical differentiation, population and gender development, infrastructure, risk management and vulnerability and employment.

Independent, but poor

Ethiopia is Africa's oldest independent country and, with the exception of a five-year occupation by Mussolini's Italy, has never been colonised. In the first part of the twentieth century Ethiopia forged strong links with Britain, whose troops helped evict the Italians in 1941 and put Emperor Haile Selassie back on his throne. During the 1960s and early 1970s British influence gave way to that of the US, which in turn was supplanted by the then-USSR.

Although relatively free from the coups that have plagued other African countries, Ethiopia's turmoil has been no less devastating. Drought, famine, war and ill-conceived policies brought millions to the brink of starvation in the 1970s and 1980s.

In 1974 this helped topple Selassie. His regime was replaced by a self-proclaimed Marxist junta under which thousands of opponents were purged or killed, property was confiscated and defence spending spiralled. With the overthrow of the junta in 1991, political and economic conditions stabilised somewhat, but not enough to restore investor confidence.

The Ethiopian People's Revolutionary Democratic Front (EPRDF) of incumbent premier Meles Zenawi won bitterly contested elections in May 2005, despite a swing to the opposition – the Alliance for Freedom and Democracy. The win paved the way for his third five-year stint as prime minister.

Claims of vote rigging accompanied the poll, and the EPRDF and the main opposition both claimed victory as the initial results were announced. Around 36 people were killed and hundreds were arrested in protests sparked by opposition allegations of electoral fraud by the ruling party.

Meles had taken part in the guerrilla campaign against the Mengistu regime, and was chosen as transitional head of state after the overthrow of the dictator in 1991. Once a Marxist-Leninist, by the 1990s he had become a champion of the free market and parliamentary democracy.

Ethiopia continues to face political uncertainties, to a large degree related to the demarcation of its border with Eritrea. The Eritrea-Ethiopia Boundary Commission ruling that the town of Badme would be located within Eritrea ignited strong opposition in Ethiopia, leading to protracted delays in the official demarcation of the border. The government has said it will not go to war over Badme, but the international community's efforts have not succeeded so far in resolving the impasse. Nor, it has to be said, have they improved relations between the countries, and in November 2006 the two countries again rejected proposals to settle the continuing border dispute. In a further complication, Ethiopia has sent troops (since 2006) to intervene on behalf of the transitional government (TG) in Somalia, while Eritrea was accused in October of arming the Islamist opponents of the TG. The United Nations Mission to Ethiopia and Eritrea (UNMEE), which had patrolled the disputed border between the two countries since 2002 was withdrawn in 2008, although the dispute rumbled on.

The African Development Bank's 2008 edition of *African Economic Outlook* (AEO) said that the key objective of the Ethiopian government as enunciated in the Plan for Accelerated and Sustained Development to End Poverty (PASDEP) for the period 2005/06–2009/10 is to achieve robust and pro-poor economic growth so as to accelerate progress towards the Millennium Development Goals (MDGs).

It went on to confirm that the economy is still dominated by agriculture, which accounted for nearly 47 per cent of GDP in 2007, down from the high of 56.7 per cent in 1996/97. The sector grew by 9.4 per cent in real terms in 2006/07, down from 10.9 per cent in 2005/06. Coffee, which remains the largest export product, exhibited output growth of 40 per cent in 2006/07. Tea, the second largest export, also performed well. The government intends to introduce a number of policy initiatives in agriculture over the next five years to address structural constraints, including building the introduction of high-yielding varieties.

KEY INDICATORS — Ethiopia

	Unit	2003	2004	2005	2006	2007
Population	m	68.42	72.03	73.03	75.07	*77.17
Gross domestic product (GDP)	US$bn	6.23	8.08	11.37	15.17	19.43
GDP per capita	US$	91	116	156	202	*252
GDP real growth	%	-3.8	11.6	10.3	11.6	11.4
Inflation	%	15.1	9.0	6.8	12.3	17.0
Industrial output	% change	0.0	6.8	6.6	7.4	0.0
Agricultural output	% change	0.0	17.3	12.0	11.2	0.0
Exports (fob) (goods)	US$m	433.0	562.8	917.3	1,024.0	0.0
Imports (cif) (goods)	US$m	1,630.0	2,104.0	3,700.9	4,105.6	0.0
Balance of trade	US$m	-1,197.0	-1,541.2	-2,783.5	-3,080.9	0.0
Current account	US$m	-180.0	-500.0	-1,567.8	-1,785.9	-881.0
Total reserves minus gold	US$m	955.6	1,496.8	1,121.5	832.7	0.0
Foreign exchange	US$m	944.8	1,485.1	1,111.0	821.6	0.0
Exchange rate	per US$	8.43	8.58	8.85	8.85	9.09

* estimated figure

Risk assessment

Economic	Fair
Political	Poor

Regional stabilityPoor

COUNTRY PROFILE

Historical profile

For millennia, Ethiopia has stood apart from the rest of Africa by virtue of its long history, rich religious and cultural heritage, unique ethnic and linguistic composition and style of government. The troubled passage of Africa's oldest independent country from feudal monarchy to something resembling a federal democracy, via two decades of brutal dictatorship, ran parallel to droughts, famines and the secession of Eritrea.

100 BC A kingdom including part of modern-day Ethiopia existed around Axum.

450 AD The kingdom was converted to Christianity and the Ethiopian church became part of the Coptic community.

1896 Italy tried to seize Ethiopia but lost the Battle of Adwa. The Italians held on to Eritrea on the Red Sea coast.

1916 Ras Tafari, later known as Emperor Haile Selassie, gained power over local lords but his appeal to the League of Nations for help against the occupying Italians went unheeded.

1936 Benito Mussolini's army invaded all of Ethiopia, which became part of Italian East Africa.

1941 British and Commonwealth troops along with the arbegnoch, Ethiopian resistance, fought the Italians.

1945 Emperor Haile Selassie returned to power after the Second World War.

1962 Eritrea was annexed by Ethiopia.

1974 Haile Selassie was deposed in coup led by Teferi Benti.

1975 Haile Selassie died in custody.

1977 Benti was killed and replaced by Colonel Mengistu Haile Mariam, who led a brutal regime known as the Dergue. At least 100,000 opponents or critics were killed.

1977 Somalia tried to annex part of Ethiopia's Ogaden region, where most people are ethnic Somalis. Cuban and Soviet troops and tanks assisted Ethiopia in repelling the Somalian invasion.

1984 Drought led to a famine in which as many as one million people may have died.

1987 A Soviet-style constitution was adopted and the People's Democratic Republic of Ethiopia was formed. The regime was supported by the Soviet Union.

1991 Rebellions in Eritrea, led by the leftist Eritrean People's Liberation Front (EPLF) and, in Tigray province, by the Tigray People's Liberation Front (TPLF) ensued. Mengistu fled to Zimbabwe as the EPLF took control of Eritrea and a TPLF-led coalition, the Ethiopian People's Revolutionary Democratic Front (EPRDF), marched into Addis Ababa.

1995 A general election was held and won by the EPRDF. The country was officially renamed the Federal Democratic Republic of Ethiopia. Negaso Gidada became president.

1998 Border disputes resulted in Eritrea and Ethiopia resuming full-scale fighting in mid-year and sporadic clashes thereafter.

1999 Eritrea refused to withdraw from the disputed Badme area.

2000 The EPRDF parties won the legislative elections. UN Mission in Ethiopia and Eritrea (UNMEE) peacekeepers opened a 1,000km cease-fire buffer zone between Ethiopia and Eritrea after the two countries signed a peace deal in Algiers, ending the two-year war.

2001 President Gidada quit the ruling coalition but finish his term in office. Girma Wolde Giorgise was elected, by parliament, to the largely ceremonial position of president.

2002 Eritrea and Ethiopia accepted a ruling on their border dispute – by the international Boundary Commission in The Hague – and a new 1,000km frontier was established. Ethiopia, ravaged by drought, requested food aid for nearly six million people.

2004 A resettlement programme started to move over two million people away from parched, over-worked highlands to the pastural, but disease rife plains of south-west Ethiopia. Long-term drought in Afar region resulted in over 350,000 people receiving food aid, when livestock deaths became widespread.

2005 The ruling EPRDF and its allies won parliamentary elections. The independent commission at the Permanent Court of Arbitration in The Hague, set up in as part of the peace deal signed in Algiers in 2000 between Eritrea and Ethiopia, ruled that Eritrea had launched unlawful attacks against Ethiopia in 1998, thereby triggering the border war between the two countries. The Ethiopian government said that it would lodge a claim for compensation. Donors put on hold US$375 million of budget support because of a government crackdown on opposition supporters.

2006 A new Alliance for Freedom and Democracy was formed by several opposition parties and rebel groups. Ethiopian troops intervened in Somalia to support the transitional government against Islamist militia forces. Ethiopia, together with Eritrea, rejected international proposals to settle their continuing border dispute.

2007 A census was undertaken in June, however, the government acknowledged that it would not be comprehensive as it did not include populations in Afar and Somali, which would be recorded separately in November. Ethiopia, which uses the Coptic calendar of 13 months and is seven years later than the Gregorian calendar, celebrated the millennium on 12 August. Parliament re-elected President Giorgise for another term in office on 9 October. Talks, set by the Ethiopia-Eritrea Border Commission, to confirm the demarcation between Ethiopia and Eritrea, failed to reach an agreement on time. The Commission considers the border it drew in 2006 to be binding in the face of the impasse. While Ethiopia and Eritrea accepted the ruling neither attempted to implement its recommendation and 1,700 UN peace-keeping troops remain in the area in a notional demilitarised zone, until at least 2008.

2008 Ethiopia severed diplomatic ties with Qatar because of 'its hostility to Ethiopa itself'. It is also believed that Ethiopia is angry with Al Jazeera television station, which is based in Doha, coverage. The Security Council terminated the UNMEE as of 31 July.

Political structure

Constitution

A constitution was adopted 8 December 1994 which established a federal system of government. The constitution formally came into force in August 1995 when the Federal Democratic Republic of Ethiopia was proclaimed.

Ethiopia comprises 11 semi-autonomous administrative regions organised loosely along major ethnic lines.

Form of state

Federal democratic republic

The executive

The role of president is largely a figurehead position. The prime minister, who is elected by parliament for a five-year term, holds executive power.

The president is elected by parliament for a six-year term.

National legislature

The Federal Parliamentary Assembly has two chambers. The Yehizbtewekayoch Mekir Bet (Council of People's Representatives) has 527 members, elected for a five-year term in single-seat constituencies. The Yefedereshn Mekir Bet (Council of the Federation) has 117 members, one each from the 22 minority nationalities and one from each professional sector of is remaining nationalities, designated by the regional councils which may elect them directly or provide their direct elections.

Last elections

15 May 2005 (parliamentary); 8 October 2001 (presidential).

Results: Presidential: Girma Wolde Giorgise was unanimously elected by parliament.
Parliamentary: the ruling EPRDF won 327 seats of 547 (with 59 per cent of the vote), CUD 109 seats, UEDF 52 seats, SPDP 24 seats, OFDM 11 seats, BGPDUF 8 seats, ANDP 8 seats, GPDM 3 seats, all others 1 seat.
Next elections
2007 (presidential); 2010 (parliamentary)

Political parties
Ruling party
Ethiopian People's Revolutionary Democratic Front (EPRDF), an alliance led by the Tigray People's Liberation Front (TPLF)
Main opposition party
Alliance for Freedom and Democracy (AFD) (formed 22 May 2006 by the CUD, UEDF and four rebel groups).

Population
77.17 million (2007)*
Last census: October 1994: 53,477,265. The third national census was taken over a nine-day period from 29 May 2007, at a cost of US$45.7 million; Afar and Somali regions were recorded separately in November.
Population density: 49.9 inhabitants per square km. Urban population: 16 per cent (1995—2001).
Annual growth rate: 2.6 per cent 1994–2004 (WHO 2006)
Internally Displaced Persons (IDP)
132,000 (UNHCR 2004)
Ethnic make-up
Oromo (40 per cent), Amhara and Tigrayan (32 per cent), Sidamo (9 per cent), Shankella (6 per cent), Somali (6 per cent), Afar (4 per cent), Gurage (2 per cent).
Religions
The Ethiopian Coptic Church is influential, particularly in the north. There is a large Muslim community in the south, made up mainly of Arabs, Somalis and Oromos. Ethiopian Orthodox (40 per cent), Muslim (40 per cent), animist and other (20 per cent).

Education
Ethiopia has one of the world's lowest school enrolment rates. The government aims to enrol 5.3 million children in primary schools by 2005. The pattern of enrolment shows large gender gaps with girls being more likely to drop out in the early stages. Oxfam estimates that fewer than one-third of boys and one-tenth of girls aged 6—11 start school and one quarter of these drop out during the first two grades. Female literacy rates are only 32 per cent and girls of primary school age work 14—16 hours a day on a variety of tasks, either helping out at home or earning an income. In regions where tuition fees have been abolished, school enrolment has increased by up to 20 per cent.
In secondary schools, English has replaced Amharic as the medium of instruction, although several local languages are also used.
Literacy rate: 42 per cent adult rate; 57 per cent youth rate (15–24) (Unesco 2005).
Pupils per teacher: 43 in primary schools.

Health
Per capita total expenditure on health (2003) was US$20; of which per capita government spending was US$12, (WHO 2006).
The government aimed at reorganising health services through a twenty-year health development strategy, with a series of five-year investment programmes; the second phase began in 2003. The system provides access to health services for only about half of the population, mainly in the urban areas. Estimates suggests that 24 per cent and 15 per cent of the population respectively had access to improved water and sanitation facilities.
In February 2005 the World Health Organisation – Global Polio Eradication Initiative (WHO – Polio Eradication) launched an Africa-wide mass polio immunisation programme, this coincided with the first case of the desease reported in Ethiopia in four years; its re-emergence was due to infected travellers. In a synchronised campaign with Somalia and Kenya, inoculation began for under fives by WHO – Polio Eradication and the country's health authorities in September 2006.
In August authorities reported a sharp increase in number of malaria cases in northern Ethiopia with 20,000 more cases in June 2005 than in June 2004.
HIV/Aids
There were 1.4 million people HIV positive in 2003, of which 770,000 were women, plus 120,000 children were HIV positive and 720,000 children were made orphans. There were 120,000 deaths due to aids in 2003.
The loss in annual GDP growth per capita was projected to be 0.6 per cent between 2002–10 due to the impact of the disease.
In Addis Ababa the prevalence rate of HIV/Aids has been falling from a high of 24 per cent in 1995 to 11 per cent in 2004.
HIV prevalence: 4.4 per cent aged 15–49 in 2003 (World Bank)
Life expectancy: 50 years, 2004 (WHO 2006)
Fertility rate/Maternal mortality rate: 5.7 births per woman, 2004 (WHO 2006); maternal mortality 18 per 1,000 live births (World Bank).
Child (under 5 years) mortality rate (per 1,000): 112 deaths per 1,000 live births; 47 per cent of children aged under five were malnourished (World Bank).
Head of population per physician: 0.03 physicians per 1,000 people, 2003 (WHO 2006)

Welfare
Ethiopia is one of the poorest countries in the world, with annual income per capita below US$100. Following the end of the border conflict with Eritrea in 2000, the government of Ethiopia started to implement an ambitious adjustment and reform programme and renewed its commitment to poverty reduction.

Main cities
Addis Ababa (capital, estimated population 3.1 million in 2005), Dire Dawa (274,252), Nazret (212,062), Gondar (154,787) Debre Zeyit (104,537).

Languages spoken
Oromigna and Tigrigna are widely spoken. English is taught in schools; as well as Arabic, French and Italian, it is used in business circles and understood in most hotels and major towns. Over 80 local languages are also spoken.
Official language/s
Amharic

Media
National news agency: Ethiopain News Agency
Other news agencies: AllAfrica: www.allafrica.com
The Reporter: http://en.ethiopianreporter.com
Walta Information Centre (WIC): www.waltainfo.com
Press
Newspaper circulation is limited to the urban literate. The government maintains a strict control over journalists and many are in exile.
Dailies: In Amharic, Addis Zemen (www.ethpress.gov.et) is a state-owned, Addis Admass (www.addisadmass.com) is privately owned. In English, the Ethiopian Herald (www.ethpress.gov.et) is a state-owned, The Africa Monitor (with The Daily Monitor, as an imprint) (www.theafricamonitor.com) is privately owned.
Weeklies: There are a few magazines published in Amharic and English, including Ethiopian Weekly Press Digest and The Sun. There are many more online publications.
Business: In English, weekly publications include Capital (www.capitalethiopia.com) and Addis Fortune (www.addisfortune.com), both provide business news and features.

Broadcasting
The national broadcaster is the Ethiopian Radio and Television Agency (ERTA) (www.erta.gov.et).
Radio: Radio services are the main medium of mass communication and sources of news and information.
The government-owned Radio Ethiopia (www.angelfire.com/biz/radioethiopia) operates nationally over several AM frequencies in 11 languages Amharic, Arabic, English, French and local languages.
The are just a few private, independent radio stations, including Radio Fanaa (www.radiofanaa.com) and Radio Jigjiga (www.radiojigjiga.com). External services are broadcast into Ethiopia by expatriates.
Television: The state-controlled Ethiopian Television (www.erta.gov.et) is a monopoly, which broadcasts to most of the country via a microwave link-up. Foreign satellite services are available from Jump TV (www.jumptv.com).
News agencies
National news agency: Ethiopain News Agency
Other news agencies: AllAfrica: www.allafrica.com
The Reporter: http://en.ethiopianreporter.com
Walta Information Centre (WIC): www.waltainfo.com

Economy
Ethiopia is one of the poorest countries in the world, despite a wealth of resources. Economic development has been retarded by various factors, including poor infrastructure, desertification, recurrent droughts, deterioration in the terms of trade and the effects of the war with Eritrea. Agriculture is the principal economic activity, accounting for around 48 per cent of GDP, 60 per cent of exports and 80 per cent of employment. Coffee is Ethiopia's largest export. The government is keen to diversify the economy.
The conclusion of peace with Eritrea brought with it the resumption of international support for the Ethiopian economy, which had been suspended due to the government's increased military expenditure and reports of human rights atrocities.
The drought of 2002–03, which caused a decline in agricultural output and water shortages, had a serious effect on the economy and necessitated a sharp increase in food aid. GDP growth contracted by -3.8 per cent in 2003, but with better weather conditions the economy improved; GDP grew by around 12 per cent in 2004, although slowing subsequently.
Despite a series of reform programmes to alleviate poverty, around 50 per cent of the population still live below the poverty line. Government plans of decentralisation, on IMF insistence, have had mixed success.

External trade
Ethiopia is a member of the Common Market of Eastern and Southern Africa (Comesa), however in May 2007 it did not have plans to join the customs union and free trade area as agreed by other member states.
Ethiopia is the origin of the coffee plant, and coffee beans are still a major export product providing over 30 per cent of the country's foreign earnings (a fall from over 60 per cent in the mid-1990s due to a slump in world prices).
Imports
Principal imports are food and live animals, petroleum and petroleum products, chemicals, machinery, motor vehicles, cereals, textiles, semi-manufactured goods and fertilisers.
Main sources: Saudi Arabia (18.1 per cent total, 2006), China (11.4 per cent), India (8.1 per cent).
Exports
Principal exports are coffee, khat, gold, leather products, live animals, oilseeds, marble and other minerals.
Main destinations: China (10.5 per cent total, 2006), Germany (8.7 per cent), Japan (7.4 per cent).

Agriculture
Farming
The agricultural sector is the mainstay of the economy, accounting for around 45 per cent of GDP, 85 per cent of employment and 62 per cent of exports. Only about two-thirds of Ethiopia's 122 million hectares of land is suitable for agriculture, of which around 15 per cent is actually cultivated. Large parts are affected by soil erosion. Intensive subsistence agriculture has depleted the soil and Ethiopia can no longer feed its population, even when the weather is good. Very little of the cultivated area is irrigated.
The chief cash crop is coffee, which accounts for around half of export earnings. Germany is the largest market for Ethiopian coffee. Falling world prices for coffee in recent years, together with severe droughts, has resulted in declining production and loss of revenues. Many growers have responded by switching to the production of qat. While coffee fell from 60 per cent of total exports to 35 per cent, export of qat increased to 15 per cent from 6 per cent.
Other cash crops include cotton and sugar. The main food crops are maize, sorghum, wheat, barley, millet and teff.
Crop production in 2005 included: 9,339,500 tonnes (t) cereals in total, 1,650,000t wheat, 2,740,000t maize, *1,800,000t sorghum, 1,090,000t barley, 2,450,000t sugar cane, *400,000t potatoes, *360,000t sweet potatoes, 1,050,275t pulses, 139,220t oilcrops, 77,000t linseed, 260,000t green coffee, *45,450t fibre crops, 75,000t treenuts, *731,000t fruit in total, 894,800t vegetables in total. Livestock production included: 606,460t meat in total, 336,040t beef, 74,000t game meat, 4,560t camel meat, 56,560t lamb, *28,650t goat meat, 77,000t game meat, 52,000t poultry, *36,624t eggs, 1,583,250t milk, *39,000t honey, 65,100t cattle hides, 6,066t goatskins, 10,080t sheepskins, *12,000t greasy wool.
* estimate
Forestry
Only 4 per cent of Ethiopia's land area is forested. Since the mid-1970s, there has been extensive deforestation with up to 75 per cent of forest cover cleared or degraded, according to the UN's Food and Agriculture Organisation (FAO). The overwhelming majority of timber production is used as domestic fuel.
Ethiopia is one of the world's largest exporters of natural gum and gum resin (gum Arabic). Between 1996–2002 it exported over 13,000 tonnes of natural gum, worth US$17 million. However, industry experts warned, in March 2006, that damage from forest fires, woodfuel harvesting and improper gum tapping was causing serious damage to the resources, added to which, resettlement programmes were also destroying woodland habitats.
Timber production in 2004 included 95,957,336 cubic metres (cum) roundwood, 2,928,000cum industrial roundwood, 17,700cum sawnwood, 4,000cum sawlogs & veneer logs, 93,400cum wood-based panels, 93,029,336cum wood fuel, 3,220,535t charcoal.

Industry and manufacturing
The industrial sector contributes 12.4 per cent of GDP and employs about 7 per cent of the workforce. Manufacturing of small handicrafts and other small industry sub-sectors make up around 7 per cent of GDP.
Industry is primarily based on the processing of agricultural raw materials. Principal among these is food processing, but textiles, handicrafts, and leather production are also significant.
Growth is constrained by a lack of raw materials, outdated machinery and techniques and the need for imports throughout the sector.

Tourism
Although visitor numbers have risen consistently each year since 1991, reaching around 200,000 in 2004, tourism is under-developed. The economic importance

of the sector and Ethiopia's potential as a destination are recognised and priority is being given to improving the infrastructure and the country's image, which has suffered from the conflict with Eritrea and natural disasters. In November 2004, Ethiopia was selected by the World Tourism Organisation as one of the first beneficiaries of the Sustainable Tourism and Elimination of Poverty initiative, which will provide experise and attract funding for tourism proposals. Tourism is expected to contribute 4.5 per cent to GDP in 2005.

Mining

The mining sector accounts for around 6 per cent of GDP.

The government says there are at least 500 tonnes of proven gold reserves in the country. Activity is limited to small-scale gold mining.

The country has substantial reserves of iron ore and untapped reserves of platinum, tantalum (used in the electronics industry), nickel, phosphate, diatomite, copper, zinc, soda ash and potash. Tantalum reserves are estimated at 25,000 tonnes at one site alone.

The output of non-metallic minerals such as limestone and marble has increased significantly.

A number of foreign mining companies have been awarded exploration concessions.

Hydrocarbons

Ethiopia does not produce oil, but there is commercial potential and foreign interest in investment in the sector is high. An exploration deal between the Ethiopian government and Petronas (Malaysia) was signed in 2003, the first of potentially many inward investments into the oil industry. Ethiopia has had to rely on imports of refined oil to meet energy requirements since the closure of the Assab refinery in 1997. Sudan became an important source of supplies in January 2005, when shipment by tanker truck along a new road commenced.

Natural gas reserves are estimated at around 115 billion cubic metres.

Ethiopia does not produce or import coal.

Energy

Ethiopia has considerable hydroelectric capacity and the Ethiopian Electric Power Corporation (EEPCO), has embarked on an extensive construction programme to provide a greater generating capacity for the country. In July 2006, a US$2 billion hydroelectric power station was official agreed between EEPCO, and Italy's Salini Construction – the Gibe 111. It will be built in the north-west where hydro capacity is greater than elsewhere in an otherwise drought-afflict country and is estimated will produce 1,870MW when it becomes fully operational after 2011.

In 2005, installed generating capacity is around 800MW. Only 17 per cent of the population has access to electricity, EEPCO electrified 80 towns between 2001–03 and the programme is ongoing. The new plant is expected to bring access to electricity up to 50 per cent and allow Ethiopia to become a net exporter of energy.

The Tis Abay II hydroelectric power station, near Lake Tana in the north-west, supplies 73MW to the Kaliti main power distribution station, operated by the EEPCO.

Ethiopia's first independent hydroelectic power station became operational in 2004. Situated in the south-west, the Gilgel Gibe provides 690MW to EEPCO.

Wood had always been a traditional source of energy and the planned expansion of hydroelectricity should reduce this and allow the many forests that have become severely depleted – and adding the desertification of Ethiopia – to recover.

Banking and insurance

Central bank

National Bank of Ethiopia

Main financial centre

Addis Ababa

Time

GMT plus three hours

The Ethiopian day officially begins at 0600 (midnight elsewhere).

Geography

Ethiopia extends inland from the Red Sea coast of eastern Africa. The country has a long frontier with Somalia near the Horn of Africa. Sudan lies to the west, Djibouti to the east, Eritrea to the north and Kenya to the south.

The country is a high central plateau, at 1,800–3,000 metres above sea level which is dissected by the Great Rift Valley that runs diagonally across the country. The tallest peak is Mount Ras Dashen, at 4,620 metres in the Simien Mountains, in the rugged north. In the north-west the Blue Nile rises in Lake Tana. The landscape in the south is flatter and more suited to agriculture.

Climate

Dependent on altitude. Lowland regions are very hot and dry throughout the year. On the plateau (including Addis Ababa) dry season from October–May with temperature range from as low as 6 degrees Celsius (C) in December to 26 degrees C in March (light rain from February–April). Temperatures can fall sharply at night during the dry season. Rainy season from June–September with average temperature 21 degrees C.

Entry requirements

Passports

Required by all. Must be valid for at least six months.

Visa

Required by all. For business visas, an application should be accompanied by a letter from a sponsoring organisation or company. For those self-employed, a letter from a solicitor, accountant or business registration authority should suffice. Visas are usually issued for a one month period; heavy penalties may be imposed for unauthorised extensions. If necessary, contact the Immigration Office for an Alien's Registration Card and an exit visa. Visa application forms can be downloaded from a number of Ethiopian embassy websites (www.mfa.gov.et/Consular_Affair_Diplomatic/Consular_Affair.php).

An international certificate of vaccination against yellow fever is required when applying.

Foreign nationals are advised to register their arrival with the consular representative of their embassy.

Currency advice/regulations

Up to Birr100 can be imported, if a visitor has a re-entry permit Birr100 may be exported, or else local currency export is prohibited.

Unlimited foreign currency may be imported but it must be declared on arrival. Export of foreign currency is allowed up to the amount declared.

Travellers cheque are accepted and are best taken as either US dollars or pound sterling.

Customs

Skins, hides and any antique articles require an export certificate. Laptop computers must be declared upon arrival and departure. Tape recorders require special customs permits.

Health (for visitors)

Health facilities are extremely limited in Addis Ababa and inadequate outside the city. Travellers should bring their own prescription drugs and a doctor's note describing the medication. If the quantity of drugs exceeds that expected for personal use, a permit from the ministry of health is required.

The altitude in Addis Ababa may cause health problems.

Mandatory precautions

A yellow fever inoculation certificate.

Advisable precautions

Visitors should be in date for the following vaccinations: yellow fever, polio, typhoid, tetanus, hepatitis A and B, meningitis.

There is a rabies risk.

Malaria prophylaxis recommended before visiting the lowlands. There is no malaria risk in Addis Ababa.

Tap water must be treated as unsafe unless boiled and filtered (bottled water is available in the main cities). Eat only well cooked meals, preferably served hot; vegetables should be cooked and fruit peeled. Dairy products are unpasteurised and should be avoided

A first aid kit that includes disposable syringes, is a reasonable precaution. Medical insurance is essential, including emergency evacuation, and an adequate supply of personal medicines is necessary.

Hotels

Hotels are available in Addis Ababa and other main centres. A service charge of 10 per cent and a tax of 2 per cent are added to bills but a small tip is usual in addition to the service charge. Payment is generally required in foreign currency.

Credit cards

Credit cards are accepted by airlines and the larger hotels only.

Public holidays (national)

Fixed dates

^7 Jan (Genna/Ethiopian Christmas Day), ^19 Jan (Timket/Epiphany), 2 Mar (Victory of Adwa Day), 28 May (Downfall of the Dergue), ^11 Sep (Enkutatash/New Year's Day), ^26 Sep (Meskel/Finding of the True Cross).

Variable dates

^Ethiopian Good Friday, ^Ethiopian Easter Day, Eid al Adha, Birth of the Prophet, Eid al Fitr.

^ Coptic Christian feasts only.

Ethiopia follows the Julian calendar, instead of the Gregorian calendar, used in most other parts of the world. The Ethiopian calendar year is divided into 13 months: 12 months of 30 days each and one month of five days (six in a leap year). The Ethiopian year commences on 11 September and runs seven years and eight months behind the Gregorian calendar.

Islamic year – 1429 (10 Jan 2008–28 Dec 2008): The Islamic year contains 354 or 355 days, with the result that Muslim feasts advance by 10–12 days against the Gregorian calendar. Dates of feasts vary according to the sighting of the new moon, so cannot be forecast exactly.

Working hours

Banking

Mon–Thu: 0800–1500; Fri: 0800–1100, 1330–1500; Sat: 0830–1100.

Business

Mon–Thu: 0830–1230, 1330–1730; Fri: 0830–1130, 1330–1730. Most private businesses also work on Saturdays.

Government

Mon–Thu: 0830–1230, 1330–1730. Fri: 0830–1130, 1330–1730.

Shops

Mon–Sat: 0800–1300, 1400–2000. Local variations.

Telecommunications

Mobile/cell phones

A GSM 900 service is available in large cities and towns only.

Electricity supply

220V, 50 cycles AC. Plugs are of the two-pin variety.

Social customs/useful tips

Handshaking is the usual mode of greeting. The first name is followed by that of the father – there are no family names. The words Ato, Woizero and Woizrity are the equivalents of Mr, Mrs and Miss respectively, and should be used when addressing people.

Smoking is not popular among traditional people, or in front of priests. Dress should be modest. Shoes are removed on entering churches/mosques. Private formal entertaining is common in Addis Ababa, and cocktail parties are not uncommon.

Ethiopian law strictly prohibits the photographing of military installations, police/military personnel, industrial facilities, government buildings and infrastructure.

Security

Crime is an increasing problem in Addis Ababa. Normal precautions should be taken.

Exercise caution if travelling to the northern Tigray and Afar regions (within 50km of the Ethiopian/Eritrean border) because of landmines and unsettled conditions in the border area. Travel to the Ogaden Region is considered very dangerous and should not be attempted. Limit road travel outside major towns to daylight hours only.

Getting there

Air

National airline: Ethiopian Airlines

International airport/s: Addis Ababa-Bole International (ADD), 8km from city, bar, restaurant, bank, post office, shops, car hire.

Airport tax: International departures US$20 in cash and exact amount, excluding transit passengers.

Surface

Road: Entry by land into Ethiopia is possible, if difficult, via Dewale and Galafi (Ethiopia-Djibouti), Moyale (Ethiopia-Kenya), Humera and Metema (Ethiopia-Sudan), Jijiga (Ethiopia-Somalia). The road linking Nairobi and Addis Ababa forms part of the Trans-East African Highway.

Rail: The rail route from Djibouti to Addis Ababa is subject to disruption.

Water: Ethiopia has been landlocked since Eritrea gained independence.

Main port/s: Until the outbreak of hostilities with Eritrea in 1998, Ethiopia relied heavily on the Eritrean ports of Assab and Massawa. Djibouti has subsequently become Ethiopia's principal trading gateway.

Getting about

National transport

Air: Ethiopian Airlines operates domestic service to main towns.

Road: An all-weather road network connects principal towns. The road system is undergoing expansion.

There are border posts at Moyale on the Kenyan border, Adwa and Adigrat near the border with Eritrea, and Dewelle for Djibouti.

Roads are impassable to Lalibela from June to September.

Drivers bringing their own vehicles to Ethiopia will require a carnet de passage.

Buses: Coach services (liable to suspension) Addis Ababa-Gondar.

Rail: A line runs from Addis Ababa to Dire Dawa (and on to Djibouti). However, visitors are advised not to use this line for security reasons.

City transport

Taxis: In Addis Ababa, the National Tour Operations (NTO) provides taxis at the main hotels and the airport, although independent and communal cabs are available. It is advisable to check the fare and the destination before entering the cab. The most reliable taxis are available from the office of the Hilton Hotel. The taxi journey from the airport to the city centre takes about 30 minutes. Tipping is not usual.

Buses, trams & metro: Journey time from airport to city centre 30 minutes.

Car hire

Car hire (with or without driver) is available in the main centres. A valid international driving licence is required. Traffic drives on the right.

Payment for car rental is generally required in foreign currency.

BUSINESS DIRECTORY

The addresses listed below are a selection only. While World of Information makes every endeavour to check these addresses, we cannot guarantee that changes have not been made, especially to telephone numbers and area codes. We would welcome any corrections.

Telephone area codes

The international dialling code (IDD) for Ethiopia is +251 followed by area code and subscriber's number.

Addis Ababa	11	Gondar	58
Awassa	46	Jimma	47
Bahir Dar	58	Mekelle	4
Dire Dawa	25	Nazareth	22

Chambers of Commerce

Addis Ababa Chamber of Commerce, PO Box 2458, Addis Ababa (tel: 515-055;

fax: 511-479; e-mail: aachamber1@telecom.net.et).

Awassa Chamber of Commerce, PO Box 167, Awassa (tel: 200-375; fax: 205-197).

Bahir Dar Chamber of Commerce, PO Box 48, Bahir Dar (tel: 200-481; fax: 201-787).

Dire Dawa Chamber of Commerce, PO Box 198, Dire Dawa (tel: 113-082; fax 112-468; e-mail: luiji@telecom.net.et).

Ethiopian Chamber of Commerce, PO Box 517, Addis Ababa (tel: 518-240; fax: 517-699; e-mail: ethcham@telecom.net.et).

Gondar Chamber of Commerce, PO Box 50, Gondar (tel: 110-320; fax: 115-656).

Mekelle Chamber of Commerce, PO Box 503, Mekelle (tel: 402-529; fax: 408-914).

Nazareth Chamber of Commerce, PO Box 36, Nazareth (tel: 112-083; fax: 122-699).

Banking

Awash International Bank SC; PO Box 12638, Bole Road, Addis Ababa (tel: 614-482/83, 612-919; fax: 614-477).

Bank of Abyssinia SC; PO Box 12947, Addis Ababa (tel: 514-130, 514-752; fax: 511-575).

Commercial Bank of Ethiopia; PO Box 255, Unity Square, Addis Ababa (tel: 511-271, 515-004; fax: 514-522, 512-166).

Construction and Business Bank, PO Box 3480, Addis Ababa (tel: 512-300; fax: 515-103).

Dashen Bank SC; PO Box 12752, Garad Building, Debre Zeit Road, Addis Ababa (tel: 661-380, 655-525; fax: 661-640, 653-037).

Development Bank of Ethiopia, PO Box 1900, Josep Broz Tito, Addis Ababa (tel: 511-188; fax: 511-606).

Wegagen Bank SC; PO Box 1018, Addis Ababa (tel: 655-015; fax: 653-330).

Central bank

National Bank of Ethiopia, PO Box 5550, Addis Ababa, Ethiopia (tel: 517-430; fax: 514-588; email: nbe.excd@telecom.net.et; internet: www.nbe.gov.et).

Travel information

Addis Ababa-Bole Airport, PO Box 978, Addis Ababa (tel: 180-455; fax: 612-533).

Antiquities Authority, National Museum of Ethiopia, PO Box 76, Addis Ababa (tel: 117-150; fax: 553-188).

Ethiopian Airlines, PO Box 1755, Bole International Airport, Addis Ababa (tel: 612-222; fax: 611-474); town office (tel: 517-000; fax: 611-474; internet: www.flyethiopian.com).

National tourist organisation offices

Ethiopian Tourism Commission, PO Box 2183, Addis Ababa (tel: 517-470, 150-609, 513-962; fax: 513-899; internet: www.visitethiopia.com).

National Tour Operations (NTO), PO Box 5709, Addis Ababa (tel: 512-955; fax: 517-688).

Other useful addresses

African Union, PO Box 3243, Addis Ababa (tel: 557-700; fax: 511-299).

British Embassy, Commercial Section, Fikre Mariam Abatechan Street, Addis Ababa (tel: 612-354; fax: 610-588).

Central Statistical Office, PO Box 1143, Addis Ababa (tel: 113-010).

Department of Immigration and Refugee Affairs, PO Box 5741, Addis Ababa (tel: 553-899).

Djibouti–Ethiopian Railway Corporation, PO Box 1051, Addis Ababa (tel: 517-250; fax: 513-533).

Ethiopian Customs Office, PO Box 3248, Addis Ababa (tel: 513-100; fax: 518-355).

Ethiopian Embassy (USA), 3506 International Drive, NW, Washington DC 20008 (tel: 202-364-1200; fax: 202-686-9551; e-mail: ethiopia@ethiopianembassy.org).

Ethiopian Investment Authority, PO Box 2313, Addis Ababa (tel: 510-033; 514-396).

Ethiopian Privatisation Agency, PO Box 11835, Ethiopian Investment Authority Building, Bole Road, Addis Ababa (tel: 521-833; fax: 513-955).

Ethiopian Private Industries' Association, PO Box 8739, Addis Ababa (tel: 512-384; fax: 552-633).

Ethiopian Television, PO Box 5554, Addis Ababa.

Ethiopian Tourist Trading Enterprise, PO Box 8640, Addis Ababa (tel: 612-277; fax: 610-500).

Maritime and Transit Services, PO Box 1186, Addis Ababa (tel: 510-666; fax: 514-097).

Ministry of Culture and Information, PO Box 1364, Addis Ababa (tel: 551-011; fax: 551-609).

Ministry of Economic Development & Co-operation, PO Box 2428, Addis Ababa (tel: 519-684; fax: 517-988).

Ministry of Foreign Affairs, PO Box 393, Addis Ababa (tel: 517-345; fax: 514-300).

Ministry of Trade and Industry, PO Box 2559, Addis Ababa (tel: 518-200; fax: 514-288).

Voice of Ethiopia, PO Box 1020, Addis Ababa.

Wildlife Conservation Department, PO Box 386, Addis Ababa (tel: 510-455; fax: 510-168).

National news agency: Ethiopain News Agency

Address: PO Box 530 Addis Ababa (tel: 155-0011; fax: 155-1609; internet: www.ena.gov.et).

Internet sites

Africa Business Network: http://www.ifc.org/abn

AllAfrica.com: http://www.allafrica.com

African Development Bank: http://www.afdb.org

ENA - Ethiopian News Agency: http://www.telecom.net.et/~ena

Ethiopian Mission to the UN: http://www.undp.org/missions/ethiopia

Ethiopian Privatisation Agency: http://www.undp.org/missions/ethiopia

Mbendi AfroPaedia (information on companies, countries, industries and stock exchanges): http://mbendi.co.za

Falkland Islands/Islas Malvinas

KEY FACTS

Official name: Falkland Islands

Head of State: Queen Elizabeth II, represented by Governor Alan Edden Huckle (from 28 Aug 2006)

Head of government: Chief Executive Dr Tim Thorogood (since 7 Jan 2008)

Area: 12,173 square km (including East and West Falkland and adjacent islands)

Population: 2,932 (2004)

Capital: Stanley

Official language: English

Currency: Falkland pound (Fl£) = 100 pence

Exchange rate: Fl£0.50 per US$ (Jul 2008); (pegged to pound sterling)

GDP per capita: US$25,000 (2003)

GDP real growth: 2.00% (2006)*

Inflation: 3.60% (2004)*

* estimated figure

COUNTRY PROFILE

Historical profile

1592 First sighted by English mariners (Captain John Davis in ship Desire – the motto of the islands became Desire the Right).

1690 The first landing was by British Captain John Strong in the ship, Welfare. The Falkland Islands were named after the then Treasurer of the Navy, Viscount Falkland.

1764 French settlement was recorded. The islands were named Les Malouines after the French town of St Malo, hence the Argentine name of Malvinas for the islands.

1765 Captain John Byron (British) took formal possession of the islands at Port Egmont.

1767 The French settlement was sold to Spain and named Puerto de la Soledad.

1770 The Spanish ousted the British from Port Egmont.

1771 The British garrison was re-established.

1774 The garrison was withdrawn, leaving a plaque 'as a mark of possession' and a flag 'left flying'.

1820 The flag of the United Provinces of La Plata (Spanish) was hoisted at Puerto de la Soledad.

1823 The governor of the islands was nominated by the United Provinces Government (but did not visit).

1824 A German merchant, Louis Vernet, was given land by grant of the Buenos Aires government and a settlement of mixed nationalities, over the next few years, was established at Puerto de la Soledad.

1828 Vernet was appointed governor by the United Provinces. He attempted to stop sealing operations by other nations.

1831 The US protested about these actions and sent USS Lexington to sack Puerto de la Soledad (with the US president's approval). The islands were again unpopulated.

1833 Port Louis (Puerto de la Soledad) was taken over by the British, asserting full rights under naval superintendents until 1842.

1842 The first British governor, Richard C Moody, took up residence.

1981 The Falkland Islands and its dependencies were designated as British Dependent Territories.

1982 Argentina invaded the Falkland Islands. The UK despatched a military force, composed of naval ships and troops. The UK recaptured the islands.

1983 The British Nationality (Falkland Islands) Act gave islanders full British citizenship.

1990s The UK and Argentina resumed diplomatic relations. Both sides agreed to a formula to protect their respective positions on sovereignty and maritime jurisdiction, while discussing other matters. The UN committee on decolonisation urged the UK and Argentina to negotiate an ending to the dispute. The UK remained adamant that the self-determination of Falkland islanders was paramount. Argentina adopted a constitutional amendment asserting its sovereignty over the islands.

1999 In an effort to improve relations, Argentine nationals were allowed to visit the islands for the first time since 1982.

2001 The UK agreed to allow Argentinean private aircraft and shipping to visit the islands.

2002 The Falkland Islands and its dependencies were designated as a self-governing British Overseas Territories.

2003 The 33rd General Assembly of the Organisation of American States (OAS) passed a statement of support for Argentina's claim to the Falkland Islands. The OAS called on Britain and Argentina to resume negotiations over the South Atlantic archipelago as soon as possible.

2004 Relations between Argentina and the UK deteriorated as Argentina banned charter flights to and from the Falklands crossing its airspace, and when an Argentinean ice breaker, the Almirante Irizar, began 'policing' a Falklands conservation zone by challenging fishing vessels, demanding details of their permits and when Argentina gave permission for Aerolineas Argentinas to begin direct flights to the Falkland Islands, without regard for any UK agreement.

2006 The twice-weekly BBC radio programme, Calling the Falklands, which had been on the air for 62 years, was terminated in March. Alan Huckle became governor.

2007 HMS Nottingham, a destroyer class ship, became the latest South Atlantic patrol ship to maintain a British maritime presence in the South Atlantic. It was joined by the protection vessel HMS Dumbarton Castle which will patrol the seas around the Falkland Islands until

2012. In March, Argentina terminated a 1995 agreement with the UK on oil exploration in the vicinity of the Falkland Islands. An agreement with BHP Billiton for at least two exploration wells to be drilled by 2010 was signed. The islands held celebrations to mark 25 years since their liberation from the Argentine invasion force.
2008 Dr Tim Thorogood became chief executive on 7 January. Following an Anglo-Argentine feasibility study, it was estimated that 20,000 unexploded ordinances have yet to be disarmed, and which 'would present significant technical challenges and risks'.

Political structure

Constitution

The current constitution dates from 1985, with amendments in 1997 and 1998. The islander's rights to self-determination are prescribed. The operations of the Governor and Executive and Legislative Councils are mandated under the constitution. A constitutional review was underway in 2008.

Defence and foreign affairs are the responsibility of the UK government.

Form of state

Overseas territory of the United Kingdom

The executive

Supreme authority is vested in the British monarch and exercised by the governor with the advice and assistance of the Executive and Legislative Councils.

The governor presides over a five-member Executive Council (three elected and two ex-officio members). The governor is obliged to consult the Executive Council, except for defence and security issues (when the Commander of the British Forces in the islands advises and directs). If the governor opposes the Executive Council an immediate report must be presented to the UK government in explanation. The governor is responsible for external affairs and the public service.

National legislature

The Legislative Council is composed of eight members (three from Camp (countryside) constituency and five from the Stanley constituency) elected by universal adult suffrage and two ex-officio members – the chief executive and the financial secretary. The council has a substantial measure of responsibility for the island's affairs.

Legal system

English common law

Last elections

17 November 2005 (legislative council)

Results: Legislative council: eight out of the ten seats were filled by election of non-partisan candidates, the remaining places being filled by ex-officio members.

Next elections

November 2009 (parliamentary)

Political situation

Along with all other British Overseas Territories a review of the Falkland Islands constitution was underway in 2008. The UK government is keen to see all territories take more responsibility for themselves, but it maintains implacable support for Falkland Islands self-determination in the face of Argentina's adamant refusal to give up any part of its claim on the Falkland Islands.

The islands are prospering with the growth in tourism, a low unemployment rate and the continued quartering of military staff. Oil and gas exploration has progressed so that by 2010 at least two test drills will be undertaken in the waters off the Falkland Islands. Other mineral rights were leased, for gold prospecting let since 2000, for which ore is expected to be shipped abroad in 2008–09.

Population

2,932 (2004)

Last census: April 2001: 2,913

Population density: 4.8 inhabitants per square km.

Annual growth rate: 1.1 per cent (2003)

Ethnic make-up

White, almost exclusively of British descent. Workers from St Helena make up about 10 per cent of the population.

Religions

Anglican, Roman Catholic, United Free Church, Evangelist Church, Jehovah's Witnesses, Lutheran, Seventh-Day Adventist.

Main cities

Stanley (capital, estimated population 2,181 in 2005)

Languages spoken

Official language/s

English

Media

Press

The two weekly newspapers are Teaberry Express (www.falklandnews.com) and Penguin News (www.penguin-news.com). Official announcements and government directives are published in periodic publications of The Falkland Islands Gazette. The Falkland Islands News Area Network (www.falklandnews.com) provides a news agency service covering local headlines and from other regional newspapers such as SAFIN Magazine, St Helena News, The Islander Newspaper and the Antarctic Sentinel.

Broadcasting

Radio: The Falkland Islands Broadcasting Service and British Forces Broadcasting Service operate a local radio station and provide 24 hours/day listening on FM and MW. Satellite radio services are also available.

Television: Apart from the BFBS which provides satellite and cable TV services primarily for the military personnel stationed on the islands, KTV (www.ktv.co.fk) also operates a satellite service which distributes nine channels including BBC, CNN, TNT and HBO.

Economy

The Falkland Islands is self-financing with an economy largely dependent on agriculture, of which fisheries is the main sector, generating over £20 million (US$39.2 million) annually. Almost 80 per cent of the total marine catch is exported to Spain. The Falkland Islands Development Corporation (FIDC) is keen to enhance the islands' development prospects through a National Aquaculture Strategy. After fishing, wool is the largest component of farming income. High quality wool is exported to the UK while FIDC is attempting to increase value added features. Other developments include a new abattoir designed to meet EU standards in order to exploit the islands' certification as a country producing organic food.

The other key element of the economy is tourism. Over 30,000 tourists typically visit each year, most arriving by cruise ships. Improved hotel accommodation and access have been included in development plans. There are regular, scheduled flights from Chile and the UK, via the RAF military airbase at Brize Norton in Oxfordshire. Although the RAF and Falkland Islands tourist board are committed to providing a comprehensive service for travellers, the route and distance still places a limitation on the numbers visiting by air.

External trade

As a UK Overseas Territory the Falkland Islands is a part of the European Union's Association of Overseas Countries and Territories (OCT Association), and some EU laws apply, specifically animal slaughter and commercial food hygiene regulations.

There are several rural associations that market local meat, wool, hides and fish.

Imports

Principal imports include fuel, food and drink, building materials and clothing.

Main sources: UK (72.5 per cent total, 2005), US (15.1 per cent), The Netherlands (8.5 per cent)

Exports

Until the arrival of the fishery, wool and sheepskins, and hides were virtually the only exports. Squid, hake, finfish and mero (toothfish) together with wool, are the main exports.

Main destinations: Spain (81.9 per cent total, 2004), US (6.0 per cent), UK (4.5 per cent)

Agriculture

Farming

Soil quality is generally poor – peat over clay (peat is used as fuel). Virtually all available land has been used for sheep farming although small areas of arable land are cultivated (eg potatoes, hay crops, vegetable crops grown by individual households).

A hydroponic garden facility constructed in Stanley yields good quality vegetable crops for local and shipping consumption.

There is an indigenous tussock (or tussac) grass (Poa Flabellata, which will grow to a height of 3–4 metres) but because of its palatability for livestock, it has been over-grazed in most places.

Constant strong winds affect the suitability of all flora, and only the hardiest will survive. Indigenous grass covering large areas is known locally as 'whitegrass' (Cortaderia Pilosa) and a heather-like plant 'diddle-dee' (Empetrum Rubrum) is common.

There are around 90 farms. The average size is 10,000ha, with an average of 6,400 sheep. Sheep stock are a Corriedale/Polwarth mixture with small admixture of other breeds, eg Romney. The average clip per sheep is over 3.55kg.

Certain sheep diseases found elsewhere (eg foot rot, skin complaints/parasites) are either absent or not considered a problem on the islands.

An abbattoir meeting EU standards was opened in 2001 and is an important part of the Islands' organic farming programme. Farmers are being encouraged to diversify. The Islands have accreditation as organic under the brand name, Falklands' Finest.

Mutton is the principal source of protein and is supplemented during winter by beef. A dairy farm on East Falkland provides an important proportion of the islands' milk. The pasture is improved by nitrogen fertiliser in quantities that would be uneconomic over a larger area.

Livestock production in 2005 included: 911t meat in total, 131t beef, 774t lamb, 105t pig meat, 7t poultry, 160t eggs 1,500t milk, 2,340t wool, greasy.

Fishing

The Interim Conservation and Management Zone inaurgurated by the British government in 1986, was substanially revised in 2005. The revised law regulates the new system of transferable fishing rights. The Falklands have managed and policed a fish reserve and generated significant revenues through the annual award of fishing licences. These go to support the islands' health, education and welfare system. They have dropped to around £15 million (US$30 million) in recent years as a result of drop in Illex (squid) catches. Squid accounts for 75 per cent of the fish taken.

The Fisheries Department monitors marine activity daily and restrictions have been imposed on seismic fleets, especially during the fishing season.

The Falkland Islands Fishing Companies Association (FIFCA) was formed in 2007 to represent the fishing industry.

Industry and manufacturing

Small industrial units serve both onshore and offshore commitments. Hand-knitted local garments are produced for sale to visitors.

The Falkland Islands' largest private company, Falkland Islands Holdings plc, is quoted on the London Stock Exchange where it began trading in 1998. Activities are mainly retail trading and provision of services to the Falkland Islands. It controls about 80 per cent of retail sales, is the agent for Land Rover, the most popular vehicle, owns the Darwin Shipping Line and operates the port in Stanley.

Tourism

Tourism is a fast-growing industry, with the attraction of wildlife and also interest in the military aspects of the 1982 Falkland Islands conflict. As sheep production becomes increasingly uneconomic, tourism is seen as a possible means of maintaining some of the outlying communities. Cruise visitors have greatly increased in recent years.

Between October 2007–April 2008, 62,200 passengers from visiting cruise ships were given clearance to land. This shows an annual growth of 21 per cent for the 2007–08 season, with a growth in passenger numbers averaging 16 per cent per annum since the 2001–02 season. Of the 46 different vessels which visited in the 2007–08 season, 10 were maiden calls.

Mining

There is speculation that the great blanket bogs which obscure much of the inland geology of the islands may hide some diamond-bearing kimberlites and exploration is under way. There has been some evidence of gold.

Hydrocarbons

In 1996, oil licences were granted by the UK government to a mixed group of international companies including Desire Petroleum, a group formed partly on behalf of the islanders. Potential reserves are estimated at up to 60 billion barrels.

The Falklands Islands Holdings company announced in June 2004 that it was forming a new oil exploration company called Falkland Oil and Gas (FOGL), in partnership with Global Petroleum and RAB Capital. With the mapping of 4,340km offshore leases FOGL believe that there is potentially 200–250 million barrels of oil in its operational areas.

Although there is potential in the oil sector in the Falkland Islands currently no oil is being produced and the islands rely on the import of petroleum products. Coal and gas is neither produced or imported.

Energy

The majority of households use oil. Stanley has a power station that generates 6.3MW of electricity at 240V/50Hz and a piped water supply. Outside Stanley settlements generate their own power and there is no public water supply.

There is a plentiful supply of peat (turf) although few houses still have peat stoves.

Three new turbines were installed in 2007 power by the Sand Bay Wind Farm. By November 2007 they produced 300,000 units of electricity, and around 25 per cent of all electricity consumed in Stanley.

Time

GMT minus four hours (GMT minus three hours April–September)

Geography

The Falklands Islands, comprising two large islands and about 700 smaller ones, are in the south-western Atlantic Ocean, about 770km (480 miles) north-east of Cape Horn, South America. They are 500km (300 miles) from the South American mainland.

The coastlines are marked by rocky headlands and sandy beaches. Vegetation comprises low grasses, ferns and shrubs. There are many small lakes and peaty pools and three rivers: the San Carlos on East Falkland and the Warrah and Chartres on West Falkland. There are hill ranges on both main islands, the highest points being Mount Usborne on East Falkland (705m) and Mount Adam on West Falkland (700m).

Hemisphere

Southern

Climate

Temperatures range from minus 6–21 degrees Celsius (C) with occasional lows of minus 10 degrees C and highs of 25 degrees C. Rainfall is around 700mm per year. Strong to gale-force winds are frequent during spring and early summer.

Entry requirements

Passports

Valid passports required by all, valid for three months.

Visa

Not required by nationals of EU/EEA countries, North America, Australasia and other commonwealth countries, Argentina, Chile, Brazil, Uruguay, Japan, Hong Kong, South Korea, Israel, Andorra, Liechtenstein, San Marino and Vatican City. For further confirmation and exceptions contact the Travel Co-ordinator in London (+44-(0)207-222-2542). Booking forms for the flight from the UK include details and purpose of visit and are required to be completed before or on arrival. All visitors are required to have a return ticket, accommodation and sufficient funds.

Currency advice/regulations
There are no restrictions on the import and export of local or foreign currency. The Falkland Islands has its own currency which is equivalent to UK sterling. The notes and coins cannot easily be exchanged for sterling or other currencies outside the Islands. Sterling is freely used on the islands and dollars are accepted.

Customs
200 cigarettes, 50 cigars, 100 cigarillos or 250 grams of tobacco; one litre of alcohol, two litres of wine; and 10 litres of beer or cider.
Import licences are required for plants, foodstuffs and firearms.

Prohibited imports
Uncooked or cured meat and plants are only allowed in under licence. Livestock is allowed on any in-coming aircraft.

Health (for visitors)

Mandatory precautions
None

Advisable precautions
Yellow fever vaccination in case of any stopover in Africa en route.
Radiation alerts are issued with local weather forecasts when the ozone hole stretches over the islands. Precautions against skin cancer should be taken with high factor suncream and clothing protection.

Credit cards

Credit cards are generally accepted at hotels and retail outlets.

Public holidays (national)

Fixed dates
1 Jan (New Year's Day), 21 Apr (Queen's Birthday), 14 Jun (Liberation Day), 8 Aug (Battle Day), 25 Dec (Christmas Day), 26 Dec (Boxing Day), 28–29 Dec (Stanley Races).

Variable dates
Good Friday, Peat Cutting Day (first Mon in Oct).

Working hours

Business
Mon- Fri: 0800-1200. 1300-1700.

Government
Mon–Fri: 0800–1200, 1300-1630.

Shops
Mon-Fri: 0900-1200, 1300-2000.

Telecommunications

Telephone/fax
Direct satellite telephone and telefax links are in operation throughout the Islands.

Postal services
A new post code for the islands has been issued through the Universal Postal Union: FIQQ 1ZZ.

Electricity supply
Voltage and plugs for electrical appliances are the same as in the UK, 240V 50Hz.

Getting there

Air
Flights to the Falkland Islands depart from RAF Brize Norton, Oxfordshire, UK, six or seven times per month. For information, contact a travel agent or the Falklands Islands Government office in London (tel: +44 (0)207-222-2542). LanChile operate weekly flights from Santiago via Puerto Montt and Punta Arenas. Details from any travel agent or from International Tours and Travel in Stanley (tel +500-22041; fax +500-22042).
International airport/s: Mount Pleasant International Airport (MPN); 56km from Stanley.
Other airport/s: Stanley Airport
Airport tax: Departure tax: £20.

Surface
Water: Cruise ships stop in at Stanley.
Main port/s: Stanley.

Getting about

National transport
Air: Depending on bookings and weather conditions, the Falkland Islands Government Air Service (FIGAS) operates daily services to the majority of settlements with a fleet of eight-passenger Britten-Norman Islander aircraft.
Road: There is a limited amount of surfaced road mainly around Stanley and Mount Pleasant. Gravel roads are a common feature.
Water: Boats may be chartered in advance by large groups; there is no regular service for small groups.

City transport
Taxis: There is a limited taxi service in Stanley and at the airport, provided by Stanley and Lowes Taxis (tel: (+500) 21381) and Cindy Cars (tel: (+500) 22123).
Buses, trams & metro: There is a bus service from the airport to Stanley, operated by Falkland Islands Tours & Travel (+500-21775).

Car hire
4X4 vehicles can be rented from Falkland Islands Company Ltd, Crozier Place, Stanley (tel: (+500) 27678).

BUSINESS DIRECTORY

The addresses listed below are a selection only. While World of Information makes every endeavour to check these addresses, we cannot guarantee that changes have not been made, especially to telephone numbers and area codes. We would welcome any corrections.

Telephone area codes
The international dialling code (IDD) for the Falkland Islands is +500 followed by subscriber's number.

Chambers of Commerce
Falkland Islands Chamber of Commerce, PO Box 378, West Hillside, Stanley (tel: 22-264; fax: 22-265; e-mail: commerce@horizon.co.fk).

Banking
Standard Chartered Bank, Box 166, Ross Road, Stanley (tel: 27-220; fax: 27-219); UK contact (tel: +44(0) 20-7280-7500).

Travel information
Falkland Islands Company Travel Services, Stanley (tel: 27-633; fax: 27-603).

Falkland Islands Government Air Service (FIGAS), c/o Falkland Islands Government, Stanley Airport (tel: 27-219; fax: 27-309; e-mail: figas@horizon.co.fk).

Falkland Islands Tourist Board, London, UK (e-mail: manager@tourism.org.fk) issues an accommodation guide.

Falkland Islands Tours & Travel (tel: 21-775; e-mail: astewart@horizon.co.fk).

RAF Brize Norton, Oxfordshire, UK (tel: +44 (0)1993-897-366).

Travel Co-ordinator, Falkland Islands Government Office, Falkland House, 14 Broadway, Westminister, London SW1H 0BH, UK (tel: (+44 -20) 7222-2542; fax: (+44-20) 7222-2375; e-mail: travel@figo.u-net.com).

National tourist organisation offices
Falkland Islands Tourist Board, Shackleton House, Stanley (tel: 22-215; fax: 22-619; e-mail: jettycentre@horizon.co.fk; internet site: http://www.tourism.org.fk).

Ministries
Chief Executive, Thatcher Drive, Stanley (tel: 27-110; fax: 27-109).

Department of Agriculture and Mineral Resources, Stanley (tel: 27-355; fax: 27-352).

Department of Civil Aviation, Stanley Airport (tel: 27-300; fax: 27-302).

Department of Education, 23 Ross Road, Stanley (tel/fax: 27-292).

Department of Fisheries, PO Box 598, Stanley (tel: 27-260; fax: 27-265).

Department of Oil, Ross Road, Stanley (tel: 27-322; fax: 27-321).

Department of Public Works, Stanley (tel: 27-193; fax: 27-191).

Governor's Office, Government House, Stanley (tel: 27-433; e-mail: gov.house@horizon.co.fk).

Treasury, Falkland Islands Government, Thatcher Drive, Stanley (tel: 27-143; fax: 27-144).

UK Government Office, Falkland House, 14 Broadway, Westminster, London SW1H 0BH, UK (tel: +44 (0)20-7222-2542; fax: +44 0)20-7222-2375; e-mail: rep@figo.u-net.com).

Other useful addresses

Attorney General, PO Box 143, Stanley (tel: 27-273/4; fax: 27-276).

British Geological Survey, Petroleum Geology Group, Murchison House, West Mains Rd, Edinburgh, EH9 3LA (tel: +44(0)131 667-1000; fax: +44 (0)131 668-4930).

Cable & Wireless, Stanley (tel: 20-800; fax 22-206).

Customs & Immigration, Stanley (tel: 27-340; fax: 27-342).

Falkland Islands Development Corporation, Stanley (tel: 27-211; fax: 27-210).

Falklands Islands Co Ltd (FIC), Crozier Place, Stanley (tel: 27-600; fax: 27-603).

Medical Services/King Edward VII Memorial Hospital, Stanley (tel: 27-415; fax: 27-416).

Meteorological Office, RAF Mount Pleasant (tel: 73-557).

Overseas Territories Department, Foreign & Commonwealth Office, King Charles St, London SW1A 2AH (tel: +44(0)20-7270-3000; fax: (0)20-7270-2086).

The United Kingdom Falkland Islands Trust (administers the Shackleton Scholarship fund), c/o 14 Broadway, Westminster, London SW1H 0BH, UK (tel: +44 (0)20-7222-2542; fax: +44 (0)20-7222-2375).

Internet sites

Falkland Islands Government: www.falklands.gov.fk

Falkland Islands information: www.falklands-malvinas.com/

Falkland Islands web portal: www.falklandislands.com

Falkland Islands News Network: www.sartma.com

United Kingdom Falkland Islands Trust: www.ukfit.org.uk

Faroe Islands

COUNTRY PROFILE

Historical profile

The first Norse settlers arrived in the Faroes from neighbouring Denmark and the Orkneys in the ninth century.

1380 Early administration was undertaken by a parliamentary body known as the Alting. The end of parliamentary procedures saw the Alting renamed the Løgting and becoming a royal court.

1397 The Faroes become a Danish province, with the political merger of Norway and Denmark into the Kalmar Union.

1849 The first Danish constitution included the Faroe Islands, administered under the Danish county Roskilde.

1939–45 The Faroe Islands were occupied by the British during the Second World War, although they remained largely self-governing; with continuous war work the economy improved steadily and was sustained.

1946 The Faroe Islands returned to Danish control. In a referendum, a very small majority voted in favour of becoming an independent state. Negotiations and diplomacy led to a home rule arrangement instead.

1948 The Home Rule Act made the Faroes security, foreign and economic affairs the responsibility of Denmark.

1998 Anfinn Kallsberg replaced Edmund Joensen as prime minister.

2001 A referendum to be held for approval of legislative amendments to enable a gradual winding-down of Denmark's authority on the islands was shelved after Denmark's Prime Minister Poul Nyrup Rasmussen said that subsidies would stop after four years if the islanders voted for independence.

2004 Jóannes Eidesgaard (JF) became prime minister, leading a coalition of the SF, the Javnaðarflokkurin (JF) (Social Democrats) and the Fólkaflokkurin (FF) (People's Party).

2006 A trust fund agreement was signed with the World Bank, whereby the Faroe Islands provides development collaboration with the Pacific island of Palau. Iceland and the Faroe Islands signed a special economic treaty granting many free trade arrangements for goods, services, capital and workers.

2008 In parliamentary elections held on 19 January, the Tjóðveldisflokkurin (TF) (Republican Party) won 23.3 per cent of the vote (8 seats out of 33), the Sambandsflokkurin (SF) (Union Party) 21 per cent (7), the FF 20.1 per cent (7), the JF 19.4 per cent (6), the Mioflokkurin (MF) (Centre Party) 8.4 per cent (3), and the Sjálvstýrisflokkurin (Home Rule Party) 7.2 per cent (2). Turnout was 89.2 per cent. Jóannes Eidesgaard remained as prime minister.

Political structure

Constitution

The Faroe Islands were administered as a Danish county until they achieved home rule in 1948. The Faroe Islands are a Danish external territory, electing two members to the Danish parliament, which maintains responsibility for constitutional, foreign and defence matters. A High Commissioner represents the Danish government and advises on joint affairs.

Form of state

Parliamentary democratic dependency

National legislature

Internal affairs are under the legislative control of the Løgting (parliament) which has 32 members elected by proportional representation (PR) in seven constituencies, with up to five supplementary seats dependent upon the numbers of people voting. The term of office is four years. Universal suffrage is 18 years.

The Landsstyri (a government of six members) is formed, based on the strength of the parties in the Løgting. The Løgmadur (prime minister) has to ratify all Løgting laws.

All Danish legislation must be submitted to the Landsstyri before becoming law.

Last elections

19 January 2008 (parliamentary)

Results: Parliamentary: the Tjóðveldisflokkurin (TF) (Republican Party) won 23.3 per cent of the vote (8 seats out of 33), the Sambandsflokkurin (SF) (Union Party) 21 per cent (7), the Fólkaflokkurin (FF) (People's Party) 20.1 per cent (7), the Javnaðarflokkurin (JF) (Social Democrats) 19.4 per cent (6), the Mioflokkurin (MF) (Centre Party) 8.4 per cent (3), and the Sjálvstýrisflokkurin (Home Rule Party) 7.2 per cent (2). Turnout was 89.2 per cent.

Next elections

January 2012 (parliamentary)

Political parties

Ruling party

Coalition government of the Javnaðarflokkurin (JF) (Social Democrats),

KEY FACTS

Official name: Føroyar (Faroe Islands)

Head of State: Queen Margrethe II of Denmark, represented by the High Commissioner Søren Christensen (from 1 Aug 2005)

Head of government: Prime Minister Jóannes Eidesgaard (JF) (from 2004; re-elected 19 Jan 2008)

Ruling party: Coalition government of the Javnaðarflokkurin (JF) (Social Democrats), Tjóðveldisflokkurin (TF) (Republican Party) and Mioflokkurin (MF) (Centre Party) (from 19 Jan 2008)

Area: 1,399 square km (18 islands)

Population: 48,353 (2004); (48,500* in 2007)

Capital: Tórshavn

Official language: Faroese, Danish

Currency: Faroese krone (FKr) (same value as Danish krone)

Exchange rate: FKr4.70 per US$ (Jul 2008)

GDP per capita: US$22,000 (2003)

GDP real growth: 10.00% (2003)

Labour force: 24,250 (2003)

Unemployment: 1.00% (2003)

Inflation: 5.10% (2003)

Balance of trade: -US$51.00 million (2003)

* estimated figure

Tjóðveldisflokkurin (TF) (Republican Party) and Mioflokkurin (MF) (Centre Party) (from 19 Jan 2008)

Main opposition party

Tjóðveldisflokkurin (TF) (Republican Party)

Political situation

Praise for the Faroe Islands' economy was forthcoming in 2008, when the US Moody's Investor Services boosted Faroe Islands foreign currency rating to AA+, in April. The strong performance of the fishing industry coupled with a decade of the islands' ability to manage economy growth, based on deep-sea fishing and the withdrawal of government guarantees and subsidies meant the economic crisis of the early 1990s was definitely over. Nevertheless Canada has only recently opened its ports to Faroe Islander prawn (shrimp) fishing fleets, closed to them since 2004 (for the second time within two years), as Canada claimed illegal fishing was depleting stocks. International negotiations begun, in 2008, are hoped will resolve the matter.

The rise in importance of oil exploration has also grown in the last decade and in February 2007 the independent company, Faroe Petroleum, was awarded rights to explore for oil and gas in regions between Scotland and the Faroe Islands. In November it agreed to sub-lease two exploration wells near the Faroe Islands to the UK's CIECO Exploration and Production.

Conservation is an important concern for Faroese but as in so many places worldwide the delicate balance between sustained growth and the natural environment always threatens to tip in favour of one or the other.

Population

48,353 (2004); (48,500* in 2007)

Last census: July 2002: 47,350

Population density: 33 inhabitants per sq km (2000).

Annual growth rate: 1.2 per cent (2003)

Ethnic make-up

Scandinavian

Religions

Evangelical Lutheran Church of Denmark (85 per cent). The Faroe Islands are a diocese under the Danish national church. Of the various smaller religious communities the largest is the Plymouth Brethren.

Health

Life expectancy: 79 years (estimate 2003)

Fertility rate/Maternal mortality rate: Two births per woman (2003)

Birth rate/Death rate: 14 births per 1,000 population; nine deaths per 1,000 population (2003).

Child (under 5 years) mortality rate (per 1,000): Seven per 1,000 live births (2003)

Main cities

Tórshavn (Thorshavn), on the island of Streymoy (capital, estimated population 18,573 in 2005), Klaksvík (4,722).

Languages spoken

Faroese (derived from Old Norse) and Danish. Icelandic, English, Norwegian and Swedish are also widely spoken and understood.

Official language/s

Faroese, Danish

Media

Press

In Faroese, the only newspapers are published daily, including Sosialurin (www.sosialurin.fo), Dimmalætting (www.dimma.fo) and Vikublaðið (www.vikublad.fo).

Broadcasting

The national, public broadcasting company is Kringvarp Føroya (www.uf.fo).

Radio: The public network Útvarp Føroya (ÚF) and three other stations broadcast on several frequencies to provide national radio coverage. Rás (www.ras2.fo), Linden Kristligt Kringvarp (www.lindin.fo) a Christian broadcast, and Sundfelli broadcast in Faroese.

Television: The public network Sjónvarp Føroya (Svf) (www.svf.fo) provides between eight hours (weekdays) up to 15 hours (weekend) with local news and information and imported, dubbed, foreign entertainment programmes.

Advertising

Print material, outdoor and television attract most advertising revenues. There is no advertising on radio, and poster sites are heavily regulated.

Economy

The economy is heavily dependent on fishing and is vulnerable to international price fluctuations. The collapse of the fishing industry in the early 1990s, due to falling world prices and catches, and the banking crisis from 1992 to 1996 devastated the Faroese economy, reducing GDP to two-thirds of its size in the 1980s. The unemployment rate was close to 20 per cent and 10 per cent of the population emigrated.

In 1998, the economy began to recover due to rising fish catches. Immigration was high, implying that many who left during the crisis returned. Oil business activities have also improved the economic situation. Economic policy focussed on free market reform and public spending reduction.

The economy grew strongly for several years until 2002, but a period of stagnation followed. Fishing went into decline again in 2003 with a drop in prices and volume. The economy contracted in 2003, recovering slowly in the following years. There was marked improvement by 2006, when GDP grew by around 10 per cent, attributed largely to increased consumption and investment, especially in the housing market. The upward trend is not expected to be sustained, because of limited production capacity and shortage of labour.

Labour market and unemployment

Unemployment has fallen sharply from 12 per cent in 1997 to 5 per cent in 1999.

External trade

As an autonomous overseas territory of Denmark the Faroe Islands negotiates it own bilateral trade agreements. It has executive and legislative powers over marine resources and trade relations. It is also a separate customs territory from Denmark and the EU.

Foreign trade is mainly with the EU countries, which receive around 80 per cent of exports. The EU accounts for around 58 per cent of imports, mainly consumer goods and raw materials.

Imports

Machinery and transport equipment, consumer goods, raw materials and semi-manufactures, fuels, fish and salt.

Main sources: Denmark (46.2 per cent total, 2005), Norway (18.2 per cent), Germany (8.2 per cent), Spain (7.5 per cent), Iceland (4.8 per cent)

Exports

Fish and fish products (over 90 per cent), stamps and ships.

Main destinations: Denmark (38.2 per cent total, 2005), UK (29.6 per cent), Nigeria (8.9 per cent), Norway (6.1 per cent), The Netherlands (4.3 per cent)

Agriculture

Farming

Sheep-rearing is an important activity on the Faroe Islands. There are 70,000 sheep ranging free on the islands, providing meat and wool for the use of the inhabitants. Cattle are also kept for milk and meat. The islands have to import meat and other agricultural products, but have become self-sufficient in milk. Increasing co-operation among agricultural organisations has been fostered to make the islands as self-sufficient as possble. Potatoes are grown and also hay for the cows reared for milk production.

Crop and livestock production in 2005 included 1,500 tonnes (t) potatoes, 591,491t meat in total, 77t beef, 521t mutton and lamb, 119t sheepskins and 10t cattle hides.

Fishing

Fishing is the dominant economic activity, acounting for 97 per cent of exports. The main fish stocks are cod, haddock and coalfish. Annual fish catches in excess of 600,000 tonnes have been the basis of sustained growth, with exports at eur80 million (US$124 million) in 2007. The rising global price of fish has also contributed to the industry's profits as well as the investment in salmon and trout sea farming. Nevertheless, the business is highly vulnerable to fluctuations in not only world prices but also in amounts caught. In 2004, the total marine fish catch was 585,835 tonnes and the total crustacean catch was 9,346 tonnes.

Industry and manufacturing
Most industrial activities are connected to the fishing sector. They include processing plants and shipyards, as well as the making of nets, ropes, etc. Small industries include breweries, building components, fibreglass boats, computer software, food and milk products, tinned fish and spun and wollen goods.

Tourism
Tourism is second in importance to fishing, but is not a major activity. Efforts have been made to develop its potential in order to help diversify the economy. Most foreign visitors come from Scandinavia.

Hydrocarbons
There is a possibility of offshore oil between the Faroe Islands and the Shetland Islands.
An agreement with the UK in 1999 established a boundary, paving the way for increased exploration activity on the Faroese side. The first exploration licences were awarded in August 2000.
Subsequent oil exploration in the waters around the Faroe Islands have produced disappointing results, but a significant oil find in UK waters near the maritime border was announced in December 2002 by a consortium led by US-based Amerada Hess, which led to an increase in exploration in 2003 and 2004. The Faroese government does not expect any oil field development before 2007. A second licensing round was launched in August 2004 and the first licences issued in January 2005.
The Faroe Islands relies on imported petroleum products. It does not currently produce or import gas and coal.

Banking and insurance
Monetary policy and administration is headed by the Danish central bank (Danmarks Nationalbank).
When the banking crisis began in 1992, there were two big banks, one small private bank and savings banks in the Faroe Islands. One of the big banks was owned by Den Danske Bank. By the end of the crisis, the small bank had gone into bankruptcy, the two big banks had merged and were taken over by the Home Rule authorities and the savings banks were still in business. The savings banks and the merged bank function as banks under the same law.
Central bank
Danmarks Nationalbank

Time
GMT (daylight saving, end-March to end-September, GMT plus one hour).

Geography
The Faroe Islands are a group of 18 islands (of which 17 are inhabited) in the North Atlantic Ocean, south-east of Iceland and north-west of the north coast of Scotland. The main island is Streymoy and nowhere on the archipelago is over 3km from the sea. The islands are rocky with little opportunity for growing crops or forestry, although grass is plentiful.
Hemisphere
Northern

Climate
Mild winters and cool summers; usually overcast; can be foggy and windy.

Entry requirements
Passports
Required by all.
Visa
Even though a Danish territory, visas for Denmark are not valid for the Faroe Islands unless specified on the permit. For a business visa, an original letter of invitation from a local company or organisation, giving details about purpose of visit and duration of stay must accompany an application, along with evidence of hotel reservations.

Health (for visitors)
As for Denmark.
Advisable precautions
Without appropriate clothing for the climate hypothermia is a hazard.

Public holidays (national)
Fixed dates
1 Jan (New Year's Day), Apr 25 (Flag Day, afternoon only), 5 Jun (Constitution Day), 28 Jul (St Olav's Eve, afternoon only), 29 Jul (St Olav's Day), 24–26 Dec (Christmas Holiday), 31 Dec (New Year's Eve).
Variable dates
Maundy Thursday, Good Friday, Easter Monday, Prayer Day (Apr/May), Ascension Day, Whit Monday.

Working hours
Banking
Mon–Fri: 0930–1600 (Thu 0930–1800).
Business
Mon–Fri: 0800–1600 or 0830–1630.
Government
Mon–Fri: generally 0900–1700.
Shops
Mon–Fri: 0800–1700 or 0900–1730, Sat: close at 1300 or 1400.

Telecommunications
Mobile/cell phones
GSM 900 services cover virtually the entire territories.

Getting there
Air
National airline: Atlantic Airways has regular flights to Denmark, Norway, Iceland, Scotland, England and Greenland.
International airport/s: Vágar Airport (FAE) on the island of Vágar, located near the town of Sørvágur, a ferry links the island to Streymoy. Facilities include bank, restaurant, bar and shops.

BUSINESS DIRECTORY

The addresses listed below are a selection only. While World of Information makes every endeavour to check these addresses, we cannot guarantee that changes have not been made, especially to telephone numbers and area codes. We would welcome any corrections.

Telephone area codes
The international direct dialling (IDD) for the Faroe Islands is +298. There are no area codes.

Useful telephone numbers
Emergency services000

Chambers of Commerce
Faroe Islands Trade Council, 12 Bryggjubakki, PO Box 259, Tórshavn 110 (tel: 353-100; fax: 353-101; e-mail: trade@trade.fo).

Banking
Central bank
Landsbanki Føroya, Müllers hús, í Gongini, PO Box 229, Tórshavn 110 (tel: 318-305; fax: 318-537; e-mail: landsbank@landsbank.fo).

Danmarks Nationalbank, Havnegade 5, DK-1093 Copenhagen (tel: (+45) 3363-6363; fax: (+45) 3363-7103; e-mail: info@nationalbanken.dk).

Travel information
Atlantic Airways, Vagar Airport, FR-380 (tel: 333-700; fax: 333-380).

Maersk Air, Aarvegur 6, PO Box 3225, FO-110 Tórshavn (tel: 333-700; fax: 318-670; e-mail: ff@olivant.fo).

Smyril Line, Jonas Broncksgota 37, PO Box 370, FO-110 Tórshavn (tel: 315-900; fax: 315-707; e-mail: office@smyril-line.fo).

Air Iceland, Vagar Airport, FO-380 Sorvagur (tel: 332-755; fax: 332-280).

The Faroe Islands Tourist Board Copenhagen, Hovedvagtsgade 8, 2, DK-1103 Copenhagen K, Denmark (tel: (+45) 3314-8383; fax: (+45) 3393-8575).

Faroe Travel, PO Box 1199, FO-110 Tórshavn (tel: 312-600; fax: 319-200).

National tourist organisation offices

Faroe Islands Tourist Board, Undir Bryggjubakka 17, PO Box 118, FO-110 Torshaven, (tel: 355-800; fax: 355-801; email: tourist@tourist.fo; internet site; www.tourist.fo).

Other useful addresses

British Consulate, Yviri vid Strond 19, PO Box 19, FR-3800 Tórshavn (tel: 313-510).

The Faroese Government, PO Box 64, FR-110 Tórshavn (fax: 314-942).

Faroese Press Agency, P/f Salvará, Tjarnardeild 12, Tórshavn.

Sjónvarp Føroya (television broadcasting), PO Box 21, FR-3800 Tórshavn (tel: 317-780).

Útvarp Føroya (general broadcasting), PO Box 328, FR-3800 Tórshavn (tel: 316-566).

Internet sites

Danish embassy with useful information on the Faroes: http://www.denmarkemb.org

Faroe business news: www.news.fo

Faroe Islands general site: www.faroe.com

Faroe Islands tourist site: www.faroeislands.com

Fiji

Fijian politics of late have been determined by the fault line that continues to divide the island nation. In simple terms, this is the ethnic division between the country's native Fijian population and the Indian population which owes its presence in Fiji to the British. Under colonial rule indentured Indian labour was introduced to Fiji to work on the sugar plantations. In the twenty first century the Indians are in a majority, a position which creates understandable unease on the part of the Fijians, while the Indians feel resentment that they have been unable to play a full part in the country's government. The *Bose Levu Vakaturaga* (Great Council of Chiefs) is the assembly of traditional chiefs of Fiji that meets annually to discuss matters of concern to the Fijian people (but not necessarily the Indian people). The Council appoints the President of Fiji – a power embodied in the 1997 constitution and seen by most Indians as excluding them from fair representation.

Communal tensions in Fiji improved after the coup in 2000. However, a rumour that President Josefa Iloilovatu was to announce his retirement in 2006 risked upsetting the delicate balance between indigenous Fijians and ethnic Indians. The president, who first came to power in July 2000 and was later re-appointed by the Great Council of Chiefs in 2001, has won the respect of many Fijians as he attempted to find common ground between the various racial and political groupings.

The expected happens

Sure enough, in December 2006, Republic of Fiji Military Forces (RFMF) Commander, Commodore Bainimarama, announced that he had assumed executive power, dismissing the elected government and declaring a state of emergency. Commodore Bainimarama later claimed to have returned executive authority to the president, with himself acting as interim prime minister. An interim government was also sworn in. Bainimarama had been critical of the elected government and, on a number of occasions had threatened to take steps to remove the government.

A pattern had thus begun to emerge in Fijian politics. In 1987 the democratic rule of Fiji had been interrupted by a military coup led by then Lieutenant Colonel Sitiveni Rabuka. A four month period of interim rule by the Governor General ended with a second coup by Rabuka on 25 September 1987. Rabuka abrogated the 1970 Constitution and declared Fiji a republic. A short period of military government, and two subsequent interim administrations followed and a new constitution was promulgated on 25 July 1990 with elections held in May 1992.

Fiji had already suffered a period of political, social and economic instability beginning in 2000, this time somewhat more dramatically, when George Speight seized control of the parliament and took hostage Prime Minister Mahendra Chaudhry and some members of his government for 56 days. The hostage-taking was followed by the purported abrogation of the 1997 Constitution; the departure of then President Mara and the installation of three successive unelected interim administrations. Rulings by the Fiji High Court and Court of Appeal that the 1997 Constitution remained the supreme law of the land led to the general elections of September 2001 and Fiji's subsequent return to parliamentary democracy under the prime ministership of Laisenia Qarase, who had led the caretaker and interim governments.

The general elections of 2001 were won by the United Fiji Party (UFP), headed by interim Prime Minister Qarase. Following these elections, and in accordance with a constitutional provision for multi-party representation in cabinet, Prime Minister Qarase invited members of the Fiji Labour Party (FLP) to join his cabinet. Qarase refused however, to include FLP leader Chaudhry in the cabinet. In November 2004, the FLP announced that they were no longer interested in participating in the Qarase-led government. Prime Minister Qarase's SDL government was returned to office with a narrow majority at the elections held in May 2006. A multi-party cabinet, including members of the FLP, was then formed.

On 5 December 2007, Bainimarama announced that he had assumed executive power, that he had dismissed the Qarase Government and declared a state of

KEY FACTS

Official name: Republic of the Fiji Islands

Head of State: President President Ratu Josefa Iloilovatu Uluivuda (from 2000; dismissed in 2006 and re-instated by the Great Council of Chiefs, 3 Jan 2007)

Head of government: Head of government: Prime Minister (interim) Commodore Voreqe 'Frank' Bainimarama (sworn in 4 Jan 2007)

Ruling party: Coalition: Fiji Labour Party (FLP) and National Alliance Party of Fiji (NAPF) (since Jan 2007)

Area: 18,333 square km (about 332 islands, 110 inhabited)

Population: 869,000 (2007)

Capital: Suva (on Viti Levu)

Official language: English, Fijian and Hindi

Currency: Fijian dollar (F$) = 100 cents

Exchange rate: F$1.48 per US$ (Jul 2008)

GDP per capita: US$3,921 (2007)

GDP real growth: -4.40% (2007)*

Labour force: 355,000 (2004)

Inflation: 4.80% (2007)

Balance of trade: -US$1.09 billion (2006)

Foreign debt: US$112.80 million (2004)

Visitor numbers: 545,000 (2006)*

* estimated figure

emergency. On 4 January, Bainimarama claimed to have returned executive power to President Iloilo and, on the following day, he assumed the office of prime minister. Bainimarama then appointed his interim government. Following the removal of the democratically elected government, not for the first time, Fiji was suspended from the Councils of the Commonwealth.

Economic consequences

The political crisis of 2000 saw the Fiji economy decline by 2.8 per cent in that year. This contraction was accompanied by substantial job losses, and migration of skilled and professional workers, the latter trend declining but persisting to the present. Since 2000, business confidence and private investment have picked up, but not to a point sufficient to drive sustained growth. Skills shortages affect most sectors of the economy, notably the construction industry. The economy recorded reasonable growth in the period 2001–04, driven by a resurgent tourism industry. Growth in 2005 was only 2.1 per cent. This decline from the high growth of 3.9 per cent in 2004 was due principally to the termination of preferential trading arrangements for sugar and garments (affecting exports to the United States), Fiji's major manufacturing and export industries.

The budget for 2007, announced in November, is the first part of a new 5-year Strategic Development Plan. The central objective of the Plan is to reach a target of 5 per cent economic growth per year. The budget estimated growth for 2006 of 3.6 per cent, driven mainly by tourism, and a projection of 2 per cent growth for 2007. Government foreign reserves were estimated to be 3.3 months of imports for 2006, and are expected to remain at similar levels for 2007. Remittances totalled FJD311 million (US$185 million) for 2005 and are now the second largest foreign exchange earner. Government debt has risen to 50 per cent of GDP, and the government intends to attempt to maintain a net deficit of not more than 2 per cent of GDP for the next five years in order to see government debt fall to 45 per cent of GDP. The 2006 budget deficit was estimated to be 3.2 per cent of GDP and the projection for 2007 is 2 per cent, in line with the plans outlined above.

Sugar isn't so sweet

Fiji also expected to feel the effects of the loss of concessions to key markets for its textiles and sugar in 2005 and 2006. The sugar industry will need to become self-reliant if it is to survive the ending of EU sugar price subsidies, expected in 2007. The costs of restructuring are high; upgrading of the sugar mills is estimated at F$126 million (US$60 million), in addition to F$40 million (US$19 million) to pay small sugar cane farmers to leave the sector and F$40 million (US$19 million) for improving transport and handling systems.

Sugar cane growers claim that the government's restructuring programme is moving forward too rapidly and infrastructural problems, such as the decrepit railways, which have contributed to the sugar industry's plight, are being neglected.

Tourism should be Fiji's success story. Travel and tourism in 2005 is estimated to have contributed 12.0 per cent to GDP, provided over 95,000 jobs (around 1 in every 3.6 jobs, according to the World Travel and Tourism Council) and generated some US$545 million. Capital investments were estimated at US$140.2 million.

Market capitalisation on the South Pacific Stock Exchange topped F$1 billion (US$585 million) for the first time in 2005, with 16 listed companies. However, the tourism industry inevitably suffers from Fiji's political instability. Australian tourists are highly sensitive to any threat of instability, while Fiji's tourist product is very similar to that offered by many of its South Sea neighbours.

KEY INDICATORS — Fiji

	Unit	2003	2004	2005	2006	2007
Population	m	0.83	0.84	0.85	0.86	0.87
Gross domestic product (GDP)	US$bn	1.79	2.63	2.82	3.17	*3.41
GDP per capita	US$	2,151	2,143	3,296	3,674	*3,921
GDP real growth	%	3.0	3.9	0.7	3.6	*-4.4
Inflation	%	3.0	2.4	2.4	2.5	4.8
Exports (fob) (goods)	US$m	442.0	703.7	698.0	711.0	*1,210.1
Imports (cif) (goods)	US$m	642.0	1,320.2	1,610.0	1,802.0	*2,890.4
Balance of trade	US$m	-200.0	-616.5	-912.0	-1,091.0	*-1,680.4
Current account	US$m	-230.0	-160.0	-476.0	-552.0	*-507.0
Total reserves minus gold	US$m	423.6	478.1	314.7	–	–
Foreign exchange	US$m	393.4	446.1	284.8	–	–
Exchange rate	per US$	1.90	1.72	1.68	1.66	1.55

* estimated figure

Risk assessment

Economic	Poor
Political	Moderate/unstable
Regional stability	Good

COUNTRY PROFILE

Historical profile

1643 The islands were first sighted by a European.
1874 Fiji became a British crown colony.
1879–1916 Over 60,000 Indian indentured labourers were imported to work on sugar plantations. The government in India stopped the recruitment of labourers.
1920 All indenture labour agreements were ended.
1963 General elections were held with the first majority Indian-led political party standing. The great council of chiefs signed the Wakaya Letter that asserted Fijian paramountcy.
1966 The Fijian Alliance Party was formed.
1968 Ratu Sir Kamisese Mara, Fiji's first prime minister was given the first instruments of independence. The Fijian Alliance Party won elections by appealing to both Indians and Fijians.
1970 On 10 October Fiji became independent and introduced a British-style political system with a new constitution. The British monarch remained Head of State, a bicameral parliament was introduced and a separate electoral roll for each ethnic group was provided.
1972 The first independent general elections were won by Ratu Mara's Fijian Alliance Party.
1977 Internal dispute between the leaders of the (ethnic Indian) National Federation Party (NFP), which had won a majority in the lower house of parliament elections resulted in a failure to form a government and Ratu Mara was recalled to power. The Fijian Alliance Party had won a majority in the upper house of parliament.

1981 The ethnic Fijian Western United Front political party was formed.
1985 The Fijian Labour Party (FLP) was formed, led by Timoci Bavadra.
1987 The NFP-FLP won the general elections and formed the first Indian-dominated government, led by Timoci Bavadra. The Alliance Party became defunct. Lieutenant Colonel Sitiveni Rabuka led two coups that overthrew the government as a republic was declared and all ties to the British monarch severed. Fiji was expelled from the British Commonwealth and overseas aid was suspended.
1990 A new constitution was promulgated and considered by foreign observers as racist, as it enshrined the supremacy of ethnic Fijians by allocating 37 seats to Fijians, 27 seats to Indians and 6 to others in the lower house of parliament.
1992 The Soqosoqo Duavata ni Lewenivanua (SDL) (Fijian People's Party), led by Rabuka won general elections. Rabuka became prime minister.
1994 The great council of chiefs appoint Ratu Sir Kamisese Mara as president.
1995 The president appoints a team to review the 1990 constitution.
1997 After three years of discussion a new non-discriminatory constitution was enacted. Fiji was re-admitted to the Commonwealth.
1999 The FLP won general elections and formed a coalition government with the Christian Democratic Alliance, Party of National Unity and the Fijian Association Party. Mahendra Chaudhry, the first Fijian of Indian descent, became prime minister. President Ratu Sir Kamisese Mara was sworn in for a five-year term.
2000 In a coup, led by George Speight, Chaudhry and his cabinet were held captive by an armed group seeking more power for ethnic Fijians and forced to resign from office. The great council of chiefs ordered President Mara to sack the government. Supporters of Speight rioted in Suva while he called for the 1997 constitution to be scrapped. The Commonwealth suspended Fiji's membership. All the hostages were freed as Commodore Frank Bainimarama seized power and restored order. President Mara retired from office and the great council of chiefs appointed the father-in-law of Speight, Josefa Iloilovatu Uluivuda (commonly known as Ratu Josefa Iloilo) as president. Laisenia Qarase was appointed prime minister of an all-Fijian interim government. The High Court ruled that the deposed government of Mahendra Chaudhry should be reinstated.
2001 The Court of Appeal ruled that the interim government was illegal, and stated that the 1997 multi-racial constitution should remain in place. President Iloilo was re-appointed by the great council of chiefs for a five-year term; he re-appointed Laisenia Qarase as caretaker prime minister. In general election, observed by the Commonwealth, Qarase's SDL won, but since it failed to secure an outright majority, it joined with the Matanitu Vanua (MV) (Conservative Alliance Party) in a coalition government. Qarase was sworn in as prime minister; his cabinet barred all ethnic Indians.
2002 Samisoni Speight Tikonasau, the brother of George Speight, was elected to parliament, reflecting the extent of George Speight's support among the voting public.
2003 A cyclone destroyed homes and flooded wide areas of the north and east of the country. The High Court ruled that the FLP should be allowed its seats in the cabinet.
2004 Ratu Sir Kamisese Mara died. The FLP declined a government role in favour of official opposition duties.
2006 Prime Minister Qarase agreed to review the Reconciliation, Tolerance and Unity Bill. President Uluivuda was re-appointed. The MV agreed to dissolve as a party and its members to merge with the ruling SDL, after it changed its stance on working to free its party members convicted of coup related offences. The ruling SDL won 36 out of 71 seats in the general elections and the FLP won 31 seats. The FLP entered into coalition with the SDL. In a bloodless, military coup d'état led by Commodore 'Frank' Josaia Voreqe Bainimarama, the president and government were dismissed. Bainimarama assumed the presidency and Jona Senilagakali Baravilala was appointed as the interim prime minister. Fiji was suspended from the Commonwealth.
2007 Under pressure from the great council of chiefs, Bainimarama reinstated Uluivuda as president on 3 January and Bainimarama became interim prime minister on 4 January. Bainimarama announced that parliamentary election would be held in 2010. Bainimarama dismisses the great council of chiefs, which refused to endorse his government and proposed vice president. A six-month long state of emergency was lifted at midnight on 7 June, re-instated in September and lifted again in October; restrictions on public gatherings and on the media were not lifted.
2008 In February Bainimarama convened a great council of chiefs with himself as chairman. On 1 July Fiji withdrew its participation in the Pacific Islands Forum – Joint Working Group on Fiji, leading to fears that the elections scheduled for 2009 would not go ahead.

Political structure

Constitution

The constitution was promulgated on 25 July 1990 and amended on 25 July 1997 to allow non-ethnic Fijians more say in government and to make multi-party government mandatory. Bars against non-Fijians becoming prime minister and president were removed.
The Court of Appeal upheld the 1997 constitution in 2001.
The constitution states any political party with more than 10 per cent of the seats in parliament must be offered a cabinet position.
Voting: universal suffrage, over 21 years.

The executive

Executive authority is vested in the president, who is elected by the Great Council of Chiefs for a maximum of two five-year terms. A presidential council advises the president on matters of national importance. The president is the commander-in-chief of the military forces.

National legislature

There is a bicameral parliament – the Senate (upper house) (34 seats – 24 appointed by the Great Council of Chiefs, nine appointed by the president, and one appointed by the council of Rotuma) and the House of Representatives (lower house) (71 seats – 23 reserved for ethnic Fijians, 19 reserved for ethnic Indians, three reserved for other ethnic groups, one reserved for the council of Rotuma constituency encompassing the whole of Fiji and 25 open seats). Members serve five-year terms.
The prime minister is usually the leader of the majority party or coalition in parliament and is appointed by the president for a five-year term. The 18-member cabinet is appointed by the prime minister from among the members of parliament and is responsible to parliament.
The Great Council of Chiefs (GCC) comprises the highest-ranking members of the traditional chief system. The composition of the GCC was changed from 24 August 2007, when the number of members was reduced from 55 to 52, made up of 42 members representing chiefs from the 14 provinces, six co-opted members, three representatives of the chiefs of Rotuma and the Fijian affairs minister. The president, vice president and prime minister are no longer members, and commoners are excluded.

Legal system

Based on the British legal system.

Last elections

6–13 May 2006 (parliamentary)
Results: Parliamentary: Soqosoqo Duavata ni Lewenivanua (SDL) (United Fiji Party) won 44.6 per cent (36 seats out of 71); Fiji Labour Party (FLP) won 39.2 per cent of the vote (31 seats); United

People's Party (UPP) 0.84 per cent (two seats); and Independents 4.9 per cent (two seats). Turn-out was 87.7 per cent.
Next elections
March 2009 (parliamentary)

Political parties
Ruling party
Coalition: Fiji Labour Party (FLP) and National Alliance Party of Fiji (NAPF) (since Jan 2007)
Main opposition party
Soqosoqo Duavata ni Lewenivanua (SDL) (United Fiji Party)

Population
869,000 (2007)
Last census: August 1996: 775,077
Population density: 44 inhabitants per square km. Urban population: 45.2 per cent (2002).
Annual growth rate: 1.0 per cent 1994–2004 (WHO 2006)
Ethnic make-up
Ethnic Fijians represent about 51 per cent of the population. Indians comprise about 44 per cent. There are also some Europeans, other Pacific islanders and Chinese.
Religions
Methodist (37 per cent), Roman Catholic (9 per cent), Hindu (38 per cent), Muslim (8 per cent).

Education
Fiji showed remarkable progress in access to basic education in the years following 1996. Basic education was boosted with the introduction of tuition assistance for primary schools in 1994. Totalling about F$4.8 million (US$2.3 million) annually, this assistance enabled primary schools to meet their annual development costs.
Primary schooling lasts for eight years; secondary education lasts for a possible seven years, with intermediate stages of four-year junior secondary, two-year senior secondary and one-year seventh form schooling. Progression through all stages culminates in examinations. Lessons are taught mainly in English but may also be taught in Fijian and Hindi.
The University of the South Pacific, which serves 10 English-speaking territories in the South Pacific, is the main provider of higher education.
Government expenditure on education increased through the 1990s and typically amounts to 16.21 per cent of the national budget.
In September 2004, the EU announced a US$44 million programme aimed at improving the quality of education in Fiji. It will assist more than 70 per cent of primary schools and 50 per cent of secondary schools.
Literacy rate: 93 per cent adult rate; 99 per cent youth rate (15–24) (Unesco 2005).
Compulsory years: 6 to 14.
Enrolment rate: 110.45 per cent gross enrolment in primary education (including repitition rates).

Health
Per capita total expenditure on health (2003) was US$220; of which per capita government spending was US$135, at the international dollar rate, (WHO 2006).
Health care facilities in Fiji are barely adequate for routine medical problems. Two major hospitals, the Lautoka Hospital and the Colonial War Memorial Hospital in Suva, provide emergency and outpatient services. Other hospitals and clinics provide only a limited range of health services.
Access to clean water is available to 47 per cent of the total population.
HIV/Aids
HIV prevalence: 0.1 per cent aged 15–49 in 2003 (World Bank)
Life expectancy: 69 years, 2004 (WHO 2006)
Fertility rate/Maternal mortality rate: 2.9 births per woman, 2004 (WHO 2006)
Birth rate/Death rate: 23 births per 1,000 population; six deaths per 1,000 population (2003).
Child (under 5 years) mortality rate (per 1,000): 16 per 1,000 live births (World Bank)

Main cities
Suva (capital, on Viti Levu, estimated population 177,300 in 2003), Lautoka (on Viti Levu, 45,700), Nadi (on Viti Levu, 32,600), Labasa (on Vanua Levu, 25,400), Nausori (on Viti Levu, 22,800).

Languages spoken
English is widely used in business circles. Fijian dialects are spoken by the indigenous Fijians (Bauan is the most spoken). The Indian community speaks Fiji-Hindi. Cantonese is also spoken.
Since 2003, compulsory classes teaching the Fijian and Hindi languages have been introduced in some primary and secondary schools in order to avert the threat of losing the ethnic languages of the country.
Official language/s
English, Fijian and Hindi

Media
Other news agencies: ABC Pacific Beat: www.radioaustralia.net.au/pacbeat
Pacific Magazine:
www.pacificmagazine.net
Press
Journalistic standards are generally regarded as vigorous.
Dailies: In English, newspapers include Fiji Daily Post (www.fijidailypost.com), with its Fijian The Fiji Times (www.fijitimes.com) has business news and Fiji Sun (www.sun.com.fj), which is a tabloid.
Weeklies: In Fijian Nai Lalakai takes stories from The Fiji Times (www.fijitimes.com/nailalakai.aspx) and Na Volasiga, covering current affairs. Two Hindi language publications include Sartaj and Shanti Dut which features national and international news. The Pacific University Journalism publishes USP Bulletin and online news (www.usp.ac.fj/journ/).
Business: In English Fiji Islands Business (www.islandsbusiness.com) and Island Business are twin publications with varing domestic or international markets.
Periodicals: In English, the monthly Pacific (www.pacificmagazine.net) has regional news articles.
Broadcasting
Radio: Radio is the most popular medium for entertainment, news and information, particularly on remote islands.
The Fiji Broadcasting Corporation (FBCL) (www.radiofiji.com.fj) network has five stations providing a range of programmes based on the Fijian-, English or Hindi-languages. The Communications Fiji Ltd (www.cfl.com.fj) has a commercial network of five stations broadcasting to difference audiences including Radio Navtarang, in Hindi and Viti FM, in Fijian and FM96 for the under 25 years age group. Another commercial station, in English, is Radio Fiji Gold (www.radiofiji.com.fj).
The UK-based BBC World Service, the French Radio Internationale and Radio Australia are broadcast through local FM relay stations.
Television: The national public TV station is Fiji TV (www.fijitv.com.fj), which also has a satellite, pay-to-view service, provided by Sky Fiji, with over 20 channels. Local programmes are provided in Fijian, Hindi and English. Services are also transmitted to other Pacific territories, for a fee.
Advertising
Local press, radio and cinema outlets, as well as a few outdoor poster and billboard sites, provide venues for advertising.

Economy
The Fijian economy has been highly dependent on sugar exports and tourism. However, the economy is relatively diverse with gold, silver and limestone mining contributing to Fijian exports. Remittances from expatriates are an important source of foreign exchange.
Confidence in Fiji as an investment destination weakened following the 2000 coup, which resulted in job losses and emigration of skilled workers. Fragile growth returned after the lifting of sanctions and the return of donor aid. Increases in consumer spending and tourism spurred GDP growth to 4.4 per

cent in 2002, but this was not sustained due to the downturn in gold and sugar production. Growth fell to 2.1 per cent by 2005, as the loss of protected sugar and textile exports took effect. Tourism, which continued to expand, cushioned the economy and is expected to form the basis of recovery.
In November 2006, a five-year strategic development plan was inaugurated with the object of reaching five per cent annual growth.
In October 2007 the EU wrote to the Interim Government informing it that the EU would be with-holding the US$6.25m allocation of aid to the sugar industry for 2006 as it was not satisfied with Fiji's progress towards a return to democracy. Payments for 2007 would depend on future progress.

External trade

Fiji is a member of the South Pacific Regional Trade and Economic Co-operation Agreement (Sparteca) along with 12 other regional nations, which allows products duty free access by Pacific Island Forum members to Australian and New Zealand markets (subject to the country of origin restrictions). It is also a member of the Melanesian Spearhead Group (with Papua New Guinea, Solomon Islands and Vanuatu) as a sub-regional trade group, whereby customs tariffs have been harmonised and a free trade agreement is in negotiation.

Imports

Principal imports are manufactured goods, petroleum products, chemicals, machinery and transport equipment and food.
Main sources: Singapore (34.5 per cent total, 2006), Australia (22.4 per cent), New Zealand (15.9 per cent).

Exports

Principal exports are raw sugar, garments, gold, timber, fish, molasses and coconut oil.
Main destinations: Australia (17.4 per cent total, 2006), US (14.4 per cent), UK (11.1 per cent).

Agriculture

Farming

The agricultural sector typically accounts for around 16 per cent of GDP and employs 40 per cent of the workforce.
Historically, 85 per cent of land is granted to Fijian clans (Mataqali) and by law cannot be sold. This has led to underutilisation of some land. The soil is generally fertile and easily worked.
In 1997 the Native Land Trust Board (NLTB) refused to renew land-leases to Indo-Fijian farmers, forcing many off the land and into the towns. As a result, production of sugar fell and in 2004 over 30 per cent of these farms were vacant. NLTB admitted that rental income had dropped significantly and in 2003 it recorded a loss. An invitation to the ex-tenants to return was ignored as many had adapted to urban life, while young ethnic Fijians did not come forward to farm.
Sugar normally accounts for half agricultural output, but has declined both in quality and quantity. The sugar industry supports about 25 per cent of the working population, consumes around 12 per cent of all goods and services and earns more than 40 per cent of export income. The Fiji Sugar Corporation aims to diversify into ethanol and to encourage other uses for spare land, especially rice (50 per cent of which is imported).
Fiji's already ailing sugar industry suffered a devastating blow in August 2004, when the World Trade Organisation (WTO) decided in favour of a case brought by Brazil, Australia and Thailand, to prevent the EU from paying preferential prices for sugar imports from developing African, Caribbean and Pacific (ACP) countries like Fiji. For nearly 20 years, Fiji's sugar industry has been totally dependent on the EU's preferential prices, which are three to four times higher than world market levels. As a result, the sugar sector is in the process of restructuring in order to respond to the end of EU sugar subsidies in 2007. This has given impetus to the government's drive to find alternatives to sugar cane production.
Production in 2005 included: 16,330 tonnes (t) cereals in total, 15,000t rice, 1,300t maize, 33,000t cassava, 1,200t okra, 80t potatoes, 6,200t sweet potatoes, 38,000t taro, 6,500t bananas, 5,200t yams, 3,662t pineapples, 2,800t tomatoes, 1,634t papayas, 700t citrus fruit, t mangoes, 182,290t oilcrops, 140,000t coconuts, 3,300t ginger, 160t pepper spice, 385t tobacco, 22,821t fruit in total, 21,200t vegetables in total, 3,000,000t sugar cane.Livestock production included: 26,511t meat in total, 8,360t beef, 3,938t pig meat, 1,000t goat meat, 13,191t poultry, 2,700t eggs, 57,000t milk, 100t honey.

Fishing

Fishing for local consumption includes skipjack, yellowfin and commercial species. Prawns and oysters are raised in fish farms. Bêche-de-Mer, shark-fins, trochus, mother-of-pearl and turtle shells are collected and sold.
The typical annual fish catch is over 44,700t with over 14,000t of other seafood. One million pieces of coral are harvested annually as well as 160,000 units, pearls and shells.
In 2004, the total marine fish catch was 41,928 tonnes and the total crustacean catch was 1,272 tonnes.

Forestry

In addition to natural rain forest, large new plantations of pine and hardwood were established in the late 1970s. There are exports of pine chips to Japan and sawn pine to Australia. The clearing of forests has caused soil erosion.
Timber imports in 2004 were US$26.6million, while exports amounted to US$23.1 million.
Estimated timber production in 2004 included 383,000 cubic metres (cum) roundwood, 346,000cum industrial roundwood, 159,000cum pulpwood round & split, 84,000cum sawnwood, 37,000cum wood fuel, 181,000cum sawlogs & veneer logs, 10,000cum wood-based panels, 37,000cum wood fuel.

Industry and manufacturing

The industrial sector as a whole accounts for 26 per cent of GDP and employs 15 per cent of the workforce. The manufacturing industry (excluding sugar milling) accounts for 13 per cent of GDP and sugar accounts for one-third of industrial output.
Sugar cane is crushed at local mills and exported as raw sugar and molasses. In June 2003, two mills were closed as part of the government's restructuring of the sector. Copra milling, which produces coconut oil and oil cake for export, is carried on at Suva and Savusavu. There are two breweries, a flour mill and a steel-rolling mill.

Tourism

Tourism is Fiji's most important economic activity and a vital contributor to the balance of payments. It accounts for 16 per cent of GDP, is the principal foreign exchange earner and gives employment to 40,000 people. The sector was seriously damaged by the coup in 2000, but recovered by 2003, when a record 430,800 visitors were recorded. Australia, from which a quarter of arrivals come, is the main market, followed by New Zealand, the US and the UK. Tourism in the rural areas and the outer islands, especially sustainable eco-tourism, is being developed. Expansion of the sector faces problems from shortage of skilled labour and pressure on available water and electricity provision.

Mining

The mining sector accounts for around 3 per cent of GDP and employs 2 per cent of the workforce.
Gold is Fiji's second largest export. Production is centred on one large mine, Vatukoula, owned by Emperor Gold Mines, which produces 120,000–160,000 ounces per annum and has reserves of around 3.5 million

ounces. Accessible ore is expected to be exhausted within 10 years. Another smaller mine at Mount Kasai is operated by Pacific Island Gold and was reopened in 1997 following a 50-year closure.

Hydrocarbons
Fiji has no proven hydrocarbons reserves, but the outlook for oil exploration is optimistic. Fiji relies entirely on imports to meet energy requirements.

Energy
A mini-hydroelectric scheme in Vanua Levu supplies electricity to 40 villages and other processing industries.

Banking and insurance
Central bank
Reserve Bank of Fiji

Time
GMT plus 12 hours

Geography
Fiji comprises more than 800 islands, of which 100 are inhabited, situated about 3,100km north-east of Australia and 5,000km south-west of Hawaii, in the Pacific Ocean. The four main islands are Viti Levu, Vanua Levu, Tavenui and Kadavu. Plains and valleys, including flood plains, and low mountains provide agricultural land. High mountains are rugged and volcanic.
Hemisphere
Southern

Climate
Hot and damp, tempered by cool winds from May–October. Maximum temperature during summer (December–April) 32 degrees Celsius (C), when hurricanes and cyclonic storms sometimes occur; rarely falls below 18 degrees C during the rest of the year.

Entry requirements
Passports
Required by all. Passports must be valid for three months beyond the the date of departure and visitors must possess sufficient funds and return/onward passage.
Visa
Visitor's visa (for stays up to four months) are issued on arrival to many foreign nationals from the Americas, Europe, Australasia and some Asian countries. Business visas, by representatives of overseas companies, from countries that do not require a visa may visit without further documentation.
Contact the nearest Fiji Consulate for further information.
Currency advice/regulations
There is no restriction on the import of local or foreign currency although it must be declared. Export of all currencies can only be up to the amount declared on entry.
Travellers cheques are accepted and are recommended in Australian dollars or pound sterling, to avoid added exchange fees.
In a review of currency designs in 2005 it was decided to retain the image of the head of the British monarch on the currency, even though Fiji has been a republic since 1987.
Customs
Personal effects allowed duty-free. Strict animal and plant quarantine regulations; fruit or plant material should not be brought in. Many agricultural and manufactured items subject to import embargoes and licensing and the list is subject to alteration. Details available from the Ministry of Commerce and Industry in Suva.
Prohibited imports
Strict animal and plant quarantine regulations apply; fruit or plant material are prohibited. Many agricultural and manufactured items are subject to import embargoes and licensing; a list and details are available from the Ministry of Commerce and Industry in Suva.

Health (for visitors)
Mandatory precautions
Vaccination certificates are required for yellow fever if travelling from an infected area.
Advisable precautions
Vaccination for diphtheria, tuberculosis, hepatitis A and B, polio, tetanus, typhoid and dengue fever. There is a rabies risk. In rural areas water should be boiled before drinking.

Hotels
There are many tourist hotels of all standards and types, frequently in scenic locations around the islands.
Tipping is not encouraged but visitors may give a gratuity for excellent service.

Credit cards
Most major credit cards accepted at hotels, restaurants, shops and rental car agencies, tours, cruises and travel agencies. American Express, Diners Club, Visa, JCB and Master Card have representatives in Suva.

Public holidays (national)
Fixed dates
1 Jan (New Year's Day), 25–26 Dec (Christmas Holiday).
Variable dates
Good Friday, Easter Monday, National Youth Day (first Fri in May), Ratu Sir Lala Sukuna Day (last Mon in May), Queen's Official Birthday (Jun/Jul), Fiji Day (Oct), Diwali (Oct/Nov), Birth of the Prophet Mohammed.
Muslim and Hindu festivals are timed according to local sightings of various phases of the moon.

Working hours
Banking
Mon–Thu: 0930–1500; Fri: 0930–1600. Foreign exchanges Mon–Fri 0830–1700; Sat: 0830–1200.
Business
Mon–Fri: 0830–1630/1700 (some business close early on Fri).
Government
Mon–Thu: 0800–1300, 1400–1630; Fri: 1400–1600.
Shops
Mon–Fri: 0800–1700; Sat: 0800–1300.

Telecommunications
Mobile/cell phones
A GSM 900 service is available throughout most of the islands.

Electricity supply
240/415V AC, with flat three-pin plug fittings. Larger hotels have 110V conversion units for electric shavers.

Social customs/useful tips
Lightweight suit and tie for men and lightweight suit or equivalent for women. It is customary to shake hands on meeting and taking leave. On social occasions punctuality is appreciated, and dress should be formal.
An invitation to a traditional village is regarded as an important occation. When visiting a bure (a native thatched cottage) shoes must be removed and head lowered when entering. Hats must be removed and an invitation to drink kava should be accepted to avoid insult.
Clothing may be casual, but should be modest: swimsuits are not acceptable anywhere except on beaches and around hotel pools.

Getting there
Air
National airline: Air Pacific
International airport/s: Nadi International (NAN), 8km north of Nadi, 200km from Suva; duty-free shop, restaurant, bank, post office, car hire.
Other airport/s: Nausori (SUV), 21km from Suva.
Airport tax: Departure tax F$30; not applicable to 24 hour transit passengers.
Surface
Water: Regular ferries operate between Kiribati, Nauru, Samoa and Tuvalu.
Main port/s: Labasa, Lautoka, Levuka, Savusavu and Suva.

Getting about
National transport
Air: Air Fiji operates several daily flights between Nadi International and Nausori Airport and most other domestic services. Air Pacific operates the main route between Nadi and Suva. Sunflower Airlines and Turtle Island Airways operate on parts of Viti Levu and are available for charter.

Helicopters can be chartered from Pacific Crown Aviation, Suva.
Road: There is a 3,300km road network, about one-third of which is metalled. On Viti Levu, a 500km coastal highway links main centres. A trans-insular road on Vanua Levu connects Labasa with Savusavu.
Buses: Air-conditioned buses operate daily between Suva, Nadi and Lautoka; fares are cheap. Air-conditioned coaches for longer distances.
Water: Small inter-island vessels operate from Suva and Lautoka. A regular ferry service connects Suva and Labasa, Ovalau and Koro Island. Ferries also connect the majority of the major coastal areas of Viti Levu and Vanua Levu with all the major islands. It is also possible to charter boats.

City transport

Taxis: Metered taxis are available in main centres. It is advisable to negotiate fares for long journeys, in advance. Journey time for a taxi from the airport to the city centre is around 10 minutes.
Buses, trams & metro: Journey time from airport to city centre 20 minutes; buses operate 0700–1830.

Car hire

Chauffeur-driven and self-drive car hire available. Current overseas or international licence acceptable for six months. Driving is on the left-hand side of the road, speed limits are 50kph in towns and villages, 80kph on highways.

BUSINESS DIRECTORY

The addresses listed below are a selection only. While World of Information makes every endeavour to check these addresses, we cannot guarantee that changes have not been made, especially to telephone numbers and area codes. We would welcome any corrections.

Telephone area codes

The international dialling code (IDD) for Fiji is +679 followed by the customer number.

Useful telephone numbers

Police, fire and ambulance: 000

Chambers of Commerce

Suva Chamber of Commerce, 7th Floor, Honson Building, Thomson Street, PO Box 337, Suva (tel: 331-3505).

Banking

Australia & New Zealand Banking Group Ltd, PO Box 179, ANZ House, 25 Victoria Parade, Suva (tel: 321-3000; fax: 330-0267).

National Bank of Fiji, 107 Victoria Parade, PO Box 1166, Suva (tel: 331-4400; fax: 330-2190, 330-2032).

Westpac Banking Corporation, 6th Floor, Civic House, Town Hall Road, Suva (tel: 330-0666; fax: 330-0718).

Central bank

Reserve Bank of Fiji, Private Mail Bag,Viti Levu Island, Suva (tel: 331-3611; fax: 330-1688; email: rbf@reservebank.gov.fj).

Travel information

Air Fiji, 185 Victoria Parade, Suva (tel: 331-5055, 331-4495; fax: 330-0771, 337-0693).

Flight information (24 hours) (tel: 672-2599).

Hotel reservations (available 24 hours on arrival concourse) (tel: 672-2433).

Nadi International Airport, Civil Aviation Authority of Fiji, Private Mail Bag (tel: 672-2500, 672-1555; fax: 652-1500, 672-3795).

Tourist information (0800–1700 hours) (tel: 672-2433).

National tourist organisation offices

Fiji Visitors' Bureau, Thomson Street, PO Box 92, Suva (tel: 330-2433; fax: 330-0970, 330-2751; e-mail: infodesk@fijifvb.gov.fj; internet site: http://www.bulafiji.com).

Ministries

Ministry of Primary Industries and Co-operatives, PO Box 358, Rodwell Road, Suva (tel: 331-1233).

Prime Minister's Office (tel: 321-1201; fax: 330-6034).

Other useful addresses

Asian Development Bank (ADB), South Pacific Regional Mission, La Casa di Andrea, Fr. Dr. W. H. Lini Highway; PO Box 127, Port Vila (tel: +678 2 23-300; fax: +678 2 23-183; email: adbsprm@adb.org; internet: www.adb.org/SPRM).

Bureau of Statistics, PO Box 2221, Government Buildings, Suva (tel: 331-5144, 331-5822; fax: 330-3656).

Commonwealth Development Corporation, 371 Victoria Parade, Suva (tel: 330-2577).

Department of Information, PO Box 2225, Government Buildings, Suva (tel: 321-1250/1; fax: 330-0776).

Fiji Posts and Telecommunications Ltd, PO Box 40, Suva (tel: 321-0329; fax: 330-5591; internet site: www.TelecomFiji.com.fj).

Fiji Trade and Investment Board, PO Box 2303, Government Buildings, Suva (tel: 331-5988; fax: 331-5783).

Forum Secretariat, Ratu Sukuna Road, Suva (fax: 330-3069).

National Marketing Authority of Fiji, PO Box 5085, Raiwaqa, Suva (tel: 338-5888).

Pacific Islands News Association Secretariat (PINS), Private Mail Bag, Level II, Damodar Centre, 46 Gordon Street, Suva (tel: 330-3623; fax: 330-3943).

Other news agencies: ABC Pacific Beat: www.radioaustralia.net.au/pacbeat
Pacific Magazine: www.pacificmagazine.net

Internet sites

Fiji government: www.fiji.gov.fj

Fiji information: www.fijiatoz.com

Tourism Council of the South Pacific: www.tcsp.com/destinations/fiji

Finland

KEY FACTS

Official name: Suomen Tasavalta: Republiken Finland (Republic of Finland)

Head of State: President Tarja Halonen (SDP) (since 2000; re-elected Jan 2006)

Head of government: Prime Minister Matti Vanhanen (since 2003; re-elected 18 March 2007)

Ruling party: Three-party coalition led by Suomen Keskusta (KESK) (Centre Party of Finland); Suomen Sosialidemokraatinen Puolue (SDP) (Social Democratic Party of Finland); Svenska Folkpartiet i Finland (SFP) (Swedish People's Party) (since 2003)

Area: 338,144 square km

Population: 5.25 million (2007)*

Capital: Helsinki

Official language: Finnish and Swedish

Currency: Euro (eur) = 100 cents (from 1 Jan 2002; previous currency markka, locked at M5.95 per euro)

Exchange rate: eur0.63 per US$ (Jul 2008)

GDP per capita: US$46,602 (2007)*

GDP real growth: 4.40% (2007)

Labour force: 2.67 million (2007)

Unemployment: 6.80% (2007)

Inflation: 1.60% (2007)

Balance of trade: US$11.86 billion (2007)

Foreign debt: US$226.51 billion (2004)

Annual FDI: US$49.50 billion (cumulative, 1995–2004, OECD); US$4.70 billion (OECD, 2004)*

* estimated figure

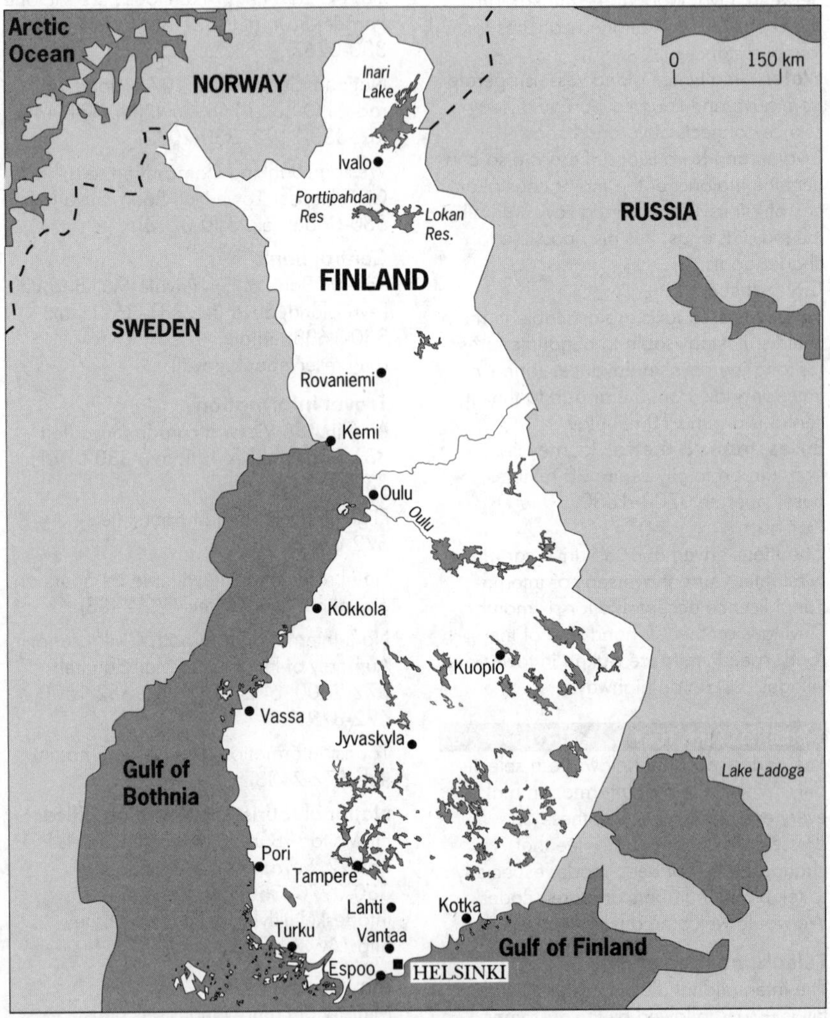

In Finland's last elections, in 2003, the rural based Suomen Keskusta (KESK) (Centre Party of Finland) won 24.7 per cent of the vote, gaining power from the previous government led by the Suomen Sosialedemokraatinen Puolue (SDP) (Social Democratic Party of Finland), which won 24.5 per cent of votes. The Centre Party formed a new coalition government with the Social Democratic Party and the Swedish People's Party. The Coalition government held 117 of the 200 seats in Parliament.

Following the election, Ms Anneli Jäätteenmäki, leader of the KESK, was elected Finland's first female prime minister. However, as a result of a scandal involving documents that were leaked during the election campaign, Ms Jäätteenmäki was forced to resign after only two months in office and was replaced by Mr Matti Vanhanen, also of the KESK and then minister of defence. Since then, support for the three main parties has remained relatively stable with 2006 opinion polls showing only little change. The next general election will be held in March 2007. President Tarja Halonen (SDP) was re-elected for a second term in the presidential election held in February 2006. Despite her popularity in opinion polls only weeks before the election, Halonen only won a by a small margin. The opposition party's candidate (Sauli Niinistö) came second and Prime Minister Vanhanen, the ruling KESK's candidate for president, came third.

Growth trend

A nation-wide strike over holiday pay and working conditions, affecting 24,000 employees in the paper-manufacturing sector, had hit Finland hard in 2005. The strike, running through May and June, cost the industry an estimated 40 million euros a day. Paper accounts for approximately one third of Finland's exports and 40–50 per cent of manufacturing output. Finland only produces around 4 per cent of the world's paper but in Europe it supplies 60 per cent of magazine paper and 20 per cent of graphic paper. Financial analysts within Finland predicted that the strike would shave 0.3 per cent off the country's GDP for every month it continued. GDP contracted in the second quarter of 2005 by 1.6 per cent, compared to first quarter figures. Nevertheless, GDP growth in 2006 rose to an estimated 3.5 per cent, consolidating the trend of 2004 (3.75 per cent) and 2005 (2.9 per cent). The Bank of Finland forecasts an average 3 per cent growth during the period 2006–08. Inflation has declined from 2.7 per cent in 2001 to 1.5 per cent in 2006, below some of the more pessimistic forecasts, but still almost double the rate seen in 2005 of 0.8 per cent. Despite high oil and energy prices and a housing-boom in the Helsinki area, inflation is estimated to remain under 2 per cent in coming years. Unemployment remains high, though decreasing, at 8.1 per cent in June 2006. According to several international estimates, significantly improved employment levels will only come about with structural changes in the labour market and in taxation. Many Finnish jobs have been moved offshore and this trend continues to threaten Finland's economy and the labour market. Reforming the labour market has been identified as a key priority for the government, although the opposition parties claim that little progress has been made so far.

Finland has few natural energy resources and in order to meet increasing energy demand the Finnish parliament voted (107–92) in May 2002 in support of a fifth nuclear reactor being built in Finland. The construction of the new reactor started in 2005 and it is expected to be operational in 2010. Finland's other energy options include increased use of natural gas and electricity imported from Russia. Finnish industry has also called for a preliminary decision to be made on a possible sixth nuclear reactor. In June, the European Environment Agency published a report that singled out Finland as one of the biggest emitters of carbon dioxide in the EU, second only to Italy. The EU is committed to reducing carbon dioxide emissions by 8 per cent of 1990 levels by 2012.

Relations with Russia

With Russia set to become Finland's biggest trading partner over the next few years (it is already its third biggest, after Germany and Sweden), Finland understandably invests a considerable amount of time on relations with its Russian neighbour. Finnish president Tarja Halonen hosted her Russian counterpart, Vladimir Putin, and visited Putin in St Petersburg in 2005. Trade and investment issues, particularly relating to Finnish investment in the neighbouring Russian Republic of Karelia, dominated talks. President Halonen politely rebuffed President Putin's efforts to garner Finnish support for Russia's quarrels with Estonia and Latvia. Russia has long complained that citizenship laws in these countries discriminate against ethnic Russian minorities.

In August, after President Putin's visit to Finland, the Russian government announced that it was in no hurry to renew Finland's lease on the Saimaa Canal, half of which runs through Russian territory. The lease expires in 2013 and Finland has been pressing for an early extension. The canal runs through formerly Finnish territory forcibly annexed by Joseph Stalin in 1940. Opinion polls indicate that between a quarter and a third of Finns surveyed wanted the return of territories lost to Russia.

Outlook

Analysts have been regularly wrong about Finland's growth prospects. The European Commission, however underestimated the potential with its forecast of 3.7 per cent GDP growth in 2006. With inflation expected to stay low and the budget to stay in surplus, Finland's prospects can only be described as good.

Risk assessment

Politics	Good
Economy	Good
Regional stability	Good

COUNTRY PROFILE

Historical profile

Before independence in 1917, Finland was controlled by Sweden and later Russia. Prior to Sweden's conquest of Finland in the 1150s, the country had been a feudal and tribal society.

1150–1293 Sweden was in control of Finland.

1362 Finland was granted the full rights of a Swedish province.

1523 Treaty gave Russia part of Karelia (area between Finland and Russia).

1721 Russia took control of the whole of Karelia.

1809 Finland was conquered by Russia.

1905–06 Strikes were held by the population demanding rights and liberties. Parliamentary government and universal suffrage were established; in 1906,

KEY INDICATORS — Finland

	Unit	2003	2004	2005	2006	2007
Population	m	5.21	5.22	5.25	5.27	*5.26
Gross domestic product (GDP)	US$bn	161.50	*186.60	195.79	210.84	245.01
GDP per capita	US$	31,773	35,670	37,320	39,828	*46,602
GDP real growth	%	2.1	3.7	2.9	4.8	4.4
Inflation	%	1.3	0.1	0.8	1.3	1.6
Unemployment	%	9.2	8.9	8.4	7.7	6.8
Exports (fob) (goods)	US$m	52,834.0	61,083.0	65,272.0	77,552.0	89,905.0
Imports (cif) (goods)	US$m	41,312.0	48,262.0	55,127.0	66,046.0	78,045.0
Balance of trade	US$m	11,522.0	12,821.0	10,145.0	11,505.0	11,860.0
Current account	US$m	6,760.0	8,400.0	9,658.0	9,550.0	11,268.0
Total reserves minus gold	US$m	10,514.9	12,318.2	10,588.3	6,494.2	7,063.1
Foreign exchange	US$m	9,544.5	11,522.0	10,143.1	6,134.6	6,689.2
Exchange rate	per US$	0.88	0.80	0.77	0.75	0.69

* estimated figure

Finland became the first European country to give votes to women.
1917 Collapse of the Russian Empire. A Finnish declaration of independence was followed by a brief civil war.
1919 Establishment of a republic; Kaarlo Ståhlberg became Finland's first president. In the following 70 years, more than 60 governments, mainly minority coalitions, held power.
1939–41 The Soviet Union invaded Finland and after the bitter conflict of the 1939–40 'Winter War', Finland entered the Second World War on the side of Nazi Germany. In December 1940, German troops were invited by the Finnish government to occupy parts of the country and Finland joined Germany's invasion of the Soviet Union in 1941.
1944 Finland signed a peace treaty with the Soviet Union and its troops withdrew from Soviet territory. Finnish troops were then engaged in the 'Lapland War' in northern Finland against withdrawing German soldiers.
1945 Following the end of the Second World War, punitive reparations and the cession of Southern Karelia and its only Arctic port, Petsamo, were forced on Finland by the Soviet Union.
1948 The Treaty of Friendship, Co-operation and Mutual Assistance was signed by Finland and the Soviet Union. It lasted until 1992 after the Soviet Union's break-up.
1956–82 The powers of the strong executive presidency allowed for in the constitution were further enhanced by President Urho Kekkonen. He was succeeded by President Mauno Koivisto in 1982.
1987 The Suomen Keskusta (KESK) (Centre Party of Finland) was replaced after 50 years in government. Conservatives were in the coalition government for the first time in 21 years. Harri Holkeri was appointed Finland's first conservative prime minister since 1946.
1994 Martii Ahtisaari was elected as president. The Suomen Kristillinen Liitto (SKL) (Christian League of Finland), which opposed EU membership, withdrew from the coalition after Finland completed negotiations on joining the EU.
1995 Finland joined the EU. The Suomen Sosialidemokraatinen Puolue (SDP) (Social Democratic Party) won the parliamentary elections and formed a coalition government, with the SDP's Paavo Lipponen as prime minister.
1999 The SDP was again returned as the strongest party in the parliamentary elections; a five-party government coalition was formed. Lipponen was re-elected as prime minister.
2000 Tarja Halonen was elected as president – Finland's first female president. The powers of the president were reduced, following the introduction of a new constitution.
2001 Finland joined other EU states to support the US's military action in Afghanistan, following the 11 September terrorist attacks.
2002 The Vitireä Liitto (VIHR) (Green League) left the coalition government after parliament voted to proceed with plans to build Finland's fifth nuclear reactor.
2003 Anneli Jäätteenmäki became Finland's first female prime minister, heading a coalition of her own KESK, which won the March parliamentary elections, the SDP and the SFP/RKP. Jäätteenmäki was forced to resigned as prime minister in June; she was unable to form a working coalition as she was seen as untrustworthy following her revelations of secret international undertakings by the former prime minister, during the election campaign. Parliament elected the defence minister, Matti Vanhanen, as prime minister.
2004 In March, former prime minister Anneli Jäätteenmäki was acquitted of charges of illegally obtaining secret documents about the Iraq War while she was opposition leader.
2005 Former prime minister, Paavo Lipponen, stepped down as party leader of the SDP; Eero Heinäluoma replaced him. The popularity of the EU fell, in line with a number of other EU member states that had rejected the new EU constitution in referenda, as a poll conducted in December showed that 49 per cent of Finns would vote 'no' to EU membership if given a choice at that time.
2006 The incumbant president, Tarja Halonen, won 46 per cent of the vote in the 15 January elections. Although this was nearly twice the number of votes of her nearest rival, Sauli Niinisto, who won 24 per cent, the constitution demanded a minimum of 50 per cent. The run-off held on the 29 January, was won by Halonen with 51.8 per cent of the vote.
2007 In parliamentary elections held on 18 March, the ruling KESK won 23.1 per cent of the vote (51 seats out of 200), only one seat more than its rival, the Kansallinen Kokoomuspuolue (KOK) (National Coalition Party). Prime Minister Matti Vanhanen (KESK) began talks with other parties immediately to form a coalition government.
2008 In July the engineering group Metso Oyj announced it will make hybrid (fuel) cars for the US Fisker Automotive company starting in 2009.

Political structure

Constitution

Finland's republican constitution, approved in 1919, was based on the principle of a unicameral parliament and a strong executive president.
In March 2000, a new constitution reduced the president's powers, and increased the role of the government – consisting of a prime minister and cabinet – who exercise power in conjunction with the president.

Form of state

Constitutional republic

The executive

The president is Head of State and is directly elected, by universal vote, for a six-year term, and is allowed to stand for office for two further consecutive terms. The president and government exercise executive power over matters of foreign policy and national security. The president is expected to approve or reject all measures adopted by the Eduskunta (parliament) within a period of three months, and if no decision is reached, a bill lapses.

National legislature

The 200-member unicameral parliament – the Eduskunta – is elected every four years by universal suffrage of all citizens aged from 18, using a system of proportional representation which takes into account the differing population densities in the 15 electoral districts. It usually meets for 120 days a year, starting in February, but can extend the session at its discretion. Any legislative proposal can be postponed until the next legislative session on a one-third vote in parliament.
The president is empowered to order elections, but the parliament decides when they are held. The parliament also appoints the prime minister and the 17 or 18 members of the Valtioneuvosto (Council of State/cabinet). Most of its members are drawn from within the parliament, but a few may come from outside. It is responsible to parliament for the general administration of the country. Because Finland has a loose, multi-party system, the cabinet always contains a coalition of parties and may be re-formed frequently.

Legal system

The legal system is based on Swedish civil law and is codified. The judicial system is divided between ordinary civil and criminal jurisdiction and special courts of litigation.
The president appoints a chancellor of justice who is not a cabinet member. His function is to oversee the Council of State and to submit an annual report on its legal conduct.
The Court of the Realm is supreme constitutional court, six of whose 13 members are elected by parliament for a term of four years. The final court for civil and criminal cases is the Korkein Oikeus (supreme court), whose president and 21 members are appointed directly by the state president; the supreme administrative court is the Korkein Hallinto-Oikeus.

Composed of 21 presidentially-appointed judges, it is the highest tribunal of administrative appeal.

Last elections

29 January 2006 (presidential); 18 March 2007 (parliamentary)

Results: Parliamentary: Suomen Keskusta (KESK) (Centre Party of Finland) won 23.1 per cent of the vote (51 seats out of 200); Kansallinen Kokoomuspuolue (KOK) (National Coalition Party) 22.3 per cent (50); Suomen Sosialidemokraatinen Puolue (SDP) (Social Democratic Party of Finland) 21.4 per cent (45); Vasemmistoliitto (VAS) (Left Alliance) 8.8 per cent (17); Vihreä Liitto (VIHR) (Green League) 8.5 per cent (15); Suomen Kristillisdemokraatit (KD) (Finnish Christian Democrats) 4.9 per cent (seven); the Svenska Folkpartiet i Finland (SFP) (Swedish People's Party) 4.5 per cent (nine); Perussuomalaiset (PerusS) (True Finns) 4.1 per cent (five). Turnout was 67.8 per cent.

Presidential: Tarja Halonen was re-elected with 46.3 per cent of the vote.

Next elections

January 2012 (presidential); March 2011 (parliamentary).

Political parties

Ruling party

Three-party coalition led by Suomen Keskusta (KESK) (Centre Party of Finland); Suomen Sosialidemokraatinen Puolue (SDP) (Social Democratic Party of Finland); Svenska Folkpartiet i Finland (SFP) (Swedish People's Party) (since 2003)

Main opposition party

Kansallinen Kokoomuspuolue (KOK) (National Coalition Party)

Population

5.25 million (2007)*

Last census: December 2000: 5,181,115

Population density: 17 inhabitants per square km.

Annual growth rate: 0.3 per cent 1994–2004 (WHO 2006)

Ethnic make-up

Virtually all the population is of Finnish origin, apart from a small foreign population of around 20,000, a small number of Romany Gypsies, a Sámi (Lapp) minority in the north and a significant Swedish-speaking minority in the west.

The Estonians are close cultural relatives of the Finns. There are some small ethnic groups related to the Finns living in Russia.

Religions

Nearly 90 per cent of the Finnish population belongs to the Evangelical Lutheran Church. The Orthodox Church accounts for most of the remainder; there are Catholic, Jewish and Pentecostal minorities.

Education

Finland achieved the highest overall scores in international tests for educational quality. Public expenditure on education amounts to 5.7 per cent of GDP. Universal primary education and gender parity, at this level and in secondary schools, have been achieved.

A sustained investment in education has resulted in high standards with the most rapid rise seen among those achieving a tertiary level qualification. The younger age groups are now more highly educated than their elders with about 83 per cent of people aged 25–34 having at least an upper secondary qualification in 1997, as against only 23 per cent of the population over the age of 65 achieving the same.

The education system consists of comprehensive secondary schools, post-comprehensive general and vocational education, higher education and adult education each lasting for three years. Vocational institutions provide initial apprenticeship training, in nearly all fields. A three-year vocational qualification gives access to all forms of higher education.

The Finnish higher education system comprises polytechnics and universities. The polytechnic system is founded on a nationwide network of 29 regional polytechnics. There are 20 universities, all of which are in the public sector. In addition to degree programmes, universities also provide adult education and various research and consultant services.

Compulsory years: 7 to 16

Enrolment rate: 99 per cent, for both boys and girls, total primary enrolment of the relevant age group. Enrolment in secondary and tertiary levels of the relevant age group was 118 per cent and 74 per cent respectively (World Bank).

Pupils per teacher: 18 in primary schools.

Health

Per capita total expenditure on health (2003) was US$2,108; of which per capita government spending was US$1,613, at the international dollar rate, (WHO 2006).

The national healthcare system is excellent and few take out private health insurance. Employers pay towards national health insurance through social security contributions. Health services have traditionally been free, but the 1990s saw changes and nominal charges introduced on a range of basic services.

HIV/Aids

HIV prevalence: 0.1 per cent aged 15–49 in 2003 (World Bank)

Life expectancy: 79 years, 2004 (WHO 2006)

Fertility rate/Maternal mortality rate: 1.7 births per woman, 2004 (WHO 2006); maternal mortality 0.06 per 1,000 live births (World Bank).

Birth rate/Death rate: 10 deaths and 11 births per 1,000 people (World Bank).

Child (under 5 years) mortality rate (per 1,000): 3.1 per 1,000 live births (World bank)

Head of population per physician: 3.16 physicians per 1,000 people, 2002 (WHO 2006)

Welfare

Finland has a well-developed system of social welfare, and the high level of support has proved to be a stabilising factor in social terms. However, the government has been forced by a steadily rising budget deficit to seek ways of cutting its social spending. Welfare spending, despite cuts, typically totals over 50 per cent of GDP. Finland has an ageing population; those aged over 65 are expected to constitute over a quarter of the population by 2030, one of the highest proportions in the world. Pension regulations have permitted earlier retirement than in many other countries. These factors, combined with high life Most Finns receive health insurance, unemployment benefit, pension and family allowances.

Main cities

Helsinki (capital, estimated population 568,676 in 2005), Esbo (230,711), Tampere (204,580) Vantaa (186,238), Åbo (177,078),

Languages spoken

Finnish belongs to the Baltic-Finnic group of the Finno-Ugric languages, which also includes Estonian and Hungarian and is also related to Sámi, the language of the indeginous people of northern Scandinavia.

English is widely understood in business circles; German and Russian are also spoken.

Official language/s

Finnish and Swedish

Media

National news agency: STT (Finnish News Agency)

Press

The constitution guarantees the freedom of the press.

Dailies: There are over 50 newspapers published daily, of which 10 are national. In Finnish, morning newspapers include Helsingin Sanomat (www.hs.fi), which has the largest subscription circulation and Aamulehti (www.aamulehti.fi) with the second highest, Borgåbladet (www.bbl.fi), Turun Sanomat (www.turunsanomat.fi). The largest circulation newspaper in Swedish is Hufvudstadsbladet (www.hbl.fi). Evening newspapers are tabloid including

Ilta-Sanomat (www.iltasanomat.fi) and Ilalehti (www.iltalehti.fi) which has the third largest circulation in Finland. There are also a number of newspapers sponsored by political parties.
Weeklies: Most daily newspapers publish a weekend edition. There are a full range of magazines for all interests, Katso (www.katso.fi) features popular entertainment, Urheilulehti (www.urheilulehti.fi) is a sports magazine and Äpy (www.apy.fi) is the country's oldest humorous magazine.
Business: Prominent publications include Kauppalehti (www.kauppalehti.fi), Talous Sanomat (www.taloussanomat.fi), and Talouselämä (www.talouselama.fi), which is a economic journal.
Periodicals: There are over 3,000 magazines on offer, most popular are of general interest.

Broadcasting

The national, public broadcaster is YLE (Yleisradio Oy) (www.yle.fi), which is funded by a licence fee. It typically attracts 44 per cent of TV viewers and over 50 per cent of radio listeners.
All analogue services were switched to digital in September 2007, allowing a mix of free-to-air and pay-TV services.
Radio: YLE operates seven radio stations through either digital or FM/MW/SW frequencies, which cater for all genres including cultural, music, talk, news, entertainment and education, in Finnish, Swedish and the Sámi-language. Radio Finland provides external services, including worldwide news in Latin.
There are many private national and local radio stations including Radio Nova (www.radionova.fi), Groove FM (www.groovefm.fi) from Helsinki, Radio 957 (www.radio957.fi) from Tampere and Radio Iskelmä (www.iskelma.net) from Lahti.
Television: There are over 20 TV stations of which the public broadcaster YLE (www.yle.fi) has six channels showing a full range of programmes. MTV3 (www.mtv3.fi) is the most popular commercial station, Nelonen (www.nelonen.fi) has 50 per cent foreign and domestic programming, Sub TV (www.subtv.fi) is aimed at the young.

Advertising

The typical adspend is over US$1 billion per annum, with over 50 per cent spent in newspapers, followed by television (20 per cent) and magazines (15 per cent).
There are restrictions on tobacco, alcohol, advertising to children and across-the-counter medicines.
Direct mail advertising and direct response advertising via printed, broadcast media and internet and mobile/cell phone are steadily increasing in market penetration.

Economy

Finland's economy collapsed in the early 1990s in the wake of the demise of the Soviet Union, but is now recognised as the most competitive country in the world. Finland responded by developing into an advanced communications and information technology centre and becoming a world leader in innovation by investing heavily in research and development (3.5 per cent of GDP) and cultivating a highly-educated workforce.
Finland is a small market-oriented economy dependent on foreign trade. Exports account for around 50 per cent of GDP. In 2006, GDP grew by 5.5 per cent, almost double the previous year's figure, reflecting a tendency to volatility.
Telecommunications, with the Nokia company at the forefront dominating the world mobile phone market, are of increasing importance as the driving force of the economy. The wood products sector, based on Finland's abundance of forests, is still, as in the past, a major contributor to the economy. Manufacturing and engineering are also of long-standing importance.

Labour market and unemployment

Women constitute 48 per cent of the labour force.

External trade

As a member of the European Union, Finland operates within a communitywide free trade union, with tariffs sets as a whole. Internationally, the EU has free trade agreements with a number of nations and trading blocs worldwide. Its economy is export-oriented, with over 40 per cent of production being shipped abroad and export trade representing 70 per cent of GDP.
Timber wood pulp and paper are Finland's core export base, while Nokia is the world's leading mobile telephony and alone represents 20 per cent of the country's exports.

Imports

Main imports are foodstuffs including grain, fuel and petroleum products, chemicals, transport equipment, machinery, textile yarn and fabrics, industrial raw materials like iron and steel.
Main sources: Russia (14.1 per cent total, 2006), Germany (13.8 per cent), Sweden (9.7 per cent).

Exports

Main exports are forestry products (Finland is the world's second largest forestry exporter, after Canada), mobile phones and wireless network technology, vehicles, machinery and equipment, biotechnology, chemicals.
Main destinations: Germany (10.6 per cent total, 2006), Sweden (10.4 per cent), Russia (10.0 per cent).

Agriculture

Farming

The opening up of Finland's agricultural sector was a major issue in the negotiations for EU membership.
Finnish agriculture is based on small family farms, with the average agricultural area of a farm about 25 hectares (ha). Forests are an integral part of the country's farms, and the average forest area of farms is 43ha. About 43 per cent of the farms produce food crops. Wheat and rye are cultivated on about 10 per cent of the arable land, and about 9 per cent is used for growing other crops including potatoes and sugar beets.
Agriculture typically contributes 1.1 per cent of GDP, although active farms employ 5 per cent of the workforce. On average, only about half of the income of farm families is obtained from agriculture, while farm forestry usually provides 10 to 15 per cent of the income.
Production is based on livestock, and about 80 per cent of the agricultural area is used as pasture or for arable fodder cropping. About 33 per cent of the farms are dairy farms. Finland is 85 per cent self-supporting in food grains, dairy products and root crops.
Fundamental reform to the Common Agricultural Policy (CAP) was introduced throughout most of the EU on 1 January 2005. The subsidies paid on farm output, which tended to benefit large farms and encourage overproduction, were replaced by single farm payments not conditional on production. This is expected to reward farms that provide and maintain a healthy environment, food safety and animal welfare standards. The changes are also intended to encourage market conscious production and cut the cost of CAP to the EU taxpayer. Finland introduced this measure on 1 January 2006.
Crop production in 2005 included: 4,105,000 tonnes (t) cereals in total, 796,300t wheat, 739,000t potatoes, 2,045,000t barley, 1,178,000t oats, 40,280t oilcrops, 1,081,000t sugar beets, 14,573t fruit in total, 229,035t vegetables in total. The estimated livestock production included: 382,095t meat in total, 93,290t beef, 198,490t pig meat, 650t lamb, 86,970t poultry, 57,900t eggs, 2,595,000t milk, 1,700t honey, 10,500t cattle hides.

Fishing

Fishing, aquaculture and fish processing are a traditional part of Finnish industries. The food fishing industry is managed in accordance with the EU's Common Fisheries Policy (CFP), which covers resource, market and structural policies including inland waters and sea fishing as well as a monitoring system. The EU Commission has ratified the structural programme for

the fisheries industry in Finland for 2000–06.
Fish farming is carried out both in the sea and in inland waters. The most important economic fish for sea fishing are Baltic herring and salmon. Although employment in the sector has dropped considerably, the catch remains stable due to the adoption of more efficient fishing techniques. The total catch is around 120,000 tonnes, of which less than a third is used for human consumption.
The annual production of farmed fish is around 17,500 tonnes consisting mainly of large rainbow trout.
In 2004, the total marine fish catch was 88,883 tonnes and the total crustacean catch was 156 tonnes.

Forestry

Nearly three-quarters of the country is covered by forest, estimated at 21.9 million hectares (ha). Forest resources have been increasing steadily, as annual growth exceeds felling and natural losses. About two-thirds of the forest area is privately-owned, mainly by small-scale farmers. Timber products account for nearly one third of export products and nearly one third of manufacturing output. There is a high level of product specialisation, aided by the fact that the transport and machinery sectors tend to cater for the forest industry. The most common species of tree growing are Scots pine, spruce and birch.
In 2004 exports amounted to US$13.6 billion, while imports were US$1.5 billion.
Production in 2004 included: 53,799,662 cubic metres (cum) roundwood, 49,280,858cum industrial roundwood, 13,544,060cum sawnwood, 24,256,858cum sawlogs and veneers, 25,024,000cum pulpwood, 2,029,000cum wood-based panels, 4,518,804cum woodfuel; 14,036,000 tonnes (t) paper and paperboard, including 723,000t newsprint, 9,301,000t printing and writing paper, 12,619,000t wood pulp, 740,000t recovered paper.

Industry and manufacturing

Industry in Finland is concentrated in three areas: paper and pulp production; machinery and other metal products; and hi-tech electronics (particularly mobile phone production). The metals, engineering and electronics sector account for over 50 per cent of the country's work force and exports. Finnish exports have underpinned its strong economy and only a severe global downturn could leave the country vulnerable, not only to industry-specific shocks affecting its three principal sectors, but also performance in its key markets.
Research and development (R&D) investment in Finland is one of the highest in the world.

Tourism

Travel and tourism is expected to contribute US$7.6 billion or 3.7 per cent of GDP in 2005, and employ 10.9 per cent of the workforce. Total exports generated are expected to reach US$5.3 billon and tourism is estimated to attract US$4.6 billion or 12.1 per cent of all captial investment.
Visitors from Sweden are the most numourus at 608,765 in 2004; the next 16 countries together accounted for almost three million visitors.

Mining

The sector accounts for only 0.3 per cent of GDP.
There are around a dozen ore mines, producing mainly chromium, mercury, zinc, silver, copper and nickel.
Deposits are small. Prospecting is being intensified to curb imports; refining technology is a major focus of development work. Outokumpu, the mining and metals group, has modernised the production facilities at its Harjavalta plant through an investment programme. The programme includes the copper smelter and nickel production line located at Harjavalta and the copper refinery located at Pori, both towns in western Finland.

Hydrocarbons

Finland has no oil resources and there are no current exploration plans. All of its oil demands are imported primarily from the North Sea, Oman and Russia. Finland imported around 200,000 barrels per day (bpd) in 2004. There are two refineries in Finland with a joint capacity of 200,000bpd, both are located on the southern coastline and oil is brought to them by sea.
Finland has no gas resources and domestic demands are imported from Russia.
Natural gas fulfils around 11 per cent of Finland's energy needs. There is interest from Finland to build a natural gas pipeline along the Baltic seabed although no terms have been made yet.
There are no coal reserves and Finland's needs are met by imports from Poland, Russia and the US. Finland consumed 5.8 million tonnes of oil equivalent in 2003.

Energy

Owing to the high proportion of energy-intensive industry, long distances between population centres and geographic situation with a cold climate, Finland's per capita energy consumption is one of the highest among International Energy Agency (IEA) countries.
There are four nuclear reactors – two Russian and two Swedish-built. Expansion of nuclear power has reduced dependence on imported coal and oil.
The fifth nuclear power plant, in Olkiluoto on the west coast, will begin construction in mid-2006, with completion and commercial electricity production of 1,600MW in 2009. The Finnish electricity company, Teollisuuden Voima Oy (TVO), will oversee construction. Nuclear power provides around 28 per cent of Finland's energy requirements.
Imatran Voima Oy (IVO), the state-owned power utility, has 12.5 per cent of the Nordic power market. Finland had two national grids which were merged in the late 1990s. The national grid operator is Fingrid. IVO and Industrial Power Group each own 30 per cent and the state 16 per cent.
Electricity demand is expected to increase at an estimated annual rate of 2–2.5 per cent by 2007, before levelling off.
Finland receives all its natural gas from Russia. To reduce its dependency on Russian supplies, one suggestion is to receive supplies from the Norwegian gas fields via a pipeline through Sweden, but the investment costs are currently too high.
Wood fuels provide Finland with around 10 per cent of the primary fuel for electricity generation and 15 per cent of the total energy requirement, one of the highest rates among the industrialised nations.
Wood-based fuels can, however, have a moisture content of up to 60 per cent which can make them difficult to burn.

Financial markets

Stock exchange

The Helsinki Stock Exchange is part of the OMX Exchanges group that owns and operates stock exchanges in six Baltic region countries. OMX provides the exchanges and the software necessary to drive the largest integrated securities market in Northern Europe.
In 2004 the value of equities turnover was US$228 billion and the number was 19 million.

Banking and insurance

There are around 341 banks in Finland. Nordea, the largest bank in the Nordic region is Finnish. Other major banks in Finland include Oko Bank, Sampo Bank and Sweden's Svenska Handelsbanken AB.

Central bank

Suomen Pankki (Bank of Finland); European Central Bank (ECB).

Time

GMT plus two hours (daylight saving, late-March to late-September, GMT plus three hours).

Geography

Finland is the fifth-largest country in Europe, but is one of the most sparsely populated. The land frontier with Sweden to

the north-west is 586km long, while the far northern border with Norway runs for 716km and the eastern border with Russia for 1,269km. Finland's western and southern shores are washed by the Baltic Sea.
The coastal regions consist of flat clay plains, where most agriculture is undertaken. The lake district, which is estimated to contain over 55,000 lakes and is densely wooded forests, occupies much of the south-east. Northern Finland is within the arctic circle and is mostly scrubland.

Hemisphere
Northern

Climate
Finland's climate varies widely across the country, with exceptionally strong differences between the summer and the winter norms. Temperatures average 5 degrees Celsius (C) in Helsinki and minus 0.4 degrees C in the north. January is the coldest of the long winter months, with an average minus 9 degrees C. Peak average temperatures in Helsinki are reached in July (18 degrees C).
Average annual rainfall in Helsinki is 675mm. Spring months are relatively dry, declining to 36mm in March, but higher rainfall starts in July, reaching a peak of around 70mm in the August–October period. Finland's snow season usually runs from November to April (although it runs up to May further north).

Dress codes
Formal dress, including dark-coloured suits for men, is normal for business purposes. In winter, heavy, warm clothing is essential for outdoor wear. A fur cap and winter boots or overshoes are also strongly recommended.

Entry requirements

Passports
Passports are required by all and must be valid for up to six months beyond the date of stay. Nationals of countries which are signatories of the Schengen Accord may visit on national IDs.

Visa
Visas are required by all except nationals of Schengen Accord countries, North America, Australasia and some Asian countries, for up to three months. All visas issued will adhere to Schengen Accord requirements. For business visas a letter of invitation from a local business contact, stating nature and duration of stay, plus proof of return/onward ticket and travel insurance, with a minimum coverage of US$25,000, or other medical insurance that covers Finland, must accompany the application.
For further information see http://formin.finland.fi/doc/eng/services/entry/main.html or contact the consular section of the nearest embassy. A Schengen visa application (offered in several languages) can be downloaded from http://europa.eu/abc/travel/ see 'documents you will need'.

Currency advice/regulations
There is unrestricted import of local and foreign currency.
Travellers cheques are widely accepted.

Customs
Personal items are duty-free. There are no duties levied on alcohol and tobacco between EU member states, providing amounts imported are for personal consumption. Visitors aged less than 22 years may not import alcohol over 22 per cent proof.

Prohibited imports
Alcohol drinks over 60 per cent by volume are prohibited. Certain plant material and food, firearms and works of art are subject to restrictions and formalities. The Finnish tourist board can provide further advice.

Health (for visitors)
Nationals of the European Economic Area (EEA) countries and Switzerland can access reduced cost and sometimes free medical treatment using a European Health Insurance Card (EHIC) while visiting the EEA. Exceptions include nationals of the 10 countries which joined the EU in 2004 whose EHIC is not valid in Switzerland. Applications for the EHIC should be made before travelling.

Mandatory precautions
No special requirements are necessary.

Advisable precautions
All imported medication that are narcotics must be accompanied by a doctor's letter. Mosquito repellent is advised for visits to the north in summer.

Hotels
In Helsinki and the surrounding area, hotels are classified into five price categories. Generally of a high standard. Rates vary depending on location, facilities and season. Accommodation should be booked well in advance, especially during summer. If accommodation is unobtainable, a place may be found through Hotellikeskus (accommodation clearing-house) at the Central Railway Station in Helsinki. Gratuities are not expected, with the exception of porters. Service is included in restaurant bills, although a little extra can be added.

Credit cards
All major international credit cards are accepted.

Public holidays (national)

Fixed dates
1 Jan (New Year's Day), 6 Jan (Epiphany), 1 May (May Day), 6 Dec (Independence Day), 24–26 Dec (Christmas Holiday).

Variable dates
Good Friday, Easter Monday, Ascension Day, Midsummer's Eve, All Saints' Day.

Working hours
Finns tend to take fairly frequent holidays during the summer months. As a result, business visits between mid-June and mid-August should be undertaken only after making sure that the other party will be available. September to May is the favoured time for business visits. Some businesses and shops close from midday on the day before public holidays.

Banking
Mon–Fri: 0915–1615. Post offices may close later than commercial, savings and co-operative banks.

Business
Mon–Fri: 0800–1600; in summer businesses frequently close at 1530.

Government
Mon–Fri: 0800–1600.

Shops
Mon–Fri: 0900–1700; Sat: 0900–1300. Large department stores and supermarkets open Mon–Fri: 0900–2000; Sat: 0900–1800.

Telecommunications

Mobile/cell phones
There are extensive GSM 900/1800 and G3 services available.

Electricity supply
220V AC, 50Hz. Continental two-pin plugs are standard.

Social customs/useful tips
Finns appreciate punctuality. A gift of flowers is usual when visiting a business partner's home for the first time. Guests should not start drinking before their hosts have proposed their health.
Tips are small, except for unusually good service.
Think twice before refusing to go to a sauna with a host, since such an invitation is seen as a gesture of confidence and friendship by your host. Business meetings are sometimes conducted in saunas.
There are strict laws on drinking and driving.

Security
Street crime is a relative rarity in Finland; normal precautions apply.

Getting there

Air

National airline: Finnair

International airport/s: Helsinki-Vantaa (HEL), 19km north of capital; facilities include banks/bureaux de change, duty-free shops, car hire, hotel reservations, VIP lounge, conference rooms and restaurants.

Other airport/s: Jyväskylä (JYV), 21km from city; Kemi (KEM), 6km from city; Kokkola (KOK), 22km from city; Oulu

(OUL), 15km south-west of city; Rovaniemi (RRVN), 10km from city; Tampere (TMP), 15km from city; Turku (TKU), 7km from city; Vaasa (VAA), 12km from city.

Airport tax: None

Surface

Road: The majority of road routes include sea ferry links from Sweden or Germany. There is a land link via Norway or Sweden to Finnish Lapland, involving travel through the Arctic Circle.

Rail: There are rail/sea links from Hamburg, Copenhagen and Stockholm to Helsinki or Turku. A rail connection to Stockholm is available from Haparanda/Tornio in the north. There are daily trains to Moscow and St Petersburg.

Water: Daily ferry services from Sweden, twice weekly from Germany and Poland. Reservations should be made in advance as these tend to be heavily booked, especially during summer and at weekends. Also regular services to Estonia and St Petersburg (Russia).

Main port/s: Helsinki, Kotka, Hamina, Mariehamn, Vaasa, Turku, Pori, Sköldvik, Rauma and Oulu.

Getting about

National transport

Air: Finland has one of the densest internal networks in Europe. Finnair provides connections between Helsinki and Ivalo, Joensuu, Jyväskylä, Kajaani, Kemi, Kittilä, Kokkola, Kuopio, Kuusamo, Lappeenranta, Mariehamn, Mikkeli, Oulu, Pietarsaari, Pori, Rovaniemi, Saonlinna, Tampere, Turku, Vaasa and Varkaus.

Road: Finland's 77,000km network of public roads include 12,000km of high-grade national highway and 30,000km of secondary routes, but there is only just over 600km of motorways. Traffic is light but distances are great, the roads remain passable at all times of the year, although weight restrictions are imposed during April and May in southern Finland and May to June in northern Finland.

Buses: Efficient coach services cover the entire country, and are the main form of transport in Lapland.

Rail: Network of around 6,000km (including 1,600km electrified), operated by state railway company, Valtionrautatiet (VR). Relatively inexpensive and there are several passes available allowing travel over a set period. Seat reservation is obligatory on special express trains. Tickets are valid for one month. Sleeper services are available on the main connections.

Water: Important method of transport, owing to large number of lakes (187,888), which cover 31,500 square km.

City transport

Taxis: Taxis have a yellow taksi sign, which is lit when the taxi is vacant. They can be hired at taxi ranks or signalled from the street. Fares are more expensive at night. Taxi drivers are not tipped.

Buses, trams & metro: An efficient and integrated bus, metro and tramway service, suburban rail lines and ferry services to Suomenlinna Islands, operates in Helsinki. A common fares system applies to all the modes (including the ferries) with a zonal flat fare and free transfer between services. Multi-trip tickets are sold in advance, as are various passes.

Regular bus services, including Finnair City Bus, operate from the airport to the city, taking 35 minutes. Some Helsinki hotels run courtesy coaches.

Car hire

Available in most major towns. Rates include maintenance and insurance. The minimum age varies (usually 20–25) and at least one year's driving experience is a requirement for all drivers. The speed limits are 50kph in built-up areas, 80kph on normal roads and 120kph on motorways. The wearing of seat belts is compulsory. The use of headlights at all times is obligatory. Traffic drives on the right. A national driving licence or International Driving Permit is required. Driving around Helsinki is not recommended due to the lack of parking spaces. Any accident involving elk or raindeer must be report to the police.

BUSINESS DIRECTORY

The addresses listed below are a selection only. While World of Information makes every endeavour to check these addresses, we cannot guarantee that changes have not been made, especially to telephone numbers and area codes. We would welcome any corrections.

Telephone area codes

The international direct dialling (IDD) code for Finland is +358, followed by area code and subscriber's number:

Hämeenlinna	3	Mikkeli	15
Helsinki	9	Oulu	8
Imatra	5	Pori	2
Joensuu	13	Rovaniemi	16
Jyväskylä	14	Tampere	3
Kotka	5	Tornio	16
Kuopio	17	Turku	2
Lahti	3	Vaasa	6

Useful telephone numbers

Emergencies 114

Chambers of Commerce

Central Chamber of Commerce of Finland, 17 Aleksanterinkalu, PO Box 1000, Helsinki 00101 (tel: 696-969; fax:650-303; e-mail: keskuskauppakamari@wtc.fi).

Central Finland Chamber of Commerce, 4 Sepänkatu, Jyväskylä 40100 (tel: 652-400; fax: 652-411; e-mail: info@centralfinlandchamber,fi).

Helsinki Chamber of Commerce, 12 Kalevakatu, Helsinki 00100 (tel: 228-601; fax: 2286-0228; e-mail: kauppakamari@helsinki.chamber.fi).

Kuopio Chamber of Commerce, 2 Kasarmikatu, Kuopio 70110 (tel: 282-0291; fax: 282-3304; e-mail: kauppakamari@kuopiochamber.fi).

Lapland Chamber of Commerce, 29 Maakuntakatu, Rovaniemi 96200 (tel: 318-877; fax: 318-885; e-mail: kauppakamari@lapland.chamber.fi).

Turku Chamber of Commerce, 1 Puolankatu, Turku 20100 (tel: 274-3400; fax: 274-3440; e-mail: kauppakamari@turku.chamber.fi).

Banking

Nordea Bank Finland, Aleksanterinkatu 36 B, Helsinki, Fin-00020 Helsinki (tel: 1651; fax: 1654-2838).

Nordic Investment Bank, Fabianinkatu 34, PO Box 249, Fin-00171 Helsinki (tel: 18-001; fax: 180-0210).

Oko Bank, PO Box 308, Fin-00101 Helsinki (tel: 4041).

Sampo Plc, Unioninkatu 22, Fin-00075 Helsinki (tel: 105-1515).

Suomen Pankkiyhdistys r y (Finnish Bankers' Association), Museokatu 8 A, Box 1009, Fin-00101 Helsinki (tel: 405-6120; fax: 4056-1291).

Suomen Säästöpankkiliitto (Savings Bank Association), Pohjoisesplanadi 35A, 00101 Helsinki 10 (tel: 13-341).

Central bank

Suomen Pankki (Bank of Finland), Rauhankatu 16, PO Box 160, FI-00101 Helsinki (tel: 108-311; fax: 174-872; e-mail: info@bof.fi); European Central Bank (ECB), Kaiserstrasse 29, D-60311 Frankfurt am Main, Germany (tel: (+49-69) 13-440; fax: (+49-69) 1344-6000).

Travel information

Finland Travel Bureau Ltd, Mail Department, PB319, 00101 Helsinki 10 (poste restante service).

Finnair, Tietotie 11A, Helsinki-Vantaa Airport (tel: 81-881; fax: 818-4401; internet site: http://www.finnair.com).

Finnish State Railways (internet site: http://www.vr.fi/e-index.htm).

Helsinki-Vantaa Airport (tel: 82-771).

Helsinki Tourist Office, Pohjoiiesesplanadi 19, Helsinki.

National tourist organisation offices

Finnish Tourist Board (Matkailun Edistamiskeskus), Töölönkatu 11, PO Box 625, SF-00100 Helsinki (tel: 4030-1211; fax: 4030-1301/1333; e-mail: mek@mek.fi; internet site: http://www.mek.fi).

Ministries

FINNIDA (Finnish International Development Agency), c/o Ministry for Foreign Affairs, Merikasarmi, Laivastokatu 22, 00160 Helsinki (tel: 134-151; fax: 629-840).

Ministry of Agriculture and Forestry, Hallituskatu 3 A, PO Box 232, 00171 Helsinki (tel: 1601 (exchange); fax: 160-2190).

Ministry of Defence, Et. Makasiinikatu 8 A, PO Box 31, 00131 Helsinki (tel: 16-161; fax: 653-254).

Ministry of Education, Meritullinkatu 10, PO Box 293, 00171 Helsinki (tel: 134-171; fax: 135-9335).

Ministry of the Environment, Kasarmikatu 25, PO Box 380, 00131 Helsinki (tel: 19-911; fax: 1991-9545).

Ministry of Finance, Aleksanterinkatu 3, PO Box 286, 00171 Helsinki (tel: 1601 (exchange); fax: 160-3120).

Ministry for Foreign Affairs, Merikasarmi, Laivastokatu 22, PO Box 176, 00161 Helsinki (tel: 134-151; fax: 1341-5070).

Ministry of the Interior, Kirkkokatu 12, 001070 Helsinki (tel: 1601; fax: 160-2927).

Ministry of Justice, Eteläesplanadi 10, PO Box 1, 00131 Helsinki (tel: 18-251; fax: 1825-7730).

Ministry of Labour, Eteläesplanadi 4, PO Box 524, 00101 Helsinki (tel: 18-561; fax: 1856-7950).

Ministry of Social Affairs and Health, Snellmaninkatu 4-6, PO Box 267, 00171 Helsinki (tel: 1601 (exchange); fax: 160-4716).

Ministry of Trade and Industry, Aleksanterinkatu 4, PO Box 230, 00171 Helsinki (tel: 1601; fax: 160-3666).

Ministry of Transport and Communications, Eteläesplanadi 16, 00130 Helsinki (tel: 1601 (exchange); fax: 160-2596).

Prime Minister's Office, Snellmaninkatu 1 A, Fin-00170 Helsinki (tel: 3589-1601).

Other useful addresses

American Embassy, Itäinen Puistotie 14B, 00140 Helsinki (tel: 171-931; fax: 635-332).

British Embassy, Itäinen Puistotie 17, 00140 Helsinki (tel: 2286-5100; fax: 2286-5262).

Confederation of Finnish Industries, Eteläranta 10, SF 00130, Helsinki 13 (tel: 661-665).

Council of State, Aleksanterinkatu 3 D, 00170 Helsinki (tel: 1601 (exchange); fax: 160-2163).

Finnish Embassy (USA), 3301 Massachusetts Avenue, NW, Washington DC 20008 (tel: 202-298-5800; fax: 202-298-6030; e-mail: info@finland.org).

Finnish Foreign Trade Association, Arkadiankatu 2, PO Box 908, 001001 Helsinki (tel: 69-591; fax: 694-0028).

Helsinki Stock Exchange, Fabianinkatu 14, 00100 Helsinki 10 (tel: 624-161).

Invest in Finland Bureau, Aleksanterinkatu 17, 00100 Helsinki (tel: 696-9125; fax: 6969-2530; internet site: http://www.investinfinland.fi).

Liiketyönantajain (Confederation of Commerce Employers), Eteläranta 10, 00130 Helsinki 13 (tel: 19-281).

Main Post Office, Mannerheimintie 11, 00100 Helsinki 10.

Meilahti Hospital Haartmanink 3, Helsinki (tel: 4711).

Nesté (largest industrial corporation), Keilaniemi, 02150 Espoo, Helsinki (tel: 4501).

Oy Suomen Tietotoimisto (news agency), Lönnrotinkatu 5, 00120 Helsinki 12 (tel: 646-224).

Statistics Finland, Työpajankatu 13, PO Box FI-00022, Helsinki (tel: 17-341; fax: 1734-2279; internet site: http://tilastokeskus.fi/index_en.html).

Suomen Työnantajain Keskusliitto (Finish Employers' Confederation) Eleläranta 10, Helsinki 13 (tel: 17-281).

Tullihallitus (Board of Customs), Erottajankatu 2, 00120 Helsinki (tel: 6141).

Ulkomaankaupan Agenttiliitto (Finnish Foreign Trade Agents' Federation) Mannerheimintie 42A 00260 Helsinki 26 (tel: 446-768).

National news agency: STT (Finnish News Agency)

Internet sites

Virtual Finland: http://virtual.finland.fi

Finnish company information (top 100 Finnish companies): www.nedecon.fi

France

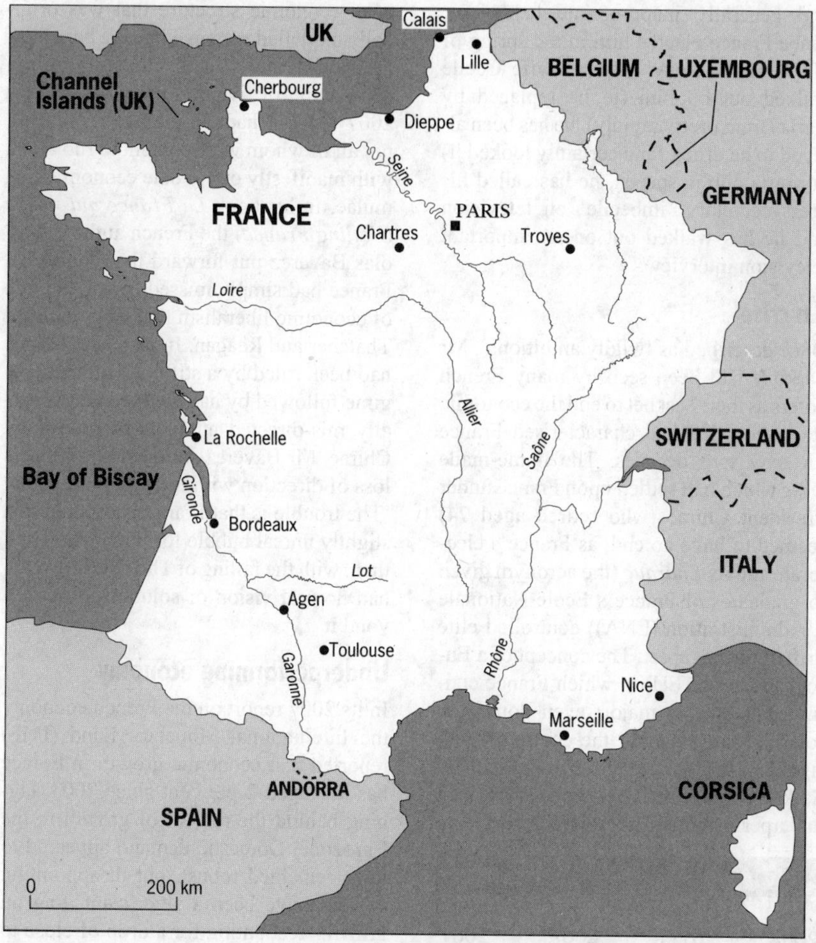

KEY FACTS

Official name: La République Française (The French Republic)

Head of State: President Nicolas Sarkozy (UMP) (from 16 May 2007)

Head of government: Prime Minister François Fillon (UMP) (appointed 17 May 2007)

Ruling party: Union pour un Mouvement Populaire (UMP) (Union for a People's Movement)

Area: 543,965 square km

Population: 61.68 million (2007)*

Capital: Paris

Official language: French

Currency: Euro (eur) = 100 cents (from 1 Jan 2002; previous currency French franc, locked at Ff6.56 per euro)

Exchange rate: eur0.63 per US$ (Jul 2008)

GDP per capita: US$41,511 (2007)*

GDP real growth: 1.80% (2007)

Labour force: 27.61 million (2006)

Unemployment: 8.30% (2007)

Inflation: 1.60% (2007)

Balance of trade: -US$1.67 billion (2006)*

Foreign debt: US$2,797.77 billion (2004)

Visitor numbers: 79.10 million (2006)*

* estimated figure

French President Nicholas Sarkozy's first year in office was marked by his rapid descent in France's presidential popularity polls. As 'Sarko' staggered from one contradiction to another, France's electorate was left confused and disappointed.

Even Sarko's sizzle...

Perhaps ill-advisedly, the 53 year old Mr Sarkozy had tried to steer a path between the authority that his position bestowed upon him, and the informality with which he sought to characterise his presidency. He succeeded in achieving neither objective: his state visit to the Vatican was best remembered for an apparent need to read text messages on his mobile telephone during his audience with the Pope. The manner of his marriage to the high-profile singer Carla Bruni called into question his judgement as press photographers were invited on the couple's honeymoon, but not to witness the marriage ceremony. Mr Sarkozy soon gained the nickname of 'hyper president' as he stumbled from one ill-thought out measure to another, barely pausing to consider how they might best be implemented. The names of his cabinet ministers, even including that of the Prime Minister Francois Fillon, rarely appear in reports in the international press. This is the case even when reforms relating to ministry-specific issues such as education and housing are announced. One of his advisers, Jaques Attali, was charged with producing a report and recommendations on economic liberalisation, very much the great white hope of Mr Sarkozy's administration. When produced, the report came up with some 300 measures, many of which were announced and later retracted; others simply never saw the light of day. In an interview, Mr Sarkozy was accused by one opposition member of displaying 'Sizzle, but no steak'.

...fizzles out

Other commentators took their criticism of Mr Sarkozy a stage further, suggesting that he was more interested in his ego than in ruling France. This posture has rightly, if unfavourably, been compared with the more self-effacing stance of M Fillon. What has also become clear are the tensions between France's ministers and the Sarko 'kitchen cabinet'. To some degree this has resulted from ministerial resentment at the treatment meted out to them by the President. The Presidential position has inevitably become isolated; much of his unpopularity is caused by his self-indulgent behaviour rather than by the reforms he has sought to put in place. After one year, one observer suggested that there were three reasons for his amazing loss of popularity. First, the economy, which has shown few signs of improvement. At the heart of France's economic malaise lies the apparent impossibility of containing the budget deficit. Second, Mr Sarkozy's often erratic views and opinions. The extent of his misjudgement can best be judged by the regularity with which apologies and corrections – both on television and in the press – have been considered necessary. Third his often arrogant personal behaviour and that of the people with which he has surrounded himself. When the chips are down, the French are a conservative bunch. They might give Mr Sarkozy the benefit of the doubt over misjudged economic reforms – but not over his 'in your face' marital behaviour and generally inappropriate behaviour. Since France elected him in the spring of 2007, Mr Sarkozy's former wife Cécile walked out on him (to be replaced by Carla Bruni pretty rapidly), he has been alleged to be drunk (and certainly looked it) during a public speech, he has called his press secretary 'imbécile' on television and he has walked out on an important television interview.

'La crise'

Once described as 'wildly ambitious', Mr Sarkozy had been seen by many French voters as their best bet to end the economic stagnation that had characterised France for over two decades. The home-made *crise* which had settled upon France under President Chirac (who retired aged 74) seemed to have no end, as France's electorate and its *Enarque* (the acronym given to graduates of France's Ecole Nationale d'Administration (ENA)) controlled elite drifted further apart. The concept of a European Union (EU) in which France continued to play a major, even dominant, role had long been at the centre of both right and left wing politics in France. Mr Sarkozy was left to cope with an underperforming economy and an electorate which – after its 2005 rejection of the proposed European Constitution – appeared to have lost faith in any European dreams. Following his 2007 election success, it also fell to Sarko to move France back on to the European agenda. This was never going to be an easy task; France by most accounts has benefited more than any other country from a European economic structure that was originally modelled very much to the benefit of France's framers in a smaller European community of five original members. By 2007 the EU had 27 member countries, not all of whom were content to rub along with manifestly out of date economic formulae. In his book *La France qui tombe* (*Falling France*) the French author Nicholas Baverez put forward the theory that France had simply missed out on the tide of economic liberalism that had produced Thatcher and Reagan. In its place, France had been ruled by a stifling Mitterand regime followed by half-hearted and generally mis-directed attempts at reform by Chirac. Mr Baverez summed up France's loss of direction with the observation that 'The trouble is that France prospered in a slightly unreal bubble for thirty years and then, with the falling of The (Berlin) Wall, had no real vision or solution to get beyond it'.

Underperforming economy

In its 2007 report on the French economy the International Monetary Fund (IMF) reported that economic growth in France has averaged 2 per cent since 2003, lagging behind the revival of growth in the Eurozone. Domestic demand appeared to have remained robust, but disappointing exports have been a significant drag on growth, accounting for a drop of close to half a percentage point of gross domestic product (GDP) per year on average. In 2007, France's annual GDP growth was 1.9 per cent, down from the 2.0 per cent of 2006. Domestic demand still remained the driver of growth. According to the IMF the drop in export growth and the continued import growth meant that France's current account deteriorated steadily, from a surplus of 1.4 per cent of GDP in 2002 down to an estimated deficit of 1.3 per cent in 2007.

Inflationary pressures also increased, but France's headline inflation still remained one of the lowest in the Eurozone. After dropping to 1.2 per cent in mid-2007, headline inflation had rebounded back up to 2.8 per cent by December 2007 reflecting the surges in food and energy prices. Unit labour costs have

KEY INDICATORS — France

	Unit	2003	2004	2005	2006	2007
Population	m	60.08	60.30	62.70	61.34	*61.68
Gross domestic product (GDP)	US$bn	1,749.30	2,002.58	2,127.17	2,252.11	2,560.26
GDP per capita	US$	29,106	32,663	33,925	36,706	*41,511
GDP real growth	%	0.5	2.3	1.2	1.9	1.8
Inflation	%	2.0	2.3	1.9	1.9	1.6
Unemployment	%	9.6	9.7	9.7	9.2	8.3
Coal output	mtoe	1.3	0.4	0.2	0.2	12.0
Exports (fob) (goods)	US$m	384,662.0	421,120.0	439,220.0	483,110.0	548,030.0
Imports (cif) (goods)	US$m	388,373.0	429,070.0	471,360.0	520,810.0	601,410.0
Balance of trade	US$m	-3,711.0	-7,940.0	-32,140.0	-37,690.0	-53,390.0
Current account	US$m	4,990.0	-5,410.0	-33,577.0	-28,192.0	-33,386.0
Total reserves minus gold	US$m	30,186.0	35,314.0	27,753.0	42,652.0	45,710.0
Foreign exchange	US$m	23,122.0	29,077.0	23,996.0	40,287.0	43,587.0
Exchange rate	per US$	0.88	0.80	0.77	0.75	0.69

* estimated figure

risen, as productivity gains have lagged wage behind inflation. Monetary conditions have tightened noticeably since 2006, reflecting European Central Bank (ECB) rate increases and, more recently, euro appreciation and the increase in risk premiums due to the fallout from the financial turbulence.

The turbulence in the financial markets appeared to have a limited impact on the domestic economy. According to the IMF, the performance of the banking sector remained solid. French banks' exposure to the US sub-prime market appears fairly limited. Nonetheless, according to the IMF, financial institutions remained vulnerable, particularly in respect of off-balance sheet exposures. The events at Banque Société Générale (SocGen) where a lone trader managed to lose an estimated US$7 billion, apart from causing his employers SocGen a few sleepless nights, revealed major shortcomings in internal control. The fraud also shone the spotlight on another of France's establishment aristocracies, the *Club des Cent* (it translates literally as the Hundred Club). SocGen's chief executive was a member of the club as well as being an *Enarque* graduate. The Paris based *International Herald Tribune* (IHT) reported in February 2008 that 'at least half of France's largest companies are run by graduates of just two schools, the Ecole Polytechnique which trains the country's top engineers, and the ENA.' The IHT went on to observe that this fact was all the more impressive since 'the two schools together produce only about 600 graduates a year'. The figure for Harvard alone in the US is 1,700 graduates each year. In a bold step, in early 2008 Mr Sarkozy gave a speech in which he undertook to reduce the number of civil servants recruited directly from the ENA, describing the move as 'a revolution to change mentalities'. Never one to do things by halves, he went on to announce that 'together we will build the public service of the twenty-first century'. But as had been so often the case with Sarkozy's reform proposals, the response from the trades unions was less than encouraging. France's largest union, the Confédération Générale du Travail, described the speech as a 'declaration of war'. In view of organised labour's response to his proposals, which included reducing the number of civil servants by 22,000 plus a further 11,200 in the education sector, Mr Sarkozy rapidly announced that he would rather discuss his proposals directly with the voters themselves. Quite how this 'discussion' was to take place was not made clear.

Recent French history no doubt weighed heavily in Mr Sarkozy's mind. Under the Chirac presidency, trades' union opposition to the reforms proposed by the then prime minister, Alain Juppé, resulted in a prolonged transport strike which quickly gathered popular support. Events were to take their toll, as parliament had to be dissolved enabling voters to express their loss of confidence in the Juppé government by voting it out of power, ushering in a socialist led government.

But what about the economy?

In 2008, annual GDP growth is projected by the IMF to reach 1.5 per cent, a lot weaker than originally anticipated. The relentless rise in oil prices, the strengthening of the euro and weakening economic prospects in partner countries will be a brake on growth. The zeal with which the government has pursued its structural reform programme appeared to have cooled off by mid-2008. At the centre of the programme had been the need to increase flexibility in labour markets, something that continued to prove elusive in 2008. Although the government has endeavoured to introduce a number of measures to make the 35-hour working week restriction less binding, these have met with some opposition. In December 2007 Mr Sarkozy had offered French companies the possibility of abolishing the constraints of the 35-hour week in return for higher wages and the agreement of the employees concerned. A similar response was the case with Mr Sarkozy's proposed labour market reforms. Other labour market initiatives included a review of the mechanism for setting the minimum wage, Salaire Minimum Interprofessionnel de Croissance (SMIC), and the merger of the unemployment and job placement agencies. Other market reforms were often as vague as they were ineffective.

The 2008 budget represented a pause in fiscal consolidation. The budget as published maintained spending restraints (including an unprecedented reduction in public employment), but these were offset by the cost of the August 2007 tax package, which left little room for deficit reductions. Over the medium term, the government aims for an annual structural adjustment of one half percentage point of GDP consistent with the longer term objective of reaching fiscal balance by 2012. A reformer at heart, paying eloquent lip service to the American model (or dream?) he so much admires, Mr Sarkozy has not been able to come to terms with the French reality. 'How does it read in Clermont Ferrand' may not trip off the tongue, but it is France's provincial industrial sector and its mollycoddled civil servants who have to decide between a stagnating status quo and the uncertain, and often contradictory, reform programme set out by Mr Sarkozy. The contradictions are also found between Mr Sarkozy's modernising, liberalising stance when in France and the protectionist, anti-globalisation position he adopts and advocates at European and international gatherings.

Club-Med anyone?

Mr Sarkozy's hyper activity again showed itself in mid-2008 as France prepared to take on the rotating EU Presidency for six months. As part of a plan clearly designed to show that France was back in a European driving seat, Mr Sarkozy risked being all things to all men. His enthusiasm flew in the face of a May 2008 Irish rejection (in a referendum) of the proposed European Constitution that looked likely to condemn greater European integration to the dustbin. Mr Sarkozy sought to heap blame and opprobrium not only on the Irish electorate (who had done no more than the Dutch and French electorates before them) but also on the European Commission (for favouring trade liberalisation at a time when the French government was intent on greater protectionism) and on the ECB for not heeding his advice on interest rate increases. At the inauguration of the French EU Presidency Mr Sarkozy had to content himself with his grandiose, but largely unpopular, concept of a Mediterranean Union (MU) to be launched at a Mediterranean summit in Paris in July 2008. The MU concept appeared to be flawed from the outset, dismissed by both Brussels Eurocrats and German diplomats alike as at best a French sideshow, at worst an attempt by France to find a platform (and maybe the money) that would enable it to be a European leader rather than continue to be an also ran.

Approval ratings probably also featured in Mr Sarkozy's political musings. In September 2007 he was scoring 57 per cent, already a 30-year low for a newly elected president. Eight months later, the figure had dropped to an unheard of 32 per cent as his ambitious reform programme came up against the embedded intransigence of French train-drivers, teachers, students, trades unions and politicians. Much of the discontent appeared to be directed against Sarko as much as against the reforms themselves. In turn, Mr Sarkozy had accused those opposed to the reforms of holding the country to hostage. Those most vociferously opposed to Mr Sarkozy's reform programme were in fact a minority of the population; the reforms only affected about half a million public employees – notably train drivers and civil servants. A sardonic *Wall Street Journal* article pointed out that the reforms, largely aimed at those public employees permitted to retire on a full pension some 20 years before the rest of the population, were also aimed at France's ballet dancers. The *Wall Street Journal* noted that the ballerinas' pension arrangements cost the nation a staggering US$8.9 billion annually. The leading article also pointed out that no livelihoods were at all likely to be threatened by Sarkozy's proposed reforms; this in the country with one of the Eurozone's highest official unemployment rates. In a 3 May editorial *The Economist* magazine in London bleakly noted that 'There is little time for him to make up lost ground. Success is not impossible. But another bad year and he risks being written off as little better than Mr Chirac'. Overcoming the effects of three decades of economic stagnation, and the mental attitudes that go with it, is no easy task.

Risk assessment

Economy	Fair
Politics	Fair
Regional stability	Good

COUNTRY PROFILE

Historical profile

After the collapse of the Visigothic Merovingian kingdom, Gaul, in the eighth and ninth centuries, became the heart of an empire ruled by the Germanic Charlemagne (Charles the Great) and encompassing parts of Western Europe. After Charlemagne's death in 814, parts of the West Frankish kingdom (most of modern-day France) were invaded by the Vikings and the Magyars before becoming a feudal lordship by the 10th century. The West Frankish kingdom eventually became the Royaume de France (Kingdom of France) and the lords appointed Hugues Capet as the first French King in 987.

1337–1453 The Hundred Years' War took place between the English and the French. The English were defeated in 1453 and driven out of Aquitaine in southern France.

1789 The lack of representation for the increasingly powerful middle class, opposition to France's absolute monarchy and economic problems led to the French Revolution and the overthrow of Louis XVI.

1792 The First Republic was declared.

1804 Napoléon Bonaparte declared himself emperor and launched a military campaign in Europe.

1815 Napoléon's defeat at Waterloo by the British, Belgians, Dutch and Prussians saw the end of his reign. Louis XVIII became King of France.

1848 An uprising led by students and workers, although quickly crushed, again led to the overthrow of the monarchy. Louis Napoléon (nephew of the first Napoléon) was elected president.

1852 Louis Napoléon declared himself emperor.

1871 France's defeat in the Franco-Prussian War resulted in the annexation of Alsace-Lorraine by the Germans.

1914 France was invaded by Germany.

1918 Following the end of the First World War and Germany's defeat, France regained Alsace-Lorraine.

1939 After Germany's invasion of Poland, France and the UK entered the Second World War by declaring war on Germany.

1940 France signed an armistice after Germany had invaded the country. The Germans installed a puppet government, the Vichy, led by Henri-Philippe Pétain. A Free French resistance movement was established in the UK under the leadership of General Charles de Gaulle.

1944 Following the liberation of France by the Allied powers, a provisional government took office under General de Gaulle.

1945 After the war in Europe ended in May, General de Gaulle retired from public office. The Fourth Republic was created with a constitution giving ultimate power to the Assemblé Nationale (National Assembly).

Between 1946 and 1958 France had 26 different governments, many including large communist elements.

1958 The Fifth Republic was created after the introduction of a new constitution, which allowed for the creation of a powerful presidency. In December, de Gaulle was elected president. France became a founder member of the forerunner of the EU, the European Economic Community (EEC), along with Belgium, Italy, Luxembourg, the Netherlands and West Germany.

1968 Discontent with low wages, lack of social reform and poor education policies led to a revolt by students and workers. The general strike was settled by the granting of generous wage rises and the student revolt collapsed, although de Gaulle's political position was fatally weakened.

1969 De Gaulle resigned from the presidency after losing a referendum on his programme for strengthening the regional government. He was succeeded by Georges Pompidou (1969–74) who was followed by Valéry Giscard d'Estaing (1974–81).

1981 François Mitterrand became the first socialist president since 1958 following Giscard d'Estaing's electoral defeat, governing with the first left-wing cabinet for 23 years.

1995 Jacques Chirac succeeded François Mitterrand as president.

2002 Euro currency replaced the franc. President Chirac defeated Le Pen in elections. Prime Minister Lionel Jospin resigned and Chirac appointed Jean-Pierre Raffarin of the Démocratie Libérale (DL) (Liberal Democracy) in his place. After legislative elections, a coalition government was formed, led by the UPM, UDF and allies.

2003 France was crippled by a series of public sector strikes over pension reform.

2004 Voting in regional elections showed national discontent with the government, resulting in the left-wing opposition carrying 21 out of the country's 22 mainland regions. Prime Minister Raffarin resigned, but was immediately re-installed by President Chirac, who instigated a major reshuffle of his government to carry it through the remaining three years of his term.

2005 France held a referendum on the European Constitution in which almost 55 per cent voted No, with 45 per cent in favour; turnout was about 70 per cent. Prime Minister Raffarin resigned the next day; Dominique de Villepin was appointed prime minister. Rioting in disadvantaged and disaffected immigrant communities broke out, first in the Paris suburb of Clichy-sous-Bois, then elsewhere in the capital and in other towns and cities. Final figures reported by the French police were 8,973 vehicles burnt and 2,888 arrests forcing the government to declared a state of emergency for several weeks.

2006 With the first cases of the dangerous N1H5 avian influenza (bird flu) found, 20 countries banned French poultry imports. France took the lead in providing 1,700 troops for UN peace-keeping duties in the Lebanon in August. France and Germany combined to apply pressure to the EU demanding tougher conditions for Turkey's proposed membership.

2007 Nicolas Sarkozy won the presidential elections in the second round on 6 May, defeating Ségolène Royal by 53 per cent of the votes to 47 per cent. He was inaugurated on 16 May. François Fillon was appointed prime minister on 17 May.

2008 President Sarkozy married Carla Bruni at the Elysée Palace on 2 February. On 4 Febuary, a special parliamentary congress voted to amend the wording in the EU constitutional treaty and omit any reference to the French constitution. This change allows France to ratify the new EU treaty without another referendum. The treaty was formally ratified on 14 February. On 23 July parliament scraped the 35-hour working week, 10 years after it was introduced. From August, companies can organise working patterns based on agreements with their workforces.

Political structure

Constitution

The 25 September 1958 constitution of the Fifth Republic maintained the original French republican ideals of liberty, fraternity and equality. It was designed to end post-war political deadlock by granting greater powers to the president. It guarantees the unity and indivisibility of the French state.

Since 1982 much administrative and financial power, traditionally held by the state, has been devolved to the 22 régions (regions) and 96 départements (departments) of metropolitan France. In March 2003, parliament approved constitutional amendments which allow all of the regions and departments a greater amount of autonomy.

In mid-2000, legislation was passed granting semi-autonomy to the island of Corsica as a single administrative unit, replacing its previous status as two standard départements. France's overseas territories are either classed as Département d'Outre-Mer (DOM) (Overseas Department) or Térritoire d'Outre-Mer (TOM) (Overseas Territory), depending on the level of autonomy.

Form of state

Semi-presidential democratic republic

The executive

Executive power is held by the president, elected by universal adult suffrage for a five-year term which can be renewed only once. A two-round voting system operates for presidential elections, with the second round a run-off between the two highest polling candidates from the first round.

The president appoints the prime minister and other members of the government, can dissolve the Assemblée Nationale and can also veto laws. In practice, the president traditionally accepts as prime minister the leader of the largest party in the National Assembly, and approves the prime minister's choice of government ministers.

The presidential term of office was reduced from seven years to five with effect from the 2002 presidential elections.

National legislature

The legislature is a bicameral Parlement (Parliament) consisting of an upper house, the Assemblée Nationale (National Assembly), and a lower house, the Sénat (Senate). The Assemblée Nationale comprises 577 deputés (deputies) elected by geographical constituencies (including 17 overseas representatives) for a five-year term while the Sénat has 321 seats, one-third of which are renewed every three years in indirect elections.

Legal system

The country has no supreme court but this role is filled by a nine-member Conseil Constitutionel (Constitutional Council). Its task is to ensure that law treaties and regulations are in keeping with the constitution and that elections are conducted in a regular manner. The highest court of appeal is the Cour de Cassation, which can overrule decisions in all lower courts, but not government legislation. Since the signing of the Single European Act in 1986, the European Court of Justice (ECJ) has been the highest authority in certain areas of French law. France also accepts International Court of Justice (ICJ) jurisdiction.

Last elections

22 April/6 May 2007 (presidential); 10/17 June 2007 (parliamentary).

Results: Presidential: Nicolas Sarkozy (Union pour un Mouvement Populaire) (UMP) (Union for a Popular Movement) won 53 per cent of the vote; Ségolène Royal (Parti Socialiste (PS) (Socialist Party)) won 47 per cent.

Parliamentary: (first round) the UMP won 39.54 per cent (98 out of 110 seats to be decided). Turnout was 60.4 per cent. (Second round):

Next elections

2012 (presidential and parliamentary)

Political parties

Ruling party

Union pour un Mouvement Populaire (UMP) (Union for a People's Movement)

Main opposition party

Parti Socialiste (PS) (Socialist Party)

Population

61.68 million (2007)*

Last census: March 1999: 58,520,688

Population density: 107 inhabitants per square km. Urban population: 76 per cent (1995–2001).

Annual growth rate: 0.4 per cent 1994–2004 (WHO 2006)

Ethnic make-up

The population is predominantly Western European. North Africans form the principal ethnic minority, with smaller communities from former French colonies in Asia and sub-Saharan Africa.

Religions

There is no state religion, but Roman Catholicism predominates (90 per cent of population), with a significant Protestant minority concentrated in southern France (2 per cent) and Muslim and Jewish communities in major urban areas (1 per cent each).

Education

Compulsory education is provided for free. Primary schooling lasts to the age of 11, after which all pupils transfer to a four-year course in secondary school. At the age of 15 there are two options: either a three-year course leading to the baccalauréate examination or a two-year vocational course. An average of 80 per cent of schoolchildren are expected to achieve the baccalauréate, which is the minimum entry qualification to university. Educational expenditure is typically equivalent to 6 per cent of gross national income.

Compulsory years: Six to 16

Pupils per teacher: 19 in primary schools

Health

Per capita total expenditure on health (2003) was US$2,902; of which per capita government spending was US$2,213, at the international dollar rate, (WHO 2006).

France's liberal state-subsidised medical system allows doctors and dentists to establish private practices. Patients, who are free to choose their own providers, are reimbursed by the state for up to 85 per cent of medical costs. The government makes full provision for people who are unable to make any contributions, by treating them as private patients covered by insurance. A survey by the Organisation for Economic Co-operation and Development (OECD) in mid-2000 showed the French healthcare system to be the best in the world in terms of diagnosis, cure and survival rates for major diseases. Official figures published in May 2004 indicated that the French health system was losing US$27,200 a minute. Proposed reforms to reduce the cost of the health system have met with vociferous opposition from doctors, nurses and health professionals. Fraud is estimated to cost the system more than US$980 million per year, and ease of access to prescription drugs is thought to be the principal reason for the fact that French consumption of drugs and medicine is more than three times the European average.

HIV/Aids

HIV prevalence: 0.4 per cent aged 15–49 in 2003 (World Bank)

Life expectancy: 80 years, 2004 (WHO 2006)

Fertility rate/Maternal mortality rate: 1.9 births per woman, 2004 (WHO 2006); maternal mortality 0.1 per 1,000 live births (World Bank).

Child (under 5 years) mortality rate (per 1,000): 4.4 per 1,000 live births (World Bank)

Head of population per physician:
3.37 physicians per 1,000 people, 2004 (WHO 2006)

Welfare
France's extensive social security system, including health insurance, family allowances and retirement insurance, covers 99.2 per cent of the population.
In common with other industrialised nations, France's ageing population is an increasing concern. The cost of pensions is set to escalate significantly from 9.8 per cent of GDP in 2001 to 13.5 per cent of GDP by 2030.

Main cities
Paris (capital, estimated population 2.1 million in 2005), Marseille (771,153), Lyon (454,478), Toulouse (402,905), Nice (344,338), Nantes (278,056), Strasbourg (268,062), Bordeaux (216,683).

Languages spoken
Breton is spoken in Brittany and Euskera (Basque) is spoken in the south-west, while in Alsace and Lorraine, in the east, German is widely spoken.
English is spoken in the business community, but an understanding of French is considered essential for visitors.
Flemish, Catalán, Occitan, Corsu, Arabic, Kabyle and Antillean are also spoken.

Official language/s
French

Media
National news agency: Agence France Presse
Other news agencies: Reuters: http://fr.reuters.com
Focus: www.focusinfo.eu

Press
French newspapers are editorially free from government control and censorship, and cover the full political spectrum.
There are 85 daily newspapers published, of which 24 are nationals. There are around 870 newspapers and 6,000 magazines published reaching over 45 per cent of adults. Regional newspapers have a larger readership than national titles.
Dailies: In French, major newspapers include Le Monde (www.lemonde.fr), Le Figaro (www.lefigaro.fr) is a conservative newspaper, Libération (www.liberation.fr) a left-wing newspaper, Ouest France (www.ouest-france.fr) has the largest circulation, Le Parisien (www.leparisien.fr) a centrist newspaper and La Croix (www.la-croix.com) a Catholic newspaper.
Weeklies: In French, the Courrier Intenational (www.courrierinternational.com), L'Epress (www.lexpress.fr) and Le Point (www.lepoint.fr) report on news and current affairs, Le Journal du Dimanche (www.lejdd.fr) is a popular Sunday newspaper. Special interest publications include Maghreb Hebdo concerning north African news and La Marseillaise a communist publication and two humourist magazines are Le Canard Enchaîné and Le Herisson. In English The Riviera Times (www.rivieratimes.com).
Business: In French, daily newspapers include Les Echos (www.lesechos.fr), La Tribune (www.latribune.fr) and Investir (www.investir.fr). Monthly publications include the popular economics magazine Capital (www.capital.fr), L'Expansion (www.lexpansion.com) and Valeurs Actuelles (www.valeursactuelles.com) a weekly and Le Revenu (www.lerevenu.com) a bi-weekly magazine. Jeune Afrique Economie is an Africa-oriented bi-weelkly.
Periodicals: In French, monthly publications include Le Monde Dipomatique (www.monde-diplomatique.fr) a left-wing magazine, Entrevue (www.entrevue.fr) a tabloid entertainment magazine, Lire (www.lire.fr) a cultural magazine and Le Nouvel Afrique Asie a left-wing third world-orientated monthly magazine. Influential women's magazines include Vogue (www.vogue.fr) and Marie Claire (www.marieclaire.fr).

Broadcasting
France is a world leader in broadcasting, providing international news and entertainment services to most continents, via radio, satellite, pay-to-view digital services and internet links.
Radio: The national public radio service is Radio France (www.radiofrance.fr) with seven stations offering a range of genre including classical, news, sport, information, culture and modern music. Radio France Internationale (RFI) (www.rfi.fr) is funded wholly by the French ministry of foreign affairs; it broadcasts worldwide in 19 languages, other than French.
Nationally, there are 17 commercial radio stations including Europe 1 (www.europe1.fr), Fun Radio (www.funradio.fr), RTL (www.rtl.fr) a major news and entertainment network, Sud Radio (www.sudradio.fr), NRJ (www.nrj.fr), a leading music network and Alouette (www.alouette.fr).
Apart from private local and regional radio stations, many are affiliates of national networks.
Television: The national public broadcaster is France Télévisions (www.francetelevisions.fr) with five networks. Some channels carry advertising. Channels are designated France 2, 3, 4, 5 and RFO (www.rfo.fr) for overseas territories. Combined, France Télévisions typically has 40 per cent of the audience share and 30 per cent of revenues.
TF1 (www.tf1.fr) is the leading commercial TV channel with typically 35 per cent audience share and almost 50 per cent of advertising revenues. Programmes include locally made and foreign imports. TFI operates a national 24-hour news channel, La Chaine Info (http://tf1.lci.fr), as well as a major digital and internet TV service, France 24 (www.france24.com), with a wide range of international news and current affairs in French, English and Arabic. All analogue services will be switched to digital services by 2011.

Advertising
The typical annual ad-spend is around eur10 billion (US$7.2 billion), of which the greater part is spent by retail advertising at over 2 billion (US$1.4 billion). Television and magazine advertising typically carry around 30 per cent of the market each.
Numerous advertising agencies operate throughout the country. Television advertising is strictly controlled, by Régie Française de Publicité (RFP), and is expensive. There is limited advertising available on radio. All other media are widely used for advertising, although newspapers and magazines dominate. There are over 50,000 poster panels available. New advertising media is available through the internet and mobile/cell phones.
Tobacco and alcohol may be advertised but only under strict rules.

Economy
France has a mixed economy with large agricultural, industrial and service sectors. In line with other mature economies, GDP is dominated by the services sector, followed by industry. The services sector annually contributes around 70 per cent to GDP. Although it accounts for a relatively low percentage of GDP (3.1 per cent), the country's agricultural heritage ensures that the sector remains politically important and can conflict with France's commitments to the EU.
The government has completed a major industrial restructuring and modernisation programme, placing particular emphasis on production for the home market and expanding export capacity. The government has traditionally played a very active role in the economy. Although the state's influence has declined in recent years due to privatisation, the state sector continues to be important.
The economic stagnation France experienced in the early part of 2005 turned around in the latter half, helped by robust domestic demand. GDP growth was 1.2 per cent in 2005 and expected to be 2.5 per cent in 2006, while inflation was 1.9 per cent, rising to 2.0 per cent in 2006 due to rising energy costs. A current account deficit of -0.3 per cent of GDP in 2004 deepened in 2005 to -1.6 per cent.

Some much-needed reforms in public finances, notably pensions, were carried through by the former government, but it is questionable whether the will remains to continue the process in other areas. A top priority of the government continues to be unemployment, which is around 10 per cent and, more worryingly, with disproportionately high youth unemployment. The government attempted to bring in reforms to labour laws in 2006 but public demonstrations forced a climb-down.

Labour market and unemployment

The French labour force totalled 14.6 million in the third quarter of 2000, while unemployment dropped from an average of 11.2 per cent in 1999 to 8.9 per cent in July 2001.

The French labour force has high productivity rates and education levels are high. Regulations on working hours and conditions are extensive and many firms experience flexibility problems, although the introduction of a 35-hour working week in late 1999 to curb unemployment was actually used by many employers to enhance flexibility by increasing the amount of part-time employment. Small- and medium-sized firms (SMEs) were required to start implementing the 35-hour week in January 2002.

In 2005, the government plans to allow employees to work longer than 35 hours.

External trade

As a member of the European Union, France operates within a communitywide free trade union, with tariffs sets as a whole. Internationally, the EU has free trade agreements with a number of nations and trading blocs worldwide. France has several overseas departments which are treated as de jure mainland France with fully implemented treaties with the EU.

France is a leading world trader; it is a major exporter of agricultural produce and processed food, its industrial base includes vehicles, aerospace and high-speed trains, telecommunications, weapons and consumer goods.

French business signed US$30 billion in trade deals with China following President Sarkozy's state visit in November 2007. China bought 160 Airbus passenger aeroplanes and two electricity generating, nuclear reactors.

Imports

Principal imports are machinery and equipment, vehicles, crude oil, aircraft, plastics and chemicals.

Main sources: Germany (16.3 per cent total, 2006), Italy (8.5 per cent), Belgium (8.3 per cent).

Exports

Principal exports include machinery and vehicles, trains and rail equipment, aircraft, plastics, chemicals and pharmaceuticals, iron and steel, food and beverages.

Main destinations: Germany (14.5 per cent total, 2006), Spain (9.9 per cent), Italy (9.1 per cent).

Agriculture

Farming

France is a major European food producer with self-sufficiency in dairy produce and is a substantial exporter of livestock produce, wine, fruit and vegetables. Agriculture contributes around 3.1 per cent to GDP and employs 5 per cent of the labour force. France is also the largest recipient of subsidies, financed through the EU's Common Agricultural Policy (CAP).

Most of French agriculture is now governed by CAP. The CAP is based on three broad principles:

- the EU is treated as a single market for agricultural produce
- EU farmers are given preference over outside suppliers
- the cost of the CAP is met by EU member governments.

Fundamental reform to the CAP was introduced in 2005, whereby subsidies paid on farm output, which tended to benefit large farms and encourage overproduction, were replaced by single farm payments not conditional on production. This is expected to reward farms that provide and maintain a healthy environment, food safety and animal welfare standards. The changes are also intended to encourage market conscious production and cut the cost of CAP to the EU taxpayer. France is due to introduce this measure in 2006.

With the growing global demand for Champagne, which reached a record of almost 151 million bottles in 2007, the government extended the growing region, officially allowing vintners within the newly expanded area to designate their sparkling wine as Champagne. An area of 33,500 hectares in north-eastern France is the only place worldwide allowed to use the coveted Appellation d'Origine Controlee (AOC) and to label its wine Champagne. The last expansion of the Champagne region was in 1927; the latest enlargement will become operational in 2009, with the new AOC Champagne expected to be ready for sale by 2019.

Crop production in 2005 included: 63,706,000 tonnes (t) cereals in total, 36,922,000t wheat, 10,357,000t barley, 13,226,000t maize, 6,347,000t potatoes, 29,030,000t sugar beets, 4,419,000t rapeseed (canola), 515,000t oats, 268,000t sorghum, 1,753,500t pulses, 24,250t citrus fruit, 6,787,000t grapes, 2,332,267t oilcrops, 20,000t tobacco, 28,000t olives, 56,500t treenuts, 2,123,000t apples, 10,339,100t fruit in total, 8,185,000t vegetables in total. Livestock production included: 6,179,379t meat in total, 1,529,000t beef, 2,257,000t pig meat, 123,000t lamb, 5,279t horsemeat, 1,971,000t poultry, 1,045,000t eggs, 26,133,000t milk, 15,000t honey, 150,000t cattle hides.

Fishing

Although oyster farming remains highly vulnerable to the risk of disease, France is the top European producer of oysters and among the first three producers of mussels (from both fishing and aquaculture).

France is also the top European producer of fresh water trout and has remained competitive with European regions with more favourable environmental conditions. Sea bass and sea bream represent the majority of marine farm production with turbot farming expanding. Only part of the production is for domestic consumption, the remainder being exported.

In 2004, the total marine fish catch was 497,231 tonnes and the total crustacean catch was 17,409 tonnes.

Forestry

Forestry is France's richest natural resource with over a quarter (15 million hectares) of metropolitan France covered by forest, giving it the largest tree-covered area in the EU. The Office National des Forêts (ONF) (National Forestry Office) manages over a quarter of this area. Forestry is concentrated in the east, south and south-west of the country, with the largest area being the Landes, coastal forests south of Bordeaux. Deciduous forests account for 61 per cent of the total, while 38 per cent are coniferous or mixed.

About 8 per cent of the wooded area is brushwood.

Although it is a net importer of sawn softwoods and pulp for its paper industry, France remains the largest producer of sawn hardwood in Europe.

The forestry industry supplies raw materials to several industries. About 60 per cent of French wood production is used in the construction industry.

Timber imports in 2004 were US$9 billion, while exports amounted to US$7.1 billion.

Production in 2004 included 34,950,000 cubic metres (cum) roundwood, 32,450,000cum industrial roundwood, 9,860,000cum sawnwood, *21,000,000cum sawlogs and veneers, *11,000,000cum pulpwood, 6,046,000cum wood-based panels, 2,500,000cum wood fuel; 52,000 tonnes (t) charcoal, 10,249,000t paper and paperboard, including 1,118,000t newsprint, 3,475,000t printing and writing paper, 2,503,000t wood pulp, 5,942,000t recovered paper.

* estimate

Industry and manufacturing

France has a broad industrial base incorporating a large capital-intensive state-owned sector, composed mainly of small- and medium-sized manufacturing enterprises, which together contribute around 25 per cent to GDP and employ 27 per cent of the labour force.

Industrial policy is generally aimed at developing the domestic market, promotion of 'new technology' sectors and internationalisation of state-owned companies.

Government protection of industry is an important economic issue and one which threatens both to retard the efficiency of domestic markets and alienate France's European partners.

Leading sectors include agri-foodstuffs, telecommunications, aerospace, motor industry, metallurgy, chemicals, parachemicals and pharmaceuticals, textiles and clothing.

Tourism

France is the world's top destination for tourists with over 80 million visitors in 2004. France launched a major PR campaign in 2003 to promote the country to the US travelling public, but while the number of long-haul visitors increased, their main destination was Paris, and so regional centres did not benefit from these arrivals. China has designated France as an approved destination for its holidaying citizens; Chinese visitors could swell France's arrival numbers by several millions.

Mining

The mining sector typically contributes 7 per cent to annual GDP and employs less than 1 per cent of the workforce. France is a significant producer of iron ore, bauxite and potash. In an effort to reduce dependence on imported minerals, exploration for lead, zinc, barium and tungsten has been intensified.

Hydrocarbons

France has around 160 million barrels of estimated oil reserves. Crude oil production has declined since about 1990 from 67,000 barrels per day (bpd) to 23,300 bpd in 2004. France is a heavy consumer of oil, amounting to two million bpd, most of which has to be imported.

France has a crude oil refining capacity of 1.9 million bpd. The largest refinery, TotalFinaElf's at Gonfreville l'Orcher, has a capacity of 343,00 bpd. France will need substantial investment to upgrade the refining sector in order to meet the EU's stringent environmental regulations.

France is a major player on world energy markets. TotalFinaElf is the fourth-largest company in the world and has assets in Africa, Latin America and the North Sea. It was created in 1999 when Total and Elf Aquitaine merged with Belgium's Petrofina.

France has around 14 billion cubic metres of estimated natural gas reserves, but production is negligible and declining. As with oil, France imports the bulk of the gas it consumes.

Coal reserves are small. Coal has gradually been replaced by nuclear power for electricity generation. The coal-mining industry ended with the closure of the last mine in 2004, but some coal is imported for the remaining coal-fired power stations and the steel industry.

Energy

Around 80 per cent of French electricity is generated by nuclear power stations. In 2007 France consumed 99.7 million tonnes of oil equivalent in nuclear energy. There are 58 nuclear reactors in France. The government plans to expand the sector with the construction of a new generation of reactors as well as upgrading existing assets. France is one of the world's largest nuclear power producers and produces enough electricity to be a net exporter.

The state-owned monopoly, Electricité de France (EdF), owns the entire transmission network and supplies 95 per cent of all electricity in the country.

In 2000, France passed legislation that began the electricity sector's liberalisation. Since then, about 1,800 large industrial and commercial consumers comprising about 30 per cent of the market have been able to choose their electricity supplier.

The second-largest electricity group is the Compagnie Nationale de Rhône (CNR), which produces about 3 per cent of France's electricity, mostly from hydroelectric plants.The other producer is Société Nationale d'Electricité et de Thermique (SNET), a subsidiary of the French coal utility, Charbonnages de France.

Financial markets

Stock exchange

The Paris Bourse is part of Euronext, an integrated cross-border single currency stock, derivatives and commodities market composed of the Brussels, Paris and Amsterdam exchanges.

Euronext is the largest European exchange in terms of cash trading volume through the central order book. It is the second-largest exchange in Europe in terms of the number and total market capitalisation of listed companies.

Banking and insurance

Central bank

Banque de France; European Central Bank (ECB)

Time

GMT plus one hour (daylight saving, late March to late October, GMT plus two hours)

Geography

France is bordered to the north by the English Channel (La Manche), and to the north-east, east and south-east by Belgium, Luxembourg, Germany, Switzerland and Italy, respectively. The Mediterranean Sea forms the southern boundary, and Spain the south-western, while the west coast faces the Atlantic Ocean.

France, the largest country in the west of Europe, has lush farming land, extensive forest and a large alluvial salt mash that makes up much of the province of the Camargue. The overall impression is of a rolling landscape from the south-west to north-east and mountainous regions for the rest of the country. There are four major river systems (the Seine, Loire, Rhone and Marne) that drain into either the Atlantic Ocean, English Channel or the Mediterranean Sea. The highest mountain, Mont Blanc (4,810 metres), is situated in the French Alps in the south-east.

Hemisphere

Northern

Climate

France has a moderate maritime climate in the north with a small temperature range and abundant rainfall. By contrast, southern France has a Mediterranean climate, with hot dry summers and mild, moist winters. Eastern France has a continental climate, with thunderstorms prevalent in summer. The average temperature in Paris in January is three degrees Celsius (C) and in July 18 degrees C. Annual rainfall in Paris is 573mm.

Dress codes

Western dress is the norm.

Entry requirements

Passports

Passports are required by all, expect nationals of EU countries with national ID cards. Passports must be valid for three months beyond the length of stay.

Visa

Required by all, except citizens of EU countries, North America, Australasia and Japan, for stays up to three months; this includes business trips by representatives of foreign entities with an invitation from a local company or organisation. Proof of adequate funds for stay, an itinerary, a guarantee of repatriation if necessary and return/onward ticket are also required.

For further exceptions, full details and a copy of the application form visit www.diplomatie.gouv.fr/thema/dossier.gb.asp and follow the path (entering France) to the database. A Schengen visa application (offered in several languages) can be downloaded from http://europa.eu/abc/travel/ see 'documents you will need'.

Currency advice/regulations
There are no limits to the amount of local or foreign currency imported or exported, although amounts exceeding eur7,600 must be declared.

Customs
Personal items are duty-free. There are no duties levied on alcohol and tobacco between EU member states, providing amounts imported are for personal consumption.
Plant material, meat products from Africa and valuable art or antique objects must be declared.

Health (for visitors)
Nationals of the European Economic Area (EEA) countries and Switzerland can access reduced cost and sometimes free medical treatment using a European Health Insurance Card (EHIC) while visiting the EEA. Exceptions include nationals of the 10 countries which joined the EU in 2004 whose EHIC is not valid in Switzerland. Applications for the EHIC should be made before travelling.

Mandatory precautions
None

Advisable precautions
There are no particular health hazards in France, although rabies is a problem in some rural areas.
Medical insurance is advisable for visitors of non-EEA countries as healthcare costs can be high. Only medication for personal use may be bought into France.

Hotels
Classified into deluxe and one- to four-star. Reservations (either direct or through centralised booking offices) should be made in advance during holiday seasons. Single rooms are rare and rates are usually quoted for double rooms. A tip of around 12–15 per cent of the bill is usual, provided no service charge has already been added.

Credit cards
All major credit cards are accepted.

Public holidays (national)
Fixed dates
1 Jan (New Year's Day), 1 May (Labour Day), 8 May (Victory Day), 14 Jul (Bastille Day), 15 Aug (Assumption Day), 1 Nov (All Saints' Day), 11 Nov (Armistice Day) and 25 Dec (Christmas Day).
The months of July and August are traditionally when the French take their holidays.

Variable dates
Easter Monday, Ascension Day, Whit Monday.

Working hours
Anyone intending to visit France for business purposes should avoid the traditional holiday month of August, when most businesses and government departments have only a skeleton staff at work.

Banking
Mon–Fri: 0900–1200 and 1400–1600.
Some banks close on Mondays and all close early on the day before a Bank Holiday.

Business
Mon–Fri: 0900–1200 and 1400–1800.

Government
Mon–Fri: 0830–1800.

Shops
Mon–Fri: 0900–1830 (most shops are closed between 1200–1430). Some shops open on Sundays and some close on Mondays.

Telecommunications
Postal services
The main Paris post office, at Louvre metro station, is open 24 hours, all year round.

Mobile/cell phones
There are 900/1800 and 3G GSM services available throughout all of the country.

Electricity supply
220V AC

Social customs/useful tips
In France, strangers and acquaintances shake hands at the beginning and end of a meeting.
Most offices traditionally have a long lunch hour, lasting from 1200 until at least 1400. Lunchtime remains a popular time for doing business, with a number of restaurants in big cities catering expressly for business clients.
French nationals must carry identification at all times. Visitors should carry their passports. Spot identity checks are not uncommon and it is illegal to be without identification.

Security
Serious crimes represent only a tiny percentage of the total number reported, while there has been a big rise in delinquency, vandalism and petty theft. Pickpockets operate particularly in train stations and subways.
France has one of the highest road accident rates in Europe.

Getting there
Air
France has a number of airports located in the various regions receiving international flights.
National airline: Air France
International airport/s: Paris-Charles de Gaulle Airport (CDG), 23km north-east of Paris. Facilities include a business centre, bank, post office, restaurants, bars, duty-free shopping, medical centre and pharmacy. Car hire is available.
Other airport/s: Orly (ORY), 14km south of Paris; Bordeaux (BOD), 12km from city; Lille (LIL), 15km from city; Lyon (LYS), 24km east of Lyon; Marseille (MRS), 24km north of city; Nice (NCE), 6km west of Nice; Toulouse (TLS), 10km from city; Biarritz (BIQ); Nantes (NTE); Perpignan (PGF) and Strasbourg (SXB).
Airport tax: None

Surface
France has good rail, road and sea connections with all surrounding countries.
Rail: The Eurostar service is provided by Belgium, UK and French railways, operating high speed rail connections between London, Paris and Brussels. Road vehicles are transported through the tunnel in Le Shuttle trains.
Water: There are regular cross channel ferries from the UK and Mediterrean ferries to Corsica, Spain (Balearic Islands) and North Africa.
Main port/s: Marseille (Europe's third-largest port), Boulogne, Nice, Calais, Dieppe, Dunkirk, Cherbourg, Le Havre, Rouen.

Getting about
National transport
Air: Paris is the most important business destination in France and is served by the two main airports, at Orly and Charles de Gaulle. Major cities are linked by Air France. Some services operate only during summer.
Road: France has the densest road network in the world. There are 806,000km of roads, including 7,100km of motorways, most of which are autoroutes à péage (toll roads).
Buses: There are good local bus services and some long-distance coach services.
Rail: French transport policy favours the railways. The Société Nationale des Chemins de Fer Français (SNCF) (French National Railroad Company) operates a nationwide network reaching to almost every part of the country. The most important rail lines radiate from Paris. Three high-speed train (TGV) lines link northern and southern France. These trains are modern and comfortable; seats can be booked in advance.
Water: There are approximately 9,000km of inland navigable waterways. Major canal areas are situated in the north and north-east of Paris, where the majority of the navigable rivers, including the Seine, the Rhine, the Midi, Brittany and the Loire are connected with canals.

City transport
Paris has one of the best urban transport networks in the world. A Carte Orange Hebdomadaire allows unlimited travel for

one week on most forms of public transport.

Taxis: From Charles de Gaulle and Orly airports to the city centre, limousines and taxis are available.

Taxis are only available from stations de taxi (taxi ranks). Day and night rates should be displayed inside the vehicle. Note that extra charges are usually levied for journeys to racecourses, stations and airports. Tipping is usually 10–15 per cent.

Buses, trams & metro: In Paris, the same tickets may be used on buses and the metro; a carnet of 10 tickets is cheaper. Buses operate between 0600–2100; some exceptional routes operate until 0030.

Car hire

All major international hire companies have offices in Paris and other main towns. Drivers must carry at all times: a passport or national ID card, a valid driving licence, car ownership papers and proof of insurance.

Traffic drives on the right. Priorité à droite applies, particularly in built-up areas – cars coming out of a side turning on the right have priority, unless suspended where a sign indicates. Speed limits: 130kph on toll motorways, 110kph on dual carriageways, 90kph on other roads and 60kph in towns. Note that these limits are reduced when wet. Speed limits for drivers who have held their licence for less than two years are 110kph on motorways, 100kph on dual carriageways and 80kph on other roads.

Wearing of seat belts is compulsory in front seats.

BUSINESS DIRECTORY

The addresses listed below are a selection only. While World of Information makes every endeavour to check these addresses, we cannot guarantee that changes have not been made, especially to telephone numbers and area codes. We would welcome any corrections.

Telephone area codes

The International direct dialling (IDD) code for France is +33, followed by area code and subscriber's number:

Paris	1
North-west (Nantes, Rouen, etc)	2
North-east (Lille, Strasbourg etc)	3
South-east and Corsica (Lyon, Marseilles, etc)	4
South-west (Bordeaux, Toulouse, etc)	5

Useful telephone numbers

Police: 17
Fire: 18
Medical emergency and ambulance: 15

Chambers of Commerce

American Chamber of Commerce in France, 156 Boulevard Haussmann, 75008 Paris (tel: 5643-4567; fax: 5643-4560; e-mail: amchamfrance@amchamfrance.org)

Assemblée des Chambres Françaises de Commerce et d'Industrie, 45 Avenue d'Iéna, PO Box 3003, 75773 Paris Cedex 16 (tel: 4069-3700; fax: 4720-6128; e-mail: contactdie@acfci.cci.fr).

Boulogne-sur-Mer Chambre de Commerce et d'Industrie, 98 Quai Gambetta, 62204 Boulogne-sur-Mer (tel: 2199-6200; fax: 2199-6201; e-mail: ccibco@boulogne-sur-mer.cci.fr).

Bordeaux Chambre de Commerce et d'Industrie, 12 Place de la Bourse, 33076 Bordeaux (tel: 5679-5000; fax: 5569-5265; e-mail: bourse@bordeaux.cci.fr).

British-French Chamber of Commerce and Industry, 31 Rue Boissy d'Anglas, 75008 Paris (tel: 5330-8130; fax: 5330-8135; e-mail: information@francobritishchamber.com).

Calais Chambre de Commerce et d'Industrie, 24 Boulevard des Alliés, PO Box 199, 62104 Calais Cedex (tel: 2146-0000; fax: 2146-0099; e-mail: ccic@calais.cci.fr).

Grenoble Chambre de Commerce et d'Industrie, 1 Place André Malraux, PO Box 297, 38016 Grenoble Cedex 1 (tel: 7628-2828; fax: 7628-2747; e-mail: ccig@grenoble.cci.fr).

Loiret Chambre de Commerce et d'Industrie, 23 Place du Martroi, 45044 Orléans Cedex 1 (tel: 3877-7777; fax: 3853-0978; e-mail: direction@loiret.cci.fr).

Lorraine Chambre de Commerce et d'Industrie, 10 Viaduc J-F Kennedy, CS 4231, 54042 Nancy Cedex (tel: 8390-1313; fax: 8328-8833; e-mail: crci@lorraine.cci.fr).

Lyon Chambre de Commerce et d'Industrie, Palais du Commerce, Place de la Bourse, 69289 Lyon Cedex 2 (tel: 7240-5858; fax: 7837-5346; e-mail: info@lyon.cci.fr).

Nantes Chambre de Commerce et d'Industrie, 16 Quai Ernest Renaud, PO Box 90517, 44105 Nantes Cedex 4 (tel: 4044-6060; fax: 4044-6090; e-mail: administrator@nantes.cci.fr).

Nice Chambre de Commerce et d'Industrie, 20 Boulevard Carabaçel, PO Box 1259, 06005 Nice Cedex 1 (tel: 0820-422-222; fax: 9313-7399; e-mail: mde.nice.carabacel@cote-azur.cci.fr).

Rennes Chambre de Commerce et d'Industrie, 2 Avenue de la Préfecture, CS 64204, 35042 Rennes Cedex (tel: 9933-6666; fax: 9333-2428; e-mail: info@rennes.cci.fr).

Rouen Chambre de Commerce et d'Industrie, Palais des Consuls, Quai de la Bourse, PO Box 641, 76007 Rouen Cedex 1 (tel: 3414-3737; fax: 3514-3838; e-mail: ccir@rouen.cci.fr).

Strasbourg Chambre de Commerce et d'Industrie, 10 Place Gutenburg, 67081 Strasbourg Cedex (tel: 0388-752-525; fax: 0388-223-120; e-mail: direction@strasbourg.cci.fr).

Banking

Association Française de Banques, 18 Rue la Fayette, 75009 Paris (tel: 4246-9259).

Banque Française du Commerce Extérieur (BFCE), 21 Boulevard Haussmann, 75009 Paris (tel: 4800-4800; fax: 4800-3970).

Banque Indosuez, 96 Boulevard Haussmann, 75008 Paris (tel: 4420-2020; fax: 4420-1522).

Banque Nationale de Paris SA, 16 Boulevard des Italiens, 75009 Paris (tel: 4014-4546; fax: 4014-5599).

Banque Paribas, 3 Rue d'Antin, 75078 Paris Cedex 02 (tel: 4298-1234; fax: 4298-0433).

Caisse Centrale des Banques Populaires, 10-12 avenue Winston Churchill, 94677 Charenton Le Pont Cedex (tel: 4039-0000; fax: 4039-3940).

Caisse d'Epargne, 19 Rue du Louvre, 75001 Paris (tel: 4041-3031; fax: 4233-4518).

Compagnie Bancaire, 5 Avenue Kléber, 75798 Paris Cedex 16 (tel: 4525-2525; fax: 4501-7805).

Compagnie Financière de Crédit Industriel et Commercial (CIC Group), Rue de la Victoire 66, 75009 Paris (tel: 4280-8080).

Crédit Agricole, Boulevard Pasteur 91-93, 75015 Paris (tel: 4323-5202).

Crédit Commercial de France (CCF), 103 Avenue des Champs-Elysées, 75008 Paris (tel: 4070-7040; fax: 4070-7353).

Crédit Foncier de France, SA, 19 Rue des Capucines, 75001 Paris (tel: 4244-8000; fax: 4244-7822).

Crédit Local de France, 7-11 Quai André Citroen, 75015 Paris (tel: 4392-7777; fax: 4592-7672).

Crédit Lyonnais SA, Boulevard des Italiens 19, 75002 Paris (tel: 4295-7000).

Crédit Mutuel, 88 Rue Cardinet, 75017 Paris (tel: 4401-1010; fax: 4401-1227).

Société Générale, Boulevard Haussmann 29, 75009 Paris (tel: 4298-2000).

Union Européenne de CIC (CIC Group), 4 Rue Gaillon, 75107 Paris Cedex 02 (tel: 4266-7000; fax: 4266-7878).

Central bank

Banque de France, 31 Rue Croix des Petits Champs, 75001 Paris (tel: 4292-4292; fax: 4292-3940; e-mail: infos@banque-france.fr).

European Central Bank, Kaiserstrasse 29, D-60311 Frankfurt am Main, Germany (tel: (+49-69) 13-440; fax: (+49-69) 1344-6000; e-mail: info@ecb.int).

Travel information

Air France (head office), 1 Place Max-Hymans, Paris 75757 Cedex 15 (tel: 4323-8181; internet site: http://www.airfrance.fr).

Airport office: 45 Rue de Paris, Roissy Charles de Gaulle, Paris 95747 (tel: 4156-7800).

Maison de la France (tourist office), 8 Avenue de l'Opéra, Paris 75001 (tel: 4296-1023; fax: 4286-8052).

Roissy Charles de Gaulle and Le Bourget airports, BP 20101, 95711 Roissy Charles de Gaulle Cedex (tel: 4862-1212, 4864-6807) (24 hours).

Ministries

Ministry of Agriculture, Fisheries and Food, 78 Rue de Varenne, 75700 Paris (tel: 4955-4955; fax: 4955-4039).

Ministry of Capital Works, Housing, and Transport, 246 Blvd Saint-Germain, 75007 Paris (tel: 4081-2122; fax: 4081-3099).

Ministry of the Civil Service, Administrative Reform and Decentralisation, 72 Rue de Varenne, 75700 Paris (tel: 4275-8000; fax: 4275-8970).

Ministry of Culture and Communication, 3 Rue de Valois, 75042 Paris (tel: 4015-8000; fax: 4261-3577).

Ministry of Defence, 14 Rue Saint-Dominique, 75700 Paris (tel: 4219-3011; fax: 4505-4091).

Ministry for the Economy, Finance and Industry, 139 Rue de Bercy, 75572 Paris Cedex 12 (tel: 5318-4000; fax: 5318-9701; internet site: www.minefi.gouv.fr).

Ministry of Employment, Rue de Grenelle, 75700 Paris (tel: 4438-3838; fax: 4438-2010).

Ministry of the Environment, 20 Avenue de Segur, 75302 Paris 07 SP (tel: 4219-2021; fax: 4219-1120).

Ministry of Foreign Affairs, 37 Quai d'Orsay, 75700 Paris (tel: 4317-5353; fax: 4551-6012).

Ministry of Industry, the Post Office and Telecommunications, 101 Rue de Grenelle, 75700 Paris 9 (tel: 4319-3636; fax: 4319-3052).

Ministry of the Interior, Place Beauvau, 75800 Paris (tel: 4927-4927; fax: 4266-1280).

Ministry of Justice, 13 Place Vendome, 75042 Paris (tel: 4477-6060; fax: 4477-6000).

Ministry of Labour and Social Affairs, 127 Rue de Grenelle, 75700 Paris (tel: 4438-3838; fax: 4056-6710).

Ministry of National Education, Higher Education and Research, 110 Rue de Grenelle, 75700 Paris (tel: 4955-1010; fax: 4955-1556).

Ministry for Relations with Parliament, 69 Rue de Varenne, 75700 Paris (tel: 4275-8000; fax: 4081-7300).

Ministry of Small- and Medium-Sized Enterprises, Trade and Artisan Activities, 80 Rue de Lille, 75700 Paris (tel: 4319-2424; fax: 4319-3767).

Ministry of Town and Country Planning, Urban Affairs and Integration, 35 Rue Saint-Dominique, 75700 Paris (tel: 4275-8000; fax: 4275-7755).

Ministry of Youth and Sport, Rue Olivier de Serres, 75015 Paris (tel: 5369-3000; fax: 5369-4370).

Prime Minister's Office, 57 Rue de Varenne, 75700 Paris (tel: 4275-8000; fax: 4544-1572).

Other useful addresses

ANIT (public information service), 8 Avenue de l'Opéra, 75001 Paris (tel: 4260-3738).

La Bourse de Paris (Stock Exchange), 39 Rue Cambon, 75001 Paris (tel: 4927-7000; fax: 4289-7868).

Bureau International des Expositions (International Exhibition Bureau), 56 Avenue Victor-Hugo, 75116 Paris (tel: 4500-3863; fax: 4500-9615).

Caisse Centrale de Co-opération Economique (CCCE), 233 Boulevard Saint-Germain, Paris (tel: 4550-3220).

Centre Française du Commerce Extérieur, 10 Avenue d'Iéna, 75116 Paris (tel: 4505-3000).

Direction Générale des Impôts, Centre des Non-Résidents, 9 Rue d'Uzés, 75094 Paris.

France Telecom, 6 Place d'Alleray, 75505 Paris Cedex 15.

French Embassy (USA), 4101 Reservoir Road, NW, Washington DC 20007 (tel: (+1-202)-944-6000; fax: (+1-202)-944-6166).

Institut National de la Statistique et des Etudes Economiques (INSEE), 18 Boulevard Adolphe Pinard, 75675 Paris Cedex 14 (tel: 4117-5050; fax: 4117-6666; internet site: http://www.insee.fr).

Invest in France Network/DATAR, 1 Avenue Charles Floquet, 75343 Paris Cedex 07 (tel: 4065-1006; fax: 4065-1240).

Service de la Répression des Fraudes et du Contrôle de la Qualité, 44 Boulevard de Grenelle, 75732 Paris.

Post Office, 52 rue du Louvre, Paris (tel: 4028-2000).

National news agency: Agence France Presse, 11–15 Place de la Bourse, 75002 Paris (tel: 4041-4646; fax: 4041-4632; www.afp.com).

Other news agencies: Reuters: http://fr.reuters.com
Focus: www.focusinfo.eu

Internet sites

Ferry information: http://seafrance.com/ferries_to_france.html

France Bottin (provides market information on France's main companies): www.bottin.fr

French electronic phonebook (searches can be conducted by name or by regions): www.epita.fr:5000/11/english.html

Tourist information: www.francetourism.com/

French Guiana

KEY FACTS

Official name: Guyane Française (French Guiana)

Head of State: President of France (Jacques Chirac), represented by Préfet Jean-Pierre Laflaquière (from Aug 2006)

Head of government: President of the General Council, Pierre Désert (since 2004); President of the Regional Council, Antoine Karam (since 1992)

Ruling party: Parti Socialiste Guyanais (PSG) (Socialist Party) (since 2000; re-elected 2004)

Area: 91,000 square km

Population: 202,000 (2008)*

Capital: Cayenne

Official language: French

Currency: Euro (eur) = 100 cents (from 1 Jan 2002; previous currency French franc, locked at Ff6.56 per euro)

Exchange rate: eur0.63 per US$ (Jul 2008)

GDP per capita: US$8,500 (2006)*

Labour force: 58,800 (2003)

Unemployment: 22.00% (2003)

Inflation: 1.50% (2003)

Balance of trade: -US$470.00 million (2003)

Foreign debt: US$1.20 billion (2003)

* estimated figure

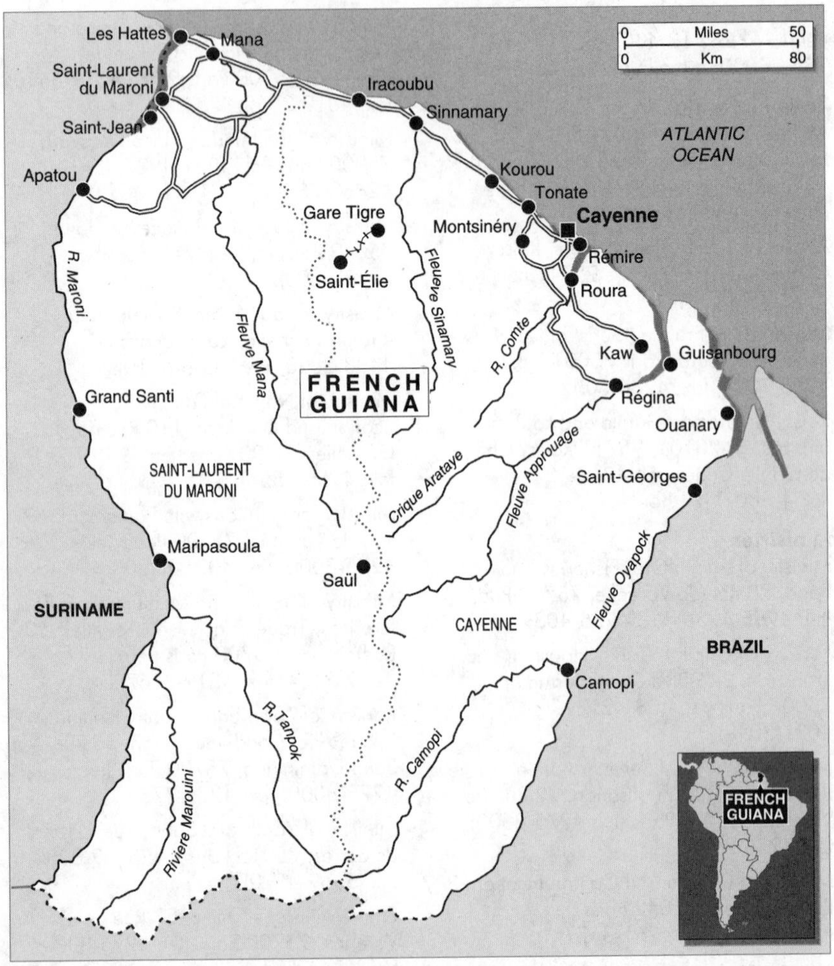

COUNTRY PROFILE

Historical profile

Carib and Arawak Indians were the original inhabitants of French Guiana.
1496 First reported European sighting.
1604 The French established their first settlement on French Guiana.
1654–1915 There were numerous changes in control between the French, British, Dutch, Brazilian and Portuguese, as well as border disputes. During this period the economy of the region came close to collapse, particularly after the abolition of slavery in 1848. Black African slaves had previously worked on French Guiana's sugar plantations.
1946 French Guiana became a French Département d'Outre-Mer (DOM) (Overseas Department).
1953 Closure of penal colony on Devil's Island.
1964 The Kourou Space Centre was established.
1974 French Guiana was further incorporated into the French political system and granted the status of region of France.
1983 French Guiana was granted devolution. A Regional Council was established under the French decentralisation policy.
1998 The Parti Socialiste Guyanais (PSG) remained the single largest party in the Regional Council after the elections.

2000 There were pro-independence demonstrations and French Guiana sought to alter its relationship as a DOM.
2002 French Guiana adopted the euro as its official currency. Arianespace launched Intelsat 904 into orbit from Kourou. The satellite provides Internet, telecommunications and television services for Europe, Africa, Central Asia and Australia.
2003 A revision to the constitution began a process of change to the political and administrative organisation with the Regional Council assuming more influence.
2004 Early elections for the Regional Council were won by the PSG with 17 seats.
2005 Arianespace and the Russian Space Agency signed an agreement for construction of the Soyuz launch pad.
2006 Jean-Pierre Laflaquière was appointed préfet. The Vega, First Stage Motor, (light-lift launcher) had a successfully take-off.
2007 On 16 May, Nicolas Sarkozy became head of state and president of the French Republic. Under a deal with the European Space Agency (ESA), a new launch pad for the Russian Soyuz space launcher was begun. The first flight of medium-lift launchers is expected in late 2008.

Political structure

Constitution

28 September 1958 (French Fifth Republic)

Under the 1946 constitution of the French Fourth Republic, French Guiana became a Département d'Outre-Mer (DOM) (Overseas Department) of France. In 1974, it was granted additional status as a region of France.

The president of France is represented by a préfet, appointed by the government in Paris. French Guiana is represented in the French National Assembly and in the French Senate by two deputies and one senator.

Since 1983, following the French government's policy of decentralisation, regional councils have been elected with powers similar to those of the regions.

The local government comprises a Conseil Régional (Regional Council) of 31-members and a 19-member Conseil Général (General Council), both directly elected for six-year terms. Since a revision to the constitution in March 2003 the political and administrative organisation has been in a state of change; the Regional Council is assuming more influence.

Form of state

Département d'Outre-Mer (DOM) (Overseas Department) of France, with additional status as a région (region) of France.

The executive

Executive power is vested in the president of France, represented by a Préfet (Commissioner), appointed by the president on the advice of the French Ministry of Interior.

National legislature

Local administration is through a directly-elected Conseil Général (General Council) of 19 members and an indirectly-elected 31-member Conseil Régional (Regional Council). Presidents of the General and Regional Councils are appointed by the members of those councils.

Two members are elected to the French National Assembly and one member to the French Senate.

Legal system

French legal system

Last elections

March 2004 (Regional Council)

Results: Regional Council: the Parti Socialiste Guyanais (PSG) (Socialist Party) won 17 seats, The Union pour un Mouvement Populaire (UMP) (Union for the Popular Movement) and Walwari Committee (aligned with the PRG in France) each won seven seats.

Next elections

Political parties

Ruling party

Parti Socialiste Guyanais (PSG) (Socialist Party) (since 2000; re-elected 2004)

Main opposition party

Union pour un Mouvement Populaire (UMP) (Union for the Popular Movement), Walwari Committee (aligned with the PRG in France)

Population

202,000 (2008)*

Last census: March 1999: 156,790

Population density: Two inhabitants per square km.

Annual growth rate: 4.6 per cent (2003)

Ethnic make-up

Black or mixed race (66 per cent), white (12 per cent), East Indian, Chinese or Amerindian (12 per cent).

There are settlements of Hmong farmers from Laos. The troubles in neighbouring Suriname encouraged thousands of Surinamese to cross the border illegally and settle. The space centre has brought in thousands of scientists who live in a community of their own.

The minimum wage has attracted not only Surinamese but also Brazilians. These clandestines (illegal immigrants) are marginalised and forced to live in the poorest areas of the country, often without work.

Religions

Roman Catholic

Education

Schooling is compulsory and French Guiana has both public and private elementary schools, a high school, and two vocational schools. The condition of schools is, however, very poor, leading students to strike.

Literacy rate: 84 per cent, male; 82 per cent, female; adult rates (World Bank).

Health

Government health planning is seriously affected by the high prevalence of sexually transmitted diseases and an endemic level of dengue fever.

Health insurance is provided by the state-sponsored social security system, financed with compulsory contributions from salaries. People are usually reimbursed on the basis of rates negotiated between care providers and the social security.

Life expectancy: 77 years (estimate 2003)

Fertility rate/Maternal mortality rate: Three births per woman (2003)

Birth rate/Death rate: 21 births per 1,000 population; five deaths per 1,000 population (2003).

Child (under 5 years) mortality rate (per 1,000): 13 per 1,000 live births (2003)

Welfare

The official unemployment rate is 22 per cent with higher rates among young people. Jobs connected with satellite launching, combined with orderly French rule and an annual financial contribution amounting to US$500 million from Paris, have provided benefits such as good roads, decent health care, and a generous social security system.

Main cities

Cayenne (capital, estimated population 55,638 in 2005), St Laurent-du-Maroni (27,429), Kourou (main town around the space centre and rapidly growing, 27,132), Matoury (36,275), Rémire-Montjoly (20,823).

Languages spoken

French and French-Creole. Some business executives speak English, although business is generally conducted in French.

Official language/s

French

Media

Press

Daily papers are Guyane-Matin, France-Guyane and La Presse de Guyane. There are no English-language newspapers. US and metropolitan French papers are available. Several periodicals are in circulation but there are no trade publications.

Broadcasting
Radio-Télévision Française d'Outre-mer (RFO) broadcast in French. There are two independent radio stations: Cayenne FM and Radio Tout Mount.

Economy
The overall economy remains underdeveloped. The main activities are fishing, which accounts for 75 per cent of exports and forestry, which is under exploited due to poor infrastructure. An expanding sawmill industry has increased the exports of hardwood logs. Eco-tourism is beginning to grow in importance, as French Guiana has large tracts of unspoilt rain forests, but few facilities to cater for all but the most hardy.
The single major contributor to the economy, accounting for 25 per cent of GDP and half of tax revenues is the Centre Spatial Guyanais (Guiana Space Centre) at Kourou, which launches commercial and government funded rockets, using either the European Ariane 5 or Russian Soyuz launchers. An estimated 24 per cent of the population work directly or indirectly in jobs connected with the space industry.
French Guiana is otherwise dependent on aid, technical assistance and imports from France. As a department of France, it receives the same benefits as mainland France: a minimum wage, free education and health care, and a large, well-paid civil service.

External trade
As a département d'outre-mer (DOM) of France, French Guiana is integrated as an outermost region of the European Union, which includes all EU trade agreements. There is heavy dependence on France for financial aid. The balance of trade deficit is mainly due to high imports of food and fuels, and undeveloped export potential.
Imports
Principal imports are food (grains, processed meat), machinery and transport equipment, fuels and chemicals.
Main sources: France (over 60 per cent), US, Trinidad and Tobago, Italy
Exports
Principal exports are shrimp, timber and rosewood essence, gold, rum and clothing.
Main destinations: France (over 60 per cent total), Switzerland (7 per cent), US (2 per cent)

Agriculture
Cultivation is limited to the coastal area. Only 0.18 per cent of the total land area is cultivated and production is dominated by crops for domestic consumption such as rice, maize and bananas, while sugar cane is grown for rum production.
A small number of cattle farms have also been established.
Estimate crop production in 2005 included: 23,500 tonnes (t) rice, 10,400t cassava, 4,100t taro, 5,350t sugar cane, 3,770t tomatoes, 4,500t bananas, 3,170t plantains, 2,175t citrus fruit, 14,500t roots and tubers, 24,590t vegetables in total. Livestock production included: 1,908t meat in total, 320t beef, 1,100t pig meat, 28t lamb and goat meat, 460t poultry, 460t eggs, 270t milk.
Fishing
The typical total annual fish catch is over 5,000mt. Shellfish, molluscs and cephalopods account for another 2,700mt per annum.
In 2004, the total marine fish catch was 2,150 tonnes and the total crustacean catch was 3,364 tonnes.
The rainforest covers around 90 per cent of the land area. Poor infrastructure means the vast timber resources have not been fully exploited. Imports and exports of timber in 2004 were both US$2.4 million; exports consisted of over 50,100 cubic metres of raw hardwood while imports were mostly processed sawnwood and wood panels used in construction.

Industry and manufacturing
The sector includes construction, shrimp processing, forestry products, rum and gold mining. Manufacturing is virtually non-existent, except for small factories processing agricultural or seafood products and a few sawmills. A tile and brick-making plant, based on important fields of red clay, operates in the Cayenne neighbourhood. Production of rum from sugar cane has declined. Industrial activity is limited to the area around the Kourou space centre.

Tourism
Tourism is an important area of the economy. The sector suffered following the 11 September 2001 terrorist attacks in the US. The prospects for eco-tourism are good.

Mining
Bauxite deposits of 42 million tonnes and kaolin deposits of 40 million tonnes have been found, but extraction is not economically viable, although kaolin mining has begun in the Mana area. There are also reserves of silica, niobium and tantalite. Gold is mined, both legally and illicitly, the latter activity on a large scale and causing serious environmental damage. Significant exploitation of the mineral resources will come about only with further improvements in infrastructure.

Hydrocarbons
French Guiana does not produce oil, gas or coal. It is heavily dependent on imports of petroleum products to meet its energy needs, importing around 6,500 barrels per day. Gas and coal are not imported.

Energy
French Guiana relies to a large extent on petroleum imports from France.

Banking and insurance
The Banque Nationale de Paris Guyane Sa (BNP Guyane) is a major commercial bank offering a wide range of services. There are branches in Cayenne, Kourou and Rémire-Montjoly.
Central bank
European Central Bank

Time
GMT minus three hours

Geography
French Guiana lies on the north coast of South America, with Suriname to the west and Brazil to the south and east. The country is largely low lying with hills no higher that 600 metres and covered in dense Amazonian rainforest that grows down to the mangrove fringed coastline.
Hemisphere
Northern

Climate
The climate is tropical. It is generally hot and humid with heavy rain. The dry season is August–December with an average temperature of 28 degrees Celsius (C). The rainy season is January–June with a temperature range of 22–32 degrees C.

Dress codes
For business meetings men should wear a lightweight or tropical suit and tie and women a lightweight suit or the equivalent.

Entry requirements
Passports
Passports are required by all except nationals of France and some francophone countries holding national identity cards. Passports should be valid for three months from the date of departure.
Visa
Required by all, except citizens of EU, North America, Australasia and Japan, for stays up to one month; this includes business trips by representatives of foreign entities with an invitation from a local company or organisation. Proof of adequate funds for stay, an itinerary, a guarantee of repatriation if necessary and return/onward ticket are also required.
For further exceptions, full details and a copy of the application form visit www.diplomatie.gouv.fr/thema/dossier.gb.asp and follow the path (entering France) to the database.
Currency advice/regulations
There are no limits to the amount of local or foreign currency imported or exported,

although amounts exceeding eur7,600 should be declared.

Travellers cheques are accepted; to avoid extra exchange fees, it is recommended that they be in euros, US dollars or pound sterling.

Health (for visitors)

Mandatory precautions

A yellow fever certificate.

Advisable precautions

Hepatitis A, B and D, typhoid and polio immunisations are recommended. Dengue fever is endemic. Malaria prophylaxis is advisable if travelling outside Cayenne. Water precautions should be taken, although tap water in Cayenne is safe. There is a rabies risk.

Hotels

There is a good standard of accommodation available in Cayenne, Kourou and St Laurent. Rates normally include service and taxes; if not, a 10 per cent tip is usual.

Public holidays (national)

Fixed dates

1 Jan (New Year's Day), 1 May (Labour Day), 8 May (Victory Day), 10 Jun (Abolition Day), 14 Jul (Bastille Day), 15 Aug (Assumption Day), 1 Nov (All Saints' Day), 11 Nov (Armistice Day), 25 Dec (Christmas Day).

Variable dates

Ash Wednesday (Carnival – Feb/Mar), Easter Monday (Mar/Apr), Ascension Day (Thur – May/June).

Working hours

Banking

Mon–Fri: 0730–1230, 1430–1730.

Business

Mon–Fri: 0800–1300, 1500–1800.

Government

Mon–Fri: 0730–1300, 1430–1830 (closed Wed and Fri afternoons).

Electricity supply

220V AC, 50 cycles

Getting there

Air

International airport/s: Cayenne-Rochambeau (CAY), 15km from city; bar, post office, shops, hotel reservations, car hire.

Airport tax: None

Surface

Road: There is a coastal road to Suriname but there is no road access to Brazil.

Water: Ferries run regularly to Suriname, and from St George to Oiapoque (Brazil).

Getting about

National transport

Air: Air Guyane, Guyane Aero Service and Heli-Inter Service serve main centres and the interior of the country. (Bookings can be made through Air France.)

Road: There are 356km of national routes and 366km of departmental roads. Cayenne district is served by a good road system, but the streets of Cayenne itself are inferior. The only major road runs from Cayenne, via Kourou, to St Laurent on Suriname border.

Buses: Scheduled services on Cayenne to St Laurent route.

Water: Major form of travel. Motor boat serves some coastal towns. River boats and small planes link interior centres with coast. 400km rivers are navigable by small ocean-going vessels and river and coastal steamers but interior connections are made by local craft.

City transport

Taxis: Taxis are available in main towns. Fares include gratuities.

Car hire

Car hire is available in Cayenne and at the airport. An international licence required.

BUSINESS DIRECTORY

The addresses listed below are a selection only. While World of Information makes every endeavour to check these addresses, we cannot guarantee that changes have not been made, especially to telephone numbers and area codes. We would welcome any corrections.

Telephone area codes

The international direct dialling (IDD) code for French Guiana is +594 followed by another 594 and the subscriber's (six digit) number.

Useful telephone numbers

Talking clock: 3699
Times of tides: 378-300
Radio taxi: 307-305, 305-225
Bus service: 314-554
Fire: 18
Police: 17

Chambers of Commerce

Guyane Chambre de Commerce et d'Industrie, PO Box 49, Hôtel Consulaire, Place de l'Esplinade, 97321 Cayenne (tel: 299-600; fax: 299-634; e-mail: contact@guyane.cci.fr).

Banking

Banque Française Commerciale, 8 Place des Palmistes, 97300 Cayenne (tel: 291-111; fax: 301-312).

Banque de la Guyane, PO Box 35, 2 Place Victor-Schloelcher, Cayenne (tel: 310-515).

Banque Nationale de Paris Guyane, 2 Place Victor-Schoelcher, Cayenne (tel: 396-300; fax: 302-308).

Crédit Agricole, Angle av L Héder et rue Damas, 97300 Cayenne (tel: 318-000; fax: 317-524).

Crédit Martiniquais, 76 Av Gal de Gaulle, 97300 Cayenne (tel: 315-700; fax: 314-801).

Crédit Populairé Caisse Crédit Mutuel, 93 rue Lalouette, 97300 Cayenne (tel: 301-523; fax: 301-765).

Central bank

Banque de France, 31 Rue Croix des Petits Champs, 75001 Paris (tel: 4292-4292, 6480-2020; fax: 4292-3940; email: infos@banque-france.fr).

European Central Bank, Kaiserstrasse 29, D-60311 Frankfurt am Main, Germany (tel: (+49-69) 13-440; fax: (+49-69) 1344-6000; email: info@ecb.int).

Travel information

Air France, Cayenne (tel: 379-899).

Air Guyane, Aéroport de Rochambeau, 97351 Matoury (tel: 356-555; fax: 356-506).

Surinam Airways, c/o Atlas Voyages, 15 Rue Louis Blanc, 97300 Cayenne (tel: 317-298; fax: 305-786).

Syndicat Autonome des Hoteliers Restaurateurs et Cafétiers de Guyane, PK 9,2 Route de Rémire, 97354 Rémire Montjoly (tel: 354-100; fax: 354-405).

Syndicats d'Initiative Office du Tourisme, 7 Av du Président Monnerville, Cayenne 97300 (tel: 312-919).

National tourist organisation offices

French Guiana Tourist Board, 12, Rue Lallouette; BP 801; 97338 Cayenne (tel: 296-500; fax: 296-501; internet: www.tourisme-guyane.com/en).

Other useful addresses

Agence Régionale pour le Développement de l'Industrie Minière (Ardim), 111 rue Christophe Colomb, 973000 Cayenne (tel: 294-575).

Centre Spatial Guyanais, Korou (tel: 326-123).

Direction Régionale de l'Industrie, de la Recherche et de l'Environnement, pointe Buzaré, PO Box 7001, 97307 Cayenne (tel: 297-530; fax: 290-734).

Radio-Télévision Française d'Outre-mer(RFO), 43 bis Rue du Dr Devèze, BP 336, 97305 Cayenne (tel: 311-500).

Internet sites

Centre Français du commerce exterieur (site in French): http://www.cfce.fr

French Guiana Consular Information: http://travel.state.gov/french_guiana.html

French Polynesia

KEY FACTS

Official name: Territoire de la Polynésie Française (Territory of French Polynesia)

Head of State: President of France (Nicolas Sarkozy), represented by Préfet Adolphe Colrat (from 12 Jun 2008)

Head of government: President of the Territorial Government Gaston Tong Sang (Union pour la Démocratie (UPLD) (Union for Democracy)) (from 15 Apr 2008)

Ruling party: Coalition led by Union pour la Démocratie (UPLD) (Union for Democracy), supported by minor parties (from 15 Apr 2008)

Area: 3,600 square km (35 islands and 83 atolls)

Population: 260,000 (end-2006)

Capital: Papeete (on Tahiti)

Official language: French and Reo Maohi (Tahitian)

Currency: Comptoirs Français du Pacifique franc (CFPf) = 100 centimes

Exchange rate: CFPf75.22 per US$ (Jul 2008); (pegged CFPf119.25 per euro)

GDP per capita: US$17,500 (2004)

GDP real growth: 4.00% (2003)

Labour force: 87,843 (2004)

Unemployment: 10.90% (2004)*

Inflation: 0.80% (2004)

Balance of trade: -US$1.50 billion (2005)

Visitor numbers: 212,000 (2004)

* estimated figure

COUNTRY PROFILE

Historical profile

French Polynesia consists of 118 islands and was settled by Polynesians betweeen 300 and 800 AD. From these islands, Hawaii, the Cook Islands and New Zealand were colonised.

1843 Tahiti, the largest island, and Moorea became French protectorates.

1880 Tahiti became a French colony. The other islands were annexed under the name Comptoirs Français de l'Océanie.

1957 The group of islands became the Territoire d'Outre-Mer (TOM, overseas territory) of French Polynesia, administered by a governor in Papeete on Tahiti.

1960 An international airport opened at Faa'a on Tahiti.

1963 French nuclear tests were conducted for the first time at Mururoa Atoll.

1977 Increased powers for the council of ministers were approved by the French government.

1984 New powers for the government, particularly in commerce, were approved by the French government.

1983 Despite strong local protests, French authorities insisted that nuclear tests would continue for 'as long as necessary'.

1984 Jurisdiction over certain local affairs (local budget, health services, primary education, culture, social welfare, public works, agriculture and sports) was conferred on the council of ministers. Gaston Flosse became president of the governing council.

1986 The Tahoeraa Huiraatira-Rassemblement pour la République (TH-RPR) (People's Servant-Rally for the Republic) won the Territorial Assembly elections.

1987 Following accusations of misappropriation of public funds, Flosse resigned as president.

1990 Amendments to the constitution augmented presidential and Territorial Assembly powers.

1996 Gaston Flosse was re-elected president. France ended nuclear testing. The French government relinquished control of all territory affairs except for defence, law enforcement, the judiciary and the local currency.

2002 An appeal court in Paris dismissed fraud accusations against President Flosse.

2004 France's President Chirac dissolved the Territorial Assembly and changed French Polynesia's status to Pays d'Outre-Mer (overseas country) (POM). Oscar Temaru (pro-independence, Tavini Huira'atira (People's Servant) (PS) was elected president of the new assembly – Assemblée de la Polynésie française (Assembly of French Polynesia). Temaru was ousted by Gaston Flosse (TH-RPR).

2005 The final result of assembly election was 27 seats for the UPLD, 27 for the TH-RPR and three for the Alliance pour la Démocratie Nouvelle (ADN) (Alliance for a New Democracy). President Flosse (TH-RPR) was ousted in a no confidence vote. Oscar Temaru (PS), leader of the pro-independence movement and supported by the ADN, was elected president. Anne Boquet became Préfet.

2006 President Temaru (PS) was ousted and Gaston Tong Sang (Tahoera'a Huiraatira (TH) (Popular Rally) was elected president, by the assembly.

2007 Nicolas Sarkozy became head of state and president of the French Republic. In the first round of the postponed presidential elections for the Territorial Assembly, the incumbent, Gaston Tong Sang received the least votes and was eliminated. In the second round, Oscar Temaru (PS) won 27 votes and Édouard Fritch (TH) 17. A group of Tong Sang supporters broke away from the ruling TH and formed a new party, the O Porinetia To Tatou Ai'a (OPTTA). The French National Assembly approved a new parliamentary voting system of proportional representation and a minimum electoral threshold in a bid to bring a measure of stability to the islands' politics.

2008 On January 31 the cabinet of President Oscar Temaru resigned. After two round in the general elections, held on 27 January and 10 February, the To Tatou Ai'a (Our Home) coalition (led by Oscar Temaru) won a total of 45.2 per cent of the vote (27 seats out of 57), the UPLD (led by Gaston Tong Sang) won 37.2 per cent (20) and the TH (led by Gaston Flosse) 17.2 per cent (10). Turnout was 76.9 per cent. A coalition of opposites, Our Home and TH voted Gaston Flosse into the presidency on 23 February, but he lost a vote of no confidence and, on 15 April, was replaced by Gaston Tong Sang (UPLD), with support from minor parties with 29 seats in parliament. On 12 June, Adolph Colrat was appointed Préfet, taking up his post by July.

Political structure

Constitution

In 1996, the French government relinquished control over all the territory's affairs except for defence, foreign affairs, law enforcement, the justice system and the local currency. France is represented by a high commissioner who has a supervisory role. The territory is represented in the French Parliament by two deputies and two senators.

The local government has control over the territory's more than three million square kilometres of sea, as well as shipping, civil aviation, work permits, mineral exploration, foreign investment and local economic affairs. Under the Statute of Autonomy, it has full control over its Exclusive Economic Zone.

French Polynesia became a Pays d'Outre-Mer (POM) (overseas country) of France in 2004 with the implementation of the Assemblée de la Polynésie française (Assembly of French Polynesia) statute. It has 57 members in the assembly representing six constituencies.

Under the autonomy law, the electoral list gaining the most votes in general elections wins a bonus of extra seats, amounting to a third of the seats in the local parliament.

Form of state

Autonomous Pays d'Outre-Mer (POM) (overseas country) of France

National legislature

The president of the council of ministers is elected by the 57-member Assemblée de la Polynésie Française (Assembly of French Polynesia), itself elected by proportional representation for a five-year term. On 26 November 2007, the French National Assembly approved an amendment to the parliamentary voting system in an attempt to streamline the chaotic nature of politics in French Polynesia. The new proportional representation system has two rounds of voting; to reach the second round any candidate must have at least 12.5 per cent of the vote from the first round and their party much achieve a minimum electoral threshold 5 per cent.

Last elections

27 January and 10 February 2008 (first and second rounds of national assembly)

Results: Parliamentary: the To Tatou Ai'a (Our Home alliance) won a total of 45.2 per cent of the vote (27 seats out of 57), the UPLD alliance won 37.2 per cent (20) and the Tahoera'a Huiraatira (Popular Rally) 17.2 per cent (10). Turnout was 76.9 per cent.

Next elections

2013 (national assembly)

Political parties

Ruling party

Coalition led by Union pour la Démocratie (UPLD) (Union for Democracy), supported by minor parties (from 15 Apr 2008)

Main opposition party

To Tatou Ai'a (Our Home) coalition

Political situation

Gaston Tong Sang's term in office as president started with a vote of no confidence in his predecessor – president for just five weeks – but within 21 days he already had to pay back favours to his supporter, with portfolios for government positions or suffer the same fate. The political instability is having an effect on the economy, apart from soaring world prices for fuel and food, tourism, a major foreign earnings industry, registered -1.5 per cent in 2007 compared to the 2006 figures.

Business leaders despair of the interminable power struggles and have pleaded for a government of unity to be formed, but these appeal have gone unheeded, as the opening of parliament in 2008 was disrupted by opposition members boycotting proceedings. Finally Préfet Anne Boquet strongly cautioned politicians about their behaviour and injudicious language.

France is preparing to sign a US$672.3 million, five-year, development pact with its POM and may be it should give sharper lessons in civic duty until French Polynesia provides a sensible, stable and forward looking government ready to invest the money.

Population

260,000 (end-2006)

Last census: 20 Aug–15 September 2007

Population density: 63 inhabitants per sq km. Urban population: 53 per cent (1995–2001).

Annual growth rate: 2.5 per cent (2003)

Ethnic make-up

Polynesian (78 per cent), Chinese (12 per cent), local French (6 per cent), metropolitan French (4 per cent).

Religions

Protestant (54 per cent), Roman Catholic (30 per cent), other (16 per cent).

Education

Enrolment rate: 116 per cent gross primary enrolment, of relevant age groups, (including repeaters) (World Bank).

Health

Life expectancy: 73 years (men) 77 years (women), 2007

Fertility rate/Maternal mortality rate: 2.04 births per woman

Birth rate/Death rate: 16.93 births per 1,000 population; 4.63 deaths per 1,000 population.

Child (under 5 years) mortality rate (per 1,000): 8.44 deaths per 1,000 live births

Main cities

Papeete (capital, on Tahiti, estimated population 26,580 in 2005), Faa'a (on Tahiti, 29,076).

Languages spoken

English is spoken, especially in tourist and business circles.

Official language/s

French and Reo Maohi (Tahitian)

Media

National news agency: L'Agence Tahitienne de Presse (Tahitipress)

Press

Dailies: There are two newspapers available, in French, La Dépêche de Tahiti (Tahiti's largest newspaper) and Les Nouvelles de Tahiti.

Weeklies: In French La Tribune Polynesienne has general interest news. In English the Tahiti Sun Press, is a free-issue publication for tourists.

Periodicals: In French, monthly magazines include L'Hebdo Maohi (www.hebdo.pf) and the Tahiti-Pacifique (www.tahiti-pacifique.com) both covering current affairs.

Broadcasting

Radio: In addition to the government-operated RFO Polynésie (www.rfo.fr/polynesie.php) service, there are a number of private radio stations operating mostly on larger, inhabited islands, including Radio Bleue, Radio Tefana Te Reo, Radio Maohi and Radio Te Vevo, which all broadcast in Tahitian.

Television: The French overseas broadcaster RFO (http://polynesie.rfo.fr) provides all local produced news and imported French programmes, as well as internet TV services.

Advertising

Advertising is available in local newspapers and all such ads, correspondence and trade literature should be in French.

Economy

The main source of revenue is financial transfers from France, which represent 30 per cent of GDP; expatriate remittances are also an important source of revenue. The government is attempting to capitalise on tourism, which is worth over US$400 million annually and brings around 230,000 visitors to the islands.

Around one million black pearls, valued at US$150 million are exported annually – French Polynesia is the Pacific region's second-largest source of loose pearls (after the Australian production of yellow pearls). Co-operatives and private producers farm quality cultured black pearls under strict guidelines introduced to maintain a healthy crop of oysters.

French Polynesia has a serious problem of unemployment, especially since France ceased its nuclear testing and withdrew most military personnel in 1996. France agreed to contribute funds as compensation for a limited period, but has since agreed that these payments be for an indefinite period.

Agriculture consists of smallholders growing fruit and vegetables, while plantations provide copra and coconut oil for export. The fisheries sector is growing. Deep-sea resources (particularly tuna) are fished, mainly by Asian fleets under licence. French Polynesia has the Pacific region's largest exclusive economic zone.

Development of the remote archipelagos (Marquesas, Australs, Tuamotu and Gambiers) has begun with the construction of more airstrips and roads to improve port facilities and public services. Capital development throughout the territory has helped create new businesses, while strengthening social services.

External trade

Imports

Main imports are foodstuffs, fuels, machinery and equipment.

Main sources: France (30.9 per cent total, 2006), Singapore (12.5 per cent), US (10.4 per cent).

Exports

Typically, the main exports are black pearls (90 per cent of total exports), coconut oil and its derivatives, copra, beer, vanilla, fish and shark meat.

Main destinations: Hong Kong (32.1 per cent total, 2006), Japan (27.8 per cent), France (13.3 per cent).

Agriculture

Farming

Accounts for 4 per cent of GDP and employs 13 per cent of the workforce. Its development is a central plank of government policy. Primary products are copra, vanilla, mother-of-pearl shells, taro and cultured pearls.

Weather permitting, local production supplies over 60 per cent of overall demand for some vegetables.

Local production supplies about 28 per cent of demand for dairy products and 83–87 per cent of demand for pork. Fruit is produced for export, for fruit juice factories, and for the local market.

Crop production in 2005 included: 87,000 tonnes (t) coconuts, 4,300t cassava, 11,310t oilcrops, 3,000t sugar cane, 3,400t pineapples, 1,370t citrus fruit, 900t potatoes, 7,200t vegetables in total, 9,440t fruit in total, 10,400t roots & tubers, 50t vanilla. Livestock production included: 1,973t meat in total, 130t beef, 1,100t pig meat, 75t goat, 665t poultry, 2,043t eggs, 1,350t milk, and 50t honey.

Fishing

Green mussel, prawn, live bait and freshwater shrimp aquaculture are under development. The fishing industry, in particular tuna, is growing. Typically, the annual catch is over 500,000mt including both fish and other seafood. The government aims to increase its commercial tuna-fishing fleet to around 150 vessels, which are to be built locally and overseas. Ship-building businesses in China and Fiji will probably be the main constructors.

Pearl farming is the second most important economic activity, after tourism, with over 800,000 harvested annually. Black pearls are the main merchandise export. They are mainly shipped to Japan and US.

Forestry

Although 70 per cent of the islands' land area is covered in forest, conditions limit exploitation to random felling, and almost all timber is imported. Plantations will yield productive forest of 11,250 hectares (ha) of Caribbean pine by 2025; 30ha of wood for local cabinet-making is planted per year.

Industry and manufacturing

The small manufacturing sector primarily processes agricultural products. It accounts for approximately 18 per cent of GDP and employs 19 per cent of the workforce.

The oil mill, Huilerie de Tahiti, purchases all copra produced and processes it into coconut oil and meal (for animal feed), soap-making and monoi (scented coconut oil). Other industries include breweries, soft drinks and fruit juice factories and power station. Several small concerns produce textiles and handicrafts.

Tourism

Tourism is the most important economic activity, accounting for a quarter of GDP, and is the primary earner of foreign income.

Mining

Reserves of phosphate are present but not exploited.

Hydrocarbons

French Polynesia does not produce oil, gas or coal. It relies on imports to meet its oil needs.

Energy

Solar energy is much used as a power source.

Banking and insurance

Although banking facilities in the principal urban centres are good, and include ATMs, financial service providers are scarce on some of the outlying islands.

Central bank

The Paris-based Institut d'Emission d'Outre-Mer (IEOM) provides all central banking services except foreign exchange reserves.

Time

GMT minus 10 hours

Geography

French Polynesia comprises several scattered groups of islands (120 islands in total) in the south Pacific Ocean, lying about halfway between South America and Australia.The Cook Islands are to the west and the Line Islands (part of Kiribati) to the north-west. The island groups in French Polynesia include the Iles du Vent (including the islands of Tahiti and Moorea) and the Iles Sous le Vent (about 160km north-west of Tahiti), which together constitute the Society Archipelago; the Tuamotu Archipelago which comprises 78 islands scattered east of the Society Archipelago in a line stretching north-west to south-east for about 1,500km; the Gambier Islands located 1,600km south-east of Tahiti; the Austral Islands lying 640km south of Tahiti; and the Marquesas Archipelago, 1,450km north-east of Tahiti.

Most islands are mountainous (volcanic) and ringed with coral reefs; the Tuamotu and Gambier groups are mainly low-lying atolls.

Hemisphere

Southern

Climate

French Polynesia is located in the tropical zone of the southern hemisphere. It has two seasons: warm and moist (Dec–Feb) average temperature 27 degrees Celsius (C); cool and dry (Mar–Nov), average temperature 21 degrees C. Rainfall varies, depending on relief of island and exposure to prevailing winds, but heaviest Nov–Mar.

Entry requirements

Passports

Required by all, valid for six months after date of departure.

Visa

Required by all, except nationals of EU, other European countries and Australia for stays up to three months and nationals of the US, Canada, New Zealand, Japan, South Korea and most Latin American countries for stays up to one month.

Currency advice/regulations

Customs

Visitors are allowed to bring 200 cigarettes, 100 cigarillos, 50 cigars or 200 grams of tobacco; one or two litres of spirits depending on strength; 50g perfume and 250ml eau de toilette; and goods to the value of CPFf5,000 duty free.

All baggage coming in from Fiji and Samoa, except hand luggage, is fumigated. Travellers should carry clothing and toilet articles for an overnight stay in their hand luggage and arrange for their hotel to collect other baggage from the airport after fumigation.

Prohibited imports

Import of foodstuffs, weapons and illegal drugs.

Health (for visitors)

Mandatory precautions

Vaccination certificate for yellow fever if travelling from an infected area.

Advisable precautions

Vaccination for diphtheria, tuberculosis, hepatitis A and B, polio, tetanus, typhoid are recommended. There is a rabies risk.

Hotels

Most of the major international hotel chains are represented. Hotels are expensive and tend to be clustered in resorts. Cheaper, but off the beaten track, are pensions (bed-and-breakfast type accommodation).

Credit cards

American Express, Diners' Club, Master Card and Visa accepted throughout Tahiti.

Public holidays (national)

Fixed dates

1 Jan (New Year's Day), 5 Mar (Missionary Day), 1 May (Labour Day), 8 May (Victory Day), 14 Jul (Bastille Day), 15 Aug (Assumption Day), 8 Sep (Autonomy Day), 1 Nov (All Saints' Day), 11 Nov (Armistice Day), 25 Dec (Christmas Day).

Variable dates

Good Friday, Easter Monday, Ascension Day, Whit Monday.

Working hours

Banking

Mon–Fri: 0800–1530.

Business

Mon–Fri: 0800–1200, 1330–1730; Sat: 0800–1200.

Government

Mon–Fri: 0800–1200, 1330–1730; Sat: 0800–1200.

Shops

Mon–Fri: 0730–1130, 1400–1700; Sat: 0730–1130.

Electricity supply

220V AC, 60 cycles (check with hotel before using appliances).

Weights and measures

Metric system

Social customs/useful tips

Tipping is not customary, and is contrary to traditional Tahitian hospitality.

Getting there

Air

National airline: Air Tahiti Nui

International airport/s: Tahiti-Faa'a International Airport (PPT), 6km from Papeete; restaurant, bank and car hire.

Airport tax: None.

Surface

Main port/s: Papeete.

Getting about

National transport

Air: There are over 25 airfields in addition to Tahiti-Faa'a International Airport. Air Tahiti operates scheduled flights to Moorea, Huahine, Raiatea, Bora-Bora, Maupiti, Rangiroa, Manihi, Takapoto, Tubuai, Nuku-Hiva (Marquesas), Ua Huka, Hiva Oa, Ua Pou, Anaa, Makemo, Hao, Rurutu and Mangareva (Gambiers) and several other atolls. Air Moorea operates daily services between Tahiti and Moorea. Both airlines also offer air taxi services, charters, circle island flights and transportation to other islands. Other air operators include Tahiti Conquest Airlines and Pacific Helicopter Tours.

Road: There are approximately 200km of road on Tahiti, including a circular 120km asphalt road around the main part of the island, and 100km of road on Moorea.

Buses: Le truck runs an unscheduled transport service between Papeete and outlying districts, leaving approximately every half hour for nearby areas and daily for distant points. The system also operates on Moorea, Bora Bora and some other islands.

Water: There is a scheduled boat service between Papeete and Moorea.

City transport

Taxis: Fares are controlled and should be displayed in each cab. In Tahiti, fares double between 2300 and 0500. Information on fares is available at GIE Tahiti Tourisme at the airport and in Papeete. The journey time from the airport to the city centre is 10 minutes.

Buses, trams & metro: Airport to city centre bus service operates 0400–2359 hours, every 15 minutes.

Car hire

There are numerous car hire establishments; rates include insurance. Drivers must hold a licence valid for at least one year and must be at least 21-years-old. Driving is on the right-hand side of the road.

BUSINESS DIRECTORY

The addresses listed below are a selection only. While World of Information makes every endeavour to check these addresses, we cannot guarantee that changes have not been made, especially to telephone numbers and area codes. We would welcome any corrections.

Telephone area codes

The international dialling code (IDD) for French Polynesia is + 689 followed by subscriber's number.

Useful telephone numbers

Police: 17
Fire: 18

Chambers of Commerce

French Polynesia Chamber of Commerce and Industry, PO Box 118, Rue Docteur Cassiau, 98713 Papeete (tel: 540-700; fax: 540-701).

Banking

Banque de Polynésie SA, PO Box 530, 355 Boulevard Pomare, Papeete (tel: 466-666; fax: 466-664).

Banque de Tahiti SA, PO Box 1602, Rue Cardella, Papeete (tel: 417-000; fax: 423-376).

Banque Socredo, PO Box 130, 115 rue Dumont d'Urville, Papeete (tel: 415-123; fax 433-661).

Central bank

Institut d'Emission d'Outre-Mer (IEOM), 5 rue Roland Barthes, 75012 Paris, France (tel : +33 1 5344-4141; fax : +33 1 4347-5134; e-mail: contact@ieom.fr).

Travel information

Air Moorea, BP 6019, Faa'a International Airport (tel: 864-141; fax: 864-299).

Air Tahiti Nui, Immeuble Dexter, Pont de l'Est, BP 1673, Papeete (tel: 460-303; fax: 460-222).

National tourist organisation offices

Tahiti Tourisme, Immeuble Paofai, Bvd Pomaré, BP 65 Papeete (tel: 505-700; fax: 436-619; e-mail: tahiti-tourisme@mail.pf; internet site: http://www.tahiti-tourisme.com).

Other useful addresses

Institut Territorial de la Statistique, BP 395, Papeete, Tahiti (tel: 437-196; fax: 427-252).

Service des Affaires Economiques, BP 82, Papeete, Tahiti.

Syndicat des Importateurs et des Négociants, PO Box 1607, Papeete, Tahiti.

Syndicat d'Initiative de la Polynésie Française, BP 326, Papeete.

National news agency: L'Agence Tahitienne de Presse (Tahitipress)

Internet sites

Tourism Council of the South Pacific: www.infocentre.com/spt.

Enterprise and development agency (in French): www.creation-entreprises.pf/

Gabon

KEY FACTS

Official name: République Gabonaise (Gabonese Republic)

Head of State: President El Hadj Omar Bongo Ondimba (PDG) (since 1967; re-elected Nov 2005)

Head of government: Prime Minister Jean Eyeghe Ndong (PDG) (appointed 20 Jan 2006)

Ruling party: Parti Démocratique Gabonais (PDG) (Gabonese Democratic Party) (since 1960; re-elected Dec 2006) with Groupe Du Rassemblement Nationale Des Bücherons-Mba Abessole (RNB-Mba Abessole) (National Woodcutters Party-Mba Abessole's Party)

Area: 267,667 square km

Population: 1.43 million (2007)*

Capital: Libreville

Official language: French

Currency: CFA franc (CFAf) = 100 centimes (Communauté Financière Africaine (African Financial Community) franc)

Exchange rate: CFAf413.80 per US$ (Jul 2008); CFAf655.96 per euro (pegged from Jan 1999)

GDP per capita: US$7,887 (2007)*

GDP real growth: 5.50% (2007)*

Labour force: 607,000 (2004)

Inflation: 5.00% (2007)

Oil production: 230,000 bpd (2007)

Balance of trade: US$4.18 billion (2006)

Foreign debt: US$3.80 billion (2004)

* estimated figure

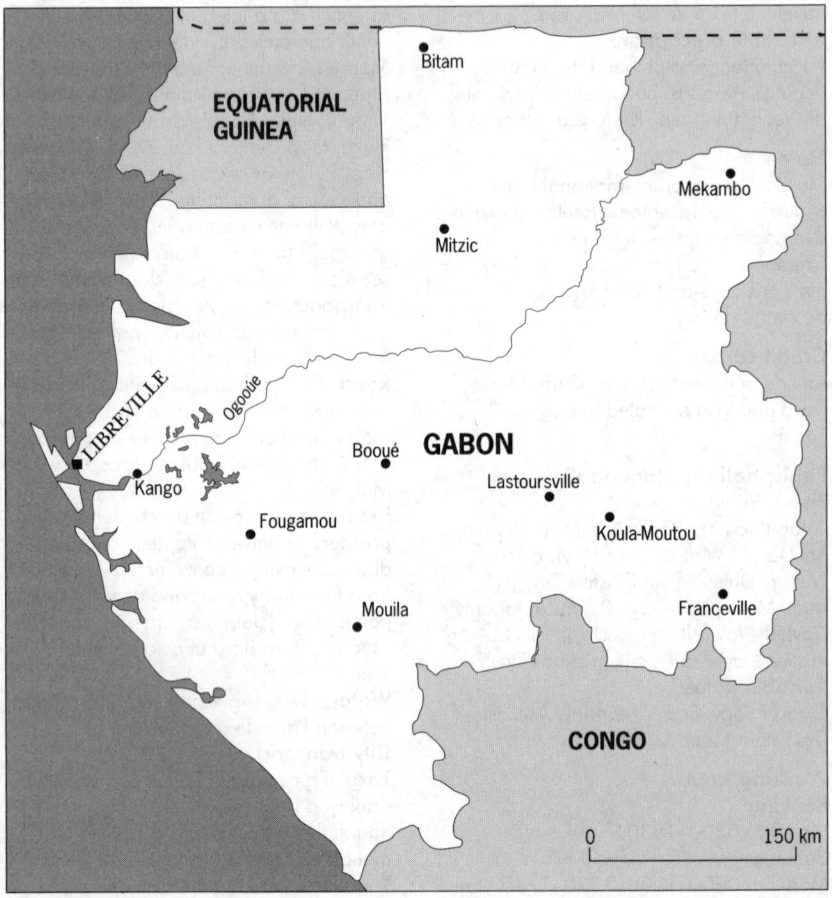

President El Hadj Omar Bongo Ondimba has been in power since 1967. There is no constitutional restriction on how long he may serve. Despite inherently unstable political conditions, a small population, abundant natural resources and considerable foreign support have helped make Gabon one of the more prosperous and stable African countries. It has maintained and conserved its pristine rain forest and rich bio-diversity. Despite the abundance of natural wealth, poor fiscal management hobbles the economy. The IMF has criticised the government for overspending on off-budget items, over borrowing from the central bank, and slipping on its schedule for privatisation and administrative reform.

Gabon has only ever enjoyed a mini-oil boom – it never amounted to much in international terms. Nevertheless, at one stage it was enough to make it Africa's fifth and OPEC's eighth, largest producer of crude. As in a number of African countries, the oil revenues have permitted the launching of a number of developments – or in some cases simply prestige – projects. Some had a solid economic foundation, others not. And despite being made up of more than 40 ethnic groups, Gabon has escaped the strife afflicting many other West African states.

Economy

According to the African Development Bank's 2008 edition of *African Economic Outlook* (AEO) Gabon's economy still largely depends on oil – 64 per cent of government revenues and 82 per cent of export revenues. The high oil prices seen in 2006 and 2007 helped increase the country's real gross domestic product (GDP) growth rate, which was 5.5 per cent in 2007. In 2007, Gabon registered per-capita GDP of US$7,887 , well above the sub-Saharan average of some US$1,500. However, analysts estimate that 60–70 per cent of Gabonese still live below the poverty line. Inflation has decreased over the last decade, with recent decreases attributed to weak private domestic demand. Inflation had dropped to 1.0 per cent in 2004, but was 5.0 per cent in 2007. Gabon, like so many African countries, aims to increase growth in the non-oil sector, especially as oil exports decline as an inevitable result of lower domestic oil production.

In addition to declining oil production, Gabon is faced with high debt payments amounting to as much as 40 per cent of the government budget. By September 2006, the International Monetary Fund (IMF) had loaned a total of US$65 million to Gabon. The World Bank currently has three active projects in Gabon, which include US$50 million in loans. The projects are aimed towards increasing natural resource management within the country. In addition, the International Finance Corporation (IFC) has invested US$256 million in the Gabonese energy sector.

The oil

Oil reserves were 2.0 billion barrels at the end of 2007, and production was 230,000. barrels per day (bpd) of crude oil, down from 235,000bpd in 2006 and well below Gabon's 1997 peak of 371,000bpd. Gabon exports the majority of its crude oil, with over half going to the United States. The remaining exports go to western Europe and Asia. In 1996, Gabon left the Organization of Petroleum Exporting Counties (OPEC), citing the organisation's high annual dues as the reason.

The need to diversify

Significant challenges remain to reduce Gabon's dependence on oil, diversify the economy, and make progress in poverty reduction. Multilateral donors are working with the government to direct Gabon's resources towards poverty alleviation, improved social outcomes and better governance. Some progress has been made in terms of human development. For example, life expectancy remains relatively high (for Africa) at 56.6 years, but infant mortality is low at 60 per 1,000, down from 88 in 1985, and 86 per cent of the population has access to safe water.

There will have to be sustained efforts to bolster non-oil revenue and improve the efficiency of public spending. By using the bulk of windfall oil revenues in the coming years to reduce domestic and external debt Gabon has the opportunity to place its public finances on a permanently sounder footing. At the same time, continued macroeconomic discipline needs to be accompanied by reinvigorating the structural reform process to accelerate the diversification of Gabon's economy and boost growth and employment in the non-oil sector.

Politics

President Omar Bongo is Africa's longest-serving head of state and one of the world's longest serving leaders. He has led Gabon since he succeeded the post-independence leader Leon M'ba in 1967. He was last re-elected for a further seven years in November 2005, receiving almost 80 per cent of the votes. International observers said the poll was largely free and fair. In 1968 he had declared Gabon a one-party state, a status which it kept until 1991. Opposition parties have so far failed to pose a serious challenge to the president's Parti Démocratique Gabonois (PDG) (Democratic Gabonese Party).

Bongo portrays himself as the custodian of Gabon's political stability and has been credited with encouraging foreign investment. His critics, however, accuse him of having authoritarian tendencies. The 2006 legislative elections confirmed the dominance of the ruling party, the PDG, which won 81 seats on 120 in the national assembly.

Risk assessment

Economic	Fair
Political	Good
Regional stability	Fair

COUNTRY PROFILE

Historical profile

Gabon's capital city, Libreville, (Freetown in translation) was founded as a settlement for freed slaves. The city is located on the site of a fort built in 1843 after a French officer succeeded in signing treaties with two local chiefs known as 'King' Denis and 'King' Louis. Libreville was later used as a base by another French officer, Pierre Savorgnan de Brazza, who set off in 1879 to spread French influence into the Congo.

The French government named a governor for Gabon in 1886 and two years later Libreville became the capital of the French Congo. In 1904 the capital was transferred to Brazzaville and Gabon became a colony in French Equatorial Africa in 1910. The northern part of the country, which was ceded to the Germans in the Cameroon in 1911, was recovered at the end of the First World War in 1918.

The region that is now Gabon was inhabited by the Omiéné by the sixteenth century. They were outnumbered by the Fang by the eighteenth century. Between the sixteenth and eighteenth centuries, Gabon

KEY INDICATORS — Gabon

	Unit	2003	2004	2005	2006	2007
Population	m	1.36	1.38	1.36	*1.40	*1.43
Gross domestic product (GDP)	US$bn	5.64	7.23	8.68	*9.55	*11.30
GDP per capita	US$	4,167	5,469	6,366	*6,835	*7,887
GDP real growth	%	2.6	1.9	3.0	*1.1	*5.5
Inflation	%	2.1	1.0	4.0	6.4	5.0
Industrial output	% change	–	3.0	3.5	-4.6	–
Agricultural output	% change	–	5.8	3.5	2.1	–
Oil output	'000 bpd	240.0	235.0	234.0	232.0	230.0
Exports (fob) (goods)	US$m	3,278.0	3,710.0	3,727.0	6,054.0	–
Imports (cif) (goods)	US$m	1,345.0	1,225.0	1,381.0	1,878.0	–
Balance of trade	US$m	1,933.0	2,485.0	2,346.0	4,176.0	–
Current account	US$m	580.0	750.0	1,662.0	1,717.0	1,450.0
Total reserves minus gold	US$m	196.6	443.4	668.6	1,113.4	1,227.2
Foreign exchange	US$m	196.3	436.9	668.1	1,112.2	1,226.0
Exchange rate	per US$	574.89	496.63	507.22	496.60	454.40

* estimated figure

was part of the Loango empire, which stretched from the Ogooué river to the Congo river.

1472 Portuguese navigators arrived in the Ogooué estuary and Gabon soon became an important centre for slave trading for the Portuguese, Dutch, British and French.

1839 Having gained a dominant position in the area and despite Fang resistance, Gabon became part of the French Congo. The French began work to abolish the slave trade.

1910 Gabon became part of French Equatorial Africa.

1939–1945 Gabon was held by the Free French.

1946 Gabon became a province of French Equatorial Africa. In gratitude for the support of the local population for the Free French, President Charles de Gaulle of France granted French citizenship to all the territory's people.

1957 Gabon gained internal autonomy.

1958 It achieved self-government within the French community.

1960 Gained full independence from France, under President Léon M'Ba. The Parti Démocratique Gabonais (PDG) (Gabonese Democratic Party) assumed power.

1964 French forces restored M'Ba to the presidency after an abortive military coup d'état.

1967 President M'Ba died. Vice President Albert-Bernard Bongo became president.

1973 Bongo was re-elected and converted to Islam, adopting the forename Omar.

1981–89 Political unrest grows as people call for more democracy.

1990 After demonstrations by students and strikes by workers, President Bongo legalised opposition parties.

1991 A new constitution was introduced that formalised the multi-party system.

1993 Bongo narrowly won the presidential election, although the opposition claimed massive electoral fraud.

1996 Parliamentary elections gave the PDG an overwhelming majority.

1998 President Bongo won another seven years in power with more than two-thirds of the vote.

1999 The country was plunged into a deep recession due to the fall in the world price of oil.

2001 The PDG won the parliamentary elections.

2002 The PDG formed a coalition with the opposition to form the government.

2003 Constitutional changes made in July allow presidents to run for office for unlimited terms. The president modified his name to El Hadj Omar Bongo Ondimba.

2004 Gabon signed separate agreements to export around one billion tonnes of iron ore as well as oil to China.

2005 In presidential elections incumbent El Hadj Omar Bongo Ondimba won 79.2 per cent of the presidential vote; Pierre Mamboundou 13.6 per cent and Zacharie Myboto 6.6 per cent. Turnout was 63.3 per cent.

2006 Omar Bongo Ondimba was sworn in as president for a third seven-year term. Jean Eyeghe Ndong (PDG) was appointed prime minister by the president. In parliamentary elections the ruling PDG won 82 out of the 120 seats, allied parties won 17, opposition 17 and independents four seats.

2008 Former foreign minister, Jean Ping was elected chairman of the African Union Commission on 1 February.

Political structure

Constitution

In 1991 a new constitution was introduced which restored multi-party elections and protected civil liberties. The constitution maintained a strong presidential role but allowed for a more influential prime minister.

In July 2003, the constitution was changed to allow presidents to run for office for unlimited number of times, and the number of presidential election rounds was reduced from two to one.

Form of state

Presidential democracy

The executive

Executive power is divided between the president, elected by universal suffrage every seven years, and the prime minister and Council of Ministers (Cabinet) who are appointed by the president.

Government members must be more than 35 years of age and have at least seven years' professional experience.

The president is head of state, head of administration and chief of the armed forces.

National legislature

Legislative power is vested in the 120-member Assemblée Nationale (national assembly), with 111 members elected for five-year terms in single-seat constituencies and nine members appointed by the president.

Members of the 91-seat Sénat (senate) are elected for six year terms by local and departmental councillors.

Legal system

The legal system is based on the French civil law system and customary law. There is judicial review of legislative acts in the Constitutional Chamber of the Supreme Court.

Last elections

27 November 2005 (presidential); 17 December 2006 (National Assembly).

Results: Presidential: incumbent El Hadj Omar Bongo Ondimba won 79.2 per cent of the vote; Pierre Mamboundou 13.6 per cent and Zacharie Myboto 6.6 per cent. Turnout was 63.3 per cent.

Parliamentary: PDG won 82 seats out of 120; RNB-Mba Abessole won 17; opposition parties including UPG 8; Union Gabonaise pour la Démocratie et le Développement (UGDD) (Gabonese Union for Democracy and Development) 4, others 5; independents 4 seats.

Next elections

2009 (senate); 2011 (national assembly); 2012 (presidential);

Political parties

Ruling party

Parti Démocratique Gabonais (PDG) (Gabonese Democratic Party) (since 1960; re-elected Dec 2006) with Groupe Du Rassemblement Nationale Des Bûcherons-Mba Abessole (RNB-Mba Abessole) (National Woodcutters Party-Mba Abessole's Party)

Main opposition party

Union du Peuple Gabonais (UPG) Union of the Gabonese People

Population

1.43 million (2007)*

Last census: December 2003: 1,269,000 (provisional)

Population density: Five inhabitants per square km. Urban population: 82 per cent of total (1995–2001).

Annual growth rate: 2.3 per cent 1994–2004 (WHO 2006)

Ethnic make-up

There are some 40 different ethnic groups, of which the Fangs are the largest (40 per cent of the total); the Bapounous (20 per cent) are also highly significant. There are some 25,000 Europeans, mainly of French nationality.

Religions

Christianity (59 per cent), mostly Roman Catholic; indigenous animist beliefs (40 per cent). There is a small Muslim community (less than 1 per cent).

Education

School is compulsory and free for all children up to the age of 16 years. Secondary education covers seven years, divided into a lower cycle lasting four years and an upper cycle lasting three years. On completion of the upper cycle, pupils take the examinations for the Baccalauréat for advancement to university. On completion of the lower cycle, pupils may opt to take a 'short' or a 'long' course of technical secondary education. The former leads to the Brevet de Technicien and the latter to the Baccalauréat technique.

Two universities – Omar Bongo University and the University of Science and Technology of Masuku (USTM at Franceville) –

as well as various independent institutions provide higher education. Universities enjoy a certain degree of autonomy, even though higher education is financed exclusively by public funds.
Public expenditure on education typically amounts to 2.5 per cent of annual GDP.
Literacy rate: 79.8 per cent, male; 62.2 per cent, female; adult rates (World Bank).
Enrolment rate: 62 per cent total primary school enrolment of the relevant age group (World Bank).
Pupils per teacher: 56 in primary schools.

Health

Per capita total expenditure on health (2003) was US$255; of which per capita government spending was US$170, at the international dollar rate, (WHO 2006).
Gabon is plagued by poor health conditions, which are aggravated by the hot and humid climate and is the country worst affected by malaria in sub-Saharan Africa.
Gabon faces a growing crisis of male impotence affecting 25 per cent of all adult men, blamed on high levels of alcohol and tobacco use.
HIV/Aids
HIV/Aids is a rapidly growing crisis the World Health Organisation (WHO) estimates that 30,000 people in Gabon are being infected with HIV each year and Gabon is beginning to experience the serious effects of the African pandemic.
Around 8,600 children have been orphaned by the disease. The main concentration of HIV/Aids cases is in the capital, Libreville. The government has launched a campaign to prevent the disease spreading further.
HIV prevalence: 8.1 per cent aged 15–49 in 2003 (World Bank)
Life expectancy: 57 years, 2004 (WHO 2006)
Fertility rate/Maternal mortality rate: 3.9 births per woman, 2004 (WHO 2006); maternal mortality 600 per 100,000 live births (World Bank).
Birth rate/Death rate: 16 deaths to 36 births per 1,000 population,
Child (under 5 years) mortality rate (per 1,000): 60 per 1,000 live births (World Bank)
Head of population per physician: 0.29 physicians per 1,000 people, 2004 (WHO 2006)

Welfare

Gabon's social welfare system, while deeply flawed, is one of the best in sub-Saharan Africa. It operates a social insurance system and healthcare system through separate funds administered by the National Social Security Fund (CNSS) and National Social Guarantee Fund (CNGS) for self-employed and state workers under contract through a pay-as-you-go system. As these funds have experienced financial difficulties and the government has undertaken to restructure them with a view to their long-term viability. Inadequate contributions have been blamed for the over-spending.
The social insurance system covers benefits including old age, disability, sickness, maternity and work injuries with provision for certain categories of self-employed workers. Old age pensions are available to men aged 55 with 20 years of insurance and 120 months of contribution during the last 10 years. It is set at a minimum of 40 per cent of average earnings during the last three or five years of pay. There is also provision for old-age settlement with a lump sum equal to 50 per cent of average monthly earnings for every six months of contribution, if the person is ineligible for pension.
Medical services are provided by hospitals and dispensaries operated by the CNSS, and by other establishments. Free maternity care is payable up to six weeks before, and eight weeks after, confinement.
A family allowance law also offers benefits to employees with one or more children under the age of 16 years. Family Allowance Benefits provide a month income for each child and a year school allowances for primary, secondary and technical school students.

Main cities

Libreville (capital, estimated population 673,995 in 2004), Port-Gentil (118,940).

Languages spoken

French is used for all documentation. The main native language is Fang, with a number of other Bantu dialects spoken.
It is essential that business visitors should be able to conduct business in French. Interpreters can be hired locally.
Official language/s
French

Media

The constitution guarantees freedom of speech and of the press, however, these are not always respected and this has led to self-censorship by local journalists.
National news agency: Agence Gabonaise de Presse (AGP)
Other news agencies: Gabonews: www.gabonews.ga
Internet Gabon: www.internetgabon.com
Press
The national press is heavily influenced by government which owns the majority of newspapers used to discredit opposition political parties and independent media.
While all newspapers may be critical of the government and political leaders, none are critical of the president. The government has shown itself to be quick to use libel laws, which can be both criminal and civil matters, and to suspend publications it deems unacceptable in their reporting.
Foreign newspapers and magazines are readily available in Libreville.
Dailies: The only newspaper is the government-owned L'Union, published in French.
Weeklies: In French, privately-owned newspapers include Le Temps which has a satirical tenor, Le Temoin covers general news and information, La Lowe, La Relance and the fortnightly Le Journal.
Business: In French, a monthly journal Business Gabon (www.gaboneco.com/busnessgabon/Business_Gabon.pdf) has business articles and information.
Periodicals: L'Union also publishes a monthly magazine, with a similar circulation. M'Bolo has three issues on holiday and travel.
Broadcasting
Gabon is developing as the centre of Francophone broadcasting for Central and West Africa, being the base of the radio service Africa No 1 and for the African operations of France's Canal Plus. The state has taken a financial interest in these broadcasting media, as well as in the main newspaper, directly and through parastatal groups. It therefore retains a high degree of control.
The government-owned, national, public broadcasting service, Radiodiffusion-Télévision Gabonaise (RTG), operates radio stations and a network of provincial stations.
Radio: RTG operates two national radio stations, based in Libreville, and a network of six regional stations broadcasting in French and local languages.
A major international station, Africa No 1, is 60 per cent government owned, with the rest owned by private Gabonese shareholders. It is in partnership with the French-owned Radio France Internationale (RFI), broadcasting throughout Africa.
Other, commercial stations include Black FM and Radio Emergence.
Television: RTG operates a network of provincial TV stations, which broadcast in French and local languages. RTG 1 is a national service, broadcast in Libreville and Franceville; while RTG 2 can be received only in the Libreville and the coastal area.
Téléafrica, is a private commercial channel that broadcasts 24 hours a day. Subscription TV is available through the French, Canal Horizons (Gabon), a channel designed to serve the whole of Francophone Central Africa.

News agencies
National news agency: Agence Gabonaise de Presse (AGP)
Other news agencies: Gabonews: www.gabonews.ga
Internet Gabon: www.internetgabon.com

Economy
Gabon is sub-Saharan Africa's fourth-largest oil exporter; revenue from oil exports, which account for around 51 per cent of GDP and 63 per cent of government income, has kept the economy afloat. However, production has been declining in recent years, while reserves (around 2.5 billion barrels) are running down. Gabon is under pressure to plan against the day when, unless new reserves are discovered, it can no longer depend on oil. The IMF, reporting in 2005 on the economy and the end of reliance on oil, observed that Gabon continued to face a 'lack of economic diversification and weak non-oil growth'.
Public sector employment and wages are considered an important inhibition on entrepreneurial enterprises, which constrains competitiveness in the non-oil sector. Domestic growth in non-oil activities has been modest and dependent on timber production (around 80 per cent of non-oil exports) and manganese (15 per cent). Both of these markets are privately exploited, volatile and subject to external pressures. The agricultural sector remains largely underdeveloped.
Gabon has been criticised by the World Bank and the IMF for poor economic management. The government has persistently failed to meet its privatisation targets. Future IMF assistance will depend on the privatisation of the remaining parastatals.
Due to its oil wealth and the small size of the population, Gabon's per capita GDP of US$5,469 is markedly higher than the US$500 average of sub-Saharan Africa. However, over 60 per cent of the population live below the poverty line, income being distributed extremely unevenly with 90 per cent of the wealth held by 5 per cent of the population. Efforts to alleviate poverty, in partnership with international donors, are taking place.

External trade
Gabon is a member of the Economic and Monetary Community Central African (Cemac), the Economic Community of Central African States (ECCAS) and the Bank of Central African States, using the CFA franc. There is a common external tariff (CET) within Cemac.
Imports
Principal imports are foodstuffs, machinery and equipment, chemicals and construction materials.
Main sources: France (40.6 per cent total, 2005), US (6.4 per cent), Cameroon (4.2 per cent)
Exports
Principal exports are crude oil (over 70 per cent of total), timber, manganese and uranium
Main destinations: US (53.5 per cent total, 2005), France (6.4 per cent), China (6.3 per cent), Trinidad and Tobago (4.0 per cent)

Agriculture
Farming
The agricultural sector in Gabon has been neglected, forcing the importation of a large percentage of the country's food needs. Only about 1 per cent of total land area is under cultivation and agriculture is further limited by the small size of the population. A shortage of cultivated lands has been the major problem facing the agricultural sector which, mostly through subsistence farming, supports a large portion of the population.
Principal cash crops are palm oil, cocoa and refined sugar, while subsistence crops are cassava, maize and plantains. Cocoa is grown mainly in Woleu Ntem province and coffee mainly in Ogooué-Ivindo, Ogooué-Lolo and Haut Ogooué provinces. Sugar cane is grown and refined by the Société Sucrérie du Haut-Ogooué (Sosuho). Annual sugar output is around 30,000 tonnes. Agrogabon set up three cattle ranches in the 1980s, importing tsetse fly-resistant cattle. They are located at Lekabi, Nyanga and N'Gounie. The only industrial-scale poultry farm is run by the Société Industrielle d'Agriculture et d'Elevage de Boumango (SIAEB).
The estimated crop production for 2005 included: 32,000 tonnes (t) cereals in total, 31,000t maize, 230,000t cassava, 155,000t yams, 2,800t sweet potatoes, 600t cocoa beans, 270,000t plantains, 13,118t oilcrops, 11,000t natural rubber, 235,000t sugar cane, 32,000t oil palm fruit, 59,000t taro, 294,000t fruit in total, 35,410t vegetables in total. Estimated livestock production included: 31,716t meat in total, 1,096t beef, 21,000t game meat, 3,080t pig meat, 960t lamb and goat meat, 3,600t poultry, 1,980t eggs, 1,575t milk.
Fishing
Gabon has well-stocked fishing grounds, which are only partially exploited. Domestic demand is estimated at around 36,000 tonnes. The typical annual catch is over 40,000 tonnes. Traditional fishing accounts for two-thirds of national fishing output. There are about a dozen fleets, most of which are foreign, engaged in industrial fishing in Gabonese waters.
In 2004, the total marine fish catch was 33,649 tonnes and the total crustacean catch was 2,533 tonnes.
Forestry
Exports of forest products amount to around US$320 million annually and timber is a source of employment for nearly a third of the working population outside the public sector. Forests cover almost 85 per cent of the land area, estimated at 21.8 million hectares (ha). Deforestation typically accounts for 0.05 per cent annually average decrease, or the equivalent of 10,000ha of forest cover.
The forestry industry is the second-largest industry in the country. Gabon commercially exploits and exports both soft and hard woods, but cultivation and processing of timber comprises the main portion of forestry activities. The country produces sawn timber, veneers and plywood. Tropical hardwood logs constitute the bulk of its roundwood exports. The potential commercial volume of live trees is estimated at 400 million cubic metres, 130 million of which is the much celebrated ebony gaboon wood.
Gabon is the fifth-largest world producer of timber, behind Finland, Canada, Sweden and New Zealand.
The forest is divided into three administrative zones. The coastal area is already fairly well exploited. The zone around Ngounie, Nyanga and Haut-Ogooué has the bulk of current activity. The Booue-Lastourville axis of the Transgabon railway is largely undeveloped. Seven large companies dominate okoume production. The largest is the majority state-owned Compagnie Forestière du Gabon (CFG).
Okoume, designated as the most important commercial timber, is selectively logged in a significant proportion of the country's forests. Exploitable forest potential is more than 300 million cubic metres. One-third of this is okoume, which is particularly suited to the production of plywood.
Timber imports in 2004 were US$6.2 million, while exports only amounted to US$319.8 million.
Timber production in 2004 included 4,570,000 cubic metre (cum) roundwood, 3,500,000cum industrial roundwood, 233,000cum sawnwood, 3,500,000cum sawlogs and veneer logs, 221,700cum wood-based panels, 1,070,000cum wood fuel, 17,400t charcoal.

Industry and manufacturing
The main industrial activities are oil refining and timber processing, although these activities are treated separately from other industry in the national accounts. The other main manufacturing sectors are

food processing, drinks and tobacco, metal transformation (primarily connected with shipyard activities and supplying the oil and wood industries) and building materials. Small sub sectors include textiles and chemicals (lubricants, paints, varnishes and detergents).
A fair proportion of the very modest industrial sector has been based on a policy of import substitution. This is now being abandoned as part of structural adjustment measures. The outlook for industry is therefore bleak even though there are plans to develop a regional export market within the Union Douanière des Etats de l'Afrique Centrale (UDEAC) (Central African Customs and Economic Union) countries. In theory, this larger potential market would allow industry to develop economies of scale that the small domestic market does not justify. In practice, however, high labour costs are likely to frustrate efforts to promote the regional market. Gabon's labour costs are high due to the well-established social security system, most of the cost of which is borne by employers, offering benefits that are not found in many other West and Central African countries.

Tourism
Gabon receives around 120,000 foreign visitors annually. However, only around 1 per cent are tourists. Nevertheless this growing sector is expected to contribute US$1.5 million in 2005, or 3.3 per cent of GDP.
The ministry of tourism is beginning to market Gabon as an eco-tourist destination. La Lopée Reserve in south-east Gabon, covering 4,940 square km, was the country's first national park. The sector has yet to be fully developed with over US$226 million or 10.1 per cent of total capital investment expected to be spent on travel and tourism in 2005. However, the high local cost of living makes it difficult to compete internationally, even though Gabon has a good hotel infrastructure, marvellous sandy beaches, generally safe bathing and many wildlife attractions. There are about 6,000 hotel beds in the country. Gabon has five game reserves: La Lopée, Mouklaba, Wonga-Wonge, Sette-Cama and Iguela.

Mining
Mining and hydrocarbons together contribute around 50 cent to GDP and employ 10 per cent of the workforce.
Gabon is one of the world's leading producers of manganese and uranium. Other areas of interest are gold and iron ore. Activity is concentrated on extraction and export of manganese ore (reserves of 200 million tonnes) and uranium (reserves of 35,000 tonnes). Both are crudely refined before export, the manganese as a 51 per cent concentrate and the uranium as 74 per cent pure yellow cake. Manganese goes mainly to Europe, but also to the US and the Far East. Uranium goes mainly to France (about 10 per cent of France's requirements), the rest to Belgium and Japan. Manganese and uranium account for 10 per cent of merchandise exports. Manganese production is declining, while large deposits of iron ore, barytes (used in paint-making) and niobium, discovered during construction of the Transgabon railway, have yet to be exploited.
There are 50 million tonnes of phosphate reserves.

Hydrocarbons
Gabon is sub-Saharan Africa's fourth-largest oil producer, after Nigeria, Angola and Equatorial Guinea. With income from oil exports representing around 40 per cent of GDP and 80 per cent of exports, Gabon's economy is highly dependent on this one commodity. The exports go primarily to Western Europe, although China has imported Gabonese crude for its growing market since February 2004.
In 2004, the proven oil reserves were 2.3 million barrels, with production at 235,000 barrels per day (bpd). Production is falling rapidly from the high of 370,000bpd in 1997.
The World Bank estimates that oil production is likely to decline by 50 per cent by 2007, which will strain government revenues. Exploration and production occurs both onshore and offshore. The country's downstream industry consists of the Sogara refinery, which has a capacity of 21,000bpd.
The government has consistently maintained a market-oriented policy towards its sizeable oil reserves and has one of the most attractive hydrocarbons codes in Africa. Under this law, the state has a minimum 25 per cent holding in all oil-producing companies operating in Gabon. Oil exploration permits are awarded under production-sharing agreements, which are individually negotiated.
Natural gas reserves totalled approximately 33.9 billion cubic metres (cum) in 2004, down from 42 billion cum in 2003, with production at around 1 billion cubic metres per annum. All gas produced in Gabon is used for electricity or refinery fuel.
Gabon does not produce or import coal.

Energy
Gabon has a total electricity generating capacity of 300MW, more than two-thirds of which is hydroelectric with the potential of around 6,000MW when fully developed. The largest hydroelectric dams are Tchimbele (69MW) and Kinguele (58MW), on the M'Bei River.
Société d'Energie et d'Eau du Gabon (SEEG) is responsible for the production and distribution of electricity and water throughout the country – 51 per cent was sold to a French consortium in 1997, representing sub-Saharan Africa's first privatisation of a water and electricity utility. Consumption is principally concentrated in the regions of Libreville, Port-Gentil and Franceville.

Banking and insurance
Central bank
Banque des Etats de l'Afrique Centrale
Main financial centre
Libreville

Time
GMT plus one hour

Geography
Gabon is an equatorial country on the west coast of Africa, with Equatorial Guinea and Cameroon to the north, and the Republic of Congo to the south and east.
The eastern boundary lies along the watershed of the Democratic Republic of Congo (DRC), so that all rivers flow broadly west through Gabon into the sea. The sandy coastal strip consists of palm-fringed bays, lagoons and estuaries. The uplands are heavily eroded by river action, and there is a wide coastal plain, which is largely alluvial in nature. The natural vegetation is dense rain forest.
Hemisphere
Straddles the equator; Liberville, the capital, is in the north.

Climate
The climate is equatorial with an annual mean temperature of 28 degrees Celsius and high levels of humidity. The rainy seasons are between October and mid-December, and between mid-January and May. The dry season is from June to September.

Dress codes
Lightweight or tropical clothing is suitable, with rainwear for the monsoon season. Businessmen should wear a lightweight or tropical suit and women a lightweight suit or equivalent.

Entry requirements
Passports
Required by all. Passports must be valid for more than six months after the date of departure.
Proof of return/onward passage is necessary.
Visa
Required by all and to be applied for before travelling. Applications for business visas require a letter from the representative's company accepting responsibility for any expenses incurred, a full itinerary and

a letter of invitation from a host company in Gabon.

Currency advice/regulations
There are no limits on the import of foreign or domestic currency, although any sum should be declared on arrival. Export of local currency, to countries outside the CFA franc zone, is limited of CFAf200,000.
Visitors are advised to carry travellers cheques in euros to avoid extra exchange fees.

Health (for visitors)
Mandatory precautions
A yellow fever vaccination certificate is required.
Advisable precautions
Immunisations are advisable for yellow fever, hepatitis A, tetanus and typhoid. There is a rabies risk.
Malaria and HIV/Aids are prevalent and standard measures should be taken to avoid these diseases.
Water which is used for drinking, brushing teeth or making ice should first be boiled. Dysentery can be caught from contaminated raw fruit and vegetables and unboiled water. Dairy products made from local milk should be avoided. Meat and fish should be well cooked and eaten hot.

Hotels
Available in Libreville, Port Gentil, Lambaréné and other main centres. Service charge is usually included in bill, if not a tip of 10–15 per cent is usual.

Credit cards
Credit cards are not widely accepted.

Public holidays (national)
Fixed dates
1 Jan (New Year's Day), 1 May (Labour Day), 16 Aug (Assumption Day), 16–18 Aug (Independence Day celebrations), 1 Nov (All Saints' Day), 25 Dec (Christmas Day).
Variable dates
Easter Monday, Whit Monday, Eid al Adha, Eid al Fitr.
Islamic year – 1429 (10 Jan 2008–28 Dec 2008): The Islamic year contains 354 or 355 days, with the result that Muslim feasts advance by 10–12 days against the Gregorian calendar. Dates of feasts vary according to the sighting of the new moon, so cannot be forecast exactly.

Working hours
Banking
Mon–Fri: 0730–1130, 1430–1630.
Business
Mon–Fri: 0730–1200, 1430–1800.
Government
Mon–Fri: 0800–1200, 1500–1800; Sat: 0800–1300.
Shops
Mon–Sat: 0800–1200, 1500–1900.

Telecommunications
Mobile/cell phones
GSM 900 services are available in the most populated areas.

Electricity supply
220-30V AC, 50 cycles. Round two-pin plugs are standard.

Social customs/useful tips
Business is conducted in French. Appointments should be made in advance. It is customary to shake hands when meeting and taking leave. Business cards are exchanged after introduction.
Gratuities are between 10–15 per cent if no service charge is included.
The lifestyles of the middle classes in Libreville, Port-Gentil and Franceville have been heavily influenced by the French, and French etiquette has been largely adopted.
As elsewhere in Africa, it is extremely unwise to attempt to photograph any military installations or troop movements, security checkpoints, etc.

Security
Crime is increasingly a problem with incidents of robbery and armed attacks, particularly around Libreville and Port-Gentil. Avoid carrying valuables or wearing jewellery in public and walking alone at night. Avoid travelling at night and always comply with the frequent police roadblocks.

Getting there
Air
National airline: Air Gabon (Compagnie Nationale Air Gabon).
International airport/s: Libreville-Léon M'Ba (LBV), 12km from city; restaurant, currency exchange; Port Gentil (POG), 4km from city.
Other airport/s: Franceville-Mvengue (MVB) has air charters. There are 65 other public and 50 private airfields linked mostly with the forestry and petroleum industries.
Airport tax: None
Surface
Road: The major routes are from the Republic of Congo, Cameroon or Equatorial Guinea. These are semi-surfaced but generally are in good condition and well maintained.
Water: There is a boat to and from São Tomé every five days.
Main port/s: The principal deep-water ports are Port Gentil, Owendo (Libreville). Mayumba and Nyanga are used for shipping timber. There is a fishing port in Libreville.

Getting about
National transport
Air: Air Gabon operates scheduled and charter flights to all main centres.
Road: There are an estimated 8,590km of roads, including 3,290km of main roads and 1,950km of secondary roads. Except for the routes Libreville-Ndende, Booué-Bitam, roads can be difficult in the rainy season. Travel by bush taxis and truck can be dangerous, especially in the rainy season.
Buses: Regular coach and minibus services link Libreville with Lambaréné, Oyem, Mouila and Bitam. Some services are subject to rainy season conditions.
Rail: Regular services operate on the Transgabon railway linking Libreville with Booué, Ndjolé and Franceville. There are two classes. The railcars are air-conditioned for some services but no refreshment or sleeping accommodation is scheduled. The rolling stock is generally new.
Water: The principal river is the Ogooué, navigable from Port-Gentil to Ndjole (310km), and serving the towns of Lambaréné, Ndjolé and Sindara.
A ferry service (taking two hours) operates between Libreville and Port-Gentil.
City transport
Taxis: Unmetered 'collective' and private taxis are available in main towns; tipping is not usual; rates vary according to the time of day. The journey from the airport to the Libreville city centre takes 10 minutes.
Car hire
Available in main towns, at airports and through hotels. International driving licence required. Charges are high.

BUSINESS DIRECTORY

The addresses listed below are a selection only. While World of Information makes every endeavour to check these addresses, we cannot guarantee that changes have not been made, especially to telephone numbers and area codes. We would welcome any corrections.

Telephone area codes
The international dialling code (IDD) for Gabon is + 241 followed by subscriber's number.

Useful telephone numbers
Police:732-036761-044
760-950720-951
Fire:18 761-520
Ambulance:732-771 762-344

Chambers of Commerce
Gabon Chamber of Commerce, Agriculture, Industry and Mines, PO Box 2234, Libreville (tel: 722-064; fax: 746-477).

Banking
Banque Gabonaise de Développement; PO Box 5, Rue Alfred Marche, Libreville (tel: 762-429, 762-489; fax: 742-699).

Banque Gabonaise et Francaise Internationale (BGFI), PO Box 2253, Blvd de l'Indépendance, Libreville (tel: 732-326, 764-035; fax: 740-894, 744-456).

Banque Internationale pour le Commerce et l'Industrie du Gabon SA, PO Box 2241, Avenue du Colonel Parant, Libreville (tel: 762-613, 763-811; fax: 746-410).

Banque Nationale du Crédit Rural, PO Box 1120, Avenue Bouët, Libreville (tel: 724-742, 766-144, 763-045; fax: 740-507).

Banque Populaire du Gabon, PO Box 6663, Blvd de l'Indépendance, Libreville (tel: 724-719; fax: 728-691).

Caisse Nationale d'Epargne, Siège Social, Libreville (tel: 766-509).

Centre de Chéques Postaux, Siége Social, Libreville (tel: 766-509).

Union Gabonaise de Banque SA, PO Box 315 & 2238, Avenue du Colonel Parant, Libreville (tel: 777-000; fax: 764-616).

Central bank

Banque des Etats de l'Afrique Centrale, Direction Nationale; PO Box 112, Libreville (tel: 761-352; fax: 744-563; e-mail: beaclbv@beac.int).

Travel information

ADL (Aeroport de Libreville), BP 363, Libreville (tel: 736-128).

Air Gabon (Compagnie Nationale Air Gabon), BP 2206, Aeroport International Léon M'ba, Libreville (tel: 730-027; fax: 731-156).

Eurafrique Voyages, BP 4026, Libreville (tel: 762-787; fax: 761-897).

Libreville Léon M'Ba International Airport, BP 363, Libreville (tel: 736-244/246/247; fax: 736-128).

Ministry of tourism

Ministry of Transport, Tourism and National Parks, BP 3974, Libreville (tel: 763-240).

Ministries

Ministry of Agriculture and Rural Development, BP 551, Libreville (tel: 721-579).

Ministry of the Arts, Culture and People Education, BP 1007, Libreville (tel: 724-028).

Ministry of Defence, Security and Immigration, BP 13493, Libreville (tel: 760-835).

Ministry of Economy, Finance, Budget and Privatisation, BP 9672, Libreville (tel: 721-571, 760-580; fax: 761-518).).

Ministry of Foreign Affairs and Co-operation, BP 2245, Libreville (tel: 762-251).

Ministry of Forestry and Environment, BP 199, Libreville (tel: 733-191).

Ministry of Higher Education, BP 3919, Libreville (tel: 763-252).

Ministry of Home (in charge of Local Collectivities and Mobile Security), BP 2110, Libreville (tel: 762-181).

Ministry of Housing, Land Registry and Town Planning, BP 512, Libreville (tel: 740-461).

Ministry of Justice, BP 547, Libreville (tel: 720-160).

Ministry of Labour and Human Resources, BP 2256, Libreville (tel: 732-739).

Ministry of Mining, Energy and Hydraulic Resources, BP 4041, Libreville (tel: 762-863).

Ministry of National Education and Professional Training, BP 6, Libreville (tel: 721-741).

Ministry of Public Health, BP 50, Libreville (tel: 762-522).

Ministry of Public Service and Administrative Reform, BP 496, Libreville (tel: 762-150).

Ministry of Shipping, BP 803, Libreville (tel: 733-210).

Ministry of Small and Medium Businesses, BP 4120, Libreville (tel: 720-636).

Ministry of Social Affairs, Family and Solidarity, BP 5684, Libreville (tel: 761-700).

Ministry of State Control, Decentralisation, Administration of Territory and Regional Integration, BP 178, Libreville (tel: 763-550).

Ministry of Trade Industry, BP 3906, Libreville (tel: 722-887).

Ministry of Youth and Sport, BP 3904, Libreville (tel: 763-576).

Other useful addresses

Compagnie Minière de l'Ogoué (Comilog), BP 578, Libreville (tel: 722-474).

Conseil Economique et Sociale de la République Gabonais, BP 1075, Libreville (tel: 762-668).

European Development Fund, BP 321, Libreville (tel: 732-250).

Gabonese Embassy (US), 2034 20th Street, NW, Washington DC 20009 (tel: (+1-202) 797-1000; fax: (+1-202) 332-0668).

Société de Développement de l'Agriculture au Gabon (Agrogabon), BP 2248, Libreville (tel: 764-082).

Société Equatoriale de Travaux Pétroliers Maritimes, BP 493, Libreville (tel: 753-509).

Société Gabonaise de Financement et d'Expansion, BP 2151, Libreville.

Société Gabonaise de Participation et de Développement, BP 1624, Libreville.

Société Gabonaise de Raffinage, BP 530, Libreville (tel: 752-365).

Société Nationale de Transports Maritimes (Sonatram), BP 3841, Libreville (tel: 740-632; fax: 745-967).

US Embassy, Boulevard de la Mer, BP 4000, Libreville (tel: 762-002).

National news agency: Agence Gabonaise de Presse (AGP)

Address: BP 168, Libreville (tel: 443507; fax: 443509; internet: www.agpgabon.ga).

Internet sites

Africa Business Network: http://www.ifc.org/abn

AllAfrica.com: http://allafrica.com

African Development Bank: http://www.afdb.org

Africa Online: http://www.africaonline.com

Mbendi AfroPaedia (information on companies, countries, industries and stock exchanges in Africa): http://www.mbendi.co.za

KEY FACTS

Official name: Republic of The Gambia

Head of State: President Yahya Abdul-Aziz Jamus Junkung Jammeh (since 1994; re-elected 22 Sep 2006)

Head of government: President Yahya Abdul-Aziz Jamus Junkung Jammeh (APRC)

Ruling party: Alliance for Patriotic Reorientation and Construction (APRC) (since 1996; re-elected Jan 2007)

Area: 11,295 square km

Population: 1.59 million (2007)

Capital: Banjul

Official language: English

Currency: Dalasi (D) = 100 butut

Exchange rate: D20.97 per US$ (Jul 2008)

GDP per capita: US$411 (2007)

GDP real growth: 7.00% (2007)

Labour force: 746,000 (2004)

Inflation: 5.00% (2007)

Balance of trade: -US$56.70 million (2005)

The Gambia

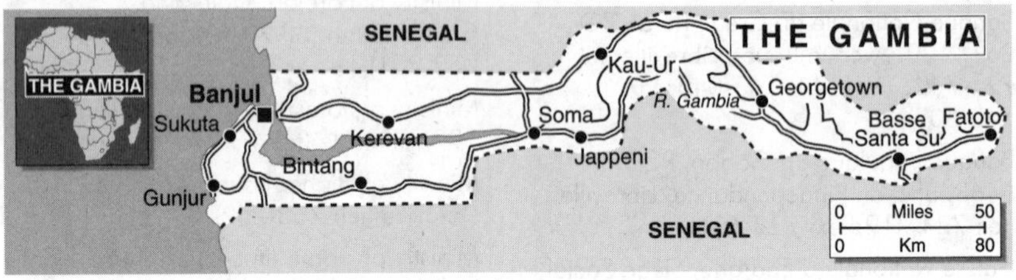

Dawda Jawara dominated politics as president from independence first as prime minister and then as elected president from 1970 when the country became a republic. After 30 years in power he was removed in a bloodless coup by Captain Yahya Jammeh in July 1994. Jammeh announced a four year programme to return The Gambia to civilian rule; a consultation process eventually produced a constitution which allows for multi-party elections and a presidential term of five years with no limit on the number of terms a president may serve. Jammeh himself, although he initially denied he would stand, won the first elections under the new constitution in 1996 with 56 per cent of the vote. The following year, his newly formed party, the Alliance for Patriotic Reorientation and Construction (APRC), won 33 seats in the 45 seat parliament.

Jammeh won the elections of 2001 with 53 per cent of the vote in the second round of voting, and the 2006 elections with an increased margin of 66 per cent. There had been a coup attempt in April 2006, which resulted in the arrest of 27 people. Preparations for the elections were controversial with the dismissal by the president of the last three chairmen of the Independent Electoral Commission and a clamp down on the freedom of the press. Never the less, the actual vote was considered to free and fair on the day although the Commonwealth Secretariat noted 'abuses of incumbency' in the lead up to the polls.

Liberal economy

The Gambia's economy is a liberal, market-based economy, underpinned by subsistence agriculture and a significant tourist industry. Groundnuts are the chief export earner and account for 6.9 per cent of GDP; services, including tourism, contribute 54 per cent. Export markets have changed in recent years from being almost exclusively the UK and other European Union (EU) countries to include Thailand and China and other West African countries such as Senegal, Guinea-Bissau and Ghana. China and Brazil have become important sources of imports.

The governor of the Central Bank of the Gambia, Momodou Bamba Saho, reported in March 2008 that he expected the economy to grow by 6.5 per cent in 2008, down from the 6.9 per cent of 2007, 'premised on decreased activity in building and construction and the groundnut trade'. He went on to say that '...the government's budget registered a surplus of 0.1 per cent of GDP including grants in 2007, while without grants, he said the budget was in deficit by 1.0 per cent. Domestic revenue rose by 13.7 per cent to D3.4 billion (US$12 million), D106.1 million higher than estimated... Preliminary balance of payments estimates for the fourth quarter of 2007 indicate an overall surplus of US$8.48 million from a surplus of US$9.34 million in the third quarter. The current account balance is expected to narrow from 12.9 per cent of GDP in 2006 to 10.1 per cent in 2007'. He also noted that external sector conditions had improved in 2007 owing to prudent monetary and fiscal policies as well as the benign global environment. Inflation, he said, is forecast at 5.0 per cent for 2008, although he warned of the risks of the continued rise in oil prices.

Human rights

A US state department (USSD) publication, *Human rights report on The Gambia*

, published in March 2008 states that 'The government's respect for the human rights of its citizens did not improve during the year (2007). Although the constitution and law provide for protection of most human rights, there were problems in many areas. Prison conditions remained poor. Arbitrary arrests and detentions continued. Security forces harassed and mistreated detainees, prisoners, opposition members, and journalists with impunity. Prisoners were held incommunicado, faced prolonged pretrial detention, and were denied due process. The government restricted freedom of speech and (the) press. Women experienced violence and discrimination, and female genital mutilation (FGM) remained a problem. Child labour and trafficking in persons also were problems.' An Amnesty International report published in 2007 similarly criticised the government. However, a USSD Internation Religious Freedom Report published in September 2007 reported that 'The Constitution provides for freedom of religion, and the Government generally respected this right in practice. There was no change in the status of respect for religious freedom covered by this report, and government policy contributed to the generally free practice of religion.' Sunni Muslims are 90 per cent of the population, Christians 9 per cent and 1 per cent indigenous animist beliefs.

Outlook

Unemployment and underemployment rates remain high; short-term economic progress depends on sustained bilateral and multilateral aid, on responsible government economic management, on continued technical assistance from the IMF and bilateral donors, and on expected growth in the construction sector.

Risk assessment

Politics	Poor
Economy	Fair
Regional stability	Fair

COUNTRY PROFILE

Historical profile

When independence came to The Gambia in 1965, there were many who doubted that Africa's newest state would hold on to her status for any appreciable length of time. The oldest and most northerly of Britain's former West African possessions, The Gambia is surrounded, except on her Atlantic seaboard, by the bigger and more populous Senegal. It is said that but for the river the country would not have existed.

1455 The Portuguese established trading stations along the River Gambia.
1889 The boundaries of The Gambia were agreed by the British and French.
1894 The Gambia became a British protectorate.
1965 Following independence, Dawda Jawara, as the head of the People's Progressive Party (PPP), became prime minister, with the British monarch as head of state.
1970 Following a referendum, The Gambia became a republic. Dawda Jawara was elected president.
1981 Around 500 people were killed when Senegalese troops intervened in support of Jawara and suppressed a coup.
1982 Senegal and The Gambia formed a confederation called Senegambia intended to integrate military, economic and political institutions.
1989 The Gambia, the subordinate partner, withdrew from Senegambia and the confederation collapsed.
1991 The Gambia and Senegal signed a treaty of friendship.
1994 President Jawara was deposed by a military coup led by Lieutenant Yahya Jammeh. The 1970 constitution was suspended and all political parties banned.
1996 A new constitution was approved giving multi-party democracy. The Alliance for Patriotic Reorientation and Construction (APRC) were formed to support Yahya Jammeh in the presidential election. Three political parties were prohibited from taking part in elections. Jammeh and the APRC were elected to the presidency and legislature, in what observers said were not free and fair elections.
2001 President Jammeh lifted the ban on opposition political parties. He was re-elected president.
2002 The centrist United Democratic Party (UDP) boycotted parliamentary elections, leaving the ruling APRC to win most seats unopposed.
2005 Border tensions rose when Gambia doubled the price of ferry crossings and Senegalese haulage firms, in protest, blockaded access routes. Senegal was effectively split in two as goods were hauled around Gambia on roads that were not all-weather and were unsuitable for heavy loads. Gambia experienced a shortage of goods in the marketplace due to the loss of revenue and blockaded imports. Nigeria, representing Ecowas mediated between the protagonists.
2006 Thousands of refugees find sanctuary in The Gambia during fighting between the Senegalese army and Casamance separatists. President Jammeh won re-election.
2007 In January the APRC won 42 out of 48 seats in the national assembly. The UDP won four seats and the National Alliance for Democracy and Development (NADD) one seat and an independent one seat.
2008 The government expelled a senior UN official, Fadzai Gwaradzimba, after she criticised the president for his widely publicised herbal cure for HIV/Aids, which he claimed could cure the disease within days.

Political structure

Constitution

The constitution was enacted in 1970, amended in 1982 and 1996.

Form of state

Democratic republic

KEY INDICATORS — The Gambia

	Unit	2003	2004	2005	2006	2007
Population	m	1.40	1.42	1.52	1.55	1.59
Gross domestic product (GDP)	US$bn	0.38	0.41	0.46	0.51	0.65
GDP per capita	US$	246	276	304	325	411
GDP real growth	%	7.4	7.7	5.1	6.5	7.0
Inflation	%	17.0	14.6	3.2	2.0	5.0
Agricultural output	% change	–	14.2	4.7	4.5	–
Exports (fob) (goods)	US$m	138.0	114.4	140.3	108.7	–
Imports (cif) (goods)	US$m	225.0	180.9	197.0	221.8	–
Balance of trade	US$m	-87.0	-66.5	-56.7	-113.2	–
Current account	US$m	-20.0	-47.0	-93.0	-58.0	-70.0
Total reserves minus gold	US$m	59.3	83.8	98.3	120.6	142.8
Foreign exchange	US$m	57.1	80.7	96.0	116.9	140.0
Exchange rate	per US$	25.95	27.31	28.25	28.25	22.00

The executive
Power rests with the president, who is elected by universal suffrage every five years. The president is both the head of state and head of government and appoints the cabinet.

National legislature
Legislative power is vested in the unicameral 53-member House of Representatives, comprising 48 members directly elected for a five-year term and five members appointed by the president.

Last elections
25 January 2007 (parliamentary); 22 October 2006 (presidential).

Results: Parliamentary: The ruling APRC won 42 seats out of 48 seats, the UDP won four seats and the National Alliance for Democracy and Development (NADD) one seat and an independent one seat. Five seats were filled by appointed members. Turnout was 41.7 per cent.
Presidential: incumbent Yahya Jammeh (APRC) won 67.3 per cent of the vote; Ousainou Darboe (UDP) won 26.6 per cent. Turnout was 59 per cent.

Next elections
2011 (presidential); January 2012 (parliamentary)

Political parties

Ruling party
Alliance for Patriotic Reorientation and Construction (APRC) (since 1996; re-elected Jan 2007)

Main opposition party
The United Democratic Party (UDP)

Population
1.59 million (2007)

Last census: April 2003: 1,364,507 (provisional)

Population density: 105 habitants per square km. Urban population: 33 per cent (1995–2001).

Annual growth rate: 3.2 per cent 1994–2004 (WHO 2006)

Ethnic make-up
Three major ethnic groups: Mandinka (42 per cent), Fula (18 per cent), Wolof (16 per cent). Other substantial ethnic groups: Jola, Serahule, Serere, Manjago, Bambara, Creole/Aku.

Religions
Muslim (90 per cent), Christian (9 per cent), animist beliefs (1 per cent).

Education
Primary schooling begins at aged seven and is free of charge and non-selective until aged 15. Secondary education is either vocational or academic. Basic vocational schools offer two-year courses and vocational secondary schools provide four-year courses. General secondary schools offer a three-year course leading to higher education provided by the University of The Gambia. The Gambia College offers vocational courses in agriculture, education, nursing, midwifery, and public health.

Literacy rate: Adult rates: 38.9 per cent, male; 31.9 per cent, female (World Bank).

Compulsory years: None

Enrolment rate: 77 per cent gross primary enrolment; 25 per cent gross secondary enrolment, of relevant age groups (including repeaters) (World Bank).

Pupils per teacher: 30 in primary schools.

Health
Per capita total expenditure on health (2003) was US$96; of which per capita government spending was US$38, at the international dollar rate, (WHO 2006). Improved water sources are available to 62 per cent of the population. Around 90 per cent of children are immunised against measles.

HIV/Aids
The Gambia has so far escaped much of the African pandemic. However, with 14 per cent of sex workers testing positive, there is a chance that the infection will spread.

HIV prevalence: 1.2 per cent aged 15–49 in 2003 (World Bank)

Life expectancy: 57 years, 2004 (WHO 2006)

Fertility rate/Maternal mortality rate: 4.6 births per woman, 2004 (WHO 2006); maternal mortality 1,100 per 100,000 live births (World Bank).

Child (under 5 years) mortality rate (per 1,000): 90 per 1,000 live births (World Bank)

Head of population per physician: 0.11 physicians per 1,000 people, 2003 (WHO 2006)

Welfare
The Gambia has two important funds, the social security fund and the housing finance fund, that receive contributions from employers and employees either directly or indirectly. The Department of Social Welfare in Banjul has been restructured with four major units covering child care, adult, elderly and disabled services. The Gambia government and the Social Security and Housing Finance Corporation (SSHFC) initiated mass housing projects including a rural electrification programme covering all major towns and villages.

Main cities
Banjul (capital, estimated population 46,700 in 2003), Serekunda (344,100), Bakau (82,300), Brikama (80,400).

Languages spoken
Mandinka, Wolof and Fula are local languages. French is taught in some secondary and high schools. German, Italian, Dutch and the Scandinavian languages are also spoken by tourism staff.

Official language/s
English

Media

Press

Dailies: In English. Daily Observer (www.observer.gm) and The Gambia Daily News (www.gambia.dk). Several online news outlets exist include Gambia News (www.gambianow.com), The Gambia Times (http://afrikanpath.com) which was launched on 5 July 2007 with local and regional news and Freedom Newspaper (www.freedomnewspaper.com).

Weeklies: The Gambia News & Report magazine, the Foroyaa (www.foroyaa.gm) is published bi-weekly and The Point Newspaper (www.thepoint.gm) thrice weekly; all are privately-owned.

Broadcasting
The state-owned Gambia Radio and Television Services (GRTS) provides a national network.

Radio: GRTS is non-commercial and broadcast in English and local languages. Other commercial stations, Radio 1 FM, West Coast Radio and City Limits Radio are privately owned.

Television: GRTS provides the only national service with a single channel which covers 60 per cent of the country. There are other private satellite, subscription channels, the most popular includes GAMTV and Premium TV Network which broadcasts throughout the coastal area.

Economy
The Gambia is classified as a low-income country with an economy which is, according to an IMF report of December 2006, at a crossroads. While the authorities have achieved macroeconomic stability since 2004, the economy is highly susceptible to external and domestic policy-induced shocks. These have included a drought, changes in groundnut marketing arrangements, a sharp drop in the exchange rate and a closure of the Gambian border with Senegal. For long-term stability the IMF recommends that the government commits the country to a reform agenda that will promote growth and reduce poverty. To do this, it will need to strengthen its governance and accountability in public finances, as well as in the central bank and improve the environment for private sector development. If the government fails to control fiscal slippage from unbudgeted expenditures it may repeat the example of lost international aid experienced in 2004. As the government failed to stay within its budget and breached IMF requirements, this prevented the EU from disbursing around US$3.8 million in a

budget support programme. A late submission to the IMF also resulted in The Gambia having to pay back in full two disbursements of over US$10 million. This in turn delayed its goal for implementation of the Heavily Indebted Poor Countries (HIPC) Initiative, to reduce payments on outstanding debts. The IMF expects the country to be back on course by the end of 2006. The HIPC Initiative and Poverty Reduction and Growth Facility (PRGF) will provide funds worth a total of US$91 million up to 2020.

In 2005 GDP growth was 5.0 per cent while inflation fell to 3.5 per cent (falling further to 2.0 per cent in the first six months of 2006). GDP growth is expected to be 4.9 per cent in 2006. The structure of the economy reflects the dominance of the services sector, which makes up over 50 per cent of GDP, and agriculture with over 30 per cent; industry, including manufacturing accounts for only 13 per cent. The fastest growing sectors in 2005 were tourism including hotels and restaurants (which have grown by an average 10 per cent since 2002), construction and telecommunications.

Agriculture, forestry and fisheries remain important sectors. Groundnuts, in the form of nuts, oil and cattle cake, accounts for 50 per cent of all exports, but the nationalisation of the industry in the 1980s, then the re-privatisation in 1996 and the introduction of new marketing regulations in February 2005, whereby the Gambian Agricultural Marketing Corporation (Gamco), was given a monopoly to market and process groundnuts, led to a somewhat disorganised industry. Crops that could not be purchased by Gamco, due to its inability to raise the finance necessary to purchase the bumper harvest, were sold, by farmers, across the border in Senegal where they fetched higher prices.

The government's general policy is to diversify and broaden the productive base of the economy and foster economic growth and development. The Economic Recovery Programme (ERP) includes institutional reform, price liberalisation and the adoption of a flexible exchange rate regime. The government recognises that to improve the potential for tourism and re-exports, the poor infrastructure must be overhauled. To this end the government has undertaken some major capital investment projects, such as a new terminal at the capital's international airport and improved port facilites.

For the Gambia to make a crucial break from past piecemeal policies that inflated then depressed the economy, it must diversify and establish the conditions that spark continued growth and reduce poverty, market forces must be allowed to determine prices and interest rates, while it ensures macroeconomic stability so that external shocks do not have a long lasting adverse effect on internal mechanisms.

External trade

As a member of the Economic Community of West African States (Ecowas), which was set up to promote economic integration among members, The Gambia is also a member of the West African Economic and Monetary Union using the common currency, the CFA franc.

It is also a member of the Economic Community of Western African States (Ecowas), which was set up to promote economic integration among members. It is a member of the Anglophone West African Monetary Zone (WAMZ), which is due to introduce a common currency. WAMZ will eventually be merged with the Francophone-members' currency to produce a single currency (the eco) for the region.

With few natural resources, foreign exchange is dependent on remittances, tourism and the export of groundnuts (both raw and processed). Geographically, The Gambia is a long wedge separating the north and south of Senegal and as a result haulage firms must cross The Gambia to avoid the long and arduous route around it. Re-exports, are estimated at 34 per cent of total imports, which supply significant foreign exchange for the Gambian economy.

Imports

Principal imports are foodstuffs, manufactured items, fuel, machinery and transport equipment that support the transit trade.

Main sources: Denmark (16.6 per cent total, 2006), US (12.0 per cent), China (9.3 per cent).

Exports

Principal exports are groundnuts (peanuts), fish, cotton lint, palm kernels and re-exports.

Main destinations: UK (49.0 per cent total, 2006), Senegal (30.8 per cent), France (4.7 per cent).

Agriculture

Farming

Agriculture remains the main sector of the economy, typically contributing around 30 per cent to GDP and employing over 70 per cent of the workforce.

Approximately 17 per cent of the total land area is cultivated. Groundnuts are cultivated on about 60 per cent of the planted area, and provide 85 per cent of official export earnings. The Gambia is the second-largest producer of groundnuts in the world, after Senegal. Production of food crops (rice, maize, millet, sorghum, cassava) is insufficient to meet local needs, but receives a great deal of official encouragement. Small-scale fruit and cotton farming are also important while some livestock is exported to neighbouring countries for breeding.

The government, backed by international development agencies and donors, is attempting to increase agricultural production. The on-going US$2.5 million Lowlands Agricultural Development Project (LADEP) is aimed at developing 6,000 hectares for cultivation and the rehabilitation of 1,500 hectares in various lowland ecologies. US$2 million has been allocated to assist women's groups engaged in sheep, goat and poultry production while US$1.5 million is dedicated to an integrated rural development scheme.

The estimated crop production in 2005 included: 212,702 tonnes (t) cereals in total, 132,494t millet, 135,697t groundnuts (in shell), 29,209t maize, *22,000t rice, *3,200t pulses, 45,059t oilcrops, *35,000t oil palm fruit, *500t seed cotton, *4,160t fruit in total, *9,000t vegetables in total. Estimated livestock production included: 6,845t meat in total, *3,240t beef, 480t pig meat, 1,150t lamb and goat meat, 975t poultry, *748t eggs, 7,700t milk, 378t cattle hides, *1,000t game meat.

* estimate

Fishing

Fishing has also increased in importance with the annual catch rising to over 22,000 tonnes. The government, with assistance from the UN Development Programme (UNDP), is encouraging improved methods and modernisation of boats. Illegal fishing by foreign trawler fleets remains a problem.

In 2004, the total marine fish catch was 28,422 tonnes and the total crustacean catch was 99 tonnes.

Forestry

Imports of forest products in 2004 amounted to US$1.7 million, while exports amounted to US$669,000.

Timber production in 2004 was 750,701 cubic metre (cum), 112,700cum industrial roundwood, 106,000cum sawlogs and veneer logs, 638,001cum wood fuel, 51,447t charcoal.

Industry and manufacturing

The industrial sector contributes around 6 per cent to GDP and employs 4 per cent of the workforce.

The manufacturing sector is small-scale and underdeveloped.

The main activities (most of which are centred around Banjul, particularly in the Kanifing Industrial Estate) include groundnut and fish processing, brewing, footwear, perfume, cement and brick production.

Tourism

The tourism sector is growing in importance in the Gambian economy with a

US$132.5 million turnover estimated for 2005, showing a growth rate of 9.3 per cent and all other indicators for the sector show increases.

An increasing number of Europeans are arriving, of whom between 50–60 per cent are British; statistics in 2005 identified The Gambia as a particularly competitive destination for British visitors and overall growth was estimated at just over 10 per cent. The travel and tourist sector contributed 16.0 per cent (2004) to GDP and employed around 118,600 people in the industry. Capital investment in 2005, in tourism, is estimated at US$11.7 million or 16.6 per cent of total investment. The government has plans to see one million visitors arriving by 2013. A new tourist residential resort development, of 130 plots, is in the planning stages.

Eco-tourism and historical sites are among the other tourist activities offered by The Gambia, although most tourists prefer the sea-and-sun holiday package. Six new hotels are scheduled for completion in 2005 and 2006. The Sheraton Hotel is due to open in mid-2006.

Environment

Concerns are mounting over the ecological effects of tourism on the local environment, particularly shore erosion and the depletion of water resources.

Mining

Most mining activity is centred on the production of industrial minerals for local consumption. The Australian Carnegie Corporation is investigating the Brufut deposits located along the coast and around 11,000 tonnes of zircon has been found. There are known deposits of kaolin, tin, ilmenite and rutile, mostly unexploited.

Hydrocarbons

The downstream industry is reliant on imported petroleum products, importing 1,940 barrels per day.

The Gambia does not produce or import gas.

Energy

There is total dependence on imported petroleum. Fuelwood is the main source of domestic energy. Hydroelectric resources are being developed on the River Gambia.

Banking and insurance

The banking sector is underdeveloped, but is growing as a result of increased economic activity and macroeconomic stability. The sector has seen consolidation, with two large mergers and privatisations.

It was announced in March 2005 that the introduction of the shared currency, the Eco, in The Gambia, Ghana, Guinea, Nigeria and Sierra Leone, which was due in July 2005, would be postponed. The currency was proposed to facilitate trade and growth with an ultimate plan to merge it with the CFA franc.

Central bank

Central Bank of The Gambia

Main financial centre

Banjul

Time

GMT

Geography

At its widest part The Gambia is only 48km wide as it straddles the River Gambia over its last 470km down to the Atlantic Ocean, where the country has a short coastline. The Gambia is the smallest country in Africa, and lies on both banks of the river, completely surrounded by Senegal. The land is low-lying, with mangroves towards the river mouth, and open savannah plains for most of the remaining land, with a maximum elevation of only 73 metres at the higher reaches of the river, in the east. During the dry season, when water levels drop, the river's width, at the capital Banjul, is only 5km across and tidal saltwater washes along its length for almost 250km turning the water brackish.

Hemisphere

Northern

Climate

Sub-tropical with distinct seasons. Dry season from November–May with temperatures around 21–27 degrees Celsius (C). The dry harmattan wind keeps the humidity low, but can obscure the sun and severely limit vision for days. Rainy season from June–October has high humidity and temperatures around 26–32 degrees C.

Entry requirements

Passports

Required by all. Passports must be valid for three months from date of departure.

Visa

Required by all, except citizens of countries with reciprocating visa-free entry for both tourism and business, (UK 30 days, others 90 days). See www.thegambia.net/visa.htm for initial details and contact the nearest embassy for confirmation All visitors must have onward/return tickets.

Currency advice/regulations

There is no restriction on the import or export of local currency – although exchanging local currency abroad may be difficult. The import of currency from Algeria, Ghana, Guinea, Mali, Morocco, Nigeria, Sierra Leone and Tunisia is prohibited. The import of all other currencies is unrestricted but must be declared; export is unlimited up to the amount declared.

Travellers cheques are accepted.

Health (for visitors)

Mandatory precautions

Yellow fever vaccination certificate required only if travelling from an infected area.

Advisable precautions

Inoculations and boosters should be current for cholera, tetanus, polio, hepatitis A, diphtheria, typhoid and yellow fever. There may be a need for vaccinations for tuberculosis, hepatitis B and meningitis. Use malaria prophylaxis (that also provide protection for hepatitis B and yellow fever) including mosquito repellents, nets and clothing that cover the body after dark. There is a risk of rabies.

HIV/Aids is prevalent. To avoid bilharzia, do not bath in fresh water lakes or rivers, use only well-maintained, chlorinated swimming pools.

Use only bottled or boiled water for drinks, washing teeth and making ice. Eat only well cooked meals, preferably served hot; vegetables should be cooked and fruit peeled. Dairy products are unpasteurised and should be avoided, unless cooked. There is a shortage of routine medications, including sun-screens, and visitors should take all necessary medicines with them. A first aid kit that includes disposable syringes, is a reasonable precaution.

Healthcare is not to Western standards and medical insurance, including emergency evacuation, is necessary.

Hotels

Book well in advance, especially if arriving during tourist season (Nov–May). Many Gambian hotels are geared to package holidays. 10 per cent tip is usual.

Credit cards

International credit cards are accepted; arrangements for hotel payment by credit cards should be arranged at the beginning of a stay. ATM exist in large towns but may be unreliable.

Public holidays (national)

Fixed dates

1 Jan (New Year's Day), 18 Feb (Independence Day), 1 May (Labour Day), 22 Jul (Revolution Day), 25 Dec (Christmas Day).

Variable dates

Eid al Adha, Good Friday and Easter Monday (Mar/April, Birth of the Prophet, Eid al Fitr.

Islamic year – 1429 (10 Jan 2008–28 Dec 2008): The Islamic year contains 354 or 355 days, with the result that Muslim feasts advance by 10–12 days against the Gregorian calendar. Dates of feasts vary according to the sighting of the new moon, so cannot be forecast exactly.

Working hours
Banking
Mon–Thu: 0800–1330; Fri: 0800–1100 in Banjul; Mon–Fri: 0800–1200, 1600–1800 elsewhere.
Business
Mon–Thu: 0800–1600; Fri: 0800–1230.
Government
Mon–Thu: 0800–1600; Fri: 0800–1230.
Shops
Mon–Thu: 0800–1700; Fri–Sat: 0800–1300.

Electricity supply
220V AC, 50 cycles, with a mix of round and flat, three pin plugs.

Social customs/useful tips
In business, the personal approach is important; handshaking is widely used and the traditional greeting is salam alaikum. Jackets and ties should be worn at meetings; women may wear trousers.
Many Gambians are Muslim and their religious customs and beliefs should be respected. There are prohibitions concerning smoking and eating in public during Ramadan.

Getting there
Air
National airline: Gambia International Airlines (GIA)
International airport/s: Banjul International (BJL), 24km from city; bar, bank, restaurant, post office, shop and business lounge including internet connections. Taxis are available to the city.
Airport tax: Arrival tax at Banjul International (BJL) airport: either US$10, UK £5 or eur10.
Surface
Road: Road access to Banjul is possible from Dakar (Senegal), by the Trans-Gambia Highway which crosses the River Gambia by ferry between Farafenni and Mansa Konko. There is an alternative car ferry crossing between Barra and Banjul.
Water: Regular ferry services run between Banjul and Dakar (Senegal).

Getting about
National transport
Road: There are over 3,000km of roads, of which 450km are paved, particularly around Banjul; unsealed roads often become impassable in the rainy season. Highways run along each bank of the River Gambia; the Trans-Gambia highway runs north to south, crossing the river at Farafenni-Mansa Konko (car ferry).
Buses: The Gambia Public Transport Corporation (GPTC) operates cheap and reliable services linking Banjul with the coastal hotel area and other main centres. There are several commercial bus services, such as Amdalaye and Transgambia services.
Water: There are around a dozen ferry crossing points where people, livestock and vehicles cross the river between the north and south shores. The Banjul-Barra ferry runs every 90 minutes (journey time 20—30 minutes) and there are small wooden ferries up-country which carry only three or four vehicles at a time.
A boat travels the length of the River Gambia, from Banjul to Basse, once a week. The journey takes about three days. It is possible to return overland by coach.
City transport
Taxis: Green (tourist) taxis have a diamond sign and a serial number on the side. They are licensed by the Gambia Tourism Authority and dedicated to serving tourists and other visitors. They are normally parked outside the hotels in the resort areas. The journey from the international airport to the city centre takes 30–40 minutes.
Yellow and Green taxis are mainly four-passenger saloon cars which run a shared taxi service between short distances or park by the roadside for individual hire.
The most common way of travelling is by collective bush taxis. These are mainly seven-passenger saloon cars, vans, minibuses and buses. They do not have a single colour and they operate a shared service between both short and long distances. It is advisable to agree the fare in advance when hiring collective taxis.
A 10 per cent tip is usual.
Car hire
International driving licence accepted for a period of three months. National licence can be used for a short visit. Traffic drives on the right.
Car hire facilities are somewhat limited and local enquiries through the tourist office are advised. Take care, there is a lack of adequate traffic signs.

BUSINESS DIRECTORY

The addresses listed below are a selection only. While World of Information makes every endeavour to check these addresses, we cannot guarantee that changes have not been made, especially to telephone numbers and area codes. We would welcome any corrections.

Telephone area codes
The international dialling code (IDD) for The Gambia is + 220 followed by subscriber's number.

Useful telephone numbers
Police: 17
Fire: 18
Ambulance (Banjul): 16

Chambers of Commerce
Gambia Chamber of Commerce & Industry, 1-3 Ecowas Avenue, PO Box 333, Banjul (tel: 4227-765; fax: 4229-671; email: gcci@qanet.gm).

Banking
Arab Gambian Islamic Bank Ltd, 7 Ecowas Avenue, Banjul (tel: 4223-773; fax: 4223-770).

First International Bank Ltd, PO Box 1997, 6 OAU Boulevard, Banjul (tel: 4202-000/5; fax: 4202-001, 4202-000).

International Bank for Commerce (Gambia) Ltd, PO Box 211, 11a Liberation Avenue, Banjul (tel: 4228-144, 4228-145; fax: 4229-312).

Standard Chartered Bank Gambia Ltd, PO Box 259, 8 Ecowas Avenue, Banjul (tel: 4228-681/4; fax: 4227-714).

Trust Bank Limited (TBL), PO Box 1018, 3-4 Ecowas Avenue, Banjul (tel: 4225-777, 4225-778/9; fax: 4225-781).

Central bank
Central Bank of The Gambia, 1-2 Ecowas Avenue, Banjul (tel: 4227-786; fax: 4226-969).

Travel information
Banjul (Yundum) International Airport, PO Box 285, Banjul (tel: 4473-000; fax: 4472-190).

Gambia International Airlines, Satellite House, PO Box 268, 68-69 Wellington Street, Banjul (tel: 4223-702, 4223-706; internet: www.gia.gm).

Gambia River Excursions, Lamin Lodge, Jangjangbureh Camp, PO Box 664 Banjul (tel: 4497-603; fax: 4495-526; internet: www.gambiariver.com).

West African Tours, PO Box 222, Serrekunda, (tel: 4495-258, 4495-532; fax: 4496-118; internet: www.westafricatours.gm).

Ministry of tourism
Department of State for Tourism and Culture, The Quadrangle, Banjul (tel: 4229-563, 4223-210).

National tourist organisation offices
Gambia Tourism Authority, Kololi, KMC, PO Box 4085, Bakau (tel: 4462-491–4; fax: 4462-487; email: info@gta.gm; internet: www.visitthegambia.gm).

Ministries
Ministry of Agriculture and Natural Resources (MANR), The Quadrangle, Banjul (tel: 4472-888; fax: 4237-034).

Ministry of Finance and Economic Affairs, The Quadrangle, Banjul (tel: 4227-221).

Other useful addresses
British High Commission, 48 Atlantic Road; PO Box 507, Fajara, Banjul, (tel: 4495-133–4; fax: 4496-134; email: bhcbanjul@gamtel.gm).

Central Statistics Office, Central Bank Building, Buckle Street, Banjul (tel: 4228-105).

Gambia Embassy (USA), Suite 905, 1156 15th Street, NW, Washington DC 20005 (tel: (+1-202) 785-1399; fax: (+1-202) 785-1425).

Gambia Hotel Association, c/o The Bungalow Beach Hotel, PO Box 2637, Serrekunda (tel: 4465-288; fax: 4466-180).

Gambia Investment Promotion and Free Zones Agency (GIPFZA), 5 Nelson Mandela Street, PO Box 757, Banjul (tel: 4222-4412, 4222-836; fax: 4222-829; e-mail: dipm.gipfza@qanet.gm; ceo.gipfza@qanet.gm).

National Investment Promotion Authority (NIPA), Independence Drive, Banjul (tel: 4228-332; fax: 4229-220).

US Embassy, 92 Kairaba Ave; PO Box 19, Fajara, Banjul (tel: 4392-856, 4392-858; fax: 4392-475; email: ambanjul@gamtel.gm).

Internet sites

Africa Business Network: www.ifc.org/abn
AllAfrica.com: allafrica.com
African Development Bank: www.afdb.org
Africa Online: www.africaonline.com
Gateway site: gambiagateway.tripod.com
Mbendi AfroPaedia (information on companies, countries, industries and stock exchanges in Africa): mbendi.co.za
The Gambia Tourism Authority: www.visitthegambia.gm
The Gambia website: www.gambia.net

Georgia

Despite a steadily improving economy, Georgia finds itself on the world's stage for all the wrong reasons. The completion of the Baku-Tbilisi-Ceyhan (BTC) oil pipeline linking Azerbaijan-owned oil fields on the Caspian Sea with the outside world, is good news, cementing Georgia's position as a regional economic player. However, stalemate was the order of the day in Georgia's attempts to bring back under its control two secessionist regions, Abkhazia and South Ossetia.

The economy strengthens

With GDP growth of around 7.6 per cent in 2006, Georgia continued to leave behind much of its post-Soviet economic blues. In December 2005, Georgia became the proud owner of its first ever international credit rating – a B+ (long-term) from Standard & Poor's. Having contracted by nearly one half in 1992, the Georgian economy has grown rapidly since 2003. Foreign direct investment (FDI) has been the main engine of Georgian growth over the past couple of years. Although Georgia is itself resource poor, the BTC consortium has invested heavily in Georgia in order to facilitate oil shipments through Georgian territory. About 15 per cent of the BTC's length runs through Georgia and during construction, Georgians made up 75 per cent of the BTC's workforce. In May 2005, the BTC was officially opened in Baku; Tbilisi currently earns US$50 million a year in transit fees. Environmentalists continue to criticise the BTC, particularly in relation to the pipeline's route through Georgia's Borjomi National Park. A second oil export route through Georgia also came online in July, the Baku-Supsa rail link, which ships Azeri oil from the Caspian to the Black Sea port of Batumi.

Economic diversification and reform

Forecasts put Georgia's GDP growth rate at 7.6 per cent for 2007. In January 2006, Russian gas prices to Georgia doubled. Russia proposes a further increase during 2007, taking the price to US$230 per 1,000 cubic meters, the highest among the states of the former Soviet Union. For this, and other trade and economic measures taken by Russia against Georgia, Georgia has threatened to withhold Russian accession to the WTO. Some analysts consider that transit revenues from the BTC oil pipeline, which bypasses Russia, will help to sustain Georgia's economy, enabling it to weather these storms. It is estimated that around 6 per cent of GDP comes from remittances by Georgians working in Russia. In 2005, net FDI in Georgia amounted to around 7 per cent of GDP, forecast to

KEY FACTS

Official name: Sak'art'velos Respublika (Republic of Georgia)

Head of State: President Mikhail Saakashvili (from 2004; re-elcted 6 Jan 2008)

Head of government: Prime Minister Lado Gurgenidze (appointed 16 Nov 2007)

Ruling party: Natshhionakhuri Modzraoba - Demokrathebi (NM-D) (National Movement - Democrats) (elected Mar 2004)

Area: 69,700 square km

Population: 4.37 million (2007)

Capital: Tbilisi

Official language: Georgian

Currency: Lari (L) = 100 tetri

Exchange rate: L1.40 per US$ (Jul 2008)

GDP per capita: US$2,355 (2007)*

GDP real growth: 12.40% (2007)

Labour force: 2.02 million (2005)

Unemployment: 13.80% (2005)

Inflation: 9.20% (2007)

Balance of trade: -US$830.00 million (2006)

Foreign debt: US$1.90 billion (2004)

Annual FDI: US$450.00 million (2005); US$133.8 million (first quarter 2006)

* estimated figure

rise to around 7.5 per cent in 2006. Flatteringly, the World Bank regards Georgia as one of the world's top economic reformers. However, the government has implemented only the easier parts of its reform agenda and Georgia still needs to focus on attracting more foreign investment to develop its manufacturing sector and diversify its export base.

Georgia has around 55 per cent of its labour force engaged in the agricultural sector, and tried hard in 2005–06 to diversify and develop its economy. In July, the IMF gave Georgia a good report card with regard to macroeconomic reform and poverty reduction. By joining the flat tax brigade and promoting privatisation of government assets, Georgia hoped to improve its business climate. In this vein, in June, a National Anti-Corruption Strategy was launched by President Mikhail Saakashvili. In October, the non-governmental organisation (NGO) Transparency International rated Georgia one of the most corrupt countries in the world (130th out of 158 countries surveyed, in descending order), although it also noted significant improvements. Tourism is viewed by the government and many businesses as a source of substantial economic growth, particularly with regards to Georgia's Black Sea coast. Soviet era elites once flocked to Georgia for its beaches, wine and cuisine. After years of decline, visitor numbers rose by 18 per cent in the first quarter of 2005 and the government is seeking to attract investment in tourist infrastructure.

Splits

Georgia had experienced a potentially rocky start to 2005 when, in February, Prime Minister Zurab Zhvania was found dead, possibly having committed suicide. Despite losing one of its leading lights, the Rose Revolution team continued to dominate the political landscape under President Saakashvili. Zhvania's successor, Zurab Noghaideli was appointed on 17 February 2005. In October 2005, the ruling party easily defeated a newly re-organised opposition alliance in five by-elections. However, by the end of October there were signs that the Rose Revolution leadership was beginning to split. The high profile foreign minister, Salome Zurabishvili, was acrimoniously sacked, prompting speculation of a new political formation in the country. Saakashvili had won the presidency by direct popular vote in January 2004. The next presidential election has been brought forward from late-2009 to late-2008 to coincide with the parliamentary elections.

Abkhazia and Ossetia

Fresh from reasserting central control over its wayward Ajaria Autonomous Republic Georgia's government had approached 2005 with cautious optimism regarding two other secessionist regions, Abkhazia and South Ossetia. The latter pair had broken away from Tbilisi in 1994 and 1992 respectively and, with Russian support, had resisted all efforts to reintegrate. With more than 200,000 ethnic Georgians expelled from their homes, from Abkhazia in particular, President Saakashvili was under pressure to re-unite Georgia. In January, Saakashvili presented a plan for the peaceful reintegration of South Ossetia into Georgia to the Parliamentary Assembly of the Council of Europe (PACE). Discontent in South Ossetia goes back to 1989 over language rights which reflect a long-held ambition to unite with the Republic of North Ossetia located on the Russian side of Georgia's northern border. A joint Georgian/Russian/South Ossetian peacekeeping operation has been in place since 1992. In September 2005, South Ossetia signed a friendship treaty with North Ossetia with the explicit goal of unification within the Russian Federation. Georgia argues that South Ossetia is an integral part of Georgia and is not ethnically distinct and has never been independent. In November 2006, Georgia condemned the claim by breakaway authorities in South Ossetia that 99 per cent of the province's population had voted in favour of independence from Tbilisi. Saakashvili did little to help negotiations by calling South Ossetia a 'criminal nest'. Georgia reportedly amassed 10,000 troops on the border of South Ossetia.

Georgia's efforts to woo Abkhazia were, if anything, even less successful. The 200,000 people of the Abkhazia region hold aspirations to regain the status of a republic which they briefly enjoyed in the 1920s. Thirty per cent of the population of Abkhazia are ethnic Russians, and Russia still retains assets in the region. However, talks on even basic issues, such as re-opening a rail-link between Georgia and Abkhazia broke down over an Abkhaz refusal to speak with Georgian negotiators. Abkhazia had, at one stage, begun moves to confiscate all property vacated by ethnic Georgians who had fled the region, and even began issuing independent passports. Georgia had stepped up its efforts to enforce a maritime blockade against Abkhazia, which resulted in the Abkhaz boycotting formal peace talks, despite pressure from Georgia, the UN, France, Germany, the US and the UK to attend. In July 2006, the Georgian parliament called for the withdrawal of Russian peacekeepers from South Ossetia and Abkhazia.

After months of negotiations, Georgia has secured a promise from Russia to vacate its remaining military bases on Georgian soil (in Batumi and Akhalkalaki), by the end of 2008. Nevertheless, Georgia very much remains in the shadow of its larger neighbour. Unsurprisingly, both

KEY INDICATORS — Georgia

	Unit	2003	2004	2005	2006	2007
Population	m	5.37	5.32	4.32	*4.40	*4.37
Gross domestic product (GDP)	US$bn	3.34	5.09	6.39	7.76	10.29
GDP per capita	US$	622	866	1,479	*1,764	2,355
GDP real growth	%	4.7	8.5	9.6	9.3	12.4
Inflation	%	4.4	5.7	8.3	9.1	9.2
Industrial output	% change	–	14.0	14.5	14.5	–
Agricultural output	% change	–	-7.9	12.0	-9.3	–
Exports (fob) (goods)	US$m	515.0	1,092.5	1,472.4	633.0	2,104.1
Imports (cif) (goods)	US$m	750.0	2,008.6	2,686.3	1,463.0	4,976.5
Balance of trade	US$m	-235.0	-916.0	-1,213.9	-830.0	-2,872.4
Current account	US$m	-290.0	-340.0	-347.0	-1,235.0	-2,028.0
Total reserves minus gold	US$m	190.7	382.9	473.2	930.8	1,361.2
Foreign exchange	US$m	185.8	371.7	472.2	929.9	1,346.3
Exchange rate	per US$	2.15	1.97	1.71	1.71	1.59

* estimated figure

Abkhazia and South Ossetia receive substantial financial, military and diplomatic support from Moscow. Russian peacekeepers, nominally part of multilateral deployments, protect the secessionists' front lines, and Russia has been happy to issue passports to Abkhaz and South Ossetians.

In front of the UN General Assembly in September, President Saakashvili went so far as to accuse Russia of trying to annex South Ossetia and Abkhazia. Despite professing respect for Georgia's territorial integrity, Russia also took care to maintain the status quo by resisting any attempt by Georgia to internationalise the conflict resolution process. In March, it moved to render toothless an agreement between Georgia and the EU over border monitoring, and in December it rejected a Georgian proposal to invite the US into the South Ossetia negotiation process. Restrictions on Georgia's freedom of movement also extended to its energy policy. In December, Russia refused to allow the transit of Kazakh natural gas through its territory into Georgia, despite willingness by Kazakhstan to facilitate the deal.

Outlook

Georgia's economy enjoyed further rapid growth in 2006. The prospect of the SCP being completed by the end of the year bodes well for FDI, and the tourism industry recovery will almost certainly gather pace. However inflation, was 8.3 per cent in 2005, will require government attention. With national elections not due until 2008, serious political upheaval is unlikely.

Risk assessment

Politics	Good
Economy	Fair
Regional stability	Poor

COUNTRY PROFILE

Historical profile

In the ninth century BC, the legendary Kingdom of Colchis was founded where Jason found the golden fleece and fell in love with Medea. Georgia is this mythical place. The country's Amirani legend parallels the Greek myth.

Georgia converted to Christianity in 330 AD.

The nineteenth century saw Georgia gradually incorporated into Russia.

1916 Georgia joined an alliance with Armenia and Azerbaijan.

1918–21 There was a brief spell of independence until Russia invaded in 1921 and Georgia was incorporated into the Soviet Union.

1940–45 An estimated 10 per cent of the population perished in the Stalin purges.

1989 The killing of 20 people by Soviet troops during a national demonstration in Tbilisi triggered the final disillusionment with communism.

1990 Following a referendum which called for independence from the Soviet Union, Zviad Gamsakhurdia was elected the first president in July. Racist policies caused problems.

1991 Independence from Russia was declared. Prime Minister Teniz Sigua resigned.

1992 Gamsakhurdia was overthrown in a coup and Eduard Shevardnadze assumed power. Parliamentary elections were held, at which Shevardnadze was elected Chairman of the State Security Council. Shevardnadze re-appointed Teniz Sigua as prime minister. After Georgian independence the northern region of Abkhazia declared itself independent of the new state. The subsequent war killed an estimated 10,000 and created 300,000 internally displaced persons (IDP).

1994 A cease-fire was signed.

1995 After surviving a car bomb assassination attempt, Shevardnadze was elected by popular vote, and the Sak'art'velos Mokalaketa Kavshiri (SMK) (Union of Georgian Citizens) secured a majority vote in the parliamentary elections. A constitution was adopted. The Abkhaz parliament rejected the proposed status of autonomous republic within Georgia.

1996 In accordance with the constitution, a National Security Council was established.

1997 A Civil Code, second only to the constitution in importance, was adopted. Capital punishment was abolished.

1998 Shevardnadze survived a second assassination attempt.

1999 Georgia became a member of the Council of Europe.

2000 President Shevardnadze won the presidential elections. He said that he would not stand for a third term.

2001 Fighting erupted between Georgian security forces and Abkhazia separatists, despite the signing of a peace agreement. Mass demonstrations followed a raid by security forces on an independent television station, which had criticised the government for corruption.

2002 US special forces arrived to help train and equip Georgian forces for counter-terrorist operations. Russia accused Georgia of harbouring Chechen militants in South Ossetia and the Pankisi Gorge. Russian President Putin warned of military action if Georgia failed to deal with them.

2003 Work began laying the Georgian section of the 1,760km Baku-Tbilisi-Ceyhan (BTC) oil pipeline. Rigged elections resulted in mass protests and the storming of the parliament. President Shevardnadze was forced to resign; Nino Burdzhanadze became acting president. The Supreme Court later annulled the election results.

2004 Mikhail Saakashvili was sworn in as president and he nominated Zurab Zhvania for the re-introduced post of prime minister. A bloc led by the President's party won all the seats in the March parliamentary elections.

2005 Prime Minister Zurab Zhvania died and Zurab Noghaideli became prime minister. The BTC oil pipeline, capable of carrying one million barrels per day of Caspian oil to Western markets, opened.

2006 Relations with Russia deteriorated as energy supplies to Georgia were interrupted and Georgia demanded withdrawal of Russian troops from South Ossetia and Abkhazia; Russia imposed embargoes on Georgian produce, transport and postal links, before and after Georgia arrested four Russians in Tbilisi on spying charges. In a referendum, over 90 per cent of South Ossetians voted for independence. Russia threatened to cut off gas supplies unless Georgia agreed to a price increase.

2007 On 5 January an agreement for a price increase was reached. A 15-day state of emergency was declared on 7 November, as opposition protesters accused the president of corruption and demanded new elections. Only state-television was allowed to report on the news, while Imedi TV, which had broadcast the views of opposition leaders, was suspended. On 8 November the president acceded to protesters' demands and called for fresh elections to be held in January 2008. A state of emergency was declared on 7 November; it was lifted on 16 November. On the same day Lado Gurgenidze was appointed prime minister by President Saakashvili, replacing Zurab Noghaideli. On 25 November President Saakashvili resigned to take part in early presidential elections. The speaker of parliament, Nino Burjanadze, became acting president.

2008, On 6 January, in presidential elections the incumbent Mikhail Saakashvili was re-elected with 53.8 per cent of the vote, his nearest rival, Levan Gachechiladze won 27 per cent. After the official results were announced Gachechiladze claimed the election had been 'falsified' and that he would challenge the result. International observers claimed the election had been democratic and that 'the outcome should be respected'. President Saakashvili was inauguarted on 20 January. Within a month of his defeat in the presidential elections, Badri Patarkatsishvili died in exile in the UK. Following police investigations it was determined that Patarkatsishvili had died of natural causes. In 21 May parliamentary elections, President Mikheil Saakashvili's Natshhionakhuri Modzraoba (NM) (United National Movement) won 59.4 per cent of the vote (and around 120 seats out of 150), the Memarjvene Opozicia (MO) (Rightist Opposition) alliance won 17.6 per cent, all other parties won less than 10 per cent of the vote. However the opposition contested the results and European observers noted irregularities. After days of fighting in South Ossetia by separatists the government sent in troops to restore order on 7 August. Fierce fighting in Tskhinvalk, the capital of South Ossetia, resulted in the Georgian air force bombing surrounding areas. The Russian region of North Ossetia reinforced the Georgian South Ossetia, with a reported 150 military units through the Roki tunnel through the Caucasus Mountains: Georgia mobilised its army. Russia officially launched a 'peace enforcement' programme in support of South Ossetia. The Russian air force bombed the Georgian town of Gori on 8 August as a convoy of Russian tanks and armoured vehicles arrived in the area. Russian troops engaged Georgian troops inside Georgia as thousands of refugees fled the area. By 22 August Russia had forced Georgian forces out of South Ossetia and adopted defensive positions within Georgia. Despite intensive international diplomatic actions to bring about a peaceful resolution Russia refused to withdraw completely and left a contingent to maintain a 'security buffer zone' of seven kilometres on either side of the South Ossetian border. The Russian president formally recognised the breakaway regions of South Ossetia and Abkhazia as independent states on 26 August.

Political structure

Constitution
The 1995 constitution provides for a presidential republic with federal elements. The country is divided into nine districts and 64 regions.

Form of state
Presidential democratic republic

The executive
The president, who is head of state and head of government, is directly elected for five years and can serve no more than two terms. The head of state holds supreme executive power, together with the cabinet of ministers.

National legislature
The unicameral Sak'art'velos Parlamenti (Georgian Parliament) has 235 members who serve a four-year term (150 elected by party list, 75 in single-seat constituencies and 10 representing displaced persons from the separatist region of Abkhazia).

Legal system
The legal system is based on the civil law system.

Last elections
21 May 2008 (parliamentary); 6 January 2008 (presidential).

Results: Parliamentary: the Natshhionakhuri Modzraoba (NM) (United National Movement) won 59.4 per cent of the vote (and around 120 seats out of 150), the Memarjvene Opozicia (MO) (Rightist Opposition) alliance won 17.6 per cent, all other parties won less than 10 per cent of the vote. Presidential: Mikhail Saakashvili won 53.5 per cent of the vote, Levan Gachechiladze won 25.7 per cent, and Badri Patarkatsishvili won 7.1 per cent; turnout is 56.2 per cent.

Next elections
2012 (parliamentary); 5 January 2013 (presidential).

Political parties

Ruling party
Natshhionakhuri Modzraoba - Demokrathebi (NM-D) (National Movement - Democrats) (elected Mar 2004)

Main opposition party
Memarjvene Opozicia (MO) (Rightist Opposition)

Population
4.37 million (2007)

Last census: January 2002: 4,371,535

Population density: 78 inhabitants per sq km. Urban population: 57 per cent urban (1995–2001).

Annual growth rate: -1.3 per cent 1994–2004 (WHO 2006)

Internally Displaced Persons (IDP) 260,000 (UNHCR 2004)

Ethnic make-up
There are over 100 different ethnic groups in the country, including Georgian (70 per cent), Armenian (8 per cent), Russian (6 per cent) and Azeri (6 per cent). Other significant ethnic groups include Abkhazians and Ossetians.

Religions
Greek Orthodoxy is the main religion. There are also Shi'ite and Sunni Muslims, Jehovah Witnesses, Jews, Armenian Gregorians, Catholics and Baptists. There is inter-communal strife between the Christian Georgians and the Ossetian and Abkhazian ethnic Muslim minorities.

Education
Elementary schooling lasts for six years followed by two years of basic education. Secondary school education lasts for three years. Technical and vocational upper secondary education takes another two to four years.

There are 26 public higher education institutions in Georgia including eight universities and 14 technical and specialised institutes. In addition, 209 private higher education institutions have been established.

Public expenditure on education typically amounts to 5.2 per cent of annual gross national income (World Bank). Loans of US$60 million from the World Bank helped reform Georgia's secondary education.

Compulsory years: 6 to 14.

Enrolment rate: 89 per cent boys; 88 per cent girls, total primary school enrolment of the relevant age group (including repetition rates) (World Bank).

Pupils per teacher: 18 in primary schools.

Health
Per capita total expenditure on health (2003) was US$174; of which per capita government spending was US$42, at the international dollar rate, (WHO 2006).

The population has 76 per cent and 99 per cent access to improved water and sanitation facilities, respectively.

HIV/Aids
HIV prevalence: 0.1 per cent aged 15–49 in 2003 (World Bank)

Life expectancy: 74 years, 2004 (WHO 2006)

Fertility rate/Maternal mortality rate: 1.4 births per woman, 2004 (WHO 2006); maternal mortality rate 70 per 100,000 live births (World Bank).

Child (under 5 years) mortality rate (per 1,000): 41 per 1,000 live births; 3 per cent of children aged under five are malnourished (World Bank).

Head of population per physician: 4.09 physicians per 1,000 people, 2003 (WHO 2006)

Welfare
Georgia has to cope not only with 58.5 per cent of its people living below the official poverty line but also an increased influx of refugees in the Pankisi Valley, 150km north of Tbilisi, inhabited largely by ethnic Chechens, known as Kists. The US Agency for International Development (USAID) has funded Georgia to implement community level activities, which benefit refugees, internally displaced people and others affected by ethnic violence and the deterioration of the social welfare system.

The benefits system includes pensions, unemployment benefits and family allowance, all paid at flat rates. The government provides 100 per cent electricity tariff discounts for war veterans and 50 per cent discounts for tax, customs, defence and security personnel.

Increased poverty in the urban areas leads to high incidence of wage and social transfer arrears. UN reports suggest that the average minimum wage is still insufficient to ensure an adequate standard of living for large parts of the Georgian population.

Main cities
Tbilisi (population 1.2 million in 2004), Kutaisi (268,800); Rustavi (181,400), Batumi (145.400).

Languages spoken
Russian and English are spoken and in the territory of Abkhazia, Abkhazian is sometimes spoken.
Official language/s
Georgian

Media
The constitution guarantees freedom of speech and of the press. However political turmoil during the 2008 presidential election saw intimidation of journalists by political leaders of on all sides of the debate.
Other news agencies: Prime-News: http://eng.primenewsonline.com
Civil Georgia: www.civil.ge
Press
There are around 200 newspapers but most are small, local and without influence. Newspapers are typically subsidized by patrons, in business and politics, and editorial independence is correspondingly compromised.
Dailies: In Georgian Sakartvelos Respublika (Republic of Georgia) (www.opentext.org.ge/sakartvelos-respublika), was the official government newspaper. Other private publications include 24 Saati (24 Hours) (www.24saati.ge), Rezonansi (Resonance). In Russian Svobodnaya Gruzia (Free Georgia) (www.svobodnaya-gruzia.com). In English The Messenger (www.messenger.com.ge).
Weeklies: In English, The Georgian Times (www.geotimes.ge) and Georgia Today (www.georgiatoday.ge).
Business: The EU-funded Georgian Economic Trends (www.geplac.org) is a quarterly with the best source of business news and information. It is published by the European Policy and Legal advice Center (Geplac) in English and Georgian.
Broadcasting
Georgian Public Broadcasting (GPB) (www.gpb.ge) provides national coverage.
Radio: The GPB (www.gpb.ge) has two radio stations, Public Radio offering a range of news, cultural and entertainment programmes and Radio Two offers Georgian music programmes, with part of the daytime schedule given over to educational, social and entertainment programmes. Private, commercial stations include, Radio Imedi (www.radio-imedi.ge) a national news and speech network and Fortuna FM (www.fortuna.ge) with local and international music of most genre.
Television: Most Georgians rely on TV to provide their news and information. The GPB (www.gpb.ge) has two TV stations, Public TV has a full range of programmes from news and current affairs to children's TV and sport and Channel Two has specialist programming but does not reach all regions of the country. There are a several commercial TV stations including Rustavi 2 (www.rustavi2.com.ge) is the most popular TV channel, Imedi TV (www.imedi.ge) and Mze TV (http://mze.ge), all providing locally produced and imported programmes.

Economy
Georgia has been slow to emerge from the aftermath of the demise of the Soviet Union, which precipitated economic collapse in the nineties. Under the aegis of the IMF and the World Bank, reforms are being pursued to restructure the economy, including privatisation of state-owned assets, which was completed in 2006. The economy is growing, but political problems have slowed progress; the ability to attract foreign investment and introduce further liberal reforms has been affected by continuing instability, particularly in connection with the South Ossetian and Abkhazian disputes and relations generally with Russia, which uses economic measures against Georgia.
Agriculture and mining are still the mainstay of the economy, accounting between them for around 40 per cent of GDP and 60 per cent of employment. Georgia nevetheless remains reliant on imports of fuel, food and pharmaceuticals to meet domestic demands. This exposes Georgia to extraneous pressures, as with the price increases imposed by Russia on gas supplies in 2006. A new gas link connecting the Caspian Sea to the Mediterranean Sea (the Baku-Tbilisi-Ceyhan pipeline), which commenced operations in 2005, crosses Georgia and is expected to ease dependence on Russia as well as contribute to the econony through transit fees.

External trade
Georgia had traditional ties with Russia which were, following the break-up of the Soviet Union, formalised through the Commonwealth of Independent States (CIS), however relations have become strained since Georgia has moved towards the West and Russia imposed restrictions on Georgian imports and transport access. The destination of exports to Russia has steadily switched to Europe and the US.
Georgia is an important transit country for goods and hydrocarbons through Central Asia.

Imports
Imports typically include fuels, machinery and parts, transport equipment, grain and other foods and pharmaceuticals.
Main sources: Russia (15.4 per cent total, 2005), Turkey (11.4 per cent), Azerbaijan (9.4 per cent), Ukraine (8.8 per cent), Germany (8.3 per cent), US (6.0 per cent)
Exports
Merchandise exported includes metal and ore, machinery, nuts and wine and aircraft.
Main destinations: Russia (18.1 per cent total, 2005), Turkey (14.3 per cent), Azerbaijan (9.8 per cent), Turkmenistan (8.9 per cent), Bulgaria (5.0 per cent), Armenia (4.7 per cent), Ukraine (4.4 per cent), Canada (4.2 per cent)
Re-exports
Fuel, citrus fruits and wine.

Agriculture
Farming
The agricultural sector typically contributes over 30 per cent to GDP and employs about 50 per cent of the workforce.
Georgia is a major agricultural producer and the warm climate favours the growing of a range of sub-tropical crops in the coastal region. Crops include tea, grapes, tobacco and fruit.
A great deal of Georgia's produce is exported to other former Soviet republics in return for much-needed supplies of manufactured goods.
Crop production in 2005 included: 712,200 tonnes (t) cereals in total, 200,000t wheat, 441,000t maize, 439,700t potatoes, 66,000t barley, 18,100t pulses, 80,000t citrus fruit, 180,000t grapes, 115,000t tomatoes, 9,336t oilcrops, 1,500t tobacco, 18,800t treenuts, 3,110t various spices, 24,000t tea, 70,000t apples, 426,800t fruit in total, 476,000t vegetables in total. Livestock production included: 111,800t meat in total, 51,000t beef, 35,400t pig meat, 9,600t lamb, 15,500t poultry, 31,470t eggs, 781,400t milk, 2,000t honey, 8,170t cattle hides, 1,404t sheepskins, 2000t greasy wool.
Forestry
Over two-fifths of the land is covered by forests and woodland, of which only a fifth is available for wood production and another fifth is classified as primeval forest untouched by man. Around 60 per cent of Georgia's trees are broadleafed, including beech, oak, hornbeam and chestnut, and the rest are coniferous, mainly spruce and pine. Forests are important to protecting soil and water. The state owns all forests by law.
Georgia produces and exports roundwood (typically 65 per cent of

forestry exports) and sawnwood (27 per cent) from hardwood species.

Industry and manufacturing

Industry accounts for a quarter of GDP and employs about 20 per cent of the workforce. Light industrial activities include food-processing and drinks production, metallurgy, shipbuilding, car production, consumer durables, garment manufacturing and oil-processing. Other industries include mining, chemicals, heavy engineering and steel-making.
Levels of self-sufficiency in the manufacturing sector are low and export manufacturing potential is limited. The sector is troubled by a periodic lack of finance, the slow pace of rehabilitation of enterprises and low levels of management.

Tourism

The tourism sector has considerable potential to expand, but is hindered by government inactivity and political instability. There were around 290,000 arrivals in 2004.

Mining

Georgia has major mineral deposits, notably manganese, copper and lead. Small quantities of iron ore are extracted.
There are reserves of about 200 million tonnes of manganese ore in Chiatura, of which 60 per cent is recoverable through underground mining and 40 per cent through open-pit mining. The Madneuli mining plant at Kazreti in southern Georgia is the country's only producer of copper concentrate. The Madneuli deposit contains the bulk of copper reserves, with reserves of around 460,000 tonnes of ore.

Hydrocarbons

Georgia has limited oil reserves, estimated at 35 million barrels, but is believed to have greater potential.
Exploration is taking place off the Black Sea coast as well as onshore. Georgia, which consumes 42,000 barrels per day (bpd), produces around 2,000 bpd and relies on imports from Russia and Azerbajian. There are two refineries.
Georgia has always been a natural transportation route for the oil from the Caspian Sea to the Mediterranean. The oil pipeline from Baku, Azerbaijan, to the Black Sea port of Supsa in Georgia, was opened in 1999. The initial capacity of the Baku-Supsa pipeline was 115,000bpd of Caspian Sea crude oil. The Baku-Tbilisi-Ceyhan oil pipeline, to carry one million barrels per day of Caspian oil to western markets, opened in 2005.
Georgia had proven natural gas reserves of around 80 million cubic metres but Georgia, is dependent on imports of natural gas from Russia.
Coal reserves are estimated at 800 million tonnes, of which over a half are located at Tkibuli-Shaorskoye.

Energy

Georgia has a generating capacity of 4.5GW, which is produced by 53 hydroelectric power stations and three thermal power plants. Fuel shortages and a deteriorating infrastructure means the electricity sector operates below capacity and there are frequent power cuts. In order to meet demand, Georgia imports electricity from Armenia, Azerbaijan and Russia and has run up considerable debt on these imports, resulting in disputes with the suppliers. Poor electricity supply and high rates have prompted widespread non-payment among Georgian electricity customers.

Financial markets

Stock exchange

The Georgian Stock Exchange (GSE) opened in August 1999. There are over 280 companies trading on the GSE.
The GSE is part of the Federation of Euro-Asian Stock Exchanges (FEAS).

Banking and insurance

The banking sector has undergone reform since 1995 and the central bank, the National Bank of Georgia (NBG), has assumed a supervisory role. The NBG has concentrated on consolidating the banking sector to clamp down on poor management, corruption and non-performing loans. It has also progressively raised the minimum capital requirement, which has caused a dramatic fall in the number of banks operating in the country and forced many to seek foreign participation to survive.

Central bank

National Bank of Georgia (NBG)

Time

GMT plus three hours

Geography

Georgia is situated in west and central Transcaucasia on both sides of the Suram range. There are frontiers with Turkey and Armenia in the south, and with Azerbaijan in the south-east. The Black Sea coast is to the west. To the west of the Surams lies the more mountainous Kura basin. The Rion, which flows westwards into the Black Sea, and the Kura which flows eastwards through Azerbaijan into the Caspian Sea, are the country's two main rivers.

Hemisphere

Northern.

Climate

Hot and humid summers and mild winters. Georgia is protected against the cold air from the north by the Great Caucasus mountains. Temperatures range from 21 degrees Celsius (C) to 33C in July and from 0C to 10C in January. The west, including the Black Sea coast, lies in a sub-tropical zone with high humidity and heavy rainfall; temperatures average 5C in winter and 22C in summer. Eastern Georgia is more equable with lower humidity; temperatures average 2–4C in winter and 20–25C in summer. The mountain regions are dryer and cooler, while above 3,600m snow and ice prevail year-round.

Entry requirements

Passports

Required by all. Passports must be valid for six months after date of departure.

Visa

Required by all, except nationals of EU countries, CIS countries (other than Russia and Turkmenistan), Canada, Israel, Japan, Switzerland and US.
Business visas may in some cases require a letter of invitation from a local company or organisation and a letter of introduction from the employer.
Do not overstay the limit of the visa. The Georgian authorities can impose heavy penalties for non-compliance, including detention, fines and deportation, and all removals at the traveller's expense.

Currency advice/regulations

There are no restrictions on the import and export of local currency. The import of foreign currency is allowed, but export is limited to US$500.
Almost all payments are made in cash (US dollar notes are the most useful). Most foreign currency can be exchanged at special exchange shops in the streets of large towns.

Customs

Small amount of personal goods duty-free. On arrival declare all foreign currency and valuable items such as jewellery, cameras, computers and musical instruments.

Health (for visitors)

A reciprocal health agreement for urgent medical treatment exists with the United Kingdom. Some proof of UK residence will be required. Rabies is a health risk.

Mandatory precautions

A vaccination certificate is required for yellow fever if travelling from an infected area.

Advisable precautions

Water precautions are recommended (water purification tablets may be useful).
It is advisable to be in date for the following immunisations: tetanus (within 10 years), typhoid fever, hepatitis A (moderate risk only), hepatitis B, meningitis.
Any required medicines should be carried by the visitor, and it could be wise to have precautionary antibiotics if going outside major urban centres.
A travel kit including a disposable syringe is a reasonable precaution.

Credit cards
Only one or two outlets in Tbilisi can handle credit cards.

Public holidays (national)
Fixed dates
1 Jan (New Year's Day), 7 Jan (Orthodox Christmas Day), 19 Jan (Orthodox Epiphany), 3 Mar (Mothers' Day), 8 Mar (Women's Day), 9 Apr (Restoration Day), 9 May (Victory Day), 12 May (St Andrew's Day), 26 May (Independence Day), 28 Aug (Orthodox Assumption of the Virgin/Mariamoba), 14 Oct (Svetitskhovloba), 23 Nov (St George's Day/Giorgoba).
Variable dates
Orthodox Easter Monday

Working hours
Banking
Mon–Fri: 0930–1730.
Business
Mon–Fri: 0900–1800.
Shops
Mon–Sat: 0900–1700.

Electricity supply
220V AC 50Hz

Weights and measures
Metric system

Social customs/useful tips
Georgians are excellent hosts. Feasting is a central part of Georgian tradition. If you go to a dinner as the guest of honour, it is not unusual to be asked to sing a song or recite a romantic poem. When Georgians show friendship, it is sincere.

Security
There is a risk of terrorist activity, especially on the border with Chechnya.There has been an increase in the number of robberies, kidnappings and assaults involving foreigners, especially business people, in and around the capital, Tbilisi. Travellers should exercise caution in crowded places and markets, and when using public transportation. It is advisable not to walk alone at night and to avoid unofficial taxis.
Travellers should avoid unnecessary travel outside Tbilisi, especially at night. Train travel to Armenia, which is prone to incidents of theft and crime, should be avoided.

Getting there
Travellers intending to stay in Tbilisi for longer than three days must register with the Ministry of the Interior.
Air
National airline: Georgian Airways.
International airport/s: Tbilisi International Airport (TBS), 18km from city centre.
Airport tax: None

Surface
Road: Highways connect Georgia to the Russian Federation via the Caucasian Road Tunnel and the Georgian Military Highway to north Ossetia.
Rail: Tbilisi has railway connections with Azerbaijan, Armenia and Iran. The conflict in Abkhazia has affected the rail link with the Russian Federation.
Water: International connections to main ports from the Black Sea ports of Odessa, Sochi, Trabzon and Istanbul. Connections are also available with the Mediterranean ports of Genoa and Piraeus.
Main port/s: The main ports are Batumi (deals mainly with oil exports), Poti and Sukhumi.

Getting about
National transport
The European Bank for Reconstruction and Development's (EBRD) plans for the transport sector include improving the maintenance of existing rail, road, port and airport systems; promoting the commercialisation and privatisation of the transport industries; developing Georgian links with the Euro-Asian corridor; encouraging better co-ordination between the Georgian transport systems and those of the other states in the region; and providing technical co-operation for policy development, structural reform, economic analysis, project specification and preparation, and economic and environmental assessment.
Road: Difficult terrain and weather conditions restrict road links. Note that reliable road maps and signposts do not exist. Independent drivers should note that fuel can be difficult to obtain without specialist local knowledge. An international driving permit is required.
Buses: Buses operate between major towns and cities. There is a small underground system in Tbilisi.
Rail: There is approximately 1,583km of track with a double-track railway between Marelisi and Sagandzile. There are regular services between Tbilisi, Azerbaijan and Russia. Reservations are required for all trains.
City transport
There are many forms of cheap public transport in Tbilisi. A knowledge of the local language with its own script could be very helpful.
Taxis: Both official and unofficial taxis are plentiful.
Fares should always be agreed in advance as fares for foreigners can be set extremely high. It is advisable to use only official taxis and not share with strangers.
Car hire
Although the roads are severely pot-holed, hiring a car and driver through your guide or business associate is the quickest form of transport. It is not recommended to drive yourself.

BUSINESS DIRECTORY

The addresses listed below are a selection only. While World of Information makes every endeavour to check these addresses, we cannot guarantee that changes have not been made, especially to telephone numbers and area codes. We would welcome any corrections.

Telephone area codes
The international direct dialling code (IDD) for Georgia is +995, followed by area code and subscriber's number:

Kutaisi	331	Tbilisi	32

Useful telephone numbers
Police: 02
Fire: 01
Ambulance: 03

Chambers of Commerce
American Chamber of Commerce in Georgia, 1 Nustubidze Street, 0177 Tbilisi (tel: 312-110; fax: 312-105; e-mail: amcham@amcham.ge).

Georgian Chamber of Commerce and Industry, 11 Chavchavadze Avenue, 0179 Tbilisi (tel: 230-045; fax: 235-760; e-mail: info@gcci.ge).

Banking
Bank of Georgia, 3 Aleksander Pushkin Street, 0105 Tbilisi (tel: 444-1729; fax: 444-182; e-mail: welcome@bog.ge).

People's Bank of Georgia, 74 Chavchavadze Avenue, Tbilisi 0162 (tel: 555-500; e-mail: info@peobge.com).

ProCredit Bank, 154 Agmashenebeli Avenue, Tbilisi 0112 (tel/fax: 202-222; e-mail: central@procreditbank.ge).

TBC Bank, 7 Marjanishvili Street, Tbilisi 0102 (tel: 777-000; fax: 772-774; e-mail: marjanishvili@tbcbank.com.ge).

United Georgian Bank, 37 Uznadze Street, Tbilisi 0102 (tel: 505-505; fax: 999-139; e-mail: admin@ugb.com.ge).

Central bank
National Bank of Georgia, 3/5 Leonidze Street, 0105 Tbilisi (tel: 996-505; fax: 999-346; e-mail: info@nbg.gov.ge).

Travel information
Georgian Airways, 12 Rustaveli Prospect, Tbilisi (tel: 485-560; fax: 999-660; e-mail: info@georgian-airways.com).

National tourist organisation offices
Department of Tourism and Resorts, 12 Kasbegi Avenue, 0061 Tbilisi (tel: 525-301)

Ministries
Ministry of Agriculture and Food, Kostava 41, Tbilisi (tel: 996-261; fax: 933-300).

Ministry of Communications and Post, 2.9 April St, Tbilisi (tel: 999-528; fax: 934-419).

Ministry of Culture, 37 Rustaveli Ave, Tbilisi (tel: 937-433; fax: 999-037).

Ministry of Defence, 2 University St, Tbilisi (tel: 303-163; fax: 983-929).

Ministry of the Economy, 12 Czhanturia St, Tbilisi (tel: 230-925; fax: 982-743).

Ministry of Education, 52 Chkheixze St, Tbilisi (tel: 958-886; fax: 770-073).

Ministry of Environmental Protection and Natural Resources, 68a Kostava St, Tbilisi (tel: 230-664; fax: 983-425).

Ministry of Finance, 170 Barnovi, Tbilisi (tel: 226-805; fax: 292-368).

Ministry of Foreign Affairs, 4 Chitadze St, Tbilisi (tel: 989-377; fax: 997-249).

Ministry of Health, 30 Gamsakhurdia Ave, Tbilisi (tel: 387-071; fax: 389-802).

Ministry of Industry, 28 Gamsakhurdia Ave, Tbilisi (tel: 931-045, 386-558).

Ministry of the Interior, 10 D/Kheivnis St, Tbilisi (tel: 996-296; fax: 986-532).

Ministry of Justice, 19 Griboedov St, Tbilisi (tel: 989-252; fax: 990-225).

Ministry of Refugees and Accommodation, 30 Dadiani St, Tbilisi (tel: 663-302).

Ministry of Social Security, Labour and Employment, 7/2 Leonidze St, Tbilisi (tel: 938-989; fax: 936-150).

Ministry of State Property Management, 64 Czhavczhavadze Ave, Tbilisi (tel: 294-875; fax: 225-209).

Ministry of State Security, 4.9 April St, Tbilisi (tel: 982-383; fax: 932-791).

Ministry of Trade and Foreign Economic Relations, 42 Kazbegi Ave, Tbilisi (tel: 389-667; fax: 398-882).

Ministry of Urbanisation and Construction, 16 V Pshavela Ave, Tbilisi (tel: 374-276; fax: 220-541).

Other useful addresses

British Embassy, GMT Plaza, 4 Freedom Square, 0105 Tbilisi (tel: 274-747; fax: 274-792; e-mail: British.Embassy.Tbilisi@fco.gov.uk).

Business Communication Centre (BCC), 47 Kostava Street, Tbilisi (tel: 988-371; fax: 987-601).

Business Support Centre (BSC) Kutaisi, 124 Rustaveli Avenue, Kutaisi (tel: 310-1001; fax: 331-1001; e-mail: BSC@iberiapac.ge).

Committee for Socio-Economic Information of Georgia, 4 K Gamsakhurdia Avenue, Tbilisi (tel: 361-450, 938-936; fax: 995-892, 995-622).

Georgian Embassy (USA), Suite 300, 1615 New Hampshire Avenue NW, Washington DC 20009 (tel: (1+202)-387-2390; fax: (1+202)-393-4537; e-mail: georgiaemb@hotmail.com).

Georgian Stock Exchange, 74a Chavchavadze Avenue, Tbilisi 0162 (tel: 220=718; fax: 251-876; e-mail: info@gse.ge).

Independent Agency for the Development of Municipal Services, 89/24 D Agmashenebeli Ave, Tbilisi (tel: 951-003; fax: 986-950).

Sakenergo (state hydroelectricity company), 1 Vekua Street, Tbilisi (tel: 989-814; fax: 940-676).

Saknavtobi (state oil company), 65 M Kostava Street, Tbilisi 0175 (tel: 942-887; fax: 332-509).

Saktransgasmretsvi (state gas company), 22 Delisi III Lane, Tbilisi (tel: 932-981; fax: 227-746).

Telecom Georgia, Tbilisi (tel: 999-197; fax: 442-929; e-mail: info@telecom.ge).

Other news agencies: Prime-News: http://eng.primenewsonline.com
Civil Georgia: www.civil.ge

Internet sites

Information on government, elected officials and economic information: www.parliament.ge

Press office of the President of Georgia: www.presidpress.gov.ge/

Georgian Investment Centre: http://web.sanet.ge/gic/

Germany

As Chancellor Angela Merkel steadily succeeded in establishing Germany as an international player rather than the sick man of Europe, so the German electorate's deep seated wariness over any international involvement began to become an embarrassment. Nowhere was this more evident than in Afghanistan where one observer described the German Nato contingent as no more than 'traffic policemen' referring to the German government's embarrassing failure to allow the troops' deployment to the front line.

Peacekeeping only?

Unquestionably, Germany's international role has grown both in importance and in status since re-unification and the fall of the Berlin Wall. However, if the country is to honour its Nato responsibilities, then it will have to address what the London *Financial Times* labelled the 'simmering opposition' to any international involvement that goes beyond peacekeeping and disaster relief. The ability of Mrs Merkel's Christlich-Demokratische Union (CDU) Christian Democrat party to address this problem is no more than expression of the CDU's tentative grip on power through an uncomfortable coalition with a left-leaning Sozialdemokratische Partei (SPD) (Social Democrat Party).

Mrs Merkel's high profile (and first) visit to Afghanistan in 2007 was designed

KEY FACTS

Official name: Bundesrepublik Deutschland (Federal Republic of Germany)

Head of State: Federal President Horst Kohler (since 1 Jul 2004)

Head of government: Chancellor Angela Merkel (CDU/ CSU) (sworn in 22 Nov 2005)

Ruling party: Coalition: Christlich-Demokratische Union Deutschlands/Christlich-Soziale Union in Bayern (CDU/CSU) (Christian Democratic Union of Germany/Christian Social Union of Bavaria) and Sozialdemokratische Partei Deutschlands (SPD) (Social Democratic Party of Germany) (formed 22 Nov 2005)

Area: 357,041 square km

Population: 82.20 million (2007)

Capital: Berlin

Official language: German

Currency: Euro (eur) = 100 cents (from 1 Jan 2002; previous currency Deutsche mark, locked at DM1.96 per euro)

Exchange rate: eur0.63 per US$ (Jul 2008)

GDP per capita: US$40,154 (2007)

GDP real growth: 2.50% (2007)

Labour force: 39.59 million (2004)

Unemployment: 8.40% (2007)

Inflation: 2.20% (2007)

Balance of trade: US$189.24 billion (2005)

Foreign debt: US$3,662.65 billion (2004)

Visitor numbers: 23.60 million (2006)*

* estimated figure

to help reverse the increasing rift between Germany's international profile and a public reluctance to see German troops taking casualties in a war that has little popular support and even less understanding. Following the disaster that was the Second World War, the German population has grown accustomed to their role as international bystanders, happy to watch other nations stand up and be counted. The perceived failure of the Iraq invasion did little to convince them otherwise, to the extent that they had become deeply suspicious of all and any overseas military commitments. Germany is one of the few European countries that still operates a conscripted military service obligation. This does little to assuage fears that 'our boys' may die in a foreign field. The renascent SPD even went so far as to mount a campaign to withdraw all German troops from Afghanistan. All sentiments which did little to improve German popularity among those Nato partners – Canada, Holland, the UK and the US – who have troops operating in the front line.

Never had it so good?

After some years in the doldrums, Germany's economy started to flex its muscles in the first half of 2008, building on the success of 2007. In its June monthly report, the Deutsche Bundesbank was able to report that overall output had risen by 1.5 per cent for the second quarter over the previous year, after taking seasonal effects into account. When adjusted for the different number of working days, gross domestic product (GDP) was in fact 2.6 per cent up on the previous year, an annual rate that compared favourably with the 1.8 per cent recorded for the preceding quarter. The International Monetary Fund (IMF) projected Germany's GDP growth rate for 2008 at 1.5 per cent as the effects of a depressed US economy and the strengthening of the Euro began to bite. The Deutsche Bundesbank had originally forecast Germany's GDP growth for 2008 at 2.0 per cent, dropping to 1.4 per cent in 2009. The generally unfavourable economic environment prevailing in mid-2008 meant that all forecasts have to be treated with some circumspection.

Industrial strength

For these reasons, the projected growth figures exceeded the forecast originally made in the Deutsche Bundesbank's macroeconomic projections for 2008. The unusually mild winter enabled German industry to process the orders received in late 2007 without impediments, and also benefited the construction sector. The buoyancy of the manufacturing and construction sectors also resulted in greater job creation, with overall employment expanding by 1.7 per cent over the previous year in the first quarter of 2008. Of all the reforms carried out by the Merkel coalition, job creation has probably been the most successful. By the beginning of 2008 there were some 700,000 fewer people out of work than in 2006, and 1.5 million fewer than in 2005 when German unemployment peaked at over 5 million. In December 2008 alone, unemployment dropped by over 75,000, the twenty-first consecutive month of falling unemployment. On a seasonally adjusted basis, according to the Bundesagentur für Arbeit (BA) (Federal Employment Agency), unemployment had dropped to 8 per cent in the first quarter, 1.5 per cent lower than the previous year and 0.6 per cent lower than in the previous quarter. The number of people in work is expected to increase to 40.3 million in 2008, with a further modest increase in 2009. The unemployment rate is forecast at 7.8 per cent in 2008 and 7.6 per cent in 2009. Germany's growth potential will depend on the extent to which skills shortages can be overcome, both by improved education and training and by increased immigration levels of skilled workers. With its low birth rate and ageing population Germany has difficulty in finding working-age people able to fill the jobs created by its resurgent economy.

Coalition differences

In its report on the German economy, the International Monetary Fund (IMF) drew attention to the potentially constraining effects of Germany's new sectoral minimum wages. Germany is one of the few European countries without a national minimum wage. Angela Merkel has consistently been opposed to the idea on the grounds that it would be detrimental to job creation, but the CDU's coalition partners, the SPD, have focussed on the adoption of a minimum wage in regional elections. The issue has probably been exaggerated in importance by both sides of the argument. A 2006 study by the Organisation for European Co-operation and Development (OECD) calculated that a minimum wage of eur4.50 per hour would only affect one per cent of full-time employees.

Inflation worries

The news on inflation was less encouraging. In the first quarter of 2008 consumer price inflation was just as high as in the final quarter of 2007, at an annual rate of 3.1 per cent. This was 0.2 per cent higher than forecast, due in large measure to increased global energy and food prices. If energy is excluded, a reasonable inflation forecast for 2008 would be as low as 1.7 per cent. The price increases resulted in a marked deterioration in primary consumption in the last quarter of 2007, from which it barely recovered in the first half of 2008. The price increases simply reduced the scope for household expenditure. German consumers are known for their caution; as consumers' price expectations became more and more pessimistic, so their

KEY INDICATORS — Germany

	Unit	2003	2004	2005	2006	2007
Population	m	82.38	82.63	82.44	82.29	82.20
Gross domestic product (GDP)	US$bn	2,400.70	2,714.42	2,791.74	2,915.87	3,322.15
GDP per capita	US$	28,710	32,695	33,865	35,432	40,154
GDP real growth	%	-0.1	1.7	0.9	2.8	2.5
Inflation	%	0.9	1.8	1.9	1.8	2.2
Unemployment	%	9.5	9.5	9.1	9.8	8.4
Natural gas output	bn cum	17.7	16.4	15.8	15.6	14.3
Coal output	mtoe	54.1	54.7	53.2	50.3	86.0
Exports (fob) (goods)	US$m	750,000	909,700	972,370	1,135,730	1,354,120
Imports (cif) (goods)	US$m	600,000	717,920	783,130	934,860	1,075,430
Balance of trade	US$m	150,000	191,780	189,240	200,860	278,690
Current account	US$m	51,760	96,410	128,379	181,200	254,520
Total reserves minus gold	US$m	50,694.0	48,823.0	45,140.0	41,687.0	44,327.0
Foreign exchange	US$m	41,095.0	39,899.0	39,765.0	37,719.0	40,768.0
Exchange rate	per US$	0.88	0.80	0.77	0.75	0.69

inclination to make major purchases also waned. What the IMF terms Germany's generally 'low reliance on credit' has helped banks to observe normal lending terms and conditions.

It was therefore left to investment to be the economy's principal stimulus. Construction investment, benefiting from the mild winter weather, increased by 4.5 per cent over the fourth quarter of 2007; expenditure on machinery and equipment also rose – by 4 per cent – in the same quarter. The commendable 2.4 per cent increase in exports of goods and services was effectively negated by a 3.5 per cent increase in imports, particularly of capital goods. Despite a further deterioration in the terms of trade, at the end of April 2008 Germany's trade surplus rose by eur2.4 billion (US$2.4 billion), to eur17.7 billion (US$17.7 billion). Industrial output in the second quarter of 2008 showed an overall increase of 5.6 per cent for the year, although the production of major items such as trains, aircraft and ships was 8.1 per cent down in the month of April 2008. Production of consumer goods also recorded sharp declines.

Germany appeared to have escaped relatively unscathed from the 2007–08 sub-prime crisis. Credit terms for German companies tightened only marginally, and for households hardly changed at all. GDP growth in Germany exceeded expectations in the first quarter of 2008, with large volumes of export orders in hand. The Deutsche Bundesbank estimated that the resilience of the German economy represented a clear counterweight to any downside risks that were likely to beset the economy in 2008.

Reforms?

What remains to be addressed by the German government and its electorate are the essential reforms needed by a burdensome health and welfare structure. Chancellor Merkel also managed to begin reforming Germany's health sector, despite strong opposition. A government health fund is to be established by 2009 which will spread healthcare contributions more evenly. Angela Merkel had originally proposed a flat-rate premium for health care contributions, replacing those based on a proportion of wages. This, combined with subsidies for the very poor (a growing concern with five million unemployed), was seen as the sort of root and branch reforms Germany badly needed across the whole spectrum of government expenditure. But such fundamental reforms not only faced resistance from the opposition, but had soon lost the support of Mrs Merkel's own party in the face of popular opposition. In what represented a major adjustment, in 2007 Germany had managed to adjust its budget, as part of an ambitious reform programme aimed at reaching a primary surplus of 3.5 per cent of GDP by 2011. Although this represented quite an achievement, the IMF has noted that longer term fiscal challenges remain, notably that of health service funding and reforms. The IMF also noted that Germany's fiscal position was moving from overall balance in 2007 to a moderate deficit in 2008. In the view of the IMF, Germany's gentle fiscal loosening should help cushion the effects of any anticipated slowdown.

Being Mrs Merkel

Angela Merkel had inherited something of a poisoned chalice from her predecessor. For a start, bringing the budget deficit to within 3 per cent of GDP (as prescribed by the EU Stability and Growth Pact) by 2007 looked to be a tall order, as did lowering Germany's record unemployment levels. Against all the odds, and some would say depite herself, Mrs Merkel achieved both of these objectives one year after being elected; Germany's budget deficit was below 3 per cent in 2006 and below 1 per cent in 2007–08 following the federal government's revenue raising measures in 2007. Germany's chronic unemployment dropped to 9.6 per cent and was under the 3.5 million mark by the end of 2007. These successes may have resulted in a cooling of Germany's reformist ambitions. Chancellor Merkel's popularity also remained strong thanks to her success in restoring Germany's relations with the US, and maintaining Germany's high – and largely favourable – European profile. As chairperson of the European Union (first six months of 2007), Mrs Merkel succeeded in getting all 27 states to agree on an environmental agenda.

Mrs Merkel can hardly be described as a charismatic leader. But she is a politician through and through, and has shown an impressive ability to achieve her objectives – and a comparable capacity to recognise and accept the unachievable. Following her election as head of the ruling coalition in 2005, most political observers expected her to have difficulty in forcing through the CDU reforming agenda. The less optimistic analysts foresaw two years of compromise (rather than achievement) followed by two years of in-fighting in the run up to the next elections. In fact, the in-fighting started earlier than expected, leaving a stark contrast between Mrs Merkel's international achievements and the continual bickering at home. Faced with trenchant opposition from the SPD, the junior partner in the ruling coalition, Mrs Merkel and her CDU party colleagues appear to have taken the path of least resistance, agreeing to increase unemployment benefits for older workers and grant cash subsidies to mothers who choose not to work. These populist moves represented a sea change in German politics, as the reforming 2010 agenda originally introduced by Mrs Merkel's pre-decessor as chancellor, Gerhard Schroeder, was not just watered down, but abandoned.

Confronted not only with the 'official' opposition headed up by the Freie Demokratische Partei (FDP) (Free Democratic Party) but also accepting that the SPD, far from supporting her reformist agenda were steadfastly opposed to it, Angela Merkel had very few options. In the opinion polls, a resurgent Left Party appeared to have replaced the Free Democrats as the true opposition, leaving open the possibility that in the next election different coalition groupings might emerge. Under this scenario, the SPD could well align itself with the Greens and the Left parties, leaving the CDU to rejoin the Free Democrats in a centre right coalition. What remains uncertain, or even unlikely, is whether any of these groupings would be able to gain the outright majority required to form a government.

Russian energy

Thanks to Mrs Merkel's diplomatic prowess, even Germany's tense relationship with Russia appeared to be improved rather than endangered. This became increasingly important as Russia began to use its energy supplies as a lever in its international relations. This is particularly important as Germany is the fifth-largest consumer of oil in the world, with consumption reaching 2.7 million barrels per day (bpd) in 2004. Due to the size of the German economy and the lack of significant domestic oil production, Germany is also one of the world's largest oil importers. The country relies upon imports for over 90 per cent of its crude oil demand. According to Eurostat, Germany imported 2.1 million bpd of crude oil during the first seven months of 2006, slightly lower than the same period in 2005; most imports came from Russia (34 per cent), followed by Norway (16 per cent), the United Kingdom (12 per cent), and Libya (12 per cent). Germany also imports large amounts of refined petroleum products. Besides coal, Germany does not possess any sizable hydrocarbon reserves, so the country must rely upon imports to meet the majority of its energy needs. The lack of domestic hydrocarbon resources has led Germany to become a world leader in the development of renewable energy technologies, with the country being the world's largest producer of bio-diesel and generator of electricity from wind.

Germany had 367 million barrels of proven oil reserves in January 2006. Most of these reserves are located in northern and north-eastern Germany. The country produced 170,000bpd of oil in 2005, of which 67,000bpd (39 per cent) was crude oil. Over half of Germany's crude oil production comes from a single field, Mittelplate, located in tidal flatlands in the North Sea. Mittelplate is a joint project of German oil and gas companies RWE and Wintershall AG. According to OGJ, Germany had 9.1 trillion cubic feet (Tcf) of proven natural gas reserves in January 2006, the third largest in the European Union, after the Netherlands and the United Kingdom. Almost all of Germany's natural gas reserves and production occur in the north-western state of Niedersachsen, between the Wesser and Elbe rivers. Germany's sector of the North Sea also contains sizable natural gas reserves, currently supporting the A6-B4 production project. However, environmental regulations have curtailed the complete exploration and development of the area. Despite the lack of domestic production, Germany is the third-largest consumer of natural gas in the world, behind the United States and Russia.

Risk assessment

Politics	Good
Economy	Good
Regional stability	Good

COUNTRY PROFILE

Historical profile

Prior to the nineteenth century, the area of modern-day Germany consisted of a series of city states forming part of the Holy Roman Empire. Following invasion by France and subsequent liberation in 1815, Prussia emerged as the most powerful state in the region.

1871 Germany was unified under the Prussian royal house of the Hohenzollerns. Wilhelm I was appointed Germany's first Kaiser. After defeating France in the Franco-Prussian War, Alsace-Lorraine was annexed by Germany.

1880–1900 After Germany became Europe's leading industrial power, it attempted to expand territorially and become a world power, establishing colonies in Africa and trying to influence politics in the Balkans.

1914–18 Germany invaded Belgium and then France. The UK intervened, but the war in France became attritional until 1917, when US troops joined British and French forces. The First World War ended in 1918 with Germany's defeat. Kaiser Wilhelm II went into exile in the Netherlands. The Weimar Republic, a federation of 19 states, was declared in November 1918.

1919 Friedrich Ebert was appointed Germany's first president. Germany was called on to make massive financial reparations and to cede Alsace-Lorraine to France and parts of the Saarland to Poland, as part of the Treaty of Versailles. The Rhineland was de-militarised and occupied by the Western European powers.

1920s Germany was gripped by an economic depression, suffering from hyper-inflation and high unemployment. As it could not afford to pay war reparations, France and Belgium occupied the industrialised Rhur as a protest.

1931 The instability of the economy and of democratic government led to the fascist National-Sozialistische Deutsche Arbeiterpartei (NSDAP) (Nationalist Socialist German Workers' Party) or Nazis, led by Austrian Adolf Hitler, becoming the largest party in the German parliament.

1933 Adolf Hitler was appointed chancellor of Germany.

1934 The Nazis consolidated their power. Hitler established himself as the führer (leader) of the Third Reich. The economy was rebuilt, all other political parties were banned and Hitler's opponents, Jews and other minorities were placed in concentration camps.

1936 German troops re-took the Rhineland and provided military aid to Spanish nationalists fighting the Spanish Civil War. Germany, Italy and Japan formed an alliance.

1938 Austria became part of the German Third Reich after its pro-Nazi chancellor, Arthur von Seyss Inquart, invited German troops into the country. Annexation of Sudetanland, Czechoslovakia.

1939 Germany signed a non-aggression pact with the Soviet Union. Britain and France declared war on Germany after German roops invaded Poland.

1940 Germany captured most of Western Europe while most of Eastern Europe had pro-German puppet governments installed.

1941 Germany invaded the Soviet Union. Following Japan's attack on Pearl Harbour, the US declared a state of war with Japan; three days later, Japan's allies, Germany and Italy, declared war on the US.

1944–45 The US, Britain and the Soviet Union liberated Nazi-occupied Europe. Adolf Hitler committed suicide in Berlin. Following the end of the Second World War, Germany was occupied by the Allied powers.

1949 The Federal Republic of Germany (FRG) was established in the western zone by unifying the British, French and American zones of control, and the German Democratic Republic (GDR) was established in the east, under the Sozialistische Einheitspartei Deutschlands (SED) (Socialist Unity Party), following failure of negotiations to establish a unified administration. Konrad Adenauer became federal chancellor. Waltar Ulbricht became general secretary of the GDR's ruling communist party until 1971 when Erich Honeker replaced him.

1951 The FRG and France merged their coal and steel industries through the European Coal and Steel Community (ECSC).

1953 Severe food shortages and the policy of 'sovietisation' in GDR led to uprisings and strikes, suppressed by Soviet troops, causing large numbers of refugees to begin fleeing to the West.

1954 The FRG was admitted to NATO.

1955 The GDR became a member of the Soviet Union's Warsaw Pact.

1957 The FRG declared Berlin its capital. Bonn became the seat of government until reunification.

1958 The FRG became a founding member of the forerunner of the EU, the European Economic Community (EEC).

1961 The GDR constructed the Berlin Wall between eastern and western sectors to stem the flow of refugees to West Berlin.

1963–66 Ludwig Erhard succeeded Adenauer as federal chancellor.

1966–69 Federal Chancellor Kurt Georg Kiesinger 's coalition comprised the two largest parties, Christlich-Demokratische Union (CDU) (Christian Democratic Union)/Christlich-Soziale Union (CSU) (Christian Social Union) and the Sozialdemokratische Partei Deutschland (SPD) (Social Democratic Party of Germany). He chose the mayor of Berlin, Willi Brandt, as his foreign minister.

1969 Willi Brandt (SPD) became chancellor, heading a coalition of SPD and Freie Demokratische Partei (FDP) (Free Democratic Party). He implemented a policy of ostpolitik, orienting FRG foreign policy towards Eastern Europe and détente with the GDR.

1971 Erich Honecker became leader of the GDR, which became one of the most hardline members of the Warsaw Pact. In the late 1980s, Honecker resisted calls for

democratisation on the Russian glasnost pattern.
1973 The FRG and GDR joined the UN.
1974 Helmut Schmidt became federal chancellor after the fall of Brandt in a security scandal. Disputes over the deteriorating economic situation, nuclear power and defence policy led to coalition instability and the withdrawal of the FDP in 1982.
1982 The CDU leader, Helmut Kohl, became federal chancellor and formed a coalition government.
1989–90 The Soviet Union withdrew support for the Honecker regime, prompting his resignation, the dismantling of the Berlin wall, democratisation of the GDR and moves towards a market economy. The reunification of Germany took place in October 1990. Helmut Kohl won the first free German election since 1931.
1994 Federal elections resulted in a narrow victory for Chancellor Kohl and his CDU-led coalition.
1998 The SPD gained the largest share of the vote in the elections. Gerhard Schröder became chancellor and formed a coalition government with Bündis 90 (Alliance 90) and Die Grünen (Greens).
1999 Germany became a founding member of the European Economic and Monetary Union (Emu). Johannes Rau was elected as federal president.
2000 Helmut Kohl resigned as chairman of the CDU following revelations about illicit funding to the party during his time as chancellor. He was replaced by Angela Merkel.
2002 Euro currency replaced the deutsche mark. Gerhard Schröder was re-elected as chancellor by one of the narrowest margins in German election history.
2003 In March, the Constitutional Court rejected a government request to ban the neo-Nazi National Democratic Party, after accusations that state agents had infiltrated the party's ranks, acting as agents provocateurs to discredit it.
2004 On 1 July, Horst Köhler took office as federal president.
2005 In July Chancellor Schröder dissolved parliament in preparation for early elections. The 18 September elections were indecisive with the CDU/CSU winning 35.2 per cent of the vote and the SPD 34.2 per cent. Angela Merkel was named chancellor on 10 October, and confirmed by a parliamentary vote in November. She leads a coalition government of CDU/CSU and SPD and is Germany's first woman chancellor, as well as the first chancellor from the former communist eastern part of Germany.
2006 Germany experienced economic recovery during the year. In January, a Russian dispute with Ukraine over gas supplies had a knock-on effect on Germany's supplies, sparking a debate over the nature of its relationship with Russia, particularly in terms of energy dependency. In July, parliament approved proposals to amend the constitution to reform the working of the federal structure. In October, the government decided that German armed forces should engage actively in an international security role.

Political structure

Constitution
Federal republic; under the 1949 Grundgesetz (constitution), Germany has a high degree of devolution.
The federal structure is formed from 16 Bundesländer (regional states), including the city of Berlin. Each state has its own constitution, an elected legislature and a government with responsibilities including education and public order.

Form of state
Federal parliamentary democratic republic

The executive
Executive authority is held by the Bundesregierung (federal government). The chief executive and head of government is the Bundeskanzler (federal chancellor), chosen by the Bundestag (lower house of the federal assembly) and usually the leader of the ruling party, who then appoints his own ministers. The Bundespräsident (federal president) is elected for a five-year term by the members of the Bundesversammlung (federal assembly), but has largely ceremonial duties.

National legislature
Federal legislative power is vested in the Bundesversammlung (federal assembly), which consists of the Bundestag (lower house) and Bundesrat (upper house). The Bundestag has 603 members elected for a four-year term to single-seat constituencies and by proportional representation, together with a speaker. The Bundesrat consists of 69 members chosen by the 16 Bundesländer (regional assemblies) and a speaker.

Legal system
The Federal Constitutional Court rules on constitutional issues, taking appeals from the lower courts. German law is largely code law that traces its roots to the Roman legal system. The court system below the Constitutional Court includes five branches: ordinary, labour, administrative, social and fiscal courts. Civil and criminal cases are normally in the jurisdiction of the ordinary court system, which is organised in local, regional and state tiers with a federal tribunal (Bundesgerichtshof), presiding over the system. Since the signing of the Single European Act in 1986, the European Court of Justice (ECJ) has been the highest court of appeal for rulings on matters affected by EU law.

Last elections
23 May 2004 (presidential); 18 September 2005 (parliamentary).
Results: Parliamentary: CDU/CSU won 35.2 per cent of the vote, 226 seats, SPD 34.2 per cent, 222 seats, FDP 9.8 per cent, 61 seats, The Left Party 8.7 per cent, 54 seats, The Greens 8.1 per cent, 51 seats. Turnout was 77.7 per cent.
Presidential: Horst Köhler was elected as federal president.

Next elections
2009 (presidential).

Political parties

Ruling party
Coalition: Christlich-Demokratische Union Deutschlands/Christlich-Soziale Union in Bayern (CDU/CSU) (Christian Democratic Union of Germany/Christian Social Union of Bavaria) and Sozialdemokratische Partei Deutschlands (SPD) (Social Democratic Party of Germany) (formed 22 Nov 2005)

Main opposition party
Freie Demokratische Partei (FDP) (Free Democratic Party).

Population
82.20 million (2007)
Last census: March 2004: 82,491,000
Population density: 235 inhabitants per square km. Urban population: 88 per cent.
Annual growth rate: 0.2 per cent 1994–2004 (WHO 2006)

Ethnic make-up
The majority of the population is Germanic. There is a small ethnic Slavonic (Sorbian) enclave in the south-east state of Saxony (approximately 60,000) and a Danish minority in the northern state of Schleswig-Holstein (approximately 50,000). There are an estimated 70,000 Sinti and Roma German nationals, mainly in the state's cities and towns . Some neighbourhoods in industrial cities are dominated by guest workers, mostly from Turkey, the Balkans and southern Europe.

Religions
The two principal religions are Roman Catholicism and Protestantism. The German Evangelical (Lutheran) church dominates in the overwhelmingly Protestant eastern, northern and central parts of the country. Members of the Catholic church form a majority in the south and west.

Education
Participation levels in primary and secondary education are almost 100 per cent, while 45 per cent attend some form of tertiary education. Approximately 4.8 per cent of GNP is spent on public education.

The public school system is administered by the individual states. Primary education is free and grants are made available for secondary education in institutions where fees are charged.
A year of kindergarten is followed by four years of primary school (Grundschule). Pupils are then screened for later admission into either advanced study or specialised and vocational training. Those in the advanced track continue at a Gymnasium to the age of 19, and then take the Arbitur comprehensive academic examination for admission to university. The majority of pupils attend vocational college after the age of 16.
In June 2004, the German cabinet agreed to give 10 of the country's leading unversities and researsh centres an extra US$2.3 billion, over five years, from 2006.
Compulsory years: Six to 16
Pupils per teacher: 17 in primary schools

Health

Per capita total expenditure on health (2003) was US$3,001; of which per capita government spending was US$2,348, at the international dollar rate, (WHO 2006).
There is no national health service, instead comprehensive healthcare is administered by the individual states. Health insurance provides 100 per cent of workers' salary for six weeks then drops to 80 per cent for 78 weeks. Health insurance also covers maternity and death benefits. Health insurance premiums, split by worker and employer in the case of those with high salaries, average 12.5 per cent of gross earnings.
HIV/Aids
HIV prevalence: 0.1 per cent aged 15–49 in 2003 (World Bank)
Life expectancy: 79 years, 2004 (WHO 2006)
Fertility rate/Maternal mortality rate: 1.3 births per woman, 2004 (WHO 2006)
Birth rate/Death rate: 8.6 births per 1,000 population; 10.3 deaths per 1,000 population (2003).
Child (under 5 years) mortality rate (per 1,000): 4.2 per 1,000 live births (World Bank)
Head of population per physician: 3.37 physicians per 1,000 people, 2003 (WHO 2006)

Welfare

Germany's health and social security systems are among the most generous in the world. Health, unemployment and retirement insurance are mandatory for most ordinary wage-earners under a wide-ranging social insurance system that has developed over more than a century. The system operates on a payroll withholding plan with contributions from workers, employers and government.
The welfare system provides assistance for all needy people who are unable to fend for themselves. There are funds for the support of widows, orphans and disabled people. The state makes available housing allowances for the poor in addition to its subsidies to low-income housing construction. The annual budget for spending in 2005 is eur1.8 billion (US$1.5 billion), plus eur3.2 billion (US$2.6 billion) to be given to local authorities for their social programme spending.
Changes to be introduced in January 2005 affect the newly unemployed and those without work for more than a year, who will receive only a flat rate benefit and any additional sum will be means tested, while measures to supervise and support those seeking work will be stepped up. These measures are being introduced to reduce the financial burden of the welfare system.
The Constitutional Court ruled that workers with children should pay a lower premium for the compulsory nursing insurance scheme than childless people.
Pensions
Of major concern is the rapidly changing demographic balance. As Germany's population continues to shrink, a smaller working population will have to bear the burden of an ever increasing number of pensioners. Pensions cost Germany the equivalent of 11–12 per cent of annual GDP and this is projected to rise to 18–19 per cent by 2040.
Contributions to the state pension scheme, which is mandatory except for workers with high salaries, range up to 18.7 per cent of gross income and are shared equally by worker and employer. The normal retirement age is 63 for men and 60 for women.

Main cities

Berlin (capital, estimated population 3.4 million (m) in 2005), Hamburg (1.8m), Munich (1.2m, Bavaria), Cologne (965,300), Frankfurt am Main (648,000), Essen (588,800), Dortmund (587,600), Stuttgart (581,100), Düsseldorf (571,966), Bremen (527,900), Hanover (516,300), Duisburg (513,400), Nürnberg (486,700), Leipzig (486,100), Dresden (473,300), Bonn (307,500), Mannheim (306,100).

Languages spoken

English is widely spoken, especially in business circles; French is also spoken, particularly in the Saarland. In the north in Schleswig-Holstein, Danish is spoken by the Danish minority and taught in schools. Regional dialects often differ markedly from standard German. There is an ongoing debate on language reform in Germany. It is almost 100 years since language laws were last comprehensively reformed.
Sorbian, North and West Frisian, Romani, Turkish and Kurdish are also spoken.
Official language/s
German

Media

The constitution guaranteed freedom of the press. Germany has several international conglomerates that produce material for all media outlets, including Bertelsmann, ProSiebenSat.1 and Axel Springer.
National news agency: DPA (Deutsche Presse-Agentur)
Other news agencies: Pressetext Deutschland (business news):www.pressetext.de
Press
There are few national newspapers, most publications are regionally based and may be distributed nationally. Although newspaper circulations at over 21 million the figure has been falling since the 1990s. There are hundreds of newspaper titles, most of which are locally produced. Tabloid newspapers are referred to as 'boulevard press'. Most newspapers are subscribed to rather than purchased daily.
Dailies: Major national publications include, in German, Bild (www.bild.de) a tabloid with the highest circulation, Süddeutsche Zeitung (SZ) (www.sueddeutsche.de), Frankfurter Allegemeine Zeitung (FAZ) (www.faz.net), Frankfurter Rundschau (www.fr-online.de) and Tageszeitung (www.taz.de).
Foreign language newspapers are published in Berlin, in French and Spanish.
Weeklies: In German, an influential newspaper with more analysis and background information is Die Zeit (www.zeit.de); other news magazines include Der Spiegel (www.spiegel.de) with the largest circulation and has an English-language edition, Stern (www.stern.de), Focus (www.focus.de) and the illustrated magazine Superillu (www.superillu.de). A few of the national dailies produce Sunday papers
Business: In German, Börsen Zeitung (www.boersen-zeitung.com) published Tuesday–Saturday is a financial newspaper, Handelsblatt (www.handelsblatt.com) and Aktiv (www.aktiv-online.info) for general business news; most national daily newspapers have sections on business and finance, including. Weekly publications include WirtschaftsWoche (www.wiwo.de) a economic magazine covering many aspects of business and Kapital, which looks at economic issues from a political standpoint; they are both

published by the GWP Media Group (www.gwp.de).
There are numerous trade and business publications. The German Institute of Business Management publishes a range of periodical of specific interest, on company law and governance.
Periodicals: There are over 800 general magazines and 1,000 specialist periodicals of offer.
In German, the monthly, NinetoFive is an imprint of WirtschaftsWoche (www.wiwo.de) with lifestyle contents for the office worker. Lieraturen (www.literaturen-online.de) is a literary monthly magazine and Brigitte (www.brigitte.de) is a women's magazine published fortnightly.
In English, Exberliner (www.exberliner.com) is published bi-monthly.

Broadcasting

Public broadcasting is funded by licence fees.
Radio: ARD (www.ard.de) is a consortium of national, public broadcasters providing a nationwide service with regional based programmes; some collaborate to produce shows of common interest. Most produce their own programmes of news and genre music. Most operate on the FM bandwidth and some are available digitally (DAB). Another public network is DeutschlandRadio (www.dradio.de) operates two national networks, with news and cultural programmes and a music channel. Deutsche Welle (www.dwelle.de) provides an international service in seven foreign languages, with news in 23 other languages, broadcasting via radio, internet and mobile/cell phones.
There are an abundance of private, commercial regional radio stations. Large media conglomerates operate radio stations and well as private interests catering for all genres.
Television: Germany has the largest and most competitive television market in Europe. Two of the largest television channel, ZDF (www.zdf.de) and ARD (www.ard.de), are national public services. ARD is a network of regional channels while ZDF is a nationwide channel that also broadcasts in Austria, Luxembourg and Switzerland. Both produce their own contents in a full range of programmes. There are private, commercial channels including Europe's largest TV, radio and production company, RTL Television (www.rtl.de), Sat.1 (www.sat1.de) and pay-to-view channels, specialising in genres such as films (Premiere (www.premiere.de)), sport (Arena (www.arena.tv)), documentaries and music. All public and private, major networks deliver German satellite TV programmes to international subscribers.
Germany plans to begin halting analogue TV transmission from 2008, as regional digital services are made available, completing the switch by 2010.

Advertising

Typical annual spending on advertising is over US$11.8 billion, of which an equal share, of 30 per cent, is divided between television and magazines, with newspapers averaging 15 per cent of the total amount.
There are regulations governing the insertion of adverts on television and radio with a limit of 20 minutes and 90 minute per working day respectively. TV programme sponsorship is permitted. Advertising by new technologies requires that they are clearly recognisable. Cinema allows tobacco advertising as well as product placing and surreptitious advertising.

Economy

Germany's GDP in 2005 was the world's third largest (after the US and Japan) at US$2.79 trillion. The economy is highly developed, with services accounting for around 70 per cent of GDP and a strong industry base of around 29 per cent, which is typically higher than some of its long-term EU partners. A World Bank report published in December 2007 stated that almost 50 per cent of the World's total GDP was produced between the US, China, Japan, Germany and India.
The reunification process, begun in 1990, revealed a gulf between west and east Germany. There was a stark divide between the strong, technologically advanced and highly competitive western Germany and the less developed, former communist economy of the east, which by 2006 had been reinterpreted. In a Germany confronting globalisation, east Germany is becoming the symbol of openness to change. Businesses see east German workers ready to change jobs, move with the work, retrain, work longer hours with less annual holidays and at salaries less than their west German counterparts.
The economy has been growing since 2003, when GDP growth was -0.1 per cent, to 0.9 per cent in 2005, and is expected to be 2.5 per cent in 2006. Domestic demand has been strong due to improved employment figures and productivity growth. Germany's trade surplus in October 2006 was a record US$23 billion, as exports rose to 22.6 per cent of GDP, and continued to surpass the US in the export of manufactured goods.
Despite the 2006 budget incorporating a 3.4 per cent deficit (contrary to EU fiscal rules on stability and growth), the government is attempting to limit spending with budget cuts in social services and a rise in VAT from 16 per cent to 19 per cent (to bring the deficit down to below 3.0 per cent). It is planning to raise the retirement age to 67 years, as a measure to counter an ageing population.
There has been a marked change in German optimism. With all the signs showing an upturn, Germany was ranked, by Ernst & Young, the best country in Europe to do business and ranked third in the world (after the US and China). Nevertheless direct foreign investment is not as strong as in the UK or France and a change in the corporate tax rate, due to be implemented in January 2007, may have an impact on the economy later.
Unemployment fell by 53,000 in November, to 3.6 million, its lowest since 1992, as industry grew and 600,000 extra jobs were created in 2007. Growth was achieved despite rising energy prices a strong euro and German inflation at its highest since 1994.

Labour market and unemployment

Approximately 42 per cent of the workforce is female. The workforce contained 39.1 million people in November 2000, and is projected to contract by 0.1 per cent per annum 2000–15.
The country has a well-educated and highly qualified workforce. Over 30 per cent of all positions are export-related.
Job creation has been hampered by structural rigidities in the labour market. Productivity is very high, but so are wage levels and related social security costs that must be borne by employers.
The unemployment situation in Germany improved rapidly over 1999 and 2000 due to high growth rates and increasing labour market flexibility, and the total number of registered unemployed in January 2001 was 4.0 million, equivalent to a rate of 9.3 per cent. This represented a fall in unemployment of 4.7 per cent from January 2000, but the rate remains higher than the European Union (EU) average of 8.2 per cent. Moreover, the national figure disguises wide regional variations, with rates of 7.2 per cent recorded in the western states in November 2000, compared to 16.3 per cent in the eastern states.

External trade

As a member of the European Union, Germany operates within a communitywide free trade union, with tariffs sets as a whole. Internationally, the EU has free trade agreements with a number of nations and trading blocs worldwide. It is Europe's leading export trader and the world's third largest vehicle exporter. Exports account for over 70 per cent of GDP

Imports

Include machinery, vehicles, chemicals, foodstuffs, textiles and metals.

Main sources: France (8.7 per cent total, 2006), The Netherlands (8.3 per cent), China (6.7 per cent).

Exports

Principal exports include machinery, vehicles, chemicals, electrical and electronic equipment and plastics.

Main destinations: France (9.6 per cent total, 2006), US (8.7 per cent), UK (7.3 per cent).

Agriculture

Farming

Germany has always provided incentives and subsidies for agriculture, which is generally regarded as a national resource.

Most of Germany's agriculture is now governed by the EU's Common Agricultural Policy (CAP). It is based on three broad principles:

- the EU is treated as a single market for agricultural produce
- EU farmers are given preference over outside suppliers
- the cost of the CAP is met by EU member governments

Fundamental reform to the CAP was introduced on 1 January 2005. The subsidies paid on farm output, which tended to benefit large farms and encourage overproduction, were replaced by single farm payments not conditional on production. This is expected to reward farms that provide and maintain a healthy environment, food safety and animal welfare standards. The changes are also intended to encourage market conscious production and cut the cost of CAP to the EU taxpayer.

Livestock production has long been the most important part of the sector, but is steadily declining.

Cereal crop production in Germany (particularly wheat) was adversely effected in June and September of 2005, by unusually hot temperatures and late summer rains respectively. Estimates for total cereal production in 2005 were more than ten per cent lower than 2004 yields.

Crop production in 2005 included: 45,803,100 tonnes (t) cereals in total, 23,578,000t wheat, 3,812,000t rye, 11,722,500t barley, 11,157,500t potatoes, 3,811,000t maize, 967,600t oats, 29,000t hops, 1,804,833t oilcrops, 25,427,000t sugar beets, 1,122,000t grapes, 4,658,700t rapeseed (canola), 1,600,000t apples, 4,248,254t fruit in total, 3,737,365t vegetables in total. Livestock production included: 6,884,060t meat in total, 1,145,000t beef, 4,505,000t pig meat, 54,000t lamb, 90,000t game meat, 27,628,000t milk, 1,054,000t poultry, 798,000t eggs, 17,000t honey, 141,000t cattle hides.

Fishing

West German sea fishing has experienced a sharp decline in recent decades. The government makes some subsidies available, but policy is largely an EU matter. The total seafood catch declined rapidly to just over 300,000 tonnes per annum during the mid 1990s. Since then catches have fallen to around 250,000 tonnes per year. Freshwater catches have also seen a drop in quantity of about one-fifth over the same period. Cuts in 2006 fishing quotas, agreed by the EU in December 2005, are expected to prolong this decline for the forseeable future.

The home ports of the east German deep-sea fishing fleets are Rostock-Marienehe and Sassnitz. The fleets work the waters off Iceland, Greenland, Labrador and Newfoundland and off the coast of West Africa. Inland fisheries account for only 4 per cent of the annual catch.

In 2004, the total marine fish catch was 218,278 tonnes and the total crustacean catch was 20,015 tonnes.

Forestry

Forest accounts for nearly a third of the land area estimated at 10.7 million hectares (ha) in 2000. These are located mainly in the south, centre and east of the country, with relatively little on the northern plain. Most of the forest area is available for wood supply. The growing stock per hectare is high and has been increasing. About 50 per cent of forests are publicly owned.

Germany has a strong forest industry and is one of the leading producers of wood-based panels and paper in the global market. The large-scale engineered wood product industry is dependent partially on sawnwood imports. Paper production is also partly based on imported wood pulp. It is one of the largest exporters and consumers of recycled paper.

Forest exports in 2004 amounted to US$15.9 billion, while imports amounted to US$15.3 billion.

Production in 2004 included 54,504,000 cubic metres (cum) roundwood, 48,657,000cum industrial roundwood, 19,850,000cum sawnwood, 32,241,000cum sawlogs and veneers, 12,695,000cum pulpwood, 14,108,000cum wood-based panels, 5,847,000cum wood fuel; 20,392,000 tonnes (t) paper and paperboard, including 2,403,000t newsprint, 7,880,000t printing and writing paper, 2,244,000t wood pulp, 13,219,000t recovered paper.

Industry and manufacturing

The industrial sector accounts for 36.2 per cent of GDP and employs approximately 36 per cent of the workforce.

Germany is a leading European producer of motor vehicles and accessories, industrial plant, machine tools, electrical goods, scientific instruments, chemicals, pharmaceuticals and consumer goods.

Traditional industries (steel, shipbuilding) have contracted because of foreign competition and weaker demand.

Some companies have moved into entirely new industries in order to take advantage of government deregulation and growth in service industries.

Strenuous efforts are being made to modernise industry in western Germany through the use of electronics and more flexible production techniques, and to restructure industry in eastern Germany which has remained uncompetitive in terms of price and quality. Worst affected areas are steel, electronics, engineering and chemicals.

High production costs in eastern Germany are preventing the region's companies from competing with their western counterparts and are contributing to a high rate of insolvencies. The number of bankruptcies in Germany grew by a record 14 per cent in 2002 as more than 37,579 businesses filed for insolvency. In early 2002, several prominent German companies were affected, including the construction company Philipp Holzmann AG and the aircraft manufacturer Fairchild-Dornier, while 2003 bankruptcies included the electronics manufacturer, Grundig. Insolvencies were most marked in construction, the main growth sector in eastern Germany. In 2004, the car manufacturer Volkswagen (VW) recorded a large decline in profits and between June and July 2005 three senior VW officials were forced to resign amid accusations of bribery.

East German industry began to show improvements in growth and productivity in the late 1990s, particularly in the electronics, food processing, printing, engineering and automotive sectors.

Industrial production rose by 1.5 per cent in September 2005, and 1.1 per cent in October 2005.

Tourism

Tourism accounts for 8 per cent of GDP and is a major employer, providing work for 2.8 million people. The main market is Europe, principally the Netherlands, followed by the UK and Switzerland. The US, which comes second after The Netherlands, is the most lucrative market. The sector is not a significant net foreign exchange earner, because so many Germans travel abroad. Foreign visitor numbers were falling by more than a million each year from 2000, when 19 million were recorded, until 2003 when 18.4 million arrivals were recorded.

Mining

The mining sector accounts for around 1 per cent of GDP and 1 per cent of the workforce.

Hydrocarbons

Germany depends heavily on oil and gas imports (approximately 96 per cent for oil and 80 per cent for natural gas).

Total estimated oil reserves stood at 200–400 million barrels in 2005, situated mainly in the north and north-east of the country.

Most of the country's natural gas requirements are imported, although offshore gas fields in the North Sea, estimated to contain 12.7 billion cubic metres (cum), began to be developed in 2000. In 2004, proved natural gas reserves stood at 200 billion cum down from the 210 billion cum in 2003; production was 16.4 billion cum in 2004. Germany is the EU's second largest consumer of natural gas, after the UK, and fourth in the world, most of which is met by imports. Around 35 per cent of gas imports derive from Russia and in January 2006, when a Russian dispute over gas supplies with Ukraine led to a temporary reduction in supplies to Germany, the German government began exploring ways to diversify its imports. In September 2005 Germany signed an agreement with Russia to build a 1,200km gas pipeline underneath the Baltic Sea, which would transport Russian gas between the Russian town of Vyborg to the German town of Greifswald. The project is set to cost US$5billion; German companies control a 49 per cent stake in the pipeline, with the remainder in Russian hands. Work began on the pipeline in December 2005 amid complaints from Poland and the Ukraine that the project is designed to bypass its consumers. Also in December 2005, the former German chancellor Gerhard Schröder accepted a top position with the North European Gas Pipeline Company, the consortium overseeing the Vyborg-Greifswald pipeline. In response, spokespersons for Germany's main opposition parties accused the former chancellor of a conflict of interest.

Coal is Germany's main hydrocarbon resource. In 2004, coal reserves stood at 6.7 billion tonnes and production totalled 54.7 million tonnes oil equivalent (toe). Germany is the biggest coal producer in Europe and seventh in the world. Eastern Germany has huge deposits of lignite as well as significant deposits of anthracite, potassium salts and uranium ore. However, there are relatively few feasibly accessible natural resources other than large supplies of black and brown coal, so Germany is largely dependent on imports.

High extraction costs mean that exploitation of small deposits of iron ore, copper, lead, tin and zinc is limited.

There is pressure to cut high-cost black coal output and jobs in the Ruhr and Saar basins as part of a drive for reduced government subsidies and more competition in energy markets.

In eastern Germany, brown coal production has been scaled back as supplies are used more efficiently in power stations and as efforts are made to curb pollution. Brown coal is regarded as a particularly dirty coal for carbon dioxide emissions and disruption of water levels would extend into The Netherlands.

Energy

There are over 2,800 power plants in Germany, including 19 nuclear reactors which provide nearly 30 per cent of Germany's electricity. Oil typically accounts for around two-fifths of energy consumption, coal for a quarter, natural gas for a fifth and nuclear energy for much of the remainder. Net energy imports account for over half of commercial energy.

Pressure from environmental groups and the Greens led the government in June 2001 to announce the gradual phasing out of nuclear power by 2021. The decision is in line with Germany's developed use of renewable energy. Revenue from an energy tax is used to fund new renewable energy projects. In 2004, renewable energy accounted for 9.8 per cent of total electricity consumption in Germany, mainly from wind power.

Financial markets

Stock exchange

There are eight German stock exchanges – located in Frankfurt, Dusseldorf, Munich, Berlin, Hamburg, Stuttgart, Hanover and Bremen. The Frankfurt Stock Exchange is the dominant trading floor with more than half the volume traded. Combined volume on the eight German exchanges exceeds that of all other European financial centres except London.

Banking and insurance

A sophisticated banking system underpins the country's economic strength.

There are three main categories: central bank; multi-purpose banks, including commercial, co-operative and (publicly owned) regional Landesbanks and savings banks; and specialist banks, including mortgage banks and instalment credit houses.

Many banks have important shareholdings in industrial companies and bankers sit on the supervisory boards of many companies.

In 2003, Josef Ackermann, the chief executive of Germany's main bank Deutsche Bundesbank, was put on trial for corruption. Although initially cleared, a retrial was ordered in December 2005 and Ackermann is facing increasing calls for his resignation.

Central bank

Deutsche Bundesbank; European Central Bank (ECB)

Time

GMT plus one hour (daylight saving, late March to late October, GMT plus two hours)

Geography

The Alps form the southern border with Switzerland and Austria. Germany's southern and eastern borders facing the Czech Republic are also demarcated by mountain ranges. The eastern border with Poland follows the Oder and Neisse rivers. The north is a low, wide coastal plain along the North and Baltic seas, which are separated by Denmark's Jutland peninsula. Germany's western borders join (in an anti-clockwise direction) the Netherlands, Belgium, Luxembourg, France and Switzerland.

Picturesque, forested highlands dominate the central and southern regions. The country is drained by the Danube, Rhine, Elbe, Weser and Oder river systems.

The highest mountain, with an elevation of 2,962 metres, is an alpine peak called Zugspitze, straddling the border with Austria. The main centres of population are concentrated in the west, along the middle and lower Rhine from Karlsruhe, near the French border, and from there northward through the highly industrialised Ruhr conurbation, to the Netherlands border. The German segment of the Rhine is 865km long, all of it navigable. On the south-east side of Europe's continental divide or watershed, the Danube flows eastward from its source in the Black Forest, through 647km of west Germany, to leave the country at the Austrian border at Passau on its way to the Black Sea. There is an important canal system allowing ships to sail from the Oder to the Elbe (to Prague).

Hemisphere

Northern

Climate

Moderate summers and rainy, bleak winters. Most of the country has a typical north-west coastal climate, heavily influenced by moist maritime air masses from the Atlantic. The eastern fringe of the country is sometimes influenced by the continental high pressure centre, making for somewhat colder winters and warmer summers. Prevailing winds are usually from the west.

Dress codes

It is customary to wear a suit and tie in banks, businesses and government offices.

Entry requirements
Passports
Required by all except citizens of Schengen agreement countries who may travel with national ID cards.
Visa
Required by all, except tourist and business visitors from EU, North America, Australasia and most of Europe for up to three months. For confirmation of exceptions and requirements see: www.auswaertiges-amt.de/ the website of the consular section of the German ministry of foreign affairs.
Germany is a member of the Schengen visa accord and all visitors that require a visa must apply to a Germany consulate; when a visa has been issued a visitor may travel to any other Schengen zone without further visas. A Schengen visa application (offered in several languages) can be downloaded from http://europa.eu/abc/travel/ see 'documents you will need'.
Currency advice/regulations
There are no restrictions on the import or export of local or foreign currency.
Customs
Personal items are duty-free. There are no duties levied on alcohol and tobacco between EU member states, providing amounts imported are for personal consumption.

Health (for visitors)
Nationals of the European Economic Area (EEA) countries and Switzerland can access reduced cost and sometimes free medical treatment using a European Health Insurance Card (EHIC) while visiting the EEA. Exceptions include nationals of the 10 countries which joined the EU in 2004 whose EHIC is not valid in Switzerland. Applications for the EHIC should be made before travelling.
Mandatory precautions
Vaccination certificates are not usually required, unless arriving from infected area.
Advisable precautions

Hotels
No official rating system. 10–15 per cent service charge. Advisable to book in advance, especially when trade fairs are being held. All major credit cards accepted.

Public holidays (national)
Fixed dates
1 Jan (New Year's Day), ^6 January (Epiphany), 1 May (Labour Day), ^15 Aug (Assumption Day), 3 Oct (German Unity Day), ^31 Oct (Day of Reformation), ^1 Nov (All Saints' Day), 25 Dec (Christmas Day), 26 Dec (Boxing Day).
Although not official holidays, many shops and businesses are also closed on Christmas Eve and New Year's Eve.
Variable dates
Good Friday, Easter Monday, ^Ascension Day, Whit Monday, ^Corpus Christi (May/Jun)
^ Holiday in certain areas only

Working hours
Banking
Mon–Fri: various hours between 0830–1300, 1400–1600; Thu: 0830–1300, 1400–1730. City centre branches do not close for lunch. Exchange bureaux: 0600–2200.
Business
Mon–Fri: usually 0800–1730.
Government
Mon–Fri: usually 0800–1700.
Shops
Mon–Fri: 0900–2000; Sat: 0900–2000.

Telecommunications
Mobile/cell phones
There are G3, 900 and 1800 services throughout the country.

Electricity supply
220V AC, 50 Hz. European-style round two-pin plugs are in use.

Social customs/useful tips
Handshaking is universal at the beginning and end of every social or business encounter. Germans acknowledge others, even strangers, with a standard greeting when entering or leaving a room, office, shop or railway compartment.
The focal point of German social life is frequently club membership. The thick web of traditional clubs, which are based on activities including pre-Lenten carnival and sports, card playing, animal husbandry and marksmanship, strongly contribute to social life. It is known as Vereinsleben, or club culture.
Germans are extremely aggressive drivers and politeness on the road is not rewarded. There is no speed limit on some parts of the autobahn (motorway network).
Verbal public insults can result in lawsuits. There are also strict laws against racial slurs, especially anti-Semitism.
Do not try to pay bill if invited to a restaurant during business hours. If dining at a German's home, it is considered impolite to arrive late; a gift of flowers is a social 'must'; do not drink until the host has his or her glass. It is regarded as bad manners to keep your hands in your pockets when talking to someone.

Getting there
Air
National airline: Lufthansa
International airport/s: Berlin airports are small and do not receive intercontinental flights, arrivals are via continental or connecting flights. A redeveloped airport accepting intercontinental flights will not be ready before 2011. Frankfurt Airport (FRA), the principal German airport, is 13km south-west of the city, facilities include banks, post office, duty-free shops, restaurants and business suites. Extensive access to the city and other German connections are provided by trains (including international rail links), buses and taxis. Car hire and limousine services are available.
Other airport/s: Bremen (BRE) 4km south of city; Berlin-Tempelhof (THF), Berlin-Tegel (TXL) and Berlin-Schönefeld (SXF). Berlin-Schönefeld, in 2006, began redevelopment to replaced Berlin's three airports with the Berlin-Brandenburg International airport to be completed by 2011; Cologne/Bonn-Konrad Adenauer (CGN) 20km north of Bonn and 14km south-east of Cologne; Düsseldorf (DUS) 8km north of city; Hamburg (HAM) 13km north of city; Hanover (HAJ) 11km from city; Leipzig/Halle (LEJ); Munich (MUC) 11km north-east of city; Nuremberg (NUE) 8km north of city; Stuttgart Echterdingen (STR) 14km south of city.
Airport tax: None.
Surface
Road: There are good quality motorways and main roads linking all surrounding countries.
Water: Ships provide regular passenger services and cruises on the Danube between Regensburg, Vienna, Bratislava and Budapest and from Passau via Austria, Slovakia, Hungary, Serbia, Bulgaria to Romania and the Black Sea.
Main port/s: Bremen, Bremerhaven, Hamburg, Kiel, Rostock, Stralsund, Wilhelmshaven and Wismar.

Getting about
National transport
Air: Frequent services link Berlin, Hanover, Cologne/Bonn, Düsseldorf, Frankfurt, Hamburg, Bremen, Munich, Nuremberg and Stuttgart. Early morning flights provide direct links between many of these centres. Domestic flights are not cheap, but competition is bringing down prices.
Road: There are over 487,000km of roads with a modern network of motorways (autobahnen) linking all cities. Secondary roads in eastern Germany may not be of comparable standard with the west.
Buses: Good nationwide coach services are operated by Deutsche Bahn (DB) and other companies.
Rail: DB runs reliable Intercity Express and Sprinter services, with high-speed trains between major cities which include faster east–west links. First and second class travel is available and it is advisable to book in advance. For long-distance travel, trains can often be a quicker option than flying.

Water: Seaports on the Baltic and North Sea coasts are linked to inland waterways and railways. Navigable inland waterways are used extensively.

City transport

There are buses, trams, metro and electric railway services in many towns.

A Welcome Card entitles travellers to 48 hours of bus and rail travel. It can be bought at hotels or VBB (bus and train) offices. Otherwise, machines dispense tickets permitting three consecutive hours' travel on buses and trains.

Taxis: Good taxi services run in all main cities. In Berlin, the metered cabs are beige Mercedes with yellow taxi signs, available outside hotels or at well-signed ranks.

Car hire

Speed limits: built up areas 50kph, normal roads 100kph, autobahns 'recommended' top speed of 130kph.

Information is available from automobile clubs such as Allgemeiner Deutscher Automobil Club eV (ADAC), Automobil Club von Deutschland eV (AvD) and Deutscher Touring Automobil Club eV.

The wearing of seat belts is compulsory.

BUSINESS DIRECTORY

The addresses listed below are a selection only. While World of Information makes every endeavour to check these addresses, we cannot guarantee that changes have not been made, especially to telephone numbers and area codes. We would welcome any corrections.

Telephone area codes

The international direct dialling (IDD) code for Germany is +49 followed by the area code:

Berlin	30	Hamburg	40
Bonn	228	Hanover	511
Bremen	421	Leipzig	341
Cologne	221	Munich	89
Dortmund	231	Münster	251
Dresden	351	Nuremberg	911
Düsseldorf	211	Potsdam	331
Essen	201	Stuttgart	711
Frankfurt (Main)	69		

Useful telephone numbers

Police: 110

Fire: 112

Chambers of Commerce

American Chamber of Commerce in Germany, 12 Rossmarkt, 60311 Frankfurt am Main (tel: 929-1040; fax: 929-10411; e-mail: info@amcham.de).

Association of German Chambers of Industry and Commerce, 29 Breite Strasse, 10178 Berlin (tel: 203-080; fax: 203-081000; e-mail: dihk@berlin.dihk.de).

Berlin Chamber of Industry and Commerce, 85 Fasanenstrasse, 10623 Berlin (tel: 315-10666; fax: 315-10166; e-mail: service@berlin.ihk.de).

British Chamber of Commerce in Germany, 60 Severinstrasse, 50678 Cologne (tel: 314-458; fax: 315-335; e-mail: info@bccg.de).

Cologne Chamber of Industry and Commerce, Unter Sachsenhausen 10-26, 50667 Cologne, (tel: 164-0551; fax:164-0129; e-mail: my@koeln.ihk.de).

Düsseldorf Chamber of Industry and Commerce, 1 Ernst-Schneider- Platz, 40212 Düsseldorf (tel: 355-70; fax: 355-7401; e-mail: ihkdus@duesseldorf.ihk.de).

Frankfurt am Main Chamber of Industry and Commerce, 4 Börsenplatz, 60313 Frankfurt am Main (tel: 219-70; fax: 219-71424; e-mail: info@frankfurt-main.ihk.de).

Hamburg Chamber of Industry and Commerce, 1 Adolphsplatz, 20457 Hamburg (tel: 361-38138; fax: 361-38401; e-mail: service@hk24.de).

Hanover Chamber of Industry and Commerce, 49 Schiffgraben, 30175 Hanover (tel: 31-070; fax: 310-7333; e-mail: schrage@hannover.ihk.de).

Munich Chamber of Industry and Commerce, 2 Max Joseph Strasse, 80333 Munich (tel: 511-6368; fax: 511-6290; e-mail: alberts@muenchen.ihk.de).

Stuttgart Chamber of Industry and Commerce, 30 Jägerstrasse, 70174 Stuttgart (tel: 200-50; fax: 200-5354; e-mail: info@stuttgart.ihk.de).

Banking

Bayerische Landesbank, 18 Briennerstrasse, 80333 Munich (tel: 217-101; fax: 217-123579; e-mail: info@bayernlb.de).

Bremer Landesbank, 26 Domshof, 28195 Bremen (tel: 332-0; fax: 332-2322; e-mail: kontakt@bremerlandesbank.de).

Commerzbank, Kaiserplatz, 60261 Frankfurt am Main (tel: 136-20; fax: 285-389; e-mail: info@commerxbank.com).

Deutsche Bank, 12 Taunuslage, 60262 Frankfurt am Main (tel: 910-00; fax: 910-34225; e-mail: deutsche.bank@db.com).

Dresdner Bank, 1 Jürgen Ponto Platz, 60301 Frankfurt am Main (tel: 263-0; fax: 263-4831; e-mail: dresdner-bank@dresdner-bank.com).

DZ Bank, Platz der Republik, 60265 Frankfurt am Main (tel: 744-701; fax: 744-71685; e-mail: mail@dzbank.de).

Hamburgische Landesbank, 50 Gerhart Hauptmann Platz, 20095 Hamburg (tel: 333-30; fax: 333-32707; e-mail: info@hamburglb,de).

Hypovereinsbank, 16 Am Tucherpark, 80538 Munich (tel: 378-0; e-mail: info@hypovereinsbank.de).

Landesbank Baden-Württemberg, 2 Am Hauptbahnhof, 70173 Stuttgart (tel: 127-0; fax: 127-3278; e-mail: kontakt@lbbw.de).

Landesbank Berlin, 171 Bundesallee, 10889 Berlin (tel: 869-801; fax: 869-83074; e-mail: information@lbb.de).

Landesbank Hessen-Thuringen, 52-58 Neue Mainzer Strasse, 60311 Frankfurt am Main (tel: 913-201; fax: 291-517; e-mail: presse@helaba.de).

Landesbank Rheinland-Pfalz, 54-56 Grosse Bleiche, 55116 Mainz (tel: 113-01; fax: 113-2724; e-mail: lrp@lrp.de).

Landesbank Saar, 2 Ursulinenstrasse, 66111 Saarbrücken (tel: 383-01; fax: 383-1200; e-mail: service@saarlb.de).

Landesbank Schleswig-Holstein, 6 Martinsdamm, 24103 Kiel (tel: 900-01; fax: 900-2446; e-mail: info@lb-kiel.de).

Norddeutsche Landesbank, 10 Friedrichwall, 30159 Hannover (tel: 361-0; fax: 361-2502; e-mail: info@nordlb.de).

Westdeutsche Landesbank, 15 Herzogstrasse, 40217 Düsseldorf (tel: 826-2449; fax: 826-9683; e-mail: presse@westlb.de).

Central bank

Deutsche Bundesbank, Wilhelm Epstein Strasse 14, 60431 Frankfurt am Main (tel: 9566-3511; fax: 9566-4679; email: presse-information@bundesbank.de).

European Central Bank (ECB), Kaiserstrasse 29, 60311 Frankfurt am Main (tel: 13-440; fax: 1344-6000; email: info@ecb.int).

Travel information

Allgemeiner Deutscher Automobil Club (ADAC), 8 Am Westpark, 81373 Munich (tel: 767-60; fax: 767-62500; e-mail: adac@adac.de).

Automobil Club von Deutschland (AvD), 16 Lyoner Strasse 60528 Frankfurt am Main (tel: 660-60; fax: 660-6789; e-mail: avd@avd.de).

Deutsche Bahn (railway operator), 2 Potsdamer Platz, 10785 Berlin (tel: 297-0; fax: 297-1961; e-mail: info@bahn.de; internet site: http://www.bahn.de/index_e.html).

Lufthansa, 2-6 Von Gablenz Strasse, 50679 Cologne (tel: 696-0; fax: 696-3002; internet site: http://www.lufthansa.co.uk).

National tourist organisation offices
Deutsche Zentrale für Tourismus, Beethovenstrasse 69, 60325 Frankfurt am Main (tel: 757-20; fax: 751-903; e-mail: info@d-z-t.com).

Ministries
Office of the Federal Chancellor, 1 Schlossplatz, 10178 Berlin (tel: 400-0; fax: 400-01818; e-mail: internetpost@bundeskanzler.de).

Ministry of Consumer Protection, Food and Agriculture, Rochusstrasse 1, 53123 Bonn (tel: 529-05291; fax: 529-4262; e-mail: internet@bmvel.bund.de).

Ministry of Defence, 18 Stauffenbergstrasse, 10785 Berlin (tel: 200-400; fax: 200-48333; e-mail: poststelle@bmvg.bund.400.de).

Ministry of Economic Co-operation and Development, 40 Friedrich Ebert Allee, 53113 Bonn (tel: 535-0; fax: 535-3500; e-mail: poststelle@bmz.bund.de).

Ministry of Economy and Labour, 36 Scharnhorststrasse, 10115 Berlin (tel: 615-0; fax: 615-7010; e-mail: info@bmwa.bund.de).

Ministry of Education and Research, 2 Heinemannstrasse, 53175 Bonn-Bad Godesberg (tel: 57-0; fax: 573-601; e-mail:bmbf@bmbf.bund.de).

Ministry of the Environment, Nature Conservation and Nuclear Safety, 6 Alexanderplatz, 10178 Berlin (tel: 305-0; fax: 305-4375; e-mail: service@bmu.de).

Ministry of Families, Senior Citizens, Women and Youth, 42 Taubenstrasse, 10117 Berlin (tel: 206-550; fax: 206-551145; e-mail: poststelle@bmfsfj.bund.de).

Ministry of Finance, 97 Wilhelmstrasse, 10117 Berlin (tel: 682-0; fax: 682-4420; e-mail: poststelle@bmf.bund.de).

Ministry of Foreign Affairs, 1 Werderscher Markt, 10117 Berlin (tel: 500-000; fax: 500-3402; e-mail: poststelle@auswaertiges-amt.de).

Ministry of Health, 78a Am Propsthof, 53121 Bonn (tel: 941-0; fax: 941-4900; e-mail: info@bmg.bund.de).

Ministry of the Interior, 101 Alt-Moabit, 10559 Berlin (tel: 681-0; fax: 681-2926; e-mail: poststelle@bmi.bund.de).

Ministry of Justice, 37 Mohrenstrasse, 10117 Berlin (tel: 202-570; fax: 259-525; e-mail: poststelle@bmj.bund.de).

Ministry of Transport, Construction and Housing, 44 Invalidenstrasse, 10115 Berlin (tel: 200-80; fax: 200-81920; e-mail: buergerinfo@bmvbw.bund.de).

Deutsche Bundestag, Platz der Republik 1, 11011 Berlin (tel.: 227-0; fax: 2273-6878 or 2273-6979; internet: www.bundestag.de).

Other useful addresses
American Embassy, 4-5 Neustädtische Kirchstrasse , 10117 Berlin (tel: 830-50; fax: 238-6290).

Aussenhandelsvereinigung des Deutschen Einzelhandels (Ave) (foreign trade association of the German retail trade), 1 Mauritiussteinweg, 50676 Cologne 1 (tel: 921-8340; fax: 921-8346; e-mail: info@ave-koeln.de).

Ausstellungs-und Messe-Ausschuss der Deutschen Wirtschaft (Auma) (trade fair industry association), 9 Littenstrasse, 10179 Berlin (tel: 240-000; fax: 240-00263; e-mail: info@auma.de).

British Embassy, 70-71 Wilhelmstrasse, 10117 Berlin (tel: 201-840; fax: 201-84123; e-mail: info@britischebotschaft.de).

Bundesagentur für Aussenwirtschaft (bfai) (German Office for Foreign Trade), 87-93 Agrippastrasse, 50676 Cologne (tel: 205-70; fax: 205-7212; e-mail: info@bfai.de).

Bundesanstalt für Arbeit (federal labour office), 106 Regensburger Strasse, 90478 Nuremberg (tel: 179-0; fax: 179-3600; e-mail: zentralamt@arbeitsamt.de).

Bundesverband der Deutschen Industrie (Bdi) (industry federation), Haus der Deutschen Wirtschaft, 29 Breite Strasse, 10178 Berlin (tel: 202-80; fax: 202-82450; e-mail: info@bdi-online.de).

Bundesverband des Deutschen Gross-und Aussenhandels (wholesale and foreign trade federation), Haus des Handels, 1A Am Weidendamm, 10117 Berlin (tel: 590-09950; fax: 590-099519; e-mail: info@bga.de).

Bundesvereinigung der Deutschen Arbeitgeberverbände (BDA) (employers' associations federation), Haus der Deutschen Wirtschaft, 29 Breite Strasse, 10178 Berlin (tel: 203-30; fax: 203-31055; e-mail: info@bda-online.de).

Büro des Beauftragten für Auslandsinvestitionen in Deutschland (foreign investment in Germany), 34 Markgrafenstrasse, 10117 Berlin (tel: 206-570; fax: 206-57111; e-mail: office@fdin.de).

Deutscher Gewerkschaftsbund (DGB) (trades unions federation), 2 Henrietta Herz Platz , 10178 Berlin (tel: 240-600; fax: 240-60324; e-mail: info@bundesvorstand.dgb.de).

Deutsches Institut für Wirtschaftsforschung (DIW) (economic research institute), 5 Königin Luise Strasse, 14195 Berlin (tel: 879-890; fax: 897-89200; e-mail: postmaster@diw.de).

Deutsche Presse-Agentur (dpa) (news agency), 38 Mittelweg, 20148 Hamburg (tel: 411-30; fax: 411-32219; e-mail: info@hbg.dpa.de).

German Convention Bureau, 48 Münchener Strasse, 60329 Frankfurt am Main (tel: 242-9300; fax: 242-93026; e-mail: info@gcb.de).

German Embassy (US), 4645 Reservoir Road, NW, Washington DC 20007 (tel: (+1-202) 298-4000; fax: (+1-202) 298-4249; e-mail: ge-embus@ix.netcom.com).

Industrial Investment Council (IIC), 57 Charlottenstrasse, 10117 Berlin (tel: 209-45660; fax: 209-45666; e-mail: info@iic.de).

Presse- und Informationsamt der Bundesregierung (government press office), 84 Dorotheenstrasse, 10117 Berlin (tel: 272-0; fax: 272-1365; e-mail: InternetPost@bundesregierung).

Statisches Bundesamt (federal statistical office), 11 Gustav Stresemann Ring, 65189 Wiesbaden (tel: 752-405; fax: 724-000; e-mail: pressestelle@stba.bund400.de; internet site: www.statistik-bund.de/e_home.htm).

Wirtschaftsförderung Berlin (Berlin Business Development Corpration), Ludwig Erhard Haus, 85 Fasanenstrasse, 10623 Berlin (tel: 399-800; fax: 399-80239; e-mail: info@wf-berlin.de).

Zentralverband der Deutschen Werbewirtschaft (ZAW) (advertising industry federation), 17 Villichgasse, 53177 Bonn (tel: 820-920; fax: 357-583; e-mail: zaw@zaw.de).

National news agency: DPA (Deutsche Presse-Agentur)

Other news agencies: Pressetext Deutschland (business news):www.pressetext.de

Internet sites
Gateway site to web directory (in German with translation facilities): www.dino-online.de/

German-British Chamber of Commerce: www.germanbritishchamber.co.uk

German Government Website: www.bundesregierung.de

Germany Business Finder: www.infospace.com/uk.telegr/intldb/bizfindint.htm?QO=DE

Germany Technical Corporation: www.gtz.de/home/english/index.html

Tourist Board: www.germany-tourism.de

Ghana

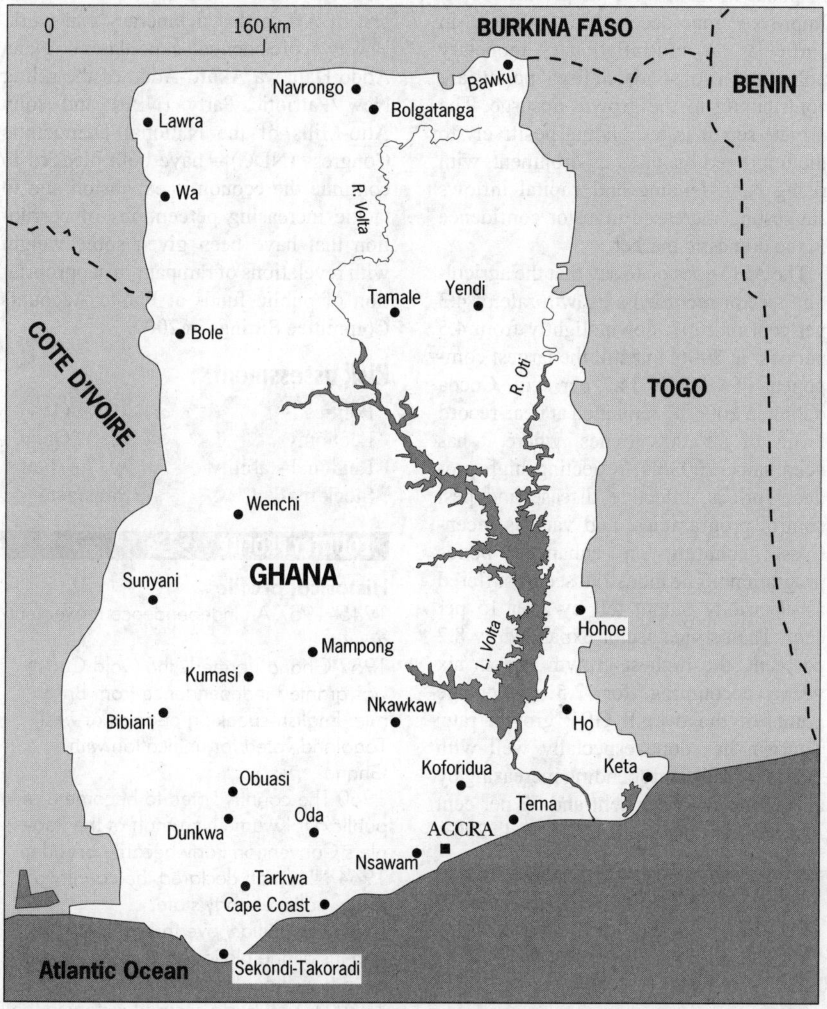

In 1966 its first president and pan-African hero, Kwame Nkrumah, was deposed in a coup, heralding years of mostly-military rule. A series of coups resulted in the suspension of the constitution in 1981 and a ban on political parties. In 1981 Flight Lieutenant Jerry Rawlings staged a second and successful coup and the country began to move towards economic stability and democracy.

A new constitution, restoring multi- party politics, was approved in 1992 when Rawlings won presidential elections. He won again in 1996, but was constitutionally prevented from running for a third term. John Kufuor defeated former vice president Atta Mills in the presidential ballot in December 2000, in a free and fair election, marking the first peaceful, democratic transfer of power in Ghana since independence.

President John Kufuor won a second term in December 2004, in a presidential poll internationally praised for being well-run and orderly. He is known as the 'Gentle Giant'. He has made economic growth a priority. During his first term, inflation and borrowing costs fell. He has also taken a leading role in mediating in regional conflicts, including those in Liberia and Côte d'Ivoire.

Natural resources

Ghana is well-endowed with natural resources: gold, timber, industrial

KEY FACTS

Official name: Republic of Ghana

Head of State: President John Agyekum Kufuor (INPP) (since 7 Jan 2001)

Head of government: President John Agyekum Kufuor

Ruling party: New Patriotic Party (NPP) (since Dec 2000)

Area: 239,460 square km

Population: 21.97 million (2007)

Capital: Accra

Official language: English

Currency: Cedi (GH¢) = 100 pesewas (re-denominated 3 July 2007)

Exchange rate: GH¢1.12 per US$ (Jul 2008) (re-denominated 3 July 2007; 4 zeros removed)

GDP per capita: US$676 (2007)*

GDP real growth: 6.40% (2007)*

Labour force: 10.60 million (2004)

Unemployment: 10.20% (2004)

Inflation: 9.60% (2007)

Balance of trade: -US$3.58 billion (2006)

Foreign debt: US$7.40 billion (2004)

Visitor numbers: 442,000 (2006)*

* estimated figure

diamonds, bauxite, manganese, fish, rubber, hydropower, petroleum, silver, salt and limestone; but even so, Ghana remains heavily dependent on international financial and technical assistance. Gold, timber, and cocoa production are major sources of foreign exchange. The domestic economy continues to revolve around subsistence agriculture, which accounts for 34 per cent of GDP and employs 60 per cent of the work force, mainly small landholders.

Will Ghana dodge the oil curse?

Oil is coming to Ghana. The Jubilee field off the coast south west of the port of Takoradi should start flowing in 2010. The operator, Anglo-Irish Tullow Oil, aims to start pumping some 120,000 barrels per day (bpd) by then, and to double output a few years later. But the question is, can Ghana avoid the corrosive effects of oil seen elsewhere in Africa? Nigeria went from a moderately prosperous country on the back of agricultural exports, to a hugely rich oil producer, to one of the most corrupt countries in the world with a poverty index not much better than Sierra Leone.

Ghana has had its fair share of coups and counter coups as well as economic woes. But since Jerry Rawlings was the first elected president to step down after his maximum two terms in office in 2000, and to be succeeded by another democratically elected president, John Kufuor, Ghana has steadily improved its economy. Kufuor is scheduled to relinquish the presidency after his two terms when elections are held in December 2008.

Economy

The African Development Bank's 2008 edition of *African Economic Outlook* (AEO) says that Ghana has exhibited a changed economic outlook, with improving growth reflecting both strong economic fundamentals and a positive response to them from the private sector. Improved macroeconomic policies, in particular an anti-inflationary monetary policy and a consolidated fiscal policy, are contributing to the growth upsurge. The private sector is responding positively to the improved business environment, with rising bank lending and capital inflows suggesting increased investor confidence in the domestic market.

The AEO goes on to say that the agricultural sector recorded a growth rate of 4.3 per cent in 2007, down slightly from 4.5 per cent in 2006, but still the largest component of GDP at 34.7 per cent. Cocoa output in 2006/07 remained at near-record levels of 600,000 tonnes, where it has been since 2003/04, reflecting high producer prices, effective disease and pest control programmes, and various incentives, including an enhanced bonus programme. The industrial sector suffered as electricity output fell by over 15 per cent. The service sector expanded by 8.2 per cent, the highest growth rate in six years, accounting for 2.5 percentage points of the overall GDP growth rate. Tourism has done especially well with visitor arrivals and spending increasing by an estimated 49 per cent and 72 per cent respectively between 2000 and 2007. There was also a sharp increase in both public and private investment.

KEY INDICATORS — Ghana

	Unit	2003	2004	2005	2006	2007
Population	m	20.25	20.35	20.89	21.42	*21.97
Gross domestic product (GDP)	US$bn	7.70	8.62	10.72	12.89	*14.86
GDP per capita	US$	384	434	513	593	*676
GDP real growth	%	4.7	5.5	5.9	6.2	*6.4
Inflation	%	27.7	12.6	15.1	10.9	9.6
Industrial output	% change	–	5.1	6.7	8.6	–
Agricultural output	% change	–	7.5	6.1	5.5	–
Exports (fob) (goods)	US$m	3,015.0	2,784.6	2,802.2	3,685.0	–
Imports (cif) (goods)	US$m	4,469.0	4,297.3	5,345.4	7,264.0	–
Balance of trade	US$m	-1,454.0	-1,512.6	-2,543.1	-3,579.0	–
Current account	US$m	130.0	110.0	-751.0	-1,381.0	-1,896.0
Total reserves minus gold	US$m	1,352.8	1,626.7	1,752.9	2,090.3	–
Foreign exchange	US$m	1,306.0	1,605.9	1,751.8	2,089.1	–
Exchange rate	per US$	8,625.00	8,930.04	9,242.50	0.92	0.95

* estimated figure

Outlook

Ghana celebrated its 50th anniversary of independence in 2007 against a background of deepening democracy and improving governance. The December 2008 elections will be crucial in showing the rest of Africa that democracy can work. The two presidential candidates – Nana Addo Dankwa Akufo-Addo of the ruling New Patriotic Party (NPP) and John Atto-Mills of the National Democratic Congress (NDC) – have both pledged to continue the economic expansion and to tackle increasing perceptions of corruption that have been given some weight with revelations of rampant misappropriation of public funds at Public Accounts Committee Sittings in 2007.

Risk assessment

Politics	Good
Economy	Good
Regional stability	Fair
Stock market	Satisfactory

COUNTRY PROFILE

Historical profile

1945–1957 An independence movement grew.

1957 Ghana (formerly the Gold Coast) was granted independence from British rule. English-speaking peoples of west Togoland voted for unification with Ghana.

1960 The country voted to become a republic. Dr Kwame Nkrumah of the People's Convention Party became president.

1964 Nkrumah declared the country a single political party state.

1966 The military overthrew Nkrumah and install the National Liberation Council, a transitional government.

1969 Dr Kofi Busia secured victory in the parliamentary elections and became prime minister.

1972 After another military coup, Col Ignatius Acheampong took control of the country.

1978 Acheampong was deposed by the military and Lt-Gen F Akuffo, previously chief of the defence staff, became president.

1979 Akuffo's government was destabled in an unsuccessful coup launched by Flt-Lt Jerry J Rawlings. Dr Hilla Limann of the People's National Party (PNP) was later elected as president. A new constitution was promulgated.

1981 Jerry J Rawlings took power through a second military coup, disolved parliament and ruled through the Provisional National Defence Council (PNDC) .

1983–89 Discontent with the regime and its economic ineffectiveness led to a series of attempted coups, student unrest and alleged anti-government conspiracies. The government attempted to impose fiscal and monetary discipline and bring the economy into alignment with market trends and influences resulting in the cedi being devalued by 6,300 per cent in 1987. Over 1.1 million Ghanaians were expelled from Nigeria and returned home, placing great strain on limited resources.
1990 A national referendum on the restoration of multi-party politics was demanded.
1992 A referendum endorsed a new constitution to allow a multi-party system. Jerry Rawlings was elected president and his National Democratic Congress (NDC) secured an overall majority in legislative elections.
1993 The constitution entered into force and the Fourth Republic was inaugurated.
1996 Jerry Rawlings won the presidential election and his party, the NDC, won the legislative elections.
2000 John Kufuor won the presidential elections and his party, the New Patriotic Party (NPP), became the largest party in parliament. He became the first elected president in Ghana's history to succeed another elected president.
2002 The ruling NPP won a by-election in the northern constituency of Bimbilla, giving it a majority in parliament. Ethnic battles in the north led to the murder of Ghana's second most important tribal king, Ya Naa Yakubu Andani of the Dagbon people. His death led to the resignation of two senior government ministers.
2004 The former president, Jerry Rawlings, testified before the National Reconciliation Commission investigating human rights offences during the early years of his rule. Incumbent John Kufuor (NPP) was re-elected president and the ruling NPP won the parliamentary elections.
2005 The first fall in HIV/Aids infection rates in five years was reported.
2006 A proposal to amend legislation to enable Ghanaians living abroad to vote in elections was the occasion for a large, peaceful demonstration in Accra. The presidential jet acquired during the Rawling presidency was sold. China promised a US$66 million loan to Ghana for development projects.
2007 The cedi was re-denominated on 3 July, when four zeros were removed and the new banknote began to be referred to as the Ghana Cedi. In July and August it was announced that 'substantial oil deposits' were found in territorial waters.
2008 Tribal violence between the Kusasi and Mamprusi people led to the deaths of 13 people in Bawku in June. A heavy military presence and a curfew was need to bring peace, while the president called for talks over a contested chieftaincy to be resolved.

Political structure

Constitution
The constitution came into force on 7 January 1993. It is based on the US model. It allows for a multi-party system.
Ghana has 10 administrative regions which are subdivided into districts.

Form of state
Unitary republic

The executive
Executive power is vested in the president, vice president and Council of Ministers; both the vice president and the Council of Ministers are appointed by the president.
The president is elected by universal suffrage for a maximum of two four-year terms.
If no candidate receives more than 50 per cent of votes in the presidential election, a new election between the two candidates with the highest number of votes is to take place within 21 days.

National legislature
Legislative power is held by a 200 member unicameral parliament, which is elected every four years by direct adult suffrage.

Legal system
The legal system is based on English common law and local customary law.

Last elections
7 December 2004 (presidential and parliamentary)
Results: Parliamentary: The NPP won 129 seats out of 230; the NDC won 94.
Presidential: John Agyekum Kufuor (NPP) was re-elected with 52.5 per cent of the vote; John Evans Atta Mills (NDC) won 44.6 per cent.

Next elections
7 Dec 2008 (parliamentary and presidential)

Political parties

Ruling party
New Patriotic Party (NPP) (since Dec 2000)

Main opposition party
National Democratic Congress (NDC)

Population
21.97 million (2007)
Last census: March 2000: 18,912,079
Population density: 79 inhabitants per square km. Urban population: 36 per cent (1995—2001).
Annual growth rate: 2.3 per cent 1994–2004 (WHO 2006)

Ethnic make-up
Akan (including Ashanti) (44 per cent), Dagomba (16 per cent), Ewe (13 per cent), Ga-Adangbe (8.3 per cent), Guan (3.7 per cent), Gurma (3.5 per cent).

Religions
Christian (43 per cent), traditional religions (38 per cent), Muslim (12 per cent). There is complete freedom of worship in Ghana.

Education
Since the government removed school fees for primary education in 2005, record numbers of children have been enrolled. Over 600,000 more children of ages 5–13 were enrolled, with girls being the greater proportion of new students. The World Bank is due to give a grant of US$11 million in 2006, to provide more teachers, build new classrooms and purchase textbooks, in recognition for the government's efforts in achieving an objective of the UN Millennium Development Goals in education.
Government expenditure on education is about a quarter of total government spending.
Ghana boasts the oldest university in sub-Saharan Africa – at Legon in Accra.
Literacy rate: 74 per cent adult rate; 92 per cent youth rate (15–24) (Unesco 2005).
Enrolment rate: 69 per cent primary enrollment (2005–06 academic year, up from 59 per cent in 2004–05) (2006).
Pupils per teacher: 33 in primary schools.

Health
Per capita total expenditure on health (2003) was US$98; of which per capita government spending was US$31, at the international dollar rate, (WHO 2006).
In August 2004 the government imposed a 2.5 per cent levy on top of a 12.5 per cent VAT to be used in a National Health Insurance.

HIV/Aids
The fragile infection rate trend was down from 3.6 per cent in 2003 to 3.1 in 2004. Officials will not laud the result as a victory until the trend shows a three-year steady decline. In the meantime infection rates of other sexually transmitter deseases (STD) are showing a rise among young people indicating unprotected sex. Authorities are planning to switch emphasis A survey in 2003 indicated there were over 350,000 people living with HIV (UNAIDS).
HIV prevalence: 3.1 per cent aged 15–49 in 2004. Prevalence in the north is lower averaging 1.8 per cent, while in the south it is 6.5 per cent (government figures).
Life expectancy: 57 years, 2004 (WHO 2006)
Fertility rate/Maternal mortality rate: 4.2 births per woman, 2004 (WHO 2006)

Child (under 5 years) mortality rate (per 1,000): 59 per 1,000 live births; 25 per cent of children aged under five are malnourished (World Bank).
Head of population per physician: 0.15 physicians per 1,000 people, 2004 (WHO 2006)

Welfare
The government's policies of structural adjustment have hit urban Ghanaians hard as the contraction of industry and the removal of state subsidies have led to increased unemployment, crime and poverty. In a bid to dampen the impact of reform, the government adopted a US$100 million Programme of Action to Mitigate the Social Costs of Adjustment (Pamscad) in the late 1990s to help cushion the shock of redundancies or redeployment as a result of the ERP. It involves 23 projects under five main categories: community initiatives, employment (including food-for-work schemes), redeployment (compensation for those made redundant), basic needs (self-help schemes) and education. Medium-term strategies are centred on the provision of primary health care.

Main cities
Accra (capital, estimated population 1.6 million in 2004), Kumasi (649,652), Tamale (278,676) Tema (209,250), Ashiaman (170,143), Obuasi (163,349), Teshi (109,927), Bolgatanga (93,100).

Languages spoken
There are over 25 major languages with numerous dialects. The principal languages spoken are Twi and Fante (spoken by the Akans), Ga, Hausa, Dagbani, Ewe and Nzema.
There is an official policy to encourage Ghanaians to be multilingual so French is also taught in most schools.
Official language/s
English

Media
Press freedom is respected and Ghana has a reputation as 'one of the most unfettered' in Africa. A government appointed commission regulates all media.
National news agency: Ghana News Agency
Press
Dailies: There are many newspapers on offer, all chasing a constricted advertising market hampered by government advertising being limited to state-owned publications and other advertisers tending to do business with only the larger publications. In English, the Daily Graphic (www.graphicghana.com) and Ghanaian Times (www.newtimesonline.com) are state-owned; the Daily Guide (http://dailyguideghana.com) is a tabloid, the conservative publication The Statesman (www.thestatesmanonline.com) is one of the oldest (although with a broken record) newspapers with a full range of articles, and the Accra Daily Mail (http://news.accra-mail.com).
Weeklies: In English, independent publications include the The Ghanaian Chronicle (www.ghanaian-chronicle.com), Ghana Palaver (www.ghana-palaver.com), with news and current affairs, Public Agenda (www.ghanaweb.com/public_agenda) is published twice weekly with social stories and The Spectator (http://spectator.newtimesonline.com) is a weekend edition of entertainment news. The Mirror is state-owned.
Business: In English, the Business and Financial Times (http://bftghanaonline.com), provides comprehensive information. Major newspapers have sections on business and finance.
Periodicals: In English, The Heritage (www.theheritagenews.com) is a month political review and the Christian Messenger is a conservative Presbyterian monthly. The Ghana Review International (http://ghanareview.com) is a foreign publication of national news.
Broadcasting
The state-run Ghana Broadcasting Corporation (GBC) is the national public operator.
Radio: GBC Radio (www.gbcghana.com) has a network of three stations with radio service in English, Hausa and other African languages and an external radio service in English, French and Hausa. Private, commercial stations include Vibe FM (www.vibefm.com.gh) Citi FM (www.citifmonline.com), Solid FM (www.mysolidonline.com) and Space FM (www.spacefmradio.com).
Television: GBC operates Ghana TV (GTV) (www.gbcghana.com), which produces 80 per cent of locally made programmes. There are several private TV stations including TV3 (www.tv3.com.gh), Crystal TV and Media TV.
News agencies
National news agency: Ghana News Agency

Economy
Agriculture is the leading economic activity and the main driver of economic growth. Cocoa, the principal crop, accounts for around 40 per cent of exports. Ghana is the world's second-largest producer of cocoa after Côte d'Ivoire. A sequence of very good years has recently resulted in record harvests, which have benefited from high prices. Other crops include oil palm, millet, sorghum and cassava. Timber exports are important, while gold mining has regained its role in the economy and become a major export in competition with cocoa. The tourism sector is expanding.
Ghana opted for debt relief under the Heavily Indebted Poor Country (HIPC) programme in 2002 and adopted a programme to tighten fiscal policies, speed up privatisation of state entities and improve social services. Since then, the economy has shown steady growth and in July 2005 the IMF and the World Bank announced US$3.5 billion in debt service relief, to run until 2020. Ghana has achieved a stable macroeconomic environment. GDP grew by 6.2 per cent in 2006, up from 5.5 per cent in 2005. Inflation, which exceeded 30 per cent in 2001, has fallen, and, despite the effects of oil price rises in 2005, was reduced to around 10 per cent in 2006.
The government deregulated domestic fuel prices and eliminated subsidies in 2004, allowing the market to find its level, while removing a drain on government expenditure. Consumer confidence has grown since 2003 and retail spending has risen accordingly, with new service industries opening.
A financial sector strategic plan, introduced in 2003, set out a blueprint for reform, particularly in regulatory and judicial restructuring, allowing for private property rights protection and competition. Further plans for the economy include the continued sale of parastatal enterprises, the removal of virtually all import restrictions and the elimination of exchange rate controls.
Ghana is seen as a safe alternative by shipping traffic to the Côte d'Ivoire, which, since 2003, has been suffering internal strife. This increased Ghana's importance as a trading hub and foreign investors became interested in developing Ghana's ports and improving trade relations. Ghana needs to improve roads and port efficiency before it can take full advantage of the situation.

External trade
Ghana is a member of the Economic Community of Western African States (Ecowas), which was set up to promote economic integration among members. It is a member of the Anglophone, West African Monetary Zone (WAMZ), which is due to introduce a common currency. WAMZ will eventually be merged with the Francophone-members' currency to produce a single currency (the eco) for the region.
Imports
Principal imports are manufacturing equipment, petroleum and foodstuffs.
Main sources: Nigeria (9.6 per cent total, 2006), China (9.5 per cent), UK (8.9 per cent).

Exports
Principal exports are gold (typically 40 per cent of total), cocoa timber, tuna, bauxite, aluminium, manganese ore and diamonds.
Main destinations: South Africa (25.8 per cent, 2006), Burkina Faso (12.6 per cent), The Netherlands (11.1 per cent).

Agriculture

Farming
Agricultural land – around 14,600 hectares (ha) – accounts for almost 65 per cent of the total land area. There is over 6330ha of arable and permanently cultivated land and around 8350ha of pastureland.
Ghana is a leading cocoa producer in the world, providing 19 per cent of the total. Cocoa still has major importance to the economy providing around 60 per cent of export earnings. Government monopoly on cocoa sales was removed in 1993; private trading companies purchase directly from farms. Since 2002 investment in cocoa production has expanded taking advantage of rising world prices. In 2005–06 production was hit by the spread of swollen shoot virus, a disease that de-foliates and eventually kills cocoa trees.
Other cash crops for export include bananas, kola nuts, limes, coffee, copra and palm kernels.
Crops grown for the local agribusiness include rubber, sugar, cotton, and oil palms.
Subsistence farming of food crops (cassava, plantains, rice, maize, sorghum, millet, yams) has been affected by prolonged drought and shortages of fertilisers, but there has been a recovery, particularly in maize and rice production.
Estimated crop production for 2005 included: 1,942,546 tonnes (t) cereals in total, 1,070,000t oil palm fruit, 1,157,621t maize, 9,738,812t cassava, 399,300t sorghum, 143,798t millet, 241,807t rice, 2,380,858t plantains, 330,000t citrus fruit, 306,220t oilcrops, 736,000t cocoa beans, 8,500t treenuts, 389,649t groundnuts (in shells),1,800t green coffee, 3,892,259t yams, 1,800,000t taro, 2,833,908t fruit in total, 642,450t vegetables in total. Livestock production included: 177,450t meat in total, 25,375t beef, 10,248t pig meat, 11,079t lamb, 11,986t goat meat, 57,000t game meat, 28,763t poultry, 25,175t eggs, 36,010t milk, 2,944t cattle hides, 1,329t sheepskins.

Fishing
The annual domestic fish catch averages 300,000 tonnes, satisfying over 75 per cent of domestic demand. Fish farms have been set up in the north in an effort to achieve total fish self-sufficiency.
Tuna is one of Ghana's non-traditional exports, but the maximum sustainable yield from the 28,000 square km territorial waters is far from being realised.
In 2004, the total marine fish catch was 313,935 tonnes and the total crustacean catch was 1,307 tonnes.

Forestry
Ghana has around 39 per cent of forest cover in addition to 37 per cent of woodland. There are over 200 species of tropical hardwood.
Most commercial forestry is concentrated in the south. The extent of productive forest reserves is put at 1.2 million hectares, containing 190 million cubic metres of potential wood volume in trees over 30cm in diameter. Timber is Ghana's third-largest export commodity. The current export level of commercially viable species and sizes (trees with diameters of 70cm or more) can only be maintained if reliance on popular hardwoods is lessened and exploitation of lesser known species is increased. Domestic demand for wood for fuel is far greater than the permissible cut of one million cubic metres.
The National Forests Protection Strategy resulted in decreasing deforestation during the 1990s. The strategy plans to make the private sector responsible for the costs of forest depletion. The Environmental Protection Agency (EPA) monitors developments and policy affecting wildlife, forests and mining activities.
A local non-government body is developing a bamboo and rattan industry instead of available timber. The project plans to develop 20,000ha of bamboo by 2007.
Timber imports in 2004 were US$69.6 million, while exports amounted to US$175.2 million.
Timber production in 2004 included 22,028,000 cubic metre (cum) roundwood, 480,000cum sawnwood, 1,350,000cum sawlogs and veneer logs, 435,000cum wood-based panels, 20,678,000cum wood fuel, 752,000t charcoal.

Industry and manufacturing

The industrial sector accounts for approximately 27.2 per cent of annual GDP and accounted for 23.4 per cent of the country's growth achieved in 2004. Services are the second largest sector in the country and accounted for 32.4 per cent of the economy and was responsible for 25.9 per cent of overall growth in 2004. Manufacturing only contributes 9.0 per cent to GDP, electricity, gas and water 2.6 per cent and construction 8.5 per cent.
The privatisation and commercialisation of Ghana's public sector since the mid-1990s led to a severe contraction in manufacturing as jobs were shed, firms liquidated and the economy flooded by cheap imports. Officials believe foreign investment offers the key to the development of the sector.
Ghana's medium-sized manufacturing industries include aluminium smelting, paper and cement manufacturing and petroleum refining. The aluminium smelter at Tema, the Volta Aluminium Company (Valco), is the country's most capital-intensive enterprise. Potential production capacity is 200,000 tonnes, but only a fraction of this has been produced in recent years.
The government is seeking to expand important agri-based industries and textile manufacturing. It is also encouraging the establishment of more industries geared to processing local raw materials to replace imported inputs.

Tourism
Tourism has developed into a major foreign currency earner and the sector is one of the fastest-growing in Africa. It accounted for 4.8 per cent of GDP in 2004 and is forecast to contribute 5.4 per cent to GDP in 2005.
An ambitious 15-year development plan, exploiting tourism as a means of improving the economy, aims to increase arrivals to one million by 2010. If this target is to be achieved, more needs to be done to improve infrastructure and travel connections. Eco-tourism sites are being developed for European and the US markets, other amenities will cater for conventions, adventure holidays and the historical slave trade heritage sites.

Mining

Mining typically accounts for 18 per cent of GDP and employs 3 per cent of the workforce. Minerals resources include gold, manganese, diamonds, bauxite, iron ore, limestone, silica, columbite, tantalite and several rich clays.
Gold is the principal mineral export and Ghana is Africa's second-largest gold producer, after South Africa. Ashanti Goldfields Corporation (AGC) accounts for 85 per cent of total output. The other major producer is the State Gold Mines Corporation. Recoverable gold reserves are estimated at 57,000 tonnes. AGC has invested US$200 million in two new mines, while Newmont (the largest mining company globally) was given the go-ahead to begin the Ahafo South Project, a greenfields site, in April 2005.
Diamonds and manganese each account for 1–2 per cent of export earnings. Diamonds (mostly industrial) are mined by Ghana Consolidated Diamonds Ltd in the Birim Basin. Ghana is the eighth-largest diamond producer in the world. Manganese ore is mined at Nsuta by the National Manganese Corporation.

Manganese production averages 280,000 tonnes per annum.
Ghana has vast bauxite reserves near Kibi, but heavy transport/extraction costs have limited commercial development of local bauxite for use by the Valco aluminium smelter.
In 2003, Ghana granted mining licences in its protected forest reserves to attract new foreign investment.

Hydrocarbons
Ghana's oil reserves are less than 16 million barrels, which is generally too small for commercial exploitation. The substantial proportion of the one million tonnes per year domestic oil requirement is generally imported from Nigeria. Petroleum products account for about a quarter of the country's energy requirements. Arco and Petro Ghana, among other companies, are drilling offshore in the South Tano area in the west of the country.
The Tema Oil Refinery (TOR) has a capacity of 45,000 barrels per day (bpd). A residual catalytic cracking (RCC) unit has been installed at TOR in order to boost productivity and produce petroleum and liquefied petroleum gas (LPG) for export.
Natural gas reserves totalled 23.52 billion cubic metres (840 billion cubic feet), which are located primarily in the Tano fields.
The West African Gas Pipline Project will link Nigeria, Ghana, Togo and Benin, supplying gas from Nigeria's gas fields. The projected was begun in 2003 with a consortium investing around US$500 million to construct the 1,000km pipeline; it is to be managed by Chevron Texaco. Construction in Ghana began in June 2005.
Ghana does not produce coal but imports minimal amounts of around 3,000 tonnes annually.

Energy
Hydroelectricity accounts for the majority of Ghana's domestic power.
The Volta River Authority (VRA) has responsibility for the development, generation and distribution of electricity. The 912MW Akosombo hydropower plant and the 160MW Kpong plant are run at capacity. Plans to build an additional station (400MW) on the Black Volta River at Bui were finally agreed in 2007. Construction of the US$600m dam started in September despite continuing concerns about the environmental and social effects of the dam. The construction is partly funded by a loan from China.
The thermal power station near Takoradi produces 300MW and is due to be linked to the natural gas pipeline, under construction, from Nigeria. Ghana currently supplies electricity to the power grids in Benin and Togo from the Akosombo Plant on the Volta River.
Western Power Company, a subsidiary of the Ghana National Petroleum Corporation (GNPC) has secured funding for two barge-mounted gas turbines in the Western Region to add to overall production.
Several reforms have transformed Ghana's energy sector and, despite controversial price hikes for domestic and commercial consumers, consumption is growing as services improve.
Ghana has plans to install electricity service to every community of over 500 people by the year 2020. The National Electrification Scheme has proceeded since 1995 and is due to be completed, in five-year phases, by 2020.

Financial markets
Stock exchange
The Ghana Stock Exchange (GSE) has two main indices, the GSE All-Share Index and the Databank Stock Index (DSI).
The GSE has not only increased turnover significantly but also produced record returns of 87 per cent in 2003 and 142 per cent in 2004.

Banking and insurance
Stability in money markets and low inflationary expectations following petroleum deregulation, led to a reduction in the prime interest rate of 16.5 per cent on 30 May 2005, down from 18.5 per cent which had remained unchanged since May 2004.
It was announced in March 2005 that the introduction of the shared currency, the Eco, in Ghana, Guinea, Nigeria, Sierra Leone and The Gambia, which was due in July 2005, would be postponed. The currency was proposed to facilitate trade and growth with an ultimate plan to merge it with the CFA franc.
Central bank
Bank of Ghana
Main financial centre
Accra

Time
GMT

Geography
Ghana's southern border is the Gulf of Guinea. To the north, east and west lie the states of Burkina Faso, Togo and Côte d'Ivoire. From north to south the country extends a distance of about 680 km.
The River Volta, which flows from the north to the south-east, is the most conspicuous landmark. There is a coastal area of thicket and mangrove which gives way in the east and north-east to more open plains and semi-deciduous forest.
To the west and north-west of the coastal strip is high forest, which still covers the greater part of Ashanti and part of the Northern Region. The forest gives way in the north to Guinea savannah woodland; the extreme north-eastern corner of Ghana forms part of the drier Sudan savannah woodland.
Hemisphere
Northern

Climate
Ghana lies entirely within the tropics. In the northern savannah the climate is hot and dry, with intermittent rainfall during March–September. In the hot and humid forest regions there are two rainy seasons, during March–June and September–November. At the coast, which is only 4.5 degrees from the Equator, the heat is intense.
The capital city, Accra, is only 65 metres above sea level. The capital's hottest month is March, with temperatures of 24–32 degrees Celsius (C); August is the coldest month, with temperatures of 21–27 C. The annual rainfall in the capital averages 865mm. The driest month is December when rainfall averages 18mm, and the wettest month is June when rainfall averages 235mm.

Dress codes
Western-style clothes are usually worn for business purposes, including shorts for outdoor occupations. On social or ceremonial occasions, traditional costume or Western-style clothes are equally acceptable.
Local dress includes the expensive, hand-woven Kente cloth for which Ghana is famous: this is worn by men like a toga.
Wearing any military clothing, such as camouflage jackets or trousers, or any clothing or items that may appear military in nature, is strictly prohibited.

Entry requirements
Passports
Required by all, except by members of the Economic Community of West African States (Ecowas) with a valid travel certificate.
Visa
Required by all, except nationals of Ecowas countries, Kenya, Zimbabwe, Egypt, Mauritius, Singapore and Hong Kong.
Visas are valid for three-month periods.
An application for a business visa must contain a letter of confirmation from the representative's employer and itinerary, plus an invitation from a local host. All visitors must have return/onward passage.
Currency advice/regulations
It is advisable to check the latest currency regulations prior to visit.
It is easy to exchange US dollar bills for cedis. Visa cards can be used to withdraw cedis from Barclays Bank automatic teller machines (ATMs).

Unlimited import of foreign currency, but it must be declared. Unused foreign currency, travellers cheques, etc, declared on arrival, can be exported. Foreign currency must be exchanged with authorised dealers only. Keep the foreign exchange form. Import of local currency is prohibited and export is limited to C5,000, which must be recorded in passport.
Unused cedis can be re-exchanged into foreign currency by local banks or the Bank of Ghana, but the declaration form T.5 must show that the monies were obtained while in Ghana from an authorised dealer in foreign exchange.

Health (for visitors)
Mandatory precautions
A yellow fever vaccination certificate must be presented on arrival. A cholera vaccination may be required, depending on local circumstances.
Advisable precautions
Cholera is seasonal. Typhoid, polio, tetanus, hepatitis A and meningitis vaccinations are recommended. A hepatitis B vaccination is recommended if staying in Ghana over six months. A vaccination for rabies is recommended if travelling to rural areas. Malaria prophylaxis should be taken as risk exists throughout the country. Water precautions are essential. There is a bilharzia risk and swimming in rivers is not advisable. HIV/Aids is present in Ghana. Guinea worm is rife and increasing in northern regions.
Emergency facilities are extremely limited. Insurance is vital and emergency evacuation should be included.

Hotels
Available in Accra, Kumasi, Takoradi and other regional capitals. Prices are high. A 10 per cent government tax is added. Tipping is permitted in hotels, restaurants, etc. It is rarely added to the bill.

Credit cards
The most widely accepted credit cards are American Express, Diners' and Visa. They may be used for payment at nearly all airlines, leading hotels and major supermarkets.
Many restaurants and airlines prefer to be paid in cash.

Public holidays (national)
Fixed dates
1 Jan (New Year's Day), 6 Mar (Independence Day), 1 May (Labour Day), 25 May (Africa Day), 4 Jun (1979 Coup Anniversary), 1 Jul (Republic Day), 25 Dec (Christmas Day), 26 Dec (Boxing Day), 31 Dec (Revolution Day).
Variable dates
Good Friday, Easter Monday, National Farmers' Day, Eid al Adha, Eid al Fitr.
Islamic year – 1429 (10 Jan 2008–28 Dec 2008): The Islamic year contains 354 or 355 days, with the result that Muslim feasts advance by 10–12 days against the Gregorian calendar. Dates of feasts vary according to the sighting of the new moon, so cannot be forecast exactly.

Working hours
Banking
Mon–Thu: 0830–1400; Fri: 0830–1500.
Business
Mon–Fri: 0800–1200, 1400–1700. Sat: 0830–1200.
Government
Mon–Fri: 0800–1230, 1330–1700.
Shops
Mon–Tue and Thu–Fri: 0800–1200, 1400–1730. Wed and Sat: 0800–1300. Closed on Sundays.

Electricity supply
220V AC, 50 cycles

Social customs/useful tips
It is traditional to arrive with a gift when accepting private hospitality, particularly in rural areas. It is customary to use the right hand when presenting an object to another person, particularly in the case of food or a gift.
In northern Ghana, where the population tends to be Muslim, Islamic customs should be respected: it is considered unclean to eat or drink with the left hand; it is insulting to point the sole of your shoe at a Muslim. Older people are treated with special respect in Ghana.
It is inadvisable for foreigners to refer to tribalism or ethnic affiliations when discussing current affairs.
Body language differences include the custom of a greater degree of physical contact – touching and holding hands – between men and between women.
Business people need patience when dealing with bureaucracy. There are regular power cuts in Accra.
There are no unusual or particularly strict laws, but foreign visitors should observe all rules and regulations as Ghana does not take ignorance of the law as an excuse for non-observance. It is prudent to carry proof of identity.

Security
Violent crime has risen, particularly in and around Accra. Visitors are advised to exercise a high level of vigilance in public areas and when travelling in vehicles. If possible, avoid travelling alone in taxis after dark. Be wary when withdrawing cash from the few cash points in central Accra. Thefts of both luggage and travel documents occur at Kotoka International Airport. Ensure your documents are kept secured (particularly when leaving the airport) and never leave your baggage unattended.
Be wary of all offers of unsolicited assistance at the airport unless from uniformed porters or officials who, as with all other permanent staff, wear a current ID card bearing their name and photograph. ID cards without photographs are not valid.
Taking photographs near sensitive installations, including military sites and government buildings, is prohibited.
Permission should be obtained before taking photographs of anyone in uniform.

Getting there
Air
National airline: Ghana International Airlines
International airport/s: Accra-Kotoka International (ACC), 5km from city; duty-free shop, bar, buffet, restaurant, bank, post office, taxis.
Airport tax: International departures C22,000; domestic departures C500.
Surface
Road: The coastal road runs from Lagos (Nigeria) through Cotonou (Benin) and Lomé (Togo) to Accra. The condition of this road is variable. A generally good road links Abidjan (Côte d'Ivoire) with Kumasi.
Main port/s: The main ports are Tema and Takoradi. Ships connect Tema, 25km east of Accra, with ports in Nigeria, Côte d'Ivoire, Cameroon and South Africa.

Getting about
National transport
Transport in northern Ghana can be more difficult than in southern Ghana.
Air: Several airlines fly domestic routes from Kotoka to Kumasi and Tamale.
Road: There are over 30,000km of classified roads — 15,000km of these are trunk roads, the remainder being feeder roads. There are also around 6,000km of unclassified tracks. Of the total road network, approximately 6,000km are paved. There are reasonable roads between Accra and the main towns.
The main routes are Accra-Tema, Accra-Takoradi, Accra-Kumasi, Accra-Koforidua, Accra-Ho. Roads are often potholed and badly marked.
Buses: State-run bus services connect major centres. They are subject to delays and cancellation and are not recommended for business users.
Rail: The total network is about 1,000km, connecting Tema-Accra through Nsawam-Koforidua-Nkawkaw (Eastern Region) to Kumasi (Ashanti Region) through to Dunkwa and Prestea, Tarkwa and Sekondi-Takoradi (Western Region). Another line runs from Huni Valley (Western Region) to Kade (Eastern Region). Two classes; air-conditioning and restaurant cars not available; sleeping accommodation available on some services.
Water: A weekly ferry, the Yapei Queen, plies Lake Volta between Yeji in the north and Akosombo, more than 200km to the

south, a two-day journey. Ferries connect Yeji with Makongo and Buipe.

City transport

Taxis: There are cheap and reliable taxis in Accra.

Tipping is not usual; taxis are unmetered – fare is by negotiation; rates are often posted in hotels.

Buses, trams & metro: The bus services in Accra are run by the city authority and private operators.

Car hire

Car hire is expensive. An international driving licence is recommended; this must be endorsed by Police Licensing Office if stay exceeds 90 days. Traffic drives on the right.

Driving at night is not advised.

BUSINESS DIRECTORY

The addresses listed below are a selection only. While World of Information makes every endeavour to check these addresses, we cannot guarantee that changes have not been made, especially to telephone numbers and area codes. We would welcome any corrections.

Telephone area codes

The international direct dialling code (IDD) for Ghana is +233, followed by area code and subscriber's number:

Accra	21	Takoradi	31
Koforidua	81	Tamale	71
Kumasi	51	Tema	22

Useful telephone numbers

Police, fire and ambulance: 999.

Chambers of Commerce

Accra District Chamber of Commerce, Trade Fair Centre, PO Box 2325, Accra (tel: 662-427).

British-Ghana Chamber of Commerce and Industry, PO Box GP 21101, Accra (tel: 674-762; fax: 296-836; e-mail: info@ghanabritishchamber.com).

Ghana National Chamber of Commerce, 65 Kojo Thompson Road, PO Box 2325, Accra (tel: 662-427; fax: 662-210; e-mail: gncc@ncs.com.gh).

Banking

Agricultural Development Bank, PO Box 4191, Cedi House, Liberia Road, Accra (tel: 662-758, 662-762; fax: 662-912, 662-846).

Amalgamated Bank Limited, PO Box C1541, C131/3 Farrar Avenue, Accra (tel: 249-690; fax: 249-697; e-mail: amalbank@ighmail.com).

Barclays Bank of Ghana Ltd, PO Box 2949, Barclays House, High Street, Accra (tel: 664-901/4, 665-382; fax: 667-420).

CAL Merchant Bank Ltd, PO Box 14596, 45 Independence Avenue, Accra (tel: 221-056, 231-098, 222-345, 221-091, 231-912-7; fax: 231-104, 231-913).

Ecobank Ghana Ltd, 19 Seventh Avenue, Ridge West, Private Mail Bag, GPO, Accra (tel: 229-532, 228-812, 221-103, 667-109; fax: 667-127, 232-086).

First Atlantic Merchant Bank Ltd, PO Box C1620, Atlantic Place, No. 1 Seventh Avenue, Ridge West, Cantonments, Accra (tel: 231-433-5, 245-647, 245-660, 232-566; fax: 231-399).

Ghana Commercial Bank Ltd, PO Box 134, Accra (tel: 664-914 (5 lines), 664-911, 664-918; fax: 662-168).

International Commercial Bank Ltd, PO Box 20057, Accra (tel: 666-190, 665-779; fax: 668-221).

Merchant Bank (Ghana) Ltd, PO Box 401, Merban House, 44 Kwame Nkrumah Ave, Accra (tel: 666-331/2, 666-336; fax: 663-398).

Metropolitan and Allied Bank (GH) Ltd, PO Box C 1778, Valco Trust House, Castle Road Branch, Cantonments, Accra (tel: 232-770, 232-776; fax: 232-728).

National Investment Bank Ltd, PO Box 3726, 37 Kwame Nkrumah Avenue, Accra (tel: 240-001, 240-024; fax: 240-030/34).

Prudential Bank Ltd, PO Box 9820, Airport, Accra (tel: 226-322, 226-803; fax: 226-803).

SSB Bank Ltd, 1 Cola Avenue, Kokomlemle, Accra (tel: 222-564/223-375/222-136; fax: 222-136).

Stanbic Bank Ghana Limited, PO Box CT 2344, Valco Trust House, Castle Road, Ridge, Accra (tel: 234-683-4, 234-679, 250-066-7, 250-070-5; fax: 234-685).

Standard Chartered Bank Ghana Ltd, PO Box 768, 3rd Floor, Accra High Street Building, Accra (tel: 664-591-8, 672-210; fax: 667-751, 663-560).

The Trust Bank Ltd, PO Box 1862, Re-insurance House, 68 Kwame Nkrumah Avenue, Accra (tel: 240-049–052; fax: 240-056, 240-059).

Central bank

Bank of Ghana, PO Box 2674, Thorpe Road, Accra (tel: 666-174; fax: 662-996; e-mail: secretary@bog.gov.gh).

Travel information

Accra Kotoka International Airport, PO Box 87, Accra (tel: 776-171).

Ghana International Airlines, Silver Star Tower, PO Box 78, Kotoka International Airport, Accra (tel: 213-555; fax: 767-744).

Ghana Tourist Development Co Ltd, PO Box 8710, Accra (tel: 772-084; fax: 772-093).

Ministry of tourism

Ministry of Tourism, PO Box 4386, Accra (tel: 666-314, 666-426; fax: 666-826).

National tourist organisation offices

Ghana Tourist Board, PO Box 3106, Accra (tel: 238-330; fax: 231-779; e-mail: gtb@africa-on-line.com.gh).

Ministries

Ministry of Communications: PO Box M.41, Accra (tel: 229-870; fax: 229-786).

Ministry of Defence, Burma Camp, Accra (tel: 774-727; fax: 773-951).

Ministry of Education, PO Box M45, Accra (tel: 662-772; fax: 664-067).

Ministry of Employment and Social Welfare, PO Box M84, Accra (tel: 665-421; fax: 667-251).

Ministry of Environment, Science and Technology, PO Box M39, Accra (tel: 662-626; fax: 666-828).

Ministry of Finance and Economic Planning, PO Box M40, Accra (tel: 665-441, 665-587, 666-512; fax: 667-069; internet: www.finance.gov.gh).

Ministry of Food and Agriculture, PO Box M37, Accra (tel: 663-036, 665-421; fax: 663-250).

Ministry of Foreign Affairs, PO Box M53, Accra (tel: 664-008; fax: 665-363; internet: www.mfa.gov.gh/).

Ministry of Health, PO Box M44, Accra (tel: 665-323; fax: 663-810).

Ministry of Information, PO Box M41, Accra (tel: 228-0211).

Ministry of Interior, PO Box M42, Accra (tel: 665-421; fax: 662-688).

Ministry of Justice & Attorney General, PO Box M60, Accra (tel: 665-051).

Ministry of Land and Forestry, PO Box M212, Accra (tel: 665-949; fax: 666-801, 666-896).

Ministry of Local Government, Rural Development and Co-op, PO Box M50, Accra (tel: 664-763; fax: 667-911).

Ministry of Mines and Energy, PO Box 40, Stadium Post Office, Accra (tel: 667-090; fax: 668-262).

Ministry of Mobilisation (tel: 665-349; fax: 667-251).

Ministry of Roads and Transport, PO Box M43, Accra (tel: 666-465; fax: 667-911).

Ministry of Tourism, PO Box 4386, Accra (tel: 666-314; fax: 666-182; e-mail: MOT@ghana.com; internet site: http://www.estghana.gov.gh; www.africaonline.com.gh/Tourism).

Ministry of Trade and Industry, PO Box M47, Accra (tel: 663-327; fax: 665-114).

Ministry of Works and Housing, PO Box M43, Accra (tel: 662-242; fax: 663-268).

Ministry of Youth and Sports, PO Box M 252, Accra (tel: 664-71; fax: 663-927).

Other useful addresses

Accra International Conference Centre, PO Box C1054, Accra (tel: 669-600; fax: 669-825).

Ashanti Goldfields Co Ltd, Gold House, Patrice Lumumba Road, Roman Ridge, PO Box 2665, Accra (tel: 772-190, 776-224, 778-155; fax: 775-947).

Association of Ghanaian Industry, PO Box 8624, Accra (tel: 777-283; fax: 773-143).

Black Star Line, PO Box 2760, Accra (tel: 776-161; fax: 775-140).

British Diplomatic Mission, Accra (tel: 221-665).

Civil Aviation Authority, Kotoka International Airport, PO Box 87, Accra (tel: 773-283).

Coffee, Sheanuts Exporters' Association, c/o Mr J W Biney, Agrotrade Ltd., PO Box 226, Accra (tel: 224-820; fax: 224-564).

Customs, Excise and Preventive Service, PO Box 68, Accra (tel: 666-841; fax: 660-019).

Department of Co-operatives, PO Box M150, Accra (tel: 666-212).

Department of Urban Roads, Ministry of Roads and Transport, PO Box 38, Accra (tel: 230-381, 223-908; fax: 234-522).

Divestiture Implementation Committee, F35/5 Ring Road East, North Labone, PO Box CT102, Cantonments, Accra (tel: 772-049, 773-119, 760-281; fax: 773-126; e-mail: dicgh@ncs.com.gh).

Export Finance Company, Bank of Ghana, PO Box 2674, Accra (tel: 666-902; fax: 662-996).

Federation of Association of Ghanaian Exporters (FAGE), c/o Kiku Ltd., PO Box M378, Accra (tel: 223-215; fax: 776-755).

Finsap Implementation Secretariat, Private Mail Bag (PMB), Ministries Post Office, Accra (tel: 666-254, 664-976; fax: 667-448; e-mail: finsap@gh.com).

Ghana Assorted Foodstuffs Exporters Assocation, PO Box 16073, Airport - Accra (tel: 220-746; fax: 223-663).

Ghana Chamber of Mines, PO Box 991, Accra (tel: 665-355; fax: 662-926).

Ghana Civil Aviation Authority, Private Mail Bag, Kotoka International Airport, Accra (tel: 776-171; fax: 773-293; e-mail: centre-GCAA@ighmail.com; internet site: http://www.gcaa.com.gh).

Ghana Cocoa Board, PO Box 933, Accra (tel: 221-212; fax: 667-104, 665-076; e-mail: cocobod@africaonline.com.gh).

Ghana Export Promotion Council, Republic House, Tudu, PO Box M 146, Accra (tel: 228-813/830/623; fax: 668-263, 233-715; e-mail: gepc@ighmail.com).

Ghana Free-Zones Board, PO Box M626, Accra (tel: 670-532/5; fax: 670-536; e-mail: freezone@africaonline.com.gh; internet site: http://www.ghanaclassified.com.ghzb).

Ghana Furniture Producers/Exporters Association, PO Box 32, Trade Fair Centre, Accra (tel: 775-311).

Ghana Highway Authority, PO Box 1641, Accra (tel: 666-591; fax: 665-571).

Ghana Investment Promotion Centre (GIPC), PO Box M193, Accra (tel: 665-125/9; fax: 663-801; e-mail: gipc@ghana.com; internet site: http://www.gipc.org.gh).

Ghana Liaison Office, Cotecna Inspection S A, 10 Drake Avenue, Airport Residential Area, PO Box C2212, Cantonments, Accra (tel: 775-698; fax: 553-522).

Ghana National Petroleum Corporation (GNPC), Private Mail Bag, Tema (tel: 232-056; fax: 774-143).

Ghana National Procurement Agency, Ministries Post Office, Private Mail Bag, Accra (tel: 220-851; fax: 221-049).

Ghana Shippers Council, Private Mail Bag, Ministries Post Office, Accra (tel: 666-915; fax: 668-768).

Ghana Stock Exchange, Marketing Department, 5th Floor, Cedi House, Liberia Road, Accra (tel: 669-914; fax: 669-913; e-mail: stockex@ncs.com.gh; internet site; http://www.gse.com.gh).

Ghana Trade and Investment Gateway Project (GHATIG), PO Box M47, Accra (tel: 663-439, 664-074; fax: 665-423; e-mail: gateway1@ghana.com).

Ghana Yam Producers and Exporters' Association, PO Box 5233, Accra (tel: 775-311; fax: 668-263).

Ghanaian Embassy (USA), 3512 International Drive, NW, Washington DC 20008 (tel: (+1-202)-686-4520; fax: (+1-202)-686-4527; e-mail: hagan@cais.com).

Horticulturists' Association of Ghana, PO Box 9303, Accra (tel: 772-139; fax: 772-350).

Institute of Economic Affairs (tel: 776-641; fax: 776-724).

Internal Revenue Services, PO Box 2202, Accra (tel: 664-961; fax: 664-938).

Organisation for Export Development for Seafood, c/o Signotrade Ltd., PO Box 16851, Accra (tel: 712-762; fax: 668-263).

Precious Metals Marketing Corporation, PO Box M108, Accra (tel: 664-931; fax: 772-350).

Private Enterprises Foundation (PEF), PO Box C1671, Cantoments, Accra (tel: 222-313; fax: 231-487).

Registar-General's Department, PO Box 118, Accra (tel: 666-469).

US Diplomatic Mission, Accra (tel: 228-440).

Vegetables Exporters' Association, c/o Ghana Export Promotion Council, PO Box M146, Accra (tel: 221-212; fax: 668-263).

Volta River Authority, PO Box MB77, Accra (tel: 664-941, 221-124; fax: 662-610; e-mail: orgsrv@accra.vra.com).

National news agency: Ghana News Agency

PO Box 2118, Accra (tel: 662-381, 665-135/6/7; fax: 669-841; email: ghnews@ghana.com; internet: www.ghananewsagency.org).

Internet sites

Africa Business Network: http://www.ifc.org/abn

Ghana Forestry Commision: http://ghanatimber.org/

AllAfrica.com: http://allafrica.com

African Development Bank: http://www.afdb.org

Mbendi AfroPaedia (information on companies, countries, industries and stock exchanges in Africa): http://mbendi.co.za

Yellow Pages: http://www.ghanaforum.com/directory.htm

Gibraltar

KEY FACTS

Official name: Gibraltar

Head of State: Queen Elizabeth II, represented by Governor Sir Robert Fulton (from 27 Sep 2006)

Head of government: Chief Minister Peter Caruana (GSD) (since 1996; re-elected Oct 2007)

Ruling party: Gibraltar Social Democrats (GSD) (since 1996; re-elected Oct 2007)

Area: 7 square km

Population: 28,779 (2005)

Capital: Gibraltar

Official language: English

Currency: Pound sterling (£) = 100 pence (the euro also circulates and is accepted informally)

Exchange rate: £0.50 per US$ (Jul 2008)

GDP per capita: US$38,322 (2004)

Unemployment: 2.00% (2003)

Inflation: 2.80% (2005)

Balance of trade: -US$193.90 million (2005)

Visitor numbers: 7.79 million (2005)

Gibraltar's future remains closely bound up with its relationship with Spain. The Cordoba Agreement (which 'freezes' the arguments over sovereignty and enables Gibraltar to develop as the hub for a potentially important development area of Spain) is certain to benefit Gibraltar's stability and its economy. There is scant possibility of Gibraltarians voting in favour of adopting Spanish sovereignty, however the option may be dressed up. But the new transport links and increased opportunities for dialogue and co-operation promise much for the international role of this small colony.

Also under the Cordoba Agreement Spain recognised Gibraltar's '350' international direct dialling code and permitted Gibraltar mobile telephone roaming in Spain.

'The Rock'

For both the British and Spanish governments, Gibraltar is an anachronism that will not go away. For twenty-first century Britain it is more of a liability than an asset, for Spanish governments, it is an annoying irritation used by each of the major parties to highlight the shortcomings of the other. The 29,400 population crammed into 2.5 square miles (6.5 square km) on Spain's southernmost point is a mixture of Italian (mostly of Genoese ancestry), Moorish (from nearby Morocco), Jewish (who had been expelled from Spain), Maltese, Portuguese and Hindi cultures – everything, in fact except Spanish. There are relatively small numbers of British residents, although an increasing number of Britons work in the colony. More than 1 per cent of the residents are millionaires from abroad, attracted by Gibraltar's Category Two tax status awarded to people with net assets of over US$3.5 million. Under this scheme qualifying residents must buy or rent a property; they then pay a maximum of US$40,000 in annual income tax.

IMF approval

In mid-2007 the government of Gibraltar announced that the International Monetary Fund (IMF) had once again endorsed Gibraltar's robust regulatory environment and anti-money laundering regime. The IMF's assessment, which resulted in the production of four reports, was carried out at the invitation of the government. The IMF came to the conclusion that 'the Gibraltar authorities are concerned with protecting the reputation and integrity of Gibraltar as a financial centre, and are cognisant of the importance of adopting and applying international regulatory standards and best supervisory practices. Gibraltar has a good reputation internationally for co-operation and information sharing'. This stamp of approval is vital for the future expansion of Gibraltar's financial sector.

For decades now has held a significant share of the global offshore sector. Developing Gibraltar as an offshore centre has been a key part of the government's strategy, even in the face of reservations and obstruction from Madrid. The advantages of offshore banking in Gibraltar include its favourable tax status (bank interest is not taxed in Gibraltar, even when paid to residents), the lack of exchange controls, communications, stable government, and EU membership. The EU's Savings Tax Directive, which came into force on 1 July 2005, means that for all citizens of EU member states there is an exchange of information between the Gibraltar authorities and the individuals' home tax authorities in regard to payments of interest and other returns on savings. Importantly, the directive does not apply to payments to corporate bodies. Gibraltar is beginning to develop corporate big business, which it is hoped will reduce the colony's reliance on providing more standard – and less remunerative – business for private clients.

Much of the banking activity in Gibraltar is directed to asset management for high-net-worth individuals, not least because Gibraltar has tried hard to attract such people with special tax regimes. In its financial services regulations, Gibraltar aims to match UK standards. An example of this is the local money laundering legislation which implemented the EU Directive and was extended as in the UK to encompass all crimes. Accordingly, all banking supervision regulations are the same as those in the UK and procedures for opening an account are much the same. Under EU legislation, a Gibraltar-licensed bank may set up branches elsewhere in Europe. Most of the twenty banks established in Gibraltar are branches of major UK, European or US banks.

No change

In parliamentary elections held on 11 October 2008 the Gibraltar Social Democrats (GSD) were re-elected with 49.3 per cent of the vote (10 seats out of 17); the Gibraltar Socialist Labour Party (GSLP) won 31.8 per cent (4 seats), the Gibraltar Liberal Party (GLP) won 13.6 per cent (3 seats); there are two ex-officio members. Turnout was 81.4 per cent.

Risk assessment

Economy	Good
Political	Good
Regional stability	Good

COUNTRY PROFILE

Historical profile

1704 Gibraltar, commonly referred to as the Rock, was captured by the UK from Spain.
1713 Gibraltar was ceded to Britain in the Treaty of Utrecht. The Treaty stipulated that the Rock would become a part of Spain if Britain gave up sovereignty.
1830 Gibraltar became a crown colony.
1869 The opening of the Suez Canal increased Gibraltar's importance in guarding the route to India and the Far East.
1939–45 Gibraltar was a busy naval base in the Second World War. After the war, Spain continued to press for the return of Gibraltar, but rejected the UK's offer to refer the matter to the International Court of Justice.
1967 More than 12,000 Gibraltarians voted to remain British; only 44 opted for Spanish rule. The dispute continued to disrupt friendly relations between Spain and UK; for a while, Spain closed the frontier. Both countries sought a peaceful settlement, and the Gibraltarian people maintained their wish to remain British.
1969 Gibraltar adopted a new constitution that devolved a measure of power from the UK to local ministers.
1975 The death of Spain's dictator, General Franco, led to more friendly relations with Spain, but there was still no resolution of the sovereignty issue.
1984 The Brussels Agreement was signed between Spain and the UK, establishing a negotiating process over the issue of Gibraltar's sovereignty.
1985 Spain lifted its border blockade.
1996 Peter Caruana was elected chief minister.
1998 Spanish proposals for joint sovereignty were rejected by the UK.
2000 The UK and Spain reached an agreement over Gibraltar's administrative status, which allowed Spanish recognition of documents and passports issued in Gibraltar. The repair of a nuclear submarine sparked protests from the Spanish government and Gibraltar's civilians.
2002 Spain and UK held talks to consider grounds for sharing sovereignty of Gibraltar. An informal referendum rejected the talks by 95:1.
2004 The 300th anniversary of the British occupation of Gibraltar was commemorated amid continued tensions with Spain. A trilateral forum, of the UK, Spain and Gibraltar, began talks on the territory's future.
2005 Cammell Laird announced it would invest US$34.9 million in its Gibraltar shipbuilding yard between 2006–08 to develop its market in super-yacht building and refitting. Gibraltarians took part in their first European elections.
2006 An agreement easing border controls and allowing flights from Spain to land in Gibraltar was reached in September. Lieutenant General Sir Robert Fulton became governor. A referendum for a new constitution was successful as 60.24 per cent of the vote agreed to the proposition. Direct passenger flights from Spain commenced .
2007 In parliamentary elections held on 11 October the GSD were re-elected with 49.3 per cent of the vote (10 seats out of 17); the GSLP 31.8 per cent (4), the Gibraltar Liberal Party (GLP) 13.6 per cent (3); there are two ex-officio members. Turnout was 81.4 per cent.

Political structure

Constitution
A new constitution was promulgated on 2 January 2007, which modernises the UK-Gibraltar relationship. Some responsibilities undertaken by the governor are limited, particularly those areas of external affairs, defence, internal security and the public service. The house of Assembly became the Gibraltar Parliament, which determines its own size and new commissions were create to undertake the appointments to the judiciary and public service and a new police authority was created, which will undertake greater local input.

Form of state
British Crown colony

The executive
The governor does not take an active role in governmental affairs. The Chief Minister is the head of the Gibraltar government and holds much of the power.

National legislature
The unicameral Gibraltar Parliament, comprises a speaker (appointed by the governor), two ex-officio members and 15 elected members serving a four-year term. All legislation is ratified by the governor.

Legal system
It is based on English common law coupled to statutes. The civil courts in Gibraltar are the Court of First Instance, the Supreme Court, the Court of Appeal and ultimately, the Privy Council in the UK.

Last elections
11 October 2007 (parliamentary)

Results: Parliamentary: the GSD were re-elected with 49.3 per cent of the vote (10 seats out of 17); the GSLP 31.8 per cent (4), the Gibraltar Liberal Party (GLP) 13.6 per cent (3); there are two ex-officio members. Turnout was 81.4 per cent.

Next elections
2011 (parliamentary)

Political parties

Ruling party
Gibraltar Social Democrats (GSD) (since 1996; re-elected Oct 2007)

Main opposition party
Gibraltar Socialist Labour Party (GSLP)

Political situation
Success of the new constitution, which gives the territory, not only increased status, but also practical power in 2007 encourages Gibraltar to apply for membership of the United Nations. This of course is yet another thorny issue for Spain that sees the territory as a wayward entity that should be firmly under its jurisdiction. But Gibraltar has an historic tie to the UK, which has consistently said it won't give away Gibraltar's future of self-determination without a referendum in agreement. In the meantime, Gibraltar is taking progressively more decisions for itself and may never want to give up its, admittedly circumscribed, freedom.

Population

28,779 (2005)

Last census: November 2001: 27,495

Annual growth rate: 0.2 per cent (2003)

Ethnic make-up
English, Italian, Maltese, Portuguese, Spanish.

Religions
Roman Catholic (77 per cent), Church of England (7 per cent), Muslim (7 per cent), Jewish (2 per cent).

Education

Gibraltar has a comprehensive system of education, based on the UK model. Bayside (merged with three separate schools), is the only secondary school for boys between the ages of 12 and 18. Westside School, the Gibraltar Girls' Comprehensive School caters for 900 students between the ages of 12 to 18. Many children are likely to receive third level education in the UK through several grant facilities, resulting in the high incidence of returning professional graduates.

Health
Health conditions are generally good and broadly comparable to most of Western Europe. Heart diseases and cancers account for most mortality. Gibraltar's health services are closely modelled on the UK's National Health Service, with which it maintains professional and service links. There is provision for a full range of primary care and secondary care services, available through the Primary Care Centre. Medical cases requiring tertiary care are usually referred to the UK or Spain. The St Bernard's Hospital is the only general hospital, with 170 beds providing outpatient services, emergency facilities and investigative facilities.
Government expenditure towards healthcare amounted is around £30 million (US$45.2 million) per annum
Life expectancy: 79 years (estimate 2003)
Fertility rate/Maternal mortality rate: 1.7 births per woman (2003)
Birth rate/Death rate: 11 births per 1,000 population; nine deaths per 1,000 population (2003).
Child (under 5 years) mortality rate (per 1,000): Five per 1,000 live births (2003)

Welfare
A social insurance funds all state pensions and benefits, with contributions and other earnings on investments meeting the cost of the scheme. The government's investment in capital projects towards social and economic development is funded by the Improvement and Development Fund, 12 per cent of which is allocated for housing.

Languages spoken
Spanish, Italian, Portuguese and Malti; English is used in schools and for official purposes.
Official language/s
English

Media
Press
Dailies: Gibraltar's oldest daily newspaper is the Gibraltar Chronicle (www.chronicle.gi).
Weeklies: There are several magazines including Panorama (www.panorama.gi), Vox (www.vox.gi), which also publishes a Spanish section, The New People (www.thenewpeople.net) with political reports and the satirical Gibraltar Inquirer (www.gibinquirer.net).
Business: The Gibraltar International (www.gibraltarfinance.com) is a quarterly magazine covering finance and business matters.
Periodicals: Magazines include the monthly Insight (www.insight-gibraltar.com) with lifestyle news and The Gibraltar Magazine (www.thegibraltarmagazine.com) with business and leisure articles.
Broadcasting
Public radio and television services are provided by the Gibraltar Broadcaster Corporation (GBC) (www.gbc.gi), funded partly by revenue from TV licence fees and also through advertising fees and the UK military broadcaster, BFBS (www.ssvc.com/bfbs).
Radio: Two station networks broadcast within the territory Radio Gibraltar (www.gbc.gi) and the BFBS Radio and Radio 2 (www.ssvc.com/bfbs). There are a number of external services from Spain that can be received.
Television: GBC (www.gbc.gi) operates one channel and BFBS offers access to pay-to-view TV and satellite services.
Advertising
All, typical media outlets offer the availability for advert.

Economy
Gibraltar has few natural resources, with almost no part of its land area capable of sustaining agriculture. It has a significant absence of heavy manufacturing activity, apart from ship repair. The economy is dependent on imports of food, consumer goods, building materials, construction equipment and fuel. As such, the economy is service-based, in particular financial, tourism (over 5 million tourists annually – including day-visitors from Spain), shipping services fees, and duties on consumer goods. The first three sectors contribute 25–30 per cent of GDP. Telecommunications accounts for another 10 per cent.
The gaming sector has been a growth industry since the first gambling business began operating in 1989. Gibraltar is an attractive home to Internet betting sites, where such businesses pay only a maximum of US$800,000 in tax annually; PartyGaming made over US$6 million in 2005, and casino games, played online, turned over hundreds of million of dollars, in 2006.
An agreement reached with Spain in 2006 finally broke a 30-year ban on flights between Gibraltar and Spain. It is expected to improve tourist arrival numbers. Spain also agreed to recognise Gibraltar's Internet suffix .gi and mobile (cell) phone signals across the border.
Gibraltar has a small population, boosted by a large pool of foreign workers recruited for the financial sector, it has an economy that is dependent on offshore financial services. As such, it is in competition with a number of tax havens within the EU and outside, and is subject to international limits on money transactions, while maintaining a reputation for probity and turning a profit. If it can successfully manage these separate aspects it should continue to flourish.

External trade
Gibraltar is a member of the European Community as an overseas territory of the UK, however it does not participate in the customs union, common commercial policy (free movement of goods do not apply), and the levy of VAT. Nevertheless community rulings are implemented through UK local legislation.
Its regular trade deficit is largely offset by invisible earnings.
Imports
Main imports are fuels, manufactured goods, and foodstuffs.
Main sources: Spain (23.4 per cent total, 2005), Russia (12.3 per cent), Italy (12.0 per cent), UK (9.0 per cent), France (8.9 per cent), The Netherlands (6.8 per cent), US (4.7 per cent)
Exports
Manufactured goods
Main destinations: UK (30.8 per cent total, 2005), Spain (22.7 per cent), Germany (13.7 per cent), Turkmenistan (10.4 per cent), Switzerland (8.3 per cent)
Re-exports
Petroleum (over 50 per cent of total), tobacco, manufactured goods and wine.

Industry and manufacturing
The shipbuilding company, Cammell Laird (Gibralter) Ltd ownes and operates the shipyard and dry dock. The port provides an important source of income. The Gibraltar government has encouraged the setting up of light industries there, by making available a package of incentives and other benefits to successful companies. Gibraltar also has a wine bottling plant and a satellite control system.
The New Harbours, a free-port zone where there are no duties or taxes on imported materials and low rates of tax on profits, comprises warehousing, industrial workshops and office space, available to rent or purchase for exporting companies.

Tourism
Tourism is a major sector of the economy and accounts for around a third of GDP. Gibraltar is known for its cheap shopping, military history, colonial architecture and beaches. Over seven million visitors arrive each year, mainly by the land route, although this number also includes

non-Gibraltarian frontier workers. Cross-border day visitors, who come primarily to shop, outnumber the traditional overnight visitors in both volume and value, resulting in a more robust economy. Cruise ship tourism is on the increase, and has been earmarked for encouragement by the authorities. Conference tourism is also being developed.

Hydrocarbons
Gibraltar does not produce oil, gas or coal. It imports petroleum products to meet its energies needs, around 4,000 barrels per day. However it does not import either gas or coal.

Banking and insurance
Gibraltar has a well-developed financial services sector, which has grown due to its independent jurisdiction under the EU's Treaty of Rome and its sound fiscal regime.
Gibralter is a signatory of a new EU tax agreement that was introduced in July 2005. It has agreed to pass on, to the tax department of an EU citizen's country, information concerning the amount of money in savings accounts, to allow tax to be levied from the account holder's home country.
There were 22 licensed banks and 18 insurance companies operating.

Offshore facilities
In 2003, the collapse of Rock Financial Services hit about 400 investors and was a blow to Gibraltar's reputation as a sound financial centre.

Time
GMT plus one hour (daylight saving, late-March to late-September, GMT plus two hours).

Geography
Gibraltar is situated at the southernmost tip of the Iberian Peninsula in southern Europe. The territory consists of a narrow peninsula running southwards from the south-west coast of Spain, to which it is connected by a sandy isthmus. About 8km (five miles) across the bay, to the west, lies Algeciras, the Spanish port, and 32km (20 miles) to the south, across the Strait of Gibraltar, is Morocco. The Mediterranean Sea is to the east.

Hemisphere
Northern

Climate
At the junction between the Mediterranean and Atlantic Ocean the climate in Gibraltar is heavily influenced by these and its local topography. Two local winds the levanter and poniente determine conditions. The easterly levanter produces warm, humid weather with sea fogs. The westerly poniente produces hot and mostly dry weather. Temperatures in summer average 25 degrees Celsius (C), although it can rise to over 30 degrees C; in winter it averages 14 degrees C.

Entry requirements
Passports
Required by all, except EU nationals travelling with valid national ID cards.

Visa
As an overseas territory of the UK, visa requirements are the same. Visas are required by all, except nationals of North America, Australasia, Japan and other EU members. For further exceptions and advice visit www.ukvisas.gov.uk/ (includes application forms). All visas must be applied for before travelling.
Gibraltar is outside the Schengen Agreement area. Visitors should ensure they have the right to return to Spain on their Schengen visa before entering Gibraltar from Spain.

Currency advice/regulations
There are no restrictions on the import or export of local or foreign currencies. Local bank notes are not accepted in the UK and should be exchanged before leaving Gibralter.
Travellers cheques are widely accepted and should be in pound sterling to avoid extra exchange fees.

Hotels
There is an official rating system in either stars or diamonds. Reservations should be made in advance, especially during summer (April–October).

Public holidays (national)
Fixed dates
1 Jan (New Year's Day), 8 Mar (Commonwealth Day), 1 May (May Day), 10 Sep (Gibraltar National Day), 25–26 Dec (Christmas).
Holidays that fall on the weekend are taken on the next Monday.

Variable dates
Good Friday, Easter Monday (Mar/Apr), Spring Bank Holiday (last Monday in May), Queen's Official Birthday (Jun), August Bank Holiday (last Monday in Aug).

Working hours
Banking
Mon–Thur: 0900–1530; Fri: 0900–1700.

Business
Mon–Fri: 0900–1700 (0800–1400, summer). Sat: 0900–1300.

Government
Mon—Fri: (winter) 0800—1615; (summer) 0730—1330.

Shops
Mon–Fri: Most shops open from 0900–1930 and some open from 0900–1300 and 1500–1900, Sat: 1000–1300.

Telecommunications
Mobile/cell phones
GSM 900 is available throughout the territory.

Electricity supply
240V AC, with UK style flat, thee-pin plugs.

Security
Violence and street crime is rare.

Getting there
Air
British Airways and Monarch Airlines operate daily direct flights from the UK.
National airline: GB Airways
International airport/s: Gibraltar (GIB) North Front airport, 1km from town centre. Facilities include duty-free shops, restaurants, bank and car hire. Taxis and hotel coaches are available. The airport is a ten minute walk from the centre of town.
Airport tax: None

Surface
Access is from Málaga, through the Spanish frontier at La Línea.
Rail: There are no railways in Gibraltar but there are links to the Spanish national railway across the border, accessible within a few minutes.
Water: There are regular ferry services from Tangier in Morocco.

Getting about
National transport
Bus and taxi services are available. Taxi drivers are obliged by law to produce, on demand, a copy of the taxi fares. Gibraltar has a total of about 45km of roads. There is no railway network.

City transport
Taxis: Taxis are available from the airport to the town centre.
Buses, trams & metro: There is a bus service which operates from the airport to the town centre, journey time 15 minutes.

Car hire
Local car hire is available. A valid EU or international driving licence and evidence of insurance are required (third party). An age limit may be imposed usually 23–70 years. Traffic drives on the right. The speed limit is 50kph (31mph), except where indicated. Dipped headlights are compulsory at night time and seat belts are compulsory.
Additional conditions apply for travel into Spain.

BUSINESS DIRECTORY

The addresses listed below are a selection only. While World of Information makes every endeavour to check these addresses, we cannot guarantee that changes have not been made, especially to telephone numbers and area codes. We would welcome any corrections.

Telephone area codes
The international direct dialling code (IDD) for Gibraltar is +350 followed by subscriber's number. (The IDD for Gibraltar is not recognised by Spain).

Chambers of Commerce
Gibraltar Chamber of Commerce, Don House, 38 Main Street, PO Box 29, Gibraltar (tel: 78-376; fax: 78-403; e-mail: gichacom@gibnet.gi).

Banking
Abbey National (Gibraltar) Ltd, 237 Main Street (tel: 76-090; fax: 72-028).

ABN Amro Bank (Gibraltar) Ltd, PO Box 100, 2-6 Main Street (tel: 79-220/79-370; fax: 78-512).

Baltica Bank (Gibraltar) Ltd, 215a Neptune House, Marina Bay (tel: 42-670; fax: 42-676).

Banco Atlántico (Gibraltar) Ltd, Eurolife Building, 1 Corral Road (tel: 40-117; fax: 40-110).

Banco Bilbao Vizcaya International (Gibraltar) Ltd, 3rd Floor, Hadfield House, Library Street (tel: 79-420; fax: 73-870).

Banco Bilbao Vizcaya (Gibraltar) Ltd, 260/262 Main Street (tel: 77-797, 77-871, 77-896).

Banco Central Sa, 198/200 Main Street (tel: 73-625, 73-650, 73-675; fax: 73-707).

Banco Español de Crédito, 114 Main Street (tel: 76-518; fax: 73-947).

Banque Indosuez, 206/210 Main Street (tel: 75-090; fax: 79-618).

Barclays Bank plc, 84/90 Main Street (tel: 78-565; fax: 79-509).

Crédit Suisse (Gibraltar) Ltd, Neptune House, Marina Bay (tel: 76-606; fax: 76-027).

Gibraltar Private Bank Ltd, PO Box 407, 10th Floor, ICC, Casemates (tel: 73-350; fax: 73-475).

Hambros Bank Ltd, PO Box 375, 32 Line Wall Road (tel: 74-850; fax: 79-037).

Hispano Commerzbank (Gibraltar) Ltd, Suite 14, 30/38 Main Street (tel: 74-199; fax: 74-174).

Lloyds Bank plc, 323 Main Street (tel: 77-373; fax: 70-023).

Midland Bank Trust Corporation (Gibraltar) Ltd, PO Box 19, Hadfield House, Library Street (tel: 79-500; fax: 72-090).

National Westminster Bank, 57 Line Wall Road (tel: 77-737; fax: 74-557).

Republic National Bank of New York (Gibraltar) Ltd, Neptune House, Marina Bay, PO Box 5578 (tel: 79-374; fax: 75-684).

Royal Bank of Scotland (Gibraltar) Ltd, 1 Corral Road (tel: 73-200; fax: 70-152).

Varde Bank International (Gibraltar) Ltd, PO Box 476, Suite E, Regal House, 3 Queensway (tel: 42-455; fax: 42-456).

Travel information
GB Airways, Iain Stewart Centre, Beehive Ring Road, Gatwick Airport, West Sussex RG6 0PB, UK (tel: (1293)664-239; fax: (1293)664-218).

London Passport Office, Globe House, 89 Ecclestone Square, London SW1V 1PN, UK (tel: (0870) 521-0410 (24-hour UK national advice line); (+44-20) 7901-2150 (international visa enquiries for British Overseas Territories. Opening hours: Mon-Fri 0730-1900; Sat 0900-1600); internet: www.passport.gov.uk; www.ukpa.gov.uk).

National tourist organisation offices
Gibraltar Tourist Board, Duke of Kent House, Cathedral Square (tel: 74-950; fax: 74-943; e-mail: tourism@gibnet.gi; internet site: www.gibraltar.gi).

Ministries
Government of Gibraltar, UK Office, 179 Strand, London WC2R 1EL, UK (tel: (+44-20) 7836-0777; fax: (+44-20) 7240-6612; e-mail: info@gibraltar.gov.uk; internet site: www.gibraltar.gov.uk).

Government Secretariat, 6 Convent Place (tel: 70-071; fax: 74-524).

Governor's Office, The Convent, Main Street (tel: 45-440; e-mail: convent@gibnet.gi).

Ministry of Tourism and Transport, Duke of Kent House, Cathedral Square (tel: 74-950; fax: 74-943).

Ministry of Trade, Industry and Telecommunications, Suite 771, Europort (tel: 52-052; fax: 71-406; e-mail: dticomm@gibnet.gi; internet site: www.gibraltar.gov.gi).

Other useful addresses
Economic Planning and Statistics Office, 6 Convent Place (tel: 75-515, 70-071).

Gibraltar Finance Centre, Suite 771, Europort (tel: 50-011; fax: 47-677; e-mail: fsc@gibnet.gi).

Gibraltar Information Bureau, Arundel Great Court, 179 Strand, London WC2R 1EH (tel: (+44-20) 7836-0777; fax: (+44-20) 7240-6612).

Gibraltar Telecommunications International Ltd, Mount Pleasant, 25 South Barrack Road (tel: 59-609; fax: 59-644).

Gibtelecom, Suite 942, Europort (tel: 52-200; fax: 71-673; internet site: www.gibtele.com).

Internet sites
Audio site – Talking about Gibraltar: www.gibnynex.gi/info/gibtalk

Business in Gibraltar: www.Gibraltarian.com/Gibraltar_business.asp

Government of Gibraltar: www.gibraltar.gov.gi

Gibraltar Broadcasting Corporation (GBC): www.gbc.gi

Offshore facilities: www.Gibraltaroffshore.com/

Greece

In Greece's September 2007 elections, Mr Karamanlis' centre-right New Democracy Party won 152 seats in Greece's 300 seat parliament, 13 down on the 2004 result, but still allowing President Karolos Papoulias to ask him to form a government. Although New Democracy polled 4 per cent less than in 2004, the principal opposition party, Pasok, also lost ground, recording its worst result since 1977. By February 2008, Mr Karamanlis' majority had been reduced to a wafer thin single seat, following the resignation from New Democracy of a deputy imputed in an unravelling corruption scandal.

The manifesto wobbles

New Democracy's election manifesto had promised reforms to the thorny problems of Greece's pensions and higher education. This was made clear in February 2008 when over 2 million Greek workers went on strike in protest at proposed government pension reforms. These include plans to merge some 170 state pension funds into a smaller number (five to six) of large units which would be entrusted to professional managers. Implicit in the reforms were proposals to reduce benefits for existing workers. Mr Karamanlis' efforts to introduce pension reforms were blighted by a concurrent series of corruption scandals involving not only senior political allies of the prime minister, but also the German industrial group, Siemens. Allegations surfaced that the German company had paid amounts up to eur100 million (US$100 million) to politicians in both the major parties. Some of the alleged bribes related to contracts for the 2004 Olympic Games. Another series of allegations related to the sale of government bonds at inflated prices to pension funds managed by government appointees.

Bucking the trend

2008 saw the longest uninterrupted period of growth Greece has known in recent years coming to an end. None-the-less, the

KEY FACTS

Official name: I Elliniki Dimokratia (The Hellenic Republic)

Head of State: President Karolos Papoulias (since Mar 2005)

Head of government: Prime Minister Costas Karamanlis (ND) (since 2004; re-elected Sep 2007)

Ruling party: Nea Dimokratia (ND) (New Democracy) (since 2004; re-elected 16 Sep 2007)

Area: 131,957 square km

Population: 11.12 million (2007)

Capital: Athens

Official language: Greek

Currency: Euro (eur) = 100 cents (from 1 Jan 2002; previous currency drachma, locked at Dr340.75 per euro)

Exchange rate: eur0.63 per US$ (Jul 2008)

GDP per capita: US$28,273 (2007)*

GDP real growth: 4.00% (2007)*

Labour force: 4.37 million (2004)

Unemployment: 8.30% (2007)

Inflation: 3.00% (2005)

Balance of trade: -US$34.25 billion (2005)

Foreign debt: US$233.10 billion (2004)

Visitor numbers: 16.04 million (2006)*

* estimated figure

economy expanded at a healthy annual rate of 3.6 per cent in the first quarter of 2008, in line with the government's forecast for the year. The government's 2008 budget, submitted to parliament in October 2008, ambitiously aimed to cut the budget deficit to 1.7 per cent of gross domestic product (GDP), with a view to balancing public finances by 2010. Luxembourg based Eurostat, the European Union (EU) statistics agency, had agreed to an upward revision of Greece's GDP by some 20 per cent. Even before the revision, the 12 year period of consistent growth around the 4 per cent mark had enabled the government to reduce unemployment and raise average incomes to 90 per cent of the EU-15 average. The budget projected a double digit increase in tax revenues against a smaller increase in government expenditure. Greece's finance minister, George Alogoskoufis saw the 2008 budget as marking the second phase of Greek fiscal consolidation, addressing the reduction of the deficits of the state health system and the state-owned enterprises.

Greece's average household borrowing levels were less than 65 per cent of the eurozone average, enabling domestic demand to remain high. The International Monetary Fund (IMF) in its mid-2008 report on the Greek economy expressed concerns that in the longer-term, Greece's persistent loss of competitiveness raised the prospect of a prolonged period of slow growth. Averting this risk would require improving cost competitiveness through wage moderation, an environment that encourages product upgrading, and a broadened effort to reform product and labour markets. In the short term, inflation remained a concern, reaching 4.4 per cent by April 2008, the highest (although not by much) rate in the eurozone (the countries that have adopted the euro as their currency). Government forecasts put inflation in 2008 at 4.0 per cent for the year, up from the 2.9 per cent recorded in 2007. Inflation has been fuelled by high wage increases, particularly in the private sector; public sector increases had been more moderate. High global energy and food prices had combined with peculiarly Greek factors such as loose controls of retail prices and increased transport costs to the tourism intensive islands. Greek productivity and competitiveness remain among the lowest in the EU. Greece also has the lowest level of exports as a proportion of total trade in the EU. Given Greece's relatively small population base, any significant economic growth will have to be more export-led; domestic demand will not provide sufficient depth in the long term. Another nagging problem is the immovably high level of the current account deficit.

Greece's financial authorities have been pursuing further fiscal consolidation with the goal of achieving a balanced budget by 2010. Given the high level of public debt and anticipated population ageing pressures, further adjustment thereafter to a surplus position will become necessary. The influx of baby boomers is expected to create problems for Greece's stretched social security system after 2015. In the meanwhile, Greece's revenue objectives for 2008–10 are ambitious; their achievement will require further revenue enhancing measures. Reforms to tax administration and expenditure management are being implemented, and will need to be broadened. A gradualist approach is being taken on pension reform. The reform agenda is narrow and the policy proposals are lacking full assessment of financing needs and cost savings. While the IMF sees a need for greater ambition, the authorities view their reform strategy as politically realistic. Structural reforms have been put in place, but impediments to higher productivity remain. Initiatives were underway to improve the business environment. However, enhancing competition and reducing labour market rigidities will remain challenges.

Banking

In its annual report, the IMF noted that the Greek banking sector appeared to be sound and in mid-2008 had remained largely unaffected by the international financial market turmoil. Greek banks have tended to focus on the twin objectives of developing their domestic business and gradual expansion in their immediate region of south-east Europe. The IMF has expressed concern that continued rapid credit growth and an increasing presence in south-eastern Europe, financed partly by wholesale funding, had increased Greek banks' exposure to credit, country, and liquidity risks.

Turkish delight

In January 2008 Mr Karamanlis made the first official visit to Turkey by a Greek prime minister since 1959. Although the landmark visit raised considerable hopes of improved relations between the two countries, it was difficult to see what the immediate results might be. There were few expectations in either Ankara or Athens that the visit would bring about any resolution of the long established animosity between Greece and Turkey. Although the climate of mutual mistrust has cooled down, this has done little to address the territorial disputes between the countries, not to mention any dialogue over the Cyprus issue. Although the political climate has not improved in practical terms, the same was no longer the case with commercial relations. A particular feature of 2007 was the continued expansion of trade and commercial ties between Greece and Turkey. Not only has a joint gas pipeline

KEY INDICATORS — Greece

	Unit	2003	2004	2005	2006	2007
Population	m	11.04	11.07	11.12	11.12	11.12
Gross domestic product (GDP)	US$bn	172.80	209.40	284.23	268.69	*314.62
GDP per capita	US$	15,881	18,722	25,560	24,157	*28,273
GDP real growth	%	4.5	4.2	3.7	4.2	*4.0
Inflation	%	3.5	3.1	3.5	3.3	3.0
Unemployment	%	9.3	10.0	9.9	8.9	8.3
Coal output	mtoe	9.7	9.5	9.6	9.3	8.1
Exports (fob) (goods)	US$m	13,040.0	15,500.0	17,631.0	20,300.0	*23,471.7
Imports (cif) (goods)	US$m	45,379.0	54,280.0	51,884.0	64,585.0	*75,100.1
Balance of trade	US$m	-32,339.0	-38,780.0	-34,253.0	-44,285.0	*-51,628.4
Current account	US$m	-10,750.0	-8,420.0	-18,235.0	-29,684.0	-43,703.0
Total reserves minus gold	US$m	4,361.4	1,191.0	506.4	565.9	631.1
Foreign exchange	US$m	3,843.3	743.7	309.1	408.3	518.2
Exchange rate	per US$	0.88	0.80	0.77	0.75	0.69

* estimated figure

been opened, by 2007, bi-lateral trade had increased to eur1.8 billion (US$1.8 billion). Turkey's Ziraat Bank planned to open two branches in Athens and in Komotini in north-eastern Greece in 2008; when completed, the total investment by the Turkish bank of eur18 million (US$18 million) would be the largest single Turkish investment in Greece. In 2006, the National Bank of Greece paid eur3.8 billion (US$3.8 billion) for the Turkish Finansbank. The trade between the two countries reflects certain imbalances in that while Turkey exports goods to Greece, Greece has focussed more on the export of capital to Turkey. Turkish investment in Greece has largely been through franchising agreements rather than through acquisition.

Risk assessment

Economy	Fair
Politics	Good
Regional stability	Good

COUNTRY PROFILE

Historical profile

Ancient Greece at one point ruled a substantial empire extending across the Middle East and Central Asia. Many features of Western civilisation can be traced to aspects of ancient Greek culture and institutions, including music, philosophy and democratic rule. The Greek monarchy later administered the eastern arm of the Roman empire. Following the fall of the Roman empire, Greece was initially ruled by the Byzantines from their capital in Constantinople (now Istanbul).

1454 After the fall of Constantinople to Suleiman the Magnificent, Greece and most of the eastern Mediterranean were occupied by the Ottoman empire.

1829 Following a war against the Ottomans lasting eight years, Greece declared its independence as a monarchy.

1913 The London Conference reduced the amount of ethnic Albanian-dominated territory of the former Ottoman Empire, Cameria (Chamouria) was granted to Greece.

1917 Greece entered the First World War on the side of the Allies and made territorial gains.

1923 Greece signed the Lausanne Peace Treaty with Turkey. The Treaty outlined the territory of each country and provided Greece with a number of islands in the Aegean Sea.

1939 Greece rejected Italy's ultimatum seeking free passage for its troops in the Second World War and repelled its attack, but was occupied by Germany. The government and the King went into exile. Mass armed resistance grew out of various political groupings.

1944 Liberation from the Nazis. The returned National Unity government under George Papandreou fought a civil war against the Communists.

1949 Constitutional monarchy was re-established. There were territorial gains from the war, the last of which was the Dodecanese islands in the south-eastern Aegean Sea.

1967–72 A military coup led by right-wing army officers deposed King Konstantinos II. An attempted counter-coup by the King failed, and he went into exile. Colonel Georgios Papadopoulos appointed himself prime minister. The regime was brutal and repressive with all political activity banned.

1973 Greece was declared a republic with Papadopoulos as president. General Demetrios Ioannides led a bloodless coup; Papadopoulos was overthrown. Partial civilian rule was allowed. General Phaidon Gizikis was appointed president.

1974 Civil war in Cyprus and the Turkish invasion of the island brought Greece close to war with Turkey and caused the downfall of the military junta. Elections resulted in a decisive victory for Nea Dimokratia (ND) (New Democracy). A referendum rejected proposals for a return to constitutional monarchy.

1975 A republican constitution providing for a parliamentary democracy was promulgated and Konstantinos Tsatsos was elected president.

1977 The ND was re-elected with a reduced majority.

1980 In May, Constantine Karamanlis was elected president. Greece joined the EU.

1981 The Panellino Socialistiko Kinima (Pasok) (Pan-Hellenic Socialist Movement) gained an absolute majority in parliament in the elections. The Pasok government, led by Andreas Papandreou, was the first socialist government in Greek history.

1985 President Karamanlis resigned and Christos Sartzetakis became president. Pasok was returned to power and implemented proposed constitutional changes. The government's programme of economic austerity became very unpopular and resulted in widespread industrial unrest.

1986 Constitutional amendments limited the powers of the president.

1989 ND won the largest proportion of votes in the elections.

1993 The ND government was forced to resign after losing its one seat parliamentary majority. Pasok regained power.

1995 Costis Stephanopoulos was elected president.

1996 Prime Minister Papandreou resigned due to ill health and Costas Simitis became prime minister. Andreas Papandreou died, ending an era of authoritarian control over Pasok, which won the parliamentary elections.

2000 Incumbent president, Stephanopoulos, was re-elected. Pasok was re-elected, becoming the first party to win three successive elections. Greece's application to join the Economic and Monetary Union (Emu) was accepted.

2001 Greece officially joined the Emu.

2002 Euro currency replaced the drachma.

2004 The ND, led by Costas Karamanlis, won the parliamentary elections.

2005 On 8 February, Karolos Papoulias was elected president; he was sworn in on 12 March. Newly introduced labour laws ended 'jobs for life'.

2006 On 17 January the prime minister announced proposals for revision of the constitution.

2007 Russia and Greece signed a US$1.2 billion pipeline deal on 15 March. The 285km pipeline will allow access for Russian oil, via Alexandroupolis on the Aegean Sea, to the huge EU market. The project is expected to be completed in 2010. In August as series of forest fires swept through areas in southern Greece and killed over 60 people and destroyed over 4,500 homes. The prime minister called an early election on 16 September and despite the critism levelled at the government for its inability in dealing with the destruction, the ruling ND won with a reduced majority, 41.8 per cent (152 seats out of 300), the main opposition, Pasok, won 38.1 per cent (102); turnout was 74.1 per cent. Costas Karamanlis resumed his post as prime minister on 18 September.

2008 The ongoing disagreement between Greece and FYROM Macedonia concerning the name Macedonia was again a cause of dissent in March. Greece threatened to block membership of NATO unless its neighbour dropped its name, Macedonia.

Political structure

Constitution

The constitution of 1975 has been revised on several occasions in line with contemporary circumstances. It sets out the rights and responsibilities of the parliament, judiciary, people and church. The constitution is enshrined in law.

In March 1986, parliament ratified changes to the 1975 constitution, limiting the president's power in relation to parliament.

Form of state

Parliamentary democratic republic

The executive

The president of the republic is Head of State, and is elected by parliament for a

five-year term, for a maximum of two terms. The president must be elected by a two-thirds majority, or on the third ballot by a three-fifths majority.
Since 1985 when presidential power was reduced, de facto executive power is wielded by the prime minister and cabinet. The cabinet is named by the prime minister.

National legislature
Legislative power rests with the 300-member unicameral Vouli ton Ellinon (parliament), elected for four years by universal and compulsory adult suffrage.

Legal system
Greek law is based on codified Roman law with the judiciary divided into civil, criminal, and administrative courts. Judicial independence is guaranteed under the constitution.

Last elections
16 September 2007 (parliamentary); 8 February 2005 (presidential).
Results: Presidential: Karolos Papoulias was elected president, receiving 279 votes in the 300-seat parliament.
Parliamentary: the ruling ND won with 41.8 per cent of the vote (152 seats out of 300); Pasok won 38.1 per cent (102); the Kommounistiko Komma Ellados (KKE) (Communist Party of Greece) won 8.2 per cent (22); the Synaspismos tis Rizospastikis Aristeras (SYRIZA) (Coalition of Left and Progressive Forces) 5.0 per cent (14) and Laikos Orthodoxos Synagermos (LAOS) (Popular Orthodox Rally) 3.8per cent (10). Turnout was 74.1 per cent.

Next elections
16 September 2007 (snap parliamentary); 2010 (presidential).

Political parties

Ruling party
Nea Dimokratia (ND) (New Democracy) (since 2004; re-elected 16 Sep 2007)

Main opposition party
Panellino Sosialistiko Kinima (Pasok) (Pan-Hellenic Socialist Movement).

Population

11.12 million (2007)
Last census: March 2001: 10,964,020
Population density: 81 inhabitants per square km. Urban population: 60 per cent (1995–2001).
Annual growth rate: 0.5 per cent 1994–2004 (WHO 2006)

Ethnic make-up
Greece is a very homogenous state and the vast majority of its citizens regard themselves as ethnic Greek. However, there are also small numbers of Turks, Pomaks, Gypsies, Vlaks and an increasing numbers of illegal Albanian economic refugees (some 300,000 are believed to live in Athens).

Religions
Over 95 per cent of the population are baptised in the Greek Orthodox Church. There are small Muslim, Catholic and Jewish communities.

Education
Primary education lasts for six years. Secondary education generally lasts for six years and is divided into two equal periods. Approximately 47 per cent of the relevant age group participate in some form of tertiary education. Overcrowded classes at public high schools and a lack of facilities mean that students take private tuition or attend night school to improve their chances of going to university, for which entrance is fiercely competitive.
Women comprise almost 60 per cent of Greek graduates.
Public education expenditure is equivalent to just over 3 per cent of GDP.
Literacy rate: 98 per cent, male; 96 per cent, female; adult rates (World Bank).
Enrolment rate: 93 per cent at primary level and 95 per cent at secondary level (of the relevant age groups).
Pupils per teacher: 14 in primary schools

Health
Per capita total expenditure on health (2003) was US$1,997; of which per capita government spending was US$1,025, at the international dollar rate, (WHO 2006).
Although basic healthcare is provided free of charge, many Greeks find standards unsatisfactory and prefer to go to private doctors and clinics, or even to pay the high cost of treatment abroad.

HIV/Aids
HIV prevalence: 0.2 per aged 15–49 in 2003 (World Bank)
Life expectancy: 79 years, 2004 (WHO 2006)
Fertility rate/Maternal mortality rate: 1.2 births per woman, 2004 (WHO 2006)
Child (under 5 years) mortality rate (per 1,000): 5.0 per 1,000 live births (World Bank)
Head of population per physician: 4.38 physicians per 1,000 people, 2001 (WHO 2006)

Welfare
Social security is handled by more than 350 state-run or state-supervised social insurance funds, which together cover almost all the Greek population. The largest of these funds is the general social security scheme, run by the Idryma Koinonikis Asfalisis (IKA) (Social Security Institute). The scheme covers 1.8 million wage earners, pays pensions and operates a network of hospitals and out patient clinics.
Parliament approved the restructuring of the debt-burdened and complex state pension system in June. Greece has a growing aged population, which will become problematic.
At 9 per cent of the total labour force, the proportion of Greek employees living in conditions of poverty is one of the highest in the EU.

Main cities
Athens (capital, estimated population 721,477 in 2005), Piraeus (172,025), Thessaloniki (356,449), Patras (164,968), Iráklion (capital of Crete, 139,798), Corinth (31,377), Lárisa (129,661), Kallithéa (108,202).

Languages spoken
Macedonian, Albanian, Turkish, Aroumanian, Bulgarian and Pomak are spoken by their resident populations. Most people in the business community also speak English, French or German.

Official language/s
Greek

Media

Other news agencies: ANA-MPA: www.ana-mpa.gr

Press
Although the media has considerable freedom, a public prosecutor may stop circulation of an edition of a newspaper on the grounds that it is blasphemous, offends public decency, reveals military or state secrets or offends the Greek president.
Dailies: There are 34 national daily newspapers and most publish Sunday editions. Most newspapers have political party affiliations.
In Greek, high circulation newspapers include Ethnos (Nation) (www.ethnos.gr), Kathimerini (Daily) (www.kathimerini.gr), To Vima, (The Tribune) (www.tovima.gr), Eleftheros Typos (Free Press) (www.e-tipos.com) and two evening publications include Eleftherotypia (Press Freedom) (www.enet.gr) and Ta Nea, (The News) (www.tanea.gr). Some offer online articles in English.
Weeklies: Many daily newspapers publish weekend editions. In Greek, To Proto Thema (www.protothema.gr) is a tabloid newspaper and Stochos (www.stoxos.gr) is a nationalist publication. In English Athens News (www.athensnews.gr); Big News Network is an internet site (www.bignewsnetwork.com).
Business: In Greek, there are several business newspapers, Naftemboriki (www.naftemporiki.gr) is a financial daily, Kerdos (www.kerdos.gr), Reporter (www.reporter.gr) reports on financial markets, others include Express (www.express.gr), Imerissia (www.imerisia.gr), Isotimia (www.isotimia.gr) and

Oikonomikos Tachydromos (http://oikonomikos.dolnet.gr), a magazine for economic and policy analysis. Regional publications include Thrakiki Agora (www.thrakikiagora.gr) and Thrakiki Gi (www.thrakikigi.gr) from Komotini in the north-east. Industry publications include Naftika Chronika (www.naftikachronika.gr) concerning Greek shipping. Some offer online articles in English.

Periodicals: In Greek, for women, monthly magazines include Gynaika, the oldest women's publication and Praktiki for articles on the home.

Broadcasting

Elliniki Radiophonía Tileórassi (ERT) (Hellenic Radio and Television) (www.ert.gr) is the state-owned, public broadcaster. It derives around 80 per cent of its funding through licence fees.

Radio: ERT (http://tvradio.ert.gr) operates five radio channels, ERA 1–5, with nationwide coverage. ERA5 is an overseas network called 'Voice of Greece', while Filia (Friendship) broadcasts to immigrants in 12 languages, mainly European but includes Arabic, providing news, information and entertainment. There are over 400 commercial radio stations, many unregulated by government, providing programmes of music, sport and news and talk.

Television: ERT (www.ert.gr) operates three TV channels; two, ET1 and NET are broadcast from Athens and ET3 broadcasts from Thessaloniki with regional programmes for Northern Greece. New technologies include ERT Digital and ERT World (via satellite) with programmes broadcast around the world.

There are dozen commercial, private, digital and satellite channels based regionally, including Mega Channel (www.megatv.com), Skai TV (www.skai.gr), ANT1 Gold (www.gold.antenna.gr), Nova Cinema (www.novacinema.gr) and Nova Sport (www.novasport.gr).

In 2008 there were no cable TV services, although two services are available via high-speed internet connections.

Advertising

Greece has a modern advertising market with a typical annual adspend of US$12.5 billion. Television and magazines account for around 30 per cent each of the total amount, with newspapers capturing around 15 per cent.

There are restrictions on advertising to children, with no ads targeting them on TV until 2200 hours. Alcohol cannot be advertised on radio or TV until 1800 and 1900 hours respectively, while tobacco advertising is completely banned on electronic media.

External poster panels are popular with an estimated 26,000 nationwide.

Economy

Greece has a mixed economy with a heavy dependence on tourism, agriculture and shipping. It has experienced strong GDP growth since the 1990s, although with mixed results. Current accounts have been in deficit since 2000, while inflation has been consistently above the 3.0 per cent peg set under the EU fiscal rules on stability and growth.

Nevertheless in 2005, GDP growth was 3.7 per cent due to domestic demand and a rise in manufactured goods as well as a liberalised financial sector and private sector credit. It is estimated that GDP growth will be 4.1 per cent in 2006. Unemployment was been around 10 per cent since 2001, but the trend is downward from 9.9 per cent in 2005 to a projected 8.8 per cent in 2007.

Greece's banking industry is a highly profitable sector, with strong capital and liquidity positions. The IMF, in a January 2007 report, considered the exposure of Greek banks to non-performing loans was high and that the trend continues. The central bank is increasing its monitoring of bank lending standards, strengthening provisioning requirements and measures to limit credit to highly indebted households. In 2006 the Bank of Cyprus made a take-over bid of around US$4.8 billion for the Athens-registered Piraeus Bank, Emporiki, which could have produced one of the largest banks in Greece, with 12 per cent of total deposits. However, the French Crédit Agricole bank finally acquired 71.97 per cent of the stock, in August. The Fitch credit rating agency increased the Emporiki Bank's Issuer Default rating from BBB to A+ and the bank's individual rating from BBB- to A.

Tourism does much to drive the economy and since the success of the Olympic games in 2004, it has remained in positive growth with a 5.6 per cent rise in 2005. In 2006 the tourist sector accounted for 18 per cent of Greek GDP growth, and employed one in five people. The number of visitors expected to arrive in 2007 is 14 million, however the tourist association has warned that the competitiveness of Greece with a strong euro may loose its market share, as visitors switch destinations to Turkey, Egypt and elsewhere. The recommendation is that the industry should cater for more than sun-seekers, with value-added activities such as archaeological tours, spas, sailing and cruises.

The export of Greek agricultural products will be enhanced following recommendations for the promotion of products with specific designation of origin, backed by EU measures to limit external copying of product and name.

Greece has the world's largest commercial fleet and is fifth overall in fleet numbers, while being ranked number one, at 14.1 per cent of global, gross tonnage. The shipping sector contributes up to 4.5 per cent of GDP and employs around 160,000 people or 4 per cent of total employment.

External trade

As a member of the European Union, Greece operates within a communitywide free trade union, with tariffs sets as a whole. Internationally, the EU has free trade agreements with a number of nations and trading blocs worldwide. It is Europe's largest producer of tobacco and the fifth largest exporter of cotton worldwide. Exports account for almost 50 per cent of Greece's GDP.

Imports

Principal imports include raw materials, fuels and lubricants, chemicals, machinery and transport equipment, foodstuffs, basic manufactures and consumer goods.

Main sources: Germany (12.6 per cent total, 2006), Italy (11.5 per cent), Russia (7.1 per cent).

Exports

Principal exports include tobacco, electrical and manufactured goods, petroleum products, chemicals, textiles and agricultural products, fruit and vegetables and live animals.

Main destinations: Germany (11.5 per cent total, 2006), Italy (11.4 per cent), Bulgaria (6.5 per cent).

Agriculture

Farming

Agriculture is an important but diminishing sector of the economy, typically contributing, around 8.3 per cent to GDP and employing around 12 per cent of the labour force.

The government's agricultural policy is, to a large extent, shaped by EU farm policies, since the bulk of Greece's net benefits from EU membership arrive in the form of price supports for farmers. Greek farms are small by EU standards, averaging less than two hectares (ha).

In January 2006, fundamental reform to the Common Agricultural Policy (CAP) was initiated to replace subsidies paid on farm output, which tended to benefit large farms and encourage overproduction, with single farm payments not conditional on production. This should reward farms that provide and maintain a healthy environment, food safety and animal welfare standards. The changes are also intended to encourage market conscious production and cut the cost of CAP to the EU taxpayer.

Main crops include wheat, barley, maize, fruit (especially olives), vegetables, oil seeds, tobacco, cotton and sugar beet.

Traditionally, farm co-operatives have played a large role in agriculture as a source of purchasing seeds, renting machinery and selling products. Larger co-operatives also handle basic processing and marketing. Attempts to restructure the co-operatives have largely failed, with weak management and widespread corruption preventing their modernisation and development.

The sector is also handicapped by weak infrastructure, low levels of technology and generally poor soil. However, with the exception of meat, dairy products and animal feeds, Greece is self-sufficient in foodstuffs.

During the summer of 2007 forest fires devasted large areas of southern Greece, with particular damage inflicted on the olive groves of Kalamata; an estimated 20 per cent of national production was lost. Production is not expected to recover fully until 2012.

Crop production for 2005 included: 4,603,200 tonnes (t) cereals in total, 1,800,000t wheat, 2,300,000t maize, 1,157,000t citrus fruit, 1,200,000t grapes, 840,000t potatoes, 220,000t barley, 1,700,000t tomatoes, 592,619t oilcrops, 123,000t tobacco, 2,200,000t olives, 2,350,000t sugar beet, 80,300t chillies & peppers, 92,400t treenuts, 1,100,000t seed cotton, 359,000t cotton lint, 3,637,300t fruit in total, 3,847,650t vegetables in total. Estimated livestock production included: 476,573t meat in total, 75,000t beef, 134,500t pig meat, 81,000t lamb, 44,000t goat meat, 134,373t poultry, 105,000t eggs, 1,975,045t milk, 15,000t honey, 12,250t cattle hides, 16,300t sheepskins, 9,600t greasy wool, 20t cocoons, silk.

Fishing

Fish production is important for domestic consumption and export. The annual freshwater fish catch is around 25,000 tonnes, with a marine catch of approximately 270,000 tonnes. Coastal fish farms produce sea bass and gilthead bream.

Although Greece has an expanding aquaculture sector, its processing and marketing sector remains underdeveloped. Following the EU's common fisheries policy, the country benefits from the EU structural fund that covers the whole sector and also includes the development of the processing and marketing of products.

In 2004, the total marine fish catch was 76,323 tonnes and the total crustacean catch was 4,417 tonnes.

Forestry

Forest and other wooded land accounts for half of the land area, with forest cover estimated at 3.5 million hectares (ha). Most of the forest is in the northern and western part of the mainland and about 90 per cent is available for wood supply. Significant quantities of roundwood production are used for fuel consumption.

More than three-quarters of the forest and other wooded land is under public ownership, and only about 20 per cent is privately owned. The forest sector is rather small and all types of forest products are imported, mainly comprising sawnwood and paper products.

Timber imports in 2004 were US$1.0 billion, while exports amounted to US$140.4 million.

Production in 2004 included 1,525,588 cubic metres (cum) roundwood, 468,678cum industrial roundwood, 380,878cum sawlogs and veneer logs, 191,080cum sawnwood, 841,778t wood-based panels, 1,056,910cum wood fuel; 266,497 tonnes (t) paper and paperboard, 43,000t printing and writing paper, 51,000t recovered paper.

Industry and manufacturing

Industry typically accounts for 25 per cent of GDP and employs 26 per cent of the labour force. Within the industrial sector, manufacturing accounts for 57 per cent of output and construction 32 per cent. The remaining 11 per cent of industrial output is accounted for by the minerals and utilities sectors.

Manufacturing, which contributes around 15 per cent to overall GDP, is dominated by small family-owned companies, most of which are situated around Athens or in export-oriented zones around the port of Thessaloniki.

The number of mergers and acquisitions of Greek firms by foreign investors has increased in recent years, with greater numbers of companies making initial public offerings (IPOs) on the Athens Stock Exchange. However, production has been sluggish and relatively few industries are competitive on a European level.

Greek industry is also less competitive compared to its EU neighbours because it has no land boundaries with the Union.

The aluminium sector, which is facing a shortage of domestic raw material, represents more than 1.5 per cent of GDP and employs approximately 40,000 workers.

Tourism

The tourist sector is Greece's biggest industry and principal source of foreign exchange earnings. In 2005 it should earn 38.6 per cent, or US$16.2 billion, in total exports. Travel and tourism is expected to generate US$23 billion, or 7.2 per cent of GDP and employ 18.2 per cent of the workforce, in 2005. The sector attracted US$5.7 billion or 10.7 per cent of total capital investment.

The government is seeking to improve quality by developing the conference and incentives market and upgrading hotels. Investment proposals for luxury leisure complexes are being encouraged.

Every year, there are around 12 million foreign visitors to Greece, with a boost of 4.52 per cent in 2004 when Greece hosted the Olympic Games in Athens.

Mining

There is a relative wealth of natural resources including large deposits of bauxite (aluminium ore), marble, lignite, magnesite, ferro-chrome, ferro-nickel, lead, zinc, uranium and manganese.

Mining activity is small-scale and the sector typically contributes only 3 per cent to GDP and employs only 1 per cent of the workforce.

New gold resources have been found at Skouries (an ancient copper mine), estimated to contain five–seven million ounces of gold.

Hydrocarbons

Greece has oil reserves of around seven million barrels (2005), produces around 6,411 barrels per day (bpd) and consumes 429,000bpd annually and is, therefore, a net importer of oil; oil provides 65 per cent of the country's fuel source. However, its importance is beginning to decline, as natural gas becomes more important.

Most domestic oil production comes from the Prinos fields, which are exploited by North Aegean Petroleum Company (NAPC) consortium.

Greece's oil industry is dominated by the state owned Hellenic Petroleum (HP), for which the government has a 27.5 per cent stake.

On the 15 March, Russia, Greece and Bulgaria signed a US$1.2 billion pipeline deal. The pipeline will run inland, from the Bulgarian Black Sea port of Burgas to Alexandroupolis, on the Aegean Sea. Russian oil will be transported via the 285km pipeline to the huge EU market, avoiding the busy Bosphorus, where oil tankers can wait for days for access to open waters. A Russian consortium will hold a 51 per cent stake in the deal to build and operate the pipeline and a joint Greek/Bulgarian consortium 24.5 per cent each. The project is expected to be completed in 2010.

HP operates a 214km oil pipeline, with a capacity to carry about 50,200bpd, from the port of Thessaloniki to Skopje in Macedonia. HP also operates three oil refineries with a combined refining capacity of 301,400bpd and a private refinery with a 100,000bpd capacity.

Total natural gas reserves stood at 990 million cubic metres (cum) in 2005. Consumption has been low, since the mid-1990s when consumption was 28.3 million cum, to 2.4 billion cum in 2003, and is projected to triple by 2015.

The Greek natural gas sector is controlled by the Greek Public Gas Company (DEPA). However, since 2004 market liberalisation has seen ownership opened to external competition.
Greece had coal reserves of 4.23 million tonnes in 2005. Reserves are comprised wholly of low quality lignite, with high extraction costs.

Energy
Greece generates approximately 50 million MW of electricity annually; around 90 per cent is thermal. Around 63 per cent of primary energy requirements are met by imported oil. Emphasis has been on developing indigenous oil resources (largely from the Prinos oil field) and expanding hydroelectric and geothermal power generation, but most future power plants will be entirely gas-fired. Growth in electricity has increased by 50 per cent since 1995 and the energy authorities estimate that it will need an extra 6,000MW of additional capacity by 2015.
The production, distribution and transmission of electricity in Greece was under the full control of the state-owned Public Power Corporation (PPC). However EU requirements for market liberalisation have compelled the government to open up ownership to competition. By 2005 state-control was 51 per cent of PPC. Although PPC has lost its monopoly it still produces 96 per cent of all electricity production.
The power network is connected to the networks of Albania, Bulgaria and Macedonia. Greece exports electricity to Kosovo in Serbia and Montenegro.
Greece is the EU's second-largest solar collector (after Germany), with 20 per cent of households using solar powered water heaters.

Financial markets
Stock exchange
The Athens Stock Exchange (Athex) is home to the Helenic Exchange (Helex), Central Securities, Athens Derivatives Exchange and the Thessalonica Exchange (TSEC).
Athex has over 300 listed companies, with the Hellenic Telecom Organisation having the most traded shares in 2005.

Banking and insurance
Liberalisation of the banking system was initiated in 1987. Interest rates are fully freed and commercial banks permitted to handle forward dealing in foreign exchange. Companies can borrow in foreign exchange without restriction.
Central bank
Bank of Greece; European Central Bank (ECB).

Time
GMT plus two hours (daylight saving, late-March to late-September, GMT plus three hours)

Geography
Greece lies in south-eastern Europe. The country consists mainly of a mountainous peninsula between the Mediterranean Sea and the Aegean Sea. It is bounded by Albania, Macedonia (FYROM) and Bulgaria to the north, Turkey to the north-east, the Aegean Sea to the east, the Sea of Crete to the south and the Ionian Sea to the west. To the south, east and west of the mainland are many Greek islands, the largest being Crete.
Hemisphere
Northern

Climate
Coastal regions and the islands have typical Mediterranean conditions, with mild, rainy winters and hot, dry, sunny summers. Rainfall comes almost entirely in the winter months, although amounts vary widely according to position and relief. Continental conditions affect the northern mountainous areas, with severe winters, deep snow cover and heavy precipitation, but summers are hot.
Athens: 9 degrees Celsius (C) (January); 28 degrees C (July); annual rainfall 414mm.

Dress codes
A suit and tie or formal clothing are necessary for business meetings, even during the hot summer months.
Women tend to dress smartly in the evening and men wear either suits or smart, casual clothes.

Entry requirements
Passports
Required by all, except nationals of EU/EEA countries, Switzerland and Monaco holding valid national identity cards. Passports must be valid for at least three months beyond length of stay.
Visa
Required by all, except nationals of Schengen agreement signatory countries and citizens of most of the Americas, Europe and many Asian countries. For confirmation of exceptions, contact the consular section of the nearest embassy. For those applying for a business visa, contact the consulate before travelling to determine requirements. A Schengen visa application (offered in several languages) can be downloaded from http://europa.eu/abc/travel/ see 'documents you will need'.
Currency advice/regulations
There are no restrictions on the import and export of local or foreign currency. Foreign currency over US$1,000 or equivalent must be declared on arrival.

Customs
Personal items are duty-free. There are no duties levied on alcohol and tobacco between EU member states, providing amounts imported are for personal consumption.
Strict regulations apply concerning the export of antiquities, including rocks from archaeological sites. Penalties range from large fines to prison terms.

Health (for visitors)
Nationals of the European Economic Area (EEA) countries and Switzerland can access reduced cost and sometimes free medical treatment using a European Health Insurance Card (EHIC) while visiting the EEA. Exceptions include nationals of the 10 countries which joined the EU in 2004 whose EHICs are not valid in Switzerland. Application for the EHIC should be made before travelling.
Mandatory precautions
Yellow fever vaccination certificate is required if travelling from infected area.
Advisable precautions
Long-term visitors should consider hepatitis A immunisation. Drinking water is not always purified .
Comprehensive travel insurance is advisable, in case of medical or other emergencies.

Hotels
Numerous hotels in all main towns, classified as de luxe, A,B,C,D and E. There is a 15 per cent service charge. A small tip will be expected. It is advisable to make reservations well in advance, especially between May and September.

Credit cards
All major credit cards are accepted.

Public holidays (national)
Fixed dates
1 Jan (New Year's Day), 6 Jan (Epiphany), 25 Mar (Independence Day), 1 May (Labour Day), 15 Aug (Assumption Day), 28 Oct (Ochi Day/National Day), 25 Dec (Christmas Day), 26 Dec (St Stephen's Day).
Variable dates
Greek Orthodox Shrove Monday, Greek Orthodox Good Friday, Greek Orthodox Easter Monday, Greek Orthodox Whit Monday, Greek Orthodox Pentecost.

Working hours
Banking
Mon–Fri: 0800–1400.
Business
Mon–Fri: generally 0800–1400 and 1700–2000; tend to close earlier during summer and on Mon and Wed afternoons.
Government
Mon–Fri: usually 0800–1500.

Shops
Mon, Wed and Sat: 0800–1400; Tue, Thu and Fri: 0800–1400 and 1800–2100.

Telecommunications
Mobile/cell phones
There are GSM roaming facilities available in 900/1800 band widths, with coverage throughout the country, including the island territories.

Electricity supply
220V AC

Social customs/useful tips
Personal contact is an important way of conducting business in Greece.
Greek bureaucracy can be slow. Identification documents and various authorisation letters or seals are necessary.
It is forbidden to photograph military installations and aircraft. Penalties for breaking the law can be severe.

Security
Visitors should be alert to the presence of pickpockets and purse-snatchers in tourist sites, particularly in Athens. As with the rest of Europe, there is a threat from terrorist activity, but Greece has its own anarchists, who occasionally engage in violence.

Getting there
Air
Greece has a strong tourist industry that relies on 80 per cent of international visitors arriving by air. Airports are located on the mainland as well as the islands.
National airline: Olympic Airways
International airport/s: Eleftherios Venizelos Airport (ATH), sited in Sparta, 27km north-west of Athens. Facilities include: business centre, shops, duty-free shops, restaurants and car hire. Further information can be obtained at www.aia.gr. Express bus routes carry passengers into Athens or the port of Pireaus.
Other airport/s: Alexandroupolis (AXD), 7km from city; Corfu (CFU), 1.6km from city; Heraklion (HER), 5km from city; Ioannina (IOA), 5km from city; Kos (KGS), 27km from city; Mykonos (JMK); Paros (PAS); Rhodes (RHO), 16km south-west of Rhodes; Thessaloniki Makedonia (SKG), 16km from city; Skiathos (JSI); Thira (JTR).
Airport tax: International eur12.5; domestic eur8.51
Surface
Road: The Greek road network is accessible via Italy, Bulgaria and Macedonia (FYROM) (border crossing at Medzitlija, near Bitola).
Rail: The Greek rail network is connected to most European routes via Italy, Bulgaria and Macedonia (FYROM). There is a daily service between Athens and Istanbul.
Water: Frequent passenger ferry services operate from Italy to Piraeus. A car ferry service runs between Ancona and Brindisi (Italy) and Igoumenitsa and Patras.
There is a ferry from Marmaris, Turkey, to the island of Rhodes.
Main port/s: Heraklion, Igoumenitsa, Patras, Piraeus, Rafina, Salonika and Volos.

Getting about
National transport
Air: As well as the international airports, there are a further 25 other airports all connected by regular services operated by Olympic Airways.
Road: There are 117,000km of roads in Greece, of which about 9,000km are unpaved. There are 470km of motorways, including a route from Athens to Thessaloniki.
Rail: Over 2,500km of track is operated by Hellenic Railways Organisation Ltd, with services to most towns.
Water: About 80km of navigable inland waterways are used, as well as several regular ferry services along the coast and connecting the various islands.
City transport
Taxis: Taxis are plentiful in Athens, but avoid rush hours. There is an extra charge for each piece of luggage, waiting time, journeys outside Athens/Piraeus and journeys after midnight. Yellow taxis run from the airport to downtown Athens.
Buses, trams & metro: There is a good, but often busy, bus network in Athens with a standard flat rate within city limits. Tickets are available at blue booths situated near the bus stops, or at many kiosks throughout the city. These tickets must be inserted into a machine inside the bus to be valid. Double-decker buses run between the airport and downtown Athens, operating every 20 minutes from 0600 until midnight.
The Attico Metro runs from 0530 to midnight daily, approximately every four minutes during rush hour and every 10 minutes at other times. Tickets must be purchased before entering the metro and must be cancelled upon entry.
An extension to the subway system was inaugurated in 2000 as part of the subway grid built for the 2004 Olympic Games.
Car hire
All major car hire companies have offices in Athens and some other main towns. Rates vary depending on size of car, length of hire and season. International driving licences are recognised, but UK, Belgian, Austrian and German full licences are also accepted. International insurance Green Card is valid, provided Greece is mentioned. The wearing of seatbelts is compulsory. Traffic drives on the right .
Extreme care is necessary if riding a motorbike.

BUSINESS DIRECTORY

The addresses listed below are a selection only. While World of Information makes every endeavour to check these addresses, we cannot guarantee that changes have not been made, especially to telephone numbers and area codes. We would welcome any corrections.

Telephone area codes
The international direct dialling code (IDD) for Greece is +30, followed by area code and subscriber's number:

Athens	210	Samos	273
Heraklion	81	Thessaloniki	31

Useful telephone numbers
Police: 100
Fire: 199
Hospitals: 106
Emergency services (24-hours; information in English, French and Greek, to request ambulances, fire department, police and coastguard): 112

Chambers of Commerce
American-Hellenic Chamber of Commerce, 109 Messoghion Avenue, 11526 Athens (tel: 699-3559; fax: 698-5686; e-mail: info@amcham.gr).

Athens Chamber of Commerce and Industry, 7 Akademias Street, 10671 Athens (tel: 360-4815; fax: 361-6408; e-mail: info@acci.gr).

British-Hellenic Chamber of Commerce, 25 Vassilissis Sophia Avenue, 10674 Athens (tel: 721-0361; fax: 722-2119; e-mail: info@bhcc.gr).

Heraklion Chamber of Commerce and Industry, 9 Koronaiou Street, 71202 Heraclion, Crete (tel: 022-9013; fax: 022-2914; e-mail: info@ebeh.gr).

Samos Chamber of Commerce and Industry, 19 Koundourioti Street, 83100 Samos (tel: 087-970; fax: 022-784; e-mail: samcci@otonet.gr).

Thessaloniki Chamber of Commerce and Industry, 29 Tsimiski Street, 54624 Thessaloniki (tel: 037-0100; fax: 037-0166; e-mail: root@ebeth.gr).

Union of Hellenic Chambers of Commerce and Industry, 7 Akademias Street, 10671 Athens (tel: 363-2702; fax: 362-2320; e-mail: hellas@uhcci.gr).

Banking
Agricultural Bank of Greece SA, Panepistimiou 23, 105-64 Athens (tel: 939-9911; fax: 323-9611).

Alpha Bank, 40 Stadiou Street, 102-52 Athens (tel: 326-0000; fax: 326-5438).

Commerical Bank of Greece, 11 Sophocleous Street, 102-35 Athens (tel: 328-4000; fax: 325-3746).

Egnatia Bank, Omirou 22, 106-72 Athens (tel: 360-6914; fax: 362-7945).

General Bank, Panepistimiou 9, 105-64 Athens (tel: 324-1289; fax: 322-2271).

National Bank of Greece, Aeolou 86, 150-51 Athens (tel: 334-1000; fax: 321-3119; internet site: http://www.nbg.gr).

Post-Office Savings Bank, Pesmazoglou 2-6, 105-59 Athens (tel: 323-0621; fax: 323-1055).

Central bank

Bank of Greece, 21 E Venizelos Avenue, GR 102-50 Athens (tel: 320-1111; fax: 323-2239; e-mail: secretariat@bankofgreece.gr).

European Central Bank (ECB), Kaiserstrasse 29, D-60311 Frankfurt am Main, Germany (tel: (+49-69) 13-440; fax: (+49-69) 1344-6000; e-mail: info@ecb.int).

Travel information

Athens Airport (East), Helliniko, 167-00 Athens (tel: 969-9111; fax: 966-6162).

Athens Airport (West), Helliniko, 167-00 Athens (tel: 936-9111; fax: 936-3328).

Athens International Airport (Eleftherios Venizelos), 5th km Spata, Loutsa Ave, 190 04 Spata (tel: 369-8300; fax: 369-8883; internet site: http://www.aia.gr).

Hellenic Chamber of Hotels, 24 Stadiou Street, 10564 Athens (tel: 331-0022/33; fax: 323-6962, 322-5449).

Olympic Airways, Syngrou Ave 96-100, 117-41 Athens (tel: 926-9111; fax: 926-7154).

Ministry of tourism

Ministry of Tourism, Amerikis 2B, 105-64 Athens (tel: 322-3111; fax: 322-4148).

National tourist organisation offices

Ellinikos Organismos Tourismou (GNTO) (Greek National Tourist Organisation), Odos Amerikis 2, Athens 10564 (tel: 322-3111/9).

Ministries

Ministry of Aegean, Syngrou Ave 49, 117-43 Athens (tel: 923-7970; fax: 923-8200).

Ministry of Agriculture, Acharnon 2, 101-76 Athens (tel: 529-1111; fax: 524-0475).

Ministry of Commerce, Caningos Square, 106-77 Athens (tel: 381-6242; fax: 384-2642).

Ministry of Culture, Bouboulinas 20, 106-82 Athens (tel: 820-1100; fax: 820-1337).

Ministry of Education and Religious Affairs, Mitropoleos 15, 101-85 Athens (tel: 325-4221; fax: 324-8264).

Ministry of Environment, Town Planning and Public Works, Amaliados 17, 115-23 Athens (tel: 643-1461; fax: 644-7608).

Ministry of Finance, Karageorgi Servias 10, 101-84 Athens (tel: 331-3400; fax: 323-8657).

Ministry of Foreign Affairs, Academias 1, 106-71 Athens (tel: 361-0584; fax: 645-0028).

Ministry of Health, Welfare and Social Security, Aristotelous 17, 101-87 Athens (tel: 524-9010; fax: 522-3246).

Ministry of Industry, Energy and Technology, Michalakopoulou 80, 101-92 Athens (tel: 748-2770; fax: 770-8003).

General Secretariat for Energy and Technology, Mesogeion Ave 14-18, 115-10 Athens (tel: 775-2221; fax: 771-4153).

Ministry of Interior, Dragatsaniou 2, 105-59 Athens (tel: 322-3521; fax: 324-1180).

Ministry of Justice, Mesogeion 96, 115-27 Athens (tel: 775-7619; fax: 779-6055).

Ministry of Labour, Pireos 40, 101-82 Athens (tel: 523-3110; fax: 524-9805).

Ministry of National Defence, Papagou Camp, Mesogeion 227-229, 154-51 Athens (tel: 646-5201; fax: 646-5584).

Ministry of National Economy: Division for Foreign Capital and Attracting Investments, Syntagma Square, 101-80 Athens (tel: 333-2000; fax: 333-2130; internet site: http://www.dos.gr/welcome_en.htm).

Division for Private Investment Policy, Syntagma Square, 101-80 Athens (tel: 333-2252/3; fax: 333-2326).

Regional Development Divisions of Attica, Thiras 60, 112-52 Athens (tel: 862-9810; fax: 862-9742).

Ministry of Press and Mass Media, Zalokosta 10, 101-63 Athens (tel: 363-0911; fax: 360-6969).

Ministry of Prime Minister's Office, Vas Sofias, 106-74 Athens (tel: 339-3000; fax: 339-3020).

Ministry of Public Order, Pan Kanellopoulou 4, 101-77 Athens (tel: 692-8510; fax: 692-1675).

Ministry of Transport and Communications, Xenofontos 13, 105-57 Athens (tel: 325-1211; fax: 324-7400).

Prime Minister's Office, Maximos Mansion, Herod Atticus 19, 106-74 Athens (tel: 671-7071; fax: 671-5799).

Other useful addresses

Athenagence (ANA) (news agency), Odos Pindarou 5, Athens 10671 (tel: 363-9816).

Athens and Piraeus Electric Railways (ISAP), Athinas 67, 105-52 Athens (tel: 324-8311; fax: 322-3935).

Athens and Piraeus Trolleys (ILPAP), Admitou 17, 104-46 Athens (tel: 821-6305; fax: 883-7445).

Athens and Piraeus Water Company (EYDAP), Oropou 156, 111-46 Athens (tel: 253-3402; fax: 253-3124).

Athens Municipal Gas Corporation (DEFA), Orfeos 2, 118-54 Athens (tel: 346-1194; fax: 346-1400).

Athens Stock Exchange, Sofokleous 10, 105-59 Athens (tel: 321-1301; fax: 321-3938; internet site: http://www.ase.gr/).

British Embassy, I Ploutarchou Street, 106-75 Athens (tel: 727-2600).

Centre for Planning and Economic Research (KEPE), Hippokratous St 22, 106-80 Athens (tel: 362-7321; fax: 361-1136; e-mail: kepe@kepe.gr).

Cotton Organisation (OBA), Syngrou Ave 150, 176-71 Athens (tel: 923-4314; fax: 924-3676).

'Democritus' Nuclear Research Centre, Ag Paraskevi, 153-10 Athens (tel: 651-8911; fax: 651-9180).

Department of Press and Information, Ministry to The Prime Minister's Office, Odos Zalokosta 10, Athens (tel: 363-0911).

Economic and Industrial Research Institute (IOBE), Tsami Karatasi 11, 117-42 Athens (tel: 924-1378; fax: 923-3977).

Export Promotion Organisation (OPE), Mar Antippa 86-88, 163-46 Athens (tel: 996-1900; fax: 991-5392).

Federation of Greek Industry (SEB), Xenofontos 5, 105-57 Athens (tel: 323-7325; fax: 322-2929).

Geological and Mineral Research Institute (IGME), Mesogion Ave 70, 115-27 Athens (tel: 779-8412; fax: 775-2211).

Greek Atomic Energy Commission, Ag Paraskevi, 153-10 Athens (tel: 651-8911; fax: 651-9180).

Greek Embassy (USA), 2221 Massachusetts Avenue, NW, Washington DC 20008 (tel: (+1-202)-939-5800; fax: (+1-202)-939-5824; e-mail: greece@greekembassy.org).

Greek Post Offices (ELTA), Apellou 1, 101-88 Athens (tel: 324-3311; fax: 324-1228).

Greek Radio and Television (ET 1), Mesogion Ave 432, 153-42 Athens (tel: 639-0772; fax: 639-0652).

Greek Radio and Television (ET 2), Mesogion Ave 136, 115-62 Athens (tel: 770-1911; fax: 777-6239).

Greek Railways Organisation (OSE), Sina 6, 106-72 Athens (tel: 362-4402; fax: 362-8933).

Hellenic Aerospace Industry (EAB), Mesogion Ave 2-4, 115-27 Athens (tel: 779-9679; fax: 779-7670).

Hellenic Centre for Investment (HCI), 3 Mitropoleos Str, GR-105 57 Athens (tel: 324-2070; fax: 324-2079).

Hellenic Organisation for Small- and Medium-Size Enterprises and Handicraft Undertakings (EOMMEX), Xenias 16, 115-28 Athens (tel: 771-5002; fax: 771-5025).

Hellenic Organisation for the Promotion of Exports (HOPE), 1 Mitropoleos Street, 10557 Athens (tel: 324-7011/16).

Hellenic Standardisation Organisation (ELOT), Acharnon 313, 111-45 Athens (tel: 201-5025; fax: 202-0776).

Hellenic Telecommunications Organisation (OTE), Kifissias 99, 151-24 Athens (tel: 611-7466; fax: 681-0899).

Hellenic Tobacco Organisation (EOK), Kapodistriou 36, 104-32 Athens (tel: 524-7311; fax: 524-7318).

National Statistical Service , Lykourgou 14-16, 101-66 Athens (tel: 324-85118; fax: 324-1098; internet site: http://www.statistics.gr/).

Panhellenic Confederation of Farmers' Co-operatives (PASEGES), Kifissias 16, 115-26 Athens (tel: 770-4737; fax: 777-9313).

Panhellenic Exporters' Association, Kratinou 11, 105-52 Athens (tel: 522-8925; fax: 522-9403).

Public Materials Administration Organisation (ODDY), Stadiou 60, 105-64 Athens (tel: 324-4231; fax: 324;2970).

Public Petroleum Corporation (DEP), Mesogion Ave 357-359, 152-31 Athens (tel: 650-1340; fax: 650-1383).

Public Power Corporation (PPC), Halkokondyli 30, 104-32 Athens (tel: 523-4301; fax: 523-5307).

Union of Commercial Agents, Voulis 15, Athens (tel: 322-3148).

Urban Transport Organisation (OAS), Metsovou 15, 106-82 Athens (tel: 883-6077; fax: 821-2219).

Other news agencies: ANA-MPA: www.ana-mpa.gr

Internet sites

Bridge to Greece and Cyprus: http://greekvillage.com/bridge/bridge.htm

EFG Eurobank Ergasias: http://www.eurobank.gr

Greek telephone directory: http://www.hellasyellow.gr/

Greenland

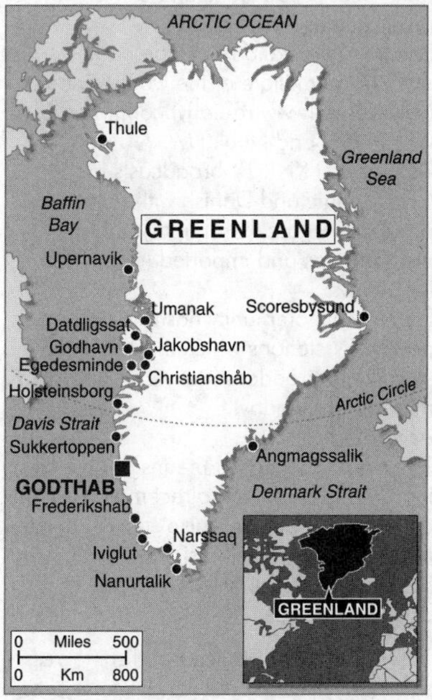

COUNTRY PROFILE

Historical profile

Settlers from Iceland arrived in 986. Greenland first came under Danish rule in the fourteenth century. All European settlers had disappeared by 1600 although native Inuit communities survived. A new Danish settlement was established in 1721.

1940 During the German occupation of Denmark in the Second World War, Greenland came under US protection. Denmark re-assumed control of Greenland but with continued military use of bases by the US and later NATO.

1953 Greenland ceased to be a colony and became an autonomous province of the Danish Kingdom under the Home Rule Constitution. Native Inuit were expelled, by Danish officials, from their ancestral lands in the north to make way for expansion of the US airbase at Thule.

1973 Greenland joined the EEC (later EU) as part of Denmark.

1979 Full home rule was granted to Greenland; Denmark retained control of constitutional matters, foreign relations and defence.

1985 Greenland left the EEC following two referenda.

1987 A disagreement with Denmark over the presence of a US military radar system in Thule led to the fall of the coalition government.

1991 Parliamentary elections resulted in a coalition government composed of the Siumit (Forward) party and the Inuit Ataqatigiit (IA) (Inuit Brotherhood).

1995 The IA formed a coalition with Attasut. Lars Emil Johansen became prime minister.

1999 The Danish High Court concluded the Inuit were illegally removed from their land around Thule in 1953, but their right to return was denied.

2000 NASA scientists found that the ice sheet which covers 85 per cent of Greenland's territory was melting by one metre per year.

2002 A coalition government was formed comprising the Siumut and IA parties; Hans Enoksen, became prime minister.

2003 The short-lived coalition collapsed amid allegations of corruption and the use of a native shaman. A new coalition of Siumut and the Atassut party formed, but it failed within months during a row over the budget. Siumut resumed its coalition with the IA. Inuits lose their appeal to the Danish Supreme Court for return of their land.

2004 Denmark signed an agreement with the US to refurbish the US airbase at Thule.

2005 Prime Minister Enoksen was returned to power in early elections, called in response to allegations of misuse of public funds by ministers and failure of budgetary discussions.

2006 Official studies declared the Greenland ice sheets were melting at an increased rate.

2007 Plans by Greenland Inuits to increase their quota for whale hunting deadlocked the International Whaling Commission negotiations. Critics accused Greenland of expanding the commercial aspects rather than for cultural and nutritional values of native whaling.

2008 The five countries surrounding the Artic met in Greenland to discuss territorial claims. The talks were aimed at reducing the detrimental effect of unrestrained exploration for oil and gas and forming an agreement concerning access to the north-west passage between the Atlantic and Pacific oceans.

KEY FACTS

Official name: Greenland (Kalaallit Nunaat)

Head of State: Queen Margrethe II of Denmark, represented by High Commissioner Søren Hald Møller (since 1 Apr 2005)

Head of government: Prime Minister Hans Enoksen (Siumut) (since 2002; re-elected 2005)

Ruling party: Coalition of Siumut (Forward) and Inuit Ataqatigiit (Inuit Brotherhood) (since 2003; re-elected 2005)

Area: 2,166,086 square km, of which 410,449 square km is not covered by permanent ice

Population: 56,969 (2005)

Capital: Nuuk (Godthåb)

Official language: Greenlandic Inuit and Danish

Currency: Danish krone (Kr) = 100 ore

Exchange rate: Kr4.70 per US$ (Jul 2008)

GDP per capita: US$20,000 (2003)

GDP real growth: 2.00% (2005)

Labour force: 32,437 (2006)

Unemployment: 7.30% (2006)

Inflation: 1.20% (2005)

Balance of trade: -US$39.00 million (2003)

Foreign debt: US$25.00 million (2003)

Visitor numbers: 14,000 (2003)*

* estimated figure

Political structure

Constitution

The Home Rule constitution, enacted on 2 June 1953, altered the status of Greenland from a colony to an autonomous province of Denmark. In 1979 full powers were granted with executive, judicial and legislative branches. Denmark retained control of constitutional matters, foreign relations and defence.

Greenland is a special cultural community in the Kingdom of Denmark.

Greenland elects two members to the Danish parliament.

Form of state

Parliamentary democratic dependency

The executive

The Danish monarch is head of state and is represented by a High Commissioner appointed by the monarch.

Executive power is exercised by a prime minister who heads the government, which is composed by the majority political party or parties in parliament.

There are seven Landsstyremaend (ministers) headed by the Landsstyreformanden (prime minister).

National legislature

The unicameral Landstingets (parliament) has 31 members, elected by proportional representation for four-year terms.

Last elections

15 November 2005 (parliamentary)

Results: Parliamentary: Siumut won 30.7 per cent of the vote (10 seats out of 31), Democrats 23 per cent (seven), Inuit Ataqatigiit 22.6 per cent (seven), Atassut 19.1 per cent (six) and Independents 4.1 per cent (one).Turnout was 74.9 per cent.

Next elections

2009 (parliamentary)

Political parties

Ruling party

Coalition of Siumut (Forward) and Inuit Ataqatigiit (Inuit Brotherhood) (since 2003; re-elected 2005)

Main opposition party

Demokraatit (Democrats)

Political situation

As global warming melts the Artic ice, the countries that surround the newly accessible land and waters free of ice may now allow possible exploitation and this has become an international bone of contention. While the US was in disagreement with Canada concerning access to the Northwest Passage as free passage for all shipping, in 2006, the Russians, using a submarine, planted its national flag on the Artic seabed and claimed an area of one million square kilometres, in August 2007. The countries, US, Russia, Canada, Norway and Denmark, sat down to discuss the future of the region in Greenland. While no immediate resolution was agreed it was expected that a final decision on exploration rights may be agreed by 2023.

Population

56,969 (2005)

Last census: July 2000: 56,124

Population density: Seven inhabitants per square km (2001) (icecap excluded).

Annual growth rate: 0.2 per cent (2003)

Ethnic make-up

Eighty-eight per cent of the population are Inuit and Greenland-born whites and the remainder are primarily Danes.

Religions

Ninety-six per cent belong to the Evangelical Lutheran Church of Denmark.

Education

US$102 million was spent on education in 2002.

Pupils per teacher: 10 in primary schools.

Health

Life expectancy: 68.9 years (estimate 2003)

Fertility rate/Maternal mortality rate: 2.4 births per woman (World Bank)

Birth rate/Death rate: 16 births per 1,000 population; eight deaths per 1,000 population (2003).

Child (under 5 years) mortality rate (per 1,000): 17 per 1,000 live births (2003)

Main cities

Nuuk (Godthåb) (capital, estimated population 14,438 in 2005), Sisimiut (Holsteinsborg) (5,335), Ilulissat (Jakobshavn) (4,352).

Languages spoken

Danish and Greenlandic Inuit, which is an eastern branch of the East-Eskimo language categorised by linguists as Inupik, which is spoken on the northern coasts of Canada and Alaska and the eastern-most tip of Siberia. Greenlanders connected with tourism often speak English.

Official language/s

Greenlandic Inuit and Danish

Media

Press

In Greenlandic (although with Danish and sometimes English online editions), there are only two newspapers, Atuagagdliutit Gronlandsposten (www.ag.gl) is published twice weekly and Sermitsiak is published weekly; Niviarsiaq is published monthly.

Dailies: There are no daily newspapers.

Weeklies:
Grønlandsposten/Atuagagdliutit and Sermitsiak.

Periodicals: Grønland is a general interest periodical, published 10 times a year.

Broadcasting

The national public broadcaster is Kalaallit Nunaata Radioa (KNR) (Greenland Broadcasting Company) with overall responsibility for radio and television services. It is financed through government funding, advertising and sponsorship and broadcasts a range of cultural, news, music and entertainment programmes.

Radio: Greenland Radio (KNR) broadcasts in Greenlandic and Danish with both local productions and Danish programmes.

Private radio stations include Radio 50Z20, an affiliate of the Danish, Radio Nyhederne (www.radionyt.com), Radio Grønnedal and Nuuk FM

Television: KNR TV broadcasts in Greenlandic and Danish with domestic productions of cultural and youth programmes and imported (mostly Danish) shows.

Each local community has one or more private TV stations which are allocated a 15-minute broadcast daily on KNR-TV (30 minutes on Sunday).

Advertising

The most widely used means of advertising are the press and direct mail. The only cinema in Greenland also shows advertising. There is no advertising on radio, and poster sites are heavily regulated.

Economy

There are over 400 licensed fishing vessels operating in Greenland, where over 90 per cent of all exports are derived from fish products, and fishing is the primary industry. Whaling is also an aspect of the industry, with around 2,700 whales caught each year. Greenland is heavily dependent on subsidies from Denmark in the form of block grants. The total financial package received from Denmark is around US$500 million annually. Greenland has been looking at other ways to make the economy more diverse, including offshore oil exploration and tourism.

Labour market and unemployment

The public sector employs almost two-thirds of all wage earners. Greenland has a literacy rate of 98 per cent.

External trade

Greenland is not a member of the European Union, despite being an overseas territory of Denmark. However, it has a fishing agreement with the EU, which allows it to sell its fish products as non-dutiable goods in the EU. It also has leased fishing rights to the EU.

While Canada provides Greenland with fresh fruit and vegetables Greenland does not produces anything that Canada does not already have, so trade is generally one-way.

Imports
Imports include machinery and transport equipment, manufactured goods, food, petroleum products.
Main sources: Denmark (66.8 per cent total, 2005), Sweden (19.3 per cent), Ireland (3.6 per cent)
Exports
Exports consist mainly of fish (cod, halibut and crabs, which accounts for approximately 45 per cent) and shrimp, which makes up over 55 per cent.
Main destinations: Denmark (65.5 per cent total, 2005), Japan (12.3 per cent), China (5.3 per cent)

Agriculture

Farming
The agricultural sector, comprising around 60 farms, is largely confined to sheep farming in the south and small-scale reindeer farming. Livestock production in 2005 included 360 tonnes of mutton and lamb. The production of lamb and reindeer meat is mainly for domestic consumption. Arable areas mainly produce hay for fodder.
Livestock production in 2005 included: 560t meat in total, 360t mutton and lamb, 20t greasy wool.
Fishing
Fishing is the mainstay of the economy, accounting for over 90 per cent of exports and giving employment to a quarter of the population. Principal products include shrimp, halibut, cod and seal. Typical annual catches include over 142,000 tonnes (t) shrimps and 197,000t fish. Halibut is increasingly important, while cod has declined in importance. Traditional sea mammal catches are typically over 2,500 whales and 115,000 seals annually.
The fishing industry employs around 6,000 people. The principal export markets are the EU, especially Denmark, and Japan.
Greenland lost the vote to have its whaling quota expanded to include 10 humpback whales, at the International Whaling Commission (IWC) meeting in June 2008. Other members considered that too much of the whale meat, 25 per cent, was sold commercially, in contravention of the IWC qualification for aboriginal or subsistence whaling. The quota for Inuit whaling 2008–12 was agreed at 212 minkes, 19 fins and two bowhead whales.
In 2004, the total marine fish catch was 70,484 tonnes and the total crustacean catch was 143,390 tonnes.

Industry and manufacturing

Industry is centred on fish processing and packaging. Most of the sector is controlled by the government-owned Royal Greenland company, which manages factories and smaller plants in both GreenInd and Denmark. Some tanning and leatherworking takes place in the south. Infrastructure improvements have provided a boost to construction activity, in particular the development of new airstrips.

Tourism

Tourism offers good potential for expansion, despite being restricted by the short season and high costs. Greenland has a lot to offer tourists: icebergs, nature, wilderness, dog-sledging, whale watching, northern lights, etc. The sector has grown in recent years as a result of the home government's policy designed to promote economic diversification and reduce dependence on Denmark. Visitor numbers have risen to around 30,000 a year, mainly from Denmark.

Mining

There are known reserves of zinc, lead, copper, cobalt, uranium, iron ore, gold and diamonds. Mineral exploration is actively encouraged and the administration has reformed its mining regulations. Large quantities of two of the world's rarest metals, niobium and tantalum, exist in Greenland.

Hydrocarbons

Greenland still hopes that oil and gas might become one of the mainstays of the economy. Oil exploration began in the 1970s. The Home Rule government is encouraging further exploration offshore of West Greenland. Arctic climate and deep waters make the task difficult. At present, Greenland relies on imports.
Greenland does not produce or import gas and coal.

Energy

Greenland is almost totally dependent on Denmark for its energy supplies. There is a hydroelectric station in Buksefjorden, which supplies Nuuk, and other hydro-electric plants are under construction or being planned.

Banking and insurance

NUNA Bank A/S is an independent bank that was formerly a subsidiary of the Danish bank Sparekasse Bikuben AS. The two banks share a strong business relationship. The other major bank in Greenland is Grønlandsbanken, which is owned by Danish banks.
Central bank
Monetary policy and administration is handled by the Danish central bank (Danmarks Nationalbank).

Time

Greenland has four time zones:
East Greenland and Scoresbysund – GMT minus one hour (daylight saving, end March to end September, GMT)
Central Greenland, Godthåb – GMT minus three hours (daylight saving, GMT minus two hours)
Western Greenland, Thule – GMT minus four hours (no daylight saving)
Danmarkshavn – GMT (no daylight saving)

Geography

Greenland is the world's largest island, although much of the surrounding seas are permently frozen forming the arctic shelf. Greenland lies in the North Atlantic Ocean, to the east of Canada and to the west of Iceland. Around 85 per cent of the landmass is permanently covered by ice up to 3,375 metres (m) thick. A snow peaked central range of mountains run north/south, with the highest peak reaching 3,200m above sea-level. There are 410,449 square km of coastland that is habitable.
Hemisphere
Northern

Climate

Arctic; temperatures at Nuuk/Godthåb vary between about minus 12 degrees Celsius (C) and 11 degrees C.

Entry requirements

Entry requirements are the same as for Denmark.
Passports
Required by all, except EU visitors travelling on national ID cards.
Visa
Even though a Danish territory, visas are not valid for Greenland unless specified in the permit. For a business visa, an original letter of invitation from a local company or organisation, giving details about purpose of visit and duration of stay must accompany an application, along with evidence of hotel reservations.
Approval must be obtained from the Greenland Home Rule administration, PO Box 1015, 3900 Nuuk, Greenland, for entry into the military defence areas including the gateways of Sondre Stromfjord and Thule (unless in direct transit to points outside the airport of Sondre Stromfjord) and entry for the purpose of mountain/glacier climbing or geological/archaeological research.

Health (for visitors)

Mandatory precautions
Vaccination certificates are not usually required.
Advisable precautions

Public holidays (national)

Fixed dates
1 Jan (New Year's Day), 6 Jan (Epiphany), 21 Jun (National Day), 24–26 Dec (Christmas).

Variable dates
Maundy Thursday, Good Friday, Easter Monday, Great Prayer Day (Apr/May), Ascension Day, Whit Monday.

Working hours
Banking
Mon–Fri: 0930–1600 (Thu 1800).
Business
Mon–Fri: 0800–1600 or 0830–1630.
Government
Mon–Fri: generally 0900–1700.
Shops
Mon–Fri: 0800–1700 or 0900–1730, Sat: close at 1300 or 1400.

Telecommunications
Mobile/cell phones
There is a 900 GSM service in populated areas only.

Electricity supply
220V AC, 50Hz.

Getting there
Air
National airline: Air Greenland
International airport/s: Kangerlussuaq (Sondre Stromfjord) (SFJ) international airport, on the west coast close to Sisimiut and the capital, Nuuk, has regular flights from Canada, Iceland and Denmark. Facilities include: bureau de change, restaurant, duty-free shops, post office and car rental.
Other airport/s: Narsarsuaq (UAK) is an airport for stopover flights between Europe and North America and internal flights, with few facilities.
Kulusuk (KUS), on the east coast receives some internal flights but most come from Iceland.
Airport tax: None
Surface
Water: Comfortable cruise ships sail during the summer season.
Main port/s: Nuuk/Godthåb

Getting about
National transport
Air: Air Greenland flies routes along the western coast from Pituffik and Qaanaaq in the north to Paamiut in the south and across to Kulusuk and Tasiilaq in the east. The regularity of services is dependent on the weather; reservations should be made well in advance. Helicopter services link other, more remote, settlements.
Road: There are virtually no roads connecting towns in Greenland. Only 60km of paved roads exist, realistically the best means of transport is the traditional sea and air travel where available.
Dog-sledges and snow mobiles can be hired for variable periods.
Water: Greenland Trade operates two passenger liners on the west coast. Villages are served by local boats, some of which are for private hire.

BUSINESS DIRECTORY

The addresses listed below are a selection only. While World of Information makes every endeavour to check these addresses, we cannot guarantee that changes have not been made, especially to telephone numbers and area codes. We would welcome any corrections.

Telephone area codes
The international direct dialling (IDD) code for Greenland is +299, followed by the subscriber's number.

Banking
Grønlandsbanken (Bank of Greenland) 29 Skibshavnsvej, PO Box 1033, DK-3900 Nuuk (tel: 347-700; fax 347-706).

Central bank
Danmarks Nationalbank, Havnegade 5, DK-1093 Copenhagen (tel: (+45) 3363-6363; fax: (+45) 3363-7103; e-mail: info@nationalbanken.dk).

Travel information
Greenland Tourism Main Office, 29 Hans Egedesvej, PO Box 1615, Nuuk DK-3900 (tel: 342-820; fax: 322-877; e-mail: info@greenland.com).

National tourist organisation offices
Greenland Tourism a/s, Main Office, PO Box 1552, 3900 Nuuk (tel: 322-888; fax: 322-877; e-mail: info@visitgreenland.com).

Ministries
Grønlands Hjemmestyre (Greenland Home Rule administration), PO Box 1015, 3900 Nuuk (tel: 345-000; e-mail: info@gh.gl; internet site: www.gh.gl).

Greenland Home Rule Government Denmark Office, Sjaeleboderne 2, 1122 Copenhagen K, Denmark (tel: (+45) 3313-4224; fax: (+45) 3332-2024).

Prime Minister's Office, Greenland Department, 3 Hausergade, DK-1128 Copenhagen K, Denmark (tel: (+45) 3393-2200).

Other useful addresses
Ministry of Foreign Affairs, Asiatisk Plads 2, DK-1448 Copenhagen, Denmark (tel: (+45) 3392-0000; internet: www.um.dk/en).

Greenland Trade Shipping Department, Grønlandshavnen, DK-9220 Aalborg Ost (tel: (+45) 9815-7677).

Kalaallit Nunaata Radioa (Grønlands Radio) (KNR) (Radio Greenland), H J Rinksvej 35, PO Box 1007, 3900 Nuuk (tel: 321-172; fax: 324-703).

Internet sites
Bureau of minerals and petroleum: http://bmp.gl/

Greenland Radio: http://www.knr.gl/

Greenland Tourism: http://www.greenland-guide.gl

Grenada

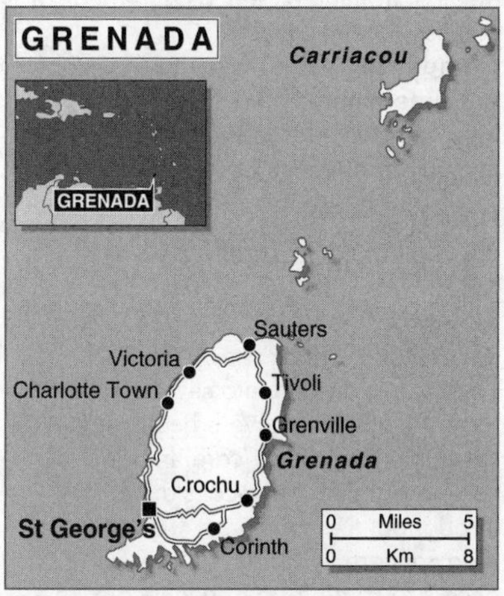

COUNTRY PROFILE

Historical profile

1762 Grenada was initially colonised by the French until captured by the British.
1783 British control of the islands was recognised.
1958 Grenada joined the Federation of the West Indies.
1967 Internal self-government was granted.
1974 Eric Gairy became prime minister of a newly independent Grenada.
1979 A coup deposed Gairy and Maurice Bishop, leading the socialist New Jewel Movement, took power.
1983 Civil disturbances, anti-government protests, media restrictions and a power struggle within the left-wing government resulted in a coup d'etat, led by General Hudson Austin, which deposed and the execution of Prime Minister Bishop and nine members of his cabinet. A US-led invasion, backed by troops from Jamaica, Barbados and other members of the Organisation of Eastern Caribbean States (OECS), arrested Austin and reinstated the 1974 constitution.
1984 The general election was won by the New National Party (NNP) led by Herbert Blaize.
1987 The National Democratic Congress (NDC) was formed.
1996 Grenada signed anti-drug trafficking treaties with the US. The appointment of Sir Daniel Williams as governor general provoked controversy, owing to his links with the NNP.
1999 The NNP won the general election, gaining every seat in the House of Representatives.
2001 Grenada was blacklisted by the OECD's Financial Action Task Force (FATF) for not doing enough to combat money laundering. A review of offshore banking was begun.
2002 The government revoked the licences of 36 offshore banks in an attempt to secure Grenada's removal from the FATF blacklist. Grenada was hit by tropical storm Lili, causing damage estimated at around 2 per cent of GDP.
2003 Grenada was removed from the FATF's blacklist. The NNP was re-elected.
2004 Thirty-years of independence were celebrated in February. Prime Minister Mitchell was accused of taking a US$500,000 bribe from a German citizen. Hurricane Ivan struck Grenada damaging 85 per cent of the island's housing.
2005 Grenada-born, army Private Johnson Beharry received Britain's highest military bravery awarded, the Victoria Cross, for his service in Iraq. Hurricane Emily struck the island in July, causing extensive damage.
2006 The EU granted eur9.3 million (US$11 million) for the rehabilitation of schools devastated by Hurricanes Ivan and Emily.
2007 The UK-based Privy Council ruled that 14 convicts, sentenced to death for the 1983 coup d'etat must be re-sentenced as the original sentencing was 'illegitimate'.
2008 Sir Eric Gairy was named as Grenada's first National Hero. He had formed the Grenada United Labour Party in 1950 and steered the island to independence in 1974, becoming Grenada's first prime minister. In the 8 July parliamentary elections the opposition NDC won 11 seats (out of 15), ousting the former ruling party, the NNP, which won four seats. Turnout was 80.3 per cent. Tillman Thomas became prime minister on 9 July.

Political structure

Form of state

Independent state; it is a member of the Commonwealth.

The executive

The British monarch is the head of state, represented by the governor general appointed by the monarch. Executive power is vested in the cabinet, led by the prime

KEY FACTS

Official name: Grenada

Head of State: Queen Elizabeth II, represented by Governor General Sir Daniel C Williams (since 1996)

Head of government: Prime Minister Tillman Thomas (took office 9 Jul 2008)

Ruling party: National Democratic Congress (NDC) (from 9 Jul 2008)

Area: 345 square km

Population: 103,000 (2005)*

Capital: St George's

Official language: English

Currency: East Caribbean dollar (EC$) = 100 cents

Exchange rate: EC$2.70 per US$ (fixed)

GDP per capita: US$4,670 (2005)

GDP real growth: 5.00% (2005)

Inflation: 3.50% (2005)

Balance of trade: -US$202.30 million (2004)

Foreign debt: US$330.00 million (2004)

* estimated figure

minister. The cabinet is appointed by the governor general on the advice of the prime minister and is responsible to parliament. Following legislative elections, the leader of the majority party or the leader of the majority coalition is usually appointed prime minister by the governor general.

National legislature

The bicameral parliament consists of a 15-member House of Representatives (members are elected by popular vote to serve five-year terms) and an upper, 13-member, Senate (10 senators appointed by the government and three by the leader of the opposition)

Legal system

The legal system is based on English common law. Grenada is responsible for its own magistrate's courts. The regional Eastern Caribbean Supreme Court is responsible for the high court and the court of appeals. The final court of appeal is to the Privy Council in the UK.

Last elections

8 July 2008 (parliamentary)

Results: Parliamentary: The NDC won 50.9 per cent of the vote (11 seats out of 15), the NNP won 47.7 per cent (four); turnout was 80.3 per cent.

Next elections

2013 (parliamentary)

Political parties

Ruling party

National Democratic Congress (NDC) (from 9 Jul 2008)

Main opposition party

New National Party (NNP)

Political situation

Prime Minister Keith Mitchell has an apparent penchant for persistent misfortune. Firstly, in 2004 he was accused of accepting US$500,000 from a German citizen in return for the post of general ambassador to Grenada and a diplomatic passport. An accusation he denied and was never proven. The second accusation is not only more convoluted but also has a wider implication if proved true.

In 2007, in a US criminal trial Prime Minister Mitchell was sited as a recipient of US$1 million from a US swindler. In the documents submitted to court it was asserted that Mitchell was or had been a US citizen. The news of this resulted in a question mark over Mitchell's Grenadian citizenship and his legitimacy as a Grenadian politician (only Grenadian citizens may be politicians). As of March 2008 the prime minister had not revealed the circumstances regarding his citizenship and whether he had revoked US citizenship at the time of his first election to the parliament of Grenada.

Population

103,000 (2005)*

Last census: May 2001: 102,632

Population density: 285 inhabitants per square km. Urban population: 38 per cent (1995—2001).

Annual growth rate: 0.3 per cent 1994–2004 (WHO 2006)

Ethnic make-up

Black (82 per cent), mixed black and European (13 per cent), European and East Indian (5 per cent) and a small number of Arawak/Carib.

Religions

Roman Catholic (53 per cent), Anglican (13.8 per cent), other Protestants (33.2 per cent).

Education

Education in Grenada is based on the English GCSE and A level system. There are several excellent local schools and an international primary school.

In total, there are 79 schools, 59 primary, 19 secondary and one tertiary institution. TA Marryshow Community College has a school of agriculture and a teacher's training college.

The St George's University School of Medicine is run by a US firm and offers medical training as well as non-medical courses.

Compulsory years: Five to 16.

Enrolment rate: 95 per cent gross primary enrolment of relevant age groups (including repeaters) (World Bank 2003).

Health

Per capita total expenditure on health (2003) was US$473; of which per capita government spending was US$348, at the international dollar rate, (WHO 2006).

Grenada is divided into seven health districts, six of which have a health centre responsible for primary care. In addition, there are several medical stations throughout the country.

Medical care is limited, but everyone has access to some form of healthcare, regardless of ability to pay.

Life expectancy: 68 years, 2004 (WHO 2006)

Fertility rate/Maternal mortality rate: 2.4 births per woman, 2004 (WHO 2006)

Birth rate/Death rate: 23 births per 1,000 population; 7.5 deaths per 1,000 population (2003).

Child (under 5 years) mortality rate (per 1,000): 18.0 per 1,000 live births (World Bank)

Welfare

The social welfare department of the ministry of labour administers social work programmes to families and gives financial aid to three private children's homes. There is also a women's shelter in the northern part of the island. There are a number of government social service agencies that monitor the welfare of children, women and those with disabilities.

Main cities

St George's (capital, estimated population 3,680 in 2005)

Languages spoken

English and French patois

Official language/s

English

Media

Freedom of the press is guaranteed by law.

Press

The monthly The Barnacle publishes business news. There are no daily newspapers. The Grenada Guardian is

KEY INDICATORS — Grenada

	Unit	2003	2004	2005	2006	2007
Population	m	0.10	0.09	*0.11	*0.11	*0.11
Gross domestic product (GDP)	US$bn	0.44	*0.44	0.50	0.56	*0.59
GDP per capita	US$	5,000	4,241	*4,797	*5,293	*5,571
GDP real growth	%	2.5	-3.2	12.1	3.0	*3.1
Inflation	%	2.8	2.3	3.5	4.3	*3.7
Exports (fob) (goods)	US$m	78.0	33.3	–	–	–
Imports (cif) (goods)	US$m	270.0	235.6	–	–	–
Balance of trade	US$m	-192.0	-202.3	–	–	–
Current account	US$m	-140.0	-50.0	-128.0	-129.0	*-138.0
Total reserves minus gold	US$m	83.2	121.7	94.3	–	110.6
Foreign exchange	US$m	83.2	121.7	94.2	0.0	110.5
Exchange rate	per US$	2.70	2.70	2.70	2.70	2.70

* estimated figure

sponsored by the Grenada United Labour political Party.
Weeklies: Weeklies include The Grenadain Voice (www.granadianvoce.com), The Grenada Informer (www.belgrafix.com) and Grenada Today.
Periodicals: The Barnacle (www.barnaclegrenada.com) is published monthly.
Broadcasting
The Grenada Broadcasting Network (GBN) (www.klassicgrenada.com) provides the national, public service, and is partly owned by the government and partly by the Caribbean Communications Network (CCN) (www.onecaribbeanmedia.net).
Radio: GBC operates two radio stations, Klassic Radio and Hott FM (www.klassicgrenada.com). Klassic Radio has 43 per cent of the audience listening figures and can be received by surrounding islands. Hott FM has a younger audience than its associate station.
Commercial radio includes City Sound FM (www.citysoundfm.com) and Voice of Grenada (www.spiceislander.com/vog), religious stations include Harbour Light Radio (www.harbourlightradio.org) and the Catholic Radio Upgrade.
Television: GBC Television (www.klassicgrenada.com) operates one channel and Gayelle TV is a the private cable service from Trinidad and Tobago.

Economy

Caribbean islands are typically subject to damage inflicted by hurricanes and Grenada is no exception, however the devastation caused by Hurricane Ivan in 2004 (200 per cent of GDP) was compounded by another, Hurricane Emily, which struck in July 2005 and caused damage particularly in rural areas. The cost of repair for both had a marked impact on Grenada's GDP growth, which drop to -3.0 per cent in 2004 (down from 2.5 per cent in 2003). Construction led the economy, not only in rebuilding (about 60 per cent of the housing stock had to be repaired), but also in anticipation of revived tourist numbers as Grenada hosted a number of second round games in the Cricket World Cup tournament in 2007 and the new stadium built for the event. However, agricultural growth lagged with nutmeg being particularly badly hit. Grenada typically produces 25 per cent of world output of nutmeg, but in 2004 exports were 1,790kg, down from 2,362kg in 2003. Cocoa is another important crop but the damage to plantations (an average 32 per cent of production) of this and nutmeg trees has focussed on the ageing population in the countryside and the lack of motivation necessary to replant what would be a long-term project. Nevertheless, the government is aware that the resuscitation of the nutmeg sector could lead agriculture out of its recession.
The IMF approved a three-year loan arrangement of just over US$15 million under its Poverty Reduction and Growth Facility (PRGF) in April 2006 to underwrite the government's medium-term economic reform programme. In May 2006, the Paris Club of debtors rescheduled outstanding debts of US$16 million, while the government signed a soft loan with the World Bank of US$3.5 million for a public sector modernisation programme.
As part of the government's reform of tax policies a valued added tax (VAT) to replace a general consumption tax, was introduced on 1 January 2008.

External trade

As a member of the Caribbean Community and Common Market (Caricom), Grenada operates within the single market (Caribbean Single Market and Economy (CSME)), which it joined by July 2006 and has a common currency as a member of the Eastern Caribbean Central Bank (ECCB). Grenada is also a member of the Organisation of East Caribbean States (OECS); set up to promote region development and economic integration.
Imports
Main imports are food, manufactured goods, machinery, chemicals and fuel.
Main sources: Trinidad and Tobago (32.7 per cent total, 2006), US (23.5 per cent), Barbados (4.6 per cent).
Exports
Main exports are bananas, cocoa, nutmeg and mace, fruit and vegetables, clothing.
Main destinations: Saint Lucia (18.2 per cent total, 2006), Antigua and Barbuda (12.4 per cent), Saint Kitts and Nevis (11.1 per cent).

Agriculture

Farming
The agricultural sector contributes around 8 per cent to GDP and accounts for around 65 per cent of exports.
Activity centres on the traditional farming of nutmeg/mace (the world's second-largest producer after Indonesia), cocoa and bananas. Nutmeg and cocoa exports have benefited from a decline in world supply due to political problems in global suppliers (Indonesia and Côte d'Ivoire), as opposed to improvements in output.
Agricultural development policy is geared towards the rehabilitation of the cocoa industry, the promotion of new export crops, greater provision of fertilisers and other inputs and privatisation of state farms.
Grenada was adversely affected by the loss of export markets in 2007, when WTO-led legislation opened up the EU banana market to worldwide suppliers.
The estimated crop production in 2005 included: 6,500 tonnes (t) coconuts, 4,380t citrus, 300t maize, 400t yams, 7,200t sugar cane, 4,100t bananas, 740t plantains, 1,900t mangoes, 1,500t avocados, 737t cocoa beans, 2,747t nutmeg, 200t other spices, 16,830t fruit in total, 4,000t roots and tubers, 2,649t vegetables in total. Livestock production included: 1,128t meat in total, 143t beef, 193t pig meat, 92t lamb & goat meat, 600t poultry, 920t eggs, 520t milk.
Fishing
There is a small fishing industry.
The typical total annual fish catch is over 2,247t. Shellfish, molluscs and cephalopods account for another 39t per annum. In 2004, the total marine fish catch was 1,985 tonnes and the total crustacean catch was 19 tonnes.

Industry and manufacturing

The industrial sector accounts for around 20 per cent of GDP, of which manufacturing constitutes around 7 per cent.
Manufacturing activities include the production of garments, beverages, flour, wheat-bran, animal feed, furniture, paints and varnishes, sugar, rum, coconut oil, lime juice and honey. Furniture, handicrafts and garments are also manufactured for export to the Caricom market.
The government is committed to achieving growth in the manufacturing sector and to this end is endeavouring to attract foreign firms to use Grenada as a base for exports to extra-regional markets. Joint ventures are encouraged between local private sector and foreign investors in order to assist local manufacturers to access capital, technology and marketing channels.

Tourism

Tourism, which accounts for around 5 per cent of Grenada's GDP and 5 per cent of the total labour force, is an increasingly important element in the economy, particularly in terms of its foreign exchange-earning capacity. After several difficult years, the sector has recovered since in 2003. The cruise market is being actively developed and a newly-constructed cruise terminal was opened in December 2004 that is part of phase one of a redevelopment site for the city of St George. The damage to accommodation caused by Hurricane Ivan in September 2004 resulted in an overall contraction of stay-over numbers for the year. The cruise-ship sector, on the other hand, recovered very quickly, recording 226,944 visitors for 2004.
The majority of visitors originate in the US, other Caribbean countries and the UK. An increasing number of visitors are coming

from the UK and Germany due to the expansion of charter flights.

Hydrocarbons
Grenada does not produce oil and relies on imports of petroleum. In March 2004, the Grenada government asked the Commonwealth Fund for Technical Co-operation (CFTC) for advice on awarding contracts for oil and gas exploration.
Grenada does not produce or import gas and coal. Trinidad and Tobago plans to build a 600 mile natural gas pipeline linking the eastern Caribbean islands, which would open possibilities of importing natural gas into Grenada.

Banking and insurance
The seven members of the Organisation of Eastern Caribbean States (OECS), Antigua and Barbuda, Dominica, Grenada, Montserrat, St Kitts and Nevis, St Lucia and St Vincent and the Grenadines, share a common currency and central bank. The British Virgin Islands and Anguilla are associate members.

Central bank
Eastern Caribbean Central Bank, St Kitts and Nevis.

Offshore facilities
The strengthening of the regulatory framework by the Grenada International Financial Services Authority (GIFSA) led to significant improvement and in 2003 Grenada was removed from the blacklist drawn up by the Organisation for Economic Co-operation and Development (OECD).

Time
GMT minus four hours

Geography
Grenada is a mountainous, heavily forested island. It is the most southerly of the Windward Islands in the West Indies. The country also includes some of the small islands known as the Grenadines, which lie to the north-east of Grenada, the largest of these being the low-lying island of Carriacou.

Hemisphere
Northern

Climate
Tropical marine with an annual mean temperature of 28 degrees Celsius. Rain occurs mainly from June–December. Driest from February–May.

Entry requirements
Passports
Required by all and must be valid for six months from the date of departure. Proof of return/onward passage is necessary.

Visa
Not required by nationals of most of the Americas, Europe, Australasia and Japan, for both tourist and business trips, valid for three months. Business visitors should supply extra information: letter of introduction from foreign company and letter of invitation from a local host. For further details and exceptions contact the consular section of the nearest High Commission or Embassy.

Currency advice/regulations
The import and export of foreign currencies is unrestricted, however large amounts should be declared.
Travellers cheques are widely accepted. To avoid extra exchange fees US dollar denominations are advised.

Health (for visitors)
Mandatory precautions
Yellow fever certificate required if arriving from an infected area.

Advisable precautions
Immunisation against hepatitis A, B and diphtheria may be recommended.
Medical attention can cost several thousand dollars and doctors often expect immediate cash payments; insurance is advisable.

Hotels
There are a wide variety of hotels from luxurious to one star. Except for town hotels, most are located near beaches, all hotels should be booked well in advance. An 8 per cent sales tax on food and beverages and 10 per cent service charge are added to the bill.

Public holidays (national)
Fixed dates
1 Jan (New Year's Day), 7 Feb (Independence Day), 1 May (Labour Day), 25 Oct (Thanksgiving Day), 25–26 Dec (Christmas).

Variable dates
Good Friday, Easter Monday (Mar/Apr), Whit Monday, Corpus Christi (May/Jun), Emancipation Day (first Mon in Aug), Carnival (two days, Aug).

Working hours
Banking
Mon–Thu: 0800–1400; Fri: 0800–1300, 1430–1700.

Business
Mon–Thu: 0800–1145, 1300–1600; Fri: 0800–1145, 1300–1700.

Government
Mon–Thu: 0800–1145, 1300–1600; Fri: 0800–1145, 1300–1700.

Shops
Mon–Fri: 0800–1145, 1300–1600; Sat: 0800–1145.

Telecommunications
Mobile/cell phones
GSM 850 900/1800/1900 services cover all of St George.

Electricity supply
220/240V AC, 50 cycles

Getting there
Air
International airport/s: Grenada International-Point Salines (GND), 8km from St George's; bureau de change, duty-free shops, restaurant, shops and car rental. Taxis are available.
Airport tax: Departure tax EC$50, payable in local currency only.

Surface
Water: Many cruise lines call at Grenada. Regular boat services from St Vincent, Martinique and Trinidad. There is a ferry service to Carriacou Island.
Main port/s: St George's.

Getting about
National transport
Road: There are approximately 1,050km of roads, of which 650km are paved, although most main roads are narrow and winding.
Buses: Public transport is provided by small private operators, with a system covering the entire country. Cheap but often slow and few run during the late afternoons, evenings and Sundays.

City transport
Taxis: Widely available. Fares are regulated.

Car hire
International licence required or local permit obtained (valid national licence must be presented to local Traffic Department), a minimum age of 25 applies. Traffic drives on the left.

BUSINESS DIRECTORY
The addresses listed below are a selection only. While World of Information makes every endeavour to check these addresses, we cannot guarantee that changes have not been made, especially to telephone numbers and area codes. We would welcome any corrections.

Telephone area codes
The international direct dialling code (IDD) for Grenada is +1 473, followed by subscriber's number.

Chambers of Commerce
Grenada Chamber of Industry and Commerce, PO Box 129, St George's (tel: 440-2937; fax: 440-6621; e-mail: gcic@caribsurf.com).

Banking
Bank of Nova Scotia, PO Box 194, Grand Anse, St George's (tel: 440-3274).

Barclays Bank, PO Box 37, Grand Anse, St George's (tel: 440-3232; fax: 440-3232).

Grenada Bank of Commerce, PO Box 4, Grand Anse, St George's (tel: 440-3521; fax: 440-4153).

Grenada Co-operative Bank, Church Street, St George's (tel: 440-2111, 440-3549; fax: 440-6600).

Grenada Development Bank, Halifax Street, St George's (tel: 440-2382/1620).

National Commercial Bank of Grenada, Halifax Street, St George's (tel: 440-3566/8).

Scotiabank, Halifax Street, St George's (tel: 440-3274).

Central bank
Eastern Caribbean Central Bank, Agency Office, Monckton Street, St George's (tel: 440-3016; fax: 40-6721).

Travel information
Grenada Hotel Association, Ross Point Inn, Lagoon Road, St George's (tel: 444-1353; fax: 444-4847).

Ministry of tourism
Ministry of Tourism, Civil Aviation, Social Security, Culture, Gender and Family, Ministerial Complex, 4th Floor, St. George's, (tel: 440-0366; fax: 440-0443).

National tourist organisation offices
Grenada Board of Tourism, PO Box 293, The Carenage, St George's (tel: 440-2279; fax: 440-6637; internet: www.grenadagrenadines.com).

Ministries
Ministry of Agriculture, Ministerial Complex, 2nd and 3rd Floors, St George's (tel: 440-27008 fax: 440-4191).

Ministry of Carriacou and Petit Martinique Affairs, Beausejour, Carriacou (tel: 443-6026; fax: 443-6040).

Ministry of Communication & Works, Ministerial Complex, 4th Floor, St George's (tel: 440-2181; fax: 440-4122).

Ministry of Education, Botanical Gardens, St George's (tel: 440-2166; fax: 440-6650).

Ministry of Finance, Trade, Industry and Planning, Financial Complex, St George's (tel: 440-2731; fax: 440-4115).

Ministry of Foreign Affairs and International Trade, Ministerial Complex, 4th Floor, St George's (tel: 440-2640; fax: 440-4184).

Ministry of Health and Environment, Ministerial Complex, 1st and 2nd Floords, St George's (tel: 440-2649; fax: 440-4127).

Ministry of Housing, Social Services and Co-operatives, Ministerial Complex, 1st and 2nd Floors, St George's (tel: 440-6917; fax: 440-7990).

Ministry of Implementation, Ministerial Complex, 6th Floor, St George's (tel: 440-2255; fax: 440-4116).

Ministry of Labour and Local Government, Ministerial Complex, 3rd Floor, St George's (tel: 440-2532).

Ministry of Legal Affairs, Attorney General's Office, Church Street, St. George's (tel: 440-2050; fax: 440-6630).

Ministry of Youth, Sports and Community Development, Ministerial Complex, 2nd Floor, St George's (tel: 440-6917; fax: 440-6924).

Office of the Prime Minister, Ministerial Complex, 6th Floor, St George's (tel: 440-2225; fax: 440-4116).

Other useful addresses
Export Development Unit, Ministry of Trade, Lagoon Road, St George's (tel: 440-2101; fax: 440-4115).

Grenada Cocoa Board, Scott St, St George's (tel: 440-2234).

Grenada Co-operative Banana Society, Scott St, St George's (tel: 440-2117).

Grenada Co-operative Nutmeg Association, PO Box 160, St George's (tel: 440-2097).

Grenada Industrial Development Corporation, Frequente Industrial Park, True Blue, St. George's (tel: 444-1035; fax: 444-4828; e-mail: gidc@caribsurf.com; internet site: www.grenadaworld.com).

Grenada International Financial Services Authority (GIFSA), PO Box 39713, Carenage (tel: 440-8717; fax: 440-4780; e-mail: grenoffshore@caribsurf.com).

Grenada Manufacturers' Council, PO Box 129, St George's (tel: 444-4485/2937; fax: 440-6627).

Grenadan Embassy (US), 1701 New Hampshire Avenue, NW, Washington DC 20009 (tel: 202-265-2561).

Other news agencies: Caribbean Net News: www.caribbeannetnews.com

Internet sites
Blue Horizons Cottage Hotel: www.cpscaribnet.com/ads/blue/blue.html

Calabash Hotel: www.cpscaribnet.com/ads/calabash/calabash.html

Coyaba Beach Resort: www.cpscaribnet.com/ads/coyaba/coyaba.html

Guadeloupe

KEY FACTS

Official name: Guadeloupe

Head of State: President of France (Nicolas Sarkozy), represented by Préfet Emmanuel Berthier since 11 Oct 2007)

Head of government: President of Conseil Général Jacques Gillot (since 23 Mar 2001); President of Conseil Régional Victorin Lurel (since 2 Apr 2004)

Ruling party: Objectif Guadeloupe

Area: 1,780 square km

Population: 445,000 (2007)*

Capital: Basse Terre

Official language: French

Currency: Euro ( ) = 100 cents (from 1 Jan 2002; previous currency French franc, locked at Ff6.56 per euro)

Exchange rate: 0.63 per US$ (Jul 2008)

GDP per capita: US$7,900 (2005)*

Balance of trade: -US$1.56 billion (2003)

* estimated figure

COUNTRY PROFILE

Historical profile

Guadeloupe is situated within the Lesser Antilles. The first inhabitants were the Arawak Indians and Carib Indians. The Carib name for the island was Karukera (island of beautiful water).

1493–1600 Columbus was the first European visitor. Spain made two attempts to colonise the islands of Guadeloupe but was unsuccessful, due to strong indigenous resistance.

1635 France conquered the islands and established its first settlement.

1654 The French welcomed a small number of Dutch who settled in Guadeloupe. They proved vital to the turnaround of Guadeloupe's economy by developing its sugar industry. Black African slaves were brought to the island to work on plantations.

1674 Guadeloupe became part of the French Crown Colonies.

1700s Guadeloupe was the scene of many battles between the French and British, who repeatedly fought for possession.

1808–1814 Guadeloupe was occupied by the British.

1816 The islands were handed back to France by the Treaty of Vienna.

1854–1885 Following the abolition of slavery in 1847, workers were brought to Guadeloupe from India. During this period, blacks were allowed to participate in Guadeloupe's political sphere and Guadeloupe was allowed representation in the French parliament.

1946 Guadeloupe became a French Département d'Outre-Mer (DOM) (Overseas Department).

1974 Guadeloupe was further incorporated into the French political system and granted the status of region of France.

1983 Guadeloupe was granted devolution. A Regional Council was established under the French decentralisation policy.

1998 Hurricane Georges wreaked havoc on the islands

1999 The Basse Terre declaration by Guadeloupe, Martinique and French Guiana called for greater local control. The country was hit by hurricane Lenny.

2002 Guadeloupe adopted the euro as its official currency. In the French presidential elections, Guadeloupe's support for Jacques Chirac was overwhelming (91 per cent of the vote).

2003 A referendum in Guadeloupe and Martinique rejected a French government-backed reform plan to streamline the system of local government and give the islands a new status. Guadeloupe's dependencies, St Barthélémy and St Martin voted to become overseas collectives.

2004 Victorin Lurel took office as president of the regional council and Jacques Gillot as president of the general council. Paul Girot de Langlade took office as préfet.

2006 Jean-Jacque Brot became préfet on 12 June.

2007 On 16 May, Nicolas Sarkozy became head of state and president of the French Republic. On 11 October Emmanuel Berthier became préfet. A new desalination unit, capable of producing 4,000 cubic metres of drinkable water from seawater, was installed on Saint Barthélémy and began production in February. Hurricane Dean destroyed 80 per cent of all banana plantations in April. St Barthélémy and St Martin, became French overseas collectives

2008 An agreement was signed in April between the governments of Guadeloupe and Dominica for the development and delivery of geothermal energy from Dominica via undersea electricity cables.

Political structure

Constitution

28 September 1958 (French Fifth Republic).

Under the 1946 constitution of the French Fourth Republic, Guadeloupe became a Département d'Outre-Mer (DOM) (Overseas Department) of France. In 1974, it was granted additional status as a region of France.

Guadeloupe is represented in the French National Assembly by four deputies and in the Senate by two senators.

Since 1983, following the French government's policy of decentralisation, regional councils have been elected with powers similar to those of the regions.

Administration is by a préfet appointed by the government in Paris.

The local government comprises a Conseil Régional (Regional Council) of 39 members and a 42-member Conseil Général (General Council), both directly elected for six-year terms.

Dependencies: Marie Galante, Les Saintes, Désirade, St Barthélémy and St Martin, Grand Bourg (on Marie Galante).

In a 2003 referendum, voters on Guadeloupe's dependencies, St Barthélémy and St Martin, approved a referendum which streamlined the islands' local government and gave them a new status as French overseas collectives in 2007.

Form of state

Département d'Outre-Mer (DOM) (Overseas Department) of France, with additional status as a région (region) of France.

Legal system

French legal system

Last elections

March 2004 (Conseil Général and Conseil Régional)

Next elections

2010 (Conseil Général and Conseil Régional)

Political parties

Ruling party

Objectif Guadeloupe

Main opposition party

Political situation

In a region dominated by either the English or Spanish language, official measures to support the Francophone West Indies now includes not only a French language training programme offered by the Université des Antilles et de la Guyane to students from the Organisation of Eastern Caribbean States (OECS) region but also a French-speaking mobile (cell) phone network set up in 2007–08, by the Digicel Group, for the French West Indies and French Guiana.

Population

452,000 (2005)*

Last census: March 1999: 422,222

Population density: 250 inhabitants per square km.

Annual growth rate: 1 per cent (2003)

Ethnic make-up

Black or mixed race (90 per cent), white (5 per cent), East Indian and others (5 per cent).

Religions

Roman Catholic (95 per cent), other: Hindu, African animist, Protestant (5 per cent).

Education

Many students pursue higher education in the islands or in France. The islands have a teacher's training college, a school of law, and a school of science.

Literacy rate: Over 90 per cent

Compulsory years: 6 to 17.

Health

In addition to several hospitals, Guadeloupe has a Pasteur Institute for the study of tropical diseases. The consumption of crack cocaine has increased steadily with a large number of drug addicts being treated regularly by the health and social services.

Life expectancy: 77.5 years (estimate 2003)

Fertility rate/Maternal mortality rate: Two births per woman (2003)

Birth rate/Death rate: 16 births per 1,000 population; six deaths per 1,000 population (2003).

Child (under 5 years) mortality rate (per 1,000): Nine per 1,000 live births (2003)

Welfare

The existence of a state homecare policy and a traditional lifestyle enable most people aged 60 and over to live at home. The people are highly dependent on French social welfare programmes and development funds. About one-third of children under the age of 17 are brought up in single-parent families. Financial assistance is often available to needy families for their children's basic needs and to enable children to attend school at an early age.

Main cities

Basse-Terre (capital,on Basse Terre, estimated population 12,046 in 2005); Les Abymes (on Grande Terre, 65,700); Pointe-à-Pitre (commercial centre, straddles islands of Grande Terre and Basse Terre, 21,580); Capesterre (on Basse Terre, 20,400).

Dependencies include Marie Galante, Les Saintes, Désirade, St Barthélémy and St Martin, Grand Bourg (on Marie Galante).

Languages spoken

French (99 per cent); Creole patois is also spoken.

Official language/s

French

Media

Press

The only daily newspaper is the regional publication France Antilles. Local newspapers include Le Journal de St Barth (www.st-barths.com/jsb/headlinesfr.html), with a weekly edition.

Broadcasting

The French overseas broadcaster RFO (www.rfo.fr) provides locally produced radio and television news (http://guadeloupe.rfo.fr) and imported French programmes, as well as internet TV services.

Radio: Private radio stations include Radio Caraibes International (www.rci.gp), NRJ Antilles (www.nrjantilles.com) and Radyo Tanbou (www.radyotanbou.com).

Economy

Guadeloupe is heavily dependent on aid from France, which has prevented any significant macroeconomic adjustment to local conditions. The services sector dominates the economy, providing almost 70 per cent of GDP and over 60 per cent of employment. Tourism is the prominent sector with most visitors originating from the US; cruise ships are providing an increasing number of tourists. Agriculture is important, sugarcane is losing its dominance and is being replaced by bananas, aubergines (eggplants) and flowers. Unemployment, particularly among the young, is high at over 25 per cent.

External trade

As a département d'outre-mer (DOM) of France, Guadeloupe is integrated as an outermost region of the European Union, which includes all EU trade agreements. The rising trade deficit is only partially offset by earnings from tourism and aid flows from France aimed particularly at lowering the unemployment rate.

Imports

Principal imports are machinery and transport equipment, foodstuffs and live animals, basic manufactures, miscellaneous manufactures, road vehicles and parts, chemicals and related products.

Main sources: France (63.0 per cent total, 2005), Germany (4.0 per cent), US (3.0 per cent), Japan (2.0 per cent), The Netherlands Antilles (2.0 per cent)

Exports

Principal exports are bananas, machinery and transport equipment, rum, basic manufactures, sugar.

Main destinations: France (60.0 per cent total, 2005), Martinique (18 per cent), US (4.0 per cent)

Agriculture

Farming

Agriculture is the main sector of the economy, contributing 15 per cent to GDP and employing 15 per cent of the population. Guadeloupe is not self-sufficient, relying heavily on food imports from France.

An estimated 36 per cent of the total area is cultivated arable land, 10 per cent is pasture and 15 per cent woodland/forest (including national park land of around 3,000 hectares).

The export of bananas has been a prime acitivity accounting for around 50 per cent of foreign earnings. The future of the banana industry, which has relied on preferential access to the EU, is threatened by a World Trade Organisation (WTO) ruling that this access is illegal and will end. The EU has agreed new tariff quotas from 2006. The number of banana producers fell from 1,000 to 400 in the period 1993–2003. In October 2003, banana producers in Martinique and Guadeloupe formed an association to seek to improve sales in France and in new markets.

Sugar, flowers and melons are also cultivated.

Crop production in 2005 included: 10,750 tonnes (t) yams, 5,135t citrus, 4,210t sweet potatoes, 800,000t sugar cane, 123,000t bananas, 9,000t plantains, 1,400t cassava, 3,070t tomatoes, 850t mangoes, 3,500t pineapples, 8t vanilla, 142,590t fruit in total, 40,144t vegetables. Livestock production included: 6,042t meat in total, 3,350t beef, 1,000t pig meat, 200t goat meat, 1,414t poultry, 1,656t eggs, 65t milk, 150t honey, 585t cattle hides.

Fishing

Offshore fishing is a traditional source of food. The main fish catch includes lobsters, crab and octopus. The sector is underdeveloped, although demand is growing.

The typical total annual fish catch is over 10,114t. Shellfish, molluscs and cephalopods account for another 714t per annum.

In 2004, the total marine fish catch was 9,400 tonnes and the total crustacean catch was 150 tonnes.

Exports of timber products in 2004 amounted to US$145,000 and imports amounted to US$30.6 million.

The estimated timber production in 2004 included 15,300 cubic metres (cum) roundwood, 300cum industrial roundwood, 1,000cum sawnwood, 300cum sawlogs and 15,000cum wood fuel.

Industry and manufacturing

The industrial sector contributes around 17 per cent to GDP and employs 15 per cent of the workforce.

Manufacturing industries are small and centre on the processing of raw materials. Main activities include sugar refining, rum distilling, food processing, cement and brick manufacture, mineral water bottling and ship repair. The construction industry employs 12 per cent of the workforce and is the third-largest sector of activity.

There is an industrial freeport at Jarry.

Tourism

Tourism is estimated to account for over 8 per cent per cent of GDP and employ more than 25 per cent of the workforce.

The sector is predicted to grow by 7.2 per cent year-on-year between 2006–15 with economic activity doubling from US$1,046 million in 2005 to US$2,004 million in 2015.

About 81 per cent of Guadeloupe's tourists come from France, 12 per cent from other European countries and 7 per cent from US.

Mining

Guadeloupe has no mineral resources.

Hydrocarbons

Guadeloupe relies entirely on imported refined oil products. It does not import coal or natural gas.

A proposed pipeline from Trinidad and Tobago to Guadeloupe and Martinique opens possibilities for the future import of natural gas.

Banking and insurance

Central bank

Caisse Centrale de Co-opération Economique; European Central Bank (ECB)

Time

GMT minus four hours

Geography

Guadeloupe is the most northerly of the Windward Islands group in the West Indies. Dominica lies to the south, and Antigua and Montserrat to the north-west. Guadeloupe is formed by two large islands, Grande Terre (mountainous) and Basse Terre, separated by a narrow sea channel, with two smaller islands, Marie Galante, to the south-east, and La Désirade, to the east. St Barthélémy and the northern half of St Maarten (the remainder being part of the Netherlands Antilles) are dependencies.

Hemisphere

Northern

Climate

Sub-tropical with annual mean temperature of 27 degrees Celsius. Levels of humidity and rainfall highest around Basse-Terre. Refreshing trade winds all year round. Humid season – hivernage – is between September and November.

Entry requirements

Passports

Required by all.

Visa

As an overseas region of France entry requirements are the same as those for France.

Visas required by all, except citizens of EU, North America, Australasia and Japan, for stays up to one month; this includes business trips by representatives of foreign entities with an invitation from a local company or organisation. Proof of adequate funds for stay, an itinerary, a guarantee of repatriation if necessary and return/onward ticket are also required. For further exceptions, full details and a copy of the application form visit www.diplomatie.gouv.fr/en/ and follow the path (going to France) on the legend.

Currency advice/regulations

There are no restrictions on the import and export of foreign currency but the amount imported must be declared. The amount of foreign currency, other than euros, that may be taken out must not exceed that imported.

ATMs are readily available. Travellers cheques in euros are accepted everywhere, however cheques in other currencies if accepted, may attract extra exchange fees.

Prohibited imports

Illegal drugs.

Health (for visitors)

Mandatory precautions

A yellow fever vaccination certificate is required if travelling from an infected area.

Advisable precautions

Hepatitis, typhoid, tetanus and polio vaccinations. Water precautions should be taken.

Hotels

There is a good range of quality hotels in Guadeloupe, as well as more basic accommodation. If a service charge is not added, a 15 per cent tip is usual.

Credit cards

Credit and charge cards are accepted in may places.

Public holidays (national)

Fixed dates

1 Jan (New Year's Day), 1 May (Labour Day), 8 May (Victory Day), 27 May (Abolition Day), 14 Jul (Bastille Day), 21 Jul (Schoelcher Day), 15 Aug (Assumption Day), ^1 Nov (All Saints' Day), 2 Nov (All Souls' Day), 11 Nov (Armistice Day), 25 Dec (Christmas).

Variable dates

Carnival (Feb, two days), ^Ash Wednesday (Feb/Mar), Good Friday (Mar/Apr), ^Easter Monday, ^Ascension Day, Whit Monday.

^ Religious holiday.

Working hours

Banking

Mon–Fri: 0800–1200, 1400–1600.

Some banks open Sat: 0800–1200, but these close 1200 Wed.

Banks close at noon on the day preceding a bank holiday.

Business

Mon–Fri: 0800–1200, 1400–1800.

Business visits are best between January–March and June–September.

Government

Mon–Fri: 0800–1300, 1500–1800.

Shops

Mon–Sat: 0800–1200, 1430–1700.

Telecommunications

Mobile/cell phones

GSM 900 and 1800 services are available on Basse Terre.

Electricity supply

220/380V AC, 50 and 60 cycles

Getting there

Air

National airline: Air Caraibes.

International airport/s: Pointe-à-Pitre Le Raizet International Airport (PTP), 3km from Pointe-à-Pitre; duty-free shop, restaurant, buffet, bank, post office, shops, hotel reservations, car hire.

Airport tax: None

Getting about

National transport

Air: Air Guadeloupe, Air St Barthélémy and Liat operate frequent services to all the dependent islands from Pointe-à-Pitre.

Road: The total network is around 3,000km – including about 500km of national highway; secondary roads can be tortuous.

Buses: There are several private bus lines that connect Pointe-à-Pitre or Basse Terre with all villages. There are no timetables; a hand gesture is needed to stop buses.

City transport

Taxis: Plentiful but generally regarded as expensive, particularly in rural areas.

Car hire

Reservations for car rental are advisable, especially between December and April. An international licence is required and one year's experience driving.

BUSINESS DIRECTORY

The addresses listed below are a selection only. While World of Information makes every endeavour to check these addresses, we cannot guarantee that changes have not been made, especially to telephone numbers and area codes. We would welcome any corrections.

Telephone area codes

The international direct dialling code (IDD) for Guadeloupe is +590, followed by another 590 and subscriber's number.

Chambers of Commerce

Basse Terre Chamber of Commerce and Industry, 6 Rue Victor Hugues, 97100 Basse Terre (tel: 994-444; fax: 812-117; e-mail: ccibt:ais.gp).

Pointe-à-Pitre Chamber of Commerce and Industry, Hôtel Consulaire, Rue Félix Eboué, 97159 Pointe-à-Pitre (tel: 937-600; fax: 902-187; e-mail: contacts@cci-pap.org).

Banking

Caisse Régionale de Crédit Agricole Mutuel de la Guadeloupe, BP 134, Zone Artisanale de Petit Perou, 97154 Pointe-à-Pitre (tel: 906-565).

Central bank

European Central Bank (ECB), Kaiserstrasse 29, D-60311 Frankfurt am Main, Germany (tel: (+49-69) 13-440; fax: (+49-69) 1344-6000).

Travel information

Air Caraibes, Morne Vergain, 97139 Abymes (tel: 824-747; fax: 824-749; e-mail: direction@aircaraibes.com).

Ministry of tourism

Bureau Industrie et Tourisme, Préfecture de la Guadeloupe, Rue de Lardenoy, 97109 Basse Terre (tel: 817-681).

Direction de la Promotion Touristique, Préfecture de la Guadeloupe, Rue Lardenoy, 97100 Basse Terre (tel: 811-560).

National tourist organisation offices

Office Départemental du Tourisme (Guadeloupe Tourism Board), 5 Square de la Banque, PO Box 1099, 97181 Pointe-á-Pitre (tel: 894-689, 820-930; fax: 838-922).

Other useful addresses

Agence pour la Promotion Industrielle de la Guadeloupe (APRIGA), BP 1229, 97184 Pointe-à-Pitre (tel: 834-897; fax: 902-187).

Chambre d'Agriculture de la Guadeloupe, 27 rue Sadi-Carnot, 97110 Pointe-à-Pitre (tel: 821-130; fax: 918-873).

Port Autonome de la Guadeloupe, Boulevard Pointe Jarry, Zone de Commerce International, Basse Terre (tel: 213-971; fax: 213-979).

Port Autonome de Pointe-á-Pitre, Gare maritime, 97165 Pointe-á-Pitre Cedex (tel: 213-900; fax: 213-969; internet site: http://www.port-guadeloupe.com).

Syndicat des Producteurs-Exportateurs de Sucre et de Rhum de la Guadeloupe et Dépendances, Zone Industrielle de la Pointe Jarry, 97122 Baie Mahault, BP 2015, 97191 Pointe-à-Pitre (tel: 266-212).

Internet sites

Local government: http://guadeloupe.pref.gouv.fr

Guam

KEY FACTS

Official name: Territory of Guam

Head of State: US President George W Bush

Head of government: Governor Felix Perez Camacho (Republican) (since 2003; re-elected 7 Nov 2006)

Ruling party: Republican Party (elected 5 Nov 2004)

Area: 549 square km

Population: 173,457 (2007)

Capital: Agaña

Official language: Chamorro and English

Currency: US dollar (US$) = 100 cents

GDP per capita: US$22,661 (2006)*

Labour force: 62,050 (2004)*

Unemployment: 7.70% (2004)

Inflation: 2.50% (2005)*

Balance of trade: -US$361.90 million (2006)

Visitor numbers: 1.21 million (2006)*

* estimated figure

COUNTRY PROFILE

Historical profile

Guam is the largest of the Marianas islands, which were occupied by the Chamorro Indians, a Malayo-Polynesian people, around 1500 BC.

1521 The Spanish seized control of Guam, which became a port of call for its galleons travelling between Mexico and the Philippines.

1898 Spain ceded Guam to the US after it lost the Spanish-American war. Guam was transformed into a strategic naval base.

1941 The US were forced out by the Japanese during the Second World War.

1944 US rule was reinstated after three years of fighting. Guam has remained an important military base since then.

1950 The Organic Act of Guam granted the island internal self-government and the islanders US citizenship, but not voting rights in US elections.

1962 The US passed the Naval Clearing Act which opened Guam's ports to foreign visitors.

1975 More than 100,000 evacuees from the fall of Vietnam were repatriated via Guam.

1996 Around 7,000 Kurdish refugees, fearing retaliation from Iraqi leader Saddam Hussein were housed on Guam.

1997 The strongest ever recorded typhoon ripped through Guam, leaving thousands homeless.

2002 Sino-Guamian economic ties were strengthened through visiting delegations to both countries. Felix Camacho (Republican) was elected governor.

Super-typhoon Pongsona struck in December.

2004 A state of emergency was declared after typhoon Tingting hit the island, leaving it almost completely flooded and was struck by super-typhoon Chaba later. The Republicans won control of the legislature from the Democrats in the parliamentary elections.

2006 On 7 November, Governor Camacho won re-election with 50 per cent of the vote.

2008 A US$1.2 billion, B-2 stealth bomber crashed on take-off from Guam; both pilots ejected safely.

Political structure

Constitution

Guam is represented by an elected non-voting delegate to the US House of Representatives; elections are every two years. Its inhabitants are US citizens but are not allowed to vote in US elections. In June 2004, a new process for the island's primary elections was approved, which prevents voters from crossing over between political parties on the ballot; voters can, however, keep their political affiliations confidential.

Form of state

Although it is administered by the department of the interior, Guam is virtually a self-governing unincorporated territory of the US.

The executive

Local executive power rests with a governor, elected by popular vote to a four-year term, who heads a cabinet made up of departmental directors.

National legislature

The 15-member legislature is elected to a two-year term by popular vote. It passes legislation on local matters.

Last elections

4 November 2004 (parliamentary); 7 November 2006 (gubernatorial).

Results: Parliamentary: the Republicans won 51.8 per cent of the vote (nine out of 15 seats); the Democrats won 48.1 per cent (six seats).

Gubernatorial: Felix Camacho (Republican) was re-elected governor with 50 per cent of the vote; Robert Underwood (Democrat) won 48 per cent.

Next elections

4 November 2008 (parliamentary); November 2010 (gubernatorial).

Political parties

Ruling party

Republican Party (elected 5 Nov 2004)

Main opposition party

Democratic Party

Political situation

The US House of Representatives passed an economic stimulus plan, whereby tax rebate cheques began to be sent to all tax payers in mid-2008, to stimulate the local economy and encourage consumer spending. Most households in Guam were looking forward to sums between US$300–600 for singles and US$1,200 for couples but 247 were disappointed when the Guam administration garnished their cheques for outstanding local tax duties.

The recovered US$100,788 was much needed, to cover costs for the Memorial Hospital, Guam Housing, an Urban Renew plan and child support.

Population

173,457 (2007)

Last census: April 2000: 154,805
Population density: 276 inhabitants per square km.
Annual growth rate: 1.5 per cent (2003)
Ethnic make-up
Native Chamorros comprise 37 per cent of the population, Filipinos (26 per cent), white (10 per cent), Chinese, Japanese, Korean and others (27 per cent). There is tension between the Chamorros and guest workers from the Philippines and other Asian countries.
Religions
Roman Catholic (85 per cent)

Education
The education system is similar to that of the US but is poorly managed, with drop-out rates at around 50 per cent. Schools lack basic equipment and essential books.
Education is a high priority for parents and is considered the key to success in Chamorro life. Despite ongoing criticisms of the flaws in the system, the government has implemented no major reforms.
Compulsory years: Five to 16

Health
With a young and growing population the government is faced with the challenge of developing a health care system that will meet their needs. Health services are funded by the US government and the World Health Organisation (WHO).
Health services are good but there is a shortage of adequately trained medical staff. Training of medical personnel was a government priority throughout 2002–05. There are high incidents of mental retardation and thyroid cancers, blamed on nuclear contamination when naval ships were sent for decontamination to Guam.
Life expectancy: 77.9 years (World Bank)
Fertility rate/Maternal mortality rate: 3.7 births per woman (World Bank)
Birth rate/Death rate: 23 births and four deaths per 1,000 population (2003)
Child (under 5 years) mortality rate (per 1,000): 6.5 per 1,000 live births (2003)

Welfare
Welfare is unevenly distributed among the population. The Chamorros are the main beneficiaries of welfare while Filipinos receive less than 10 per cent of government money, however in a 2005 a survey over 50 per cent found to be homeless were Chamorros.

Main cities
Agaña (capital, estimated population 3,923 in 2005), Tamuning (11,361), Mangilao (9,116), Barrigada (4,860), Yigo (8,677)

Languages spoken
English, Chamorro, Chinese, Japanese and Korean.
Official language/s
Chamorro and English

Media
Other news agencies: ABC Pacific Beat: www.radioaustralia.net.au/pacbeat
Pacific Magazine: www.pacificmagazine.net
Press
The Guam Business News is a monthly publication.
Dailies: In English the Pacific Daily News (www.guampdn.com) is the only national newspaper. The US Navy has its own publication Navigator with news and stories relevant to its readership.
Weeklies: There are several weeklies available. In English, Micro Call, Guam Shopper's Guide, Pacific Crossroads, Pacific Voice (published on Sundays for the Catholic community), Pacific Sunday News and Tropic Topics. In Japanese, Guam Shinbun and Guam Kyodo News Service, which provides a facsimile news service twice daily for the Japanese community and tourists. In Korean, the Korean Community News and Korean News.
Business: Guam Business News is a monthly publication.
Periodicals: In English, Latte Magazine is a quarterly, featuring contemporary life and multiculturalism; Micronesica is a bi-annual and Manila, Manila is a glossy news and lifestyle magazine catering to the Filipino community.
Broadcasting
The US Federal Communications Commission is responsible for broadcasting regulations.
Radio: There are several radio stations, the largest are K57 (KGUM) (www.k57.com) and KAUM (www.kuam.com), with news and talk shows, and these are parts of larger broadcasting media enterprises. KTKB Mega Mixx (www.ktkb.com) and Loud Radio 88 (http://loudradio88.homestead.com) are private stations. Several Christian radio stations provide music and entertainment, Light 91, Joy 92 and Adventist World Radio.
Television: Commercial TV stations include K57 (www.k57.com) and KAUM (www.kuam.com), with locally produced news and imported entertainment programmes. A cable service is provided by MSNBC KUAM (www.msnbc.msn.com)

Economy
Guam remains one of the most prosperous islands in the Pacific and has the second highest GDP per capita of the region, Hawaii having the highest. About 60 per cent of Guam's income comes from US federal spending, particularly in defence facilities. In early 2006, it was announced that 8,000 troops will be re-deployed (from Okinawa, Japan) to Guam in 2008, and it is anticipated that it could add around US$15 billion to military spending (spread over 2006–16). Most of these funds will be spent on housing and other military facilities. However general infrastructure will benefit from more investment. In response, the real estate sector has grown, which is increasing speculation in new developments on the island and construction is increasingly being felt on GDP growth.
Nevertheless, tourism is the largest sector in the economy and has experienced a resurgence since 2003, when Japanese visitor numbers had fallen below one million (a figure typical of the early 1990s). In 2005 Japanese tourists accounted for 78 per cent of all tourists. Guam is increasingly being seen as a reasonable destination for Japanese visitors on a limited budget. Tourism accounts for around 35 per cent of total employment.
Aside from tourism, the only other significant source of income is the fishing industry, although the cement and construction industries have continued to prosper due to the constant ravaging of buildings and infrastructure by natural disasters.

Labour market and unemployment
About 31 per cent of local employment is with either US or territorial government while tourism accounts for a third of private sector employment. There are migrant workers from the Philippines and other Asian countries. Civilian pay by the military is typically twice that in the civilian economy.

External trade
Guam exports free of duty to a number of countries, including Australia, Japan and the US.
Imports
Main imports are petroleum and petroleum products, food and manufactured goods.
Main sources: Singapore (50 per cent total, 2005), South Korea (21.4 per cent), Japan (14.0 per cent), Hong Kong (4.6 per cent)
Exports
Main exports are onstruction materials, fish, food and beverage products.
Main destinations: Japan (67.2 per cent total, 2005), Singapore (7.1 per cent), UK (4.8 per cent)
Re-exports
Food re-exports for distribution throughout the Pacific provide the mainstay of export income along with refined petroleum products.

Agriculture

Farming

The agriculture sector typically accounts for 7 per cent of gross island product (GIP). Most agricultural activity is part-time market gardening on smallholdings.

In March 2004, a fungus infected thousands of betel nut trees in the southern parts of Guam and scientists feared it could spread to other types of palm tree. More than 3,000 infected trees were destroyed.

Estimated crop production in 2005 included: 53,000 tonnes (t) coconuts, 6,890t oilcrops, 5,164t vegetables in total, 2,400t watermelons, 2,350 roots & tubers, 100t sweet potatoes, 180t citrus fruit, 120t tomatoes, 2,685t fruit in total, 152t treenuts, 5,162t vegetables in total.

Estimated livestock production included: 202t of meat in total; 7t beef, 11t goat meat, 140t pig meat, 43t poultry, 700t eggs and 12t honey.

Fishing

Fishing is an important source of protein. Future areas for growth include salmon and trout farming. Typical annual catches include 200t freshwater fish, 280t marine fish, and 28t of all other seafood.

In 2004, the total marine fish catch was 178 tonnes.

Industry and manufacturing

Industry typically accounts for 15 per cent of GDP and employs about 3 per cent of the labour force. Most industrial goods are imported.

Main industries include US military, tourism, construction, transshipment services, concrete products, printing and publishing, food processing and textiles.

Government policy is attempting to focus on attracting foreign investment, particularly from Asian manufacturers, in order to develop the industrial base.

Tourism

Tourism is still Guam's most important economic activity. The government is seeking to expand into new markets in Europe and Asia, including China, and to diversify Guam's tourism product, especially into sports tourism.

Among Guam's natural attractions are it's unspoilt coral reefs, white sand beaches, lagoons and waterfalls. The brown tree snake, accidentally introduced in the 1940's has, however, decimated its bird-life and eradication programmes are carried out regularly. Guam is ideal for water sports including surfing, canoeing, jet skiing, and deep-sea fishing, in waters that are clear and warm. On the land, there are seven golf courses and good hiking tracks. It is one of the best diving destinations in the world with shipwrecks and coral reefs. On Cocos Island, two miles off the Southern tip of Guam there is a Spanish galleon wreck with billions of dollars worth of treasure that has still to be recovered.

Environment

In May 2005 a US research study confirmed that Guam had received measurable radioactive fallout during nuclear testing from 1946–62. The government confirmed that residents would be eligible under the Radiation Exposure Compensation Act. Radioactive polution was also acknowledged in Apra Habour, caused when military ships were decontaminated by washing down after testing.

Military expansion of the Andersen Air Force Base will cause the loss of some pristine native forest at a time when several endangered bird species are being reintroduced into the area.

Mining

Mining contributes less than 5 per cent to GDP. Rock and cement production supplies the construction industry.

Hydrocarbons

Guam does not produce or refine oil, it relies entirely on imports. Around 20,000 barrels per day of refined oil products, mainly jet fuel, gasoline and distillate are imported. Guam does not produce or import gas or coal.

Energy

A petroleum refinery has been in operation since the 1970s.

Banking and insurance

Central bank

Federal Reserve Bank of San Francisco

Time

GMT plus ten hours

Geography

Guam is the southernmost and largest of the Marianas, situated about 2,170km (1,350 miles) south of Tokyo, Japan, and 5,300km (3,300 miles) west of Honolulu, Hawaii.

The island consists of two ancient volcanoes of which the southern peak is 407 metres at its tallest. In the north and between the summits are limestone plateaux with deep gorges that drop to the narrow coastal shelf.

The world's deepest chasm in the deepest ocean, the Marianas Trench, lies around 400km south-west of Guam.

Hemisphere

Northern

Climate

Guam is warm and humid with temperatures averaging between 24–30 degrees Celsius. Dec–May is generally cooler and drier. Rainfall, up to 300mm per month, averages 2,000mm per annum. The heaviest rainfall is usually between Jul–Sep. There are occasional tropical storms. The tropical humidity is tempered somewhat by the prevailing north-westerly trade winds.

Dress codes

Informal, lightweight clothing is acceptable.

Entry requirements

Passports

Required by all.

Visa

US entry requirements apply. Visas required by all, except US citizens and foreign nationals of countries that have visa free entry to the US and are in possession of machine readable passports with biometric data, under the Visa Waiver Program (VWP) introduced in 2005. All other visitors and passport holders must apply for a visa. Visas, for both tourism and business, are valid for up to 90 days. A return/onward ticket is also required. Further information can be found at http://travel.state.gov/ including information on temporary business visas. More detailed information can be found at http://uscis.gov/graphics/services/visa_info.htm.

Currency advice/regulations

There are no restrictions on import or export of foreign or local currency. However amounts over US$10,000 or equivalent must be declared.

Customs

Personal items are duty-free.

Prohibited imports

Plant material, meat products, illegal drugs and any material that breaches US copyright laws.

Health (for visitors)

Mandatory precautions

Vaccination certificates required for yellow fever if travelling from infected area.

Advisable precautions

Dengue fever is endemic; it is advisable to cover up at dawn and dusk and prophylaxis should be used. Vaccinations for diphtheria, tuberculosis, hepatitis A and B, tetanus, typhoid fever should be considered. No cases of polio have been reported since the 1990s. There is a rabies risk in rural areas.

Ciguatera poisoning is possible if eating tropical reef-fish – toxins are not removed through cooking – avoiding barracuda, grouper, snapper and amberjack will reduce the risk.

Medical insurance is necessary as all healthcare costs are high. All continuous medication should be carried along with its packaging and prescription.

Public holidays (national)

Fixed dates

1 Jan (New Year's Day), 4 Jul (US Independence Day), 21 Jul (Liberation Day), 2

Nov (All Souls' Day), 11 Nov (Veterans' Day), 8 Dec (Lady of Camarin Day), 25 Dec (Christmas).

Variable dates

Martin Luther King Day (third Mon in Jan), President's Day (second Mon in Feb), Guam Discovery Day (first Mon in Mar), Good Friday, Memorial Day (last Mon in May), Labour Day (first Mon in Sep), Columbus Day (first Mon in Oct), Thanksgiving Day (fourth Thu in Nov).

Working hours

Banking

Mon–Thu: 1000–1500; Fri: 1000–1800; Sat 0900–1200. ATMs are available.

Business

Mon–Fri: 0730/0830–1730/1800; Sat: 0830–1200.

Government

Mon–Fri: 0730/0830–1730/1800; Sat: 0830–1200.

Shops

Mon–Fri: 0800–1700; Sat: 0800–1300.

Telecommunications

Mobile/cell phones

GSM 1900 and 850 services cover most of the island.

Electricity supply

110V AC, 60Hz

Weights and measures

US system

Getting there

Air

Korean Air, Continental Micronesia, All Nippon Airlines, Japan Airlines and Palau Micronesia Air all serve Guam.

International airport/s: The Antonio B Won Pat International Airport (GUM), 11km from Agaña; duty-free shop, first-class lounge, restaurant, currency exchange, hotel reservations and car hire.

Airport tax: None

Surface

Main port/s: Apra Harbour.

Getting about

National transport

Road: The roads and highways are third-rate and bumpy, with some 600km surfaced.

Buses: A reasonable service connects almost all villiages, however services do not run on Sundays or public holidays.

Taxis: Are readily available and fares are metered.

City transport

Car hire

Available through most major companies. In general, charges are based on time, mileage and insurance. An international driving licence is required.

BUSINESS DIRECTORY

The addresses listed below are a selection only. While World of Information makes every endeavour to check these addresses, we cannot guarantee that changes have not been made, especially to telephone numbers and area codes. We would welcome any corrections.

Telephone area codes

The international direct dialling code (IDD) for Guam is +1 671, followed by subscriber's number.

Chambers of Commerce

Guam Chamber of Commerce, 173 Aspinall Avenue, Ada Plaza Center, PO Box 283, Agana 96932 (tel: 472-6311; fax: 472-6202; e-mail: gchamber@guamchamber.com.gu).

Banking

Bank of Hawaii, PO Box BH, Agaña 96910 (tel: 4779-781; fax: 4777-533).

First Commercial Bank, 1st Floor, 330 Hernan Cortes Ave, Agaña 96910 (tel: 4726-864/5; fax: 4778-921).

Union Bank of California NA, 194 Hernan Cortes Ave, Agaña 96910 (tel: 4778-811; fax: 4723-284).

Central bank

Federal Reserve System, 20th Street and Constitution Avenue, NW, Washington DC 20551 (tel: (202) 452-3000; fax: (202) 452-3819).

Travel information

Dive Rota, PO Box 941, Rota MP 96951 (email: mark@diverota.com; internet: www.diverota.com).

Freedom Air, PO Box 1578, Hagatna, 96932 (tel: 647-8360/1; fax; 472-8080; email: freedom@ite.net).

National tourist organisation offices

Guam Visitors Bureau, PO Box 3520; 401 Pale San Vitores Road, Tamuning 96913 (tel: 646-5278/9; fax: 646-8861: internet: www.visitguam.org).

Other useful addresses

Guam Economic Development Authority, Suite 911, ITC Building, 590 South Marine Drive, Tamuning, Guam 96911 (tel: 649-4141; fax: 649-4146).

Other news agencies: ABC Pacific Beat: www.radioaustralia.net.au/pacbeat

Pacific Magazine: www.pacificmagazine.net

Internet sites

The Pacific Daily News: www.guampdn.com

KUAM Broadcasting News: www.kuam.com

US Office of Insular affairs: www.doi.gov/oia

Guatemala

KEY FACTS

Official name: República de Guatemala (Republic of Guatemala)

Head of State: President Álvaro Colom (from 14 Jan 2008) (UNE)

Head of government: President Álvaro Colom (from 14 Jan 2008)

Ruling party: Unidad Nacional de la Esperanza (UNE) (National Union of Hope) (elected Sep 2007)

Area: 108,890 square km

Population: 13.31 million (2007)

Capital: Guatemala City

Official language: Spanish

Currency: Quetzal (Q) = 100 centavos

Exchange rate: Q7.41 per US$ (Jul 2008)

GDP per capita: US$2,532 (2007)*

GDP real growth: 5.70% (2007)*

Labour force: 4.76 million (2004)

Unemployment: 3.70% (2004)

Inflation: 6.80% (2007)

Balance of trade: -US$5.88 billion (2006)

Foreign debt: US$5.97 billion (2004)

Visitor numbers: 1.50 million (2006)*

* estimated figure

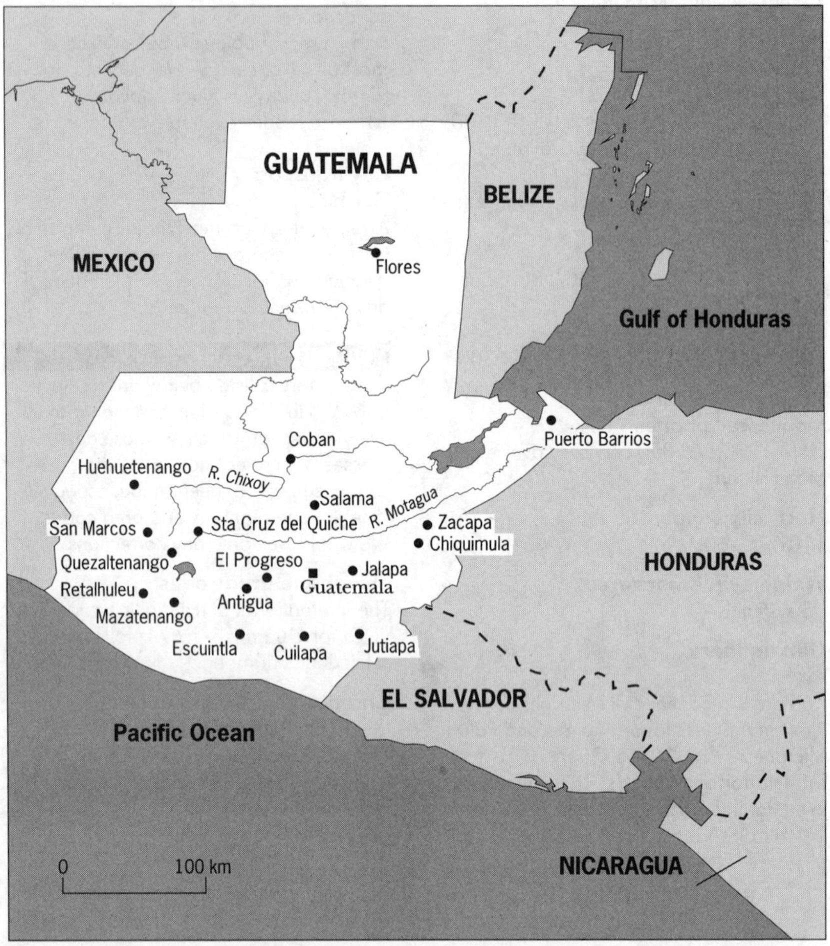

Guatemala elected a new president in 2007. Center-left candidate Alvaro Colóm Caballeros won the second round of voting in November 2007. Colóm defeated his opponent, former General Otto Pérez Molina, who stood on a platform that promised to tackle Guatemala's high poverty, crime, and murder rates. It was the third attempt at the presidency on the part of Colóm, a Mayan priest and successful businessman. Mr Colóm proposed greater social expenditure to fight poverty and create more jobs, which in the Guatemalan context sounded pretty woolly stuff. Sr Pérez Molina had pledged a more heavy-handed approach to solving the high crime and murder rates, saying he would deploy the army, double the police force, and reinstate the death penalty. Pérez Molina served in the military during Guatemala's long civil war and some voters suspected his election might return the country to a time of corrupt military rule. The best-known presidential candidate was Nobel Prize laureate Rigoberta Menchú who, despite her fame, only managed to obtain some 3 per cent of the total vote. For the second round of the presidential poll there were 30,000 Guatemalan police on duty and nearly 20,000 international observers present. Each candidate had, predictably, promised to alleviate Guatemala's poverty; salaries average around US$200 a month.

Commonplace crime

Prior to the first round of voting, 38 people had been killed and more than 61 violent attacks on candidates and political activists were reported. By the time the election was over, at least 50 candidates for both local and legislature seats, party activists and their family members had been murdered. Violent crime is a commonplace in Guatemala, with some 5,000 murders annually many related to drug trafficking and corruption. Both candidates had promised to crack down on crime.

In addition to electing their president, Guatemala's voters were choosing 158 national legislators and 332 local mayors.

The Rios Montt Affair

In a further development, in early 2007 Spain demanded the extradition of seven former members of Guatemala's government to face trial in Spain. Spain's highest court ruled that cases of genocide committed abroad could be judged in Spain, even if no Spanish citizens were involved. The Spanish extradition request makes specific reference to former military rulers Rios Montt and Oscar Mejia. They, and others, are wanted in connection with a series of kidnappings, mass murders and torture of Mayan Indians during Guatemala's 36 year long civil war which ended in the mid-1990s. Even though two of the men sought for extradition are in custody in Guatemala, it is thought unlikely that the extradition requests will bear fruit.

The US government, which had openly supported Ríos Montt during his regime, somewhat belatedly stated that it would be difficult to maintain a normal relationship with the ex-ruler due to his human rights record. Nor is Ríos Montt a friend to big business, whose leaders prefer candidates who would attract rather than upset foreign investors. Some human rights activists wanted to see Ríos Montt run in the presidential election – and lose. Any defeat at the polls would be seen as dealing a blow to his power and influence. However, the ruling in favour of Ríos Montt indicated pro-military leanings among members of the highest court and did not bode well for legal efforts that seek justice for Guatemala's human rights violators. By his election to the legislature in late 2007, Mr Montt effectively saw off his legal opponents. In Guatemala, legislators have immunity from prosecution.

Growth grows

According to the United Nations Economic Commission for Latin America and the Caribbean (ECLAC), the Guatemalan economy grew by 5.5 per cent in 2007 thanks to the buoyancy of private consumption, which was boosted by large inflows of family remittances (12.5 per cent of GDP). Those inflows went some way towards financing the country's large trade deficit (about 17 per cent of GDP). The current account deficit (5 per cent of GDP) was more than covered by foreign direct investment and other capital inflows. The yearly inflation figure to November was 9.1 per cent, mostly owing to supply factors, so the 2007 inflation target of 4–6 per cent was not met.

For 2008, the authorities project GDP growth of 5.0 per cent, an inflation rate between 3.5 per cent and 5.5 per cent and a central government deficit of 1.6 per cent of GDP. The new government took office in January 2008, and was expected to comply with the commitment to maintain macroeconomic stability and give greater priority to social policies. It had to face the public security problems and construct legal standards to enable the authorities to have access to stable and sufficient revenue. Guatemala's tax burden stood at 12 per cent of GDP, well below the average for Latin America and the Caribbean.

Up to September 2007, total government revenue in real terms rose by 9 per cent (compared with 11 per cent in 2006), boosted by economic growth. In real terms, current expenditure increased by 8 per cent and capital expenditure by 17 per cent. Particularly significant was the growth of physical investment as a result of new public works projects. As a result, the government deficit in 2007 was slightly above the 2006 figure of 1.9 per cent of GDP. A one-year extension was agreed for the extraordinary tax imposed temporarily to support the peace agreements (IETAP), which is due to expire at the end of 2007. It will generate revenue equivalent to 1 per cent of GDP for the 2008 budget.

In the course of the year, in order to counter inflationary pressures, the monetary authorities made five increases of 0.25 points each to the monetary policy rate, which stood at 6.25 per cent in December. International reserves rose, mostly because of disbursements from government external borrowing; this was reflected in an increase in public external debt of US$300 million. A proportion of the resulting resources was held in central bank deposits, so fiscal policy contributed to holding back the growth of the money supply. Open-market operations were continued, albeit at a lower rate than in 2006. In October, the year-on-year variation of means of payment in real terms was 4 per cent, while variation in credit to the private sector was 12 per cent for local-currency and 34 per cent in terms of foreign currency. This was beyond the range established in the monetary programme, due to lower financial costs and the relative stability of the nominal exchange rate. Up to November, the central bank did not intervene in the exchange market. In comparison with 2006, the quetzal experienced a slight real effective appreciation (0.5 per cent). However, the appreciation was significant (12 per cent)

KEY INDICATORS — Guatemala

	Unit	2003	2004	2005	2006	2007
Population	m	12.22	12.39	13.72	*12.98	*13.31
Gross domestic product (GDP)	US$bn	24.70	27.45	31.79	30.21	*33.69
GDP per capita	US$	1,941	1,953	2,317	*2,326	*2,532
GDP real growth	%	2.4	2.6	3.2	5.2	*5.7
Inflation	%	5.6	7.0	9.1	6.6	6.8
Industrial output	% change	–	0.9	2.9	5.5	–
Agricultural output	% change	–	3.7	3.3	1.8	–
Exports (fob) (goods)	US$m	2,787.0	3,429.5	3,437.0	6,025.2	*4,489.5
Imports (cif) (goods)	US$m	6,300.0	7,189.1	8,827.0	11,068.7	*10,981.1
Balance of trade	US$m	-3,513.0	-3,759.6	-5,390.0	-5,043.6	*-6,491.6
Current account	US$m	-1,060.0	-1,150.0	-1,393.0	-1,510.0	-1,685.0
Total reserves minus gold	US$m	2,833.2	3,426.3	3,663.8	3,914.9	4,129.9
Foreign exchange	US$m	2,825.0	3,418.3	3,657.3	3,909.3	4,125.6
Exchange rate	per US$	7.91	7.94	7.69	7.69	7.60

* estimated figure

with regard to the average for the period 2000–06.

Lending and private investment

Despite the suspension of two banks (one in October 2006 and the other in January 2007), several bank mergers have taken place since October 2006 in response to the strategy of national banks to increase their solvency. Non-performing loans and loans in arrears, as a percentage of the total credit portfolio, fell from 5.9 per cent in 2006 to 5.3 per cent in 2007.

GDP growth in 2007 was due to buoyant construction and transport and communications, which posted growth rates of around 15 per cent. Construction was boosted by increased public investment and the expansion of credit to the private sector. Growth in the transport and communications sector was mainly attributable to investment by telecommunications enterprises. Agriculture grew by 4 per cent thanks to a recovery of traditional crops. Coffee production climbed as its prices picked up on the international markets, while sugar production rose owing to increased demand in the light of higher export quotas under the Dominican Republic-Central America-United States Free Trade Agreement (CAFTA-DR). Manufacturing growth remained modest at 3 per cent.

Inflation on the up

Inflation gathered pace during 2007 to reach a year-on-year increase of 9.1 per cent in November, compared with 5.8 per cent at the end of 2006. The main determinants were supply factors such as the price rises in petroleum and its derivatives as well as in food (partly offset by the relative stability of the exchange rate). In October, food prices chalked up year-on-year increase of 14.0 per cent, partly due to the harvest losses in the wake of high rainfall.

In 2007, the minimum daily wage was 44.58 quetzals for agricultural activities and 45.82 quetzals for non-agricultural activities. In September 2007, the cost of the basic basket of foods was 55.16 quetzals a day. Real minimum wages fell by 1 per cent. According to the three employment surveys carried out by the Social Research and Study Association (ASIES), half of companies reported employment as unchanged. However, there was a rise in the number of companies reporting an increase in the number of jobs (from 27 per cent in January to 36 per cent in September).

Exports and imports both rise...

The value of merchandise exports climbed by 16 per cent in 2007, mainly on the strength of the increase in traditional exports (especially banana and coffee). The best performances by non-traditional exports were fruits, vegetables and legumes, as well as other food products (in terms of volume) and mineral products (by volume).

Up to August, external sales of clothing showed a decline (-28 per cent). The value of merchandise imports expanded by 15 per cent. Main examples included purchases of durables (24 per cent) and construction materials (35 per cent). The oil bill continued to grow and represented 18 per cent of total imports. Revenues from family remittances amounted to US$4.2 billion. The rate of growth of remittances fell from 21 per cent in 2006 to 17 per cent in 2007. This reduced buoyancy is a reflection of rising unemployment, lower wages for Guatemalan emigrants working in the troubled construction industry in the United States and the recent toughening of the migration policy in that country. Income from remittances remains a key factor in financing the wide goods and services deficit. The current account deficit was amply covered by capital inflows, causing international reserves to swell by US$170 million.

Risk assessment

Politics	Fair
Economics	Good
Regional stability	Good

COUNTRY PROFILE

Historical profile

1523–24 Pedro de Alvarado defeated the indigenous Mayan civilisation and created Guatemala as a Spanish colony.
1821 The Central American provinces (Costa Rica, Guatemala, Honduras, Nicaragua and El Salvador) declared independence from Spain.
1822 Central American confederation annexed itself to the Mexican Empire, under General Agustín de Iturbde, later Emperor Agustín I.
1823 Agustín I was overthrown and Mexico became a republic. The Central American states formed the United Provinces of Central America.
1825 Costa Rica, Guatemala, Honduras, Nicaragua and El Salvador formed the Central American Federation (CAF).
1838 The CAF was dissolved and Guatemala became a fully independent republic.
1844–65 Guatemala was ruled by conservative dictator Rafael Carrera.
1873–85 Liberal, Rufino Barrios, became president, he attempted to modernise the country by developing an army and introducing coffee plantations.
1930 General Jorge Ubico began his repressive dictatorship.
1941 Guatemala declared war on the Axis Powers.
1944 Ubico was overthrown in a popular revolution. Juan José Arevalo headed a new government that introduced social reforms, including a social security system and land redistribution.
1951 Jacobo Arbenz Guzmán became president and stepped up the reforms.
1954 A US-backed coup d'état, led by Colonel Carlos Castillo Armas and prompted by the US United Fruit Company when disused land it owned was nationalised overthrew the democratically elected government. A military dictatorship was installed.
1957 Castillo Armas was assassinated.
1958 Miguel Ramon Ydígoras Fentes took control and his autocratic rule led to a failed military revolt by junior officer in 1960. Most leaders of armed insurrection for the next 36 years of civil war were part of this group.
1963 Enrique Peralta became president following a coup and civilian administration was completely assumed by the military whose power and influence increased. Widespread repression of opposition groups increased as leaders were targetted for assassination or 'disappearance'. Insurgents countered with sabotage and violent guerrilla tactics.
1966 Civilian rule was restored when César Méndez, Revolucionario Partido (PR) (Revolutionary Party) was elected president. Nevertheless, the military launched a major counterinsurgency campaign, which crippled the guerrilla movement in the countryside.
1970 Carlos Arena, backed by the military and the US, was elected president.
1976 An earthquake struck just south-west of Guatemala City that killed around 27,000 people and left one million citizens homeless.
1978–1984 Over 90 per cent of all atrocities occurred during this time as government forces and insurgents battled. The most frequent victims were the ethnic Mayan population who were attacked by both sides and accused of being collaborators or sympathisers of the opposition.
1980 Thirty seven people died, in the Spanish Embassy siege in Guatemala City, when Mayan peasant farmers were protesting about military repression.
1981 Left-wing insurgent groups unified to become Unidad Revolucionaria Nacional Guatemalteca (URNG) (National Guatemalan Revolutionary Unit).
1982 General Efraín Ríos Montt seized power in a military coup. His dictatorship

was in power during the bloodiest period of the civil war.
1983 Montt was ousted by General Mejía Victores, who declared an amnesty on guerrillas.
1985 Marco Vinicio Cerezo was elected president and Democracia Cristiana Guatemalteco (DCG) (Guatemalan Christian Democracy) won legislative elections.
1989 An attempt to overthrow Cerezo failed.
1991 Jorge Serrano Elias was elected president.
1993 Serrano's attempt to impose an authoritarian regime led to mass demonstrations and he was forced to resign. Ramiro de Leon Carpio was elected president by the legislature.
1994 Peace talks began between the government and the URNG.
1995 The URNG declared a cease-fire. The UN and the US criticised the government for widespread human rights violations and the deaths of more than 200,000 civilians during the civil war.
1996 After a civil war lasting 36 years, a peace treaty was signed. Alvaro Arzú and his Partido de Avanzada Nacional (PAN) (National Advancement Party) won the subsequent presidential and National Congress elections. Arzú began a purge on senior military officers implicated in human rights violations.
1999 A UN-sponsored investigation found that the security forces were responsible for 93 per cent of all human rights atrocities committed during the civil war and that the military had overseen 626 massacres in Mayan villages. Alfonso Portillo of the Frente Republicano Guatemalteco (FRG) (Guatemalan Republican Front) was elected president.
2000 Portillo was sworn in as president.
2001 A foreign exchange law allowed the free circulation of US dollars from May and citizens and companies were allowed to hold US dollar bank deposits without prior authorisation. The government paid US$1.8 million in compensation to the families of 226 victims killed by soldiers and death squads in the village of Las Dos Erres in 1982.
2003 Teachers, striking over demands for salary increases and improvements to the school system, disrupted international air travel and access to seaports. The ruling FRG was defeated by the Gran Alianza Nacional (GANA) (Grand National Alliance) in the parliamentary elections. Óscar Berger Perdomo (GANA) won the presidential run-off election on 28 December.
2004 Berger was sworn in as president on 14 January. Former dictator, Ríos Montt, was put under house arrest on charges of inciting a riot, and genocide relating to atrocities carried out when he was in power. The State accepted responsibility for more human rights violations during the civil war; US$3.5 million was paid out to victims in July. In September, 11 people were killed as demonstrators clash with police.
2005 In March, the government signed the Central American Free Trade Agreement (Cafta) with the US and five of the Central American and Caribbean states, amid anti-US demonstrations. Hurricane Stan hit the region in October causing 699 deaths, over 35,000 homes were destroyed and there were numerous landslides and extensive flooding. In the US, in November, Guatemala's top anti-drugs investigator was arrested on drug trafficking charges.
2006 In January, manslaughter charges against Ríos Montt were dropped. However, in December Spain requested that he, and several other military rulers, be extradited to face charges of genocide and atrocities carried out during the 36-year long civil war; the request was denied.
2007 In parliamentary elections held on 9 September the opposition Unidad Nacional de la Esperanza (UNE) (National Union of Hope) won 48 seats out of 158, the ruling GANA 37, the Partido Patriota (PP) (Patriotic Party) 30, the FRG 15; turnout was 60.5 per cent. Two rounds of presidential elections were held on 9 September and 4 November. Álvaro Colom (UNE) won 28.2 per cent of the vote in the first round but this was not enough for an outright victory. In the second round Colom won with 52.82 per cent of the vote; his nearest rival Otto Pérez Molina (PP) won 47.18 per cent. Turnout was 48.3 per cent.
2008 Álvaro Colom Caballeros was sworn in as president on 14 January.

Political structure

In addition to their unicameral national parliaments, El Salvador, Guatemala, Honduras, Nicaragua, Panama and Dominican Republic also return directly-elected deputies to the supranational Central American Parliament.

Constitution

The constitution, which came into effect in 1986 (replacing the 1966 constitution suspended in 1982), created a representative system of government in which power is exercised equally by the legislative, executive and judicial arms. Guatemala is divided into 22 provinces, subdivided into municipalities.

Form of state

Presidential democratic republic

The executive

Executive power is held by the president, directly elected for four years, assisted by a vice president and an appointed cabinet.

National legislature

Legislative power is vested in the 80-member unicameral Congreso de la República (Congress), elected every four years, of which 64 seats are elected in departmental congressional districts and 16 in a nationwide ballot. Electoral suffrage is universal for all aged 18 years or over. Congress approves laws by means of an absolute majority, except those involving constitutional change or any international treaty or agreement affecting the sovereignty of the state; these must secure a two-thirds majority. Congress is responsible for all electoral matters, for approving the budget and decreeing taxes and for conferring honours. Congress meets on 15 June each year and ordinary legislative sessions last four months.

Legal system

Guatemala has a civil law system with judicial review of legislative acts. The Supreme Court serves as the highest appeal court in the country; there is also a separate Court of Constitutionality and a Supreme Electoral Tribunal. The country does not accept the compulsory jurisdiction of the International Court of Justice.

Last elections

9 September 2007 (parliamentary); 9 September/4 November 2007 (presidential).

Results: Presidential: (first round), Álvaro Colom (Unidad Nacional de la Esperanza (UNE) (National Union of Hope)) won 28.2 per cent of the vote, Otto Pérez Molina (Partido Patriota (PP) Patriotic Party)) 23.5 per cent, Alejandro Giammattei (GANA) 17.2 per cent. All other candidates won less than 10 per cent. Turnout was 60.5 per cent. Second round, Álvaro Colom won 52.82 per cent, Otto Pérez Molina won 47.18 per cent. Turnout was 48.3 per cent.
Parliamentary: Unidad Nacional de la Esperanza (UNE) (National Union of Hope) won 22.8 per cent of the vote (48 seats out of 158), GANA 16.5 per cent (37); Partido Patriota (PP) (Patriotic Party) 15.9 per cent (30); Frente Republicano Guatemalteco (FRG) (Guatemalan Republican Front) 9.8 per cent (15), Encuentro por Guatemala (EG) (Encounter for Guatemala) 6.7 per cent (4); Partido Unionista (PU) (Unionist Party) 6.1 per cent (8), Centro de Acción Social (CASA) (Social Action Centre) 4.9 per cent (5); Partido de Avanzada Nacional (PAN) (National Advancement Party) 4.6 per cent (4), and Union del Cambio Nacionalista (UCN) 4.1 per cent (4). Turnout is 60.5 per cent.

Next elections

2011 (president and parliament)

Political parties
Ruling party
Unidad Nacional de la Esperanza (UNE) (National Union of Hope) (elected Sep 2007)
Main opposition party
Gran Alianza Nacional (GANA) (Grand National Alliance)

Population
13.31 million (2007)
Last census: November 2002: 11,237,196
Population density: 101.8 inhabitants per square km. Urban population: 40 per cent (1995–2001).
Annual growth rate: 2.3 per cent 1994–2004 (WHO 2006)
Ethnic make-up
A high proportion of the population belongs to 22 Mayan ethno-linguistic groups, conserving the cultural heritage of their ancestors. Their numbers are disputed but they constitute at least 45 per cent of the population and possibly as much as 60 per cent. Many of the inhabitants of the Caribbean coast are of Afro-Caribbean origin.
Religions
The constitution guarantees freedom of worship. Catholicism is the most widespread religion, although large numbers of conversions have been made in recent years by Protestant churches, including mainstream non-conformists and US-based fundamentalist sects. Protestant leaders claim to have converted some 30 per cent of the population and are playing an increasingly active role in the country's politics. Some indigenous communities hold services combining Catholicism with pre-Columbian rites.
Education
Elementary education is free and lasts for six years and secondary education, which begins at age 13, for a further six years, divided into two three-year courses. There are five universities, three of which are private, located in Guatemala City and Quetzaltenango, the country's second-largest city.
Literacy rate: 70 per cent adult rate; 80 per cent youth rate (15–24) (Unesco 2005).
Compulsory years: Seven to 14 in urban areas only.
Enrolment rate: 90 per cent total primary enrolment of the relevant age group; 26 per cent total enrolment in secondary schools, of the relevant age group; enrolment in tertiary education is less than 10 per cent.
Pupils per teacher: 35 in primary schools.

Health
Per capita total expenditure on health (2003) was US$235; of which per capita government spending was US$93, at the international dollar rate, (WHO 2006). Healthcare remains inadequate with 80 per cent of spending and hospitals confined in the two major cities.
HIV/Aids
HIV prevalence: 1.1 per cent aged 15–49 in 2003 (World Bank)
Life expectancy: 68 years, 2004 (WHO 2006)
Fertility rate/Maternal mortality rate: 4.5 births per woman, 2004 (WHO 2006); maternal mortality 2.9 per 1,000 live births (World Bank).
Child (under 5 years) mortality rate (per 1,000): 35 per 1,000 live births; 44 per cent of children aged under five are malnourished (World Bank).

Welfare
Social security, which is compulsory, covers health and hospital care as well as industrial accidents, disability and widowhood for registered workers. All employers with five or more workers are required by law to register with the State Institute of Social Security.

Main cities
Guatemala City (capital, estimated population 964,823 in 2005), Mixco (297,039), Villa Nueva (218,513), Quezaltenango (112,121).

Languages spoken
Approximately 22 Indian languages are widely spoken throughout the highlands, including Quiché, Cakchiquel, Mam and Kekchi. About 40 per cent of all Guatemalan children enter school with no knowledge of Spanish.
English is spoken in almost all tourist areas.
Official language/s
Spanish

Media
The constitution guarantees freedom of the press. Private, independently owned media outlets dominate the market.
Press
Most of Guatemala's media is privately owned. Journalists have reported incidents of intimidation particularly following articles exposing corruption.
Dailies: In Spanish, national newspapers include Prensa Libre (www.prensalibre.com), La Hora (www.lahora.com.gt) and El Periodico and are broadsheets with articles on business and finance, while Siglo Veintiuno (www.sigloxxi.com) is a tabloid style newspaper.
Regional newspapers, in Spanish, include El Metropolitano (www.elmetropolitano.net) with local editions in five cities. Other local publications such as Diario de Centroamérica (www.dca.gob.gt), Nuestro Diario (www.nuestrodiario.com) and El Qeutzalteco (www.elquetzalteco.com.gt) are tabloid style newspapers.
In English, the Guatemala Times (www.guatemala-times.com) is an online publication.
Broadcasting
The state-owned Radiodifusión y Televisión Nacional operates public broadcasting.
Radio: The state-owned Radio TGW (www.radiotgw.gob.gt) operates a network of five radio stations, providing news, educational and cultural programmes, however it has low audience numbers. It competes with dozens of commercial stations, located regionally and locally and many of them broadcasting at least part of the time in indigenous languages. In Spanish, news and information stations include Emiroras Unidas (http://radio.emisorasunidas.com), a national network, Radio Sonora (www.sonora.com.gt) and Radio Punto (www.radiopunto.com).
Christian churches operate several radio stations which broadcast from rural areas, including Radio Cultural TGN (www.radiocultural.com), broadcasting in several languages.
Television: There is no public TV. The majority of commercial TV is owned by a few elites. TV channels broadcasting on terrestrial and satellite include Canal 3 (www.canal3.com.gt), Televisiete (www.canal7.com.gt), Vea Canal (www.veacanal.com), Guatevision (www.guatevision.com), TeleOnce, Trecevision and Latitud.
The Comtech cable TV channel operates Claro TV (www.comtech.net.gt) in Guatemala City.

Economy
The economy of Guatemala has grown steadily if somewhat slowly since 2001, but is still the largest economy in Central America. In 2005, GDP growth was 3.2 per cent and is expected to continue at the same rate in 2006. Despite inflation at 9.1 per cent, due in some part to higher global oil prices in 2005, it is likely to fall below 6.0 per cent in 2006.
The agricultural sector accounts for over 20 per cent of GDP and employs around half the workforce. This means however that Guatemala is heavily reliant on world demand and is sensitive to external shocks and natural disasters. Coffee has been the mainstay of the economy but low global prices deflated the sector and it was only in 2005 that prices began to improve. Guatemala produced 3,675 bags of coffee (220,500 tonnes), in 2004–05, but

has since reduced its production in the face of chronic global overproduction.
The Inter-American Development Bank estimated that in 2006 migrant workers sent some US$3,610 million to their families in Guatemala.
The IMF has applauded the determination with which the government has set about achieving its primary goals of creating a stable macroeconomic environment and reducing the public deficit. Strong policies in the areas of fiscal deficit reduction, financial sector restructuring and structuring reforms to boost growth and reduce poverty should help improve domestic confidence, and through it increase private investment levels. The World Bank has warned that the perception of corruption and weak integrity in some public institutions could pose additional difficulties.

External trade

Guatemala is a member of the Central America Free Trade Agreement (DR-Cafta), which includes the Dominican Republic, Costa Rica, El Salvador and Honduras and the US; it is working to remove all tariffs and barriers between members by 2024. It is also a member of the Central American Common Market (CACM), along with Costa Rica, El Salvador, Honduras and Nicaragua.

Imports

Principal imports are foodstuffs including grain, fuels, vehicles, clothing and other consumer goods, and construction materials.

Main sources: US (31.2 per cent total, 2006), Mexico (8.3 per cent), China (6.1 per cent).

Exports

Principal exports are coffee (typically around 40 per cent of annual total), light assembly products, processed food, textiles, sugar, rum, bananas, cardamom and cut flowers.

Main destinations: US (44.7 per cent total, 2006), El Salvador (11.9 per cent), Honduras (7.2 per cent).

Agriculture

Farming

Guatemala's most important economic sector is agriculture. The sector accounts for approximately 25 per cent of total GDP and employs about half of the country's total workforce. Despite the agricultural sector's high employment level, the number of jobs in the sector is falling due to increased mechanisation. Approximately 17 per cent of Guatemala's total land mass is cultivated arable land, 10 per cent pasture and 35 per cent forest.
Throughout the 1990s, Guatemala was relatively successful in establishing agricultural diversification, in an effort to buttress export earnings against commodity price fluctuations. It also sought to encourage the development of processing and packaging plants so as to upgrade the value of farm exports. Most of this took place in the highland areas where there is a good supply of land and labour. The production of fresh and frozen vegetables and ornamental plants and flowers has been particularly successful.
Production is mainly export-oriented, the major cash crops being coffee (the largest single earner of foreign exchange), sugar cane, bananas, cotton, cardamom (Guatemala accounts for over 90 per cent of world trade in cardamom) and tobacco. Vegetables such as mangetout, broccoli and asparagus, as well as a wide variety of fruits, are exported to the US and Europe.
Coffee growers plan to double the country's production between 1998–2008. Coffee has suffered from poor global commodity prices, although rising output has helped offset some of the losses.
Maize is the main food crop, although rice and wheat are also grown. Agricultural produce also includes cocoa, beans and flowers.
Foreign investment has so far been limited as a result of the absence of a domestic land market. Land is regarded as an indication of wealth and most owners leave it fallow if they choose not to plant. Land distribution is uneven, with just under 80 per cent of all farms under 3.5 hectares (ha) and 1 per cent over 2,500ha. Most foreign participation is concentrated on the non-traditional agricultural crops now emerging as major export earners.
Estimated crop production in 2005 included: 1,171,788 tonnes (t) cereals, 1,072,310t maize, 18,000,000t sugar cane, 282,923t potatoes, 600,000t oil palm fruit, 34,926t rice, 1,000,000t bananas, 268,000t plantains, 252,877t citrus fruit, 187,000t mangoes, 20,540t tobacco, 187,229t tomatoes, 144,966t oilcrops, 132,105t pulses, 216,600t green coffee, 2,105t cocoa, 49,823t natural rubber, 1,995,469t fruit in total, 976,777t vegetables in total. Estimated livestock production included: 248,022t meat in total, 63,000t beef, 26,000t pig meat, 1,208t lamb, 471t goat meat, 2,344t horsemeat, 155,000t poultry, 85,000t eggs, 270,000t milk, 1,500t honey, 8,880t cattle hides.

Fishing

Guatemala's typical catch is approximately 14,300 tonnes (t), 9,800t freshwater fish inclusive.
In 2004, the total marine fish catch was 3,192 tonnes and the total crustacean catch was 3,325 tonnes.

Forestry

Approximately 35 per cent of Guatemala's total land mass is covered by forests. Some 20 per cent of Guatemala's land area is protected against industrial exploitation.
Softwood conifers account for 22 per cent with broad-leaved species, including valuable hardwoods such as mahogany, cedar and rosewood, accounting for the rest. Other forest products include rubber and chicle, an important chewing gum base, which is extracted in the forested Petén region.
The majority of timber production is consumed as domestic fuel, while a modest amount of sawnwood is exported. Much of the domestic demand for paper is met by imports.
Timber imports in 2004 were US$217.6 million, while exports amounted to US$35.6 million.
Timber production in 2004 included 16,324,873 cubic metres (cum) roundwood, 419,000cum industrial roundwood, 366,000cum sawnwood, 404,000cum sawlogs & veneer logs, 43,400cum wood-based panels, 15,904,542cum wood fuel, 7,000t charcoal.

Industry and manufacturing

Guatemala has a well developed industrial sector and the sector as a whole contributes approximately one fifth to GDP in a typical year. Industry contributes around 20 per cent to GDP (manufacturing contributes around 14 per cent) and employs 15 per cent of the workforce. Industry is primarily involved in activities related to agricultural inputs for major firms involved in food and drink processing, rubber, textiles, pottery, paper and pharmaceuticals. Other important industries are the assembly of electronic products, manufacture of furniture, canned goods, oil refining, cement, metals (especially steel), electrical goods assembly, plastics, chemicals, fertilisers and cigarettes.
Social and industrial unrest, high energy costs, shortages of imported materials and a slump in private and public investment have severely hampered industrial production. However, major government house building and infrastructural repair plans since the end of the civil war seem to have given a signficant boost to the construction industry, although construction as a proportion of GDP has shrunk in recent years.

Tourism

The tourism industry of Guatemala has achieved steady growth in recent years. The sector now accounts for 6.9 per cent of total GDP and 6 per cent of total employment.
Guatemala relies on its ecology and Mayan ruins to attract visitors. Visitor numbers, which stood at 632,683 in 1998, two years after the end of the civil war, jumped to 818,645 the following year,

reaching 884,190 in 2002. The following year saw a slight fall, attributed to signs of instability and lack of tourist events, but in 2004 the figure rose once more, to 1,004,000. The largest market for Guatemalan travel and tourism in recent years has been El Salvador, though the US and Canada overtook that country in 2003.

Mining

The Alta Verapaz copper mine represents the main mining operation in Guatemala. In addition to copper, tungsten and antimony there are also exploitable reserves of marble and sulphur. Deposits of lead, zinc, gold and silver are also known to exist.

Lead is mined at Ballena and Penasco by Cía Minas de Oriente SA (Minersa). Reserves are estimated at 2.2 million tonnes and contain 86 grammes per tonne of silver. Minas de Guatemala operates the Annabella and Los Lirios antimony and tungsten mines, producing about 1,800 tonnes per month of ore (6 per cent antimony, 0.5 per cent lead). The Oxec copper mine, worked by Transmetales in Alta Verapaz, has a capacity of 150,000 tonnes per year. The country's major mineral resource is laterite, with the El Estor deposits estimated at 50 million tonnes.

In August 2005 the World Bank was crtiticised for its role in funding a gold mining project in Guatemala. The Bank was criticised for not consulting the local community properly and for failing to evaluate the humanitarian or environmental implications of the proposed facility.

Hydrocarbons

Guatemala is the only oil producing country in Central America. The country's proven oil reserves stand at 526 million barrels, though actual reserves are thought to be as much as 1 billion barrels. Guatemala produces 19,800 barrels per day (bpd), a decrease on the 21,080 bpd figure recorded in 2003. The majority of production occurs in the northern jungle areas, near to the border with Mexico. Development of the industry has been slow due to the reluctance of foreign companies to invest in the area owing to political unrest and unfavourable terms.

Guatemala refines oil imported primarily from Venezuela with favourable terms due to the San José pact.

Gas reserves amounted to 3.08 billion cubic metres in 2003. Although some areas are still to be properly surveyed. In December 1999, Guatemala and Mexico signed a protocol for the construction of a natural gas pipeline from southern Mexico to Guatemala. The pipeline is part of a wider Central America gas pipeline network and will meet the initial demand estimated at about 1.1 million cubic metres per day. It offers the potential to reduce the region's reliance on seasonally-dependent hydroelectric power. Guatemala does not consume or import natural gas.

Guatemala typically imports over 220,000 tonnes of coal annually. Coal is mainly used for primary energy production. Guatemala does not produce coal.

Energy

Guatemala retains a total electricity generation capacity of approximately 1.3GW. The San José power station is Central America's largest coal-fired power plant. A 300MW thermal power plant owned by the Decasa consortium is under construction, the first phase of which was came on-line in 2003. A 165MW thermal plant owned by the US's Duke Energy was completed in mid-2003.

Financial markets

Stock exchange

A national stock exchange, the Bolsa de Valores Nacional (BVN), was established in Guatemala City in 1987. It is under common ownership with one share per associate, and trades mainly in government bonds and debt. Until the privatisation programme began in the 1990s, few private stocks and shares were traded, a reflection of how exclusive and restricted the business establishment in Guatemala was. The privatisation of state-owned assets has been carried out through the exchange. There is also an agricultural stock exchange (Bolsa Agrícola Nacional).

Banking and insurance

The Guatemalan banking and financial services sector is organised under a central banking system, above which is the higher authority of the Monetary Board. There are 35 private commercial banks in Guatemala, but the banking market is dominated by a handful of large institutions. Some 40 per cent of total assets are in the hands of the five largest banks. Guatemala is no longer on the OECD Financial Action Task Force (FATF) list of non-co-operative countries regarding money laundering.

Central bank

Banco de Guatemala

Offshore facilities

Time

GMT minus six hours

Geography

Guatemala has five distinct geographical zones. The first is the lowland Pacific strip running the length of the coastline, where the climate is tropical and summer rains are heavy. Most of the country's large sugar, banana and cotton farms are based here. Some 50km in from the coast the land rises to form the first of two mountain ranges running north-west to south-east. This range includes a string of volcanoes. A plateau formed by a series of volcanic basins at an average height of 1,500 metres above sea level forms the third zone; the capital, Guatemala City, and most of the country's population are to be found here.

Another mountain range with peaks of over 4,000 metres forms the basis of the north-west highlands, tapering down to the border with Honduras and El Salvador at its south-east extremity, where most of the country's more than four million indigenous people live. Beyond the mountains the land falls rapidly into a flat expanse of tropical forest. This area, which accounts for the northern part of the departments of Izabal, El Quiche, and Alta Verapaz and all the 36,400 square km of El Petén department, remains one of the region's last wildernesses.

Hemisphere

Northern

Climate

The climate varies with altitude but is essentially sub-tropical with little variation between the seasons. The hottest month is May when the average daily minimum and maximum temperatures are 16 degrees Celsius (C) and 29 degrees C. The coldest month is January when the temperature varies between 12 degrees C and 23 degrees C. The driest month is February and the wettest June, when there is an average of 274mm of rainfall.

Dress codes

Guatemalans are generally conservative in dress. Tropical lightweight suits are the accepted dress in business circles in the capital. Extremes of fashion should be avoided.

Entry requirements

Passports

Required by all.

Visa

Visas are not required by most nationals of the Americas, EU, Australasia, and a few Asian countries, for between 1–3 months.

A business visa, requiring additional information to the visitor's visa, must be applied for before arrival. The application should include a company letter as proof of business intentions.

Currency advice/regulations

No restrictions on import/export of foreign currency. There is free circulation of US dollars.

Health (for visitors)

Mandatory precautions

Cholera and yellow fever vaccination certificates are required from citizens of infected countries.

Advisable precautions
Malaria is prevalent in the low-lying areas outside the city, prophylaxes are recommended. Dengue fever is endemic, although there is no preventive medication, mosquito repellent and clothing covering as much skin as possible at dawn and dusk should help. Inoculations are recommended against typhoid, hepatitis A and B and typhoid.
Guatemalan hospitals are reluctant to give medical treatment unless a patient has medical insurance, so evidence of insurance cover should be carried at all times. State-funded hospitals are regarded as understaffed, ill-equipped and often unhygienic. Private clinics should be used where possible.
Bottled water should be used. Milk is often unpasteurised and should be boiled; avoid dairy products which are likely to have been made from unboiled milk. Only eat hot well-cooked meat and fish. Pork, salad and mayonnaise carry increased risk. Vegetables should be cooked and fruit peeled. There is a rabies risk.

Hotels
In the main cities there are a range of good hotels, the range can be limited in provincial towns. Most charge 20 per cent room tax; 10 per cent is added where service charges are not levied.

Public holidays (national)
Fixed dates
1 Jan (New Year), 1 May (Labour Day), 30 Jun (Army Day), 15 Aug (Assumption Day), 15 Sep (Independence Day), 20 Oct (Revolution Day), 1 Nov (All Saints' Day), 24 Dec (half-day), 25 Dec, 31 Dec (half-day).
Variable dates
Easter (Wed–Fri; Mar/Apr)

Working hours
Banking
Generally Mon–Fri: 0900–1500.
Business
Mon–Fri: 0800–1600. Private companies Mon–Fri: 0800–1200, 1400–1800.
Government
Mon–Fri: 0800–1600.
Shops
Shopping centres (Mon–Sun) 0900–2000.

Telecommunications
Mobile/cell phones
GSM 850/1900 services are available.

Electricity supply
110V AC, 60 cycles

Social customs/useful tips
Customs and social mores tend to mirror those of Catholic Europe or the more conservative southern states of the United States. Punctuality is not one of most Guatemalans' strongest points, although Western propensity for good time keeping is recognised in their phrase 'English time'.

Security
Security in the capital has become much more of a problem in recent years as street crime and house break-ins have risen. Armed mugging and gratuitous violence is common and most companies have armed guards and watchmen.

Getting there
Air
National airline: TACA – an amalgamation of the flag airlines of Guatemala (Aviateca), Costa Rica (Lacsa) and Nicaragua (Nica).
International airport/s: Guatemala City-Aurora (GUA), 6km from the city; duty-free shop, bank, bar, restaurant, bank, hotel reservations, post office, shops, car hire.
Airport tax: Departures tax US$30; not applicable to 24 hour transit passengers.
Surface
Road: The Pan-American Highway runs through the country from Mexico to El Salvador, stretching 511km. There are other roads from El Salvador, Honduras and Mexico and there is a route via Melchor de Mencos from Belize. Plans for any journey should be made in the light of prevailing road conditions.
Rail: It is possible to use scheduled train services but some of these are often subject to suspension.
Main port/s: Champerico, Puerto Barrios, San José, Santo Tomás de Castilla and the Quetzal Port.

Getting about
National transport
Air: TACA operates a domestic service to major centres.
Road: Total network is 13,238km, only 26 per cent of which is paved; using unpaved roads can be difficult. Paved roads are of fair quality.
Buses: Bus services connect major towns.
City transport
Taxis: There is a good taxi service in Guatemala City. Fares are generally negotiated but there are set rates for journeys from the airport to certain destinations. Tipping (5–10 per cent) is discretionary.
Buses, trams & metro: Numerous services within Guatemala City – said to be (outside usual rush hours) less crowded than some cities.
Car hire
Any valid licence is usually acceptable. Many of the international rental agencies have offices both at La Aurora airport and in Guatemala City centre.

BUSINESS DIRECTORY
The addresses listed below are a selection only. While World of Information makes every endeavour to check these addresses, we cannot guarantee that changes have not been made, especially to telephone numbers and area codes. We would welcome any corrections.

Telephone area codes
The international direct dialling code (IDD) for Guatemala is +502, followed by subscriber's number. Telephones and faxes have been eight digits since Septermber 2004.

Chambers of Commerce
American Chamber of Commerce in Guatemala, Avenida las Americas 18-81, Zona 14, 01014 Guatemala City (tel: 2363-1774; fax: 2367-3414; e-mail: director@amchamguate.com).

Guatemala Chamber of Commerce, 10a Calle 3-80, Zona 1, 01001 Guatemala City (tel: 2253-5353; fax: 2220-9393; e-mail: info@camaradecomercio.org.gt).

Banking
Banco Nacional de Desarrollo Agrícola (BANDESA), 9 Calle 9-47, Zona 1, 01001.

Banco Nacional de la Vivienda (BANVI), 6 Ave 1-22, Zona 4, 01004.

Credito Hipotecario Nacional, 7 Ave 22-77, Zona 1, 01001.

Banco de Occidente, 7 Ave 11-15, Zona 1, 01001.

Banco del Agro, 9 Calle 5-39, Zona 1, 01001 (tel: 2251-4026; fax: 2230-0322).

Banco del Café SA, Ave La Reforma 9-00, Zona 9, 01009.

Banco del Quetzal SA, Plaza El Robel, 7 Ave 6-26, Zona 9, 01009.

Banco Granai & Townson SA, 7 Ave 1-86, Zona 4, 1004.

Banco Industrial SA, 7 Ave 5-10, Zona 4, 01004.

Citibank, Ave La Reforma 15-45, Zona 10, 01010.

Lloyds Bank International, 6 Ave 9-51, Zona 9, 01009.

Central bank
Banco de Guatemala, 7 Avenida 22-01, Zona 1, PO Box 365, 01001 Guatemala City (tel: 2230-6222; fax: 2253-4035; email: webmaster@banguat.gob.gt).

Travel information
Asociación Guatemalteca de Agentes de Viajes (AGAV) (Guatemalan Association of Travel Agents), 6a Avenida 8-41, Zona 9, Apdo 2735, Guatemala City.

TACA, Avenida Hincapié 12-22, Aeropuerto La Aurora, Zona 13,

Guatemala City (internet (including email) www.taca.com).

National tourist organisation offices
Instituto Guatemalteco de Turismo (INGUAT) (Guatemalan Tourism Institute), 7 Avenida 1-17, Zona 4, Centro Cívico 01004, Guatemala City (tel: 2331-1333; fax: 2331-8893; e-mail: inguat@guate.net; internet: www.visitguatemala.com).

Ministries
Ministry of Agriculture, Livestock and Food, Avenida Reforma 4-47, Zona 10, Guatemala City.

Ministry of Communications, Transport and Public Works, Avenida Reforma 4-47, Zona 10, Guatemala City (tel: 2362-6051; fax: 2362-6059).

Ministry of Culture and Sport, 5 Calle 4-33, Zona 1, Plaza Rabi, Guatemala City.

Ministry of Defence, Avenida Reforma 4-47, Zona 10, Guatemala City (tel: 2360-9907; fax: 2360-9909).

Ministry of Economy, 8 Avenida 10-43, Zona 1, Guatemala City (tel: 2238-3331/2/3; fax: 2251-5055).

Ministry of Education, Avenida Reforma 4-47, Zona 10, Guatemala City.

Ministry of Employment and Social Security, 14 Calle 5-49, Zona 1, Edificio Nasa, Guatemala City (tel: 2230-5592/4; fax: 2251-3559).

Ministry of Energy and Mines, Diagonal 17, 29-78, Zona 11, Guatemala City (tel: 2477-0382, 2476-0680).

Ministry of Finance, Entre 8 Avenida y 21 calle, Zona 1, Centro Cívico, Guatemala City (tel: 2230-5180, 2230-5202; fax: 2251-6514).

Ministry of Foreign Affairs, Avenida Reforma 4-47, Zona 10, Guatemala City.

Ministry of Health and Social Assistance, Avenida Reforma 4-47, Zona 10, Guatemala City (tel: 2232-4509).

Ministry of the Interior, Avenida Reforma 4-47, Zona 10, Guatemala City.

Other useful addresses
Agroindustrias de Exportación, 14 Calle 7-46, Zona 10, Guatemala City

Asociación de Gerentes de Guatemala, 10a Calle 3-17, Zona 10, Edificio Aseguradora General, Nivel 70, Apartado Postal 2373, Guatemala City, 01010.

Bolsa Agrícola Nacional, 4a Calle 6-55, Zona 9, Guatemala City.

Bolsa de Valores Global, Av La Reforma 9-76, Zona 9, Edificio SCI Centre, Nivel 70, Guatemala City, 01009.

Bolsa de Valores Nacional, SA, 7a Av 5-10, Zona 4, Centro Financiero, Torre II, Nivel 20, Guatemala City, 01004.

British Embassy, Edificio Torre Internacional, Nivel 11, 16 Calle 0-55, Zona 10, Guatemala City (tel: 2367-5425–9; fax: 2367-5430; email: embassy@intelnett.com).

Centro de Investigaciones Económicas Nacionales (CIEN), 5 Av 15-45, Zona 10, Centro Empresarial, Torre 1, Of 302, Apartado Postal 260-C, Guatemala City.

Centro Nacional de Promoción de las Exportaciones, 6A Avenida Torre Profesional, Zona 14, Apdo 1237, Guatemala City.

Comité Co-ordinador de Asociaciones Agrícolas, Comerciales, Industriales y Financieras (CACIF), Ruta 6 9-21, Zona 4, Nivel 90, Guatemala City.

Coperex (international marketing fair), 8 Calle 2-33, Zona 9, Parque de la Industria, Guatemala City.

Dirección General de Radiodifusión y Televisión Nacional, 5a Avenida Zona 1, Guatemala City.

Empresa Eléctrica de Guatemala (EEGSA), 8a Calle y 6a Avenida Esquina, Zona 1, Guatemala City.

Empresa Municipal de Agua (Empagua), 7a Avenida 1-20, Zona 4, Edificio Torre Café, Nivel 16, Guatemala City.

Fundación para el Desarrollo de Guatemala (FUNDESA), Parque Gerencial Las Margaritas, Diagonal 6, 10-65, Zona 10, Of 402, Guatemala City.

Guatemala–US Trade Association (GUSTA), 299 Alhambra Circle, Suite 207, Coral Gables, Florida 33134, USA (tel: (+1-305) 443-0343; fax: (+1-305) 433-0699).

Guatemalan Embassy (USA), 2220 R Street, NW, Washington DC 20008 (tel: (+1-202) 745-4952; fax: (+1-202) 745-1908; e-mail: info@guatemala-embassy.org).

Inforpress Centroamericana, 9a Calle A 3-56, Guatemala City 01001.

Instituto Centroamericano de Investigación y Tecnología Industrial (ICAITI), Avenida La Reforma 4-47, Zona 10, Guatemala City.

Instituto Nacional de Electrificación (INDE), 7a Avenida 2-29, Zona 9, Guatemala City.

International Investment Securities Corporation, Edificio Galerías Reforma 8-60, Zona 9, Torre 1, Nivel 90, Guatemala City.

Telgua (Empresa de Telecomunicaciones de Guatemala), 5 Calle Avenida Reforma, Zona 9, Guatemala City (tel: 2331-8999/6599, 2230-1050).

United States Department of Commerce, Guatemala Desk, Department of Commerce H3025, Washington DC 20230, USA (tel: (+1-202) 377-2627; fax: (+1-202) 377-3718).

US Embassy, Avenida La Reforma 7-01, Zona 10, Guatemala City.

Other news agencies: Inforpress (in Spanish and English): www.inforpressca.com

Prensa Latina (from Cuba, in six languages): www.prensa-latina.com.ar

Internet sites
Guatemalan portals: http://mi-guatemala.tripod.com

http://www.elcafecito.com/Zonas_geograficas/Paises/Guatemala

Business information: http://www.tradepoint.org.gt

Guinea

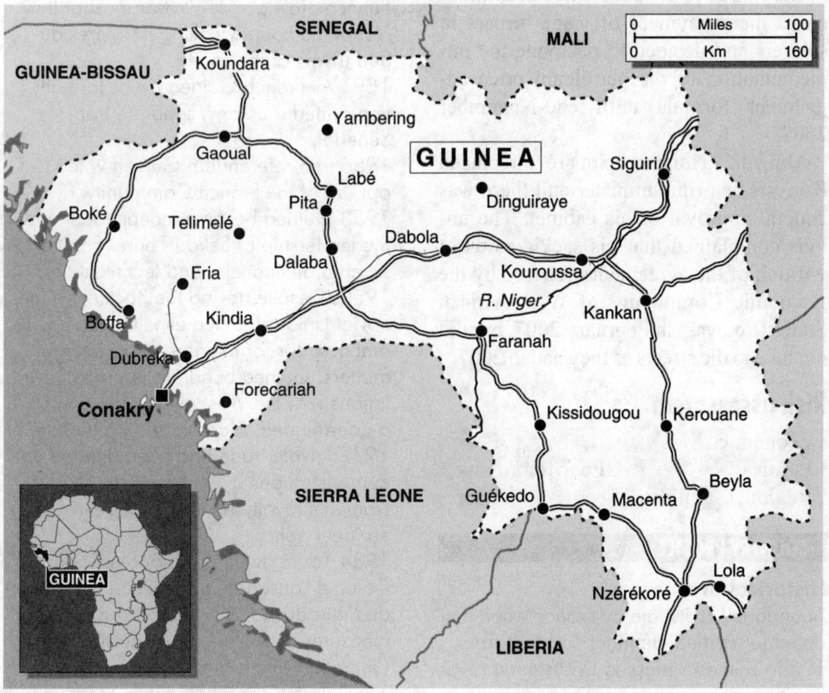

Guinea's mineral wealth makes it potentially one of Africa's richest countries, yet its people are among the poorest in West Africa. Acute economic problems, instability among its neighbours and uncertainty over a successor to its authoritarian president have prompted a European think-tank, the International Crisis Group (ICG), to warn that Guinea risks becoming a failed state.

The London *Financial Times*, in an article on 5 August 2008 quoted Tom Albanese, chief executive of Rio Tinto, as saying 'without doubt, the top undeveloped tier-one iron ore asset in the world' was the Simandou iron ore project in Guinea. The mine should be producing by 2018 and could eventually produce up to 170 million tonnes of iron ore a year. Rio Tinto, according to the *Financial Times*, is expected to spend some US$6 billion on constructing the mine and a 750km rail track to the coast. However, it appeared in August that Tinto had become a pawn in a power struggle between President Lansana Conté and one of his ministers, Mamady Sam Soumah. Saumah was sacked, reinstated and sacked again in a row over the iron ore concession given to the mining company.

Musical chairs

President Lansana Conté had seized power in a bloodless coup in 1984 and has ruled with an iron fist ever since. In 2003 he won a third term in a poll which was boycotted by the opposition. Voters in a referendum had backed the removal of a two-term limit which would have forced him to retire. Critics said the move was a constitutional coup which would ensure that he remained president for life. The next elections are due in 2010. However, the president is said to be ailing and analysts believe he may be replaced before then.

Conté says he was born in the 1930s. After serving in the French army he returned home and became chief of staff in 1975. He seized power after President Sekou Touré's death in 1984, suspended the constitution, freed political prisoners and encouraged exiles to return. By 1992 he had organised a return to civilian rule,

KEY FACTS

Official name: République de Guinée (Republic of Guinea)

Head of State: President General Lansana Conté (PUP) (since 1984; re-elected 2003)

Head of government: Prime Minister Ahmed Tidiane Souaré (appointed 21 May 2008)

Ruling party: Parti de l'Unité et du Progrès (PUP) (Party of Unity and Progress) (since 1995; re-elected 2002)

Area: 245,857 square km

Population: 9.96 million (2007)*

Capital: Conakry

Official language: French

Currency: Guinean franc (Gf)

Exchange rate: Gf4,502.50 per US$ (Jul 2008)

GDP per capita: US$473 (2007)*

GDP real growth: 1.50% (2007)

Labour force: 4.00 million (2004)

Inflation: 22.80% (2007)*

Balance of trade: US$104.00 million (2005)

Foreign debt: US$3.54 billion (2004)

* estimated figure

proceeding to win a presidential poll in 1993 and parliamentary elections in 1995.

Critics say he has lost popularity and has become increasingly isolated. Supporters say he has won a war against dissidents. Conté, who is a diabetic and a chain smoker, rarely makes public appearances. There is no obvious successor to the ailing leader.

Ruled by strong-arm leaders since independence, Guinea has been seen as a bulwark against instability in neighbouring Liberia, Sierra Leone and Côte d'Ivoire. However it has also been implicated in the conflicts that have ravaged the region.

Economy

According to the World Bank, Guinea's growth performance since the late 1990s has been well below its potential, especially in view of the country's natural resource endowments. Guinea's social indicators compare poorly with neighbouring countries, although significant strides have been made in primary education and access to safe water.

The International Monetary Fund (IMF) said in 2008 that the economic stabilisation policies in 2007 had been broadly successful. Fiscal and monetary discipline helped stem inflation, and economic activity made a timid recovery. Fiscal targets were broadly achieved, in spite of a revenue shortfall, and the absence of central bank financing of the government kept monetary expansion under control.

Guinea has continued to experience social and political instability, which has been compounded by the impact of the world food and fuel price increases. The threat of a general strike led the government to concede significant mitigating measures for civil servants after petroleum prices were increased by 63 per cent in April 2008. Mounting tensions between President Conté and Prime Minister Kouyaté (whom he had appointed to appease civil protests in early 2007) wound up with the dismissal of the latter on 20 May 2008. Following subsequent unrest in the military, the authorities accommodated the repayment of wage arrears to soldiers and decided to postpone the implementation of the petroleum price adjustment formula until end-November 2008.

Ahmed Tidiane Souaré replaced Kouyaté as prime minister and there was general approval of his cabinet. The unions complained that his sacking was in volition of the agreement brokered by the Economic Community of West African States (Ecowas) in February 2007, but did not take to the streets as they had in 2007.

Risk assessment

Economic	Poor
Political	Poor/Improving
Regional stability	Poor

COUNTRY PROFILE

Historical profile

Abandoned to its fate by France when it opted for immediate independence in 1958, Guinea struggled to sustain a revolutionary approach to independence. It remained isolated – even from its West African neighbours – for decades while its rulers sought to establish some form of representative democracy that worked in the African context. Nor has the ideological path followed by Guinea since independence been well received by its citizens, who only needed to look at neighbouring countries such as Senegal to see the more immediate and tangible attractions of laissez-faire capitalism.

From the thirteenth to fifteenth centuries Guinea was part of the Mali empire which covered a large part of West Africa.

1450s The coastal region began to be settled by European traders.

1849 The French declared the area around Boké a protectorate. France's influence grew as it took over most of the rest of the country calling it Rivières du Sud (rivers of the south).

1891 As French Guinea it was formally constituted a colony, separate from Senegal.

1956 In a referendum Guinea voted to opt out of the French Community.

1958 Guinea became independent under the leadership of Sekou Touré. France severed all financial and technical ties.

1960s Despite having the backing of the Soviet Union, Guinea expelled the Soviet ambassador for interference in internal matters. Guinea began to improve its relations with the West although it remained a non-aligned, Marxist, one-party state.

1977 Private trade had been banned until demonstrations by traders in the market women's revolt, led to a change in government policy.

1984 Touré died. In a bloodless coup, Colonel Lansana Conté became president and introduced IMF-backed austerity measures as well as a new currency, the Guinean franc, which replaced the syli.

1990 A new constitution was approved.

1993 Conté won the presidency in multi-party elections, which were marred by killings and alleged fraud.

1995 The Parti de l'Unité et du Progrès (PUP) (Party of Unity and Progress), led by President Conté, won the multi-party legislative elections.

1996 As much as a quarter of the army mutinied due largely to low pay.

1998 President Lansana Conté was re-elected.

1999 Lamine Sidime (PUP) was appointed prime minister.

2001 The government accused neighbouring Liberia and rebels from Sierra Leone of aiding its army mutineers and attempting to destabilise the country. The number of displaced peoples, locally and from abroad, grew. There were rebel attacks along the borders between Guinea and Liberia, and Sierra Leone. A constitutional referendum permitted Conté to retain the presidency and run for a third and extended term (from five to seven years).

2002 The ruling PUP won parliamentary elections, delayed by two years allegedly due to the fighting between Guinea and Sierra Leone, and Liberia.

2003 Incumbent Lansana Conté won the presidential elections. The National Assembly voted unanimously for an amnesty

KEY INDICATORS — Guinea

	Unit	2003	2004	2005	2006	2007
Population	m	8.40	8.47	9.28	9.64	*9.96
Gross domestic product (GDP)	US$bn	3.47	3.51	3.33	3.14	*4.71
GDP per capita	US$	413	403	359	325	*473
GDP real growth	%	3.6	1.2	3.3	2.1	*1.5
Inflation	%	12.9	17.5	31.4	34.7	*22.8
Industrial output	% change	–	2.9	4.0	5.0	–
Agricultural output	% change	–	4.1	4.0	4.2	–
Exports (fob) (goods)	US$m	835.0	725.6	807.0	1,073.6	*1,145.4
Imports (cif) (goods)	US$m	670.0	688.4	703.0	939.8	*1,029.5
Balance of trade	US$m	165.0	37.2	104.0	-89.4	*-82.5
Current account	US$m	-120.0	-190.0	-133.0	-185.0	*-433.0
Exchange rate	per US$	1,995.00	2,405.00	5,556.00	5,556.00	4,242.70

* estimated figure

for those convicted of political crimes, allowing them to stand for positions in national politics.
2004 Cellou Dalein Diallo was named prime minister in December.
2005 The President escaped an assassination attempt when shots were fired at his motorcade in the capital, Conakry.
2006 A five-day general strike took place in February. In March the president attended a Swiss medical clinic for treatment of his chronic diabetes. President Conté sacked Prime Minister Diallo on 5 April, just hours after signing a decree to increase Diallo's power to assumed more control of key ministerial portfolios. Diallo's sacking, for 'gross misconduct' came just as a cabinet reshuffle would have marginalised Conté's closest supporters and highlighted the power struggle underway in government, between the ailing president's inner circle. Presidency Secretary-General Fode Bangoura was seen to lead the counterattack and the restoration of Conté's supremacy. In May, government restucturing led the post of prime minister to be removed and responsibilities given to other expanded ministries. Bangoura became the Minister of Presidential Affairs, with control of the military and the economy.
2007 A general strike (from 10–28 January) called in an attempt to depose President Conté, disrupted the vital bauxite industry and caused the president to dismissed his long-term supporter, Fode Bangoura, in an effort to placate the unions. Eventually the president agreed to fill the empty post of prime minister and Eugène Camara was appointed as prime minister, on 9 February. However, the announcement of Camara, a close, hard-line supporter of the president, sparked riots in the capital and caused concern about the deteriorating political situation among Guinea's neighbours. On 12 February, martial law, with a 20-hour-a-day curfew, was imposed to curb violence that had broken out as another national general strike resumed and opposition and union leaders called on the president to step down from office. On 26 February, Lansana Kouyaté, a candidate acceptable to the opposition, was appointed as prime minister; the general strike was called off.
2008 President Conté sacked Prime Minister Lansana Kouyate, on 21 May, sparking riots in the capital city. Ahmed Tidiane Souaré was appointed as prime minister. Souaré announced his new cabinet on 19 June. Ten of the cabinet served in the cabinet of the Lansana Kouyaté; four of the 36 members are women.

Political structure

Constitution
The constitution was promulgated in 1990. In 2001 a constitutional amendment revised the length of the presidential term from five years to seven, with no legal limit to the number of terms a president may sit.

Form of state
Republic

The executive
Prior to the constitutional amendments, made in 2001, the president was elected for a five-year term, renewable only once. Following the changes, the mandate increased to a seven-year term with no legal limit as to the number of times that it could be renewed.
The prime minister and the Council of Ministers are appointed by the president.

National legislature
The unicameral Assemblée Nationale Populaire (People's National Assembly) has 114 deputies serving five-year terms.

Legal system
The legal system is based on French civil law, customary law and decree.

Last elections
21 December 2003 (presidential); 30 June 2002 (parliamentary) (originally scheduled for November 2000).
Results: Presidential: incumbent Lansana Conté won 95.6 per cent of the vote and Mamadou Bhoye Barry 4.4 per cent; turnout was 82.8 per cent.
Parliamentary: the ruling Parti de l'Unité et du Progrès (PUP) (Party of Unity and Progress) won 61.5 per cent of the vote; Union pour le Progrès et le Renouveau (UPR) (Union for Progress and Renewal) 21.7 per cent; the opposition boycotted the election; the turnout was low.

Next elections
2010 (presidential)

Political parties

Political parties were legalised from 1992.

Ruling party
Parti de l'Unité et du Progrès (PUP) (Party of Unity and Progress) (since 1995; re-elected 2002)

Main opposition party
Rassemblement du Peuple Guinéen (RPG) (Rally of the Guinean People).

Population

9.96 million (2007)*
Last census: December 1996: 7,156,406 (provisional)
Population density: 28 per square km. Urban population: 28 per cent (1995–2001).
Annual growth rate: 2.4 per cent 1994–2004 (WHO 2006)
Internally Displaced Persons (IDP) 100,000 (UNHCR 2004)

Ethnic make-up
Fulani (35 per cent), Malinke (30 per cent), Soussou (20 per cent).

Religions
Islam (85 per cent), a small number of Roman Catholics (8 per cent) and traditional beliefs (7 per cent).

Education

Guinea shows an upward trend in gross enrolment rate with increasing demand for teachers, school facilities, and other resources. The government has initiated the third phase of the project Basic Education for All (2001—2012) focussing on increased access, improved quality and efficiency through decentralisation processes. Despite significant urban/rural and gender disparities in enrolment ratios, there is overall improvement. The crisis in teacher supply persists despite the World Bank and the government's intensive teacher-training programme (FIMG), which had planned recruitment of approximately 6,000 teachers for the entire 1998-2001 period.
Government expenditure on education is about 25–26 per cent of the total national budget.
Enrolment rate: 45.2 per cent net enrolment in primary; 11.9 per cent net enrolment in secondary schooling (World Bank).
In rural areas the enrolment rate for girls remains at only 26 per cent.
Pupils per teacher: 49 in primary schools.

Health

Per capita total expenditure on health (2003) was US$95; of which per capita government spending was US$16, at the international dollar rate, (WHO 2006).
Improved water sources and sanitation facilities are available to 48 per cent and 58 per cent of the population, respectively.
In August 2004 epidemeiologists of the Global Polio Eradication Initiative announced that new cases of polio had been confirmed in Guinea. The infection is believed to have spread from Northern Nigeria.

HIV/Aids
HIV/Aids infection is currently concentrated in urban areas. Overall 2.8 per cent of pregnant women, 42 per cent of sex workers and 2.5 per cent of young adults (aged 15–24) are HIV positive. With governmental initiatives and local education, it is hoped to avert a potential pandemic if the rates in rural areas follow the urban trend.
HIV prevalence: 3.2 per cent aged 15–49 in 2003 (World Bank)
Life expectancy: 53 years, 2004 (WHO 2006)

Fertility rate/Maternal mortality rate: 5.8 births per woman, 2004 (WHO 2006); maternal mortality 620 per 100,000 live births (World Bank).
Child (under 5 years) mortality rate (per 1,000): 109 per 1,000 live births; 23 per cent of children under aged five are malnourished (World Bank).
Head of population per physician: 0.11 physicians per 1,000 people, 2004 (WHO 2006)

Welfare
Guinea's social insurance system provides coverage for unemployed people, pensions, old-age benefits and survivor benefits (payable to widows, orphans and dependant relatives). Old age pensions are applicable to all those aged 55 and over. The system also provides sickness and maternity benefits as well as allowance for those families with children under the age of 17.

Main cities
Conakry (capital, estimated population 1.4 million in 2005), Nzérékoré (177,855), Kankan (141,446), Kindia (160,884).

Languages spoken
African languages are in daily use. English is seldom used.
Official language/s
French

Media
The government maintains a tight control of the media, with censorship of newspapers and controls to close private radio stations and interrupt international relays, while the military has a secure hold of the national broadcaster.
National news agency: Agence Guineenne de Presse
Other news agencies: APA: www.apanews.net
Panapress: www.panapress.com
Press
The high cost of printing hampers and restricts independent publishing and disrupts regular print runs.
In French, the only business publication is the Sud Economic (http://sud-economie.press-guinee.com), other general news publications include Le Diplomate (www.nouvelle-tribune.com), L'Enqueteur (http://enqueteur.boubah.com), La Nouvelle Tribune (www.nouvelle-tribune.com), L'Observateur (www.observateur-guinee.com) and Le Populaire (http://lepopulaire.press-guinee.com). The Sanakou (http://sanakou.press-guinee.com) is published in Labé. The Le Lynx (www.mirinet.net.gn/lynx) is an independent satirical weekly.
Broadcasting
Radio: The state-owned, commercial Radiodiffusion-Télévision Guinéenne (RTG) operates Radio Guinenne in several languages including French, English, Arabic, Portuguese and a series of Radio Rurale in local languages. Private stations include Familia FM, Liberte FM, Radio Nostralie Guinea and Soleil FM. Radio France Internationale and BBC World Service can both be received.
Television: The state-owned, commercial Radiodiffusion-Télévision Guinéenne (RTG) has one channel.
News agencies
National news agency: Agence Guineenne de Presse
Other news agencies: APA: www.apanews.net
Panapress: www.panapress.com

Economy
Rich in minerals and fertile land, Guinea is a potentially wealthy country, but remains one of Africa's more underdeveloped economies. The country possesses major mineral, hydropower and agricultural resources. With 50 per cent of the world's bauxite reserves, Guinea is the world's second largest bauxite producer. Mining of bauxite and also of iron and other minerals accounts for 80 per cent of foreign earnings.
Political instability, corruption and poor resource management have adversely affected the business environment in Guinea.
Efforts to improve economic management under the terms of an IMF Poverty Reduction and Growth Facility (PRGF), which ran from May 2001 to May 2004, were only partially successful. The IMF suspended the PRGF in December 2002 because of the failure to meet key performance criteria. While there had been some growth in 2002, the economic situation deteriorated in 2003 with weakening GDP growth and rising inflation, which continued through 2004 and into 2005. Expenditure cuts frequently targeted non-defence expenditure, undermining the government's ability to reach its poverty alleviation targets. Continuing border security problems and political uncertainty have added to the government's difficulties. Further efforts to establish control of the economy with tighter policies and reforms are being made in co-operation with the IMF.
The situation is partly offset by donor support and debt relief.
Despite liberalising the investment environment, Guinea is still dependent on primary commodities and lacks the capital and infrastructure to diversify the country's export markets as well as provide for the domestic market. Dependence on the export of bauxite and other minerals exposes the economy to fluctuations in world prices, creating potential problems for sustainable economic development.

External trade
Guinea is a member of the Economic Community of Western African States (Ecowas), which was set up to promote economic integration among members. It is a member of the Anglophone, West African Monetary Zone (WAMZ), which is due to introduce a common currency. WAMZ will eventually be merged with the Francophone-members' currency to produce a single currency (the eco) for the region.
Guinea has around 50 per cent of the world's reserves of bauxite and is the second largest supplier of bauxite. Although diamond exports are rising, the balance of payments situation is precarious, despite large volumes of concessionary assistance from the World Bank, IMF and foreign aid donors.
Imports
Principal imports are petroleum products, metals, machinery, transport equipment, textiles, foodstuffs and grain.
Main sources: China (8.5 per cent total, 2005), US (7.3 per cent), France (7.2 per cent), Côte d'Ivoire (5.2 per cent), Italy (4.7 per cent), Belgium (4.1 per cent)
Exports
Exports are dominated by bauxite and alumina (up to 90 per cent of total), gold, diamonds, coffee, fish, fresh fruit and vegetables.
Main destinations: Russia (14.6 per cent total, 2005), South Korea (11.3 per cent), Spain (10.2 per cent), Ukraine (7.9 per cent), US (6.1 per cent), Ireland (6.0 per cent), France (5.7 per cent), Germany (5.0 per cent), Belgium (4.5 per cent)

Agriculture
Traditional farming generates around 23 per cent of GDP and around 67 per cent of the population is engaged in subsistence farming.
Only 7 per cent of land is cultivated, although there is considerable potential for development.
Main cash crops are sugar cane, groundnuts, oil palm, cotton, citrus fruits and coffee. Main subsistence crops are rice (60 per cent of cultivated land), cassava, maize and vegetables.
Output has stagnated due to transport problems, low levels of mechanisation, poor marketing and a lack of vital inputs. Although infrastructural projects have rectified some problems, the country is in need of further investment to improve roads linking agricultural areas to domestic and foreign markets.
The fishing, forestry and livestock sectors are small. There is potential for lucrative

fishing but the fishing fleet suffers from lack of funds.

Estimated crop production in 2005 included: 1,142,000 tonnes (t) cereals in total, 900,000t rice, 1,350,000t cassava, 135,000t fonio, 430,000t plantains, 853,000t oil palm fruit, 150,000t bananas, 1,480,000t roots and tubers, 210,000t citrus fruit, 169,877t oilcrops, 1,800t tobacco, 20,500t green coffee, 2,500t cocoa beans, 22,500t coconuts, 164,000t mangoes, 280,000t sugar cane, 40,000t seed cotton, 15,000t cotton lint, 3,360t natural rubber, 1,106,000t fruit in total, 482,200t vegetables in total. Livestock production included: 58,435t meat in total, 35,483t beef, 1,990t pig meat, 4,535t lamb, 6,021t goat meat, 4,000t game meat, 5,050t poultry, 18,585t eggs, 94,956t milk, 600t honey, 6,501t cattle hides, 775t sheepskins.

Fishing

In 2004, the total marine fish catch was 88,550 tonnes.

Forestry

The value of exports in 2004 amounted to US$8.2 million, while imports amounted to US$3.4 million.

Production in 2004 included 12,286,470 cubic metres (cum) roundwood, 651,000cum industrial roundwood, 26,000cum sawnwood, 138,000cum sawlogs and veneers, 11,635,470cum wood fuel; 304,007t charcoal.

Industry and manufacturing

The industrial sector contributes around 4 per cent to GDP and employs 5 per cent of the workforce.

Apart from aluminium smelting, it is small-scale and designed to meet local requirements. Aluminium smelting from locally mined bauxite is being modernised with French aid.

The other main industries, textiles, food processing and plywood, are handicapped by supply bottlenecks and shortages of skilled labour.

The investment code and economic liberalisation are expected to attract more foreign capital.

Tourism

Tourism is undeveloped, lacking appropriate infrastructure and attracting only small numbers of visitors. The potential importance of the sector is recognised by the authorities who plan to develop it. Tourism is expected to contribute 5.7 per cent to GDP in 2005.

Mining

Mining is the most dynamic sector of the economy, accounting for around 30 per cent of GDP and almost all export earnings. It is rich in uranium, titanium, copper, manganese, iron ore, gold and diamonds. Around 8 per cent of the workforce is employed in the sector. A mining code introduced in 1995 renewed foreign interest in the mining sector, offering a range of guarantees and tax incentives to foreign investors, who may own up to 85 per cent of any venture.

Bauxite accounts for around 20 per cent of GDP and around 90 per cent of exports. 650,000 tonnes of alumina are produced from the country's single refinery at Fria. The largest bauxite producer is the Sangarédi mine, operated by Compagnie des Bauxites de Guinée (CBG), a joint venture between the government and Halco. CBG has an annual production capacity of 14 million tonnes.

Diamond reserves are estimated at 40 million carats (93 per cent gem quality). The Aredor diamond mine, near Banankore, is 50 per cent owned by the government and 50 per cent by a consortium led by Bridge Oil of Australia and produces around 25,000 carats per year. Diamond mining capacity in Guinea is far lower than recorded exports. It is thought that many gems exported from Guinea have been smuggled from neighbouring countries into Guinea. Key sites of precious stones include Siguiri, Mandiana, Dinguiraye, Kissidougou and Kérouané, and along the rivers of Baoulé, Milo and Diani.

On 2 August 2007, the Australian minerals exploration company, Murchison United, announced a significant deposit of uranium in the southeast of Guinea, near Firawa.

Hydrocarbons

Oil is not produced in Guinea, but exploration for offshore petroleum is under way. Partners Houston's SCS Corp and US Oil Corp have obtained exclusive rights for exploration of offshore Guinea. Guinea relies on imports of refined oil products, importing 8,300 barrels per day.

Guinea does not produce or import natural gas or coal.

Energy

There is considerable potential for hydropower from several large rivers, as yet untapped.

The country imports oil to run power stations.

The Garafiri Dam, with power production capacity of 75MW, was built by France at a cost of US$211 million.

Banking and insurance

It was announced in March 2005 that the introduction of the shared currency, the Eco, in Guinea, Ghana, Nigeria, Sierra Leone and The Gambia, which was due in July 2005, would be postponed. The currency was proposed to facilitate trade and growth with an ultimate plan to merge it with the CFA franc.

Central bank

Banque Centrale de la République de Guinée

Main financial centre

Conakry

Time

GMT

Geography

Guinea lies on the west coast of Africa, with Sierra Leone and Liberia to the south, Senegal to the north, and Mali and Côte d'Ivoire inland to the east.

The country is curved in shape, with Sierra Leone occupying a large chunk of the central region. It can be divided into four geographic zones: the furthest from the coast is bio-diverse rain forest, which turns into savannah in the centre. There is a northern hill region and a coastal zone with an Atlantic coast of 320km. The highest mountain is Mont Nimba (1,752 metres), which is at the centre of an internationally recognised nature reserve, on the border with Côte d'Ivoire and Liberia.

There are 22 rivers that begin life in Guinea, including the Senegal, Gambia and Niger rivers.

Hemisphere

Northern

Climate

The climate is tropical and humid. In the south the rainy season falls in June–October; rainfall is particularly heavy in Conakry, average temperatures range from 22–30 degrees Celsius (C). The dry season is from November–April, likely temperature range 24–35 degrees C. The north is generally cooler and drier.

Entry requirements

Passports

Required by all and must have six months validity from the date of departure.

Visa

Required by all except nationals of some African countries. Applications for visas must be made to a Guinea Consulate before travelling. Business visas should included proof of sufficient funds, a business letter with a full itenerary, and an invitation from a local company or organisation. Contact the nearest embassy for further details.

Currency advice/regulations

There are no restrictions on the import of foreign currency but the amount must be declared; export may not exceed the amount imported. It is a requirement to exchange an amount of foreign currency into Gf, depending on the length of stay. Local currency up to Gf1,000 may be imported provided a valid declaration for its previous export can be provided.

Traveller's cheques have limited outlets in banks and large hotels. To avoid extra exchange fees US dollars and Euros are recommended.

Health (for visitors)
Mandatory precautions
Yellow fever vaccination certificate.
Advisable precautions
Malaria prophylaxes are essential as risk exists throughout the country. Immunisations or booster shots are necessary for diphtheria, tetanus, polio, hepatitis A, typhoid and yellow fever. Vaccinations may be needed for hepatitis B, TB, meningitis and cholera. Rabies is a risk in rural areas.
Use only bottled or boiled water for drinks, washing teeth and making ice. Eat only well cooked meals, preferably served hot; vegetables should be cooked and fruit peeled. Avoid pork, salad and food from street vendors. A full first-aid kit would be useful.

Hotels
Limited first-class accommodation is available in Conakry and Kankan; good hotels are expensive. Hotel bills may be paid in foreign currency or by credit card. A service charge is usually included in the bill. Tipping is optional.

Public holidays (national)
Fixed dates
1 Jan (New Year's Day), 1 May (Labour Day), ^15 Aug (Assumption Day), 27 Aug (Anniversary of Women's Revolt), 28 Sep (Referendum Day), 2 Oct (Republic Day), 1 Nov (All Saints' Day), 25 Dec (Christmas).
Variable dates
^Easter Monday, Eid al Adha, Birth of the Prophet, ^Ascension Day, Day after the Night's Vigil (Nov), Eid al Fitr (three days).
^ Christian holiday only
Islamic year – 1429 (10 Jan 2008–28 Dec 2008): The Islamic year contains 354 or 355 days, with the result that Muslim feasts advance by 10–12 days against the Gregorian calendar. Dates of feasts vary according to the sighting of the new moon, so cannot be forecast exactly.

Working hours
Banking
Mon–Fri: 0800–1230, 1430–1700.
Business
Mon–Thu: 0830–1730; Fri: 0800–1300.
Government
Mon–Thu: 0800–1500; Fri: 0800–1300; Sat: 0800–1500.

Telecommunications
Mobile/cell phones
GSM 900 services are available.

Electricity supply
220V AC, 50 cycles

Social customs/useful tips
Showing respect for people will enhance your regard. Always greet people and never go straight into conversation without pleasantries beforehand. It is considered polite to use people's titles.

Security
Visitors are advised not travel to border areas where security is weak and there is a risk of kidnapping.
Always carry an identity card or passport, if stopped you are obliged to show ID.
Pickpocketing, muggings and armed break-ins occur in the city; avoid carrying valuables in public and remain vigilant.
There are numerous confidence tricksters typically attempting to dupe foreigners into buying precious gems (which, even if authentic, need export licences), gold and counterfeit goods.

Getting there
Air
National airline: Air Guinée (government owned) flies domestic routes only. International flights are regional or European.
International airport/s: Conakry (CKY), 13km from city, bank, and car hire. Taxis are to city.
Airport tax: None
Surface
Road: Best route is the coastal road from Sierra Leone (Freetown) to Conakry. Roads from Ganta (Liberia) to N'zérékoré and from Mali (to Kankan and Siguiri) can be difficult.

Getting about
National transport
Air: Air Guinée operates regular domestic service between Conakry, Boké, Kankan, Kissidougou, Labé, Macenta, N'zérékoré, Siguiri.
Road: A few main roads are surfaced, eg from Conakry north to Kindia and Kissidougou, and parts of the road east to Freetown in Sierra Leone. Most roads are laterite and become impassable during the rainy season (Jun–Oct).
Buses: Coach services include Conakry-Kindia-Gaoual and Dabola-N'zérékoré.
Rail: Narrow-gauge railway from Conakry to Kindia and Kankan, which is in poor condition.
City transport
Taxis: Available in Conakry, limited availability elsewhere; can be hired from hotels by the hour or day. Standard fares apply within towns, but for longer journeys fares should be agreed in advance. Tipping is optional.
Car hire
International and national driving licence required. Driving outside city limits with chauffeur and special authorisation only.

BUSINESS DIRECTORY

The addresses listed below are a selection only. While World of Information makes every endeavour to check these addresses, we cannot guarantee that changes have not been made, especially to telephone numbers and area codes. We would welcome any corrections.

Telephone area codes
The international dialling code (IDD) for Guinea is + 224, followed by subscriber's number.
All telephone/fax numbers became eight digits from December 2005.

Chambers of Commerce
Guinea Chamber of Commerce, Industry and Handicrafts, PO Box 545, Conakry (email: cciag@sotelgui.net.gn).

Banking
Banque Internationale pour le Commerce et l'Industrie de la Guinée SA; PO Box 1484, Avenue de la République, Conakry (tel: 3041-2908/3643).

Banque Islamique de Guinee; PO Box 1247, 6è Avenue de la Republique, Conakry (tel: 3041-4581, 3046-2075).

Banque Populaire Maroco-Guineenne; PO Box 4400, Avenue de la Republique, Conakry-360 (tel: 3041-1599/2360/2552).

Ecobank-Guinee; PO Box 5687, Avenue de la Republique, Conakry (tel: 3045-5876).

International Commercial Bank; PO Box 3547, Cité Chemin de Fer, Conakry (tel: 3041-2590.

Société Générale de Banques en Guinée; PO Box 1514, Kaloum Coronthie Immeuble Boffa, Cité Chemin de Fer, Conakry (tel: 3041-1746).

Union Internationale de Banque en Guinée UIBG; PO Box 324, Angle 5è Boulevard, 6è Avenue de la République, Conakry (tel: 3041-2096/4309).

Central bank
Banque Centrale de la République de Guinée; PO Box 622, 3 Boulevard du Commerce, Conakry (tel: 3041-2651; fax: 3041-4898).

Travel information
Air France, BP 590, Ave de la Republique, Conakry (tel: 3046-4535)

Air Guinée, Route du Niger, BP 12, 12 Côte Commissariat Central, Conakry (tel: 3045-3662).

Other useful addresses
Bureau Veritas, BP 1451, Conakry (tel: 3044-1841, 3044-2202; fax: 3041-2112).

Chambre Economique de Guinée, BP 609, Conakry.

Comité d'Etat pour la Co-opération avec l'Europe Occidentale, Conakry.

Direction Nationale des Marchés Publics et du Portefeuille de l'Etat (privatisation office), La Division du Portefeuille du Ministère des Finances, avenue de la République, Face á l'Hôpital Ignace DEEN, BP 2006, Conakry (tel: 3041-3957; fax: 3041-4220).

ENTRAT (state forwarding firm), BP 315, Conakry.

Entreprise Nationale Import–Export (Importex), BP 152, Conakry (tel: 3044-2813, 3044-2809).

French Commercial Department, Ambassade de France, BP 373, Conakry (tel: 3041-1605, 3041-1655; fax: 3041-2708).

Guinea Embassy (US), 2112 Leroy Place, NW, Washington DC 20008 (tel: (+1-202) 483-9420; fax: (+1-202) 483-8688; e-mail: emgui@sysnet.net).

Office National des Hydrocarbures (Onah), Conakry.

L'Office de Promotion des Investissement Privés – Guichet Unique (OPIP) (assistance for foreign investors), BP 2024, Conakry (tel: 3045-1830, 3041-4985; fax: 3041-3990; e-mail: dg@opip.org.gn).

Port Autonome, BP 805, Conakry (tel: 3044-2728, 3044-2737; fax: 3041-4564).

Radio-Télévision Guinéenne (RTG), BP 391, Conakry.

Statistical Office, Bureau du Premier Ministre, Conakry (tel: 3044-2148).

National news agency: Agence Guineenne de Presse

Address: BP 1535; Anciens locaux d'Enelgui, 2ème boulevard, 5ème avenue, Conakry (tel: 144-434; 430-549; email: info@agpguinee.net)

Internet sites

Africa Business Network: www.ifc.org/abn

AllAfrica.com: http://allafrica.com

African Development Bank: www.afdb.org

Africa Online: www.africaonline.com

Mbendi AfroPaedia (information on companies, countries, industries and stock exchanges in Africa): http://mbendi.co.za

Online news www.guineenews.org/

Guinea-Bissau

KEY FACTS

Official name: República da Guiné-Bissau (Republic of Guinea-Bissau)

Head of State: President João Bernardo Vieira (since 1 Oct 2005)

Head of government: Martinho Carlos Correia (PAIGC) (from 6 Aug 2008)

Ruling party: Coalition government: Partido Africano da Independência de Guiné e Cabo Verde (PAIGC) (African Independence Party of Guinea and Cape Verde), Partido para a Renovaçao Social (PRS) (Party for Social Renewal) and Partido Unido Social Democrático (PUSD) (United Social Democratic Party) (from 17 Apr 2007)

Area: 36,125 square km

Population: 1.67 million (2007)*

Capital: Bissau

Official language: Portuguese

Currency: CFA franc (CFAf) = 100 centimes (Communauté Financière Africaine (African Financial Community) franc).

Exchange rate: CFAf413.80 per US$ (Jul 2008); CFAf655.95 per euro (pegged from Jan 1999)

GDP per capita: US$206 (2007)*

GDP real growth: 2.50% (2007)*

Labour force: 695,000 (2004)

Inflation: 3.40% (2005)

Balance of trade: US$82.00 million (2006)

Foreign debt: US$765.00 million (2004)

Visitor numbers: 246,000 (2006, including visiting expatiates)

* estimated figure

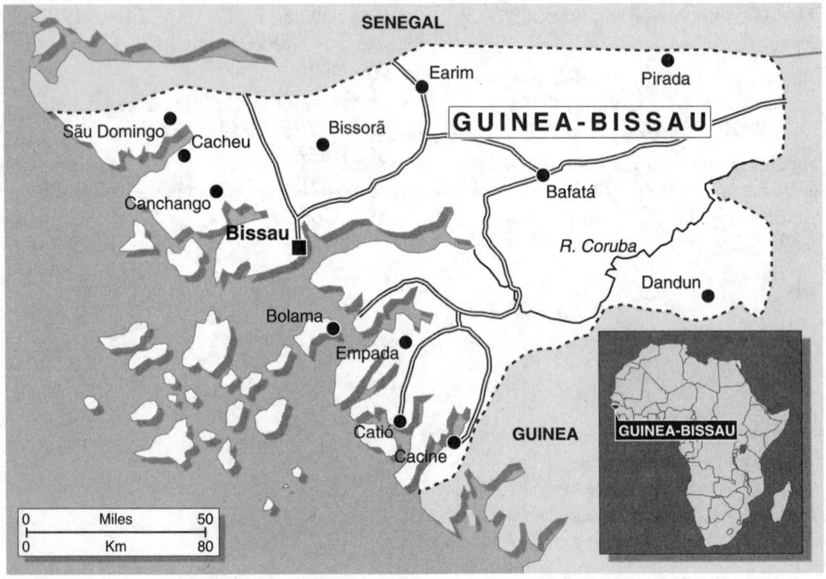

The small (under 2 million population) country of Guinea-Bissau has seen numerous coups attempts and uprisings since its independence from Portugal in 1974. With poor infrastructure and low social indicators, Guinea-Bissau is one of the poorest countries in the world, ranking 172 of 177 countries. Visitors to the capital, Bissau, can be forgiven for forgetting that not one, but two wars ever took place here at all. This resilient people seem to bear no grudges and no scars and are, on the contrary, remarkably calm, civil and kind. Many of the country's problems can be traced back to the damaging effects of war. In 1953, before the war of liberation, more than a million acres were under cultivation; 20 years later the figure had dropped to some 300,000 acres. Guinea-Bissau is still trying to overcome the effects of this long period of political instability and economic stagnation that followed the civil war of 1998–99. After a coup in 2003 and parliamentary elections in 2004, a new government was nominated in May 2004 and presidential elections were held in October 2005, bringing João Bernardo Vieira to power as president and Carlos Gomes Junior was nominated by the assembly as prime minister.

Junior was sacked by the president in November and replaced by Aristides Gomes, who in turn was replaced by Marthinho Ndafa Cabi in March 2007. The formation of the three party coalition, called the 'Stability pact', which nominated him as prime minister had briefly reassured the country's donors that the country could be entering an era of relative political calm. He lasted until 6 August 2008 when Martinho Carlos Correia became prime minister after the Partido Africano da Independência de Guiné e Cabo Verde (PAIGC) (African Independence Party of Guinea and Cape Verde) withdrew from the coalition on 25 July.

Economy

Guinea-Bissau ranks among the lowest 10 countries in the world on the human development index. More than two-thirds of the population of approximately 1.6 million live below the poverty line, in a country where per capita GDP is US$206 (2007). The inequality of income distribution is one of the most extreme in the world.

The country's industrial base was virtually destroyed in the war; enterprises remain severely undercapitalised because of confiscations and looting during the conflict, the infrastructure has deteriorated and electricity production is intermittent at best. As a result, there has been minimal private investment.

Economy

There is no short term fix for Guinea-Bissau. Because of high costs, the development of petroleum, phosphate and other mineral resources is not a near-term prospect. Never-the-less, there has been a gradual economic recovery since 2007, thanks in part to increased agricultural production as normal rains returned. Broad money grew by 25 per cent in 2007, somewhat faster than initially projected. Central bank accumulation of foreign assets and higher credit to the private sector helped push up domestic liquidity. As expected, the external current account deficit (excluding official current transfers) narrowed to 12.5 per cent of GDP in 2007, from 27 per cent in 2006, reflecting higher exports of cashews, some from the previous year's stock.

Inflation

According to the International Monetary Fund (IMF) Guinea-Bissau's 12-month inflation rate rose to 9.3 per cent by end-2007, from 3.2 percent at end-2006, driven mainly by a 14 per cent rise in food prices. Annual inflation has remained high in 2008, at 9.1 per cent at end-May, while food prices rose 15.5 per cent during the period. Because Guinea-Bissau relies heavily on imports, international price developments explain a large part of domestic price inflation, but recent evidence also points to domestic factors as possible causes of the recent rise in inflation. The trend since 2007 of inflation being higher in Guinea-Bissau than in the region as a whole suggests the country's inflation has a large idiosyncratic component. Prices for local goods were also higher than for imported goods throughout 2007.

Outlook

Although risks are tilted to the downside, the economic outlook for 2008 remains positive. Real GDP growth is still expected to increase to over 3 per cent in 2008, based on a slight increase in cashew production and increasing construction activity. Inflation, on the other hand, is now expected to be higher than expected; given international price projections for food and fuel products, inflation for 2008 would average about 6 per cent, compared to the projected 3.3 per cent. The external current account deficit will also be higher-than-expected owing to higher food and fuel imports.

Risk assessment

Economic	Improving
Political	Poor
Regional stability	Fair

COUNTRY PROFILE

Historical profile

1400s Until Portuguese traders first came to Guinea-Bissau, the country was part of the Mali empire.
1915 The Portuguese had colonised only the coastal regions until the nineteenth century but finally gained control of the interior. Unlike its other colonies, Portugal made little attempt to develop the then Portuguese Guinea.
1956 The liberation movement, PAIGC was founded.
1973 A unilateral declaration of independence was proclaimed on 24 September, by which time nearly all the necessary preparations for government had been made by the rebels. PAIGC dropped the name Portuguese Guinea in favour of Guinea-Bissau. Amilcar Cabral was assassinated
1974 Portugal long refused to relinquish power, extending Africa's longest war of independence, but finally granted it after the fall of Marcello Caetano, in Lisbon, in April. Luis Cabral, (brother of the PAIGC leader Amilcar Cabral), became president.
1980 PAIGC was committed to the unification of Guinea-Bissau and Cape Verde, but this aim was dropped when a military coup d'état led by João Bernardo Vieira, who replaced Cabral.
1990 Parliament revoked the PAIGC sole legitimate party status.
1994 Vieira was elected president in the first free elections and PAIGC won the parliamentary elections.
1997 Formal entry to the Communauté Financière Africaine when the CFA franc replaced the peso as national currency.
1998 A civil war began. General Ansumane Mane attempted a coup against Vieira following an army uprising, when Vieira had tried to sacked the general for smuggling arms into the neighbouring Senegalese province of Casamance. Senegalese and Guinea troops supported the government and after a month of fighting a cease-fire was agreed, in July.
1999 Ecowas forces arrived to keep the peace, but fighting broke out again and President Vieira was ousted. Malam Bacai Sanha became interim president. The Partido para a Renovaçao Social (PRS) (Party for Social Renewal) won the parliamentary elections.
2000 Kumba Ialá (Yala), leader of the PRS, was elected president.
2003 President Kumba Ialá was deposed in a bloodless coup.
2004 The opposition PAIGC won the parliamentary elections and Carlos Gomes Júnior, was sworn in as prime minister.
2005 Former military leader and deposed president, João Bernardo 'Nino' Vieira (who had returned from exile in Portugal), won the presidential election runoff and almost immediately sacked the government of Prime Minister Junior and Aristides Gomes was named as prime minister.

KEY INDICATORS — Guinea-Bissau

	Unit	2003	2004	2005	2006	2007
Population	m	1.51	1.38	1.59	*1.62	*1.67
Gross domestic product (GDP)	US$bn	0.28	0.28	0.30	*0.31	*0.34
GDP per capita	US$	183	208	190	*189	206
GDP real growth	%	-1.2	4.3	3.2	*1.8	*2.5
Inflation	%	0.6	0.3	3.4	*1.9	*3.7
Industrial output	% change	–	2.5	4.5	6.0	–
Agricultural output	% change	–	6.0	6.0	5.5	–
Exports (fob) (goods)	US$m	71.0	83.0	101.0	110.0	–
Imports (cif) (goods)	US$m	59.0	58.0	112.0	28.0	–
Balance of trade	US$m	12.0	25.0	-11.0	82.0	–
Current account	US$m	-300.0	-240.0	-11.0	*-35.0	-6.0
Total reserves minus gold	US$m	164.4	227.2	79.8	82.0	112.9
Foreign exchange	US$m	163.2	226.6	79.2	81.5	112.8
Exchange rate	per US$	574.89	496.63	507.22	496.60	454.40

* estimated figure

2006 The cashew crop, a major source of foreign income, suffered a major setback as world prices slumped and farmers were left with crops they could not sell. The World Bank suspended a US$15 million funding for infrastructure, due to a lack of transparency in contracts. Other funding, of over US$66 million, will continue to support projects in health and the environment. Guinea-Bissau was rated as 172 out of 176 in the United Nations Development Programme (UNDP) human development index, which determines a country's progress towards the millennium goals of, among others, longer life, a descent standard of living, schooling and human rights.
2007 In March, Prime Minister Aristides Gomes resigned, following a no-confidence vote in the legislature. Martinho Ndafa Kabi took office as prime minister. A law was passed in December that guaranteed amnesty to the perpetrators of violence committed between 1980–2004 during the period of political unrest.
2008 An aeroplane loaded with 600kg of cocaine from South America was seized by police at the international airport on 14 July. The plane had fake Red Cross markings and was abandoned shortly after arrival. Several foreign nationals were arrested within 10km of the airport. The president appointed Carlos Correia as prime minister on 6 August.

Political structure

Constitution
The 1984 constitution has been revised five times. The 1999 amendment reserves the highest posts in the country for 'native Bissau-Guineans'.
Form of state
Unitary republic
The executive
Executive power rests with the president, who is the head of state and serves a five-year term. The president appoints the prime minister, who presides over the Council of Ministers.
National legislature
The Assembleia Nacional Popular (National Assembly) has 102 seats and is elected for a five-year term.
Legal system
The legal system is based on the 1984 constitution, revised in 1993.
Last elections
19 June/24 July 2005 (presidential); 28/30 March 2004 (parliamentary).
Results: Presidential: former president João Bernardo Vieira was elected president with 52.4 per cent of the run-off vote. Malam Bacai Sanhá (PAIGC) was runner-up with 47.6 per cent. Turnout was 78.6 per cent.
Parliamentary: PAIGC, won 45 seats out of 100, the PRS 35 seats; PUSD 17 and União Eleitoral (UE) (Electoral Union) two seats. Turnout was 76.2 per cent.
Next elections
2009 (parliamentary); 2010 (presidential).
Political parties
Ruling party
Coalition government: Partido Africano da Independência de Guiné e Cabo Verde (PAIGC) (African Independence Party of Guinea and Cape Verde), Partido para a Renovaçao Social (PRS) (Party for Social Renewal) and Partido Unido Social Democrático (PUSD) (United Social Democratic Party) (from 17 Apr 2007)
Main opposition party
Partido Unido Social Democrático (PUSD) (United Social Democratic Party)

Population

1.67 million (2007)*
Last census: December 1991: 983,367
Population density: 31 per square km. Urban population: 32 per cent (1995–2001).
Annual growth rate: 2.9 per cent 1994–2004 (WHO 2006)
Ethnic make-up
Balanta (30 per cent), Fula (20 per cent), Manjaca (14 per cent), Mandinga 13 per cent, Papel 7 per cent.
Religions
Some 65 per cent of the population are animist, 30 per cent Muslim and 5 per cent Christian.

Education

Literacy rate: 59 per cent, total; 26.2 per cent female adult rates (World Bank).

Health

Per capita total expenditure on health (2003) was US$45; of which per capita government spending was US$21, at the international dollar rate, (WHO 2006).
Improved water sources are available to 49 per cent of the population.
HIV/Aids
HIV prevalence: 2.8 per cent (UNAIDS estimate 2004)
Life expectancy: 47 years, 2004 (WHO 2006)
Fertility rate/Maternal mortality rate: 7.1 births per woman, 2004 (WHO 2006); maternal mortality 910 deaths per 100,000 live births (World Bank).
Child (under 5 years) mortality rate (per 1,000): 126 per 1,000 live births (World Bank).
Head of population per physician: 0.12 physicians per 1,000 people, 2004 (WHO 2006)

Main cities

Bissau (capital, estimated population 452,640 in 2005), Bafatá (26,312), Gabú (12,255), Catió (7,279), Canchungo (6,282).

Languages spoken

Crioulo (a hybrid of medieval Portuguese and local words) is the common language. Balanta, Bijago and Fulani are also spoken. French is more widely spoken than English. All correspondence and documentation should be in Portuguese and French.
Official language/s
Portuguese

Media

Despite the constitution guaranteeing freedom of the press, the government has not always respected this and journalists are known to practice self-censorship. Journalists that have reported on drug trafficking have been subject to harassment.
The small and weak media scene is hampered by the country's financial constraints.
National news agency: ABMP (Agência Bissau Media e Publiçacões)
Other news agencies: Bissau Digital: www.bissaudigital.com
Guine-Bissau: www.guine-bissau.com
Press
Newspaper and magazines include No Pintcha, Correio de Bissau Fraskera and Banobero.
Broadcasting
The state-owned Radio Televisao de Guinea-Bissau (RTGB) is the public broadcaster.
Radio: RTGB operates the only Radiodifusão Nacional public radio station. International radio is provided by RTP in Portuguese and RFI in French. Private radio stations include Radio Pidjiquiti, Bombolom FM, both very popular, and Voice of Quelele.
Television: The state-owned RTGB broadcasts locally. RTP Africa is funded by Portugal, with donated equipment, but managed locally by Bissau-Guineans.
News agencies
National news agency: ABMP (Agência Bissau Media e Publiçacões)
Other news agencies: Bissau Digital: www.bissaudigital.com
Guine-Bissau: www.guine-bissau.com

Economy

Guinea-Bissau is one of the poorest countries in the world. GDP per capita in 2007 was only US$206; around 75 per cent of the population live below the poverty line, surviving through subsistence farming. The informal economy has been estimated as larger than the legal market.
The military conflict of 1998–99 damaged the infrastructure, much of which has yet to be repaired, although several donors are providing assistance.The economy

was further damaged in the ensuing political unrest, which disrupted business activities.

Since the coup in 2003, there has been some improvement. World Bank and African Development Bank (ADB) loans have helped to underpin the economy. The government restored central control of the economy in 2004 and has made efforts to improve collection of tax revenues and to reduce expenditures. After two years of negative growth, GDP grew by 4.3 per cent in 2004 and 3.5 per cent in 2005.

The main economic activities are farming and fishing. Crops include cashew nuts, peanuts, rice and palm kernels.

Guinea-Bissau is the world's fifth largest producer of cashew nuts, which account for 90 per cent of exports. Excellent harvests in recent years facilitated the government's restabilisation efforts, but world demand for cashews declined sharply in 2006 and prices collapsed.

External trade

As a member of the Economic Community of West African States (Ecowas), Guinea-Bissau is also a member of the West African Economic and Monetary Union using the common currency, the CFA franc.

Guinea-Bissau has a large trade deficit and heavy dependence on foreign aid and credits. In 2006 the government set the selling price of cashew nuts for farmers at twice the market price and sales plummeted until farmers were forced to sell at knock-down prices as buyer went elsewhere for their supplies, this resulted in widespread hunger as farmers were unable to sell their crops.

Imports

Principal imports are fuel and energy, foodstuffs, transport equipment, capital goods.

Main sources: Italy (25.3 per cent total, 2005), Senegal (18.6 per cent), Portugal (15.8 per cent), Côte d'Ivoire (4.3 per cent)

Exports

Principal exports are cashew nuts (Guinea-Bissau is the eighth largest supplier of cashew nuts worldwide), shrimp, with small quantities of peanuts, palm kernels and sawn timber. Fish is harvested by foreign trawlers, who pay for fishing rights.

Main destinations: India (72.0 per cent total, 2005), Nigeria (17.1 per cent), Ecuador (4.0 per cent)

Agriculture

Farming

The agricultural sector (including fishing) is the principal economic activity, accounting for around 60 per cent of GDP and over 70 per cent of total export earnings and employing 70 per cent of the workforce.

Only 9 per cent of total area is cultivated; inland areas are largely savannah, coastal areas are forest and mangrove swamps. Construction of a bridge on the Mansoa river between Dakar and Bissau improved links between Cacheu and Oio regions (which produce half of the country's agricultural output) and markets.

There are chronic food shortages, despite the emphasis on food self-sufficiency and co-operative farming.

The main food crop is paddy rice (19 per cent of cultivated land); other food crops include millet, sorghum, plantains, root crops, some maize and groundnuts.

Other cash crops include palm kernels, coconuts, tobacco, sugar.

The crop production for 2005 included: 212,538 tonnes (t) cereals in total, *81,000t cashew nuts, 39,835t maize, *38,000t cassava, 23,359t sorghum, 98,340t rice, *39,000t plantains, *45,500t coconuts, *80,000t oil palm fruit, *8,200t citrus fruit, *20,527t oilcrops, *76,420t fruit in total, *25,500t vegetables in total. Livestock production included: 19,973t meat in total, 5,247t beef, 11,540t pig meat, 1,716t lamb and goat meat, 1,470t poultry, 1,176t eggs, 19,030t milk, 65t honey, 1,193t cattle hides, 195t sheepskins.

* estimate

Fishing

The fishing sector is important. Exports of fish and shellfish are expected to increase as the country's large marine resources are exploited. The European Development Fund gave US$35 million in aid to develop the fishing industry, including an ice-making plant. Fish worth between US$300–600 million are caught in the waters each year, but value added production on-shore is minimal.

More investment is needed to refurbish the main port, damaged during the civil war, to enable fish processing for export to Europe or to neighbouring countries for processing and re-export.

In 2004, the total marine fish catch was 5,820 tonnes and the total crustacean catch was 30 tonnes.

Forestry

Production in 2004 included 592,000 cubic metres (cum) roundwood, 170,000cum industrial roundwood, 15,700cum sawnwood, 40,000cum sawlogs and veneers, 422,000cum wood fuel.

Industry and manufacturing

The industrial sector contributes around 12 per cent to GDP and employs 10 per cent of the workforce. Production is mostly agri-related: processing groundnuts, fish processing, rice dehusking, sugar refining. There is also a large brewery plant, a small Citroën assembly plant, brick making and textile industries. Since the end of the civil war, there has been a drive to modernise transport facilities.

Tourism

The sector is undeveloped, with only around 1,000 visitors per year, mostly for fishing or hunting.

Mining

The main barrier to investment in the mining sector is the country's poor infrastructure.

Test drilling at the Farim phosphate deposit indicated it was commercially viable with high phosphate recovery rates (84.1 per cent).

Hydrocarbons

Guinea-Bissau imports all its petroleum needs. Offshore oil exploration has been undertaken recently and while some oil deposits have been found they are not yet commercially viable. More test drilling will be carried out in 2006.

Gas and coal are neither produced or imported.

Energy

Electricity generating capacity stands at around 15MW following investment in four 1MW generators from China and three small generators from Libya since 2002. The country has an electricity deficit that may be eased by a proposed Ecowas plan to create an electricity network incorporating regional producers.

Guinea-Bissau is dependent on imported oil while hydroelectric potential remains largely untapped.

Banking and insurance

Central bank

Banque Centrale des Etats de l'Afrique de l'Ouest

Main financial centre

Bissau

Time

GMT

Geography

Guinea-Bissau lies on the west coast of Africa, with Senegal to the north and Guinea to the east and south. The terrain is mainly low coastal plain with thick forest and mangrove swamps, rising to hills in the east, where savannah prevails; the highest elevation is approximately 300 metres. Guinea-Bissau also includes Bolama island and the Bijagós archipelago of 15 main islands, lying over 40km out in the Atlantic Ocean.

Hemisphere

Northern.

Climate

Tropical with rainy season from mid-May to November and dry season from

December–April. Average temperatures range from 20–38 degrees Celsius (C) in April–May, and from 15–33 degrees C in December–January. High humidity from July–September.

Entry requirements

Passports

Required by all, valid for six months.

Visa

Required by all, except nationals of Ecowas countries for stay of one month. Applications for business visas should include a letter from the visitor's company accepting responsibility for any expenses incurred, and a full itinerary. For further details, contact the nearest embassy.

Currency advice/regulations

Import and export of local currency is prohibited. There is no restriction on the import of foreign currency, but amounts should be declared; export of foreign currency is allowed up to the declared amount.

Health (for visitors)

Medical facilities are limited.

Mandatory precautions

Yellow fever vaccination certificate.

Advisable precautions

Malaria prophylaxes are essential as risk exists throughout the country. Immunisations or booster shots are necessary for diphtheria, tetanus, polio, hepatitis A, typhoid and yellow fever. Vaccinations may be needed for hepatitis B, TB, meningitis and cholera. Rabies is a risk in rural areas.

Use only bottled or boiled water for drinks, washing teeth and making ice. Eat only well cooked meals, preferably served hot; vegetables should be cooked and fruit peeled. Avoid pork, salad and food from street vendors. A full first-aid kit would be useful.

Hotels

Accommodation is very limited and difficult to obtain at short notice. Reservations should be made well in advance, preferably through business contacts. Hotel tariffs are liable to change at short notice.

Credit cards

Credit cards cannot be used.

Public holidays (national)

Fixed dates

1 Jan (New Year's Day), 20 Jan (Death of Amilcar Cabral), 8 Mar (Women's Day), 1 May (Labour Day), 3 Aug (Colonisation Martyrs' Day), 24 Sep (National Day), 14 Nov (Readjustment Movement Day), 25 Dec (Christmas Day).

Variable dates

Eid al Adha, Eid al Fitr

Islamic year – 1429 (10 Jan 2008–28 Dec 2008): The Islamic year contains 354 or 355 days, with the result that Muslim feasts advance by 10–12 days against the Gregorian calendar. Dates of feasts vary according to the sighting of the new moon, so cannot be forecast exactly.

Working hours

Banking

Mon–Fri: 0830–1430.

Business

Mon–Fri: 0830–1430.

Government

Mon–Fri: 0830–1430.

Shops

Mon–Fri: 0730–1230, 1430–1830.

Telecommunications

Telephone/fax

Communications are poor.

Mobile/cell phones

GSM 900 roaming facilities are available.

Getting there

Air

International airport/s: Bissau-Osvaldo Vieira Airport (OXB), 8km from city. Taxis and minibuses are available to take visitors to the city.

Airport tax: None.

Surface

Road: The road from Guinea is mostly paved; however, that which is not, from the border to Labé, gets boggy in the rainy season. Petrol is readily available only in the cities.

A 720-metre bridge over the Mansoa river has improved the traffic flow on the trans-African coastal road between Dakar, Senegal and Bissau.

Water: There are sea links between Cape Verde and Guinea-Bissau.

Main port/s: Bissau

Getting about

National transport

Air: There are no mainland internal flights. Flights go between Bissau and Bubaque Island and a small plane flies to Orango Island from Bissau.

Road: Total road network is over 3,250km, of which about a third is all-weather.

Buses: Minibuses operate on the main roads.

Taxis: Long-distance taxis leave from the market square in Bissau.

Water: Boats serve most towns on the coast and up-river. Tickets available from the Guinémar Office.

City transport

Taxis: Taxis are available in Bissau and serve all main towns.

BUSINESS DIRECTORY

The addresses listed below are a selection only. While World of Information makes every endeavour to check these addresses, we cannot guarantee that changes have not been made, especially to telephone numbers and area codes. We would welcome any corrections.

Telephone area codes

The international dialling code (IDD) for Guinea-Bissau is + 245 followed by subscriber's number.

Chambers of Commerce

Guini-Bissau Associação Comercial, Industrial e Agricola, PO Box 88, Bissau (tel: 222-276).

Guini-Bissau Camara do Comercio, Industria e Agricultura, PO Box 361, Bissau (tel: 212-844; fax: 201-602).

Banking

Central bank

Banque Centrale des Etats de l'Afrique de l'Ouest, Direction Nationale, Avenue Amilcar Cabral 124, PO Box 38, Bissau (tel: 215-548; fax: 201-305).

Ministries

Ministry of Economy and Finance, Rua Justino Lopes 74A, Bissau (tel: 203-495; fax: 203-496).

Ministry of Finance, Avenue Domingos Ramos, Caixa Postal 67, Bissau (tel/fax: 201-037).

Ministry of Mines and Energy, Caixa Postal 387, Bissau.

Other useful addresses

Empresa Nacional de Comércio Geral, CP 5, Bissau (tel: 212-925).

Empresa Nacional de Pesquisas e Exploração Petroliferas e Mineiras (Petrominas), 58 Rua Eduardo Mondlane, Bissau (tel: 212-279).

Guinea-Bissau Embassy (USA), 15929 Yukon Lane, Rockville MD 20855 (tel: (+1-202) 947-3958).

Guinémar Office, 21A Rua Guerra Mendes, Bissau.

Petroguin, Caixa Postal 387 Bissau (tel: 221-155, 222-625; fax: 221-155, 222-625).

Radiodifusão Nacional da República da Guiné-Bissau, CP 191, Bissau.

National news agency: ABMP (Agência Bissau Media e Publicações)

CP1069; Rua Euardo Mondlane 52, Bissau (tel: 206-147; email: agenciabissau@agenciabissau.com; internet: www.agenciabissau.com).

Internet sites

Africa Business Network: http://www.ifc.org/abn

AllAfrica.com: http://allafrica.com

African Development Bank: http://www.afdb.org

Africa Online: http://www.africaonline.com

Guyana

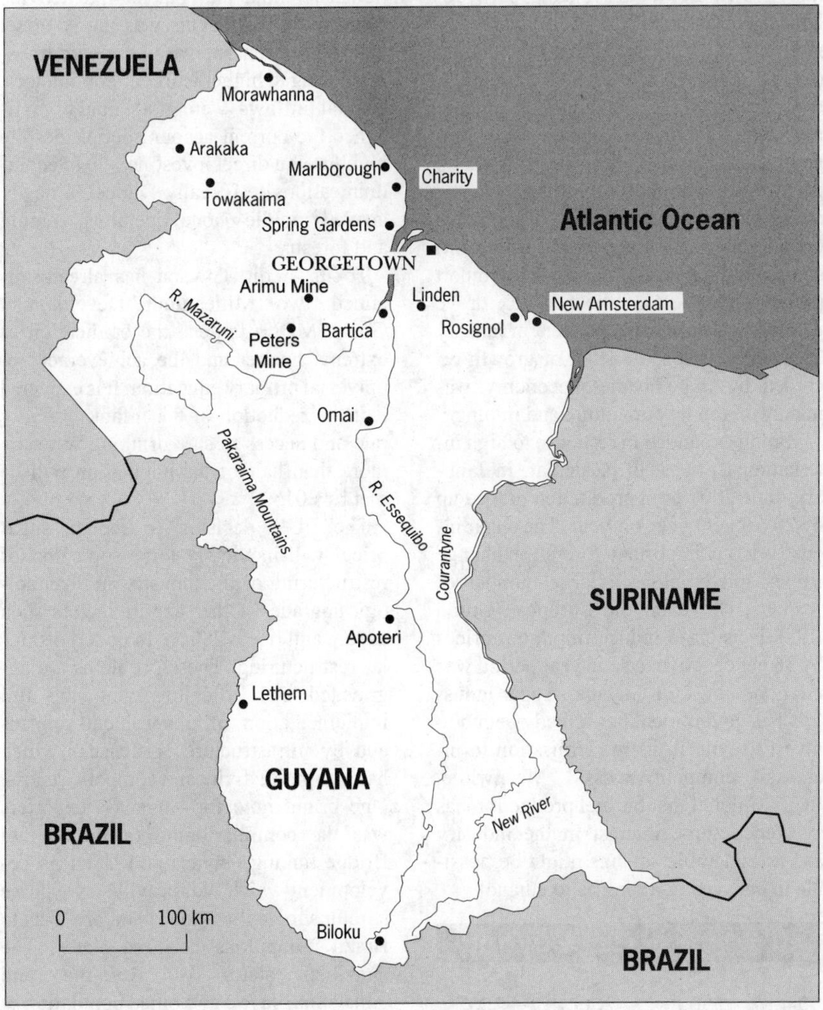

The thirtieth anniversary was marked in 2008 of an event that put Guyana on the international map for all the wrong reasons: the mass suicide of 913 people in the religious community known as Jonestown. In November 1978, California Congressman Leo Ryan had arrived in Guyana to find out exactly what was going on in Jonestown and interview its inhabitants. The cult had re-located from California to Guyana following and a US inland revenue service (IRS) investigation and indictment. The investigation did not get very far, however: after having his life threatened by a cult member during the first day of his visit, Mr Ryan decided to cut his trip short and return to the US with some Jonestown residents who also wished to leave. As they prepared to board their plane, a group of Jonestown guards opened fire on them, killing Congressman Ryan and four others. Some members of Ryan's party escaped, however. James Jones told his followers that Mr Ryan's murder would make it impossible for their commune to continue functioning. Rather than return to the United States, he announced, the cult would make the ultimate sacrifice. The cult's followers were given a deadly concoction and Mr Jones decided to shoot himself.

KEY FACTS

Official name: Co-operative Republic of Guyana

Head of State: President Bharrat Jagdeo (PPP/Civic) (since 1999; re-elected 28 Aug 2006)

Head of government: Prime Minister Samuel A A Hinds (since 1997)

Ruling party: People's Progressive Party/Civic (PPP/Civic) (re-elected 28 Aug 2006)

Area: 214,970 square km

Population: 761,000 (2007)

Capital: Georgetown

Official language: English

Currency: Guyana dollar (G$) = 100 cents

Exchange rate: G$203.20 per US$ (Jul 2008)

GDP per capita: US$1,365 (2007)*

GDP real growth: 5.40% (2007)

Labour force: 334,000 (2004)

Unemployment: 30.00% (2005)* (includes underemployment rate)

Inflation: 12.20% (2007)

Balance of trade: -US$94.40 million (2005)

Foreign debt: US$1.33 billion (2004)

* estimated figure

The US government saw fit to investigate the suicide, presumably since virtually all the dead were US citizens. In 1980, the House Select Committee on Intelligence determined that the CIA had no advance knowledge of the mass murder-suicide. The year before, the House Foreign Affairs Committee had concluded that the Jonestown – a settlement in the jungle – cult leader, Jim Jones suffered extreme paranoia. The committee released a 782 page report, but for reasons best known to itself, kept more than 5,000 pages secret.

VAT introduced

The events of 1978 are long forgotten by most Guyanese. Following the 2006 elections, Guyana was able to focus on the continued need to reform and restructure its economy. According to the United Nations Economic Commission for Latin America and the Caribbean (ECLAC) in 2007 the economy registered an estimated annual growth rate of 4.5 per cent, similar to the 2006 figure of 4.7 per cent. Inflation rose to 10.4 per cent, well up on the 4.2 per cent of 2006, largely due to the one-off effect of the introduction of value added tax (VAT) in January 2007. ECLAC noted that despite the increase in revenue from this tax, Guyana's fiscal deficit widened. The current account deficit remained high at 27.9 per cent of GDP, reflecting the capital and intermediate goods imports associated with private and public investment projects as well as the unfortunate combination of high import prices and deterioration in tourism earnings. This lead to a balance of payments deficit of some US$54 million, contrasting with the surplus of US$45 million recorded in 2006). ECLAC estimated that the Guyanese economy would grow at an annual rate of some 3.5 to 4 per cent in 2008.

Despite the higher-than-expected increase in revenue from VAT the fiscal deficit widened to 12.1 per cent of GDP (11.9 per cent in 2006). This was party down to rapid growth in capital spending, partly related to the Cricket World Cup, and the upgrade of the Guyana Sugar Corporation (GUYSUCO), an investment to modernise the state owned sugar monopoly in order to reduce production costs and enhance competitiveness. Inflation accelerated from 4.2 per cent in 2006 to 10.4 per cent in 2007 owing to the combined effect of the introduction of VAT (at a rate of 16 per cent) and rapidly increasing oil and food import prices. The effect of the new tax drove monthly inflation to 6.6 per cent in January 2007. The reasonable level of growth recorded by the Guyanese economy was mainly driven by agriculture and mining.

Mining expanded in response to high international prices. In particular, in January–June 2007 gold production picked up by 20 per cent year-on-year. The sugar industry is an important foreign exchange earner and employs a large number of workers. However, the European Union (EU) decision to reduce minimum prices by 36 per cent over a four-year period was not good news for Guyana's sugar industry. The government has already begun to invest heavily in its modernisation to increase competitiveness. Meanwhile, ECLAC noted that biofuel production has awakened some interest in the industry and considerable savings might be possible in converting molasses to ethanol.

Guyana's current account deficit is large, at around US$250 million or 27.9 per cent of GDP in 2007, (20.1 per cent in 2006). During January–June travel and tourism receipts dropped by 6 per cent, as the expected earnings from the Cricket World Cup failed to materialise. The number of actual visitors was below expectations, as India and Pakistan exited the tournament early. This was partly offset by a 25 per cent increase in inward transfers owing to higher workers' remittances. Capital inflows were not enough to finance the current account deficit despite high foreign direct investment in telecommunications (especially Digicel, a newly arrived mobile-phone operator), mining and forestry.

To its credit, Guyana has already attained two Millennium Development Goals (MDG) targets, the eradication of extreme hunger and the achievement of universal primary education. It is expected that the reduction of the infant mortality rate and access to safe drinking water by more than half of the population will be met by 2015.

The EU's decision to reduce sugar prices will inevitably force some sort of restructuring of the industry and technology upgrades. Other export sectors such as rum and rice will have to undergo similar restructuring. These problems are aggravated by difficulties with the full implementation of government reforms and by infrastructure bottlenecks which hamper productivity and competitiveness. One bright note for Guyana's exporters was the commissioning of the Takutu Bridge linking Guyana and Brazil, a development which will provide a welcome stimulus for selling goods and products to Brazil's populous northern states. The Brazilian states of Roraima and Amazonia, have a combined population of six million.

KEY INDICATORS — Guyana

	Unit	2003	2004	2005	2006	2007
Population	m	0.83	0.87	0.76	0.76	0.76
Gross domestic product (GDP)	US$bn	0.85	0.79	0.18	0.89	*1.04
GDP per capita	US$	1,029	1,024	1,081	*1,170	*1,365
GDP real growth	%	0.2	1.6	-1.9	5.1	*5.4
Inflation	%	5.8	4.7	6.9	6.6	*12.2
Exports (fob) (goods)	US$m	500.0	570.2	587.2	594.8	–
Imports (cif) (goods)	US$m	575.0	650.1	681.6	792.4	–
Balance of trade	US$m	-75.0	79.9	-94.4	-197.6	–
Current account	US$m	-80.0	-90.0	-156.0	-172.0	-189.0
Total reserves minus gold	US$m	276.4	231.8	251.9	279.6	313.0
Foreign exchange	US$m	271.6	224.7	251.4	278.1	312.5
Exchange rate	per US$	179.00	179.00	201.69	201.69	204.20

* estimated figure

Risk assessment

Economy	Improving
Politics	Fair
Regional stability	Fair

COUNTRY PROFILE

Historical profile

The area before European settlement was inhabited by semi-nomadic, hunter-gatherer Amerindian tribes, notably Arawaks and Caribs.

1498 Christopher Columbus first sighted Guyana.

1616 The Dutch built the first fort.

1640 The first African slaves arrived to work on sugar plantations. Settlements

grew up in Essequibo, Demerara and Berbice and were sustained by trade through the Dutch West Ind
ia Company.
1763 The Berbice slave rebellion began on one plantation and spread to others along the Berbice river.
1781–1803 The Three colonies of Essequibo, Demerara and Berbice, passed into the hands of the English, briefly to the French, back to the Dutch, then the English, then the Dutch and lastly back to the English.
1814 After the Napoleonic Wars the colonies of were ceded to Britain.
1831 The British administration merged the three colonies into British Guiana, but retained the Dutch administrative, legislative and legal system.
1834 Britain abolished slavery in all its territories. Many Indian and smaller numbers of Chinese and Japanese indentured labourers were brought to work on the estates.
1920 Indentureship ended.
1953 The General election was won by the People's Progressive Party (PPP), led by Cheddi Jagan and Forbes Burnham. The British government deemed the government as pro-Communist and suspended the constitution. The PPP spilt and Burnham founded the People's National Congress/Reform (PNC) party.
1957 and 1961 The PPP won both general elections. Support began to grow for independence.
1964 Guyana's political system was generally viewed as fraudulent with Guyana a de facto one-party state and an 'administrative dictatorship'.
1965 The PPP won most seats in the general election, however a coalition of PNC and another minor, conservative, party formed a government. Burnham became prime minister and stayed in post in an increasingly authoritarian manner, until 1980
1966 Guyana gained independence.
1971 A UN tribunal convened to try and resolve the long-standing border dispute with neighbouring Venezuela concerning the oil-rich Essequibo region.
1980 A new constitution introduced the post of executive president, and Forbes Burnham became the first.
1985 President Burnham died. Desmond Hoyte became president. The one-party state and radical socialism was gradually replaced by a market economy. Austerity measures introduced in the late 1980s resulted in great civil unrest.
1992 The National Assembly and Regional Council were elected in the first free and fair general elections. Hoyte lost the presidency to former Marxist, Dr Cheddi Jagan (PPP).
1997 A PPP/Civic (PPC/C) coalition won the election, but PNC refused to accept the election results. Cheddi Jagan died in March. Samuel Hinds became president until December when Jagan's widow Janet was elected president.
1998 After boycotting parliament since the 1997 election, the PNC returned to the National Assembly, following intervention by the Caribbean Community (Caricom), which carried out an independent audit of the election results and brokered an accord with the PNC, which also catered for a new constitution and fresh elections.
1999 Janet Jagan resigned the presidency due to ill-health; she was succeeded by Bharrat Jagdeo.
2000 Guyana had an agreement with the Canadian oil company CGX Energy to drill within waters also claimed by neighbouring Suriname. Suriname gunboats raided the exploration oil-rig sparking international tension; diplomatic proposals for joint exploration and exploitation failed.
2001 The general election was won by President Jagdeo's ruling PPP/C.
2002 A high-profile television presenter, Mark Benschop, was charged with treason after he was accused of inciting demonstrators to storm the presidential offices compound. The demonstrators were complaining of discrimination against Afro-Guyanese.
2003 A UN tribunal convened and tried, without success, to resolve the maritime border dispute with Suriname.
2004 CGX Energy announced it had begun exploration of inshore waters along the Cortenyne Coast, with drilling in the disputed Berbice area to start by September. A key witness in the trial of home affairs minister Ronald Gajraj was shot dead before he could testify about allegations of extra-judicial killings. The minister had stepped down after several months of procrastination and opposition inquiry. Guyana joined 12 South American countries in the launch of an economic and political bloc called the South American Community of Nations.
2005 Severe flooding in January affected half the country's population. By March, the economic effect was shown to be a 2.2 per cent reduction in the year's economic growth, costing the nation about US$65 million. In April Ronald Gajraj was reinstated as home affairs minister, following a ruling by a presidential commission acquitting him of any wrongdoing, however the decision to reinstall the minister provoked international criticism. In May, Gajraj resigned his position.
2006 On 22 April, the agriculture minister, Satyadeow Sawh, was murdered. In elections on 28 August, President Jagdeo was re-elected with 54.6 per cent of the vote his PPP/C party won a majority with 36 seats in the 65-member parliament.
2007 The UN ruled that both Suriname and Guyana should share the oil-rich offshore territory.
2008 Gunmen attacked the village of Lusignan, east of the capital, in January, firing into several houses, killing 11 people, including five children. Angry villagers block the main east-west highway in protest at what they said was too little done to combat gangs in the area. There was fear that the attack was racially motivated as the village is predominantly ethnic Indian and the attackers were from the ethnic African community.

Political structure

Constitution

The constitution was enacted in 1980, a decade after Guyana became a co-operative republic and 14 years after joining the Commonwealth.
Guyana is divided into 10 regions, each headed by a chairman who presides over a regional democratic council. Local communities are administered by village or city councils.

Form of state

Co-operative republic

The executive

Executive power rests with the president, who appoints and supervises the prime minister and other ministers. The president is the presidential candidate chosen by the major party in the National Assembly. Most cabinet ministers are also members of the National Assembly; the constitution limits non-member technocrat ministers to five. Technocrat ministers serve as non-elected members, allowing them to debate, but not to vote.

National legislature

The unicameral National Assembly comprises 40 members chosen on the basis of proportional representation from national lists named by the political parties and an additional 25 members, who are elected by regional administrative districts. The president may dissolve the Assembly and call new elections at any time, but no later than five years from its first sitting.

Legal system

Guyana's legal system is based on Roman Dutch law modified by English common law. The country has a series of magistrates' courts and further appellate courts, a Court of Appeal, headed by a chancellor of the judiciary, and a High Court, presided over by a chief justice. The chancellor and the chief justice are appointed by the president.
An ombudsman investigates complaints against government departments or other authorities.

Last elections
28 August 2006 (presidential and parliamentary)
Results: Presidential: incumbent Bharrat Jagdeo (PPP/C) won 64.6 per cent of the vote; Robert Corbin (PNCR/1G) won 34 per cent; Raphael Trotman (Alliance for Change) won 8.1 per cent.
Parliamentary: PPP/C won 54.6 per cent of the vote (36 seats out 65); PNCR/1G 34 per cent (22 seats); Alliance for Change won 8.4 per cent (five seats); two other parties won one seat each. Turnout was 68.8 per cent.
Next elections
2011 (general)

Political parties
Ruling party
People's Progressive Party/Civic (PPP/Civic) (re-elected 28 Aug 2006)
Main opposition party
People's National CongressReform/One Guyana (PNCR/1G)

Population
761,000 (2007)
Last census: September 2002: 751,223
Population density: Four inhabitants per square km. Urban population: 38 per cent (1995–2001).
Overall population density is low although population distribution is very uneven with a high concentration of people along the coastal strip and many inland areas virtually uninhabited. More than one-quarter of the total population live in the capital, Georgetown.
Annual growth rate: 0.3 per cent 1994–2004 (WHO 2006)
Ethnic make-up
East Indian (51 per cent) (resident mostly in agricultural areas) and Afro-Guyanese (30 per cent) (resident mostly in towns) make up the majority. The remainder are of Chinese and European heritage, or Amerindians, most of whom live in the west and south or on reserves.
The main groups of Amerindians are Arawak, Carib, Wapisiana and Warao. The Caribs include Akawaio, Macushi, Patamona and Waiwai.
Religions
Christian (approximately 50 per cent), Hindu (35 per cent) and Muslim (10 per cent).

Education
Education includes primary school, four to six years of secondary school and between three to four years of higher academic or practical education. Students are usually expected to remain in the school system until the age of 16. There are around 900 schools in Guyana.
Increased access to secondary education is supported by two bilateral funded education projects – the Guyana Education Access Programme (GEAP) and the Guyana Building Equity Project (GBET). In 2000 about 53 per cent of children had access to secondary education compared to 35 per cent between 1993–1999.
A five-year project funded by the British Department for International Development (DfID) is due for completion in 2005. The project focusses on improving school infrastructure, teaching and overall management of the education system. It should enable all Guyanese children to have access to quality education.
Literacy rate: 98.7 per cent, total; 98.3 per cent, female: adult rates in 2002 (World Bank).
Compulsory years: Five to 14
Enrolment rate: 97.4 per cent net primary enrolment (World Bank).

Health
Per capita total expenditure on health (2003) was US$283; of which per capita government spending was US$233, at the international dollar rate, (WHO 2006).
The government has stepped up provisions for drugs and medical supplies in all hospitals and health centres including facilities in the Georgetown Public Hospital Corporation (GPHC).
Improved water sources are available to 48 per cent of the population.
HIV/Aids
By 2001 46 per cent of sex workers were living with HIV/Aids and the probability of the virus passing into the wider population is considered by UNAID/WHO as high.
HIV prevalence: 3.2 per cent aged 15–49 in 2003 (World Bank)
Life expectancy: 63 years, 2004 (WHO 2006)
Fertility rate/Maternal mortality rate: 2.2 births per woman, 2004 (WHO 2006)
Birth rate/Death rate: 9 deaths and 18 births, per 1,000 population (World Bank).
Child (under 5 years) mortality rate (per 1,000): 52 deaths per 1,000 live births; 12 per cent of children aged under five are malnourished (World Bank).

Welfare
The government has been developing new housing schemes, including distributing over 20,000 housing lots for a Low Income Settlement Project. The private sector has also been encouraged to assist in the development of the housing sector.

Main cities
Georgetown (capital, estimated population 227,700 in 2003), Linden (44,300), New Amsterdam (32,500).

Languages spoken
Guyana is the only English-speaking country in South America. Urdu, Hindi, Amerindian languages and Creole are also spoken. Along the Brazilian border, many Guyanese also speak Portuguese.
Official language/s
English

Media
National news agency: GINA (Government Information Agency)
Press
Dailies: In English, the Guyana Chronicle (www.guyanachronicle.com) is state-owned, private newspapers include Stabroek News (www.stabroeknews.com) and Kaieteur News (www.kaieteurnews.com).
Weeklies: All daily newspapers publish a weekend edition. In English, other newspapers include The Catholic Standard and the Mirror (www.mirrornewsonline.com) published twice weekly.
Broadcasting
The state-owned National Communications Network (NCN) (www.ncnguyana.com) operates radio and television services.
Radio: The (NCN) (www.ncnguyana.com) operates two radio stations, Hot FM (http://98hotfm.co.gy) broadcasting modern music. The Voice of Guyana (http://voiceofguyana.com) broadcasts internationally (http://vog560am.co.gy).
Television: The (NCN) (www.ncnguyana.com) operates a public TV station (http://ncn.co.gy). A number of TV channels are received from neighbouring countries. There are international satellite TV channels available.

Economy
Guyana found difficulty in moving away from typical colonial dependency on primary industries after Independence in 1966. But since the early 1990s it has been attempting to transform itself from a state dominated to largely free-market economy. The external debt burden has been reduced by US$1 billion and with negotiated loan repayments to the Paris Club of foreign debtors, debt servicing in 2006 was 20 per cent of GDP, down from the 94 per cent in 1992. The Inter-American Development Bank is expected to write-off debts of US$460 million in 2007. Nevertheless, Guyana is included in the Heavily Indebted Poor Country initiative (HIPC), whereby for future loans the government undertakes macroeconomic reforms to control the economy, improve the accountability and transparency of the public sector and deliver public services, including health, education and a water supply. Raising the standards of living is important, with around 40 per cent of the population living below the poverty line.
The steep rise in global oil prices since 2004 and severe flooding in January 2005, which inundated coastal areas

and caused 70,000 people to flee, causing damage estimated at US$465 million, impacted on the GDP growth rate. It was 1.6 per cent in 2004, but fell to -3.0 per cent in 2005; it is expected to recover to 0.7 per cent in 2006 and is projected to rise to 3.2 per cent in 2007, barring external shocks.

Agriculture plays a large role in Guyana's economy, accounting for over 30 per cent of GDP, services account for over 40 per cent and industry 25 per cent, of which manufacturing is 10 per cent. Sugar is the principal crop and the sector employs around 30,000 people. However new European Union (EU) policies on sugar purchases caused production to fall when prices were cut. In 2006, the EU provided a loan of eur5.6 million (US$7 million) to upgrade the Enmore sugar factory, which will add value to the crop. Sugar production grew by 9.8 per cent to 259,588 tonnes in 2006, 13,000 tonnes more than in 2005. Livestock and forestry both registered growth in 2006 of 2 per cent and 5 per cent respectively.

Mining is an important sector, with bauxite as the leading mineral, followed by gold. Venezuela supplies most of Guyana's fuel needs, although Russian oil companies have been investing in exploring for oil.

The government has implemented tax reforms and a value added tax was introduced on 1 January 2007, set at 16 per cent.

Despite the government priority of promoting foreign investment and membership of the Caribbean Community (Caricom) inward investment has been slow. Social and political unrest between ethnic divisions of the country has proved a deterrent to foreign investors.

The Inter-American Development Bank estimated that in 2006 migrant workers sent some US$270 million to their families in Guyana.

External trade

Along with 11 other members of the Caribbean Community and Common Market (Caricom), Guyana operates within the single market (Caribbean Single Market and Economy (CSME)), which became operational on 1 January 2006. CSME includes the free movement of goods and services, a common trade policy and external tariff.

Despite good export earnings for sugar in 2006 (US$145 million, up from US$118 million in 2005) the long-term prospects for the industry are deteriorating as preferential European Union sugar imports are curtailed by 2010. The export value of timber and fishing have increased but the government may halt the export of raw materials in favour of some processing within the country to boost value and foreign exchange.

Imports

Fuels and lubricants (typically up to 40 per cent of total), machinery and transport equipment, consumer goods, food and chemicals.

Main sources: Trinidad and Tobago (33.6 per cent total, 2006), US (27.2 per cent), China (5.1 per cent).

Exports

Sugar (over 40 per cent of total), bauxite and alumina, shrimps, rice, rum, timber, diamonds and gold.

Main destinations: UK (20.4 per cent total, 2006), Canada (18.0 per cent), US (15.5 per cent).

Agriculture

Farming

Agriculture is a very important economic activity in Guyana. The sector employs approximately 35 per cent of the workforce and contributes a similar amount to the country's total GDP.

The sugar industry is an important export earner, responsible for around 46 per cent of total exports. Rice accounts for 12 per cent of Guyana's export earnings and 19 per cent of its agricultural contribution to GDP.

About 2 per cent of the total land area is under cultivation. Cultivation of cash crops is confined to the alluvial coastal plain.

The main cash crops are sugar, rice and shrimps. In July 2004 the European Union (EU) decision to cut the price of imported sugar, by up to 20 per cent in 2005 and 33 per cent in 2007, sparked demonstrations of the visiting EU delegation. The EU proposal would mean a cut of US$0.10 per pound and could cost Guyana over US$37 million. Ironically the changes came in a year of a bumper sugar crop, when Guyana Sugar Corporation (GuySuCo) reported that 324,940 tonnes, the second highest production in 15 years had been harvested.

Guyana is self-sufficient in sugar, rice, vegetables, fish, meat and fruit and increased government investment in the sector has improved production of many other products. Cassava is the principal crop grown in the interior.

Emphasis is also being placed on the cultivation of oil palms, soya beans and corn, and on the development of dairy farming.

There is a national herd of livestock of between 200,000–250,000 head which are ranched on the Rupununi savannah in the south-east.

The estimated crop production in 2005 included: 3,000,000 tonnes (t) sugar cane, 501,500t rice, 29,000t cassava, 45,000t coconuts, 12,200t citrus fruit, 17,000t bananas, 1,300t pulses, 40,300t roots and tubers, 6,420t oilcrops, 68,371t fruit in total, 41,800t vegetables in total. Estimated livestock production included: 26,660t meat in total, 1,750t beef, 700t pig meat, 520t lamb, 260t goat meat, 23,430t poultry, 465t eggs, 30,000t milk, 74t honey.

Fishing

The fishing industry represents a valuable source of income to the economy of Guyana. Produce is sold on both domestic and international markets and the industry employs approximately 5 per cent of the country's total workforce.

Guyana is the region's largest exporter of shrimp, which make up 14 per cent of total exports. Government initiatives in the fishing sector include the improvement of fisheries management and the encouragement of investment in unexploited marine stocks. The typical annual fish catch is over 55,000mt, of which 27,000mt is shellfish.

In January 2004, Guyana obtained certification to export fishery products to European countries.

In 2004, the total marine fish catch was 37,312 tonnes and the total crustacean catch was 18,605 tonnes.

Forestry

Guyana is one of the most densely forested countries in the world. Approximately 95 per cent of the country's total land mass is covered by forest and woodland.

All the forests are state-owned. Sawnwood and plywood are the principal forest products; pulp and paper, however, are imported.

Timber imports in 2004 were US$3.8 million, while exports amounted to US$29.3 million.

Timber production in 2004 included 1,347,302 cubic metres (cum) roundwood, 481,000cum industrial roundwood, 36,000cum sawnwood, 100,000cum pulpwood, 366,000cum sawlogs & veneer logs, 54,000cum wood-based panels, 866,302cum wood fuel, 21,718t charcoal.

Industry and manufacturing

The expansion of the industrial sector has traditionally been hampered by a lack of domestic energy supplies together with a dearth of technical and managerial personnel. At present the sector contributed roughly 10 per cent of total GDP and employs approximately 10 per cent of the total work force.

Previously, a serious shortage of foreign exchange had also caused the closure of many firms relying on imported inputs. However, the government is trying to expand the country's industrial base with a policy of diversification and greater encouragement of foreign investors to work with the predominant state sector. Guyana's manufacturing industry is dominated by the processing of raw materials. Activity related to the mining sector (predominantly bauxite, gold and diamonds) and the processing of agricultural products such as sugar, rice, coconuts and timber, together account for about three-quarters of manufacturing activity. The remainder is accounted for by small-scale import substitution production for the local market. A shortfall in investment is a recurring problem.

In December 2003, Guyana and Trinidad and Tobago concluded an agreement to import raw sugar from Guyana in 2004, to meet the additional requirements of the sugar refinery operated by the Sugar Manufacturing Company Limited (SCML).

Tourism

The tourism industry in Guyana is growing relatively quickly, but the industry's potential remains to be fully exploited. The sector is increasing in importance as an economic activity and currently contributes 9.3 per cent to GDP while accounting for 7.7 per cent of total employment.

Development is at an early stage with much work to be done to establish the necessary infrastructure and conditions. There are problems of safety and waste management. Eco-tourism is seen as the way forward. Visitor numbers declined sharply in the 1990s and did not recover until 2000. Numbers are still struggling to return to the 1994 level of 113,000 arrivals. There were 100,911 visitors in 2003 and this figure rose again to 126,200 in 2004. Most visitors are overseas Guyanese and Caribbean nationals.

Environment

In mid-January 2005 severe rains and flooding caused extensive damage to Guyana's infrastructure, killing dozens and leaving around 20,000 people temporarily homeless as they waited for flood waters to subside.

Mining

Both mining and quarrying are of great importance to Guyana's economy. Both activities combined, amount to 25 per cent of total GDP and account for approximately 12 per cent of the country's total work force.

Annual gold production averages 440,000 ounces, 70 per cent of which comes from Omai Gold Mines, a US$300 million venture. Cambior and Golden Star Resources – Canadian companies – own 65 per cent and 30 per cent of Omai, respectively, and the Guyana government owns 5 per cent. In mid-2003, residents of western Guyana began legal action against Omai for allegedly allowing a dam to collapse on the Essequibo river in 1995, pouring 2.9 million cubic metres of cyanide-tainted slurry into the river. Around 23,000 residents supporting the writ want Omai to pay US$2 billion in damages and are demanding an end to the dumping of toxic waste into the river. A similar writ was issued in 2000, but was thrown out by the courts on technical grounds.

Royalties paid to Guyana's Gold Board are linked to world gold prices. An estimated one-fifth of gold production is smuggled across the borders to Venezuela, Brazil and Suriname by local miners. There is also inefficient alluvial mining by some 10,000 miners using dredgers and suctions.

Bauxite is the country's most important mineral, typically accounting for around a quarter of total export earnings. Production slumped in the early 1980s, prompting the government to seek outside help for the management of the industry.

There are known deposits of kaolin, molybdenum, uranium, copper, semi-precious stones, talc, soapstone and high-silica sand, which the government would like to develop.

In a typical year, Guyana's gold production is estimated to be 384,000 ounces.

Hydrocarbons

After four years of contention, in 2007, a UN tribunal made a decision concerning the disputed oil-rich territory clamed by both Guyana and Suriname. The ruling declared that both countries were entitled to explore the region off the Atlantic coastline with Guyana being granted 33,152 square kilometres. An estimate of the recoverable oil is 2 billion cubic metres (15 billion barrels) and 1.19 trillion cubic metres of gas.

The disputed maritime area included an oil-rich concession granted to a Canadian company, with the agreement on both sides a surge in exploration by other oil companies is expected.

Energy

Guyana continues to be heavily dependent on imported oil from both Venezuela and Trinidad and Tobago in order to meet its energy needs. The country does have considerable potential for hydroelectric power generation however.

The International Development Association (IDA) has financed a project to evaluate Guyana's petroleum reserves, and a licence has been given to Petrel USA, to explore for offshore oil.

Guyana Electricity Corporation (GEC) is government-subsidised, and much of its financing is from the Inter-American Development Bank (IDB). A number of the GEC's existing thermal stations are being rehabilitated.

The GEC's commissioning of the US$17 million 22MW Wartsila generating plant has brought total capacity in the Demerara system up to 94MW, which is sufficient to meet peak demand.

Banking and insurance

Guyana's banking and financial services industry is concentrated in the capital Georgetown. The Central Bank of Guyana regulates the industry.

Central bank

Bank of Guyana

Main financial centre

Georgetown

Time

GMT minus four hours.

Geography

A plain about 15km wide runs along the 320km northern (Atlantic) coast and extends west into Venezuela and east into Suriname. This strip, which lies some 1.5 metres below sea level and is protected by a system of dykes, is intensively farmed and contains 90 per cent of the population. To the south of this area the land is mountainous, heavily forested and covered with a network of fast-flowing rivers with numerous rapids and falls, including the Kaietur Falls on the Potaro River which is seven times higher than Niagara. There are substantial reserves of bauxite, gold and diamonds in this area. To the south-west along the border with Venezuela is a region of upland savannah, the Rupununi, where the rest of the population, predominantly Amerindian, engages in limited agriculture and cattle-raising.

Hemisphere

Northern.

Climate

The climate is tropical, with a mean monthly temperature of 26–28 degrees Celsius (C) throughout the year on the coast (28 degrees C in the interior). Temperatures of above 32 degrees C or below 24 degrees C at any time of day or any season are rare. Rainfall is between 200–280mm per year on the coast, mainly in two sharply defined wet seasons, May to August and November to January. In the south there is a single rainy season from April to September, but rainfall is lower – averaging 150mm per year.

Dress codes

Among local businessmen the shirtjac suit – based upon a civilian version of the bush jacket – is widely worn in preference to the traditional business suit. It is perfectly acceptable to wear an open-necked shirt without a jacket on all but the most formal of occasions, but shorts are frowned upon.

Entry requirements
Passports
Required by all and valid for at least six months beyond intended stay.
Visa
Visas are required by all, except nationals of North America, Western Europe, Australasia, some Asian and all Caricom countries. For full details see: www.guyana.org/govt/visa_requirements.html.
Currency advice/regulations
The import and export of local currency is limited to G$200. The import of foreign currency is unlimited, subject to declaration on arrival; export is limited to amount declared.

Health (for visitors)
Mandatory precautions
A yellow fever vaccination certificate is required if arriving from an infected area.
Advisable precautions
Vaccination against yellow fever is encouraged for travellers to rural areas.
There is a risk of malaria in some areas of the interior, and adequate precautions should be taken. Water in urban areas is chlorinated, but typhoid is a risk in rural areas so drinking water should be boiled; bottled water is widely available. Dairy products are likely to be made from unpasteurised milk.
Various hepatitis strains are common. B and D stains are endemic in the Amazon basin and precautions are necessary. Tropical parasites, TB, and dengue fever all occur in certain areas. Professional advice concerning precautions should be sort before travelling to Guyana.
Hospital conditions may not match those in developed countries; health insurance, including repatriation is recommended.
Travellers should carry enough prescription and medical supplies for the duration of their stay.

Hotels
Hotels are available in Georgetown, Linden and New Amsterdam. Rooms are generally in short supply. A 10 per cent tip is usual.

Public holidays (national)
Fixed dates
1 Jan (New Year's Day), 23 Feb (Republic Day), 1 May (Labour Day), 5 May (Arrival Day), 26 May (Independence Day), 25–26 Dec (Christmas).
When a public holiday falls on a Sunday, the following Monday is taken as the holiday.
Variable dates
Holi (Hindu, Mar), Good Friday, Easter Monday, Caricom Day (first Mon in Jul), Liberty Day (first Mon in Aug), Diwali (Hindu, Oct/Nov), Eid al Adha, Birth of the Prophet.
Hindu and Muslim festivals are timed according to local sightings of various phases of the moon.

Working hours
Banking
Mon–Thu: 0800–1230; Fri: 0800–1230, 1500–1700.
Business
Mon–Thu: 0800–1600; Fri: 0800–1200.
Government
Mon–Thu: 0800–1200, 1300–1630; Fri: 0800–1200, 1300–1530.
Shops
Mon–Fri: 0800–1130, 1300–1600; Sat: 0800–1130.

Electricity supply
Electricity supply is not standardised; Georgetown generally 110V AC 60Hz, but some supplies are 220V AC, 50Hz. Elsewhere supply is 110V AC at either 50 or 60 cycles.

Weights and measures
The metric system is official, but imperial measures are often preferred.

Social customs/useful tips
Business is often conducted in a relaxed atmosphere and an emphasis is placed upon personal contact. At the same time, careful observance of polite formalities such as handshaking and formal use of titles (such as Mr, etc) is appreciated. All officials should be treated with careful respect. Attention to detail in the making and keeping of appointments is also appreciated, although punctuality may not be reciprocated.
Invitations to the homes of business contacts are regularly offered since Guyanese pride themselves upon their hospitality. It is customary for visitors to return the invitation in a hotel or to a restaurant.
Hotel and restaurant staff and taxi drivers customarily receive a 10 per cent tip; airport porters are tipped by the bag.

Security
The streets of Georgetown can be unsafe after dark due to street robbery, and the use of taxis is recommended. Ostentatious display of wealth such as expensive wristwatches or jewellery and the carrying of large amounts of cash should be avoided. As in all cities, it is unwise to leave articles unattended in parked cars or hotel rooms.

Getting there
Air
International airport/s: Cheddi Jagan International Airport (GEO), 40km from Georgetown; bank, duty free, restaraunts and car hire.
Airport tax: G$4,000 for international departures; not applicable to transit passengers.
Surface
Road: A coastal road runs from the Suriname border to Georgetown, via a ferry across the Berbice River at New Amsterdam.
Entry from Brazil is possible at Lethem where international border controls are in place. A bridge being constructed across the Takutu river will eventually connect Bonfim in Roraima State (Brazil) to Lethem. There are unsealed roads in current use. There are no road connections to Venezuela.
Water: There is a ferry service between Guyana-Suriname.
Main port/s: Georgetown, New Amsterdam and Springlands.

Getting about
National transport
Air: Air travel is the only efficient method of reaching the interior of the country. Trans Guyana Airways operates both regional and interior flights, but occasionally permits are needed from the ministry of the interior for non-nationals. Early booking is essential.
Charter facilities are available at Georgetown. Larger towns and mining companies have airports or landing strips.
Road: There are all-weather, asphalt roads along the coast and some brick roads inland. A coastal road links Georgetown, Rossignol, New Amsterdam and the Suriname border. Another coast road runs west from Georgetown, via the Demerara River, to Parika. A sealed highway to the Brazilian border via Lethem is in the initial stage of construction; only unsealed roads exist currently.
Buses: Buses are operated privately and run regularly and are generally reliable (although crowded). Services run along the coast. Private tapir minibuses, mine buses and bush buses (into the interior) are also available.
Rail: There is no passenger rail service, although some mining companies have private goods lines.
Water: Passenger and cargo vessels travel up the Demerara, Essequibo and Berbice rivers, and also along the coast between the rivers. Ferries link Parika-Bartica on the Essequibo River; Rosignol-New Amsterdam on the Berbice River; Corriverton-Suriname on the Corentyne River. These services include New Amsterdam-Ituni, Georgetown-Bartica, Rosignol-New Amsterdam. River taxis (small wooden boats) service the same areas as the ferries. The taxis are faster and more expensive, they may also be chartered.
City transport
Taxis: Taxis are widely available in major towns and can be found on ranks. They have standard fares for inner city journeys;

fares for longer trips should be negotiated in advance. A 10 per cent tip is usual. For early morning flights from Timehri, make taxi arrangements the previous day.

Buses, trams & metro: Minibuses are a cheap mode of transport. They connect Timehri airport with Georgetown and are safe in the day. At night it is wiser to use a taxi.

Car hire

Car hire facilities are limited. They are available in Georgetown but must be booked well in advance. An international driving licence is required. Traffic drives on the left.

BUSINESS DIRECTORY

The addresses listed below are a selection only. While World of Information makes every endeavour to check these addresses, we cannot guarantee that changes have not been made, especially to telephone numbers and area codes. We would welcome any corrections.

Telephone area codes

The international dialling code (IDD) for Guyana is +592, followed by subscriber's number:

Chambers of Commerce

Berbice Chamber of Commerce, 12 Chapel Street, New Amsterdam, Berbice (tel: 227-6340; fax: 226-4535).

Georgetown Chamber of Commerce and Industry, PO Box 10110, 156 Waterloo Street, North Cummingsburg, Georgetown (tel: 225-5864; fax: 226-3519; e-mail: info@georgetownchamberofcommerce.org)

Banking

Bank of Baroda, Avenue of the Republic & Regent Street, Georgetown (tel: 226-4005).

Bank of Nova Scotia, Regent & Hinck Streets, Georgetown (tel: 640-312; fax: 225-7985).

Citizens Bank Guyana Ltd, 201 Camp & Charlotte Sts, Georgetown (tel: 226-1705/6; fax: 226-1719).

Demerara Bank Ltd, 230 Camp St & South Rd, Georgetown (tel: 225-0610/9; fax 225-0601).

Guyana Bank for Trade & Industry, 47-48 Water Street, Georgetown (tel: 226-8430/9; fax: 227-1612).

Guyana Co-operative Agricultural & Industrial Development Bank, 126 Barrack & Parade Streets, Kingston, Georgetown (tel: 225-8806/9; fax: 226-8260).

Guyana National Co-operative Bank, Lombard & Cornhill Streets, Georgetown (tel: 225-7810/9).

National Bank of Industry & Commerce, 38-40 Water Street, Georgetown (tel: 226-4091/5; fax: 227-2921).

Central bank

Bank of Guyana, 1 Church Street & Avenue of the Republic, PO Box 1003, Georgetown (tel: 226-3250; fax: 227-2965; e-mail: comminications@bankofguyana.org.gy).

Travel information

Air Services Ltd, Wights Lane, Kingston, Georgetown (tel: 226-1767, 226-5759).

Guyana Overland Tours, PO Box 10173, 6 Avenue of the Republic, Robbstown, Georgetown (tel: 226-9876).

Roraima Airways, 101 Cummings Street, Georgetown (tel: 225-9647; fax: 225-9646).

Tourism Association of Guyana, 228 South Road, Lacytown, Georgetown (tel: 225-0807; fax: 225-0817).

Ministry of tourism

Ministry of Tourism, Industry and Commerce, 229 South Road, Lacytown, Georgetown (tel: 226-8629; fax: 225-9898; e-mail: ministry@mintic.gov.gy).

National tourist organisation offices

Guyana Tourism Office, Sophia Exhibition Complex, Georgetown (tel: 223-6351 fax: 231-6351).

Ministries

Ministry of Agriculture, Regent Road, Bourda, Georgetown (tel: 223-7844; fax: 225-0599; e-mail: moa@sdnp.org.gov.gy).

Ministry of Amerindian Affairs, 236 Thomas and Quamina Streets, Georgetown (tel: 227-5067; fax: 223-1616; e-mail: moaa@networksgy.com).

Ministry of Culture, Youth and Sports, 71 Main Street, Georgetown (tel: 227-7866; fax: 226-8549; e-mail: psmincys@guyana.net.gy).

Ministry of Education, 26 Brickdam, Stabroek, Georgetown (tel: 223-7900; fax: 225-8511; e-mail: moegyweb@yahoo.com).

Ministry of Finance, Main Street, Kingston, Georgetown (tel: 225-6088; fax: 226-1284; e-mail: guyanadmd@solutions2000.net).

Ministry of Fisheries, Crops & Livestock, Regent Road, Bourda, Georgetown (tel: 226-1565; fax: 227-2978; e-mail: minfci@sdnp.org.gy).

Ministry of Foreign Affairs, 254 South Road & New Garden Street, Georgetown (tel: 226-9080; fax: 223-5241; e-mail: minfor@sdnp.org.gy).

Ministry of Foreign Trade, 254 South Road & New Garden Street, Georgetown (tel: 226-1607; fax: 223-0900; e-mail: moftic@moftic.gov.gy).

Ministry of Health and Labour, Brickdam, Stabroek, Georgetown (tel: 226-1560; fax: 225-4505; e-mail: moh@sdnp.org.gy).

Ministry of Home Affairs, Brickdam, Stabroek, Georgetown (tel: 225-7270; fax: 227-4806).

Ministry of Housing and Water, 41 Brickdam, Stabroek, Georgetown (tel: 225-7192; fax: 227-3455; e-mail: housing@guyana.net.gy).

Ministry of Information, Area B Homestretch Avenue, Georgetown (tel: 226-8996; fax: 226-4003; e-mail: gis@sdnp.org.gy).

Ministry of Labour, Human Services and Social Security, 1 Water and Cornhill Streets, Stabroek, Georgetown (tel: 225-0655; fax: 227-1308; e-mail: nrdocgd@sdnp.org.gy).

Ministry of Legal Affairs, 95 Carmichael Street, Georgetown (tel: 223-7355; fax: 227-5419).

Ministry of Local Government and Regional Development, Fort Street, Kingston, Georgetown (tel: 225-8621; fax: 226-5070).

Ministry of Parliamentary Affairs, Office of the President, New Garden Street, Georgetown (tel: 226-6453).

Ministry of Public Service Management, 164 Waterloo Street, Georgetown (tel 227-1193; fax: 227-2700; e-mail: psm@sdnp.org.gy).

Ministry of Transport and Hydraulics, Wights Lane, Kingston, Georgetown (tel: 226-1875; fax: 225-8395; e-mail: minoth@networksgy.com).

Office of the President, New Garden Street, Bourda, Georgetown (tel: 225-1573; 227-3050; e-mail: op-iu@sdnp.org.gy).

Office of the Prime Minister, Wights Lane, Kingston, Georgetown (tel: 226-6695; fax: 226-7573; pmoffice@sdnp.org.gov.gy).

Other useful addresses

Association of Non-Traditional Exporters of Guyana (ANTEG), (tel: 226-0779; fax: 226-1063),

Bauxite Industry Development Co, 71 Main Street, Georgetown (tel: 225-7780; fax: 226-7413).

British High Commission, 44 Main Street, PO Box 10849, Georgetown (tel: 226-5881; fax: 225-0671; e-mail: bhcguyana@networksgy.com).

Caribbean Community Secretariat, PO Box 10827, Turkeyen, Georgetown (tel: 222-0001; fax: 222-0171; e-mail: info@caricom.org).

Consultative Association of Guyanese Industry, East Street, PO Box 10730, Georgetown.

Forest Products Association of Guyana (tel: 226-9848).

Forestry Commission, 1 Water Street, Georgetown (tel: 226-7271; fax: 226-8956; e-mail: forstry@sdnp.org.gy).

Geology and Mines Commission, PO Box 1028, Brickdam, Georgetown (tel: 225-3047; fax: 225-2274; e-mail: ggmc@sdnp.org.gy).

Guyana Broadcasting Corporation, PO Box 10760, Georgetown (tel: 226-9231).

Guyana Embassy (USA), 2490 Tracy Place, NW, Washington DC 20008 (tel: (+1-202) 265-6900; fax: (+1-202) 232-1297; e-mail: guyanaemb@aol.com).

Guyana Export Promotion Council, Sophia National Exhibition Park, Sophia, Georgetown (tel: 225-9443, 227-3394, 226-8526; fax: 226-3400).

Guyana Manufacturers' Association (GMA), 62 Main Street, Georgetown (tel: 227-4295; fax: 227-0670).

Guyana Mining Enterprise Ltd, Linden, Georgetown.

Guyana Office for Investment, Go-Invest, 190 Camp & Church Streets, Georgetown (tel: 225-0658, 227-0653; fax: 225-0655).

Guyana Rice Producers' Association (tel: 226-4411, 227-6957).

Guyana Rice Board, 1-2 Water Street, Georgetown (tel: 226-6822).

Guyana State Corporation, 45-47 Water Street, Georgetown (tel: 226-0530).

Guyana Sugar Corporation, 201 Camp Street, Cummingsburg, PO Box 10547, Georgetown (tel: 226-0571; fax: 225-7274).

Institute of Private Enterprise Development, (IPED), Georgetown (tel: 225-8949, 225-3067, 226-4765).

New Guyana Marketing Corporation, Robb Street, Georgetown.

Omai Gold Mines Limited, 176-D Middle Street, Cummingsburg, Georgetown (tel: 226-8129, 226-5898; fax: 226-6468).

Private Sector Commission (PSC), Georgetown (tel: 225-7170, 64-603; fax: 227-0725).

Public Corporations Secretariat, PO Box 1020, 45-7 Water Street, Georgetown (tel: 226-0536/9).

Shipping Association of Georgetown, 28 Main and Holmes Streets, Georgetown (tel: 226-2632).

United States Embassy, 31 Main Street, Georgetown (tel: 225-4900; fax: 225-8497).

National news agency: GINA (Government Information Agency)

Other news agencies: Caribbean Net News: www.caribbeannetnews.com

Guyana Journal: www.guyanajournal.com

Internet sites

Berbice online newspaper: http://www.berbicenews.com

Guyana News and Information: http://www.guyana.org/

Economic Commission for Latin America and the Caribbean: http://www.eclac.cl/index1.html

Inter-American Development Bank: http://www.iadb.org

Organisation of American States: http://www.oas.org

Latin World: http://www.latinworld.com

Latin Trade Online://www.latintrade.com

Local web directory: http://sdnp.org.gy/guylink.html

Haiti

KEY FACTS

Official name: République d'Haiti (Republic of Haiti)

Head of State: President René Préval (since 14 May 2006)

Head of government: Prime Minister Michèle Pierre-Louis (from 31 Jul 2008)

Ruling party: Coalition led by Fwon Lespwa (Front for Hope) (formed 6 June 2006)

Area: 27,750 square km

Population: 8.63 million (2007)*

Capital: Port-au-Prince

Official language: French and Creole

Currency: Gourde (G) = 100 centimes

Exchange rate: G38.85 per US$ (Jul 2008)

GDP per capita: US$630 (2007)*

GDP real growth: 3.20% (2007)*

Labour force: 3.77 million (2004)

Inflation: 9.00% (2007)*

Balance of trade: -US$945.00 million (2006)

Foreign debt: US$1.20 billion (2004)

* estimated figure

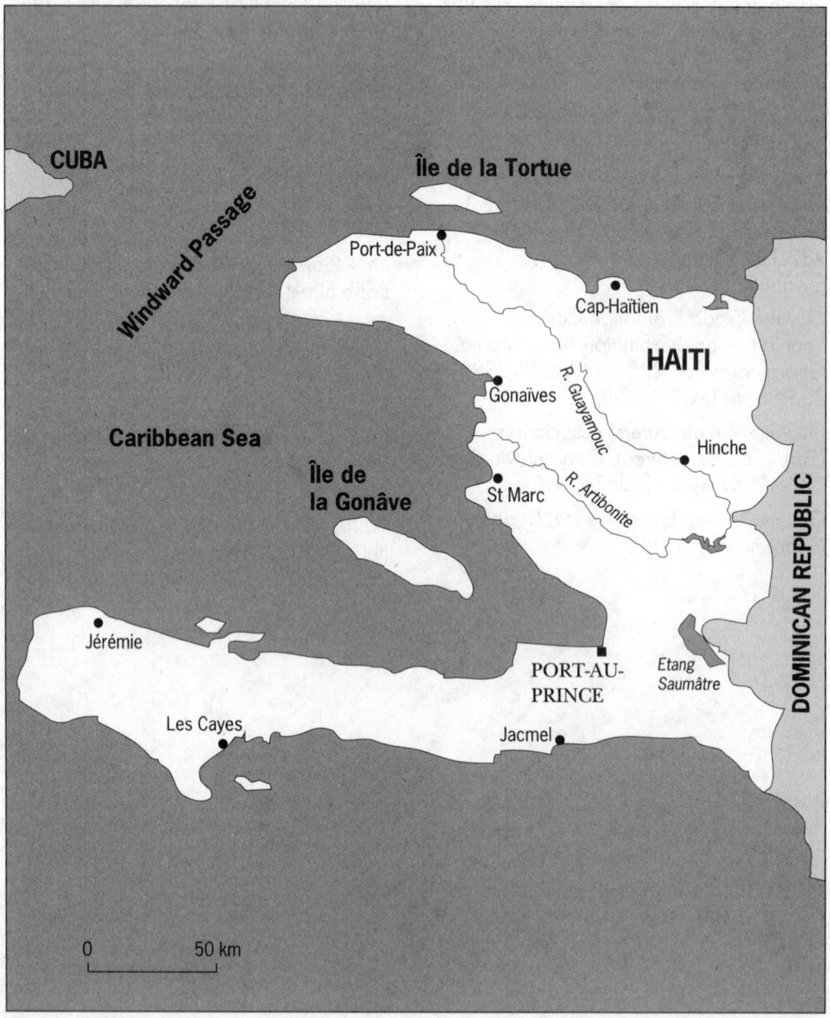

The one-year extension of the mandate of the United Nations Mission in Haiti, and the ratification of commitments undertaken by bilateral and multilateral donors, are encouraging signs of a consolidation of efforts to provide co-operation to Haiti. In 2007 the Haitian economy recorded positive GDP growth of 3.3 per cent for the third year running. However, several economic sectors turned in less than brilliant performances, suggesting that the economic recovery has not fully taken hold. Local supply remains limited, partly due to shortcomings in infrastructure (particularly in terms of energy) that may become systematic bottlenecks blocking a sustained economic recovery. GDP growth of 4 per cent is projected for 2008, and the International Monetary Fund (IMF) estimates that growth could rise to 4.0 per cent or more, assuming stronger budget execution, continued improvement in security conditions, increased private investment, and growth benefits from improved US market access (especially textiles) under the Haitian Hemispheric Opportunities through Partnership (HOPE) Act. But the Bank acknowledges that even at this rate it will take many years for Haiti to catch up the ground lost in previous years, amid political instability and poor governance.

Haiti's economy has contracted, in per capita terms, in three of the last four decades. Real per-capita GDP fell by an average of 1 per cent per year from 1961 to 2000, resulting in an overall decline of 45 percent over the period.

No longer a basket case

In November 2007 the Haitian government completed a comprehensive strategy paper that sets out the main development challenges facing Haiti and the government's strategic priorities for addressing them. The Document de Stratégie Nationale pour la Croissance et la Réduction de la Pauvreté (DSNCRP) (National Strategy for Growth and Poverty Reduction Document), was developed through a broad consultative process under the guidance of the ministry of planning and external co-operation. The DSNCRP outlines three strategic pillars for action. These are:

- enhancing human development, with a focus on improving delivery of basic services
- strengthening democratic governance, particularly by improving security and the justice system
- promoting four specific vectors of growth

The vectors of growth identified by the strategy are agriculture and rural development, tourism, infrastructure, and science and technology. The DSNCRP also emphasises the importance of a stable macroeconomic framework and sound management of public resources, which depend on good governance and transparency.

Encouragingly, the 2006/07 fiscal year, which was the first full budget cycle managed by the government authorities that took office in May 2006, was positive in terms of the main macroeconomic indicators. Inflation was lower than in the year earlier period, while the fiscal deficit (1.6 per cent of GDP) was covered without recourse to the central bank. The balance-of-payments current account also posted a surplus and the levels of net international reserves would cover over three months of imports for the first time in 10 years. The authorities also finalised Haiti's Poverty Reduction and Growth Strategy Paper, although this had to be approved by the executive branch and parliament, and is pending validation by the IMF and the World Bank.

Expectations for 2008 will inevitably be affected not only by those factors but also by other political changes. The need for constitutional reform (repeatedly called for by President René Préval) and the presumable renewal of members of the Electoral Council in the run up to the senatorial by-elections are the main issues in a dispute that could weaken the country's political stability if a consensus is not reached

In the 2006/07 fiscal year, there was a considerable delay in budget implementation throughout the period. The largest items of expenditures (37 per cent of total spending) were paid out in the last few months (especially in September).

The results of economic policy were in keeping with the guidelines laid down in the Poverty Reduction and Growth Facility (PRGF) agreed with the IMF. The fiscal situation significantly improved in real terms, both in revenue (6.7 per cent) and expenditure (23.3 per cent). This generated a deficit of 1.6 per cent of GDP, following the virtually balanced result of the previous year. The current surplus (0.6 per cent of GDP) was the result of the favourable performance of indirect taxes (8 per cent). Stricter control of tax evasion, fraud and corruption also had a positive effect. Apart from September, when the central bank had to intervene by selling US$10 million of currency, the gourde continued to appreciate in nominal and real terms thanks to inflows of foreign exchange in the form both of remittances and external co-operation, and contained import demand.

Capital expenditure booms

The positive GDP result (3.3 per cent) was attributable to the performance of agriculture, construction (4.5 per cent) and trade services (19.4 per cent). Agriculture fared well thanks to favourable weather conditions, while construction was supported by investments in public works and trade benefited from the upturn in consumption resulting from remittances and small but segmented increases in employment. As for investment, higher capital expenditure in the public sector (up by 202 per cent in real terms) had an extremely positive effect on the overall indicator. October-to-October inflation (8.1 per cent) was considerably lower than the 10.3 per cent recorded at the end of the previous year, partly thanks to greater control by the authorities but mainly due to the effects of currency appreciation. This is demonstrated by the fact that the price of the basket of local goods rose by 8.4 per cent, while the basket of imported goods increased by just 2.7 per cent. This result cushioned the fall in real wages (with the increase of 8.2 per cent lower than that of the 12.5 per cent recorded in 2006). Despite this, job creation is still lagging.

The US$99 million surplus on the balance-of-payments current account was due to net transfers (particularly remittances) totalling US$1.1 billion and a US$74 million reduction in the trade deficit. There was a net decrease in imports, both in terms of value (-8 per cent) and volumes (-13 per cent). The rise in import prices combined with a slight fall in export prices to bring down the terms of trade (-6.2 per cent). The capital flight trend in banking services changed direction to post US$11 million in net inflows, while official funds saw a rise in outlays (up from US$99 million to US$146 million) in the form of loans, and an increase in debt servicing (from US$57 million to US$75 million).

KEY INDICATORS — Haiti

	Unit	2003	2004	2005	2006	2007
Population	m	8.38	8.67	8.33	8.48	*8.63
Gross domestic product (GDP)	US$bn	2.70	3.54	3.98	4.66	*5.43
GDP per capita	US$	440	419	478	550	*630
GDP real growth	%	0.7	-3.5	0.4	2.3	*3.2
Inflation	%	32.3	27.1	15.8	14.2	*9.0
Exports (fob) (goods)	US$m	298.0	338.1	381.0	384.0	–
Imports (cif) (goods)	US$m	1,140.0	1,085.0	1,302.0	1,329.0	–
Balance of trade	US$m	-842.0	-746.9	-921.0	-945.0	–
Current account	US$m	-33.0	-15.6	-27.0	-19.0	*11.0
Total reserves minus gold	US$m	62.0	114.4	133.1	253.1	443.2
Foreign exchange	US$m	61.6	114.4	120.7	245.1	435.6
Exchange rate	per US$	38.00	38.88	37.65	37.65	36.75

* estimated figure

Meanwhile, net international reserves (US$290 million) were more than twice the level recorded in 2006.

Risk assessment

Politics	Fair
Economy	Fair
Regional stability	Good

COUNTRY PROFILE

Historical profile

1492 Christopher Columbus landed and named the island Hispaniola, or 'little Spain'.
1496 The Spanish established the first European settlement in the western hemisphere at Santo Domingo, now the capital of the Dominican Republic.
1697 The island of Hispaniola was divided between France and Spain. The western half became Haiti.
1801 A former black slave, Toussaint Louverture, led a guerrilla rebellion, conquering Haiti, abolishing slavery and proclaiming himself governor general of all Hispaniola. He was captured by the French and died in their custody.
1804 Independence was declared by former slave Jean-Jacques Dessalines, who declared himself emperor. There were various monarchical periods until 1859.
1806 Dessalines was assassinated and Haiti became divided into the black-controlled north and the mulatto-controlled south.
1818–43 Pierre Boyer unified Haiti, but excluded blacks from power.
1915 The US invaded Haiti claiming it was protecting its property and investments threatened by clashes between blacks and mulattos.
1934 The US withdrew its troops.
1956 François 'Papa Doc' Duvalier, a voodoo physician, seized power in a military coup and became president in the following year.
1964 Duvalier declared himself president-for-life and established a dictatorship with the help of the violent Tontons Macoute militias.
1971 Duvalier died and was succeeded by his son, the 19-year-old Jean-Claude 'Baby Doc' Duvalier, who declared himself president-for-life.
1986 Baby Doc fled Haiti amid riots and a multitude of coup attempts. Lieutenant General Henri Namphy assumed power as the head of a governing junta.
1988 Leslie Manigat became president but was overthrown in a coup led by Brigadier General Prosper Avril, who installed a civilian government under military control.
1990 Jean-Bertrand Aristide was elected president.
1991 Aristide was expelled from the country following a military coup. The new junta promised elections at a future date. The US, France and Canada suspended aid to Haiti and refused to recognise the new government.
1993 The UN imposed sanctions on Haiti after the military regime rejected an accord designed to facilitate Aristide's return to power.
1994 After US forces removed the military government of General Raoul Cedras, Aristide returned from exile and was reinstalled as president. He was not permitted by law to stand for re-election in 1995.
1995 René Preval was elected to replace Aristide.
1997 US troops left Haiti. Prime Minister Rosny Smarth resigned.
1999 President Préval dissolved the legislature and a Provisional Electoral Council (CEP) was created to organise elections; Jacques Eduard Aléxis was appointed prime minister and a government was sworn in.
2000 The Fanmi Lavalas (FL) (Lavalas Family) party won control of the Senate and President Jean-Bertrand Aristide won the controversial presidential election.
2001 President Jean-Bertrand Aristide was sworn in; he appointed Jean-Marie Chéréstal as prime minister. Aristide agreed to hold new parliamentary elections in return for the OAS helping Haiti to obtain US$500 million of suspended aid. There was an unsuccessful coup attempt.
2002 Prime Minister Chéréstal resigned amid allegations of corruption and incompetence. Aristide appointed Yvon Neptune as prime minister. In November, there were violent clashes between government and opposition factions, attacks by government loyalists on civic groups and armed anti-government gangs. Opposition groups and US officials said the elections due by the end of the year should not proceed since security has worsened.
2004 The escalating violent protests in Haiti stemmed from disputed elections in 2000, which the opposition says were rigged. The opposition rebels, led by Guy Philippe, gained control of several towns, and on 29 February, President Jean-Bertrand Aristide resigned and left the country; Chief Justice Boniface Alexandre was sworn in as caretaker president. The UN approved a multi-national security force to restore law and order. On 9 March, Gérard Latortue was named as prime minister and on 17 March, a government of national unity was sworn in. Hurricane Mitch struck in May devastating large areas of Haiti and leaving a death toll of around 2,000. A UN force assumed Haiti peacekeeping duties in June. In August, the US made available US$9 million to Haiti to assist in election preparations for 2005; an agreement was signed between Haiti, the UN and the Organisation of American States (OAS) for the organisation of the elections. In September, Hurricane Jeanne swept through Haiti, killing as many as 1,500 Haitians.
2005 UN peacekeepers cracked down on violence between supporters and opponents of ousted president Jean-Bertrand Aristide. Presidential and legislative elections, scheduled to be held in November, were postponed to the following month and then to January 2006.
2006 General Urano Teixeira Da Matta Bacellar, head of the UN peacekeeping force, was found dead in his hotel room on 8 January. Presidential and legislative elections finally took place on 7 February. Former president René Préval won the presidential election with 51.2 per cent of the vote; he was sworn in on 14 May. Fwon Lespwa (Lespwa) (Front de l'Espoir) won the largest share of votes in both rounds of parliamentary elections in the Senate and the Chamber of Deputies. Jacques-Edouard Alexis became prime minister on 17 May and formed a six-party coalition cabinet under Lespwa leadership in June.
2008 Prime Minister Jacques-Édouard Alexis lost support in the Senate on 12 April, following widespread rioting over soaring food prices and the perceived lack of government action to increase national food production. The Senate unanimously voted for Alexis' dismissal and unanimously ratified the nomination of Ericq Pierre as prime minister. However, on 13 May the chamber of deputies rejected Pierre, prolonging the time the country was without a government. On the 7 May the Senate ratified (17-0) the nomination of Ericq Pierre as prime minister. On May 12, however, he was rejected (51-35) by the Chamber of Deputies. On May 25 President Préval nominated Robert Manuel as his new candidate for the position but he was judged unacceptable; finally Michèle Pierre-Louis was proposed. She was finally chosen by both houses of parliament on 31 July; she is also only the second female to be given the premiership.

Political structure

Constitution

Under the 1987 constitution, executive power is held by an elected president, serving a five-year term, and a cabinet of ministers.

Form of state

Republic

The executive

The president is elected for a five-year term by universal suffage. A president may be elected for a maximum of two, non-continuous terms. The prime minister is appointed by the president whose decision is ratified by the senate.

National legislature

The bicameral National Assembly consists of an 83-member House of Representatives, elected every four years in single-seat constituencies, and a 27-member Senate, elected for six years (one-third renewed every two years) in single-seat constituencies.

Legal system

Haiti's judicial system is based on the French Napoleonic Code. Judges are appointed by the president. The supreme court is the Court de Cassation, which may make rulings on constitutional matters. There is a court of appeal and civil courts in the major administrative centres.

Last elections

7 February 2006 (presidential); 7 February/21 April 2006 (parliamentary).

Results: Presidential: René Préval (Lespwa) won 51.21 per cent of the vote; Leslie Manigat (RDNP) won 12.4 per cent and Charles Henry Baker (Respect) 8.2 per cent

Parliamentary: In the Senate, Fwon Lespwa (Lespwa) (Front de l'Espoir) (Front for Hope) won 13 out of 30 seats. In the Chamber of Deputies, Lespwa won 23 out of 99 seats; Fusion des Sociaux-Democrates Haitienne (Fusion of Haitian Social Democrats) won 17 seats; Union Nationale Chrétienne pour la Reconstruction d'Haiti (Christian National Union for the Reconstruction of Haiti) 12 seats; Alliance Démocratique (Alyans) (Democratic Alliance) 10 seats; Oganizasyon Pèp Kap Lité (Struggling People's Organization) 10 seats.

Next elections

2010 (parliamentary); 2011 (presidential)

Political parties

Ruling party

Coalition led by Fwon Lespwa (Front for Hope) (formed 6 June 2006)

Main opposition party

Population

8.63 million (2007)*

Last census: January 2003: 8,373,750

Population density: 283 inhabitants per square km. Urban population: 36 per cent (1994–2000).

Annual growth rate: 1.4 per cent 1994–2004 (WHO 2006)

Ethnic make-up

Approximately 95 per cent are Afro-Caribbean; the remainder are white or of mixed race.

Religions

Roman Catholic (80 per cent), Protestant (16 per cent). Around half the population also practices voodoo, an African-derived belief.

Education

Only 20 per cent of the population complete primary schooling which is theoretically compulsory and the pass rate for secondary school exams is 7–8 per cent. Secondary education is provided by the state and lycées (private secondary schools). There are also vocational training and domestic science establishments. There is a state-run university and an administration and management institute (which offers courses in medical subjects, agricultural and veterinary sciences, law, economics and ethnology) and an Institute of Administration and Management.

Literacy rate: 52 per cent adult rate; 66 per cent youth rate (15–24) (Unesco 2005).

Compulsory years: 6 to 15.

Enrolment rate: 64 per cent total primary school enrolment of the relevant age group (including repetition rates) (World Bank).

Pupils per teacher: 35 in primary schools.

Health

Per capita total expenditure on health (2003) was US$84; of which per capita government spending was US$32, at the international dollar rate, (WHO 2006).

According to the UN's food aid agency, in April 2006, over 50 per cent of women suffer from anaemia, most of which is often caused by insufficient iron in their generally poor diet, plus worm infestation and malaria. The percentage of pregnant women suffering from anaemia is even higher at two out of three and is the leading cause of spontaneous miscarriage and infant mortality during delivery.

The vaccination coverage for children has been irregular and accounts for only 25 per cent. There have been nationwide campaigns to inoculate children under the age of 10 years; 53 per cent of all children had been vaccinated in 2002.

Improved water sources and sanitation facilities are available to 46 per cent and 28 per cent of the population, respectively.

Medical provision is good for those who can afford it.

HIV/Aids

HIV/Aids has become a leading cause of death, and urban infection rates are over twice the number of rural population infection rates.

For the first time, in June 2004, a joint mission was undertaken by the UN and UNAids, who have sent teams into the field with peacekeepers, in an attempt to limit HIV in a conflict zone. This initiative is designed to pre-empt the spread of the desease before the main contingent of peacekeepers arrive. There are fears that as 1 in 20 Haitians are HIV positive and with the arrival of a peacekeeping force with an almost inevitable sex-industry that will develop, Haiti could become a flashpoint of transmission. UNAids provides condoms, education and testing services to the peacekeepers.

HIV prevalence: 5.6 per cent aged 15–49 in 2003 (World Bank).

Life expectancy: 55 years, 2004 (WHO 2006)

Fertility rate/Maternal mortality rate: 3.9 births per woman, 2004 (WHO 2006)

Birth rate/Death rate: 34 births per 1,000 population; 13.4 deaths per 1,000 population (2003).

Child (under 5 years) mortality rate (per 1,000): 76 per 1,000 live births (World Bank)

Welfare

Since 80 per cent of Haiti's population live below the poverty line and its social and economic indicators remain far lower than the average for Latin America and the Caribbean, the country is not eligible for the IMF's Heavily Indebted Poor Countries (HIPC) debt relief initiative.

In the public sector, still only 20 per cent of resources go to rural areas, where approximately two-thirds of the people live.

Poor welfare provision is one factor which causes migration both from the countryside to the capital and out of the country. As many as 330,000 Haitians are thought to be living in the US.

Incidences of crime and violence are very high in Haiti. The strengthening of the Haitian police force with improvements in the penal system is likely to improve the situation. The government will need to spread the cost of maintaining social welfare services including those on education, health, water, sanitation and family planning with private sectors.

Main cities

Port-au-Prince (capital, estimated population 1.2 million in 2005), Carrefour (438,057), Delmas (375,218), Cap Haïtien (134,163), Pétionville (106,369).

Languages spoken

Official language/s

French and Creole

Media

Freedom of the press was a casualty of political instability, nevertheless, as the situation improved self-censorship has remained as journalists avoided reporting on politicians and commercial sponsors.

National news agency: Agence Haitienne de Presse

Press

Dailies: In French, private newspapers include Le Nouvelliste (www.lenouvelliste.com) and Le Matin (www.lematinhaiti.com).

Weeklies: In French, Haiti Progrès (www.haiti-progres.com) has online editions in English and Creole.
Business: In French, Haiti en Marche (www.haitienmarche.com) is a weekly newspaper.

Broadcasting
The Conseil National des Télécommunications (www.conatel.gouv.ht) is responsible for broadcasting regulations. The national, public broadcaster is Radio Télévision Nationale d'Haiti (RTNH).
Radio: With a low literacy rate radio is the principal medium for news and information. There are over 250 radio stations in operation in both private and public service. The government-owned Radio Nationale d'Haiti (www.radionationalehaiti.net) broadcasts in French. Private, independent radio stations include Radyo Atlantik (www.atlantikhaiti.com), Radio Metropole Haiti (www.metropolehaiti.com) and Signal FM (www.signalfmhaiti.com).
Television: Télévision Nationale D'Haiti (www.tnh.ht) has a tie-in with the pay-to-view Jump-TV, the international TV cable and satellite service. Private, commercial TV stations include Télé-Haiti (www.telehaitionline.com), which is a cable station relaying captured satellite signals on four channels, Tele Quisqueya Saint-Marc (TQ) (www.haitipal.com/tq) and PVS Antenne.

Economy
Haiti is the poorest country in the western hemisphere. Three-quarters of the population live below the poverty line, with more than half subsisting on less than US$1 a day. Unemployment is high at around 65 per cent, illiteracy is estimated at around 50 per cent, epidemics and malnutrition are widespread and population growth is running at 2 per cent per year. Haiti's public sector is in disarray and the country's infrastructure network is badly fragmented and in need of significant investment.
The key to Haiti's future economic development lies in the government's ability, under President Préval, who was sworn in in May 2006, to implement the structural changes necessary to satisfy the international community's conditions for releasing millions of US dollars in aid. Political infighting and uncertainty have delayed the implementation of important structural reforms.
The elections in 2005 led to a climate of uncertainty and instability. GDP was 1.5 per cent and inflation 16.8 per cent. Nevertheless, the agriculture sector grew by 2.6 per cent and construction by 3 per cent. The star performer was the maquila-dominated textile industry, which grew by 3.6 per cent and increased exports by around a third.
Funding for utilities, job creation and humanitarian aid was channeled through the Haiti Interim Co-operation Framework (ICF), although additional funds to extend it until the end of 2007 are uncertain.
Haiti was approved as eligibile for the Heavily Indebted Poor Countries (HIPC) Debt Initiative in April 2006.
The Inter-American Development Bank estimated that in 2006 migrant workers sent some US$1,650 million to their families in Haiti.

External trade
Although Haiti is member of the Caribbean Community (Caricom), it did not adopt the single market and economy (CSME), which was ratified by 12 other member states on 1 January 2006.
International aid of over US$1 billion and remittances, estimated at around US$1 billion in 2006, are vital elements of the economy.

Imports
Main imports are foodstuffs, manufactured goods, machinery and transport equipment, fuels and raw materials.
Main sources: US (49.3 per cent total, 2005), The Netherlands Antilles (12.0 per cent), Colombia (3.2 per cent)

Exports
Main exports are clothing, mangoes, manufactures, leather and raw hides, seafood and cocoa.
Main destinations: US (80.8 per cent total, 2005), Dominican Republic (6.9 per cent), Canada (4.0 per cent)

Agriculture
Farming
Agriculture accounted for around 27 per cent of GDP in 2004 and employs two-thirds of the working population. The main cash crops are coffee, sisal and sugar.
An estimated 47 per cent of the total land area is cultivated and 20 per cent is pasture. Subsistence farming and animal husbandry predominate. Only 10 per cent of cultivation is carried out on large plantations. Maize, rice, sorghum, millet, beans, fruit and vegetables are grown. Production is largely outside the cash economy. Recurrent drought, insufficient irrigation, low producer prices and a weak infrastructure have kept production levels down and necessitated the import of foodstuffs, particularly cereals.
Estimated crop production in 2005 included: 1,080,000 tonnes (t) sugar cane, 199,000t yams, 398,000t cereals in total, 198,000t maize, 330,000t cassava, 11,500t potatoes, 180,000t maize, 170,000t sweet potatoes, 102,000t rice, 290,000t bananas, 280,000t plantains, 28,000t green coffee, 59,000t citrus fruit, 11,689t oilcrops, 984,000t fruit in total, 199,550t vegetables in total. Livestock production included: 99,893t meat in total, 42,500t beef, 33,000t pig meat, 780t lamb, 6,000t goat meat, 5,600t horsemeat, 8,413t poultry, 5,050t eggs, 69,700t milk, 850t honey, 6,314t cattle hides.

Fishing
The total annual fish catch is typically around 5,000 tonnes, three-quarters of which is through marine fishing. Around 10 per cent is exported.
In 2004, the total marine fish catch was 5,700 tonnes and the total crustacean catch was 2,000 tonnes.

Forestry
Forests cover around 88,000 hectares (ha) or 1 per cent of the total land area. This compares to around 40 per cent of land area in 1940. Deforestation is causing serious soil erosion and desertification. The rapid decline of the forests is partly due to the demand for fuel wood. There are no large-scale forest industries. The local demand for industrial wood and paper products is mainly met by imports. Timber imports in 2004 were US$11.4 million, while exports amounted to US$24,000.
Timber production in 2004 included: 2,231,557 cubic metres (cum) roundwood, 239,000cum industrial roundwood, 13,800cum sawnwood, 224,000cum sawlogs and veneer logs, 1,992,557cum wood fuel, 28,002t charcoal.

Industry and manufacturing
Industry accounted for around16 per cent of GDP in 2004 and employed 10 per cent of the workforce. It is concentrated in Port-au-Prince.
Besides the traditional food processing, construction and textile industries, there is an important artisan manufacturing sector producing handicrafts, such as baskets, leather goods, brushes, and rugs. Manufacturing operations are concentrated in electronic and electrical equipment, sporting goods, toys and garments. Haiti is the world's leading producer of baseballs and one of the Caribbean's largest suppliers of garments and electronic components to the US market. There is very little production for local consumption.
Manufacturing output in Haiti continues to suffer in an uncertain political and business climate and international pressures for massive internal structural reforms.

Tourism
Tourism continues to be hurt by Haiti's unsettled conditions. The importance of the once-thriving sector to the economy is recognised and efforts are being made to revive it. Cruise ship arrivals account for the majority of visitors. Tourism is

expected to contribute around 2.2 per cent to GDP in 2005.

Mining
The mining and export of bauxite ceased in 1983 with the closure of Reynolds mine at Miragoane. There are known, but not commercially viable, deposits of copper, silver, gold, marble, lignite and natural asphalt.

Hydrocarbons
Haiti relies on the import of petroleum products to meet domestic demand. Most of this is supplied by Mexico and Venezuela, which sell oil to 11 Caribbean and Central American countries on favourable terms under the San José Pact of 1980 . Haiti does not import gas or coal.

Energy
The electricity supply is restricted to main towns. Haiti experiences power cuts on a regular basis.
Local wood provides three-quarters of total energy and is a major cause of deforestation and soil erosion.

Banking and insurance
The banking sector is underdeveloped and in disarray. The crowding out of private sector credit has undermined the banks' ability to function as an important part of the economy. Few people have bank accounts and the large informal sector and black market tends to keep the savings ratio and therefore banks' capital at low levels.

Central bank
Banque Nationale de la République d'Haiti.

Main financial centre
Port-au-Prince

Time
GMT minus five hours.

Geography
Haiti occupies the western part of the Caribbean island of Hispaniola (the Dominican Republic occupies the remaining two-thirds), and some smaller offshore islands. Cuba is to the west and is less than 80km away.
Much of Haiti's land area is covered by mountains, which rise up to about 3,000 metres. Environmental damage caused primarily by population pressure has reduced the area of forests to about 6–8 per cent of land area. A number of rivers flow vigorously during the rainy season only, and there are large lakes in the centre of the country close to the border with the Dominican Republic.

Hemisphere
Northern

Climate
Year-round temperatures in Port-au-Prince varies only slightly from 24–27 degrees Celsius (C). The rainy season is from May–November. The climate is tropical, with the rainy seasons in October–November and May–June. May is the wettest month (231mm average rainfall) and December to February the driest and coldest. Temperatures vary from around 22 degrees C on the coast in January to 34 degrees C in July.

Dress codes
Jackets (tropical weight) and ties are normally worn for business. Swimwear is only worn at beaches and pools. Dresses of at least knee-length are recommended for women.

Entry requirements

Passports
Passports are required by all and must have at least six months validity beyond the date of departure. Proof of return/onward passage is required.

Visa
Required by all. Business and tourist visas are not required by citizens of North America or Argentina.
Business visitors from other destinations should supply a letter of introduction from their company and proof of sufficient funds for length of stay. For further information contact the nearest embassy.

Currency advice/regulations
There are no restrictions on the import or export of foreign or local currency. Nevertheless, amounts over G200,000 should be declared.
Travellers cheques are widely accepted, however it is difficult in banks, hotels and shops to exchange foreign currency other than US dollars.

Health (for visitors)
The rate of HIV/Aids is high and precautions should always be taken.

Mandatory precautions
Yellow fever vaccination is required if arriving from an infected area.
Anti-malaria precautions are essential.
Tap water is not safe to drink, and therefore ice, salads, raw vegetables and unpeeled fruits are suspect.

Advisable precautions
Inoculations against typhoid, polio and tetanus are recommended. Malaria prophylaxis and a mosquito net may be necessary. There is a very high prevalence of HIV/Aids. Use only bottled or boiled water for drinks, washing teeth and be wary of ice in restaurants. Eat only well cooked meals, preferably served hot; vegetables should be cooked and fruit peeled.
Medical facilities are very limited and offer a poor standard of care. Adequate supplies of essential medicines should be carried by visitors, with their prescription details. Local emergency services are inadequate, so full travel insurance, which includes emergency medical evacuation, should be obtained.

Hotels
There is not a good range of accommodation, the best hotels are in the capital and in tourist resorts. Hotels are fully booked during Carnival. There is a government tax of 10 per cent and hotels add a 5 per cent service charge to bills.

Credit cards
Major credit cards are accepted.

Public holidays (national)

Fixed dates
1 Jan (Independence Day), 2 Jan (Ancestors' Day), 14 Apr (Pan American Day), 1 May (Labour Day), 18 May (Flag and University Day), 15 Aug (Assumption Day), 17 Oct (Dessalines Day), 24 Oct (United Nations Day), 1 Nov (All Saints' Day), 2 Nov (All Souls' Day), 18 Nov (Vertières Battle Day), 25 Dec (Christmas Day).

Variable dates
Carnival (two days, Feb), Ash Wednesday, Good Friday (Mar/Apr), Ascension Day, Corpus Christi (May/Jun).

Working hours

Banking
Mon–Fri: 0900–1300, 1500–1700; Sat: 0900–1300.

Business
Mon–Fri: 0800–1600. (Visits are best arranged between November–March).

Government
Mon–Fri: 0800–1400.

Telecommunications

Mobile/cell phones
There is a 850 GSM service in operation.

Electricity supply
110-220V AC

Weights and measures
Officially the metric system is in force but many US measures are also used.

Social customs/useful tips
Careful observance of polite formalities such as handshaking, direct eye contact, formal use of titles such as Monsieur, etc, is essential, and offence may be taken if they are not observed. All officials should be treated with careful respect.

Security
Crime is widespread and often violent. The kidnapping of foreign nationals for ransom money is increasingly common. Random shootings, during robbery, has become more common, and pickpockets are numerous. Do not leave property in vehicles and always travel with doors locked and windows up. Armed hold-ups of vehicles take place, even in daylight, in busy parts of Port-au-Prince.

Some areas of Port-au-Prince should be avoided at all times. Whenever possible avoid going out after dark.
Whenever possible leave documents in a safety deposit box.

Getting there

Air

National airline: Haiti Trans Air offers limited flights to the US.

International airport/s: Port-au-Prince International Airport (PAP), 10km from city; duty-free shop, bar, bank, car hire. Cap-Haitien (CAP), 10km from the city.

Airport tax: Departure tax US$30 and security charge G10, excluding transit passengers.

Surface

Road: Access is possible from Dominican Republic, although sometimes, bureaucratic delays can occur.

Main port/s: Port-au-Prince, Cap Haitien, Gonaives.

Getting about

National transport

Air: Caribintair flies to Cap Haitien. Other towns can be reached from Port-au-Prince by charter flights.

Road: The total road network is around 4,000km, although not all passable/practicable in wet weather. There are surfaced roads from Port-au-Prince to Cap Haitien, Jacmel and Les Cayes.
Camionettes (large, out-of-town taxis) are available.

Buses: Unscheduled services operate from Port-au-Prince to Les Cayes, Jacmel, Jérémie, Hinche, Port de Paix and Cap Haitien.

City transport

Taxis: Publiques (shared taxis) can be identified by red ribbon in the window and registration number beginning 'P'. Tipping is not usual.

Car hire

Cars can be hired in Port-au-Prince and Petionville, at the airport and from hotels. International licence is required. Petrol is hard to find outside cities. Hire cars have registration numbers beginning with 'L'.

BUSINESS DIRECTORY

The addresses listed below are a selection only. While World of Information makes every endeavour to check these addresses, we cannot guarantee that changes have not been made, especially to telephone numbers and area codes. We would welcome any corrections.

Telephone area codes

The international direct dialling code (IDD) for Haiti is +509, followed by subscriber's number.

Chambers of Commerce

Haiti Chamber of Commerce and Industry, Boulevard Harry Truman, PO Box 982, Port-au-Prince (tel: 222-8661; fax: 222-0281; e-mail: ccih@acn2.net).

Banking

Banque Commerciale d'Haiti, Champ de Mars, Port-au-Prince.

Central bank

Banque de la République d'Haiti, Rues des Miracles et du Magasin de l'Etat et , PO Box 1570, Port-au-Prince (tel: 299-1200; fax: 299-1045; e-mail: webmaster@brh.net).

Travel information

Air Haiti, 35 ave Marie-Jeanne, Port-au-Prince.

Association Hotelière et Touristique d'Haiti, Hotel Montana, rue F. Cardozo, route de Pétionville, BP 2562, Port-au-Prince.

National tourist organisation offices

Office National du Tourisme d'Haiti, Avenue Marie Jeanne, Port-au-Prince (tel: 223-5631).

Ministries

Ministry of Economy and Finance, Palais des Ministères, Port-au-Prince.

Ministry of Information and Co-ordination, 300 Route de Delmas, Port-au-Prince.

Other useful addresses

Association des Industries d'Haiti (ADIH), Delmas 31 et 33, Etase Galeria 128, BP 2568, Port-au-Prince.

Association des Producteurs Agricoles (APA), c/o Chambre de Commerce et d'Industrie d'Haiti, blvd Harry S. Truman, Cite de l'Exposition, Port-au-Prince.

Centre de Promotion des Investissements et des Exportations Haitiennes (Prominex), Angle rue Lamarre et ave John Brown, Port-au-Prince.

Haitian Embassy (USA), 2311 Massachusetts Avenue, NW, Washington DC 20008 (tel: (+1-202) 332-4090; fax: (+1-202) 745-7215; e-mail: embassy@haiti.org).

Haitian International Business Center, 444 Brickell Avenue, Brickell Suite 650, Miami, Florida 33131, USA (tel: (+1-305) 374-8300).

National news agency: Agence Haitienne de Presse

Other news agencies: Caribbean Net News: www.caribbeannetnews.com

Haiti Press Network (in French): www.haitipressnetwork.com

Haitian Times: www.haitiantimes.com

Internet sites

Embassy of Haiti: www.haiti.org

Haiti Business Directory: www.ascnet.net/haiti/directory.htm

Haiti website (in French): www.haitiwebs.com/

Latin America Network Information Center: www.lanic.utexas.edu

Honduras

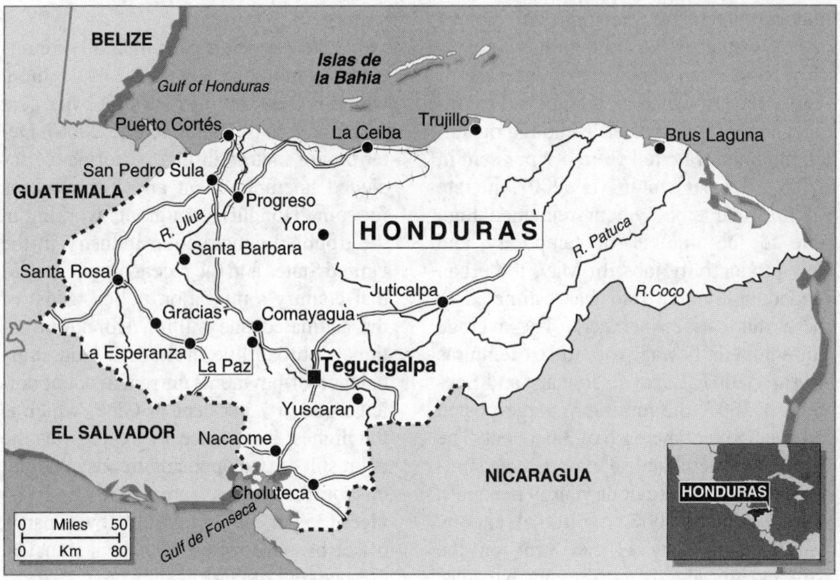

Honduras has one of the highest incidences of poverty and inequality in the Western hemisphere. The situation of the poor, who usually live off small-scale agriculture in rural areas, was aggravated by the disaster caused by Hurricane Mitch in 1998. After this massive loss of life and assets, Honduras embarked on a very ambitious Poverty Reduction Strategy (PRS) in consultation with civil society and donors, agreeing to a set of actions aimed at reducing the incidence of extreme poverty by half by 2015.

In 2005 Hondurans elected José Manuel 'Mel' Zelaya of the Liberal Party as president in the seventh successive peaceful, democratic change of government since 1982. Sr Zelaya's margin of victory was a mere 4 per cent, the smallest margin in Honduran electoral history.

The Zelaya administration has made poverty reduction its top priority, endorsing the PRS. The four pillars identified by the President for his administrative mandate (January 2006 to January 2010) were the creation of equitable economic growth for employment generation, good governance through state modernisation and civic participation, environmental protection and risk management and the development of human capital.

We've never had it so good

In 2007, according to the United Nations Economic Commission for Latin America and the Caribbean (ECLAC) the Honduran economy expanded by 6 per cent, with per capita GDP growth of 12 per cent over the preceding five years. This performance was attributable to the impact of family remittances, which accounted for 25 per cent of GDP, on private consumption, as well as the private construction boom following the expansion of bank credit. Inflation increased to an annual rate of 9.6 per cent in November well up on the 5.3 per cent registered at the end of 2006, which was outside the target range of 4 per cent to 6 per cent. The government deficit widened from 1.3 per cent of GDP in 2006 to 2.4 per cent in 2007. The unprecedented trade deficit of 32 per cent of GDP, along with the income balance deficit, was only partly financed by current transfers. The balance-of-payments current account posted a significant deficit, corresponding to 7 per cent of GDP.

For 2008, according to ECLAC, the authorities have projected GDP growth of 5.5 per cent and established a target range of 5 per cent to 6 per cent for inflation. February 2007 saw the conclusion of the Poverty Reduction and Growth Facility (PRGF)

KEY FACTS

Official name: República de Honduras (Republic of Honduras)

Head of State: President José Manuel Zelaya Rosales (since 27 Jan 2006)

Head of government: President José Manuel Zelaya Rosales

Ruling party: Partido Liberal de Honduras (PLH) (Liberal Party of Honduras) (elected 27 Nov 2005)

Area: 112,088 square km

Population: 7.51 million (2007)*

Capital: Tegucigalpa

Official language: Spanish

Currency: Lempira (L) = 100 centavos

Exchange rate: L18.89 per US$ (Jul 2008)

GDP per capita: US$1,635 (2007)*

GDP real growth: 6.30% (2007)*

Labour force: 2.67 million (2004)

Unemployment: 28.50% (2004)

Inflation: 6.90% (2007)

Balance of trade: -US$3.49 billion (2006)

Foreign debt: US$6.33 billion (2004)

Visitor numbers: 739,000 (2006)*

* estimated figure

agreement with the International Monetary Fund (IMF). In the period up to August 2007, total real government revenues rose by 17 per cent, due to both increased economic activity and improved tax receipts. Real current expenditure climbed by 15 per cent in the same period, due to wage increases. For 2007 as a whole, the primary deficit was expected to widen considerably (to 1.6 per cent of GDP), as was the overall central government deficit. Additionally, the authorities were still faced with resolving the financial problems of state-owned enterprises in the electric power and telecommunications sectors. In the period 2003–05, electricity utility ENEE posted financial losses of US$120 million a year. In 2007, relief on the servicing of public external debt amounted to US$233 million, with US$118 million used to finance spending associated with the poverty reduction strategy.

Boom sectors fuel inflation

The most buoyant sectors in 2007 were construction and telecommunications. Construction grew by 11 per cent on the strength of the boom in private activity, mainly residential projects and buildings for agro-industrial use. Transport and telecommunications also performed well. Growth in industry (5 per cent) was driven by the non-metals sector and cement production. The basic metal industry recorded a decline. Agriculture expanded by only 3 per cent, due in part to climatic events such as the tropical storm Felix that struck mainly the north west of Honduras in September.

According to ECLAC, inflation increased to reach a 12 month annual rate of 9.6 per cent in November, compared to 5.3 per cent at the end of 2006. This was mainly due to higher prices for petroleum and its derivatives, and also for maize and wheat. The situation was partly offset by the stability of the exchange rate against the US dollar. In November, the food sector recorded an annual price increase of 15.9 per cent, which inevitably had an impact on the basic basket. Although the unemployment rate fell from 4.9 per cent in 2006 to 4.1 per cent in May 2007, the rate of informal employment remained high due to the number of temporary and low-productivity jobs. In May, the urban underemployment rate was estimated to be as high as 25 per cent. The average minimum daily wage rose to 101 lempiras in early 2007. Between January and September 2007, the minimum wage posted an average real increase of 3 per cent. The growth of merchandise exports was similar to that of the previous year (9 per cent). Up to August 2007, traditional exports had expanded by 11 per cent on the strength of sales of coffee and bananas, while non-traditional exports were less buoyant, at only 7 per cent. *Maquila* value added rose by 10 per cent, compared with an average growth rate of 15 per cent for the three-year period between 2004 and 2006. Between January and July, exports of clothes to the United States market were 8.8 per cent higher than in the year earlier period (following the 4 per cent decline recorded in 2006). Imports, boosted by the real appreciation of the lempira, grew by 22 per cent in the same period. Purchases of capital goods for metallurgical projects, communications and construction expanded by 35 per cent, followed by consumer goods (25 per cent). Oil represented 18 per cent of total imports.

In 2007, revenues from family remittances amounted to US$2.64 billion, which represented growth of 12 per cent (compared with 35 per cent in 2006). Determining factors in this performance included unemployment and lower wages for some Honduran emigrants working in the troubled construction industry in the United States and the recent toughening of that country's migration policy. Most of the estimated one million Honduran nationals abroad live in the US. Honduras' balance-of-payments current account deficit stood at 7 per cent of GDP, which is the highest level since 1996, and was the net result of two opposing trends: a deficit on non-factor and factor goods and services (35 per cent of GDP) that was partly offset by the surplus of current transfers (28 per cent of GDP).

Risk assessment

Economy	Good
Politics	Good
Regional stability	Good

KEY INDICATORS — Honduras

	Unit	2003	2004	2005	2006	2007
Population	m	6.86	6.94	7.22	*7.36	*7.51
Gross domestic product (GDP)	US$bn	7.00	7.37	8.29	10.76	*12.28
GDP per capita	US$	997	1,035	1,148	*1,462	*1,635
GDP real growth	%	2.0	4.2	4.1	6.3	*6.3
Inflation	%	6.8	8.1	8.8	5.6	*6.9
Industrial output	% change	–	3.2	5.8	5.2	–
Agricultural output	% change	–	7.0	0.5	8.1	–
Exports (fob) (goods)	US$m	1,396.0	2,411.2	2,647.8	1,930.0	2,120.1
Imports (cif) (goods)	US$m	2,994.0	3,678.5	4,187.5	5,418.0	–
Balance of trade	US$m	-1,598.0	-1,267.3	-1,539.7	-3,488.0	–
Current account	US$m	-310.0	-430.0	-33.0	-508.0	-1,225.0
Total reserves minus gold	US$m	1,430.0	1,970.4	2,327.2	2,628.5	2,526.8
Foreign exchange	US$m	1,417.1	1,956.9	2,314.6	2,615.5	2,513.1
Exchange rate	per US$	17.43	18.20	18.90	18.89	18.89

* estimated figure

COUNTRY PROFILE

Historical profile

1821 The Central American provinces (Costa Rica, Guatemala, Honduras, Nicaragua and El Salvador) declared independence from Spain.

1822 Central American confederation annexed itself to the Mexican Empire, under General Agustín de Iturbde, later Emperor Agustín I.

1823 Agustín I was overthrown and Mexico became a republic. The Central American states formed the United Provinces of Central America.

1825 Costa Rica, Guatemala, Honduras, Nicaragua and El Salvador formed the Central American Federation (CAF).

1838 The CAF was dissolved and Honduras became a fully independent republic.

1840–1957 Honduras was ruled by a military and civilian élite.

1957 The first democratic presidential election was won by Ramon Villeda Morales, a popular moderate reformist.

1963 Morales was ousted by Colonel Osvaldo Lopez Arellano in a military coup. Military rule continued until 1980.

1969 Honduras and El Salvador fought what became known as the 'soccer war', which was prompted by land disputes and El Salvador's win in the World Cup play-offs between the two countries. Over 3,000 people died.
1981 Presidential elections were won by Roberto Suazo Cordova of the Partido Liberal de Honduras (PLH) (Liberal Party of Honduras), although real power remained in the hands of the army under General Gustavo Alvarez.
1985 José Azcona Hoyo (PLH) won the presidential election, following a change in the constitution which limited the presidency to a maximum of one term.
1989 Rafael Leonardo Callejas Romero of the Partido Nacional (PN) (National Party), the right-wing opposition party, was elected president.
1993 Carlos Roberto Reina Idiáquez (PLH) won the presidential election.
1997 Carlos Roberto Flores Facussé (PLH) was elected president.
1998 Honduras was severely affected by Hurricane Mitch – around 11,000 people were killed and 1.3 million left homeless.
1999 The constitution was amended to make the president the commander-in-chief of the armed forces.
2001 Ricardo Maduro Joest (PN) was elected president and the PN won the legislative elections.
2002 Honduras renewed diplomatic ties with Cuba, with whom it had broken relations in 1961. Persistent drought and the decline in world coffee prices left around 300,000 Hondurans suffering from hunger.
2003 After prisoners rioted, the government was accused of overcrowding prisons without solving the crime epidemic.
2004 More than 100 prisoners, many of them gang members, were killed in a fire at San Pedro Sula prison. Honduran troops withdrew from Iraq.
2005 The PLH won the presidential and legislative elections.
2006 Manuel Zelaya Rosales (PLH) was inaugurated as president. The Central American Free Trade Agreement (Cafta) came into effect.
2007 In October after eight years of conflict, the International Court of Justice ruled on a new maritime boundary between Honduras and Nicaragua. The result gives both countries equal access to the rich fishing grounds and oil and gas exploration waters in the area.
2008 From 31 May Tegucigalpa's international airport was closed to larger passenger aircraft. Honduras signed a free trade agreement with Taiwan on 15 July.

Political structure

In addition to their unicameral national parliaments, El Salvador, Guatemala, Honduras, Nicaragua, Panama and Dominican Republic also return directly-elected deputies to the supranational Central American Parliament.

Constitution

The constitution was promulgated in 1982 and amended in 1999, making the president the commander-in-chief of the armed forces.
Voting is by secret ballot and is compulsory for all citizens aged 18 or over. Members of the security forces are barred from voting. Municipal elections and elections of representatives in the 18 departments are held every two years.

Form of state

Presidential democratic republic

The executive

Power is divided between a strong executive, a unicameral national assembly and an independent judiciary. The president, three vice presidents and members of the national assembly serve parallel four-year terms. Presidents are not allowed to stand for re-election to a second term in office.

National legislature

Limited legislative functions are vested in the 128-member National Congress, elected by proportional representation every four years. Seats are distributed according to a complex system of proportional representation. The National Assembly appoints supreme court justices, who administer the judiciary.

Legal system

The legal system is based on Roman and Spanish civil law. Honduran laws are set out in the 'Cordigoes' or codes. The civil code covers dealings between people. The business code covers all matters relating to business while the penal code covers crime and punishment. The legal system is in desperate need of reform.

Last elections

27 November 2005 (presidential and parliamentary)

Results: Presidential: José Manuel Zelaya Rosales (PLH) won 50 per cent of the votes; Porfirio Lobo Sosa (PNH) won 46.2 per cent.
Parliamentary: Partido Liberal de Honduras (PLH) (Liberal Party of Honduras) won 62 seats out of 128; Partido Nacional de Honduras (PNH) (National Party of Honduras) won 55 seats; Partido de Unificación Democrática (PUD) (Democratic Unification Party) 5 seats. Turnout was 46 per cent.

Next elections

2009 (presidential and parliamentary)

Political parties

Ruling party

Partido Liberal de Honduras (PLH) (Liberal Party of Honduras) (elected 27 Nov 2005)

Main opposition party

Partido Nacional de Honduras (PNH) (National Party of Honduras)

Population

7.51 million (2007)*

Last census: July 2001: 6,071,200 (provisional)

Population density: 56 inhabitants per square km. Urban population: 54 per cent of total (1995—2001).

Annual growth rate: 2.6 per cent 1994–2004 (WHO 2006)

Ethnic make-up

Around 90 per cent are mestizos, with minorities of Indians, blacks, whites and others. The largest indigenous group is the Garifuna, descendants of African slaves and Arawak Indian women from San Vicente, who live along the north coast. The Miskitos live in the Mosquitia – wetland, rainforest country – and the Lencas live around Copan.

Religions

More than 90 per cent of the population are Roman Catholics. There is freedom of worship.

Education

Primary education is compulsory and free of charge. Secondary education, from 13 years to 17 years, is not compulsory.

Literacy rate: 80 per cent adult rate; 89 per cent youth rate (15–24) (Unesco 2005).

Compulsory years: Seven to 12

Enrolment rate: 110 per cent gross primary enrolment, of the relevant age group (including repetition rate); 32 per cent gross secondary enrolment; 9 per cent gross tertiary enrolment (World Bank).

Pupils per teacher: 35 in primary schools

Health

Per capita total expenditure on health (2003) was US$184; of which per capita government spending was US$104, at the international dollar rate, (WHO 2006).
In Honduras the quality of, and access to, healthcare is directly tied to income levels. Adequate health care is available to those able to pay the high cost. Health care for the urban and rural poor is limited.
The ministry of health manages 28 hospitals with 4,093 beds. There are also 31 hospitals managed by the private sector. The private sector generally concentrates on individual care and does not participate in general public sector health activities. A national policy was formulated to make sure people have access to safe, quality drugs. This policy however, has not been implemented.
The relatively young population places an extra burden on health facilities. Nearly two-thirds of the population have no access to essential drugs.

Infectious and parasitic diseases are the leading causes of death. Gastroenteritis and tuberculosis are serious problems. Approximately one-third of the population has no access to safe water or sanitation facilities.

HIV/Aids

The disease is spread predominantly through heterosexual intercourse. A study showed that the HIV prevalence in female sex workers was over 10 per cent (USCF – Centre for HIV Information, 2005).

HIV prevalence: 1.8 per cent aged 15–49 in 2003 (World Bank)

Life expectancy: 67 years, 2004 (WHO 2006)

Fertility rate/Maternal mortality rate: 3.6 births per woman, 2004 (WHO 2006); maternal mortality 110 per 100,000 live births (World Bank).

Child (under 5 years) mortality rate (per 1,000): 32 per 1,000 live births; 25 per cent of children aged under five are malnourished (World Bank).

Welfare

Honduras is classified as a low-income country by the World Bank – 50 per cent of its inhabitants live below the poverty line. Social security benefits, mainly for pensions and health care, cover around 12 per cent of the Honduran population and account for around 1 per cent of GDP. Social security is mainly limited to urban centres. About 80 per cent of those covered live either in the capital, Tegucigalpa, or in the northern city of San Pedro Sula.

Organised social security started operations in 1962. Contributors are covered for general illness, maternity, accidents at work, professional illnesses, invalidity, old age and funeral expenses. There is no unemployment benefit.

Dependants, who account for 60 per cent of those covered, get some access to health care and pensions. Children under five years get free health treatment and wives of contributors receive maternity care in hospitals run by the social security institute. The widows of contributors receive pensions and there are more restricted pensions for widowers. Orphans, usually up to the age of 14 years, receive some support.

Main cities

Tegucigalpa (capital, estimated population 1.3 million in 2003), San Pedro Sula (505,200), La Ceiba (116,700).

Languages spoken

English is common in some parts of the north coast and the Caribbean Islas de la Bahía.

Official language/s

Spanish

Media

While the constitution guarantees freedom of speech and the press, there are punitive defamation laws that tend to restrict journalism and journalists are known to practice self-censorship. Journalists reporting on corruption, drug trafficking and human rights abuses have been targeted not only for harassment but also by laws that require them to divulge their sources. Media outlets have been the object of political attacks with death threats issued to journalists and managers. Corruption of the media has also included bribes to journalists, selective government advertising and access and denial of public officials.

In 2005, the Supreme Court declared that defamation laws that protected public officials were unconstitutional.

Press

Ownership of newspapers in held by a few conglomerates with political and economic ties to the elite.

Dailies: The most popular newspapers are, in Spanish, El Heraldo (www.heraldohn.com) and El Tiempo (www.tiempo.hn), others include La Tribuna (www.latribuna.hn) and La Prensa (www.laprensahn.com). Articles include financial and business news.

Weeklies: In Spanish, government announcements are published in La Gaceta.

In English, Honduras This Week (www.marrder.com/htw) covers news from Central America.

Broadcasting

Radio and television play a key role in Honduras, where literacy is around 60 per cent. Television is all privately owned and operated; there is one state-owned radio station.

Radio: There are five stations broadcasting nationally and over 280 local radio stations.

The biggest stations include Radio HRN (www.radiohrn.hn), Radio América (www.radioamerica.hn) and Power FM (www.powerfm.hn). The public radio network broadcasts under the collective name of Radio Corporación.

Television: There are six nationwide TV stations and some with more than one channel. The ones with the biggest market share are Televicentro (www.televicentrotv.net) with several channels and digital services and CBC Canal 6 (www.noti6.com), Vica TV (www.vicatv.hn) and Soptel Canal 11 (www.canal11.hn).

Economy

Honduras is one of the most impoverished and backward countries in the western hemisphere. Over 60 per cent of the population live below the poverty line; income inequality is considerable and increasing.

Unemployment is high at over 25 per cent. Although the economy is currently experiencing modest growth, the changes in GDP remain too sluggish to support major reductions in poverty. Some of Honduras's heavy debt burden has recently been written off, but it remains to be seen how much of this relief will be used to benefit social and economic improvement.

Honduras has diversified away from its former dependence on bananas and coffee. In addition to timber, cultivated shrimps and melons, an important maquila clothes-manufacturing industry has developed with US investment and for export mainly to the US. Remittances from expatriate workers, mainly in the US, are a vital source of foreign exchange, as is the tourism sector, which is growing in importance. The Inter-American Development Bank estimated that in 2006 migrant workers sent some US$2,359 million to their families in Honduras. Honduras is closely tied to the US, which is the principal market for its exports and the main source of investment and aid.

Although the disastrous effects of Hurricane Mitch in 1998, which cost an estimated US$3 billion, are still felt, the economy has grown steadily over the past few years. Economic restructuring is a priority, as Honduras attempts to diversify its export markets away from dependency on agriculture and remain in favour with multilateral organisations and international financiers. This has involved an increasingly unpopular privatisation programme in which prices have risen while incomes dropped. Successive governments have tried to promote private investment, but have been hampered by bureaucracy, an overvalued national currency and civil wars in each of the three neighbouring countries.

External trade

Honduras is a member of the Central America Free Trade Agreement (DR-Cafta), which includes Dominican Republic Costa Rica, El Salvador, Guatemala and the US; it is working to remove all tariffs and barriers between members by 2024.

A maquila industry, which began in the late 1980s, produces clothing for export, mainly to the US. Other non-traditional exports include the cultivation of oriental crops, farmed shrimps and melons. Remittances are estimated at over US$2 billion in 2006 (or more than 20 per cent of GDP).

Imports

Principal imports are petroleum, machinery and vehicles, industrial raw materials and foodstuffs.

Main sources: US (53.1 per cent total, 2005), Guatemala (6.5 per cent), El Salvador (4.1 per cent)
Exports
They include coffee, shrimp and lobster, bananas, palm oil, fruit and vegetable, timber and gold.
Main destinations: US (72.2 per cent total, 2005), Guatemala (2.9 per cent), El Salvador (2.9 per cent),

Agriculture

Farming

Agriculture is one of the most important economic activities in Honduras. The sector accounts for around 80 per cent of total exports, constitutes 20 per cent of total GDP and employs 57 per cent of the country's workforce.
Sugar cane, bananas (grown on the northern lowland) and coffee are the main agricultural exports. The government is encouraging the growth of new banana varieties but it is likely to be a number of years before new crops become profitable exports.
Hurrican Mitch devastated the agricultural sector in 1998 and just about wiped out the banana and coffee plantations. Further damage to the coffee sector occurred due to low world prices and ongoing drought. The price of a pound of robusta fell to around US$0.17 cents, the lowest for 30 years. By the end of December 2004 prices were back at over US$1 per pound.
Other agricultural exports include frozen meat, wood, cotton and tobacco.
The main food crops are maize, rice, sorghum and beans. Production of these staples has steadily risen, though food imports are still necessary to meet domestic demand.
Emphasis has been on land reform and the cultivation of new crops such as cocoa, allspice, cardamom, melons and citrus fruits.
Crop production in 2005 included: 5,625,450 tonnes (t) sugar cane, 1,233,000t oil palm fruit, 568,973t maize, 13,700t rice, 190,640t green coffee, 678t cocoa beans, 36,051t sorghum, 21,469t potatoes, 887,072t bananas, 284,994t plantains, 205,920t oilcrops, 308,994t citrus fruit, 153,252t tomatoes, 6,154t tobacco, 1,696,578t fruit in total, 634,365t vegetables in total. Livestock production included: 223,442t meat in total, 72,878t beef, 9,013t pig meat, 85t lamb, 193t goat meat, 140,711t poultry, 40,912t eggs, 1,761,950t milk, 117t honey, 9,520t cattle hides.

Fishing

Honduras' annual fish catch is typically over 18,000mt, of which approximately 12,000mt is shellfish. The country's main fish export is lobster, harvested by divers who spend up to seven hours a day on the sea bed. The lobsters are mainly exported to the US. Legislation requires all divers to undergo specific instruction and boat owners to hold licences to carry trained divers only. The government is expected to promote the potential of Honduras' fishing industry in order to attract investment and curtail growing unemployment along the country's coasts which has forced fishermen to dive for lobsters. Improved regulation would benefit the lobster colonies which are in danger of being depleted. Honduras also has a well-established shrimp farming industry. In 2004, the total marine fish catch was 10,587 tonnes and the total crustacean catch was 4,163 tonnes.

Forestry

Honduras does not have a great deal of energy resources and consequently wood is widely used as an inexpensive form of fuel. This has led to a widespread problem of deforestation in Honduras.
During 1990–95, the average rate of deforestation was 2.3 per cent, the third highest rate in the Western hemisphere after Haiti and Paraguay. Although it is estimated that 7.4 million hectares of land were covered by forest in 1987, annual deforestation in the 1980s was thought to be in the region of 70,000 hectares.
Since then the government has been keen to redress the rate of deforestation through education and development programmes.
The government has promoted the protection of Honduras' forests by agreeing with foreign companies such as Stone Container Corporation (US), to establish a comprehensive forestry management plan enabling Honduras to increase the size of its forest coverage.
In a typical year, exports of forest materials amount to US$43.1 million, while imports amount to US$100 million.
Production in 2004 included 9,619,212 cubic metres (cum) roundwood, 920,000cum industrial roundwood, 437,000cum sawnwood, 920,000cum sawlogs & veneer logs, 9,000cum wood-based panels, 8,699,212cum wood fuel; 3,000 tonnes (t) charcoal, 95,000t paper and paperboard, including 12,000t newsprint, 13,000t printing and writing paper, 7,000t wood pulp, 51,000t recovered paper.

Industry and manufacturing

Honduras's industrial sector is the smallest in Central America and contributes in the region of 27 per cent to total GDP. Approximately 15 per cent of Honduras' workforce is employed in the sector.
Government responsibility for the industrial sector has traditionally been divided between the ministry of economy's general directorate of industry, the central bank and various other official institutions.
In the late 1980s, government introduced policies aimed at stimulating Honduran labour-intensive industries, especially agro-industry, while boosting investment and exports to combat high unemployment. The authorities since then have continued to try and release Honduras from dependency on certain commodities such as bananas and coffee.
Virtually no production equipment is produced in Honduras and capital goods must be imported from foreign suppliers. The demand for capital goods cannot be funded without the government's help and the need to expand the country's industrial base is being frustrated by financial constraints.
Manufacturing remains heavily dependent on imports of capital goods, raw materials and foreign technology; the biggest growth in the sector has been the maquiladora (in-bond assembly and manufacturing) industries. The four main areas of manufacturing in Honduras are concentrated around food processing, agro-export, maquila and chemicals. However, capacity utilisation is still low on account of Honduras' narrow domestic market and lack of international competitiveness.
The key to helping the growth of the Honduran industrial sector has been the government-backed free trade zones (FTZ) and privately funded Export Processing Zones (EPZs). Roughly 90 per cent of all merchandise currently manufactured in the zones is clothing. Cloth is manufactured in the US and exported to Honduras from where it is then re-exported as garments, often duty free, to the US.

Tourism

The tourism industry of Honduras continues to expand. The sector now constitutes 10.4 per cent of the country's total GDP and accounts for 8.5 per cent of total employment.
Travel and tourism is an increasingly important economic activity, with the environment and Mayan remains as major attractions. Despite the 11 September 2001 terrorist attacks in the US and local problems, visitor numbers continued to rise annually. 549,500 arrivals were recorded in 2002, compared with 517,914 in 2001, a trend which continued in 2003. In 2004, the total rose once again, with 688,200 people visiting Honduras. Over half of the visitors come from other Central American countries.

Mining

At present the mining sector employs approximately 2 per cent of Honduras' total workforce. The country has large reserves of tin, iron, copper and coal. There are small reserves of gold, silver, lead and zinc that are extracted for export.

Hydrocarbons

Honduras does not produce oil at present, despite extensive offshore exploration aimed at locating deposits. Purchases of foreign oil are the country's main import. Apart from wood, primary energy output is limited to hydroelectric energy and vegetable residues, mainly bagasse (the waste left over from sugar cane once the juice is extracted). The first oil exploration licensing round was started in 2001. The area of a border dispute between Honduras and Nicaragua has possible large oil reserves. The area was opened for bidding by Nicaragua in 2002 without the dispute being resolved. Honduras imports all its oil needs and has no refining capacity. Honduras is neither a producer nor an importer of natural gas.

Energy

In recent years, emphasis has been placed on offshore oil exploration and the development of Honduras' significant hydropower potential. At present, approximately a quarter of the country's energy requirements are imported.
The 292MW El Cajón hydroelectricity plant, and a second hydroelectric dam at Río Lindo/Yojoa, are meeting all the country's electricity needs as well as exporting power to Nicaragua, Costa Rica, El Salvador and Guatemala.
The electricity grids of Honduras and El Salvador have been linked in order to increase export trade in power.

Banking and insurance

The regulators of the banking and financial services sector of Honduras retain tight restrictions on bank ownership of fixed assets and limits on buying corporate shares. Foreign banks wishing to set up in Honduras must obtain approval from the president. Domestic and foreign-owned banks operate under identical rules, and historically there has been little difference in the type of business they conduct.

Central bank
Banco Central de Honduras

Main financial centre
Tegucigalpa

Time

GMT minus six hours

Geography

Honduras is in the middle of the Central American isthmus. It has a long northern coastline on the Caribbean Sea and a narrow southern outlet to the Pacific Ocean. Guatemala is to the west, El Salvador to the south-west and Nicaragua to the south-east. Covering 112,088 square km, Honduras is the second largest country in Central America after neighbouring Nicaragua. Much of the country is covered by thick forests and mountains, while around a quarter of the land is suitable for farming. Apart from a low coastal plain in the north-east, the country is crossed by numerous ranges of mountains and hills. The highest peak is the Cerro de las Minas at 2,866 metres in the western Sierra de Celaque.

Hemisphere
Northern.

Climate

Honduras has a tropical climate on the coast and a temperate climate in the mountainous interior. Temperatures in the capital Tegucigalpa, at 960 metres, are usually between 15 degrees Celsius (C) and 30 degrees C. Rain falls throughout the year on the north coast, while the rest of the country has heaviest rains between May and November. The average rainfall is 3,037mm per year. During the rainy season, May–November, the climate is temperate; in March and April the warm days are punctuated by cool nights; and in December–February it is cool and dry during the day, but chilly at night. The best time to visit is April–May.

Entry requirements

Passports
Required by all, valid for three months on arrival.

Visa
Visas are not required by nationals of most of the Americas and Europe (excluding Schengen agreement states), Australasia, Japan and some other Asian countries. Business visas should be accompanied by a company letter as proof of business intentions, and a full itinerary. For confirmation and requirements, contact the local embassy.

Currency advice/regulations
There are no restrictions on the import and export of local and foreign currency. US dollars should be declared on arrival; re-export is allowed up to the declared amount.

Health (for visitors)

Mandatory precautions
A yellow fever vaccination certificate is required if arriving from an infected area.

Advisable precautions
Typhoid, tetanus and polio vaccinations are advisable. There is a risk of malaria, especially in rural areas – prophylaxis is recommended. Water precautions are essential throughout the country.

Hotels

Hotel standards are reasonable in Tegucigalpa and San Pedro Sula. Hotel bills are subject to 16 per cent sales tax.

Public holidays (national)

Fixed dates
1 Jan (New Year's Day), 14 Apr (Americas Day), 1 May (Labour Day), 15 Sep (Independence Day), 3 Oct (Morozán Day), 12 Oct (Columbus Day), 21 Oct (Armed Forces Day), 25 Dec (Christmas Day).

Variable dates
Maundy Thursday, Good Friday.

Working hours

Banking
Mon–Fri: 0900–1500.

Business
Mon–Fri: 0800–1200, 1330/1400–1700; Sat: 0800–1100.

Government
Mon–Fri: 0800–1200, 1330/1400–1700; Sat: 0800–1100.

Electricity supply

110 or 220V AC, 60 cycles.

Social customs/useful tips

Handshaking is the main form of greeting. Embracing is frowned upon by both men and women.
Mothers are regarded as the leading family figures. It is a grave offence to insult someone's mother. Women rather than men are often the principal family breadwinners. Grandparents and elders are highly respected. The extended family plays an important social role by providing a sense of unity.
It is customary to send flowers to the hostess if invited to dinner or as a guest to someone's home.
Professional persons should be addressed by their title. Graduates are known as Licenciados.

Security

There is widespread petty and violent crime, including armed robbery, car hijacking, burglary and sexual assaults. Visitors are advised to exercise vigilance and caution in all areas, not to carry large amounts of money, take only what is necessary, keep the rest deposited at the hotel and not to resist robbery attempts.

Getting there

Air

National airline: Sol Air.

International airport/s: Tegucigalpa-Toncontín (TGU), 5km from city; duty-free shop, bar, restaurant, bank, post office, vaccination centre, shops, car hire.

Airport tax: US$32.

Surface

Road: It is possible to reach Tegucigalpa via the Pan-American Highway from Goascorán (on the border with El Salvador) and from El Espino and Guasaule (on the border with Nicaragua). Bus services run from most Central American countries. Entry from Guatemala is possible via the Western Highway.

Main port/s: Ampala, La Ceiba, Cortés, Roatan, Castilla, Tela, Lorenzo.

Getting about

National transport

Air: Isleñas Airlines, Sosa Airlines and Rollins Air are the three local airlines, operating numerous flights between Tegucigalpa, San Pedro Sula, Roatan, La Ceiba, Trujillo and Tela. To reach more remote areas using other services, local enquiries should be made.

Road: Network of 10,468km, concentrated along coast (roughly San Pedro Sula to Trujillo) and the area between San Pedro Sula and Tegucigalpa and the Guatemalan border. The main highways are paved, although roads are of varying quality. Travel on unpaved roads is not recommended.

Buses: Frequent services San Pedro Sula to Tegucigalpa; also linking with Juticalpa, Danlí, Choluteca.

Rail: There are passenger train services in the north, running between San Pedro Sula, Puerto Cortés and Tela, although they are somewhat ramshackle and the service is slow.

Water: Water transport is commonly used to travel between Honduras, the Caribbean islands and the bay islands. In Mosquitia almost all transport is along the waterways due to poor road infrastructure.

City transport

Taxis: Can be hailed, ordered by telephone or found at ranks; also possible to hail and share a taxi; fares by negotiation (sometimes a flat rate). Tipping is not usual.

Buses, trams & metro: Buses stop outside the entrance to the Toncontín international airport. All buses in and around the capital operate between 0500 and 2100.

Car hire

A national or international licence is required. Rental cars are available in Tegucigalpa, San Pedro Sula, La Ceiba and on the island of Roatán.

BUSINESS DIRECTORY

The addresses listed below are a selection only. While World of Information makes every endeavour to check these addresses, we cannot guarantee that changes have not been made, especially to telephone numbers and area codes. We would welcome any corrections.

Telephone area codes

The international direct dialling code (IDD) for Honduras is +504 followed by the customer number.

Chambers of Commerce

American-Honduran Chamber of Commerce, Hotel Honduras Maya, PO Box 1838, Tegucigalpa (tel: 232-7043; fax: 232-2031; e-mail: amcham@t.hn2.com).

Cortes Camará de Comercio e Industrias, 17 Avenida Circunvalación, PO Box 14, San Pedro Sula (tel: 553-0761; fax: 533-3777; e-mail: ccic@ccihonduras.org).

Honduras Federación de Camarás de Comercio e Industrias, Edificio Castañito, Bulevar Morazan, Tegucigalpa, PO Box 3393 (tel: 232-6083; fax: 232-1870; e-mail: fedecamara@sigmant.hn).

Tegucigalpa Camará de Comercio e Industrias, Bulevar Centramérica, PO Box 3444, Tegucigalpa (tel: 232-4200; fax: 232-0159; e-mail: infoccit@ccit.hn).

Banking

Banco Atlantida SA, PO Box 3164, Plaza Bancatlan, Tegucigalpa (tel: 321-742; fax: 321-273).

Banco CentroAmericano de Integración Económico, Edificio Midence Soto, Nivel 10, PO Box 772, Tegucigalpa, M D C Honduras (tel: 372-230; fax: 311-906).

Banco Continental SA, PO Box 390, San Pedro Sula, Cortes (tel: 531-310; fax: 522-750).

Banco del Comercio SA (Bancomer), PO Box 160, San Pedro Sula, Cortes (tel: 533-600; fax: 533-128).

Banco de El Ahorro Hondureño SA, PO Box 3185, Tegucigalpa (tel: 375-161; fax: 374-638).

Banco de Honduras SA, PO Box 3434, Tegucigalpa (tel: 326-122; fax: 326-164).

Banco de la Exportación SA (Banexpo), PO Box 3988, Tegucigalpa (tel: 394-256; fax: 394-265).

Banco de las Fuerzas Armadas SA (Banffaa), PO Box 877, Tegucigalpa (tel: 312-051; fax: 313-832).

Banco de Los Trabajadores SA, PO Box 3246, Tegucigalpa (tel: 379-501; fax: 378-422).

Banco de Occidente SA, PO Box 3284, Tegucigalpa (tel: 370-310; fax: 370-486).

Banco del País SA, PO Box 314, San Pedro Sula, Cortes (tel: 525-202; fax: 525-229).

Banco Hondureño del Café (Banhcafe), PO Box 583, Tegucigalpa (tel: 328-370; fax: 328-332).

Banco Financiera Centroamericana SA (Ficensa), PO Box 1432, Tegucigalpa (tel: 381-661; fax: 381-630).

Banco La Capitalizadora Hondureña SA (Bancahsa), PO Box 344, Tegucigalpa (tel: 371-171; fax: 372-775).

Banco Mercantil SA (Bamer), PO Box 116, Tegucigalpa (tel: 320-006; fax: 323-137).

Banco Sogerín SA, PO Box 440, San Pedro Sula, Cortes (tel: 533-888; fax: 572-001).

Lloyds Bank, PO Box 3136, Tegucigalpa (tel: 366-864; fax: 366-417).

Central bank

Banco Central de Honduras, PO Box 3165, Tegucigalpa MDC (tel: 237-2270; fax: 237-1876; e-mail: webmaster@mail.bch.hn).

Travel information

National tourist organisation offices

Instituto Hondureño de Turismo, Col San Carlos, Edificio Europa, PO Box 3261, Tegucigalpa (tel: 222-2124 ext 502; fax: 222-2124 ext 501; e-mail: tourisminfo@iht.hn).

Ministries

Ministry of Agriculture, Boulevard Miraflores, Tegucigalpa, MDC (tel: 32-8394; fax: 325-375).

Ministry of Culture, Arts and Sport, Ave La Paz, Tegucigalpa, MDC (tel: 369-738; fax: 369-738).

Ministry of Defence, 4c, 5a Tegucigalpa, MDC (tel: 380-065; fax: 380-238).

Ministry of Education, 1C 2-3A Comaguela (tel: 228-517; fax: 374-312).

Ministry of External Relations, Antigua Casa Presidencial, Centro Civico Gubernamental, Tegucigalpa, MDC (tel: 343-297; fax: 341-484).

Ministry of Health, 3C 4A Tegucigalpa, MDC (tel: 228-518; fax: 384-141).

Ministry of Industry, Trade and Tourism, 5A, 4C Edif Salame, Tegucigalpa, MDC (tel: 382-025; fax: 372-836).

Ministry of Labour and Social Security, 7C 2-3 Ave Comayaguela (tel: 379-778; fax: 223-220).

Ministry of Natural Resources and Environment, Barrio la Fuente, Tegucigalpa, MDC (tel: 375-664; fax: 375-726).

Ministry of Public Works, Transport and Housing, Barrio la Bolsa, Comayaguela (tel: 33-7690; fax: 252-227).

Presidential Office, Palacio José Cecilio del Valle, Bd Juan Pablo II, Tegucigapa, MDC (tel: 326-282; fax: 31-0097).

Other useful addresses

Asociación Nacional de Industriales, Boulevard los Proceres, 4a Avenida, Colonia Lara, Tegucigalpa.

Asociación Hondureña de Productores de Café (Coffee Producers' Association), 10a Avenida, 6a Calle, Apdo 959, Tegucigalpa.

British Embassy, Edif Palmira, 3rd Floor, Colonia Palmira, Tegucigalpa (tel: 320-612, 320-618; fax: 325-480).

Consejo Hondureño de la Empresa Privada, Barrio la Plozuela, 5th Floor, Edificio San Miguel, Tegucigalpa.

Corporación Nacional de Inversiones (CONADI), Apdo 842, Tegucigalpa (tx: 1192).

División Estudios Económicos, Banco Atlántida, Apdo 57-C, Boulevard Centroamérica, Tegucigalpa.

Home Office, Palacio Nacional, 2o Piso, Tegucigalpa, MDC (tel: 228-604; fax: 37-1121).

Honduran Embassy (US), 3007 Tilden Street, NW, Washington DC 20008 (tel: (+1-202) 966-7702; fax: (+1-202) 966-9751; e-mail: embassy@hondurasemb.org).

Honduras Stock Exchange, PO Box 161, San Pedro Sula (tel: 534-410; fax: 534-480).

Secretary of the Treasury, 3C, 5A Tegucigalpa, MDC (tel: 220-111; fax: 382-309).

Secretaria de Planificación y Presupuesto (SECPLAN), 2 Avenida 9 y 10 Calle Comayaguela, Tegucigalpa.

US Embassy, Avenida La Paz, Apdo 26-C, Tegucigalpa (tel: 323-120; fax: 320-027).

Internet sites

Cámara de Comercio e Industrias de Cortes (Cortes Chamber of Commerce and Industry) (local, national and international business issues in Spanish only): http://www.123.hn/

Honduras yellow pages: http://www.only-honduras.com

Latin America Network Information Center: http://www.lanic.utexas.edu/

Hong Kong

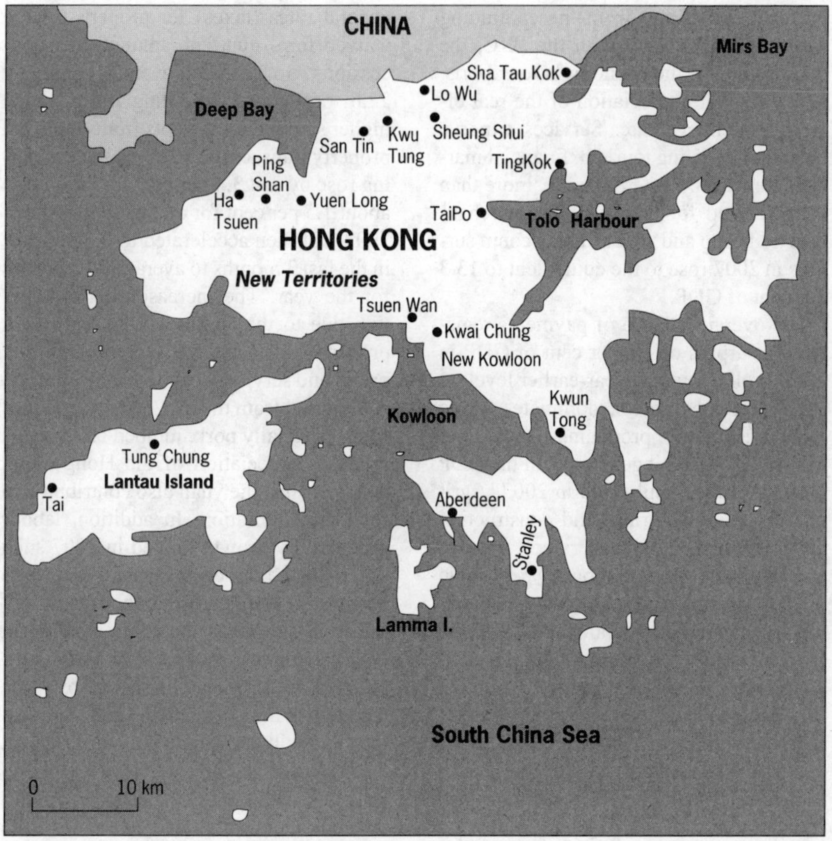

Whatever hopes Hong Kong's voters might hold for eventual democracy, these (however slender) were kept alive in December 2007 when pro-democracy candidate Anson Chan won a by-election against the Beijing backed candidate Regina Ip. In their hearts, however, Hong Kong Chinese know that Beijing is unlikely ever to loosen its grip on Hong Kong, whatever the result of local elections. These fears were endorsed in January 2008 when Beijing set out its proposals for Hong Kong's 'democracy'. In a curate's egg response to Hong Kong's request for full democracy, Beijing set out a timetable for the direct popular election of Hong Kong's chief executive: this would not happen until there had been two more five-year chief executive terms of office. In short, no joy until 2017, and even then all candidates would have to be approved by Beijing. The Beijing government knows full well that any ground ceded to Hong Kong's democracy lobby will create problems elsewhere, not least in Tibet. The Chinese government also needs to maintain an unflinching position in discussions with Taiwan.

The good times return

The response of the Beijing government to Hong Kong's persistent demands for greater democracy had to be answered by the current chief executive, Donald Tsang, who has held the post since 2005. Perceived locally as a Chinese puppet, it fell to Mr Tsang to hold the line; he was helped, however, by the strength of the Hong Kong economy and the feel-good effect that accompanied it. According to the Asian Development Bank's (ADB) *Asian Development Outlook* Hong Kong's economy grew by 6.3 per cent in 2007,

KEY FACTS

Official name: Xianggang Tebie Xingzhengqu (Hong Kong Special Administrative Region (SAR) of China)

Head of State: State President Hu Jintao (elected 15 Mar 2003)

Head of government: Chief Executive Donald Tsang (from 21 Jun 2005, re-elected 25 March 2007)

Ruling party: There is no official ruling party; all candidates and parties must receive official approval from the Zhongguo Gongchandang (Chinese Communist Party).

Area: 1,070 square km (including 235 islands)

Population: 6.97 million (2007)*

Capital: The Legislative Council building is situated in the central district of Victoria, on Hong Kong Island

Official language: Chinese (Mandarin, Beijing dialect de jure; Cantonese de facto) and English

Currency: Hong Kong dollar (HK$) = 100 cents

Exchange rate: HK$7.79 per US$ (Jul 2008)

GDP per capita: US$29,650 (2007)*

GDP real growth: 6.30% (2007)*

Labour force: 3.71 million (2004)

Unemployment: 4.10% (2007)

Inflation: 2.00% (2007)

Balance of trade: -US$7.63 billion (2005)

Foreign debt: US$59.21 billion (2004)

Visitor numbers: 15.82 million (2006)*

* estimated figure

decelerating from about 7 per cent in the previous two years. Growth was largely driven by domestic demand; private consumption increased by 7.8 per cent and contributed 4.5 percentage points to GDP growth. This spending was supported by a strong labour market and buoyant asset markets. Unemployment fell to 4.0 per cent, the lowest level since the end of British rule in 1998, and average monthly wages rose by 4.6 per cent in the third quarter from a year earlier. As a consequence of strong employment, rising incomes, and increasing tourist arrivals, the volume of retail sales rose by 10.5 per cent last year, nearly double the rate of 2006. Buoyant asset markets boosted household wealth and thus supported consumption growth. The index of share prices rose by 39 per cent in 2007, despite a market retreat in the last 2 months of the year. The property market also revived, helped by lower mortgage interest rates and improved incomes. House prices rose by 11.5 per cent in 2007 and the number of residential property transactions surged by about 50 per cent.

Investment in building and construction rebounded to register growth of 0.2 per cent, after falling for several years, while investment in machinery and equipment rose by 6.6 per cent. Relatively low real interest rates supported both consumption and investment growth. Given that the US and Hong Kong dollars are linked, interest rates in Hong Kong generally follow those in the US. Consequently, nominal interest rates declined in the second half of 2007. Real rates tended to fall faster, especially in the fourth quarter when inflation started to pick up. Net exports of goods and services in real terms, on the other hand, declined for the first time since 2001. Exports of both goods and services increased by 7.9 per cent, outpaced by imports, which rose by 8.9 per cent. Re-exports, accounting for 96 per cent of total merchandise exports, grew by 10.8 per cent, benefiting from the continuing surge in global trade with the PRC, the main source of the economy's re-exports, and a gradual depreciation of the real effective exchange rate. Services exports, bolstered by rising tourism, financial market activity, and external trade, more than compensated for the widening merchandise trade gap and the current account surplus in 2007 rose to the equivalent to 13.3 per cent of GDP.

The overall balance of payments registered a surplus of 7.1 per cent of GDP in 2007, well above the year-earlier level.

The services sector dominates Hong Kong's economy, producing over 90 per cent of GDP, and it generated all the GDP growth on the supply side in 2007. Agriculture, manufacturing, and construction all contracted. Among services, finance and insurance grew by about 19 per cent in 2007, reflecting strong expansion in banking and buoyant financial market activity, much of it involving fund-raising for PRC companies. Yuan-denominated banking services also expanded. Other services activities to perform well were real estate and business services; import and export trade services; and hotels, restaurants, and retail trading (the last group benefiting from healthy consumer and tourist spending).

KEY INDICATORS — Hong Kong

	Unit	2003	2004	2005	2006	2007
Population	m	7.39	7.84	6.84	6.90	*6.97
Gross domestic product (GDP)	US$bn	158.60	163.01	177.78	190.00	*206.71
GDP per capita	US$	23,125	23,667	26,000	27,499	*29,650
GDP real growth	%	2.1	8.1	7.5	7.0	*6.3
Inflation	%	-2.6	-0.4	0.9	2.0	2.0
Unemployment	%	7.8	6.7	5.7	4.8	4.1
Coal output	mtoe	6.6	6.6	6.7	7.0	7.0
Exports (fob) (goods)	US$m	224,040	260,263	289,579	317,600	345,979
Imports (cif) (goods)	US$m	208,100	269,575	297,206	331,634	365,679
Balance of trade	US$m	15,940.0	-9,312.0	-7,627.0	-14,033.0	-19,701.0
Current account	US$m	16,180.0	15,870.0	20,268.0	22,936.0	*25,459.0
Total reserves minus gold	US$m	118,360	123,540	124,240	133,170	152,640
Foreign exchange	US$m	118,360	123,540	124,240	133,170	152,640
Exchange rate	per US$	7.70	7.79	7.80	7.77	7.79

* estimated figure

Low inflation, high surplus

Solid economic growth strengthened the fiscal position in the fiscal year 2007 (ended 31 March 2008). The fiscal surplus rose to an estimated 7.2 per cent of GDP, even after income tax rates were cut and general rates (taxes) for properties were waived for 3 quarters, among other concessions. Government revenues surged by 22.6 per cent, benefiting from much higher stamp duty receipts from stock and property transactions. Government spending rose by just 3.4 per cent. Inflation was about 1.5 per cent for the first 9 months of 2007, but then accelerated to 3.5 per cent in the last 3 months to average 2.0 per cent for the year. The increase after October was due to the ending of the waiver on property rates and an increase in food prices and services costs. Much fresh food is imported from the PRC, where prices of food, especially pork, jumped last year. A gradual depreciation of the Hong Kong dollar against the yuan also contributed to food price inflation. In addition, labour productivity growth dipped in 2007 such that rising labour costs began to put some upward pressure on inflation.

Key assumptions include a slowing in PRC economic growth in 2008 and a sharp pullback in US growth, followed by some recovery in the US in 2009. Others are that the yuan will appreciate gradually against the US dollar and that the Hong Kong dollar's link with the US dollar will be maintained. Domestic interest rates are expected to continue to decline this year alongside those in the US. The government projects that the budget will turn to a small deficit in the 2008 financial year and return to surplus the following fiscal year. The 2008 budget lowers personal and corporate income taxes by 1 percentage point to 15.0 per cent and 16.5 per cent, respectively. The projected budget turnaround to a deficit from last year's surplus is expected to provide support for domestic demand.

In line with a weaker US dollar, the ADB expects the Hong Kong dollar to depreciate against many currencies, supporting exports to Asian and other markets. On the balance of these influences, the ADB expects GDP growth to decline to 4.5 per cent in 2008 and then to lift to 4.8 per cent in 2009 if a recovery gets under way in industrial economies. The ADB notes that inflation jumped to 6.3 per cent in February 2008, the highest rate in about 10 years, propelled in part by some one-time factors. Housing has the biggest weighting in the composite consumer price index and rents for private housing are rising sharply along with property values. The price of imported food, the second-largest component in the index, is also moving up. The expected weaker US dollar and firmer yuan will raise import prices and the tight labour market will put some upward pressure on inflation.

Risk assessment

Politics	Fair
Economy	Good
Regional stability	Fair

COUNTRY PROFILE

Historical profile

1839 China impounded opium stocks and blocked further shipments. Major traders, Jardine Matheson, called on the British government to exert its right to trade. The Royal Navy blockaded Chinese ports, sparking the first Opium War.
1842 China ceded Hong Kong to Great Britain under provision of the Treaty of Nanking, following defeat in the first Opium War, which it fought to wipe out the illicit smuggling of opium into the country. Hong Kong was already a sizeable local fishing community with 3,000 inhabitants and 2,000 fishermen. Hong Kong became an important British naval base and attracted merchants from mainland China allowing the colony to become an important regional entrepôt.
1856–60 The second Opium War was fought in which the British and French defeated China.
1860 The Kowloon Peninsula was acquired under the Convention of Peking.
1898 The New Territories were leased from China for a period of 99 years.
1900s Immigration from the mainland increased as social turmoil due to the Boxer rebellion and general insecurity in China grew, while the prospects of employment in Hong Kong's light industries increased.
1937 Outbreak of the Sino-Japanese War. As the Japanese army advanced further into China, more Chinese fled to Hong Kong. It is estimated that over 500,000 Chinese entered the territory at this time.
1941 Hong Kong fell to the Japanese.
1945 After Japan's defeat in the Second World War, Britain resumed control of the territory.
1984 The UK conceded that from July 1997, on the expiry of the lease on the New Territories, China would regain sovereignty over the whole of Hong Kong. The Sino-British Joint Declaration contained detailed assurances on the future of Hong Kong.
1997 Hong Kong became a Special Administrative Region (SAR) of the People's Republic of China in an arrangement to last for 50 years. The Hong Kong stock market crashed; a fear that currency speculators would trade the Hong Kong dollar down in value prompted authorities to raise interest rates.
1998 Only 23 per cent of eligible voters turned out to choose an 800-member election committee with powers to nominate the chief executive and 10 legislators. The election process was criticised as complicated and undemocratic. Hong Kong International Airport on Lantau Island, the largest civil engineering project in history, was opened.
1999 Beijing redefined the constitution, ruling who had the right to live in Hong Kong. This constitutional change sparked protests.
2000 There was a low turnout in the elections which saw the Democratic Party (DP) lose a seat to the pro-Beijing Democratic Alliance for the Betterment of Hong Kong (DAB) in the Legislative Council (LegCo).
2001 Chief Secretary Anson Chan, holder of the SAR's second most powerful office, resigned, amid concerns that pressure from Beijing had made her position unsustainable. Donald Tsang replaced Chan as chief secretary.
2002 Chief Executive Tung Chee Hwa was appointed for a second five-year term.
2003 The flu-like killer disease, Severe Acute Respiratory Syndrome (Sars), spread to Hong Kong from mainland China. Around 500,000 people protested over a proposed anti-subversion law, which many believe threatened basic rights; another demonstration of 50,000 people called for universal suffrage and the dismissal of Chief Executive Tung Chee-hwa.
2004 Chinese legislators ruled out direct elections for a Hong Kong leader in 2007.
2005 Chief Executive Tung Chee-hwa resigned due to ill health; he was replaced by Chief Secretary Donald Tsang. The legislative council rejected an electoral reform package proposed by Tsang.
2006 A goods and services tax was introduced, but met with widespread opposition and was later abandoned.
2007 On 25 March Donald Tsang won a second term as chief executive. The former colonial official, Ms Anson Chan, won a seat in the legislature in December. She won with 55 per cent of the vote against China-backed Regina Ip (43 per cent) and six other candidates. Ms Chan has campaigned for universal suffrage and full democracy. Donald Tsang submitted his report on democratic reform in Hong Kong to Beijin in December.
2008 One of the largest gem auctions ever was held in May, at which US$60 million stones were sold including a 101.27 carat diamond which sold for over US$6 million. It was the largest colourless diamond to be auctioned since 1990 and the new Hong Kong owner will have the right to name it.

Political structure

Constitution

The Basic Law, promulgated by the People's Republic of China (PRC) in 1990, effectively became Hong Kong's constitution after sovereignty of the former British colony was handed over to mainland China in July 1997. The Basic Law pledges to maintain Hong Kong's economic, social and political distinctiveness for a period of 50 years after the handover to the PRC, under the principle of 'one country, two systems'. Foreign affairs and defence are the responsibility of the central government in Beijing.

Form of state

Special Administrative Region (SAR) of the People's Republic of China

The executive

Hong Kong is administered by a Beijing-appointed chief executive, who represents the Chinese Politburo. Tung Chee Hwa was appointed chief executive by a 400-member Selection Committee in 1996, assuming the role in July 1997.
The 13-member Executive Council (ExCo) serves in an advisory role for the Chief Executive. Under the terms of the Basic Law, an 800-member 'election committee', mostly selected from the business community via functional constituencies, will nominate future chief executives.

National legislature

The 60-seat unicameral LegCo comprises 24 members directly elected by geographical constituency, 30 members indirectly elected to represent professional and other functional constituencies, and six indirectly elected by the 800-member 'election committee'.
The first term was two years from 1998 to 2000; subsequent terms are four years.

Legal system

Under the Basic Law, Hong Kong's legal system is guaranteed independence from the Chinese judiciary. A Hong Kong Court of Final Appeal replaced the Privy Council in the United Kingdom as the highest court. The autonomy of this institution was seriously undermined in 1999 after a bitter dispute between the executive and the court over the migration of dependants from mainland China, in which China's legislature, the National People's Congress (NPC), overruled the Court of Final Appeal. However, the government in Beijing declared that recourse to the NPC would be kept a rare and exceptional act, and has not been invoked since.

Last elections

12 September 2004 (Legislative Council); 25 March 2005 (chief executive).

Results: Legislative Council: The pro-government parties won 35 seats out of 60; the pro-democracy parties won 25 seats. Turnout was 55.6 per cent.

Chief executive: the 800-member election committee re-elected Donald Tsang by 649 votes to 123 for Alan Leong.

Next elections

September 2008 (Legislative Council)

Political parties

Ruling party

There is no official ruling party; all candidates and parties must receive official approval from the Zhongguo Gongchandang (Chinese Communist Party).

Main opposition party

There is no formal opposition.

Population

6.97 million (2007)*

Last census: March 2001: 6,708,389

Population density: 6,865 inhabitants per square km (2000), one of the highest in the world.

Annual growth rate: Projected growth 1 per cent per annum (2000–15).

Ethnic make-up

Approximately 98 per cent of the population is of Chinese descent. There are Caucasian, Indian and Filipino minorities, perhaps totalling more than 200,000, but many of these are seasonal migrant workers.

Religions

Buddhism and Taoism (74 per cent); Confucianism, Islam and Hinduism (17 per cent); Christianity (9 per cent). There are places of worship for most other religious groups. Falun Gong, the sect banned in mainland China, is legal in Hong Kong.

Education

Primary education is provided free in all government schools and in most government-assisted schools from the ages of six to 11 years. Secondary schools are divided into junior and senior levels, for 12–14-year-olds and 15–16-year-olds, respectively. The secondary school system consists of Anglo-Chinese grammar schools, Chinese middle schools, secondary technical schools and pre-vocational schools. There are a number of universities, several of which used to be technical colleges. After the British handover in 1997, 24 of Hong Kong's 124 secondary schools which taught in English were ordered to change to Cantonese.

Government expenditure on education amounts to over 20 per cent of the SAR government budget. The largest proportion of the budget is spent on basic education, accounting for 68.8 per cent of total spending on education.

Literacy rate: 93.8 per cent total, 90.1 per cent female; adult rates (World Bank).

Health

Government efforts have been mainly geared to the continuous development of the primary health care services.

Eighteen health centres and 18 visiting health teams provide services to the elderly and their carers. There are three types of hospital in Hong Kong: public, government-assisted and private. Provision of hospital service at nominal cost is made universally accessible to all people. Hong Kong's health care service faces a huge financial strain due to its ageing population and escalating medical costs.

Life expectancy: 80.1 years (estimate 2003)

Fertility rate/Maternal mortality rate: 1.0 birth per woman; maternal mortality 5.6 per 100,000 total births (World Bank).

Birth rate/Death rate: 7.9 births and 5 deaths and per 1,000 people (World Bank)

Child (under 5 years) mortality rate (per 1,000): 2.7 per 1,000 live births (World Bank)

Welfare

The social security schemes available in Hong Kong cover a broad range of developmental, support and remedial services, and financial assistance to those in need. The Comprehensive Social Security Assistance Scheme is means-tested and non-contributory. The Scheme provides cash assistance to individuals and families to meet their basic and essential needs. The recipients are also helped through various initiatives to establish self-reliance. The Social Security Allowance Scheme aims to meet the special needs of the elderly and people with disabilities. The Accident Compensation Schemes provide short-term assistance to families or individuals in cases of reduced or lost earnings.

Main cities

Xianggang (Victoria, Hong Kong Island) (estimated population 1.0 million (m) in 2005); Juilong (Kowloon) (2.0m); Tuen Mun (522,370), Sha Tin (475,177), Fanling (321,650)

Languages spoken

Cantonese is the Chinese language spoken at home by more than 90 per cent of the population. Mandarin Chinese (Putonghua), the official language of the People's Republic of China, is widely understood.

English is universally understood in business and commerce.

Official language/s

Chinese (Mandarin, Beijing dialect de jure; Cantonese de facto) and English

Media

The freedom on the press is guaranteed in basic law.

National news agency: Xinhua News Agency, Hong Kong Branch

Other news agencies: Hong Kong China News Agency (HKCNA): www.chinanews.com.hk

Press

Hong Kong has retained its press freedom since being reunited with China and is a major centre for print journalism with one of the world's largest press industries. It does not impose prior censorship on its newspapers or television and radio news reports.

Dailies: There are over 50 daily newspapers, most of which are published in Chinese.

In English, the South China Morning Post (www.scmp.com) has the largest circulation, China Daily (www.chinadaily.com.cn) is published by the Chinese communist party.

In Chinese, broadsheets include Ming Pao (www.mingpaonews.com) and Sing Tao (www.singtao.com). Newspapers considered pro-Beijing include Ta Kung Pao (www.takungpao.com.hk), Sing Pao (www.singpao.com) and Wen Wek Po (www.wenweipo.com). The newspapers with the highest circulations are tabloid and informal, including The Sun (http://the-sun.on.cc), the Oriental Daily and Apple Daily (http://home.atnext.com).

Weeklies: In Chinese and with the highest circulation Next Magazine (http://next.atnext.com) is tabloid in style that not only covers entertainment but also current affairs, economic and business issues. Others include Easy Finder (http://face.atnext.com), East Touch, East Week and Him Magazine (www.him.com.hk). The only Chinese newsweekly, Yazhou Zhoukan (Asia Weekly) (www.yzzk.com) has broad contents of economic and international news.

Business: In English, the free-issue The Standard (www.thestandard.com.hk) covers financial markets and news and the Far Eastern Economic Review (Feer) (www.feer.com), is an influential monthly covering all aspects of the news throughout Asia. In Chinese newspapers include Hong Kong Commercial Daily (www.hkcd.com.hk) with the largest circulation in Mainland China, Hong Kong Economic Journal (www.hkej.com) and Hong Kong Economic Times cover financial news.

Periodicals: There are over 500 periodicals in circulation. In English, the monthly

Prestige Hong Kong (www.prestigehk.com), is a glossy lifestyle and society magazine and Muse (www.musemag.hk) covers art and culture.

Broadcasting
The Hong Kong Broadcasting Authority (BA) is responsible for regulating and licensing all broadcasting outlets, while standards are maintained by the Television and Entertainment Licensing Authority (TELA).
The government-funded, but independent, Radio Television Hong Kong (RTHK) (www.rthk.org.hk) provides public broadcasting.
Radio: RTHK (www.rthk.org.hk) provides seven radio channels (RTHK Radio 1–6 and Radio Putonghua), with a full range of locally produced programmes in Cantonese, English and Mandarin. RTHK Radio 6 relays the BBC World Service. There are two private, commercial radio stations. Commercial Radio Hong Kong (CRHK) (www.crhk.com.hk) has three channels and a full range of programmes to rival RTHK. The other station is Metro (www.metroradio.com.hk) with three channels, Metro- Finance, Showbiz and Plus.
Television: RTHK (www.rthk.org.hk) produces locally made educational, entertainment and news and current affairs programmes that are shown on other TV stations.
The two private, free-to-air TV stations are Asia Television (ATV) and Television Broadcasts (TVB), each with one channel in English and one in Chinese. There are several subscription networks which between them offer over 200 channels, showing locally produced and international programmes, the largest of which is Cable TV Hong Kong (www.cabletv.com.hk), which produces more programmes than any other broadcaster.

Advertising
Advertising is available in the press, on commercial radio and TV, in cinemas and on poster sites, with direct mail and news technology. Advertising expenditure is equivalent is typically over 1 per cent of GDP.

Economy
Hong Kong's economy is concentrated around its services sector, which contributes over 87 per cent of GDP, of which trade and financial services account for 50 per cent and 40 per cent respectively. There has been strong GDP growth since 2003/04 when it jumped to 8.6 per cent then fell back slightly in subsequent years. GDP growth in 2006 was 6.8 per cent and is predicted to be 5.4 per cent in 2007. The rise in growth has been attributed, by the IMF, to strong mainland-related exports and domestic demand. In turn, the rate of unemployment has improved so that it is at its lowest level since the 1990s, at 4.8 per cent in 2006 and projected to be 4.4 per cent in 2007. Inflation has remained low by world standards only reaching 0.9 per cent in 2005 and rising to 2.0 per cent in 2006.
The Hong Kong dollar is the official currency which is pegged to the US dollar, but since the Chinese government freed the renminbi from its fixed rate to the US dollar and as more mainland Chinese visitors have been arriving the renminbi has grown in acceptance.
In the medium term, the economy of Hong Kong faces financial integration with mainland China. The extent of current integration is still relatively small, although observers believe that a fluid convergence should be achieved. Hong Kong's ability to manage Chinese domestic savings intermediation could be its key role.

External trade
Hong Kong, as an independent customs territory separate from the rest of China and can enter into international commercial and economic agreements on it own behalf. As an economic entity it participates in full membership of a number of international organisations including the Asia Pacific Economic Cooperation forum (APEC).
Under the Closer Economic Partnership Arrangement (CEPA), Hong Kong has a trade alliance with China's nine southernmost provinces and Macau through the pan-Pearl River Delta (PRD) trade bloc, which has been described as 'the largest and most export-oriented of China's regions' with a regional GDP of over US$270 billion. It has a free trade agreement with China, which allows the trade of goods of Hong Kong origin entry at zero tariff, as well as preferential treatment in 27 service sectors.
Hong Kong's manufacturing base has relocated to mainland china where raw materials are readily available and concurrently, its service industry has grown, in part to compete against China's own growing financial centres.

Imports
Main imports are petroleum, raw materials and semi-manufactures, capital goods and foodstuffs.
Main sources: China (45.3 per cent total, 2006), Japan (10.6 per cent), Taiwan (7.7 per cent).

Exports
Exports include electrical machinery and appliances – telecommunications, sound recording and electronic components – textiles, clothing, footwear, watches and clocks, toys, plastics, precious stones and printed material.
Main destinations: China (46.3 per cent total, 2006), US (14.8 per cent), Japan (4.8 per cent).

Re-exports
These include consumer goods, clothing, electrical machinery and appliances.

Agriculture
Agriculture accounts for around 0.1 per cent of GDP. The land area is mountainous, with fertile soils when they are watered. Agricultural land, including 600 hectares of orchards, accounts for 7 per cent of the total land area.
Main crops include sweet potatoes, yams, taro, sugar cane, white cabbage, flowering cabbage, lettuce, chinese kale, radishes and watercress.
Hong Kong has a fishing fleet of about 4,900 vessels, most of which are mechanised. The fishing sector employs about 24,000 fishermen, who are provided with training organised by the Agriculture and Fisheries Conservation Department (AFCD) in order to enhance the competitiveness of the sector. Pond and marine fish farming in the New Territories accounts for 3 per cent of total production. Seafood production can reach up to 200,000 tonnes per annum. Freshwater fish production is more limited, typically 4,000 tonnes or less per annum. In addition, Hong Kong imports in the region of 60,000 tonnes of freshwater fish per annum and some 500,000 tonnes of seafood, of which 300,000 tonnes are typically re-exported.
In 2004, the total marine fish catch was 152,674 tonnes and the total crustacean catch was 5,950 tonnes.

Industry and manufacturing
Industry accounts for around 11 per cent of GDP and employs 18 per cent of the workforce. The relocation of manufacturing operations from Hong Kong to mainland China is causing a long-term decline in the sector. The re-export sector, in contrast, has grown due to growing consumer demand and industrial production on the mainland.

Tourism
Tourism is the most important sector of the economy. It was affected by the Sars outbreak in 2003, which reduced visitor numbers, particularly from mainland China, its largest market. A prompt, vigorous and imaginative strategy quickly reversed the initial impact to such effect that the sector boomed in 2004 with a 40.4 per cent increase in visitor numbers. The impetus was mainly due to an increase in tourists from mainland China, who comprised 56 per cent of the 21,810,630

arrivals. The upward trend increased in 2005.
Infrastructure and attractions are being expanded, especially in connection with the new Disneyland opened in September 2005. Tourism is expected to contribute two per cent to GDP in 2005.

Environment
Hong Kong is suffering air pollution as a result of pollution from southern China; visibility has declined over the past 30 years and continues to worsen. Although Hong Kong has sharply reduced its own emissions, it lies at the southern end of a vast industrial conurbation that includes Guangzhou and Shenzhen.

Mining
Mining accounts for less than 0.05 per cent of GDP, producing mainly kaolin (around 44,500 tonnes) and feldspar (around 5,500 tonnes).

Hydrocarbons
Hong Kong relies entirely on imports of hydrocarbons.
Natural gas is brought to Hong Kong via the pipeline from the South China Sea offshore gas field and is used for power generation.
Annual coal imports of around nine million tonnes meet 20 per cent of energy consumption.

Financial markets
Stock exchange
The Hong Kong Stock Exchange is the world's seventh largest in terms of capitalisation and the second largest in Asia, ranking only behind Japan.

Banking and insurance
Domestic banks in Hong Kong have tended to rely on the property sector for their earnings. Mortgages and other property-related lending still account for 40 to 50 per cent of total loans. Banking practice codes were revised in 2001 to make banking more transparent and consumer friendly. In 2002, some of the criteria for entry to the banking sector were relaxed. The aim was to attract a wider range of domestic and international banks to become involved in the SAR.
Hong Kong is an excellent location for insurers and has the largest number of insurance companies in Asia. Mainland Chinese insurers are linking up with foreign insurers in Hong Kong to cater for China's insurance market. By 2003, there were around 7,000 insurance establishments in the SAR with a total premium income of US$7 billion. French AXA group, the world's biggest insurance company, has its regional headquarters in Hong Kong.

Central bank
Hong Kong has no finance ministry or official central bank. The Hong Kong Monetary Authority (HKMA) oversees the monetary and banking system.
Main financial centre
Central District

Time
GMT plus eight hours

Geography
Hong Kong comprises some 235 islands and islets and a portion of the Chinese mainland, adjoining China's southern province of Guangdong. It consists of three areas: Hong Kong Island, the Kowloon Peninsula and the New Territories, which account for 92 per cent of the territory. About 75 per cent of Hong Kong's land is unsuitable for food production, consisting of hills that rise from sea level to 900 metres.
Hemisphere
Northern

Climate
Hong Kong is subtropical and monsoonal. Summer (May to mid-September) is hot and humid with a risk of typhoons. July and August can be very hot. Autumn (September to December) is generally sunny, but drier, and the most pleasant time of year. Winter (December to February) is dry, but can get uncomfortably cold, with an average temperature of 15 degrees Celsius (C). Spring (March and April) is moderately warm and damp. The average annual temperature is about 23 degrees C, while rainfall averages 2,224mm per year, and humidity is often above 83 per cent.

Dress codes
Business dress is formal as appearance is taken seriously. Very smart dress is also de rigueur for ladies; skirts are advisable, rather than trousers.

Entry requirements
Passports
A valid passport is required by all. Passports must be valid for six months after arrival.
Visa
Visas required by all, with some exceptions see www.immd.gov.hk/ehtml/hkvisas.htm for further details.
Business and tourist visas are considered the same, up to the minimum time allowed to visit. For further clarification email: enquiry@immd.gov.hk; or contact the local Chinese embassy.
Regulations regarding entry into Hong Kong are extensive owing to the high level of illegal immigration. Travellers are advised to obtain up-to-date information before any journey.
Prohibited entry
Currency advice/regulations
There are no currency restrictions.
Travellers cheques are readily accepted.
Customs
Personal effects are duty-free. Visitors wishing to purchase ivory products in Hong Kong will need an export licence from the Hong Kong authorities, and will also need to show an import licence for their final destination.
Prohibited imports
Illegal drugs, fireworks, firearms, counterfeit items, textiles, ivory products, animals and plants, game, meat and poultry. Live animals are strictly controlled. Antibiotics may not be imported without an accompanying doctor's letter .
Visitors entering from China should expect searches for fireworks.

Health (for visitors)
Mandatory precautions
Yellow fever and cholera inoculation if travelling from infected areas.
Advisable precautions
Vaccinations are recommended for diphtheria, tuberculosis, hepatitis A and B, polio, tetanus and typhoid. Dengue fever is increasing, however the risk of malaria has been reduced. Tap water is safe to drink.
A HK$580 fee is imposed on any visitor who has to use accident and emergency hospital services. Medical insurance is recommended.

Hotels
A wide range of hotels are available; advance bookings are recommended between May–November. A 10 per cent service charge and 5 per cent tax are added to hotel bills.

Credit cards
Major international credit cards are widely accepted, although cash prices may be lower.

Public holidays (national)
Fixed dates
1 Jan (New Year's Day), 5 Apr (Ching Ming/Tomb Sweeping Day), ^1 May (Labour Day), 1 Jul (HKSAR Establishment Day), 1 Oct (National Day), 25–26 Dec (Christmas).
^ Holidays falling on Sunday are taken on Monday.
Variable dates
Chinese New Year (Jan/Feb, three days), Good Friday and Easter Monday (Mar/Apr), Birth of Buddha (May), Tuen Ng (Dragon Boat festival, May/Jun), Chinese Mid-Autumn Festival (Sep/Oct), Chung Yeung Festival (Oct).

Working hours
Banking
Mon–Fri: 0900–1630; Sat: 0900–1230.

Business
Mon–Fri: 0900–1300, 1400–1700; Sat: 0900–1300.
Government
Mon–Fri: 0900–1300, 1400–1700; Sat: 0900–1230.
Shops
Central District 1000–1900; Causeway Bay and Wanchai 1000–2130; Tsimshatsui East 1000–1930; Tsimshatsui, Yaumatei and Mong Kok 1000–2100. Most department stores and shops open Sundays. Some Japanese stores close one day per week, and street markets operate all day and into the night.

Telecommunications
Mobile/cell phones
GSM 900/1800 services are available throughout the islands and territories.

Electricity supply
200V AC, 50Hz. No uniformity in plug design.

Weights and measures
Metric system (Imperial system and local units also in use).

Social customs/useful tips
Western influence in Hong Kong has produced ways of doing business that are similar to other major business capitals. However, behind the facade of modern office blocks and neon-lit shopping malls, ancient Chinese customs still survive and have become part of the life of the foreign community.
Business cards are handed out liberally as a method of developing a network of professional contacts. A Chinese translation on the reverse side is a worthwhile addition. Use both hands when offering a business card, as passing it with one hand is seen as impolite.
Appearances of wealth are considered important in a territory that is dedicated to making money. Business contacts are ostentatiously wined and dined. Most entertaining is done in restaurants. It is considered bad manners to divide the bill after a meal. If you go to a dinner as the guest of honour, you should rise and thank the host briefly for his hospitality.
Personal friendships and family ties oil the wheels of business. The wealthy keep a high social profile, donating large sums of money to charity.
Punctuality is helpful as most people have packed days, although some allowances are made for the heavy traffic.
Policemen who speak English have a red shoulder badge.

Security
The level of crime against visitors is relatively low. Theft, mainly by pickpockets, is a problem on the streets.

Getting there
Air
National airline: Cathay Pacific Airways
International airport/s: Hong Kong International (HKG), 34km from the centre. Post office, bank, bureau de change, restaurants/cafeterias, duty free shop, taxis.
Airport tax: HK$120, excluding transit passengers.
Surface
The business district and commercial centre of Hong Kong is located on Hong Kong island. Kowloon and the new territories across the harbour are part of the Asia mainland, with road links providing connections.
Road: Bus services link Guangzhou to the Hong Kong border.
Rail: The Kowloon-Canton Railway Corporation (KCR) is the main carrier of passengers to and from China, with express trains serving Kowloon-Guangzhou and Kowloon-Lowu.
Water: Hovercraft services operate four times a day to and from Guangzhou and several times daily to and from Zhuhai. There are frequent daily services to and from Macao by hovercraft (75 minutes), jetcats (75 minutes), high speed ferry (90 minutes) and jetfoil (60 minutes).
Main port/s: Victoria Harbour (Hong Kong Island) and Tolo Harbour (New Territories).

Getting about
National transport
Air: Dragonair flies to 23 mainland Chinese destinations, as well as other regional capitals in Asia.
Hong Kong maintains separate immigration and customs policies from the mainland and flights between them are treated as international and not domestic flights.
Road: Hong Kong's road network is extensive and of high quality but often congested in central areas.
Buses: Bus services are inexpensive and convenient.There are three main private bus companies, China Motor Bus (CMB), Citybus and Kowloon Motor Bus (KMB, Kowloon only), and private minibus services.
Rail: There are three rail systems which operate outside urban areas. The KCR runs a passenger service between Kowloon and Guangzhou (China) and a suburban service to the new towns of the north-eastern New Territories; KCR also operates the Light Rail Transit network in the north-western New Territories; a cable-hauled funicular railway operates on Hong Kong Island between Garden Road in the Central District to Victoria Gap on the Peak.
The Airport Express is a dedicated high-speed train link, with a journey time of 24 minutes from central Hong Kong to the airport. Operating hours: 0550–0115 daily.
Water: There are extensive ferry, hovercraft, hydrofoil and coastal services between the islands of Hong Kong.
City transport
Taxis: Metered taxis (that calculate time and distance) are readily available in most areas of the territory. They carry four to five passengers. Cabs are painted green and silver in the New Territories, and red and silver in town. Hong Kong taxis are reasonably priced. It is advisable to have the destination written in Chinese. Tips are discretionary. Taxi drivers retain odd cents of change as a matter of course. A ride to or from the airport– Central District will include an extra toll charge of HK$30 plus any tunnel tolls.
Buses, trams & metro: There are regular shuttle buses to and from the airport to both Central District (Hong Kong Island) and Tsimshatsui (Kowloon). They are cheaper than taxis and serve five routes every 12–15 minutes. Airport bus routes A11 and A12 operate 0600–2359 hours to Central District, journey time 70 minutes.
Trams: A flat fare system operates on Hong Kong Island's double-decker five-line tram system. The trams are crowded at rush hour, but afford good views of Hong Kong at other times.
Ferry: There are regular ferry services across the narrow strip of water from Star Ferry terminal at the north of Hong Kong Island to Kowloon.
Car hire
A valid driving licence issued in the country of origin may be used for up to 12 months. Parking difficulties and traffic congestion should be taken into account when planning to drive in Hong Kong. Chauffeur-driven and self-drive car hire is available.

BUSINESS DIRECTORY

The addresses listed below are a selection only. While World of Information makes every endeavour to check these addresses, we cannot guarantee that changes have not been made, especially to telephone numbers and area codes. We would welcome any corrections.

Telephone area codes
The international direct dialling code (IDD) for Hong Kong is +852, followed by subscriber's number.

Useful telephone numbers

Emergencies	999
Directory enquiries	108
Problems	109
International calls	010
Calls to China	012
Collect (reversed charge) calls	011

Tourist information 2801-7177
International direct dialling code enquiries 013

Chambers of Commerce

American Chamber of Commerce in Hong Kong, 1904 Bank of America Tower, 12 Harcourt Road, Central (tel: 2526-0165; fax: 2810-1289; e-mail: amcham@amcham.org.hk).

British Chamber of Commerce in Hong Kong, Emperor Group Centre, 288 Hennessy Road, Wan Chai (tel: 2824-2211; fax: 2824-1333; e-mail: info@britcham.com).

Banking

Bank of East Asia Ltd, GPO Box 31, 10 Des Voeux Road, Central (tel: 2842-3200; fax: 2845-9333).

Bank of China (Hong Kong) Ltd; Bank of China Tower, 1 Garden Road, Hong Kong (tel: 2826-6350; fax: 2530-3875).

DBS Bank (Hong Kong) Ltd, 99 Queen's Road Central, Central (tel: 2218-2706).

Hang Seng Bank Ltd, Hang Seng Bank Headquarters, 83 Des Voeux Road, Central (tel: 2825-5111; fax: 2845-9301).

HSBC, 1 Queen's Road, Central (tel: 2822-1111; fax: 2868-1646; internet: www.hsbcnet.com).

Nanyang Commercial Bank Ltd, 151 Des Voeux Road, Central (tel: 2852-0888; fax: 2815-3333).

Shanghai Commercial Bank Ltd, 12 Queen's Road, Central (tel: 2841-5415).

Wing Lung Bank Ltd, 45 Des Voeux Road, Central (tel: 2826-8333; fax: 2810-0592).

Central bank

Hong Kong Monetary Authority, 3 Garden Road, Central (tel: 2878-8196; fax: 2878-8197; e-mail: hkma@hkma.gov.hk).

Travel information

Cathay Pacific Airways, Swire House, 9 Connaught Road, Central (tel: 2747-5000; fax: 2810-6563).

Hong Kong Automobile Association, March Road, Wanchai (tel: 2574-3394).

Star Ferry Concourse, Kowloon; Shop 8, Basement Jardine House, Central (tel: 2801-7177 (visitor hotline); fax: 2810-4877).

National tourist organisation offices

Hong Kong Tourist Association (HKTA), 9-11th Floor, Citicorp Centre, 18 Whitfield Road, North Point (tel: 2807-6543, 2807-6177 (tourist information); fax: 2807-6582; internet site: http://www.hkta.org).

Other useful addresses

Agriculture and Fisheries Department, 13/F Canton Road Government Offices, 393 Canton Road, Kowloon (tel: 2733-2174; fax: 2311-3731).

Banking, Securities, Insurance & Companies Division, 24th Floor Admiralty Centre, Tower II, Central (tel: 2527-8337; fax: 2865-6146).

Buildings Department, 3-12/F Murray Building Garden Road, Central (tel: 2848-2327; fax: 2840-0451).

Business and Industrial Trade Fairs Ltd, 51 Gloucester Road, Wanchai (tel: 2865-2633; fax: 2866-1770, 2865-5513).

Census and Statistics Department, Wanchai Tower 1, 12 Harbour Road, Wanchai (tel: 2823-4807).

Chinese Manufacturers' Association of Hong Kong, 3rd and 4th Floor CMA Bldg, 64 Connaught Road, Central (tel: 2545-6166).

Civil Aviation department, 46/F Queensway Government Offices, 66 Queensway (tel: 2867-4332; fax: 2869-0093).

Consumer Council, 22/F, K Wah Centre, 191 Java Road, North Point (tel: 2856-3113; fax: 2856-3611).

Department of Health, 17 & 21/F Wu Chung House, 213 Queen's Road East, Wan Chai (tel: 2961-8989; fax: 2836-0071).

Environmental Protection Department, 24-28/F Southorn Centre, 130 Hennessy Road, Wan Chai (tel: 2835-1018; fax: 2838-2155).

Exchange Fund Division, 24th Floor Admiralty Centre, Tower II, Central (tel: 2529-0024; fax: 2865-6146).

Federation of Hong Kong Industries, 4/F Hankow Centre, 5-15 Hankow Road, Kowloon (tel: 2723-0818).

Finance Branch, Government Secretariat, Central Government Offices, Lower Albert Road, Central (tel: 2810-2540; fax: 2810-1530).

Hong Kong Convention & Incentive Travel Bureau (trade fairs), 35th Floor Jardine House, Central (tel: 2801-7111; fax: 2810-4877).

Hong Kong Exporters' Association, Room 825 Star House, 3 Salisbury Road, Tsim Sha Tsui, Kowloon (tel: 2730-9851).

Hong Kong Government Industry Department, 'One-Stop' Unit, 14th Floor, Ocean Centre, 5 Canton Road, Kowloon (tel: 2737-2434; fax: 2730-4633).

Hong Kong Economic and Trade Office, 6 Grafton Street, London W1S 4EQ (tel: (+044-20) 7499-9821; fax: (+044-20) 7495-5033; email: general@hketolondon.gov.hk).

Hong Kong Industrial Estates Corporation, 107 Estate Centre Building, 19 Dai Cheong Street, Tai Po Industrial Estate, Tai Po, New Territories (tel: 2664-1183).

Hong Kong Productivity Council, 78 Tat Chee Avenue, HKCP Bldg, Kowloon (tel: 2788-5678).

Hong Kong Standards and Testing Centre, 10 Dai Wang Street, Tai Po Industrial Estate, Tai Po, New Territories (tel: 2667-0021).

Hong Kong Telecom Association, GPO Box 13461 (tel: 2881-2333; fax: 2881-2332).

Hong Kong Trade Development Council, Research Department, 36-39/F Office Tower, Convention Plaza, 1 Harbour Road, Wan Chai (tel: 2584-4333; fax: 2824-0249; internet site: http://www.tdc.org.hk/).

Industry Department, 14/F Ocean Centre, 5 Canton Road, Tsim Sha Tsui (tel: 2737-2216; fax: 2377-0730).

Labour Department, 16/F Harbour Building, 38 Pier Road, Central (tel: 2852-3511).

Securities & Futures Commission, 38/F Two Exchange Square, 8 Connaught Place (tel: 2840-9202; fax: 2845-9553).

Stock Exchange of Hong Kong Ltd, 1/F, 1 and 2 Exchange Square, 8 Connaught Place, PO Box 8888 (tel: 2522-1122; fax: 2868-1308).

Telecommunications Authority, 29th Floor, Wu Chung House, 213 Queens Road East, Wan Chai (tel: 2961-6333; fax: 2803-5110).

Trade Department, Ocean Centre, 5 Canton Road, Kowloon (tel: 2722-2333).

US General Consulate, 26 Garden Road (tel: 2523-9011; fax: 2845-1598).

Visa Office, Ministry of Foreign Affairs, 5th Floor, Lower Block, 26 Harbour Road, Wanchai (tel: 2835-3794).

National news agency: Xinhua News Agency, Hong Kong Branch

Other news agencies: Hong Kong China News Agency (HKCNA): www.chinanews.com.hk

Internet sites

Economic Services Bureau: www.info.gov.hk/esb/content.htm

Hong Kong Airport: www.hongkongairport.com

Hong Kong Shipping directory: www.info.gov.hk/mardep/sdfiles/shipdir.ht

Hong Kong Statistics: www.info.gov.hk/censtatd/eindex.htm

Hungary

Hungary marked the fiftieth anniversary of the bloody Hungarian revolution in 2006. Hopes that the anniversary would be a genuine cause for celebration were to prove misplaced. In 1956 Hungarians were struggling against Soviet control with the world watching as students lobbed Molotov cocktails at Soviet tanks in the Budapest streets. In 2006, more prosaically, the government was battling European Union (EU) budget directives. EU accession, secured in 2004, has helped Hungary attract greater international interest, both political and financial. With a population of only just over 10 million, Hungary is a country sometimes in danger of being overlooked – but 2005 had propelled it into the limelight with a visit from the British prime minister, Tony Blair, and a prime ministerial meeting with the US President, George W Bush. Ferenc Gyurcsány, the prime minister, seized on this 50-minute conversation to bolster his international image and exhorted Bush to join Hungary for its imminent anniversary celebrations.

Disturbances

Things started to go wrong in September 2006; small scale protests began in response to the introduction of Prime Minister Ferenc Gyurcsány's economic austerity measures (notably higher taxes). These measures were a key part of the government's Convergence Plan, which is designed to reduce the budget deficit and eventually bring Hungary into the eurozone. The Convergence Plan, which was approved by the European Commission in September 2006, also requires extensive structural reform of the public sector.

Unrest increased when a recording was anonymously leaked to the media in which Mr Gyurcsány was reported to have said that his party had lied to the electorate. Mr Gyurcsány had been speaking to a closed meeting of his Magyar Szocialista Párt (MSzP) (Hungarian Socialist Party) Caucus in May. Following the leak of the recording, Mr Gyrucsány published the text of the speech on his website. He and others complained that his speech had been misrepresented. A demonstration turned violent with approximately 60 people injured. Smaller demonstrations continued over the period leading up to the 1 October local elections.

The governing coalition performed worse in the local elections than expected,

KEY FACTS

Official name: Magyar Köztársaság (Republic of Hungary)

Head of State: President László Sólyom (since Aug 2005)

Head of government: Prime Minister Ferenc Gyurcsány (MSzP) (since 2004; elected 23 Apr 2006)

Ruling party: Coalition: Magyar Szocialista Párt (MSzP) (Hungarian Socialist Party) and Szabad Demokratak Szovetsege (SzDSz) (Alliance of Free Democrats) (since 2002; re-elected Apr 2006)

Area: 93,033 square km

Population: 10.06 million (2007)*

Capital: Budapest

Official language: Hungarian (Magyar)

Currency: Forint (Ft)

Exchange rate: Ft144.25 per US$ (Jul 2008)

GDP per capita: US$13,762 (2007)*

GDP real growth: 1.30% (2007)*

Labour force: 4.24 million (2007)

Unemployment: 7.40% (2007)

Inflation: 7.90% (2007)*

Balance of trade: -US$1.15 billion (2006)

Foreign debt: US$74.92 billion (2004)

Visitor numbers: 9.26 million (2006)*

* estimated figure

but Budapest and seven other large cities were nonetheless retained. In October 2006, Mr Gyurcsány sought and won a confidence vote in Parliament by 207 votes to 165. Opposition-organised protests continued for some time. These peaked in late October, following government celebrations marking the 50th anniversary of the 1956 Hungarian uprising. Violence broke out again on this occasion. The opposition called on the crowd of around 100,000 to continue to protest until the prime minister resigned and also called for a referendum on education, health, pensions and land reform. Smaller protests continued until a large rally organised by the main opposition party, Fidesz-KDNP (Coalition of Fidesz-Magar Polgári Szövetség (Fidesz-Hungarian Civic Union), and some smaller demonstrations were held on 4 November, the anniversary of the return of Soviet troops to Budapest in 1956. There was no further violence and no major demonstrations. But the events had made it clear that Hungary's political divisions continue to run deep.

Economy

EU membership has brought palpable benefits to Hungary, boosting agricultural incomes, helping GDP growth and pumping regional and structural aid into the country. The economy grew at an estimated rate of 4.5 per cent in 2006, continuing Hungary's strong growth trend (2004 – 4.0 per cent, 2005 4.1 per cent) and maintaining its strong status among the newer EU members. In 2006 inflation fell to an estimated 3.5 per cent, virtually unchanged from the 3.5 per cent of 2005. Hungary's GDP per capita dipped slightly, to US$ 10,296 from US$10,814 in 2005. In terms of purchasing power, per capita income continued to rise. Hungary continued to flout the EU stability and growth pact, which lays down a deficit limit of 3 per cent of GDP as a prerequisite to entering the eurozone. Hungary had planned to convert to the single currency in 2010. However, there were real concerns that it would not meet the deficit targets for entering the Exchange Rate Mechanism II (ERM II) by 2008. Hungary needs to spend two years in the ERM II before converting to the euro in 2010. A significant factor in the imbalance was the demand by Eurostat, the EU's statistical information service, that Hungary incorporate its expensive motorway construction figures into the budget. It had cunningly tried to isolate these figures, exploiting the project's status as a public/private partnership. This factor alone raised the 2005 deficit by 1.9 per cent of GDP. The true arithmetic only emerged when the national bank revealed that the government had been massaging the figures.

The appointment of a new finance minister, Janos Veres, in April 2005 seemed to signal official recognition that state spending had to be reined in. However, such measures have not materialised. EU commissioner for economic and monetary affairs, Joaquin Almunia, has taken a dim view of the Hungarians' failure to control their budget. With others, he has warned that tight fiscal discipline will be the only way to regulate the books. As Hungary is not yet a member of the eurozone, it is not liable for formal sanctions. However, other punishments are possible, such as withholding structural funds: Almunia has not ruled this out.

Mr Gyurcsány's efforts to make Hungary more attractive to investors by offering tax incentives and a simplification of bureaucracy, appears to be paying off. For now, Hungary is reaping great rewards from foreign investors who appreciate the relatively low labour costs, relatively skilled workforce and sound infrastructure that the country has to offer. Since 2004 foreign investment has been responsible for the creation of over 14,000 jobs. However, the country cannot afford to be complacent, as other eastern European countries are hot on Hungary's heels, eager to offer even greater savings to overseas companies. Hungary particularly has to look out for Slovakia, Romania, Poland and the Czech Republic. Competition for labour is focussed not only on cost but on the quality of the workforce.

2006 elections

Prime Minister Gyurcsány was re-elected in parliamentary elections in April. Rioting had followed his admission in September that he lied about the economy during the election, but he defied demands for his resignation. On 6 October he won a vote of confidence in parliament.

Social problems

In 2004 Hungary took one step towards tackling one of its most entrenched social problems: the widespread discrimination experienced by its Roma population. Livia Jaroka was elected as the first Romany MEP. It was a fitting move considering that Europe had just entered the Decade of Roma Inclusion (2005–15), in which eight nations are participating: Hungary, Romania, Croatia, Bulgaria, the Czech Republic, Slovakia, Serbia, Montenegro and Macedonia. Roma people, who account for 7 per cent of Hungary's population and over 10 million people in Europe, are often forced to live in utterly wretched conditions. They suffer astronomically high levels of joblessness: in some areas unemployment rates have reached 100 per cent. The average jobless figure among Roma is seven times the Hungarian average. Roma suffer discrimination and segregation in

KEY INDICATORS — Hungary

	Unit	2003	2004	2005	2006	2007
Population	m	10.04	10.12	10.10	10.08	*10.06
Gross domestic product (GDP)	US$bn	83.04	100.70	111.57	112.92	*138.39
GDP per capita	US$	8,272	10,129	11,049	11,206	*13,762
GDP real growth	%	2.9	4.0	4.2	3.9	*1.3
Inflation	%	4.6	6.8	3.6	3.9	*7.9
Unemployment	%	5.9	6.1	7.2	7.5	7.4
Industrial output	% change	–	4.7	6.9	5.4	–
Agricultural output	% change	–	37.9	-10.9	2.6	–
Coal output	mtoe	2.8	2.9	2.0	2.1	2.9
Exports (fob) (goods)	US$m	40,000.0	55,368.0	61,847.0	74,348.0	–
Imports (cif) (goods)	US$m	44,500.0	58,290.0	63,836.0	75,494.0	–
Balance of trade	US$m	-4,500.0	-2,922.0	-1,989.0	-1,146.0	–
Current account	US$m	-7,450.0	-8,930.0	-7,457.0	-7,352.0	*-7,750.0
Total reserves minus gold	US$m	12,737.0	15,908.0	18,539.0	21,527.0	23,970.0
Foreign exchange	US$m	12,015.0	15,312.0	18,283.0	21,316.0	23,773.0
Exchange rate	per US$	216.92	202.52	195.85	192.27	176.03

* estimated figure

education, housing and healthcare. One in five Roma children is written off as having learning difficulties and relegated to sink classes. Jaroka has raised the profile of this persecuted minority and in 2005 some progress was made. In Miskolc, in the east of the country, the Chance for Children organisation proposed to the courts that the segregation of white and Roma children in the school system was illegal. The local administration was acquitted but publicity from the case contributed to the amendment of the Education Act, passed in December 2005. This change will prevent schools selecting pupils along ethnic lines, and will prioritise places for disadvantaged children, predominantly Roma. In the same month, the Roma Rendôrök Országos Egyesülete, or National Roma Police Association, was inaugurated. This is the first such organisation in the world and hopes to break down the deep mutual distrust that exists between the legal authorities and Hungary's ethnic minorities.

Outlook

Hungary's political immaturity risks minimising the substantial economic progress that the country has made, posting a consistently high growth rate while containing inflation to acceptable levels. Hungary is by no means alone in its inability to contain the budget deficit – a number of EU members would face similar difficulties if they were to wish to join the eurozone now.

Risk assessment

Politics	Fair
Economy	Good
Regional stability	Good

COUNTRY PROFILE

Historical profile

The Hungarians (Magyars) are a Turkic or Finno-Ugrian people who settled on the Hungarian plains in the seventh century AD.

From the mid-eighteenth century, Hungary, together with Austria and a large area of central and eastern Europe, was part of the dual monarchy ruled by the Habsburgs.

1914–18 After the assassination of Archduke Ferdinand, the heir to the Austro-Hungarian throne, Austro-Hungary declared war on Serbia in June 1914, with the support of Germany. In November 1918, after the Austro-Hungarian empire was defeated in the First World War, Hungary declared its independence, King Karl IV stood down as head of state of Hungary and the Entente powers carved-up Hungary as a punishment for its role in the First World War, taking two-thirds of its territory and nearly 60 per cent of its pre-war population.

1919 Communists seized power and declared the Hungarian Soviet Republic but were defeated by Admiral Miklos Horthy, who governed as Regent from 1920 until 1944.

1920 Hungary signed the Treaty of Trianon, confirming its territorial losses to Romania, Yugoslavia, Czechoslovakia and Austria.

1939–45 Hungary allied with Germany and acquired territory through the partitioning of Czechoslovakia and the Axis invasion of Yugoslavia. Having sought to break the alliance, Hungary was occupied by Germany in 1944 before being invaded by the Soviets later in the same year. Following the end of the Second World War, Hungary's territory was reduced to pre-war boundaries and severe reparations exacted.

1947 Communists were the largest single party in the general election.

1949 The People's Republic was established. With Matyas Rakosi as prime minister, purges and political trials on the Stalinist model followed. Agriculture was reorganised on the Soviet pattern and industry was nationalised.

1953 The more liberal Imre Nagy became prime minister, before being replaced by communist András Hegedüs in 1958.

1956 Support for liberals grew among the population but turned into violence. Nagy became prime minister for eleven days before the Soviet Union intervened militarily. The communist Magyar Szocialista Mukaspart Partja (MSzMP) (Hungarian Socialist Workers' Party), returned to power with János Kádár as prime minister.

1958 Nagy was executed in Romania for his part in the 1956 Hungarian uprising. Árpád Szákasits, as chairman of the Presidential Council, became the head of state.

1960s Kádár introduced a number of minor liberal reforms such as dismantling collective farms, raising wages and introducing some intellectual freedom.

1988 Dissatisfaction among party members with the remoteness of the leadership led to the resignation of Kádár and moves towards 'Socialist Pluralism'.

1989 The MSzMP was re-named the Magyar Szocialista Párt (MSzP) (Hungarian Socialist Party). Mátyás Szürös became Hungary's interim president.

1990 First free multi-party parliamentary elections for 43 years resulted in the formation of a coalition government led by József Antall of the Magyar Demokrata Fórum (MDF) (Hungarian Democratic Forum).

1994 The general election resulted in a coalition government led by Gyula Horn of the MSzP.

1998 The centre-right Fiatal Demokraták Szövetsége-Magyar Polgári Párt (Fidesz-MPP) (Federation of Young Democrats-Hungarian Civic Party), led by Viktor Orbán, unexpectedly won the general election.

1999 Hungary became one of the first former Soviet satellite states to join NATO.

2000 Ferenc Mádl was elected president by parliament, replacing Árpád Göncz who had been president since 1990.

2001 The government introduced the Status Law, providing the four million ethnic Hungarians in neighbouring countries the right to work and study in Hungary.

2002 After parliamentary elections, Péter Médgyessy (leader of MSzP) was sworn in as prime minister of a coalition government, comprising MSzP and Szabad Demokratak Szovetsege (SzDSz) (Alliance of Free Democrats).

2003 In the EU membership referendum, turnout out was only 46 per cent; 84 per cent of voters said yes to membership.

2004 Hungary joined the EU. After the ruling MSzP withdrew support from him, Prime Minister Péter Medgyessy resigned. Ferenc Gyurcsány became prime minister.

2004 A proposal to grant citizenship to ethnic Hungarians born overseas was approved by 51.5 per cent in a referendum. However the vote was invalidated by low turn-out.

2005 László Sólyom became president.

2006 Prime Minister Gyurcsány was re-elected in the parliamentary elections. Rioting followed his admission that he had lied about the economy during the election, but he defied demands for his resignation. He later won a vote of confidence in parliament.

2007 On 20 December Hungary became a member of the European Union Schengen area whereby all travellers may cross borders without a passport or visa.

2008 An agreement for visa-free visits of citizens to the US was signed on 14 March 2008.

Political structure

Constitution

In 1989 the 1949 constitution was amended so that Hungary was formally re-titled the Hungarian Republic, concluding 40 years as a People's Republic.

Under the amended constitution, Hungary has a multi-party system.

Supreme power is vested in parliament.

The Constitutional Court has the power to overturn decisions or decrees that are considered unconstitutional.

Form of state

Parliamentary democratic republic

The executive
The prime minister is chosen by the National Assembly and heads the executive Council of Ministers or cabinet. The prime minister's control of the cabinet has been enhanced by the creation of a minister for the prime minister's office.
The president is also elected by the National Assembly for a five-year term. The president has no executive power, and is not able to dissolve parliament.
National legislature
Legislative power is vested in the unicameral Országgyüles (National Assembly), elected every four years, which enacts the constitution and laws, determines the state budget and elects the president of the republic, the prime minister and the Council of Ministers. The Országgyüles contains 386 deputies, of whom 176 are elected from single-member constituencies.
Legal system
The legal system is based on the amended 1949 constitution.
Civil and criminal cases are brought before district and county courts and the Supreme Court in Budapest. District courts are courts of first instance whereas county courts may act either as courts of first instance or as appeal courts. The Supreme Court is usually an appeal court, but can also take cases submitted to it by the Public Prosecutor and act as a court of first instance. All courts of first instance have one professional judge and two lay assessors. Appeal courts have three professional judges. The district and county judges are elected by district or county councils. All members of the Supreme Court are elected by parliament.
Last elections
9/23 April 2006 (parliamentary); 7 June 2005 (presidential)
Results: Presidential: In the election by parliament, László Sólyom (Independent) won with 185 votes; Katalin Szili (MSzP) won 182 votes.
Parliamentary: MSzP won 185 seats out of 386; Fidesz-KNDP won 164 seats; SzDSz 18 seats; joint MSzP/SzDSz candidates won six seats; MDF 11 seats. Turnout was 67.8 per cent.
Next elections
2010 (presidential and parliamentary).

Political parties
Ruling party
Coalition: Magyar Szocialista Párt (MSzP) (Hungarian Socialist Party) and Szabad Demokratak Szovetsege (SzDSz) (Alliance of Free Democrats) (since 2002; re-elected Apr 2006)
Main opposition party
Fidesz-KDNP (Coalition of Fidesz-Magar Polgári Szövetség (Fidesz-Hungarian Civic Union) and Kereszténydemokrata Néppárt (KDNP) (Christian Democratic People's Party).

Population
10.06 million (2007)*
Last census: February 2001: 10,198,315
Population density: 110 inhabitants per square km. Urban population: 65 per cent (1995–2001).
Annual growth rate: -0.2 per cent 1994–2004 (WHO 2006)
Ethnic make-up
The population is almost entirely made up of ethnic Hungarians. Small groups of Germans, Slovaks, Romanians, Serbs and Gypsies (Roma) make up about 4 per cent of the population. Roma are not recognised as an official ethnic group, although they are estimated to number between 360,000 and 600,000.
Religions
There is no official national religion. Roman Catholic (67.5 per cent), Calvinist (20 per cent) and Lutheran (5 per cent). There are approximately six million Roman Catholics, two million Calvinists, 430,000 Lutherans, and 80,000 Jews in Hungary.

Education
Compulsory education starts at six years of age and most children complete secondary education. There are four types of secondary school, offering either academic or vocational education. Apprentice training schools are attached to factories and agricultural co-operatives. There are 57 higher education institutes, including 10 universities and nine technical universities. Some privatisation of education is taking place as church and other private schools are created. Public expenditure on education is equivalent to around 5 per cent of annual gross national income (GNI), and includes subsidies to private education at the primary, secondary and tertiary levels.
Literacy rate: 99.4 per cent total, 99.2 per cent female, adult rates in 2002 (World Bank).
Compulsory years: Six to 18
Enrolment rate: 89.7 per cent net primary enrolment, 84.9 per cent net secondary enrolment (World Bank 2003).
Pupils per teacher: 12 in primary schools.

Health
Per capita total expenditure on health (2003) was US$1,269; of which per capita government spending was US$919, at the international dollar rate, (WHO 2006).
The health system is run by the State Health Fund, an entity with substantial operational autonomy and no effective accountability. It is financed by payroll taxes of 15 per cent from employers and 4 per cent from employees, although transfers from the budget have been necessary due to a large funding gap.
Service delivery remains poor. Although healthcare is free in Hungary, patients regularly hand over cash bribes to poorly-paid medical staff in order to gain proper access. There are reports of doctors recommending dangerous treatments in exchange for bribes. A major area of concern is the heavy subsidisation of medicine, which patients often obtain freely and then sell on.
HIV/Aids
HIV prevalence: 0.1 per cent aged 15–49 in 2003 (World Bank)
Life expectancy: 73 years, 2004 (WHO 2006)
Fertility rate/Maternal mortality rate: 1.3 births per woman, 2004 (WHO 2006); maternal mortality 15 per 100,000 live births (World Bank).
Child (under 5 years) mortality rate (per 1,000): 7.7 per 1,000 live births (World Bank)
Head of population per physician: 3.33 physicians per 1,000 people, 2003 (WHO 2006)

Welfare
Economic reforms have included a pioneering reorganisation of the pension system, with a new 'multi-pillar' system launched in 1996, supported by a World Bank US$150 million loan. Employees make mandatory contributions to the existing pay-as-you-go (PAYG) system and to a fully funded second pillar, based on a system of personal savings accounts held in privately managed pension funds. Those joining the work force after June 1998 were obliged to participate in the new system. In 2001, the government made both systems voluntary. The new scheme has proved highly popular. The largest private pension fund is managed by Nationale-Nederlanden (NN), with 257,000 members and Ft4 billion (US$16.4 million) in managed assets. Social security contributions on salaries are paid by the employer (39 per cent) and by the employee (10 per cent). Employer contributions must also be made to the unemployment solidarity fund (4.5 per cent) and by the employee (1.5 per cent).

Main cities
Budapest (capital, estimated population 1.7 million in 2005), Debrecen (213,692), Miskolc (180,012), Szeged (169,198), Pécs (161,355), Györ (130,480), Nyíregyháza (120,880), Székesfehérvár (106,951).

Languages spoken
Slovak, Croatian, Serbian, Slovene, Romani are also spoken.

The main foreign language is German, followed by English, Russian and French.

Official language/s

Hungarian (Magyar)

Media

National news agency: Magyar Távirati Iroda (MTI) (Hungarian News Agency): http://english.mti.hu

Other news agencies: Havaria Press (in Hungarian): www.havariapress.hu

Press

Foreign ownership dominates the print media and all newspapers are privately owned. While the market in tabloid news is growing, quality newspapers are in decline.

Dailies: There are over 30 dailies of which 10 are national newspapers. Local newspapers have a strong market lead and national broadsheets are considered partisan.

In Hungarian, the most popular national newspaper is the free issue Metro (www.metro.hu); the most popular quality newspapers are the Népszabadság (www.nol.hu) and Magyar Nemzet (www.mno.hu), with Magyar Hírlap (ww.magyarhirlap.hu), Népszava (www.nepszava.hu) and Reggel (www.reggel.hu), which include articles on business and finance.

Weeklies: In Hungarian, magazines for news and current affairs include 168 Óra (www.168ora.hu), Hírek (www.miep.hu), Magyar Demokrata (www.demokrata.hu) and HVG (http://hvg.hu); for women, Hölgyvilág (www.holgyvilag.hu), Nok Lapja (www.nlcafe.hu); Hócipo (www.hocipo.hu) is a satirical magazine.

Business: In Hungarian, the leading business and financial newspapers are the Napi Gazdaság (www.napi.hu), Magyar Tokepiac (www.magyartokepiac.hu) and Világgazdaság (www.vilaggazdasag.hu). Magazines include Adó (www.ado.hu) and Bank & Tözsde (www.bankestozsde.hu).

In English, the weekly Budapest Business Journal (www.bbj.hu), has a round up of news and comprehensive industry and company information.

Periodicals: In Hungarian the monthly Közéleti Krónika (www.kronika.matav.hu) covers general interest.

Broadcasting

The state-owned media has lost its monopoly and, since 1996, most of its market. Its reputation has been damaged with accusation of political interference by government.

Radio: The state-run Magyar Rádió (www.radio.hu) operates three national public stations, Bartok (www.mr3-bartok.hu), Kossuth (www.mr1-kossuth.hu) and Petofi (www.mr2.hu), which include specialist interest broadcasts of parliamentary proceedings and religion. The two private, national commercial stations Danubius (www.danubius.hu) and Sláger (www.slager.hu) are also those with the highest listener figures. There are many local radio stations, either private, public and community, with intense competition for listeners.

Television: Television is the most popular medium for news, information and entertainment.

Magyar Televízió (MTV) (www.mtv.hu) has two channels M1 and M2. Funding for these services is provided by government grants and advertising revenue. MTV is chronically under-funded and the quality and quantity of programming is weak. Private commercial TV is led by RTLKlub (www.rtlklub.hu) and TV2 (http://tv2.hu), which offer a wide range of locally produced programmes and well as imported TV shows. Hir TV (www.hirtv.net) is a 24-hour news channel. There are dozens of pay-to-view TV channels offering programmes in most genres.

Advertising

The professionalism of advertising has grown rapidly since the 1990s and services include traditional ad campaigns and new technologies.

Advertising space can be purchased directly on television and radio, in cinemas, newspapers, magazines and posters. The advertising of tobacco, alcohol and medicines is regulated under a code of ethics and edicts.

Economy

Hungary has a market economy with a large industrial base and heavy dependence on foreign trade. Since the mid-1990s, Hungary has boasted one of the most successful growth rates in Central Europe. In 2004, exports and investment began to replace domestic consumption as the main drivers of growth. Exports increased by 15 per cent in 2004, followed by 11.4 per cent in 2005. The private sector accounts for around 80 per cent of GDP, with a high level of foreign ownership and foreign investment.

In 2006, the economy was overtaken by a crisis in government spending, which had been in the making for some time, but ignored by both the authorities and investors. Over the years, government spending on public services has been high, while revenue collection and expenditure controls have been inefficient, resulting in a burgeoning budget deficit. By 2006, the deficit approached 10 per cent. Investors became impatient and the stock market and currency lost value. Furthermore, the EU Commission, exasperated by unrealistic budget forecasts, rejected the latest economic plan, dashing Hungary's hopes of joining the eurozone in 2010. To stabilise the economy and meet EU requirements, the government introduced an austerity programme of tax increases and spending curbs to reduce the deficit to three per cent in 2008, together with proposed public service reforms. It is likely that these measures will not be sufficient and that more action will be needed to achieve the targets. The immediate effect will be a decline in growth from around four per cent in 2006 to 2.5 per cent in 2007. Membership of the eurozone may not be attainable before 2013.

Despite Hungary's tribulations, investor confidence in the longer-term outlook remains high, while the economy continues to benefit from the financial benefits of EU membership.

Labour market and unemployment

Approximately 45 per cent of the workforce is female. The labour market contained approximately 5 million workers in 1998, out of 7 million people of employable age (15–64).

Approximately 37 per cent of the labour force is employed in industry (including manufacturing and construction), 12 per cent in agriculture, 10 per cent in commerce and 8 per cent in transport and communications. There has been rapid growth in tertiary sector employment.

Unemployment fell from 9.7 per cent in 1999 to 6.5 per cent in 2000, but is over 20 per cent in some eastern cities. About 25 per cent of those unemployed are classified 'long-term unemployed'.

In the period January to July 2000, the average gross monthly wage reached US$275.6. In 2000, gross average wages increased by 13.5 per cent in nominal terms. In January 2001, the government raised the minimum wage from Ft25,000 (US$84) a month to Ft40,000 (US$138).

External trade

As a member of the European Union, Hungary operates within a communitywide free trade union, with tariffs sets as a whole. Internationally, the EU has free trade agreements with a number of nations and trading blocs worldwide.

The economy is dependent on export trade, of which 75 per cent goes to the EU, mainly Germany. Major sectors include vehicle assembly and electronics which account for a third of exports. Hungarian wine and fruit are consumed throughout the EU.

Imports

Principal imports are capital goods, machinery and equipment, fuels and electricity, food products, raw materials, energy (natural gas and electricity).

Main sources: Germany (27.3 per cent total, 2006), Russia (8.0 per cent), Austria (6.3 per cent).

Exports

Principal exports are machinery and equipment, manufactures goods, foodstuffs and agricultural produce, raw materials, energy (refined oil and electricity).

Main destinations: Germany (29.5 per cent total, 2006), Italy (5.5 per cent), Austria (4.8 per cent).

Agriculture

Farming

The agricultural sector contributes 7 per cent to GDP and employs around 12 per cent of the workforce. Agriculture and animal husbandry dominate in the Great Plain in central and eastern Hungary. The western region of Transdanubia – which includes Lake Balaton, the largest lake in Central Europe – is dominated by intensive agriculture and animal husbandry.

Farming is largely socialised; co-operatives are the dominant form of production.

The agriculture and food industry produces on average 50 per cent more food than is consumed domestically. Principal crops include wheat, maize, barley, sugar beet and potatoes. The livestock sector is also important. Crop cultivation, especially wheat, maize, potatoes, fruit and vegetables, accounts for around half of Hungary's agricultural output. Processed and unprocessed meat, dairy products and wine are the other main products.

The agriculture and food industry produces, on average, 50 per cent more than is needed for domestic consumption.

After EU accession in 2004, Hungary is eligible for EU agricultural subsidies and rural development through the Common Agricultural Policy (CAP). However, it will only receive the full amount by the end of a 10-year transition period in 2013.

During its transitional entry stage Hungary has decided to implement the reform of the CAP on 1 January 2009. The reform was introduced throughout most of the EU on 1 January 2005, when subsidies on farm output, which tended to benefit large farms and encourage overproduction, were replaced by single farm payments, not conditional on production. The change is expected to reward farms that provide and maintain a healthy environment, food safety and animal welfare standards. The changes are also intended to encourage market conscious production and cut the cost of CAP to the EU taxpayer.

Crop production in 2005 included: 16,149,350 tonnes (t) cereals in total, 5,079,000t wheat, 9,000,000t maize, 1,196,000t barley, 607,220t potatoes, 815,000t grapes, 285,000t tomatoes, 115,000t chillies & peppers, 657,048t oilcrops, 295,000t rapeseed (canola), 12,000t tobacco, 3,108,150t sugar beets, 720,000t apples, 157,000t oats, 1,882,500t fruit in total, 2,091,500t vegetables in total. Livestock production included: 1,034,495t meat in total, 55,000t beef, 482,830t pig meat, 1,165t lamb, 480,000t poultry, 180,200t eggs, 2,043,000t milk, 20,500t honey, 385t sheepskins, 5,000t greasy wool, 7,000t cattle hides.

Fishing

Hungary is a landlocked country and although there is some fishing from lakes and rivers, most of the country's consumption needs are met through imports. Fish production in Hungary is mostly concentrated in the available 140,000 hectares (ha) of natural water and 20,000ha of man-made fishponds. The fish production sector primarily involves common carp and African catfish and remains a small and special sub-sector of agriculture. The sector traditionally supports less than 0.5 per cent of the total labour force and contributes below 2 per cent of the total for agricultural production. Annual consumption per capita is typically less than 3kg.

Forestry

Forests account for a fifth of Hungary's land area but the industry amounts to only 0.3 per cent of GDP. Forestry agriculture largely concentrates on production using hardwood species of trees, mostly being used for energy purposes. Oak and black locust are most prevalent. The state owns about 58 per cent of forests and and employs 20,000 workers on this land. Hungary is a net importer of all primary forest products as a result of not undertaking softwood and pulp production.

Exports of forest products in 2004 amounted to US$641 million, while imports were valued at US$1.1 billion.

Production in 2004 included: 5,660,300 cubic metres (cum) roundwood, 2,988,300cum industrial roundwood, 1,575,000cum sawlogs and veneers, 204,800cum sawnwood, 653,300cum pulpwood, 638,300cum wood-based panels, 2.672,000cum woodfuel; 579,000 tonnes (t) paper and paperboard, 248,000t printing and writing paper, 378,000t recovered paper.

Industry and manufacturing

Mechanical engineering, chemicals, pulp and paper industries, as well as the iron and steel industry and metal processing are particularly successful sectors. Other industries include building materials, food processing and textiles. One of the fastest growing sectors in Hungary, as the country moves away from heavy industry, is motor vehicle components and assembly.

Foreign direct investment (FDI) has contributed greatly to industrial output in Hungary, concentrating in areas such as machinery, vehicles, computers, telecommunications equipment, electrical and electronic goods. These successes have been concentrated in a relatively small number of capital-intensive companies. Analysts warn that Hungary could be in danger of developing a two-tier economy, with a prosperous, predominantly foreign-owned sector of larger enterprises and a struggling, locally- owned sector of small- and medium-sized enterprises (SMEs).

In the past, government policy focussed on the development of heavy industry and agriculture. In the late-1990s, this shifted towards the development of SMEs. These account for 45 per cent of GDP and represent 69 per cent of employment. The main problem facing smaller enterprises is the growing black market. This is due to a constantly changing and, thus far, largely unfavourable tax system in which evasion is widespread. Law-abiding SMEs are finding it difficult to compete with black market labour. In order to help compensate for this, the government has tried to promote entrepreneurial SMEs through tax cuts and better access to credit.

Tourism

Since 1988, Hungary has seen an unprecedented tourist boom as package tourists and international convention delegates take advantage of competitive prices, relatively crime-free streets and a rich and varied cultural scene. Most visitors are from Germany and Austria, but there are increasing numbers from Poland, America and Japan. The sector accounts for almost 10 per cent of GDP and employs 10–13 per cent of the workforce. The sector has traditionally played an important role in Hungary's foreign exchange revenues.

Emphasis is on three fields of tourism – conference, spa, and exclusive tourism, particularly equestrian tourism.

Tourist arrivals numbered 3 million in 2004, up slightly from the previous year.

Mining

The mining sector accounts for 5 per cent of GNP and employs 3 per cent of the workforce.

Hungary is a major European producer of bauxite, and also a small-scale producer of lignite and manganese ore. In the Northern Hills, iron ore and copper are mined.

Hydrocarbons

Hungary is a small-scale producer of coal, oil and natural gas. In the Great Plain in central and eastern Hungary, there are natural gas and oil deposits and

brown coal is mined in the Northern Hills region. Hungary has 102.5 million barrels of oil reserves, producing around 41,000 barrels per day (bpd). Hungry is the largest oil producer in North Central Europe. Hungry has one oil refinery with a capacity of 161,000 bpd, US$59 million has been invested to create a new hydrodesulfurisation unit in line with EU standards for low sulphur gasoline and diesel.
Proven reserves of natural gas stand at around 1.2 trillion cubic feet. Hungary relies heavily on imports of natural gas from Russia. Domestic consumption and production of natural gas are projected to rise 30 per cent and fall 20 per cent respectively by 2010. Gas storage capacity is well developed and can hold 120 days of peak winter imports.
Coal reserves totaled 3.3 billion tonnes in 2004; coal production was 2.9 million tonnes oil equivalent. Hungarian coal tends to be high in sulphur and ash, making it difficult to expand coal production and conform to EU environmental norms. Only the country's lignite reserves offer any possibility for an expansion in domestic production.

Energy
Hungary is around 50 per cent dependent upon imported oil and gas from Slovakia and, to a lesser extent, the Middle East. Electricity is imported via a grid from Vinnitsa in Ukraine. Hungary has one nuclear power plant near Paks in central Hungary. The plant provides 40 per cent of domestic energy needs and is dependent on enrichment and processing facilities from the Russian Federation. There are also three privately-owned small hydroelectric power plants in Hungary, based at Hernádviz, Kisköre and Tiszalök, although these provide limited electricity. There are plans to implement geothermal energy in addition to the wind generators which have been operating since 2000.

Financial markets
Stock exchange
The Budapest Stock Exchange (BSE), the first of the former socialist Central and Eastern European exchanges to reopen, was formally re-established in 1990.

Banking and insurance
Hungary has the most developed financial sector in Eastern Europe, with the Magyar Nemzeti Bank (MNB) (National Bank of Hungary) (central bank) playing an important role in economic and financial management of the economy. The country privatised banking services from 1994–97 in order to attract foreign investment. About 30 of the 38 banks in Hungary are foreign-owned and are led by the OTP Bank (formely known as the National Savings Bank). Foreign-owned banks control 90 per cent of the country's total banking assets. OTP Bank, with an extensive branch network, offers banking for the general public, and also foreigners needing foreign exchange accounts.
Foreign trade and currency transactions are conducted by the Magyar Külkereskedelmi Bank (MKB) (formerly the Hungarian Foreign Trade Bank) and by some other banks.
The Central-European International Bank is an internationally active offshore bank owned by the central bank and six foreign banks.
Hungary adopted a German model for the banking system in 1999, allowing banks to engage in both commercial and investment banking.

Central bank
Magyar Nemzeti Bank (MNB) (National Bank of Hungary)

Main financial centre
Budapest

Time
GMT plus one hour (daylight saving, late March to late October, GMT plus two hours)

Geography
Hungary is a landlocked country in central Europe surrounded by the Alps, the Carpathians and the Dinaric Mountains. The Danube and Tisza rivers run through the country, which is bounded by Slovakia to the north, Ukraine to the north-east, Romania to the east, Serbia, Croatia and Slovenia to the south and Austria to the west.
The River Danube forms Hungary's north-western border with Slovakia and then flows south through Budapest, bisecting the country. More than half of the land surface consists of plains less than 200 metres above sea level. The highest point is Kekes at 1,015 metres in the Matra hills to the north, while the lowest point is on the southern edge of Szeged along the River Tisza (the longest tributary of the Danube) at 77 metres.
The major regions of the country are: the Pannonian or Great Hungarian Plain (central and eastern Hungary), east of the River Danube and also drained by the Tisza; Transdanubia (western Hungary, including Lake Balaton, the largest lake in central Europe); the Little Hungarian Plains in the north-west between the mountains and the Danube; and along Hungary's northern border are the Matras, foothills of the Carpathian Mountains.

Hemisphere
Northern

Climate
The temperate continental climate of Hungary is under the varying influence of three climatic zones: continental, Atlantic and Mediterranean. The annual median temperature in Budapest is 11 degrees Celsius (C). The warmest month is July, with an average of 22 degrees C, the coldest January, with minus 1 degrees C. Averaging 1,988 hours of sunshine a year, Hungary experiences more sun than most of the countries in Western Europe. Average annual rainfall is 630mm, but distribution is unpredictable. Most rain usually falls in May and June, but the south-west regions may have more in October. May is the wettest month, and September the driest. The central parts of the Great Plains are the driest with 200–500mm, the hilly western area of Koeszeg and Sopron the wettest with 900–1,000mm.

Dress codes
Hungarians used to dress more formally than West Europeans, but blazers, sports coats and flannels are as acceptable as lounge suits for visiting businessmen. Do not be offended if Hungarians ask where you bought your clothes or how much they cost.
Advisable clothing: medium to heavy-weight and heavy topcoat for winter; light-weight clothing for summer. A raincoat will be needed in spring and autumn.

Entry requirements
Passports
Passport required by all; must be valid for six months beyond date of departure.

Visa
Required by all, except nationals of EU and Schengen area signatory countries, North America, Australasia and Japan. For further exceptions contact the nearest embassy. A Schengen visa application (offered in several languages) can be downloaded from http://europa.eu/abc/travel/ see 'documents you will need'. Business trips may be made visa-free, or on short-term visas. For terms and conditions see: www.mfa.gov.hu/kum/en/bal/ and follow links to consular services.
Transit passengers must have onward/return passage.

Currency advice/regulations
The import and export of local currency is limited to Ft200,000, provided the amount is declared. The import of foreign currency is unlimited, although amounts over Ft1 million must be declared. The export of foreign currency cannot exceed the amount imported and must be exported no later than three months after import. There is no compulsory money exchange on departure, however only 50 per cent of a visitor's forints can be re-exchanged (up to a limit of US$450, and with exchange receipts) at any authorised bureaux de change, or branch of the National Savings Bank.

Customs
Personal items are duty-free. There are no duties levied on alcohol and tobacco between EU member states, providing amounts imported are for personal consumption.

Health (for visitors)
Nationals of the European Economic Area (EEA) countries and Switzerland can access reduced cost and sometimes free medical treatment using a European Health Insurance Card (EHIC) while visiting the EEA. Exceptions include nationals of the 10 countries, which joined the EU in 2004, whose EHIC is not valid in Switzerland. Applications for the EHIC should be made before travelling.
Mandatory precautions
There are no special requirements.
Advisable precautions
There are no specific precautions necessary although a hepatitis A immunisation might be useful.

Hotels
There is a full range of hotels in Budapest. Reservations can be made in advance directly or through IBUSZ.
All hotels charge a 1–2 per cent tourism tax for guests staying more than one night. Tipping usually 10–15 per cent.
Good hotels are concentrated in Pest, the business half of Budapest.

Credit cards
Credit cards are accepted and can be used for cash advances.

Public holidays (national)
Fixed dates
1 Jan (New Year's Day), 15 Mar (National Day), 1 May (Labour Day), 20 Aug (National Constitution/St Stephen's Day), 23 Oct (Remembrance Day), 1 Nov (All Saints' Day), 25–26 Dec (Christmas).
Variable dates
Easter Monday, Whit Monday.

Working hours
Banking
Mon–Thu: 0800–1500; Fri: 0800–1300.
Business
Mon–Thu: 0800–1600.
Government
Mon–Fri: 0800–1630.
Shops
Mon, Tue, Wed & Fri: 1000–1800, Thu: 1000–2000, Sat: 1000–1300.
Shops may have varied opening hours. Food shops open at 0600–0700 and may not close until 2000.

Telecommunications
Mobile/cell phones
There is a GSM dual band of 900 and 1800 with coverage throughout the country.

Electricity supply
220V AC, 50 cycles

Social customs/useful tips
Business people are expected to dress smartly. Local business people are generally friendly and hospitable and it is usual for visitors to be invited to lunch or dinner in a restaurant. Business cards are widely distributed and visitors are advised to have a supply available in Hungarian. Best months for business visits are September to May and appointments should always be made. Interpreter and translation services may be booked through travel agents. In business Hungarians expect people to speak their mind. Giving and receiving gifts is very common; take promotional gifts with you.
Punctuality is appreciated.
If you are invited to a Hungarian home, take flowers for the hostess and wine or liquor for the host.
Hungarian law requires visitors to carry passports or other ID at all times.

Security
There has been an increase in street crime in Budapest, although levels are still below those in many Western capitals. Bag-snatching and pickpocketing are common in Budapest. Criminals at times pose as police officers, and credentials should be requested for inspection.

Getting there
Air
National airline: Malév (Hungarian Airlines)
International airport/s: Budapest-Ferihegy (BUD, 16km from city; duty-free shop, restaurants and bar, bank/bureaux de change, tourist information centre, post office and car hire. Scheduled bus services run to the city centre; minibuses run to and from any address in the city. The 93 bus runs an express service between the underground terminus at Kobánya-Kispest and the Ferihegy terminals; a pre-purchased or season ticket is required. Taxis are available at all times.
Airport tax: None
Surface
Hungary is included in the Pan-European Corridor 5 scheme. The project has some 3,270km of railways, linking Kiev in the Ukraine with western Europe via Italy, and 2,850 of new and upgraded roads.
Water: A hydrofoil service is available on the Danube between Vienna and Budapest in the summer. Ships provide regular passenger service and cruises starting at Passau and Regensburg (Germany) to Budapest, passing through Austria and Slovakia. There are also links with the rivers Rhine and Main and the Black Sea.

Getting about
National transport
Road: Generally the road system is good. Tolls are payable on some roads and all motorways for which season tickets can be purchased. There are eight arterial roads: all but the M8 start from central Budapest. From Budapest the two main highways are the M1 to Györ (then to Austria) and the M7 along Lake Balaton. The M3 connects Budapest with eastern Hungary.
Buses: Budapest is linked to all major towns. Tickets are available from Volán offices throughout the country.
Rail: Services are operated by MÁV. All cities are linked by efficient services, but facilities are often inadequate. Supplements are payable on intercity (IC) and express trains and reservations are compulsory on IC trains and recommended for express trains, particularly in summer. Tickets and seat reservations can be bought 60 days in advance at domestic railway stations.
Water: Ferries run several times daily between Budapest and Visegrád over the summer; one service extends to Esztergom.
City transport
Most government offices, business centres and main hotels are located in Pest, on the eastern side of the Danube. The public transport system is good and it is rarely necessary to take a taxi, especially as the city centre is quite compact.
Buda, the hilly, western part of the city, is more difficult to get around without a car.
Taxis: Taxis are available from ranks, by telephone or can be hailed in the street. Taxis are metered. Avoid all unmarked cabs as they not only demand payment for mileage covered, but also for the return journey to their starting point.
A taxi from the airport to the centre of Budapest takes between 40 minutes and one hour; always agree your fare in advance. Non-airport taxis are plentiful and inexpensive although rates vary widely (watch out for meters being on the 'night' rate during the day). Tipping of 15–20 per cent is expected.
Buses, trams & metro: There is good public transport in all the main towns, including tramways in some.
Budapest has bus, trolleybus, tramway, suburban railway (HEV), a three-line metro and boat services. The metro has ticket barriers at all stations. The bus-trolleybus-tramway system has pre-purchase flat fares with ticket puncher on board. Day passes and season tickets are available for all the transport modes in the city. Trams and buses generally run from 0430–2300. Some night services also operate. The metro runs from 0430–2310; stations are identified by a large 'M'.

Trains: Main railway stations: Déli Pu (Southern RW Terminal), Krisztina krt 37/a, Budapest I.
Keleti Pu (Eastern RW Terminal), Baross Tér (tel: 142-9150).
Nyugati Pu (Western RW Terminal), Teréz krt 111 (tel: 122-7860).
Ferry: The Danube provides a ready highway for ferries and sightseeing cruises.

Car hire

Hire cars are available from the airport, hotels and IBUSZ travel company. The speed limit is 50kph in built up areas, 90kph on main roads, 110kph on highways and 130kph on motorways. There is an absolute ban on drinking and driving, headlights must be kept dipped, mobile phones can only be used with headsets and seat belts are compulsory. An international driving licence is recommended. For travel on the M1 and M3 motorways, drivers require a motorway vignette, obtainable from the Hungarian Auto Klub, petrol stations, post offices, and some motorway access points; without one, drivers may be fined.

BUSINESS DIRECTORY

The addresses listed below are a selection only. While World of Information makes every endeavour to check these addresses, we cannot guarantee that changes have not been made, especially to telephone numbers and area codes. We would welcome any corrections.

Telephone area codes

The international direct dialling code (IDD) for Hungary is +36, followed by area code and subscriber's number:

Budapest	1	Pecs	72
Debrecen	52	Salgotarjan	32
Gyor	96	Szeged	62
Miskolc	46	Szekesfehervar	22
Nyiregyhaza	42	Szombathely	94

Useful telephone numbers

Ambulance, Police, Fire: 112
24-hour emergency service (English-speaking): 118-8212
24-hour multi-lingual crime reporting service: 0800—2000: 438-8080; after hours: 06-80-660-044
Fotaxi (tel: 222-2222)
City Taxi (tel: 211-1111)
Volantaxi (tel: 166-6666)

Chambers of Commerce

American Chamber of Commerce in Hungary, 10 Deak Ferencu utca, 1052 Budapest (tel: 266-9880; fax: 266-9888; e-mail: info@amcham.hu).

Borsod-Abauj-Zemplen County Chamber of Commerce and Industry, 1 Szentpali u, 3530 Miskolc (tel: 328-539; fax: 328-722; e-mail: bokik@mail.bokik,hu).

British Chamber of Commerce in Hungary, 6 Bank utca, 1054 Budapest (tel: 302-5200; fax: 302-3069; e-mail: bcch@bcch.com).

Budapest Chamber of Commerce and Industry, Krisztina krt 99, 1016 Budapest (tel: 488-2000; fax: 488-2119; e-mail: bkik@bkik.hu).

Czongrád Chamber of Commerce and Industry, 2-4 Tisza Lajos krt, 6701 Csongrád (tel: 426-343; fax: 426-149; info@csmkik.hu).

Fejér County Chamber of Commerce, 4-6 Hosszusetater, 8000 Székesfehérvár (tel: 510-310; fax: 510-312; e-mail: fmkik@mail.fmkik.hu).

Gyor-Moson-Sopron County Chamber of Commerce and Industry, 10/A Szent Istvan ut, 9021 Gyor (tel: 520-202; fax: 520-291; e-mail: kamara@gymskik.hu).

Hajdu-Bihar County Chamber of Commerce and Industry, 10 Petofi ter, 4025 Debrecen (tel: 500-721; fax: 500-720; e-mail: info@hbkik.hu).

Hungarian Chamber of Commerce and Industry, 6-8 Kossuth Lajos ter, 1055 Budapest (tel: 474-5101; fax: 474-5105; e-mail: mkik@mkik.hu).

Pecs-Baranya Chamber of Commerce and Industry, 36 Majorossy I ut, 7625 Pécs (tel: 507-149; fax: 507-152; e-mail: pbkik@pbkik.hu).

Pest County Chamber of Commerce and Instry, 40 Vaci utca, 1051 Budapest (tel: 317-7666; fax: 317-7755; e-mail: titkarsag@pmkik.hu).

Sopron Chamber of Commerce and Industry, 14 Deak ter, 9400 Sopron (tel: 523-570; fax: 523-581; e-mail: k-kamara@sopron.hu).

Vas County Chamber of Commerce and Industry, 2 Honved ter, 9700 Szombathely (tel: 312-356; fax: 316-936; e-mail: vmkik@vmkik.hu).

Veszprem Chamber of Commerce, 3 Budapesti u, 8200 Veszprém (tel: 429-008; fax: 412-150; e-mail: vkik@iveszpremikamara.hu).

Zala County Chamber of Commerce and Industry, 24 Petofi Sandor ut, 8900 Zalaegerszeg (tel: 550-514; fax: 550-525; e-mail: zmkik@zmkik.hu).

Banking

General Banking and Trust Co Ltd, Markó ut 9, H-1055 Budapest (tel: 269-1450; fax: 260-1440).

Magyar Külkereskedelmi Bank (commercial bank), St István ter 11, H-1821 Budapest (tel: 269-0922; fax: 269-0959).

OTP Bank, Nádor ut 16, H-1876 Budapest (tel: 153-1444; fax: 112-6858).

Raiffeisen Bank, PO Box 173, H-1054 Budapest (tel: 484-4400; fax: 484-4444).

Central bank

Magyar Nemzeti Bank (National Bank of Hungary), 1054 Szabadság tér 8-9, 1850 Budapest (tel:428-2752; fax: 302-3000).

Travel information

Ferihegy International Airport flight enquiries (tel: 157-7155); passenger service (tel: 157-8555; fax: 157-8993).

Hungarian Automobile Club, Francis ut 38, Budapest XIV (tel: 691-8310).

IBUSZ – Hungarian Travel Agency (main Budapest office), Tanács krt 3/c, Budapest VII (tel: 142-3140).

Lufthansa Airport Office (tel: 157-0290, 157-6506; fax: 157-6192); town office, V ci utca 19-21, Budapest (tel: 266-4511; fax: 266-8669).

Malév Hungarian Airlines, (headquarters), 1097 Könyves Kálmán Krt 12-14 (tel: 235-3535); (customer service) Váci út 26, Budapest 11532 (tel: 235-3222; fax: 235-3244; email: centrum@malev.hu).

Police Tourinfo Office (service in English and German), Vigado Utca 6, 1051 Budapest.

Secretariat of the Hungarian Tourist Council, 6th floor, Margit krt 85, H-1024 Budapest (tel: 1175-1682; fax: 1175-38190).

National tourist organisation offices

Tourinform (Hungarian Tourist Board), Suto ut 2, H-1052 Budapest (tel: 117-9800; fax: 117-9578; e-mail: tourinform@mail.hungarytourism.hu; internet site: http://www.hungarytourism.hu).

Ministries

Ministry of Agriculture and Regional Development, Kossuth Lajos tér 11, H-1055 Budapest (tel: 302-0000; fax: 302-0402).

Ministry of Defence, Balaton ut 7-11, H-1055 Budapest (tel: 332-2500; fax: 311-0182).

Ministry of Economic Affairs, Honved U 13-14, H-1055 Budapest (tel: 302-2355; fax: 302-2394; internet site: http://www.gm.hu/english).

Ministry of Education, Szalay U 10-14, H-1055 Budapest (tel: 302-0600; fax: 302-2002).

Ministry of Environmental Protection, Fo ut 44-50, H-1011 Budapest (tel: 457-3300).

Ministry of Finance, József Nádor tér 2-4, H-1051 Budapest (tel: 118-2066, 138-2633; fax: 118-2570).

Ministry of Foreign Affairs, Bem rkp 47, H-1027 Budapest (tel: 458-1000; fax: 155-9693).

Ministry of Health, Arany János u 6-8, H-1051 Budapest (tel: 332-3100; fax: 302-0925).

Ministry of Home Affairs, József Attila u 2-4, H-1051 Budapest (tel: 331-3700, 332-5790; fax: 118-2870).

Ministry of Justice, Kossuth Lajos ter 4, H-1055 Budapest (tel: 268-3003).

Ministry of Transport, Telecommunications & Water Management, Dob ut 74-81, H-1077 Budapest (tel: 322-0220, 341-4300; fax: 322-8695).

Office of the President, Kossuth Lajos Ter 3-5, Budapest (tel: 268-4000).

Pressinform (information bureau for foreign journalists), Budakeszi ut 41, H-1021 Budapest (tel: 175-1890; fax: 175-1178).

Prime Minister's Office, Kossuth Lajos tér 1-3, H-1055 Budapest (tel: 268-3000; fax: 268-3050).

Other useful addresses

Allami Biztosító (state insurance company), Ullöi ut 1, H-1813 Budapest (tel: 117-8566).

Amex, Deak Ferenc ut 10, 1050 Budapest (tel: 117-8008).

British Embassy, 6 Harmincad utca, Budapest 1051 (tel: 266-2888; fax: 429-6360).

Budapest Stock Exchange, Deak Ferenc ut 5, H-1052 Budapest (tel: 117-5226; fax: 118-1737; internet site: www.fornax.hu/fmon/index.html).

Central Statistical Office, International Relations Department, Keleti Károly utca 5–7, , PO Box 51, H-1525 Budapest (tel: 212-6136; fax: 212-6378; internet site: www.ksh.hu/eng/index.htm).

Federation of Scientific and Technical Societies (MTESZ), Kossuth Lajos tér 6–8, Budapest V (tel: 153-3333).

Hungarian Aluminium Industrial Co Ltd (Hungalu), Privatisation Directorate, Room 419, 85 Margit krt, Budapest 1024 (tel: 175-6528; fax: 175-5802).

Hungária Biztositó (Hungária Insurance Company), Bánk ut 17–6, H-1115 Budapest (tel: 182-0750).

Hungarian Embassy (USA), 3910 Shoemaker Street, NW, Washington DC 20008 (tel: (+1-202) 362-6730; fax: (+1-202) 686-6412; e-mail: office@huembwas.org).

Hungarian Foundation for Enterprise Promotion, Etele ut 68, Budapest H-1115 (tel: 203-0348/60; fax: 203-0377).

Hungarian Investment and Trade Development Agency (ITD), Euro Information Correspondence Centre, Dorottya ut 4, 1051 Budapest (tel: 118-1712/6064; fax: 118-6198; e-mail: itdheicc@mail.datanet.hu; internet site: www.itd.hu/index.htm).

Hungarian Privatisation and Foreign Investment, APV, Pozsonyi ut 56, H-1133 Budapest (tel: 269-8600; fax: 267-0079).

Hungary EU Energy Centre (Thermie), Konyves Kalman Krt 76, 1087 Budapest VIII (tel: 269-9067, 133-1304; fax: 269-9065).

Hungexpo International Fair Centre, Dobi Istvan ut 10, Budapest X.

Magyar Tavirati Iroda (Hungarian news agency) (MTI), Fem utca 507, 1016 Budapest (tel: 155-6722).

Mineralimpex Hungarian Oil and Gas Co, Benczur u 13, 1068 Budapest (tel: 131-6720; fax: 153-1779, 142-3584).

US Embassy, Szabadsag ter 12, 1054 Budapest (tel: 267-4400; fax: 269-9326 or 269-9337 (Consular Section).

National news agency: Magyar Távirati Iroda (MTI) (Hungarian News Agency): http://english.mti.hu

Other news agencies: Havaria Press (in Hungarian): www.havariapress.hu

Internet sites

Budapest Network: www.budapestnetwork.com

Budapest Sun: www.budapestsun.com

Hungary Network: www.hungary.com

Online financial journal: www.portfolio.hu/en

Virtual Hungary: virtualhungary.com

Iceland

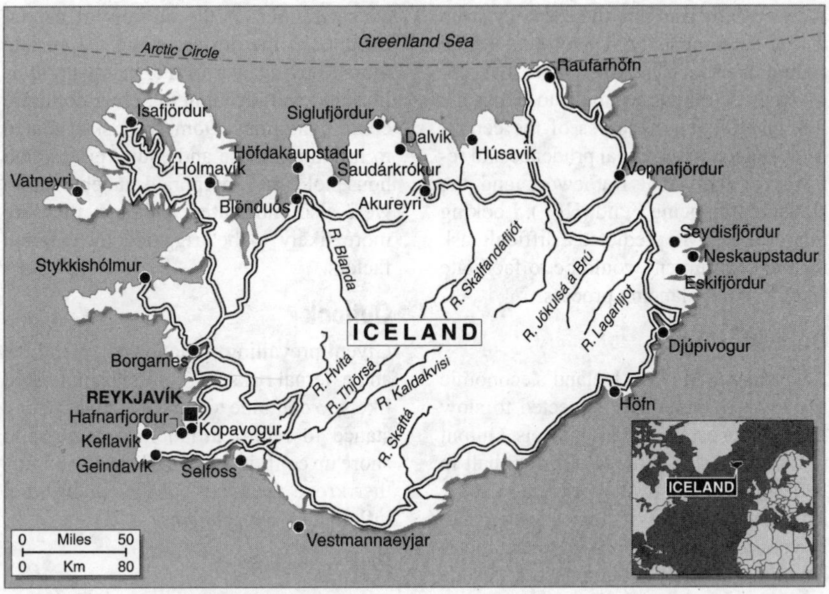

How the mighty are fallen! In 2007 what seemed to have got Iceland into so much economic trouble so quickly, was its over dependence on foreign capital. Iceland's bold economic development strategy did not come undone as a direct result of the US sub-prime crisis; the crunch came when its investors became concerned that they might no longer have access to credit on international markets, and decided to rein in. The first shock came in July 2007 when there was panic selling of the krona to the extent that dealing was suspended on Iceland's interbank foreign currency exchange markets.

Blame it on the cod

The apparent trigger was a bigger than expected cut in Iceland's permitted cod quota for the following year. The response confirmed both the importance of cod fishing to the economy and Iceland's reluctance to seek membership of the European Union (EU). Popular sentiment has it that Iceland's membership of the European Free Trade Association (EFTA) (the other three members are Norway, Liechtenstein and Switzerland) provides it with most of the advantages of EU membership without the constraints. None the less, despite this relatively straightforward explanation of Iceland's economic crunch, the prime minister (and governor of Iceland's central bank), Davíd Oddsson, persisted in seeking an explanation of the crisis in a hedge fund conspiracy theory. With its small population and total reserves of less than US$5 billion, the theory may be plausible, but is none the less unlikely.

Nordic cavalry

Iceland's government and Sedlabanki Íslands (Central Bank of Iceland) could hardly claim total surprise. Between 2000 and 2007 domestic credit had more than quadrupled as a percentage of GDP. To prevent capital flight, interest rates had been pushed up to an annual 15 per cent, where they stayed into mid-2008; hardly conducive to an economic kick-start. In a show of Nordic confidence three European central banks came to the rescue of beleaguered Iceland and its currency the krona in May 2008. The central banks of Sweden, Denmark and Norway came up with a US$2.3 billion rescue plan in the form of swap agreements that would enable the Central Bank of Iceland to have access to US$500 million from each of them. The krona rose by almost 5 per cent against the euro following the

KEY FACTS

Official name: Lyoveldio Island (Republic of Iceland)

Head of State: President Ólafur Ragnar Grímsson (since 1996; re-elected 26 Jun 2004)

Head of government: Prime Minister Geir Hilmar Haarde (SSF) (since 15 Jun 2006)

Ruling party: Coalition led by Sjálfstaeðisflokkurinn (SSF) (Independence Party) with Samfylkingin (SF) (Social Democratic Alliance) (formed 22 May 2007)

Area: 103,100 square km

Population: 313,000 (2006)

Capital: Reykjavík

Official language: Icelandic

Currency: Icelandic krona (Ikr) = 100 aurar

Exchange rate: Ikr79.18 per US$ (Jul 2008)

GDP per capita: US$63,830 (2007)

GDP real growth: 3.80% (2007)

Labour force: 174,300 (2006)

Unemployment: 1.00% (2007)

Inflation: 5.30% (2007)

Balance of trade: -US$1.48 billion (2005)

announcement of the arrangement. This reversed the trend of the first half of the year during which time the krona had dropped by as much as 26 per cent over the year. At its July 2008 meeting, the board of governors of the central bank decided to hold the bank's interest rate at 15.5 per cent.

The IMF

In its consultation report of May 2008 the International Monetary Fund (IMF) surprisingly re-iterated that the battered Icelandic economy was both prosperous and flexible. The IMF noted that Iceland's per capita income was among the highest, and income inequality among the lowest in the world. Labour and product markets were open and flexible, institutions and policy frameworks strong, and the government's debt very low. Management of natural resources has enabled Iceland to diversify the economy and help ensure sustainability. Against this backdrop, in the view of the IMF, the long-term economic prospects for the Icelandic economy remained enviable.

Nonetheless, the IMF went on to note that in mid-2008 Iceland's economy was at a difficult and uncertain turning point. The long home-grown, foreign-funded boom was coming to an end. Its legacies were overstretched private sector balance sheets, large macroeconomic imbalances, and a continued high dependence on foreign financing. With tightening global liquidity conditions and fragile market sentiment, Iceland's banks have also come under significant pressure; in response, the banks have started to slow lending growth and rationalise balance sheets. As liquidity constraints became tighter, the overheated economy showed signs of cooling.

In response to these intensifying external pressures, the central bank tightened the policy rate, enhanced liquidity provision to reduce pressures in foreign exchange and domestic markets, and improved its foreign exchange liquidity access by entering into the currency swap rescue agreements with the three Nordic central banks. The government has expressed its willingness both to boost the foreign exchange reserves of the central bank and to pursue fiscal prudence and reforms of the fiscal framework and the Housing Financing Fund (HFF). Looking forward, the IMF predicted a difficult task for the government would be to facilitate an orderly rebalancing process.

Outlook

According to the IMF Iceland's economic activity was inevitably expected to slow from its unsustainably high levels. Output was projected to come to a virtual halt in 2008 and contract by 2–3 per cent in 2009, led by a shrinking of domestic demand. Private consumption was set to decline as lending conditions tighten, real estate prices correct, private sector balance sheets retrench, and purchasing power decreases. Public sector and aluminium related investment will only partially offset the expected fall in other investments. Inflation was expected to remain above target well beyond 2008, reflecting the krona depreciation, high inflation expectations, and continued global inflationary pressures. The combination of a widening output gap and falling house prices were expected to bring inflation down. However, this outlook is based on the assumption that the exchange rate is broadly stable going forward, which is by no means certain.

The IMF expected the uncertainties surrounding Iceland's economic outlook to remain unusually large, with significant downside risks determined by external considerations. If the outflow of capital continues, the krona could depreciate more (moving ever further below its equilibrium level), leading to tighter domestic credit conditions. Domestic risks (related to inflation, house and equity prices, and household and corporate indebtedness) were also substantial, although they are more likely to be triggered by external factors.

Outlook

Given prevailing inflationary pressures and external risks, the central bank looked likely to continue to pursue its tight policy stance to return inflation to target and shore up confidence in the krona. Any further krona decline would inevitably fuel inflationary expectations.

Risk assessment

Economy	Fair
Politics	Good
Regional stability	Good

KEY INDICATORS — Iceland

	Unit	2003	2004	2005	2006	2007
Population	m	0.29	0.29	0.30	0.31	0.31
Gross domestic product (GDP)	US$bn	9.67	12.38	16.08	16.68	20.00
GDP per capita	US$	33,317	43,576	53,623	54,205	63,830
GDP real growth	%	4.1	5.7	7.5	4.4	3.8
Inflation	%	2.0	3.1	4.0	6.8	5.3
Unemployment	%	3.3	3.1	2.1	1.3	1.0
Exports (fob) (goods)	US$m	2,520.0	2,897.0	3,107.0	3,477.0	4,792.0
Imports (cif) (goods)	US$m	2,900.0	3,415.0	4,590.0	5,716.0	6,181.0
Balance of trade	US$m	-380.0	-519.0	-1,482.0	-2,239.0	-1,388.0
Current account	US$m	-430.1	-670.0	-2,618.0	-4,232.0	-3,125.0
Total reserves minus gold	US$m	792.3	1,046.0	1,035.7	2,301.3	2,578.7
Foreign exchange	US$m	764.6	1,017.3	1,009.1	2,273.2	2,549.1
Exchange rate	per US$	75.99	70.14	70.78	69.53	62.93

COUNTRY PROFILE

Historical profile

Settled by Norwegians and Celtic (Scottish and Irish) immigrants during the late ninth and tenth centuries, Iceland boasts the world's oldest parliament, the Althingi. Iceland was under Norwegian, then Danish, rule from the thirteenth century. The severity of Iceland's terrain was frequently compounded by natural disasters leading, in the nineteenth century, to large-scale emigration to the USA and Canada. The island was granted its own constitution in the 1840s.

1903 Iceland was granted Home rule from Denmark.

1918 Iceland became a sovereign state in union with Denmark.

1940 Germany invaded Denmark. British troops were stationed in Iceland.

1944 Iceland terminated the convention linking it with Denmark and declared itself a republic.

1948 Iceland joined the International Whaling Commission (IWC).

1949 Iceland joined NATO and the Council of Europe. A large US airbase was established at Keflavík.

1953 Iceland became a founding member of the Nordic Council.

1959–71 The Coalition of Independence and Social Democratic Parties remained in power.
1960s–70s Iceland's unilateral extensions of its territorial waters to protect its fishing grounds led to the 'Cod Wars' with the UK, and in 1976, caused a temporary break in diplomatic relations, the first such break between NATO members.
1980 Vigdís Finnbogadóttir was elected president, the world's first popularly elected female head of state.
1985 Iceland was declared a nuclear-free zone, barring entry to all nuclear weapons.
1987 Thorsteinn Pálsson was appointed prime minister.
1991 Iceland quit the International Whaling Commission (IWC) after the organisation refused to consider Icelandic proposals for moderate catch quotas.
1996 Ólafur Ragnar Grímsson was elected president, replacing Vigdís Finnbogadóttir, who stepped down after 16 years in office.
1999 The elections again returned a centre-right coalition of Sjálfstaeðisflokkurinn (SSF) (Independence Party) and Framsóknarflokkurinn (FSF) (Progressive Party).
2000 Ólafur Ragnar Grímsson was unopposed in the presidential elections.
2002 Iceland's bid to rejoin the IWC, without signing up to the moratorium on commercial whaling, was rejected.
2003 Prime Minister Oddsson's SSF won the May parliamentary elections.
2004 Incumbent Ólafur Ragnar Grímsson was re-elected in the presidential elections. Halldór Ásgrímsson (FSF) became prime minister.
2005 The government granted Bobby Fischer, the chess grandmaster and US fugitive of 10 years, Icelandic citizenship.
2006 Halldór Ásgrímsson resigned as prime minister and Geir Haarde (SSF) replaced him. The US closed its naval base at Kevlavik.
2007 In the 12 May general election, the SSF won 25 seats and retained power.
2008 Bobby Fischer, former world chess champion and naturalised citizen, died on 18 January. Plans to extend commercial whaling in summer 2008 were likely to be confirmed. Whaling had been resumed in 2006 and quotas only issued if a demand for whale meat was realised. Quotas for around 100 minke and a few fin whales will be issued by the government.

Political structure

Constitution

The constitution was adopted 17 June 1944.
The parliament and office of president jointly exercise legislative power, with due adherence to the constitution. The judiciary is guaranteed independence.
Elections are by proportional representation with universal direct suffrage over the age of 18.
The constitution recognises the Evangelical Lutheran Church as the state church.

Form of state

Parliamentary democratic republic

The executive

Executive power is vested jointly in the offices of the president as Head of State, and prime minister as head of government (appointed by the president) and the cabinet (appointed by the prime minister and approved by parliament).
Any citizen aged over 35 may become president, by popular vote (if more than one candidate stands for the post; without a challenge a candidate is duly elected without a vote).

National legislature

Legislative power is held jointly by the president and the 63-member Althingi (parliament). Members are elected for a four-year term by proportional representation.
The president is head of state, directly elected for a four-year term.

Legal system

The legal system is based on the 1944 constitution; the civil law system is based on Danish law.

Last elections

26 June 2004 (presidential)l; 12 May 2007 (parliamentary)

Results: Presidential: Ólafur Ragnar Grímsson won 85.6 per cent of the vote; Baldur Ágústsson won 12.5 per cent and Ástthór Magnússon 1.9 per cent; turnout was 62.6 per cent.
Parliamentary: Sjálfstæðisflokkurinn (SSF) (Independence Party) won 36.6 per cent of the vote (25 seats out of 63); Samfylkingin (SF) (Social Democratic Alliance) won 26.8 per cent (18 seats); Vinstrihreyfingin - grænt framboð (VG) (Left-Green Movement) 14.3 per cent (nine); Framsóknarflokkurinn (FSF) (Progressive Party) 11.7 per cent (seven); and Frjálslyndiflokkurinn (FF) (Liberal Party) 7.3 per cent (four). Turnout was 83.6 per cent.

Next elections

June 2008 (presidential); May 2011 (parliamentary).

Political parties

Ruling party

Coalition led by Sjálfstaeðisflokkurinn (SSF) (Independence Party) with Samfylkingin (SF) (Social Democratic Alliance) (formed 22 May 2007)

Main opposition party

Framsóknarflokkurinn (FSF) (Progressive Party)

Population

313,000 (2006)

Last census: July 2000: 281,154
Population density: 2.7 per square km.
Urban population: 93 per cent (1995—2001).
Annual growth rate: 1.0 per cent 1994–2004 (WHO 2006)

Ethnic make-up

Almost the entire population are descendants of Norwegians and Celts.

Religions

Lutherans (96 per cent), Protestants and Catholics (3 per cent).

Education

Pre-schooling is offered to children aged between one and six years when compulsory primary education begins. This leads into lower secondary school until aged 16 when students choose upper secondary education – either academic grammar or comprehensive schooling or vocational industrial or specialised training. Upper secondary education covers four years and is open to anyone who has completed compulsory school. Grammar and comprehensive attainment leads to higher education facilities at age 20.
Icelandic municipalities are responsible for delivering education in different regions.
There are eight higher education institutions in Iceland, most of which are run by the state and require no tuition fees. Private parties with state support run three institutions that charge tuition fees. About 16 per cent of Icelandic students in higher education study abroad.
The total public expenditure in education is typically 5—6 per cent of GDP.
Compulsory years: Six to 16.
Enrolment rate: 99 per cent net primary enrolment; 85.3 per cent net secondary enrolment (World Bank 2003).

Health

Per capita total expenditure on health (2003) was US$3,110; of which per capita government spending was US$2,598, at the international dollar rate, (WHO 2006).
The country is divided into health care regions, each with their own primary health care centres, some of which are run jointly with the local community hospital; hospitalisation is free of charge. The number of Icelandic physicians has increased steadily during the last decade.

HIV/Aids

HIV prevalence: 0.2 per cent aged 15–49 in 2003 (World Bank)
Life expectancy: 81 years, 2004 (WHO 2006)
Fertility rate/Maternal mortality rate: 2.0 births per woman, 2004 (WHO 2006)

Child (under 5 years) mortality rate (per 1,000): 3.0 per 1,000 live births (World Bank)
Head of population per physician: 3.62 physicians per 1,000 people, 2004 (WHO 2006)

Welfare
Iceland follows the Nordic social security system, which aims to provide universal social welfare and health services.
The social security system covers pension, occupational injury, health and maternity insurance. Most pensions are covered by private pension funds. There is generous coverage for maternity leave for both men and women.
Special attention has been given to women's employment and special grants have been provided to women for running businesses.

Main cities
Reykjavík (capital, estimated population 114,661 in 2005), Kópavogur (26,754), Hafnarfjörður (21,820), Akureyri (16,221).

Languages spoken
The Icelandic language belongs to the North Germanic branch of the Indo-European family.
Official language/s
Icelandic

Media
The constitution guarantees freedom of the press.
Press
Dailies: In Icelandic popular newspapers include Morgunbladid (www.mbl.is), Frettabladid (www.visir.is), DV (www.dv.is) is an evening newspaper.
Weeklies: In Icelandic, regional newspapers include FréttirW0 (www.sudurlandid.is/Eyjafrettir) from Sudland, Vikurfrettir (www.vf.is), from Sudurnes, Tidis (www.patreksfjordur.is), from Vestfirdir and Skessuhorn (www.skessuhorn.is) from Vesturland. Sed og Heyrt is a tabloid magazine.
Business: In Icelandic, Viðskiptablaðið (www.vb.is), is a daily, Markadurinn (http://vefmidlar.visir.is), is published weekly. Marine industry publications include Aegir and Fiskifrettir.
Periodicals: In Icelandic, the monthly Mannlíf (www.mannlif.is) covers news and current affairs and for women, Birtingur (www.birtingur.is) is published 10 times a year.
Broadcasting
The Ríkisútvarpið (RÚV) (Icelandic National Broadcasting Service) is the public network providing services from a number of regional centres.
Radio: RÚV (www.ruv.is) operates two radio stations Rás 1 and Rás 2. The largest private commercial radio network is Bylgjan (http://lettbylgjan.is).
Television: Sjónvarpið/RÚV (www.ruv.is) operates the national television service and locally producing Icelandic language shows as well as transmitting imported TV shows. It transmits for around eight hours per day during the week and 16 hours per day during the weekend. Private commercial TV stations includes Stöð 2 (www.stod2.visir.is) with five channels and Skjárinn (http://skjarinn.is) with three channels.
Advertising
Although the market is very small the advertising market is very dynamic with ads being placed in all media including new technologies. The print media typically accounts for over 50 per cent of the market. The quality of locally produced television advertising material is very high by international standards.
There is a total ban on advertising alcohol and tobacco and restrictions on advertising over the counter medicines. Outdoor advertising is limited by environmental laws, however billboards are popular. Information can be obtained from Association of Icelandic Advertising Companies.

Economy
Iceland has an open market economy based largely on fishing (although cod stocks are diminishing), tourism (expanding fast) and aluminium smelting (based on abundant geothermal power and water). It has a small population (299,815 in 2005) and one of the highest per capita GDP rates in Europe (US$35,700 in 2005).
The economy has been experiencing an upsurge since 2004 when it recorded a GDP growth of 8.2 per cent, with good growth of 5.6 per cent in 2005 and 4.0 per cent in 2006. The growth is credited to the expansion of the aluminium sector and strong domestic demand, fuelled by a record high current account deficit and inflation. In December 2006, the central bank was obliged to raise its interest rate to a record high of 14.25 per cent, in an attempt to curb the annual inflation rate which was running at an average 5.9 per cent. The bank's inflationary target is 2.5 per cent; the measures brought the rate down to 2.9 per cent in February 2007.
The fishing industry typically makes up around 60 per cent of exports and contributes 10 per cent of GDP. However, the level of cod catches are falling, which has had a knock-on effect for the processing industry. The large fish processing company, Samherji, moved its operations from Dalvík to Grimsby in the UK, an EU member-state, in 2006. Not only was the move necessary to take advantage of lower wages (lower by 30–40 per cent), but also for lower transport costs, at half Samherji's usual expenditure. It was also advantageous to dissipate the negative effect of the strong krona on exports, which were particularly vulnerable in 2006, so much so that there was consideration of joining the European Monetary Union (EMU) and adopting the euro as the national currency. However, the proposal was finally dismissed as the interest rate set by EMU was considered to be counterproductive to Iceland's monetary policy.
The Alcoa Fjaroaal aluminium smelter plant is due to become operational in 2007. The national power company, Landsvirkjun, is building a number of dams to supply the water for the plant and has had to counter opposition from environmentalists. The employment opportunities created by the plant are considered to outweigh environmental considerations. Once exports of aluminium start in 2007 it is expected that fish related exports and aluminium will be 50 per cent of exports each.

Labour market and unemployment
Iceland has a well-educated workforce of approximately 141.7 million in 2000. The rate of unemployment decreased from 2.5 per cent in 1998 to 1.9 per cent in 1999. There are labour shortages in fish processing and construction.

External trade
Iceland is a member of the European Economic Area agreement which maintains an internal market with, while not joining, the EU. The EU consults EEA members before making its decisions on community legislation. The EEA agreement allows freedom of movement of goods (excluding, to a significant degree, agriculture and fisheries), persons, services and capital.
Export trade accounts for 80 per cent of GDP. In an attempt to move away from primary industries, which are subject to world prices and dwindling stocks, Iceland has developed interests in financial services, software production and biotechnology.
Imports
Principal imports include capital goods, vehicles, consumer goods, petroleum, foodstuffs and clothing.
Main sources: US (13.1 per cent total, 2006), Germany (12.4 per cent), Norway (7.2 per cent).
Exports
Fish and marine products (over 50 per cent), manufactured goods and minerals – aluminium, ferrosilicon, diatomite.
Main destinations: The Netherlands (16.6 per cent total, 2006), UK (15.6 per cent), Germany (15.0 per cent).

Agriculture
Farming
Some 20 per cent of Iceland's land area is suitable for the raising of livestock and for fodder production. Only 6 per cent of the area is used for the cultivation of, principally, hay and potatoes, and the rest is used for livestock.
Arable land is scarce, but good grazing allows for self-sufficiency in meat (mostly lamb), milk, poultry, eggs, cheese and butter.
The sector is small-scale, heavily subsidised and organised into co-operatives. High import tariffs protect domestic production from foreign competition.
Estimated crop production in 2005 included: 12,000 tonnes (t) potatoes, 1,300t tomatoes, 1,000t cucumbers, 800t cabbages, 20t fruit in total, 4,010t vegetables in total. Livestock production included: 25,900t meat in total, 3,200t beef, 5,200t pig meat, 8,500t lamb, 5,800t poultry, *2,600t eggs, 112,000t milk, 500t cattle hides, *1,920t sheepskins, 800t greasy wool.
* estimate
Fishing
Fishing replaced farming early in this century as the dominant sector of the economy. The fishing industry (including processing) is the single most important export earner, accounting for 60 per cent of Iceland's exports. The large modernised trawler fleet supplies over 110 freezing plants, which produce white fish fillets, frozen shrimps, capelin, scampi, scallops, fish oil and fish meal.
The Icelandic Freezing Plants Corporation and Iceland Seafood Ltd are the leading fish exporters.
There is rapid growth of inland and offshore fish farming.
In September 2007 fishing quotas for Atlantic cod were drastically reduced due to the falling number of young fish stocks. The decision by the government to cut back on the country's biggest export earner is expected to have a big impact, on not only fishermen's livelihoods but also the short- to medium-term outlook for the industry. While the measures should preserve the industry the long-term outlook will be of a reduced fishing fleet.
In 2004, the total marine fish catch was 1,965,103 tonnes and the total crustacean catch was 21,486 tonnes.
Forestry
Forest exports in 2004 amounted to US$430,000, while imports amounted to US$76.4 million.

Industry and manufacturing
The industrial sector contributes 26 per cent to GDP and employs 30 per cent of the workforce.
It is centred on fish and food processing. A salmon fish processing plant on Iceland's east coast is the first to use state-of-the-art technology to process salmon for export to the EU and US.
Other major industrial activity focusses on aluminium smelting, ferro-silicon alloys, diatomite production and light manufacturing. The demands of the fishing industry have lead to developments in the country's computer, software and electronics industries and have also encouraged developments in biotechnology and pharmaceuticals.
With abundant hydroelectric and geothermal power in Iceland has led to power-intensive industries, the largest of which is aluminium smelting. In June 2007 the US-owned Alcoa smelter opened in eastern Iceland, with a capacity of 314,000 tonnes annually when fully operational.

Tourism
Tourism is an increasingly important sector, accounting for 13 per cent of foreign exchange earnings and 4.5 per cent of GDP. A growing proportion of arrivalsare winter visitors. The Nordic countries, North America and particularly the UK are the main markets. The industry is well organised and expanding, catering largely to adventure and eco-tourists.
Whale-watching, which attracts around 25 per cent of tourists, is growing in popularity. The decision to resume whale-hunting in 2003 hurt Iceland's image abroad and has given rise to fears that it could undermine the more lucrative tourist sector.
Travel and tourism is expected to provide US$1.8 billion or 7.1 per cent of GDP and employ over 20 per cent of the workforce, in 2005. The sector is expected to attract US$659 million or 18.7 per cent of total capital investment for 2005.

Hydrocarbons
Iceland does not produce any hydrocarbons. It consumes both coal and oil to meet domestic energy demands. Iceland does not consume natural gas. It consumes around 15,760 barrels per day (bpd) of refined oils. Iceland is dependent on these oils to fuel its cars, transportation system and fishing trawlers. Iceland also consumes approximately 139,700 tonnes of coal annually. With the government having an official policy to replace fossil fuels with hydrogen fuels, the consumption of oil and coal is likely to decrease as this industry grows.

Energy
Rapid development of cheap hydroelectric and geothermal power has led to self-sufficiency in energy requirements.
Geothermal energy accounts for 54 per cent of Iceland's energy consumption while hydro-energy accounts for 17 per cent. Imported energy (oil and coal) serve 29 per cent of domestic energy needs. It is estimated that only 12 per cent of Iceland's energy potential has been harnessed. Iceland aims to become the first fossil-fuel free economy by 2020 and plans to develop a fully hydrogen-powered transport system by 2035.
Around 85 per cent of homes have geothermal heating. The fishing fleet remains dependent on imported oil.

Financial markets
Stock exchange
The Iceland Stock Exchange (ICEX) has benefited from joining the Norex Alliance. Its trading system has been upgraded in order to cope with increased demand.

Banking and insurance
In addition to the central bank, there are four commercial banks operating: the Búnadarbanki Íslands (Agricultural Bank), Icebank Ltd, Islandsbanki Ltd and Landsbanki Íslands (National Bank of Iceland) are privately owned.
Kaupthing, an investment bank, and the Búnadarbanki merged in May 2003 to form the Kaupthing Búnadarbanki.
Central bank
Sedlabanki Íslands (Central Bank of Iceland)

Time
GMT

Geography
Iceland comprises one large island, with an area of 103,000 square km, and numerous smaller ones, situated near the Arctic Circle in the North Atlantic Ocean. The main island lies about 300km (190 miles) south-east of Greenland, about 1,000km (620 miles) west of Norway and about 800km (500 miles) north of Scotland. The Gulf Stream keeps Iceland warmer than might be expected.
A geologically young island, Iceland is volcanically and geothermally active. The largest volcanoes are Hekla and Snaefellsness. The terrain has a rugged aspect. As much as half of it is mountainous lava desert and wasteland. The central highlands are barren and interspersed with mountains and glaciers. 11 per cent of Iceland is covered by glaciers. The most extensive glacier, located in the south-east of the island, is Vatnajökull, which covers an area of 8,500 square km. The highest point in Iceland, Hvannadalshnúkur, which rises to 2,119m, is in this region. There are numerous lakes and fast-flowing, unnavigable rivers, some of which rise in the glaciers, while others are spring-fed. The coastline is irregular, with bays and

fjords, affording good natural harbours, though some parts are sandy with lagoons. The populated areas are restricted to less than a fifth of the land, around the coasts and in the valleys, especially in the Reykjavik area.
The largest islands are the Westmann Isles to the south, Hrísey to the north and Grímsey in the Arctic Circle.

Hemisphere
Northern.

Climate
Temperate, with mild but stormy winters and cool summers. Rainy in the south. Average temperatures vary between about minus 1 and 12 degrees Celsius.

Dress codes
Medium-weight throughout year, plus a topcoat and raincoat for winter.

Entry requirements

Passports
Required by all, except nationals of Nordic and Schengen Accord countries. Passports must be valid three months after date of departure.

Visa
Required by all, except nationals of EU/EEA and other European countries, North America, Australasia and some Latin American and Asian countries. For a full list of exceptions visit: www.utl.is/english. A Schengen visa application (offered in several languages) can be downloaded from http://europa.eu/abc/travel/ see 'documents you will need'.

Currency advice/regulations
There are no restrictions on the import and export of local and foreign currency.

Customs
Visitors may bring in personal effects and limited quantities of tobacco products and alcohol free of duty. Fishing and riding equipment must be accompanied by a certificate of disinfection issued by an authorised veterinary authority.

Health (for visitors)
Nationals of the European Economic Area (EEA) countries and Switzerland can access reduced cost and sometimes free medical treatment using a European Health Insurance Card (EHIC) while visiting the EEA. Exceptions include nationals of the 10 countries which joined the EU in 2005 whose EHIC is not valid in Switzerland. Applications for the EHIC should be made before travelling.

Mandatory precautions
There are no compulsory vaccinations.

Advisable precautions
Travellers should have up-to-date tetanus and polio immunisations.

Hotels
Most towns have hotels and guest houses. Between June and September university hostels and boarding schools are also used as hotels. Some hostels and many farms provide bed and breakfast service. The rating system is one-star (basic) to five-star (luxury). Tipping is not customary.

Credit cards
All major credit cards, such as American Express, Diners', Eurocard, Visa and Master Card, are accepted.

Public holidays (national)

Fixed dates
1 Jan (New Year's Day), 1 May (Labour Day), 17 Jun (National Day), 24 Dec (Christmas Eve, from mid-day), 25 Dec (Christmas Day), 26 Dec (Boxing Day), New Year's Eve (from mid-day).

Variable dates
Maundy Thursday, Good Friday, Easter Monday, First Day of Summer, Ascension Day, Whit Monday, Commerce Day (first Mon in Aug).

Working hours

Banking
Mon–Fri: 0915–1600 (winter), 0800–1600 (summer), plus 1700–1800 on Thu (Co-operative Bank, National Bank, Agricultural Bank (Kringlam).

Business
Mon–Fri: usually 0900–1700.

Government
Mon–Fri: usually 0900–1700.

Shops
Mon–Fri: 1000–1800. Most also open Sat 1000–1400/1600 (winter only, Oct to end May). Kiosks remain open until 2330 or even later.

Telecommunications

Mobile/cell phones
GSM 900/1800 services are available in populated areas.

Electricity supply
220V AC

Social customs/useful tips
Icelanders are generally self-confident, self-reliant and reserved. However, once the initial contact has been made people are more than likely to be friendly. Handshaking is customary on arrival and departure.

Getting there

Air
National airline: Icelandair
International airport/s: Keflavík International Airport (KEF), 51km south-west of Reykjavík; bank, restaraunts, shops, car hire.
Airport tax: A security fee of Ikr620 (Ikr285 for children two to 12 years of age) is charged on departure.

Surface
Water: There are ferry services to Iceland from Denmark, Norway and the Shetland Isles.

Getting about

National transport
Air: Air Iceland and Landsflug operate domestic services throughout the island to destinations which link with regional carriers in the west, north and east of the country. Light aircraft readily available for charter and sightseeing.
Road: There are approximately 1,350km of roads. Main highways (approximately one quarter of total) follow the coastline and are hard-surfaced; the rest are gravel-surfaced. Regular coach services link even the remote inland areas.
Water: Regular cargo coastal services link all major ports. Passenger and car ferries sail several times a day between Reykjavík and Akranes and between Thorlakshöta and Vestmannaeyian.

City transport
Taxis: These are used extensively and usually summoned by telephone, although they can be hailed in the street. The journey time from the airport to the city centre is about 40 minutes.
Buses, trams & metro: There are excellent regular services covering the centre and suburbs of Reykjavík. There is a standard fare for any length of journey, even if it involves more than one bus route. Journey time from the airport to the city centre is about 45 minutes.

Car hire
Car hire is available in Reykjavík and several other towns. Rates vary depending on the type of car. Minimum age 20 years, and an international driving licence is usually required. Advance reservations are necessary between June and August. Self-drive cars not recommended as a method of national transport as road surfaces tend to be poor.

BUSINESS DIRECTORY

The addresses listed below are a selection only. While World of Information makes every endeavour to check these addresses, we cannot guarantee that changes have not been made, especially to telephone numbers and area codes. We would welcome any corrections.

Telephone area codes
The international direct dialling code (IDD) for Iceland is +354, followed by subscriber's number.

Chambers of Commerce
Iceland Chamber of Commerce, House of Commerce, Kringlan 7, 103 Reykjavík (tel: 510-7100; fax: 568-6564; e-mail: info@chamber.is).

Banking
Kaupthing Búnadarbanki, Austurstraeti 3, 101 Reykjavík (tel: 525-6000; fax: 525-6209).

Íslandsbanki (Bank of Iceland), Kringlunni, 155 Reykjavík (tel: 560-8000; fax: 560-8150).

Landsbanki Íslands (National Bank of Iceland), Laugavegur 77, 155 Reykjavík (tel: 560-6400; fax: 552-9882; internet site: http://www.landsbanki.is).

Central bank

Sedlabanki Íslands, Kalkofnsvegi 1, 150 Reykjavík (tel: 569-9600; fax: 569-9605; e-mail: sedlabanki@sedlabanki.is).

Travel information

Airport Authority, Leifur Eiriksson Passenger Terminal, Keflavík Airport, 235 Keflavík.

BSI Travel (buses), Umferdarmidstödin v/Hringbraut, 101 Reykjavík.

Icelandair (Flugleidir), Reykjavík Airport, Reykjavík IS-101 (tel: 505-0200; fax: 505-0300; internet site: http://www.icelandair.com).

National tourist organisation offices

Icelandic Tourist Board, Laekjargotu 3, 101 Reykjavík (tel: 535-5500; fax: 535-5501; e-mail:info@icetourist.is).

Ministries

Ministry of Agriculture, 4th Floor, Sölvhólsgötu 7, 150 Reykjavík (tel: 560-9750; fax: 552-1160).

Ministry of Commerce and Industry, Arnarhváli, 150 Reykjavík (tel: 560-9070, 560-9420; fax: 562-1289).

Ministry of Communication, Hafnarhúsinu vio Tryggvagötu, 150 Reykjavík (tel: 560-9630; fax: 562-1702).

Ministry of Culture and Education, Sölvhólsgötu 4, 150 Reykjavík (tel: 560-9504; fax: 562-3068).

Ministry of the Environment, Vonarstraeti 4, 150 Reykjavík (tel: 560-9600; fax: 562-4566).

Ministry of Finance, Arnarhválli, 150 Reykjavík (tel: 560-9200; fax: 562-8280).

Ministry of Fisheries, Skúlagötu 4, 150 Reykjavík (tel: 560-9670; fax: 562-1853).

Ministry for Foreign Affairs, Rauoarásti\01g 25, 150 Reykjavík (tel: 560-9900; fax: 562-2373, 562-2386).

Ministry for Foreign Affairs, Trade Department, Hverfisgata 115, 105 Reykjavík (tel: 560-9930; fax: 562-4878).

Ministry of Health and Social Security, Laugavegi 116, 150 Reykjavík (tel: 560-9700; fax: 551-9165).

Ministry of Industry, Arnarhváli, 150 Reykjavík (tel: 560-9420; fax: 562-6859).

Ministry of Justice, Arnarhváli, 150 Reykjavík (tel: 560-9010; fax: 552-7340).

Ministry of Social Affairs, Hafnarhúsinu vio Tryggvagötu, 150 Reykjavík (tel: 560-9100; fax: 552-4804).

Office of the Prime Minister (Stjórnarráoshúsinu vio Laekjargötu), 150 Reykjavík (tel: 560-9400, 560-9403; fax: 562-4014, 562-8626).

Other useful addresses

Association of Icelandic Importers, Exporters & Wholesale Merchants, (Félag Islands Storkaupmanna), Húsi verslunarinnar, 103 Reykjavík (tel: 567-8910; fax: 468-8441).

British Embassy, Laufásvegur 31, PO Box 460, 101 Reykjavík (tel: 550-5100; fax: 550-5105; e-mail: britemb@centrum.is).

Customs Department, Tolhusid, Tryggvagata 19, 150 Reykjavík (tel: 560-0300; fax: 562-5826).

Embassy of the United States of America, Laufásvegur 21, Reykjavík (tel: 629-100; fax: 29-139).

Export Council of Iceland, Lagmuli 5, Box 8796, 129 Reykjavík (tel: 568-8777; fax: 568-9197).

Federation of Icelandic Co-operative Societies (Samband of Iceland), Import Division, v/Holtavegur, 104 Reykjavík (tel: 568-1266; fax: 568-0290).

Icelandic Embassy (USA), Suite 1200, 1156 15th Street, NW, Washington DC 20005 (tel: (+1-202)-265-6653; fax: (+1-202)-265-6656; e-mail: icemb.wash@utn.stjr.is).

Icelandic Energy Marketing Agency, Haaleitisbraut 68, 103 Reykjavík (tel: 515-9000; fax: 515-9003; e-mail: landsvirkjun@lv.is).

Iceland Management Association, Ananaust 15, 121 Reykjavík (tel: 562-1066).

Invest in Iceland Bureau (privatisation and foreign investment), Hallveigarstigur 1, PO Box 1000, IS-121 Reykjavík (tel: 511-4000; fax: 511-4040; internet site: http://www.invest.is/us/index.htm; e-mail: Invest@icetrade.is).

National Economic Institute (for information on economic development corporations), Thjodhagsstofnun, Kalkofnsvegi 1, Reykjavík (tel: 569-9500; fax: 562-6540).

Retailers' Association of Iceland, Hus Verslunarinnar, Kringlan 7, 103 Reykjavík (tel: 568-7811; fax: 568-5569).

Samband islenskra auglysingastofa (Association of Icelandic Advertising Companies), Borgartún 35, 105 Reykjavík (tel: 562-9588; internet: www.sia.is/SIA/English).

Statistical Bureau in Iceland, Hagstofa Islands, Skuggasund 3, 150 Reykjavík (tel: 560-9800; fax: 562-8865; internet site: http://www.statice.is/).

Internet sites

Iceland Reporter: www.centrum.is/icerev

Iceland websites: www.iceland.vefur.is

The Trade Council of Iceland: www.icetrade.is

KEY FACTS

Official name: Republic of India (also known as Bharat, local-language name)

Head of State: President Pratibha Patil (from 25 Jul 2007)

Head of government: Prime Minister Manmohan Singh (since 22 May 2004)

Ruling party: Coalition led by the Indian National Congress (INC) (formed 22 May 2004)

Area: 3,287,590 square km

Population: 1.12 billion (2007)*

Capital: New Delhi

Official language: Hindi and English; 15 other languages are recognised for official use in regional areas.

Currency: Rupee (Rs) = 100 paisa

Exchange rate: Rs42.76 per US$ (Jul 2008)

GDP per capita: US$978 (2007)*

GDP real growth: 9.20% (2007)*

Labour force: 482.42 million (2004)

Unemployment: 9.20% (2004)

Inflation: 6.40% (2007); 12.0% (Jul 2008)*

Oil production: 807,000 bpd (2007)

Balance of trade: -US$64.91 billion (2006)

Foreign debt: US$117.20 billion (2004)

Visitor numbers: 4.45 million (2006)*

Annual FDI: US$11.00 billion (2006)*

* estimated figure

India

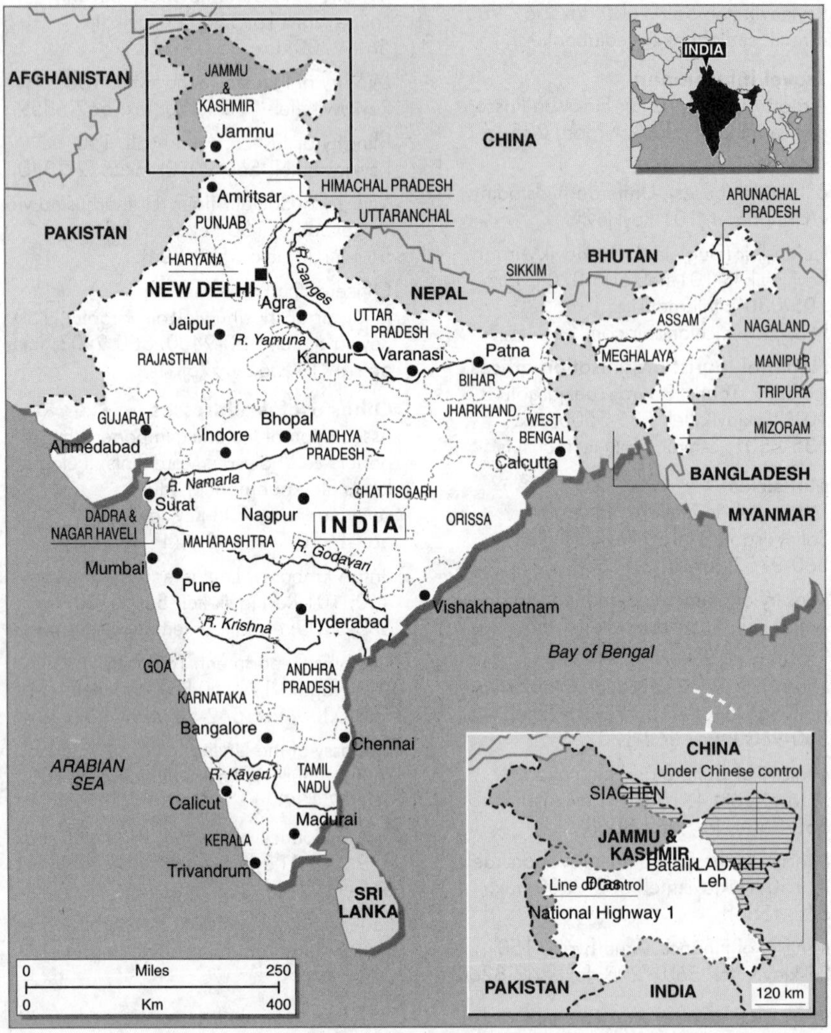

In 2007 India, the world's largest democracy, continued to impress. In the 15 years since its massive economy began to be liberalised the reach of India's economy became a commonplace in international business circles. This was perhaps best symbolised by the purchase, from Ford USA, of the Jaguar and Land Rover motor car companies by India's Tata group. However, the sheer size of India's economy allows it to ignore a number of unwelcome home truths.

Unreformed and unwilling

In a March 2008 article, the London *Economist* published an extensive critique of the Indian economy entitled *What's holding India back?* The article drew attention to the government's failure to include a number of items such as states' deficits and food and fuel subsidies in the March 2008 budget. The *Economist* calculated that this represented the exclusion of items adding up to 3.1 per cent of GDP. According to the *Economist*, in this respect India was in a far worse position than other 'big' emerging economies (viz China) which had been less complacent. Central to any attempt at reform in India is its omnipresent civil service, estimated to be some 10 million strong. Although civil service pay awards have performance strings attached, these are seen more as aspirational than as essential. India's reforming prime minister, Manmohan Singh, has achieved a great deal since taking office in 2004, but there is till a long way to go. Government pay rises are seen as the birthright of a civil service renowned for its bureaucracy as well as its petty corruption. In another article, the *Economist* quoted Mr lance Pritchett of the Kennedy School of Government in Harvard as saying that India's public sector was 'one of the world's top ten problems, of the order of AIDS and climate change'. Ironically, the elite India Administrative Service (IAS) which is India's decision making/taking service, would in many respects stand comparison with many senior civil service cadres. Numbering only 5,600, its district magistrates – more often known as 'district offices' – can find themselves running areas and populations the size of small countries. The IAS can trace its origins back to the once respected Indian colonial service, a position in which it was often harder to obtain than in the administrative class of the home civil service. As the Indian economy has increased, so has the size of the IAS; but there are those in India who hold it responsible for the failure of the Indian government to wholeheartedly adopt economic liberalisation.

Optimism?

In its Asian Development Outlook for 2008, the Asian Development Bank (ADB) observes that over the past decade, India has undergone a transformation and climbed to a high-growth path as macroeconomic and structural reforms reduced regulation, improved the business environment, and opened the economy to greater competition. Yet it still needs to focus on certain key areas with the potential to push growth to a higher plateau. The most crucial are enhancing the policy and regulatory framework to encourage the private sector and reining in fiscal deficits. A dynamic private sector that creates jobs, increases productivity, and invests in the economy plays a crucial role in bolstering growth. Removing the bottlenecks to private sector growth and competition in India could, in the opinion of the ADB, well generate an additional 2 per cent of gross domestic product (GDP) growth.

Saved by services

According to the ADB's economists, India's impressive economic performance of the past few years continued in 2007, although GDP growth slowed from 9.6 per cent in fiscal year (FY) 2006 to 8.7 per cent in FY 2007 (ended March 2008). The deceleration, reflecting tightened monetary policies, touched all sectors Industry, contributing about 29 per cent of GDP, and a major driver of growth in FY 2006, eased a little. Key factors were weaker growth in consumer spending, constrained by inflationary pressure and higher borrowing costs. The slowdown was led primarily by a decline in consumer durables production, but other manufacturing industries as well as mining and energy (oil, coal and electricity) also made weaker contributions.

Agriculture, accounting for about 18 per cent of GDP, witnessed a sharp drop in growth levels, from 3.8 per cent in FY 2006 to 2.6 per cent in FY 2007. The reduction came mainly from a poor winter crop. The low growth rate also reflected falling levels of public investment and ancillary services. In response to falling agricultural growth, the government has set a goal of doubling growth from 2 per cent a year over the last decade to 4 per cent in the 11th Five-Year Plan (2007–12) by bridging the gap between potential and actual yields.

The key contributor to India's growth was the services sector, which generated an impressive 53 per cent of GDP and continued its rapid growth, at 10.7 per cent in FY 2007. It was led by the trade, hotel, transport and communications sub sectors. The finance, insurance, real estate and business services sub sectors remained healthy despite a decline in growth. Growth in the hitherto booming construction sector decelerated from 12 per cent in FY 2006 to 9.6 per cent in FY 2007 as a result of hardening lending rates and less expansive lending policies by the ReserveBank of India (RBI) (central bank).

Growth in India's economy was driven by domestic demand, which remained strong despite rising inflation. Robust growth in real wages and remittances also buttressed consumption. Demand for consumer durables, such as automobiles, motorcycles and scooters, was particularly affected by the rising costs of borrowing. Government consumption spending also fell, from 6.2 per cent in FY 2006 to 5.5 per cent in FY 2007, in keeping with rationalisation of expenditure and deficit commitments made under the Fiscal Responsibility and Budget Management Act of 2003. Investment was the fastest-growing component of domestic demand. Growth in bank credit to commercial enterprises subsided in the second half of FY2007.

Problems with the dollar?

The surge in capital inflows continued unabated on account of economic performance, healthy productivity growth, tightening financial integration with

KEY INDICATORS — India

	Unit	2003	2004	2005	2006	2007
Population	m	1,068.50	1,088.06	*1,096.92	*1,108.00	*1,123.97
Gross domestic product (GDP)	US$bn	603.30	694.70	780.78	877.22	1,098.95
GDP per capita	US$	539	608	*712	792	*978
GDP real growth	%	7.4	7.3	9.2	9.7	9.2
Inflation	%	4.6	3.8	4.2	6.2	6.4
Industrial output	% change	–	8.6	9.0	10.6	–
Agricultural output	% change	–	0.7	2.3	2.7	–
Oil output	'000 bpd	793.0	819.0	784.0	807.0	801.0
Natural gas output	bn cum	30.1	29.4	30.4	31.8	30.2
Coal output	mtoe	172.2	191.0	199.6	209.7	208.0
Exports (fob) (goods)	US$m	62,952.0	69,180.0	104,780.0	127,090.0	–
Imports (cif) (goods)	US$m	79,658.0	89,330.0	156,334.0	191,995.0	–
Balance of trade	US$m	-16,706.0	-20,150.0	-51,554.0	-64,905.0	–
Current account	US$m	6,850.0	2,050.0	-6,854.0	-9,800.0	-19,345.0
Total reserves minus gold	US$m	98,938.0	126,593.0	131,924.0	170,738.0	266,988.0
Foreign exchange	US$m	97,617.0	125,164.0	131,018.0	170,187.0	266,553.0
Exchange rate	per US$	46.81	45.26	44.43	44.50	39.34

* estimated figure

world markets, and a wide interest rate differential relative to the rest of the world.

The RBI has been attempting to control money supply growth to maintain price stability, while seeking to ensure credit market and interest rate conditions that support investment in the context of relative stability in the exchange rate. But it has had limited success. While the rupee weakened slightly in the latter part of FY 2007, it appreciated by about 13 per cent against the US dollar and by about 7 per cent on average for the year in real effective terms. The steep and unexpectedly large cuts in US interest rates in early 2008 created a much larger differential with Indian lending rates, which are among the highest in Asia. The pressure mounted on the RBI to cut its rates even though high inflation meant that there is no room for easing its policy.

The RBI's tight monetary stance brought down inflation in manufactured goods but after October 2007 this was outweighed by rising food and energy prices. Inflation, as measured by year-on-year growth in the wholesale price index, reached 4.6 per cent in February 2008 creeping toward the RBI's target limit of 5 per cent. In early March 2008, the first of the monthly readings on inflation jumped to 5.9 per cent, a 10-month high, driven by further food price increases. India is the largest importer of edible oils in the world with more than 40 per cent of its domestic demand met through imports. Reflecting the tight global situation and adversely affected by domestic supply constraints, food prices rose faster than inflation. The government responded by increasing subsidies on food items, controlling exports, and subsidising imports.

Revising the road map

The Indian government, like many others, appeared to be wrong footed by the rapidity of fuel and food price rises. In addition to their inevitably inflationary effect, the risk of popular discontent began to make itself apparent, with sporadic popular protests breaking out. Finance minister Palaniappan Chidambaram indicated that he intended to ask the 13th Finance Commission to provide a revised road map, to take into account off-budget subsidies on oil, food, and fertiliser (which has been funded by bond issues). Appreciation of the local currency against the US dollar has also hurt Indian exporters. Merchandise exports grew by 21.6 per cent in the first 10 months of FY 2007 when expressed in US dollars. However, this reflected the sharp appreciation of the rupee more than any actual increase in exports, the growth of which, in rupee terms, was a more modest 7.7 per cent. The slowdown was evident most notably in chemicals, engineering goods, textiles, and readymade garments and handicrafts.

The growth of goods imports, at 29.6 per cent in US dollar terms in the first 10 months of FY 2007, was also overstated when compared to its rupee value (14.7 per cent). Non-oil imports of capital goods, chemicals, edible oils, and precious and semiprecious stones provided the main stimulus for the growth of imports, which rose by 36.1 per cent, while oil imports went up by 16.5 per cent. The net effect of all this was an almost 50 per cent widening of the US dollar trade deficit from a year earlier. Preliminary balance of payments estimates indicated that the current account deficit would be about 1.9 per cent of GDP, higher than the 1.1 per cent recorded in FY 2006.

Although the trade deficit widened significantly, it was offset by a strong rise in the inflow of remittances and an increasing surplus from exports of services such as software and business services.

The Indian stock market kept up its 3 year bull run in 2007 with a marked increase in portfolio investment by foreign institutional investors, though they remained relatively small players. The Sensex stock market index had shown increased volatility since early January 2007 and in line with stock markets throughout the world, the Indian market fell by about 25 per cent in the first three months of 2008. The Indian government's budget position has improved markedly since the adoption of the Fiscal Responsibility and Budget Management Act, which envisaged an annual reduction of at least 0.3 percentage points in the fiscal deficit. Buoyancy in tax collections allowed for a reduction in the deficit in FY 2007 to an estimated 3.1 per cent of GDP, marginally below target. The federal budget for FY 2008 projected a further decline to 2.5 per cent, and proposed a rationalisation of the income tax structure by raising tax exemption limits and by restructuring tax slabs. The corporate tax rates remained the same.

Populist budget

The 2008 budget will probably be the last before the general elections in 2009, and for this reason adopted a more populist stance on spending for health, education and rural infrastructure, in line with the 11th Plan strategy of inclusive growth. A central feature of the stance was a farm-loan waiver estimated at Rs600 billion, or almost 1 per cent of GDP. Alarmingly, funding of the waiver was not included in the budget.

Concluding its review of the Indian economy, the ADB notes that the federal deficit figures did not present India's complete fiscal picture for four key reasons. First, the deficit incurred by state governments was excluded. Second, the civil service pay increase recommended by the Sixth Pay Commission (which in fairness, was announced after the budget), would cost the federal government up to US$3.1 billion in FY 2008 if implemented; this was not provided for. Third, the cost of various off-budget items, such as oil bonds and losses of state owned electricity companies, were excluded. Fourth, isolating domestic prices from rising international food prices would require additional budget financing during the year. Adding in all these four items would lift the total general government deficit significantly. These exclusions, continued to add to a public debt that is equivalent to a staggering 80 per cent of GDP, among the world's highest. Interest payments were projected to rise by 11 per cent in FY 2008 and to equal just over 30 per cent of expected total revenue receipts.

Risk assessment

Economy	Good
Politics	Good
Regional stability	Fair

COUNTRY PROFILE

Historical profile

1200 The start of five-and-a-half centuries of Muslim rule over the region, beginning with the Sultanate era.

1757 The region gradually came under the influence of British rule after the battle of Plassey.

1858 India came under the direct rule of the British crown after a failed mutiny.

1885 The Indian National Congress was founded by Indian nationalists.

1920s Nationalist leader, Mohandas Karamachand Gandhi, launched a campaign of civil disobedience against British rule.

1942 Congress launched its 'Quit India' campaign.

1947 The Union of India was granted independence by Britain. Hundreds of thousands died during communal violence following independence. Jawaharlal Nehru of the Congress became India's first prime minister. The Hindu ruler of Muslim-majority Jammu and Kashmir joined secular India rather than Islamic

Pakistan when the subcontinent was partitioned at the end of British rule. India and Pakistan went to war in Kashmir. A peace agreement was signed.
1948 Gandhi was assassinated by a Hindu fundamentalist.
1950 India became a republic. It remained a member of the Commonwealth. The constitution of India was adopted. France transferred sovereignty of Chandernagore to India.
1954 France ceded its four remaining Indian settlements (Pondicherry, Yanam, Mahe and Karaikal).
1961 Indian forces overran the Portuguese territories of Goa, Daman and Diu and they were annexed by India.
1962 India lost a border war with China.
1964 Nehru died and was succeeded by Lal Bahadur Shastri.
1965 India and Pakistan fought a second war over Kashmir.
1966 Shastri died and Nehru's daughter, Indira Gandhi, became prime minister.
1971 India-Pakistan war over East Pakistan (later Bangladesh). A Treaty of Friendship was signed with the Soviet Union.
1972 The Simla peace agreement set a new Line of Control (LoC) in Kashmir, separating India- and Pakistan-controlled areas.
1974 India exploded its first nuclear device in underground tests.
1975 Indira Gandhi was found guilty of instigating electoral malpractice and was barred from office.
1977 Congress lost elections for the first time.
1980 Indira Gandhi was reinstated as prime minister heading a Congress splinter group, Congress (Indira). There followed years of widespread political and religious disturbances in several states.
1984 Indira Gandhi was assassinated by her Sikh bodyguard after troops stormed the Golden Temple, the Sikhs' most holy shrine, to arrest Sikh separatists. Her son, Rajiv Gandhi, was sworn in as prime minister. Widespread violence continued.
1987 India deployed peace-keeping troops in Sri Lanka.
1989 After an election in which over 100 people died, VP Singh was sworn in as prime minister. His government was the first minority government in Indian history.
1990 The Indian army opened fire in Srinagar during a protest against a crackdown on separatism, killing 38 and giving impetus to rebel campaigns. Singh resigned in November. Chandra Shekhar was sworn in as prime minister. Indian troops withdrew from Sri Lanka. Muslim separatists, trained and armed by Pakistan, began a campaign of violence in Kashmir.
1991 Shekhar resigned, and the reformist government of PV Narashima Rao came to power. Rajiv Gandhi, the former prime minister, was assassinated by Sri Lankan Tamil separatists while electioneering.
1996 Following the general elections, the post-independence Nehru/Gandhi dynasty came to an end with the defeat of Congress. The largest single party in parliament became the Hindu fundamentalist Bharatiya Janata Party (BJP) (Indian Nationalist Party), which attempted and failed to form a government, after which the United Front (UF), a 13-party coalition, succeeded.
1997 Kocheril Raman Narayanan became India's tenth president, after five years as vice president. He was the first Dalit (untouchable) to become president. The UF government was toppled after Congress withdrew its support in the lower house.
1998 A coalition government led by the BJP was formed and Atal Behari Vajpayee was appointed prime minister. India and Pakistan each conducted underground nuclear tests, leading to widespread international condemnation and US sanctions.
1999 Prime Minister Vajpayee made a historic bus ride to Pakistan for a peace summit with Prime Minister Nawaz Sharif. Vajpayee lost a confidence vote, but was reaffirmed, following general elections. Pakistan and India fought a brief war in Kargil in Indian-controlled Kashmir.
2000 India celebrated the birth of its one billionth citizen. New states – Chattisgarh (part of Madhya Pradesh), Uttaranchal (in the north) and Jharkand (part of the eastern state of Bihar) – were created.
2001 The US lifted sanctions on Pakistan and India as a reward for supporting its attacks on Afghanistan. There was an unsuccessful terrorist attack on India's parliament, which India blamed on Pakistan and imposed sanctions.
2002 Rebels thought to be from Pakistan attacked an Indian army camp in Kashmir, killing more than 30 people. India threatened retaliation and moved troops to the border. The tension eased when India lifted its five-month ban on direct flights to Pakistan and ordered its naval battleships back to port. A P J Abdul Kalam was sworn in as president.
2003 India and China reached a de facto agreement over the status of Tibet and Sikkim in a cross-border trade agreement. The Indian and Pakistani armies began a cease-fire across the LoC dividing the disputed state of Kashmir and the Himalayan glacier of Siachen.
2004 Prime Minister Vajpayee visited Pakistan on his first visit since 1999, and met President Musharraf. In their first talks with the Indian government, Kashmiri separatist leaders agreed that all violence in the Himalayan region should stop. The Indian National Congress (Congress) won the parliamentary elections and Manmohan Singh was named prime minister. An earthquake off the island of Sumatra caused a tsunami that devastated coastal areas in the region. The final toll for India was estimated to be 12,407 dead or missing, 647,599 displaced.
2005 The first bus-link for 57 years between divided Kashmir began. India, along with Bangladesh, Bhutan, Maldives, Nepal, Pakistan and Sri Lanka, signed the South Asia Free Trade Agreement (SAFTA).
2006 The third bus link between India and Pakistan was launched, providing the first direct link across the divided Punjab since partition in 1947. Agreement was reached with the US giving India access to American civilian nuclear technology.
2007 In July, Pratibha Patil became India's president and first female Head of State. She was elected by state and federal parliaments with 65.8 per cent of the vote; Bhairon Singh Shekhawat won 34.2 per cent. In August severe monsoon flooding in Bihar caused death and destruction and left around 11 million Indian villagers affected. India celebrated 60 years of independence from Britain.
2008 The first passenger train since 1965 began operations between Dhaka (Bangladesh) and Kolkata on 14 April. A number of Indian cities have been targetted by Islamist bombs, killing dozens and injuring many more. The tension between Hindus and Muslems have been blamed for the violence. The government won a vote of confidence after the Communist Party of India (CPI) withdrew it support from the coalition government, in protest at India's civilian nuclear co-operation deal with the US.

Political structure

Constitution

The Constitution of India was inaugurated on 26 January 1950. The Preamble declares that the people of India solemnly resolve to constitute a 'sovereign socialist secular democratic republic' and to secure to all its citizens, justice, liberty, equality and fraternity. India has 28 self-governing states and seven union territories with a federal form of government. Any citizen aged 18 years and over is eligible to vote. India is the world's largest democracy.

Form of state

Secular, democratic republic

The executive

Executive power lies with the prime minister, who is appointed by the president, who has a largely ceremonial role and serves a five-year term. The prime minister nominates a 20-member Council of Ministers (cabinet).

National legislature

Parliament consists of two houses, the 545-member Lok Sabha (House of the People) (lower house), and the 245-member Rajya Sabha (Council of States) (upper house).

Members of the Lok Sabha are directly elected for a maximum five-year term by universal adult suffrage, except for two who are nominated by the president.

Members of the Rajya Sabha are elected by the state assemblies for six years (one-third being replaced every two years), except for 12 who are nominated by the president.

The legislative field is divided between the Union (central government) and the states. The Union possesses exclusive powers to make laws with respect to matters grouped under 97 headings in the constitution, including foreign affairs, defence, citizenship and trade with other countries. The Union territories are administered by the federal government based in New Delhi. Major legislation requires passage through both houses of parliament.

Each state has its own governor and elected state assembly, with a chief minister and council of ministers. Policy in areas such as agriculture, education and law and order are determined at the state level.

Legal system

The legal system is based on English common law. There is limited judicial review of legislative acts.

The judiciary is independent and known for delivering verdicts which may not necessarily please the government in power. The Chief Justice presides over the Supreme Court, which is the highest court in the land. Each state has its own high court.

Last elections

20 April/10 May 2004 (parliamentary); 21 July 2007 (presidential).

Results: Parliamentary: INC won 145 seats out of 545 (26.8 per cent of the vote); its allies 73 (8.7 per cent); the BJP 138 (22.2 per cent); its allies 48 (14.1 per cent); the Communist Party of India (Marxist) 43 (5.7 per cent), the Samajwadi Party 36 (5.3 per cent), the Bahujan Samaj Party 19 (5.3 per cent) and the Communist Party of India 10 (1.4 per cent).

Presidential: Pratibha Patil won 65.8 per cent of the vote; Bhairon Singh Shekhawat won 34.2 per cent.

Next elections

2012 (presidential); 2009 (parliamentary)

Political parties

Ruling party

Coalition led by the Indian National Congress (INC) (formed 22 May 2004)

Main opposition party

Bharatiya Janata Party (BJP) (Indian People's Party)

Population

1.12 billion (2007)*

Last census: March 2001: 1,028,610,328

Population density: 337 inhabitants per square km.

Annual growth rate: 1.7 per cent 1994–2004 (WHO 2006)

Ethnic make-up

Indo-Aryan (72 per cent), Dravidian (25 per cent), Mongoloid and others (3 per cent).

Religions

Hindu (84 per cent), Muslim (13 per cent), Christian, Sikh, Buddhist, Jain.

Education

A Constitutional Amendment act passed in 2001 made education for all children aged six to 14 a fundamental right. The government earmarked 8 per cent of GNP for education, of which at least 50 per cent would be allocated to primary education. The government is also aiming for universal elementary education by 2010. Accordingly, the department of elementary education and literacy was allocated Rs4,900 crore (US$1,067 million) for 2002/03.

Primary education up to the age of 14 is compulsory in most states and lasts for eight years. Lower primary education between aged six and 11 is free in all states, but upper primary education from 11 to 14 years is free in only 12 states.

Secondary and higher education spending is forecast at Rs49.5 billion (US$1 billion) in 2003/04, of which, Rs17.7 billion (US$388 million) is allocated to higher education spending.

Gender differences, ethnic minorities, caste discrimination and regional disparities have contributed largely to wide inequalities in the development of basic education between Indian states. Independent surveys at the grassroots level show that despite the rhetoric of policy makers, expenditure in the education sector has been falling and typically 6,600,000 working children are still denied the right to primary education. Micro-level strategies for basic education in rural areas are developed through concerted co-operation between local communities, NGOs, government, and international donors.

Literacy rate: 61 per cent adult rate (Unesco 2005)

Compulsory years: Six to 14. Compulsory education is enforced in eight States/Union Territories (UT) when it covers entirely primary schooling; in four States/UT compulsory education is only enforced between ages six to 11; while in March 2003, the ministry of education confirmed that as many as 20 States/UT had not introduced any measure of compulsion.

Enrolment rate: 92 per cent gross primary enrolment; 58 per cent for upper primary enrolment.

Pupils per teacher: 62 in primary schools.

Health

Per capita total expenditure on health (2003) was US$82, of which per capita government spending was US$20, (WHO 2006).

The size and complexity of the Indian population renders universal healthcare difficult to achieve.

India, with its large migrant workforce, is one of only two countries that exports polio (the other is Nigeria), according to the World Health Organisation – Global Polio Eradication Initiative (WHO – Polio Eradication). In particular the state of Uttar Pradesh, where the disease is endemic, saw an outbreak infecting over 400 people in 2006, which was spreading into neighbouring states. India represented 28 per cent of worldwide polio cases in 2006 an increase of 3 per cent from 2005.

In 2004 a new drug treatment for tuberculosis, the first in 40-years, which kills one million sufferers in India and 10 million worldwide, was announced. The medication was developed, and will be manufactured, in India as part of its positioning as a major location for cost-effective, bio-medical research.

In 2006, by October, there had been outbreaks of dengue fever in New Dehli, with around 5,000 cases and 100 deaths; in Kerala up to 20,000 people had been affected by chikungunya fever (carried by mosquitoes) and in the northern states of Bihar and Uttar Pradesh and the area bordering Nepal, Japanese encephalitis had killed almost 400 people.

In October 2007 the government launched a plan for insurance covering disability, health and life for India's 400m working poor. The plan is part of the government's 'New Deal' for rural India.

HIV/Aids

The World Bank warned India that without greater measures to prevent the spread of HIV through the use of condoms, infections rates and subsequent deaths from Aids could surpass all other pathogens. Indian authorities say infection rates are falling, though critics claim that the factors that lead to high rates in sub-Saharan Africa are all present in India: large pools of

migrant labour, large numbers of prostitutes and stigma about sex and the Aids disease. Condom use has levelled out at 50 per cent and without an increased use new infections could grow by 3 million before 2013. Nationwide policies to tackle the disease are not apparent, with each state tackling the threat locally and some seemingly unable to change old habits.
A UNAids report, published in May 2006, claimed that there were 5.7 million people HIV positive in India, overtaking the 5.5 million infected in South Africa.
In April 2005 the head of the UN backed Global Fund to Fight Aids, Tuberculosis and Malaria, Richard Feacham, said official Indian statistics on the disease were wrong. Stating that Indian had more infections than registered, due to underreporting and that India's infection rates had surpassed that of South Africa. He rejected India's estimate of 5.1 million HIV sufferers, saying that the etimate was a 'conservative figure based on limited data', and he did not believe that India had adequate surveillance measures. The Global Fund has contributed US$265 million for Aids control (2004–09). The government increased the Naco spending to US$95.8 million, however it is estimated that per capita spending on Aids control in India is only US0.29, half the rate spent in Thailand.
While India's infection rate is only 1 per cent, in some of its most populous states the infection rates are up to 20 per cent. The UK endorsed the Naco assertion that more foreign aid would be spent on HIV/Aids sufferers. Of the £123 million (US$219), donated by the UK to fight the disease, £95 million (US$169 million) is still scheduled to be spent by March 2007.
HIV prevalence: 0.9 per cent aged 15–49 in 2003 (World Bank)
Life expectancy: 62 years, 2004 (WHO 2006)
Fertility rate/Maternal mortality rate: 3.0 births per woman, 2004 (WHO 2006); maternal mortality 410 per 100,000 live births (World Bank).
Birth rate/Death rate: 9 deaths to 27 births per 1,000 head of population.
Child (under 5 years) mortality rate (per 1,000): 63.0 per 1,000 live births; 45 per cent of children aged under five are malnourished (World Bank).
Head of population per physician: 0.6 physicians per 1,000 people, 2005 (WHO 2006)

Welfare

The between 60–115 million children toiling as bonded workers in India. Most are agricultural labourers while others work in factories or as domestics. The majority of these children are Dalit caste (the untouchables) and may be bound to their employer for years to pay back loans incurred by their parents. While these children are working they do not attend school which perpetuates their deprivation in later life.
The are estimates of between 60–115 million children toiling as bonded workers in India. Most are agricultural labourers while others work in factories or as domestics. The majority of these children are Dalit caste (the untouchables) and may be bound to their employer for years to pay back loans incurred by their parents. While these children are working they do not attend school, which perpetuates their deprivation in later life.
Homeless children, widows, the elderly, and the disabled (who often occupy the strata of the most destitute people in India) do not have any explicit protection in the constitution, and consequently not enough demand for any government - (whether local, state or national) to extend care to them. The National Nutrition Mission, distributes food grains at subsidised prices to poor families.
World Bank estimates that India has 40 per cent of the World's poor. The government estimates that 85 per cent of the population is in need of some form of welfare support; 25 per cent of the population belongs to either scheduled castes (SC) or scheduled tribes (ST) and these people have been ascribed special welfare measures. The National SC and ST Finance and Development Corporation provides funds for developing entrepreneurial and other skills.
The central government's expenditure on social services accounts for 1.66 per cent of GDP. India's population suffers periodic problems of floods, droughts and other natural disasters.

Pensions

The 2003/04 budget planned a massive overhaul of the pension system. From 1 January 2004, new employees in the public and private sector stopped paying into state pensions and were made to pay into privately managed funds.
The public sector finance organisation, Life Insurance Corporation of India (LIC), also ran a new pension scheme, the The state-subsidised scheme will be available to workers above the age of 55, guaranteeing an annual return of 9 per cent and a maximum pension of Rs2,000 (US$43) per month.
An assurance scheme called Janaraksha has been designed by the LIC to provide life insurance for farmers and workers with irregular incomes.

Main cities

New Delhi (capital, estimated population 10.4 million (m) in 2004); Mumbai, capital of Maharashtra state (12.6m) (was Bombay, renamed 1995); Kolkata, capital West Bengal state (4.9m) (was Calcutta, renamed 1999); Bangalore (name changing to Bengaluru 1 Nov 2006), Karnataka state (4.6m); Chennai, capital of Tamil Nadu state (4.5m) (was Madras, renamed in 1995); Ahmadabad, Gujarat state (3.7m); Hyderabad, capital of Andhra Pradesh state (3.7m); Kanpur, Uttar Pradesh state (2.7m); Pune, Maharashtra state (2.7m), Sûrat (2.6m), Jaipur (2.5m), Lakhnau (2.3m), Nâgpur (2.2m).

Languages spoken

Hindi is spoken by almost a third of the population. English is widely spoken and is often the main language of business, with over 350 million Indians using it as the lingua franca. Most central government documents are in both Hindi and English. Government policy is to encourage wider use of Hindi.
There are 15 local official languages in the various states, of which the most widely spoken are Punjabi, Telugu, Bengali, Marathi, Tamil, Urdu and Gujarati. There are 1,652 languages spoken throughout the country.
In August a ruling by the mayor of Mumbai, Shubha Raul, made Marathi the official language of local government in Mumbai. Concern was expressed by a number of elected officials with a limited grasp of Marathi, who felt they would be put at a disadvantage. There was also concern that the move would hamper Mumbai's aspirations of becoming an international financial centre, and that it would encourage a resurgence of regional politics. All documents for the Municipal Corporation of Greater Mumbai (BMC) have to be written in Marathi.

Official language/s

Hindi and English; 15 other languages are recognised for official use in regional areas.

Media

The government guarantees the freedom of the press. The market is huge and has been expanding as the economy has grown.
Other news agencies: There are over 40 domestic news agencies.
Press Trust of India: www.ptinews.com
United News of India: www.uniindia.com

Press

India has a large middle class and newspaper circulation has expanded with new titles being added.
Dailies: Newspaper titles may be published in English and a local language, editions in English have national readerships, whereas local language newspapers are often regionally limited.
Circulation figures for top newspapers are in the millions.

In English, The Times of India (http://timesofindia.indiatimes.com) is the leading broadsheet, followed by Hindustan Times (http://timesofindia.indiatimes.com), The Hindu (www.thehindu.com), New Delhi Times (www.newdelhitimes.org) and Early Times (www.earlytimes.in).
Regional newspapers include The Indian Express (www.indianexpress.com) and The Asian Age (www.asianage.com) from New Delhi, The Statesman (www.thestatesman.net) and The Telegraph (www.telegraphindia.com) from Kolkata, Kashmir Observer (www.kashmirobserver.com) from Srinagar and Deccan Herald (www.deccanherald.com) from Bangalore.
Weeklies: There are no major national weeklies, but a huge number of all genre published at local level.
Business: There are several financial and business newspapers, including, in English, Mint (www.livemint.com), is a national newspaper, regional newspapers include The Economic Times (http://economictimes.indiatimes.com) and The Financial Express (www.financialexpress.com) are based in Mumbai and Business Line (www.blonnet.com) is based in Chennai. Business Today (http://businesstoday.digitaltoday.in) is a national magazine.
Periodicals: In English, the monthly Diplomatist (www.diplomatist.com) covers international relations and trade, Frontline covers news and current affairs, published fortnightly, the monthly Verve (www.verveonline.com) is the oldest publication for women.

Broadcasting

Radio: India has the largest radio network, worldwide. It has hundreds of FM radio stations, broadcasting, most music programmes, in local languages Only All India Radio (http://allindiaradio.org) the public network, with over 200 local stations may broadcast the news. Major commercial networks include Radio Mirchi (www.enil.co.in) with a network of 32 stations and Radio City (www.radiocity.in) with 18 stations. Meow FM is a talk radio station in Delhi and Mumbai for women.
Television: The national, public broadcaster is Noordarshan (www.ddindia.gov.in) with eight regional centres. There are large media groups that operate TV channels, including Zee TV (www.zeetelevision.com), Star TV (http://starnews.indya.com) and Sun Network (www.sunnetwork.org), which broadcast via satellite and cable, with schedules including locally produced and imported TV shows. India has the largest cable TV market in the world, with over 60 million subscribers.

Advertising

The Advertising Standards Council of India (ASCI) has codes of practice some of which are voluntary. Advertising is available throughout traditional media as well as new technologies. Outdoor advertising is subject to certain restrictions.

Economy

The US based Goldman Sacks Bank forecast, in January 2007, that India could overtake the US and become the world's second largest economy, after China, by 2042. A World Bank report published in December 2007 stated that almost 50 per cent of the World's total GDP was produced between the US, China, Japan, Germany and India.
Since 2002 its economy has been growing by around 8 per cent and it has been little effected by the sharp rise in global oil prices and falling US dollar. The IMF considers the economic expansion should be sustained in the medium-term if economic reforms, that were begun in the mid-1990s, are maintained. However, it remains to be seen how the central government manages the consensus for reform among all its diverse associates and states. It is expected that reforms in privatisation, labour law and reduced public ownership of banks will be difficult to achieve.
The government is focussing on four main policy objectives: achieving fiscal sustainability while financing development; managing price stability; fostering a deeper and broader financial sector; and promoting job-intensive growth.
Services provide over 50 per cent of GDP and agriculture almost 20 per cent, whereas industry supplies 27 per cent, of which manufacturing is around 16 per cent. In 2005, the agricultural sector grew by 2.3 per cent while both industry, manufacturing and services all grew by over 9 per cent. Agriculture employs around 60 per cent of the workforce and the government is attempting to increase growth, necessary to achieve food security, by providing farmers with cheap credit and an expansion of the rural jobs guarantee scheme.
There has been a large increase in the number of small- to medium-sized Indian companies that are competing on the world market, with Indian entrepreneurs buying internationally recognised companies. India experienced greater outflow of FDI then inward investment in 2006. This has allowed Indian corporations access to western markets and advanced technology. India, it would appear, is beginning to compete with the West for 'intellectual capital' by investing in value-added, technology intensive industries, at home and abroad, which utilises the graduates of its new universities and the successful Indian diaspora.
Manufacturing companies have emerged as efficient, low cost producers with the potential for further growth matched by India's outlook for advancement.
Around 22 per cent of the population are in poverty; measures undertaken through the Millennium Development Goals have improved literacy and increased enrolment of girls in schools, however, there is still more to be achieved in reducing child mortality and immunisation. Nevertheless, India believes that with sustained growth it can reduce poverty to a low single digit number within two generations.
The inflation rate rose to 11 per cent for y-o-y to 7 June 2008, the highest rate since 1995. Interest rates have broken the government's target of 5.0–5.5 per cent per annum. The central bank raised key lending rates, to combat inflation, by 25 base points to 8 per cent in June 2008. Rising costs in fuel and food are responsible for the interest rate hikes.

External trade

India is a member of South Asia Association for Regional Co-operation, which operates a preferential trading arrangement (Sapta) that covers 6,000 products. In 2004 the South Asia Free Trade Area was agreed by Sapta, to be implemented between the seven member states (India, Pakistan, Bhutan, Nepal, Bangladesh, Sri Lanka and Maldives) by 2012.
Traditional products such as jewellery and gems (around 80 per cent of cut diamonds worldwide were produced in India), textiles, clothes and footwear, foodstuffs, metal manufacture and leather products remain leading exports but the rapidly growing softwear sector including IT services in outsourced call centres have assumed a large proportion of export trade.

Imports

Main imports include crude oil, machinery, precious stones, fertiliser and chemicals
Main sources: China (9.0 per cent total, 2006), Saudi Arabia (6.2 per cent), US (5.7 per cent).

Exports

Principal exports include textiles, gem stones and jewellery, engineering goods, organic chemicals and leather manufactures.
The multinational clothing company GAP halted sales of a child's smock blouse following documentary evidence of illegal forced child labour in factories sanctioned to make its clothing.
Main destinations: US (15.4 per cent total, 2006), UAE (9.5 per cent), China (6.4 per cent).

Agriculture

Farming

Agriculture accounts for around 21 per cent of GDP. Main crops are wheat, rice, pulses, tea, sugar cane, cotton, jute, coffee, oilseeds, tobacco, rubber and potatoes. The southern state of Kerala accounts for 93 per cent of the natural rubber production. Dairy farming has made India self-sufficient in milk powder and butter (ghee).

Domestic demand and consumption patterns within the country have shifted from cereals to non-cereals including oilseeds, pulses, fruits, vegetables and dairy products. This shift calls for diversification of agricultural production and rural development to sustain future growth. While emphasis on minimum price support for rice and wheat has been beneficial, crop diversification and removal of restrictions on stock limits allowing greater flexibility in marketing are some of the key issues requiring more attention.

Of the 181 million hectares (ha) of agricultural land available, 162 million ha is arable and 11 million ha is permanent pasture. Land legislation has ensured that agriculture remains a fragmented sector, with the typical holding about one hectare. The land ceiling does not extend to farmland used for the cultivation of plantation crops, such as tea, coffee and rubber. Other problems for the sector include a lack of technological modernisation and infrastructural bottlenecks related to irrigation and rural electrification.

Use of improved seed varieties, irrigation and fertilisers has made India self-sufficient in most grains. Land for extending cultivation is limited, but there is scope for productivity improvements in other crops.

The sector is dependent on annual monsoon levels and if rains are poor during the July sowing season production can suffer.

In a move to improve the income of the poorest farmers the government, in its 2008 budget, cancelled the debt of small farmers, in a scheme of loan cancellations costing US$15 billion.

During the 2007–08 winter, the heaviest snowfalls since the 1970s buried the desert habitat of the rare Himalayan pashmina goat that produces exceptionally fine wool. As winter stocks of fodder ran out the goats began to starve and by February official figures reported 600 had died, and many more in remote areas were endangered.

Crop production ('000) in 2005 included: 233,960 tonnes (t) cereals in total, 72,000t wheat, 129,000t rice, 232,320t sugar cane, 5,600t soya beans, 6,400t rapeseed (canola), 1,460t barley, 14,500t maize, 9,000t millet, 8,000t sorghum, 6,700t cassava, 25,000t potatoes, 9,500t coconuts, 9,034t oilcrops, 16,820t bananas, 10,800t mangoes, 14,600t pulses, 275t green coffee, 831t tea, 1,053t various spices, 780t natural rubber, 51,000t pepper spice, 4,575t fibre crops, 7,500t seed cotton, 2,475t cotton lint, 1,900t jute, 598t tobacco, 47,031t fruit in total, 80,529t vegetables in total. Livestock production ('000) included: 6,297t meat in total, 1,494t beef, 1,488t buffalo, 497t pig meat, 239t lamb, 475t goat meat, 1,965t poultry, 2,492t eggs, 91,940t milk, 52t honey, 77t silk cocoons, 129t goatskins, 56t sheepskins, 404t cattle hides.

Fishing

India's share in the world seafood market largely depends on its shrimp exports. The crustacea catch is typically around 600,000 tonnes, and the fish catch is typically around six million tonnes, the export value of which is approximately US$65 million and US$80 million respectively. The government has given increased attention to the development of other fishery resources including squid, cuttlefish and fin fish. Export of frozen items has enabled India to penetrate into markets of Western Europe, North America and South-east Asia.

About a third of exports comprise low-value fin fish varieties and another third are frozen shrimp. Japan remains the largest importer of Indian sea food, although the emergence of the South-east Asian market due to import liberalisation has boosted the industry. The US is also a major buyer of frozen seafood, accounting for around 15 per cent of the value of marine products exported.

The sector is likely to witness steady growth as the organised corporate sector has become increasingly involved in the preservation, processing and export of coastal fish. The introduction of several resource specific vessels will enlarge the scope of marine fish landings.

In 2004, the total marine fish catch was 2,342,138 tonnes and the total crustacean catch was 464,138 tonnes.

Forestry

India has vast and diverse forest resources, comprising around 22 per cent of the total land area and ranging from tropical moist and dry deciduous types to evergreen, alpine, thorn and mangrove forests. Forest cover is estimated at 64 million hectares (ha). India has more than 12 million ha of forest plantations, used mainly for fuel consumption. There are about 80 national parks and around 450 wildlife sanctuaries.

Wood is an important source of fuel: India is the world's largest consumer of fuelwood. India has a very low level of industrial wood consumption in per capita terms. The forestry industry consists of small production units with low operating efficiency. There is an acute shortage of raw material, particularly for the manufacture of pulp and paper.

Total imports of forest products in 2004 amounted to US$1.59 billion, while exports amounted to US$259.6 million.

Production ('000) in 2004 included 322,985 cubic metres (cum) roundwood, 19,146cum industrial roundwood, 17,500cum sawnwood, 18,350cum sawlogs and veneers, 621cum pulpwood, 2,341cum wood-based panels, 303,839cum wood fuel; ('000) 1,714 tonnes (t) charcoal, 4,145t paper and paperboard, including 700t newsprint, 1,530t printing and writing paper, 3,425t paper pulp, 850t recovered paper.

Industry and manufacturing

Industry contributed 27 per cent to GDP in 2004. Heavy industry has traditionally been dominated by large state-controlled enterprises. With the steady removal of protection by the state since the early 1990s, these lost some ground to smaller enterprises. Main heavy industries include steel, chemicals, cement and heavy engineering. Further developments in petrochemicals and fertilisers are expected.

Textiles account for 35 per cent of India's export earnings.

Small companies are moving into high-technology products including computers, as well as traditional light engineering and textiles. Import controls have been relaxed on raw materials and services necessary for increased export trade. The entire system of industrial licensing has been revised to promote freer competition and many companies are now turning to private capital markets for expansion funding.

Tourism

Tourism is the third-largest foreign exchange earner and is growing at more than 6 per cent per year. The sector accounted for 4.9 per cent of GDP in 2004. About six per cent of the workforce is employed in the sector.

There were 3.91 million arrivals in 2005, an increase of 13.2 per cent on 2004, despite the impact of the December 2004 tsunami on the region.

Environment

Since 2002 the number of Indian tigers has fallen drastically from 3,642 to 1,411, due to poaching and urbanisation. India is home to 40 per cent of the World's tigers and has 23 tiger reserves in 17 states. The government sponsored a protection unit in 2007, but wildlife experts have said that urgent efforts should be made to save more tigers with inviolate areas and well armed forest guards. The poaching is for body parts for Chinese medicine, with tiger pelts valued up to US$12,500 in China.

Mining

India is well-endowed with mineral resources, mainly iron ore, manganese, uranium, good-quality bauxite (an estimated 2.65 billion tonnes of reserves, the world's fourth largest) and chromite, but they are not fully exploited. Other minerals present include lead, zinc, tin, silver, mercury and cobalt.

Most of India's raw materials are for domestic consumption. The only exports of any significance are iron ore, mica and manganese ore. India's major markets for iron ore are Japan, South Korea and China. India's reserves of copper, zinc and lead are of relatively low quality.

Hydrocarbons

India had 5.4 billion barrels of oil reserves in 2005 and produced 837,000 barrels per day (bpd). Most of the oil reserves are located in the Mumbai High, Upper Assam, Cambay, Krisha-Godavari and Cauvery basins. Oil consumption, which averaged around 2.5 million bpd in 2005, is expected to grow to 3.9 million bpd by 2010, requiring net imports of at least 3 million bpd. Oil accounts for around a third of total energy consumption. In an effort to reduce dependence on imports, India is encouraging further exploration and production. India has a refinery capacity of 2.3 million bpd.

India had natural gas reserves of 920 billion cubic metres in 2004 and produced 29.1 billion cubic metres. Over two-thirds of India's gas reserves are located in the Mumbai High basin and Gujarat. Total gas consumption was 32.1 billion cubic metres and is projected to rise by around five per cent a year. Much of this increase is attributed to increased use of gas in electricity power generation. Consumption could be higher, but problems in financing liquefied natural gas (LNG) import projects have led to downward revisions of forecasts. The government is improving and expanding the infrastructure to meet the growing demand for natural gas.

India had total coal reserves of 92.4 billion tonnes in 2004 and produced 189 million tonnes oil equivalent (mtoe). India is the world's third-largest coal producer after China and the US. The main coal fields are in Bihar, West Bengal and Madhya Pradesh. Around 90 per cent of coal is produced by Coal India Ltd (CIL). Consumption was around 205 mtoe in 2004. Power generation accounts for around 70 per cent of coal consumption; the second-largest consumer is heavy industry. Consumption is forecast to rise to around 387 million tonnes by 2010.

Energy

India has installed electricity generating capacity of 126GW (78GW thermal, 26GW hydroelectric and 2.5GW nuclear). A new, and controversial dam in the western state of Gujarat, began generating electricity in January 2007. The dam is the centre of a network of reservoirs and canals of Sardar Sarovar, one of India's longest rivers and was first proposed in the 1950s but was subject to long legal battles before completion. Water and power (1450MW) are destined for the central and western regions.

Although 80 per cent of the population has access to electricity, the supply is unreliable and interruptions are frequent. Government policy is to increase capacity by 100GW by 2012 to keep pace with rapid industrialisation and bring electricity to the whole country.

More efficient stoves, solar cookers and biogas plants are being developed to address the problem of energy shortages. Other renewable sources are being explored, including wind and solar generators.

Financial markets

Stock exchange

India has 24 stock exchanges. The main ones are The Stock Exchange, Mumbai and the National Stock Exchange, both of which are fully automated.

Banking and insurance

Indian banking has traditionally been strongly directed from the centre; even private sector banks (excluding foreign banks) are required to lend to national priority projects. In February 2005 the remaining 27 banks in government hands were given freedom to manage themselves, including the ability to acquire foreign assets and close down unprofitable accounts. The government had nationalised the country's 14 major domestic banks in 1969. Since the mid-1980s there has been a relaxation and improved profitability due to the deregulation of interest rates and the removal of credit allocation obligation, except for quotas for priority sectors. Reforms made since the mid-1990s have led to a growth in private sector banking activity.

Financial reforms implemented in 2001 focussed on tightening regulations on capital adequacy, income recognition, non-performing assets (NPAs), disclosure and transparency in accounting and risk management. The 2002 budget allowed foreign banks to establish subsidiaries in India for the first time, and sector caps on portfolio investments made by foreign institutional investors were eased.

Central bank

The Reserve Bank of India (RBI) controls India's financial system on a day-to-day basis.

Main financial centre

Mumbai is the main financial centre; New Delhi, Kolkata and Chennai are also important.

Time

GMT plus 5.5 hours

Geography

India is a bounded by Pakistan in the north-west, China in the north, the Himalayan Kingdoms of Nepal (administered by China) and Bhutan in the north and north-east. Bangladesh is surrounded on three sides by a bulge of Indian states that border China in the north-east and Myanmar in the east to south, with the Bay of Bengal separating it from the mainland. In the Indian Ocean India's neighbours are Sri Lanka and the Maldives.

India is a large landmass with four distinct regions. The northern Himalayan regions rise to a peak of 7,757 metres before falling away towards the east. The great rivers, Ganges and Brahmaputra begin life in these mountains before draining through a flat alluvial plain into the Bay of Bengal. On the other side of the country, the Great Indian or Thar Desert separates India and Pakistan. In the south the Deccan tableland is bordered by ranges of hills, the Western and Eastern Ghats and Nilgiri Hills in the south, and their coastal belts.

Hemisphere

Northern

Climate

India's winter is January–February, with hot weather increasing from March–May, south-western monsoons from June–September, and post monsoons or north-east monsoons in the southern peninsula from October–December. Temperatures vary from sub-zero in the far north during winter to constant tropical heat in southern regions. Average summer temperatures on the plains are approximately 27 degrees Celsius.

Dress codes

Dress is mostly informal in India except in winter months in New Delhi, where suits and coats are more usually worn. Women are expected to dress with modesty even in very hot weather. Businessmen can expect to wear suits and ties to meetings all year as most buildings have air conditioning.

Entry requirements

Passports

Required by all.

Visa
Required by all, and must be obtained before travelling as visas cannot be issued on arrival. Foreign nationals arriving on long-term, multiple visas are required to register with the nearest Foreigners Regional Registration Officer within 14 days of arrival. Those overstaying their visa entitlement will be fined and may be prosecuted.
For business visas a letter, issued by the local host company or organisation, giving details of itinerary, and traveller's company, a summary of purpose of trip, and the acceptance of full responsibility for any expenses incurred during the term of stay, should be submitted with the application. Business visas, valid for 10 years with multiple entries, are available to foreign businessmen who have set up or intend setting up joint ventures in India. For further details of various visas and restrictions see www.indianembassy.org or www.hcilondon.net. Nationals of Pakistan and Bangladesh are advised to seek further advice before travelling to, or via, India.
Prohibited entry
Currency advice/regulations
Import and export of local currency is prohibited; the exception is rupees that visitors may take to Nepal – notes must be less than Rs100, and Bangladesh and Sri Lanka – up to Rs20 per person.
Import of foreign currency is unlimited; amounts below US$1,000 (or equivalent) need not be declared, however, amounts over US$5,000 must be declared and registered on a encashment certificate on arrival. Export of foreign currency is limited to the amount declared, therefore all currency transaction receipts should be retained.
Travellers cheques are widely accepted. Currency may only be exchanged at banks or authorised money changers.
Customs
The export of products over 100 years old need a permit. Animal products from endangered species are illegal.

Health (for visitors)
Mandatory precautions
Vaccination certificates for yellow fever if travelling from an infected area.
Advisable precautions
Vaccinations for cholera, dysentery, Japanese B encephalitis and typhoid are recommended. Other vaccinations that may be recommended are diphtheria, tuberculosis, hepatitis A and B, meningitis and tetanus. Malaria, hepatitis B, dengue and chikungunya fever are caused by mosquitoes, precautions including mosquito repellents, nets and clothing covering the body, should be used, especially at night. There is a risk of rabies in rural areas.
Polio is endemic in certain states and precautions, including booster shots, should be taken.
Use only bottled or boiled water for drinks, washing teeth and making ice. Eat only well cooked meals, preferably served hot; vegetables should be cooked and fruit peeled. Avoid pork and salad and food from street vendors. A full first-aid kit would be useful.
Locally manufactured Western proprietary medicines are easily obtainable, but visitors on regular medication should bring their own supplies – amounts for the length of the visit only.

Hotels
International-standard accommodation is widely available. Hotel bills must be paid in foreign exchange or in rupees proved to have been purchased in India with foreign exchange. Hotels in main cities are usually heavily booked, and it is advisable to book well in advance.
Extra charges may be applied to hotel bills, including variable service charges plus 10 per cent expenditure tax and 15 per cent luxury tax.

Credit cards
Major credit cards are accepted by larger hotels, travel agencies and airline offices, as well as some larger stores. The Central Card is issued by the Reserve Bank of India and is widely accepted.

Public holidays (national)
Fixed dates
1 Jan (New Year's Day), ^26 Jan (Republic Day), ^15 Aug (Independence Day), ^2 Oct (Mahatma Gandhi's Birthday), 26 Nov (Guru Nanak's Birthday), 25 Dec (Christmas Day).
Variable dates
Good Friday (Mar/Apr), Mahavira's Birthday (Feb/Mar), Holi (Hindu, Mar), Sri Rama's Birthday (Apr), Buddha Purnima (May), Vijaya Dasami/Dussera (Sep/Oct), Diwali (Hindu, Oct/Nov), Eid al Adha, Eid al Fitr, Islamic New Year, Birth of the Prophet Mohammed.
^ Recognised official national holiday.
All other holidays are either state, religious or informal holidays and may be observed at locally determined times dependent on sightings of various phases of the moon, or by adherents only.

Working hours
Banking
Mon–Fri: 1000–1400; Sat: 1000–1200, in New Delhi, Kolkata and Chennai. Mon–Fri: 1100–1500; Sat: 1100–1300 in Mumbai.
Business
Mon–Fri: 1000–1700, in New Delhi and Chennai; 0930–1700 in Kolkata; 1000–1730 in Mumbai.
Government
Mon–Fri: 1000–1730, in New Delhi, Kolkata and Chennai; 0930–1630 in Mumbai.
Shops
Mon–Fri: 0930–1930 in New Delhi; 1000–1830 in Kolkata; 1000–1830 in Mumbai; 0900–1930 in Chennai.

Telecommunications
Mobile/cell phones
There are 900 and 1800 GSM services available, most are regionally based within cities and towns.

Electricity supply
Usually 220V AC, 50Hz; some areas have a DC supply for domestic use. Plugs used are of the round two- and three-pin type.

Weights and measures
Metric system

Social customs/useful tips
Namaste is the usual greeting (palms together as in prayer). Visiting cards are exchanged – use the right hand when giving or receiving items. It is not customary for business associates to be entertained at home. Hotels, which provide virtually the only bars in India, require non-resident foreigners to pay their bills in foreign currency.
Business and official contacts are addressed by their last name – Sri (Mr), Srimati (Mrs or Ms).
Cows are sacred to Hindus, and many Hindus are vegetarian. Sikhs and Parsees do not smoke tobacco. Muslims do not eat pig's flesh in any form, and orthodox Muslims do not drink alcoholic beverages. Officially the government follows a strictly secular policy, with religion considered a private affair.

Security
Generally, travel in India is quite safe, but travel to Jammu and Kashmir regions is not recommended. Mumbai is the safest city in India. Its police force is known to be the most efficient in the country. It is reasonably safe to travel by taxi until midnight anywhere in the city except slums and red-light districts.

Getting there
Air
National airline: Air India (Air India and Indian Airlines, which flies domestic routes, are to merge in mid-2007).
International airport/s: There are five international airports: Indira Gandhi International (DEL), 20km south of Delhi; Sahar International (BOM), 36km north of Mumbai; Netaji Subhas Chandra Bose International (CCU), 27km north-east of Kolkata; Meenambakkam (MAA), 14km south-east of Chennai; Patna (PAT), 8km from Patna. Dabolim (GOA) airport receives international chartered flights.

All international airports have duty-free shopping, bars, restaurants, currency exchanges, post offices and business centres that include telecommunications and rest facilities.

Airport tax: International flights, Foreign Travel Tax (FTT) Rs500; neighbouring countries only, FFT Rs150; excluding transit passengers.

Surface

Road: Overland access is possible through Nepal and Bangladesh, there is only one access point from Pakistan at Wagah – it may be dangerous crossing the border at any other place. The status of border crossing points and opening hours should be checked before travelling.

Rail: Rail connections exist between India and Bangladesh, although the journey is difficult.

The train service between Pakistan and India was restored in 2004 – one train a week between Lahore in Pakistan and Attari in India.

Main port/s: India has 12 major ports: five on the east coast, Kolkata-Haldia, Paradip, Visakhapatnam, Chennai and Tuticorin and seven on the west coast, Kandla, Mumbai, Jawaharlal Nehru, Mormugao, New Mangalore and Cochin.

Getting about

National transport

Air: The only time-efficient way to get between the large cities and even some smaller ones is by plane. The cost of air travel is reasonable and there are several domestic carriers. Airline tickets may now be bought at the airport, at least one hour before a flight.

Smoking and drinking are banned on board all internal flights.

Road: There are two million kilometres of road, including 833,000km of surfaced roads and 35,000km of national highways connecting main cities. Chauffeur driven cars can be hired in the big cities.

Buses: A number of long-distance express bus services operate, and air conditioning is becoming increasingly available. Poor roads make travel uncomfortable.

Rail: The Indian rail network covers over 64,000km and is the main form of domestic transport. Rail connections are available between all major towns and cities, with air-conditioned coaches and sleeper accommodation available on some routes. Some train journeys take 24 hours or more.

Water: There are coastal shipping and ferry services.

City transport

Taxis: Local taxis of varying standards are usually available. In main cities, metered taxis may not always show current rates, and fares should be negotiated in advance. Tipping is officially discouraged, but is practiced.

Other transport includes motorised trishaws.

Buses, trams & metro: There are over 40 stations in the New Delhi metro network, which will eventually cover 60km and is due to be completed by 2010. The first section of elevated track was opened in 2002 and in July 2005 another 11km stretch of underground lines, from the government areas of the capital, via the commercial area, to the old city, was opened. A completed 32km section was opened in December 2005. When completed it is expected to cut a journey across the city from one hour at rush-hour, to 15 minutes.

There are surburban metro systems in Mumbai, Kolkata and Chennai (a monorail rapid transit system).

Car hire

Self-drive hire cars are available in Mumbai and chauffeur-driven car hire is available in main cities.

BUSINESS DIRECTORY

The addresses listed below are a selection only. While World of Information makes every endeavour to check these addresses, we cannot guarantee that changes have not been made, especially to telephone numbers and area codes. We would welcome any corrections.

Telephone area codes

The international direct dialling (IDD) code for India is +91, followed by area code and subscriber's number:

Ahmedabad	79	Jammu	191
Amritsar	183	Kolkata	33
Bangalore	80	Lucknow	522
Bhopal	755	Madurai	452
Chandigarh	172	Mumbai	22
Chennai	44	Nagpur	712
Cochin	484	New Delhi	11
Goa	832	Patna	612
Hyderabad	40	Pune	212
Jaipur	141	Rajkot	281
Jallunder	181	Varanasi	542
Kanpur	512	Vishakhapatnam	891

Useful telephone numbers

Police:100
Ambulance:102
Fire:101
Operator:199
Directory enquiries:197
International enquiries:187
Call booking:186

Chambers of Commerce

American Chamber of Commerce in India, Maurya Sheraton Hotel, Sardar Patel Marg, New Delhi 110021 (tel: 2302-3102; fax: 2302-3109; e-mail: usamcham@bol.net.in).

Associated Chambers of Commerce and Industry of India, 147B Gautam Nagar, Gulmohar Enclave, New Delhi 110049 (tel: 2651-2477; fax: 2651-2154; e-mail: assocham@sansad.nic.in).

Bengal National Chamber of Commerce and Industry, 23 RN Mukherjee Road, Kolkata 700001 (tel: 248-2951; fax: 248-7058; e-mail: bncci@bncci.com).

Bombay Chamber of Commerce and Industry, Mackinnon Mackenzie Building, Shoorji Vallabhdas Road, Mumbai 400001 (tel: 2261-4681; fax: 2262-1213; e-mail: bcci@bombaychamber.com).

Cochin Chamber of Commerce and Industry, Bristow Road, PO Box 503, Cochin 682003 (tel: 266-8650; fax: 266-8651; e-mail: chamber@md2.vsnl.net.in).

Federation of Indian Chambers of Commerce and Industry, Federation House, Tansen Marg, New Delhi 110001 (tel 2373-8760; fax@ 2332-0714; e-mail: ficci@ficci.com).

Goa Chamber of Commerce and Industry, Goa Chamber Building, Rua de Ormuz, Panaji-Goa 403001 (tel: 222-4223; fax: 242-9010; e-mail: gcci@sancharnet.in).

Gujarat Chamber of Commerce and Industry, Ashram Road, PO Box 4045, Ahmedabad 380009 (tel: 658-2301; fax: 658-7992; e-mail: gcci@gujaratchamber.org).

Indian Chamber of Commerce and Industry, Indian Chamber Road, Mattancherry, PO Box 236, Cochin 682002 (tel: 222-4335; fax: 222-4203; e-mail: mail@iccicochin.com).

Madras Chamber of Commerce and Industry, Karumuttu, 634 Anna Salai, Chennai 600035 (tel: 2434-9452; fax: 2434-9164; e-mail: mascham@md3.vsnl.net.in).

Mahratta Chamber of Commerce, Industries and Agriculture, 14 Tilak Road, Pune 411002 (tel: 444-0371; fax: 444-7902; e-mail: mccipune@vsnl.com).

PHD Chamber of Commerce and Industry, PHD House, opposite Asian Games Village, New Delhi 110016 (tel: 685-2416; fax: 686-3135; e-mail: phdcci@del2.vsnl.net.in).

Rajasthan Chamber of Commerce and Industry, Chamber Bhawan, MI Road, Jaipur 302003 (tel: 256-163; fax: 256-1419; e-mail: info@rajchamber.com).

Banking

Allahabad Bank, 2 Netaji Subhas Road, Kolkata 700 001 (tel: 220-0283; fax:

221-4598; email: homktg@allahabadbank.co.in).

Bank of Baroda, Suraj Plaza-1, Sayaji Ganj, Baroda 390 005 (tel: 361-852; 362-395).

Bank of India, Express Towers, Nariman Point, Mumbai 400 021(tel: 2202-3020; fax: 2202-3167; email: cmdboi@bom5.vsnl.net.in).

Canara Bank, Canara Bank Buildings, 112 Jayachamarajendra Road, PO Box 6648, Bangalore 560 002 (tel: 222-1581; fax: 222-2704; email: canbank@blr.vsnl.net.in).

Central Bank of India, Chandermukhi, Nariman Point, Mumbai 400 021 (tel: 2202-6428).

Corporation Bank, Mangalore 575 001 (tel: 426-416; fax: 441-208; email: corpho@corpbank.com).

ICIC, 163 Backbay Reclamation, Mumbai 400 020 (tel: 2202-5115; fax: 2204-6582).

Oriental Bank of Commerce, Harsha Bhawan, E-Block, Connaught Place, New Delhi 110 001 (tel: 2332-3444; fax: 2371-3244; email: obc@obcindia.com).

Punjab National Bank, 5 Sansad Marg, New Delhi 110 066 (tel: 2371-6032; fax: 2332-1305; email: pnbibd@ndf.vsnl.net.in).

State Bank of India, Madame Cama Road, PO Box 10121, Mumbai 400 021 (tel: 2202-2059; fax: 2204-0073).

Union Bank of India, Union Bank Bhavan, 239 Vidhan Bhavan Marg, Nariman Ponit, Mumbai 400 021 (tel: 2202-4647, 2202-6049; email: ibdhelpdesk@unionbankofindia.co).

Central bank

Reserve Bank of India, Central Office Building, Shahid Bhagat Singh Road, Mumbai 400 001 (tel: 286-1602; fax: 266-2105; e-mail: helpprd@rbi.org.in).

Travel information

Indian Airlines, Airlines House, 113 Gurdwara Rakabganj Road, New Delhi 110 001 (tel: 2335-7307; fax: 2371-9484).

Ministry of tourism

Department of Tourism of the Government of India, Ministry of Tourism, Transport Bhawan, 1 Parliament Street, New Delhi 110001 (tel: 371-0379; fax: 371-0518; internet: www.tourismindia.com).

National tourist organisation offices

India Tourism Development Corporation Ltd, SCOPE Complex, Core VIII, 6th Floor, 7 Lodi Road, New Delhi 110003 (tel: 436-0303; fax: 436-0233).

Ministries

Ministry of Agriculture, Krishi Bhavan, Dr Rajendra Prasad Road, New Delhi 110 001 (tel: 2378-2691; fax: 2338-8006).

Ministry of Chemicals and Fertilisers, Shastri Bhavan, Dr Rajendra Prasad Road, New Delhi 110 001 (tel: 2338-6519; fax: 2338-6364).

Ministry of Civil Aviation, Rajiv Ghandi Bhavan, Safdarjung Airport Complex, New Delhi 110 003 (tel: 2463-2991; fax: 2461-0354; e-mail: secy@civilav.delhi.nic.in).

Ministry of Commerce and Industry, Udyog Bhavan, Rafi Marg, New Delhi 110 001 (tel: 2301-0261; fax: 2301-4418; e-mail: commerce@hub.nic.in).

Ministry of Communications, Dak Bhavan, Parliament Street, New Delhi 110 001 (tel: 2371-0350; fax: 2371-2333).

Ministry of Consumer Affairs, Food and Public Distribution, Krishi Bhavan, Dr Rajendra Prasad Road, New Delhi 110 001 (tel: 2338-5723; fax: 2378-2213).

Ministry of Defence, South Block, New Delhi 110 011 (tel: 2301-6220; fax: 2301-5403).

Ministry of the Environment and Forests, Paryavaran Bhavan, CGO Complex, Lodhi Road, New Delhi 110 003 (tel: 2436-1896; fax: 2436-2222; e-mail: secy@menf.delhi.nic.in).

Ministry of External Affairs, South Block, New Delhi 110 011 (tel: 2301-6660; fax: 2301-0700).

Ministry of Finance, North Block, New Delhi 110 001 (tel: 2301-2810; fax: 2301-3289; internet site: http://wwwmnic.in/finmin/).

Ministry of Health and Family Welfare, Nirman Bhavan, Maulana Azad Road, New Delhi 110 011 (tel: 2301-4751; fax: 2301-6648).

Ministry of Heavy Industries and Public Enterprises, Udyog Bhavan, Rafi Marg, New Delhi 110 001 (tel: 2301-4598; fax: 2301-3086; e-mail: nic-dpe@hub.nic.in).

Ministry of Home Affairs, North Block, New Delhi 110 001 (tel: 2301-1011; fax: 2301-5750).

Ministry of Human Resource Development, Shastri Bhavan, Dr Rajendra Prasad Road, New Delhi 110 001 (tel: 2378-2698; fax: 2338-1355; e-mail:ksm@sb.nic.in).

Ministry of Information and Broadcasting, Shastri Bhavan, Dr Rajendra Prasad Road, New Delhi 110 001 (tel: 2338-4782; fax: 2378-3513).

Ministry of Labour, Shram Shakti Bhavan, Rafi Marg, New Delhi 110 001 (tel: 2371-7515; fax: 2371-1708; e-mail: labour@lisd.delhi.nic.in).

Ministry of Law, Justice and Company Affairs, Shastri Bhavan, Dr Rajendra Prasad Road, New Delhi 110 001 (tel: 2338-7557; fax: 2338-4241; e-mail: lawmin@caselaw.delhi.nic.in).

Ministry of Mines, Shastri Bhavan, Dr Rajendra Prasad Road, New Delhi 110 001 (tel: 2338-3082; fax: 2338-6402; e-mail: dom@sb.nic.in).

Ministry of Ocean Development, Mahasagar Bhavan, CGO Complex, Lodhi Road, New Delhi 110 003 (tel: 2436-0874; fax: 2436-0779).

Ministry of Parliamentary Affairs, Parliament House, New Delhi 110 001 (tel: 2301-7798; fax: 2301-7726; e-mail: parlmin@sansad.nic.in).

Ministry of Petroleum and Natural Gas, Shastri Bhavan, Dr Rajendra Prasad Road, New Delhi 110 001 (tel: 2338-3100; fax: 2338-6550).

Ministry of Power, Shastri Bhavan, Dr Rajendra Prasad Road, New Delhi 110 001 (tel: 2371-4168; fax: 2371-7519).

Ministry of Railways, Rail Bhawan, Parliament Street, New Delhi 110 001 (tel: 2338-2323; fax: 2330-3871).

Ministry of Science and Technology, Technology Bhavan, New Mehrauli Street, New Delhi 110 016 (tel: 2301-4999; fax: 2686-3847).

Ministry of Space, Lok Nayak Bhavan, New Delhi 110 003 (tel: 2469-7130; fax: 2461-7377).

Ministry of Surface Transport, Transport Bhavan, Parliament Street, New Delhi 110 001(tel: 2371-4095; fax: 2373-1270).

Ministry of Textiles, Udyog Bhavan, Rafi Marg, New Delhi 110 001 (tel: 2301-3779; fax: 2301-3711).

Ministry of Tourism, Transport Bhawan, Parliament Street, New Delhi 110 001 (tel: 2338-4173; fax: 2338-5115).

Ministry of Urban Development and Poverty Alleviation, Nirman Bhavan, Maulana Azad Road, New Delhi 110 011 (tel: 2301-8495; fax: 2301-4459; e-mail: muae@urban.delhi.nic.in).

Ministry of Water Resources, Shram Shakti Bhawan, Rafi Marg, New Delhi 110 001 (tel: 2371-4200; fax: 2371-0253; e-mail: webmaster@mowr.delhi.nic.in).

Ministry of Youth Affairs and Sport, Shastri Bhavan, Dr Rajendra Prasad Road, New Delhi 110 001 (tel: 2338-4183; e-mail: web.yas.@sb.nic.in).

Prime Minister's Office, South block, New Delhi 110 011 (tel: 2301-2312; fax: 2301-6857).

Other useful addresses

Asian Development Bank, India Resident Mission, 37 Golf Links, New Delhi 110 003 (tel: 2469-2578; fax: 2463-6175; e-mail:adbinrm@mail.asiandevbank.org).

British Deputy High Commission, Maker Chambers IV, 222 Jamnalal Bajaj Road, PO Box 11714, Nariman Point, Mumbai 400021 (tel: 2283-0517, 2283-2330, 2283-3602; fax: 2202-7940).

British High Commission, Shanti Path, Chanakyapuri, New Delhi 110 021 (tel: 2687-2161; fax: 2687-2882).

British Deputy High Commission, 1 Ho Chi Minh Sarani, Kolkata 700016 (tel: 242-5171; fax: 242-3435).

British Deputy High Commission, 24 Anderson Road, Chennai 600006 (tel: 827-3136/7; fax: 826-9004).

British Trade Office, 37/7 Cunningham Road, Bangalore 560052 (tel: 2220-4844; fax: 2220-4855).

Delhi Stock Exchange Association Ltd, 3 and 4/4B Asaf Ali Rd, New Delhi 110 002 (tel: 2327-9000/1302; fax: 2332-6182).

Delhi Tourism and Transport Development Corporation Ltd, 18A DDA, SCO Complex, Defence Colony, New Delhi 24 (tel: 2461-4354; fax: 2469-7352).

Department of Atomic Energy, South Block, New Delhi 110 011 (tel: 2301-1773; fax: 2301-3843).

Department of Electronics, Electronics Niketan, 6 CGO Complex, New Delhi 110 003 (tel: 2436-3101; fax: 2436-3083).

Federation of Indian Exports Organisation (FIEO), 56 Asiad Village, New Delhi 110 016 (tel: 2649-3220).

Foreign Investment Promotion Board, Prime Minister's Office, South Block, New Delhi 110 011 (tel: 2301-7839; fax: 2301-6857).

India Investment Centre, Jeewan vihar Building, Sansad Marg, New Delhi 110 001 (tel: 2373-3673; fax: 2373-245).

Indian Airlines, Stores and Purchases Department, Safdarjung Airport, New Delhi 110 003 (tel: 2461-1293; fax: 2462-1776; e-mail: sinha.ial@gems.vsnl.net.in).

Indian Embassy (USA), 2107 Massachusetts Avenue, NW, Washington DC 20008 (tel: (+1-202) 939-7000; fax: (+1-202) 265-4351; e-mail: indembwash@indiagov.org).

Infrastructure Leasing and Financial Services, East Court, Zone VI, 4th Floor, India Habitat Centre, Lodhi Road, New Delhi 110 003 (tel: 2463-6637/41/42).

Power Grid Corporation of India Ltd, 10th Floor, Hemkunt Chambers 89, Nehru Place, New Delhi 110 019 (tel: 2622-2995, 2646-6806; fax: 2647-3332, 2642-8357).

Silk and Rayon Export Promotion Council, Resham Bhavan 78, Veer Nariman Rd, Mumbai 400020 (tel: 2294-792).

State Trading Corporation of India, Jawahar Vyapar Bhavan, Tolstoy Marg, New Delhi 110 001 (tel: 2331-3177; fax: 2332-6741).

The Stock Exchange (BSE), Phiroze Jeejeebhoy Towers, Dalal Street, Mumbai 400001 (tel: 2272-1233/4; fax: 2272-1552; e-mail: info@bseindia.com; internet site: http://www.bseindia.com).

Trade Development Authority, PO Box 767, Bank of Baroda Building, Parliament St, New Delhi 110 001 (tel: 2332-0214).

US Embassy, Shanti Path, Chanakyapuri, New Delhi 110 021(tel: 2687-6500; fax: 2687-6579, 2687-0031 (Consular Section)).

Other news agencies: There are over 40 domestic news agencies.

Press Trust of India: www.ptinews.com

United News of India: www.uniindia.com

Internet sites

Explore India: http://www.exploreindia.com

General Information: http://www.hcidhaka.org

India Department of Commerce: http://www.nic.in/eximpol/

India On-line: http://indiaonline.com/index.html

Indian business: http://www.indiamart.com/allindia/

Indian company information: http://www.tradeaccess.com/general.htm

Indian Economy and Business links: http://www.ib-net.com/links/economy.htm

India Opportunity: http://www.DocuWeb.ca/India

Indian Press Information Bureau: http://www.nic.in/India-Image/PIB/

Indian weather service: http://weather.nic.in

Indonesia

The death of former president Suharto in early 2008 left Indonesians with mixed feelings. Indonesia's one time strongman was both revered as the architect of Indonesia's growth and dismissed as one of the twentieth century's most successful criminals. As Indonesia entered seven days of official mourning, Suharto's daughter Siti Hariyanti 'Tutut' Rukmana asked Indonesians to forgive her father for his mistakes. Indonesians are a sentimental lot, and it was not long before calls for Suharto's alleged crimes to be forgiven gathered pace.

Ten years on

In 1998 Indonesia had found itself bruised and battered by the Asian financial crisis which knocked over 13 per cent off gross domestic product (GDP) and left it with zero growth in 1999. The crisis, which shook financial markets around the world, caused institutional investors to withdraw millions of dollars from emerging markets, not least Indonesia. After an interregnum of political uncertainty, President Susilo Bambang Yudhoyono assumed power in September 2004 in Indonesia's first ever presidential election, unseating the incumbent Megawati Sukarnoputri. Mr Yudhoyono's first years as president were marked with some success. He received international plaudits for reaching a peace agreement with separatist rebels in the turbulent Aceh province. Maintaining some degree of economic stability is also seen as an achievement. Indonesia has, over the past three years, suffered an unprecedented series of natural disasters, including the *tsunami* of December 2004 in Aceh, the Nias earthquake of March 2005, the May 2006 earthquake in Yogyakarta and Central Java, and the July 2006 earthquake and *tsunami* in West Java. In addition, avian influenza has already claimed more Indonesian lives than in any other country. Despite these natural disasters, Indonesians had become used to economic growth – in the 30 years leading up to the 1998 Asian financial crisis, the Indonesian economy achieved an average growth rate of over 7 per cent as the Suharto regime opened up the economy and investment billions flowed in. Under Suharto's perceptive, if corrupt, patronage Indonesia's ethnic Chinese came to dominate the economy. Ironically, Chinese economic success was not matched with any social advancement; the Chinese were never granted more than second class citizen status.

Growth maintained

By 2007 both development spending and poverty eradication funding had returned to pre-Asian financial crisis levels; Indonesia had an additional US$15 billion to spend on development in 2008 as a result of reducing fuel price subsidies and generally prudent fiscal management. Expectations of continued economic growth were realised in 2007 with an acceleration to 6.3 per cent, well above the 5-year average of 5.5 per cent and the best growth rate since 1996, before the crisis. According to the Asian Development Bank (ADB) in its *Asian Development Outlook*, the main drivers of growth were private consumption, supported by private investment, and an expansion of exports. Growth in fixed capital formation increased to 9.2 per cent in 2007, although most went to buildings (76 per cent in real terms) and only 14 per cent to machinery and equipment. The fixed capital investment-to-GDP ratio increased to 24.9 per cent in 2007, up 5.4 percentage points over 4 years. The improvement in investment was underpinned by an increase in domestic credit, and by falling inflation and interest rates. The lower inflation and interest rates also helped push up consumer spending, with private consumption increasing by 5.0 per cent in 2007 and making the biggest contribution to GDP growth. The contribution to GDP growth from net exports partly reflected a rise in exports owing to the boom in world commodity prices. Higher GDP growth was accounted for mainly by the services sector, with transportation and communications, and electricity, gas and water supply recording double digit growth. The rapid expansion of telecommunications services owes much to growing demand for mobile telephone and Internet services, which have been expanding by 40–50 per cent a year. The expansion of utilities was due mainly to a 30

KEY FACTS

Official name: Republik Indonesia (Republic of Indonesia)

Head of State: President Susilo Bambang Yudhoyono (since Oct 2004)

Head of government: President Susilo Bambang Yudhoyono

Ruling party: Coalition led by Partai Golongan Karya (Golkar) (Party of the Functional Groups) (since Oct 2004)

Area: 1,919,443 square km (17,508 islands)

Population: 224.94 million (2007)*

Capital: Jakarta, on Java

Official language: Bahasa Indonesia

Currency: Rupiah (Rp) = 100 sen

Exchange rate: Rp9,148.00 per US$ (Jul 2008)

GDP per capita: US$1,925 (2007)*

GDP real growth: 6.30% (2007)*

Labour force: 108.99 million (2004)

Unemployment: 11.80% (2005)

Inflation: 6.40% (2007)*

Oil production: 969,000 bpd (2007)

Balance of trade: US$29.65 billion (2006)

Foreign debt: US$141.50 billion (2004)

Visitor numbers: 4.87 million (2006)*

* estimated figure

per cent rise in gas usage as the state-owned electricity company switched to gas from more expensive fuels, and to a government drive to get consumers to shift from subsidised kerosene to non-subsidised liquefied petroleum gas.

Manufacturing output growth of 4.7 per cent reflected higher growth in machinery, food, rubber, and paper products, offset in part by declining output for textiles, refined petroleum products, and liquefied petroleum gas. The increase in food, rubber, and paper products was stimulated by higher world prices. Reduced output for textiles is a sign of declining competitiveness in this labour-intensive industry.

Agricultural output growth at 3.5 per cent was driven by a 4.8 per cent increase in rice production and higher world prices for plantation crops such as palm oil and rubber. Mining and quarrying grew by just 2.0 per cent, despite considerably higher prices for oil and gas (which account for 55 per cent of this sub sector's output). This weakness was largely due to a 1.2 per cent decline in oil and gas extraction caused by years of under-investment in the sector.

Reflecting an easing in the global economy in late 2007, year-on-year GDP growth slipped to 6.3 per cent in the fourth quarter from 6.5 per cent in the third. Year-on-year inflation declined from a peak of 18.4 per cent in late 2005 to 6.6 per cent at end-2007, as the impact of a 126 per cent rise in fuel prices in October 2005 faded. Amid some volatility, inflation remained within Bank Indonesia's (central bank) target range of 5–7 per cent during the year, averaging 6.4 per cent. While movements in food prices and seasonal factors contributed much to the volatility, a combination of factors ranging from higher global non-food commodity prices, a depreciating rupiah, and a steady increase in domestic demand kept inflation from declining further.

Energy supplies decline

According to the *US Oil & Gas Journal* (OGJ), Indonesia had 4.4 billion barrels of proven oil reserves as of end 2007. Oil production in Indonesia has decreased steadily during the last decade, owing to disappointing exploration efforts and declining production at Indonesia's large, mature oil fields. In October 2001, Indonesia's oil sector experienced significant reforms with the passage of the new Oil and Gas Law No. 22/2001. The law forced state-owned oil company Pertamina to relinquish its role in granting new oil development licences and limited the company's monopoly in upstream activities. Pertamina's regulatory and administrative functions were transferred to the new regulatory body, Badan Perlaksanaan Minyak Gas, or BP Migas. Pertamina was formed into the limited liability company PT Pertamina (Persero) by presidential decree in 2003, although it remains a state-owned entity. PT Pertamina has been laying the groundwork for full privatisation to take place at some point in the future.

Indonesia's oil sector is dominated by several international oil companies (IOCs). The single largest oil producer is Chevron, which controls Caltex Pacific and Unocal's former Indonesian assets. BP, ConocoPhillips, ExxonMobil, and Total are also significant oil producers in the country, with China's state-owned companies PetroChina and China National Offshore Oil Corporation (CNOOC) also having a considerable presence. The liberalisation of Indonesia's downstream oil and gas sector has been under discussion for several years. Pertamina maintained its retail and distribution monopoly for petroleum products until July 2004, when the first licences for retail sale of petroleum products were granted to BP and Petronas of Malaysia. However, PT Pertamina maintains a dominant position in Indonesia's downstream sector, operating all eight of the country's refineries. The government is still promising to open the sector to full competition, although progress has been slow to date. Indonesia historically has maintained consumption subsidies for domestic retail fuel consumers, with products being sold at a discount from world market prices. After a series of modest increases in petroleum prices over the past few years, President Yudhoyono announced a sharp reduction of subsidies in September 2005. Prices of retail gasoline and diesel rose by an average of 125 per cent as a result. Despite this one-time move, fuel consumption subsidies still take up a sizeable portion of government expenditures.

According to the US Energy Information Administration (EIA), Indonesia is the tenth largest holder of proven natural gas reserves in the world and the single largest in the Asia-Pacific region. According to the Indonesian government, more than 70 per cent of the country's natural gas reserves are located offshore, with the largest reserves found off Natuna Island, East Kalimantan, South Sumatra, and West Papua (previously known as Irian Jaya). As with the oil sector, Indonesia's natural gas sector underwent reforms with the passage of the Oil and Gas Law No. 22/2001. State-owned Pertamina was forced to relinquish its monopoly status in upstream natural gas projects, and BP Migas now holds primary regulatory authority in the sector. PT Pertamina, the limited liability corporation that was formed from its predecessor, remains an important player in Indonesia's natural gas exploration and production activities. PT Pertamina and six major international companies dominate Indonesia's natural gas industry, accounting for more than 90 per cent of the country's production. The six companies are: Total, ExxonMobil, Vico (a BP-ENI joint venture), ConocoPhillips, BP and Chevron. Natural gas transmission and distribution activities are carried out by the state-owned utility Perusahaan Gas Negara (PGN). Historically, Indonesian natural gas production has been geared toward export markets, but the country has made an effort to shift natural gas toward domestic uses in recent years as a substitute for the country's declining oil output. However, Indonesia's limited natural gas transmission and distribution network remains an obstacle to further domestic consumption.

Outlook

With presidential elections not due until 2009, and no concerted opposition to face, the Yudhoyono administration is expected to stay the course. Credit rating Moody's has noted that Indonesia's improving political stability could be blown off course over the longer term if there is any return to zero growth and low levels of investment. There also remains a pressing need for the Yudhoyono administration to get to grips with a range of reforms that would address issues such as customs and excise duties, labour laws, land acquisition rights and the legal system as a whole. Indonesia also needs to diversify from its traditional dependence on extractive industries such as oil, gas and minerals. This is easier said than done: Indonesia's ports are a long way from the key US and European markets. Principal competitors in this field such as China and Vietnam still have cheaper labour costs and an increasingly better educated work force. But unless major enterprises are privatised, they will lack the agility to respond to market requirements and changes. None the less, Indonesia's democracy has proved remarkably resilient. That political stability now needs to be converted to economic stability.

Risk assessment

Economy	Good
Politics	Fair
Regional stability	Good

COUNTRY PROFILE

Historical profile

It is thought that Negroid peoples came to Irian Jaya, from East Africa around 30,000 years ago. Melanesians arrived later; the resultant population migrated throughout the islands of what is now Indonesia. Later settlers arrived from India, Burma and China. Islam spread to Indonesia as a result of the strong trading links with the Arabian Peninsula.

1511 The Portuguese arrived in Indonesia, looking for spices. The Spaniards followed, bringing Christianity to the region.

1799 The Dutch gained control of the territory through the United East India Company. They gradually extended their control throughout the entire region. The Portuguese maintained East Timor.

1924 The Partai Kommunis Indonesia (PKI) (Indonesian Communist Party) was established. It was first active among trade unionists and rural villagers. The rural areas came to be the PKI's main power base.

1942–45 The islands of the Dutch East Indies were occupied by the Japanese. After the Second World War the Dutch regained control. Nationalist leader Ahmed Sukarno returned from internal exile and organised the fight for independence from Dutch colonial rule.

1945 In a speech in July Sukarno urged the adoption of the Panca Sila (Five Principles) as the ideological basis of the new state. The five principles were nationalism, internationalism (or humanitarianism), democracy, social justice, and belief in God.

1949 After four years of insurgency The Netherlands recognised the independence of Indonesia. A federal constitution was introduced, giving limited self-government to the 16 constituent regions. Ahmed Sukarno as leader of the Partai Nasional Indonesia (PNI) Indonesian Nationalist Party, assumed the presidency. The Dutch retained control of West Papua; the Portuguese retained control of East Timor.

1950 The constitution was dissolved and the country adopted a unitary political structure. Sukarno was elected president.

1955 Sukarno won Indonesia's first general election. Political instability prompted Sukarno to dissolve parliament and a period of autocratic rule ensued.

1962 Dutch authority for West Papua was passed to UN administration.

1963 Authority for West Papua was transferred to Indonesia.

1964 Indonesia laid claim to areas of Borneo which had been granted to Malaysia on its independence, leading to a three-year guerrilla conflict on the Malaysian border, which severely damaged the Indonesian economy.

1965 A failed coup d'état by the PKI resulted in the deaths of hundreds of thousands of left-wing activists.

1967 Sukarno transferred full emergency power to General Suharto, commander of the Indonesian armed forces.

KEY INDICATORS — Indonesia

	Unit	2003	2004	2005	2006	2007
Population	m	219.75	221.78	219.21	222.05	*224.94
Gross domestic product (GDP)	US$bn	208.30	254.30	286.96	364.38	*436.94
GDP per capita	US$	946	1,165	1,309	1,640	*1,925
GDP real growth	%	3.4	5.1	5.7	5.5	*6.3
Inflation	%	6.6	6.1	10.5	13.1	6.4
Unemployment	%	10.5	9.2	11.8	10.6	*7.6
Industrial output	% change	–	3.9	5.0	4.7	–
Agricultural output	% change	–	4.1	2.8	3.0	–
Oil output	'000 bpd	1,179.0	1,126.0	1,136.0	1,071.0	969.0
Natural gas output	bn cum	72.6	73.3	76.0	74.0	66.7
Coal output	mtoe	70.5	81.4	83.2	119.9	27.8
Exports (fob) (goods)	US$m	61,053.0	69,860.0	86,224.0	103,514.0	118,014.0
Imports (cif) (goods)	US$m	32,551.0	45,070.0	63,856.0	73,868.0	84,930.0
Balance of trade	US$m	28,502.0	24,790.0	22,368.0	29,646.0	33,083.0
Current account	US$m	7,250.0	7,280.0	307.0	10,836.0	11,009.0
Total reserves minus gold	US$m	34,962.0	34,952.0	32,989.0	41,103.0	54,976.0
Foreign exchange	US$m	34,742.0	34,724.0	32,774.0	40,866.0	54,737.0
Exchange rate	per US$	8,674.50	8,934.84	9,130.00	9,098.10	9,327.50

* estimated figure

1968 General Suharto became president.
1975 Portugal granted independence to its colony of East Timor.
1976 East Timor was invaded by Indonesia and became a province. This annexation was never officially recognised by the UN.
1985 Australia recognised Indonesia's incorporation of East Timor.
1997 The South-East Asian economic crisis caused the rupiah to plummet in value.
1998 Suharto, re-elected in March, was forced to resign on 21 May after accusations of corruption and widespread public disturbances as the country's economy reached near collapse. He was succeeded by Bacharuddin Jusuf Habibie.
1999 A UN sponsored referendum on independence was supported by the population of East Timor. Anti-independence militia rampage through East Timor until UN administration is imposed and the Indonesian government agreed to grant it independence. Abdurrahman Wahid was elected president of Indonesia by the People's Consultative Assembly.
2000 Ex-president Suharto's legal trial, on corruption charges, collapsed. Ethnic, religious and separatist violence in several provinces grew.
2001 The IMF halted further loans citing the government's inability to tackle corruption. Wahid was voted out of office for his alleged involvement in two financial scandals. Vice President Megawati Sukarnoputri was sworn in as president.
2002 Indonesia, Malaysia and the Philippines signed a pact to counter terrorism. The government and separatist rebels in Aceh province signed a peace agreement giving greater autonomy and free elections to Aceh in exchange for disarmament by rebels. Constitutional changes included the posts of president and vice president to be by popular vote. A bomb planted by Islamic fundamentalists on the island of Bali, and targetted at Western tourists, killed 202 people. The International Court of Justice awarded the disputed islands of Sipadan and Ligitan to Malaysia.
2003 The Aceh peace accord failed; martial law was imposed. Three Bali bomb suspects were found guilty and sentenced to death.
2004 Susilo Bambang Yudhoyono won the presidential elections. An earthquake off the island of Sumatra caused a devastating tsunami that struck coastal areas throughout the region, particularly the peninsula of Aceh on Sumatra island. The final estimate for Indonesia was 167,000 dead or missing and 572,126 displaced.
2005 Warships were dispatched to the Ambalat region of the Sulawesi Sea off the east coast of Borneo when Royal Dutch/Shell, under an agreement with Malaysia, started to explore for oil; Indonesia claims the region as its own and had signed a similar deal in 2004 with US Unocal Corp for hydrocarbon exploration. An agreement was signed between the leaders of Indonesia and Timor-Leste, recognising the location of their shared land border. The government withdrew the last troops from Aceh province, following the disbanding of the military wing of the Gerakan Aceh Merdeka (GAM) (Free Aceh Movement) a few days earlier.
2006 Legislation was introduced extending partial home rule to Aceh. Local elections were held in Aceh for a governor and other officials.
2007 In July the European Union banned all Indonesian airlines from EU air space, citing safety concerns, and warned its citizens not to use these airlines elsewhere in the world. See Getting There. The governor of Jakarta was directly elected for the first time on 8 August.
2008 Former president (1967–98) Suharto died on 27 January. In May, the government was forced to raise subsidised fuel prices by around 30 per cent, in line with global prices, prompting civil unrest.

Political structure

Constitution

The system of government is based on the 1945 constitution which underlines the unity of Indonesia as a republic, supplemented by the General Elections Law of 1969.

The constitution provides for five branches of government: the president, the Dewan Perwakilan Rakyat (DPR) (House of People's Representatives), the Supreme Audit Board, the Supreme Court and the Supreme Advisory Council. Despite geographic diversity and the limited reach of the political centre, Indonesia has not implemented a federal system, an option tarnished by association with the colonial era under Dutch rule. Instead, each of the 27 provinces is headed by a governor who is responsible to the president through the minister of home affairs, and represents the central government in his province. The north Sumatran province of Aceh, the territory of Jogjakarta in central Java, and the capital, Jakarta, have a special status.

Since 1985, by law, all major organisations, including political parties, religious groups and trade unions, must include acknowledgement of Pancasila (the Five Principles) as their sole guiding ideology in their constitutions. It emphasises tolerance among different religious groups and a political system based on consensus.

All Indonesian citizens over the age of 17 are eligible to vote, as well as those citizens under the age of 17 who are married. To stand for election, a citizen must be at least 21 years old.

In August 2002, 14 amendments were made to the constitution, to take effect with the next elections. The revisions included the abolition of the reservation of 38 parliamentary seats for military personnel.

In July 2003, parliament passed legislation setting the parameters for the first direct presidential election.

Form of state

Democratic republic

The executive

Executive power rests with the president, who serves a five-year term. Under the constitutional amendments introduced in August 2002, the president and the vice president are to be directly elected by the people, rather than being appointed by the Majelis Permusyawaratan Rakyat (MPR) (People's Consultative Assembly). The president is also head of government and can deploy direct legislative powers. The cabinet is appointed by the president; it may be partisan or largely composed of technocrats without an independent power base.

National legislature

The MPR has 700 members, comprising 135 regional representatives, 65 representatives of professional groups and the 500 members of the DPR.

The MPR is to be restructured in 2004. Within the DPR, the 500 members are elected via proportional representation for a five-year term. The constitutional reforms agreed in 2002 will mean that after the 2004 elections, the armed forces will no longer appoint any members of parliament and all members will be directly elected.

All statutes and the state budget must be approved by the DPR, which has the right to initiate legislation. Draft legislation is submitted to the DPR by the government, and passes through four stages: an explanation of the proposed legislation, a general debate, discussions between the appropriate commission of the DPR and the government, and a final debate and vote. Legislation that is approved is sent to the president for enactment. The Supreme Audit Board is responsible for auditing the state's finances and reporting the results of its investigations to the DPR.

Legal system

The judicial powers of the state are exercised by the Supreme Court.

Last elections

5 July/20 September 2004 (presidential); 5 April 2004 (parliamentary).

Results: Presidential: in the run-off on 20 Sep 2004, Susilo Bambang Yudhoyono won 60.9 per cent of the vote and the incumbent, Megawati Sukarnoputri, won 39.1 per cent.

Parliamentary: Golkar 21.6 per cent (128 seats); PDI-P won 18.5 per cent (109 seats).

Next elections

2009 (parliamentary and presidential)

Political parties

Ruling party

Coalition led by Partai Golongan Karya (Golkar) (Party of the Functional Groups) (since Oct 2004)

Main opposition party

Partai Demokrasi Indonesia Perjuangan (PDI-P) (Indonesian Democratic Party - Struggle)

Population

224.94 million (2007)*

Last census: June 2000: 206,264,595

Population density: 116 inhabitants per square km. Urban population: 42 per cent (1995–2001).

Annual growth rate: 1.3 per cent 1994–2004 (WHO 2006)

Ethnic make-up

Although 95 per cent of the population are of Malay origin, there are some 300 minorities, including Melanesian, Proto-Austranesian, Polynesian and Micronesian; there are approximately four million ethnic Chinese. Indonesia encompasses the Islamic people of Aceh on the northern tip of Sumatra, the densely populated main island of Java, the tourist resorts of Bali, the island of Flores and the primitive tribes of Irian Jaya in the east.

Religions

Islam (87 per cent), Christianity (10 per cent), Hinduism (mainly in Bali) (2 per cent) and Buddhism (1 per cent). Indonesia has the world's largest Muslim population, although Hindu-derived and indigenous religious variations are common. Religious violence has spread in line with political uncertainty. Animist beliefs are held in remote areas.

Education

Free universal primary education has been a long-term aim of the government. Almost 100 per cent of eligible children attend such schools, compared to only 40 per cent when President Suharto came to power in 1968. The overall literacy rate has increased by 31 per cent, up from 54 per cent in 1970.

Secondary education consists of two three-year cycles; over 50 per cent of eligible students are in secondary education. Tertiary education has also expanded, with 11 per cent of eligible students in school, up from 1 per cent in the late 1960s. The vast majority of tertiary institutions are privately owned, although there is a network of state institutions around the country. The quality of these universities and colleges varies enormously and large numbers of Indonesian students go overseas for their tertiary education. Despite improvements, the Indonesian education system is not supplying enough technicians and scientists for the country's ambitious plans.

Public expenditure on education typically amounts to 1.4 per cent of annual GDP. In April 2003, the Islamic Development Bank approved a US$31 million loan to Indonesia to finance university expansion.

Literacy rate: 88 per cent adult rate; 98 per cent youth rate (15–24) (Unesco 2005).

Compulsory years: 7 to 16

Enrolment rate: 113 per cent gross primary enrolment of the relevant age group (including repeaters); 56 per cent gross secondary enrolment (World Bank).

Pupils per teacher: 22 in primary schools.

Health

Per capita total expenditure on health (2003) was US$113; of which per capita government spending was US$40, (WHO 2006).

While basic healthcare has improved immeasurably over the past 30 years, it remains an urban rather than rural phenomenon. Inadequate numbers of trained staff remain the rule. Expatriates and wealthier Indonesians usually go to Singapore or Australia for operations. State healthcare is rudimentary. According to government figures, there are about 1,350 hospitals in Indonesia with 110,200 beds. There are approximately 0.7 hospital beds per 1,000 people, which is low even by regional standards (India has 0.8 beds per 1,000).

Improved water sources are available to 74 per cent of the population.

There were cases of polio reported to the World Health Organisation – Global Polio Eradication Initiative in 2006; the country had previously been free of the disease and its re-emergence was due to infected travellers.

HIV/Aids

HIV prevalence: 0.1 per cent aged 15–49 in 2003 (World Bank)

Life expectancy: 67 years, 2004 (WHO 2006)

Fertility rate/Maternal mortality rate: 2.3 births per woman, 2004 (WHO 2006); maternal mortality 230 per 100,000 live births (World Bank).

Child (under 5 years) mortality rate (per 1,000): 31 per 1,000 live births; 27.3 per cent of children aged under five are malnourished (World Bank).

Head of population per physician: 0.13 physicians per 1,000 people, 2003 (WHO 2006)

Welfare

Although poverty has been greatly reduced, the decline in living standards during the economic contraction of 1998 has yet to be reversed. The government has no plans to provide comprehensive welfare for the country's population of over 200 million. Instead, the government attempts to subsidise the cost of living of the poor through price controls, although these are being phased out in line with IMF commitments on goods such as kerosene. The state-run Workers' Accident Insurance and Provident Fund (Jamsostek) is the only form of social security in Indonesia. The insurance covers accident, sickness, pensions, unemployment, health and housing benefits. Outside Jamsostek there are other welfare programmes provided by private insurance companies, but they are not compulsory.

Main cities

Jakarta (capital, on island of Java, estimated population 9.0 million (m) in 2004); Surabaya (3.1m); Bandung (2.8m); Medan (2.2m) on Sumatra; Palembang (1.5m) on Sumatra; Tangerang (1.3m), Semarang on Java (1.3m); Ujung Pandang (Makassar) on Sulawesi (Celebes) (1.3m); Banjarmasin (568,800); Samarinda (508,900) and Pontianak (506,300) on Kalimantan (Borneo); Denpasar on Bali (502,100); Jogjakarta on Java (484,200).

Languages spoken

Bahasa Indonesia has existed as an official language for the past 70 years, and is still in the process of developing, with new words constantly being added. For simplicity's sake, the use of English words is common, particularly in the banking, insurance and technology sectors. However, the government wishes to promote Indonesian language development and reduce the use of foreign words.

English is widely spoken in government and business circles and by the younger generation. Many older Indonesians speak Dutch as a second language.

Each ethnic group has its own language. Altogether, more than 580 languages and dialects are spoken, including Javanese, Sundanese, Arabic and Chinese.

Official language/s

Bahasa Indonesia

Media

The constitution provides for freedom of the press and speech, however, the government has occasionally restricted these rights. The Constitution Court struck down several laws in 2006–07 that criminalised defamation of the government, president and vice president, which had been used to curtail reporting. The government restricts the movement of journalist around the country and special permits must be obtained to visit, for example, West Papua.

National news agency: Antara National News Agency
Other news agencies: Indoexchange (for stock market news): www.indoexchange.com
Press
Dailies: In Indonesian, the largest newspapers include Kompas (http://kompas.com), Media Indonesia (www.mediaindonesia.com), Koran Tempo (www.korantempo.com), Republik (www.republika.co.id), Pos Kota (www.poskota.co.id) and Rakyat Merdeka (www.rakyatmerdeka.co.id) a tabloid. In English The Jakarta Post (www.thejakartapost.com), which includes business and financial news.
There are many more regional and local newspapers available.
Weeklies: In Indonesian, magazines include Tempo (www.tempointeractive.com) with English online edition, Gatra (www.gatra.com) for news and current affairs, Tabloid Nova (www.tabloidnova.com) and Hanyawanita (www.hanyawanita.com), is for women.
Business: In Indonesian, newspapers and magazines include Bisnis Indonesia (http://web.bisnis.com), Bisnis Bali (www.bisnisbali.com) and SWA (www.swa.co.id); the JIEF Economic Monthly (www.jief.biz) is also in Japanese and Warta Ekonomi (www.wartaekonomi.com). In English, publications include the Standard Trade and Industry Directory of Indonesia Indonesian Commercial Newsletter.
Periodicals: In Indonesian, the monthly Femina (www.femina-online.com) is for women. Intisari is a science monthly. In English, the quarterly Inside Indonesia (http://insideindonesia.org) has in-depth articles on politics and social issues and the monthly Latitudes Magazine has features on culture, travel and the arts.
Broadcasting
The government bans live news coverage and relayed international live news programmes on radio and television. However, digital news via the internet is a growing market.
Radio: There are many radio stations operating in FM and AM frequencies. A few digital audio broadcasting (DAB) stations have begun operations in Jakarta and Surabaya, since 2006.
The national public broadcaster is Radio Republik Indonesia (RRI) (www.rri-online.com), with six networks including the international channel, Voice of Indonesia. Private, commercial stations include Kiss FM (www.kissfm.co.id), Oz Radio Bali (www.ozradio.net) and Radio Otomotion (www.otomotionfm.com) for news.
Television: There are around a dozen national TV networks competing with the publicly owned Televisi Republik Indonesia (TVRI), (www.tvri.co.id), which broadcast free-to-air, cable and satellite TV.
Major private TV channels include RCTI (www.rcti.tv) with a variety of locally produced shows including news, entertainment and religion. With similar content, SCTV (www.sctv.co.id) is known for its soap operas (entertaining serials?) and Indosiar (www.indosiar.com) known for its cultural programmes and foreign language dramas.
Advertising
With a population of over 220 million, advertising revenue per annum is around US$11.6 billion. All traditional outlets are available plus new technologies.
Television advertising must be 100 per cent Indonesian resourced, through agencies, actors and location, unless a government waver is agreed and the product or service is an international brand or icon.

Economy
The economy, which had been struggling for several years, following the Asian financial crisis in 1997, has been making modest progress. GDP growth was around 3.5 per cent between 2001–03 but it picked up in 2004 and has remained at over 5.0 per cent since. Inflation, which peaked at 18.0 per cent in October 2005, due to the steep rise in global oil prices, was brought under control by a tight monetary policy that slowed domestic demand. Annual inflation eventually averaged 10.5 per cent in 2005, as unemployment rose to 11.8 per cent.
The service sector vies with industry, 45 per cent and 40 per cent respectively, to provide the major proportion of GDP. Agriculture provides 14 per cent, a figure that has been steadily falling since 1985.
Indonesia produced 1.1 million barrels of oil per day in 2005, contributing US$19.2 billion or 22.5 per cent of total export earnings and around 30 per cent of government revenues. Industry produces electrical appliances, rubber products and textiles for export, while agriculture exports include timber and rice.
Despite the introduction of a number of macroeconomic reforms, which has improved the economy, Indonesia is still vulnerable to external shocks such as the global financial turmoil of mid-May 2006 and the loss of confidence by domestic investors, coupled with a lack of FDI. As well as natural disasters (much of Indonesia is subject to frequent earthquakes), 80 per cent, or US$4.7 billion, of the reconstruction cost of homes and infrastructure damaged during the 2001 tsunami has been spent and it is estimated that reconstruction following the June 2006 Yogyakarta earthquake will be another US$3 billion.
Indonesia's long-term sovereign credit ratings were lifted by Standard & Poors in July 2006; the foreign currency improved to BB-, while the local currency rating rose to BB+.
In October 2006 Indonesia paid back the outstanding US$3.2 billion of the US$11.1 billion loan, incurred during the 1997 financial crisis, four years ahead of schedule.
The IMF has commended Indonesia's achievements in making steady economic progress and noted that it has returned to pre-crisis levels of real GDP growth, with a declining trend of public debt and improved creditworthiness.

Labour market and unemployment
The Indonesian labour market is estimated to be approximately 90 million people. Approximately 40 per cent of the workforce is female. The unemployment rate was estimated at 10.5 per cent in 2003.
Economic opportunities for the educated are few and unemployed university graduates constitute a significant proportion of those without work. Around 43 per cent of the country's jobless live in rural areas.
The minimum wage in manufacturing is not more than a few dollars a day. Low wages and the employment of children in factories and workshops have in the past led to sweat shop allegations against Indonesia by labour groups in developed countries. However, there has been a growth in employment, although the rate of underemployment remains high; nearly 45 million people worked less than 35 hours per week in the late 1990s. Progress is slow as there are approximately 2.5 million new entrants into the labour force each year. Lower wages and overheads in Indonesia were largely responsible for increased investment in the consumer electronics and home appliances sector during the 1980s and 1990s.

External trade
Indonesia is a member of the Asian and Pacific Economic Co-operation (Apec) and belongs to the Asian Free Trade Area (AFTA) operated by the Association of South East Asian Nations (ASEAN), which was set up to attract foreign direct investment (FDI) and the elimination of tariffs within the membership.
The US-owned Freeport-McMoran mine Grasberg, located in Papua, contains the largest single reserves of copper and gold in the world.
Indonesia became a net importer of oil in 2004 as production fell.
Imports
Main commodities include machinery and equipment, petroleum and chemicals, foodstuffs.

Main sources: Singapore (16.4 per cent total, 2006),China (10.9 per cent), Japan (9.0 per cent).

Exports

One of the most successful export sectors has been consumer electronics and home appliances. Major exports also include oil and gas, plywood, textiles and rubber, copper, gold and other minerals.

Main destinations: Japan (21.6 per cent total, 2006), US (11.1 per cent), Singapore (8.9 per cent).

Agriculture

Farming

Agriculture accounts for around 15 per cent of GDP and employs 48 per cent of the labour force. Agricultural products make up 25 per cent of non-oil export earnings.

After planting more high-yield varieties, investing in irrigation systems, doubling the use of fertilisers and trebling the use of pesticides, Indonesia has achieved self-sufficiency in rice. Poor harvests can still result in rice and other cereals having to be imported to rebuild stocks.

Cassava, maize, sugar, sweet potatoes, bananas and many other fruits and vegetables are grown for local consumption.

Self-sufficiency in sugar is a government goal.

It is estimated that there are 1.2 million clove farmers. Indonesia consumes 95 per cent of worldwide clove production, used in the manufacture of kretek (clove/ tobacco mix) cigarettes. The clove cigarette industry is one of the country's major employers and the government has tariffs in place to restrict the import of cloves, mainly from Madagascar and Zanzibar, in an attempt to maintain its sustainability when over 80 per cent of the cloves consumed is home grown.

Large estates that have undergone rehabilitation produce coffee, tea, rubber, coconuts and palm oil nuts, mostly for export.

Indonesia is the world's largest producer of coconuts and the second-largest of palm oil, copra and natural rubber. It is the third-largest in rice, coffee and cocoa.

Crop production in 2005 included: 65,313,711 tonnes (t) cereals in total, 54,088,468t rice, 11,225,243t maize, 19,424,708t cassava, 1,901,802t sweet potatoes, 1,072,040t potatoes, 4,874,439t bananas, 1,469,000t groundnuts, 310,721t pulses, 2,071,084t citrus fruit, 16,285,000t coconuts, 64,425,500t oil palm fruit, 626,872t tomatoes, 16,156,856t oilcrops, 141,000t tobacco, 601,272t cocoa beans, 700,045t green coffee, 25,600,000t sugar cane, 1,437,665t mangoes, 2,066,000t natural rubber, 2,387t vanilla, 260,000t kapok fruit, 1,100,514t chillies, 164,817t tea, 14,747,491t fruit in total, 7,609,427t vegetables in total.

Livestock production included: 2,392,180t meat in total, 447,570t beef, 40,240t buffalo meat, 566,500t pig meat, 123,190t sheep and goat meat, 1,213,110t poultry, 1,030,590t eggs, 915,300t milk, 58,560t cattle hides.

Fishing

Foreign aid organisations have assisted the government in rehabilitating the fishing sector. Foreign fishing trawlers are not permitted to operate in Indonesian waters, as these would obstruct traditional coastal fishermen.

Indonesia's fishing industry is plagued by corruption and illegal fishing methods, such as the use of bottle bombs to increase the size of the catch. Ineffective monitoring of fishing techniques means that these practices are likely to continue.

Shrimp and tuna fish are important exports. Other species include scad, Indian mackerel and sea catfish. Indonesia is the fifth largest producer of tuna in the world and has become one of the world's biggest exporters of shrimps and prawns.

In 2004, the total marine fish catch was 3,832,290 tonnes and the total crustacean catch was 328,590 tonnes.

Forestry

Forest products are the third most important export earner. Indonesia has some of the world's largest remaining reserves of tropical hardwoods. Legislation aims to reduce the rate of felling and to ban the export of logs, and has increased the proportion used locally in timber processing.

Illegal logging remains a problem and has doubled the deforestation rate. It is estimated that Indonesia is losing up to two million hectares (ha) of forest annually. It was estimated that 300,000cum of hardwood is illegally felled each year in the state of New Guinea and shipped to China for processing. Indonesia's decentralisation programme could worsen the situation since local governments do not have the ability to manage their resources effectively. The military have also been implicated in the illegal logging trade with corruption and entrenched interests underpinning the activity. Indonesia is under pressure from international organisations to reform its forestry policy and to control the unprecedented rate at which its forests are depleted.

Exports in 2004 totalled to US$4.9 billion, while imports amounted to US$1.3 billion.

Production in 2004 included 109,060,284 cubic metres (cum) roundwood, 3,248,500cum industrial roundwood, 6,250,000cum sawnwood, 26,000,000cum sawlogs and veneers, 3,248,000cum pulpwood, 7,329,000cum wood-based panels, 79,563,784cum wood fuel, 74,452 tonnes charcoal.

Industry and manufacturing

Industry contributes around 44 per cent of GDP and employs 15 per cent of the workforce.

In the oil-rich 1970s, Indonesia operated a highly protected industrialisation policy with heavy state involvement on both a regulatory and investment front. Declining export revenues from oil and gas in the mid-1980s led to a reversal of this policy. Industry was progressively deregulated and foreign investment encouraged in previously protected areas.

Non-traditional export industries were promoted – initially garments and shoes, later electronics, chemicals and minerals. The government also successfully encouraged investment in automobile manufacturing, air and sea transportation, power, communications and highways.

Tourism

The tourist sector, which grew to 5.1 million visitors in 2000, was hit by a series of disasters which reversed the upward trend. Following the 11 September 2001 terrorist attacks in the US came the Bali bombing in October 2002. The impact especially of the latter event promised to be less damaging than was expected, but signs of recovery in early 2003 were negated by the Iraq war, the Sars outbreak and the terrorist attack on the Marriott Hotel in Jakarta. Visitor numbers, which stood at around five million in 2002, fell to 4.4 million in 2003. The setback was temporary. Despite the introduction of a new visa policy in February 2004, the sector recovered quickly, recording 5.3 million arrivals in 2004. Then, in October 2005, another bomb in Bali set back the industry yet again. The government, which recognises the importance of tourism to the economy and actively promotes the sector, aims to attract 10 million visitors by 2009.

The biggest market is Singapore, which accounted for 1.6 million arrivals, followed by Malaysia, Japan, Australia and Taiwan.

Tourism had been expected to contribute 3.1 per cent to GDP in 2005.

Environment

Indonesia is ranked first in the world for its range and variety of corals, and together with the Philippines, Australia, Papua New Guinea and Solomon Islands for coral reef fish species.

In November 2007 Indonesia was warned by Greenpeace that the drainage of peat wetlands in favour of plantations producing palm oil (used in foods and bio-fuel) was causing greater release of carbon dioxide (a greenhouse gas) than forest clearances by burning alone. Indonesia is planning to become the world's leading producer of palm oil, with a huge project planned for Borneo. In the face of international critisism of deforestation, and Indonesia's ranking as the world's third largest greenhouse emitter, around 80 million trees were planted nationwide in November.

Mining

The archipelago of Indonesia produces tin, copper and chromium ore. Indonesia is the world's second-largest producer of tin (after China), producing typically 46,000 tonnes of tin concentrate. In addition to other precious metals, it is also a major producer of copper, bauxite and nickel. Mining and quarrying typically account for around 13 per cent of GDP. Mining's share of GDP has fallen continuously in recent years as production has dropped in response to depressed world prices. Increasing world demand for copper and rising prices have encouraged mines to be restarted and new mines opened.

The government is eager to increase investment in gold, copper and nickel exploitation, although complex issues are involved in mineral exploitation throughout the archipelago. Indonesia is by far the largest gold producing nation in Asia and one of the top 10 producers in the world. Gold is mined at Lebong Tandai in Sumatra and is produced as a by-product from the Freeport copper mine in the highlands of Irian Jaya. Most of Indonesia's gold mines have a short life span. Instability, particularly in separatist areas such as Aceh and Papua, has halted exploration projects in the past. The majority of gold comes from PT Freeport's mining facility in Irian Jaya.

Nickel is mined from new, large deposits in central Sulawesi and Irian Jaya; much of it becomes ferro-nickel and nickel matte, primarily for export. Bauxite production is carried out at Asahan in north Sumatra, for export to Japan.

Tin mining is carried out by state-owned PT Tambang Timah and joint-venture company PT Koba Tin (25 per cent owned by PT Tambang Timah and 75 per cent owned by Iluka Mining Corporation). PT Tambang Timah is the world's largest tin producer, producing tin from Bangka Island, including dredging operations at Karimun and Kundur islands in the Riau Province. The company has tin reserves estimated at around 382,000 tonnes, of which 60 per cent is located offshore.

Hydrocarbons

The role of oil and gas peaked in the early 1980s when it contributed over four-fifths of total exports. Although oil and gas earnings are still significant, their contribution to GDP is declining.

The oil sector remains very important and Indonesia is the major oil producer in South-east Asia. Oil accounts for 17 per cent of exports. In March 2004, Indonesia became a net importer of crude oil, which could continue if investment levels remain low.

Indonesia had proven reserves of 4.7 billion barrels in 2004 and produced 1.26 million barrels per day.The state-owned oil company, Pertamina, dominates the sector, although foreign involvement has steadily increased. In the downstream sector, Indonesia has eight refineries with a combined capacity of 1,056,000bpd.

Indonesia had proven natural gas reserves of 2.56 trillion cubic metres in 2004 and produced 73.3 billion cubic metres. Natural gas is supplied from two very large fields at Arun in North Sumatra and Badak in East Kalimantan, although large offshore discoveries have been made around the Natuna Islands in the South China Sea; nearly all is liquefied.

Large-scale systematic coal operations began in 1980 and Indonesia is now the world's third-largest coal producer. Indonesia had coal reserves of 5.0 billion tonnes in 2005. Coal output was around 81.5 million tonnes. Coal is one of the top 10 non-oil exports.

Lower grade lignite prevails (59 per cent) followed by sub-bituminous (27 per cent) and bituminous and anthracite (14 per cent). The state-owned PT Tambang Bukit Asam produces around nine million tonnes per year from four open cast mines. The rest is produced by private coal companies.

Energy

Indonesia has installed electricity-generating capacity of around 25GW, generated mainly by oil-fired plants and some hydro-power. Projects are planned to develop coal and gas-fired and hydro-electric power generation in order to preserve oil for export.

The sector has suffered from under-investment in generating equipment, with the result that, while demand continues to increase, supply is erratic

Financial markets

Stock exchange

The Jakarta Stock Exchange (JSE) is small by regional standards and has attracted little attention from global investors. It has around listed 300 companies, all domestic.

Banking and insurance

In July 2006 the central bank announced plans to restructure the banking system by limiting the number of banks investors may control to one. The Indonesia Bank Restructuring Agency (IBRA) was given the task of enhancing public confidence in the banking industry, which had reached a low in 2002, before the sale of Bank Central Asia (BCA), Indonesia's largest bank. Following the sale the IMF commended the government's restructuring policies, which restored solvency to the banking system with net earnings becoming positive for the first time since the 1998 Asia economic crisis. It also advised the government to strengthening standards of corporate governance within the sector. Indonesia was removed from the OECD Financial Action Task Force (FATF) list of non-co-operative countries on money laundering in early 2005.

Central bank

Bank Indonesia

Main financial centre

Jakarta

Offshore facilities

Time

Indonesia has three time zones.

Java, Sumatra, west and central Kalimantan and Madura: GMT plus seven hours – West Zone

Bali, south and east Kalimantan, Sulawesi: GMT plus eight hours – Central Zone

Aru, Kai, Moluccas, Tanimbar, Irian Jaya: GMT plus nine hours – East Zone

Geography

The Indonesian archipelago has 17,508 islands and is the largest in the world, extending about 5,150km (3,200 miles) from Sumatra in the west to Irian Jaya, the western half of New Guinea, in the east. The main islands are Sumatra, Java, Bali, Sulawesi (the Celebes) and Timor. Kalimantan, the Indonesian part of Borneo island shared with Malaysia and Brunei, forms a major part of Indonesian territory. Now independent, the former Portuguese colony of East Timor became the youngest province in 1976. Indonesia's neighbours are Malaysia, Singapore, Papua New Guinea, the Philippines and Australia.

Part of the so-called volcanic 'ring of fire' on the Pacific rim, Indonesia has hundreds of volcanoes, 70 of them still active, and hardly a year passes without a major eruption. Earthquakes are also frequent, but rarely cause significant damage.

The country has the world's second largest area of primary rainforest after Brazil, with species of plant and animal life as diverse as anywhere on the planet. On Borneo alone, there are 3,000 different tree species. It also has an extraordinary diversity of animal life, with an estimated 500 species of mammals, including tigers, elephants, hairy rhinoceros, warthogs, small leopards, civets, mouse deer, orangutans, baboons and monkeys. Birds of Paradise, hornbills, peacocks and cockatoos are among the 1,500 species of known birds. The Komodo dragon is three metres long and weighs up to 150kg. It is the world's largest lizard and it is found only on the east Indonesian island of Komodo.

Hemisphere

Straddles the equator

Climate

All of the islands in the archipelago lie within the tropical zone, with average temperatures of 26 degrees Celsius (C). The dry season usually lasts from May to September, the wet season from October to April. In the hill regions west of Jakarta, average temperatures drop to a pleasant 21 degrees C. Indonesia straddles the equator and days are all the same length and rain is frequent. Yearly rainfall in Jakarta is about 300mm and humidity is more than 80 per cent. The islands east of Bali have a much drier climate, and tropical vegetation and jungles give way to rocky savannahs.

Dress codes

Foreigners are expected to dress for business as they would at home, despite the heat, although men can get away without ties and jackets during the day. Formal attire includes suits, or traditional batik shirts. Women are advised to dress conservatively as do their Indonesian counterparts. Proper decorum should especially be observed when visiting places of worship.

Entry requirements

Passports

Required by all and must have at least six months validity from date of entry, with proof of return/onward passage and sufficient funds for length of stay.

Visa

Required by all.
Nationals of Apec countries may obtain business visas for up to six months depending on the country of origin. Travellers should contact an Indonesian Consulate for details.
Business visitors arriving from countries with reciprical visa-free facilities on short-term visits need to supply an itinery, letter of business intent from their employer and a letter from a local sponsor.
All other visitors should contact an Indonesian Consulate for visa details.

Currency advice/regulations

The import of local currency is limited to Rp50,000 and must be declared, amounts over Rp10 million must be authorised; export is limited to the amount declared on import. Import and export of foreign currency is unlimited.
Major currencies or travellers cheques may be exchanged at most banks, except in the provinces. It is advisable to carry rupiahs in sufficient amount before travelling to outer provinces or minor towns.

Customs

Personal effects are allowed entry; cameras must be declared. Video cameras, tape recorders, binoculars, portable radios, typewriters and sports equipment may be imported on condition that they are exported on departure.

Prohibited imports

These include illegal drugs and narcotics, firearms, ammunition, TV sets, pornography, publications in Chinese characters and Chinese medicine.

Health (for visitors)

Mandatory precautions

Vaccination certificates for yellow fever if travelling from infected area.

Advisable precautions

Vaccinations that are necessary include: cholera, diphtheria, tetanus, hepatitis A, polio and typhoid. Vaccinations that may be advised include: hepatitis B, tuberculosis, Japanese B encephalitis and rabies.
Anti-malarial precautions should be taken; the use of mosquito nets and repellents and covering up the body after dark can help avoid malaria, hepatitis B and dengue fever. Only well-maintained and chlorinated swimming pools are safe in which to swim.
Use only bottled or boiled water for drinks, washing teeth and making ice. Eat only well cooked meals, preferably served hot; vegetables should be cooked and fruit peeled. Avoid dairy products, salad and food from street vendors. A full, first-aid kit would be useful.
Medical insurance is essential, including emergency evacuation, and an adequate supply of personal medicines is necessary.

Hotels

International-standard hotels have air-conditioning and often business centres, where translation and secretarial services are normally available. A 10 per cent service charge is normally added to the bill, so tipping with small change is usual. Where no service charge has been added, a tip of 5–10 per cent would be appropriate.

Credit cards

Credit and charge cards are widely accepted and ATMs are available in city centres.

Public holidays (national)

Fixed dates

^1 Jan (New Year), ^17 Aug (Independence Day), ^25 Dec (Christmas Day).

Variable dates

^Chinese New Year (Jan/Feb), Nyepi (Hindu New Year, Mar/Apr), Waisak Day (Birth of the Lord Buddha, May), Good Friday (Mar/Apr), Ascension Day, Eid al Adha, Islamic New Year, Birth of the Prophet Mohammed, Ascent of Prophet Mohammed, ^Eid al Fitr (two days).
^Official national holidays, holidays that fall on Friday are taken the next day. The remainder, Muslim, Hindu and Christian, are informal holidays taken by adherents.
Islamic year – 1429 (10 Jan 2008–28 Dec 2008): The Islamic year contains 354 or 355 days, with the result that Muslim feasts advance by 10–12 days against the Gregorian calendar. Dates of feasts vary according to the sighting of the new moon, so cannot be forecast exactly.

Working hours

Banking

Mon–Fri: 0830–1530/1730; Sat: 0930–1230. Hotel banks may remain open longer.

Business

Mon–Fri: 0800–1600; Sat: 0830–1230. Fri: it is difficult to make an appointment after 1100 although businessmen sometimes meet people in the late afternoon and early evening.

Government

Mon–Thu: 0800–1500; Fri: 0800–1130; Sat: 0800–1400.

Shops

0800/1000–2100/2200 (some close at 1730).

Telecommunications

Mobile/cell phones

There are limited 900/1800 GSM services around Jakata. A G3 system in planned.

Electricity supply

Generally 220V 50Hz, with two-pronged plug. However, some hotels in the provinces may still be using 110V AC, 50Hz. It is better to check before using an appliance.

Weights and measures

Metric system

Social customs/useful tips

Indonesia is predominantly Muslim and alcohol is not considered essential to social intercourse. Care should be taken to respect Muslim, Hindu and other religious conventions. Footwear should be removed before entering places of worship and temples and sometimes also private homes.
Handshaking with the right hand is customary both for men and women. It is conventional to shake hands and give a slight bow with the head on meeting and taking leave. Punctuality is appreciated on social occasions.
Pork is forbidden for the Muslim population and beef for the Balinese Hindus. Do not start to consume food or drink until invited by the host to do so.
Pribumi is used to describe anything indigenous or native to Indonesia, and occurs

in commercial or business contexts with reference to local participation, local capital investment or local loans.

In Indonesia, Western-style beckoning is considered rude; instead, turn your hand palm down, and waggle your fingers – like an upside-down wave. Putting your hands on your hips is considered an overt sign of aggression or contempt.

The word 'no' is regarded as impolite; often people use the word belum, which means 'not yet'.

Security

Since 2000, Indonesia has been experiencing unrest and violence. There has been sectarian and ethnic strife in Aceh, Irian Jaya, Central and West Kalimantan, Maluku, North Maluku, Central and South Sulawesi and tension in West Timor.

Since October 2002, terrorist attacks have deliberately targetted Western tourists.

Getting there

Air

National airline: Garuda Indonesia (GA) and Merpati Nusantara Airlines (MZ). In July 2007 the European Union banned all Indonesian airlines from EU air space, due to safety concerns and warned its citizens not to use these airlines elsewhere in the world.

International airport/s: Soekarno-Hatta International (CGK), 28km north-west of Jakarta, banks/bureaux de change, a post office, duty-free shops, gift shops, 24-hour restaurants, snack bars, car hire and 24-hour medical/vaccination facilities; Denpasar Bali Ngurah Rai International (DPS), 13km south-west of the city, is the main airport on Bali; Bandung Husein (BDO); Cirebon Penggung (CBN); Ketapang (KTG); Pontianak Supadio (PNK); Semarang Uani (SRG); Surabaya Juanda (SUB).

Airport tax: International departures: Rp100,000.

Surface

Water: High-speed ferries run between Sumatra and Malaysia. Routes are either Medan–Penang or Dumai–Melaka. There are also services between Mandalo (Sulawesi) and the Philippines. Maritime piracy is a problem in some Indonesian waters.

Main port/s: Tanjung Priok, Jakarta; Tanjung Perak, Surabaya; Belawan, on Sumatra.

Getting about

National transport

Air: Garuda Indonesia operates extensive domestic services, including daily services between Jakarta, Surabaya and Medan. Other routes are also served by Sempati Air and Merpati Nusantara Airlines.

Road: Extensive road network includes over 370,000km of road, 25 per cent of which is surfaced. A 525km highway links key areas in Jambi and South Sumatra. Motorways and toll roads are good, but roads are narrower and poorly maintained in rural areas and remote regions. Secondary roads are frequently impassable in the rainy season. Driving outside major cities at night can be hazardous.

Buses: Express coach services link the main cities. Local bus services are inexpensive, but their use is complicated, they are often crowded, and service may be interrupted in the rainy season.

Rail: The rail network, limited to Java, Sumatra and Madura, comprises 8,600km of track. Java and parts of Sumatra have air-conditioned express rail services with sleeping and dining cars only between major cities. Fares are comparatively cheap but higher on air-conditioned trains. There are several trains daily from Jakarta to Bandung and Surabaya. Ordinary services can be slow, with many stops.

Water: There are extensive scheduled and non-scheduled inter-island sailings.

City transport

Roads in major cities are good.

Taxis: Taxis are plentiful but in various states of disrepair. Wherever possible, opt for Blue Bird or Silver Bird taxis and check the driver switches on the meter before starting the journey.

Taxis can be obtained at hotels, airports and railway stations. From Sukarno-Hatta airport to Jakarta, taxis add a surcharge and toll.

There are metered taxis only in Jakarta, Surabaya, Bandung, Solo, Semarang and Jogjakarta, but it may be necessary to insist on the use of the meter. Fares are very reasonable. Taxis may also be hired by the hour, which is less expensive for longer journeys.

In Jakarta it can be difficult to hail taxis, so engage one at the hotel and retain it until returning. A 10 per cent tip is usual.

There are also minicabs for two passengers, the bemo (small bus) which plies regular routes, and the becak, all of which need advance bargaining to come to a mutually accepted fare.

From city centre to Jakarta Soekarno-Hatta airport taxi journey times are about 45 minutes.

Buses, trams & metro: Journey time on the bus from city centre to Jakarta Soekarno-Hatta International Airport is about 60 minutes.

Car hire

Car hire, mostly chauffeur-driven, is available in major towns and cities. Except for international car hire operators which accept credit cards, full payment for car hire is made up-front. Traffic drives on the left. Driving at night can be dangerous outside major urban areas as it is common to encounter drivers who do not use their lights.

BUSINESS DIRECTORY

The addresses listed below are a selection only. While World of Information makes every endeavour to check these addresses, we cannot guarantee that changes have not been made, especially to telephone numbers and area codes. We would welcome any corrections.

Telephone area codes

The international direct dialling (IDD) code for Indonesia is +62, followed by the area code and subscriber's number:

Balik Papan	542	Manado	431
Bandung	22	Medan	61
Banjarmasin	511	Padang	751
Denpasar	361	Palembang	711
Jakarta	21		

Useful telephone numbers

Police: 110
Ambulance:118
Fire113
Directory (local):108
Directory (other Indonesian):106
International information102
International operator:101
Domestic connections:100

Chambers of Commerce

American Chamber of Commerce in Indonesia, World Trade Centre, Jalan Jend Sudirman Kav 29-31, Jakarta 12920 (tel: 526-2860; fax: 526-2861; e-mail: info@amcham.or.id).

Bali Chamber of Commerce and Industry, Gedung Merdeka, Jalan Surapati 7, Denpasar 80232 (tel: 233-053; fax: 227-020; e-mail: kadin_bali@balinetwork.com).

British Chamber of Commerce in Indonesia, World Trade Centre, Jalan Jend Sudirman Kav 31, Jakarta 12920 (tel: 522-9453; fax: 527-9135; e-mail: bisnis@britcham.or.id).

Indonesian Chamber of Commerce and Industry, Menara Kadin Indonesia, Jalan HR Rasuna Said X-5 Kav 2-3, Jakarta 12950 (tel: 916-5535; fax: 527-4485; e-mail: info@kadin.net.id).

Jakarta Chamber of Commerce and Industry, Majapahit Permai B21-23, Jalan Majapahit 18-22, PO Box 3077, Jakarta 10160 (tel: 380-8091; fax: 384-4549; e-mail: kadin_jkt@indosat.net.id).

Banking

Bank Dagang Nasional Indonesia (BDNI), Jl Hayam Wuruk No 8, Jakarta (tel: 231-1221/0530/0886; fax: 380-5725).

Bank Danamon, Jl Kebon Sirih No 15, Jakarta 10340 (tel: 231-1331, 230-1901/2; fax: 230-1883/5).

BankExim, Jl Lapangan Setasiun No 1, Jakarta 11110 (tel: 692-3122, 690-0991; fax: 692-3047, 690-5328).

Bank Internasional Indonesia (BII), Jl MH Thamrin Kav 22 No 51, Jakarta Pusat (tel: 230-0888/0666; fax: 230-1426).

Bank Mandiri, Jakarta (e-mail: corp.communications@bankmandiri.co.id; internet site: http://www.bankmandiri.co.id).

Bank Negara Indonesia (BNI), Jl Jend Sudirman Kav 1, Jakarta 10220 (tel: 251-1946; fax: 251-1214).

Bank Umum Nasional, 135 Jl Senen Raya, Jakarta 10410 (tel: 231-2828; fax: 231-2929).

Indonesian Bank Restructuring Agency, Komplek Bank Indonesia, Jl Budi Kemuliaan, Building D, 10th Floor, Jakarta (fax: 231-1478).

PT Bank Pembangunan Indonesia, JL RP Soeroso No 2-4, Jakarta 10011 (tel: 230-1908; fax: 230-1242/3, 230-0154).

PT Bank Bali Tbk, 17th Floor, Gedung Bank Bali, Jalan Jenderal Sudirman Kav 27, Jakarta 12920 (tel: 523-7899; fax: 250-0811).

Central bank

Bank Indonesia, 2 Jalan MH Thamrin, Jakarta 10110 (tel: 381-7187; fax: 350-1867; e-mail: humasbi@bi.go.id).

Travel information

Bouraq Indonesia Airlines, PO Box 2965, Jalan Angkasa 1-3, Kernayoran, Jakarta 10720 (tel: 629-5289; fax: 629-5364).

Garuda Indonesia, Jl. Merdeka Selatan 13, Jakarta 10110 (tel: 380-1901; fax: 380-6652; internet site: http://www.garuda-indonesia.com).

Merpati Nusantara Airlines, PO Box 323, Jalan Angkasa 2, Jakarta 10013 (tel: 413-608; fax: 420-7311).

National tourist organisation offices

Direktorat Jenderal Pariwisata Indonesia (Directorate-General of Tourism), 16/19 Jalan Medan Merdeka-Barat, Jakarta 10110 (tel: 386-0934; fax: 386-0828; internet site: http://www.tourismindonesia.com).

Ministries

Ministry of Agriculture, Jalal Harsono RM 3, Ragunan, Pasar Minggu, Jakarta 12550 (tel: 781-5380; fax: 781-6385).

Ministry of Defence, Jalal Medan Merdeka Barat 13-14, Jakarta 10110 (tel: 384-0889; fax: 384-5178).

Ministry of Economy, Jalal Lapangan Banteng Timur 2-4, Jakarta 10310 (tel: 319-01152; fax: 319-01151).

Ministry of Education, Jalal Jend Sudirman, Senayan, Jakarta (tel: 573-1618; fax: 573-6870).

Ministry of Energy and Mineral Resources, Jalal Medan Merdeka Selatan 16, Jakarta 10110 (tel: 380-4242; fax: 384-7461).

Ministry of Finance, Jalall Lapangan Banteng Timur 2, Jakarta 10170 (tel: 344-9230; fax: 381-4324).

Minstry of Fisheries and Maritime Affairs, Jalal Veteran, 3rd Floor, Jakarta (tel: 385-7009; fax: 344-6733).

Ministry of Foreign Affairs, Jalal Taman Pejambon 6, Jakarta 10111 (tel: 344-1508; fax: 385-1193).

Ministry of Forestry and Estate Crops, Jalal Jend Gatot Subroto, Senayan, Jakarta (tel: 573-1820; fax: 570-0226).

Ministry of Health, Jalal HR Rasuna Said Blok X-5 Kav 4-9, Jakarta 12950 (tel: 520-1590; fax: 520-1591).

Ministry of Home Affairs, Jalal Medan Merdeka Utara 7, Jakarta 10110 (tel: 384-2222; fax: 385-1193).

Ministry of Justice and Human Rights, Jalal HR Rasuna Said Kav 4-5, Kuningan, Jakarta (tel: 525-3006; fax: 525-3090).

Ministry of Manpower and Transmigration, Jalal Taman Makam Pahlawan 17, Jakarta (tel: 798-9912; fax: 799-2629).

Ministry of Political, Social and Security Affairs, Jalal Medan Merdeka Utara 7, Jakarta 10110 (tel: 384-9453; fax: 345-0918).

Ministry of Religious Affairs, Jalal Lapangan Banteng Barat 3-4, Jakarta 10710 (tel: 381-1679; fax: 381-1436).

Ministry of Resettlement and Regional Infrastructure, Jalal Pattimura 20, Kebayoran Baru, Jakarta 12110 (tel: 720-3962; fax: 726-0769).

Ministry of Social Affairs, Jalal Rasuna Said blok X-5 Kav 4-9, Jakarta 12950 (tel: 310-3781; fax: 310-3783).

Ministry of Trade and Industry, Jalal Jend Gatot Subroto Kav 52-53, Jakarta 12950 (tel: 525-6548; fax: 522-9592).

Ministry of Welfare, Jalal Salemba Raya 28, Jakarta 10430 (tel: 310-3781; fax: 310-3783).

Other useful addresses

Asean Secretariat, 70 A Jalan Sisingamangaraja, Jakarta 12110 (tel: 726-2991, 724-3372; fax: 724-3504, 739-8234; e-mail: asean.or.id).

Asian Development Bank, Indonesia Resident Mission, Gedung BRI II, 7th Floor, Jl. Jend Sudirman Kav. 44-46, Jakarta 10210 (tel: 251-2721; fax: 251-2749; e-mail: adbirm@mail.asiandevbank.org).

Badan Ko-ordinasi Penanaman Modal (BKPM) (Co-ordinating Board for Capital Investment), Jalan Jend Gatot Subroto 44, Jakarta Selatan (tel: 525-4981, 525-4619; fax: 525-4945).

Badan Pelaksana Bursa Komoditi (ICEB) (Indonesian Commodity Exchange Board), Bursa Building, 2nd and 4th floors, Jalan Medan Merdeka Selatan 14, Jakarta 10110 (tel: 371-921; fax: 380-4426).

Badan Pelaksana Pasar Modal (BAPEPAM) (Capital Market Operation Board), Jalan Medan Merdeka Selatan 14, Jakarta 10110 (tel: 365-509).

Business Advisory Services, Kuningan Plaza Building, Jalan Rasuna Said Kav C-11-14, Jakarta (tel: 517-7295).

Central Bureau of Statistics, Jl Dr Sutomo 18, Jakarta (tel: 372-808; internet site: http://www.bps.go.id).

Commander-in-Chief of the Armed Forces, ABRI Headquarters, Mabes ABRI Cilangkap, Jakarta Timur (tel: 384-2679, 840-1243; fax: 380-6711).

Indonesia-British Business Association, C/O Ernst & Young International, Jakarta Stock Exchange Building 23rd Floor, J1 Jenderal Sudirman, Kav 52-53, Jakarta 12190 (tel: 515-1984; fax: 515-1985).

Indonesia Science Institute, Jl Jend. Gatot Subroto No. 10, Jakarta 12710 (tel: 525-1831).

Indonesian Bank Restructuring Agency, Komplek Bank Indonesia, JL Budi Kemuliaan, building D, 10th Floor, Jakarta (fax: 231-1478).

Indonesian Embassy (USA), 2020 Massachusetts Avenue, NW, Wasahington DC 20036 (tel: (+1-202) 775-5200; fax: (+1-202) 775-5365; e-mail: indonesia@dgs.dgsys.com).

Jakarta Stock Exchange (JSE), Jalan Mendeka Selatan 14, Jakarta Pusat (internet site: http://www.jsx.co.id).

Office of the National Land Agency (BPN), Jl Sisingamangaraja 2, Jakarta Selatan (tel: 722-2420, 739-3939).

US Embassy, Medan Merdeka Selatan 5, Jakarta (tel: 344-2211; fax: 386-2259; e-mail: jakconsul@state.gov; internet site: http://www.usembassyjakarta.org).

National news agency: Antara National News Agency

Other news agencies: Indoexchange (for stock market news): www.indoexchange.com

Internet sites

IndonesiaNet Business Centre: http://www.indonesianet.com/

Iran

KEY FACTS

Official name: Jomhoori e Islami e Iran (Islamic Republic of Iran)

Head of State: President Mahmoud Ahmadinejad (since 6 Aug 2005)

Head of government: President Mahmoud Ahmadinejad

Ruling party: Conservative coalition, led by the Combatant Clergy Society (elected 7 May 2004)

Area: 1,648,195 square km

Population: 70.88 million (2007)*

Capital: Tehran

Official language: Farsi (Persian)

Currency: Rial (IR) 10 rials = 1 toman

Exchange rate: IR9,143.00 per US$ (Jul 2008)

GDP per capita: US$4,149 (2007)*

GDP real growth: 5.80% (2007)*

Labour force: 24.55 million (2004)

Unemployment: 11.20% (2005)

Inflation: 17.50% (2007)*

Oil production: 4.40 million bpd (2007)

Balance of trade: US$17.74 billion (2006)

Foreign debt: US$13.40 billion (2004)

* estimated figure

Iran in 2008 caused an international stir about its nuclear intentions by test-firing ballistic missiles in an exercise, carried out by the elite Revolutionary Guard, to demonstrate how Iran might retaliate if attacked by Israel, or even the US. It was unlikely that Israel would take any pre-emptive action against Iran without US support, but unlike the US, Israel saw Iran's nuclear ambitions as a matter of life or death and could not afford to take any chances. The relationship – or lack of one – between Iran and the US continues to be one of the watching world's major pre-occupations. One well-place US observer was quoted in late 2006 as saying: ' Iraq is the disaster we have to get rid of, and Iran is the disaster we have to avoid'. The appointment of Robert Gates, a former Central Intelligence Agency (CIA) director as Secretary of Defence, replacing Donald Rumsfeld, and the recommendations of the Iraq Study Group that the US should re-establish relations with Iran, represented an important change in the Middle East dynamic, and in Iran's position. Before the loss of its majority in Congress, the Republican administration's priorities were to destabilise the Iranian government and prevent it from developing, or acquiring a nuclear bomb. At stake was Iran's claim that it had the right to develop nuclear power. Iran first began its nuclear programme in 1974, froze it in 1979 and resumed operations in 1992. The stated intent has been since 1974 that Iran wants to build nuclear power stations, not nuclear weapons. The US, EU and the Atomic Energy Agency (IAEA) point out that, as a signatory of the Nuclear non-Proliferation Treaty (NPT), Iran is bound to open its facilities to international inspection. This inspection regime was instituted with the intent of preventing the development of nuclear arsenals by states other than the 'official' nuclear states – the US, Britain, France, China and Russia.

Politics

In parliamentary elections held on 16 March 2008, candidates with a conservative affiliation won most seats. This was mostly because the reformists had seen most of their candidates disqualified from standing; however, they still comprise 15 per cent of the new parliament, which sat for the first time on 27 May. Analysts note that the number of reformists elected will be strengthened by the number of independents, many of whom are actually reformists who ran as independents rather than be disqualified from standing in the election.

The moderate conservatives are lead by the MP for the religious city of Qom, Ali Larijarni, who had headed Iran's nuclear negotiations until sacked by President Ahmadinejad in 2007. He was elected to the influential position of parliamentary speaker and is likely to play a strong role in restraining the government. He is also said to be considering standing in the presidential elections due in 2009. If so, his position as speaker is likely to stand him in good stead in the lead up to the elections.

In August 2008, in a rare and surprising move, Iran's supreme leader, Ayatollah Ali Khamenei called upon Mr Ahmadinejad to prepare for another term as president. Without mentioning any names the Ayatollah said accused some 'bullying and brazen countries and their worthless followers (of wanting) to impose their will on the Iranian nation'. Critics have accused the president of being a foreign policy hardliner and for causing controversy abroad by calling for the destruction of Israel, and refusing to negotiate on uranium enrichment.

President Ahmadinejad adopts confrontational rhetoric on a range of international issues, particularly the international community's concern with the nature of Iran's ongoing nuclear programme. There is considerable uncertainty – in and outside Iran – as to whether Mr Ahmadinejad's stance is determined by his international inexperience, a misunderstanding of events, or the simple wish to establish Iran as an equal player on the regional, or international, stage.

Continuing growth

Iran's GDP grew by a healthy 5.8 per cent in 2007, unchanged from 2006. Iran has registered consistently high GDP growth figures since 2002 (5 per cent). High oil prices in 2006 and 2007 have helped, although the distribution of income has remained unequal. GDP per capita in dollar terms rose from US$3,197 in 2006 to US$4,149 in 2007. Iranian oil production in 2007 was 4.40 million barrels of oil per day (bpd), up from 4.34 million bpd in 2006. The increase in the price of oil contributed to the 22 per cent in exports in 2006.

Despite these higher oil revenues, Iran's high budget deficit remains a chronic problem, due in part to the country's large-scale state subsidies on foodstuffs and gasoline. In mid-2006, the Iranian government was still undecided how to handle gasoline subsidies. Iran's legislators stated their opposition to providing the additional US$3.5 billion necessary to pay for imports through the end of the fiscal year in March 2007.

Iran subsidises the price of oil products heavily, which contributes to rising domestic consumption. Iran's existing oilfields have a natural decline rate estimated at 8 per cent onshore and 10 per cent per year offshore. Currently, according to the EIA, Iran exports around 2.5 million bpd of oil, of which OECD countries import 60 per cent (or 1.6 million bpd).

Additionally, also according to the *Oil and Gas Journal*, Iran has an estimated 970 trillion cubic feet (Tcf) in proven natural gas reserves, giving it the world's second largest reserves behind Russia.

By any international standards, the Iranian economy is opaque and inefficient. Large state-owned enterprises dominate key industry sectors, and organisations controlled by charitable religious foundations also account for a large share of GDP. The private sector is generally confined to small- and medium-sized enterprises. The IMF has recommended that earlier efforts at economic reform be renewed to improve economic performance. President Ahmadinejad was elected on the promise of a return to 'revolutionary values' and improved income redistribution but has not advanced this systematically to date. Ultimately, decisions of the Supreme Leader and the Expediency Council will decide economic direction. While high oil prices in recent years have assisted economic growth the levels of inflation and unemployment remain high.

Job-seekers

Around 750,000 people each year join the labour market. Unemployment is officially around the 10 per cent mark, although unofficial sources put the figure higher at 14–15 per cent. President Ahmadinejad came to power pledging to tackle unemployment, but with a population where the under-30s constitute more than two-thirds of the total, short-term job creation has not been the solution.

Avoiding sanctions

Ever since the US named Iran as one of the original 'axis of evil' countries supposedly supporting terrorism it has attempted to impose tough sanctions through the United Nations. The January 2008 draft resolution was weaker than the US would have liked, but represented a moderate increase, and was agreed by both China and Russia. Resolution 1803 included urging governments to withdraw financial backing from firms trading with Iran, inspect

KEY INDICATORS — Iran

	Unit	2003	2004	2005	2006	2007
Population	m	66.26	67.42	68.60	69.48	*70.88
Gross domestic product (GDP)	US$bn	137.10	163.41	188.48	222.13	*294.09
GDP per capita	US$	1,853	2,473	2,748	3,197	4,149
GDP real growth	%	4.5	6.6	4.4	5.8	*5.8
Inflation	%	16.0	15.6	12.1	11.8	*17.5
Industrial output	% change	–	7.0	10.9	7.0	–
Agricultural output	% change	–	2.2	10.0	4.0	–
Oil output	'000 bpd	3,852.0	4,081.0	4,049.0	4,343.0	4,401.0
Natural gas output	bn cum	81.5	85.5	87.0	105.0	111.9
Exports (fob) (goods)	US$m	28,283.0	38,790.0	55,265.0	67,682.0	–
Imports (cif) (goods)	US$m	29,547.0	31,300.0	44,302.0	49,943.0	–
Balance of trade	US$m	-1,264.0	7,490.0	10,963.0	17,739.0	–
Current account	US$m	2,060.0	8,740.0	14,038.0	20,650.0	30,465.0
Exchange rate	per US$	8,137.00	8,545.00	9,230.00	9,230.00	9,332.00

* estimated figure

cargo going into and out of the country, and requests the International Atomic Energy Agency (IAEA) to report on whether Iran has complied with demands to suspend uranium enrichment.

In October 2007 the US had taken matters into their own hands by imposing unilateral sanctions on Bank Mellat, Bank Melli and the Sederat Bank. However, the banks have managed, after an initial setback, to circumvent the sanctions largely by establishing links with small- and medium-sized banks. Other companies have become adept at avoiding sanctions, and the 2008 push to privatise a number of state-owned companies may tempt international corporations to invest, particularly those from China, India, Russia, South Africa and Malaysia.

Privatisation

In 2008 Iran stepped up plans to privatise national industries including airlines, banking, shipping, steel and telecommunications. Three new investment banks – Amin, Novin and Pasargad – started operations in early 2008, with a remit 'to do what other investment banks all over the world do' said deputy finance minister, Heidari Kord Zangeneh, in an interview with the London *Financial Times*. Iran's economy has been dominated by the state sector and has been trying to sell off non-strategic state-companies, but has been largely unsuccessful until recently.

Risk assessment

Politics	Poor
Economy	Fair/opaque
Regional stability	Poor

COUNTRY PROFILE

Historical profile

Formerly one of the greatest empires of the ancient world, in the seventh century, Persia (renamed Iran in 1935) was one of the first countries to be occupied by Islamic armies. It has since maintained a distinct cultural identity within the Islamic world by retaining its own calendar, language and distinctive styles in arts and literature, and adhering to the Shi'a interpretation of Islam. The poet, Omar Khayam, whose poems have been translated into many languages, was born in Persia in the latter part of the eleventh century.

1907 A constitution was introduced, which limited the royal absolutism of the ruler. An Anglo-Russian agreement (annulled after the First World War) divided Iran into spheres of influence, one Soviet and the other British.

1909–13 Following the discovery of a large oil field in Masjet Soleiman, the Anglo-Persian Oil Company (APOC) was founded in 1909. A licence to search for, refine, produce and export oil, was granted to the APOC in 1913. (The APOC changed its name to the Anglo-Iranian Oil Company (AIOC) in 1935; the AIOC was a British enterprise, owned jointly by the private sector and the British government. Later, the company was renamed British Petroleum (BP)).

1921–26 A Cossack officer, Reza Khan, carried out a military coup, becoming prime minister in 1923. Parliament subsequently proclaimed him the Shah, to be called Reza Shah Pahlavi, ushering in the Pahlavi era. His eldest son, Mohammed Reza was proclaimed crown prince.

1935 Persia was renamed Iran.

1941 In the Second World War, after Reza Shah demonstrated allegiance to Germany, the British and Soviets entered Iran and removed him from power. They permitted his son, Mohammad Reza Shah Pahlavi, to succeed to the throne.

1949 The power of the Shah was increased following an attempted assassination by the Tudeh communist party, which was then banned.

1950 Mohammed Mosaddeq, a leading advocate of oil nationalisation, was installed as prime minister, following the assassination of his predecessor.

1951 Iran's Assembly approved the nationalisation of the oil industry, which was formerly controlled by Britain. As a result, Britain boycotted the purchase of Iranian oil. A contest for control of the government began between the young Shah and the nationalistic Mosaddeq.

1953–54 Mainly due to oil interests, the British persuaded the US to help the Shah remove Mosaddeq. Large sectors of Iranian public opinion condemned the US and Britain for this coup and Mosaddeq became a folk hero of Iranian nationalism. Drilling concessions were granted to eight foreign oil companies.

1963 The Shah assumed complete control of the government and launched a programme of land reform and social and economic modernisation. He used the Secret Police (SAVAK) to control opposition to his reforms.

1978 Following several years of growing opposition to the Shah's rule, martial law was imposed.

1979 The Shah was overthrown by forces loyal to the exiled religious leader, Ayatollah Khomeini, who became Valy e Faqih (supreme spiritual leader) of Iran. The Shah and his family were forced into exile in Egypt. The Islamic Republic of Iran was proclaimed following a referendum. Fifty-two staff members at the US Embassy in Tehran were taken hostage by Islamic militants, who demanded the extradition of the Shah from the US, where he was having medical treatment.

1980 Abolhassan Beni Sadr was elected president. The former shah died of cancer.

1980–88 The Iran-Iraq War broke out after Iraq invaded Iran over disputed border areas.

1981 The US Embassy hostages in Tehran were released.

1989 After Ayatollah Khomeini's death, Ali Akbar Hashemi Rafsanjani was sworn in as president, a post which had previously been largely ceremonial, and Khomeini's position as Supreme Leader was taken by the former president, Ayatollah Ali Khamenei.

1990 A peace agreement with Iraq was signed.

1995 Oil and trade sanctions were imposed by the US, which alleged that Iran had sponsored terrorist groups throughout the region, had sought to acquire nuclear arms and destabilise the Middle East peace process.

1996 In the general election, the Combatant Clergy Society (CCS) retained its position as the largest single group.

1997 Many people were surprised when Mohammad Khatami, a moderate cleric, was elected president.

2000 Elections to an expanded Majlis returned a majority for reformist candidates. Ayatollah Ali Khamenei halted a bill that would have revived Iran's banned reformist newspapers. In December, the Oil Stabilisation Fund (OSF) was established, to use money accumulated when oil prices rise above a set level, to level out fluctuations in prices and to promote the private sector.

2001 President Khatami was re-elected for a second term. Saudi Arabia and Iran signed a security accord to combat terrorism, drug trafficking and organised crime.

2002 Iran released nearly 700 Iraqi prisoners held since the 1980–88 war. President Bush included North Korea with Iran and Iraq in an 'axis of evil' due to their supposed development of Weapons of Mass Destruction (WMD). Iran began construction of its first nuclear reactor.

2003 Student-led protests were held in Tehran against the clerical establishment. Parliament passed a bill guaranteeing free parliamentary elections. Iran came under pressure from the International Atomic Energy Agency (IAEA) over its nuclear energy programme. Subsequent IAEA inspections concluded there was no evidence of a weapons programme. A major earthquake hit the city of Bam in the south-east, killing 40,000 people and leaving the city in ruins.

2004 Over a third of parliament resigned in February after the Council of

Guardians upheld the disqualification of more than 2,000 prospective reformist candidates hoping to stand in the elections. Iran failed to fully co-operate with an IAEA enquiry into its nuclear activities. Run-off parliamentary elections were won by the conservatives. As part of a deal with the EU, Iran agreed to suspend most of its uranium enrichment programme.
2005 Three villages were destroyed and 40 badly damaged when an earthquake struck central Iran. Mahmoud Ahmadinejad was elected president. He caused international concern when he suggested that Israel should be wiped off the map. A new natural gas pipeline between Iran and Azerbaijan was begun.
2006 The UN Security Council voted to impose sanctions over Iran's refusal to stop uranium enrichment.
2007 Bank Sepah was blacklisted by the US. The state-owned bank was accused of being the 'financial lynchpin' in Iran's efforts to procure material for its missile programme. A US intelligence report said Iran had stopped work on a nuclear weapon in 2003 due to international opposition and that it would not be likely to produce enriched uranium before 2010–15. The report did not reflect a 2005 US intelligence report that claimed Iran was 'determined to develop nuclear weapons'.
2008 President Ahmadinejad visited Iraq on 2 March, the first visit by a president since the Iran/Iraq war in the 1980s. In parliamentary elections held on 16 March, candidates with a conservative affiliation won most seats. Iran test fired nine missiles on 9 July, including Shahab 3, which, with a range of over 2,000 kilometres, could reach Israel. On 10 July French oil company, Total, announced it would not be investing in Iran because it was too risky. The company had been considering an investment in developing gas fields in the south of the country.

Political structure

Constitution

Iran became an Islamic Republic in April 1979, having previously been a monarchy under the Shah. The constitution of the Islamic Republic was formally adopted in December 1979. The constitution also provides for representation in the Majlis Shura-e-Islami (Islamic Consultative Assembly) of non-Islamic minorities, Zoroastrians, Jews and Christians. However, power is wielded mainly by the Shi'a clergy.

Form of state

Islamic republic

The executive

The Wali Faqih (Supreme Leader of the Islamic Revolution) retains overall control of all branches of government, including the judiciary and the revolutionary guard. He declares war and peace and can veto presidential nominations. His role combines spiritual leader, theological protector and supreme authority. The structure of the constitution is effectively split between the president, who is elected every four years, and the Supreme Leader, who has overall control. The Supreme Leader, in his role as theological protector, appoints the Council for the Protection of the Constitution. All legislation adopted by the Majlis Shura-e-Islami is scrutinised by the council to ensure that it is in keeping with Islamic principles and laws. The council consists of six religious lawyers.
The Council of Guardians, composed of 12 jurists and clerics, has supervisory powers over elections and a right of veto over all legislation if it does not conform with Islamic law and the constitution. It is independent of the Supreme Leader.
In 1986, the Expediency Council was established to mediate between the Majlis and the Council of Guardians. It is designed to resolve political decisions which cannot be solved through the main channels, but it is controlled by the spiritual leader.
A further adjunct to the Supreme Leader's power is the Assembly of Experts which consists of 83 clerics who elect the next Supreme Leader, interpret the constitution and approve Majlis decisions. The cumulative effect of this plethora of legislative institutions is that despite the enhancement of the president's power, following reform in 1989, he remains tightly constrained by these institutional checks and balances.

National legislature

The 290-member Majlis Shura-e-Islami is elected every four years. Although MPs are technically independent, the Majlis is now very loosely divided along party political lines between the conservative clergy groupings and the reformist May 23 Front, named after the day of President Khatami's victory in 1997. The Majlis is elected by universal suffrage, with a voting age of 15.

Legal system

The judiciary is organised independently of the other branches of government. There are two types of courts: public and special. The Penal Courts, Special Civil Court and Islamic Revolution Courts adjudicate on the basis of Islamic laws, fixed since 1979 for a wide range of crimes.

Last elections

17/24 June 2005 (presidential); 16 March 2008 (parliamentary).

Results: Presidential: Mahmoud Ahmadinejad won 61.7 per cent of the vote in the second round; Akbar Hashemi Rafsanjani won 35.9 per cent. Turnout was 59.6 per cent.
Parliamentary: candidates with a conservative affiliation won most seats.

Next elections

2012 (parliamentary); 2009 (presidential).

Political parties

Ruling party

Conservative coalition, led by the Combatant Clergy Society (elected 7 May 2004)

Main opposition party

May 23 Front, of which the largest grouping is the Mosharekat (Participation) Front

Population

70.88 million (2007)*

Last census: October 1996: 60,055,488

Population density: 65 per cent (1995–2001).

Annual growth rate: 1.2 per cent 1994–2004 (WHO 2006)

Ethnic make-up

The population is predominantly Persian (55 per cent), with the second largest group being Azeris, concentrated in the north-west. There are also Afghans (approximately two million Afghan refugees were repatriated by the UN refugee organisation in 2002), Kurds, Baluchis, Lurs, Turkmen, Arabs and nomads.

Religions

Islam of the Twelver Shi'a sect is dominant. A Sunni Muslim minority is concentrated in fringe areas of Iran. There are also small Baha'i, Christian, Jewish and Zoroastran communities.

Education

Government expenditure on education was 37.2 per cent of the annual budget in 1999/2000, with 7.4 per cent for higher education and 4.0 per cent for research. Education is compulsory for eight years from the ages of six. This is not fully effective in rural areas. Primary education is free and lasts for five years. Secondary education begins at 11 years and lasts for up to seven years, with a first course of three years and a second course of four years.
Secondary education is split between intermediate (or 'guidance') schools and secondary schools. There are also technical, business and other specialised vocational schools.
Iran has 116 higher education institutes, 23 of which are full universities. Enrolment in the universities accounts for 68 per cent of Iran's 123,000 students, with the remainder enrolled in other institutes of higher education. Secondary education (Reform system) covers three years and a one-year pre-university programme.
Higher education is provided by comprehensive universities, specialised universities, universities of technology, medical universities, teacher training centres and private institutions. The Islamic Open

University was established in 1981. It has around 100,000 students in 70 Iranian cities and towns. In addition, there are 131 teacher-training colleges, 107 teacher colleges for rural areas, 10 colleges for technical and vocational teachers, and 19 institutes of technology.
Education became a state monopoly following the 1979 Revolution, but a law passed in 1987 provided for the creation of private schools under certain conditions. To keep pace with population growth, 10,000 new university educated teachers are required each year.
Literacy rate: 78.1 per cent total; 71.4 per cent female, adult rates in 2002 (World Bank).
Compulsory years: 6 to 14.
Enrolment rate: 98 per cent total primary enrolment of relevant age group; 77 per cent total secondary enrolment (World Bank).
Pupils per teacher: 30 in primary schools.

Health

Per capita total expenditure on health (2003) was US$498; of which per capita government spending was US$235, at the international dollar rate, (WHO 2006).
The combined ministry of hygiene, medical care and education is the authority responsible for health and medical care, controlling all related offices and organisations in the private sector as well as those directly funded by the state. The Social Security Organisation (SSO) offers health insurance and runs 60 hospitals, 260 clinics and 30 medical record registration offices in the country.
Iran has adequate healthcare facilities in the cities, although it is generally insufficient in rural areas. The government has, however, created a large number of health clinics in small towns, as well as in villages, to serve the population of the surrounding area. The ministry has undertaken a national hygiene campaign by setting up 'hygiene houses' in many villages and towns. In 2000, only 80 per cent of Iranians had access to health services.
Drug abuse is a serious problem in Iran, due to imports of cheap heroin and opium from Afghanistan, and there are an estimated two million drug addicts.

HIV/Aids

Intravenous drug users in Iranian prisons accounted for 65 per cent of HIV infections in the country. A programme has been implemented, by non-governmental agencies, working to reduce the harm of HIV/Aids among this group.
Rates of HIV/Aids infection among tuberculosis patients also rose and reached 4.2 per cent by mid-2001 (UNAID/WHO).
HIV prevalence: 0.1 per cent aged 15–49 in 2003 (World Bank)
Life expectancy: 70 years, 2004 (WHO 2006)
Fertility rate/Maternal mortality rate: 2.1 births per woman, 2004 (WHO 2006); maternal mortality 37 deaths per 100,000 live births (World Bank).
Child (under 5 years) mortality rate (per 1,000): 33 per 1,000 live births; 11 per cent of children aged under five are malnourished (World Bank).
Head of population per physician: 0.45 physicians per 1,000 people, 2004 (WHO 2006)

Welfare

A large number of organisations, usually autonomous, are responsible for social welfare. Various foundations manage sequestered property worth billions of US dollars. They are responsible for the care of families of men killed in the war with Iraq, for war refugees and for rural development. At the local level in the cities and towns, mosque committees (komitehs) have funds, which are made available for poorer families. The country's rationing system, that includes giving coupons for limited quantities of staple foods and other items at heavily subsidised prices, is also run through mosques.
Iran's Social Security Organisation (SSO) provides a list of services, including survivor's pension, subsidies to large families, retirement, unemployment and disability benefits.
The social security scheme covers some 260,000 factories, workshops and offices.
The Foundation for the Refugees of the Imposed War operates under the authority of Iran's ministry of labour and social affairs. It is responsible for the welfare of over two million of the country's internal refugees, or displaced persons, from the Iran-Iraq war.

Main cities

Tehran (capital, estimated population 7.5 million (m) in 2005), Mashhad (2.3m), Esfahan (1.5m), Tabriz (1.2m), Shiraz (1.2m), Karaj (2.5m), Ahvaz (1.0m).

Media

The government maintains strict control of the media and imposes censorship, particularly of material with Western influence and any divergence from religious regulations. In 2007 the US-based human right's watchdog, Freedom House, rated Iran as 'not free', with one of the lowest scores worldwide, as all publications must be licensed and can be subject to closure, with criminal penalties for journalists for reporting 'propaganda against the state' and the intimidation of publishers, editors and journalist has included detaining, fines and in some cases torture.
National news agency: IRNA (Islamic Republic News Agency): www2.irna.ir
Other news agencies: IRIB: www.irib.ir
Iranian Students News Agency (ISNA): http://isna.ir
Press TV: www.presstv.com

Press

There are a large number of daily and weekly newspapers, which had a wide range of political stances; however since 2006 the government began a crack down on reformist publications. Newspapers are challenged by a falling readership, the small advertising market and the shortage of imported and locally produced paper.
Dailies: In Farsi, the main conservative newspapers include Kayhan (www.kayhannews.ir) the oldest and run by the office of the supreme leader, Resalat (www.resalat-news.com), favours a market economy, and Jomhouri Eslami (www.jomhourieslami.com), is linked to Ayatollah Ali Khamene'i with radical views on foreign policies. Jaam e Jam (www.jamejamonline.ir), has the largest circulation and is published by IRIB. Reformist newspapers include Etemaad (www.etemaad.com) and Aftab e Yazd (www.aftab-yazd.com). In English, Iran News (www.irannewsdaily.com), the Tehran Times (www.tehrantimes.com), is government-run, Iran Daily (www.iran-daily.com), is published by IRNA.
Weeklies: Magazines tend to be special interest publications. In Farsi, the Chelcheragh (www.40cheragh.org) is a social magazine and Gozaresh (www.gozaresh.com), covers computers and technology.
Periodicals: The quarterly Azari Majedi (www.azarmajedi.com) in Farsi, English and French, for articles on culture, the monthly Donya e Bazi (www.dbazi.com) covers computer games.

Broadcasting

The national public broadcaster is the Islamic Republic of Iran Broadcaster (IRIB) (www.irib.ir).
Radio: The state-run IRIB (www.irib.ir) has eight national networks with provincial services and an external service that broadcasts in 27 languages.
Television: Around 80 per cent of the population watch TV, with the youth TV having the largest audience. The state-run IRIB (www.irib.ir) has four national networks with provincial services, plus an international channel and three satellite channels. IRIB also has a motion picture production company, Sima Film. In 2007, an alternative, state-run TV network, Press TV (www.presstv.com), based in Tehran, with 24-hour news was introduced.

Economy
There are serious concerns about the sustainability of Iran's economic growth because of its high dependence on oil exports and their internationally governed prices. The economy is protected by high external tariffs, price controls, subsidies and a banking system which lacks liquidity. There are also concerns at the government's apparent willingness to print money to finance state-owned industries' deficits.
Politically-run state conglomerates, bonyads, dominate the economy, particularly the non-oil sector. They are allocated two-thirds of the budget each year and own or control all the country's transport, oil, petrochemical and mining companies. Despite this, the private sector remains surprisingly resilient. Many new private sector companies have been formed since the revolution. The government hopes that Iranian expatriates will form the spearhead of 'foreign' private-sector investment in the development of manufacturing capacity. The government also hopes to increase Iran's industrial competitiveness and exports by encouraging privatisation.
Since the steep rise in oil prices in 2005, Iran's economy has been enhanced by oil revenue by some US$36.8 billion in 2005, and with an estimated US$48.8 billion in 2006. The economy as a whole registered 5.4 per cent GDP growth in 2005 and an estimated 6.0 per cent in 2006. The service sector accounted for 46 per cent of GDP, while industry supplied 44 per cent, of with manufacturing was 10 per cent; agriculture accounted for 10 per cent in 2005 and all sectors grew by around 10 per cent.
Iran has to find employment for around 750,000 new workers each year, which puts a strain on an economy that is heavily skewed by its oil sector and has high rates of inflation – 13.0 per cent in 2005 and 10.2 per cent in 2006. The private sector does not act in a free market, there are extensive price controls and rates of return and large state subsidies for energy products. Among the noteworthy export products that do not belong to the petrochemical industry, are pistachio nuts (14.5 million tonnes exported in 2005), highly prized carpets, and motor vehicles. Iran has the largest vehicle assembly plant in the Middle East and is planning to expand its exports to Venezuela, India, China and Belarus.
The government has begun to address some of its macroeconomic problems, by reassessing priorities to reduce social and regional disparities with sustained growth and jobs creation. However, in the short term the price of basic foodstuffs have risen, as well as imported refined oil. A new value added tax (VAT) is proposed for mid-2007/08.
In December 2006, the government announced that it would no longer trade its oil for US dollars but instead shift its foreign currency reserves to the euro. This has been in response to US pressure on the Iranian economy due to its nuclear development plans. Foreign-held assets in dollars have been steadily moved out of dollars since 2003. The government has also requested its business community to open letters of credit in euros. As a measure of popular sentiment concerning the growing rift between Iran and the world community, and the general rate of inflation, the sale of gold coins has increased; their value jumped by 32 per cent alone between February–April 2006.

External trade
Iran belongs to the Economic Co-operation Organisation (ECO), with seven nations of Central Asia with Turkey and Pakistan. The ECO has plans to create a free trade zone. Iran also has bilateral trade agreements with, among others, Venezuela, Cuba, Iraq and South Africa.
Oil accounts for around 60 per cent of GDP and 80 per cent of export revenues. Shortages of foreign currency have produced a boom in counter (barter) trade, which obscures the extent of foreign trade.

Imports
Main imports include industrial raw materials (iron and steel) and intermediate goods, electrical and electronic equipment, foodstuffs and other consumer goods, technical services and military supplies.
Main sources: China (6.0 per cent total, 2006), France (5.4 per cent), India (3.7 per cent).

Exports
Crude oil, petroleum products; non-oil items, include iron and steel, organic chemicals, carpets, pistachio nuts, dates and caviar.
Main destinations: Japan (23.9 per cent total, 2006), Italy (10.7 per cent), France (6.9 per cent).

Agriculture
Since the 1979 revolution, land ownership has been in dispute. Meanwhile, people have moved from the countryside to the city. This has left a shortage of agricultural labour, despite high unemployment in the economy as a whole. On many farms, particularly those in the private sector near Tehran, immigrant Afghan workers have replaced Iranians.
Since it was set up in the 1980s, the Bonyad-e Mostazafin (Foundation for the Oppressed and Deprived) has brought new facilities, especially water, electricity and roads, to thousands of rural villages. Government efforts to stimulate sluggish private investment in agriculture have made little headway. As half of Iran's farmers belong to 3,000 rural co-operatives, grouped into 180 unions and benefiting from cheap credit made available by the state, they are reluctant to embrace private sector competition.
The government wants to reduce the import bill for food and agricultural inputs. Iran imports large quantities of meat, rice, vegetables, oil, sugar and tea, as well as cattle fodder, fertilisers, machinery and tractors. It is encouraging the expansion of cotton and sugar cane plantations, livestock production and downstream processing industries for these products.
The crop production for 2005 included: 22,410,000 tonnes (t) cereals in total, 14,500,000t wheat, 4,200,000t potatoes, 2,900,000t barley, 3,500,000t rice, 6,500,000t sugar cane, 4,850,000t sugar beets, 1,500,000t maize, cassava, 450,000t seed cotton, 120,000t cotton lint, 695,000t pulses, 434,000t treenuts, 3,825,000t citrus fruit, 190,000t pistachios, 2,800,000t grapes, 4,200,000t tomatoes, 105,000t chillies & peppers, 83,960t oilcrops, 21,000t tobacco, 41,000t olives, 52,000t tea, 2,400,000t apples, 880,000t dates, 90,000t figs, 13,143,110t fruit in total, 13,495,000t vegetables in total. Livestock production included: 1,685,620t meat in total, 320,000t beef, 12,320t buffalo meat, 388,880t lamb, 105,000t goat meat, 844,740t poultry, 610,000t eggs, 5,980,000t milk, 36,000t honey, 42,300t cattle hides, 64,800t sheepskins, 75,000t greasy wool, 6,000t cocoons, silk.

Fishing
There are few river systems in Iran, and most freshwater fishing is for subsistence purposes. There is commercial fishing on the Persian Gulf and the Caspian Sea. Iran produces around 444,000 tonnes of seafood per year. Main species are sturgeon, tuna, mackerel, shrimps, lobsters and crayfish. Iran produces around 90 per cent of the world's caviar. Fish farming is an increasingly important activity. In 2004, the total marine fish catch was 306,937 tonnes and the total crustacean catch was 6,636 tonnes.

Forestry
There is some forestation in the north of the country, near the Caspian Sea, but limited commercial exploitation is generally for domestic purposes only.
Forest product exports in 2004 were US$9.4 million, while imports amounted to US$634.5 million.
Production in 2004 included 820,000 cubic metres (cum) roundwood, 743,000cum industrial roundwood, 68,000cum sawnwood, 274,000cum sawlogs & veneer logs, 240,000cum

pulpwood, 665,000cum wood-based panels, 77,000cum wood fuel; 3,000 tonnes (t) charcoal, 415,000t paper and paperboard, including 50,000t newsprint, 70,000t printing and writing paper, 290,000t paper pulp, 80,000t recovered paper.

Industry and manufacturing

The government's goal in the past has been to build up basic industries as a means of import substitution and to develop a broad industrial base to reduce reliance on oil. The government has also given priority to the development of downstream industries in the oil and gas sectors and to the development of mining and metals processing.

Tehran and Isfahan are the main industrial centres. The largest industrial conglomerate is the National Iranian Industries Organisation (NIIO), a state-owned group which is directly responsible for 90 companies in manufacturing, engineering and trading. The NIIO companies are in nine industrial groups: textiles and leather, chemicals, pharmaceuticals, food, electrical goods, construction and cellulose. Industry accounted for 41 per ecnt of GDP in 2004.

Tourism

Iran's potential as a major tourist destination has been impeded by inadequate accommodation standards and travel restrictions, as well as a generally poor image abroad. Nevertheless, visitor numbers have grown in recent years. The authorities recognise the value of tourism and in 2004 announced a long-term programme to develop the sector, while reducing state involvement. An integrated tourism body was created in May 2004. Obstacles to visitors are being eased and pricing differentials eliminated. Tourism is expected to contribute 3.6 per cent to GDP in 2005.

Environment

In January 2008, for the first time in living memory temperatures snow fell in the country's southern deserts, as temperatures dropped to a low of -24 degrees Celsius.

Mining

Iran is one of the world's 15 major mineral-rich countries and the mining sector employs directly over 107,000 workers. Production has a market value of over US$4 billion. The government is trying to encourage private investment in mineral exploration and production.

The majority of the large-scale mines and major industries, including steelworks, copper, lead and zinc, are partially or totally state-owned. The government has sought to develop the country's abundant mineral resources as an alternative to oil- and gas-based industrial development. However, as in other sectors, expansion of mineral production has suffered from shortages of foreign currency for machinery and spare parts, power cuts, and the lack of mining experts. Consequently, Iran is still obliged to import many raw materials, which it could produce from its own resources, given appropriate investment and manpower skills.

The Iranian government has strongly encouraged foreign investment on 'buy-back' terms that enables foreign investors to recoup capital through receipt of the project's output. Substantial improvement is targetted for the non-ferrous metals sector including aluminium, copper and zinc. Iran has 60 lead and zinc mines, 30 coal mines, 20 copper mines and 40 deposits of chromite, fluorene and sulphur. It also has an important industrial mineral sector, and is the third largest producer of gypsum in the world.

Hydrocarbons

The ministry of oil is responsible for state companies which control the oil, gas and petrochemicals sectors. They are the National Iranian Oil Company (NIOC), the National Iranian Gas Company (NIGC) and the National Petrochemical Company (NPC). Iran's total oil reserves were estimated at 132.5 billion barrels in 2004, 11.1 per cent of the world's total. At current rates of production, Iran's oil reserves should last until at least the middle of the 21st century and there are hopes of finding new oil fields in Iranian territorial waters in the Caspian Sea; Iran's Caspian oil reserves could amount to around 15 billion barrels, although this is dependent on an agreement on boundaries by the littoral states. The government hopes to attract foreign investment in order to raise production capacity to 5.6 million bpd by 2010 and 7.3 million bpd by 2020.

Iran's Opec quota was 3.96 million bpd in 2005. Iran exports 2.5 million bpd, around half of which goes to Asia, with the rest destined for Europe and Africa.The constitution prohibits granting oil licences on a concessionary basis or in the form of a direct equity stake. International oil companies are involved in developing Iran's oil fields on a buyback basis. This entails the contractor funding all investments in an oil field in return for an allocated production share from the state-owned NIOC. The operation of the oil field is transferred to the NIOC once the contract is completed.

In the downstream sector, petrochemicals are being developed as part of the government's strategy to add value to hydrocarbon exports. Iran is the second largest petrochemical producer in the region, after Saudi Arabia, with output of 20 million tonnes in 2005, expected to rise to 27 million tonnes by 2007. Iran is encouraging foreign investment into the petrochemical industry.

Proven gas reserves were 27.5 trillion cubic metres in 2003, with production at 85.5 billion cubic metres. Natural gas accounts for around 50 per cent of Iran's total energy consumption. The government is keen to expand export markets, particularly in Asia. The massive South Pars gas field, which is shared with Qatar, is being developed in 25 stages over 25 years.

Iran produces around one million tonnes per year (tpy) of coal and consumes approximately 1.6 million tpy.

Iran's first mechanised underground coal mine is at Tabas. It produces around 1.5 million tonnes of coking coal for steel production each year.

Energy

Iran has an electricity generating capacity of 31GW, over 90 per cent of which is produced by thermal power stations and the remainder by hydroelectricity. Iran's demand is growing rapidly at around 7.5 per cent per annum and this will require a doubling of electricity generating capacity by 2012. The government has set up a number of build-operate-transfer (BOT) contracts to generate foreign investment in the electricity sector. However, it appears unwilling to break up or privatise the state-controlled Tavanir organisation, which operates as a monopoly in the power sector.

In 1998, the Russian government announced that it would honour a contract worth US$780 million to build two nuclear reactors near the Iranian port of Bushehr. Ukraine had previously pulled out after US pressure. In 2001, Russia agreed to help develop Iran's nuclear generating capacity, particularly the continuing development of the first Bushehr reactor. The US has raised strong objections over the development of nuclear power in Iran, claiming that it will be used for military purposes and the construction of nuclear warheads. The Iranian government insists the Bushehr reactors are for domestic energy consumption and has stood by the terms of the Nuclear Non-Proliferation Treaty, of which Iran is a signatory.

Financial markets

Stock exchange

The Tehran Stock Exchange (TSE) was established in 1968.

Banking and insurance

Before the revolution, Iran's banking system was handicapped by the small number of banks, by heavy indebtedness (both to the central bank and to foreign creditors) and by the high levels of

non-performing assets, a legacy of the virtual absence of regulatory controls under the Shah's regime. After the reorganisation in 1979, the sector's weakness was further aggravated by economic recession, the freezing of Iranian assets held abroad and the long war with Iraq.
The government recognises that the state-owned banking system is unable to provide sufficient credit for economic growth. Non-banking credit institutions (NBCIs) will legally do what bazaaris have been doing for two decades. Foreign banks, a number of which have a representative office in Tehran, became more active as oil exports revived and financing became available for the reconstruction programme. Reconstruction requires imported goods and services. French banks are keen to regain the dominance they enjoyed in foreign trade financing in Iran before 1983, when France's supply of weapons to Iraq caused a breakdown in relations between France and Iran. Several French banks are on the approved list of the National Iranian Oil Company (NIOC). The most active are Banque Paribas, Société Générale and Banque Nationale de Paris.
As part of the 2000—04 economic development programme, the banking sector is being opened up to foreign participation and in 2002, Bank Markazi (the central bank) agreed to license the first fully foreign-owned banks since the 1979 revolution.
Bank Sepah was blacklisted by the US. The state-owned bank was accused of being the 'financial lynchpin' in Iran's efforts to procure material for its missile programme.

Central bank

Bank Markazi Jomhouri Islami Iran

Main financial centre

Tehran

Time

GMT plus 3.5 hours

Geography

Iran is a large and varied country. Much of it is desert wilderness, with mountainous regions along the western borders with Iraq and in the north with Turkey. Around 11 per cent of Iran is forested, notably in the northern regions of the Caspian Sea and Zagros mountains.
By the early part of the twentieth century, the majority of the population were villagers living in fertile fringes of Iran's great central plateau, which is made up of vast sand and salt deserts. However, rapid urbanisation, especially the growth of the capital Tehran, has changed the distribution of the population and the activities in which it is engaged.
Water is scarce in most of Iran and its availability dictates the density of the population in settled areas. There are very few towns of any size in central and eastern Iran, although there are lush oases scattered across the sand and salt deserts. There is a traditional system of subterranean water channels, cut from the water tables in mountains for irrigation.

Hemisphere

Northern

Climate

The climate for most of the country is dry and hot in summer before abruptly changing to a bitterly cold winter. The best season for visiting is around the Persian New Year (Nowruz). Temperatures range from 51 degrees Celsius (C) in summer at the head of the Gulf to minus 14 degrees C in winter in the interior. The mean temperatures are 3 degrees C in January and 29 degrees C in July. The Gulf area becomes very hot and humid in summer.

Dress codes

Since the 1979 Islamic Revolution, ties are shunned by Iranians but suits are acceptable. Informal dress is acceptable for men (not shorts). Women should always dress discreetly in public and avoid make-up.
Iranian women are required to cover all their hair and to disguise the shape of their bodies by wearing long, loose fitting clothes. Men can be stopped for having inappropriate hairstyles. Punishment can take the form of imprisonment, lashes or fines.

Entry requirements

Passports

Required by all, valid for six months beyond period of visit.

Visa

Visas are required by all, except nationals of Turkey and some other countries subject to change, and are valid for 30 days. Business visas must have an invitation letter from a local, sponsoring company, to be submitted to the foreign ministry in Tehran for approval. When authorised, the host company can obtain a reference number which is forwarded to the applicant. After one week, the visitor should contact the consulate quoting the reference number, and confirm the approval. Once confirmed, the application and documents can be submitted to the consular section for further action.

Prohibited entry

Israeli citizens or anyone with Israeli stamps in their passport will be rejected.

Currency advice/regulations

Import and export of local currency is limited to IR200,000. No restrictions on the import of foreign currency, but over US$1,000 must be declared on arrival; export is limited up to amount declared. Currency should be exchanged by authorised banks and exchange dealers and the receipts presented on departure.

Customs

The export of all antiques (over 50 years old) is prohibited, including gems, coins, handwritten manuscripts and other artifacts.

Prohibited imports

The import of all alcohol, firearms and ammunitions, video tapes and obscene publications.

Health (for visitors)

Mandatory precautions

A yellow fever certificate is required if travelling from an infected area. An AIDS certificate is required if staying more than three months.

Advisable precautions

Cholera is a high risk and precautions are required. Typhoid, dysentery and typhoid fever are common.

Hotels

The situation and status of hotels should be carefully checked. The use of the name of an international management chain does not imply a current connection with the chain, but may indicate only a previous link or the usual name by which the hotel is known. Most hotels are utilitarian. Evening entertainment is very rare.

Credit cards

Mastercard and visa are accepted in major locations.

Public holidays (national)

Fixed dates

11 Feb (Victory of Islamic Revolution, 1979), 20 Mar (Oil Nationalisation Day), 1 Apr (Islamic Republic Day), 2 Apr (Public Outing Day), 4 Jun (Death of Imam Khomeini), 5 Jun (Anniversary of Uprising against the Shah).

Variable dates

Nowruz (Persian New Year), Martyrdom of Imam Hassan Mojtaba, Martyrdom of Imam Reza, Martyrdom of Hazrat Fatemeh, Birthday of Imam Ali, Prophet Mohammad received his calling, Birthday of Imam Mahdi (12th Imam), Martyrdom of Imam Ali, Eid al Fitr, Martyrdom of Imam Sadegh, Eid e Ghorban (Eid al Ahda), Eid e Ghadir Khom, Tassoua, Ashura, Arbeen, Demise of Prophet Mohammad, Martyrdom of Imam Reza.
Iran uses the solar Persian calendar, which differs from the Gregorian calendar: there are 31 days in each of the first six months of the Persian calendar, 30 days in each of the next five months and 29 days in the last month, except in leap year when it has 30 days.
The Persian calendar dates from the Arab/Muslim invasion and the introduction of Islam into the country. The calendar (known as the Hejrieh Shamsi) is very precise; it was devised by the renowned

Persian mathematician, Omar Khayyam. The months are: Farvardin, Ordibehesht, Khordad, Tir, Mordad, Shahrivar, Mehr, Aban, Azar, Day, Bahman, Esfand. The Iranian calendar year was briefly changed in commemoration of the 2,500th anniversary of the Persian Empire in 1971. The year was changed from 1350 Hejrieh Shamsi to 2530 Melli (national). This calendar was unpopular and the nation reverted to the old calendar soon afterwards.

Persian year 1385: 21 March 2006 to 20 March 2007 (year 1386: 21 March 2007 to 22 March 2008).

Working hours

Friday is the Muslim day of religious observance (weekly holiday).

Banking

Sat–Wed: 0800–1700; Thu: 0800–1200; closed on Friday.

Business

Sat–Wed: 0700/0800–1300, 1600–1900. Closed on Thursday and Friday.

Government

Sat–Wed: 0700/0800–1300, 1600–1900. Closed on Thursday and Friday.

Shops

Sat–Wed: 0800–2000; Thu: 0800–1200; most bakeries and some food shops stay open on Fridays while the rest close.

Electricity supply

230V AC, 50 cycles

Weights and measures

Metric system

Social customs/useful tips

Visitors for business engagements are expected to arrive on time for appointments. However, it is by no means uncommon to be kept waiting, or even for appointments to be cancelled without notice.

The Gulf is never called Arabian, but is usually identified as Persian.

Normal Muslim customs prevail within most areas of the country. Alcohol is forbidden, although tolerance is shown to non-Muslims who may drink it at home.

Women must sit at the back of buses.

Men and women who are not married must not touch, therefore a business deal with a woman may not be sealed with a handshake.

Business negotiations can take a long time. A good lawyer and a detailed contract are essential.

Prostitution, casual sex and especially homosexual sex, are punishable with death or long prison sentences. Foreign visitors are not exempt from these laws.

Security

There is little violent street crime in Tehran, but visitors should take great care of their wallets and bags. Keep passports separate from other valuables.

Getting there

Air

National airline: IranAir

International airport/s: Mehrabad (THR), 5km west of Tehran, with duty-free shop, restaurant, bank, post office, shops; Shiraz (SYZ), 15km from city, with currency exchange, post office, shops.

Airport tax: Departure tax: IR70,000.

Surface

Road: There are roads from Iraq, Turkey, Armenia, Afghanistan and Pakistan, although these routes are not always passable.

Rail: There is a link with Turkey and Syria. A rail route runs nearly 300km from Mashhad into Turkmenistan, crossing the border at Sarakhs to join the Soviet-era Turksib railway at Tedzhen.

Water: Ferries run between Iran and United Arab Emirates, Manama (Bahrain) and Kuwait City.

Main port/s: The large ports on the Gulf include the country's main oil terminal at Kharg Island, the largest port Khorramshahr, Bandar Shahid Rajai, Bushehr, Bandar Khomeini and Chah Bahar. The main ports on the Caspian Sea are Bandar Anzali and Bandar Nowshahr.

Getting about

National transport

Air: IranAir and Aseman Airlines run frequent services between most cities and Tehran.

Road: Surfaced roads serve main centres; condition of secondary roads may vary.

Buses: There is an extensive, comfortable and cheap bus network that runs throughout the country. Scheduled long-distance coach services vary in their routes, but usually travel between all the main towns.

Rail: Rail services on the 5,500km network may vary, but there are usually various classes of service, with sleeping accommodation, air-conditioning and restaurant services available.

City transport

Taxis: Taxis are not metered and frequently shared. Those hired by telephone or by hotels are more expensive. Tipping is not expected.

Car hire

An international driving licence (along with two photographs) is required.

BUSINESS DIRECTORY

The addresses listed below are a selection only. While World of Information makes every endeavour to check these addresses, we cannot guarantee that changes have not been made, especially to telephone numbers and area codes. We would welcome any corrections.

Telephone area codes

The international direct dialling (IDD) code for Iran is +98, followed by area code and subscriber's number:

Abadan	631	Isfahan	311
Ahvaz	611	Kerman	342
Arak	262	Mashad	511
Babol	111	Shiraz	711
Bakhtaran	431	Tabriz	411
Hamadán	811	Tehran	21

Useful telephone numbers

Ambulance: 123

Fire: 125

General emergencies: 123

Police: 110

Traffic accidents: 197

Chambers of Commerce

Iran Chamber of Commerce, Industries & Mines, 254 Taleghani Avenue, Tehran 15814 (tel:8884-6031; fax: 8882-5111; e-mail: info@iccm.org).

Irano-British Chamber of Commerce, Industries and Mines, 254 Taleghani Avenue, Tehran 15814 (tel 8881-0525; fax: 8881-0526; e-mail: info@ibchamber.org).

Shiraz Chamber of Commerce, Industries and Mines, Zand Street, Shiraz 71356-53564 (tel: 2230-4415; fax: 2233-1220; e-mail: info@sccim.com).

Tehran Chamber of Commerce, Industries and Mines, 254 Taleghani Avenue, Tehran 15814 (tel: 8884-6031; fax: 882-5111; e-mail: info@tccim.com).

Banking

Bank Maskan, Ferdowsi Avenue, PO Box 11365-3499, Tehran (tel: 6670-9658; fax: 6670-9684; e-mail: info@bank-maskan.ir).

Bank Mellat, Head Office Bldg, 327 Taleghani Ave, 15817 Tehran (tel: 8296-2700).

Bank Melli Iran, Ferdowsi Avenue, PO Box 11365-171, Tehran (tel: 3231; fax: 3391-2813).

Bank Refah Kargaran, 40 Northern Shirazi Street, Mollasadra Avenue, Tehran (tel: 8804-2926; fax: 8804-2926).

Bank Saderat Iran, Sepehr Tower, 43 Somayeh Avenue, PO Box 15745-631, Tehran (tel: 8829-9469; fax: 8883-9534).

Bank Sepah, Imam Khomeini Square, PO Box 11364-9569, Tehran (tel: 6674-3761; fax: 6674-3282; e-mail: info@banksepah.ir). (Bank Sepah was blacklisted by the US. The state-owned bank was accused of being the 'financial lynchpin' in Iran's efforts to procure material for its missile programme.)

Bank Tejarat, PO Box 11365-5416, 130 Taleghani Avenue, Nejatoullahie, 15994

Tehran (tel: 8882-6690; fax: 8889-3641).

Central bank
Bank Markazi Jomhouri Islami Iran,PO Box 11365-8551, Tehran (tel: 29-951; fax: 673-5674;e-mail: g.secdept@cbi.ir).

Travel information
Irpedia, 6 Kachouee Avenue, Chamran Highway, Tehran (tel: 200-8189; e-mail: info@irpedia.com).

Pars Tourist Agency, Zand Sreet 71358, Shiraz (tel: 222-3163; fax: 224-0645; e-mail: info@key2persia.com).

Ministry of tourism
Ministry of Culture and Islamic Guidance, Baharestan Square, Kamal-al-Molk Avenue, Avenue Kamalolmolk, Tehran (tel: 3851-2583; fax: 3311-7535).

National tourist organisation offices
Iran Tourist Co, 257 Motahari Avenue, Tehran 15868 (tel: 8873-6762/5; fax: 8873-6158; e-mail: info@irantouristco.com; internet site: http://www.irantouristco.com).

Ministries
Ministry of Commerce, 492 Valieasr Avenue, Tehran (tel: 8889-3553; fax: 8890-3943).

Ministry of Foreign Affairs, Imam Khomeini Square, Tehran (tel: 6673-9191; fax: 6674-3149; e-mail: matbuat@mfa.gov.ir).

Ministry of Information and Communication Technology (MICT), Sharlati St, PO Box 15875-4415, 16314 Tehran (tel: 8846 9000; fax: 8846 8131).

Ministry of Petroleum, Hafez Crossing, Taleghani Street, Tehran (tel: 6615-2606; fax: 6615-4977; e-mail: public-relations@mop.ir).

Ministry of Science, Research and Technology, Unit 2, Ostad Nejatollahi Street, Teheran (tel: 8890-2024; fax: 8890-2027; e-mail: msrt@mche.or.ir).

Other useful addresses
Export Promotion Centre of Iran, PO Box 11-48, Tajrish, Tehran (tel: 2205-1437; fax: 2205-1438; e-mail: epc-iran@epc-iran.com).

Iranian Interests Section (USA), 2209 Wisconsin Avenue, NW, Washington DC 20007 (tel:(+1-202)-965-4990; fax: (+1-202)-965-1073; e-mail: requests@daftar.org).

National Iranian Oil Company (NIOC), Taleghani Avenue, PO Box 1853, Tehran (tel: 6615-2275; fax: 6641-0916; e-mail: public-relation@nioc.com).

Statistical Centre of Iran, Dr Fatemi Ave, PO Box 14155-6133 Tehran (tel: 8896-5061; fax: 8896-5070; e-mail: sci@sci/org.ir).

Tehran Stock Exchange, 228 Hafez Avenue, Tehran (tel: 6670-4130; fax:6670-2524; e-mail: info@tse.ir).

National news agency: IRNA (Islamic Republic News Agency): www2.irna.ir

Other news agencies: IRIB: www.irib.ir

Iranian Students News Agency (ISNA): http://isna.ir

Press TV: www.presstv.com

Internet sites
Customs Administration: http://www.irica.gov.ir

General information: http://www.salamiran.org

General political information: http://www.netiran.com

Islamic Republic News Agency: http://www.irna.ir

Iraq

KEY FACTS

Official name: Al Jumhouriya al Iraqia (The Republic of Iraq)

Head of State: President Jalal Talabani (PUK) (since Apr 2005; re-elected 22 Apr 2006)

Head of government: Prime Minister Nouri al Maliki (Dawa) (appointed 22 Apr 2006)

Ruling party: Coalition: Government of National Unity led by United Iraqi Alliance (since 20 May 2006)

Area: 434,924 square km

Population: 27.50 million (2007)* (Figure includes the UN estimated 4.6 million living in exile)

Capital: Baghdad

Official language: Arabic and Kurdish

Currency: New Iraqi dinar (ID) 1,000 fils

Exchange rate: ID1,155.05 per US$ (Jul 2008); (Iraqi Central Bank auction rate) (New Iraqi dinar since 2003)

GDP per capita: US$2,900 (2007)*

GDP real growth: 5.00% (2007)*

Labour force: 7.23 million (2004)

Unemployment: 27.50% (2007)* (Average figure, does not include underemployment)

Inflation: 12.28% (2007)

Oil production: 2.15 million bpd (2007)

Balance of trade: US$11.82 billion (2006)*

Foreign debt: US$125.00 billion (2004)

* estimated figure

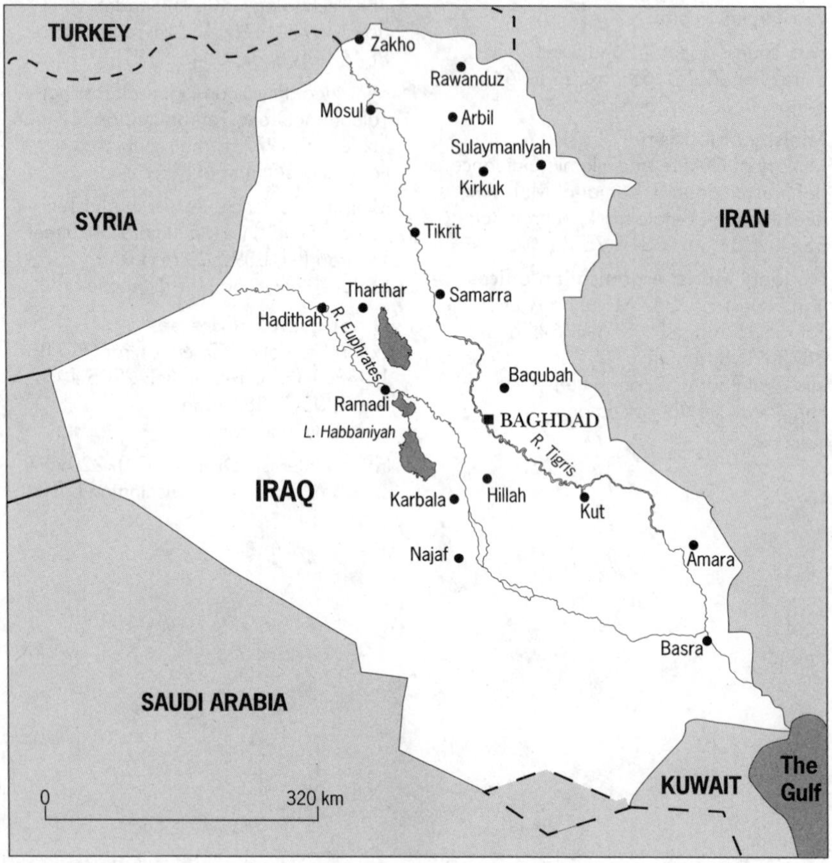

March 2008 marked the fifth anniversary of the invasion of Iraq by US lead coalition forces. For the coalition, the problem had changed: the challenge now was not how coalition forces might successfully enter Iraq, but how they could leave it. Over the five years the US and its allies had struggled to cope not only with a manifestly incompetent US secretary of defence, but also with the absence of any cogent strategy to deal with an increasingly successful al Qaeda influenced insurgency. The result was that the coalition was unable to provide the most basic function of any government: security for the population.

Five years on

Writing in the *International Herald Tribune*, Frederick Kagan of the American Enterprise Institute noted that perhaps the most surprising development of the Iraqi war has been the transformation of the US military into a tolerably effective counter-insurgency force. What Mr Kagan describes as the 'intellectual framework' for the policy came from Generals Petraeus and Odierno. Not that the policies adopted were new; the idea of involving local communities as an intelligence network was first developed by British colonial forces in Malaysia in the 1950s. The 'surge' concept also meant deploying more troops. Pre-war planning had provided for less than half the number of troops that independent analysts considered necessary. From 2004 to 2007 the insurgents were able to take advantage of the shortfall. Once that deficiency was at least partially remedied, things began to change.

The end of 2007 saw some fragile signs that inter-sectarian peace, if not being totally restored, was at least gaining a toe-hold in Iraq. Some reports estimated that the death toll in Baghdad had dropped by 50 per cent over the second half of the year. Barricades were slowly being dismantled and refugees – some 2 million people are estimated to have left Iran since the US led invasion – were beginning to return. The US based humanitarian group Human Rights Watch attributed much of the influx to an increasingly hostile attitude to Iraqi refugees in neighbouring countries.

As he approached the end of his deployment in Iraq, General David Petraeus, the US forces commander in Iraq, could take some satisfaction from the improvement in the security situation. Although parts of the country remained dangerous, the fact was that Iraqi cities such as Ramadi and Ghazaliya and many more had become much safer. The much criticised surge appeared to have worked, as shops and restaurants began to flourish and the popularity of the al Qaeda insurgency appeared to be waning.

An insecure economy?

In 2007 the World Bank acknowledged that Iraq's long prevalent insecurity had seriously hampered Iraqi reconstruction and investment, resulting in low oil production and slower economic growth. To make matters worse, shortages of key commodities had contributed to a rise in inflation in 2006. Encouragingly, inflation dropped during the first part of 2007. None the less, Iraq's economic prospects for 2007 and beyond continued to depend on the precariously improved security situation. Provided the planned investments in the oil sector were realised, a gradual expansion of oil production ought to be feasible. However, there were significant downside risks, including from volatile oil prices, and the uncertainties surrounding the political and security situation.

Iraq's 2007 budget allowed for an ambitious investment programme; but much progress needed to be made in improving a slow project implementation rate. Current spending, including on wages and pensions, also needed to be contained in order to maintain fiscal sustainability.

IMF support

An International Monetary Fund (IMF) endorsed stand-by arrangement (SBA) for Iraq had been approved in December 2005. The arrangement originally ran until March 2007, but was extended up to September 2007. The first and second reviews of the arrangement were completed in August 2006, and the third and fourth reviews were concluded in March 2007. The SBA supported a programme aimed at maintaining macroeconomic stability, paving the way for sustainable growth, and achieving external debt sustainability. Iraq continued to view the SBA as precautionary. Of equal importance for Iraq was the Paris Club's agreement in November 2004 to an 80 per cent debt reduction for Iraq, to be achieved in three stages. The first and second stages each comprised a 30 per cent reduction. The final stage comprised an additional 20 per cent reduction, and will depend on the completion, by the end of December 2008, of the final review of arrangements with the IMF.

The backdrop to Iraq's economic development remained Iraq's serious, if improving, security problems. These worsened living conditions, adversely affected economic activity, and had encouraged the emigration of professionals and skilled labour, although by early 2008 there were signs that this trend had been reversed.

The 2004 United Nations Development Programme survey of living conditions had highlighted Iraq's poor scores on the Millennium Development Goals, with widespread malnutrition, low primary school enrolment, and high child mortality. Although the survey has not since been updated, the results from the 2007 Iraq Poll had provided indications of further deterioration in living conditions.

Flight

The United Nations' refugee agency has estimated that over four million Iraqis are displaced, including some 1.9 million inside Iraq and over two million in neighbouring countries. The large numbers of refugees are putting a strain on Iraq's neighbouring countries (the bulk of the refugees – probably around 1.2 million, have made their way to neighbouring Syria; a further 750,000 have fled to Jordan). When asked to indicate 'how things are going in their lives these days?' 60 per cent of respondents in the 2007 Iraq Poll answered 'very bad' or 'quite bad', more than double the 29 per cent recorded in 2004 and 2005. More than three quarters of Iraqis said that jobs were hard to find, which supported the official under-employment estimates ranging from 30 to 50 per cent. The availability of clean water, medical care, and basic goods and services had, after some improvement in 2005, all deteriorated. Three out of five Iraqis considered the conditions of local schools to be bad, more than twice as many as in 2004. When asked about the 'biggest single problem facing Iraq' more than half of the respondents to the 2007 Iraq Poll mentioned security, followed by political and military issues (26 per cent), social issues (12 per cent), and economic issues (9 per cent).

Annual consumer price inflation increased to 66 per cent in January 2007, double the 31.5 per cent registered at the end of 2005, reflecting shortages of key commodities, primarily fuel. Core inflation (excluding fuel and transportation) also remained high at about 32 per cent. The growth of money supply was, however, well below the level of inflation in

KEY INDICATORS — Iraq

	Unit	2003	2004	2005	2006	2007
Population	m	24.70	25.39	26.56	27.50	*27.50
Gross domestic product (GDP)	US$bn	21.58	33.70	30.60	87.90	*55.44
GDP per capita	US$	844	1,303	1,063	*2,900	0
GDP real growth	%	-9.5	37.3	34.0	*1.9	*5.0
Inflation	%	34.0	27.0	37.0	*31.9	12.3
Oil output	'000 bpd	1,344.0	2,027.0	1,820.0	1,999.0	2,145.0
Natural gas output	bn cum	–	–	–	–	–
Exports (fob) (goods)	US$m	16,543.0	17,780.0	23,697.4	30,529.4	–
Imports (cif) (goods)	US$m	21,680.0	19,570.0	20,002.2	18,707.5	–
Balance of trade	US$m	-5,137.0	-1,790.0	369.5	11,821.9	–
Current account	US$m	–	–	–	1,252.0	–
Total reserves minus gold	US$m	–	–	12,104.1	19,535.4	–
Foreign exchange	US$m	–	–	11,439.9	18,839.2	–
Exchange rate	per US$	0.31	1,450.00	1,314.65	1,314.65	1,216.70

* estimated figure

2006. Following an intensified policy effort to bring inflation under control, the annual inflation rate had declined to 38 per cent in May 2007; core inflation also decreased to 21 per cent in May 2007. Fuel shortages reportedly declined somewhat in the first months of the year, contributing to the narrowing of the gap between headline and core inflation. In June, however, fuel shortages worsened again and headline inflation increased to 46 per cent; core inflation continued to decline to 19 per cent.

Oil

After more than a decade of sanctions and two Gulf Wars, Iraq's oil infrastructure needs modernisation and investment. Despite a large reconstruction effort (including Iraq Relief and Reconstruction Fund (IRRF) support of US$1.72 billion), the industry has not been able to meet its targets since 2004. The EIA gloomily noted that in 2007, Iraq's petroleum sector faced technical challenges across the board, in procuring, transporting and storing crude and refined products, as well as managing pricing controls and imports, fighting smuggling and corruption, improving budget execution, and managing the sustainability of operations.

A further challenge to the development of the oil sector is that resources are not evenly divided across sectarian and demographic lines. Most known hydrocarbon resources remain concentrated in the Shiite areas of the south and the ethnically Kurdish north, with few resources in control of the Sunni minority. For this reason a legal framework for investment in the hydrocarbon sector remains a main policy objective. The EIA notes that various US government agencies, multilateral institutions and other international organisations all concur that long-term Iraq reconstruction costs could reach US$100 billion or higher, of which it is estimated that over a third will go to the oil, gas and electricity sectors. In addition, the World Bank estimates that at least US$1 billion in additional revenues needs to be committed annually to the oil industry just to sustain current production.

Estimating the reserves

According to the US *Oil and Gas Journal*, in 2007 Iraq's proven oil reserves were 115 billion barrels, although these statistics have not been revised since 2001 and are largely based on seismic data from the 1970s. Since 2006, multinational oil companies have re-examined seismic data and conducted comprehensive surveys of Iraq's hydrocarbons reserves in locations throughout the country. Geologists and consultants have estimated that relatively unexplored territory in the western and southern deserts may contain an estimated additional 45 to 100 billion barrels of recoverable oil. While internal Iraqi estimates have ranged into the hundreds of billions of barrels of additional oil, the seismic data under review by a host of international firms seem to be pointing to more conservative, but significant, increases. Iraq has the lowest reserve to production ratio of the major oil-producing countries.

The majority of the known oil and gas reserves in Iraq form a belt that runs along the eastern edge of the country. The EIA reports that Iraq has some 9 fields that are considered 'super giants' (with over 5 billion barrels of reserves) as well as 22 known 'giant' fields (with over 1 billion barrels). According to independent consultants, the cluster of super giant fields of south-eastern Iraq forms the largest known concentration of such fields in the world and accounts for 70 to 80 per cent of Iraq's proven oil reserves. An estimated 20 per cent of oil reserves are in the north of Iraq, near Kirkuk, Mosul and Khanaqin. Control over rights to reserves is a source of controversy between the ethnic Kurds and other groups in the area.

The Western Desert is of interest to oil prospectors as well as to the sectarian groups occupying these areas where there is no active oil production. Minor oil formations beneath western territory have been known of for decades, but little has been done in the way of development. Much of this area is just now undergoing exploration, although it belongs to the same geological formation as the Saudi Arabian deposits. According to an Egyptian news source from February 2007, a test well at the Akkas field in the Al Anbar province is flowing at rates equivalent to larger fields elsewhere in Iraq.

Production

The EIA reports that in 2006, Iraq's upstream crude oil production averaged 2.0 million barrels per day (bpd), down from the notional capacity of 2.8 to 3.0 million bpd in pre-invasion January 2003. Estimates of Iraq's current production levels vary and metering systems have been put in place at Basrah to improve export accounting. The EIA reported differences in daily production volumes ranging between 100,000 to 300,000bpd. Historically, two-thirds of production came from the southern fields and the remainder from the north-central fields near Kirkuk. At present, the majority of Iraqi oil production comes from just three giant fields: North and South Rumaila and Kirkuk. The Rumaila fields, operated by Iraqi parastatal South Oil Company, along with a ring of nearly a dozen smaller fields, including Subha, Luhais, West Qurna and Az Zubair, have been producing 1.5 to 1.9 million bpd; close to pre-war levels. Conversely, average production at Kirkuk and the northern fields of around 200,000bpd is only a fraction of the pre-war peak of around 680,000bpd, due to reservoir damage from gas and water injection. In May 2007, the Iraq oil ministry reported that total production from the northern fields was 206,000bpd, all of which went to domestic consumption. Iraq's inability to secure crude pipelines in the north has meant that exports are generally routed through the southern port of Basrah, crude oil exports have fallen from a post-war high of around 2.0 million bpd in 2004, to an average of 1.5 million bpd in 2006.

Iraq's draft Hydrocarbon Law, which was first presented to the upper house of parliament for review in February 2007, was central to the development of the oil and gas industry. The draft law focused on upstream development and laid out the conditions for investment and international participation in the sector. The law also detailed a governance model which included the proposed re-establishment of the former Iraq National Oil Company (INOC) and a central regulatory body.

According to the OGJ, Iraq's proven natural gas reserves are 112 trillion cubic feet (Tcf). Probable reserves have been estimated at closer to 275–300 Tcf and work is currently underway to update hydrocarbon reserve numbers. Iraq's proven gas reserves are the tenth largest in the world, and two-thirds of resources are associated with oil fields including Kirkuk, as well as the southern Nahr (Bin) Umar, Majnoon, Halfaya, Nassiriya, the Rumaila fields, West Qurna, and Az Zubair.

According to the EIA's International Energy Annual report, natural gas production in Iraq has steadily declined over the past decade-and-a-half, reportedly due to an associated fall in oil production and deterioration of gas processing facilities. In 2005, dry natural gas production was approximately 87 billion cubic feet (Bcf); down from 215 Bcf in 1989. In late 2006, the oil ministry reported that natural gas production was averaging 900 million cubic feet (Mcf) in the south (associated) and 490 Mcf in the north. Approximately 60 per cent of associated natural gas production is flared, due to a lack of sufficient infrastructure to utilise it for consumption and export.

Risk assessment

Economy	Improving
Politics	Poor
Regional stability	Fair

COUNTRY PROFILE

Historical profile

1920 Iraq was placed under British mandate.
1921 Amir Faisal ibn Hussain (a member of the Arab Hashemite dynasty) was proclaimed Iraq's first King.
1932 Iraq became an independent state.
1933 King Faisal died and was succeeded by his son, Ghazi.
1939 King Ghazi was killed in a car crash and was succeeded by the infant Faisal II, whose uncle, Prince Abd al Ilah, acted as regent.
1953 King Faisal II assumed full powers.
1958 A military coup overthrew the monarchy and a republic was proclaimed.
1963 Pan-Arab elements in the armed forces staged a coup and formed a government under Colonel (later Field Marshal) Abd as Salem Muhammad Aref
1966 Aref was killed in an airplane crash and was succeeded by his brother.
1968 Major General Abd ar Rahman Muhammad Aref was removed from office in a coup organised by the Hizb al Ba'ath al Arabiyah al Ishtiraki (Ba'ath) (Socialist Arab Rebirth Party). The Ba'ath government was headed by Major General Ahmad Hassan al Bakr (a former prime minister) and supreme authority was vested in the Revolutionary Command Council (RCC).
1970 The RCC and the leader of the Kurdistan Democratic Party (KDP) signed a peace agreement.
1972 Iraq nationalised the Iraq Petroleum Company (IPC).
1979 The vice president of the RCC, Saddam Hussein (already the real power in Iraq), replaced Al Bakr as president.
1980–88 The Iran-Iraq War broke out after Iraq invaded Iran over a disputed border area.
1988 A chemical attack ordered by Saddam Hussein on the northern Kurdish town of Halabja, killed 5,000 people.
1990 The Iraqi invasion of Kuwait was condemned by the international community which, led by the US, deployed armed forces to Saudi Arabia. Following the invasion, the United Nations Security Council (UNSC) imposed an arms embargo and economic sanctions on Iraq (Resolution 661) and passed Resolution 678, which authorised member states to use force if Iraq had not withdrawn from Kuwait by 15 January 1991.
1991 The Gulf War started on 16 January. Coalition forces launched an aerial bombing campaign against Iraqi forces in Kuwait and Iraq and US-led ground forces (from around 30 countries, including Syria, Egypt and Morocco) liberated Kuwait.
The UN maintained the arms embargo and economic sanctions on Iraq after the end of the War in an attempt to force it to disarm of weapons of mass destruction (WMD). After a Kurdish and Shi'a Muslim-led uprising was brutally quashed by Saddam Hussein's regime, the US, UK and France imposed 'no-fly zones' on Iraq to protect the Kurds in the north and the Shi'as in the south. The UN adminstered the three northern provinces of Dahuk, Arbil and As Sulaymaniyah, which allowed the Kurds to develop their own semi-autonomous Kurdish enclave, with its own parliament.
1993 The US launched 24 cruise missiles at targets in Baghdad after an alleged Iraqi plot to assassinate former US president George Bush was uncovered.
1994 Saddam Hussein appointed himself prime minister as well as president.
1995 The population voted in a referendum on Saddam Hussein's presidency and, inevitably, supported him. The Iraq oil-for-food programme, administered by the UN, began.
1996 Saddam Hussein's son-in-law, his brother and their families, were granted asylum in Jordan; the two men were subsequently promised a pardon by Saddam Hussein, but were killed on their return to Baghdad. Saddam Hussein's eldest son, Uday, survived an assassination attempt.
1998 Various disputes arose between Iraq and the UN over UN inspections to verify the termination of Iraq's WMD programme; Saddam Hussein excluded the weapons inspectors from Iraq. As a result, the US and the UK launched their largest military attack against Iraq since the Gulf War, bombing installations throughout Iraq.
1999 The spiritual leader of the Shi'a community, Ayatollah Mohammed Sadiq al Sadr, was assassinated in Najaf.
2000 In his capacity as head of the Organisation of the Petroleum Exporting Countries (Opec), President Hugo Chávez Frías of Venezuela travelled overland to Baghdad – the first democratically elected head of state to enter Iraq since the Gulf War.
2001 Five UN officials working for the UN oil-for-food programme were expelled by Iraqi authorities on charges of spying.
2002 A presidential referendum extended Saddam Hussein's rule for a further seven years. US President Bush demanded that Hussein must prove to the UN weapons inspectors that he had disposed of his WMD, as stipulated in the UN resolution after the First Gulf War, if not the US would launch a war against Iraq. The UK prime minister, Tony Blair, confirmed his support for the US. UN weapons inspectors were allowed into Iraq for the first time in four years, however the information they were shown was not sufficient to convince the US that there were no WMD. President Bush included Iraq, North Korea with Iran and a list of countries that supported terrorism as an 'axis of evil'.
2003 After diplomatic efforts to force Iraq to disarm failed and the expiry of an US ultimatum giving Hussein and his sons 48 hours to leave the country, US-led coalition forces invaded Iraq. Within 20 days central Baghdad was under US control and the Hussein government had collapsed. The Ba'ath party was abolished, together with institutions of the former regime. The UN Security Council lifted economic sanctions and a 25-member Iraq Governing Council (IGC) was appointed, with a rotating nine-member presidency. Hussein's sons, Uday and Qusay, were killed in a battle with US troops attempting to arrest them. The leader of the Shi'as, Ayatollah Mohammed Baqr al Hakim, was killed in Najaf. An amended US resolution on Iraq, legitimising the US-led administration, was approved by the UN, which stressed early transfer of power to the Iraqis. The security situation deteriorated as guerrilla warfare intensified. At the end of the year, Saddam Hussein was captured in Tikrit.
2004 After the president of the IGC was killed in a car bomb attack, Iyad Allawi (a Shi'a) was designated prime minister in May and Ghazi al Yawar (a Sunni tribal leader) was chosen as president. An interim 36-member cabinet was appointment to governed Iraq until elections for a fully independent government could be held; it had power-sharing responsibilities with the US-led multinational forces in matters of security. The US handed over sovereignty to the Iraqi interim government. Hussein was transferred into Iraqi legal custody. There was heavy fighting for more than a week in an uprising against coalition troops by Shi'a militia loyal to radical cleric, Moqtada al Sadr, in the holy city of Najaf.
2005 An estimated eight million people voted in the elections for a Transitional National Assembly. Many Sunni Moslems boycotted the elections, and the Shi'a United Iraqi Alliance won most seats. Iraq's first freely elected parliament in half a century began its opening session after a series of explosions targetted the gathering. Kurdish leader Jalal Talabani was named president. Former president, and

Sunni leader, Ghazi al Yawar, and Shi'ite leader, Adel Abdul Mahdi, were named as deputies. The Shi'ite leader, Ibrahim Jaafari, was named prime minister. The Kurdish parliament unanimously elected Massoud Barzani as president of the autonomous region of Kurdistan. In his trial, former president, Saddam Hussein, was accused, along with seven others, of murdering 148 people in 1982 in the Shi'a town of Dujail. It was adjourned for 40 days after defence lawyers said they needed more time to examine the prosecution's documents. Although it resumed on time it was adjourned again, after one of the defendants said that he had been unable to replace his original attorney, who had been murdered. Parliamentary elections were held.
2006 After several months in which no progress was made in forming a new government, the interim prime minister, Ibrahim Jaafari, relinquished office under intense pressure and was replaced by his colleague in the Islamic Dawa Party (a leading party within the Shi'ite grouping United Iraqi Alliance), Nouri al Maliki. A coalition government was sworn in. The chief judge in Saddam Hussein's trial, Abdullah al Amiri, was removed by the government, which said the judge was 'no longer neutral', after he made court statements that Saddam had not been a dictator; he was replaced by Muhammad al Uraiybi. Saddam Hussein was executed by hanging, after being found guilty of crimes against humanity. An unauthorised recording of the event, showing him being taunted by his captors, was broadcast on the Internet.
2007 US President Bush dispatched further troops, specifically to police Baghdad. The full contingent of 21,500 soldiers had arrived by May. Civilian deaths in the four weeks before the initial troop arrivals in February were 1,440, which dropped to 265 in the following four weeks. There was a record number of 44 car bombs in February but a decline in violence was recorded as Iraqi-US forces targetted the followers of the Shi'a cleric, Moqtada al Sadr, known as the Mahdi army, as its leadership fled to Iran. New, permanently manned, combat outposts were established inside neighbourhoods to provide timely security responses and intelligence gathering. Former vice president, Taha Yassin Ramadan, was executed for crimes against humanity in March. His original sentence of life imprisonment was increased following an appeal by the prosecution. The Sunni Accordance Front suspended its participation in cabinet at the end of June, leaving just Shi'a and Kurdish members in both the cabinet and parliament. Official figures showed a drop in the number of civilian deaths from 1,900 in May to just over 1,200 in July. Between January and August, 17 government members either quit or suspended their involvement in the government; this left the Unity Government without any Sunni members and left it weak and vulnerable. Four car-bombs exploded in a concerted attack on a Kurdish religious sect, the Yazidi, in August, killing over 250 and injuring over 350 people. US military officials blamed al Qaeda for the atrocity. However, there was a drop of over 50 per cent in the number of Iraqi civilians killed by violence September, and, at 884 was the lowest level for 12 months. There were also fewer US deaths. In October, the Kurdish government, in northern Iraq, signed four exploration and two refinery contracts, worth about US$800 million, with several international energy companies. The deals were signed ahead of Iraqi national oil and gas laws and increased tension between the central government and the Kurdish territory.
2008 Final approval by the presidency council (on 3 February) of legislation passed in January allows for former Ba'ath party members to return to public life. On 11 February Russia announced that it was writing off US$12 billion of debt which had built up under Sadam Hussain. President Ahmadinejad of Iran began a 2-day visit on 2 March, the first visit by a president since the Iran/Iraq war in the 1980s. The Christian Archbishop of Mosul, Paulos Faraj Rahho, was kidnapped and later found dead on 13 March. The leader of al Qaeda in Iraq, Ahmed Ali Ahmed (known as Abu Omar) was sentenced to death on 18 May for the murder of Archbishop Rohho. A US audit of reconstruction projects undertaken in Iraq concluded that millions of dollars were wasted on projects that were incomplete due to rising costs, poor performance and delays, mostly from violence. Four representatives of the militant cleric Moqtada al Sadr political bloc were replaced in cabinet on 19 July, as six representatives of the principal Sunni bloc rejoined the Shi'a-led government, after a year-long break after a row over power-sharing and security force operations against Sunni militias. Parliament approved a draft law for provincial elections, to be held on 1 October, despite a boycott by the Kurdish bloc and a few Shi'a MPs.

Political structure

Constitution

A public referendum approved a new permanent constitution on 15 October 2005. It came into effect when the elections for the Council of Representatives took place on 15 December 2005.
The constitution declares that the Republic of Iraq is an independent, sovereign nation, and its system of governance is democratic, federal, and representative (parliamentary). Islam is the official religion of the state and is a basic source of legislation. Iraq is part of the Arab nation and the Islamic world.
Universal suffrage begins at aged 18.
The country is divided into 18 provinces (muhafazat, singular muhafazahW0): al Anbar, al Basrah, al Muthanna, al Qadisiyah, An Najaf, Arbil, As Sulaymaniyah, At Ta'mim, Babil, Baghdad, Dahuk, Dhi Qar, Diyala, Karbala', Maysan, Ninawa, Salah ad Din and Wasit.

Form of state

Republic, federal

The executive

Executive authority consists of the Presidency Council, the Council of Ministers, presided over by the prime minister.
The Presidency Council consists of the president and two deputies; they are elected by the national assembly.

National legislature

The unicameral Majlis al Watani (National Assembly), with 275 members. There is a 115-seat Kurdish parliament in the semi-autonomous northern governorates.

Legal system

Under the constitution the Judiciary is independent and represented by courts of different kinds and levels, issuing their rulings according to law. No authority can interfere in the judiciary or in the affairs of justice.
The Federal Judiciary includes the Supreme Judiciary Council, and the Supreme Federal Court.The Iraqi court system is divided into the Civil Courts, Courts of Personal Status, and Criminal Courts.

Last elections

15 December 2005 (National Assembly).
Results: Parliamentary: United Iraqi Alliance won 48.19 per cent of the votes (128 seats out of 275); Kurdistani Gathering won 21.67 per cent (53 seats); Tawafoq Iraqi Front 15.09 per cent (44 seats); National Iraqi List 8.02 per cent (25 seats); Hewar National Iraqi Front 4.10 per cent (11 seats); Islamic Union of Kurdistan 1.29 per cent (five seats); Liberation and Reconciliation Gathering 1.07 per cent (three seats); Progressives 1.19 per cent (two seats); other parties one seat each. Turnout was 79.63 per cent.

Next elections

1 October 2008 (provincial); 2009 (presidential and parliamentary)

Political parties

Ruling party

Coalition: Government of National Unity led by United Iraqi Alliance (since 20 May 2006)

Main opposition party
Hizb al Fadhila al Islamiyah (Islamic Virtue Party)

Population

27.50 million (2007)* (Figure includes the UN estimated 4.6 million living in exile)
Last census: October 1997: 19,184,543 (excluding data for autonomous northern regions)
Population density: 49 inhabitants per square km. Urban population: 68 per cent (1995–2001).
Annual growth rate: 3.0 per cent 1994–2004 (WHO 2006)

Ethnic make-up
Arabs comprise 75 per cent of the population, with Kurds representing a further 20 per cent (mostly located in northern Iraq) and Turkmen, Assyrian and other minorities making up the remaining 5 per cent.

Religions
Shi'a (also known as Shi'ite, Shiite, Shi'is) Muslims are the largest religious group, comprising 54 per cent of the population. Sunni Muslims were politically dominant in the Saddam Hussein period, although accounting for only 42 per cent of the total. There is a significant number of Christians and a small number of Yazidis and others.

Education
After the 2003 Iraq War, attempts began to re-build Iraq's education system, as the US Agency for International Development (USAID) granted US$2 million to provide immediate educational needs.
Free education is provided for children between the ages of six and 18.
Literacy rate: 40.1 per cent total, 24.1 per cent female, adult rates in 2002 (World Bank).
Compulsory years: Six and 12
Enrolment rate: 46 per cent in primary education. Only 37 per cent of girls attend school. (Unicef, 2008)
Pupils per teacher: 20 in primary schools.

Health
Per capita total expenditure on health (2003) was US$64; of which per capita government spending was US$33, at the international dollar rate, (WHO 2006).
In 2007 there was an outbreak of cholera in the north with at least 2,000 cases and several fatalities. The UK-based charity Oxfam warned that only 30 per cent of the population had access to clean water and only around 40 per cent had access to sewage facilities.
In 2008 it was estimated the around 50 per cent of registered physicians had left the country due to sectarian threats and violence.

HIV/Aids
HIV prevalence: 0.1 per cent aged 15–49 in 2003 (World Bank)
Life expectancy: 55 years, 2004 (WHO 2006)
Fertility rate/Maternal mortality rate: 4.7 births per woman, 2004 (WHO 2006)
Child (under 5 years) mortality rate (per 1,000): 102 per 1,000 live births (World Bank)
Head of population per physician: 0.66 physicians per 1,000 people, 2004 (WHO 2006)

Welfare
Iraq is struggling to repair its social infrastructure, welfare and pensions are being administered in an ad hoc manner until the newly elected government can get to grips with the economy and implement nationwide policies.
All political parties, during the January 2005 election campaign, advocated the introduction of comprehensive state subsidies and welfare measures and to aleviate the widespread poverty the government may have to invest heavily in its welfare programmes.
In 2008 there were an estimated 1.9 million internally displaced persons.

Main cities
Baghdad (capital, estimated population 6.9 million (m) in 2005), Mosul (1.1m), Basra (1.1m), Arbil (910,381), Kirkuk (618,149), Sulaymaniyah (683,261).

Media

The media has been liberated from official sanctions and there has been a rapid growth in all mediums. Private media outlets are typically linked to political, religious and ethnic groupings.
Other news agencies: Nina (National Iraqi News Agency): www.ninanews.com
Voices of Iraq: www.aswataliraq.info

Press
Dailies: In Arabic, newspapers with the highest circulations include Al Mada (www.almadapaper.com), Al Sabah (www.alsabaah.com), Al Mashriq (www.al-mashriq.net), Al Ahali (www.ahali-iraq.net). In Kurdish, Al Ittihad (www.alitthad.com) and Khabat (www.xebat.net), published by the Kurdistan Democratic Party. Iraqi newspapers with English online editions include Al Sabah and Azzaman (www.azzaman.com).

Broadcasting
The Iraqi Media Net (www.iraqimedianet.net) is the national public radio and television broadcaster.
Radio: The Republic of Iraq Radio (www.iraqimedianet.net), known as Iraqi Radio has two networks RI 1 and H Quraan. There are many local radio stations in operation, including Radio Annas (www.radioannas.com), Al Huda Radio (www.al-hodaonline.com), Radio Sawa (www.radiosawa.com) and Radio Nawa Kurdish (www.radionawa.com). There are international services provided by France, UK and the US available via local relays.
Television: Around 70 per cent of the TV audience watch satellite TV with pan-Arab stations taking the majority share of ratings. Iraqi Media Net (www.iraqimedianet.net) operates three channels of Al Iraqiya TV, TV2 and Sports TV. Private stations include Al Sharqiya (www.alsharqiya.com) and Al Sumaria (www.alsumaria.tv). In the semi-autonomous Kurdistan there are three satellite stations, Kurdistan Satellite Channel (www.kurdistan.tv), KurdSat (www.kurdsat.tv) and Zagros (www.zagrostv.com).

Economy

The economy is still faced with enormous difficulties and although the government is attempting to rectify the lack of infrastructure and security, it has limited scope for success. The continuing insurgency is creating internal pressures that are impinging on the economy. There have been sharp price rises in food, fuel and electricity, transportation costs and communications and the growing shortage of these commodities has had a knock-on effect with inflation running at 31.6 per cent in 2005 and jumping to 53.4 per cent by March 2006.
Overall, GDP growth was only 3.7 per cent in 2005, down from a spectacular 37.3 per cent in 2004, following the regime change and before the increased terrorism began to curb free trade. While Iraq has oil reserves of 15.5 billion tonnes, its production of 1.8 million barrels per day (bpd), was a fall of 9.5 per cent on the 2.0 million bpd of 2004 and growth depends on peace and stability coupled with improved infrastructure. In February 2007, the government set before parliament plans to guarantee that oil revenue would be shared among the three principal ethnic groups. It is hoped this measure will ensure unity and a cessation in sectarian bloodshed as current oil fields are located in the predominately Shi'a region in the south while the best prospects for oil in the future are in the Kurdish region of the north.
The new government took several months to be composed and in that time some macroeconomic measures agreed with the IMF were missed, which delayed the implementation of the debt reduction agreement with the Paris Club of foreign debtors. The first two stages reducing the debts by 30 per cent each time had been

achieved by December 2005. The final stage, with a 20 per cent reduction is planned by December 2008.
Iraq's economy cannot grow with any degree of uniformity until internal security can be assured and citizens can go about their daily lives without fear of death or injury. Until then, whatever progress is achieved is at risk from the insurgency and any objective analysis can only consider what was, is and with luck may be.

External trade
In 2005 the Greater Arab Free Trade Area (Gafta) was ratified by 17 members, including Iraq, creating an Arab economic bloc. A customs union was established whereby tariffs within Gafta will be reduced by a percentage each year, until none remain. In July 2007 Iraq was still in negotiation with WTO for membership.
Iraq has an open trade investment regime whereby a customs duty of 5 per cent is levied on all import goods, except primary commodities such as food, medicines, clothing and humanitarian items.

Imports
Commodities include food, medicines and manufactured goods.
Main sources: Syria (26.8 per cent total, 2006), Turkey (20.7 per cent), US (11.9 per cent).

Exports
Main exports include crude oil (over 80 per cent), non-oil item include raw materials food and live animals.
Main destinations: US (46.7 per cent total, 2006), Italy (10.7 per cent), Canada (6.2 per cent).

Agriculture
Farming
The area of cultivatable land in Iraq is estimated to be around 12 million hectares (ha). About four million ha of this arable land consists of rain-fed agriculture and the remaining eight million depends on irrigation. Less than 50 per cent of this land is actually cultivated. However, irrigation systems are badly in need of repair and salinity is increasingly affecting large areas of arable land.
The most important crops are barley and wheat (yields of each exceed one million tonnes in a good year) and rice; and after cereals, which account for most of the arable land, cotton, dates, vegetables and fruit.
Historically, dates were the most valuable exports after oil (with an annual value of around US$75 million). Production plummeted due to the war with Iran (1980–88), and to pollution which affected millions of trees in the south, following the 1991 Gulf War.

Fishing
There is a small fishing industry, mostly based on the Tigris and Euphrates rivers. Without import and export activities it will remain insignificant.
In 2004, the total marine fish catch was 3,126 tonnes and the total crustacean catch was 30 tonnes.

Forestry
Forests cover around 800,000ha, or 1.8 per cent of the land area and are mainly confined to the northern part of the country. There is no significant commercial exploitation.

Industry and manufacturing
Iraq's major industries centre on the petroleum, chemical, textile, construction and food processing sectors. Much of Iraq's industrial base was affected by war and sanctions. Before the 1991 Gulf War, Iraq was second only to Saudi Arabia in terms of oil production and reserves. Iraq's oil industry was boosted and re-invested into by the UN oil-for-food programme, although it was far from pre-1991 levels. During 2004 and 2005 there were efforts to re-build Iraq's industrial and manufacturing base, particularly in oil production.

Tourism
Tourism could bring a great deal of revenue into the economy. Since August 2003, the Baghdad Institute for Tourism and Hotels is offering a graduation class to the country's travel industry.

Mining
The mining sector contributes about 8 per cent to GDP and employs 4 per cent of the working population.
Iraq has huge resources of phosphates and its sulphur reserves are among the world's largest; there is significant potential for sulphur exports.
Other minerals include glass sand, raw materials for the construction industry, and modest quantities of iron ore, lead, copper and gypsum.

Hydrocarbons
Iraq had proven oil reserves of 15.5 billion tonnes of oil in 2005; production was 2.3 million barrels per day (bpd) at the end of 2007, just above the 2003 pre-invasion level.
There are also proven natural gas reserves of 3.1 trillion cubic metres (cum) in 2005, just under 15 per cent of global reserves. About 70 per cent of Iraq's natural gas supplies are by-products of oil production. Prior to the 1991 Gulf War, Iraq was producing up to 20 billion cum of natural gas per annum, but this fell sharply during 1991–2002.The largest gas fields are in the north at Kirkuk, and in Rumaila and Zubair in the south.
Iraq has some small low-grade coal deposits, with some limited exploitation before 1990 suppling the domestic chemicals industry. These mines are thought to have fallen into disuse following the destruction of industrial capacity and imposition of UN sanctions.

Energy
Much of Iraqi's national power grid, including 20 power stations, was destroyed or damaged by coalition bombing in the 1991 Gulf War. Further damage was done during the 2003 Iraq War when the Baghdad power grid was badly damaged. By July 2003, it was estimated that no more than 3,600MW of electricity was being generated. Another 2,000MW is required to meet the country's needs in the short-term. By December 2005 5 per cent of the population had electricity for 24 hours/7 days a week, 40 per cent had more than eight hours per day and 15 per cent had only 2–4 hours per day. As an indicator of the quality of modern life, more has to be done to improve the service for most of the population to benefit.

Financial markets
Stock exchange
The Iraq Stock Exchange (ISX), was re-opened on 24 June 2004. It is an independent, self-regulating institution with the Iraq Securities and Exchange Commission overseeing proceedings.
The initial plan was to relist 10–15 stocks per month. Companies have to have their accounts verified and international auditors and major shareholders have to be vetted to exclude former regime members.
The exchange processed the 589 million shares traded on the first day manually and will continue to do so until the contract for new electronic equipment is fulfilled.

Banking and insurance
The banking systems, according to the IMF in 2005, is weak and barely functioning. It comprises the Central Bank of Iraq and 26 chartered banks. Two state-owned banks, the Rafidain and Rashid Banks, account for over 90 per cent of the commercial banking assets and 75 per cent of the local branch network. These institutions are heavily over-staffed with too many staff under-skilled and the government may invite foreign involvement in restructuring them. It may also amalgamate four of the smaller, and specialised banks into two regional development banks and well establishing new Islamic banks.
In 2003, the Trade Bank of Iraq (TBI) was established to provide financial and related services to facilitate imports and exports. It is independent of the Central Bank of Iraq.
The authorities will be implementing international accounting and auditing standards, and improving disclosure requirements, to adhere to recognised practices in good governance.

Central bank
Central Bank of Iraq

Time
GMT plus three hours (daylight saving, April–September, GMT plus four hours)

Geography
Iraq is bounded by Turkey to the north, Iran to the east, Kuwait to the south-east, and Saudi Arabia, Jordan and Syria to the west. There is also a neutral zone between Iraq and Saudi Arabia administered jointly by the two countries with Iraq's portion covering 3,522 square km. The country's most fertile area and heartland is the flood plain of the Tigris and Euphrates rivers, which flow in parallel for most of their length from the Turkish and Syrian borders respectively, to the Gulf. The north-east of Iraq is mountainous while the large western desert area is sparsely populated and undeveloped.

Hemisphere
Northern

Climate
There is an excessively hot sub-tropical period with no rainfall from May–September (38–49 degrees Celsius (C)). Dry and pleasantly warm from October–April (20–25 degrees C), with occasional heavy rain. Continental conditions affect the northern mountainous areas which experience severe winters, but the southern plains have warm winters with some rain and very hot, dry summers. The temperature in Baghdad ranges from between 4 degrees C and 16 degrees C in January, to between 24 degrees C and 33 degrees C in July and August. Average annual rainfall is 300mm.

Dress codes
Conservative and modest dress should be worn in public in conformity with local Islamic traditions. Safari suits or short-sleeved suits are acceptable for men at work or at informal meetings; lounge suits in light materials are worn for formal meetings and in the evening.

Entry requirements
All requirements are subject to change and should be thoroughly checked before departure.

Passports
Passports are required by all.

Visa
There are only a few countries designated to issue visas and only to certain authorised visitors. See Entry Visa Regulations in the consular section at www.iraqembassy.org for a list.

Prohibited entry
Nationals of Israel and holders of passports with evidence of travel in Israel are denied entry.

Currency advice/regulations
A currency declaration form must be completed on arrival and departure. The import and export of local currency is restricted to small coins only. The import of foreign currency is unlimited but amounts must be declared. Export cannot exceed the amount declared on entry. Travellers cheques are little used.

Customs
Beyond the allotted duty-free allowance, the total value of imports must not exceed ID100. Electrial goods (not for personal use), commercial artifacts and fruits and plant material are subject to import duty. The export of antiques and artefacts is prohibited.

Health (for visitors)
Travellers should be aware of the poor capacity of Iraqi hospitals to extend medical care and that communications and essential services, including power and water cannot be relied on. Comprehensive medical insurance covering repatriation is essential. There are severe shortages of essential drugs. Detailed health advice should be sought before visiting Iraq.

Mandatory precautions
A certificate of vaccination against yellow fever, if travelling from an infected area.

Advisable precautions
Precautions should include vaccinations, or booster shots, for typhoid, diphtheria, tetanus, polio and hepatitis A; some vaccines may be advised including hepatitis B, TB, cholera and rabies. Anti-malarial precautions should be taken; the use of mosquito nets and repellents and covering up the body after dark can help avoid malaria and hepatitis B.

All water should be regarded as being potentially contaminated. Water used for drinking, brushing teeth or making ice should be boiled or otherwise sterilised. Dairy products are likely to be unpasteurised and should be avoided. Eat only well-cooked meat and fish, preferably served hot. Vegetables should be cooked and fruit peeled. Pork, salad and mayonnaise may carry increased risk.

Hotels
There are few and should be booked in advance. Payment in hard currency is required and a 10 per cent service charge is added.

Credit cards
Not in use.

Public holidays (national)

Fixed dates
1 Jan (New Year's Day), 17 Apr (FAO Day), 1 May (Labour Day), 14 Jul (Republic Day).

Variable dates
Eid al Adha (four days), Islamic New Year, Birth of the Prophet, Eid al Fitr (two days).

Islamic year – 1429 (10 Jan 2008–28 Dec 2008): The Islamic year contains 354 or 355 days, with the result that Muslim feasts advance by 10–12 days against the Gregorian calendar. Dates of feasts vary according to the sighting of the new moon, so cannot be forecast exactly.

Working hours
The weekly closing day is Friday.

Banking
Sat–Wed: 0800–1230; Thur: 0800–1100. During Ramadan: 0800–1000.

Business
Sat–Wed: 0800–1400; Thursday: 0800–1300.

Government
Summer hours: Sat–Wed: 0800–1230; Thu: 0800–1100. Winter hours: Sat–Wed: 0830–1430 Thu: 0830–1330.

Shops
Small shops tend to open very early, close during the middle of the day and then re-open from around 1600–1900 or later. Food markets open around 0900 and close at mid-day or when supplies are exhausted.

Telecommunications

Mobile/cell phones
GSM 900 services are available. Numbers begin 7801/2/3/4, plus 6 digits.

Electricity supply
220V AC, 50 cycles

Weights and measures
Metric system.

Social customs/useful tips
Traditional Islamic culture predominates, with Quranic law playing an active role in the day-to-day life of the country. Visitors should be careful to respect this and act accordingly. They should always address their hosts by full name and title. Traditional Arab hospitality is generally offered. In business meetings formal courtesies are expected. Visiting cards are regularly exchanged and these should be printed in Arabic as well as English. Meetings may not always be on a one-to-one basis and it is often difficult to confine conversation to the business in hand, as many topics may be discussed in order to assess the character of potential business partners. Patience and good humour are required.

Always refer to the stretch of water south of Iraq as the Arabian Gulf or the Gulf – never the Persian Gulf.

It is unwise to discuss religion or politics, and desirable to have an informed view on contemporary issues (such as Israel) in case such subjects arise.

During the Ramadan fasting month, both smoking and drinking in public are forbidden.

Security

Visitors should keep in touch with developments in the Middle East as any increase in regional tension might affect travel advice. The security situation in Iraq remains dangerous with insurgent forces targetting coalition interests and personnel as well as international agencies, such as the UN and the Red Cross. There are daily bombings in central and southern Iraq.

Getting there

Air

National airline: Iraqi Airways

Scheduled flights, in August 2006, were still being planned.

International airport/s: Baghdad International Airport (BGW), 18km west of Baghdad; Basra International Airport.

Other airport/s: Smaller airfields exist at Hadithah, Kirkuk and Mosul.

Airport tax: Departure tax: ID2,000.

Surface

Road: The only two borders open are the highway from Amman, Jordan, to Baghdad (2,331km across the desert) and from Turkey via the road through Zakho and Mosul; this crosses Iraqi Kurdistan territory and the Kurds sometimes impose taxes on goods carried.

Travel by road remains hazardous and is not recommended.

Rail: The line between Mosul and Aleppo, Syria was reopened, although the service was suspended.

Water: All ports remain closed to civilian traffic.

Main port/s: Umm Qasr and Khor al Zubair are the major commercial ports.

Getting about

National transport

Air: Services are subject to US military restrictions. Prior to 2003 Iraqi Airways flew from Baghdad to Basra. There are domestic airports at Mosul and Kirkuk.

Road: Despite the Iraq War, the country's 40,800km road system is in relatively good condition with 84 per cent paved.

Rail: Prior to 2003, the rail network included three-class services with sleeping accommodation, restaurant cars and air-conditioning. Rail links between most major centres include Baghdad-Mosul, Baghdad-Arbil and Baghdad-Basra.

City transport

Taxis: Prior to 2003, taxis were available in major cities and at hotels. There were shared and regular taxis. There was a standard fare system and taxis were meters. A surcharge was made after 2200 hours. Fares should be clearly agreed in advance. Tipping is not expected.

Car hire

BUSINESS DIRECTORY

The addresses listed below are a selection only. While World of Information makes every endeavour to check these addresses, we cannot guarantee that changes have not been made, especially to telephone numbers and area codes. We would welcome any corrections. Readers should be aware that the details following may not be current. Telephone numbers probably won't work.

Telephone area codes

The international direct dialling code (IDD) for Iraq is +964, followed by area code and subscriber's number:

Baghdad	1	Mosul	60
Basra	40	Najaf	33
Erbil	66	Nasiriya	42
Kirkuk	50	Sulayimaniya	53
Kut	23	Tikrit	21

Useful telephone numbers

Police: 104
Fire: 115
Ambulance: 122
Emergency hospital: 719-5191
Operator: 537-2191
Directory enquiries: 102
International operator: 105

Chambers of Commerce

Federation of Iraqi Chambers of Commerce, Sadoon Street, PO Box 3388 Al-Alwia, Baghdad (tel: 718-7348; fax: 718-1115; e-mail: union@uruklink.net).

Baghdad Chamber of Commerce, Mustansir Street, PO Box 24168 Almsarif, Baghdad (tel: 887-6111; fax: 887-9563).

Basrah Chamber of Commerce, Al-Azizyah Street, Alashad, Basrah (tel: 211-343; fax: 212-478).

Mosul Chamber of Commerce, Khalid Ibn Al-Waleed, PO Box 35, Mosul (tel: 774-771; fax: 771-359).

Banking

Bank of Baghdad, PO 3192, Alawiyah (tel: 822-7083).

Credit Bank of Iraq, PO Box 3420, Baghdad (tel: 360-0494).

Dar Es Salaam Investment Bank, PO Box 3067, Alawiyah (tel: 360-4646).

Industrial Bank of Iraq, al Khullani Square, PO Box 5825, Baghdad (tel: 887-2181).

Iraq Middle East Investment Bank, PO Box 10379, Baghdad (tel: 360-4242).

Rafidain Bank, New Banks' Street, Massarif, PO Box 11360, Baghdad (tel: 887-0522: fax: 415-8616).

Rashid Bank, PO Box 7177, Tourism Building, Haifa Street, Baghdad (tel: 884-5287, 885-3433; fax: 882-6201).

Central bank

Central Bank of Iraq, PO Box 64, Rashid Street, Baghdad, Iraq (tel: 886-5171; fax: 886-6802).

Travel information

Baghdad International Airport, Baghdad (tel: 887-2500, 886-3999; fax: 887-5808).

Ministries

Ministry of Foreign Affairs (email: press@iraqmofamail.net; internet: wwww.iraqmofa.net).

Directorate of Foreign Economic Relations, Ministry of Trade, Khulafa Street, al Khullani Square, Baghdad (tel: 887-2682).

Ministry of Industry and Military Industrialisation, Nidhal Street, near Sa'adoun Petrol Station, Baghdad (tel: 887-2006).

Ministry of Oil, al Mansour, PO Box 6178, Baghdad (tel: 541-0031).

Other useful addresses

Iraqi Embassy (in the UK), 169 Knightsbridge, London SW7 1DW (tel: (+44-20) 7602-8456 and 7581 2264; fax: (+44-20) 7589-3356).

Iraqi Embassy (in the USA), 1801 P Street, NW, Washington, DC 20036 (tel: (+1-202) 483 7500; internet: www.iraqiembassy.org).

Iraq National Oil Company, al Khullani Square, PO Box 476, Baghdad (tel: 887-1115).

Iraqi Federation of Industries, Iraqi Federation of Industries Building, al Khullani Square, Baghdad.

Other news agencies: Nina (National Iraqi News Agency): www.ninanews.com

Voices of Iraq: www.aswataliraq.info

Internet sites

Guide to Iraqi businesses: www.iraqdirectory.com

Iraq Stock Exchange: www.isx-iq.net

Iraq portal: www.portaliraq.com

Ireland

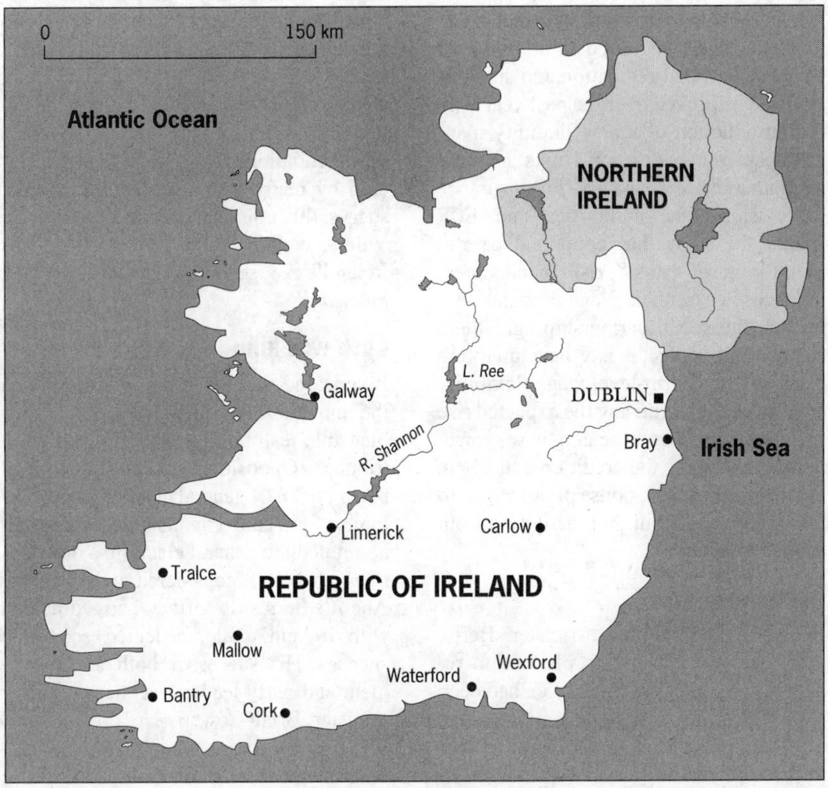

KEY FACTS

Official name: Éire (Ireland)

Head of State: President Mary McAleese (since 1997; returned unopposed Oct 2004)

Head of government: Prime Minister Bertie Ahern (leader of Fianna Fáil) (since 1997; re-elected 24 May 2007)

Ruling party: Coalition government led by Fianna Fáil (FF) (Soldiers of Destiny), Comhaontas Glas (Green Party) (Greens) and two independents (since 2002; re-elected 24 May 2007)

Area: 70,283 square km

Population: 4.32 million (2007)*

Capital: Dublin

Official language: Irish (Gaelic) and English

Currency: Euro (eur) = 100 cents (from 1 Jan 2002; previous currency, punt, locked at IR£0.79 per euro)

Exchange rate: eur0.63 per US$ (Jul 2008)

GDP per capita: US$59,924 (2007)

GDP real growth: 5.30% (2007)*

Labour force: 1.90 million (2004)

Unemployment: 4.60% (2007); in June 2008 the actual number of unemployed (217,400) rose to the highest since September 1998.

Inflation: 2.70% (2007)

Balance of trade: US$37.65 billion (2005)

Foreign debt: US$944.95 billion (2004)

Visitor numbers: 8.00 million (2006)*

* estimated figure

In 2008 Ireland found itself, almost unwittingly, at the centre of European politics when its voters, in a referendum, rejected the proposed, watered down, European Union (EU) Lisbon Treaty that had come to replace the originally tabled European constitution. The constitution itself had been rejected by voters in France and Holland. Voting in critical European referenda has become something of an Irish speciality. Irish voters had initially rejected the 2001 Treaty of Nice which allowed EU enlargement, approving it on a second vote.

A Euro-muddle

A second referendum originally mooted for mid-2008 was indefinitely delayed as it became unclear what, if anything, would happen if Irish voters rejected it for a second time. The legal position in such a situation was perfectly clear: there would be no Lisbon Treaty, according to the European Commission's spokeswoman in Ireland, Ruth Deasy. Public opinion surveys in Ireland had suggested that its voters had little knowledge of the treaty, and even less of why they should approve it. Officials in Brussels had been at pains to point out to the Irish that it ill became a country that had gone from being one of the poorest members of the EU when it joined in 1973 to third place in terms of purchasing power to reject the treaty. These arguments were largely lost on an Irish electorate that in 2008 had become more concerned with falling property values than with European harmonisation. The ungainly drafting of the Lisbon Treaty did little to help: the treaty itself looked like the proverbial horse designed by a committee, a series of complicated, bureaucratic amendments to the original constitution with no obvious rationale or narrative. The clearest feature of the proposed treaty was its lack of clarity. It did however serve to cause concern among those Irish voters that bothered to read it, over issues such as taxation and the possible erosion of Ireland's national sovereignty and its cherished neutrality.

Between 1995 and 1999 Ireland had the fastest growing economy in the developed world. In 2006, Ireland's GDP grew at three times the rate of the eurozone average. If the economy grew, so did a number of worrying social problems, not least drug-taking. It is estimated that there are some 75,000 cocaine users in the republic. Ironically, the end of the Northern Ireland conflict allowed drug taking and dealing to grow unchecked as paramilitary vigilante policing ended. In the early twenty-first century Ireland could claim Europe's fastest growing death rate due to illegal drugs.

IMF approval

In its annual report on the Irish economy, the International Monetary Fund (IMF) noted that Ireland's economic performance remained impressive, saying somewhat ominously that in recent years economic growth had become became increasingly reliant on house building. Competitiveness eroded somewhat, though it is still broadly appropriate. The rise in euro area interest rates has prompted a welcome cooling of the housing market, which will help to rebalance economic growth and reduce inflation, though there is a risk of a sharper slowdown. The key policy challenges are therefore to support adjustment to sustainable growth. The IMF expressed concern over the introduction of measures that weaken the underlying fiscal position. In the view of the IMF over the medium term, it will be important to improve the quality of spending and review the tax base. As age-related spending is destined to rise considerably in the long term, improving the public understanding of fiscal pressures and a better approach to pension planning would be needed.

The IMF had noted that Ireland's banks had large exposures to the property market, but stress tests suggested that cushions are adequate to cover a range of shocks. Financial regulation and supervision had improved over the past year with the introduction of a new liquidity management framework for banks and the strengthening of capacity for insurance supervision. The authorities and IMF shared the view that continued careful monitoring of banks' risk management practices is essential. Wage moderation – in both the social partnership agreement and the public sector pay benchmarking exercise – and firm-level wage flexibility are crucial to minimising the expected rise in unemployment and seizing new growth opportunities. As the credit crunch began to bite in early 2008, house prices began to fall sharply, and building activity all but ground to a halt.

Ahern goes

In April 2008 Prime Minister Bertie Ahern announced that he planned to resign in early May. Mr Ahern, 56, had been *taoiseach* (prime minister) since June 1997 and had been a member of the Irish Parliament for 31 years. The announcement came a day after Mr Ahern began a court challenge to limit the work of a public inquiry probing planning corruption in the 1990s. The tribunal was probing Mr Ahern's personal finances. Mr Ahern had been leader of his party, Fianna Fáil, since 1994 and headed up a coalition government.

Mr Ahern had played a key role in the negotiations leading up to the Northern Ireland Good Friday Agreement of 1998, which finally brought a degree of peace to the province. When the peace talks held in the Northern Ireland Parliament Stormont were in their crucial final stages, he returned from his mother's funeral to rejoin the negotiations. Mr Ahern was considered by many to be the republic's most successful politician since Eamon De Valera, winning three elections. He was Ireland's second-longest serving *taoiseach*.

Cash was king

It appeared that Mr Ahern had bowed to the inevitable following seemingly implausible testimony to an anti-corruption tribunal. Opposition deputies, who had narrowly lost a general election in 2007 to Fianna Fáil, called on his successor to call an immediate general election, a development that was considered unlikely. Mr Ahern's terms in office had coincided with Ireland's unprecedented economic success. His successor both as government and party leader, was deputy prime minister, Brian Cowen.

The investigation into Mr Ahern's affairs focussed on secret cash payments he allegedly received from businessmen in the mid-1990s. When the *Irish Times* published details of the payments in September 2006, Mr Ahern had claimed on national television and in parliament to have received just two major payments from personal friends totalling US$96,000 in December 1993 and January 1994. Having first insisted that he was broke at the time, he later admitted he already had an office safe full of money as well as a bank loan.

The investigation subsequently uncovered undocumented cash deposits running up to December 1994 allegedly involving Mr Ahern. The total 1994 value of the deposits – which were reportedly held in accounts controlled by Mr Ahern, his daughters, his former girlfriend and his local party office – allegedly exceeded 450,000 Irish pounds (US$880,000). Mr Ahern's defence was badly weakened when his former office secretary was reduced to tears on the stand as she denied, then admitted, taking £15,500 (US$30,500) to deposit in accounts

KEY INDICATORS — Ireland

	Unit	2003	2004	2005	2006	2007
Population	m	3.93	4.02	4.13	4.24	*4.32
Gross domestic product (GDP)	US$bn	148.60	153.70	200.77	219.37	*258.57
GDP per capita	US$	39,030	44,888	48,604	51,800	59,924
GDP real growth	%	3.6	5.1	5.5	5.7	*5.3
Inflation	%	4.1	2.3	2.2	2.7	2.9
Unemployment	%	4.8	4.5	4.4	4.4	4.6
Exports (fob) (goods)	US$m	92,695.0	98,745.0	102,934.0	104,667.0	115,517.0
Imports (cif) (goods)	US$m	52,789.0	59,183.0	65,286.0	72,779.0	84,226.0
Balance of trade	US$m	39,906.0	39,562.0	37,649.0	31,888.0	31,292.0
Current account	US$m	-2,140.0	-2,660.0	-5,233.0	-9,136.0	-11,685.0
Total reserves minus gold	US$m	4,079.0	2,831.0	779.0	720.0	779.0
Foreign exchange	US$m	3,425.0	2,324.0	514.0	494.0	591.0
Exchange rate	per US$	0.88	0.80	0.77	0.75	0.69

* estimated figure

controlled by Mr Ahern and his two daughters in 1994. Polls had revealed that half Ireland's electorate did not believe Mr Ahern's testimony.

Outlook

Taking over from Mr Ahern proved no easy task for Mr Cowen. Unemployment had begun to register as a major problem as Ireland's construction based economy faltered. Lower growth rates cut tax revenues, pushing Ireland's budget deficit up towards the 3 per cent limit imposed by the European Commission. Ireland's relations with the Commission had also become more complex. The Lisbon Treaty had been defeated by a majority of 53 per cent in the referendum; this despite the fact that the net benefit of EU membership to each member of the population was eur10,000 (US$19,600). The uncharismatic Mr Cowen is faced with a very uncertain future, both politically and economically.

Risk assessment

Economy	Good
Politics	Fair
Regional stability	Good

COUNTRY PROFILE

Historical profile

In the twelfth century, the Norman invasion began a long period of foreign domination. Over the centuries, Irish Catholic hostility increased along with English control, following the seizure of land, the Protestant Reformation and the loss of religious and political freedoms.

1801 Ireland was united with Great Britain through the Act of Union.

1840s The potato crop was blighted over several years, leading to severe famine. Combined with emigration, this reduced the population by one-third. The decade also saw the beginnings of a republican movement.

1916 The British army suppressed the republican Easter Rising, provoking the formation of Sinn Féin (Ourselves alone).

1919–21 The Anglo-Irish War was fought against British troops and police by the military arm of Sinn Féin, the Irish Republican Army (IRA).

1921 Partition saw 26 southern counties form the Irish Free State under the British crown, while the six north-eastern counties remained part of the UK.

1922 The Dáil Eireann (Irish parliament) ratified the treaty establishing the Free State, sparking a civil war with nationalists, who advocated full independence, led by Eamonn De Valera.

1927 De Valera entered parliament as the head of the newly-created Fianna Fáil (Soldiers of Destiny).

1932 Fianna Fáil won the elections. De Valera began to work towards full independence from Britain.

1937 The constitution was promulgated, abolishing the Free State and declaring Ireland as an independent state.

1938 Douglas Hyde became the country's first president, with De Valera as prime minister.

1939–45 Ireland remained neutral during the Second World War, but many Irishmen fought in the British Army acting on behalf of the Irish state.

1948 Fianna Fáil lost the election and De Valera was replaced by John Costello.

1949 A republic was proclaimed and Ireland left the Commonwealth. Partition remained contentious and the IRA mounted a terrorist campaign for reunification with the six northern counties.

1955 Ireland joined the UN.

1957 De Valera was voted back into office as prime minister; he said that the union of Northern Ireland with the Republic could not be achieved through violence.

1959 De Valera became president.

1973 Ireland joined the forerunner of the EU, the European Economic Community (EEC). Fianna Fáil, the traditional party of government, lost power in the general election and Jack Lynch resigned. Liam Cosgrave formed a coalition between his party, Fine Gael, and the Labour Party. The IRA became active again after a long period of decline as fighting intensified in the North due to oppression of Catholics under the Unionist-run regime and later, direct rule from London.

1977 Fianna Fáil won the general election and Jack Lynch again became prime minister.

1980s None of a succession of elections produced a single-party majority government.

1985 The Ango-Irish Agreement established regular participation by the Irish government in political, legal, security and cross-border matters in Northern Ireland.

1990 The first left-winger and the first woman, Mary Robinson, was elected to the presidency.

1992 In a referendum, Irish voters agreed to loosen the abortion laws, enabling women to travel abroad to have an abortion.

1993 The Downing Street Declaration by the Irish and British governments offered talks to all parties in Northern Ireland if they renounced political violence.

1995 A referendum to change the 1937 constitution narrowly approved the lifting of the ban on divorce.

1997 Mary McAleese, who lives in Northern Ireland, became the first British subject to be elected president of the Irish Republic.

1998 In a referendum, nearly 95 per cent of voters approved the Good Friday Agreement, which entailed Ireland giving up its constitutional claim to Northern Ireland.

2001 In a referendum, Ireland voted against the Treaty of Nice, which proposed enlargement of the EU to include up to 13 new member states.

2002 Euro currency replaced the punt. After parliamentary elections, Bertie Ahern was confirmed as prime minister and formed a coalition government led by Fianna Fáil. At the second attempt, Ireland voted 63 per cent in favour of the EU's Treaty of Nice, on a turnout of 48 per cent.

2004 As holder of the EU presidency, it hosted ceremonies to welcome the EU's 10 new member states. On 1 October, President Mary McAleese was returned unopposed for a second term.

2005 Irish was adopted as an official working language of the EU. In the Irish-speaking, mainly western, districts (Gaeltacht), English has been removed from road signs and official maps.

2006 Former prime minister, Charles Haughey, died on 13 June, aged 80. In December an official tribunal found that he had 'accepted bribes and followed unethical business practices' and accepted 'cash from wealthy businessmen over a 17-year period, including eight years as Taoiseach'.

2007 In the 24 May general elections, Fianna Fáil won 77 seats (out of 166) and just failed to achieve an outright majority, prompting coalition talks. On 13 June, the Green party and two independents agreed to a government coalition.

2008 Bertie Ahern resigned as prime minister on 7 May and Brian Cowen (leader of Fianna Fáil) was elected prime minister by parliament. On 13 June, in a referendum held on the reform of the expanded EU, voters rejected the Lisbon Treaty by 53.4 per cent to 46.6 per cent. The treaty was designed to provide a streamlined European Commission, a new president of the European Council, removal of the national veto in more policy areas and a European foreign minister. By June, 14 countries out of 27 had ratified the treaty by acts of parliament but a referendum in Ireland was mandatory, as constitutional changes were required to conform to the treaty.

Political structure

Constitution

The constitution was drawn up in 1937. The Uchtarán na Eireann (president), directly elected every seven years, is guardian of the constitution, and may submit a bill to the people in a referendum or to the Supreme Court if it is felt that legislation might contravene the constitution. The constitution was amended three times by referendum in the 1990s, to loosen anti-abortion laws, legalise divorce and give up Ireland's territorial claim to Northern Ireland in favour of the principle of unity by consent.

Form of state

Parliamentary democratic republic

The executive

Executive power is exercised by the cabinet, led by the Taoiseach (prime minister) who is appointed by the president on the recommendation of the Dáil Eireann (House of Representatives).

National legislature

Legislative power is vested in the bicameral Oireachtas (National Parliament), consisting of the Seanad Eireann (Senate) and the Dáil Eireann.

The Dáil is the main legislative body and has the responsibility of electing the cabinet, which must consist of not less than seven and no more than 15 members. There are 166 members of the Dáil, who are elected by proportional representation every five years.

The Seanad, with 60 members, is elected by a system of electoral colleges, its periods corresponding with that of the Dáil. It can delay a bill for up to 90 days or suggest changes, but cannot block it permanently. The taoiseach nominates 11 Seanad members, 43 are elected by panels representing vocational and cultural interests and six are elected by Ireland's universities.

Legal system

The Irish constitution declares that every person living in Ireland has certain fundamental personal rights, listed in articles. Every constitutional right has the same status and value, however when a conflict arises between constitutional rights the courts have the prerogative to adjudicate which constitutional right is more important in which particular case. Much civil and criminal law is derived from English common law and remains in force if it is consistent with the Constitution.

The courts are made up of District, Circuit and the High Court. District Courts deal with summary offences and minor civil cases. Circuit Courts deal with civil cases of a more serious nature and criminal cases are presented before a judge with a jury of 12 citizens.

The High Court, has full jurisdiction in civil and criminal cases and can act as an appeal court from the Circuit Court. When exercising criminal jurisdiction, it is called the Central Criminal Court. Under the Offences Against the State Act 1939, Special Criminal Courts were set up; these sit without a jury.

The Supreme Court, the court of final appeal, consists of a Chief Justice and five other judges who can hear appeals on all High Court decisions. It is also the final arbiter on the interpretation of the constitution.

Last elections

October 2004 (no presidential elections were held as Mary McAleese was the only candidate); 24 May 2007 (parliamentary).

Results: Parliamentary: Fianna Fáil won 41.6 per cent (78 seats out of 166), Fine Gael 27.3 per cent (51), Labour Party 10.1 per cent (20), Greens 4.7 per cent (six), Sinn Féin 6.9 per cent (four), Progressive Democrats 2.7 per cent (two), Independents 5.7 per cent (5).

Next elections

2011 (presidential); 2012 (parliamentary).

Political parties

Ruling party

Coalition government led by Fianna Fáil (FF) (Soldiers of Destiny), Comhaontas Glas (Green Party) (Greens) and two independents (since 2002; re-elected 24 May 2007)

Main opposition party

Fine Gael (FG) (United Ireland Party)

Population

4.32 million (2007)*

Last census: April 2002: 3,917,203

Population density: 54 inhabitants per square km. Urban population: 59 per cent of total (1995–2001).

Annual growth rate: 1.3 per cent 1994–2004 (WHO 2006)

Ethnic make-up

Ireland is predominantly white. Only recently has it seen non-white immigration.

Religions

Roman Catholic (95 per cent); Church of Ireland (2.8 per cent); Presbyterian (0.4 per cent) Jewish (0.1 per cent); others (0.3 per cent); no religion (1.2 per cent).

Education

Education is divided into three levels: primary, secondary and tertiary. Primary schooling (including, although not compulsory, infant pre-schooling from age four), lasts for eight years. Secondary schooling starts age 12 for either five or six years, and includes a junior and a senior cycle with examinations at the end of each. About 81 per cent of Irish students complete the senior cycle and almost 50 per cent go on to tertiary education, which can be either academic or vocational. Ireland has a higher proportion of graduates with scientific skills in the 25–34 age group than any other OECD member, except Japan.

Compulsory years: Six to 15.

Enrolment rate: 105 per cent gross primary enrolment of relevant age group; 118 per cent gross secondary enrolment (including repeaters) (World Bank).

Pupils per teacher: 22 in primary schools.

Health

Per capita total expenditure on health (2003) was US$2,496; of which per capita government spending was US$1,968, at the international dollar rate, (WHO 2006).

Eight regional health boards administer Ireland's health system, which is funded by the central government, through the department of health, which in turn is under the control of the minister of health. Various community welfare services operate for the chronically sick, the elderly and the disabled. Almost 38 per cent of the population – those on lower incomes – receive medical services free of charge. The remainder receive public hospital services for a minimum charge. Charges are also made to the better-off for visits to the family doctor and to hospital consultants.

HIV/Aids

HIV prevalence: 0.1 per cent aged 15–49 in 2003 (World Bank)

Life expectancy: 78 years, 2004 (WHO 2006)

Fertility rate/Maternal mortality rate: 1.9 births per woman, 2004 (WHO 2006); maternal mortality, 5 per 100,000 live births (World Bank).

Child (under 5 years) mortality rate (per 1,000): 5.1 per 1,000 live births (World Bank)

Head of population per physician: 2.79 physicians per 1,000 people, 2004 (WHO 2006)

Welfare

Social insurance is compulsory for employees and the self-employed. The principal benefits are unemployment, disability and maternity payments plus pay-related benefits to supplement those on low incomes, invalidity pension (for those on disability benefit), widows' payments (contributory and non-contributory), orphans' payments, deserted wives' payments, old age pensions (contributory and non-contributory), medical treatment benefits, including dental and optical, an occupational injuries scheme and certain free schemes for the elderly. Employees in the private sector contribute at the highest rate.

Main cities

Dublin (capital, estimated population 1.0 million in 2004), Cork (193,400), Limerick (84,900), Galway (67,200), Waterford (47,800).

Languages spoken

Official documents are printed in both English and Irish.

Five per cent of the population speak Irish as their first language.

Official language/s
Irish (Gaelic) and English

Media
Press
In 2007 less than 50 per cent of the population read a daily newspaper, however, access of newspaper websites rose by 27 per cent.
There are over 50 newspapers and over 100 magazines. The circulation figures for morning newspapers have remained stable but figures for evening newspapers have been falling.
Dailies: The newspapers with the highest circulations are the Irish Independent (www.independent.ie), The Irish Times (www.irishtimes.com) and the Irish Examiner (www.irishexaminer.com). The free issue Metro (www.metroireland.ie) has taken a lead in circulation figures in Dublin.
Weeklies: In Gaelic Foinse (www.foinse.ie) is published in Galway. In English, Woman's Way (www.harmonia.ie) is the leading woman's magazine, An Phoblacht Republican (www.anphoblacht.com) takes with an Irish Republican perspective on national and international affairs. A number of local or regional newspapers, owned by few conglomerates including North West of Ireland Printing and Publishing (www.nwipp-newspapers.com) published weeklies such as Donegal News and GaelicLife and Independent News and Media. (www.independent.ie). Other smaller newspapers include Waterford Today (www.waterford-today.ie), Limerick Post (www2.limerickpost.ie) and Anglo Celt (www.anglocelt.ie) from Cavan. There are also many specialist, genre magazines available.
Business: Dublin has a small number of business publications. The weekly newspaper Sunday Business Post (www.sbpost.ie) provides Ireland's financial, political, The monthly Marine Times (www.marinetimes.ie) covers the fishing industry and aquaculture industries and communities and ShelfLife (www.mediateam.ie) for retail news. A magazine aimed at directors Decision (www.decisionireland.com) is published six times a year.
Periodicals: The monthly Image (www.image.ie) is a glossy women's magazine. U (www.harmonia.ie) is a tabloid, published fortnightly. Of general interest, the scholarly History Ireland (www.historyireland.com) and Irish Roots Magazine (www.irishrootsmedia.com) on genealogy and ZenthOptimedia (www.zenithoptimedia.com.sg) publishes entertainment guides GV Magazine and Newsline.

Broadcasting
The Broadcasting Authority is responsible for regulating public and private broadcasting. Broadcasting laws lay down rules regarding the balance of news and current affairs and culture in broadcasting, in addition to the prohibition of matters which the minister for telecommunications considers likely to promote or incite crime. Radio Telefís Éireann (RTE) (www.rte.ie) is the national public broadcaster, funded by a license fee and advertising revenue.
Radio: There are around 60 radio stations located around the country. Almost three million adults listen to the radio every day and of the top 20 shows, 18 are broadcast by RTE (www.rte.ie), which has four networks including popular music, classical and cultural, talk and an Irish-language station. Private, commercial radio includes Today FM (www.rte.ie), NewsTalk (http://newstalk.ie) and 98FM (www.dublins98.ie) from Dublin, Red FM (www.redfm.ie) from Cork and Galway Bay FM (www.galwaybayfm.ie).
Television: The RTE (www.rte.ie) has two television channels (RTE 1 and Network 2) and provides locally produced shows as well as imported programmes. It has a 57 per cent share of the advertising market and its main local competitor TV3 (www.tv3.ie) has 20 per cent, followed by TG4 (www.tg4.ie) the Irish language station. Overall, RTE's principal competition is from UK digital TV providers.
Digital TV is received by 58 per cent of households, but free-to-air digital services is expected to begin in 2009. One-third of homes are cabled, however satellite TV is becoming popular, carrying further UK channels.
Advertising
Annual adspend is typically around US$19 billion. Promotion of tobacco products is banned, and the advertising of alcohol is strictly controlled. Commercials on TV and radio are limited to 10 per cent of transmission time. Newspapers, magazines, posters and films are also widely used. Information is available from the Advertising Standards Authority in Dublin.

Economy
Ireland has continued, since the 1990s, its impressive economic expansion with GDP growth at 5.5 per cent in 2005 and an estimated 5.3 per cent in 2006. Per capita income, at US$48,604 in 2005, has overtaken the EU average with a real growth rate of 3.3 per cent, while inflation remained low at 2.4 per cent in 2005–06. However, the Organisation of Economic Co-operation and Development (OECD) has warned that Ireland is vulnerable not only to external shocks but also to some home grown ones as well. Reform of the electricity and telecommunications sector is desirable, to prevent competition from being stifled. Infrastructure needs to be upgraded and scientific education and innovation fostered through public spending.
The tight labour market could prevent expansion in the future. Immigration is currently alleviating supply bottlenecks but in the long-term, measures to increase female participation should be undertaken.
The largest domestic worry reported was the housing market which had tripled in real value since 1997. Nevertheless, a property crash is thought unlikely.
Ireland has an open economy with principle exports in goods and services producing 50 per cent of GDP, of which tourism, as the major service industry, typically contributes over 4 per cent of GDP. Exports in 2005 amounted to almost US$103 billion, while imports amounted to just over US$65 billion.
Juxtaposed with high-tech industries, is an agricultural sector that accounts for 8 per cent of GDP, 7 per cent of exports and employs 7.5 per cent of the workforce.
Ireland has a highly skilled labour pool. A national development plan is focussed on IT, life-sciences, medical technologies, engineering, financial and international services, Internet based activity and digital business. Of the more than 1,100 foreign-owned companies operating in Ireland around 50 per cent are US based, and the combined number of UK and German companies make up around 25 per cent. Those industries that have shown most growth in exports are computers and electrical machinery and chemical and pharmaceuticals products.

External trade
As a member of the European Union, Ireland operates within a communitywide free trade union, with tariffs sets as a whole. Internationally, the EU has free trade agreements with a number of nations and trading blocs worldwide.
International trade accounts for around 150 per cent of GDP. It is an exporter of electronic and IT equipment and pharmaceutical and biotechnology products produced by multinational and start-up hi-tech companies utilising a highly educated workforce.
Ireland is the fourth largest producer of salmon in Europe and exports 60 per cent of its meat production.
Imports
Imports consist of data processing equipment, other machinery and equipment, chemicals, petroleum and petroleum products, textiles and clothing.
Main sources: UK (31.7 per cent total, 2006), US (11.3 per cent), Germany (8.2 per cent).

Exports
Exports consist mainly of machinery and equipment, computers, chemicals, pharmaceuticals, live animals and animal products and natural gas (to Northern Ireland).
Main destinations: US (18.3 per cent total, 2006), UK (17.5 per cent), Belgium (16.0 per cent).

Agriculture
Farming
Agricultural earnings equate to over 8 per cent of annual GDP and around 7 per cent of export earnings. The sector employs 7.5 per cent of the labour force.
With its temperate climate and relatively high levels of rainfall, Ireland is suited to stock raising, with the result that there is a predominance of livestock production in Irish agriculture. Approximately 70 per cent of all land is devoted to pasture while 10 per cent is tilled. Irish farms tend to be owner-occupied, with an average size of just over 25 hectares.
Agriculture policy is dominated by the EU and its Common Agricultural Policy (CAP). Ireland is a major beneficiary of EU farm subsidies. Fundamental reform to the Common Agricultural Policy (CAP) was introduced on 1 January 2005 in Ireland. The subsidies paid on farm output, which tended to benefit large farms and encourage overproduction, were replaced by single farm payments not conditional on production. This is expected to reward farms that provide and maintain a healthy environment, food safety and animal welfare standards. The changes are also intended to encourage market conscious production and cut the cost of CAP to the EU taxpayer.
Ireland is a net exporter of agricultural goods. Main exports include meat, vegetables, milk, butter and alcoholic beverages. Main agricultural imports include rice and maize.
The proposed first trials of generically modified potatoes, in 2006, caused protests from environmentalists, who claimed that Ireland's reputation as a 'clean, green' producer could be lost.
Estimated crop production in 2005 included: 1,856,400 tonnes (t) cereals in total, 1,027,000t barley, 1,500,000t sugar beets, 723,000t wheat, 500,000t potatoes, 14,000t pulses, ,660t oilcrops, 15,000t apples, 106,000t oats, 22,700t fruit in total, 221,660t vegetables in total.
Estimated livestock production included: 977,005t meat in total, 563,200t beef, 207,500t pig meat, 70,000t lamb, 131,680t poultry, 32,000t eggs, 5,500,000t milk, 200t honey, 64,750t cattle hides.

Fishing
The sea fishing industry makes an important contribution to the agricultural economy. Mackerel accounts for about 35 per cent of total catch, and is the most important species landed.
In 2004, the total marine fish catch was 243,496 tonnes and the total crustacean catch was 22,646 tonnes.

Forestry
With forest cover estimated at 659,000 hectares (ha), it occupies less than a tenth of the total land area. Though Ireland is traditionally one of Europe's least forested countries, massive afforestation programmes have contributed to an annual average increase of 3.03 per cent, the equivalent of 17,000ha of forest cover. Private ownership in new planting areas has been rising with around two-thirds of the forest remaining under state ownership. Employment in the forest and wood products industry is about 13,000.
Most of the forest is available for wood supply. Roundwood production has considerably increased with the expansion of forest cover. Much of the production consists of softwood logs for the domestic sawn wood and panel industry. Ireland imports most of its paper and sawn wood. Exports of forest materials in 2004 amounted to US$475.9 million, while imports amounted to US$902.8 million.
Production in 2004 included 2,562,035 cubic metres (cum) roundwood, 2,542,489cum industrial roundwood, 938,959cum sawnwood, 1,722,636cum sawlogs & veneer logs, 722,009cum pulpwood, 841,093cum wood-based panels, 19,546cum wood fuel.

Industry and manufacturing
The industrial sector accounts for 24 per cent of GDP, 80 per cent of the value of annual exports and approximately 27 per cent of employment.
Ireland's indigenous manufacturing base is relatively small. Traditional industries, such as food and beverages, textiles, paper, non-metallic minerals and machinery, dominate, although there has been rapid growth in new export-oriented chemicals as well as electronic engineering industries. Most of the new capital and skill-intensive industries are subsidiaries of large US and European multinationals and are heavily reliant on imported primary and intermediate inputs.
US Wyeth Pharmaceuticals is investing US$1 billion in a factory in the world's largest integrated biotechnology campus at Grange Castle in Dublin, which opened in September 2005. Wyeth will produce infant vaccines, antibiotics and an arthritis treatments.

Tourism
Tourism has grown at a rapid rate since 1990, the number of visitors doubling to 6.6 million by 2004. The sector contributes around 4.5 per cent of GDP and gives employment to 140,000 people. All parts of the Republic benefit from the expansion of tourism, which has become an important factor in regional development, bringing employment and business to otherwise economically-deprived areas. Dublin has become a major short city-break destination. The UK is the main source of visitors. US tourists is the next largest and the most lucrative market. Vastly improved air connections, as well as sea links, have assisted Ireland's tourist explosion. The authorities are concerned about the cost and quality of the tourism product and are seeking to sharpen the sector's competitiveness.

Mining
Mining accounts for about 1 per cent of GNP and 1 per cent of the workforce. Europe's largest zinc and lead deposits are located at Navan, County Meath, and are operated by Tara Mines. Production has continued since the mid-1970s.
Ireland is Europe's leading producer of zinc. There are also reserves of gypsum, barytes, dolomite, silica sand, limestone, coal, marble and small amounts of silver. Gypsum is extracted from an open-pit at Knocknacran, Co Monaghan. Gold and base metals have been discovered at Clontibret, County Monaghan.
A zinc mining project at Lisheen, county Tipperary, began production in 2000. The US$280.5 million project is a joint venture between Ivernia West, an Irish exploration company, and Anglo-American, the South African company. The two ore deposits, containing 19 million tonnes of recoverable reserves, have been producing 1.5 million tonnes of ore or 160,000 tonnes of zinc a year since 2000.

Hydrocarbons
Dependence on imported petroleum has been reduced due to the exploitation of domestic gas and peat reserves. No significant hydrocarbon reserves have been found. In 2003, the Irish government adjusted the regulations for exploration and production in a bid to encourage new investment in the oil industry.
Natural gas represents around 23 per cent of primary energy consumption. Ireland's total proven gas reserves amounted to 19.8 billion cubic metres in 2004. However, Ireland still continues to import around 80 per cent of its gas demand, primarily from Britain. The government plans to become self sufficient in gas by 2007; this will be when the Corrib and Sevens Head gas field comes online. Indigenous reserves of natural gas are

located in the Kinsale Head gas field and the smaller Ballycotton field off the Cork coast.
Coal is not produced in Ireland but is imported.

Energy
Ireland has the only stand-alone electricity and gas grid in the EU, although new projects will increase the country's interdependence with the UK and the rest of Europe. It has an installed capacity of 4,600MW, with peak demand of 3,800MW. It is one of the fastest growing energy markets in Europe, with demand increasing by 5 per cent a year from the mid-1990s.
A natural gas pipeline project linking the country to the UK will provide security of supply and meet growing demand from industry and power generation.
Dependence on imported petroleum has been reduced due to the exploitation of domestic gas and peat reserves. Peat continues to provide around 550MW of generated electricity and is also used in significant quantities as a domestic fuel.

Financial markets
Stock exchange
The Irish Stock Exchange (ISE) has faced severe constraints on growth as, like many small markets in the euro-zone, Irish equities have suffered as institutions re-locate assets. This reduced the weighting of Irish stocks as they no longer had to match their liabilities with assets, but bought euro-based equities which no longer represent a currency risk.
The ISE launched the Irish Enterprise Exchange (IEX) in April 2005, designed to offer a trading forum for local and smaller companies within Ireland.

Banking and insurance
The two top Irish banks, Allied Irish Banks (AIB) and the Bank of Ireland, dominate the domestic market.
There is evidence of intensified competition within the domestic Irish market, with domestic and international newcomers. Domestically, certain building societies and banks have been looking to increase their value to shareholders through mergers and diversification of services.
Banking competition from abroad is mainly from the UK. However, the Irish banking system is widely regarded as overcrowded and may be in need of consolidation if its long-run competitiveness is to be sustained. Higher inflation and worries about European interest rates have dampened the short-term outlook for Irish equities.
Central bank
Central Bank of Ireland; European Central Bank (ECB).

Time
GMT (daylight saving, end March to end October, GMT plus one hour)

Geography
Ireland is situated in the north-west of Europe, bordered in the east by the Irish Sea, in the west by the Atlantic Ocean and in the south by the Celtic Sea. The landmass is bounded by mountains and has a low-lying central plain.
The island of Ireland consists of 32 counties, of which six, in the north east, belong to Northern Ireland, part of the United Kingdom.
Hemisphere
Northern

Climate
Ireland is in the temperate zone, with moderate south-westerly winds, influenced by the warm waters of the Gulf Stream, which produce a mild climate with rain throughout the year and annual rainfall varying between 800–1,200mm. The driest months are May and June.
The coldest months are January and February, when temperatures average between 4 and 7 degrees Celsius (C); the warmest months are July and August, when temperatures average between 14 and 17 degrees C.

Dress codes
While dress tends to be informal, business people normally wear suits, and evening social events can be quite formal. A medium-weight raincoat is advised throughout the year.

Entry requirements
Passports
Required by all, except UK-born nationals, who require official photographic identification, and other EU visitors with a valid national ID card.
Visa
Visas are not required by nationals of the EU, the Americas, Australasia and many Asian countries. For confirmation see www.irlgov.ie/iveagh and see Service. Other business travellers should contact the consulate of the nearest Irish Embassy for further information.
Currency advice/regulations
The import of local and foreign currency is unrestricted.
Travellers cheques are widely accepted.
Customs
Personal items are duty-free. There are no duties levied on alcohol and tobacco between EU member states, providing amounts imported are for personal consumption.
Prohibited imports
A wide range of items, including firearms, offensive weapons, ammunition and explosives, pornography, meat and meat products, live or dead animals (including birds and poultry), hay and straw (including used in packing) and endangered species.
UK residents only may be accompanied by a domestic dog, which has its necessary passport of health.

Health (for visitors)
Nationals of the European Economic Area (EEA) countries and Switzerland can access reduced cost and sometimes free medical treatment using a European Health Insurance Card (EHIC) while visiting the EEA. Exceptions include nationals of the 10 countries, which joined the EU in 2004, whose EHIC is not valid in Switzerland. Applications for the EHIC should be made before travelling.
Mandatory precautions
There are no requirements.
Advisable precautions
Travel insurance for those not entitled to free emergency cover.

Hotels
Classified into three categories: Star A, B and C. Reservations should be made in advance. Tipping: 10 per cent is customary.

Credit cards
All international credit and debit cards are widely accepted. ATMs are available in most town.

Public holidays (national)
Fixed dates
1 Jan (New Year's Day), 17 Mar (St Patrick's Day), 25–26 Dec (Christmas).
Variable dates
Good Friday, Easter Monday, May Bank Holiday (first Mon in May); June Bank Holiday (first Mon in Jun), Summer Bank Holiday (first Mon in Aug), Halloween Bank Holiday (last Mon in Oct).

Working hours
Banking
Mon–Fri: 0900–1600 (banks open later one evening a week, in Dublin on Thursdays until 1700, may vary in other cities).
Business
Mon–Fri: 0900–1700.
Government
Mon–Fri: 0915–1300, 1415–1715.
Shops
Mon–Fri: 0900–1730; late night shopping in city centres usually occurs once a week when shops are open to 2100.
Supermarkets Mon–Wed: 0830–1900; Thu–Sat: 0830–2100/2000/1900; Sun: 1200–1800.

Telecommunications
Mobile/cell phones
GSM 900/1800 operate throughout the country.

Internet/e-mail

Electricity supply

220V AC, with UK style, flat, three-pin plugs.

Social customs/useful tips

The hold of the Catholic Church over Ireland has diminished in recent years and the country now has an air of moderate social liberalism, although there are more conservative attitudes in rural areas.

Smoking is banned in pubs and restaurants.

Getting there

Air

National airline: Aer Lingus

International airport/s: Dublin (DUB), 10km north of city. Airport express coaches and taxis are available to the city centre.

Shannon (SNN), 26 km from Limerick. Bus services are available every hour to and from both Limerick and Clare, (60 minutes duration). A daily express coach travels between both Shannon and Limerick, or Galway. A taxi service is also available to Limerick.

Airport facilities at both airports include duty-free shopping, bank, bureau de change, bar, restaurant and tourist information centre.

Other airport/s: Cork (ORK), 5 km from city; Horan (NOC) at Knock, Co Mayo, Connaught Province.

Airport tax: None

Surface

Road: Bus Éireann and National Express operate services from London, and many other UK centres, to Dublin and other destinations.

Rail: Most rail-ferry services to Ireland depart from London. There are a number of services across the Northern Ireland border including the regular, direct intercity Belfast-Dublin service (duration 2.15 hours).

Water: In addition to conventional ferry crossings, there are high-speed catamaran sailings. Routes include links with Scotland, England and Wales to alternative destinations in Ireland. Continental connections include routes to north-western France.

Rail links provide connections from the major seaports.

Main port/s: The main ports are Dun Laoghaire, Dublin, Rosslare and Cork.

Getting about

National transport

Air: Daily services between Dublin and Shannon, and Dublin and Cork operated by Aer Lingus. Also one flight daily between Dublin and Horan Airport, Knock. Charter services are available. Domestic airports include Waterford (WAT), Galway (GWY), Sligo (SXL), Carrickfinn (CFN) and Kerry (KIR). In addition, there are also various small airstrips which receive passenger services.

Road: The Irish road network carries the overwhelming part of Irish imports and exports. A good highway system links all cities.

Buses: Bus Éireann is the national bus line, with services all over the south and north. Winter bus schedule is often drastically reduced and many routes simply disappear after September.

Rail: Ireland's rail network is not extensive. Irishrail is the main operator, with routes which fan out from Dublin.

Water: There are ferry services to outlying islands off the west coast and across rivers.

City transport

Taxis: Taxis in Ireland tend to be expensive. There are metered taxis in Cork, Dublin, Galway and Limerick, but in other places fares must be agreed beforehand. If a taxi is booked by telephone there may be a small pick-up charge.

Buses, trams & metro: There are comprehensive bus services in all towns and cities, combined in Dublin with a fast, surburban rail service, the Dart.

Two tram services – the Luas – were inaugurated in 2004. The red line runs from Connelly Street in Dublin's city centre, west then south-west, to Tallaght. The green line runs from St Steven's Green, in the administrative district of Dublin, south to Cherrywood.

Car hire

Available in all main towns, but heavy demand during tourist season. All international hire companies are represented in Ireland. Drivers must be aged between 21 and 75. A national or international driving licence is required and the driver is generally required to have had at least two years experience. Speed limits 30mph (48kph) in built-up areas and 60mph (96kph) on main roads. Driving is on the left.

BUSINESS DIRECTORY

The addresses listed below are a selection only. While World of Information makes every endeavour to check these addresses, we cannot guarantee that changes have not been made, especially to telephone numbers and area codes. We would welcome any corrections.

Telephone area codes

The international direct dialling (IDD) code for Ireland is +353 followed by area code and subscriber's number:

Cork	21	Mullingar	44
Donegal	73	Shannon	61
Dublin	1	Sligo	71
Galway	91	Tipperary	62
Kilkenny	56	Waterford	51
Killarney	64	Wexford	53
Limerick	61	Wicklow	404

Chambers of Commerce

American Chamber of Commerce Ireland, 6 Wilton Place, Dublin 2 (tel: 661-6201; fax: 661-6217; e-mail: ifo@amcham.ie).

Chambers of Commerce of Ireland, 17 Merrion Square, Dublin 2 (tel: 661-2888; fax: 661-2811; e-mail: info@chambersireland.ie).

Cork Chamber of Commerce, Fitzgerald House, Summerhill North, Cork (tel: 450-9044; fax: 450-8568; e-mail: info@corkchamber.ie).

Dublin Chamber of Commerce, 7 Clare Street, Dublin 2 (tel: 644-7200; fax: 676-6043; info@dublinchamber.ie).

Dun Laoghaire Rathdown Chamber of Commerce, Kilcullen House, 1 Haigh Terrace, Dun Laoghaire (tel: 284-5066; 284-5034; e-mail: info@dirchamber.ie).

Dundalk Chamber of Commerce, Hagan House, Ramparts Road, Dundalk (tel: 933-6343; fax: 933-2085; info@dundalk.ie).

Limerick Chamber of Commerce, 96 O'Connell Street, Limerick (tel: 415-180; fax: 415-785; e-mail: info@limchamber.ie).

Mullingar Chamber of Commerce, ACC House, Dominick Street, Mullingar (tel: 44-044; fax: 44-045; e-mail: info@mullingar-chamber.ie).

Sligo Chamber of Commerce and Industry, 16 Quay Street, Sligo (tel: 916-1274; fax: 916-0912; e-mail: sligochamber@eircom.net).

Waterford Chamber of Commerce, Georges Street, Waterford (tel: 311-136; fax: 876-002; e-mail: info@waterfordchamber.ie).

Wexford Chamber of Industry and Commerce, The Ballast Office, Crescent Quay, Wexford (tel: 22-226; fax:241-70; e-mail: info@wexchamber.iol.ie).

Banking

Allied Irish Bank Ltd, Bankcentre, PO Box 452, Ballsbridge, Dublin 4 (tel: 660-0311; fax: 668-2508).

Allied Irish Investment Bank plc, Bankcentre, Ballsbridge, Dublin 4 (tel: 660-4733).

Bank of Ireland, Lower Baggot Street, Dublin 2 (tel: 661-5933; fax: 661-5671).

The Institute of Bankers in Ireland (banking association), Nassau House, Nassau Street, Dublin 2 (tel: 679-3311).

Investment Bank of Ireland Ltd, 26 Fitzwilliam Place, Dublin 2 (tel: 661-6433; fax: 661-6433).

National Irish Bank, 7/8 Wilton Terrace, Dublin 2 (tel: 678-5066; fax: 661-3324).

Ulster Bank, 33 College Green, Dublin 2 (tel: 677-7623).

Ulster Investment Bank Ltd, 2 Hume Street, Dublin 2 (tel: 661-3444; fax: 676-3021).

Central bank

Central Bank and Financial Services Authority of Ireland, PO Box 559, Dame Street, Dublin 2 (tel: 434-4000; fax: 671-6561; e-mail: enquiries@centralbank.ie).

European Central Bank (ECB), Kaiserstrasse 29, D-60311 Frankfurt am Main, Germany (tel: (+49-69) 13-440; fax: (+49-69) 1344-6000; e-mail: info@ecb.int).

Travel information

Aer Lingus, Head Office Block, Dublin Airport (tel: 705-2222; fax: 705-3832; internet site: www.aerlingus.ie).

Cork Airport (tel: 431-3131; internet: www.corkairport.com)

Dublin Airport (tel: 814-1111; internet: www.iol.ie).

Irishrail (internet: www.iarnrodeireann.ie and www.irishrail.ie)

Ryanair, Corporate Head Office Building, Dublin Airport (tel: 844-4489, 844-4400; fax: 844-4402; internet: www.ryanair.com).

Shannon Airport (tel:712-000; internet: www.shannonairport.com).

Ministry of tourism

Department of Arts, Sport and Tourism, 23 Kildare Street, Dublin 2 (tel: 631-3800; fax: 661-1201; internet: www.arts-sport-tourism.gov.ie).

National tourist organisation offices

Irish Tourist Board, Baggot Street Bridge, Dublin 2 (tel: 676-5871, 661-6500; fax: 676-4764, 676-4765; internet site: www.irland.ie).

Ministries

Department of Agriculture and Food, Agriculture House, Kildare Street, Dublin 2 (tel: 607-2000; internet: www.agriculture.gov.ie).

Department of Defence, Colaiste Caoimhin, Mobhi Road, Glasnevin, Dublin 9 (tel: 804-210; fax: 804-5000; email: info@defence.irlgov.ie).

Department of Education and Science, Marlborough Street, Dublin 1 (tel: 889-6400; email: info@education.gov.ie).

Department of Enterprise, Trade and Employment, 23 Kildare Street, Dublin 2 (tel: 631-2121; fax: 631-2827; email: info@entemp.ie).

Department of Environment, Heritage and Local Government, Custom House, Dublin 1 (tel: 888-2000; internet: www.environ.ie).

Department of Finance, Government Bldgs, Upper Merrion Street, Dublin 2 (tel: 676-7571; fax: 678-9936; email: webmaster@finance.irlgov.ie).

Department of Foreign Affairs, 80 St Stephen's Green, Dublin 2 (tel: 478-0822; fax: 478-1484; internet: http://foreignaffairs.gov.ie).

Department of Transport, Transport House, 44 Kildare Street, Dublin 2 (tel: 670-7444; email: info@transport.ie).

Department of Taoiseach, Government Buildings, Upper Merrion Street, Dublin 2 (tel: 662-4888; fax: 678-9791; email: webmaster@taoiseach.gov.ie).

Department of Arts, Sport and Tourism, 23 Kildare Street, Dublin 2 (tel: 631-3800; fax: 661-1201; internet: www.arts-sport-tourism.gov.ie).

Other useful addresses

Central Statistics Office, Skehard Road, Cork (tel: 359-000; fax: 359-090; internet site: www.cso.ie).

Confederation of Irish Industry, Confederation House, Kildare Street, Dublin 2 (tel: 660-1011).

Enterprise Ireland, Glasnevin, Dublin 9 (tel: 808-2000; fax: 808-2020; internet site: www.enterprise-ireland.com).

IDA Ireland (Industrial Development Agency), Wilton Park House, Wilton Place, Dublin 2 (tel: 668-6633; fax: 660-3703).

Irish Business and Employers' Confederation, 84 Lower Baggot Street, Dublin 2 (tel: 660-1011; fax: 660-1717).

Irish Embassy (USA), 2234 Massachusetts Avenue, NW, Washington DC 20008 (tel: (+1-202) 462-3939; fax: (+1-202) 232-5993; e-mail: embirlus@aol.com).

Provincial Newspapers' Association of Ireland, 33 Parkgate Street, Dublin 8 (tel: 679-3679).

RTÉ (Irish broadcasting), Donnybrook, Dublin 4 (tel: 208-3111; fax: 208-3080; internet: rte.ie)

The Stock Exchange, 24-28 Anglesea Street, Dublin 2 (tel: 677-8808; fax: 677-6045).

Internet sites

Access Ireland: www.visunet.ie

Business information: www.factfinder.ie

Doras web directory: www.doras.ie

Ireland On-Line: www.home.iol.ie

Irish Government website: irlgov.ie

Irish Times: www.irish-times.com

Irish trade web (information on Irelands' top 1000 companies): www.itw.ie

Israel

KEY FACTS

Official name: Medinat Israel (State of Israel)

Head of State: President Shimon Peres (Likud) (since July 15 2007)

Head of government: Prime Minister Ehud Olmert (elected 28 Mar 2006).

Ruling party: Coalition government: Kadima (Forward), Labour (Ha-Avoda), Shas (Ha-Sfarradim Shomrey Torah) (World Union of Sephardi Torah Keepers) and Gimla'ey Yisrael LaKneset (GIL) (Israeli Pensioners for the Knesset) (Age) (since 4 May 2006).

Area: 20,700 square km (excluding occupied territories)

Population: 7.21 million (2007)*

Capital: Jerusalem (Israel regards the entire city as its capital although it is not recognised by the UN); Tel Aviv, administrative and diplomatic centre

Official language: Hebrew

Currency: New shekel (NIS) = 100 agorot

Exchange rate: NIS3.41 per US$ (Jul 2008)

GDP per capita: US$22,475 (2007)*

GDP real growth: 5.30% (2007)

Labour force: 2.89 million (2007)

Unemployment: 7.30% (2007)

Inflation: 0.50% (2007)

Balance of trade: -US$5.52 billion (2007)

Foreign debt: US$74.46 billion (2004)

* estimated figure

The state of Israel marked its sixtieth anniversary of statehood in 2008. The creation of this unique country was essentially a Jewish European concept, which did not take into account Palestinian rights or sensibilities, not to mention basic living requirements. Sixty years on, this fundamental flaw continued to dog Israel's history and prospects.

Confused history

Israel's short history as a nation state has been anything but straightforward. Layer of history is laid upon layer, and alongside each comes a confusion of Zionist ideology and blurred history, the role of the *kibbutzniks*, the role of the British during the mandate and, the elephant in the cupboard, Israel's relationship – or the lack of one – with Palestine and the Palestinians. In 1969, Prime Minister Golda Meir had rashly claimed that 'there were no such things as Palestinians', an attitude subsequently adopted in varying degrees by many Israeli chroniclers and historians. If the Palestinians indeed did not exist, then as a non-existent body even in 2008 they certainly continued to put up a pretty good show. Many Israeli attitudes and beliefs were based on the assumption that the over half million Arabs who fled their villages during the 1947–49 period did so of their own volition, or at least did so believing that they would soon be able to return. In fact, as contemporary records amply documented, most of the Palestinians were expelled by Israeli forces and those that did leave 'voluntarily' did so as refugees fearing for their lives. It was not until the late 1980s that Israeli historians began to come to terms with what were uncomfortable truths, often facing vehement opposition from a wide range of Israeli society. The 1967 Arab Israeli war, quickly branded as the semi-biblical 'six-day war' had infused both individual Israelis and the Israeli body-politic with a new-found confidence and disregard for their nation's more obvious shortcomings. The occupation of Sinai, Gaza, Golan and the West Bank appeared, at the time, to have provided Israel with a long needed security. Bolstered by the post-1967 euphoria, Israelis failed to accept that in any occupied territory the occupiers, however legitimate or otherwise their claims may be, are responsible for the welfare and the quality of life of the occupied. In 2008 the failure to recognise this simple truth still lay at the heart of Israel's problems.

Security?

If victory in the six-day war was meant to guarantee Israel's security, the reverse turned out to be the case, as Palestinian nationalism became increasingly rampant and violent. Israel, the nation that had inspired so much idealism, became to be seen, not only by Palestinians, as an insensitive, uncaring occupying power. Israeli nationalism is itself a complex phenomenon, buttressed by countless external forces, of which what became to be known as the US *Israel lobby*, ensuring that Israel continued to receive unquestioning support, practically, militarily and financially, was by far the most important. The Israel lobby embraced not only American Jews, but also groups from the Christian Zionist Right, closely allied to President George Bush. In this respect it resembled other powerful US lobbies entrenched in the fabric of US politics such as the National Rifle Association. In most respects, however, the Israel lobby's characteristics were those of typical US interest groups.

There is, however, one significant difference: few other interest groups have the ability to determine, or even derail, US foreign policy. US support of Israel, and by implication its tacit opposition to the establishment of a Palestinian state has managed to provoke the anger and dismay of most of its regional allies, notably Saudi Arabia, Egypt and Jordan. This was particularly the case in 2006 when Israel unleashed a hugely disproportionate response in Lebanon to Hezbollah's kidnapping of two Israeli soldiers.

When it comes to the practicalities of US support for Israel, the sums are impressive. US aid to Egypt amounts to US$20.00 per head each year; US aid to Israel is 25 times greater, at US$500 per head. Additionally, and uniquely, Israel receives what is classed as a 'lump sum cash transfer', money for which Israel is not held to account and can use as it sees fit. Some estimates put at US$100 billion the total amount of US aid to Israel in its brief history. The US is also able to turn a selective blind eye to Israeli shortcomings: despite imposing sanctions on countries that refuse to ratify the Chemical and Biological Weapons Conventions, the US has never sought to require Israel to do so.

Olmert on the way out

By mid-2008, historians had already decided not to give outgoing prime minister Ehud Olmert of the Kadima Party a glowing final report. He will probably best be remembered for his disastrous conduct of the 2006 Lebanon war (although much of the blame lay with an incompetent military). Olmert's reputation was further tarnished by a series of alleged financial scandals that began to close in on him. Public support for Mr Olmert had consistently been below 40 per cent for the first half of 2008, plummeting even further by mid-year as support for the Likud's Mr Netanyahu seemed steadily to rise. Despite his mishandling of the war, as his term in office gradually unravelled, Mr Olmert appeared to have grasped the inevitability of a two-state solution if Israel's survival were to be guaranteed. Badly weakened, and lacking in political support, Mr Olmert was unable to do much about seeking the solution he had come to see as inevitable. First, because in Israel he had to spend too much time looking over his shoulder; second, because the only dialogue he was able to undertake was with Mahmoud Abbas, the President of the Palestinian Authority, himself holed below the water-line following a Hamas *coup d'état* in Gaza, home to one and a half million Palestinians. This left Mr Abbas and his Fatah supporters controlling only the West Bank; even that control was tenuous, as Islamist extremists often ran riot in the West Bank.

Hamas does not even deign to recognise Israel or its right to exist. It has also refused to accept any of the previous agreements that Israel had entered in to with the Palestinian Authority. In mid-2008 much looked likely to depend on the manner in which Mr Olmert's successor was chosen, and the identity of that successor. There looked to be four principal candidates, of whom the Kadima Party's Tipi Livni (and Israel's foreign minister) seemed to be the front runner. The Labour Party's leader Ehud Barak, the other pragmatic candidate shared Ms Livni's advocacy of a two-state solution, in contrast with Kadima transport minister Shaul Mofaz, whose opposition to any accommodation with the Palestinians is shared by the Likud party's leader, Benjamin Netanyahu.

The so-called November 2007 US brokered peace summit between Olmert and Abbas had achieved very little. Neither leader commanded much authority at home, something they both shared with their host, US President George W Bush. The most noteworthy feature of the summit was the number of Arab leaders that saw fit to attend, seen by most observers as an effort to demonstrate Sunni cohesion against potential Shia initiatives. For this reason, the most notable absentees from the gathering were the Shia Iranians, regarded by both Israel and the Palestinian Authority as a threat to their collective existence. The March 2008 surge in fighting in Gaza caused Mr Abbas to withdraw from later talks.

The lack of any cogent Israeli dialogue with Hamas, possibly combined with diminished Israeli intelligence resources in Gaza, lead to an embarrassing loss of face for Israel when in January 2008, Hamas, despite warnings from the Egyptian side in late-2007, allowed the wall constituting the boundary with Egypt to be knocked down, permitting tens of thousands – possible more – Gazan Palestinians to stream through and purchase food and other requisites lacking in Gaza from Egyptian shops in the border towns of Rafah and al Arish. Palestinian exhilaration at the snoop thus cocked at Israel represented a political coup for Hamas as well as a mounting threat to Israeli security through Gaza's increasingly ineffective borders.

KEY INDICATORS — Israel

	Unit	2003	2004	2005	2006	2007
Population	m	6.61	6.70	6.72	7.05	*7.21
Gross domestic product (GDP)	US$bn	109.04	117.55	129.84	142.25	161.94
GDP per capita	US$	16,501	17,695	19,308	20,177	*22,475
GDP real growth	%	0.9	4.3	5.2	5.2	5.3
Inflation	%	1.6	-0.4	1.3	2.1	0.5
Unemployment	%	11.3	10.4	9.0	8.4	7.3
Exports (fob) (goods)	US$m	29,320.0	36,167.0	39,746.0	43,724.0	50,242.0
Imports (cif) (goods)	US$m	32,270.0	38,564.0	43,780.0	46,958.0	55,760.0
Balance of trade	US$m	-2,950.0	-2,397.0	-4,034.0	-3,234.0	-5,518.0
Current account	US$m	1,372.0	2,955.0	4,277.0	8,546.0	4,993.0
Total reserves minus gold	US$m	26,315.1	27,094.4	28,059.4	29,153.2	28,518.5
Foreign exchange	US$m	25,778.4	26,616.0	27,839.0	29,011.0	28,406.0
Exchange rate	per US$	4.60	4.48	4.22	4.19	3.99

* estimated figure

The Gaza-Egyptian border is some 250km long; its porosity not only enabled arms and other *matériel* to be smuggled in to Gaza; it also strengthened the links between Hamas and the Muslim Brotherhood, of which it is an offshoot. The border breach did little to improve Israeli-Palestinian relations, with each side blaming the other for allowing it to happen in the first place, although some doubt had to hang over the sincerity of the Egyptian protests. The importance of the January events was to show that Hamas was able to act with some impunity when it wished to do so. They did little to improve the lot of Palestinians either in Gaza or the West Bank.

In March 2008 fighting between Israel and Gaza escalated following a rocket attach that killed an Israeli citizen in the border town of Siderot. The Israeli response, borne of frustration rather than strength, killed over 100 Palestinians and caused the death of a further two Israeli soldiers. B'Tselem, an Israeli human rights group estimated that since June 2007 Israel had killed some 350 Gazans, including more than 100 civilians and children.

What remained clear was that any meaningful discussions with its Arab neighbours will depend on the clear acceptance of agreed Israeli borders on the one hand, and on the recognition of Palestinian rights and compensation on the other. In 2008 Israelis showed a greater degree of uncertainty about their country's future than at any time since its creation. That uncertainty not only relates to Israel's relations with its neighbours, but also to the sort of country in which they wish to live.

Economy strengthens

In January 2008 the International Monetary Fund (IMF) reported that strong macroeconomic conditions and sound domestic policies had significantly improved Israel's growth performance and prospects but vulnerabilities remained.

Despite the war in Lebanon with Hezbollah in 2006, according to the IMF Israel's gross domestic product (GDP) growth averaged about 5.25 per cent during the 2006/07 financial year. Buoyant world trade propelled exports and investment, fostering strong employment growth – which was also supported by welfare reform – and private consumption. Some Israeli banks announced losses on mortgage-related US assets but the effect on profitability and capital had been small. Nor had Israeli banks been experiencing funding pressures, as they relied almost exclusively on deposits from the public. Isreali authorities did not expect a fall-out of the financial turmoil on the Israeli banking system that could adversely affect its ability to support the domestic economy.

Monetary policy successfully stabilised inflation expectations, even though inflation has frequently been outside the 1–3 per cent target range on account of exchange rate changes. Lately, inflation had been undershooting the 1–3 per cent target, largely reflecting the sheqel's appreciation against the US dollar, but at end 2007 was rising again. By November, prices stood just under 3 per cent above the end-2006 level. Thus, the IMF expected Israel's economic activity to remain strong, even if somewhat less buoyant than in the past. Domestic preconditions for continued output growth remained in place. Specifically, GDP growth was broad based, families' real incomes continued to rise, including those of the poor; corporate profitability and balance sheets had also improved. The IMF considered the economy's competitiveness to remain solid. It noted, however, that capacity constraints were beginning to bind, notably in the market for highly skilled employees. Accordingly, the ministry of finance and Bank of Israel (BoI) foresaw 4.2 per cent and 4.4 per cent real GDP growth, respectively, for 2008. Taking into account the latest developments and prospects, the IMF struck a less optimistic note, projecting 3.8 per cent GDP growth.

Risk assessment

Politics	Fair
Economy	Fair
Regional stability	Poor

COUNTRY PROFILE

Historical profile

The struggle between the Israelis and the Palestinians over historic claims to land is one of the most enduring of all the world's conflicts.

1917 The Balfour Declaration suggested the establishment in Palestine of a national home for the Jewish people.

1922 The Council of the League of Nations assigned to Britain a mandate for the Ottoman Arab territory of Palestine, a region that covered present-day Israel and Jordan, plus the Golan Heights region (claimed by Syria). The British divided the mandate into two parts, designating all lands west of the Jordan River as Palestine and those east of the river as Transjordan. The League of Nations mandate also addressed the goal of restoring a Jewish homeland in Palestine.

1929 Riots in Jerusalem between Arab Palestinians and Jews were sparked by a dispute over the use of the western wall of the Al Aqsa Mosque (the site is sacred to Muslims, and Jews claim it as part of their temple).

1936–39 The Arab Higher Committee opposed Jewish immigration to Palestine and the Peel Commission concluded that the mandate in Palestine was unworkable. Legislation limiting the number of Jewish immigrants into Palestine was introduced by the British government.

1945–46 Many Jews who had survived the Nazi German Holocaust arrived in Palestine and Jewish extremists began to oppose Britain's immigration legislation. Transjordan became independent and was later re-named Jordan.

1947 Britain decided to leave Palestine and called on the UN to make recommendations. The UN adopted Resolution 181, which called for the establishment of both Jewish and Arab states within Palestine. A partition plan was drawn up, based solely on population, with Jerusalem as an international zone under UN jurisdiction. The Jews agreed to the partition; the Arabs refused.

1948 Conflict ensued between Arabs and Jews. Jewish leaders announced the formation of the State of Israel, open to the immigration of Jews from all countries. Egypt, Iraq, Lebanon, Syria and Jordan joined Palestinian and other Arab guerrillas and invaded Israel. The armistice agreements extended the territory under Israel's control beyond the UN partition boundaries. Many Arabs fled Israel to become refugees in the surrounding Arab countries, ending the Arab majority in the new Jewish state.

1956 Egypt blockaded the Red Sea port of Eilat and Israeli forces attacked and occupied the Sinai peninsula, later being joined by Britain and France, which sought to regain control of the Canal Zone. In the face of strong international opposition, particularly from the US, all three withdrew their forces.

1967 After Egypt again blockaded Eilat, Israel launched and won the Six Day War against Egypt, Jordan and Syria, taking control of the Sinai peninsular and the Gaza Strip, which had been Egyptian territory, together with the Golan Heights, formerly claimed by Syria, and the West Bank, including East Jerusalem, which had been united with Jordan since 1950. Around 300,000 Palestinian Arabs fled to Jordan.

Israel's settlement policy started; it occupied the Sinai peninsular, the Golan Heights, the Gaza Strip and the West Bank, including East Jerusalem, re-unifying the city; the Jews transferred to these areas became known as settlers and

the territories became known as the occupied territories.
1968–70 The War of Attrition was a limited war fought between Egypt and Israel, initiated by Egypt as a way to recapture the Sinai from Israel. The war ended with frontiers at the same place as when the war started.
1973 Lebanon was used by the Palestinians as a base for activities against Israel. In retaliation, Israeli commandos raided Beirut, killing three associates of Palestine Liberation Organisation (PLO) chairman, Yasser Arafat. In the 6 October War (also known as the Yom Kippur War), Egypt and Syria invaded Israel to reclaim some of the land lost in the Six Day War, but despite some early strategic gains by Egypt and Syria, Israel counter-attacked and repelled the invasion, re-conquering the Golan Heights from Syria.
1978 Prime Minister Menachim Begin and Egyptian Prime Minister Anwar Sadat signed peace accords at Camp David in the US. Israel agreed to withdraw from the Sinai.
1981 Israel annexed East Jerusalem and the Golan Heights.
1982–85 The Sinai peninsular was returned to Egypt in 1982. Israel launched a full-scale invasion of Lebanon. Despite subsequently withdrawing from most of the territory, Israel maintained some troops in Lebanon in order to help secure its own northern border. 1987 The Palestinians launched an intifida (uprising) against the Israelis.
1988 The Harakat al Muqawama al Islamia (Hamas) (Islamic Resistance Movement) was formed and began armed resistance to Israeli rule in the occupied territories of the West Bank and Gaza Strip.
1989 Mass immigration, of Jews from the Soviet Union, began; many settled in the occupied territories.
1991–93 Israel and the PLO conducted secret negotiations in the Norwegian capital of Oslo, crafting an interim peace accord, which was signed in the US. The Oslo Peace Accords laid the basis for transfer of authority from the Israeli military administration to the PLO in the Gaza Strip and an undefined area around the town of Jericho in the West Bank. President Ezer Weizman took office.
1995–96 A follow-up treaty, Oslo II, (known collectively, with the first, as the Accord), was signed. It envisaged Palestinian autonomy, with Israeli troop units withdrawn from the West Bank. Yasser Arafat was elected president of the Palestinian Legislative Council (PLC), the assembly of the Palestinian National Authority (PNA).
2000 President Ezer Weizman resigned and Moshe Katsav, (Likud party), was elected president. Israel withdrew its forces from southern Lebanon without reaching an agreement with Syria on the future of the Golan Heights. The Camp David summit aimed a pushing forward the Accord failed when no agreement could be reached; the Palestinians claimed sovereignty over all of east Jerusalem, including Judaism's holiest place Temple Mount. The right-wing opposition leader, Ariel Sharon, made a provocative visit to Palestinian controlled Temple Mount (called al Haram as Sharif by Arabs) and the second intifada was launched. A total blockade was imposed by Israel on the West Bank and Gaza.
2001 Ariel Sharon was elected prime minister. He declared the PNA a terrorist-supporting organisation and launched Operation 'Defensive Shield', invading the PNA-controlled West Bank and Gaza Strip, attacking its institutions and besieging Yasser Arafat's headquarters.
2002 Saudi Arabia proposed a peace initiative, whereby Israel could have normal relations, peace and security with the Arab world if Israel withdrew from captured territories and agreed to recognise a Palestinian state. Israel began building a 640km security barrier, claiming it was the only way to control the infiltration of militant terrorists.
2003 US President Bush unveiled the Middle East Road Map to Peace, to run between 2003–05, with a cease-fire, an end to Jewish settlements in the occupied territories and the creation of an independent Palestinian state. However neither side kept to its timetable and it, de facto, failed.
2004 The International Court of Justice ruled that the West Bank security barrier was illegal, and that construction should halt. President Yasser Arafat died in November. In December, Sharon's minority coalition narrowly avoided collapse after he dismissed four Shinui ministers who had voted against the 2005 budget bill.
2005 Israel's parliament approved Sharon's new coalition government on 10 January. On 8 February, Sharon and the newly elected Palestinian president, Mahmoud Abbas, signed a truce that planned to bring to an end four years of violence between the two countries. Egypt and Jordan agreed to return their ambassadors to Israel. On 20 February, the cabinet approved the removal of Jewish illegal settlers from the Gaza Strip and part of the West Bank. Hamas bombed targets in Israel claiming it was not party to the truce. Abbas ordered a crackdown and sacked senior security chiefs. On 21 August Israeli troops began clearing Jewish settlements from Gaza. Most commercial buildings were left standing but some homes and synagogues were destroyed. In November Sharon left the Likud, a party he had helped found, to form a centrist party, Kadima, which would be aligned between the right-of-centre Likud and Labour on the left. Sharon suffered a minor stroke on 18 December. On 19 December, Binyamin Netanyahu was elected leader of Likud.
2006 Sharon suffered a massive stroke on 4 January; his deputy, Ehud Olmert, took over as acting prime minister. Olmert was asked by the Kadima party to stand in as party chairman. The 28 March elections were won by Kadima with 28 seats, Labour won 20 and the former ruling Likud party won 11. On 11 April, the cabinet declared that Sharon, in a coma since his stroke, was 'permanently incapacitated' and Olmert became prime minister. In June, Israel became a member of the International Red Cross, however, after a dispute over the use of the traditional red cross and crescent symbols, Israel decided to use a diamond-shaped red crystal. In July, Hezbollah paramilitary forces based in southern Lebanon crossed the border and captured two Israeli soldiers. Israel retaliated by invading Lebanon on 12 July, in an attempt to retrieve its soldiers; it inflicted massive damage, especially in the south, to infrastructure with thousands of homes destroyed and hundreds of civilian casualties. The conflict lasted for 34 days, however the Israeli soldiers were not recovered.
2007 Raleb Majadele (Labour) was appointed to the cabinet on 12 January, he is the first Arab Muslim to hold office in Israel. On 17 January, General Halutz resigned as head of Israel's armed forces following an enquiry into the conduct of the 2006 invasion of Lebanon which criticised its poor planning, strategy and execution. A criminal inquiry to determine Ehud Olmert's role in the privatisation of Bank Leumi will be held and if indicted he will be forced to resign as prime minister. The president took a leave of absence to defend himself against criminal charges of rape and sexual harassment. In the first round of the presidential election held by parliament on 13 June, Shimon Peres won 58 votes (out of 120), Reuven Rivlin 37, Colette Avital 21. In the second round, Rivlin and Avital withdrew and Peres won with 86 votes. Moshe Katsav resigned as president on 29 June; Peres replaced him on 15 July. Binjamin Netanyahu was re-elected leader of the right-wing Kilud party.
2008 Ehud Olmert announced on 30 July that he will step down as prime minister by 19 September, due to a damaging corruption case.

Political structure
Constitution
Israel passed the Law and Administration Ordinance on attaining independence, in 1948. In the Declaration of the Establishment of the State of Israel that embodied the principals of law, it was recognised that these principals would evolve in time and circumstances.
Basic laws set out the powers of the executive, legislative and judicial branches. The country functions without a written constitution as Israel's founders wanted to avoid creating problems between religious and secular Jews and between Jews and the non-Jewish minority.
Form of state
Parliamentary democracy
The executive
Executive power rests with the government (a cabinet of ministers), headed by a prime minister as head of government. The government may determine its own agenda and executive procedures.
The prime minister is directly elected for four years and cannot be deposed from office without fresh elections.
The prime minister chooses members of the cabinet from either inside or outside the Knesset (parliament). The cabinet is responsible to the Knesset.
The president is Head of State and has a largely ceremonial role; elected every five years for a maximum of two terms.
National legislature
The 120-seat unicameral Knesset is elected by proportional representation for a maximum of four years. The country is divided into six mezoh (administrative districts).
Legal system
The law is based on English common law, components of Jewish religious law and some features of other systems, as appropriate.
The judiciary has constitutionally guaranteed independence. The court system has three levels: the Supreme Court, district courts and magistrates' courts. The court system does not employ juries in Israel. There is also a separate system of limited and specific tribunals that deal with military, labour law and religious, civil matters.
Last elections
28 March 2006 (parliamentary); 31 June 2007 (presidential).
Results: Parliamentary: Kadima (centrist) won 28 seats out of the 120 seats of the Knesset, Labour (centre-left) 20, Shas (ultra-authodox) 13, Yisrael Beitenu (Russian emigres, far-right) 12, the former ruling Likud party won 11 seats, Arab parties 10, other parties 26; turnout was 62.3 per cent.
Presidential: (first round) Shimon Peres won 58 votes (out of 120), Reuven Rivlin 37, Colette Avital 21. Second round: Rivlin and Avital withdrew and Peres won 86 votes.
Next elections
2007 (presidential); 2010 (parliamentary)

Political parties
Ruling party
Coalition government: Kadima (Forward), Labour (Ha-Avoda), Shas (Ha-Sfarradim Shomrey Torah) (World Union of Sephardi Torah Keepers) and Gimla'ey Yisrael LaKneset (GIL) (Israeli Pensioners for the Knesset) (Age) (since 4 May 2006).
Main opposition party
Likud

Population
7.21 million (2007)*
Last census: November 1995: 5,548,523 (including residents of East Jerusalem and Israelis in Palestinian territories).
Population density: 302 inhabitants per square km. Urban population: 92 per cent (1995–2001).
Annual growth rate: 2.4 per cent 1994–2004 (WHO 2006)
Ethnic make-up
European, Middle Eastern and North African Jews, Arabs and Druze.
Religions
The Jewish, Muslim, Catholic, Greek Orthodox, Druze, Protestant and Baha'i faiths are all represented. Non-Jews make up 18 per cent of the population. They include 635,000 Muslims, 105,000 Christians (almost all Arabs) and 78,000 Druze. The ultra-orthodox Jewish, or charedi, population has nearly doubled since 1990 to about 600,000, or 10 per cent of Israel's population.

Education
Education is provided free of charge and is organised by the state. Primary schooling lasts until aged 11.
Secondary schools are divided into four groups: state schools, which are attended by the majority, state religious schools, Arab and Druze schools and Torah schools for ultra-orthodox Jews. Youth Aliya schools specialise in educating new immigrants.
Demand for tertiary education consistently outstrips domestic supply, so that more Israelis study at universities abroad than at home, giving the country a ratio of graduates that is one of the highest in the world.
Public expenditure on education typically amounts to around 8 per cent of GDP.
Literacy rate: 95 per cent adult rate; 100 per cent youth rate (15–24) (Unesco 2005).
Compulsory years: Five to 16
Enrolment rate: 98 per cent total primary enrolment, of relevant age group (including repeaters); 88 per cent total secondary enrolment (World Bank).
Pupils per teacher: 14 in primary schools

Health
Per capita total expenditure on health (2003) was US$1,911; of which per capita government spending was US$1,303, at the international dollar rate, (WHO 2006).
The ministry of health, the large municipalities, private, non-profit institutions and health insurance funds cater to different medical facilities. Companies are required to contribute to insurance for their employees to cover hospital treatment. The Histadrut (General Federation of Labour) whose members include 90 per cent of Jewish workers, provide sickness benefits and medical care. About 95 per cent of the population are covered by a health insurance plan.
Smoking is prevalent among 45 per cent of men and 30 per cent of women causing health hazards. It is estimated that 99 per cent of the population have access to safe water and sanitation facilities are universal. By 2002, 95 per cent of children aged under 12 years were immunised.
HIV/Aids
HIV prevalence: 0.1 per cent aged 15–49 in 2003 (World Bank)
Life expectancy: 80 years, 2004 (WHO 2006)
Fertility rate/Maternal mortality rate: 2.8 births per woman, 2004 (WHO 2006); maternal mortality 5 per 100,000 live births (World Bank).
Birth rate/Death rate: 6 death and 21 births per 1,000 people (World Bank)
Child (under 5 years) mortality rate (per 1,000): 5.0 per 1,000 live births (World Bank)
Head of population per physician: 3.82 physicians per 1,000 people, 2003 (WHO 2006)

Welfare
There is a state-sponsored social welfare system, the National Insurance Institute, which covers the entire population. It is largely financed by compulsory monthly fees collected under the National Insurance Law, with the government providing the remaining funds. The system provides pensions, general disability payments, work injury compensation, child support and other allowances. The Institute also reimburses employers for salaries paid to employees during annual military reserve duty. Citizens disabled during military service are entitled to additional benefits from the defence ministry.

Main cities
Jerusalem (capital, estimated population 700,745 in 2005). Israel regards the

entire city as its capital, but its claim to East Jerusalem, captured by Arab forces in 1948 but recaptured by Israel in 1967, is disputed by Palestinians and a number of other countries.

The diplomatic centre is Tel Aviv (estimated population 365,677 in 2005). Other cities include Haifa (273,877), Ashdod (207,268), Bersheva (191,349) and Netanya (170,332).

Media

Other news agencies: Israel National News: www.israelnationalnews.com
Israel News Agency (INA): www.israelnewsagency.com
Israeli News Now: www.israelinewsnow.com
PR Newswire: www.prnewswire.co.il

Press

The press has more freedom than in any of its neighbours and the government respects its media.

The mix of newspapers reflects the diversity of the population with Hebrew national dailies vying with Arabic, English and the Russian language newspapers for their readership, although non are exclusive and crossover readership is common.

Dailies: In Hebrew Yediot Aharonot (www.ynet.co.il), a tabloid has the largest circulation, Haaretz (www.haaretz.co.il), has a reputation for quality reporting, Maariv (www.nrg.co.il) is a popular tabloid. In English The Jerusalem Post (www.jpost.com), is a broadsheet and Vesti is a popular Russian language newspaper.

Weeklies: In Arabic Kul al Arab (www.kul-alarab.com) is a popular publication of news and current affairs.

Business: In Hebrew, Globes (www.globes.co.il), with an English online edition, is a weekly publication along with The Marker (www.themarker.com). An online site Bull (www.bull.co.il) covers news from the stock market.

Periodicals: In English and German, Challenge (www.challenge-mag.com), is a magazine concerning the Israeli-Palestinian conflict, published six times a year.

Broadcasting

The Israel Broadcasting Authority (IBA) (www.iba.org.il) is the national, public broadcaster, which is funded by licence fees, sponsorship and radio adverts.

Radio: The IBA (www.iba.org.il) operates a network referred to as Kol Yisrael (Voice of Israel), of eight different stations, the four popular, domestic services include in Hebrew (Network A, B and C) broadcasting news, talk radio, music and (Network D) is an Arabic service. There is also a station for recent immigrants to Israel broadcasting in 13 languages, predominantly Russian. The other three are devoted to classical music, education and Jazz.

Independent radio stations include Arutz 7 (www.inn.co.il) a national network, all other stations are locally based including 90FM (www.90fm.co.il) in Jerusalem, Galgalatz (http://glz.msn.co.il) in Beersheva and Radio Haifa (http://1075.fm).

Television: The IBA (www.iba.org.il) has two channels, one broadcasting in Hebrew and the other in Arabic. There are other, pubic commercial stations including Channel 2, with weekly schedules operated by Keshet TV (www.keshet-tv.com) and Reshet TV (www.rashet.tv), Channel 10 (www.nana10.co.il) and Israel Plus (www.israel-plus.com) which broadcasts in Russian. There are several cable services and one local satellite service, Yes (www.yes.co.il). Other, international satellite services are available.

Advertising

Besides television, radio and press, there is cinema screen advertising, as well as limited poster and illuminated sign facilities. Newspapers accounts for the single largest share of adspend although revenues are falling as TV's share is increasing. New technologies are beginning to claim their own share of advertising venue.

Economy

Israel has a thriving modern economy, based on high technology and communications industries, which is orientated towards exports. The markets for its products lie outside the Middle East, mainly in North America, western Europe and east Asia. The US is the principal market. As well as high technology equipment, the main exports are cut diamonds, agricultural produce and pharmaceuticals. Israel is a world centre for cutting and polishing of diamonds. The trade and processing of diamonds accounted for almost US$6.6 billion in exports in 2006; the industry is one of the country's largest. Israel benefits from stong overseas investment, despite the instability of the region, as well as tax revenues, high personal consumption levels and substantial aid from the US.

Israel is reliant on imports for raw materials and oil. Grains also have to be imported, although Israel is otherwise self-sufficient in other agricultural produce.

Israel experienced a recession in 2001–02, due to a downturn in the exports markets, but since 2003 has returned to growth: compared with less than one per cent in 2003, GDP grew by 5.5 per cent in 2005. The turn-around was effected by a programme of budget cuts, tax incentives, reduction of state participation in industry and investment in infrastructure. The recovery has proceeded regardless of the threat from the occupied territories. The former dependence on Palestinian labour has been replaced by increased use of 'guest workers' from China, Thailand and Eastern Europe.

External trade

Israel had bilateral free trade agreements with, among others, the EU, Turkey, the US, Canada and Mexico.

Exports provide over 95 per cent of GDP, of which 40 per cent is achieved by hi-tech industry output and pharmaceutical companies producing generic medicines and cut and dressed precious and semi-precious gems and pearls provides over 35 per cent. The trade and processing of diamonds accounted for almost US$6.6 billion in exports in 2006; the industry is one of the country's largest. Israel has a free trade agreement with the US and is also a signatory of the Euro-Mediterranean Partnership agreement, which provides for the introduction of free trade between the EU and 10 Mediterranean countries, by 2012.

Imports

Principal imports include raw materials, military equipment, investment goods, rough diamonds, fuels, grain and consumer goods.

Main sources: US (12.4 per cent total, 2006), Belgium (8.2 per cent), Germany (6.7 per cent).

Exports

Principal exports are machinery and equipment, software, cut diamonds, agricultural products, chemicals, textiles and clothes.

Main destinations: US (38.4 per cent total, 2006), Belgium (6.6 per cent), Hong Kong (5.9 per cent)

Agriculture

Farming

The agricultural sector contributes around 2 per cent to GDP and employs 5 per cent of the working population.

Israel is largely self-sufficient in food, importing some cereals, sugar beet and animal feeds. Food, beverages and tobacco are exported.

Farms are relatively small but mostly part of kibbutzim (larger co-operatives) or moshavim (co-operative smallholder villages), sharing machinery etc. The kibbutz and moshav movement formed the backbone of early Jewish settlement in Palestine before the State's creation in 1948. The Keren Kayemeth Le Yisrael (Jewish National Fund) was created in 1901 to buy land for the settlers. Since 1948 it has become involved in land development, especially land reclamation and forestry.

Israel's agricultural miracle of the 1950s and early 1960s, with annual growth levels of around 12 per cent, was based on intensive irrigated farming, the rise in domestic demand from new immigrants and the expansion of export markets. From the late 1960s, growth slowed to stagnation by the 1980s. Many blamed the bureaucratic marketing organisations for stifling incentives and others blamed an overemphasis on heavily irrigated cash crops, such as cotton, which have become increasingly costly to produce and are vulnerable to international competition.

The major crops are fruits (30 per cent of total production), vegetables (14 per cent) and livestock (42 per cent).

About 40 per cent of farm produce is sold locally, 26 per cent to industry for processing and another 26 per cent is exported directly.

Of the total cultivated land area (4,400 square km), over half is under irrigation. The general trend in agriculture is towards greater mechanisation and many agricultural workers have transferred to industry.

Estimated crop production in 2005 included: 316,400 tonnes (t) cereals in total, 190,000t wheat, 80,000t maize, 570,000t potatoes, 21,301t sweet potatoes, 36,000t sorghum, 10,700t barley, 95,000t bananas, 14,930t pulses, 545,000t citrus fruit, 14,300t dates, 95,000t grapes, 405,000t tomatoes, 29,965t oilcrops, 50,000t olives, 335,000t watermelons, 5,500t treenuts, 125,000t apples, 65,000t seed cotton, 20,000t cotton lint, 118,000t chillies & green peppers, 1,175,300t fruit in total, 1,669,895t vegetables in total. Estimated livestock production included: 576,700t meat in total, 82,000t beef, 18,100t pig meat, 5,130t lamb, 2,570t goat meat, 468,820t poultry, 90,700t eggs, 1,240,025t milk, 3,200t honey, 810t sheepskins, 880t greasy wool, 6,200t cattle hides.

Fishing

There is some fish farming; approximately 85 per cent of the total catch of fish is consumed locally.

In 2004, the total marine fish catch was 2,288 tonnes and the total crustacean catch was 59 tonnes.

Forestry

Between 60,000–70,000 tonnes of timber are harvested annually. Imported forest products amounted to US$759.3 million in 2004, while exports were US$44.7 million.

Timber production in 2004 included 27,000 cubic metre (cum) roundwood, 24,957cum industrial roundwood, 10,619cum sawlogs and veneer logs, 7,169cum pulpwood, 181,000cum wood-based panels, 2,043cum wood fuel.

Industry and manufacturing

The sector contributes around 17 per cent to GDP and employs 28 per cent of the working population.

The growth sectors are the capital intensive, science-based industries, such as aircraft (executive jets and fighters), electronics (telecommunications equipment), biotechnology, agricultural technology, chemicals and mining.

A wide range of goods are made or assembled for the domestic market, including cars, commercial vehicles, electrical goods, paper and paper products.

Israeli governments have historically worked with trade unions and employers to plan economic policy. Key policy elements have been to build up basic industry with state or trade union funds and high-tech industries that are either state-owned (a spin-off from the important arms industry) or privately-owned, but which benefit from government incentives aimed specifically at attracting foreign technology. Industry has long been supported with protective tariffs and subsidies, but Israel is progressively exposing its domestic market to competition from abroad as a result of growing trade with the EU and the US. Exports are vitally important to Israeli industry on account of the small size of the domestic market.

The strength of the Israeli manufacturing industry is increasingly in high technology. Traditional industries, such as food processing, textiles, metals, rubber and plastics and chemicals, are well developed but the future manufacturing base is likely to be in heavy and hi-tech industries, particularly the defence industry. Government policy is to shift from low value labour intensive industries to high value hi-tech industries. These have become increasingly important as labour-intensive industries such as the textile industry relocate to more competitive economies such as Jordan, Egypt and Turkey where labour costs are lower.

In 2005 the government embarked on its largest privatisation programme since the late 1990s. A stake of 30 per cent of Bezeq Israel Telecom was sold to a private consortium headed by media mogul Haim Saban, for US$970 million.

Tourism

The tourism industry is affected by the ongoing domestic terrorism since 2000. It has been estimated that up to 2 out of 3 anticipated visitor arrivals failed to arrive. Luxury hotels, built in anticipation of the greater numbers, have been standing empty as the industry restructures itself. Numbers are increasing as the focus of marketing has turned to Jewish and Christian pilgrims, cultural tourists and secular visitors who now see the destination as a country with localised violence.

In 2003 Israel joined the Euromed Heritage Programme, a computerisation project, sponsored by the EU, which focusses on cultural tourists of archaeology, arts and history, promoting sites through the internet. Israel and Jordan have a joint marketing arrangement to package resorts for overseas visitors, such as cruise ships visiting the Gulf of Aqaba.

Travel and tourism is expected to add US$3 billion or 2.4 per cent of GDP in 2005 and employ 8.3 per cent of the total work force. Tourism should generate US$3.6 billion in total exports and is part of the reason that in 2005 it is estimated to have attracted US$2.7 billion or 13.3 per cent of total investment.

Mining

The mining sector typically contributes 1 per cent to GDP and employs 1 per cent of the workforce.

There are vast reserves of potash, bromine and periclase in the area of the Dead Sea, the world's most saline lake, and deposits of 600 million tonnes of phosphate rock in the Negev Desert. These evaporites are produced for fertilisers and industrial minerals. Phosphates are mined at Oron (around 1.2 million tonnes per annum); potash is extracted from the Dead Sea at Sodom (approximately 3.5 million tonnes per annum). Israel is the world's second-largest producer of bromine and produces 20 per cent of world output.

Hydrocarbons

Israel does not produce oil and for political and security reasons is reluctant to obtain its hydrocarbons from one single source, particularly one from the Middle East. Currently Israel obtains the majority of its oil from Russia and central Asia – Turkmenistan and Kazakhstan. Other sources include Mexico, Egypt, Angola and the UK. It imports around 300,000 barrels per day (bpd) and it is estimated to have around four million barrels of oil reserves located underneath gas reserves. There has been significant oil exploration onshore and in the Mediterranean (with the drilling of over 350 wells). In May 2004 a deposit to the east of Kfar Saba was discovered with an estimated billion barrels of oil. Israel has two oil refineries, at Haifa and Ashdod, with a joint capacity of 220,000bpd, this supplies all of the country's refined oil needs. If the Israeli-Palestinian conflict is resolved then Israel could provide an alternative route for oil exports from the Gulf to the West. At present, oil exports travel through the Suez canal or around southern Africa. Israel has an estimated 600 million tonnes of recoverable oil shale, producing

around 9,000bpd. This reserve is located mainly in the Rotem basin region.
Natural gas reserves are estimated at 90–141 billion cubic metres (cum), found in deposits off the Israeli coast and Gaza Strip coast.
Israel has plans to increase the percentage of natural gas in its energy mix. The Yam Thetis group, constructed a gas production and distribution facility delivering gas from the Mari field (offshore) to the coast and production began in December 2004.
Approximately 32 per cent of Israel's energy requirements is met by coal. Israel does not produce coal but imports it primarily from South Africa, Columbia, Australia and Indonesia.

Energy

The Israel Electric Corporation (IEC) is the public utility company responsible for generating and supplying energy to the country. Israel has 9.1GW of installed electricity generating capacity, 70 per cent of which comes from coal-fired power stations, 25 per cent from oil-fired stations and the remainder by gas-oil and independent power producers (IPPs). Approximately 97 per cent of fuel requirements are met from imports.
The government forecasts that the country will need to expand capacity to 15.3GW by 2010. This will require an estimated US$1.3 billion investment in the sector. To do this, the government hopes to increase the participation of the private sector, with the aim of 10 per cent of electricity to be generated by IPPs.
The IEC has begun the process of converting diesel-powered generators to natural gas. It hopes to generate 40 per cent of its energy from gas by 2006. It is also in the process of acquiring new gas turbines, which will increase generating capacity by 650MW.
A new coal-fired power station in Ashkelon with sophisticated anti-pollution measures is expected to come online by 2009 and add 1,220MW to total generating capacity.
Solar power is widely used for domestic hot water heating, but not for the commercial generation of electricity.

Financial markets

Stock exchange

Israel's stock market is the Tel Aviv Stock Exchange (TASE).

Banking and insurance

The government introduce structural reforms to the banking system in 2005 with the legislation to break the dominance of the largest banks over capital markets. It is intended to open up the banking sector to foreign competition. The top two banks, Hapoalim and Leumi, will be required to sell their mutual funds before 2009 and provident funds by 2008. Smaller institutions have longer to do the same.

Central bank

The Bank of Israel (BOI), Jerusalem. It has the sole right to issue currency, create and implement monetary policy, regulate and supervise commercial and other banks, control foreign exchange, maintain foreign currency reserves and publish the only representative exchange rate for the shekel versus foreign currencies.

Main financial centre

Tel Aviv

Time

GMT plus two hours (daylight saving GMT plus three hours)

Geography

Israel is at the eastern end of the Mediterranean Sea, with a coastline of about 270km from the Lebanese border in the north to the north-eastern tip of the Sinai Desert in the south. Israel has borders with Lebanon in the north, Syria in the north-east, Jordan in the east and south-east and Egypt is in the south west. There is a short coastline on the Gulf of Aqaba in the south
Within these internationally recognised borders there are disputed borders between Israel and State of Palestine. Gaza is a strip (around 40km wide) of coastline in the south-west and the West Bank is an area west of the Jordan River, containing Jerusalem and areas west and north of the city, the borders of which have been in dispute since the Six Day War in 1967.
The country can be divided into four regions, the coastal plain, the central highlands, the Jordan Rift Valley (which includes Lake Tiberias (also known as the Sea of Galilee in the bible and Lake Kinneret by Israelis) and the Negev Desert (an area including the Dead Sea, the lowest land point on the planet at 399 metres below sea level). The desert comprises over half the country's landmass and is an extension of the greater Sinai Desert.

Hemisphere

Northern

Climate

Two climates exist, Mediterranean in the north and an arid sub-tropical in the south. Jerusalem, situated in the central highlands, has summer temperatures in July–August of 19–29 degrees Celsius (C) and 6–14 degrees C in winter (December–January). Tel Aviv on the coast has a more humid climate with summer temperatures of 24–35 degrees C and 19–30 degrees C in winter. Eilat, on the Gulf of Aqaba, records the hottest average summer temperatures of 40 degrees C.

Dress codes

Business dress is fairly relaxed, except on formal occasions. In Jerusalem even in the height of summer a sweater is often necessary at night. Tel Aviv, along the coast, is far more humid and evenings are warmer.
It is recommended that business women should wear respectable clothing; bare arms, trousers and short skirts may cause offence to some community members.

Entry requirements

Passports

All travellers require passports with at least six months validity from the date of entry; proof of return/onward passage and sufficient funds for stay are also required.
The Israeli Ministry of the Interior insists that Israeli citizens holding dual nationality must enter and leave Israel on their Israeli passport.
NB When crossing into Israel from any border other than the West Bank, it is important to note that an Israeli stamp, or exit stamp from any of the neighbouring countries, will mean entry is barred to almost any other Arab country. It is possible to request that the passport should not be stamped and a separate form is stamped instead and attached to the passport; the form can be removed when exiting the country.

Visa

Israel has agreements with 65 countries for visa-free travel, including most citizens from Europe, the Americas, Australasia and some Asian countries. Transit passengers with onward passage within 24 hours do not require visas. Contact the nearest Israeli consulate for further information.

Prohibited entry

Persons carrying a Palestinian identity number will not be permitted to enter Israel through Ben Gurion International Airport if their last departure was through the Allenby Bridge or Rafah border crossings.

Currency advice/regulations

There are no restrictions on the import of local and foreign currencies but amounts to be exported should not exceed the amount imported.
Money should only be changed at authorised exchanged outlets.
Travellers cheques are widely accepted.

Customs

Video cameras and other electronic items must be declared on entry.

Prohibited imports

Fresh meat and fruit and vegetables from Africa.

Health (for visitors)

Mandatory precautions

There are no vaccinations required.

Advisable precautions

Inoculations and boosters should be current for tetanus and hepatitis A. There

may be a need for vaccinations for typhoid, tuberculosis, diphtheria and hepatitis B. Rabies is a risk.
Mains water is normally safe to drink but readily available bottled water is advised for the first few weeks of a visit.
A supply of any regular medicines required should be carried, with their prescription details; medical insurance, which includes emergency evacuation, is recommended.

Hotels
There are plenty of hotels in business and tourist centres. Service charge of 15 per cent usually added to bill. Settlement of bills in foreign currency will avoid payment of local taxes. Many hotels quote prices in US dollars.

Credit cards
All major credit and charge cards are widely accepted. ATMs are widely available.

Public holidays (national)
Fixed dates
Variable dates
Purim (Mar), First day of Passover (Apr), Last day of Passover (Apr), Independence Day (May), Shavuot (Pentecost) (Jun), Tisha B'Av (Aug), Rosh Hashanah (Jewish New Year) (Sep/Oct), Yom Kippur (Day of Atonement) (Oct), First day of Succoth (Feast of Tabernacles) (Oct), Last day of Sukkot (Oct), Shemini Atzeret (Celebration of Renewal and Thanksgiving) (Oct).
The Jewish calendar is based on the lunar and solar cycle. Each month begins with a new moon and runs for either 29 or 30 days; this results in years that are either 12 or 13 months long. The Jewish new year begins in March or April.
The Jewish religious day is Saturday – the Sabbath – which begins at nightfall on Friday until nightfall on Saturday. Most public services and shops close early on Friday.
Muslim and Christian holidays are also observed by their respective populations. Thus, depending on the district, the day of rest falls on Friday, Saturday or Sunday.
Jewish year – 5767 (23 Sep 2006–12 Sep 2007): the Jewish calendar is lunar and loses approximately 12 days per year against the Gregorian calendar, therefore every three years a leap or intercalary month is inserted to re-align the calenders.

Working hours
Banking
Sun–Fri: 0830–1200; Sun/Tue/Thu: 1600–1800.
Business
Sun—Thu: 0800–1730. On Fridays, some businesses stay open until 1230, but most close all day.
Government
Sun–Thu: 0730–1430 (Jun—Oct); 0730–1300, 1345–1600 (Nov–May). All government offices close on Friday afternoon and all day on Saturday.
Shops
Sun—Fri: 0800—1900; some shops close 1300—1600. Jewish shops observe closing time near sunset Friday evenings; Arabic stores are closed on Friday; Christian shops are closed on Sunday. Shops in hotels are often open until midnight.

Telecommunications
Mobile/cell phones
There are GSM 900/1800 roaming facilities available, with coverage throughout Israel and the West Bank.

Electricity supply
220V AC, 50 cycles. Most sockets are round and three-pronged so a European adaptor is necessary.

Weights and measures
Metric system, but area is usually measured in dunam (1,000 sq metres).

Social customs/useful tips
People are hospitable and informal and culturally diverse. Jewish traditions and customs are generally adhered to.
Israel is largely secular in character and Mediterranean in style. The Jewish Sabbath, from Friday dusk until Saturday dusk is, however, widely observed. Shops close on Friday and do not open again until Sunday morning. Most cinemas and restaurants are closed on Friday night. In most cities over the Sabbath there is no public transport (except for taxis), postal service, or banking service. Some religious sections in Jerusalem and the Tel Aviv suburb of Bnei Brak, as well as Tel Aviv's main street, Rehov Dizengoff, are closed to traffic. The same is true on six Jewish religious holidays.
Punctuality is not a strong point and business visitors should not be surprised to be kept waiting. Business meetings are less formal in character than in northern Europe but the normal courtesies are observed.
It is considered by many a violation of the Sabbath to smoke in public places such as restaurants and hotels.

Security
Security is tight owing to the threat of terrorist activity, and delays in the ongoing peace process have increased tensions. Business travellers often encounter delays because of security alerts. Prolonged questioning and detailed searches may take place at the time of entry and/or departure. Do not leave bags unattended.
In Jerusalem, tourists should exercise caution at religious sites on holy days. Visitors are advised to avoid demonstrations and areas where large crowds are gathering. The theft of passports, credit cards and valuables from public beaches is commonplace. Visitors should carry passports at all times as a form of identity. Money and valuables should be kept out of sight.

Getting there
Air
National airline: El Al
El Al has an intensive security check and passengers are advised to arrive for flights in plenty of time.
International airport/s: Ben Gurion International (TLV), 20km south-east of Tel Aviv (50k west of Jerusalem); duty-free shop, ATMs, currency exchange, bar, restaurant, hotel reservations, post office, shops, car hire. A rail service to Tel Aviv operates between 0300–0000, journey time 15 minutes. Taxis and buses are available to Jerusalem and Tel Aviv.
Other airport/s: Eilat Central Airport (ETH)
Airport tax: None
Surface
Road: Tourists from Jordan can cross into Israel after obtaining a 'bridge pass' from the Jordanian Interior Ministry in Amman. It is also possible to cross the border at Eilat on the Red Sea coast. The road and bus route, via Cairo and Rafa (Gaza Strip), has been closed.
There is an exit tax of US$16 at all land border crossings.
Water: There are ferry services from Piraeus (Greece) and Larnaca (Cyprus) to Haifa.
Main port/s: Haifa, Ashdod and Eilat.

Getting about
National transport
Air: Arkia operate daily services from Tel Aviv to Jerusalem, Haifa, Eilat, and other major cities.
Road: Main roads are good. Maximum speed 90km per hour.
Buses: Buses connect all centres of population; they are frequent and cheap but can be crowded. Buses do not operate from sunset on Friday to sunset on Saturday.
Rail: Services between Tel Aviv and Haifa (hourly). Seats can be reserved. No service Friday evenings or Saturday.
City transport
Taxis: Taxis are metered but flat rates often apply so it is advisable to check before any long trips.
From Ben Gurion airport to Tel Aviv centre takes about 30 minutes.
Many offices close on Fridays and consequently traffic flows are better.
For inter-city travel (including Saturdays), sherut (share taxis) run between central points in main cities and are not expensive. Some sherut companies, including Arieh and Aviv, will accept advance bookings.

Car hire
International companies have offices in main cities and at Ben Gurion airport. Drivers must be over 21 years and have an international credit card and national or international licence. Seat belts are compulsory for drivers and front-seat passengers. Most road signs on major roads are in English.

BUSINESS DIRECTORY
The addresses listed below are a selection only. While World of Information makes every endeavour to check these addresses, we cannot guarantee that changes have not been made, especially to telephone numbers and area codes. We would welcome any corrections.

Telephone area codes
The international direct dialling (IDD) code for Israel is +972, followed by area code and subscriber's number:

Afula	4	Kfar Saba	9
Ashdod	8	Natanya	9
Ashkelon	8	Nazareth	4
Beersheva	8	Raanana	9
Briei Brak	3	Ramat Gan	3
Eilat	8	Rehovot	8
Haifa	4	Safed	4
Holon	3	Tel Aviv	3
Jerusalem	2		

Useful telephone numbers
International operator: 188
Directory enquiries: 144
Collect calls: 142
Overseas operator: 188
Ambulance: 101
Fire: 102
Police: 100
Correct time: 155

Chambers of Commerce
America-Israel Chamber of Commerce and Industry, 35 Shaul Hamelech Boulevard, PO Box 33174, Tel Aviv 61333 (tel: 695-2341; fax: 695-1272; email: amcham@amcham.co.il).

British-Israel Chamber of Commerce, 29 Hamered Street, PO Box 50321, Tel Aviv 61502 (tel: 510-9424; fax: 510-9540; email: isrbrit@bezeqint.net).

Federation of Israeli Chambers of Commerce, 84 Ha'ashmonaim Street, PO Box 20027, Tel Aviv 61200 (tel: 563-1020; fax: 561-9027; chamber@chamber.org.il).

Haifa and the North Chamber of Commerce and Industry, 53 Ha'atzmaut Road, PO Box 33176, Haifa 31331 (tel: 862-6364; fax: 864-5424; email: main@haifachamber.org.il).

Banking
Bank Hapoalim BM, 50 Rothschild Blvd, Tel Aviv 66883 (tel: 567-5777; fax: 567-6015; internet site: www.bankhapoalim.co.il).

Bank Leumi Le-Israel BM, 24-32 Yehuda Halevi St, Tel Aviv 65546 (tel: 514-8111; fax: 566-1872).

The First International Bank of Israel Ltd, Shalom Tower, 9 Ahad Haam St, Tel Aviv 65251 (tel: 519-6111; fax: 510-0316).

Investec Bank (Israel) Ltd; PO Box 677, 38 Rothschild Boulevard, Tel Aviv 61006 (tel: 564-5645; fax: 564-5210).

Israel Discount Bank Ltd, 27-31 Yehuda Halevi Street, Tel Aviv 65136 (tel: 514-5555; fax: 514-5346; internet site: www.discountbank.net).

Union Bank of Israel Ltd, 6-8 Ahuzat Bayit Street, Tel Aviv 65143 (tel: 519-1111; fax: 519-1421).

Central bank
Bank of Israel, PO Box 780, Kiryat Ben-Gurion, Jerusalem 91007 (tel: 655-2211; fax: 652-8805; e-mail: webmaster@bankisrael.gov.il).

Travel information
Arkia Israeli Airlines Ltd, (Charter Airline), Sde Dov, PO Box 39301, Tel Aviv, 61392 (tel: 690-2222; fax: 699-1512).

Automobile and Touring Club of Israel (MEMSI), 20 Harakevet Street, PO Box 65144, Tel Aviv 65117 (tel: 564-1122; fax: 566-0493).

Bus Station, Levinsky and Levanda intersection, Nava Sha'anan, Tel Aviv.

Dan Co-operative Society for Public Transport Ltd. (City buses), 39 Shaul Hamelech Blvd., Tel Aviv, 64928 (tel: 693-3333; fax: 693-3511).

Egged Israel Transport Co-operative Ltd (Intercity buses), 142 Petach Tikvah Road, Tel Aviv, 64921 (tel: 692-2211; fax: 696-5354).

El Al Israel Airlines Ltd, Ben Gurion Airport, Lod, 71285 (tel: 971-6111; fax: 972-1442; internet site: www.elal.co.il).

Israel Airports Authority, Ben Gurion Airport, PO Box 137 70100 (tel: 975-5555; fax: 973-1650; www.iaa.gov.il).

Israel Ports and Railway Authority, 74 Derech Petach Tikva, POB 20121, Tel Aviv, 61201 (tel: 565-7000; fax: 512-1048).

Israel Railways, PO Box 18085, Tel Aviv, 61180 (tel: 542-1515; fax: 695-8176).

Ministry of tourism
Ministry of Tourism, 24 King George Street, PO Box 1018, Jerusalem 94262 (tel: 675-4811; fax: 625-3407; e-mail: doar@tourism.gov.il; internet site: www.travelnet.co.il).

Ministries
Prime Minister's Office, 3 Kaplan Street, PO Box 187, Kiryat Ben-Gurion, Jerusalem 91919 (tel: 670-5555; fax: 651-2631; email: markal@pmo.gov.il).

Ministry of Agriculture, Agricultural Centre, PO Box 50200, Bet-Dagan (tel: 948-5555; email: pniot@moag.gov.il).

Ministry of Communications, 23 Jaffa Street, Jerusalem 91999 (tel: 670-6320; fax: 670-6372; email: intmocil@moc.gov.il).

Ministry of Construction and Housing, Kiryat Hamemshala, PO Box 18110, Jerusalem 91180 (tel: 584-7211; fax: 581-1904).

Ministry of Defence, Kaplan Street, Hakirya, Tel-Aviv 61909 (tel: 569-2010; fax: 691-6940).

Ministry of Education, 34 Shivtei Israel Street, PO Box 292, Jerusalem 91911 (tel: 560-2222; fax: 560-2223; email: info@education.gov.il).

Ministry of the Environment, 5 Kanfei Nesharim Street, Givat Shaul, PO Box 34033, Jerusalem 95464 (tel: 655-3777; fax: 653-5934).

Ministry of Finance, 1 Kaplan Street, Kyriat Ben-Gurion, PO Box 13195, Jerusalem 91008 (tel: 531-7111; fax: 563-7891; email: webmaster@mof.gov.il).

Ministry of Foreign Affairs, Hakirya, Romema, Jerusalem 91950 (tel: 530-3111; fax: 530-33367; email: markal@mofa.gov.il; internet site: (Information) www.israel.org).

Ministry of Health, 2 Ben-Tabai Street, PO Box 1176, Jerusalem 91010 (tel: 670-5705; fax: 623-3026).

Ministry of Industry and Trade, 30 Agron Street, PO Box 299, Jerusalem 91002 (tel: 622-0220; fax: 624-5110).

Ministry of the Interior, 2 Kaplan Street, PO Box 6158, Kiryat Ben-Gurion, Jerusalem 91061 (tel: 670-1411; fax: 670-1628).

Ministry of Justice, 29 Salah A-din Street, Jerusalem 91010 (tel: 670-8511; fax: 628-8618; email: feedback@justice.gov.il).

Ministry of Labour and Social Welfare, 2 Kaplan Street, PO Box 915, Kiryat Ben-Gurion, Jerusalem 91008 (tel: 675-2311; fax: 675-2803).

Ministry of National Infrastructure, 216 Jaffa Street, Jerusalem 91130 (tel: 500-6777; fax: 500-6888).

Ministry of Public Security, Kiryat Hamemshala, PO Box 18182, Jerusalem 91181 (tel: 530-9999; fax: 584-7872).

Ministry of Religious Affairs, 236 Jaffa Street, PO Box 13059, Jerusalem 91130 (tel: 531-1171; fax: 531-1183; email: tsibor@religinfoserv.gov.il).

Ministry of Science, Culture and Sport, Kiryat Hamemshala Hamizrahit, POB 49100, Jerusalem 91181 (tel: 541-1111).

Ministry of Transport, 97 Jaffa Street, Jerusalem 91000 (tel: 622-8211; fax: 622-8693).

Office of the President, 3 Hanassi Street, Jerusalem 92188 (tel: 670-7211; fax: 561-0037).

The Knesset, Kiryat Ben-Gurion, Jerusalem 91950 (tel: 675-3333; fax: 652-1599).

Other useful addresses

Administration of Rabbinical Courts, 9 Koresh Street, Jerusalem 91012 (tel: 624-8603; fax: 624-5019).

British Embassy, 192 Hayarkon Street, Tel Aviv 63405 (tel: 524-9171; fax: 524-3313).

Central Bureau of Statistics, 3 Kaplan Street, PO Box 187, Kiryat Ben-Gurion, Jerusalem 91919 (tel: 655-3553; fax: 655-3325).

Israeli Academy of Sciences and Humanities, Albert Einstein Square, Talbieh, PO Box 4040, Jerusalem 91040 (tel: 563-6211).

Israel Airports Authority, Ben Gurion Airport (tel: 971-2804; fax: 971-2436). For information on taxes and tariffs (tel: 971-5596).

Israel Convention Bureau (ISCOB), Israel Tourism Administration, PO Box 1018, Jerusalem.

Israeli Broadcasting Authority, Klal Building, 97 Jaffa Street, PO Box 6387, Jerusalem 91063 (tel: 529-1888).

Israel Chemicals Ltd, 123 Hahashmonaim Street, Tel Aviv, 67133 (tel: 563-0232; fax: 561-5391).

Israel Electric Corporation Ltd, 2 Hahagana Boulevard, Haifa, 35254 (tel: 854-8548; fax: 853-8149).

Israel Fuel Corporation Ltd (Delek), Prof. Y. Kaufman Street, PO Box 50250, Tel Aviv, 61500 (tel: 591-5555; fax: 510-2072).

Israel Land Administration (part of the National Infrastructure Ministry), 6 Shamai Street, POB 2600, Jerusalem 94631 (tel: 520-8422; fax: 523-4960).

Israel Shipyards Ltd, Po Box 10630, Haifa Bay, 26118 (tel: 846-0245; fax: 841-0572).

Israel Telecommunication Corporation, PO Box 1088, Jerusalem, 91010 (tel: 539-5333; fax: 625-2506).

Israel Trade Fairs Centre/Israel Convention Centre, PO Box 21075, 61210 Tel Aviv (tel: 422-422).

Israeli Embassy (US), 3514 International Drive, NW, Washington DC 20008 (tel: (+1-202) 364-5500; fax: (+1-202) 364-5560; email: ask@israelemb.org).

Manufacturers' Association of Israel, Industry House, PO Box 50022, 29 Hamered Street, Tel Aviv (tel: 650-121).

National Coal Supply Corporation Ltd, 155 Bialik Street, Ramat Gan, 52523 (tel: 751-2261; fax: 751-0119).

National Insurance Institute, 13 Weizmann Blvd, Jerusalem 91909 (tel: 670-9211; fax: 670-9792).

National Water Company (Mekorot), 9 Lincoln Street, Tel Aviv, 67134 (tel: 623-0555; fax: 623-0833).

Oil Refineries Ltd, PO Box 4, Industrial Zone, Haifa, 31000 (tel: 878-8111; fax: 872-8319).

Ormat Industries Ltd, Po Box 68, Szydlowksi Road, New Industrial Area, Yavne, 70650 (tel: 433-777; fax: 439-901).

Pama Development for Energy and Sources, PO Box 20118, 14 Kalman Magen Street, Tel Aviv, 61200 (tel: 695-8129; fax: 695-8131).

Paz Oil Company Ltd, PO Box 434, 4 Hagefen Street, Haifa, 31003 (tel: 856-7111; fax: 852-2390).

Postal Authority, 237 Jaffa Street, Jerusalem 91999 (tel: 629-0800; fax: 629-0921).

State Comptroller, POB 1081, Jerusalem 91010 (tel: 531-5111).

Tahal Consulting Engineers Ltd (Water), PO Box 11170, 54 Ibn Gvirol Street, Tel Aviv, 61111 (tel: 692-4434; fax: 696-9969).

The Tel Aviv Stock Exchange (TASE), 54 Ahad Ha'am Street, Tel Aviv 65202; PO Box 29060, Tel Aviv 61290 (tel: 567-7411; fax: 510-5379; internet site: www.tase.co.il).

Zim Israel Navigation Co. Ltd, 7-9 Pal Yam Avenue, Haifa, 31000 (tel: 865-2111; fax: 865-2956).

Other news agencies: Israel National News: www.israelnationalnews.com

Israel News Agency (INA): www.israelnewsagency.com

Israeli News Now: www.israelinewsnow.com

PR Newswire: www.prnewswire.co.il

Internet sites

Mercantile Discount Bank: www.mercantile.co.il

Yellow and White Pages: www.yellowpages.co.il

Italy

In a December 2007 editorial entitled *The Italian Slob* the London *Times* described Italy as 'the nation that defined the good life', going on to say that Italy now needed to 'learn how to live it'. The editorial described Italy as a country 'mired in an hysterical identity crisis', itself quoting an editorial in Italy's prestigious daily *La Repubblica* which referred to Italy's 'explosion of provincialism' and as being 'traumatised by the fear of decline'.

What decline?

Some of Italy's decline is undeniable. In 2007, for the first time, Spain's gross domestic product (GDP) per capita overtook that of Italy. International investment in Spain is put at nearly US$50 billion, three times greater than Italy's US$17 billion. In 2007, the UK, where the number of days lost to strikes once caused it to be known as the 'sick man of Europe', in 2007 lost only 26 days annually. In Italy the figure was 120 days. Comparing Italian sloth with Spanish commercial energy, the *Times* editorial highlighted a number of melancholy statistics. Italian members of parliament, with free cinema and football tickets cost the nation more than those of France and Spain combined. The

KEY FACTS

Official name: Repubblica Italiana (Italian Republic)

Head of State: President Giorgio Napolitano (elected 10 May 2006)

Head of government: Prime Minister Silvio Berlusconi (from 15 Apr 2008)

Ruling party: Coalition supporting Silvio Berlusconi, led by Popolo della Libertà (PdL) (People of Freedom) with Lega Nord per l'Indipendenza della Padania (Lega Nord) (Northern League for the Independence of Padania) and Movimento per l'Autonomia (MpA) (Movement for Autonomy) (from 14 Apr 2008)

Area: 301,277 square km

Population: 58.67 million (2007)

Capital: Rome

Official language: Italian

Currency: Euro (eur) = 100 cents (from 1 Jan 2002; previous currency lira, locked at L1,936.27 per euro) (Campione d'Italia, an Italian enclave near Lake Lugano in Switzerland, uses the Swiss franc, although the euro also circulates)

Exchange rate: eur0.63 per US$ (Jul 2008)

GDP per capita: US$35,872 (2007)

GDP real growth: 1.50% (2007)

Labour force: 24.70 million (2007)

Unemployment: 6.00% (2007)

Inflation: 2.00% (2007)

Oil production: 122,000 bpd (2007)

Balance of trade: US$4.24 billion (2007)

Foreign debt: US$1,639.05 billion (2004)

Visitor numbers: 41.10 million (2006)*

* estimated figure

presidential palace, the Quirinal, costs Italians four times as much to run as the UK's Buckingham Palace. According to one book on the topic, Italy boasts the highest number of official chauffeur driven cars in Europe. Alitalia, the national airline has not made a profit in years, yet retains the symbolism of bygone years when national airlines were subsidised along with railways. Italy's pervasive sense of decline has not been helped by its continued dependence on an increasingly geriatric bunch of politicians. Mr Prodi is 68, Silvio Berlusconi is 71. Even more worryingly, Italy's unemployment rate of 7 per cent (and Italian statistics always have to be treated with some care) puts it 77th in the international league tables. Italy's unofficial, or 'black' economy is the highest in Europe, an estimated 60 per cent above the Organisation for European Co-operation and Development (OECD) average. According to the London *Economist* in 2005 only half of Italy's registered companies made any profits at all.

IMF uneasiness

The International Monetary Fund (IMF) rarely throws its hands up in the air when it comes to making an annual assessment of a member nation's economy. The announcement in February 2008 by Mr Alessandro Leipold, Chief of the Fund's 2008 Consultation Mission to Italy, was hardly positive. It baldly stated that: 'The IMF mission that visited Italy over the past 10 days for the planned 2008 Article IV Consultation discussions gathered much useful information and evaluations of Italy's economic situation. In the current political context it was not, however, in a position to hold forward-looking policy discussions. The mission will thus return to Rome when political circumstances allow for such discussions'.

While the reasons for the IMF's hesitation focussed on Italy's political uncertainties at the time, Italy's central bank, the Banco d'Italia, portrayed a relatively upbeat picture in its analysis of the economy in 2007, observing that in 2007 the Italian economy grew at a slower rate than the average in the rest of the euro area (1.5 as against 2.8 per cent), the pattern since the mid-1990s. Services accounted for almost all of the expansion, while industrial activity contracted from the beginning of the year, contrary to the trend in the other main European countries. A less unfavourable picture of the Italian industrial cycle in 2007 emerged based on the indicators for turnover and orders, which appeared better placed to capture the effects of progressive internationalisation and shift in the composition of output towards higher-quality goods, which industrial production statistics only partly took into account.

Banco de Italia optimism

The bank went on to note that Italy's rate of inflation in 2007 averaged 1.8 per cent, as measured by the index of consumer prices for the entire resident population. The average result masked divergent trends over the year. After falling below 2 per cent in the first nine months of 2007, inflation rose sharply in the fourth quarter, as in the rest of the euro area, driven by the surge in food and energy prices. The moderation of domestic costs, in particular the lack of wage pressures and the appreciation of the euro, helped curb the increase in the prices of the other components.

A solid export performance, fuelled by the expansion of outlet markets and the enhanced competitiveness of Italian firms provided the main contribution to growth. By contrast, domestic demand failed to strengthen sufficiently. The growth in household expenditure remained low, reflecting primarily the protracted weakness of disposable income, which since 1991 has grown in real terms at an annual average rate of just 0.3 per cent (compared with 1 per cent in Germany and 2.2 per cent in France). In 2007 the uncertainty engendered by the effects of the crisis in the international financial markets and the erosion of purchasing power associated with the acceleration in prices in the fourth quarter also had a significant impact. In addition, the boost provided by capital gains, which in the early 2000s had been very substantial in the housing ma4rket, weakened.

Since the final quarter of 2007 the economic situation was considered by the Bank to have deteriorated: the rate of inflation had risen, driven by persistent increases in the prices of food and energy commodities; confidence among households and firms had eroded, in response to the uncertain world economic outlook. Based on the most recent indicators, the acceleration in GDP recorded in the first quarter of 2008, which offset the equivalent decline in the previous quarter, appeared to be partly temporary.

In 2007 Italian households' expenditure increased by 1.4 per cent in real terms; although rising slightly, the rate of growth was around half the average recorded during the upswing of the second half of the 1990s. The largest contribution to the increase came from spending on services, which rose by 2.1 per cent. Purchases of semi-durable and especially of durable goods also sustained household expenditure. In contrast, spending on non-durable goods fell by 0.3 per cent, owing in part to the stagnation of food purchases, which in the second half of the year were held down by price increases for raw materials.

KEY INDICATORS — Italy

	Unit	2003	2004	2005	2006	2007
Population	m	57.48	57.31	58.08	58.44	58.67
Gross domestic product (GDP)	US$bn	1,465.90	1,672.30	1,772.77	1,858.34	2,104.67
GDP per capita	US$	25,137	29,219	30,525	31,802	35,872
GDP real growth	%	0.4	1.2	0.1	1.8	1.5
Inflation	%	2.8	2.3	2.2	2.2	2.0
Unemployment	%	8.9	8.0	7.7	6.7	6.0
Oil output	'000 bpd	107.0	104.0	118.0	111.0	122.0
Natural gas output	bn cum	13.7	13.0	12.0	11.0	8.9
Exports (fob) (goods)	US$m	290,231.0	336,400.0	372,750.0	418,074.0	502,384.0
Imports (cif) (goods)	US$m	289,017.0	329,300.0	372,690.0	430,585.0	498,142.0
Balance of trade	US$m	1,214.0	7,100.0	60,000.0	-12,510.0	4,242.0
Current account	US$m	-21.9	*-24,820.0	-28,426.0	-47,566.0	-47,250.0
Total reserves minus gold	US$m	30,366.0	27,859.0	25,515.0	25,662.0	28,385.0
Foreign exchange	US$m	26,056.0	24,011.0	23,528.0	24,413.0	27,319.0
Exchange rate	per US$	0.88	0.80	0.77	0.75	0.69

* estimated figure

Prodi goes...

In his end of year news conference, then Prime Minister Romani Prodi announced that Italy's budget deficit would be 2 per cent of Italy's GDP, significantly lower than the official government target of 2.4 per cent. Mr Prodi had inherited a budget deficit of over 4 per cent, although it gradually emerged that the situation was perhaps not as bad as expected. The improvement was attributed to greater than anticipated government revenues, in turn due to improved tax collections. Government collections rose by an impressive US$35 billion, this following an increase of US$35 billion in 2006.This was good news for the government, but improved taxation is never an electoral 'plus'. Mr Prodi also projected that Italy's economic growth would slow to 1.5 per cent in 2008, down from the 1.9 per cent figure of earlier official estimates. Despite the generally upbeat picture of 2008, Italian data for the first part of 2008 proved to be more negative, causing most analysts to lower their growth forecasts to around the 1 per cent mark. This might well prove to be optimistic as most of Europe risked slipping into recession in 2008. For over a decade, Italy's economic growth has been below that of its EU partners. Mr Prodi, also claimed that Italy would not be damaged by the US inspired credit crunch. Mr Prodi's precarious nine party coalition although it lasted for 20 months, a long time by Italian standards, never looked likely to stay the course. Its undoing was the unpopular presence of Italian troops in Afghanistan.

...and Berlusconi comes (not again?)

Despite Silvio Berlusconi's scandal ridden record as prime minister in his earlier terms of office, he did at least establish an Italian political record by going the distance and lasting the full five years of his electoral term. His election victory in April 2008 was more a victory of illusion than of substance. Hopes that Rome's mayor, the youthful (he is 52) Walter Veltroni might mount a plausible challenge proved short lived. Mr Veltroni seemed to be stronger on form than on substance. Italian voters appeared to feel that at least with Mr Berlusconi, they knew what they were likely to be getting, even if it did boil down to cosmetic surgery and a reputation as a septuagenarian seducer. None the less, it seemed to many observers somewhat paradoxical that Mr Berlusconi was asking Italy's voters to support him as he endeavoured to overcome problems many of which were of his own creation. Analysts could only point to two Berlusconi reforms. One, the so called Maroni law, revised pensions by raising the retirement age from 57 to 60. The other, the Biagi Law, allowed employers to offer their employees more flexible contracts. It did appear to improve employment prospects, but under the Prodi coalition government, a number of these benefits were wiped out as Italy's trade unions fought back. Otherwise, Italy's public finances worsened under Mr Berlusconi.

Most Italians' fears began to be borne out when Mr Berlusconi's first measures in government were the closure of the office of Italy's high commissioner against corruption and altering legislation to avoid the embarrassment of facing further corruption charges himself. After his strong anti-corruption talk during a short election campaign, Mr Berlusconi's post election priorities appeared to have been revisited. Evading the wider canvas of privatisation and liberalisation of Italy's creaking government and economy, Mr Berlusconi showed few signs of having changed his spots. Adopting the simple philosophy of changing, rather than breaking the law where convenient, appeared central to the Berlusconi political philosophy, although it had never appeared in his election manifesto.

Risk assessment

Politics	Fair
Economy	Fair
Regional stability	Good

COUNTRY PROFILE

Historical profile

By the 400s BC the Roman state – comprising several cities in close association – had begun its expansionist policy that transformed it from a vigorous republic to an empire that encompassed most of Europe, North Africa, the Middle East and some of Asia Minor. It eclipsed all previous empires and influenced the peoples of Europe for many centuries.

By the fifth century AD, little of the Roman Empire survived and the peninsula became a feudal society before being conquered by invading armies.

The prestige of the Roman Empire lingered on and endowed the leaders of the Christian Church with a status that probably would have been lacking otherwise.

The city states of Italy in the Middle Ages were vibrant, rich and centres of education and industry. Pre-eminent among them were Venice and Genoa (powerful maritime trading centres), Florence (a centre for trade and artistic merit) and Rome (the seat of the Pope). With divided loyalties and rivalries the independent states on the peninsular were unable to resist concerted invasion by predatory outsiders.

1796–1806 The French, under Emperor Napoléon Bonaparte, occupied Italy. The country was carved up to be ruled by Napoléon, his relatives and Pope Pius VII.

1814–15 Following Napoléon's defeat by the Austrians, British, Prussians and Russians, Italy returned to its feudal status under the terms of the Congress of Vienna. Regions of northern Italy were also handed to Austria.

1848 A rise in nationalism and rebellion against Austrian rule began, known locally as the Risorgimento (Revival). A key figure in this process was Giuseppe Garibaldi.

1859—61 A partly unified Italy was created under the King of Sardina (Sardina, Piedmont, Genoa, Savoy), Vittorio Emmanuelle II.

1870. Italian nationalists liberated Rome from French rule and proclaimed it the capital of a unified Italy under Vittorio Emmanuelle II.

1889—90 Italy established colonies in Africa through military conquest, namely in Somalia and Eritrea.

1901 Italy secured a territorial concession in the Chinese city of Tientsin

1911—12 Italy gained Tripolitania and Cyrenaica (later Libya) and the Dodekanesa (Dodecanese) Islands from the Ottoman Empire.

1916–18 Italy eventually fought alongside the Allies in the First World War. Ensuing disorder and economic weakness fostered the rise of Benito Mussolini and the Partito Nazionale Fascista (PNF) (National Fascist Party).

1919 Italy gained Trentino-Südtirol (South Tyrol), the Istrian peninsula and Trieste, which had been parts of the Austro-Hungarian Empire, under the terms of the Treaty of Versailles. Italian nationalists later seized control of the former Austro-Hungarian city of Fiume (now Rijeka), in the face of Yugoslav claims.

1922 After Italian fascists marched on Rome, Mussolini and the PNF were invited to form a government by the Italian King, Vittorio Emmanuele III.

1924–26 Mussolini increased his prime ministerial powers, effectively making his rule a dictatorship.

1929 Three Lateran Treaties granted Roman Catholicism special status in Italy. The Vatican City state, under the rule of the Pope, was created within Rome.

1935–36 Italy invaded Abyssinia (now Ethiopia).

1936 Italy supported General Franco's nationalists in the Spanish Civil War, until they won in 1939.

1940–42 Italy was part of the Axis powers, assisting Nazi Germany's military campaigns in Europe and Africa. It also invaded British Somaliland in East Africa in 1940.
1943 Allied forces invaded southern Italy and its African colonies. Mussolini was removed from government, imprisoned, and Pietro Badoglio was appointed prime minister. After escaping from prison, Mussolini declared the creation of the Repubblica Sociale Italiana (Social Republic of Italy) in German-controlled northern Italy.
1945 The fascist regime collapsed as the allies liberated the whole of Italy. Mussolini was executed by Italian partisans.
1946 In May, Vittorio Emmanuele III abdicated from the Italian throne and was temporarily replaced by Umberto II. After a referendum the Italian monarchy was abolished and a republic was declared. Enrico De Nicola was appointed as temporary head of state.
1948 De Nicola was elected the Republic's first president. The constitution, which established a parliament, was promulgated.
1949–82 There followed a succession of short-lived coalitions involving the Democrazia Cristiana (DC) (Christian Democrats) and up to four other major parties, frequently producing several regroupings and new cabinets in a year.
1978 Former prime minister and then president of the DC, Aldo Moro, is assassinated by the Red Brigades.
1983–87 Bettino Craxi, of the Partito Socialista Italiano (PSI) (Italian Socialist Party), headed what was then the longest-running post-war Italian government.
1989 The DC returned to government and Giulio Andreotti became prime minister for the third time.
1992–93 Italy had two prime ministers in two years, Giuliano Amato and Carlo Azeglio Ciampi. Both were forced to resign after political and corruption scandals.
1994 Silvio Berlusconi, of the Forza Italia (FI) (Go Italy!) – a party he largely created and funded, was elected prime minister in March and resigned in December. A transitional government was formed led by independent Lamberto Dina.
1996 The centre-left Ulivo (Olive Tree) coalition won the parliamentary elections and the coalition's leader, Romano Prodi, was appointed prime minister.
1997 A constitutional reform commission, drawn from both houses of parliament, altered the Italian political system by introducing direct elections for the office of president.
1998 The Democratici di Sinistra's (DS) (Democrats of the Left) Massimo d'Alema succeeded Romano Prodi, who resigned after parliament rejected the budget.
1999 The government fell and d'Alema resigned. He was reinstated by the newly-elected president, former prime minister Ciampi.
2000 D'Alema resigned and was replaced by Giuliano Amato, heading a new centre-left 12-party coalition government.
2001 The Casa delle Libertà (House of Freedom) coalition won the elections and Silvio Berlusconi became prime minister for a second time. Voters approved a referendum on constitutional changes to give more power to the regions.
2002 The euro currency replaced the lira. A controversial bill, allowing Berlusconi to retain control of his media empire, was passed in parliament.
2003 Berlusconi went on trial on corruption charges for allegedly bribing judges, it was suspended as parliament granted immunity from prosecution while in office to five of the most senior figures in government. The Parmalat dairy food-manufacturing giant – one of Italy's blue-chip companies – was declared insolvent when a US$11 billion-plus accountancy fraud was discovered.
2004 The Constitutional Court threw out the immunity from prosecution law and the prime minister's trial resumed in April.
2005 In March an Italian secret service agent was shot dead in Iraq by American troops during a hostage rescue operation, prompting massive street demonstrations. Romano Prodi, became leader of the renamed centre-Left bloc, L'Unione (The Union), formerly Ulivo. In December Antonio Fazio, governor of the Bank of Italy, resigned and was replaced by Mario Draghi. Plans, proposed by the Berlusconi government, to reformed the electoral system whereby all parliamentary seats be determined by proportional representation and only parties that won a minimum of 2 per cent of the vote would be allocated seats, passed through both chambers of parliament.
2006 On 10 April, in national elections, the coalition L'Unione, led by Romano Prodi won 49.8 per cent (348 out of 630 seats) while the ruling coalition Casa delle Libertà won 49.7 per cent (281 seats) in the Chamber of Deputies. In the Senate, L'Unione won 49 per cent (158 out of 315 seats), the Casa delle Libertà won 50.2 per cent (156 seats). Turnout was 84 per cent. Berlusconi refused to concede defeat until 2 May, even though Italy's highest court had confirmed Prodi's victory on 19 April. On 10 May, Giorgio Napolitano was elected president, by the Electoral College, with 543 votes (out of 1,009). He was the first former Communist to be elected president of Italy. On 26 June, a remarkable 54 per cent of the electorate turned out to vote in a referendum on far-reaching constitutional changes. The proposals, which would have given the prime minister and the regions increased powers, was rejected by a 61.7 per cent majority.
2007 Romano Prodi resigned as prime minister on 21 February, following a surpise defeat in the senate for his foreign policy, in particular sending more troops to enhance Nato's deployment in Afghanistan. On 24 February, the president refused to accept Prodi's resignation and asked him to submit to a vote of confidence in both chambers of the parliament, which was won, 162–157 in the upper house, on 28 February. Walter Veltroni won the 16 October elections to become leader of the Democratic party.
2008 Prime Minister Prodi resigned after losing a parliamentary vote of no-confidence. On 30 January the president asked Franco Marini to form an interim government. However when Marini failed President Napolitano dissolved parliament on 6 February and early elections were held on 13 April. In the general elections, the three-party coalition supporting Silvio Berlusconi won a combined 46.81 per cent of the votes (340 seats out of 630), the two-party coalition supporting Walter Veltroni won 37.54 per cent (239). On 8 May Silvio Berlusconi was sworn into office as prime minister and head of the country's 62nd post-war government. The cabinet in June resurrected the 2003 proposal to grant the highest-ranking state officials immunity from prosecution, including Prime Minister Berlusconi during their mandate. Both houses of parliament must approve the move, but similar legislation has been overturned by the constitutional court.

Political structure

Constitution

Under the terms of the 1948 constitution, Italy's legislative power is held by a bicameral parliament.

Italy is divided into 20 regions which enjoy a large degree of autonomy. Each region has a regional council elected every five years by universal suffrage.

In 2001, the constitution was amended by the federalist reform bill which increased the decision-making power of the regions.

In 2005 proportional representation was introduced to elect both houses of parliament.

Form of state

Parliamentary democratic republic

The executive

Executive power is held by the prime minister, who is usually the leader of the largest party in the lower house of the

parliament, and by a cabinet of ministers chosen by him.
The president, who must be more than 50 years old, holds a seven-year term of office and is elected by an electoral college consisting of both chambers of parliament and regional representatives. From the presidential term due to start in 2006, presidents will be directly elected. The president nominates a number of Supreme Court judges and has the power to dissolve parliament but has no other executive powers.

National legislature
Parliament consists of the Camera dei Deputati (Chamber of Deputies) and the Senato della Repubblica (Senate of the Republic). The chamber of deputies comprises 630 members, of which 475 are directly elected and the remainder are elected be proportional representation.
The senate has 315 members, of which 83 are elected be proportional representation and the remainder by direct popular vote. In addition there are several senators-for-life who are former presidents of the Republic. Members of both houses are elected for five-year terms.

Legal system
The legal system is based on the constitution of 1948.
The Constitutional Court, set up in 1955, is the final arbiter of the constitutionality of laws and decrees. It defines the powers of the state and regions and passes judgements in disputes between them. It can also try the president and government ministers. The court consists of 15 judges. Five are appointed by the president, five by parliament and the remainder by the highest law and administrative courts.
The highest court of cassation is divided into 23 appeal court districts, with three other sections. These are then further divided into 159 tribunal districts which, together, are divided into 899 magistracies. There are 90 first degree assize courts and 26 assize courts of appeal.

Last elections
13-14 April 2008 (parliamentary); 10 May 2006 (presidential).
Results: Presidential: Giorgio Napolitano, elected president by the Electoral College, with 543 votes (out of 1009).
Parliamentary (Chamber of Deputies): the three-party coalition supporting Silvio Berlusconi won 46.81 per cent of the votes (340 seats out of 630), the two-party coalition supporting Walter Veltroni won 37.54 per cent (239), the Unione di Centro (UdC) (Union of the Centre) won 5.62 per cent (36), the Südtiroler Volkspartei (SVP) (South Tyrolean People's Party) 0.4 per cent (two). No other party won enough votes to achieve any seats.
Senate: Silvio Berlusconi's coalition won 47.32 per cent of the votes (171 seats out of 309), Walter Veltroni's coalition won 38.01 per cent (130), the UdC won 5.69 per cent (three), others including SVP won 2.78 per cent (five). Turnout was around 80 per cent.

Next elections
April 2013 (parliamentary); 2011 (presidential).

Political parties

Ruling party
Coalition supporting Silvio Berlusconi, led by Popolo della Libertà (PdL) (People of Freedom) with Lega Nord per l'Indipendenza della Padania (Lega Nord) (Northern League for the Independence of Padania) and Movimento per l'Autonomia (MpA) (Movement for Autonomy) (from 14 Apr 2008)

Main opposition party
Opposition in the chamber of deputies and the senate – coalition led by Partito Democratico (PD) (Democratic Party) with Italia dei Valori (IdV) (Italy of Values)

Population

58.67 million (2007)
Last census: October 2001: 57,110,144
Population density: 196 inhabitants per square km (2000). Urban population: 67 per cent.
Annual growth rate: 0.1 per cent 1994–2004 (WHO 2006)

Ethnic make-up
Centuries of colonisation have meant that Italy has many ethnic heritages and groups, including Arberesh (Albanian) (around 100,000, mainly in southern Italy), French (around 100,000, mainly in Valle d'Aosta), German (around 290,000, mainly in Trentino-Alto Adige), Friulian (around 600,000, mainly in Friuli-Venezia Giulia), and Greek (around 4,000, mainly in Calabria). The country has been a destination for immigrants from all over the world. There are an estimated one million foreigners residing in Italy.

Religions
97.5 per cent Roman Catholic.

Education

Schooling is free of charge and compulsory from age six. Primary schooling lasts until age 11 years, and lower secondary schools from age 11 to 14 years. Only the first year of upper secondary schooling is compulsory.
Higher secondary schools, from age 14, provide five-year courses in the arts, sciences and teacher training. Specialised secondary schools run four-year courses, and vocational and professional training programmes lasting for three and five years, respectively.
Graduation from higher secondary school automatically gives a student a place at university. Besides universities, a wide range of professional training establishments also provide higher education.
Most of the existing universities were directly established by the state, although some private institutions are recognised.
There are 51 state universities and three technical universities.
Public expenditure on education typically amounts to 4.9 per cent of annual gross national income.
Literacy rate: 98.5 per cent total; 98.2 per cent female, adult rates (World Bank).
Compulsory years: Six to 15
Enrolment rate: 101 gross primary enrolment of relevant age group (including repeaters); 95 per cent gross secondary enrolment (World Bank).
Pupils per teacher: 11 in primary schools

Health

Per capita total expenditure on health (2003) was US$2,266; of which per capita government spending was US$1,703, at the international dollar rate, (WHO 2006).
The healthcare system is regionally based, providing universal coverage free of charge at the point of service. There are deep regional inequalities in healthcare expenditure and in supply and utilisation of healthcare services.
Healthcare is financed through general taxation collected centrally, various other regional taxes and users' payments, which replaced the previous system of social health insurance contributions. In 2000, the National Health Fund was replaced by the National Solidarity Fund, which was developed to transfer funds to the regions unable to raise sufficient resources. The Fund was authorised to spend 10 per cent of the overall regional funding.

HIV/Aids
HIV prevalence: 0.5 per cent aged 15–49 in 2003 (World Bank)
Life expectancy: 81 years, 2004 (WHO 2006)
Fertility rate/Maternal mortality rate: 1.3 births per woman, 2004 (WHO 2006); maternal mortality 11 per 100,000 live births (World Bank).
Birth rate/Death rate: 10 deaths to nine births per 1,000 people (World Bank)
Child (under 5 years) mortality rate (per 1,000): 4.3 per 1,000 live births (World Bank)
Head of population per physician: 4.2 physicians per 1,000 people, 2004 (WHO 2006)

Welfare

Italy has a fully comprehensive social security system with benefits covering unemployment, retirement pensions, disability,

family allowances and health services. The social security system is financed by contributions made by the state, employers and employees, and forms part of the government's overall budget.
The pension system is contribution-based calculated on the basis of the social security contributions paid over the course of working life. The system assures equal benefits for both public and private sector employees. There is increasing government expenditure on old-age pensions and survivorship annuities due to its ageing population.
There have been promising developments in the regulation of family allowances and income maintenance programmes. The Family Allowance fund, replaced by the Family Unit Allowance, differentiates the allowance in relation to the number of members of the family and the make-up of the family unit's income.

Pensions

The long-awaited pension reform bill was passed in July 2004. Italy was spending 14 per cent of GDP on pensions and the bill is expected to save 0.7 per cent of GDP annually from 2013–30.
The requirements for employees will be that they must pay 40 years of contributions into the fund before receiving benefits at aged 57, or retire later at aged 60 with a minimum 35 years contributions. This reform will be implemented by 2008.

Main cities

Rome (capital, estimated population 2.5 million in 2004), Milan (1.2 million), Naples (991,700), Turin (856,000), Palermo (651,500), Genoa (602,500), Bologna (369,300), Florence (351,600), Bari (311,900), Catania (305,900), Venice (265,700).

Languages spoken

German is spoken in South Tyrol on the Austrian border. Slovene is spoken by a minority in Trieste. French is spoken in the Val d'Aosta, bordering France and Switzerland. Albanian is spoken in some areas of Basilicata, Calabria and Sicily. An increasing number of business people also speak English, replacing French as the second commercial language.

Official language/s

Italian

Media

National news agency: ANSA (Agenzia Nazionale Stampa Associata)
Other news agencies: AGI (Agenzia Giornalistica Italia) (in Italian): www.agenziaitalia.it

Press

There are approximately 125 newspapers, which reach 42.5 per cent of the adult population, and an estimated 10,000 magazines.
Italy's press is highly regionalised and controlled directly or indirectly by either major media groups, political parties or corporate entities. The Agnelli family (which owns Fiat) controls the Turin-based La Stampa, Milan's Corriere della Sera and the sports daily Gazzetta dello Sport; the multinational, Ferruzzi group owns Il Messagero in Rome and Italia Oggi; Fininvest controls the Milan-based Il Giornale; Carlo de Benedetti, chairman of Gruppo Editoriale L'Espresso, owns La Repubblica and over 12 regional newspapers.
Dailies: There are around 150 dailies newspapers, of which 20 are distributed nationally. In Italian, those with the highest circulations include, Il Corriere della Sera (Evening Courier) (www.corriere.it), La Repubblica (www.repubblica.it), La Stampa (The Press) (www.lastampa.it) and Il Messaggero (www.ilmessaggero.it). All regions produce their own dailies including Barisera (www.barisera.it) in Puglia, L'Arena (www.larena.it) in Verona, Gazzetta del Sud (www.gazzettadelsud.it) in Sicily and In Umbria (www.inumbria.it) in Perugia. Free issue newspapers have become popular and many centres have their own editions within a national format (www.epolis.sm). Italy does not have tabloid newspapers but the sports newspaper La Gazzetta dello Sport (www.gazzetta.it) has one of the largest circulations.
Weeklies: There are over 50 weekly magazines, with an average of 15 million copies produced. In Italian, general interest weeklies and special interest magazines include Gente (People), Panorama, Famiglia Cristiana (www.sanpaolo.org/fc), for Roman Catholic views and Oggi (Today), Panorama (http://www.panorama.it) and L'Espresso (http://espresso.repubblica.it) for news and current affairs.
Business: In Italian, there are several newspapers from Milan, including the respected Milano Finanza (www.milanofinanza.it), Il Sole 24 Ore (www.ilsole24ore.com), 24 Minuti (www.24minuti.ilsole24ore.com) and Affari Italiani (www.affaritaliani.it), which also offers tabloid news and from Naples Il Denaro (www.denaro.it) and in German Sudtiroler Wirtschaftszeitung (www.swz.it) from South Tyrol. In Italian, weekly magazines include Il Mondo (www.ilmondo.rcs.it) concerned with the economy, business and politics and a supplement of La Repubblica (www.repubblica.it), Affari & Finanza.
Periodicals: There are around 100 monthly magazines published catering for all genres. In recent years 'gossip' magazines such as, in Italian, Gossip News (www.gossipnews.it) and Kiss Me (www.kissme.it), have grown in popularity. Mondodori Media (www.mondadori.it) publishes a range of general periodicals on life-style, consumer, cuisine, entertainment and commercial interests including Grazia, and Cucina, other publications include Donna Moderna (www.donnamoderna.com).

Broadcasting

The national public broadcaster is Rai (Radiotelevisione Italiana) (www.rai.it).
Radio: There are numerous radio stations, of which over a dozen form national networks. Rai (www.rai.it) has three stations which offer entertainment, culture and news from parliament. National commercial stations include 105 Classic (www.105classics.net), CNR (www.radiocnr.it), a news network, Radio Cuore (www.radiocuore.it) and Radio Italia (www.radioitalia.it) is a community radio station.
Television: Rai (www.rai.it) has three channels (Rai Uno, Due, Tre) and has a market share of around 50 per cent, with funding derived from public funding (through TV licences, general taxes and donations) and advertising, providing locally produced and imported programmes. The main competitors are Mediaset (www.mediaset.it), owned by Silvio Belusconi, the biggest national, commercial network with three channels and La7 (www.la7.it).
Analogue transmissions are due to end in 2010, in favour of digital terrestrial transmission. There are many cable TV and Satellite, pay-to-view broadcasting is almost entirely provided by US-based Sky; , ing locally produced and imported programmes.

Advertising

Typical annual expenditure on advertising is US$10.7 billion, of which over 50 per cent is spent on television ads, with newspapers only accounting for 20 per cent.
There are regulations restricting advertising during children's programmes and cartoons of less than 30 minutes, nor must children appear in broadcast adverts. Tobacco is banned completely.
There are a range of regulations that allow advertising for alcohol and pharmaceuticals on TV.

Economy

Italy is western Europe's fourth-largest economy, although a lower growth rate in the size of the working population and a history of low domestic investment have meant that GDP growth has lagged behind its continental partners for some time. In 2005 GDP growth was only 0.5 per cent but with a modest increase of 1.7 per cent estimated for 2006. Inflation has remained low at the EU set level of less than 3.0 per cent since 2000. Unemployment averaged 8.0 per cent for the same

period and it was estimated to have fallen to 7.0 in 2006, showing signs of a strengthening economy.
Italy is a large industry-based economy with a heavy dependence on imported energy. Traditionally, the government has been significantly involved in industry through large state holding companies. However, a privatisation programme started in 1992 continues to reduce the government's role in the economy.
The services sector, particularly tourism, is important to overall economic performance. Tourism is Italy's third biggest source of foreign income after manufacturing of machinery and textiles and clothing. Florence alone receives over seven million visitors a year. The country's south, the Mezzogiorno, has much lower per capita income levels and higher unemployment rates than the more industrialised north, despite many years of heavy government subsidies. The severe regional imbalances in Italy's labour market are a serious problem for the economy.
Italy's decision to join the euro improved investor confidence significantly.

External trade

As a member of the European Union, Italy operates within a communitywide free trade union, with tariffs sets as a whole. Internationally, the EU has free trade agreements with a number of nations and trading blocs worldwide.
Exports provide over 50 per cent of GDP, of which manufactured goods represents around 97 per cent despite lacking most raw materials and energy needed to sustain the trade; nevertheless it is renowned for its luxury goods and quality manufacture. Italy is the world's second largest exporter of wine and Europe's premier exporter of rice, fruit and vegetables.

Imports

Main imports are capital goods, consumer products, chemicals, transport equipment, energy products, minerals and non-ferrous metals, textiles and clothing, food, wine tobacco and raw materials.
Main sources: Germany (16.4 per cent total, 2006), France (9.1 per cent), China (5.2 per cent).

Exports

Main exports are engineered and electrical products, textiles and fashion clothing, precision machinery, armaments, vehicles and transport equipment, pharmaceuticals and chemicals; food, beverages and tobacco; minerals, plastics and non-ferrous metals.
Main destinations: Germany (13.1 per cent total, 2005), France (11.6 per cent), US (7.5 per cent).

Re-exports

Re-fined oil and petroleum products

Agriculture

Farming

Italian farming is characterised by substantial regional differences. Farms in the north are closer to their counterparts in north European countries – in terms of technology, culture and economy – than Italian farmers in the south. Italy's programme for developing the south of the country includes drainage and irrigation schemes, and building up co-operatives and integrated agribusiness ventures to improve trading opportunities.
The country has gradually adapted and delegated much of its farm policy to the EU, through the Common Agricultural Policy (CAP). Fundamental reform to the CAP was introduced on 1 January 2005 in Italy. The subsidies paid on farm output, which tended to benefit large farms and encourage overproduction, were replaced by single farm payments not conditional on production. This is expected to reward farms that provide and maintain a healthy environment, food safety and animal welfare standards. The changes are also intended to encourage market conscious production and cut the cost of CAP to the EU taxpayer.
Only 20 per cent of Italy is fertile arable land and farms are mostly small-scale. Regions with the most labour intensive farms are Sicily and Apulia. Capital intensive farms are most common in the northern province of Emilia Romagna, but the overall proportion of agricultural employment is the same in the north and south.
In mountain areas, which stretch throughout the peninsula and on the islands, agricultural activity concentrates on forestry and livestock. The climate is ideal for vineyards and Italy vies with France as one the world's biggest wine producers.
The plains of the north and of Apulia, the heel of Italy, are also important areas for wheat, olives and fruit. Half of total agricultural income is generated in the Po valley and the plains in the north. The area produces the entire rice crop, cereals such as wheat and corn, fodder and livestock. In central Italy, wine-making and wheat-growing are the main activities.
Most citrus fruit and olives are grown in the south, where vegetables and cereals are also grown.
Crop production in 2005 included: 21,401,177 tonnes (t) cereals in total, 7,530,133t wheat, 10,622,000t maize, 1,188,676t barley, 1,370,000t rice, 1,810,086t potatoes, 3,836,793t citrus fruit, 9,256,814t grapes, 7,814,899t tomatoes, 1,167,189t oilcrops, *110,000t tobacco, 307,471t treenuts, 4,114,293t olives, *12,000,000t sugar beets, 377,598t chillies & peppers, 587,876t soya beans, 2,194,875t apples, 19,203,132t fruit in total, 16,686,924t vegetables in total. Livestock production included: 4,098,800t meat in total, 1,180,000t beef, 3,200t buffalo meat, 1,550,000t pig meat, 62,000t lamb, 3,600t goat meat, *1,000,000t poultry, 225,000t rabbit meat, 700,000t eggs, 11,602,050t milk, 9,000t honey, *132,000t cattle hides, *48,000t horsemeat, *11,000t greasy wool, *60t cocoons, silk.
* estimate

Fishing

The fishing industry has a turnover of around US$4 billion, but it remains a neglected sector of the economy. Sicily and the Adriatic coast produce 76.4 per cent of the country's fish. The most important fish commercially are sardines and anchovies.
In 2004, the total marine fish catch was 168,095 tonnes and the total crustacean catch was 17,025 tonnes.

Forestry

Forest and wooded land account for less than 40 per cent of land area. Sixty per cent of the forest is available for wood supply. Broadleaved species account for 66 per cent of the growing stock, the main species being beech, deciduous and evergreen oaks, poplars and chestnut. Common coniferous species include pine, Norway spruce and European larch.
Italy is one of the major consumers, producers and traders of forest products in the EU. It accounts for nearly ten per cent of EU total paper and wood-based panel production.
Exports of forest material in 2004 amounted to US$4.3 billion, while imports amounted to US$9.5 billion.
Production in 2004 included 8,697,393 cubic metres (cum) roundwood, 2,883,316cum industrial roundwood, 1,448,398cum sawlogs and veneers, 1,580,000cum sawnwood, 533,175cum pulpwood, 5,596,000cum wood-based panels, 5,814,077cum woodfuel; 9,667,000 tonnes (t) paper and paperboard, (including 193,000t newsprint), 3,110,000t printing and writing paper, 657,000t wood pulp, 5,474,000t recovered paper.

Industry and manufacturing

The industrial sector contributes approximately 32 per cent to GDP and employs 33 per cent of the labour force. Subdivided by sector, manufacturing contributes approximately 26 per cent to annual GDP, with construction accounting for a further 6 per cent.
Problems in the sector include growing competition in traditional products from developing countries, and the small share of the export market taken by value added high technology products. Efforts to attract industrial investment to the depressed

southern region have met with only partial success, despite large subsidies.
Industrial production grew by only 0.7 per cent in 2004 and is estimated to have declined by 1.7 per cent in 2005.

Tourism
Italy's important tourist sector, which accounts for 6.2 per cent of GDP and gives employment to around two million people, was badly hit by the 11 September 2001 terrorist attacks in the US. Recovery was obstructed by the Iraq war and the SARS outbreak in 2003. The strengthening of the euro vis-a-vis other currencies has added to the sector's difficulties, deterring US and Japanese tourist in particular. Arrivals from Germany, the biggest market, have also shown a decline.
China has designated Italy as an approved destination for its holidaying citizens and it has already become one of the top three in Europe; Chinese visitors could swell Italy's arrival numbers by millions.

Mining
The mining sector accounts for only 0.5 per cent of GDP and employs a similar percentage of the workforce. Italy has relatively poor mineral resources, although large quantities of iron ore and pyrites, mercury, lead, zinc, bauxite, aluminium, sulphur, gravel, alabaster and marble exist.
Sardinia (Cagliari, Sassari and Iglesias) is the main mining area and holds the only large sulphur deposit in Europe, but mining it is not economically viable. Bauxite is mined mainly in Abruzzi, Campania and Apulia, though output has dropped due to falling demand from the aluminium industry. Output of lead, zinc and particularly copper have all increased. Quarrying activity is strong, with marble and gravel much in demand for the construction and road building industries.

Hydrocarbons
Italy relies heavily on energy imports (85 per cent of domestic requirements). However, a plan is under way to develop indigenous resources, as well as the use of coal and natural gas.
Proven oil reserves stood at 700 million barrels in 2004, producing 107,000 barrels per day (bpd). Italy consumes 1.9 billion bpd and is one of the largest oil importers in Europe with 90 per cent of its consumption dependent on imports. It imports approximately 1.8 million bpd, mostly from Libya (28.3 per cent of oil imports) and Iran (17.2 per cent). Italy also has a refining capacity of 2,292,000bpd.
Italy, one of the largest per capita oil consumers in Europe, sought to decrease its reliance on oil imports by developing other fuel sources in the 1990s. To promote this diversification the government adjusted fuel taxes, with the duty on oil rising by between 33–61 per cent. Domestic taxes on natural gas will increase by only 5 per cent, with petrol replacement gas tax actually set to fall by 23 per cent.
Italy produces 13.0 billion cubic metres of gas annually (2004) from reserves of 170 billion cubic metres (2004), most of which are in and off Sicily. At current rates of consumption this is only enough to supply Italy's needs for another twenty years.
Natural gas use has increased significantly since the 1990s and accounts for 30 per cent of the country's total energy consumption. According to Snam, the company responsible for supplying and transporting methane gas throughout Italy, natural gas will generate 60 per cent of the country's electricity by 2010.
Domestic production meets 40 per cent of domestic demand, with the remainder imported under long-term contracts from the countries of the former Soviet Union, Algeria and the Netherlands. Future supplies are likely to be diversified as plans to build a US$5.5 billion gas pipeline between Libya and Sicily become reality. The 600km pipeline, which opened in October 2004, will deliver a total of 10 billion cubic metres per year to Italy. Snam also signed a 25-year contract with Norway in October 2001 to receive six billion cubic metres of natural gas per year through existing pipelines.
Most domestic coal production is used in electricity generation, although coal accounts for only 8 per cent of total domestic energy consumption. Italy consumed 17.1 million tonnes of oil equivalent in 2004.
Russia's decision to cut off gas supplies to Ukraine on 1 January 2006 caused alarm in Italy, as a sizeable portion of its import network is dependent upon Ukrainian transnational pipelines.

Energy
Ente Nazionale per L'Energia Elettrica (Enel), the former state-owned energy monopoly, was privatised in November 1999.
It owns 85 per cent of Italy's electrical generating capacity, although the government restructured the company in 2002. Enel also sold off some of its regional electricity distribution networks to municipal companiess.
Italy has four nuclear power stations, all of which are owned by Enel. Following a public vote in 1987, which decided against the use of nuclear power, none of the plants are currently in operation. They are not expected to be reopened.
Electricity needs are met by buying extra power generated by France's nuclear reactors.

Banking and insurance
Scandal hit the Central Bank in July 2005 when the governor, Antonio Fazio, refused to allow a cross-border banking takeover and was subsequently placed under investigation in two criminal inquiries. He refused to resign for several months, receiving strong support from one of Italy's governing parties, the Lega Nord, and the Catholic Church, but was eventually replaced by Mario Draghi in December. Unlike Mr Fazio, who held an open-ended mandate, Mr Draghi will serve a six-year term, renewable once.

Central bank
Banca d'Italia; European Central Bank (ECB).

Time
GMT plus one hour (daylight saving, late March to late October, GMT plus two hours)

Geography
Italy consists of a peninsula stretching from southern Europe into the Mediterranean and includes a number of adjacent islands, including Sicily in the south-west and Sardinia in the west. The country stretches 1,200km from north to south and has 7,456km of coastline.
The distinctive boot-shaped peninsula is dominated by two extensive mountain ranges, accounting for about 75 per cent of the land area. The Alps form a natural barrier separating Italy from Slovenia in the north-east, Austria and Switzerland in the north and France in the north-west. The Apennines form the backbone of the peninsula.
Italy experiences frequent minor earthquakes, especially in the south, and its active volcanoes include Vesuvius in the Naples district, Etna in Sicily and Stromboli in the Aeolian Islands.
Two autonomous countries lie within Italy's frontiers, the Vatican City in Rome, home of the Holy See, and the tiny republic of San Marino in the north-east.

Hemisphere
Northern

Climate
While Italy lies in a temperate zone, the climates of the north and south vary. Summers are uniformly hot, although summers in the south can be extremely hot and dry. In the winter, the south is generally mild, while the north can be extremely cold – particularly near the Alps and Po Valley. Temperatures range from about 4–30 degrees Celsius.

Dress codes
Particular attention is paid to dress, although dress codes are not rigid. Most businessmen wear suits and ties during business hours.

Entry requirements
Passports
Required by most; passports must be valid for three months from arrival. Nationals of countries which are signatories of the Schengen Accords, which includes most EU/EEA member states, San Marino and Croatia, may visit on national IDs.
Visa
No visa requirements for citizens of most of Europe, the Americas, Australasia and some Asian countries, visiting for up to 90 days. For a full list, and further information for those citizens not included on the list of visa-free travel, visit www.ambwashingtondc.esteri.it and see consular services. A Schengen visa application (offered in several languages) can be downloaded from http://europa.eu/abc/travel/ see 'documents you will need'.
Business travel is also allowed for those enjoying visa-free travel. Those who do not have visa-free arrangements must provide a letter from their employer guaranteeing travel expenses, including full itinery and purpose of the trip. Letters of invitation from all Italian companies to be visited, and a current (not over 90 days) Visura Camerale issued by the Italian Chamber of Commerce should be attached; a return/onward ticket must be produced before collection of the passport and visa from the issuing consulate; which may request any additional documents at its discretion.
Within eight days of arrival in Italy the visa traveller must appear before local police authorities to receive a Residency Permit and will also need to show proof of health insurance.
Currency advice/regulations
Import and export of local and foreign currency up to eur12,000 (or foreign equivalent) is permitted. Imports and export of amounts greater than this must be declared within 48 hours of arrival or departure.
Travellers cheques are widely accepted.
Customs
Personal items are duty-free. There are no duties levied on alcohol and tobacco between EU member states, providing amounts imported are for personal consumption.

Health (for visitors)
Nationals of the European Economic Area (EEA) countries and Switzerland can access reduced cost and sometimes free medical treatment using a European Health Insurance Card (EHIC) while visiting the EEA. Exceptions include nationals of the 10 countries, which joined the EU in 2004 whose EHIC is not valid in Switzerland. Applications for the EHIC should be made before travelling.
Mandatory precautions
None.
Advisable precautions
No special immunisations are needed. Pharmacists are usually open from 0830 to 1300 and 1600 to 2000.

Hotels
Classified into five star categories. Rates are fixed by the Provincial Tourist Board, and vary according to class, season, services available and locality. A service charge of 15–18 per cent is added to bills, but additional tips are also expected for individual services. Restaurants expect 15 per cent on top of the bill.

Credit cards
International credit cards are widely accepted.

Public holidays (national)
Fixed dates
1 Jan (New Year's Day), 6 Jan (Epiphany), 25 April (Liberation Day), 1 May (Labour Day), 2 Jun (National Day), 15 Aug (Assumption Day), 1 Nov (All Saints' Day), 8 Dec (Immaculate Conception), 25–26 Dec (Christmas).
Variable dates
Easter Monday

Working hours
Business travellers would do best to avoid August when Italians desert the stifling heat of the big cities for the beaches and mountains. The mass exodus usually begins in mid-July and lasts at least until after the Ferragosto festival (August 15). Most factories, government offices, shops and restaurants close for all of August or are run by minimal staff.
The afternoon siesta is still very much part of the Italian way of life in Rome and the south. In northern Italy, there is a trend towards standard European business hours of 0900 to 1700, at least in offices.
Banking
Mon–Fri: 0830–1300; 1500–1600.
Banks in tourist areas may not close for lunch.
Business
Northern Italy: 0930–1300 and 1400–1800.
Central and southern Italy: 0830–1245 and 1630–2000.
Government
Post offices: Mon–Fri: 0830–1345 and Sat: 0830–1200; central city post offices stay open until 2100.
Government offices: Mon–Sat: 0830–1345.
Shops
Mon–Sat: 0830–1230, 1500–1800; Sat: 0900–1230.

Telecommunications
Mobile/cell phones
There are 3G, 900/1800 GSM services throughout the country.

Electricity supply
220V AC, 50Hz

Social customs/useful tips
Italians always shake hands on meeting and leaving. Exchanging business cards is also normal practice as it helps to reinforce the informal network of personal contacts which permeates Italian business. Businessmen prefer that written communication, either by e-mail, facsimile or letter, be sent before a telephone discussion. Personal titles are considered important, although often more prestigious than professionally accurate. Small luxury goods are frequently exchanged as gifts in business. Smoking is still fashionable, with fewer restrictions than in many other Western countries.
Italians are required to carry identification on them at all times and foreigners are recommended to do likewise.

Security
Handbag snatching and pickpocketing are widespread, particularly in popular tourist spots in Rome and Naples. It is advisable not to wear conspicuous jewellery or carry personal valuables. In general the level of violent crime is low, but drug-related crime is on the increase in Milan, Rome and Naples. With this in mind, visitors to Rome are advised to avoid the streets around the central railway station at night.

Getting there
Air
National airline: Alitalia
International airport/s: Leonardo da Vinci (Fiumicino) Rome (FCO) 26km south-west of Rome. There is a direct rail link to the central railway station (duration 35 minutes), and express buses into Rome. Licensed, metered taxis are also available to the city.
Milan Malpensa (MXP) 45km north-west of Milan. Both airport facilities include duty-free shops, bar, restaurant, car hire, bank, bureau de change and business centre.
Other airport/s: Pisa (PSA), 2km from city, (an hour by train from Florence); Turin International (TRN), 16km north-west of city; Venice Marco Polo (VCE), 13km north-west of city; Bologna G Marconi (BLQ); Milan Linate (LIN); Naples Capodichino (NAP); Genoa Cristoforo Colombo (GOA); Palermo (PMO).
Airport tax: None

Surface

Italy is included in the Pan-European Corridor 5 scheme. The project has some 3,270km of railways, linking Kiev in the Ukraine with western Europe via Italy, and 2,850 of new and upgraded roads.

Road: Italy can be entered by road from France, Switzerland, Austria and Slovenia. However, several passes are closed during winter. In addition to the Riviera coastal motorway, access from France and Switzerland is maintained via the St Bernard, Mont Blanc and Fréjus tunnels.

Rail: There are daily services, run by Ferrovie dello Stato (FS) (Italian State Railways) that run from France, Switzerland and Austria, which are linked to the European rail network.

The high-speed Lyon-Turin Ferroviaire rail link, consisting of two linked tunnel sections, which are due to join the north-south, east-west transport network hub in Lyon, is expected to be completed by 2012.

Water: There are regular ferry service connections to Greece, Albania, North Africa, Croatia and France.

Main port/s: Genoa, Trieste, Augusta, Taranto, Leghorn, Savona, Ancona, Bari, Brindisi, Civitavecchia, Venice, La Spezia, Naples, Palermo (Sicily), and Cagliari and Porto Torres (Sardinia).

Getting about

National transport

Air: Alitalia and Aero Transporti Italiani (ATI) operate services connecting Rome to most major towns. Alisarda operates services connecting Rome, Milan and Turin with Sardinia.

Road: There is a road network of over 300,000km, of which 6,000km are motorways (autostrade) with tolls, connecting most cities.

Buses: Extensive bus services, operated by several companies, link all major towns.

Rail: Trenitalia operates an extensive network in all regions. Express trains, which provide buffet carriages, have seats to be booked in advance. Larger railway stations provide left luggage, banks, ATMs and refreshment facilities.

Water: Ferryboat and hydrofoil services linking the mainland with Sicily, Sardinia and the smaller islands are operated by several lines including the State Railways.

City transport

Taxis: Available in all towns and tourist resorts, usually in ranks at railway stations, or can be called by phone. Fares vary considerably, and unmetered cabs should be avoided. Drivers round up their fares; gratuities are not necessary.

Buses, trams & metro: All major cities have bus services with one standard fare. Day and monthly tickets are available. Bus tickets can also be bought in packs of five and then fed into a machine upon boarding.

There are metros in Rome and Milan with standard single fares as for buses. In Milan tickets last for 70 minutes and can be used on both metro lines and all bus routes. A daily or monthly ticket usable for all Rome services is available. The metro journey from Malpensa international airport, Milan, to the city centre takes around 30 minutes.

Tram services are available in Milan, Naples and Turin.

Car hire

Self-drive cars are available; the daily rate depends on the engine size, plus an additional charge per kilometre. Special weekly tariffs are available. VAT is charged. Official translation of driving licence required. Driving is on the right. Maximum speed is 50kph in towns, 90/110kph on country roads and 130kph on motorways. There are legal obligations for wearing seat belts while driving and warning waistcoats (fluorescent jackets) when leaving a vehicle during a breakdown or emergency.

Road signs are international.

BUSINESS DIRECTORY

The addresses listed below are a selection only. While World of Information makes every endeavour to check these addresses, we cannot guarantee that changes have not been made, especially to telephone numbers and area codes. We would welcome any corrections.

Telephone area codes

The international direct dialling code (IDD) for Italy is +39, followed by area code, including the first zero:

Bologna	051	Pisa	050
Capri	081	Rome	06
Florence	055	Trieste	040
Genoa	010	Turin	011
Milan	02	Venice	041
Naples	081	Verona	045

Useful telephone numbers

Police, fire and ambulance: 113

Chambers of Commerce

American Chamber of Commerce in Italy, 1 Via Cantù, 20123 Milan (tel: 869-0661; fax: 805-7737; email: amcham@amcham.it).

Brescia Camera di Commercio, 3 Via Orzinuovi, 25125 Brescia (tel: 351-41; fax: 351-4222; email: brescia@bs.camcom.it).

British Chamber of Commerce for Italy, 12 Via Dante, 20121 Milan (tel: 877-798; fax: 8646-1885; email: bcci@britchamitaly.com).

Florence Camera di Commercio, 3 Piazza dei Giudici, 50122 Florence (tel: 2795-1; fax: 2795-259; email: info@fi.camcom.it).

Genoa Camera di Commercio, 4 Via Garibaldi, 16124 Genoa (tel: 270-41; fax: 270-4300; email: camera.genova@ge.camcom.it).

Milan Camera di Commercio, 9b Via Meravigli, 20123 Milan (tel: 8515-1; fax: 8515-4232; email: infohighway@mi.camcom.it).

Naples Camera di Commercio, 2 Via S Aspreno, 80133 Naples (tel: 760-7111; fax: 552-6940; email: segretaria.generale@na.camcom.it)

Padua Camera di Commercio, 34 Via E Filiberto, 35122 Padua (tel:; fax: 820-8290; email: info@pd.camcom.it).

Rome Camera di Commercio, 147 Via De' Burrò, 00186 Rome (tel: 520-2630; fax: 520-82617; email: info@rm.camcom.it).

Treieste Camera di Commercio, 14 Piazza della Borsa, 34121 Trieste (tel: 670-1111; fax: 670-1321; email: info@ts.camcom.it).

Turin Camera di Commercio, 24 Via San Francesco da Paola, 10123 Turin (tel: 571-6405; fax: 571-6404; email: urp@to.camcom.it).

Unione Italiana delle Camere di Commercio, Industria, Artigianato e Agricoltura, 21 Piazza Sallustio, 00187 Rome (tel: 470-41; fax: 470-4240; email: segretaria.generale@unioncamere.it).

Venice Camera di Commercio, 2032 Via XXII Marzo, San Marco, 30124 Venice (tel: 786-111; fax: 786-330; email: segretaria.generale@ve.camcom.it).

Verona Camera di Commercio, 96 Corso Porta Nuova, 37122 Verona (tel: 808-5011; fax: 594-648; email: cciaavr@vr.camcom.it).

Banking

Banca Commerciale Italiana, Via del Corso, 226 C.A.P. 00186 Rome (tel: 67-121; fax: 6712-4925).

Banca di Napoli, Via Toledo 177–188, 80132 Naples (tel: 791-1111).

Banca Nazionale del Lavoro, Via Vittoro Veneto 119, 00187 Rome (tel: 47-021; fax: 4702-6263).

Banca Nazionale dell'Agricoltura SPA, Via Salaria 231, 00199 Rome (tel: 85-881; fax: 8588-3396).

Banca Popolare Commercio E Industria Scarl, Via Casifina 1790, 00132 Rome (tel: 207-1712; fax: 207-2676).

Banca di Roma, Via del Corso 320, 00186 Rome (tel: 67-071; fax: 6707-3783).

Cassa di Risparmio di Roma, 320 Via del Corso, 00186 Rome (tel: 67-071; fax: 6707-3783).

Cassa di Risparmio di Torino, 31 Via XX Settembre, 10121 Torino (tel: 57-661; fax: 638-203).

Credito Italiano, 00144 Piazzale dell'Industria 46 (tel: 54-631; fax: 5423-7006).

European Investment Bank, via Saroagna 36, 100187 Rome (tel: 47-191; fax: 487-3438).

Istituto Centrale Delle Banche Di Credito Cooperativo, Via Torino 146, 00184 Rome (tel: 47-161; fax: 4716-5583).

Istituto Di Credito Delle Casse Di Rigparmio Italiane, Via San Basilo 15, 00187 Rome (tel: 47-151).

Mediocredito Centrale, Via Piemonte 51, 00187 Rome (tel: 47-911; fax: 479-1626).

Nuovo Banco Ambrosiano, Piazza Paolo Ferrari 10, 20121 Milan (tel: 85-941).

Central bank

Banca d'Italia, Via Nazionale 91, 00184 Rome (tel: 47-921; fax: 479-22983; internet: www.bancaditalia.it).

European Central Bank (ECB), Kaiserstrasse 29, D-60311 Frankfurt am Main, Germany (tel: (+49-69) 13-440; fax: (+49-69) 1344-6000; email: info@ecb.int).

Travel information

Alitalia (Linee Aeree Italiane), Centro Direzionale, Viale Alissandro Marchetti, 111, Rome 100148 (tel: 709-2780; fax: 709-3065).

Leonardo da Vinci (Fiumicino) Airport, Via dell'Aeroporto di Fiumicino 320, PO Box 68, 00050, Fiumicino (tel: 5951; fax: 595-5707; email: info@adr.it; internet: www.adr.it).

Milan Malpensa Airport, 21010 Varese (tel: 7485-2200; fax: 7485-4010: email: communication@sea-aeroportimilano.it; internet: www.sea-aeroportimilano.it/eng).

Ministry of tourism

Ministry of Industry and Tourism, Via Molise 2, 00187 Rome (tel: 47-051; fax: 4705-2215).

National tourist organisation offices

Ente Nazionale Italiano per il Turismo (ENIT), 2/6Via Marghera, 00185 Rome (tel: 49-711; fax: 446-3379; email: sedecentrale@cert.ent.it; internet: www.enit.it).

Ministries

Ministry of Agriculture and Forests, Via XX Settembre 20, 00187 Rome (tel: 46-651; fax: 592-314).

Ministry of Defence, Via XX Settembre 8, 00187 Rome (tel: 488-2126; fax: 474-7775).

Ministry of Education, Viale Trastevere 76/A, 00153 Rome (tel: 58-491; fax: 580-3381).

Ministry of Employment and Social Welfare, Via Flavia 6, 00187 Rome (tel: 46-831; fax: 4788-7174).

Ministry of the Environment, Piazza Venezia 11, 00187 Rome (tel: 70-361; fax: 678-3844).

Ministry of Equal Opportunities, c/o Presidenza del Consiglio dei Ministry, Palazzo Chigi, 00187 Rome (tel: 67-791; fax: 678-3998).

Ministry of Finance, Viale Europa 242, 00144 Rome (tel: 59-971; fax: 501-5714).

Ministry of Foreign Affairs, Piazzale della Farnesina, 00194 Rome (tel: 36-911; fax: 323-6258).

Ministry of Foreign Trade, Viale America 341, 00144 Rome (tel: 59-931; fax: 5964-7504).

Ministry of Health, Viale dell'Industria 20, 00144 Rome (tel: 59-941; fax: 5964-7649).

Ministry of Industry and Tourism, Via Molise 2, 00187 Rome (tel: 47-051; fax: 4705-2215).

Ministry of the Interior, Piazzale del Viminale, 00184 Rome (tel: 6451; fax: 482-5792).

Ministry of Justice, Via Arenula 71, 00186 Rome (tel: 68-851; fax: 5227-8550).

Ministry of Posts and Telecommunications, Viale America 201, 00144 Rome (tel: 59-581; fax: 594-274).

Ministry of Public Administration, Palazzo Vidoni, Corso Vittorio Emanuele 116, 00186 Rome (tel: 680-031).

Ministry of Public Works, Piazza Porta Pia 1, 00198 Rome (tel: 44-121; fax: 4426-7275).

Ministry of Transport, Piazza della Croce Rossa 1, 00161 Rome (tel: 84-901; fax: 4424-1539).

Ministry of the Treasury and Budget, Via XX Settembre 97, 00187 Rome (tel: 47-611; fax: 488-2146).

Ministry for University, Scientific and Technological Research, Piazzale Kennedy 20, 00144 Rome (tel: 59-911; fax: 591-5493).

Office of the President, Palazzo del Quirinale, 00187 Rome (tel: 4699).

Prime Minister's Office, Palazzo Chigi, Piazza Colonna 370, 00187 Rome (tel: 67-791; fax: 678-3998).

Other useful addresses

Borsa Valori di Milano, Piazza Degli Affari, 20100 Milan (tel: 8534).

British Embassy, Via XX Settembre 80/A, 00187 Rome (tel: 482-5551, 482-5441; fax: 487-3324).

Commissione Nazionale per le Società e la Borsa (Commission for Companies and the Stock Exchange), Milan (tel: 877-841).

Confederazione Generale dell'Industria Italiana (General Confederation of Italian Industry), Viale dell'Astronomia 30, 00144 Rome (tel: 59-031).

Confederazione Generale Italiana del Commercio (General Confederation of Italian Commerce), Piazza G.C. Belli 2, Rome (tel: 588-783, 580-192).

Ente Nazionale Idrocarburi (ENI), Piazzalo E. Mattei, 00144 Rome (tel: 59-001).

Ente Partecipazioni e Finanziamento Industria Manifatturiera (EFIM), Via XXIV Maggio 43–45, 00187 Rome (tel: 47-101).

Istituto Nazionale di Statistica (ISTAT) (national statistics office), Via Cesare Balbo 16, 00100 Rome (tel: 46-731; fax: 4673-4177).

Istituto per la Ricostruzione Industriale (IRI) Via Vittorio Veneto 85, 00187 Rome (tel: 47-271).

Istituto Nazionale per il Commercio Estero (Italian government agency for promotion of foreign trade), 21 Via Liszt, 00100 Rome (tel: 59-921).

Italian Embassy (US), 3000 Whitehaven Street, NW, Washington DC 20008 (tel: (+1-202) 612-4400; fax: (+1-202) 518-2154; email: stampa@itwash.org).

US Embassy, Via Vittorio Veneto 119A, 00187 Rome (tel: 46-741; fax: 4674-2356).

National news agency: ANSA (Agenzia Nazionale Stampa Associata). Via della Dataria 94, 00187 Rome (tel: 678-6161).

Internet sites

City of Venice Gateway: www.venetia.it

City of Florence information: www.aboutflorence.com

Gateway site of servers listed by city (launches into Italian language sites): www.cilea.it/WWW-map

Italian Central Bank: www.bancaditalia.it

Italian Statistics: www.istat.it

Italian Embassy in the US (includes economic and trade data) www.italyemb.org

Ministry of Foreign Affairs: www.esteri.it/eng/index/htm

The Uffizi Museum: www.uffizi.firenze.it

Jamaica

KEY FACTS

Official name: Jamaica

Head of State: Queen Elizabeth II (since 1952); represented by Governor General Kenneth Hall (appointed Feb 2006)

Head of government: Prime Minister Bruce Golding (from 11 Sep 2007)

Ruling party: Jamaica Labour Party (JLP) (from 3 Sep 2007)

Area: 10,989 square km

Population: 2.69 million (2007)*

Capital: Kingston

Official language: English

Currency: Jamaican dollar (J$) = 100 cents

Exchange rate: J$72.06 per US$ (Jul 2008)

GDP per capita: US$4,172 (2007)*

GDP real growth: 1.40% (2007)*

Labour force: 1.36 million (2004)

Unemployment: 15.00% (2004)

Inflation: 9.30% (2007)

Balance of trade: -US$2.88 billion (2006)

Foreign debt: US$4.84 billion (2004)

Visitor numbers: 1.68 million (2006)*

* estimated figure

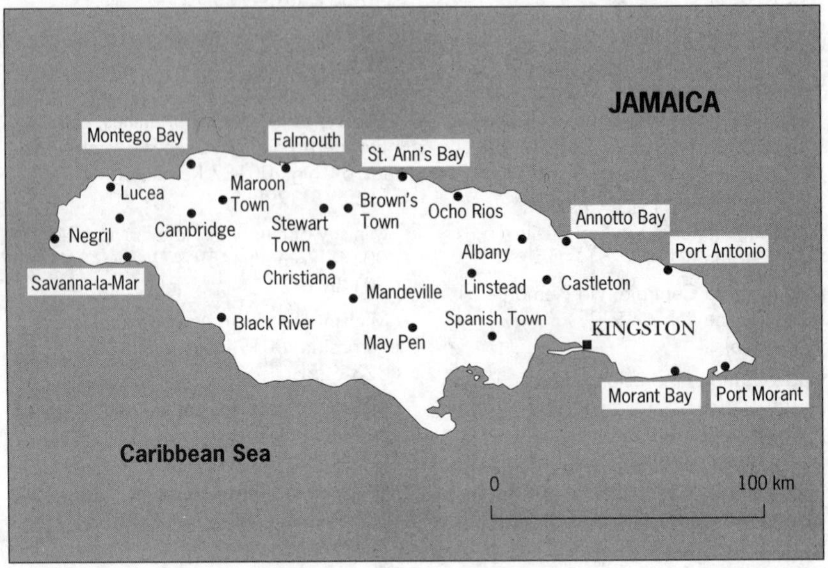

For all the wrong reasons, Jamaica was highlighted as the murder capital of the Caribbean after the death on 18 March 2007 of Pakistan's cricket coach, Bob Woolmer. Rumour and innuendo swept the country and cast a pall over the Cricket World Cup (CWC). It was not until over a year later that it was finally confirmed that he had died of natural causes. In the meantime, damage had been done to the country's tourism industry, and the CWC fizzled out into a win for Australia who beat Sri Lanka in a lack lustre final.

Hard fought elections

Mrs Simpson Miller, of the People's National Party (PNP), who had been prime minister for 18 months, initially said that the election results were too close to call. Some seats, she said, would need a recount. In the end, the Jamaica Labour Party (JLP) won with 50.1 per cent of the vote to the PNP's 49.8 per cent. The JLP was back in power after 18 years, with Bruce Golding as prime minister.

The JLP had campaigned on a manifesto of reform of the health and education sectors as a means of tackling the country's poverty situation, but at the same time promising to continue with the previous government's strict fiscal policy. It has also said that it aims to divest the government of a number of state-owned organisations, while injecting greater private sector participation and dynamism into the economy.

Growth slows

Gross domestic product (GDP) slowed in 2007, to 1.4 per cent from 2.5 per cent in 2006. According to the Caribbean Development Bank's (CDB) *Annual Economic Review* for 2007 several factors, primarily external, undermined a more favourable performance. A faltering US economy characterised by a weakened dollar and sub-prime mortgage market turbulence coupled with spiralling energy costs and the impact of hurricane Dean weighed heavily on the country's growth momentum.

Agricultural supply shortages precipitated by severely adverse weather conditions, together with rising import costs and marginal depreciation of the domestic currency, led to a pick-up in inflation. In the monetary system, while credit growth was robust, excess liquidity conditions triggered Central Bank intervention and a marginal tightening of monetary policy.

Hurricane damage led to a loss of critical export capacity, especially in the agriculture and mining sectors, while a reduction in tourist arrivals and remittance inflows contributed to a worsening of the current account balance. Continued strong foreign direct investment (FDI) in the telecommunications and tourism sectors partly offset this loss. The fall off in tourist arrivals (after record growth of 12.3 per cent in 2006) was put down to a number of factors, including a new passport regime put on US citizens travelling abroad, the depressed economic situation in the US and a weakening US dollar, and a sharp rise in regional transport costs.

While the services sector continued to grow in 2007, although less strongly than in 2006, agricultural output fell by 1.1 per cent, following abnormally high growth of 15.9 per cent in 2006. This volatility reflects the sector's vulnerability to natural hazards such as hurricanes, and low levels of private and public sector investment. Banana, coffee and sugar production were particularly badly affected by hurricane Dean in 2007.

On the plus side, an additional 150,000 tonnes of capacity in alumina was constructed at the Jamalco aluminium refinery, part of a planned doubling of production to 2.8 million tonnes announced in 2005.

Outlook

The CDB outlook for the Jamaican economy is still relatively upbeat. The JLP administration has signalled it's strong intention of tackling the debt overhang through creative approaches while bolstering the country's finances through tax reform and the divestment of unproductive or loss-making state assets. The high crime rate has over the years put off investors and must be rectified.

Risk assessment

Economy	Improving
Politics	Fair
Regional stability	Good

COUNTRY PROFILE

Historical profile

1494 Jamaica was sighted by members of an expedition led by Christopher Columbus.
1509 Jamaica was occupied by Spaniards. Most of the indigenous Arawak community died from exposure to European diseases. African slaves were brought in to work on the sugar plantations.
1655 The British captured the island. Jamaica became a slave-based economy producing sugar and some coffee for export.
1692 Jamaican capital, Port Royal, sunk into the sea after an earthquake and Spanish Town became the new capital.
1834 Abolition of slavery.
1865 A major revolt against Jamaican landowners among freed slaves living in hardship was brutally put down by the British. The local legislature surrendered its powers and Jamaica became a crown colony.
1870 Plantations began to replace sugar cane with banana production, due to increased sugar beet production in Europe.
1884 A new constitution marked the revival of Jamaican autonomy.
1930s The worldwide economic depression and greater international competition undermined the Jamaican sugar industry.
1938 Popular uprisings caused by unemployment and resentment of racial British policies led to the establishment of the People's National Party (PNP) by Norman Manley.
1944 Universal adult suffrage was introduced and a new constitution allowed for the election of the House of Representatives.
1958 Jamaica became part of the attempted West Indies Federation.
1962 At the insistence of Prime Minister Alexander Bustamante, Jamaica left the West Indies Federation and gained separate independence as a member of the British Commonwealth. Kingston became the capital city.
1968–69 Protests against poor housing conditions turned into serious riots in Kingston.
1972 Michael Manley became prime minister and pursued a policy of economic self-reliance.
1976 The PNP won another term following elections marked by violence and proceeded to nationalise businesses and build closer ties with Cuba.
1980 Edward Seaga became prime minister and reversed the nationalisation policies of the previous government. The US granted the Seaga government substantial aid after it distanced itself from Cuba.
1988 Hurricane Gilbert caused an estimated US$3 billion damage to much of the island.
1989 The PNP ousted the JLP in elections, returning Michael Manley as prime minister. Manley, however, chose to continue Seaga's policy.
1992 Manley retired on health grounds and was succeeded by Percival Patterson.
1993 The PNP was returned to office with an increased majority.
1997 The PNP won a third term in office.
1999 Protests against a new fuel tax spilled over into rioting in several areas. The Jamaican Defence Force (JDF) was ordered onto the streets to tackle the high rate of crime.
2001 Violence broke out in Kingston. There were gun battles between the police and gangs with political links. The army was called out after 25 people had been killed.
2002 The ruling PNP won parliamentary elections.
2004 Extra police were drafted into St James, the island's tourism capital, in July, to tackle the escalating crime wave. The business community pledged J$200,000 (US$3,289) worth of petrol each month to aid the police. Ivan, the worst hurricane since 1988, struck Jamaica on 12 September, damaging thousands of homes and killing 15 people.
2005 Jamaica and Venezuela signed a US$200 million agreement on 23 August

KEY INDICATORS — Jamaica

	Unit	2003	2004	2005	2006	2007
Population	m	2.66	2.68	2.66	2.67	*2.69
Gross domestic product (GDP)	US$bn	8.10	8.93	9.40	10.39	*11.21
GDP per capita	US$	2,763	3,237	3,532	3,887	*4,172
GDP real growth	%	1.9	2.5	1.4	2.5	*1.4
Inflation	%	16.7	11.5	15.3	8.6	9.3
Unemployment	%	11.8	12.2	11.2	10.3	9.9
Exports (fob) (goods)	US$m	1,368.0	1,586.1	1,664.3	1,984.0	–
Imports (cif) (goods)	US$m	3,813.0	3,525.9	4,245.5	4,868.0	–
Balance of trade	US$m	-2,445.0	-1,939.8	-2,581.2	-2,884.0	–
Current account	US$m	-850.0	-1,150.0	-1,053.0	-1,197.0	-1,623.0
Total reserves minus gold	US$m	1,194.9	1,846.5	2,169.8	2,318.4	–
Foreign exchange	US$m	1,194.8	1,846.4	2,169.8	2,318.2	–
Exchange rate	per US$	54.83	60.12	67.13	66.92	71.28

to modernise and expand the Petrojam oil refinery in Kingston.
2006 In February, Portia Simpson-Miller, the local government minister, was elected to succeed Prime Minister PJ Patterson as president of the PNP, opening the way for her to become prime minister on 30 March.
2007 In September parliamentary elections, the opposition JLP won 50.1 per cent, 33 seats (out of 60); the ruling PNP won 49.8 per cent (27). Turnout was 60.4 per cent. Bruce Golding became prime minister.
2008 The government announced, on 23 April, that it was prepared to legalise casinos, despite strong opposition from religious groups.

Political structure

Constitution

Jamaica is a parliamentary democracy and independent state within the Commonwealth. The British monarch is the titular head of state and is represented by a governor general appointed on the advice of the prime minister. The governor general's role is mainly ceremonial and is guided in most cases by the prime minister, who as head of government effectively exercises executive power. Duties include appointing the leader of the opposition from among members of parliament who do not support the government. The governor general must have no affiliation with any political party while holding office.
Local governments in the 14 parishes are due for election every three years. The minimum voting age is 18. Voting is by secret ballot and the candidate who wins the most votes in each constituency is elected in a first-past-the-post electoral system.

Form of state

Constitutional monarchy

The executive

The head of state is the British monarch who is represented by the Governor General of Jamaica. The prime minister is selected by the governor general from the House of Representatives as the member best able to command the support of the House. Executive power rests with the cabinet – made up of the prime minister and at least 11 ministers. Cabinet ministers are chosen by the prime minister.

National legislature

The legislature is a bicameral parliament. It consists of a 60-member House of Representatives, elected every five years, and a 21-member Senate, appointed to a parallel term. The prime minister, who is also leader of the majority in the House of Representatives, appoints 13 senators, while the remaining eight are named by the leader of the opposition. The Senate mainly reviews legislation passed by the House of Representatives, although it can also initiate legislation, except on financial matters.
Voting must be held within three months of the dissolution of parliament. There have been eight parliaments since 1962, when Jamaica became the first English-speaking West Indian island to gain independence from the UK.

Legal system

The judiciary is headed by a Supreme Court and a Court of Appeal. The governor general, acting under the guidance of a six-member Privy Council based in London, UK, can grant pardons to convicted criminals. The final appeal is to the Judicial Committee of the Privy Council in the UK.

Last elections

3 September 2007 (parliamentary)
Results: Parliamentary: the Jamaica Labour Party (JLP) won 50.1 per cent (33 seats out of 60), People's National Party (PNP) won 49.8 (27 seats). Turnout was 60.4 per cent.

Next elections

2012 (parliamentary)

Political parties

Ruling party

Jamaica Labour Party (JLP) (from 3 Sep 2007)

Main opposition party

Jamaica Labour Party (JLP)

Population

2.69 million (2007)*
Last census: September 2001: 2,607632
Population density: 209 inhabitants per square km. Urban population: 56 per cent of total population.
Annual growth rate: 0.7 per cent 1994–2004 (WHO 2006)

Ethnic make-up

Afro-Caribbean (90.9 per cent), East Indian (1.3 per cent), European (0.2 per cent), Chinese (0.2 per cent), mixed (7.3 per cent) and other (0.1 per cent).

Religions

Jamaica is home to a number of Christian denominations, mostly Protestant (over 61 per cent of the population). These include the Church of God (21 per cent), Baptist (9 per cent), Anglican (6 per cent) and Seventh-Day Adventist (9 per cent) churches. Roman Catholics (4 per cent) and spiritual cults (35 per cent) make up the other principal religious groups.

Education

The quality of schooling has slowly deteriorated over the last 20 years as debt reduction and other fiscal issues take higher priority. Jamaica's education system is based on the British system. Schooling consists of a two year pre-primary from aged 4, then a compulsory primary cycle of six years. Secondary schooling is divided into three phases, at the end of each, students either leave or move up to the next grade. They enter a 'first cycle' secondary school for three years, then a sixth form education of two-years and finally a 'second cycle' secondary school of two years; GSE 'O' and 'A' level examinations conclude the latter two. The education system accommodates a variety of public and private schools.
The main beneficiary of the government's spending on education is the primary school system, which enjoys a higher per capita expenditure than secondary and tertiary education.
Free places are offered in secondary schools through an annual common entrance examination, but a shortage of places has meant that not all children who qualify can be accommodated.
Post-secondary education is available at three universities and a number of community and teacher-training colleges. Opportunities for tertiary education remain limited, with only 8 per cent of high school graduates going to university or other higher institutions.
The primary and secondary education system was affected by the structural adjustment programme agreed with the IMF during the 1990s, which resulted in general cutbacks in social services expenditure. However, education has also benefitted from direct support from multilateral institutions. In 1996, the World Bank initiated a US$28 million student loan project, and has sponsored reform of secondary education. In 2000, the Inter-American Development Bank (IDB) approved a US$31 million loan to support the development of the primary school system.
Literacy rate: 88 per cent adult rate; 95 per cent youth rate (15–24) (Unesco 2005).
Compulsory years: Six to 12
Enrolment rate: 101 per cent gross primary enrolment, of relevant age group (including repeaters) (World Bank)
Pupils per teacher: 31 in primary schools.

Health

Per capita total expenditure on health (2003) was US$216; of which per capita government spending was US$109, at the international dollar rate, (WHO 2006).
Jamaica's health care is affordable and improving dramatically; increasing life expectancy and lowering infant mortality rates to some of the best figures in the Caribbean. Unfortunately, money has been taken out of the funding for the public education system.
Improved water sources and sanitation facilities are available to 71 per cent and

84 per cent of the population, respectively.

HIV/Aids

HIV prevalence: 1.2 per cent aged 15–49 in 2003 (World Bank)

Life expectancy: 72 years, 2004 (WHO 2006)

Fertility rate/Maternal mortality rate: 2.4 births per woman, 2004 (WHO 2006)

Birth rate/Death rate: 17.4 births per 1,000 population; 5.4 deaths per 1,000 population (2003).

Child (under 5 years) mortality rate (per 1,000): 17 per 1,000 live births (World Bank)

Head of population per physician: 0.85 physicians per 1,000 people, 2003 (WHO 2006)

Welfare

Welfare is provided under the National Insurance Scheme (NIS) and the Social Assistance Programme. The NIS is contributory and provides protection against loss of income for men aged 18 to 70 years and women aged 18 to 65 years. There has also been multilateral involvement in welfare provision, including a US$20 million Jamaica Social Investment Fund (JSIF) initiated by the World Bank in 1996. JSIF is part of a national programme aimed at eliminating poverty and generating social funds. The Bank has initiated a social assessment programme for the inner cities, to allow the JSIF to target poverty more effectively.

The Jamaican government has mobilised support from several non-governmental organisations and other charities towards the administration of social security and welfare measures. It is open to collaboration and partnership with stakeholders, both locally and abroad to improve the quality of services delivered to the poor. Such organisations include, Food for the Poor, which was involved in a massive programme to build 2,000 homes for poor families across Jamaica.

Main cities

Kingston (capital, estimated population 701,063 in 2005), Portmore (124,050), Montego Bay (108,968), Spanish Town (97,729).

Languages spoken

English and a local patois, influenced by Elizabethan English.

Official language/s

English

Media

The media is free from censorship, athough the government has wide involvement in television, it has little control over radio and none in the print media.

National news agency: Jamaica Information Service

Press

Dailies: There of the three dailies, two are published in the morning, The Jamaica Gleaner (www.jamaica-gleaner.com) and The Jamaica Observer (www.jamaicaobserver.com), The Jamaica Star (an afternoon tabloid) (www.jamaica-star.com).

Weeklies: There are several publications for local communities as well as one national newspaper, Sunday Herald (www.sunheraldja.com), North Star Times and Mandeville Weekly. The Xtra-News (www.xnewsjamaica.com) is an entertainment magazine.

Business: The monthly Investor's Choice magazine serving a diverse audience. Daily and weekly newspapers have local business news articles.

Periodicals: A monthly magazine, The Commentator (www.thecommentatorjm.com) publishes submitted articles on a variety of historical and current topics.

Broadcasting

Radio: All radio stations are independently owned and commercially operated. RJR Communications Group (www.rjrgroup.com) operates Radio Jamaica with a network of three stations including RJR (www.rjr94fm.com) for news and talk radio, Fame FM (www.famefm.fm) for innovative music and Hitz 92. Other stations include NewsTalk (www.newstalk.com.jm), Kool 97 FM (http://kool97fm.com) and Irie FM (www.iriefm.net).

Television: There are three TV stations in operation, of which TVJ (www.televisionjamaica.com) and CVM TV (www.cvmtv.com) are the other major broadcasters providing locally produced and imported TV programmes, Love TV (www.love101.org) is a religious broadcaster. Cable and satellite TV is available for subscribers, including CETV, Hype TV and RJR (http://rjrgroup.com).

Advertising

Radio, television, the press and billboards are the major advertising media. Although radio and local TV provide the widest ranging of media options, new technologies such as the internet are attracting more advertisers and advertising revenue.

Economy

Agriculture, tourism and the bauxite-alumina industry have dominated Jamaica's economy. More recently the services sector has gained in importance. Sugar, and later banana production, used to produce much of Jamaica's earnings during the pre-independence era, but with diversification it now exports bananas, coffee, citrus fruit, onions, peppers and other vegetables as well as beverages including rum, beer and carbonated drinks.

Tourism and related services are of particular importance, accounting for around 65 per cent of GDP; visitor numbers in 2006, which jumped by 15.3 per cent on the previous year, passed the three million mark. Remittance earnings, particularly from emigrants in the US, Canada and UK, are an important source of foreign exchange. The Inter-American Development Bank estimated that in 2006 migrant workers sent some US$1,770 million to their families in Jamaica.

Jamaica is an open and import-dependent economy, vulnerable to the effects of oil and commodity prices on its balance of trade. Like other Caribbean countries, it suffers from periodic hurricanes and flooding. Hurricane Ivan, which devastated many areas and crops in September 2003, is estimated to have cost Jamaica US$362 million. The sharp rise in the price of oil in 2005 highlights Jamaica's vulnerability to forces beyond its control. The combined effects of energy price increases and unfavourable weather conditions adversely impacted on growth in 2004 and 2005. Performance in most sectors improved in 2006 with better weather for agriculture and falling oil prices.

The business environment continues to be affected by high levels of petty and organised crime, with observers monitoring the murder rate as closely as more orthodox indicators.

External trade

Along with 11 other members of the Caribbean Community and Common Market (Caricom), Jamaica operates within the single market (Caribbean Single Market and Economy (CSME)), which became operational on 1 January 2006. CSME includes the free movement of goods and services, a common trade policy and external tariff.

There is a heavy reliance on commodity exports while its dependency on energy imports continues to cause severe balance of payments difficulties, although the PetroCaribe Energy Co-operation Agreement with Venezuela helps to ease these difficulties.

Imports

Principal imports are foodstuffs, petroleum, capital goods and industrial supplies, vehicles, machinery and transport equipment, construction materials and consumer goods.

Main sources: US (39.3 per cent total, 2006), Trinidad and Tobago (13.9 per cent), Venezuela (5.9 per cent).

Exports

Principal exports are alumina, bauxite and chemicals, rum, coffee, sugar, bananas and yams, manufactured clothes.

Main destinations: US (30.2 per cent total, 2006), Canada (15.6 per cent), China (15.2 per cent).

Re-exports

Re-exports including chemicals, machinery, transport equipment and miscellaneous manufactures represent 3.5 per cent of total value.

Agriculture

Farming

The agricultural sector, including forestry and fishing, typically contributes 6.9 per cent to GDP and employs approximately 19 per cent of the workforce. Agricultural production is often affected by adverse weather conditions. Blue Mountain coffee, one of the most expensive in the world, is grown in Jamaica.

Estimated crop production in 2005 included: 1,900,000 tonnes (t) sugar cane, 22,000t sweet potatoes, 222,500t citrus fruit, 4,000t potatoes, 125,000t bananas, 21,000t plantains, 20,571t pineapples, 15,000t cassava, 1,000t maize, 2,700t green coffee, 1,150t cocoa beans, 23,120t oilcrops, 148,000t yams, 170,000t coconuts, 19,300t tomatoes, 10,400t pimento & allspice, 1,800t tobacco leaves, 464,404t fruit in total, 196,504t vegetables in total. Estimated livestock production included: 102,923t meat in total, 14,500t beef, 5,490t pig meat, 1,559t goat meat, 81,321t poultry, 5,765t eggs, 28,500t milk, 1,000t honey, 1,430t cattle hides.

Fishing

Although most fishing is for domestic consumption, inland commercial fishing could be developed. The local freshwater fish industry has been able to increase production of fish in smaller ponds and cut its production cost by 30 per cent, thanks to new technology. Traditional ponds which occupy vast acreages, produce a negligible 6.25 fish per square metre. Latest technology put to use at the Longville Park fish farm, which consists of four concrete-lined ponds approximately 250 square metres in size with automated systems to monitor oxygen levels in the water and feeding, is likely to increase production up to 125 fish per square metre. Estimates show that annual output could increase to 6.6 million pounds of freshwater fish, enabling Jamaica to compete on the world market.

The typical annual marine fish catch is 4,660mt and 560mt shellfish.

In 2004, the total marine fish catch was 8,646 tonnes and the total crustacean catch was 300 tonnes.

Forestry

Exports of timber products in 2004 were US$162,000, while imports amounted to US$64.8 million.

Production in 2004 included 852,496 cubic metres (cum) roundwood, 282,400cum industrial roundwood, 66,200cum sawnwood, 132,400cum sawlogs and veneers, 570,096cum wood fuel, 8,848t charcoal.

Industry and manufacturing

Overall performance of the manufacturing and processing sectors was estimated to have increased by 4.4 per cent from January to September 2004 over the same period in 2003. The industrial sector typically contributes 35 per cent to GDP, of which manufacturing contributes 12 per cent. The sector employs around 8 per cent of the workforce.

The growth in cement production, in line with increased construction, and food processing were 2004 production leaders.

Agro-industries dominate the manufacturing sector, particularly textiles, sugar refining, paper products, cigarettes and alcohol, particularly rum and beer. Of these the textile industry has declined under the impact of competition from producers with freer trade links to the US, such as Mexico.

Other important manufacturing industries (most of which are foreign-owned and heavily dependent on imported materials and components) include chemicals, machinery and tools, glass, cement and metal products. Industry in Jamaica has suffered from difficulty in competing with more efficiently produced imports. Other problems include the high cost of security due to instances of drug contamination of exports by smugglers.

The main capital-intensive industries are petroleum refining at Kingston (capacity 34,200 barrels per day), and the refining of bauxite for export. The emphasis of industrial policy during the 1990s was on expanding facilities at the Kingston and Montego Bay free zones, encouraging foreign investment in export-based manufacturing and exploiting opportunities offered under the Caribbean Basin Initiative (CBI).

In 2003, Alcoa Inc, the world's leading supplier of alumina, completed a 250,000 tonne expansion project at the Jamalco refinery at a cost of US$115 million. The revised tax arrangements, along with the expansion, lowered costs at the refinery by approximately 30 per cent.

Further expansion of the Jamalco's Clarendon refinery was announced in July 2005 when a plan was agreed by Alcoa and the Jamaica government. This will add 1.5 million tonnes per year (mtpy) of capacity at a cost of US$1.2 billion, bringing the total capacity to 2.8 mtpy. The construction costs include a new power station and high hurricane wind and earthquake protection.

Total bauxite and alumina production in Jamaica for 2004 was 13.25 million tonnes and 4.02 million tonnes respectively.

Tourism

Tourism is Jamaica's principal economic activity. Outstanding tourist numbers in 2003 were surpassed in 2004 with over 1.28 million visitors arriving. Of these over 70 per cent were from the US and 17 per cent from Europe. Cruise shipping fell slightly with 414 ships arriving between January–September 2004, disembarking almost one million visitors.

Tourist growth in 2005 registered 8 per cent for the first four months of the year. China has designated Jamaica as an approved destination for its holidaying citizens; Chinese visitors could swell arrival numbers by many thousands.

Mining

The mining sector generates around half of export earnings and contributes approximately 9 per cent to GDP. Mining and quarrying employs approximately 1 per cent of the workforce.

Activity is centred on the extraction of bauxite and alumina refining. Known reserves of bauxite are around two billion tonnes, although most is of relatively low quality. Other minerals exploited include gypsum, marble, silica and clays.

On 20 June 2005 a bilateral agreement was signed between China and Jamaica to, establish a bauxite mining and alumina refinery facility, projected to process 1.4 million tonnes of alumina a year.

Hydrocarbons

Jamaica derives around 96 per cent of its energy requirements from imported oil. Early attempts, in the 1970–80s, to find commercially exploitable deposits of oil and gas were unsuccessful; any deposits found were too costly to retrieve. However in November 2004 the government launched an offer for licences to explore four onshore and 22 offshore blocks in Jamaica's exclusion zone. New technology and more experience has led to the belief that any viable deposits may now be exploitable.

Jamaica does not produce coal but imports around 54,000 tonnes per annum.

Energy

Almost all the country's energy needs are imported. Oil is supplied at concessionary rates by Mexico and Venezuela. There is a strategy to move from oil to liquefied natural gas as the country's main source of energy for electricity generation. The major consumer is the alumina industry, where energy accounts for up to 40 per cent of production costs.

The potential for hydroelectric schemes is small and most electricity is generated in oil-fired power stations.

Banking and insurance

The banking sector has undergone extensive restructuring since 1997, when the government intervened to prevent a complete collapse of the country's financial institutions. The sector's problems arose from a lack of proper risk management which created inherent weaknesses. These were exposed when the monetary authorities raised interest rates to stem the tide of inflation causing asset values to plummet. The restructuring of the financial sector was completed by the Financial Sector Adjustment Company (Finsac) in March 2002 at an estimated cost of around 30 per cent of GDP. In the restructuring process, Finsac merged banks and sold them to the Royal Bank of Trinidad and Tobago. Consequently, foreign banks have a high presence in Jamaica, controlling around 80 per cent of total bank deposits.

Central bank

The Bank of Jamaica

Time

GMT minus five hours

Geography

Jamaica, with an area of 10,989 square km, is the third largest island in the Caribbean. Covered with dense tropical vegetation, it is 234km long and 82km across at the widest point. The island lies about 145km south of Cuba and 160km west of Hispaniola. Mountain ranges snake across the island from south-east to north-west, with many long spurs to north and south. The highest summits are at the eastern end of the island, with the Blue Mountain Peak the tallest at 2,256 metres. The longest river, the Rio Minho, flows south from its source in the centre of the country, and is 92km long.

Hemisphere

Northern

Climate

Jamaica is around 5 degrees south of the Tropic of Cancer and has a maritime tropical climate characterised by warm trade winds. Average coastal and lowland temperatures are around 27 degrees Celsius, with little seasonal variation. Mean annual rainfall is about 200mm, with the main rainy season in October and a second one in May. Jamaica may be subject to the tropical storms and hurricanes typical of the Caribbean basin weather system.

Dress codes

Dress codes are mainly informal. Officials wear a jacket and tie or loose-fitting lightweight clothes when the climate is hot and humid. A sweater is rarely needed, even on cooler evenings. Light rainwear is useful. On social occasions, dress as for business meetings unless otherwise indicated.

Entry requirements

Passports

Required by all, valid for six months from date of departure, except nationals of the US and Canada, who require only proof of identity and nationality, (all US and Canadian nationals require a passport for re-entry to their country from January 2007).

Visa

No visa requirements for nationals of EU/EEA countries, North America, Australasia, and some Latin American and Asian countries. For details, see www.jhcuk.com/newguide-fr.html. Business visas require a letter from the employer, an itinerary and evidence of sufficient funds.

Currency advice/regulations

The import and export of local currency is prohibited. The import and export of foreign currency is allowed, subject to declaration.

Prohibited imports

Obscene images and publications. The following items are restricted and require permits: meat, ground provisions, fruit and vegetables, pharmaceuticals, firearms, used tyres, two-way radios, coconut derivatives, motor vehicles, explosives, bulk alcohol, sugar, human remains, pesticides and live animals.

Health (for visitors)

Mandatory precautions

A yellow fever vaccination certificate is required if arriving from an infected area.

Advisable precautions

Hepatitis A and B, tetanus, TB, typhoid and polio vaccinations are recommended. Drinking water from the public supply is safe.

Foreigners visiting the island can use public health services, but are advised to seek private medical attention. Insurance to cover the latter which can be expensive is highly recommended.

Hotels

Hotels and guest houses are graded and mostly geared towards holidaymakers. There are also numerous resort villas and apartments.

Public holidays (national)

Fixed dates

1 Jan (New Year's Day), 23 May (Labour Day), 1 Aug (Emancipation Day), 6 Aug (Independence Day), 25–26 Dec (Christmas).

Variable dates

Ash Wednesday, Good Friday, Easter Monday, National Heroes' Day (third Mon in Oct).

Working hours

Banking

Mon–Thu: 0900–1400; Fri 0900–1500. Branches of some banks open on Sat.

Business

Mon–Fri: 0830–1630/1700. Some offices open Sat.

Government

Mon–Fri: 0830–1630/1700. Some offices open Sat.

Shops

Mon–Sat: 0830–1630/1700.

Electricity supply

110/220V AC, 50 cycles

Social customs/useful tips

Appointments should be made in advance. Punctuality is appreciated. An additional 10 per cent tip is usual, even where a 10–15 per cent service charge is billed automatically. Penalties for drug offences are severe, with possession of even small quantities possibly leading to imprisonment. Luggage should be packed without the help of others and only your own should be carried through customs.

Security

It is advisable not to walk around after dark due to street crime. Some parts of Kingston are considered dangerous even during the daytime, avoid exploring nightlife away from main hotels and restaurants, unless accompanied by Jamaican friends. Only taxis, authorised by the Jamaica Union of Travellers Association (Juta) should be used and preferably ordered through hotels.

Getting there

Air

National airline: Air Jamaica.

International airport/s:

Kingston-Norman Manley International (KIN), 17km south-east of city, duty-free shop, bars, restaurants, bank, post office, car hire.

Other airport/s: Montego Bay-Sangster International (MBJ), 3km north of Montego Bay.

Airport tax: J$1,000.

Surface

Water: The island has several ports catering for international shipping and local ferries.

Main port/s: Kingston, Montego Bay, Ocho Rios and Port Antonio.

Getting about

National transport

Air: Air Jamaica serves several destinations. TimAir Ltd and International Air Link provide charter services.

Road: There is an extensive network of surfaced, all-weather roads, accounting for 70 per cent of the total of around 18,000km.

Buses: Minibuses in towns are generally cheap but crowded; in the country they are often considered slow, crowded and sometimes dangerous. There are regular, scheduled services over longer distances (eg Kingston-Montego Bay; journey time varies, to some extent dependent on route).

Rail: Jamaica has 272km of track. Passenger services have been suspended since 1992. A privately-owned portion of the network is used for transport of bauxite.

City transport

Taxis: All taxis have red PPV plates. It is advisable to negotiate fares (J$) in advance. Taxis in Kingston no longer use meters. A 10 per cent tip is usual.

Car hire

Widely available. International or national licence accepted; traffic drives on the left.

BUSINESS DIRECTORY

The addresses listed below are a selection only. While World of Information makes every endeavour to check these addresses, we cannot guarantee that changes have not been made, especially to telephone numbers and area codes. We would welcome any corrections.

Telephone area codes

International direct dialling code (IDD) for Jamaica is +1 876, followed by subscriber's number.

Chambers of Commerce

American Chamber of Commerce of Jamaica, Le Méridien Jamaica Pegasus Hotel, 81 Knutsford Boulevard, Kingston (tel: 929-7866; fax: 929-8597; e-mail: info@amchamjamaica.org).

Jamaica Chamber of Commerce, 85a Duke Street, Kingston (tel: 922-0150; fax: 924-9056; e-mail: jamcham@cwjamaica.com).

Montego Bay Chamber of Commerce and Industry, 4-7 Overton Plaza, PO Box 213, Montego Bay (tel: 952-6045; fax: 952-2784).

Banking

National Investment Bank of Jamaica, 32 Trafalgar Road, Kingston 10 (tel. 929-9050).

Bank of Nova Scotia Jamaica, Scotia Centre, Port Royal Street, Kingston (tel: 922-1000).

CIBC Jamaica, 23-27 Knutsford Boulevard, Kingston 5 (tel: 929-9310).

Citibank N.A., 63-67 Knutsford Boulevard, Kingston 5 (tel: 926-3270/3285; fax: 929-3745).

National Commercial Bank of Jamaica, The Atrium, 32 Trafalgar Road, Kingston 10 (tel: 929-9050).

RBTT Bank Jamaica, 17 Dominica Drive, Kingston 5 (tel: 960-2340; e-mail: rbtt@cwjamaica.com).

The Financial Sector Adjustment Company, PO Box 54, 76 Knutsford Boulevard, Kingston 5: (tel: 906-1809; fax: 906-1822; info@FINSAC.com).

Trafalgar Commercial Bank, 60 Knutsford Boulevard, Kingston 5 (tel: 929-3383, 929-3511, 929-3521; fax: 929-3654).

Central bank

Bank of Jamaica, Nethersole Place, PO Box 621, Kingston (tel: 922-0750; fax: 922-0854; e-mail: info@boj.org.jm).

Travel information

Air Jamaica Ltd, 72–76 Harbour St, Kingston (tel: 922-3460; fax: 967-3125; pr@airjamaica.com).

Jamaica Hotel and Tourist Association, 2 Ardenne Road, Kingston 10 (tel: 926-3635; fax: 929-1054; e-mail: info@jhta.org).

National tourist organisation offices

Jamaica Tourist Board, Knutsford Boulevard, Kingston 5 (tel: 929-9200; fax: 929-9375; e-mail: info@visitjamaica.com).

Ministries

Office of The Prime Minister, Jamaica House, 1 Devon Road, Kingston 6 (tel: 927-9941/3; fax: 929-0005).

Ministry of Agriculture, Hope Gardens, Kingston 6 (tel: 927-1731/45; fax: 927-1904).

Ministry of Education and Culture, 2 National Heroes Circle, Kingston 4 (tel: 922-1400/19; fax: 967-1837).

Ministry of Finance and Planning, 30 National Heroes Circle, Kingston 4 (tel: 922-8600/15; fax: 922-7097).

Ministry of Foreign Affairs and Foreign Trade, 21 Dominica Drive, Kingston 5 (tel: 926-4220/8; fax: 929-5112; e-mail: mfaftjam@cwjamaica.com).

Ministry of Health, Oceana Hotel Complex, 2 King Street, Kingston (tel: 967-1092; fax: 967-7293).

Ministry of Industry, Commerce and Technology, 36 Trafalgar Road, Kingston 10 (tel: 929-8990/9; fax: 960-1623; e-mail: gojmii@infochan.com).

Ministry of Labour and Social Security, 1f North Street, Kingston (tel: 922-9500, 967-1900; fax: 922-6902).

Ministry of Land and Environment, 2 Hagley Park Road, Kingston 10 (tel: 926-1590, 926-7008; fax: 926-2591; e-mail: mehsys@hotmail.com).

Ministry of Local Government, Youth & Community Development, 85 Hagley Park, Kingston 10 (tel: 754-0994; fax: 960-0725).

Ministry of Mining and Energy, 36 Trafalgar Road, Kingston 10 (tel: 926-9170/7; fax: 968-2082; e-mail: hmme@cwjamaica.com).

Ministry of National Security and Justice, Mutual Life Building, North Tower, 2 Oxford Road, Kingston 5 (tel: 906-4908/33; fax: 906-1724; e-mail: inform@infochan.com).

Ministry of Tourism and Sports, 64 Knutsford Boulevard, Kingston 5 (tel: 920-4956; fax: 920-4944; e-mail: opmt@cwjamaica.com).

Ministry of Transportation and Works, 1c-1f Pawsey Place, New Kingston (tel: 754-1900; fax: 927-8763).

Ministry of Water and Housing, 7th Floor, Island Life Building, 6 St Lucia Avenue, Kingston 5 (tel: 754-0973; fax: 754-0975; e-mail: prumow@cwjamaica.com).

Attorney General's Department, Mutual Life Building, North Tower, 2 Oxford Road, Kingston 5 (tel: 906-2416/7) and 79-83 Barry Street, Kingston (tel: 922-6140; fax: 922-5109).

Other useful addresses

All-Island Jamaica Cane Farmers' Association, 4 North Ave, Kingston 4 (tel: 922-3010; fax: 922-077).

Banana Export Co (BECO), 10 South Ave, Kingston 4 (tel: 922-5490).

British High Commission, Trafalgar Road, PO Box 575, Kingston 10 (tel: 926-9050; fax: 929-7869).

Cabinet Office, 1 Devon Road, Kingston 10 (tel: 927-9941/3; fax: 929-8459).

Cocoa Industry Board, Marcus Garvey Drive, PO Box 68, Kingston 15 (tel: 923-6411).

Coffee Industry Board, Marcus Garvey Drive, Kingston 15 (tel: 923-7211).

Jamaica Bauxite Institute, Hope Gdns, PO Box 355, Kingston 6 (tel: 927-2073; fax: 927-159).

Jamaica Exporters' Association (JEA), 13 Dominica Drive, PO Box 9, Kingston 5 (tel: 929-1292; fax: 929-831).

Jamaica Information Service, Kingston (tel: 926-3740, 926-3590; fax: 926-715).

Jamaica Manufacturers' Association, 85a Duke Street, Kingston (tel: 922-8880/2).

Jamaica Promotion Corporation (Jampro Limited), 35 Trafalgar Road, Kingston 10 (tel: 929-9450, 929-9452/6; fax: 924-9650; e-mail: jamprouk@investjamaica.com).

Jamaica Stock Exchange, 40 Harbour Street, Kingston (tel: 922-0806; fax: 922-6966; e-mail: info-jse@jamstockex.com).

Jamaican Embassy (USA), 1520 New Hampshire Avenue, NW, Washington DC 20006 (tel: (+1-202)-452-0660; fax: (+1-202)-452-0081; e-mail: emjam@sysnet.net).

Kingston Free Zone, Lot 27, Shannon Drive, Kingston 15 (tel: 923-5274).

The Planning Institute of Jamaica, 39 Barbados Ave, Kingston 5 (tel: 926-1480; fax: 926-4670).

US Embassy, Mutual Life Centre, 2 Oxford Road, Kingston 5 (tel: 929-4850).

National news agency: Jamaica Information Service

Other news agencies: Caribbean Net News: www.caribbeannetnews.com

Jamaica New Bulletin: (www.jamaicanewsbulletin.com)

Internet sites

Export Jamaica: http://www.exportjamaica.org

Jamaica Stock Exchange: http://www.jamstockex.com

CVM Television: http://www.cvmtv.com/top_news1.htm

Jamaica and Jamaican Top 5 Sites: http://www.top5jamaica.com

Jamaicamarket (business gateway): http://www.jamaicamarket.com

Jamaica Promotions Corporation (Jampro) (export and investment promotion agency): http://www.investjamaica.com

Japan

KEY FACTS

Official name: Nippon or Nihon (Japan)

Head of State: Emperor Tsegu no Miya Akihito (since 1989)

Head of government: Prime Minister Yasuo Fukuda (LDP) (from 25 Sep 2007)

Ruling party: Coalition: Liberal Democratic Party (LDP) and New Komeito Party (NKP) (since 2001; re-elected Sep 2005)

Area: 377,728 square km (3,900 small islands)

Population: 127.76 million (2007)*

Capital: Tokyo

Official language: Japanese

Currency: Yen (¥)

Exchange rate: ¥106.73 per US$ (Jul 2008)

GDP per capita: US$34,312 (2007)

GDP real growth: 2.10% (2007)

Labour force: 66.66 million (2004)

Unemployment: 3.90% (2007)

Inflation: 3.00% (2006)

Balance of trade: US$93.96 billion (2005)

Foreign debt: US$1,544.83 billion (2004)

Visitor numbers: 7.33 million (2006)*

* estimated figure

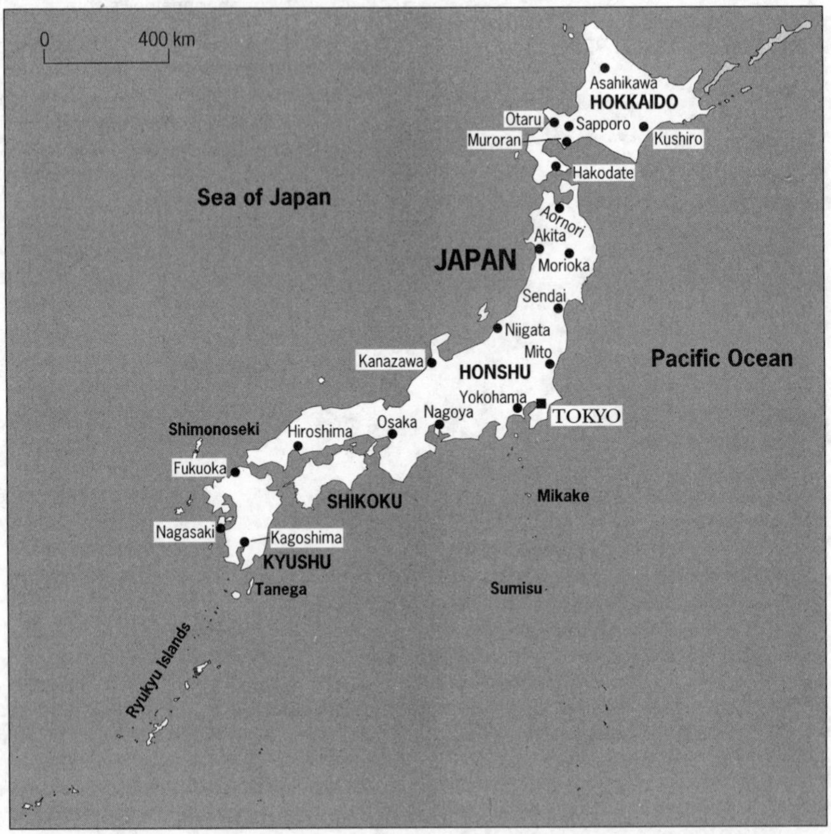

With a sigh of relief, Japan saw the July 2008 G8 summit end in Hokkaido without too many disagreements or demonstrations, with nothing more controversial to announce than what the world's leaders called a 'shared vision' on climate change, despite developing nations declining to sign up to suggested emissions targets. Leaders who attended the three-day summit also discussed Zimbabwe, and the global rise in food and energy prices.

Consensus first

In most respects the Hokkaido gathering summed up the Japanese approach to international gatherings. The discussions at the Windsor Hotel, close to Lake Toyako, saw the heads of the United States, Japan, Germany, France Britain, Italy, Canada and Russia joined by no less than 14 other heads of state in what was the largest ever G8 meeting. Despite the best efforts of police and immigration authorities in Japan, several thousand foreign demonstrators had joined forces with home-grown protesters to protest against anything and everything from global warming to banning cluster bombs, poverty and even the G8 itself. Encompassing all these desires and emotions, one banner unveiled at a protest event in the nearby city of Sapporo declared: 'No to the hypocritical G8 Summit promoting the destruction of the global environment'. Another simply stated: 'Down with imperialism'. Earlier protests had been relatively relaxed.

For the Japanese authorities, making sure that the demonstrations did not disrupt or disturb the G8 summit seemed almost to matter more than the outcome of the discussions themselves. The G8's shared vision may have echoed well around the salons of the Windsor Hotel, but it had little impact around the world. But at least there had been no embarrassment, or worse still, loss of face for the host nation.

Weak all round

According to the Bank of Japan (BoJ), in mid-2008 Japan's economic growth had been sluggish against a backdrop of high energy and materials prices and weaker growth in exports. In muted vein, the Bank reported that the pace of increase in Japanese exports had slowed and business fixed investment had been levelling off, as corporate profits decreased mainly due to a deterioration in the terms of trade. Private consumption had been relatively weak, mainly due to sluggish growth in household income and the increase in prices of petroleum products and food. The recovery in housing investment had stalled and public investment, meanwhile, had been sluggish. With these developments in demand both at home and abroad, production growth had been relatively weak. While growth looked likely to remain sluggish for the time being, Japan's economy was expected to return to a moderate growth path as international commodity prices levelled out and overseas economies began to move out of their deceleration phase.

Fukuda struggles

The blandness of the Hokkaido G8 summit was in many respects a reflection of the weakness and ineffectual position of Prime Minister Yasuo Fukuda and his Liberal Democratic Party (LDP) government. In mid-2008 the prospects of Mr Yasuo leading his party or its coalition to victory in Japan's next general election looked pretty remote. Mr Fukuda's popularity ratings in mid-2008 were lower even than his deeply unpopular predecessor Mr Shinzo Abe. The 71 year old Mr Fukuda's inability to out-manoeuvre his opposition leader, the younger Mr Ichiro Ozawa, was in some measure a reflection of the LDP's political ineptitude. Mr Fukuda seemed to have the uncanny knack of walking into self-made political traps; he also appeared to have little idea how to get out of them.

Modest growth prospects

The Bank of Japan expected growth in Japanese exports to remain only modest in 2007–08, due to the slowdown in overseas markets. Growth in domestic private demand also looked likely to be sluggish, as corporate profits were expected to decrease and real household income was likely to remain relatively weak. Public investment, meanwhile, was projected to drop. In the light of these developments in demand, production was also expected to remain relatively weak.

On the price front, the three-month rate of increase in domestic corporate goods prices had been high, mainly due to the rises in international commodity prices. At the end of 2007, the year-on-year rate of increase in consumer prices (excluding fresh food) was around 2 per cent against a general background of increased prices of petroleum products and food. Domestic corporate goods prices were likely to continue increasing, but in the view of the Bank of Japan, the pace of increase is likely to slow, with the year-on-year rate of increase in consumer prices expected to increase initially, but to moderate gradually thereafter, reflecting international developments in the prices of both energy and food.

'Accommodative' financiers

The environment for corporate finance has been what the Bank of Japan described as 'accommodative' on the whole. Credit demand in the private sector has been increasing moderately. Issuing conditions for bonds has also been generally favourable, although tightening for firms with low credit ratings and in selected industries. The amount outstanding of lending by private banks, notably of lending to large firms, has been increasing, although that of lending to small and medium-sized firms falling. In the view of the Bank of Japan, the financial position of most Japanese companies continued to be favourable in late 2007, but that of small and medium-sized firms had deteriorated somewhat. In the foreign exchange and capital markets, long-term interest rates have fallen and the yen has depreciated against the US dollar. Meanwhile, stock prices remained at around the same level in mid-year.

Modest slowdown

The International Monetary Fund (IMF) adopted a similar stance, noting that Japan appeared to be headed for a modest slowdown, although there remained risks from the global economy. Fallout from the US sub-prime mortgage crash has been limited and activity supported by strong exports to non-US destinations. Gross domestic product (GDP) growth is expected to moderate to slightly below potential in 2008–09 in line with lower global demand and the less favourable terms of trade. Headline CPI inflation has edged up, reflecting higher commodity prices, but wages remain sluggish, and inflation risks so far appear contained. Risks to the growth outlook have become more balanced in recent months, although considerable uncertainty remains, particularly regarding global commodity prices and their effects on the economy.

Strong tax collections and cuts in public works have trimmed the fiscal deficit in recent years, but public debt remains high. The government was targeting a primary deficit (excluding social security) of 0.5 per cent of GDP in 2008 (Japan's fiscal year (FY) begins in April) and is aiming for primary balance by 2011. Assuming

KEY INDICATORS — Japan

	Unit	2003	2004	2005	2006	2007
Population	m	127.65	127.94	127.75	127.75	*127.76
Gross domestic product (GDP)	US$bn	4.33	4,623.40	4,557.12	4,377.05	4,383.76
GDP per capita	US$	32,859	36,575	35,672	*34,264	*34,312
GDP real growth	%	2.5	2.6	1.9	2.4	2.1
Inflation	%	-0.2	-0.7	-0.6	0.3	1.3
Unemployment	%	5.3	4.7	4.4	4.1	3.9
Coal output	mtoe	0.7	0.7	0.6	0.7	0.8
Exports (fob) (goods)	US$m	471,934	539,000	567,570	615,800	678,090
Imports (cif) (goods)	US$m	382,959	406,870	473,610	534,500	573,340
Balance of trade	US$m	88,975	132,130	93,960	81,300	104,750
Current account	US$m	136,240	171,810	165,690	170,437	210,490
Total reserves minus gold	US$m	663,289	833,891	834,275	879,682	952,784
Foreign exchange	US$m	652,790	824,264	828,813	874,936	948,356
Exchange rate	per US$	113.48	108.14	120.35	117.24	113.35

only a slight cyclical downturn, the 2008 deficit target should be maintained even if tax revenue falls short. Thereafter, a more ambitious strategy would be desirable so as to place public debt on a firmly downward path.

With limited scope for further expenditure cuts, fiscal consolidation will require comprehensive tax reform including raising the consumption tax. The tax reform debate has moved slowly. Nonetheless, the government's FY 2009 plan to end earmarking of gas taxes is welcome. The government also intends to increase its contribution to the basic pension, which will require additional revenue. In light of these plans, various tax reform options are on the table. A consumption tax hike may become more palatable if it is linked to the need to fund social security spending and this opportunity to raise the consumption tax rate should be seized.

Japan's underlying inflation is still about zero and the BoJ can afford to hold interest rates steady until concerns over domestic activity and the global economy have eased. However, prices have begun to rise, and to guide inflation expectations, the BoJ is improving communication about the future conduct of monetary policy. The yen remains market-determined and has appreciated by about 10 per cent in real effective terms since mid-2007, although IMF estimates suggest that it remains undervalued relative to its longer-term equilibrium.

Japan was not a major sub-prime player and the financial system has escaped serious damage, with the BoJ's flexible liquidity management keeping money markets stable. The authorities remain vigilant to risks from further global market disruptions, as well as from a slowing economy. Banks' end-year results already incorporate additional information on structured holdings as called for by the Financial Stability Forum (FSF). In the view of the IMF, bolstering capital cushions and improving risk management would help to further strengthen the financial system and enhance financial intermediation.

Japanese practices

The period since Japan entered its long spell of near recession in the late-1980s, had seen significant changes in Japanese working methods and company structures. New hirings were generally on a contractual basis rather than on the traditional 'job for life' Japanese model. There was resultant insecurity – both on the part of workers with short term contracts and on the part of full time employees who feared that they might be changed to temporary contracts. The overall fear of unemployment meant that many workers worked – unofficially – longer, unpaid, hours than those stipulated in their contracts. On paper, the Japanese do not appear to work particularly long hours – 1,780 hours per annum according to the London *Economist* magazine. This is actually less than in the US, where the figure is 1,800 hours pa, but more than the 1,440 hours worked in Germany. The difference is that in Japan extra, unpaid and unrecorded hours were worked by as much as 30 per cent of the workforce. The average for these workers was 60 hours per week. In 2007 the social implications of this situation were beginning to be recognised, although even blue chip Japanese companies had long been happy to allow the situation to continue.

The importance of gas

According to the US *Oil &Gas Journal*, Japan had about 1.4 trillion cubic feet (Tcf) of proven natural gas reserves as of January 2006. Despite limited natural gas resources, Japan is an important natural gas consumer (90.2 billion cubic metres (bcm) in 2007, compared with Indonesia's consumption of 33.8 bcm), and imports virtually all of its natural gas from other countries. Lacking international pipeline connections, all of Japan's imports come in the form of liquefied natural gas (LNG). Japan began importing LNG from Alaska in 1969, making it one of the first countries to pioneer LNG trade. Today, Japan is the largest importer of LNG in the world.

As with the oil industry, Inpex and the companies created from the former Japan National Oil Company are the primary actors in Japan's upstream natural gas sector. Besides Inpex, various other Japanese companies are involved in natural gas exploration and production efforts, primarily overseas. Because Japan is the world's largest LNG buyer, the country has a robust LNG infrastructure, most of which is owned and operated by local power generation companies. Osaka Gas, Tokyo Gas, and Toho Gas are Japan's largest retail natural gas companies, with a combined share of about 75 per cent of the retail market. Although Japan is a large natural gas consumer, it has a limited natural gas pipeline transmission system. This is partly due to geographical constraints posed by the country's mountainous terrain, but it is also the result of previous regulations that limited investment in the sector. Reforms enacted in 1995 and 1999 have helped to open the sector to greater competition, and a number of new private companies have entered the industry since the reforms.

The lack of oil

In an effort to mitigate the country's lack of domestic oil resources, Japanese oil companies have sought participation in exploration and production projects overseas. In May 2006, Japan's minister of trade, economy and industry announced a long-term strategy that urges Japanese companies to increase energy exploration and development projects around the world to help secure a stable supply of oil and natural gas. Furthermore, he announced a goal of Japan importing 40 per cent of its oil needs from Japanese-owned concessions by 2030, up from the current level of about 15 per cent.

One of Japan's largest investments in oil projects overseas was in the Neutral Zone (sometimes called the Divided Zone) between Kuwait and Saudi Arabia. However, the Japanese-owned Arabian Oil Company (AOC) lost its concession in the Saudi portion of the Neutral Zone in 2000. AOC also controlled 40 per cent of the Kuwaiti portion of the project, as the operator of the Khafji and Hout oil fields. However, this concession expired in January 2003, although AOC continues to operate in the Kuwaiti portion of the Neutral Zone under a service contract. While AOC does not hold an equity stake in the project, it continues to receive about 50,000barrels per day (bpd) of oil from the joint development, although this figure is much smaller than the previous amount received from the Saudi concession

Inpex was awarded a US$2 billion contract to develop the large Azadegan oil field in Iran in 2004, which is estimated to hold 6 billion barrels of recoverable oil reserves. Inpex was the operator of the project and held a 75 per cent stake. However, in October 2006, the state-owned National Iranian Oil Company (NIOC) slashed Inpex's share to 10 per cent, after the Iranian government complained the Japanese company had not developed the oil field quickly enough. The future status of the Azadegan project remains unclear, and NIOC is reportedly in discussions with other oil companies to develop the oil field (aside from the Gulf, Japanese companies have also sought equity participation in oil projects in the Caspian Sea region). In 2002, Inpex acquired a 10 per cent stake in the Azeri-Chirag-Guneshli (ACG) Project in Azeri territory of the Caspian Sea. The ACG oil fields currently produce around

420,000bpd of oil and hold between 5.4–6.9 billion barrels of recoverable reserves. While Inpex holds a 10 per cent stake in the ACG project, Japan does not currently import any crude oil from Azerbaijan or the Caspian region. Inpex has also held an 8 per cent interest in the North Caspian Sea Block of the Kashagan offshore oil field in Kazakhstan since 1998.

Another region where Japanese companies have been involved in exploration and production activities is the Russian Far East, primarily through the Sakhalin-I and -II oil and natural gas projects. Japan's Sakhalin Oil and Gas Development Company (SODECO), a consortium of public and private Japanese oil companies, holds a 30 per cent interest in the Sakhalin-I project. Oil production at Sakhalin-I began in 1999, and is reached around 250,000bpd at the end of 2006. Japanese officials are keeping a close eye on ongoing projects in Russia. The Sakhalin-II project, in which Mitsui and Mitsubishi hold a combined 45 per cent stake, recently experienced problems with its environmental licence. Russian authorities have also complained about Sakhalin-I's escalating costs. Japan is also carefully observing Russian plans to build an oil pipeline to the Pacific coast, for which Russia has yet to choose a final destination. Beijing has lobbied for the ESPO (Eastern Siberia Pacific Coast) route to pump oil to China, although Russian officials have said they favour a route that would allow exports to both China and Japan.

Risk assessment

Economy	Good
Politics	Fair
Regional stability	Good

COUNTRY PROFILE

Historical profile

1600 The unification of Japan began in the Tokugawa period (1600–1868), during which a national administrative hierarchy was formed.
1868 The restoration of the imperial family from political obscurity ended the Tokugawa shogunate and began the Meiji era. Key reforms were initiated to orient Japan to the West and end centuries of isolation.
1894 Japan defeated imperial China in a brief war.
1895 China ceded Taiwan to Japan and allowed Japan to trade in China.
1904–05 Japan went to war with Russia and won.
1910 After three years of fighting, Japan annexed Korea.
1914—19 Japan had limited participation in the First World War on the side of Britain and the allies. The Treaty of Versailles gave Japan some territory in the Pacific.
1920—32 Since the late 1920s, extreme nationalism had increased. In 1931, Japan invaded Manchuria, renaming it and installing a puppet regime. The Japanese prime minister was assassinated in 1932 by ultra-nationalists. The military held increasing influence in the country.
1938–41 Japanese forces occupied large parts of China and south-east Asia, forcing the British out of Singapore, Malaysia and Hong Kong.
1945 Following its defeat in the Second World War, the subsequent armistice ceded control over many of Japan's outer islands, and the country was placed under US military occupation.
1947 A new democratic constitution was enacted, renouncing all military activity outside Japan.
1951 Following the signing of the peace treaty, Japan regained its sovereignty. Sovereignty over the Tokara Archipelago and the Amami islands were also restored.
1955 The Liberal Democratic Party (LDP) was formed by a coalition of centre-right groups.
1956 Japan joined the UN.
1964 Prime Minister Hayato Ikeda was succeeded by Eisaku Sato, who was to become the longest-serving prime minister in Japanese history, remaining in office until 1972.
1972 The Bonin Islands and the remainder of the Ryukyu Islands (including Okinawa), which had been under US administration since 1945, were finally returned to Japan.
1976 Following the resignation of Sato's successor, Kakuei Tanaka, in 1974, Tanaka was arrested on charges of accepting bribes. The scandal damaged the LDP, which, in the elections, lost its overall majority for the first time.
1983 Following seven years of judicial proceedings, Kakuei Tanaka was found guilty of accepting bribes. Tanaka began appeal proceedings and refused to resign his legislative seat, forcing a premature general election.
1986 The LDP recovered its absolute majority in the Diet.
1987 The high court upheld the 1983 decision, finding Tanaka guilty of accepting bribes.
1989 The Showa era ended with the death of Emperor Hirohito, who had reigned since 1926. He was succeeded by his son, Akihito, beginning the Heisei era.
1993 The LDP lost its majority in the lower house in the national election and a coalition government was formed.
1994 Tomiichi Murayama, leader of the Social Democratic Party of Japan (SDPJ), became Japan's fourth prime minister in a year.
1996 The LDP won the general election.
1997 Ryutaro Hashimoto of the LDP returned for his second term as prime minister. The economy entered a severe recession.
1998 Keizo Obuchi succeeded Hashimoto, who resigned following his party's defeat in the upper house election.
2000 Obuchi died and was replaced by Yoshiro Mori. The LDP lost its parliamentary majority, forcing Prime Minister Mori to rely on coalition partners. Mori survived the first in a series of votes of no-confidence.
2001 Mori was rocked by scandals and an unpopular image, he resigned as prime minister and party leader. Junichiro Koizumi was elected as the LDP's new president and became prime minister. He helped turn around the fortunes of the LDP as it won Tokyo's metropolitan elections. The LDP coalition won the upper house elections.
2002 Koizumi's opinion poll ratings plummeted as his 'reform' agenda prove unpopular.
2003 The LDP was re-elected in the parliamentary elections.
2004 The opposition won the upper house partial elections; however, the LDP-led coalition retained its majority in both houses. Japanese non-combat troops are sent to Iraq. Huge earthquakes killed 30 people in the north.
2005 Parliament was dissolved and an early election, after the prime minister's proposals to privatise Japan Post was defeated in the upper house. The LDP won an increased majority in the Diet, gaining 47 seats, while the main opposition, DPJ, lost 63 seats. Turnout was 67.51 per cent. Relations with China were strained as a result of controversial Japanese textbooks, Koizumi's visits to a war shrine commemorating war criminals and China's exploration of disputed areas of the East China Sea.
2006 In September, Shinzo Abe won LDP leadership elections and became party president. On 26 September, Koizumi resigned from the premiership and was replaced by Shinzo Abe. Legislation converting the Japan Defence Agency into a ministry of defence was passed in December.
2007 In July, the ruling LDP lost its majority in the upper house (Shugi-in) parliamentary elections. The opposition DPJ won 60 seats to achieve an overall number of 109 members. Satsuki Eda (DPJ)

became president of the upper house after a unanimous vote in August; he was the first non-LDP president in over 50 years and the first opposition politician to become president. Shinzo Abe resigned as prime minister in September and Yasuo Fukuda (LDP), was appointed as his successor.

2008 Indigenous people of the northern island of Hokkaido, the Ainu, were given full recognition by the government on 6 June. Prime Minister Fukuda lost a vote of confidence in the upper house, in June, but won the same vote in the lower house. On 18 June Japan and China agreed to the joint development of a gas field in the East China Sea, which had been a protracted bilateral dispute.

Political structure

Constitution

The Japanese constitution came into force in 1947. It may be amended only if the proposed alteration is passed with a two-thirds majority by the Diet (parliament) and then submitted to the people for ratification, either in a referendum or election.

Japan is a parliamentary democracy based on universal adult suffrage. Religion and state are constitutionally separate.

Since the crown prince and his siblings have no male children, in November 2004, the ruling Liberal Democratic Party (LDP) had begun to consider constitutional changes that would allow a woman to ascend to the imperial throne.

Form of state

Constitutional monarchy

The executive

Executive power is vested in the cabinet, which consists of the prime minister and not more than 20 ministers of state (including ministers without portfolio and the chief cabinet secretary) and is collectively responsible to the Diet.

By convention, the chosen president of the majority party becomes prime minister; the Emperor appoints the prime minister, who must already have been approved by the Diet. The prime minister appoints the cabinet, the majority of whom must be members of the Diet; the cabinet remains collectively responsible to the Diet.

The Emperor is the head of state under the constitution, but has only formal powers related to government.

National legislature

The Diet (parliament) is the highest organ of state power and the sole lawmaking authority, comprising two houses.

The 480-member Sangi-in (House of Representatives) (lower house), with 300 members elected in single-member constituencies and 180 by proportional representation; all members serve for four-year terms.

The 242-member Shugi-in (House of Councillors) (upper house), with 98 members elected by proportional representation and 144 elected in multi-member constituencies; all members serve for a fixed six-year term, with half the number of members elected every three years. The chamber cannot be dissolved by the prime minister.

Both houses must be in agreement for legislation to be enacted, althoug when the Diet is in deadlock the lower house takes precedence.

Legal system

The judiciary is independent, but the role of bureaucratic interpretation and the reluctance of the Japanese to get involved in litigation mean that judges are less influential than in Western democracies. All judicial power is vested in the Supreme Court and four types of inferior court – High, District, Family and Summary Courts.

The judges of the Supreme Court, except the chief judge, who is appointed by the Emperor, are appointed by the cabinet. The judges of inferior courts are also appointed by the cabinet, but only from a list of persons nominated by the Supreme Court.

Last elections

11 September 2005 (parliamentary; lower house); 29 July 2007 (parliamentary; upper house).

Results: Parliamentary (House of Representatives): the Liberal Democratic Party (LDP) won 296 seats out of 480; Democratic Party of Japan (DPJ) 113; New Komeito Party (NKP) 31; Japanese Communist Party (JCP) nine; and Social Democratic Party (SDP) seven.

Parliamentary (House of Councillors): the DPJ won 60 seats (to achieve an overall number of 109); the LDP won 37 (83); the NKP won nine (20); the JCP won three (seven); the SDP won two (four); others nine (14). Turnout was 58.6 per cent.

Next elections

2009 (parliamentary)

Political parties

Ruling party

Coalition: Liberal Democratic Party (LDP) and New Komeito Party (NKP) (since 2001; re-elected Sep 2005)

Main opposition party

Democratic Party of Japan (DPJ).

Population

127.76 million (2007)*

Last census: October 2000: 126,925,843

Population density: 337 inhabitants per square km. Urban population: 79 per cent (1995—2001).

Annual growth rate: 0.2 per cent 1994–2004 (WHO 2006)

Ethnic make-up

Japan is generally recognised to be racially homogenous, however there are small numbers of Ainu (indigenous people) and almost one million Koreans.

The 1980s saw an influx of illegal immigrants into Japan, notably from the Philippines. Immigration levels have remained low relative to other industrialised countries, with non-Japanese making up only 2 per cent of the population.

Religions

Shintoism and Buddhism (majority), Christianity (minority). Many people profess both Shintoism and Buddhism, observing Shinto rites for birth and marriage and Buddhism for funerals. Both religions continue to play a significant role in cultural, philosophical and even business and political spheres. There are approximately 1.7 million Christians.

Education

Japan follows the American educational cycle of 6-3-3-4 years, where the six, elementary (primary) years and three junior high school years are free of charge and mandatory.

Even though competition is fierce, 97 per cent of students enrol for non-compulsory high school at aged 15. Valued places in prestigious high schools virtually guarantee a direct path into universities and other institutes of higher education. High school lasts for three years. There are a number of private international schools. At 62.6 per cent, Japan has the highest rate, of any industrialised country, for students going into higher education. There are three types of institutes of higher education: university, junior college and technical college.

There are also kindergartens for pre-school children, and miscellaneous schools for vocational and practical training, and special education schools for the physically and mentally handicapped.

Admission is highly competitive at every stage of schooling and there have been many critics who question whether the intensive school curriculum enables students to confront a dynamic, modern world. Changes have been introduced to encourage a greater flexibility in both teaching and learning. The academic year has been amended to five days a week and 210 days a year.

Public expenditure on education typically amounts to 3.6 per cent of annual gross national income.

Compulsory years: Six to 15

Enrolment rate: 101 per cent gross primary enrolment, 103 gross secondary enrolment; of the relevant age groups (including repeater) (World Bank).

Pupils per teacher: 19 in primary schools

Health

Per capita total expenditure on health (2003) was US$2,244; of which per capita government spending was US$1,818, at the international dollar rate, (WHO 2006).

Medical facilities in Japan are excellent, with around 97 per cent of all medical services covered by plans such as National Health Insurance, which is also available to foreigners with residence or work visas.

Japan has a low fertility rate reflecting trends in all developed countries as its population ages rapidly. In a February 2005 study the recorded number of Japanese men fell by 0.01 per cent, as the population rose by 0.05 per cent, these figures are the smallest seen (apart from the war years when statistics of military deaths were withheld) since records began in 1920. The fall in the number of men could be explained by many working abroad, however what is sure is the number of Japanese aged over 65, in 2004, reached a record high of 19.5 per cent, as those aged under 14 fell to an all-time low of 13.9 per cent. The concerns in the changing demographics has prompted reform of the state pension where amendments implemented in 2004 steadily reduce benefits, as premiums increase.

HIV/Aids

There are signs that the sexual behaviour of youth in Japan could be changing significantly and putting this group at greater risk of HIV infection.

HIV prevalence: 0.1 per cent aged 15–49 in 2003 (World Bank)

Life expectancy: 82 years, 2004 (WHO 2006)

Fertility rate/Maternal mortality rate: 1.3 births per woman, 2004 (WHO 2006); maternal mortality eight per 100,000 live births (World Bank)

Birth rate/Death rate: 1.26. In 2007 forecasters said the population could fall by 20 per cent by 2050.

Child (under 5 years) mortality rate (per 1,000): 3.1 per 1,000 live births (World Bank)

Head of population per physician: 1.98 physicians per 1,000 people, 2002 (WHO 2006)

Welfare

Japan's social security system is divided into five parts: public assistance, welfare services, social insurance (medical care, pensions, child allowances, unemployment insurance and workers' accident compensation), public health, public service pensions and assistance for war victims.

There are some 26,000 social welfare institutions (excluding day nursery facilities), of which around 16,600 are public and 9,400 private.

Pensions

The falling birth rate and ageing population has increased the pressure on the pension scheme, which relies on contributions paid by those working, too many of whom have opted out.

The welfare ministry estimates that social security costs will increase fourfold by 2025, from ¥65 trillion (US$608 billion) in 1995 to ¥274 trillion (US$2.6 trillion) in 2025. To compound the problem, the stagnating economy in the 1990s resulted in a huge pension liabilities gap – underfunded pension liabilities are thought to total ¥419 trillion (US$3.9 trillion). To fill the gap, the government has raised corporate taxes and scaled back the benefits.

The pension reform bill was opposed by those who claimed that the underlying assumptions on which it was based were flawed. About 40 per cent of self-employed workers are said to have failed to pay contributions, many believe they would be unlikely to see any retirement benefits. Without a unified pension, which covers all workers, the funding remains problematic, although a sales tax has been proposed to add to the funding.

Family support

A social security reform bill was passed in June 2004, in which corporate tax will be increased gradually from 13.58 per cent in 2004 to 18.3 per cent in 2017, while benefits will be reduced, with payments at only 50 per cent of the average take-home pay. Opposition say increased tax will encourage employers to hire part-time workers who are covered by another scheme.

Main cities

Tokyo, on Honshu, (capital, estimated population 8.3 million (m) in 2004); Yokohama, (3.5m); Osaka (2.6m) Nagoya, (2.2m), Sapporo (1.9m), Kobe (1.5m), Ome (1.5m), Kyoto (1.5m), Fukuoka (1.4m), Kawasaka (1.3m), Hiroshima (1.1m), Sendai (1.0m), Kitakyushu (1.0m).

Languages spoken

It is hard to operate in Japan without some knowledge of Japanese or the services of an interpreter.

Pupils are taught English in school for seven years but this involves a formal grammatical knowledge rather than spoken English.

Official language/s

Japanese

Media

Other news agencies: Jiji Press (in Japanese): www.jiji.com

Kyodo News: http://home.kyodo.co.jp

Nikkei Net (business and stock market news): www.nni.nikkei.co.jp

Press

Around 80 per cent of the population read a daily newspaper, of which there are over 120 to choose from, with a combined publish run of around 70 million. In the largest markets, such as Tokyo, there can be three editions published per day. Nevertheless, the number of subscribers is declining and this trend is expected to continue.

Dailies: In Japanese (with English online editions) the major nationals include Yomiuri Shimbun (www.yomiuri.co.jp/dy), the leading newspaper with a circulation of around 10 million and is affiliated to Nippon TV, Asahi Shimbun (www.asahi.com/english) is affiliated to Asahi TV and Mainichi Shimbun (http://mdn.mainichi.jp) is affiliated to TBS. Other major newspapers are regionally based including Hokkaido Shimbun (www.hokkaido-np.co.jp), The Kyoto Shimbun (www.kyoto-np.co.jp) and Sankei Shimbun (www.sankei-kansai.com) from Osaka.

The Japan Times (www.japantimes.co.jp) is the only exclusively English language newspaper published, while Japan Today (www.japantoday.com) is a comprehensive online publication.

Weeklies: Some Japanese newspapers publish an English weekly edition. The Tokyo Journal (www.tokyo.to), Tokyo Weekender (www.weekender.co.jp) and Metropolis (www.metropolis.co.jp), are published for foreigners living in Japan, and in particular the capital.

There are weekend or Sunday editions of daily newspapers, including. Aera (www3.asahi.com) and Sekai (www.iwanami.co.jp).

Business: In Japanese, the Nikkan Kogyo Shimbun (www.nikkan.co.jp) and Nihon Keizai Shimbun (www.nikkei.co.jp) are leading financial newspapers from Tokyo of which The Nikkei Weekly (www.nikkei4946.com) is the English-language weekly edition of the latter.

All quality newspapers cover business and economic news.

A trade-press of 7–8,000 publications covers most aspects of business and the economy.

The Japan Economic Institute of America (www.jei.org) publishes articles and analysis of the business environment from a US perspective.

Periodicals: Japanese Anime and Manga magazines featuring illustrative, cartoon stories are very popular and cater for all ages.

Broadcasting

NHK (Nippon Hoso Kyokai) (www.nhk.or.jp) is only one of five national terrestrial broadcasters all of which compete strenuously for audiences. TBS (www.tbs.co.jp) provides national radio and television services.

Radio: NHK (www.nhk.or.jp) has a network of three stations, Radio 1 for news a talk radio, Radio 2 for cultural and educational programmes and FM Radio for classical music. It also operates an external network, Radio Japan; the First Services broadcasts in Japanese and English to Asia and the Second Service which broadcasts in 20 other languages throughout Asia. There are numerous commercial radio stations located regionally including Tokyo FM (www.tfm.co.jp) TBS Radio (www.tbs.co.jp/radio), FM Cocolo (www.cocolo.co.jp) from Osaka, Zip FM (http://zip-fm.co.jp) from Nagoya and FMii (www.fmii.co.jp) from Morioka. The American Forces Network (AFN) operates from US military bases, offering English-language programmes from Yokata Air Base (www.yokota.af.mil/afn). Digital radio services are available, provided by all major broadcasters.

Television: NHK (www.nhk.or.jp) is the only public TV service, funded largely by a licence fee. It is at the forefront in providing new technological transmissions and analogue signals will be completely replaced by digitals signals by 2011. Japan was the first country to introduce high definition (HD) TV services and NHK has a channel exclusively for these transmissions. Of the other major national TV networks all are commercial, including Nippon Television Network (NTV) (www.ntv.co.jp), the Tokyo Broadcasting System (TBS) (www.tbs.co.jp), Fuji Television (www.fujitv.co.jp) and TV Asahi (www.tv-asahi.co.jp).

Locally produced TV programmes dominate the schedules and foreign shows may have an influence on production although they do not get screened.

Millions of viewers subscribe to cable and satellite TV.

Advertising

The advertising industry is governed by self-regulations. All the traditional advertising outlets are available through the press, commercial radio, TV and cinemas as well as outdoor advertising sites. New technologies are an important source of new advertising revenue.

Economy

Finally, in 2007, the government can sigh with relief that the economy has recovered enough to report that the country's recession and deflation is finally behind it. The recovery began in 2002 but took several years to expand. A World Bank report published in December 2007 stated that almost 50 per cent of the World's total GDP was produced between the US, China, Japan, Germany and India.

The Bank of Japan increased its base lending rate of 0.0 per cent to 0.25 per cent in July 2006 – the first rise since 2000. Japanese businesses were borrowing more on capital investment in property, which in 2005 was the primary element that underpinned the 2.6 per cent GDP growth (a figure that was revised down to 1.9 per cent, by the Bank of Japan in late 2006). Exports also played an important role in the expansion but the bank wanted to avoid the havoc that over-investment in stocks and land last caused in the 1990s. Job prospects and capital investment grew in 2006 and corporate confidence had returned to both large and small firms.

While company profits rose by 15 per cent in 2006, domestic demand remained stubbornly low, wages did not increase significantly and households have had to spend more on living. Energy prices rose in line with the global price of oil. Consumer spending typically accounts for 57 per cent of GDP but until profits are translated into earnings this may remain static, or even fall.

Projected growth for 2006 is 3.0 per cent, and 2.0 per cent in 2007; inflation is expected to rise slowly as industry picks up. The IMF recommends that the government should implement fiscal consolidation and boost productivity through structural reforms for non-inflationary growth.

Japan has the second-largest economy in the world. While it is heavily industrialised, with a free market economy producing competitive international trade, it also has a highly protected agricultural sector with subsidies that produce high prices for the consumer. Only 15 per cent of Japan's land is arable, but it produces around 40 per cent of the country's agricultural needs.

Japan is extremely dependent on imported energy and minerals. Since the energy shock of the 1970s it has reduced its dependency on petroleum from 75 per cent to around 57 per cent currently.

After a decade of stagnation the economy has now been growing in its longest post-war expansion Nevertheless international observers are still cautious in overstating the recovery until it has shown more signs of a typical, fully engaged economy.

External trade

Japan is a member of the Asia-Pacific Economic Co-operation (Apec) which is a forum for discussing regional economic, investment and trade matters. It does not belong to any free trade zone but does have bilateral trade agreements with several countries worldwide.

Japan has the world's largest fishing fleet and account of around 15 per cent of the global catch; the Japanese consume more seafood than any other nation. Japan is the second largest producer of paper (after the US).

The open market economy is predicated on external trade, providing around 25 per cent of GDP, allowing purchase of the mass of raw materials that Japan does not possess; the majority of exports are finishes goods.

Imports

Principal imports are fuels, industrial raw materials, machinery and equipment, textiles, foodstuffs – rice, grains, fish products, meat products, chemicals and non-ferrous ores and ash.

Main sources: China (20.5 per cent total, 2006), US (11.8 per cent), Saudi Arabia (6.4 per cent).

Exports

Principal exports are vehicles and transport equipment, semiconductors, electronic and electrical machinery, optical and measuring equipment.

Main destinations: US (22.5 per cent total, 2006), China (14.3 per cent), South Korea (7.8 per cent).

Agriculture

Farming

The agricultural sector accounts for approximately 1.5 per cent of GDP and employs around 7 per cent of the workforce (down from 50 per cent at the end of the Second World War). Most people in farm employment supplement their income with non-farm employment.

Only about 15 per cent of the land area is available for agriculture and stock-rearing and this is constantly in demand for residential use. Agriculture is highly intensive, making considerable use of technology and capital investment.

Wet cultivation of rice is the main activity (virtually self-sufficient), with a trend toward production of beef, citrus fruits and tobacco. Wheat, barley, soya beans, potatoes, sweet potatoes, vegetables, fruit, tea and silkworms are also produced.

The price of rice has declined and it is difficult for the paddy farmers to make a profit. In addition, consumers' tastes have changed and they are eating more potatoes, bread, pasta and noodles instead of rice.

Japanese farming is heavily protected by government subsidies and high import tariffs, despite the fact that Japan is dependent on food imports. The political influence of farmers has frequently stalled free trade negotiations with other countries which are deemed as competitors to the Japanese farming sector.

Crop production in 2005 included: 12,051,450 tonnes (t) cereals in total,

10,989,000t rice, 2,900,000t potatoes, 1,050,000t sweet potatoes, 4,374,800t roots and tubers, 1,370,000t citrus fruit, 2,200,000t cabbages, 224,300t grapes, 760,000t tomatoes, 47,647t oilcrops, 49,000t tobacco, 1,350,000t sugar cane, 4,200,000t sugar beets, 230,000t soya beans, 100,000t tea, 870,000t apples, 3,623,400t fruit in total, 11,593,600t vegetables in total. Livestock production included: 3,000,185t meat in total, 500,000t beef, 1,250,000t pig meat, 1,240,015t poultry, 2,465,000t eggs, 8,255,000t milk, *3,300t honey, 7,000t horsemeat, 31,500t cattle hides, 600t cocoons, silk.
* estimate

Fishing
Japan is one of the world's great fishing nations and there are some 3,000 fishing ports dotted around its coasts. Its methods of driftnet fishing, which drags up sea fauna indiscriminately from the ocean, have been criticised throughout the world. The establishment of 200-mile economic zones at sea by a number of countries has meant that Japan has had to go further afield for fishing grounds: half the catch now comes from outside Japanese waters and Japanese boats have increasingly been accused of predatory practices.
Fishing contributes substantially to domestic food supply and export earnings. Japanese fishermen catch pollack, pilchards, cod, salmon, mackerel and other fish throughout the north and central Pacific, and are second only to the former USSR in whaling. The total annual marine catch can be up to seven million tonnes per year, with a further 5 per cent of demand imported. Aquaculture is well developed and there are inshore fisheries for squid, clams, crustaceans, shallow-water fish and dolphins.
Japan remains a whaling nation and has been criticised for using overseas aid to manipulate countries into voting in favour of maintaining whaling in international waters. The typical import value of aquatic mammals amount to over US$176 million yearly, while total fish imports average over US$2 billion.
The Japanese whaling fleet set sail in November 2007, with a quota to kill up to 1,000 whales. There was considerable international condemnation, especially from the US, Australia and New Zealand, of the inclusion of humpback and fin whales in the numbers to be killed. There had been a moratorium on commercial whaling since 1986, and on the killing of humpback whales 1963. The Japanese maintain that they are whaling in the name scientific research. By April 2008, the fleet had failed to reach its quota due to interference by anti-whaling activists, who took direct action to disrupt whaling.
In 2004, the total marine fish catch was 3,093,405 tonnes and the total crustacean catch was 143,287 tonnes.

Forestry
Japan is heavily forested, with forests covering around 66 per cent of the total land area. The variation in climate across Japan means that the country enjoys a diverse range of forests. Plantations account for around 44 per cent of total forested area. About 42 per cent of forests are in public ownership.
Japan is a major consumer of wood and paper products. Despite being heavily forested, Japan is one of the world's largest importers of forest products and by far the largest importer of tropical logs and wood products. The production costs involved in the extraction of Japanese wood are high, so the country is forced to rely on imports. Exports of forest materials typically amount to around US$950 million, while imports amount to over US$10 billion.
Production in 2004 included: 15,729,419 cubic metres (cum) roundwood, 15,615,000cum industrial roundwood, 13,603,000cum sawnwood, 12,015,000cum sawlogs and veneers, 3,600,000cum pulpwood, 5,288,000cum wood-based panels, 114,419cum woodfuel; 37,000 tonnes (t) charcoal, 29,253,000t paper and paperboard, including 3,695,000t newsprint, 9,734,000t printing and writing paper, 10,654,000t paper pulp, 14,841,000t recovered paper.

Industry and manufacturing

The industrial sector contributes approximately 40 per cent of GDP. Manufacturing employs nearly 24 per cent of the workforce, compared to 16 per cent in the US and an average of 18 per cent in OECD countries. In the past, industry has benefited from innovative technology and, in some less competitive sectors such as chemicals, aircraft and software, from considerable financial backing from the government. Japan has also traditionally led the world in automated production processes, which has helped to reduce the industrial workforce and redeploy workers into the tertiary sector.
Factory production shrank by 2 per cent in January 2008, from a 1.6 per cent growth in December 2007. The recession in the US and a slower demand for electronics in Asia and Europe were blamed for the fall. Japan's export driven economy could suffer further from falling global demand, which may result in a fall in wage growth and less domestic consumption.
One of the main long-term problems in Japanese industry is its productivity. The Nikkei-300 non-financial companies have typically had a return on equity of just 4 per cent, compared to 20 per cent in the US. Since the mid-1990s, Japanese industry has failed to produce a positive spread between cost of capital and return on capital.
Part of the root cause of inefficiency is the prevailing culture. The Japanese are admired for their discipline and patience, but these qualities have not resulted in increased productivity; and whereas Japanese product innovation and development is excellent, sales and marketing have lagged behind. In uncompetitive, protected sectors, firms have paced their development to keep step with the slowest.
Although the government, as well as companies themselves, is coming round to seeing the benefit of alliances with foreign firms in order to compete on the international stage, the process is slow. Moreover, communication issues surrounding Japan's complex corporate culture can act as something of a barrier to merger and acquisition activities between Japanese and foreign firms.
Nevertheless, as the cross-holding structure typical of Japan's famous keiretsu groups (business networks which own stakes in one another as a means of mutual security) unravels, Japanese firms in general are coming under pressure to prioritise profits over their traditional relationships. Firms kept alive by their banks after they have lost all hope of financial viability – often termed the 'zombies' by Asian business journalists – will need to be closed or merged in order to restore investor confidence in the industrial sector.

Tourism

Taiwan and Korea are the main sources of tourists to the country. Tourist arrivals in 2004 numbered 5,702,400. The tourism sector was worth 3.5 per cent of GDP in 2005, providing 2,737,000 jobs and involving 4.3 per cent of the workforce.

Mining

Mining accounts for 0.5 per cent of GDP and 1 per cent of total employment. There are few exploitable mineral resources. Molybdenum, manganese, zinc, copper and iron are mined on a small scale. Japan is self-sufficient in sulphur and limestone.

Hydrocarbons

Japan has the thid highest oil consumption in the world and relies heavily on imports, particularly from the Middle East. In 2005 talks were held with Russia on arrangements to transport oil via a new pipeline, from Eastern Siberia to the Pacific Ocean and Japan. The first stage of construction is due to be completed in 2008 with no timetable yet agreed for the second and final phase. There is some dispute over the exact routing of the pipeline, with Japan aggrieved at Chinese

involvement. Capacity is expected to reach 1.6 million bpd.
Japan and China are also locked in talks about exploration of gas fields in the East China Sea. This could boost reserves and contribute to sourcing Japan's annual gas consumption of 72.2 billion cubic metres.
In 2002 Japan closed its coal mines. It is a large coal importer, using the fuel for 20 per cent of its energy needs. Japan produced a mere 0.7 million tonnes oil equivalent in 2004, while it used 120.8 million tonnes. In 2004, it had only 359 million tonnes of proven coal reserves.

Energy
Japan is reliant on imported energy and is among the top five biggest energy users in the world. Japan has a total generating capacity of around 230GW. Around 60 per cent of total generation is produced by thermal plants, 30 per cent by nuclear reactors, 8 per cent by hydroelectric dams and the rest from geothermal, solar and wind power. Japan is already the third largest nuclear consumer and is set to increase its reliance on nuclear energy even further. The government plans to build up to 12 additional nuclear reactors by 2010 to add to the current total of 52. There are plans to expand nuclear power generation by 30 per cent.
Liquefied natural gas (LNG) is also likely to become an important source of energy for electricity generation in the long-term.
Japan's electricity prices are among the highest in the world, but prices are falling due to cuts in capital investment. The country is served by 10 vertically integrated utility companies which have monopolies over different regions; Japan has no national grid. The regional organisation of grids is an impediment due to the limited number of inter-connections. In 2005 the utilities market was deregularised and made more efficient, leading to significant price cuts.
The Japanese government is committed to energy efficiency.

Financial markets
Stock exchange
The Tokyo Stock Exchange's (TSE). The Nikkei index rose by 23 per cent over 2005, while the topix (Tokyo Stock Price Index) rose by 30 per cent.

Banking and insurance
In the 1990s the bubble burst in the Japanese economy and banks were the major casualties. They became burdened with huge amounts of non-performing loans (NPL) and bad debt.
In efforts to bounce back and also to prevent future risk, a series of mergers and takeovers took place in the banking sector. The fifteen banks that had existed during the financial crash were reduced to four. The biggest bank, Mizuho Bank, was created when Dai-Ichi Kangyo Bank, Fuji Bank and the Industrial Bank of Japan merged. The other three are: Mitsubishi Tokyo Financial Group, Sumitomo Mitsui Banking and the United Financial of Japan Group (UFG). However, the biggest 'bank' in the world is the Japanese post office, which is in the process of privatisation.
The Bank of Japan (BoJ) was granted independence from the government in 1998. However, in 2005 the government applied acute pressure to the BoJ to ensure that it did not raise interest rates above zero before economic growth was proven to be steady. The finance ministry reacted to the BoJ's reluctance by threatening to rescind its independence. The government's distrust of the Bank's monetary policy stems from 2000 when the Bank prematurely raised interest rates against the will of domestic finance officials and the IMF.
Central bank
Bank of Japan.
Main financial centre
Tokyo, Osaka and Nagoya.

Time
GMT plus nine hours

Geography
Japan lies off the north-east coast of Asia and consists of four main islands – Hokkaido, Honshu, Shikoku and Kyushu – and thousands of smaller islands running in an arc from north (latitude 45 33'N) to south (latitude 24 25'N). Japan is mainly mountainous with only 29 per cent of the national land area consisting of plains and basins. It has about 10 per cent of the world's active volcanoes and its highest mountain, Mount Fuji (3,776 metres), is a dormant volcano. Japan occupies less than 0.3 per cent of the earth's total land area: it is only 4 per cent of the size of the United States and one and a half times bigger than the United Kingdom.

Climate
The general climate is temperate, except for part of Hokkaido in the north and some of the southernmost islands. Spring is March–May, with average temperatures of 6 degrees Celsius (C) (minimum) and 21 degrees C (maximum). The rainy season is mid-June–mid-July. Summer is June–August, with temperatures between 20 degrees C and 28 degrees C. Autumn is September–November, with temperatures ranging from 10 degrees C to 24 degrees C. Rainfall is heaviest June and August–September. Winter is December–February, with temperatures from minus 5.1 degrees C to 16 degrees C.
Annual rainfall is 1,000–2,500mm. South and central Japan can be subject to typhoons in late summer and early autumn.

Dress codes
In modern Japan, dark business suits and Western dress are the normal rule.
Traditional Japanese dress consisted of kimonos for both men and women. On for formal occasions women often wear kimonos, while men usually wear morning dress, but occasionally also wear kimonos for weddings etc.

Entry requirements
Passports
Required by all. Passports must be valid for the duration of stay.
Visa
No visa requirements for citizens of most of Europe, the Americas, Australasia and some Asian countries, visiting for up to 90 days. For a full list, and application form, plus further information for those citizens not included on the list of visa-free travel, see www.mofa.go.jp/j_info/visit/visa/index.html.
Business travel is allowed for those enjoying visa-free travel for the minimum period. Those who do not must provide business letters, itinerary and invitations from Japanese hosts.
Foreigners arriving in Japan (both visitors and residents) are fingerprinted and photographed. The move was introduced in November 2007 as an anti-terrorist measure.
Currency advice/regulations
There are no restrictions on currency import or export. However, amounts in excess of ¥1 million (or equivalent) must be declared. All money exchanged must be through authorised banks and money changers. The money exchange counter at Narita airport is open from 0900–2300.
Travellers cheques are accepted in larger bank branches, hotels and duty-free shops. To avoid extra exchange fee, US dollars and Japanese yen are best.
Customs
Personal effects duty-free. Visitors may purchase souvenir items (pearls, cameras, transistor radios) free of sales tax at designated shops, but they must be taken out of the country within six months.
Prohibited imports
Firearms, ammunition, illegal drugs, pornography including films. Counterfeit or altered currencies. Animal, plant/soil and food products.

Health (for visitors)
There are no mandatory precautions. Japan has extensive health facilities with high standards, although medical services are expensive and insurance is essential.

The International Association of Medical Assistance to Travellers provide English speaking doctors.

Advisable precautions
Inoculations may be useful for the occasional occurrence of typhoid hepatitis A and C and TB.

Hotels
Hotels should be booked well in advance. Service charges and taxes are added to the bill, and tipping is not customary. In addition to Western-style hotels, there are traditional Japanese-style inns (ryokan) in Tokyo and Osaka.

Credit cards
International credit and charge cards are widely accepted. ATMs, may not accept foreign cards, although Citbank ATMs do and are open 24 hours.

Public holidays (national)
Fixed dates
31 Dec–3 Jan (New Year holidays), 11 Feb (Foundation Day), 29 Apr (Greenery Day), 3–5 May (Constitution Day/Citizens' Day of Rest/Children's Day), 20 Jul (Marine Day), 15 Sep (Respect for the Aged Day), 23 Sep (Autumnal Equinox), 3 Nov (Culture Day), 23 Nov (Labour Thanksgiving Day), 23 Dec (Emperor's Birthday).

With the exception of New Year's Day, if a holiday falls on a Sunday, the following day is treated as a holiday instead. When there is a single day between two national holidays, it is also taken as a holiday.

Avoid visits during Golden Week (Apr–May) and the Obon festive season (late Jul–third week in Aug), when everywhere is very crowded.

Variable dates
Coming of Age Day (Seijin-no-hi) (Jan), Vernal Equinox (Shunbun-no-hi) (Mar), Physical Fitness Day (Oct).

Working hours
Banking
Mon–Fri: 0900–1500.

Business
Mon–Fri: 0900–1700; Sat: 0900–1200 (most companies close on Saturdays).

Government
Mon–Fri: 1000–1700; Sat: 1000–1200.

Shops
1000–1900 (many closed on Wed or Thu).

Telecommunications
Mobile/cell phones
3G services are available in most cities.l

Electricity supply
100V AC, 60 cycles in west Japan (Osaka) and 100V AC, 50 cycles in east Japan (Tokyo), with flat two-pin plug fittings.

Weights and measures
Metric system

Social customs/useful tips
The Japanese are a polite and reserved people. They do not expect overseas visitors to understand or adopt their customs – but they do value courtesy and friendliness and efforts to follow their customs are appreciated. The suffix san is added to the surname (ie Suzuki-san instead of Mr Suzuki) in polite conversation.

In most Japanese homes, in Japanese-style inns and frequently in traditional restaurants, it is taboo to wear outdoor shoes; instead slippers are provided. It is considered bad etiquette to step on the door sill or the borders of the tatami mats.

Japan has become thoroughly Westernised on the surface but the people still celebrate numerous traditional festivals. These range from the informal – cherry blossom viewing in the spring and kite flying – to formal festivals such as celebrating a person's coming of age.

The Japanese insist on punctuality and punctiliousness in business behaviour. It is essential to carry meishi or name cards (preferably with your name in Japanese on the reverse). When receiving name cards at formal meetings, the correct procedure is to study them carefully and then place them in front of you on the table. Seating arrangements are particularly important in Japan. The place of honour is generally that furthest from the door.

Gift giving is a pleasant Japanese custom and for Japanese businessmen the exchange of gifts at New Year is very important. Ideally, gifts should consist of something personal, and be given, unopened, at the start of meetings. Whisky is now so widely sold and discounted in Japan that it is not a particularly attractive gift. When receiving gifts the Japanese practice is to treat them as objects of great reverence, but never to open them in front of the donor.

Late night business entertainment is common, but being invited to a Japanese home is rare. Restaurants are the usual venue for private social entertaining. Drinking has its own rituals: it is bad manners for a visitor to pour a drink for himself. It is impolite to blow your nose in public. Kissing in public, standing too close to someone while talking and eating while walking down the street are also considered impolite. Do not point with your index finger – use the whole hand, palm turned upwards, in a flowing movement.

Security
Japanese cities are safe despite recent increases in crime. Burglaries are uncommon. Late night travel is usually perfectly safe, even for unaccompanied women, though drunks are to be avoided.

Getting there
Air

National airline: Japan Airlines (JAL); Japan Air System (JAS); All Nippon Airways (ANA)

International airport/s: Tokyo International, Narita (NRT), 60km east of Tokyo, with duty-free shops, bank/bureau de change (0900–2300), car hire, restaurants and tourist information centres with multilingual staff. There is a free shuttle bus connecting the two terminals.

Osaka Kansai International (KIX), 50km south-west of city; duty-free shops, car hire, banks/bureaux de change, tourist information (0900–2100) and bar/restaurant. Travel time by Nankai Express to Nama station in central Osaka 29 minutes. Tickets for trains, which connect with the Shinkansen Bullet train network, must be pre-booked.

Fukuoka, Itazuke (FUK), 10km from city; Nagoya, Komaki (NGO), 18km from city; Kagoshima (KOJ), 6km from city; Kumamoto (KMJ), 8km from city; Okinawa (OKA) 3km from Naha; Osaka International (OSA); Kobe; Kyoto.

Limousine bus services link Kansai International Airport with Osaka city centre and various other points including Kobe, Hikone and Nara.

Other airport/s: Haneda (HND), the former international airport, serves largely as a domestic airport, 19km south of Tokyo. China Airlines flights from Taipei, Taiwan, arrive here.

Airport tax: Tokyo Narita International Airport levies a tax of ¥2,040, which is usually included in the ticket price.

Getting about
National transport

Air: Most domestic flights from Tokyo to Osaka and other Japanese cities are from Haneda, 19km from Tokyo. Extensive air services provided by a number of local airlines link all main cities and provincial towns. Tickets can be purchased by automatic machines at Tokyo and Osaka International Airports' domestic departure counters.

Road: Road transport is the main form of domestic access. The network consists of 1.2 million km of road. There are good motorways linking Tokyo, Osaka, Kobe, Hiroshima, Yamaguchi, Shimonoseki, Moji, Fukuoka, Kumamoto and Morioka. Tolls are payable on certain roads.

Long-distance travel by road is not recommended (travel time from Tokyo to Nagasaki by car is 18 hours, by train 9 hours and by plane less than 2 hours), road signs are in Japanese and roads are frequently very crowded outside main cities.

Buses: An extensive network of frequent coach services link main centres via express motorways, but visitors are advised against coach travel in view of language difficulties and the complexity and number of routes available.

Rail: Japan Railways run national routes from the terminal located beneath the airport.

It is easy to travel by rail to all regions. Express and limited express trains are best for intercity travel with very frequent services run on the main routes. Shinkansen, the Bullet Trains, are the fastest, with compartments for wheelchair passengers, diners and buffet facilities. Supplements are payable on the three classes of express train and in green (first-class) cars of principal trains, for which reservations must be made well in advance; two pieces of ordinary luggage may be carried free, but there are restrictions on size and weight. Other types of train include Tokkyu (Limited Express), Kyuko (Express), Kaisoku (Rapid Train) and Futsu (Local Train). For short-distance trains, tickets can only be bought at vending machines outside train stations.

Long-distance one-way tickets generally do not permit stopovers and ticket refunds are not made after the time of the planned journey. Foreign visitors can make considerable savings by buying a Japan Rail exchange voucher, which is sold only outside Japan.

All Japan Railways (JR) stations display station names in both Japanese and Roman letters. The station's name is at the top centre of the signboard, in large letters; the names of the previous station and the next station are at the bottom of the signboard, in smaller letters.

Water: Jetfoil services to Kobe. There is also a jetfoil from Kansai International Airport to Osaka Port, with a journey time of around 40 minutes.

City transport

Taxis: Metered taxis can be easily hired in large cities at hotel entrances or by flagging them down in the street, but do not try to open or close the driver-controlled passenger door. Tipping is not required.

Journey times: from Narita International Airport to Tokyo city centre around 90 minutes; from Kansai International Airport to Osaka city centre about 60 minutes.

There is a surcharge after 2200 and an additional time charge is levied for traffic jams. Taxis are five times more expensive than trains.

Few taxi drivers understand foreign languages or read Roman lettering, so it is advisable to have your destination, including the name of a nearby landmark, written down in Japanese, along with the telephone number if possible. Hotels can often help with this. A map showing the location of the destination is also helpful.

Buses, trams & metro: Limousine buses depart several times an hour from Narita airport to city-centre hotels; journey time is about two hours. There is also a bus to the Tokyo City Air Terminal (TCAT). Tickets for all services can be bought in the terminals.

Buses can be confusing and are best used with someone who knows the system.

Efficient underground railway services operate in Tokyo, Yokohama, Osaka, Kyoto, Kobe, Nagoya, Sapporo and Fukuoka, with station names displayed in Roman as well as Japanese lettering.

Trains: JR and Keisei railway lines provide frequent services from Narita airport to the city centre, journey time 60—90 minutes.

Car hire

An international driving licence is required. Driving is on the left. Chauffeur-driven cars are often recommended for visitors without command of Japanese and knowledge of the area, as traffic and navigation can be difficult. Symbolic road signs have the expected international meanings, but few signs are written in the Roman alphabet. A red triangle with white script means 'stop', while a white triangle with a red border and blue script means 'proceed slowly'.

BUSINESS DIRECTORY

The addresses listed below are a selection only. While World of Information makes every endeavour to check these addresses, we cannot guarantee that changes have not been made, especially to telephone numbers and area codes. We would welcome any corrections.

Telephone area codes

The international direct dialling (IDD) code for Japan is +81, followed by area code and subscriber's number:

Fukuoka	92	Nagoya	52
Hiroshima	82	Okayama	862
Kawasaki	44	Osaka	66
Kobe	78	Sapparo	11
Kyoto	75	Tokyo	3
Nagasaki	958	Yokohama	45

Useful telephone numbers

Emergency
Police: 110.
Ambulance/Fire: 119
Overseas calls
Tokyo to south-east Asia: 3211-4211.
Tokyo operator: 0051.
Tokyo telegraph office: 3211-5588.
Nagoya telegraph office: 203-3311.
Osaka telegraph office: 228-2151.

Chambers of Commerce

American Chamber of Commerce in Japan, Masonic 39 MT Building, 2-4-5 Azabudai, Minato-ku, Tokyo 106-0041 (tel: 3433-5381; fax: 3433-8454; e-mail: info@accj.or.jp).

British Chamber of Commerce in Japan, Kenkyusha Eigo Centre Building, 1-2, Kagurazaka, Shinjuku-ku, Tokyo 162-0825 (tel: 3267-1901; fax: 3267-1903; e-mail: info@bccjapan.com).

Fukuoka Chamber of Commerce and Industry, 2-9-28 Hakata-ekimae, Hakata-ku, Fukuoka 812-8505 (tel: 441-1110; fax: 474-3200; e-mail: fksomu@fukunet.or.jp).

Kobe Chamber of Commerce and Industry, 6-1 Minato-jima Naka-machi, Chuo-ku, Kobe 650-8543 (tel: 303-5801; fax: 303-2312; e-mail: info@kcci-iic.ne.jp).

Nagoya Chamber of Commerce and Industry, 2-10-19 Sakae, Naka-ku, Nagoya (tel: 223-5611; fax: 231-6768; e-mail: info@nagoya-cci.or.jp).

Yokohama Chamber of Commerce and Industry, 2 Yamashita-cho, Naka-ku, Yokohama 231-8524 (tel: 671-7400; fax: 671-7410; e-mail: info@yokohama-cci.or.jp).

Banking

Mitsubishi Tokyo Financial Group, 1-3-2 Nihonbashi-Hongkucho, Chuo-ku, Tokyo (tel: 3245-1111; fax: 3246-1708); 7-1 Marunouchi 2-chome, Chiyoda-ku, Tokyo 100 (tel: 3240-1111; fax: 3211-6645).

Mizuho Bank, 1-1-5 Uchisaiwaicho, Chiyoda-ku, Tokyo 100 (tel: 3596-111).

Sumitomo Mitsui Banking Corporation, 1-2 Yurakucho, 1-chome, Chiyoda-ku, Tokyo 100-0006 (tel: 2501-1111).

Central bank

Bank of Japan (Nippon Ginko), 2-1-1 Nihonbashi-Hongokucho, Chuo-ku, Tokyo 103 (tel: 3279-1111; fax: 3277-1473).

Travel information

Japan Airlines (JAL), Tokyo Building, Marunouchi 2-7-3, Chiyoda-ku, Tokyo 100 (tel: 3284-2610; fax: 3284-2659; internet site: http://www.spin.ad.jp/jal/home-e.html).

Japan Automobile Federation, Shiba-Koen, 3-5-8 Minato-ku, Tokyo 105 (tel: 3436-2811).

Tourist Information Centre, 1-6-6 Yurakucho 1-chome, Chiyoda-Ku, Tokyo 100 (tel: 3502-1461); Kyoto Tower Building, Higashi-Shiokojicho, Shimogyo-ku, Kyoto 600 (tel: 371-5649).

Japan Travel Phone is a nationwide telephone service for English-language assistance and travel information. Available from 0900–1700 daily, the service is toll-free from outside Tokyo or Kyoto: information on eastern Japan: 0088-222-800 (or 0120-222-800); information on western Japan: 0088-22-4800 (or 0120-444-800). Tokyo: 3503-4400. Kyoto: 371-5649. Tokyo; French-language assistance: 3503-2926.

Tokyo: Japan Railways (JR) English-language information service, (Mon–Fri, except holidays) 1000–1800; reservations cannot be accepted by telephone service: 3423-0111. (Narita Express has a free phone connection to this service).

National tourist organisation offices

Japan National Tourist Organisation, 2-10-1 Yuraku-cho, Chiyodaku, Tokyo (tel: 3201-3331; fax: 3201-3347; internet: www.jnto.go.jp).

Ministries

Ministry of Agriculture, Forestry and Fisheries, 1-2-1 Kasumigaseki, Chiyoda-ku, Tokyo 100-8950 (tel: 3502-8111; fax: 3592-7697; e-mail: white56@maff.go.jp).

Ministry of Education, Culture, Sports, Science and Technology, 3-2-2 Kasumigaseki, Chiyoda-ku, Tokyo 100-8959 (tel: 3581-4211; fax: 3595-2017).

Ministry of the Environment, 1-2-2 Kasumigaseki, Chiyoda-ku, Tokyo 100-8975 (tel: 3581-3351; e-mail: MOE@eanet.go.jp).

Ministry of Foreign Affairs, 2-2-1, Kasumigaseki, Chiyoda-ku, Tokyo 100-8919 (tel: 3580-3311; fax: 3581-2667; e-mail: webmaster@mofa.go.jp).

Ministry of Health, Labour and Welfare, 1-2-2 Kasumigaseki, Chiyoda-ku, Tokyo 100-8916 (tel: 5253-1111; fax: 3501-2532).

Ministry of Justice, 1-1-1 Kasumigaseki, Chiyoda-ku, Tokyo 100-8977 (tel: 3580-4111; fax: 3592-7011; e-mail: webmaster@moj.go.jp).

Ministry of Land, Infrastructure and Transport, 2-1-3 Kasumigaseki, Chiyoda-ku, Tokyo 100-8918 (tel: 5253-8111; fax: 3580-7982; e-mail: webmaster@mlit.go.jp).

Ministry of Public Management, Home Affairs, Posts and Telecommunications, 2-1-2 Kasumigaseki, Chiyoda-ku, Tokyo 100-8926 (tel: 5253-5111; fax: 3504-0265; e-mail: feedback@mpt.go.jp).

Defence Agency, 5-1 Ichigaya, Honmura-cho, Shinjuku-ku, Tokyo 162-8801 (tel: 3268-3111; e-mail: info@jda.go.jp).

National Public Safety Commission, 2-1-2 Kasumigaseki, Chiyoda-ku, Tokyo 100-8974 (tel: 3581-0141).

Prime Minister's Office, 1-6-1, Nagata-cho, Chiyoda-ku, Tokyo 100-8914 (tel: 3581-2361; fax: 3593-1784).

Other useful addresses

Asian Development Bank, Japanese Representative Office, Second Floor, Yamato Seimei Building, 1-7 Uchisaiwaicho 1-Chome, Chiyoda-ku, Tokyo 100 (tel: 3504-3160; fax: 3504-3165; E-mail: adbjro@mail.asiandevbank.org).

Association for the Promotion of International Trade, Nihon Building, 6-2 Otemachi 2-chome, Chiyoda-ku, Tokyo (tel: 3245-1561).

British Embassy, No 1 Ichiban-cho, Chiyoda-ku, Tokyo 102 (tel: 3265-6340; fax: 5275-0346).

Council of All-Japan Exporters' Association, Kikai Shinko Kaikan Building, 5-8 Shibakaen 3-chome, Minato-ku, Tokyo.

Defence Agency, 9-7-45 Akasaka, Minato-ku, Tokyo 107-0052 (tel: 3408-5211; fax: 3408-6480).

Economic Planning Agency, 3-1-1 Kasumigaseki, Chiyoda-ku, Tokyo 100-0013 (tel: 3581-0261; fax: 3581-0838).

Environment Agency, 1-2-2 Kasumigaseki, Chiyoda-ku, Tokyo 100-0013 (tel: 3581-3351; fax: 3502-0308).

Fair Trade Commission, 2-2-1 Kasumigaseki, Chiyoda-ku, Tokyo 100-0013 (tel: 3581-5471; fax: 3581-1963).

Federation of Economic Organisations (Keidanren), 9-4 Othe-machi 1-chome, Chiyoda-ku 100, Tokyo (tel: 3279-1411; fax: 5255-6250).

Hokkaido Development Agency, 3-1-1 Kasumigaseki, Chiyoda-ku, Tokyo 100-8922 (tel: 3581-9111; fax: 3581-1208; e-mail: info1@had.go.jp).

House of Councillors, 1-7-1 Nagata-cho, Chiyoda-ku, Tokyo 100-0014 (tel: 3581-3111; fax: 3581-2900).

House of Representitives, 1-7-1 Nagata-cho, Chiyoda-ku, Tokyo 100-0014 (tel: 3581-5111; fax: 3581-2900).

Imperial Household Agency, 1-1 Chiyoda, Chiyoda-ku, Tokyo 100-0001 (tel: 3213-1111; fax: 3282-1407).

Japan Commercial Arbitration Association, Tosho Building, 2-2 Marunouchi 3-chome, Chiyoda-ku, Tokyo (tel: 3214-0641).

Japan Committee for Economic Development, Kogo Club Building 4-6 Marunouchi 1-chome, Chiyoda-ku, Tokyo (tel: 3211-1271).

Japan External Trade Organisation (JETRO), 2-5 Toranomon 2-chome, Minato-ku 105, Tokyo (tel: 3582-5511).

Japan Federation of Economic Organisations (Keidanren), 9-4 Otemachi 1-chome, Chiyoda-ku, Tokyo (tel: 3279-1411).

Japan Federation of Importers' Organisation, Nihombashi Daiwa Building, 1-6-1 Nihombashi Hon-Cho, Chuo-ku, Tokyo (tel: 3270-2020).

Japan Federation of Smaller Enterprise Organisation, 8-4 Nihonbashi Kayaba-cho 2-chome, Chuo-ku 103, Tokyo (tel: 3669-6862; fax: 3668-2957).

Japan Foreign Trade Council, World Trade Centre Building, 4-1 Hamamatsu-cho 2-chome, Minato-ku 105, Tokyo (tel: 3435-5952; fax: 3435-5979).

Japan Guide Association (interpreter and translation services), Shin Kokusai Building, 4-1 Marunouchi 3-chome, Chiyoda-ku, Tokyo (tel: 213-2706).

Japan International Co-operation System, 5th Floor, Shinjuku Sanshin Bldg, 4-9 Yoyogi 2-chome, Shibuya-ku, Tokyo 151 (tel: 5981-5988; fax: 5981-5994).

Japan Productivity Centre, 1-1 Shibuya 3-chome, Shibuya-ku 150, Tokyo (tel: 3409-1111; fax: 3409-4128).

Japan Securities Dealers Association, 5-8 Nihombashi Kayabacho 1-chome, Chuo-ku, Tokyo (tel: 3667-8459; fax: 3666-8009).

Japanese Embassy (USA), 2520 Massachusetts Avenue, NW, Washington DC 20008 (tel: (+1-202) 238-6700; fax: (+1-202) 328-2187).

Kansai Economic Federation, Nakanoshima Centre Bldg, 2-27 Nakanoshima 6-chome, Kita-ku, Osaka 530 (tel: 253-2351; 253-1678).

Management and Co-ordination Agency, 3-1-1 Kasumigaseki Chiyoda-ku, Tokyo 100-0013 (tel: 3581-6361; fax: 3593-1620).

Okinawa Development Agency, 1-6-1 Nagata-cho, Chiyoda-ku, Tokyo 100-0014 (tel: 3581-2361; fax: 3581-4783).

Science and Technology Agency, 2-2-1 Kasumigaseki, Chiyoda-ku, Tokyo 100-8966 (tel: 3581-5271; fax: 3593-1371; e-mail: www@sta.go.jp).

Statistics Bureau & Statistics Centre Management & Coordination Agency, 19-1

Wakamatsu-cho, Shinjuku-ku, Tokyo 162 (tel: 3202-1111; fax: 5273-1180).

Supreme Court, 4-2 Hayabusa-cho, Chiyoda-ku, Tokyo 102-0092 (tel: 3264-8111; fax: 3221-8975).

Tokyo International Trade Fair Commission, 7-24 Harumi 4-chome, Chuo-ku, Tokyo 103 (tel: 3666-0141, 3531-3371; fax: 3663-0625).

Tokyo Stock Exchange, 2-1 Nihombashi Kabutocho 1-chome, Chuo-ku, Tokyo (tel: 3666-0141; fax: 3663-0625, 3666-0141; internet site: http://www.tse.or.jp).

West Japan Railway Company, 4-24 Shibata 2-chome, Kita-ku, Osaka 530-8341 (tel: 375-8981; fax: 375-8919).

World Trade Centre of Japan, 4-1 2-chome Hamamatsu-cho, Minato-ku, Tokyo (tel: 3435-5651).

Other news agencies: Jiji Press (in Japanese): www.jiji.com

Kyodo News: http://home.kyodo.co.jp

Nikkei Net (business and stock market news): www.nni.nikkei.co.jp

Internet sites

Asahi Shimbun: http://www.adv.asahi.com/english

Japan access: http://www.keidanren.or.jp/A2J/index.html

Japan Company Record: http://www.japancompanyrecord.com/

Japan Hotel Association: http://www.j-hotel.or.jp

Japan Information Network: http://jin.jcic.or.jp

Japan Statistics: http://www.stat.go.jp/1.htm

JETRO Homepage (Japanese Trade Promotion): http://www.jetro.go.jp

Sanwa Bank: http://www.sanwabank.co.jp

Jordan

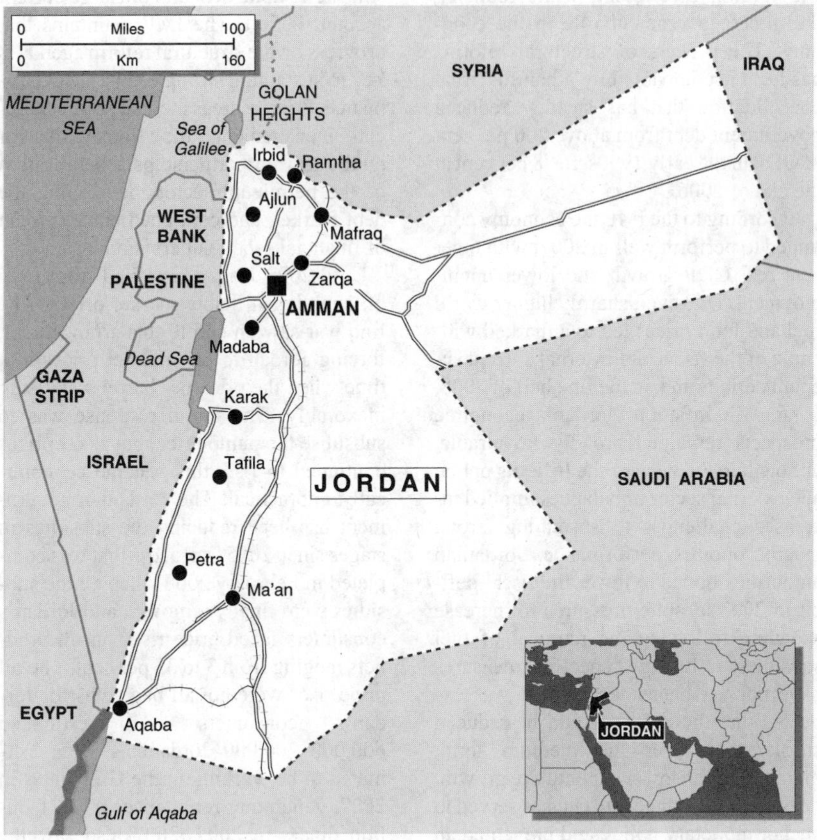

Jordan was once described as a 'dynastic accident' rather than a country. In many ways its survival as a body politic has been more 'miraculous' than that of Israel. That it has survived is very much the legacy of its former King Hussein, father of today's ruler, King Abdullah. What King Hussein sought was the survival of his Hashemite dynasty rather than simply the survival of Jordan as a state. Surrounded by zealots, Jordan's success has been its realism rather than any fanaticism.

Elections

Jordan held what it looks upon as general elections in November 2007. Somewhat predictably, representatives of the tribes and families loyal to the ruling Hashemite dynasty again won the majority of seats contested in the House of Deputies. Mr Nader Dahabi was appointed prime minister, the King mandating him to progress social and economic reforms, particularly energy security through alternative and renewable resources including nuclear energy. Economic growth and enhancing the competitiveness of the national economy were 'prerequisites for security and social stability'. Technocrats, including senior civil servants and academics, are strongly represented in Cabinet.

Jordan First

The ambitious Jordan First initiative of King Abdullah has changed the focus of Jordanian politics on to the domestic issues of the economy, and social and political development. Since King Abdullah's 'Amman Message' in 2004, Jordan has also actively promoted its version of moderate Islam and interfaith understanding. It's nearness to Iraq, and the presence of

KEY FACTS

Official name: Al Mamlaka al Urduniya al Hashemiya (The Hashemite Kingdom of Jordan)

Head of State: King Abdullah II (crowned Feb 1999)

Head of government: Prime Minister Nader al Dahabi (from 22 Nov 2007)

Ruling party: National Constitutional Party (NCP) (pro-monarchy coalition formed from a union of nine centrist parties)

Area: 91,860 square km

Population: 5.73 million (2007)*

Capital: Amman

Official language: Arabic

Currency: Jordanian dinar (JD) = 1,000 fils

Exchange rate: JD0.70 per US$ (Jul 2008)

GDP per capita: US$2,795 (2007)*

GDP real growth: 5.70% (2007)*

Labour force: 1.80 million (2004)

Unemployment: 15.00% (official, 2004); 30.00% (unofficial, 2004)

Inflation: 5.40% (2007)*

Balance of trade: -US$7.03 billion (2006)

Foreign debt: US$7.32 billion (2004)

Visitor numbers: 3.23 million (2006)*

* estimated figure

large numbers of Iraqi refugees in Jordan has inevitably placed Jordan in the front line of terrorist offensives. Jordan has been the target of numerous terrorist incidents in recent years, including the 2005 bombing of three Amman hotels, in which 60 people were killed. Jordan also has a large Palestinian population with more than one and a half million Palestinian refugees. Significantly, Jordan is one of only two Arab states (the other is Egypt) that has a peace treaty with Israel, concluded in 1994.

Frail economy

Jordan is one of the few Middle Eastern states that has absolutely no oil. Its only natural resources are potash and phosphate. The population is urbanised at around 80 per cent, and is one of the youngest among lower-middle income countries, with 38 per cent under the age of 14. Although demographic growth, currently at around 2.6 per cent per year, is slowing, the total population is expected to reach almost 7 million by 2015.

The Jordanian economy is small and narrowly based. Jordan's main exports include clothing, pharmaceutical products, phosphate, potash and fertilisers. Traditionally, Jordan has benefited greatly from remittances from a large expatriate professional community. It is also a significant recipient of foreign aid, which has been vital over the years to further Jordan's social welfare and development programmes. Despite the unsettled regional environment, Jordan has made progress towards achieving some degree of macroeconomic stability. Fiscal consolidation, combined with prudent monetary, privatisation and exchange rate policies, and a rescheduling and restructuring of external debt has led to an improved macroeconomic environment in recent years. Structural reforms are aimed at promoting private sector-led growth and foreign investment, while reducing the direct government role in the economy. The process of structural reforms has been accompanied by a painful fiscal consolidation that has steadily reduced government debt from above 200 per cent of GDP in the early 1990s, to 78 per cent at the end of 2006.

According to the IMF the economy continued to perform well in 2007, with 6 per cent real GDP growth and lower unemployment. However, sharply higher world fuel and food prices led to a marked widening of the fiscal and external current account deficits and, in the first half of 2008, a jump in inflation. Jordan's economic prospects remained broadly favourable, although in the view of the IMF, its public and external sector imbalances implied increased challenges to sustaining strong macroeconomic performance. Jordanian authorities hoped to lower the fiscal deficit in 2008, despite pressures to increase spending following the removal of fuel subsidies. Although specific measures have not yet been identified, it was expected that the deficit would be reduced substantially over the medium term, mainly through lower expenditure growth.

Jordan's exchange rate peg has served to anchor monetary policy and prevented an even larger deterioration of the current account in 2007, when there was upward pressure on the dinar. The planned tightening of fiscal policy in 2008 will also help narrow the fiscal and external imbalances and bring inflation down. Significant further fiscal consolidation is needed over the medium-term to reduce the still-high public debt and the large current account deficit. The IMF maintains that progress on the structural reform agenda is key to sustaining strong economic performance. Priority areas include public financial management, the framework for public-private partnerships, liberalisation of the petroleum sector, developing the debt market, and continued enhancement of financial sector supervision.

Until 2003 Jordan benefited from Iraqi oil supplies at below market prices. The Iraq war saw an end to this arrangement, forcing Jordan to pay market prices at a time when the price per barrel was rising inexorably. The initial response was to subsidise the pump price, but as oil prices continued to rise, this became economically impractical. The Jordanian government has been reducing the subsidies in stages since 2005, a process that was completed in February 2008 when all the subsidies were finally removed, and Jordan's consumers faced price rises on oil products ranging from 3 to 33 per cent. The oil price rises were not all bad news for Jordan's consumers. An estimated 600,000–700,000 Jordanians were estimated to be working in the Gulf states in 2007, generating remittances of 2.21 billion dinars in 2007. 2007 also saw the level of remittances overtake that of foreign direct investment (FDI) which dropped to US$1.83 billion in 2007, well down on the US$3.2 billion recorded in 2006.

Jordan is a member of the World Trade Organisation (WTO) and has concluded free trade agreements with the United States, the European Union, Singapore and a number of Arab countries, including Bahrain, Egypt, Morocco, Syria, Tunisia and the United Arab Emirates.

KEY INDICATORS Jordan

	Unit	2003	2004	2005	2006	2007
Population	m	5.56	5.80	5.49	5.60	*5.73
Gross domestic product (GDP)	US$bn	10.13	11.50	12.71	14.10	*16.01
GDP per capita	US$	.1,820	1,947	2,317	2,519	*2,795
GDP real growth	%	3.1	6.7	7.2	6.3	*5.7
Inflation	%	2.5	3.4	3.5	6.3	*5.4
Industrial output	% change	–	13.3	9.8	11.4	–
Agricultural output	% change	–	2.2	3.7	5.4	–
Exports (fob) (goods)	US$m	3,085.0	3,200.0	4,301.4	5,204.4	*5,700.0
Imports (cif) (goods)	US$m	5,480.0	7,600.0	9,317.3	10,260.2	12,021.0
Balance of trade	US$m	-2,395.0	-4,400.0	-5,015.9	-5,055.9	-6,321.6
Current account	US$m	1,120.0	-90.0	-2,260.0	-1,598.0	-2,769.0
Total reserves minus gold	US$m	5,194.3	5,266.6	5,250.3	6,722.0	7,542.0
Foreign exchange	US$m	5,193.1	5,246.8	5,249.5	6,720.4	7,539.4
Exchange rate	per US$	0.71	0.71	0.71	0.71	0.71

* estimated figure

Risk assessment

Economy	Good
Political	Fair
Regional stability	Poor

COUNTRY PROFILE

Historical profile

1928 Transjordan obtained qualified independence in a treaty with Britain.
1946 Transjordan achieved full independence as the Hashemite Kingdom of

Jordan under the Emir, who took the title of King Abdullah.
1948 Jewish leaders announced the formation of the State of Israel in British-mandate Palestine and thousands of Palestinian Arabs fled to Jordan and the West Bank.
1950 A post-war agreement united Jordan with the part of Palestine remaining in Arab hands (the West Bank, including East Jerusalem, but excluding the Gaza Strip).
1951 King Abdullah was assassinated and was succeeded by his son, Talal bin Abdullah.
1952 Hussein bin Talal formally took power as King Hussein after his father, Talal bin Abdullah, stepped down due to mental illness.
1956 King Hussein banned political parties.
1957 British troops completed their withdrawal from Jordan.
1967 Six Day War. Israel occupied the West Bank and Gaza Strip and re-unified Jerusalem; around 300,000 Palestinian Arab refugees entered Jordan.
1970 Civil war (Black September) between the Jordanian army and Palestinians followed airplane hijackings by the Palestine Liberation Organisation (PLO) resistance group. The PLO was forcefully expelled from its bases in Jordan and moved to Lebanon
1972 An attempted military coup was thwarted.
1974 Jordan and other Arab countries recognised the PLO as the sole legitimate representative of the Palestinian people.
1978–84 The House of Representatives (parliament) was temporarily replaced during these years by a National Consultative Council appointed by the King.
1986 King Hussein severed political links with the PLO and ordered its main offices to shut.
1988 The House of Representatives was dissolved, prior to King Hussein's announcement of the severance of all administrative and legal ties with the West Bank. The King publicly backed the Palestinian intifada against Israeli rule.
1989 The first general elections since 1967 were contested only by independent candidates.
1992 Parliament authorised political parties for the first time since they were banned by King Hussein 36 years previously.
1993 Multi-party elections were held.
1994 The Jordan-Israel Peace Treaty was signed at Wadi Araba, Jordan, following the opening of the first border crossing between Aqaba (Jordan) and Eilat (Israel).
1997 The parliamentary elections were boycotted by nine opposition parties, led by the Islamic Action Front (IAF). The Islamists said the electoral law favoured the rural constituencies, where support for the King was strong, over the towns, where nearly half of Jordan's population lived. The elections were won by the National Constitutional Party (NCP), a pro-monarchy coalition formed from the union of nine centrist parties.
1999 King Hussein appointed his eldest son, Abdullah bin Hussein, as crown prince and heir, replacing Prince Hassan, the King's brother, who had been appointed crown prince in 1965. King Hussein, who had been treated for cancer for many years, died, and Abdullah bin Hussein was sworn in as King.
2000 King Abdullah II made a historic visit to the state of Israel. Jordan joined the World Trade Organisation (WTO).
2002 Senior US diplomat, Laurence Foley, was shot dead outside his home in Amman. Many political activists were arrested.
2003 King Abdullah II ratified an amended law adding six women members to the women's share in parliament. Independent candidates, allies of the King, won two-thirds of the seats in the parliamentary elections. The King appointed Faisal al Fayez as prime minister and three female ministers.
2004 The Wahdah Dam project was launched. Israel and Jordan agreed a joint project to build a desert science centre on their shared border.
2005 Jordan returned its ambassador to Israel after a truce was signed by Israel and Palestine.
2007 New entry regulations were introduced stemming the flow of refugees from Iraq; over one million Iraqis took up residence since 2003. In parliamentary elections independent candidates won 104 out of 110 seats, the Islamic Action Front won 6; turnout was 54 per cent. Nader al Dahabi was named prime minister.
2008 Queen Rania, wife of King Abdullah, set up a YouTube video-sharing website to answer questions from her English-speaking audience about Arab stereotypes. By July, two million people had watched items on her website.

Political structure

Constitution

Under a revised constitution of January 1952, the throne passes by male descent to heirs above the age of 18. A Regent or Council of Regency exercises power on behalf of the heir if he is below the age of 18 on succeeding to the throne. King Hussein's youngest brother, Prince Hassan, was Crown Prince between 1964–99, but in January 1999, a change was made to the constitution. The constitution previously required the meeting of a 'family council' to discuss a change of succession. Under the revision, King Hussein directly appointed his eldest son, Abdullah bin Hussein, as the new Crown Prince.
Jordan is divided into eight governorates, each headed by a governor and consisting of districts, sub-districts and counties. At local government level there are 152 municipalities, including Greater Amman, and 340 village councils. Local affairs are managed by city or village councils. Councils are under the supervision of the ministry of municipal and rural affairs.
A national charter, published by King Hussein in 1991, enshrined the principle of political freedom. It also underscored the ultimate power of the monarchy.
In February 2003, King Abdullah II ratified an amended law adding six women members to the parliament.

Form of state

Monarchy with limited parliamentary democracy.

The executive

The King is head of state and commander-in-chief of the armed forces.
The King has the power to declare war or conclude peace treaties, order elections, inaugurate, adjourn and prorogue the lower house of parliament as well as to appoint the prime minister, cabinet and speaker of the upper house of parliament.

National legislature

Legislative power rests with the al Ayan council (Senate/upper house) – 50 members appointed by the King – and the House of Representatives (lower house) – 110 members elected by universal suffrage for a four-year term.
Eighteen seats in the House of Representatives are reserved for Christians, Circassians and Bedouins. Six seats are reserved for women.
Individual ministers or governments may be removed from office on a vote of no-confidence by the House of Representatives.

Legal system

Judges are appointed by royal decree and are independent of the legislature and the executive. The King has the right of clemency and must confirm death sentences.

Last elections

20 November 2007 (parliamentary)
Results: Parliamentary: independent candidates that are allied to King Abdullah won 104 out of 110 seats, the Islamic Action Front won 6; turnout was 54 per cent.

Next elections

2011 (parliamentary)

Political parties

Ruling party

National Constitutional Party (NCP) (pro-monarchy coalition formed from a union of nine centrist parties)

Main opposition party
Islamic Action Front (IAF) (the political wing of the Muslim Brotherhood)

Population
5.73 million (2007)*
Last census: October 2004: 5,100,981
Population density: 53 inhabitants per square km. Urban population: 79 per cent (1995—2001).
Annual growth rate: 3.1 per cent 1994–2004 (WHO 2006)
Ethnic make-up
The population is predominantly Arab, with small minorities of Circassians, Armenians and Kurds. No official figures are kept but it is generally accepted that Palestinians constitute 60 to 70 per cent of Jordan's population.
Religions
Over 80 per cent of the population are Sunni Muslims. There is a Christian minority, mainly Roman Catholic, Coptic and Greek Orthodox, and smaller numbers of other Muslims.

Education
The government has instituted a programme to revise and upgrade the state school system, involving teacher retraining, new curricula and substantial school construction. University students tend to concentrate on science, mathematics and computer programming. Consequently, Jordan has a steady supply of young people with the necessary skills in computer programming, as well as those with training in basic technical education.
Literacy rate: 91 per cent adult rate; 99 per cent youth rate (15–24) (Unesco 2005).
Compulsory years: 6 to 14; elementary aged 6–11 and preparatory 12–14.
Enrolment rate: 70 per cent for boys and 72 per cent for girls total primary school enrolment, (including repetition rates) of the relevant age group (World Bank estimates 1994–2000).
Pupils per teacher: 21 in primary schools.

Health
Per capita total expenditure on health (2003) was US$440; of which per capita government spending was US$199, at the international dollar rate, (WHO 2006).
Improved water sources and sanitation facilities are available to 99 per cent and 96 per cent of the population, respectively.
HIV/Aids
HIV prevalence: 0.1 per cent aged 15–49 in 2003 (World Bank)
Life expectancy: 71 years, 2004 (WHO 2006)
Fertility rate/Maternal mortality rate: 3.4 births per woman, 2004 (WHO 2006); maternal mortality 41 per 100,000 live births (World Bank).
Birth rate/Death rate: 4 deaths and 30 births per 1,000 population.
Child (under 5 years) mortality rate (per 1,000): 23 per 1,000 live births (World Bank)
Head of population per physician: 2.03 physicians per 1,000 people, 2004 (WHO 2006)

Welfare
Social security in Jordan has few beneficiaries relative to contributing workers and it only first started paying benefits in 1995.
All workers in non-government establishments that employ more than five persons are obliged to contribute to the state social security fund. Those in smaller establishments may contribute voluntarily.
Lump-sum payments and hospital expenses are made in the case of work-related injury, death and retirement pensions. The Social Security Corporation (SCC) provides two types of insurance — old age disability and work-related injuries insurance. It collects revenues directly from wages and is not reliant on the government budget. It covers both the private sector and any public employees hired after 1995.

Main cities
Amman (capital, estimated population 1.3 million in 2004), Zarqa (512,200), Irbid (267,200), Aqaba (100,700), Salt (66,200), Mafraq (67,400).

Media
Press
A press and publications law was passed in late 1992. The law banned a wide range of items including those which harm the King or his family or reveal information about the armed forces. The ban on hurting national unity, insulting Arab or Muslim heads of state or transgressing so-called 'public ethics' caused the most controversy.
The law also forced all Jordanian journalists to become members of the Jordan Press Association and denies them the right to protect their sources. The law came as media activity surged with a dozen newspapers licensed or applying for licences and the legalisation of domestic satellite dishes opening Jordanians to uncensored world television.
The Jordan News Agency (Petra) provides news to local and foreign media. The Ministry of Information, which Petra had been a part of, ceased to exist in early 2002. A new media policy is being drawn-up by the Jordanian Media Higher Council, which was established in December 2001.
Dailies: Jordan has both Arabic and English dailies, all published nationally. The Arabic newspapers are Sawt al Shaab, al Ra'i Daily (both government-owned), al Dustour, al Aswaq and al Arab Alyawm. The English newspapers are Arab Daily, Assabeel Jordan Times and Jordan Times.
Weeklies: There are several weeklies in Arabic, including Akhbar al Usbu, Amman al Masa, Assabeel Weekly and al Hawadith. English language weeklies include The Star and there is also a French weekly supplement to The Jordan Times.
Broadcasting
Broadcasting is run by state bodies and the press is licensed by the government. Restrictions on the press eased considerably in the early 1990s and many areas have been opened to active discussion. A certain amount of self-censorship remains and some subjects – including information on military and security establishments and criticism of the royal family – are strictly taboo.
Radio: The state radio service broadcasts domestic and external programmes in Arabic and English.
Television: The state television service runs one Arabic channel and one foreign channel which broadcasts programmes in English, French and Hebrew.
Advertising
Advertising is handled through the private sector, and appears in newspapers and on the television and radio.

Economy
Jordan is poor in resources: it lacks oil, water is scarce and agricultural land is limited. Its geographic location at the centre of the Middle East means that its fortunes are strongly influenced by regional circumstances. Unlike many Arab states, Jordan has strong trade links with its neighbours. Intra-Arab trade and remittances from overseas workers, especially those in the Gulf states, make a significant contribution to the economy. Jordan has long served as a transit route for goods destined for Iraq, from which it formerly received subsidised oil. The consequences of the 2003 Iraq War on the Jordanian economy from lost export opportunities, higher oil import costs and reduced foreign direct investment has been estimated to be as high as US$1.5 billion.
Nevertheless, prudent policies and structural reforms have secured a degree of stability. GDP is growing by around 6 per cent a year.
Since 2000, Jordan has followed a strategy of diversifying its economic base. A reform programme was launched at the end of 2001, the chief priorities of which were improvements in welfare services, education and water resources. Economic policies are designed to strengthen

economic growth, maintain financial stability and a solid external reserve position and reduce public indebtedness through continued fiscal consolidation.

A privatisation programme was cautiously initiated in the 1990s, particularly in the hotel and tourism sector. With a budget deficit that reached US$609 million in 2002, there was a serious need for fiscal prudence and the government turned to privatisation and negotiation with its international creditors as the primary methods of balancing the budget. Jordan secured financial loans from the US and the EU to support its economic reform and development programmes.

In addition to substantial remittances from expatriate workers, tourism is a major earner of foreign exchange. Visitor numbers increased in 2006 by 13 per cent to 6.5 million. Jordan exports potash and phosphate, its only natural resources, and also fertilisers, pharmaceuticals, clothing and fruit, but is dependent on imports, especially of basic foodstuffs and oil and runs a large trade deficit.

External trade

Jordan has signed the Agadir Agreement which proposes to set up a free trade zone (FTZ) between Egypt, Jordan, Tunisia and Morocco. In 2005 the Greater Arab Free Trade Area (Gafta) was ratified by 17 members, including Jordan, creating an Arab economic bloc. A customs union was established whereby tariffs within Gafta will be reduced by a percentage each year, until none remain.

It is also a signatory of the Euro-Mediterranean Partnership agreement, which provides for the introduction of free trade between the EU and 10 Mediterranean countries, including Jordan, by 2012.

Imports

Main imports are crude oil, textiles, machinery, vehicles, capital goods and manufactured goods.

Main sources: Saudi Arabia (25.6 per cent total, 2006), China (10.4 per cent), Germany (7.8 per cent).

Exports

Main exports are manufactured clothing, phosphates, fertilisers and potash, vegetables, manufactured goods and pharmaceuticals.

Main destinations: US (25.1 per cent total, 2006), Iraq (12.3 per cent), India (7.7 per cent).

Agriculture

Farming

Agriculture contributed around two per cent to GDP in 2004, compared with around five per cent in 1994. Jordan became a net importer of foodstuffs when it no longer had access to its principal growing areas on the West Bank of the River Jordan. More than 91 per cent of the total land area is classified as desert and only 6 per cent is cultivable. The sector is vulnerable to drought. Extreme variations in seasonal rainfall in the highland areas lead to severe fluctuations in yields from year to year. Highland farmers are one of the poorest groups in the country. Irrigated farming in the Jordan Valley has been a success in production terms, but marketing has suffered from periods of overproduction and fluctuations in exports.

Jordan has two distinct agricultural zones: the irrigated Jordan Valley and the rain-fed highlands. Government policy has been to encourage intensive fruit and vegetable growing in the Jordan Valley, both for local consumption and as a major export earner, and to boost cereal and fodder production in the highlands in an effort to reduce a high food import bill. Farming is a private sector activity, but the state-owned Agricultural Marketing and Processing Company (AMPC) plays a regulatory role in fresh produce imports. The government buys cereal and fodder crops at fixed prices, with prices of other crops set according to supply and demand.

Since 1986, state land in southern Jordan has been leased to private farmers for sophisticated irrigation projects conceived at a time when the Arab world was placing heavy emphasis on food self-sufficiency. The projects rely on ground water reserves and there is increasing concern that the benefits of increased production are outweighed by the depletion of scarce water supplies.

Crop production in 2005 included: 82,568 tonnes (t) cereals in total, 33,154t wheat, 13,101t maize, 131,020t potatoes, 34,524t barley, 35,276t bananas, 41,136t apples, 2,100t tobacco, 73,990t olives, 133,043t citrus fruit, 31,751t grapes, 408,396t tomatoes, 5,200t dates, 4,234t pulses, 16,301t oilcrops, 2,232t treenuts 289,524t fruit in total, 1,055,867t vegetables in total. Livestock production included: 131,942t meat in total, 4,750t beef, 4,000t lamb, 1,500t goat meat, 121,260t poultry, 35,100t eggs, 252,668t milk, 200t honey, 57,140t sheepskins, 1,950t greasy wool.

Fishing

Jordan's only seaboard is in the south at Aqaba, on the Red Sea. The number of fishermen and vessels is negligible and the catches are consumed locally for the most part. A number of fish farming projects have been started, but with little success. The level of the Jordan river is frequently very low, contributing to the difficulties of fish farming. The majority of Jordan's fish for consumption is imported. In 2004, the total marine fish catch was 144 tonnes.

Forestry

Active afforestation programmes are under way in some areas in an effort to control soil erosion and desertification.

Exports in 2004 amounted to US$38.4 million largely based on paper pulp, while imports of most forest materials amounted to US$249.9 million. There is little commercial exploitation of forests.

Production in 2004 included 241,198 cubic metres (cum) roundwood, 4,000cum industrial roundwood, 253,302cum wood fuel; 33,192 tonnes (t) charcoal, 25,300t paper and paperboard, 1,600t printing and writing paper.

Industry and manufacturing

Jordan's geographical location has affected its trade and industrial development. The Iran-Iraq war (1980–88) and the Gulf War (1991), as well as the Israeli-Palestinian crisis, have restricted Jordan's trade. It is therefore understandable that the government believes that industrial expansion depends on developing new overseas markets beyond the region. The minerals sector has successfully developed secure markets in the Indian sub-continent and in South-East Asia. Most other Jordanian industry relies on highly volatile Arab markets. State industries have become a particular burden, with the Jordanian Water Authority accumulating debts of US$113 million.

With the loss of exports of manufactured goods to Iraq, there was a 6 per cent drop in output in 2003.

Tourism

Tourism is the most important sector of the economy. The sector accounts for about 10 per cent of GDP and is the second highest earner of foreign exchange. Jordan has been experiencing a growth in tourism inspite of the regional conflicts. New resorts are being built along the Dead Sea and Gulf of Aqaba with luxury hotels, international retail outlets, sports facilities, entertainment centres and private residences. The resort of Ras al Yamaniya in Aqaba has been designated a duty-free zone to attract both visitors and investment. Urban regeneration has also been included in plans, by the antiquities ministry, to market Jordan, with Amman and Petra rivalling its coastal resorts as top holiday destinations.

In 2003 Jordan joined the Euromed Heritage Programme, a computerisation project, sponsored by the EU, which focuses on cultural tourists of archaeology, arts and history, promoting sites through the internet.

There were 2.8 million visitors in 2004, compared with 2.3 million in 2003.

Environment
Water is the single greatest challenge to Jordan's long-term well-being. The available figures on supply and demand present a disturbing picture. Agriculture remains the largest consumer of water resources, accounting for over 70 per cent of total water use. The acute water shortage means that Jordan is heavily reliant on ground water, of which 45 per cent is irreplaceable. In the long-term, water consumption at the present rates cannot be sustained. With an increasing population rate in Jordan, the government has estimated that per capita water supply will fall from the current 200 cubic metres per person to only 91 cubic metres by 2025.
A programme of dam building has improved supply but it is clear that a solution to the problem will have to come from better regional arrangements for water sharing. Jordan receives 215 million cubic metres annually from Israel through dams and pipelines. The Israeli-Palestinian conflict has not disrupted these water supplies and the government has done its utmost not to offend Israel over the conflict in order to prevent a repeat of Israel's decision in 1999 to cut water supplies to Jordan .
The building of the Wahdeh (formerly known as Maqarin) dam on the Jordanian-Syrian border cannot proceed without the agreement of Israel, which stands to lose water as a result of the project.
The water and irrigation ministry has invested some US$5billion to boost supply, which will be invested in a number of projects until 2010.

Mining
The Jordanian government earmarked the mining and minerals industry as a priority sector for investment and development.
The Natural Resources Authority (NRA) is the main policy-making body in the mineral sector, which promotes investment and undertakes operations. The agency has benefited from the UN Conference on Trade and Development's (Unctad) technical assistance and is able to attract foreign investment into the sector. The NRA has identified a range of metallic and non-metallic minerals, of which Jordan has substantial reserves. The EU is funding a project to identify the economic potential of non-oil mineral resources, including copper, a granitoid complex and ornamental stone.
The phosphate and potash industries in Jordan are key contributors to the economy. The Eshidiya deposit owned by Jordan Phosphate Mining Corporation (JPMC) has a proved phosphate reserve of 1,200 million tonnes. The Arab Potash Company (APC), which accounts for 4.4 per cent of the world's total potash production, produces 1.8 million tonnes of potash annually in Jordan. Almost 1.4 million tonnes is exported to 28 countries (mostly Asian).
The Jordan Safi Salt Company (Jossco) produces 1.2 million tonnes per year of industrial salt. Jordan is also an important exporter of calcium carbonate to other Middle Eastern states. Mineral production is largely of industrial minerals derived from the overlying sediments and volcanics. The most important mineral resources, which merit development and provide investment opportunities, are silica sand, tripoli, gypsum, ornamental stone (Ajlun limestone) and zeolite.

Hydrocarbons
Jordan, unlike its neighbours Iraq and Syria, is not blessed with huge gas or oil reserves and has to import the bulk of its oil requirements to meet domestic demand. The country is untypical of the Middle East in that its economy is not directly linked to the fluctuations of the international oil market.
Proven oil reserves are small and there is no oil production. The government encourages foreign oil companies to undertake exploration. Long-held hopes of a good oil find that could bring prosperity have not been achieved so far, but there are indications of a sizeable reserve in the Azraq area. The rising oil prices are an added inducement to the government and the industry to step up exploration of Jordan's potential.
Jordan has 6.5 billion cubic meters (cum) of natural gas reserves. Jordan currently produces around 849,000cum per day of natural gas from the Risheh field. The Risheh field provides gas to a thermal power station, which generates around 12 per cent of Jordan's electricity. Jordan is already receiving natural gas from Egypt through a pipeline which will connect Egypt, Jordan, Syria, Lebanon, Iraq and Europe when completed.
Jordan does not produce or import coal.

Energy
Government policy has been to restrain energy consumption while increasing efforts to develop domestic energy sources and lessen dependence on oil imports. Domestic oil production falls well below energy demand estimated to be equivalent to two million barrels per year.
The state-owned Jordan Electricity Authority (JEA) is the main electricity producer, with two major plants: the Hussein Thermal Power Station outside Amman and the Aqaba Thermal Power Station in the south. Total installed capacity is around 1600MW. Responsibility for distribution of electricity lies with the Jordan Electric Power Company (Jepco) and the Irbid District Electricity Company (Ideco).
In 2001, Jordan, Syria and Egypt inaugurated a US$300 million electricity line linking the grids of the three countries.
Gas finds in the Risha area of north-eastern Jordan in the early 1990s have enabled the country to reach 25 per cent self-sufficiency in electricity generation, equivalent to 6,570MWH. The Risha field itself produces around 12 per cent of Jordan's electricity needs through two 30MW gas turbines connected to the national grid. Major expansion in Jordan's power generating capacity will continue to depend on imported oil.

Financial markets
Stock exchange
The Amman Stock Exchange (ASE) was established in 1976 and is claimed to be one of the most efficient in the Middle East.

Banking and insurance
Central bank
Central Bank of Jordan (CBJ)
Main financial centre
Amman

Time
GMT plus two hours (daylight saving GMT plus three hours)

Geography
Jordan is bounded by Syria to the north, Iraq to the east, Saudi Arabia to the south and Israel, the West Bank and Gaza Strip to the west. The only access to the sea is at Aqaba at the northern tip of the Gulf of Aqaba and about 400km south of the capital Amman.
There are three major geographical regions – the Jordan Rift Valley, the Eastern Uplands and the desert. Settlement is concentrated in northern and central sections of the uplands which run in a narrow strip from the Syrian border in the north to the Shubak/Petra area in the south.
Hemisphere
Northern

Climate
The climate is Mediterranean with dry, warm to hot summers and wet, mild to cool winters. There are noticeable variations due to altitude with temperatures in the Jordan Valley and Aqaba region around 10 degrees Celsius (C) higher on average than the highlands area throughout the year. Daytime temperatures in the highlands range from 25 to 32 degrees C in summer and from 7 to 15 degrees C in winter. Rainfall ranges from 40cm annually in the northern highlands to 10cm in the south and 20cm in the Jordan Valley.

Dress codes
Lightweight clothing is needed during the hottest months and warm clothing in winter when snow is not uncommon. Both

men and women should dress discreetly in public.

Entry requirements

Passports

Required by all and must have at least six months validity.

Visa

Required by all, except most citizens of the Middle East. Many nationals may obtain a visa at the port of entry (for stays up to 14 days) and all others must apply in advance. Visit www.mfa.gov.jo and follow path from Ministry to Consular Affairs Department, for a full list of each category. Business visas should be applied for in advance and require a business letter outlining purpose of visit and an itinerary. Visas are not issued at the King Hussein Bridge across the Jordan River from Israel.

Currency advice/regulations

There are no restrictions on the import or export of foreign or local currency. Travellers cheques are accepted in banks.

Prohibited imports

Illegal drugs. Firearms require export permission for country of origin and prior approval for import into Jordan. Permitted weapons must be transported as baggage.

Health (for visitors)

Mandatory precautions

There are no automatic health checks at entry points, but travellers arriving from areas with infectious diseases such as cholera are expected to have had appropriate vaccinations. Travellers coming from an infected area require a yellow fever vaccination certificate.

Advisable precautions

Vaccination against typhoid, polio and hepatitis is advisable. Tap water is generally of a good standard, but short-stay visitors may prefer bottled water.

Hotels

There is a good selection of hotels in Amman. A number of new hotels are being built in Amman, around the Dead Sea and in Aqaba. The main tourist centres are Aqaba and the ancient city of Petra. A service charge of 10–12 per cent is usually added to the bill plus a government tax of 10 per cent on all services at three-, four- and five-star hotels and restaurants.

Extra tips are discretionary. Porters' and drivers' tips are about 8 per cent.

Credit cards

Major credit cards are accepted at hotels and restaurants.

Public holidays (national)

Fixed dates

1 Jan (New Year's Day), 30 Jan (King Abdullah II's Birthday), 1 May (Labour Day), 25 May (Independence Day), 14 Nov (King Hussein's Birthday), 25 Dec (Christmas Day).

Variable dates

Eid al Adha (four days), Islamic New Year, Birth of the Prophet, Ascent of the Prophet, Eid al Fitr (three days).

Islamic year – 1429 (10 Jan 2008–28 Dec 2008): The Islamic year contains 354 or 355 days, with the result that Muslim feasts advance by 10–12 days against the Gregorian calendar. Dates of feasts vary according to the sighting of the new moon, so cannot be forecast exactly.

Working hours

Friday is the official day of rest.

Banking

0830–1230 (Sat–Thu); some banks open for two hours in the afternoon, generally from 1500–1700.

Business

Summer: 0800–1300, 1500–1900 (Sat–Thu); winter: 0800–1330 (Sat–Thu). During Ramadan, most firms operate only from 0900–1600. Christian businesses may close on Sunday afternoon.

Government

0800–1400 (Sat–Thu).

Shops

0800–2000/2100 or 0930–1330, 1530–1800 daily. Some shops close Fridays and public holidays.

Telecommunications

Mobile/cell phones

GSM 900 and 1800 services cover almost all of the country.

Internet/e-mail

Internet access is available in Amman, Aqaba and other major business districts.

Electricity supply

Domestic 220V, 50 cycles AC. Industrial 220–380V 50 cycles AC.

Lamp sockets are screw-type, and there is a wide range of wall sockets. Bring a universal adapter.

Weights and measures

Metric system. Land is measured in dunums (1,000sq metres).

Social customs/useful tips

Jordanian society operates a mixture of traditional and modern attitudes and habits, and a foreigner needs to be aware which apply in any given situation. Business appointments are usually respected, though most people keep an open door and interruptions must be expected. All meetings are prefaced by an extended exchange of pleasantries allowing both sides the chance to assess each other. Tea and coffee are offered in all offices, and should be accepted; however, on the third or fourth appointment during a morning it is acceptable to excuse oneself and accept just a glass of water. It is still not customary to refer directly to a man's wife unless you have actually met her; it is safer to enquire after the welfare of 'the family'. It is forbidden to eat, drink or smoke in public in daylight hours during Ramadan.

Handshaking is the customary form of greeting. Jordanians are proud of their Arab culture and are hospitable and courteous. A small gift is quite acceptable in return for hospitality.

Islam plays an important role in society. Be discreet when drinking alcohol and do not drink in public places. Women are expected to dress modestly, and for both women and men beachwear must only be worn on the beach or by the poolside.

Security

Visitors should keep in touch with developments in the Middle East as any increase in regional tension might affect travel advice.

Street crime is rare in Jordan, with mugging virtually unheard of. However, housebreaking and car theft is on the increase and reasonable precautions must be observed. There are occasional small-scale bomb attacks against cinemas and nightclubs in Amman. Women do not usually walk alone in Amman after about 2200, but driving alone is safe. A woman alone wanting a taxi late at night is advised to telephone a taxi office with which she is familiar.

Getting there

Air

National airline: Royal Jordanian Airlines

International airport/s: Amman-Queen Alia International (AMM), 32km east of Amman (35 minutes from city centre).

Airport tax: Departure tax: JD4

Surface

Road: King Hussein Bridge is the only way to cross the Jordan river from Israel, and only the official minibus services are allowed to cross it. There are also buses and taxis from Syria, where the only border crossing point is at Ramtha/Der'a. There are a number of routes into Jordan from Jeddah and Riyadh in Saudi Arabia.

Rail: There is an elderly and decrepit rail link between Damascus (Syria) and Mecca (Saudi Arabia), via Amman but the journey time can be two–three times the length of time taken to drive the same route.

Water: There are ferry services, including car ferries, between Aqaba and Nuweiba in Egypt.

Main port/s: Aqaba is the country's only port.

Getting about

National transport

Air: The only internal air route is between Amman and Aqaba. Royal Jordanian

Airlines operate regular flights. Arab Wings offer a charter service.
Road: The road network is good, with well-surfaced main roads connecting all the major towns and cities.
Buses: The Jordanian Express Tourist Transport Company (Jett) runs extensive services.
Rail: The rail network is no longer viable for the traveller.
Water: There are no passenger services along the Jordan river.

City transport

Taxis: Metered taxis are readily available in Amman and other cities (do not let your driver forget to switch on his meter). Can be hired for the journey or the day for an agreed sum. Do not use a taxi without a meter before agreeing the fare with the driver. There are also many service taxis offering a standard charge for any journey. Since there are few street names outside Amman, destinations are generally described in relation to landmarks. Tipping is approximately 10 per cent.

Car hire

National or international driving licence required. Driver must be at least 25 years old and not over 60. Speed limit is 100kph. Insurance is compulsory.

BUSINESS DIRECTORY

The addresses listed below are a selection only. While World of Information makes every endeavour to check these addresses, we cannot guarantee that changes have not been made, especially to telephone numbers and area codes. We would welcome any corrections.

Telephone area codes

The international direct dialling (IDD) code for Jordan is +962 followed by the area code:

Amman	6	Madaba	8
Aqaba	3	Mafraq	4
Balga (Salt)	5	Zarqa	9
Irbid	2		

Useful telephone numbers

Ambulence193
Fire 193
Police192

Chambers of Commerce

American Chamber of Commerce in Jordan, 23 Salem Al-Hindawi Street, Shmeisani, PO Box 840817, Amman 11184 (tel: 565-1860; fax: 565-1862; e-mail: mail@jaba.org.jo).

Amman Chamber of Commerce, Al-Sharif Shaker Bin Zaid Street, PO Box 287, Amman 11118 (tel: 566-6151; fax: 566-6155; e-mail: info@ammanchamber.org.jo).

Amman Chamber of Industry, 2nd Circle Amman, PO Box 1800, Amman 11118 (tel: 464-3001; fax: 464-7852; e-mail: aci@aci.org.jo).

Aqaba Chamber of Commerce, PO Box 12, Aqaba 77110 (tel: 201-2235; fax 201-3070; e-mail: ask@index.com.jo).

Federation of Jordanian Chambers of Commerce, Al-Sharif Shaker Bin Zaid Street, PO Box 7029, Amman 11118 (tel: 566-5492; fax: 568-5997; e-mail: fjcc@nets.com.jo).

Irbid Chamber of Commerce, PO Box 13, Irbid (tel: 724-2077; fax: 724-2072; e-mail:icc@go.com.jo).

Jerash Chamber of Commerce, PO Box 195, Jerash (tel/fax: 635-1278).

Madaba Chamber of Commerce, PO Box 120, Madaba (tel: 544-120; fax: 545-878).

Mafraq Chamber of Commerce, PO Box 21, Mafraq (tel: 623-4197; fax: 623-1135).

Zarqa Chamber of Commerce, PO Box 77, Zarqa (tel: 385-3307; fax: 385-4617).

Banking

Arab Bank Plc, PO Box 950545, 11195 Amman (tel: 560-7231; fax: 560-6793; e-mail: international@arabbank.com.jo).

Arab Banking Corporation (Jordan), PO Box 926691, 11190 Amman (tel: 5 66-4183; fax: 568-6291; e-mail: info@arabbanking.com.jo).

Arab Jordan Investment Bank, PO Box 8797, 11121 Amman (tel: 560-7126; fax: 568-1482; e-mail: info@ajib.com).

Bank of Jordan, PO Box 2140, 11181 Amman (tel: 569-6277; fax: 569-6291; boj@go.com.jo).

Cairo Amman Bank, PO Box 950661, 11195 Amman (tel: 461-6910; fax: 464-2890; e-mail: cainfo@ca_bank.com.jo).

Export and Finance Bank, PO Box 941283, 11194 Amman (tel: 569-4250; fax: 569-2062; e-mail: info@efbank.com.jo).

Housing Bank for Trade and Finance, PO Box 7693, 11118 Amman (tel: 560-7315; fax: 567-8121; e-mail: quality@hbtf.com.jo).

Jordan Gulf Bank, PO Box 9989, 11191 Amman (tel: 5 60-3931; fax: 566-4110; e-mail: jgb@jkbank.com.jo).

Jordan Investment and Finance Bank, PO Box 950601, 11195 Amman (tel: 566-5145; fax: 568-1410; e-mail: jifbank@jifbank.com.jo).

Jordan Kuwait Bank, PO Box 9776, 11191Amman (tel: 568-8814; fax: 569-5604; e-mail: webmaster@jkbank.com.jo).

Jordan National Bank, PO Box 3103, 11181 Amman (tel: 562-2282; fax: 562-2281; ingo@inb.com.jo).

Union Bank for Saving and Investment, PO Box 35104, 11180 Amman (tel: 560-7011; fax: 566-6149; e-mail: info@unionbankjo.com).

Central bank

Central Bank of Jordan , PO Box 37, 11118 Amman (tel: 463-0301–10; fax: 463-8889; e-mail: banksuper@cbj.gov.jo).

Travel information

Royal Jordanian Airlines, PO Box 302, Amman (tel: 672-872).

Ministry of tourism

Ministry of Tourism & Antiquities, PO Box 224, Amman (tel: 464-2311/4; fax: 464-8465; e-mail: tourism@mota.gov.jo).

National tourist organisation offices

Jordan Tourism Board, PO Box 830688, Amman 11183 (tel: 567-8294; fax: 567-8295; e-mail: jtb@nets.com.jo; internet: www.see-jordan.com).

Ministries

Ministry of Agriculture, University of Jordan Street, PO Box 2099, Amman (tel: 568-6431, 568-6151; fax: 568-6310).

Ministry of Awqaf and Islamic Affairs, POB 659, Amman (tel: 566-141; fax: 560-2254).

Ministry of Communications and Postal Affairs, PO Box 35214 (tel: 560-7111; fax: 560-6233).

Ministry of Culture, PO Box 6140, Amman (tel: 463-6392/3569-6588; fax: 569-6598).

Ministry of Defence, PO Box 80, Amman (tel: 464-1211, 462-2131; fax: 464-2520).

Ministry of Development Affairs, PO Box 1577, Amman (tel: 464-361; fax: 464-8825).

Ministry of Education, PO Box 1646, Amman (tel: 847-671; fax: 566-6019).

Ministry of Energy and Mineral Resources, PO Box 2310 (tel: 586-3326/9; fax: 586-5714, 581-5615).

Ministry of Finance, PO Box 85, Amman (tel: 463-6321, 463-6502, 463-7781/2; fax: 464-3132, 464-3121).

Ministry of Foreign Affairs, 3rd Circle, PO Box 35217, Amman (tel: 464-4361, 464-4311; fax: 464-8825; internet www.mfa.gov.jo/).

Ministry of Health, PO Box 86, Amman (tel: 566-5131; fax: 568-8373).

Ministry of Industry and Trade, PO Box 2019, Amman (tel: 560-7191; fax: 560-3721).

Ministry of Information, PO Box 1794, Amman (tel: 464-1467; fax: 464-8895).

Ministry of the Interior, PO Box 100, Amman (tel: 463-8849, 566-3111, 569-1141; fax: 560-6908).

Ministry of Justice, PO Box 6040, Amman (tel: 566-3101; fax: 568-0238).

Ministry of Labour, PO Box 9052, Amman (tel: 560-7481; fax: 566-7193).

Ministry of Municipal, Rural and Environmental Affairs, 3rd Circle, PO Box 1799, Amman (tel: 464-1393/7; fax: 467-2135).

Ministry of Parliamentary Affairs, Jabal, Amman (tel: 464-1211; fax: 464-2520).

Ministry of Planning, PO Box 555, Amman (tel: 464-4466/7; fax: 464-9341).

Ministry of Public Works and Housing, PO Box 1220, Amman (tel: 585-0470, 585-0479; fax: 585-7590).

Ministry of Social Development, PO Box 6720, Amman (tel: 593-1391; fax: 567-3198).

Ministry of Supply, PO Box 830, Amman (tel: 560-2121, 560-2135; fax: 560-4691).

Ministry of Tourism & Antiquities, PO Box 224, Amman (tel: 464-2311/4; fax: 464-8465; e-mail: tourism@mota.gov.jo).

Ministry of Trade and Industry, PO Box 2019, Amman (tel: 663-191; fax: 603-721).

Ministry of Transport, PO Box 35214, Amman (tel: 551-8111; fax: 552-7233).

Ministry of Water and Irrigation, PO Box 2412, Amman (tel: 568-0100, 568-0117; fax: 567-9143).

Ministry of Youth, PO Box 1794 (tel: 604-701; fax: 604-717).

Prime Minister's Office, PO Box 80, Amman (tel: 641-211; fax: 642-520).

Other useful addresses

Amman Financial Market (AFM), PO Box 8802, Amman (tel: 660-170; fax: 686-830).

Amman World Trade Centre, PO Box 962140, Amman (tel: 560-5791/2; fax: 560-5793).

Arab Potash Company (APC), PO Box 1470, Amman (tel: 566-6165; fax: 567-4416).

British Embassy, PO Box 87, Abdoun, Amman (tel: 592-3100; fax: 592-3759; e-mail: british@nets.com.jo).

British Embassy, Commercial Section, PO Box 6062, Amman (tel: 592-3100; fax: 592-3759; e-mail: becommercial@nets.com.jo).

Chief of the Royal Court, PO Box 80, Amman (tel: 464-1211, 462-7421; fax: 464-2520).

Civil Aviation Authority, PO Box 7547, Amman (tel: 92-282; fax: 891-653).

Customs Department, PO Box 90, Amman (tel: 463-8358; fax: 464-7791; internet site: www.customs.gov.jo).

Indo-Jordan Chemicals Company, PO Box 926787, Amman (tel: 568-5732; fax: 568-5730).

Institution for Standards and Metrology, PO Box 941287, Amman 11194 (tel: 568-0139; fax: 568-1099).

Investment Promotion Council, PO Box 893, Amman 11821 (tel: 553-1081/2/3; fax: 552-1084; e-mail: ipc@amra.nic.gov.jo).

Jordan Dead Sea Industries Company (JODICO), PO Box 941260, Amman (tel: 569-941; fax: 569-5939).

Jordan Europe Business Association, PO Box 910751, Amman (tel: 568-5433; fax: 566-6550).

Jordan Export Development and Commercial Centres Corporation (JEDCO), PO Box 7704, Amman (tel: 560-3507; fax: 568-4568; internet site: www.jedco.gov.jo).

Jordan Fertilisers Industrial Company, PO Box 409, Aqaba (tel: 201-4156; fax: 201-7008).

Jordan Magnesia Company (JORMAG), PO Box 941260, Amman (tel: 569-5941; fax: 569-5939).

Jordan Phosphate Mines Company (JPMC), PO Box 30, Amman (tel: 560-7141; fax: 568-2290).

Jordanian Business Association, PO Box 926182, Amman (tel: 568-0855; fax: 566-0663).

Jordanian Embassy (USA), 3504 International Drive, NW, Washington DC 20008 (tel: (+1-202) 966-2664; fax: (+1-202) 966-3110; e-mail: hkjembassydc@aol,com).

National Electric Power Company (NEPCO), PO Box 2310, Amman 1181 (tel: 558-615; fax: 518-336).

Nippon Jordan Fertilisers Company Ltd., Po Box 926861, Amman (tel: 569-1708; fax: 568-4127).

US Embassy, PO Box 354, Jabal, Amman 11118 (tel: 592-0101; fax: 592-0163).

Internet sites

Arabia On-line: www.arabia.com

ArabNet: www.arab.net/

Global Chamber of Commerce: www.gcc.net

Jordan information site: www.kinghussein.gov.jo

KEY FACTS

Official name: Kazakstan Respublikasy (Republic of Kazakhstan)

Head of State: President Nursultan Äbishuly Nazarbayev (since Apr 1990; re-elected 4 Dec 2005)

Head of government: Prime Minister Karim Masimov (appointed 10 Jan 2007)

Ruling party: Nur-Otan (Fatherland's Ray of Light) (since Oct 1999; re-elected 18 Aug 2007) (re-named from Otan, Dec 2006)

Area: 2,717,300 square km

Population: 15.12 million (2007)*

Capital: Astana (seat of government) (renamed 1998; formerly called Akmola; inaugurated as the new capital 1997); Almaty (formerly Alma Ata, commercial capital)

Official language: Kazakh

Currency: Tenge (T) = 100 tein (introduced Nov 1993)

Exchange rate: T120.19 per US$ (Jul 2008)

GDP per capita: US$6,868 (2007)*

GDP real growth: 8.50% (2007)*

Labour force: 7.60 million (2004)

Unemployment: 8.40% (2005)

Inflation: 10.80% (2007)

Oil production: 1.49 million bpd (2007)

Balance of trade: US$14.64 billion (2006)

Foreign debt: US$26.03 billion (2004)

Annual FDI: US$4.27 billion (2004)

* estimated figure

Kazakhstan

Kazakhstan is a strategically located country in Central Asia with enormous natural resources. Those resources, plus a relatively stable political system, have enabled the economy to become larger than all the other Central Asian states combined. Kazakhstan narrowly missed making the list of the 50 largest world economies for both imports and exports in 2007, but with continued development of its natural resources in early 2008 Kazakhstan looked certain to break into the top 50 before long.

A downturn in growth

The Asian Development Bank (ADB) reports that after nearly a decade of GDP growth averaging 10 per cent, a sudden halt in capital to domestic banks, due to global financial market turmoil, triggered a sharp reduction in lending activity and a downturn in growth. An increase in inflation and a drop in foreign exchange reserves added to difficulties. Any further deceleration in growth is expected to be checked by increased oil income, a healthy fiscal position, and still-strong foreign reserves. Key challenges are keeping non-oil growth out of a slump, managing banking sector external debt, and lowering inflation. Long-term prospects remain positive, given the substantial oil wealth.

The middle of 2007 was a turning point for the economy, bringing new macroeconomic difficulties to this petroleum-rich country. In the first half of the year, GDP had grown by 10.2 per cent, but international financial turbulence sharply reduced capital inflows, which in turn restricted bank lending and slowed economic activity: GDP growth fell markedly to 5.8 per cent in the fourth quarter. Expansion for the year was estimated by the ADB to be 8.5 per cent. Rapid growth in 2000–04 had been driven primarily by rising oil production and large hydrocarbon investments that were financed by inflows of foreign direct investment. However, rapid development of the country's non-oil economy has become the main engine of growth since 2005, especially construction and services, and was mostly financed by borrowing from domestic banks.

Blame it on the banks

Kazakh banks mostly borrow from abroad to finance their lending, since the domestic deposit base is small. External debt has surged in recent years and by end-September 2007 it amounted to US$93.9 billion, including US$28.4 billion of intra-company loans among oil companies. The private portion amounted to US$62.5 billion (equal to about 60 per cent of GDP) with the bulk of this resulting from the rapid expansion of borrowing by local banks after 2004. Heavy external borrowing allowed domestic banks to keep fuelling their lending activity, which more than quadrupled between 2004 and mid-2007. In this rapid expansion of credit, local banks became overexposed to the country's booming real estate market, with some 70 per cent of loans (reportedly) directly or indirectly connected to the sector. The phenomenon experienced by Kazakhstan for the past few years, in which credit boom and rising real estate prices were interlinked and mutually reinforcing, acted as a financial accelerator, risking a housing market bubble and over-indebtedness of businesses and households.

From August 2007, local Kazak banks had difficulties in accessing funds from the international markets. This raised their borrowing costs and precipitated a liquidity squeeze, which both reduced their ability to service their foreign debt and led to a sharp increase in domestic interest rates. As a consequence, bank loans to the domestic economy grew by only 1.8 per cent in the fourth quarter. Without access to bank financing, many construction companies suspended activities, and the real estate market stagnated.

To ease the situation the National Bank of Kazakhstan (NBK), as lender of last resort, opened a short-term credit line for liquidity support. It injected around US$18 billion into the banking system in August and September 2007, mainly through repurchase agreements and foreign exchange swaps. Money market rates moved from about 6 per cent in June to 12 per cent by end-2007. The NBK's credit to banks, however, fell from about US$2.2 billion at end-August to US$0.6 billion by year-end. To avoid a collapse in the real estate market and an economic recession in general, the government allocated US$4 billion of budget funds as a rescue package: US$1 billion was used in 2007, with the rest to be taken up in 2008. Rumours about a banking crisis and a housing crash, along with a dearth of information, caused a steep depreciation of the domestic currency, the tenge. At end-August, during a public holiday, the tenge slumped from T125 to US$1 to T150–170 in private foreign exchange offices throughout the country. NBK intervened to support the currency to bring the rate back to T120 to US$1, holding it stable through year-end. In its rescue operations, NBK's foreign exchange reserves dropped by US$6 billion in the period August–October 2007, but reserves subsequently increased up to January 2008.

Inflation on the rise

Consumer price inflation in September 2007 moved into double digits for the first time in seven years. Kazakhstan's end year inflation rate reached 18.8 per cent, pushing annual average inflation to 10.8 per cent. Prices of vegetable oil, bread, and flour were the chief culprits in food price inflation. During 2007, the price of vegetable oil doubled, and those of flour and bread rose by two thirds and by one half, respectively.

Various factors played a part in the climbing prices. Externally, these were, in the main, escalating global food prices. Internally, these were excessive domestic demand fuelled by a rapid money expansion, real wages that rose faster than labour productivity, increases in utility and transport fares, and structural rigidities that limited competition. In response to the surge in inflation, the government introduced a raft of measures including a ban on vegetable oil and oilseed exports; the elimination of duties on imports of vegetable oil and the reduction of duties on imports of other important foodstuffs.

It's all about oil

The US Energy Information Administration (EIA) reports that Kazakhstan has the Caspian Sea region's largest recoverable crude oil reserves, and its production accounts for over half of the roughly 2.8 million barrels per day (bpd) currently being produced in the region (including regional oil producers Azerbaijan, Uzbekistan and Turkmenistan). Kazakhstan oil exports are the foundation of the country's economy and have ensured that average real GDP growth has stayed above 9 per cent for the last 6 years. Real GDP growth during 2007 averaged 9.5 per cent.

Perhaps surprisingly, Kazakhstan's combined onshore and offshore proven hydrocarbon reserves have not been accurately surveyed, but have been estimated to be between 9 and 40 billion barrels (estimated by the EIA to be somewhere between those of Algeria and Libya). Kazakhstan produced approximately 1.45bpd of oil in 2007 and consumed 250,000bpd, resulting in petroleum net exports of around 1.2 million bpd. EIA expects oil production in Kazakhstan to reach 1.54 and 1.71 million bpd in 2008 and 2009, respectively. Increased oil production in recent years has been the result of an influx of foreign investment into Kazakhstan's oil sector. International projects have taken the form of joint ventures with Kazmunaigaz (formerly Kazakhoil), the national oil company, as well as production-sharing agreements (PSAs), and exploration/field concessions. The majority of the growth will come from four enormous fields: Tengiz, Karachaganak, Kurmangazy and Kashagan.

Kazakh oil exports are growing rapidly, with current infrastructure delivering it to

KEY INDICATORS — Kazakhstan

	Unit	2003	2004	2005	2006	2007
Population	m	13.50	13.89	15.09	15.11	*15.12
Gross domestic product (GDP)	US$bn	29.70	43.24	57.12	91.00	*103.84
GDP per capita	US$	1,948	2,715	3,786	5,363	*6,868
GDP real growth	%	9.5	9.4	9.7	10.6	*8.5
Inflation	%	6.1	6.9	7.6	8.6	10.8
Unemployment	%	8.6	8.0	8.4	*7.4	–
Industrial output	% change	–	11.2	10.3	13.4	–
Agricultural output	% change	–	-0.1	7.3	6.0	–
Oil output	'000 bpd	1,106.0	1,295.0	1,364.0	1,426.0	1,490.0
Natural gas output	bn cum	12.9	18.5	23.5	23.9	27.3
Coal output	mtoe	43.2	44.4	44.0	49.2	29.9
Exports (fob) (goods)	US$m	13,233.0	20,603.1	28,300.6	38,762.0	48,439.1
Imports (cif) (goods)	US$m	91,440.0	13,817.6	17,978.8	24,120.0	33,208.4
Balance of trade	US$m	-78,207.0	6,785.6	10,321.8	14,642.0	15,140.7
Current account	US$m	-272.6	920.0	-735.0	-1,795.0	*-6,851.0
Total reserves minus gold	US$m	4,236.2	8,473.1	6,084.2	17,750.8	15,776.8
Foreign exchange	US$m	4,235.0	8,471.9	6,083.0	17,749.5	15,775.4
Exchange rate	per US$	149.55	136.41	125.33	125.33	120.75

world markets through the Black Sea (via Russia), the Gulf (via swaps with Iran), to the north, pipeline and rail (through Russia), and now to China in the east.

Nazarbayev reconsiders

During 2007, Kazakh authorities announced they would review all energy and mineral resources contracts in a bid to generate more revenue and diversify the sources of investment. President Nursultan Nazarbayev signed an amendment into law in October 2007 that allows the government to unilaterally break contracts with oil companies, possibly motivated in part by frustration over delays with the Kashagan project. The new law, which became effective in November 2007, gave Kazakhstan two paths to terminate contracts with energy companies. One option forces the company into negotiations with the government, and the other option allows for the repudiation of the contract with a notice period of only two months.

In response to concern about Kazakhstan's investment climate, the tax ministry proposed reforming the foreign investment structure. Within one month, however, the government decided to drop a proposal that would have turned the PSA regimes into a concession-type system, allowing the country to change tax rates and contract terms more easily.

Gas exports begin

In 2007 gas production increased by over 8 per cent from 2006. In 2007, the the US based *Oil and Gas Journal* revised upwards its estimate of proved natural gas reserves in Kazakhstan to 100 trillion cubic feet (Tcf), putting the country on par with Turkmenistan. Most of Kazakhstan's natural gas reserves are located in the west of the country, with roughly 25 per cent of proven reserves situated in the Karachaganak field.

Kazakhstan produces about as much natural gas as it consumes, although following maintenance at Tengiz and Karachaganak in the last couple years, the country is poised to become a net exporter in 2008. The Kazakhstan energy ministry estimated that production during 2007 totalled 1,037 billion cubic feet (Bcf), over 70 per cent of which was produced by international consortia at the Tengiz and Karachaganak fields.

Risk assessment

Economy	Fair
Politics	Fair
Regional stability	Fair

COUNTRY PROFILE

Historical profile

1822–1915 Tsarist Russia deposed the khans, took control of the Kazakh tribes and established the garrison town of Verny, now Almaty. Russian and Ukrainian peasants were brought in to settle the Kazakh lands and the first industrial enterprises were set up.

1916–17 The population joined the other Central Asian republics in a violent uprising against Russian rule, which was suppressed. After the October Revolution in Russia, the Russian ruler, Lenin, gave the peoples of Central Asia the right of self-determination.

1920s–30s Kazakhstan was granted autonomous status as part of the USSR in 1920. Soviet nationalities policy under the direction of Joseph Stalin saw Soviet rule enforced from Moscow by Red Army troops who put down Muslim revolts throughout Central Asia after the Russian civil war. Industrialisation and collectivisation of agriculture began. One million mainly nomadic Kazakhs died of starvation in the central government's campaign to enforce permanent settlements and build collective farms.

1930s–40s Kazakhstan was granted full Soviet Socialist Republic status in 1936. The country was transformed into a major producer of non-ferrous metals, coal and oil, as well as a region of developed agriculture.

1940s–50s Koreans, Crimean Tatars, Germans and others were forcibly moved to Kazakhstan. The first nuclear test explosion was carried out in 1949 at Semipalatinsk in eastern Kazakhstan.

1950s–60s Russian President Nikita Khruschev's 'Virgin Lands' scheme began. It brought agriculture to much of the Kazakh steppe and made the Kazakhs a minority in their own republic, as Russian and Ukrainian settlers were sent to run the collective farms. In 1961, the first manned spacecraft took off from Baykonur cosmodrome in central Kazakhstan.

1986 Riots in Almaty over the replacement of Dinmukhamed Kunayev (an ethnic Kazakh) with Gennady Kolbin (an ethnic Russian) as head of the Kommunisticheskaya Partiya Kazakhstana (KPK) (Communist Party of Kazakhstan) were the first signs of ethnic and nationalist unrest in Central Asia.

1989 Nursultan Nazarbayev, an ethnic Kazakh, was appointed leader of the KPK. Kazakh was declared an official language and Russian a language of inter-ethnic communication.

1990 Kazakhstan's Supreme Soviet appointed Nazarbayev as the country's first president and declared state sovereignty.

1991 Nazarbayev won uncontested presidential elections. President Nazarbayev had supported Gorbachev's efforts to keep the Soviet Union intact and Kazakhstan was the last Soviet Republic to declare full independence. Kazakhstan joined the Commonwealth of Independent States (CIS), an association which grew out of the remnants of the Soviet Union. The President signed a decree closing the Semipalatinsk nuclear testing ground.

1992 Kazakhstan became a member of the UN.

1993 A programme of national privatisation began.

1994 The first multi-party parliamentary elections were held for a full-time professional legislature, the Kenges (parliament). Results returned a predominantly pro-Nazarbayev assembly. Uzbekistan signed an economic, military and social co-operation treaty with Kazakhstan and Kyrgyzstan.

1995 President Nazarbayev dissolved parliament following a ruling by the Constitutional Court that the 1994 parliamentary elections were invalid. The president's term of office was extended to 2000 and a referendum endorsed the introduction of a new constitution.

1996 Uzbekistan, Kazakhstan and Kyrgyzstan agreed to create a single economic market.

1997 Oil agreements were signed with China. Kazakhstan's capital was moved from Almaty to Akmola, formerly known as Tselinograd.

1998 The new capital was renamed Astana. The constitution was amended to extend the presidential term from five to seven years and to remove the upper age limit for a president.

1999 Presidential elections were brought forward from 2000; Nazarbayev was re-elected after his main rival was barred from standing. International observers claimed there were serious irregularities in the parliamentary elections. An attempt by ethnic Russians in north-east Kazakhstan to form a separate state failed.

2000 A law was passed granting Nazarbayev life-long powers and privileges. Belarus, Kazakhstan, Kyrgyzstan, Russia and Tajikistan (formerly the Customs Five) established the Eurasian Economic Community (EEC). Internal security and border controls were increased following incursions by Islamic militants from Kyrgyzstan and Uzbekistan.

2001 The country's first major pipeline running from the large Tengiz oil field to the Black Sea was opened. Nazarbayev purged the government of officials accused of joining the newly formed Democratic Choice reform movement. Pope John Paul II paid his first visit to Kazakhstan. Tajikistan, China, Russia,

Kazakhstan, Kyrgyzstan and Uzbekistan formed the Shanghai Co-operation Organisation (SCO) and agreed to fight ethnic and religious militancy, while promoting investment and trade.
2003 A bill allowing private ownership of land was passed. Russia, Ukraine, Kazakhstan and Belarus signed an economic union treaty.
2004 A deal was signed with China on the construction of an oil pipeline to the Chinese border. Nazarbayev's Otan (Fatherland) party was re-elected in the 19 September Majlis elections; international observers considered them flawed.
2005 In January, Democratic Choice, one of the main opposition parties, was ordered by the court to be dissolved because it had encouraged protests against the parliamentary election results. Nursultan Nazarbayev was re-elected president on 4 December.
2006 Galymzhan Zhakiyanov,one of the founders of the Democratic Choice Party, was released from prison in January. The opposition leader, Altynbek Sarsenbaiuly (True Bright Path party), was murdered in February. Asar (All Together), the small political party of President Nazarbayev's daughter, merged with the president's ruling party, Otan, in September. In December, two other small parties merged with Otan, which was re-named Nur-Otan (Fatherland's Ray of Light).
2007 In January, Daniyal Akhmetov resigned as prime minister and was replaced by Karim Masimov. Amendments to the constitution were adopted by parliament and parliament called on the president to implement the new constitution by dissolving parliament and calling early elections in June. General elections, held in August, ratified the constitution and the ruling Nur-Otan won 88.1 per cent and all available seats (98); turnout was 64.6 per cent. The Organisation for Security and Co-operation in Europe (OSCE) elected Kazakhstan, its first ex-Soviet republic, to be its president in 2010. Criticism of the decision came from human-rights groups that claimed Kazakhstan did not observe OSCE commitments domestically.
2008 The newly elected president of Russia, Dmitry Medvedev, chose Kazakhstan as his first official destination in May. Talks with President Nazarbayev centred on urging that Kazakhstan-produced oil should be routed through Russia to the energy hungry markets in Europe.

Political structure

Constitution

On 21 May 2007 amendments to the constitution were approved by parliament. Some presidential power was transferred to parliament, whereby it now influences the formation of government, the constitutional court and the central election committee. The number of Majilis (lower house) members was increased to 154: 98 deputies by proportional representation (with 10 per cent reserved for women), nine seats exclusively reserved for ethnic representatives. Elections for the Majilis are to be five-year terms. The president can now become involved with political parties during his time in office. Parliament voted to allow President Nazarbayev an exception from the two-term restriction and allow him to stand for a third term, while presidential terms will be reduced from seven years to five, from 2012. The majority parliamentary party will determine the government. State funding of political parties was introduced for parties that received over 7 per cent of the popular vote in previous elections. Political candidates may only use specifically allocated election funds but media coverage will be granted to all candidates. The role of the Senate (upper house) will assume full powers when the Majilis is in recess. The president shall appoint 15 senators (instead of seven). The power and independence of the judiciary was increased.

Form of state

Secular democratic republic

The executive

The power of the executive was redistributed in 2007. The president is elected for seven years (to be reduced to five-year terms from 2012). The prime minister and the Council of Ministers are appointed by the president and approved by parliament.

National legislature

Legislative power is vested in a bicameral parliament. The Majilis (lower house) agrees the appointment of the prime minister and influences the formation of the government, the constitutional court and the central election committee. There are 154 Majilis members, with 98 elected by proportional representation from closed lists, nine ethnic representatives appointed by the president (chosen from an unelected body called the Assembly of the People of Kazakhstan) and 47 Maslikhats (representatives of elected local governments). Majilis members are elected for five-year terms.
The senate may assume the power of the Majilis when it is in recession. It has 39 members; the president appoints 15 senators; other members are popularly elected to serve six-year terms.

Legal system

The legal system is based on the civil law system. The country has a Supreme Court (44 members), and a Constitutional Council (seven members).

Last elections

18 August 2007 (parliamentary); 4 December 2005 (presidential).
Results: Parliamentary: (Majilis) the Nur-Otan won 88.1 per cent and all available seats (98); Zhalpyulttyk Sotsial-Demokratiyalyk Partiya (Nationwide Social Democratic Party) 4.6 per cent; Qazaqstan Demokratiyalyk Partiya Ak Zhol (Democratic Party of Kazakhstan Bright Path) 3.2 per cent; turnout was 64.6 per cent.
Presidential: Nursultan Äbishuly Nazarbayev was re-elected with 91 per cent of the votes; Zharmakhan Tuyakbai won 6.6 per cent. Turnout was 76.8 per cent.

Next elections

18 Aug 2007 (parliamentary); 2012 (presidential).

Political parties

President Nazarbayev's ruling party, Otan (Fatherland), merged with the small Asar (All Together), Civic and Agrarian parties in 2006, and was re-named Nur-Otan (Fatherland's Ray of Light). The defunct Civic Party and Agrarian Party had jointly contested the 2004 election as the Agrarian and Industrial Union of Workers Bloc.

Ruling party

Nur-Otan (Fatherland's Ray of Light) (since Oct 1999; re-elected 18 Aug 2007) (re-named from Otan, Dec 2006)

Main opposition party

Qazaqstan Kommunistik Partiyasi (QKP) (Communist Party of Kazakhstan); Qazaqstannyn Demokratiyalyk Tandau (QDT) (Democratic Choice of Kazakhstan).

Population

15.12 million (2007)*
Last census: February 1999: 14,953,126
Population density: Six inhabitants per square km (one of the most sparsely populated countries in the world). Urban population: 56 per cent (1995–2001).
Annual growth rate: -0.8 per cent 1994–2004 (WHO 2006)

Ethnic make-up

Kazakh (Qazaq) (45 per cent, principally in the south), Russian (36 per cent, principally in the north), Ukrainian (5 per cent), German (4 per cent), Uzbek (2 per cent), Tartars (2 per cent), Uighur (1 per cent), Korean (0.6 per cent).

Religions

Muslim (47 per cent), Russian Orthodox (44 per cent), Protestant (2 per cent) and other (7 per cent). Kazakhstan is officially a secular state along Turkish lines. Kazakhs are predominantly Islamic (Sunni), while Russians belong to the Orthodox Church. Islam, not of a fundamentalist nature, is strongest in the countryside. North American and

European evangelical organisations are very active throughout the country.

Education

Although the 99 per cent literacy rate claimed by the Soviet authorities for Central Asia was exaggerated, particularly in rural areas, education in Central Asia surpasses that of neighbouring countries to the south.

Primary education starts from the age of six and lasts for four years followed by basic secondary education for five years and general secondary, which is not compulsory, lasting for another two years. Secondary professional education is offered in special professional or technical schools, lyceums or colleges and vocational schools. The Academy of Sciences in Almaty is the republic's principal college of higher education. Several private institutions offering higher education have been licensed. The Academy of Sciences is the republic's principal college of higher education.

All classes are now officially conducted in Kazakh, but many schools have been allowed to continue teaching in Russian after strong Russian protests. The argument is somewhat academic, however, as most educated Kazakhs converse in Russian and all ethnic groups are eager to learn English. Plans to introduce the Latin script, bringing the republic closer to Turkey, are unlikely to be realised for some years.

Literacy rate: 99 per cent adult rate; 100 per cent youth rate (15–24) (Unesco 2005).

Compulsory years: Six to 15

Enrolment rate: 89 per cent, total primary school enrolment of the relevant age group, including repetition rates (World Bank estimates 1994–2000).

Pupils per teacher: 18 in primary schools.

Health

Per capita total expenditure on health (2003) was US$315; of which per capita government spending was US$180, at the international dollar rate, (WHO 2006).

Kazakhstan's healthcare system is highly decentralised with a separate development model for every region. Public funds available for reforming the system are limited and do not cover the basic needs of the population, including access to primary healthcare services.

The healthcare services sector consists of public and private providers, including hospitals, offices and clinics of medical doctors, other specialised healthcare facilities and health insurance providers. The number of public hospitals has fallen leaving 63.8 beds available per 10,000 people. This reduction corresponded to a growth of small out-patient facilities (so-called family healthcare units); with the network numbering 1,752 facilities. The number of private hospitals has increased by over 30 per cent since 2000. More than half of private clinics and hospitals concluded contracts with regional healthcare departments to provide certain medical services to be paid from regional state budgets.

In the Semipalatinsk area in northern Kazakhstan, a former nuclear testing area, cases of cancer and birth defects are widespread. During the Soviet era, the military tested the local population before and after nuclear tests to assess the consequences of exposure to radiation. The high levels of plutonium in the soil stem from the numerous tests and cause, among other things, immune-deficiency which is passed from generation to generation.

Respiratory diseases are the most common illnesses because of the republic's myriad environmental problems.

Improved water sources are available to 91 per cent of the population.

A US$65 million clean water programme began in October 2003. Funds to provide improved water supplies to over 500,000 people, in four regions of Kazakhstan, was jointly provided by the Asian Development Bank (ADB), the Islamic Development Bank and the government – US$34.6 million, US$9.5 million, US$20.9 million respectively. The average per capita investment for water services is US$125 for surface facilities such as construction of pumping stations and treatment facilities and US$90 for groundwater services including repairing pipes, sewage and wastewater drainage. Hygiene and sanitation education programmes will run along with the infrastructure programme and work is expected to be completed by 2009.

HIV/Aids

HIV prevalence: 0.2 per cent aged 15–49 in 2003 (World Bank)

Life expectancy: 61 years, 2004 (WHO 2006)

Fertility rate/Maternal mortality rate: 1.9 births per woman, 2004 (WHO 2006); maternal mortality 70 per 100,000 live births (World Bank).

Child (under 5 years) mortality rate (per 1,000): 63 per 1,000 live births; 4.2 per cent of children aged under five are malnourished (World Bank).

Head of population per physician: 3.54 physicians per 1,000 people, 2003 (WHO 2006)

Welfare

The former Soviet Union developed an extensive welfare system, but price liberalisation has rendered pensions, unemployment benefit and money paid out to single parent families virtually worthless. Most Kazakhstanis hold down two or three jobs and rely heavily on privately grown food. The government has said it intends to cushion low-income groups from the heaviest blows of economic reform, but is under pressure not to stretch the budget for fear of hyperinflation.

Kazakhstan has emerged as a role model in pension reform in the Commonwealth of Independent States (CIS). In January 1998, a pay-as-you-go (PAYG) system was replaced with a privately managed and fully-funded system (similar to that introduced by Chile in the 1980s). Under the new system, employees pay a compulsory 10 per cent of their wages into a personal retirement account. This is in addition to existing pension liabilities funded through a 15 per cent payroll tax which will be cut to 5 per cent by 2009. The reform initially increased the pension fund deficit, as the state had to make up for the contributions that were diverted to the private funds. In 1998, the World Bank approved a US$300 million loan to support the government's efforts to finance the transition to a fully-funded pension system by financing part of the estimated 1.7 per cent of GDP fiscal deficit. Nevertheless, the programme is regarded as highly successful, with participation levels and the yields on investments remaining high.

By the end of 2001, the assets accumulated in Kazakhstan's pension funds reached T182.5 billion (US$1.2 billion). At the same time, the share of state pension funds fell from 39 per cent to 32 per cent over 2001. On the other hand, the minimum capital required to invest in private pension funds doubled in 2000 to T180 million (US$1.2 billion), leading to the merger of private funds with stronger institutions, and the share of private funds grew to 68 per cent in 2001.

Main cities

Astana (capital, estimated population 343,250 in 2005); Almaty (commercial capital, 1.2 million); Karaganda (404,881); Shymkent (373,658); Taraz (352,769); Pavlodar (309,723), Semey (269,759).

Languages spoken

Kazakh (Turkic) is only spoken by around 40 per cent of the population. Russian is the language of inter-ethnic communication, spoken by two-thirds of the population and used in everyday business.

Official language/s

Kazakh

Media

Although the constitution guarantees freedom of the press, private owned and opposition media outlets are subject to harassment and censorship. Presidential prerogative includes his private life, health and financial dealings being designated state secrets and criminal charges can be incurred for 'insulting' the president and public officials. The government has control of most printing presses and transmission facilities for radio and television.

National news agency: Kazinform

Other news agencies:

Interfax-Kazakhstan: www.interfax.kz

Press

According to government statistics, there are 990 privately owned newspapers and 418 privately owned magazines. Most are supportive of the government with members of President Nazarbayeva's family owning some of the largest circulating newspapers.

Dailies: There are several daily and weekly newspapers in both Russian and Kazakh including: Kazakhstanskaya Pravda (www.kazpravda.kz), Karavan (www.caravan.kz), Ekspress-K (www.express-k.kz), Vremya (www.time.kz), Liter (www.liter.kz) and Zhas Alash (www.zhasalash.kz).

Business: In Cyrillic, Delovaya Nedelya (www.dn.kz), Panarama (www.panorama.vkkz.com) are Russian-language publications. The US-based news agency EIN News (www.einnews.com) also provides business and economic news, in English.

Broadcasting

A law was introduced in 2002 requiring that at least 50 per cent of all television and radio broadcasts must be in the Kazakh language other languages include Russian and Chinese. The Turkish Radio and Television Corporation (TRT) also broadcasts programmes for Kazakhstan.

Radio: Kazakh Radio is state-run, private stations including Europa Plus (www.europaplus.kz) with a nationwide network, Khabar Hit FM and Russkoye Radio-Aziya are owned by President Nazarbayeva's daughter. Other, private stations include Radio 31 (www.31.kz/radio31), Radio Tekc (www.radiotex.net) and Auto Radio (www.avtoradio.kz).

International radio networks including the BBC (www.bbc.co.uk/worldservice) and Radio Free Europe (www.rferl.org) are available.

Television: Of there are five television channels available all are either government owned by family members of President Nazarbayeva. The state-run Kazakh TV has two channels. The Khabar news agency owns Khabar TV (www.khabar.kz), Yel Arna (for cultural programmes) and Caspionet (www.caspionet.kz) a satellite station. KTK (www.ktk.kz) is a commercial channel. Other private stations include Channel 31 TV (www.31.kz), Alma TV, the first cable TV station in Almaty and Perviy Kanal Evraziya a local channel.

Imported US TV programmes are popular.

Economy

Kazakhstan's attempt to introduce a free market economy, as well as political stability, initially left the economy in turmoil in 1992–98. Energy shortages were commonplace and the reliance on Russian export routes stifled oil and gas earnings.

Macroeconomic and currency stability were evident by 2000, due to oil revenue. GDP has shown strong growth since 2000 of over 9 per cent each year until 2005 when it was 9.4 per cent; it is expected to grow by 8.3 per cent in 2006. Oil exports typically represent over 30 per cent of GDP growth. Such exports grew by 37.4 per cent in 2005 and are estimated to have grown by 25.9 per cent in 2006. This growth coincided with record world prices for petroleum and Kazakhstan has reaped enormous oil revenue. This, coupled with a rapid growth in non-oil revenues, led to a substantial expansion of budgetary expenditure and increased fiscal surplus. Government spending has expanded, averaging around 20 per cent, since 2003. The highest rates of growth were on housing and agriculture.

The unemployment rate has been around 8 per cent per annum; there has been a 30 per cent increase in pensions and public sector salaries, resulting in inflation rising from 6.9 per cent in 2004 to 7.6 per cent in 2005 and projected to remain around 8 per cent in 2006/07.

Kazakhstan has significant deposits of petroleum, gas, and minerals including coal, iron ore, copper, zinc, uranium, and gold. Agriculture products include dairy goods, leather, meat, wool and grain (Kazakhstan is the seventh-largest producer of wheat in the world, typically producing 15–16 million tonnes per annum). The banking sector remains strong, which has contributed to growing public confidence. The country's strong macroeconomic performance resulted in the foreign currency debt rating of BBB- (Standard and Poor's). The monetary policy has been well managed and government has adopted an openness to foreign investment and implemented market economy reforms in currency convertibility, while controlling an allocation of resources.

External trade

Kazakhstan was still in negotiation to join the World Trade Organisation (WTO), in July 2007. It belongs to the Eurasian Economic Community (EurAsec or EAEC), which was set up in 2000 to promote a customs union between its six member states (Belarus, Kazakhstan, Kyrgyzstan, Russia, Tajikistan, and Uzbekistan) and among other objectives, to introduce standardised currency exchange and rules for trade in goods and service. The EAEC evolved out of the Commonwealth of Independent States (CIS) Customs Union and has begun the process of merging with the Central Asian Co-operation Organisation (CACO).

Kazakhstan has plentiful natural resources, including oil and gas, coal, copper, silver, uranium and zinc, all of which are export commodities. Around 50 per cent of all exports is oil, which provides 30 per cent of GDP. As the manufacturing sector is underdeveloped imports are dominated by capital and consumer goods.

Imports

Principal imports include machinery and equipment (over 40 per cent), vehicles, machinery, iron and steel, appliances and electronic products and fuel.

Main sources: Russia (38.3 per cent total, 2006), China (8.1 per cent), Germany (7.6 per cent)

Exports

Principal exports are dominated by primary products including oil and oil products (over 50 per cent), ferrous metals (around 25 per cent), chemicals, machinery, grain, wool, meat and coal.

Main destinations: Italy (18.0 per cent total, 2006), Switzerland (17.6 per cent), Russia (9.8 per cent).

Agriculture

Farming

Agriculture contributes approximately 8.5 per cent to GDP and employs a quarter of the working population.

Kazakhstan's farming area constituted 16 per cent of the former Soviet Union's farm land. The cultivation of the 'Virgin Lands' in the north during the Soviet period introduced a high level of mechanisation and Kazakhstan used to provide around 14 per cent of Soviet grain.

There are still many problems in the agricultural sector, including weaknesses in input supply (such as fertilisers), poor incentives for farm production and failure to restructure farm enterprises. Privatisation is proceeding slowly. Small-scale private farming has been introduced in the south, while production in the north remains more centralised. While agricultural land may be leased long-term, attempts to introduce private land ownership is unpopular.

Irrigated land in the south and east produces fruit, vegetables, sugar beet, rice, tobacco, mustard and natural rubber. Wheat, cotton and oilseeds are the main crops produced. Dairy farming, horse breeding and sheep breeding are also undertaken.

Crop production in 2005 included: 13,737,600 tonnes (t) cereals in total,

11,070,000t wheat, 1,546,000t barley, 2,520,000t potatoes, 307,000t rice, 510,000t maize, 145,000t oats, *28,000t grapes, 163,485t oilcrops, 517,000t tomatoes, 310,800t sugar beets, 77,000t chillies & peppers, *14,000 tobacco, 350,000 seed cotton, *100,000t cotton lint, 150,000t apples, 256,500t fruit in total, 2,840,900t vegetables in total. Livestock production included: 768,800t meat in total, 345,000t beef, 207,000t pig meat, 110,000t lamb, 7,500t goat meat, 43,000t poultry, 55,000t horsemeat, 141,005t eggs, 4,712,700t milk, *1,000t honey, *41,800t cattle hides, 10,600t sheepskins, 29,200t greasy wool.

* estimate

Fishing

In the north-eastern part of Kazakhstan cold water fish are found in the River Ob catchment area, including the Altai Mountains drainage of the Irtysh River, mountain rivers of the Tien Shan range and in Lake Balkhash, which has a mix of cold water and temperate water fish stocks.The fishing of streams and rivers is largely unmanaged, but considerable effort has been put into maintaining reasonably high fish catches in some lakes and reservoirs. Kazakhstan has concentrated largely on the exploitation of indigenous fish stocks. The typical annual fish catch is over 31,000mt.

Forestry

Forest and other wooded land account for a small part of the total. Forests cover around 12.1 million hectares, which has increased by an average of 2.22 per cent per annum.

The increasing demand for forest products is met by imports, mainly from the Russian Federation, with imports in 2004 valued at US$239 million and exports at US$5.4 million.

Estimated production in 2004 included 300,800 cubic metres (cum) roundwood, 129,900cum industrial roundwood, 103,920cum sawlogs and veneer logs, 265,084cum sawnwood, 10,375t wood-based panels, 170,900cum wood fuel; 58,000 tonnes (t) paper and paperboard.

Industry and manufacturing

The share of industry, including mining, in GDP in 2004 was estimated at 39.5 per cent. The sector grew by 10.6 per cent in 2004.

Kazakhstan inherited a well-developed industrial base from the Soviet era. The principal activities are in minerals, petrochemicals, food processing, machinery and light industry.

Tourism

Kazakhstan's considerable tourist potential is being actively developed by the government, which has accorded it priority status. A Law on Tourism Activities was promulgated and a five-year Tourist Development Plan adopted in 2001, with the object of presenting a positive image of the country, building essential infrastructure and ensuring visitor safety. Visitor numbers and revenues have risen. There were 106,486 arrivals in 2004, an increase of 19.2 per cent over the previous year. Tourism contributed 1.6 per cent to GDP in 2004. Attractions include the Silk Road, adventure and eco-tourism. Air connections are being improved — Air Astana has opened direct routes to major European cities as well as Seoul and Bangkok.

Environment

The Aral Sea was subject to a loss of up to 50 per cent of its water, dropping by up to 19 metres, due to the overuse of water from the two main rivers which fed into it. A World Bank funded project to build, reconstruct and rehabilitate waterworks along the river Syr Darya has reversed the damaged in the northern section of the sea. A sluice will be installed to supply water to the parched southern section. Plans are underway to improve irrigation in the farmland around the sea. Potentially, revenue may be earned from the sale of hydroelectic power.

Mining

Mining contributes around 15 per cent to GDP and employs 8 per cent of the workforce.

Rich in mineral resources, Kazakhstan produces 40 per cent of the world's chrome ore, second only to South Africa. There are also important deposits of iron ore, nickel, cobalt, vanadium, titanium, copper, lead, wolfram, zinc, gold, silver, tin, tungsten, molybdenum, uranium, cadmium, bismuth, pyrophyllite, barite, phosphorites, magnesium, phosphorous, asbestos, rare earths and sizeable manganese deposits in eastern and northern Kazakhstan. There are significant bauxite reserves in southern Kazakhstan.

Hydrocarbons

Kazakhstan was the former-Soviet Union's second-largest oil producer after Russia, and is believed to have the world's largest untapped oil and gas reserves. Since independence, the government has concentrated its efforts on attracting foreign investment to this sector.

Kazakhstan has proven oil reserves of 9.0 billion barrels. Total reserves are thought to be far higher. Foreign investment has flooded into the booming oil sector and since 1992 oil production has increased by over 50 per cent to 1.2 million barrels per day (bpd). Around 75 per cent of production is exported and accounts for around a quarter of GDP. In March 2007, KazMunaiGas, the 60 per cent state-owned oil company, announced net profits for 2006 of US$972 million, an increase on 2005 of 180 per cent, although total production had only increased by 2 per cent.

There are three major refineries at Pavlador, Atyrau and Shymkent with a joint capacity of 345,093 bpd. The downstream sector, which is unattractive to foreign investors, continues to be state-controlled.

Kazakhstan has proven natural gas reserves of 1.9 trillion cubic metres and produces 16.2 billion cubic metres a year. A lack of sufficient pipeline infrastructure has meant that Kazakhstan has not reached its full potential in natural gas exploitation. The government has targeted the sector for expansion. The completion of the 635km Karachaganak-Atyrau pipeline in 2003 allows Kazakhstan to export limited quantities of gas and other hydrocarbons.

Kazakhstan has recoverable reserves of coal of 37.5 billion tonnes and produces 95 million tonnes per year. Coal is the largest domestic source of energy. Output and consumption of coal have declined since independence. Around 28 million tonnes of coal are exported, mainly to Russia and Ukraine. Many of the high-cost underground coal mines have been closed, and its more competitive surface mines have been purchased and are operated by international energy companies.

Energy

Kazakhstan has a total electricity generating capacity of 17.4GW produced mainly by coal-fired power plants, but with an increasing proportion from five hydroelectric power stations. The sector is faced with large amounts of inefficient or redundant equipment and needs considerable investment if it is to reverse the decline in output and halt the frequent power stoppages experienced since independence.

Kazakhstan closed down its only nuclear station in 1999. The government is considering the construction of a new 1,500MW nuclear power plant in the south-east near Lake Balkash by 2012.

Financial markets

Stock exchange

The Kazakhstan Stock Exchange (KSE) was launched in September 1997.

Banking and insurance

In the early 1990s, Kazakhstan had a liberal banking policy which allowed the emergence of many banks which were under-capitalised and badly managed.

Central bank

National Bank of Kazakhstan

Following the National Bank of Kazakhstan's transition to international accounting standards, it announced on 29 January 2003 that it will no longer set the exchange rate for the tenge for accounting purposes.

Time

Western Kazakhstan: GMT plus four hours
Central Kazakhstan, Astana: GMT plus five hours
Eastern Kazakhstan, Almaty: GMT plus six hours

Geography

Kazakhstan, in Central Asia, is a landlocked country but with a coastline on the Caspian Sea, (the largest lake in the world). It is the second-largest country in the region, extending some 1,900km (1,200 miles) from the Volga river in Europe, in the west, to the Altai mountains, in the east, and about 1,300km (800 miles) from the Siberian plain in the north to the Central Asian deserts in the south. Kazakhstan's 2.7 million square km are equivalent to the size of Western Europe and comprise rolling steppes to the north, desert to the south and part of the western edge of the Tien Shan mountains to the south-east.

Kazakhstan is bordered by the Russian Federation to the north, China to the east, Kyrgyzstan, Uzbekistan and Turkmenistan to the south. In the south-west there is almost a 1,000km coastline on the Caspian Sea. Half of the Aral Sea lies within Kazakhstan, the other half in Uzbekistan.

Hemisphere

Northern

Climate

The temperature varies greatly from temperate steppe in the north to desert in the south. Temperatures in southern Kazakhstan average minus 3 degrees Celsius (C) in January and 29 degrees C in June. Average temperatures in Almaty range from minus 5 degrees C to 35 degrees C. Rainfall averages 200–300mm per annum in the north of the country and 400–500mm in the south.

Dress codes

Not overly formal during business hours, although women must dress modestly. Formal wear may be expected when visiting the theatre or attending a dinner party. Shorts should not be worn except in a sporting environment.

Entry requirements

Passports

Required by all visitors, valid for six months beyond intended length of stay.

Visa

Required by all, except nationals of CIS countries and Turkey. Business visas are issued after an invitation from a local company has been registered with the consular department of the Ministry of Foreign Affairs in Kazakhstan. When authorised, the host company obtains a reference number which is forwarded to the applicant who submits the application form along with a business letter of intent, a full itinerary and an undertaking of financial responsibility for expenses incurred by the representative. Details can be obtained from the consular section of the nearest embassy.

Tourist visits over five days require registration by the local authorities on arrival.

Currency advice/regulations

There are no restrictions on the import and export of local currency. Import of foreign currency is allowed subject to declaration on arrival; export is limited to amount declared.

Customs

A customs declaration form must be completed on arrival and retained until departure. Items for declaration are articles intended for personal use (currency, jewellery, cameras, computers, etc), which must be exported when leaving. It is advisable to keep receipts for goods purchased locally.

Prohibited imports

Military weapons and ammunition, illegal drugs, pornography, live animals, photographs or printed material detrimental to the image of Kazakhstan, loose pearls or anything carried for a third party.

Health (for visitors)

Mandatory precautions

Vaccination certificates are required for yellow fever if travelling from an infected area. For stays over one month and applications for visas for stays over three months, an AIDS certificate is required.

Advisable precautions

It is advisable to be in date for the following immunisations: polio (within 10 years), tetanus (within 10 years), typhoid fever, TB, hepatitis A, tick-borne encephalitis. Anti-malarial precautions advisable. Any medicines required by the traveller should be taken by the visitor, and it could be wise to have precautionary antibiotics if going outside major urban centres. A travel kit including a disposable syringe is a reasonable precaution. Water precautions recommended: water purification tablets may be useful or drink bottled water. Rabies is a health risk.

Hotels

Advisable to book at least a month in advance through Intourist or other specialist travel agents. There are many luxury Western-style hotels in Almaty. Gratuities are becoming more customary, particularly in international hotels.

Credit cards

More widely accepted than anywhere else in Central Asia; as well as being welcomed in shops and hotels, they can be used for cash advances.

Public holidays (national)

Fixed dates

1–2 Jan (New Year), 8 Mar (Women's Day), 22 Mar (Nauryz Meyrami/Traditional Spring Holiday/Persian New Year), 1 May (Unity Day), 9 May (Victory Day), 30 Aug (Constitution Day), 25 Oct (Republic Day), 16 Dec (Independence Day).

Variable dates

Eid al Adha

Working hours

Banking

Mon–Fri: 0930–1730.

Business

Mon–Fri: 0900–1800.

Government

Mon–Fri: 0900–1730.

Shops

Mon–Sat: 0900–1700.

Electricity supply

220V AC.

Social customs/useful tips

Kazakhistanis are very hospitable and courteous. It is best to book appointments for meetings in the morning. Cancellation, even at the last minute, is fairly common. Russian is the everyday business language. Business and politics are intertwined, with negotiations and deals often 'arranged'.

Security

It is unwise to venture out on the streets alone at night. Dress inconspicuously as wealthy-looking foreigners can be a target for muggers.

It may be preferable to travel by intercity bus rather than train, as robberies are making rail travel increasingly hazardous.

Getting there

Air

Almaty is the principal gateway to the country and well-served, with the most developed air routes through Turkey and Russia.

National airline: Air Astana.

International airport/s: Almaty International (ALA), 10km north-east of the city; hotel, car hire, duty-free shops, cafeterias. Atyrau International (GUW), 8km west of the city; bank, post office, restaurant, car hire. Astana (TSE), 17 km south of the city; facilities include duty-free shop and restaurant. Buses and taxis connect to the city centre.

Other airport/s: There are fifteen other airports.

Airport tax: None

Surface

Road: There are generally good international road connections to the surrounding countries. The north-east area is well served by roads to the Urals and the North Caucasus.

The Regional Road Corridor Improvement Project, estimated at US$18 billion, to improve Central Asian roads, airports, railway lines and seaports and provide a vital transit route between Europe and Asia was agreed, on 3 November 2007. Six new transit corridors, between Afghanistan, Azerbaijan, China, Kazakhstan, Kyrgyzstan, Mongolia, Tajikistan and Uzbekistan, of mainly roads and rail links, will be constructed, or existing resources upgraded, by 2013. Half the costs with be provided by the Asian Development Bank and other multilateral organisations and the other half by participating countries.

Rail: A railway line was completed in 1991 between Almaty and Urumchi in China. There are also rail connections to Russia, Kyrgystan and Turkmenistan. A new railway line is being built to connect Iran and Turkey with Kazakhstan.

Foreign visitors should use caution when travelling by train, other than the Almaty-Moscow line, as violent crime against westerners is on the increase.

Main port/s: Aktau (formerly Shevchenko) on the Caspian Sea is the main oil port and trans-shipment centre.

Getting about

National transport

Air: There are fifteen domestic/local airports located around the regions that are served by scheduled internal flights. It should be noted that maintenance procedures for aircraft on internal flights may not conform to internationally accepted standards.

Planes and helicopters can be chartered for nominal prices provided you have a good local contact.

Road: Primary and secondary roads are of poor quality, particularly in desert and semi-desert regions. However, the Oral region is well served by road links to the Urals, European Russia and the North Caucasus. Road transport is subject to cancellation and delay. Passengers are advised to travel in groups. Petrol supplies are adequate. Kazakhstan has 189,000km of paved and gravelled roads, 108,100km of unpaved roads and 80,900km of earth roads.

Buses: There are regular bus services between all the main cities.

Rail: Rail links are extensive but slow. There are 14,460km of railway, excluding industrial lines, in Kazakhstan. The Turksib railway connects Almaty with the Trans-Siberian line to the north at Novisibirsk, while the principal rail connection with Moscow runs through Chimkent and Uralsk.

City transport

Taxis: Unless Russian or Kazakh is spoken, ensure any taxi taken is booked through the hotel reception desk and that the price is agreed beforehand.

Buses, trams & metro: Swift and cheap trolley-bus and bus network in Almaty.

Car hire

A national driver's licence with an authorised translation or an international driving permit is required.

BUSINESS DIRECTORY

The addresses listed below are a selection only. While World of Information makes every endeavour to check these addresses, we cannot guarantee that changes have not been made, especially to telephone numbers and area codes. We would welcome any corrections.

Telephone area codes

The international direct dialling code (IDD) for Kazakhstan is +7, followed by area code and subscriber's number:

Almaty	3272	Shimkent	3252
Astana	3172	Uralsk	3112
Karaganda	3212	Ust-Kamenogorsk	3232
Petropavlovsk	3152	Zhezkazgan	3102

Useful telephone numbers

Police: 02

Fire: 01

Ambulance: 03

Chambers of Commerce

Almaty Chamber of Commerce and Industry, 45 Tole bi Street, Almaty 480091 (tel: 620-301; fax: 611-404; e-mail: alcci@nursat.kz).

American Chamber of Commerce in Kazakhstan, 531 Seifullina Prospect, Almaty 480091 (tel: 587-938; fax: 587-939; e-mail: information@amcham.kz).

East Kazakhstan Chamber of Commerce and Industry, PO Box 177, 3 Novatorov Street, Ust-Kamenogorsk 492000 (tel: 265-310; fax:267-247; e-mail@cci@ustk.kz).

Kazakhstan Union of Chambers of Commerce and Industry, 26 Masanchi Street, Almaty 480091 (tel: 920-052; fax: 507-029; e-mail: tpprkaz@online.ru).

North Kazakhstan Chamber of Commerce and Industry, 112 Mira Street, Petropavlovsk 642015 (tel: 460-568; fax: 465-443; e-mail: tpp@petropavl.kz).

Semipalatinsk Chamber of Commerce and Industry, 92/22 Abai Street, Semipalatinsk 490050 (tel/fax: 627-887; e-mail: tpp@relcom.kz).

South Kazakhstan Chamber of Commerce and Industry, 31 Tauke khan Street, Shimkent 486050 (tel: 211-405; fax: 211-403).

West Kazakhstan Chamber of Commerce and Industry, 67 Kuibyshev Street, Uralsk 417000 (tel: 504-440; fax: 513-537; e-mail: zktpp@kaznet.kz).

Banking

ATF Bank, 100 Furmanov Str, 480091 Almaty (tel: 503-765; fax: 501-995).

Bank Centercredit, 100 Shevchenko Street, 480072 Almaty (tel: 634-605, 680-140; fax: 507-813).

Central Asian Bank for Co-operation and Development, 115-a Abay Ave, Almaty (tel: 422-737; fax: 428-627).

Demir Kazakhstan Bank, 61A Kurmangazy Street, 480091 Almaty (tel: 508-550, 508-527; fax: 508-525).

Export-Import Bank of Kazakhstan, 118 Pushkin Street, 480021 Almaty (tel: 622-815, 633-767, 634-300; fax: 631-985).

Halyk Savings Bank of Kazakhstan; 97 Rozybakieva St, 480046 Almaty (tel: 509-991; fax: 679-738).

Kazkommertsbank, 135 Gagarin Avenue, 480060 Almaty (tel: 585-101; fax: 585-281; internet site: http://www.kkb.kz).

Temirbank, 68/74 Abay Ave, 480008 Almaty (tel: 587-888; fax: 590-529; e-mail: board@temirbank.kz; internet site: http://www.temirbank.kz).

Central bank

National Bank of Kazakhstan, 21 Koktem-3, 480090 Almaty (tel: 504-631; fax: 506-090; e-mail: info@nationalbank.kz).

Travel information

Aeroflot, 111 Zhibek Zhola Street, Almaty (tel: 390-594).

Air Kazakhstan, 59 Mira Street, 480003 Almaty (tel: 335-518; fax: 335-506).

Flight information (24 hours) (tel: 541-555).

Intourist, Hotel Ostrar, Gogolya 65, Almaty (tel: 330-045, 330-076).

Almaty Airport, Mailin Street 2B, 480040 Almaty (tel: 571-300; fax: 571-281).

Astana International Airport, PO Box 1968, 473026 Astana (tel: 333-709; fax: 333-741).

Kazakhstan Tourist Agency, 22 Kosmonautov Street, 480083 Almaty (tel: 390-318; fax: 390-257).

Travel Bureau, Hotel Irtysh, Ulitsa Abai 97, Semipalatinsk, Almaty (tel: 447-529, 447-531).

National tourist organisation offices
Department of Tourism, 4 Republic Square, Almaty 4860065 (tel/fax: 620-030; e-mail: dep_tour@nursat.kz; internet: www.kaztour.kz).

Ministries
Ministry of Agriculture, 49 Abai Street, 473000 Astana (tel: 323-763; fax: 324-541).

Ministry of Culture, Information and Public Accord, 22 Beibitshilik Street, 473000 Astana (tel: 322-495; fax: 326-203).

Ministry of Defence, 49 Auezova Street, 473000 Astana (tel: 337-845;fax: 337-892).

Ministry of Economy and Trade, 2 Beibitshilik Street, 473000 Astana (tel/fax: 333-003).

Ministry of Education and Science, 83 Kenesary Street, 473000 Astana (tel: 322-540; fax: 326-482).

Ministry of Employment and Social Security, 2 Manasa Street, 473000 Astana (tel: 153-602; fax: 341-270).

Ministry of Energy and Mineral Resources, 37 Beibitshilik Street, 473000 Astana (tel: 337-133; fax: 337-164).

Ministry of Finance, 60 Republic Avenue, 473000 Astana (tel: 334-186;fax: 280-321).

Ministry of Foreign Affairs, 10 Beibitshilik Street, 473000 Astana (tel: 327-669; fax: 327-667).

Ministry of Internal Affairs, 4 Manasa Street, 473000 Astana (tel: 343-601; fax: 341-738).

Ministry of Justice, 45 Pobeda Street, 473000 Astana (tel: 391-213; fax: 321-554).

Ministry of Natural Resources and Environmental Protection, 81 Karl Marx Street, 475000 Kokshetau (tel: 54-265; fax: 50-620).

Ministry of State Revenues, 48 Abai Avenue (tel: 326-951;fax: 326-963).

Ministry of Transport and Communications, 49 Abai Street, 473000 Astana (tel: 326-277; fax: 321-058).

Prime Minister's Office, 11 Beibitshilik Street, 473000 Astana (tel: 320-985;fax: 152-028).

Other useful addresses
Atomic Energy Agency, 13 Republic Square, 480013 Almaty (tel: 637-626; fax: 633-356).

Board for Investment Projects, Department of Transport, Room 124, Gogol Str 86, 480091 Almaty (tel: 323-661, 324-769; fax: 322-679, 324-449).

Business Communication Centre, 89 Michurina Street, Almaty 480059 (tel: 476-803, 347-549; fax: 347-798).

Centre for Economic Reforms, 4 Republic Square, Almaty (tel: 621-836).

Committee for the use of Foreign Capital, 152 Bogenbai Batyr, 3rd Floord, Ablay Khan Street 97, 480091 Almaty (tel: 627-326; fax: 696-152).

Kazakh Centre of Business Co-operation 'Atakent', 42 Timiryazeve Street, Almaty 480058 (tel: 473-113; fax: 509-238).

Kazakh Embassy (USA), 1401 16th Street, NW, Washington DC 20036 (tel: (+1-202)-232-5488; fax: (+1-202)-232-5845; e-mail: kazakh@intr.net).

Kazakhgas, 521 Seifullin Street, Almaty (tel: 324-288; fax: 325-442).

Kazakhstan Caspishelf, 211 Mukhanov Street, Almaty (tel: 416-034; fax: 416-430).

Kazakhstan Commerce (import-export), Zhibek Zholy 64, 480002 Almaty (tel: 333-871; fax: 331-483).

Kazakhstan Foreign Trade Organisation, v/o Kazakhintorg, Gogolya 111, Almaty (tel: 328-381).

Kazakhstanmunaigas (oil and gas refining), 458 Seifullin Street, Almaty (tel: 695-800; fax: 626-630).

Kazakh Academy of Sciences Engineering Institute, 80 Bogenbay Batyr Street, Almaty 480100 (tel: 541-281; fax: 695-769).

Kazakhstan Stock Exchange, Ulitsa Timipiazeva 42, Almaty (tel: 441-043; fax: 447-809).

Kazakh State TV and Radio, Ulitsa Mira 175, Almaty (tel: 633-716).

Kazchrome Transnational Corporation, 56 Kunaev Street, Almaty, 480002.

KazMunayGaz, 142 Bogenbai Batyr Street, 470091 Almaty (tel: 626-080; fax: 695-405).

Kazpisprom (a joint-stock company representing food producers), 92 Internatsionalnaya Street, Almaty (tel: 629-482; fax: 628-652).

Kaztag (state news agency), 77 Ablai Han Street, Almaty (tel: 625-037).

Kazvetmet (represents metal producers), 111 Gogol Street, 480003 Almaty (tel: 622-318; fax: 328-488).

Market Economy Group (privatisation committee), President's Office, Government House, Almaty (tel: 621-022).

State Property and Privatisation Committee, Ministry of Finance, 36 Auezov Street, 473024 Astana (tel: 334-397; fax: 320-937).

Union of Manufacturers and Businessmen, 4/450 Republic Square, Almaty (tel: 622-307; fax: 665-490).

National news agency: Kazinform

Other news agencies:
Interfax-Kazakhstan: www.interfax.kz

Internet sites
Kazakhstan local navigator: http://reenic.utexas.edu/reenic/countries/kazakhstan/kazakhstan/html

Kazakhstan government website: http://www.president.kz/

Kenya

KEY FACTS

Official name: Jamhuri ya Kenya (Republic of Kenya)

Head of State: President Mwai Kibaki (Narc) (re-elected 27 Dec 2007)

Head of government: Prime Minister Raila Odinga (ODM) (from 13 Apr 2008)

Ruling party: Orange Democratic Movement (ODM) (elected 27 Dec 2007)

Area: 582,646 square km

Population: 34.65 million (2007)

Capital: Nairobi

Official language: KiSwahili and English

Currency: Kenyan shilling (Ksh) = 100 cents (convertible with currencies of Tanzania and Uganda)

Exchange rate: Ksh66.30 per US$ (Jul 2008)

GDP per capita: US$845 (2007)*

GDP real growth: 6.90% (2007)*

Labour force: 16.94 million (2004)

Inflation: 9.70% (2007)*

Balance of trade: -US$2.30 billion (2006)

Foreign debt: US$6.79 billion (2004)

* estimated figure

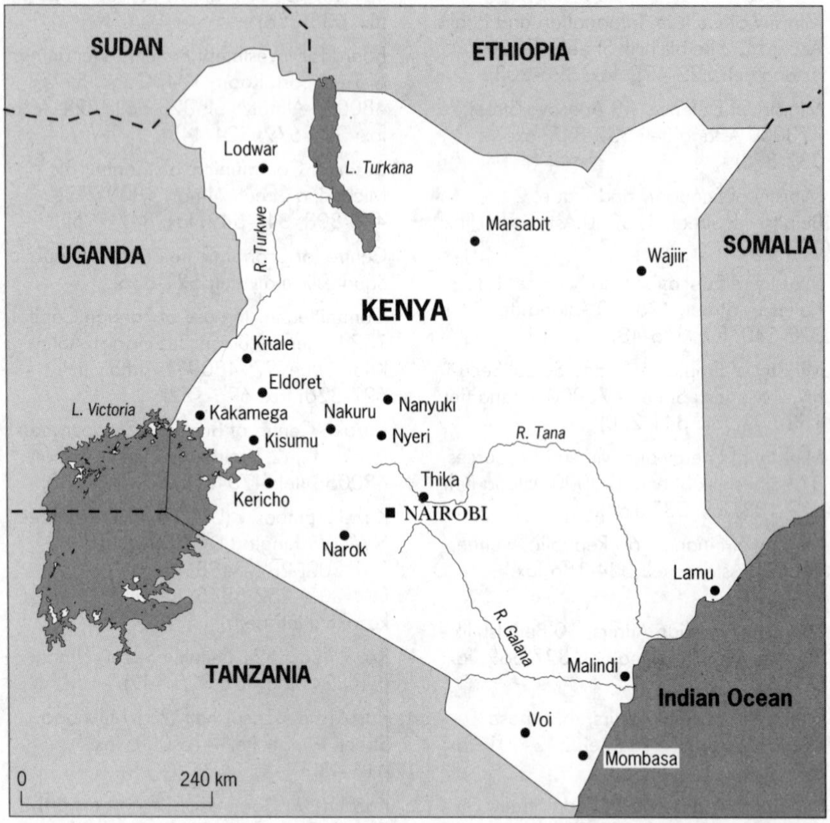

Almost ten years on from the powerful explosions that rocked the American embassies in Nairobi and Dar es Salaam (Tanzania) in August 1998, Kenyans were again mourning their dead in early 2008. This time it wasn't international terrorism but Kenyan tribalism that caused the devastation.

Disappointed, but not surprised

The elections for president and parliament held on 27 December 2007 were closely contested with more candidates standing than ever before – 2,548 candidates stood for the 210 parliamentary seats. Turnout was over 70 per cent; 60 per cent of the previous members lost their seats, including 20 cabinet ministers. The Orange Democratic Movement (ODM) won 99 seats while the president's Party of National Unity coalition (PNU) won 43 seats. The presidential result announced was 47 per cent (4,584,721 votes) for incumbent Mwai Kibaki of the PNU and 44 per cent (4,352,993) for Raila Odinga of the ODM. Observers, both domestic and international, denounced the presidential counting as flawed and there were violent protests from ODM supporters. The violence spread across the country and although the actual number will probably never be known, it is estimated that as many as 1,500 lives were lost, and up to 600,000 people displaced.

A team of eminent persons appointed by the African Union (AU), led by former UN secretary general, Kofi Annan, with Graça Machel and former Tanzania president Benjamin Mkapa, helped negotiate a settlement. President Kibaki, who had been inaugurated immediately after the elections, eventually agreed to appoint Raila Odinga as prime minister of a coalition government. Political analysts said they were saddened and disappointed by violence that had followed the elections, but not surprised.

Economy to decline?

The Kenyan economy suffered a sever shock from the ethnic violence following the elections. Tourism figures dropped immediately and will take time to recover. International confidence has been damaged and tribal rivalries reignited. Kenya had previously been showing steady growth – growth in 2007 was 6.9 per cent compared to 6.1 per cent in 2006. According to *African Economic Outlook* (AEO), published jointly by the African Development Bank (AfDB) and the Organisation for Economic Co-operation and Development (OECD) in 2007, this reflected broad-based growth in most sectors. Under the Economic Recovery Strategy (ERS) which ended in 2007, investor confidence was restored, farm prices improved, and rural electrification proceeded in many parts of the country. Before the eruption of the crisis following the disputed presidential election, the economy appeared to be on track to maintain or improve upon its performance in 2007. However, now it appears probable that growth in 2008 will be much less than expected. The implementation from 2008 of *Vision 2030*, a strategy comprising five-year development plans, the first of which provides for increased investments in infrastructure and other key sectors, should provide continued impetus for growth.

Still corrupt

It is salutary to read in the 1980 edition of *Africa Review* that the then presidency of Daniel arap Moi was going to be remembered for ridding Kenya of 'corruption, nepotism, bribery and related practices'. It was said at the time, 'not a day went by' without some new 'probe' or 'investigation'. Over a quarter of a century later little appears to have changed in the Kenyan approach to election and government. Reflecting President Mwai Kibaki's election platform, anti-corruption measures dominate political and structural reform.

In early 2006 finance minister David Mwiraria resigned after being accused, with other senior officials, of being involved in a scam to received money for security contracts. Former anti-corruption ombudsman, John Githongo, who fled to exile in the UK in February 2005, was asked by parliament to return to Nairobi to give evidence. His report on corruption, which was leaked to the press, said that his attempts to investigate the Anglo-Leasing scandal had been blocked by four ministers, including Mr Mwiraria.

Kenya's greatest weakness is still its level of corruption in the highest places, actual and percieved. Major lenders such as the World Bank, International Monetary Fund (IMF), the US, Japan and the UK, have all at one time or another withdrawn or stopped aid funds. In April 2007, the IMF released funds of US$56.8 million, the first for over two years. It also extended Kenya's Poverty Reduction and Growth Facility (PRGF) programme to the end of November to enable time to complete the third review on Kenya's performance. These funds followed two weeks after a change of heart by the World Bank, which made Kenya the first country to have its Country Assisstance Strategy (CAS) updated. Although the IMF had overlooked some of its key demands in unlocking its funding, it did insist that its demands that ministers, permanent secretaries and heads of state firms declare their wealth was the basis for the waiver.

When tackled on a perceived slowness of economic reform, Kibaki's government had pleaded the large amount of time devoted to constitutional reform, capacity constraints in key ministries, and the slow resumption of donor budgetary assistance. Progress in implementing structural reforms has been mixed. There have been delays in implementing reforms in the areas of public expenditure, the financial sector and parastatals. The lack of progress in moving toward a comprehensive medium-term expenditure framework and instituting a more robust expenditure management system is attributable to organisational and capacity constraints at the ministry of finance. Parastatal reforms suffered from a lack of consensus on the objectives and modalities for privatisation.

The domestic revenue effort has been strengthened and expenditure restructuring and management reforms accelerated. Domestic borrowing targets have been relaxed somewhat. Although these changes will result in a moderate increase in domestic budgetary resources and in an improvement in the productivity of public spending, public investment will be scaled down over the medium-term compared to original assumptions.

The medium-term macroeconomic framework has been modified to take account of the more difficult environment now foreseen for the medium-term. The terms of trade are now projected to deteriorate moderately instead of producing the modest gains envisaged earlier. Donor assistance will fall significantly short of earlier expectations and key reforms in the financial and parastatal sectors have been crowded out of the legislative agenda by constitutional reform deliberations.

The eventual lowering of the domestic debt ratio to GDP remains the key focus of the economic programme. To preserve some essential social and economic programme in the face of slow donor support, domestic borrowing will exceed expectations, but in the short-term be broadly unchanged at 22 per cent of GDP

KEY INDICATORS — Kenya

	Unit	2003	2004	2005	2006	2007
Population	m	32.39	33.52	33.45	34.05	*34.65
Gross domestic product (GDP)	US$bn	14.30	16.10	18.73	22.82	*29.30
GDP per capita	US$	385	482	560	*670	*845
GDP real growth	%	1.9	3.1	5.8	6.1	*6.9
Inflation	%	3.6	11.5	10.3	14.4	*9.7
Industrial output	% change	–	3.4	1.4	2.0	–
Agricultural output	% change	–	1.4	0.7	3.0	–
Exports (fob) (goods)	US$m	2,411.0	2,589.0	2,820.0	3,502.0	–
Imports (cif) (goods)	US$m	3,564.0	4,190.0	5,065.0	6,768.4	–
Balance of trade	US$m	-1,153.0	-1,601.0	-2,245.0	-3,266.4	–
Current account	US$m	132.4	-136.7	-260.6	-525.7	*-1,014.0
Total reserves minus gold	US$m	1,481.9	1,519.3	1,798.8	2,415.8	3,355.0
Foreign exchange	US$m	1,461.0	1,499.0	1,780.6	2,396.0	3,334.6
Exchange rate	per US$	76.79	77.37	69.55	69.55	62.95

* estimated figure

compared with the original target of 24.7 per cent. Some crowding out of private activity is expected, as the public sector will absorb a sizeable proportion of projected financial savings. The domestic debt-ratio is expected to decline thereafter.

Outlook

Before the December 2007 elections polls suggested that many Kenyans consider life to be worse under the then Narc government than under Moi. The resulting ousting of so many long standing members of parliament and ministers was an encouraging demonstration f democracy at work. However, until the pervasive taint of corruption can be removed from Kenyan politics and public life, the country will struggle to reach levels of investment and efficiency it needs to develop and meet the needs of its growing population.

Risk assessment

Politics	Poor
Economy	Poor
Regional stability	Fair

COUNTRY PROFILE

Historical profile

Following the troubled Mau Mau years of the 1950s and the struggle to win independence from a then reluctant Britain and an even more reluctant white settler minority, Kenya managed to establish some sort of economic and political stability, despite a number of crises. Since independence, Kenya was run mostly by a Kikuyu hierarchy with one or two non-Kikuyus taking leading roles from time to time, perhaps the most notable being former President Daniel arap Moi, who demonstrated remarkable political durability.

From the mid-nineteenth century British interest in the region grew, in 1895 Kenya was declared a British protectorate, and a crown colony in 1920. White settlers established large farms from early in the twentieth century.

1944 The Kenyan African Union (KAU) was formed to voice local demands for the return of native lands.

1947 KAU was led by Jomo Kenyatta, a prominent member of the Kikuyu tribe.

1952 A state of emergency was announced in response to guerrilla activity by the Kikuyu-led secret society, the Mau Mau. More than 13,500 Africans were killed during the uprising, compared to less than 100 Europeans.

1953 The KAU was suspended. Kenyatta was detained.

1957 Africans were elected to the Legislative Council and offered ministerial posts.

1960 A new constitution gave Africans a majority in the Legislative Council. The KAU split: the Kenya African National Union (Kanu) (which had a strong Kikuyu and Luo membership) and the Kenya African Democratic Union (Kadu) were established.

1961 Kenyatta was freed and became president of Kanu and leader of an all-party African government.

1963 The Republic of Kenya was proclaimed and Kenyatta became president.

1964 Kadu was dissolved.

1978 Jomo Kenyatta died and was succeeded as president by Daniel arap Moi.

1979, 1983 and 1988 Only Daniel arap Moi stood in the presidential elections and was elected unopposed.

1992 After a lengthy period in, effectively, a one-party state, multi-party elections were held and President Moi was re-elected.

1997 President Moi and Kanu won the presidential and parliamentary elections.

1998 Terrorists blew up the US embassy in Nairobi, 244 people were killed and over 4,000 people were injured.

2001 President Daniel arap Moi appointed the opposition National Development Party (NDP) leader, Raila Odinga, to his 26-member cabinet, forming Kenya's first coalition government. International aid was withheld by the IMF when the government failed to implement anti-corruption measures.

2002 The NDP and Kanu announced a merger in the run-up to the general election. Uhuru Kenyatta became Kanu's presidential candidate, leading to a wave of defections, including Raila Odinga. Emilio Mwai Kibaki of the opposition, National Rainbow Coalition (Narc), won the presidential elections with 62.3 per cent of the vote.

2003 A draft constitution was presented to parliament, proposing a number of reforms.

2004 The deadline for the enactment of the long-awaited new constitution, which proposed restricting presidential powers and creating a post of prime minister, was missed. In a corruption survey Kenya was rated 129 worst, out of 146, by the watchdog Transparency International, which said the problem remained 'rampant'.

2005 A referendum on constitutional changes held on 22 November was lost by the government as the Liberal Democratic Party (LDP) members of the ruling Narc coalition voted against it. On 23 November, President Kibaki dismissed his entire cabinet; a new cabinet was named on 7 December. On 21 December, justice and constitutional affairs minister, Martha Karua, was asked to prepare a bill for a new constitution.

2006 On 1 February, finance minister, David Mwiraria, resigned in a corruption scandal. The police raided and closed down the premises of the Standard Media Group on 2 March, drawing widespread international condemnation. The Chinese president, on a visit to Kenya in April, signed an offshore oil exploration agreement with Kenya. On 24 November, Uhuru Kenyatta was replaced as Kanu chairman by Nicholas Biwott; on 27 December, the High Court blocked the elections, pending a hearing of a challenge by Kenyatta.

2007 On 3 June a new political party was formed out of the ruling Kanu coalition and other pro-Kibaki political parties, to be known as Kanu-Kenya. In presidential elections held on 27 December the incumbent Mwai Kibaki (Party of National Unity coalition) won 46.6 per cent of the vote, his nearest rival Raila Odinga (ODM) won 44.3 per cent; Kalonzo Musyoka (ODM-K) won 8.9 per cent. Widespread rioting broke out following the results and while international observers reported that polling had been 'relatively orderly and generally positive', the chief EU monitor said the Electoral Commission of Kenya had 'not succeeded in establishing the credibility of the tallying process…' The result was denounced as rigged by the opposition ODM. President Kibaki was sworn in on 30 December.

2008 It was estimated that around 1,500 people died in the violence that followed the December 2007 elections and 600,000 people were displaced in January and February as distrust increased between the main tribal groups. President Kibaki opened the 10th parliament on 6 March. He called for members to become 'ambassadors of peace' in their constituencies and urged them to pass the four bills (the National Accord and Reconciliation Bill, the Constitutional Amendment Bill, the Truth Justice and Reconciliation Bill and the Ethnic Commission Bill) which form part of the Annan-brokered agreement signed on 1 February. MPs agreed the power-sharing deal. The new cabinet was announced on 13 April by President Kibaki, naming Raila Odinga as prime minister.

Political structure

Constitution

The constitution was promulgated in 1963. In 1997, a number of constitutional changes took place; these allowed the formation of a coalition government, the review of the constitution by an independent commission and increased the number of directly elected seats in the Kenyan National Assembly from 188 to 210. A further 12 seats are nominated by the government.

A constitutional amendment affirming the National Assembly's supremacy and curbing the powers of the presidency was approved in 1999. This removed the president's right to appoint the clerk of the house, enabling the legislature to appoint and dismiss the clerk, who is no longer answerable to the president's office. The clerk manages everything from the National Assembly's agenda to its budget.
The country is divided into seven provinces run by provincial commissioners appointed by the president. The provinces are divided into districts run by district commissioners. Towns and districts have municipal and country councils, which are partly elected and partly nominated, but the commissioner has wider powers than the councils. The Nairobi area has a separate government-appointed city commission.

Form of state
Republic

The executive
Executive power in Kenya is in the hands of the president, assisted by the vice president and cabinet, both named by the president.

National legislature
The unicameral Bunge (National Assembly) has 224 members: 210 elected in single-seat constituencies for a five-year term, 12 members are appointed by the president and there are two ex officio members, who are the speaker of the parliament and the attorney general.

Legal system
Kenya's legal system is based on English common law, Islamic law and tribal law, with a High Court and Court of Appeal. The Chief Justice of the Court of Appeal is appointed by the president.

Last elections
27 December 2007 (presidential and parliamentary)
Results: Presidential: Mwai Kibaki won 46 per cent of the vote, Raila Odinga won 44 per cent, all other candidates won less than 10 per cent. These results were published by the Electoral Commission on 8 January 2008.
Parliamentary: Orange Democratic Movement (ODM) won 99 seats (out of 224); Party of National Unity (PNU) 43, Orange Democratic Movement-Kenya (ODM-K) 16, Kenya African National Union (Kanu) 14, Safina 5, all other parties won less than 5 seats.

Next elections
2012 (presidential and parliamentary)

Political parties

Ruling party
Orange Democratic Movement (ODM) (elected 27 Dec 2007)

Main opposition party
Kenya African National Union (Kanu)

Population

34.65 million (2007)
Last census: August 1999: 28,686,607
Population density: 52 inhabitants per square km. Urban population: 31 per cent (1995–2001).
Annual growth rate: 2.4 per cent 1994–2004 (WHO 2006)

Internally Displaced Persons (IDP)
350,000 (UNHCR 2004)

Ethnic make-up
Kenya is a multi-cultural society. Most of Kenya's people belong to 13 ethnic groups although there are a further 27 smaller groups. The majority of Kenyans belong to Bantu tribes such as the Kikuyu (22 per cent), Luhya (14 per cent) and Kamba (11 per cent). The Luo (13 per cent) are of Nilotic origin, as are the smaller Kalenjin (12 per cent), Maasai, Turkana and others.
The Kikuyu live in the central highlands and have traditionally been dominant in commerce and politics, although this is changing. A small European settler population remains in the highlands, involved in farming and commerce. In the north live the Somalis and the nomadic Hamitic peoples (Turkana, Rendille and Samburu); Kamba and Maasai peoples are concentrated in the south and eastern lowlands, and the Luo live around Lake Victoria.

Religions
Protestant (38 per cent), Roman Catholic (28 per cent), animist (26 per cent), Muslim (6 per cent), others (including small Hindu, Sikh and Jain minorities) (2 per cent).

Education

Education has expanded rapidly since independence in 1963. The number of primary schools has more than doubled, while that of secondary schools has increased eighteen-fold. Enrolment at primary schools has declined by 20 per cent since 1980, when the gross enrolment rate was 115 per cent (including repeaters).
Primary education begins at the age of six and is provided free of charge at state schools, however the lack of state funds compels schools to charge fees for books, electricity, water and upkeep, forcing children of poor families to either abandon learning early on or develop an erratic attendance record.
It has been estimated by Oxfam that 75 per cent of children aged six to 11 will enrol for school by 2015.
Secondary school enrolment has grown since 1980, when it was 20 per cent, but still covers only a small proportion of the relevant age group.
The present government, elected in December 2002, has pledged to introduce universal, free and compulsory primary education, an aim which will require higher levels of expenditure then currently spent.
Literacy rate: 84 per cent adult rate; 96 per cent youth rate (15–24) (Unesco 2005).
Enrolment rate: 85 per cent gross primary enrolment of the relevant age group (including repititions); 24 per cent gross secondary enrolment (World Bank).
Pupils per teacher: 31 in primary schools.

Health

Per capita total expenditure on health (2003) was US$65; of which per capita government spending was US$25, (WHO 2006).
Improved water sources are available to 48 per cent of the population.
There were cases of polio reported to the World Health Organisation – Global Polio Eradication Initiative (WHO – Polio Eradication) in 2006; the country had previously been free of the disease and its re-emergence was due to infected travellers. In a synchronised campaign with Ethiopia and Somalia, inoculation began for under fives by WHO – Polio Eradication and the country's health authorities in September 2006.
In October 2007, it was estimated that around 10 per cent of the population were suffering from diabetes, but only 3.5 per cent were diagnosed. Around 85 per cent of the cases were type II diabetes, linked to an unhealthy diet of too much starchy food, high in sugars, salts and fats, and lack of exercise.

HIV/Aids
The number of HIV positive cases have fallen from a high of 4.5 million in 2000 to 2.1 million in 2004. HIV testing also improved with a 10-fold increase between 2002–04. Kenyan businesses were rated as best in the region for having HIV prevention programmes and providing their workers with condoms. In June 2006 the fee for anti-retroviral (ARV) drugs was removed in hospital and public clinics; this is expected to boost the number of Aids sufferers who undertake the course of treatment.
The national level of HIV/Aids infections is mixed, in urban areas rates have declined, however, infection figures for rural areas have yet to peak. Added to which, food shortages due to East Africa's worst drought in a decade, hampers Aids patients with their ARV treatment.
The annual loss in terms of GDP per capita growth are projected to be 1.3 per cent per annum between 2000–10. Households, in which one family member dies of Aids, are estimated to lose between 49–78 per cent of their annual income.

Kenya's Population Council has reported that many women surveyed, knowing they were HIV positive had not disclosed their condition to their partners for fear of violence or abandonment.
The Kenyan government's annual expenditure on HIV/Aids amounts to 6.5 per cent of the annual healthcare budget.
HIV prevalence: 4 per cent (2006), down from 14 per cent in 1997 (UNAids 2006).
Life expectancy: 51 years, 2004 (WHO 2006)
Fertility rate/Maternal mortality rate: 5.0 births per woman, 2004 (WHO 2006); maternal mortality 590 per 100,000 live births (World Bank).
Child (under 5 years) mortality rate (per 1,000): 79 per 1,000 live births (World Bank)
Head of population per physician: 0.14 physician per 1,000 people, 2004 (WHO 2006)

Welfare

Approximately 47 per cent of the total population is under 15 years. Around 50 per cent of the population is thought to live on less than US$1 a day. Around 80 per cent of the population is at risk from drought, famine and HIV/Aids.
A social security system, administered separately from the government budget, covers only government employees and workers in the small modern sector of the economy. The welfare system is financed by the National Social Security Fund (NSSF), set up in 1965. The NSSF has approximately 2.7 million members. In theory, social security contributions are compulsory and are deducted from wages at source. Deductions range from one-thirtieth to one-tenth of earnings. The employer pays half of each employee's contribution. In practice, few families or small businesses enrol their servants or workers. In November 2001, President Moi announced the establishment of a mandatory National Social Health Insurance (NSHI) scheme that would cover all Kenyans.
Social security benefits are limited to survivor's benefit (paid on the death of contributor), invalidity benefit, withdrawal benefit (a fixed sum paid on retirement) and an emigration grant. There is no unemployment benefit. Every Kenyan is entitled to supplementary health benefit under the National Hospital Insurance scheme, founded in 1966.

Main cities

Nairobi (capital, estimated population 2.8 million in 2005, some 1,650 metres above sea-level), Mombasa (795,174), Nakuru (276,263), Kisumu (394,684), Eldoret (230,351), Ruiru (225,794)

Languages spoken
KiSwahili is the lingua franca. In addition, most tribes have their own language. English is universally used in business and spoken by most people in the tourist industry. Other languages are Gikuyu, Kiluhya, Dholuo, Kikamba, Maasai and Somali.
Official language/s
KiSwahili and English

Media

The press is lively and mostly free but can be subjected to extra-legal intimidation if it incurs the wrath of the authorities.
In August 2007 President Kibaki refused to sign a bill which could have forced reporters to reveal their sources. The bill was returned to parliament. Kenya has a lively media which has exposed corruption in government in the past.
National news agency: Office of Public Communications
Press
Dailies: The Nation Media Group publishes the independent Daily Nation (www.nation.co.ke) in English and in KiSwahili Taifa Leo, other private publications include, in English, The Standard (www.eastandard.net) which is the oldest newspapers; the Kenya Times (www.timesnews.co.ke) and The People Daily are owned by political entities.
Weeklies: Some daily newspapers publish weekend editions, others include Coastweek (www.coastweek.com) from Mombassa and the Weekly Advertiser.
Business: The Nation Media Group publishes the Business Daily (www.bdafrica.com) and the weekly The East African (www.theeastafrican.co.ke). The Business Mirror is a fortnightly, promotional trade publication. The Centre for Business Information in Kenya (CBIK) (www.epckenya.org) publishes a number of specific marketing, sales, exports and business information pamphlets.
Periodicals: There are a number of general and specialised periodicals.
Broadcasting
The Kenya Broadcasting Corporation (KBC) (www.kbc.co.ke) is the state-run radio and television provider.
Radio: With high levels of poverty radio is the principal medium for news and information and with the significant expansion of FM radio, particularly ethnic stations which have increased public participation through call-in programmes radio provides an important medium for public debate. KBC (www.kbc.co.ke) operates extensive national services in English, Hindi, KiSwahili and 14 other local languages. Private radio stations include Capital FM (www.capitalfm.co.ke), Kiss FM (www.kissfm.co.ke) and a Christian station Family FM (www.familykenya.com). Coro FM and Radio Citizen in Kikuyu and East FM in Hindi.
Television: KBC (www.kbc.co.ke) operates one channel with programmes in KiSwahili and English it also runs Metro TV with a younger target audience. The satellite channel, Kenya Television Network (KTN) (www.ktnkenya.tv) broadcasts imported and locally produced programmes. Other, private TV stations include the Christian Family TV (www.familykenya.com), Stella TV and NTV (http://politics.nationmedia.com) run by Nation Media Group.
The Africa-wide Business Africa (www.business-africa.net) broadcasts news and business items over the internet in French and English.
News agencies
National news agency: Office of Public Communications

Economy

The widespread violence that erupted after the December 2007 presidential elections caused the Kenyan shilling to drop 7 per cent against the US dollar, while the scheduled weekly tea auction – the biggest in the world – had to be postponed. Tourism and agriculture are the country's largest foreign currency earners and the violence disrupted both markets with tourists advised not to visit – January is the most popular month for visitors – and exports halted either on the farm or at the port of Mombasa. Business representatives warned the government that it would lose around US$30 million per day through lost tax revenues for every day companies had to remain closed. On 3 January 2008 the credit ratings agency Standard & Poors downgraded Kenya's sovereign credit rating to B+, saying 'the longer the situation remains unresolved, the likelier it is to affect Kenya's domestic debt market and balance of payments'.
Kenya is a predominantly rural, low income economy and is heavily indebted to international lenders. Seventy-five per cent of the land area is arid or semi-arid, leading to high concentrations of population, notably in the large shanty towns that skirt the major cities such as Nairobi. Agriculture dominates employment, with at least 80 per cent of the population engaging in subsistence farming; the sector contributes around 26 per cent to GDP. Available arable land is scarce and output depends on a climate which frequently brings drought.
Despite this, Kenya is probably the most developed economy in East Africa. Industrial activity is more diversified than in neighbouring countries and includes more private sector involvement. Industries include food processing, tobacco, beverages and transport. There is a strong

service sector, mainly tourism and financial services, which contributes the bulk of GDP and is a major source of employment and foreign exchange.

The economy has made moderate progress, aided by a domestic austerity programme, but population growth threatens to overtake economic advances. Large current account deficits have been partly funded by foreign borrowing.

After a sluggish period, the economy has picked up, with GDP increasing from 1.9 per cent in 2003 to six per cent in 2006. While the trend is forecast to continue, business confidence is being eroded by mounting levels of violence.

A serious obstacle to Kenya's development is the level of corruption and nepotism, in both government and business. It has resulted in the suspension of aid from several international donors.

External trade

Kenya is a member of the East African Economic Community (EAC) (with Tanzania and Uganda), which was set up to provide a unified approach to development in trade, politics, investment, industrial development and social progress, between member states. Kenya is also a member of the Common Market for Eastern and Southern Africa (Comesa), and operates within a free trade zone with 13 of the 19 member states.

Around 65 per cent of all exports are fresh flowers, fruit and vegetables which are flown to European markets hours after harvesting. In 2006 around 50 per cent of all agricultural produce, valued at over US$200 million were exported to the UK; horticulture provided the second largest foreign earnings after tourism.

Imports

Principal imports are machinery and vehicles, petroleum, iron and steel, resins and plastics.

Main sources: UAE (11.9 per cent total, 2006), India (8.9 per cent), China (8.4 per cent).

Exports

Principal exports are tea (typically over 25 per cent of total), horticultural products and coffee. Other exports include petroleum products, fruit and vegetables, cement and sisal.

Main destinations: Uganda (15.8 per cent total, 2006), UK (10.2 per cent), US (8.1 per cent).

Agriculture

Farming

Agriculture accounted for around 16 per cent of GDP in 2004. The sector generates 60 per cent of export earnings and gives employment to 62 per cent of the workforce. Less than 20 per cent of Kenya's land surface is arable. There is an acute shortage of arable land and uneven distribution has resulted in most farmers working plots of two hectares or less. Population growth and rapid urbanisation place increasing pressure on food production and distribution to meet demand at affordable prices. In addition, there is an ecological risk to some of the most fertile areas of western and central Kenya, which are already severely overpopulated. Given the pressure on the land, increased food production depends on the development of new high-yielding crops.

The principal cash crops are tea, coffee (mainly arabica grown by smallholders), sugar, cotton, pyrethrum, sisal, tobacco, pineapples and wattle. Kenya produces high quality coffee, an average of one million bags per annum. In 2005 the government relaxed the rules under which coffee farmers could sell their crops to agents rather than to national auction houses. Production of coffee has dropped from 118,000 tonnes in 1987 to 50,000 tonnes in 2003 and the changes are expected in increase competition and farmer's income. Horticultural produce is increasingly important and it is the second-largest export earner after tea with flowers making up the largest share (close to 40,000 tonnes).

Primary and processed agricultural products account for over 55 per cent of export earnings. Subsistence farming comprises more than half of output. Maize is the most important food crop. Sorghum, cassava, beans and fruit are also grown. Inadequate storage facilities, little irrigation, recurrent drought and lack of incentives and land have restricted growth.

The government's goal during the 1990s was to maintain at least 5 per cent annual growth in agricultural output to the end of the century. However, production has been consistently behind these targets, achieving only 2.9 per cent in the decade since 1995. Population has outpaced food production, the shortfall having to be met through imports mainly fro Asia.

Estimated crop production in 2005 included: 2,798,500 tonnes (t) cereals in total, 2,200,000t maize, 4,660,995t sugar cane, 380,000t wheat, 630,000t cassava, 1,000,000t potatoes, 580,000t sweet potatoes, 510,000t plantains, 463,250t pulses, 260,000t tomatoes, 39,262t oilcrops, 20,000t tobacco, 50,820t green coffee, 295,000t tea, 118,000t mangoes, 600,000t pineapples, 23,000t treenuts, 2,206,600t fruit in total, 1,581,810t vegetables in total. Estimated livestock production included: 497,685t meat in total, 319,000t beef, 19,800t camel meat, 18,525t pig meat, 34,200t lamb, 36,300t goat meat, 19,800t camel meat, 54,000t poultry, 60,720t eggs, 2,965,700t milk, 21,500t honey, 40,950t cattle hides, 11,550t goatskins, 6,840t sheepskins.

Fishing

Kenya has a coastline of 680km, as well as territoral waters in Lake Victoria and Lake Takana. Some 20,000 small fishermen along the coast complained in 2008 that large foreign boats were depriving them of their living. Although 60 boats, mostly from Europe and the Far East, have been licensed to fish, local fisherman estimate that some 200 boats are fishing in a single season. Most of the ships target prawns, yellow fin tuna and sharks. A report by the UK's Department for International Development (DFID), shows that Kenya losses about US$5m through illegal fishing by foreign boats each year.

In a meeting of African ministers in Namibia, held on 2 July, members discussed illegal and unregulated fishing, which is estimated to cost Africa US$1 billion per annum in lost revenue and the threat to stocks and local artisan fishing. In 2004, the total marine fish catch was 6,213 tonnes and the total crustacean catch was 1,228 tonnes.

Forestry

Kenya has only 2 per cent of forest cover. Deforestation is a major problem along with desertification in northern regions. Fuel wood and charcoal meet more than 75 per cent of the domestic energy requirement, however, the government is attempting to protect timber resources which are being depleted from excessive demands. The government estimates that only 70 per cent of Kenya's wood fuel demands are met by regenerative growth. The need for land is placing increasing pressure on Kenya's forestry reserves.

Imports of forest materials in 2004 were US$75.3 million, while exports amounted to US$21.4 million.

Production in 2004 included 22,161,621 cubic metres (cum) roundwood, 1,792,000cum industrial roundwood, 241,000cum sawlogs and veneer logs, 391,000cum pulpwood, 78,000cum sawnwood, 83,000t wood-based panels, 20,369,621cum wood fuel; 17,700 tonnes (t) charcoal, 164,700t paper and paperboard (including 11,000t newsprint), 14,700t printing and writing paper, 123,000t paper pulp, 38,000t recovered paper.

Industry and manufacturing

Industry accounted for around 20 per cent of GDP in 2004, with manufacturing contributing over 13 per cent.

Foreign investment, particularly from the UK, Japan and US, plays a significant role. Emphasis is on developing joint venture, export-oriented industries and encouraging greater utilisation of local raw materials and other inputs. Large sections of industry continue to operate well below full capacity as a result of import controls, rising costs and marketing difficulties. Rainfall can also have an impact on the sector's performance, with power shortages and reduced agricultural production during drought causing knock-on effects for manufacturing.

The manufacturing sector has been affected by power shortages, a fall in the growth of foreign direct investment (FDI) and rising costs of fuel imports. However, it remains the most developed manufacturing sector in East Africa.

Principal industries include food and tobacco processing, beverages, chemicals, machinery and transport equipment, textiles, glass, vehicle assembly and construction materials.

The public sale of shares in the mobile/cell phone company Safaricom, which was set at Ks5, when they went on sale on 9 June 2008, rose by 60 per cent in one day to Ks8. It was Kenya's record biggest stock market flotation and earned the government around US$833 from its 25 per cent stake in the company. The sale was over-subscribed by more than 500 per cent, with those successful receiving around 20 shares. Safaricom, with profits of US$370 million in 2007, is East Africa's most profitable company.

Kenya's mobile/cell phone market has only a take-up of 33 per cent, with further room for growth.

Tourism

Tourism is the country's largest foreign exchange earner and is expected to contribute 5.3 per cent to GDP in 2005. Kenya's tourist assets are its wildlife, mostly accessible through a system of parks and reserves, extensive white sand beaches protected by coral reefs, and dramatic scenery from deserts to tropical rain forest. Tourism is recognised as a means of poverty reduction and private sector growth. To this end, Kenya and the EU formed the Kenya Trust Fund in 2002 to finance tourism development and the marketing and promotion of tourism.

Since 2004, the sector has recovered from the damage it suffered as a result of terrorist attacks in 1998 and 2002. Vigorous promotion, together with the lifting of warning alerts by other governments, has resulted in an escalation in the number of visitors mainly from Europe and Asia in 2004 and 2005. The growth of the market has exceeded the availability of accommodation. Attention is being turned to developing Kenya from a mass market to a high-value destination.

The violence following the presidential elections in early 2008 impacted badly on tourism as an estimated one million visitors cancelled their holidays. Tourism is the country's premier foreign income earner – providing more than the combined amount from tea and horticulture. Visitor numbers had doubled between 2004–07, but in January 2008, 85 per cent of the usual number was lost, which had a direct impact on employment with the loss of 20,000 jobs and a further 80,000 indirect jobs by March. An estimated US$1 billion was lost, with a fall in investor confidence, according to the finance minister.

Mining

Mining accounts for just 1 per cent of GDP. The sector is dominated by the production of industrial minerals such as soda ash, flourspar, kaolin and some gemstones. Gold is also produced in small quantities by artisanal gold miners. The government's policy is to encourage private sector participation in further exploration, prospecting and development of the mineral resources sector.

The most promising mining prospects are within the licences held by the Canadian mining company Tiomin Resources for deposits covering four areas – Mambrui, Sokoke, Vipingo and Kwale – which hold 12 per cent of the world's rutile and ilmenite resources.

Hydrocarbons

Kenya oil requirements are met by imports,which accounted for around 22.5 per cent of total imports in 2005. Kenya imports about two million tonnes of crude oil per year, mainly from the United Arab Emirates, but recovers some foreign exchange by exporting refined productsto Uganda, Rwanda, Zambia and Tanzania. Kenya has a 90,000bpd capacity oil refinery at Mombasa, but even after investment in improvements the refinery still produces around 60 per cent below capacity.

There has been limited exploration for oil since 1954, mainly in the Rift Valley and the north-eastern provinces,without tangible results. Interest has been ignited by discoveries in Sudan, which shares Kenya's geology, and by the rise in world oil prices. Companies from a number of countries, including China, are becoming increasingly involved in the possibility of locating reserves of oil and also gas and the search is also being extended offshore to the Lamu basin.

Kenya does not produce or import natural gas.

Kenya has plans to diversify its fuel sources for electricity generation and is searching for coal in the Mui and Mutitu basins in Mwingi and Kitui districts.

Energy

Kenya has a total generating capacity of 1,032MW. A further 423MW by 2006 is planned to meet increasing demand caused by a growing economy. Hydroelectric and geothermal power supplies around 25 per cent of energy needs. Electricity is supplied inland by hydroelectric plants in the Tana river basin, by the geothermal station at Olkaria, and at Kipevu, on the coast, by a 75MW oil-fired plant which was opened in 1999. This is irregularly supplemented by a bulk supply of 30MW from Owen Falls in Uganda, under a 50-year agreement signed in 1958.

In July 2004, the World Bank approved a credit of US$80 million for Kenya's energy sector recovery project, which aims to support efficient expansion of power generation capacity to meet the economy's projected supply deficits by 2006/07and to improve access to electricity to the urban poor.

Financial markets

Stock exchange

In 2005 the Nairobi Stock Exchange (NSE) had 48 equity listings with a market capitalisation of US$6 billion. The NSE is small and somewhat speculative. It was established in 1954 and is sub-Saharan Africa's fourth-largest bourse. It originally operated as an association of stockbrokers with no trading floor until October 1991. The introduction of the trading floor has led to a substantial increase in trading volumes and dramatic upward movement in the various indexes. In 1995, foreign investors were allowed back into the NSE for the first time in 30 years. The NSE has been instrumental in enabling the public and private sectors in Kenya to raise large amounts of capital for expansion projects and for the financing of new businesses.

The public sale of shares in the mobile/cell phone company Safaricom, which was set at Ks5, when they went on sale on 9 June 2008, rose by 60 per cent in one day to Ks8. It was Kenya's record biggest stock market flotation and earned the government around US$833 from its 25 per cent stake in the company. The sale was over-subscribed by more than 500 per cent, with those successful receiving around 20 shares.

Banking and insurance

Kenya contains a thriving community of foreign banks, which were attracted during the 1970s and 1980s by its reputation for political and commercial stability, good telecommunications infrastructure and the large number of multinationals based in the country. However, the sector is plagued by high levels of non-performing loans which threaten to undermine banking liquidity, affecting the wider economy.

Central bank
Central Bank of Kenya

Main financial centre
Nairobi

Time
GMT plus three hours

Geography
Kenya lies on the east coast of Africa. It is bounded by Ethiopia and Sudan to the north, Uganda and Lake Victoria to the west, Tanzania to the south and Somalia and the Indian Ocean to the east.
From the Indian Ocean, the land rises gradually through dry bush to the arable land of the highlands. The highest peak is Mount Kenya at 5,200 metres. The west of the country is dissected by the Great Rift Valley, partly filled by a chain of lakes.

Hemisphere
Straddles the equator

Climate
The climate is tropical in low-lying districts, especially along the coast, but is more temperate on the plateau and in the highlands. Kenya has two rainy seasons when temperatures can fall sharply: the long rains from April to June and the short rains in October and November. The hottest month is February, with temperatures of 20–30 degrees Celsius (C), while the coolest month is July, with temperatures of 11–22 degrees C. Nairobi, at an altitude of 1,661 metres, has a mean annual temperature of 17 degrees C and annual rainfall averaging 864mm.

Dress codes
A lightweight suit, collar and tie or other formal clothing should be worn for business meetings. Despite a hot tropical climate, nights can be cool and it is advisable to have a sweater to cover day wear, which should be light cotton casual at the coast. Warmer clothing is needed especially in June and July. Evening dress should normally be smart casual. Nairobi is considerably cooler than Mombasa.

Entry requirements
Passports
Required by all, valid for three months from date of entry.

Visa
Required by all, with the exception of nationals of some Commonwealth and other countries. Visas may be obtained from Kenyan missions or at the port of entry, although nationals of certain specified countries nationals must apply well in advance for referral to Nairobi. For a full list of each category and further details, visit www.kenyaembassy.co.uk.

Currency advice/regulations
There are no restrictions on the import and export of local and foreign currencies, subject to declaration of amounts in excess of Ksh100,000.
US dollar or other hard currency travellers cheques are recommended.

Health (for visitors)
Mandatory precautions
Yellow fever vaccination certificate if arriving from an infected area.

Advisable precautions
Yellow fever, typhoid, tetanus, hepatitis A, meningitis and polio vaccinations. Malaria prophylaxis necessary for coastal and other lower altitude regions. Water precautions should be taken – bilharzia is present. Rabies is a risk in rural areas and vaccinations must be administered following a bites from any mammal.

Hotels
There is a wide range available in main centres. It is advisable to book well in advance during peak season (November–April).

Credit cards
Major cards are widely accepted.

Public holidays (national)
Fixed dates
1 Jan (New Year's Day), 1 May (Labour Day), 1 Jun (Madaraka Day), 10 Oct (Moi Day), 20 Oct (Kenyatta Day), 12 Dec (Independence/Jamhuri Day), 25–26 Dec (Christmas).
Holidays falling on a Sunday are observed the following Monday.

Variable dates
Good Friday, Easter Monday, Eid al Fitr.

Working hours
Banking
Mon–Fri: 0900–1400. Open first and last Sat in each month 0900–1100.
Barclays Bank, Kenyatta Avenue, Nairobi, open daily for foreign exchange until 1600.
Airport banks are open until midnight every day.

Business
Mon–Fri: 0800–1300, 1400–1700; Sat: 0830–1200/1230. Mombasa offices normally open and close half-an-hour earlier.

Government
Mon–Fri: 0800–1300, 1400–1700; Sat: 0830–1200/1230. Mombasa offices normally open and close half-an-hour earlier.

Shops
Mon-Fri: 0800–1700; Sat: 0830–1300. Many shops open outside these hours.

Electricity supply
230/240V AC, 50 cycles. Subject to power surges outside main centres.
Sockets are usually three-pin square (British type).

Social customs/useful tips
Personal contact is an important way of doing business in Kenya.
Bureaucracy can be frustratingly slow, although persistence pays. Going in person to the relevant office is often the best way of getting things done. Government and commercial offices are within easy walking distance of the main hotels.
Outside the major towns local customs vary from place to place. In the game parks and bush, some tribes do not like being photographed, although in areas where tourism is more developed, some tribe members will allow photographs for a fee. Visitors to game parks should not leave their vehicles without permission from the guide. There is a large Arab influence on the coast and most hotels display government signs saying nudity is banned. Topless bathing for women is, however, tolerated in areas where there are large concentrations of hotels.
Kenyans are friendly and open, and the greeting, jambo, will be returned with a smile.
It is prohibited to photograph the president or his residence, military, police or related installations.

Security
Security is not a problem in the major towns during the day but flashy displays of jewellery are not recommended. Do not carry large amounts of cash.
Nairobi is practically deserted after 2200. Walking around the African quarters of town without a guide or in the shanty towns around the capital is not advised. Visitors are advised to avoid political meetings and demonstrations.
Incidents of armed car-hijacking are prevalent in Nairobi and Mombasa.
Do not attempt to escape from hijackers or resist their demands.

Getting there
Air
National airline: Kenya Airways
International airport/s: Nairobi – Jomo Kenyatta International (NBO), 17km from city, duty-free shop, bar, restaurant, buffet, bank, post office, shops, car hire.
Other airport/s: Mombasa – Moi International (MBA), 13km south-east of city, duty-free shop, bar, restaurant, bank, post office, shops, car hire. Medium-sized airports have also been developed at Eldoret, Kisumu and Malindi.
Airport tax: US$20, usually included in ticket price.

Surface
Road: Entry by road from Uganda, Ethiopia, Sudan and Tanzania can be difficult. Regulations and conditions should be checked with Kenyan authorities before travelling.

An all-weather road links Nairobi to Addis Ababa (Ethiopia) and there is a 590km road link between Kitale and Juba (Sudan).
In rural areas, some of the unsurfaced roads can be difficult in wet weather.
Rail: A 1,085km main line runs from the port of Mombasa through Nairobi, Nakuru and Eldoret to Uganda. There is also a link to Moshi (Tanzania).
Main port/s: Mombasa

Getting about

National transport

Air: Kenya Airways operates regular services linking Mombasa, Malindi, Kisumu and other major centres with Nairobi. Local light aircraft companies fly regular services to smaller airfields, such as Lamu, a tourist attraction on the coast.
Charter flights are also available to game reserves, such as Maasai Mara, and main centres.
Road: The growth in road transportation has led to overloading of some highways, and both the maintenance and improvement of these routes have been neglected. This also applies to roads which come under the jurisdiction of town authorities.
Nearly all main towns are connected by good surfaced roads. In rural areas some of the unsurfaced roads can be difficult in wet weather.
Long-distance (Peugeot) taxi service operates between towns. Cars can be shared, although it is not generally recommended.
Buses: Coach services operate on all major routes between towns and cities and into Tanzania, Ethiopia and Uganda.
Rail: The Kenya Railways system comprises approximately 1,920km of one metre gauge single track.
There are departures daily, with first- and second-class service, from Nairobi to Mombasa; the overnight service is popular. Journey time is approximately 14 hours. Trains often run late, but are fairly comfortable. It is advisable to book sleeping compartments in advance.
Two Uganda-Kenya railway agreements were signed in April 2006. In Uganda a concession agreement covers the freight services of Uganda Railways Corporation (URC), while an Interface agreement covers matters common to the Kenya freight and passenger concession and the Uganda freight concession. The Rift Valley Railways Consortium (RVRC) will invest US$15 million over the first five years and a further US$75 million over the remainder of the agreement in Uganda and US$45 and US$300 million respectively in Kenya.

City transport

Taxis: Available in most major towns. Some licensed taxis are metered and often shared, with fares according to time and distance. Fares for long trips should be agreed in advance.
Buses, trams & metro: Good and fairly cheap services operate regularly in Nairobi and Mombasa and between towns and cities, as well as across the borders to Tanzania, Ethiopia and Uganda. Minibuses and vans (matatu) are unregulated and can be overcrowded; they are not recommended for visitors.

Car hire

Can be hired from travel operators and hotels in Nairobi, Mombasa and Malindi. A national or international driving licence which has been held for at least two years without endorsements, including the period of visit to Kenya, is required .

BUSINESS DIRECTORY

The addresses listed below are a selection only. While World of Information makes every endeavour to check these addresses, we cannot guarantee that changes have not been made, especially to telephone numbers and area codes. We would welcome any corrections.

Telephone area codes

The international direct dialling (IDD) code for Kenya is +254, followed by area code and subscriber's number:

Eldoret	53	Malindi	42
Garissa	46	Mombasa	41
Kajiado	45	Nairobi	20
Kericho	52	Naivasha	50
Kisumu	57	Nakuru	51
Kwale	40	Voi	43

Chambers of Commerce

Kenya National Chamber of Commerce & Industry, Ufanisi House, Haile Selassie Avenue, PO Box 47024, Nairobi (tel: 220-867; fax: 334-2934; e-mail: kncci@swiftkenya.com).

Banking

African Banking Corporation Ltd, PO Box 46452, Mezzanine Floor, ABC-Bank, Koingange Street, Nairobi (tel: 223-922, 251-540/1, 226-712, 248-978; fax: 222-437).

Barclays Bank of Kenya Ltd, PO Box 30120, Barclays Plaza, Loita St, Nairobi (tel: 214-270, 313-405; fax: 213-915, 215-418).

The Co-operative Bank of Kenya Ltd, PO Box 48231, Union Towers, Kenya-Re Plaza - Taifa Rd, Moi Ave, Nairobi (tel: 225-579, 228-453/7, 251290/9; fax: 229-38, 246-635, 227-747).

Commercial Bank of Africa Ltd, Commercial Bank Building, Standard/Wabera Streets, Nairobi (tel: 228-881; fax: 335-827, 340-157).

Development Bank of Kenya Ltd, PO Box 30483, Finance House, Loita Street, Nairobi (tel: 340-401, 340-402, 340-403; fax: 338-426).

Imperial Bank Ltd, PO Box 44905, 8th Floor, IPS Bldg, Kimathi St, Nairobi (tel: 252-175/6/7/8, 252-184/5, 225-060; fax: 230-994, 250-137).

Investments & Mortgages Bank Ltd, PO Box 30238, I & M Bank House, 2nd Ngong Avenue, Nairobi (tel: 711-994-8, 310-105-7; fax: 713-757, 716-372).

Kenya Commercial Bank Ltd, PO Box 48400, Moi Avenue, Nairobi (tel: 339-441; fax: 215-565).

National Bank of Kenya Ltd, PO Box 72866, National Bank Building, Harambee Avenue, Nairobi.

Standard Chartered Bank Kenya Ltd, PO Box 30003, Stanbank House, Moi Avenue, Nairobi (tel: 330-200, 331-210; fax: 214-086).

Central bank

Central Bank of Kenya, Haile Selassie Avenue, PO Box 60000-0200 Nairobi (tel: 286-1000; fax: 340-192; e-mail: info@centralbank.go.ke).

Travel information

Automobile Association of Kenya, AA House, Embakasi, PO Box 40087, Nairobi (tel: 825-060; fax: 825-068; e-mail: aakenya@africaonline.co.ke).

Air Kenya, Wilson Airport, PO Box 30357, Nairobi (tel: 605-745; fax: 602-951; e-mail: resvns@airkenya.com).

Kenya Airways, Airport North Road, Embakasi, PO Box 19142, Nairobi (tel: 642-2000; fax: 823-488).

Kenya Railways, PO Box 30121, Nairobi (tel: 221-211; fax: 340-049).

Ministry of tourism

Ministry of Tourism and Wildlife, Utalii House, Uhuru Highway, PO Box 30027, Nairobi (tel: 333-555; fax: 318-045; e-mail:info@tourism.go.ke).

National tourist organisation offices

Kenya Tourist Board, Kenya-Re Towers, Ragati Road, PO Box 30630, Nairobi (tel: 711-262; fax: 719-925; e-mail: info@kenyatourism.org).

Ministries

Ministry of Agriculture, Livestock Development and Marketing, Kilimo House, Cathedral Road, PO Box 30028, Nairobi (tel: 718-870; fax: 725-774).

Ministry of Commerce and Industry, Co-operative House, Haile Selassie Avenue, PO Box 30430, Nairobi (tel: 340-010, 340-224; fax: 218-845).

Ministry of Energy, Nyayo House, Kenyatta Avenue, PO Box 30582, Nairobi (tel: 333-551).

Ministry of the Environment and Natural Resources, Kencom House, Moi Avenue, PO Box 30126, Nairobi (tel: 229-261).

Ministry of Finance, Treasury House, Harambee Avenue, PO Box 30007, Nairobi (tel: 338-111; fax: 330-426).

Ministry of Information and Broadcasting, Jogoo House 'A', Taifa Road, PO Box 30025, Nairobi (tel: 334-688; fax: 340-659).

Ministry of Planning and National Development, PO Box 3007, Nairobi (tel: 338-111; fax: 330-426).

Ministry of Transport and Communications, Transcom House, Ngong Road, PO Box 52692, Nairobi (tel: 729-200; fax: 726-362).

Office of the President, Harambee House, Harambee Avenue, PO Box 30510, Nairobi (tel: 227-411; fax: 723-666).

Other useful addresses

Africa Growth Fund, PO Box 34045, Nairobi (tel: 721-566; fax: 722-240).

African Project Development Facility, International House, PO Box 46534, Nairobi.

Agricultural Development Corporation, PO Box 30367, Nairobi (tel: 338-530).

Attorney-General's Office, State Law Office, Harambee Avenue, PO Box 40112, Nairobi (tel: 227-461; fax: 211-082).

British High Commission, Bruce House, Standard Street, PO Box 30465, Nairobi (tel: 335-944; fax: 333-196); Commercial Section, Upper Hill Road, PO Box 30133, Nairobi (tel: 714-699; fax: 719-082; e-mail: bhctrade@users.africaonline.co.ke).

Capital Markets Authority (CMA), Re-Insurance Plaza, Taifa Rd, PO Box 74800, Nairobi (tel: 221-910/869; fax: 216-681).

Central Police Station, University Way, Nairobi (tel: 222-222).

Central Reference Library, Ministry of Information, Department of Information, PO Box 8053 or 30025, Nairobi (tel: 223-201).

Communications Commission of Kenya (CCK), 5th Floor, Longonot Place, Kijabe Street, PO Box 14448, Nairobi 00800 (tel: 240-165, 250-173, 310-083/4; fax: 252-547; internet site: http://www.cck.go.ke).

Customs and Excise, PO Box 40160, Nairobi.

Development Finance Company of Kenya, Finance House, Loita Street, PO Box 30483, Nairobi (tel: 340-401; fax: 338-246).

East African Report on Trade and Industry, PO Box 30339, Nairobi.

Economic Development for Equatorial and Southern Africa, PO Box 56038, Nairobi (tel: 822-920/4; fax: 822-925/907).

Executive Secretariat and Technical Unit (ESTU), Anniversary Towers, University Way, 7th Floor, PO Box 34542, Nairobi (tel: 222-127/57/68; fax: 216-945).

Export Processing Zones Authority (EPZA), British American Centre, Mara Rd, PO Box 50563, Nairobi (tel: 712-800/6; fax: 713-704).

Export Promotion Council (EPC), Anniversary Towers, 1st Floor, University Way, PO Box 40247, Nairobi (tel: 228-534/5; fax: 218-013).

Federation of Kenya Employers (FKE), Argwings Kodhek Road, PO Box 48311, Nairobi (tel: 721-929; fax: 721-948).

General Post Office, Kenyatta Avenue, Nairobi.

Horticultural Crops Development Authority (HCDA), Uniafric House, Koinange St, PO Box 42601, Nairobi (tel: 337-381/3).

Industrial and Commercial Development Corporation, Uchumi House, Nkrumah Avenue, PO Box 45519, Nairobi (tel: 229-213; fax: 333-880).

Industrial Promotion Services Ltd, IPS Building, PO Box 30500, Nairobi (tel: 228-026, 728-207; fax: 214-563).

International Finance Corporation, View Park Towers, PO Box 30577, Nairobi (tel: 224-726; fax: 219-980).

Kenya Association of Manufacturers (KAM), Mpaka Rd, Westland, PO Box 30225, Nairobi (tel: 746-005/7; fax: 746-028).

Kenya Association of Tour Operators (for information on conference facilities throughout Kenya), PO Box 48461, Nairobi (tel: 227-005).

Kenya External Trade Authority, PO Box 43137, Nairobi (tel: 226-016).

Kenya Investment Authority, National Bank of Kenya Building, Harambee Avenue, PO Box 55704, Nairobi (tel: 221-401; fax: 243-862; e-mail: info@investmentkenya.com).

Kenya Power Company Limited, Stima Plaza, Kolobot Road, PO Box 47936, Nairobi (tel: 741-181/9; fax: 337-351).

Kenya Revenue Authority, Tax Programmes and New Business Initiatives, Nairobi (tel: 715-428; fax: 715-432).

Kenya Tea Development Authority, Commonwealth House, Moi Avenue, Nairobi (tel: 221-441).

Kenyan Embassy (USA), 2249 R Street, NW, Washington DC 20008 (tel: (+1-202)-387-6101; fax: (+1-202)-462-3829; e-mail: info@kenyaembassy.com).

Kenyatta International Conference Centre, PO Box 30746, Nairobi (tel: 332-383).

Nairobi Stock Exchange, Kimathi Street, IPS Building, 2nd Floor, PO Box 43833, Nairobi (tel: 230-692; fax: 224-200).

US Embassy, Corner Moi and Haile Selassie Avenues, PO Box 30137, Nairobi (tel: 334-141; fax: 340-838).

National news agency: Office of Public Communications

Address: PO Box 45617; KICC Building, 3 Floor, 8 Harambee Ave, 00100 Nairobi (tel: 202 224-0488; fax: 202 240-600; email: comms@comms.go.ke).

Internet sites

Africa Business Network: http://www.ifc.org/abn

AllAfrica.com: http://allafrica.com

African Development Bank: http://www.afdb.org

Africa Online: http://www.africaonline.com

KenyaWeb: http://www.kenyaweb.com/

Mbendi AfroPaedia (information on companies, countries, industries and stock exchanges in Africa): http://mbendi.co.za

KEY FACTS

Official name: Ripaberikan Kiribati (Republic of Kiribati) (pronounced Kiribas)

Head of State: President (Beretitenti) Anote Tong (BTK) (elected 2003; re-elected 17 Oct 2007)

Head of government: President (Beretitenti) Anote Tong

Ruling party: Boutokan te Koaua (BTK) (Pillars of Truth) (since 2003; re-elected Aug 2007)

Area: 810 square km (33 islands and atolls)

Population: 98,000 (2007)*

Capital: Bairiki (on Tarawa)

Official language: I-Kiribati, English

Currency: Australian dollar (A$) = 100 cents)

Exchange rate: A$1.03 per US$ (Jul 2008)

GDP per capita: US$686 (2007)*

GDP real growth: 2.00% (2007)*

Inflation: 0.20% (2007)*

Balance of trade: -US$45.00 million (2005)

Foreign debt: US$15.70 million (2003)

* estimated figure

Kiribati

COUNTRY PROFILE

Historical profile

Micronesians from the South Pacific settled Kiribati between 200 and 500 AD. Kiribati (pronounced Kiribas) is made up of 33 low-lying coral atolls and is sub-divided into three main groups known as the Gilbert Islands, the Phoenix Islands and the Line Islands.

1892 Kiribati became part of the British colony of the Gilbert and Ellice Islands and was administered by the West Pacific High Commission in Fiji.

1942 The islands were occupied by the Japanese during World War II.

1963 Transition to independence began, with the formation of legislative and executive councils under the supervision of a British governor general.

1975 Ellice Islands seceded and formed the separate entity of Tuvalu.

1979 Became the fully independent Republic of Kiribati.

1982–91 Iremia Tabai won the first three post-independence presidential elections in 1982, 1983 and 1987. Constitutional restrictions prevented Tabai contesting the 1991 elections which were won by Teatao Teannaki.

1994 Teburoro Tito of the Mwaneaaban te Mauri Party (MMP) was elected president.

1995 The government unilaterally moved the international date line east to ensure the country's collection of islands were designated as lying within the same day.

1997 China built a satellite-tracking base on Kiribati's main atoll on a 15-year lease.

1998 President Tito was elected to his second term.

2000 The Caroline Island was the first inhabited place to greet the new millennium, the name of the island was changed in celebration of the event.

2001 The Pacific Islands Forum, of which Kiribati is a member, completed its negotiations to bring 14 Pacific island countries into a free trade agreement, known as the Pacific Islands Countries Trade Agreement (PICTA). The government of President Tito suffered heavy losses in the second round of parliamentary elections.

2002 Parliament passed newspaper registration laws, giving powers to ban the publication of newspapers that face complaints.

2003 Teburoro Tito (MMP) won presidential elections. President Tito lost a motion of no confidence and parliament was dissolved. In the general elections the ruling, MMP, won 16 seats, the Boutokaan te Koaua (BTK) (Pillars of Truth) won 17. Anote Tong (BTK) was elected president. Kiribati established diplomatic relations with Taiwan, but also offered to honour the lease of the satellite tracking station with China, but China rejected the offer, dismantled the station and severed diplomatic relations.

2005 Kiribati joined the International Whaling Commission in January.

2006 Kiribati designated an area of 184,700 square km in the Phoenix Islands as the world's third largest marine reserve. Kiribati appealed to the United Nations for action on global warming amid concerns about rising sea levels.

2007 In two rounds of parliamentary elections held in August, the results were, BTK won 18 seats, MTM seven and independents 19 seats. In presidential elections held in October, incumbent Anote Tong won about 65 per cent of the vote, the next closest rival, Nabuti Mwemwenikarawa, won about 33 per cent. A new cabinet was sworn in on 23 October.

2008 In February, the Phoenix Islands Protected Area was increased to 410,500 square kilometres to become the world's largest marine reserve.

Political structure

Constitution

The 1979 constitution created an independent republic with a president as head of state, executive government, judicature and public service. A provision for citizenship of Kiribati also includes special status of Banaba and Banabans, as well as fundamental rights of freedom for individuals.

Form of state

Independent democratic republic; it is a member of the Commonwealth.

The executive

Executive power is exercised by a popularly elected beretitenti (president), for a four-year term, limited to three terms. The president is elected by the people from among three candidates nominated by the Maneaba (house of assembly) from its ranks. The president is head of state and head of government and appoints a cabinet composed of a president, vice president, 10 ministers from the house of assembly and an ex officio attorney general.

National legislature

The unicameral Maneaba (house of assembly) consists of 46 members elected

for four-year terms in multi-seat constituencies. One appointed member represents the Banaban community (most of whose inhabitants were evacuated from the Banada Island during phosphate mining and now live on Rabi Island in Fiji). The speaker is an appointed post from outside the membership of the house of assembly and the attorney general is an ex officio post.
Universal suffrage begins at aged 18.
Last elections
17 Oct 2007 (presidential); 22/30 August 2007 (parliamentary).
Results: Parliamentary: (the combined result of rounds one and two) the BTK won 18 seats, MTM seven and independents 19 seats.
Presidential: incumbent Anote Tong (BTK) won 65 per cent of the vote; Nabuti Mwemwenikarawa won 43.5 per cent; and Banuera Berina (Maurin Kiribati Pati) (MKP)) won 9.1 per cent. Turnout was around 50 per cent.
Next elections
2011 (presidential and parliamentary)

Political parties
Ruling party
Boutokan te Koaua (BTK) (Pillars of Truth) (since 2003; re-elected Aug 2007)
Main opposition party
Maneaban te Mauri (MTM) (Protect the Maneaba)

Population
98,000 (2007)*
Last census: November 2000: 84,494 (provisional)
Population density: 123 inhabitants per square km. Urban population: 39 per cent (1995—2001).
Annual growth rate: 2.2 per cent 1994–2004 (WHO 2006)
Ethnic make-up
Predominantly Micronesian, with some Polynesian.
Religions
Roman Catholic (52 per cent), Protestant (Congregational) (40 per cent), Seventh-Day Adventist, Islam, Baha'i Faith, Latter-day Saints and Church of God.

Education
The Junior Secondary School (JSS) programme aims to provide universal access to basic secondary education. Almost all the outer islands (except Teraina and Tabuaeran) and South Tarawa have junior secondary schools.
Higher education, including both university level programmes and post-secondary vocational/technical training, is provided by the government and the regional institution, University of the South Pacific (USP). The government also operates two tertiary institutions on South Tarawa: Tarawa Technical Institute and Kiribati Teachers College.
Literacy rate: 92.2 per cent, adult rate.
Compulsory years: six to 15
Enrolment rate: 67.8 per cent gross school enrolment.

Health
Per capita total expenditure on health (2003) was US$253; of which per capita government spending was US$233, at the international dollar rate, (WHO 2006).
The government has collaborated with the World Health Organisation (WHO) to strengthen its primary healthcare services. WHO's technical support has brought down the infant mortality rate and increased life expectancy.
Improved water sources are available to 47 per cent of the population.
There is one general hospital in Tarawa and a number of health centres in the more populated islands. There are few doctors. Medical facilities are of the most basic kind and there are no pharmacies.
Excessive alcohol consumption has become a very severe problem both socially and medically. Diabetes linked to a western diet is widespread.
HIV/Aids
There has been a significant increase in infections on Tarawa.
Life expectancy: 65 years, 2004 (WHO 2006)
Fertility rate/Maternal mortality rate: 4.1 births per woman, 2004 (WHO 2006)
Birth rate/Death rate: 31 births per 1,000 population; 8.6 deaths per 1,000 population (2003).
Child (under 5 years) mortality rate (per 1,000): 49 per 1,000 live births (World Bank)

Welfare
The government has instituted a bonding system requiring all trained personnel to serve the country for at least the same number of years that it has funded their training. The retirement age, which was previously 50 years for all government employees, has been increased to 60 years for doctors and 55 for other categories.

Main cities
Bairiki, (capital, on Tarawa, estimated population 30,600 in 2005), Bikenibeu (on Tarawa, 7,704).

Languages spoken
English is used for official communications and is widely understood in the capital, Tarawa. It is used less on the outer islands where i-Kiribati is the norm. In the i-Kiribati language the letters 'ti' are pronounced 's' (Kiribati is pronounced Kiribas).
Official language/s
I-Kiribati, English

Media
Despite the lack of independent news outlets the government-owned radio and newspaper provide an appropriate level of press freedom.
Other news agencies: ABC Pacific Beat: www.radioaustralia.net.au/pacbeat
Pacific News: www.pacificmagazine.net
Press
Since 2002, the Newspaper Registration Amendment Bill allows publications to be deregister and stopped when faced with complaints.
Weeklies: The government-owned Te Uekera is published in I-Kiribati and English. An independent newspaper, Kiribati New Star, began publication in 2004.
Periodicals: There are no newsagents and only limited copies of overseas papers and magazines are sold in shops. Religious organisations publish newsletters and periodicals in I-Kiribati with local news and stories relevant to their readership. Te Itoi ni Kiribati and Kaotan te Ota for Catholic and Protestant communities respectively.

KEY INDICATORS Kiribati

	Unit	2003	2004	2005	2006	2007
Population	m	0.10	0.10	–0.09	*0.10	*0.10
Gross domestic product (GDP)	US$bn	0.08	0.07	0.06	*0.06	*0.07
GDP per capita	US$	727	760	596	*658	*686
GDP real growth	%	2.5	1.8	-0.2	*2.4	*2.0
Inflation	%	1.4	2.3	-0.5	*-0.2	*0.2
Exports (fob) (goods)	US$m	6.0	17.0	4.0	–	–
Imports (cif) (goods)	US$m	44.0	62.0	77.0	–	–
Balance of trade	US$m	-38.0	-45.0	-73.0	–	–
Current account	US$m	-10.0	-10.0	-22.0	-17.0	*-21.0
Exchange rate	per US$	1.55	1.28	1.28	1.28	1.16

Broadcasting

Kiribati is a member of the Commonwealth Broadcasting Association (www.cba.org.uk), which promotes best practices in broadcasting.

Radio: The only radio stating in operation is Radio Kiribati broadcasting in AM and FM, which provides a national, public network. External services from the BBC and VOA may be received on short-wave radios.

Economy

Kiribati lacks both human and natural resources; the infrastructure is weak, the islands remote and the soil is poor and frequent droughts. This, together with a traditional land tenure structure, makes the islands unconducive to large-scale agricultural activity. However, Kiribati used to export phosphate from Banaba Island until the deposits were exhausted in 1979 and the Revenue Equalization Reserve Fund (RERF), which was financed by phosphate earnings, continues to be important to Kiribati and held over US$400 million in 2004. Income from the RERF enables the government to cover fiscal deficits and to buffer year-to-year movements on the current account. Almost all manufactured goods are imported, and with only small exports of copra, the annual trade balance is consistently in deficit (US$51.1 million in 2004). Despite this, thanks to the large foreign holdings in the RERF, official reserves remain high at around US$359 million.

Kiribati's large (around 3.5 million square kilometres – some six times the area of France) Exclusive Economic Zone (EEZ) is a major source of fishing licence revenue. GDP growth fell in 2006 to around one per cent, from 2.5 per cent in 2003, but inflation was low, copra prices were high and income from the RERF went up to A$25 million (US$34 million).

Official development assistance amounts is US$15–20 million per year, mainly donated by Japan, the UK, Australia and New Zealand.

Kirimati (Christmas) Island has been used for landings of unmanned space shuttles operated by the Japan Aerospace Exploration Agency. Japan is leasing land on Kirimati to build a spaceport, and according to the agreement will spend US$12.9 million over the period 1999–2012. Japan is also funding the building of a storage and handling area at the island's fishing port. Game fishing and birdwatching have also been attracting visitors to the island.

Kiribati's development strategy, as set out in its National Development Strategy 2004–07, covers six key sectors: economic growth, fair distribution, public sector performance, conservation of physical assets, equipping the population to manage change and the sustainable use of financial reserves by ministries. According to the Asian Development Bank (ADB), Kiribati's prospects in the medium term will be hampered by lack of private sector development, overdependence on the government, pressures of population growth and associated low youth employment opportunities.

External trade

Kiribati is a member of the South Pacific Regional Trade and Economic Co-operation Agreement (Sparteca) along with 12 other regional nations, which allows products duty free access by Pacific Island Forum members to Australian and New Zealand markets (subject to the country of origin restrictions).

Much of Kiribati's foreign revenue is provided through leased fishing rights, remittances and international aid and operates with a trade deficit that is not balanced by export trade.

Imports

Principal imports are fuel, vehicles, machinery, food, manufactured goods, miscellaneous manufactures and chemicals.

Main sources: Australia (33.5 per cent total, 2006), Fiji (27.5 per cent), Japan (18.4 per cent).

Exports

Principal exports are copra (over 60 per cent), aquarium fish, dried shark fins and seaweed.

Main destinations: US (26.2 per cent total, 2006), Belgium (24.6 per cent), Japan (16.4 per cent).

Agriculture

Farming

The agricultural sector accounts for about 15 per cent of GDP and around 60 per cent of exports.

Agricultural development is limited by poor soil quality. There are commercial and government-owned copra plantations on Teraina (Washington) and Tabuaeran (Fanning) islands, but peasant smallholdings are more usual. Most copra is exported to Europe by the Copra Co-operative Society (CCS).

Flour, sugar and rice are replacing the traditional breadfruit and taro in the national diet, increasing reliance on imports.

Estimated crop production in 2005 included: 103,000 tonnes (t) coconuts, 13,390t oilcrops, 2,000t taro, 5,000t bananas, 6,400t fruit in total, 9,800t roots and tubers, 230t treenuts, 5,900t vegetables in total. Estimated livestock production included: 1,335t meat in total, 875t pig meat, 459t poultry and 240t eggs.

Fishing

There are programmes to upgrade subsistence fisheries to small commercial enterprises.

Deep-sea fishing is carried out by foreign fleets under licence in the immense Kiribati Exclusive Economic Zone (EEZ).

In September 2006, a second Kiribati and EU contract under which Spanish, French and Portuguese purse seine and long-line fishing boats are to be allowed to catch tuna in the EEZ. The latest deal emphases the promotion of sustainable and responsible fishing.

Typically, the annual catch for home consumption is over 32,000t including both fish and other seafood.

In 2004, the total marine fish catch was 25,500 tonnes and the total crustacean catch was 140 tonnes.

Industry and manufacturing

Small-scale manufacturing industries include clothing, furniture and handicrafts.

Tourism

Tourism plays a minor role in the Gilbert Islands but in the northern Line Islands tourism has a high priority. A growing number of tourists visit the rare seabird colonies situated on Kirimati (Christmas Island).

Attractions include World War Two battle sites, game fishing, ecotourism, and the Millennium Islands, situated just inside the International Date Line and the first place on earth to celebrate the New Year. There are also opportunities for fishing, surfing and diving, although there are not many organised activities.

Access to Kiritimati has been aided by a weekly charter flight from Honolulu.

Environment

The South Pacific Regional Environment Programme (SPREP) reported in 1999 that, due to global warming, two uninhabited islands in the Kiribati group, Tebua Tarawa and Abanuea, had disappeared beneath the waves, others have almost gone, and the main islands suffer severe floods from high tides.

The Phoenix Islands Protected Area, the world's largest marine reserve of 410,500 square kilometres was created by Kiribati in February 2008. It includes the planet's biggest intact coral archipelagos with an estimated 120 species of coral, 520 species of fish, some of which have only recently been discovered, large sea turtle populations and important seabird nesting sites.

Hydrocarbons

Kiribati does not produce any hydrocarbons and does not import natural gas or coal. It relies entirely on imports of distillate, jet fuel and gasoline to meet its fuel requirements.

Energy

Annual electricity production and consumption is about 6.5 million kW.

Banking and insurance
There is no central bank in Kiribati and the sole commercial bank is the Bank of Kiribati. The government does not buy and sell foreign exchange.

Time
GMT plus twelve hours

Geography
Kiribati comprises 33 atolls in three principal groups, within an area of about 3.6 million square km (two million square miles) in the mid-Pacific Ocean. The country extends about 3,870km (2,400 miles) from east to west and about 2,050km (1,275 miles) from north to south. Nauru lies to the west and Tuvalu and Tokelau to the south.
Most islands are low-lying coral outcrops covered in poor soil, except for Banaba, which rises to 80m with good planting. Kiribati has no hills or freshwater streams on any of its islands and relies on wells and stored rainwater.
Hemisphere
Straddles the equator, with most islands in the southern hemisphere.

Climate
Temperatures range from 25–33 Celsius. The wet season extends from Dec–May and rainfall variation is high in most of the islands. A gentle breeze from the easterly quarter is predominant. The westerly gale (Oct–Mar) can be unpleasant.

Entry requirements
Passports
Required by all and must have six months validity from date of arrival.
Proof of return/onward passage and sufficient funds are also required.
Visa
Required by all, except citizens of UK and most Commonwealth countries and Pacific Islanders, for up to either 20 or 30 days, dependent on business, tourist and nationality criteria. Contact the nearest consulate for further information (some details are given at www.embassy-avenue.jp/kiri/visa/index.html). Citizens of Australia, Japan and US require visas.
Currency advice/regulations
There are no restriction on the import or export of foreign or local currencies Travellers cheques in Australian dollars avoid extra exchange fees; they are accepted in main banks and some shops.
Customs
Personal effects are allowed duty-free.
Strict quarantine laws govern the import of plants, or parts of plants, vegetable matter or soil, clay or earth, animals and/or animal products.
Visitors are not allowed to take out of the country human remains, artefacts over 30 years old, traditional fighting swords, traditional tools, dancing ornaments or suits of armour.
Prohibited imports
Firearms, ammunition, explosives and indecent publications.

Health (for visitors)
Mandatory precautions
Vaccination certificate for yellow fever is required if travelling from an infected zone.
Advisable precautions
Vaccination for diphtheria, tuberculosis, hepatitis A and B, polio, tetanus, typhoid are recommended. There is also a rabies risk. It is advisable to boil water before drinking. Dengue fever is occasionally reported.

Hotels
In addition to the islands' four hotels, there are rudimentary rest houses. All hotels provide laundry services. Travellers cheques are seldom accepted.
A 10 per cent service charge is added to all hotel bills. Tipping is not customary.

Public holidays (national)
Fixed dates
1 Jan (New Year's Day), 8 Mar (Women's Day), 18 Apr (Health Day), 12 Jul (Independence Day – three days), 7 Aug (Youth Day), 7 Oct (Education Day), 25–26 Dec (Christmas).
Variable dates
Good Friday and Easter Monday (Mar/Apr) Gospel Day (Jul), Human Rights Day (Dec).

Working hours
Banking
Mon–Fri: 0930–1500 for all branches of Bank of Kiribati except Bikenibeu which opens from 0900–1400 and Kiritimati Island branch which opens between 1230 and 1330.
Business
Mon–Fri: 0800–1230, 1330–1615.
Government
Mon–Fri: 0800–1230, 1330–1615.
Shops
Shopping on Tarawa is very limited.
Mon–Sat: 0700–1900 (some shops open until 2030).

Telecommunications
Telephone/fax
A telephone service is available throughout urban Tarawa. Radio telephone links available to most outer islands.
Mobile/cell phones
There is a limited GSM 900 service available.

Electricity supply
240V AC, 50 cycles. Appliances with the standard Australian type three-pin plug will operate within South Tarawa.

Weights and measures
Metric system (Imperial units also used).

Social customs/useful tips
In official correspondence i-Kiribati adopt the western convention of signing their names with initials and surname, but it is customary (and more polite) to address people by their first name.
Women should not go out in shorts or short dresses especially on the outer islands. Bikinis should not be worn.

Getting there
Air
National airline: Air Kiribati
International airport/s: Bonriki International (TRW) on Tarawa.
Airport tax: Departure tax A$20; except transit passengers.
Surface
Government ships operate between Fiji and Kiribati. The remoteness of the islands restricts the number of large vessels which call. The international ports are Betio (on Tarawa), Banaba and Kirimati.

Getting about
National transport
Air: Air Kiribati provides inter-island plane connections several times a week to most of the islands. Charter flights can be arranged.
Road: There are 30km of asphalt road on Tarawa and Christmas Island.
Buses: A large fleet of privately owned buses operates an efficient and inexpensive mode of public transport from the airport to the main centres on South Tarawa. They may be flagged down anywhere on the main road; users may get off anywhere they wish. Buses operate daily from Betio to Buota 0600–2100.
Water: Passenger ferries operate between the islands.
City transport
Taxis: Taxis are available on Tarawa but cannot be booked, nor do they have meters. Charges are high.
Car hire
An international driving licence is required. Driving is on the left side of the road. In general, car hire is available on urban Tarawa and Kiritimati only.

BUSINESS DIRECTORY
The addresses listed below are a selection only. While World of Information makes every endeavour to check these addresses, we cannot guarantee that changes have not been made, especially to telephone numbers and area codes. We would welcome any corrections.

Telephone area codes
The international direct dialling (IDD) code for Kiribati is +686, followed by subscriber's number.

Useful telephone numbers
Fire, police, ambulance: 999
Tungaru Central Hospital, Nawerewere, South Tarawa: 28-100.

Chambers of Commerce
Kiribati Chamber of Commerce, PO Box 550, Betio, Tarawa (tel: 26-351; fax: 26-332; e-mail: kcc@tski.net.ki).

Banking
Bank of Kiribati Ltd, PO Box 66, Bairiki, Tarawa (tel: 21-095; fax: 21-200; e-mail: bankofkiribati@tksl.net.ki).

Development Bank of Kiribati, PO Box 33, Bairiki, Tarawa (tel: 81-224; fax: 81-444; e-mail: bokxmas@tksl.net.ki).

Travel information
Air Kiribati, PO Box 274, Bikenibeu, Tarawa (tel: 28-088/093; fax: 26-204).

Air Marshall, PO Box 104, Bairike, Tarawa (tel: 21-578; fax: 21-579).

Air Nauru, Tobaraoi Travel, Tarawa (tel: 26-567; fax: 26-000).

Air Tungaru Corporation, PO Box 274, Bikenibeu, Tarawa (tel: general 28-088; reservations 21-214).

Authentic Atoll Tours, PO Box 296, Bangantebure, Bikenibeu, Tarawa (tel and fax: 28-454).

Tarawa Agency, PO Box 274, Bikenibeu, Tarawa (tel: 28-088, 28-165; fax: 28-216).

National tourist organisation offices

Kiribati Visitors Bureau, PO Box 261, Bikenibeu, Tarawa (tel: 28-287/288; fax: 26-193).

Ministries
Ministry of Commerce, Industry and Tourism, PO Box 510, Betio, Tarawa (tel: 26-157, 26-158; fax: 26-233).

Ministry of Education, Bikenibeu, Tarawa (tel: 28-091; fax: 28-222).

Ministry of Environment, Bairiki, Tarawa (tel: 21-099; fax: 21-120).

Ministry of Finance and Economic Planning, PO Box 67, Bairiki, Tarawa (tel: 21-082; fax: 21-307).

Ministry of Foreign Affairs, PO Box 68, Bairiki, Tarawa (tel: 21-342; fax: 21-466; email: mfa@tskl.net.ki).

Ministry of Health and Family Planning, Bikenibeu, Tarawa (tel: 28-081; fax: 28-152).

Ministry of Line and Phoenix Group, Bairiki, Tarawa (tel: 21-449).

Ministry of Trade, Industry and Labour, Bairiki, Tarawa (tel: 21-097; fax: 21-167).

Ministry of Transport and Communications, Betio, Tarawa (tel: 26-435; fax: 26-193).

Ministry of Works and Energy, Betio, Tarawa (tel: 26-192; fax: 26-343).

Other useful addresses
Abamakoro Trading Ltd, PO Box 492, Betio, Tarawa (tel: 26-568; fax: 26-415).

Asian Development Bank (ADB), South Pacific Regional Mission, La Casa di Andrea, Fr. Dr. W. H. Lini Highway; PO Box 127, Port Vila (tel: (+678-2) 23-300; fax: (+678-2) 23-183; email: adbsprm@adb.org; internet: http://www.adb.org/SPRM).

British High Commission, PO Box 61, Bairiki, Tarawa (tel: 21-327; fax: 21-488).

Broadcasting and Publications Authority, PO Box 78, Bairiki, Tarawa.

General Post Office, Bairiki (tel: 21-080).

Kiribati Co-operative Wholesale Society (tel: 26-092; fax: 26-224).

Kiribati National Library and Archives, PO Box 6, Bairiki, Tarawa (tel: 21-245; fax: 28-222).

Kiribati Shipping Corporation, PO Box 495, Betio, Tarawa (tel: 26-195; fax: 26-204).

Office of the Attorney General, Bairiki, Tarawa (tel: 21-242).

Philatelic Bureau, Ministry of Transport and Communications, PO Box 494, Betio, Tarawa (tel: 26-515; fax: 26-193).

Telecom Kiribati Ltd, PO Box 72, Bairiki, Tarawa (tel: 21-287; fax: 21-010).

Tungaru Central Hospital, Bikenibeu, Tarawa (tel: 28-081).

Other news agencies: ABC Pacific Beat: www.radioaustralia.net.au/pacbeat

Pacific News: www.pacificmagazine.net

Internet sites
South Pacific Tourism Organisation: http://www.tcsp.com/kiribati/index.html

Kiribati homepage: http://www.trussel.com/f_kir.htm

Government site: http://www.tskl.net.ki/kiribati/

North Korea

In September 2008 speculation about the health of North Korea's leader, Kim Jong Il was intense. Kim's absence from unexpectedly small-scale celebrations of his country's sixitieth anniversary – a significant milestone in the country's history – suggested that his condition was serious. Reports in South Korean newspapers claimed that he had collapsed. North Korean media had not reported any public appearances by the 60 year old leader since August 2008. South Korean intelligence services also reported that Kim was suffering from chronic heart disease and diabetes.

Succession

Since North Korea (officially the Democratic People's Republic of Korea (DPRK)) was founded in 1948 under soviet stewardship, it has known only two leaders: Kim Il Sung and, following his death in 1994, his son, Kim Jong Il. Kim had not missed any of the ten previous military parades celebrating major anniversaries. He had, however, been known to disappear from public view for extended periods when North Korea's international situation risked worsening. By mid-2008, North Korea's nuclear disarmament negotiations had reached something of stalemate, and tensions with the US and its allies had increased. Often at such times Kim would avoid public appearances to attract international attention and increase North Korean fears of an American invasion.

The Korean peninsula was controlled by the Japanese police and army from 1910–45. Nationalist movements were suppressed ruthlessly, doing little to foster a love of the Japanese on the part of the

KEY FACTS

Official name: Chosun Minchu-chui Inmin Konghwa-guk (Democratic People's Republic of Korea) (DPRK)

Head of State: Kim Jong-il formally assumed power and was elected General Secretary of the KWP in 1997. In 1998, his father, Kim il-Sung, who died in 1994, was named President of North Korea for life.

Head of government: Prime Minister Kim Yong Il (appointed 11 Apr 2007)

Ruling party: Chosun Rodongdang (Korean Workers' Party) (KWP)

Area: 122,400 square km

Population: 23.10 million (2006)*

Capital: Pyongyang

Official language: Korean

Currency: Won (W) = 100 chon)

Exchange rate: W142.45 per US$ (Jul 2008); (based on central bank dealing; floating exchange rate from mid-2003)

GDP per capita: US$1,700 PPP (2005)

GDP real growth: 1.00% (2005)

Labour force: 11.70 million (2004)

Balance of trade: -US$1.38 billion (2005)

Foreign debt: US$12.00 billion (2003)

* estimated figure

Korean people. At the end of the Second World War, Russian troops entered Korea from the north and American troops from the south, each establishing its own, rival, government. The Russians brought with them a resistance leader, Kim il-Sung, father of the current President Kim Jong-il, who became head of the Democratic People's Republic of Korea (North Korea) in September 1948. From June 1950 the communist regime in the north attempted to reunite Korea by force, but the fighting – in which Chinese 'volunteers' arrived in numbers to oppose US-led United Nations forces – achieved nothing. An armistice signed at Panmunjon in July 1953 left the border in much the same state – along the 38th parallel – as it had been at the beginning of what later became known simply as the Korean War.

North Korea originally adopted Marxism-Leninism as its ruling philosophy. In 1972, however, the ruling philosophy was refined into the so-called *Juche* ideology, based on somewhat nebulous tenets of self reliance largely inspired by the rambling writings of Kim il-Sung. *Juche*, it was claimed, was a people centred ideology aimed to 'realise the independence of the masses'. However, the people the new ideology appeared to be centred around were North Korea's ruling family and its cronies.

More Kims to come

With a population of some 23 million, North Korea has for long been the most highly organised communist country in the world. Every North Korean is a member of one or more organisations. Approximately 2 million people are members of the Korean Workers Party (KWP) which has long played a leading – if increasingly rubber stamp – role in the country's politics. Enormous attention has traditionally been given to mass mobilisation and ideological exhortation, although hunger and health now prevail much more in most of the population's mind.

There are reports that the 'Dear Leader' Kim Jong-il's personal credibility is in ruins and the regime is teetering on the edge. This is in part for personal reasons – in 2004 his favoured mistress died of breast cancer – and economic. Food levels are minimal. The Japanese foreign ministry compiled an analysis which concluded that there were 'signs of instability' and that the fight to succeed Kim would be explosive. The leader is thought to prefer his 24-year old son with his favourite mistress, Kim Jong-chol, and has been grooming him for succession. Jong-chol went to school in Switzerland under an assumed name. There have been rumours of gun battles between the Kim family, specifically between the heir and Kim il-Sung's illegitimate son, contesting the succession.

The economy dwindles

North Korea has not disclosed official economic data since 1965, although South Korea's figures for North Korean GDP indicate a rise of 2.2 per cent in 2004. However, the economy has been shrinking for over ten years since collapse in the 1990s and is in a fragile state, kept alive only by aid donations. The country has been crippled by industrial stagnation and famine, exacerbated by its vast defence spending and an intensification of military exercises. Goods are mass produced at low quality and rationed. The concentration of economic policy on the development of heavy industry reflected the continued implementation of outdated former Soviet-style priorities, wholly unsuited to present conditions.

Foreign investment in industry, construction, technology and tourism is officially encouraged, but there have been few firms willing to invest in North Korea.

In 2005 finance officials pushed for further modernisation of national companies and discussed ways to bring in more foreign direct investment to the failing economy. Exports between the two Koreas, for the first six months of 2005, grew by 40 per cent, to a level of US$453 million. These financial exchanges, a large part of which comprise aid, is politically motivated – southern businesses operate at a loss thinking to pave the way to reunification of the peninsula. Fibre optic cables were laid to link the two Koreas in 2005, facilitating communication between divided families, and it was agreed that plans for two linking roads and two railways would also be unveiled. There is some evidence of North Korea's modernisation – internet access, a few bars and restaurants and even the sight of one or two hamburgers for sale. A middle class market is emerging.

Food shortages

North Korea faces a serious and on-going humanitarian situation, with severe food shortages. The UN World Food Programme made a global appeal for increased funds in 2005 saying that food was getting ever-more scarce in the region. The programme currently feeds a staggering 6.5 million in North Korea but only has enough aid now to feed 3.6 million on half rations. The price of key commodities was becoming too high for cash-strapped pockets. Political tussles have complicated food aid provision, with the US slashing donations. Japanese donors also became hesitant in the face of reawakened tensions about Japanese hostages captured during the Cold War by North Korea years ago.

Nuclear defence or bargaining chip?

Two theories are advanced as to why North Korea persists in maintaining and developing an expensive nuclear arsenal and missile system. The optimists view is that if rice was Kim il-Sung's idea for the formation of socialism in North Korea, missile development was its means of survival. The late 'great leader' had decreed that 'Rice is Socialism' and that North Korea as a Socialist country would triumph only when its people were well fed. Under Kim il-Sung, North Korea's hills and small mountains were deforested to plant rice. Agricultural experts dared not challenge the great leader's policy, even though the North Korean climate was ill-suited for rice farming. Meanwhile, instead of building up conventional military and weaponry, Kim il-Sung concentrated

KEY INDICATORS — North Korea

	Unit	2003	2004	2005	2006	2007
Population	m	22.47	22.69	22.86	23.01	23.11
Gross domestic product (GDP)	US$bn	10.13	–	–	–	–
GDP per capita	US$	800	–	–	–	–
GDP real growth	%	1.0	–	–	–	–
Exports (fob) (goods)	US$m	1,200.0	–	1,380.0	–	–
Imports (cif) (goods)	US$m	2,100.0	–	2,713.0	–	–
Balance of trade	US$m	-900.0	–	-1,375.0	–	–
Exchange rate	per US$	2.20	2.20	142.45	–	–

on developing the means of mass destruction, which would be more effective for his brinkmanship policy.

The optimistic view is that Pyongyang will continue to make food aid a condition for de-militarisation and normalisation in the Beijing meetings. A more pessimistic theory, prevailing since the Iraq war is that the investment in nuclear weapons is an end in itself, a non-negotiable deterrent and guarantor of the regime's continued hegemony over its starving people.

Kim il-Sung's strategy to develop weapons of mass destruction, however, may prove to be an ineffective and costly one after all. If the US goes ahead with its plan to deploy laser weapon technology in the Korean peninsula, Pyongyang's missile would be rendered ineffective as a major threat or as a leverage tool for negotiations.

Any significant de-militarisation programme would create problems of another kind for North Korea. The de-mobilisation of its million strong armed forces – in 2004 one of the largest armies in the world – would have disastrous social consequences. Redundant soldiers would have no jobs to go to, creating the risk for the government of widespread social unrest and a reduced capability to maintain control. A US based human-rights group has estimated that there are already some 20,000 political prisoners in North Korea.

Outlook

North Korea remains something of an international enigma, with scant prospect of an improvement in its economic prospects. The chasm between the richest and poorest is likely to widen as some liberalisation is undertaken. Defectors have claimed that the as many as 200,000 people suspected of political crimes are detained in remote labour camps. There are reports that prisoners often do not receive trials, and some die from torture and ill-treatment. International human rights groups have alleged that North Korea executes political prisoners, opponents of the regime and repatriated defectors. A principle of 'collective retribution' is said to operate in the DPRK, where the families of transgressors are also subjected to punishment, imprisonment or relocation to remote areas.

Once infrastructure is restored, the DPRK, with its low-cost, relatively educated and very well disciplined workforce, might conceivably become a centre for competitively priced exports to Russia and China. A priority for the country would be to forge economic and investment ties with neighbouring countries to get a foot in the door of the world economy.

Risk assessment

Politics	Poor
Economics	Poor
Regional stability	Good

COUNTRY PROFILE

Historical profile

1910 Japan formalised its annexation of Korea after gaining responsibility for its security following victory in the Russo-Japanese war of 1905.
1919 Japan suppressed the mass March First movement for self-determination.
1930s–1940s Japan imposed measures designed to assimilate the Korean population, including the outlawing of the Korean language and family names. Korea suffered under military occupation but gained the benefits of forced industrialisation.
1945 Liberation at the hands of Allied forces was a prelude to partition of the peninsula as the victorious powers encouraged friendly governments north and south of the 38th parallel. The US occupied the south while the north was taken over by the Soviet Union. As the two powers did not wish to give independence to Korea, feeling that the Korean people needed political and social re-education, a line of demarcation was established.
1947 The Chosun Rodongdang (Korean Workers' Party) (KWP) was established by Kim il-Sung (known as the 'Great Leader').
1948 The Democratic People's Republic of Korea (DPRK) was established as an independent communist state.
1950 North Korea, backed by Soviet and Chinese Communist forces, invaded South Korea. War ensued.
1953 A cease-fire was signed on 27 July; a peace treaty was never signed.
1972 A constitution was laid down.
1994 Kim il-Sung, who spent his last two decades in power, died. He was succeeded by his son Kim Jong-il (known as the 'Dear Leader').
1995–96 Floods destroyed 16 per cent of arable land.
1997 Kim Jong-il formally assumed power. He was elected general secretary of the KWP.
1998 Kim il-Sung, who died in 1994, was named president of North Korea for life.
1999 The head of UN World Food Programme (WFP) warned of imminent famine.
2000 Australia, the Philippines and Italy restored diplomatic ties with DPRK. South Korea President Kim Dae-Jung visited Pyongyang and met Kim Jong-il in an unprecedented and much fêted meeting of the two Koreas' leaders. The then US secretary of state, Madeleine Albright, visited Kim Jong-il. North Korea and the UK established diplomatic relations.
2001 An EU delegation held talks with Kim Jong-il. Talks started by the US administration in 2000 were suspended. Talks on opening the first land route between the Republic of Korea and Korea DPR broke down. After the worst winter in 50 years and a summer drought harvests were devastated, the UN WFP called for over US$300 million in food aid.
2002 US President George W Bush included North Korea with Iran and Iraq in an 'axis of evil' due to their development of Weapons of Mass Destruction (WMD). There were real developments in inter-Korean relations — the two sides agreed to resume the engagement process after the South Korean envoy, Lim Dong-won visited DPRK. The accord included plans for economic co-operation, continuing family reunions and a revival of a cross-border railway project linking the two countries. At the height of the famine, UN estimates one-third of the population received food aid and half the population were malnurished.
2003 China began talks in an effort to persuade North Korea to end its nuclear arms programme. All 687 KWP candidates , standing unopposed, won 100 per cent of the votes in elections to the National Assembly. Pak Pong Ju became premier.
2004 A train carrying volatile materials exploded killing at least 161 people and injuring over 1,000. South and North Korea temporarily opened their borders. The Gyeongui railway line was under refurbishment and a new line, Donghae Bukbu (Tonghae Pukpu), began construction. Japan resumed its food aid in August.
2005 North Korea launched a short-range missile in a test-fire in the general direction of Japan. In international talks, led by an agreement was reached whereby the nuclear weapons programme would be terminated in return for aid and security guarantees. The DPRK later demanded a civilian nuclear reactor; which was rejected. In December, further negotiations were rejected by North Korea, unless assets frozen in September in a Macau bank, which the US had accused, along with DPRK, of laundering millions of US dollars worth of counterfeit and illegally earned money; the effect of which was to deny DPRK access to the international banking system.
2006 The North Korea government listed its central bank on the London Stock exchange in an attempt to circumvent financial sanctions and had by May sold an

estimated US$28 million in gold bullion on international markets. On 9 October a limited nuclear explosion of less than one kiloton was detonated in North Korea, resulting in international financial sanctions being imposed.
2007 In January the US accused the UN of allowing aid funding to be 'perverted for the benefit of the Kim Jong Il regime' instead of being spent on the people of DPRK. The UN responded by suspending all payments until an audit was completed. On 13 February, DPRK and representatives of the six-country negotiation group signed an agreement whereby two contentious nuclear reactors in North Korea would be closed down, which international inspectors would verify, in return for the supply of 50,000 tonnes of heavy fuel oil, plus food and other aid. It will also allow DPRK access to the international banking system and a formal end to the 1950–53 Korean war. North and South Korea resumed ministerial meetings following the nuclear closure deal. On 11 April, Pak Pong Ju was replaced as prime minister by Kim Yong Il. In July, UN inspectors confirmed that the Yongbyon nuclear reactor had been shut down. Other nuclear facilities, grouped around North Korea's weapons programme, are due to be closed later as the agreed international aid is delivered. Floods in August killed over 100 people and left 300,000 people temporarily homeless; the government requested humanitarian aid as many crops were destroyed. A summit of leaders of North and South Korea took place on 2 October in Pyongyang. The three-day talks were aimed at a 'peace settlement together with economic development'. The South Korea delegation included industrialists, bureaucrats, poets and clerics. US technicians began the process of disabling the nuclear complex in November. The end-of-year deadline to disclose its nuclear programme was missed, although the dismantling of the Yongbyon nuclear facility was begun on time. However, without the written disclosure analysts say North Korea's commitment to a non-nuclear status remains in doubt.
2008 On 26 June President George W Bush of the US announced that the US would remove North Korea from its list of state sponsors of terrorism, and exempt it from the Trading with the Enemy Act. However, no sooner had he done so than he issued an executive order to keep a number of the sanctions in place, and in mid-August it was announced that the US would not afterall remove North Korea from the list. The removal is dependent on North Korea disabling its nuclear facilities. President Kim did not appear at the 9 September military parade to celebrate the country's 60th birthday, leading to reports that he had suffered a stroke.

Political structure

Constitution

Under the terms of the 1972 constitution, nominal political authority is held by a unicameral Supreme People's Assembly (SPA).
Local government is vested in nine provincial and three municipal elected people's assemblies.
Government at all levels is dominated by the Chosun Rodongdang (Korean Workers' Party) (KWP).

The executive

The head of state holds executive power and governs in conjunction with a Central People's Committee and an appointed Administrative Council (cabinet).
The head of state is no longer president since the title was given to Kim il-Sung, after he had died, for life.
Kim Jong-il was given administrative powers in 1994 and formally assumed power as head of state after being elected general secretary of the ruling KWP in 1997.

National legislature

The SPA exercises legislative power. Its 687 members are elected every four years from a single list of candidates.
The SPA, which elects a standing committee to represent it when not in session, also elects the head of government.

Legal system

The legal system is based on the German civil law system with Japanese influences and Communist legal theory.

Last elections

3 August 2003 (parliamentary)
Results: 687 candidates chosen by the ruling Chosun Rodongdang (Korean Workers' Party) (KWP), standing unopposed, won 100 per cent of the votes each; turnout was 99.9 per cent.

Next elections

Political parties

No political parties, other than the KWP, are permitted to operate.

Ruling party

Chosun Rodongdang (Korean Workers' Party) (KWP)

Population

23.10 million (2006)*
Last census: December 1993: 21,213,378
Population density: 186 inhabitants per square km.
Annual growth rate: 0.8 per cent 1994–2004 (WHO 2006)

Ethnic make-up

The Korean DPR (DPRK) has a highly homogeneous population descended from migratory groups who entered the Korean Peninsula from Siberia, Manchuria and inner Asia. There is a small Chinese community and a few ethnic Japanese.

Religions

The constitution provides for 'freedom of religious belief' but, in practice, organised religious activity is discouraged, except for certain government-sponsored religious groups. Traditional religions are Buddhism, Confucianism, Daoism, Shamanism and Chondogyo.

Education

The is a national Education for All Forum (EFA) that organises consultations with organisations such as the Youth League, the Women's Union and the Academy of Educational Science.
Education in Korea consists of six years of elementary education, three years of junior high school, three years of senior high school, and four years of college education. The government has established a free educational system and plans to extend this to the remote areas of the country. However, school attendance in some areas has reportedly dropped to between 60—80 per cent, due to extreme economic hardship not only, in families through lack of food, but also in school facilities with inadequately trained teachers, poor heating and scarce learning materials.
Competition for college entry is fierce. There are three universities. These are the Kim Il-Sung, Kim Chaek Polytechnic and Korryo-Songgyungwan. There are also around 280 colleges.
It is common for students to opt for military service after graduation. This is not compulsory, but can positively affect an individual's future career.
Literacy rate: 95–99 per cent, adult rate.

Health

There is an extensive, free medical care system, but the quality of care has declined.
Per capita total expenditure on health (2003) was US$74; of which per capita government spending was US$68, at the international dollar rate, (WHO 2006).
Water and sanitation sector, one of the key priority areas, remains poorly funded at only 18 per cent of the requirement.
A nutrition survey conducted by Unicef, in 2002, indicated that 40 per cent of children under five were chronically malnourished or stunted (a fall from the previous high of 45 per cent in 2000) and in 2003 nationwide, 5 million people, especially children, the elderly and pregnant females were dependent on foreign food aid. The mortality rate for those aged under 5 was 55 per 1,000 children; maternal mortality continues to increase as estimates show that the nutritional status of some 480,000 pregnant and nursing women is poor.

Life expectancy: 66 years, 2004 (WHO 2006)
Fertility rate/Maternal mortality rate: 2.0 births per woman, 2004 (WHO 2006)
Birth rate/Death rate: 17.6 births per 1,000 population; seven deaths per 1,000 population (World Bank 2003).
Child (under 5 years) mortality rate (per 1,000): 42 per 1,000 live births (World Bank 2004)

Welfare
A large segment of the civilian population rely on the government-run public distribution system. In 2003 the meagre food ration was further reduced to 250–380 grammes per person daily – half the minimum daily energy requirement. People are required to rely on independently procured supplements; families in urban, industrial areas have fared worst.

Main cities
Pyongyang (capital, estimated population 3.5 million (m) in 2005), Kaesong (1.9m), Hamhung (724,720), Ch'ongjin (705,850), Namp'o (2.3m), Sunch'on (423,790), Wonsan (350,179).

Languages spoken
English, amoung other international languages, is used in business.
Official language/s
Korean

Media
Press
Dailies: These include Rodong Shinmun, Minju Choson, Rodong Chongnyon and Pyongyang Times. The Korean News Service in Tokyo also provides an internet service Korean News at www.kcna.co.jp/index-e.htm.
Business: The Foreign Trade Publishing House publishes a monthly journal, Foreign Trade of the DPRK, which includes listings of specialised corporations, giving telegraphic and telex addresses.
Periodicals: A semimonthly, Tokyo-based unofficial mouthpiece of the Korea DPR government, The People's Korea, reports on Korean affairs.
Broadcasting
Radio: National and locally-produced programmes are widely disseminated (factory, outdoor loudspeakers); there are external services in several languages.
Television: There are two stations, plus a third channel at weekends. Viewing foreign channels is illegal for Korean DPR nationals.

Economy
North Korea has probably the world's most highly centralised planned economy. The concentration of economic policy on the development of heavy industry reflects the continued implementation of outdated Soviet-style priorities, wholly unsuited to present conditions. However, under-investment and lack of spares has led to a moribund industrial sector that is considered beyond rescue. Energy output is, likewise, declining.
Agricultural output in 2006 was hampered by severe floods and a drought that followed resulted in a twelth year of food shortages. Vast defence spending, an intensification of military exercises and the provocative development of nuclear weapons is distorting social provision. North Korea relies on foreign food aid and energy supplies for survival.
Foreign investment in industry, construction, technology and tourism is officially encouraged, but there have been few firms willing to invest in North Korea. Without investment in infrastructure, North Korea, with its low-cost, relatively educated workforce, cannot become the centre for competitively-priced exports to Russia and China that its geographic location could provide.
Rapprochement with South Korea could help rescue the economy, as two-way trade between the two Koreas, which was legalised in 1988, consists of joint venture projects mostly with Japan-based Koreans. Only about half consisted of commercial trade, the rest comprising aid and co-operative projects.

External trade
North Korea's foreign trade accounts for less than 10 per cent of GDP. There is a special economic zone, Rajin-Sonbong, near Rason on the north-eastern border with China and Russia, allowing free trade access in return for investment.
The Kaesong Industrial Region is an economic development zone where South Korean companies have set up manufacturing facilities. The zone is expected to be completed by 2012 and employing around 700,000 people.
The trade in illicit drugs is thought to be an important source of foreign currency within the grey economy.
Imports
Vital supplies of food aid are still required. Main imports are petroleum and coking coal, crude rubber, alloying elements, sulphur, halite, grain, cotton, sugar and palm oil
Main sources: China (39.8 per cent total, 2006), South Korea (26.2 per cent), Russia (8.3 per cent).
Exports
Commodity exports are clothing, iron and steel, armaments, machinery and equipment, non-ferrous metals, manufactured goods, fireproof bricks, anthracite, magnetite cakes, cement, magnesia clinker and machine tools.
Main destinations: China (37.3 per cent total, 2006), South Korea (25.4 per cent), Japan (9.8 per cent).

Agriculture
Farming
The agriculture sector accounts for an estimated 30 per cent of GDP and is thought to employ 43 per cent of the workforce.
Agriculture is mostly practised on large-scale collective and state farms, which have been fatally mismanaged. Main crops are rice, maize and potatoes. Other crops include wheat, barley, rape, sugar, millet, sorghum, pulses, sweet potatoes, vegetables, tobacco and silkworms. Extra grain supplies are necessary. Since the mid-1990s, North Korea has been affected by adverse climatic conditions, with a series of floods and droughts destroying crops. Other problems affecting the sector include severe deforestation, which has caused silting of rivers, a lack of fertilisers and pesticides and low levels of mechanisation. This has led to a serious food deficit at a time when North Korea's increasing political isolation has affected aid flows.
Crop production in 2005 included: 4,461,000 tonnes (t) cereals in total, 2,500,000t rice, 1,600,000t maize, 2,070,000t potatoes, 175,000t wheat, *360,000t sweet potatoes, *310,000t pulses, 19,500t treenuts, 95,000t garlic, *68,640t oilcrops, 65,400t tobacco, 669,000t apples, *36,000t seed cotton, *12,000t cotton lint, *60,000t chillies & peppers, *360,000t soya beans, 1,420,000t fruit in total, 3,996,900t vegetables in total. Livestock production included: 250,219t meat in total, 22,050t beef, 167,500t pig meat, 998t lamb, 11,250t goat meat, 47,500t poultry, 136,000t eggs, *94,000t milk, *1,500t cocoons, silk.
* estimate
Fishing
In 2004, the total marine fish catch was 174,400 tonnes and the total crustacean catch was 16,000 tonnes.
Forestry
Imports of forest materials in 2004 were US$32.1 million, while exports amounted to US$6.1 million.
Estimated production in 2004 included 7,237,495 cubic metres (cum) roundwood, 1,500,000cum industrial roundwood, 1,000,000cum sawlogs and veneer logs, 391,000cum pulpwood, 280,000cum sawnwood, 5,737,495cum wood fuel; 148,178 tonnes (t) charcoal, 80,000t paper and paperboard 106,000t recovered paper.

Industry and manufacturing
The industrial sector accounts for an estimated 20 per cent of GDP and is thought

to employ a similar percentage of the workforce.
Major manufacturing activities have been diversified to include production of steel, iron, non-ferrous metals, machinery and equipment, fertilisers, plastics and cement. Light industrial products include silk, cotton and rayon textiles, chemicals, processed food, machine tools, hardware and machinery.
Development projects in western and eastern industrial zones have included a vinalon factory in Sunchon with productive capacity of 100,000 tonnes per annum, a potash fertiliser complex in Sariwon, a coal mining complex in Anju, steel complexes in Nampo and Chongjin and synthetic rubber plants in Hamhung and Namhung.
Two production centres are planned at the port cities of Nampo and Wonsan to supplement a free-trade zone in the Rajin-Sonbong area bordering China and Russia, which has little infrastructure to support its industry. The new centres will specialise in consumer product exports by foreign companies and will be located near population centres.
Hyundai, South Korea's largest conglomerate, has developed DPRK's largest industrial complex, costing US$5 billion and located in Kaesong.
The Korean Friendship Association organises business trips to DPRK (see internet sites)

Tourism
Tourism is recognised as a means of earning foreign exchange and visitors, with the exception of Americans, are allowed into the country. The sector is undeveloped. Infrastructure is lacking, entry procedures are protracted, the cost, which includes mandatory minders, is high, and movements are tightly controlled. Arrivals, organised as package tours, are mainly by cruise ships, but a land route, via the Demilitarised Zone, opened in 2003. The main markets are South Korea, China and Japan. Around 2,000 visitors come from western countries. South Korea is actively engaged in consolidating tourism between the two countries for political reasons.

Mining
The mining sector is thought to account for some 10 per cent of GDP and to employ 5 per cent of the workforce. North Korea is well-endowed with mineral resources, including refractory clays, phosphates, sulphur and graphite and ores of iron, magnesium, tungsten, copper, lead, zinc, silver, gold, magnesite and nickel. Non-ferrous metals are an important foreign exchange earner, with 70 per cent of zinc, lead and copper production in the Hamhung district.

Hydrocarbons
North Korea has no proven reserves of oil or natural gas. North Korea relies on imports of oil for its requirements, mainly for transportation purposes, but does not import natural gas.
North Korea has coal reserves conservatively estimated at around 1.0 billion tonnes, with annual production at over 100 million tonnes. Small amounts of coal are imported. Coal supplies over 85 per cent of domestic primary energy consumption.

Energy
Electrical generating capacity is 9.5GW, two-thirds of which is provided by hydropower and the rest by coal-fired plants. Capacity is under-uttilised and consumption has declined over the years. Infrastructure, including power plants and the transmission grid, have deteriorated. Blackouts and supply shortages are frequent.
Construction of the first reactor to replace an existing plant, said to be capable of producing plutonium, was expected to begin in late 2002, but following opposition from the US after it was reported that North Korea had not discontinued its nuclear weapons programme, plans for two reactors were shelved.

Banking and insurance
There are no private banks in North Korea. The euro replaced the US dollar as the official foreign exchange currency in 2002; the Japanese yen is an unofficial exchange currency.

Central bank
Central Bank of the Peoples' Repubic of Korea

Main financial centre
Pyongyang

Time
GMT plus nine hours

Geography
North Korea occupies the northern part of the Korean peninsula, bordered to the north by the People's Republic of China and to the south by South Korea. It has a series of mountain ranges, covering up to 80 per cent of the land, across the Korean peninsula and includes all the tallest peaks of over 2,000 metres. A ridge of mountains, the Nangnim Range, runs north-south and makes communication between the east and west coast difficult. Most of the habitable areas are either in the lowlands or the coastal plains, which are, in turn, limited; the two largest plains – P'yongyang and Chaeryng – are only 500 square kilometres each. Most rivers run in a westerly direction due to the lie of the mountains. The Yalu River is the longest at 790km and flows west into Korea Bay in the Yellow Sea.

Hemisphere
Northern

Climate
Winters are cold, with temperatures ranging from minus 3 degrees Celsius (C) to minus 8 degrees C in January and falling as low as minus 20 degrees C at night. Summers are warm and humid, with an average temperature in August of 25 degrees C. Most rainfall is from June–September.

Entry requirements
Passports
Required by all.

Visa
Required by all. Applications for visas should be made well in advance. It is impossible to visit Korea DPR except by official invitation or by joining group tours from certain countries. Contact the nearest embassy for further details.

Currency advice/regulations
Import and export of local currency is prohibited. Import and export of foreign currency is unlimited, but must be declared. The euro has replaced the US dollar as the official foreign exchange currency; all other currencies will be exchanged at unfavourable rates.

Customs
Single shot cameras, laptop computers (without internet connections) and personal electronic music players are allowed but must be declared.

Prohibited imports
Illegal drugs, firearms and explosives, animals, plants, video cameras, camera lens over 150mm and pornography. Any mass printed documents, literature, audio and videotapes, compact discs and letters deemed political or intended for religious proselytising are also prohibited.
Mobile telephones and global positioning satellite systems and radios are not permitted and must be deposited on entry and collected on departure at the Customs checkpoint.

Health (for visitors)
Mandatory precautions
No compulsory vaccinations.

Advisable precautions
Malaria and cholera are a risk and precautions are essential. Vaccinations against diphtheria, hepatitis A and B, Japanese B encephalitis, polio, tuberculosis, tetanus and typhoid are recommended. Rabies is a risk.
There is a foreigners' hospital in Pyongyang, with higher standards then elsewhere in North Korea where hospitals often lack heat, medicine and supplies and suffer from frequent power loss and outbreaks of infection. In these hospitals one should avoid any invasive surgery. It is strongly recommend that visitors obtain

comprehensive health insurance before travelling to DPRK, including emergency medical evacuation as necessary.
All medication necessary should be taken (in their original packaging) in sufficient quantities, as it is not possible to purchase supplies locally.
Drink only bottled or sterilised water, avoid dairy products, which are probably unpasturised. Eat only hot, cooked meat, fish and vegetables, or peeled fruit, and avoid pork, salads and mayonnaise.

Hotels

Pyongyang has deluxe hotels that are equivalent to Western 3 stars hotels. Hotels outside Pyongyang are not as well developed but include the traditional Korean hotel Minsok.

Credit cards

The main hotels in Pyongyang will take credit and debit cards (Visa and Mastercard but not American Express).
Travellers' cheques are not accepted. Hotels generally insist on full payment in advance when checking-in.
Tipping is officially frowned upon, but is increasingly expected by some hotel staff.

Public holidays (national)

Fixed dates

1 Jan (New Year's Day), 16–17 Feb (Kim Jong-il's Birthday), 15 Apr (Kim il-Sung's Birthday), 25 Apr (Army Day), 1 May (Labour Day), 27 Jul (Victory Day), 15 Aug (Liberation Day), 9 Sep (Independence Day), 10 Oct (Foundation of the Korean Workers' Party), 27 Dec (Constitution Day).

Working hours

Banking

0900–1700. The Trade Bank of the DPRK situated near Kim Il-Sung Square in Sungni Street, Pyongyang, is open in the morning every day except Sunday.

Business

0800–1200, 1300–1700.

Government

0800–1200, 1300–1700.

Shops

1000–1800.

Telecommunications

Mobile/cell phones

In 2004, the use of mobile phones was banned.

Electricity supply

The electric current on the national grid is 220V AC and 60Hz. 220V and 110V power points are available in hotels.

Weights and measures

Metric system

Social customs/useful tips

Koreans give a short bow or nod as a sign of respect when greeting or departing, although foreigners are usually greeted with a handshake.
When anything is handed over to or received from another person, including business cards, it is polite to use both hands. The card should be read and not immediately put away.
The surname precedes the given name in Korean, but may be transposed for the benefit of foreigners.
Chopsticks should never be placed upright in rice: this is only done at funerals.
In homes and traditional restaurants, shoes are removed and slippers worn.
The Korean word for 'four' is similar to that for death and considered unlucky.
Many public buildings and all hospitals omit the fourth floor.
Names should never be written in red ink, a traditional symbol of death.

Security

Government agencies closely supervise visitors to North Korea. Hotel rooms, telephones and fax machines may be monitored, and personal possessions in hotel rooms may be searched. Photographing roads, bridges, airports, railway stations, or anything other than designated public tourist sites may be perceived as espionage and could result in confiscation of cameras and film or even detention.

Getting there

Air

It is essential to reconfirm ticket bookings for a journey some days in advance, as an issued air ticket does not guarantee a seat, unless it has been confirmed and endorsed prior to travel. For most travellers this will be done by their travel agents or inviting organisation in the DPRK.
National airline: Air Koryo
International airport/s: Sunan (FNJ), 24 km from Pyongyang.
Airport tax: None.

Surface

Rail: Rail services operate to/from Beijing and Moscow. Cargo trains started running between North and South Korea on 11 December 2007.
Main port/s: Chongjin, Haeju, Hungnam, Najin, Nampo, Wonsan. The two Koreas are discussing expansion of shipping routes. Nampo and Wonsan may become special import-export zones.

Getting about

National transport

It can be difficult to reach many areas of the interior, although the system is developing.
Air: Air Koryo operates domestic services.
Road: The road network (75,112km) includes motorways between Pyongyang and Wonsan and Pyongyang and Nampo.
Rail: The rail network is estimated at 8,533km, 89 per cent of which is electrified, with two classes of accommodation. Rail travel is slow.
Water: Rivers, canals and sea transport provide important internal links.

City transport

Taxis: Taxis are available and should be booked through the hotel.
Buses, trams & metro: There is a four-line underground system in Pyongyang with a hub at Jonu Station.

BUSINESS DIRECTORY

The addresses listed below are a selection only. While World of Information makes every endeavour to check these addresses, we cannot guarantee that changes have not been made, especially to telephone numbers and area codes. We would welcome any corrections.

Telephone area codes

The international direct dialling (IDD) code for PDR Korea is +850, followed by area code and subscriber's number.
Pyongyang2Hamchon9

Banking

Changgwang Credit Bank Chukzen 1-dong, Mangyongdae District, Pyongyang (fax: 381-4793).

Credit Bank of Korea, Chongryu 1-Dong, Munsu Street, Otan-dong, Central District, Pyongyang (tel: 381-8285; fax: 381-7806).

Foreign Trade Bank of the Democratic People's Republic of Korea, FTB Building, Jungsong dong, Central District, Pyongyang (tel: 381-5270; fax: 381-4467).

The International Industrial Development Bank, Mansu-dong, Central District, Pyongyang (tel: 381-8610).

Korea Daesong Bank, Segori-dong, Gyongheung Street, Pyongyang.

Korea Joint Bank, Ryugyong 1 dong, Pothonggang District, Pyongyang (tel: 381-8151; fax: 381-4410).

Koryo Bank, Pong-Hwa Dong, Potonggang District, Pyongyang (tel: 381-8168; fax: 381-4033).

Central bank

Central Bank of the Democratic People's Republic of Korea, Mansu-dong, 58-1 Sungri Street, Central District, Pyongyang, (fax: 381-4624).

Travel information

Air Koryo, Sunan Airport, Sunan District, Pyongyang (fax: 381-4410 ext 4625).

Kumgangsan International Tourist Company, Central District, Pyongyang (fax: 381-2100).

Tourist Advertisement and Information Agency, Songuja-dong, Mangyongdae District, Pyongyang

Ministry of tourism

National tourist organisation offices

State General Bureau of Tourism of the DPRK, Central District, Pyongyang.

Other useful addresses

Committee for the Promotion of International Trade of the Democratic People's Republic of Korea, Central District, Pyongyang.

Foreign Languages Publishing House, Sosong District, Pyongyang.

Foreign Trade Publishing House, Pyongyang District, Pyongyang.

Korea-Europe Technology & Economy Services, 15 Sojae-chon, Konguk-dong, Potonggang District, Pyongyang (e-mail: ketes@ketes.org).

Korean Central News Agency (KCNA), Potonggang District, Pyongyang.

Korean Committee for Solidarity with World People, 8-120 Yonggwang Street, Central District, Pyongyang.

Korean General Company for Economic Co-operation, Central District, Pyongyang.

Korean General Merchandise Export and Import Corporation, Central District, Pyongyang.

Korean Publications Exchange Association, PO Box 222, Pyongyang 20691.

Korean Publications Export and Import Corporation, Central District, Pyongyang.

Permanent Representative of the DPRK to the United Nations, 515 East 72nd Street, 38-F, New York, NY 10021 (tel: (+1-212) 972-3106; fax: (+1-212) 972-3154; email: prkun@undp.org).

Internet sites

Korean Friendship Association (for business trips): www.korea-dpr.com

Koryo Group, British company in Beijing, China, arranging tourism to North Korea: www.koryogroup.com

South Korea

NORTH KOREA

Sea of Japan

Ch'orwon

Kangnung
Ch'unch'on

SEOUL

Wonju
Samch'ok

Suwon

Ch'ungju

Yellow Sea

Ch'onan

Yongju

Ch'ongju

Andong

Taejon

SOUTH KOREA

Pohang

Kunsan

Taegu
Kyongju

Chonju

Ulsan

Kwangju
Namwon
Chinju

Masan

Sunchon

Pusan

Korea Strait

Cheju

JAPAN

0 75 km

KEY FACTS

Official name: Daehan Min-kuk (Republic of Korea)

Head of State: President Lee Myung-bak (Hannara Dang (HD) (Grand National Party) (sworn in 25 Feb 2008)

Head of government: Prime Minister Han Seung-soo (HD) (since 25 Feb 2008)

Ruling party: Hannara Dang (HD) (Grand National Party) (since 9 Apr 2008)

Area: 99,091 square km

Population: 48.55 million (2007)

Capital: Seoul

Official language: Korean

Currency: Won (W) = 100 chon

Exchange rate: W1,013.85 per US$ (Jul 2008)

GDP per capita: US$19,751 (2007)

GDP real growth: 4.90% (2007)

Labour force: 23.99 million (2007)*

Unemployment: 3.30% (2007)

Inflation: 2.50% (2005)

Balance of trade: US$33.47 billion (2005)

Foreign debt: US$308.70 billion (2007)*

Visitor numbers: 6.16 million (2006)*

Annual FDI: US$4.30 billion (2005)

* estimated figure

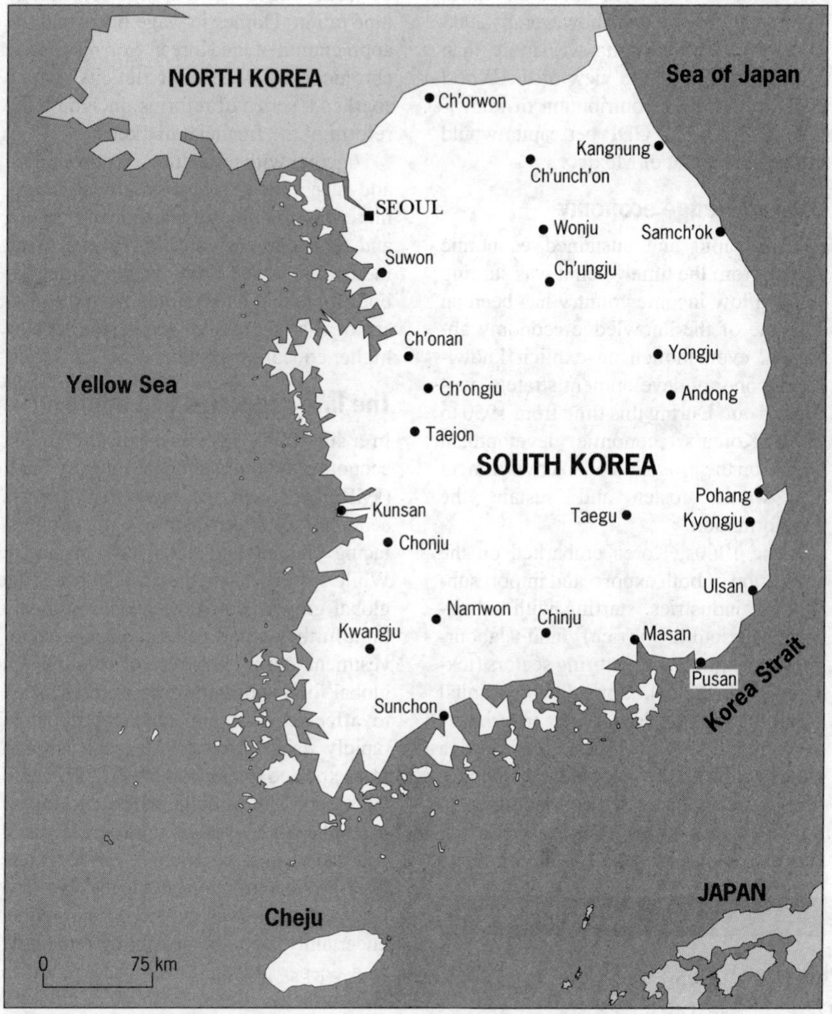

When South Korea's presidential race officially began in November 2007, it was already clear that the conservative candidate, Lee-Myung-bak was a frontrunner. Mr Lee had every interest in registering as a presidential candidate, not least to protect himself against any possible legal action that might arise from accusations made by a former business associate that he was involved in business fraud. Although prosecutors had already cleared Mr Lee of any involvement in a failed company, rumours and allegations remained in the election run-up period.

Being Mr Lee

Following his election victory in December 2007, Mr Lee was eventually sworn in as South Korea's seventeenth president in late February 2008. His inauguration went with more of a whimper than a bang. This reflected the low level of support that Mr Lee could command within his own party, the Hannara Dang (HD) (Grand National Party. Earlier in February an enquiry had cleared Mr Lee of any wrongdoing. Mr Lee, a former executive in a construction company and mayor of Seoul had led in the opinion polls throughout the election

campaign as voters made the economy their principal concern and saw in Mr Lee, nicknamed 'the bulldozer', a pragmatic technocrat rather than a charismatic politician. Mr Lee's manifesto included bold promises to return South Korea back to 7 per cent annual growth and to reduce the country's administrative bureaucracy. But public concern over his ministerial appointments caused no less than three of his appointees to resign even before he took office. Mr Lee's first weeks in power were hardly promising: opposition politicians from the United Democratic Party boycotted the National Assembly over a beef import dispute with the US (South Koreans considered US beef to be tainted with 'mad cow' disease) which threatened to derail a free trade agreement with the US; and South Korea's ambassador to Japan was recalled in protest at Japanese intransigence over sovereignty of the miniscule Dokdo islands. The shooting of a South Korean tourist near Mount Kumgang in North Korea had also put Mr Lee in a difficult position in pursuing improved relations with the North.

Amazing growth

In a 2006 review of the Korean economy, the World Bank noted that the Republic of Korea had experienced rapid and sustained economic growth over four decades. In the aftermath of World War II, Korea's GDP per capita was comparable to levels in the poorer countries in Africa. Then the Korean War, from which South Korea emerged in 1953, made conditions even worse; Korea was considered by many to be a hopeless case after four years of mass destruction. However, after 45 years, Korea's GDP per capita has increased more than 11-fold, to over US$12,000, which is on par with the medium economies of the European Union. Significantly, the contribution of knowledge has been a key factor in Korea's miracle of rapid economic growth. By comparison, Mexico's GDP per capita in 1960 was about 2.5 times larger than that of Korea; however, by 2003 Korea's GDP per capita was more than twice Mexico's. In the view of the World Bank, without the contribution of knowledge, Korea's real GDP per capita would still be below that of Mexico.

The knowledge economy

Korea's rapid and sustained economic growth from the time when it was starting out as a low income country has been an outcome of the knowledge economy approach, even though an explicit knowledge economy development strategy was not laid out. During this time from 1950 to 1997, Korea's economic development hinged on the provision of an environment that would foster and sustain the transformation.

In the 1960s, Korea embarked on the promotion of both export- and import substitution industries, starting with subsistence agriculture (rice) and labour-intensive light manufacturing sectors (textiles and bicycles). Considerable capital accumulation and investment in primary education during this period allowed a gradual shift up the value-added chain toward more sophisticated commodities.

In the 1980s, Korea undertook efforts to ensure a market-conducive environment by deregulating various sectors and liberalising trade. Concurrently, it expanded higher education while investing in indigenous research and development through the establishment of the National Research and Development Programme.

Korea continued to pursue high-value-added manufacturing in the 1990s by promoting indigenous high-technology innovation. Domestic wage hikes and the appreciation of the Korean won resulted in chronic current account deficits, which sparked a series of reforms, including the reform of the financial market.

Together with the setting up of a modern and accessible information infrastructure, there was continued expansion of research and development capabilities in Korean industries, which drew on the skilled labour force that had resulted from the government's aggressive expansion of the higher education system.

The IMF's concerns and approval

In a July 2008 assessment of the Korean economy, the International Monetary Fund (IMF) expressed the view that Korea's economy was, like many Asian countries, facing challenging global circumstances. While exports have shown resilience, the global growth slowdown would probably limit further export gains and constrain investment during the rest of 2008. High global food and fuel prices were expected to affect consumption and contribute to rapidly rising prices. As a result, growth was expected to moderate to 4.1 per cent in the second half of 2008, before picking up in 2009, while weaker domestic demand and stabilising commodity prices were likely to slow inflation later in the year. The IMF's outlook was subject to substantial uncertainty, with the possibility remaining of a deeper global slowdown, a return to more volatile global financial conditions, or still higher oil prices.

In this context, in the view of the IMF South Korea's macroeconomic policies should focus on controlling inflation. In particular, ensuring that inflation expectations remain well-anchored is critical for sustained strong economic growth. Should inflation begin to moderate and the economy remain soft, there may be scope for more accommodative macroeconomic policies. Korea's flexible exchange rate regime, with intervention limited to smoothing excessive volatility, has served the country well in the past and continues to be appropriate.

Healthy finances?

While the Korean financial system remains healthy, the ongoing global

KEY INDICATORS — South Korea

	Unit	2003	2004	2005	2006	2007
Population	m	47.57	47.72	48.14	48.30	48.55
Gross domestic product (GDP)	US$bn	608.10	679.70	791.57	888.44	957.05
GDP per capita	US$	10,641	14,098	16,444	18,395	19,751
GDP real growth	%	3.1	4.6	4.2	5.1	4.9
Inflation	%	3.3	3.6	2.8	2.2	2.5
Unemployment	%	3.4	3.7	3.7	3.5	3.3
Coal output	mtoe	1.5	1.4	1.3	1.3	1.3
Exports (fob) (goods)	US$m	193,817	257,745	288,996	331,842	378,982
Imports (cif) (goods)	US$m	178,827	219,584	255,523	303,937	349,573
Balance of trade	US$m	14,990	38,161	33,473	27,905	29,409
Current account	US$m	12,110	26,820	14,981	5,385	5,954
Total reserves minus gold	US$m	155,284	198,996	210,317	238,882	262,150
Foreign exchange	US$m	154,508	198,175	209,967	238,387	261,770
Exchange rate	per US$	1,194.23	1,145.47	940.05	925.14	930.10

financial turmoil has raised some modest concerns. International credit market stresses have underlined that banks reliant on wholesale funding may be exposed to greater liquidity risk. Korean banks are beginning to diversify their funding sources and supervisors are increasingly focused on limiting such risks. International experience suggested that enhanced contingency planning would also help. Bank loan quality is strong but an economic slowdown could reveal some vulnerabilities, particularly in small- and medium-sized enterprise (SME) lending, which merited continued close attention. Short-term external debt has risen sharply in recent years, as a counterpart to hedging activity, and more recently, with foreign purchases of sovereign bonds. This debt should be monitored, but its sources and uses are very different from those of a decade ago, and risks remain moderate.

Looking ahead, structural changes to the financial sector will present both challenges and opportunities. Increased financial sector competition, in light of the legal framework taking effect in 2009, should contribute to growth, but will require financial oversight to meet new regulatory challenges, including risks from more complex institutions and products.

Mr Lee's government appropriately aimed to address structural challenges to Korea's impressive growth record, including through deregulation, privatisation, and tax cuts. Plans for any tax cuts should be in the context of a broader tax reform plan that concretely addresses long-run fiscal pressures, notably those associated with an aging population.

Risk assessment

Economy	Good
Politics	Fair
Regional stability	Fair

COUNTRY PROFILE

Historical profile

1910 Japan formalised its annexation of Korea after gaining responsibility for its security following victory in the Russo-Japanese war of 1905.
1919 Japan suppressed the mass March First movement for self-determination.
1930s–1940s Japan imposed measures designed to assimilate the Korean population, including the outlawing of the Korean language and family names. Korea suffered under military occupation but gained the benefits of forced industrialisation.
1945 Liberation at the hands of allied forces was a prelude to partition of the peninsula as the victorious powers encouraged friendly governments north and south of the 38th parallel. The US occupied the south while the north was taken over by the Soviet Union. As the two powers did not wish to give independence to Korea, feeling that the Korean people needed political and social re-education, a line of demarcation was established.
1947 The Chosun Rodongdang (Korean Workers' Party) (KWP) was established by Kim il-Sung (known as the 'Great Leader').
1948 The Democratic People's Republic of Korea (DPRK) was established as an independent communist state.
1950 DPRK, backed by Soviet and Chinese Communist forces, invaded South Korea. War ensued.
1953 A cease-fire was signed on 27 July; a peace treaty was never signed.
1972 A constitution was laid down.
1994 Kim il-Sung, who spent his last two decades in power, died. He was succeeded by his son Kim Jong-il (known as the 'Dear Leader').
1995–96 Floods destroyed 16 per cent of arable land resulting in severe famine.
1997 Kim Jong-il formally assumed power. He was elected general secretary of the KWP.
1998 Kim il-Sung, who died in 1994, was named president of DPRK for life. Famine relief was supplied by the UN. A rocket was fired by DPRK which over flew Japan and crashed into the Pacific Ocean. DPRK claimed it was a satellite and not a missile.
2000 Australia, the Philippines, UK and Italy restored diplomatic ties with DPRK. South Korea President Kim Dae-Jung visited Pyongyang and met Kim Jong-il in an unprecedented and much fêted meeting of the two Koreas' leaders. US secretary of state, Madeleine Albright, visited Kim Jong-il. Family reunions were allowed between the north and south after separations since the Korean War.
2001 An EU delegation held talks with Kim Jong-il. After the worst winter in 50 years and a summer drought harvests were devastated, the UN WFP called for over US$300 million in food aid.
2002 US President George W Bush included DPRK with Iran and Iraq in an 'axis of evil' due to their development of Weapons of Mass Destruction (WMD). Naval skirmishes between DPRK and South Korea in the Yellow Sea, were the worst since 2000, killing over 30 sailors on both sides. Nevertheless, there was agreement to resume the engagement process with plans for economic co-operation, continuing family reunions and a revival of a cross-border railway project. At the height of the famine, UN estimated one-third of the population had received food aid and half the population was malnourished. Junichiro Koizumi, the Japanese prime minister visited, the first to do so. The abduction of Japanese citizens was at the forefront of the talks. DPRK admitted to its secret nuclear weapons programme, and resumed construction of its nuclear reactor. Inspectors from the UN's International Atomic Energy Agency (IAEA) were expelled.
2003 DPRK resigned from the international treaty for the Nuclear Non-proliferation Treaty (NPT). All 687 KWP candidates, standing unopposed, won 100 per cent of the votes in elections to the National Assembly. Pak Pong Ju became premier. International talks begin in an attempt to curb DPRK nuclear aspirations.
2004 A train carrying volatile materials exploded killing at least 161 people and injuring over 1,000. South and DPRK temporarily opened their borders. The Gyeongui railway line was under refurbishment and a new line, Donghae Bukbu (Tonghae Pukpu), began construction. International talks attempting to curb DPRK nuclear aspirations failed.
2005 DPRK claimed it had nuclear weapons for self-defence. DPRK launched a short-range missile in a test-fire in the general direction of Japan. In a fourth round of international talks, an agreement was reached whereby the nuclear weapons programme would be terminated in return for aid and security guarantees. The DPRK later demanded a civilian nuclear reactor, which was rejected. The assets of a Macao bank were frozen including those of DPRK, which the US accused of laundering millions of US dollars worth of counterfeit and illegally earned money; the effect of which was to deny DPRK access to the international banking system. The DPRK rejected further negotiations unless their assets were released.
2006 The DPRK government listed its central bank on the London Stock exchange in an attempt to circumvent financial sanctions and sold an estimated US$28 million in gold bullion on international markets. Long- and medium-range missiles were tested, prompting widespread international condemnation A limited nuclear explosion of less than one kiloton was detonated in DPRK, resulting in international financial sanctions being imposed.
2007 In January the US accused the UN of allowing aid funding to be 'perverted for the benefit of the Kim Jong Il regime' instead of being spent on the people of DPRK. The UN responded by suspending all payments until an audit was completed. On 13 February, DPRK and representatives of the six-country negotiation group signed an agreement; two contentious nuclear reactors in DPRK would be

closed down and would be verify by international inspectors, in return for the supply of 50,000 tonnes of heavy fuel oil, plus food and other aid. The DPRK would also be allowed access to the international banking system and a formal end to the 1950–53 Korean War. North and South Korea resumed ministerial meetings following the nuclear closure deal. In April, Pak Pong Ju was replaced as prime minister by Kim Yong Il. In May, the first passenger trains crossed the north-south border since 1953. In July, the IAEA confirmed that the Yongbyon nuclear reactor had been shut down. Other nuclear facilities, grouped around DPRK's weapons programme. Floods in August killed over 100 people and left 300,000 people temporarily homeless; the government requested humanitarian aid as many crops were destroyed. A summit of leaders of North and South Korea took place. The South Korea delegation included industrialists, bureaucrats, poets and clerics. US technicians began the process of disabling the nuclear complex in November. The end-of-year deadline to disclose its nuclear programme was missed, although the dismantling of the Yongbyon nuclear facility was begun on time. However, without the written disclosure analysts say DPRK's commitment to a non-nuclear status remained in doubt.
2008 In March and April the relations between DPRK and South Korea deteriorated when DPRK expelled managers of joint industrial enterprises and test fired short-range missiles. South Korea sent warships into northern waters. On 26 June DPRK sumitted the declaration on its nuclear activities to China. The US lifted its sanctions and announced that DPRK would be removed from countries designated as a state sponsor of terrorism.

Political structure

Constitution

A new constitution, allowing direct presidential elections and thus providing a framework for civilian rule, took effect in 1988 after receiving overwhelming approval in a referendum. The constitution removed the president's sweeping emergency powers that included the right to dissolve parliament. It also enhanced the authority of the legislature and judiciary. It provided for more civil liberties, including restoration of habeas corpus, while the National Assembly was empowered to supervise and investigate state affairs. Free presidential elections replaced the electoral college system, which had favoured the ruling party candidate. In addition, the constitution requires that the armed forces must maintain political neutrality.
The constitution provides for greater checks and balances among the executive, legislative and judiciary powers. A Board of Audit and Inspection was set up to monitor all government expenditure, revenue and agencies. The chairperson is appointed by the president but only with the National Assembly's approval.
A constitutional court has judgement on the constitutionality of any legislation.

Form of state

Democratic republic

The executive

Executive power is held by the president, who is popularly elected for a single term of five years and governs with the assistance of the State Council, normally composed of 15–30 ministers and headed by the prime minister. The State Council is appointed by the president on the advice of the prime minister. It does not have to be composed entirely of members of the National Assembly. No active member of the armed forces may serve on the State Council.
The president has veto power over legislation, but the National Assembly can override this by a two-thirds vote.
Other presidential powers include the appointment of officials such as judges, ministers, the mayors of five cities (Seoul, Pusan, Taegu, Inchon and Kwangu) and the governors of nine provinces.

National legislature

Legislative power is exercised by the unicameral Kuk Hoe (National Assembly), which, under the 1988 constitution, must have no fewer than 200 members, serving four-year terms.

Legal system

There is a three-tier legal system, headed by a Supreme Court. This Court is composed of a chief justice (for a six-year term) and 13 justices (on recommendation by the chief justice), all appointed by the president, with the consent of the National Assembly. Below the Supreme Court are High Courts (intermediate appelate courts) and, below these, District Courts. High Courts and District Courts are divided into geographic districts. Korea also has a number of specialised courts, such as a Family Court and an Administrative Court.

Last elections

9 April 2008 (parliamentary); 19 December 2007 (presidential).
Results: Parliamentary: the HD won 153 seats (out of 299), the United Democratic Party (UDP) 81, the Liberty Forward Party (LFP) 18, pro-Park Geun-hye coalition 14, Creative Korea Party 3, independents 25. Presidential: Lee Myung-bak (HD) won 48.7 per cent of the vote, ahead of Chung Dong-young (Daetonghap Minju Sindang, (United New Democratic Party) (UNDP)) with 26.1 per cent and Lee Hoi Chang (independent) with 15.1 per cent.

Next elections

December 2012 (presidential); 2012 (National Assembly).

Political parties

Ruling party
Hannara Dang (HD) (Grand National Party) (since 9 Apr 2008)
Main opposition party
United Democratic Party (UDP)

Population

48.55 million (2007)
Last census: November 2000: 46,136,101
Population density: 479 inhabitants per square km. Urban population: 82 per cent (1995—2001).
Annual growth rate: 0.7 per cent 1994–2004 (WHO 2006)

Ethnic make-up

Koreans, although apparently homogeneous, have complex ethnic origins, with much genetic input from the nomadic tribes of Mongolia and Central Asia. There are over 25,000 Chinese, the only major foreign ethnic community besides the 37,000 US troops stationed in South Korea. In addition, there are some 230,000 migrant labourers from a variety of countries such as Kazakhstan, Morocco and China. There is also a growing number of refugees who have escaped from the harsh conditions of North Korea.

Religions

There is no state religion and the country is tolerant of various religious faiths. Although census and churchgoing data conflict, the most recent information available indicates that up to 49 per cent of the population professes to be Christian, 47 per cent Mahayana Buddhist, 3 per cent Confucianist.

Education

Public expenditure on education amounts to 3.6 per cent of GDP. Universal primary education and gender parity, at this level and in secondary schools, have been achieved.
Primary schooling lasts until a child is 12, middle secondary schooling lasts for three years, these constitute compulsory education. Upper secondary high schools offer either, an academic, special purpose (combined academic and vocational courses), or a wholly vocational programme, lasting for three years.
There are five types of public and private teriary institutions including junior colleges and universities.
Literacy rate: 98 per cent, male; 96.8 per cent, female; adult rates (World Bank).
Compulsory years: 6 to 15
Enrolment rate: 110 per cent, gross primary enrolment, of relevant age group

(including repeaters); 102 per cent, gross secondary enrolment (World Bank).
Pupils per teacher: 31, in primary schools

Health
Per capita total expenditure on health (2003) was US$1,074; of which per capita government spending was US$531, at the international dollar rate, (WHO 2006).
There are around 19,500 private clinics complementing the country's hospitals, of which a significant number are university-affiliated. Improved water sources and sanitation facilities are available to 92 per cent and 63 per cent of the population resectively.
Life expectancy: 77 years, 2004 (WHO 2006)
Fertility rate/Maternal mortality rate: 1.2 births per woman, 2004 (WHO 2006); maternal mortality 20 deaths per 100,000 live births (World Bank).
Birth rate/Death rate: 6 deaths and 14 births per 1,000 population (World Bank estimates).
Child (under 5 years) mortality rate (per 1,000): 5 per 1,000 live births (World Bank)

Welfare
The National Basic Livelihood Protection Law makes social assistance a legal right for the unemployed, based on a concept of 'productive welfare' which combines means-testing with self-support plans to facilitate re-entry to the workforce.
Public pensions provision, introduced in 1988, is set to increase as the system confronts an ageing population with a 12-fold increase in the expected number of beneficiaries by 2010. Contributions will have to double to 18 per cent of salary to maintain an actuarial balance, according to the Organisation for Economic Co-Operation and Development (OECD). The South Korean government may consider alternative options, such as privately-managed pensions funds, paid into by the allowances firms are obliged to award departing employees.

Main cities
Seoul (capital, estimated population 10.1 million (m) in 2005), Pusan (3.7m), Inch'on (2.7m), Taegu (2.6m), Taejeon (1.5m), Kwangju (1.4m), Seongnam (1.0m), Ulsan (1.1m), Koyang (1.0m).
In 2007, the government will start building a new administrative capital in Chungcheongnam-do province, to the south of Seoul; the first ministries and government departments will move in 2012; the city should be complete by 2030.

Languages spoken
The Korean language is a member of the Altaic family with origins in Mongolia. Approximately 60 per cent of the vocabulary is borrowed from Chinese. The written language employs its own phonetic character system, Hangul.
English is spoken to a limited extent in government and business circles. The older generation often speak Japanese.
Official language/s
Korean

Media
The Korean media, reputedly notorious for their appetite for influence, are thought, by civic campaigners, to be a constituency in need of urgent reform. Efforts made in the past to curtail publishers and their various backers have not succeeded. The sector has a long tradition of collaborating with South Korea's authoritarian regimes and is sensitive about criticism of bias.
Press
Much of the Korean press is controlled by industrial conglomerates. Readership is high and there are over 100 national and local dailies to choose from.
Dailies: The 'Big Three' nationals published in Seoul are Chosun Ilbo (http://english.chosun.com) is considered a conservative publication, JoongAng Ilbo (http://joongangdaily.joins.com) and Donga Ilbo (http://english.donga.com), take an independent line. In Korean, other regional publication include from Pusan Pusan Ilbo (www.busanilbo.com), Kookje Shinmun (www.kookje.co.kr); from Inch'on Inchon Ilbo (http://news.itimes.co.kr); from Taegu Kyongbuk Ilbo (www.kyongbuk.co.kr), Maeil Shinmun (www.imaeil.com) and Morning News (www.morningnews.co.kr). In English, The Seoul Times (www.theseoultimes.com).
Weeklies: Many foreign magazines have Korean sections, local news magazines include Korea Newsreview, which publishes articles from the government-owned Korea Herald (www.koreaherald.co.kr), in English.
Business: In Korean, Hankyung (www.hankyung.com), Financial News Daily (www.fnnews.com), Seoul Economic Daily (www.hankooki.com) and Maeil Business Newspaper (http://news.mk.co.kr, with online English edition. Most national newspapers also provide business news some with online English editions.
Periodicals: Dong-A Herald is a bimonthly student newspaper. The Granite Tower is a monthly English language tabloid.

Broadcasting
Radio: The public service is the Korea Broadcasting System (http://english.kbs.co.kr), which operates six networks including Radio Korea International (http://world.kbs.co.kr) offering programmes in 11 languages.
There are over 200 local radio stations some of which are relayed nationwide. Around 30 per cent of all stations are privately owned and commercial. There are national networks that are educational and religious. The American Forces Network (AFN) Korea (http://afnkorea.net) is operated by the US military.
Television: There are over 30 television stations run by the country's networks, of which the most important are Korea Broadcasting System (KBS) and Munwha Broadcasting Corporation (MBC). The longest-running stations are KBS 1, 2, 3 (an educational station), MBC and AFKN-TV (operated by the US military for its personnel and their dependants). Other networks operating in South Korea include Asia-Pacific broadcaster Arirang TV, which provides English-language programming, the youth-oriented Mnet, Korea Music Television, Seoul Broadcasting System (SBS) and the News Channel of Korea. Around 90 per cent of the population subscribe to cable TV.
Advertising
Commercial advertising may be placed in the press, on radio and television and in cinemas, as well as on public billboards and posters. The Korea Broadcasting Advertising Corporation (Kobaco) is authorised as the sole media representative responsible for over 50 broadcasting stations in television, radio and digital services. It publishes a document setting out all advertising requirements Introduction to broadcast advertising in Korea.

Economy
Economic growth over the past 30 years has been spectacular. Starting from a low base comparable to the poorest economies of the time, South Korea has become an advanced economy ranked eleventh in the list of largest global economies. It weathered the Asian economic criss of 1997–99 and managed to avoid most of the shocks that hit many other east Asian economies in 2001/02 due to its highly diversified industrial base and large domestic market. By 2005, GDP growth was 3.8 per cent and was forecast to increase by around five per cent in 2006. Inflation remained low at 2.7 per cent in 2005, as did unemployment at 3.7 per cent.
South Korea is a major exporter of manufactured electronic products. Massive capital investment and education, begun in the mid-1970s, provided the county with

large numbers of well-qualified engineers to work in the expanding electronics sector. South Korea held 60 per cent of the global market share in flash memory products in 2006. In the medium-term the electronics sector is expected to decrease as US demand slows. Electronics accounted for 40 per cent of all exports in 2005.

South Korea is China's largest foreign direct investor, as it has shifted basic production to take advantage of lower unit costs. China has also become South Korea's largest foreign direct investor, with US$1.2 billion in 2004.

South Korea's total lack of hydrocarbons will always be a concern and means that all oil and natural gas have to be imported, making the economy vulnerable to oil price rises. Nevertheless, the strong won allowed it to ride the global oil price rise in 2005 and achieve a US$33.5 billion trade balance. The economy is sound and in a good position to weather most shocks.

External trade

South Korea is a member of the Asia-Pacific Economic Co-operation (Apec) forum, which is a group of 21 countries that border the Pacific. The objective of Apec is to facilitate trade, economic growth and investment in the region.

South Korea is the world's leading semiconductor manufacturer and as a whole the manufacturing sector provides 40 per cent of GDP. Other sectors include steel making, shipbuilding, vehicle assembly and textile manufacture.

Imports

Principal imports are machinery, electronics and electronic equipment, petroleum, steel, plastics, transport equipment, iron and steel.

Main sources: Japan (18.5 per cent total, 2005), China (14.8 per cent), US (11.8 per cent), Saudi Arabia (6.2 per cent)

Exports

Principal exports are semiconductors, telecommunications equipment, vehicles, computers, steel, ships and petrochemicals.

Main destinations: China (21.8 per cent total, 2005), US (14.6 per cent), Japan (8.5 per cent), Hong Kong (5.5 per cent)

Agriculture

Farming

The agricultural sector accounts for around 3.7 per cent of GDP and employs 15 per cent of the workforce. Farming remains essentially subsistence-based and is inherently uncompetitive. While, by comparison, farmers are richer than their counterparts elsewhere in Asia, the average farm holding is big enough to support only a small family and the disparity in incomes between the urban and rural populations is growing.

Price-support policies for farmers are being reduced in line with South Korea's international commitments. Increasing the average size of farms and decoupling production decisions from government aid are likely to be vital in promoting efficiency in farming.

The main crops grown are rice, sweet potatoes, barley, soya beans and a wide range of fruit and vegetables. Despite considerable efforts, the country depends on imports for animal feed grains. Ginseng, tobacco, pears and processed noodles are among South Korea's exports.

Crop production in 2005 included: 6,759,006 tonnes (t) cereals in total, 6,418,000t rice, 3,300,000t cabbages, 670,000t potatoes, 290,000t sweet potatoes, 420,000t chillies & peppers, 350,000t garlic, 33,900t treenuts, 581,000t citrus fruit, 360,000t grapes, 400,000t tomatoes, 38,720t oilcrops, *35,666t tobacco, 125,000t soya beans, 380,000t apples, 2,487,000t fruit in total, 12,160,000t vegetables in total. Livestock production included: 1,739,729t meat in total, 229,000t beef, 1,050,000t pig meat, 3,300t goat meat, 450,024t poultry, 598,000t eggs, 2,237,665t milk, 29,000t honey, 37,746t cattle hides.

Fishing

The fishing industry is an important source of export earnings but international restriction of fishing zones has limited potential growth. South Korean fishing vessels are mostly active in the South Pacific. The annual catch, of which some 60 per cent is marine fish, totals up to 2.6 million tonnes.

In 2004, the total marine fish catch was 1,066,541 tonnes and the total crustacean catch was 82,100 tonnes.

Forestry

Forests, around half of which are conifer, cover some 65 per cent of the total land area. Much of the forest owes its existence to large-scale replanting programmes implemented after the Second World War and since the end of the Korean War in 1953. The latter conflict, together with logging under the Japanese occupation, and demand for fuelwood, badly degraded the native forest.

South Korea and Indonesia have an agreement for forestry co-operation. This involves projects such as tree planting, fighting forest fires, skills development and eco-tourism investment.

Exports of forest materials in 2004 amounted to US$1.9 billion, while imports amounted to US$3.9 billion.

Production in 2004 included 4,552,202 cubic metres (cum) roundwood, 2,089,000cum industrial roundwood, 4,366,000cum sawnwood, 3,860,000cum wood-based panels, 289,000cum sawlogs & veneers, 1,400,000cum pulpwood, 2,463,202 cum wood fuel, 6,000 tonnes (t) charcoal, 10,511,000t paper and paperboard (including 1,679,000t newsprint), 2,475,000t printing and writing paper, 545,000t paper pulp, 6,875,000t recovered paper.

Industry and manufacturing

Korea's industrialisation programme made it the world's eleventh richest economy during the 1990s, when it became the world's largest shipbuilder and producer of DRAM memory chips, the fourth biggest car exporter and the sixth largest steelmaker. The industrial sector accounts for around 40 per cent of GDP and employs around a fifth of the workforce.

The manufacture of iron and steel products, the automobile industry, shipbuilding, petrochemicals and electronics continue to be central to export-led growth. Other main products include fertilisers and other industrial chemicals, rubber, synthetic and natural textiles, garments, footwear and processed foods.

The industrial structure continues to be haunted by the legacy of rapid state-guided industrialisation protected from overseas competition. The government has struggled to limit the economic power of the 30 largest leading companies (chaebol), which still dominate national industry.

Tourism

Tourism is an important and growing industry. New hotels, both de luxe and budget class, have opened and more are being built throughout the country. New resort complexes are under construction. There were 5.8 million visitor arrivals in 2004. Tourism is expected to contribute 1.6 per cent to GDP in 2005.

Mining

There are no significant mineral resources. South Korea relies mainly on imports to meet its increasing domestic demand. The major mineral imports are iron ore, copper and zinc ore concentrates. Cement is a major export commodity to the US, as there is surplus in the domestic market.

LG-Nikko Copper Incorporated, a joint venture established by LG and Japan Korea Joint Smelting Company, a Japanese consortium, is the only copper smelting and refining operation in South Korea. Each company was obliged to invest US$20 million in the joint venture that took control of LG's Changhang and Onsan copper smelting and refining operations, which had an estimated value of US$830 million.

Domestic iron ore supplies only about one per cent of South Korea's needs. The Pohang Iron and Steel Company (Posco), the largest crude steel producer in South Korea and the only integrated iron and steel producer, formed a strategic alliance with Nippon Steel Corp, to expand research and development, and also encouraged other Asian companies to join the alliance. Posco employs more than 5,000 employees at production plants in Pohang and Kwangyang, producing more than 23.4 million tonnes of steel products annually for customers in over 60 countries. Its products range from electrical steel sheets to stainless steel products.
The only lead and zinc mine, at Kumba, supplies about 10 per cent of the demand for lead and zinc concentrates. Korea Zinc, which is one of the largest primary zinc producers in the world, completed the expansion of its zinc plant complex at Onsan, and is able to produce over 350,000 tonnes per year. Young Poong Corporation, its parent company, increased zinc metal output at the Sukpo zinc refinery, in the North Kyongsang Province, by over 198,300 tonnes per year.
The non-metal mineral sector accounts for 51.9 per cent of the total mining industry. Other industrial mineral production includes limestone, silica stone, kaolin, serpentine, feldspar and zeolite. Major imports consist of potash, asbestos and manganese ores and concentrates.

Hydrocarbons
South Korea has no domestic oil reserves. Oil consumption was 2.1 million bpd in 2004, making it the world's seventh largest consumer and fourth largest importer. The country has built up strategic petroleum reserves which cover 90 days of imports, in order to offset any disruption to supply. The state-owned Korea National Oil Corporation (KNOC) has, in an effort to secure the country's oil supply, bought up stakes in oil companies throughout the world and is involved in 18 foreign exploration and production projects. South Korea has an oil refining capacity of 2.6 million barrels per day (bpd).
Domestic gas production began in November 2003 with KNOC's development of a small natural gas field, located offshore in the south-east. The development supplies just 2 per cent of the country's total demand for natural gas. South Korea has relied on imports of liquefied natural gas (LNG) to provide it with gas since 1985, when the Korea Gas Corporation (Kogas) was formed. Consumption of natural gas, which has increased in recent years, typically amounts to 18.7 billion cubic metres. Indonesia and Malaysia provide most of South Korea's LNG, other sources being Brunei, Australia and Qatar. LNG is the fastest growing energy source in South Korea.
Coal supplies around 21 per cent of South Korea's energy needs. Domestic production has declined from 10 million tonnes in the mid-1980s to less than 4 million tonnes in 2004. Domestic coal production is of low-quality anthracite used in residential heating and small boilers. Steam coal for power supply and metallurgical coal for steelmaking come mainly from China and Australia, where the Korean Electric Power Corporation (Kepco) has invested in a number of mines.

Energy
South Korea has over 50GW of generating capacity, supplied mainly by thermal and nuclear power . The government projects electricity demand will rise by an average annual rate of 3.4 per cent between 2002 and 2015.
The privatisation of the state-owned electricity utility, Korean Electric Power Corporation (Kepco), has moved at a slow pace due to strong opposition from the trade unions.

Banking and insurance
The 1997/98 financial crisis revealed underlying structural problems in South Korea's banking system. The crisis led to the creation of the Financial Restructuring Committee (FRC), which reported a large ratio of non-performing loans (NPLs) to total loans and poor accounting standards. The government was forced to nationalise the country's five largest banks so that by 2002/03 at 7.5 per cent, South Korea had the second-lowest NPL ratio in East Asia after Hong Kong. The estimated recovery rate on South Korean NPLs is 35 per cent, compared to Singapore and Hong Kong at 75 per cent and 50 per cent respectively.
Although the financial system is in better health, controversies linger over bank privatisation. Arguments also surround banking regulation, with President Roh reluctant to allow the chaebol to regain their influence over the sector. Roh favours increasing the powers of independent directors and shareholders as well as encouraging greater foreign ownership, although there is little foreign interest in South Korea's banking sector which is seen as risky.
Another pressing concern for the government is consolidating the banking sector into three or four large banks.
Central bank
Bank of Korea
Main financial centre
Seoul

Time
GMT plus nine hours
Geography
South Korea forms the southern part of the Korean peninsula, in north-east Asia, with the Democratic People's Republic of Korea to the north. To the west is the Yellow Sea, the East China Sea is to the south and the Sea of Japan is to the east. The Korea Strait separates the peninsula from Japan in the south-east. The country's portion of the peninsula is dominated by rugged terrain and mountains, culminating in the T'aebaek-sanmaek mountain range which runs from north to south along the eastern coast. Two major rivers originate in this range, the Naktong flowing to the Korea Strait and the Han river to the Yellow Sea. Plains are few and far between, mostly concentrated in the west, with the coastal strips in the east and south typically narrow. There are a number of islands off the southern and western coasts. Of these the largest is Cheju, over 1,800 square km in size and home to South Korea's highest peak, Mount Hallasan (1,950 metres).
Hemisphere
Northern

Climate
Winters are dry and very cold, with temperatures well below 0 degrees Celsius (C) between December–February. Korean summers are typically hot and humid, with monsoon rains, tropical storms and occasional typhoons from June–September. The average July temperature range is 22–29 degrees C. The narrow southernmost coastal plain has the mildest climate and is home to vegetation such as bamboo and evergreen oak.

Entry requirements
Passports
Required by all and must be valid for six months from the date of departure.
Visa
Not required by tourists from North America, Japan, Australia and many citizens of EU for up to 60 days. See http://english.tour2korea.com and the link to Entry Info for a full list and entitlements. For business travellers and those not eligible for visa-free travel, visit www.mofat.go.kr/me/index.jsp and see visa control. Applications must be submitted to the nearest Korean consulate.
Prohibited entry
Currency advice/regulations
The import of local and foreign currency greater than US$10,000 must be declared; permission for the export of local and foreign currency larger than US$10,000 (or equivalent, including travellers cheques) must be obtained from customs or the Bank of Korea; export is

limited to the amount declared on arrival. Exchange receipts should be retained for verification.
Travellers cheques are accepted in banks, hotels and larger shops in major towns.

Customs

Personal effects are duty free, including high-value items (cameras, watches etc) which should be recorded on a baggage declaration form on arrival.
A certificate from the Cultural Properties Preservation Bureau is necessary for exporting antiques. Permission for trade imports or exports must be obtained from the trade and industry ministry or from authorised foreign exchange banks, and certain items may be restricted or prohibited (such as ginseng and cuttlefish).

Prohibited imports

Illegal drugs and pornography. Firearms and ammunition, fruit, vegetables soil and seeds all require licences, obtained before arrival.

Health (for visitors)

Health facilities in South Korea are generally good. The high level of pollution may be a serious problem for those suffering from respiratory conditions.

Mandatory precautions

An HIV/Aids-free certificate is required for stays of over three months.

Advisable precautions

Vaccinations are recommended for diphtheria, tuberculosis, hepatitis A and B, Japanese B encephalitis, polio, tetanus and typhoid. There is rabies risk and travellers should avoid stray animals.

Hotels

Luxury hotels include a 10 per cent service charge in the bill. Tipping is not usual, although it is on the increase in Western-style hotels.

Credit cards

Major hotels accept credit cards, but check when booking which ones are accepted for settlement of hotel bills. Also accepted in major department stores, supermarkets etc.
The Korea Travel Card, a pre-paid debit card allows visitors to pay for goods and services throughout the country at favourable rates. The card is obtained through tourist outlets.

Public holidays (national)

Fixed dates

1 Jan (New Year's Day), 1 Mar (Independence Movement Day), ^1 May (Labour Day), 5 May (Children's Day), 6 Jun (Memorial Day), 17 Jul (Constitution Day), 15 Aug (Liberation Day), 3 Oct (National Foundation Day), 25 Dec (Christmas Day).
^ Bank and business organisations holiday.
The summer vacation is the last week in July and the first week in August.

Variable dates

Soellal (Lunar New Year, Jan/Feb, three days), Birth of Buddha (May), Chu'seok (Harvest Moon Festival, Sep/Oct, three days).

Working hours

Banking

Mon–Fri: 0900–1700.

Business

Mon–Fri: 0900–1800.

Government

Mon–Fri: 0900–1800.

Shops

Sun–Sat: 1030–2000 (department stores, closed one day per month, typically Mon, different stores choose different days). Small shops open from early morning till late evening every day of the week.

Telecommunications

Mobile/cell phones

There are 3G GSM services available.

Electricity supply

220V AC, 60 cycles, with round two-pin plugs.

Weights and measures

Metric system used in commerce; local system also in use, especially relating to land and buildings.

Social customs/useful tips

Korean surnames precede given names, and given names are never used alone, except by intimates. The family names, 'Kim', 'Lee' and 'Park', cover more than half the population and may have variant spellings. Business associates are normally addressed by title (eg Director Kim or Manager Lee).
Business entertaining usually takes place in restaurants and wives do not participate. Business visitors should carry a good supply of business cards, which are exchanged on introduction. Hotels can provide bilingual business cards overnight.
Note the official romanisation of Korean words has been altered to more accurately reflect pronunciation (eg Gimpo international airport rather than Kimpo, Busan instead of Pusan and Gimchi instead of Kimchi, Korea's signature spiced cabbage dish). However, the former romanisations are still widely used, with some major newspapers declaring a complete boycott of the new system.
Business etiquette is very formal. Punctuality and a smart appearance are important. Jackets and ties are required, even in summer. However, the ritual of getting drunk with a potential business partner may be expected. You should appear respectful at all times and keep smiling even if negotiations are slow. Business associates like to spend time getting to know you. Confirm agreements in writing. It is impolite to refuse food or drink. Use the right hand when giving or receiving. Outdoor shoes should never be worn inside a house.
There are certain areas, particularly near the demilitarised zone, where entry and photography are forbidden.

Getting there

Air

National airline: Korean Air and Asiana Airlines

International airport/s: Seoul-Inchon International Airport (ICN), 40km west of Inchon and 52km from Seoul. Facilities include, duty-free shopping, restaurant, bar, banks, business centre, medical services and car hire. It is connected to the city by rail, taxi (30–60 mins) buses and ferry. Pusan (PUS) 27km from city, with flights arriving mainly from Japan. Cheju (CJU) on the island of Cheju.

Airport tax: Departure tax: W10,000, not applicable to transit passengers.

Surface

Road: There are no land borders with any other country except North Korea; all border crossing are closed.

Rail: Cargo trains started running between North and South Korea on 11 December 2007.

Water: There is a daily ferry service between Pusan and Shiminoseki, Japan.

Main port/s: Pusan, Inchon, Masan, Ulsan, Mokpo, Kunsan, Yosu.

Getting about

National transport

Air: Gimpo Airport, located close to Gimpo, west of Seoul, is used for all domestic flights. Korean Air operates daily services between Seoul and Pusan (50 minutes), Taegu, Cheju, Ulsan and Kwangju, with less frequent services to other centres. Other services are provided by Asiana Airlines. Expect to be searched for firearms when embarking on internal flights.

Road: The road network contains more than 60,000km of highways and lesser roads. More than half of roads are paved. Major cities are linked by motorways, but minor roads may be poorly maintained. Pusan is over five hours distant from Seoul by road, compared to four hours by rail.

Buses: Air-conditioned express Chwasok buses operate between major cities, in competition with trains. Villages are often connected by a network of local buses.

Rail: Korean National Railroads offers normal and super-express trains between major cities. The super-express train (Saemaul-ho) runs between Seoul and Pusan, Chongju, Yosu and Inchon. Timetables and station signs are often in English.

Many trains have sleeping and dining cars.

Water: Various services are available. Mokpo and Pusan are linked by a steamer service twice weekly. The Angel Line, a hydrofoil service, runs between Pusan and Yosu five times daily, via Chongmy. The island of Cheju is linked to the mainland by daily ferries, including car ferries, three times per week.

City transport

Public transport in Seoul is well-developed, but becomes crowded at rush-hour.

Taxis: Registered taxis carry meters and are clearly marked on the roof. Taxis are plentiful, and available at ranks, by telephone or hailed in the steet. A 20 per cent surcharge applies between 0000–0400. Taxi drivers suspend use of meters for journeys outside town, so negotiate the fare for such trips in advance. It is advisable to carry written instructions in Korean if possible.

Buses, trams & metro: The Korean Air limousine shuttle bus calls at 20 Seoul locations, including major hotels.

City buses, though cheap and convenient, are crowded. Purple and white buses have few seats. Green and beige 'seat buses' make fewer stops and are more comfortable and air-conditioned. Tokens are available at most stops. There are English-language signs on city-centre buses only.

Seoul has an extensive metro system with eight lines accessing most parts of the city and provides a rapid means of travelling between places. First and last trains are around 0500–2400 depending on individual lines. Comprehensive information is given at www.seoulmetro.co.kr/eng/ with maps and related links. Signs are in English and Korean.

Pusan, Daegu and Incheon have metro systems and Gwangju and Daejeon have systems under construction.

Car hire

International driving licences are acceptable, but chauffeur-driven car hire is recommended in the main cities.

BUSINESS DIRECTORY

The addresses listed below are a selection only. While World of Information makes every endeavour to check these addresses, we cannot guarantee that changes have not been made, especially to telephone numbers and area codes. We would welcome any corrections.

Telephone area codes

The international direct dialling (IDD) code for the Republic of Korea, is +82, followed by area code and subscriber's number:

Inchon	32	Seoul	2
Pusan	51	Taegu	53

Useful telephone numbers

Police: 112
Fire: 119
Medical emergency 1339
Directory inquiries: 114
International calls: 1035/1037
Tourist helpline: 1330

Chambers of Commerce

American Chamber of Commerce in Korea, 4501 Trade Tower, 159-1 Samsung-dong, Kangnam-gu, Seoul 135-729 (tel: 564-2040; fax: 564-2050; e-mail: info@amchamkorea.org).

British Chamber of Commerce in Korea, 21/F Seoul Finance Centre, 84 Taepyoung-ro 1-ga, Chung-gu, Seoul 100-101 (tel: 720-9406; fax: 720-9411; e-mail: bcck@bcck.or.kr).

European Union Chamber of Commerce in Korea, Kyobo Building, 1 Chongro 1-ga, Chongro-gu, Seoul, 110-714 (tel: 725-9880; fax: 725-9886; e-mail: eucck@eucck.org).

Inchon Chamber of Commerce and Industry, 447 Nonhyon-dong, Namdong-gu, Inchon 405-300 (tel: 810-2800; fax: 810-2807; e-mail: ebiz@incci.co.kr).

Korea Chamber of Commerce and Industry, 45 Namdaemunro 4-ga, Chung-gu, Seoul 100-743 (tel: 316-3114; fax: 771-3267; e-mail: info@korcham.net).

Pusan Chamber of Commerce and Industry, 853-1 Pomchon-dong, Pusanjin-gu, Pusan 614-021 (tel: 645-7771; fax: 645-3003; e-mail: julyjang@pcci.or.kr).

Taegu Chamber of Commerce and Industry, 107 Sinchon 3-dong, Tong-gu, Taegu 701-023 (tel: 755-0041; fax: 795-5774; e-mail: mrlee@dcci.or.kr).

Banking

Bank of Seoul, 10-1, 2-ka, Namdaemun-ro, Chung-gu, Seoul (fax: 756-6389).

Cho Hung Bank Ltd., 14, 1-ka, Namdaemun-ro, Chung-gu, Seoul (tel: 733-2000; fax: 732-0835).

Citizens National Bank, 9-1, 2-ka, Namdaemun-ro, Chung-gu, Seoul (fax: 757-3679).

Commercial Bank of Korea, 111-1, 2-ka, Namdaemun-ro, Chung-gu, Seoul (tel: 754-3920; fax: 754-9203).

Export-Import Bank of Korea, 16-1, Yoido-dong, Youngdungpo-gu, Seoul 150-010 (tel: 779-6114; fax: 784-1030).

Hanil Bank, 130, 2-ka, Namdaemun-ro, Chung-gu, Seoul (fax: 754-0479).

Hana Bank, 101-1, 1-ga Ulchiro, Chung-gu, Seoul 100-191 (tel: 754-2121; fax: 756-6358).

Korea Development Bank, 10-2, Kwanchul-dong, Chongro-gu, Seoul (tel: 398-6369; fax: 720-0015).

Korea Exchange Bank, 181, 2-ka, Ulji-ro, Chung-gu, Seoul.

Korea First Bank, 100 Kongpyong-dong, Chongro-gu, Seoul (tel: 733-0070; fax: 736-8092).

Shinhan Bank, 120, 2-ga, Taepyung-ro, Chung-gu, Seoul (tel: 756-0505; fax: 774-7013).

Central bank

Bank of Korea, 110, 3-KA Namdaemun-ro, Chung-ku, Seoul 100-794 (tel: 759-4114; fax: 759-4060; e-mail:bokdplp@bok.or.kr).

Travel information

Korea Automobile Association, 1, PO Box 2008, Seoul (tel: 785-5051).

Korean Air, 41-3 Seosomun-Dong, Chung-gu, Seoul (tel: 755-2221; fax: 751-7799; internet: www.koreanair.com).

Ministry of tourism

Ministry of Culture and Tourism, 82-1 Sejongno, Chongno-gu, Seoul (tel: 736-7946; fax: 736-8513).

National tourist organisation offices

Korean National Tourism Organisation (KNTO), 40 Cheongyecheonmo, Chung-gu, Seoul 100-180 (tel: 729 9497; fax: 319 0086; e-mail: webmaster@mail.knto.or.kr; internet site: www.tour2korea.com).

Ministries

Ministry of Agriculture and Forestry, 1 Jungang-dong, Kwachon, Kyongki-do 427-760 (tel: 500-1587; fax: 503-7249; e-mail: webmaster@maf.go.kr).

Ministry of Construction and Transportation, 1 Jungang-dong, Kwachon, Kyongki-do 427-712 (tel: 504-9031; fax: 504-6825; e-mail: webmaster@moct.go.kr).

Ministry of Culture and Tourism, 82-1 Sejongno, Jongno-gu, Seoul 110-703 (tel: 3704-9114; fax: 3704-9119; e-mail: webmaster@mct.go.kr).

Ministry of Defence, 1 Yongsan-dong, Yongsan-gu, Seoul 140-701 (tel: 795-0071; fax: 703-3109; e-mail: cyber@mnd.go.kr).

Ministry of Education and Human Resources Development, 77-6 Sejong-no, Jongno-gu, Seoul 110-760 (tel: 3703-2114; fax: 2100-6133; e-mail: webmaster@moe.go.kr).

Ministry of Environment, 1 Jungang-dong, Kwachon, Kyongki-do 427-729 (tel:

2110-6546; fax: 504-9206; e-mail: shinae@me.go.kr).

Ministry of Finance and Economy, 1 Chungang-dong, Kwachon City, Kyonggi-Do, Seoul (tel: 503-7171; fax: 502-0193; internet site: www.mofe.go.kr/mofe/eng).

Ministry of Finance, Jungang-dong, Kwachon, Kyongki-do 427-725 (tel: 503-9032; fax: 503-9033; e-mail: fppr@mofe.go.kr).

Ministry of Foreign Affairs and Trade, Doryeom-dong Jongno-gu Seoul 110-787 (tel: 100-2114; fax 100-7999:email: web@mofat.go.kr; internet: www.mofat.go.kr/me/index.jsp).

Ministry of Gender Equality, 77-6 Sejong-no, Jongno-gu, Seoul 110-760 (tel: 3703-2500; fax: 2106-5145; e-mail: webadmin@moge.go.kr).

Ministry of Government Administration and Home Affairs, 77-6 Sejong-no, Jongno-gu, Seoul 110-760 (tel: 3703-2114; fax: 3703-5502; e-mail: webmaster@mogaha.go.kr).

Ministry of Government Legislation, 77-6 Sejong-no, Jongno-gu, Seoul 110-760 (tel: 3703-2114; fax: 738-2649; e-mail: lawinfo@moleg.go.kr).

Ministry of Health and Welfare, 1 Jungang-dong, Kwachon, Kyongki-do 427-760 (tel: 503-7524; fax: 504-6418; e-mail: m_mohw@mohw.go.kr).

Ministry of Information and Communication, 100 Sejong-no, Jongno-gu, Seoul 110-777 (tel 750-2114; fax: 750-2915; e-mail: webmaster@mic.go.kr).

Ministry of Justice, 1 Jungang-dong, Kwachon, Kyongki-do 427-760 (tel: 503-7023; fax: 2110-3079; webmaster@moj.go.kr).

Ministry of Labour, 1 Jungang-dong, Kwachon, Kyongki-do 427-716 (tel: 2110-2114; fax: 503-9772; e-mail: webmaster@molab.go.kr).

Ministry of Maritime Affairs and Fisheries, 50 Chungjeongno, Saedaemun-gu, Seoul 120-715 (tel: 3148-6114; fax: 3148-6044; e-mail: webmaster@momaf.go.kr).

Ministry of Planning and Budget, 520-3 Banpo-dong, Seocho-gu. Seoul 137-756 (tel: 3480-7990; fax: 3480-7600; e-mail: nara@mpb.go.kr).

Ministry of Science and Technology, 2 Jungang-dong, Kwachon, Kyongki-do 427-715 (tel: 503-7600; fax: 503-7673; e-mail: webadmin@most.go.kr).

Ministry of Trade, Industry and Energy, 1 Jungang-dong, Kwachon, Kyongki-do 427-760 (tel: 2110-5061; fax: 503-9496; e-mail: webmocie@mocie.go.kr).

Ministry of Unification, 77-6 Sejong-no, Jongno-gu, Seoul 110-760 (tel: 3703-2433; fax: 739-5047; e-mail: webmaster@unikorea.go.kr).

Other useful addresses

Association of Foreign Trading Agents in Korea, 218 Hangangro 2-ka, Youngsan-gu, Seoul (tel: 792-1581; fax: 749-1830).

Board of Audit and Inspection, 25-23 Samchong-dong, Jongno-gu, soul (tel: 721-9114; fax: 721-9299).

British Embassy, 4 Chung-dong-Chung-gu, Seoul (tel: 735-7341/3; fax: 736-6241).

Customs Administration, 71 Nonhyun-dong, Kangnam-gu, Seoul (tel: 512-0011; fax: 512-2322).

Economic Planning Board, 1 Chungang-dong, Kwach'on City, Kyonggi, Seoul (tel: 503-7171).

Emergency Planning Committee, 1 Chungang-dong, Kwachon-City, Kyonggi-Do (tel: 503-7723; fax: 503-7727).

Fair Trade Commission, 1 Chungang-dong, Kwachon-City, Kyonggi-Do (tel: 503-7171; fax: 504-5144).

Foreign Investment Policy Division, Rm 203, Complex No 3, 1 Chungang-dong, Kwacheon City, Kyongki-do (tel: 503-9276/7; fax: 503-9324).

Institute of Foreign Affairs and National Security, 1376-2 Seocho-dong, Seocho-gu, Seoul (tel: 571-1020; fax: 571-1019).

Invest Korea, Kotra Bldg 300-9 Yomgok-dong, Seocho-gu, Seoul 137-70 (tel: 3460-7545; fax: 3460–7946; internet: www.investkorea.org).

Korean Exhibition Centre, 65 Samsung-dong, Gangnam-gu, Seoul (tel: 553-7907/8; fax: 557-5784).

Korean Foreign Trade Association, TCPO Box 100, Seoul (tel: 551-5114; fax: 551-5100/5200).

Korean Information Service, 82-1 Sejongno, Jongno-gu, Seoul 110-703 (internet site: www.korea.net).

Korean Republic Embassy (US), 2450 Massachusetts Avenue, NW, Washington DC 20008, USA (tel: (+1-202) 939-5600; fax: (+1-202) 797-0595; e-mail: information_usa@mofat.go.kr).

Korea Stock Exchange, 33, Yoido-dong, Youngdeungpo-gu, KR-Seoul 150-010 (tel: 780-2271; fax: 786-0263; internet site: www.kse.or.kr/e_index.html).

Korean Trade Promotion Corporation, CPO Box 1621 10-1, 2-ka Hoehyun-dong, Chung-gu, Seoul (tel: 753-4180/9; internet site: www.kotra.or.kr/eng/index.php3).

Meteorological Administration, 1 Songwall-dong, Jongno-gu, Seoul (tel: 738-0345; fax: 723-8731).

National Statistical Office, Hanta Building, 645-15 Yoksam-dong, Kangnam-gu, Seoul (tel: 222-1901; fax: 538-3874; internet site: www.nso.go.kr/eindex.htm).

National Tax Administration, 108-4 Susong-dong, Jongno-gu, Seoul (tel: 397-1200; fax: 720-0278).

Overseas Aircargo Service Inc, 1–6 Fl. Daishin Bldg, 93–62 Bukchang-dong, PO Box 2757, Chung-gu, Seoul (tel: 753-8374/6; fax: 756-9400).

Rural Development Administratin, 250 Socun-dong, Suwon-City, Kyonggi-Do (tel: 292-4370; fax: 292-4163).

Securities Exchange Commission, 28-1 Yoido-dong, Yongdongpo-gu, Seoul (tel: 785-7593; fax: 785-3475).

Small and Medium Business Administration, 2 Chungang-dong, Kwachon-City, Kyonggi-Do (tel: 509-7114; fax: 503-7941).

Internet sites

Asiana Airlines: http://us.flyasiana.com

EC21 (Internet trade site): www.ec21.net

Korea Air: www.koreanair.com

Korea Asset Management Corporation: www.kamco.or.kr/eng/index.htm

Korea Infogate: www.koreainfogate.co.kr

Korean Travel (internet: http://english.tour2korea.com/).

Inchon International Airport, www.airport.or.kr/eng/airport/

Samsung Economic Research Institute: www.koreaeconomy.org

Kosovo

Former Serbian leader, Slobodan Milosevic, had revoked Kosovo's autonomy in 1989 and repressed Kosovo's ethnic Albanians, who make up most of its population. For the foreseeable future, most analysts consider, Kosovo's economy will remain dependent on aid and its security will continue to be assured by 16,000 NATO troops and its political affairs overseen by the European Union.

In early 2008 Kosovo's ethnic Albanian leadership declared independence from Serbia, with the backing of Washington and the European Union (EU). Kosovo soon found itself with what the New York Times described as '... the harsh uncertainties of a newborn nation', a nation not recognised by Serbia, Russia or (at least at the time of the declaration) some European countries.

Even if Kosovo found it possible to overcome the political hurdles, its economy had been so devastated by war that it was forced to import staples like milk and meat. Depressingly, Kosovo was ranked by Berlin based Transparency International, as the world's fourth most corrupt economy, after Cameroon, Cambodia and Albania. If Kosovo can build a successful economy it may have a chance of becoming a fully fledged country and stabilising the Balkans. Meanwhile, imports run at about US$1.9 billion a year, but exports are a paltry US$130 million.

COUNTRY PROFILE

Historical profile

1389 The battle of Kosovo was lost by the Serbian people and the Turkish Ottoman empire began a 500-year rule. During this time the demographics changed from Christian Serbs to Muslim Albanians.
1912 During the Balkan Wars Serbia regained control of Kosovo.
1918 Kosovo became part of the Kingdom of Serbs, Croats and Slovenes.
1941 During World War Two the Italian army controlled the entire region.
1945 The Federal People's Republic of Yugoslavia was formed into a communist republic by Josip Broz Tito, and included the province of Kosovo with its own constitutional rights.
1974 Yugoslavia increased the autonomy of constituent republics, allowing Kosovo de facto self-government.
1980 Tito died.
1987 Serbian nationalist politician, Slobodan Milosevic, incited Serbian Kosovans to protest at alleged harassment by the majority ethnic Albanians.
1989 Yugoslav president Milosevic stripped Kosovo of its constitutional rights.
1990 Ethnic Albanians declared Kosovo independent. The Yugoslav government dissolved the Kosovo government and sacked 100,000 workers, which led to a general strike.
1991 Two major Yugoslav republics (Slovenia and Croatia) declared their independence. Slovenia became independent with little dispute. Croatia with its 12 per cent Serbian population fought the remaining Yugoslav army and evicted its Serbs to gain its independence. The Yugoslav government in Belgrade began a process of disenfranchising Albanian Kosovans by closing down schools and marginalising the Albanian language.
1992 Macedonia and Bosnia and Hercegovina (BiH) declared their independence. Nationalist and ethnic tensions in BiH, the most ethnically diverse Yugoslav republic, stained until the territory erupted into war. Thousands died in 'ethnic cleansing' as one faction tried to clear a region of civilians of any other faction, as a million people were displaced. Ibrahim Rugova was elected president of the self-proclaimed Republic of Kosovo.
1996 The Ushtria Çlirimtare e Kosovës (UÇK) (Kosovo Liberation Army) began attacking Serbian police.
1998 Confrontation between Serbian forces and the UÇK increased culminating in a brutal crackdown by Serbian police and paramilitary units which resulted in massacres and thousands of civilians driven from their homes. NATO gave the Milosevic government an ultimatum to halt the crackdown or risk air attacks.
1999 An international peace deal failed and NATO began air attacks on Serbia in March. In June Serbia agreed to withdraw troops and the UN Kosovo Peace Implementation Force (Kfor) began peace-keeping operations as the UN Interim Administration Mission in Kosovo (UNMIK) came into operation, charged with determining the future of Kosovo. The

KEY FACTS

Official name: Republic of Kosovo

Head of State: President Fatmir Sejdiu (LDK) (from 9 Jan 2008)

Head of government: Prime Minister Hashim Thaçi (PDK) (from 11 Nov 2007)

Ruling party: Coalition led by Partia Demokratike e Kosovës (PDK) (Democratic Party of Kosovo) with Lidhja Demokratike e Kosovës (LDK) (Democratic League of Kosovo) and Kosova Demokratik Türk Partisi (KDTP) (Turkish Democratic Party of Kosovo) (from 11 Nov 2007)

Area: 10,887 square km

Population: 2.00 million * (2007)

Capital: Pristina

Official language: Albanian, Serbian (English is the official language of the UN Interim Administration Mission in Kosovo (UNMIK))

Currency: Euro (eur) = 100 cents

Exchange rate: eur0.63 per US$ (Jul 2008)

GDP per capita: US$877 (2007)

GDP real growth: 3.00% (2006) (estimate 3.5% 2007)

Unemployment: 50.00% * (2007) (UN Development programme)

Inflation: 1.50% (2006) (estimate 2.0% 2007)

Aid flow: US$1.65 billion (Between 1998–2005 EC funding)

* estimated figure

UÇK agreed to disarm, while Serbians fled the province in the face of revenge attacks.
2000 Local elections, were won by the Lidhja Demokratike e Kosovës (LDK) (Democratic League of Kosovo), led by Ibrahim Rugova.
2002 The parliament elected Ibrahim Rugova as president and Bajram Rexhepi of the Partia Demokratike e Kosovës (PDK) (Democratic Party of Kosovo) was elected prime minister of a power-sharing 10-member cabinet.
2003 Official negotiations between Kosovo and Serbia began. Conditions for the talks to determine Kosovo's final status were announced by the UN in December.
2004 In parliamentary elections the LDK won and incumbent President Ibrahim Rugova was re-elected. Ramush Haradinaj became prime minister. Serbian Kosovans boycotted the elections. The worst inter-ethnic violence since 1999 erupted in Mitrovica, with up to 22 people killed and hundreds injured.
2005 Prime minister Haradinaj resigned on 8 March and Adem Salihaj replaced him.
2006 President Ibrahim Rugova, died on 21 January. He was considered a moderate Kosovan leader and his death, just as negotiations on the future of Kosovo were about to start, was a setback. He was succeeded by Fatmir Sejdiu. Agim Çeku became prime minister on 10 March. Joachim Rucker took office as the head of UNMIK on 1 September.
2007 In April the UN Special Envoy Martti Ahtisaari submitted a Comprehensive Proposal for the Kosovo Status Settlement (the Ahtisaari Plan) for the independence of Kosovo which also focused on protecting the rights, identity and culture of Kosovo's non-Albanian communities, including establishing a framework for their active participation in public life. Ahtisaari also proposed that Kosovo become independent, subject to a period of international supervision. In July Agim Çeku said that no unilateral declaration of independence would be made (by ethnic Albanian leaders) without the support of the EU and US. During the first round of talks in September, concerning the future of Kosovo, no agreement was reached: Serbian authorities offered broad autonomy and the province's ethnic Albanians demanded full independence. Parliamentary elections, held on 11 November, were won by the PDK with 34.3 per cent of the vote (37 seats out of 120), led by Hashim Thaçi, former leader of the UÇK.
2008 On 9 January President Sejdiu resigned from office and took part in fresh elections, held on the same day, under Kosovo's new constitutional framework. After three rounds he won a simple majority of 61 votes to become president for a second time. On 17 February the Kosovo Assembly declared independence for Kosovo, in line with the Ahtisaari Plan. Serbia took control of the 50km railway line from Lesak-Zvecan in the ethnic Serb dominated northern region on 3 March. The new constitution came into force at midnight on 15 June and the Kosovo government took over most of the powers previously held by the UN. The EU was to deploy a 2,200 Law and Order Mission (Eulex) at the same time, but this was blocked by Russia as the move was still to be approved by the UN. Ethnic Serbs insist that the new constitution does not apply to them and as a last act of the outgoing government in Serbia, the Serbian minister for Kosovo set up a new parliament in the divided city of Mitrovica for minority Serbs. The new Kosovan Serb Assembly may challenge the legitimacy of the Kosovan Assembly and entrench de facto partition of Kosovo. The issuing of Kosovan passports began in July.

Political structure

Constitution

An interim constitutional framework was ratified in 2001 providing legitamacy for the provisional institutions of self-government, with deferral to the UN Special Representative based on the UN Security Council Resolution 1244.
A draft constitution was being prepared in February 2008.

Form of state

Parliamentary democracy

The executive

The president is elected by parliamentary members for a term of three years. The president represents the country in foreign affairs and in domestic matters acts on the advice of the prime minister and cabinet. The executive branch of government is headed by the prime minister, deputy prime ministers and all other ministers.

National legislature

The unicameral Assembly of Kosovo (Kuvendi i Kosovës) has 120 members; 100 seats directly elected by the Albanian majority population, 10 seats are reserved for Serbs and 10 seats for all other nominated ethnic groups. Legislative power is vested in the assembly and government.

Last elections

17 November 2007 (parliamentary); 9 January 2008 (presidential).
Results: Parliamentary: the Partia Demokratike e Kosovës (PDK) (Democratic Party of Kosovo) won 34.3 per cent of the vote (37 seats out of 120), the Lidhja Demokratike e Kosovës (LDK) (Democratic League of Kosovo) 22.6 per cent (25), the Aleanca Kosova e Re (AKR) (New Kosovo Alliance) 12.3 per cent (13), the Lidhja Demokratike e Dardanisë-Unioni Shqiptare DemoKristiane LD-USDK (Democratic League of Dardania-Albanian Union of Christian Democrats) 10 per cent (11), and the Aleanca për Ardhmërinë e Kosovës (AAK) (Alliance for the Future of Kosovo) 9.6 per cent (10); 20 seats were reserved for minorities. Turnout was 40.1 per cent.
Presidential: round one, Fatmir Sejdiu won 62 votes (not two-thirds of the vote and enough for an outright win), Naim Maloku won 37 votes; round two, Sejdiu won 61 votes, Maloku won 37 votes; round three (a simple majority for a win), Sejdiu won 61 votes.

Political parties

Ruling party

Coalition led by Partia Demokratike e Kosovës (PDK) (Democratic Party of Kosovo) with Lidhja Demokratike e Kosovës (LDK) (Democratic League of Kosovo) and Kosova Demokratik Türk Partisi (KDTP) (Turkish Democratic Party of Kosovo) (from 11 Nov 2007)

Main opposition party

Lidhja Demokratike e Kosovës (LDK) (Democratic League of Kosovo)

Population

2.00 million * (2007)
Last census: 1991: 1,956,000 (during political troubles)
2001: 2,400,000 (estimate: Office for Security and Co-operation in Europe)
Population density: 202 per square km

Ethnic make-up

Estimated demographics: Albanian (92 per cent) Serbian (5.3 per cent) and others (Croats, Roma, Turks) (2.7 per cent).

Religions

Muslim 90 per cent, the majority of which are Sunni, Christian Orthodox 5 per cent.

Education

Before 1991 educational institutions were administered independently of Serbian influence by Kosovan authorities, which were at liberty to construct a national curriculum and system of education. All levels of education were provided in the Albanian and Serbian languages and schools were charged with maintaining levels of instruction for all minority communities. Enrolment rates where typically almost 100 per cent and this resulted in literacy levels that matched the average of surrounding territories. From 1991, the independence of Kosovo's education service was abolished by Serbian authorities, which closed down schools and dismissed over 14,000 primary and 4,000 secondary school teachers plus over 860 university lecturers of Albanian ethnicity and required all teaching to be in the Serbian language. A parallel schooling system developed whereby Serbian schools were

enhanced at the expense of Albanian schools which began to lag behind in books and equipment. Albanian students were denied access to Serbian libraries and so took up informal learning provided by sacked teachers. However, at this time Serbian investment was cut due to the economic crisis following the conflict in Croatia and even the Serbian schools became poorly stocked and maintained.
The University of Pristina was badly damaged by vandalism and looting during the NATO attacks on Serbia in 1999, but was finally reopened to all students by 2000. Around 45 per cent of all schools were severely damaged or destroyed and many were within minefields which prevented their use until cleared. When the 2000/01 school-year began only around 50 per cent of school students attended remedial classes; the percentage began to rise as facilities improved. Apart from war damage, the previous nine years of under-investment also added to the problems of rehabilitation for the UN Administration authorities (UNMIK).
UNMIK began the reconstruction of the educational system with a three-way split into priority areas of consideration, which included the physical (buildings, books and equipment), legal aspects (new teaching structures that provided for or moderated opposing orthodoxy) and academic reform (curricula development and educational management). Teacher training was implemented under UN-sponsored programmes from 2004/05.
Finding an ongoing consensus was hampered in 2006 following the Serbian constitutional referendum (that excluded Kosovans), which voted to enshrine the Cyrillic alphabet as the official script for all territories; Albanians use the Latin script.
In 2007 Unesco stated that less than 10 per cent of 3–6 year olds had access to early childhood education, with the majority of facilities located in larger urban areas.
The conflict with Serbia led to a massive population shift from the country to towns and resulted in the overcrowding of many primary schools, which have had to operate at least a two shift system.
Literacy rate: 89.8 per cent female rate; 97.7 per cent male. Around 14 per cent of rural females are illiterate (Unesco 2007).
Compulsory years: Six to 14
Enrolment rate: 97.5 per cent (Albanian), 99 per cent (Serbian), 77 per cent (all others, of which only 69 per cent female) (Unesco 2007).
Pupils per teacher: The average was 19 per class (in primary schools) before 1999; the average has increased to 35 students per class.

Health
Kosovo, as one of the poorest territories in Europe has, as a UN report in 2007 reported, 37 per cent of the population living in poverty and 15.2 per cent in absolute poverty. The healthcare system is chronically under funded with a lack of medical equipment and drugs. Poorly educated mothers and lack of access to facilities has resulted in Kosovo having the highest fertility rate in Europe, and also the highest maternal mortality rate, despite 95 per cent of all births taking place in medical facilities. Measures to reach UN Millennium Development Goals (MDG) have been included in necessary restoration policies since 1999. Childhood immunisation reached levels of 90 per cent by 2007, although parents in some minority ethnic communities delayed vaccinations.
In 2005 a total of 72.4 per cent of the population had access to clean water, of which 96 per cent were urban dwellers, around 70 per cent of total households were connected to the sewage system, of which 95 per cent were urban dwellers.

HIV/Aids
The young have not been or are poorly informed about HIV/Aids, sex education and the risks of drugs. Less than 41 per cent of sexually active young people used a condom, according to a 2007 Unesco report.
Life expectancy: 68.8 years (67.8 male; 69.9 female) (2006 Kosovo Government)
Fertility rate/Maternal mortality rate: Separate figures from Serbia for Kosovo are unavailable.
Child (under 5 years) mortality rate (per 1,000): 69 per 1,000 (estimated, Unicef 2006)
Head of population per physician: 1 doctor per 840 head of population (2004, Kosovo Statistics Office)

Welfare
At a time when Europe's populations are ageing Kosovo's average age is 22–23 years, with around 33 per cent less than 15 years old. This group will be an ongoing burden of responsibility for the government to educate, find work and house at a time of economic hardship. There is no social welfare although international donors provide funds for programmes to aid the vulnerable. There are high levels of unemployment and poor prospects for improvement.

Main cities
Pristina (capital, 600,000 population), Mitrovica (67,900), Caglavica.

Languages spoken
Albanian, Serbian, Bosniak and Turkish. Since the arrival of the UN English has increased in popularity.

Official language/s
Albanian, Serbian (English was the official language of the UN Interim Administration Mission in Kosovo (UNMIK))

Media
National news agency: Kosova Press
Other news agencies: Kosovalive: www.kosovalive.com
Kosova Information Center: www.kosova.com

Press
Periodicals: UNMIK started the publication of a quarterly Focus (www.euinkosovo.org) with a variety of background articles on people and events in Kosovo.

Broadcasting
The national, public broadcaster is RTK (www.rtklive.com).
Radio: RTK operates two stations, Radio Kosova and Radio Blue Sky. Other, private radio stations in operation include Radio Dukagjini (www.radio-dukagjini.com), Radio Kim (www.kimradio.net) and Radio Tema (www.radiotema.net).

External trade
As a member of the Central European Free Trade Agreement (Cefta) Kosovo has free trade agreements (FTA) with Albania, Croatia, Bosnia and Hercegovina and (FYROM) Macedonia.
Major trading partners by percentage include, 53 per cent Balkans Region, 18 per cent Turkey, 14 per cent US and 15 per cent rest of the world

Exports
Principal exports are metals (including scrap) (35 per cent), timber (18 per cent), food (11 per cent).
Main destinations: Balkans region (53 per cent), Turkey (18 per cent), US (14 per cent) and rest of the world (15 per cent).

Agriculture
Farming
Of the 1.1 million hectares (ha) of Kosova land, 53 per cent (577,000ha) is arable. Over 85 per cent is privately owned, however the average size of land per rural household in 3ha. Of the arable land 51 per cent is grain, 45 per cent pastures and meadows, 2 per cent orchards and less than 1 per cent vineyards. Principal crops are wheat, corn, potatoes, watermelons and lucerne (animal fodder).
The government regards small farms as less than 5ha and large farms over 5ha, around 96 per cent of farming households work small farms. Many farms were abandoned in 1999 and rural infrastructure is in disrepair. There is an urgent need to modernise traditional practices that provide little more than subsistence production. Around 65 per cent of the

working population is employed in agriculture, providing 30 per cent of GDP. Kosovo has fallen from being a net exporter of agriculture products to foodstuffs accounting for around 30 per cent of all imports, the largest single import segment. Since the early 1990s the number of livestock has fallen and the trend has continued. From 2003 small farms have mostly invested in beef cattle, donkeys and bee hives; larger farms have invested in breeding pigs and donkeys, all other farm animals have fallen in number. Government statistics acknowledge that all but the largest of farms fail to keep records and the number of animals reported may be incorrect.
Typical production per annum includes: wheat 1,500,000 tonnes, milk 244,000 tonnes, meat 20,000 tonnes, wine 112 million litres and eggs 269 million.

Forestry

Forests represent an important resource but historic mismanagement has resulted in heavy degradation; the high demand for timber following the conflict with Serbia has increased the pressure on forestry's long-term sustainability.
Timbered areas make up 47 per cent of all land, of which forests are 460,800ha. Around 62 per cent of forests are publicly owned. Forest products, before the break-up of Yugoslavia, were a significant export sector. In 2007 manufactured products included doors, window frames and furniture, although exports remain limited.
Typical annual production is approximately 222,000 square metres felled for construction and woodfuel.

Industry and manufacturing

Industrial development was historically dictated by the economic interests of firstly Yugoslavia and later Serbia, with widespread exploitation of natural resources. Mining and forestry products formed the majority of intra-exports.
Due to war damage and the lack of investment in what were state-owned industries and manufacturing, food processing, tobacco, wood processing and textiles were all disrupted and non-productive by 2006. Privatisation was begun but the problems may be long term as poor transport infrastructure, with 25 per cent of the road network in serious need of remedial work, a serious impediment to redevelopment.
Kosovo has limited water resources, as most rivers run out of the country, any process that requires water to facilitate production will be severely hampered.

Tourism

There is little opportunity for tourism.

Environment

The US committed an initial US$15.5 million to repairing war damage, which included water contamination, minefields and unexploded ordinance (UXO). In 2007, the ongoing clearance programme concentrated on unmarked minefields and UXO in forested areas.
Archaic communist industrial practices degraded land, water and air quality and until production plants are either upgraded or closed the pollution is likely to continue. A government environmental plan was proposed in 2006 to introduce legislation to develop policies and guidelines for international funding and donor communities to deal with the problems and plan for the future. It was also recognised that a full inventory of fauna and flora for Kosovo was needed.
Kosovo, in 2006, had one national park and 11 natural reserves, 37 natural monuments and two protected landscapes totalling 46,000ha (4.27 per cent of the country). The richest area for wildlife is the Sharr Mountains and the Bjeshkët e Nemuna area.
Rivers around industrial regions are heavily polluted and denuded of aquatic life.
Energy production is the major polluter in Kosovo, producing acid rain and contaminated water with high concentrates of phenols.

Mining

The large industrial complex of Trepca, near the town of Mitrovica, is a conglomerate of 40 mines, foundries, refineries and subsidiary plants. It has one of Europe's richest deposits of lignite, lead, zinc and non-ferrous ores, as well as gold, silver and over 1.6 billion tonnes of coal, valued at an estimated eur13 billion (US$18.9 billion). However, the only railway capable of transporting coal is through Serbia and an alternative route through Albania or Macedonia is not expected for many years. Trepca had previously been the source of much of former Yugoslavia's mining wealth and after the 1999 conflict was realised as Kosovo's principal economic asset, despite the need for investment to revitalise its infrastructure.
Geophysical studies undertaken in 2007 showed a high potential for larger than already known gold, nickel and chrome deposits.
There are large stocks of decorative stone, including onyx, white, grey and black marble, gray granite and other stone such as gneiss, magnesite, quartzite and porphyry which may have an important as export goods, but have yet to be fully exploited.

Energy

The Kosovo Energy Corporation (KEK) was scheduled to produce 4,483GW of electricity and import 497GW in 2008. The World Bank committed US$5 million in December 2007 to support the KEK to clean up a gasification plant, including the containment, packaging and removal from site of toxic and waste materials including benzene, ammonia and oily compounds. Long-term energy development and electricity supply is also being provided for as Kosovo's national power grid is brought up to international standards. Around 97 per cent of all electricity is generated by lignite. Two generating plants close to the open cast lignite mines of Bardhi and Mirash burn 7 million tonnes to provide up to 710MW per annum. Energy production is the major polluter in Kosovo, producing acid rain and contaminated water with high concentrates of phenols.

Banking and insurance

The World Bank is providing grants and technical assistance to the Central Banking Authority to oversee the financial system and provide stability and development, including supervision of banks and non-bank financial institutions (insurance and pension funds).

Central bank

Central Bank of Kosovo

Main financial centre

Pristina

Time

GMT plus one hour (daylight saving, late March to late October, GMT plus two hours)

Geography

This land-locked country, roughly square in shape standing on a corner is surrounded by Serbia from the north to the south-east, Macedonia (FYROM) in the south, Albania to the west and Montenegro in the north-west. The average altitude is 800 metres above sea level, however, there are several mountain ranges encircling the country, with the highest ranges in the south-west, north-west and north. The highest mountain, Gjeravica, in Peja in the south-west, is 2,656 metres high, with deep, wide valleys and the largest river, the White Drin at 122 km, flowing down into the central plain, on which most of the urban areas are located. The largest lake, Gazivoda, in Mitrovica, is 9.1 square km.

Hemisphere

Northern

Climate

With a continental climate summers in Kosovo are warm and winters are cold. Temperature ranges average from +30 degrees Celsius (summer July–August) to

-10 degrees C (winter December–January). Snowfalls are typical between November and March even on the lowland flat plains. The large mountain ranges also produce local variations and rainfall distributions.

Entry requirements

Passports

Required by all and must be valid for up to 90 days from date of entry.

Serbian authorities will not allow entry to Serbia from Kosovo, unless as a through journey from Albania or Macedonia, or as part of a return journey.

Visa

As of February 2008, for visits of less than 90 days, visitors with US passports do not require visas. EU citizens from countries that recognised Kosovo's independence also do not require visas. All other visitors and those staying over 90 days must provide documentary evidence for purpose of visit, such as employment or education. A 90-day entry stamp will be issued at the border.

For further information see www.unmikonline.org/regulations/ADMDIRECT/2005/ADE2005_08.pdf or visitors should contact the consular section of their own ministry of foreign affairs for advice.

Currency advice/regulations

The banking system is embryonic and a cash economy exists so visitors should expect to travel with enough cash for their stay. There are a few ATMs in Pristina; credit cards are not widely accepted.

The Serbian dinar is in use in Serbian-populated regions.

Customs

UNMIK has been responsible for customs, before trained Kosovan officials are deployed.

Consumer items are limited and should be declared, including jewellery, only two cameras (including a video camera allowed), binoculars, one bicycle and camping equipment, electronic equipment such as laptops and musical players. Sporting equipment may have added restrictions and further information should be obtained.

Prohibited imports

Regulations may be altered with little notice, check details before travelling. Weapons and ammunitions. Animals may be imported with a vet certificate and proof of healthy condition.

Health (for visitors)

Mandatory precautions

None

Advisable precautions

It is advisable to be in date for the following immunisations: diphtheria, polio and tetanus (within 10 years), typhoid fever, hepatitis A (moderate risk only), hepatitis B and tuberculosis; rabies is a risk. Crimean Congo Haemorrhagic Fever (CCHF) is endemic, particularly in the central Kosovo region and visitors suffering from flu-like systems with a red rash or bleeding in the mouth should seek medical advice.

The health system is severely under funded and care may not reach visitors expectations, so comprehensive travel insurance, including medical evacuation, should be purchased before travelling. There is a shortage of medicines and visitors should travel with all necessary medications for the duration of their stay.

Hotels

There are no four- or fire-star hotels, Pristina has the largest stock of hotels, but elsewhere there is little choice beyond mid-range and budget accommodation.

Credit cards

Are not widely accepted.

Public holidays (national)

Public holidays that fall at the weekend are taken on the following Monday.

Fixed dates

1–2 January (News Year), 7 January (Orthodox Christmas), 17 February (Independence Day), 1–2 May (Labour Day), 28 November (Flag Day), 25 December (Christmas Day)

Variable dates

Orthodox Christmas, Easter Monday, (first Monday in May), Start of Ramadan, Eid al Fitr, Eid al Adha.

Working hours

Banking

Mon–Fri 0800–1900; Sat 0800–1500; a few open on Sun.

Business

Mon–Fri: 0700/0800–1500/1600.

Government

In 2008 no information was available.

Shops

In 2008 no information was available.

Telecommunications

Mobile/cell phones

There is an uneven coverage of GSM 900/1800 services.

Electricity supply

220 volts AC, 50Hz.

Social customs/useful tips

Doing business can be protracted due to cumbersome official bureaucracy.

Avoid taking photographs of military installations and obvious war damage.

Security

In 2008, landmines and unexploded ordinance (UXO) still posed a threat, particularly in border areas with Albania, the Dulje Pass area (in central Kosovo) and in the west and south of the country. All roads and tracks have been cleared.

Political demonstrations have been known to spill over into violence and should be avoided. Criminal activity is largely centred on pickpockets and theft of vehicles, particularly four-wheel drive and luxury cars.

Getting there

Air

National airline: Kosova Airlines (HHI)

International airport/s: Pristina International Airport (PRN), 18km south-west of the capital, with a business lounge, duty free, restaurants, car hire and banking. Taxis from the airport are available between 0500–2230 for a 20 minute journey; airport buses start running two hours before the first flights at 0500 up to 2300.

Airport tax: A eur15 departure tax is typically included in the price of a ticket.

Surface

Road: There are several frontier posts between Serbia, a few between Albania and Macedonia of which delays are common due to the poor road conditions.

Rail: The railway system operates an irregular service and should not be considered reliable.

Getting about

National transport

Road: There is a 1,925km network of two-lane main and secondary roads of which 1,576km is paved, but even the standard of this is fair to poor and conditions deteriorate in rural areas and after bad weather.

Rail: The railway system operates an irregular service and should not be considered reliable. A 300km single-track railway runs north-south and from the north to the east-west. These are part of the railway that ran from Serbia to either Macedonia or Albania through Kosovo. Domestic services are poor and slow in winter and prone to delays.

City transport

Taxis: As most people's first choice for any distance most taxis are marked and have metres. The destination should be written in Albanian, as English is not spoken by all and the condition of taxis and standard of driving varies.

Buses, trams & metro: Public transport is limited.

Car hire

International car hire firms offer modern vehicles from Pristina and its airport. The European Green Card vehicle insurance is not valid in Kosovo and vehicle insurance, preferably comprehensive, is necessary and should be purchased before driving. It is unlikely that credit cards or travellers cheques will be accepted everywhere so sufficient euro should be carried to pay for insurance and petrol.

Traffic and local drivers may pose a hazard to unwary foreign drivers and

travelling at night can be risky. Fuel, although widely available, varies in quality. In summer during dry hot weather there is a danger of forest fires and care must be taken when driving through wooded areas and lighted cigarette ends should not be thrown away.
Note that Serbian car hire firms do not permit their rented vehicles to enter Kosovo.

BUSINESS DIRECTORY

Telephone area codes
The international direct dialling code (IDD) for Kosovo is +381, followed by 38 area code for Pristina and then the subscriber's number. By mid-2008 area codes for the rest of Kosovo are still being determined.

Useful telephone numbers
Emergency number: 112
Police: 92
Fire service: 93
First aid: 94

Chambers of Commerce
Kosovo Chamber of Commerce, Mother Theresa No 20, Pristina 10000 (tel: +381 224-741; fax: +381 224-299; email: info@oek-kcc.org; internet: www.oek-kcc.org).

Banking
Bank for Business, UÇK Street No 41, 10000 Pristina (tel: 244-666).

Economic Bank, Migjeni Street No 1, 10000 Pristina (tel: 244-396).

KASA Bank, Rexhep Luci Street No 5, 10000 Pristina (tel: 246-180).

New Bank of Kosova, Nëna Terezë Street No 49a, Pristina 10000 Pristina (tel: 223-976).

ProCredit Bank, Skenderbeu Street, 10000 Pristina (tel: 240-248).

Raiffeisen Bank Kosovo UÇK Street No 51, 10000 Pristina (tel: 226-400/1

Central bank
Central Bank of Kosovo, 33 Garibaldi Street, Pristina (tel: 222-055; fax: 243-763; email: publicrelations@bpk-kos.org; internet: www.cbak-kos.org).

Travel information
Kosova Airline, Vellusha e Poshtme 17, Te Kino Rinia (tel: 249-184/5; fax: 249-186; email: info@kosovaairlines.com; internet: www.flyksa.com).

Kosovo Railways, Sheshi i Lirisë pn, Fushë Kosovë (tel: 536-355; fax: 536-307; email: info@kosovorailway.com; internet: www.kosovorailway.com).

Ministries
Ministry of Trade and Industry, Perandori Justinian Street, Pejton Square, 3–5 Pristina (tel: 38 20 036-015; internet: www.mit-ks.org)

Other useful addresses
Auditor General, Gazmend Zajmi No 59, 10000 Pristina (internet: www.ks-gov.net/oag).

Community Development Fund Rruga Perandori Justinian No 4, Pristina (tel: 249-677/8; fax: 249-679; internet: www.kcdf.org).

Constitutional Secretariat, New Bld, 8th Floor, Office 803, Skenderbeg Square, 10000 Pristina (tel: email: info@kushtetutakosoves.info; internet: www.kushtetutakosoves.info).

Economic Initiative for Kosovo (ECIKS), Nussdorfer Strasse 20–23, A-1090 Vienna, Austria (+43 1-890-5026; internet: www.eciks.org).

British Consulate, Ismail Qemajli 6, Arbëri Dragodan, Pristina (tel: 254-700; fax: 249-799; email: britishoffice.pristina@fco.gov.uk).

Independent Media Commission, Gazmend Zajmi Street, No 1 Pristina (tel: 245-031; fax: 245-034; email: info@imc-ko.org; internet: www.imc-ko.org).

Investment Promotion Agency of Kosovo, Perandori Justinian No 3-5, Qyteza Pejton, Pristina (tel/fax: 38 200-360; email: infor@invest-ks.org; internet: www.invest-ks.org).

National Assembly (Media Office), Mother Theresa No 20, Pristina 10000 (tel: 211-186/189; fax: 211-188; internet: www.assembly-kosova.org).

Statistics Office of Kosovo, Zenel Salihu Street No 4, Pristina (tel: 235-111; fax: 235-545; email: esk@ks-gov.net; internet: www.ks-gov.net/esk).

United Nations Development Programme (UNDP), (internet: www.ks.undp.org).

National news agency: Kosova Press

Other news agencies: Kosovalive: www.kosovalive.com

Kosova Information Center: www.kosova.com

Internet sites

Department of Tourism, Visit Kosovo, (internet: www.visitkosova.org).

Hotel Pristina: www.hotelprishtina.com

Grand Hotel Pristina: www.grandhotel-pr.com

Kosovo Force (KFOR): www.nato.int/KFOR

Kosovo map: http://kosova.org/maps/atlas/index.asp

Kosovo postal codes: http://kosova.org/docs/pdf/Kodet_Postare.pdf

Kosova Tourism Association: www.kotas-ks.org

Ministry of Trade and Industry, (internet: www.mti-ks.org).

OSCE: http://www.osce.org/kosovo

Republic of Kosovo Assembly: www.assembly-kosova.org

UNMIK: www.unmikonline.org

Kuwait

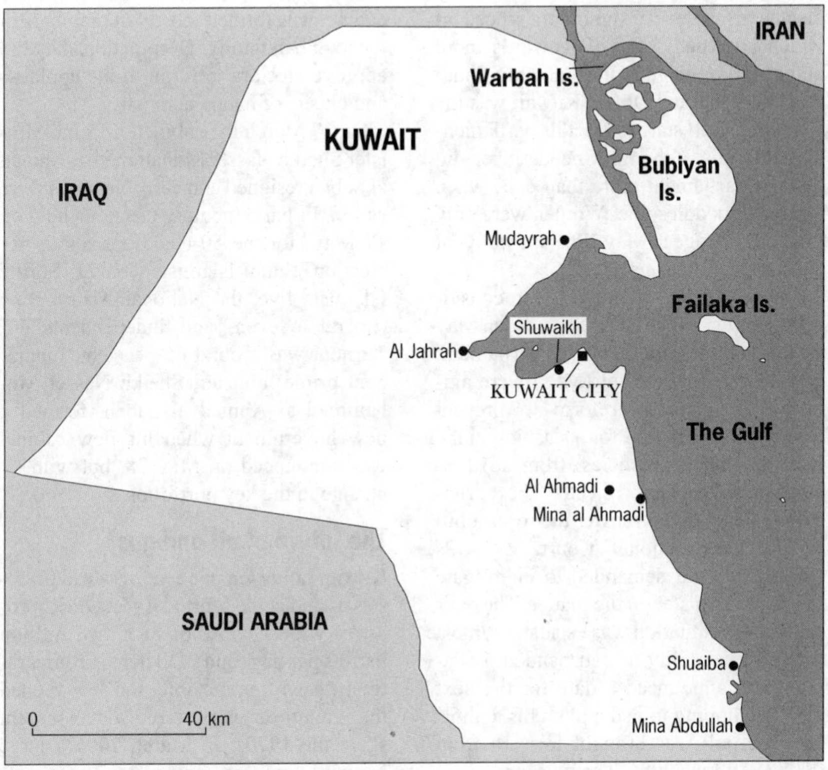

Kuwait has a strong economy. Its stock market performs well, it benefits from continuously high oil prices, and it enjoys political stability. With all of the pieces of the economic puzzle in place, this could be the perfect time for the country to start diversifying away from oil in order to limit dependence on this limited natural resource and ensure future growth.

In a September 2007 report on the Kuwaiti economy, Crédit Suisse noted that in the 1990s, Kuwait was faced with three major impacts: the Iraqi invasion, the drop of oil prices and the securities market crash – all of which had taken a toll on the country's economy. Today, Kuwait has fully recovered from these past issues and the economic forecast for the country looks good. 'Today, Kuwait is in very strong shape', according to Crédit Suisse. The Swiss bank envisages great opportunities for Kuwait's economy. The long history of the Kuwaiti stock market has produced experienced investors who are not interested in a 'quick buck'. 'They are thinking long-term and invest accordingly, which creates stability'. Besides that, Kuwait's stock market has a good record of paying solid dividends to investors. 'Kuwait's current account balance is 50 per cent of its GDP – unlike any other market in the region and probably the largest in the world,' say the bank's analysts. Moreover, in May 2007 Kuwait broke away from the fixed link to the US dollar. This move will enable Kuwait to mitigate the risk of import inflation due to the weakening of the US dollar.

A future with less oil?

Oil prices have been rising higher than most analysts expectations. That upward trend is, in the view of many analysts more than likely to persist. 93 percent of Kuwait's population is employed directly by the government. The huge public sector is feeding off the results of the country's enormous oil reserves. These reserves

KEY FACTS

Official name: State of Kuwait

Head of State: Sheikh Sabah al Ahmed al Jabir al Sabah (since 25 Jan 2006)

Head of government: Prime Minister Sheikh Nasser al Mohammad al Ahmad al Sabah (appointed 7 Feb 2006)

Ruling party: 16-member Council of Ministers (appointed 2006)

Area: 17,818 square km (including neutral zone)

Population: 3.31 million (2007)

Capital: Kuwait City

Official language: Arabic

Currency: Kuwaiti dinar (KD) = 1,000 fils

Exchange rate: KD0.26 per US$ (Jul 2008)

GDP per capita: US$33,634 (2007)*

GDP real growth: 4.60% (2007)*

Labour force: 1.12 million (2004)

Unemployment: 2.20% (2004)

Inflation: 4.90% (2007)*

Oil production: 2.63 million bpd (2007)

Balance of trade: US$32.30 billion (2005)

Foreign debt: US$15.02 billion (2004)

* estimated figure

enable the government to guarantee each Kuwaiti a lifetime job, independent of their qualifications, ability and even performance. Therefore, what sounds like a great blessing for its population may turn out to be a handicap in a few decades.

The need for an oil-rich country to diversify away from its biggest source of profit is not as far fetched as it might seem. In fact, most other countries in the GCC are already thinking of the next generations when oil will become a scarce commodity. Dubai and Qatar, for example, are promoting tourism and developing their non-oil sector by investing in their infrastructure. While developing a private sector is the best option for a strong future, changing attitudes and years of reliance on the government could present a different set of problems. Changes on such a scale could place the Kuwaitis at a great disadvantage in their own country.

On 15 January 2006 the Emir, Sheikh Jaber al Ahmad al Ahmad al Sabah, died, leaving behind 23 sons and 15 daughters. He had ruled the country of 2.7 million people since 1977. He was automatically succeeded by his cousin, the elderly and wheelchair-bound crown prince, Sheikh Sa'ad al Abdullah al Sabah. No sooner was he instated than the government plotted to remove him on the grounds of ill health, and replace him with Sheikh Sabah al Ahmad al Jabir al Sabah, the then prime minister. However, just in time, Sheikh Sa'ad offered his abdication. The new emir, Sheikh Sabah al Ahmed, had previously held the post of foreign minister for four decades, establishing a solid reputation. He appointed his brother, Sheikh Nawaf al Ahmed, as the new crown prince and his nephew Sheikh Nasser Muhammad al Ahmed as prime minister.

The deposition process which had been set in motion against Sheikh Sa'ad would have been constitutional and democratic. The full legal process may have been avoided but even so, the fact that the will of the ruling dynasty was overturned by elected officials set a significant precedent which unsettled some of Kuwait's more authoritarian neighbours – notably Saudi Arabia, Qatar and Oman. Kuwait was the first Arab Gulf state to elect its parliamentary officials, although Sheikh Jaber did dismiss parliament more than once when it proved meddlesome. Women were only granted suffrage in May 2005 and political parties are still illegal.

The succession dilemma led to considerable unrest which came to a head in May 2006 when the emir dismissed parliament. Members of parliament (MPs) were agitating for electoral reform to prevent fraud, notably calling for a slashing in the number of constituencies, from 25 divisions to five. They rejected the parliament's decision to transfer the reform bill to the Constitutional Court; 29 MPs walked out and demanded to interrogate the prime minister on the matter. The emir felt that the situation was escalating into a crisis of instability. He suspended parliament and announced a date for the next election, hoping to make plain his authority. The poll was brought forward from 2007 to 29 June 2006. The vote, perceived as a referendum on electoral reform, generated a greater degree of activism and campaigning than usual. This could have been for two historic reasons: it was the first national election in which women could participate and the first widely discussed and debated by Kuwait (internet) bloggers. Reformist candidates fared particularly well and will form a front against the conservative ruling family. The energy and cabinet ministers, suspected of fraud, lost their jobs although the newly elected cabinet was formed mostly of members of the al Sabah family. Despite this, they did approve electoral reform, to the applause and cheers of happy activists.

On 17 March the cabinet of Prime Minister Sheikh Nasser Muhammad al Ahmad al Sabah resigned and early elections were called. In parliamentary elections held on 17 May (for the 50 elective seats up for election) Sunni Islamists won 21, Shi'ite Islamists five, the National Action Bloc (liberals) seven, and independents 17. Turnout was around 65 per cent. Incumbent prime minister, Sheikh Nasser Muhammad al Ahmad al Sabah, formed a new government when his new cabinet was announced on May 28, but with no change in the key portfolios.

The future of oil and gas

Kuwait holds ten per cent of world oil reserves and is the fourth largest OPEC producer with a quota of over two million barrels per day (bpd). Oil here is comparatively easily extractable and has funded the country's very rapid development since the 1970s. In March 2006 a large new oil and gas field was discovered, which is expected to expand the country's gas industry by around 990 million cubic metres of gas reserves and over 10 billion barrels of oil. The gas find is something of a reassurance as earlier talks to import gas from Qatar and Iran had run into difficulties. However, the suspension of parliament and instability surrounding the succession led to setbacks with the US$8.5 billion Project Kuwait, the deal which proposes to allow foreign oil companies into the country. It is expected that foreign money and expertise will enable production to soar from 2.5 million to 4 million bpd by 2025. Whether or not the deal goes ahead will have an impact on world oil prices but it has not yet been properly debated by parliament.

Economic developments

Generally the Kuwaiti oil-based economy is on a sound footing; one indicator of wealth is the ratio of cars to people which is 2:1. However, in March 2006 stock markets across the region fell by as much as 12 points. Kuwait suffered least and the

KEY INDICATORS — Kuwait

	Unit	2003	2004	2005	2006	2007
Population	m	2.37	2.39	2.99	3.18	*3.31
Gross domestic product (GDP)	US$bn	38.85	41.75	*80.78	98.72	*111.34
GDP per capita	US$	16,388	19,559	27,006	31,014	*33,634
GDP real growth	%	2.7	7.2	*10.0	6.2	*4.6
Inflation	%	2.1	1.8	*4.1	3.0	*4.9
Oil output	'000 bpd	2,238.0	2,424.0	2,643.0	2,704.0	2,626.0
Natural gas output	bn cum	8.3	9.7	9.7	12.9	12.6
Exports (fob) (goods)	US$m	21,794.0	30,221.0	44,430.0	58,638.0	–
Imports (cif) (goods)	US$m	9,882.0	10,920.0	12,230.0	14,350.0	–
Balance of trade	US$m	11,912.0	19,301.0	32,200.0	44,288.0	–
Current account	US$m	9,424.0	18,162.0	34,308.0	50,996.0	*52,734.0
Total reserves minus gold	US$m	7,577.0	8,241.9	8,862.8	12,566.0	16,660.0
Foreign exchange	US$m	6,640.5	7,347.4	8,380.4	12,177.6	16,285.0
Exchange rate	per US$	0.30	0.29	0.29	0.28	0.27

downturn in prices was an inevitable and healthy correction to runaway prices fed by high oil profits. In August 2006, the Kuwait Finance House (KFH) developed a way for investors to hedge foreign exchange risk while keeping within *Sharia* (Islamic law). Hedging had been viewed by Muslims as a form of gambling, which is outlawed under *Sharia*. Therefore, KFH's announcement could prove very lucrative. In September 2006 the Kuwait Investment Authority communicated plans to buy a US$719 billion share in the Industrial and Commercial Bank of China, when that bank sets out the biggest initial public offering (IPO) in history.

On 1 January 2008, a common market bwtween Bahrain, Kuwait, Oman, Qatar, Saudi Arabia and UAE, the six wealthiest Gulf states came into being. Citizens of these countries can now travel between and live in any of the six states, where they may find employment, buy properties and businesses and use the educational and health facilities freely.

Sheikh Saad al Abdullah al Salim al Sabah, who had briefly been Emir of Kuwait in 2006 before ill-health led to his resignation, died on 13 May 2008. He had been much admired and liked by Kuwaitis.

Risk assessment

Politics	Good
Economy	Good
Regional stability	Fragile

COUNTRY PROFILE

Historical profile

1899 The Sheikh accepted British protection in order to counter the spread of Turkish influence. It also granted control of external relations to Britain.
1918 The end of the First World War saw the finish of what was already only nominal Turkish control over Kuwait.
1938 Oil was first discovered in Kuwait. Further exploration was interrupted by the Second World War.
1940s–50s Drilling resumed after the War and Kuwait soon developed into a thriving commercial centre. The government began using oil revenues to develop the country's infrastructure and a modern and comprehensive welfare system.
1961 Kuwait's status as a British protectorate ended and it became an independent country. The ruling Sheikh became the Emir and assumed full executive power. Iraq claimed Kuwait as part of its territory, but backed down after British military intervention.
1963 The constitution was promulgated and National Assembly elections were held.
1976 The Emir suspended the National Assembly; he said it was not acting in the country's interests.
1977 In December Sheikh Jaber al Ahmad al Sabah succeeded his cousin, Sheikh Sabah al Salem al Sabah as Emir.
1980 In the Iran-Iraq War, Kuwait supported Iraq.
1981 The National Assembly was recalled, but was again dissolved in 1986.
1985 The Emir survived an assassination attempt.
1990 Iraq invaded Kuwait and the Emir and cabinet flet to Saudi Arabia. The invasion was condemned by the international community which, led by the US, deployed armed forces to Saudi Arabia. UN Resolution 678 authorised member states to use force if Iraq did not withdraw by 15 January 1991.
1991 Iraq did not withdraw its forces when required. The Gulf War commenced with an airborne bombing campaign against Iraqi positions in Kuwait. US-led alliance ground forces entered Kuwait and force Iraq to retreat. Iraq agreed to accept all UN resolutions concerning Kuwait.
1992 The Emir was pressurised into allowing National Assembly elections, in which the opposition fared well.
1999 Islamists and liberals swept to victory in parliamentary elections. A draft law granting women full political rights, including the right to vote, was narrowly rejected by parliament. The National Assembly was suspended by the Emir, following a dispute over the misprinted state edition of the Qur'an.
2001 The Constitutional Court refused to grant women the vote.
2002 The Emir suffered a brain haemorrhage; he received treatment in London.
2003 US troops and allies massed in the border area of Kuwait before invading Iraq. Islamist and pro-government candidates were successful in parliamentary elections; liberal candidates had the major losses. Emir Sheikh Jaber appointed his brother, Sheikh Sabah al Ahmad al Jabir al Sabah, as prime minister, separating the post from the role of heir to the throne for the first time since independence.
2005 The constitution was amended, giving women the right to vote and stand for parliament. For the first time, two women were named as members of the national assembly in June and women were granted the right to take part in parliamentary elections in 2007, providing they abided by Islamic law.
2006 Emir Sheikh Jaber died on 14 January. Sheikh Sabah al Ahmad al Sabah became Emir instead of Crown Prince Sheikh Sa'ad al Abdullah al Sabah, who had been heir apparent since 1978, but who was not well enough to take up the position. Sheikh Nasser al Mohammad al Ahmad was appointed prime minister on 7 February. Women voted for the first time in a March council by-election. On 21 May, the Emir dissolved parliament and scheduled new elections for 29 June, in which members opposed to the government's stance on electoral reform won 33 out of 50 elected seats. A new reform bill agreed by parliament in July, and later ratified be the Emir, reduced the number of parliamentary constituencies from 25 to five.
2007 A member of the ruling family, Sheikh Talal Nasser al Sabah, was sentenced to death for drug trafficking and money laundering offences; three other defendants were sentenced to life and two to seven-years imprisonment. On 4 February, the cabinet of Prime Minister Sheikh Nasser al Mohammad al Ahmad resigned and was re-appointed to form another cabinet which took office on 6 March. In May, as a counter-inflationary measure, the central bank ended the dinar's peg to the US dollar, adopted in 2003, in favour of a basket of currencies.
2008 On 1 January, a common market was created by Bahrain, Kuwait, Oman, Qatar, Saudi Arabia and UAE, the six wealthiest Gulf states. Citizens of these countries are now allowed to travel between and live in any of the six states, where they may find employment, buy properties and businesses and use the educational and health facilities freely. On 17 March the cabinet of Prime Minister Sheikh Nasser Muhammad Al Ahmad Al Sabah resigned and early elections were called. Emir Sheikh Saad al Abdullah al Salim al Sabah died on 13 May. In parliamentary elections held on 17 May (for the 50 elective seats up for election) Sunni Islamists won 21, Shi'ite Islamists five, the National Action Bloc (liberals) seven, and independents 17. Turnout was around 65 per cent. Incumbent Prime Minister Sheikh Nasser Muhammad Al Ahmad Al Sabah formed a new government when his new cabinet was announced on May 28, but with no change in the key portfolios.

Political structure

Constitution

The constitution was enacted on 29 January 1963. It authorises the ruling al Sabah family to choose an Emir, who holds executive power and can proclaim legislation by decree.

The constitution ascribes the political system as democratic, with sovereignty residing in the people. Impartial personal liberty and equality of rights and duties before the law are guaranteed.

The Emir or one-third of the national assembly may propose amending the Constitution by deleting or adding new ones, except for the Emiri System and the principles of liberty and equality unless to increase provisions. Approval by a two-thirds majority is required for such a bill to succeed.
Males aged over 21 may vote; to include women aged over 21 from 2007.

Form of state
Constitutional monarchy (Emirate)

The executive
Executive power resides with the Emir, who is Head of State and appoints a prime minister, acceptable to the national assembly. In consultation with the prime minister the Emir appoints the Council of Ministers, who may not be members of parliament, although they assume ex officio membership during their term of office.
The Emir rules by decrees agreed by the Council of Ministers and, approved by parliament. He is also supreme commander of the armed forces.
Since 2003, the office of prime minister has been separated from the office of the Crown Prince, allowing greater independence of the legislature.

National legislature
The parliament is the unicameral Majlis al Umma (national assembly) of 50 elected members for four-year terms, plus 15 appointed ex officiocabinet ministers.

Legal system
The Judiciary is based on Egyptian laws, derived from French law. The legal system is a mix of Sharia (Islamic law) and Napoleonic law.
In 1960, a unified judicial system was adopted, establishing different levels of courts. There are three separate divisions including the Courts of First Instance subdivided into criminal, commercial and civil boards, the Constitutional Court and the Court of State Security. The judiciary is administered by a council of seven senior judges and minister.

Last elections
17 May 2008 (parliamentary)
Results: Parliamentary: (of the 50 elective seats up for election) Sunni Islamists won 21, Shi'ite Islamists five, the National Action Bloc (liberals) seven and independents 17. Turnout was around 65 per cent.

Next elections
2012 (parliamentary)

Political parties
No political parties are allowed, although informal groupings exist.
The largest such groupings are the Islamic Patriotic Coalition (a Shi'a fundamentalist group), two Sunni fundamentalist groups, the Islamic Constitutional Movement and the Islamic Popular Grouping (also known as the Salafi). The Kuwait Democratic Forum is the largest secular political group and has liberal and Arab nationalist opinions.

Ruling party
16-member Council of Ministers (appointed 2006)

Population
3.31 million (2007)
Last census: April 1995: 1,575,570
Population density: 102 inhabitants per square km. Urban population: 96 per cent (1995–2001).
Annual growth rate: 4.1 per cent 1994–2004 (WHO 2006)

Ethnic make-up
Kuwaiti (37 per cent), other Arab (35 per cent), south Asian (9 per cent) and Iranian (4 per cent).

Religions
Sunni Muslim (45 per cent), Shi'ite Muslim (30 per cent), other Muslims (10 per cent); others, including Christian, Hindu and Parsi (15 per cent).

Education
There is state and private education at all levels; state schools are single-sex and only private schools may be co-educational. Tuition in the state sector is in Arabic.
Compulsory schooling begins at aged six and lasts until students have completed two four-year cycles in, first, elemental then intermediate schools. The last four-year cycle is not compulsory; as with the previous two stages, it is free of charge.
Pre-primary schools (also funded by the state) cater for four- to six-year-olds.
Public expenditure on education is typically equivalent to around 5 per cent of annual GNP and included subsidies to private education at primary, secondary and tertiary levels. Average public expenditure was estimated at 39.6 per cent of GNP per capita for primary level students, 5.5 per cent for secondary level and a higher expenditure of 87.9 per cent for tertiary level students.
Literacy rate: 83 per cent adult rate; 93 per cent youth rate (15–24) (Unesco 2005).
Compulsory years: Six to 14
Enrolment rate: 77 per cent gross primary enrolment of relevant age group (including repeaters); 65 per cent gross seconday enrolment (World Bank).
Pupils per teacher: 14 in primary schools

Health
Per capita total expenditure on health (2003) was US$567; of which per capita government spending was US$440, at the international dollar rate, (WHO 2006).
Kuwait offers free, high quality health services through its clinics and hospitals, but charges for certain medical services for some residents and expatriates. The Ministry of Public Health (MPH) manages the health system and provides care on a referral basis through a network of local clinics, general and specialised services.
Life expectancy: 77 years, 2004 (WHO 2006)
Fertility rate/Maternal mortality rate: 2.3 births per woman, 2004 (WHO 2006); maternal mortality 5 per 100,000 live births (World Bank).
Birth rate/Death rate: 3 deaths and 20 births per 1,000 people (World Bank)
Child (under 5 years) mortality rate (per 1,000): 8.0 per 1,000 live births; 2 per cent of children aged under five years are malnourished (World Bank).
Head of population per physician: 1.53 physicians per 1,000 people, 2001 (WHO 2006)

Welfare
The social insurance system was set up as a basic scheme to include all employees with an addition supplementary scheme covering only those employees with an average monthly income above KD1,250.
Disability benefits are provided up to 60-years of age. The survivor pension amounts to 33.3–100 per cent of the deceased person's earnings according to number of widows and family dependants. A widow or widower receives a minimum monthly benefit.

Pensions
The old age pension is calculated on the number of years of contribution, the age at retirement and average earnings. It is set at a minimum of 65 per cent, and by a maximum benefit of 95 per cent, of the last monthly earnings.

Main cities
Kuwait City (capital, estimated population – excluding urban areas – 17,188 in 2005), Salimiya (125,603), Jaleeb (91,197), al Kreen (69,996).

Media
In 2008 Kuwait was ranked first for press freedom among all Arab states, by the Amman Centre of Human Rights Studies. A press law prohibits references to God and the prophet Mohammed. Criticism of the Emir, the constitution, the judiciary and the 'tenets and mores of the society' can be prosecuted and imprisoned thus self-censorship is practised.
National news agency: Kuwait News Agency (Kuna): www.kuna.net.kw

Press
The Ministry of Information issues licences to newspaper publishers.
Dailies: In Arabic, Al Qabas (www.alqabas.com.kw), Al Rai al Amm

(www.alraialaam.com), Al Watan (www.alwatan.com.kw), Annarar (www.annaharkw.com), Al Anba (www.alanba.com.kw), Al Seyassah and Al Taleea. In English Al Watan Daily (www2.alwatan.com.kw), Kuwait Times (www.kuwaittimes.net) and Arab Times (www.arabtimesonline.com).

Weeklies: In Arabic, Al Nahda (www.al-nahda.com) and Al Mujtammaa (www.almujtamaa-mag.com) cover for current affairs.

Business: There are three regional business magazines which provide local and regional news on financial and business news, the Lebanon-based Al Iktissad Wal Aamal (www.iktissad.com), the UAE based Zawya (http://www.zawya.com) and the monthly Investors (http://mosgcc.com/english) published by the Gulf Co-operation Council. Local daily newspapers also publish business news.

Periodicals: In Arabic, the cultural review magazines Dar al Yaqza (www.alyaqza.com), Al Arabi (www.alarabimag.com) and Anhar (www.anhaar.com) are published monthly. The Quarterly Thouq (www.thouq.com) is a glossy magazine on fashion and lifestyles.

Broadcasting

State-run radio and television is operated by the Ministry of Information.

Radio: Radio Kuwait is the national public radio station providing several services of news, sports, religion, traditional and pop music and programmes in English. The only other local radio station is the private Marina FM (www.marinafm.com). Foreign radio stations available include the UK's BBC and BFBS, the US AFN and the French Monte Carlo Doualiya. There are numerous satellite radio stations available.

Television: The state-run Kuwait Televion has four channels, KTV1–4. Other, private broadcasters include the Al Watan (www.watan.tv), Al Resalah (www.alresalah.net), a religious channel and the first satellite TV service Al Rai, funded by the Al Rai Media Group (www.alraimedia.com) which has nation-wide interests in TV, radio, publishing and advertising. Minority satellite TV interests include Bahry TV (www.bahry.com) with marine programmes and CNBC Arabiya (www.cnbcarabia.com) for business programmes. There are other smaller, local TV services available.

Advertising

Foreign firms must work through local agents and distributors, or joint ventures to advertise in Kuwait. In April 2007, 70 per cent of all advertising revenue was channelled through newspapers. Direct marketing through the mail has become popular along with internet sites. Satellite television is an effective tool for reaching conservative Kuwaiti and expatriate women in the privacy of their own homes.

Economy

Once described as 'an oil well masquerading as a country', Kuwait is vastly wealthy. The Kuwait Investment Company (KIC) is one of the most respected global financial institutions and other state organisations, such as the Kuwait Petroleum Corporation (KPC), are recognised as major global investors.

The economy is centred on the oil and natural gas industries, which account for over 50 pert cent of GDP. Production of oil is around 2.6 million barrels per day (bpd). There are plans to increase output to around 4 million bpd by 2020. Oil accounts for 70 per cent of government income. Due to record high oil prices in recent years, export revenue doubled from US$21.8 billion in 2003 to US$44.4 billion in 2005, when the balance of trade surplus increased to US$32.2 billion.

Official estimates of oil reserves were 99 billion barrels, or around 10 per cent of the world's total reserves, but in January 2006 it emerged that reserves were nearer 50 billion barrels, only half of which were proven. In July 2006, it was reported that, after 60 years, production from the Burgan oilfield, the second largest in the world and Kuwait's main source of oil, had begun to decline in 2004 from its peak of 2 billion bpd.

The volatility of Kuwait's neighbour, Iraq, as well as legal and administrative barriers to investment, have discouraged large-scale foreign undertakings in Kuwait's upstream oil operations. The overt presence of the state in the economy (80 per cent) distorts the country's macroeconomic adjustment and has led to sharp imbalances.

Recent high oil prices have strengthened the economy. GDP grew was 8.5 per cent in 2005. The main risk to the economy, and it has been judged by analysts as unlikely, would be a sharp fall in the price of oil, which is projected to fall only gradually. Kuwait's macroeconomic performance has been strong. Structural reforms have been initiated to foster non-oil growth and generate employment opportunities for Kuwaitis, while limiting public sector expenditure.

The government is managing an economy, in the short- to medium-term, with large fiscal and external current account surpluses, growing national savings and improved trading, both with Iraq and other Gulf states.

Savings – 10 per cent of all government revenue and any fiscal surpluses – are being set aside in the Reserve Fund for Future Generations (RFFG). The reserves are managed by the Kuwait Investment Authority.

External trade

Kuwait is a member of the trading bloc, the Gulf Co-operation Council (along with Bahrain, Oman, Qatar, Saudi Arabia, and the UAE), and the Pan-Arab Free Trade Area (Gafta), which operates a customs union and free trade zone.

Around 90 per cent of all exports are oil and gas, while 90 per cent of all imports are consumer goods.

Imports

Food, construction materials, vehicles and parts, consumer goods and clothing.

Main sources: US (14.1 per cent total, 2006), Japan (7.8 per cent), Germany (7.7 per cent).

Exports

Petroleum, refined oil-related and by-products, predominately plastics and fertilizers and electrical and electronic equipment.

Main destinations: Japan (20.3 per cent total, 2005), South Korea (16.1 per cent), Singapore (9.7 per cent).

Agriculture

Kuwait remains dependent on food imports. The sector as a whole accounts for only 0.4 per cent of GDP.

Estimated crop production in 2005 included: 3.400 tonnes (t) cereals in total, 2,000t barley, 800t maize, 600t wheat, 22,000t potatoes, 16,000t dates, 64,000t tomatoes, 16,000t eggplants, 34,000t cucumbers, 7,000t chillies & peppers, 16,926t fruit in total, 211,020t vegetables in total. Livestock production included: 74,585t meat in total, 1,760t beef, 490t camel meat, 29,750t lamb, 42,000t poultry, 22,000t eggs, 44,636t milk, 281t cattle hides, 10,500t sheepskins.

Fishing

Fish stocks have recovered after war-related pollution reduced stocks in the early 1990s. Fish forms a relatively major part of the national diet, and domestic production can satisfy only 40 per cent of domestic requirements.

In 2004, the total marine fish catch was 3,032 tonnes and the total crustacean catch was 1,666 tonnes.

Industry and manufacturing

Industrial areas are located in Shuaiba, Mina Abdullah (both in south Kuwait) and Shuwaikh. Efforts to foster growth of non-oil industries have been hindered by the small size of the domestic market and a lack of natural resources other than hydrocarbons. Industry has been growing very slowly as a proportion of GDP, to between 11 and 13 per cent of total output.

Tourism
Kuwait adopted a long-term strategy in 2004 to develop tourism as part of its economic diversification objectives. The sector has been dominated by official and business visitors and entry has been difficult. The priority is to improve domestic tourism (73 per cent of Kuwait residents travel abroad each year) and increase arrivals from other Gulf states. Visa regulations were eased in March 2004 to make Kuwait more accessible to overseas tourists. Kuwait has few tourist attractions, but is engaged on an ambitious programme to expand resort and leisure facilities, including the development of Failaka Island and the Sulaibikhat coast.
Travel and tourism is estimated to have contributed 1.5 per cent of GDP and employ 7.6 per cent of the work force. It was set to attract US$433.8 million or 10.9 per cent of total capital investment in 2005. The sector generates around US$2.6 billion in export revenue.

Hydrocarbons
Kuwait is the third largest oil producer in the Middle East. In 2004, it had 99 billion barrels of proven oil reserves, more than 8 per cent of the world total and output was 2.42 million barrels per day (bpd). Reserves are sufficient to last 100 years at current rates of extraction. Kuwait invested some US$15 billion over the period 1995–2005 to increase its crude oil output to 3.5 million bpd. Kuwait's Opec quota was 2.207 million bpd in March 2005; it has plans to increase its output to 4.0 million bpd.
In 2005 Kuwait signed agreements with two consortia to develop refining and marketing ventures in China and India, and Project Kuwait, a plan to revitalise a group of oil fields, at an estimated US$9 billion.
Kuwait has let a contract to Hyundai to build storage tanks for 11 million barrels of crude oil for export and refining. The contract is worth US$1.25 billion.
There are also plans to modernise three refineries to increase total domestic processing capacity to 1.0 million bpd from 800,000bpd and to allow for environmentally cleaner products.
Natural gas reserves stood at 1.57 trillion cubic metres (cum) in 2004 and gas production totalled 9.7 billion cum. Although all gas produced is 'associated gas' produced alongside oil, Kuwait possibly found its first gas field in 2004. However it may take several years before production can begin. Currently all natural gas production (9.7 billion cum in 2004) is consumed domestically. With the proposed Qatar-Kuwait gas pipeline project expecting completion in early 2006, Qatar expects to be able to sell 15 million tonnes of gas per year to Kuwait.
Kuwait does not produce or import coal.

Financial markets
Stock exchange
The Kuwait Stock Exchange (KSE).
The stock price index increased by 34 per cent in 2004 due to the buoyant economy and abundant liquidity.

Banking and insurance
The IMF, Financial System Stability Assessment (FSSA), reported that the banking system was well capitalised with no immediate threat of instability. The capital adequacy ratio (CAR) was positive and quality assets were improving profits and returns on equity, which were increasing significantly. The financial institutional framework has been strengthened.
Central bank
Central Bank of Kuwait
Main financial centre
Kuwait City

Time
GMT plus three hours

Geography
Kuwait lies at the north-west corner of the Gulf. To the south and south-west it shares a border with Saudi Arabia, and to the north and west with Iraq.
Kuwait is mainly flat desert with a scattering of oases. From east to west, the country is about 208km and from north to south, 185km. The al Mutla ridge is the only significant geographic feature. The desert is generally gravelly.
Hemisphere
Northern

Climate
Kuwait is less humid than other Gulf countries. However, the coast is more humid than inland, although the temperatures are lower.
Kuwait has four seasons. Mid-February to mid-April is spring; April to September (summer) is very hot (up to 49 degrees Celsius (C) in the shade); autumn is around mid-September to mid-November. The winter months are usually pleasant, with daytime temperatures around 18 degrees C and cold nights. Sandstorms occur, particularly in spring. Kuwait has an annual rainfall ranging from 10mm to 370mm which falls almost entirely between the months of November and April.

Dress codes
Lightweight or tropical clothes are worn in the summer, although in winter months a medium-weight jacket and a jumper are advisable. Women should dress modestly. A long-sleeved shirt and tie should be worn at business meetings but a jacket may be carried. On social occasions dress as for business meetings, unless otherwise indicated.

Entry requirements
Passports
Passports are required by all, and must be valid for six months from date of entry.
Visa
Required by all, except citizens of Gulf Co-operation Council countries. All other visitors should contact the nearest Kuwaiti Consulate for current exceptions and requirements.
Business visas, obtained before travelling, require an invitation from a sponsor in a local company or organisation. When completed it should be submitted to the issuing embassy, along with a business letter from the employer giving an account of the visitor's position and role within the foreign company, and full itinerary with purpose of visit and length of stay.
Tourist visas can be obtained at ports of entry, by nationals of the US, Western Europe, South East Asia and Australasia.
Currency advice/regulations
There are no restrictions on local and foreign currency imports or exports.
Customs
Personal effects and a limited supply of tobacco are duty-free.
Prohibited imports
Alcohol, illegal drugs, pornographic and/or politically subversive materials; pork products in any form; all non-tinned food and fresh fruit, vegetables and shellfish. Products that originate from Israel.

Health (for visitors)
Health facilities are excellent.
Mandatory precautions
There are no compulsory vaccinations.
Advisable precautions
Recommended immunisations are hepatitis A, polio and tetanus. There is a risk of rabies.

Hotels
Most visitors are business travellers.
Five-star hotels have swimming pools and exercise/gymnasium facilities. Small tip for porters is customary. There is usually a 15 per cent service charge.

Credit cards
Major credit cards (American Express, Diners Club, Visa and Mastercard or Access) accepted at all hotels and many restaurants and shops.

Public holidays (national)
Fixed dates
1 Jan (New Year's Day), 25 Feb (National Day), 26 Feb (Liberation Day), 1 Jul (Bank Holiday).
Variable dates
Eid al Adha (four days), Islamic New Year, Birth of the Prophet, Ascent of the Prophet, Eid al Fitr (three days).

Islamic year – 1429 (10 Jan 2008–28 Dec 2008): The Islamic year has 354 or 355 days, with the result that Muslim feast advance by 10–12 days against the Gregorian calendar each year. Dates of the Muslim feast vary according to sightings of the new moon, so cannot be forecast exactly.

Working hours

Friday is the Muslim day of religious observance (weekly holiday).

Banking
Sun–Wed: 0800–1200; Sun–Wed, Ramadan: 0900–1230.

Business
Sat–Wed: 0830–1400; some businesses work 1700–2000.

Government
Sat–Wed, winter: 0700–1430; Sat–Wed (summer): 0700–1400; Ramadan: 0900–1300.

Shops
Sat–Thu: 0800–1230, 1630–2100.

Telecommunications

Mobile/cell phones
There are GSM roaming facilities available, with coverage throughout the country. The ministries of communications and commerce announced their intention to auction a 26 per cent share in the Third Mobile Telecommunications Company on 10 July 2007.

Electricity supply

240V AC; plug fittings normally three-pin flat type (British).

Weights and measures

Metric system (local units are also in use).

Social customs/useful tips

Appointments should be made in advance. Punctuality is appreciated. Personal introductions are advantageous. If the visiting executive is a woman, this must be clearly stated in initial correspondence. On the street, women should not respond to approaches by men and should avoid eye contact.
Men shake hands on meeting and taking leave. Conference visits are an accepted way of doing business and other visitors may be present. The host may hold several conversations at the same time. It is not customary to start talking business immediately. Business cards should have an Arabic translation on the reverse side. Islamic conventions apply. At meetings it is polite to drink coffee or tea when offered. It is the convention to use the right and not the left hand when shaking hands, eating, and passing or receiving anything. Almost everything may stop five times a day for prayers. Some people prefer not to shake hands with those of the opposite sex. When sitting cross-legged on sofas or cushions, soles of the feet must not be shown. A man should not enquire about another man's wife, only about the children. Pork and alcohol are forbidden.
Gratuities are around 10 per cent. Bargaining is not as common as in other countries. There are many restrictions on photography.

Security

Visitors should keep in touch with developments in the Middle East as any increase in regional tension might affect travel advice.
Kuwait is relatively safe but take normal travel precautions. Like the rest of the Middle East, there is a threat to westerners from possible terrorist attacks. Mines remain a problem outside Kuwait City.

Getting there

Air
National airline: Kuwait Airways.
International airport/s: Kuwait International (KWI), 16km south of city; duty-free shop, restaurant, banks, hotel reservations, post office, car hire. Taxis and hotel courtesy buses are available.
Airport tax: Departure tax: KD2, except transit passengers remaining in the airport.

Surface
Road: There are excellent roads from the Saudi Arabian and Iraqi borders.
Main port/s: Several commercial shipping lines call in at Kuwait City.

Getting about

National transport
Road: A network of 3,800km of good paved roads and expressways link towns.
Buses: Nationwide service operated by Kuwait Transport Company, generally rated good and inexpensive.
Rail: In February 2008 a plan to build a US$11 billion rail network was announced. The plan includes a metro system for Kuwait city.

City transport
Taxis: Taxis are not metered. Both private and shared taxis, which are orange and operate on set routes, are available. Taxis are more expensive from hotel ranks. There is a standard taxi fare in Kuwait City and drivers do not expect a tip. If hiring a taxi for a day or half-day agree the fare in advance. Call taxis are reliable and widely used.

Car hire
Locally approved/inspected international driving licence (valid for duration of entry permit) and insurance with Gulf Insurance Company or Kuwait Insurance Company are essential. Driving is on the right.

BUSINESS DIRECTORY

The addresses listed below are a selection only. While World of Information makes every endeavour to check these addresses, we cannot guarantee that changes have not been made, especially to telephone numbers and area codes. We would welcome any corrections.

Telephone area codes

The international direct dialling code (IDD) for Kuwait is +965, followed by subscriber's number.

Useful telephone numbers

Ambulance: 777
Telephone enquiries: 101
Directory enquiries: 023 or 244-4777

Chambers of Commerce

American Business Council of Kuwait, PO Box 29992, Safat 13159 (tel: 564-3149; fax: 563-8012; e-mail: abckuwait@hotmail.com).

Banking

Al-Ahli Bank of Kuwait KSC, PO Box 1387 Safat-13014, Mubarak Al-Kabir St, Kuwait City (tel: 241-1101/2; fax: 242-4557).

Commercial Bank of Kuwait SAK, PO Box 2861 Safat-13029, Mubarak Al-Kabir St, Kuwait City (tel: 241-1001; fax: 245-0150).

Gulf Bank KSC, PO Box 3200 Safat-13032, Raed Centre next to Awadi Tower, Kuwait City (tel: 244-9501; fax: 244-5212).

Industrial Bank of Kuwait KSC, PO Box 3146, Safat 13032, Kuwait City (tel: 245-7661; fax: 246-2057).

National Bank of Kuwait SAK, PO Box 95 Safat-13001, Ali Awadi Tower, Ahmed Al-Jaber St, Kuwait City (tel: 242-2011; fax: 246-4156).

Central bank

Central Bank of Kuwait, PO Box 526, Abdulla Al-Salem Street, Safat 13006, Kuwait City (tel: 244-9200; fax: 244-0887; cbk@cbk.gov.kw).

Travel information

Gulf Automobile Association, PO Box 827, Safat, Kuwait City (tel: 242-3864, 243-8640).

Kuwait Airways, PO Box 394, Safat, Kuwait International Airport, Safat 13004, Kuwait (tel: 434-5555; fax: 431-9204; internet site: www.kuwait-airways.com).

Kuwait International Airport (tel: 473-3625).

Touristic Enterprises Co (TEC), PO Box 23310, Safat 13094, Kuwait City (tel: 806-806, 565-0111; fax: 565-0514; internet: www.kuwaittourism.com).

Ministry of tourism

Tourism Department, Ministry of Information, PO Box 193, Safat, Kuwait City (tel: 242-7141).

Ministries

Ministry of Awqaf and Islamic Affairs, PO Box 13, 13001 Safat, Kuwait City (tel: 248-0000; fax: 243-3750).

Ministry of Communications, PO Box 318, 13004 Safat, Kuwait City (tel: 481-9033; fax: 484-7058).

Ministry of Defence, PO Box 1170, 13012 Safat, Kuwait City (tel: 484-8300; fax: 483-7244).

Ministry of Education, PO Box 7, 13001 Safat, Kuwait City (tel: 483-6800; fax: 483-7829).

Ministry of Electricity and Water, PO Box 12, 13001 Safat, Kuwait City (tel: 537-1000; fax: 537-1420).

Ministry of Foreign Affairs, PO Box 3, 13001 Safat, Kuwait City (tel: 242-5141; fax: 241-2169; e-mail: info@mofa.org).

Ministry of Health, PO Box 5, 13001 Safat, Kuwait City (tel: 246-2900; fax: 243-2288).

Ministry of Higher Education, PO Box 27130, 13132 Safat, Kuwait City (tel: 240-1300; fax: 245-6319).

Ministry of Information, PO Box 193, 13002 Safat, Kuwait City (tel: 241-5300; fax: 241-9642; e-mail: info@moinfo.gov.kw).

Ministry of Interior, PO Box 12500, 71655 Safat, Kuwait City (tel: 243-3804; fax: 243-6570).

Ministry of Justice, PO Box 6, 13001 Safat, Kuwait City (tel: 248-0000; fax: 243-3750).

Ministry of Oil, PO Box 5077, 13051 Safat, Kuwait City (tel: 241-5201; fax: 241-7088).

Ministry of Planning, PO Box 15, 13001 Safat, Kuwait City (tel: 242-8200; fax: 240-7326).

Ministry of Public Works, PO Box 8, 13001 Safat, Kuwait City (tel: 538-5520; fax: 538-0829).

Ministry of Social Affairs & Labour, PO Box 563, 13006 Safat, Kuwait City (tel: 248-0000; fax: 241-9877).

Other useful addresses

British Embassy, PO Box 300, 13003 Safat (tel: 240-3334; fax: 240-7395).

Central Tenders Committee, PO Box 1070, 13011 Kuwait City (tel: 243-1719; fax: 241-6574).

Council of Ministers, PO Box 1397, 13014 Safat (tel: 245-5333; fax: 245-5002).

General Secretariat, PO Box 1397, Safat 13014 (tel: 245-5333; fax: 245-5002).

Kuwait Foreign Trading, Contracting & Investment Co, PO Box 5665, Kuwait 13057 (tel: 244-9031).

Kuwait International Fair Co, PO Box 656, Safat, Kuwait City (tel: 245-8560/1/2/3/4/5).

Kuwait National Industries Co, PO Box 417, Safat, Kuwait City (tel: 815-466, 812-455).

Kuwait National Petroleum Company, PO Box 70, 13001 Safat (tel: 326-2616; fax: 326-0280).

Kuwait Oil Company (KOC), PO Box 9758, 61008 Ahmadi (tel: 398-9111; fax: 398-3661).

Kuwait Parliament, The National Assembly (tel: 245-5422; fax: 243-9032).

Kuwait Petroleum Corp, PO Box 26565, Safat, Kuwait City (tel: 245-5455; fax: 246-7159).

Kuwaiti Embassy (USA), 2940 Tilden Street, NW, Washington DC 20008 (tel: (+1-202)-966-0702; fax: (+1-202)-364-2868).

National Housing Association, PO Box 23385, 13094 Safat (tel: 471-7844; fax: 242-8801).

Petrochemical Industries Board Co, PO Box 1084, Safat, Kuwait City (tel: 242-2141; fax: 246-0224).

Shuaiba Area Authority, PO Box 4690, Safat (tel: 960-903).

National news agency: Kuwait News Agency (Kuna): www.kuna.net.kw

Internet sites

Business News, Arabia online: www.arabia.com

Gulf Business Explorer: www.igulf.com

Kuwait Information: www.kuwait-info.org

Kyrgyzstan

In the parliamentary elections of December 2007, the newly formed pro-presidential party, Ak Zhol Eldik Partiyasy (Ak Zholor) (Bright Path Popular Party), obtained 49 per cent of the vote, achieving an overwhelming victory. Election observers and opposition politicians claimed that there had been irregularities, referring to ballot stuffing and falsified election returns. Kyrgyzstan's election rules require political parties to obtain 5 per cent of the republic's 2.7 million registered voters and 0.5 per cent of the total electorate in each of the nine voting regions. Of the 12 parties running for election, at the first count only Ak Zholor looked certain to qualify, causing concern that Kyrgyzstan's traditionally open political system might become, de facto, a one party system much on the lines of neighbouring Kazakhstan. Fortunately, the Supreme Court revoked the 0.5 per cent aspect of the presidential requirement and Ata Menken Socialist Party (Fatherland Socialist Party) won several seats.

Volatility

Kyrgyzstan's political situation has been volatile since the Tulip Revolution of March 2005, when protesters ousted Kyrgyzstan's long-time leader and brought a new president to power. Since then, the president's stand-off with parliament, packed with deputies from the former era, has fuelled political instability, as prime ministers came and went. This may provide the government with a base on which to advance economic reforms. Since stabilising the economy following the Russian economic crisis of 1998, it has grown by about 5 per cent a year, with the traditionally strong sectors of agriculture and mining leading the way. However, according to the Asian Development Bank (ADB) in its 2008 *Asian Development Outlook* in recent years these two traditional sectors began to lag behind other rapidly growing sectors such as construction, power, and service sub-sectors of transportation, communications and trade. In 2006 and 2007 the Kyrgyz Republic's economic performance has been strong. The ADB notes that the growth base continued to broaden towards non-gold sectors, mainly non-gold industry, construction and services, which have been developing strongly and most substantially contribute to gross domestic product (GDP) growth.

Strong growth

Despite the continuing political tensions, the ADB notes that the Kyrgyz economy grew strongly in 2007, driven by services, construction and manufacturing. Inflation, particularly for food products, jumped in the second half of the year. The

KEY FACTS

Official name: Kyrgyz Respublikasy (Kyrgyz Republic)

Head of State: President Kurmanbek Bakiyev (elected 10 Jul 2005)

Head of government: Acting Prime Minister Iskenderbek Aidaraliyev (appointed 28 Nov 2007)

Ruling party: Ak Zhol Eldik Partiyasy (Ak Zholor) (Bright Path Popular Party) (from 16 Dec 2007)

Area: 198,500 square km

Population: 5.25 million (2007)*

Capital: Bishkek (formerly Frunze)

Official language: Kyrgyz, Russian

Currency: Som (S) = 100 tyin

Exchange rate: S35.30 per US$ (Jul 2008)

GDP per capita: US$713 (2007)*

GDP real growth: 8.20% (2007)

Labour force: 2.36 million (2004)

Unemployment: 18.00% (2004)

Inflation: 10.20% (2007)

Balance of trade: -US$581.00 million (2006)

Foreign debt: US$1.97 billion (2004)

* estimated figure

authorities resumed their efforts to improve the business environment and to attract foreign investment. Prudent macroeconomic management will be critical for continued rapid growth, especially in light of the economy's vulnerability to external shocks. According to data from the National Statistics Committee, GDP grew by 8.2 per cent, well above the recent trend. The strong performance was all the more encouraging because the Kumtor gold mine, the largest single contributor to GDP, had not fully recovered from an accident in 2006 and operational problems in 2007, which led to a marginal fall in output.

Excluding gold production, the economy grew by 8.7 per cent in 2007. This strong performance was driven by a 12.4 per cent expansion in services, which contributed about two thirds of GDP growth. Industry (excluding gold) grew by 12.5 per cent, contributing about one quarter of GDP growth and reflecting a marked 20.2 per cent expansion in construction activity and gains in processing industries and utilities. Agriculture, which suffers from weak productivity, continued to expand at a muted 1.5 per cent.

On the demand side, private consumption in 2007 continued to be the main engine of growth, invigorated by rising real incomes, including those from remittances and from the shadow economy, which is estimated at a disproportionate 50–60 per cent of official GDP. Although initial data showed a healthy net inflow of foreign direct investment (FDI), the preliminary official data on fixed investment estimated growth to be only 3.7 per cent for the year.

Inflation worries

Inflation accelerated, notably in the second half. From an average of 4.0 per cent over the last 5 years, in 2006 it averaged 10.2 per cent for the whole year, soaring to 20.1 per cent at end-2007, the highest rate since 2000. For food products, particularly bread and cereals, the largest rise in prices was seen in October–November 2007. The continued decline in the area planted to grain (estimated at around 20 per cent over the last 7 years), falling yields, together with unfavourable weather conditions in 2007, lowered domestic grain production, of which wheat production fell by 16 per cent. The country imported approximately 360,000 tons of wheat in 2007 (the equivalent of nearly half domestic production), with most of that coming from Kazakhstan. As bread and other wheat-related products make up a large share of the consumption basket, the sharp rise in global wheat prices has boosted inflation. Other price increases were also important, notably for natural gas, with supplies from Uzbekistan almost doubling in price to US$100 per 1,000 cubic meters in 2007.

Wage increases as high as 30 per cent; and escalating price expectations by producers late in the year, as well as agriculture's supply constraints, also had an impact on inflation. The World Bank estimates that 40 per cent of Kyrgyzstan's population live below the poverty line, and with bread accounting for about a third of spending on food, the rising prices of wheat affect more acutely the population's poorer groups. The authorities have responded with a combination of administrative and economic policy measures under the direction of a newly established Food Security Council, chaired by the prime minister. Plans are in hand to develop a food security strategy that envisages stockpiling grain reserves of 100,000–150,000 tons, protecting the most vulnerable groups of the population, improving the provision of agricultural inputs, and enhancing the incentive structure for farmers.

The more buoyant economic activity of recent years and large foreign exchange inflows – especially in the form of remittances and foreign capital due to tourism – led the National Bank of the Kyrgyz Republic (NBKR), the central bank, to increase its purchases of foreign exchange in order to limit the nominal appreciation of the som.

Concerned with continued inflation pressure in the second half of the year, the ADB notes that in late-2007 Kyrgyzstan's monetary authorities sharply reduced their interventions in late 2007, allowing a notable nominal appreciation of the som against the US dollar. Apart from the impact of world prices on its major imports, Kyrgyzstan has so far been little affected by adverse global economic developments. However, the ADB notes that for this small open economy, economic developments in its large regional partners, such as Kazakhstan and the Russian Federation, become of particular importance, and are a potential source of risks. The adverse effects would be felt through weaker exports, slower capital inflows and investment activity, and potentially lower employment opportunities for Kyrgyz workers and weaker remittance inflows.

KEY INDICATORS — Kyrgyzstan

	Unit	2003	2004	2005	2006	2007
Population	m	5.16	5.32	5.15	5.20	*5.25
Gross domestic product (GDP)	US$bn	1.80	2.21	2.46	2.84	3.75
GDP per capita	US$		425	477	546	*713
GDP real growth	%	5.2	6.0	-0.2	3.1	8.2
Inflation	%	3.3	4.1	4.3	5.6	10.2
Industrial output	% change	–	4.1	-10.9	-7.4	–
Agricultural output	% change	–	4.1	-4.2	1.5	–
Exports (fob) (goods)	US$m	590.0	646.7	687.0	906.0	1,337.0
Imports (cif) (goods)	US$m	717.0	775.1	1,106.0	1,792.4	2,635.5
Balance of trade	US$m	-127.0	-128.4	-419.0	-886.5	-1,298.5
Current account	US$m	-50.0	-70.0	-57.0	-186.0	-244.0
Total reserves minus gold	US$m	364.6	548.7	569.7	764.3	1,107.2
Foreign exchange	US$m	354.3	528.8	564.5	731.1	1,093.4
Exchange rate	per US$	44.99	42.56	38.25	38.25	34.54

* estimated figure

Risk assessment

Economy	Good
Politics	Fair
Regional stability	Fair

COUNTRY PROFILE

Historical profile

1700s–1800s After being invaded by the Arabs, Mongols and the Chinese, Kyrgyzstan was ruled by the Khanate of Kokand (part of modern-day Uzbekistan).

1876 Tsarist troops conquered Kokand and incorporated Kyrgyzstan into the Russian empire.

1916–17 Following the suppression of rebellion in Central Asia against Russian rule and the outbreak of civil war after the

October Revolution in Russia, many Kyrgyz crossed the eastern border into China.
1918 Parts of Kyrgyzstan were absorbed into Russian-controlled Turkestan.
1920s–30s Soviet nationalities policy under the direction of Joseph Stalin saw Soviet rule enforced from Moscow by Red Army troops who put down Muslim revolts throughout Central Asia after the Russian civil war. All arable and grazing lands were consolidated into large state-owned farms, upsetting the traditional Kyrgyz way of life, based on nomadic livestock-herding. The Kyrgyz Communist Party was established as the sole legal party.
1924 Kyrgyzstan was designated the Kara-Kyrgyz Autonomous Region (renamed Kyrgyz Autonomous Region in 1925) and absorbed into the Russian Socialist Federated Soviet Republic (RSFSR).
1926 The Kyrgyz Autonomous Region was upgraded to an Autonomous Soviet Socialist Republic (ASSR).
1936 Kyrgyzstan became a constituent republic within the Union of Soviet Socialist Republics (USSR).
1940s–80s Kyrgyzstan was an important source of raw materials to the Soviet Union.
1990 The Kyrgyz and Uzbek population rioted in ethnically-divided Osh in southern Kyrgyzstan. Askar Akayev was appointed chairman of the Kyrgyz Socialist Republic.
1991 Kyrgyzstan was the first Central Asian republic to declare independence from the USSR. Akayev stood alone in the country's presidential elections. Kyrgyzstan joined the Commonwealth of Independent States (CIS).
1992 An economic reform programme was launched.
1993 Kyrgyzstan adopted its first post-Soviet constitution allowing for a parliamentary system of government. The som replaced the rouble as the unit of currency.
1994 Akayev won a resounding referendum victory, giving him the mandate to make the legislature a bicameral body. Uzbekistan signed an economic, military and social co-operation treaty with Kazakhstan and Kyrgyzstan.
1995 Akayev was re-elected for a second five-year term.
1996 A referendum gave the president the authority to appoint all top officials; parliamentary approval is only required for prime ministerial candidates. Uzbekistan, Kazakhstan and Kyrgyzstan agreed to create a single economic market.
1998 Constitutional changes were approved to change former communist farm collectives to private land ownership – the first time this was attempted by a Central Asian state. Kyrgyzstan became a member of the World Trade Organisation (WTO), the first of any former Soviet Union republics to join.
2000 President Akayev was elected for a third term, contrary to the constitution and amid allegations of electoral irregularities. The elections were followed by the harassment and imprisonment of opposition leaders and the closure of opposition newspapers. The presidents of Belarus, Kazakhstan, Kyrgyzstan, Russia and Tajikistan (formerly the Customs Five) established the Eurasian Economic Community (EEC).
2001 Akayev announced that he would not stand for re-election in the 2005 presidential election. Tajikistan, China, Russia, Kazakhstan, Kyrgyzstan and Uzbekistan formed the Shanghai Co-operation Organisation (SCO) and agreed to fight ethnic and religious militancy, while promoting investment and trade.
2002 Prime Minister Kurmanbek Bakiyev resigned and Nikolai Tanayev was named as his replacement. Opposition protesters marched in the capital, demanding the President's resignation.
2003 President Akayev's constitutional reforms, which included extending the president's term of office were endorsed by 80 per cent of voters; the opposition said they restricted civil liberties and consolidated power in the hands of the president. Widespread voting irregularities were reported by International observers. Parliament granted President Akayev and two other Soviet era Communist leaders lifelong immunity from prosecution.
2005 In February, numerous independent and opposition candidates were barred from standing in parliamentary elections which sparked widespread demonstrations. In March, protests increased during the second round of voting as demonstrators occupied government buildings in the south and calls were made for President Akayev to resign. When protesters occupied official buildings in the capital Akayev fled to Moscow; he resigned in April. The supreme court cancelled the results of the parliamentary elections, although later elected members took their seats. The acting president, Kurmanbek Bakiyev, won a landslide victory in the July presidential elections and was sworn in on 6 August. Feliks Kulov became prime minister in August and a new cabinet was sworn in on 20 December.
2006 On 9 November, President Bakiyev signed a new constitution after a week of mass protests for constitutional reforms and action to combat crime and corruption. Kyrgyzstan became a member of the World Trade Organisation (WTO) on 20 November. In December, he accepted the resignation of the entire cabinet in his long-running dispute with parliament. Parliament revised the latest constitution, reinstating some presidential powers concerning government appointments. President Bakiyev nominated Feliks Kulov as prime minister, but parliament rejected the candidate twice.
2007 Parliament approved President Bakiyev's nomination of Azim Isabekov as prime minister in January, but he resigned in March, following disagreement with Bakiyev over the make-up of the cabinet. Almazbek Atambayev became prime minister. The opposition, led by Feliks Kulov, mounted protest demonstrations in Bishkek in April, demanding the president's resignation. In the September constitutional referendum, 75 per cent of voters agreed to the change in voting laws from first-past-the-post to party-list voting, as well as the endorsement of constitutional changes, agreed in 2005, but which had been invalidated by the Constitutional Court. The international observer group, Organisation of Security and Co-operation in Europe (OSCE), reported that there had been 'numerous irregularities' with the referendum. The changes were adopted in October and the president called an early election for December. In October Prime Minister Atambayev and his cabinet resigned; Iskenderbek Aidaraliyev became acting prime minister. On 16 December, in parliamentary elections, the ruling Ak Zhol Eldik Partiyasy (Ak Zholor) (Bright Path Popular Party) won over 48 per cent of the vote. A presidential ruling required any political party to achieve a threshold 5 per cent of the national vote, of which 0.5 per cent of the vote had to be in every district in the country, to win seats. As no other party managed this Ak Zholor would have had a clean sweep and taken all 90 seats. However, the Supreme Court revoked the 0.5 per cent aspect of the presidential requirement and Ata Menken Socialist Party (Fatherland Socialist Party) won several seats. International observers criticised the elections due to the problems in vote counting and the de-registration of leading candidates.
2008 Fourteen medical professionals were charged in March with malpractice and negligence, following the infection of 42 children with the HIV virus, as a consequent of injections and blood transfusions.

Political structure

Constitution

The constitution was adopted in 1993 (amended in 1998, 2003 and 2007). It defines Kyrgyzstan as a sovereign, unitary, democratic and secular republic. All land, airspace and natural resources are the property of the state unless assigned for private usage. Discrimination on the grounds of language is forbidden. There is universal direct adult suffrage by secret ballot.

There are six administrative oblasts (regions): Chu, Issyk-Kul, Osh, Talas, Jalal-Abad and Naryn. The capital, Bishkek, has special status and is not included in any oblast.

The 2003 consitutional referendum gave local authorities more power.

The 19 September 2007 consitutional referendum agreed by 75 per cent to the change in voting laws from first-past-the-post to party-list voting, as well as the constitutional changes, agreed in 2005, but which had been invalidated by the Constitutional Court.

Form of state

Republic

The executive

The directly elected president is constitutionally limited to a maximum of two consecutive five-year terms.

The constitution states that the president must be able to speak the Kyrgyz language. The president has the authority to appoint all top officials, except the prime minister, for whom parliamentary approval is needed.

National legislature

The Jogorku Kenesh (Supreme Council), established in 1994, has two chambers. The upper house, Myizam Chygaruu Jyiyny (Legislative Assembly), has 60 members, elected for a five-year term, 45 in single-seat constituencies and 15 by proportional representation. The lower house, El Okuldor Jyiyny (People's Representatives Assembly), has 45 members, elected for a five-year term in single-seat constituencies.

In a 2003 referendum, the parliament was slated to become unicameral with 75 deputies, however the political upheaval of 2005 halted this process.

Legal system

The legal system is based on a civil law code. There are three ultimate legal authorities: the Constitutional Court, the Supreme Court and the Higher Arbitration Court. All are composed of judges with a 15-year term of office who must be approved by the national legislature and the executive. The Constitutional Court rules on the constitutionality of central and local government legislation and on the validity of elections. The Supreme Court is the highest court of appeal for civil, criminal and administrative cases previously heard in oblast, district, city and military courts. The Higher Arbitration Court oversees and rules on the operation of the regional and City of Bishkek arbitration courts.

Last elections

10 July 2005 (presidential); 16 December 2007 (parliamentary).

Results: Presidential: Kurmanbek Bakiyev with 88.9 per cent of the vote; Tursunbai Bakir uulu came second with 3.8 per cent. Turnout was 74.6 per cent.

Parliamentary: the ruling Ak Zhol Eldik Partiyasy (Ak Zholor) (Bright Path Popular Party) won 47.8 per cent of the vote and the majority of the 90 seats; Ata Menken Socialist Party (Fatherland Socialist Party) won 9.3 per cent and several seats. Turnout was over 60 per cent.

Next elections

2010 (presidential and parliamentary)

Political parties

Ruling party

Ak Zhol Eldik Partiyasy (Ak Zholor) (Bright Path Popular Party) (from 16 Dec 2007)

Main opposition party

Population

5.25 million (2007)*

Last census: March 1999: 4,822,938

Population density: 26 inhabitants per square km. Urban population: 35 per cent (1995—2001).

Annual growth rate: 1.4 per cent 1994–2004 (WHO 2006)

Ethnic make-up

Kyrgyz (54.0 per cent, originally a nomadic people of Turko-Mongolian origin who still dominate in rural areas), Russians (12.0 per cent), Ukrainians (2.5 per cent), Germans (2.0 per cent), Kazakh, Uighurs and others (29.5 per cent).

Religions

Predominantly Muslim (Sunni) (70 per cent of the population). There are also Russian Orthodox and Baptist churches.

Education

Primary education lasts for three years between the ages of seven and 10. Secondary education comprises of compulsory basic secondary (five years) and non-compulsory complete secondary (two years) which gives access to higher education. Vocational education is provided by professional schools which lasts for one-and-a-half years for those with complete secondary education.

There are 51 higher education institutions, of which 26 are run by the government. There are 13 non-governmental and 12 private higher education institutions.

Compulsory years: Seven to 15

Enrolment rate: 104 per cent gross primary enrolment of relevant age group (including repeaters); 79 per cent gross seceondary enrolment (World Bank).

Pupils per teacher: 20 in primary schools.

Health

Per capita total expenditure on health (2003) was US$161; of which per capita government spending was US$66, at the international dollar rate, (WHO 2006).

The healthcare system in Kyrgyzstan continues to be based on practices developed in the Soviet era, which concentrate on primary care and are cost-inefficient. The primary health sector has been supported by international donors, including the International Development Association (IDA), Asian Development Bank (ADB) and the German and Swiss governments, to resist the tide of an overall decline. Primary healthcare has slowly been re-formed, by local people identifying their own needs and devising methods to improve health generally. Despite the best efforts of local committees, a scandal in the hospital system resulted in a known 78 babies and some of their nursing mothers being infected with the HIV virus during to poor hygiene and corrupt practises in 2006. It has been recognised that the millions of dollars spent in international aid in prevention programmes in Kyrgyzstan the health system was of more danger than the disease.

A mandatory medical health insurance fund provides for 70 per cent of the population, covering 65 hospitals and 350 groups of family doctors. In-patient treatment is provided through a system of referrals throughout several levels of the system. Patients are entitled to essential drugs free of charge. Medical equipment supplies only 20 per cent of the needs of medical institutions. Kyrgyzstani clinics and hospitals use outdated equipment, 75 per cent of which needs to be replaced or upgraded. There is a shortage of affordable drugs and vaccines and most of the drugs are imported by small traders who do not conform to strict safety rules.

HIV/Aids

HIV prevalence: 0.1 per cent aged 15–49 in 2003 (World Bank)

Life expectancy: 63 years, 2004 (WHO 2006)

Fertility rate/Maternal mortality rate: 2.6 births per woman, 2004 (WHO 2006); maternal mortality 65 per 100,000 live births (World Bank).

Child (under 5 years) mortality rate (per 1,000): 59 per 1,000 live births; 7 per cent of children aged under five are malnourished (World Bank).

Head of population per physician: 2.51 physicians per 1,000 people, 2003 (WHO 2006)

Welfare

Like many other former Soviet countries, Kyrgyzstan has a large and complex social benefit system. Social spending, including expenditures of the social fund, makes up 28 per cent of the government budget and 7 per cent of GDP. Although the government budget subsidises the social fund, the payroll tax and the total costs of pensions are high. Pensions are often below subsistence level and the government believes that the current pension system is financially unsustainable. It is looking at cutting costs, preferably by reducing the number of beneficiaries, and aims to move to a system with a minimal state pension and a service pension based on payments into a pension insurance scheme.

Around 44.5 per cent of the population live below the poverty line. The aim of the Participatory Poverty Alleviation Programme (PPAP), set up by the UN Development Programme (UNDP), in co-operation with President Akayev's administration, is to reduce poverty in the country by 10 per cent by 2010.

Main cities

Bishkek (formerly Frunze) (capital, estimated population 843,240 in 2005); Osh (207,078).

Languages spoken

Kyrgyz is a Turkic language. Russian is widely spoken, even among ethnic Kyrgyz.

Official language/s

Kyrgyz, Russian

Media

A rise in pressure on the media in recent years from informal government censorship and large fines from legal action for slander has resulted in self-censorship in editorial content and a financial burden on media entities.

National news agency: Kabar: http://en.kabar.kg

Other news agencies: AKIpress: www.akipress.com

24.Kg: http://eng.24.kg

Press

Several daily and weekly newspapers include in Russian, Slovo Kirgyzstana, Vecherni Bishkek (www.vb.kg), Komsomolskaya Pravda (KP) (www.kp.kg), Moya Stoltisa Novosti (MSN) (www.msn.kg), Obshchestvennyy Reyting (www.pr.kg). In English The Times of Central Asia (www.timesca-europe.com) with regional news.

Broadcasting

Kyrgyz National TV and Radio Broadcasting Corporation is state-run. The government maintains control of broadcasting through licenses which can be revoked if political comment becomes provoking. Live broadcasts are restricted in what can be reported.

Radio: The state-run Kyrgyz Radio Broadcasting Corporation operates Radio 1 and 21 Vek. Most private stations operate from Bishkek, including AutoRadio, Europa Plus, Radio Max (www.max.kg) Ekho Bishkeka and Russkove Radio.

Television: There Kyrgyz National TV operates two channels. Other private stations include NTS (www.nts.kg), Piramida, Independent Bishkek TV and Broadcasts are in Kyrgyz and Russian. Osh TV is an independent TV company broadcasting in the southern regions of the country mostly in the Uzbek language.

Advertising

There is an active advertising sector using print media and billboards in particular, but services are also available in broadcast media.

Economy

Kyrgyzstan is one of the poorer countries of the former Soviet Union and was affected more than most by the loss of subsidies from Russia following independence. Prior to this, Kyrgyzstan was an important source of raw materials for the Soviet Union. However, demand from Russia for raw materials decreased dramatically and after independence Kyrgyzstan had to create new markets.

It is a recipient of international funds from the World Bank and the Asian Development Bank (ADB) and also receives assistance from the EU and bilateral aid from Japan, US, Germany and other European countries. It has received a number of IMF loans, as part of a US$102 million Poverty Reduction and Growth Facility (PRGF) agreement. The IMF and the Paris Club of foreign debtors agreed to write off US$500 million of debt between 2004–05.

In 2005, the economy stagnated with a -0.6 per cent growth, however it is expected to rebound with GDP growth of 4.0 per cent in 2006. The unemployment rate has slowly risen since 2001, reaching 9.7 per cent in 2005. At the same time GDP per capita also rose from US$308 in 2001 to US$528 in 2006. Kyrgyzstan is still classed as a poor country but with, as yet, largely un-exploited mineral wealth. It has significant deposits of coal, gold, uranium, antimony, and other rare-earth metals. Metallurgy is the government's objective for attracting foreign direct investment (FDI), which rose by 27 per cent in 2004. Production increased accordingly, however, gold production was interrupted in 2005 as the Kumtor gold mine suffered a serious accident.

The government is committed to the formation of a market economy, and the IMF has commended it on its success in carrying forward financial, fiscal and structural reforms. In 2006 further tax reforms included improvements to the administration.

The economy is structured with services providing 45 per cent of GDP, agriculture 34 per cent and industry 21 per cent, of which manufacturing was 14 per cent; only the service sector experienced positive growth in 2005.

The geography of Kyrgyzstan gives it plentiful water resources, couple with the mountainous terrain it will enable it to produce and export large quantities of hydroelectric energy in time.

This country has much of offer, it is struggling under the burden of external debt at 79 per cent of GDP (2005), but the government is attempting to bring it under control and with the right amount and quality of outside help it could thrive.

External trade

In 2007, Kyrgyzstan was still the only Central Asian country to be a member of the World Trade Organisation (WTO). It also belongs to the Eurasian Economic Community (EurAsec or EAEC), which was set up in 2000 to promote a customs union between its six member states (Belarus, Kazakhstan, Kyrgyzstan, Russia, Tajikistan, and Uzbekistan) and among other objectives, to introduce standardised currency exchange and rules for trade in goods and service. The EAEC evolved out of the Commonwealth of Independent States (CIS) Customs Union and has begun the process of merging with the Central Asian Co-operation Organisation (CACO).

Imports

Main imports are food, oil and gas, machinery and equipment, chemicals and foodstuffs.

Main sources: China (43.2 per cent total, 2005), Russia (19.8 per cent), Kazakhstan (11.9 per cent), Turkey (4.5 per cent)

Exports

Principal exports include primary minerals include mercury, antimony and rare-earth metals, chemicals, electricity and engineering goods, paper and timber products, agricultural products include woolens, vegetable oil, rice and meat.

Main destinations: UAE (35.6 per cent total, 2005), Russia (18.6 per cent), China (13.4 per cent), Kazakhstan (12.6 per cent)

Agriculture

Farming

Agriculture is one of Kyrgyzstan's main sources of wealth, accounting for around 37 per cent of GDP and employing approximately 48 per cent of the labour force.

The total area of agricultural land is 10 million hectares (ha), but only 7 per cent is cultivated.

The main products are tobacco (55,000 tonnes per annum), wool, cotton, leather, silk, meat, grain (especially barley), fruit and vegetables.

Livestock production accounts for about 60 per cent of gross agricultural income. Kyrgyzstan is the third-largest wool producer in the former Soviet Union. Only 15 per cent is processed locally. Vegetable oil, milk products and baby foods are imported.

There are no price regulations and there is no duty on export products. Since the amendment of the constitution in 1998 to allow for the full private ownership of land, the government has worked on a plan to auction land under the Land Redistribution Fund (which administers about 25 per cent of all arable land) and to implement a scheme to eliminate the state monopoly on seed production. The government lifted the moratorium on free land sales in 2001.

Crop production in 2005 included: 1,631,615 tonnes (t) cereals in total, 953,000t wheat, 1,141,000t potatoes, 233,000t barley, 432,000t maize, 167,000t tomatoes, 46,304t oilcrops, 289,076t sugar beets, 132,600t seed cotton, 48,000 cotton lint, 16,300t tobacco, 25,000t garlic, 160,430t fruit in total, 831,900t vegetables in total. Livestock production included: 195,720t meat in total, 95,300t beef, 38,000t lamb, 7,100t goat meat, 25,300t pig meat, 25,000t horsemeat, 4,900t poultry, 18,600t eggs, 1,178,000t milk, 1,500t honey, 150t silk cocoons, 9,880t cattle hides, 5,670t sheepskins, 10,000t greasy wool.

Fishing

Fishing remains important for domestic consumption, but fish stocks have been drastically reduced by irrigation, pollution and a lack of investment. The typical annual catch is 200million tonnes.

Forestry

Forests cover four per cent of Kyrgyzstan's land area, or 7,000 square km. Conifers account for 40 per cent of forest composition. Almost half of the forests are mature and over-mature stands. All forests are state-owned. Despite commercial potential, there are no significant forest industries, although Kyrgyzstan has a co-operation agreement with Switzerland for forestry development.

The total forested area has remained stable for several decades and could probably absorb higher levels of exploitation. The government aims to increase production, both to meet domestic needs and to export to other Central Asian countries.

Imports of forest materials in 2004 were US$20.5 million, while exports amounted to US$781,000.

Production in 2004 included 27,300 cubic metres (cum) roundwood, 9,300cum industrial roundwood, 22,000cum sawnwood, 4,650cum sawlogs and veneers, 18,000 cum wood fuel.

Industry and manufacturing

The industrial sector contributes around 21 per cent to GDP, with manufacturing accounting for 13.6 per cent.

Prior to independence, Kyrgyzstan was a significant producer of agricultural machinery, military equipment and medical supplies. Since fundamental manufacturing inputs came from other parts of the former Soviet Union, independence severely impacted upon the size of the industrial base.

Tourism

The geographical remoteness of Kyrgyzstan is an immediate obstacle to growth in the tourist sector, but the country's attractions should encourage international tourist demand. In 2001, the government initiated measures to develop the potentially lucrative tourist sector, but has been slow to build on them. Internal unrest and unsatisfactory infrastructure and services have also impeded significant progress. Despite its immediate shortcomings, Kyrgyzstan tourism should benefit from the country's natural beauty, historical sites and some of the highest mountains in the world.

Mining

Kyrgyzstan has deposits of gold, mercury, antimony, wolfram, tungsten, lead, zinc, uranium, rock salt and gypsum. Uranium oxide and molybdenum are produced at the Kara-Balta combine (Chu Valley). Metallic antimony (7,800 tonnes per year (tpy)) and antimony oxide (6,000 tpy) produced at the Kadamzhay combine (Osh Region), account for 13 per cent of world supply. Mercury is produced at the Khaidarkan combine (Osh Region), accounting for 21 per cent of world output.

Kyrgyzstan has impressive reserves of tin and tungsten, which are concentrated in the Sary-Dzhaz river basin, in the east of the country, and have been prospected and prepared for commercial development.

Kyrgyzstan attracts foreign mining and metallurgical companies due to its lax environmental laws. Large mining and metallurgical plants have failed to take into account the hazards of mercury, cyanide, acids and other toxic substances used in the ore refining and enrichment process. This has caused environmental disasters and poses a threat to the health of workers and the local population.

Antimony manufactured at the Kadamzhay combine suffers from high production costs and is unable to compete with relatively cheap antimony available from Chinese producers. Three other undeveloped reserves include Nichkesu (with estimated reserves of 100,000 tonnes), Savoyardy (90,000 tonnes) and Aktyub (30,000 tonnes).

The Russian, Kyrgyzstani and Kazakhstani governments have co-operated to step up the extraction and processing of raw uranium. The state-owned Khaidarkan combine in the Osh region is the only mercury producer in Kyrgyzstan. It is responsible for the improvement of ore enrichment technology and the development of the Novoye deposit, which has a high concentration of mercury, antimony and fluoride.

Most of the gold reserves are concentrated in lode deposits. With substantial deposits in the Talas mountains in the north and the Batken region in the south, together with relatively low production costs, gold is a key export for Kyrgyzstan. The Kumtor gold mine is one of the 10 largest in the world, accounting for around 30 per cent of exports and 11 per cent of GDP. Kumtor has reserves of 514 tonnes of gold. The mine typically has an annual production of 18.9 tonnes of gold; this level of production will be sustainable until 2010–13. The Kumtor Gold Company, a joint venture between Canada's Cameco and state-owned Kyrgyzaltyn, provides around 95 per cent of Kyrgyzstani gold.

Hydrocarbons

Kyrgyzstan has proven oil reserves of 40 million barrels and estimated reserves of over 2 billion barrels. Kyrgyzstan produces around 4,400 barrels per day (bpd). Domestic consumption is 11,000bpd. The downstream industry consists of one crude oil refinery at Dzhalal-abad, south of Bishkek, which was built in 1997 and has a capacity of 10,000bpd, although supplies of crude are unreliable and the refinery operates below capacity.

Kyrgyzstan has estimated gas reserves of 7.1 billion cubic metres. Gas exploitation is small due to the difficulties involved in recovering reserves. Annual domestic production of 100 million cubic metres only supplies a fraction of the 1.9 billion cubic metres consumed annually. Most gas is imported by Uzbekistan.

Coal reserves are estimated at 1.3 billion tonnes. There are sizeable coal deposits in Shurab, Kyzyl-Kiya, Naryn and Kok-Yangak. Further coal could be extracted from the Kara-Keche deposit in northern Kyrgyzstan, but it would need foreign investment to cover the US$52 million required for development.

Energy

Kyrgyzstan has an electricity generating capacity of 3.6GW. Hydropower stations account for around 80 per cent of electricity generated. There are 18 hydropower stations and two thermal power stations.

Kyrgyzstan supplies small quantities of electricity to Kazakhstan and Uzbekistan, in return for oil, gas and coal imports.

Financial markets

Stock exchange

Central Asia's second stock exchange, the Kyrgyzstan Stock Exchange (KSE), was established in 1995. Despite trading being very thin, it is playing a growing role in ensuring that scarce financial resources are directed towards areas of highest economic return. The KSE was accepted into the Federation of Euro-Asian stock exchanges in the same year

Banking and insurance

During the final years of the Soviet Union, the banking sector was one of the first economic activities to be liberalised. Upon independence in 1991, Kyrgyzstan had a large number of small banks, many of which offered limited services and had poor ratios of reserves to deposits. Of the Central Asian countries, Kyrgyzstan has made the best progress towards tighter regulation and supervision of banks, although it continues to fall short of the progress made by the Baltic states and Eastern European countries.

Kyrgyzstan adopted the Basle capital requirements in 1995, since when the minimum capital requirement has been increased in stages. As regulation of the system has tightened, so the number of banks has fallen. Simultaneously, privatisation has progressed in Kyrgyzstan to the extent that less than 10 per cent of the banking market is controlled by state banks. Furthermore, 16–17 per cent of the market is controlled by the three foreign banks with a presence in the country. The largest investment bank is the Kairat Bank.

The Law on Banks and Banking Activity, enacted in 2003, strengthened the regulatory powers of the central bank to ensure good management and corporate governance in banks, improve financial disclosure, and control insider dealing.

Central bank

National Bank of the Kyrgyz Rebublic

Time

GMT plus five hours

Geography

Kyrgyzstan is a relatively small, landlocked country situated in eastern central Asia. There are border crossings with the People's Republic of China to the east and south-east, Kazakhstan to the north, Tajikistan to the south and south-west and Uzbekistan to the west.

The Tian Shan mountains, with glaciers, fast flowing rivers and deep lakes, account for most of the country's high alpine terrain, except for the eastern edge of the steppe bordering Kazakhstan and the fertile Osh Valley to the west. Lake Issyk-Kul in the north-east of the country is the second deepest crater lake in the world.

Hemisphere

Northern

Climate

Temperature varies from the temperate steppe to sub-zero temperatures in the mountains (Bishkek: minus 5–35 degrees Celsius). Depending on terrain, annual rainfall varies from 170mm and 265mm.

Dress codes

Dress in the business community is informal, European style.

Entry requirements

Passports

Passports are required by all and must be valid for a minimum of six months at the time of entry.

Visa

Required by all except some nationals of former communist states. For tourist purposes, it is advisable to obtain visas in advance even though some nationals can obtain a visa on arrival, without a letter of invitation.

For most visitors tourist and business visas require an invitation from a local sponsor or company or government organisation. Business visas require confirmation of the contacts to be met and their business addresses and telephone numbers. These should be submitted to the issuing embassy, along with a business letter from the employer giving an account of the visitor's position and role within the foreign company, and full itinerary with purpose of visit and length of stay. For individual business travellers, visa support is required from the Ministry of Foreign Affairs. More information should be gathered from the nearest consulate.

CIS transit visas are no longer valid to enter neighbouring countries; a visa for each state should be obtained in advance.

Currency advice/regulations

Only Kyrgyz residents may import and export local currency.

The import of foreign currency is unlimited but must be declared; export is limited to the amount declared.

Travellers cheques, in US dollars, have limited acceptance in banks in the capital.

Customs

A customs declaration form is issued on arrival and must be surrendered on departure; declare all foreign currency and valuable items such as jewellery, cameras, computers, etc.

Prohibited imports

Illegal drugs, precious metals and artefacts, fur, fruit and vegetables and printed material, including photographs, which are detrimental to Kyrgyzstan.

Firearms, ammunition, works of art and antiques and live animals are subject to special permits.

Health (for visitors)

A reciprocal health agreement for urgent medical treatment exists with the UK. Proof of UK residence will be required.

Mandatory precautions

Vaccination certificates are required for yellow fever if travelling from an infected area.

Advisable precautions

Water precautions are recommended: water purification tablets may be useful or drink bottled water. It is advisable to be in date for the following immunisations: polio (within 10 years), tetanus (within 10 years), typhoid fever, tuberculosis, hepatitis A (moderate risk only), hepatitis B, tick-borne encephalitis.

Any medicines required by the traveller should be stocked by the visitor, and it would be wise to have precautionary antibiotics if going outside major urban centres. A travel kit including a disposable syringe is a reasonable precaution. There is a risk of rabies.

Hotels

It is advisable to book in advance through specialist travel agents. Tips are becoming customary.

Credit cards

Credit cards are accepted in larger hotels and banks in Bishkek.

Public holidays (national)

Fixed dates

1 Jan (New Year's Day), 7 Jan (Orthodox Christmas Day), 8 Mar (Women's Day), 21 Mar (Noruz/Persian New Year), 24 Mar (National Day), 1 May (Labour Day), 5 May (Constitution Day), 9 May (Victory Day), 31 Aug (Independence Day), 7 Nov (Socialist Revolution Day).

Variable dates

Eid al Adha, Eid al Fitr.

Islamic year – 1429 (10 Jan 2008–28 Dec 2008): The Islamic year contains 354 or 355 days, with the result that Muslim feasts advance by 10–12 days against the Gregorian calendar. Dates of feast vary according to the sighting of the new moon, so cannot be forecast exactly.

Working hours

Banking

Mon–Fri: 0930–1730.

Business

Mon–Fri: 0900–1800.

Government

Mon–Fri: 0900–1800.

Shops

Mon–Fri: 0900–1700.

Telecommunications
Mobile/cell phones
GSM 900 and 1800 services are available in populated areas only.

Electricity supply
220V AC

Social customs/useful tips
There are many customs and traditions to be understood. Alcohol is available and smoking is widespread. Gratuities are becoming more customary, particularly in international hotels.

Security
Western nationals have been advised to be vigilant if staying in Kyrgyzstan. Close proximity to Afghanistan and the presence of Western troops in the country could make foreign travellers a target of Islamic rebels. Travellers have been particularly advised to stay away from the southern provincial capital of Osh and especially the surrounding area.
It is unwise to venture out on the streets alone at night. Keep expensive jewellery, watches, cameras, etc, out of sight. Avoid parks at night and use registered taxis only.

Getting there
Air
National airline: Kyrgyz Aba Zholdoru (Kyrgyzstan Airlines)
International airport/s: Bishkek-Manas airport (FRU), 30km north of city, bureau de change, duty-free shops, post office, restaurants.
Almaty International Airport (ALA), 10km north-east of the city. Facilities include VIP lounge, car hire, duty-free shops, restaurant and post office.
Airport tax: US$10
Surface
Road: There are roads and border crossings with China, Kazakhstan, Tajikistan and Uzbekistan. Roads can be hazardous in winter. The border crossings in the south-west of the country are considered insecure due to the activity by Islamic rebels.
The Regional Road Corridor Improvement Project, estimated at US$18 billion, to improve Central Asian roads, airports, railway lines and seaports and provide a vital transit route between Europe and Asia was agreed, on 3 November 2007. Six new transit corridors, between Afghanistan, Azerbaijan, China, Kazakhstan, Kyrgyzstan, Mongolia, Tajikistan and Uzbekistan, of mainly roads and rail links, will be constructed, or existing resources upgraded, by 2013. Half the costs with be provided by the Asian Development Bank and other multilateral organisations and the other half by participating countries.
Rail: Bishkek is linked by rail to Central Asia's transport hub, Tashkent, in Uzbekistan.

Getting about
National transport
Air: Kyrgyz Aba Zholdoru operates domestic services. There are regular flights from Bishkek to Osh.
Road: There are 21,000km of roads, only about 50 per cent of which are in reasonable condition. Travel by road is generally difficult because of the terrain and in spring, landslides are common in mountain areas, especially around Osh. Travel by horseback in the mountains. There are few garage facilities on the main roads to and from Bishkek. Care should be taken when travelling by road, especially if a breakdown is involved. Driving during the winter months in private vehicles can be hazardous and some routes could be closed at times. Taxis and private drivers are often willing to provide inter-city services at reasonable prices.
Buses: There are regular and convenient bus services between major towns and cities.
Rail: The only line in use for passenger services is the 340km line in the north of the country, which connects to the Kazakhstani border at both ends and passes through Bishkek. The service is unreliable and is not widely used.
City transport
Taxis: Few taxis have meters and a price should be agreed beforehand. It is sometimes possible to hire private cars, but visitors are recommended to travel only in official taxis.
Buses, trams & metro: Cheap trolley-buses. Service 153 from Bishkek-Manas airport to city centre, every 15 minutes.
Car hire
A national licence with authorised translation or an international driving permit is required. A rented car is often accompanied by a driver.

BUSINESS DIRECTORY
The addresses listed below are a selection only. While World of Information makes every endeavour to check these addresses, we cannot guarantee that changes have not been made, especially to telephone numbers and area codes. We would welcome any corrections.

Telephone area codes
The international direct dialling (IDD) code for Kyrgyzstan is +996, followed by area code and customer's number:

Bishkek	312	Osh	322

Useful telephone numbers
Fire: 101
Police: 102
Ambulance (free): 103
Ambulance (private): 151

Chambers of Commerce
Bishkek Chamber of Commerce, Industry and Hanicraft, 539 Jibek-Jolu, Bishkek (tel: 670-113; fax: 660-048; e-mail: bishkekchamber@netmail.kg).

Kyrgyzstan Chamber of Commerce and Industry, 107 Kievskaya Street, Bishkek 720001 (tel: 210-565; fax: 210-575; e-mail: cci-kr@imfiko.bishkek.su).

Banking
Bakai, 75 Isanov Street, Bishkek 720001 (tel: 660-610; 660-612; e-mail:bank@bakai.kg).

Demir Kyrgyz International, 245 Chui Boulevard, Bishkek 720040 (tel: 610-610; fax: 610-444; e-mail: dkib@demirbank.com.kg).

Eridan, 57 Kalyk-Akieva Street, Bishkek 720001 (tel: 650-610; fax: 650-654; e-mail: eridanbank@infotel.kg).

Kairat, 390 Frunze Street, Bishkek 720033 (tel: 218-932; fax: 218-955; e-mail: kairat@kairatbank.kg).

Kurulush, 28 Manas Street, Bishkek 720391 (tel: 219-736; fax: 219-743; e-mail: kurulush@bank.kg).

Kyrgyzstan, 54 Togolok Moldo Street, Bishkek 720001 (tel: 219-598; fax: 610-220; e-mail: akb@elcat.kg).

Central bank
National Bank of Kyrgyz Republic, 101 Umetalieva St, 720040 Bishkek (tel: 669-011; fax: 669-176; internet: www.nbkr.kg).

Travel information
Airport 'Manas', Bishkek 720062 (tel: 313-593; fax: 313-040; e-mail: manas@ch2m.bishkek.su).

AKC Kyrgyz Concept, 1000 Razzakova Street, Bishkek 720001 (tel 210-556; fax: 660-220; e-mail: akc@mail.elcat.kg).

Kyrgyzstan Aba Joldoru (national airline), Airport 'Manas', Bishkek 720062 (tel: 257-755; fax: 257-162; e-mail: mana@ch2m.bishkek.su).

Kyrgyzstan Airlines (domestic services), Airport 'Manas', Bishkek 720062 (tel: 696-600).

National tourist organisation offices
Kyrgyz State Agency for Tourism and Sport, 17 Togolok Moldo Street, Bishkek 720033 (tel: 220-657; fax: 212-845).

Ministries
Ministry of Agriculture and Water Resources, 96a Kievskaya Street, Bishkek 720040 (tel: 221-435; fax: 226-784).

Ministry of Environmental Protection, 131 Isanova Street, Bishkek 720033 (tel: 219-737; fax: 216-763).

Ministry of Finance, 58 Erkindik Boulevard, Bishkek 720002 (tel: 228-922; fax: 227-404, 620-955).

Ministry of Foreign Affairs, 59 Razzakopva Street, Bishkek 720040 (tel: 220-545; fax: 263-639).

Ministry of Foreign Trade and Industry, 106 Chui Boulevard, Bishkek 720002 (tel: 223-866; fax: 220-793, 252-747).

Ministry of Justice, 37 Orozbekova Street, Bishkek 720040 (tel: 228-489; fax: 261-115).

Ministry of Transport and Telecommunications, Isanova Street, Bishkek 720017 (tel: 216-672; fax: 213-667).

Other useful addresses

British Embassy, 173 Furmanova Street, Alma Ata, Kazakhstan (accredited to Kyrgyzstan) (tel: (7-3272) 506-191; fax: (7-3272) 506-260).

Free Economic Zone General Directorate, 303 Manas Street, Bishkek 720026 (tel: 670-511; fax: 670-512).

Goskominvest (State Committee on Foreign Investments and Economic Co-operation), 58A Erkindik Boulevard, Bishkek 720002 (tel: 223-292; fax: 620-017; e-mail:satc@imfiko.bishkek.su).

Kyrgyzstan Embassy (USA), 1732 Wisconsin Avenue, NW, Washington DC 20007 (tel: (+1-202) 338-5141; fax: (+1-202) 338-5139; e-mail: embassy@kyrgyzstan.org).

Kyrgyzvneshtorg (Foreign Trade Association), 276 Abdymomunova Street, Bishkek 720033 (tel: 215-701; fax: 620-836).

National Statistical Committee of the Kyrgyz Republic, 374 Frunze Street, Bishkek 720033 (tel: 226-363; fax: 220-759; e-mail: zkudabaev@nsc.bishkek.su).

State Property Fund, 57 Erkindik Boulevard, Bishkek 720002, (tel: 227-706; fax: 660-236; e-mail: spf@imfiko.bishkek.su).

Stock Exchange, 172 Moskvskaya Street, Bishkek 720010 (tel:665-059; fax: 661-595; e-mail: kse@kse.kg).

US Embassy, 171 Mira Boulevard, Bishkek 720016 (tel: 551-241; fax: 551-264; e-mail: mukambaevaibx@state.gov).

National news agency: Kabar: http://en.kabar.kg

Other news agencies: AKIpress: www.akipress.com

24.Kg: http://eng.24.kg

Internet sites

The Times of Central Asia: http://www.times.kg

Government of Kyrgyzstan (list of departments in Cyrillic script, email addresses in Latin script): http://kenesh.bishkek.gov.kg/

Laos

KEY FACTS

Official name: Saathiaranarath Prachhathipatay Prachhachhon Lao (Lao People's Democratic Republic)

Head of State: President Choummaly Sayasone (since 8 Jun 2006)

Head of government: Prime Minister Bouasone Bouphavanh (since 8 Jun 2006)

Ruling party: Lao People's Revolutionary Party (LPRP)

Area: 236,800 square km

Population: 6.14 million (2007)*

Capital: Vientiane

Official language: Lao (English is the business language of the Lao government)

Currency: New kip (Nk) = 100 at

Exchange rate: Nk8,632.00 per US$ (Jul 2008)

GDP per capita: US$656 (2007)*

GDP real growth: 7.50% (2007)*

Labour force: 2.93 million (2004)

Unemployment: 2.40% (2005)*

Inflation: 4.50% (2007)

Balance of trade: -US$435.00 million (2006)

Foreign debt: US$3.00 billion (2004)*

Visitor numbers: 672,000 (2005)

* estimated figure

Until it came under the control of the French in the late nineteenth century, Laos was called Lane Xang Hom Khao (One Million Elephants under a White Parasol). Following the ignominious defeat of the French at Dien Bien Phu, the 1954 Geneva Accords granted full independence to Laos. Laos may have gained independence, but not much more as it fell into a civil war which was soon adopted as a proxy East–West conflict, pitting the US and Thailand against Vietnam and the (then) socialist bloc. Poor, underdeveloped Laos soon assumed an exaggerated importance in the geo-political balance as its long-suffering population found themselves on the receiving end of full-scale American bombing sorties. Communist victories in Vietnam and elsewhere left battle-scarred Laos – which had by now become the Lao People's Democratic Republic – little choice but to lick its wounds and count the cost.

Peace, but no dividend

According to World Bank figures, in the 1990s and early 2000s the Lao PDR's economy grew at an annual average rate of 6.3 per cent and the poverty incidence rate had fallen from 46 per cent of the population in 1992–93 to 35 per cent by

2002–03. During the Asian economic crisis at the end of the 1990s Laos' inflation climbed to an annual 110 per cent and growth fell back to 4 per cent. In the 2000s growth resumed at some 6 per cent annually and over the period 2000–06 inflation dropped from over 15 per cent to a more manageable 6 per cent as GDP growth edged up towards 8 per cent.

According to the Asian Development Bank in its 2008 *Asian Development Outlook*, mining and hydropower kept the economy growing at a rapid rate in 2007 and the outlook was for further growth at a more moderate pace in 2008–09. Inflation decelerated to its lowest level in years, although it began to pick up in late 2007. The Lao government has improved trade and investment conditions in its effort to join the World Trade Organisation by 2010. But more needs to be done to spur development of the private sector, as well as agriculture, to boost employment and reduce poverty. In 2007, Laos' GDP growth according to the World Bank remained strong, at over 7 per cent annually. National output expanded in the mining and processing industries, in agriculture, the construction of new hydropower projects and in tourism and other services. Laos benefits from being surrounded by prosperous, fast-growing economies.

According to the ADB, the economy grew by 8.0 per cent in 2007 (a figure one per cent higher than that quoted by the World Bank) and well above the 6.8 per cent average of 2002–06. For a seventh consecutive year, industry recorded double-digit growth (14.0 per cent in 2007), as output from hydropower plants and mining continued to expand. Industry has grown to account for nearly one third of the economy, a result of strong external demand for the country's hydropower and minerals (mainly gold and copper).

The services sector grew by 7.2 per cent in 2007. Tourist arrivals rose by about 15 per cent to an estimated (and record) 1.4 million. Tourism continued to attract significant investment in accommodation and other facilities. Agriculture and forestry, which

support more than four fifths of the population and is still the biggest sector, grew by 2.7 per cent, hurt by drought in some provinces. The expansion of hydropower and mining is underpinned by increasing inflows of foreign direct investment (FDI). Rubber plantations, small-scale manufacturing, and tourism also attracted similar investment. In 2007, gross FDI increased by nearly 20 per cent to US$770 million.

Merchandise exports in nominal terms rose by an estimated 50.6 per cent in 2007, reflecting buoyant exports of copper and gold, which account for about 60 per cent of total exports. Other exports are clothing, electricity, and agricultural products. Imports fell by 1.7 per cent as a result of reduced purchases of heavy machinery as a major hydropower project neared completion, and the closure of some clothing factories, which rely heavily on imported raw materials. A small trade surplus and rising tourism earnings helped narrow the current account deficit to 15.0 per cent of GDP. After inflows of FDI and grants, the overall balance of payments recorded a surplus. External reserves increased by US$203 million to US$530 million by December 2007, equal to almost 6 months of non-resource imports.

Despite the robust economic growth, inflation slowed, averaging 4.5 per cent in 2007. Prices started to pick up in the fourth quarter, though. The decline in inflation partly reflected government subsidies for paddy production and greater efforts at land reform, which stimulated supply of rice. Economic projections are based on the assumptions that the government will maintain its efforts to meet targets of the Sixth Socioeconomic Development Plan 2006–10, which in turn aims to achieve an annual average GDP growth of 7.5–8.0 per cent over the 5 year period.

Robust economic growth is expected in neighbouring trading partners such as China and Thailand should support demand for the country's main exports. The 1,080 megawatt Nam Theun 2 hydropower project is scheduled to be completed in 2009, and construction is under way on several other power projects due to start production between 2011 and 2015. Imports are forecast to rise significantly in 2008 as demand increases for construction materials to build new hydropower and mining projects, and imports of consumer goods increase as a result of reductions in tariffs under Association of Southeast Asian Nations (Asean) Free Trade Area commitments.

The clothing industry has been in decline since the phasing out of quotas in the European Union market in 2004. It is also hurt by rising transportation costs for imported raw materials. Several factories were closed in 2007 and the outlook for the industry is grim. Tourism, though, is expected to maintain solid growth. The performance of agriculture, as usual, depends largely on the weather.

Outlook

The ADB sees Laos' GDP growth edging down to just below 8 per cent in 2008–09. The current account deficit is forecast to remain at over US$500 million, although that would represent a declining percentage of the rising GDP. Inflows of grants and FDI should cover the external financing requirement. Inflation is expected to accelerate to 5–6 per cent in the forecast period because of rising prices for imported goods, including fuel, and the rapid growth in money supply. A value added

KEY INDICATORS — Laos

	Unit	2003	2004	2005	2006	2007
Population	m	5.57	5.69	*5.92	*6.03	*6.14
Gross domestic product (GDP)	US$bn	1.81	2.51	*2.89	3.46	*4.03
GDP per capita	US$	325	416	*487	*573	*656
GDP real growth	%	5.5	6.0	*7.1	8.1	*7.5
Inflation	%	15.5	11.2	7.2	6.8	4.5
Industrial output	% change	–	11.7	16.0	16.5	–
Agricultural output	% change	–	2.9	2.6	2.0	–
Exports (fob) (goods)	US$m	345.0	365.5	*659.0	996.0	–
Imports (cif) (goods)	US$m	555.0	579.5	*1,116.0	1,384.0	–
Balance of trade	US$m	-210.0	-214.0	-457.0	-388.0	–
Current account	US$m	-120.0	-200.0	-576.0	*-435.0	-93.0
Total reserves minus gold	US$m	208.6	223.3	234.3	328.4	532.6
Foreign exchange	US$m	189.5	207.9	220.2	313.7	517.1
Exchange rate	per US$	7,741.00	7,862.00	9,721.00	9,721.00	9,401.50

* estimated figure

tax (VAT) approved in 2006 is expected to be put into effect in 2009.

Risk assessment

Economy	Good
Politics	Fair
Regional stability	Good

COUNTRY PROFILE

Historical profile

Between the fourth and eighth centuries, communities along the Mekong river began to form into townships, called muang.
1353 This development culminated in the formation of the Lane Xang (the million elephants) Kingdom by King FaNgum and established Xieng Thong, now known as Luang Prabang as capital of Lane Xang Kingdom.
1548–71 During the reign of King Setthathirat, the capital was moved to Vientiane. During this period the That Luang Stupa, a venerated religious shrine and a temple to house the Phra Keo, the Emerald Buddha, were constructed.
1641 A Dutch merchant of the East India Company, Geritt Van Wuysthoff established the first European contact with the Kingdom. Later, Italian missionaries visited.
1893 Laos was put under French administration.
1945 Laos was briefly occupied by the Japanese towards the end of the Second World War.
1950 Laos was granted semi-autonomy as an associated state within the French union.
1954 Laos gained independence and became a constitutional monarchy. Civil war began between monarchists and communists of the Pathet Lao.
1960s Laos was subjected to intensive bombing by the US in its war against the North Vietnamese in one of the worst aerial bombardments in world history.
1973 The Vientiane cease-fire agreement led to renewed divisions between royalists and communists.
1975 The Pathet Lao (the Lao Communist movement) won the civil war. The Lao People's Democratic Republic (LDPR) was proclaimed by a National Congress of People's Representatives. Pathet Lao was renamed the Lao People's Revolutionary Party (LPRP), which became the sole legal political party. Kaysone Phomvihane was appointed prime minister and began a policy of socialist transformation of the economy.
1979 The government modified its approach following widespread food shortages and an exodus of Laotian refugees to Thailand.
1986 Laos introduced market reforms, encouraged by Soviet leader Mikhail Gorbachev.
1989 The first elections since 1975 were held, although all candidates had to be vetted by the LPRP. The LPRP retained power.
1991 A security and co-operation pact was signed with Thailand. A new constitution was promulgated. Kaysone Phomvihane became president and General Khamtai Siphandon became prime minister.
1992 President Phomvihane died. Siphandon became head of the LPRP.
1995 A 20-year aid embargo was lifted by the US.
1997 Laos became a member of the Association of South-east Asian Nations (Asean). The Asian financial crisis undermined the value of the kip.
1998 Khamtai Siphandon became president.
2000 Anti-government demonstrations erupted and a series of terrorists bomb blasts killed over a dozen people. Laos celebrated 25 years of communist rule, in December.
2001 Boungnang Vorachith was appointed prime minister and Khamtai was re-elected president. The death penalty was introduced for the possession of more than 500 grammes of heroin. The UN's World Food Programme (WFP) launched a three-year programme to feed 70,000 malnourished children in Laos.
2002 The LPRP was re-elected; Khamtai Siphandon was re-elected president.
2003 As part of reforms pledged to foreign donors in 2000, Laos' one-party parliament began a process of amending its constitution, to decentralise power.
2005 In April the World Bank approved funds for the construction of the US$1.2 billion, Nam Theun Two hydroelectric dam; the foundation stone was laid in November. According to a UN report, the poppy crop in Laos was reduced by 73 per cent since 1998 and the number of opium addicts had fallen by 42,000 to 21,000.
2006 President of the ruling LPRP Khamtay Siphandone resigned and was succeeded by Choummaly Sayasone; Bouasone Bouphavanh was appointed prime minister. A new bridge was opened across the Mekong River in the central region of Savannakhet.
2007 Former General Vang Pao, a leader among the ethnic Hmong people was arresting in the US in July, accused of planning a coup to overthrow the Lao government. The Hmong people backed the US in the Vietnam War during the 1960s and aid agencies in the region have reported that they have been subjected to human right's abuses since then.
2008 Plans to increase the area of forest to 18.7 million hectares were confirmed by the government in July. Deforestation has reduced natural forests from 41 per cent of the country in 2002 to a current 35 per cent, due to changes in agriculture, hydroelectric projects, mining and illegal logging.

Political structure

Constitution

The first constitution was endorsed in August 1991, enshrining the single-party rule of the Lao People's Revolutionary Party (LPRP).
The country is divided into provinces, municipalities, districts and villages. Each of these has a local administrative structure that is subject to the laws and policies of the national government.
Laos' one-party parliament is in the process of amending its constitution in a move towards decentralisation.

The executive

The president, elected by the National Assembly every five years, is the head of state.
The head of government is the prime minister, who is appointed by the president. The Council of Ministers is also appointed by the president.

National legislature

The legislature is unicameral. The Sapha Heng Xat (National Assembly) increased from 109 to 115 members (in 2006), directly elected for a five-year term.
The Lao People's Revolutionary Party (LPRP) Congress meets every five years. The last Congress was held in April 2006.

Last elections

8 June 2006 (presidential); 30 Apr 2006 (parliamentary)
Results: Presidential: Choummaly Sayasone was elected by the National Assembly.
Parliamentary: the Lao People's Revolutionary Party (LPRP) (the only legal party allowed) won 113 seats (out of 115), two independents.

Next elections

2007 (parliamentary); 2011 (presidential)

Political parties

Effective political power is exercised by the leadership of the sole legal political organisation, the Lao People's Revolutionary Party (LPRP).

Ruling party

Lao People's Revolutionary Party (LPRP)

Population

6.14 million (2007)*
Last census: March 1995: 4,574,848
Population density: 23 inhabitants per square km (2000). Urban population: 24 per cent (1995–2001).

Annual growth rate: 2.4 per cent 1994–2004 (WHO 2006)
Ethnic make-up
There are three main ethnic groups: the Lao Loum (lowlanders), the Lao Theung (semi-nomadic people who live mainly on the mountain slopes) and the Lao Soung (hill tribes and minority elements).
Religions
The Lao Theung and the Lao Soung are animist, but the great majority of Lao are Theravada Buddhists; there are some Christians.

Education

Nearly 60 per cent of teachers in primary and secondary schools are underqualified.
Secondary education starts at the age of 11 and is divided into three-year lower secondary school and three-year upper secondary school. Higher education is provided by the National University of Laos, which has merged with 10 higher education institutions located in Vientiane. There are also higher technical institutes and teacher training colleges.
Public expenditure on education typically amounts to 2.1 per cent of annual gross national income. In 2001, the Asian Development Bank approved a US$20 million loan to support a project partly that will enable over 550,000 children, especially girls and ethnic minorities to receive better primary education. The government is expected to fund the balance with the help of other international donors and complete the project by end-2007./10/04
Literacy rate: 66 per cent adult rate; 79 per cent youth rate (15–24) (Unesco 2005).
Compulsory years: Primary education is compulsory between the ages of six and 11.
Enrolment rate: 112 per cent gross primary enrolment of the relevant age group (including repeaters); 29 per cent gross secondary enrolment (World Bank).
Pupils per teacher: 30 in primary schools.

Health

Per capita total expenditure on health (2003) was US$56; of which per capita government spending was US$22, at the international dollar rate, (WHO 2006).
Improved water sources and sanitation facilities are available to 90 per cent and 46 per cent of the population, respectively.
HIV/Aids
HIV/Aids infection is one of the major public health challenges in the country, affecting almost all provinces and populations and is expected to triple in the next 20 years, unless preventive measures are undertaken.
HIV prevalence: 0.1 per cent aged 15–49 in 2003 (World Bank)
Life expectancy: 59 years, 2004 (WHO 2006)
Fertility rate/Maternal mortality rate: 4.7 births per woman, 2004 (WHO 2006); maternal mortality 650 per 100,000 live births (World Bank).
Child (under 5 years) mortality rate (per 1,000): 82 deaths per 1,000 live births; 40 per cent of children under aged five are malnourished (World Bank).

Welfare

About 40 per cent of the population live in poverty. The country is covered under the Asian Development Bank (ADB's) poverty reduction strategy that focusses on rural development, regional integration, human resource development, sustainable environmental management and private sector development. To achieve this, the ADB has lent Lao PDR about US$45—55 million annually on concessional terms for the period 2002–04, in addition to other technical assistance grants. Another US$1 million grant is provided by the Japan Fund for Poverty Reduction to help the landless poor increase their participation in farm-based production.

Main cities

Viangchan (Vientiane) (capital, estimated population 287,579 in 2005), Savannakhet (155,974), Louangphrabang (110,380).

Languages spoken

The adopted business language of the Lao government is English. Widely spoken languages other than Lao are: Thai, English, Vietnamese, Chinese, Russian, German, and to a much lesser extent, French; plus tribal languages.
Official language/s
Lao (English is the business language of the Lao government)

Media

National news agency: KPL (Khaosan Pathet Lao)
Press
Dailies: In Lao, the Vientiane Mai (www.vientianemai.net) is state-run; Pasason (www.pasaxon.org.la) is owned by the Laos Communist Party. In English Vientiane Times (www.vientianetimes.org.la) is published biweekly and in French Le Renovateur (www.lerenovateur.org.la) are both state-owned.
Broadcasting
Lao National Radio (www.lnr.org.la) operates two nationwide stations FM1–2, relayed by satellite on FM and AM frequencies. Foreign radio can also be received. Although all domestic Lao National TV (TVNL) is owned by the state viewers have unrestricted access to foreign TV via satellite and internet channels.

Economy

Laos is one of the poorest countries in the world. A third of the population exists outside the money economy and 80 per cent depend on subsistence agriculture; rice production accounts for around 45 per cent of GDP.
Laos remains heavily dependent on aid, with the largest multilateral donor, the Asian Development Bank (ADB), lending around US$80 million annually and the World Bank providing US$40 million. Total foreign assistance amounts to approximately US$250 million a year and accounts for over 20 per cent of GDP and over 60 per cent of the capital budget.
Laos had moved away from a centrally controlled economy to a market orientated system in 1986, with the introduction of the New Economic Mechanism (NEM), which allowed farmers to own land and sell produce at market prices as state-owned firms lost their subsidies and fixed prices. Structural reforms included real market exchange rates, removal of trade barriers and import tariffs and free access to imports and credit for the private sector. As part of the agreement with the World Bank, Laos agreed to expand its fiscal and monetary reforms, privatise state firms and strengthen the role and organisation of the banking sector. In return, investment, particularly in several hydroelectric power plants has been key in returning revenue to the government, from exports of energy.
Despite the economic reforms, the economy is still burdened by its low productivity, poor infrastructure and a dominant public sector. Tourism is beginning to have a marked impact as its share of GDP increases and has become an important source of foreign exchange.

External trade

Laos belongs to the Association of South East Asian (Asean) Free Trade Area (Afta) and maintains a list of goods that have preferential import duties between members and a programme of tariff reductions due to be introduced in the next few years. In 2007, Laos did not belong to the WTO although it has begun negotiations to join.
There are transit agreements with Vietnam, Cambodia and Thailand allowing cargo, by bonded customs carriers, to pass by cross-border highways from the coast to landlocked Laos.
Imports
Principal imports are vehicles, capital goods, food and consumer goods.
Main sources: Thailand (69.0 per cent total, 2006), China (11.4 per cent), Vietnam (5.6 per cent).

Exports
Principal exports are electricity (typically 40 per cent of total), garment and small-scale manufacturing, timber products, coffee and tin.
Main destinations: Thailand (41.3 per cent total, 2006), Vietnam (9.7 per cent), China (4.1 per cent).

Agriculture
Agriculture contributes around 47 per cent of GDP and employs over 80 per cent of the workforce.
Rice, the main crop, is cultivated in irrigated lowland paddies and on drier hill farms.
Other crops include maize, sweet potatoes, cassava, pulses, groundnuts, fruit, vegetables, sugar cane, coffee, tobacco and cotton. Livestock raised includes cattle, buffaloes, pigs, goats and poultry.
Crop production in 2005 included: 2,560,000 tonnes (t) cereals in total, 2,350,000t rice, 210,000t maize, 60,000t cassava, 248,000t sweet potatoes, 48,000t bananas, 16,500t pulses, 70,500t citrus fruit, 9,632t oilcrops, 34,500t tobacco, 23,400t green coffee, 230,000t sugar cane, 350t tea, 7,000t seed cotton, 2,333t cotton lint, 206,100t fruit in total, 774,600t vegetables in total.
Livestock production included: 89,291t meat in total, 22,500t beef, 18,623t buffalo meat, 28,000t pig meat, 518t goat meat, 19,650t poultry, 12,805t eggs, 1,973t cattle hides.

Forestry
Exports of forest materials in 2004 were US$62.7 million, while imports amounted to US$1.7 million.
Plans to increase the area of forest to 18.7 million hectares were confirmed by the government in July 2008. Deforestation has reduced natural forests from 41 per cent of the country in 2002 to a current 35 per cent, due to changes in agriculture, hydroelectric projects, mining and illegal logging.
Production in 2004 included 6,320,214 cubic metres (cum) roundwood, 392,000cum industrial roundwood, 182,000cum sawnwood, 13,000cum wood-based panels, 260,000cum sawlogs and veneers, 5,928,214 cum wood fuel;18,486t charcoal.

Industry and manufacturing
The industrial sector accounts for around 27 per cent of GDP and employs over 10 per cent of the workforce.
There is no heavy industry. The production of tin concentrates is the main industrial activity. Other major industries include textiles, bricks, cement, minerals and hydroelectricity.
Small-scale manufacturing industries produce beer, cigarettes, detergents, rubber footwear, plywood, matches, salt, animal feed, veterinary products, handicrafts, alcoholic beverages and soft drinks.
The growth sectors are garments, wood products, handicrafts and light industry, including vehicle assembly.

Tourism
Tourism is an increasingly important contributor to GDP and the balance of payments. The sector has strengthened steadily since the mid-1990s. There were 894,000 arrivals in 2004, an increase of 33 per cent over 2003. Around three-quarters of visitors came from the region, with Thailand in the lead. Tourism is expected to contribute 5.5 per cent to GDP in 2005.

Mining
Mining together with hydrocarbons contributes around 5 per cent to GDP. The sector employs 1 per cent of the workforce.
As with other economic sectors in Laos, resources have not been optimised because of bureaucracy, lack of infrastructure and inefficiency.
Principal minerals include tin, high-grade iron ore, gold, copper, potash, limestone, manganese, lead, zinc, gypsum and bauxite.
There is great potential for the extraction of gold, and explorations have been conducted by Pan Australian and CRA Exploration of Australia (a subsidiary of Rio Tinto Zinc), both in joint ventures with the Laos government. Commercial interest in gold mining has surged following the success of the Sepon project – 80 per cent Oxiana Resources and 20 per cent Rio Tinto – which started gold and copper production in 2003.

Hydrocarbons
Laos does not produce any hydrocarbons. It relies on imports of petroleum products to meet domestic consumption levels. Laos does not import either coal or natural gas. Several Thai companies are developing open-cast lignite mines.

Energy
Laos has installed electricity generating capacity of 700MW, supplied mainly by hydropower. Supply is restricted mainly to the capital. Laos exports electricity to its neighbours, mainly Thailand and China. The government envisages expansion of capacity by constructing more dams around Laos over time as a means of earning revenue from increased exports of electricity. In 2005, construction began on the World Bank-supported but controversial Nam Theu Two hydropower project, which will add 1,070MW to capacity, much of which will be exported to Thailand; it is expected to be completed by 2009.
The Asian Development Bank puts Laos' hydropower potential at 18,000MW, which could earn around US$20 billion a year.

Banking and insurance
Since the early 1990s, the number of banks in Laos has more than doubled, with a corresponding rise in business. There are eight state-run commercial banks, two joint venture banks, seven foreign banks and 32 private non-bank foreign exchange bureaux operating in Laos. Banks are gradually adopting commercial lending practices. Restructuring from September 2002 includes the phased recapitalisation of the state commercial banks, the merger of two smaller banks and a rationalisation of banking operations.

Central bank
Banque de la RDP Lao (Bank of Lao PDR)

Time
GMT plus seven hours

Geography
Laos is a landlocked country in south-east Asia, bordered by the People's Republic of China to the north, Vietnam to the east, Cambodia to the south, Thailand to the west and Myanmar (Burma) to the north-west.
It is largely a mountainous country with the Annam Range running like a spine down the length of the country producing a natural barrier, with only three mountain passes into Vietnam. The highest mountain is Pou Bia at 2,817m in the northern central region. In the south and west, along the Mekong River, large alluvial plains provide much of the country's agricultural produce. The Mekong runs for 1,805km through Laos and provides much of its border with Thailand.

Hemisphere
Northern

Climate
Most of the year is hot and humid. The climate is monsoonal and has three distinct seasons. The hot dry season begins in February, with temperatures up to 40 degrees Celsius (C), only broken by the odd shower of rain. A build-up of storm activity in April–May with increasing humidity heralds the wet season during June–October, typified by a more consistent pattern of rain and cloudy days through June, July and August. There can be as much as 250mm rainfall per month. Temperatures average 29 degrees C. During this time, the Mekong River rises and flooding of the surrounding area is not uncommon. The cool, dry season arrives in November with lower temperatures and reduced humidity. Average temperature may drop to 14–15 degrees C. The cool weather can continue until

February. Always cooler in the mountains, especially at night.

Entry requirements
Passports
Required by all, valid for six months beyond departure date.
Visa
Tourist visas are only obtained abroad through a Laotian consulate or accredited tour operator and must be used within two months. However they can be issued for immediate use at most ports of entry for periods of up to 15 days. Business visas are only issued from Laos and require a completed application form with a letter of invitation from a local company or entity. Further information should be sought through the nearest embassy.
Currency advice/regulations
Import and export of local currency is prohibited; there are no restrictions on foreign currency but amounts over US$2,000 must be declared.
Travellers cheques are not widely accepted, the Thai baht and US dollar are easiest to exchange.
Customs
It is forbidden to take any antiques or Buddha images over 50-years-old out of the country. Such items brought into Laos from other countries have to be declared at Customs.

Health (for visitors)
Laos has few hospitals and medical facilities.
Mandatory precautions
Vaccination certificates for yellow fever if travelling from an infected area.
Advisable precautions
Anti-malaria precautions; malaria is endemic in many areas of Laos but is not found in Vientiane. Mosquito repellent is recommended as dengue fever can be caught in Vientiane all year round. Immunisations against diphtheria, hepatitis A and B, Japanese B encephalitis, TB, tetanus, polio and typhoid. Rabies is a health risk.
Comprehensive health insurance, including provision for air evacuation, is strongly advised.

Hotels
The hotel sector is at an early stage of development and is at present restricted mainly to Vientiane, Luang Prabang and Vang Vieng, where there are a number of tourist-standard and luxury hotels. Visitor accommodation around the country is in short supply, the main resource being village hostels and guesthouses, where available.

Credit cards
Major credit cards are accepted by main hotels and some restaurants. The handling fee of 1.5–3.0 per cent is generally passed on to the customer.

Public holidays (national)
Fixed dates
1–2 Jan (New Year's Day/National Day), 6 Jan (Pathet Lao Day), 20 Jan (Army Day), 8 Mar (Women's Day), 22 Mar (People's Party Day), 13–15 Apr (Lao New Year), 1 May (Labour Day), 1 Jun (Children's Day), 13 Aug (Day of the Free Laos), 12 Oct (Day of Liberation), 2 Dec (Republic Day).
Variable dates
Chinese New Year (Feb), Birth of Buddha (May), Buddhist Fast begins (Jun/Jul), Buddhist Fast ends (Oct).

Working hours
Banking
Mon–Fri: 0800–1200, 1330–1730.
Business
Mon–Sat: 0800–1200, 1300–1600.
Government
Mon–Sat: 0800–1200, 1400–1700.
Some ministries close at 1130 for lunch; others work a half-day Saturday.
Shops
(Mon–Sun) 0900–1700.

Telecommunications
Mobile/cell phones
There are GSM 900/1800 services available in major cities only.

Electricity supply
220V 50Hz. Power outlets are two-prong round or flat sockets.

Weights and measures
Metric system (local units also in use).

Social customs/useful tips
The generally accepted form of greeting among Lao people is the nop, performed by placing one's palms together in a position of praying at chest level, but not touching the body. The higher the hands, the greater the sign of respect. Nonetheless, the hands should not be held above the level of the nose. The nop is accompanied by a slight bow to show respect to persons of higher status and age. It is also used as an expression of thanks, regret or saying goodbye. But with Western people, it is acceptable to shake hands.
Since the head is considered the most sacred part of the body and the soles of the feet the least, one should not touch a person's head nor use one's foot to point at a person or any object. It is forbidden for a woman to touch a Buddhist monk.
Men and women rarely show affection in public.

Getting there
Air
National airline: Lao Airlines
International airport/s: Vientiane-Wattay International Airpirt (VTE), 4km from city centre.
Airport tax: Departure tax US$10
Surface
Road: The Mitraphap (Friendship) Bridge over the Mekong River at Nong Khai, situated 14km east of Vientiane, provides the first modern road link with Thailand. It also gave Laos road access to a port for the first time.
There are road crossings from all surrounding countries, although the roads via Cambodia and Myanmar are not recommended due to poor security. Road No 1 runs from Thailand, through Laos, to China; road No 9 runs from Thailand, through Laos, to Vietnam.
Major infrastructure and construction of the Chiang Rai-Kunming Road Improvement Project is underway. When complete, it will involve over 1,220km of road along the north axis of the subregion, and will provide road links from Yunnan Province, Laos, to Bangkok in Thailand.
Rail: A railway line runs up to the border of Laos near Vientiane, although it does not run in Laos.
Water: From Kunming or Xishuangbanna, China, it is possible to travel by boat along the Mekong river south into Bokeo Province.

Getting about
National transport
It is relatively easy to travel in northern Laos but in the south, public transport is extremely erratic.
Air: Travel by air is the most convenient means of transportation within Laos. Lao Aviation flies daily from Vientiane to Luang Prabang, Savannakhet, Xieng Khouang, Pakse and Oudomsay. There are several flights a week to Luang Namtha, Sayaboury, Houeixay, Sam Neua, Saravane, Lak Xao, Muangkhong and Attapeu.
Road: Laos has 18,153km of national roads, 2,500km of which are paved. The most important road is route No 13 which runs north-south from China to Cambodia. It links Pak Mong in the north with Khong in the south, passing through major urban areas of Luang Prabang, Vientiane, Savannakhet and Champassack.
Buses: There are services between main centres.
Rail: A line from Vientiane to Nong Khai is operating, including air-conditioned coaches.
Water: River transport is important, especially on the Mekong River, which flows through 1,865km of Laos.
City transport
The easiest way to travel around town is with a car and driver, usually arranged through your hotel.

Taxis: Three-wheeled tuk-tuk (motorcycle taxis) are easily found.

Taxis are available in Vientiane, but often operate along certain routes in the manner of buses. Individual hire may require negotiation. Tipping is discouraged.

Car hire

Arrangements are generally made through hotels.

BUSINESS DIRECTORY

The addresses listed below are a selection only. While World of Information makes every endeavour to check these addresses, we cannot guarantee that changes have not been made, especially to telephone numbers and area codes. We would welcome any corrections.

Telephone area codes

The international dialling code (IDD) for Laos is +856 followed by area code (Vientiane only) and subscriber's number: Vientiane21

Useful telephone numbers

Police: 191
Police (Immigration Office) emergency number: 212-520
Fire: 190
Ambulance: 195
International Medical Clinic: 214-018, 214-022, 214-025

Chambers of Commerce

Lao National Chamber of Commerce, Phonphanao village Saysettha, PO Box 4596, Vientiane (tel: 452-579, 453-311; fax: 452-580; e-mail: laocci@laotel.com).

Banking

Banque de la République Democratique Populaire Lao, PO Box 19, Rue Yonnet, Vientiane (tel: 213-109, 213-110; fax: 213-108).

Banque Pour Le Commerce Exterieur La; PO Box 2925, N 1 Pang Kham Rd, Vientiane (tel: 213-200; fax: 213-202).

Joint Development Bank Ltd; 75/15 Lane Xang Ave, Vientiane (tel: 213-536; fax: 213-530).

Lane Xang Bank Ltd; 6-80 Setthathiilath, Vientiane (tel: 213-400, 212-186, 212-108, 212-105; fax: 213-404).

Vientiane Commercial Bank Ltd; 33 Lane Xang Ave, Hatsady, Chanthaboury, Vientiane (tel: 222-700; fax: 213-513).

Central bank

Banque de la République Democratique Populaire Lao, PO Box 19, Rue Yonnet, Vientiane (tel: 213-109; fax: 213-108; e-mail: bol@pan-laos.net.la).

Travel information

Lao Aviation, 2 Pangkham Road, PO Box 4169, Vientiane (tel: 212-055; fax: 212-056).

Ministry of tourism

Ministry of Trade and Tourism, Vientiane (tel: 412-003, 412-436; fax: 412-434).

National tourist organisation offices

National Tourism Authority of Lao PDR, PO Box 3556, PO Box 3556, Lane Xang Avenue, Vientiane (tel: 212-248, 212-251; fax: 212-769).

Ministries

Department of Foreign Trade, Ministry of Industry and Commerce, Vientiane.

Ministry of Agriculture and Forestry, Vientiane (tel: 412-358).

Ministry of Commerce and Tourism, Vientiane (tel: 107-484).

Ministry of Communications, Transport, Post and Construction, Vientiane (tel: 412-281); Foreign Relations Department (tel: 412-267).

Ministry of Defence, Vientiane (tel: 412-803); Foreign Relations Departments (tel: 412-805, 412-810).

Ministry of Education, Vientiane (tel: 216-000); Foreign Relations Department (tel: 216-005).

Ministry of External Economic Relations, Foreign Investment Adviser, Vientiane (tel: 169-804).

Ministry of Finance, Vientiane (tel: 412-142, 412-404, 412-417).

Ministry of Foreign Affairs, Vientiane (tel: 414-002, 414-003).

Ministry of Industry and Handicrafts, Vientiane (tel: 413-000, 413-004, 413-006); (Electricity Division) (tel: 413-010; fax: 413-013); (Industry Division) (tel: 414-332); (Geology and Mines Division) (tel: 212-080, 212-082; fax: 222-539).

Ministry of Information and Culture, Vientiane (tel: 212-898, 212-402); (Foreign Relations Director) (tel: 212-409).

Ministry of the Interior, Vientiane (tel: 212-503, 212-501); (Foreign Relations Division) (tel: 212-554).

Ministry of Justice, Vientiane (tel: 414-101).

Ministry of Labour and Social Welfare, Vientiane (tel: 213-001, 213-002).

Ministry of Public Health, Vientiane (tel: 412-985, 214-046).

Other useful addresses

ASEAN Investment Promotion Agency, Foreign Investment Management Committee in charge of Promotion Administration and Investment Services, Luang Prabang Road, Vientiane (tel: 216-663; fax: 215-491).

ASEAN Secretariat, 70 A J1 Sisingamangaraja, Jakarta 12110, Indonesia (tel: (+62-21) 726-2991, 724-3372; fax: (+62-21) 724-3504, 739-8234; e-mail: asean.or.id).

British Embassy, Commercial Section, 1031 Wireless Road, Bangkok 10330, Thailand (tel: (+66-2) 253-0191; fax: (+66-2) 255-8619).

British Trade Office, Vientiane, Pandit J Nehru Road, PO Box 6626, Vientiane (tel: 413-606; fax: 413-607).

Foreign Investment Management Committee, Luang Prabang Road, Vientiane (tel: 216-662, 216-663, 217-009, 217-018); fax: 215-491, 217-007, 217-013).

Lao Embassy (USA), 2222 S Street, NW, Washington DC 20008 (tel: (+1-202) 332-6416; fax: (+1-202) 332-4923).

Lao Import-Export Company, 43-47 Lanexang Road, Vientiane.

Lao National Radio, Vientiane (tel: 212-428, 212-429, 212-431, 212-430).

Lao National Television Channel 9, Vientiane (tel: 412-182).

Lao Water Authority, Commercial Division, Vientiane (tel: 412-885; fax: 414-378).

United Nations Development Programme (UNDP), Phon Kheng Road, PO Box 345, Vientiane (tel: 4101, 5605; fax: 5001).

US Embassy, Thatdam Bartholonie Road, Bane Thatdam, Vientiane (tel: 213-966, 212-581, 212-582, 212-585).

National news agency: KPL (Khaosan Pathet Lao)

Internet sites

Asian Development Bank: http://www.adb.org/lrm

Laos Business Centre: http://www.asiadragons.com/

Laos website: http://laos.asiaco.com/

Web directory: http://www.angelfire.com/ca/laoscom/

Web directory: http://www.laoworld.com/

Worldwide Gazeteer — Laos: http://www.c-allen.dircon.co.uk/Countries/Laos.htm

Latvia

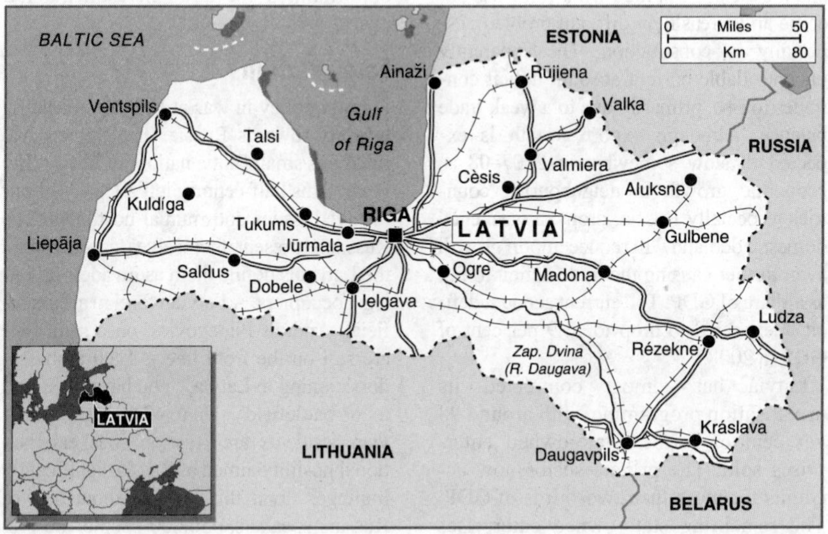

In the final quarter of 2007 Latvia's gross domestic product (GDP) growth, according to Latvijas Statistika, was revised down to 8 per cent. However, taken at constant prices, Latvia's GDP actually declined between the third and fourth quarters of 2007, by an estimated 0.23 per cent. When seen against the backdrop that in the third quarter of 2007 the Latvian economy was still growing at a quarterly rate of 2.8 per cent (or around 11 per cent at an annualised rate) meant that to proceed from this to an annualised negative growth rate of around 1 per cent represented rapid deceleration. This raised the question as to whether Latvia had, by the end of 2007, actually gone in to recession. Some analysts considered that Latvia, probably in the company of other Baltic states, had already indeed gone into recession.

Politics

Following the collapse of the Emsis government in October 2004, Aigars Kalvitis (Tautas Partija (TP) (People's Party)) succeeded in drawing together a broad centre-right coalition consisting of the TP, the Zaïo un Zemnieku Savienîba (ZZS) (Greens and Farmers Union), Latvijas Pirmâ Partija (LPP) (Latvia's First Party) and Jaunais Laiks (JL) (New Era). The new government, the third since the October 2002 parliamentary election, took office in December 2004. Given the size of the coalition as well as ideological and personality differences between the parties, the coalition remained unstable and divided. In April 2006, New Era, Latvia's leading anti-corruption party, left the coalition after Prime Minister Kalvitis had rejected its demand to expel the LPP from the coalition following a corruption scandal. The remaining three party coalition continued as a minority government until October 2006, the end of the mandate period.

In the October 2006 election, the ruling coalition won a slim majority of one parliamentary seat but chose to consolidate their majority by inviting the nationalistic Tevzemei un Brivibai/LNNK (TB/LNNK) (For Fatherland and Freedom/LNNK) to join the coalition. The coalition government continued to be led by Mr Aigars Kalvitis. This was the first time a sitting government had been re-elected in Latvia and was taken to be a sign that domestic politics were becoming more stable.

In the May 2007 presidential elections the parliament elected Valdis Zatlers as president with 59 votes, Aivars Endzins won 39 votes. President Zatlers took office on 8 July.

KEY FACTS

Official name: Latvijas Republika (Republic of Latvia)

Head of State: President Valdis Zatlers (from 8 July 2007)

Head of government: Prime Minister Aigars Kalvitis (since 2004; re-elected 2006)

Ruling party: Coalition government, comprising Tautas Partija (TP) (People's Party), Latvijas Pirmâ Partija (LPP) (Latvia's First Party) and Zaïo un Zemnieku Savienîba (ZZS) (Union of Greens and Farmers) Apvienîba Tçvzemei un Brîvîbai/Latvijas Nacionala Konservativa Partija (TB/LNNK) (Union for the Fatherland and Freedom/Latvian National Conservative Party) (since 2002; re-elected 7 October 2006)

Area: 64,589 square km

Population: 2.28 million (2007)*

Capital: Riga

Official language: Lettish

Currency: Lats (Ls) = 100 santims

Exchange rate: Ls0.44 per US$ (Jul 2008)

GDP per capita: US$11,985 (2007)*

GDP real growth: 10.20% (2007)*

Labour force: 1.30 million (2004)

Unemployment: 8.80% (2004)

Inflation: 10.10% (2007)*

Balance of trade: -US$2.97 billion (2005)

Foreign debt: US$7.37 billion (2004)

Annual FDI: US$4.00 billion

* estimated figure

In November 2007 Aleksejs Loskutovs, a leading anti-corruption investigator was sacked. In an interview he commented that the reason for his arrest 'has to be the good results of our work'. Large street demonstrations resulted in his reinstatement. On 5 December Prime Minister Kalvitis resigned amid allegations of corruption and Ivars Godmanis was appointed prime minister.

Economy

Latvia's economic growth outstripped that of other new European Union (EU) members while – at least until 2003 – inflation remained subdued. GDP growth in 2007 was 10.2 per cent, after a temporary rise in 2006 of 11.9 per cent . Sound macro-economic policies and far reaching economic reforms, re-enforced by Latvia's accession to the EU in 2004 and entry into the Exchange Rate Mechanism 2 (ERM2) in April 2005, have supported this performance. Despite these advances, Latvia's annual gross domestic product (GDP) per capita (US$11,985 in 2007) remains one of the lowest in the EU. This, combined with the rising inflation rate (10.1 per cent in 2007), higher current account deficits and sharply expanding gross external debt is enough to give the International Monetary Fund (IMF) cause for concern. Strong inflation still risks hindering progression to the single currency. The Maastricht treaty sets maximum inflation levels at 1.5 per cent more than the average of the bottom three inflation rates among EU countries. Currently, this would equate to about 3.5 per cent, well below Latvia's high rates. The inflation rate, along with rising wages, could also jeopardise the country's competitiveness.

Latvia's unemployment rate has dropped steadily since 2000 and was estimated at 5.2 per cent in 2006, declining further in 2007. Latvia has experienced large scale emigration since the country joined the EU in 2004, and the lack of a skilled work force has become an increasingly difficult problem, especially in construction. The apparently uncontrollable current account deficit continues to rise, primarily due to a weak trade balance. Although export growth is expected to slow somewhat in 2007–08 as economic growth in neighbouring countries, especially Russia, drops, a weakened domestic demand will reduce import growth even further causing the trade deficit to fall as a share of GDP. The current account deficit is expected to drop to 11.9 per cent of GDP in 2008.

Latvia has almost completed its privatisation programme, with around 98 per cent of former state-owned enterprises sold. The private sector now accounts for more than two-thirds of GDP. The remaining state-owned enterprises are mainly large infrastructure companies. Many of these enterprises operate at a loss, thus dragging down their potential sale price. Terms and conditions for privatisation have been drafted for the oil transit firm Ventspils Nafta but for as long as Russia continues to block the flow of Russian oil through the pipeline to Ventspils port, the government will have difficulty in attracting suitable investors.

Latvia has attracted substantial foreign direct investment (FDI) since independence, with Denmark being the biggest investor. In 2006 the net inflow of FDI was around US$530 million, accounting for approximately 30 per cent of GDP. FDI is expected to drop to in 2007 and 2008 as opportunities for large investments fall away.

KEY INDICATORS — Latvia

	Unit	2003	2004	2005	2006	2007
Population	m	2.30	2.26	2.31	2.29	*2.28
Gross domestic product (GDP)	US$bn	9.70	13.63	15.83	20.10	*27.34
GDP per capita	US$	4,078	5,822	6,862	8,760	*11,985
GDP real growth	%	7.5	8.0	10.2	11.9	*10.2
Inflation	%	2.7	6.3	6.7	6.5	*10.1
Unemployment	%	8.7	8.8	8.9	6.8	6.0
Exports (fob) (goods)	US$m	2,743.0	4,185.0	5,306.0	6,140.0	8,143.0
Imports (cif) (goods)	US$m	3,921.0	6,935.0	8,272.0	11,271.0	14,822.0
Balance of trade	US$m	-1,178.0	-2,749.0	-2,966.0	-5,131.0	-6,679.0
Current account	US$m	-910.0	-1,680.0	-2,010.0	-4,479.0	-6,381.0
Total reserves minus gold	US$m	1,432.4	1,912.0	2,232.1	4,353.4	5,553.4
Foreign exchange	US$m	1,432.2	1,911.7	2,231.9	4,353.1	5,553.3
Foreign direct investment (FDI)	US$bn	–	0.7	4.0	–	–
Exchange rate	per US$	0.56	0.52	0.54	0.54	0.48

* estimated figure

Foreign affairs

Foreign policy in was at first dominated by hostility towards Russia. The Soviets had ruled this small Baltic nation for nearly fifty years. This half-century left a legacy of unresolved issues and mutual hostilities. The Russians present themselves as liberators; the Latvians define them as invaders and illegal occupiers. A Latvian foreign affairs official, Andrejs Pildegovics, once said, 'We are still on the front line… I tell ambassadors coming to Latvia, 'You have been sent to the battlefield''. Up to 40 per cent of Latvian residents are Russian speakers. National hostility aimed at Russia significantly impinges upon this group. About half of Russian speakers, 450,000 people, are precluded citizenship and the right to vote, be a teacher or civil servant, because they have not passed, or have refused to sit, an official language and history test. One of the questions in this test requires the candidate to acknowledge that Latvia was occupied by Russia.

Looking West

Having joined the EU in 2004, on 20 December 2008 Latvia became a member of the Schengen Area whereby all travellers may cross EU borders without a passport or visa, and then on 12 March, it signed an agreement with the US for visa-free visits of citizens to the US. Also in early 2008 the parliament approved the EU's Lisbon Treaty for community constitutional reforms.

The US is an important ally for a country with a population of only some 2.28 million. The EU, however, has maintained a discrete distance, not wishing to jeopardise its relations with Russia.

Risk assessment

Politics	Good
Economy	Slowing
Regional stability	Good

COUNTRY PROFILE

Historical profile

Before being occupied by the Germans in the thirteenth century, Latvia had been an

important Baltic trading route and was a largely feudal and tribal society.
1561 Latvia came under Polish rule after the Livonian Order appealed to Poland-Lithuania for protection from Russia's Ivan the Terrible.
1620s Following the Polish-Swedish war, most of Latvia came under Swedish rule, except Courland in western Latvia where the dukes of Jelgava maintained allegiance to Poland until 1709.
1700–21 Russia's Peter the Great destroyed Swedish power in the Great Northern War. Latvia became part of the Russian empire.
1795 Apart from a brief period of French occupation in 1812, Courland was under Russian control until 1915 when the Germans occupied the province.
1914–18 During the First World War, Latvia alternated between Russian and German control five times. It was under Bolshevik Russian control in late 1918 by which time Latvian independence had been declared by nationalists.
1919 Joint British and German forces expelled Bolshevik Russian forces and democratic rule was introduced.
1922 A constitutional parliament, with proportional representation, was adopted.
1934–39 Prime Minister Karlis Ulmanis declared a state of emergency, suspended parliament and banned all political parties. In 1936, he assumed the title of president, becoming an autocratic ruler.
1939 Through the German and Soviet Ribbentrop-Molotov pact, Latvia was forcibly incorporated back into the Soviet Union.
1940 Latvia was incorporated as a constituent republic of the USSR.
1941 The Germans invaded and occupied Latvia.
1944 The Soviet Union liberated Latvia from German rule.
1945–80s The mass deportation to Siberia of Latvian citizens by Stalin, following the war, resulted in an influx of Russian nationals as the Soviet Union introduced collective farming and developed heavy industries in the country.
1991 Soviet troops were deployed in Riga after multi-party elections had removed the Latvijas Komunistiska Partija (LKP) (Latvian Communist Party) from office the previous year. Following the Soviet Union's withdrawal due to international pressure, Latvia declared its independence.
Anatolijs Gorbunov of the Latvijas Tautas Fronte (LTF) (Latvian Popular Front) became head of state as chairman of the Latvian Supreme Council. Ivars Godmanis, also of the LTF, became head of government as the chairman of the Council of Ministers.
1993 A coalition led by Latvijas Cels (LC) (Latvia's Way) formed a government with the Latvijas Zemnieku Savienîa (LZS) (Latvian Farmers' Union). The 1922 Satversme (constitution) was fully reinstituted. Guntis Ulmanis of the LZS was elected the first post-Soviet Latvian president. The LC's Valdis Birkavs was appointed prime minister.
1995 Parliamentary elections led to political turmoil as the ruling LC lost its dominant position and no single party held a majority. A six-party coalition government was eventually formed, dominated by the two largest parties, the centrist LC and the left-wing Democrâtiskâ Partija 'Saimnieks' (DPS) (Master Democratic Party). After wrangling and negotiation, Andris Skele of the LC was appointed prime minister.
1996 President Ulmanis was re-elected by the Saeima (parliament) for a second term of four years.
1998 Latvians narrowly backed the liberalisation of the country's citizenship laws in a referendum held alongside general elections. A centre-right coalition was formed, with Vilis Kristopans of the LC as prime minister.
1999 Latvia became a member of the World Trade Organisation (WTO), the first of the Baltic states to join. Independent Vaira Vike-Freiberga was elected president. The minority centre-left coalition headed by Vilis Kristopans fell and a majority coalition government was formed under Prime Minister Andris Skele.
2000 Skele's coalition collapsed over plans to privatise the Latvian Shipping Company (Lasco).
2002 The president invited Einars Repše and his Jaunais Laiks (JL) (New Era) to formed a coalition government following the general elections. It included Latvijas Pirmâ Partija (LPP) (Latvia's First Party), Zaïo un Zemnieku Savienîba (ZSS) (Green and Farmers Union) and the Apvienîba Tçvzemei un Brîvîbai'/Latvijas Nacionala Konservativa Partija (TB/LNNK) (Union for the Fatherland and Freedom/Latvian National Conservative Party).
2003 President Vaira Vike-Freiberga was re-elected. In a referendum 67 per cent voted to join the EU.
2004 The ruling coalition collapsed; Prime Minister Repše's resigned. Indulis Emsis (ZZS) became prime minister and formed a minority coalition government. Latvia joined NATO and the EU. The government's draft budget was rejected and Emsis resigned. Aigars Kalvitis became prime minister.
2005 A EU constitution was ratified by parliament.
2006 Citizenship laws were seen as more pressure on the minority Russian community. The ruling coalition won a majority in parliamentary elections.
2007 In March, Latvia signed a treaty with Russia defining their mutual border. In May the parliament elected Valdis Zatlers as president with 59 votes, Aivars Endzins won 39 votes. President Zatler took office on 8 July. Aleksijs Loskutovs, a leading anti-corruption investigator was sacked; large street demonstrations resulted in his reinstatement. Prime Minister Kalvitis resigned on 5 December amid allegations of corruption and Ivars Godmanis was appointed prime minister. On 20 December Latvia became a member of the European Union Schengen area whereby all travellers may cross borders without a passport or visa.
2008 An agreement for visa-free visits of citizens to the US was signed on 12 March. The parliament approved the EU's Lisbon Treaty for community constitutional reforms.

Political structure

Constitution

In 1993, the Constitutional Law supplemented the 1922 constitution. The constitution provides for basic rights and freedoms.

Latvian citizens 18 years and over and those resident in Latvia before 27 June 1940, are eligible to vote.

Form of state

Parliamentary democratic republic

The executive

Executive powers are vested in the Cabinet of Ministers, nominated by the prime minister and appointed by and accountable to, parliament. The Cabinet of Ministers is led by the prime minister, who is appointed by the president.

The president is elected by parliament for a four-year term.

National legislature

Legislative authority is vested in a 100-member unicameral Saeima (parliament), directly elected for a four-year term by proportional representation.

Parties must receive at least 5 per cent of the national vote to gain seats in the Saeima.

Legal system

The legal system is based on a civil law system. The appointment of judges to the Supreme Court is confirmed by the Saiema.

Last elections

31 May 2007 (presidential); 7 October 2006 (parliamentary).

Results: Presidential: President Vaira Vike-Freiberga was re-elected by a vote of 88–6 in parliament.

Parliamentary: Tautas Partija (TP) (People's Party) won 23 out of 100 seats; Zaïo un Zemnieku Savienîba (ZZS) (Greens and Farmers Union) 18; Jaunais Laiks (JL) (New Era) 18; Tautas Saskanas Partija (TSP) (People's Harmony Party) 17; Latvijas Pirmâ Partija (LPP) (Latvia's First Party) 10; Tevzemei un Brivibai/LNNK

(TB/LNNK) (For Fatherland and Freedom/LNNK) 8; Par Cilvçka Tiesibam Vienota Latvija (PCTVL) (For Human Rights in a United Latvia) 6. Turnout was 62.2 per cent.

Next elections

2010 (parliamentary)

Political parties

Ruling party

Coalition government, comprising Tautas Partija (TP) (People's Party), Latvijas Pirmâ Partija (LPP) (Latvia's First Party) and Zaïo un Zemnieku Savienîba (ZZS) (Union of Greens and Farmers) Apvienîba Tçvzemei un Brîvîbai/Latvijas Nacionala Konservativa Partija (TB/LNNK) (Union for the Fatherland and Freedom/Latvian National Conservative Party) (since 2002; re-elected 7 October 2006)

Main opposition party

Jaunais Laiks (JL) (New Era)

Population

2.28 million (2007)*

Last census: March 2000: 2,377,383

Population density: 37.5 inhabitants per square km. Urban population: 69 per cent (1995–2001).

Annual growth rate: -0.9 per cent 1994–2004 (WHO 2006)

Ethnic make-up

Latvian (56 per cent), Russian (32 per cent), Belarussian (4 per cent), Ukrainian (3 per cent), Polish (2 per cent), Lithuanians (1 per cent). The Latvian parliament revised naturalisation laws in 1998 to speed up the integration of Latvia's 680,000 non-citizens, mostly ethnic Russians. Citizenship is granted to stateless children, even if their parents are not citizens, provided they have lived in Latvia for at least five years. Most ethnic Russians must still pass language examinations to become citizens.

Religions

Predominantly Protestant (Lutheran), with a Roman Catholic minority in the east of the country. Orthodox Christianity is the most common religious denomination among Russians in Latvia.

Education

Education has traditionally been important in Latvia and a high level of education enabled Latvia to become a centre of the Soviet communications and electronics industries.

For those who live in rural Latvia, educational opportunities are limited. About 25 per cent in the 18–24 age group receive only a basic education.

Basic education lasts for nine years. From this, students are channelled into either 1) a basic vocational school for a two-year course from age 16; or 2) a vocational school from age 15 for three years; or 3) a vocational secondary school at age 15 for four years. Each vocational school course has its relevant qualifications. Students undertaking academic study progress to a general secondary school from age 16 for four years. Students who graduate from either the general or vocational secondary school may undertake higher education.

There are four universities and a number of other higher education institutions in Latvia. All universities and 17 other higher education institutions are state-run. In addition, there are a number of private institutions of which 10 are state-recognised. Higher education institutions confer academic degrees and professional higher education qualifications.

Latvia has a higher proportion of undergraduates than many countries (including Japan, Poland and the Czech Republic). Engineering and science courses are well established, while commercial courses such as law, accountancy and business management, although in their infancy, are growing in popularity.

Annual total expenditure on education is around 7 per cent of GDP.

Literacy rate: 100 per cent adult rate; 100 per cent youth rate (15–24) (Unesco 2005).

Compulsory years: Seven to 18.

Enrolment rate: 96 per cent gross primary enrolment of the relevant age group (including repeaters); 84 per cent gross secondary enrolment (World Bank).

Pupils per teacher: 13 in primary schools.

Health

Per capita total expenditure on health (2003) was US$678; of which per capita government spending was US$348, at the international dollar rate, (WHO 2006).

The Latvian healthcare system is set to become more expensive with the introduction of more payment-based services. However, the country has one of the highest ratios of doctors to population in the world.

Healthcare has largely deteriorated in Latvia. This has been due to a lack of primary healthcare provision, an over-stretched network of small hospitals, overstaffing and over-specialisation, the lack of modern management systems and the use of hospitals as dumping grounds for people with social rather than medical problems.

HIV/Aids

HIV prevalence: 0.6 per cent aged 15–49 in 2003 (World Bank)

Life expectancy: 71 years, 2004 (WHO 2006)

Fertility rate/Maternal mortality rate: 1.3 births per woman, 2004 (WHO 2006); maternal mortality 45 per 100,000 live births (World Bank).

Child (under 5 years) mortality rate (per 1,000): 10 per 1,000 live births (World Bank)

Head of population per physician: 3.01 physicians per 1,000 people, 2003 (WHO 2006)

Welfare

The social security system provides a state pension. There is provision for a social insurance fund. The pension system is a fund-based one, with three tiers composed of a modified pay-as-you-go (PAYG) system stronger links with contributions, a mandatory state-funded system of privately managed savings accounts and voluntary privately managed pensions.

A private pension fund law came into effect at the beginning of 1998. The legislation regulates private pension funds, which are supervised by the state insurance inspection department. Banks, life insurance companies, brokerages and investment companies are permitted to operate private pension funds, which allow saving in addition to the state pension scheme.

In 2001, the government introduced mandatory contributions for those who are subject to state pension insurance and under the age of 30, but optional for those aged between 30—49 years; the scheme is likely to be transferred to private companies. Annual total expenditure on social welfare is around 14 per cent of GDP.

Main cities

Riga (capital, estimated population 753,478 in 2005), Daugavpils (115,430), Liepaja (86,114), Jelgava (63,063), Jurmala (56,384), Ventspils (43,180), Rezekne (40,242).

Languages spoken

Russian, English and German are widely spoken (over 80 per cent of Latvians speak both Lettish and Russian); Lettish is required for citizenship. Belarusian, Ukrainian, Polish and Yiddish are also spoken. Some 150,000 Latvians speak Latgalian. A law passed in February 2004 requires at least 60 per cent of teaching at minority schools to be in Latvian.

Official language/s

Lettish

Media

National news agency: LETA (Latvian News Agency)

Other news agencies: BNS: www.bns.lv Delfi (in Latvian and Russian):www.delfi.lv

Press

After spectacular growth since 1995, consolidation became the typical development. The small press market is separated into two languages Latvian and Russian.

Dailies: In Latvian, Diena (www.diena.lv) is a prestigious, independent newspaper,

which owns several local newspapers, as does Neatkariga Rita Avize (NRA) (www.nra.lv) which owns the evening tabloid Vakara Zinas among others, Latvijas Avize (www2.la.lv) is a daily tabloid. The free newspaper 5 Min (published by Diena) has been steadily increasing its circulation since 2005.
In Russian Vesti Segodnja (Today's News) (http://rus.delfi.lv/news/press/vesti), is the largest circulating newspaper; Chas (www.chas-daily.com) from Rida and Ventspils (www.ventspils.lv) from Ventspilis.
Weeklies: In English, the independent weekly The Baltic Times (www.baltictimes.com) provides news from the region; Tovary Optum is published in Russia.
Business: In Latvian, the newspapers Dienas Bizness (www.db.lv), and in Russian Biznez I Baltiya (www.bb.lv), plus the magazine Kapitals (www.kapitals.lv) in Latvain provide comprehensive news and views on business and financial matters. Some daily newspapers include business articles.
Periodicals: There are around 190 magazine titles on offer of which Lilit (www.lilita.lv) is a leading women's monthly magazine.

Broadcasting

Radio: The national, public Latvian Radio (www.radio.org.lv) operates four stations, including Radio 1 and 2, plus Klasika and Latvia International. Private, commercial stations includes Gold FM (www2.goldfm.lv) and Radio Naba (www.naba.lv) from Riga, the public Saldus Radio (www.saldus.lv) and Alise Plus (www.aliseplus.lv) from Daugavpils in Russian.
Television: Private, commercial television dominates the market. TV3 Latvis (www.tv3.lv), launched in 1998, with programmes in Latvian, became the leading TV station in September 2007 overtaking the previous leader, Latvian Independent Television (LNT) (www.lnt.lv). The national, public Latvian Television (LTV) (www.ltv.lv) operates LVT 1 and 7, with 70 per cent funding provided by the government and the remainder by advertising and sales. Russian-based channels, although popular with large parts of the population, have increasingly faced opposition as the government – through its control of transmission rights – attempts to limit Russian influence on Latvia.

Advertising

Television advertising accounts for around 35 per cent of adspend with the print media accounting for over 40 per cent, of which newspapers account for 30 per cent. All tobacco advertising in banned and alcohol may only be advertised through printed material.

Economy

Latvia has continued its strong growth since independence in the early 1990s; GDP growth was 10.2 per cent in 2005 and the IMF is concerned that it has reached its capacity and is at risk of overheating. Unemployment was estimated at 8.5 per cent in 2005, showing a slight decrease from the previous year. Although it could have been far higher if Latvia had not lost a significant number to migration. Domestic demand expanded due to real wage growth, EU-funded spending and financial deepening, which all contributed to accelerated growth. However, liabilities in credit and high inflation, as well as an increasing current account deficit, may undermine Latvia's intentions of joining the European Monetary Union (Emu) and adopting the euro in 2008.
Inward investment was roughly eur4 billion (US$5 billion) in 2005, with investors wishing to be present in the rapidly growing Baltic market and giving them a strategic location to take advantage of opportunities in Russia and other Commonwealth of Independent States.
Nevertheless, while Latvia successfully reoriented the destination of its exports from former Soviet Union markets to western markets, it failed to transform is product base. Over 35 per cent of exports is timber produced in the huge forests that cover around 40 per cent of the land. Exports that were concentrated in high resource and labour intensive products (30 per cent timber) and utilising low-technology and low skilled workers have been reduced, but still outpace highly skilled workers and value added production techniques. The move to increase the degree of skills and performance has not kept pace with other Baltic economies.

External trade

As a member of the European Union, Latvia operates within a communitywide free trade union, which sets import tariffs as a whole. The EU has free trade agreements with a number of nations and trading blocs worldwide.
Latvia has to import all of its energy and raw material, as it does not possess any except timber, which is the single largest product, exported as either logs, finished panels or charcoal. External trade accounts for over 75 per cent of Latvia's GDP.

Imports

Principal imports are fuels and vehicles, iron ore, steel and capital goods.
Main sources: Germany (15.5 per cent total, 2006), Lithuania (13.0 per cent), Russia (7.8 per cent).

Exports

Principal exports are timber (typically over 35 per cent of total), machinery, electrical and electronic and equipment, iron and steel, textiles and foodstuffs.
Main destinations: Lithuania (14.7 per cent total, 2006), Estonia (12.7 per cent), Germany (10.1 per cent).

Agriculture

Farming

Latvia's agricultural sector still has remnants of the old Soviet central planning system and has suffered during the transition to a capitalist economic environment. With the majority of output going to the food processing sector, demand has fallen considerably. With agriculture employing over 15 per cent of the workforce, its problems are becoming increasingly significant politically. The agriculture sector is also hugely disadvantaged by the subsidies that the EU pays to its own farmers under the Common Agricultural Policy (CAP). Latvia itself is not due to benefit from CAP policies until 2013.
During its transitional entry stage Latvia has decided to implement the reform of CAP on 1 January 2009. The reform was introduced throughout most of the EU on 1 January 2005, when subsidies on farm output, which tended to benefit large farms and encourage overproduction, were replaced by single farm payments, not conditional on production. The change is expected to reward farms that provide and maintain a healthy environment, food safety and animal welfare standards. The changes are also intended to encourage market conscious production and cut the cost of CAP to the EU taxpayer.
The sector is dominated by dairy farming, pig-breeding, grain production and potatoes. Latvia is self-sufficient in the production of cattle and dairy products, pork, sugar beet, flax and potatoes. Any surplus is exported to Russia, other republics of the CIS and the EU.
The reform of the agricultural sector has proceeded at a faster rate than in either Lithuania or Estonia and 95 per cent of agricultural production comes from the private sector. Crops cover about 28 per cent of the total land area and permanent pastures about 13 per cent.
Decreases in agricultural output have been caused by the structural reforms in the sector, a lack of modern technology and the money to buy it, problems in the distribution of produce – particularly from the small private farms – and an absence of bank credit combined with high interest rates.
Stock-breeding contributes over 50 per cent of gross agricultural production; however, this means that large amounts of

fodder must be imported. Consequently the structure of the agricultural sector is changing with greater emphasis placed on grain production.
Apple production recorded a dramatic drop from 36,000 tonnes (t) in 2003 to 6,918t in 2004 while cash crops, particularly rapeseed, increased from 13,000t to 130,000t between 2001–05.
Crop production in 2005 included: 1,003,500 tonnes (t) cereals in total, 479,000t wheat, 710,000t potatoes, 281,000t barley, 130,000t rapeseed (canola), 100,000t oats, 49,810t oilcrops, 478,736t sugar beets, 7,000t apples, 19,000t fruit in total, 177,600t vegetables in total. Livestock production included: 74,650t meat in total, 22,000t beef, 37,500t pig meat, 450t lamb, 14,500t poultry, 32,045t eggs, 790,500t milk, 800t honey, 2,546t cattle hides, 12,400t sheepskins.

Fishing
Latvia's extensive coastline provides large fish catches. Principal catches include sprat, Baltic Sea pilchards, Riga Gulf pilchards, cod and salmon. Typical annual catches amount to some 145 million tonnes per year (tpy).
Thirty per cent of total fish production is used domestically while 70 per cent is exported. In October 2005, Latvia held discussions with Joe Borg, EU Commissioner for Fisheries, about conservation methods to protect overexploited and depleted cod stocks in the Baltic Sea.
In 2004, the total marine fish catch was 121,347 tonnes and the total crustacean catch was 3,202 tonnes.

Forestry
With forests covering approximately 40 per cent of total land area, forestry has the potential to become one of the most important sectors of the economy. About 60 per cent of the forest is classified as soft wood (66 per cent pine forest and 34 per cent spruce) with the remaining hardwood mainly birch. Reforestation following cutting is compulsory.
Latvia's rich and extensive forests are mainly in areas of low population, making the felling, processing and export of timber relatively easy. There is potential to harvest 8.3 million cubic metres of timber a year, half of which would be available for pulp production. The timber and furniture industry accounts for about 8 per cent of GDP and employs around 51,000 people. Timber and furniture exports grew substantially in the 1990s and currently comprise around 25 per cent of total exports. In particular, growth in exports to the EU is the result of higher wood exports.
There are about 2,500 forest industry companies in Latvia, all but a few in private ownership; the majority concentrate on sawn wood milling, wood panel production and furniture. Progress in the timber industry has been made since independence, although there is still a lack of finance, management and design skills and many production techniques remain inefficient. Pulp and paper production does not meet domestic demand. Even though Latvia is one of the top five countries in Europe in terms of forest resources per capita, it lacks a large processing plant for pulp and paper production, and consequently a large proportion of raw timber produce is exported to the pulp mills of Sweden.
Exports of forest material in 2004 amounted to US$1.0 billion, while imports amounted to US$302.2 million.
Production in 2004 included 12,754,000 cubic metres (cum) roundwood, 11,784,000cum industrial roundwood, 7,892,000cum sawlogs and veneers, 3,988,000cum sawnwood, 3,292,000cum pulpwood, 394,200cum wood-based panels, 970,000cum woodfuel.

Industry and manufacturing
The industrial sector accounts for 25.3 per cent of GDP and employs around 30 per cent of the work force.
Total manufacturing output declined in the late 1990s with food-processing hit particularly. Many Latvian food producers do not yet meet EU specifications and are therefore limited to less lucrative domestic or CIS markets such as Russia. Machinery and equipment manufacture also suffered.
Latvia is one of the most heavily industrialised areas of the former Soviet Union. A well-developed infrastructure and a broadly diversified industrial base includes both light and heavy industries including high-technology manufacturing and shipbuilding. Main industries are mechanical engineering, metal working, textiles and the food industry. Forestry, paper, chemicals, petrochemicals and communications are also important. The textiles sector is successful and export-focussed (82 per cent).
The manufacturing industry is concentrated on the production of railway carriages, buses, mopeds, washing machines and telephone systems. Mineral fertilisers are also produced. Riga, Liepaja and Ventspils are the principal industrial centres.
Industrial production increased by an estimated 8.5 per cent in 2004.
IT and telecommunications are expanding sectors, with a growth rate averaging 25 per cent over the past ten years. Banking, transport and logistics services also contribute significantly to the ecomony.

Tourism
Interest in tourism grew again after Latvia's independence in 1991 and there has been substantial investment. However, the sector is still underdeveloped, comprising only 1.3 per cent of GDP in 2005. The sector employs 14,000 people, which amounts to 1.2 per cent of the total workforce. The short summer season is a barrier to development. Tourist arrivals numbered 850,000 in 2004, up from 509,000 in 2000.

Mining
Mineral resources include limestone, clay for cement industry, dolomite, gypsum, sand for glass, clay for pottery, sand for silicate products, sand and gravel. The few minerals found in Latvia are used as building materials.
Mining and the quarrying of mineral resources account for approximately 0.5 per cent of annual GDP and have a negligible impact on the economy.

Hydrocarbons
Latvia is reliant on hydrocarbons imports, receiving most of its needs from Belarus, Russia and Lithuania. As it has no refining capacity it imports petroleum products.
Latvia's Ventspils port was Russia's primary northern crude oil export terminal. However, Russia has constructed its own terminal in order to avoid the transit fees. This will probably decrease Latvia's Russian export volumes.
Latvia does not have any natural gas resources and is reliant on Russian imports of gas to meet domestic demand. In 2005 Gazprom, Russia's huge state-owned gas company, announced plans to significantly increase prices to Ukraine and other Baltic states including Latvia. This led to temporary disruptions in supply.
Latvia does not produce coal but does produce around 500,000 tonnes of peat per annum. Coal imports come mostly from Poland.

Energy
Hydroelectric power provides 68 per cent of Latvia's power needs. However, its hydroelectric and thermal power plants do not provide the country with enough power to meet requirements.
The government adopted an energy development plan in the mid-1990s which should make Latvia 85 per cent energy self-sufficient by 2010, through modernising existing plants and building new thermal and hydroelectric capacity. However, much of the development is dependent on foreign investment. Most of Latvia's main hydroelectric stations are based on the Daugava River. State-owned Latvenergo is the operator of all of Latvia's hydro and thermal power plants.

Some 40 per cent of Latvia's electricity needs is imported from Estonia and Lithuania. The Baltic states are seeking to create a single Baltic electricity market, to integrate with Western European markets. In April 2003, power companies from Latvia, Estonia and Finland signed an agreement to lay a 315-MW underwater electricity cable between Finland and Estonia. The line, known as 'Estlink', is intended to supply Nordic countries with secure and efficient electricity generated in the Baltic states. The project is expected to cost US$117 million and to be ready by the close of 2006. Once the project is completed, Latvia should benefit from enough electricity to meet its rising needs, and enable better electricity integration of the Baltic and Nordic regions. The cable should reduce dependency on Russian supplies.

Latvia has the largest wind energy station in the Baltics, with a peak output of 2.5 million kilowatt hours of electricity per year (enough for over 1,500 households). The German energy company Preussen Elektra funded 70 per cent of the plant, which has a minimum operating life of 20 years. Over 500MW of wind energy is technically possible in the country, with only 20MW installed so far. National legislation facilitates investment in renewable energy.

Financial markets

Stock exchange

The Riga Stock Exchange (RSE) was officially re-opened in 1995. The official RSE index is known as the DJRSE.

Banking and insurance

The Bank of Latvia, the national central bank, is independent and manages the monetary supply and instigates governmental financial policy. The Financial Capital Markets Commission audits commercial banks. In the early 1990s most state banks were privatised and the sector proliferated. 1995 and 1998 saw major crises in the sector, involving mass insolvency and closures. Since then, regulation has been improved to stabilise Latvian banking and encourage investment by the West. Western owned banks control much of the country's finances. There are over 20 banks in operation.

Central bank

Latvijas Banka (Bank of Latvia)

Offshore facilities

Riga is popular with Russians seeking safe dollar accounts. Russian-linked banks have become influential in the sector.

Time

GMT plus two hours (daylight saving, late March to late September, GMT plus three hours)

Geography

Latvia is situated in north-eastern Europe on the east coast of the Baltic Sea. It is slightly larger than Switzerland at 64,589 sq km and is bordered by Estonia to the north, the Russian Federation to the east, Belarus to the south-east and Lithuania to the south and south-west. With rolling plains and gentle hills, half the country is less than 90 metres above sea level.

There are over 2,300 lakes and 12,000 rivers; the longest is the River Daugava. The largest lake is Lake Lubans which stretches over 81 square km. Latvia's highest point is in the south-east of the country where Latgale Upland reaches 289 metres.

Hemisphere

Northern

Climate

Temperate climate, but with considerable temperature variations. Mildest areas along the Baltic coast. Summer is warm with relatively mild weather in spring and autumn. Summer sunshine may be nine hours a day. Winter, which lasts from November to mid-March, can be very cold. Rainfall is distributed throughout the year with the heaviest rainfall in August. Snowfalls are common in winter months.

Dress codes

Warm clothing is essential in winter as are a raincoat and umbrella during spring and summer. Business dress is conservative but relatively informal, with a jacket and tie expected for meetings.

Entry requirements

Passports

Required by all and must be valid for at least six months. For identification purposes, a photocopy of the passport should be carried at all times.

Visa

Required by all, except nationals of EU and Schengen area signatory countries, North America, Australasia and Japan. For further exceptions contact the nearest consulate or see www.am.gov.lv/en/service/ for a full list. A Schengen visa application (offered in several languages) can be downloaded from http://europa.eu/abc/travel/ see 'documents you will need'. All visitors must have valid travel health insurance, including emergency repatriation cover.

Currency advice/regulations

There are no restrictions on import and export of local and foreign currency. Travellers cheques, in freely convertible currencies, preferably US dollars and euros, are accepted.

Customs

Personal items are duty-free. There are no duties levied on alcohol and tobacco between EU member states, providing amounts imported are for personal consumption.

It is advisable to declare valuable items such as jewellery, cameras, computers and musical instruments. Ensure that the declaration is stamped by the customs officials.

A certificate must be obtained to export of art objects over 50 years old.

Prohibited imports

Illegal drugs; guns and ammunition (without a police import permit); fresh meat.

Health (for visitors)

Nationals of the European Economic Area (EEA) countries and Switzerland can access reduced cost and sometimes free medical treatment using a European Health Insurance Card (EHIC) while visiting the EEA. Exceptions include nationals of the 10 countries, which joined the EU in 2004, whose EHIC is not valid in Switzerland. Applications for the EHIC should be made before travelling.

Mandatory precautions

There are no special requirements.

Advisable precautions

It is advisable to be in date for the following immunisations: tuberculosis, hepatitis A and diphtheria.

Any medicines required by the traveller should be taken by the visitor, and it could be wise to have precautionary antibiotics if going outside major urban centres. Rabies is endemic.

A travel kit including a disposable syringe is a reasonable precaution. It is recommended to drink bottled water. The tap water is occasionally yellow.

Hotels

Riga has business-class hotels. Tips are included in restaurant bills.

Credit cards

Credit and charge cards are accepted in large hotels and restaurants and some shops. ATMs are widely found in towns and cities.

Public holidays (national)

Fixed dates

1 Jan (New Year), 1 May (Labour Day), 4 May (Restoration Day), 23 Jun (Ligo Day/Midsummer's Eve), 24 Jun (St John's Day/Summer Solstice), 18 Nov (National Day), 25–26 Dec (Christmas/Winter Solstice).

Variable dates

Good Friday, Easter Monday.

Working hours

Banking

Mon–Fri: 0900–1700. Some banks are open between 0900–1300 on Saturdays.

Business

Mon–Fri: 0830/0900–1730/1800.

Government

Mon–Fri: 0900–1700.

Shops
Mon–Fri: 1000–1900, Saturday: 1000–1600. Grocery and department stores are usually open from 0800 until 1900. There are quite a few food stores in Riga that provide 24-hour service.

Telecommunications
Mobile/cell phones
GSM 900/1800 services are available throughout most of the country.

Electricity supply
220V AC, 50 Hz. European-style two-pin plugs are in use.

Social customs/useful tips
Latvians can be reserved and formal, but hospitable. When meeting, shake hands and slightly nod your head. If invited to a private home, it is usual to bring flowers for the hostess. Business cards are widely used.
The informal custom of overcharging foreigners (particularly by taxi-drivers) has developed since 1991.
Taxi fares do not usually include a tip, whereas restaurant bills usually do.
Tipping is generally expected. Carry small-denomination US dollar bills as well as local currency for tips, taxis etc.
Reference to Russia and Russians should be avoided, at least until you are sure of the ethnic background of your host. Many Latvians have strong feelings about Russia as many have relatives who were sent to Siberia during the Soviet period. It is also wise not to ask your host what they did before independence, as they may think you are asking whether they were in the Communist Party or even if they were sent to Siberia.

Security
As living standards have dropped, so the crime rate has risen since independence. Care should be taken not to display valuables when walking around the city.
When walking, travellers should be alert to the threat of pickpocketing and other forms of theft. Always avoid unlit streets and parks at night, and be extra vigilant if walking alone.
Wherever possible, guarded car-parks should be used and valuables kept out of sight.

Getting there
Air
National airline: Air Baltic (ABC)
International airport/s: Riga International (RIX) 8km west of Riga; facilities include currency exchange, car hire, post office, business lounge and duty-free. A courtesy shuttle bus and the number 22a bus (tickets available from the post office) run to city centre hotels; alternatively taxis are located in front of the terminal building, and the journey takes about 15 minutes.
Airport tax: None
Surface
Road: There are roads leading from all the surrounding countries, however not all have customs control and it is advisable to determine which border crossing has this facility before undertaking a fruitless journey. Visit http://www.transit.lv/ for details of the country's road network.
Rail: The Berlin to St Petersburg service passes through Daugavpils in south-eastern Latvia. Trains also link Riga with Moscow, St Petersburg and Minsk.
Water: There are direct ferries to Riga from Travemünde in Germany and Stockholm in Sweden.
Main port/s: Warm-water ports at Riga and Ventspils and Liepaja, (designated a Special Economic Zone (SEZ)).

Getting about
National transport
Air: Daily flights operate between Riga and Liepaja regional airport in the west.
Road: Latvia has a good road network, although secondary roads are in a variety of conditions.
Buses: The extensive bus network is a better form of transport than trains.
Rail: Riga is connected to all major towns and there are some cross country services. The railway terminal in Riga is Stacijas Laukums.
City transport
Taxis: Taxis can be flagged down or hired from taxis stands. All taxis have metres that should be used; there is a surcharge between 2200–0600. Some taxis accept credit cards and display a credit card sticker. Tipping is not usual.
Buses, trams & metro: There is an economic and extensive transport system, including buses, trams and trolley buses operating between 0530–2330 in Riga. In addition, some trolley bus and tram routes run an hourly night service. Tickets can be purchased from the driver or conductor. Routes are displayed on the Riga city map, available from most city kiosks.
Car hire
There are a number of international car hire firms in Riga. Either an international driving licence or an EU pink format licence is necessary and drivers have to be over 21 years old. Cars with drivers are also available. Traffic drives on the right, seat belts must be worn and car headlights must remain on at all times. Alcohol consumption and mobile phone use by drivers is strictly prohibited. Speed limits are 50kph in urban areas and 90kph on open roads.

BUSINESS DIRECTORY
The addresses listed below are a selection only. While World of Information makes every endeavour to check these addresses, we cannot guarantee that changes have not been made, especially to telephone numbers and area codes. We would welcome any corrections.

Telephone area codes
The international direct dialling (IDD) code for Latvia is +371, followed by area code

Daugavpils	54	Rezekne	46
Jelgava	30	Riga	not required
Liepaja	34	Ventspils	36

Useful telephone numbers
Fire brigade: 01
Police: 02
Ambulance: 03
National telephone operator: 116
International telephone operator: 115
Train information: 1181

Chambers of Commerce
American Chamber of Commerce in Latvia, 4 Torna iela, Riga 1050 (tel/fax: 721-2204; e-mail: amcham@amcham.lv).

British Chamber of Commerce in Latvia, Valdemara Centres, 21 Kr Valdemara iela, Riga 1010 (tel: 703-5202; fax: 703-5318; e-mail: info@bccl.lv).

Latvian Chamber of Commerce and Industry, 35 Kr Valdemara iela, Riga 1010 (tel: 722-5595; fax: 782-0092; e-mail: info@chamber.lv).

Banking
Hansabank, 26 Kalku Street, Riga LV-1050 (tel: 702-44444; fax: 702-4400; e-mail: info@hansabanka.lv).

Latvijas Krājbanka, 1 Palasta Street, Riga LV-1954 (tel: 709-2020; fax: 721-2083).

Parex Banka, 3 Smilsu Street, Riga LV-1522 (tel: 701-0000; fax: 701-0001; e-mail: inquiry@parex.lv).

Saules Bank, 16 Smilsu Street, Riga (tel: 702-0500; fax: 702-0505; e-mail: office@saules.com).

Unibanka, 23 Pils Street, Riga (tel: 721-5555; fax: 721-5566; e-mail: atsauksmes@unibanka.lv).

Central bank
Latvijas Banka, K Valdemara iela 2a, LV-1050, Riga (tel: 702-2300; fax: 702-2420; e-mail: info@bank.lv).

Travel information
Air Baltic Corporation (ABC), Riga International Airport, Riga LV-1053 (tel: 207-777; fax: 207-505); Kalku iela 15, Riga LV-1050 (tel: 207-777; fax: 722-8284).

LDZ (Latvian Railways), 3 Gogola Street, Riga, LV-1547 (tel: 723-1181; fax:

782-0231; International booking: 721-664; internet: www.ldz.lv).

Latvian Tourism Development Agency, Pils laukums 4, Riga (tel: 722-9945; fax: 750-8468; e-mail: tda@latviatourism.lv).

Lidosta Airport flight enquiries (tel: 207-009; fax: 348-654).

Lufthansa Airport Office (tel: 207-183; fax: 207-026); city centre, Kr Barona iela 7-9, Riga LV-1442 (tel: 728-5614; fax: 782-8199).

Polish Airlines, Maza Pils iela 5, Riga LV 1863 (tel: 724-2870; fax: 724-2869).

Riga International Airport Information (tel: 720-7009; internet site: http://www.riga-airport.com).

Riair (Rigas Aeronavijas), 1 Melluzu Street, Riga LV-1067 (tel: 720-7325; fax: 786-0189).

Riga Bus Station (Autoosta) (tel: 721-3611, 721-3826).

Riga Tourist Information Centre, 22 Skarnu iela (tel: 722-1731; fax: 722-7680; internet: www.rigatourism.com).

SAS, Kalku iela 15, Riga LV 1050 (tel: 721-6139; fax: 722-4282).

Ministry of tourism

Ministry of Environmental Protection and Regional Development, Peldu iela 25, Riga (tel: 702-6492; fax: 782-0442; e-mail: tourism@varam.gov.lv).

National tourist organisation offices

Latvian Tourist Board, Riga 800 Office, Torna iela 4, 1B-103, Riga LV-1050 (tel: 732-0550; fax: 732-0609; e-mail: ltboard@latnet.lv; internet: www.latviatourism.lv).

Ministries

Department of Citizenship and Immigration, 6 Raina Blvd, Riga LV-1181 (tel: 721-9181; fax: 782-0156).

Latvian Customs Department Kr Valdemara iela 1a, Riga LV-1841 (tel: 732-0928; fax: 732-2440).

Ministry of Agriculture, Republikas Laukums 2, Riga LV-1981 (tel: 702-7107; fax: 702-7512).

Ministry of Culture, Kr Valdemara iela 11a, Riga LV-1364 (tel: 722-4772; fax: 722-7916).

Ministry of Defence, Kr Valdemara iela 10-12, Riga LV-1010 (tel: 721-0124; fax: 783-0236).

Ministry of Economics, Brivibas Boulevard 55, LV 1519 Riga (tel: 701-3109; fax: 728-0882); Department of Energy Development (tel: 728-7730, 722-0151; fax: 733-8026, 722-4794).

Ministry of Education, Vajnu iela 2, 1098 Riga (tel: 722-2415; fax: 721-3992; e-mail: vetpmu@com.latnet.lv).

Ministry of Environmental Protection and Regional Development, Peldu St 25, 1494 Riga (tel: 722-3612; fax: 782-0442; e-mail: Saule@varam.gov.lv).

Ministry of Finance, Smilsu iela 1, Riga LV-1919 (tel: 722-6672; fax: 721-1140); World Bank Technical Unit (tel: 722-0348; fax: 782-0168).

Ministry of Foreign Affairs, 36 Brivibas bulv, Riga LV-1395 (tel: 701-6210; fax: 728-2121; e-mail: info@info.gov.lv; internet site: http://www.mfa.gov.lv).

Ministry of the Interior, Raina bulv 6, Riga LV-1533 (tel: 728-7260; fax: 721-2255).

Ministry of Justice, Brivibas bulv 34, Riga LV-1536 (tel: 728-2607; fax: 728-5575).

Ministry of Transport, Gogola iela 3, 1743, Riga (tel: 702-8214; fax: 721-7180).

Ministry of Welfare, Skolas iela 28, Riga LV-1331 (tel: 729-2800; fax: 727-6445).

State Property Fund (privatisation), Ministry of Economics, 36 Brivibas Boulevard, LV 1519 Riga (tel: 213-501; fax: 280-882); external department (tel: 722-5426; fax: 828-223).

Other useful addresses

Association of Insurers, Valnu iela 1, Riga LV-1912 (tel: 722-4375, fax: 724-3286).

Baltic Data House Ltd (marketing research), Akas iela 5/7, Riga LV-1050 (tel: 227-6144; fax: 227-6246, 934-6442).

British Council, Blaumena iela 5a, LV-1050 Riga (tel: 232-0468; fax: 883-0031).

British Embassy, 5 Alunana iela, Riga LV-1010 (tel: 733-8126/31; fax: 733-8132).

Business Centre (to use fax, telex, xerox, e-mail, typing, international telephone) 55 Elizabetes, Hotel 'Latvia' (tel: 722-2211).

Central Statistical Bureau of Latvia, Lacplesa Str, 1 Riga (tel: 727-0126; fax: 782-0166; internet site: www.csb.lv/avidus.cfm).

Commercial Port of Riga, Eksporta iela 6, Riga LV-1242 (tel: 732-5350; fax: 783-0051).

Commercial Port of Ventspils, Dzintaru iela 22, Ventspils LV-3602 (tel: 22-821; 21-231).

Committee for Television & Radio Broadcasting, Doma Laukums 8, Riga LV-226935 (tel: 227-906; fax: 200-025).

Consular Department, Elizabetes iela 57, Riga (tel: 728-6815; 928-7398 (24 hours); fax: 782-8274).

Department of Customs, Kr Valdemara iela 1a, Riga LV-1181 (tel: 721-9639; fax: 733-1123; e-mail: pmlp@pmlp.gov.lv).

Enterprise Support Centre, Perses Str 2, 1011 Riga (tel: 722-7623, 728-9328; fax: 782-0442); External Adviser (tel: 701-3161; fax: 782-8251, 728-0882).

Fire Protection Agency, 5 Maskavas Street, Riga (tel: 220-1322).

Government Information Agency, 36 Brivibas bulv, Riga LV-1070 (tel: 728-2828; fax: 728-4450).

Interlatvija Foreign Trade Association, Komunaru Bulv 1, 226010 Riga (tel: 332-952, 333-597; fax 226-070).

International Advertising Association, Liela Pils iela 9, Riga LV-1755 (tel: 722-8361; fax: 722-9252).

Komunalprojekts AS, 148A Brivibas Blvd, Riga LV 1012 (tel/fax: 237-6920).

Latvian Association of Civil Construction Engineers, 22/24 Grecinieku Street, Riga LV 050 (tel: 721-2661; fax: 722-4832).

Latvian Association of Traders, Kr Barona 48/50, LV-1011 Riga (tel: 721-7372; fax: 782-1010).

Latvian Business Consultants' Association, Jauniela 24, Riga LV-1050 (tel: 722-0320, 782-0076; fax: 722-8926).

Latvian Business Union (commercial information), Bungada PO Box 475, 226001 Riga (tel: 320-888; fax: 217-633).

Latvian Development Agency, Business Information Institute, 2 Perses Street, Riga LV-1442 (tel: 728-3425; fax: 782-0458; e-mail: invest@lda.gov.lv; internet site: www.lda.gov.lv).

Latvian Embassy (USA), 4325 17th Street, NW, Washington DC 20011 (tel: (+1-202) 726-8213; fax: (+1-202) 726-6785; e-mail: embassy@latvia-usa.org).

Latvian Foreign Trade Centre, 2 Elizabetes Street, Riga (tel: 732-0619, 732-1818, 732-2816; fax: 783-0035, 732-3313).

Latvian Privatisation Agency, Kr Valdemara Street 31, Riga LV-1887 (tel: 732-2281, 733-2082; fax: 783-0363; e-mail: lpa@mail.bkc.lv).

Latvian Retailers' Association, Kr Barona iela 48/50, Riga LV-1011 (tel: 721-7372; fax: 782-1010).

Latvian State Radio, 8 Doma Laukums (tel: 720-6722; fax: 720-6709, 782-0216).

Liepaja Special Economic Zone Authority, 4 Feniksa iela, LV-3401 Liepaja (tel: 26-605; fax: 80-252).

Main Post Office, Brivibas Bulvaris 21, Riga (tel: 224-155; fax: 733-1920).

National Environmental Health Centre, 7 Klijanu Street, Riga (tel: 237-7473; fax: 237-5940).

Port of Liepaja, Feniksa iela 4, Liepaja LV-3400 (tel: 342-5887; fax: 789-3418).

Public Investment Unit, Brivibas Blv. 36, 1519 Riga (tel: 701-3122; fax: 782-0458).

Riga City Council, 3 kr Valdemara Street, Riga LV-1539 (tel: 232-0680; fax: 222-0785).

Riga Fairs, Conferences & Exhibitions (tel: 213-637).

Riga Commercial Port, 5a Katrinas Street, Riga LV-1227 (tel: 732-9224; fax: 783-0215; e-mail: rto@mail.bkc.lv).

Rigas Ostas Parvalde (Riga Port Authority), 6 Eksporta St, Riga LV-1010 (tel: 732-2644; fax: 783-0051).

Riga Stock Exchange, Doma Laukums 6, Riga LV-1885 (tel: 721-2431, 722-9449; fax: 722-4515).

Saeima (Parliament), 16 Jekaba (tel: 732-2938; fax: 721-1611).

US Embassy, Raina Bulvaris 7, LV-1050 Riga (tel: 721-0005, 722-0367, 722-9709; fax: 722-6530).

Ventspils Free Port Authority, 8 Uzavas Str, Ventspils LV3601 (tel: 362-2586; fax: 362-1297).

Ventspils Tirdznecibas Osta (Ventspils Commercial Port), 20a Dzintaru Street, Ventspils LV-3602 (tel: 366-8778; fax: 362-1231).

World Trade Centre, Elizabetes iela 2, Riga LV-1340 (tel: 322-242; fax: 7830-0385).

National news agency: LETA (Latvian News Agency)

Other news agencies: BNS: www.bns.lv

Delfi (in Latvian and Russian):www.delfi.lv

Internet sites

Baltic News Service: http://www.bns.ee

Business in the Baltic States: http://www.binet.lv/english/database

Latvian information: http://www.ciesin.ee/LATVIA/

Pirma banka: http://www.rkb.lv

Trasta Komercbanka: http://www.tkb.lv

Lebanon

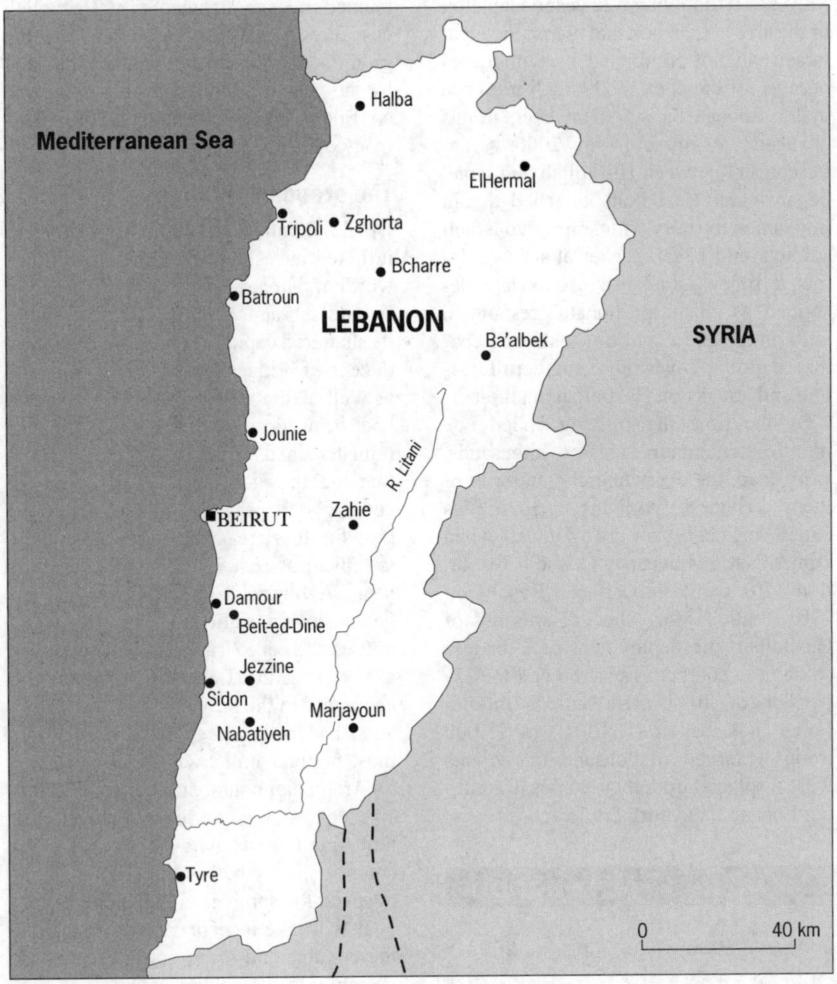

KEY FACTS

Official name: Jumhouriya al Lubnaniya (Republic of Lebanon)

Head of State: President Michel Suleiman (from 25 May 2008)

Head of government: Prime Minister Fouad Siniora (since 2005: re-appointed 25 May 2008)

Ruling party: A national unity government, with members from all political and religious blocs (from 11 Jul 2008)

Area: 10,452 square km

Population: 3.75 million (2007)*

Capital: Beirut

Official language: Arabic

Currency: Lebanese pound (LL) = 100 piastres

Exchange rate: LL1,507.50 per US$ (Jul 2008)

GDP per capita: US$6,569 (2007)*

GDP real growth: 4.00% (2007)*

Labour force: 1.73 million (2005) (In addition there are an estimated one million foreign workers)

Unemployment: 20.00% (2005)*

Inflation: 4.00% (2007)

Balance of trade: -US$6.09 billion (2005)

Foreign debt: US$15.84 billion (2004)

Visitor numbers: 1.06 million (2006)*

* estimated figure

Like a number of flashpoint countries, Lebanon's biggest problem is that of its neighbours. Long seen by Syria as a vassal state, Lebanon has also had to cope with the mistrust of its neighbour to the south, Israel. As if that were not enough, Lebanon also had to come to terms with the volatile presence of Hezbollah in its midst. Although the Shi'ite grouping was thought to be governed and directed from Syria, its operational base and the country within which it exercised greatest political influence, was Lebanon.

Lebanese confidence, and much of its infrastructure, had been once again destroyed in 2006 by what was seen by most of the international community as a completely disproportionate response from Israel to the capture of two Israeli troops by Hezbollah.

Hariri death still not resolved

In 2005, after 29 years of occupation, Syrian troops and intelligence corps had withdrawn from Lebanese soil. Throughout this period, Syria had dominated Lebanese politics and Lebanon's economy. The withdrawal, called a 'redeployment' by Syria, was precipitated by the assassination of former prime minister Rafik Hariri on 14 February 2005. Hariri had been expected to do well in elections scheduled for May. Although Hariri had accommodated himself to Syrian hegemony in the past, he had begun to take a more nationalistic line, calling for an end to Syria's domination. This change had been precipitated by a Syrian-orchestrated extra-constitutional extension of Lebanese president Emile Lahoud's term, due to expire in 2004. After Hariri's assassination, hundreds of thousands of Lebanese, from the country's often divided Muslim and Christian communities, took to the streets in Beirut, demanding an end to the Syrian presence and calling for justice. Most Lebanese suspected that Hariri had been assassinated on orders from Damascus, either by Syrian agents or members of the pro-Syrian Lebanese security services. A UN tribunal was set up to investigate the death. In September 2008 UN secretary general, Ban Ki-moon, said that he would discuss with Lebanese authorities the timing of the start of operations of the international tribunal that will try former Rafik Hariri's suspected assassins. Ban told Lebanese daily *An-Nahar* correspondent in New York that he had given instructions to UN personnel to continue administrative preparations to officially start the work of the tribunal. He said he was working on obtaining more contributions to finance the tribunal, though there was currently enough money for the first 12 months of the court's operations.

Israel invades

Sporadic clashes between Israel and Hezbollah had been part of Lebanese daily reality since Israel's withdrawal from the occupied zone in Southern Lebanon in May 2000 (following a 22 year occupation of the area). Lebanon had maintained that Israel had not completed its withdrawal because of the continued Israeli presence in the Shebaa Farms. However, things changed radically on 14 July 2006. A major conflict between Hezbollah and Israel began when Hezbollah launched a raid into Israeli territory, kidnapped two Israeli soldiers and began rocket attacks on Israeli territory. Israel, in a reaction later described as 'disporportionate' responded with an air and naval blockade of Lebanon, a ground invasion of southern Lebanon and attacks on Hezbollah positions.

By the time the fighting ended one month later, hundreds, if not thousands, were dead, the overwhelming majority of them Lebanese civilians. Hostilities ended officially on 14 August when United Nations Security Council Resolution 1701 came into effect. Resolution 1701 called for the disarming of Hezbollah, the deployment of Lebanese soldiers to southern Lebanon and the expansion of the United Nations Interim Force in Lebanon (UNIFIL) to 15,000 troops. Hundreds of thousands of civilians were displaced from their homes in southern Lebanon and northern Israel.

The indifferent morale of the Israeli forces was not boosted by the resilience and determination of Hezbollah, reversing the roles traditionally seen in the region. The conflict also seriously weakened Prime Minister Olmert; embarrassingly for Israel, the two kidnapped soldiers were not returned, and by mid-2008 still remained in Hezbollah captivity. Hezbollah casualties were never known, but the group's confidence was hugely boosted by the war – to the extent that it became confident enough to challenge the legitimacy of Lebanon's government.

The economy

Israel's month-long offensive in Lebanon inflicted an estimated billions of dollars worth of damage and once again Lebanon found itself appealing for funds to rebuild its shattered capital. Thousands of homes, dozens of bridges and hundreds of roads, as well as the siege of ports and airports had been destroyed. Lebanese finance minister Jihad Azour was quoted as saying that the Israeli offensive had killed the country's hopes for robust economic growth. 'It is a real pity ... we were hoping to achieve at least five per cent growth this year,' Azour said. The offensive had targeted power stations, factories, warehouses and cargo trucks, in what was seen as a war against Lebanon's civilians and economy. In the previous five years, Lebanon had managed to raise itself to the most popular holiday destination among its Arab neighbours, but the Israeli offensive led to a mass exodus of some one million Arab tourists, who had flocked to the country shortly before the conflict began to spend the summer in Lebanon.

'It will take a second Hariri to rebuild the country and bring confidence by investors into the country again,' one high placed civil servant commented. As prime minister 1992–98 and 2000–04, Rafik Hariri had been credited by many with Lebanon's 'economic miracle' – the booming recovery of the country after nearly two decades of civil war. Although Hariri's policies substantially increased Lebanon's public debt and he himself attracted criticism for virtually combining his roles as business magnate and prime minister, his assassination led many to fear that Lebanon's economy might collapse.

Lebanon's gross domestic product, was 4.0 per cent in 2007. Inflation had looked to run out of control, rising from -0.7 per cent in 2005 to 5.6 per cent in 2006, but then steadied at 4.0 per cent in 2007. Exports were US$4,077 thousand in 2007,

KEY INDICATORS — Lebanon

	Unit	2003	2004	2005	2006	2007
Population	m	4.04	4.43	3.65	*3.70	*3.75
Gross domestic product (GDP)	US$bn	19.62	21.90	21.43	*22.76	*24.64
GDP per capita	US$	4,858	5,225	5,863	*6,146	*6,569
GDP real growth	%	1.0	5.0	1.0	*0.0	*4.0
Inflation	%	2.5	3.0	-0.7	5.6	4.0
Industrial output	% change	–	12.4	-0.3	-1.0	–
Agricultural output	% change	–	-3.2	1.4	-6.0	–
Exports (fob) (goods)	US$m	971.0	1,783.0	2,278.0	3,207.0	4,077.0
Imports (cif) (goods)	US$m	6,525.0	8,162.0	8,368.0	9,345.0	11,926.0
Balance of trade	US$m	-5,554.0	-6,379.0	-6,090.0	-6,138.0	-7,850.0
Current account	US$m	-2,460.0	-3,130.0	-2,517.0	-1,372.0	-2,634.0
Total reserves minus gold	US$m	12,519.4	11,734.6	11,887.1	13,376.4	12,909.9
Foreign exchange	US$m	12,460.8	11,672.4	11,828.7	13,313.3	12,844.1
Exchange rate	per US$	1,507.50	1,515.04	1,512.00	1,512.00	1,512.00

* estimated figure

however imports had rocketed to US$11,926 thousand. GDP per capita remained virtually unchanged, at US$6,569 in 2007.

Outlook

The election of General Michel Suleiman on 25 May 2008 at last allowed Prime Minister Siniora to announce the formation of a national unity government with members from all political and religious blocs and once again one of the Arab world's most resilient countries could start to rebuild. In a boost to morale, the world famous Baalbeck Festival took place in early August, after a two year gap, giving hope to Lebanon's beleaguered peoples.

Risk assessment

Politics	Fair
Economy	Fair
Regional stability	Poor

COUNTRY PROFILE

Historical profile

1926 The constitution was approved and the Lebanese Republic declared.
1940 Lebanon came under the control of the Vichy French government.
1941 After occupation by Free French and British troops, independence was declared.
1943 France agreed to the transfer of power to the Lebanese government with effect from 1944.
1948 A major influx of Arab refugees from Palestine built tensions between Christian Maronites and Muslim Shi'as.
1958 The first civil war erupted between Muslim and Christian groups
1964 Yasser Arafat established a Palestine Liberation Organisation (PLO) stronghold in Lebanon.
1970 Anti-Israeli terrorist attacks from Lebanese bases increased after the PLO was expelled from Jordan. Israeli retaliations further alienated leftist Muslims from conservative Maronites (the largest Christian sect) and undermined governmental legitimacy, with nine changes in three years.
1975 Full-scale civil war erupted between Muslims (with PLO aid) and Christians. Southern Lebanon and the western half of Beirut became bases for the PLO and other Muslim militias, while the Christians controlled East Beirut and the Christian section of Mt Lebanon.
1976 A 30,000-strong Arab Deterrent Force was established to restore peace.
1978 In reprisal for an attack by Palestinians based in Lebanon, Israel invaded and occupied the south of the country; the UN called on Israel to withdraw its troops; it handed over the territory to the mainly Christian Lebanese militia.
1982 Hizbollah (Party of God) was formed by Muslim clerics, backed by Iran and Syria, to respond to the Israeli invasion of Lebanon and to advocate the establishment of an Islamic government (it became a political movement in 1985 and entered parliament in 1992). Israel launched a full-scale invasion after an assassination attempt on Shlomo Argov, its ambassador to the UK. Syria, which maintained a large army in Lebanon, unsuccessfully fought Israel. Christian Phalangist militiamen, with Israeli compliance, massacred more than 1,000 Palestinian refugees in the Sabra and Shatila camps. A Western multinational force monitored the evacuation of the PLO to Tunis.
1983 Hostilities between Israel and Lebanon ended. Syrian forces remained in Lebanon.
1985 Despite withdrawing from most of the territory, Israel maintained some troops to support the mainly Christian South Lebanon Army (SLA) (a militia set up and supported by Israel) in order to help secure its own northern border.
1986–90 Factional conflict worsened as various efforts at national reconciliation failed. Lebanon had two governments – one mainly Muslim in West Beirut, headed by Salim al Huss, the other, Christian, in East Beirut, led by the Maronite Commander-in-Chief of the Army, General Michel Aoun.
1989 Under the Ta'if Accord, a government of national reconciliation was formed with an equal number of Christian and Muslim members. Elias Hrawi was elected president.
1990 The civil war ended and General Aoun fled.
1992 President Hrawi appointed Rafik al Hariri as prime minister, heading a cabinet of technocrats. Al Hariri, a rich businessman, born in Sidon but with Saudi Arabian nationality, became the mastermind behind the reconstruction of Lebanon.
1993–97 The Oslo Peace Accords laid the basis for transfer of authority from the Israeli military administration to the PLO in the Gaza Strip and an undefined area around the town of Jericho in the West Bank. A follow-up treaty, Oslo II, envisaged Palestinian autonomy, with Israeli troop units withdrawing from the West Bank. Yasser Arafat was elected president of the Palestinian Legislative Council (PLC), the assembly of the Palestinian National Authority (PNA). Attacks and reprisals continued between Hizbollah and Palestinian guerrillas, and Israel.
1998 The National Assembly elected army chief of staff, General Émile Lahoud, as president, replacing Elias Hrawi. Following the resignation of Prime Minister al Hariri, Salim al Huss was appointed to the post.
2000 The Israeli army withdrew from southern Lebanon and the SLA disbanded. Sporadic clashes continued between Hizbollah and Israeli forces. Rafik al Hariri won convincingly at the elections and was re-appointed prime minister.
2003 Israeli warplanes and artillery attacked suspected Hizbollah positions in the disputed Shebaa Farms area in south Lebanon in retaliation for guerrilla attacks.
2004 On 3 September, parliament approved extending pro-Syria President Émile Lahoud's six-year term by three years.
In September, UN Security Council resolution 1559 demanded that Syrian soldiers leave Lebanon and that Hizbollah disarm. Rafik al Hariri opposed the extension of Lahoud's term and stood down as prime minister; Omar Karami was nominated for the post.
2005 On 14 February, former prime minister Rafik al Hariri was assassinated in a car bomb attack. Syria was accusated of supporting the perpetrators. On 28 February, thousands of protesters gathered in Beirut, demanding the withdrawal of Syrian troops; the pro-Syrian government of Prime Minister Omar Karami resigned. The presidents of Lebanon and Syria agreed that Syrian troops would withdraw to the Bekaa valley in eastern Lebanon. A protest held in Beirut on 8 March, organised by Hizbollah to show loyalty to Syria, countered weeks of anti-government and anti-Syrian protests. President Lahoud reappointed Karami as prime minister but he resigned again on 13 April, after failing to form a new government. On 15 April, Najib Mikati became the new prime minister and named a cabinet on 19 April, in which both pro-Syrian and anti-Syrian ministers held important posts. The last Syrian troops pulled out of Lebanon on 26 April. In parliamentary elections, held between 29 May–3 July, Hariri-Jumblatt, the bloc led by Sa'ad al Hariri (son of Rafik al Hariri), won 72 seats, the Shi'a Muslim bloc of Amal and Hizbollah won 35 seats and the anti-Syrian Michel Aoun and allies won 21 seats. Fouad Siniora became prime minister on 30 June. He formed a cabinet which mostly included those opposed to Syrian involvement in Lebanon but also included – for the first time – ministers of the Hizbollah and Amal movements. On 1 September four pro-Syrian generals were charged with the assassination of Rafiq al Hariri, following the findings of the UN's chief investigator.
2006 Following the publication of cartoons showing images of the Prophet Mohammed, in Denmark, demonstrators

attacked and burned the Danish embassy in Beirut in February. A Hezbollah paramilitary force crossed into Israel and captured two Israeli soldiers in July and caused Israel to retaliate by bombing targets throughout southern Lebanon. Much damage was done to the infrastructure and villages in the country while many inhabitants were displaced. In August Israeli troops invaded the Lebanon as it tried to retrieve its soldiers and inflicting maximum damage on Hizbollah and its organisation. In August, after 34 days of fighting and the death of approximately 1,000 Lebanese, mostly civilians, a truce was agreed. Israeli troops withdrew and the Lebanese army deployed, for the first time in decades, along the border with Israel. Hizbullah claimed the war was 'a strategic and historical victory for Lebanon against the Israeli enemy'. In November plans for a UN tribunal to prosecute the suspects in the Rafik al Hariri slaying caused ministers of Hizbollah and the Amal movement to resign.

2007 At an international donor conference held in Paris in January, US$7.4 billion was pledged to aid the reconstruction of war inflicted damage and the debt incurred during the conflict. The anti-Syrian politician, Antoine Ghanim, was assassinated by a car-bomb, on 19 September. Syria denied responsibility. The death of Ghanim reduced the number of anti-Syrian members of parliament within a week of presidential elections. Several more assassinations of anti-Syrian parliamentary members reduced the government's majority.The lack of a quorum on 25 September forced the first vote in parliament to elect a president to be postponed to 23 October; this in turn was postponed to 12 November. For the third time, a vote to choose the next president was postponed until the 21 November. President Émile Lahoud will resign on 24 November. A compromise candidate for president, Michel Suleiman, gained backing from all political parties. However, as a serving military officer the constitution must be amended to allow his candidacy. Requirements for support include a shortened presidential term in office, from 2013 to 2009, and an appointed prime minister with neutral allegiances. Presidential elections were postponed three times in December.

2008 Elections for president were twice postponed in January, and again on 9 February and 11 March. General Michel Suleiman was finally elected president on 25 May; he received 118 votes out of 127 and was sworn in immediately. On 11 July Prime Minister Siniora announced the formation of a national unity government with members from all political and religious blocs. The Baalbeck Festival took place in early August, after a two year gap. An agreed common border will be formally demarcated between Lebanon and Syria, in a move to improve diplomatic relations.

Political structure

Constitution

The constitution was enacted in May 1926, and has since been amended on five occasions. A key amendment agreed under the Ta'if Agreement of 1989 reduced the authority of the president by transferring executive power to the cabinet. The prime minister must be a Sunni Muslim, with the cabinet made up of equal numbers of Muslims and Christians.

Form of state

Republic

The executive

As head of state, the president is elected for a single six-year term by parliament and should be a Maronite Christian. Since 1990, however, Syria has effectively chosen the president and thereby alienated large parts of the Christian community. Under the consitution, the president chooses the prime minister upon recommendation from the parliament. In reality, Syria decides who is appointed to the position. The prime minister, who must be a Sunni Muslim, is responsible for choosing members of the 30-member Council of Ministers (cabinet). Ministers may be selected from inside or outside parliament. President General Émile Lahoud's six-year term of office, which was due to end in November 2004, was extended by parliament by three years.

National legislature

The Majlis al Nuwab (unicameral National Assembly) has 128 members, elected for a term of five years by the religious communities: Maronites (34), Sunnites (27), Shi'ites (27), Greek Orthodox (14), Greek Catholics (eight), Druzes (eight), Armenian Orthodox (five), Alaouites (two), Armenian Catholics (one), Protestants (one), Christian Minorities (one).

Legal system

The legal system is based on the 1926 constitution and the Commercial Code, the Civil Procedure Code, the Criminal Procedure Code and the Penal Code. French law has had a lasting impact on local legislation, while Ottoman law and Islamic law have also influenced Lebanon's legal system. Civil law is based on the Code of Obligations and Contracts and the Land Ownership Law. Various branches of the legal framework are being revised and updated. Lebanon has an independent judiciary.

Last elections

29 May–3 July 2005 (parliamentary); 15 October 1998 (presidential).

Results: Parliamentary: The Hariri-Jumblatt alliance won a total of 72 seats out of 128, an alliance of Amal and the Hizbollah won 35 seats, and Aoun's Free Patriotic Movement and its allies won 21 seats.

Presidential: General Émile Lahoud was elected president by the National Assembly. In 2004 Lahoud's term in office was extended until 2007 at the insistence of the Syrians.

Next elections

2007 (presidential); 2010 (parliamentary).

Political parties

Ruling party

A national unity government, with members from all political and religious blocs (from 11 Jul 2008)

Main opposition party

Population

3.75 million (2007)*

Last census: November 1970: 2,126,325 (excluding Palestinian refugees in camps)

Population density: 90 per cent (1995—2001).

Annual growth rate: 1.4 per cent 1994–2004 (WHO 2006)

Ethnic make-up

The Lebanese belong to a single ethnic grouping, Levanto Arab, which encompasses the people of the Levant coast from northern Syria to southern Palestine. Armenians and Kurds have settled in Lebanon and there are Syrian troops and many Syrian workers.

Religions

There are 17 recognised religious groupings in Lebanon. Five predominate: Shi'a Muslims, Sunni Muslims, Maronite (Catholic) Christians, Greek Orthodox Christians and Druze.

Education

Education is mainly run by private enterprises and the religious sector. State schools exist and are free of charge. Primary education lasts for nine years.

The civil war severely disrupted state education at all levels and by the end of the civil war in 1990, 1,270 schools throughout the country needed rehabilitation at an estimated cost of US$65 million. Public expenditure on education is equivalent to approximately 2.5 per cent of annual GNP.

There is a government-run Lebanese National University, but the major universities continue to be operated by the US, France and Egypt. There are over 10 universities in Beirut.

Literacy rate: 86.1 per cent total, 81.4 per cent female, adult rates (World Bank).

Compulsory years: None

Enrolment rate: 111 per cent total primary enrolment of the relevant age group (including repetition rates); 81 per cent total secondary enrolment (World Bank).

Health

Per capita total expenditure on health (2003) was US$730; of which per capita government spending was US$214, at the international dollar rate, (WHO 2006).
A Social Security Fund covers the health expenses of workers.

HIV/Aids

HIV prevalence: 0.1 per cent aged 15–49 in 2003 (World Bank)

Life expectancy: 70 years, 2004 (WHO 2006)

Fertility rate/Maternal mortality rate: 2.3 births per woman, 2004 (WHO 2006); maternal mortality 100 per 100,000 live births (World Bank).

Child (under 5 years) mortality rate (per 1,000): 27 per 1,000 live births; 3 per cent of children aged under five are malnourished (World Bank).

Head of population per physician: 3.25 physicians per 1,000 people, 2001 (WHO 2006)

Welfare

Since 1963, Lebanon has operated a social insurance system offering lump sum benefits only. Social insurance covers employees in industry, commerce and agriculture, but excludes temporary agricultural employees and those previously entitled to special benefits under the labour code.
In 1999, old age pensions were available to men aged over 60, but compulsory for those aged over 64. The benefit included a lump sum amount equivalent to the average monthly earnings during the last 12 months or the final month. The rate for disability benefit is a lump sum equal to the final month's earnings multiplied by the number of years in service. Widows receive 25 per cent of their former spouse's benefit. There are no sickness or maternity benefits. Workers receive medical benefits for up to 26 weeks or 52 weeks in special cases. Family allowances are employment-related and are available to employees with a non-working wife or with one to five children. The maximum monthly allowance is equivalent to 75 per cent of the minimum wage.

Main cities

Beirut (capital, estimated population 1.2 million in 2004), Tripoli (212,900), Sidon (149,000), Zahlé (76,600).

Media

Press of the press is practiced but there are laws forbidding defaming the president and other heads of states and inciting sectarian strife.

National news agency: NNA (National News Agency): www.nna-leb.gov.lb

Other news agencies: Central News Agency: www.almarkazia.com

Press

Dailies: In Arabic An Nahar (www.annahar.com), Al Safir (www.assafir.com), Al Anwar (www.alanwar.com), Al Diyar (www.journaladdiyar.com), Al Mustaqbal (http://almustaqbal.com) with affiliation to the Future Movement. In Armenian Aztag Daily (www.aztagdaily.com). In French L'Orient-Le Jour (www.lorient-lejour.com.lb) is the country's fifth-largest newspaper. In English The Daily Star (www.dailystar.com.lb).

Weeklies: In Arabic, Al Shiraa Magazine (www.alshiraa.com) and Al Afkar (www.alafkar.net) for politics; Al Noujoum (www.alnoujoum.com) for celebrity news and Al Jaras (www.aljaras.com) for entertainment news. In French, L'Hebdo Magazine (www.magazine.com.lb) for news and current affairs and La Revue du Liban (www.rdl.com.lb) is a news review In English Monday Morning (www.mmorning.com) for general news.

Business: In Arabic Al Markazia (www.immarwaiktissad.com) with articles on finance and current affairs and the monthly Al Iktissad Wal Aamal (www.iktissad.com) covers Arab business and economic news. In English, the UK-based monthly magazine Executive (http://executive-magazine.com) offers articles on Lebanese world of commerce in major sectors.

Periodicals: Monthly women's magazines include Snob Magazine (www.snobmagazine.com) in Arabic, is aimed at a young female audience and in French, Femme (www.femmemag.com.lb) is aimed at an older readership while Noun (www.noun.com.lb) is aimed at a sophisticated female market. In Arabic, Al Mustiqbal Al Arabi (www.caus.org.lb) is an academic publication on Arab matters.

Broadcasting

The Lebanese Broadcasting Company (LBCI) is privately owned. In 1996, Lebanon banned broadcasts of political programmes and news by about 50 private television stations and 150 radio stations and ordered them to close. Political broadcasting is restricted to four TV stations and three radio outlets controlled by the pro-government establishment.

Radio: The government gives permission to operators to broadcast and limits which station may broadcasts the news.
Radio Liban (www.96-2.com) is state-run with nationwide reception. There are many private, commercial stations including Mix FM (www.mixfm.com.lb), NBN (www.nbn.com.lb) and NRG Beirut (www.nrjlebanon.com). International broadcasts are relayed through local stations.

Television: Viewing of satellite and cable television is widespread.
Tele-Liban is the state-run channel. Other, private, commercial channels include the Lebanese Broadcasting Corporation (LBC) (www.lbcgroup.tv) the market leader with regional and international coverage through satellite transmissions. Its political stance is towards the Christian community. Future Television (www.future.com.lb) is affiliated to a Sunni Muslim political movement (Tayyar Al Mustaqbal (Future Movement). Orange TV (www.otv.com.lb) is a publicly owned station which began broadcasting in 2007. Al Manar (www.almanar.com.lb) is a station affiliated to the Hezbollah. The Lebanon-based news station Al Jaheed (www.akjadeed.tv) broadcasts throughout the region.
Cable Vision (www.cablevision-leb.net) is the largest of the cable TV services.

Advertising

The local advertising and marketing industry is well developed. Television accounts for around 60 per cent of adspend; print media accounts for 30 per cent, with the majority being channelled into national newspapers and radio and billboards accounting for the remainder.

Economy

The Lebanese economy was shattered, in 2006, following the Israeli invasion in July and August, when damage estimated at US$3.6 billion was inflicted on the infrastructure. GDP growth dropped from a modest 1.0 per cent in 2005 to –5.0 per cent in 2006. Inflation, which had been 0.3 per cent in 2005 rose to an estimated 4.8 per cent in 2006.
Lebanon has a strong tradition as an open market, trade-orientated economy. In 2005 the service sector contributed over 70 per cent of GDP (mainly banking and tourism), while industry provided 21 per cent, of which manufacturing was 12 per cent, and agriculture provided the remaining 9 per cent.
The vulnerabilities of the economy in 2005 were due to government debt, which rose to 175 per cent of GDP, despite government spending being reined in, taxes increased and state enterprises sold.
In January 2007, a major donor's conference was held, the government had hoped to raise US$9 billion to pay for repairs and cut the public debt; US$1.9 billion was pledged in soft loans and new aid but was contingent on Lebanon's meeting agreed benchmarks in implementing its proposed five-year economic and social reform programme.

External trade

In 2005 the Greater Arab Free Trade Area (Gafta) was ratified by 17 members, including Lebanon, creating an Arab economic bloc. A customs union was established whereby tariffs within Gafta will be reduced by a percentage each year, until none remain. It is also a signatory of the Euro-Mediterranean Partnership agreement, which provides for the introduction of free trade between the EU and 10 Mediterranean countries, by 2012.

In July 2007, Lebanon was close to full membership of the WTO, having progressed to the outline phase for terms of membership.

Around 65 per cent of GDP is provided by foreign trade, with recent growth in the IT (information technology) sector, although financial services still provide the lion's share.

Imports

Major imports include petroleum products, vehicles, medicine, clothing, meat and live animals, consumer goods, paper, textiles, tobacco.

Main sources: Syria (11.5 per cent total, 2006), Italy (9.7 per cent), US (9.3 per cent).

Exports

Commodity exports include gems and jewellery, electrical and electronic equipment, minerals such as salt and sulphur, iron and steel, consumer goods and construction materials.

Main destinations: Syria (26.3 per cent total, 2006), UAE (11.8 per cent), Switzerland (7.9 per cent).

Agriculture

The agricultural sector has still not recovered from the effects of the civil war. In 2004, it accounted for around seven per cent of GDP, compared with 12 per cent in 1994. Annual output is less than a fifth of pre-war levels, with only about 30 per cent of domestic demand for food and food products being met.

While agricultural exports have shown signs of recovery, they earn only around US$233 million compared with expenditure of US$1.5 billion on imports of agricultural produce. Main goods for export are surplus products such as apples, citrus fruit and potatoes.

Agricultural and farming activities are in private hands. The land tenure system and difficult terrain have resulted in the majority of farmland being divided into small relatively uneconomic units. This has acted as a disincentive to investment in irrigation and mechanisation. The government provides little aid to the sector, which has had to compete with heavily subsidized produce from other countries.

Lebanon's membership of the Greater Arab Free Trade Agreement (Gafta), which came into effect in January 2005, could expose the sector to further pressures.

The relatively mild climate allows for diversified agricultural production. Main crops: wheat, barley, maize, vegetables, potatoes, fruit, olives, tobacco. Farmers have started the cultivation of advanced cash crops, such as avocados and flowers.

Goats, cattle and sheep are the main types of livestock raised in Lebanon.

One-third of Lebanon's land is cultivable with 400,000 hectares of arable land, of which 25 per cent is irrigated. The main agricultural areas are the Beka'a valley, the Akkar plain, the coastal plain and the foothills of the central mountain range. Most of these areas were badly affected by war. Agriculture in the south and in the Beka'a valley was particularly affected.

Agriculture remains an important source of income in rural areas, and although it is difficult to estimate the number of full-time farmers, most families conduct or participate in agriculture as a part-time activity.

The estimated crop production for 2005 included: 144,700 tonnes (t) cereals in total, 120,000t wheat, 355,000t potatoes, 339,000t citrus fruit, 110,000t grapes, 220,000t tomatoes, 41,889t oilcrops, 72,000t bananas, 13,500t tobacco, 10,000t figs, 180,000t olives, 29,840t treenuts, 140,000t apples, 891,600t fruit in total, 808,100t vegetables in total. Estimated livestock production included: 201,260t meat in total, 52,500t beef, 1,320t pig meat, 14,740t lamb, 2,700t goat meat, 130,000t poultry, 47,100t eggs, 323,600t milk, 970t honey, 4,500t cattle hides, 2,010t sheepskins, 1,970t greasy wool, 50t cocoons, silk.

Fishing

Despite Lebanon's extensive coastline, commercial fishing remains a minor activity, contributing less than one per cent to GDP annually.

In 2004, the total marine fish catch was 3,491 tonnes and the total crustacean catch was 60 tonnes.

Forest cover amounts to less than 8 per cent of total land area.

Imports of forest materials in 2004 amounted to US$253.7 million, while exports were US$12.1 million.

Estimated timber production in 2004 included 88,732 cubic metres (cum) roundwood, 9,100cum sawnwood, 46,300cum wood-based panels, 7,150cum sawlogs and veneers, 81,582 cum wood fuel; 11,351t charcoal.

Industry and manufacturing

Industry and manufacturing is small to medium scale. The sector accounts for around 12.6 per cent of GDP and employs 18 per cent of the workforce. The main products are building materials, textiles and clothing, food processing and furniture.

Construction employs about 6 per cent of the workforce. Industry provides more than 40 per cent of Lebanon's merchandised export earnings.

Tourism

Tourism has recovered from the devastation of the civil war and Lebanon's popularity as a destination has been restored. By 2003, despite the Iraq War, visitor numbers were returning to pre-war levels. Around 1 million arrivals were recorded and the rising trend continued into 2004, when 1,278,000 arrivals were recorded. The sector's contribution to GDP continues to increase, although, at 12 per cent, it is still short of the 19.4 per cent attained in 1974.

The sector suffered a setback in 2005, precipitated by the assassination early in the year of Rafik al Hariri and the subsequent political instability. Year-on-year visitor numbers fell by around 14 per cent for the period January to September. There were signs of recovery in September. The longer-term prospects for the sector are not expected to be damaged by the events of 2005, although there is a growing need for lower-cost accommodation and better air connections.

The main market is Saudi Arabia, followed by Kuwait and Jordan, but increasing numbers of Europeans are rediscovering Lebanon. Asia is another growing market for the Lebanon.

The sector is concentrated on Beirut and the surrounding region. The attractions and infrastructure of the rest of the country remain to be developed.

The sector gives employment to around 24,000 people, double the pre-war level.

Mining

Lebanon has few natural resources. There are minor deposits of high-grade iron ore, asphalt, coal, lignite, phosphates and salt, all of which are exploited for internal consumption. There are also quarries for building-stone, and sand and lime suitable for use in construction.

Hydrocarbons

Lebanon relies on the import of refined oil to meet domestic demand. Initial studies indicate the presence of offshore oil and gas reserves. Several international companies have shown interest, but exploration has not been initiated yet. With the surge in fuel costs that grew in world demand in 2005, the search for hydrocarbons is likely to accelerate. With its eyes on this prospect, the government is drafting legislation to regulate the sector. It has been speculated that Lebanon could recover up to 90,000 barrels per day from any reserves.

Lebanon does not produce natural gas. A gas pipeline from Syria to Lebanon which feeds a major power station in northern Lebanon becan suppling gas in May 2005.
Lebanon does not produce coal, but imports around 2.0 tonnes per annum.

Energy
Electricity supply is highly inefficient and expensive. Outages are a regular feature of life. Electricité du Liban (EDL), the state-owned electricity provider, operates at an annual loss of US$400 million a year. Electricity is produced using imported fuel oil, which accounts for around 70 per cent of EDL's total costs. A kilowatt is three times more expensive in Lebanon than in Egypt, Syria or Turkey. EDL is scheduled to be partially privatised under a law passed in 2002.
Lebanon is seeking to convert from fuel oil to natural gas for electricity generation. Like oil, natural gas has to be imported. A pipeline giving access to Syrian gas at preferential prices was completed in March 2005, but commencement of supply has been held up. Other sources under discussion in 2005 were Egypt, through the Arab natural gas pipeline, and Qatar.

Financial markets
Stock exchange
The Beirut Stock Exchange (BSE) is one of the smallest in the region and its performance is poor compared to other emerging markets.

Banking and insurance
Before the civil war, Lebanon was the unrivalled financial centre in the Middle East. Lebanon's free exchange system, strict secrecy laws, and strong currency all served to attract regional and international institutions and customers. Favourable economic and financial conditions following the end of the civil war initially led to an improved monetary and banking situation. However, lack of dynamism in the sector has since discouraged most foreign investors.
Central bank
Banque du Liban (BDL) (Bank of Lebanon)
Main financial centre
Beirut

Time
GMT plus two hours (daylight saving GMT plus three hours)

Geography
Lebanon stretches approximately 140km along the eastern shore of the Mediterranean, bounded by Syria to the north and east and Israel to the south. Its terrain is mountainous, dominated by the parallel ranges of the Lebanon in the west and the Anti-Lebanon in the east, which run north-east to south-west. Between these ranges lies the Beka'a valley, broad in the north, narrowing in the south. The coastal plain is defined by the Lebanon range which in places plunges into the sea, dividing the coastal strip into segments. The major cities are: Tripoli in the north, Beirut on one of the wider segments halfway down the coast and Sidon and Tyre in the south.
Hemisphere
Northern

Climate
In the summer, temperatures range between 20–30 degrees Celsius (C); Beirut averages 27 degrees C. The coastal region is humid in the summer months. In the winter, temperatures in the coastal region range between 10–16 degrees C and it becomes colder inland. Snow is usual on mountains. Most rain falls between November and March. Lebanon enjoys an essentially Mediterranean climate with mild, rainy winters and long warm summers. It almost never rains between June and October, and there is an average of 300 sunny days every year. In summer it is possible to escape the heat and humidity of the coast and go to the mountains. Average annual rainfall is 893mm in Beirut, mostly occurring in winter.

Dress codes
Formal clothing is required for business meetings. Women should dress modestly.

Entry requirements
Passports
Required by all and must have six months validity from date of visit.
Visa
Required by all, with a few exceptions for regional nationals. Contact the nearest consulate for confirmation. Those who apply for a business visa must submit a business letter from the visitor's company with a letter or fax from a local business contact stating the purpose of the trip.
Prohibited entry
Entry is refused to holders of Israeli and Palestinian passports, holders of passports containing a visa for Israel, valid or expired, used or unused, and passports with entry stamps to Israel.
Currency advice/regulations
There are no restrictions on the import and export of local or foreign currencies. Travellers cheques are not suitable for Lebanon as it takes two weeks for cheques to clear.
Customs
Duty-free allowances include amounts of alcohol, tobacco and perfume. Personal belonging may not exceed LL200,000. Antiques require export permits.
Prohibited imports
Firearms, ammunition, illegal drugs and pornography.

Health (for visitors)
Mandatory precautions
Vaccination certificates for yellow fever are required if travelling from an infected area. There are no other mandatory vaccinations required to enter Lebanon.
Advisable precautions
It is recommended that visitors have preventative vaccinations for polio, typhoid, tetanus and hepatitis A.
Lebanon's medical services are generally modern, with most doctors speaking French or English. The private hospitals are the best, but more expensive, and it is recommended that insurance is taken out by all visitors.

Hotels
The ministry of tourism assesses the quality of hotels and publishes an annual report. A full range of hotels were available before the Lebanese/Israeli conflict of 2006.

A 15 per cent service charge is usually added to the bill, with additional tipping optional.

Credit cards
International credit cards are accepted throughout the capital, and in the more developed areas across the country. ATMs are plentiful

Public holidays (national)
Fixed dates
1 Jan (New Year's Day), ^9 Feb (Feast of St Maroun), 1 May (Labour Day), 6 May (Martyrs' Day), ^15 Aug (Assumption Day), ^1 Nov (All Saints' Day), 22 Nov (Independence Day), ^25 Dec (Christmas Day).
^ Observed by adherents only.
Holidays that fall at the weekend are taken on the Monday following.
Variable dates
Orthodox Christmas (Jan), Orthodox Easter (Mar/Apr, Fri–Mon), Eid al Adha (three days), Islamic New Year, Ashura (two days), Birth of the Prophet, Eid al Fitr (three days).
Islamic year – 1429 (10 Jan 2008–28 Dec 2008): The Islamic year contains 354 or 355 days, with the result that Muslim feasts advance by 10–12 days against the Gregorian calendar. Dates of feasts vary according to the sighting of the new moon, so cannot be forecast exactly.

Working hours
Banking
Mon–Fri: 0800–1230; Sat: 0800–1200.
Business
Mon–Fri: 0900–1600.
Government
Mon–Fri: 0800–1400; Sat: 0800–1300.

Shops
Mon–Sat: 0800–1900. Some shops open on Sundays.

Telecommunications
Mobile/cell phones
GSM 900 services cover the entire country.

Electricity supply
110V or 220V AC, 50 cycles. Supply is subject to fluctuations and blackouts. It is advisable to use a stabiliser when operating more advanced electronic equipment.

Weights and measures
Metric system

Social customs/useful tips
Punctuality is expected for business appointments but is less strictly observed for social engagements. The usual form of greeting is to shake hands. It is the custom to offer coffee or tea to visitors and it is considered rude to refuse. Muslim traditions are observed.
During Ramadan (the four weeks prior to the Eid al Fitr holiday) employees tend to work shorter hours. It is advisable to avoid business trips at this time.

Security
Visitors should keep in touch with developments in the Middle East as any increase in regional tension might affect travel advice.
Security in Lebanon is likely to remain hostage to the regional tensions over the Israeli-Palestinian and Iraqi conflicts. Visitors are advised to carry their passports.

Getting there
Air
Runways at Beirut airport sustained damage during the conflict in 2006. It is estimated that repairs will be completed by November 2006.
National airline: Middle East Airlines (MEA).
International airport/s: The Rafik Hariri International Airport (renamed in June 2006) (BEY), is 16km from Beirut, with duty-free shops, VIP lounge, post office, restaurant bureau de change, hotel reservation and car hire.
Airport tax: Departure tax: LL100,000 first class, LL75,000 business class, LL50,000 economy class passengers
Surface
Road: Road access is possible through Turkey via Aleppo and Syria via the Bekaa valley. No access is possible via Israel.
Water: A ferry operates between Larnaca in Cyprus and Beirut.
Main port/s: Beirut, Tripoli, Saida (Sidon), Jounieh, Tyre and Byblos.

Getting about
National transport
Air: There are no domestic flights.
Road: Some 6,000km of roads and highways, excluding municipal roads. There are two international motorways with a total length of 570km. Some 40 per cent of the road network is in poor condition. New routes were under construction prior to the 2006 conflict with Israel.
Buses: Buses travel between Beirut and other major towns around the country. There are only limited daily departures.
Rail: There is no passenger railway network in Lebanon.
City transport
Taxis: There are taxis available throughout Beirut and most of the country. Service taxis usually follow established routes where one person will often share the taxi with up to four other passengers. Share taxis will stop on request. Ordinary taxis are not restricted to a set route and will take passengers anywhere in the country. The government has fixed charges for airport taxis.
Buses, trams & metro: A few buses are available to certain destinations. Not recommended for foreign visitors.
Car hire
There are several international car hire companies in Beirut, usually offering competitive rates. Rental companies can also provide drivers with their cars.

BUSINESS DIRECTORY

The addresses listed below are a selection only. While World of Information makes every endeavour to check these addresses, we cannot guarantee that changes have not been made, especially to telephone numbers and area codes. We would welcome any corrections.

Telephone area codes
The international direct dialling (IDD) code for Lebanon is +961, followed by area code:

Grand Beirut	1	Tripoli	6
Kerswan / Jbeil	9	Tyre	7
Sidon	7	Zahle	8

Chambers of Commerce
American Lebanese Chamber of Commerce,1153 Foch Street, PO Box 175093, Beirut (tel: 985-330; fax: 985-331; e-mail: amchamlb@cyberia.net.lb).

Beirut and Mount Lebanon Chamber of Commerce, Industry and Agriculture, Sanayeh, 1 Justinien Street, PO Box 11-1801, Beirut (tel: 353-390; fax: 353-395; e-mail: info@ccib.org.lb).

Federation of the Chambers of Commerce, Industry and Agriculture in Lebanon, Sanayeh, 1 Justinien Street, PO Box 11-1801, Beirut (tel: 745-288; fax: 341-328; e-mail: fccial@cci-fed.org.lb).

Sidon and South Lebanon Chamber of Commerce, Industry and Agriculture, Boulevard Maarouf Saad, PO Box 41, Sidon (tel: 720-123; fax: 722-986; e-mail: chamber@ccias.org.lb).

Tripoli and North Lebanon Chamber of Commerce, Industry and Agriculture, Bechara Khoury Street, PO Box 47, Tripoli (tel: 425-600; fax: 442-042; e-mail: comindeg@adm.net.lb).

Banking
ABN-AMRO Bank Lebanon, ABN AMRO Tower, Charles Malek Avenue, Achrafieh, Beirut (tel: 219-200; fax: 217-756/7).

Arab African International Bank, Riad El Solh, beirur (tel: 980-162/3, 980-264/5; fax: 633-912).

Bank of Beirut; PO Box 11-7354, Bank of Beirut sal Bldg, Foch Street, Beirut Central District, Beirut (tel: 738767/68; fax: 602166).

Banque Audi, Banque Audi Plaza, Bab Idriss, 2021 8102 Beirut (tel: 200-250, 331-600; fax: 339-220).

British Arab Commercial Bank Ltd, ARESCO Centre, Banque du Liban Street, PO Box 113-5495, Hamra, Beirut (tel: 602-437; fax: 602-438).

HSBC Bank Middle East Ltd, PO Box 11-1380, St Georges Bay, Minet el Hosn, Beirut (tel: 377-477, 369-900; fax: 372-362).

Banque Libano-Française, PO Box 11808, Beirut Liberty Plaza Bldg, Roma Street, Ras Beirut, Beirut (tel: 791332; fax: 340355).

BLOM Bank, BLOM Banks's Bldg, Rashid Karami St, Verdun, Beirut, Lebanon (tel: 743-300, 738-938; fax: 738-946).

Banque de la Méditerranée; Méditerranée Group Building, Clemenceau Street, Kantari Beirut, 2022 9302 Beirut (tel: 373-937; fax: 362-706).

Central bank
Banque du Liban, PO Box 11-5544, Masraf Loubane Street, Beirut (tel: 750-000; fax: 478-2740; e-mail: bdlit@bdl.gov.lb).

Travel information
Middle East Airlines, PO Box 206, Beirut International Airport.

Tourist Police (343-209).

Trans Mediterranean Airways, PO Box 11-3018, Beirut International Airport.

Ministry of tourism
Ministry of Tourism, Information Services, 550 Central Bank Street, PO Box 11-5344, Beirut (tel: 354-764; fax: 343-279; e-mail: mot@

lebanon-tourismgov.lb; internet: www.destinationlebanon.gov.lb).

Ministries

Ministry of Agriculture, Georges Jaber Building, Badaro Street, Beirut (tel: 455-613; fax: 455-475; e-mail: ministry@agriculture.gov.lb).

Ministry of Defence, Yarzé, Beirut (tel: 452-963; fax: 457-920).

Ministry of the Displaced, Old Sidon Road, Damour (tel: 840-474; fax: 840-476; e-mail: mod@dm.net.lb).

Ministry of Economy and Trade, Assaf Building, Rue Artois, Beirut (tel: 340-504; fax: 354-640; e-mail: postmaster@economy.gov.lb).

Ministry of Education and Higher Education, Rue Georges Piko, Beirut (tel: 744-251; fax: 371-079).

Ministry of Electricity and Water Resources, Shiah, Beirut (tel: 565-040; fax: 449-639).

Ministry of the Environment, 550 Central Bank Street, Beirut (tel: 524-999; fax: 524-555).

Ministry of Finance, MOF Building, Riyad el Solh Square, Beirut (tel: 981-001; fax: 642-762; e-mail: infocenter@finance.gov.lb).

Ministry of Foreign Affairs, Rue Sursock, Beirut (tel: 334-400; fax: 584-098).

Ministry of Health, Museum Street, Beirut (tel: 615-701; fax: 645-099).

Ministry of Industry, Rue Sami Solh, Beirut (tel: 427-247; fax: 427-112).

Ministry of Information, Rue Hamra, Beirut (tel: 351-032; fax: 423-189).

Ministry of the Interior, Rue des Arts et Métiers, Sanayeh, Beirut (tel: 981-270; fax: 751-622).

Ministry of Justice, Rue Sami Solh, Beirut (tel: 425-670; fax: 422-957).

Ministry of Labour, Shiah, Beirut (tel: 556-831; fax: 556-832).

Ministry of Posts and Telecommunications, Rue Sami Shoh, Beirut (tel: 888-100; fax: 423-005; e-mail: webmaster@mpt.gov.lb).

Ministry of Public Works and Transport, Fiyadieh, Hazmieh, Beirut (tel: 458-975; fax: 459-434).

Ministry of Social Affairs, Rue Badaro, Beirut (tel: 395-561; fax: 396-148).

Ministry of Sports and Youth, Campus of Unesco, Beirut (tel: 790-529; fax: 840-440).

Ministry of Tourism, 550 Central Bank Street, Beirut (fax: 340-940; e-mail: mot@lebanon-tourism.gov.lb).

Office of the President, Presidential Palace, Beirut (tel: 220-0000; fax: 425-395).

Office of the Prime Minister, Riyad el Sol Square, Beirut (tel: 862-001; fax: 869-630).

Other useful addresses

Assocation of Lebanese Industrialists, PO Box 1520, Chamber of Commerce and Industry Building, Justinian Street, Beirut (tel: 350-280; fax: 351-167).

Board for Foreign Economic Relations, PO Box 11-5344, Beirut (tel: 483-391/5

British Embassy, Commercial Section, PO Box 60180, Coolrite Building, Autostrade, Jal El Dib, Beirut (tel: 406-330, 405-033, 402-035; fax: 402-033).

Council for Development and Reconstruction (CDR), Tallet El Serail, Beirut Central District (tel: 643-981; fax: 647-947, 864-494, 865-630).

Electricité du Liban, Nahr Street, Beirut (tel: 442-720; fax: 583-084).

Higher Council for Privatisation, Grand Serail, Beirut Central District, Beirut (tel: 987-500; fax: 983-061).

International Fairs and Promotions, SARL, PO Box 55576, Beirut.

Investment Development Authority of Lebanon, Presidency of the Council of Ministers, Liberty, Lyon Street, PO Box 113-7251, Sanayeh, Beirut (tel: 344-676, 344-403; fax: 344-463, 347-397).

Lebanese Embassy (USA), 2560 28th Street, NW, Washington DC 20008 (tel: (+1-202) 939-6300; fax: (+1-202) 939-6324; e-mail: info@lebanonembassy.org).

Solidére (development company for rebuilding Beirut), Industry and Labour Bank Building, Riyadh El-Solh Street, PO Box 11-9493, Beirut (tel: 346-891, 646-137/8/9; fax: 646-136).

National news agency: NNA (National News Agency): www.nna-leb.gov.lb

Other news agencies: Central News Agency: www.almarkazia.com

Internet sites

Investment Development Authority of Lebanon (IDAL): www.idal.com.lb

Lebanon Online: www.lebanon.com

Ministry of Economy and Trade: www.economy.gov.lb

Ministry of Tourism: www.lebanon-tourism.gov.lb

Lesotho

KEY FACTS

Official name: Kingdom of Lesotho

Head of State: King Letsie III (since 7 Feb 1996)

Head of government: Prime Minister Bethuel Pakalitha Mosisili (LCD) (since 1998; re-elected Feb 2007)

Ruling party: Lesotho Congress for Democracy (LCD) (re-elected Feb 2007)

Area: 30,355 square km

Population: 2.41 million (2007)*

Capital: Maseru

Official language: Sesotho and English

Currency: Loti (maloti, plural) (L) = 100 lisente; has parity with the South African rand, which is legal tender.

Exchange rate: L7.55 per US$ (Jul 2008)

GDP per capita: US$665 (2007)*

GDP real growth: 4.90% (2007)*

Labour force: 770,000 (2004)

Inflation: 8.00% (2007)

Balance of trade: -US$668.00 million (2006)

Visitor numbers: 357,000 (2006)*

Annual FDI: US$78.00 million (2006)

* estimated figure

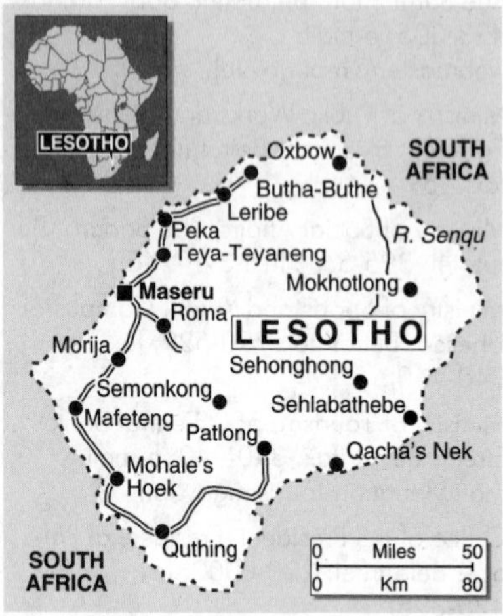

Water is the one resource that Lesotho has in abundance. Lesotho's water resources far exceed its possible future requirement, even allowing for possible future irrigation projects and for general development and improvement of living standards. Other than that, Lesotho can be summed up as a small, landlocked country, entirely surrounded by South Africa, with no substantial natural resources other than water. More than 85 per cent of the population of 2.45 million lives in rural areas, engaged mainly in agriculture, which contributes about 14 per cent of GDP, and informal activities. Then in 1986 the Lesotho Highlands Water Project (LHWP) Treaty was signed by the governments of Lesotho and the Republic of South Africa and Lesotho found itself with the largest construction site on the continent.

Lesotho's 'white gold'

Much of the tiny country of Lesotho, with its spectacular canyons and thatched huts, remained untouched by modern machines until the early 1990s when major construction work began to create the LHWP. This huge development is primarily to provide revenue for Lesotho from the provision of water to Guateng province in South Africa. Guateng generates some 60 per cent of South Africa's industrial output, 80 per cent of its mining output and is where over 40 per cent of its population lives.

The latest phase of the LHWP, which delivers water from the highlands of Lesotho to South Africa's Vaal river system, and generates hydropower for Lesotho, was inaugurated by King Letsie of Lesotho and President Mbeki of South Afric in March 2008.

In his speech at the inauguration ceremony at Mohale dam, Mbeki described the LHWP as a bi-lateral project to harness a natural resource, Lesotho's 'white gold', for the benefit of both countries. 'For South Africa,' he said 'the project brings improved security of water supply for both economic and domestic use, and will undoubtedly help to meet the increasing water demand for many years to come.' He went on to say '…Lesotho enjoys the benefits of new infrastructure, including roads, expanded communication and electricity systems, health facilities, job opportunities, improved water supply and sanitation to numerous communities, and many additional secondary benefits associated with a huge capital investment with its revenue streams. The project not only sustains the development of both countries in significant ways, but provides a show piece for the region and the rest of the continent of mutually beneficial co-operation.'

The economy improves

Lesotho has also made considerable gains in macroeconomic stability since 2004. Since the 3.7 per cent annual GDP growth rate recorded in 2005, growth soared 7.2 per cent in 2006, before dropping back to a more consistent 5.1 per cent in 2007. Since 2000 the positive impact from the construction of the LHWP, which supplies water to South Africa, and a small but rapidly growing manufacturing sector (principally textiles) have contributed to economic growth. As a result of the African Growth and Opportunity Act (AGOA) and duty and quota-free access to US markets, the garment industry became the largest single employer. The phasing out of quotas under the Multi-Fibre Agreement (MFA), has inevitably had a negative impact.

Lesotho's GDP per capita was US$632 in 2006 and estimated at US$712 in 2007.

About 35 per cent of the labour force is unemployed or under-employed. Estimated HIV/AIDS adult prevalence is 31 per cent.

The government's fiscal position and the external current account have improved markedly, the inflation rate has slowed – holding at 6.0 per cent in 2007 – and net international reserves have increased. However, poverty remains widespread. Growth has been weakened by the cumulative impact of several shocks: a substantial real appreciation of the exchange rate of the South African rand, to which the Lesotho loti is pegged; the removal of textile quotas by industrial countries; a continuing decline in the terms of trade; and persistent drought.

Lesotho's economic prospects could be affected by further trade preference erosion, a declining trend in revenue receipts from the Southern African Customs Union (Sacu) – essentially a free trade area comprised of Botswana, Lesotho, Namibia, South Africa and Swaziland – and falling remittances from Lesotho workers in South Africa as the South Africans seek to have more of their nationals employed in the mines. The number of Basotho mine workers in South African mines fell from an average of 96,000 in 1997 to 62,000 in 2002 and has continued to fall. Lesotho is facing the challenge of restoring external competitiveness and promoting rapid and broad-based growth to reduce poverty. With the country's commitment to keep the loti pegged to the rand, the burden of safeguarding macroeconomic stability will necessarily fall on fiscal policy and accelerating structural reforms to restore competitiveness.

Southern trade

Lesotho is a small, open, low-income economy with very close financial and commercial ties to South Africa. It is a member of Sacu and the (Southern Africa) Common Monetary Area (CMA). Trade among Sacu countries is free of tariffs and duties. Trade with South Africa accounts for about two-thirds of Lesotho's external trade, and foreign direct investment (stock) from South Africa is about 20 per cent of Lesotho's gross domestic product. Lesotho's banking system comprises four banks, three of them South African. Workers' remittances from South Africa and receipts of Lesotho's share of Sacu revenue constitute a significant part of national income.

The authorities have reformed public expenditure management and the financial sector and privatised public enterprises. The introduction of value added tax (VAT) and the creation of the Lesotho Revenue Authority (LRA) have helped to raise non-Sacu revenue.

Hereditary monarchy

King Letsie III has no legislative or executive powers. The monarchy is now hereditary, under the terms of the constitution, which came into effect after the March 1993 election. The monarch is a 'living symbol of national unity'; under traditional law the college of chiefs has the power to determine who is next in the line of succession, and who shall serve as regent in the event that the successor is not of mature age.

Letsie III succeeded his father, King Moshoeshoe, who was dethroned and exiled in 1990, but returned to Lesotho in 1992. Letsie III abdicated and his father was reinstated as monarch in 1995, but already there was a strong movement towards constitutional government. Letsie III was restored as king in 1996 after his father died in a car accident. Basutoland was renamed the Kingdom of Lesotho upon independence from the UK in 1966 under King Moshoeshoe. In 1998, violent protests and a military mutiny following a contentious election prompted a brief but bloody intervention by South African and Botswana military forces under the aegis of the Southern African Development Community.

In the February 2007 parliamentary elections, the ruling Lesotho Congress for Democracy (LCD) won 61seats (out of 120) in the national assembly, and Prime Minister Bethuel Pakalitha Mosisili of the LCD was set for another term in office.

Risk assessment

Politics	Fair
Economy	Fair
Regional stability	Good

COUNTRY PROFILE

Historical profile

A fight for survival brought the African nation-state of Basutoland into existence in the nineteenth century; the fight for survival still characterises the Kingdom of Lesotho. When the Zulu-Mfecane swept over South Africa in the early nineteenth century the mountain fastness of present-day Lesotho offered a defensive position to its inhabitants and a refuge to people of very diverse origins up-rooted from elsewhere.
A local chief, Moshoeshoe 1 (1831–70), took his chance to prove himself as one of the outstanding empire-builders of nineteenth century Africa. Through shrewd diplomacy and military ability, but especially as a gifted administrator, creating a reform model for traditional government. Moshoeshoe succeeded in defending his people and expanding his domain. For some time he could even defend his state against the advancing Boers, but at last, against their never ending land hunger, broke down. An unjust peace after military defeat in 1866 forced the Basuto to hand over half their agricultural lands to the Orange Free State.
When Britain responded to Moshoeshoe's pleas for British rule and protection a part of the lost territory was restored, but a disappointingly small portion. It needed

KEY INDICATORS — Lesotho

	Unit	2003	2004	2005	2006	2007
Population	m	2.41	2.59	2.36	2.36	*2.45
Gross domestic product (GDP)	US$bn	0.88	1.40	1.49	1.49	*1.60
GDP per capita	US$	364	652	631	632	*712
GDP real growth	%	4.2	2.3	3.7	7.2	*5.1
Inflation	%	7.6	5.5	3.4	6.1	*6.0
Industrial output	% change	–	3.0	–	11.4	–
Agricultural output	% change	–	0.2	2.8	1.7	–
Exports (fob) (goods)	US$m	422.0	484.5	673.0	693.6	–
Imports (cif) (goods)	US$m	738.0	730.9	1,251.0	1,360.6	–
Balance of trade	US$m	-316.0	-246.4	-578.0	-656.2	–
Current account	US$m	-150.0	-59.0	-45.0	66.0	89.0
Total reserves minus gold	US$m	460.3	502.8	519.1	658.4	–
Foreign exchange	US$m	454.4	496.7	513.5	652.7	–
Exchange rate	per US$	7.56	6.19	7.23	7.23	6.84

* estimated figure

another desperate fight, the Gun War of 1880, to convince the British government that rule by South Africa's whites was not acceptable to Moshoeshoe's nation and London arranged for direct rule through its representative in South Africa, the High Commissioner in Cape Town.
1600s Modern-day Lesotho was settled by the Sotho people; the area was already home to the San people.
1800s European traders and missionaries arrived in the area, and were soon followed by the Boers on their Great Trek. The Boer trek coincided with the expansion of the Zulu state. King Moshoeshoe the Great ensured the survival of his people by taking them to a mountain stronghold in about 1820. The policy of assisting refugees on condition that they help in defence proved successful – by 1842 the King's people numbered around 40,000 and were protected by outlying refugee settlements.
1870 By the time King Moshoeshoe died, a Basuto nation of 150,000 had been established.
1910 After annexing Basutoland, the British established the Basutoland National Council comprising members nominated by chiefs.
1960 After a new constitution was introduced, elections were held, which were won by the Basutoland Congress Party (BCP) ahead of the Basutoland National Party (BNP) led by Chief Leabua Jonathan.
1965 The BCP lost the election to the BNP; Chief Jonathan became the first prime minister of the Kingdom of Lesotho. King Moshoeshoe II was stripped of most of his powers.
1966 Independence was granted.
1970 The constitution was suspended and opposition political parties banned.
1986 The government of Chief Leabua Jonathan was overthrown in a military coup by Major General J M Lekhanya. A military government chaired by Lekhanya ruled Lesotho in co-ordination with King Moshoeshoe II and a civilian cabinet appointed by the King. The new regime was more amenable to South Africa's wishes.
1990 A constituent assembly was set up to frame a new constitution; a timetable was announced for a return to civilian rule. King Moshoeshoe II was stripped of his executive and legislative powers and exiled by Lekhanya.
1991 Lekhanya was overthrown by a group of military officers led by Major General Elias Ramaema who took control. Because Moshoeshoe II initially refused to return under the new rules of the government in which the King was given only ceremonial powers, Moshoeshoe's son was installed as King Letsie III.
1992 King Moshoeshoe returned from exile as a common citizen, in a deal with the military regime.
1993 A new constitution was adopted leaving the King as ceremonial head of the country. Elections signalled a return to democracy; the BCP won a convincing victory. King Letsie III became a purely constitutional monarch.
1994 After growing unrest, King Letsie III suspended the constitution. King Moshoeshoe, in collaboration with military supporters staged a coup but it was thwarted within a month. The settlement eventually negotiated allowed for both the re-establishment of parliamentary rule and King Letsie abdicated in favour of King Moshoeshoe.
1996 King Moshoeshoe II was killed in a road accident and was again succeeded by his son, who was sworn in as King Letsie III.
1997 King Letsie III was formally crowned.
1998 The Lesotho Congress for Democracy (LCD) won the elections. The result was rejected by opposition groups. After riots broke out in Maseru and reports circulated of an imminent military coup, 800 South African and Botswanan soldiers entered Lesotho with the aim of restoring order. The Interim Political Authority (IPA) was created to work alongside the government to prepare for elections.
2000 King Letsie III married Karabo Motsoeneng.
2001 President Thabo Mbeki of South Africa visited Lesotho to mend diplomatic relations and develop economic links. Twenty-seven LCD members of parliament quit the party to form the Lesotho People's Congress (LPC).
2002 The first chamber of parliament was enlarged from 80 seats to 120.
2003 Families displaced by the Lesotho Highlands Water Project (LHWP), and resettled in the Maseru district, won a ruling that improvements to their schools should be made by the project's authority.
2004 Prime Minister Mosisili declared a state of emergency and appealed for food aid. The first phase of the LHWP was officially opened.
2006 Foreign Minister Monyane Moleleki was shot and wounded by a gunman. The Lesotho Promise, one of the world's largest diamonds, was sold uncut for US12.4 million. To celebrate 40 years of independence, Lesotho adopted a new flag to show it was 'at peace with itself and its neighbours' and replaced the one adopted in 1986 after a coup.
2007 In parliamentary elections, the ruling LCD won 61seats (out of 120) in the national assembly. The most severe drought since the 1970s, caused widespread hunger, exacerbated by a drop in food production due to HIV/Aids and forced a state of emergence to avert famine, as the UN World Food Programme called for international aid. The annual cereal harvest was less than 25 per cent of the country's needs.
2008 The European Investment Bank (EIB) agreed a loan of US$22 million, on 26 July, for 50 per cent of the cost of the expansion and rehabilitation of wastewater and sanitation facilities in the capital.

Political structure
Constitution
A new constitution was adopted in 1993, which redefined the role of the monarchy and altered the legislative branch of the government.
The King, who is head of State, has no executive or legislative authority.
Form of state
Constitutional monarchy
The executive
Executive power is vested in the prime minister, leader of the majority parliamentary party, and the cabinet appointed by the prime minister.
National legislature
Legislative power is held by a bi-cameral National Assembly.
The first chamber, the Assembly has 120 seats, 80 of which are elected by a simple majority in single-member constituencies, while 80 seats are chosen by proportional representation through party lists.
The second chamber (Senate) is made up of 22 hereditary principal chiefs and 11 members are appointed by the King, on advice from the prime minister.
All members serve for a maximum 5-year term.
Legal system
The legal system is based on English common law and Roman-Dutch law.
Last elections
17 February 2007 (parliamentary)
Results: Parliamentary: the LCD won 61out of 120 seats; National Independent Party (NIP) 21; the All Basotho Convention (ABC) 17; Lesotho Workers' Parthy 10; all other parties won less than five seats.
Next elections
2012 (parliamentary)

Political parties
Ruling party
Lesotho Congress for Democracy (LCD) (re-elected Feb 2007)
Main opposition party
All Basotho Convention (ABC)

Population
2.41 million (2007)*
Last census: May 1996: 1,960,069
Population density: 66 inhabitants per square km. Urban population: 29 per cent of the total population (1995–2001).

Annual growth rate: 0.7 per cent 1994–2004 (WHO 2006)

Ethnic make-up

The Basotho nation is an amalgam of mainly Sesotho-speaking people. Some 45 per cent of the population is of Nguni origin. A number of smaller groups, including San Griqua, Indian and European, have also become naturalised Basotho.

Religions

Christianity (approximately 80 per cent, mainly Roman Catholic), various traditional beliefs and others (20 per cent).

Education

Primary education is free from the age of six.

Public expenditure on education typically amounts to around 8.5 per cent of gross national income (GNI). Lesotho has one university, located in the capital, Maseru.

Literacy rate: 81 per cent adult rate (Unesco 2005)

Compulsory years: Six to 13

Enrolment rate: 108 per cent gross primary enrolment, of the relevant age group (including repeaters); 31 per cent gross secondary enrolment (World Bank).

Pupils per teacher: 46 in primary schools.

Health

Per capita total expenditure on health (2003) was US$106; of which per capita government spending was US$84, at the international dollar rate, (WHO 2006).

HIV/Aids

The HIV prevalence is one of the highest in the world. The government has undertaken a scheme to offer HIV counseling and testing for every household by 2007; seven thousand people will be trained in medical care and for the purpose of the campaign.

Lesotho has record success by exceeding epectations in its participation of the UN sponsored '3 by 5' campaign (worldwide, providing three million HIV sufferers with antiretroviral drugs by 2005).

HIV prevalence: 25 per cent in 2005

Life expectancy: 41 years, 2004 (WHO 2006)

Fertility rate/Maternal mortality rate: 3.5 births per woman, 2004 (WHO 2006); maternal mortality 530 per 100,000 live births (World Bank).

Child (under 5 years) mortality rate (per 1,000): 79 per 1,000 live births; 16 per cent of children aged under five are malnourished (World Bank).

Head of population per physician: 0.05 physicians per 1,000 people, 2003 (WHO 2006)

Main cities

Maseru (capital, estimated population 267,652 in 2005), Maputsoa (97,296), Mafeteng (75,939), Teyateyaneng (37,239).

Languages spoken

English becomes the medium of instruction from the fifth year of primary education.

Official language/s

Sesotho and English

Media

National news agency: LENA (Lesotho News Agency)

Press

Journalists and the print media are frequently subject to defamation lawsuits, which hampers their freedom to report. High publishing costs keep the number of publications limited and all on offer are weeklies.

In English, Informative News (www.informativenews.co.ls) is a business magazine published on Friday. For general news, The Mirror and Public Eye (www.publiceye.co.ls). In Sesotho Makatolle, MoAfrica and Mohlanka. Mopheme (The Survivor) is published in Sesotho and English.

Broadcasting

Radio: Radio provides the majority of the population with news, information and entertainment.

The national, state-run Radio Lesotho (www.radioles.co.ls) has programmes in Sesotho and English (in educational shows during the school year). There are several private radio stations including Lesotho NBS (www.radiolesotho.co.ls), PC FM (www.pcfm.co.ls), Joy Radio, Mo Afrika FM and Catholic Radio.

Television: The national, state-run Lesotho Television has a limited service. The South African Broadcasting Corporation (SABC) (www.sabc.co.za) is available.

News agencies

National news agency: LENA (Lesotho News Agency)

Economy

Lesotho is a small, land-locked country, inside South Africa, with no major natural resources other than its rivers. Lesotho sells water and hydroelectric power to South Africa. The Lesotho Highlands Water Project, currently under construction, is one of the largest and most ambitious multi-purpose water schemes anywhere in the world, which, once complete, will provide South Africa with 79 cubic metres of water a second, by diverting the flow of the Senqu river and its tributaries northwards to South Africa. By 2044, revenues are predicted to contribute some 5 per cent to Lesotho's annual GDP. The first phase of the project was officially opened in March 2004.

Although the majority of the population live in rural areas, agriculture's share of the economy has declined in recent decades to around 17 per cent of GDP. In addition to the longer-term problem of soil erosion, the sector has been stricken alternately by drought and excessive rainfall since 2002. There has been a loss of manpower and farming skills due to the depredations of HIV/Aids. Almost one in three people suffers from HIV/Aids in Lesotho, which adversely affects both domestic and public economies.

The textile and clothing industry, which accounts for a fifth of GDP, was badly affected by the phasing out of the multi-fibre agreement in 2004 and by competition from China, causing a slump in employment and exports. By 2006, the clothing industry was being revitalised, mainly by new markets for ethical clothing.

The main support of the economy has for long been remittances from migrant workers employed in South Africa, but this source of revenue is declining, as South Africa reduces its reliance on imported labour. Remittances currently account for around 25 per cent of GDP.

Social indicators remain poor with around two-thirds of the population living below the poverty line. In 2005, the World Food Programme estimated that 500,000 people were in need of food aid.

External trade

Lesotho 's economy is heavily influenced by South Africa; all foreign trade is either with South Africa or has to pass through it to reach other markets. Lesotho is a member of the Southern African Customs Union (Sacu), with South Africa, Namibia, Swaziland and Botswana. Sacu sets customs duties for commodities passing between member states and members share the common pool of customs and excise revenue on all external trade.

Lesotho is also a member of the Southern African Development Community (SADC), the objectives which include reduction in trade barriers, achieving regional development and economic growth and evolving common systems and institutions.

Lesotho produces more denim jeans (over 26 million pairs each year) than any other country in Africa. This is despite the fall in sales and the temporary loss of jobs following the end of the Multi-Fibre Agreement (MFA) in 2005, which saw world sales of Asian garments eliminate many markets for African manufacturers.

Imports

Principal imports include petroleum, food, building materials, machinery and vehicles, pharmaceuticals and medical products.

Main sources: US (84.0 per cent total, 2005), Belgium (12.8 per cent), Canada (2.4 per cent)

Exports
Principal exports are electricity and water (to South Africa), garment manufactures, vehicles parts, wool and mohair, food and live animals.
Main destinations: Hong Kong (43.6 per cent total, 2005), China (35.4 per cent), Germany (8.4 per cent)

Agriculture
The agricultural sector has traditionally been a major contributor to the economy. A series of programmes were implemented from 1996 to boost agricultural development through commercialisation and privatisation. Progress has been slow and the IMF reported in 2005 that agriculture suffered from structural weaknesses that included poor farming techniques, soil erosion, lack of water in lowland areas and lack of access to agri-finance.
There are a number of factors constraining development such as the government's heavy involvement in production, marketing and processing of the sector. This involves controlling commodity prices as well as containing imports and exports. These policies have deterred private sector involvement and hampered growth. The country also faces a severe lack of land suitable to arable farming as well as poor soil fertility and unreliable rainfall. Poverty is widespread in rural areas, where households rely on miners' remittances to remain in operation. As more workers are being laid off in South African mines the agricultural sector is finding it hard to maintain production levels enough to feed the population.
Moreover, the construction of the Mohale dam as part of the Lesotho Highlands Water Project (LHWP) has meant flooding the most fertile land area, the only region producing a food surplus. The World Bank maintains that the US$55 million earned from water sales to South Africa will far exceed the US$2 million value of Mohale valley crops. Farmers from the Katse Dam area have been given food aid and skills training and communities have been resettled. Environmental organisations expressed concern over increased unemployment, food insecurity and water shortages downstream due to dams.
The estimated crop production for 2005 included: 247,550 tonnes (t) cereals in total, 51,000t wheat, 150,000t maize, 90,000t potatoes, 46,000t sorghum, 11,400t pulses, 13,000t fruit in total, 18,000t vegetables in total. Estimated livestock production included: 22,220t meat in total, 8,710t beef, 2,775t pig meat, 3,900t game meat, 3,100t lamb, 1,935t goat meat, 1,800t poultry, 1,512t eggs, 23,750t milk, 1,876t cattle hides, 620t sheepskins, 3,900t game meat, 2,600t greasy wool.

Industry and manufacturing
The industrial sector as a whole typically contributes around 40 per cent of GDP and employs around 26 per cent of the labour force.
Most firms are small and are in joint ventures with the Lesotho National Development Corporation (LNDC). Production is largely for export (clothing, footwear, textiles) or import substitution (food processing, bricks). Other enterprises include handicrafts, ceramics and furniture making. Pharmaceuticals and leather/hide processing are under development.
Industrial production grew by 2.6 per cent and manufacturing by 3.0 per cent in 2004.

Tourism
The Lesotho Tourism Development Corporation (LTDC) provides the direction for the tourism sector. It's strategy is to develop village based facilities where visitors can experience traditional customs and lifestyles. The country is also being marketed for the eco-tourist and those enjoying activity holidays.
The Lesotho highlands are the main tourist attraction as well as the world heritage site of Maloti/Drakensberg, which has been given a US$15 million grant, by the World Bank, to protect its bio-diversity.
Travel and tourism is expected to contribute over US$223 million, or 2.6 per cent of GDP in 2005 and employ around 27,000 workers. The sector is estimated to attract over 11 per cent of total capital investment, at almost US$70 million in 2005.

Mining
The diamond industry is mainly based on the Letseng la Terae mine. Letseng Diamonds and the New Mining Corporation each have a 38 per cent share in the project while the government retains a 24 per cent share. The mine produces just three carats per 100 tonnes, compared to the global average of 50–100 carats per 100 tonnes. Production costs are at least 10 times greater than the world average. However, Letseng la Terae continues to be in operation due to the high number of large diamonds produced.

Hydrocarbons
Lesotho does not produce any hydrocarbons. Explorations for oil took place in 1970 however this proved unsuccessful and no further attempts have been made. Currently it imports refined oil, primarily from South Africa.
Coal consumption makes up for 87 per cent of Lesotho's energy requirements and is also imported from South Africa.

Energy
The electricity supply is the responsibility of the Lesotho Electricity Corporation (LEC), and most of its power requirements are supplied by South Africa.
The first phase of an ambitious US$8 billion Lesotho Highlands Water Project (LHWP) should produce enough hydroelectricity to meet almost all Lesotho's needs.

Banking and insurance
Restructuring of the banking sector in the 1990s has strengthened the position of Lesotho's banking sector by improving asset management and the capital base of domestic banks. Along with the liberalisation of interest rates, restructuring has enabled domestic banks to respond to interest rate movements in South Africa and strengthened the Central Bank's ability to influence the money supply.
Central bank
Central Bank of Lesotho

Time
GMT plus two hours

Geography
Lesotho is a landlocked country, entirely surrounded by South African territory. It is a mountainous land situated at the highest part of the Drakensberg escarpment on the eastern rim of the South African plateau. To its west, the land falls through foothills to a lowland area where the majority of the population lives. Three large rivers, the Orange, the Caledon and the Tugela, rise in the mountains and flow through it.
Hemisphere
Southern

Climate
Temperate climate with well-marked seasons.
More than 85 per cent of the country's rainfall – averaging 700mm in mountain areas – falls from October to April. Spring comes in August. Summer from November–January with average temperature 27 degrees Centigrade (C), rising to 32 degrees C in lowland areas.
Autumn days are warm. Winter from May–July with temperatures as low as minus 7 degrees C in lowlands and minus 18 degrees C in highlands.
Snowfalls can occur on the highlands at any time of the year.

Dress codes
In summer, light, loose clothing is most comfortable, but include a raincoat.
Spring and autumn clothing should include a jersey for the cool evenings.
Heavy woollens, vests, windcheaters, socks and jackets are a must in winter.
Warm clothing is also essential for a journey into the Maloti where severe weather

conditions can be encountered any time of the year.

Entry requirements
Passports
Required by all.
Visa
Required by all, except those (mostly Commonwealth) countries listed on the internet at www.lesotholondon.org.uk, in the consular section. Further information may be requested through the consulate, or application forms downloaded from consulate websites, within applicant's country.
Currency advice/regulations
There are no restrictions on the import or export of local or foreign currency. The South African rand is interchangeable with the loti in Lesotho, but the loti cannot be used in South Africa.
Travellers cheques are widely accepted.
Customs
Personal items are exempt from duty.
Prohibited imports
Alcohol and firearms

Health (for visitors)
Mandatory precautions
Yellow fever vaccination for visitors from infected areas.
Advisable precautions
Immunisation and booster shots are advised for diphtheria, tetanus, typhoid and hepatitis A. Tuberculosis, polio and hepititis B may be advised. Malaria is not common. There is a rabies risk in rural areas. There is a very high prevalence of HIV/Aids.
Sun-burning is a problem for visitors at higher altitudes and sunscreens are recommended.
All medication necessary should be brought by a visitor.

Hotels
There are a number of comfortable, international-class hotels in Maseru. Throughout the rest of the country, accommodation ranges from medium-sized hotels to smaller tourist lodges.

Credit cards
Major credit and charge cards have acceptance.

Public holidays (national)
Fixed dates
1 Jan (New Year's Day), 11 Mar (Moshoeshoe's Day), 1 May (Workers' Day), 25 May (Heroes' Day), 17 Jul (King Letsie III's Birthday), 4 Oct (Independence Day), 24–25 Dec (Christmas).
Variable dates
Good Friday, Easter Monday, Ascension Day.

Working hours
Banking
Mon, Tue, Thu, Fri: 0830–1530; Wed: 0830–1300; Sat: 0830–1100.
Business
Mon–Fri: 0800–1245, 1400–1630; Sat: 0800–1300.
Government
Mon–Fri: 0800–1245, 1400–1630.
Shops
Mon–Fri: 0800–1700; Sat: 0800–1300.

Telecommunications
Mobile/cell phones
GSM 900 services are available in larger populated areas.

Getting there
Air
National airline: South African Airways provide regular scheduled flights via Johannesburg.
International airport/s:
Maseru-Moshoeshoe I (MSU), 18km south of Maseru. All international flights are via South Africa.
Airport tax: International departures M20; transit passengers are exempt.
Surface
Road: There are three good tarred roads from South Africa into the western region, via the Maseru Bridge, Ficksburg Bridge (both open 24 hours) and Caledonsport (open daytime only). With the implementation of the Highlands Water Project, the road network has being expanded.
There are several other border crossings but with limited opening hours.
A road tax of M5 exists for visitors leaving Lesotho by light vehicles.
Rail: Only freight traffic is carried on the rail system that links to the South African system via Maseru.

Getting about
National transport
Air: Charter flights are difficult to find. South African companies may provide a service.
Road: Over 3,500km of tarred, gravel and dirt roads. Approximately 500km are tarred.
Roads are being continuously upgraded, and tarred roads connect main towns in seven out of 10 districts.
Buses: A good service provided by mainly privately owned buses. Coach services operate Maseru-Welkom; Maseru-Qacha's Nek.
Car hire
Drivers must hold an international driving licence. Driving is on the left and seat belts are compulsory.
In winter, antifreeze is a wise precaution for all cars with watercooled engines. Chains are useful in mud and snow. Petrol can be obtained in all District Headquarter towns but is not easily obtainable elsewhere.
For visitors using their own vehicles information should be obtained from Lesotho Tourist Board Information Office (www.lesotho.gov.ls).

BUSINESS DIRECTORY

The addresses listed below are a selection only. While World of Information makes every endeavour to check these addresses, we cannot guarantee that changes have not been made, especially to telephone numbers and area codes. We would welcome any corrections.

Telephone area codes
The international dialling code (IDD) for Lesotho is +266 followed by the subscriber's number.

Useful telephone numbers
Queen Elizabeth II Hospital:312-501
Police:123
Fire brigade:122
Ambulance:121

Chambers of Commerce
Lesotho Chamber of Commerce & Industry, PO Box 79, Fairways Centre, Kingsway Avenue, Maseru 100 (tel: 2232-3482; fax: 2231-0414; e-mail: lcci@lesoff.co.za).

Banking
Lesotho Bank Ltd; PO Box 1053, Kingsway, Maseru 100 (tel: 2231-4333; fax: 2231-0348).

Barclays Bank plc, PO Box 115, Kingsway, Maseru (tel: 2231-2423; fax: 2231-0068).

NedBank, 1st Floor, Standard Bank Bldg, Kingsway, PO Box 1001, Maseru 100 (tel: 2232-2696; fax: 2231-0025).

Central bank
Central Bank of Lesotho, PO Box 1184, Corner Airport and Moshoeshoe Roads, Maseru 100 (tel: 2231-4281; fax: 2231-0051; email: cbl@centralbank.org.ls/).

Travel information
Ministry of tourism
Ministry of Tourism, Environment and Culture, PO Box 52, Maseru 100 (tel: 2231-3034).

National tourist organisation offices
Lesotho Tourist Development Corporation, PO Box 1378, Maseru 100 (tel: 2231-2427; fax: 2232-3674; email: touristinfo@ltdc.org.ls; internet: www.ltdc.org.ls).

Ministries
Minister to the Prime Minister, PO Box 527, Maseru 100 (tel: 2231-1000; fax: 2231-0102).

Ministry of Agriculture, Co-ops, Marketing and Youth Affairs, PO Box 24, Maseru 100 (tel: 2232-3561; fax: 2231-0349).

Ministry of Defence and Public Service, PO Box 527, Maseru 100 (tel: 2231-1000; fax: 2231-0102).

Ministry of Education and Manpower Development, PO Box 47, Maseru 100 (tel: 2231-3045; fax: 2231-0206).

Ministry of Finance and Economic Planning, PO Box 395, Maseru 100 (tel: 22311-101; fax: 2231-0157).

Ministry of Foreign Affairs, PO Box 1378, Maseru 100 (tel: 2231-1150; fax: 2231-1150).

Ministry of Health and Social Welfare, PO Box 514, Maseru 100 (tel: 2232-4404; fax: 2231-0467).

Ministry of Home Affairs and Local Government, Rural and Urban Development, PO Box 174, Maseru 100 (tel: 2232-3771; fax: 2231-0319).

Ministry of Information and Broadcasting, PO Box 36, Maseru 100 (tel: 2232-3561; fax: 2231-0003).

Ministry of Justice, Human Rights, Law and Constitutional Affairs, PO Box 402, Maseru 100 (tel: 2232-2683).

Ministry of Labour and Employment, Private Bag A116, Maseru 100 (tel: 2232-2565).

Ministry of Natural Resources, PO Box 426, Maseru 100 (tel: 2231-3632).

Ministry of Tourism, Sports and Culture, PO Box 52, Maseru 100 (tel: 2231-3034).

Ministry of Trade and Industry, PO Box 747, Maseru 100 (tel: 2232-2138; fax: 2231-0326).

Ministry of Transport and Telecommunications, PO Box 413, Maseru 100 (tel: 2232-3691).

Ministry of Works, PO Box 20, Maseru 100 (tel: 2231-1362; fax: 2231-0125).

Other useful addresses

British High Commission, PO Box 521, Maseru 100 (tel: 22313-961; fax: 2231-0120).

Lesotho Embassy (USA), 2511 Massachusetts Avenue, NW, Washington DC 20008 (tel: (+1-202) 797-5533; fax: (+1-202) 234-6815).

Lesotho National Development Corporation, Private Mail Bag A96, Maseru 100 (tel: 2231-2012; fax: 22310-038; internet site: www.lndc.org.ls).

Lesotho National Insurance Corporation, Private Bag A96, Maseru 100 (tel: 2231-3031; fax: 2231-0007).

Livestock Marketing Corp, PO Box 800, Maseru (tel: 2232-2444) (sole marketing concern for all livestock and products, including mohair).

Multilateral Investment Guarantee Agency (MIGA), 1818 H Street NW, Washington DC 20433, USA (tel: (+1-202) 473-1079; fax: (+1-202) 334-0265).

Radio Lesotho, PO Box 552, Maseru (tel: 2232-3561).

Statistics Bureau, PO Box 455, Maseru (tel: 2232-3852).

Trade Promotion Unit, Ministry of Trade and Industry, PO Box 747, Maseru (tel: 2232-3414; fax: 2231-0121).

National news agency: LENA (Lesotho News Agency)

Address: PO Box 36; Lerotholi Street, Maseru 100 (tel: 2232-5317; fax: 2232-6408; internet: www.lena.gov.ls).

Internet sites

Africa Business Network: www.ifc.org/abn

AllAfrica.com: http://allafrica.com

African Development Bank: www.afdb.org

Africa Online: www.africaonline.com

Public Eye (on-line edition of daily newspaper): www.publiceye.co.ls

Lesotho news agency: www.lena.gov.ls/news.htm

Mopheme newspaper: www.lesoff.co.za/news/

Lesotho Council of Non-Governmental Organisations (LCN): www.lecongo.org.ls/

Lesotho Government online: www.lesotho.gov.ls

Liberia

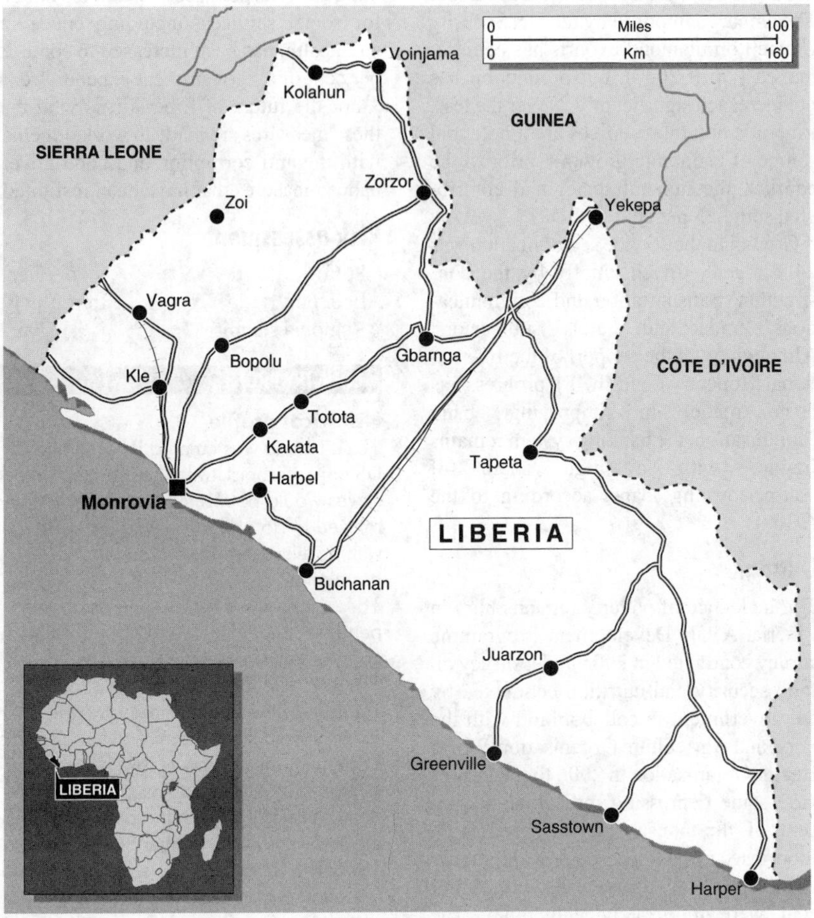

KEY FACTS

Official name: Republic of Liberia

Head of State: President Ellen Johnson-Sirleaf (since 16 Jan 2006)

Head of government: President Ellen Johnson-Sirleaf

Ruling party: Unity Party (UP)

Area: 111,370 square km

Population: 3.75 million (2007)

Capital: Monrovia

Official language: English

Currency: Liberian dollar (L$) = 100 cents (new Liberian $ banknotes introduced Mar 2000)

Exchange rate: L$63.25 per US$ (Jul 2008)

GDP per capita: US$195 (2007)

GDP real growth: 9.40% (2007)

Labour force: 1.33 million (2004)

Unemployment: 85.00% (2005)*

Inflation: 11.20% (2007)

Balance of trade: -US$3.93 billion (2004)

Foreign debt: US$3.00 billion (2004)*

* estimated figure

In a July 2006 visit to Liberia, the then president of the World Bank Paul, Wolfowitz said that 'The challenges that lie ahead are formidable, but the opportunities are even larger'. He said of the 2005 presidential election that had brought President Ellen Johnson-Sirleaf to power that it had been 'a tough but a fair election – hard-fought over compelling issues, which now provide a clear mandate for the government and a map for progress and action. It's often said – and said with good reason – that it's hard to make democracy work in poor countries, particularly in the aftermath of conflict. But the voters of Liberia have shown that it can be done. Supported by the public's clear demand for change, your courageous President has charted an ambitious course – she is determined to bring real improvements in the lives of Liberians.

'When the public chooses a grandmother to lead change, you know that something special must be happening. That is just one more unique aspect of this country. An electorate that recognised the wisdom of experience – an electorate that recognised the reasoning that allows your President to embrace differences and have the confidence to reach out. To reach out across party lines, to reach out across the entire nation, and commit Liberia to a course of reconciliation.'

Economic growth

Indeed, in its 2008 edition of *African Economic Outlook* (AEO), the African Development Bank reported that with the help of the international community, which had deployed peace-keepers and police to support the stability of the country's political and security situation, the economy was improving steadily. Despite the constraints of a collapsed infrastructure, degraded institutional capacity and loss of experienced and skilled manpower, the economy, said the AEO, was rebounding strongly. Real GDP growth has risen year-on-year since 2004 and was estimated to be 9.4 in 2007 and was expected to rise to 9.2 per cent in 2008. A key challenge is the deteriorating current account. Although export volumes are expected to improve, more needs to be done to compensate for the larger share of imports in the economy.

The government has made efforts to improve governance, but more still needs to be done on the 'very weak' indicators, including corruption, that have historically driven conflict in the country. The poverty and social situation remains dire, and there needs to be a more concerted effort at improving health and education, especially technical skills and vocational training.

The mainstay of the Liberian economy is agriculture, which in 2006 contributed around 68.9 per cent of aggregate GDP and which is a major component of the economy's revitalisation. Growth is led by commercial rubber and timber production, although the sector is the primary source of livelihood for the majority of the population. The high prices or rubber and palm oil on the international market have led to an increase in investment, although the scarce resources available to smallholders and a poor transportation network have hampered their ability to get produce to market. Agriculture also suffers from low productivity, as technology has remained stagnant for decades. This has been compounded by a dual land tenure system, formal and customary, which restricts land ownership for both Liberians and foreigners. This had been one of the prime causes of the civil conflict.

Mining was a mere 0.1 per cent of GDP in 2004/05 and did not contribute in 2006. The embargo imposed by the UN Security Council on diamond exports has been removed (April 2007), but production has not increased significantly. Never the less, Liberia's natural resources are a potential source of economic growth – prior to the conflict, the mineral sector had contributed some 25 per cent to GDP.

Growth in the service sector in 2006 was 24 per cent, driven chiefly by the construction, transportation and communications, trade and hotels sub-sectors. Although, with the support of the International Monetary Fund (IMF), progress has been made in improving bank capitalisation, the banking system remains fragile, with a high share of non-performing loans, according to the AEO.

Outlook

The incidence of poverty remains high in Liberia. A UN Development Programme survey conducted in 2005 and a survey on food security and nutrition conducted by the government in collaboration with the Food and Agriculture Organisation/World Health Organisation in 2006 together provide some depressing indicators: 11 per cent of the households surveyed were food-insecure, 40 per cent were highly vulnerable to food insecurity and 41 per cent were moderately vulnerable. The World Bank estimates that over three-quarters of Liberia's 3.75 million people live below the poverty line of US£1 per day. In an endeavour to rectify this the government adopted a short-term national poverty reduction plan to tackle the country's massive unemployment. It also re-allocated resources in the 2007 budget to pro-poor sectors, and the budget for social services, including education and health, has been increased to some 25 per cent of all government expenditure.

For the future of Liberia it is vital that these measures are made to work, together with the anti-corruption and good governance measures that have been instituted.

Risk assessment

Politics	Fair
Economy	Improving
Regional stability	Fair

KEY INDICATORS — Liberia

	Unit	2003	2004	2005	2006	2007
Population	m	3.53	3.85	3.28	3.58	3.75
Gross domestic product (GDP)	US$bn	0.42	0.50	0.53	0.61	0.73
GDP per capita	US$	120	127	161	171	195
GDP real growth	%	-5.0	21.8	9.5	7.8	9.4
Inflation	%	15.0	7.8	6.9	7.2	11.2
Exports (fob) (goods)	US$m	–	103.8	131.3	157.8	–
Imports (cif) (goods)	US$m	–	289.7	278.8	401.4	–
Balance of trade	US$m	–	-185.9	-147.5	-243.6	–
Current account	US$m	–	-258.7	-279.6	-368.7	-224.0
Total reserves minus gold	US$m	7.4	18.7	25.4	72.0	119.4
Foreign exchange	US$m	7.3	18.7	25.4	71.9	119.3
Exchange rate	per US$	54.35	54.50	58.00	58.00	59.15

COUNTRY PROFILE

Historical profile

1822 Liberia was created by a number of US philanthropists with the idea that freed slaves would be resettled in Africa. Many refused to go and those who did were met with hostility from the indigenous population.

1847 Liberia was established as an independent state. The US did not formally recognise this status until 1862.

1944–71 Under President William Tubman of the True Whig party (which monopolised power from early in Liberia's existence), the country received massive foreign investment, but this only exacerbated tension between the descendants of the settlers and the indigenous people.

1963 The local people were enfranchised – around 97 per cent of the total population.

1971 Tubman was succeeded by William Tolbert.

1980 Following protests against the government the previous year, Tolbert's government was overthrown in a coup led by Master Sergeant Samuel Doe, who survived several coup attempts and won an 'election' held in 1985. His government proved widely unpopular.

1984 New multi-party constitution.

1990 Opposition groups, led by Prince Johnson and Charles Taylor overran most of Liberia and captured Monrovia. With Johnson and Taylor both claiming the presidency, the West African peacekeeping force, the Economic Community of West African States Monitoring Group (Ecomog), installed Amos Sawyer as head of an Interim Government of National Unity (IGNU). Taylor's National Patriotic Front of Liberia (NPFL) controlled around 90 per cent of Liberia; the remnants of

Doe's supporters and Johnson's forces were both encamped within the capital.
1993 After a period of heavy fighting, a UN-sponsored peace accord was signed, calling for the creation of a six-month transitional government representing the IGNU, the NPFL and Doe's supporters and the United Liberation Movement for Democracy (Ulimo).
1994–95 Several agreements were reached, none of which brought a final peace.
1996 An attempt to arrest one faction leader for breaking the truce led to two weeks of serious street fighting in Monrovia until Ecomog regained control. Following the renewed conflict, both the faction leaders and Ecowas agreed to hold elections in 1997.
1997 Charles Taylor and his NPFL won a landslide victory.
1999 The Ghanaian and Nigerian troops, who were part of Ecomog, withdrew from Liberia.
2000 President Charles Taylor announced that his government was forming a new army.
2001 There were rebel attacks on the border between Guinea and Liberia and Liberia closed its border with Sierra Leone.
2002 A state of emergency was declared after rebels (Liberians United for Reconciliation and Democracy (LURD)) attacked a town near the capital, Monrovia.
2003 The UN Security Council extended its arms embargo against Liberia for 12 months and added an export ban on unsawn timber. In June, foreign nationals were evacuated from Monrovia amid fighting by LURD rebels in their campaign against President Taylor, who, despite pressure from the US, initially refused to resign. President Taylor eventually accepted Nigeria's asylum offer. West African peacekeepers entered Monrovia and on 8 August President Taylor submitted his resignation and named his vice president Moses Blah to take over on 11 August when he left for Nigeria. The government and two rebel groups selected Gyude Bryant, chairman of the Liberia Action Party (LAP), to head Liberia's interim post-war administration; he was sworn in on 14 October.
2004 In February, international donors pledged more than US$500 million in reconstruction aid. The UN Security Council voted in March to freeze the assets of former president Charles Taylor.
2005 The first elections since the end of the civil war were held in October; in the presidential run-off on 8 November Ellen Johnson-Sirleaf (Unity Party) (UP) defeated George Weah (Liberal Party) (LP), becoming the first woman president in Africa. On 21 December, the UN Security Council extended its ban on arms sales to Liberia for a further 12 months and the sale of diamonds and timber for a further six months.
2006 Ellen Johnson-Sirleaf was inaugurated as president on 16 January. A Truth and Reconciliation Commission was launched in February and commenced work in June. In March, former president Charles Taylor was extradited from Nigeria into UN custody in Sierra Leone and indicted for war crimes; in June, he was transferred to The Hague for trial by the UN-backed Special Court. In December, the government concluded a mineral concession agreement with Mittal Steel.
2007 Personal banking arrived in the north-east border region of Ganta, with the opening of the first bank after 16-years of civil war, when most banks outside the capital region were looted and left defunct. With chronic lack of social welfare, high unemployment and a devastated infrastructure, the president appealed for debt relief and funds to kick-start the economy, at a partnership conference in February. Liberia inherited debts of US3.7 billion; an unsustainable amount the World Bank said was 30 times the country's annual export earnings and eight times greater than its GDP. The US had granted US$500 million in aid and agreed to cancel US$391 million in debt, then pledged US$200 million in further funds. The World Bank planned to cancel US$466 million, while it was undertaking talks with other debt holders to cancel a further US$781 million. On 27 April, the UN lifted a ban on the export of diamonds which had been imposed in 2001. In July the government lifted the moratorium on the mining, sale and export of diamonds. The vital Mano River bridge connecting Sierre Leone with Liberia was officially reopened in June.
2008 US President George W Bush became the first US president to visit for 30 years when he arrived on 21 February. The first census since 1984 was undertaken in March.

Political structure

Constitution

The multi-party 1984 constitution, approved by referendum, replaced the 1847 constitution which was suspended in April 1980.

The executive

Executive power rests with the president, elected by universal adult suffrage for a term of six years; the maximum number of terms is two. The president is head of state, head of government and commander-in-chief of the armed forces.
The president must be a natural-born Liberian citizen of not less than 35 years of age, the owner of unencumbered property valued at not less than US$25,000 and resident in Liberia 10 years prior to the elections.

National legislature

Formerly, legislative power was held by the 26-member Senate (elected for a term of nine years) and the 64-member House of Representatives (elected for a term of six years).
The National Transitional Legislative Assembly (NTLA), installed in October 2003, comprises 76 members.

Legal system

Liberia has a dual system of statutory law based on Anglo-American common law for the modern sector and customary law based on unwritten tribal practices for the indigenous sector.

Last elections

11 October/8November 2005 (presidential); 11 October 2005 (Senate and House of Representatives).
Results: First round presidential: George Weah (Congress for Democratic Change) (CDC) won 28.3 per cent; Ellen Johnson-Sirleaf (UP) 19. 8 per cent; Charles Brumskine (LP) 13.9 per cent; Winston Tubman (National Democratic Party of Liberia) (NDPL) 9.2 per cent; and Varney Sherman (Coalition for the Transformation of Liberia) (Cotol) 7.8 per cent. Run-off: Ellen Johnson-Sirleaf 59.4 per cent; George Weah 40.6 per cent.
House of Representatives: CDC won 15 seats (out of 64), LP 9 seats, UP 8 seats, Cotol 8 seats, Alliance for Peace and Democracy (APD) 5 seats, the National Patriotic Party (NPP) 4 seats.
Senate: Cotol won 7 seats (out of 30), NPP 4 seats, CDC 3 seats, LP 3 seats, UP 3 seats, and APD 3 seats.

Next elections

2011 (presidential and House of Representatives); 2014 (Senate)

Political parties

Ruling party

Unity Party (UP)

Main opposition party

Liberty Party (LP)

Population

3.75 million (2007)
Last census: February 1984: 2,101,628
Population density: 32 inhabitants per square km. Urban population: 45 per cent.
Annual growth rate: 4.6 per cent 1994–2004 (WHO 2006)

Internally Displaced Persons (IDP)

500,000 (UNHCR 2004)

Ethnic make-up

Indigenous tribes (95 per cent), Americo-Liberians (5 per cent).

Religions

Christianity (68 per cent), traditional beliefs (18 per cent), Muslim (14 per cent).

Education
Primary education lasts for six years ending at age 12. Junior secondary school last for three years before successful students can progress onto senior secondary school for a further three years.
Higher education is provided principally by the Uninversity of Liberia in Monrovia, the African Methodist Episcopal University and Cuttington University College.
Literacy rate: 56 per cent adult rate; 71 per cent youth rate (15–24) (Unesco 2005).
Compulsory years: Six to 16.

Health
Per capita total expenditure on health (2003) was US$17; of which per capita government spending was US$10, at the international dollar rate, (WHO 2006).
In November 2007, the health minister estimated that the country had only one-tenth of the doctors needed for its post-conflict society. Of the 120 doctors in post, 70 were foreign doctors serving with international medical organisations and charities. Other healthcare professionals needed included nurses, midwives and laboratory technicians. Under-funding and lack of opportunity has led most trained healthcare workers to emigrate and many doctors resident in Liberia prefer to live in the coastal region leaving rural areas without medical cover. The government has offered a gratuity of US$1,000 (five times the current average salary) for any doctor who accepts assignments inland.
HIV/Aids
Altogether there were 96,000 adults, of which 54,000 women, and 8,000 children under the age of 15, living with HIV/Aids in 2003. Deaths from Aids totalled 7,200 and there were 36,000 orphans aged 0–17 created in 2003 (UCSF).
HIV prevalence: 5.9 per cent aged 15–49 in 2003 (World Bank)
Life expectancy: 42 years, 2004 (WHO 2006)
Fertility rate/Maternal mortality rate: 6.8 births per woman, 2004 (WHO 2006)
Child (under 5 years) mortality rate (per 1,000): 157 per 1,000 live births (World Bank).
Head of population per physician: 0.03 physicians per 1,000 people, 2004 (WHO 2006)

Main cities
Monrovia (capital, estimated population 550,200 in 2003), Zwedru (35,300), Buchanan (27,300).

Languages spoken
English is the business language. There are three main Liberian dialects – Golla, Bassa, Kpelle, Kru and Vai.
Official language/s
English

Media
The state of media in Liberia is still struggling to repair not only the damaged technology but also the proficiency and of the profession. Installations were either destroyed or looted during the civil war and the professionalism of journalists was corrupted as patronage was bestowed on only those that supported the former regime of Charles Taylor.
Other news agencies: APA: www.apanews.net
Panapress: www.panapress.com
Press
Since the former president Taylor's departure, several independent newspapers have started publication.
Dailies: In English The Inquirer (www.theinquirer.com.lr), The News (www.thenews.com.lr), The Analyst (www.analystliberia.com), Daily Observer (www.liberianobserver.com) and Poll Watch are all published in Monrovia.
Weeklies: The private publication, The Heritage, is published in Monrovia.
Broadcasting
State-owned TV and radio suffered particularly from looting in the civil war and lost its TV and FM radio transmitters in 1991. The Liberia Broadcasting System (LBS) has one FM small transmitter that can reach only Monrovia, and no television.
The LCN controls a TV and radio network which uses the frequency 89FM, previously used by LBS, and which, by law, belongs to the state.
Radio: The public, Liberia Broadcasting System (ELBS) (www.liberiabroadcastingsystem.com) has a limited service but provides programmes in local languages, English and French. Others radio services include Star Radio (www.starradio.org.lr), Unmil Radio (http://unmil.org) operated by the United Nations mission, Sky FM and two Christian stations. Community radio services are operated, supported by international entities.
Television: There are three, private TV stations, Clar TV, Power TV and Real TV.
News agencies
Other news agencies: APA: www.apanews.net
Panapress: www.panapress.com

Economy
The many years of mismanagement, before the election of the National Transitional Government in 2003, left Liberia with a massive external debt of around US$3.7 billion, or 800 per cent of GDP, or 3,000 per cent of total export earnings. Since January 2006, when President Johnson-Sirleaf, a former World Bank economist was elected, there has been a concerted effort to strengthen economic performance.
The reconstruction of the economy will continue to need significant external support, both financial and technical. However, donor funds, in 2006, were entirely spent outside the government budget and until improved governance and strengthened budget planning is achieved they were unlikely to be reallocated.
In January 2007 the government appealed to the IMF for an upper credit tranche programme as measures to establish a tract record for debt relief under the Highly Indebted Poor Country (HIPC) initiative had been achieved. Each month, Liberia makes a total of US$100,000 in debt repayment to the IMF, World Bank and African Development Bank.
As the country begins its reconstruction, imports far outstrip exports and an annual trade deficit of around 30 per cent of GDP exists. Macroeconomic reforms achieved greater revenue income, which rose by 82 per cent in 2006/07, including anticorruption measures and a sponsored audit. GDP grew by 5.3 per cent in 2005, to 7.8 per cent in 2006 and is projected to rise by 7.9 per cent in 2007, led in most part by the construction industry.
Rubber accounted for over 85 per cent of total exports, and earned US$141 million in 2006, but was only the second major export until 2003 when the principle export was timber. There was a United Nations embargo on Liberian timber exports until mid-2005; the company which had a monopoly on timber production was covertly owned by the former president, Charles Taylor and since his demise the sector has languished. However the industry is expected to make a significant contribution to GDP in the medium-term.
Inflation dropped from a high of 15.0 per cent in 2003 to single digits in 2005; the October 2006 rate was 5.9 per cent. Although unemployment was estimated to be around 85 per cent in early 2007, Liberia suffers from a lack of educated and trained workers, most of whom left the country during the civil war. Most industries are in the hands of foreign owners and the country urgently requires investment. High grade iron ore deposits have become depleted, leaving only medium or low grade ore. The diamond industry is expected to attract much international investment as the country becomes ever more stable.
Around US$14 million is earned from the 1,800 maritime licences issued. At around 35 per cent of the total, Liberia has the

world's second largest registered fleet (after Panama).
Liberia has a long way to go before the years of mismanagement are repaired, but the reforms undertaken since January 2006 have laid solid groundwork.

External trade
Liberia is a member of the Economic Community of Western African States (Ecowas), which was set up to promote economic integration among members. It has expressed an interest in joining four other Anglophone-members, in setting up a single currency, which will eventually be merged with the Francophone-members' currency to produce a single currency (the eco) for the region.
UN embargoes on diamond and timber exports were lifted on 21 June 2006 and 27 April 2007 respectively. The government has encouraged foreign direct investment (FDI) in mining with a US$1 billion deal negotiated with Arcelor Mittal Steel in July 2007.

Imports
Principal imports include fuels, chemicals, machinery, transportation equipment, manufactured goods and foodstuffs.
Main sources: South Korea (37.9 per cent total, 2005), Japan (21.1 per cent), Singapore (14.2 per cent), Croatia (4.7 per cent)

Exports
Principal exports rubber, timber, iron, diamonds, cocoa and coffee.
Main destinations: Belgium (41.4 per cent total, 2005), Spain (11.6 per cent), US (9.1 per cent), Malaysia (5.5 per cent), Thailand (4.6 per cent), Poland (4.6 per cent), Germany (4.4 per cent)

Agriculture
Farming
Hit by hostilities and migration from rural areas, production has been reduced from pre-war levels. Agriculture is still the most important sector of the economy, contributing approximately 35 per cent to GDP and employing 55 per cent of the workforce.
One of the country's principal cash crops is rubber, which provides a large proportion of exports. Although mostly grown in foreign-owned plantations, smallholders are responsible for over half the total acreage planted.
Coffee, cocoa and timber are also grown for export, but, as with rubber, earnings have been reduced due to falling world prices. Palm oil is produced mostly for the domestic market. The main food crops are rice, cassava and sweet potatoes, followed by eddoes and yams. The government had attempted to improve production to reduce the need for imports of rice which have become necessary to meet domestic demand.
The estimated crop production for 2005 included: 110,000 tonnes (t) rice, 490,000t cassava, 25,500t taro, 20,000t yams, 19,000t sweet potatoes, 110,000t bananas, 42,000t plantains, 3,500t pulses, 543,500t roots and tubers, 7,000t citrus fruit, 49,950t oilcrops, 174,000t oil palm fruit, 1,500t cocoa beans, 3,200t green coffee, 115,000t natural rubber, 255,000t sugar cane, 20,000t yams, 169,200t fruit in total, 76,000t vegetables in total. Estimated livestock production included: 21,896t meat in total, 1,000t beef, 4,400t pig meat, 6,500t game meat, 1,316t lamb and goat meat, 8,680t poultry, 4,520t eggs, 715t milk.
Commercial ocean fishing is a growing activity, particularly fishing for shrimps. In 2004, the total marine fish catch was 6,189 tonnes and the total crustacean catch was 52 tonnes.

Forestry
Despite international sanction prohibiting timber exports, imposed in 2001, revenue from the trade in timber played a vital role in providing funding to ex-president Charles Taylor, for illicit arms imports during the civil war.. Following his defeat, all sanctions were lifted in February 2006; at which time steps were undertaken to control the exploitation of forest recourses, including the cancellation of all previous logging concessions. The Forestry Development Authority began by introducing new, transparent contracts and a forestry reform programme.
The export of forest products dropped from US$289.5 million in 2002 to US$43.5 million in 2004, while imports grew from US$243,000 to US$2 million in the same period.
Estimated production in 2004 included 5,912,817 cubic metres (cum) roundwood, 337,000cum industrial roundwood, 157,000cum sawlogs and veneer logs, 20,000cum sawnwood, 30,000t wood-based panels, 5,575,817cum wood fuel; 183,382t charcoal.

Industry and manufacturing
The small industrial sector contributes 4.9 per cent to GDP. The manufacturing sector is relatively underdeveloped, contributing 4 per cent to GDP. Activity is mainly confined to textiles, food and rubber processing, wood products, cement and chemicals.
The sector has been weakened by the country's upheavals, which damaged infrastructure and deterred investment. Growth in the sector is in any case constrained by the small size of the domestic market, the need to import practically all raw materials, shortage of skilled labour and financial problems.

Tourism
In April 2003, Liberia requested the UN Scientific and Cultural Organisation (UNESCO) to add two Liberian sites, Sarpo National Park and Providence Island, to The World's Cultural Heritage.

Mining
Prior to the civil war, Liberia was one of the world's major producers of iron ore (mainly extracted from mines at Mount Nimba, Mano River and Bong), which accounted for around 30 per cent of GDP. Production ceased completely as a result of the war. Efforts are being made to revive the sector. In August 2005, an agreement was entered into with the Mittal Steel Company to develop reserves and associated infrastructure in western Liberia.
Diamonds are mined, previously earning Liberia an estimated US$300 million annually. During the war, factions exploited production. Current production figures are hard to gauge due to the allegations of diamond smuggling with Sierra Leone, Guinea and Côte d'Ivoire. Liberia's diamond exports, along with timber, have been subject to UN economic sanctions since 2001, because of misuse of the revenues. Foreign investors, anticipating future stability, are showing interest in the sector.
A deal between the Israeli Diamond Institute (IDI) and the government was signed, whereby diamond experts from IDI will help in the search for local diamonds. The agreement was the first since a moratorium on mining, sales and export of Liberian diamonds was lifted by the UN, imposed in 2001 in an effort to halt the trade in 'blood diamonds' used to fund the civil war.

Hydrocarbons
There are no known oil or gas reserves in Liberia. There is potential in the territorial waters in the Gulf of Guinea. Investigation is at an early stage. The National Oil Company of Liberia has signed several exploration agreemnents since 2004, but with small and sometimes obscure companies. Liberia relies on imports from neighbouring countries for its petroleum requirements. The sole refinery at Monrovia was mothballed in 1984.
Liberia does not produce or import gas and coal.

Energy
The electricity generation and supply infrastructure was wrecked early in the civil war. Privately-owned generators are the only source of electricity for those who can afford them. It is not expected that grid supplies will be available for at least five years. The state-owned Liberian Electricity Corporation (LEC) estimates that it will need in excess of US$100 million to

repair the system. As a step towards reconstruction of the sector, the LEC is undergoing a process of liberalisation, including staff restructuring, under the auspices of the EU.

In July 2006 a report by Ecowas describes Liberia's energy situation as 'desperate' and estimated that the shattered infrastructure would need US$1 billion to undertake eight major projects putting the system back into commission. While Ecowas attempts to attract donor investors, electricity is expected to be imported from Côte d'Ivoire to be supplied to four border towns.

Banking and insurance

The civil war has led to a virtual collapse of the banking system and lending services have declined dramatically. The country's five commercial banks have found it hard to attract capital savings, as the public and businesses have tended to hoard money rather than put it in banks due to a general crisis of confidence in the banking system. The subsequent lack of liquidity in the banking sector has led to a wide spread between the average deposit and lending rates. Lack of affordable bank credit has hampered growth across the economy, particularly the agricultural sector. Unless the government can ensure political stability and security and a policy is instituted to increase bank savings, Liberia's banking sector will remain in the doldrums.

Central bank

In October 1999 the National Legislature enacted a law creating the Central Bank of Liberia, which replaced the National Bank of Liberia. Monetary authority functions are undertaken by the central government.

Main financial centre

Monrovia

Time

GMT

Geography

Liberia lies on the west coast of Africa, with Sierra Leone and Guinea to the north and Côte d'Ivoire to the east.

Liberia's coastline extends for about 580km, over half of which comprises sandy beaches. The terrain is generally low-lying. Lagoons, creeks and mangrove swamps punctuate the low coastal plain, behind which the land rises to a gently rolling, grassy plateau. Further inland, in the north-east, is mountainous, where the highest point in the country at 1,380m is Mount Wuwve. The plateau and mountain regions are home to approximately 40 per cent of Africa's rainforest.

Hemisphere

Northern

Climate

Hot and tropical with high levels of humidity (85–90 per cent) and there is little temperature variation throughout the year. Average temperatures range between 20–22 degrees Celsius (C) at night and 28–32 degrees C during the day. Wet season lasts from May–October with especially heavy rain June–July.

Entry requirements

Passports

Required by all, valid for six months from date of entry.

Visa

Required by all, except nationals of Ecowas countries, Israel, South Korea and Thailand.

Currency advice/regulations

There are no restrictions on import and export of local or foreign currencies. US dollars are legal tender.

Health (for visitors)

Mandatory precautions

Yellow fever vaccination certificate is required.

Advisable precautions

Typhoid, hepatitis A, tetanus and polio vaccinations are recommended. Malaria prophylaxis should be taken as risk exists throughout the country. There is a rabies risk. Drinking water should be boiled and filtered.

Hotels

The airport hotel and other major hotels in Monrovia should be booked in advance. Rates are expensive and tipping is optional.

Credit cards

There is limited acceptance of credit cards.

Public holidays (national)

Fixed dates

1 Jan (New Year's Day), 11 Feb (Armed Forces Day), 15 Mar (J J Roberts' Birthday), 12 Apr (National Redemption Day), 14 Apr (Fast and Prayer Day), 14 May (National Unification Day), 26 Jul (Independence Day), 24 Aug (Flag Day), 29 Nov (President Tubman's Birthday), 25 Dec (Christmas Day).

Variable dates

Decoration Day (Mar), Fast and Prayer Day (Apr), Thanksgiving Day (Nov)

Working hours

Banking

Mon–Thu: 0900–1200; Fri: 0800–1400.

Business

Mon–Fri: 0800–1200, 1400–1600.

Government

Mon–Fri: 0800–1200, 1300–1600.

Shops

Mon–Sat: 0800–1300, 1500–1800.

Telecommunications

Telephone/fax

The service is 100 per cent automatic but very limited outside Monrovia. In 2006, land line numbers (six digits, starting with a two) not yet restored.

Mobile/cell phones

Cell phone numbers (seven plus seven digits, six plus five digits) are working.

Weights and measures

Imperial system

Security

Crime is high in the capital, Monrovia, with theft and assault prevalent, particularly at night.

Getting there

Air

International airport/s: Monrovia-Roberts International (ROB), 60km from city; duty-free shop, bar, restaurant, buffet, post office, shops.

Airport tax: US$25

Surface

Road: The vital Mano River bridge connecting Sierra Leone with Liberia was officially reopened in June 2007.

Getting about

National transport

Air: Air taxi companies charter planes between Monrovia and airfields throughout the country.

Road: A network of 10,000km covers most areas, although many roads are untarred. Main highways are: Monrovia-Sanniquellie (with a branch Ganta-Harper) and Monrovia-Buchanan.

Rail: There are no passenger railways.

Water: Freight/passenger services between Monrovia and Buchanan.

City transport

There are buses and taxis available from the airport to the city centre.

Taxis: Zoning system in operation. Negotiate fares in advance for long-distance journeys. Tipping is not usual.

Car hire

Chauffeur-driven or self-drive cars are available in Monrovia. International driving licence or national driving licence with permit (valid for up to 30 days) accepted. Traffic drives on the right. Self-drive cars are not generally recommended.

BUSINESS DIRECTORY

The addresses listed below are a selection only. While World of Information makes every endeavour to check these addresses, we cannot guarantee that changes have not been made, especially to telephone numbers and area codes. We would welcome any corrections.

Telephone area codes
The international dialling code (IDD) for Liberia is +231, followed by subscriber's number.
In late-2006 land-line telephone numbers (6 digits beginning with a 2) were still not functioning. Cell phone numbers (7 + 7 digits and 6 + 5 digits) were working.

Chambers of Commerce
Liberia Chamber of Commerce, Capitol Hill, PO Box 92, Monrovia (tel: 223-738).

Banking
Liberian Bank for Development and Investment (LBDI), Corner of Randall and Ashmun Streets, PO Box 547, Monrovia (tel: 227-140; fax: 226-939).

International Bank (Liberia) Limited; 64 Broad Street, Monrovia (tel: 227-438; fax: 226-092/3).

Liberian Trading and Development Bank Ltd, PO Box 293, Tradevco Building, Ashmun Street, 1000 Monrovia 10 (tel: 226-072, 226-074; fax: 226-471).

Central bank
Central Bank of Liberia: PO Box 2048, Warren and Carey Streets, Monrovia (tel: 226-991; fax: 226-144).

Travel information
Ministry of tourism
Ministry of Information, Cultural Affairs and Tourism, United Nations Drive, Capitol Hill, PO Box 10-9021, 1000 Monrovia 10 (tel: 226-269; fax: 226-069; e-mail: webmaster@liberia.net).

Ministries
Ministry of Commerce, Industry, PO Box 10-9041, 1000 Monrovia 10 (tel: 226-283).

Ministry of Finance, Bureau of Customs and Excise, PO Box 10-9013, 1000 Monrovia 10.

Ministry of Foreign Affairs, PO Box 10-9002, 1000 Monrovia 10 (tel: 226-763, 221-029, 221-751).

Ministry of Information, Culture and Tourism, PO Box 10-9021, Capitol Hill, 1000 Monrovia 10 (tel: 226-045, 226-269, 227-349; fax: 226-045).

Ministry of Justice, Bureau of Immigration, PO Box 10-9006, Broad Street, 1000 Monrovia 10.

Ministry of Lands, Mines and Energy, PO Box 10-9024, 1000 Monrovia 10 (tel: 226-281, 221-580, 221-488, 221-460).

Ministry of Planning and Economic Affairs, PO Box 10-9016, 1000 Monrovia 10 (tel: 226-962, 227-987, 222-121, 222-331, 223-208, 221-971).

Ministry of Youth and Sports, PO Box 10-9040, 1000 Monrovia 10 (tel: 226-284).

Other useful addresses
ELTV (Liberian television system), PO Box 594, Monrovia.

Liberian Development Corporation, PO Box 9043, Monrovia.

Liberian Embassy (USA), 5201 16th Street, NW, Washington DC 20011 (tel: (+1-202)-723-0437; fax: (+1-202)-723-0436; e-mail: info@liberiaemb.org).

Liberian News Agency (LINA), Ministry of Information, PO Box 9021, Capitol Hill, Monrovia (tel: 222-229).

National Investment Commission, PO Box 10-9043, 1000 Monrovia 10 (tel: 226-685, 226-575).

National Ports Authority, PO Box 14, Monrovia.

Statistics Bureau, PO Box 9016, Monrovia (tel: 222-622).

Internet sites
Africa Business Network: www.ifc.org/abn

African Development Bank: www.afdb.org

Africa Online: www.africaonline.com

AllAfrica.com: http://allafrica.com

Mbendi AfroPaedia (information on companies, countries, industries and stock exchanges in Africa): http://mbendi.co.za

Libya

KEY FACTS

Official name: Al Jamahiriya al Arabiya al Libiya ash Shabiya al Ishtirakiya al Uzma (The Great Socialist People's Libyan Arab Jamahiriya)

Head of State: Leader of First of September Revolution Colonel Muammar al Qadafi (since Sep 1969)

Head of government: Secretary of the General People's Congress Muftah Mohammed Kaiba (from 3 Mar 2008)

Ruling party: There are no official political parties

Area: 1,775,500 square km

Population: 6.09 million (2007)*

Capital: Tripoli

Official language: Arabic

Currency: Libyan dinar (LD) = 1,000 dirhams

Exchange rate: LD1.17 per US$ (Jul 2008)

GDP per capita: US$9,372 (2007)*

GDP real growth: 6.80% (2007)*

Labour force: 1.98 million (2004)

Unemployment: 30.00% (2004)

Inflation: 6.70% (2007)*

Oil production: 1.85 million bpd (2007)

Balance of trade: US$19.97 billion (2005)

Foreign debt: US$4.07 billion (2004)

* estimated figure

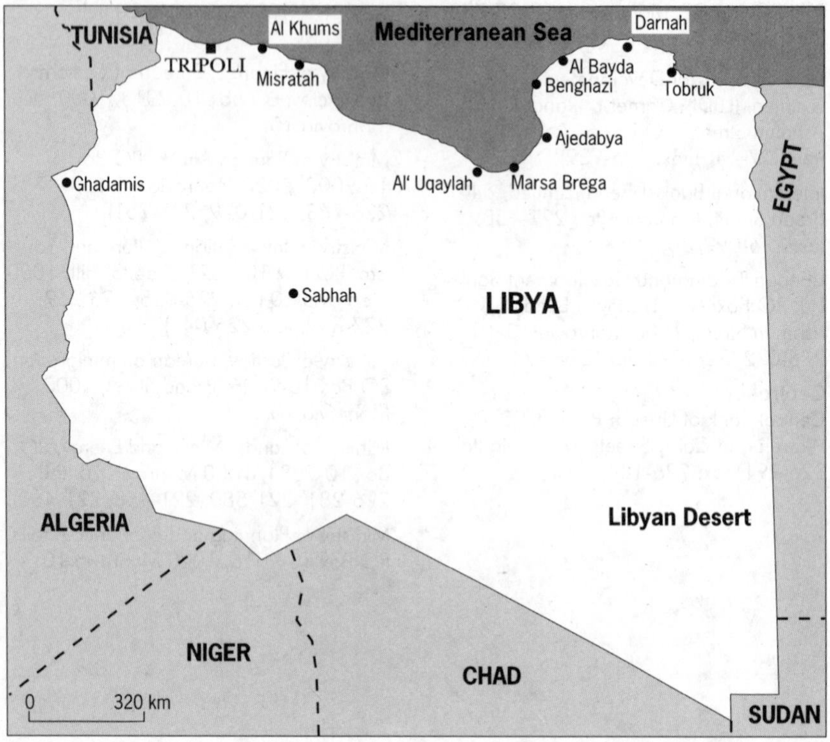

Libya, a former Roman colony, is a mostly desert country which saw invasions by Vandals, Byzantines, Arabs, Turks and, more recently, Italians before gaining independence in 1951. Its people are 97 per cent Berber and Arab, Sunni Muslims.

Oil was discovered in 1959, and in a short space of time the country was transformed into a wealthy monarchy. Ten years later King Idris was overthrown in a coup led by the 27-year-old Muammar Abu Minyar al Qadafi, and Libya embarked on a radically new chapter in its history. Over the years Qadafi has supported a broad range of militant groups, including the Irish Republican Army (IRA) and the Palestine Liberation Organisation (PLO). Qadafi's son Sayf al Islam Qadafi is said to be behind the drive to break Libya's isolation. Sayf has denied reports that he is being groomed to succeed his father.

Libya's economy faces the problem of all oil dependent countries – its growth, government investment programmes and macroeconomic indicators are all subject to changes in the price of oil. Another problem, typical of countries making the transition to a market economy is that its weak institutions, unsuitable legal system and structural rigidity slow down the reforms needed.

Libya's main problem, however, has been the international economic sanctions imposed by the United Nations and the US. In this respect, a milestone was reached in May 2006 when US President George W Bush announced that he was re-establishing a fully normalised diplomatic relationship with Libya after 30 years of embargoes and isolation. Libya had enjoyed the ignominy of being a state sponsor of terror, along with other pariah states: Iran, Syria, North Korea, Sudan and Cuba. However, Qadafi has proved a useful ally in the US-led War on Terror and Libya is a vital source of oil fields for US oil firms.

The lifting of sanctions by the US has meant that the oil industry can begin to expand again. Production capacity had fallen to 1.73 million barrels per day (bpd) in 2007, from 3.3 million bpd in 1970. There had been a chronic shortage of spare parts and regular maintenance; a lack of foreign and local investment had led to a drop in new exploration.

By 2006 the oil and gas sector, which dominates the economy, was contributing 74 per cent of GDP, compared to 2001 when the non-oil sector had contributed 62.5 per cent. The lifting of sanctions, especially by the US, opened the way for new exploration by foreign firms and the upgrading and maintenance of old oilfields.

As reported in the 2008 edition of *African Economic Outlook* (AEO), the government is increasingly favouring structural reforms, especially gradual state withdrawal from productive sectors, a reduced role in the economy and greater transparency in public affairs. The reforms involve diversification, privatisation and reform of the banking and financial sector.

Unlike other transition economies in the early 1990s, Libya has a healthy financial situation allowing it to build the safety nets needed to cushion the effects of transition

Oil and gas potential

A report by Harvard professor, Michael Porter, commissioned by Gadafi, was good news for the world's energy consumers, as Libya is set to meet much energy demand. The long embargo means that not all reserves have been exploited. In January 2006 the multinational oil company ExxonMobil signed a major exploration contract for the Cyrenaica Basin. They were followed by ConocoPhilips, Marathon Oil and Amerada Hess, who, as part of the Oasis Group, paid US$1.3 billion to re-enter the country. A handful of Japanese firms, Royal Dutch Shell and British Gas, have also signed contracts. British company BP began talks over a liquefied natural gas deal to supply the US and European markets.

In March 2006 the French nuclear energy body, the CEA, agreed on a joint nuclear technology research project with Libya, so long as Qadafi's regime continued to meet the strict accountability standards of the International Atomic Energy Agency.

US based Human Rights Watch was permitted into the country in January 2006 and noted that some improvements have been made in relation to citizens' rights and freedoms. However they also expressed concern over ongoing torture, oppression and political detentions. The Libyan government has withdrawn its participation in IMF's Heavily Indebted Poor Countries (HIPC) Initiative on grounds of insufficient political support for ratification. It is preparing its own debt relief plan.

Oil, again

The Libyan economy still depends primarily upon revenues from the oil sector, which contribute practically all export earnings and about one-quarter of GDP. These oil revenues and its small population give Libya one of the highest per capita GDPs in Africa, but little of this income flows down to the lower orders of society.

Economy

The economy remains largely state controlled. The country faces a long road ahead in liberalising the socialist-oriented economy, but initial steps – including applying for membership of the World Trade Organisation (WTO), reducing some subsidies, and announcing plans for privatisation – are laying the groundwork for a transition to a more market-based economy. The non-oil manufacturing and construction sectors, which account for about 20 per cent of GDP, have expanded from processing mostly agricultural products to include the production of petrochemicals, iron, steel, and aluminum. Climatic conditions and poor soils severely limit agricultural output, and Libya imports about 75 per cent of its food.

Some progress has been made on the reform front. Measures taken include the adoption of laws to encourage domestic and foreign private investment, the adoption of a new tax law, the removal of customs duty exemptions enjoyed by public enterprises, the reduction in tariff rates, and the preparation of a new banking law that gives the Central Bank of Libya greater independence. A privatisation plan (not including the utilities, the oil and gas sector, and the air and maritime transportation sectors) has been initiated. It involves the sale of 360 economic units.

Politics

A staunch Arab nationalist, Libyan leader Colonel al Qadafi's attempts to forge unity with other Arab states have met with little success. In the 1990s he turned to Africa and proposed a United States of Africa. The concept later found form as the African Union, replacing the by then somewhat tarnished Organisation of African Unity.

From the earliest days of his rule following his 1969 military coup, Colonel al Qadafi has held absolute power. He espouses his own political system, the Third Universal Theory. This is a combination of socialism and Islam derived in part from tribal practices and is supposed to be implemented by the Libyan people themselves in a unique form of 'direct democracy'. Qadafi has always seen himself as a revolutionary and visionary leader. He used oil funds during the 1970s and 1980s to promote his ideology outside Libya, supporting subversives and terrorists abroad to hasten the end of Marxism and capitalism. In addition, beginning in 1973,

KEY INDICATORS — Libya

	Unit	2003	2004	2005	2006	2007
Population	m	5.63	5.81	5.85	5.97	*6.09
Gross domestic product (GDP)	US$bn	14.53	29.12	41.69	49.72	*57.06
GDP per capita	US$	2,583	5,121	7,121	8,327	*9,372
GDP real growth	%	3.3	0.9	6.3	5.2	*6.8
Inflation	%	-2.1	-1.0	2.0	3.4	*6.7
Oil output	'000 bpd	1,488.0	1,607.0	1,702.0	1,835.0	1,848.0
Natural gas output	bn cum	6.4	7.0	11.7	14.8	15.2
Exports (fob) (goods)	US$m	14,527.0	18,650.0	25,849.0	37,473.0	–
Imports (cif) (goods)	US$m	6,663.0	7,224.0	11,174.0	13,219.0	–
Balance of trade	US$m	7,864.0	11,426.0	17,675.0	24,254.0	–
Current account	US$m	3,640.0	7,450.0	14,945.0	25,646.0	24,278.0
Total reserves minus gold	US$m	19,584.0	25,689.0	39,508.0	59,289.0	79,405.0
Foreign exchange	US$m	18,310.0	24,336.0	38,235.0	57,907.0	77,897.0
Exchange rate	per US$	1.27	1.27	1.28	1.28	1.22

* estimated figure

he engaged in military operations in northern Chad's Aozou Strip – to gain access to minerals and to gain influence in Chadian politics – but was forced to retreat in 1987.

Outlook

Much remains to be done to transform Libya's economy into one that is market-based and Libya's large fiscal surpluses present a good opportunity to speed up economic reforms while maintaining macroeconomic stability. To control the large non-oil deficit, the non-oil tax base must be strengthened, including by reducing tax exemptions and streamlining spending.

The substantial oil windfall projected over the medium term should be largely saved, or partly used to finance human capital investment and structural reform measures, including restructuring public enterprises and the civil service. There is a need to address the rigidities arising from the mechanical distribution of oil revenues between capital and current expenditures.

Risk assessment

Economic	Fair
Political	Fair
Regional stability	Fair

COUNTRY PROFILE

Historical profile

1510 During the struggle between Hapsburg Spain and the Ottoman Turks for supremacy in the Mediterranean, Spanish forces captured and largely destroyed Tripoli.
1524 Tripoli was entrusted to the Knights of St John of Malta.
1551 The Knights were driven out of Tripolitania by the Turks who began consolidating their control over the Maghreb region. The three provinces of Tripolitania, Cyrenaica and Fezzan were joined into one regency in Tripoli by the Ottomans.
1711–1835 Although nominally part of the Ottoman empire, the Turks in effect gave way to the local Karamanli dynasty until 1835, when the Turks strengthened their control again. The local rulers levied a toll on every Christian fleet using the Mediterranean.
1870–1911 The area was dominated by the Sanusi religious order, although the Turks and the Italians continued to invade periodically.
1911–42 By the time of the First World War in 1914, an Italian force had taken control of the coastal towns. After the War, Italy captured the Libyan nationalist hero, Omar Mukhtar, hanging him in 1931. Italy introduced an Italianisation programme.
Italy's colonisation of Libya ended when the Italians and Germans lost the war in the Western Desert. The British took over Tripolitania and Cyrenaica and the French took over the Fezzan.
1951 Libya was granted independence under King Idris (originally Mohammed Idris al Sanusi, a member of the Sanusi religious order).
1955 Oil exploration started.
1959 Oil was discovered.
1961 King Idris opened a 167km pipeline, which linked important oil fields in the interior to the Mediterranean Sea, making it possible for Libya to export oil.
1969 As pan-Arabism swept the Arab world, Colonel Muammar al Qadafi seized power as Leader of the Revolution. Most economic activities were nationalised, including the oil industry.
1970 The government closed the British airbase in Tobruk and the US Air Force base in Tripoli. Property belonging to Italian settlers was nationalised.
1971 The Federation of Arab Republics (FAR), comprising Libya, Egypt and Syria, was approved by national referendum, but was never realised.
1972 Libya and Egypt agreed to merge into a single state; the plans were abandoned.
1973 Qadafi announced a cultural revolution in which people's committees were established throughout the country. Libyan forces invaded the Aozou Strip in northern Chad.
1974 A plan to unify Libya and Tunisia was agreed, but never implemented.
1977 Qadafi set up the General People's Congress (GPC) and the country was renamed the Great Socialist People's Libyan Arab Jamahiriya.
1980 An agreement to merge Libya and Syria was made, but failed to materialise.
1981 The US shot down two Libyan aircraft which challenged its warplanes over the Gulf of Sirte, claimed by Libya as its territorial waters.
1984 Police Constable Yvonne Fletcher was killed during demonstrations outside the Libyan embassy in London. The UK suspended diplomatic relations with Libya.
1986 In an unsuccessful attempt to bring down the Qadafi regime, the US launched a major airstrike on Tripoli, causing substantial damage. The US claimed its raids were in response to an alleged Libyan involvement in the bombing of a nightclub in Berlin, which was used by US military personnel. The US imposed economic sanctions against Libya.
1988 Libyan terrorists were blamed for the bomb which destroyed a Pan Am passenger aircraft over Lockerbie in Scotland.
1989 Algeria, Libya, Mauritania, Morocco and Tunisia formed the Arab Maghreb Union.
1992 UN sanctions were imposed on Libya for refusing to hand over two men suspected of the Lockerbie bombing.
1994 Libya returned the Aozou Strip to Chad.
1995 Qadafi ordered the expulsion of 30,000 Palestinians in protest at the Oslo accords signed by the Israeli government and the Palestine Liberation Organisation (PLO).
1999 UN and EU sanctions were suspended after Libya agreed to arrest and extradite Lockerbie bombing suspects. The UK re-established diplomatic links with Libya.
2000 Qadafi visited Arab states in North Africa and the Middle East, seeking to promote Arab co-operation. Libya was one of the key signatories to the creation of the African Union (AU).
2001 Abdelbaset Ali Mohmed al Megrahi, a Libyan intelligence agent, was found guilty of the Lockerbie bombing in a Scottish court based in The Netherlands, while his co-accused, al Amin Khalifa Fhimah, was acquitted. The US imposed a five-year extension to sanctions against Libya.
2002 Megrahi's appeal failed and he was sentenced to life imprisonment in a Scottish jail.
2003 Libya was chosen to chair the UN Human Rights Commission. The Libyan government and lawyers representing families of Lockerbie bombing victims signed a compensation agreement worth US$2.7 billion. Libya formally took responsibility for the bombing before the UN Security Council. The UN Security Council voted to lift the 11-year-old sanctions against Libya (already suspended). Libya announced that it would abandon its programmes to develop weapons of mass destruction (WMD).
2004 Libya agreed to compensate families of victims of the 1989 bombing of a French passenger aircraft and to pay US$35 million to victims of the bombing of a Berlin nightclub in 1986. The UK prime minister, Tony Blair, met Colonel al Qadafi, the first visit of this kind since 1943. UN sanctions were finally lifted in February, and in April, US President Bush eased sanctions against Libya as a reward for giving up WMD. On 29 June, the US and Libya restored diplomatic relations after a break of 24 years, and US economic sanctions were lifted in September. President Chirac of France visited Libya, the first visit by a French president since 1951.
2005 Libya officially opened to tourist visitors. Leases on 26 oil fields were allocated to foreign companies.

2006 The US restored full diplomatic relations with Libya and in June rescinded Libya's designation as a state sponsor of terrorism.
2008 On 3 March Muftah Mohammed Kaiba became secretary of the General People's Congress. The youngest son of Muammar al Qadafi was arrested and held for two days. He and his wife were charged with bodily harm, threatening behaviour and coercion for allegedly striking two of their staff. In retaliation, the offices of two Swiss companies in Tripoli were ordered to close and visas for Swiss tourist were halted.

Political structure

Constitution
Libya has no constitution. In 2000, 14 ministries were abolished and their powers devolved to provincial committees or other bodies.

Form of state
Jamahiriya, or state of the masses.

The executive
Libya has no official head of state, but Colonel Muammar al Qadafi exercises absolute authority in his role as Leader of the First of September Revolution. Federal executive power is exercised by the General People's Committee (GPC) (council of ministers). The Secretary General of the GPC is a post broadly equivalent to that of prime minister.

National legislature
Political power is vested in the General People's Congress (GPC).
Libya is officially run by popular committees and congresses. Each sends delegates to the GPC, which approves laws and sets policy guidelines. There are 300 congresses, each having an executive popular committee, which can effectively take some decisions at a local level.

Legal system
The Libyan legal system is based on Sharia (Islamic law) and the Italian civil law system. There are separate religious courts and no constitutional provision for judicial review of legislative acts. The judicial system consists of the Supreme Court, courts of appeal, courts of first instance and summary courts. Libya has not accepted compulsory International Court of Justice (ICJ) jurisdiction.

Political parties

Ruling party
There are no official political parties

Main opposition party
The two most active internal opposition movements are the Islamic Liberation Party and the Muslim Brotherhood. The main exiled opposition is the US-based National Front for the Salvation of Libya (NFSL).

Population
6.09 million (2007)*
Last census: August 1995: 4,404,986
Population density: Three inhabitants per square kilometre. Urban population: 88 per cent (1995–2001).
Annual growth rate: 2.0 per cent 1994–2004 (WHO 2006)

Ethnic make-up
Berber-Arab (97 per cent). There are small communities of Greeks, Maltese, Italians, Egyptians, Pakistanis, Turks, Indians and Tunisians.

Religions
Sunni Muslim (97 per cent). A third of Libya's Muslims are affilitated to the Sanusi religious sect, which had fought against European colonialism in the first half of the twentieth century.

Education
Libya has paid particular attention to its education system, with the aim of reducing illiteracy and improving the education available to women.
Education is free for all children during the compulsory years. Secondary schooling begins at aged 15 and the curriculum is divided into three- or four-year courses and comprises a number of secondary school types including both academic and specialised or vocational centres. English and Arabic are the main languages for instruction.
Higher education is offered in 14 universities and 54 higher vocational institutes.
Literacy rate: 82 per cent adult rate; 97 per cent youth rate (15–24) (Unesco 2005).
Compulsory years: 6 to 15.

Health
Per capita total expenditure on health (2003) was US$327; of which per capita government spending was US$206, at the international dollar rate, (WHO 2006).
The government provides free health services to all its citizens. UN sanctions had a detrimental impact on the quality and access to healthcare provision and many medical services and pharmaceutical products became unavailable. With the lifting of sanctions in 2004, it is expected that these shortcomings will be overcome quickly. Many Libyans have typically sort medical treatment in Tunisia, Egypt or in Western Europe. There are two large hospitals in Tripoli and Benghazi.

HIV/Aids
HIV prevalence: 0.3 per cent aged 15–49 in 2003 (World Bank)
Life expectancy: 72 years, 2004 (WHO 2006)
Fertility rate/Maternal mortality rate: 2.9 births per woman, 2004 (WHO 2006); maternal mortality 0.75 per 1,000 live births (World Bank).
Child (under 5 years) mortality rate (per 1,000): 13 per 1,000 live births; 5 per cent of children aged under five are malnourished (World Bank).

Welfare
The government is theoretically committed to full provision of welfare services to all Libyan nationals. In reality, parts of the population are often not covered by welfare provisions. The most common welfare benefit is housing to those in need. The government provides a national social security system covering pensions and other social insurance, but the availability of such services regularly depends on annual oil receipts, which make up a large proportion of total government revenues.

Main cities
Tripoli (capital, estimated population 1.2 million in 2004), Benghazi (734,900), Al-Khums (Homs) (195,000), Misratah (Misurata) (345,566), Al-Marj (164,700), Tobruk (152,200).

Media

Press
Newspapers and periodicals are published by the official Jamahiriya News Agency (Jana) and Trades Unions. The main newspapers are Al-Fajr Al-Jahid and Shu'un Libiyah. A number of weekly, fortnightly, monthly and occasional periodicals are also produced. These include Al Sidra Magazine, Ath-Thaqafa Al-Arabiya (Arab Culture), Ad-Daawa Al-Islamia (Islamic Call) and the monthly Risala Al-Jihad (Holy War Letter) in Arabic, English and French.

Broadcasting
The broadcast media is controlled by the state-owned Great Socialist People's Libyan Arab Jamahiriya Broadcasting Corporation.
Radio: Programmes are broadcast in Arabic and English from Tripoli and Benghazi.
Television: The television service broadcasts in Arabic, but there are also channels which broadcast in Italian, English and French.

Economy
The economy depends heavily on revenues from its oil sector, exports provided US$29 billion or 68.0 per cent of GDP in 2005. The sharp rise in oil prices in 2005 increased the overall fiscal surplus to 32.5 per cent of GDP. However oil production only grew by 1.5 per cent in 2005 due to capacity constraints. The non-oil sector grew by 4.5 per cent, with strong growth in tourism, transportation and construction.
The domestic economic conditions have been improving since late 2003, when UN trade sanctions, imposed in response to Libya's refusal to hand over two security

agents suspected of the bombing in 1988 of a PanAm jet over Lockerbie in Scotland, were lifted. Broad money grew by 29 per cent, reflecting a remonetization of the economy, with greater bank credit for public enterprises.

Some problems within the economy have yet to be addressed. It is still, largely, state controlled with minimal diversification with around 75 per cent of all employment in the public sector. Nevertheless Libya has liberalised its banking sector, given more independence to the Central Bank of Libya, with authority to allow foreign banks to operate, and enacted anti-money laundering laws. A privatisation programme has been broadened to include health, insurance, transport and downstream oil activities.

In the short- to medium-term, the economy can rely on the hydrocarbon sector to achieve economic growth. The country offers vast potential, with only 25 per cent of the land area offered for exploration in 2004–05. Libya has indicated a desire to attract US$10 billion worth of foreign direct investment (FDI) in the hydrocarbon sector by 2010. There is production in petrochemicals, iron, steel, and aluminium.

Climatic conditions and poor soils severely limit agricultural output, and Libya imports about 75 per cent of its food requirements; import restrictions, particularly on food, have been eased.

The Great Man-Made River (GMR) project consists of more than 1,300 wells, most over 500 metres deep, and supplies 6.5 million square metres of freshwater per day to the capital and other major cities. The project supplies much needed water from underground aquifers beneath the Sahara to the Mediterranean coast.

External trade

Libya is a member of the Common Market of Eastern and Southern Africa (Comesa) with 19 other country members. Comesa's objective is to formulate a large economic and trading union which will be able to promote the interests of all members.

Libya led the move towards a customs union, to be set up by the end of 2008, in which the same tariffs will be applied to all external goods, while internal capital goods and raw materials move freely, with intermediate and finished products attracting a 10 per cent and 25 per cent tax respectively. Not all Comesa member states will be able to adopt the customs union without harming their economies but most have signed the agreement.

Libya is also a member of the Arab Maghreb Union (AMU) and the Pan-Arab Free Trade Area (Gafta) which operates a customs union whereby tariffs within Gafta will be reduced by a percentage each year, until none remain.

Libya has limited agricultural land and is required to import 75 per cent of its food needs, however this is adequately covered by its huge hydrocarbons reserves that accounts for over 95 per cent of total export earnings. The remaining exports are primary mining products.

Imports

Goods imported include machinery, vehicles, semi-finished goods, food and consumer products.

Main sources: Italy (18.7 per cent total, 2006), Germany (7.7 per cent), China (7.5 per cent).

Exports

Principal commodities are crude oil, refined petroleum products and natural gas, gypsum, limestone and salt.

Main destinations: Italy (37.4 per cent total, 2006), Germany (14.8 per cent), Spain (7.8 per cent).

Agriculture

Farming

Agriculture is estimated to account for 5 per cent of GDP and to employ 18 per cent of the labour force.

The cultivated land is only 1.2 per cent of the total land area and over 80 per cent of all agricultural production is concentrated around oases and the northern coastal regions, especially near Benghazi and Tripoli. Less than 1 per cent of land is irrigated.

Climatic conditions and irrigation problems limit output. Over 70 per cent of food requirements are imported. Libya is self-sufficient in fruit and vegetables, dairy products and poultry. The main crops are potatoes, wheat, barley, dates, tomatoes, almonds, oats, olives, citrus fruits and groundnuts.

The huge Great Man-Made River (GMR) phased project delivers 3.68 million cubic metres of water from underground reservoirs in the Sahara to Libya's main cities and 135,000 hectares of cultivable land. The irrigation will allow an increase the land available for agriculture. Small farms for food for local comsumption will be encouraged along with large farms that are expected to grow wheat and corn and fruits for export markets.

The estimated crop production in 2005 included: 213,465 tonnes (t) cereals in total, 125,000t wheat, 195,000t potatoes, 190,000t tomatoes, 80,000t barley, 19,375t pulses, 25,000t treenuts, 150,000t dates, 71,350t citrus fruit, 30,000t grapes, 46,500t oilcrops, 180,000t olives, 345,700t fruit in total, 869,900t vegetables in total. Estimated livestock production included: 142,170t meat in total, 6,300t beef, 27,370t lamb, 6,000t goat meat, 3,700t camel meat, 98,800t poultry, 60,000t eggs, 203,408t milk, 800t honey, 5,635t sheepskins, 9,500t greasy wool.

Fishing

The total annual catch is typically 33,000 tonnes, of which up to 6,000 tonnes are exported with a total value of between US$15–30 million. Most of the catch is taken by artisanal boats with nets or hooks. There is negligible freshwater fishing, although the government has attempted to stock reservoirs with fish. Libya has a number of fish canning plants, which can tuna and sardines. Fishmeal is also produced.

Small quantities of fish are exported to Greece, Malta and Tunisia. There is a tuna cannery at Zanzur, and sardine canneries at Zuara and Khoms.

In 2004, the total marine fish catch was 46,073 tonnes.

Forestry

Libya is very lightly forested, with less than 1 per cent of total land area covered by forest and woodland, from which small quantities of sawn timber and paper are produced. The majority of domestic demand for industrial wood products is met by imports. Experiments have been undertaken into tree planting, to halt the advance of the desert, but with mixed success; there has been some development of orchards.

Industry and manufacturing

The industrial sector is estimated to contribute 18 per cent to GDP and to employ 15 per cent of the workforce. Virtually all industry was state-owned until the privatisation of state entities – excluding utilities and the gas and oil sectors – began in 2004.

Traditionally the industrial sector was limited to small-scale processing operations, mostly in food, wood and paper, textiles and soap. However, traditional small-scale agri-allied industries have given way to the growth of import substitution industries (such as building materials manufacture) and heavy industries (such as petrochemicals, iron and steel, concrete pipes and vehicle assembly). The National Petrochemicals Company (Napectco) has built up a substantial petrochemicals capacity since the late 1970s using local feedstock. The large Marsa Brega complex is owned by Napectco which hosts a number of plants producing petrochemicals, ethanol, ammonia and urea. Much industrial investment has gone into expanding capital intensive chemicals capacity as a means of increasing the value added content of exports.

Major metal smelting projects have been impeded by low incomes and depressed world prices in recent years. Other constraints to development are insufficiently trained Libyan manpower and the small domestic market.

Tourism

After the rapprochement with the West achieved in 2003 and the lifting of US sanctions in February 2004, Libya officially opened to tourism on 26 February 2005.

Travel sanctions and political isolation was an obstacle to the revival of Libya's tourism sector. Its tourist infrastructure was neglected for many years and, while new resort and hotel projects have been initiated, more investment is needed to upgrade old resources. The Mediterranean beaches and ancient historical sites, together with its proximity to Europe and other developed North African tourist destinations, provide the country with good potential for expanding visitor numbers.

Capital investment in travel and tourism is expected to reach US$1.2 billion or 31.2 per cent of total capital investment, and the sector's share of GDP is growing, from a low 1–2 per cent of GDP in 2004 to an estimated 3.2 per cent in 2005.

Mining

Major mineral deposits include iron ore (which supplies the steel complex at Misurata), potassium, magnesium, sulphur, gypsum and phosphate. There are also potential uranium deposits. Commercial exploitation of minerals is restricted by high development costs.

Salt and construction materials are produced, but large reserves of iron ore at Wadi Shatti remain undeveloped, although this is being reconsidered.

Hydrocarbons

Libya is Africa's third-largest oil producer after Nigeria and Algeria, it is ninth in the world and is one of Europe's biggest African suppliers. Italy, Germany, Spain and France are the main export markets. However, the oil fields operated by the government are estimated to be undergoing a natural 8 per cent per annum production decline. This has made Libya increasingly reliant on foreign companies and their skilled workers.

Proven oil reserves stood at 39.1 billion barrels in 2004, or approximately 3.3 per cent of the world's total reserves. Production was around 1.6 million barrels per day (bpd) in 2004 of which 1.34 million bpd are exported; there are plans for production to increase to two million bpd by 2010 and three million bpd by 2015.

In 2005, the Libyan government sold, by competition, rights to 26 oil fields to various international companies. An initial US$103 million for the leases will be followed by a percentage of the production of recovered oil.

Libya has three domestic refineries, with a combined capacity of approximately 343,000bpd, nearly twice the volume of domestic oil consumption.

Libya's gas reserves were estimated at 1.49 trillion cubic metres (cum) in 2004. Annual gas production was 7.0 billion cum in 2004. Further expansion in gas production remains a high priority for the authorities. The government appears to favour more gas consumption domestically, which could in turn make more oil available for exports. Moreover, with the increasing attractiveness of gas as a source of fuel, Libya's vast gas reserves are widely seen as a major export commodity to European countries.

Libya does not produce coal.

Energy

Electricity production capacity is 4.6GW with an added 3.3GW for peak periods. The vast majority of electricity is provided by oil-fired power plants.

Power demand is growing rapidly at 6–8 per cent per annum. The government hopes to double generating capacity by 2020.

Several plans to add generating stations and upgrade and extend the supply system have all been hampered by funding problems encountered by the state power supplier General Electricity Company (GECOL).

Banking and insurance

Libya's banking sector was in the early stages of privatisation in 2005. Initially five, state-owned, banks will have 50 per cent of their stock offered to foreign banks that may participate as minority shareholders, although being allowed to influence management. Foreign banks will also be permitted to begin retail operations in Libya.

Central bank

Central Bank of Libya

Main financial centre

Tripoli

Time

GMT plus three hours

Geography

Libya is the fourth-largest country in Africa. It extends along the Mediterranean coast of North Africa with Tunisia and Algeria to the west, Niger and Chad to the south, Egypt to the east, and Sudan to the south-east. Most of the country is part of the Sahara Desert. Only the narrow coastal strip receives sufficient rainfall to be suitable for agriculture and it is here that 90 per cent of the population live.

In 1984, the Great Man-Made River Project was begun and when completed will transport daily 6.5 million cubic metres of fresh water, drawn from Sahara Desert aquifers in the south, to the coast in the north. The aquifer water is estimated to be over 40,000 years old. The irrigation will allow an increase in the land available for agriculture.

Hemisphere

Northern

Climate

The coastal areas enjoy a temperate Mediterranean climate. Summer (May–September) temperatures are up to 40 degrees Celsius (C), while winter (November–April) temperatures reach 25–32 degrees C during daytime but can fall to 4–5 degrees C at night. Otherwise, with 90 per cent of the country desert, very hot days (to 50 degrees C), cold nights and sandstorms are likely in May–June. There is low rainfall, mainly between October and March in the highlands and semi-desert.

Dress codes

A lightweight suit or jacket and trousers are advised. A tie and a long-sleeved shirt should be worn at business meetings, but a jacket is not essential. Women should dress modestly, covering their arms and knees.

Entry requirements

Passports

Required by all. From 11 November 2007 all foreign passports require an Arabic translation. Visitors are advised to contact a Libyan consulate or tourist office for the latest official ruling before travelling.

Visa

Required by all and valid for three months. Exceptions granted for citizens of most Middle East countries, and a few other, African, states. For further information contact the nearest Libyan consulate. All visitors must have an invitation from a Libyan contact – these can be obtained from a Libyan travel agent or Embassy – and essential information on the documentation must have Arab translations. Business visitors should be sponsored by a Libyan company, which will organise the issue of a business visa.

Prohibited entry

Nationals of Israel and passport holders with Israeli visas may be refused entry, check status with a Libyan Consulate.

Currency advice/regulations

Import and export of local currency is prohibited. The import of foreign currency is unlimited but must be declared; export is limited to the amount declared.

Travellers cheques are not readily accepted. Carrying cash is the only realistic option, and the favoured currency is the US dollar. Penalties for the use of unauthorised currency dealers are severe.

Customs
There are strict customs regulations about the import or export of firearms, religious materials, antiquities and medications.

Prohibited imports
Alcohol and illegal drugs

Health (for visitors)
Mandatory precautions
Yellow fever vaccination certificate is required if travelling from an infected areas.

Advisable precautions
Vaccinations or booster shots are advised for typhoid, tetanus and hepatitis A. Other immunisation that may be advised are polio, TB, diphtheria, and hepatitis B. Malaria prophylaxis is recommended for visits to certain areas.
Avoid drinking tap water.
If necessary medication is brought by a visitor should be accompanied by a letter of explanation. A first-aid kit would be useful.

Hotels
Tripoli has a range of hotels.

Credit cards
Credit cards are not accepted.

Public holidays (national)
Fixed dates
9 Feb (Ashura), 3 Mar (Declaration of the People's Authority Day), 11 Jun (Evacuation Day), 1 Sep (Revolution Day), 7 Oct (Friendship Day), 26 Oct (Day of Mourning).

Variable dates
Eid al Adha (two days), Islamic New Year, Eid al Fitr (two days).

Islamic year – 1429 (10 Jan 2008–28 Dec 2008): The Islamic year contains 354 or 355 days, with the result that Muslim feasts advance by 10–12 days against the Gregorian calendar. Dates of feasts vary according to the sighting of the new moon, so cannot be forecast exactly.

Working hours
Friday is the Muslim holy day and all offices, businesses and banks are closed. The oil industry is also closed on Saturday.

Banking
Sat–Wed: 0800–1500 (winter); Sat–Wed: 0800–1200 and 1600–1700, Thu: 0800–1200 (summer).
Hours may be reduced during Ramadan.

Business
Sat–Thu: 0800–1600 (winter); Sat–Thu: 0700–1400 (summer).

Government
Sat–Thu: 0730–1430 (winter); Sat–Thu: 0700–1400 (summer).

Shops
Shops are mainly open 0800–1800, often closing for a few hours during the middle of the day.

Telecommunications
Mobile/cell phones
GSM 900 services are limited to populated areas.

Electricity supply
110 or 220V AC

Social customs/useful tips
Alcohol is banned throughout Libya and visitors arriving with alcohol will have it confiscated. Women often do not attend Arab social or business meetings, despite gender equality enshrined in the constitution.
Photography of public buildings and anything of military or security interest is not permitted. It is best to avoid criticism of the country, its leadership or Islam while in Libya since this could potentially result in a heavy-handed response from the authorities.
During Ramadan, eating, drinking and smoking in public is banned throughout the hours of daylight. Islamic and Arab customs prevail and must be respected by visitors. Pork is forbidden by Muslim law. Food is traditionally eaten with the right hand only.

Security
Crime is growing in Libya. The most common crimes are car theft and theft of items left in vehicles. Muggings have occurred on the beaches. Travel to remote areas is best undertaken in groups.

Getting there
Air
National airline: Libyan Arab Airlines.
International airport/s: Tripoli International airport (TIP), 35km from the city, facilities include duty-free shops, restaurants, post office and bank.
Benina International (BEN), 19km from Benghazi; Sebha (SEB), 11km from town.
Airport tax: Departure tax LD6, except for transit passenger.

Surface
Road: There are entry points via Tunisia and Egypt by the main coast road, Algeria (via Sabhah and Ghat) and Niger and Chad (via Sabhah).
Water: There are ferry services from Malta to Tripoli. There are also occasional services from Casablanca (Morocco) and Alexandria (Egypt).
Main port/s: Benghazi, Misratah, Marsa Brega and Tripoli (free port).

Getting about
National transport
Air: Libyan Arab Airlines operates an hourly shuttle between Tripoli and Benghazi. Other scheduled routes include all major centres. Buraq Air also provides internal flights.
Road: There is a surfaced road system comprising an estimated 32,000km linking all main centres. The main roads include the 1,820km national coast road from the Tunisian border to the Egyptian border; Sabhah-Ghat; Tripoli-Sabhah; Agedabia-Kufra; Sabhah-Chad and Niger borders. Many rural roads have improved due to the infrastructure work carried out for the Great Man-Made river project.
Buses: There are services between main centres.
Rail: There has been no railway in operation since 1965 when the network was broken-up. There are plans to construct a new east-west railway line from the Tunisian border to Tripoli, extending it along the coast to Misratah and then on to Egypt via Tobrok. Another railway line is planned to run north-south from Misratah to Sabhah, and then on to Chad, however these projects are still little beyond their planning stages and may take several years before fruition. Meanwhile Libya has let contracts with private foreign companies to supply crossing and pointwork for the proposed east-west line.

City transport
Taxis: Yellow government taxis are generally cheaper than private taxis. It is advisable to negotiate the fare in advance. Taxis are often on a shared basis.
Buses, trams & metro: State-run bus services operate in Benghazi and Tripoli. They can be unreliable and overcrowded.

Car hire
There are car hire agencies in Tripoli and Benghazi, although rates can be quite high. Cars with drivers can be hired.

BUSINESS DIRECTORY
The addresses listed below are a selection only. While World of Information makes every endeavour to check these addresses, we cannot guarantee that changes have not been made, especially to telephone numbers and area codes. We would welcome any corrections.

Telephone area codes
The international direct dialling code (IDD) for Libya is +218, followed by area code and subscriber's number:

Benghazi	61	Tobruk	87
Misratah	51	Tripoli	21

Chambers of Commerce
Benghazi Chamber of Commerce, Trade, Industry and Agriculture, Issabri Street, PO Box 208, Benghazi (tel: 80-971; fax: 80-761; e-mail: benghaziccia@netscape.net).

Misurata Chamber of Commerce, Trade, Industry and Agriculture, Souweihli Street, PO Box 84, Misurata (tel: 616-497; fax: 620-340; e-mail: info@ccimisrata.org).

Tobruk Chamber of Commerce, Industry and Agriculture, Alfadel Abu Omar

Street, PO Box 868, Tobruk (tel/fax: 24-835).

Tripoli Chamber of Commerce, Trade, Industry and Agriculture, 6 Najd Street, PO Box 2321, Tripoli (tel: 333-6855; fax: 333-2655).

Union of Chambers of Commerce, Trade, Industry and Agriculture, PO Box 12556, 26 Bandong Street, Tripoli (tel: 444-1613; fax: 444-1457; e-mail:unionchamber@hotmail.com).

Banking
Libyan Arab Foreign Bank, PO Box 2542, That al-Imad Administrative Complex, Tripoli (tel: 335-0155, 335-0160, 335-0086/7; fax: 335-0164/8).

Sahara Bank, PO Box 270, 10 First of September Street, Tripoli (tel: 333-9804; fax: 333-7922).

Wahda Bank, PO Box 452, Sharia Gamal Abd an-Naser, Benghazi (tel: 222-4122; fax: 222-4122, 222-4709).

Umma Bank Sal, PO Box 685, 1 Giaddat Omar El-Mokhtar Street, Tripoli (tel: 333-4031/35, 444-2541, 444-2544; fax: 333-2505, 444-2476).

Central bank
Central Bank of Libya, PO Box 1103, Tripoli (tel: 333-3591; fax: 444-1488; e-mail: info@cbl-ly.com).

Travel information
Libyan Arab Airlines, PO Box 2555, Haiti Street, Tripoli (tel: 602-093, 608-860; fax: 2-230-970; internet: www.libyanarabairline.com).

National tourist organisation offices
General People's Committee of Tourism, PO Box 82063, Tripoli (tel: 333-6452, 333-7576; fax: 334-2709; internet: www.libyan-tourism.org).

Other useful addresses
General National Organisation for Industrialisation, PO Box 4388, Tripoli (tel: 44-680, 34-995).

Kufrah & Serir Authority, Council of Agricultural Development, Benghazi.

National Oil Corporation, PO Box 2655, Tripoli (tel: 46-180).

National Trade Union Federation, PO Box 734, Tripoli.

Internet sites
Qadafi's official website: www.algathafi.org

Africa Business Network: www.ifc.org/abn

African Development Bank: www.afdb.org

Africa Online: www.africaonline.com

AllAfrica.com: http:// allafrica.com

Buraq Air: www.buraqair.com

Libya on the Web: www.libyaweb.com/news.htm

Libyans Online: www.libyaonline.com

Libyan Mission at United Nations: www.un.int/libya/

Azar Libya Travel and Tour Company: www.angelfire.com/az/azartours/index.html

Juddaim Tourism Service: www.libya-juddaim.com/eng/index.html

Caravanserai Tours: www.caravanserai-tours.com

Liechtenstein

KEY FACTS

Official name: Fürstentum Liechtenstein (The Principality of Liechtenstein)

Head of State: Prince Hans-Adam II (titular), (since 1989; on 15 Aug 2004, Crown Prince Alois became acting Head of State)

Head of government: Prime Minister Otmar Hasler (FBP) (since 2001; re-elected Apr 2005)

Ruling party: Coalition led by Fortschrittliche Bürgerpartei (FBP) (Progressive Citizens' Party) with Vaterländische Union (VU) (Patriotic Union) (FBP since 2001; re-elected 2005, VU since 2005)

Area: 160 square km

Population: 35,322 (2007)*

Capital: Vaduz

Official language: German

Currency: Swiss franc (Swf) = 100 centimes/rappen (the euro also circulates informally)

Exchange rate: Swf1.02 per US$ (Jul 2008)

GDP per capita: US$25,000 (2004)*

Labour force: 29,000 (2004)*

Unemployment: 3.30% (2006)

Inflation: 1.00% (2004)*

Balance of trade: US$1.55 billion (2003)

Visitor numbers: 51,051 (2005)

* estimated figure

COUNTRY PROFILE

Historical profile

Independence in 1719 was followed in the early nineteenth century by a period of French domination, then close connection with Austria until 1918.
1938–70 Fortschrittliche Bürgerpartei (FBP) (Progressive Citizens' Party) was the majority party in the coalition government.
1970–74 Vaterländische Union (VU) (Fatherland Union) was the majority party in coalition, followed by FBP in the 1974 elections.
1978 Liechtenstein was admitted to the Council of Europe. A VU-led coalition was formed.
1984 Prince Hans-Adam II took over executive power from his father. Women were granted the vote in national elections, but not in local elections.
1986 Women were given to right to vote in all elections.
1989 The VU gained a majority of one seat.
1993 FBP became the largest party
1997 The VU gained an outright majority, the first by any party for over 60 years, and Mario Frick became prime minister.
2001 FBP was elected and Otmar Hasler became prime minister.
2002 The OECD included Liechtenstein on a list of seven states that were failing to meet international standards on financial transparency and information exchange. An agreement with Monaco over the prevention of money laundering and terrorist financing was signed.
2003 In a referendum, 64 per cent of voters agreed to give Prince Hans-Adam II more power, including the right to dismiss any government deemed incompetent. The vote followed a long-standing dispute between parliament and the monarch, who had threatened to leave the country if his constitutional reform proposals were not adopted.
2004 Liechtenstein adopted a new aubergine-coloured flag. On 15 August, Prince Hans-Adam II handed over day-to-day responsibility for running the country to his son, Prince Alois. Prince Hans-Adam II remains head of state.
2005 Otmar Hasler of the ruling Fortschrittliche Bürgerpartei (FBP) (Progressive Citizens' Party) was re-elected with 48.7 per cent of the vote (12 seats out of 25). A coalition with the Vaterländische Union (VU) (Fatherland Union) was formed.
2006 Liechtenstein celebrated its bi-centenary of its admission to the Confederation of the Rhine in 1806. At the newly determined 160 square km, the size of the country was found to be greater than previously thought, after its borders were re-measured.
2007 In March, the Swiss army, on night manoeuvres, accidentally tracked up to 2km into Liechtenstein before the error was noticed and the 171-man company returned to their own lands.
2008 An international arrest warrant was issued for the former employee of the LGT Bank, who allegedly sold client details to foreign government. Germany, the UK and several other countries, have used these records to pursue tax evasion by their citizens. An official announcement in August, stated that Liechtenstein would modify its banking rules to allow 'comprehensive co-operation' with foreign finance ministries on tax issues. However, 'a culture of privacy' would still be maintained and this may hamper prospects for Liechtenstein's removal from the OECD's list of countries considered unco-operative tax havens.

Political structure

Constitution

The constitution dates from 1921.Voting rights for women on national issues were granted in 1984, and on local matters two years later.
In 2003, a constitutional referendum gave Prince Hans-Adam II power to veto the decisions of parliament and to sack the government, and powers over the appointment of judges, but it took away his right to rule by emergency decree for an unlimited period and to nominate government officials.

Form of state

Absolute monarchy (since 2003)

The executive

The head of state is the monarch. The 2003 referendum conferred on the monarch the power to veto the decisions of parliament and to sack the government.

National legislature

The constitution provides for a unicameral Landtag (parliament) with 25 seats, elected by proportional representation in two multi-seat constituencies, for a four-year term. The Landtag elects a five-member government, which is thereafter officially approved by the head of state.

Legal system
The monarch appoints the country's judges.
Last elections
13 March 2005 (parliamentary); March 2003 (constitutional referendum).
Results: Parliamentary: the ruling FBP was re-elected with 48.7 per cent of the vote (12 seats out of 25), the VU 38.2 per cent (10), and the Freie Liste (Free List) 13 per cent (three). Turnout was 86.5 per cent.
Constitutional referendum: 64 per cent of voters were in favour of constitutional changes.
Next elections
2009 (parliamentary)

Political parties
Ruling party
Coalition led by Fortschrittliche Bürgerpartei (FBP) (Progressive Citizens' Party) with Vaterländische Union (VU) (Patriotic Union) (FBP since 2001; re-elected 2005, VU since 2005)
Main opposition party
Freie Liste (Free List)
Political situation
The Liechtenstein banking system, which is closely tied into the Swiss banking system, had a reputation for discretion that bordered on the secretive. But in 2007 that reputation took a beating when stolen account details were sold by an ex-LGT (Liechtenstein Global Trust) bank employee to around a dozen major foreign tax departments. While most observers questioned the morality of buying stolen goods, none of the tax authorities were in the least bit apologetic and all began to investigate the status of assets belonging to their nationals.
The Liechtenstein authorities have condemned the actions of the recipients of the information, calling their actions 'offensive' and a violation of its sovereignty. However, Germany, whose citizens represent around 40 per cent of all bank depositors, threatened to increase punitive measures if an agreed method of preventing tax evasion schemes could not be found; this threat was echoed in the US.

Population
35,322 (2007)*
Last census: December 2000: 33,307
Population density: 200 per square km.
Annual growth rate: 1.3 per cent (2003)
Ethnic make-up
Alemannic (87.5 per cent), Italian, Turkish and other (12.5 per cent).
Religions
Roman Catholic (80 per cent), Protestant (7.4 per cent).

Education
Primary education lasts for five years.
Secondary education, starting at aged 12, is provided through three school types: Oberschule, Realschule and Gymnasium. Each is geared to the attainment outcomes expected of their students.
On completing four years (compulsory) secondary education, a lower secondary school certificate is awarded. Realschule students either undertake a one year technical or vocational course leading to specialised schools of further education, or an academic course to attain the lower level Matura Certificate. Students of the Gymnasium complete a four year academic course, attaining the higher grade Matura Certificate which is recognised for university entrance either at home or in Switzerland, Austria and Germany.
Compulsory years: Seven to 16.

Health
Life expectancy: 79 years (estimate 2003)
Child (under 5 years) mortality rate (per 1,000): 10 deaths per 1,000 live births.

Main cities
Vaduz (capital, estimated population 4,999 in 2005), Schaan (5,717), Triesen (4,787), Balzers (4,486), Eschen (4,090).

Languages spoken
Allemannish – a dialect of German – is also spoken.
Official language/s
German

Media
Press
There two dailies newspapers are Liechtensteiner Vaterland (www.vaterland.li) and Liechtensteiner Volksblatt (www.volksblatt.li) and one weekly Liewo Sonntagszeitung which is published on Sunday.
Dailies: Two main dailies include the Liechtensteiner Vaterland (Vaduz) and Liechtensteiner Volksblatt (Schaan).
Weeklies: Liechtenstein News is the official weekly newspaper, providing tourist and hotel information in the principality.
Broadcasting
Radio Liechtenstein (www.radio.li) has a network of seven stations. Swiss radio signals are readily received in Liechtenstein including RTSI (www.rtsi.ch) and DSR, with seven stations. RTSI also broadcasts TV programmes.
Advertising
The Media Commission has the authority to implement the Television and Radio Act. While there are few restrictions, tobacco advertising is banned and alcohol restricted in all media outlets and advertising must not be misleading or aggressive.

Economy
Liechtenstein has a highly industrialised, export-based economy with a well-developed banking sector. It ranks as one of the wealthiest countries per capita in the world. There is close economic interdependence with Switzerland through a customs and currency union.
It is home to 15 banks, including LGT (Liechtenstein Global Trust), owned by the royal family. Liechtenstein receives about 30 per cent of its GDP from financial services. The tourism sector is an important earner of foreign exchange and the services sector enjoyed rapid expansion during the latter part of the 1990s. Over half of the workforce is employed in the services and industry, while 40 per cent of GDP is generated by industry and manufacturing. Around 30,000 businesses are registered in Liechtenstein, which is is not far short of one business per resident.
There is an extremely high ratio of self-financing enjoyed by domestic businesses plus their ability, if necessary, to fall back on private wealth. A number of companies are research-focussed and are considered world leaders in their particular specialisms.
In 2004, the Organisation for Economic Co-operation and Development (OECD) named Liechtenstein as an unco-operative tax haven and threatened sanctions for refusing to toughen laws and provide more information to tax officials from industrialised nations. The threat was rejected, as low taxes and bank privacy are the basis for Liechtenstein's prosperity. After strong pressure from EU members and in company with Switzerland, Andorra, Monaco and San Marino, Liechtenstein agreed to put in place equivalent measures to those being applied by EU's member states, in regards to taxation of income from savings.

KEY INDICATORS — Liechtenstein

	Unit	2003	2004	2005	2006	2007
Population	m	–0.03	0.04	0.0	–	0.04
Gross domestic product (GDP)	US$bn	0.82	0.88	–	–	–
GDP per capita	US$	25,000	25,000	25,000	25,000	25,000
Inflation	%	–	1.0	1.0	1.0	1.0
Exchange rate	per US$	1.32	1.24	1.25	1.25	1.25

External trade
Liechtenstein is also one of the four members of the European Free Trade Association (EFTA) and European Economic Area (EEA) which allows access to the internal EU market and takes around 70 per cent of Liechtenstein's exports.
While the industrial sector produces goods of high value it is the financial services and tourism that make the most significant contributions to the balance of payments.
Imports
Main imports include agricultural products, raw materials, machinery, metal goods, textiles, foodstuffs and vehicles.
Main sources: EU, Switzerland
Exports
Principal commodities include small speciality machinery, audio, video and vehicles parts, dental and optical products, prepared foodstuffs, ceramics, hardware and electronic equipment.
Main destinations: EU (typically over 60.0 per cent in total – Germany (24 per cent) Austria (10 per cent), France (9 per cent), Italy (7 per cent), UK (5 per cent)), US (18.9 per cent), Switzerland (15.7 per cent)

Agriculture
Farming
Agriculture is small-scale, employing only about 1.7 per cent of the population (350 workers). Activity is concentrated on dairy farming and farming of fodder cereals although vegetable cultivation and wine production are also undertaken. Utilising methods such as technical rationalisation and intensive cultivation, yields have been steadily increasing. Production typically includes 150 tonnes (t) grapes and 12,000t milk.
42 per cent of the principality is forested land. The forestry industry has grown since the late 1990s, doubling production to 22,167 cubic metres (cum) industrial roundwood and 18,000cum sawlogs and veneer logs by 2002, and maintaining production of 4,000cum fuel wood annually. 0.3 per cent of the agicultural sector are employed in forestry.

Industry and manufacturing
Industry and trade employs about 45 per cent of the workforce. Owing to lack of raw materials and a small domestic market, the sector is export-based and centred on specialised and high-technology production. Manufacturing is centred on machine building, precision engineering and metal working industries. There are also traditional industries such as chemicals (mainly pharmaceuticals), textiles, ceramics and food processing. The production of materials for dental medicine, of microsections for optics and electronics, the manufacture of preserves and deep-frozen products, upholstery, and varnishes, have all attained growing importance. Liechtenstein is the world's largest exporter of false teeth.

Tourism
Liechtenstein receives around 50,000 tourist arrivals each year, mainly from Germany and Switzerland. There has been a steady decline in number of arrivals, down from 78,000 in 1990 and 59,000 in 1995. In recent years stays in the towns have risen, while those in the mountains have fallen. The Prince's art collection includes over a thousand works including some by Van Dyck and Rubens. A portion of the £300 million collection is on display to the visiting public.

Hydrocarbons
Liechtenstein does not produce any hydrocarbons and relies entirely on imports, primarily from the EU. Liechtenstein imports around 90 per cent of its total energy needs. 46 per cent of Liechtenstein's primary energy consumption is met by oil imports. Gas contributes 27 per cent of energy consumption.

Energy
Liechtenstein is dependent on imported energy, which supplies 90 per cent of its needs. The remainder is sourced from domestically generated hydropower (75 per cent) and wood (25 per cent). The country has ratified the Kyoto Protocol. The government has pledged to source 10 per cent of domestic energy requirements from renewable sources particularly biomass and solar.

Banking and insurance
Three main banks are in operation: Liechtensteinische Landesbank, LGT Bank in Liechtenstein and Verwaltungs und Privat-Bank (VP Bank) AG. These have a close association with the Swiss banking system. Secrecy laws are strict although new legislation has put an end to the old anonymous numbered accounts.
There is a total of 17 banking institutes in operation.
Liechtenstein is a signatory of an EU tax agreement introduced in July 2005 in a number of non-EU countries. Liechtenstein will impose a withholding tax, up to 35 per cent, to be passed to the tax department of an EU citizen's country, but retaining the anonymity of the saver. This means that the relevant EU country will not be informed about the amount of money in its citizens' bank accounts.
Liechtenstein has also agreed to supply information on tax fraud, for criminal or civil trials, and notify EU member states about additional malpractices.
In April 2005, a banking ombudsman was appointed in Liechtenstein, ending years of reliance on the Swiss banking ombudsman.
The insurance sector is a recent development. Eight companies make up the Liechtenstein Insurance Association, formed in 1998.
Central bank
Centrum Bank AG
Offshore facilities
Liechtenstein is a major international offshore financial centre, and the largest single supplier of fiduciary funds in Europe.

Time
GMT plus one hour (daylight saving, late March to late October, GMT plus two hours)

Geography
Liechtenstein is a tiny, land-locked country, surrounded by Switzerland (to the west and south) and Austria (to the east). The area of the principality is 160 square km. The river Rhine forms Liechtenstein's western frontier.
The western part of Liechtenstein is lowland, situated in the Rhine flood-plain. This has been drained, providing a wide range of soil types suitable for agriculture. The eastern half of the country is in the foothills of the Rhätikon mountains (Raetian Alps), which rise to snowy Alpine peaks. The highest point is the Grauspitz at 2,599m. Coniferous forests and alpine meadows cover the lower slopes. There are three main valleys in the mountains. The river Samina crosses the range south to north to join the Ill river in Austria.
Hemisphere
Northern

Climate
Varies with altitude, generally mild and often windy. Average summer temperature 17 degrees Celsius (C). Average winter temperature 1 degree C.

Dress codes
Medium-weight throughout the year, with a topcoat for winter.

Entry requirements
Passports
Swiss regulations apply. Passports are required by all, except nationals of EU countries. Passports must be valid for three months beyond intended stay.
Visa
Swiss regulations apply. Visas are required by all, except nationals of EU/EEA countries, Australasia, North America, Japan and some other countries. Contact the nearest embassy or consulate for details.
A business visa for a citizen of a non-exempt country requires a letter of invitation from or evidence of correspondence with a Swiss company presented to the local Swiss embassy.

Currency advice/regulations
There are no restrictions on the import and export of local and foreign currencies.

Customs
Restricted amounts of alcoholic beverages, tobacco and gifts (up to value of Swf300) may be imported duty free.

Health (for visitors)
Nationals of the European Economic Area (EEA) countries and Switzerland can access reduced cost and sometimes free necessary medical treatment using a European Health Insurance Card (EHIC) while visiting the EEA. Applications for the EHIC should be made before travelling.
The EHIC of nationals of the 10 countries which joined the EU in 2005 are not valid in Switzerland.

Mandatory precautions
None

Advisable precautions
Up-to-date tetanus and polio immunisations.

Hotels
Tips are included in hotel and restaurant bills.

Public holidays (national)

Fixed dates
1 Jan (New Year's Day), 2 Jan (St Berchtold's Day), 6 Jan (Epiphany), 2 Feb (Candlemas), 19 Mar (Feast of St Joseph), 1 May (Labour Day), 15 Aug (Assumption Day), 8 Sep (Nativity of Our Lady), 1 Nov (All Saints' Day), 8 Dec (Immaculate Conception), 24–26 Dec (Christmas), 31 Dec (New Year's Eve).

Variable dates
Shrove Tuesday, Good Friday, Easter Monday, Ascension Day, Whit Monday, Corpus Christi (May/Jun).

Working hours

Banking
Mon–Fri: 0800–1630.

Business
Mon–Fri: 0800–1200 and 1330–1730.

Government
Mon–Fri: 0800–1630.

Shops
Mon–Fri: 0800–1200, 1330–1830; Sat: 0800–1600.

Getting there

Air

International airport/s: There are no airports in Liechtenstein. The nearest international airport is Zürich-Unique (ZRH), Switzerland, approximately 130km from Vaduz. Travel to Liechtenstein can then be continued by road, rail or bus; an autoroute connects Zürich with Liechtenstein.

Surface

Road: Good road access from Switzerland and to a lesser extent Austria. Autoroute (N13) extends along Liechtenstein's Rhine border to Lake Constance, Austria and Germany in the north, continuing southwards towards St Moritz. In the west there are autoroutes to Zürich, Bern and Basel.
Motorway connections: Balzers, Vaduz, Schaan, Bendern, Ruggell.

Rail: The nearest rail stations to Vaduz are at Sargans and Buchs, in St Gallen, Switzerland. Another rail station is at Feldkirch in Austria.

Getting about

National transport

Buses: All villages can be reached by bus service.

Rail: Restricted rail network, with stations at Nendelny and halts at Schaan and Schaanwald.
Nearest main rail stations are at Buchs and Sargans in St Gallen, Switzerland, and Feldkirch in Austria.

City transport
There are regular and inexpensive bus services, and easily obtainable taxi services. Tipping is not customary.

Car hire
Service offered by Avis (Vaduz), Europcar (Eschen-Nendeln) and Nolo (Balzers). Driver must have held a valid driving licence for at least one year and be over 20 years of age. Speed limit 50kph in city, 80kph outside. Traffic drives on the right.

BUSINESS DIRECTORY

The addresses listed below are a selection only. While World of Information makes every endeavour to check these addresses, we cannot guarantee that changes have not been made, especially to telephone numbers and area codes. We would welcome any corrections.

Telephone area codes
The international direct dialling (IDD) code for Liechtenstein is +423, followed by subscriber's number.

Chambers of Commerce
Liechtenstein Chamber of Commerce and Industry, Altenbach 8, 9490 Vaduz (tel: 237-5511; fax: 237-5512; e-mail: info@lihk.li).

Banking
Centrum Bank AG, Heiligkreuz 8, FL-9490 Vaduz (tel: 235-8585; fax: 235-8686).

LGT Bank in Liechtenstein AG (prior to Jan 1996, known as BIL GT Group), Herrengasse 12, FL-9490 Vaduz (tel: 235-1122; fax: 235-1522).

Verwaltungs und Privat-Bank AG, Im Zentrum, Aeulestrasse 6, FL-9490 Vaduz (tel: 235-6655; fax: 235-6500).

Central bank
Liechtensteinische Landesbank, 44 Städtle, PO Box 384, FL-9490 Vaduz (tel: 236-8811; fax: 236-8822; e-mail: llb@llb.li).

Travel information

National tourist organisation offices
Liechtenstein Tourism, Städtle 38, PO Box 139, FL-9490 Vaduz (tel: 239-6300; fax: 239-6301; e-mail: info@tourismus.li).

Other useful addresses
Amt für Volkswirtschaft (national statistics office), Kirchastrasse 7, FL-9490 Vaduz (tel: 236-6871; fax: 236-6889).

Liechtenstein Embassy (USA), 633 Third Avenue, 27th Floor, New York, NY 10017 (tel: (+1-202)-599-0220; fax: (+1-202)-599-0064).

Postillion-Reisen AG, Landstrasse 9, FL-9494 Schaan (tel: 26-565; fax: 27-037).

Presse-und Informationsamt, Regierungsgebäude, FL-9490 Vaduz (tel: 236-6111; fax: 236-6460).

Internet sites
Liechtenstein News: http://www.news.li

Tourism information: http://www.tourismus.li/

Lithuania

KEY FACTS

Official name: Lietuvos Respublika (Republic of Lithuania)

Head of State: President Valdas Adamkus (since 12 Jul 2004)

Head of government: Prime Minister Gediminas Kirkilas (LSDP) (since Jul 2006)

Ruling party: LSDP-led coalition

Area: 65,200 square km

Population: 3.38 million (2007)

Capital: Vilnius

Official language: Lithuanian

Currency: Litas (plural Litai) (Lt) = 100 cents

Exchange rate: Lt2.17 per US$ (Jul 2008)

GDP per capita: US$11,354 (2007)*

GDP real growth: 8.80% (2007)

Labour force: 1.83 million (2004)

Unemployment: 5.00% (2005)

Inflation: 5.80% (2007)

Balance of trade: -US$5.36 billion (2006)

Foreign debt: US$9.07 billion (2004)

Annual FDI: US$773.00 million (2004)

* estimated figure

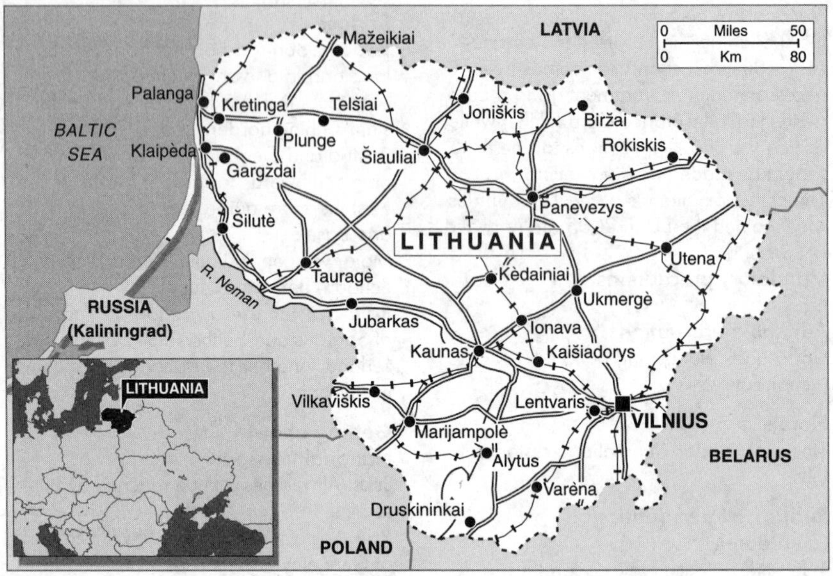

In April 2008 Lithuania's already high inflation rate continued to rise. The annual rate rose to 11.3 per cent, its highest since January 1997, up from 10.8 per cent in February, according to data released by the Lithuanian statistics office. Lithuania is struggling to get its inflation rate, which is one of the fastest growing in the European Union (EU), under control. In early 2008 rising prices lead to teachers' strikes over pay increases and helped provoke a no-confidence vote in parliament which Prime Minister Gediminas Kirkilas managed to survive. Meanwhile the finance ministry raised its 2008 inflation forecast to 9.2 per cent.

It was expected that the Lithuanian economy would keep growing in 2008, even if at a much slower rate. Some analysts considered that Lithuania was the only Baltic state in which the economy was likely to grow both in 2008 and in 2009. One Lithuanian bank forecast that in 2008 the Lithuanian economy would grow by 3.8 per cent, in 2009 by 1.9 per cent, and in 2010 by 2.9 per cent.

Politics proceed

Lithuania's politics, like those of its neighbours, have been heavily influenced by the Baltic's state's nearness to Russia and the resultant importance of accession to both the EU and the North Atlantic Treaty Organisation (Nato), both of which have been achieved. Lithuania's first presidential election was held in 1993 and was won by the former Communist Algirdas Brazauskas. He was succeeded in 1998 by the centrist Valdas Adamkus. Adamkus then lost in the January 2003 election to Rolandas Paksas. But almost as soon as Paksas' term of office started, allegations began to emerge concerning the financing of his presidential campaign and his doubtful contacts with individuals in Russia. Following a parliamentary investigation Mr Paksas was impeached by the Lithuanian parliament in April 2004 and on the same day parliament adopted a resolution appointing parliamentary chairman (speaker), Arturas Paulauskas, as acting president. Valdas Adamkus was re-elected president of Lithuania in June 2004.

Algirdas Brazauskas led broadly centre-left governments from mid-2001 until he resigned as prime minister in June 2006. Intense inter-party negotiations then led to a minority coalition government (led by Lietuvos Socialdemokratu Partija (LSDP) (Social-democratic Party of Lithuania)) under former minister of national defence Gedminias Kirkilas being approved by the parliament on 19 July 2006. Mr Kirkilas' government included ministers from his own LSDP, the Farmers' Party, and the Liberal Centrist Party. A new minority coalition government, headed by Prime Minister Kirkilas took office in July 2006, retaining the support of the opposition Conservative party on major issues until September 2007. On January 28, 2008 the Social Liberal party joined the coalition to expand it to 72 votes.

When Lithuania gained independence from the former Soviet Union in 1990, it soon became clear that unlike political independence, the social and economic changes did not immediately bring greater well being for the general good. On the contrary, the poles of wealth and poverty became more distant from each other. While the *nouveau* rich and successful became even richer, state employees and public servants risked becoming the new *lumpenproletariat*.

The shadow of Russia

Lithuania has for a very long time lived in the shadow of Russia, the big bear on its doorstep. However, recent years have seen the former soviet satellite state break free from the shackles of Moscow, by and large, though remnants of the Russian regional power's iron fist remain. Lithuania's embrace of the West and in particular the EU, has allowed the small state to look forward to charting its own future course in the world.

Lithuania was the first of the Soviet republics to breakaway from the then USSR, declaring its independence first in March 1990, and then again in 1991 when a referendum was held, overwhelmingly in favour of independence. Moscow refused to recognise the new state until after its own change of government in 1991. The last Russian troops withdrew from Lithuania in 1993. Lithuania has subsequently restructured its economy and joined both Nato and the EU in 2004. A slow starter in the westernisation and modernisation of its economy, Lithuania has caught up rapidly.

Rebounding

The EU has provided Lithuania with a development budget for the period 2007–13 of US$15 billion, a 56 per cent increase on the budget for 2004–06. Confirming the budget, the then prime minister, Algirdas Brazauskas, told President Adamkus that for every one litas Lithuania puts into the EU budget it will get back five. Lithuania will also get the EU structural aid of eur220 million and eur50 million to assist in the closing of its nuclear station Ignalina.

The country has rebounded from the 1998 Russian financial crisis. Since joining the EU labour migration has contributed to the decline in unemployment. However, structural imbalances in the labour market persist. Long-term unemployment remains a serious problem. High taxes to fund social insurance benefits hamper job creation and contribute to unemployment and tax avoidance. Gross average wages have risen significantly, reflecting a combination of a shortage of qualified labour, higher profitability in the private sector, and government efforts to attract and retain a skilled public sector labour force.

Growing domestic consumption and increased investment have furthered recovery. Trade has been increasingly oriented toward the West. Privatisation of the large, state-owned utilities, particularly in the energy sector, has been successful. Foreign government and business support have helped in the transition from a Soviet-style command economy to a market economy.

Lithuania is an upper middle-income country with an estimated GDP per capita of US$11,354 in 2007. Foreign direct investment (FDI) from EU member states, the Nordic countries in particular, has risen. However, despite remarkable progress over recent years the country is still among the poorest of EU members with less than half (48 per cent) of the EU-25 average purchasing power. Despite an unfavourable external environment, notably stagnating markets in the EU, Lithuania's real growth remained robust at 8.8 per cent in 2007, after strong growth in 2006 of 7.7 per cent.

After almost two years of deflation, consumer prices surged in 2004 because of record-high oil prices and the one-time effect of EU accession. In 2007, Lithuania's 12-month average inflation of 8.8 per cent was higher than the EU reference value, which is the average of the three lowest rates adjusted by an extra 1.5 percentage points. Keeping inflation under control is crucial for Lithuania's adoption of the euro. In May 2006, Lithuania's application to join the eurozone was rejected after narrowly missing the inflation target. Then it missed the 1 January start date for joining the European Monetary Union (Emu), due to a higher than planned inflation rate.

On the other hand, Lithuania has made visible progress in improving its business climate. According to the World Bank, Lithuania was among the top 10 reformers of an investment climate and in the top 20 in terms of creating a business environment. However, in addition to improving its business climate and adopting competitive tax rates, Lithuania has to make substantial efforts to attract foreign investments to sustain sufficient financing of the current account.

Outlook

The next presidential election is scheduled for June 2009. Liberal democrats are

KEY INDICATORS — Lithuania

	Unit	2003	2004	2005	2006	2007
Population	m	3.48	3.49	3.42	3.39	3.38
Gross domestic product (GDP)	US$bn	17.95	22.50	25.67	29.76	*38.34
GDP per capita	US$	5,156	6,404	7,494	8,768	*11,354
GDP real growth	%	6.0	6.6	7.6	7.7	*8.8
Inflation	%	-0.4	1.2	2.7	3.8	5.8
Unemployment	%	10.5	8.0	5.0	3.8	4.3
Industrial output	% change	–	8.8	7.0	7.0	–
Agricultural output	% change	–	-0.7	4.0	4.0	–
Exports (fob) (goods)	US$m	7,906.0	9,273.8	11,789.3	14,150.6	–
Imports (cif) (goods)	US$m	9,600.0	11,590.4	14,632.3	18,359.8	–
Balance of trade	US$m	-1,694.0	-2,316.6	-2,843.0	-4,209.3	–
Current account	US$m	-1,290.0	-1,910.0	-1,831.0	-3,218.0	-4,988.0
Total reserves minus gold	US$m	3,372.0	3,512.6	3,720.2	5,654.4	7,565.8
Foreign exchange	US$m	3,371.9	3,512.5	3,720.1	5,654.3	7,565.6
Exchange rate	per US$	3.03	2.62	2.67	2.67	2.39

* estimated figure

seeking the re-election of former president Rolandas Paksas, who was in office until 2004, when parliament tried to impeach him. He had allegedly told his biggest financial supporter – Russian businessman Yuri Borisov – that his phone was bugged. Impeachment was sought on the grounds that Paksas had revealed a state secret. No one seemed to deny that the state was eavesdropping on Borisov, or say for what reason it might have been, and the Supreme Court threw out the case for lack of evidence. This leaves the field clear for Paksas, spoken of as 'the daredevil of Lithuanian politics', to make a political comeback, something the liberal democrats are urging him to do. Still in his forties, he is politically a youngster compared to septuagenarian Adamkus.

On the economic front Lithuania continues to make good progress. The country has certainly responded to the macroeconomic demands placed upon its political and business elite since in acceding to full membership of the European Union. The IMF has predicted continued high GDP growth rates.

Risk assessment

Politics	Good
Economy	Fair
Regional stability	Good

COUNTRY PROFILE

Historical profile

The Grand Duchy of Lithuania was in union with Poland from 1569; it was annexed by Russia between 1772 and 1795.
1795–1914 Lithuania became part of the Russian empire.
1914–18 The Russians were driven out of Lithuania by the Germans in the First World War.
1918 Lithuania declared independence.
1922 A constitution declared Lithuania a parliamentary republic with the Seimas as the parliamentary organ.
1926 In a military coup, Antanas Smetona came to power as the head of an authoritarian regime.
1940 Lithuania was invaded and occupied by the Soviet Union.
1941 Lithuania was occupied by the Germans, until it was re-annexed by the Soviets in 1944.
1988 A nationalist movement, the Lithuanian Reform Movement (Sàjudis), was set up by a group of writers and intellectuals; at a mass rally in Vilnius, the leaders declared that the USSR occupied Lithuania illegally.
1989 Parliament approved the declaration of Lithuanian sovereignty, stating that Lithuanian laws take precedence over Soviet laws.
1990 Sàjudis won the elections (the first free elections for 50 years). Vytautas Landsbergis was elected chairman of parliament, which declared Lithuania's independence. Fearing the impact that this would have on nationalist demands in the other Baltic republics, the Soviet Union immediately imposed an economic blockade; Lithuania agreed to suspend independence, pending talks.
1991 Talks with Moscow failed and the economy faced turmoil; Landsbergis ended the suspension of the declaration of independence. A referendum was held, resulting in an overwhelming vote for independence. Following a failed coup in Moscow, the USSR recognised Lithuania's independence. Lithuania, together with Latvia and Estonia, were admitted to the UN.
1992 A new constitution introducing a presidency was adopted by referendum. The Lietuvos Demokratine Darbo Partija (LDDP) (Democratic Labour Party of Lithuania) won more seats than Sàjudis in the elections – the LDDP was the first former communist party to return to power in central and eastern Europe.
1993 Algirdas Brazauskas, the former Lietuvos Komunistu Partija (LKP) (Lithuanian Communist Party) first secretary, won direct presidential elections and appointed Adolfas Slezevicius prime minister. Following the defeat of the Sàjudis organisation in the 1992 elections, the Homeland Union was established.
1996 Allegations of corruption led to the removal of Slezevicius and Mindaugas Stankevicius was appointed prime minister. After elections, the Tevynes Sajunga (TS) (Homeland Union) formed a centre-right coalition government with the Lietuvos Kricioniu Demokratu Partija (LKDP) (Lithuanian Christian Democratic Party) and the Lietuvos Centro Sajunga (LCS) (Centre Union of Lithuania). Gediminas Vagnorius was appointed prime minister.
1998 Valdas Adamkus was elected president.
1999 Vagnorius resigned, Rolandas Paksas substituted until a new government, under the leadership of Andrius Kubilius, came to power.
2000 Following the parliamentary elections, a minority coalition government was established, which included the Lietuvos Liberalu Sajunga (LLS) (Lithuanian Liberal Union), LCS and the Modernuju Kriscioni Demokratu Sajunga (MKDS) (Modern Christian-Democratic Union) with the support of other smaller parties. Rolandas Paksas, leader of the LLS, was again appointed prime minister.
2001 Prime Minister Rolandas Paksas' coalition government was brought down over differences about energy sector privatisations. A coalition government was formed, led by the Lietuvos Socialdemokratu Partija (LSDP) (Social-democratic Party of Lithuania). The LSDP's Algirdas Brazauskas was appointed prime minister.
2002 The litas was re-pegged from the US dollar to the euro.
2003 Rolandas Paksas won the presidential election. Algirdas Brazauskas was re-appointed prime minister on 4 March. In a referendum on membership of the EU, 90 per cent voted in favour; turnout was 60 per cent.
2004 Lithuania joined NATO and the EU. Parliament impeached President Paksas following an inquiry that concluded his alleged links with Russian organised crime was a threat to national security. Valdas Adamkus was re-elected president in June and inaugurated. In the parliamentary elections, the Darbo Partija (DP) (Labour Party), won 39 seats, however this did not reached the necessary 71 for an absolute majority. A coalition government was formed including the DP, LSDP, Naujoji Sajunga (NS) New Union and non-aligned members of parliament; Algirdas Brazauskas was re-appointed prime minister.
2005 The president declined an invitation to attend the ceremony in Moscow celebrating the end of the Second World War. A Russian fighter plane crashed into Lithuanian territory and sparked diplomatic tensions. It was later discovered to have been caused by a technical malfunction and human error.
2006 Prime Minister Brazauskas's government resigned after the DP withdrew its support in protest against the president's statement that he did not trust two DP cabinet members. Gediminas Kirkilas was confirmed as prime minister.
2007 Lithuania missed the 1 January start date for joining the European Monetary Union (Emu), due to a higher than planned inflation rate. On 20 December Lithuania became a member of the European Union Schengen area whereby all travellers may cross borders without a passport or visa.
2008 An agreement for visa-free visits of citizens to the US was signed on 14 March 2008. Parliament passed a law in June making it an offence to display Soviet or Nazi images including flags, emblems and badges displaying swastikas or the hammer and sickle.

Political structure

Constitution

The constitution was adopted on 25 October 1992.

The written constitution has precedence over all subsequent laws unless amended by referendum. The office of the president, parliamentary democracy and an independent judiciary are all guaranteed under the constitution, along with specific citizens' rights.

Form of state

Parliamentary democratic republic

The executive

The head of state is the president, who is directly elected for a maximum of two five-year terms. The president can dissolve parliament if it refuses to appoint a new government or, at the latter's request, if the parliament passes a vote of no confidence. The president cannot use this power during the last six months of the presidential term of office, or if an early election has taken place during the previous six months.

The prime minister is appointed or dismissed by the president, with the approval of the Seimas. Ministers are appointed and dismissed by the president on the recommendation of the prime minister.

National legislature

The 141-member Seimas (parliament) is elected on a partly proportional, partly constituency system for a four-year term. The Seimas, on a two-to-three majority vote of its members, can decide to hold early elections.

Universal suffrage is from aged 18.

There are 56 municipalities, of these, 44 are districts and 12 are towns or cities. They are managed by municipal councils, elected for a three-year terms, and by a mayor appointed by the relevant council.

Legal system

The Lithuanian legal code is based on civil law system with no judicial review of legislative acts. The court system consists of district and county courts, the Court of Appeal and the Supreme Court as well as the Administrative Court. The president participates in the process of appointment and dismissal of judges. Moreover, the president has the right to apply to the Constitutional Court concerning the conformity of the legal acts passed by the government. Judges are independent in administering justice.

Last elections

13/27 June 2004 (presidential); 10/24 October 2004 (parliamentary).

Results: Presidential: Valdas Adamkus won 52.6 per cent of the vote; Kazimiera Prunskiene won 47.4 per cent. Turnout was 52.4 per cent.

Parliamentary: DP won 28.46 per cent of the vote (39 seats out of 141); the 'Working for Lithuania'coalition 20.65 per cent (31); TS 14.73 per cent (25); the 'For Order and Justice' coalition 11.36 per cent (10); LCS 9.18 per cent (18); and VNDPS 6.6 per cent (10). Turnout was 45.9 per cent.

Next elections

October 2008 (parliamentary); 2009 (presidential)

Political parties

Ruling party

Lietuvos Socialdemokratu Partija (LSDP) (Social-democratic Party of Lithuania)-led coalition

Main opposition party

Darbo Partija (DP) (Labour Party)

Population

3.38 million (2007)

Last census: April 2001: 3,483,972

Population density: 56.7 inhabitants per square km. Urban population: 69 per cent (1995–2001).

Annual growth rate: -0.6 per cent 1994–2004 (WHO 2006)

Ethnic make-up

Lithuanian (80.1 per cent), Russian (9.1 per cent), Polish (7 per cent), Belarussian (1.5 per cent) and others (2.3 per cent). There are long-standing cultural and political links with Poland, and many Poles live in the southern Vilnius region where they are in the majority, and have their own schools and newspapers.

Religions

Roman Catholic (primarily), Lutheran, Russian Orthodox, Protestant, Evangelical Christian Baptist, Muslim, Jewish.

Education

Primary school starts at age seven and is compulsory. There are three types of school, run by the state: primary (attended for four years), middle (five years) and secondary (three years). There are 17 higher education institutions in Lithuania. Vilnius University, founded in 1579, is the oldest university in Eastern Europe and also the largest in Lithuania.

Literacy rate: 100 per cent adult rate; 100 per cent youth rate (15–24) (Unesco 2005).

Compulsory years: Seven to 14

Enrolment rate: 98 per cent gross primary enrolment of relevant age group (including repeaters); 86 per cent secondary enrolment and 31 per cent at tertiary level (World Bank).

Pupils per teacher: 16 in primary schools.

Health

Per capita total expenditure on health (2003) was US$754; of which per capita government spending was US$573, at the international dollar rate, (WHO 2006).

Lithuania is suffering from a lack of primary healthcare provision and an overstretched network of small hospitals and large polyclinics. Over-specialisation of staff, low-quality equipment and a lack of investment have also put a strain on the health system.

The private sector accounts for only 2–3 per cent of total healthcare in Lithuania. Private clinics can charge 60 per cent more for any treatment than those funded by the state. The Lithuanian government sees these clinics as a threat to the state health care system.

HIV/Aids

HIV prevalence: 0.1 per cent aged 15–49 in 2003 (World Bank)

Life expectancy: 72 years, 2004 (WHO 2006)

Fertility rate/Maternal mortality rate: 1.3 births per woman, 2004 (WHO 2006); maternal mortality 18 per 100,000 live births (World Bank).

Child (under 5 years) mortality rate (per 1,000): 8.0 per 1,000 live births (World Bank).

Head of population per physician: 3.97 physicians per 1,000 people, 2003 (WHO 2006)

Welfare

The government is introduced a multi-pillar pension system, with voluntary public pension contributions for workers in 2004. A 2000 law enforces private voluntary pension funds.

The social security system provides pensions, sickness allowance, maternity and child care benefits and unemployment benefit. Small family grants are also provided that are not subject to means-testing. Contributions to the Lithuanian Social Insurance Fund are tax deductible. Employers contribute 30 per cent of the payroll of the company and employees pay 1 per cent of their wages.

Main cities

Vilnius (capital, estimated population 556,723 in 2005), Kaunas (367,483), Klaipeda (190,722), Siauliai (131,071), Panevezys (117,732).

Languages spoken

By law, all transactions, contracts and company returns must be in Lithuanian. English is widely spoken by business people. Other languages spoken include Russian, Polish, Belarusian, Ukrainian, German and Yiddish.

Official language/s

Lithuanian

Media

Press

The state-owned news agency ELTA serves the local press in Lithuanian and Russian. The Baltic News Service provides an English-language news service to the three Baltic republics.

Dailies: Dailies include Lietuvos Rytas (Lithuania's Morning), Kauno Diena, Klaipeda, Siauliu Krastas, Vakarines Navjienos and Respublika (Republic).

Weeklies: English-language weeklies include The Baltic Times and Lithuanian Weekly. Other Lithuanian language publications include the national weekly 7 menodienos, Kalba Vilnius for entertainment and Lietuvos Sportas is published three times in the week.
Business: Business publications include a fortnightly economics magazine Lietuvos Ukis and the business paper Verslo Zinios.
Broadcasting
The state-owned enterprise Lietuvos Radio ir Televizijos Centras (LRTC) is responsible for the broadcasting of state and commercial television and radio programmes.
There are three national commercial channels and one state-owned national channel in Lithuania, as well as seven regional stations.
Television: The privately owned TV channel LNK leads the market with an estimated 29.2 per cent audience share, followed by TV3 (27.5 per cent) and LTV (23.6 per cent). Baltijos TV (BTV) is a private channel with national coverage which is gaining in popularity.
Advertising

Economy
The economy has been marked by clear indications of healthy growth which can be traced back to the structural reforms begun in the 1990s. GDP growth in 2005 was 7.3 per cent, with an expected rate of 6.8 per cent in 2006 showing a continued strong level of growth since 2000. The growth was largely driven by wage rises (20 per cent in 2006) that fuelled household consumption by 12.6 per cent and in retail, construction and wholesale trade. However a corresponding rise in inflation spoiled Lithuanian plans of joining the European Monetary Union (EMU), which it had declared its intentions of joining, on 1 January 2007. Nevertheless, the budget surplus grew by 0.02 per cent of GDP as revenues increased by 27 per cent through better tax collection, particularly value added tax (VAT).
The economy is structured with services providing 63 per cent of GDP, agriculture 6 per cent and industry 31 per cent, of which, manufacturing is 19 per cent. All sectors grew in 2005, particularly industry and manufacturing.
Exports to the EU accounted for 63 per cent in 2005 and 21 per cent to Russia and the Commonwealth of Independent States (CIS).
Privatisation has been completed for many state-owned entities including those in the energy production and distribution sector, telecommunications and banking. The national railway remains state-owned.
It is predicted that economic activity will cool as the credit boom slows and consumers begin to get a handle on their personal debt. If this is proved the case then Lithuania may avoid a hard landing as its fully integrated, open market economy adapts to life in a freewheeling world.

External trade
As a member of the European Union, Lithuania operates within a communitywide free trade union, with tariffs sets as a whole. Internationally, the EU has free trade agreements with a number of nations and trading blocs worldwide.
Despite the poor balance of trade, exports account for 115 per cent of GDP, of which around 10 per is provided by forest and timber products. Industrial production is in food processing, shipbuilding and manufacturing, with a growing interest in information technology (IT)
Around 12 per cent of GDP is provided by fees for transit of oil from Russia to western Europe.
Imports
Principal imports include fuels and oil, vehicles, machinery and equipment, chemicals, textiles and clothing and metals.
Main sources: Russia (24.3 per cent total, 2005), Germany (14.9 per cent), Poland (9.6 per cent).
Exports
Principal exports are mineral products (over 20 per cent), textiles and clothing, machinery and electronic equipment, chemicals, timber products and foodstuffs.
Main destinations: Russia (12.8 per cent total, 2006), Latvia (11.1 per cent), Germany (8.7 per cent).

Agriculture
Farming
Agricultural land constitutes 53.4 per cent of total land area, estimated at 3.4 million hectares (ha). The industry employs about 18 per cent of the total labour force and contributed 6.2 per cent of GDP in 2004.
Main products include grain, potatoes, sugar beet and dairy products, meat and silk.
Land restitution began soon after independence in 1990, with the creation of 104,000 private family farms. The break up of state-owned farms into small plots, the limited availability of capital and a lack of business skills have slowed the recovery and development of the agricultural sector.
The agriculture ministry has embarked on the EU's Special Accession Programme for Agriculture and Rural Development (SAPARD) programme covering the period to 2007 and is intending to utilise EU funds to restructure the sector. Lithuania will not be eligible for full EU agricultural subsidies and rural development aid through CAP until 2013. During its transitional entry stage Lithuania has decided to implement the reform of the CAP on 1 January 2009. The reform was introduced throughout most of the EU on 1 January 2005, when subsidies on farm output, which tended to benefit large farms and encourage overproduction, were replaced by single farm payments, not conditional on production. The change is expected to reward farms that provide and maintain a healthy environment, food safety and animal welfare standards. The changes are also intended to encourage market conscious production and cut the cost of CAP to the EU taxpayer.
Lithuania's European and transatlantic integration will significantly increase competitive pressures on its agriculture, with a large proportion of exports heading to the US. It has adopted the Swedish model of organic farming with policies that draw heavily on bilateral international projects.
Environmental factors continue to affect agricultural reforms – 50 to 70 per cent of nitrogen and 10 to 20 per cent of phosphorus found in surface waters originated in farming activities.
Crop production in 2005 included: 2,914,832 tonnes (t) cereals in total, 1,475,000t wheat, *1,000,000t potatoes, 975,498t barley, 103,837t rye, *200,000t rapeseed (canola), 57,500t pulses, 77,109t oilcrops, 881,000t sugar beets, 104,500t oats, 5,800t flax, 45,965t fruit in total, 366,400t vegetables in total. Livestock production included: 216,700t meat in total, 60,000t beef, 110,000t pig meat, 1,000t lamb, 45,000t poultry, 50,000t eggs, 1,300,000t milk, 1,100t honey, 7,600t cattle hides.
*estimate
Fishing
The opportunity to export fishery products to the EU market without any tariff barriers has attracted the interest of its seafood processing industry.
Redfish, mackerel, cod, red plaice, black halibut and shrimp are caught in the high seas. Baltic Sea catches include cod, sprat, Baltic sprat, plaice, turbot, salmon and smelt.
In 2004, the total marine fish catch was 149,013 tonnes and the total crustacean catch was 7,057 tonnes.
Forestry
Forest and other wooded land accounts for a third of the land area, with forest cover estimated at 1.9 million hectares (ha). Most of the forest is available for wood supply. About 80 per cent of the forest area is owned by the state, although private ownership has been rising since the early 1990s. Consumption of forest products per capita is below the European average level.
The sawmill industry, which exports half of its production, contributes largely to the national economy. Large volumes of

roundwood, comprising mostly pulpwood, are exported mainly to Sweden and Germany. Although pulp and paper production is one of the oldest industries in Lithuania, most of the internal demand for high quality paper is met by imports. Chemical timber, furniture, wood-fibre and wood-chipboards are also produced, with chipboard materials in particular having strong export potential. Sawn hardwood is also used in the domestic furniture industry.

Exports of forest material in 2004 amounted to US$335.7 million, while imports amounted to US$320.1 million. Production in 2004 included 6,120,000 cubic metres (cum) roundwood, 4,860,000cum industrial roundwood, 3,420,000cum sawlogs and veneers, 1,450,000cum sawnwood, 1,430,000cum pulpwood, 393,000cum wood-based panels, 1,260,000cum woodfuel.

Industry and manufacturing

The industrial sector accounted for 33.6 per cent of GDP of which, 20.8 per cent was manufacturing in 2004; it employs around 40 per cent of the workforce.

Main industries are shipbuilding, consumer electronics, metalworking, machine building, machine tools, scientific instruments, sulphuric acid, paper, meat, dairy products, food processing, textiles, clothing and furniture. One of Lithuania's priorities is the development of light industry, particularly furniture, using natural wood products.

The principal branches of existing light industry in Lithuania are textiles and knitwear, with the largest leather and footwear enterprises in Vilnius, Kaunas and Siauliai. Other areas offering potential for growth include electronics.

The EU has stressed the need for Lithuania to speed-up restructuring of the industrial sector, particularly food processing and agricultural industries.

In 2005, the World Bank ranked Lithuania in its Doing Business Economy Ranking 15 for ease of doing business and 37 for starting a business, out of 155.

Industrial production increased by 7 per cent in 2004.

Tourism

Lithuania's tourist facilities are improving and around 1.2 million tourists visit Lithuania annually. Travel and tourism is expected to contribute US$431 million, or 1.6 per cent to GDP. While total exports in tourism is expected to earn US$1 billion, it is only expected to attract US$656 or 10 per cent of total capital investment. The country's main foreign tourism markets are neighbouring countries from the former Soviet bloc – Russia, Latvia and Poland. The fastest growing markets are Latvia, Germany, Scandinavian and Asian countries.

There are a number of tourist centres, including Trakai, the medieval capital of Lithuania, in the country's lake district. Apart from the castle, there is potential for watersports. The coastal resort of Palanga boasts sandy beaches as well as health and spa facilities. Birstonas on the bank of the Nemunas River is also a centre for spa treatments. Five national and nearly 30 regional parks are classified as protected areas.

Mining

Lithuania is famous for its high quality deposits of amber which supply the local jewellery industry. Amber deposits have been found in the coastal region of Curonian Bay and Juodkrante. The Juodkrante site covers 82 hectares; amber deposits are estimated at 112 tonnes.

Lithuania also has large reserves of high-quality iron ore in the south, but extraction is not economically viable.

Other raw materials found in small quantities include limestone, dolomite, gypsum, clay, sand and gravel.

Hydrocarbons

Lithuania's oil reserves have been falling since the 1990s. However exploration is under way and Lithuania estimates that it has 55.5 million cubic metres (cum) of oil onshore, and 36–72 million cum offshore. In 2004, production dropped by 21.1 per cent on the 469,800cum in 2003. This was due to the limited reserves, maturing fields and difficulties putting new fields online. The oil in production and the reserves found so far are high quality, light crude, which is easy to convert into refined products.

The country imports most of its domestic consumption oil needs of approximately 67,000 barrels per day (bpd) from Russia, via the Druzhba pipeline.

Lithuania is home to the only oil refinery in the Baltics – the Mazeikiu refinery which has a capacity of 263,000bpd and is one of the most efficient in the former Soviet Union. On 2002, 27 per cent of the Mazeikiu refinery was sold to Russia's second largest oil company, Yukos.

Lithuania's natural gas situation is similar to that of oil: the country has scarce reserves and is heavily dependent on Russian imports to meet the country's domestic consumption demand of 3.2 billion cubic metres per annum. In September 2005 Germany and Russia announced an agreement for a gas pipeline, to supply Russian gas to Western Europe, to be build under the Baltic Sea and bypassing Lithuania. Relations between Russia and Lithuania have been strained and West European countries are keen that their supplies of gas are not impeded by any such strain. For Lithuania's part, any plan to become the hub for gas supplies to the EU is threatened by this arrangement, as well as the implicit risk to its own supplies from Russia.

Nevertheless major infrastructure upgrading projects are under way at several Lithuanian ports.

Lithuania has reduced consumption, but still imports small quantities of coal from Poland and Russia.

Energy

The Lithuanian energy sector is dominated by Lietuvos Energija, the largest electric power company in the country. The company is 96.2 per cent state-owned, with a minority stake held by Sweden's Vatenfall. The company is structured into separate companies, responsible for generation, distribution and transmission. A privatisation programmed began in January 2004, paving the way for the complete privatisation of the electricity sector by 2010.

The ageing Ignalia nuclear power plant, similar in construction to the Chernobyl facility is being decommissioned as part of the EU accession agreement. Almost US$200 million in international grants was raised to help finance the closing down of the first reactor in January 2005. The closure date for the second reactor is 2009.

Financial markets

Stock exchange

The Nacionaline Vertybiniu Popieriu Birza (NVPB) (National Stock Exchange of Lithuania) is in Vilnius. The NVPB is a non-profit organisation with 136 shareholders, modelled on the French system.

Banking and insurance

Lithuania has a two-tier banking system whereby the commercial and central bank functions of the state bank are separated. Foreign-owned banks may operate in the country. Commercial banking operations have been removed from the central bank, which has assumed the government's responsibility for setting interest policy. The Lietuvos Zemes Ukio Bankas (LZUB) (Lithuanian Agricultural Bank) was sold by the government in early-2002 — the end of state involvement in commercial banking.

Central bank

Lietuvos Banka (LB) (Bank of Lithuania)

Main financial centre

Vilnius

Time

GMT plus two hours (daylight saving, late March to late October, GMT plus three hours)

Geography
Lithuania is the largest of the three Baltic states, situated on the eastern coast of the Baltic Sea in north-eastern Europe. It is bordered by Latvia to the north, Belarus to the south-east, Poland to the south-west and the Russian Federation to the west. There is a dense network of waterways, the main river being the Nemunas, which flows south to north into the Baltic Sea. There are many lakes in the northern regions of the Baltic Highlands. The highest point is Juozapine Hill (294 metres) in the east of the country.

Hemisphere
Northern

Climate
Lithuania enjoys one of the mildest climates along the Baltic coast. Summer sunshine may last nine hours a day, but winters can be very cold. Annual rainfall averages 490mm and humidity 80 per cent.

Dress codes
Warm clothing is necessary in winter. Business dress is conservative but relatively informal, with a jacket and tie expected for meetings. A raincoat is useful during spring and autumn.

Entry requirements
Passports
Required by all.

Visa
Required by all, except nationals of EU and Schengen area signatory countries, North America, Australasia and Japan. For further exceptions contact the nearest embassy. A Schengen visa application (offered in several languages) can be downloaded from http://europa.eu/abc/travel/ see 'documents you will need'.

Business visas for all other nationals must be applied for with an invitation from a local company or organisation and certified by the migration authorities in Lithuania (stamped and signed by a migration officer). A business letter, by the visitor's company, giving purpose of visit and full itinerary should also be included.

Currency advice/regulations
Import of local currency is unlimited but export is limited to Lt5,000. Import and export of foreign currency is unlimited although any amount over the equivalent of Lt40,000 must be declared.

Travellers cheques are not widely accepted.

Customs
Personal items are duty-free. There are no duties levied on alcohol and tobacco between EU member states, providing amounts imported are for personal consumption.

Prohibited imports
Military and hunting firearms, ammunition, fishing equipment require a permit. Meat and dairy products; illegal drugs are prohibited.

Health (for visitors)
Nationals of the European Economic Area (EEA) countries and Switzerland can access reduced cost and sometimes free medical treatment using a European Health Insurance Card (EHIC) while visiting the EEA. Exceptions include nationals of the 10 countries, which joined the EU in 2004, whose EHIC is not valid in Switzerland. Applications for the EHIC should be made before travelling.

Mandatory precautions
Vaccination certificates are required for cholera or yellow fever if travelling from an infected area.

Advisable precautions
It is advisable to be in date for the following immunisations: polio (within 10 years), tetanus (within 10 years), typhoid fever, hepatitis A (moderate risk only).

It is recommended that bottled water is used for drinking; tap water is occasionally brown.

Hotels
There are many hotels in Vilnius. Some have been restored or taken over. Most ask for payment in hard currency. Western-class hotels charge Western prices. Tipping is not widely practised.

Credit cards
Major credit cards are accepted in hotels, restaurants and shops. ATMs are found in many centres.

Public holidays (national)
Fixed dates
1 Jan (New Year), 16 Feb (Independence Day), 11 Mar (Restoration Day), 1 May (Labour Day), 8 May (Mother's Day), 26 May (Jonines), 6 Jul (Statehood Day), 15 Aug (Assumption Day), 1 Nov (All Saints' Day), 25–26 Dec (Christmas).

Variable dates
Easter (two days)

Working hours
Banking
Mon–Fri: 0900–1700. Some banks open on Sat: 0900–1300.

Business
Mon–Fri: 0900–1300 and 1400–1800; lunch break 1300–1400.

Shops
Mon–Fri: 1000–1400 and 1500–1900; Sat: 1000–1600.

Telecommunications
Mobile/cell phones
A GSM network covers the republic's eight largest cities.

Electricity supply
220V AC, 50Hz. European plugs are required.

Social customs/useful tips
Social behaviour is fairly informal. Lithuanians are open and hospitable. Straight professional questions receive straight answers. Business cards are used widely and shaking hands is the common form of greeting and farewell. Most Lithuanians are punctual – being late for a meeting can be a bad start.

Tipping has become more widespread, with waiters often expecting generous tips from westerners – avoid leaving hard currency.

Lithuanian-Russian relations are not as tense as those between Estonians and Latvians and Russians, although care should be taken when discussing Russia and its role in the region. Lithuanians also dislike being described as members of the Baltic states, rather than Lithuanian.

Security
Compared to other European capitals, the crime rate in Vilnius is relatively low, but street crime does occur. Make use of hotel safe deposit boxes and be careful not to show valuables when walking around the city. Car theft is common.

Getting there
Air
National airline: FlyLAL (Lithuanian Airlines)

International airport/s: Vilnius International (VNO), 5km from city; facilities include business and VIP lounges, duty-free shops, car hire, post office, bureau de change, restaurants, first aid. Taxis and buses are available.

Airport tax: Departure tax Lt60

Surface
Road: Lithuania has a good network of interconnecting roads, providing links to neighbouring countries.

Rail: There is a well developed rail network with Vilnius as the hub for rail connections in the region. There are train connections with Poland through Grodno in Belarus. There are regular trains to Russia (Moscow and St Petersburg). Rail travel between Lithuania, Latvia and Estonia can be slow.

Water: There are several regular ferry services from the main port of Klaipeda to UK, Russian Federation, Germany, Poland and Sweden. There are also many more irregular sea links to other foreign ports.

Getting about
National transport
Air: There are three domestic airports at Palanga, Kaunas and Siaulai but they have limited services.

Road: Paved roads are generally in good condition, however rural unpaved roads

can be hazardous. There is a modern four-lane motorway connecting Vilnius with Kaunas, Laipeda and Panaeveys.
Buses: Buses are convenient and the cheapest way to travel as trains do not serve every town and village.
Rail: The rail system is being upgraded. Twice daily trains connect Vilnius with the Baltic coast.
Water: There is a coastal ferry linking Klaipeda and the Curonian Spit. There is also a dense network of rivers, the longest of which is the Nemunas River – total length 973km, 475km of which is in Lithuania – which is suitable for navigation in parts.

City transport

Taxis: Taxis display an illuminated Taksi sign and can be flagged down in the street or found at taxi-stands or booked by telephone. Meters should be in operation and visitors can insist that they be used. If not, fares must be negotiated and avoided being paid for in hard currency. Taxis are always more expensive from the airport, railway station, cathedral and the Vilnius Department Store.
Buses, trams & metro: There is a choice of buses and trolley buses within the city. Tickets can be purchased from kiosks (spaudos kioskas) and drivers; they must be inserted into a validating machine on board. Services operate from 0600 to 0030 or 0100.
The Vilnius railway station is a cosmopolitan marketplace and terminus, but it is not safe for visitors at night.

Car hire

Many of the major car rental companies operate in Lithuania. There are winter (Oct–Mar) and summer (Apr–Sep) speed limits on motorways: 110kph (winter), 130kph (summer); 90kph (all year) on open roads and 60kph on urban roads. National driving licences with photo IDs are required. Seat belts are compulsory and drink/driving is prohitited. Traffic drives on the right. It is advisable to make sure hire vehicles have an alarm and steering lock.
Drivers must pay a fee to use any road leading to Vilnius old town.

BUSINESS DIRECTORY

The addresses listed below are a selection only. While World of Information makes every endeavour to check these addresses, we cannot guarantee that changes have not been made, especially to telephone numbers and area codes. We would welcome any corrections.

Telephone area codes

The international direct dialling code (IDD) for Lithuania is +370, followed by area code and subscriber's number:
Kaunus37Panevezys45
Klaipeda46Siauliai41
Palanga460Vilnius5

Useful telephone numbers

Directory enquiries: 09
International operator: 8-194
Fire: 01
Police: 02
Ambulance (greitoji pagalba): 03
Vilnius City Road Police, Giraites 3: 631-168

Chambers of Commerce

American Chamber of Commerce in Lithuania, 5 Lukiskiu Street, 2600 Vilnius (tel: 261-1181; fax: 212-6128; e-mail: acc@acc.lt).

Association of Lithuanian Chambers of Commerce, Industry and Crafts, 9 J Tumo-Vaizganto Street, 2001 Vilnius (tel: 261-2102; fax: 261-2112; e-mail: info@chambers.lt).

British Chamber of Commerce in Lithuania, 21 T Sevcenkos Street, 2009 Vilnius (tel: 239-2316; fax: 239-2301; e-mail: info@bccl.lt).

Kaunas Chamber of Commerce, Industry and Crafts, PO Box 2111, 8 K Donelaicis Street, 3000 Kaunas (tel: 229-212; fax: 208-330; e-mail: chamber@chamber.lt).

Klaipeda Chamber of Commerce, Industry and Crafts, 17 Danes Street, 5800 Klaipeda (tel: 390-861; fax: 410-626; e-mail: klaipeda@chambers.lt).

Panevezys Regional Chamber of Commerce, Industry and Crafts, 34 Respublikos Street, 5319 Panevezys (tel: 463-687; fax: 462-227; e-mail: panevezys@chambers.lt).

Siauliai Regional Chamber of Commerce, Industry and Crafts, 88 Vilniaus Street, 5400 Siauliai (tel: 525-504; fax: 523-903; siauliai@chambers.lt).

Vilnius Regional Chamber of Commerce, Industry and Crafts, 31 Algirdo Street, 2600 Vilnius (tel: 213-5550; fax: 213-5542; e-mail: vilnius@chambers.lt).

Banking

Bankas Snoras, 7A Vivulskio Street, 2600 Vilnius (tel: 216-2795).

Lietuvos Zemes Ukio Bankas (Lithuanian Agricultural Bank), Totoriu 4, 2600 Vilnius.

Lithuanian Commercial Banker's Association, Vilniaus 4/35, Vilnius 2001.

Lithuanian Development Bank, Stulginskio 4-7, 2600 Vilnius.

Lietuvos Taupomasis Bankas (Lithuanian Savings Bank), Savanoriu pr 19, 2015 Vilnius.

Lietuvos Valstybinis Komercinis Bankas (Lithuanian State Commercial Bank), Jogailos 14, 2001 Vilnius.

Vilniaus Bankas (commercial bank), Gedimino Avenue 12, 14, 2600 Vilnius.

Central bank

Lietuvos Bankas (Bank of Lithuania), 6 Gedimino Avenue, LT-01103 Vilnius (tel: 268-0029; fax: 262-8124; e-mail: info@lb.lt; internet: www.lb.lt).

Travel information

FlyLAL, 4 Gustaicio Avenue LT-02512 Vilnius (tel: 252-5555; email: info@flylal.com).

Krantas Travel Operator, 5 Teatro Street, LT-91247 Klaipeda (tel: 395-215)

Lithuanian Tourism Association, Pylimo 6, 2001 Vilnius.

Travel Bureau, Lietuva Hotel, Ukmerges 20, Vilnius.

Vilnius International Airport, Rodunios kelias 10A, LT- 02189, Vilnius (tel: 230-6666; fax: 232-9122; email: airport@vno.lt).

Vilnius Tourist Information Centre, (J-3) Didzioji 31, Town Hall, Vilnius (tel: 262-6470; email: turizm.info@vilnius.lt).

National tourist organisation offices

Lithuanian State Department of Tourism, A Juozapaviciaus 13, LT-09311 Vilnius (tel: 210-8796: fax:210-8753; email: vtd@tourism.lt; internet: www.tourism.lt).

Ministries

Ministry of Agriculture, Gedimino Avenue 19, LT-2025 Vilnius (email: zum@zum.lt).

Ministry of Culture, J Basanaviciaus Street 5, LT-5683 Vilnius (email: culture@muza.lt).

Ministry of Defence, Tortoriu 25/3, LT-2001 Vilnius (email: vis@kam.kam.lt).

Ministry of the Economy, Gedimino Avenue 38/2, LT-2600 Vilnius (email: pr@po.ekm.lt).

Ministry of Education and Science, A Volano Street 2/7, LT-2691 Vilnius (email: smmin@smm.lt).

Ministry of the Environment, A Jaksto Street 4/9, LT-2694 Vilnius (email: info@aplinkuma.lt).

Ministry of Finance, J Tumo-Vaizganto Street 8a/2, LT-2600 Vilnius (email: finmin@finmin.lt).

Ministry of Foreign Affairs, J Tumo-Vaizganto Street 2, LT-2600 Vilnius (email: urm@urm.lt).

Ministry of Health, Vilniaus Street 33, LT-2001 Vilnius (email: ministerija@sam.lt).

Ministry of the Interior, Sventaragio Street 5, LT-2600 Vilnius (email: infoskyrius@vrm/lt).

Ministry of Justice, Gediminio Avenue 30/1, LT-2600 Vilnius.

Ministry of Social Welfare and Labour, A Vivulskio Street 11, LT-2693 Vilnius (email: post@socmin.lt).

Ministry of Transport, Gediminio Avenue 17, LT-2679 Vilnius (email: transp@transp.lt).

Office of the President, S Daukanto Square 3, LT-2008 Vilnius (email: info@president.lt).

Office of the Prime Minister, Gedimino Avenue 11, LT-2039 Vilnius (email: kanceliarija@lrvk.lt).

Other useful addresses

Association of Light Industry Enterprises of Lithuania, Saltonishkiu 29/3, 2677 Vilnius.

Association of Lithuanian Entrepreneurs, A Jakshto 9, 2600 Vilnius.

BNS (English-language Baltic news service), Konarskio 49, Vilnius.

British Embassy, Antakalnio 2, Vilnius 2055 (tel: 222-070/1; fax: 727-579; e-mail: BE-VILNIUS@post.omnitel.net).

Central Post Office, Gedimino 7, Vilnius.

Commercial Court of the Republic of Lithuania, Gedimino pr 39/1, 2640 Vilnius.

Confederation of Lithuanian Industrialists, Saltonishkiu 19, 2600 Vilnius.

Construction Production Certification Centre, Linkmenu 28, 2600 Vilnius.

Department of Customs, A. Jaksto 1/25, 2600 Vilnius (internet: (foreign trade database) www.cust.lt/).

Department of Statistics, Gedimino pr 29, 2746 Vilnius.

ELTA Lithuanian News Agency, Gedimino Ave 21/2, Vilnius 2600.

Energy Agency, A Vienuolio 8/4, 2600 Vilnius.

Lithuanian Builders' Association, Vytauto 14/2, 2000 Vilnius.

Lithuanian Building Industry Association, Sevcenko 19, 2000 Vilnius.

Lithuanian Construction Association, Raugyklos 15, 2600 Vilnius.

Lithuanian Development Agency, Investment, Marketing and Public Relations Departments, Sv Jono Str 3 2600 Vilnius (email: lda@lda.lt; internet: www.lda.lt); Export Department, Algirdo 31, 2600 Vilnius (email: lda@lda.lt).

Lithuanian Economic and Foreign Investment Development Agency (FIDA), J Jasinskio 9, 4th floor, 2600 Vilnius.

Lithuanian Embassy (USA), 2622 16th Street, NW, Washington DC 20009 (tel: (+1-202) 234-5860; fax: (+1-202) 328-0466; email: info@ltembassyus.org).

Lithuanian Export Promotion Agency, J Tumo-Vaizganto 8a/2, 2739 Vilnius (email: lepa.epd@post.omnitel.net).

Lithuanian Free Market Institute, Birutes 56, 2600 Vilnius.

Lithuanian Information Institute, Kalvariju 3, 2659 Vilnius.

Lithuanian International Trade Agency, V Kudirkos st 18, 2600 Vilnius (email: LAITA@post.omnitel.net).

Lithuanian Investment Agency (LIA), Sv Jono 3, 2600 Vilnius.

Lithuanian Manufacturers' Confederation, Saltonishkiu 19, 2687 Vilnius.

Lithuanian Privatisation Agency, Gedimino 38/2, 2600 Vilnius.

Lithuanian Road Administration, State Property and Service Division, 36/2 Basanaviciaus Street, Vilnius LT-2009.

Lithuanian Standardisation Board, A Joksto g 1/25, 2600 Vilnius.

Lithuanian Television & Radio Broadcasting, Konarskio 49, 2674 Vilnius.

Privatisation Agency, Gedimino Prosp 38/2, Vilnius.

Securities Commission, Ukmerges g 41, 2600 Vilnius.

State Competition and Consumer Protection Office, Gedimino pr 38/2, 2600 Vilnius.

State Patent Bureau, Algirdo g 31, 2600 Vilnius.

State Quality Inspectorate, Gedimino pr 19, 2600 Vilnius

State Tax Inspection, Sermuksniu st 6, 2600 Vilnius.

Vilnius City Administration, Gedimino ave 9, 2600 Vilnius.

Internet sites

Lithuania on-line: www.aiva.lt/lol

Official travel guide: www.travel.lt

Port of Klaipeda: www.portofklaipeda.lt/en.php

Yellow pages: www.yellowpages.lt

Luxembourg

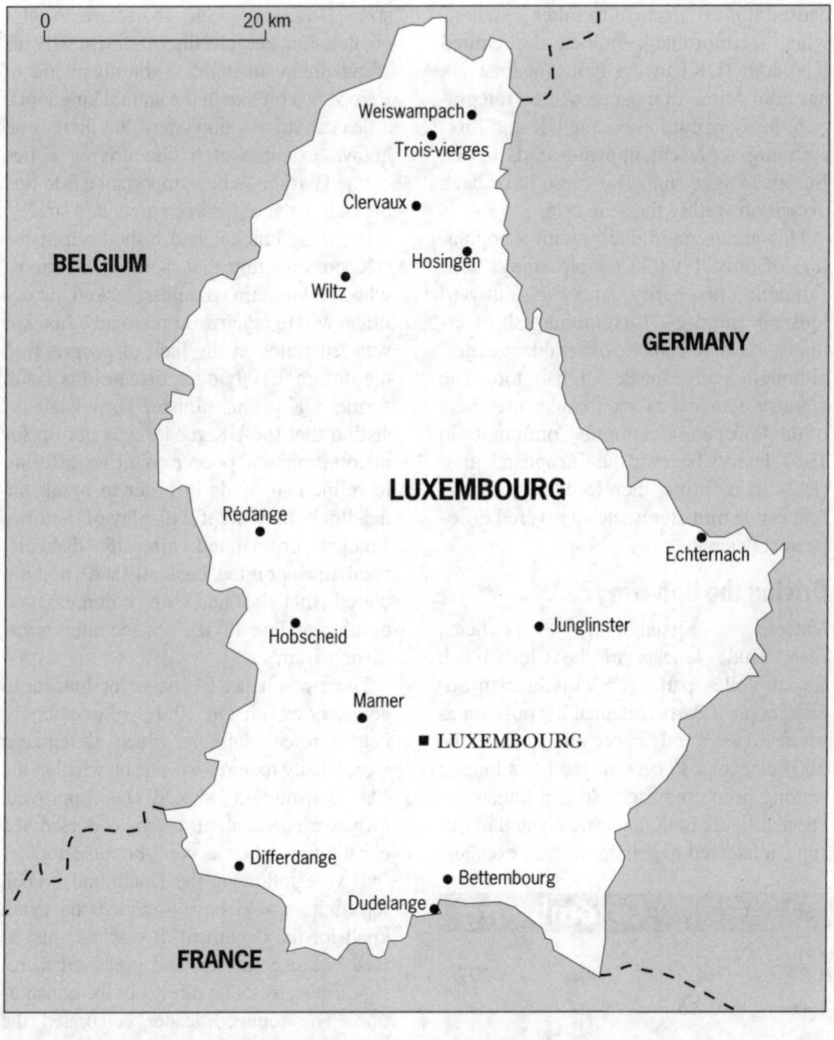

According to the Organisation for Economic Co-operation and Development (OECD), Luxembourg's economy has enjoyed a strong performance since the 2006 Survey. The economy grew by 4.5 per cent in 2007, faster than in most other OECD countries, with relatively moderate national headline inflation of just over 2 per cent. The general government had a surplus of 3 per cent of gross domestic product (GDP), while the current account surplus was around 10 per cent of GDP. The main driver of economic growth has been the financial sector, which has continued to sharply expand its activity and now accounts for nearly 30 per cent of GDP. Collective investment funds registered in Luxembourg hold assets of eur2 trillions, about one-fourth of investment funds' assets in Europe. Private banking is also an important source of activity, with the third largest market share worldwide after Switzerland and the Caribbean Islands. There have been important beneficial effects of this expansion. Not only has the financial sector created large numbers of jobs, it has also been a significant purchaser of business services supplied by other sectors, such as legal services and real estate. Other

KEY FACTS

Official name: Groussherzogtom Lëtzebuerg, Grossherzogtum Luxemburg, Grand-Duché de Luxembourg (The Grand Duchy of Luxembourg)

Head of State: Grand Duke Henri of Luxembourg (acceded Oct 2000)

Head of government: Prime Minister Jean-Claude Juncker (CSV) (elected 1995; re-elected Jun 2004)

Ruling party: Coalition led by Chrëschtlich Sozial Vollekspartei (CSV) (Christian Social People's Party) with the Demokratesch Partie (DP) (Democratic Party) (since 1999; the CSV was re-elected Jun 2004)

Area: 2,586 square km

Population: 479,000 (2007)*

Capital: Luxembourg-Ville

Official language: Lëtzebuergish (Luxembourgish); French and German are the administrative languages.

Currency: Euro (eur) = 100 cents (from 1 Jan 2002; previous currency Luxembourg franc, locked at Lf40.34 per euro)

Exchange rate: eur0.63 per US$ (Jul 2008)

GDP per capita: US$104,673 (2007)*

GDP real growth: 5.40% (2007)

Labour force: 301,000 (2004)

Unemployment: 4.40% (2007)

Inflation: 2.30% (2007)

Balance of trade: -US$4.21 billion (2005)

Annual FDI: US$57.00 billion (OECD, 2004)*

* estimated figure

positive effects have boosted the rest of the economy, such as knowledge, skill and location spillovers. The budget has benefited from dynamic tax revenues paid by the financial sector, together with temporary and recurrent positive revenue surprises from other sources. This has supported the expansion of the public sector, although its size has declined in relation to GDP.

The OECD goes on to note that Luxembourg's real growth is projected to weaken in 2008, reflecting the international financial crisis. The fall in international equity prices has led to a decline in the nominal amount of assets held by investment funds, hurting commission fees. New net inflows into investment funds have also slowed, due to the change in investor sentiment. Employment in the financial sector remained strong last year, perhaps because firms have been hoarding hard-to recruit skilled staff, but this could change rapidly if the banking sector feels a durable squeeze on earnings. A contraction similar to that following the bust of the dotcom bubble would lead to a painful adjustment. A fall of net inflows of funds into the Luxembourg financial sector would have large spillover effects on the domestic economy, as financial institutions would reduce their purchases of goods and services from other sectors and lower their payments of tax receipts based on the size of assets under management. While the unfolding of the financial turmoil is uncertain, it is likely that the economic and financial slowdown currently under way will mean that tax receipts will suffer in 2008; this should be relatively easy to absorb, however, given the healthy position of the general government last year (a surplus of 3 per cent of GDP) and does not call for immediate fiscal restraint measures designed to tighten fiscal policy.

Procommunitaire Luxembourg has always been a staunch supporter of European integration. There have been moments when national interest has caused this enthusiasm to falter – such as when it improbably joined the United Kingdom (UK) in the battle against tax harmonisation. In most respects – integration, the constitution etc the UK and Luxembourg represent opposite ends of the European spectrum. But these have been exceptions rather than the rule.

This green grand duchy with a population of only 479,000 people enjoys considerable prosperity and an outward looking mindset. Luxembourgish, German and French are the official languages, although many speak English too. The country was one of six founder members of the European Economic Community in 1957, later to become the European Union (EU). It is fitting, therefore, that the current prime minister is such a revered European statesman.

Driving the lion crazy?

Veteran Luxembourg politician Jean-Claude Juncker of the Chrëschtlich Sozial Vollekspartei (CSV) (Christian Social People's Party) retained his position as prime minister and finance minister after the 2004 elections, to become the EU's longest serving prime minister. He is a hugely respected figure both domestically and in Europe, a talented negotiator and an excellent linguist, fluent – like many of his compatriots – in five languages. Juncker was one of the chief architects of the Maastricht Treaty, especially the Economic and Monetary Union sections. Thanks to the personal qualities and depth of economic understanding of this leading personality Luxembourg has enjoyed a greater platform in European affairs than would be usual for a country of its size. However, with characteristic eloquence, Juncker tells the Continent why his grand duchy matters: 'institutional life of Europe is a bit like in the animal kingdom – a flea can drive a lion crazy, but there is no known example of a lion driving a flea crazy. That shows how important it is to find the right balance between great and small'.

In 2005, Juncker had lashed out at the UK, commenting that 'some delegations, who shall remain nameless, lacked the political will to reach an agreement'. Juncker was frustrated at the lack of progress on the future EU budget discussions, with former UK prime minister Tony Blair insisting that the UK rebate was not up for negotiation, and poorer countries offering to relinquish funds in order to break the deadlock. In a forceful display of rhetoric, Juncker proclaimed himself 'disheartened, disappointed, basically sad', and declared that he had 'no comment, no opinion and no advice' for the uncompromising Blair.

There was better EU news for Juncker to come, however. On 10 July Luxembourg held a referendum, in which all citizens were legally required to vote, on whether the EU constitution should be approved. Fifty-six per cent of voters endorsed the constitution – just as well, because another 'no' vote following the Dutch and French rejections would have sounded the death knell for the document. It was also just as well because Juncker had promised to resign if his electorate threw out the constitution. The relieved leader celebrated the result, which he described as 'the popular will of a small state but a great nation'.

With growing political and economic integration in the EU, Luxembourg could potentially benefit from European regionalism, as it is located in the centre of the European geographical area with the highest economic activity. However, future developments in EU policy in regard to financial operations could also deprive Luxembourg of substantial earnings which are an integral part of its economy.

The economy recovers

After several years of sluggish growth the Luxembourg economy is enjoying a recovery. Economic growth (GDP) was 5.4

KEY INDICATORS — Luxembourg

	Unit	2003	2004	2005	2006	2007
Population	m	0.45	0.46	0.46	0.47	0.48
Gross domestic product (GDP)	US$bn	25.64	31.14	36.62	42.51	*50.16
GDP per capita	US$	56,754	69,929	80,080	89,923	*104,673
GDP real growth	%	1.2	4.4	4.0	6.1	*5.4
Inflation	%	2.5	2.2	2.5	2.7	2.3
Unemployment	%	3.8	4.2	4.2	4.0	4.4
Exports (fob) (goods)	US$m	10,000.0	13,714.0	14,400.0	16,383.0	18,418.0
Imports (cif) (goods)	US$m	13,600.0	16,871.0	18,605.0	20,795.0	23,131.0
Balance of trade	US$m	-3,700.0	-3,157.0	-4,205.0	-4,411.0	-4,712.0
Current account	US$m	2,560.0	2,250.0	4,309.0	4,389.0	4,746.0
Total reserves minus gold	US$m	279.9	298.4	241.1	218.1	143.6
Foreign exchange	US$m	178.7	139.3	166.7	156.0	93.8
Exchange rate	per US$	0.88	0.80	0.77	0.75	0.69

* estimated figure

per cent in 2007, up on the 4.0 per cent in 2006, and again above expectations. Growth continues to be generated by increased exports and corporate investment. The manufacturing sector is enjoying the return of lost business confidence and orders look to be high. Although Luxembourg's record of attracting foreign direct investment (FDI) is good, it has been advised that it should tackle labour market reform, to help attract new businesses.

Unemployment appears to be growing steadily, with 4.4 per cent in 2007. The labour market is in need of reform to render it more flexible. High energy prices in 2005 had a negative impact on domestic private consumption and exports were affected by weak foreign markets.

Monetary policy

The European Central Bank (ECB) took over responsibility for Luxembourg's monetary policy from the Banque Centrale du Luxembourg (BCL) (Central Bank of Luxembourg) when the country joined the European Economic and Monetary Union (Emu) in January 1999. The ECB's main role is to encourage price stability of the euro currency, aiming for low inflation and low interest rates. To maintain price stability of the euro, the ECB aims for an inflation rate of 2.0 per cent across the eurozone. The ECB has had a difficult time trying to maintain the eurozone annual inflation rate at the 2 per cent target. Luxembourg's inflation in 2007 was 2.3 per cent, and is not predicted to change much in 2008.

Outlook

With one of the world's highest GDP per capita – estimated at US$104,673 in 2007, continuous economic growth over the past ten years and low inflation, Luxembourg's economy is strong and diversified. Luxembourg is undergoing growing political and economic integration in the EU. However, future developments in EU policy in regard to financial operations could also deprive Luxembourg of substantial earnings which are an integral part of its economy. The IMF is confident of good economic growth in Luxembourg.

Risk assessment

Politics	Good
Economy	Good
Regional stability	Good

COUNTRY PROFILE

Historical profile

Modern-day Luxembourg was occupied by the Burgundians, Prussians, Spanish and French until the nineteenth century, when it came under German and Dutch control.

1867 Luxembourg was granted independence.

1914–18 Luxembourg was occupied by the Germans.

1921 The Belgian-Luxembourg Economic Union (BLEU) was formed.

1940–45 Nazi Germany occupied Luxembourg.

1948 The Benelux Economic Union (Benelux) was inaugurated between Belgium, Luxembourg and the Netherlands and became effective in 1960, establishing the three countries as a single customs area in 1970.

1949 Luxembourg became a founding member of NATO.

1957 Luxembourg became one of the founder members of the forerunner to the EU, the European Economic Community (EEC).

1964 Grand Duchess Charlotte abdicated after a reign of 45 years and was succeeded by her son, Prince Jean.

1974 After being in power since 1918, the Chrëschtlich Sozial Vollekspartei (CSV) (Christian Social People's Party) was defeated by the Demokratesch Partie (DP) (Democratic Party) in general elections.

1979 The CSV regained power.

1990 Luxembourg was an original signatory of the Schengen Agreement to remove all border controls.

1994 Jean-Claude Juncker became prime minister.

1999 A CSV/DP coalition government was formed after the CSV failed to win enough seats in the parliamentary elections to have an outright majority. Juncker remained as prime minister.

2000 Grand Duke Jean abdicated and was succeeded by his son, Prince Henri.

2002 Euro currency replaced the Luxembourg franc. Luxembourg was named by a French parliamentary committee as a haven for tax evasion and money laundering.

2003 After EU talks on new rules for the taxation of savings invested abroad, in January, Luxembourg won the right to decide when they would drop the withholding tax and begin exchanging information.

2004 The Chrëschtlich Sozial Vollekspartei (CSV) (Christian Social People's Party) was re-elected in the parliamentary elections on 13 June.

2005 On 10 July, voters in Luxembourg approved the European constitution by 57 per cent to 43 per cent.

2006 Arcelor, Luxembourg's premier steel manufacture was sold to the Indian-owned Mittal Steel, for US$34 billion, which created one the world's largest steel manufacturer.

2008 President Chavez of Venezuela, announced in April that the Luxembourg-based, and Argentine-owned steel maker, Ternium, would be nationalised to bring a key industry under state ownership and drive its socialist economy.

Political structure

Constitution

The constitution was adopted in 1868 and has been amended on four occasions (1919, 1994, 1996 and 1998). It can be amended when at least two thirds, of a minimum 75 per cent of parliamentary members, vote in agreement. A plebicite must ratify the amendment.

The constitution sets out the role of the hereditary crown as Head of State, and the rights of citzens before the law.

Universal direct suffrage for all those registered and over the age of 18.

Form of state

Parliamentary democratic monarchy

The executive

Executive power is vested in the Grand Duke and exercised through the constitution and the law.

The Council of Ministers is led by the prime minister, who is chosen by the Grand Duke, and must have the support of the Chamber of Deputies.

National legislature

Legislative power is exercised by a unicameral 60-member Châmber vun Députéirten / Chambre des Députés (Chamber of Deputies), which is elected for a five-year term by proportional representation in four multi-seat constituencies. A 21-member Council of State, chosen by the Grand Duke, acts as an advisory body and has some legislative functions.

Legal system

Loosely based on Napoleonic code, of inquisitorial justice. The highest court is th Superior Court of Justice. Justices of the peace, district court judges and members of the Superior Court are appointed for life by the Grand Duke. Special laws regulate military tribunals. Administrative courts have jurisdiction over tax and administrative matters. There is a Constitutional Court that decides on the conformity of laws within the constitution. The Grand Duke has the authority to revoke or reduce penalties awarded by judges.

Last elections

13 June 2004 (parliamentary).

Results: Parliamentary: the CSV won 36.1 per cent of the vote (24 seats out of 60), LSAP/POSL 23.4 per cent (14), DP 16.1 per cent (10), Déi Gréng (Green Party) 11.6 per cent (seven) and Aktiounskomitee fir Demokratie an Rentengerechtigkeet (ADR) (Action Committee for Democracy and Pensions Justice) 10 per cent (five).

Next elections
2009 (parliamentary).

Political parties
Ruling party
Coalition led by Chrëschtlich Sozial Vollekspartei (CSV) (Christian Social People's Party) with the Demokratesch Partie (DP) (Democratic Party) (since 1999; the CSV was re-elected Jun 2004)
Main opposition party
Lëtzeburger Sozialistesch Arbechterpartei or Parti Ouvrier Socialiste Luxembourgeois (LSAP/POSL) (Luxembourg Socialist Workers' Party)

Population
479,000 (2007)*
Last census: February 2001: 439,539
Population density: 166 inhabitants per square km. Urban population: 92 per cent of total (1995—2001).
Annual growth rate: 1.4 per cent 1994–2004 (WHO 2006)
Ethnic make-up
The inhabitants of Luxembourg are mostly of German and French origin, but have a distinct national consciousness. From just under 20 per cent in 1970, the percentage of foreign residents has risen to over 30 per cent. The Portuguese, who account for over 10 per cent of the total population, form the largest foreign community. The second largest immigrant community comes from Italy (5 per cent).
Religions
Approximately 97 per cent of the population is Roman Catholic.

Education
Primary education lasts for six years, until the age of 12. Instruction is initially given in German, and French is added in the second year. Secondary education can be obtained through either a lLycé, or Lycé Technique. The first offers general and technical schooling, for up to seven years with an initial period of three years then an advanced (and non-compulsory) programme of four years. The Lycé Technique offers complete seven-year courses. French replaces German in the classroom at secondary schooling.
Higher education in the Grand Duchy is limited in scope. Approximately 4,000 students attend foreign universities, predominantly in Belgium and France.
Compulsory years: Six to 15.
Enrolment rate: 85 per cent net primary enrolment (Unicef).

Health
Per capita total expenditure on health (2003) was US$3,680; of which per capita government spending was US$3,341, at the international dollar rate, (WHO 2006).
HIV/Aids
HIV prevalence: 0.2 per cent aged 15–49 in 2003 (World Bank)
Life expectancy: 79 years, 2004 (WHO 2006)
Fertility rate/Maternal mortality rate: 1.7 births per woman, 2004 (WHO 2006)
Child (under 5 years) mortality rate (per 1,000): 4.9 per 1,000 live births (World Bank)
Head of population per physician: 2.66 physicians per 1,000 people, 2003 (WHO 2006)

Welfare
The social security system was built in several stages. It has been extended to include both the socio-professional categories and at risk groups. The minimum wage, which functions as a mechanism to guarantee resources, consists of a supplementary benefit paid up to a threshold determined according to the composition of the household. The benefit is awarded irrespective of the causes of the situation of need. Sickness benefits, in which patients pay only a small part of medical costs, as well as birth, family and unemployment payments, are included in the plans. Housing conditions are generally comparable to those found in other Western European countries. There has been some difficulty in assimilating the many thousands of foreign workers and their families.
Luxembourg conforms to the EU provisions dealing with social security based on the principle of free movement of workers within the EU that enables its workers to accept a job in another member state without suffering any inequality with regard to social security. The EU social security arrangements aim to co-ordinate the national social security schemes in all the member states of the EU and the European Economic Area (EEA).
The social security system covers benefits for sickness and maternity, pensions, insurance against accidents at work and occupational diseases, unemployment benefits and family allowances. The scheme is compulsory and covers all persons in paid employment as well as self-employed workers in the country. Half of the contribution due is payable by the worker and half by the employer. There is no contribution towards industrial accident insurance, family benefits or unemployment benefit. Contributions are payable for sickness and maternity insurance, disability insurance, old-age and survivor's pension, amounting to a certain percentage of his/her remuneration.

Main cities
Luxembourg-Ville (capital, estimated population 76,258 in 2005), Esch-sur-Alzette (27,559), Dudelange (18,036), Differdange (18,477).

Languages spoken
Official language/s
Lëtzebuergish (Luxembourgish); French and German are the administrative languages.

Media
Press
Dailies: Principal dailies include Luxemburger Wort (La Voix du Luxembourg), Tageblatt-Zeitung fir Letzebuerg, Lëtzebuerger Journal and Zeitung vum Letzebuerger Vollek. The French Le Républicain-Lorrain, which has an extensive Luxembourg section, is also widely read.
Weeklies: Include Télécran (entertainment), Contacto and Revue covering issues of general interest.
Business: There are numerous journals and magazines including d'Letzebuerger Land, l'Echo de l'Industrie, De Letzeburger Merkur, Luxembourg Business and Luxemburg News.
Periodicals: Those featuring general interest, current affairs and women's issues include Foyer de la Femme, Gaart an Heem, Grénge Spoun and Select Magazine.
Broadcasting
Compagnie Luxembourgeoise de Télédiffusion, the operator of Radio-Télé Luxembourg (RTL), operates 14 television channels in six countries and 18 radio stations across eight countries.
Advertising
There is commercial advertising on radio, TV and billboards.

Economy
Luxembourg is well situated at the heart of the EU, it benefits from its location as a centre for the regional labour market, European regionalism and membership of the euro-zone. The financial sector dominates the economy and has led the way to renewed economic activity since 2003. There were some 155 banks, mostly foreign owned, in Luxembourg in 2005, and the sector has moved away for traditional banking services to investment fund industry (IFI). It is a sound and well supervised sector that should remain resilient to adverse shocks. Strong banking commissions gained by IFIs suggests continued diversification of earning and stability.
Services typically contribute 80 per cent of GDP with industry providing around 20 per cent of which manufacturing is about 12 per cent; agriculture provides less than 1 per cent.
The strong GDP growth of 4.0 per cent in 2005 is expected to be maintained in 2006, although the fiscal deficit which widened in 2005 to 2.3 per cent of GDP and was driven by social expenditure growth, was exacerbated by the unemployment rate of 4.2 per cent.

The IMF warned that Luxembourg's public pension system was becoming unsustainable as cross-border employment was lowering the current pension dependency ratio and raising future liability.
Luxembourg's structural unemployment has been influenced by factors in neighbouring countries, which has resulted in an influx of foreign workers, who have been competing successfully with resident workers for the limited supply of available jobs. Efforts to minimise social expenditure could be damaged if the escalating unemployment is not addressed.

External trade

As a member of the European Union, Luxembourg operates within a communitywide free trade union, with tariffs sets as a whole. Internationally, the EU has free trade agreements with a number of nations and trading blocs worldwide.
The traditional steel industry provides around 10 per cent of GDP, despite depleted iron ore reserves. Hi-tech industries have grown in importance; nevertheless, the financial services sector provides around 275 per cent of GDP.

Imports

Imports include petroleum, gas, vehicles, iron ore, minerals, metals, foodstuffs and quality consumer goods.
Main sources: Belgium (34.0 per cent total, 2006), Germany (25.8 per cent), France (11.5 per cent).

Exports

Commodities include iron and steel, electrical and electronic equipment, machinery, glass, ceramics and plastics.
Intermediate manufactured products account for around 80 per cent of total exports.
Main destinations: Germany (24.6 per cent total, 2006), France (16.7 per cent), Belgium (12.3 per cent).

Agriculture

Farming

The country has gradually adapted and delegated much of its farm policy to the EU, through the Common Agricultural Policy (CAP). Fundamental reform to the CAP was introduced on 1 January 2005 in Italy. The subsidies paid on farm output, which tended to benefit large farms and encourage overproduction, were replaced by single farm payments not conditional on production. This is expected to reward farms that provide and maintain a healthy environment, food safety and animal welfare standards. The changes are also intended to encourage market conscious production and cut the cost of CAP to the EU taxpayer.
Farming is concentrated on barley, oats and potatoes in the north, and fruit and grapes in the east.
Although agricultural output has tripled since the 1980s, its contribution to GDP has in the same period declined from 4 per cent in mid-1970s to around 1 per cent in late 1990s. The number of farms declined from 5,173 in 1980 to 2,950 in 1998 as high agricultural production costs and high employment in Luxembourg caused more people to leave the farming industry and farmland has subsequently been converted to other uses. This trend slowed in 2003–04 as the economy slowed and jobs were not so readily available. Three-quarters of the land is cultivated. Pasture accounts for 55 per cent of all cultivated farmland.
Food and wine account for about 1.9 per cent of exports.
Crop production in 2005 included: 160,264 tonnes (t) cereals in total, 70,460t wheat, 14,916t rapeseed (canola), 19,370t potatoes, 52,208t barley, 1,350t pulses, 10,700t apples, 22,836t grapes, 5,668t oilcrops, 36,290t fruit in total, 16,880t vegetables in total. Livestock production included: 48,615t meat in total, 17,000t beef, 14,500t pig meat, 85t lamb, 16,700t poultry, 272,000t milk, 3,200t cattle hides.

Fishing

Luxembourg does not have any significant freshwater fishing industry.

Forestry

Largely driven back to the least productive soil and escarpments where viable development is precluded, woods cover some 89,000 hectares or around a third of the country. Extending over 4,500 hectares, the forest of Gruenwald is the largest continuous wooded area in the Grand Duchy.
Forestry only plays a very modest role in the overall economy, the commercial explotation of private forests and those subject to the system of forest tenure only represent on average between 0.1 per cent and 0.2 per cent of GDP.

Industry and manufacturing

As with the agricultural sector, Luxembourg's industrial base has declined in proportion to the dominant services sector and accounts for only 30 per cent of GDP. The country's principal industries include steel, chemicals, rubber, plastics, processing, glass, aluminium, metalworking and vehicle spares manufacture.

Tourism

Tourism is becoming a most important area of the economy and is being actively promoted by the government. In 2005 travel and tourism is expected to contribute US$1.2 billion or 3.4 per cent of GDP and employ over 12 per cent of the workforce. It should also attract US$496 million, or 6.4 per cent of total capital investment.
The Dutch have traditionally been the main visitors followed by the Belgians, Germans, French and British. Luxembourg receives the largest number of tourists in the region, followed by the Ardennes and Mëllerdall.

Mining

Iron ore, discovered around 1850, made the fortune of modern Luxembourg's economy. The steel industry still serves as one of the most important sector of the economy, although its share of GDP fallen has since the early 2000s.

Hydrocarbons

Luxembourg does not have any oil, natural gas or coal reserves. The country imports all its hydrocarbons, totalling 52,300 barrels per day (bpd) of refined oil products, 1.2 billion cubic metres of natural gas and 127,000 tonnes of coal. These imports come primarily from the EU.

Energy

There is heavy dependence on imported energy, mainly from Belgium and Germany. Luxembourg has a hydroelectric dam at Vianden, but still imports electricity. There are no nuclear power plants. Of the 6.1 billion KW hours consumed annually, only 648 million KW is generated in Luxembourg.

Financial markets

Stock exchange

The principal source of growth in the domestic economy has been the financial services sector. The main activities are banking and investment fund management.
The Luxembourg Stock Exchange trades every working day.

Banking and insurance

Luxembourg has a large banking sector. Activity is oriented towards wholesale banking services, with a large concentration of German and Scandinavian banks serving corporate customers in Europe. Private banking has rapidly increased. Banking accounts for around 16 per cent of GDP and employs 10 per cent of the workforce. Luxembourg's banking secrecy laws were a source of complaint abroad, however new rules allow authorities to investigate as necessary. There is concern that EU requirements for the deduction of a withholding tax from all foreign accounts will adversely affect the sector.

Central bank

The European Central Bank (ECB) acts as the central bank, issuing notes and coins and determining interest rates.

Time

GMT plus one hour (daylight saving, late March to late October, GMT plus two hours)

Geography
Luxembourg is a landlocked country in Western Europe, bounded by Belgium on the north and west, Germany to the east and France to the south. Luxembourg consists mainly of the upper basins of the Sauer (Sûre) and Alzette rivers. The highest point is Buurgplaatz (559 metres), in the Ardennes Plateau in the north. The southern two-thirds of the country is a rolling plateau, the Bon Pays.
Hemisphere
Northern

Climate
Luxembourg's climate is temperate, without extremes. Sea winds (south-west and north-west) shed a great part of their moisture before reaching the Luxembourg frontiers. May to mid-October is suitable for vacations; July and August are the warmest; May and June are the sunniest months; in September and October there is often an 'Indian summer'.

Dress codes
Medium-weight clothing is required throughout the year. A raincoat is useful.

Entry requirements
Passports
Passports are required by nationals of most countries. Exceptions include holders of national identity cards issued to nationals of some European countries.
Visa
Required by all, except nationals of Europe, North America, Australasia, or Japan. For a full list of visa-free citizens visit www.luxembourg-usa.org/consindex.html. Schengen visas cover all entry needs; for those requiring a business visa, a letter of business references and proof of sufficient funds to cover the cost of your intended stay should accompany the application. A Schengen visa application (offered in several languages) can be downloaded from http://europa.eu/abc/travel/ see 'documents you will need'.
Currency advice/regulations
There are no restrictions on the movement of local or foreign currencies.
Customs
Personal items are duty-free. There are no duties levied on alcohol and tobacco between EU member states, providing amounts imported are for personal consumption.
Passengers carrying weapons and transiting Luxembourg must hold an Autorisation de Transit d'Armes certificate issued by the Luxembourg Ministry of Justice.

Health (for visitors)
Nationals of the European Economic Area (EEA) countries and Switzerland can access reduced cost and sometimes free medical treatment using a European Health Insurance Card (EHIC) while visiting the EEA. Exceptions include nationals of the 10 countries, which joined the EU in 2004, whose EHIC is not valid in Switzerland. Applications for the EHIC should be made before travelling.
Mandatory precautions
None
Advisable precautions
It is recommended that travellers have up-to-date tetanus and polio immunisations.

Hotels
A one-to five-star rating system is partially in operation. Bills include the service charge. Tipping is optional.

Credit cards
All main credit cards are accepted.

Public holidays (national)
Fixed dates
1 Jan (New Year's Day), 1 May (May Day), 23 Jun (National Day), 15 Aug (Assumption Day), 1 Nov (All Saints' Day), 25-26 Dec (Christmas).
If a holiday falls on a Sunday, the Monday following is usually a holiday as well (maximum two per annum).
Variable dates
Carnival (Feb), Good Friday, Easter Monday, Ascension Day, Whit Monday, Luxembourg City Fair Day (Luxembourg City only, Sep).

Working hours
Banking
Mon–Fri: 0900–1630.
Business
Mon–Fri: 0800–1800, lunch 1200–1400.
Government
Mon–Fri: 0800–1800, lunch 1200–1400.
Shops
There are large variations in shop hours, but they are generally open 0900–2000, closed Mon morning.

Electricity supply
220V AC

Weights and measures
Metric system

Social customs/useful tips
Punctuality is appreciated. Business people are expected to wear suits. It is advisable to make prior appointments and business cards are widely used.

Security
Luxembourg has a low crime rate. However, during the tourist season pickpocketing and theft from vehicles do occur.

Getting there
Air
National airline: Luxair
International airport/s: Luxembourg-Findel (LUX), 5km east of city; restaraunts, post office shops, car hire.
Airport tax: None
Surface
Road: There are good road links with Brussels, Trier, Paris, Frankfurt and Saarbrücken. Luxembourg has open borders with all its immediate neighbours, namely Germany, France and Belgium.
Rail: There are rail connections with Brussels, Frankfurt, Amsterdam, Basle and Paris.

Getting about
National transport
Network tickets (billets réseaux), which allow unlimited travel for one day on all forms of transport throughout Luxembourg, are also available.
Road: Luxembourg has an extensive network of roads and motorways, all of which are paved.
Buses: Bus services link most towns and villages.
Rail: There are 280km of railway track. State-run railway services link the capital with most main towns.
City transport
Taxis: There is a metered taxi service with a minimum charge. Tipping is usually 10 per cent.
Buses, trams & metro: Regular flat-fare bus service operates in Luxembourg city. Tickets are valid for one hour or 10km and also allow connections with out-of-city connections.
Car hire
Car hire is available from the airport and hotels.

BUSINESS DIRECTORY

The addresses listed below are a selection only. While World of Information makes every endeavour to check these addresses, we cannot guarantee that changes have not been made, especially to telephone numbers and area codes. We would welcome any corrections.

Telephone area codes
The international direct dialling (IDD) code for Luxembourg is +352, followed by subscriber's number.

Chambers of Commerce
American Chamber of Commerce in Luxembourg, 6 Rue Antoine de Saint Exupéry, PO Box 542, L-1432 Luxembourg (tel/fax: 431-756; e-mail: info@amcham.lu).

British Chamber of Commerce for Luxembourg, 6 Rue Antoine de Saint Exupéry, L-1432 Luxembourg (tel: 465-466; fax: 220-384; e-mail: info@bcc.lu).

Luxembourg Chamber of Commerce, 7 Rue Alcide de Gaspari, L-2981 Luxembourg (tel: 423-939; fax: 438-326; e-mail: chamcom@cc.lu).

Banking

Association des Banques et Banquiers, 59 Boulevard Royal, PO Box 13, L-2010 Luxembourg (tel: 29-501, 463-6601; fax: 460-921).

Banque Continentale du Luxembourg SA, 2 Boulevard Emmanuel Servais, L-2535 Luxembourg (tel: 474-491; fax: 477-688-333).

Banque de Luxembourg SA, 80 Place de la Gare, BP 2221, L-1022 Luxembourg (tel: 499-241; fax: 494-820).

Banque et Caisse d'Epargne de l'Etat, 1 Place de Metz, PO Box 2105, L-2954 Luxembourg (tel: 4015-1; fax: 4015-2099; e-mail: info@bcee.lu).

Banque Générale du Luxembourg, Boulevard JF Kennedy, L-2951 Luxembourg (tel: 47-991, 42-421; fax: 4799-2579).

Banque Internationale à Luxembourg SA BIL), 2 Boulevard Royal, L-2953 Luxembourg (tel: 45-901; fax: 4791-2010).

Banque Nationale de Paris SA, 22-24 Boulevard Royal, L-2952 Luxembourg-Ville (tel: 47-641; fax: 26-480).

Caisse Centrale Raiffeisen SC, 28 Boulevard Royal, BP 111, L-2011 Luxembourg (tel: 462-151).

Fortuna, Société Co-opérative de Credit et d'Epargne, 128-132 Boulevard de la Pétrusse, BP 1203, L-1012 Luxembourg (tel: 488-888).

Kredietbank SA Luxembourgeoise, 43 Boulevard Royal, L-2953 Luxembourg (tel: 47-971; fax: 472-667).

Société Générale Bank and Trust, 11 Avenue Emile Reuter, PO Box 1271, L-2420 Luxembourg (tel: 479-3111; fax: 228-859; e-mail:sgbt.lu@socgen.com).

Société Nationale de Credit et d'Investissement, 7 Rue du St Esprit, BP 1207, L-1012 Luxembourg (tel: 461-9711).

Central bank

Banque Centrale du Luxembourg, 2 Boulevard Royal, L-2983 Luxembourg (tel: 4774-1; fax: 4774-4910; email: info@bcl.lu).

European Central Bank (ECB), Kaiserstrasse 29, D-60311 Frankfurt am Main, Germany (tel: (+49-69) 13-440; fax: (+49-69) 1344-6000; email: info@ecb.int).

Travel information

Luxair, Luxembourg Airport, 2987 Luxembourg (tel: 798-2311; fax: 443-2482e-mail: information@luxair.lu).

Luxembourg Airport, PO Box 635, L-2016 Luxembourg (tel: 2464-1; fax: 2464-2464; e-mail: mail@lux-airport.lu).

Luxembourg City Tourist Office, Place d'Armes, L-1136 Luxembourg (tel: 222-809; fax: 474-818; e-mail: touristinfo@luxembourg-city.lu).

Ministry of tourism

Department of Tourism, 6 Avenue Emile Reuter, L-2937 Luxembourg (tel: 478-4751; fax: 474-011; e-mail: info@mdt.public.lu).

National tourist organisation offices

Office National du Tourisme, Gare Centrale, Box 1001, L-1010 Luxembourg (tel: 4282-821; fax: 4282-8238; e-mail: info@visitluxembourg.lu).

Ministries

Ministère des Affaires Etrangères, du Commerce Extèrieur et de la Coopèration, 5 Rue Notre-Dame, L-2913 Luxembourg (tel: 4781; fax: 461-720).

Ministère de l'Agriculture, de la Viticulture et du Developpement Rural, 1 Rue de la Congrègation, L-2913 Luxembourg (tel: 4781; fax: 464-027).

Ministère de l'Amenagement du Territoire, 18 Montèe de la Pètrusse, L-2946 Luxembourg (tel: 4781; fax: 408-970).

Ministère de la Culture, 20 Montée de la Pétrusse, L-2912 Luxembourg (tel: 4781; fax: 402-427).

Ministère de l'Economie, 19-21 Boulevard Royal, L-2914 Luxembourg (tel: 478-4100; fax: 460-448).

Ministère de l'Education Nationale et de la Formation Professionnelle, 29 rue Aldringen, L-2926 Luxembourg (tel: 4781; fax: 478-5113).

Ministère de l'Education Physique et des Sports, 66 route de Treves, L-2916 Luxembourg (tel: 4781; fax: 434-599).

Ministère de l'Energie, 19 Boulevard Royal, L-2449 Luxembourg (tel: 4781).

Ministère de l'Environnement, 18 Montèe de la Pètrusse, L-2918 Luxembourg (tel: 4781; fax: 400-410).

Ministère de la Famille, 14 Avenue de la Gare, L-2919 Luxembourg (tel: 4781; fax: 478-6570).

Ministère des Finances, 3 rue de la Congregation, L-2931 Luxembourg (tel: 4781; fax: 475-241).

Ministère de la Fonction Publique et de la Réforme Administrative, Plateau du St Esprit, L-2011 Luxembourg (tel: 4781; fax: 478-3122).

Ministère de la Force Publique, Plateau du St Esprit, Bâtiment Vauban, L-2915 Luxembourg (tel: 4781; fax: 462-682).

Ministère de l'Intèrieur, 19 Rue Beaumont, L-2933 Luxembourg (tel: 4781; fax: 418-46).

Ministère de la Jeunesse, 26 Rue Zithe, L-2943 Luxembourg (tel: 4781; fax: 467-454).

Ministère de la Justice, 16 Boulevard Royal, L-2934 Luxembourg (tel: 4781; fax: 227-661).

Ministère du Logement, 6 Avenue Emile Reuter, L-2942 Luxembourg (tel: 4781; fax: 478-4840).

Ministère de la Promotion Féminine, 33 Boulevard Prince Henri, L-2919 Luxembourg (tel: 4781; fax: 41-886).

Ministère de la Santé, 57 et 90 Boulevard de la Pétrusse, L-2320 Luxembourg (tel: 4781; fax: 484-903).

Ministère de la Sécurité Sociale, 26 Rue Zithe, L-2936 Luxembourg (tel: 4781; fax: 478-6328).

Ministère des Transports, 19-21 Boulevard Royal, L-2938 Luxembourg (tel: 4781; fax: 464-315).

Ministère des Travail et de l'Emploi, 26 rue Zithe, L-2939 Luxembourg (tel: 4781; fax: 478-6325).

Ministère des Travaux Publics, 4 Boulevard FD Roosevelt, L-2940 Luxembourg (tel: 4781; fax: 462-709).

Other useful addresses

Bourse de Luxembourg SA (stock exchange), 11 Avenue de la Porte-Neuve, L-2227 Luxembourg (tel: 477-9361; fax: 22-050; internet site: http://www.bourse.lu/).

Board of Economic Development, 19-21 Boulevard Royal, L-2914 Luxembourg (tel:478-4135/4141; fax: 460-448).

Confédération du Commerce Luxembourgeois, 23 Allée Scheffer, L-2520 Luxembourg (tel: 473-125).

Fédération des Industriels Luxembourgeois, 7 Rue Alcide de Gasperi, L-1615 Luxembourg (tel: 435-366; fax: 438-326).

Foires Internationales de Luxembourg, L-2088 Luxembourg (tel: 043-991; fax: 0439-9315).

Groupement des Industries Sidérurgiques Luxembourgeoises (Federation of Iron and Steel Industries in Luxembourg), 3 Rue Goethe, PO Box 1704, L-1637 Luxembourg (tel: 480-001).

Luxembourg Embassy (USA), 2200 Massechusetts Avenue, NW, Washington DC 20008 (tel: (+1-202)-265-4171; fax: (+1-202)-328-8270; e-mail: info@luxembourg-usa.org).

Offshore Company Registration Agents (Luxembourg) SA, PO Box 878, 19 Rue Aldringen, L-1118 Luxembourg (tel: 224-286; fax: 224-287).

Press and Information Service of the Government, 43 Boulevard Roosevelt, L-2450 Luxembourg (tel: 478-224, 478-321; fax: 470-285, 20-090).

Radio Télé-Luxembourg (RTL), Villa Louvigny, L-2850 Luxembourg (tel: 476-6242; fax: 4766-2737).

Service Central de la Statistique et des Etudes Economiques (STATEC), 6 Boulevard Royal, L-2013 Luxembourg (tel: 4781; fax: 464-289; internet site: http://statec.lu/).

Société Européenne des Satellites (SES), Château de Betzdorf, L-6815 Luxembourg (tel: 710-725/1; fax: 725-227; internet site: http://www.astra.lu).

Internet sites

Complete list of banks in Luxembourg: http://www.bank.lu

Government statistics: http://statec.gouvernement.lu

Luxembourg weekly publication (in English): http://www.352.lu

Luxembourg government: http://gouvernement.lu

The Station Network, online information (in English): http://www.station.lu

Web directory: http://Luxembourg.lu/

Macao (China)

COUNTRY PROFILE

Historical profile

1513 The first group of Portuguese arrived at the entrance to the Pearl River, the area that is now Macao.
1557 The colony of Macao was founded by the Portuguese with the apparent approval of the Chinese authorities.
1845 After years of Chinese rule, the Portuguese expelled the Chinese and announced Macao a free port. The territory enlarged to include the islands of Taipa and Coloane.
1860 The Portuguese introduced gambling licences to the territory.
1887 Macao's status was recognised by the Treaty of Amity and Commerce, signed between Portugal and China.
1939–45 Macao remained neutral during the Second World War and its economy prospered.
1976 The Portuguese government declared Macao a special territory and granted it a high degree of independence.
1987 The Sino-Portuguese Joint Declaration on the Question of Macao was signed.
1999 China resumed control over the territory. Edmund Ho Hau Wah became the first chief executive, as Macao became a Special Administrative Region (SAR) of China.
2001 The Associação de Novo Macau Democrático (ANMD) (New Democratic Macao Association), won two of the 10 directly-elected seats in the legislature.
2002 As part of the move to liberalise the gambling sector, Macao issued three casino licences to private operators. This broke the monopoly of self-made billionaire and the world's most successful casino operator, Stanley Ho Hung San.
2003 Severe Acute Respiratory Syndrome (Sars) spread around the region early in the year.
2004 Edmund Ho was re-elected chief executive. The American owned and operated, Sands Macao Casino, opened with more gaming tables than any other single casino in the world.
2005 In parliamentary elections the pro-democracy group, ANMD, won 18.8 per cent of the votes. The Banco Delta Asia had accounts containing around US$7 million, linked to North Korea, frozen by the US, after the bank was branded a 'primary money-laundering concern', as having dealt in counterfeit and illicitly earned money. For almost a year before the suspension over US$49 million were transmitted through the bank on behalf of North Korean Daedong Credit Bank.
2006 Revenues from gaming, amounting to US$5.51 billion in the first 10 month, outstripped the amount earned by the US home of gambling, Las Vegas. More Casinos are due to be opened in 2007.
2008 The Macau government announced plans to curb further casino development.

Political structure

Constitution

The Basic Law, promulgated by the People's Republic of China (PRC) in 1993, effectively became Macao's Constitution after sovereignty of the former Portuguese Special Territory was handed over to PRC in December 1999. The Basic Law pledges to maintain Macao's economic, social and political distinctiveness for a period of 50 years after the handover to the PRC, under the principle of 'one country, two systems'.

Under the Basic Law, members of the executive and legislature must be permanent Macao residents. Private property, free speech and freedom of conscience are guaranteed.

Form of state

Special Administrative Region (SAR) of the People's Republic of China.

The executive

Under the terms of the Basic Law of Macao SAR (MSAR), executive power is vested in the chief executive, except in foreign affairs and defence, which are the responsibility of the People's Republic of China (PRC) government.

The chief executive, appointed by PRC after local consultation and who must have been a resident for at least 20 years, serves a five-year term, limited to two consecutive terms. An Executive Council of 10, appointed by the chief executive, consists of five MSAR departmental heads, three MSAR legislators and two other representatives.

National legislature

The Legislative Assembly has 29 members, of whom seven are government appointees, 10 are indirectly elected by business associations, and 12 are directly elected. The chief executive has the power to remove members and dissolve the

KEY FACTS

Official name: Macao Special Administrative Region of China (Macao SAR)

Head of State: State President Hu Jintao (since Mar 2003)

Head of government: Chief Executive Edmund Ho Hau Wah (appointed Dec 1999; re-elected Aug 2004)

Ruling party: There are no political parties: there are 12 popularly elected seats in the legislature, an additional 10 seats are filled by business and special interest groups, and 7 seats are appointed by Macao's chief executive.

Area: 29 square km (Macao peninsula, Taipa and Coloane islands)

Population: 540,000 (2007)*

Capital: Macao City

Official language: Chinese (Mandarin, Beijing dialect de jure; Cantonese de facto) and Portuguese

Currency: Pataca (Pa) = 100 avos

Exchange rate: Pa8.03 per US$ (Jul 2008); (the pataca is pegged to the Hong Kong dollar at Pa1.03)

GDP per capita: US$36,357 (2007)

GDP real growth: 27.30% (2007)

Labour force: 310,000 (2007)

Unemployment: 3.10% (2007)

Inflation: 5.60% (2007)

Balance of trade: -US$3.94 billion (2006)

Visitor numbers: 26.99 million (2007)

* estimated figure

Legislative Council under conditions of political deadlock.

Last elections

25 September 2005 (parliamentary)

Results: Parliamentary: Associação de Novo Macao Democrático (ANMD) (New Democrat Macao Association) won 18.8 per cent of the votes (two seats), Associação dos Cidadãos Unidos de Macao (ACUM) (United Citizens Association of Macao) 16.58 per cent (two seats), União para o Desenvolvimento (UPD) (Union for Development) 13.29 per cent (two seats), União Promotora para o Progresso (UNIPRO) (Union for Promoting Progress) 9.6 per cent (two seats). Other parties one seat each. Turnout was 58.4 per cent.

Next elections

September 2009 (parliamentary)

Political parties

There are no formal political parties. However, pro-Chinese associations control a majority of the Assembly's elective seats. A number of civic associations exist. The Associacao de Novo Macao Democratio (ANMD) (New Democratic Macao Association) has a significant presence in the Assembly.

Ruling party

There are no political parties: there are 12 popularly elected seats in the legislature, an additional 10 seats are filled by business and special interest groups, and 7 seats are appointed by Macao's chief executive.

Population

540,000 (2007)*

Last census: August 2001: 435,235

Population density: Over 20,000 inhabitants per square km. Urban population: 99 per cent.

Annual growth rate: 1 per cent (2003)

Ethnic make-up

Approximately 96 per cent of the territory's inhabitants are Chinese (mostly Cantonese from Guangdong province); the remainder are Mavanese (mixed Portuguese and Chinese).

Religions

Chinese Buddhism (45 per cent), Christianity (Roman Catholicism) (15 per cent).

Education

Primary education begins at age six and lasts until age 12. There are three stages of secondary schooling, beginning with junior, lasting for three years, then senior for two years and finally a pre-university one-year course. The first 10 years of education are free of charge.

Teaching may be given in Chinese, English or Portuguese.

Some 25 per cent of Macao's inhabitants attend any of 83 primary schools, 40 secondary schools, nine vocational technical colleges or nine institutes of higher education. The University of Macao has approximately 3,500 students in 80 undergraduate and post-graduate degree subjects.

Literacy rate: 94.3 per cent total, 91.7 per cent female, adult rates (World Bank).

Enrolment rate: 84.1 per cent net primary enrolment; 62.3 per cent net secondary enrolment (government statistics, 2005).

Pupils per teacher: 21.2 in primary/secondary schools; 9.3 in higher education.

Health

Macao's population is young, with around 60 per cent between the ages of 15 and 50. Approximately 9 per cent of the government budget is allocated to healthcare.

KEY INDICATORS — Macao (China)

	Unit	2003	2004	2005	2006	2007
Population	m	0.44	0.45	0.50	0.52	0.54
Gross domestic product (GDP)	US$bn	6.76	*8.16	11.60	14.40	*14.20
GDP per capita	US$	18,500	18,096	25,126	30,013	36,357
GDP real growth	%	9.0	28.0	2.8	17.0	27.3
Inflation	%	-2.6	1.0	4.3	5.2	5.6
Unemployment	%	6.3	4.9	4.1	3.8	3.1
Exports (fob) (goods)	US$m	2,360.0	2,506.0	2,478.0	2,559.0	–
Imports (cif) (goods)	US$m	2,530.0	3,115.0	5,270.0	6,496.0	–
Balance of trade	US$m	-170.0	-610.0	-2,792.0	-3,937.0	–
Current account	US$m	3,160.0	4,240.0	3,367.0	2,946.0	–
Total reserves minus gold	US$m	4,340.0	5,440.0	6,690.0	9.1	13.2
Foreign exchange	US$m	4,340.0	5,440.0	6,690.0	9.1	13.2
Exchange rate	per US$	7.98	8.00	8.03	–	–

* estimated figure

Life expectancy: 79.3 years (estimate 2003)

Fertility rate/Maternal mortality rate: 1.2 births per per woman (World Bank)

Child (under 5 years) mortality rate (per 1,000): Six per 1,000 live births (World Bank).

Welfare

Unemployment benefits, old age pensions and invalid benefits are administered by the Social Security Fund, which is financed through employer and employee contributions as well as government subsidies. Public assistance centres are co-ordinated by the Macao Social Welfare Institute in conjunction with the Church and other civilian organisations.

Main cities

Macao City (capital, estimated population 421,662 in 2005).

Languages spoken

Only 1.8 per cent of the population speak Portuguese. English is widely spoken and used in business and tourist circles.

Official language/s

Chinese (Mandarin, Beijing dialect de jure; Cantonese de facto) and Portuguese

Media

Freedom of the press is guaranteed under the law and the government respects this. China's official Xinhua state news agency operates as the Liaison Offices of the Central People's Government for Macau and regulates broadcasting media.

Press

Dailies: In Portuguese, publications include Hoje Macau (www.hojemacau.com), Jornal Tribuna de Macau (www.jtm.com.mo) and Ponto Final. In Chinese, publications include Macao Daily News (www.macaodaily.com), with the highest circulation, the privately owned Va Kio (www.vakiodaily.com) and Jornal Va Kio, Ou Mun, Si Man, Tai Chung Pou and Seng Pou. The Macau Post Daily (www.macaupostdaily.com) is the oldest English language newspaper.

Weeklies: There are several magazines catering for all interests.

Business: In English, Macau Business (www.macaubusiness.com) is a monthly publication with sections dedicated to specific business interests such as banking, gaming and property. In Chinese Business Intelligence (www.bizintelligenceonline.com).

Periodicals: In Portuguese Revista Macau (www.revistamacau.com) is a quarterly magazine covering cultural matters. Inside Asian Gaming (www.asgam.com) is a monthly publication concerned with industry development.

Broadcasting
Teledifusão de Macau (TDM) (www.tdm.com.mo) is the public broadcaster.
Radio: TDM (www.tdm.com.mo) operates Radio Macau in Cantonese and Portuguese. Radio Villa Verde (www.am738.com) is an independent station.
Overseas radio stations from China and Hong Kong are available.
Television: TDM (www.tdm.com.mo) operates two channels, broadcasting in Cantonese and Portuguese. There are several private TV stations broadcasting, via digital cables or satellite, which provide international programmes, including Macao Cable (www.macaucabletv.com) and Villa Verde Ltd.

Economy
Macao has grown rapidly since the mid-1980s but it wasn't until 1999 when it reverted to Chinese ownership that its economy was given encouragement to expand, not only economically, but with 2.9sq km of reclaimed land in 2006 it was joined with the island of Coloane to become one landmass, and increased Macao's area be 18 per cent. The Cotai Strip is a huge development, due to be completed by 2009, of hotels and casinos, which will caters for the two dominant industries in Macao, tourism and gambling.
The economy has been galvanised since gambling licences were granted to international firms for the first time in 2001, along with tourist visas issued to mainland Chinese citizens, to visit the only place in the country with legalised gambling. In 2004, the American owned and operated Sands Macao Casino opened with more gaming tables than any other single casino in the world. Casino operators must pay 35 per cent of gross revenue, a special gaming tax and a premium for their gaming concession and pay 1.6 per cent of their gross revenue to the Macao Foundation (a social fund to promote cultural activities). Macao's GDP, in 2004, rose by 28 per cent, fuelling further growth in casinos. GDP growth in 2005 was 2.8 per cent and was expected to grow by over 10 per cent in 2006. Inflation rose to 5.41 per cent in the first nine months of 2006, due to increased operating costs for companies and an expansion of subsistence expenses for the general public.
Industry revenues from gaming in 2006, amounting to US$5.51 billion in the first 10 months, outstripped the amount earned by casinos in the US home of gambling, Las Vegas. Around 95 per cent of gamblers were residents of Hong Kong, China and other Asian countries. It is expected that more Western gamblers will visit Macao in future, particularly when the Cotai Strip is fully functioning. With gambling revenue projected to rise annually by 25 per cent, investment in the industry is expected to reach US$25 billion by 2011. Gaming revenues in 2007 reached record levels of more than US$10 billion (Pa83.8 billion) rivaling greater Las Vegas area (in the US) for gaming income.
This much development has put a strain on employment, with demand outstripping skills. In 2006 the workforce was 260,000 but an estimated 400,000 are needed by 2010.
Despite the strong growth over the last few years, some analysts warn that the industry is overheating and that a glut of casinos could lead to a collapse. Nevertheless, operators are banking on the desire of the 100 million Chinese residents living within three hours drive, or the one billion a short flight away from their gaming tables, willing to take a chance.
China has established its second-largest Special Economic Zone in Zhuhai (on the mainland adjacent to Macao), which has powerful business links with Macao.
Macao offers tax and other incentives for investment in tourism and hotels, the electronics manufacturing industry, fishing industry and property development. It has certain competitive advantages over Hong Kong. For example, wage costs, factory rentals, office space and residential accommodation cost about half – in some cases a third – of Hong Kong equivalents. Lower operating costs in Zhuhai, particularly in labour-intensive processes, have led to a migration of many enterprises, particularly textile manufacturers, to Zhuhai, although more sophisticated, capital-intensive processes have tended to remain in Macao.
Shipping facilities have been upgraded with the construction of the Ka Ho port which has a container terminal and an oil terminal.

External trade
Under the Closer Economic Partnership Arrangement (CEPA), Macau has a trade alliance with China's nine southernmost provinces and Hong Kong through the pan-Pearl River Delta (PRD) trade bloc.
Imports
Principle imports include raw materials and semi-manufactured goods, foodstuffs, tobacco, capital goods, mineral fuels and oils and alcohol.
Main sources: China (45.2 per cent total, 2006), Hong Kong (10.2 per cent), Japan (8.4 per cent).
Exports
Principal exports include clothing, textiles, footwear, toys, electronics, machinery and parts and textile yarns.
Main destinations: US (44.1 per cent total, 2006), China (14.8 per cent), Hong Kong (11.3 per cent).

Agriculture
The agriculture and fishing sectors typically account for 0.1 per cent of GDP and 0.2 per cent of the workforce.
Soils are generally meagre and there is little agricultural production. Macao imports its food and water requirements, mainly from China.
Fish, prawns and other sea foods are trawled for local consumption and export. In 2004, the total marine fish catch was 1,020 tonnes and the total crustacean catch was 440 tonnes.

Industry and manufacturing
The textile and garment industries provide the bulk of Macao's exports, although they are subject to limitations such as EU quotas and some producers have been moving to Zhuhai. Other main products include toys, printing and packaging, leather products, electronics and opticals, food and beverages, furniture, woodware and ceramics.

Tourism
Tourism is enjoying a boom, by March 2006 visitor arrivals had reached 1.8 million, recording a 18.2 per cent annual growth rate. Visitors from mainland China grew by 26.2 per cent and same-day visitors (from Hong Kong and cruise ships – mainly from China) grew by 52.5 per cent.
The island is small with a limited selection of visitor attractions, however it has a liberal and experienced gambling culture. The casinos that operate are large and sophisticated with business regimes to match any in Las Vegas. Cultural, leisure and business tourism, underpinned by major infrastructure work, are being developed. Tourism and gaming account for over 50 per cent of GDP and employ around 40 per cent of the workforce.

Hydrocarbons
Macao does not produce any hydrocarbons. Macao relies on the import of refined oil to meet its domestic demand. It does not import natural gas.
Macao consumes small quantities of imported coal.

Energy
Companhia de Electricidade de Macao (Macao Electricity Company) is the concessionary for production, transmission and distribution of electricity. Two thermal power stations on Coloane Island meet about 80 per cent of the total requirements, the remainder being imported from neighbouring Zhuhai City in mainland China.

Banking and insurance
Since China took control of Macao in 1999, new banking laws intended to attract more foreign banks and allow a full range of offshore banking services have been enacted to ensure participation in financing the development of southern China. Macao enjoys some of the most liberal financial systems in the world.
Central bank
There is no central bank. The Monetary Authority of Macao (known as Autoridade Monetária e Cambial de Macao until 2000) is the monetary and foreign exchange authority of the territory.
Main financial centre
Macao City

Time
GMT plus eight hours

Geography
Macao comprises the peninsula of Macao and two nearby islands: Taipa, linked to the mainland by a bridge, and Coloane, which is connected to Taipa by a causeway. The territory lies opposite Hong Kong on the western side of the mouth of the Xijiang (Sikiang) river.
Hemisphere
Northern

Climate
Subtropical and monsoonal. Winter (November–April) is cool and dry, with an average temperature of 14–23 degrees Celsius (C). Summer (May–September) is hot, humid and rainy, with an average temperature of 27 degrees C. October and November are somewhat less humid. Average annual rainfall ranges from 1,000–2,000mm; monsoon rains from May–October.

Entry requirements
Passport and visa regulations are liable to change at short notice.
Passports
Valid passport required by all except holders of a Hong Kong Identity Card (HKIC) and nationals of China with a China Identity Card.
Visa
Required by all, except citizens of many European and Asian countries, North America and Australasia, arriving as tourists. Requirements for business visas should be obtained from the nearest Chinese consulate, well in advance of a business visit.
Currency advice/regulations
There are no restrictions on the import and export of local and foreign currencies.
Customs
Personal effects are allowed duty-free. Macao is a free port and there are no import duties, except on electrical appliances and equipment, which are subject to a 5 per cent ad valorem duty.
Registration is required for all imports and an import licence for goods subject to consumption tax, such as beverages, coffee, rice, salt, sugar, wheat, matches, tobacco, bricks, cement and mineral oils, gases, vehicles. There are no export duties on articles purchased in Macao.
As inward and outward travel is generally through Hong Kong, export/import regulations of Hong Kong must be observed.

Health (for visitors)
Mandatory precautions
No compulsory vaccinations are required.
Advisable precautions
Vaccinations for diphtheria, tuberculosis, hepatitis A and B, Japanese B encephalitis, polio, tetanus and typhoid. Rabies is a risk.

Hotels
There are around 9,000 hotels rooms. A 10 per cent service charge and 5 per cent tax are added to the bill. It is customary to leave a small tip.

Credit cards
Most major credit cards are widely accepted.

Public holidays (national)
Fixed dates
1 Jan (New Year's Day), 5 Apr (Qing Ming Festival), 1 May (Labour Day), 1 Oct (National Day of China), 2 Nov (All Souls' Day), 8 Dec (Immaculate Conception), 20 Dec (Macao Special Administrative Region Establishment Day), 22 Dec (Winter Solstice), 24–25 Dec (Christmas).
Variable dates
Chinese New Year (Jan/Feb), Easter, Birth of Buddha (Apr/May), Dragon Boat Festival (May/Jun), Mid-Autumn Festival (Sep/Oct), Chung Yeung Festival (Oct).

Working hours
Banking
Mon–Fri: 0930–1600; Sat: 0930–1230.
Business
Mon–Fri: 0900–1300, 1500–1730; Sat: 0900–1230.
Government
Mon–Fri: 0930–1800.
Shops
Mon–Sat: 1000–1900.

Electricity supply
220V AC, 50Hz in new buildings and 110V AC for most domestic supply, with various types of plug fittings.

Weights and measures
Metric system

Social customs/useful tips
It is customary to shake hands on meeting and taking leave.

Getting there
Air
National airline: Air Macau
International airport/s: Macao International (MFM), on Taipa Island, seven km south of the city.
The airport is linked to Macao via a four-lane motorway and to mainland China via a dual-lane highway. Estimated travelling time into central Macao is 10 minutes and 20 minutes to the Chinese border.
Airport tax: Pa90, paid in local currency.
Surface
Road: Macao is connected to mainland China by a short causeway. Two bridges, the Friendship and Lotus, the latter carrying a six-lane highway, link the island of Taipa with the Zhuhai Special Economic Zone.
Water: Most visitors enter via Hong Kong. There are over 100 scheduled sailings both ways during the day, and jetfoils operate round the clock (journey time 55 minutes). It is advisable to book in advance.
Main port/s: Macao harbour.

Getting about
National transport
Buses: Bus services operate 0700–2400, with services between the ferry pier and the city centre and the islands.
Rail: The proposed light rail system will connect all major ports and tourist attractions along the coast of the Macao Peninsula and the new town, Cotai, terminating at Macao International Airport. The light rail system will also connect to the inter-city express railway transport system proposed by mainland China.
City transport
Central Macao is tiny and easily walkable. It is possible to hire two-passenger triciclos (pedal rickshaws), although they are unsuitable for climbing the hills. It is advisable to agree the fare before starting the journey.
Taxis: Taxis are inexpensive and readily available. Licensed, metered taxis are mostly painted black with cream-coloured tops. Radio taxis are painted yellow.
Buses, trams & metro: Good local bus services. Transmac AP1 service runs from airport to city centre every 30 minutes, journey time 30 minutes; STCM service 21 runs every 20 minutes, journey time 30 minutes.
Car hire
Car hire is available. Driving is on the left. An international driving permit is required. The minimum driving age is 21.

BUSINESS DIRECTORY
The addresses listed below are a selection only. While World of Information makes every endeavour to check these

addresses, we cannot guarantee that changes have not been made, especially to telephone numbers and area codes. We would welcome any corrections.

Telephone area codes

The international direct dialling code (IDD) for Macao is +853, followed by subscriber's number.

Useful telephone numbers

Medical emergencies: 999
Police tourist hotline: 112
Fire: 999

Chambers of Commerce

Macao Chamber of Commerce, Edificio ACM, 175 Rua de Xangai, Macao (tel: 576-833; fax: 594-513; e-mail: acm@macauweb.com).

Banking

Banco Comercial de Macau SA, Rua da Praia Grande No 22, PO Box 545, Macao (tel: 569-622; fax: 580-967).

Banco Delta Asia SARL, 79 Avenida Conselheiro Ferreira de Almeida, Macao (tel: 559-898; fax: 570-068).

Banco Weng Hang SARL, 241 Avenida de Almeida Ribeiro, Macao (tel: 335-678; fax: 576-527).

Luso International Banking Ltd, 47 Avenida Dr Mário Soares, Macao (tel: 378-977; fax: 578-517).

Tai Fung Bank Ltd, Tai Fung Bank Headquarters Building, 418 Alameda Dr Carlos d'Assumpção, Macao (tel: 322-323; fax: 570-737).

Central bank

Monetary Authority of Macao, Calçada do Gaio 24-26, Macao City (tel: 568-288; fax: 325-432; e-mail: general@amcm.gov.mo).

Travel information

Administração de Aeropoertos (tel: 711-808; fax: 711-803).

Air Macao (tel: 396-5555; fax: 396-6866).

East Asia Airlines (tel: 790-7040).

Far East Jetfoils (tel: 790-7093).

Flight information (24 hours) (tel: 861-111).

Macao International Airport, R Dr Pedro Jose Lobo, 1—3, Edif Luso Internacional, 26 o andar, Macao (tel: 511-213; fax: 338-089; e-mail: aacm@aacm.gov.mo).

Sociedade de Turismo e Diversoes de Macao, 9 Largo do Senado, Macao (tel: 315-566; fax: 510-104).

National tourist organisation offices

Macau Government Tourist Office, PO Box 3006, 9 Edifício Largo do Leal Senado (tel: 375-156, 561-167, 555-424, fax: 510-104).

Other useful addresses

Coastal International Exhibition Co Ltd, Room 3808, China Resources Building, 26 Harbour Road, Wanchai, Hong Kong (tel: (+852) 2827-6766; fax: + 852 2827-6870; e-mail: general@coastal.com.hk).

Macao Business Support Centre (tel: 728-212; fax: 727-123, 728-213; e-mail: mbsc@ipim.gov.mo).

Macao Commercial Association (Associacão Comercial de Macão), Edifício ACM, Rua da Xanghai, 5th Floor (tel: 576-833; fax: 594-513).

Macao Export Promotions Department, 1-3 Rua Pedro José Lobo, International Building (tel: 78-221).

Macao Importers and Exporters' Association, Av do Infante D Henrique No 60-62, 30 o andar, Centro Comercial Central, Macao (tel: 553-187, 375-859; fax: 512-174; e-mail: aeim@macau.ctm.net).

Macao Industrial Association, PO Box 70, Travessa da Praia Grande No. 56 (tel: 574-125; fax: 578-305).

Macao Statistics Department, PO Box 3022, Ground Floor, Rua Inácio Baptista, 4D-6, Seaview Garden (tel: 550-935; fax: 307-825; internet site: http://www.dsec.gov.mo).

Macao Trade and Investment Promotion Institute, 1—3 Rua Dr Pedro Jose Lobo (7th/8th Floor) (e-mail: ipim@ipim.gov.mo); Investment Promotion (tel: 340-090, 712-660; fax: 712-659; internet site: http://www.ipim.gov.mo); Trade Promotion: (tel: 378-221, 710-528; fax: 590-309).

Internet sites

Macao Environment Council: http://www.ambiente.gov.mo

Macao government: http://www.macau.gov.mo

Macao Tower Convention and Entertainment Centre: http://www.gaming-exhibition.com

Macedonia

KEY FACTS

Official name: Republika Makedonija (Former Yugoslav Republic of Macedonia) (FYROM)

Head of State: President Branko Crvenkovski (since May 2004)

Head of government: Prime Minister Nikola Gruevski (from Aug 2006)

Ruling party: Coalition: For a Better Macedonia (made up of 19 parties) led by Vnatrešno-Makedonska Revoluciona Organizacija-Demokratska Partija za Makedonsko Nacionalno Edintsvo (VMRO-DPMNE) (Internal Macedonian Revolutionary Organisation-Democratic Party for Macedonian National Unity) (since 2006; re-elected 1 Jun 2008)

Area: 25,713 square km

Population: 2.05 million (2007)*

Capital: Skopje

Official language: Macedonian and Albanian.

Currency: Macedonian denar (Md) = 100 deni

Exchange rate: Md38.32 per US$ (Jul 2008); (pegged to the euro; trades around Md60 per euro)

GDP per capita: US$3,102 (2006)

GDP real growth: 5.00% (2007)*

Labour force: 974,000 (2004)

Unemployment: 37.50% (2005)*

Inflation: 2.20% (2007)

Balance of trade: -US$1.36 billion (2006)

Foreign debt: US$1.86 billion (2004)

Annual FDI: US$88.80 billion (2004)*

* estimated figure

According to the US based Heritage Foundation, Macedonia still has one of the lowest per capita GDPs in Europe, extremely high unemployment, and worrisome levels of corruption. The high level of informal economic activity also remains a concern. The Heritage Foundation goes on to note that Macedonia's economy is 61.1 per cent free, which makes it the world's 71st freest economy. Its overall score is 0.5 percentage point higher than last year, reflecting improved scores in four of the 10 economic freedoms. Macedonia is ranked 31st out of 41 countries in the European region, and its overall score is lower than the regional average.

Macedonia scores above the world average in five areas: business freedom, trade freedom, fiscal freedom, financial freedom and monetary freedom. Personal and corporate income tax rates are very low, although total tax revenue is somewhat high as a percentage of GDP. Inflation is moderate but has risen recently.

Macedonia has relatively low scores in three areas: government size, property rights and freedom from corruption. Government expenditures are high. Property rights are not secure, especially in contrast with other states in Europe, largely because the court system is prone to corruption, political interference, and inefficiency, partially as a result of political turmoil.

Small countries like Macedonia are inevitably dependent on their neighbours. Few more so than landlocked Macedonia. Positioned between a largely hostile Greece, underdeveloped Albania, unstable Kosovo, less than sympathetic Serbia and a Bulgaria with pre-occupations of its own, Macedonia could risk feeling sorry for itself. But the Macedonians are a tough lot – after all, Alexander the Great was a Macedonian, still known as 'Alexander the Macedonian' in Iran. Macedonia has received deserved praise both for economic and political achievements and was accepted as a candidate for EU membership on 17 December 2005.

International setbacks

Macedonia's bid to join Nato was vetoed by Greece at Nato's April 2008 meeting. Greece has consistently objected to the use of the name 'Macedonia' as it considers it could lead to confusion with its own province of Macedonia. As a result Prime Minister Nikola Gruevski called early general elections for April 2008 (they had not been due until 2010) in order to secure an absolute majority. He campaigned on promises not to submit to Greek pressure to change the country's name, to legislate for reforms necessary to join the EU, to tackle corruption and to reform the economy.

The result of the election was a win for Mr Gruevski's coalition of 19 parties, For a Better Macedonia, (led by Vnatrešno-Makedonska Revoluciona Organizacija-Demokratska Partija za Makedonsko Nacionalno Edintsvo (VMRO-DPMNE) (Internal Macedonian Revolutionary Organisation-Democratic Party for Macedonian National Unity)) with 48.3 per cent of the vote (64 seats out of 120 in parliament). However, fighting had disrupted the voting and both the Organisation for Security for Co-operation in Europe (OSCE) and the EU expressed concern. Although the VMRO-PDMNE coalition won an increased majority, the poll was a setback for Macedonia. Prime Minister Gruevski never-th-less set out an ambitious programme of economic development and political reform.

The economy

Macedonia's gross domestic product (GDP) growth rose to 5.0 per cent in 2007, up from 3.7 per cent in 2006. Inflation fell to 2.2 per cent from the 3.2 per cent recorded in 2006. However, unemployment in 2007 remained stubbornly high, at around the 35.0 per cent. GDP per capita in 2007 was US$3,467.

Politics

When the Macedonian government and ethnic Albanian rebels signed up to the Ohrid Peace Agreement in August 2001, it was agreed that dozens of changes to Macedonia's law code and constitution would have to be made in the interests of inter-communal harmony. Many of these, some of them potentially explosive, were addressed in 2005. In March, local elections were held – the first within new electoral boundaries drawn up under the Ohrid framework. The new boundaries were designed to accurately reflect Albanian majorities in many western towns and the March elections threatened to inflame nationalist sentiment within the titular Macedonian community. However, the election had been generally violence-free and earned praise from the EU. The OSCE noted some problems but approved overall conduct. A second potentially divisive issue was overcome in July, when parliament passed a law allowing for the flying of the Albanian flag in majority Albanian districts.

In November 2005, the European Commission had delivered a positive report on Macedonia's EU membership prospects, and recommended that EU leaders accept it as a candidate state. The UN Special Envoy to neighbouring Kosovo also lavished praise on Macedonia, citing it as a shining example of conflict resolution and post-conflict recovery. In December, EU leaders formally accepted Macedonia as a candidate state for membership, despite French reservations over the EU's capacity to absorb new members.

Outlook

Throughout the country high unemployment threatens to detract from Macedonia's efforts to stabilise its post-conflict politics and join the EU. The postponed language bill, which is supposed to help solve the issue of the Albanian language's status in Macedonia once and for all, still has to be addressed. There is pressure from the Macedonian nationalist opposition to further postpone or even sideline the bill permanently.

Further difficulties are predicted in Macedonia's judicial sphere. The NGO, the International Crisis Group (ICG), points to the risks involved in a decision by the ICTY to allow, in 2006, the Macedonian courts to deal with pending war crimes charges against four Macedonian nationals. The ICG suggests that the Macedonian judiciary is at present incapable of dealing with the trials, a point already foreshadowed by the EU Commission in November 2005. Such trials could present a welcome boost to the anti-government nationalist forces.

Risk assessment

Politics	Poor
Economy	Poor
Regional stability	Fair

COUNTRY PROFILE

Historical profile

Macedonia has been occupied by the Greeks, Romans, Bulgarians, Byzantines, Serbs and the Ottoman Turks. It is jokingly known as the home of both the fruit salad of the same name, and Alexander the Great (known in Iran as Alexander of Macedonia).

1371 The Ottoman Turks conquered the area and retained control until the nineteenth century.

1893 The Vnatrešno-Makedonska Revoluciona Organizacija (VMRO) (Internal Macedonian Revolutionary Organisation) was founded to gain independence from the Ottoman Empire.

1912–13 During the Balkan conflicts, the Turks were driven out and the area was

KEY INDICATORS Macedonia

	Unit	2003	2004	2005	2006	2007
Population	m	2.13	2.13	2.04	*2.04	*2.05
Gross domestic product (GDP)	US$bn	4.70	5.44	5.78	6.34	*7.50
GDP per capita	US$	1,900	2,295	2,836	3,102	3,647
GDP real growth	%	3.0	2.3	3.8	3.7	*5.0
Inflation	%	2.5	-0.3	0.5	3.2	2.2
Unemployment	%	37.0	36.7	37.5	36.0	34.9
Industrial output	% change	–	0.7	4.5	2.8	–
Agricultural output	% change	–	6.2	3.1	0.6	–
Exports (fob) (goods)	US$m	1,358.0	1,629.0	2,041.0	2,396.3	–
Imports (cif) (goods)	US$m	2,324.0	2,677.0	3,228.0	3,681.5	–
Balance of trade	US$m	-966.0	-1,048.0	-1,187.0	-1,285.2	–
Current account	US$m	-149.0	-414.8	-81.4	-23.7	*-202.0
Total reserves minus gold	US$m	897.7	905.0	1,228.5	1,750.6	2,082.3
Foreign exchange	US$m	897.4	904.2	1,227.7	1,747.6	2,080.8
Foreign direct investment (FDI)	US$bn	9,460.0	155.9	100.0	351.0	–
Exchange rate	per US$	53.91	47.00	47.12	47.12	42.43

* estimated figure

divided between Serbia and Greece, with a small section being retained by Bulgaria.
1918 Macedonia became part of the new Kingdom of Serbs, Croats and Slovenes along with parts of Bosnia-Hercegovina, Croatia, parts of Dalmatia, Montenegro, Serbia, Slavonia and Slovenia.
1929 The Kingdom was renamed Yugoslavia.
1941–45 Macedonia was occupied by Bulgaria, under German direction. The Partisans, led by Josip Broz Tito – also leader of the Communist Party of Yugoslavia (CPY) – eventually liberated the whole of Yugoslavia.
1945 Following the end of the Second World War, Macedonia became one of the constituent republics of a federated Yugoslavia. Tito assumed power and a Soviet-style constitution was adopted. The other republics were Bosnia-Hercegovina, Croatia, Slovenia, Montenegro, Serbia and the two autonomous regions of Vojvodina and Kosovo.
1953 Constitutions adopted in 1953, 1963 and 1974 increased the autonomy extended to the constituent republics.
1990 Following the collapse of communism in Yugoslavia, Macedonia held its first multi-party elections and the VMRO became the largest party in parliament.
1991 The first multi-party National Assembly was officially constituted. After a referendum in which the people voted overwhelmingly in favour of Macedonian sovereignty and independence, Macedonia declared its independence.
1992 Kiro Gligorov, the former communist leader, was elected president. A new currency, the denar, was adopted on 26 April.
1993 Greece showed consternation over Macedonia's choice of name and flag which the Greek government argued were a claim on its northern province of Macedonia. To accommodate Greek concerns, Macedonia eventually agreed to join the UN with the temporary prefix of 'Former Yugoslav Republic (of Macedonia (FYROM))' and an alternative national flag design was introduced.
1994 Kiro Gligorov was re-elected president. Greece imposed a partial trade embargo on Macedonia.
1995 An accord resulting in a normalisation of relations between Greece and Macedonia ensured that Macedonians had access to the northern Greek port of Thessaloniki, their nearest outlet to the sea.
1998 A coalition government under the leadership of Ljubco Georgievski was formed after elections.
1999 Amid accusations of electoral irregularities from the opposition, Boris Trajkovski of the Vnatrešno-Makedonska Revoluciona Organizacija-Demokratska Partija za Makedonsko Nacionalno Edintsvo (VMRO-DPMNE) (Internal Macedonian Revolutionary Organisation-Democratic Party for Macedonian National Unity) was elected president.
2000 A coalition government was formed and led by Prime Minister Georgievski.
2001 There were clashes between ethnic Albanian guerrillas and police in Tetovo and other parts of Macedonia. A cease-fire was brokered and a NATO force was sent to Macedonia to supervise the collection of arms handed in by ethnic Albanian rebels. The Ohrid Agreement was signed in August, paving the way for political reforms to enhance the status of the ethnic Albanian population within Macedonia. In April, the Macedonian government signs a Stabilisation and Association Agreement (SAA) with the EU, aimed at bringing Macedonia into line with EU political, economic and social norms.
2002 After parliamentary elections, the Socijaldemockratski Sojuz na Makedonija (SDSM) (Social Democratic Alliance of Macedonia) leader, Branko Crvenkovski, became prime minister, heading a multi-ethnic, 10-member coalition government.
2003 The EU took over NATO's military mission in Macedonia in March to oversee implementation of the Ohrid Agreement. On 4 April, Macedonia joined the World Trade Organisation (WTO).
2004 President Boris Trajkovski died in a plane crash in February; Parliament Speaker Ljupco Jordanovski became acting president. On 22 March, Macedonia formally submitted its application to join the EU. In the first round of presidential elections on 14 April, Prime Minister Branko Crvenkovski won 42.9 per cent of the vote; he went on to win the second round on 28 April and was sworn in as president on 12 May. Hari Kostov became prime minister and formed a new government. In November, an opposition-backed referendum designed to repeal the laws giving minority Albanians in Macedonia greater autonomy, failed after a low turnout; the unexpected announcement by the US to recognise Macedonia by its constitutional name, the Republic of Macedonia, just prior to the referendum was widely credited with helping to defeat the referendum; Prime Minister Kostov resigned as a result of disputes within the ruling coalition and on 26 November, Vlado Buckovski was named as prime minister.
2005 In March, local elections were held, the first under redrawn electoral boundaries, as stipulated in the Ohrid Agreement. Despite fears of inter-communal tension, EU oberservers reported a high turnout and few irregularities. The leaders of the EU member states agreed to granted EU candidate status to Macedonia in December.
2006 The opposition VMRO-DPMNE won most votes in the general elections with 32.5 per cent (44 out of 120 seats), the ruling SDSM won 23.3 per cent (32). Turnout was 56 per cent.
2007 The name of Skopje's airport was proposed to be changed in January to Aleksandar Makedonski (Alexander of Macedonia, or Alexander the Great) Airport. This provoked criticism from Greece which disputes the exploitation of what it sees as its heritage and cultural iconography.
2008 The ongoing disagreement between Greece and FYROM Macedonia concerning the name Macedonia was again a cause of dissent in March. Greece threatened to block membership of NATO unless its neighbour dropped its name, Macedonia. NATO believes membership for Macedonia will avert a division within Macedonia, whereby the Slav majority in the east parts company from the Albanian minority in the west. Following months of deadlock concerning the rights of the country's minority Albanian community, parliament was dissolved and early parliamentary elections were scheduled for 1 June. In these elections, the coalition of 19 parties, For a Better Macedonia, led by Prime Minister Nikola Gruevski's VMRO-DPMNE, won 48.3 per cent of the vote (64 seats out of 120), the Sun – Coalition for Europe, won 23.4 per cent (28 seats); turnout was 58 per cent.

Political structure

Constitution

Under the constitution, adopted on 17 November 1991, the Former Yugoslav Republic of Macedonia (FYROM) is a sovereign, independent, democratic and socially responsive state. There is universal suffrage from age 18. The constitution guarantees the free expression of national identity, the rule of law (including international law) and the legal protection of property. The principles of a free commercial market, urban and rural planning and environmental protection are also enshrined in the constitution.
Constitutional amendments to give the ethnic Albanian minority more rights were endorsed by parliament in November 2001.

Form of state

Parliamentary democratic republic

The executive

The executive is headed by the president, directly elected every five years. The prime minister appoints a cabinet of 20 ministers, who must be approved by a majority of the country's national assembly.

National legislature
The national legislature is the unicameral Sobranje (National Assembly). The Sobranje has 120 members elected every four years, 85 by direct election and 35 by proportional representation.
Legal system
Judicial powers are vested in courts which are nominally independent of government under the terms of the 1991 constitution. In practice, the judiciary remains politicised, especially in cases involving ethnic Albanians and other minorities. All civil and criminal cases are dealt with by courts of general jurisdiction. The Supreme Court is the highest court. Elected by parliament, the Judicial Council appoints and dismisses all judges and other judicial officials. The judicial system is the administrative responsibility of the justice ministry. There is a public prosecutor. The Constitutional Court decides on the conformity of national legislation with the 1991 constitution.
Macedonia is aiming to harmonise its laws and judicial standards with those of the EU and the Council of Europe, but progress is slow.
Last elections
14/28 April 2004 (presidential); 1 June 2008 (parliamentary).
Results: Presidential: Branko Crvenkovski won 60.6 per cent; Sasko Kedev won 39.4 per cent.
Parliamentary: the coalition of 19 parties, For a Better Macedonia, (led by VMRO-DPMNE) won 48.3 per cent of the vote (64 seats out of 120), the Sun – Coalition for Europe, won 23.4 per cent (28 seats), the Bashkimi Demokratik për Integrim, (BDI) won 11.13 per cent (13), the Partia Demokratike Shqiptare (PDS) (Democratic Party of Albania) won 10.5 per cent (13), all other parties won less than 2 per cent. Turnout was 58 per cent.
Next elections
2009 (presidential); 2012 (parliamentary)

Political parties

Ruling party
Coalition: For a Better Macedonia (made up of 19 parties) led by Vnatrešno-Makedonska Revoluciona Organizacija-Demokratska Partija za Makedonsko Nacionalno Edintsvo (VMRO-DPMNE) (Internal Macedonian Revolutionary Organisation-Democratic Party for Macedonian National Unity) (since 2006; re-elected 1 Jun 2008)
Main opposition party
Coalition of nine parties led by Za Makedonija Zaedno (For Macedonia Together) multi-ethnic 10-member coalition led by the Socijaldemockratski Sojuz na Makedonija (SDSM) (Social Democratic Alliance of Macedonia)

Population
2.05 million (2007)*
Last census: November 2002: 2,022,547
Population density: 79 inhabitants per square km. Urban population: 62 per cent of total (1994–2000).
Annual growth rate: 0.4 per cent 1994–2004 (WHO 2006)
Internally Displaced Persons (IDP)
3,000 (UNHCR 2004)
Ethnic make-up
Macedonian (63 per cent), Albanian (30 per cent), Turkish (4 per cent), Romanian (3 per cent). The Albanians are concentrated in Tetovo, Gostivar and other parts of the north-west.
Religions
The official religion is Macedonian Orthodox Christianity, which is practised by approximately two-thirds of the population. Muslims (over a quarter of the population) and Roman Catholics practise openly.

Education

The educational system is entirely state-controlled. During the 1990s, independence from Yugoslavia meant an end to federal subsidies, resulting in declining educational provision in Macedonia. Politically, the issue of ethnic Albanian access to higher education in the Albanian language has been the cause of great controversy and even violence in Macedonia.
Primary schooling lasts for eight years and is followed by attendance at either a general secondary school for academic students or at a variety of technical, specialist or vocational schools. After four years, in whichever mode of school, students must undertake examination before advancement to the second, three-year stage. Courses may last until students are aged 19.
There are three universities in Macedonia: Skopje, Bitola and Tetovo. The Albanian-language University at Tetovo is legalised and classified by parliament as an accredited private institution.
Compulsory years: Seven to 15.
Enrolment rate: 99 per cent total primary enrolment of relevant age group (including repetition rates); 63 per cent total secondary enrolment (World Bank).

Health

Per capita total expenditure on health (2003) was US$389; of which per capita government spending was US$329, at the international dollar rate, (WHO 2006).
The standard of state healthcare is low compared to the rest of the former Yugoslavia, the basic healthcare infrastructure has declined mainly due to the lack of funds to replace essential equipment and retain doctors in the state sector.
Healthcare provision has increasingly involved extra charges, notably for medication, leading to a large black market in healthcare services. Most healthcare professionals are either in semi-private or private practice and some parts of the healthcare system have been privatised.
Externally, Macedonia received considerable international aid for local healthcare during the 1990s.
Improved water sources and sanitation facilities are available to 99 per cent of the population.
HIV/Aids
HIV prevalence: 0.1 per cent aged 15–49 in 2003 (World Bank)
Life expectancy: 72 years, 2004 (WHO 2006)
Fertility rate/Maternal mortality rate: 1.5 births per woman, 2004 (WHO 2006); maternal mortality three per 100,000 live births (World Bank).
Child (under 5 years) mortality rate (per 1,000): 10 per 1,000 live births; and 5.9 per cent of children aged under five are malnourished (World Bank).
Head of population per physician: 2.19 physicians per 1,000 people, 2001 (WHO 2006)

Welfare

Welfare provision was heavily subsidised by budgetary transfers from outside Macedonia during the Yugoslav period, when retirement pensions and other welfare benefits were relatively generous at around 80 per cent of average monthly income. Consequently, the state pension fund experienced major financial problems after independence. Welfare benefits declined sharply, aggravated by spells of high inflation. The IMF and other official creditors have made loans available in recent years for the state pension fund and unemployment benefit outlays. The foreign exchange remittances of emigrants plays a major role in the economic support of many Macedonians.

Main cities

Skopje (capital, estimated population 460,239 in 2005), Bitola (70,423), Kumanovo (80,173), Prilep (68,472), Tetovo (51,258).

Languages spoken

Macedonian (Slavic) is written using the Cyrillic alphabet.
The Albanian minority campaigned successfully to have its language officially recognised as the country's second language. Turkish, Serbian, Croatian and Romani are also spoken.
English, French and German are often understood.
Official language/s
Macedonian and Albanian.

Media

Press

Dailies: Nearly all newspapers are privately-owned. The most widely-read dailies, Nova Makedonija, Dnevnik, Vecer, the Albanian-language Flaka e Vellazerimit and the Turkish-language Birlik are 33 per cent state-owned. Other national newspapers include Denes, M-Express, Nova and Utrenski Vesnik. Major daily news services in Macedonia are available online from the Macedonian Media (http://www.makedonija.com), Macedonian Information Center (http://www.makedonija.com/mic/index.html) and the Macedonian Information and Liason Service (http://www.soros.org.mk/mn/mils.html).

Weeklies: During the 1990s, there was a proliferation of new weekly and periodical titles, but the finances of many are extremely precarious. Some have had to turn to foreign funding sources, notably the Soros Foundation, which has also provided economic aid to the Macedonian government. Weekly publications include Economic Press featuring economics and finance. Other weekly publications include the bi-weekly FORUM magazine, Makedonsko Sonce (English/Macedonian) and Start in Macedonian.

Periodicals: The government has provided resources for a number of high quality English-language titles, notably Balkan Forum.

Broadcasting

Makedonska Radio Televizija (MKRTV) (Macedonian Radio and Television) is the state broadcasting monopoly. As in other former Yugoslav republics, government control of TV and radio broadcasting is tight. However, radio broadcasting has been liberalised and a number of smaller privately-owned broadcasters have been established.

Other than MKRTV, Bulgarian, Serbian, Albanian, Turkish and Greek broadcasting output is easily available in Macedonia. Satellite dish and VCR ownership is also growing very fast.

Economy

There were two major challenges facing the government in 2006 which were interrelated and interdependent: sustained growth and high unemployment. The economy has been showing steady signs of improvement, sustained and growing, after a decade since 1993/04 when the new currency (denar) was introduced and macroeconomic stabilisation was largely achieved.

In 2005, the service sector accounted for 59 per cent of GDP, agriculture 12 per cent and industry 29 per cent, of which manufacturing was 18 per cent. GDP growth was 3.8 per cent and was expected to be 4.0 per cent in 2006 as well as 2007. Unemployment was exceptionally high at 36.7 per cent and the IMF, in an October 2006 country report, recommended that more structural reforms should be undertaken to 'improve the quality of institutions', such as judicial reform, government transparency and a liberalised telecommunications industry. A functioning market economy should be fostered through labour market reforms, the IMF has suggested to include a lower tax wedge and the removal of tax discrimination for part-time workers. The financial sector needed bank consolidation and revised banking laws with enhanced supervision.

Macedonia has weathered trade embargoes, hyperinflation in the early 1990s, regional conflict and an internal security crisis, all of which hampered the creation of a market economy. However, it has yet to overcome an ageing industrial infrastructure from years of under-investment and the lack of job opportunities which lead many skilled workers to migrate. In November 2005, the EU Commission recommended that Macedonia be granted EU candidate status, with one of the conditions being the continuation of economic reforms. Joining the EU club may provide the lasting stability and opportunity that Macedonia needs to grow.

External trade

Export trade represents a high proportion of the economy and provides 107 per cent of GDP. Macedonia has signed a Stabilization and Association Agreement with the EU and has duty free access to EU markets. It is expected to become a full EU member by 2010.

The garment manufacturing sector has grown steadily and in 2007 was the largest single employer of industrial workers (over 30 per cent). However, most manufacturing is subcontracted and garments are intermediate goods with imported fabric being sewn for international firms who retail clothes elsewhere at the lowest price.

Macedonia is set to earn annual transit fees from the new 895km Balkan oil pipeline (AMBO), from Burgas, on the Black Sea (Bulgaria) to the port of Vlore, in southern Albania. The trilateral agreement contract was signed on 31 January 2007; the project is estimated to cost is US$1.2 billion and has a supply target of 750,000 barrels per day with construction due to begin in late 2008.

Imports

Principal imports are hydrocarbons, machinery iron, steel and chemicals, foodstuffs and vehicles.

Main sources: Russia (15.1 per cent total, 2006), Germany (9.8 per cent), Greece (8.5 per cent).

Exports

Principal exports are garments, tobacco, food and beverages, machinery and equipment, iron and steel and chemicals.

Main destinations: Serbia and Montenegro (23.2 per cent total, 2006), Greece (15.6 per cent), Germany (15.0 per cent).

Agriculture

Farming

The agricultural sector accounts for 13 per cent of GDP and employs 30 per cent of the workforce.

Agricultural land totals 1.3 million hectares (ha), of which approximately half is cultivable and half is pasture. Macedonia has propitious conditions for agriculture and is nearly self-sufficient in food production. The private sector accounts for over 75 per cent of agricultural production.

The government has allowed a systematic break-up of the old agrokombinats, or collectivised farms. As a result, privately owned farms now account for 90 per cent of annual output, although each farm is rarely more than 25ha. New private company formation in agriculture is also growing rapidly.

On the negative side, the state still directly controls 30 per cent of all arable land, or around 300,000ha. Markedly less productive than the private sector, state farms and co-operatives are scheduled to be privatised in due course, although this remains politically controversial. Local agriculture is one of the few sectors of interest to potential foreign investors due to the cultivation of higher value cash crops (particularly tobacco) with ready markets in the EU, and cheap labour costs. Economically, the government now regards agriculture as a major area for future growth and development, including increased foreign direct investment (FDI).

Crop production in 2005 included: 628,486 tonnes (t) cereals in total, 329,871t wheat, 137,000t maize, 220,000t potatoes, 135,571t barley, 27,714t pulses, 5,147t treenuts, 248,000t grapes, 113,000t tomatoes, 28,000t tobacco, 14,000t olives, 52,200t sugar beets, 82,400t apples, 110,000t chillies and peppers, 394,695t fruit in total, 446,380t vegetables in total. Livestock production included: 28,416t meat in total, 10,000t beef, 10,000t pig meat, 7,500t lamb, 4,000t poultry, 19,000t eggs, 263,000t milk, 1,000t honey, 1,520t cattle hides, 1,140t sheepskins, 3,176t greasy wool.

Macedonia has a small fishing industry, which catches freshwater fish for domestic consumption.

Forestry

Forest and other wooded land account for about two-fifths of the land area, equivalent to approximately 906,000ha. More than four-fifths of the forest is available for wood supply. Forest resources supply an active forestry industry producing approximately 774,000 cubic metres (cum) of timber per annum.

Forest wood is mainly used for fuel, while hardwood processed in local sawmills is largely exported. Domestic demand for softwoods and paper is met by imports.

Annual exports of forest products amount to US$8.1 million while imports amount to US$68.6 million in 2004.

Production in 2004 included 831,000cum roundwood, 132,000cum industrial roundwood, 27,919cum sawnwood, 126,000cum sawlogs and veneers, 699,000cum woodfuel.

Industry and manufacturing

Industry and manufacturing account for nearly 35 per cent of GDP. Macedonia retains a relatively industrialised economy inherited from the Yugoslav period. During the 1990s, the collapse of the Yugoslav market and subsequent regional conflict, the loss of former Soviet markets, the Greek economic blockade and resultant energy shortages all had devastating consequences for Macedonian industrial output.

Although privatisation of smaller industries has been largely completed, sell-offs of larger industries are still at an early stage. State industries suffer from overstaffing, slow growth, a slow rate of change in the structure of production and ailing technology.

Industrial production in 2004 was stagnant at 0.0 per cent.

Tourism

Macedonia's nascent tourist industry is primarily based at the lakeside town of Ohrid. Summer tourism is concentrated around the lakes and the national parks. Lakes Ohrid, Prespa, Dojran and Mavrovo cover a total water surface of 679 square km.

Winter tourism is developing in several ski resorts; there are 14 mountain massifs with peaks over 2,000 metres and perpetual Alpine climatic conditions. Both summer and winter tourism offer good potential for development.

Interesting archaeological sites exist, as well as numerous mosaics, frescoes and icons, the earliest dating from Roman times, in monasteries, churches and mosques. The old part of Ohrid town is a UN Educational, Scientific and Cutural Organisation (Unesco)-protected World Heritage Site, as is the lake itself.

Macedonia's tourism sector suffered heavily during the war in Kosovo (1999) and inter-ethnic fighting within Macedonia itself (2001). Tourist arrivals increased by 6.8 per cent in 2003, compared to 2002.

Environment

The Vardar, Macedonia's main river, collects the waste from several towns with no treatment facilities before flowing through Greece to the Aegean Sea. A system for monitoring the waterways and a project for communal water treatment for six towns have been initiated by the Macedonian government.

Macedonia and Albania participate in the Lake Ohrid Conservation Project (LOCP) which is a bilateral project supported by the World Bank.

Mining

Macedonia is an important producer of metals and mines significant quantities of copper and lead-zinc ores, ferroalloys and some silver. There is also some chromium production from reserves that overlap with those of nearby Albania. The aluminium and copper ore production is centred on Alumina AD in Skopje and 'Bucim' Radovis DM in Radovis respectively. There is also significant quarrying of decorative and architectural building stone.

The mining sector in Macedonia has had little chance for growth due to regional instability and depressed market conditions. The various conflicts in the former Yugoslavia have created a regional dislocation of transportation of cargoes on the Danube river, shifting the route of exports through the port of Thessaloniki in Greece at a huge cost. This financial burden has diminished Macedonia's production of hot and cold rolled steel to about 30 per cent of capacity, and the export of finished products by Balkan Steel International (BSI).

However, it was not regional dislocation that affected some companies that have traditionally exported through Greece. Their production fell or ceased due to shortage of foreign investment and adverse market conditions. Foreign investment and participation has been restricted to the steel industry (Duferco and BSI), petroleum refining (Hellenic Petroleum) and cement (Titan Cement and Holderbank Financiere Glaris).

Hydrocarbons

Macedonia has no significant domestic production of oil, requiring imports to supply domestic consumption. The oil distribution network is largely state-run. The refining company Okta runs the country's oil refineries. Hellenic Petroleum owns 54 per cent of Okta while the other 46 per cent is state owned. Russian oil companies have expressed an interest in purchasing Macedonia's oil refineries with the 2004 privatisation plan. In December 2004, Macedonia signed a US$1.2 billion agreement with Bulgaria and Albania that provided for the construction of a trans-Balkans oil pipeline. The pipeline will connect the Black Sea with the Adriatic, via the Bulgarian port of Burgas and the Albanian port of Vlores, and will transport Russian and Caspian oil that would otherwise flow through the Bosphorus. The pipeline is expected to be completed by 2008.

The country does not produce or import significant quantities of natural gas. However Macedonia is planning to use natural gas as its main source of energy in the future, so it is interested in improving natural gas transportation. The reconstruction of the existing Skopje-Oblic (Pristina) gas pipeline is planned to meet the growing natural gas demand. Macedonia has a gas pipeline of 100km in length from Deve Bair to Skopje with a connection to the international gas pipeline in Bulgaria that supplies Greece with natural gas. The pipeline transfers over 800 million cubic metres per annum as part of a wider Russian gas export pipeline network in the Balkan region.

Macedonia has large reserves of coal, estimated at more than one billion tonnes, which should last for the foreseeable future at the annual production rate of 8.9 million tonnes. Most local coal output is low grade lignite which is used extensively for domestic energy production. Higher quality anthracite coals and coke (approximately 130,000 tonnes per annum) have to be imported for some primary electricity generation and the local metallurgical industry.

Energy

Four-fifths of energy needs are satisfied by domestic production of thermoelectric and hydroelectric power; the deficit is imported from Serbia and Montenegro and Bulgaria.

A number of new hydroelectric power plants are being built and plans are being considered by the government to modernise some of Macedonia's older power plants.

Financial markets

Stock exchange

The Macedonia Stock Exchange (MSE) was co-founded by eight commercial banks and two new brokerage companies in 1995. Its significance has grown thanks to privatisation, but it remains a limited source of investment.

Banking and insurance

There are seven major public lending and savings banks in Macedonia, as well as several smaller private commercial credit banks. The sector is dominated by Stopanska Banka, which has approximately 65 per cent of domestic banking assets and 50 per cent of banking deposits.

The republic has a tiered banking structure. The Narodna banka na Republika Makedonija (NBRM) (National Bank of the Republic of Macedonia) is responsible for the money supply, the liquidity of financial institutions and foreign currency transactions and reserves. The banking system requires a major overhaul. Competition is being introduced with the emergence of private credit institutions such as Uniprokom. International institutions are providing loans.

Central bank

Narodna banka na Republika Makedonija (NBRM) (National Bank of the Republic of Macedonia)

Time

GMT plus one hour (daylight saving, late March to late September, GMT plus two hours)

Geography

Situated in south-eastern Europe on the Balkan peninsula, Macedonia, or Vardar Macedonia, is part of a wider historical and geographical region of the same name. Part of this ancient territory, known as Pirin Macedonia, is situated in modern-day Greece. Roughly rectangular in shape, Macedonia is bordered by Serbia to the north (Kosovo province to the north-west and Serbia to the north-east), Albania to the west, Bulgaria to the east and Greece to the south. Geographically, the republic is dominated by the Balkan Mountains and the Vardar River, which flows north-west to south-east.

Macedonia's strategic importance is out of all proportion to its small size, population and economic resources. On the negative side, its small size and lack of direct access to the sea makes Macedonia very vulnerable to its stronger neighbours in the southern Balkans.

Macedonia's major geographic characteristics are two large inland lakes, Ohrid and Prespa, which are shared with Albania and Greece. Lake Ohrid is a Unesco-designated World Heritage Site.

Hemisphere

Northern

Climate

The river valleys of Vardar and Strumica are temperate Mediterranean, as is the eastern region. Western and northern regions are temperate continental. However, temperatures may vary from 40 degrees Celsius (C) in the summer to minus 30 degrees C in the winter. Rainfall averages 742 millimetres annually, but around 450 millimetres in Skopje which has about 100 days of rain annually. Skopje can be very hot in the summer and shrouded in mist in the winter.

Dress codes

Informal dress is tolerated in Macedonia, but should be avoided in business contexts, notably in Skopje.

Entry requirements

Passports

Required by all, with three months validity beyond date of stay.

Visa

Required by all, except nationals of EU/EEA and most CIS countries, US, New Zealand, Japan, Malaysia, Israel, Botswana, Argentina, Cuba and Barbados. Visitors should contact the nearest consulate to confirm their visa status and requirements before travelling.

Business visas require a letter of invitation from a local company, submitted with the application.

Prohibited entry

Currency advice/regulations

There are no restrictions on the import and export of local or foreign currency.

Health (for visitors)

Medical care in private facilities or by private practitioners is not covered by insurance. Foreigners are entitled to medical care in state medical facilities and those staying for a year or more have a right to full medical coverage. Temporary visitors and those in transit are entitled to basic necessities and emergency first-aid treatment, but payment in cash is expected, regardless of insurance cover.

Mandatory precautions

None

Advisable precautions

Vaccinations are recommended for hepatitis A and, if expecting to eat or drink outside main hotels and restaurants, typhoid. Food and water precautions should be observed. Public health is poor in certain parts of Macedonia.

Hotels

There are around 90 hotels in Macedonia. There is one first-class hotel, in Skopje.

Public holidays (national)

Fixed dates

1–2 Jan (New Year), 6-7 Jan (Orthodox Christmas), 14 Jan (Orthodox New Year's Day), 8 Mar (Women's Day), 1 May (Labour Day), 24 May (SS Cyrilus and Methodius Day), 2 Aug (Ilinden Day), 8 Sep (Independence Day), 11 Oct (National Day).

Variable dates

Orthodox Easter Monday, Eid al Adha, Eid al Fitr.

Working hours

Banking

Mon–Fri: 0730–1930; Sat: 0800–1300.

Business

Mon–Fri: 0800–1600 or 0830–1630.

Government

Mon–Fri: 0700–1500 or 0730–1530.

Shops

Mon–Fri: 0800–1200 and 1700–2000/2100, but many shops open throughout day; Sat: 0800–1500.

Telecommunications

Mobile/cell phones

GSM 900 roaming facilities are available with coverage throughout the country. Services are provided by Cosmofon and MobiMak.

Electricity supply

220V AC 50Hz with two large round prongs.

Weights and measures

Metric system.

Social customs/useful tips

Macedonians are a friendly people, although less gregarious then their Serbian neighbours in the Balkans. Similar to the Bulgarians, they are also practically minded.

Political discussions of any sort are best avoided altogether by foreigners. There are strict laws against drinking and driving, speeding and other traffic offences. They are rigorously enforced.

Security

Car theft is very common. Local ownership of firearms is high. Visitors are advised to keep themselves informed of political developments.

Getting there

Air

National airline: Makedonski Aviotransport (MAT) (Macedonian Airlines)

International airport/s: Skopje (SKP), 25km from city, post office, restaurants, duty-free shop; Ohrid (OHD, 10km from city.

Air traffic control systems are not up to European standards and the airports are by-passed by many international carriers and used primarily by regional airlines.

Airport tax: None.

Surface

Road: Bus services operate along the main routes connecting Albania, Bulgaria, Greece and Serbia.

Rail: Several international railway lines pass through Skopje, including the Ljuljan-Athens and Budapest-Athens services. Intercity trains provide connections between Skopje and Belgrade (Serbia) and Thessaloniki (Greece).

Getting about

National transport

Air: There are no regular scheduled flights, although occasional flights between Ohrid and Skopje are available.

Road: There are 4,876km of modernised roads. The main road is between Ohrid and Tetovo.

Rail: There are 922km of railway lines, of which 231km are electrified. The main terminals are at Skopje, Bitola and Gevgelija on the Greek border, Kicevo in the west of the country and Kriva Palanka on the Bulgarian border.

City transport

Taxis: Good service operating in all main cities. Licensed taxis are metered, but the fare should be agreed before the journey. A 10 per cent tip is usual. Unmarked taxis should be avoided.

Buses, trams & metro: Most city centres are served by trams, and the suburbs by buses. The service is generally cheap and regular.

Car hire

Limited availability in Skopje, but very expensive. Special insurance is required for travel to certain parts of the country. An international driving licence is required. Hired cars generally have to be paid for in foreign exchange.

BUSINESS DIRECTORY

The addresses listed below are a selection only. While World of Information makes every endeavour to check these addresses, we cannot guarantee that changes have not been made, especially to telephone numbers and area codes. We would welcome any corrections.

Telephone area codes

The international direct diallng code (IDD) for Macedonia is +389 followed by the area code and subscriber's number:

Gostivar	42	Prilep	48
Kicevo	45	Skopje	2
Kochani	33	Tetovo	44
Kumanovo	31	Veles	43

Useful telephone numbers

Police: 92
Fire: 93
Ambulance: 94
Time: 95
Telegrams: 96
Telephone service: 977
Report emergencies: 985
Emergency road service: 987
Telephone information: 988

Chambers of Commerce

American Chamber of Commerce in Macedonia, 13 Juli Street 20, 1000 Skopje (tel: 3123-873; fax: 3123-872; e-mail: contact@amcham.com.mk).

Economic Chamber of Macedonia, Dimitrie Cupovski Street 13, PO Box 324, 1000 Skopje (tel: 3118-088; fax: 3116-210; e-mail: ic@ic.mchamber.org.mk).

Skopje Regional Chamber, Partizanski Odredi Boulevard 2, PO Box 509, 1000 Skopje (tel: 3112-511; fax: 3116-419; e-mail: regkomsk@regkom.org.mk).

Banking

Balkanska Banka, 6 Maksim Gorki, Skopje (tel: 3127-155; fax: 3132-186).
Eksport Import Banka, Dame Gruev 14, PO Box 836, Skopje (tel: 3133-411; fax: 3112-744; e-mail: info@eximpb.com.mk).

Invest Banka , Makedonija 9/11, Skopje (tel: 3114-166; fax: 3135-528).

Izvozna i Kreditna Banka, 11 Oktomvri 8, Skopje (tel: 3122-207; fax: 3122-393).

Komercijalna Banka, Kej Dimitar Vlahov 4, PO Box 563, Skopje (tel: 3112-077; fax: 3111-780; e-mail: international@kb.com.mk).

Kreditna Banka Skopje, Dame Gruev, Skopje (tel: 3116-433; fax: 3116-830).

Makedonska Banka, Bul. VMRO 3-12/2, Skopje (tel: 3117-111; fax: 3117-191; e-mail: info@makbanka.com.mk).

Radobank, Jurij Gagarin 17, Skopje (tel: 3393-300; fax: 3380-453; e-mail: radobank@radobank.com.mk).

Sileks Banka, Gradski Zid, Blok 9, Lokal 5, Skopje (tel: 3115-288; fax: 3114-891).

Stopanska Banka, 11 Oktomvri 7, Skopje (tel: 3191-191; fax: 3114-503; e-mail: sbank@stb.com.mk).

Teteks Bank, Naroden Front 19a, Skopje (tel: 3127-449; fax: 3131-419).

Tutunska Banka, 12 Udarna brigada bb, PO Box 702, Skopje (tel: 3105-600; fax: 3164-068; e-mail: tbanka@tb.com.mk).

Zemjodelska Banka, Vasil Glavinov 28/2, Skopje (tel: 3112-699; fax: 3224-844).

Central bank

National Bank of the Republic of Macedonia, PO Box 401, Kompleks banki bb, 1000 Skopje (tel: 3108-108; fax: 3108-357; e-mail: governorsoffice@nbrm.gov.mk).

Travel information

Macedonian Airlines (MAT), Vasil Glavinov 3, Skopje (tel: 3292-333; fax: 3229-576; e-mail: mathq@mat.com.mk).

Ohrid Airport, PO Box 134, Ohrid (tel: 252-820; fax: 252-840; e-mail: ohdap@airports.com.mk).

Skopje Airport, Skopje (tel: 148-300; fax: 148-360; e-mail: skpap@airports.com.mk).

Tourist Association of Skopje, Dame Gruev Gradski, Blok 3, PO Box 399, Skopje (tel: 3118-498; fax: 3230-803; e-mail: info@skopjetourism.org).

Ministries

Ministry of Agriculture, Forestry and Water, Leninova 2, Skopje (tel: 3134-477; fax: 3211-997).

Ministry of Culture, Bul. Ilinden bb, Skopje (tel: 3118-022; fax: 3127-112).

Ministry of Defence, Orce Nikolov bb, Skopje (tel: 3119-872; fax:3 221-808; e-mail: info@morm.gov.mk).

Ministry of Economy, Bote Bocevski bb, Skopje (tel: 3113-705; fax: 3111-541; e-mail: ms@mt.net.mk).

Ministry of Education and Science, Dimitrija Chupovski 9, Skopje (tel: 3117-277; fax: 3118-414; e-mail: contact@mofk.gov.mk).

Ministry of Environment and Urban Planning, Drezdenska 52, Skopje (tel: 3366-930; fax: 3366-931; e-mail: info@moe.gov.mk).

Ministry of Finance, Dame Gruev 14, Skopje (tel: 3117-288; fax: 3117-280).

Ministry of Foreign Affairs, Dame Gruev 6, Skopje (tel: 3110-330; fax: 3115-790; e-mail: mailmnr@mnr.gov.mk).

Ministry of Health, Vodnjanska bb, Skopje (tel: 3147-147; fax: 3113-014).

Ministry of Internal Affairs, Dimce Mircev bb, Skopje (tel: 3117-222; fax: 3112-468).

Ministry of Justice, Dimitrija Chupovski 9, Skopje (tel: 3117-277; fax: 3226-975).

Ministry of Labour and Social Policy, Dame Gruev 14, Skopje (tel: 3117-288; fax: 3118-242).

Ministry of Local Self-Government, Dimitrija Chupovski 9, Skopje (tel: 3117-288; fax: 3211-764)

Ministry of Transport and Communications, Crvena Skopska Opstina 4, Skopje (tel: 3128-200; fax: 3118-144).

Prime Minister's Office, Bul. Ilinden bb, Skopje (tel: 3115-389; fax: 3113-512).

Other useful addresses

Bank Rehabilitation Agency, Kompleks banki bb, Skopje (tel: 3126-323; fax: 3121-250).

British Embassy, Dimitrija Chupovski 26, 4th Floor, Skopje (tel: 3116-772; fax: 3117-005; e-mail: beskopje@mt.net.mk).

Customs Administration, Lazar Licenovski 13, Skopje (tel: 3224-467; fax: 3237-832).

Fund for National and Regional Roads, Dame Gruev 14, Skopje (tel: 3118-044;

fax: 3220-535; e-mail: tanjam@.mpt.net.mk).

Macedonia Telecommunications, Orce Nikolov bb, Skopje (tel: 3141-000; fax: 3120-244).

Macedonian Embassy (USA), 3050 K Street, NW, Washington DC 20007 (tel: (+1-202)-337-3063; fax: (+1-202)-337-3093; e-mail: rmacedonia@aol.com).

Macedonian Stock Exchange, Mito Hadzivasilev 20, Skopje (tel: 3122-055; fax: 3122-069; e-mail: mse@unet.com.mk).

Privatisation Agency of the Republic of Macedonia, PO Box 410, Nikola Vapcarov 7, Skopje (tel: 3117-564; fax: 3126-022; e-mail: agency@mpa.org.mk).

Skopje Fair, Belasica bb, PO Box 356, Skopje (tel: 3118-288; fax: 3117-375; e-mail: skfair@mt.net.mk).

Skopje Free Economic Zone, Salvador Allende 73, Skopje (tel: 3176-170; fax: 3177-101; e-mail: sfez@mol.com.mk).

US Embassy, Bul. Ilinden bb, Skopje (tel: 3116-180; fax: 3117-103).

Internet sites

Privatisation Agency of the Republic of Macedonia: http://www.mpa.org.mk

Economic Chamber of Macedonia: http://www.mchamber.org.mk

Government of FRY Macedonia: http://www.gov.mk/english

Agency of Information: http://www.sinf.gov.mk/defaulten.htm

National Bank of the Republic of Macedonia: http://www.nbrm.gov.mk

Macedonian Stock Exchange: http://www.mse.org.mk

Republic of Macedonia News Collection: http://b-info.com/places/Macedonia/republic/news/

Madagascar

Madagascar launched it ambitious Madagascar Action Plan (MAP) in 2007. This bold plan aims to strengthen the economy over 2007–12 by continuing structural reforms, diversifying and achieving its Millennium Development Goals (MDG).

Madagascar has made significant progress in terms of macroeconomic stabilisation and structural reform. Political stability has been broadly restored following the disputed 2001 presidential elections and the ensuing political crisis. Since that time, the authorities have taken measures to re-establish investor confidence and re-invigorate private sector growth. It is now counting on budgetary consolidation, expansion of the financial sector, a new Poverty Reduction and Growth Facility (PRGF), and the start of the Trade Integration Mechanism (TIM), which it hopes will mitigate the effects on the economy of the end of the Multi-Fibre Arrangement (MFA)

The economy

Gross domestic product (GDP) growth in 2007 was estimated at 7.32 per cent, a healthy increase over 2006 (5.47 per cent). Although GDP growth has averaged high rates since 2003, Madagascar's GDP per capita has remained stubbornly low – at US$431 in 2007. Inflation dropped from the 13.8 per cent recorded in 2005 to an estimated 10.3 per cent in 2007, but still alarmingly high. A number of key structural reforms have been implemented, albeit with significant delays, in particular in the area of public enterprise reform and the draining fight against corruption. However, Madagascar's economy remains vulnerable to shocks, including cyclones, and policy slippages. Progress in domestic revenue mobilisation and in strengthening the budget process has also remained modest, reflecting in part the country's limited institutional capacity.

In the medium term, real growth is expected to average six per cent per annum and fiscal consolidation is projected to continue, driven by an improvement of the revenue performance and modest expenditure increases. The current account position should also improve over the medium-term. While remaining fragile, the external debt position should remain sustainable, provided the authorities continue to limit new external financing to grants and to highly concessional loans. There are several risks to this outlook however, especially in the external sector, where the impact of the expiry of preferential agreements on textiles (MFA) exports could turn out to be larger than currently expected.

The government is committed to contain inflation, preserve Madagascar's competitiveness, and gradually build-up official reserves. This, together with accelerated progress on structural reforms and the assistance of the donor community, will be crucial for Madagascar to attain macroeconomic stabilisation.

Containing inflation hinges on the steadfast and timely implementation of tight monetary and fiscal policies as well as on the evolution of the world prices of oil and rice. Madagascar's revenue

KEY FACTS

Official name: Repoblikan'i Madagasikara (Republic of Madagascar)

Head of State: President Marc Ravalomanana (TIM) (since 2002; re-elected Dec 2006)

Head of government: Prime Minister Charles Rabemananjara (appointed 20 Jan 2007)

Ruling party: Tiako i Madagasikara (TIM) (I Love and Care for Madagascar) (from 2002; re-elected Sep 2007)

Area: 592,000 square km (the world's fourth-largest island)

Population: 18.61 million (2007)*

Capital: Antananarivo

Official language: Malagasy, French, English (from 2007)

Currency: Ariary (MGA) = 5 iraimbilanja

Exchange rate: MGA1,575.50 per US$ (Jul 2008)

GDP per capita: US$431 (2007)*

GDP real growth: 6.30% (2007)

Labour force: 8.31 million (2004)

Inflation: 10.30% (2007)

Balance of trade: -US$709.00 million (2006)

Visitor numbers: 312,000 (2006)*

* estimated figure

performance remains weak – reflected in a relatively low revenue-to-GDP ratio.

The International Monetary Fund (IMF) has encouraged the central bank to take further steps to improve the effectiveness of monetary policy and to be more proactive in managing liquidity. It has endorsed the authorities' flexible exchange rate policy, which limits exchange market intervention to smoothing operations, and agreed that the current exchange rate appears to be broadly appropriate.

Madagascar's limited absorptive and institutional capacity has adversely affected the implementation of structural reforms. Shortcomings in economic and social data hamper policy formulation and implementation. It will be important to continue to build national ownership of policies through a close dialogue with civil society. Better alignment of technical assistance with policy priorities will be crucial.

Having discarded past socialist economic policies, Madagascar now follows a World Bank and IMF led policy of privatisation and liberalisation. This strategy has placed the country on a slow and steady growth path from an extremely low level. Agriculture, including fishing and forestry, is a mainstay of the economy, accounting for more than one-fourth of gross domestic product and employing 80 per cent of the population. Deforestation and erosion, aggravated by the use of firewood as the primary source of fuel are serious concerns. Poverty reduction and combating corruption will be the centrepieces of economic policy for the next few years.

Formerly an independent kingdom, Madagascar became a French colony in 1896, but regained its independence in 1960. In the December 2006 presidential elections Marc Ravalomanana won a second term as president with 54.8 per cent of the vote, large enough not to need a second round of voting. This victory was particularly sweet after his plane had been shot at in a supposed attempted military coup by General Andrianafidisoa the month before. The September 2007 parliamentary elections were won by the ruling Tiako i Madagasikara (TIM) (I Love and Care for Madagascar) with 106 seats out of 127, thereby consolidating the position of Prime Minister Charles Rabemananjara, who had been appointed 20 January 2007.

Outlook

World Bank support for the Madagascar Action Plan, and a new Country Assistance Strategy (CAS) for 2007–11 should enable Madagascar to achieve significant growth in 2008.

Risk assessment

Politics	Fair
Economy	Fair
Regional stability	Fair

COUNTRY PROFILE

Historical profile

1500 The first Europeans landed in Madagascar.

1790s King Andrianampoinimerina unified the Merina tribe which soon became the island's dominant tribe, controlling nearly half of Madagascar.

1820 Britain signed a treaty recognising Madagascar as an independent state under Merina rule.

1890 An Anglo-French treaty gave control of the island to France.

1894 Queen Ranavalona III was forced to abdicate and Madagascar was declared a French colony.

1947 After several decades of growing resentment and resistance to French rule, an insurrection was crushed by France with the loss of several thousand lives.

1960 The Republic of Madagascar (known between 1960–72 as the Malagasy Republic) gained full independence. Philibert Tsiranana became president.

1972 Tsiranana was forced from office; he was replaced by General Gabriel Ramantsoa.

1975 After a short tussle between pro- and anti-government forces a military coup replaced Ramantsoa with Didier Ratsiraka. The country was renamed the Democratic Republic of Madagascar.

1992–93 Following three years of protests and civil disturbances after Ratsiraka's third presidential election victory, a referendum endorsed a multi-party constitution which enshrined a unitary state and reduced the powers of the president. In the presidential election Ratsiraka was defeated by Albert Zafy.

1997 Didier Ratsiraka beat Albert Zafy in the presidential election.

2000 Ratsiraka and his party retained considerable political power, after 70 per cent of the electorate boycotted local elections.

2001 Both candidates, Ratsiraka and Marc Ravalomanana, declared themselves winners in the presidential election.

2002 Civil disturbance accompanied the heated debate about the prospective winner of the presidential election. Ravalomanana was declared the winner by the Constitutional High Court in April, following a recount. Ravalomanana was recognised by the US as Head of State. Didier Ratsiraka fled to the Seychelles. President Marc Ravalomanana's Tiako i Madagasikara (TIM) (I Love and Care for Madagascar) won the parliamentary elections.

2003 Prime Minister Jacques Sylla announced a new cabinet.

2004 The IMF agreed to write off debts of US$2 billion. Madagascar joined the Southern African Development Community (SADC).

2006 The president's plane was shot at as he returned home from France as General Andrianafidisoa (Fidy) attempted a military coup claiming the 2001 presidential election was illegitimate. President Ravalomanana won a second term in the

KEY INDICATORS — Madagascar

	Unit	2003	2004	2005	2006	2007
Population	m	17.28	17.66	17.82	*17.96	*18.61
Gross domestic product (GDP)	US$bn	4.74	4.46	5.03	5.47	*7.32
GDP per capita	US$	274	251	282	*331	*431
GDP real growth	%	9.6	5.3	4.6	5.0	*6.3
Inflation	%	1.0	13.8	18.4	10.7	*10.3
Industrial output	% change	–	6.6	6.1	2.7	–
Agricultural output	% change	–	3.1	2.5	2.2	–
Exports (fob) (goods)	US$m	700.0	868.2	834.0	975.0	–
Imports (cif) (goods)	US$m	985.0	1,147.0	1,427.0	1,684.0	–
Balance of trade	US$m	-285.0	278.8	-592.0	709.0	–
Current account	US$m	-270.0	-370.0	-524.0	*-476.0	-626.0
Total reserves minus gold	US$m	414.3	503.5	481.3	583.2	846.7
Foreign exchange	US$m	414.2	503.3	481.2	583.1	846.6
Exchange rate	per US$	6,040.00	7,562.50	2,030.00	2,030.00	1,786.00

* estimated figure

3 December presidential election with 54.8 per cent of the vote.
2007 The president appointed General Charles Rabemananjara as prime minister in January. The cyclone season, which devastated parts of Madagascar, was the worst on record. In the April referendum on constitutional amendments, 70 per cent of the voters supported increasing presidential powers. Parliamentary elections, held in September, were won by the ruling TIM (106 seats out of 127). A US$3.3 billion nickel cobalt mine was opened in Tamatave.
2008 The UN launched an appeal to help the 332,391 people left homeless by Cyclone Ivan, one of the largest ever recorded. The first barrels of crude oil since the 1940s was produced, gaining record prices. Madagascar issued 19 offshore exploration licenses, between August 2007–March 2008.

Political structure

Constitution
Constitutional reforms in 1995 and 1998 gave the president the power to appoint or dismiss the prime minister and presidential terms in office were limited to three.
Form of state
Republic
The executive
Under the constitution the prime minister is head of government and exercises virtually all executive power. The president is directly elected for five years.
National legislature
Legislative power is vested in a 127-member Antenimieram-Pirenena (Assemblée Nationale) (National Assembly), elected for five years by proportional representation. The Senate, has 90 members, two-thirds of which are appointed by an electoral college, and the remainder nominated by the president, all serving six years.
Last elections
23 September 2007 (national assembly); 3 December 2006 (presidential).
Results: Parliamentary: the ruling Tiako i Madagasikara (TIM) (I Love and Care for Madagascar) won 106 seats out of 127, Fanjava Velogno won 2, all other minor parties won one seat each.
Presidential: Marc Ravalomanana won 54.8 per cent of the vote, a majority large enough to avoid a second round; Jean Lahiniriko won 11.68 per cent, Roland Ratsiraka won 10.9 per cent. Turnout was 61.45 per cent.
Next elections
2012 (parliamentary); 2011 (presidential)

Political parties

Ruling party
Tiako i Madagasikara (TIM) (I Love and Care for Madagascar) (from 2002; re-elected Sep 2007)
Main opposition party

Population

18.61 million (2007)*
Last census: August 1993: 12,238,914
Population density: 24 inhabitants per square km. Urban population: 25 per cent (2003).
Annual growth rate: 3.0 per cent 1994–2004 (WHO 2006)
Ethnic make-up
The population comprises 18 separate ethnic groups, all deriving in varying degrees from Malayo-Indonesian origin, with African and Arab influences a particular feature in coastal areas. The Merinas (central highlands) represent about 26 per cent of the total, while the Betsimisaraka on the east coast account for 15 per cent and the Betsileo (southern highlands) 12 per cent. The other main groups are the Antankarana (north), Sakalava (west) and Mahafaly and Antandroy (far south). There is long-standing rivalry between the highland groups (particularly the Merina) and those of the coastal regions.
Religions
Traditional beliefs (45 per cent), Christianity (about 45 per cent), Islam (7 per cent).

Education

Primary education lasts for five years. Secondary schooling is divided into two, beginning with a four-year programme. When completed students may continue in either an acedemic or technical programme, for a further three years. Education may be given in either French or Madagasy.
The majority of those who do not attend school or who withdraw early come from the poorest sections of the population and those living in rural areas; illiteracy rates in women are a higher among the youngest; and nearly half of school age children are not enrolled in schools.
Public expenditure is around 3 per cent of GDP, of which around 40 per cent is spent on primary and 35 per cent on secondary education. Higher education expenses amount to only 0.5 per cent of GDP.
Literacy rate: 68.1 per cent total, 61.6 per cent female; adult rates (World Bank).
Compulsory years: Six to 11.
Enrolment rate: 120 per cent gross primary enrolment of relevant age group (including repeaters), World Bank.
Pupils per teacher: 47 in primary schools.

Health

Per capita total expenditure on health (2003) was US$24; of which per capita government spending was US$15, at the international dollar rate, (WHO 2006).
About 60 per cent of the population live within 5km of, or about one hour's walk from, a public health centre.
Vaccination facilities remain poor with only 61 per cent of children immunised against measles, before aged one year. More than three-quarters of the people have no ready access to drinking water.
HIV/Aids
The government has a national Aids policy that covers all economic sectors.
HIV prevalence: 1.7 per cent aged 15–49 in 2003 (World Bank)
Life expectancy: 57 years, 2004 (WHO 2006)
Fertility rate/Maternal mortality rate: 5.3 births per woman, 2004 (WHO 2006); maternal mortality 488 per 100,000 live births (World Bank).
Child (under 5 years) mortality rate (per 1,000): 78 per 1,000 live births (World Bank)
Head of population per physician: 0.29 physicians per 1,000 people, 2004 (WHO 2006)

Welfare

In 2004, three separate cyclones, including Cyclone Gafilo, estimated to have been the worst cyclone in 20 years, killed over 100 people and damaged more than 117,000 hectares of farmland as well as many schools and healthcare centres. Total damage from Cyclone Gafilo was estimated, by Government, at US$250 million.

Main cities

Antananarivo (capital, and principal business centre, estimated population 1.6 million in 2005); Toamasina (Tamatave), (200,568); Antsirabé (176,933); Fianarantsoa (160,550); Mahajanga (Majunga) (134,600), Majunga (149,863); Toliara (formerly Tuléar) (113,014); Antsiranana (formerly Diégo-Suarez) (80,001).

Languages spoken

French is the usual business language and the medium for all documentation.
Very little English is spoken.
Official language/s
Malagasy, French, English (from 2007)

Media

Press
Dailies: The 1990 law on press freedom was followed by a boom in privately-owned newspapers and encouraged more critical political reporting by the print media. Daily newspapers in French include the privately owned Midi Madagasikara and Madgascar Tribune and the Antananarivo daily L'Express de Madagascar. Other popular dailies are Gazetiko and Maresaka.
Weeklies: Weeklies include a Roman Catholic publication Lakroa (Cross)

covering rural and remote areas and a bi-weekly Telo Nohorefy. Dans les media demain (In The Media Tomorrow) is a privately-owned Antananarivo weekly news digest with a large circulation in the Madagascan diaspora. Feon'ny Merina (Voice of the Merina) promotes the interests of Merina people of Malay origin.

Periodicals: Monthly magazines are Jureco and the news magazine Revue de l'Ocean indien covering other Indian Ocean islands.

Broadcasting

State monopoly of radio and television has been abolished. Radio-Télévision-Antenne 2 Malagasy (RTM) and Radio Madagasikara broadcast in Malagasy and French. There are several private stations as well as state radio and television.

Radio: Echo du Capricorne is a weekly radio broadcast dealing with Madasgascar in general, presented in both Malagasy and French.

Economy

From a GDP growth of almost -12 per cent in 2002, Madagascar recovered quickly as its political situation stabilised. Since then it has had healthy GDP growth – in 2005 it was 4.6 per cent and is expected to be 4.7 per cent in 2006. Inflation was high at 18.14 per cent in 2005, due mainly to rising global oil prices, but it had fallen to 10.6 per cent by September 2006.

The service sector is the major provider of the economy at 56 per cent, agriculture provides 28 per cent and industry 15.9 per cent, of which manufacturing is 14 per cent.

Madagascar produces around 1,800–2,000 tonnes of vanilla a year. However, processed vanilla beans earned US$600 per kilo in 2003–04, but in 2006 the price had dropped to US$20–30. Overseas competition comes from new plantations and synthetic vanilla.

Liberalised foreign exchange was introduced in 2002, with the removal of import licences and the ending of some state monopolies. The IMF advises more reforms of the taxation system, to achieve a consistent and predictable environment which avoids ad hoc exemptions.

Macroeconomic development and reforms resulted in progress as investor confidence and private investment has grown. The economy still needs help through loans and grants from international donors and Madagascar took advantage of niche opportunities in aid-funded areas such as infrastructure, education, health, mining, energy, tourism, agriculture (including cotton and non-traditional exports) and consumer goods.

In one of the world's poorest countries, around 70 per cent of the population live below the poverty line. Madagascar has reached the set conditions for aid under the enhanced Heavily Indebted Poor Countries (HIPC) Initiative, which will allow it to borrow funds backed by the Initiative's guarantee.

In 2006, oil was discovered offshore and with projected production of 60,000 barrels per day by 2010, energy analysts are predicting annual revenue of US$1 billion. Madagascar joined the Extractive Industries Transparency Initiative (EITI) a 'forum of oil producers and consumers seeking to promote accountability in oil revenue' which should supply the necessary support in Madagascar's efforts to strengthen public financial management.

External trade

Madagascar was one of the founding members of the Common Market of Eastern and Southern Africa (Comesa), and operates a free trade area (FTA) with eight out of the 20 Comesa members. Internal duties were eliminated in 2000 and a common external tariff is set to be implemented in 2008.

A series of natural disasters struck in 2007, causing first drought in the south, then widespread flooding after seven cyclone systems hit the island, which damaged infrastructure and left around 500,000 people in need of humanitarian aid. The destruction will have a knock-on effect on exports of both raw materials and goods.

Madagascar is one of the World's largest exporter of vanilla (it lost its pre-eminence in 2000 when a cyclone destroyed much of its production). It has significant reserves of minerals and ores; investment in mineral extraction was bolstered in May 2007 when the African Development Bank agreed to a US$150 million loan to develop the Ambatovy nickel plant.

Imports

Principal imports are petroleum, capital goods, consumer goods and foodstuffs and vehicles.

Main sources: China (17.8 per cent total, 2006), Bahrain (16.4 per cent), France (13.2 per cent).

Exports

Principal exports are coffee, vanilla, textiles, sugar, metals and minerals and petroleum products.

Main destinations: France (39.5 per cent total, 2006), US (15.0 per cent), Germany (6.0 per cent).

Agriculture

The agricultural sector dominates the economy. With a growth rate of 3.1 per cent in 2004, it contributed 28.8 per cent to GDP and employs around 75 per cent of the working population. Madagascar has a wide range of soil types.

Main cash/export crops are prawns, coffee, cotton, cloves and vanilla, production of which has fluctuated due to recurrent droughts and cyclones. Vanilla used to be the country's main export crop but increased competition worldwide has reduced exports. Around 1,800–2,000 tonnes of vanilla a year is produced, but its cultivation has suffered a drop in value due to overseas competition from new plantations and synthetic vanilla. Processed vanilla beans earned US$600 per kilo in 2003–04, while in 2006 the price had dropped to US$20–30.

Main food crops are rice, maize, bananas and sweet potatoes. Groundnuts, pineapples, coconuts and sugar are also grown, mostly for internal use. The decline in coffee prices led to many growers switching production to rice, increasing production by 5 per cent, and making Madagascar self-sufficient in rice (the staple diet of the country) for the first time since the mid-1970s, with annual production at around 3.0 million tonnes per year.

Divestiture of vanilla, cotton and sugar parastatals was expected to encourage greater foreign investment. However, as vanilla prices fell from US$450—500 per kilo in 2003, to US$30 in 2007, financial co-operatives kept several thousand vanilla farmers afloat.

The livestock sector is dominant in the west and south of the country.

Estimated crop production in 2005 included: 3,390,646 tonnes (t) cereals in total, 200,000t taro, 349,646t maize, 2,191,420t cassava, 280,500t potatoes, 542,234t sweet potatoes, 3,030,000t rice, 290,000t bananas, 101,610t pulses, 84,500t coconuts, 97,900t citrus fruit, 29,182t oilcrops, 1,326t tobacco, 4,500t cocoa beans, 65,000t green coffee, 3,000t vanilla, 15,500t cloves, 1,600t pepper spice, 4,790t other spices, 2,459,705t sugar cane, 17,000t sisal, 36,800t fibre crops, 210,000t mangoes, 890,600t fruit in total, 343,610t vegetables in total. Estimated livestock production included: 297,067t meat in total, 146,625t beef, 4,000t game meat, 70,000t pig meat, 8,616t lamb and goat meat, 67,160t poultry, 19,436t eggs, 535,000t milk, 3,930t honey, 20,700t cattle hides, 816t goatskins, 416t sheepskins, 50t cocoons, silk.

Fishing

Since 1996, prawns have been the number one export earner, with around 7,000 tonnes of prawn exports earning revenues of over US$60 million per annum.

In a meeting of African ministers in Namibia, held on 2 July, members discussed illegal and unregulated fishing, which is estimated to cost Africa US$1 billion per annum in lost revenue and the threat to stocks and local artisan fishing. In 2004, the total marine fish catch was 83,083 tonnes and the total crustacean catch was 14,375 tonnes.

Forestry

Only 15 per cent of Madagascar's ancient forest remains. Deforestation has left the hills exposed to the wind and rain which strips away the soil. Forest preservation and the creation of national parks are receiving large-scale international support.

Exports of timber production in 2004 was US$18.7 million while imports amounted to US$15 million.

Production in 2004 included 10,952,970 cubic metres (cum) roundwood, 183,000cum industrial roundwood, 893,200cum sawnwood, 160,100cum sawlogs and veneers, 5,000cum wood-based panels, 10,769,870cum woodfuel, 871,934t charcoal.

Industry and manufacturing

The industrial sector contributes around 16 per cent of GDP and employs around 9 per cent of the workforce.

Industry is dominated by food processing and the manufacture of textiles for international markets. Other major sectors include rice milling, sugar refining, distilling, oil-seed crushing, meat, fruit and vegetable canning, processing of cashew nuts, fruit juices, milk products and jams, cigarettes, soap and rope manufacturing, cotton spinning and brewing. Major capital-intensive industries are oil refining, fertiliser and cement production.

There are 150 firms based in industrial free zones, representing mainly textile, food processing and information technology, and creating 6,000 jobs in the Antananarivo area alone. Many textile companies in Mauritius are relocating to Madagascar due to the cheaper labour rates.

Tourism

Tourism is the second most important foreign exchange earner, after textile exports. The sector is expected to earn US$152.7 million, contribute 3 per cent of GDP in 2005, and attract 11.6 per cent of all capital investment. Travel and tourism is predicted to employ over 450,000 people, or provide one in every 18 jobs.

France is the main market and adventure and eco-tourism are the main attractions. There is considerable potential for expansion of the sector in these and other activities, such as coastal resorts, but inadequate infrastructure and low investment are a hindrance to becoming truly competitive with more established Indian Ocean destinations.

Environment

Madagascar has plants and wildlife found nowhere else on earth, and growth of both tourism and mining needs to be controlled to protect the fragile ecosystems.

Mining

Excluding gold and gem production by artisinal miners, mining contributes less than 1 per cent of GDP and employs 1 per cent of the workforce. If the informal sector is included, the contribution to GDP is around 3 per cent.

Madagascar is rich in mineral resources, although it is still only a minor mineral producer by regional standards. There are sizeable deposits of a number of minerals, industrial ores and precious and semi-precious gemstones including chrome ore, mica, graphite, gold, bauxite, uranium, iron ore, ilmenite/titanium, quartz, nickel, copper, lead, platinum, labradorite, rock-crystal, rhodolite, marble, garnets, emeralds, rubies and sapphires. There are known deposits containing 100 million tonnes of bauxite and 400 million tonnes of iron ore, although these have not been developed due to the country's poor infrastructure. Only chrome, mica and graphite have been exploited to any great extent, and export earnings from these are limited due to lack of demand. The world's largest known emerald cluster was discovered in Madagascar in 1996.

The region of Ilakaka in the southern interior has around 50 per cent of the world's sapphire reserves, while there are small quantities of semi-precious stones (garnets and amethysts) mined for export.

The state-owned Société Kraomita Malagasy (Kraoma) is Madagascar's main chromite producer. It extracts around 40,000 tonnes of concentrates and 80,000 tonnes of lumpy ore per year from the Andriamana complex and a further 20,000 tonnes from the Behandrinana mine.

There are some 100,000 individual gold miners and small syndicates. Although the government tolerates this form of mining, it is worried about its ecological effects which include a high level of mercury leaking into streams and rivers.

The country also produces graphite, 66 per cent of which comes from the Gallois mine. It exports up to 15,000tpy, mostly to UK, US and Germany.

Hydrocarbons

Madagascar does not produce oil, however exploration has shown that deposits of oil are evident. There are eight international oil companies exploring offshore blocks, including ExxonMobile, Norsk-Hyfro and Aminex.

There is one refinery in Toamasina with a capacity of around 15,000 barrels per day (bpd).

Madagascar relies on importing both crude and refined oil and a small amount of coal; it does not import natural gas.

Energy

The majority of the country's energy needs are supplied by imported fuel.

Besides fuelwood, hydropower is the main domestic energy source. Some mines and factories have their own small diesel or stream-powered generators. Construction of the country's second dam, at Ankorahotra, has been suspended pending evaluation of the oil fields.

Banking and insurance

Moves to strengthen banking supervision have been enhanced through the IMF backed Financial Sector Assessment Program.

Central bank

Banque Centrale de la République Malgache

Time

GMT plus three hours

Geography

Madagascar is situated in the western Indian Ocean, about 500km east of Mozambique in southern Africa. It comprises the island of Madagascar itself and several much smaller offshore islands. Madagascar is the fourth-largest island in the world. The terrain is dominated by a chain of mountains running the length of the island, with broad lowlands to the west and a narrow strip of lowlands to the east.

The highlands, which occupy around half of the total area, rise to 1,800m. A rift valley runs from north to south and includes lake Alaotra, which, at 40km in length, is the largest body of water in the country. The capital, Antananarivo, is located on the plateau.The highest elevations face east, forming an escarpment above the eastern lowlands. The east coast is narrow, averaging about 50km in width, and is heavily forested. The mountains slope gradually down towards the broad west coast, which is given over to savannah; unlike that of the east coast, the coastline is indented and provides harbourage.

The highest point of the island (2,880m) is in the Tsaratanana Massif at the northern end of the island. The coastline is contoured and is home to the natural harbour of Antsiranana. The southern end of the island is semi-desert with cactus-like plant species, which are unique to Madgascar. Rivers flowing east from the highlands are short and fast with waterfalls. Those flowing down the gentler western terrain are longer and slower-moving.

Hemisphere
Southern

Climate
Tropical, cooler in highlands. The summer period spans the months of November to April. Numerous areas have their own micro-climates – the highlands are subject to mild freshness in the winter, while the eastern parts of the island experience high temperatures and humidity, with barren and arid conditions dominating the western sector.

In Antananarivo, the hottest month is December (15–28 Celsius (C)), coldest July (9–19 C). The wettest month is January. Winter in the capital lasts from April to October, when it is cold and dry.

Madagascar falls within the cyclone belt and cyclones tend to occur during the rainy season December–March, which is hotter than the rest of the year. It is rainy until June or July on the east coast and is very hot throughout the year. It is drier on the west coast.

Dress codes
In Antananarivo, in the winter months, normal weight clothing is suitable, with a woollen sweater/cardigan recommended. In the summer men should wear tropical suits and women, cotton dresses. On the coast, tropical clothing is recommended all year round.

Entry requirements
Passports
Required by all, valid for six months after date of entry.
Visa
Required by all, along with proof of return/onward passage. A business visas requires a letter of recommendation from the employer, confirming the traveller's business activity and financial responsibility, to be submitted with the application.
Currency advice/regulations
Import of local currency is limited to MGA1,000; visitors are not allowed to export local currency. There is no limit on import of foreign currency, subject to declaration on arrival, and export is allowed up to the declared amount.

Health (for visitors)
Mandatory precautions
Yellow fever vaccination certificate required if arriving from an infected area.
Advisable precautions
Typhoid, polio, tetanus and hepatitis A vaccinations recommended. Malaria risk exists throughout the country and prophylaxis is necessary. There is a rabies risk. Water precautions should be taken.

Hotels
Good hotels are available in Antananarivo, Toamasina, Nosy Be, Ste Marie and Taolanaro. A service charge is added to bills at some hotels. Discretionary tipping is usual.

Credit cards
Credit cards are of limited use in Madagascar and few establishments accept them.

Public holidays (national)
Fixed dates
1 Jan (New Year's Day), 29 Mar (Commemoration Day – 1947), 1 May (Labour Day), 26 Jun (Independence Day), 15 Aug (Assumption Day), 1 Nov (All Saints' Day), 25 Dec (Christmas Day), 30 Dec (Republic Day).
Variable dates
Easter Monday, Ascension Day, Whit Monday.

Working hours
Banking
Mon–Fri: 0800–1100, 1400–1600.
Business
Mon–Fri: 0830–1200, 1400–1800.
Government
Mon–Fri: 0800–1200, 1400–1800.
Shops
Mon–Fri: 0800–1200, 1400–1800.

Telecommunications
Postal services
Air mail is advised. Surface mail can take between three and four months.

Electricity supply
110 or 220V AC, 50 cycles; also 380V AC, 50 cycles

Getting there
Air
National airline: Air Madagascar
International airport/s:
Antananarivo-Ivato (TNR), 14km from the city; restaurant, currency exchange.
Airport tax: None.
Surface
Water: There are few scheduled sea passages.
Main port/s: Toamasina (Tamatave), on the east coast, is the island's main port. It is used by numerous foreign shipping lines. Mahajanga (Majunga) is the west coast's main port. Antseranana (Diégo-Suarez) is in the extreme north of the island, and Toliara (Tuléar) is on the south-west coast.

Getting about
National transport
Air: Air Madagascar and TAM airlines fly more than 60 domestic routes. There are connections between all major towns, apart from Antsirabe. Air travel is the most used and generally recommended form of transport. There are over 100 airfields on the island, although many are just airstrips.
Road: Generally poor and in need of repair, and only passable in good weather (the dry season).
Fairly well-maintained main roads leave Antananarivo – the N4 to Mahajanga (Majunga), the RN2 to Toamasina (Tamatave), and the RN7 plateau route south to Fianarantsoa.
Rail: Two classes; light refreshments may be available; air-conditioning available on first-class trains.
Routes are: between Toamasina and Antsirabe, via Antananarivo, incorporating a connection between Moramanga and Lake Alaotra; and between Fianarantsoa and Manakara on the east coast. Daily services operate on most routes.
City transport
Taxis: Flat fare system for short journeys in most towns, otherwise by negotiation; tipping is not usual.
Car hire
Available in main centres. International driving licence required.

BUSINESS DIRECTORY

The addresses listed below are a selection only. While World of Information makes every endeavour to check these addresses, we cannot guarantee that changes have not been made, especially to telephone numbers and area codes. We would welcome any corrections.

Telephone area codes
The international dialling code (IDD) for Madagascar is +261 20 followed by operator and area codes and subscriber's number:

Antananarivo	22	Nosy-Be	86
Antsiranana	82	Toamasina	53
Fianarantsoa	75	Toliara	18
Mahajanga	62		

Useful telephone numbers
Police: 17
Fire: 18
Ambulance: 357-53

Chambers of Commerce
Antananarivo Chamber of Commerce, Industry and Agriculture, 20 Rue Paul Dussac, PO Box 166, 101 Antananarivo 101 (tel: 202-11; fax: 20213).

Antsiranana Chamber of Commerce, Industry and Agriculture, 3 Rue Colbert, PO Box 76, Antsiranana 201 (tel: 223-72; fax: 294-03).

Madagascar Federation of Chambers of Commerce, Industry and Agriculture, 20 Rue Paul Dussac, PO Box 166, Antananarivo 101 (tel: 20-211; fax: 20-213).

Mahajanga Chamber of Commerce, Industry and Agriculture, Boulevard Poincaré, PO Box 52, Mahajanga 401(tel: 226-21).

Nosy-Be Chamber of Commerce, Industry and Agriculture, Cours de Hell, PO Box

11, Nosy-Be 207 (tel: 610-26; fax: 610-56).

Toamasina Chamber of Commerce, Industry, Handicrafts and Agriculture, 4 Rue de Commerce, PO Box 108, Toamasina 501 (tel: 323-45; fax: 320-25).

Banking

BMOI, Place de l'Indépendence, BP 25 bis, Antananarivo 101 (tel: 346-09; fax: 346-10; e-mail:bmoi.sm@simicro.mg).

Bank of Africa-Madagascar, 2 Place de l'Independance, BP 183, Antananarivo 101 (tel: 391-00/; fax: 294-08).

Banque SBM Madagascar, 1 Rue Andrianary Ratianarivo Antsahavola, Antananarivo 101 (tel: 666-07; fax: 666-08).

BFV-Société Générale, 14 Lalana Jeneraly Rabehevitra, BP 196, Antananarivo 101 (tel: 206-91; fax: 345-54).

BNI-Crédit Lyonnais Madagascar, 74 Rue du 26 Juin 1960, BP 174, Antananarivo 101 (tel: 228-00; fax: 337-49).

Investco Southern Investment Bancorp, Immeuble NIAG, 8 Lalana Rainizanabololona, BP 8510, Antanimena, Antananarivo 101 (tel: 648-20; fax: 613-29).

Union Commercial Bank SA, 77 Rue Solombavambahoaka Frantsay, Antsahavola, BP 197, Antananarivo 101 (tel: 272-62; fax: 287-40).

Central bank

Banque Centrale de Madagascar, Avenue de la Révolution Socialiste, PO Box 550, Antananarivo (tel: 234-65; fax: 345-32; e-mail: b.c.m@simicro.mg).

Travel information

Air Madagascar, 31 Avenue de l'Indépendance, Analakely, Antananarivo 101 (tel: 222-22; fax: 337-60; e-mail: commercial@airmadagascar.com)

Association des Agences de Voyages de Madagascar, 5 Rue Ravveloary, Antananarivo (tel: 656-31; e-mail: aavm@wanadoo.mg).

Air Mauritius, 77 lalana Solombavabahoaka, Frantsay, Antsahavola, Antananarivo (tel: 359-00; fax: 357-73).

Réseau National des Chemins de Fer, BP 259, Soarano, Antananarivo (tel: 205-21).

Ministry of tourism

Ministry of Culture and Tourism, Rue Fernand Kasanga, BP 610, Tsimbazaza, Antananarivo (tel: 668-05; fax: 789-53; e-mail: mct@tourisme.gov.mg).

National tourist organisation offices

Maison du Tourisme de Madagascar (Madagascar Tourist Office), Place de l'Indépendance, Antaninarenina, PO Box 3224, Antananarivo (tel: 351-78; fax: 695-22; e-mail: mtm@simicro.gov.mg).

Ministries

Ministry of Private Sector Development and Privatisation, Comité de Privatisation, Zone III 1er étage, Ampefiloha, Antananarivo (tel: 666-67; fax: 601-38; e-mail: magpriv@dts.mg).

Other useful addresses

Agence Nationale d'Information 'Taratra' (ANTA), 3 rue du R P Callet, BP 386, Antananarivo (tel: 211-71).

Association of the Hotel Industry of Madagascar (SIHM), c/o Sofitrans – Soarano, Antananarivo (tel: 223-30).

Comité de Privatisation, Secrétariat Technique á la Privatisation Immeuble FIARO, Zone III 1er étage, Ampefiloha, 101 Antananarivo (fax: 2260-138).

Customs Services, Ivato Airport, Antananarivo (tel: 440-32).

Institut National de la Statistique et de la Recherche Economique (DGBDE), Direction Générale, BP 485, Antananarivo (tel: 216-52).

Madagascan Embassy (US), 2374 Massachusetts Avenue, NW, Wasghington DC 20008 (tel: (+1-202)-265-5525; fax: (+1-202)-265-3034; e-mail: malagasy@embassy.org).

Office Militaire National pour les Industries Stratégiques (monitors major industrial projects), 21 Lalana Razanakombana, Antananarivo.

Société d'Etude et de Réalisation pour le Développement Industriel, BP 3180, Antananarivo (tel: 213-35).

Syndicat de l'Industrie Hôteliére de Madagascar, BP 341, Antananarivo (tel: 202-02).

Internet sites

Africa Business Network: www.ifc.org/abn

African Development Bank: www.afdb.org

Africa News Online: www.allafrica.com

Africa Online: www.africaonline.com

Mbendi AfroPaedia (information on companies, countries, industries and stock exchanges in Africa): http://mbendi.co.za

Malawi

KEY FACTS

Official name: Dziko la Malawi (Republic of Malawi)

Head of State: President Bingu wa Mutharika (DPP) (sworn in 24 May 2004)

Head of government: President Bingu wa Mutharika

Ruling party: A coalition led by United Democratic Front (UDF) with the Mgwirizano (Unity) coalition, National Democratic Alliance (NDA), Alliance for Democracy (AFORD) and 38 non-partisan parliamentary members (elected 20 May 2004)

Area: 118,484 square km

Population: 13.39 million (2007)*

Capital: Lilongwe

Official language: English

Currency: Kwacha (K) = 100 tambala

Exchange rate: K140.52 per US$ (Jul 2008)

GDP per capita: US$264 (2007)*

GDP real growth: 7.40% (2007)

Labour force: 5.35 million (2004)

Inflation: 8.00% (2007)*

Balance of trade: -US$439.00 million (2006)

Foreign debt: US$3.42 billion (2004)

* estimated figure

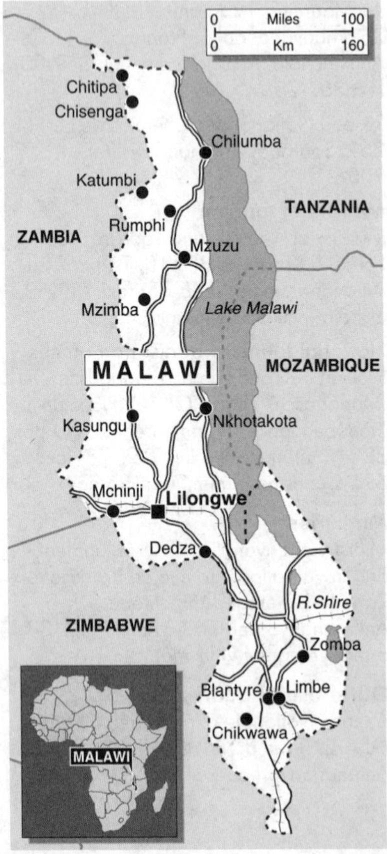

Under president-for-life, Kamuzu Banda, Malawi surprised many other African states by the way it forged ahead with scant regard for the dictates of the Organisation for African Unity (fore-runner of the African Union) – particularly over Malawi's relationship with apartheid South Africa. Dr Banda was the ultimate pragmatist – accepting South African aid and military support but never compromising on the issue of apartheid. In 2007 Malawi was once again amazing other African states.

Political muddle and meddling

President Bingu wa Mutharika came to power in May 2004 as the United Democratic Front (UDF) candidate, supported by then president Bakili Muluzi. However, within a year he had fallen out with Mr Muluzi and left to form his own party, the Democratic Progressive Party (DPP). Now Muluzi wants to come back and stand in the next elections scheduled for 2009. However, according to the constitution he cannot stand again after two consecutive terms in office, although his lawyers argue that after a five year gap he can run again. In April 2008, he was opposed in his bid to stand again by a member of his own party, James Phiri, who argued that it would be against the 'spirit of the constitution'. Muluzi is reported to have said that as he 'cannot fail to deflate a tyre I personally inflated', the 'tyre' in question being President Mutharika.

Then there were the shenanigans over the 2007/08 budget, which in 2007 took over four months to pass. Opposition MPs had refused to discuss the budget until MPs who had switched parties to the president's DPP were expelled; they were granted an injunction barring the speaker of parliament from reconvening the house in order to begin the budget debate. The injunction was overturned by the Supreme Court of Appeal and parliament was free to meet again and the budget eventually passed. The debacle led to the delay of a number of bills and the wrangling over section 65 of the constitution, which allows for the speaker to declare a seat vacant of any MP who crosses the floor, continued in early 2008.

The 2008 edition of *African Economic Outlook* (AEO), published jointly by the African Development Bank and Organisation for the Economic Co-operation and Development (OECD), has said that although growth picked up in the previous 4–5 years, it will still take some time before this translates into improved poverty outcomes. It goes on to state that '...2007 saw continued stronger economic growth of 6.8 per cent, following an exceptionally high 7.9 per cent in 2006, as the country begins to benefit from several years of prudent financial and macroeconomic management. Interest rates are now beginning to fall, and the share of credit extended to the private sector has risen as the public sector no longer crowds out private investment. The successful deployment of a national fertiliser subsidy, coupled with consistent rains across most of the country, resulted in a bumper harvest of maize, the most important staple crop. Thus, reduced food security challenges together with improved central budget discipline led to a reduction in inflation to 8.6 per cent in 2007 – the lowest in more than two decades.'

Outlook

The AEO forecasts that in order to sustain rapid economic growth, the country will need to address more effectively the structural constraints to increased private investment, such as lack of skills and low productivity, weaknesses in the business environment, and infrastructural constraints.

Risk assessment

Politics	Poor
Economy	Improving
Regional stability	Good

COUNTRY PROFILE

Historical profile

In the eighth century, the Bantu people of Nyasaland began trading with Portuguese merchants on the east African coast.

1891 The British declared the area a protectorate and in the wake of David Livingstone's explorations, an increasing number of Europeans went to Nyasaland, particularly missionaries. The settlers expropriated land and imposed taxes which led to ever growing numbers of Africans working in settler plantations or emigrating to the then Rhodesia or South Africa.

1950s Opposition to colonial rule, which had begun in the southern highlands, became more widespread. The Nyasaland African Congress was established to oppose the planned Central African Federation (CAF) with Northern and Southern Rhodesia, and the heavy-handed interference by white settlers in traditional agricultural methods.

1954 The Nyasaland African Congress grew rapidly upon the return from Britain of Dr Hastings Kamuzu Banda; within a year the colonial authorities had jailed him and other leaders.

1961 The authorities released Dr Banda and invited him to London for a constitutional conference, at which Nyasaland was promised eventual independence regardless of constitutional developments in the rest of the CAF. Elections followed, which Dr Banda's Malawi Congress Party (MCP) won.

1963 The CAF was officially dissolved, paving the way for independence in Nyasaland a year later, with Dr Banda as Prime Minister.

1966 Nyasaland became a republic and was renamed Malawi; Dr Banda became president.

1971 Banda declared himself president for life.

1978 Dr Banda and the MCP won the first election since independence.

1992 Catholic bishops condemned Banda and the one-party state and sparked mass demonstrations; humanitarian aid to the country was cut off.

1993 A referendum overwhelmingly backed a multi-party option and political parties began to develop.

1994 The United Democratic Front (UDF) beat the MCP in multi-party legislative elections and Bakili Muluzi became president. Dr Banda retired.

1995 Banda was acquitted of ordering the murder of three government ministers, he later apologising for any suffering he may have 'unknowingly caused'.

1997 Hastings Banda died in South Africa, where he was being treated for pneumonia.

1999 The UDF won the parliamentary elections and Muluzi retained the presidency for the last, five-year term.

2000 Corruption scandals began to threaten aid flow. Muluzi was forced to dismiss his government.

2002 Malawi's bishops condemned Muluzi's rule, warning that it was becoming a dictatorship. International aid was suspended due to a lack of reform and transparency. A drought caused widespread hunger; food aid was supplied by the UN.

2004 The government offered anti-retroviral drugs to HIV/Aids sufferers, free of charge. The 20 May presidential elections were won by Bingu wa Mutharika (UDF), while the Malawi Congress Party (MCP) won most seats in the parliamentary elections. The elections were not considered free and fair by observers. A coalition government was formed led by the UDF.

2005 Mutharika resigned from the UDF, claiming it was hostile to his anti-corruption campaign and formed a new group, the Democratic Progressive Party (DPP). Parliament began impeachment proceedings against the president for corruption, however by June he had survived the threat and many in the UDF, which sponsored the bill, resigned from the party. There was a UN humanitarian appeal for US$88 million in food aid to feed five million due to failed crops and a regional drought, but by October, the fund had only reached US$28 million. The DPP won a number of by-elections, in what was seen as rebuke for the UDF, in support of the president.

2006 Vice President Cassim Chilumpha was arrested and charged with treason; it was alleged that he had hired a South African assassin to kill the president. Former president Bakili Muluzi was arrested for corruption, fraud and theft during his time in office. The maize harvest was expected to be the largest since 2001, due to increased rainfall and a programme of government-sponsored fertiliser and seed distribution. The harvest should provide more than 10 per cent over the national annual requirement. In October international news was concentrated on the adoption of a Malawian baby by the US singer, Madonna.

KEY INDICATORS — Malawi

	Unit	2003	2004	2005	2006	2007
Population	m	11.65	11.65	12.86	*13.12	*13.39
Gross domestic product (GDP)	US$bn	1.70	1.91	2.08	3.16	*3.54
GDP per capita	US$	146	151	161	*241	*264
GDP real growth	%	4.9	4.3	2.1	7.8	*7.4
Inflation	%	9.6	11.6	12.3	13.9	*8.0
Industrial output	% change	–	10.2	15.4	10.1	–
Agricultural output	% change	–	2.7	-9.1	10.9	–
Exports (fob) (goods)	US$m	435.0	503.4	514.0	467.0	–
Imports (cif) (goods)	US$m	505.0	521.1	984.0	906.0	–
Balance of trade	US$m	-70.0	-17.7	-470.0	-439.0	–
Current account	US$m	-180.0	-363.0	-336.0	-195.0	–
Total reserves minus gold	US$m	126.5	133.3	158.9	133.8	216.6
Foreign exchange	US$m	122.6	128.6	154.6	129.6	212.9
Exchange rate	per US$	96.83	107.50	139.45	139.45	139.40

* estimated figure

2007 The 2007/08 budget debate by parliament did not start until 22 August after 60 members of the opposition parties UDF and MCP defected to the ruling DPP. The Supreme Court gave the Speaker powers to expel the defecting MPs, throwing into doubt the deleative strengths of the parties.
2008 In January, the government ended diplomatic relations with Taiwan, in favour of ties with China, stating it recognised Taiwan as 'an inalienable part of China's territory'. Aid, worth several billion US dollars, offered by China is thought to have persuaded Malawi to transfer its endorsement. Former president, Bakili Muluzi began a legal challenge on 15 July, to allow him to stand for election as president in 2009, on the grounds that a president who has been out of office for two consecutive five-year terms is allowed to run again. Observers have alleged that personal animosity between Muluzi and the incumbent president is a likely motive for this move.

Political structure

Constitution
The constitution dates from 1966. A multi-party political system was adopted in 1994.
Malawi is divided into 24 administrative divisions.

Form of state
Republic

The executive
The president is both the head of state and the head of government. The president names the 36-member Cabinet and is elected by popular vote for a five-year term.

National legislature
The unicameral 193-member National Assembly is elected by popular vote to serve a five-year term.

Legal system
The legal system is based on English common law.

Last elections
20 May 2004 (presidential and parliamentary)
Results: Presidential: Bingu wa Mutharika (UDF) won with 35.9 per cent of the vote, followed by John Tembo (MCP) with 27.1 per cent, Gwanda Chakuamba of the Mgwirizano Coalition with 25.7 per cent and Brown Mpinganjira (NDA) with 8.7 per cent.
Parliamentary: the MCP won 60 seats out of 193, the UDF 49 and the Mgwirizano Coalition 28, the National Democratic Alliance (NDA) 8, Alliance for Democracy (AFORD) 6, non-partisans 38.

Next elections
2009 (presidential and parliamentary)

Political parties
Ruling party
A coalition led by United Democratic Front (UDF) with the Mgwirizano (Unity) coalition, National Democratic Alliance (NDA), Alliance for Democracy (AFORD) and 38 non-partisan parliamentary members (elected 20 May 2004)

Main opposition party
Malawi Congress Party (MCP)

Population

13.39 million (2007)*
Last census: September 1998: 9,933,868
Population density: 87 inhabitants per square km. Urban population: 15 per cent (1995–2001).
Annual growth rate: 2.4 per cent 1994–2004 (WHO 2006)

Ethnic make-up
Chewa (60 per cent), Lomwe (18 per cent), Yao (13 per cent), Ngoni (7 per cent).

Religions
Christianity (80 per cent), Islam (13 per cent), traditional beliefs (7 per cent).

Education

Primary education lasts for eight years. Junior secondary school follows, and if successful, students may progress to the senior secondary school, of which each stage lasts for two years. Instruction is given in English.
Educational attainment, defined as completion of standard eight (at the end of primary school), is only 11.2 per cent. While education is free, provision has not kept up with demand. In some rural areas children have to walk up to 13km to the nearest school. The government's decision to provide free primary education has brought a crisis in the system, placing severe restrictions on its education budget. Secondary schools have less than half the teachers they need and about two-thirds of these are not trained to teach at secondary level. The government proposes to convert Malawi Distance Education Centres (DECs) into Community Day Secondary Schools (CDSS) in order to alleviate the shortage of secondary school teachers.
The University of Malawi typically has approximately 3,000 students, with roughly 1,000 new enrolments every year.
Literacy rate: 62 per cent adult rate; 73 per cent youth rate (15–24) (Unesco 2005).
Compulsory years: 5 to 13.
Enrolment rate: 134 per cent gross primary enrolment, of relevant age group (including repeaters); 29 per cent gross secondary enrolment (World Bank).
Pupils per teacher: 59 in primary schools; in some classes the ratio has increased to 96:1 due to Aids related illness among teachers.

Health

Per capita total expenditure on health (2003) was US$46; of which per capita government spending was US$16, at the international dollar rate, (WHO 2006).
Malaria is endemic; around four million new cases are reported each year. Malaria accounts for 18 per cent of all hospital deaths and 40 per cent of all outpatients visits. A programme to reduce the effect of the disease includes the provision of insecticide treated nets, more access to prompt treatment for children and increased availability of insulin potentiation therapy for pregnant women.
Malawi experienced a severe drought and locust plagues in 2004–05 that left in October 2005, over 4.6 million people short of food. The UK has provided around US$18 million in food aid and in September 2005 announced it will provide an extra £5 million (US$9.1 million) to feed those affected by food shortages. The aid will provide 60,000 tonnes of maize from South Africa, and funds for Unicef to feed 3,500 severely malnourished children as well as subsidies for farmers to buy high-yield maize seed for next year's harvest.
Both the president and the UN World Food Programme have declared Malawi, to be in crisis. Funds required for food-aid are put at US$88 million but only US$28 million, has been pledged by international donors.

HIV/Aids
There were over one million children and adults infected, of which over 50 per cent are females (2005).
With the most productive section of the population at the highest risk from HIV infection in one of Africa's poorest countries, there is concern at the long-term effect on the country's political stability, social cohesion and economic growth. Women, are the country's subsistence farmers, have been hard hit by the disease, which has had a catastrophic impact on agricultural output. It has been estimated that between a quarter and a half of civil servants may die from Aids by 2010, and the government's ability to implement health policies will be severely hampered in coming years.
Aids is the leading cause of death for those aged 20–49, with an estimated 50,000–70,000 adult and child deaths annually, and has left thousands of child-led households. Up to 70 per cent of hospital beds are occupied by patients who are HIV positive. The growing impact of Aids related deaths has driven up the state's health spending on the army and civil service by an estimated 50 per cent,

diminishing the amount available to other section of the population.

In 2004 long-term funding was provided, by international donors, to provide more health workers, disease control, HIV testing, mother-to-child infection reduction and to dispense free antiretroviral drugs to HIV/Aids sufferers. Foreign donors had suspended aid funding in 2001 due to corruption and mismanagement and new funding is offered with the proviso of independent vetting.

HIV prevalence: 15 per cent of 15–49 year olds; 8.4 per cent national prevalence and 24 per cent females of reproductive age (The Global Fund).

Life expectancy: 41 years, 2004 (WHO 2006)

Fertility rate/Maternal mortality rate: 6.0 births per woman, 2004 (WHO 2006)

Child (under 5 years) mortality rate (per 1,000): 112 deaths per 1,000 live births (World Bank)

Head of population per physician: 0.02 physicians per 1,000 people, 2004 (WHO 2006)

Welfare

Around 65 per cent of the population lives below the poverty line and deaths from Aids has killed many family breadwinners, fractured families and left communities vulnerable to social disintegration.

In 2002, the government launched a Poverty Reduction Strategy Paper (PRSP) to gain unqualified relief on its US$2.5 billion foreign debt under the controversial Highly Indebted Poor Countries (HIPC) initiative. Malawi launched its war on poverty at a time when the country was facing a severe food shortage. Two subsequent years of poor harvests and a drought in 2005 increased food shortages and threatens millions of people with starvation.

Main cities

Lilongwe (capital, estimated population 656,549 in 2005), Blantyre (691,348), Mzuzu (130,205), Zomba (97,663).

Languages spoken

English is the primary language in business. Chewa (or Chichewa, literally, language of the Chewa) is the major national language; Nyanja, Yao and Tumbuka are also spoken.

Official language/s

English

Media

Press

Dailies: The Nation is the most important daily in Malawi. Others include The Daily Times, The Independent, The Malawi Times, The Malawi News, The Enquirer and NewsdayWO.

Broadcasting

Radio: Domestic radio services are broadcast in English and Chichewa by Malawi Broadcasting Corporation. There is a small number of independent FM stations.

Television: Malawi TV broadcasts for a limited time during the day.

Economy

The country's economy has strengthened as a three-year (2005–08) arrangement under the IMF and the World Bank approved Poverty Reduction and Growth Facility (PRGF) of US$55.9 million to assist the government's economic reforms and poverty reduction programmes has been implemented. The external shock of rising global oil prices had an adverse effect on the country's GDP growth, which was only 1.9 per cent in 2005 but was expected to be between 6–8 per cent in 2006 as markets stabilised. Domestic debt fell to 20 per cent of GDP in 2005/06, despite an increase in inflation of food prices as a prolonged drought reduced the maize harvest; non-food inflation was contained. The food crisis in 2004–05 exposed around half the population to food shortages although humanitarian support averted a greater crisis. In 2006 the bumper maize harvest ended the crisis as prices returned to seasonal norms. Malawi needs around 2 million metric tonnes (mt) of maize annually and had a surplus of 1.5 million mt in 2007. A donation of 10,000mt was made to Lesotho and Swaziland, which continued to be hit by drought.

As Malawi met the Heavily Indebted Poor Countries (HIPC) completion point in August 2006, it became eligible for further relief. In September 2006, Malawi's creditors allowed debt relief of US$646 million under the enhanced HIPC initiative, which is an amount equivalent to US$3.1 billion in nominal terms of actual dollar value over a period of time. The IMF believes this initiative will save an average of US$50 million per year in debt service payments by 2020, an amount equivalent to around 2.5 per cent of annual GDP for the 2001–09 period and 1.2 per cent of annual GDP for the 2010–20 period. The country's annual service payments on outstanding debt is estimated to average US$5 million (2005–25).

The service sector provides 46 per cent of the economy, agriculture 35 per cent and industry 19 per cent, of which manufacturing is 13 per cent. The principal agricultural export product is tobacco which provides 60 per cent of foreign exchange. However, due to low prices in 2006 production is expected to fall in 2007.

National development is hampered by poor road infrastructure and a low-skilled labour force, which has deterred foreign investment. Structural adjustment has not yet led to an increase in private domestic savings, which have diminished partly due to the HIV/Aids pandemic. Nevertheless the improvements in the economy and the projected increase in per capital income of US$171, for 2007, is an encouraging sign.

External trade

Malawi was one of the founding members of the Common Market of Eastern and Southern Africa (Comesa), and operates a free trade area (FTA) with eight out of the 20 Comesa members. Internal duties were eliminated in 2000 and a common external tariff is set to be implemented in 2008. Malawi is also a member of the Southern African Development Community (SADC), the objectives of which include reducing trade barriers, achieving regional development and economic growth and evolving common systems and institutions.

Malawi's major exports are tobacco (newly industrialising countries are increasingly important destinations for its export) and tea, which are susceptible to external shocks such as droughts and fluctuating world prices.

Imports

Principal imports are petroleum, food, products, semi-manufactures, consumer goods and vehicles.

Main sources: South Africa (35.9 per cent total, 2006), Mozambique (12.5 per cent), UAE (6.0 per cent).

Exports

Principal exports are tobacco (60 per cent), tea, sugar, cotton, coffee, peanuts, wood products and garments.

Main destinations: South Africa (22.2 per cent total, 2006), UK (13.2 per cent), Germany (10.5 per cent).

Agriculture

Farming

The agricultural sector is the most important single sector of the economy, accounting for 39.1 per cent of GDP in 2004 and employing over 85 per cent of the workforce. The sector consists of two modes of production: smallholders, growing mainly food crops such as maize and groundnuts but also tobacco, and estate farmers, growing cash crops for export. Other food crops include cassava, millet, sorghum and rice. Tobacco production generates about 70 per cent of the country's exports.

Formerly a food exporter, Malawi has become a net importer due to the rising population, adverse weather conditions (especially drought), a decline in farming subsidies and smallholders switching to tobacco as their preferred crop.

In the long term, the country needs more investment in food production. Much of the investment in agriculture in the past has been directed at improving export-oriented production, while food production has been neglected.
Donors have been reluctant to give aid for investment due to the lack of transparency in previous years. The government and donor agencies will need to work together to ensure a more even pattern of investment in farming.
Estimated crop production in 2005 included: 1,860,200 tonnes (t) cereals in total, 1,750,000t maize, 2,600,000t cassava, 1,800,000t potatoes, 50,000t rice, 360,000t bananas, 300,000t plantains, 254,800t pulses, 55,754t oilcrops, 69,500t tobacco, 3,000t green coffee, 50,000t tea, 3,540t various spices, 2,100,000t sugar cane, 20t vanilla, 878,400t fruit in total, 309,800t vegetables in total. Estimated livestock production included: 59,284t meat in total, 15,990t beef, 21,000t pig meat, 6,612t goat meat, 15,280t poultry, 19,500t eggs, 35,000t milk, 1,560t cattle hides, 1,157t goatskins.

Fishing

Malawi has the western and southern shores of Lake Malawi, one of the world's largest lakes. The fishing industry is an important sector, providing much needed protein. Production can vary between 50–65,000 tonnes per year although catches have been falling since 1990 and as a consequent fish imports have increased.
The African Development Fund (ADF) has released US$10.5 million to increase fish resources in five Lake Malawi districts. Part of the money has been used to fund the Lake Malawi Artisanal Fisheries Development Project to assist local fishermen.

Forestry

Around 35 per cent of Malawi's land area is forested and there are significant areas of plantation forests. There are nine national parks and game reserves and a large number of forest reserves which provide varying levels of protection against deforestation. However, during 1990–2000, forest cover disappeared at a rate of 2.41 per cent per year, one of the highest rates of deforestation in the world. This is largely due to the use of wood for fuel for domestic and industrial uses.
Exports of forest products amounted to US$2.0 million, while imports were US$11.3 million.
Estimated timber production in 2004 included 5,621,655 cubic metre (cum) roundwood, 520,000cum industrial roundwood, 45,000cum sawnwood, 130,000cum sawlogs and veneer logs, 17,500cum wood-based panels, 5,101,655cum woodfuel, 426,494t charcoal.

Industry and manufacturing

The industrial sector contributes around 15 per cent to GDP and employs 15 per cent of the workforce. The industrial sector is centred on agri-processing.
The major constraints on growth are the country's relatively limited resource base, small domestic market and difficulties in importing raw materials and intermediate goods.
Industrial production grew by 6.3 per cent 2004.

Tourism

Tourism is being developed with foreign involvement. The country has much to offer the tourist with various landscapes including forests, lakes and mountains. There are several national parks, game reserves, and a friendly population. Travel and tourism is expected to contribute US$71 million or 3.7 per cent of GDP and employ around 133,000 people in 2005. The sector is estimated to attract US$5.5 per cent of all capital investment and generate 12.5 per cent of all exports. However attractive the country may be, Malawi's infrastructure is poor and off-putting to all but the most intrepid. The Department of Tourism has been criticised for being ineffective and lacking a national plan to market Malawi, which means that much revenue is being lost. In 2005, many visitors will also be uneasy at visiting while around half the population is malnourished and many are starving. The tourist sector may have to forego growth until the drought and famine have ended.

Mining

The sector is underdeveloped, but has potential in the extraction of heavy mineral sand, bauxite, phosphate, uranium and rare earth elements.
There are three heavy mineral sand deposits with considerable titanium resources: Tengani with over 100 million tonnes of heavy minerals, Mpyukyu/Kachulu with over four million tonnes of ilmenite, 300,000 tonnes of zircon and 10,000 tonnes of rutile and beach deposits along the shores of Lake Malawi.
The Australian owned Kayelekera uranium deposits has reserves of 11,000 tonnes of uranium ore at 0.16 per cent grade. The mine's total capital costs are estimated at up to US$65 million, while the revenue from the mine's 10-year lifespan is estimated to average between US$30–34 million per year.

Hydrocarbons

Malawi has no known oil or natural gas reserves, although there is a possibility of oil reserves beneath Lake Malawi. The government is trying to promote exploration in this area but has so far been unsuccessful. Malawi is dependent on importing refined oil products from its neighbours, mainly of gasoline and distillate. Most of the country's fuel imports are supplied via Tanzania, and South African ports and delivered by tanker.
Malawi does not import natural gas. In 2004 a study looked into the feasability of a new 248-mile fuel pipeline between the Mozambican port of Nacala and the town of Liwonde in Malawi.
There are very small coal reserves in Malawi and the Mchenga coal mine still produces below capacity. Malawi hopes to develop its coal mining industry and increase production at Mchenga in order to become self sufficient.

Energy

Malawi has around 285MW of electricity generating power, although distribution is hampered by serious disruptions caused by crumbling infrastructure and poor investment. Only 4 per cent of the population has access to electricity and only 1 per cent of these live in rural areas, compared to an average accessibility rate of 20 per cent for the whole of the Southern African Development Community (SADC).
All liquid fuels are imported, except for a small amount of ethanol produced from sugar cane. Imported liquid fuels are blended 4:1 with ethanol. Approximately 90 per cent of energy requirements are met by wood-burning. A planting programme has had to be implemented to replace dwindling resources with shortages becoming acute in the southern region. Fuel price rises have increased pressure on wood resources.

Financial markets

Stock exchange

The Malawi Stock Exchange (MSE) was established in 1996. It is one of the smallest in the world and sees little activity.

Banking and insurance

The banking system is underdeveloped and the vast majority of lending is to the government and parastatals. There is little lending to private individuals. There are five commercial banks in operation in Malawi. Although the sector is open to foreign participation, few foreign banks have shown an interest in establishing operations in Malawi.

Central bank

Reserve Bank of Malawi

Main financial centre

Blantyre and Lilongwe

Time

GMT plus two hours

Geography

Malawi is a landlocked country in southern central Africa, with Zambia to the

west, Mozambique to the south and east, and Tanzania to the north.
A fifth of the country is covered by lakes, including one of the largest in Africa, the 580km-long Lake Malawi (formerly Lake Nyasa), which borders on Tanzania and Mozambique. The lake is situated in the north-south Rift Valley and is drained by the Shire river, which flows south to meet the Zambezi in Mozambique. The terrain beyond the Rift Valley comprises plateaux and mountains, ranging from 1,000m to 3,000m high, with lower-lying land in the south. There are forests in the northern mountain areas. The Mulanje Massif, at 3,002m (Sapitwa Peak) the highest point in Malawi and central Africa, lies in the southern area, near Blantyre.

Hemisphere
Southern

Climate
On the shores of Lake Malawi and upper Shire River, the weather is pleasantly warm most of the year, hotter in the rainy season. It is more temperate in the highlands and on the plateaux, with cool nights all year. Around the lower Shire River and the south, it is more tropical and very hot during the rains.
The May–August period is cool and dry (the Chiperoni wind can be chilly during July and August). The hottest months are September–November. The rainy season is November–April.

Dress codes
There are no restrictive dress codes and resort wear is informal. Travellers are advised to respect local sensibilities, especially when visiting remote areas. Formal attire is usual for business.

Entry requirements
Passports
Required by all, valid for six months beyond date of departure.
Visa
Required by all, except nationals of most EU and Commonwealth countries, Japan and US. For further details contact the nearest consulate.
All travellers must have return/onward passage.
Currency advice/regulations
There are no restrictions on the import of local currency, but export is limited to K200. There are no restrictions on the import of foreign currency, subject to declaration, and export is limited to the amount declared on arrival.
Travellers cheques and all major currencies are accepted by banks, authorised hotels and other institutions. Recommended travellers cheques are South African rand, UK sterling, euros and US dollars.

Customs
Health (for visitors)
Healthcare and facilities are basic and expatriate residents usually travel to South Africa when in need of anything but the most straightforward medical care. Medical insurance including emergency evacuation should be arranged prior to travel.
Mandatory precautions
Yellow fever vaccination certificate is required if arriving from an infected area.
Advisable precautions
Typhoid, polio, tetanus and hepatitis A vaccinations. HIV/Aids is endemic and precautions must be taken. Take malaria prophylactics and use mosquito nets at night when provided, as well as insect repellents, especially in lower-lying areas. Cholera and rabies are a risk in some areas; vaccinations are only recommended for those at particularly high risk. Bilharzia is an increasing problem, visitors should only swim in designated areas or in swimming pools.
Although tap water is safe to drink in Lilongwe, Blantyre, Limbe and Zomba, water should be boiled or purifying tablets used in rural areas.
It is advisable to carry a sterile first aid kit including syringes, as well as any prescribed medicines.

Hotels
Good hotels available in all main commercial centres. However, space can be limited so reservations should be made well in advance and a booking confirmation obtained. A 10 per cent service charge and government tax are added to bills, and a small tip is occasionally expected.

Credit cards
Credit cards are accepted in major hotels, restaurants and car hire companies in Blantyre and Lilongwe.

Public holidays (national)
Fixed dates
1 Jan (New Year's Day), 15 Jan (John Chilembwe Day), 3 Mar (Martyrs' Day), 1 May (Labour Day), 14 Jun (Freedom Day), 6 Jul (Republic Day), 25–26 Dec (Christmas).
If a public holiday falls on a Saturday, the preceding day will be a holiday; if on a Sunday, the next day will be a holiday.
Variable dates
Easter, Mothers' Day (second Mon in Oct), Arbor Day (second Mon in Dec).

Working hours
Banking
Mon–Fri: 0800–1400.
Business
Mon–Fri: 0730–1700, with one-hour lunch break 1200–1300.
Government
Mon–Fri: 0730–1700, with one-hour lunch break 1200–1300.
Shops
Mon–Fri: 0800–1700; Sat: 0800–1200.

Telecommunications
Telephone/fax
The telephone system is poor.
Mobile/cell phones
GSM 900 services are available throughout much of the country.

Electricity supply
230V/50Hz.

Security
Normal precautions should be taken. Travel after nightfall should be avoided.

Getting there
Air
National airline: Air Malawi.
International airport/s:
Lilongwe-Kamuzu International (LLW), 26km north of the city; bars, restaurants, bank, post office, shops, car hire.
Airport tax: US$30, paid in US dollars.
Surface
The lake-ship-road-rail Northern Corridor route to Dar es Salaam (Tanzania) carries half of Malawi's fuel imports. It has the potential capacity to carry up to two-thirds of foreign freight.
Road: Road border points with Zambia, Mozambique and Tanzania open 0600—1800. To bring a vehicle into Malawi, either a carnet de passage is required, or a temporary import permit (TIP) which can be obtained at border posts for a small fee. There are two main routes from Zambia: via Chipata on the Lilongwe to Lusaka road and, further north, via Chitipa on the Karonga to Nakonde road. Entry from Tanzania is via the Songwe river bridge, north of Kaporo. Roads also link with Mozambique.
Rail: Link with Nacala (Mozambique), but capacity is severely limited by poor track condition.

Getting about
National transport
Air: Air Malawi flies regular services linking Lilongwe, Blantyre, Mzuzu, Karonga, Nyika National Park and the southern lakeshore. There are also charter services to several locations.
Road: There are around 28,000km of roads with major highways linking main centres. The standard of the surfaces is variable and can be poor.
Buses: The bus network covers most of the country. Luxury coaches operate on the Blantyre-Zomba-Lilongwe route.
Rail: There is a limited rail network, largely used for freight. Passenger services are slow and crowded and not suitable for tourists.

Water: A passenger ferry boat operates on Lake Malawi travelling between Monkey Bay in the south and Chilumba in the north, stopping regularly in between. The round trip operates weekly.

City transport

Taxis: Taxis operate in the main towns, but are scarce. Fares should be agreed in advance of journey.

Buses, trams & metro: There are regular bus services in and between the main centres, including luxury services between Lilongwe and Blantyre and Lilongwe and Mzuzu.

Car hire

Car hire is available in main cities. Demand is high so cars should be booked in advance. Self-drive cars are hired at a daily rate, which includes the first 40km. A full international driver's licence is required and a minimum age of 25 with two years' driving experience. Seat belts must be worn in the front seats. Traffic drives on the left. General speed limit of 80kph, and 60kph in urban areas.

Chauffeurs charge a daily rate plus overtime after 1600 and at lunch-time.

BUSINESS DIRECTORY

The addresses listed below are a selection only. While World of Information makes every endeavour to check these addresses, we cannot guarantee that changes have not been made, especially to telephone numbers and area codes. We would welcome any corrections.

Telephone area codes

The international direct dialling code (IDD) for Malawi is +265, followed by the subscriber's number.

Useful telephone numbers

International operator: 102
Domestic operator: 0
Directory enquiries: 191
Emergencies (Blantyre, Lilongwe): 199

Chambers of Commerce

Central Region Chamber of Commerce, PO Box 31357, Lilongwe (tel: 1759-593; fax: 1758-982; e-mail: crcci@sdnp.org.mw).

Malawi Confederation of Chambers of Commerce and Industry, Masauko Chipembere Highway, Chichiri Trade Fair Grounds, PO Box 258, Blantyre (tel: 1671-988; fax:1671-147; e-mail: mcci@eomw.net).

Northern Region Chamber of Commerce, Private Bag 135, Mzuzu (tel: 3133-415; fax: 1334-619; e-mail: nrcci@sdnp.org.mw).

Southern Region Chamber of Commerce, PO Box 258, Blantyre (tel/fax: 1675-113; e-mail: srcci@sdnp.org.mw).

Banking

CBM Financial Services Limited, PO Box 2619, Victoria Avenue, Blantyre (tel: 1621-280; fax: 1624-525).

Stanbic Malawi, PO Box 1111, Capital City, Blantyre (tel: 6120-144; fax: 1620-117).

Finance Bank of Malawi, PO Box 421, Finance House, Victoria Avenue, Blantyre (tel: 1624-799; fax: 1622-957; email: makhan@malawi.net).

First Merchant Bank Limited, PO Box 122, First House, Glyn Jones Road, Blantyre (tel: 1622-787; fax: 1621-978).

Investment & Development Bank of Malawi, PO Box 358, Indebank House, Kaushong Road, Top Mandala, Blantyre (tel: 1620-055; fax: 1623-353).

Loita Investment Bank Ltd, Loita House, Victoria Avenue; Private Bag 389, Chichiri, Blantyre 3 (fax: 1622-683).

Malawi Savings Bank, PO Box 521, Umoyo House, Blantyre (tel: 1625-111 fax: 1621-929).

National Bank of Malawi, PO Box 945, Victoria Avenue, Blantyre (tel: 1620-622; fax: 1620-464).

Central bank

Reserve Bank of Malawi, Convention Drive, City Centre, PO Box 30063, Lilongwe 3 (tel: 1770-600; fax:1 772-752; e-mail: webmaster@rbm.mw).

Travel information

Air Malawi, PO Box 84,4 Robins Road, Blantyre (tel: 1820-811; fax: 1820-042; e-mail: it@airmalawi.net).

Malawi Railways, PO Box 5492, Limbe (tel: 1640-844; fax: 1640-683).

Ministry of tourism

Ministry of Information and Tourism, Tourism House, Convention Drive, PO Box 326, Lilongwe (tel: 1775-499; fax: 1770-650; e-mail: psinfo@sdnp.org).

National tourist organisation offices

Malawi Tourism Association, Aquarius House, PO Box 1044, Lilongwe (tel: 1770-010; fax: 1770-131; e-mail: mta@malawi.net).

Ministries

Ministry of Economic Planning and Development, PO Box 30136, Capital City, Lilongwe 3 (tel: 1782-300; fax: 1782-224).

Ministry of Energy and Mining, Private Bag 309, Lilongwe 3 (tel: 1784-178; fax: 1784-236).

Ministry of Lands and Valuation, Tikwere House, Private Bag 311, Lilongwe 3 (tel: 1780-755; fax: 1780-727).

Ministry of Physical Planning and Surveys, PO Box 30385, Capital City, Lilongwe 3 (tel: 1784-655).

Ministry of Trade and Industry, PO Box 30366, Lilongwe 3 (tel: 1732-711; fax: 1732-551).

Other useful addresses

Agricultural Development & Marketing Corporation (ADMARC), PO Box 50512, Limbe (tel: 1640-500; fax: 1640-486).

Civil Service Commission, PO Box 30133, Capital City, Lilongwe 3 (tel: 1783-811).

Electricity Supply Commission of Malawi, PO Box 2047, Blantyre (tel: 1622-000; fax: 1622-008).

European Development Fund, Lingadzi House, PO Box 30102, Lilongwe 3 (tel: 1730-255).

Geological Survey Department, PO Box 27, Zomba (tel: 1522-166; fax: 1522-716).

Immigration Office, PO Box 331, Blantyre (tel: 1623-777; fax: 1623-065).

Malawi Broadcasting Corporation, PO Box 30133, Chichiri, Blantyre 3 (tel: 1671-222; fax: 1671-257).

Malawi Bureau of Standards, PO Box 946, Blantyre (tel: 1670-488; fax: 1670-756).

Malawi Development Corporation, Development House, PO Box 566, Blantyre (tel: 1620-100; fax: 1620-584).

Malawi Embassy (USA), 2408 Massachusetts Avenue, NW, Washington DC 20008 (tel: (+1-202)-797-1007; fax: (+1-202)-265-0976; e-mail: embassy@malawi.org).

Malawi Export Promotion Council, Delamere House, Victoria Avenue, PO Box 1299, Blantyre (tel: 1620-499).

Malawi Investment Promotion Agency, Private Bag 302, Lilongwe 3 (tel: 1780-800; fax: 1781-781).

Malawi Iron and Steel Corporation, PO Box 2165, Blantyre (tel: 671-455).

National Statistical Office, PO Box 333, Zomba (tel: 1522-377; fax: 1523-130).

Registrar General's Department (Companies etc), Private Bag 100, Blantyre (tel: 1635-077; fax: 1640-877).

United Nations Development Programme, Resident Representative, PO Box 30135, Capital City, Lilongwe 3 (tel: 1783-500; fax: 1783-637).

Internet sites

Africa Business Network: http://www.ifc.org/abn

AllAfrica.com: http://allafrica.com

African Development Bank: http://www.afdb.org

Africa Online: http://www.africaonline.com

Malaysia

Political discourse in Malaysia has long been restricted, not only by prohibitive legislation, but by traditional respect for cultural, ethnic and religious differences. The lack of upward pressure on government has occasionally been broken, but for the most part there has been a reluctance by Malaysia's younger generations to become engaged in civil society.

Elections and protest

The principal division, some would say fault line, of Malaysian society has always been its ethnicity. The country's principal ethnic groups – Malays, Chinese and Indians – have clung to their own political parties, schools, newspapers and even, in the case of the Malays, their own separate Islamic legal system. This de facto segregation was seen by many as the optimum formula for a uniquely Malaysian social harmony. 2007 revealed this 'harmony' as more of a standoff, as years of muted tensions began to boil over into the electoral mix. The Malaysian government was in some ways distanced from the cause of the discontent, if not its effect. In November 2007 the Indian community, constituting less than 10 per cent of the population, announced that they were bringing a US$4 trillion lawsuit against the British government for bringing them to Malaysia (Malaya as it was then known) as indented labourers and 'exploiting them for 150 years and allowing them to be marginalised'. A street demonstration lead by the Hindu Rights Action Force (Hindraf) was the first ethnically motivated street demonstration in Kuala Lumpur for more than four decades.

During 2007 the tensions that had built up within Malaysia's ethnic communities had become blurred with more general dissatisfaction at the government of Prime Minister Abdullah Badawi who, on taking power, had promised to get rid of corruption and make Malaysia's government more accountable. In November 2007, as the elections approached, a grouping of activist groups from across Malaysia's political spectrum organised demonstrations demanding clean and fair elections. Other demonstrations focussed on the rising food and fuel prices which by late 2007 had become a global problem. The general malaise forced the government, in February 2008, to dissolve parliament and call a general election.

The opposition parties hoped to take advantage of the general dissent and at least make something of a dent in the ruling National Front coalition's decades' long grip on power. It was accepted that the ruling coalition which had held the reins since 1957, would probably hold on to a majority in parliament. The immediate objective of the opposition parties was to obtain a minimum of one third of the federal parliament's seats, which would deprive the government of the ability, among other measures, to amend the constitution. In 50 years the National Front had amended the constitution 40 times. The ruling coalition was led, and effectively controlled, by the Pertubuhan Kebangsaan Melayu Bersatu (United Malays National Organisation) (UMNO), headed by Mr Abdullah, with some nine-tenths of the parliamentary seats and controlling all but one of the 13 state governments. In the vanguard of the opposition was the multi-ethnic Parti Keadilan Rakyat (PKR) (People's Justice Party) which had allied itself in the election with the Chinese Parti Tindakan Demokratik (PTD) (Democratic Action Party) and the conservative Parti Islam se Malaysia (PAS) (Islamic Party of Malaysia).

Mr Baddawi had been accused by some opposition politicians of having slept through his period of government. As the election results came in, it became clear that during the campaign Mr Baddawi had been asleep at the wheel. The National Front managed to retain its majority with a 51.2 per cent vote, but it had indeed lost its two-thirds majority for the first time since 1969. Just as chastening for the National Front was the loss of control of four of the largest states – Selangor, Penang, Kedah and Perak. The opposition had already controlled Kelantan, so after the election a total of five of Malaysia's 13 states had fallen to the opposition.

Quoting figures from the Bank Negara Malaysia (the central bank), the Asian Development Bank (ADB) in its 2008 *Asian Development Outlook* puts Malaysia's

KEY FACTS

Official name: Persekutuan Tanah Malaysia (Federation of Malaysia)

Head of State: Yang di Pertuan Agong (traditional ruler) Sultan Mizan Zainal Abidin ibni Almarhum Sultan Mahmud al Muktafi Billah (from 26 Apr 2007)

Head of government: Datuk Seri (Prime Minister) Abdullah Ahmad Badawi (since 2003; re-elected 10 Mar 2008)

Ruling party: Barisan Nasional (BN) (National Front) multi-racial coalition of 14 parties, led by Pertubuhan Kebangsaan Melayu Bersatu (United Malays National Organisation) (UMNO) (re-elected 8 Mar 2008)

Area: 330,434 square km

Population: 26.84 million (2007)*

Capital: Kuala Lumpur; Putrajaya (administrative capital)

Official language: Bahasa Malaysia

Currency: Ringgit (also known as Malaysian dollar) (M$) = 100 sen

Exchange rate: M$3.24 per US$ (Jul 2008)

GDP per capita: US$6,948 (2007)

GDP real growth: 6.30% (2007)

Labour force: 11.01 million (2004)

Unemployment: 3.50% (2005)

Inflation: 2.10% (2007)

Oil production: 755,000 bpd (2007)

Balance of trade: US$28.68 billion (2006)

Foreign debt: US$53.36 billion (2004)

Visitor numbers: 17.55 million (2006)*

* estimated figure

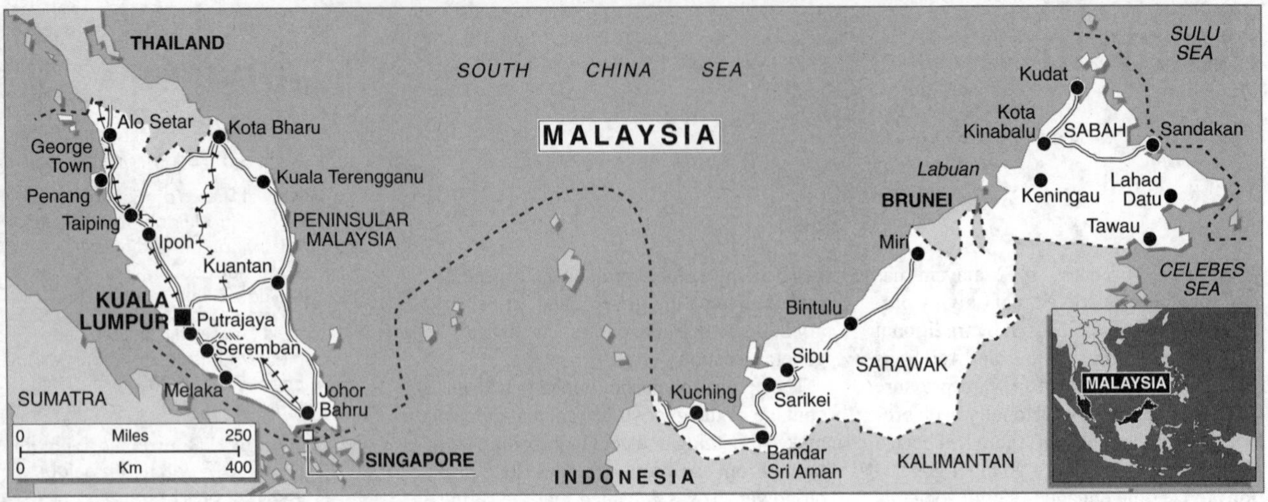

GDP growth for 2007 at 6.3 per cent, up from the 5.9 per cent recorded in 2006. According to the ADB, Malaysia's growth was driven mainly by domestic demand, which offset slower goods and services exports growth. Private consumption jumped 11.7 per cent driven by pay increases for government officials, stable interest rates, and favourable commodity prices. Public consumption also grew, to 6.4 per cent from 5.0 per cent a year earlier. Gross investment finally started to recover after the 1997 crisis, reaching 10.2 per cent in 2007 – more than triple the annual average over the last five years. FDI rose by 54 per cent, amounting to US$9.4 billion in 2007. On the supply side, the growth was broad based. The services sector continued to perform well (9.7 per cent growth), and mining sector and construction rebounded after a few years of negative growth. Reflecting slowing exports, the manufacturing sector expanded only 3.1 per cent, the slowest pace since 2001. Agricultural sector growth also slowed, to 2.2 per cent, mainly from sluggish rubber production.

Malaysia's current account surplus remained high, at 15 per cent of GDP in 2007.

Gross export growth slowed to 2.7 per cent, compared to an average of 12.1 per cent during 2002–06. Electronic and electrical exports, which typically account for about 60 per cent of Malaysia's total manufactured exports, decreased by 4.2 per cent. Slowing electronic exports were partially offset by agricultural and commodity products that expanded 14.5 per cent due mainly to higher commodity prices. Exports to the US dropped 14.5 per cent in 2007. Exports to Singapore, which re-exports many Malaysian products to the US, also fell, by 2.5 per cent. Exports to China increased dramatically by 24.3 per cent, as did those to Japan (5.8 per cent), and the EU (3.8 per cent). The balance of payments position remained favourable with reserves rising by the end of February 2008 to US$116.1 billion, equivalent to 9.6 months of retained imports and 6.8 times the short term external debt. Total external debt as a per centage of GDP continued to fall, to 31.3 per cent for 2007.

Inflation began to show signs of rising in late 2007. Annual inflation for the year remained moderate at 2.7 per cent, down from 3.6 per cent in 2006. However, the monthly CPI for food and non-alcoholic beverages increased from 2.3 per cent in June 2007 to 4.2 per cent in February 2008 driven by high commodity prices. Furthermore, although fuel price subsidies were reduced in 2005 and 2006, subsidies were maintained in 2007, suggesting that further adjustment would be needed. The Malaysian ringgit continued to appreciate against the US dollar. By the end of March 2008, the ringgit stood at M$3.18 per US dollar, having appreciated from M$3.53 and M$3.31 at the end of June and December 2007, respectively. However, compared to other East Asian currencies, Malaysia's real effective exchange rate has appreciated only modestly. Meanwhile, the key policy interest rate has been maintained at 3.5 per cent since its last change in April 2006.

The fiscal deficit amounted to 3.2 per cent of GDP in 2007, just below the figure recorded for 2006. Malaysia's fiscal policy has been expansionary, with increases in spending for emoluments, agriculture and rural development, trade and industry, transport, education, and housing. Government is aware of the need for fiscal consolidation although the budget for 2008 leads to further fiscal expansion.

Federal government domestic debt in 2007 reached 42.3 per cent, which is high relative to other East Asian countries.

The oil

According to the US Energy Information Administration (EIA) and based on information provided by the US *Oil & Gas Journal* (OGJ), Malaysia held proven oil reserves of 3.0 billion barrels as of January 2007, down from a peak of 4.6 billion barrels in 1996. The majority of the country's oil reserves are located off the coast of peninsular Malaysia, and tend to be of high quality. Malaysia's benchmark crude stream, Tapis Blend, is very light and sweet with an API gravity of 44 degrees and sulphur content of 0.08 per cent by weight.

Several new oil production projects have come online during the last few years, although Malaysia's oil output declined somewhat in 2006. Average production for 2006 stood at 798,000 barrels per day (bpd), down 7 per cent from 2005 levels. During 2006, Malaysia consumed an estimated 515,000bpd of oil, with net exports of about 283,000bpd.

Malaysia's national oil company, Petroleam Nasional Berhad (Petronas), dominates upstream and downstream activities in the country's oil sector. Petronas is the only remaining wholly state-owned enterprise in Malaysia, and is the single largest contributor of government revenues. Petronas holds exclusive ownership rights to all exploration and production projects in Malaysia, and all foreign and private companies must operate through production sharing contracts (PSCs) with the national oil company. Malaysia's oil reserves have declined in recent years, despite growth in exploration. Petronas and its various PSC partners have been most active exploring offshore areas, especially in deepwater zones that pose high operating costs and require substantial technical expertise. Despite several new projects that are set to come on stream in the next several years, the EIA forecasts that Malaysia's oil production will fall to 693,000bpd in 2008, a 13 per cent decrease from 2006 levels.

According to the OGJ, Malaysia held 75 trillion cubic feet (Tcf) of proven natural gas reserves as of January 2007. While much of the country's oil reserves are found off Peninsular Malaysia, much of the country's natural gas production comes from Eastern Malaysia, especially offshore Sarawak.

Natural gas production has risen steadily in recent years, reaching 2.2Tcf during 2004, up 47 per cent since 2000. Domestic natural gas consumption has also increased substantially, with 2004 consumption at about 1.2Tcf, or about 61 per cent higher than 2000 levels. Malaysia is a significant net exporter of natural gas, primarily in the form of liquefied natural gas (LNG). In 2005, Malaysia exported just over 1Tcf of LNG, mostly to Japan, South Korea, and Taiwan.

Risk assessment

Politics	Fair
Economy	Good
Regional stability	Good

COUNTRY PROFILE

Historical profile

1511 The Portuguese took control of Malaysia's south-western state, Malacca, as part of their plans to monopolise the South-East Asian spice trade.
1641 Control of Malacca fell to the Dutch who came to control the entire spice trade.
1786 A port was established in Malacca as part of the British East India Company.
1795 The British took full control of Malacca.
1824 The Anglo-Dutch treaty peacefully divided rule of the Peninsula between the Dutch and the British, with the British in control of Malacca.
1826 The states on Malacca, Penang and Singapore were combined to form the Straits Settlements.
1870's Britain brought the Malay states under direct rule. The Pangkor agreement signed with Malay leaders gave the British more control of the territory.
1896 The Malay states were grouped together under a British general. During British control, public services, rubber and tin production were developed. The British brought Indian and Chinese labourers to the country to help with construction projects, altering the country's ethnic make-up.
1939–45 Malaysia was overrun by the Japanese. After their defeat, the British resumed control, but the Straits Settlements were abolished.
1948 The Federation of Malaya, comprising the 11 states of Peninsular Malaysia, was formed.
1951 Pressured by strong Malay nationalism, the British were forced to introduce elections.
1955 The first federal elections were held.
1957 Malaya was granted independence from the British. It remained part of the Commonwealth.
1963 The state changed its name to Malaysia, when Singapore, Sabah and Sarawak joined the federation.
1965 Singapore seceded from Malaysia.
1977 Expulsion of the chief minister of Kelantan from the Parti Islam se Malaysia (PAS) (Islamic Party of Malaysia) resulted in violent demonstrations, the imposition of direct rule in Kelantan and the expulsion of PAS from the ruling Barisan Nasional (BN) coalition.
1981 Dr Mahathir Mohamad succeeded Hussein Onn as leader of the BN party and was formally elected as prime minister.
1986 Mahathir Mohamad was re-elected in the general election, despite internal party conflict caused by the resignation of the deputy prime minister, Musa Hitam.
1988 Constitutional amendments limiting the power of the judiciary to interpret laws were approved. The Security Law was introduced removing the right of persons detained under the Internal Security Act to have recourse to the courts.
1990 Mahathir Mohamad was re-elected.
1995 Mahathir Mohamad was elected for a third term.
1997–98 Severe worldwide financial volatility caused massive capital flight from Malaysia and the ringgit plunged. The authorities imposed capital controls and a selective exchange rate regime against the advice of the IMF. Mahathir sacked his chosen successor, finance minister Anwar Ibrahim, after disagreements regarding economic management and political manoeuvring by some of Anwar's supporters. Anwar was arrested for corruption and sexual misconduct.
1999 Anwar was imprisoned. General elections returned the Pertubuhan Kebangsaan Melayu Bersatu (UMNO) (United Malay National Front)-controlled BN to power and brought Mahathir Mohamad's fourth election as prime minister, avowedly his last.
2001 The new federal territory of Putrajaya was created. Malaysian King, Sultan Salahuddin Abdul Aziz Shah of Selangor, one of nine hereditary rulers, died. The Conference of Rulers chose Syed Sirajuddin, the Raja of Perlis state, as the new King.
2002 King Syed Sirajuddin formally took office. Indonesia, Malaysia and the Philippines signed a pact to counter terrorism and to stop a network that is believed to be trying to turn all three into a single Islamic state.
2003 Mahathir Mohamad, who had been prime minister for 22 years, retired on 31 October. The deputy prime minister,

KEY INDICATORS — Malaysia

	Unit	2003	2004	2005	2006	2007
Population	m	24.41	24.65	25.95	26.39	*26.84
Gross domestic product (GDP)	US$bn	103.70	117.78	130.84	156.09	186.48
GDP per capita	US$	4,042	4,625	5,042	*5,914	*6,948
GDP real growth	%	5.2	7.1	5.2	5.9	6.3
Inflation	%	2.0	1.4	3.0	3.6	2.1
Unemployment	%	3.6	3.6	3.6	3.3	3.2
Oil output	'000 bpd	875.0	912.0	827.0	747.0	755.0
Natural gas output	bn cum	53.4	53.9	59.9	60.2	60.5
Exports (fob) (goods)	US$m	104,999.0	123,500.0	135,495.0	160,842.0	176,403.0
Imports (cif) (goods)	US$m	83,617.0	99,300.0	110,543.0	124,144.0	139,075.0
Balance of trade	US$m	21,382.0	24,200.0	24,952.0	36,698.0	37,328.0
Current account	US$m	13,381.0	15,670.0	19,902.0	25,313.0	26,045.0
Total reserves minus gold	US$m	44,515.0	66,384.0	69,858.0	82,132.0	101,019.0
Foreign exchange	US$m	43,466.0	65,409.0	69,377.0	81,724.0	100,635.0
Exchange rate	per US$	3.80	3.80	3.51	3.55	3.32

* estimated figure

Abdullah Ahmad Badawi, was immediately appointed to be his successor.
2004 The ruling BN coalition was re-elected in the March parliamentary elections. On 26 December, an earthquake off the island of Sumatra caused a tsunami, which devastated coastal areas in the region. The final estimate for Malaysia was 75 dead or missing, 5,000 displaced.
2005 Malaysia's large population of illegal foreign workers was targeted for identification and removal, leaving the country short of labourers. A state of emergency was declared in August, in response to the worst pollution since 1997, emanating from forest fires in Indonesia.
2006 Sultan Mizan Zainal Abidin ibni Almarhum Sultan Mahmud al Muktafi Billah Shah of Terengganu took office as the thirteenth Yang di Pertuan Agong (traditional ruler), and Head of State, a position he will hold until 2011 when the next Conference of Rules choose another candidate.
2007 In April, Sultan Mizan Zainal Abidin was proclaimed king.
2008 On 13 February, the prime minister dissolved parliament for early elections a year before required. With no obvious reason for the dissolution it was speculated that Badawi wanted a further mandate before an expected downturn in the economy and any stringent and unpopular measures he may be required to introduce. In the parliamentary elections held on 8 March, the ruling BN coalition (of 14 parties) was re-elected with 50.3 per cent of the vote (140 seats out of 222, a fall from the previous 198 seats); the opposition Barisan Rakyat (People's Front) coalition (of three parties) won 46.75 per cent (82 seats). Abdullah Ahmad Badawi was sworn in as prime minister on 10 March. Anwar Ibrahim of the Parti Keadilan Rakyat (PKR) People's Justice Party, the opposition leader, was arrested on 16 July on charges of sodomy. Many claim the charges are politically motivated as the PKR has provided a successful challenge to the ruling BN. On 26 August Anwar Ibrahim won a landside victory in the Penang by-election (around 31,195 to the BN candidate's 15,805).

Political structure

Constitution

In 1992, the powers granted to the country's traditional rulers upon independence were modified to the advantage of the federal government.

In 1994, a Constitutional Amendment Bill reduced the power of the monarchy.

Each of the 13 states of the federation has its own constitution and legislative assembly. Malacca, Penang, Sabah and Sarawak are each headed by a governor appointed for a four-year term by the King. A Council of State or cabinet has executive authority in the state, and each state has a legislature which legislates on matters not reserved for the federal parliament.

Form of state

Federative republic; constitutional elective monarchy.

The executive

The supreme head of state, the Yang di-Pertuan Agong (King), is elected every five years by a Conference of Rulers (nine hereditary state rulers). The non-executive Conference of Rulers is made up of the Sultans of Kedah, Perak, Johor, Selangor, Pahang, Trengganu and Kelantan, the Besar of Negeri Sembilan and the Raja of Perlis.

Power is concentrated at the federal level of government in Kuala Lumpur, where a Federal Executive Council, or cabinet, is formed by the party or parties with a working majority in the Dewan Rakyat, the lower house of the federal parliament. The federal government and its premier deal with all federal matters.

National legislature

The bicameral parliment (the federal parliament) consists of the 222-member Dewan Rakyat (House of Representatives), elected every five years by universal suffrage, and the 69-member Dewan Negara (Senate) with two elected members from each state and 43 appointed by the King; senators serve a six-year term. Legislative power rests with the federal parliament, although the Dewan Negara can delay ordinary bills for up to a year. Supply bills, such as the budget, can be delayed for up to one month. The head of state can delay assent to legislation.

Legal system

The basis of the legal system is English common law.

The judiciary underwent major changes in the 1990s. By 1995, the jury system had been completely abolished. Constitutionally, judicial powers have been reduced to the advantage of the Executive. A code of conduct has been established for judges.

Controversy has surrounded Malaysia's retention of the death penalty for certain offences.

Two states, Kelantan and Terengganu, have tried to implement a moderate form of Sharia (Islamic law). This move has been blocked by the federal government. The Federal Court is Malaysia's highest judicial authority, although the King may grant pardons.

Last elections

8 March 2008 (parliamentary)

Results: Parliamentary: the ruling Barisan Nasional (BN) (National Front) coalition (of 14 parties) was re-elected with 50.3 per cent of the vote (140 seats out of 222); the opposition Barisan Rakyat (People's Front) coalition (of three parties) won 46.75 per cent (82 seats).

Next elections

March 2013 (parliamentary)

Political parties

Ruling party

Barisan Nasional (BN) (National Front) multi-racial coalition of 14 parties, led by Pertubuhan Kebangsaan Melayu Bersatu (United Malays National Organisation) (UMNO) (re-elected 8 Mar 2008)

Main opposition party

Barisan Rakyat (People's Front) coalition led by Parti Tindakan Demokratik (PTD) (Democratic Action Party), with Parti Islam se Malaysia (PAS) (Islamic Party of Malaysia) and Parti Keadilan Rakyat (PKR) (People's Justice Party).

Population

26.84 million (2007)*

Last census: July 2000: 23,274,690

Population density: 71 inhabitants per square km. Urbanisation is spreading rapidly, with 58 per cent of the population urbanised by 2001, compared to 34 per cent in 1970.

Annual growth rate: 2.3 per cent 1994–2004 (WHO 2006)

Ethnic make-up

Malaysia is a multi-racial country, including Malay (50 per cent), Chinese (27 per cent) and Indian (9 per cent).

The political dominance of Malays, the 'bumiputeras' prominent in the civil service, military, and education, is accepted by the Chinese and Indian communities in exchange for relative freedom in the private sector. The Kadazans are the principal ethnic group in the state of Sabah, while the Ibans, Bidayuhs and Melanaus predominate in the state of Sarawak. Approximately one million Indonesians work in Malaysia.

Religions

The official religion is Islam (55 per cent), although Malaysia is constitutionally committed to being a secular state. Buddhism, Taoism, Confucianism, Ancestor Worship, Hinduism, Christianity and Sikhism are also practised. The constitution guarantees freedom of religion.

Malays are generally Muslim. Most of the Chinese are Buddhist or Taoist, a few are Christian. The majority of Indians are Hindu, but some are Muslim, Christian or Sikh. Eurasians are predominantly Christian.

Education

Compulsory education covers six years of primary education and three years of lower secondary education.

There is selective entry for upper secondary school that lasts two years for both academic schools and vocational training. Pre-university education lasts for a further year. Higher education is provided by universities, polytechnics and colleges. There are a few private universities with three foreign universities in the country including the Monash University, Curtin University and Nottingham University-Malaysian campus.

Public expenditure on education typically amounts to 4.9 per cent of annual gross national income.

Literacy rate: 89 per cent adult rate; 97 per cent youth rate (15–24) (Unesco 2005).

Compulsory years: 6 to 16.

Enrolment rate: 98.7 per cent net primary enrolment; 69.9 per cent net secondary enrolment (World Bank).

Pupils per teacher: 19 in primary schools.

Health

Per capita total expenditure on health (2003) was US$374; of which per capita government spending was US$218, at the international dollar rate, (WHO 2006).

The Ministry of Health estimates that expenditure on health will reach 7 per cent of GDP by the year 2020. The government allocated a sum of M$5.8 billion (US$1.5 billion) to support the construction of a number of new hospitals and health clinics in 2001. The World Health Organisation's (WHO) assistance to Malaysia for technical co-operation and improving national health strategies amounted to US$1.7 million.

Public hospitals treat about 24.3 million outpatients and 1.5 million inpatients yearly. 55 per cent of doctors are engaged in private practice although only 30 per cent of the population seek medical attention from them. There are 111 public hospitals with seven private medical institutions nationwide with a total of 33,338 beds. Public sector doctors are generally concentrated in urban areas. The government has also made a special allocation of M$1.74 billion (US$46 million) towards improving the rural health services. There is increasing pressure on consumers to draw up individual financing plans through health insurance schemes and managed care organisations.

In 2002, 92 per cent of children were immunised against measles before aged one year.

HIV/Aids

HIV prevalence: 0.4 per cent aged 15–49 in 2003 (World Bank)

Life expectancy: 72 years, 2004 (WHO 2006)

Fertility rate/Maternal mortality rate: 2.8 births per woman, 2004 (WHO 2006)

Child (under 5 years) mortality rate (per 1,000): 7 deaths per 1,000 live births; 19 per cent of children aged under five were malnourished (World Bank)

Welfare

Malaysia's system of social welfare is not comparable to Western standards, but considerable legislation exists in health and safety, and protection for workers against arbitrary dismissal. The Employees Provident Fund (EPF) and Social Security Organisation (SSO) each have approximately 8.5 million contributors. There are also non-profit-making voluntary organisations and ethnic associations that do much community work among Malays, Chinese and Indians.

Main cities

Kuala Lumpur (capital, estimated population 1.4 million in 2005); Kelang (859,864); Johor Bahru (capital of Johor, 416,364); Ipoh (capital of Perak, 690,118); Kelang (859,864), Petaling Jaya (576,077), Kuantan (338,790), Kuching (capital of Sarawak, 154,652); Kota Kinabalu (capital of Sabah, 201,218).

Languages spoken

Bahasa Malaysia is the national language; it is almost identical to Bahasa Indonesia, the official language of Indonesia. English is common in commerce and industry. Chinese dialects (Cantonese, Mandarin and Hokkien) are widely used in Malaysia, and Tamil and Punjabi among Indians. Other languages include Itan Dusan and Bajau.

Official language/s

Bahasa Malaysia

Media

The state exercises some control over print and broadcast media both in terms of ownership and legislative restrictions and regulations. All printed publications are required to have their licences renewed annually. This provides ample incentive for most to limit their criticism of the government. Malaysia's first satellite television service was launched in late 1996; a team of monitors was appointed to censor the 22 channels and control content. Malaysia's information policymakers have not been chary of enforcing political goals through and in the media. The Islamic PAS' party organ, Harakah, was virtually banned in 2000, although the Internet version of the newspaper is still running. A number of journalists, including the editor of Harakah and a Canadian citizen working as local bureau chief for the Far Eastern Economic Review, have been harassed or temporarily imprisoned. The government tends to rely on the mainstream media as its propaganda vehicle. Prominent media groups include Malaysian Resources Corporation (MRCB), which also has power and financial service interests. MRCB has a 50 per cent interest in the main private TV station, Sistem Televiseyen Malaysia (TV3) and a 40 per cent interest in the New Straits Times Publishing Group.

Press

Until 1986, the media was relatively free compared to other developing countries. Local and foreign publications were allowed to publish items critical of government policies. However, the government continued to increase controls on both the local and foreign press over the years. The Printing Presses and Publications Act of 1984, enabled the government to ban any publication, following its amendment in 1987. The legislation allows the imprisonment of people who write and print 'false' news and bars courts from challenging publishing bans. The government controls or owns many of the daily and periodical publications.

Dailies: There are 19 daily newspapers: eight Chinese, five English, four Malay and two Tamil. Circulation is high and sales of newspapers are increasing. Main newspapers are The New Straits Times (English), The Malay Mail (English), Business Times (English), Utusan Malaysia (Malay), Sarawak Tribune, Nanyang Siang Pau (Chinese) Kwong Wah Yit Poh (Chinese) and Tamil Nesan (Tamil). Daily Express is an independent national newspaper of East Malaysia.

Weeklies: New Sunday Times is published on Sundays.

Business: Business publications include the daily Business Times, Banker's Journal Malaysia, Malaysian Industry and The Planter.

Periodicals: Anjung Seri and Mastika are widely read domestic magazines.

Broadcasting

The 1998 Broadcasting Act allowed greater government controls over all radio and television programmes. Under the legislation, Malaysia's information minister has the power to revoke broadcasting licences.

Radio: The state-owned Radio Television Malaysia (RTM) has a virtual radio monopoly. There are four government radio networks broadcasting in the various languages (Bahasa Melayu, Chinese, English and Tamil). In Kuala Lumpur, a visitor can tune in to the Federal Capital radio station.

Television: There are four nationwide TV channels. Two are government-run (TV1 and TV2) and two privately run (TV3 and NTV7). There is also an additional private television station, MetroVision, which only operates in the Klang Valley, which

includes Kuala Lumpur. MEGA TV, a cable network is also available in the country.
Satellite is received from the Malaysia East Asia Satellite (Measat). Measat has two in-orbit communications satellites. A third satellite is planned for 2004 as more satellite capacity is necessary. Demand for the service is high – the first consignment of 7,000 receivers was sold within days. Measat Broadcast Network Systems includes 22 local and foreign channels under the brand name Astro. The government has a 15 per cent stake in Measat Broadcasting through which it hopes to retain strong control over local media; over 100 staff are employed to monitor the content of the 22 channels. Some media production companies and media content providers, including firms active in media entertainment and animation, have moved into the Multimedia Super Corridor (MSC), a 750 square km development zone near Kuala Lumpur.

Advertising

There are a number of well established advertising agencies in Malaysia, including several which have arrangements with international advertising companies. The majority of newspapers and periodicals accept advertising, although government regulations can restrict content and presentation. The Commercial Division of the Ministry of Information is responsible for radio and TV advertisements. Outdoor and cinema advertising is widespread; direct mail is available, but multi-lingualism can restrict its use. Advertising in the country's 420 or so cinemas is limited to consumer goods. Middle-class spending patterns predominate, with some 80 per cent of the population thought to occupy this category.
Advertising spending already totalled US$600 million, or almost 1 per cent of GDP, in the mid-1990s, and has been growing since. Television typically accounts for 36 per cent of this, newspapers 53 per cent and magazines 6 per cent.

Economy

Malaysia is abundantly endowed with natural resources – rubber, palm oil, tin, timber, pepper, oil and gas – and has a stable and fast-growing economy, with wealth from basic resources channelled into diversification through a rapidly expanding industrial sector. The Malaysian economy is one of the cornerstones of south-east Asia and is geared towards attracting foreign investment, especially in the new knowledge-based industries. Malaysia has a high level of technological development, including e-commerce. Industry provides over 50 per cent of GDP, with services providing around 40 per cent and agriculture less than 10 per cent.
In 2005, GDP growth was 5.3 per cent, a fall from the 7.1 per cent in 2004, due in part from a weakened external demand for electronic products and the rise in global oil prices. However the reduced growth rate was ameliorated by a rise in private consumption (growing annually at 4.5 per cent) along with private fixed investments. Malaysia relies heavily on oil and natural gas revenue and the high world prices boosted its trade and current account balances by US$4 billion each in 2005. GDP growth is estimated to be 5.5 in 2006.
The currency, the ringit, was removed from the exchange rate peg on 21 July 2005 and slowly appreciated against the US dollar, growing by about 2.25 per cent.
Other macroeconomic fundamentals were positive, although unemployment rose to 3.5 per cent as the growth in the workforce match growth in employment. Inflation rose sharply in 2005 to 13 per cent, as bank interest rates were lifted for the first time since 1999.
Exports of electronic products are likely to lead a forcast expansion in GDP growth of 5.8 per cent in 2007, despite problems for domestic industries which must compete with state enterprises. Spending in China and the US is expected to sustain the growth and encourage private investment. Nevertheless private consumption, and household debt which has risen to 61.5 per cent of GDP, could cause some concern in the medium-term. The objective of the government's national development policy (NDP) is for Malaysia to become a fully developed nation by the year 2020, not only economically, but throughout society. The government's main priority is to improve its human capital in order to remain regionally competitive. Economic diversification is also being encouraged. Five-year development plans have transformed the economy over the last decade from a low-technology commodity-based environment to one where manufacturing and the services sectors are employing higher and more sophisticated technology.

External trade

Malaysia belongs to the Association of South East Asian (Asean) Free Trade Area (Afta) and maintains a list of goods that have preferential import duties between members and a programme of tariff reductions due to be introduced in the next few years.
Malaysia is a major exporter of manufactured goods, including semiconductor devices and electronic, electrical goods and appliances; it is a major destination for outsourced commodities and the government is encouraging the expansion of hi-technology and software products to provide more skilled employment.
Malaysia is also a world leading producer of rubber, palm oil and cocoa and a major exporter of tropical timber.

Imports

Main imports include electrical and electronic equipment, machinery, petroleum products and plastics, vehicles, iron and steel products and chemicals.
Main sources: Japan (13.2 per cent total, 2006), US (12.5 per cent), China (12.1 per cent).

Exports

Main exports are appliances and equipment, petroleum and liquefied natural gas, timber and wood products, palm oil, rubber, textiles and chemicals.
Main destinations: US (18.8 per cent total, 2006), Singapore (15.4 per cent), Japan (8.9 per cent).

Agriculture

Farming

Agriculture contributes around 9.5 per cent to GDP. Labour shortages and migration from rural to urban areas are contributory factors in the decline of the sector in recent decades. Over 20 per cent of the total land area is cultivated. Malaysia is the world's largest producer of palm oil and natural rubber, the latter accounting for around 25 per cent of world production. Most rubber production (97 per cent) occurs in Peninsular Malaysia. Smallholders account for 69 per cent of output. The government is looking to upgrade the sector from small-scale farming to high-scale farming involving the use of technology.
The government has encouraged diversification away from rubber, the colonial-era staple export, into palm oil production; Malaysia now accounts for over half of world output. World Bank aid has supported government initiatives to improve productivity, increase diversification and alleviate poverty in the agricultural sector. In line with the government's emphasis on new sources of growth within the sector, the production of selected Malaysian tropical fruits and flowers has made a particular contribution. Production and export of cocoa and pepper have increased, as newly planted areas have improved yields. Other main crops are coconuts, sugar cane, tobacco, vegetables, coffee, tea, maize and groundnuts. Sugar cane and tea are grown as plantation crops; for the rest, smallholders account for most cultivation.
The government is trying to encourage higher yields in rice, the main subsistence crop. The formerly state-owned Bernas group, a monopoly rice importer, has entered into joint ventures with Marditech, the commercial arm of the Malaysian

Agricultural Research and Development Institute (Mardi), in a drive to produce high-class rice that could rival Thai varieties. The dominance of smallholdings in rice cultivation remains the biggest barrier to advanced rice cultivation.

The state-run Palm Oil Research Institute of Malaysia (Porim) is attempting to genetically modify the oil palm, in order to create more palm olein, used as refined cooking oil in India and China.

In June 2008 the government announced that more rice would be grown in Sarawak to boost domestic supplies in the face of global price rises of 70 per cent. Malaysia imports over 20 per cent of its rice needs and will divert land assigned for palm oil cultivation to make up national shortfalls.

Estimated crop production in 2005 included: 2,231,000 tonnes (t) rice, 1,200,000t sugar cane, 430,000t cassava, 530,000t bananas, 710,000t coconuts, 75,650,000t oil palm fruit, 30,700t citrus fruit, 320,000t pineapples, 17,034,410t oilcrops, 13,850t tobacco, 33,423t cocoa beans, 40,000t green coffee, 3,900t tea, 1,174,600t natural rubber, 21,000t pepper spice, 5,700t various spices, 2,500t ginger, 1,317,350t fruit in total, 511,000t vegetables in total. Livestock production included: 1,197,673t meat in total, 4,535t buffalo meat, 21,254t beef, 205,500t pig meat, 1,144t lamb and goat meat, 965,000t poultry, 453,000t eggs, 45,125t milk, 3,374t cattle hides.

Fishing

Malaysia typically produces 1.5 million tonnes of fish and other aquatic life per year. It imports about 100,000 tonnes and exports over twice this amount, but the bulk of production is destined for domestic consumption. The main species of fish catch are freshwater fish; marine fish, squid, cuttlefish, octopus, shrimps and prawns. Malaysia is also experimenting with fish-farming.

In 2004, the total marine fish catch was 1,128,781 tonnes and the total crustacean catch was 93,364 tonnes.

Forestry

Around 58 per cent of Malaysia is covered by natural forest. Some 14 million hectares (ha), or 43 per cent of total land area, are within designated Permanent Forest Estates, designed to ensure sustainable forestry. Of these some 10.5 million ha are productive forest, the remainder being protected. More than three million ha are designated as conversion forests, which will eventually be cleared and put into alternative use.

Malaysia is one of the world's largest exporters of tropical hardwood; Sarawak is the most important timber-producing area. New markets have been found in the Middle East. The sector is moving away from upstream operations into those with more value added, including furniture making (25 per cent of total exports), plywood (23 per cent), and sawn timber (17 per cent).

Malaysia is a member of the International Tropical Timber Organisation (ITTO) and is committed to sustainable forest management. Rattan, rubber and bamboo are alternatives to logging.

Import of forest materials in 2004 amounted to US$1.5 billion, while exports amounted to US$3.5 billion.

Timber production in 2004 included 25,116,279 cubic metre (cum) roundwood, 5,598,000cum sawnwood, 22,000,000cum sawlogs and veneer logs, 6,963,000cum wood-based panels, 3,119,279cum woodfuel; 27,480 tonnes (t) charcoal, 978,000t paper and paperboard, (including 250,000t newsprint), 185,000t printing and writing paper, 123,700t wood pulp, 650,000t recovered paper.

Industry and manufacturing

Manufacturing makes the largest contribution to the economy, accounting for over 30 per cent of GDP and 80 per cent of export earnings. Heavy industries based on the country's natural resources have been developed. The promotion of small- and medium-sized firms has been ephasised and measures taken to disperse industries to less developed states.

Conglomerate groups, often politically well-connected, used to control large parts of Malaysian industry.

The recession tamed some of the excesses of this system. Many have been restructured and the old management replaced.

Tourism

Tourism is expected to contribute 5.3 per cent to GDP in 2005. The sector is the second most important foreign exchange earner, after industry. Tourism has been accorded priority status by the government to improve foreign exchange earnings, and to provide employment opportunities.

Visitor numbers fell sharply from 13.3 million in 2002 to 10.6 million in 2003 in the wake of the Sars scare, but rebounded in 2004 to 15.7 million. The majority of visitors to Malaysia traditionally come from other Asean nations. The government wants to attract more long-haul tourists from Europe and Australia.

Mining

The leading minerals mining firm, the Malaysia Mining Corporation (MMC), is trying to diversify away from tin and is prospecting for base and precious metals on the east coast of peninsular Malaysia.

Gold mining has been revived and the Penjom mine accounts for 70 per cent of annual gold production. Malaysia produces around 4,000kg of gold per year. Other resources mined include iron ore, bauxite and copper.

There are undisclosed reserves of gold and antimony in Bau in Sarawak. MMC has also found reserves of copper, silver, gold and bismuth in Pahang state and deposits of alluvial gold in Kelantan state.

The mining sector output is declining, mainly as a result of falling tin, copper and petroleum output.

Hydrocarbons

Malaysia has proven oil reserves of three billion barrels and production of around 775,000 barrels per day (bpd) of crude oil. Domestic consumption is estimated at 519,000bpd. Malaysia exports 270,000bpd, mainly to Japan, Singapore, South Korea and Thailand. There are six refineries with a total refining capacity of 545,000bpd. Oil reserves are in decline.

Most oil production is concentrated in offshore activities around the Malaysian peninsula. A new deep water discovery will help boost reserves and increase production in the near future.

Malaysia has natural gas reserves totalling 2.41 trillion cubic metres and production of 53.4 billion cubic metres per annum, more than double domestic consumption. Most of the surplus gas is converted into liquefied natural gas (LNG) and exported to Japan, South Korea and Taiwan. Malaysia accounts for almost a fifth of global exports of liquefied natural gas (LNG).

Malaysia has proven coal reserves of 275 million tonnes, mainly located on Sarawak.

Energy

Malaysia's total installed generating capacity is 14GW, of which 86 per cent is supplied by thermal plants and the rest by hydropower. Around 52 per cent of demand comes from the industrial sector, 25 per cent from transportation, 12 per cent from commercial sectors and 11 per cent from residential users. It is estimated that demand will have risen by over 8 per cent per annum between 2002 and 2005.

Development of the coal reserves and hydropower potential is intended to diversify sources of energy and reduce the use of gas in thermal generation. Reducing the number of national blackouts Malaysia suffers is a priority.

Five independent power producers (IPPs) supply power alongside the established utilities in Sarawak, Sabah and Peninsular Malaysia.

Financial markets

Stock exchange

Since 1996, foreign companies have been able to list shares on the Kuala Lumpur Stock Exchange (KLSE), which is

one of the world's most important commodity trading centres.
The Malaysia Monetary Exchange (MME) trades interest rate and currency futures, and is distinct from the Kuala Lumpur Options and Financial Futures Exchanges (Kloffe).
The Malaysian Exchange of Securities Dealings and Automated Quotations (Mesdaq) is an over-the-counter market designed to generate venture capital for high-technology companies.

Banking and insurance
Bank Negara Malaysia ordered a major consolidation programme in 2001. This involved creating 10 institutions from 31 commercial banks, 19 financial companies and 12 merchant banks. By end-2001, 51 financial institutions had successfully merged. As a result, Malaysia's banking system is well-capitalised to meet future demands for capital expenditure.
Central bank
Bank Negara Malaysia
Offshore facilities
Measures to enhance development of Labuan island, Malaysia's offshore banking centre, are planned. Approximately 1,000 financial institutions already have a presence in Labuan.

Time
GMT plus eight hours

Geography
Malaysia comprises 13 states in the Malay Peninsula situated south of Thailand, including Sabah and Sarawak states on the north coast of the island of Borneo, which is separated from the Peninsula by the South China Sea. Peninsular Malaysia extends 740km from Perlis state in the north to Johor state in the south. Sabah and Sarawak stretch some 1,120km from Tanjung Datu (Sarawak) in the west to Hog Point (Sabah) in the east.
Malaysia has a land frontier with Thailand to the north, is bordered by the Republic of Singapore to the south and by the Indonesian island of Sumatra across the Straits of Malacca to the west. Other important neighbours are the Philippines and Brunei which separates Sabah and Sarawak.
Hemisphere
Northern

Climate
The climate is tropical with high temperatures and high humidity throughout the year. Relative humidity averages about 80 per cent annually.
Average daily temperatures 21–32 degrees Celsius (C) in the lowlands; in the hill resorts they average 18–24 degrees C but can be as low as 16 degrees C.
November–February is the rainy season for the east coast of Peninsular Malaysia, the north-eastern part of Sabah and western part of Sarawak. In some years, rainfall is concentrated in short periods and some flooding can occur.
During the months of April, May and October, the west coast of the peninsula experiences occasional thunderstorms in the afternoons. Showers are heavy but they clear up as quickly as they come.
Rainfall averages around 2,300mm a year.

Dress codes
Lightweight clothing is worn all year. The dress code tends to be conservative and although jackets are not usually worn in offices, a tie and long-sleeved shirt are normal. For formal meetings, a full suit is required. Government officials often wear a safari-style short-sleeved suit. In deference to the Islamic culture, western business women should dress modestly at all times.

Entry requirements
Passports
Required by all, and must be valid six months from date of departure.
Visitors must have proof of return/onward passage and enough money to finance their stay.
Visa
Social visas are not required by nationals of most countries although the length of stay permitted varies by nationality. There are a number of exceptions, particularly African countries, and for a full list go to http://malaysia.embassyhomepage.com/malaysia_visa_malaysian_embassy_london_uk.htm
There are two categories: a visa with reference (VWR), issued in Malaysia and appropriate for business travellers, and a visa without reference (VWTR), issued in overseas countries. All visitors with a VWTR must enter Malaysia through an airport only.
A visitor's pass issued for entry into the Malaysia peninsular is not valid for entry into Sabah and Sarawak.
Prohibited entry
Holders of Israeli passports.
Currency advice/regulations
The import of local currency is limited to M$1,000, the import of foreign currency in amounts over M$1,000 or equivalent must be declared using a Travellers Declaration Form (TDF), which can be obtained from airports, tourist offices or Malaysian diplomatic missions. Export of local and foreign currency is limited to the amount declared on arrival.
Customs
Personal items and a limited amount of tobacco and alcohol may be imported duty-free.
Prohibited imports
Illegal drugs, firearms and ammunition, daggers and knives and pornographic materials. Malaysia enforces a very strict drug trafficking policy that includes capital punishment.

Health (for visitors)
Mandatory precautions
Valid certificate of vaccination against yellow fever if travelling from infected area.
Advisable precautions
Vaccinations are advisable for diphtheria, tuberculosis, typhoid, hepatitis A and B, Japanese A encephalitis, tetanus and polio. Tap water is boiled by many people before drinking, although it is generally regarded as safe.
There is a malaria risk in Sabah (northern Malaysia) and the eastern Malaysia province of Sarawak. There is a rabies risk.
Visitors with respiratory problems may be put at risk from the poor air quality caused by pollution.

Hotels
There are a range of good hotels in all main cities. A 5 per cent tax and 10 per cent service charge is added to hotel and restaurant meals. Tipping is not encouraged.

Credit cards
Extensive acceptance of all major cards, particularly in urban centres and hotels. Travellers cheques are also widely accepted.

Public holidays (national)
Fixed dates
1 Jan (New Year's Day), 1 May (Labour Day), 31 Aug (National Day), 25 Dec (Christmas Day).
Holidays falling on Sunday are celebrated the next day.
Malaysia's multi-ethnic and multi-religious population celebrates a variety of holidays – federal, Muslim, Christian, Buddhist, Hindu and others.
In addition to federal holidays, each state has 3–4 additional holidays, one of which is the birthday of its ruler.
1 Feb (City Day) is a holiday in the Federal Territory of Kuala Lumpur.
Variable dates
Chinese New Year (two days, Jan/Feb), Birth of Buddha (Apr), The King's Birthday (first Sat in Jun), Divali (Hindu, Oct/Nov), Eid al Adha, Islamic New Year, Birth of the Prophet Mohammed, Eid al Fitr (two days).
Islamic year – 1429 (10 Jan 2008–28 Dec 2008): The Islamic year contains 354 or 355 days, with the result that Muslim feasts advance by 10–12 days against

the Gregorian calendar. Dates of feasts vary according to the sighting of the new moon, so cannot be forecast exactly.

Working hours

The Muslim weekly holiday is Thursday afternoon and Friday and is observed in the states of Johor, Kedah, Kelantan, Perlis and Terengganu. Other states have a Saturday–Sunday weekend.

Banking

Mon–Fri: 0930–1600, Sat: 0930–1130 (second and fourth Sat only).
Mon–Fri: 0800–1200, 1400–1600; Sat: 0800–1100 in Sabah only.

Business

Mon–Fri: 0900–170; Sat: 0900–1300, Malaysia Peninsular, times vary in East Malaysia.

Government

Mon–Fri: 0830–1630 in most provinces. Sat–Wed: 0830–1630; Thu 0830–1230 in Kedah, Kelantan and Terengganu.

Shops

Usually 1000–2200 (department stores and supermarkets), 0930–1900 (shops) in Peninsular Malaysia; Mon–Sat: 0800–1830 in Sabah; Mon–Fri: 0900–1800, Sat: 0900–1300 in Sarawak.

Telecommunications

Mobile/cell phones

There are 3G, 900 and 1800 GSM services available in most populated areas.l

Electricity supply

220V AC, 50Hz. Three-pin square plug fittings and bayonet-type light fittings are generally used.

Weights and measures

Metric system

Social customs/useful tips

Appointments should be made in advance and punctuality is important. It is customary to shake hands on meeting and taking leave, although Muslim women avoid shaking hands with men and vice versa.
Business cards are exchanged after introduction. By tradition, Malaysians are hospitable, open people and prefer to avoid arguments, which are seen as distasteful.
Avoiding loss of face is an important consideration in business negotiations.
Malaysians place great importance on the correct use of titles. Tunku or Tengku indicates hereditary royalty; Tun denotes membership of a high order of chivalry. Tan Sri an Datuk (or Datuk Seri or Dato) indicate knighthood. Tuan or Encik is the equivalent of Mr, Puan of Mrs, Cik of Miss.
Visitors should be aware of the conventions of Muslims, Buddhists and Hindus, and other religious and ethnic groups.
Muslims are not permitted to drink alcohol or eat pork. The fasting month of Ramadan is strictly observed. Use right hand only for receiving anything (food, drink, money etc) and for eating. Refusal of offered refreshment is considered discourteous. It is customary to bargain when shopping, except in department stores.
Tipping is officially discouraged but is seen in the capital.
The authorities have a very strict attitude to drug abuse and there can be a mandatory death sentence for anyone, including foreigners, who is convicted of possession of even a very small amount of narcotics.
Other punishments include whipping, in addition to any custodial sentence. Warning notices about dadah (drugs) are prominently displayed at the airport.

Security

Street crime is low compared with European cities, but is increasing. Bag snatching is becoming common generally, as is passport theft on aircraft and in airport buildings. Possessions should not be left unattended, even in vehicles with a locked boot. Credit card fraud is becoming more common, and care should be taken when paying by this method.
Visitors are advised to avoid street gatherings and demonstrations which could place them at risk, especially if gatherings lack police permission.

Getting there

Air

National airline: Malaysian Airlines (MAS).
International airport/s: Kuala Lumpur International Airport (KUL), 55km south of the city, near Putrajaya, duty-free shop, restaurant, ATMs, bank, business facilities, post office, shops, car hire. Taxis must be pre-paid in the airport arrivals area (travel time 40 minutes). There is also a 24-hour express bus service to and from the city centre (journey time 60 minutes). A high speed rail service, (the KLIA Ekspres), provides access to the city in 28 minutes. Tickets can be purchased onboard or at the KL air terminal office.
Kota Kinabalu (BKI), 7km from city, situated on the northern coast of Sabah state is the principal international airport of Sabah on the north-eastern part of Borneo Island of East Malaysia. Facilities include duty free, bank, restaurant and bars. Taxis have prices for zoned trips.
Other airport/s: Penang (Bayan Lepas) (PEN), 16km south of Georgetown, capital of small island off the north-west coast of the peninsula, duty-free shop, bar, restaurant, currency exchange, hotel reservations, shops, car hire; Kuantan (KUA), 16km from city; Kuching (KCH), 11km from the city, (situated in the west of Sarawak on the island of Borneo) and receives a limited number of international flights.
Airport tax: International departure tax: M$45

Surface

Road: There are two Asian highways that pass through Malaysia. The AH2 and AH18 combined, runs north-south along the eastern seaboard, from Thailand to Singapore.
The state of Johor is linked to Singapore by a causeway.
It is also possible to cross the land border between Malaysia and Indonesia between Pontianak in Kalimantan and Kuching in Sarawak.
Rail: A railway line runs from Singapore to Kuala Lumpur, Butterworth, and on into Thailand.
Water: The main ferry crossing from Singapore is between North Changi and Tanjung Belungkor. High-speed ferries run between Sumatra and Malaysia; routes are either Medan–Penang or Dumai–Melaka. A ferry from Port Kelang, Kuala Lumpur's port, goes to Belawan, on Sumatra. Yachts sail irregularly between Langkawi in Malaysia and Phuket in Thailand.
There are ferry connections between Brunei and Sabah.

Getting about

National transport

Air: There are over 20 domestic airports. MAS operates extensive network services to main centres and, particularly in Sabah and Sarawak, smaller towns.
Road: About 80—90 per cent of the 43,818km road network in Peninsular Malaysia is paved. All major cities and towns are linked by roads although in the monsoon season driving can be difficult.
Buses: Most long-distance bus services operate from Kuala Lumpur to all major cities and town. The buses are fast, economical and reasonably comfortable. Seats can be reserved. On many routes buses are air-conditioned, which cost a little more than the regular buses. In Sabah and Sarawak rural services are provided by four-wheel-drive vehicles.
Taxis: In almost every town there are long-distance taxi offices or teksi (taxi) ranks. They wait for the full complement of four passengers before leaving.
Rail: The capital city is the hub of the national railway system, which is modern, comfortable and economical. Day and night services link major cities in Peninsula Malaysia.
There is a line which branches off the Singapore-Kuala Lumpur-Butterworth-Thailand line at Gemas and runs through Kuala Lipis up to the north-east corner of Malaysia, near Kota Baharu. There are other branch lines which are not used very much.

There are express and ordinary trains. Express trains are air-conditioned and are generally first- and second-class only, and on night trains there is a choice of sleepers or seats.
Rail passes are only available to foreigners and can be purchased at a number of main railway stations.
Water: The Straits Steamship Company operates a passenger service between Port Kelang and Sabah and Sarawak every nine to 10 days. There are frequent ferry services between Penang and Butterworth. There are boats between the Peninsula and offshore islands, and along the rivers of Sabah and Sarawak.

City transport

Taxis: Travel vouchers for airport taxis are available at the airport counters at fixed rates.
Between midnight and 0600, an extra surcharge of 50 per cent applies. There is an extra charge for telephone bookings.
Taxi coupons at fixed prices to various destinations in the city and its vicinity are available at Platform Four of the Kuala Lumpur railway station.
There are bicycle rickshaws in many towns.
Buses, trams & metro: Kuala Lumpur has a 29km, fully automated, driverless, three line, light rail transit (LRT) system (known locally as the Putra, after its original operators): the Kelana Jaya Line, the Ampang Line and the Sri Petaling Line. There are other rail services within the city, including a monorail, a commuter service and two high-speed airport rail links.
Trains: The express rail link between central Kuala Lumpur and the international airport opened in April 2002.

Car hire

Car hire is available in all main cities. Driving is on the left-hand side of the road, and the use of seat belts in front seats is obligatory. International driving licences are required. Chauffeur-driven cars are available.

BUSINESS DIRECTORY

The addresses listed below are a selection only. While World of Information makes every endeavour to check these addresses, we cannot guarantee that changes have not been made, especially to telephone numbers and area codes. We would welcome any corrections.

Telephone area codes

The international direct dialling (IDD) code for Malaysia is +60, followed by area code and subscriber's number:

Ipoh	5	Melaka	6
Johor Bahru	7	Penang	4
Kota Kinabalu	88	Port Dickson	6
Kuala Lumpur	3	Sandakan	89
Kuantan	9	Sibu	84
Kuching	82	Taiping	5

Useful telephone numbers

Emergency	999
Operator (trunk call enquiries)	102
Directory	103
International service	108
Tourist Police	243-5522

Chambers of Commerce

American Malaysian Chamber of Commerce, Amoda Building, 22 Jalan Imbi, 55100 Kuala Lumpur (tel: 2148-2407; fax: 2148-8540; e-mail: info@amcham.com.my).

British Malaysian Chamber of Commerce, c/o British High Commission, 185 Jalan Ampang, 50450 Kuala Lumpur (tel: 2163-1784; fax: 2163-1781; e-mail: britcham@bmcc.org.my).

Kuala Lumpur Chamber of Commerce, 79 Kompleks Damai, Jalan Datuk Haji Eusoff, Kuala Lumpur (tel: 4042-4711; fax: 4042-1540; e-mail: dpmmbkl@tm.net.my).

Malay Chamber of Commerce Malaysia, Plaza Pekeliling,2 Jalan Tun Razak, 50400 Kuala Lumpur (tel: 4041-8522; fax: 4041-4502; e-mail: wmaster@dpmm.org.my).

Malaysian International Chamber of Commerce and Industry, Plaza Mont' Kiara, 2 Jalan Kiara, 50480 Kuala Lumpur (tel: 6201-7708; fax: 6210-7705; e-mail:micci@micci.com).

Banking

Affin Merchant Bank Berhad, PO Box 1124, 27th Floor, Menara Boustead, 69 Jalan Raja Chulan, 50200 Kuala Lumpur (tel: 2070-8080; fax: 2070-7592).

Bumiputra-Commerce Bank Berhad, 6 Jalan Tun Perak, 50050 Kuala Lumpur, (tel: 2693-1722; fax: 2698-6628).

Bank Kerjasama Rakyat Malaysia Bhd, Bangunan Bank Rakyat, Jalan Tangsi, 50480 Kuala Lumpur (tel: 2612-9600; fax: 2612-9576).

Bank Muamalat Malaysia Berhad, Menara Bumiputra, 21, Jalan Melaka, PO Box 10407, 50913, Kuala Lumpur (tel: 2698-8787; fax: 2692-2000).

Bank Pembangunan & Infrastruktur Malaysia Berhad, PO Box 12352, Menara Bank Pembangunan, Jalan Sultan Ismail, 50774 Kuala Lumpur (tel: 2615-2020; fax: 2692-8520).

Bank Islam Malaysia Berhad, Level 11, Darul Takaful, Jalan Sultan Ismail, 50734 Kuala Lumpur (tel: 2616-8000; fax: 2698-0587).

Bank Simpanan Nasional, Wisma BSN, 117 Jalan Ampang, 50450 Kuala Lumpur (tel: 2162-3222; fax: 2710-7252).

Citibank Berhad, PO Box 10112, 165 Jalan Ampang, 50450 Kuala Lumpur (tel: 232-5334; fax: 232-8763).

Malayan Banking Berhad, PO Box 12010, 100 Jalan Tun Perak, 50050 Kuala Lumpur (tel: 2070-8833; fax: 2070-2611).

Bank Negara, Jalan Dato Onn, 50480 Kuala Lumpur (tel: 2698-8044; fax: 2691-2990).

Sabah Development Bank, PO Box 12172, 88824 Kota Kinabalu; SDB Tower, Wisma Tun Faud Stephens, Km 2.4, Jalan Tuaran, Sabah (tel: 232-177; fax: 261-852).

Southern Bank Bhd, Wisma Genting, Jalan Sultan Ismail, Peti Surat 12281, Kuala Lumpur (tel: 263-7000; fax: 232-5008).

Standard Chartered Bank, 2 Jalan Ampang, 50450 Kuala Lumpur (tel: 232-6555; fax: 238-3295).

Central bank

Bank Negara Malaysia, Jalan Dato' Onn, PO Box 10922, Kuala Lumpur 50929 (tel: 2698-8044; fax: 2691-2990; e-mail: info@bnm.gov.my).

Travel information

Automobile Association of Malaysia, E-7-4, Megan Avenue 1, 189 Jalan Tun Razak, 50400 Kuala Lumpur (tel: 2162-5777; fax: 2162-5358; email: mru@aamhq.po.my; internet: www.aam.org.my).

KLIA Ekspres, Express Rail Link Sdn Bhd, L2, KL City Air Terminal, KL Sentral Station, 50470 Kuala Lumpur (tel: 2267-8088, customer enquiry: 2267-8000; fax: 2267-8910; email: air-rail@KLIAekspres.com; internet: www.kliaekspres.com).

Malaysia Airlines, Main Ticket Office, Bangunan MAS, Jalan Sultan Ismail, 50250, Kuala Lumpur (tel: 7846-3000; fax: 2162-9025; email customer@mas.com.my; internet: www.malaysiaairlines.com).

Rapid KL (Public Transport) 1 Jalan PJU 1A/46, Off Jalan Lapangan Terbang, Sultan Abdul Aziz Shah, 47301 Petaling Jaya, Selangor (tel: 7650-7788; fax: 7625-6667; email: suggest@rapidkl.com.my; internet: www.putralrt.com.my).

National tourist organisation offices

Malaysia Tourism Promotion Board, 17th Floor, Menara Dato' Onn, Putra World Trade Centre, 45, Jalan Tun Ismail, 50480 Kuala Lumpur (tel: 2615-8188; fax: 2693-5884; email: enquiries@tourism.gov.my; internet: www.tourism.gov.my).

Ministries

Ministry of Agriculture, Wisma Tani, Jl Sultan Salahuddin, 50624 Kuala Lumpur (tel: 2617 -5000; fax: 2691-3758; email: matdaud@agri.moa.my).

Ministry of Culture, Arts and Heritage, TH Perbadanan Tower, Maju Junction, 10110 Jl Sultan Ismail , 50694 Kuala Lumpur (tel: 2612-7600; fax: 2693-5114, 2697-6100; email: info@heritage.gov.my).

Ministry of Defence, Jl Padang Tembak, 50634 Kuala Lumpur (tel: 292-1333, 230-1033; fax: 298-4662, 298-5372).

Ministry of Domestic Trade and Consumer Affairs, Lot 2G3, Presint 2, Federal Goverment Administrative Centre, 62623 Putrajaya (tel: 8882-5500 ; fax: 8882-5763; email: nsuzana@kpdnhep.gov.my).

Ministry of Education, Level 5, Block E8 Parcel E, Federal Goverment Administrative Centre, 62604 Putrajaya (tel: 8884-6000; fax: 8889-5235; email: julina@bdpk.moe.gov.my).

Ministry of Energy, Water and Communications, Block E4/5, Government Complex, Parcel E , Federal Government Administrative Centre, 50668 Kuala Lumpur (tel: 8883-6000; fax: 8889-5235; email: norliza@ktak.gov.my).

Ministry of Entrepreneur Development and Co-operative Development, Lot 2G6, Precint 2, Federal Goverment Administrative Centre, 62100 Putrajaya (tel: 8880-5100; fax: 8880-5106; email: webmaster@mecd.gov.my).

Ministry of Federal Territories, Level 3, West block , Perdana Putra Building , Federal Government Administrative Centre, 62502 Putrajaya (tel: 8889-7844 ; fax: 8888-9140; email: admin@kwp.gov.my).

Ministry of Finance, Finance Ministry Complex, Precint 2, Federal Government Administrative Centre, 62592 Putrajaya (tel: 8882-3000; fax: 8882-3892/3894; email: webmaster@treasury.gov.my).

Ministry of Foreign Affairs, Wisma Putra , No 1, Jl Wisma Putra, Precint 2, 62602 Putrajaya (tel: 8887-4000/ 4570, 8889-2476; fax: 8889-1717/2816; email: webmaster@kln.gov.my; internet: www.kln.gov.my).

Ministry of Health, Block E1, E6, E7 and 10, Parcel E, Federal Government Administrative Centre, 62590 Putrajaya (tel: 8883-3888; fax: 2698-5964; email: iadam@moh.gov.my).

Ministry of Home Affairs, Block D2, Parcel D, Federal Government Administrative Centre, 62546 Putrajaya (tel: 8886-3000; fax: 8889-1613; email: pro@moha.gov.my).

Ministry of Human Resources, Level 6-9, Block D3, Parcel D, Federal Government Administrative Centre, 62502 Putrajaya (tel: 8886-5000; fax: 8889-2381; email: ksm@mohr.gov.my).

Ministry of Housing and Local Government, Level 3-7, Block K, Pusat Bandar Damansara, 50782 Kuala Lumpur (tel: 2094-7033; fax: 2094-9720; email: pro@kpkt.gov.my).

Ministry of Information, Angkasapuri, Bukit Putra, 50610 Kuala Lumpur (tel: 2282-5333; fax: 2282-1255; email: webmaster@kempen.gov.my).

Ministry of Internal Security, Level 3, Block D1 and D2, Parcel D, Federal Government Administrative Centre, 62546 Putrajaya (tel: 8886 8000; fax: 8889 1730; email: pro@mois.gov.my).

Ministry of Natural Resources and Environment, 13th Floor, Wisma Tanah,, Jl Semarak, 50574 Kuala Lumpur (tel: 2692-1566; fax: 2693-2166; email: webmaster@nre.gov.my).

Ministry of Plantation Industries and Commodities, Level 6–13, Lot 2G4, Precinct 2, Federal Government Administrative Centre, 62654 Putrajaya (tel: 8880-3300; fax: 8880-3482; email: info@kppk.gov.my).

Ministry of Rural and Regional Development, Level 5-9, Block D9, Parcel D, Federal Government Administrative Centre, 62606 Putrajaya (tel: 8886-3500/3700; fax: 8886-3801; email: webmaster@rurallink.gov.my).

Ministry of Science, Technology and Innovations, Level 1-7, Block C5, Federal Government Administrative Centre, 62662 Putrajaya (tel: 8885-8000; fax: 8888-9070; email: webmaster@mosti.gov.my).

Ministry of Transport, Level 5-7, Block D5, Parcel D, Federal Government Administrative Centre, 62502 Putrajaya (tel: 8886-6000/2597; fax: 8889-1569; email: saptuyah@mot.gov.my).

Ministry of Works, Level 4, Block B, Kompleks Kerja Raya, Jl Sultan Salahuddin, 50580 Kuala Lumpur (tel: 2711-1100/ 9309; fax: 2711-6612; email: pro@kkr.gov.my).

Ministry of Women, Family and Community Development, Level 1-6, Block E, Government Office Complex , Kompleks Pejabat Kerajaan Bukit Perdana, Jl Dato' Onn, 50515 Kuala Lumpur (tel: 2693-0095, 2693-0401; fax: 2693-4982; email: info@kpwkm.gov.my).

Ministry of Youth and Sports, Lot G4, Precinct 4, Federal Government Administrative Centre, 62570 Putrajaya (tel: 8871-3333; fax: 8888-8767; email: webmaster@kbs.gov.my).

Prime Minister's Department, Perdana Putra Building, Federal Government Administrative Centre, 62502 Putrajaya (tel: 8888-8000; fax: 8888-3444; email: ppmnun@pmo.gov.my).

Other useful addresses

Advertising Standards Authority of Malaysia, c/o Coopers and Lybrand, Hong Kong Bank Building, Leboh Pasar, Kuala Lumpur.

Asean Investment Promotion Agency, Malaysian Industrial Development Authority, 6th Floor, Wisma Damansara, Damansara Heights, PO Box 10618, 50720 Kuala Lumpur.

Asean Secretariat, 70 A Jl Sisingamangaraja, Jakarta 12110, Indonesia (tel: (+62-21) 726-2991, 724-3372; fax: (+62-21) 724-3504, 739-8234; internet: www.asean.or.id).

British Council, Jalan Bukit Aman, PO Box 10539, 50916 Kuala Lumpur.

British High Commission, PO Box 11030, 50732 KL; 185 Jalan Ampang, 50450 Kuala Lumpur (tel: 2170-2200; (Consular Section, tel: 2170-2345; email: consular2.kualalumpur@fco.gov.uk)).

British Malaysian Industry & Trade Association (BMITA), PO Box 12574, 50782 Kuala Lumpur.

Capital Issues Committee, Kementerian Kewangan, 11th Floor, Block 9, Khazanah Malaysia, Jl Duta, Kuala Lumpur.

Department of Immigration, Level 1-7 (Podium) Block 2G4, Precinct 2, Federal Government Administration Centre, 62550 Putrajaya, Federal Territory (tel: 8880-1000; fax: 8880-1200; internet: www.imi.gov.my).

Federal Land Development Authority, (FELDA), Wisma Felda, Jalan Perumahan Gurney, 54000 Kuala Lumpur (tel: 2693-5066; fax: 2692-0087; email: unitit.felda@felda.net.my).

Federation of Malaysian Manufacturers, Tingkat 7 Balai Felda, Jalan Gurney Satu (1), 54000 Kuala Lumpur (tel: 2698-7772; fax: 2693-0018; email: tohit.1@felda.net.my).

Foreign Investment Committee, Economic Planning Unit, Prime Minister's Dept, Jl Dato' Onn, Kuala Lumpur (tel: 230-0133).

Bursa Malaysia, (Kuala Lumpur Stock Exchange), Exchange Square, Bukit Kewangan, 50200 Kuala Lumpur (tel:

2034-7000; fax: 2732-0069; email: enquiries@bursamalaysia.com).

Malaysian Embassy (US), 2401 Massachusetts Avenue, NW, 20008 (tel: (+1-202) 328-2700; fax: (+1-202) 483-7661; email: mwwashdc@erols.com).

Malaysian Export Trade Centre, Ministry of Trade and Industry, Wisma PKNS, Jl Raja Laut, 50350.

Malaysian Industrial Development Authority (MIDA), Blk 4, Plaza Sentral, Jalan Stesen Sentral 5, Kuala Lumpur Sentral, 50470 Kuala Lumpur (tel: 2267-3633; fax: 2274-7970; email: promotion@mida.gov.my; internet: www.mida.gov.my).

Sarawak Economic Development Corporation, PO Box 400; 6-11th Floor, Menara SEDC, Jalan Tunku Abdul Rahman, 93902 Kuching, Sarawak, (tel: 416-777; fax: 424-330; email: ssedc@po.jaring.my; internet: www.sedc.com.my).

Securities Commission, 3 Persiaran Bukit Kiara, Bukit Kiara, 50490 Kuala Lumpur (tel: 6204-8510; fax: 6201-5078; internet: www.sc.com.my).

Internet sites

Malaysia Homepage: www.jaring.my

Malaysia portal: www.mycen.com.my

Malyasia yellow and white pages: www.tpsb.com.my/thome.htm

Maldives

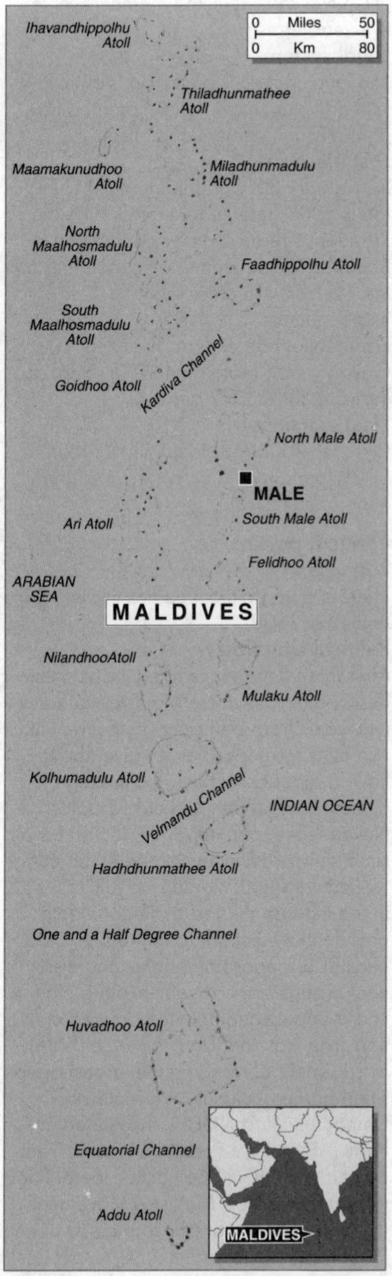

COUNTRY PROFILE

Historical profile

1887 The islands were placed under British protection, with internal self-government.

1932 The first democratic constitution was proclaimed. The sultanate became an elected position.

1953 The Maldives became a republic and a member of the Commonwealth as the sultanate was abolished. However, the sultanate was restored within months.

1965 Gained full independence as a sultanate and left the Commonwealth.

1968 Following a referendum, the country reverted from a sultanate back to a republic. Ibrahim Nasir became president.

1975 The UK pulled out of its military base on Addu atoll. A proposal from the USSR to take over the base was rejected.

1978 Nasir retired and Maumoon Abdul Gayoom was elected president.

1980s The expansion in the tourist industry resulted in the growth in the economy. An industrial zone was established on Gan.

1982 Rejoined the Commonwealth.

1988 An attempt by Sri Lankan Tamil mercenaries to depose the government was thwarted with the help of Indian army forces.

1994 Non-party elections to the Majlis (parliament) were held.

1997 A new constitution was passed.

1998 President Maumoon Abdul Gayoom was re-elected for a fifth consecutive term in office.

1999 Forty non-partisan members were elected to the Majlis.

2002 The Maldivian and Indian governments began working together to implement a plan for poverty reduction in the Maldives.

2003 Riots broke out in Malé when prison inmates protested at alleged torture. President Gayoom won a sixth term with over 90 per cent of the vote.

2004 A special Majlis was formed to consider constitutional changes proposed by the President, including limiting his powers and allow the formation of political parties. A referendum agreed to a presidential and parliamentary style of government. An earthquake off the island of Sumatra caused a tsunami that devastated coastal areas in the region, including 20 inhabited islands of the Maldives. The final toll in the Maldives was estimated at 108 dead or missing and 29,577 displaced.

2005 In parliamentary elections, all candidates for the 42 seats ran officially as

KEY FACTS

Official name: Divehi Raajjeyge Jumhooriyyaa (Republic of Maldives)

Head of State: President Maumoon Abdul Gayoom (since 1978)

Head of government: President Maumoon Abdul Gayoom

Ruling party: There are no political parties in the Majlis, until Mar 2009

Area: 298 square km (1,190 tiny atoll islands) – Malé: 1.5 square km

Population: 345,000 (2007)

Capital: Malé, on Malé Island

Official language: Dhivehi (Maldivian)

Currency: Rufiyaa (MRf) = 100 laari

Exchange rate: MRf12.80 per US$ (Jul 2008)

GDP per capita: US$3,040 (2007)

GDP real growth: 6.60% (2007)

Labour force: 128,000 (2004)

Unemployment: 0.05% (2004)

Inflation: 5.00% (2007)*

Balance of trade: -US$590.00 million (2006)

Foreign debt: US$472.00 million (2007)

* estimated figure

independents and parliament unanimously voted in favour of introducing multiparty politics. Five political parties registered including Dhivehi Rayyithunge Party (DRP) (Maldivian Peoples Party), the president's party, Islamic Democratic Party (IDP), Adhaalath Party (AP) (Justice Party) and Maldivian Democratic Party (MDP). Mohamed Nasheed (known as Anni) returned from exile to register the MDP; he was later arrested for terrorism and sedition.

2006 The South Asia Free Trade Agreement (Safta), came into effect; signatories included Maldives, Bhutan, Bangladesh, India, Nepal, Sri Lanka and Pakistan. Nasheed (MDP) was released from jail.

2007 A referendum, to determine a presidential or parliamentary system of rule, was held on 18 August; 60 per cent of the vote, agreed to a presidential system and endorsed President Gayoom's continued administration. As a threat to the principal industry in the Maldives, a bomb exploded in Malé on 29 September, injuring 12 foreign tourists. Over a dozen militant jihadi suspects were arrested or were later wanted for the bombing.

2008 In January, an assassin failed to kill President Gayoom, when a boy scout wrestled a knife from the attacker's hand. A new constitution was ratified on 7 August which introduced key democratic changes, including multi-party presidential elections, the separation of power and a bill of rights.

Political structure

Constitution

The constitution dates from 1997, which provides power to the executive, the legislature and the judiciary, while these powers are vested from the people. The president also derives influence from the constitutional role as 'supreme authority to propagate the tenets of Islam'.

However critics argue that supreme power under the constitution is held by the president, who can appoint and dismiss the top posts in all branches of the administration. The constitution, it is argued, does not provide a guarantee that individuals' rights are not subject to subordinate laws and government practices.

In 2007 constitutional changes included the introduction of a US-style presidential form of government, where the president can only hold office for two terms and the introduction of a multiparty parliament.

In January 2008 the gender bar that allowed women to serve in the Majlis but not become a presidential candidate, was removed. A new constitution was ratified on 7 August which introduced key democratic changes, including multi-party presidential elections, the separation of power and a bill of rights.

Voting: universal suffrage over 21 years. Local authority is vested in atoll chiefs and island headmen appointed by the president.

The executive

Executive power is held by the president, who is head of state and head of government, commander-in-chief of the armed forces, minister of defence and national security, and minister of finance and treasury.

The president is nominated by the legislature, who is the only candidate offered in a yes/no referendum to the people, for a renewable five-year term. The president has the sole power to summon the Majlis which can alter the constitution by majority vote. A government is appointed and chaired by the president; cabinet ministers are not required to be members of the Majlis.

National legislature

The unicameral Majlis (parliament) has 50 members, 42 are elected and eight are appointed by the president. Each of the 20 administrative atolls has a quota of two members, with the capital Malé also given two seats. Elected members serve five-year terms.

Legal system

The legal system is based on Islamic law with admixtures of English common law, primarily in commercial matters.

Last elections

22 January 2005 (parliamentary); 17 October 2003 (referendum confirming the President's re-election by parliament).

Results: Parliamentary: all candidates for the 42 seats ran officially as independents.

Presidential referendum: President Gayoom won more than 90 per cent of the vote; turnout 77 per cent.

Next elections

October 2008 (presidential); 31 March 2009 (parliamentary, the first multiparty general elections)

Political parties

Ruling party

There are no political parties in the Majlis, until Mar 2009

Political situation

After three decades of rule by one president, politicians in the Maldives, so long held back from participating in civic life, can be forgiven for being naïve about how to mount an effective campaign to defeat the man they see as a dictator. Nevertheless, one important lesson for all such activists is encapsulated in the adage 'united we stand, divided we fall'.

In the lead up the first multi-candidate presidential election, to be held in October 2008, opposition parties and dissident groups came together with a plan to find a single candidate to contest the election. The National Unity Alliance (NUA), was formed, comprising the largest opposition parties including the Maldivian Democratic Party (MDP), the Adhaalath Party (AP) (Justice Party) the Islamic Democratic Party (IDP), the Social Liberal Party (SLP) and the New Maldives Movement (NMM), a party that was formed by three former cabinet ministers.

Before a unity candidate could be found the IDP and SLP left the alliance and Mohamed Nasheed (known as Anni), of the largest grouping, MDP, had alienated broad support within his party when he said he would be prepared to be the running mate of Dr Hassan Saeed (a faction member of the president's ruling Dhivehi Rayyithunge Party (DRP) (Maldivian

KEY INDICATORS — Maldives

	Unit	2003	2004	2005	2006	2007
Population	m	0.28	0.29	0.34	0.34	0.34
Gross domestic product (GDP)	US$bn	1.25	0.78	0.80	0.91	1.05
GDP per capita	US$	3,900	2,318	2,376	2,629	3,040
GDP real growth	%	8.4	8.8	-4.5	19.1	6.6
Inflation	%	-1.5	6.4	3.3	3.7	5.0
Industrial output	% change	–	12.8	3.0	10.6	–
Agricultural output	% change	–	2.7	4.0	-0.7	–
Exports (fob) (goods)	US$m	110.0	175.4	153.2	215.9	–
Imports (cif) (goods)	US$m	395.0	564.8	655.5	815.3	–
Balance of trade	US$m	-285.0	-389.4	503.2	-599.5	–
Current account	US$m	-30.0	-90.0	-274.0	-369.0	–
Total reserves minus gold	US$m	159.5	203.6	186.3	231.4	308.4
Foreign exchange	US$m	156.7	200.7	183.6	228.5	305.3
Exchange rate	per US$	12.78	12.80	12.80	12.80	12.80

Peoples Party). Some MDP party members left in disgust and the party was felt undermined.
In turn the NUA was gravely weakened and the prospect of each opposition party proposing their own candidate could seriously undermine the its chances of winning with the vote split so many ways.

Population
345,000 (2007)
Last census: March 2000: 270,101
Population density: 897 inhabitants per sq km. Urban population: 28 per cent (1995–2001). Malé is one of the most densely populated cities in the world.
Annual growth rate: 2.8 per cent 1994–2004 (WHO 2006)
Ethnic make-up
The majority of the population are Sinhalese or Dravidian, with significant Arab and smaller African minorities.
Religions
Islam (Sunni majority)

Education
Primary education is provided through either private or state schools; lessons are given in English, Arabic and Dhivehi.
The curriculum, for segregated (by gender) secondary education, is based on the British system and many schools prepare students to sit the General Certificate of Education at 'O' level and a few for 'A' level examinations. Students have to travel abroad for higher education.
President Gayoom has made improving education levels his top priority. There is an ongoing teacher training programme due to the shortage of qualified teachers. Typically 2.4 per cent of the GNP is spent on primary education.
Literacy rate: 97.2 per cent total; adult rates (World Bank).
Enrolment rate: 98 per cent net primary enrolment (Unicef).
Pupils per teacher: 24 in primary schools.

Health
Per capita total expenditure on health (2003) was US$364; of which per capita government spending was US$324, at the international dollar rate, (WHO 2006).
The Maldives has significantly improved health services and severe diseases such as malaria, childhood tuberculosis and leprosy have been eradicated.
There are two hospitals on the main island and six regional hospitals serving all the remaining islands. In addition, there are 45 health centres and 36 health posts serving the islands.
By 2002, 99 per cent of children were immunised against measles before aged one year.

HIV/Aids
The first Maldivian with HIV was identified in 1991. There have been six deaths as a result of Aids. Although the HIV rate is very small, the Maldives is particularly vulnerable to the spread of the virus due to the high number of migrant workers that pass through the islands. Drug usage among young people is also on the rise.
Life expectancy: 67 years, 2004 (WHO 2006)
Fertility rate/Maternal mortality rate: 4.1 births per woman, 2004 (WHO 2006)
Child (under 5 years) mortality rate (per 1,000): 55 per 1,000 live births; 45 per cent of children aged under five are malnourished (World Bank).
Head of population per physician: 0.92 physicians per 1,000 people, 2004 (WHO 2006)

Welfare
Due to the highly dispersed character of the country, it is difficult for the government to ensure that everyone receives benefits. The ministry of women's affairs and social welfare has responsibility for administering the welfare programme that covers women, children, the disabled and unemployed.

Main cities
Malé (capital, estimated population 82,726 in 2005).

Languages spoken
The Maldivian language is Indo-Aryan.
Official language/s
Dhivehi (Maldivian)

Media
The government retains the power to close media outlets critical to its regime which has resulted in media self-regulation.
Press
There are several newspapers publishing in the Divehi language, and some with English online editions, including Haveeru (www.haveeru.com.mv) and Miadhu (www.miadhu.com.mv), Aafathis Daily News (www.aafathisnews.com.mv), is one of the oldest local newspapers and Haama Daily (www.haamadaily.com).
Broadcasting
Radio: There are only four radio stations broadcasting, two government owned, Voice of Maldives (www.vom.gov.mv) and Radio Eke and two private DhiFM (http://dhifm95.com) and Capital Radio (http://capital956.fm). An overseas radio operated by expatriates opposed to the government of President Gayoom broadcasts over the internet, Radio Minivan (www.minivannews.com).
Television: The only local television service, TVM Maldives, is government-run. Satellite TV is available.

Economy
The economy has grown by an average 7.5 per cent since 1995, with the tourist industry providing 28 per cent of GDP and over 60 per cent of foreign exchange earnings. The December 2004 tsumani which killed over 100 people and caused over US$300 million in damaged property impacted severly on tourism. Government policy has been to set up resorts on uninhabited islands, preserving a desert island atmosphere. The environmental impact of global warming is a concern as 80 per cent of the island area is only up to one metre above the sea level – hence the high level of destruction by the tsumani.
GDP growth in 2005 fell by 3.6 per cent. However, in 2006, as tourists returned to the islands and reconstruction and new resort construction proceeded, growth grew by an estimated 18 per cent. The down side of all the building was a widening of the trade deficit as a result of the import of goods and construction materials, just at a time when global oil prices rose sharply.
The small population is hard pressed to fill all the jobs the expansion has produced and unemployment is negligible.
Development of the tourism industry has required investment in infrastructure and modern passenger boats.
As an Islamic nation, the Maldives receives aid from Kuwait and Saudi Arabia. President Gayoom has also managed to harness a steady flow of Japanese aid. In addition, development funding comes from the UK and Australia.
The largest project undertaken by the Maldives is the ongoing Hulhumalé infrastructure project, reclaiming land for development for domestic, commercial and industrial expansion. The new island is located in the Kafuul Atoll close to Malé, the capital city. Reclamation began in 1997 at an initial cost of US$11 million.

External trade
The Maldives is a member of South Asia Association for Regional Co-operation, which operates a preferential trading arrangement that covers 6,000 products. In 2004 the South Asia Free Trade Area (Safta) was ratified, to be implemented between the seven member states (India, Pakistan, Bhutan, Nepal, Bangladesh, Sri Lanka and Maldives) by 2012.
Fishing is a major industrial sector, which provides export commodities, as well as revenue from licensed fishing rights to foreign fleets. Manufactured garments and boat building are important products. Agriculture is inadequate and staple foods must be imported.

Imports

Main imports are petroleum, food, intermediate and consumer goods, capital machinery and vehicles.

Main sources: Singapore (23.9 per cent total, 2006), UAE (21.1 per cent), India (9.4 per cent).

Exports

Main exports include fish, garments and boats.

Main destinations: Thailand (26.0 per cent total, 2006), Japan (15.0 per cent), Sri Lanka (12.8 per cent).

Agriculture

Agriculture, including fishing, accounts for around 15 per cent of GDP and employs 40 per cent of the labour force. Farming is at subsistance level on small-holdings, confined to field crops and fruit trees, with no livestock. Main crops are coconuts, bananas, watermelon, sweet potato, cucumber, cassava, pumpkin, cabbage and yam. Approximately 6 per cent of the total land area is under cultivation. The soil is shallow and highly alkaline, with poor water-retaining properties.

The UN Food and Agriculture Organisation (FAO) reported that food production in 2005 was severely reduced by the damage caused by the December 2004 tsunami. Floods inundated the islands and around 50 per cent of agricultural field plots on 53 of the 199 inhabited islands were lost through saline intrusion. Many fruit bearing trees such as coconuts, mangoes and bananas were uprooted.

Crop production in 2005 included: 15,827 tonnes (t) coconut, 16t sweet potatoes, 35t taro, 2,058t oilcrops, 6,579 roots & tubers, 2,000t treenuts, 3,930t bananas, 12,930t fruit in total, 27,030t vegetables in total. Meat production is about 1,000t per annum.

Fishing

The fishing sector, providing 11 per cent of GDP, is second to tourism in importance in the economy. Fish provide the main source of protein for the population with a 126,000mt annual catch. Fishing employs over 20 per cent of the workforce.

The tsunami caused US$14 million worth of damage or destruction to boats, harbours and jetties.

In 2004, the total marine fish catch was 153,394 tonnes.

Tourism

Tourism is the main economic activity. It contributes around 30 per cent of GDP and is the principal source of foreign exchange and revenue. The most important market is Italy, with around a quarter of visitors, followed by the UK, Germany and Japan. Tourist arrivals have risen at an annual average rate of 17 per cent. Receipts from tourism have not kept pace with the increased numbers, due to decline in spending per visitor. In 2003, there were 563,593 visitors, compared with 484,680 in 2002. While by 18 December 2004 visitor arrivals reached a record 600,000, six days later, the Asian tsunami struck, wrecking much infrastructure, causing an estimated US$10 million worth of damage and impacting severely on visitor numbers in 2005.

Environment

It has been reported that the beaches of one-third of the Maldives' 200 inhabited islands could be swept away by rising sea levels, as global warming melts the fringes of polar ice caps. Another issue affecting the Maldives is the depletion of fresh water aquifiers which threatens water supply.

Hydrocarbons

The Maldives do not produce any oil and rely on imports of refined oil products, mainly of distillate and jet fuel, to meet domestic energy requirements.

The Maldives do not produce or import natural gas or coal.

Energy

The Maldives has installed generating capacity of around 106MW, supplied by oil. Around half the capacity is concentrated in resort areas. The State Electricity Company (Stelco) generates a third of the supply; the rest is supplied by Island Development Committees and private generators.

Banking and insurance

Central bank

Maldives Monetary Authority

Time

GMT plus five hours

Geography

The Republic of Maldives is one of the smallest countries in the world. Situated in the Indian Ocean, it lies about 675km (420 miles) south-west of Sri Lanka. The northern tip of the Maldives is about 600km south of India. Over 99 per cent of the territory is sea.

The Maldives consists of around 1,190 small islands grouped into 26 atolls, running north to south in a double chain 823km long and 129km wide. The total land area is around 298 square km. Most of the islands are coral outcrops perched on a submarine mountain range, although some are only sandbars. They are low-lying, reaching no higher than two metres above sea level. They are at risk of flooding from natural causes, most recently the tsunami of December 2004.

The geography of the country can be affected in that islands can disappear as a result of flooding, as well as from erosion. The potential effects of global warming on sea levels puts the continued physical existence of the archipelago at risk.

Around 200 islands are inhabited. Many of these are covered by tropical vegetation, including coconut palms and breadfruit trees, while the uninhabitated islands are given over to scrub. Few islands in the archipelago are longer than 2km, the longest being Hithadhoo, which is 8km long. While most form atolls enclosing shallow lagoons, several are single islands with coral beaches.

Hemisphere

Northern

Climate

There is year-round sunshine, with temperatures ranging 26–30 degrees Celsius. Most rainfall occurs during the south-west monsoon season from April–October.

Entry requirements

Passports

Required by all, valid for six months.

Visa

Visas are issued free to all visitors on arrival at the airport in Malé for visits of up to 30 days (visas may be extended for a minimum of three months on payment of a fee). Proof of return/onward passage is necessary.

Currency advice/regulations

There are no restrictions on the import and export of local and foreign currencies.

Customs

Personal effects are allowed duty-free. Tortoise and articles produced using tortoise shells may not be exported.

Prohibited imports

Alcohol, pork, pharmaceuticals and goods at variance with Islamic culture are prohibited or subject to restrictions. Pornographic material may not be imported.

Health (for visitors)

Mandatory precautions

Vaccination certificate required for yellow fever if travelling from an infected area.

Advisable precautions

Anti-malarial precautions, outside Malé. Hepatitis A and B, tetanus and typhoid. There is a rabies risk.

Visitors are advised to use mosquito repellent, a mosquito net at night, and wear clothing covering as much skin as possible.

Hotels

The Maldives are a popular tourist destination. There are numerous first class hotels and island resorts.

Credit cards

All major credit cards, including American Express, Visa and MasterCard, are widely accepted on the islands.

Public holidays (national)
Fixed dates
1 Jan (New Year's Day), 26–27 Jul (Independence Days), 3 Nov (Victory Day), 11–12 Nov (Republic Day).
Variable dates
Hajj Day (Jan), Eid al Adha, Islamic New Year, National Day, Birth of the Prophet, Start of Ramadan, Eid al Fitr (End of Ramadan), Huravee Day (Jul), Martyrs' Day (Sep).
Islamic year – 1429 (10 Jan 2008–28 Dec 2008): The Islamic year contains 354 or 355 days, with the result that Muslim feasts advance by 10-12 days against the Gregorian calendar. Dates of feasts vary according to the sighting of the new moon, so cannot be forecast exactly.

Working hours
Banking
Sun–Thu: 0800–1330.
Business
Sun–Thu: 0730–1430. During the month of Ramadan 0900–1300.
Government
Sun–Thu: 0730–1430.
Shops
Sat–Thu: 0930–2300; Fri: 1400–2300.

Telecommunications
Telephone/fax

Weights and measures
Metric system

Social customs/useful tips
Alcohol can only be consumed in holiday resorts.

Getting there
Air
National airline: Island Aviation Services
International airport/s: Malé International Airport (MLE), on Hulule Island, 2km north-east of Malé; post office, bank, restarurants, duty-free shop.
Airport tax: US$12, usually included in price of ticket.
Surface
Main port/s: Gan, Uligamu and Malé.

Getting about
National transport
Air: Island Aviation Services operates regular domestic flights between Malé and island airports at Gan, Kaadedhdhoo, Kadhdhoo and Hanimaadhoo. Charter planes are also available.
Water: There is a public boat service from the airport to Malé city centre, with a journey time of 15 minutes. Resort islands have regular ferry services. Local boats can be hired; rates are negotiable. Charter vessels are available.

City transport
Due to the small size of the islands, there is little need for transportation. It is possible to walk to all places within the small area of Malé.
Taxis: Taxis are available in Malé.

BUSINESS DIRECTORY

The addresses listed below are a selection only. While World of Information makes every endeavour to check these addresses, we cannot guarantee that changes have not been made, especially to telephone numbers and area codes. We would welcome any corrections.

Telephone area codes
The international direct dialling code (IDD) for the Maldives is +960, followed by subscriber's number.

Useful telephone numbers
Police: 119
Fire: 118
Ambulance: 102

Chambers of Commerce
Maldives National Chamber of Commerce and Industry, G Viyafaari Hiya, Ameenee Magu, PO Box 92, Malé 2004 (tel: 332-6634; fax: 331-0233; e-mail: mncci@dhivehinet.net.mv).

Banking
Bank of Ceylon, 2 Boduthakurufaanu Magu, Malé (tel: 332-3045; fax: 332-0575; e-mail: bcmale@dhivehinet.net.mv).

Bank of Maldives, 11 Boduthakurufaanu Magu, Malé (tel: 333-0100; fax: 332-8233; e-mail: bmla@dhivehinet.net.mv).

Habib Bank Ltd, Ground Floor, Ship Plaza, 1/6 Orchid Magu , Malé (tel: 332-2051; fax: 332-6791; e-mail: hbmale@dhivehinet.net.mv).

State Bank of India, Boduthakurufaanu Magu, Malé (tel: 332-0860; fax: 332-3053; e-mail: sbimale@dhivehinet.net.mv).

Central bank
Maldives Monetary Authority, 3rd Floor, Umar Shopping Arcade, Chandhanee Magu, Malé 20156 (tel: 3312-343; fax: 3323-862; e-mail: mail@mma.gov.mv).

Travel information
Island Aviation Services, Malé (tel: 333-5566; fax: 331-4806; e-mail: sales@island.com.mv).

Maldives Tourism Promotion Board, 12 Boduthakurufaanu Magu, Malé (tel: 332-328; fax: 332-3229; e-mail: mtpb@visitmaldives.com).

Malé International Airport, Malé (tel: 332-5511; fax: 333-1515; e-mail: info@macinet.net).

Ministry of tourism
Ministry of Tourism, 2/F Ghazi Building, Orchid Magu, Henveiru, Malé (tel: 313-461).

Ministries
Ministry of Atolls Development, Faashanaa Bdg, Boduthakurufaanu Magu, Malé (tel: 332-3070; fax: 332-7750; e-mail: info@atolls.gov.mv).

Ministry of Communication, Science and Technology, 12 Boduthakurufaanu Magu, Malé (tel: 333-1695; fax: 333-1694; e-mail: secretariat@mcst.gov.mv).

Ministry of Economic Development and Trade, Ghazee Bdg, Ameeru Ahmed Magu, Malé (tel: 332-3668; fax: 332-3840; e-mail: contact@trademin.gov.mv).

Ministry of Fisheries, Agriculture and Marine Resources, Ghazee Bdg, Ameeru Ahmed Magu, Malé (tel: 332-2625; fax: 332-6558; e-mail: it@fishagri.gov.mv).

Ministry of Health, Ameenee Magu, Malé (tel: 332-5311; fax: 332-7793; e-mail: moh@dhivehinet.net.mv).

Ministry of Higher Education, Employment and Social Security, Haveeree Hingun, Malé (tel: 331-7172; fax: 333-1578; e-mail: admin@employment.gov.mv).

Ministry of Women's Affairs and Social Security, Umar Shopping Arcade, Chandhanee Magu, Malé (tel: 332-5956; fax: 331-6237; e-mail: info@urcmaldives.gov.mv).

Other useful addresses
Attorney General's Office, Huravee Bdg, Malé (tel: 332-3809; fax: 331-4109).

Maldives National Ship Management Ltd, 2/F, Ship Plaza, Male (tel: 332-3871; fax: 332-4323; e-mail@ mnfl@dhivehinet.net.mv).

Maldives Association of Tourism Industry, Gadhamoo Bdg, Boduthakurufaanu Magu, Malé (tel: 332-6640; fax: 332-6641).

Maldives Traders' Association, G Viyafaari Hiyaa, Meenee Magu, Malé (tel: 332-6634; fax: 332-1889).

State Trading Organisation, Haveeree Higun, Malé (tel: 332-3279; fax: 332-5218; e-mail: sto@dhivehinet.net.mvo).

Internet sites
Maldives Consular Information: http://www.travel.state.gov/maldives.html

Maldives news online: http://maldivesculture.com

Mali

KEY FACTS

Official name: République du Mali (Republic of Mali)

Head of State: President Amadou Toumani Touré (since 2002; re-elected Apr 2007)

Head of government: Prime Minister Modibo Sidibé (appointed 27 Sep 2007)

Ruling party: The Congrès pour la Démocratie et le Progrès (CDP) (Alliance for Democracy and Progress) coalition led by Alliance pour la Démocratie en Mali-Parti Pan-Africain pour la Solidarité et la Justice (ADEMA-PASJ) (Alliance for Democracy in Mali-African Party for Solidarity and Justice) with Union pour la République et la Démocratie (URD) (Union for the Republic and Democracy) and Rassemblement National pour la Démocratie (RND) (National Assembly for Democracy) (from 22 July 2007)

Area: 1,241,238 square km

Population: 12.00 million (2007); (12,324,029 (2008) estimate)

Capital: Bamako

Official language: French

Currency: CFA franc (CFAf) = 100 centimes (Communauté Financière Africaine (African Financial Community) franc). New notes were issued in 2005.

Exchange rate: CFAf413.80 per US$ (Jul 2008); CFAf655.95 per euro (pegged from Jan 1999)

GDP per capita: US$517 (2007)

GDP real growth: 2.50% (2007)

Labour force: 5.75 million (2004)

Inflation: 2.50% (2007)

Balance of trade: -US$1.53 billion (2004)

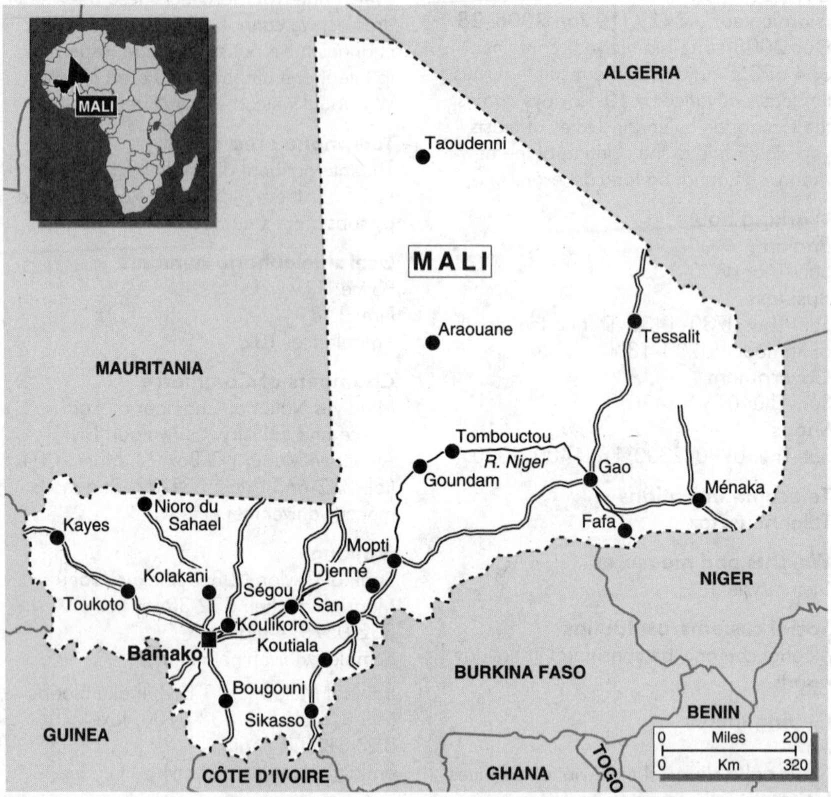

Present day Mali is the result of shifting boundaries left by ancient empires going back to the fourth century, and France, which conquered Mali in the middle of the 19th century. In 1958 it was proclaimed the Sudanese Republic and the following year it became the Mali Federation, after uniting with Senegal. However, Senegal seceded and Mali became independent in 1960.

In 1985 Mali fought a brief border war with Burkina Faso, and relations continue to be strained. In the early 1990s the army was sent to the north to quell a rebellion by Tuareg tribes over land, cultural and linguistic rights. Then again, in 2006, the Tuaregs attacked government barracks in the north in May. The government signed a peace agreement (the Algiers Agreement), mediated by Algeria, with the rebels in July 2006. Mali remained relatively peaceful until May 2007 when a dissident Tuareg rebel, Ibrahim Ag Bahanga, attacked an army post in Tinzaoutene. The government eventually asked Iyad Ag Ghaly, the leader of the Alliance Démocratique de 23 Mai 2006 pour le Changement to mediate in finding a solution. Most Tuareg rebels have now surrendered their weapons and are in Kidal in the north.

It is, however, among the poorest countries in the world, with 65 per cent of its land area desert or semi-desert. Economic activity is largely confined to the riverine area irrigated by the Niger. About 10 per cent of the population is nomadic and some 80 per cent of the labour force is engaged in farming and fishing. Industrial activity is concentrated on processing farm commodities. Mali is heavily dependent on foreign aid and is vulnerable to fluctuations in world prices for cotton, its main export, along with gold. Worker remittances and external trade routes for the landlocked country have been jeopardised by continued unrest in neighbouring Côte d'Ivoire.

Encouraging growth

The outlook for the medium term is encouraging – growth in 2006 and 2007 was 5.3 per cent and 4.2 per cent respectively, according to the African Development Bank. Agricultural production, particularly cereals, should rebound following adequate rainfall, resulting in a reversal of recent inflation. The terms of trade have begun to improve, notably with respect to gold prices. Mali has told the International Monetary Fund (IMF) that it remains fully committed to completing the privatisation of the Compagnie Malienne pour le Développment des Textiles (its textile development company) by 2008 and attaches high priority to financial sector reforms. A revised timetable for reform of the cotton sector, postponing privatisation until 2008, has been approved. The issues centre on whether to sell assets by zoning or equity in new subsidiary companies, creating a regulatory framework, and strengthening the role of cotton producers in downstream activities. The privatisation of other non-financial sector companies is proceeding, albeit with some technical delays. Restructuring of the Énergie du Mali remains a priority.

To sustain growth at an average of approximately six per cent per annum over the medium term, Mali will focus its policies and reforms on improving efficiency and competitiveness, particularly through structural reforms in the cotton and banking sectors and the strengthening of public finances and public institutions. The current account deficit is expected to narrow as the terms of trade gradually improve and gold exports increase as a result of the opening of new mines.

Politics

Mali has achieved a remarkable political transformation with an increasingly strong democratic process taking root throughout the 1990s, culminating in the peaceful transfer of power between two democratically elected leaders in 2002. The third multi-party government since President Amadou Toumani Touré took office in June 2002 was formed in 2004. This placed Mali among those African countries moving to a democratic political system, and it is hoped will provide a strong platform for moving ahead on economic and institutional reforms.

The April 2007 elections saw the re-election of President Amadou Toumani Touré with 71.20 per cent of the vote; Ibrahim Boubacar Keïta came second with 19.15 per cent. Turnout was a disappointing 36.2 per cent. Secure in his position until 2012, President Touré will be more able to implement a number of controversial policies, including strengthening security in the north of the country, and his ambitious poverty-reduction programme.

Long periods of military rule in Mali over the years left the country devoid of mature politicians capable of running the country. Amadou Toumani Touré, the army general credited with rescuing Mali from military dictatorship and handing it back to its people, first come to power in 1991, overthrowing military ruler Moussa Traoré after his security forces killed over 100 pro-democracy demonstrators. He gained widespread respect, and the nickname 'soldier of democracy', for handing power to elected civilians the next year. Born in 1948, Touré belongs to no official party but went into the first round of the elections in 2002 with the backing of numerous support groups and 22 minor parties.

Risk assessment

Economic	Improving
Political	Satisfactory
Regional stability	Poor

COUNTRY PROFILE

Historical profile

900 Modern-day Mali was part of the empire of Ghana.
1250s Sundiata Keita, leader of the Mandinka people, established the Empire of Mali, which stretched from the Atlantic to the present-day borders of Nigeria and controlled most trans-Sahara trading routes by the fourteenth century.
1464 The Songhai Empire, centred around Gao, overwhelmed the Mali Empire and began to conquer the Sahel.
1591 After a Moroccan invasion, the Songhai Empire collapsed.
1890s Mali became a French colony.
1960 Mali gained independence from France as part of the Federation of Mali, which was dissolved a few weeks later when Senegal broke away. The Republic of Mali was established and Modibo Keita became the country's first president.
1968 Keita was overthrown by a military coup, led by Moussa Traoré, who became president.
1977 Protests erupted following Keita's death in prison.
1979 A new constitution provided for elections in which Traoré was elected as president.
1985 A border war erupted between Mali and Burkina Faso, but was ended after intervention by other African states.
1991 Following pro-democracy demonstrations, Traoré was deposed by a military coup. A 25-member military/civilian Transitional People's Salvation Committee came to power, led by Lieutenant Colonel Amadou Toumani Touré.
1992 Touré resigned and did not stand in the elections he organised. Alpha Oumar Konaré was democratically elected president.
1995 A peace agreement with Tuareg rebels led to the return of thousands of refugees from neighbouring African states.
1997 President Konaré was re-elected..

KEY INDICATORS — Mali

	Unit	2003	2004	2005	2006	2007
Population	m	11.68	11.79	12.48	13.90	*12.00
Gross domestic product (GDP)	US$bn	3.69	4.86	5.41	6.22	*6.75
GDP per capita	US$	316	404	434	487	*517
GDP real growth	%	5.6	2.2	6.1	4.3	*2.5
Inflation	%	-0.8	-3.1	6.4	1.9	*2.5
Industrial output	% change	–	-0.3	8.6	5.0	–
Agricultural output	% change	–	-4.7	3.0	4.4	–
Exports (fob) (goods)	US$m	680.0	323.0	1,100.9	1,550.4	–
Imports (cif) (goods)	US$m	630.0	1,858.0	1,245.5	1,475.4	–
Balance of trade	US$m	50.0	-1,535.0	-144.6	75.0	–
Current account	US$m	-210.0	-230.0	-437.6	-302.0	*-446.0
Total reserves minus gold	US$m	908.7	1,040.7	854.6	969.5	1,087.1
Foreign exchange	US$m	894.6	1,026.2	841.2	955.4	1,071.9
Exchange rate	per US$	574.89	496.63	507.22	496.60	454.40

* estimated figure

1999 Traoré was sentenced to death for corruption, but his sentence was commuted to life imprisonment by Konaré, who announced that he would not contest the next presidential election
2000 Mande Sidibe, a former IMF official, was appointed prime minister.
2001 Konaré announced the indefinite postponement of a constitutional referendum which proposed granting him immunity from prosecution.
2002 Amadou Toumani Touré won the presidential election and named Ahmed Mohamed Ag Hamani as prime minister. The Constitutional Court reversed the outcome of the parliamentary elections. In October, the government resigned without explanation and a new government of national reconciliation took over.
2003 The IMF announced that Mali was to benefit from debt relief amounting to approximately US$675 million under the enhanced Heavily Indebted Poor Countries (HIPC) initiative.
2004 Ousmane Issoufi Maïga replaced Hamani as prime minister.
2006 Tuareg rebels, demanding greater autonomy, attacked government barracks in the north. The government signed a peace agreement, mediated by Algeria, with the rebels.
2007 In April, President Amadou Toumani Touré was re-elected with 71.20 per cent of the votes; Ibrahim Boubacar Keïta, president of the national assembly, was runner-up with 19.15 per cent. Turnout was 36.2 per cent. In the two rounds of parliamentary election in July, the Congrès pour la Démocratie et le Progrès (CDP) (Alliance for Democracy and Progress) coalition led by Alliance pour la Démocratie en Mali-Parti Pan-Africain pour la Solidarité et la Justice (ADEMA-PASJ) (Alliance for Democracy in Mali-African Party for Solidarity and Justice) won 92 seats (out of 160). The ruling Espoir 2002 (Hope 2002) renamed Front pour la Démocratie et la République (FDR) (Front for a Democratic Republic) won 11 seats. Turnout was low at 33.39 per cent. Prime Minister Ousmane Issoufi Maïga resigned and Modibo Sidibé was appointed as his replacement on 27 September.

Political structure

Constitution

A referendum held in January 1992 approved a constitution establishing multi-party rule.

A two-round voting system for electing parliamentarians was established.

In 1997, a new electoral code introduced an Independent National Electoral Commission (CENI) comprising 34 members: 10 representatives of government services, 10 from civil society and 14 from the political parties (seven from the opposition and seven from the parliamentary majority).

Other changes included the authorisation of independent candidacies, the reduction in the number of voters per polling station to 700 and an increase in the number of deputies in the National Assembly from 116 to 147. The principle of sponsoring presidential candidates was ended, and correspondence or proxy voting and eligibility for other African nationals were annulled.

Administratively, Mali is divided into eight regions and the capital district of Bamako, each under the authority of an appointed governor.

Form of state

Republic

The executive

The directly-elected president serves a five-year term, with a limit of two terms. The president is head of state and commander-in-chief of the armed forces. The president appoints the prime minister and chairs the Council of Ministers.

National legislature

Mali has a 147-member National Assembly with a five-year term. Election is direct and by party list. The head of government is the prime minister.

Legal system

Based on French civil law system and customary law. The legal system is constitutionally independent of the executive.

Last elections

1/22 July 2007 (parliamentary); 29 April 2007 (presidential).

Results: Parliamentary: the Alliance pour la Démocratie en Mali-Parti Pan-Africain pour la Solidarité et la Justice (Adema-PASJ) (Alliance for Democracy in Mali-African Party for Solidarity and Justice) won 55 seats; the Union pour la République et la Démocratie (URD) (Union for the Republic and Democracy) 36; Rassemblement National pour la Démocratie (RND) (National Assembly for Democracy) one (these parties form the Congrès pour la Démocratie et le Progrès (CDP) (Alliance for Democracy and Progress) coalition. The Rassemblement Pour le Mali (RPM) (Party for Mali) won 11 seats; the Parti pour la Renaissance Nationale (Parena) (Party for a National Rebirth) four, (these parties form the coalition Front pour la Démocratie et la République (FDR) (Front for a Democratic Republic) formerly called Espoir 2002 (Hope 2002); the Solidarité Africaine pour la Démocratie et l'Indépendance (Sadi) (African Solidarity for Democracy and Independence) four; independents 12 and undecided 37 seats. Turnout was 33.39 per cent.

Presidential: Incumbent Amadou Toumani Touré won 71.20 per cent of the vote; Ibrahim Boubacar Keïta won 19.15 per cent. Turnout was 36.2 per cent.

Next elections

July 2012 (parliamentary); 2012 (presidential)

Political parties

Ruling party

The Congrès pour la Démocratie et le Progrès (CDP) (Alliance for Democracy and Progress) coalition led by Alliance pour la Démocratie en Mali-Parti Pan-Africain pour la Solidarité et la Justice (ADEMA-PASJ) (Alliance for Democracy in Mali-African Party for Solidarity and Justice) with Union pour la République et la Démocratie (URD) (Union for the Republic and Democracy) and Rassemblement National pour la Démocratie (RND) (National Assembly for Democracy) (from 22 July 2007)

Main opposition party

Alliance pour la Démocratie en Mali-Parti Pan-Africain pour la Liberté, la Solidarité et la Justice (ADEMA) (Alliance for Democracy in Mali)

Population

12.00 million (2007); (12,324,029 (2008) estimate)

Last census: April 1998: 9,790,492

Population density: Eight inhabitants per square km. Urban population: 31 per cent (1995–2001).

Annual growth rate: 2.9 per cent 1994–2004 (WHO 2006)

Ethnic make-up

Mande (50 per cent), Peul (17 per cent), Voltaic (12 per cent).

Religions

Muslim (90 per cent), indigenous beliefs (9 per cent), Christian (1 per cent).

Education

Primary schooling is divided into two stages, with the first and compulsory stage lasting until aged 13, followed by three years of basic education. At age 16 students may follow either an academic path in a general secondary school, for three years, or specialised education through a technical secondary school, for either two or three years. Four year vocational courses are also available.

Mali has one of the highest pupil-teacher ratio in the world, with an average of around 80 pupils per teacher.

Literacy rate: 19 per cent adult rate; 24 per cent youth rate (15–24) (Unesco 2005).

Compulsory years: Seven to 13

Enrolment rate: 29 per cent net primary enrolment (Unicef)

Pupils per teacher: 80 in primary schools.

Health

Per capita total expenditure on health (2003) was US$39; of which per capita government spending was US$22, at the international dollar rate, (WHO 2006). Improved water sources and sanitation facilities are available to 65 per cent and 30 per cent of the population respectively. In August 2004 epidemiologists of the Global Polio Eradication Initiative announced that new cases of polio had been confirmed in Mali. The infection is believed to have spread from Northern Nigeria.

HIV/Aids

There are an estimated 100,000 people living with HIV/Aids in Mali – 5,000 are under the age of 15. Mali has so far escaped much of the African pandemic. The African Development Fund (ADF) provided US$12.1 million for a programme to reduce the prevalence rate from 1.9 per cent in 2003 to 1 per cent by 2008. The money will be used to improved testing for the disease, antiretroviral drugs and training medical and research workers to monitor and manage the pandemic.

HIV prevalence: 1.9 per cent aged 15–49 in 2003 (World Bank)

Life expectancy: 46 years, 2004 (WHO 2006)

Fertility rate/Maternal mortality rate: 6.8 births per woman, 2004 (WHO 2006)

Child (under 5 years) mortality rate (per 1,000): 122 per 1,000 live births; 25 per cent of children aged under five are malnourished (World Bank).

Head of population per physician: 0.08 physicians per 1,000 people, 2004 (WHO 2006)

Welfare

In the mid-1990s, it was estimated that 72.8 per cent of the population lived on less than US$1 per day and over 90 per cent lived on less than US$2 per day. The distribution of wealth in Mali is highly unequal and the highest 10 per cent of the population owns 56.2 per cent of the wealth.

In over 70 districts in Mali, one million people were affected by swarms of locust and suffered acute food shortages. Emergency food aid was provided from reserves while government officials estimated over 440,000 tonnes of the 2004 harvest to have been destroyed.

Main cities

Bamako (capital and main business centre, estimated population 1.5 million in 2005); Sikasso (160,904); Gao (152,265), Ségou (149,530), Mopti (131,530).

Languages spoken

Tamazight (the Berber language) is recognised as a national language. Tamazight belongs to the Afro-Asiatic family and is related to ancient Egyptian and Ethiopian. Arabic, Bambara, Fulani, Senoufo and Dogon are commonly spoken. Very little English is spoken.

Official language/s

French

Media

Press

Dailies: Dailies include L'Essor, Info-Matin, Le Soir de Bamako and Sud-info.

Weeklies: Eighteen opposition parties launched a weekly paper, La Voix de l'Opposition in 1998. Other weeklies published from Bamako include Aurore, Carcan, Carrefour, Les Echos, Independent, Scorpion, Le Malien Magazine, Soudanais, Tambour, Temps and Le Zenith.

Periodicals: Periodicals include the bi-monthly Cauris and Courrier (irregular).

Economy

Mali is one of the world's poorest countries and is heavily dependent on foreign aid. In 2005/06 the cereal crop, along with a buoyant gold sector, a principal foreign exchange earner which strengthened trade, and improving debt relief, showed an overall growth in its economic performance. GDP growth was 6.1 per cent in 2005 and expected to be 5.1 per cent in 2006. Total revenue from grants should provide 56.8 per cent of GDP in 2006. Inflation fell to 5.0 per cent in 2005 and is expected to fall further as the economy improves.

The economy is vulnerable to price fluctuations in the world price of cotton, its main export. The state-owned cotton company is being prepared for privatisation by 2008 but needs to undergo further structural reform to improve its finances. It will be broken down into four regional ginning operations, under the guidance of an appointed privatisation expert.

In co-operation with the IMF, the government has implemented various structural adjustment programmes to diversify the economy and the country's export markets.

Gold mining has attracted an increasing number of foreign investors. Under the auspices of IFI, Mali authorities continue to reduce budget deficits, cut the operating losses of state enterprises and liberalise the economy.

China has taken an increasingly important role in infrastructure projects and joint venture companies in Mali which led to the opening of a Chinese investment centre in 2002. Joint large-scale construction projects include irrigation infrastructure, a bridge across the Niger River, a conference centre, a national stadium in the capital, Bamako, and four regional stadia.

External trade

As a member of the Economic Community of West African States (Ecowas), Mali is also a member of the West African Economic and Monetary Union using the common currency, the CFA franc. Ecowas was set up to promote economic integration among members.

Its primary exports, cotton and gold, are subject to world prices and along with livestock sales provide 80–90 per cent of export earnings in 2006. Remittances constitute an important portion of foreign revenue.

Imports

Principal imports are petroleum products, machinery and equipment, construction materials, foodstuffs and textiles.

Main sources: France (13.1 per cent total, 2005), Senegal (13.1 per cent), Côte d'Ivoire (8.5 per cent)

Exports

The main exports are cotton, gold and livestock.

Main destinations: China (25.2 per cent total, 2005), Pakistan (12.8 per cent), Thailand (8.7 per cent), Taiwan (6.7 per cent), Italy (4.5 per cent)

Agriculture

Farming

Agriculture is the mainstay of the economy, contributing around 35 per cent of GDP, employing 73 per cent of the workforce (largely at subsistence levels) and accounting for about 45 per cent of agricultural exports. Only about 2 per cent of the total land area is cultivated, but approximately 20 per cent of the total land area along the Niger River is suitable for cultivation, with the most productive areas lying between Bamako and Mopti. Principal food crops are millet, sorghum, paddy rice, maize and groundnuts. Supported by foreign aid, the government has co-ordinated a programme to expand production of rice as a staple food. There is a regular food deficit due to recurrent drought, crop smuggling and an inefficient marketing and distribution system. The main export crops are cotton, groundnuts, cereals, fresh fruit and vegetables. Mali is Africa's second-largest cotton producer. Livestock exports have experienced growth in recent years following the abolition of export taxes on livestock. The livestock sector is a mainstay of the economy in the northern half of the country and contributes 20 per cent to GDP. Recent desertification caused by deforestation and global warming has shifted herding activity southwards.

In 2004, the worst locust plague for 15 years attacked crops across much of west Africa and the Sahel region of southern Sahara. The UN has organised a nine-country response group with

Morocco and Algeria sending aid of vehicles and pesticide but, a year after the warning was first given, it has been estimated that only 3 per cent of the 4.3 million hectares that required spraying has been treated. Mauritania is the hatching ground for the largest swarms although the insects are breeding elsewhere in the region. In Mali, the damage caused by locust swarms, together with poor rainfall, decimated livestock herds in 2004.

Estimated crop production in 2005 included: 2,845,005 tonnes (t) cereals in total, 974,676t millet, 459,463t maize, 74,500t sweet potatoes, 664,083t sorghum, 718,086t rice, 600,000t seed cotton, 113,300t pulses, 146,500t roots and tubers, 102,480t oilcrops, 1,004t tobacco, 360,000t sugar cane, 32,000t fruit in total, 333,000t vegetables in total.

Estimated livestock production included: 248,477t meat in total, 97,760t beef, 36,000t lamb, 18,000t game meat, 48,510t goat meat, 18,000t game meat, 7,552t camel meat 36,000t poultry, 10,080t eggs, 608,440t milk, 300t honey, 15,040t cattle hides, 8,352t sheepskins, 6,930t goatskins.

Fishing

Fishing is an important livelihood along the Niger River. The annual fish catch is around 100,000 tonnes, of which 20 per cent is exported, mainly to Côte d'Ivoire. Production, through artisanal fishing, is vulnerable to drought, pollution and man-made obstructions across the river.

Inland fisheries have been targeted for development as part of the national poverty reduction strategy. Fish processing and packaging centres and 10,000ha fish ponds plus supporting developments are among the undertakings. A US$22 million package of support was provided in 2004 by the African Development Bank.

Forestry

Timber imports in 2004 were US$5.3 million, while exports amounted to US$1.4 million.

Estimated timber production in 2004 included 5,378,031 cubic metre (cum) roundwood, 412,900cum industrial roundwood, 12,800cum sawnwood, 4,965,131cum woodfuel.

Industry and manufacturing

The industrial sector is growing, contributing around 26 per cent to GDP in 2004. Manufacturing is concerned mainly with agricultural processing for domestic consumption and export. Other industries include soft drinks, textiles, soaps, plastics, cigarettes, cement, bricks and agricultural tools and equipment. Activity is concentrated in Bamako.

Around 90 per cent of production is accounted for by state enterprises, although rationalisation and privatisation plans are likely to continue.

Tourism

Toursim is an increasingly important sector of the economy, third only to gold and cotton. It is expected to contribute 3.5 per cent to GDP in 2005. Around 200,000 visitors arrive each year. Infrastructure is being expanded to cater for the industry.

Mining

The mining sector typically contributes around 10 per cent to GDP and employs 0.5 per cent of the workforce. Gold is Mali's principal mineral resource and since the late 1990s has replaced cottojn and livestock as the country's largest export earner .

Following the introduction of new mining laws in 1991, which helped expand gold production, Mali has become Africa's third largest gold producer after Ghana and South Africa. Total gold reserves are estimated at up to 700 tonnes and geologists claim there is potential for further discoveries. However, commercial exploitation is hampered by the lack of adequate physical infrastructure. Gold represents 80 per cent of the country's total mineral production.

The first privately owned gold mine was opened by BHP-Utah at Syama in 1990, but following operational difficulties it was sold to Randgold of South Africa in 1996. The mine underwent an investment programme and production peaked at 6.1 tonnes in 1999. However, in January 2001, Randgold decided to mothball Syama after extensive flooding led to financial losses.

Opened in 1997, the Sadiola Hill open-cast mine, owned by AngloGold, IAMGold and the Mali government, has estimated reserves of around 130 tonnes. With average annual production estimated at around 10 tonnes per annum until 2010, it is the second largest gold mine in Africa and one of the biggest and lowest cost gold mines in the world.

The Yatela gold mine – owned jointly by AngloGold (40 per cent), IAMGold (40 per cent) and the Mali government (20 per cent) – lies 35km to the north of Sadiola, and was officially opened in September 2002. It has reserves of over 72 tonnes with estimated average annual production of 6 tonnes over a period of 12 years. In 2002, it produced 6.8 tonnes of gold.

The Morila gold mine, opened in early 2001, is forecast to produce an average of 10 tonnes per year over a period of 14 years and is jointly owned by Rangold (40 per cent), AngloGold (40 per cent) and the Mali government (20 per cent). In 2002, Morila produced 15.2 tonnes of gold. Feasibility studies are being conducted on the re-opening of the Kalana gold mine which could produce an estimated 430kg per annum. There are also large unexploited deposits at Kodieran (43 tonnes), Loulo (30.1 tonnes), Segala (15.4 tonnes) and Tabakto (1 tonne).

Artisanal gold mining has been practised in Mali for around 1,000 years and represents 0.6 per cent of GDP and employs around 150,000 seasonal workers. Much of this kind of mining is performed without permits and is generally dangerous.

Phosphate production is around 10,000 tonnes per annum. Small quantities of salt, limestone and uranium are also mined. There are known deposits of bauxite, manganese, iron and tin, and prospecting for lithium, diamonds and copper is under way. Lack of adequate infrastructure has deterred commercial exploitation.

Hydrocarbons

There are no known oil or gas resources in Mali. Petroleum products are imported from the SIR refinery at Abidjan, Cote d'Ivoire, and the SAR refinery at Dakar, Senegal. Typically 4,000 barrels per day (bpd) of refined oil are imported. Mali has no refining capacity.

Energy

Mali is reliant on imported petroleum, although sufficient electricity is produced to meet local demand. Bamako is supplied with hydroelectric power from the dam at Selingué. Most other towns rely on diesel generators.

The Manantali dam in south-west Mali began producing hydroelectricity in 2002, 13 years after it was completed.

Financial markets

Stock exchange

Malian shares are listed on the regional stock exchange (bourse) which opened in Abidjan, Côte d'Ivoire, in 1998. The exchange also lists shares from companies registered in Benin, Burkina Faso, Côte d'Ivoire, Niger, Senegal and Togo. The seven members of the bourse are also members of the Economic and Monetary Union of West Africa (UEMOA) as well as being members of the Economic Community of West African States (Ecowas).

Banking and insurance

Mali has an undeveloped banking sector with just nine banks and two financial institutions. Three of the banks are majority owned by the state while the state owns a minority share in three others. There are three privately owned banks. In recent years, the sector has undergone liberalisation.

Central bank

Banque Centrale du Mali

Main financial centre
Bamako

Time
GMT

Geography
Mali is a landlocked country in West Africa, with Algeria to the north, Mauritania and Senegal to the west, Guinea and Côte d'Ivoire to the south, and Burkina Faso and Niger to the east.
Mali is a landlocked country in West Africa, with Algeria to the north, Mauritania and Senegal to the west, Guinea and Côte d'Ivoire to the south, and Burkina Faso and Niger to the east.
There are three distinct topographic regions. The north is the arid Saharan zone, the semiarid Sahel (an Arab word to describe a border or margin) of savannah and scrubland in the centre, and in the south the fertile and cultivated Sudanese zone. The land rises from the south, typically flatland, through rolling plains to high plateaux in the north. Rugged hills no higher than 1,000 metres line the north-east boundary with Mauritania. The Niger River is 1,693 kilometres long and runs through most of the central and southern region and is considered by Malians as the country's lifeblood as it provides drinking water, aquaculture, irrigation and transport.
Hemisphere
Northern

Climate
There is considerable variation between southern, central and northern areas, rain being rare and sporadic in the far north, Sahara region. Bamako's rainy season runs from June to October with humidity reaching 80 per cent and temperatures ranging from 20 degrees Centigrade (C) to 36 degrees C. The warm, dry season runs from November to February followed by a hot, dry season between February and May with average temperatures of 35 degrees C.

Entry requirements
Passports
Required by all. Passport must be valid six months from date of entry.
Visa
Required by all; there are a few exceptions such as citizens of Ecowas countries. For further details and exceptions visit www.maliembassy-addis.org with its link to consular services. Business visas also require a covering company letter declaring the purpose of the trip and proof of return/onward passage.
Currency advice/regulations
The import and export of local currency is unlimited. Import and export of foreign currency is unlimited however amounts over the equivalent of CFAf25,000 must be declared.
Travellers cheques are accepted in banks.
Customs
Personal belongings and a small amount of tobacco and alcohol are permitted duty free. Cameras and films must be declared.
Sporting firearms and plants, excluding fruit and vegetables, need a certificate of import.
Prohibited imports

Health (for visitors)
Mandatory precautions
Yellow fever vaccination certificate is required by all.
Advisable precautions
Typhoid, tetanus, hepatitis A and polio vaccinations are recommended. Malaria prophylaxis should be taken as risk exists throughout the country. There is a rabies risk. Water precautions must be taken.

Hotels
There are only a few good hotels available and these can be expensive.

Credit cards
Major international credit and charge cards have limited acceptance in major hotels in the capital.

Public holidays (national)
Fixed dates
1 Jan (New Year's Day), 20 Jan (Armed Forces Day), 26 Mar (Day of Democracy), 1 May (Labour Day), 25 May (Africa Day), 22 Sep (Independence Day), 25 Dec (Christmas Day).
Variable dates
Easter Monday, Eid al Adha, Birth of the Prophet, Eid al Fitr.
Islamic year – 1429 (10 Jan 2008–28 Dec 2008): The Islamic year contains 354 or 355 days, with the result that Muslim feasts advance by 10–12 days against the Gregorian calendar. Dates of feasts vary according to the sighting of the new moon, so cannot be forecast exactly.

Working hours
Banking
Mon–Fri: 0730–1300; Mon–Thur 1400–1630; Fri 1500–1730.
Business
Mon–Thu: 0730–1230, 1300–1600. Fri: 0730–1230, 1430–1730.
Government
Mon–Thu, Sat: 0730–1430, Fri: 0730–1230.

Telecommunications
Telephone/fax
The internal service is unreliable.
Mobile/cell phones
GSM 900 services are available in the larger urban areas only.

Electricity supply
220V AC, 50 cycles.

Getting there
Air
National airline: Air Mali.
International airport/s: Bamako (BKO), 15km from city.
Airport tax: CFAf2,500 is payable on domestic flights; CFAf8,000 on international flights within Africa; and CFAf10,000 is payable for flights outside Africa. The airport tax may be collected at time of ticket sale and does not apply to transit passengers on the same flight and for children under two years.
Surface
Road: Good road from Niger (Niamey); condition of routes from Côte d'Ivoire and Burkina Faso varies; those from Senegal and Algeria are not generally recommended.
Rail: There is a regular twice weekly rail service from Senegal (Dakar) to Bamako (with sleeping and restaurant cars and facility for conveying vehicles). Journey takes up to 29 hours.
Main port/s: River ports of Bamako, Mopti, Tombouctou and Gao on the Niger.

Getting about
National transport
Air: There are no scheduled services between Bamako and other towns. Charter of light aircraft available from Société des Transports Aériens (STA). Tombouctou Air Service provides domestic flights.
Road: Main roads run from Sikasso and Bougouni in the south to Bamako, and from Bamako to Mopti and on to Gao via a tarred road. Conditions of roads are variable and secondary roads can be difficult.
Buses: Cheap but generally uncomfortable. Services run from Bamako to all main towns.
Rail: Main routes: Bamako-Koulikoro (59 km); Bamako-Kayes (494km). There are two classes: sleeping and restaurant facilities. Some air-conditioned cars are available.
Water: Three river steamers operate up and down the River Niger betwen August and late December, linking Koulikoro, Mopti, Tombouctou and Gao. Four classes are available, but first-class cabins must be booked in advance through SMERT, the tourist organisation.
City transport
Taxis: Cheap and widely available but not metered. Official standard fare system in Bamako. Tipping is not usual.
Car hire
International driving licence recommended. Hired cars are usually Renaults or Peugeots.

BUSINESS DIRECTORY

The addresses listed below are a selection only. While World of Information makes every endeavour to check these addresses, we cannot guarantee that changes have not been made, especially to telephone numbers and area codes. We would welcome any corrections.

Telephone area codes

The international dialling code (IDD) for Mali is +223, followed by subscriber's number.

Useful telephone numbers

Police: 17
Fire: 18
Ambulance: 225-002

Chambers of Commerce

Mali Chamber of Commerce and Industry, Place de la Liberté, BP 46, Bamako (tel: 222-9645; fax: 222-2120; e-mail: ccim@cefip.com).

Banking

Bank of Africa Mali, BP 2249, 418 Avenue de la Marne, Bamako (tel: 222-4672, 222-4088; fax: 222-4653).

Banque Commerciale du Sahel; BP 2372, 127 Rue, Bozola, Bamako (tel: 210-195/97, 225-536; fax: 222-5543, 222-0135).

Banque de Développement du Mali, BP 94, Ave Modibo Keita, Quartier du Fleuve, Bamako (tel: 222-2050, 222-4088; fax: 222-5085, 222-4250).

Banque de l'Habitat du Mali, BP 2614, Rue de Métal Soudan, Quartier du Fleuve, Bamako (tel: 222-9190, 222-9342; fax: 222-9350).

Banque Internationale du Mali; BP 15, Blvd de l'Indépendance, Bamako (tel: 222-5111, 222-5066; fax: 222-4566).

Banque Internationale pour le Commerce et l'Industrie du Mali; BP B72, Bd du Peuple, Immeuble Nimagala, Bamako (tel: 223-3370; fax: 223-3373).

Banque Malienne de Crédit et de Dépôts, BP 45, Avenue Modibo Keïta, Bamako (tel: 222-5336; fax: 222-7950).

Banque Nationale de Développement Agricole - Mali; BP 2424, Immeuble Dette Publique, Bamako (tel: 222-6464, 222-6611 fax: 222-2961).

Ecobank-Mali; BP 1272, Quartier du Fleuve, Place de la Nation, Bamako (tel: 223-3300; fax: 223-3305).

Central bank

Banque Centrale des Etats de l'Afrique de l'Ouest, Direction Nationale, PO Box 206, Avenue Moussa Travele, Bamako (tel: 222-3756; fax: 222-4786).

Travel information

Air Mali, Immeuble Scif, Square Lumumba, BP 27, Bamako (tel: 225-741/42; fax: 222-349).

Commissariat au Tourisme, BP 191, Bamako (tel: 225-673).

Delta Voyages SA, Immeuble Gamby (ex BNDA), BP 5005, Bamako (fax: 231-272).

Timbuctours, BP 222, Bamako (tel: 225-315).

Ministry of tourism

Ministry of Crafts Industry and Tourism, BP 2211, Bamako (tel: 223-6344, 223-6450; fax: 223-8201).

Ministries

Ministry of Agriculture, Breeding and Fishing, BP 61, Bamako (tel: 222-2979, 222-2785, 222-3006).

Ministry of Economy and Finances, BP 776, Bamako (tel: 222-9918, 222-8353; fax: 229-4440).

Ministry of Education, BP 71, Bamako, (tel: 222-2450; 222-2125; fax: 223-0545).

Ministry of Foreign Affairs, Bamako (fax: 230-327, 225-226).

Ministry of Industry and Trade, BP 1759, Bamako (tel: 221-6399, 222-8353; fax: 221-3114).

Ministry of Labour and Public Works, BP 80, Bamako, (tel: 222-4819; 222-1117; fax: 222-6548).

Ministry of Overseas Aid and International Co-operation, Bamako, (tel: 222-5092; 223-0056).

Other useful addresses

Direction Nationale du Plan et de la Statistique, Koulouba, Bamako (tel: 222-2753).

Government Press Office, Bamako, (tel: 222-0733).

Radiodiffusion-Télévision Malienne, BP 171, Bamako (tel: 222-2474).

Mali Embassy (USA), 2130 R Street, NW, Washington DC 20009 (tel: (+1-202) 332-2249; fax: (+1-202) 332-6603; e-mail: info@maliembassy-usa.org).

Internet sites

Africa Business Network: http://www.ifc.org/abn

African Development Bank: http://www.afdb.org

AllAfrica.com: http://www.allafrica.com

Africa Online: http://www.africaonline.com

Mbendi AfroPaedia (information on companies, countries, industries and stock exchanges in Africa): http://mbendi.co.za

Malta

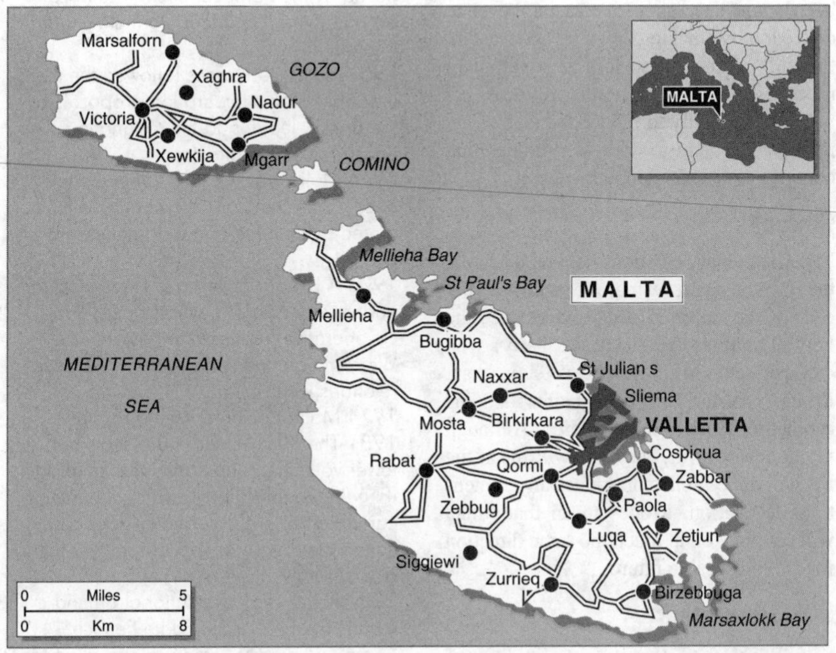

KEY FACTS

Official name: Republic of Malta

Head of State: President Edward Fenech Adami (since 4 Apr 2004)

Head of government: Prime Minister Lawrence Gonzi (re-appointed 12 Mar 2008)

Ruling party: Partit Nazzjonalista (PN) (Nationalist Party) (since 1998; re-elected 8 Mar 2008)

Area: 316 square km

Population: 410,000 (2007)*

Capital: Valletta

Official language: Malti and English

Currency: Euro ( ) = 100 cents (from 1 Jan 2008)

Exchange rate: 0.63 per US$ (Jul 2008)

GDP per capita: US$18,089 (2007)

GDP real growth: 3.80% (2007)

Labour force: 153,000 (2004)

Unemployment: 6.30% (2007)

Inflation: 0.70% (2007)

Balance of trade: -US$1.20 billion (2005)

* estimated figure

Positioned as it is between Europe (Sicily) and Africa and astride the great trade routes from the eastern Mediterranean to the exit to the Atlantic at Gibraltar, Malta was always going to be either a strategic asset in someone else's portfolio of territories, or a key refuelling stop on everybody else's trade routes. The Phoenicians, no slouches when it came to international trading, were in Malta around 1000 BC, the Greeks came in 736 BC, when it was named Melita. There was a period of Byzantine rule from the fourth to the ninth century, and then a long period of Arab rule when most of the population became Muslims and spoke Arabic. The Arabs were followed by the Sicilian Normans (who restored Christianity), the Angevines, Hohenstaufen and the Aragonese towards the end of the thirteenth century. Spain gave the islands to the Knights of St John who built the city of Valletta, named after Jean Parisot de la Valette. The French under Napoleon captured the islands in 1798, and the British took the islands two years later when Malta became a British protectorate, and then part of the British Empire in 1814 (as part of the Treaty of Paris); it became fully independent in 1964. It is no wonder that the Maltese are now an adaptive, tough people.

All change

On 1 January 2008 Malta changed its currency when it adopted the euro. The International Monetary Fund (IMF), in a report published in May 2008, warned that although the adoption of the euro can be seen as a landmark in Malta's growth-oriented reform agenda, it must also be aware that cost-competitiveness in some traditional exports will wane. At the same time, the opening of Malta's market and EU membership will facilitate an upward shift in the value-added and quality export sectors.

Malta has experienced a three-year expansion, financed mostly by foreign direct investment (FDI) and export diversification. New export-oriented activities such as pharmaceuticals, on-line gaming and financial and business services have contributed to a drop in the external account deficit to 5.5 per cent of GDP. Tourism has received a boost from an increase in arrivals on low-cost airlines. Labour costs, however, have risen more than productivity, which will likely contribute to a rise in inflation. While the government recognises the need for Malta to improve labour productivity, it has been reluctant to take politically sensitive restructuring decisions. There remain high levels of consumer expectations and social security expenditure that appears unsustainable in the longer term.

Malta has no significant natural resources (except for some limited fishing) and is totally dependent on oil imports for its energy needs. With a population of just over 400,000, Malta also has a very small internal market. Its economy is dependent on export-oriented industries (especially electronic components and clothing) with tourism, the single largest foreign currency earner, accounting for a quarter of Malta's gross domestic product (GDP). GDP grew by 3.8 per cent in 2007, up from the 3.4 per cent in 2006. The manufacturing industry is characterised by some 400 medium-to large-sized export-oriented firms, mostly foreign-owned, and a large number of micro and small enterprises geared to the domestic market. The services sector remains the prime driver of economic growth in Malta. Financial services and telecommunications have increased in importance in recent years and there has been greater activity in the construction industry due to a boom in house prices. Incentives have been introduced to attract foreign investment and to encourage offshore business and financial houses to use Malta as a base for operations in Europe and the Mediterranean. An international free port operates successfully as a central Mediterranean transshipment hub, although competition from other Mediterranean free ports has been increasing.

Restoring sustainability to the public finances continues to be a major challenge for the ruling Partit Nazzjonalista (PN) (Nationalist Party) government. Although there has been some success in increasing revenue collection by cracking down on tax evasion, this still contributes to loss in government revenues. Further economic reforms are needed, especially to reduce the size of the public sector and to address rigidities that continue to reduce competitiveness.

Outlook

In parliamentary elections held on 8 March, the PN won a narrow majority with 49.3 per cent of the vote (35 seats out of 69), the Partit Laburista (PL) (Labour Party) won 48.8 per cent (34); turnout was 93 per cent. Prime Minister Lawrence Gonzi and his cabinet took office on 12 March. Although the tightness of the majority will mean the PN will not be able to introduce any contentious legislation, it does mean that Malta will continue on in much the same direction for the foreseeable future.

Risk assessment

Politics	Good
Economy	Good
Regional stability	Good

COUNTRY PROFILE

Historical profile

1814 Malta became a crown colony of the UK, with limited self-government.
1942 The islanders were awarded the George Cross for heroism during a three-year siege and severe bombing by Germans and Italians in the Second World War.
1947 Malta was granted full internal self-government.
1956 In a referendum, a majority voted in favour of integration with the UK as proposed by the Partit Laburista (Malta Labour Party) (MLP) under Dominic (Dom) Mintoff.
1959–62 Disturbances followed the rejection of Mintoff's integration proposals by the British, leading to his resignation. The British reinstated direct rule.
1964 Malta was granted full independence within the Commonwealth, reinforced by defence and aid treaties with UK.
1971 A Labour government was elected under Dom Mintoff , who signed co-operative treaties with Eastern and Western countries and established close relations with Libya.
1974 Malta declared itself a republic.
1981 The MLP gained more seats but fewer votes than the Partit Nazzionalista (PN) (Nationalist Party), which mounted a campaign of civil disobedience and boycotted the House of Representatives for over a year.
1987 Following constitutional amendments, the PN, led by Eddie Fenech Adami, worked to maintain non-aligned status, while seeking closer ties with the West.
1990 Malta applied to join the EU.
1996 The EU application was frozen by Alfred Sant (MLP) when he took office as prime minister.
1998 Prime Minister Fenech Adami (PN) renewed the island's application to join the EU.
2000 Malta was placed in the first wave of EU accession candidate countries.
2003 A referendum produced a 53.6 per cent vote in favour of EU membership; turnout was 91 per cent. The ruling PN won the parliamentary elections.
2004 Prime Minister Fenech Adami stepped down and Lawrence Gonzi was sworn in as prime minister. Eddie Fenech Adami took office as president. Malta joined the EU on 1 May.
2005 The Maltese parliament ratified the European constitution in a unanimous vote.
2006 Increasing numbers of illegal immigrants from Africa forced Malta to seek stronger commitment from EU partners.
2007 On 10 July EU officials formally invited Malta to join the third stage of the European Monetary Union (EMU). On 20 December Malta became a member of the European Union Schengen area

KEY INDICATORS — Malta

	Unit	2003	2004	2005	2006	2007
Population	m	0.40	0.40	0.40	0.41	*0.41
Gross domestic product (GDP)	US$bn	4.64	5.39	5.67	6.39	7.42
GDP per capita	US$	11,705	13,734	14,342	15,716	*18,089
GDP real growth	%	2.8	1.5	2.2	3.4	3.8
Inflation	%	2.0	2.7	2.5	2.6	0.7
Unemployment	%	5.6	5.7	7.1	7.3	6.5
Exports (fob) (goods)	US$m	2,000.0	2,688.3	2,458.1	2,948.2	3,237.9
Imports (cif) (goods)	US$m	2,800.0	3,559.6	3,662.3	4,154.3	4,541.1
Balance of trade	US$m	-800.0	-871.3	-1,204.2	-1,206.1	1,303.2
Current account	US$m	-280.0	-560.0	-595.0	-426.0	*-459.0
Total reserves minus gold	US$m	2,728.7	2,699.7	2,576.4	2,876.8	3,785.4
Foreign exchange	US$m	2,624.5	2,589.4	2,473.0	2,865.0	3,662.0
Exchange rate	per US$	0.37	0.34	0.33	0.32	0.30

* estimated figure

whereby all travellers may cross borders without a passport or visa.
2008 On 1 January, Malta adopted the euro as its official currency. In parliamentary elections held on 8 March, the PN won 49.3 per cent of the vote (35 seats out of 69), the MLP won 48.8 per cent (34); turnout was 93 per cent. Prime Minister Lawrence Gonzi and his cabinet took office on 12 March.

Political structure

Constitution
The independence constitution of 1964 was amended on 13 December 1974, to provide for the creation of the office of president to replace that of governor general.
Form of state
Parliamentary democratic republic; it is a member of the Commonwealth.
The executive
The House of Representatives elects the president as constitutional head of state for a five-year term. The president appoints the prime minister and, on the latter's advice, the cabinet, which holds executive power.
National legislature
Legislative power is vested in the unicameral Kamra tar-Rapprezentanti (house of representatives) (69 members elected for five years by universal adult suffrage on a plurality basis). Should a party polling a majority of votes fail to gain a majority of seats in the House, extra seats are allocated until a majority of one seat is achieved.
Legal system
The judiciary is independent. Public law is based on English common law.
Last elections
29 March 2004 (presidential); 8 March 2008 (parliamentary).
Results: Presidential: Edward Fenech Adami won 33 out of 65 votes in the election by the House of Representatives. Parliamentary: PN won 49.3 per cent of the vote (35 seats out of 69); PL won 48.8 per cent (34). Turnout was 93 per cent.
Next elections
2013 (parliamentary); 2009 (presidential).

Political parties

Ruling party
Partit Nazzjonalista (PN) (Nationalist Party) (since 1998; re-elected 8 Mar 2008)
Main opposition party
Partit Laburista (PL) (Labour Party)
Political situation
Malta looked outward in 2007 as it prepared to join all the other European countries in the eurozone. From the formal application submitted on 26 February, through its final acceptance in July, to the release of newly minted Maltese euro coins, bearing the image of the Maltese Cross in time for 1 January 2008, when Malta dropped the Maltese Lira. While the change has come at an opportune time, when the euro, in April 2008, is pegged at is highest ever, it also has a negative impact on tourists visiting from outside the eurozone. Nevertheless, Malta sees itself as a fully paid up member of the European Union and the long-term benefits of this should far outweigh drawbacks in the loss of short-term foreign earnings.
Having got the country into the EU and geared up the mechanism for the new currency the electorate, by a wafer-thin majority, decided to heap faint praise on the Nationalist party and let it carry on until perhaps something else, more spectacular, comes along and they can really make up their minds who they want to govern. Until then better the devil you know…

Population

410,000 (2007)*
Last census: November 1995: 378,132
Population density: 1,184 inhabitants per square km. Urban population: 91 per cent.
Annual growth rate: 0.7 per cent 1994–2004 (WHO 2006)
Ethnic make-up
Most Maltese are descendants of Phoenicians, with strong elements of Italian and other Mediterranean influences.
Religions
Roman Catholic (98 per cent).

Education

Primary education lasts for six years; secondary schooling lasts for five years, divided into a three-year orientation cycle and a two-year cycle of specialisation.
There are two types of secondary education schools – junior Lyceums and area secondary schools; following either of these leads to a choice between academic or technical courses. Over 54 per cent of students continue with their education and training after the age of 16. Church schools are funded through the government and tuition is free.
Higher education is mainly provided by the University of Malta. The quality of education in Malta is high and attracts students from the Mediterranean and the Middle East.
Literacy rate: 92.6 per cent total; 93.4 per cent female, adult rates (World Bank).
Compulsory years: Five to 16.
Enrolment rate: 108 per cent (boys); 107 per cent (girls) gross primary enrolment of the relevant age group (including repetition rates) (World Bank).

Health

Per capita total expenditure on health (2003) was US$1,436; of which per capita government spending was US$1,150, at the international dollar rate, (WHO 2006).
Public hospital services are adequate although there have been concerns over the long waiting times. Total bed capacity is around 2,000. An increasing number of doctors are resigning due to poor working conditions and wages. Due to the low numbers of doctors, some health centres have stopped operating on a 24-hour basis.
In 2002, a programme of refurbishment and modernisation was undertaken in all government hospitals.
HIV/Aids
HIV prevalence: 0.2 per cent aged 15–49 in 2003 (World Bank)
Life expectancy: 79 years, 2004 (WHO 2006)
Fertility rate/Maternal mortality rate: 1.5 births per woman, 2004 (WHO 2006)
Child (under 5 years) mortality rate (per 1,000): 5.0 per 1,000 live births (World Bank).
Head of population per physician: 3.18 physicians per 1,000 people, 2003 (WHO 2006)

Welfare

The Maltese welfare system is poised for reform. There is a significant welfare gap in society.
The social security contribution rate paid by every Maltese employer is 10 per cent. The self-employed pay a rate of 15 per cent.
In January 2002, a Care Allowance was introduced for children living in institutions. This allowance was extended to foster parents.

Main cities

Valletta (capital, estimated population 7,170), Birkirkara (22,685), Mosta (18,416), Qormi (18,100), Mosta (18,416), Sliema (12,380), Zabbar (15,452).

Languages spoken

Malti, English and some Italian; most business correspondence is in English.
Official language/s
Malti and English

Media

Press
Dailies: The major dailies include The Malta Independent (English), The Times (English), In-Nazzjon (Maltese), L-orizzont (Maltese).
Weeklies: The Malta Independent on Sunday (English), The Sunday Times (English), Il-Mument (Maltese), It-Torca (Maltese).
Business: The Malta Business Weekly (English, published every Thursday).

Broadcasting
Supervised by Malta Broadcasting Authority. Xandir Malta (part of TeleMalta Corp) broadcasts two radio services (Radio Malta) and a TV service (Television Malta). Private broadcasting services have been introduced following a liberalisation of media laws. Six private radio stations are already in operation. Over 20 Italian TV stations are received in Malta, and many satellite stations are available through a cable television network.

Advertising
Advertisements can be placed on radio and TV through Xandir Malta in Gwardamangia. Newspapers, periodicals, cinemas and poster sites also available.

Economy
Economic growth was negative between 2003–04 but recovered in 2005; IMF registered GDP growth of 1.0 per cent, although Malta's own statistics registered 2.5 per cent, due to a revision in measuring methods. The growth was due to improved domestic demand and strengthening investment. However, the economy has suffered since 2003 when visitor numbers began to fall; it registered a reduction of 2.4 per cent in 2005. Tourism is one of the country's principal industries, accounting for around 30 per cent of GDP, and a drop in growth impacts heavily on related sectors such as transport, hotels and restaurants and telecommunications. In 2007, a major low-cost airline began operations from the UK to Malta and around 100,000 extra visitors are expected. While this is good news for a stagnant hotel sector the price of domestic properties is also expected to rise and exclude young Maltese residents from buying their own homes.

Export of manufactured goods, particularly semi-conductors which account for 75 per cent of all sales, is the other prime industry. Measures designed to increase the competitiveness of Maltese exports and to widen the range of incentives available to the industrial investor are given priority and to encourage offshore business and financial houses to use Malta as a base for operations in Europe and the Mediterranean.

Transport-related services, such as transshipment and ship repair, are important to the economy. Malta is a 'flag of convenience' state and has been under pressure from the EU to comply with EU maritime standards.

Even before joining it in 2004, Malta's economy was closely integrated into the European Union (EU), and has benefited from EU development funds to improve its infrastructure.

In per capita terms, Malta is one of the most affluent EU members, although it is also the smallest. The narrow range of foreign exchange earning sectors and the small domestic market make Malta vulnerable to external shocks.

A key requirement for Malta to be able to adopt the euro by 2007 is the reduction of the budget deficit, for which it has undertaken measures. Government spending was reduced by 1.9 per cent in 2005 as part of fiscal consolidation. Despite crackdowns, tax evasion still contributes to a loss in government revenues. The government also plans reduce the size of the public sector and labour costs, which remain high, compared to the general level of productivity.

External trade
As a member of the European Union, Malta operates within a communitywide free trade union, with tariffs sets as a whole. Internationally, the EU has free trade agreements with a number of nations and trading blocs worldwide.

Manufactured commodities provide 75 per cent of total exports, while the tourist sector provides 30 per cent of GDP.

Malta's has the world's fourth largest merchant fleet in the world and is actively encouraging growth in international banking and financial services and developing an offshore tax haven.

Imports
Principal imports are petroleum and vehicles, foodstuffs, electrical and electronic components, machinery, beverages and tobacco, manufactured and semi-manufactured goods.

Main sources: Italy (38.3 per cent total, 2006), UK (10.1 per cent), France (9.5 per cent).

Exports
Major exports include manufactured electrical and electronic items, general machinery, clothes and books.

Main destinations: France (15.0 per cent total, 2006), Germany (12.8 per cent), Singapore (12.7 per cent).

Re-exports

Agriculture
Farming
The agricultural sector accounts for around 2.5 per cent of GDP and employs less than 2 per cent of the population. Agricultural production supplies only about 20 per cent of Malta's food needs. There is a limited area of land available for agriculture and freshwater supplies are scarce. Potatoes and onions are the largest vegetable crops; potatoes are also the largest export crop. Grapes are the largest fruit crop and flower cultivation is flourishing.

Malta has decided to implement the reform of the EU Common Agricultural Policy (CAP) on 1 January 2007. The reform was introduced throughout most of the EU on 1 January 2005, when subsidies on farm output, which tended to benefit large farms and encourage overproduction, were replaced by single farm payments, not conditional on production. The change is expected to reward farmers who provide and maintain a healthy environment, food safety and animal welfare standards. The changes are also intended to encourage market conscious production and cut the cost of CAP to the EU taxpayer.

The estimated crop production for 2005 included: 11,600 tonnes (t) cereals in total, 9,400t wheat, 25,000t potatoes, 2,694t grapes, 388t figs, 14,657t tomatoes, 8,199t fruit in total, 58,017t vegetables in total. Livestock production included: 18,838t meat in total, 1,290t beef, 8,470t pig meat, 138t lamb and goat meat, 7,547t poultry, 6,140t eggs, 46,760t milk, 1,350t rabbit.

Fishing
Around 1,000 tonnes of marine fish are landed annually, while acquaculture produces 2,000 tonnes. Around 370 people are registered as full-time fishermen, with 300 registered fishing vessels in operation. Another 1,500 boats are owned by part-time fishermen.

In 2004, the total marine fish catch was 1,103 tonnes and the total crustacean catch was 26 tonnes.

Timber imports in 2004 were US$85 million, while exports amounted to US$1 million.

Industry and manufacturing
The industrial sector contributes approximately 30 per cent to GDP and employs 35 per cent of the labour force.

Manufactures include textiles, clothing, synthetic fibres, footwear, wines and beer, furniture, electronic goods, automobile components, measuring/controlling equipment and tobacco products.

Ship-repairing is an important foreign exchange earner, but the Malta Drydocks company suffered falling revenues during the 1990s as worldwide shipping activity declined. As a result, the government has decided to end subsidies to both the Malta Drydocks and Malta Shipbuilding companies by 2008.

Tourism
The Maltese economy is heavily dependent on tourism, which is expected to contribute around 32 per cent to GDP in 2005. The impact of the 2001 terrorist attacks in the US, compounded by the Iraq War and the Sars outbreak in 2003, resulted in a decline in visitor numbers, but there were signs of recovery in 2004. The UK is the main market and continues to show growth, although this has been offset by falling numbers from the next most important sources of visitors, Germany,

Italy and France. Niche tourism, in particular diving, English-language learning and conferences, is being developed. The majority of tourists arrive by air, but cruise ship visits have risen and a terminal is under construction to foster this trend.

Mining
Malta has no exploitable natural resources.

Hydrocarbons
Malta does not possess any natural energy resources and all energy sources have to be imported. Malta has, over the years, built up a preferential arrangement with Libya for the import of crude petroleum. Energy-related imports account for some 7 per cent of total imports.
Exploration for oil and gas has been conducted offshore for a number of years, but no commercial reserves have been identified.

Financial markets
Stock exchange
The Malta Stock Exchange (MSE) was set up in 1992 to encourage private investment in a range of commercial and government stocks. It has grown rapidly as a result of strong domestic and offshore investment interest, with total market capitalisation of over US$3.7 billion.

Banking and insurance
There are two major commercial banks — Bank of Valletta and the HSBC Bank Malta plc.
Central bank
Central Bank of Malta

Time
GMT plus one hour (daylight saving, late March to late October, GMT plus two hours)

Geography
The largest and only inhabited islands of the Maltese archipelago in the Mediterranean are Malta, Gozo and Comino. The main island, Malta, lies 93km (58 miles) south of the Italian island of Sicily and 290km (180 miles) north of the Libyan coast, with Tunisia to the west.
Malta is typically limestone rock with a series of low hills and slopes running toward the north-west and low-lying land to the south-east. The soil can be thin producing heathland, while terraced hills produce much of Malta's agricultural produce.
Hemisphere
Northern

Climate
Mediterranean, with hot summers and warm winters. Temperatures range from about 29 degrees Celsius (C) down to about 10 degrees C. January and February are the coldest months, July and August the hottest. August and September tend to be hot and humid, but usually with sea breezes in evening.

Dress codes
European clothing is suitable for winter, spring and autumn; tropical weight for summer.

Entry requirements
Passports
Required by all, excepted for citizens of EU and EEA with national ID cards. Passports must be valid for three month beyond the length of stay.
Visa
Required by all, except nationals of EU and Schengen area signatory countries, North America, Australasia and Japan. For further exceptions contact the nearest embassy or see www.foreign.gov.mt and follow the link to travel advice. A Schengen visa application (offered in several languages) can be downloaded from http://europa.eu/abc/travel/ see 'documents you will need'.
Currency advice/regulations
The import and export of local currency is limited to Lm5,000; the import of export of foreign currency is unlimited.
Travellers cheques are widely accepted.
Customs
Personal items are duty-free. There are no duties levied on alcohol and tobacco between EU member states, providing amounts imported are for personal consumption.

Health (for visitors)
Nationals of the European Economic Area (EEA) countries and Switzerland can access reduced cost and sometimes free medical treatment using a European Health Insurance Card (EHIC) while visiting the EEA. Exceptions include nationals of the 10 countries, which joined the EU in 2004, whose EHIC is not valid in Switzerland. Applications for the EHIC should be made before travelling.
Advisable precautions
There are no special requirements.

Hotels
Classified from five-star to one-star. All hotel staff speak English and many are multi-lingual.

Credit cards
All major credit and debit cards are accepted; ATMs are widely available.

Public holidays (national)
Fixed dates
1 Jan (New Year's Day), 10 Feb (St Paul's Shipwreck), 19 Mar (St Joseph's Day), 31 Mar (Freedom Day), 1 May (Labour Day), 7 Jun (Commemoration of the 1919 Uprising), 29 Jun (Feast of St Peter and St Paul), 15 Aug (Assumption Day), 8 Sep (Victory Day), 21 Sep (Independence Day), 8 Dec (Immaculate Conception), 13 Dec (Republic Day) and 25 Dec (Christmas Day).
Variable dates
Good Friday

Working hours
Banking
Mon–Fri: 0830–1230; Sat: 0830–1200. Summer and winter opening hours may vary.
Business
Mon–Fri: 0830–1245 and 1430–1730.
Government
Mon–Fri: 0745–1230 and 1315–1715 (Jun to Sep Mon–Fri: 0730–1330).
Shops
Mon–Sat: 0900–1300 and 1600–1900.

Telecommunications
Mobile/cell phones
GSM 900 and 1800 services are available throughout the islands.

Electricity supply
240V AC

Weights and measures
The metric system is the main one in use. Sometimes the imperial system is also used and, on rare occasions, the old local measures.

Getting there
Air
National airline: Air Malta.
International airport/s: Malta (MLA) at Luqa, 5km from Valletta, facilities include bureau de change, duty-free shops, car hire and restaurant. Taxis and buses are available.
Airport tax: None
Surface
Water: There are regular car ferry services from Sicily and the Italian mainland.

Getting about
National transport
Air: Internal flights (by helicopter) operate between Malta and Gozo.
Buses: Regular bus services run from Valletta to most towns and villages on Malta and Gozo.
Water: Gozo Channel Company operates a regular round-the-clock daily ferry service between Malta and Gozo.
City transport
Metered taxis are available.
Car hire
Self-drive cars are available at daily, weekly and monthly rates with unlimited mileage and fully comprehensive insurance. A national or international driving licence is required, which must be endorsed at the Police Licensing Office, Floriana. Speed limits are 40kph in built-up areas and 64kph elsewhere. Driving is on the left.

BUSINESS DIRECTORY

The addresses listed below are a selection only. While World of Information makes every endeavour to check these addresses, we cannot guarantee that changes have not been made, especially to telephone numbers and area codes. We would welcome any corrections.

Telephone area codes

The international direct dialling (IDD) code for Malta is +356 followed by subscriber's number.

Useful telephone numbers

Police: 191
Ambulance: 196
Fire brigade: 199
Directory enquiries: 190
Overseas operator: 194
Time check: 195

Chambers of Commerce

Malta Chamber of Commerce and Enterprise, Exchange Buildings, Republic Street, Valletta VLT 05 (tel: 2123-3873; fax: 2124-5223; e-mail: admin@chamber.org.mt).

Maltese-American Chamber of Commerce, Exchange Buildings, Republic Street, Valletta VLT 05 (tel: 2124-7233; fax: 2124-5223; e-mail: president@malta-uschamber.com).

Banking

APS Bank ltd, 275 St Paul Street, Valletta VLT 07 (tel: 247-547; fax: 238-698).

Bank of Valletta Ltd, 58 Zachary Street, Valletta VLT 04 (tel: 243-261/7; fax: 230-894).

Bank of Valletta Group, BOV Centre, High Street, Sliema, SLM 16 (tel: 336-224; fax: 346-160; internet site: www.bov.com).

HSBC Bank Malta plc, 233 Republic Street, Valletta VLT 05 (tel: 485-713; fax: 489-425).

HSBC Bank Malta (Overseas) plc, 15 Republic Street, Valletta VLT 05 (tel: 249-801/4; fax: 249-805).

Investment Finance Bank Ltd, 168 Strait Street, Valletta VLT 07 (tel: 232-017, 233-349; fax: 242-014).

Lombard Bank (Malta) Ltd, Lombard House, 67 Republic Street, Valletta VLT 05 (tel: 248-411/8; fax: 246-600).

Valletta Investment Bank Ltd, 144 St Christopher Street, Valletta VLT 02 (tel: 2235-246; fax: 234-419).

Central bank

Central Bank of Malta, Pjazza Kastiija, Valletta CMR 01 (tel: 2550-0000; fax: 2550-2500; e-mail: info@centralbankmalta.com).

Travel information

Air Malta, Head Office, Malta International Airport, Gudja (tel: 2299-9984, 2299-9885; fax: 2299-9368; internet site: http://www.airmalta.com).

Malta International Airport Ltd, Luqa LQA 05 (tel: 249-600; fax: 243-042; internet site: http://www.maltairport.com).

National tourist organisation offices

Malta Tourism Authority, 280 Republic Street, Valletta CMR 02 (tel: 224-444, 225-048/9; fax: 220-401; e-mail: info@visitmalta.com; internet site: http://www.visitmalta.com).

Ministries

Ministry of Investment, Industry and Information Technology, 168 Triq id-Dejqa, Valletta CMR 02 (tel: 2122-6808; fax: 2125-0700; email: miti@gov.mt).

Ministry of Foreign Affairs, Palazzo Parisio, Merchants Street, Valletta CMR 02 (tel: 2124-2853; fax: 2123-5032; email: info.mfa@gov.mt).

Ministry of Finance, Maison Demandols, South Street, Valletta CMR 02 (tel: 2124-9640/6; fax: 2122-4667; email info.mfin@gov.mt).

Ministry of Resources and Infrastructures, Block B, Floriana CMR 02 (tel: 2122-2378; fax: 2124-3306).

Other useful addresses

British High Commission, Whitehall Mansions, Ta'Xbiex Seafront, Ta'Xbiex, MSD 11, (tel: 2323-0000; fax: 622-001).

Department of Industry, St George's, Canon Road, St Venera (tel: 446-259).

Department of Information, Auberge de Castille, Valletta (tel: 225-241, 224-901; fax: 237-170).

Department of Trade, Lascaris, Valletta (tel: 224-411).

Embassy of the United States of America, PO Box 535, Valletta CMR O1 (tel: 2561-4000; fax: 2124-3229; email: usembmalta@state.gov).

Hotels and Restaurants Association, 7 Frederick Street, Valletta (tel: 336-843; fax: 237-253).

Malta Broadcasting Authority, National Rd, Blata 1-Bajda (tel: 221-281).

Maltacom (telecommunications), Spencer Hill, Marsa HMR12 (postal address: PO Box 40, Qormi, QRM01) (tel: 240-000; fax: 246-369; e-mail: mcintrel@maltacom.com; internet site: www.maltacom.com).

Malta Development Corporation, PO Box 141, Marsa GPO 01; head office: Triq I-Industrija, Qormi (tel: 441-888; fax: 441-887; e-mail: info@mdc.com.mt; internet site: www.investinmalta.com).

Malta Drydocks, The Docks (tel: 822-451, 822-491; fax: 800-021).

Malta Export Trade Corporation, Trade Centre, PO Box 8, San Gwann SGN 01 (tel: 446-186/7/8; fax: 496-687; internet site: www.metco.com.mt/main.htm).

Malta Federation of Industry, Development House, St Anne Street, Floriana VLT 01 (tel: 222-074, 234-428; fax: 240-702).

Malta Financial Services Centre (MFSC), Attard (tel: 441-155; fax: 441-188).

Malta Freeport Corporation Ltd, Freeport Centre, Port of Matrsaxlokk, Kalafrana BBG 07 (tel: 650-200; fax: 684-814).

Malta Investment Management Co Ltd (MIMCOL), Trade Centre, San Gwann Industrial Estate, Birkirkara SGN09 (tel: 497-970; fax: 499-568).

Malta Maritime Authority, Maritime House, Lascaris Wharf, Valletta VLT 01 (tel: 250-360/4; fax: 250-365).

Malta Shipbuilding Co Ltd, Marsa (tel: 220-051, 237-297; fax: 240-930).

Malta Stock Exchange, Pope Pius V Street, Valletta VLT 11 (tel: 244-051/5; fax: 244-071).

Malta Trade Fairs Corporation, The Fair Grounds, Naxxar NXR 02 (tel: 410-371/4; fax: 414-099).

Maltese Embassy (US), 2017 Connecticut Avenue, NW, Washington DC 20008 (tel: (+1-202) 462-3611; fax: (+1-202) 387-5470; e-mail: malta_embassy@compuserve.com).

Parliamentary Secretariat for Maritime and Offshore, House of Four Winds, Valletta (tel: 241-570).

Privatisation Unit, Ministry of Finance and Economic Affairs, Trade Centre, San Gwann Industrial Estate, San Gwann SGN 09 (internet site: www.maltacom.com).

Sea Malta Co Ltd, Sea Malta Building, Flagstone Wharf, Marsa HMR 12 (tel: 232-230/9; fax: 225-776).

Internet sites

Malta Government: http://www.magnet.mt/

Marshall Islands

COUNTRY PROFILE

Historical profile

The Marshall Islands comprise over a thousand flat coral islands of white sand beaches and lagoons.

1788 The Marshall Islands were named after Captain John Marshall, who visited the islands on his way to China from Botany Bay.

1886 Germany established a protectorate over the Marshall Islands.

1914 The islands were captured from Germany by Japan.

1935 The Japanese transformed the islands into a military base.

1944 Allied troops occupied the islands.

1945 After the end of the Second World War, control of the Marshall Islands was granted to the US.

1946 The Marshall Islands were used as a nuclear testing ground by the US.

1947 Marshall Islands became one of six entities in the Trust Territory of the Pacific Islands (TTPI) established by the UN with the US as the Trustee.

1962 The US ended nuclear testing on the islands.

1965 The Congress of Micronesia was established, with representatives from all TTPI islands.

1978 The Marshall Islands first constitution was adopted.

1979 The government of the Marshall Islands was officially established and the islands became self-governing. Amata Kabua was elected president.

1982 The official title of the islands became the Republic of the Marshall Islands (RMI).

1983 RMI voters approved the Compact of Free Association (CFA) with the US.

1986 The US Congress approved the CFA. The RMI was granted sovereignty, aid and US defence, in return for continued US military missile testing.

1990 The UN Security Council formally ended the trusteeship.

1991 The RMI joined the UN.

1995 President Kabua was re-elected for the fourth time.

1996 Amata Kabua died. He was succeeded by his cousin, Imata Kabua

1999 The United Democratic Party (UDP) won the general election.

2000 Kessai Note (UDP) was elected president.

2001 Former inhabitants of Bikini and the Enewetak atolls were awarded over US$1 billion in compensation for hardship suffered when they were evacuated and resettled in the 1940s to allow US nuclear tests on the islands.

2003 The RMI concluded negotiations with the US on the provisions of the CFA.

2004 Kessai Note was re-elected as president.

2006 Justin deBrum, a leading politician and presidential candidate died.

2007 In general elections held on 19 November the ruling UDP won 14 seats (out of 33) and the opposition coalition United People's Party (UPP) and Aelon Kein Ad (AKA) (Our Islands) won 17, independents won the remaining seats. The OECD removed RMI from the blacklist of unco-operative tax havens.

2008 On 7 January the parliament elected Litokwa Tomeing (UPP/AKA) as president by 18 to 15 votes and replaced the incumbent Kessai Note. President Tomeing and his cabinet were sworn in on 14 January.

Political structure

Constitution

The constitution was adopted in 1979. Under the Compact of Free Association (CFA), the Marshall Islands have control over all domestic and foreign affairs with the exception of defence which is the responsibility of the US.

Universal suffrage begins at aged 18.

Form of state

Self-governing territory in free association with the US.

The executive

Executive power rests with the president and the cabinet. The president is both head of state and head of government, elected by parliament for a four-year term. The president appoints the cabinet from members of the Nitijela (parliament).

National legislature

The bicameral system of government includes the Nitijela (lower house), with 33 senators of the Nitijela elected from 24 constituencies, for four-year terms. The Nitijela holds legislative power and elects the president.

The upper house, Council of Iroij (council of chiefs) is an advisory body, of 12 tribal chiefs, with consultative authority on matters relating to land and customs, who serves four-year terms.

Last elections

7 January 2008 (presidential); 19 November 2008 (parliamentary).

Results: Presidential: Litokwa Tomeing (UPP/AKA coalition) won 18 votes, Kessai Note won 15

KEY FACTS

Official name: Republic of the Marshall Islands

Head of State: President Litokwa Tomeing (UPP/AKA) (from 7 Jan 2008)

Head of government: President Litokwa Tomeing

Ruling party: Coalition of the United People's Party (UPP) and Aelon Kein Ad (AKA) (Our Islands) (14 Jan 2008)

Area: 183 square km consisting of 29 atolls and 1,225 islets

Population: 52,700 (2007)*

Capital: Majuro (on Majuro atoll)

Official language: Marshallese, English

Currency: US dollar (US$) = 100 cents)

GDP per capita: US$2,836 (2007)

GDP real growth: 1.70% (2007)

Labour force: 14,677 (2006)

Unemployment: 34.00% (2006)

Inflation: 3.00% (2005)*

* estimated figure

Parliamentary: UDP won 14 seats (out of 33) and the opposition coalition of United People's Party (UPP) and Aelon Kein Ad (AKA) (Our Islands) won 17, independents won the remaining.

Next elections
2011 (parliamentary and presidential)

Political parties

Ruling party
Coalition of the United People's Party (UPP) and Aelon Kein Ad (AKA) (Our Islands) (14 Jan 2008)

Main opposition party
United Democratic Party (UDP)

Political situation
RMI, along with its five Pacific nations partnership that make up a group membership of the International Whaling Commission (IWC), drew wrath (although not retaliation) from New Zealand when it voted in favour of Japan's pro-whaling declaration, in June 2006. In the face of generous financial aid for Pacific islands from Japan, the Australian environment minister embarked on a whistle-stop tour of IWC members in an attempt to shore up support for a full ban, which ultimately failed. In the financial year 2008 per capita aid was US$1,548, provided by the US, Taiwan and Japan.
The November 2007 parliamentary elections resulted in two firsts. For the first time an unprecedented number of independent members were elected, leaving the government to be formed by a coalition, also for the first time. The result was determined as a reaction by many landowners to the previous government's agreement with the US to lease, long-term, Kwajalein Atoll for missile testing. The landowners have consistently rejected the agreement for leasing the atoll until 2086 and say that unless there is an improvement in terms of conditions the agreement must end in 2016.

Population
52,700 (2007)*
Last census: June 1999: 50,848
Population density: 282 inhabitants per square km (2000). Urban population: 66 per cent (1995–2001).
Annual growth rate: 1.7 per cent 1994–2004 (WHO 2006)
Ethnic make-up
Micronesian
Religions
Christian (mostly Protestant).

Education
Enrolment rate: 134 per cent (boys); 133 per cent (girls), gross primary enrolment of the relevant age group (including repetition rates) (Unicef).

Health
Per capita total expenditure on health (2003) was US$477; of which per capita government spending was US$461, at the international dollar rate, (WHO 2006).
Over 80 per cent of children are immunised against measles. RMI has the highest per capita rate of leprosy in the world.
Life expectancy: 62 years, 2004 (WHO 2006)
Fertility rate/Maternal mortality rate: 4.4 births per woman, 2004 (WHO 2006)
Birth rate/Death rate: 34 births per 1,000 population; five deaths per 1,000 population (2003).
Child (under 5 years) mortality rate (per 1,000): 53 per 1,000 live births (World Bank)

Main cities
Majuro (capital, on Majuro atoll, Dalap-Uliga-Darrit Municipality, estimated population 25,400 in 2004), Ebeye, on Kwajalein, (9,935), Darrit (7,263), Rairok (5,409).

Languages spoken
There are two main Marshallese dialects from the Malayo-Polynesian family.
Marshallese is used by the government. English is taught in the schools and is widely spoken. Japanese is also spoken.
Official language/s
Marshallese, English

Media
Other news agencies: ABC Pacific Beat: www.radioaustralia.net.au/pacbeat
Pacific Magazine:
www.pacificmagazine.net
Press
The Marshall Islands Journal (www.marshallislandsjournal.com) containing items in both Marshallese and English, is published every Friday and the government published Marshall Islands Gazette has official news.
Broadcasting
The government-owned radio station V7AB and MBC Television station are the only national broadcasters. Micronesia Heatwave is a commercial radio station and V7AA is a religious station.
Pay-to-view, cable TV is available in some areas.

Economy
The Marshall Islands has a limited revenue base; most income is derived from payment by the US under the Compact of Free Association (CFA), which came into effect in 2004, and commits the US to long-term financial support, international aid and a few commercial ventures. With an initial US$29 million, the US will be contributing US$7 million a year to the Intergenerational Investment Fund (IIF) until 2023, and together with government contributions the Fund should be able to provide investment in the islanders' future. The government employs over 60 per cent of the workforce; unemployment is as high as 34 per cent. Agriculture is a small sector of GDP, of largely subsistence products such as breadfruit, taro and pandanus; small quantities of commercial copra are processed but with limited means of trade. The Marshall Islands licenses ships as a flag of convenience and has around 1,200 ships registered, making it the fifth largest fleet in the world and earning about US$1 million annually.
GDP growth in 2005 was 3.5 per cent, an increase on the -1.5 per cent growth rate in 2004.
Hopes that the defunct tuna industry will revive were given a boost in 2006 as a Chinese company announced plans to process skipjack tuna for the Asian market. Initially 500 jobs are expected to be created and should provide a much needed lift to local businesses.
In December 2006, the European Union granted US$625,000 as a first payment of aid, to pay for training programmes for non-governmental organisations. In 2007 two other grants will provide solar power

KEY INDICATORS — Marshall Islands

	Unit	2003	2004	2005	2006	2007
Population	m	0.06	0.06	0.06	0.06	0.06
Gross domestic product (GDP)	US$bn	0.12	0.11	0.14	0.15	0.16
GDP per capita	US$	1,600	1,800	2,271	*2,540	2,696
GDP real growth	%	4.1	4.5	1.1	*3.0	3.5
Inflation	%	2.5	2.4	4.4	4.3	2.4
Exports (fob) (goods)	US$m	14.2	15.7	17.0	16.0	–
Imports (cif) (goods)	US$m	77.5	73.1	99.0	99.0	–
Balance of trade	US$m	-63.3	-71.6	-82.0	-83.0	0.0
Current account	US$m	26.0	16.0	9.0	7.0	7.0
Exchange rate	per US$	1.00	1.00	1.00	1.00	1.00

* estimated figure

installations for schools and homes on outlying islands.
The use of the US dollar as the country's currency acts as a partial shield to major macroeconomic fluctuations, and compliance with CFA guidelines has helped promote responsible economic policies. The public sector will continue driving the economy over the medium term. Over the long term, the government has the fiscal challenge of managing the adjustment to a decline in CFA funds and placing government revenues on a sustainable basis.

External trade

The Marshall Islands (RMI) is a member of the South Pacific Regional Trade and Economic Co-operation Agreement (Sparteca) along with 12 other regional nations, which allows products duty free access by Pacific Island Forum members to Australian and New Zealand markets (subject to the country of origin restrictions).
Semi-manufactured goods, assembled in the islands, enjoy preferential access to US markets under the Compact of Free Association. Light manufacturing includes soap, cooking oil, salad oil, margarine, and cosmetics, using local processed coconut oil.

Imports

Principal imports, which far outstripping exports, are foodstuffs, petroleum, machinery and equipment, beverages and tobacco.
Main sources: US, Japan, Australia, New Zealand, Singapore, Fiji, China, Philippines

Exports

Principal exports are copra cake, coconut oil, handicrafts and fish
Main destinations: US, Japan, Australia, China

Agriculture

Farming

Subsistence farming of taro, breadfruit, bananas, yams, sweet potatoes and vegetables, along with pig and poultry raising, is the main occupation. Large areas of potentially arable land remain uncultivated.
Crop production in 2005 included: 15,000 tonnes (t) coconuts and 1,950t oilcrops; livestock production is only adequate to maintain farming families.

Fishing

Fishing, particularly tuna, is important, supplying the principal source of protein as well as export revenues. A dozen longline tuna boats built with Asian Development Bank money almost doubled the fleet in the mid-1990s. Tuna is supplied to the country's tuna processing factory, located at Majuro.
A Hawaiian company, Black Pearl Inc, noted after extensive research the potential for breeding black pearl oysters. Some farms have opened but it will be several years before they can compete with world market leaders. Seaweed farming may offer an alternative. Typical pearl and shell harvest production is 100,000 units per annum.
In 2004, the total marine fish catch was 47,172 tonnes.

Industry and manufacturing

Small-scale industries include handicrafts, fish processing, copra processing, bakeries and boat building and repairs. A tuna processing factory which opened in 1999 was a significant addition to industry.
The Marshall Islands Ports Authority agreed with the Ching Fu Shipyard of Taiwan to locate a floating drydock in Majuro in 2005, which is the largest ship repair facility in the central Pacific.

Tourism

Tourism is relatively undeveloped, although there is potential for growth. Visitor numbers are negligible – less than 1,400 tourists in 2004; business visitors numbered around 2,250. In general, there was a slow but steady growth in the number of holidaymakers until 2001, peaking at 1,483, but falling to 1,380 in 2003. The main market is Japan, followed by the US.

Mining

Small mineral deposits exist, but exploitation is hampered by a shortage of land to accommodate the displaced population and doubts about economic viability. Extraction of phosphate occurs at Ailinglaplap.

Hydrocarbons

The Marshall Islands rely entirely on the import of hydrocarbons from the US and Australia. Fossil fuels make up 99 per cent of the Marshall Island's total energy production.

Banking and insurance

Growth in the Marshall Islands' banking sector is limited by the size of its population. Commercial bank lending in 2004 was some US$45 million while deposits were substantially greater at US$81 million.

Time

GMT plus twelve hours

Geography

The Marshall Islands are located in the area of the Pacific Ocean known as Micronesia (which includes Kiribati, Tuvalu and other territories). The islands lie about 3,200km (2,000 miles) south-west of Hawaii and about 2,100km (1,300 miles) south-east of Guam.
The Marshall Islands comprises around 1,200 coral islands and islets, of which five are single islands, the rest combining into 29 atolls. The territory extends over 750,000 square km of sea area in two parallel chains: Ratak (Sunrise) to the east and Ralik (Sunset) to the west. Total land mass of the system is around 183 square km. The mean height is two metres. The atolls are narrow and encircle large lagoons. Beaches are white sand.

Hemisphere

Northern

Climate

Tropical climate. Warm and humid, temperatures 23–30 degrees Celsius, humidity around 80 per cent. High temperatures are cooled by trade winds. Rainfall variable, minimum 250mm per year, can occur in downpours. Hurricanes are possible.

Entry requirements

Passports

Required by all, valid for six months beyond date of departure.

Visa

Required by all, except nationals of the US, Federated States of Micronesia and Palau. Tourist and business visas are issued on arrival for stays up to three months.
All visitors must have proof of adequate funds and return/onward passage. Special regulations may apply to some non-tourist destinations. Further information can be obtained through www.rmiembassyus.org.

Health (for visitors)

Mandatory precautions

Advisable precautions

Vaccinations for hepatitis A and B and typhoid are recommended; those for tetanus and diphtheria should be updated as needed.

Hotels

There are a number of first class and other hotels, mainly on Majuro and Ebeye, and guesthouses, which are more widely distributed.

Credit cards

Visa, Mastercard and American Express are accepted by most major businesses.

Public holidays (national)

Fixed dates

1 Jan (New Year's Day), 1 Mar (Nuclear Survivors Day), 1 May (Constitution Day), 21 Oct (Compact Day), 17 Nov (President's Day), 25 Dec (Christmas Day).
Some dates vary from island to island.

Variable dates

Fishermen's Day (first Fri in Jul), Rijerbal/Labour Day (first Fri in Sep), Manit/Customs Day (last Fri in Sep), Gospel Day (first Fri in Dec).

Working hours
Banking
Mon–Fri: 1000–1500; Fri: 1000–1800.
Business
Mon–Fri: 0800–1700.
Government
Mon–Fri: 0800–1700.
Shops
Mon–Sat: 0800–2000; (Sun) 0800–1800.

Telecommunications
Telephone/fax
International satellite links provide fax and Internet facilities. Communication with the outer islands is by radio.
Postal services
There are US Postal Service offices on Majuro and Ebeye.
Mobile/cell phones
Cellular service is available on Maburo, Ebeye and Kwajalein.

Social customs/useful tips
In business an informal attitude prevails. Appointments should be made. Business cards are exchanged. Business is usually conducted in English. Permission should be sought before taking photographs of people. The minimum drinking age is 21 years. Swimsuits, shorts or short skirts should not be worn in urban areas. Tipping is optional.

Getting there
Air
National airline: Air Marshall Islands.
International airport/s: Amata Kabua International International (MAJ), 25km from Majuro. There are buses, taxis and hotel transport from the airport to the city.
Airport tax: US$15.
Surface
Main port/s: Majuro and Kwajalein.

Getting about
National transport
Air: Air Marshall Islands flies services to most of the atolls.
Road: The main roads on the major islands are paved. Others are stone-, coral- or laterite-surfaced roads and tracks.
Water: The government operates several vessels, which link the islands on an irregular schedule. Inter-island cruises are available and boats can be hired privately.
City transport
Taxis: Taxis are plentiful and relatively cheap, but usually operate on a shared basis.
Car hire
There are many car hire operators. Driving is on the right.

BUSINESS DIRECTORY

The addresses listed below are a selection only. While World of Information makes every endeavour to check these addresses, we cannot guarantee that changes have not been made, especially to telephone numbers and area codes. We would welcome any corrections.

Telephone area codes
The international direct dialling (IDD) code for Marshall Islands is +692 followed by area code and subscriber's number:

Ebeye	329	Majuro	625.

Chambers of Commerce
Majuro Chamber of Commerce, PO Box 1318, Majuro 96960 (tel: 625-3051; fax: 625-3343; e-mail: majurochamber@hotmail.com).

Banking
Bank of Marshall Islands, PO Box J, Majuro 96960 (tel: 625-3636; fax: 625-3661; e-mail: bankmar@ntamar.com).

Travel information
Air Marshall Islands, PO Box 1319, Majuro 96960 (tel: 625-3731; fax: 625-37; e-mail: amisales@ntamar.net).
Marshall Islands Visitors Authority, PO Box 5, Majuro 96960 (tel: 625-6482; fax: 625-6771; e-mail: tourism@ntamar.com).

Ministry of tourism
Ministry of Resources and Development, Tourism Office, PO Box 1727, Majuro 96960 (tel: 625-6482; fax: 625-3218).

Other useful addresses
Marshall Islands Embassy (USA), 2433 Massachusetts Avenue, NW, Washington DC 20008 (tel: (+1-202)-234-5414; fax: (+1-202)-232-3236: e-mail: info@rmiembassyus.org).

Other news agencies: ABC Pacific Beat: www.radioaustralia.net.au/pacbeat

Pacific Magazine: www.pacificmagazine.net

Internet sites
Website of the Marshall Islands: http://www.rmiembassyus.org/

The Pacific business centre: http://cba.hawaii.edu/pbcp/

Martinique

COUNTRY PROFILE

Historical profile

1493 Columbus was the first European visitor.
1635 The island was settled by the French – in the face of indigenous Indian hostility.
1700s The island was seized by the British several times.
1763 Marie-Josephe Rose Tascher de la Pagerie – Napoleon's Empress Josephine – was born at Les Trois Ilets.
1814 The British gave up their attempts to control the island and it became a French possession under the Treaty of Paris.
1848 The Emancipation Proclamation abolished slavery in the West Indies.
1902 St Pierre was destroyed by an eruption of the volcano Mount Pelée.
1946 Martinique became a French Département d'Outre-Mer (DOM) (Overseas Department).
1974 Martinique was further incorporated into the French political system and granted the status of region of France.
1983 Martinique was granted devolution. A Regional Council was established under the French decentralisation policy.
1999–2001 The presidents of the regional assemblies of Martinique, Guadeloupe and French Guiana called for more autonomy from France.
2002 Martinique adopted the euro as its official currency.
2003 A referendum in Guadeloupe and Martinique rejected a French government-backed reform plan to streamline the system of local government and give the islands a new status.
2004 Martinique was the first port of call for Cunard's newest, and largest, cruise ship, Queen Mary II. It continues to call regularly and is expected to boost the island's tourism. Yves Dassonville took over as Préfet, replacing Michel Cadot.
2005 A visit by French interior minister, Nicolas Sarkozy, was postponed following the announcement by the French president that a controversial law, which required the teaching of the French colonial era as positive, would be revoked. Sarkozy was a member of the conservative-led government that passed the law. Protests by Martinique islanders, led by Aime Cesaire had been planned.
2007 On 16 May, Nicolas Sarkozy became head of state and president of the French Republic. In July Ange Mancini was appointed Préfet. An earthquake of 7.4 magnitude, struck off the north-west coast on 29 November. Damage was limited to two collapsed buildings and loss of electricity to a third of the island.
2008 The poet, Aime Cesaire, a leading figure of not only the local but also the wider, international black empowerment and cultural community, died on 17 April. President Sarkozy led the mourners in a state funeral in Fort-de-France.

Political structure

Constitution

28 September 1958 (French Fifth Republic)
Under the 1946 constitution of the French Fourth Republic, Martinique became a Département d'Outre-Mer (DOM) (Overseas Department) of France. In 1974, it was granted additional status as a region of France.
Martinique is represented in the French National Assembly by four deputies and in the Senate by two senators.
Administration is by a préfet appointed by the government in Paris.
Since 1983, following the French government's policy of decentralisation, regional councils have been elected with powers similar to those of the regions.
Local administration is through a Conseil Régional (Regional Council) of 41 members and a 45-member Conseil Général (General Council), both directly elected for six-year terms.

Form of state

Département d'Outre-Mer (DOM) (Overseas Department) of France, with additional status as a région (region) of France.

The executive

The island is administered by a préfet (commissioner), appointed by the central government in Paris.

National legislature

Legal system

French law applies. The country has no supreme court but this role is filled by a nine-member Conseil Constitutionel (Constitutional Council). Its task is to ensure that law treaties and regulations are in keeping with the constitution and that elections are conducted in a regular manner. The highest court of appeal is the Cour de Cassation, which can overrule decisions in all lower courts, but not government legislation. Since the signing of the Single European Act in 1986, the European Court of Justice (ECJ) has been the highest authority in certain areas of French law.

Last elections

28 March 2004 (Conseil Régional).

KEY FACTS

Official name: Martinique

Head of State: President of France, (Nicolas Sarkozy, from 16 May 2007), represented by Préfet Ange Mancini (since 18 Jul 2007)

Head of government: President of Conseil Général Claude Lise (since 22 Mar 1992); President of Conseil Régional Alfred Marie-Jeanne (since 1998; re-elected 2004)

Ruling party: L'Alliance Mouvement pour l'Indépendence de la Martinique (MIM)/Conseil National des Comités Populaires (CNCP) (since Mar 2004)

Area: 1,100 square km

Population: 399,000 (2007)*

Capital: Fort-de-France

Official language: French

Currency: Euro ( ) = 100 cents (from 1 Jan 2002; previous currency French franc, locked at Ff6.56 per euro)

Exchange rate: 0.63 per US$ (Jul 2008)

GDP per capita: US$14,400 (2003)*

Labour force: 136,200 (2004)

Unemployment: 21.70% (2005)

Visitor numbers: 484,000 (2005)

* estimated figure

Results: MIM/CNCP won 28 seats out of 41; Convergence Martiniquaise (nine seats); Les Forces Martiniquaises de Progrès (four seats).

Next elections

2010

Political parties

Ruling party

L'Alliance Mouvement pour l'Indépendence de la Martinique (MIM)/Conseil National des Comités Populaires (CNCP) (since Mar 2004)

Main opposition party

Convergence Martiniquaise

Political situation

A referendum on a French government proposal held in Martinique in 2003 seemed straightforward. The proposal was twofold. First, it would streamline the local government apparatus and reduce the number of elected offices. The second effect would be a change in Martinique's relationship with France, which would effectively reduce its standing as a region of France. The proposal was made in response to a call made in 1999—2000 for more independence.

However, the proposal was rejected and the failure was thought to be due to voters' worry that any change in their status would ultimately result in a withdrawal of French central government funds needed, most particularly, for social security.

Population

399,000 (2007)*

Last census: March 1999: 381,325

Population density: 282 inhabitants per sq km.

Annual growth rate: 0.6 per cent (2003)

Ethnic make-up

African and mixed race (90 per cent), white (5 per cent), East Indian and others (5 per cent).

Religions

Roman Catholic (85 per cent), Protestant (10 per cent), Islam, Hindu, pagan African (5 per cent).

Education

There is 42 per cent enrolment in education for the 20- to 24-year age groups with a high rate of unemployment among them.

Literacy rate: 98 per cent, adult rate (2003)

Health

Water for consumption is subject to intensive controls and is of high quality.

There are three public hospitals including one teaching hospital, and three private clinics.

HIV/Aids

Martinique has a departmental Aids control scheme.

Life expectancy: 79 (estimate 2003)

Birth rate/Death rate: 15 births per 1,000 population; 6.4 deaths per 1,000 population (2003).

Child (under 5 years) mortality rate (per 1,000): 7.4 per 1,000 live births (2003)

Welfare

With unemployment ranging between 30 and 35 per cent among the youth, there has been a noticeable increase in the number of people calling for independence from France. The French social security system guarantees a high minimum wage, a 35-hour working week, five-week vacations, a 40 per cent incentive on salary and other social benefits.

Main cities

Fort-de-France (capital (prefecture), estimated population 96,400 in 2003), Le Lamentin (36,400), Le Robert (21,800), Schoelcher (21,400), Sainte Marie (20,600, Le Francois (19,000).

Languages spoken

French and Creole patois (developed from French, English, Spanish and some African languages). English is widely understood.

Official language/s

French

Media

Press

In French, France Antilles is the only daily newspaper, which belongs to a French-based publishing house. Weekly publications include Le Progressiste, Aujourd'hui Dimanche, Justice, Le Naif and Antilla.

Broadcasting

The French overseas broadcaster RFO (www.rfo.fr) provides locally produced radio and television news (http://martinique.rfo.fr) and imported French programmes, as well as internet TV services.

Radio: Apart from the public RFO Martinique radio broadcasts, Radio Caraibes International (http://rci.fm) and NRJ Antilles (www.nrjantilles.com) are private radio stations.

Economy

The local economy represents no more than 25 per cent of GDP, while French funding accounts for the remaining 75 per cent. Martinique has an open market economy, primarily based on bananas and light industry. Agriculture provides about 6 per cent of GDP and light industry over 11 per cent, however tourism is becoming increasingly dominant, providing around 10 per cent of GDP in 2006, but with projected growth of 60 per cent by 2016. The tourist sector is a major employer and key source of foreign exchange and Martinique has not only increased its share of the cruise ship industry but has also become a leading provider of luxury holiday venues.

A French government's 15-year economic development plan for the dependent territories, published in 2002, has led to greater improvements in infrastructure and has improved the island's investment climate.

Among the improvements is the construction of a land and sea transport terminal, next to Pointe Simon Cruise Terminal, which integrates water taxis and public transport and a lagoon resort and spa at Cap Est.

External trade

As a département d'outre-mer (DOM) of France, Martinique is integrated as an outermost region of the European Union, which includes all EU trade agreements. The large trade deficit is only partly offset by invisible earnings from tourism, workers' remittances from abroad, and French aid aimed at developing the tourist trade and reducing unemployment.

Imports

Principal imports are petroleum products, crude oil, foodstuffs, construction materials, vehicles, clothing and other consumer goods.

Main sources: France (62 per cent), Venezuela (6.0 per cent), Germany (4.0 per cent), Italy (4.0 per cent), US (3.0 per cent)

Exports

Principal exports are refined petroleum products, bananas, rum and pineapples.

Main destinations: France (45 per cent), Guadeloupe (28 per cent)

Agriculture

Farming

Once the mainstay of economy, the agricultural sector has declined in recent years. It employs 10 per cent of the workforce and contributes 7 per cent to GDP. Around 48 per cent of total land area is cultivated, 25 per cent is forest and 19 per cent savannah. The majority of farms are privately run by smallholders. Activity is centred on the production of pineapples and bananas, mainly for industrial processing and export.

Crops such as sweet potatoes, yams, manioc, beans, cabbages and tomatoes are grown primarily for domestic consumption. Small quantities of aubergines and limes are exported. Virtually all the island's meat requirements are met by imports.

The future of the important banana industry, which has relied on preferential access to the EU, is threatened by a World Trade Organisation ruling that this access is illegal and must end. The EU has agreed new tariff quotas which were introduced from 2006. The number of banana

producers fell from 1,200 to 750 in the period 1993–2003. In October 2003, banana producers in Martinique and Guadeloupe formed an association to seek to improve sales in France and in new markets.
Estimated crop production in 2005 included: 7,500 tonnes (t) yams, 1,200t sweet potatoes, 193,000t sugar cane, 300,000t bananas, 18,000t plantains, 1,410t citrus, 1,150t coconuts, 6,700t tomatoes, 18,000t pineapples, 337,970t fruit in total, 30,300t roots and tubers, 30,500t vegetables in total. Livestock production included: 4,890t meat in total, 1,800t beef, 1,650t pig-meat, 250t lamb, 1,050t poultry, 1,500t eggs, 2,200t milk.

Fishing

Fishing (lobster, crayfish, crab, clams) is undertaken all year round. The typical total annual fish catch is over 6,250t. Shellfish, molluscs and cephalopods account for another 909t per annum.

Industry and manufacturing

Major industries include an oil refinery (capacity 17,000 barrels per day (bpd)), a cement works, rum distilling, sugar refining, dairy produce, fruit canning, soft drinks manufacture, mineral water bottling and a polyethylene plant.
Industrial development has been poor and centres mainly on the manufacture of consumer goods for the local market. Five industrial zones have been set up and tax exemptions introduced to encourage light industrial development.

Tourism

Tourism is becoming increasingly dominant, providing around 10 per cent of GDP in 2006, but with projected growth of 60 per cent by 2016. The tourist sector is a major employer and key source of foreign exchange and Martinique has not only increased its share of the cruise ship industry but has also become a leading provider of luxury holiday venues.

Mining

Martinique has no mineral resources.

Hydrocarbons

Martinique does not produce any hydrocarbons and relies on imports of crude oil.
Martinique does not produce or import coal or natural gas. A proposed pipeline from Trinidad and Tobago to Martinique and Guadeloupe opens possibilities for the future import of natural gas.

Energy

Electricity production: 585 million kW. There is one refinery and two thermal power stations. Together, SARA (Société Anonyme de Raffinerie des Antilles) and EDF (Electricité de France) employ 900 people.

Banking and insurance

Central bank

Caisse Centrale de Co-opération Economique; European Central Bank (ECB)

Time

GMT minus four hours

Geography

Martinique is one of the Windward Islands in the West Indies, with Dominica to the north and St Lucia to the south. The island, which has an area of 1,100 square km, is bounded to the west by the calm Caribbean Sea and to the east by the choppier Atlantic Ocean.
The terrain rises from the south to the mountainous centre and the north. The highest point in the island, situated in the north, is an active volcano, Mount Pelée, which reaches 1,397m. The mountain areas are covered with rainforest. The Lamentin Plain, an area of hills and valleys, occupies the centre of the island. The northern beaches consist of volcanic ash and are grey, while those in the south, where the Salines Beach is located, are sandy and white. The southern Atlantic coastline is protected by coral reefs.

Hemisphere

Northern

Climate

Sub-tropical with an annual mean temperature of 26 degrees Celsius. Rain heaviest in the north. Rainy season from June–October. The island's temperature is moderated by trade winds.

Entry requirements

Passports

Required by all, valid for three months beyond the date of departure.

Visa

Required by all, except citizens of EU, North America, Australasia and Japan. Business visas require an invitation from a local company or organisation. Proof of adequate funds for stay, an itinerary, a guarantee of repatriation if necessary and return/onward ticket are also required.

Currency advice/regulations

There are no restrictions on the import and export of local and foreign currencies, but amounts in excess of eur7,600 must be declared.

Health (for visitors)

Mandatory precautions

A yellow fever vaccination certificate is required if travelling from an infected area.

Advisable precautions

Hepatitis, typhoid, tetanus and polio vaccinations. Water precautions should be taken.

Hotels

There is a 5 per cent room tax. If service charge is not added, 15 per cent tip is usual.

Public holidays (national)

Fixed dates

1 Jan (New Year's Day), 1 May (Labour Day), 8 May (Victory Day), 22 May (Abolition of Slavery), 14 Jul (Bastille Day), 21 Jul (Schoelcher Day), 15 Aug (Assumption Day), 1 Nov (All Saints' Day), 11 Nov (Armistice Day), 25 Dec (Christmas Day).

Variable dates

Carnival (four days, Feb), Good Friday, Easter Monday, Ascension Day, Whit Monday.

Working hours

Banking

Mon–Fri: 0800–1200, 1400–1700. Banks close at noon on day preceding a bank holiday.

Business

Mon–Fri: 0800–1200, 1430–1700; Sat: 0800–1200.

Government

Mon–Fri: 0730–1300, 1500–1730.

Shops

Mon–Fri: 0900–1300, 1500–1800; Sat: 0900–1300.

Telecommunications

Telephone/fax

There is a 100 per cent automatic service.

Electricity supply

220V AC, 50 cycles

Getting there

Air

National airline: Air Caraibes.
International airport/s: Lamentin (FDF), 11km from Fort-de-France; restaurant, banks, shops, car hire.
Airport tax: None.

Surface

Main port/s: Fort-de-France is the only commercial port; other ports of entry include St Pierre, Anse Mitan and Le Marin.

Getting about

National transport

Road: Well-developed network of more than 2,000km of roads, three-quarters of which are paved and the rest gravel and earth.
Water: There are regular ferry services (vedettes) from Fort-de-France to Pointe de Bout and Anse Mitan.

Car hire

There are ample car rental facilities. A valid driving licence is required and also, for periods beyond 20 days, an international licence.

BUSINESS DIRECTORY

The addresses listed below are a selection only. While World of Information makes every endeavour to check these addresses, we cannot guarantee that changes have not been made, especially to telephone numbers and area codes. We would welcome any corrections.

Telephone area codes
The international direct dialling code (IDD) for Martinique is +596, followed by subscriber's number.

Useful telephone numbers
Ambulance: 15
Fire brigade: 18
Police: 17

Chambers of Commerce
Martinique Chamber of Commerce and Industry, 50 Rue Ernest Deproge, PO Box 478, Fort-de-France 97241 (tel: 552-800; fax: 606-668; e-mail: info@martinique.cci.fr).

Banking
Banque des Antilles Françaises, 34 rue Lamartine, BP 582, 97200 Fort-de-France (tel: 739-344; fax: 635-894).

Banque Française Commerciale, 6-10 rue Ernest Deproge, 97200 Fort-de-France (tel: 638-257).

Banque National de Paris, Avenue des Caraibes, 97200 Fort-de-France (tel: 737-111).

Chase Manhattan Bank, Place de Monseigheur Romero, 97200 Fort-de-France (tel: 602-424).

Crédit Martiniquais, rue de la Liberté, Fort-de-France (tel: 701-240).

Institut d'Emission des DOM (IEDOM), Boulevard General de Gaulle, BP 512, 97206 Fort-de-France (tel: 594-400; fax: 594-404).

Société Générale de Banque aux Antilles, rue de la Liberté, BP 408, 97200 Fort-de-France (tel: 716-983).

Central bank
European Central Bank (ECB), Kaiserstrasse 29, D-60311 Frankfurt am Main, Germany (tel: (+49-69)-13-440; fax: (+49-69)-1344-6000; e-mail: info@ecb.int).

Travel information
Agence Régionale pour le Développement du Tourisme de la Martinique (ARDTM), 4 Rue de l'école Hotellière, Anse Goureaud, 97233 Schoelcher (tel: 616-177; fax: 612-272).

Air Caraibes, Morne Vergain, 97139 Abymes (tel: (0590)-824-747; fax: (0490)-824-749; e-mail: direction@aircaraibes.com).

Délégation Régionale au Tourisme, 41 Rue Gabriel Péri, 97200 Fort-de-France (tel: 393-767; fax: 730-096).

Fort-de-France Office du Tourisme, 76 rue Lazare Carnot, 97206 Fort-de-France (tel: 602-773; fax: 602-795; e-mail: info@tourismefdf.com).

Lamentin Airport, 97200 Lamentin (tel: 421-600; fax: 421-877).

National tourist organisation offices
Comité Martiniquais du Tourisme, Immeuble Le Beaupré, Pointe de Jaham, 97233 Schoelcher (tel: 616-177; fax:612-272; e-mail: infos.cmt@martiniquetourisme.com).

Other useful addresses
Agence pour le Développement Economique de la Martinique, Immeuble Nayaradou, Plateau de Cluny, 97233 Schoelcher (tel: 734-581; fax: 724-138).

Bureau del'Industrie de l'Artisanat, Préfecture, 97262 Fort-de France (tel: 713-627).

Chambre Départementale d'Agriculture, Place D'Armes, BP 312, 97286 Lamentin Cedex (tel: 517-575; fax: 519-342).

Chambre des Métiers, 2 Rue du Temple, Morne Tartenson, BP 1191, 97249 Fort-de-France (tel: 713-222; fax: 704-730).

Post Office, 132 boulevard Pasteur, Fort-de-France (tel: 599-600).

Préfecture, rue Victor Severe, BP 647-648, 97262 Fort-de-France (tel: 631-861; fax: 714-029; internet site: http://www.martinique.pref.gouv.fr/pages/somangl.html).

Internet sites
Regional Council of Martinique: http://www.cr-martinique.fr/anglais/accueil_anglais.html

Martinique Promotion Bureau: http://www.martinique.org

Martinique Shipping Services: http://www.marship.fr

Mauritania

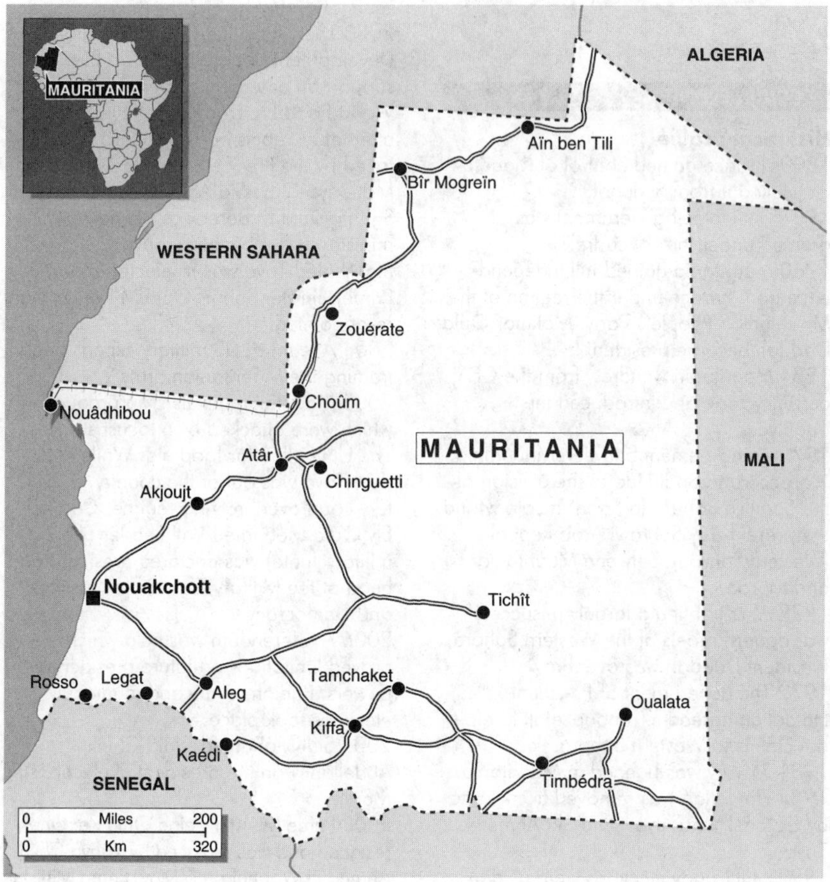

Barely eighteen months after he had won elections in March 2007, President Sidi Ould Cheikh Abdallahi was overthrown and Mauritania was back in the land of coups and counter-coups the population had so hoped to have left behind. Mauritania is huge, its geography apparently purposeless. Three quarters of Mauritanians live along the northern banks of the Senegal River. The Sahel droughts have driven many thousands of peasants and nomads into the shanty-towns around Nouakchott, and if it isn't the floods then it's the locusts that do the damage.

This time the coup had been triggered by the president's attempt to dismiss the military's top commanders, including the head of the presidential guard, General Mohamed Ould Abdelaziz, after reports that the military had been behind the mass resignation of 48 MPs from the ruling party. Instead, he and Prime Minister Yahia Ould Ahmed el Ouakef were rounded up and imprisoned. The prime minister was briefly released but rearrested three days later on his way to Nouadhibou to address a rally against the coup, or to flee the country (Nouadhibou is close to the border with Morocco).

An 11-member military council is currently (August 2008) governing the country, after what was the fifth coup since independence in 1960. The 2007 elections had been the first to elect a civilian head of state in 47 years. The coup leaders have promised to hold 'free and transparent' elections as soon as possible and to 'relaunch …the democratic process…to bring for the future a continued and harmonious functioning of all the constitutional powers'. The coup received general

KEY FACTS

Official name: République Islamique Arabe et Africaine de Mauritanie (Islamic Republic of Mauritania)

Head of State: President of the High Council of State: General Mohamed Ould Abdel Aziz. (from 6 Aug 2008)

Head of government: Prime Minister Moulaye Ould Mohamed Laghdaf (appointed 14 Aug 2008)

Ruling party: All members of parliament are independents

Area: 1,030,700 square km

Population: 2.96 million (2007)*

Capital: Nouakchott

Official language: Hassani Arabic and Wolof

Currency: Ouguiya (UM) = 5 khoums

Exchange rate: UM230.25 per US$ (Jul 2008)

GDP per capita: US$931 (2007)*

GDP real growth: 0.90% (2007)*

Labour force: 1.27 million (2004)

Unemployment: 20.00% (2004)

Inflation: 7.20% (2007)*

Balance of trade: US$607.00 million (2006)

Foreign debt: US$2.30 billion (2004)

* estimated figure

international condemnation from, amongst others, the African Union and United Nations.

Prior to the coup, an International Monetary Fund (IMF) report in May 2008 had been quietly up-beat on Mauritania's future. It said that despite a steeper-than-expected decline in oil production reflecting persistent technical problems and a difficult external environment, Mauritania's macroeconomic performance over the previous few years had been good. Real non-oil GDP growth was estimated to have increased to 59 per cent in 2007, driven by a rebound in agriculture and new mining projects. The current account had deteriorated, reflecting higher food prices and lower oil exports. The gross international reserves position, however, had strengthened to 1.9 months of imports of goods and services at end-December 2007.

Performance criteria and benchmarks under the Poverty Reduction and Growth Facility (PRGF) were successfully met by the end of December 2007. Poverty related spending had exceeded the programme target as pro-poor spending accelerated towards the end of 2007.

Outlook

The authorities have engaged in a comprehensive reform agenda to stimulate non-oil growth and reduce poverty in the context of the PRGF-supported programme. In particular, they intend to improve infrastructure, enhance competitiveness, promote private sector development, improve fiscal management, fight corruption, maintain macroeconomic stability and increase government's efficiency in delivering public services. To support their development plan, the authorities successfully organised a consultative group meeting in Paris in December 2007, where they received financial pledges amounting to US$2.1 billion. The key to all this is, of course, the resolution of the political situation and the holding of free and fair elections.

Risk assessment

Economy	Fair
Politics	Poor
Regional stability	Fair

COUNTRY PROFILE

Historical profile

1800s France gained control of Mauritania, ruling it from Senegal.
1957 Limited self-government was granted under the Loi cadre.
1960 Mauritania gained full independence from France under the regime of the Mauritanian People's Party. Mokhtar Ould Daddah became president.
1974 Mauritania withdrew from the CFAf currency zone and introduced the ouguiya.
1975 An agreement between Mauritania, Morocco and Spain led to the division of the Spanish Sahara (a Spanish colony and the present-day Sahrawi Arab Republic (Western Sahara)) between Mauritania and Morocco.
1978 After fighting a largely unsuccessful war against rebels of the Western Sahara, President Daddah was overthrown.
1979 The government of President Haidallah agreed to renounce all territorial claims to Western Sahara.
1981 Slavery was banned in Mauritania.
1984 Haidallah was removed from office by Colonel Maaouya Ould Sid'Ahmed Taya.
1992 Multi-party elections were held in which President Taya was returned to office.
1996 The governing Parti Républicain Démocratique et Social (PRDS) (Social and Democratic Republican Party) won the elections.
1997 President Taya was re-elected.
1999 Full diplomatic relations were established with Israel. After criticism by Iraq, the foreign ministry announced that Mauritania had severed its relations with Iraq.
2001 The PRDS was re-elected.
2002 Famine increased due to three years of drought.
2003 The OPEC Fund for International Development donated US$300,000 to support an emergency operation by the World Food Programme (WFP). A coup attempt by rebels in Nouakchott was foiled by the President's troops. President Maaouya Ould Sid'Ahmed Taya named Sghair Ould M'Bareck as the new prime minister. Incumbent Maaouya Ould Sid'Ahmed Taya was re-elected president. Prime Minister Sghair Ould M'Bareck was re-appointed.
2004 A team of US military experts began training the Mauritanian army.
2005 Mauritania lost its crop production, which were attacked by a locust swarms. The UN called for food aid. While President Taya was out of the country, a military coup overthrew his regime. Colonel Ely Ould Mohamed Vall (leader of the military Junta) was declared president and head of the Military Council for Justice and Democracy.
2006 A referendum was held which approved limitations on future presidential powers. Parliamentary and municipal elections took place.
2007 Sidi Mohamed Ould Cheikh Abdellahi won the presidential elections in March.
2008 Prime Minister Zeine Ould Zeidane resigned and was replaced by Yahya Ould Ahmed El Waghef on 6 May. Prime Minister el Waghef resigned on 3 July, he was re-appointed and re-formed his government on 15 July. A coup d'etat led by General Mohamed Ould Abdel Aziz removed President Abadellahi and Prime Minister El Waghef from power on 6 August. A military council was established to begin 'dialogue with all political parties and all civic institutions in organising' new presidential elections to 're-launch' the 'democratic process'. Within a week two-thirds of members of parliament had signed a document in support of the coup. A High Council of State was established, led by General Abdel Aziz. Moulaye Ould Mohamed Laghdaf was appointed prime minister on 14 August. Former prime minister El Waghef was arrested, released and then rearrested a few days later on 20 August.

Political structure

Constitution

A new constitution was approved in 2006; a president is limited to two consecutive

KEY INDICATORS — Mauritania

	Unit	2003	2004	2005	2006	2007
Population	m	2.82	2.83	2.82	*2.89	*2.96
Gross domestic product (GDP)	US$bn	1.04	1.51	1.86	2.71	*2.76
GDP per capita	US$	370	462	658	*921	*931
GDP real growth	%	5.4	5.2	5.4	11.7	*0.9
Inflation	%	5.5	10.4	12.1	6.2	7.2
Exports (fob) (goods)	US$m	355.0	408.0	604.0	1,812.0	–
Imports (cif) (goods)	US$m	360.0	925.0	1,177.0	1,205.0	–
Balance of trade	US$m	-5.0	-517.0	-573.0	607.0	–
Current account	US$m	-110.0	-290.0	-877.0	-36.0	*-184.0
Exchange rate	per US$	266.42	265.93	270.80	270.80	252.54

* estimated figure

terms in office, which are cut from six to five years and there is a presidential age limit of 75 years. The oath of office includes a vow not to alter these changes.

Form of state
Islamic republic

The executive
The president is the head of state and is elected by universal suffrage for five-year terms. The president appoints the prime minister and presides over the Council of Ministers, who are recommended by the prime minister and appointed by the president. The president is the supreme chief of the armed forces.

The president, after consultation with the prime minister and the presidents of the assemblies, may pronounce the dissolution of the National Assembly.

National legislature
Legislative power is vested in a bicameral parliament, with the 81-member al Jamiya al Wataniyah (national assembly, the lower house) being directly elected every five years, and a 56-member Majlis al Shuyukh (senate, the upper house), indirectly elected every six years.

The prime minister, under the authority of the president, defines the policy of the government, divides the tasks among the ministers and directs and co-ordinates the action of the government.

Legal system
The legal system is based on the 1991 constitution and is strongly influenced by Sharia (Islamic law).

Last elections
11/25 March 2007 (presidential); 19 November/3 December 2006 (parliamentary)

Results: Presidential (first round): Sidi Mohamed Ould Cheikh Abdellahi won 24.8 per cent of the vote; Ahmed Ould Daddah 20.7 per cent; Zein Ould Zeidane 15.3 per cent; Messaoud Ould Boulkheir 9.8 per cent; Ibrahima Moctar Sarr 7.9 per cent; Saleh Ould Mohamedou Ould Hanenna 7.7 per cent. Turnout is 70.1 per cent.

Parliamentary: Regroupement des Forces Démocratiques (RFD) (Rally of Democratic Forces) won 15 out of 95 seats; Union des Forces du Progrès (UFP) (Union of Forces for Progress) won eight seats; Parti Republicain Démocratique et Renouvellement (PRDR) (Republican Party for Democracy and Renewal) seven seats; other parties, including Alliance Populaire pour le Progrès (APP) (Alliance for Popular Progress) 24 seats, and independents 41seats.

Next elections
2011 (parliamentary); 2012 (presidential).

Political parties

Political parties were legalised in July 1991 but were forbidden to be organised on racial or regional lines, or to be opposed to Islam.

Ruling party
All members of parliament are independents

Main opposition party

Population

2.96 million (2007)*

Last census: November 2000: 2,548,157

Population density: Two inhabitants per square km. Urban population: 59 per cent.

Annual growth rate: 2.9 per cent 1994–2004 (WHO 2006)

Ethnic make-up
The population comprises a majority of Arabised Moors. The rest are ethnically linked with the peoples of Senegal and Mali. Moor-black (40 per cent), Moor (30 per cent), black (30 per cent).

Religions
Islam (99 per cent) is the state religion.

Education

Primary schooling lasts for six years. Progression to secondary education is through a competitive entrance examination. Secondary schooling lasts for six years, divided into two three-year cycles. Each stage requires further examination and students may graduate from either with academic or technical qualifications.

Public expenditure on education typically amounts to around 5 per cent of gross national income (GNI).

Literacy rate: 41 per cent adult rate; 50 per cent youth rate (15–24) (Unesco 2005).

Compulsory years: Six to 16.

Enrolment rate: 87 per cent (boys); 82 per cent (girls) gross primary enrolment of the relevant age group (including repeaters), (Unicef).

Pupils per teacher: 50 in primary schools.

Health

Per capita total expenditure on health (2003) was US$59; of which per capita government spending was US$46, at the international dollar rate, (WHO 2006).

By 2002, 81 per cent of children were immunised against measles. Improved water sources and sanitation facilities are available to 37 per cent and 33 per cent of the population, respectively.

HIV/Aids

HIV prevalence: 0.6 per cent aged 15–49 in 2003 (World Bank)

Life expectancy: 58 years, 2004 (WHO 2006)

Fertility rate/Maternal mortality rate: 5.7 births per woman, 2004 (WHO 2006)

Child (under 5 years) mortality rate (per 1,000): 77 per 1,000 live births; 32 per cent of children aged under five are malnourished (World Bank).

Head of population per physician: 0.11 physicians per 1,000 people, 2004 (WHO 2006)

Main cities
Nouakchott (administrative capital, estimated population 719,167 in 2005); Nouadhibou (formerly Port-Etienne, 89,772), Rosso (59,592), Adel Bagrou (58,429).

Languages spoken
French is usually spoken in business circles; English is rarely spoken. Hassani Arabic, Pulaar, Soninke and Wolof are the major languages in everyday use.

Official language/s
Hassani Arabic and Wolof

Media

Press
The only daily newspaper is Ach-Chaab printed in both Arabic and French. There are a large number of weekly papers. Issues of weekly newspapers are routinely seized under Article 11 of the 1991 Press Law, which allows government to censor arbitrarily publications that attempt any open criticism of state action.

Pre-publication censorship, the arrest of journalists and bans of newspapers are very common government actions in Mauritania. The weekly Rajoul al-Chari has been under attack and the independent weekly Le Calame has faced suspension. Other newspapers targetted by the government include La Tribune and the weekly Al Alam.

Agence Mauritanienne d'Information (http://www.mauritania.mr/ami) in Nouakchott is the official government press agency that publishes the daily editions of Chaab newspapers (circulated in Arabic), Horizons (French) and the official Bulletin of the Agency.

Broadcasting
Office Mauritanien de Radiodiffusion et de Télévision (OMRT) broadcasts in Arabic and French.

Economy

Before the August 2005 military coup the economy was given mixed praise and caution by the IMF. After the regime change Mauritania requested a revised three-year arrangement, to run October 2006–September 2009, under the Poverty Reduction and Growth Facility (PRGF) for support of its plans to establish a sound economic environment. As measures had been successful in achieving previously set fiscal and monetary targets to reduce inflation to less than 10 per cent in the first half of 2006 it was granted.

GDP growth was 5.4 per cent in 2005 a figure that had remained consistent since 2003, however, despite the regime change and any expected disruption, GDP growth in 2006 was estimated to have jumped to 13.9 per cent. Inflation fell correspondingly from 12.1 per cent in 2005 to 6.4 per cent in 2006. Exports increased by about one-third as imports decreased, which contained the fiscal deficit.

Mauritania began producing oil in 2006. However initial production of 75,000 barrels per day (bpd) in March dropped to 30,000bpd in the third quarter of 2006.

The country joined the Extractive Industries Transparency Initiative (EITI) a 'forum of oil producers and consumers seeking to promote accountability in oil revenue' as part of the IMF sponsored growth programme, in September 2005

The IMF advised that oil funds should be used in accordance with Mauritania's own poverty reduction strategy plans, with a fund for investment in future generations. Since the coup the new authorities have agreed, more-or-less, the IMF analyses of the economy. A new committee monitors its efforts for good governance and an inspector general has been appointed to oversee public spending.

External trade

Mauritania is a member of the Arab Maghreb Union (AMU) (with Morocco, Tunisia, Algeria and Libya), however no economic integration or free trade agreement has been achieved between members.

In 2006, exports of crude oil began, averaging 75,000 barrels per day and an agreement was signed with the European Union to allow EU fishing fleets access to Mauritanian waters for eur516 million (US$700 million) over 2006–12.

Imports

Principal imports are capital machinery and equipment, petroleum products, vehicles, foodstuffs and consumer goods.

Main sources: France (11.9 per cent total, 2006), China (8.2 per cent), Belgium (6.9 per cent).

Exports

Principal exports are fish and fish products, crude oil, iron ore and gold.

Main destinations: China (26.2 per cent total, 2006), Italy (11.8 per cent), France (10.2 per cent).

Agriculture

Farming

Production of food crops is restricted to irrigated land in the south along the north bank of the Senegal River. Three years of drought created serious food shortages as yields for millet and sorghum dropped by over 60 per cent in 2002; agricultural growth in 2003 was only 0.2 per cent. This rose to 3.7 per cent in 2004 as harvests improved. International aid and imported cereals have been vital in supplementing the main food crops – millet, sorghum, rice, maize, potatoes and dates.

Most of Mauritania consists of arid and semi-arid land and although it is unsuitable for crops, livestock rearing is an important sector. Nomadic herders comprise around 10 per cent of the population, although their numbers are dwindling. In 2005 Oxfam stated intermittent droughts since 2000 have affected nomadic herders and northern farming families, leading to food crises and a need of food and farming aid.

In late 2004 large plagues of locust attacked crops across much of west Africa and the Sahel region of southern Sahara. Initial fears of widespread destruction of harvests did not occur however food prices had spiralled during the threat and only returned to expected norms after early rains in May 2005.

Estimated crop production for 2005 included: 76,469 tonnes (t) cereals in total, 55,000t rice, 4,412t maize, 2,200t potatoes, 2,200t sweet potatoes, 14,966t sorghum, 24,000t dates, 44,500t pulses, 1,500t oilcrops, 2,500t yams, 27,100t fruit in total, 4,200 vegetables in total. Estimated livestock production included: 89,349t meat in total, 23,000t beef, 22,000t camel meat, 24,750t lamb, 13,800t goat meat, 4,320t poultry, 5,270t eggs, 348,800t milk, 3,420t cattle hides, 3,300t sheepskins, 1,656t goatskins.

Fishing

Fishing contributes up to 10 per cent of GDP and provides around 45 per cent of export earnings as well as being an important source of food for Mauritanians. The coastal waters are among the richest in the world and joint venture fishing is one of the most important foreign exchange earners. The catch is mainly deep sea species and shellfish – particularly shrimp for the Japanese market.

In 2004, the total marine fish catch was 177,127 tonnes and the total crustacean catch was 1,812 tonnes.

Forestry

The majority of timber production is used as domestic firewood.

Timber imports in 2004 were US$4.5 million, while exports amounted to US$0.5 million.

Timber production in 2004 included 1,587,039 cubic metre (cum) roundwood, 6,000cum industrial roundwood, 1,581,039cum woodfuel; 152,030t charcoal.

Industry and manufacturing

The industrial sector contributes around 10 per cent to GDP and employs 5 per cent of the workforce.

The most important activities are fish freezing and processing and the treatment of locally mined iron ore. There are also various small import substitution industries (brewing, footwear, dairy processing etc), oil refining and a sugar refinery in Nouakchott.

Industrial production increased by 2 per cent in 2003.

Tourism

The tourism sector is underdeveloped. Revenues from the sector are estimated at an annual US$20 million. Most foreign visitors are business travellers to Nouakchott, drop-in visitors crossing the border from Senegal or occasional desert safari enthusiasts.

Mining

The mining sector contributes around 13 per cent to GDP, employs 5 per cent of the working population and generates 42 per cent of export earnings.

The annual output of iron ore is around 12 million tonnes, of which about 11 million tonnes is exported – 36 per cent to France, 26 per cent to Italy, 16 per cent to Belgium, 8 per cent to Germany, 4 per cent to Spain and 4 per cent to the UK.

The iron mines are located in the Tiris region in the north and are owned and operated by Société Nationale Industrielle et Minière (SNIM). Other mineral resources include copper (at Akjoujt); gold (also near Akjoujt); phosphates (deposits at Bofal), diamonds and uranium.

Hydrocarbons

Currently Mauritania does not produce hydrocarbons but this will change in 2006 when the Chinguetti oil field begins production. It is expected to produce around 75,000 barrels per day (bpd) and the field should last for eight years.

Other oil and gas fields will come online before 2008, including the Tiof oil field, with reserves of 350 million barrels, the Banda field with 85–140 billion cubic metres, and the Pelican field with 28–42 billion cubic metres, of gas reserves. More exploration of offshore sites is underway.

A new ministry of oil and energy was set up in March 2005.

Mauritania has one refinery, the Somir Refinery, at Nouadhibou. This runs on Algerian crude and is operated by an Algerian company.

Mauritania imports small amounts of coal.

Energy

Primary energy resources consist of non-commercial biomass, mostly fuel wood. Over half of the installed generating capacity is provided by hydroelectric dams. There is small-scale thermal electricity (generating capacity 110MW), the majority of which is provided by isolated diesel generators.

Completion of work on the Manantali dam, on the Senegal river, has led to an increase in hydroelectric power supply to Mauritania, Senegal and Mali, with five generators supplying around 40MW each.

The Société Mauritanienne d'Electricité (Maurelec) is responsible for electricity generation, transmission and supply. The electricity network serves only a few people in urban areas.

Banking and insurance

In recent years, Mauritania's banking sector has undergone liberalisation with the government selling its equity stake in commercial banks, making the sector more competitive. Reform of the banking sector has led to limits on bank lending and to new laws on debt recovery.

Domestic confidence in the banking sector remains low and 60 per cent of cash is still not placed in banks. However, this represents an enormous opportunity for the banking sector to increase savings and improve liquidity. An increase in the number of bank branches and the introduction of micro-banking schemes may transform the sector in coming years.

Central bank

Banque Centrale de Mauritanie

Main financial centre

Nouakchott

Time

GMT

Geography

Mauritania lies in north-west Africa, with the Atlantic Ocean to the west, Algeria and Western Sahara/Morocco to the north, Mali to the east and south, and Senegal to the south.

Mauritania extends over an area of 1,030,700 square km, around 75 per cent of which is covered with sand and scrub. South-west-facing scarps in the huge plains are home to oases. The general flatness is relieved by rocky plateaux, which rise to 500–600m. These are cut by ravines and punctuated by isolated peaks. The country's highest point is Kediet Ijill, which reaches 915m. The plateaux drop gradually north-eastwards to the Empty Quarter, heralding the onset of the Sahara. Westwards, between the plateaux and the Atlantic Ocean, the terrain alternates between areas of plains and dunes, which increase in size and movement to the north. The only area of permanent vegetation is in the south along the Senegal river, which forms the frontier with Senegal.

Hemisphere

Northern

Climate

The climate is hot and dry. The hottest month in Noukachott is September (24–34 degrees Celsius (C)); the coldest is December (12–29 degrees C); the wettest month is August.

Entry requirements

Passports

Required by all.

Visa

Required by all, except citizens of neighbouring states, contact the consular section of the nearest embassy for confirmation of exclusions. Business travellers may visit with a tourist visa, obtained in advance. An application should include a bank letter showing sufficient funds for the length of trip, an employer's letter of accreditation and an invitation from a local company or organisation.

All travellers must have return/onward passage.

Currency advice/regulations

Unlimited foreign currency may be imported, but the amount must be declared on arrival. Unexchanged foreign currency may be exported. Declaration forms must be produced on departure. Import and export of local currency is strictly forbidden. Controls are constantly subject to modification.

Health (for visitors)

Mandatory precautions

Yellow fever vaccination certificate required if arriving from an infected area.

Advisable precautions

Yellow fever, hepatitis A, tetanus, typhoid and polio vaccinations. Malaria prophylaxis should be taken.

Water precautions are advisable. There is a rabies risk.

Hotels

Accommodation is limited and visitors should book well in advance. A service charge is normally included in the bill, otherwise a 15 per cent tip is usual.

Credit cards

Only accepted in main hotels.

Public holidays (national)

Fixed dates

1 Jan (New Year's Day), 1 May (Labour Day), 25 May (Africa Day), 10 Jul (Armed Forces Day), 28 Nov (Independence Day).

Variable dates

Eid al Adha, Islamic New Year, Birth of the Prophet, Eid al Fitr.

Islamic year – 1429 (10 Jan 2008–28 Dec 2008): The Islamic year contains 354 or 355 days, with the result that Muslim feasts advance by 10–12 days against the Gregorian calendar. Dates of feasts vary according to the sighting of the new moon, so cannot be forecast exactly.

Working hours

Banking

Sun–Wed: 0800–1115; 1430–1630; Thu: 0800–1500.

Business

Sat–Wed: 0800–1500; Thu: 0800–1300. Some stop for a lunch-time break (usually 1200–1300 or 1500).

Government

Sat–Wed: 0800–1500; Thu: 0800–1300.

Shops

Sat–Thu: 0800–1200; 1430–1800.

Telecommunications

Telephone/fax

International telephone facilities are available in Nouakchott and Nouadhibou.

Electricity supply

127/220V AC, 50 cycles. Plugs and sockets mostly two-pin (round).

Getting there

Air

National airline: Air Mauritanie

International airport/s: Nouakchott (NKC), 4km from city; Nouadhibou (NDB), 4km from city; .

Airport tax: UM270.

Surface

Road: Crossing the Mali and Western Sahara/Morocco borders may present difficulties and the Algerian frontier is closed. The best route is via Senegal. A surfaced road exists from Dakar (Senegal) to Nouakchott.

Main port/s: Nouadhibou and Nouakchott

Getting about

National transport

Air: Air Mauritanie provides mainly weekly services between most main centres.

Road: Most roads linking major centres are adequate, although four-wheel drive vehicles are recommended. Minor roads are usually impassable after the rainy season. There is a paved road between Rosso (on the Senegal River, where a ferry connects with the road to Dakar) and Akjoujt, via Nouakchott, and another, La Route de l'Espoir, running from Nouakchott to Mali.

Rail: A track runs inland from the coast (Nouakchott-Zouerate), mainly for freight, but there are some passenger services (single-class) scheduled; motor vehicles are sometimes carried.

City transport

Taxis: Taxis are numerous in the main towns. They are not metered, but the fares are standardised, although they should be checked before departure. A small tip is usual. Taxis can be rented by the hour.

Car hire

Cars can be rented in Nouakchott, Nouadhibou and Atar. An international or national driving licence is required. Out of town, a four-wheel drive vehicle with chauffeur, although expensive, is recommended.

BUSINESS DIRECTORY

The addresses listed below are a selection only. While World of Information makes every endeavour to check these addresses, we cannot guarantee that changes have not been made, especially to telephone numbers and area codes. We would welcome any corrections.

Telephone area codes

The international dialling (IDD) code for Mauritania is +222, followed by subscriber's number.

Chambers of Commerce

Mauritania Chamber of Commerce, Industry and Agriculture, Avenue de la République, PO Box 215, Nouakchott (tel: 525-2214; fax: 525-3895; e-mail: ccia@mauritel.mr).

Banking

Banque Mauritanienne pour le Commerce International, PO Box 622, Immeuble Afarco, Avenue Gamal Abdel Nasser, Nouakchott (tel: 525-4349; fax: 525-2045).

Banque Nationale de Mauritanie; PO Box 614, Avenue Gamal Abdel Nasser, Nouakchott (tel: 525-2602; fax: 525-3397).

Central bank

Banque Centrale de Mauritanie, PO Box 623, Avenue de l'Indépendence, Nouakchott (tel: 525-2206; fax: 525-2759; e-mail: info@bcm.mr).

Travel information

Air Mauritanie, Avenue Gamal Abdel Nasser, PO Box 41, Nouakchott (tel: 525-2721; e-mail: resa@airmauritanie.mr).

Ministry of tourism

Ministry of Trade, Handicrafts and Tourism, Directorate of Tourism, PO Box 246, Nouakchott (tel: 525-1367; fax: 525-1057).

National tourist organisation offices

Office National du Tourisme, PO Box 2884, Nouakchott (tel: 529-0344; fax: 529-0528; e-mail: ont@mauritel.mr).

Ministries

Ministry of Economic Affairs and Development, BP 238, Nouakchott (tel: 525-1612; fax: 525-5110; e-mail: infomaed@mauritania.mr).

Ministry of Education, PO Box 227, Nouakchott (tel: 525-8445; fax: 525-1222).

Ministry of Finance, PO Box 197, Nouakchott (tel: 525-4397; fax: 525-3114; e-mail: sidahd@mauritania.mr).

Ministry of Fishing and Maritime Economy, PO Box 137, Nouakchott (tel: 525-9970; fax: 525-3146).

Ministry of Foreign Affairs and Co-operation, PO Box 230, Nouakchott (tel: 525-2682).

Ministry of Health and Social Affairs, PO Box 169, Nouakchott (tel: 525-2052).

Ministry of Infrastructure and Transport, PO Box 237, Nouakchott (tel: 525-3337).

Ministry of the Interior, Post and Telecommunications, PO Box 195, Nouakchott (tel: 525-2020).

Ministry of Mines and Industry, PO Box 199, Nouakchott (tel: 525-3086; fax: 525-6937; e-mail: mmi@mauritania.mr).

Ministry of Trade, Artisans and Tourism, PO Box 182, Nouakchott (tel: 525-1057).

Ministry of Rural Development and Environment, PO Box 366, Nouakchott (tel: 525-1500; fax: 525-7574).

Prime Minister's Office, PO Box 237, Nouakchott (tel: 525-3337).

Other useful addresses

Centre d'Information Mauritanien pour le Developpement Economique et Technique, PO Box 2119, Nouakchott (tel: 525-8738; fax: 525-8648; e-mail: cimdet@pacdet.org).

Confédération Générale des Employeurs de Mauritanie (CGEM), PO Box 383, Nouakchott (tel: 525-2160; fax: 525-3301).

Fédération des Industries et Armement de Pêche (FIAP), PO Box 43, Nouadhibou (tel: 574-5089; fax: 574-5430).

Fédération des Industries et des Mines (FIM), PO Box 5501, Nouakchott (tel: 525-0304; fax: 525-6955).

Mauritanian Embassy (USA), 2129 Leroy Place, NW, Washington DC 20008 (tel: (+1-202)-232-5700; fax: (+1-202)-319-2623).

Mauritanienne d'Entreposage des Produits Pétroliers (MEPP), Nouakchott (tel: 525-2646; fax: 525-4608; e-mail: mepp@mauritel.mr).

National Statistics Office, BP 240, Nouakchott (tel: 525-5031; fax:525-5170; e-mail: webmaster@)ons.mr).

Internet sites

Africa Business Network: http://www.ifc.org/abn

AllAfrica.com: http://allafrica.com

African Development Bank: http://www.afdb.org

Africa Online: http://www.africaonline.com

Mbendi AfroPaedia (information on companies, countries, industries and stock exchanges in Africa): http://mbendi.co.za

Mauritius

KEY FACTS

Official name: Republic of Mauritius

Head of State: President Sir Anerood Jugnauth (from 7 Oct 2003)

Head of government: Prime Minister Navin Ramgoolam (AS) (5 Jul 2005)

Ruling party: Alliance Sociale (AS) (Social Alliance) (elected 3 Jul 2005)

Area: 1,865 square km

Population: 1.26 million (2007)*

Capital: Port Louis

Official language: English and French

Currency: Mauritian rupee (MR) = 100 cents

Exchange rate: MR26.55 per US$ (Jul 2008)

GDP per capita: US$5,520 (2007)

GDP real growth: 4.60% (2007)

Labour force: 546,000 (2004)

Unemployment: 8.80% (2007)*

Inflation: 10.70% (2007)

Balance of trade: -US$794.60 million (2005)

Foreign debt: US$2.29 billion (2004)

Visitor numbers: 906,971 (2007)

* estimated figure

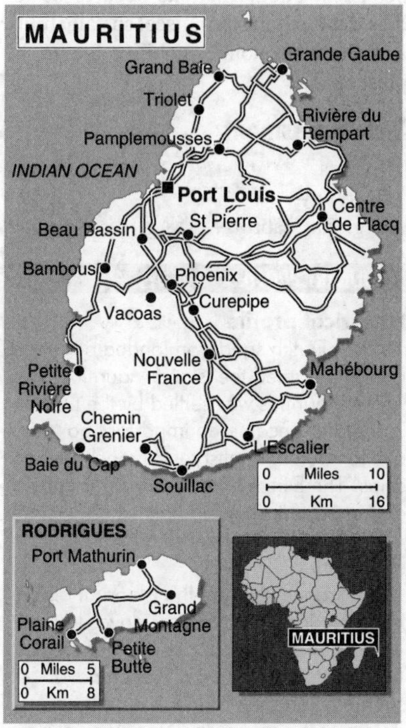

Mauritius did well in 2007, in large part driven by a boom in the tourism sector, which in turn led to growth in the construction industry, and to an increase in the level of employment. However, by the middle of 2008, tourism, particularly long-distance tourism such as that to Mauritius, was feeling the effect of the sharp increase in the cost of oil, reflecting on transport not only of the tourists themselves, but also of so much of the trappings of tourism.

Mauritius is one of the most densely populated countries in the world. It seems incredible, in the 21st century, to think that in the early 1970s economists were predicting that the island community would experience a demographic nightmare of Malthusian proportions. But Mauritius' population growth was contained as the birth rate fell from over 3.0 per cent to less than 1.5 per cent. The rest, as they say, is economic history.

According to the 2008 edition of *African Economic Outlook* (AEO), a joint publication of the African Development Bank and Organisation for Economic Co-operation and Development, the economy of Mauritius is expected to grow by about 5 per cent in 2008 and 2009. However, it remains vulnerable to external shocks such as high oil and other commodity prices. And a further adverse performance in the sugar sector could result in slower growth. The good external competitiveness of Mauritius in 2007 was also the result of the past nominal and real depreciation of the rupee against the currencies of its main trading partners. But the rupee stabilised towards the end of the year, and even appreciated against some major currencies.

The AEO points out that although Mauritius has based its development on preferential access to European markets, an important development has been the amendment of the 2004 banking act to allow for Islamic banking. The Finance Act 2007 defines Islamic banking business as any financial business, the aims and operations of which are, in addition to the conventional good governance and risk management rules, consonant with the ethos and value system of Islam. An Islamic deposit means a sum of money or monetary equivalent of goods or services received by or paid to any person under which the receipt and repayment shall be in accordance with the terms of an agreement made on any basis including custody or profit sharing. The Central Bank of Mauritius became an assiociate member of the Islamic Financiasl Services Board in November 2007 and any bank in Mauritius can now opt to offer Islamic banking through a special window, or by launching a full fledged Islamic bank.

The decision by the European Union (EU) to reduce the guaranteed price of sugar to the African, Caribbean and Pacific producers has led to the restructuring of the sugar industry. Mauritius is in the process of becoming a competitive producer of refined sugar and derivative products based on sugar cane.

According to the World Bank, gross domestic product (GDP) growth for 2007 is estimated at 4.6 per cent, up on the 3.7 per cent of 2006. This is still respectable by the standards of the region. Mauritius is highly vulnerable to changes in the world trade regime. According to one estimate, the ending of Multi-Fibre Agreement (MFA) in January 2005 and the phasing out of sugar preferences by 2008 could cost Mauritius as much as 8–9 per cent of GDP, 20 per cent of exports, and 40 per cent of government revenue. But while these developments add some urgency, Mauritius' very success in adapting to changing conditions is proof against a drop in the economy.

The World Bank acknowledges that the challenge which Mauritius now faces has not come as a surprise. Over the past decade, the groundwork has been laid to move the economy toward more knowledge- and skill-intensive activities and higher-value-added financial and business services. Successive governments have been implementing Mauritius' vision for its future, restructuring and downsizing sugar and textiles, putting in place enabling legislation for offshore financial services, and drawing FDI into the IT sector with a state-of-the-art, fibre optic wired Cyber Tower. While the July 2005 election brought a change in government, no fundamental shift in Mauritius' development strategy was anticipated.

Remarkably, Mauritius's development has been financed almost entirely from domestic savings, which have been channelled through an efficient domestic banking system. Foreign direct investment (FDI) has played a minor role.

The government's development strategy centers on expanding local financial institutions and building a domestic information telecommunications industry. Mauritius has attracted more than 9,000 offshore entities, many aimed at commerce in India and South Africa, and investment in the banking sector alone has reached over US$1 billion.

Politics

Mauritius has a multiparty democratic system. Former prime minister, Navin Ramgoolam of the Social Alliance, returned to power after defeating Paul Bérenger of the Mauritian Militant Movement in elections in July 2005. Ramgoolam promised to tackle rising inflation and unemployment. To this end, he advocates trade agreements that give preference to Mauritian exports, including sugar and textiles. Born in 1947, Ramgoolam first served as prime minister between 1995 and 2000. He is a doctor and lawyer.

Outlook

Mauritius is one of the key regional economies that are growing at an impressive rate, encouraged by growing political stability and financial prudence. Since independence in 1968, it has experienced a significant transformation, moving from an economy that was almost entirely dependent on sugar cane cultivation and sugar manufacturing to one that has benefited from an export-led growth strategy. Small-businesses in particular are thriving in this environment, accounting for an ever-greater proportion of available jobs.

Mauritius's immediate and medium-term macroeconomic challenges are threefold. First, there is a need to diversify and transform the economy, especially in light of the loss of trade preferences in the sugar and textile sectors. Second, Mauritius must undertake structural reforms to increase labour market flexibility. Third, persistent budget deficits need to be reduced if medium-term fiscal sustainability and macroeconomic stability are to be preserved.

Risk assessment

Politics	Good
Economy	Good
Regional stability	Good

KEY INDICATORS — Mauritius

	Unit	2003	2004	2005	2006	2007
Population	m	1.22	1.23	1.24	1.25	*1.26
Gross domestic product (GDP)	US$bn	5.51	6.06	6.21	6.31	6.96
GDP per capita	US$	4,447	4,829	5,011	5,043	5,520
GDP real growth	%	4.8	4.4	3.0	3.7	4.6
Inflation	%	7.7	8.5	9.5	5.6	10.7
Unemployment	%	7.7	8.4	9.6	9.2	*8.5
Industrial output	% change	–	1.6	-1.4	-0.1	–
Agricultural output	% change	–	3.1	3.5	-3.9	–
Exports (fob) (goods)	US$m	1,600.0	2,012.0	2,143.7	2,263.0	–
Imports (cif) (goods)	US$m	1,800.0	2,245.0	2,938.4	3,329.0	–
Balance of trade	US$m	-200.0	-233.0	-794.6	-1,066.0	–
Current account	US$m	100.0	30.0	-216.9	-336.0	-549.0
Total reserves minus gold	US$m	1,577.3	1,605.9	1,339.9	1,269.9	1,780.3
Foreign exchange	US$m	1,519.2	1,544.7	1,289.2	1,226.3	1,739.9
Tourist numbers	'000	702.0	718.9	761.1	788.3	907.0
Exchange rate	per US$	27.55	27.50	32.57	32.57	28.80

COUNTRY PROFILE

Historical profile

1598 A Dutch squadron landed at Grand Port and named the island Mauritius.

1638 Mauritius was settled by the Dutch. The island became an important port of call for Dutch, English and French trading ships. The Dutch introduced sugar cane and imported slaves to harvest it.

1710 The Dutch abandoned their settlement.

1721 France claimed the island; it also imported large numbers of slaves to harvest sugar cane, cotton and other crops.

1810 Britain defeated a French naval squadron and the island was ceded to Britain at the end of the Napoleonic Wars.

1835 Slavery was abolished. Most freed slaves left the plantations and settled in coastal towns; workers had to be imported from the Indian sub-continent to take their place, most of whom opted to remain on the island at the end of their contracts.

1936 The Labour Party (LP) was formed and organised strikes and protests between 1937–45.

1953 A group of Mauritians under Seewoosagur Ramgoolam rose to the leadership of the LP, which won the elections to the Legislative Council. Most Creoles joined the Parti Mauricien Social-Démocrate (PMSD) (Social Democratic Party of Mauritius).

1959 New political parties emerged including the Muslim Committee of Action (CAM). CAM formed an alliance with the LP.

1968 Mauritius gained independence from Britain.

1969 Ramgoolam's LP-CAM (Muslim) ruling alliance was strengthened when a coalition with the PMSD was formed. In response, the Mouvement Militante Mauricien (MMM) (Mauritian Militant Movement) was established.

1982 The LP lost power as the MMM, in alliance with the Parti Socialiste Mauricien (PSM), gained power under the premiership of Anerood Jugnauth.
1983 The MMM split and Jugnauth formed the Mouvement Socialiste Mauricien (MSM) (Mauritian Socialist Movement) which formed a government with the LP.
1990 The MMM and the MSM formed a political alliance and aimed to transform Mauritius into a republic.
1992 Cassam Uteem was elected president.
1995 An alliance of the LP and the MMM, led by Navinchandra Ramgoolam and Paul Berenger, won the parliamentary elections. Ramgoolam became prime minister.
1997 The LP-MMM coalition broke up when the MMM left government and became the official opposition. Even so, the LP continued to hold an outright majority in the legislature and for the first time since independence, Mauritius was governed by a single party. Cassam Uteem was re-elected president.
2000 The opposition, MSM/MMM, won the parliamentary election. Sir Anerood Jugnauth, leader of the MMM, became prime minister for the second time. Mauritius revived a claim to sovereignty over Diego Garcia, the British Indian Ocean Territory.
2001 The WTO trade policy review encouraged Mauritius to further liberalise and diversify its economy. A constitutional amendment was introduced, allowing Rodrigues Island to have two representatives in the National Assembly and its own regional assembly.
2002 President Uteem resigned and Vice President Angidi Chettiar became interim president, but he also resigned; both men had refused to sign into law controversial anti-terrorism legislation. The National Assembly elected Karl Offman as president. On Rodrigues Island, the Rodrigues People's Organisation (RPO) won 10 seats out of 18 and the Mouvement Rodriguais (MR) (Rodrigues Movement) won eight seats in the first Rodrigues Regional Assembly election. The Rodrigues Regional Assembly opened with Jean Daniel Spéville as chief commissioner.
2003 Serge Clair became chief commissioner of Rodrigues Island. Sir Anerood Jugnauth resigned and Paul Bérenger replaced him as prime minister. Sir Anerood Jugnauth was appointed as president.
2005 In parliamentary elections the opposition Alliance Sociale (AS) (Social Alliance) won 49 per cent of the vote (38 out of 62 constituencies) and the incumbent coalition MSM and MMM won 43 per cent (22). Turnout was 81.5 per cent. Navin Ramgoolam (AS) became prime minister.
2006 Former residents of Diego Garcia, in the Chagos Archipelago, evicted by the British, for the island to be turned into a US military air base, in the 1960s and living since in Mauritius, which also claims Diego Garcia, won the right to visit their island.
2007 The British High Court ruled that families of the expelled Diego Garcia islanders could return home.
2008 The Le Morne Mountain was added to the list of Unesco World Heritage sites in July. The mountain was an important site of shelter and became a symbol of freedom for runaway slaves fleeing the eastern slave trade in the 18 and 19 centuries.

Political structure

Constitution

Mauritius is a republic with a president as head of state.
The president is elected by a simple majority of all the members of the National Assembly for a five-year term. The National Assembly is the supreme body that votes laws. The president's agreement and signature is required to sign legislation into law.

Form of state

Republic

The executive

Executive power is vested in the prime minister, leader of the majority parliamentary party.
There is a Council of Ministers consisting of the prime minister and not more than 24 other ministers.

National legislature

The unicameral National Assembly has 62 seats elected by universal adult suffrage for five years.
For the purpose of electing members of the National Assembly, the island of Mauritius is divided into 20 three-member constituencies.
The island of Rodrigues returns two members.
The official language of the National Assembly is English but any member may address the Chair in French.

Last elections

3 July 2005 (parliamentary): February 2002 (presidential).
Results: Presidential: the National Assembly elected Karl Offman as president. Parliamentary: Alliance Sociale (AS) (Social Alliance) won 49 per cent of the vote (38 out of 62 constituencies) and the coalition of MSM and MMM won 43 per cent (22). Turnout was 81.5 per cent. Condidates for the remaining eight seats in the 70-member National Assembly were nominated by the electoral board, giving representation in parliament to showing high but unsuccessful placings.

Next elections

2007 (presidential); 2010 (parliamentary).

Political parties

Ruling party

Alliance Sociale (AS) (Social Alliance) (elected 3 Jul 2005)

Main opposition party

Coalition of Mouvement Socialiste Mauricien (MSM) (Mauritian Socialist Movement) and Mouvement Militante Mauricien (MMM) (Mauritian Militant Movement)

Population

1.26 million (2007)*
Last census: July 2000: 1,178,848
Population density: Population density: 588 per square km. The population densities of the island of Mauritius and the island of Rodrigues are 624 and 345, respectively. Urban population: 42 per cent (1995—2001).
Annual growth rate: 1.1 per cent 1994–2004 (WHO 2006)

Ethnic make-up

Indentured workers were brought from India to work on sugar estates and their descendants form a majority of the population, followed by Creoles (of mixed, predominantly African, origin), Muslim Indians, Chinese and Europeans. Hindu Indo-Mauritian (51 per cent), Creole (27 per cent), Muslim Indo-Mauritians (17 per cent), Chinese (2 per cent).

Religions

Hinduism (51 per cent), Christianity (Roman Catholic) (31.3 per cent), Muslim (16.6 per cent).

Education

Education is modelled on the English school system. Primary schooling lasts for six years until the age of 12; lower secondary schooling lasts for five years and upper secondary schooling for a further two years. Examinations are undertaken at each transition.
The expenditure allocated to education by central government was 16 per cent (Unicef estimates 1992–1999).
Literacy rate: 85.3 per cent total; 82.3 per cent female, adult rates (World Bank).
Compulsory years: Five to 12.
Enrolment rate: 93.6 per cent net primary enrolment, of the relevant age group; 62.9 per cent net secondary enrolment (World Bank).
Pupils per teacher: 24 in primary schools.

Health

Per capita total expenditure on health (2003) was US$430; of which per capita government spending was US$261, at the international dollar rate, (WHO 2006).

Life expectancy: 72 years, 2004 (WHO 2006)
Fertility rate/Maternal mortality rate: 2.0 births per woman, 2004 (WHO 2006)
Child (under 5 years) mortality rate (per 1,000): 16 deaths per 1,000 live births; about 15 per cent of children aged under five are malnourished (World Bank).
Head of population per physician: 1.06 physicians per 1,000 people, 2004 (WHO 2006)

Main cities
Port Louis (capital, estimated population 147,251 in 2005), Beau Bassin/Rose Hill (107,716), Vascoas-Phoenix (118,421), Curepipe (84,057), Quatre Bornes (79,504).

Languages spoken
Creole and Bhojpuri are the predominant languages in everyday life.

Official language/s
English and French

Media
Press
Several daily newspapers including Le Mauricien, l'Express, The Sun and some weekly newspapers and periodicals are in circulation.

Broadcasting
Mauritius Broadcasting Corporation (MBC) operates two TV and three radio channels. Broadcasts in English, French, Creole, Hindi, Tamil, Telegu, Marathi, Urdu, Chinese, Gujarati and Bhojpuri. French pay-TV station Canal Plus and Sky News from the UK British Sky Broadcasting Corporation have been transmitting programmes since 1995.
Radio: Radio Sugar FM is the main station, operated by MBC.

Economy
The economy was knocked off tract in 2006 as a result of the phasing out of textile and sugar trade preferences, especially with the European Union, and the rise in the global price of oil. Domestically, economic activity was sluggish. GDP growth was 3.5 per cent in 2005 and was expected to fall to 2.7 in 2006.
The end of textile quotas led to an industry contraction of 18 per cent between 2001–04 and 12 per cent in the first quarter of 2005 with unemployment rising by 13 per cent. As a result, in 2007, it was announced that seven of the 11 current sugar refineries will be closed and the remaining will be converted into 'flexi-factories'. Sugar plantations will be increased from 50–80 per cent of total land cultivated and the sugar will be processed into ethanol and other by-products to alleviate the islands' energy needs. The redevelopment, estimated at eur301 million (US$397 million), provided through EU assistance will create a temporary loss of sugar production and this coupled with the loss of textile manufacturing earnings, has caused a projected GDP growth of no greater than 1.2 per cent until 2011, and then only if the textile and sugar sectors regain their competitiveness.
The service sector provides 66 per cent of GDP, agriculture 6 per cent and industry 28 per cent, of which manufacturing is 20 per cent. Tourism is an important sector and one the government regards as a growth industry. It has increased the number of airlines allowed to arrive in high-season, while encouraging conference and retail investment. Other sources of growth include information technology and telecommunications as Mauritius offers a home to call centres and software development companies; although neither are expected to be big income earners they could boost overall economic productivity.

External trade
Mauritius was one of the founding members of the Common Market of Eastern and Southern Africa (Comesa), and operates a free trade area (FTA) with eight out of the 20 Comesa members. Internal duties were eliminated in 2000 and a common external tariff is set to be implemented in 2008. Mauritius is also a member of the Southern African Development Community (SADC), the objectives of which include reducing trade barriers, achieving regional development and economic growth and evolving common systems and institutions.
The importance of sugar as an export commodity has been replaced by services exports which generate more than 33 per cent of total foreign exchange earnings, as tourism contributes the largest and growing share.

Imports
Principal imports are manufactured goods, manufacturing equipment, foodstuffs, petroleum products and chemicals.
Main sources: France (14.3 per cent total, 2006), India (13.6 per cent), China (8.6 per cent).

Exports
Principal exports are clothing and textiles, sugar, cut flowers and molasses.
Main destinations: UK (32.4 per cent total, 2006), France (15.1 per cent), UAE (11.4 per cent).

Agriculture
Farming
The agricultural sector contributes around 6 per cent to GDP and employs 13 per cent of the workforce.
Sugar cane cultivation dominates the sector. Approximately 70 per cent of all cultivated land is devoted to the crop, and the sugar industry as a whole employs the majority of the workforce and accounts for 3 per cent of GDP. Cultivation is undertaken both on large plantations and by smallholders.
The other major export crop is tea, grown by tenant farmers. Mauritius is the fourth-largest producer of tea per capita in the world. Around 75 per cent of tea production (green leaf) is controlled by the Tea Development Authority, whose commercial activities are privately run.
Tobacco is grown for the home market.
Main food crops include potatoes and other vegetables, output of which is sufficient to meet domestic demand.
Much of the island's meat requirement is imported. Around 75 per cent of food requirements are also imported.
Estimated crop production in 2005 included: 190 tonnes (t) maize, 5,200,000t sugar cane, 130t cassava, 175t taro, 12,300t potatoes, 500t sweet potatoes, 12,100t bananas, 410t citrus fruit, 13,200t tomatoes, 4,560t pineapples, 516t oilcrops, 480t tobacco, 673t various spices, 1,450t tea, 17,820t fruit in total, 72,727t vegetables in total. Livestock production included: 32,467t meat in total, 2,500t beef, 825t pig meat, 232t lamb and goat meat, 28,279t poultry, 5,200t eggs, 4,000t milk.

Fishing
All fish-farming production and 90 per cent of marine fishing provides about 40 per cent of the nutritional requirement of the Mauritian population. Commercial aquaculture includes cultivation of giant freshwater prawns and oysters. Mauritius is a hub for longline tuna fishing fleets that dock to offload their cargo on to freezer ships for transhipment and provides the local economy with foreign currency.
Total fish catches amount to over 10,000 tonnes per year with another 70 tonnes of other sea food. Over 70,000 cultivated oysters are produced each year.
Sports fishing has become a major influence, along with reef diving, which not only drives the local tourist industry but also employs boats and crews formerly used in fishing that were less capable of competing with modern replacement ships and mechanisation.
In a meeting of African ministers in Namibia, held on 2 July, members discussed illegal and unregulated fishing, which is estimated to cost Africa US$1 billion per annum in lost revenue and the threat to stocks and local artisan fishing.
In 2004, the total marine fish catch was 9,880 tonnes and the total crustacean catch was 40 tonnes.

Forestry
The annual value of exports in 2004 amounted to US$1.5 million, while imports amounted to US$52 million.
Annual estimated production: 13,500 cubic metres (cum) roundwood, 3,000cum sawnwood, 5,000cum sawlogs and veneers, 6,000cum woodfuel, 100mt charcoal.

Industry and manufacturing
The industrial sector contributes around 30 per cent to GDP and employs 28 per cent of the workforce.
The industrial sector is based on the Export Processing Zones (EPZ) which were opened in the 1970s to take advantage of the preferential treatment which Mauritius receives under the Cotonou Agreement.
Production of textiles, and in particular knitwear, has become the most significant EPZ industry, and Mauritius is the world's third-largest exporter of pure new wool products. The EPZ textiles industry employs 91 per cent of the industrial workforce, accounts for 68 per cent of EPZ enterprises and 80 per cent of EPZ exports. The EPZs generate 23 per cent of GDP. In 2001, the knitwear industry moved towards high-fashion apparel as part of the effort to modernise.
Diversification is being encouraged to help get over the loss of preferential treatment in textiles. Other industries include the manufacture of watches and clocks, jewellery, spectacle frames and leather goods.
Informatics Park for foreign companies specialising in information technology was opened in 1994. Mauritius has plans to develop into a 'cyber island' and will receive assistance from the IMF as part of its upgrade.

Tourism
Tourism is the third most important source of foreign exchange. The sector is expected to account for 14.5 per cent of GDP in 2005.
There are around 105 registered hotels with around 11,000 total room capacity. Twenty new hotels are planned by 2016 at the total cost of US$450 million. Saturation point is near and there is a risk of environmental damage if development is not managed and contained accordingly.
There were 718,861 visitor arrivals in 2004, compared with 702,018. Europe is the main market, especially France, which accounts for more than a quarter of visitors, followed by South Africa.

Hydrocarbons
There are no known oil or gas reserves in Mauritius, which is reliant on imports to meet its energy needs. Refined oil products supply 84 per cent of Mauritius' energy needs and 19,600 barrels per day (bpd) were imported in 2001. Imports of petroleum products are handled by the State Trading Corporation. Mauritius does not import natural gas.
Mauritius does not produce coal, but imports it to meet 5 per cent of its energy requirements. In 2001 it imported 383,000 short tonnes.

Energy
Local electricity supply is largely from diesel powered thermal stations. There has been rapid development of electricity generation from bagasse (refuse produced in sugar-making). Hydroelectricity plants produce 25 per cent and bagasse 15 per cent of electricity.

Financial markets
Stock exchange
The Stock Exchange of Mauritius (SEM) was established by the government in July 1989 with five companies listed.
The stock market was opened to international investors in 1994.
There are ambitions to become a regional exchange, supplemented by offshore funds and listings from mainland Africa. In 1996 a central depository and settlement system was introduced. A new Securities Act also brought the framework up to world standards.
A weighted index, the SemDex, was introduced in 1998. In June 2003, market capitalisation was US$1.6 billion, with 38 listed companies. Foreign investors do not need approval to trade shares unless investment is for the purpose of management of a Mauritian company or for a holding over 15 per cent of a sugar company.

Banking and insurance
In 1989 tax and duty incentives were introduced for foreign banks licensed to engage in offshore banking. Mauritius launched Africa's first offshore banking centre at the end of 1989 which continues to expand.
Central bank
Bank of Mauritius.
Main financial centre
Port Louis.

Time
GMT plus four hours

Geography
Mauritius lies in the Indian Ocean. The principal island, from which the country takes its name, lies about 800km (500 miles) east of Madagascar. The other main islands are Rodrigues, the Agalega Islands and the Cargados Carajos Shoals (St Brandon Islands).
The island of Mauritius is volcanic with a coastal plain sharply rising to a plateau of 275–580 metres (m). Piton de la Rivière Noire is the highest peak, at 828m and the Grand River South East is the longest river. Coral reefs surround the island from hundreds of metres to several kilometres off the coast.
Hemisphere
Southern

Climate
Maritime – tropical in summer (November–April), and sub-tropical for the rest of the year. High humidity especially in inland areas. Summer temperatures average 25–30 degrees Celsius (C) with maximum 35 degrees C in February. Highest rainfall occurs in summer (when cyclones are likely). From May–November, drier and warm with temperatures 19–27 degrees C. Lowest rainfall from September–November. Inland areas generally 5 degrees C cooler than coast and with higher rainfall.

Entry requirements
Passports
Passports must be valid for six months from date of entry.
Visa
Required by all except citizens of most Commonwealth countries, plus EU, US and others. For a full list and further information see www.gov.mu/portal/site/passportSite and follow link from passport and visa requirements. Business travellers may visit with a tourist visa, obtained in advance. An application should include details of sufficient funds for the length of trip, an employer's letter of accreditation and an invitation from a local company or organisation.
All travellers must have return/onward passage.
Currency advice/regulations
The import and export of local and foreign currency is unlimited.
Travellers cheques are accepted in banks, hotels and authorised dealers.
Prohibited imports
Sugar cane, invertebrates and soil micro-organisms and illegal drugs.
Firearms and ammunition require import permits and must be declared on arrival.

Health (for visitors)
Mandatory precautions
Yellow fever and cholera vaccination certificates are required if arriving from infected areas.
Advisable precautions
Typhoid, tetanus, hepatitis A and polio vaccinations. Water precautions should be taken.

Hotels
There is a wide choice available but relatively expensive. A value added tax of 15 per cent is added to hotel and restaurant bills. Tip is not compulsory.

Credit cards
International credit and charge cards are acceptable in many establishments. ATMs are available.

Public holidays (national)
Fixed dates
1–2 Jan (New Year), 1 Feb (Abolition of Slavery Day), 12 Mar (National Day), 1 May (Labour Day), 2 Nov (Arrival of Indentured Labourers), 25 Dec (Christmas Day).
Variable dates
Thaipoosam Cavadee (Jan/Feb), Chinese New Year (Jan/Feb), Maha Shivaratri (Feb/Mar), Ougadi (Mar/Apr), Ganesh Chaturthi (Aug/Sep), Diwali (Oct/Nov), Eid al Fitr.
There are a diversity of cultures, each with their own set of holidays. Muslim, Buddhist and Hindu festivals are timed according to local sightings of the moon and its phases.

Working hours
Banking
Mon–Thu: 0915–1515; Fri: 0915–1530; Sat: 0915–1115. Some banks open Mon–Fri: 0900–1700.
Business
Mon–Fri: 0830–1615, Sat: 0900–1200.
Government
Mon–Fri: 0900–1600; Sat 0900–1200 (minimal staff only).
Shops
Mon–Sat 0930–1930.

Telecommunications
Mobile/cell phones
GSM 900 and 3G services cover almost the entire area of Mauritius and Rodrigues.

Electricity supply
220V AC, 50 cycles.

Weights and measures
The metric system is in general use, but certain obsolete French measures are still used in connection with the measurement of land.

Getting there
Air
National airline: Air Mauritius.
International airport/s: Sir Seewoosagur Ramgoolam International (MRU) 3km from Mahébourg, 48km south-east of Port Louis; duty free, currency exchange, post office, shops, car hire, banks.
Airport tax: Departure tax: MR500
Surface
Main port/s: Port Louis is the island's only commercial port with five deep water quays. Its free port status underpins the island's offshore banking system.

Getting about
National transport
Air: Air Mauritius operates inter-island service between Mauritius and Rodrigues and Réunion. Two Air Mauritius Bell Jet helicopters are available for transfer from airport to hotel and tours.
Road: There is an extensive network throughout the island. About 93 per cent of the road network is paved. Occasional congestion. A dual highway links Port Louis and Phoenix, Port Louis and Mapou/Pamplemousses.
Buses: Good bus services cover the main island.
City transport
Taxis: Operate in all towns, villages and resorts. Generally unmetered so it is advisable to agree a fare before starting the journey. Tipping is not usual.
Car hire
Widely available. International or foreign licence accepted; traffic drives on the left.

BUSINESS DIRECTORY

The addresses listed below are a selection only. While World of Information makes every endeavour to check these addresses, we cannot guarantee that changes have not been made, especially to telephone numbers and area codes. We would welcome any corrections.

Telephone area codes
The international dialling code (IDD) for Mauritius is +230, followed by subscriber's number.

Useful telephone numbers

Emergency	999
Fire	995
Police	208-7018

Chambers of Commerce
Mauritius Chamber of Commerce and Industry, 3 Royal Street, Port Louis (tel: 208-3301; fax: 208-0076; e-mail: mcci@intnet.mu).

Banking
African Asian Bank Limited, Office 5, 8th Floor, Max City Building, Corner Louis Pasteur & Remy Ollier Streets, Port Louis (tel: 240-7002, 240-7350; fax: 240-7009).

Bank of Baroda, African Asian Bank Limited, PO Box 553, Sir William Newton Street, Port Louis (tel: 208-1504; fax: 208-3892).

Bank of Mauritius, PO Box 29, Sir William Newton Street, Port Louis (tel: 202-3800; fax: 208-9204).

Banque Nationale de Paris Intercontinentale, 1 Sir William Newton Street, Port Louis (tel: 208-4147/8/9, 208-4151/2; fax: 208-8143).

Delphis Bank Limited, 16 Sir William Newton Street, Port Louis (tel: 208-5061; fax: 208-5388).

Development Bank of Mauritius Ltd, PO Box 157, Chaussée, Port Louis (tel: 208-0241; fax: 208-8498).

Indian Ocean International Bank Ltd, 34 Sir William Newton Street, Port Louis (tel: 208-0121; fax: 208-0127).

Mauritius Commercial Bank Ltd, 9-15 Sir William Newton St, Port Louis (tel: 202-5000; fax: 208-7054).

South East Asian Bank Ltd, 26 Bourbon Street, PO Box 13, Port Louis (tel: 208-8826/7/8, 212-2884/6/7; fax: 208-8825).

State Bank of Mauritius Ltd, PO Box 152, State Bank Tower, 1 Queen Elizabeth II Ave, Port Louis (tel: 202-1111; fax: 202-1234).

Central bank
Bank of Mauritius, Sir William Newton Street, Port Louis (tel: 208-4164 fax: 208-9204; e-mail: bomrd@bow.intnet.mu).

Travel information
Air Mauritius, Rogers House, 5 President John F. Kennedy Street, PO Box 441, Port Louis (tel: 208-7700; fax: 208-8331).

Ministry of tourism
Ministry of Tourism, Emmanuel Anquetil Bldg, Sir Seewoosagur Ramgoolam St, Port Louis (tel: 201-2286).

National tourist organisation offices
Mauritius Tourism Promotion Authority, 11th Floor, Air Mauritius Centre, President John Kennedy Street, Port-Louis (tel: 210-1545; fax: 212-5142; e-mail: mtpa@intnet.mu; Internet: www.mauritius.net).

Ministries
Ministry of Agriculture and Natural Resources, NPF Bldg, 9th Floor, Port Louis (tel: 212-7946; fax: 212-4427).

Ministry of Arts, Culture, Leisure and Reform Institutions, Government Centre, Port Louis (tel: 201-2032).

Ministry of Civil Service Affairs and Employment, Government Centre, Port Louis (tel: 201-1035; fax: 212-9528).

Ministry of Co-operatives and Handicraft, Life Insurance Corporation of India Bldg, 3rd Floor, John Kennedy St, Port Louis (tel: 208-4812; fax: 208-9265).

Ministry of Economic Planning and Development, Emmanuel Anquetil Bldg, Sir Seewoosagur Ramgoolam St, Port Louis (tel: 201-1576; fax: 212-4124).

Ministry of Education and Science, Sun Trust Bldg, Edith Cavell St, Port Louis (tel: 212-8411; fax: 212-3783).

Ministry of Energy, Water Resources and Postal Services, Government Centre, Port Louis (tel: 201-1087; fax: 208-6497).

Ministry of the Environment and Quality of Life, Barracks St, Port Louis (tel: 212-8332; fax: 212-9407).

Ministry of External Affairs, Government Centre, Port Louis (tel: 201-1416; fax: 208-8087).

Ministry of Finance, Government Centre, Port Louis (tel: 201-1145; fax: 208-8622).

Ministry of Fisheries and Marine Resources, Port Louis.

Ministry of Health, Emmanuel Anquetil Bldg, Sir Seewoosagur Ramgoolam St, Port Louis (tel: 201-1910; fax: 208-0376).

Ministry of Housing, Lands and Town and Country Planning, Moorgate House, Port Louis (tel: 212-6022; fax: 212-7482).

Ministry of Industry and Industrial Technology, Government Centre, Port Louis (tel: 201-1221; fax: 212-8201).

Ministry of Information, Government Centre, Port Louis (tel: 201-1278; fax: 208-8243).

Ministry of Internal and External Communications, Emmanuel Anquetil Bldg, 10th Floor, Sir Seewoosagur Ramgoolam St, Port Louis (tel: 201-1089; fax: 212-1673).

Ministry of Justice, Jules Koenig St, Port Louis (tel: 208-5321).

Ministry of Labour and Industrial Relations, Ming Court, cnr Eugène Laurent and GMD Atchia Sts, Port Louis (tel: 212-3049; fax: 212-3070).

Ministry of Local Government, Government Centre, Port Louis (tel: 201-1215).

Ministry of Manpower Resources and Vocational and Technical Training, Jade House, Remy Ollier St, Port Louis (tel: 242-1462).

Ministry for Rodrigues Island, Fon Sing Bldg, Edith Cavell St, Port Louis (tel: 208-8472; fax: 212-6329).

Ministry of Social Security and National Solidarity, cnr Maillard and Jules Koenig Sts, Port Louis (tel: 212-3006).

Ministry of Trade and Shipping, Government Centre, Port Louis (tel: 201-1067; fax: 212-6386).

Ministry of Women's Rights, Child Development and Family Welfare, Rainbow House, cnr Edith Cavell and Brown Sequard Sts, Port Louis (tel: 208-2061; fax: 208-8250).

Ministry of Works, Treasury Bldg, Port Louis (tel: 208-0281; fax: 212-8373).

Ministry of Youth and Sports, Emmanuel Anquetil Bldg, Sir Seewoosagur Ramgoolam St, Port Louis (tel: 201-1242; fax: 212-6506).

Prime Minister's Office, Government Centre, Port Louis (tel: 201-1001; fax: 208-8619).

Other useful addresses

British High Commission, Commercial Section, 7th Floor, Les Cascades Building, Edith Cavell Street, Port Louis (tel: 208-9850/1; fax: 212-8470).

Export Processing Zone Development Authority, 5th Floor, Les Cascades, Edith Cavell St, Port Louis (tel: 212-9760; fax: 212-9767).

Mauritius Embassy (USA), Suite 441, 4301 Connecticut Avenue, NW, Washington DC 20008 (tel: (+1-202) 244-1491; fax: (+1-202) 966-0983; e-mail: mauritius.embassy@prodigy.net).

Mauritius Employers' Federation, Cerné House, Chausse, Port Louis (tel: 212-1599; fax: 212-6725).

Mauritius Export Processing Zone Association, 42 Sir William Newton St, Port Louis (tel: 208-5216; fax: 212-1853).

Mauritius Free Port Authority, 2nd Floor, Deramann Tower, Sir William Newton St, Port Louis (tel: 212-9627; fax: 212-9629).

Mauritius Industrial Development Authority, Level 2, BAI Bldg, 25 Pope Hennessy St, Port Louis (tel: 208-7750; fax: 208-5965; e-mail: mida@media.intnet.mu).

Mauritius Offshore Business Activities Authority, 1st Floor, Deramann Tower, 30 Sir William Newton St, Port Louis (tel: 212-9650; fax: 212-9459).

Mauritius Standards Bureau, Ministry of Industry and Industrial Technology, Réduit (tel: 454-1933; fax: 464-7675).

Internet sites

Africa Business Network: www.ifc.org/abn

AllAfrica.com: http://allafrica.com

African Development Bank: www.afdb.org

Business Directory: www.mauritius.co.uk/

Mbendi AfroPaedia (information on companies, countries, industries and stock exchanges in Africa): http://mbendi.co.za

Mexico

KEY FACTS

Official name: Estados Unidos Mexicanos (United Mexican States)

Head of State: President Felipe de Jesús Calderón Hinojosa (took office on 1 Dec 2006)

Head of government: President Felipe Calderón (PAN) (from 1 Dec 2006)

Ruling party: Partido Acción Nacional (PAN) (National Action Party) (since 2000, re-elected 6 Jul 2006)

Area: 1,958,201 square km

Population: 105.37 million (2007)

Capital: Mexico City (DF)

Official language: Spanish

Currency: Mexican peso (Mex$) = 100 centavos

Exchange rate: Mex$10.20 per US$ (Jul 2008)

GDP per capita: US$8,479 (2007)*

GDP real growth: 3.30% (2007)

Labour force: 40.74 million (2004)

Unemployment: 3.20% (2004); 25.00% (underemployment, 2004)

Inflation: 3.90% (2007)

Oil production: 3.48 million bpd (2007)

Balance of trade: -US$7.84 billion (2006)

Foreign debt: US$138.69 billion (2005)

Visitor numbers: 21.40 million (2006)*

* estimated figure

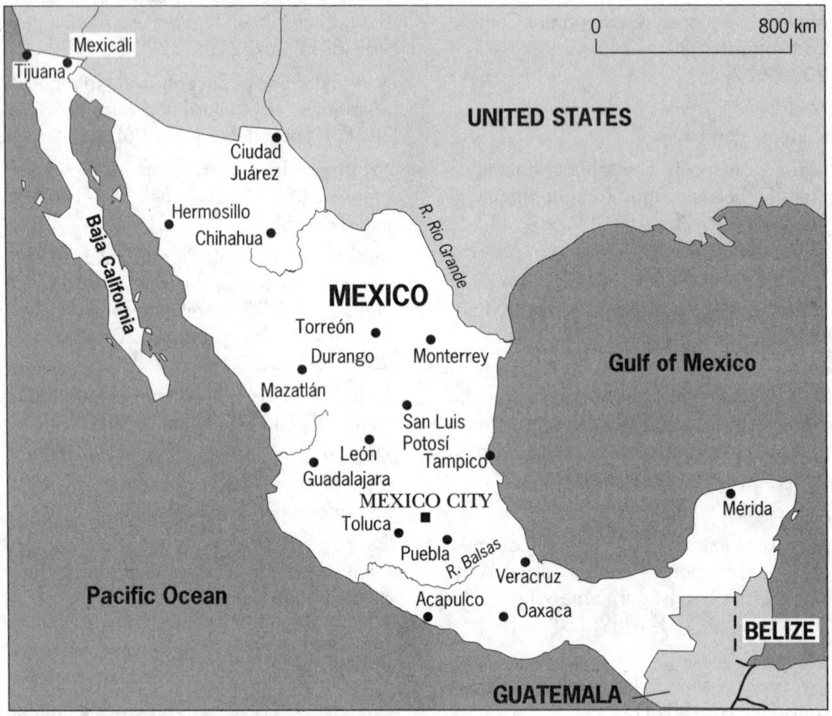

For Mexico, the fast rising prices of food products in late 2007 and early 2008 continued to pose problems for Mexico's poor and, in consequence, for its government. Some 40 per cent of Mexico's population is poor and an estimated 18 per cent is considered to live in extreme poverty. In early 2007, rises in tortilla prices had forced President Calderón to adopt emergency measures including an increase in duty-free imports of corn.

Stable growth, government cuts

In 2006 Mexico received US$18.9 billion in foreign direct investment, positioning it fourth among emerging economies, behind China, Russia and Turkey. According to the World Bank Mexico's positive and stable economic performance together with the official decision to combat poverty has permitted a rise in per capita income levels, though poverty and inequality indices are still very high. According to official estimates, per capita income is US$7,870, Latin America's highest, life expectancy at birth is 75 years and the percentage of school-age children attending schools is 98 per cent. Between 1996 and 2005, Mexico reported an average per capita income growth of 2 per cent annually. Recently Mexico's economic growth has been relatively stable, nearing 3 per cent annually between 2000 and 2007. In order to insure a robust creation of employment opportunities and reduce poverty rates significantly, Mexico needs to improve its competitiveness.

Ironically, in mid-2007 President Calderón's principal concern had been a possible fall in the price of oil. Traditionally, oil has accounted for around 30 per cent of Mexico's fiscal revenues. The 2007 budget had been based on a price of US$42.50 per barrel of exported oil. The government had established a new US$6.2 billion oil stabilisation fund to offset any further drops in the oil price. Mr Calderón had also introduced austerity measures that included a 10 per cent cut in salaries for senior government officials (including his own) that were expected to save as much as US$2.3 billion in 2007. A World

Bank study published in 2006 indicated that the net worth of Mexican billionaires rose to 6 per cent of GDP in 2006, up from a figure of 4 per cent in 2000. The increased wealth was largely created by stock market gains and booming corporate earnings. Worryingly, much of this wealth arose from monopoly enterprises – in one high profile instance, the giant food processor Gruma controls some 70 per cent of Mexico's cornmeal and tortilla market.

Budget concerns

Mexico's 2007 budget had anticipated slower growth in the US economy. It also initially foresaw an inflation rate of 3 per cent for the year despite the fact that core inflation had risen to 3.6 per cent in 2006. According to the United Nations Economic Commission for Latin America and the Caribbean, (ECLAC/CEPAL) private consumption increased by around 4 per cent following increased employment and credit levels. Inflation was by now expected to be around 4 per cent, as a result of higher international prices for food and energy, as well as rises in some domestic prices. Although the floods that struck the Tabasco and Chiapas regions in the final quarter of 2007 affected over a million people, the likely consequences for Mexico's economic growth in 2008 were expected to be marginal.

In 2008, ECLAC saw the Mexican economy growing at the same rate of 3.3 per cent, following the launch of the National Infrastructure Programme 2007–12. Under the programme, planned expenditure for the period was US$232 billion, representing an increase of 50 per cent over the level seen under the previous administration of president Vicente Fox where growth rates averaged below 2 per cent. Infrastructure development was seen by the Calderón administration as a way to address the regional inequalities that had caused the social unrest that expressed itself during the 2006 election period. Public-sector revenues had increased by 2.4 per cent between January and September 2007, as oil revenues dropped by 4.6 per cent, while non-oil revenues rose by 6.4 per cent. Oil revenues declined as a result of the 22.6 per cent fall in hydrocarbon duties and facilities due to lower natural gas prices, smaller volumes of extracted crude and a fall in the amount paid in tax. In contrast, the revenues of the parastatal enterprise Petróleos Mexicanos (PEMEX) grew by 66.4 per cent in real terms as the price of petroleum rose to US$56.37 per barrel by the end of the third quarter, which was much higher than the US$42.5 per barrel set out in the general economic policy guidelines, but as it turned out, much less than the prices being realised by the middle of 2008, which reached twice the guideline price. There were two main factors behind the expansion of non-oil revenues: first, the considerable increase in duties and facilities, and second, higher receipts from income tax, VAT and the special tax on production and services. In the case of VAT, the improvement was due to increased sales. As for the special tax on production and services, it was due to increased receipts from alcoholic beverages and tobacco. Higher than-expected receipts made it possible to raise real budgetary expenditure in the public sector by 2.7 per cent between January and September, at the time of a 5.2 per cent rise in current expenditure and, above all, a 15 per cent rise increase in capital expenditure. Physical investment expanded by 2.5 per cent to represent 15.8 per cent of programmable spending. Public-sector borrowing requirements are estimated to stand at 1.6 per cent of GDP, which is double the amount recorded in 2006. In September, Congress approved an amended version of the fiscal reform initiative proposed by the executive. Once the law was adopted, the government expected tax revenues to rise by 1.1 per cent of GDP in 2008, and by up to 2.1 per cent in 2012.

A key factor in Mexico's economic activity was the slowdown in demand from the United States, which failed to be offset the higher sales of cars and other durables to Japan and the European Union. Internal demand, following six months of extremely slow growth, was estimated to have gradually expanded in the second half of the year in response to the recovery in employment and credit. The positive performance in terms of supply was spearheaded by services, which grew by around 4 per cent as a result of the good results in communications and transport, as well as financial services and insurance. Manufacturing lost momentum due to reduced production of wood and wood products, textiles and clothing and other manufactures, while production increased in machinery and equipment, paper, printing and publishing and non-metallic minerals. Particularly striking was the 10.3 per cent annual expansion (October to October) of automobile production, especially for the export market. Mexico's employment rate dropped, as unemployment rose from 3.6 per cent of the economically active population (EAP) between January and September 2006 to 3.8 per cent in the same period of 2007. According to the national survey on occupation and employment, 11.2 per cent of the EAP were in critical employment conditions in the third

KEY INDICATORS **Mexico**

	Unit	2003	2004	2005	2006	2007
Population	m	102.60	102.80	103.09	104.22	*105.37
Gross domestic product (GDP)	US$bn	626.10	683.51	767.69	840.01	893.37
GDP per capita	US$	6,006	6,506	7,447	8,060	*8,479
GDP real growth	%	1.3	4.4	2.8	4.8	3.3
Inflation	%	4.5	4.7	4.0	3.6	3.9
Unemployment	%	2.4	2.7	3.6	3.6	–
Industrial output	% change	–	4.2	1.6	5.0	–
Agricultural output	% change	–	3.2	-1.5	4.8	–
Oil output	'000 bpd	3,789.0	3,824.0	3,759.0	3,683.0	3,477.0
Natural gas output	bn cum	36.4	37.1	39.5	43.4	46.2
Coal output	mtoe	5.0	4.3	4.8	5.3	9.2
Exports (fob) (goods)	US$m	164,240.0	187,999.0	214,233.0	250,292.0	–
Imports (cif) (goods)	US$m	169,634.0	196,810.0	221,820.0	256,131.0	–
Balance of trade	US$m	-5,394.0	-8,811.0	-7,587.0	-5,839.0	–
Current account	US$m	-8,560.0	-8,710.0	-4,897.0	-2,220.0	-7,370.0
Total reserves minus gold	US$m	58,956.0	64,141.0	74,054.0	76,271.0	87,109.0
Foreign exchange	US$m	57,740.0	62,778.0	73,015.0	75,448.0	86,309.0
Exchange rate	per US$	10.81	11.29	10.97	10.85	10.82

* estimated figure

quarter of the year, while almost 27 per cent were in informal employment. As a result of the slower economic pace in the US, the growth rate of the value of exports more than halved from 19.8 per cent between January and September 2006 to 6.6 per cent in the same period of 2007. At the same time, there were striking increases in imports of consumer goods (15.1 per cent) and capital goods (11.6 per cent). All of the above generated a trade deficit that was US$5.633 billion wider than it was in the period January–September 2006.

Oil on the wane

According to the US Energy Information Authority (EIA), by 2007 Mexico's oil production had begun to decrease, as production at the giant Cantarell field declined. The oil sector continued to generate over 10 per cent of export earnings.

According to the US based *Oil and Gas Journal* (OGJ), Mexico had 12.2 billion barrels of proven oil reserves as of end January 2007. Most reserves consist of heavy crude oil varieties, with a specific gravity of less than 25 degrees API. The largest concentration of remaining reserves occurs offshore in the southern part of the country, especially in the Campeche Basin. There are also sizable reserves in Mexico's onshore basins in the northern parts of the country.

In 2007, Mexico was the sixth-largest producer of oil in the world. The country produced an average of 3.71 million barrels per day (bpd) of total oil liquids, down from 3.63 million bpd in 2006. Of Mexico's oil production, about 88 per cent is crude oil and condensate, the rest consisting of natural gas liquids (NGL) and refinery gain. Many analysts believe that Mexican oil production has peaked, and that the country's production will continue to decline in the coming years. Based on its December 2007 Short Term Energy Outlook, EIA forecasts that Mexico will produce 3.32 million bpd in 2008. According to Petróleos Mexicanos (PEMEX) Mexico's state-owned petroleum company, Mexico's reserves/production ratio (based on previous-year production levels) fell from 20 years in 2002 to 10 years in 2006. It is generally considered that Pemex does not have sufficient funds available for exploration and investment to reverse the decline, owing to the larger amount of its revenues that the company transfers to the federal government.

Mexico had some 13.01 trillion cubic feet (Tcf) of proven natural gas reserves as of end-2007. According to Pemex, the Southern Region of the country contains the largest share of proven reserves. However, the Northern Region will likely be the centre of future reserves growth, as it contains almost ten times as much probable and possible natural gas reserves as the Southern Region. In 2007, Mexico produced 46.2 billion cubic metres (bcm) of natural gas, while consuming 54.1bcm. Pemex reported that Mexico imported 451 million cubic feet per day (MMcf/d) of natural gas in 2006.

Mexico's natural gas production has grown in recent years, following steady declines during the late 1990s. During that time, natural gas consumption has grown steadily, driven mostly by the electricity sector, whose share of total natural gas consumption increased from 16 per cent in 1996 to 32 per cent in 2006. Pemex itself is the single largest consumer of natural gas, representing around 40 per cent of domestic consumption in 2006.

Risk assessment

Economy	Good
Politics	Good
Regional stability	Good

COUNTRY PROFILE

Historical profile

The Olmecs inhabited the country around 3,500 years ago, their civilisation reaching its peak about 1200 BC. By AD 500–600, the Mayas had risen to prominence and Teotihuacan (where Mexico City now stands) was thriving, with 200,000 inhabitants.

1519 The Spanish, and Hernan Cortés, arrived. The Aztecs were the dominant culture.

1810–21 The Spanish colony became independent. Conflicts with the US and France ensued.

1876–1910 The Porfirio Díaz dictatorship, known as the Porfiriato, led to a series of revolutions and coups.

1911 Díaz resigned and was replaced by Francisco Madero, one of the revolutionary leaders.

1911–17 A period of civil war, with revolutionary peasant leaders Francisco Villa and Emiliano Zapata refusing to back the government.

1914 General Venustiano Carranza seized power, preventing the re-emergence of the Porfiriato.

1917 The institution of Mexico's modern liberal constitution which enshrined land reform and labour rights.

1920 Carranza was assassinated. Civil war broke out.

1929 President Plutarco Elías Calles created the Partido Nacional Revolucionario (PNR) (National Revolutionary Party), a multi-class party that developed institutionalised mechanisms which enabled and controlled popular participation in government.

1934 General Lázaro Cárdenas became president and restructured the PNR, renaming it the Partido de la Revolución Mexicana (PRM) (Party of the Mexican Revolution). He also created official unions for workers and peasants, which were controlled by the official party.

1939 Disenchanted middle-class conservatives launched the Partido de Acción Nacional (PAN) (National Action Party).

1940 Leon Trotsky was assassinated in Mexico.

1946 Miguel Alemán became president and renamed the ruling party the Partido Revolucionario Institucional (PRI) (Institutional Revolutionary Party), signifying the final transition from the ideals of the revolution to liberal capitalism and a corporatist state.

1968 Growing disenchantment with authoritarian politics and rising urban poverty led to a series of mass demonstrations, culminating in a massacre of several hundred peaceful demonstrators, most of them young students.

1970 Luis Echeverría Alvarez became president, seeking to calm political turbulence through increased state spending and bolstering the power of trade unions.

1976 José López Portillo was appointed president. Oil revenues were used to borrow additional capital to initiate a rapid transition towards industrial development.

1982 An economic recession in the US, high international interest rates and falling oil prices sparked a debt crisis in which Mexico was unable to obtain enough loans to service existing debts and ran out of money. A programme of economic stabilisation and structural adjustment was initiated under the administration of President Miguel de la Madrid, creating divisions within the PRI.

1988 The PRI split. The left-wing corriente democrática joined a coalition of minor parties to back the candidacy of Cuauhtémoc Cárdenas, son of former president, Lázaro Cárdenas, in the presidential elections. Despite massive electoral fraud, Cárdenas still managed to come second behind the PRI's Carlos Salinas de Gortari.

1992 As part of Mexico's commitments in the run-up to the signing of the North American Free Trade Agreement (Nafta), Salinas effectively repealed Article 27 of the Mexican Constitution which had guaranteed land reform.

1994 The Zapatistas led an uprising in Chiapas in response to the treatment of

indigenous peasants and neo-liberal economic policy. The Zapatistas attracted worldwide sympathy and attention was fixed on the effects of economic policy and Nafta on the growing number of Mexico's poor. The PRI's presidential candidate, Luis Donaldo Colosio, was murdered; many believed the killing was carried out by members of his own party.
1994 Ernesto Zedillo of the PRI won the presidential election amid accusations of dirty tricks and vote-buying.
1997 Mid-term congressional elections left the PRI as the biggest single party in the lower house of Congress, but denied it an absolute majority. A deal was struck between the left-wing Partido de la Revolución Democrática (PRD) (Party of the Democratic Revolution) and the traditionally conservative Partido Acción Nacional (PAN), as well as two smaller parties, giving the opposition its first taste of real power.
2000 PAN won the elections, and the PRI lost the presidency and its majority in the Senate, as well as its status as the party with the largest number of seats in the lower house. The break with PRI rule was historic as the party, including its previous incarnations, had enjoyed continuous office since 1929.
2001 The Senate unanimously approved a constitutional bill granting autonomy to indigenous people, opening the way for peace talks with the Zapatista rebels, although this fell short of the demands of the Zapatistas.
2002 Roberto Madrazo won the elections for the leadership of PRI.
2004 A federal investigation was ordered into the unsolved murder of 250 women, over a ten-year period, in the border town of Ciudad Juarez. Around 250,000 people demonstrated in Mexico City, against official ineffectiveness in the face of violent crime and kidnappings.
2005 Six prison officers were murdered and all high security jails were put on high alert, following an escalation of tension between the authorities and drug gangs. Mexico City mayor Andrés Manuel López Obrador was stripped of his immunity from prosecution in a land expropriation dispute, but the case was later dropped.
2006 Felipe de Jesús Calderón Hinojosa narrowly won the presidential election with 35.88 per cent of votes, defeating his rival Andrés Manuel López Obrador with 35.31 per cent. Despite the challenge to the result, the Federal Election Tribunal confirmed Calderón's victory. President declared war on drug cartels with a new federal police force and the deployment of thousands of troops to the western state of Michoacán.
2007 In February, over 75,000 people protested in Mexico City and more in other locations, at the rapid rise in prices of basic foodstuff. Tortillas, the staple food particularly among the poor, rose by 40 per cent in the previous months and at a rate far quicker that inflation in general. The price increases were largely due to the cost of maize imports from the US where such produce has been redirected for use in bio-fuel.
2008 The death toll of 1,400, due to organised drug cartels, was recorded in the first five months and was 4,000 since the beginning of the police crackdown in 2006. In July, the navy seized a makeshift submarine smuggling almost six tonnes of cocaine to the US, while the army seized 12 tonnes of marijuana in Tijuana.

Political structure

Constitution

The political system established by the 1917 constitution emphasises presidential power.
Mexico is a federal republic of 31 states and one federal district (Mexico City). States are divided into municipalities. State governors are directly elected every six years. Deputies of state legislatures hold office for three years. The states are empowered to raise taxes and introduce and enforce state laws.
In order to register for federal elections, political parties must have a total of at least 65,000 party members and must have 3,000 supporters per state in at least 16 states or 300 party members per constituency in at least half of the constituencies which return deputies elected by majority vote. Alternatively, a party may be allowed conditional registration if it has been active for four years. This conditional registration can be converted to official registration if the party then obtains at least 1.5 per cent of the vote. In 1989, a law was adopted giving a party obtaining 35 per cent of the vote in a general election an absolute majority in the chamber of deputies.

Form of state

Federal presidential democratic republic

The executive

The president is directly elected by majority vote for a period of six years and takes office on 1 December of the election year, but is unable to stand for a second term. The president is assisted by a cabinet (usually 19 members), one of whom is the governor of the Federal District (the administrative area which includes the capital, Mexico City), the attorney general for the country as a whole and the attorney general for the Federal District. The cabinet is appointed by the president.
The president also appoints the judges of the supreme court and higher courts of justice, the senior officers of the armed forces and diplomats, but these appointments are subject to approval by the Senate.

National legislature

The Congreso de la Union (congress) is a bicameral legislature consisting of the 500-member Camara de Diputados (chamber of deputies), elected for a three-year term, and the 64-member Camara de Senadores (senate), whose members are elected every six years. Members of both chambers are ineligible for immediate re-election.
The senate is elected by majority vote and is composed of two members for each of the 31 states and two members for the Distrito Federal (federal district – Mexico City).
Of the deputies, 300 are elected by majority vote and 200 by proportional representation of political party lists.
A permanent committee, composed of 15 deputies and 14 senators, acts in place of the Congress when the Congress is in recess.

Legal system

Under the 1917 constitution, the judiciary is independent of the executive and legislative bodies, but in practice the judiciary tends not to oppose the president.
The judicial system is divided into federal and state judiciaries.
The federal system has both ordinary and constitutional jurisdiction. It consists of the 21-member supreme court (which deals with penal, administrative, civil and labour cases), collegiate circuit courts (cases regarding an individual's constitutional rights) and unitary circuit courts (appeals). There are 12 collegiate circuits and nine unitary circuits. There are 68 district courts.

Last elections

2 July 2006 (presidential and parliamentary)
Results: Chamber of Deputies: Partido Acción Nacional (PAN) (National Action Party) won 41.2 per cent of votes (206 out of 500); Alianze por el Bien de Todos (ABT) (Alliance for the good of all) (including Partido de la Revolución Democrática (PRD) (Party of the Democratic Revolution) 25.4 per cent (127) and Convergencia (C) (Convergence)) 29.0 per cent (159); Alianza por México (AM) (Alliance for Mexico) (including Partido Revolucionario Institucional (PRI) (Institutional Revolutionary Party) 20.6 per cent (103) and the Partido Verde Ecologista de México (PVEM) (Green Ecologist Party of Mexico)) 28.2 per cent (122); Partido Neuva Alianza (PNA) New Alliance Party 4.5 per cent (9); Partido Alternativa Socialdemócrata y Campesina (PASC) (Social Democratic and Peasant Alternative Party) 2.1 per cent (4).
Senate: PAN won 34.1 per cent (11 seats out of 128); ABT 29.8 per cent (36), AM

27.4 per cent (38), PNA 4.2 per cent (1), PASC 2.0 per cent (1).
Presidential: Felipe de Jesús Calderón Hinojosa narrowly won with 35.88 per cent of votes; Manuel López Obrador won 35.31 per cent.

Next elections
2009 (parliamentary); 2012 (presidential)

Political parties

Ruling party
Partido Acción Nacional (PAN) (National Action Party) (since 2000, re-elected 6 Jul 2006)

Main opposition party
Alianze por el Bien de Todos (ABT) (Alliance for the good of all) coalition (including Partido de la Revolución Democrática (PRD) (Party of the Democratic Revolution) 25.4 per cent (127) and Convergencia (C) (Convergence))

Population

105.37 million (2007)
Last census: February 2000: 97,483,412
Population density: 51 inhabitants per square km (2000). Urban population: 74 per cent (1995–2001).
Annual growth rate: 1.5 per cent 1994–2004 (WHO 2006)

Ethnic make-up
Mestizo (mixed Indian-European) (55 per cent), Amerindian (29 per cent), European origin (16 per cent).

Religions
Roman Catholic (89 per cent), Protestant (6 per cent).

Education

Compulsory education is provided free of charge. Primary schooling lasts for six years; secondary education (which begins at age 12), is divided into two cycles of three years. Students either follow an academic or technical programme of education, which can lead on to higher education or specialised training.
In 1985, the government reorganised state education with priority given to literacy. A high proportion of spending has traditionally gone into higher education, with much of this devoted to adult literacy. While higher education has received relatively strong funding, the school system suffers from low teachers' pay, a consequent lack of teacher motivation and poor equipment. There is a high student drop-out rate from schools. Legal restrictions on religious education have reduced the willingness of the Catholic Church to provide education on a fee-paying basis. However, the falling birth rate has relieved some pressure on the school system. The student-teacher ratio, which reached a high point of 35.67 in 1964, improved during the 1980s and 1990s and was 27 by 2002.
At university level the private sector is active, although most Mexicans still attend state universities where fees are low. Standards are variable but often good. However, only a minority of students attending university complete their studies.
Literacy rate: 91 per cent adult rate; 97 per cent youth rate (15–24) (Unesco 2005).
Compulsory years: Six to 16
Enrolment rate: 106 per cent gross primary enrolment of relevant age group (including repeaters); 64 per cent gross secondary enrolment; 16 per cent in tertiary education (World Bank).
Pupils per teacher: 27 in primary schools (World Bank)

Health

Per capita total expenditure on health (2003) was US$582; of which per capita government spending was US$270, at the international dollar rate, (WHO 2006).
By 2002, 96 per cent of infants aged less than one year had been immunised against measles. Access to clean drinking water is available to over 80 per cent of the population.
About half of the hospitals belong to the Instituto Mexicano del Seguro Social (IMSS) (Mexican Institute for Social Security).

HIV/Aids
HIV prevalence: 0.3 per cent aged 15–49 in 2003 (World Bank)
Life expectancy: 74 years, 2004 (WHO 2006)
Fertility rate/Maternal mortality rate: 2.3 births per woman, 2004 (WHO 2006)
Child (under 5 years) mortality rate (per 1,000): 23 per 1,000 live births; about 7.5 per cent of children aged under five are malnourished (World Bank).

Welfare

Social welfare is administered primarily by the IMSS and financed by contributions from employees, employers and the government. Some institutions, such as Petróleos Mexicanos (Pemex) (Mexican Petroleum), the military and the Federal Electricity Commission, have their own systems. About half of the working population is covered by social security. There is no unemployment benefit.
Since 1997, Mexicans have been able to sign up with private pension fund administrators, bypassing the IMSS, notorious for its inefficiencies as a state operator. The previous government led by the Partido Revolucionario Institucional (PRI) (Institutional Revolutionary Party) transferred the pension system from a state-funded pay-as-you-go basis to a scheme where private fund administrators compete for workers' pension contributions.

Main cities
Mexico City (capital, estimated population 8.5 million in 2005; 2,240 metres above sea-level), Ecatepec (2.0m), Guadalajara (1.6m), Puebla (1.4m), Ciudad Juárez (1.4m), Tijuana (1.5m), Nezahualcóyotl (1.2m), Monterrey (1.1m), León (1.2m), Zapopan (1.2m), Naucalpan (865,256), Tlalnepantla (699,847), Guadelupe (776,098), Acapulco (743,112), San Luis Potosí (721,619), Aguascalientes (707,964), Chihuahua (751,100), Merida (750,855).

Languages spoken

Native American languages spoken include Náhuati, Maya and Zapoteco.
Some English is spoken in business centres.

Official language/s
Spanish

Media

Press
Dailies: There are several Spanish language dailies published from Mexico City and other regions, the most influential being Excélsior, La Crónica de Hoy, El Debate, Diario de Chihuahua, El Diario de Yucatan, Frontera, El Heraldo de Chihuahua, El Heraldo de México, El Imparcial, El Día, El Independiente, El Informador, La Jornada, Kesher Editorial, La Mañana, El Mañana, Mural, Reforma, El Universal, Uno más uno, El Norte and Novedades.
English language publications include a daily colour tabloid El Nacional, Diario de Juárez, Público, The News and the bi-lingual Novedades Quintana Roo (Spanish, English).
The sport papers Esto and Ovaciones have the largest circulations.
Weeklies: Gringo Gazette is an English language bi-weekly newspaper covering local news, recreation, entertainment, and community events in southern Baja.
Business: Business publications include El Financiero and the daily El Economista.

Broadcasting
Radio: Over 800 commercial and 45 cultural radio stations. Radio VIP in Mexico City broadcasts in English.
The largest radio station is Radio Centro. Approximately a third of the population owns a radio set.
Television: Most Mexicans have access to a television set. There are over 400 television stations. The largest is Televisa, a private company, which closely follows the government line but operates independently. It has four channels, one of which is broadcast nationally. The company estimates that its main news programme, 24 Hours, reaches an average of 14 million viewers. The second largest station, Channel 13, estimates that its main news programme, 7 Days, is watched on average by six million people.

Advertising

Annual advertising expenditure is equivalent to 1.2 per cent of GDP. Most international advertising companies have offices in Mexico City. Television advertising dominates the sector, but billboards are popular. This is partly because restrictions on tobacco and alcohol advertising do not apply to billboards, and partly owing to the high population density in the three main cities, especially Mexico City, which contains half the country's 15,000 billboards.

Economy

The economy has drawn praise from the IMF as it recovered since 2003, and achieved much of the government's objectives. GDP growth was 3.0 per cent in 2005 and was expected to rise to 4.0 per cent in 2006. Inflation fell to an estimated 3.3 in 2006 while unemployment in the formal sector increased by over 6.5 per cent in June, its fastest rise since 2001. Public debt and the fiscal deficit both continued to decline as high global oil prices, as well as non-oil revenues, strengthened. Mexico is a large oil producer with exports accounting for just under one-third of government revenue.

One-tenth of the population live and work abroad, remittances from Mexican expatriates, mostly in the US, reached US$23.5 billion in 2006 and outstripped the value of the tourist sector.

Mexico's membership of the North American Free Trade Agreement (NAFTA) since 1994 has encouraged massive inflows of foreign direct investment (FDI), which in turn have transformed Mexico into a manufacturing base serving not only its large domestic market but more particularly its huge neighbour, the US market. Virtually all the world's major companies are now present in Mexico. Asian electronics companies, for instance, proliferate in the state of Baja California, which is host to a multitude of operations run by companies based in the Far East. The rise of Chinese exports to the US is beginning to have an adverse affect on Mexican exports.

Despite this, the services sector has steadily risen, providing 70 per cent of GDP and growing by 3.9 per cent in 2005. Industry constitutes 26 per cent, of which manufacturing accounts for 18 per cent. Agriculture provides only 3.8 per cent of GDP and fell by 1.5 per cent in 2005.

Mexico has largely de-coupled its economy from Brazil, and now has much stronger ties with the US. Underpinning this has been a shift from an oil-based economy to a manufacturing-based economy, driven by the initial growth of the maquiladoras (in-bond assembly lines) and the development of import-export business, particularly in the car and light manufacturing industries.

The overall expansion of the Mexican economy has increased jobs in the formal sector and bolstered disposable income. Together with a strong peso, this led to a surge in imports, although high oil export prices have limited the deterioration of the trade deficit. Oil exploration is underway as the ratio of proven oil reserves to production falls and reduced oil revenue has an adverse effect on the economy.

The OECD 2005 Economic Policy Reforms made a number of employment related recommendations including making the school system more effective, eliminating barriers to the telecommunications sector, easing restrictions on FDI, reforming the tax system and improving the 'rule of law'.

External trade

Mexico is a member of the North American Free Trade Agreement (Nafta), with the United States and Canada. Mexico has also signed free trade agreements with the European Union, the Central American Free Trade Agreement (DR-Cafta) and Japan.

The economy is heavily dependent on trade, and foreign trade accounts for around 60 per cent of GDP, of which 80 per cent is carried on with the US. There are free economic zones, Maquiladoras, where semi-manufactured and duty-free goods are assembled and shipped directly to the US. A leading Maquiladoras product was finished garments but heavy competition from Asian manufacturers has resulting in a drop in production since 2005.

Mexico is a leading world exporter of many minerals and agricultural products as well as petroleum and natural gas. Over two million vehicles were assembled in Mexico in 2006, with most destined for the US and Canada.

Imports

Principal imports are metalworking machines, steel mill products, agricultural machinery, electrical equipment, capital machinery for car assembly and aircraft building and parts.

Main sources: US (50.9 per cent total, 2006), China (9.5 per cent), Japan (6.0 per cent).

Exports

Principal exports are manufactured and assembled goods, petroleum and oil products, vehicles and auto parts, silver, cotton, corn, oranges and other fruits, vegetables and coffee, mercury, zinc and fluorite.

Main destinations: US (84.8 per cent total, 2006), Canada (2.1 per cent), Spain (1.3 per cent)

Agriculture

Farming

Approximately 5 per cent of Mexico's total GDP is attributable to the agricultural sector. Despite this relatively low percentage contribution to GDP, the labour intensive nature of the agricultural sector ensures that it employs up to a quarter of the total workforce.

Farming is small-scale and frequently inefficient. About 50 per cent of total cultivatable land (estimated at 19 million hectares) is held by ejidos, rural communities farming on small individual/collective lots. There are few large commercial farms except in export-oriented vegetable-producing regions of the north-west. The principal food crops are maize (over 50 per cent of harvested area and 60 per cent of total grain production), sorghum, wheat, rice, barley, potatoes, soya beans and dry beans. The production of basic foodstuffs can be severely affected by drought, insufficient irrigation (less than 30 per cent of cultivated land is irrigated) and underdeveloped marketing and infrastructural back-up. Supplies of food grain in particular have not kept up with the demands imposed by rapid population growth. Principal export crops are coffee, cotton, fresh fruit, honey, sugar, tobacco and tomatoes. Exports of cattle are also important.

Mexico's membership of the North American Free Trade Agreement (Nafta) has affected the farming sector, with the US dominating trade. In the five years prior to the implementation of Nafta in January 1994, farm output grew by 3.85 million tonnes, compared to an increase of just 2.1 million tonnes in the five years after the agreement came into effect. Between 1995 and 2001, the value of farm imports from the US increased from US$3.3 billion to US$7.4 billion, while Mexico's farm exports to the US grew from US$3.8 billion to US$5.3 billion. Mexico has become increasingly dependent on US food imports and by 2002 imported 95 per cent of the soya beans, 59 per cent of the rice and 40 per cent of the beef consumed domestically.

President Fox's pro-Nafta approach has come under increasing criticism from the Mexican public. Farmers fear that the subsidies to US's farmers will put them out of business. In January 2003, tariffs on 80 agricultural imports from the US and Canada were lifted as part of Nafta's provisions. Farmers' unions called on the government to renegotiate the trading rules, but the government refused and offered to negotiate a package of compensatory policies instead.

Crop production in 2005 included: 31,250,884 tonnes (t) cereals in total, 20,500,000t maize, 3,000,000t wheat,

1,109,420t barley, 6,300,000t sorghum, 1,734,810t potatoes, 2,026,610t bananas, 959,000t coconuts, 45,126,500t sugar cane, 310,861t green coffee, 48,405t cocoa beans, 2,148,130t tomatoes, 21,895t tobacco, 6,475,411t citrus fruit, 146,636t fibre crops, 333,501t oilcrops, 22,500t natural rubber, 1,040,390t avocados, 1,503,010t mangoes, 1,853,610t chillies and peppers, 456,638t grapes, 14,758,654t fruit in total, 10,013,516t vegetables in total. Livestock production included: 5,040,237t meat in total, 1,543,090t beef, 1,058,205t pig meat, 42,140t lamb, 41,626t goat meat, 2,272,080t poultry, 1,906,476t eggs, 10,028,233t milk, 56,808t honey, 5,661t sheepskins, 4,282t greasy wool, 7,350t goatskins, 176,230t cattle hides.

Fishing

Mexico's level of fish production is relatively high, with demand being met almost entirely by domestic production. Imports represent only 8.2 per cent of total seafood consumption.

Shrimps, tuna, mackerel, bass, perch, bonito, shark, oysters have risen in importance in the Mexican fishing sector. The leading fish producing states – Sinaloa, Sonora, Baja California, Veracruz and Baja California Sur – contribute to approximately 65.2 per cent of the country's total catch. Annually 70 per cent of the total catch comes from the Pacific Ocean compared to 30 per cent from the Gulf of Mexico, Caribbean and non-coastal states.

In 2004, the total marine fish catch was 1,079,326 tonnes and the total crustacean catch was 79,897 tonnes.

Forestry

Approximately 55.2 million hectares of Mexico's total landmass is covered by forests and the country is endowed with vast resources of soft and hard woods. Around 4 per cent of the country's total forested area is protected.

Most forestry products are produced for domestic consumption, mainly softwood sawnwood and wood-based panels. Timber imports in 2004 were US$3.3 billion, while exports amounted to US$312.3 million.

Timber production in 2004 included 45,181,734 cubic metre (cum) roundwood, 6,913,000cum industrial roundwood, 2,962,000cum sawnwood, 5,737,000cum sawlogs and veneer logs, 954,000t pulpwood, 430,000cum wood-based panels, 38,268,734cum woodfuel; 100,000 tonnes (t) charcoal, 4,391,000t paper and paperboard, (including 252,000t newsprint), 759,000t printing and writing paper, 375,000t paper pulp, 920,000t recovered paper.

Industry and manufacturing

The industrial sector is an important economic activity in Mexico, accounting for a significant proportion (29 per cent) of total GDP. About one fifth of total employment is accounted for by the sector.

The maquiladoras (in-bond assembly lines) make, assemble or process components and raw materials bought 'in-bond' from the US which are then re-exported duty-free. The growing importance of maquiladora exports to the US has made the Mexican economy more exposed to US demand. The US economic slowdown in 2001 and 2002 led to a contraction in the maquiladora sector.

Tourism

Mexico's tourism industry continues to grow strongly and the country remains Latin America's premier tourist destination. Travel and tourism now accounts for 14.5 per cent of total GDP and 14.2 per cent of total employment. Capital investment in the industry has also increased significantly in recent years and now accounts for 10.4 per cent of total capital investment in the economy.

Mexico rode out the effects of events such as the 11 September 2001 terrorist attacks in the US, suffering only a slight fall in visitor numbers to 19.8 million in 2002, while revenues increased. The sector was in recovery by 2004 and the prospects for considerable expansion are encouraging, with 20,237,400 people visiting the country in 2004 alone. This stability has been partly due to more Americans, wishing to avoid overseas travel and to holiday closer to home, visiting Mexico, many by cruise ships.

Environment

In November 2007, the worst flooding in recorded history struck in the southern state of Tabasco affecting more that two million people and trapping around 300,000 in their homes. With 70 per cent of the state underwater it was estimated that the entire state's crop production was lost. Dozen of people were killed in neighbouring Chiapas State where the rain caused mud slides and buried a village. When foreign aid began to arrive distribution was found to be particularly difficult as the roads were unusable.

Mining

Mining is an important industry in Mexico and the country is a major producer of gold, silver and base metals. Mexico accounts for approximately 17 per cent of total world production of silver, 38 per cent of celestite production and 29 per cent of bismuth production. The mining sector continues to attract significant foreign investment, the vast majority of which comes from the US and Canada.

There are four major domestic producers: Industrias Peñoles, Grupo Industrial Menera Mexico, Empresas Frisco and Luismin. The main mining states are Sonora, Coahuila, Zacatecas, Chihuahua, Baja California Sur, San Luis Potosí, Durango and Guanajuato.

Hydrocarbons

Mexico is a significant producer of oil, with large proven reserves of 14.8 billion barrels. The country has the fourth largest proven reserves in the Western Hemisphere and produces some 3.8 million barrels per day (bpd). Net exports of oil amount to approximately 1.7 million bpd, the vast majority of which (79 per cent) is exported to the US.

Oil revenues account for one-third of total government income. Although Mexico is not a member of the Organisation of the Petroleum Exporting Countries (OPEC), government policy has often been to cut production in line with OPEC targets in an effort to increase world prices.

Most oil fields lie in or near the Gulf of Mexico. The largest producing field is within the Gulf of Campeche, which produces, on average, 65 per cent of total oil output. Mexico has the eleventh-largest refining capacity in the world which has improved the country's export potential. Mexico has six refineries with a total capacity of 1.5 million bpd. The government plans to increase refinery capacity by 350,000bpd in 2006.

Mexico has proven gas reserves of 420 billion cubic metres with production of 37.1 billion cubic metres. Most gas production is associated with oil extraction. Gas production is increasingly unable to fulfil domestic demand and Mexico is likely to import an increasing amount of gas from the US. However, Petróleos Mexicanos (Pemex), the state oil corporation, believes that by 2008, gas production will have increased by 50 per cent over 1999 levels. Although Pemex dominates the upstream gas industry, the downstream sector has undergone liberalisation since the passing of the 1995 Natural Gas Law, which allows private companies to participate in gas transportation, storage and distribution.

Mexico has proven coal reserves of 1.2 billion tonnes, mostly located in Coahuila in the north-east. Most is used for steel production and electricity generation. Coal-fired generators supply 10 per cent of Mexico's electricity output.

Energy

Mexico's capacity for electricity generation is approximately 45.9GW, an increase on recent years. Approximately 83 per cent of total electricity generated comes from conventional thermal sources, 9 per cent from hydroelectricity and 5 per cent from

nuclear power, while 3 per cent is derived from other renewables. Mexico's energy minister has stated that the country will need to spend about US$51 billion over the next 10 years in order to meet demand for electricity in the country. This would mean the construction of an extra 28GW of electricity generation capacity. Plans to construct three nuclear plants have been delayed, although the Laguna Verde plant has already been charged with radioactive materials. Hydroelectricity consumption is constant; nuclear energy consumption is declining marginally.
There has been considerable congressional opposition to President Fox's moves to privatise the electricity sector, including his moves to decrease subsidies for electricity charges to consumers. However, independent power producers (IPPs) have become a major source of investment in the Mexican electricity sector.

Banking and insurance
Mexico's banking and financial services sector is now well established, following privatisation in 1990. The sector had previously been nationalised in 1982. There are three main types of account held in Mexican banks; peso denominated checking accounts, US dollar checking accounts and certificates of deposit
Banco de México issues currency, controls monetary policy and is responsible for exchange rates and national reserves. Participation of the private sector is encouraged in a capital market involving leasing, mutual funds, insurance and brokerage. The banking crisis of 1995 caused by the turmoil of peso devaluation, resulted in the closure of several banks. The government was forced to inject huge amounts of emergency capital into the system. Mexico had 44 banks, 13 of which were government-owned.
Banamex is the country's largest bank, and comprises the operations of Citigroup and Banacci, which merged in August 2001.

Central bank
Banco de México

Main financial centre
Mexico City

Time
Central Mexico: GMT minus six hours (daylight saving, minus five hours)
Northern Mexico: GMT minus seven hours (daylight saving, minus six hours)
Sonora State: GMT minus seven hours (no daylight saving)
Baja State: GMT minus eight hours (daylight saving minus seven hours)

Geography
Mexico has a northern frontier of 2,400km with the US and a southern frontier of 885km with Guatemala and Belize. It has a coastline of 2,780km on the Gulf of Mexico and the Caribbean and of 7,360km on the Pacific and the Gulf of California.
Mexico comprises a great variety of terrain, ranging from swamp to desert, from tropical lowland jungle to high alpine vegetation and from thin, arid soils to others so rich that they can support three crops a year. More than half the country is at an altitude of over 1,000 metres and much is over 2,000 metres.
The centre is flanked by an eastern and a western range of mountains running roughly parallel to the coasts. The northern part of the plateau is low, arid and thinly populated. The southern section of the central plateau is crossed by a volcanic range of mountains. The mountainous southern end of the plateau, the heart of Mexico, has ample rainfall and although comprising only 14 per cent of the land, it holds nearly half the country's population. Mexico City lies in a small high basin measuring 50 square km.

Hemisphere
Northern

Climate
Varies with altitude. Tropical southern region and coastlands are hot and wet, while the highlands of the central plateau are temperate. Temperature in Mexico City ranges from 5–25 degrees Celsius (C) with occasional sharp frosts in winter (December–February).
Climate and vegetation depend on altitude. The tierra caliente (hot area) takes in the coastal and plateau lands below 750 metres. The tierra fria (cold zone) is from 2,000 metres upwards. The climate of the inland highlands is mostly mild, but with sharp changes of temperature between day and night, sunshine and shade.
Generally, winter is the dry season and summer the wet season. There are only two areas where sufficient rain falls all year round. The first lies south of Tampico, the capital of Tamaulipas state, along the lower slopes of the Sierra Madre Oriental and across the isthmus of Tehuantepec into Tabasco state, and the second along the Pacific coast state of Chiapas. The two areas represent about 12 per cent of the total surface area. Apart from these favoured regions, the rest of Mexico is arid.

Dress codes
People generally dress smartly in Mexico City. Shorts are worn only at holiday resorts. Dress codes for business and leisure are usually the same as those of Europe. There is little central heating and moderately warm clothing is needed in the winter, particularly at night. The capital, Mexico City, is 2,240 metres above sea level. At lower altitudes temperatures can be very high and lightweight clothing is essential.

Entry requirements
Requirements for Mexico are complex and comprehensive guidance should be obtained from consular sections of local embassies before departure, any infringement of regulations can result in fines and expulsion.

Passports
Required for all.

Visa
The regulations for entry into Mexico are complex and visitors are advised to confirm all aspects of visa requirements before travelling. Visas are not required by those using a tourist card, which are issued only to tourists and are valid for 30 days. All other visitors require visas. Business visas are divided into two, 'lucrative' and 'non-lucrative', and applications must be accompanied by a business letter of accreditation stating the nature of business, proof of sufficient funds for length of stay and a full itinerary, plus an invitation from a local company. See www.inm.gov.mx and follow the links, in English, to I would like to visit Mexico for full details, or www.mexonline.com for more general information.

Currency advice/regulations
The import and export of local currency is unrestricted up to the equivalent amount of US$10,000; amounts greater than this must be declared. The import of foreign currency is unlimited but must be declared as export is limited to the amount declared on arrival. The export of gold coins is prohibited.
Many establishments in cities or tourist areas accept payment in US dollars.
Travellers cheques in US dollars are readily accepted in most banks, hotels and commercial outlets.

Customs
There are sometimes rigorous searches for drugs, firearms or large sums of currency, and expensive jewellery or electronic equipment may attract attention and demands for customs duty. There are restrictions on the import of motor vehicles.

Prohibited imports
Fresh meat, particularly pork, fish, fruit, vegetables, flowers and seeds are prohibited unless a permit is obtained before travelling. Firearms and ammunition require an import licence.
Archaeological artifacts may not be exported.

Health (for visitors)
Mandatory precautions
A yellow fever vaccination certificate is required if arriving from an infected area.

Advisable precautions
Diphtheria, tuberculosis, hepatitis A and B, typhoid, tetanus and polio

vaccinations. Malaria risk exists in some rural areas – prophylaxis recommended. There is a rabies risk. Dengue fever is endemic in northern regions.
Bottled water and water supplied from taps marked 'drinking/sterilised water' in hotels can be drunk without precautions. All other water should be regarded as potentially contaminated.
Mexico City is at 2.250 metres (7,400ft), and visitors may take some time to acclimatise to the altitude. The levels of pollution in Mexico City are extremely high and cab be a health threat.
Health insurance is advised. Medical facilities are good and pharmacies are permitted to diagnose and treat minor ailments.

Hotels

There are six classified types of hotels, of five stars and an additional Gran Turismo, with maximum rates set by the government.
Mexico City is one of the biggest cities in the world, so location is very important. The main hotels are in the business, financial and commercial area along Reforma Avenue. It is advisable to book in advance expecially during the high season and to confirm the booking in writing. There is a levy of 15 per cent VAT and 2 per cent accommodation tax added to bills – unless the visitor is from overseas travelling for meetings and conventions and fairs, who have confirmed their migatory status, use a credit card and make their arrangements through the event's organisers then VAT is exempt. Tipping is usually 10 per cent.

Credit cards

Visa and Mastercard are readily accepted, however there is a government tax of 6 per cent on transaction. ATMs are widely available.

Public holidays (national)

Fixed dates
1 Jan (New Year's Day), 5 Feb (Constitution Day), 21 Mar (Birthday of Benito Juárez), 1 May (Primero de Mayo), 5 May (Battle of Puebla Day), 1 June (Navy Day), 20 Nov (Revolution Day), 25 Dec (Christmas Day).
Religious holidays are celebrated by adherents.
Variable dates
Carnival (Jan/Feb, five days)

Working hours

Hours of business in Mexico City are variable and hours in other parts of the country vary considerably according to the climate and local custom.
Banking
Mon–Fri: 0900–1600; larger branches in Mexico city may opened Mon–Fri: 0800–1900; Sat 0800–1200. Small town branches may only open Mon–Fri 0800–1330.
Business
Mon–Fri: 0800–1800; lunch is taken anywhere between 1300–1500, for up to two hours.
Government
Mon–Fri: 0800–1500.
Shops
Mon–Sat: 1000–1800/1900.

Telecommunications

Mobile/cell phones
GSM 900 and 1900 services are available in highly populated areas only.

Electricity supply

120V AC, 60 cycles. Two-pin flat plugs (as in USA) are used.

Social customs/useful tips

During the working day moderate punctuality is appreciated although some lateness is tolerated. It is acceptable to arrive late for evening social occasions which often continue well into the night.
Mexicans are patient, courteous and hospitable and will often treat visiting foreigners with polite reserve. An effort to speak Spanish is much appreciated. Otherwise it is advisable not to presume too much until you know the people concerned fairly well.
Tipping in hotels, restaurants and bars is expected since service charges are not added to the bill. A normal tip is 15 per cent. If service has been very good, 20 per cent should be given.

Security

It is unwise to carry large sums of money or valuables in Mexico City, where the number of assaults is rising.
Visitors should be wary of walking through neighbourhood streets during festivities. Many Mexicans own guns and they tend to fire them in the air to celebrate, especially towards evening.
Armed robbery in urban areas is a risk. Short-term opportunistic kidnapping is common. Visitors should exercise care when using ATMs.

Getting there

Air
National airline: Aeroméxico (AM) and Mexicana (MX)
International airport/s: Mexico City-Benito Juárez (MEX), 13km south of city; duty-free shops, restaurants, bank, bureau de change, 24-hour refreshments, chemist, tourist information, 24-hour left luggage, post office, first aid (with vaccinations for cholera and yellow fever available) car hire.
A taxi to the city takes about 45 minutes. Prepaid taxi tickets are available from the 'Authorised Taxi Service' booth in baggage reclaim; authorised taxis are white and mustard yellow with an aeroplane logo. Travellers are strongly advised to take an authorised, prepaid taxi and to always lock taxi doors when inside.
Major hotels run shuttle minibuses from the airport. There is also a train and regular airport bus to the city centre.
Other airport/s: Acapulco (ACA) 26km from city; Guadalajara (GDL) 20km from city; Monterrey (MTY) 24km from city. All include restaurant, bank and car hire facilities; and access by taxi and bus.
Airport tax: Approximately US$21, which may be included in the ticket price, transit passengers are exempt.
Surface
Road: There are roads into Mexico from the US, Belize and Guatemala. Drivers should note that permission is required to bring a car into Mexico for longer than 72 hours.
Rail: Connections with Mexico can be made from any city in the US or Canada. All trains are provided with pullman sleepers, restaurant cars and club cars and most are air conditioned.
Water: Regular passenger ships run from the US and South America. There are also riverboat services from Flores and Tikal (Guatemala) to Palenque, Chiapas in Mexico. Enquire locally for further details.
Main port/s: Gulf of Mexico coast: Altamira, Cd del Carmen, Coatzacoalcos, Pto Madero, Tampico, Veracruz; Pacific coast: Acapulco, Ensenada, La Paz, Lázaro Cardenas, Mazatlán, Manzanillo, Puerto Vallarta, Salina Cruz, Santa Rosalia.

Getting about

National transport
Air: There is a comprehensive network of daily scheduled services between main commercial centres.
Road: There are 95,000km of paved roads, about half of which are operated by the federal government, and the other half by the state governments. There are also more than 5,600km of toll roads, which are operated by private companies. Mexico's roads carry more than 85 per cent of the nation's overland freight and almost all intercity passengers.
Buses: There are three kinds, first- and second-class and local. It is advisable to book seats in advance in Baja California. Buses with odd numbers run north-south, while even numbered run east-west. Peribus services circulate Mexico City.
Rail: Rail services include special first-class, regular first-class and second-class. Routes include Guadalajara to Mexico City; Monterrey to Mexico City; Mexico City to Veracruz to Tapachula; Cuidad Juárez to Chihuahua. Services are slower than buses but electrification is in progress. There are sleeper services

between Mexico City and Guadalajara, Monterrey, Veracruz, Ciudad Juárez, Chihuahua, Mérida. It is advisable to book well in advance.
Water: There are regular ferries from the mainland at Quaymas in Sonora, to Santa Rosalía in Baja California Sur. There are services to the Caribbean Islands of Isla Mujeres and Cozumel.

City transport

Taxis: Taxis are usually fitted with meters, but these are often not used. Agree fare in advance. No tip is necessary.
Fixed route taxis can be identified by lime-green colour, rank taxis by coral and those with no fixed route by yellow. There are around 17 fixed routes. The number of fingers held out of a taxi window indicates the number of seats left.
Special tourist taxis, turismo, have English-speaking drivers.
The safest means of transport is a taxi de sitio – dial-a-cab services which charge about double the metered street taxi rates, but which are still cheap by international standards. These can be found outside every hotel.
It is best to carry a map of Mexico City as taxi drivers cannot be relied on to know their way around the huge city.
Buses, trams & metro: The Mexico City Metro, with eight lines, is excellent, but often crowded. Runs 0500–0000 Mon–Sat; opens 0700 (Sun). Maps are not displayed at all stations, but can be obtained at Insurgentes station.
There is also a small tramway network, and extensive bus and trolley bus services. The latter system has been modernised, and also has a flat fare. There is a state-run bus and trolley bus service in Guadalajara, with trolley buses running in tunnels, and also extensive private bus services.
The Monterrey City metro system (called Metrorrey) has two lines with 25 stations, with more under construction, which runs from Sun–Sat: 0500–2400.

Car hire

Car hire is widely available, with or without a driver, but often expensive. A foreign licence is acceptable. Car hire is not recommended for business travellers or tourists because of excessive traffic, aggressive drivers, and counter-pollution measures which mean that on certain days of the week, driving is off limits.

BUSINESS DIRECTORY

The addresses listed below are a selection only. While World of Information makes every endeavour to check these addresses, we cannot guarantee that changes have not been made, especially to telephone numbers and area codes. We would welcome any corrections.

Telephone area codes

The international direct dialling (IDD) code for Mexico is +52, followed by area code and subscriber's number:

Acapulco	744	Mexico City	55
Chihuahua	614	Monterrey	81
Ciudad Juárez	656	Oaxaca	951
Durango	618	Puebla	222
Guardalajara	33	Tampico	833
León	477	Torreón	817
Mérida	999	Veracruz	229

Useful telephone numbers

Police060
Fire/ambulance078
Highway emergency078
Locatel (service to locate missing persons or stolen cars)(55) 5658-1111.
Sectur (24-hour help to tourists in trouble) (55) 5250-0123

Chambers of Commerce

American Chamber of Commerce Mexico, Lucerna 78, Colonia Juarez, 06600 México, DF (tel: 5141-3800; fax: 5703-3908; e-mail: amchammx@amcham.com.mx).

British Chamber of Commerce in Mexico, 30 Río de la Plata, 6500 México, DF (tel: 5256-0901; fax: 5211-5451; e-mail: britchamexico@britchamexico.com).

Chihuahua Cámara Nacional de Comercio, Servicios y Turismo, 1800 Avenida Cuauhtemoc, 31020 Chihuahua (tel: 416-0000; fax: 415-1928; e-mail: cfn@infosel.net.mx).

Confederación de Cámaras Nacionales de Comercio, Servicios y Turismo, 144 Balderas, Colonia Centro, 06079 México, DF (tel/fax: 5722-9300; e-mail: sistemas@concanacored.com).

Guadalajara Cámara Nacional de Comercio, Servicios y Turismo, 4095 Avenida Vallarta, Fraccionamiento Camino Real, 45000 Guadalajara (tel: 3880-9090; fax: 3880-9097; e-mail: direccion@canacogdl.com.mx).

Juarez Cámara Nacional de Comercio, Servicios y Turismo, 4505 Avenida Henry Dunant y Avenida M Diaz, 32315 Ciudad Juarez (tel: 113-707; fax: 112-674; e-mail: canacojr@hotmail.com).

Mexico City Cámara Nacional de Comercio, 42 Paseo de la Reforma, Colonia Centro, 06048 México, DF (tel: 535-2502; fax: 703-2958; e-mail: presidencia1@ccmexico.com.mx).

Puebla Cámara Nacional de Comercio, Servicios y Turismo, 2704 Avenida Reforma, 72160 Puebla (tel: 480-705; fax: 480-800; e-mail: canacopu@axtel.net.mx).

Banking

Banamex, Actuario Robero Medellin 800, Colonia Santa Fé, 01219 México, DF (tel: 1226-2639; tel: 5999-2888).

Bancomer, Montes Urales 620,Colonia Lomas de Chapultepec, 11000 México, DF (tel: 5201-2264; fax: 5238-7790).

Banorte, Periférico Sur 4355, Colonia Jardines en la Montaña, 14210 México, DF (tel: 5169-9300; fax: 5169-9460).

Bital, Paseo de la Reforma 156, Juarez, 06600 México DF (tel: 5721-5715; fax: 5721-3846).

Santander Mexicano, Prolongación Paseo de la Reforma 500, Colonia Lomas de Santa Fé, 01210 México, D F (tel: 5257-8000; fax: 5629-4742).

Scotiabank Inverlat, Manuel Avila Camacho 1, 11009 México, DF (tel: 5229-2053; fax: 5395-9050).

Central bank

Banco de México, Avenida 5 de Mayo 1, Colonia Centro, Delegación Cuauhtémoc, 06059 (tel: 5237-2000; fax: 5237-2070; e-mail: sidaoui@banxico.org.mx).

Travel information

Benito Juárez International Airport, Av Capitán Carlos León s/n Col Peñón de los Baños Del Venustiano Carranza, México, DF CP 15620 (tel: 5571-3600; fax: 5726-0107).

Fondo Nacional de Fomento al Turismo (FONATUR) 22nd Floor, Insurgentes Sur 800, Colonia del Valle, 03100 México DF (tel: 5687-0567/8; fax: 5687-5058, 5682-5058; email: ibotas@fonatur.gob.mx; internet: www.fonatur.gob.mx).

Infotour, Zona Rosa, Amberes 54, Mexico City (tel: 5525-9380).

Ministry of tourism

Secretaría de Turismo (SECTUR) Presidente Mazaryck 172, Colonia Polanco, 11570 México DF (tel: 5250-8555; fax: 5250-4406 (general enquiries), 5254-0942 (marketing), email: correspondencia@mexico-travel.com; internet: www.mexico-travel.com).

National tourist organisation offices

Consejo de Promoción Turística de México, Mariano Escobedo 550, 11580 Mexico DF (tel: 5258-1090/2; email: cptmex@infosel.net.mx; internet: www.visitmexico.com).

Ministries

Ministry of Agrarian Reform (SRA), Tepozteco 36, 1er Piso, Col Vertiz Narvarte, 03020 Mexico (tel: 5579-6094; fax: 5579-3767).

Ministry of Agriculture, Rural Development and Livestock (SAGAR), Av Insurgentes Sur

476, 50. piso, Col Roma Sur, 06700 Mexico (tel: 5584-0808; fax: 5584-1177).

Ministry of Communication and Transport (SCT), Xola y Av Universidad, Cuerpo C, PB, Col Narvarte, 03028 Mexico (tel: 5538-5148; fax: 5519-9748).

Ministry of Defence (SEDENA), Blvd Manuel Avila Camacho y Av Industria Militar, Col Lomas de Sotelo, 11600 Mexico (tel: 5395-6766; fax: 5557-1370).

Ministry of Education (SEP), Brasil 31, PB oficina 115, Col Centro, 06029 Mexico (tel: 5329-6827; fax: 5329-6822).

Ministry of Energy (SE), Av Insurgentes Sur 552, 1er. Piso, Col Roma Sur, 06769 Mexico (tel: 5584-4304; fax: 5564-9782).

Ministry of Finance and Public Credit (SHCP), República de El Salvador 47, PA, Col Centro, 06080 Mexico (tel: 5709-6675; fax: 5709-3272).

Ministry of Fishing, Environment and Natural Resources (SEMARNAP), Anillo Periférico Sur 4209, 3er Piso, Col Jardines en la Montaña, 14210 Mexico (tel: 5628-0891; fax: 5628-0780).

Ministry of Foreign Affairs (SRE), Eje Central Lázaro Cardenas 257, ala 'A', 1er Nivel, Col Guerrero, 09600 Mexico (tel: 5782-3660; fax: 5327-3025).

Ministry of Health (SSA), Lieja 8, 50 piso, Col Juárez, 06600 Mexico (tel: 5553-7670; fax: 5286-5497).

Ministry of the Interior (SG), Abraham Gonzalez 48, PB, Col Juárez, 06699, Mexico (tel: 5535-2718; fax: 5535-9952).

Ministry of Labour and Social Welfare (STPS), Periférico Sur 4271, Edificio A, 1er Nivel, Col Fuentes del Pedregal, 14149, Mixico (tel/fax: 5645-3715).

Ministry of Naval Affairs (SM), Eje 2 Oriente 861, Tramo Heroica Escuela Naval Militar, Col Los Cipreses, Coyoacan, 04830 Mexico (tel: 5684-8188; fax: 5679-6411).

Ministry of Social Development (SEDESOL), Av Constituyentes 947-B, PB, Col Belén de las Flores, 01110 Mexico (tel: 5515-4508; fax: 5272-0118).

Ministry of Trade and Industry (SECOFI), Av Alfonso Reyes 30, 20 piso, Col Condesa, 06140 Mexico (tel: 5729-9193; fax: 5729-9314).

Other useful addresses

Asociación Nacional de importadores y Exportadores de la República Mexicana, Monterrey 130, Col Roma Sur, 06700, Mexico, DF (tel: 5564-9379; fax: 5584-5317).

Asociación Nacional para el Fomento de las Exportaciones Mexicanas, Ed de las Instituciones 702, Ocampo 250 Poncente Apartado 64100, Monterrey NL (tel: 5428-010, 422-143, 422-154; fax: 528-207).

Asociación de Personal Técnico para Conferencias Internacionales AC, Universidad 1855-502, Mexico 20, DF (tel: 5550-0170).

British Embassy, Lerma 71, Col. Cuauhtemoc, 06500 Mexico City (207-2569, 207-2089/2149; fax: 5207-2593, 207-7672).

Comptroller General (SECOGEF), Av Insurgentes Sur 1735, PB Ala Norte, Oficina 39, Col Guadalupe Inn, 01020 Mexico (tel: 5662-2762; fax: 5662-4511).

Confederación de Cámaras Industriales de los Estados Unidos Mexicanos, Manuel Maria Contreras 133, 8, Cuauhtemoc, 06597, Mexico DF (tel: 5546-9053; fax: 5535-6871).

Consejo Nacional de Comercio Exterior, Tiaxcala 177 Desp 803, Apartado 06100, Mexico DF (tel: 5286-8744, 286-8798; fax: 5211-8465).

Dirección General de Telecommunicaciones, Lázaro Cárdenas 567 11 Piso Ala Norte, Col Navarate, 03020 Mexico, DF (tel: 5519-4049, 530-3492, 519-0908; fax: 5559-9812).

Instituto de Intérpretes y Traductores SA, Rio Rhin 40, 06500 Mexico 5, DF (tel: 5566-7722, 566-8312).

Instituto Mexicano del Petróleo, Avenida Eje Central Lázaro Cardenas 152, 07730 Apartado 14-805, Mexico 14, DF (tel: 5567-6600).

International Telegraph Office, Balderas 14-18 Colon, Mexico DF.

Mexican Embassy (USA), 1911 Pennsylvania Avenue, NW, Washington DC 20006 (tel: (+1-202) 728-1600; fax: (+1-202) 728-1698; e-mail: mexembusa@aol.com).

Mexican Investment Board MIB, Paseo de la Reforma No. 915, Lomas de Chapultepec, 11000 Mexico (tel: 5202-7804; fax: 5328-9930).

Mexican Stock Exchange, Paseo de la Reforma 255, Colonia Cuauhtemoc, 06500 Mexico (tel: 5726-6600; fax: 5726-6805).

Pemex (Petróleos Mexicanos), Avenida Marina Nacional 329, Mexico 17, DF (tel: 5250-2611, 254-2044).

Public Telex Office, Vallejo y Norte 45, Mexico 2, DF/San Bartolo Naucaplan, Mexico 16, DF.

Secretariat of State for Commerce and Industrial Development, Alfonso Reyes 30, Mexico, DF (tel: 5286-1823, 211- 0036; fax: 5286-0804).

Secretariat of State for Energy, Mines and Federal Industry, Insurgentes Sur 552, 3, 06769 Mexico, DF (tel: 5564-9790; fax: 5574-3396).

Secretariat of State for Finance and Public Credit, Palacio Nacional, 1 Patio Mariano, 06066 Piso ofna 3045, Mexico, DF (tel: 5518-5420; fax: 5542-2821).

US Embassy, PO Box 3087, Paseo de la Reforma 305, Colonia Cuauhtemoc, 06500 Mexico City, DF (tel: 5211-0042; fax: 5207-8938).

Internet sites

Communicación Mass Media de Mexico (Spanish): http://www.mexnews.com

Comprehensive information site: http://www.mexonline.com

Central bank http://www.banxico.org.mx

El Heraldo newspaper http://www.heraldo.com.mx

General directory http://www.mexicoweb.com.mx

General guide http://www.mexconnect.com

Mexicana: airline http://www.mexicana.com

Mexican government agencies, chambers of commerce and other trade institutions (English) http://www.mexicosi.com

Statistics: http://www.inegi.gob.mx

Stock exchange http://www.bmv.com.mx

Travel & tourism information http://www.go2mexico.org.mx

Travel & tourism information http://www.visitmexico.com

Federated States of Micronesia

KEY FACTS

Official name: Federated States of Micronesia

Head of State: President Immanuel Manny Mori (elected and sworn in 11 May 2007)

Head of government: President Manny Mori

Ruling party: All parliamentary members sit as independents

Area: 607 volcanic islands and coral atolls with land area of just over 700 square km

Population: 124,141 (2004)

Capital: Palikir (in Pohnpei state)

Official language: English (nationwide); each state has its own official language including Pohnpeian, Ulithian, Woleaian, Yapese, Kosraean and Chuukese.

Currency: US dollar (US$) = 100 cents

GDP per capita: US$2,300 (2006)

GDP real growth: 3.00% (2005)

Unemployment: 16.00% (2004)

Inflation: 1.50% (2004)

Balance of trade: -US$118.70 million (2004)

COUNTRY PROFILE

Historical profile

The Federated States of Micronesia (FSM) comprises four island states – the capital state of Pohnpei (formerly Ponape), Chuuk (known until 1990 as Truk), Yap and Kosrae. These were formerly Japanese League of Nations mandated islands.

1947 The islands became part of the UN's Trust Territory of the Pacific Islands (TTPI), administered by the US under a UN mandate.

1978 the FSM gained sovereignty following a constitutional convention and referendum.

1979 On implementing the FSM constitution, former districts became States of the Federation.

1982 FSM signed a 15-year Compact of Free Association (CFA, referred to as the Contract) with the US, which would retain responsibility for foreign affairs and defence.

1986 The Contract was implemented.

1990 The US Trusteeship was ended by the UN Security Council.

1991 The federation joined the UN.

1999 Talks on the relationship between the US and FSM following the ending of Contract began.

2001 The Contract was extended for a further two years

2002 The super-typhoon Chata'an devastated the island of Chuuk, killing 37 people and destroyed homes and crops. US federal funds were provided to help recovery and rebuilding.

2003 In FSM congressional elections, Joseph J Urusemal was elected as president. A US$3.5 billion, 15-year, Contract was signed with the US.

2004 The super-typhoon Sudel devastated the island of Yap destroying 1,500 homes and utility facilities.

2005 In parliamentary elections, 10 non-partisan congressional candidates were elected.

2006 China pledged around US$3.0 million in grant assistance to FSM. The first project to be undertaken with the funds is the Pohnpei State Administration building.

2007 FSM and the US Peace Corps celebrated 40 years of partnership in regional development. Parliamentary elections were held on 6 March. Congress elected Manny Mori as president on 11 May.

2008 The conman, Peter Foster, was jailed in Brisbane Australia for money laundering and defrauding the Bank of FSM of around US$580,000.

Political structure

Constitution

The constitution was promulgated in 1979, it guarantees fundamental human rights and established a separation of powers. Each state has a constitutional government with an elected governor and lieutenant governor. The US is responsible for defence and security issues.

Each state has its own constitution with a elected legislature, governor and power for implementing its own budget.

Form of state

A Federation of four states – Pohnpei, Chuuk, Kosrae and Yap; a self-governing territory in free association with the US.

The executive

The president and vice president are elected from a group of four senators, one nominated from each state, for a four-year term. The president is Head of State and head of government but does not exercise executive power, which is retained by the congress.

The president appoints a cabinet of supporters and technocrats.

National legislature

The unicameral congress has 14 non-partisan members; 10 members are elected in single seats constituencies for two-year terms (five from Chuuk, three from Pohnpei, one from Yap and one from Kosrae), four members are elected by proportional representation, one from each state, for four-year terms – these members provide the pool from which a president and vice president are chosen by congress members.

The congress exercises executive and legislative power.

Last elections

6 March 2007 (parliamentary); 11 May 2007 (presidential, in congress).

Results: Parliamentary: non-partisan candidates were elected to the 14 seats. Presidential: Immanuel 'Manny' Mori was elected by parliament.

Next elections

2009 (parliamentary); 2011 (presidential, in congress).

Political parties
There are no political parties; political allegiances follow family and island-related dynamics.
Ruling party
All parliamentary members sit as independents
Political situation
The newly elected president of FSM, Manny Mori, has had to adopt a stern domestic strategy to revitalise the economy of FSM, by imposing sanctions on the state of Chuuk, which by population and geography is the largest island, but is also habitually the most profligate. For decades Chuuk has run a fiscal deficit that has threatened to ruin the fragile economy of the entire federation. As President Mori is from Chuuk, where there were high hopes his election would provide extra cash to bail it out, his task has been to impose a harsh budget that cracked down on fiscal mismanagement and slashed its bloated state bureaucracy.
In an effort to remove the reliance of FSM on the funding by the Compact of Free Association (with the US), President Mori set up a National Trade Facilitation Committee (NTFC) in January 2008. One of the committee's first objectives was to formulate a comprehensive trade police to be used when FSM participates in international trade negotiations. Mori is also targeting FSM's need for foreign direct investment and China is rapidly become the country's high-profile donor. Self sustaining development would also include the world's most productive tuna resources and tourism. The project for an underwater, telecommunications optic cable had, by January 2008, secured the US$15 million necessary for phase one of the project. At the same time Mori has his eye on making FSM the agricultural centre of the region, not only to feed the growing domestic population but also the US military bases in Guam. The plans include investment in infrastructure and education with the re-opening of an abandoned agricultural and technical college on Pohnpei.

Population
124,141 (2004)
Last census: April 2000: 107,008
Population density: 169 inhabitants per square km. Urban population: 29 per cent (1995–2001).
Annual growth rate: 0.4 per cent 1994–2004 (WHO 2006)
Ethnic make-up
The population is composed of nine Micronesian and Polynesian groups.
Religions
Roman Catholic (50 per cent), Protestant (47 per cent).

Education
The education system is modelled after the US educational system. Over 30 per cent of the population attend secondary schools. Private elementary and secondary schools also exist, sponsored by religious groups. Although the College of Micronesia-FSM provides two- and three-year programmes, most students prefer to enrol in US tertiary educational institutions. The Micronesia Maritime and Fisheries Academy in the State of Yap was set up to provide effective training in maritime and fisheries technologies, to cater for the growing demand for trained personnel in the expanding fishing industry.
Compulsory years: 6 to 14.
Enrolment rate: 142 per cent gross primary enrolment, of relevant age groups (including repeaters) (World Bank 2003).

Health
Per capita total expenditure on health (2003) was US$270; of which per capita government spending was US$238, at the international dollar rate, (WHO 2006).
There are inadequate primary health care facilities, with little secondary and tertiary-level treatment facilities. In some states there are shortages of essential medical supplies including contraceptives. As a result patients have little choice but to travel to health facilities overseas. Government funds are channelled towards curative services rather than preventative and primary health care. The Asian Development Bank has granted loans for training health workers, improving medical supplies and extending a limited health insurance scheme to provide broader and universal coverage.
Life expectancy: 70 years, 2004 (WHO 2006)
Fertility rate/Maternal mortality rate: 4.3 births per woman, 2004 (WHO 2006)
Birth rate/Death rate: 25.1 births per 1,000 population; 4.9 deaths per 1,000 population (2005).
Child (under 5 years) mortality rate (per 1,000): 30.2 per 1,000 live births (2005)

Welfare
Although the FSM does not produce a poverty profile as such, recent household income and expenditure surveys suggest that around 40 per cent of households could be considered as low income. Despite some remittances from overseas migrants, the number of low income households is still high. The lowest income households are on the outer islands where opportunities for formal sector employment and commercial activities are few.

Main cities
Palikir (capital, in Pohnpei State, estimated population 6,645 in 2005), Weno (on Chuuk) (13,758), Nett (7,365), Kitti (7,049), Tol (on Chuuk) (4,747), Tonoas (4,140), Kolonia Town (on Pohnpei) (5,360).

Languages spoken
English is the lingua franca of the country. Yap has four languages: Yapese, Ulithian, Woleaian, and Satawalese; Pohnpei languages are Pohnpeian, Nukuoroan and Kapingamarangian, Chuukese in Chuuk and Kosraean in Kosrae. Other spoken languages include: Pingelapese, Ngatikese, Mokilese, Puluwatese and Mokilese.
Official language/s
English (nationwide); each state has its own official language including Pohnpeian, Ulithian, Woleaian, Yapese, Kosraean and Chuukese.

Media
Other news agencies: ABC Pacific Beat: www.radioaustralia.net.au/pacbeat
Pacific Magazine:
www.pacificmagazine.net
Press
There are no daily newspapers but various weeklies, the Pohnpei Business News, The Island Tribune and Micronesia Weekly cover a range of subjects. The federal government publishes The National

KEY INDICATORS — Federated States of Micronesia

	Unit	2003	2004	2005	2006	2007
Population	m	0.12	0.12		0.11	0.11
Gross domestic product (GDP)	US$bn	0.28	*0.23	–0	–0	0.26
GDP per capita	US$	2,000	*2,090		0	2,172
GDP real growth	%	2.4	-3.3	–	–	-3.2
Inflation	%	1.5	1.5		–	3.3
Total reserves minus gold	US$m	89.6	54.8	–	–	48.5
Foreign exchange	US$m	87.8	52.9	–	–	46.4
Exchange rate	per US$	–0	–0	1.00	–0	–0

* estimated figure

Union, with information bulletins, every fortnight, while state governments produce their own newsletters.

Broadcasting

Radio: There is a radio stations in each state, operated by both the government and a religious organisation through FSM Telecommunications (www.fm/radio.htm). Broadcasts are transmitted in English and the main local dialects.

Television: The government runs the only TV coverage on the islands KPON TV (on Pohnpei), TTKK TV (on Chuuk) and WAAB TV (on Colonia).

Economy

Fishing and subsistence farming are the main economic resources. Marine products generate almost all export revenues. Tourism is being developed, but the remoteness of the islands is an impediment. The economy is dependent on US financial support. In May 2003, the US and the FSM agreed a new Compact of Free Association (CFA), which guarantees grant assistance until 2023 and provides for a trust fund, expected to generate enough income to enable the FSM to offset the loss of CFA revenue from 2024. The US government has control over the administration of the trust fund until 2023. All earnings from the trust fund will remain untouched until 2023 and will be reinvested.

External trade

The FSM is a member of the South Pacific Regional Trade and Economic Co-operation Agreement (Sparteca) along with 12 other regional nations, which allows products duty free access by Pacific Island Forum members to Australian and New Zealand markets (subject to the country of origin restrictions).

FSM has an exclusive economic zone of almost 3 million square km of the Pacific Ocean and fish exports accounts for 80 per cent of export trade, mainly to Japan; it also has a bilateral trade agreement with the European Union regarding tuna fisheries.

Imports

Principal imports are food, manufactured goods, machinery, equipment and beverages. Imports are approximately three times larger than exports.

Main sources: US (39.7 per cent total, 2006), Japan (8.8 per cent), Australia (4.2 per cent), Hong Kong (3.6 per cent).

Exports

Principal exports are fish, garments, bananas and black pepper. Some beef, fruit and vegetables are also exported.

Copra was formerly Yap's principal export, but this has been overtaken by betel nut and pepper leaf, traditionally, used in chewing. A 'chew' consists of a betel nut wrapped in pepper leaf with a touch of lime powder made from burned coral; the combination stains teeth red and betel nut is described as mildly narcotic.

Main destinations: Japan, US, Guam

Agriculture

Farming

The agricultural sector contributes approximately 17 per cent to GDP. Subsistence farming is the main occupation and provides most of the food consumed in the territory.

Estimated crop production in 2005 included: 11,800 tonnes (t) cassava, 40,000t coconuts, 3,000t sweet potatoes, 2,000t bananas, 300t plantains, 3,100t vegetables, 90t rice, 33t cocoa beans, 295t other fresh fruit. Livestock production included: 245t beef, 13t goat meat, 873t pig meat and 135t poultry meat.

Fishing

Fishing is the mainstay of the economy and generates most of the country's export revenues. International fishing fleets pay to fish in FSM's rich territorial waters, including one of the world's best tuna grounds. However, the sector is dominated by foreign owned companies operating offshore and so employs few local people.

The Pohnpei State government expanded its local fishing industry in 2003, using vessels which had been donated by the government of the Republic of Korea.

Fishing provides a primary source of protein for the local population.

FSM also typically harvests 150,000 pearls annually.

In 2004, the total marine fish catch was 29,184 tonnes and the total crustacean catch was 25 tonnes.

Industry and manufacturing

Small-scale industries include handicrafts, fish processing, bottling, copra processing, bakeries and boat building. The Pohnpei Agricultural and Trade School runs a small coconut products plant, which makes 'Oil of Ponape' toiletries.

Most private sector activity is in retail and wholesale trade which are dependent on demand generated by government spending.

Tourism

Tourism accounts for only 6 per cent of GDP, but is a significant foreign exchange earner. The Asian Development Bank has identified tourism as one of FSM's highest potential growth industries, although the cost of airfares is seen as a hiderance to expansion. Tourist numbers have been down, a trend that began in 2000 and although there was a recovery with 14,038 tourist arrivals in 2002 by 2004 numbers were as low as 10,000 people.

FSM is particularly attractive to divers and in 2004 tourist hotels related to the activity had an 80 per cent occupancy rate while general resorts reported typical occupancy rates of around 40 per cent.

The region's most spectacular scenery is underwater. The island of Chuuk has an underwater-wreck-museum where more than 60 Japanese ships, as well as planes, that were sunk during the Second World War are open to divers to view.

Mining

Small mineral deposits exist, but there are doubts about the economic viability of commercial exploitation, which would be hampered by a shortage of land to accommodate any displaced population.

Banking and insurance

There are three commercial banks which serve the four states: Bank of the Federated States of Micronesia, Bank of Guam and the Bank of Hawaii. A government chartered FSM Development Bank is the main financial institution used to foster the growth of new business ventures and private sector development.

Time

GMT plus 12 hours

Geography

The Federated States of Micronesia (FSM), together with Palau, form the archipelago of the Caroline Islands, about 800km east of the Philippines. It is a group of 608 small islands, only four large islands are inhabited, in an area over 2.5 million square kilometres of Pacific Ocean.

Most of the islands are little more than sandy coral outcrops, while others are high rise volcanic peaks covered with forests, or mangroves along shorelines and lagoons.

Hemisphere

Northern

Climate

Warm and humid, temperatures 23–30 degrees Celsius with humidity around 80 per cent. Rainfall is variable, but the minimum is generally 250mm per annum. Hurricanes are possible.

Entry requirements

Passports

Required by all except US citizens with proof of citizenship. Passports must be valid for 120 days beyond date of entry.

Visa

Not required by US citizens with proof of adequate funds. Entry permits granted to all others with proof of return/onward passage and adequate funds for stays up to 30 days. Business visits need an entry permit, (see www.visit-fsm.org/visitors/permit.pdf).

Currency advice/regulations

No restrictions on import and export of local or foreign currency.

Travellers cheques and credit/charge cards are accepted in visitor orientated businesses.

Health (for visitors)

Mandatory precautions

Vaccination certificates required for yellow fever if travelling from infected area.

Advisable precautions

Vaccinations for diphtheria, tuberculosis, hepatitis A and B, polio, TB, tetanus, typhoid and paratyphoid are advisable.

Leprosy has been endemic for generations.

Water precautions are necessary. There is a cholera risk due to lack of access to safe water. There is a rabies risk.

Hotels

Hotels tend to be low rise, resort style. There is no star ratings. There is a 6 per cent accommodation tax on Pohnpei and 10 per cent on Yap; Chuuk and Kosrae do not levy a tax.

Credit cards

Limited to certain businesses and hotels in the state centres.

Public holidays (national)

Fixed dates

1 Jan (New Year's Day), 10 May (FSM Constitution Day), 24 Oct (United Nations Day), 3 Nov (National Day), 25 Dec (Christmas Day).

Variable dates

Good Friday (Mar/Apr)

Working hours

Banking

Mon–Thurs: 0930–1430; Fri: 0930–1600.

Business

Mon–Fri: 0800–1700.

Government

Mon–Fri: 0800–1700.

Shops

Mon–Sat: 0800–2000; Sun 0900–1030.

Telecommunications

Postal services

Mobile/cell phones

A GSM 900 service exists on the inhabited islands.

Electricity supply

110 volt and US type outlets are used.

Social customs/useful tips

Tips are neither expected nor encouraged.

Getting there

Air

National airline: None but the US owned Continental Micronesia Airlines operates throughout Micronesia with connections to Hawaii and Guam.

International airport/s: Pohnpei (PNI), 5km south of Kolonia Town.

Other airport/s: Chuuk (TKK), Yap (YAP), Kosrae (KSA).

Airport tax: Departure tax: Pohnpei US$10, Chuuk US$15, Kosrae US$10, Yap none.

Getting about

National transport

A trip to the outer islands can be complicated and arrangements should be made at least several months in advance.

Air: Pacific Missionary Aviation (PMA) in Yap State and in Pohnpei State provide domestic air services. There are airstrips in the outer islands of Ulul and Ta in Chuuk State.

Road: The road network has been upgraded in many areas through a resurfacing programme begun in the late 1990s.

Taxis: Inexpensive and readily available in most centres.

Water: Passenger and freight services between the islands and atolls are provided by state-owned vessels. The frequency of inter-island services is governed by weather conditions; it is best to contact the FSM visitor's board for current information (www.visit-fsm.org).

City transport

BUSINESS DIRECTORY

Telephone area codes

The international direct dialling (IDD) code for the FSM is +691, followed by area code and subscriber's number:

Chuuk	330	Pohnpei	320
Kosrae	370	Yap	350

Useful telephone numbers

Pohnpei

Police: 320-2221

Fire: 320-2223

Ambulance: 320-2213

Chuuk

Police: 330-2223

Fire: 330-2222

Ambulance: 330-2444

Kosrae

Police: 911

Fire: 370-3333

Ambulance: 370-3012

Yap

Police: 911

Fire: 350-2415

Ambulance: 350-3446

Chambers of Commerce

Chuuk Chamber of Commerce, PO Box 700, Weno, Chuuk 96942 (tel: 330-2318; fax: 330-2314).

Kosrae Chamber of Commerce, PO Box 1075, Tofol, Kosrae 96944 (tel: 370-2044; fax: 370-2066; e-mail: kosraecci@mail.fm).

Pohnpei Chamber of Commerce, PO Box 405, Kolonia, Pohnpei 96941 (tel: 320-2452; fax: 320-5277).

Banking

Bank of the Federated States of Micronesia, PO Box BF, Tofol, Kosrae, 96944 (tel: 320-2850; fax: 370-3568; email: bofsmhq@mail.fm).

FSM Development Bank, Box M, Kolonia, Pohnpei State, 96941 (tel: 320-2840; fax: 320-2842)

Bank of Guam, Chuuk Office (tel: 330-2567; fax: 330-2640).

Bank of Hawaii, Kosrae Office (tel: 370-3230; fax: 370-2027).

Travel information

Chief of Immigration, Office of the Attorney General, Palikir, Pohnpei 96941 (tel: 320-5844; fax: 320-2234).

National tourist organisation offices

National Visitors Board, PO Box PS-12, Palikir, Pohnpei, 96941 (tel: 320-5133; fax: 320-3251; email: fsminfo@visit-fsm.org; internet: www.visit-fsm.org).

Ministries

Department of Foreign Affairs and Trade, Pacific Islands Branch, R G Casey Building, John McEwan Crescent, Barton ACT 0221, Australia (fax: (+62-2) 6261-2332).

Secretary for Foreign Affairs, Pohnpei (tel: 320-2641; fax: 320-2933).

Secretary for Economic Affairs, Pohnpei (tel: 320-2646; fax: 320-5854).

Other useful addresses

British Embassy, PO Box No 61, Bairiki Tarawa (tel: 21-327; fax: 21-488).

Chuuk State Government, Weno, Chuuk State, 96942.

FSM Public Information Office, FSM Government, Box P.S. 34, Palikir, Pohnpei, 96941.

Kosrae State Government, Tofol, Kosrae, 96944.

Office of the Governor, Yap State Government, PO Box 39, Colonia, Yap, 96943.

Pohnpei State Government, Kolonia, Pohnpei, 96941.

The Secretary of Finance, PO Box P.S. 158, Palikir, Pohnpei, 96941 (tel: 320-2640; fax: 320-2380).

Other news agencies: ABC Pacific Beat: www.radioaustralia.net.au/pacbeat

Pacific Magazine: www.pacificmagazine.net

Internet sites

FSM Telecom: http://www.telecom.fm

Government website: http://www.fm.org

Tourist information: http://www.visit.micronesia.fm

US Office of Insular affairs: http://www.doi.gov/oia

Moldova

Moldova's economy is 58.4 per cent free, according to the 2008 assessment of the US based Heritage Foundation, which makes it the world's 89th freest economy. Its overall score is 0.8 percentage point lower than last year, reflecting lower scores in five of the 10 economic freedoms. Moldova is ranked 36th out of 41 countries in the European region, and its overall score is lower than the regional average. Moldova scores slightly above the world average in trade freedom, business freedom, labour freedom, and fiscal freedom, and property rights. The average tariff rate is low, but non-tariff barriers include burdensome regulations and restrictive customs.

Since independence in 1991 Moldova has been subject to a potentially lethal cocktail of adverse internal and external conditions. Civil war, drought, the collapse of markets in the former Soviet Union and increases in the costs of imported oil and gas have all hurt hard.

Once ruled by Romania the present day Moldavans retain close linguistic, cultural and historic ties with its neighbour. Romania lies to the east and to the west is Ukraine, but in truth it is the influence of Russia that predominates. The largest successor state to emerge from the former Soviet Union remains all-powerful in the region and its heavy hand is still felt throughout Moldovan political and economic life on a day-to-day basis.

Moldova became part of the Soviet Union at the close of the Second World War and Russian troops were stationed in the country. At the time of the break-up of the USSR and the creation of the Russian Federation in 1991, Moldova, along with the other Russian satellite states, became independent. Moldova's Slavic population seized the opportunity to declare the territory east of the Dniestr River the Republic of Transdniestr. Although Russian troops pulled out of Moldova, they remain in the breakaway territory, which is now under the *de facto* rule of an elected pro-Russian 'president', Igor Smirnov. Transdniestr remains internationally unrecognised, except of course, by Russia. This made, until 2008 when Russia declared South Ossetia and Abhazia independent, one of the few – if any – pirate states in the world.

But it kicked off with something like eighty per cent of Moldovan heavy and light industry on its soil, which didn't do any harm. And the rest of Moldova could easily be held to ransom by the breakaway republic as virtually all raw materials had to pass through Transdniestr en route to Moldova. Nor was the presence of the Russian Fourteenth army on their soil too much of a worry. The continued re-election of Smirnov has been criticised by both Moldovan President Vladimir Voronin and his supporter in the dispute, Romanian President Traian Basescu.

While Transdniestr continues to look to Russia, the ethnic Moldovans in the western territory, though under a pro-Russian Communist government from 2001–05, now favour ties with the West. Neighbouring Romania joined the European Union (EU) at the beginning of 2007. Though Moldova was the first of the former Soviet satellite states to elect a Communist government after the break-up of the USSR, the same government has carried out a complete U-turn. Voronin's Partidul Comunistilor din Moldova (PCM) (Communist Party of Moldova), elected in 2001, changed its politics but not its name, campaigned in the 2005 election on a pro-Western platform, and was re-elected.

KEY FACTS

Official name: Republica Moldoveneasca (Republic of Moldova)

Head of State: President Vladimir Voronin (leader of PCM) (since 2001; re-elected 4 Apr 2005)

Head of government: Prime Minister Zinaida Greceanîi (PCM) (appointed by the president 21 Mar 2008)

Ruling party: Partidul Comunistilor din Moldova (PCM) (Communist Party of Moldova) (since 2001; re-elected 6 Mar 2005)

Area: 33,700 square km

Population: 3.39 million (2007)*

Capital: Chisinau (Kishinev)

Official language: Moldovan (in latin script)

Currency: Leu (L) = 100 bani

Exchange rate: L9.73 per US$ (Jul 2008)

GDP per capita: US$1,248 (2007)*

GDP real growth: 5.00% (2007)*

Labour force: 2.21 million (2004)

Inflation: 12.60% (2007)

Balance of trade: -US$1.64 billion (2007)

Foreign debt: US$1.87 billion (2004)

* estimated figure

Expensive energy

President Traian Basescu of Romania has assured Voronin that he will not allow Moldova to suffer from Russia's move to phase out the supply of subsidised gas for ex-Soviet states. Announced by Russia's state gas supplier Gazprom, it is seen as a means to put pressure on countries such as Moldova, who are seeking closer relations with the West. Basescu said that the Romanian government is ready to offer Moldova gas and electricity 'if the prices charged by Russia rise excessively'.

A faltering economy

GDP growth in 2006 was 3.0 per cent well down on the 7.0 per cent of 2005 due to insufficient investment and external shocks such as higher gas import prices and temporary bans placed by Russia again in 2006 (from March through to November) on key Moldovan agricultural produce, including wine. With exports to Russia back on track, it is expected that real GDP growth will have risen to around 5.5 per cent in 2007. Inflation for 2006 was estimated to be 11.5 per cent. Fiscal policy continued to support efforts to bring inflation down.

The government implemented a ruling that all goods entering Ukraine through the breakaway region of Transdniestr must have Moldovan custom stamps. The measures were intended to stop smuggling and had the backing of the EU, US and the OSCE but angered the Transdniestr leadership. In September, a referendum in 2006 in Transdniestr voted to claim independence from Moldova and eventually to become a region of Russia. Russia had suspended imports of Moldovan meat and wine, claiming a lack of quality but lifted the ban in November. Observers considered Russia had attempted to pressurise Moldova in its attempt to join the WTO, after Moldova threatened to block Russia's bid for membership.

The International Monetary Fund (IMF) had said in December 2005 that growth was likely to slow marginally over the next several years, given the impact of higher energy prices and emerging tightness in adjacent labour markets. Avoiding a more pronounced slowdown would depend on a continued recovery in investment, particularly of the private sector. The IMF has suggested that fiscal policy in 2007–08 should remain cautious both to support lower inflation and to avoid crowding out private sector investment. As general government expenditure had risen from around 33 per cent of GDP in 2003 to about 37 per cent in 2005, it was now time to examine carefully the quality and composition of government spending.

The 2006 budget had contained several positive structural features. A number of tax exemptions were eliminated; the government began to repay outstanding credits to the central bank and transfers of central bank profits would now take place only once a year on the basis of audited accounts. The budget also began to accumulate resources needed to help settle outstanding arrears to external creditors.

The IMF said the reform of public administration was exceptionally important to improve the business environment. Moldova could count on the support of its international development partners in this effort, which began with reviews of all levels of the central public administration.

Outlook

In some respects the economic outlook for Moldova can be said to have improved. The IMF forecasts a decline in the rate of inflation, with consumer prices dropping slightly. However, work remains to be done to keep the rate of inflation to a minimum, as particularly strong inflationary pressures are likely to come into play in the country and the surrounding region as uncontrollable energy prices continue to spiral upwards.

Risk assessment

Politics	Fair
Economy	Fair
Regional stability	Poor

KEY INDICATORS — Moldova

	Unit	2003	2004	2005	2006	2007
Population	m	4.23	4.21	3.39	*3.39	*3.39
Gross domestic product (GDP)	US$bn	2.09	2.60	2.99	3.36	*4.23
GDP per capita	US$	493	716	883	*991	*1,248
GDP real growth	%	6.0	7.0	7.5	4.0	*5.0
Inflation	%	18.0	12.3	11.9	12.7	12.6
Unemployment	%	2.0	2.0	8.1	–	–
Industrial output	% change	–	5.0	7.2	-10.0	–
Agricultural output	% change	–	13.7	-1.7	2.0	–
Exports (fob) (goods)	US$m	790.0	1,030.0	1,104.4	1,044.0	1,360.7
Imports (cif) (goods)	US$m	1,403.0	1,830.0	2,295.2	2,684.0	3,676.7
Balance of trade	US$m	-613.0	-800.0	-1,190.8	-1,640.0	-2,316.0
Current account	US$m	-140.0	-180.0	-242.0	-404.0	-746.9
Total reserves minus gold	US$m	302.3	470.3	597.5	775.5	1,333.6
Foreign exchange	US$m	302.2	470.2	597.4	775.3	1,333.5
Exchange rate	per US$	13.50	12.33	13.03	13.03	0.69

* estimated figure

COUNTRY PROFILE

Historical profile

Moldova is a remnant of the medieval principality of Moldavia (later called Bessarabia). Once part of Romania, Moldova maintains close ties with Romania and a majority of Moldovans consider themselves to be ethnic Romanians.

1940 The Moldovan Soviet Socialist Republic (SSR) was established within the Soviet Union. The Moldovan SSR included land annexed from Romania and the Ukraine, providing much of the basis for the inter-communal strife.

1989 Achieved de facto independence from the former Soviet Union.

1990 Moldova's attempts to become an independent republic were hindered by the country's economic weaknesses and its strained relations with Russia. Ethnic Russians proclaimed the 'Transdniestr Republic' on the left bank of the Dniestr River.

1991 Civil war erupted between the Transdniestr separatists and Moldova. Russian troops were deployed in Moldova to oversee a cease-fire agreed between the warring factions. Moldova formally declared its independence, with Mercea Snegur as the country's first president, and joined the Commonwealth of Independent States (CIS).

1992 Moldova was recognised by the UN. The Partidul Popular Crestin-Democrat (PPCD) (Christian-Democrat People's Party) resigned from government. A new coalition government took office.

1994 Moldova pursued a pro-Western policy and entered into NATO's Partnership for Peace (PfP) programme. The extreme left Partidul Democrat Agrar din Moldova (PDAM) (Agrarian-Democratic Party of Moldova) won the elections. A new consitution was introduced.
1996 Petru Lucinschi won the presidential elections.
1998 The Partidul Comunistilor din Moldova (PCM) (Communist Party of Moldova) won the biggest share of the vote in the parliamentary elections, but was unable to form a government as it was short of an absolute majority in the Parlamentul (Parliament). Right-wing parties, which had finished behind the PCM in the elections, joined together and formed a coalition government, led by Ion Ciubuc.
1999 The government collapsed. Its successor, an alliance of several centrist and centre-right parties also collapsed, following defections and a no-confidence vote. A non-affiliated government emerged, led by Dumitru Braghis.
2000 Against President Lucinschi's wishes, Moldova was transformed into a parliamentary republic — giving the parliament the opportunity to elect the president instead of election by popular vote. Parliament failed to elect a new president when neither candidate received the 61 votes required for outright victory.
2001 The PCM won the parliamentary elections and Vasile Tarlev was appointed prime minister. Vladimir Voronin, leader of the PCM, was elected president by parliament. Russia committed itself to removing troops from Moldova by 2002 as drawn up by the Organisation for Security and Co-operation in Europe (OSCE). Moldova joined the World Trade Organisation (WTO). Igor Smirnov was re-elected as self-styled president of the breakaway Transdniestr region.
2002 The announcement of plans to make Russian an official language and compulsory in schools sparked months of mass protests which ended only when the scheme was shelved. The OSCE deadline for the withdrawal of Russian troops from Transdniestr was extended until the end of 2003.
2003 Moldova was told it must meet at least three conditions in order to restore relations with the World Bank: to elaborate a poverty reduction strategy, resume relations with the IMF and solve a dispute between the government and Unión Fenosa (a Spanish company which owns three Moldovan energy distribution networks).
2004 In Transdniestr, the Russian and Ukrainian-speaking autonomous territory, closed several schools using the Moldovan language and Latin instead of Cyrillic script. Economic sanctions were imposed by Moldova, which also withdrew from talks with Russia regarding the territory.
2005 The ruling PCM and President Vladimir Voronin were re-elected. Vasile Tarlev was reappointed as prime minister. Gazprom doubled the price of gas and cut off supplies when Moldova refused to pay.
2006 The halted gas supplies impacted the flow through Moldova to Germany. An agreement was reached with phased price increases. Transdniestr reacted badly to a new law that all goods entering Ukraine through Transdniestr must have Moldovan custom stamps, to foil smuggling. In reprisal, Russia suspended imports of Moldovan meat and wone, claiming a lack of quality but lifted the ban after Moldova threatened to block Russia's bid for membership of the WTO. A referendum in Transdniestr voted for independence from Moldova and eventually to become a region of Russia.
2008 On 19 March, Vasile Tarlev resigned as prime minister. The president nominated Zinaida Greceanîi as prime minister on 21 March and her government was approved by parliament on 31 March.

Political structure

Constitution

The 1977 constitution was replaced in August 1994, establishing the country as a 'presidential, parliamentary republic' based on political pluralism and 'the preservation, development and expression of ethnic and linguistic identity'. The constitution enforces the separation of judicial, legislative and executive powers.
Moldova's independence and neutrality are enshrined in the constitution, as are the rights of all ethnic minorities.
For administrative purposes Moldova is divided into 40 districts (raioane) and 10 cities. Gagauz-Yeri and Transdniestr are guarenteed autonomous status, although the unrecognised separatist government of Transdniestr also claims outright independence.

Form of state

Parliamentary democratic republic

The executive

Executive power is held by the president of the republic, who must approve legislation and may also propose it. The president nominates the prime minister and government.
Candidates for the presidency must be over 35 years of age, resident in the country for at least 10 years and speakers of the national language. The president is elected for a term of four years by the parliament. The president is limited to two consecutive terms of office.

National legislature

The 101-member Parlamentul (parliament) is the legislative body with the power to appoint the president. It can also approve or reject presidential nominations for the prime minister and government.
The government must be appointed within 30 days of parliamentary elections or fresh elections must be called.
The term of parliament is four years, with elections by direct universal suffrage for all those aged over 18 years, with a proportional representation electoral system.
There are two parliamentary sessions per year (February—July and September—December), although an extraordinary session may be called at the request of the president of the republic or by the chair of parliament.

Legal system

The legal system is based on civil law. The Constitutional Court is the highest legal authority. It reviews the legality of legislative acts and must validate the election of the president and all members of parliament. Its independence is guaranteed by the constitution and judges, once selected, cannot be removed without their consent. The Constitutional Court consists of six judges, two each appointed by the president, parliament and Higher Council of Magistrates, all for a six-year term.
The rest of the justice system is administered by the Supreme Court, Appeals Court and lesser courts. Following recommendation by the Higher Council of Justice, the judges of the Supreme Court are appointed by parliament, and those of all lesser courts by the president of the republic, all for a renewable term of five years.
The Higher Council of Magistrates consists of 11 members, of which five (the minister of justice, the president of the Supreme Court, the president of the Court of Appeal, the president of the Court of Business Audit and the prosecutor general) are automatic members, a further three are judges appointed by the Supreme Court and three are academic lawyers appointed by parliament.

Last elections

4 April 2005 (presidential); 6 March 2005 (parliamentary).
Results: Presidential: Vladimir Voronin, leader of the PCM, was re-elected by parliament, winning 75 votes against one for Gheorghe Duca.
Parliamentary: the ruling Partidul Comunistilor din Moldova (PCM) (Communist Party of Moldova) was re-elected with 46.1 per cent of the vote (about 56 seats out of 101), the Democratic Moldova bloc 28.4 per cent (about 34) and the Partidul Popular Crestin Democrat (PPCD) (Christian Democrat People's Party) 9.1 per cent (about 11). Turnout was 63.7 per cent.

Next elections
2009 (parliamentary and presidential)

Political parties
Ruling party
Partidul Comunistilor din Moldova (PCM) (Communist Party of Moldova) (since 2001; re-elected 6 Mar 2005)
Main opposition party
Partidul Popular Crestin Democrat (PPCD) (Christian Democrat People's Party)

Population
3.39 million (2007)*
Last census: October 2004: 3,388,071 (provisional)
Population density: At 132 people per square km, Moldova is the second smallest republic of the Newly Independent States (NIS) but has the highest population density. Urban population: 45 per cent (1995—2001).
Annual growth rate: -0.3 per cent 1994–2004 (WHO 2006)
Internally Displaced Persons (IDP)
1,000 (UNHCR 2004)
Ethnic make-up
The high number of ethnic Ukrainians and Russians in Moldova stems from the former Soviet Union's forced emigration policies in an attempt to dilute the ethnic Moldovan population. There are internal disputes with ethnic Russians and Ukrainians in the separatist Transdniestr region and with Gagauz Turks in the south.
Ethnic groups in Moldova include: Moldovan/Romanian (64.5 per cent); Ukrainian (13.8 per cent); Russian (13 per cent); Gagauz (3.5 per cent); Bulgarian (2 per cent); and others (3.2 per cent).
Religions
Christianity is the majority religion in Moldova, the principal denomination being the Eastern Orthodox Church (98.5 per cent). The Gagauz also adhere to Orthodox Christianity despite their Turkic roots. There are Romanian and Turkish liturgies in Moldova, but the Russian Orthodox Church (Moscow Patriarchy) has jurisdiction.
Although there are an estimated 20,000 Roman Catholics in Moldova, the Moldovan branch of the Roman Catholic Church, founded in 1848, has few active congregations. Approximately 1.5 per cent of the population is Jewish.

Education
Primary education lasts for four years, at aged 10 students move on to secondary school for seven or eight years. This is divided into five years of lower secondary school and may be followed by two or three years of upper secondary school, following either technical or academic programmes, leading to either higher education or further training. Lessons may be given in either Romanian or Russian.
There are several private higher education institutions.
Before the collapse of the Soviet Union, Moldova's education system was completely integrated into the Soviet system. This meant that most teaching was in the Russian language. Since independence, the curriculum has become much more focussed on Moldovan history and culture. The Moldovan government has restored the Romanian language in schools and added courses in Romanian literature and history to the curriculum. The governments of Romania and Moldova established strong ties between their education systems. Several thousand Moldovan students have attended school in Romania, and the Romanian government has donated textbooks to replace Soviet-era books.
The government's decision to introduce Russian in primary schools as a mandatory subject in January 2002 was a cause of much controversy. In February 2002, the government announced that the Russian language lessons would be optional.
Literacy rate: 99 per cent adult rate; 100 per cent youth rate (15–24) (Unesco 2005).
Compulsory years: 6 to 15.
Enrolment rate: 97 per cent total primary enrolment of the relevant age group (including repetition rates); 81 per cent secondary enrolment (World Bank).
Pupils per teacher: 23 in primary schools.

Health
Per capita total expenditure on health (2003) was US$177; of which per capita government spending was US$96, at the international dollar rate, (WHO 2006).
By 2002, 94 per cent of infants aged less than one year had been immunised against measles.
HIV/Aids
HIV prevalence: 0.2 per cent aged 15–49 in 2003 (World Bank)
Life expectancy: 67 years, 2004 (WHO 2006)
Fertility rate/Maternal mortality rate: 1.2 births per woman, 2004 (WHO 2006)
Birth rate/Death rate: 15.27 births and 12.79 deaths per 1,000 people (2005 estimates)
Child (under 5 years) mortality rate (per 1,000): 40.42 per 1,000 live births (2005)
Head of population per physician: 2.64 physicians per 1,000 people, 2003 (WHO 2006)

Welfare
A social insurance system covers old age pensions, worker's disability, survivors, sickness and maternity benefit and family allowance, plus unemployment payments. Contributions are obtained from workers at 1 per cent of earnings (23 per cent for self-employed); 29–30 per cent employer's payroll, dependent on industry or enterprise; central government pays ad hoc flat-rate payments; regional (Republics), local authorities and employers can also provide supplementary benefits, from their own budgets, for specific needs.
Moldova remains one of the poorest countries in the region and pensioners remain particularly disadvantaged, accounting for 20 per cent of the population. The government intends to introduce private pensions to supplement the current state pension system. In 1999, legislation on private pensions allowed for the establishment of both open and closed pension funds based on voluntary contributions.
Pensions
The minimum retirement age is 62 years with a full pension dependent on 32 years of insurance cover.

Main cities
Chisinau (Kishinev) (capital, estimated population 664,325 in 2005), Tiraspol (183,678), Balti (143,630), Tighina (123,038).

Languages spoken
The 1994 constitution states that Moldovan is the country's official language, although it allows for the use of other languages in the country's ethnic minority areas. Officially known as 'limba moldoveneasca' (language of Moldova), Moldovan is a dialect of Romanian. Russian is the first language of about one-third of the population, and is more universally spoken than Moldovan. Most people are bilingual.
The government attempted to introduce a language law in 1989 which would force government officials to speak both Moldovan and Russian. Since many Russian-speakers could not speak Moldovan and needed time to learn the language, the parliament decided in 1994 to postpone the law indefinitely. The law was a major factor in accelerating the separatist movements of the Russian-speaking Transdniestr region and of the Gagauz-Yeri minority who speak Gagauz (a Turkish dialect). Other minority languages include Ukrainian and Bulgarian.
The government's decision, although later annulled, to introduce Russian in primary schools as a mandatory subject in 2002 was the cause of much controversy.
Official language/s
Moldovan (in latin script)

Media
Despite the guarantees of free expression enshrined in the constitution, following the election of the Communist Party to power in 2001 the media sector has been

subjected to growing administrative and legal pressures designed to exercise control over it. There is, in reality, little real independence within the media, particularly the state-owned media. Whether privately or publicly owned, editorial interference by political and business interests is commonplace.

Press

In 2002, 180 newspapers and magazines were in publication, of which some 100 had national circulation, and 80 local circulation. Around 20 per cent of those with national circulation were partly funded by the state. Political parties published some 15 per cent and the rest were under private or corporate ownership.

A poll commissioned by the Independent Journalism Centre showed that 44 per cent of Moldovans do not read a newspapaer at all, and a further 20 per cent read one less than once a week.

Dailies: Nezavisimaia Moldova is a Russian-language daily of the Government of the Republic of Moldova. Chisinau News is one of the most widely read dailies. Other general interest newspapers include the Romanian-language Jurnal de Chisinau and the Russian-language Kommersant Moldoviy, Kishinyovskie Novosti, Komsomolskaya Pravda, Moldavskie Vedomosti and Novaya Gazeta.

Business: Publications include the Russian-language Delovaya Gazeta and Ekonomicheskoe Obozrenie and the Romanian-language business magazine Observator Economic.

Periodicals: The East-West Observer is an English-language monthly newspaper.

Broadcasting

Radio and televison broadcast licences are issued by the Broadcast Co-ordinating Council (BCC). Licences are issued on the basis of a number of criteria encompassing the plurality of options, equality in the treatment of participants, the quality and diversity of programming, free competition, domestic broadcast productions and the impartiality and independence of broadcast programmes.

Radio: There are some 115 private local radio and television stations; a number of these cover about 70 per cent of the country including Chisinau Municipality's 'Antena C' and the private stations HitFM and Russkoe Radio.

Television: In addition to the public televison station Moldova 1, Russia's public broadcaster ORT and Romania's TVR also have national coverage in Moldova.

Economy

Moldova experienced two major external shocks in 2006 which are predicted to have long-lasting effects. At a time when Moldova had to deal with a high rise in imported natural gas supplies, the import of Moldavian wine was banned by Russia on health grounds. Wine exports to Russia represent 80 per cent of all exports and 19 per cent of GNP. These setbacks are likely to reduce GDP growth by 2–3 per cent in 2007–08.

The service sector provides 58 per cent of GDP, agriculture 17 per cent and industry 25 per cent, of which manufacturing accounts for 17 per cent. Thre is rich agricultural land in Moldova, producing a wide variety of produce.

Economic objectives set out under the IMF Poverty Reduction and Growth Facility (PRGF) were achieved through dedicated adherence to the programme.

The overarching objective for Moldova's future is its integration into the European Union (EU) and the economic measures implemented from 2005 are designed to enhance its appeal to the EU, despite being the poorest country in Europe.

Moldova has reasonable social indicators, including a low level of illiteracy and long life expectancy but poverty is a serious problem with around 80 per cent of the population living below the poverty line.

Macroeconomic policies, designed to achieve a free-market economy, are aimed at reducing poverty and improving the country's prospects. GDP growth in 2005 was 7.0 per cent and is expected to grow by 3.0 per cent in 2006. Inflation was expected to fall to a single digit but may remain around the 11.9 per cent recorded in 2005.

The rate of unemployment is unknown as internationally recognised statistical data has yet to be gathered comprehensively.

External trade

Moldova is a member of the Central European free trade agreement (Cefra) which, by 2007, following the loss of those countries that had joined the European Union, has left eight country members, most located in the Balkans (except Moldova).

Moldova has traditional ties with Russia which were, following the break-up of the Soviet Union, formalised through the Commonwealth of Independent States (CIS). However since 2005 relations have become strained as Russia has exerted economic pressure on Moldova by doubling the price of Russian natural gas and banning Moldovan imports, particularly wine which represented almost 15 per cent of GDP; around 80 per cent of the country's wine exports were destined for Russia. In 2006 exports to the European Union grew to 38 per cent of total, worth eur1.2 billion (US$1.5 billion). Remittances represent an important aspect of foreign earnings, estimated at US$400–500 million annually.

Imports

Natural gas and petroleum, machinery and equipment, chemicals, textiles and consumer goods.

Main sources: Ukraine (19.2 per cent total, 2006), Russia (15.5 per cent), Romania (12.8 per cent).

Exports

Exports include wine and agricultural foodstuffs, textiles and machinery.

Main destinations: Russia (17.3 per cent total, 2006), Romania (14.8 per cent), Ukraine (12.2 per cent).

Agriculture

Farming

Agriculture remains a key sector of the national economy. The sector contributes around a fifth of GDP and is a considerable source of export revenue. It employs over 40 per cent of the working population. Moldova's main resources are its climate and the rich black chernozem soil covering 75 per cent of the land, making it ideal for growing wine grapes, tobacco, sugar beet and for raising dairy cattle. Grains, vegetables and fruits are also important. The animal husbandry sector specialises in the breeding of livestock, pigs and poultry.

The majority of production continues to be from state farms and co-operatives, although as the land reform programme progresses this is expected to change. Agro-industrial complexes are dominant in meat and dairy production. Pork is the main domestic protein source. A quarter of total meat production is exported.

There are around 150 wineries in Moldova and 170,000 hectares (ha) of vineyards. The wine making industry has attracted foreign investment and is dependent upon markets in the CIS. The majority of annual sugar exports go to former Soviet republics. Moldova is also a major tobacco producer.

Crop production in 2005 included: 2,830,300 tonnes (t) cereals in total, 1,840,000t maize, 690,000 t wheat, 318,000t potatoes, 260,000t barley, 907,000t sugar beets, 600,000t grapes, 138,410t oilcrops, 150,000t pulses, 21,100t treenuts, 338,000t apples, 95,000t tomatoes, 18,000t chillies & peppers, 10,200t tobacco, 1,024,710t fruit in total, 380,800t vegetables in total.

Livestock production included: 86,300t meat in total, 23,000t beef, 38,000t pig meat, 2,500t lamb, 22,200t poultry, 37,426t eggs, 628,000t milk, 2,200t honey, 960t sheepskins, 3,230t cattle hides.

Fishing

Only 20 fish species, including crucian carp, perch, bream and soodak, are of any commercial importance. Most of the fish resources are concentrated in natural and artificial lakes devoted to fish breeding.

Forestry

Forest and wooded land account for about one-tenth of the land area, with forest cover estimated at 325,000 hectares (ha). All forests in Moldova are state-owned. About two-thirds of the forest is available for wood supply, while the rest is protected and conserved. Timber includes oak, beech and ash.

Production is mostly for domestic consumption. More than half of all wood consumed is used as fuel or processed into charcoal. The forestry industry faces a shortage of raw materials and is not sufficient to meet the domestic markets. Moldova imports sawnwood and paper. Wood and wood products account for around four per cent of annual GDP. Moldova typically produces approximately 500,000 cubic metres of timber per annum.

Timber imports in 2004 were US$29.3 million, while exports amounted to US$3.7 million.

Industry and manufacturing

Industry accounts for around 25 per cent of GDP. A large proportion of industrial production is concentrated in the breakaway Transdniestr region, where most of Moldova's electricity, metallurgy and metallurgical equipment are produced.

The agro-industrial complex is at the heart of the economy, carrying out the production, transportation, processing, storage and sale of agricultural products. Other industries include electronics, machine tools, tractors, agricultural engineering, building materials, chemicals and furniture manufacture.

Tourism

Tourism is at an early stage of development. The economic value of tourism is recognised and efforts are being made to entice visitors from outside the traditional east European market. Visitor numbers have fallen in recent years: here were around 17,000 arrivals in 2004 compared with 19,000 in 2000. Moldova lacks obvious tourist attractions, so the country's rural charms are being exploited with village holidays, hunting and vineyard tours. The small size of the country is presented as an advantage, allowing all of it to be toured in a short time. Conference and other business tourism is also being encouraged. New infrastructure is being constructed and old stock renovated.

Hydrocarbons

Total domestic oil reserves are minimal with limited production capacity. The Valenskoye field has commercial reserves of around 73 million barrels, which Moldova is planning to exploit in partnership with foreign investors. Potential production is estimated at 732,000 barrels per year. Moldova imports some 22—29 million barrels of oil annually to meet its consumption requirements, which were projected to reach an estimated 25,000 barrels per day (bpd) in 2005. Although Moldova had traditionally imported most of its oil products from Russia, estimates show that supplies from Romania and Ukraine meet nearly 99 per cent of current oil demand.

Gas reserves are estimated at 25 billion cubic metres. Moldova imports three million cubic metres of natural gas annually from Russia, 40 per cent of which goes to the industrialised Transdniestr region. The monopoly domestic gas distributor Moldova-Gaz is heavily indebted to Gazprom, the Russian gas monopoly, with supplies being suspended on occasion to force payment.

Moldova has substantial reserves of coal (10 million tonnes), which should last for the foreseeable future at recent low rates of production. Most production is low-grade bituminous (tar) coal, used in construction rather than power generation. For energy purposes, Moldova imports approximately 420,000 tonnes of hard coal per annum.

Energy

Moldova has limited electricity generating capacity. Although it has three power stations with a total capacity of 301MW, part of the equipment is worn out and must be replaced. Much capacity is in the disputed province of Transdniestr.

Moldova is trying to conserve energy and to develop alternative power sources — solar, wind and geothermal.

Financial markets

Stock exchange

Moldova's embryo economy has yet to develop recognisable financial markets. With founding capital of US$60,000 the Moldova Stock Exchange (MSE) was established in 1993 and began activity in 1995. There are over 1,000 companies listed on the MSE, of which 500 are traded regularly, although most of these are small- or medium-sized.

Banking and insurance

Central bank

Banca Nationala a Moldovei (BNM) (National Bank of Moldova)

Time

GMT plus two hours (daylight saving, late March to late October, GMT plus three hours)

Geography

Moldova is a landlocked country in south-eastern Europe, bordered to the north, east and south by Ukraine and to the west by Romania. Most of the country consists of flat plains with low hills. Approximately 11 per cent of Moldova is forested.

Moldova is a fertile plain with small areas of hill country in the centre and north. The main rivers are the Dniestr, which flows through the eastern regions and on into the Black Sea, and the Prut, which marks the western border with Romania and which joins the Danube at the southern tip of Moldova.

The separatist Republic of Transdniestr (not officially recognised) lies between the eastern Ukrainian border and the Dniestr River.

Hemisphere

Northern

Climate

With a temperate, continental climate Moldova has long hot summers and chilly winters. Average temperatures vary between minus 2 degrees Celsius (C) and 22 degrees C. Extremes of temperature can reach 35 degrees C during summer and minus 25 degrees C (with a good deal of ice and snow) in the winter. Average annual rainfall is 500–550mm in the northern and central areas and 450mm in the south.

Dress codes

Business dress is usually quite conservative, but not excessively formal.

Entry requirements

Passports

Required by all. Passports must be valid for at least six months after the date of departure.

Visa

Required by all except CIS nationals. Visit www.consularassistance.com/consular.html for the requirements and a visa application form, to be submitted to the nearest consulate for processing. Limited stay visas can be obtained at Chisinau airport and some major road crossings from Romania; however, these cost more than those organised in advance. Arrival by train requires a visa before travelling.

Currency advice/regulations

The import and export of local currency is unlimited; the import of foreign currency is unlimited but the amount must be declared and export is limited to the amount declared.

Travellers cheques are not in general use, although some banks may exchange them.

Customs

A small amount of personal goods are allowed in duty-free. On arrival declare all valuable items such as jewellery, cameras, computers and musical instruments.

Health (for visitors)

Mandatory precautions

Vaccination certificates for cholera and yellow fever are mandatory if travelling from an infected area. Any person applying for a visa for a stay of more than three months must present a certificate showing that the individual is HIV negative. Only tests performed at clinics approved by the Moldovan government are accepted.

Advisable precautions

It is advisable to be in date for the following immunisations: diphtheria, polio and tetanus (within 10 years), typhoid fever, hepatitis A (moderate risk only), hepatitis B, tuberculosis and tick-borne encephalitis. Healthcare is free in Moldova (although medicines must be purchased). There are chemists where you can buy basic drugs (aspirin, etc), but it is wise to take a supply of frequently used medicines with you, including precautionary antibiotics if travelling outside main urban areas. A travel kit, including disposable syringes, is a reasonable precaution. There is a rabies risk. Water precautions are recommended and water purification tablets may be useful.

Credit cards

Credit cards are not in general use, some banks may accept them.

Public holidays (national)

Fixed dates

1 Jan (New Year's Day), 8 Mar (Women's Day), 1 May (Labour Day), 9 May (Victory Day), 27 Aug (Independence Day), 31 Aug (Limba Noastra/National Language Day), 14 Oct (Chisinau City Day).

Variable dates

Religious holidays are celebrated by adherents (Orthodox Christmas and Easter).

Working hours

Banking

Mon–Sat: 0930–1730 for banks; 0900–1800 for bureau de change.

Business

Mon–Fri: 0900–1800.

Government

Mon–Fri: 0900–1800.

Shops

Mon: 0800–1700, Tue–Sat: 0800–2100.

Telecommunications

Mobile/cell phones

GSM 900 services available throughout most of the country.

Electricity supply

220V AC 50 Hz.

Weights and measures

Metric system

Social customs/useful tips

Business appointments are essential and punctuality appreciated. Business cards are usually exchanged. There are many customs and traditions to be understood. Gratuities are becoming more customary, particularly in international hotels.
Take flowers if invited to someone's home and leave shoes at the door.

Security

Although safer than many Western cities, the streets of Chisinau have become more dangerous since independence, particularly after dark. Care should be taken to avoid unlit areas, even in the city centre. There are few embassies in Chisinau (no British Embassy, for instance). Before departure to Moldova, visitors are advised to check with their own ministry of foreign affairs for information on who to contact in the case of an emergency. The British Foreign & Commonwealth Office (FCO), for example, advises its nationals to contact the British Embassy in Bucharest in Romania.
Avoid all travel in the eastern region of Transdniestr.

Getting there

Air

National airline: Air Moldova; services are not extensive with international flights to Europe only.

International airport/s: Chisinau International (KIV), 13km south-east of the city with duty-free and bank. Taxis and a regular bus service are available to the city (travel time 15–25 minutes).

Airport tax: Departure tax: US$12.

Surface

Road: The principal route runs from Odessa in the Crimea into Moldova through Tiraspol, north to Chisinau, Bel'tsy and then back into Ukraine.
Buses run to Chisinau from Bucharest, Romania.

Rail: The Moldovan rail network is connected to that of Ukraine, Romania and Russia. The principal rail routes connect Chisinau with Tiraspol and Ukraine to the east, and Lasi in Romania to the west. The journey time to Bucharest is approximately 11.5 hours, to Moscow 22 hours and Sofia 23 hours. First-class sleeping carriages, booked in advance from Chisinau station, are recommended.

Water: The Dniestr River flows into the Black Sea in Ukraine, near the port of Odessa. It is used more for industrial transportation than for passengers.

Getting about

National transport

Road: The road network, although extensive, is in need of significant investment and repair. The main routes run from Kagul to Chisinau via Komrat and from Chisinau to Lipkany via Bel'tsy. Roads from Tiraspol in Transdniestr to Chisinau and other destinations in the rest of Moldova may be subject to closure due to conflict in the breakaway region.

Buses: There are buses between larger towns.

Taxis: Can be hired by the hour, prices should be negotiated before travelling.

Rail: Most larger towns are connected by rail. Lines run north-south from Kagul and the southern border with Ukraine to Lipkany and the northern border with Ukraine. Owing to the Transdniestr conflict, routes from Chisinau and Kagul to Tiraspol and Bendery are liable to disruption.

Water: The Dniestr River runs parallel to Moldova's eastern border, and is extensively used, although mostly for industrial rather than passenger transport.

City transport

The names of streets are in both Moldovan and Russian.

Taxis: Taxis are widely available and can be picked up at stands or hailed anywhere in the city.

Car hire

Vehicles with a driver or for self-drive are readily available; an international driving permit is required.

BUSINESS DIRECTORY

The addresses listed below are a selection only. While World of Information makes every endeavour to check these addresses, we cannot guarantee that changes have not been made, especially to telephone numbers and area codes. We would welcome any corrections.

Telephone area codes

The international direct dialling (IDD) code for Moldova is +373, followed by the area code and subscriber's number:

Chisinau	22	Bendery	282
Bel'tsy	231	Tiraspol	284

Useful telephone numbers

Ambulance: 903
Fire: 901
Police: 902
Operator assistance for international telephone calls: 071

Chambers of Commerce

American Chamber of Commerce in Moldova, Joly Alon Hotel, 37 Maria Cebotari Street, Chisinau 2012.

Moldova Chamber of Commerce and Industry, 151 Stefan cel Mare Street, Chisinau 2004 (tel: 221-552; fax: 234-425; e-mail: president@chamber.md).

Banking

Banca Comerciala Romana SA Sucursala, 32A Tricolorului Street, Chisinau 2012 (tel: 220-549; fax: 223-509; email: bcr@cni.md).

Banca Sociala, 61 Banulescu-Bodoni Street, Chisinau 2006 (tel: 221-481; fax: 224-230).

BTR Moldova, 18 Renasterii Street, Chisinau 2005 (tel: 201-100; fax: 201-101; e-mail: office@btr.md).

Businessbanca, 9 Alexandru cel Bun Street, Chisinau 2012 (tel: 223-338; fax: 222-370).

Chisinau Municipal Bank, 83 Stefan cel Mare Avenue, Chisinau 2012 (tel/fax: 228-090).

Comertbank, 63 Columna Street, Chisinau 2001 (tel: 541-356; fax: 543-151; e-mail: combank@chmoldpac.md).

Energbank, 78 Vasile Alexandri Street, Chisinau 2012 (tel: 544-377; fax: 253-409).

Export - Import, 6 Stefan cel Mare Avenue, Chisinau 2001 (tel: 272-583; fax: 546-234; e-mail: exim@eximbank.com).

Finance and Trade Bank, 26 Pushkin Street, Chisinau 2012 (tel: 227-435; fax: 228-253; e-mail: fincom@fcb.mldnet.com).

International Commercial Bank (Moldova), 108 Mitropolit Dosoftei Street, Chisnau 2012 (tel: 226-025; fax: 225-053; e-mail: info@icbsb.md).

Investprivatbank, 34 Sciusev Street, Chisinau 2001 (tel: 274-386; fax: 540-510; email: bnc@ipb.mldnet.com).

Mobiasbanca, 65 Tighina Street, Chisinau 2001 (tel/fax: 541-974; email: info@bcmobias.moldova.su).

Moldindconbank, 38 Armeneasca Street, Chisinau 2012. (tel: 225-521: fax: 279-195; email: computer@micb.net.md).

Moldova - Agroindbank, 9 Cosmonautilor Street, Chisinau 2006 (tel: 222-770; fax: 242-454).

PetrolBANK, 33 Ismail Street, Chisinau 2001 (tel: 500-101; fax: 548-827; email: juri@petrolbank.com).

Savings Bank, 115 Columna Street, Chisinau 2012 (tel: 244-722; fax: 244-731; email: bem@cni.md).

Unibank, 26 Pushkin Street, Chisinau 2012 (tel: 225-586; fax: 220-530).

Universalbank, 180 Stefan cel Mare Avenue, Chisinau 2004 (tel: 246-406; fax: 246-489; email:stabil@mail.universalbank.md).

Victoriabank, 141 August 31 Street, Chisinau 2004 (tel: 233-065; fax: 233-933; email: mail@victoriabank.md).

Central bank

Banca Nationala a Moldovei, 7 Renasterii Avenue, Chisinau 2006 (tel: 221-679; fax: 220-591; e-mail: webmaster@bnm.org).

Travel information

Air Moldova, Aeroportul Chisinau, MD 2026, Chisinau (tel: 529-356; fax: 525-064; internet: www.mdv.md).

Ministry of tourism

Ministry of Culture and Tourism, Piata Marii Adunari 1, MD-2033, Chisinau (tel: 227-620; fax: 232-388).

National tourist organisation offices

National Tourism Agency, 180 Stefan cel Mare Street, Office 901 Chisinau MD 2004, (tel: 210 774; internet www.turism.md).

Ministries

Ministry of Agriculture and Food Industry, 162 Stefan cel Mare Boulevard, Chisinau (tel: 233-427; fax: 232-368).

Ministry of Culture, 1 Piata Marii Adunari Nationale, Chisinau (tel: 227-620; fax: 232-388).

Ministry of Defence, 84 Vasile Alexandri Street, Chisinau (tel: 781-156; fax: 233-507).

Ministry of Economy and Reforms, Piata Marii Adunari Nationale 1, 277033 Chisinau (tel: 221-133; fax: 234-064).

Ministry of Education, 1 Piata Marii Adunari Nationale (tel: 233-151; fax: 233-474).

Ministry of Finance, Cosmonautilor Street, 277012 Chisinau (tel: 233-575; fax: 228-610).

Ministry of Foreign Affairs, 1 Piata Marii Adunari Nationale, Chisinau (tel: 233-940; fax: 232-302).

Ministry of Foreign Economic Relations, Piata Marii Adunari Nationale 1, Chisinau 277033 (tel/fax: 234-628).

Ministry of Health, 1 Vasile Alexandri Street, Chisinau (tel: 721-010; fax: 738-781).

Ministry of Industry and Trade, 69 Stefan cel Mare Boulevard, Chisinau (tel: 233-556; fax: 227-346).

Ministry of Internal Affairs, 75 Stefan cel Mare Boulevard, Chisinau (tel: 221-201; fax: 222-723).

Ministry of Justice, 82, 31 August Street, Chisinau (tel: 233-340; fax: 234-797).

Ministry of Labour, Social Protection and Family, 1 Vasile Alexandri Street, Chisinau (tel: 737-572; fax: 723-000).

Ministry of National Security, 166 Stefan cel Mare Boulevard, Chisinau (tel: 239-454; fax: 242-018).

Ministry of Privatisation and State Property Administration, 26 Puskin Street, Chisinau (tel: 234-350; fax: 234-336; internet site: http://privatization.md).

Ministry of Territorial Development, Public Utilities and Construction, 3 Gheorghe Tudor Street, Chisinau (tel: 259-111; fax: 259-499).

Ministry of Telecommunications and Informatics, 134 Stefan cel Mare Boulevard, Chisinau (tel: 221-001; fax: 241-553).

Ministry of Transport and Road Construction, 12/A Bucuriei Street, Chisinau (tel: 629-450; fax: 624-875).

Other useful addresses

British Embassy (there is no British representative in Moldova but the British Embassy in Moscow has some responsibility), Commercial Department, Kutuzovsky Prospeckt 7/4, Moscow 121248 (tel: 956-7477; fax: 956-7480).

Business Centre of Moldova Ltd., Stefan cel Mare 180, Room 303, 277004 Chisinau (tel: 247-914; fax: 247-915).

Department of Civil Protection and Exceptional Situations, 69 Cheorghe Asachi Street, Chisinau (tel: 233-430; fax: 233-430).

Department of Customs Control, 65 Columna Street, Chisinau (tel: 549-460; fax: 263-061).

Department of Energy Resources and Fuel, 50 Eminescu Street, Chisinau (tel: 221-010; fax: 222-264).

Department of Environmental Protection, 73 Stefan cel Mare Boulevard, Chisinau (tel: 226-161; fax: 233-806).

Department of National Relations, 109/1, Alexei Mateevici Street, Chisinau (tel: 240-292; fax: 243-610).

Department of Publishing, Polygraphy and Trade of Books, 180 Stefan cel Mare Boulevard, Chisinau (tel: 246-525).

Department of Standards, Metrology and Technical Control, 48 Serghei Lazo Street, Chisinau (tel: 247-991; fax: 222-321).

Department of Statistics, 124 Stefan cel Mare Avenue, Chisinau 227001 (tel: 233-549; fax: 545-162).

MoldEnergo, 78 Vasile Alexandri Str, 277012 Chisinau (tel: 221-065; fax: 253-142).

Moldexpo International Exhibition Centre, 1 Ghioceilor, 277008 Chisinau (tel: 627-416; fax: 627-420).

Moldovan Foreign Trade Organisation, ul Sadovaya 65, 277018 Chisinau (tel: 244-436; fax: 223-226).

Moldova-Gaz, 38 Albisoara Str, 277005 Chisinau (tel: 256-778; fax: 240-014).

Moldova Stock Exchange, 73 Stefan cel Mare, 277001 Chisinau (tel: 265-554; fax: 228-969).

Moldovan Embassy (USA), 2101 S Street, NW, Washington DC 20008 (tel: (+1-202) 667-1130; fax: (+1-202)

667-120-4; e-mail: moldova@dgs.dgsys.com).

Moldsilva (Forestry Association), 124 Stefan cel Mare Blvd, 277012 Chisinau (tel: 262-256; fax: 223-251).

National Association of Banks, 7 Renasterii Str, 277006 Chisinau (tel: 225-177; fax: 229-382).

National Foreign Trade Company (Moldova-EXIM), 65 Mateevici Str, 277012 Chisinau (tel: 223-226; fax: 244-436).

National Fuel Association, 90 Columna Str, 277001 Chisinau (tel: 223-078; fax: 240-509).

State Company Teleradio Moldova National TV and Radio, 64 Hincesti Highway, 277028 Chisinau (tel: 721-077, 721-863).

Internet sites

Business information: http://www.infomarket.md

Business network: http://www.mbinet.md

Chamber of Commerce: http://www:chamber.md

Freezone and export processing: http://www:moldova-freezone.com

General information (in Moldovan - Romanian): http://www.moldova.md

General government and economy: http://www.moldova.org

IMF Moldova office: http://www.imf.md

Internet resources directory: http://www.ournet.md

Ministry of Economy - Trade department: http://www.trade.moldova

Moldovan parliament: http://www.parlament.md

National Bank rates: http://www.mldnet.com

Monaco

KEY FACTS

Official name: Principauté de Monaco (The Principality of Monaco)

Head of State: Prince Albert II (acceded to the throne 6 Apr 2005)

Head of government: Minister of State Jean-Paul Proust (since 2005; re-elected 2008)

Ruling party: Coalition of the Union pour Monaco (Union for Monaco), led by Union pour la Principauté (UP) (Union for the Principality), with Union Nationale pour l'Avenir de Monaco (UNAM) (National Union for the Future of Monaco) and Promotion de la Famille Monégasque (PFM) (Promotion of the Monegasque Family (since 2003; re-elected February 2008)

Area: 2 square km

Population: 32,000 (2005)*

Capital: Monaco-Ville

Official language: French and Monégasque

Currency: Euro (eur) = 100 cents

Exchange rate: eur0.63 per US$ (Jul 2008)

GDP per capita: US$30,000 (2006)*

Labour force: 30,540 (2003)

Unemployment: 3.10% (2003)

* estimated figure

COUNTRY PROFILE

Historical profile

1297 Francois Grimaldi led a group of partisans into Monaco, which has been ruled by the family ever since.
Honore II signed a treaty of friendship with France, guaranteeing the independence of the principality.
1814 The principality was re-established after its abolition during the French Revolution.
1861 Its independence was guaranteed under French protection. The first constitution was introduced.
1918 Louis, the heir to the throne, was a bachelor and the next male in line to succeed if Louis died without an heir was a German prince, the Duke of Urach. France would not countenance a German monarch and therefore imposed a constitutional provision that only the monarch's own children could inherit the throne.
1949 Prince Rainier III, embodying divine right, succeeded to the throne.
1956 Prince Rainier married the US actress, Grace Kelly.
1962 A constitution was enacted that allowed for sharing of legislative powers between the monarch and elected national council; principle of divine right was abolished.
1982 Princess Grace was killed in a car accident.
1988 The Union Nationale et Démocratique (UND) (National and Democratic Union) won the elections.
1993 The UND was defeated by two lists of candidates, known as Liste Campora and Liste Medecin.
1993 Monaco was admitted to the UN.
1998 UND won the elections.
2000 France threatened to take legislative measures against Monaco unless it clamped down on money laundering activities.
2001 France and Monaco reached an agreement on money laundering. As part of the co-operative, Monaco agreed to work more closely with the Financial Oversight Commission (FOC) to revise rules governing investment management companies.
2002 Monaco adopted the euro as its official currency. Parliament changed the 1918 law of succession, allowing one of Prince Rainier's daughters, either Caroline or Stephanie – to be followed by one of their children – to succeed Albert if he died without a legitimate heir. Liechtenstein concluded an agreement with Monaco over the prevention of money laundering and terrorist financing.
2003 The Union pour Monaco (UPM) (Union for Monaco) alliance, led by Stephané Valeri, won a landslide majority in the parliamentary elections, ending the 40-year rule of the UND.
2004 Prince Rainier was diagnosed with heart problems.
2005 Prince Rainier III died on 6 April. He had come to the throne in 1949 and was the longest serving monarch in Europe. Prince Albert II was enthroned on 12 July. Jean-Paul Proust was appointed as minister of state.
2008 In the 3 February parliamentary elections, the ruling Union pour Monaco (Union for Monaco) coalition won 21 out of 24 seats, the Rassemblement et Enjeux pour Monaco (REM) (Rally and Issues of Monaco) won three seats and the Monaco Ensemble (Monaco Together) failed to win any. Turnout was 76.9 per cent.

Political structure

Constitution

Under the 1962 constitution, Monaco is governed under the authority of the monarch, a minister of state and a unicameral National Council.
Only Monégasques may vote.
In 2002, parliament passed a change to the 1918 law of succession. Princesses Caroline or Stephanie may inherit if Prince Albert dies without a legitimate heir. The line of succession will pass down through the line of whichever Princess assumes the title. An agreement with France allows Monaco to remain an independent country in the event of a lack of heir to succeed to the Principality.

Form of state

Parliamentary democratic monarchy

The executive

The monarch is the head of state. The monarch nominates the minister of state from a list of three French diplomats submitted by the French government. As head of the Council of Government (three members appointed by the monarch), the minister of state exercises executive power under the monarch.
The laws are initiated by the monarch; the Council of Government prepares draft legislation in his name; the National

Council passes laws and the national budget (in public session); the monarch alone promulgates laws which are then published in the Journal de Monaco.
The government is assisted by two consultative bodies: the Council of State and the Economic Council.

National legislature
Legislative authority resides with the 18-member Conseil National (national council) elected every five years by universal adult suffrage. The National Council has no power to topple the government.

Legal system
Although judicial authority is vested in the monarch, it is delegated to the courts and tribunals, which dispense justice in the monarch's name, but completely independently (there is no minister of justice in the Principality).

Last elections
3 February 2008 (parliamentary)
Results: Parliamentary: The Coalition of the Union pour Monaco (Union for Monaco), led by Union pour la Principauté (UP) (Union for the Principality), with Union Nationale pour l'Avenir de Monaco (UNAM) (National Union for the Future of Monaco) and Promotion de la Famille Monégasque (PFM) (Promotion of the Monegasque Family) won 52.2 per cent of the vote (21 seats out of 24), the Rassemblement et Enjeux pour Monaco (REM) (Rally and Issues of Monaco) 40.49 per cent (three seats), Monaco Ensemble (Monaco Together) 7.31 per cent (no seats). Turnout was 76.9 per cent.

Next elections
2013 (parliamentary)

Political parties

Ruling party
Coalition of the Union pour Monaco (Union for Monaco), led by Union pour la Principauté (UP) (Union for the Principality), with Union Nationale pour l'Avenir de Monaco (UNAM) (National Union for the Future of Monaco) and Promotion de la Famille Monégasque (PFM) (Promotion of the Monegasque Family (since 2003; re-elected February 2008)

Main opposition party
Union nationale et démocratique (UND) (National and Democratic Union)

Political situation
There was a landslide majority for the UPM alliance, led by Stephané Valeri, in the 203 parliamentary elections that ended the 40-year rule of the UND. The UND, which had held all the seats in the previous parliament, only managed to hold on to three seats. The swing in favour of the UPM was largely due to the increasing unpopularity of the UND leader, Jean-Louis Campora, who had served as parliamentary speaker for 30 years. Campora lost his seat in the election. Turnout was 80 per cent, but only around 20 per cent of the total population is eligible to vote due to the constitutional nationality requirements.

Population

32,000 (2005)*
Last census: June 2000: 32,017 (provisional)
Population density: 16,410 inhabitants per sq km.
Annual growth rate: 1.1 per cent 1994–2004 (WHO 2006)

Ethnic make-up
According to the 2000 census, around 7,000 of the total population are Monégasques, 11,000 French, 7,000 Italian and some 2,000 British.

Religions
The state religion is Catholicism, but religious freedom is guaranteed by the constitution. Other religions practised are Anglicanism, Baha'i, Judaism, Protestantism.

Health

Per capita total expenditure on health (2003) was US$4,487; of which per capita government spending was US$3,403, at the international dollar rate, (WHO 2006).
Life expectancy: 82 years, 2004 (WHO 2006)
Fertility rate/Maternal mortality rate: 1.8 births per woman, 2004 (WHO 2006)
Child (under 5 years) mortality rate (per 1,000): 4.0 per 1,000 live births (World Bank)

Main cities

Monaco-Ville (capital, estimated population 1,400 in 2003), Monte Carlo (15,400), La Condamine (14,600).

Languages spoken

Italian and English are widely spoken and understood. The traditional Monégasque language is spoken by the older generation of Monégasques and is taught in schools. Ligurian and Occitan are also spoken.

Official language/s
French and Monégasque

Media

Press
The official Journal de Monaco is a journal published weekly by the ministry of state,
The independent, Mediterraneum Editions (www.mediterra.com), publishes newspapers in several languages, including the in-house publications, in English The Monaco Times (www.mctimes.com) in Italian, Il Corriere di Monaco (www.corrieremonaco.com) and in German Monaco Zeitung. In French, Monaco Hebdo covers current affairs. Regional newspapers with sections devoted to Monaco include Nice-Matin, Gazette Monaco-Côte d'Azur, Monaco Actualité and Monte Carlo Méditerranée.

Broadcasting
The influence of Monaco on media broadcasting is high due, not only to its extensive radio network, but also as host to one of the oldest television awards festival.
Radio: Radio Monte Carlo (RMC) (www.rmc.fr) broadcasts throughout France and northern Italy with external services in 12 languages. The service it began, transmitting to the Arab world, Monte Carlo Doualiva, was taken over by Radio France Internationale. Riviera Radio (www.rivieraradio.mc), based in RMC studios, broadcasts in English 24 hours per day. Evangelical programmes are broadcast by shortwave in numerous foreign languages by Trans World Radio (www.twr.org).
There are also a number of private, commercial FM stations including Nostalgie (www.nostalgie.fr), Radio Monaco (www.radio-monaco.com) and Radio Classique (www.radioclassique.fr).
Television: The commercial station TMC Monte Carlo (www.tmc.tv) broadcasts popular imported films and shows as well as local news programmes. The government also operates a localised TV station, Monaco Info, showing cultural and magazine style programmes, for a limited number of hours each week.

Economy

Monaco enjoys a small, open and diversified economy based on tourism, the convention business, banking and insurance, but with a significant industrial sector.
Government revenue is derived from value added tax (VAT) levied on hotel, banking and commercial services (55 per cent) and state monopolies such as telecommunications, the post office and tobacco industry (16 per cent); gambling revenue accounts for only 4 per cent. Until the first statistical survey is published in 2007, information and detail on Monaco's economy, GNP and GDP is unavailable. It is thought that financial services accounts for 50 per cent of GDP
Although Monaco is not a member of the EU, France's membership gives it access to the European marketplace. Monaco adopted the euro as its official currency at the same time as France.
The late Prince Rainier endeavoured to broaden the base of the local economy, notably with the Fontvieille development of 22 hctares of reclaimed land to the west of the old town, which is now a centre for light industry and low-cost housing. Monaco's total area has been increased by one-tenth by this project.

Monaco is diversifying into the knowledge-based industry, aiming to become a European leader in multimedia, the Internet and telecommunications.
In June 2004, Monaco agreed to operate equivalent measures to those applied by EU's member states regarding taxation of income from savings, beginning in 2005.

External trade

Monaco has a free trade and customs union with France, which operates within the European Union and, by extension, effects Monaco. France collects and rebates Monegasque trade duties. Virtually all foreign trade is within the service sector including financial, commercial and tourism. Many companies are registered, for tax reasons, in Monaco, which does not publish official statistics.

Imports

Fuels, food, vehicles and consumer goods.

Exports

Financial services
There is no commercial agriculture in Monaco.

Industry and manufacturing

Around 200 firms employing 4,000 people typically account for about 33 per cent of GDP. Main products are cosmetics, healthcare, pharmaceuticals, precision instruments, glass, plastics, electrical goods, electronics, textiles and food processing. Also important are construction and public works.

Tourism

Tourism contributes around 25 per cent of GDP. Monaco attracts around 260,000 tourists annually. Most visitors are day trippers. The casino and the annual Grand Prix motor race are major attractionons. The oceanographic museum, formerly directed by Jacques Cousteau, is one of the most renowned institutions of its kind in the world.
Monaco is expanding its conference and exhibition activities to enhance its appeal to the business travel market.

Energy

Monaco is entirely reliant on imports from France to meet its energy requirements. The Société Monégasque de l'Electricité et du Gaz is responsible for distribution.

Banking and insurance

There are nearly 50 banks and around 20 other financial institutions catering to 130,000 clients worth US$78 billion. In addition to commercial and retail services, Monaco has in recent decades increasingly provided private banking and wealth management services. Monaco's banking system operates under French banking law and is subject to regulation by the Banque de France.
Monaco's reputation as a tax haven with a secretive banking system has made enemies in other jurisdictions, which accuse Monaco of abetting money-laundering and tax evasion. Monaco has been resistant to pressure to be more be more rigorous and transparent in its dealings, but does take action against money-laundering under existing legislation. In addition, mutual assistance agreements to exchange information on money-laundering have been concluded since 2001 with several countries, including France, Spain, Belgium, and Switzerland .
Monaco was obliged to accede to the EU Savings Tax Directive, which took effect in July 2005. Under the withholding tax option, Monaco's banks and financial institutions will automatically deduct tax, initially 15 per cent rising to 35 per cent by 2011, from income earned on interest and other savings of EU citizens and transfer it to the national tax departments. Monaco will be able to retain its banking secrecy by being allowed to withhold information on non-residents' savings. Monaco has also agreed to supply information on tax fraud, for criminal or civil trials, and notify EU member states about additional malpractices.

Central bank

European Central Bank
Monaco does not have a central bank, but monetary links to France have included acceptance of French currency and subsequently the euro as legal tender, while financial institutions located in Monaco have access to the Banque de France on the similar terms to French banks.

Main financial centre

Monaco-Ville

Time

GMT plus one hour (daylight saving, late March to late September, GMT plus two hours)

Geography

The Principality of Monaco is a small enclave in south-eastern France, close to the French-Italian frontier. It comprises a narrow, 4km stretch of Mediterranean coastline with an area of 1.9 square km, situated at the foot of the Alpes Maritimes, which gives it a rocky aspect on the landward side. The highest point is Mont Agel, which reaches 140m.
Monaco is divided into four main localities: the old fortified town of Monaco-Ville, where the palace and cathedral are located; La Condamine, the harbour and business area; Monte Carlo, the resort and main residential area; and Fontvieille, an area of 0.33 square km recovered from the sea in recent years for light industry and residential development.

Hemisphere

Northern

Climate

The climate is Mediterranean with mild winters and warm summers. The hottest months are July and August, with average temperatures of 25 degrees Celsius.

Entry requirements

Passports

Required by all, except nationals of EU/EEAcountries, Switzerland, Andorra and San Marino, valid for three months beyond date of departure.

Visa

Not required for visits up to three months provided visitors arrive from France and adhere to French entry requirements.
French visas are required by all, except citizens of EU, North America, Australasia and Japan, for stays up to three months; this includes business trips by representatives of foreign entities with an invitation from a local company or organisation. Proof of adequate funds for stay, an itinerary, a guarantee of repatriation if necessary and return/onward ticket are also required.

Currency advice/regulations

There are no restrictions on the import or export of local and foreign currencies.

Health (for visitors)

Mandatory precautions

None

Advisable precautions

Up-to-date tetanus and polio immunisations.

Hotels

Classified into one- to four-star and predominantly four-star/luxury categories. Monaco has around 2,500 hotel rooms, most of which are four-star. The occupancy rate is around 50 per cent.

Credit cards

All credit cards are accepted.

Public holidays (national)

Fixed dates

1 Jan (New Year's Day), 26–27 Jan (Feast of St Dévote), 1 May (Labour Day), 31 May (Prince Albert Day),15 Aug (Assumption Day), 1 Nov (All Saints' Day), 19 Nov (National Day/ Fête du Prince), 8 Dec (Immaculate Conception), 25 Dec (Christmas Day).

Variable dates

Easter Monday, Ascension Day, Whit Monday, Corpus Christ (May/Jun).

Working hours

Banking

Mon–Sat: 0900–1200 and 1400–1630 (except Saturday afternoons preceding Bank Holidays). Banque Franco-Portugaise, Monte Carlo, is open on Saturdays.

Business
Mon–Fri: 0900–1200 and 1400–1700.
Government
Mon–Fri: 0930–1230 and 1330–1700.
Shops
Mon–Sat: 0900–1230 and 1500–1830.

Telecommunications
Telephone/fax
Mobile/cell phones
GSM 900 serivice is available throughout the territory with a 3G service planned.

Security
Monaco has relatively low rates of crime. Pickpockets operate in train stations and subways.

Getting there
Air
The nearest international airport is at Nice (NCE) in France, 22km from Monaco. There is a heliport in Monte Carlo (MCM), from which Heli-Air Monaco and Monacair operate.
Airport tax: None.
Surface
Road: There are good road links between Monaco and France. No formalities are required to cross the border.
Rail: Monaco is well-served by rail links between and to cities in France, Italy and Switzerland. Daily and over-night through trains transit the Principality. The TGV Méditeranée operates between Monaco and Paris
Water: Harbours at Condamine (Hercule port) and Fontvieille can accommodate yachts. Larger vessels can anchor in the bay of Monaco.

Getting about
National transport
There are around 50km of roads and 1.6km of railways (operated by Société Nationale des Chemins de Fer Français).
Buses: There are regular bus services within Monaco, as well as to neighbouring French centres. A direct service is available from Nice Airport to Monaco, stopping at a number of hotels.
City transport
Taxis: Taxis are available around the clock in the Avenue de Monte Carlo and from the railway station. There are taxi ranks at Fontvieille, Place des Moulins, Avenue de la Costa and Beach Plaza.
Buses, trams & metro: Buses operate every five minutes from Monaco-Ville to the casino and every 10 minutes to the railway station and the beaches.

BUSINESS DIRECTORY

Telephone area codes
The international direct dialling (IDD) code for Monaco is +377, followed by an eight-digit number.

Useful telephone numbers
Police (emergencies):17 (switchboard): 9315-3015

Ambulance/Fire services (emergencies): 18 (switchboard):9330-1945

Medical/paramedic team/ambulance: 9375-2525

Doctor or chemist on duty:9325-3325

Main Post Office, Palais de la Scala: 9325-1111.

Chambers of Commerce
Monaco Economic Development Chamber, 11 Rue du Gabian, BP 653, MC 98013 Monaco (tel: 9798-6868; fax: 9798-6869; e-mail: info@cde.mc).

Banking
Banque Franco Portugaise (BFP), 5 Av Princesse Alice, MC 98000 (tel: 9350-1115; fax: 9350-1921).

Banque Générale du Commerce, 2 Av des Spélugues, Monte Carlo (tel: 9350-1762).

Banque Internationale de Monaco, Sporting d'Hiver, 2 Av Princesse Alice, Monte Carlo (tel: 9216-5757; fax: 9216-5750).

Barclays Bank plc, 31 Av de la Costa, Monte Carlo (tel: 9315-3535; fax: 9325-1568).

Crédit Foncier de Monaco, 11 Bd Albert 1er, MC98000 (tel: 9310-2000; fax: 9310-2350).

Société Générale, 16 Ave de la Costa (tel: 9315-5700); also at 17 Bd Albert 1er (tel: 9350-8692).

Société Monégasque de Banque Privée, 9 Boulevard d'Italie, MC 98000 (tel: 9315-2323).

Central bank
European Central Bank (ECB), Kaiserstrasse 29, D-60311 Frankfurt am Main, Germany (tel: +49(69)13-440; fax: +49(69)1344-6000; e-mail: info@ecb.int).

Travel information
Automobile Club of Monaco, 23 Boulevard Albert 1er, Monaco (tel: 9315-2600; fax: 9325-8008; e-mail: info@acm.mc).

Gare de Monaco, 26 Avenue Prince Pierre, Monaco (tel: 9310-6015; e-mail: info@monaco-gare.com).

Heli-Air Monaco, Héliport de Monaco, Quartier de Fontvieille, Macono (tel: 9205-0050; fax: 9205-0051; e-mail: helico@heliairmonaco.com).

Monacair, Héliport de Monaco, Quartier de Fontvieille, Monaco (tel: 9797-3900; fax: 9797-3909; e-mail: accueil@monacair.mc).

Compagnie des Autobus de Monaco (CAM), 3 Avenue Président J F Kennedy, Monaco (tel: 9770-2222; fax: 9770-2223).

Service de la Marine, Direction des Ports, 6 Quai Antoine, PO Box 468, Monaco (tel: 9315-8678; fax: 9315-3715; e-mail: marine@gouv.mc).

National tourist organisation offices
Direction du Tourisme et des Congrès, 2a Boulevard des Moulins, Monaco (tel: 9216-6116; fax: 9216-6000; e-mail: dtc@monaco-tourisme.com).

Other useful addresses
Centre de Congrès, Bd Louis II, Monaco (tel: 9310-8400).

Centre d'Informations Administratives, 23 Av Prince Héréditaire Albert, Monaco (tel: 9315-4026).

Centre de Presse, 4 Rue des Iris, Monte Carlo (tel: 9330-4227).

Centre de Rencontres Internationales, Ave d'Ostende, Monaco (tel: 9310-8600).

Comité des Fêtes, Monaco-ville (tel: 9330-8004).

Direction de l'Expansion Economique, 'Le Concorde', 11 Rue du Gabian, PO Box 665, Monaco (tel: 9798-6868; fax: 9798-6869; e-mail: info@cde.mc).

Directorate of Fiscal Services, 57 Rue Grimaldi, MC98000 (tel: 9315-8122; fax: 9205-8155).

Douanes, 7 Av Président JF Kennedy, Monaco (tel: 9330-2600).

Mairie de Monaco, Monaco-ville (tel: 9315-2863).

Ministère d'Etat, Monaco-ville (tel: 9315-8000).

Monte Carlo Casino, Place du Casino, Monaco (tel: 9216-2000; fax: 9216-3862; e-mail: mrk.jeux@sbm.mc).

Monte Carlo Main Post, Square Beaumarchais (Palais de la Scala) (tel: 9350-6987).

Radio Monte Carlo (RMC), 16 Bd Princesse Charlotte, Monte Carlo (tel: 9315-1617).

Service de l'Urbanisme et de la Construction, 23 Av Prince Hérditaire Albert, Monaco (tel: 9315-8000).

Télé Monte Carlo, 16 Bd Princesse Charlotte, Monaco (tel: 9315-1415).

Internet sites
Banking and investment advice: www.cmb.mc

Monaco online: www.monaco.mc/

Monte Carlo web directory: http://monte-carlo.mc/

KEY FACTS

Official name: Mongol Uls (The State of Mongolia)

Head of State: President Nambaryn Enkhbayar (MPRP) (elected 22 May 2005, inaugurated 24 Jun 2005)

Head of government: Prime Minister Sanjaagiin Bayar (from Nov 2007)

Ruling party: Nambaryn Enkhbayar (Mongolian People's Revolutionary Party) (MPRP) (since 2006; re-elected 20 May 2008)

Area: 1,565,000 square km

Population: 2.63 million (2007)

Capital: Ulaanbaatar (Ulan Bator) (formerly Urga)

Official language: Khalkha Mongolian

Currency: Tugrik (Tug)

Exchange rate: Tug1,156.50 per US$ (Jul 2008)

GDP per capita: US$1,486 (2007)*

GDP real growth: 9.90% (2007)*

Labour force: 1.35 million (2004)

Inflation: 9.00% (2007)

Balance of trade: US$57.00 million (2006)

Foreign debt: US$1.30 billion (2004)

* estimated figure

Mongolia

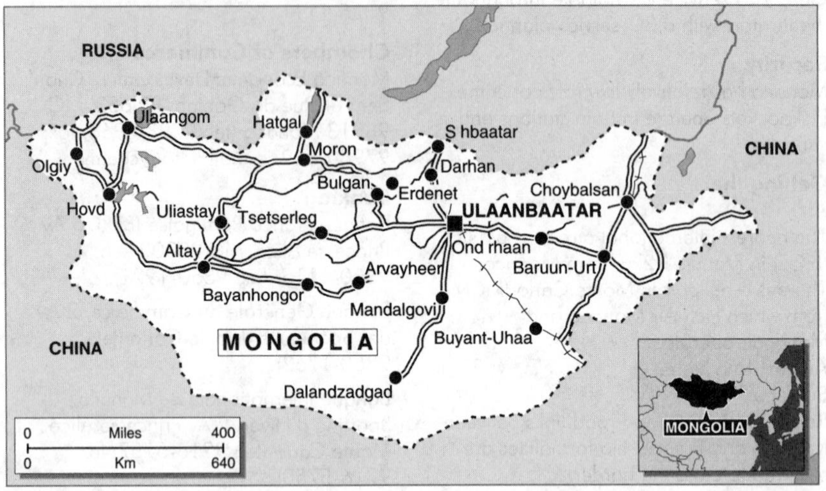

Mongolia's June 2008 elections proved to be something of a surprise for observers and participants alike. The election outcome produced a unique scenario in which the once again victorious communist party – Nambaryn Enkhbayar (Mongolian People's Revolutionary Party) (MPRP) – with 76 seats sought to find a way in which the humiliated opposition could be given a larger token presence in the assembly. Over half Mongolia's population is made up of nomadic herdsmen who, the election results suggested, had little sympathy with the opposition's modernising ambitions. In the event the prime minister designate (although Bayar was already prime minister he had previously been nominated rather than elected), Sanjaagiin Bayar, was offering to find a legally acceptable way to give an additional 15 seats to the opposition to avoid giving the impression that Mongolia had reverted to one-party rule. Mongolia's opposition leaders had other ideas, claiming that even were such an offer to be made, they would not necessarily accept it. Some opposition politicians had indicated that they might boycott parliament and even take the government to court rather than accept the overwhelming outcome of the elections.

Things took a turn for the worse after riots in Ulan Bator produced a number of fatal casualties. President Nambaryn Enkhbayar declared a state of emergency after the headquarters of the ruling party was set on fire. Other demonstrators forced their way in to the General Election Commission offices to demand that officials resign over what they considered to be voting irregularities. Five people were killed in the riots and another 300 injured as the capital city was sealed off, a curfew announced and roadblocks erected to enforce the blockade. International election monitors claimed that the election had been fairly conducted. Until the 2008 election, Mongolia's politics had been remarkably tranquil.

Described by Sir Fitzroy Maclean as 'The Back of Beyond', Mongolia is famed for its legendary thirteenth century conqueror Ghengis Khan, who created the largest empire in history. However, since the break-up of this huge alliance, the country was ruled for 200 years by China and for 70 years by the Soviets. Having experienced years of glorious empire, foreign rule and communism, in 1990 the country took a new path and adopted democracy. The political process has been dynamic of late with the election of a new president, popular demonstrations, and the arrival of a new prime minister after mass cabinet resignations. In 2005, the country was catapulted into the world media, albeit briefly, by the visit of US President W George Bush.

Politics

Mass protests in Kyrgyzstan in March 2005 which precipitated the fall of that government inspired reformists in Mongolia to also turn out and line the streets of the capital Ulaanbaatar. Protesters toasted the Kyrgyzstan rebels as allies, and demanded another set of government elections and a crackdown on corrupt practices.

In May 2005 the former communist party, Mongolian People's Revolutionary Party (MPRP), candidate and one-time prime minister Nambaryn Enkhbayar was elected as president, winning 53 per cent of the vote. Turnout was a healthy 75 per cent. As prime minister, Enkhbayar had courted the youth vote by performing on stage alongside platform-heeled Mongolian pop group Lipstick. He was a self-confessed fan of UK prime minister Tony Blair, duly hiring a British spin-doctor and describing the MPRP as 'communist monsters'. The Buddhist Enkhbayar is a talented and bilingual scholar, having translated novels by British authors such as Charles Dickens and Virginia Woolf. The Mongolian presidential role is more figurehead than ruler, but Enkhbayar's importance may be heightened by the current of popular dissatisfaction and the fact that the government is formed of a coalition.

At the beginning of 2006, 10 MPRP ministers – more than half of the cabinet – resigned, thus forcing the coalition government to disband and the prime minister, Tsakhia Elbegdorj, to resign. The MPRP criticised Elbegdorj for high inflationary rates and inadequate economic growth. Popular protests were held in the freezing cold streets of Ulaanbaatar, some in support of and some against the prime minister. All, however, called for an end to corruption and for the country's endemic poverty to be addressed. There is a feeling in the country that the poor have been forgotten since the fall of the communist regime, and that divisions of wealth have widened.

Two weeks after this mass resignations Miyeegombo Enkhbold, chairman of the MPRP, was named as the new prime minister, ending the interval of political turmoil. A party official was quoted as saying of the new leader: 'He's known as someone who doesn't talk much, but does the work'. Enkhbold was replaced as prime minister in November 2007 when Sanjaagiin Bayar was nominated as prime minister until the elections were held in June 2008.

Economy

The International Monetary Fund (IMF) said in 2008 that Mongolia's economy had performed well in recent years. Aided by a sharp run-up in the international prices of copper and gold, real GDP growth has averaged almost 9 per cent since 2004, while per capita income has more than doubled, but is still only US$1,486 annually. Although the upturn in performance was initially driven by developments in the mining sector, growth has spread to other sectors, including construction and financial services. High mineral prices and improvements in tax administration have generated rapid growth in government revenues, and the budget recorded significant surpluses over the past three years.

Growth picked up to 10 per cent in 2007, while signs of overheating became increasingly apparent in the second half of the year. Inflation rose from 6 per cent (year-on-year) in June 2007 to 21 per cent in March 2008. The inflationary pressures reflected a relaxation of monetary and fiscal policies, large increases in prices for food and fuel, and transportation capacity constraints.

Foreign direct investment (FDI) in the mining sector has been a primary driver of growth, helped by opening of a new gold mine. The 18 per cent growth in the agricultural industry also contributed to budgetary success. Tourism also helped pour money into the country after a poor year in 2003 due to the Sars crisis.

The Mongolian economy can be volatile as it is so heavily reliant on agriculture and fluctuating world commodity prices. Extreme weather conditions have been known to wipe out annual crops. For this reason the IMF have recommended that Mongolia diversify its economy and switch to more reliable bases of income.

Over a third of the population exist in conditions of poverty and the level of unemployment is high. Agriculture, to a large extent livestock production, still accounts for more than a fifth of GDP. Some 40 per cent of the Mongolian labour force continues to be employed in mostly nomadic livestock herding (35 million heads in 2006). The share of services has increased significantly over the last years and now exceeds 50 per cent. Industry and particularly mining (together a quarter of GDP) have consolidated their share in recent years. Industry also includes wool and cashmere processing, leather goods production, food processing, construction, and, in recent years, garments. Today 80 per cent of GDP is generated by the private sector (compared with 10 per cent in 1990).

Outlook

Mongolia has long had good reason to worry about China's long term plans. Only 40 per cent (or less) of the world's Mongols live in Mongolia; another 40 per cent live in Inner Mongolia, an autonomous region of China. Mongolian propaganda has long expressed fears over annexation by China.

Mongolia's medium-term economic outlook is favourable. High mineral prices

KEY INDICATORS — Mongolia

	Unit	2003	2004	2005	2006	2007
Population	m	2.58	2.61	2.56	2.59	*2.63
Gross domestic product (GDP)	US$bn	1.13	1.63	2.09	3.16	*3.90
GDP per capita	US$	438	512	817	1,216	*1,486
GDP real growth	%	5.5	10.6	6.6	8.6	*9.9
Inflation	%	4.7	5.0	12.1	5.0	9.0
Industrial output	% change	–	14.9	-2.2	7.3	–
Agricultural output	% change	–	17.7	9.2	9.7	–
Exports (fob) (goods)	US$m	501.0	853.0	1,037.0	1,543.0	*1,889.0
Imports (cif) (goods)	US$m	659.0	1,000.0	1,159.0	1,486.0	*2,117.3
Balance of trade	US$m	-158.0	-147.0	-122.0	57.0	*-228.3
Current account	US$m	-70.0	-40.0	-29.0	222.0	*-23.0
Total reserves minus gold	US$m	236.1	236.3	430.3	926.0	1,195.6
Foreign exchange	US$m	235.9	236.1	430.1	925.8	1,195.4
Exchange rate	per US$	1,125.50	1,185.30	1,165.00	1,165.00	1,169.30

* estimated figure

have spurred minerals exploration and re-energised plans to exploit very large untapped deposits of copper, gold, coal, uranium, and other minerals. With the expected opening of the new Oyu Tolgoi copper and gold mine in 2011, real GDP growth is projected to pick up from around 7-9 per cent in 2008-10 to 12-14 per cent in 2011-12. With strong policy implementation, it should be possible to bring inflation down to a single digit by end-2008 and to maintain a rate of 5-6 per cent over the medium term.

Risk assessment

Politics	Good
Economy	Fair
Regional stability	Fair

COUNTRY PROFILE

Historical profile

1206-63 Mongol tribes were unified under the leadership of Temujin, later called Genghis Khan. With his cavalry army, he invaded China and occupied Peking and build the largest land empire ever. His offspring increased the empire by invading much of Russia and defeating the armies of most of eastern Europe, including Hungary and Poland. The onslaught stopped just 40 miles short of Venice when the Mongol commander Subutai was order to return home.
1368 The Mongols were force out of Peking by Chinese troops as the Mongol empire collapsed.
1380 The Russian, Prince Dmitriy Donskoy, defeated the Golden Horde (troops of Genghis Khan's oldest son, Juchi, in Russia), as Chinese troops destroyed Karakorum, the Mongol capital.
1636 Inner Mongolia was formed by the conquest of the southern Mongols by the Chinese Manchu empire.
1691 Outer Mongolia was formed when the Manchu empire offered protection to the northern Mongols.
1911 Following the republican revolution, Mongolian princes declared the province's independence.
1921 The Mongolian People's Party was founded and a Provisional People's government was established.
1924 The Mongolian People's Republic was proclaimed.
1928–1960 The Soviet Union (USSR) influenced the governing of Mongolia as ideological and repressive communist rule was instigated. Historical and cultural heritage were undermined, as family names were prohibited, monasteries destroyed and lamas murdered.
1961 Mongolia became a member of the UN, and was accorded diplomatic recognition by West European states.
1987 Mongolia was finally granted diplomatic recognition by the US.
1991 Mongolia's main backer, the USSR, disintegrated, ending decades of economic and political support for the country.
1992 A new constitution was introduced, establishing Mongolia as a democratic parliamentary state. Mongolia's official title became the State of Mongolia.
1997 Natsagiin Bagabandi of the Mongol Ardyn Khuv'sgalt Nam (Mongolian People's Revolutionary Party) (MPRP) (formerly the Mongolian People's Party), was elected president.
1999 Rinchinnyamiyn Amarjargal became prime minister.
2000 The MPRP won the parliamentary elections. Nambariin Enkhbayar, leader of the MPRP, was elected prime minister by the Great Hural.
2001 The incumbent president, Natsagiin Bagabandi of the MPRP, was re-elected.
2002 Prime Minister Mikhail Kayanov of Russia visited Mongolia to boost economic co-operation between the two countries.
2003 Two Mongolians, who visited northern China, became the country's first confirmed Severe Acute Respiratory Syndrome (Sars) cases.
2004 The World Bank endorsed a new Country Assistance Strategy (CAS) and US$18 million urban water credit. On 20 August, parliament appointed Tsakhiagiyn Elbegdorj (Ekh Oron-Ardchilan (Motherland Democratic Coalition) (MDC)) as prime minister and parliament approved his cabinet.
2005 Nambaryn Enkhbayar (MPRP) won the presidential elections.
2006 Ten ministers, members of the MPRP, resigned accusing the coalition government of not doing enough to counter corruption and poverty. Parliament voted to dissolve the coalition government. Miyeegombo Enkhbold (MPRP) was endorsed by parliament as the new prime minister. With 38 of parliament's 76 seats the MPRP is the largest party, but will still needs the support of minor parties in order to form a coalition government; the MDC has 34 seats.
2007 On 22 November, Sanjaagiin Bayar was elected by parliament as prime minister.
2008 In parliamentary elections held on 20 May, the ruling Mongol Ardyn Khuv'sgalt Nam (Mongolian People's Revolutionary Party) (MPRP) won 53.4 per cent of the vote, the Mendsaikhany Enkhsaikhan (Democratic Party) (Democrats) won 19.7 per cent, Bazarsad Jargalsaikhan (Republican Party) won 13.9 per cent and Badarch Erdenebat (Motherland Party) won 11.4 per cent. Turnout was 74.9 per cent. Prime Minister Sanjaagiin Bayar remained in office. The elections were widely contested and although election observers reported no major problems with the new voting system, the results sparked violent protests over claims that they had been rigged. After four deaths and hundreds injured, a four-day state of emergency was imposed. In July, at the opening of parliament, the 25 Democrat members staged a walkout and brought the session to a halt.

Political structure

Constitution

The constitution entered into force on 12 February 1992. A January 1998 constitutional amendment stated that legislators were eligible to serve concurrently as prime minister or as other ministers. The January amendment was later effectively nullified by the Constitutional Court ruling of 24 November 1998 that prohibited members of the People's Great Hural from holding cabinet posts. On 15 March 2000, the Constitutional Court cancelled amendments to the 1992 constitution, which had been approved by the People's Great Hural, and later vetoed by the president.

Form of state

Parliamentary republic

The executive

The head of state is the president, nominated by parties in the People's Great Hural, and elected by popular vote for a four-year term.

National legislature

The legislature, the 75-member unicameral People's Great Hural, is directly elected every four years by all citizens over 25-years-old. The People's Great Hural elects a prime minister and appoints a cabinet, in consultation with the president.

Legal system

A mixture of Russian, German and US law.

Last elections

22 May 2005 (presidential); 20 May 2008 (parliamentary).

Results: Presidential: Nambaryn Enkhbayar (MPRP) won 53.4 per cent of the vote and Mendsaikhany Enkhsaikhan (MDC) 20 per cent; turnout was 74.9 per cent.

Parliamentary: the Nambaryn Enkhbayar (Mongolian People's Revolutionary Party) (MPRP) won 53.4 per cent of the vote, the Mendsaikhany Enkhsaikhan (Democratic Party) won 19.7 per cent, Bazarsad Jargalsaikhan (Republican Party) won 13.9 per cent and Badarch Erdenebat (Motherland Party) won 11.4 per cent. Turnout was 74.9 per cent.

Next elections

June 2008 (parliamentary); 2009 (presidential).

Political parties
Ruling party
Mongol Ardyn Khuv'sgalt Nam (Mongolian People's Revolutionary Party) (MPRP) (since 2006; re-elected 20 May 2008)
Main opposition party
Ekh Oron-Ardchilan (Motherland Democratic Coalition) (MDC)

Population
2.63 million (2007)
Last census: January 2000: 2,373,493
Population density: 2 inhabitants per square km. Urban population: 57 per cent (1995—2001).
Annual growth rate: 1.0 per cent 1994–2004 (WHO 2006)
Religions
Tibetan Buddhist Lamaism and Shamanism, Islam (4 per cent) – there is no state religion.

Education
Primary schooling lasts for four years until aged 12. Secondary education is divided into four years compulsory lower secondary schooling for students aged 12–16 years and two years upper secondary for those aged 16–18 years. Only students of upper secondary schools progress to higher education. Technical and vocational schools admit graduates of both lower and upper secondary schools.
Government and private institutions provide higher education and offer BA, MA and PhD degrees.
Public expenditure on education typically amounts to 5.7 per cent of annual gross national income.
Literacy rate: 98 per cent adult rate; 98 per cent youth rate (15–24) (Unesco 2005).
Compulsory years: Eight to 16.
Enrolment rate: 88 per cent gross primary enrolment, of relevant age group (including repeaters); 56 per cent gross secondary enrolment (World Bank).
Pupils per teacher: 31 in primary schools.

Health
Per capita total expenditure on health (2003) was US$140; of which per capita government spending was US$90, at the international dollar rate, (WHO 2006).
About 98 per cent of infants aged less than one year are immunised against measles.
HIV/Aids
HIV prevalence: 0.1 per cent aged 15–49 in 2003 (World Bank)
Life expectancy: 65 years, 2004 (WHO 2006)
Fertility rate/Maternal mortality rate: 2.4 births per woman, 2004 (WHO 2006); maternal mortality 150 per 100,000 live births (World Bank).
Child (under 5 years) mortality rate (per 1,000): 56 per 1,000 live births; 12.5 per cent children under aged five were malnourished (World Bank).
Head of population per physician: 2.63 physicians per 1,000 people, 2002 (WHO 2006)

Welfare
Growing unemployment and a weak social safety net remain the country's prime concern. About 36 per cent of Mongolia's population still live below the official poverty line. Many poor are unable to work and rely on social security to meet their basic needs. In 2001, the Asian Development Bank (ADB) granted two loans totalling US$12 million to strengthen Mongolia's social security services. The first loan of US$8 million will be used to support policy and legal reforms to enhance the delivery of social welfare services and strengthen social insurance schemes. A second ADB loan of US$4 million will invest in projects such as nursing homes, services for the disabled and day care centers. The government aims to replace the large centralised institutions with smaller community-based nursing homes and day care centers. The Government is providing co-financing of US$2 million. The Ministry of Social Welfare and Labour as the executing agency will implement the project over five years, until end October 2006. ADB has also provided a US$600,000 technical assistance grant financed by the Japanese Government.
More than 100,000 people are registered as disabled by Mongolia's Ministry of Social Welfare and Labor. About 40,000 disabled people, who are capable of working, remain jobless.

Main cities
Ulaanbaatar (which translates as 'Red Hero') (Ulan Bator) (formerly Urga) (capital, estimated population 904,802 in 2005), Erdènèt (88,243), Darhan (62,696).

Languages spoken
Russian is the principal foreign language, although English is being encouraged. Kazak is also spoken in western Mongolia.
Official language/s
Khalkha Mongolian

Media
Press
The newspapers with the largest circulations are the government Odriyn Sonin, successor to the state-owned Ardyn Erh (established in 1990) and Zasgiyn Gazryn Medee (weekly), Nügel Buyan (police) and Ulaanbaatar (local government). The party newspapers Ardchilal (MNDP), Ug (MSDP) and Unen (MPRP) appear less frequently.
English-language weekly newspapers include the Mongol Messenger and the on-line publication Mongolia This Week (http://www.mongoliathisweek.mn).
Broadcasting
Radio: Services are broadcast in Mongolian and also Russian, Chinese, English, French, Japanese and Kazakh.
Television: Thanks to satellite relays 100 per cent of the population can receive Mongolian programmes. Russian television is received by satellite ground stations all over the country and US television in Ulaanbaatar for a few hours daily.
Kazakhstan Television is available in the predominantly Kazakh Bayan-Olgiy aimak of western Mongolia.

Economy
The economy has been through hard times but at last 2005–06 showed a marked improvement driven largely by the sevenfold increase in the global price of copper and the higher price for gold, two of Mongolia's principal exports. However, the manufacturing sector had to contend with the end of textile and clothing quotas, which resulted in many factories closing and leaving a significant number of workers, around 10,000, unemployed. Between 2000–04 clothing exports accounted for 11.3 per cent of GDP, in 2005 clothing exports to the US fell by 40 per cent and total clothing exports dropped by almost 60 per cent. GDP growth in 2005 was 6.2 per cent and was expected to be over 7.0 per cent in 2006. Inflation spiked in 2005 through higher energy costs and food prices, reaching 17.5 per cent in June, although the year-on-year rate was 12 per cent and was expected to be 7.0 per cent in 2006. In 2005, the service sector accounted for 51 per cent of the economy, agriculture 22 per cent and industry 27 per cent, of which manufacturing was 4 per cent.
Tourism is growning, with 330,000 visitors arriving and spending over US$200 million in 2005. Foreign direct investment (FDI) in tourism is estimated to be 1.1 per cent of total FDI and 10 per cent of GDP.
Mongolia relies on imports of oil and natural gas from Russia and is vulnerable to external shocks. It has done much to embrace the practices of a free-market economy, by privatising state-owned enterprises but it also has a substantial grey economy, estimated to be as much as 50 per cent of GDP, and the authorities have much more to do to bring this money into the financial system.
Along with government spending, which was curbed in 2005, increased corporate tax and higher commodity prices turned a budget deficit in 2004 into a 2.9 per cent surplus, which is expected to increase to 9.0 per cent in 2006. Mongolia paid

US$300 million to Russia as reimbursement before Russia wrote-off Mongolia's long-standing US$10 billion debt for loans received during the Soviet era. Mongolia's debt burden was halved at the end of 2003 and is estimated to have fallen to 32 per cent of GDP by 2006.
Mongolia not only has extensive deposits of minerals that include gold, copper, coal, tin, tungsten and molybdenum, it also has huge unspoiled areas of land. In the western region around 30 per cent of the national livestock, which is being raised in traditional methods, could supply meat to most of Central Asia, as well niche markets in the West as organic meat.
The National Development Strategy (NDS) lays down development objectives and strategies, including human development, the environment and a public investment programme, to be implemented over the 15 years to 2022. Japan and the Asian Development Bank have provided US$1.8 million towards a US$2.12 project to harmonise investment planning under the NDS.

External trade

Mongolia does not belong to any regional trade community but it does have bilateral agreements with India, Russia and the US.
The economy is underpinned by sales in primary products, in particular copper, gold, molybdenum, tin and tungsten, which represents 20 per cent of GDP.
Mongolia is dependent on remittances.

Imports

Main imports are petroleum, electricity, machinery and equipment, vehicles, food products, consumer goods, chemicals, building materials, sugar and tea.
Main sources: Russia (36.9 per cent total, 2006), China (27.2 per cent), Japan (6.6 per cent).

Exports

The main export products are copper, gold, cashmere, livestock, animal products, wool, hides, fluorspar and other non-ferrous metals.
Main destinations: China (67.8 per cent total, 2006), Canada (11.1 per cent), US (7.7 per cent)

Agriculture

Farming

Agriculture accounted for around 21per cent of GDP in 2004 and employed 40 per cent of the workforce.
Major crops include barley, potatoes and wheat. Primary meat products include beef and veal, chicken, horse, camel, lamb and pork. The major agricultural exports are carded hair, wool sheepskins, beef and fine animal hair.
Crop production in 2005 included: 143,450 tonnes (t) cereals in total, 140,000t wheat, 85,000t potatoes, 4,300t treenuts, 1,600t oats, 125t fruit in total, 55,650t vegetables in total. Livestock production included: 195,407t meat in total, 47,000t beef, 300t pig meat, 67,000t lamb, 35,000t goat meat, 38,000t horsemeat, 7,500t camel meat, 450t eggs, 359,000t milk, 10t honey, 11,200t cattle hides, 10,160t goatskins, 19,800t sheepskins, 15,000t greasy wool.

Forestry

Industry and manufacturing

The industrial sector contributes around 28 per cent to GDP and employs 12 per cent of the workforce. Industrial activity is centred on Ulaanbaatar and other main cities and is based mainly on agricultural products and mining. Products include bricks, cement, lime, sawn timber, scoured wool, felt, felt boots, woollen fabric, leather footwear, soap, flour, garments, matches, bakery goods, confectionery, meat products, beer and vodka.
In 2004, industrial expansion increased by around five per cent compared with less than two per cent the previous year, due to an expansion of gold mining output.

Tourism

The tourist sector has recovered from the disappointing results of 2003, occasioned by the Sars outbreak. Visitor arrivals increased by 67 per cent in 2004. The improvement is expected to continue.

Mining

The mining sector's contribution to GDP increased from 10 per cent to 20 per cent by 2004.
Mongolia boasts one of the richest reserves of mineral resources in the world, but economic mismanagement and a shortage of infrastructure have hindered exploitation.
The Erdenet copper-molybdenum complex, an open-pit mining and concentrating development 340km from Ulaanbaatar, accounts for a large proportion of exports by value. Copper reserves are large enough for another 60 years.
Other mines include fluorspar at Bor-Ondör and gold at Ih-altat. Gold mining has increased significantly since 1990. Mongolia has approximately 2,000 tonnes of gold reserves. Major gold-producing areas are Naran, Tolgoi and Zamar.
Other minerals present include iron, zinc, silver, tungsten, tin, lead and graphite, but production levels are limited by inefficient extraction methods.
Mineral products account for around 40 per cent of the country's total exports. Almost all of Mongolia's copper concentrates are exported to Russia and China.
A law passed in 1995 permits full foreign ownership of mining ventures in Mongolia, including those involving precious metals. Gold producers are no longer forced to sell to the Mongolian central bank at prices below the prevailing international price.
The first foreign investment gold mine, Boroo Gold, opened in 2004 and immediately pushed up Mongolia's output by 40 per cent.

Hydrocarbons

Mongolia does not produce oil or natural gas. Mongolia has no oil refineries and imports refined oil to supply its domestic demand, mainly from Russia; over half of these imports are gasoline. Over 550,000 tonnes of oil products are consumed annually. Exploration is taking place and small reserves of oil have been identified.
Mongolia has sizeable deposits of coal and produces around 5.6 million tonnes a year, most of which is lignite. Coal accounts for around 80 per cent of primary energy consumption. Mongolia exports around 11,000 tonnes of coal a year.

Energy

Mongolia has an electricity capacity of 788MW, derived mainly from coal-fuelled thermal power stations. Intermittent shortage of fuels for dump trucks and railway locomotives and station maintenance difficulties result in frequent power cuts and low generation totals.

Financial markets

Stock exchange

The Mongolian Stock Exchange in Ulaanbaatar was founded in 1991.

Banking and insurance

There is a two-tier banking system. Mongolia's first private commercial bank, the Central Asia Bank (CAB), established in 1992, collapsed in 1996 due to bad debt and poor management. The Reconstruction Bank of Mongolia was established as a universal commercial bank in 1997.
In 2003, two banks were sold: the AG Bank to the Japanese-based H S Securities for US$6.9 million, following a three-year restructuring programme and the Trade and Development Bank of Mongolia, sold for US$12.23 million, to the Swiss-based Banca Commerciale Lugano and US-based Gerald Metals.

Central bank

Bank of Mongolia

Main financial centre

Ulaanbaatar

Time

GMT plus eight hours

Geography

Mongolia is a landlocked country in central Asia, with Russia to the north and the

People's Republic of China to the south, east and west.
The land consists of a plateau that rises to between 914–1,524 metres with mountain ranges running from the west to north-east. The tallest mountains are the Altai Mountains in the south-west, which rise to 4,267 metres. The large, flat plains of the centre, east and south-east include untracked Steppes and the arid Gobi desert. The largest rivers are the Selenge Mörön and its tributary, the Orhon Gol, which crosses the border into Russia in the north.

Hemisphere

Northern

Climate

Summers are warm and wet, and winters extremely cold. In Ulaanbaatar, winter temperatures range from minus 4 degrees Celsius (C) to minus 50 degrees C, with an average of minus 26 degrees C in January; in summer temperatures range from 0–40 degrees C, with an average of 17 degrees C in July. Relative humidity ranges from 65 per cent (July–August) to 75 per cent (November–February). Rainfall is low, with an average of 233mm per year in Ulaanbaatar (two-thirds of which falls June–August) and 116–344mm per year elsewhere. On average, there are 250 cloudless days a year.

Entry requirements

Passports

Required by all and must have six months validity from the date of entry to Mongolia.

Visa

Required by all, with some exceptions see: www.un.int/mongolia and follow the link to visa and travel for further information. Business and tourist visitors staying for more than 30 days are referred to as temporary residents and apply with a non-tourist visa; a local contact or business partner will increase the chance of visa approval. When granted, visitors must register with the Foreign Citizens Bureau in Ulaanbaatar within seven days of arrival. Visitors who need to register must de-register before leaving Mongolia, at the Office of Immigration, Naturalization and Foreign Citizens. After de-registering, an 'exit visa' from the consular department of the Mongolian Ministry of Foreign Affairs will be issued.
Contact the nearest consulate for further advice and to confirm all aspects of visa requirements before travelling.

Currency advice/regulations

The import of local currency is limited to Tug815 and must be declared. The import of foreign currency is limited to US$2,000 or its equivalent. The export of local and foreign currency is limited the amount declared on arrival.
Travellers cheques have limited use in the capital, cheques in US dollars are easiest to exchange.

Customs

Importation of pornography and export of valuable antiques is strictly prohibited. Customs regulations are enforced by strict examinations. Firearms for sporting purposes require a licence. Import allowances included 200 cigarettes and two litres of alcohol.

Health (for visitors)

Mandatory precautions

No vaccination certificates are required.

Advisable precautions

Immunisations for typhoid, TB, hepatitis A and B are necessary while tetanus, diphtheria and polio vaccinations should be up-to-date. Rabies is a risk, particularly in rural areas.
There is a shortage of routine medications and visitors should take all necessary medicines with them. A first aid kit that includes disposable syringes, is a reasonable precaution. Use only bottled or boiled water for drinks, washing teeth and making ice. Eat only well cooked meals, preferably served hot; vegetables should be cooked and fruit peeled. Dairy products are unpasteurised and should be avoided, unless cooked.
Healthcare is not to Western standards and medical insurance, including emergency evacuation, is necessary.

Hotels

There are a number of suitable hotels for foreign visitors in Ulaanbaatar, but in the provinces facilities are basic.

Credit cards

International credit and charge cards are accepted in major city centres.

Public holidays (national)

Fixed dates

1 Jan (New Year's Day), 8 Mar (Women's Day), 1 Jun (Mothers' and Childrens' Day), 11–13 Jul (Naadam), 26 Nov (Independence Day).

Variable dates

Bituum and Tsagaan Sar (Lunar New Year) (Jan/Feb/Mar, three days)

Working hours

Banking

Mon–Fri: 0930–1230; 1400–1500.

Business

Mon–Fri: 0900–1800.

Government

Mon–Fri: 0900–1800.

Shops

Mon–Sat: 1000–1800 (some food shops stay open later). Some open Sunday.

Telecommunications

Mobile/cell phones

GSM 900 services are available in large urban areas only.

Electricity supply

240V AC, 50Hz

Weights and measures

Metric system.

Getting there

Air

National airline: MIAT (Mongolian Airlines)

International airport/s: Ulaanbaatar Buyant-Ukhaa (ULN), 15km from city, facilities include duty-free shops, bank, restaurant and car hire. Taxis and buses provide access to the city, travel time 15–30 minutes.

Airport tax: Departure tax of US$12

Surface

Road: While there are many roads that cross the borders from China and Russia only a few are designated for international visitors and permission must be obtained from Mongolian authorities to cross, before travelling.
The Regional Road Corridor Improvement Project, estimated at US$18 billion, to improve Central Asian roads, airports, railway lines and seaports and provide a vital transit route between Europe and Asia was agreed, on 3 November 2007. Six new transit corridors, between Afghanistan, Azerbaijan, China, Kazakhstan, Kyrgyzstan, Mongolia, Tajikistan and Uzbekistan, of mainly roads and rail links, will be constructed, or existing resources upgraded, by 2013. Half the costs with be provided by the Asian Development Bank and other multilateral organisations and the other half by participating countries.

Rail: Ulaanbaatar is served by the Trans-Mongolian Railway connecting Moscow and Beijing, with an express train that runs once a week. International trains have restaurant and sleeping cars.
There are frequent delays on the routes to Beijing and Siberia. Trains operate on summer and winter schedules, alternating in May and October.

Getting about

National transport

Air: MIAT operates an extensive domestic network. Regular air services provide the only feasible means of long-distance internal travel, although delays and cancellations are frequent. There are officially 21 airports, but only eight have paved runways.

Road: There are 46,700km of roads and tracks. Only 3 per cent of roads are paved (mainly around the cities). Many of the unpaved roads and cross-country tracks are impassable during the summer, because of flooding or waterlogging. The poor railway network dictates that roads provide the only access routes to 16 of Mongolia's 21 provinces.

Buses: Inter-urban bus services are available, with many long-distance bus routes, but their use is unfeasible due to the distances involved.

Rail: In addition to the cities served by the Trans-Mongolian Railway (Sühbaatar, Darhan, Ulaanbaatar, Dzamyn-Uüd and Saynshand), there are branch lines to various industrial centres and mining towns, including Erdenet, Baganuur and Bor-Ondör. Total network 1,815km.

City transport

Taxis: Taxis are available for journeys from the airport to the city centre, with a journey time of 15 minutes.

Buses, trams & metro: There are trolley-buses and buses. Service 11 operates 0600–2200 from airport to city centre, journey time 30 minutes.

Car hire

A hire car with driver is the only option as local knowledge of conditions is vital; hires can be arranged by most hotels or tourist organisations in Ulaanbaatar.

Rates vary from fixed hourly, daily, weekly or monthly hire.

Off-road vehicles can be hired from specialist suppliers but a local licence is required, this can be obtained, for a fee, using a valid national or international licence.

BUSINESS DIRECTORY

The addresses listed below are a selection only. While World of Information makes every endeavour to check these addresses, we cannot guarantee that changes have not been made, especially to telephone numbers and area codes. We would welcome any corrections.

Telephone area codes

The international direct dialling code (IDD) for Mongolia is +976, followed by area code and subscriber's number:

Ulaanbataar 11

Useful telephone numbers

Police: 102

Fire: 101

Ambulance: 103

Car hire

Ulaanbaatar

Car Base: (tel: 379-965).

Chambers of Commerce

Mongolian National Chamber of Commerce & Industry, 11 J Sambuu Street, Ulaanbaatar 38 (tel: 312-501; fax: 324-620; e-mail: info@mongolchamber.mn).

Ulaanbaatar Chamber of Commerce, Box 254, Ulaanbaatar 210136 (tel; 329-912; fax: 311-385; e-mail: ubcc@magicnet.mn).

Banking

Agricultural Bank, PO Box 185, Peace Avenue, Ulaanbaatar (tel: 457-880; fax: 458-670); e-mail: haab@magicnet.mn).

Anod Bank of Mongolia, PO Box 361, 18 Commerce Street, Chingeltei, Ulaanbaatar (tel: 327-566; fax: 313-070); e-mail: anod@magicnet.mn).

The Bank of Mongolia, Baga Toiruu-9, Ulaanbaatar (tel: 322-166; fax: 311-471).

Credit Bank, Suknbaatar Square, 20A, Ulaanbaatar (tel: 321-897; fax: 321-897).

Erelbank Ltd, Chingis Avenue, Khan-uul District, Ulaanbaatar (tel: 343-387; fax: 343-567).

Golomt Bank of Mongolia, PO Box 22, 4th Floor, Sukhbaatar Square 3, Central Place of Culture, Ulaanbaatar (tel: 311-530; fax: 312-307).

Mongol Post Bank, PO Box 874, Kholboochdiin Street 4, Ulaanbaatar (tel: 310-301; fax: 328-501).

Savings Bank, 6 Commerce Street, Ulaanbaatar (tel: 327-467; fax: 327-467).

Trade & Development Bank of Mongolia, 7 Commerce Street, Ulaanbaatar (tel: 327-020; fax: 312-418).

Ulaanbaater City Bank, PO Box 370, Baga toiruu 15, Ulaanbaatar (tel: 312-155; fax: 311-067).

Zoos Bank, 6 Choimbalin, Chingeltei, Ulaanbaatar (tel: 329-537; fax: 329-537).

Central bank

Bank of Mongolia, Baga Toiruu 9, Ulaanbaatar 46 (tel: 310-392; fax: 311-417; email: feprmd@mongolbank.mn).

Travel information

Flight information (0800-2200 hours) (tel: 119).

Juulchin, Ulaanbaatar (tel: 320-246, 328-428).

MIAT Head Office, MIAT Building, Buyant-Ukhaa 45, Ulaanbaatar 210134 (tel: 379-935, 984-070; fax: 379-919; email: contact@miat.com; internet: www.miat.com).

Ulaanbaatar Buyant-Ukhaa Airport, Ulaanbaatar 34 (tel: 379-986; fax: 379-744).

National tourist organisation offices

Mongolian Tourism Association, Room 318, Trade Union Building, Sukhbaatar Square 11, Ulaanbaatar 38 (tel/fax: 327-820; internet: www.travelmongolia.org)

Ministries

Ministry of Finance, Ulaanbaatar 46.

Ministry of Foreign Relations, Ulaanbaatar 11.

Ministry of Trade and Industry, 11 Sambuu St, Ulaanbaatar 46 (tel: 706-146; fax: 326-325).

Other useful addresses

British Embassy, 30 Enkh Taivry Gudamzh, PO Box 703, Ulaanbaatar 13 (tel: 458-133; fax: 458-036; email: britemb@mongol.net).

Mongol An Corporation, Baigal Ordon, Ulaanbaatar 38 (tel/fax: 360-067).

Mongolian Business Development Agency (MBDA), U Barsbold (fax: 311-092; email: mbda@magicnet.mn).

Mongolian Embassy (US), 2833 M Street, NW, Washington DC 20007 (tel: (+1-202) 333-7117; fax: (+1-202) 298-9227; email: monemb@aol.com).

Mongolian Stock Exchange, Sukhbaatar Square 14, Ulaanbaatar (tel: 310-501; fax: 325-170; email: msebatj@magicnet.mn).

The Permanent Mission of Mongolia to the United Nations, 6 East 77th street, New York, NY10021-1704 (tel: (+1-212) 861-9460; fax: (+1-212) 861-9464; email: mongolia@un.int).

School of Economic Studies (Economic Institute), National University of Mongolia (fax: 325-349; email: suvd@magicnet.mn).

State Statistical Board, Ulaanbaatar 11 (fax: 324-518).

Internet sites

Guide to Mongolia (with links): http://www.mongoliaonline.com

Mongolian Stock Exchange: http://mse.com.mn

Parliament of Mongolia: http://www.parl.gov.mn/english.htm

School of Economic Studies: http://www.ses.edu.mn

State Property Committee: http://www.spc.gov.mn

Montenegro

Two years after gaining formal independence from Serbia, in 2007 Montenegro's economy was functioning at full capacity, with growth rates forecast to exceed 7 per cent by the end of 2008. Nearly 85 per cent of the capital value of Montenegrin companies was already privatised. The banking sector, telecommunications, oil distribution and import services were all privately owned. Growth has been mainly driven by foreign direct investment (FDI). In 2006, according to Montenegro's central bank, FDI had reached US$680 million, six times higher than in 2004. In the first half of 2007, FDI increased by 78 per cent and Montenegro had one of the highest FDI per capita rates in Europe at US$ 1,100.

In contrast, Montenegro's business environment is still weak if measured by its international ranking, despite a significant improvement since independence. Montenegro ranks a lowly 81st in the world according to the World Bank's *Ease of doing business index*. Long licensing procedures, the severe difficulties faced when registering a property, a bureaucratic trading environment, and a high level of difficulty in enforcing commercial contracts, remain significant disadvantages in Montenegro's business environment.

Affected by international financial turbulence, Montenegro's asset prices have soared in the last two years, leading to a remarkably rapid growth of credit which has further fuelled investment in real estate. Rapid credit growth suggests an overheating economy. Positively, Montenegro's growth has not been adversely affected by inflationary pressures. Retail inflation peaked slightly above the central bank's expectations, particularly in the electricity sector which has not yet been opened up to competitive mechanisms and price liberalisation. Electricity shortages have also occurred despite tariff increases.

Economic reforms, such as the privatisation of state-owned assets and a greater freedom of foreign trade and investment, have contributed to a stable macroeconomic position. The budget has remained in surplus.

An independence referendum in Montenegro had long appeared unstoppable and finally took place in May 2006, as planned by the Đukanovic government. Opinion polls in 2005 had consistently reported 41–44 per cent support for independence, with around 38 per cent against. This breakdown approximately reflected the ethnic make-up of Montenegro, with people identifying themselves as Montenegrin generally more independence-minded than those identifying themselves as Serbian. It was ironic that the 16 per cent of the population who identified themselves as Bošniak or Albanian appeared to have the casting vote. The recommendation of the Venice Commission's advisory report, published in December 2005, that Montenegrin citizens living in Serbia not be allowed to vote in the referendum was predicted to favour the independence camp. Such Montenegrins were considered more likely to vote against independence.

The economy

Montenegro achieved real GDP growth of over 5.7 per cent in 2006. Growth took place across all the sectors of the economy: industrial production, tourism, forestry, construction and transportation. Industrial output growth has been low due to supply problems in the energy sector.

Independence and significant tourism potential have generated impressive investor interest in Montenegro and started a recovery with growth which reached 7.5 per cent in 2007. But strong growth, and the exuberance it has generated, has brought its own problems. There are signs of overheating, with inflation and wages picking up, and the current account deficit soaring. Vulnerabilities are also building up with rapid credit growth weakening private sector balance sheets, an expansive fiscal stance, and an asset price boom.

The current account deficit is expected to widen further in 2007 to 37 per cent of GDP driven by high investment (spurred by foreign direct investment, which has hovered around 24 per cent of GDP in the past few years) and low savings associated with wealth effects and galloping credit expansion. The share of foreign credits in

KEY FACTS

Official name: Republika Crna Gora (Republic of Montenegro) (ROM)

Head of State: President Filip Vujanovic (since 2002; elected 11 May 2003)

Head of government: Prime Minister Milo Djukanovic (from 20 Feb 2008)

Ruling party: Koalicija za Evropsku Crnu Goru (KECG) (Coalition for European Montenegro, comprising Demokratska Partija Socijalista (DPS) (Democratic Party of Socialists) and Socijaldemokratska Partija (SDP) (Social Democratic Party)(elected 10 September 2006)

Area: 14,026 square km

Population: 674,686 (2006)*

Capital: Podgorica (administrative); Cetinje (cultural).

Official language: Montenegro Serbian (Lekavian dialect)

Currency: Euro (eur) = 100 cents (from 1 Jan 2002; previous currency Deutsche mark, locked at DM1.96 per euro)

Exchange rate: eur0.63 per US$ (Jul 2008)

GDP per capita: US$3,284 (2005)

GDP real growth: 4.30% (2005)

Unemployment: 22.30% (2004)

Inflation: 3.40% (2007)

Annual FDI: US$1.35 billion (2006)

* estimated figure

the financing of the current account deficit has risen. Rising labour costs have been eroding competitiveness.

Rapid credit growth is testing the capacity of the young banking system to prudently assess and manage credit risks. Banking regulation and supervision is relatively strong, but very fast credit expansion tests the capacity of the banks and has been taking its toll on banks' financial indicators.

Fiscal policy is adding to demand pressures. Strong revenue performance has boosted the fiscal surplus, but tax cuts have weakened the impact of automatic stabilisers. A general public sector wage increase of 30 per cent, which is being implemented in steps starting from October 2007, has added to demand pressures providing an unhelpful fiscal stimulus.

Outlook

Free of the yoke of federation, Montenegro can focus on developing its economy as it wishes. The reluctance of the EU and its members to commit to investment should also be less of a problem for a genuinely independent Montenegro.

Risk assessment

Politics	Fair
Economy	Fair
Regional stability	Fair

COUNTRY PROFILE

Historical profile

1878 Following the collapse of the Ottoman Empire, of which Montenegro had been an autonomous region, the independence of the principality of Montenegro was recognised under international treaties.
1910 Prince Nikola became king and helped lead the Balkan forces that pushed the European boundaries of the Ottoman Empire back to north of Constantinople.
1914–18 As a supporter of the Allies (Entente Powers), Montenegro was occupied by Austro-Hungarian troops.
1918 The defeat of the Austro-Hungarian empire during the First World War saw the creation of the Kingdom of the Serbs, Croats and Slovenes, encompassing Bosnia and Hercegovina (BiH), Croatia, parts of Dalmatia and Macedonia, Montenegro, Serbia, Slavonia and Slovenia. King Nikola was deposed when, during the Podgorica People's Assembly, Montenegro voted for a union with the Kingdom of Serbia.
1919 The Kingdom of Serbs, Croats and Slovenes became a semi-autonomous region of Hungary.
1929 Following disputes between Serbs and Croats, King Alexander assumed dictatorial powers and the country was renamed Yugoslavia.
1941–45 During the Second World War parts of Yugoslavia were occupied by the Germans, Italians, Hungarians and Bulgarians.
1945–46 Following the end of the war, Serbia and Montenegro became two of the constituent republics of a federated Yugoslavia. The other republics were Bosnia and Hercegovina (BiH), Croatia, Macedonia, Slovenia and the two autonomous regions of Vojvodina and Kosovo. As the leader of the Yugoslav Communist Party (YCP), Josip Broz Tito became head of state and a Soviet-style constitution was adopted. The Serbian state and Belgrade, as the federation's capital, were the primary focus of economic and political control and the majority of the officers of the Yugoslav military were from Serbia and Montenegro.
1980 Tito died. A system of collective (rotating) presidency was adopted; ethnic tensions began to re-surface.
1989 The Serbian nationalist, Slobodan Milosevic, became president of the Republic of Serbia.
1991 Slovenia and Croatia and later Macedonia declared their independence from Yugoslavia.
1992 BiH declared its independence. Bosnian Serbs (who made up 30 per cent of the population) backed by the remaining Yugoslav federation, declared their own independence from BiH, claiming 65 per cent of the territory. The degree of inter-ethnic violence that followed, including 'ethnic cleansing', had not been seen in Europe since the Second World War. The UN imposed economic sanctions against Serbia and Montenegro, the only two Yugoslavian republics remaining.
1997 Milo Djukanovic (prime minister of Montenegro since 1994) became president of Montenegro, after defeating a pro-Milosevic candidate. Milosevic was named president of what remained of Yugoslavia.
1998 NATO began airstrikes against military targets. NATO peace-keepers moved into Kosovo.
1999 NATO extended airstrikes to include mainly Serbian infrastructure. Politically, Montenegro began to distance itself from Serbia declaring it was not a party to the conflict in Kosovo.
2002 Demokratska Lista za Evropsku Crnu Goru (DLECG) (Democratic List for a European Montenegro) coalition, led by the Demokratska Partua Socualista Crne Gore (DPS) (Democratic Socialist Party), won the parliamentary elections. Milo Djukanovic (DPS) resigned from the presidency to become prime minister and former prime minister Filip Vujanovic, took over as acting president. The euro was adopted as the official currency.
2003 Yugoslavia was abolished and replaced with a looser federation of its two member states, Serbia and Montenegro. Yugoslav President Kostunica stepped down and was replaced as Head of the State of Serbia and Montenegro by Svetozar Marovic, a Montenegrin. Filip Vujanovic was elected president of Montenegro.
2006 In a referendum on independence, 55 per cent voted to sever the union with Serbia. Montenegro formally declared itself an independent state and also became a member of the United Nations. In

KEY INDICATORS — Montenegro

	Unit	2003	2004	2005	2006	2007
Population	m	0.64	0.63	0.65	6.54	0.66
Gross domestic product (GDP)	US$bn	-0	-0	44.98	48.46	*2.97
GDP per capita	US$	0	0	0	0	*3,800
GDP real growth	%	–	4.0	5.4	5.7	*7.5
Inflation	%	–	2.4	3.4	2.1	3.4
Exports (fob) (goods)	US$m	–	–	–	594.0	–
Imports (cif) (goods)	US$m	–	–	–	1,342.0	–
Balance of trade	US$m	–	–	–	-748.0	–
Current account	US$m	–	–	–	*-755.0	-1,102.0
Total reserves minus gold	US$m	63.7	81.8	204.0	432.7	732.6
Foreign exchange	US$m	63.7	81.8	204.0	432.7	722.0
Foreign direct investment (FDI)	US$bn	–	–	1.0	1.4	–
Exchange rate	per US$	-0	-0	0.77	0.75	0.69

* estimated figure

the first independent parliamentary elections the ruling coalition claimed victory. Prime Minister Djukanovic resigned and Zeljko Sturanovic (DPS) was appointed as his replacement. Montenegro joined NATO.
2007 A Stabilisation and Association Agreement (SAA) between the European Union and Montenegro, the first step in the process for accession to the EU, was signed in October. The agreement requires constitutional and judicial reforms to comply with EU membership.
2008 On 31 January Prime Minister Sturanovic resigned due to ill health; Milo Djukanovic became prime minister on 20 February. In presidential elections held on 6 April, incumbent, Filip Vujanovic (DPS) won 51.89 per cent of the vote, his nearest rival Andrija Mandic (Serb List) won 19.55 per cent.

Political structure

Constitution
Passed in 1992.
The constitution may be amended if 10,000 voters, not less than 25 deputies or the president and prime minister submit a proposal, which is subsequently agreed by two-thirds of the Assembly members.
Form of state
Democratic, social and ecological state
The executive
The president of the republic is elected by universal suffrage for a term of five years. A president is limited to two terms in office.
The president has the right to refer adopted laws back to the Assembly for review; if the new legislation is passed for a second time the president must promulgate the law. The president names a successor if a prime minister loses the confidence of the Assembly.
A new law governing presidential elections was enacted in December 2007. All candidates must collect signatures from 1.5 per cent of registered voters to achieve a place in the ballot.
National legislature
The parliament, Skupština Republike Crne Gore, or Assembly, is unicameral with 77 members. Deputies are elected, by universal suffrage of those aged 18 years and over, to the Assembly for four-year terms.
The government is headed by a prime minister, who proposes a cabinet that is agreed by the Assembly.
All government policies and laws must be agreed by the Assembly; without agreement the prime minister must resign and be replaced by another candidate.
Legal system
The rule of law is mandated in the constitution.
The legal system is independent and autonomous. The law is administered by a judge and jury in public, where citizens have the right to legal assistance. The Supreme Court is the highest court of law. Capital punishment is reserved for the most serious offences.
Last elections
6 April 2008 (presidential); 10 September 2006 (parliamentary).
Results: Presidential: Filip Vujanovic (DPS) won 51.89 per cent of the vote, Andrija Mandic (Serb List) 19.55 per cent, Nebojša Medojevic (Movement for Changes) 16.64 per cent, Srdan Milic (Socialist People's Party) 11.92 per cent.
Parliamentary: KECG won 41 seats (out of 81); SL won 12 seats; Pokret za Promjene (PzP) (Movement for Change) 11 seats; and a coalition led by SNP 11 seats. Turnout was 70.3 per cent.
Next elections
2013 (presidential); 2010 (parliamentary).

Political parties

Ruling party
Koalicija za Evropsku Crnu Goru (KECG) (Coalition for European Montenegro, comprising Demokratska Partija Socijalista (DPS) (Democratic Party of Socialists) and Socijaldemokratska Partija (SDP) (Social Democratic Party)(elected 10 September 2006)
Main opposition party
Srpska Lista (SL) (Serbian List),coalition led by Srpska Narodna Stranka (SNS) (Serbian People's Party).

Population

674,686 (2006)*
Last census: November 2003: 620,145
Ethnic make-up
Montenegrin (43.2 per cent), Serbian (32.0 per cent), Bosniak (7.7 per cent), Albanian (5.3 per cent), Croats (1.1 per cent) all others (10.7 per cent).
Religions
Orthodox Christian, Muslim and Roman Catholic.

Education

Compulsory education is provided free by the state. Lessons are taught in Serbian and Albanian, although under the constitution lessons may be taught in the language of any ethnic group.
Cyrillic and Latin text have equal standing under the constitution.
Secondary education may continue from three–four years and culminates in a matura graduation certificate, which allows acceptance at a university. There is only one university, in Podgorica, that provides higher education and post-graduate education.
Compulsory years: 7 to 16

Health

Healthcare is publicly financed for children, expectant mothers and the elderly, under the constitution.
Since 1992, the extent and quality of healthcare provision has sharply deteriorated. However, a well-developed private healthcare system has emerged for the better-off. Largely free at the point of delivery and funded by a universal social insurance tax levied on all employees and employers, public healthcare provision require all kinds of charges, most notably for imported medications.
HIV/Aids
There have been few cases of HIV/Aids recorded since the first case was diagnosed in Montenegro in 1989. Nevertheless, the Global Fund to Fight Aids provided US$2.9 million, for a national strategy to combat the disease including prevention measures and diagnostic and antiretroviral treatment for the years 2006–2010.

Welfare

The constitution declared that a mandatory insurance scheme provides all employees and their family all forms of social security. The state is required to provide for the old, infirm and incapable.

Main cities

Podgorica (capital, 141,854 in 2005), Nikšic (58,031), Pljevlja (18,943), Bijelo Polje (17,460).

Languages spoken

Serbian and Albanian
Official language/s
Montenegro Serbian (Lekavian dialect)

Media

Press
Dailies: Pobjeda and Monitor are published in Podgorica.
Broadcasting
There is one radio and television network based in Podgorica, Radio Televizija Crna Gora (RTCG) (Radio Televison of Montenegro).

Economy

Since Montenegro opted to represent itself as an independent country in 2005, the economy and state institutions have worked hard to achieve a good record for its first year in operation.
The IMF, which reviewed the economy just as Montenegro spilt from Serbia were enthusiastic that it could achieve its goals of sustained increases in GDP growth, employment and real income. Montenegro is in the process of creating a fully functioning free-market economy, with over 80 per cent of former state-owned businesses and property privatised. GDP growth was 3.1 per cent in 2005 and was expected to grow by 5.5 per cent in 2006, while inflation should fall from 3.4 per cent to 2.6 per cent in the same period.
Standard and Poor's, the sovereigns ratings agency, gave Montenegro a BB+

credit rating in 2005. Montenegro's commitment to joining the European Union and adopting the euro (in March 2002) has concentrated the focus of the economy towards flexibility in all aspects, such as labour, corporate, fiscal and financial structures, so as to encourage diversification. As yet, high unemployment at 22.3 per cent, (a figure estimated in 2004 for Serbia and Montenegro) is still characteristic of an earlier economic regime.

The economy is composed of a 56 per cent service sector, industry 28 per cent and agriculture 15 per cent. There are large deposits of bauxite which provides the core of Montenegro's industrial base, however, high production costs have hampered continued growth. Tourism is now a major component of GDP with annual growth of 10 per cent and attracts the largest share of foreign direct investment.

External trade

Montenegro has bilateral free trade agreements with the EU, European Free Trade Association (Efta), Russia and countries of Central and South-Eastern Europe (Cefta).

While Montenegro has an established industrial sector based on bauxite mining and aluminium production, tourism has become the principal foreign exchange earner.

Imports

Main imports include petroleum and lubricants, vehicles and machinery, capital machinery, manufactured goods, chemicals, food and live animals and raw materials.

Main sources: Italy (14.4 per cent of 2004 total), Slovenia (12.6 per cent), Bosnia- Hercegovina (9.1 per cent).

Exports

Principal exports include aluminium, manufactured goods, food and live animals and raw materials.

Main destinations: Italy (41.9 per cent of 2004 total), Greece (15.7 per cent), Switzerland (9.6 per cent).

Agriculture

Farming

Around 1 per cent of the workforce is employed in the fishing industry.

Fishing

Around 1 per cent of the workforce is employed in the fishing industry.

Forestry

Montenegro, when it committed itself to eco-friendly development in its 1992 constitution, reflected what is a coincidence of history and geography. Its forests had not been plundered during eras of autocracy so that a largely pristine ecosystem is available for sustainable development including tourism and timber production.

Forest and woodland cover over half the total area of land – 743,609 hectares (ha), of which forest cover is 620,872ha. The majority of forests are state-owned – 500,041ha – while 243,568ha are privately owned. There is an estimated 72.1 million square metres of standing stock, of which conifers amount to 30 million square metres.

State ownership protects forests from over-exploitation, with sustainable objectives for timber production.

Industry and manufacturing

The manufacturing industry is one of the largest employers, followed by retail and transport.

Tourism

Montenegro has been successful in attracting European visitors and headed the list of the worlds fastest growing tourist destinations, by the World Travel and Tourism Council. Tourism accounts for 14.8 per cent of GDP, providing more than 22,000 jobs.

Environment

The constitution mandates that the environment is protected from exploitation.

Mining

There are large deposits of bauxite; aluminium accounts for around 25 per cent of Montenegro's industrial output and almost 75 per cent of export earnings. The first and largest bauxite mines are in Nikšic, employing about 1,400 workers. There are coal mines in Plijevlja but they are chronically underfunded and in need of investment to increase production. There are shale deposits but Montenegro does not have the technology to exploit them.

Hydrocarbons

There are coal mines in Plijevlja but are chronically underfunded and in need of investment to increase production. There are shale deposits but Montenegro does not have the technology to exploit them.

Energy

Montenegro imports around a third of its annual electricity needs. It depends on imported oil and gas despite increased utilisation of local resources of hydroelectric power, which accounts for 76 per cent of electricity generation. There is a coal-fired power station at Plievlja.

Much of Montenegro's energy sector has been weakened by neglect, lack of investment and war damage. In 2006, the government increased the price of electricity to boost revenue for rehabilitation and redevelopment. Long-term investment is planned for the development of hydroelectric plants between Montenegro, Serbia and Bosnia and Hercegovina at Buk Bijela on the river Drina.

Financial markets

Stock exchange

The Montenegroberza stock exchange was founded in 1993 and became fully operational in 1995 and the New Securities Exchange (NEX Montenegro), was founded in 2001. Both trade shares in private companies, public investment funds and old currency savings bonds. Their transactions totalled over 66,770 and the volume of trade in the first eight monts of 2005 was over eur114.6 million (US$144.7 million), over twice the total volume in 2004.

Banking and insurance

Central bank

Centralna Banka Crne Gore

Main financial centre

Podgorica

Time

GMT plus two hours, (daylight saving GMT plus one hour, end March to end of October).

Geography

Montenegro is somewhat diamond in shape with a tiny, 25km, border with Croatia in the west. It has a much longer, 225km, border with Bosnia and Herzegovina from the west to the north. Serbia has a 203km border on its east to south east and Albania has a 172km border along the south. Lastly, it has a 294km coastline along the Adriatic Sea from the south west to west.

The name Montenegro (Crne Gora) means black mountain and, from the sea, must seem like a solid rock formation. High limestone mountains overshadow the shoreline, rising sharply from the narrow coastal plain (no wider than 10km), which is dotted with many bays and coves. The mountains form a tableland that lacks the soil to sustain much life as rainwater is quickly drained through porous rocks. At 2,522m the highest peak is Bobotov Kuk, in the north west of the country, in high mountains, that stretch along the border with Bosnia and Hercegovina. A matching mountain range lies along the Albanian border. These mountain ranges generally rise to over 2,000m in height, but then 60 per cent of the country is above 1,000m, nevertheless the northern region is futile pasturelands. Over 80 per cent of the country is forest, much of it primeval.

There are three main rivers running north/south – Piva, Tara and Lim – added to which are 40 lakes, the largest of which is Skadar, which spans the border with Albania. The river Tara has a 82km long, 1300m deep canyon, which is the world's second deepest chasm (after the US Grand Canyon).

Hemisphere

Northern

Climate
The climate is dictated by the geography. Mediterranean climate allows coastal summer temperatures to reach 26 degrees Celsius (C), falling to 12 degrees C in winter. The tableland has a continental climate, when summer temperatures can reach 40 degrees C and drop during winter as low as 5 degrees C. In the alpine, snowcapped northern mountains winters are cold, temperatures can fall to minus 7 degrees C and summers cool at 20 degrees C.

Entry requirements
Passports
Required by all
Visa
Requirements for Montenegro have yet to be published – the following were appropriate for the union of Serbia and Montenegro and should only be considered as guidelines. Contact a Montenegro Consulate for further information.
Visas are required by all, with the exception of most European, North American and Australasian visitors for both business and tourist reasons. Visitors arriving via Serbia require a visa.
Those visitors that require visas should contact the nearest embassy or consulate for an application form. Business travellers in this category will require a letter of invitation from a local company giving the nature of business, duration of visit and a full itinerary, plus a letter from the employing company confirming details; and proof of sufficient funds for living expenses and medical insurance.
Currency advice/regulations
The import of local and foreign currency is unlimited but must be declared; export is limited to the declared amount.

Hotels
There are a wide range of hotels ranging from luxury to family-run pensions. The ministry of tourism began a system of star rating, but by August 2006 had not completed the process.
Hotel reservations should be made in advance, especially during summer.

Credit cards
Major international credit and charge cards are accepted.

Public holidays (national)
Fixed dates
1 Jan (New Year), 1 May (Labour Day), 9 May (Victory Day), 13 Jul (National Day), 29 Nov (Republic Day).
Variable dates
Orthodox: Christmas (three days), and Easter (two days); Bayram (Feast of the Sacrifice, first day of Ramadam)
These religious holidays are based on the lunar calendar.

Working hours
Banking
Mon–Fri: 0830–1630
Business
Mon–Fri: 0800–1500.
Government
Mon–Fri: 0730–1530.
Shops
Mon–Fri: generally in larger towns: 0800–2000 (some shops may close between 1200–1700); Sat: 0800–1500.

Telecommunications
Mobile/cell phones
There are GSM 900/1800 services that cover almost all of the country.

Electricity supply
220V, 50Hz with European flat and round, two-pin plugs.

Weights and measures
Metric system

Getting there
Air
National airline: Montenegro Airlines
International airport/s: Podgorica International airport (TGD), 12km from the city. A new terminal, opened in May 2006, includes bureau de change, restaurant, shops and an information centre. Taxis and buses are available to the city.
Other airport/s: Tivat Airport, on the Adriatic Coast, caters largely for tourist flights from Europe.
Airport tax: Departure tax: eur16, in cash.
Surface
Road: There are border crossings from Croatia at Debeli and Brijeg, from Albania at Bozaj, several from Bosnia and Hercegovina at Vilusi, Vracenovici, Scepan Polje and Metaljka and from Serbia at Bijelo Polje.
Vehicle owners must pay a toll on entering Montenegro.
Rail: There are links to Serbia via Belgrade and Albania via Skadar.
Water: There are regular ferry services from Italy.
Main port/s: Bar, Kotor and Zelenika

Getting about
National transport
Road: There are over 5,000km of roads but only 60 per cent are paved and are not maintained to a high standard. Two major roads that provide access around the country are the Adriatic Highway which runs along the coast from Ulcinj to Igalo and the motorway, with tolls, from Petrovac to the Serbian border at Bijelo Polje, via Podgorica.
Buses: Bus services link most towns and cities.
Rail: There are almost 250km of railways, with most lines running from the coast in the south west to the Serbian border in the north east. All lines run into Podgorica, of which one rail link terminates at Nikšic.
City transport
There are bus services in Podgorica.
Taxis: City taxis have meters, although if not in use negotiate a price before travelling.
Car hire
There are several local and international car hire firms in Montenegro, with cars available at the airport and in large towns.
An international driving licence is necessary, along with insurance. Traffic drives on the right, with speed limits at 120kph on motorways, 100kph on other main roads. Road signs are likely to be in Cyrillic script.

BUSINESS DIRECTORY
The addresses listed below are a selection only. While World of Information makes every endeavour to check these addresses, we cannot guarantee that changes have not been made, especially to telephone numbers and area codes. We would welcome any corrections.

Telephone area codes
The international direct dialling (IDD) code is +381, followed by area code and subscriber's number:

Podgorica	81

Useful telephone numbers

Ambulance	94
Fire	93
Police	92

Chambers of Commerce
Montenegro Chamber of Economy, 29 Novaka Miloseva, 81000 Podgorica (tel: 230-545; fax: 230-943; e-mail: pkcg@cg.yu).

Banking
Atlasmont Banka, 4 Stanka Dragojevica St, Podgorica (tel: 407-200; fax: 665-451; e-mail: office@atlasmont.cg.yu).

Crnogorska Komercijalna Banka (Commercial Bank of Montenegro), Moskovska bb, 81000 Podgorica (tel: 404-232; fax: 404-277: email: info@ckb.cg.yu).

NLB Montenegrobanka, 46 Bulevar Stanka Gragojevica, 81000 Podgorica (tel: 402-212; fax: 402-212; e-mail: info@montenegro-banka.com).

Podgoricka Banka, 8a Novaka Miloseva Street, 81000 Podgorica (tel: 224-555; fax: 405-100; email: pgbanka@cg.yu).

Central bank
Centralna Banka Crne Gore (CBCG) (Central Bank of Montenegro), Bulevar Svetog Petra Cetinjskog 7, Podgorica (tel: 403-191; fax: 664-140; e-mail: info@cb-cg.org).

Travel information

Automobile Association of Montenegro, Podgorica (AMSCG), (tel: 225-493, 224-467).

Montenegro Airlines, Slobode 23, Podgorica (tel: 664-411/433/455; email: office.podgorica@mgx.cg.yu).

National Tourist Organization of Montenegro, Omladinskih Brigada 7, 81000 Podgorica (tel: 230-959; fax: 230-979; e-mail: tourism@cg.yu)

Zeljeznica Crne Gore (Montenegro railways), Trg Golootockih Zrtava 13, 81000 Podgorica (tel: 441-302; fax: 633-957; email: zcq-uprava@cg.yu).

Tivat Airport, PP24, 85320 Tivat (tel: 670-960; fax: 670-950; internet: www.aptivat.com).

Ministry of tourism

Ministry of Tourism, Rimski trg 46, Kancelarija br 8 Podgorica (tel: 482-145; e-mail: ministarstvo.turizma@mn.yu; internet: www.mturizma.cg.yu; www.visit-montenegro.org).

National tourist organisation offices

National Tourism Organisation, Omladinskih Brigada 7, 81000 Podgorica (tel: 230-959, 230-981; fax: 230-979; email: tourism@cg.yu; internet: www.visit-montenegro.com

Ministries

Ministry of Agriculture, Forestry and Water Management, Podgorica (tel: 482-109; fax: 234-306; email: milanm@mn.yu).

Ministry of Culture and Media, Podgorica (tel: 231-561; fax: 231-540; email: marinko_vorgic@min-kulture.mn.yu).

Ministry of Economics, Podgorica (tel: 242-104, 482-112; fax: 242-028; email: minprivrede@mn.yu).

Ministry of Education and Science, Podgorica (tel: 405-301; fax: 405-334; email: mpin@cg.yu).

Ministry of Environmental Protection and Physical Planning, Podgorica (tel: 482-220; fax: 34-131; email: milenaz@mn.yu).

Ministry of Finance, Stanka Dragojevica br 2, Podgorica (tel: 242-835; fax: 224-450; email: mf@mn.yu).

Ministry of Foreign Affairs, Stanka Dragojevica 2, Podgorica (tel: 246-357, 201-530; fax: 224-670; email: mip.ministar@mn.yu).

Ministry of Health, 46 Romas Square, Podgorica (tel: 234-056, 482-346; fax: 242-762; email: tijanak@mn.yu).

Ministry of Interior, Podgorica (tel: 241-252, 349-000; email: mup.kabinet@cg.yu).

Ministry for International Economic Relations, Stanka Dragojevica br 2, 81000 Podgorica (tel: 225-568; 225-591; email: mierei@mn.yu).

Ministry of Justice, Vuka Karadzica 3, 81000 Podgorica (tel: 507-552; fax: 407-522; email: pravda@cg.yu).

Ministry of Labour and Social Welfare, Podgorica (tel: 234-252; fax: 482-443).

Ministry of Maritime Affairs and Transportation, Rimski trg 46, 81000 Podgorica (tel: 234-179; fax: 234-331; email: mps@mn.yu).

Ministry of Minority Protection, Podgorica (tel: 482-126; fax: 234-198; email: min.manj@cg.yu).

Other useful addresses

Agency of Montenegro for Economic Restructuring and Foreign Investment, Jovana Tomasevica bb, 81000 Podgorica, Montenegro (tel: 242-640; fax: 245-756; email: anaz@mn.yu).

Aluminium Industry of Montenegro (tel: 620-616; fax: 620-955; e-mail: kap.board@cg.yu).

Vektra Montenegro (management, transportation, storage, international trade), Vuka karadzica 10, 81000 Podgorica (tel: 624-500; fax: 625-335; e-mail: office@vektra.cg.yu; internet: www.vektra.cg.yu).

Directorate for Construction of Highways in Montenegro, Podgorica (tel: 625-110, 625-102; fax: 624-353).

Montenegro Development Fund, Bulevar Rvolucije 9, 81000 Podgorica (tel: 245-973; email: fzcrg@cg.yu; internet: www.fzrcg.cg.yu).

Montenegrin Investment Promotion Agency (MIPA), Podgorica (e-mail: info@mipa.cg.yu; internet: www.mipa.cg.yu).

Montenegro Stock Exchange, Cetinjski put 2a (Zgrada Vektre) 81000 Podgorica (tel: 205-940, 205-960; fax: 205-920; internet: www.montenegroberza.com).

National Statistics Office, Proleterske No 2, Street IV, Podgorica (tel: 241-206; fax: 241-270; email: statistika@cg.yu; internet: www.monstat.cg.yu).

New Securities Exchange Montenegro (NEX Montenegro), Miljana Vukova bb, 81000 Podgorica (tel: 230-670, 230-690, 210-170; fax: 230-640; internet: www.nex.cg.yu).

Internet sites

Customs Administration: www.djp.gc.yu

Government of Montenegro: www.vlada.cg.yu/eng

Official Gazette: www.sllrcg.cg.yu

Montenegro tourism: www.visit-montenegro.com

Montenegro Business Alliance: www.visit-mba.org

Montserrat

COUNTRY PROFILE

Historical profile

1493 Montserrat was first sighted by Columbus.
1632 Britain gained possession of the island and English and Irish Catholic settlers from the Protestant island of St Kitts and Nevis colonised Montserrat.
1648 There were some 1,000 Irish families on the island.
1651 The first slaves were brought to the island and the economy became based on sugar.
1871–1956 Montserrat was part of the Leeward Islands, and then became a British Dependent Territory.
1958–62 Montserrat was part of the Federation of the West Indies. From 1960 the island had its own administrator (the title was changed to governor in 1971).
1990 A new constitution was adopted.
1995 The Soufriere Hills volcano began to erupt.
1997 Massive volcanic eruptions destroyed the capital Plymouth, the airport and the port, and left the southern half of the island uninhabitable. Nineteen people were killed, thousands were left homeless and the population fell to around 4,000 as many fled to Britain and nearby Caribbean islands. David Brandt replaced Bertrand Osborne as chief minister.
1998 Reconstruction work began under the UK's Sustainable Development Plan.
1999 The UK government announced volcanic activity had dropped to safe levels. Evacuees began to return. With the loss of four and a half of the original seven constituencies, new election rules were introduced, and all national legislature seats became single-seat, first-pass-the-post constituencies.
2000 The growth of a new lava dome at the Soufriere Hills volcano once again threatened the island.
2002 A constitutional review was begun.
2003 There was another major eruption at the Soufriere Hills volcano.
2004 In March, there was an increase in volcanic activity and people in the evacuation zone were told to leave the area immediately. Deborah Barnes-Jones was sworn in as governor. The US Department of Homeland Security removed the temporary protected status of US-based Montserratians.
2005 The new airport was opened allowing access for international visitors.
2006 In parliamentary elections although the Movement for Change and Prosperity (MCAP) won most seats, it did not win enough for an outright majority. The New People's Liberation Movement (NPLM) and the Montserrat Democratic Party (MDP)) coalition formed the government. Lowell Lewis (MDP) was elected chief minister by his coalition colleagues.
2007 Peter Waterworth was sworn in as governor on 27 July.

Political structure

Constitution
The 1989 Constitution sets out the legal framework for all executive and legislative power, which came into force in 1990. Montserrat is an internally self-governing British Overseas Territory.

Form of state
British Caribbean dependency

The executive
The British monarch is Head of State and is represented by a governor, who is responsible for defence, internal security (including the police force), external affairs, the public service and international financial services.
The governor chairs meetings of the Executive Council (ExCo), which consists of the governor, attorney general, financial secretary, chief minister and three other ministers, elected from the LegCo.

National legislature
The Legislative Council (LegCo) has seven members, elected for a five-year term in single-seat constituencies, as well as two ex-officio members, and two appointed members.

Last elections
31 May 2006 (parliamentary)
Results: Parliamentary: MCAP won 36.1 per cent of the vote (four out of nine seats); the NPLM won 29.4 per cent (three seats); MDP 24.4 per cent (one seat); and an independent 10.1 per cent (one seat). Turnout was 78 per cent.

Next elections
2011

Political parties

Ruling party
Coalition led by the New People's Liberation Movement (NPLM), with the Montserrat Democratic Party (MDP) and an independent (from June 2006)

Main opposition party
Movement for Change and Prosperity (MCAP)

Political situation
The Montserrat Development Corporation (MDC) was formed in 2007 and is expected to facilitate the building of a new central town at Little Bay, in the north of

KEY FACTS

Official name: Montserrat

Head of State: Queen Elizabeth II; represented by Governor Peter Waterworth (since 27 Jul 2007)

Head of government: Chief Minister Lowell Lewis (MDP) (from Jun 2006)

Ruling party: Coalition led by the New People's Liberation Movement (NPLM), with the Montserrat Democratic Party (MDP) and an independent (from June 2006)

Area: 102 square km

Population: 9,538 (2007)* (Many citizens left the island when volcanic eruptions began in 1995; numbers have yet to return to former levels).

Capital: Plymouth – destroyed by volcano in 1997; temporary headquarters at Brades while Little Bay is being developed as the new capital.

Official language: English

Currency: East Caribbean dollar (EC$) = 100 cents

Exchange rate: EC$2.70 per US$ (fixed)

GDP per capita: US$7,485 (2004)

GDP real growth: -2.83% (2006)

Labour force: 4,520 (pre-1997 eruption)

Unemployment: 6.00% (2003)

Inflation: 1.00% (2006)

Balance of trade: -US$20.60 million (2004)

Foreign debt: US$8.90 million (2003)

Visitor numbers: 15,700 (2003)

* estimated figure

the island. The MDC will form partnerships with private and public sectors organisations to redevelop the island, the first to be the new capital. Local businesses have already begun to relocate and what began as temporary accommodation is quickly becoming permanent.
Local seismic predictions stated in 2008 that, in the short-term, further eruptions from the still active volcano are likely to remain localised and relatively calm. For a decade the value of land has been depressed but local residents are beginning to notice that foreign visitors are buying up land for redevelopment as holiday homes and worrying that if this trend continues those in exile will never be able to return home.

Population
9,538 (2007)* (Many citizens left the island when volcanic eruptions began in 1995; numbers have yet to return to former levels).
Last census: May 2001: 4,491
Population density: 94.1 inhabitants per square km, prior to the volcanic eruptions in 1995.
Annual growth rate: 4.2 per cent (2003)
Ethnic make-up
Afro-Caribbean (95 per cent), white (5 per cent).
Religions
Anglican, Methodist, Roman Catholic, Pentecostal, Seventh-Day Adventist.

Education
Montserrat has a high level of literacy. Primary education formally begins at the age of five and continues until the age of 11. The state provides for a full five-year secondary education. Secondary schools offer programmes for academic entry courses to higher education and technical, vocational skills training. The University of the West Indies School of Continuing Studies offers university level courses.
The Montserrat Community College project, which is jointly funded by the EU and the UK-based Department for International Development (DfID), will cost EC$6 million (US$1.8 million). The new college will include classrooms, laboratories, library and offices.
Compulsory years: 2 to 16.

Health
Periodic volcanic eruption has wreaked havoc with health service maintenance, record keeping, and the overall collection of information. The immunisation programme continued to operate well throughout the volcanic emergency.
Life expectancy: 78 years (estimate 2003)
Fertility rate/Maternal mortality rate: 1.8 births per woman (2003)
Birth rate/Death rate: 17.6 births per 1,000 population; 7.3 deaths per 1,000 population (2003).
Child (under 5 years) mortality rate (per 1,000): 7.8 per 1,000 live births (2003)

Welfare
Montserrat remains dependent on the British government for budgetary aid and to finance its capital programmes. Previous Public Sector Investment Programmes were aimed at developing critical infrastructure in the habitable North. The emphasis was on accommodating the displaced population on the island and providing housing for a number of migrant workers from neighbouring Caribbean islands. The British Government has approved £10 million (US$ 14 million) for housing over a period of five years (2001–2006).
The Social Welfare System in Montserrat has developed a comprehensive Poverty Protection Programme providing various forms of assistance to its people.

KEY INDICATORS — Montserrat

	Unit	2003	2004	2005	2006	2007
Population	m	*0.01	*0.01	*0.01	*0.01	–
GDP per capita	US$	3,400	–	–	–	–
GDP real growth	%	1.2	4.3	–	–	–
Inflation	%	2.6	–	–	–	–
Exports (fob) (goods)	US$m	0.7	4.8	1.8	–	–
Imports (cif) (goods)	US$m	17.0	25.4	26.2	–	–
Balance of trade	US$m	-17.0	-20.6	-24.4	–	–
Current account	US$m	–	–	-15.7	–	–
Total reserves minus gold	US$m	15.2	14.1	13.9	14.5	–
Foreign exchange	US$m	15.2	14.1	13.9	14.5	–
Exchange rate	per US$	2.70	2.70	2.70	–	–

Main cities
Plymouth (estimated population 3,500 before being evacuated in 1996 (due to volcanic activity); by the end of 1997, the city had been destroyed by volcanic eruptions).
Interim government buildings have been built at Brades Estate, in the Carr's Bay/Little Bay vicinity at the north-west end of Montserrat.

Languages spoken
Official language/s
English

Media
Press
The only newspaper is the weekly The Montserrat Reporter (www.themontserratreporter.com).
Broadcasting
Radio: The public radio service ZJB (www.zjb.gov.ms) has a full range of programmes with news, music and regular reports on volcanic activities.
Television: There are two private, cable TV channels, both operated by foreign services.

Economy
Volcanic activity between 1995–97 left around half of the island uninhabitable as two-thirds of the population fled as the economy fell into ruin.
Intensive reconstruction efforts have helped pull the island out of a deep and prolonged recession, aided by US$33 million in funds from the UK Department for International Development (DfID).
By 2004 Montserrat had recorded three years of sustained growth as real GDP grew by 4.3 per cent. The growth was registered in the construction of hotels and restaurants, wholesale and retail trade and transport and government sectors, which were indicative of the rise in activity in the tourist sector.
Tourism has slowly begun to recover as visitor numbers increase. The government has the tourist industry at the centre of Montserrat's recovery and allocated US$2.6 million to fund projects in its Tourism Repositioning Strategy, 2004–06.
Discussions on the Country Policy Plan (CPP) with UK authorities produced assistance, over 2004–07, from the DfID to complete the new airport, support private sector development, tourism, housing, improve the road network and develop Little Bay as the new capital.
Agricultural production was affected by ash from the 2004 eruption of the Soufriere Hills volcano, which damaged 95 per cent of the crops in the ground.
The Montserrat Development Corporation (MDC) was formed in 2007 and is expected to facilitate the building of a new central town at Little Bay, in the north of

the island. The MDC will form partnerships with private and public sectors organisations to redevelop the island, the first to be the new capital. Local businesses have already begun to relocate and what began as temporary accommodation is quickly becoming permanent.
Local seismic predictions stated in 2008 that, in the short-term, further eruptions from the still active volcano are likely to remain localised and relatively calm. For a decade the value of land has been depressed but local residents are beginning to notice that foreign visitors are buying up land for redevelopment as holiday homes and worrying that if this trend continues those in exile will never be able to return home.

External trade

As a British Overseas Territory, Montserrat is a member of the association of overseas countries and territories (OCTs) with formal relations with the European Union, which provides, among others, investment in economic and sustainable development.
Remittances and tourism provide the majority of foreign earnings, however there is an intractable large trade deficit, caused by the need to import most basic commodities.

Imports

Main imports include petroleum, lubricants, and related materials, machinery and vehicles, foodstuffs and manufactured goods.

Main sources: US, UK, Trinidad and Tobago, Japan, Canada

Exports

Commodity exports include light manufactures, agricultural produce and quarried stone.

Main destinations: US, Antigua and Barbuda, UK

Agriculture

The agricultural sector was declining prior to the volcanic eruptions (1995–97), when approximately 25 per cent of land area was cultivated. There was a further setback when the Soufriere Hills volcano erupted in April 2004, covering 95 per cent of planted crops with ash. Agriculture used to contributed around 4 per cent to GDP, employing 5 per cent of the labour force. The main crops have traditionally been potatoes, tomatoes, carrots, cabbages, cucumbers, sweet potatoes and string beans.
The evacuation order issued in 1996 forced farmers to abandon fields in the danger zone, which was still in place in 2005; those entering the area face legal action.
Output in the agricultural sector has been reduced to merely producing goods for domestic consumption. With the south of the island destroyed by the volcano, land has become a precious commodity. Much of the land in the north is unsuitable for farming. Development efforts now focus on high-yield crops and restoring self-sufficiency in vegetables and livestock.
Estimated crop production in 2005 included: 140 tonnes (t) potatoes, 20t sweet potatoes, 150t bananas, 140t mangoes, 100t tomatoes, 150t bananas, 80t citrus, 15t chillies & peppers, 710t fruit in total, 475t vegetables in total. Estimated livestock production included: 900t meat in total, 720t beef, 60t pig meat, 48t lamb and goat meat, 72t poultry, 63t eggs, 2,250t milk.
The typical total annual fish catch is 50t.

Industry and manufacturing

The industrial sector used to account for around 19 per cent of GDP and 10 per cent of employment and included rum, textiles and electronic appliances. After the electronic component assembly plant and the rice milling factory were forced to close due to the volcanic eruptions, the manufacturing sector's share of GDP fell from 5.9 per cent to less than 1 per cent.
Manufacturing output is concentrated on two small furniture businesses.
Construction is the largest sector of the economy – mainly due to the demand for housing and basic infrastructure. This has been bolstered by substantial grants from the British government.
Discussions are being held with an Irish company with a view to establishing a factory to utilise volcanic ash in manufacturing roofing slates and other building construction materials for export.

Tourism

The tourism sector used to contribute around a fifth of GDP and was a major foreign exchange earner. After the volcanic eruptions began in 1995, the sector virtually disappeared, mainly due to the destruction of Plymouth, the island's capital, and the main airport. Despite continued volcanic activity, reconstruction of the infrastructure and marketing of the island's attractions have been a priority. A new airport opened in Gerald on 11 July 2005. Scheduled, daily flights to Antigua and St Maarten connect with international flights from North America and Europe. The airport is open to charter flights from other Caribbean islands.
Growing numbers of tourists are attracted to Montserrat by the live volcano. The main viewing point is the Montserrat Volcanic Observatory where the pyroclastic flows of lava can be observed. Total visitor arrivals are increasing, albeit from a low start base. Visitors from the English-speaking Caribbean make up around 40 per cent of stay-over tourist arrivals.

Hydrocarbons

Montserrat does not produce any hydrocarbons and imports and consumes around 400 barrels per day (bpd) of refined oil products. Supplies come from the US and Trinidad and Tobago.
Montserrat does not import either natural gas or coal.

Banking and insurance

The banking sector was severely effected by the volcano eruption, which destroyed the buildings of the country's main banks. Barclays Bank pulled out of the island while the Royal Bank of Canada reduced its range of services. The locally-owned Bank of Montserrat continues to operate.
The seven members of the Organisation of Eastern Caribbean States (OECS), Antigua and Barbuda, Dominica, Grenada, Montserrat, St Kitts and Nevis, St Lucia and St Vincent and the Grenadines, share a common currency and central bank. The British Virgin Islands and Anguilla are associate members.
Montserrat has implemented the new EU tax directive, introduced in July 2005, as a British Caribbean Dependency. Details of all EU nationals' deposits will be forwarded to the tax department of the relevant EU country, allowing tax to be levied in their home country.
Montserrat has also agreed to supply information on tax fraud, for criminal or civil trials, and notify EU member states about additional malpractices.

Central bank

The Eastern Caribbean Central Bank, St Kitts & Nevis

Offshore facilities

The government is trying to promote offshore banking on the island.

Time

GMT minus four hours

Geography

Montserrat is one of the Leeward Islands in the West Indies. It is a mountainous, volcanic island, which lies about 55km (35 miles) north of Basse Terre, Guadeloupe, and about 43km (27 miles) south-west of Antigua.

Hemisphere

Northern

Climate

The island has tropical weather with a mean temperature of 30 degrees Celsius and low humidity due to tradewinds. There is little variation throughout the year. The wettest months are from September–November, and the driest from February–June.

Dress codes

Casual lightweight clothing, and during the winter months a light jacket or sweater for the late evening is advisable.

Entry requirements

Passports

Required by all and valid for six months.

Visa

Required by all, except nationals of most EU and Commonwealth countries, North America, Japan and a number of other countries and territories. An onward/return ticket, proof of accommodation and sufficient funds for the stay are required.

Currency advice/regulations

There are no restrictions on import and export of local or foreign currencies, subject to declaration on arrival and limited to declared amount on departure.

Health (for visitors)

Mandatory precautions

Yellow fever vaccination certificate if arriving within six months from an infected area.

Those arriving from areas of known epidemics, including cholera must have vaccination certificates.

Advisable precautions

Typhoid and polio vaccinations are recommended. Tap water is considered safe.

Credit cards

Few shops, hotels or restaurants accept credit cards.

Public holidays (national)

Fixed dates

1 Jan (New Year's Day), 17 Mar (St Patrick's Day), 25–26 Dec (Christmas), 31 Dec (Festival Day).

Variable dates

Good Friday, Easter Monday, Labour Day (first Mon in May), Whit Monday, August Monday (first Mon in Aug).

Working hours

Banking

Bank of Montserrat: Mon, Tue, Thurs: 0800–1400; Wed 0800–1300; Fri: 0800–1500.

Royal Bank of Canada: Mon–Thurs: 0800–1400; Fri 0800–1500.

Business

Mon–Fri: 0800–1200, 1300–1600. Some businesses close early Wed: 0800–1200, and some open Sat: 0800–1230.

Government

Mon–Fri: 0800—1600.

Shops

0800–1600. Most shops close early in the afternoon on Wednesday and Saturday.

Telecommunications

Telephone/fax

A 100 per cent automatic system.

Electricity supply

220V AC, 60 cycles; also 400V, three-phase.

Social customs/useful tips

A tip of 10 per cent, in hotels and restaurants, is usual.

Getting there

Air

International airport/s: Gerald's Airport (MNI), 2km from Little Bay; restaurant, shop, car hire.

Airport tax: Caricom nationals US$13; other nationals US$21.

Surface

Water: The ferry service between Montserrat and Antigua was discontinued following the opening of Gerald's Airport in July 2005.

Getting about

National transport

Due to volcanic activity, much of the south of the island is designated as an Exclusion Zone, to which entry is banned. Maps of affected areas are available on arrival.

Road: Before the eruption of Soufriere Hills volcano in 1995, there were 269km of roads, of which 203km were paved. The roads in the Exclusion Zone in the south were ruined and many in the rest of the island suffered considerable damage.

Buses: Buses are privately owned and readily available.

City transport

Taxis: Readily available. Legal fixed-rate system.

Car hire

Temporary licences can be obtained on production of national licence. Traffic drives on the left.

BUSINESS DIRECTORY

The addresses listed below are a selection only. While World of Information makes every endeavour to check these addresses, we cannot guarantee that changes have not been made, especially to telephone numbers and area codes. We would welcome any corrections.

Telephone area codes

The international direct dialling code (IDD) for Montserrat is +1 664, followed by subscriber's number.

Chambers of Commerce

Montserrat Chamber of Commerce and Industry, PO Box 384, Brades (tel: 491-3640; fax: 491-3639; e-mail: chamber@candw.ag).

Banking

Bank of Montserrat, PO Box 10, St Peters (tel: 491-3843; fax: 491-3163; e-mail: bom@candw.ag).

Royal Bank of Canada, PO Box 222, Brades (tel: 491-2426; fax: 491-3391; e-mail: rbcmont@candw.ag).

Central bank

Eastern Caribbean Central Bank, Agency Office, PO Box 484, 2 Farara Plaza, Brades (tel: 491-6877; fax: 491-6878; e-mail: eccbmni@candw.ms).

Travel information

Carib Aviation, VC Bird International Airport, PO Box 318, St Johns, Antigua (tel: (+1-268) 481-2401; fax: (+1-268) 481-2405; email: operationsmanager@carib-aviation.com).

Carib World Travel, Redcliffe Street, PO Box W122, Antigua (tel: (+1-268) 460-6103; fax: 480-2995; email: info@carib-world.com).

Montserrat Aviation Services, PO Box 257, Brades (tel: 491-2533; fax: 491-7186; email: monair@candw.ms).

National tourist organisation offices

Montserrat Tourist Board, 7 Farara Plaza, Buildings B&C: PO Box 7, Brades (tel: 491-2230 fax: 491-7430; e-mail: info@montserrattourism.ms).

Ministries

Governor's Office Lancaster House, Olveston (tel: 491-2688/9; fax: 491-8867; e-mail: govoff@cnadw.ag).

Ministry of Finance, Government Headquarters, Brades (tel: 491-2356/2777/3057; fax: 491-2367; e-mail: minfin@candw.ag).

Other useful addresses

British High Commission, 11 Old Parham Road, Box 483, St John's, Antigua (tel: (+1-268) 462-0008; fax: (+1-268) 562-2124; e-mail: britishh@candw.ag).

Development Unit, Government Headquarters, Brades (tel: 491-2066/2557; fax: 491-4632; e-mail: devunit@candw.ag).

Financial Services Commission, Phoenix House, PO Box 188, Brades (tel: 491-6887/8; fax: 491-9888; e-mail: fscmrat@candw.ag).

Montserrat government in UK, 7 Portland Place, London W1B 1PP. (tel: (+44-(0)20) 7031-0317; fax: (+44-(0)20) 7031-0318; e-mail: j.panton@montserratgov.co.uk).

National Development Foundation Montserrat Ltd, PO Box 337, Davy Hill (tel: 491-3070; fax: 491-6566; e-mail: mon;ndf@candw.ag).

Other news agencies: Caribbean Net News: www.caribbeannetnews.com

Internet sites

Montserrat info: http://www.volcano-island.com.

Montserrat Volcano Observatory (MVO): http://www.mvo.ms

Morocco

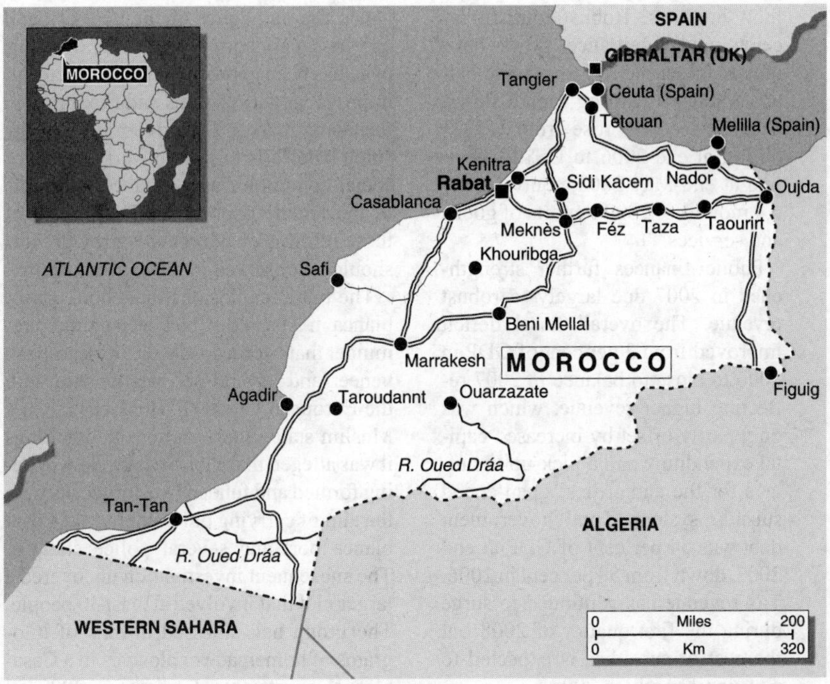

Tangiers stands just 14km from Europe; it is best known for the smuggling of drugs and illegal immigrants. In early 2008 however, and after years of discussions, the Tangier Med project 40km to the east of Tangier was finally taking shape. The port and associated industrial area will cost some US$2 billion to construct and it is hoped that when it is completed it will attract development to the so far under-developed northern area of Morocco.

The economy

Growth has been insufficient to significantly reduce poverty and unemployment. It averaged three per cent annum over the last decade. Recurrent droughts contribute to increasing poverty in rural areas. The unemployment rate remains high, particularly in urban areas. Although the growth of the non-agricultural sector has become more resilient to agricultural output shocks, it is insufficient to significantly reduce unemployment.

Non-agricultural GDP growth reached 6.6 per cent in 2007, although overall real GDP slowed to 2.7 per cent due to a sharp fall in cereal production. Growth in 2008 has been strong, driven by a rebound in agriculture, continued strong private investment, and vibrant activity in construction and services. Sound macroeconomic policies combined with sustained structural reforms and the opportunities provided by globalisation have resulted in a gradual improvement in living standards and per capita income. However, unemployment, notably among the youth, remains a challenge.

The International Monetary Fund (IMF) reported in July 2008 that consumer price inflation remains low, in part because administered prices have not been adjusted since the beginning of 2007. Year-on-year consumer price inflation was 2 per cent in 2007, down from about 3 per cent in 2006, and would have been higher if there had been full pass-through of world oil and commodity prices on administered prices. Inflation has picked up in 2008, reaching 3.7 per cent in April 2008, driven mainly by sharply rising food prices.

KEY FACTS

Official name: Al Mamlaka al Maghrebia (The Kingdom of Morocco)

Head of State: King Mohammed VI (since 1999)

Head of government: Prime Minister Abbas El Fassi (from 19 Sep 2007)

Ruling party: Coalition government led by Hizb al Istiqlal (Istiqlal) (Indpendence Party) (since 2002; re-elected 2007)

Area: 711,000 square km

Population: 30.73 million (2007)*

Capital: Rabat (official, diplomatic) Casablanca (commercial centre)

Official language: Arabic

Currency: Dirham (Dh) = 100 centimes

Exchange rate: Dh7.25 per US$ (Jul 2008); (roughly pegged at Dh10 per euro, which circulates widely)

GDP per capita: US$2,389 (2007)

GDP real growth: 2.20% (2007)*

Labour force: 12.46 million (2004)

Unemployment: 12.10% (2004)

Inflation: 2.00% (2007)

Balance of trade: -US$11.62 billion (2006)

Foreign debt: US$17.67 billion (2004)

Visitor numbers: 6.56 million (2006)*

* estimated figure

KEY FACTS

Official name: Western Sahara

(The legal status of the territory and the issue of sovereignty are unresolved; they are contested by Morocco and the Polisario, which in Feb 1976, formally proclaimed a government-in-exile of the Sahrawi Arab Democratic Republic (SADR)).

Head of State: President Mohammed Abdelazziz (Polisario) (since 1982)

Head of government: Prime Minister Abdelkader Taleb Oumar (from Oct 2004)

Ruling party: Independence movement – Frente para la Liberación de Saguia al Hamra y Río de Oro (Polisario) (Popular Front for the Liberation of Saguia al Hamra and Río de Oro)

Area: 266,000 square km

Population: 273,008 (2006)*

Capital: Laayoune (El Aaiún)

Official language: Arabic and Spanish

Currency: Moroccan dirham (Dh) = 100 centimes; the currency used in the Occupied Zone

Exchange rate: Dh8.59 per US$ (Jan 2007); (roughly pegged at Dh11 per euro, which circulates widely)

Labour force: 12,000 (2004)*

Aid flow: US$10.00 million (annually)*

* estimated figure

The report goes on to say that Morocco's external position is sound. Exports have performed well, although imports have been rising even faster, with robust demand for capital and consumer goods, greater food imports to offset the drop in cereal production, and the sharp rise in the world prices of petroleum and food products. Robust tourism receipts and remittance flows have mostly offset the negative trade balance, and with strong capital flows, external reserves rose from US$22 billion at end-2006 to US$26.5 billion at end-May 2008, equivalent to 6.4 months of 2009 imports of goods and services.

Public finances further strengthened in 2007 due largely to robust revenue. The overall fiscal deficit improved from 2 per cent of GDP in 2006 to close to balance in 2007 reflecting higher revenue, which was only partly offset by increased capital expenditure and a pick-up in outlays for the authorities' open-ended subsidy system. Total government debt was 54 per cent of GDP at end 2007, down from 58 per cent in 2006. Tax revenue has continued to surge during the first quarter of 2008 but the cost of subsidies is expected to rise significantly in 2008.

Monetary policy remained geared toward maintaining low and stable inflation, in the context of the exchange rate peg. The central bank has left its key policy rate unchanged at 3.25 per cent since early 2007, and lowered reserve requirements from 16.5 per cent to 15 per cent in December 2007 because of reduced bank liquidity. Monetary aggregates continued their strong rise, with broad money up by 15 per cent (year-on-year) at end-April 2008, and private credit rising by 28 per cent. The current level of the dirham's exchange rate is broadly in line with economic fundamentals.

Large state-owned enterprises have been privatised and remaining public enterprises are being restructured or prepared for privatisation. In the area of trade liberalisation, the implementation of the association agreement with the EU, Morocco's main trading partner, is proceeding as scheduled. Most Favoured Nation tariffs have been reduced to a maximum of 10 per cent for goods freely traded with the EU. Morocco is bidding for membership of the EU, but there appears to be little enthusiasm for the idea within Europe itself. It has been accorded the status of non-Nato ally by Washington, which has praised its support for the US-led war on terrorism. The financial sector is being strengthened. The imminent promulgation of a new central bank and banking laws will further enhance the autonomy of the central bank and its supervisory power. A new labour code has been approved and is expected to improve labour relations and flexibility in the labour market. The government is pursuing its efforts to fight poverty, improve social conditions, and enhance the rights of the female population. The impact of these reforms on Morocco's growth rates should be observed in the medium-term.

The bomb explosions that shook Casablanca in April 2007 had been a timely reminder that Morocco, despite its European veneer and 'would-be' relationship with the European Union (EU) is very much a Muslim state. Shortly after the bombings it was alleged that a terrorist group was being formed and funded by Moroccans with the aim of carrying out bombings at Casablanca port and several police stations. The subsequent investigation uncovered a larger plot that involved at least 30 people. The group had amassed dozens of kilograms of homemade explosives in a Casablanca apartment. Earlier in 2007 al Qaeda had announced that it had set up a cell in north Africa.

Police arrested 31 suspects, who were questioned by judges in preliminary court hearings. One specialist on Islamism in Morocco, said that he found it hard to imagine that this group did not have any foreign links.

Politics

The Kingdom of Morocco is the most westerly of the North African countries known as the Maghreb. Strategically situated with both Atlantic and Mediterranean coastlines, but with a rugged mountainous interior, the country remained independent for centuries while developing a rich culture blended from Arab, Berber, European and African influences.

The king has said the fight against poverty is a priority, earning him the name 'guardian of the poor'. Officials cite improved access to basic services in shanty towns and among the rural poor. But some non-government organisations say little has changed beyond the statistics, with poverty still widespread and unemployment remaining high.

One of the King's key reforms has been the *Mudawana*, a family law which grants more rights to women. The king maintains it is in line with Koranic principles but it has been opposed by religious conservatives.

In parliamentary elections which took place in September 2007 33 parties and 6,600 candidates participated and the Istiqlal won most votes, to retain power and become the governing coalition party. Its partner in the outgoing government, the USFP lost 12 seats. The turnout, at 37 per cent, was the lowest in Morocco's history. The opposition Parti de la Justice du Développement (PJD) (Justice and Development Party), an Islamic group, had been expected to win the most votes.

Morocco needs to achieve sustained high rates of growth in non-agricultural output. In the context of its increasing integration into the world economy, accelerated structural reforms and fiscal consolidation are essential elements.

Outlook

Morocco still has a long way to go if it is to reach European levels. It faces problems typical for developing countries: restraining government spending, reducing constraints on private activity and foreign trade, and achieving sustainable growth. Long-term challenges include preparing the economy for freer trade with the US and EU, improving education and job prospects for Morocco's youth, and raising living standards. The 2007 bomb attacks give cause for concern; Morocco, with its significant European based tourist industry, is an obvious target for errant terrorists,

Risk assessment

Politics	Fair
Economy	Fair
Regional stability	Fair

COUNTRY PROFILE

Historical profile

1777 Morocco was the first country to recognise the newly sovereign USA. The Treaty of Peace and Friendship between the two countries (negotiated in 1787) is the longest unbroken US treaty relationship.
1860 Spain declared war in a dispute over the Ceuta enclave and won a further enclave and an enlarged Ceuta.
1884 Spain created a protectorate in coastal areas of Morocco.
1904 France and Spain agreed on respective zones of influence in the country.
1912 Morocco became a French protectorate under the Treaty of Fez. Spain continued to operate its coastal protectorate.
1923 France, Spain and Britain set up the international zone of Tangier.
1921–26 A rebellion in the Rif mountains, led by Abdel Krim, was eventually quelled by French and Spanish troops.
1943 The Istiqlal (Parti de l'Istiqlal) (Independence Party) was founded and an independence struggle began.
1956–57 Independence was granted by France and Spain. Tangier became Moroccan once more. Spain kept its two coastal enclaves. Sultan Sidi Mohammed ben Youssef adopted the title of King Mohammed V and established an hereditary monarchy.
1961 Mohammed V died and was succeeded by King Hassan II. He introduced political liberalisation.
1963 The first general elections were held.
1965 Following student riots and civil unrest, the King declared a state of emergency and suspended parliament.
1971 There was a failed attempt to depose the King and to establish a republic.
1972 A constitution was adopted.
1973–76 The Frente Popular para la Liberación de Saguia el Hamra y Río de Oro (Polisario) (Popular Front for the Liberation of Saguia el Hamra y Río de Oro), formed with Algerian support, aimed at an independent state in Spanish Sahara, a territory south of Morocco, controlled by Spain. King Hassan ordered a 350,000-strong Green March into the territory, attempting to annex it for Morocco. Spain agreed to withdraw from the region (later to become Western Sahara) and to transfer it to joint Moroccan-Mauritanian control. Polisario announced the formation of the Saharawi Arab Democratic Republic (SADR) and formed a government-in-exile. Western Sahara was divided betweem Morocco and Mauritania. Fighting continued between Moroccan military and Polisario forces.
1977 Morocco left the Organisation of African Unity (OAU) in protest at the SADR's admission to the body.
1983 Relations between Morocco and Algeria improve.
1988 Full diplomatic relations with Algeria were resumed.
1991 A UN-monitored cease-fire began in Western Sahara.
1998 The moderate socialist Union Socialiste des Forces Populaires (USFP) (Socialist Union of Popular Forces) won the elections and formed a government.
1999 King Hassan II died suddenly and his son, Mohammed VI, acceded him.
2000 King Mohammed VI began a process of modest political liberalisation.
2002 King Mohammed married Salma Bennani, a 24-year-old computer engineer; the marriage to a commoner was a break with Royal Moroccan tradition. Morocco occupied the tiny, uninhabited island of Leila or Isla del Perejil (Parsley Island) off its coast and owned by Spain, and prompted an international spat. After the general election, the two main parties – the USFP and Istiqlal – formed a coalition government. Driss Jettou was appointed prime minister.
2003 Senegal and Morocco signed agreements on closer co-operation. There

KEY INDICATORS — Morocco

	Unit	2003	2004	2005	2006	2007
Population	m	30.36	29.89	30.14	*30.44	*30.73
Gross domestic product (GDP)	US$bn	44.50	50.06	51.62	65.41	*73.43
GDP per capita	US$	1,527	1,629	1,713	*2,149	*2,389
GDP real growth	%	5.5	3.5	1.7	8.0	*2.2
Inflation	%	1.2	2.0	1.0	3.3	2.0
Unemployment	%	11.4	11.1	11.3	9.6	–
Industrial output	% change	–	4.9	3.9	4.6	–
Agricultural output	% change	–	1.9	-15.2	23.0	–
Exports (fob) (goods)	US$m	8,172.0	9,744.0	10,288.0	11,913.0	–
Imports (cif) (goods)	US$m	13,263.0	16,238.0	20,582.0	23,534.0	–
Balance of trade	US$m	-5,091.0	-6,494.0	-10,294.0	-11,621.0	–
Current account	US$m	1,590.0	922.0	1,018.0	1,856.0	*-71.0
Total reserves minus gold	US$m	13,851.0	16,337.0	16,187.0	20,341.0	24,123.0
Foreign exchange	US$m	13,634.0	16,107.0	16,008.0	20,182.0	23,980.0
Exchange rate	per US$	9.50	8.87	8.59	8.44	7.83

* estimated figure

were suicide bombings in Casablanca killing 41 and injuring many more.
Anti-terriosm laws were enacted and a campaign against extremists undertaken. Crown Prince Moulay Hassan was born.
2004 An earthquake in the north killed over 500 people. A free trade agreement was signed with the US after Morocco had been designated a major non-NATO ally.
2005 Prime Minister Jettou announced that Morocco wanted to establish a TGV (French high-speed train service) by 2015, between Casablanca, Marrakech and Agadir. Hundreds of migrants from sub-Saharan Africa attempted to force their entry into the Spanish enclaves of Melilla and Ceuta but were repelled and later were deported from Morocco. An official commission reported that human rights abuses during the rule of King Hassan II included almost 600 deaths.
2006 A meeting to try and revive the Arab Maghreb Union (AMU), to tackle regional security, was held. The AMU has been hampered for a decade by the dispute between Morocco and Algeria over the future of Western Sahara.
2007 Morocco proposed the Sahara autonomy plan which would allows Morocco and Polisario to discuss the future of Western Sahara without pre-conditions. The UN and US welcomed the new proposal. UN-sponsored talks regarding the plan failed to achieve agreement. In parliamentary elections, 33 parties and 6,600 candidates participated and the Istiqlal won most votes, to retain power and become the governing coalition party. Its partner in the outgoing government, the USFP lost 12 seats. The turnout, at 37 per cent, was the lowest in Morocco's history.

Political structure

Constitution

Adopted 10 March 1972; amended 1992 and 1996.
The constitution prohibits a one-party political system.
The King is Amir al Moumineen (Commander of the Faithful), hereditary head of state and supreme commander of the armed forces. He appoints the cabinet on the recommendation of the prime minister.
The King is empowered to declare a state of emergency and dissolve parliament if necessary.

Form of state

Constitutional monarchy

The executive

The King holds executive power, which is delegated to the prime minister and cabinet.

National legislature

Legislative powers are exercised by the bicameral Barlaman (parliament).
The 325-member Majlis al Nuwab (assembly of representatives, lower house) is directly elected for a five-year term in multi-seat constituencies. A national list for the remaining 30 seats are reserved for women.
The 270-member Majlis al Mustasharin (assembly of counsellors) is indirectly elected by local and national members of electoral colleges for nine-year terms; ever three years 90 members are re-elected.
The lower house debates legislation presented to it by the government; approved legislation is automatically promulgated after one month.
The upper house has the power to caution or censure the government. Cautioning motion must be signed by at least one-third of members and must be approved by an absolute majority. A censure motion must be brought by one-third of counsellors and must be approved by a two-third majority. A censure motion requires the government to resign.

Legal system

The legal system is based on Islamic law and a combination of French and Spanish civil law codes. The Supreme Court is responsible for reviewing government legislation.

Last elections

7 September 2007 (parliamentary)
Results: Parliament: Hizb al Istiqlal (Indpendence Party) won 10.7 per cent of the vote (52 seats out of 325), the Parti de la Justice et du Développement (Justice and Development Party) 10.9 per cent (46), Mouvement Populaire (People's Movement) 9.3 per cent (41), Rassemblement National des Indépendents (National Rally of Independent) 9.7 per cent (39), Union Socialiste des Forces Populaires) (Socialist Union of People's Forces) 8.9 per cent (38), Union Constitutionelle (Constitutional Union) 7.3 per cent (27), Parti du Progrès et du Socialisme (Party of Progress and Socialism) 5.4 per cent (17), the alliance Union PND-Al Ahd (Union-Al Ahd) 5.5 per cent (14); all other parties and independents won less than 5 per cent of the vote and less than 10 seats. Turnout was 37 per cent.

Next elections

2012 (parliamentary)

Political parties

Ruling party

Coalition government led by Hizb al Istiqlal (Istiqlal) (Indpendence Party) (since 2002; re-elected 2007)

Main opposition party

Parti de la Justice et du Développement (PJD) (Justice and Development Party) (Islamists)

Population

30.73 million (2007)*
Last census: September 2004: 29,680,069
Population density: 68 inhabitants per square km (2001). Urban population: 55.1 per cent of the total (2004 census).
Annual growth rate: 1.4 per cent (2004 census); 1.6 per cent 1994–2004 (WHO 2006)

Ethnic make-up

Mostly Berbers and Arabs. There is a small Jewish minority and an estimated 60,000 foreign residents, mainly of French, Spanish and Italian origin.

Religions

Islam is the state religion. Sunni Muslim (98 per cent). There are small minority Jewish and Roman Catholic communities.

Education

The illiteracy rate is as high as 83 per cent among women in rural areas. The government aims to increase the literacy to 76 per cent by 2010. Public expenditure on education is about 5 per cent of annual Gross National Income (GNI) and includes subsidies to private education at all levels.
Primary, or first stage education lasts until the age of 12, then students move onto second stage until aged 15, when they choose between an academic general secondary school or a technical secondary school for three years. At aged 18 the academic students undertake the Baccalauréat for progression to higher education. Technical students may undertake a further two years study in their specialised skill.
Higher education is provided by 13 universities, specialised schools and institutes under the supervision of the National Ministry of Education. Besides a traditional system of higher education, there are 28 executive training institutes (Etablissements de Formation des Cadres), which provide specialised training under the direct control of ministerial departments. There are also eight Grandes Ecoles d'Ingénieurs (engineering schools). A private university opened in September 1994. Universities are mainly public institutions with budgetary autonomy.
In 2003, schools began to teach Tamazight, the Berber language which predates Arabic in north Africa; children will have to learn using Arabic, Latin and Berber scripts.
Literacy rate: 51 per cent adult rate; 70 per cent youth rate (15–24) (Unesco 2005).
Compulsory years: 7 to 14.
Enrolment rate: 86 per cent gross primary enrolment of relevant age group (

including repeaters); 39 per cent gross secondary enrolment (World Bank).
Pupils per teacher: 28 in primary schools.

Health

Per capita total expenditure on health (2003) was US$218; of which per capita government spending was US$72, at the international dollar rate, (WHO 2006).
It is estimated that less than 20 per cent of Moroccans have access to healthcare. Public hospitals are free, but patients must buy medicine and pay for certain services, such as X-rays. Medical fees are reimbursed only for children. There are basic health services in rural areas, including local dispensaries, rural hospitals and provincial hospitals. Government policy specifically targets the reduction of infant deaths, the provision of family planning services, nutrition awareness programmes and campaigns against malaria and tuberculosis.

HIV/Aids
HIV prevalence: 0.1 per cent aged 15–49 in 2003 (World Bank)
Life expectancy: 71 years, 2004 (WHO 2006)
Fertility rate/Maternal mortality rate: 2.7 births per woman, 2004 (WHO 2006); maternal mortality 230 per 100,000 live births (World Bank).
Birth rate/Death rate: Seven deaths and 25 births per 1,000 head of population (World Bank).
Child (under 5 years) mortality rate (per 1,000): 36 per 1,000 live births (World Bank)
Head of population per physician: 0.51 physicians per 1,000 people, 2004 (WHO 2006)

Welfare

There is a stark contrast between the living standards of the rural and urban population. In 2004, 19 per cent of the population lived below the poverty line. In rural areas over a third of the population are classified as poor.
Morocco's social security system is based on the Caisse Nationale de la Sécurité Sociale (CNSS) (National Social Security Fund), which is funded by subscribers' contributions and interest on investments. All salaried workers in industry, commerce and services must belong to the CNSS. Civil servants belong to a similar scheme, run by the Caisse Nationale des Organismes de Prévoyance Sociale (CNOPS).
In cases of illness or accident, an employee can receive 50 per cent of salary after the eighth day. The employee can claim this benefit for up to 52 weeks every two years. Maternity benefit, equal to 50 per cent of salary, is paid for up to 10 weeks. The invalidity pension is equal to 50 per cent of salary for someone who has worked between five and 15 years. If a worker dies, the family is entitled to a payment equal to two months' salary. Old age pensions, equal to 50 per cent of salary, are payable to employees who have contributed for at least 15 years. The retirement age is 60. A pension is paid to the family of a deceased retired worker, provided they had worked for more than 15 years.

Main cities

Rabat (capital, estimated population 1.9 million (m) in 2005), Casablanca (commercial centre, 3.5m), Fez (1.2m), Marrakesh (969,420), Agadir (2.0m), Tangier (851,321), Meknès (587,315), Oujda (456,524), Kenitra (428,181).

Languages spoken

Business literature and correspondence should be in French or Arabic.
Arabic is spoken in general. French is taught in school and is more commonly spoken in government, business and among the Moroccans elite.
There are three main dialects of Tamazight (the Berber language) spoken all over the country. Tamazight belongs to the Afro-Asiatic family and is related to ancient Egyptian and Ethiopian.
Berber groups and their dialects: Shleuh (Ishalhiyan), in the High Atlas, Tashalhit dialect; Imazighen (Imazighen), Middle Atlas/Eastern High Atlas, Tamazight dialect; Rifans (Irifiyan), Northern Morocco, Tarifit dialect.
In the north, Spanish is widely spoken, while in the bigger cities like Casablanca, English is very common.

Official language/s
Arabic

Media

The government uses the media to strengthen national unity and aid cultural, economic and social development. This has meant extending the state media network to remote areas, improving training and modernising technical equipment. The government owns the official news-agency, Maghreb Arab Presse. While print media is predominantly independent, electronic media remains largely under government control.

Press
Dailies: Principal newspapers in Arabic, French and English include the government owned Al Anbaa, Le Matin du Sahara et du Maghreb, Maroc Hebdo, La Nouvelle Tribune, La Gazette du Maroc, Al Annbaa, Al Jarida Al Maghribia, Al Bayane, Morocco Today and News Express. On-line news services include the daily French (www.)marocnews.com.
Business: Numerous periodicals are available in French and Arabic, including the business weekly La Vie Economique. l'Economiste carries financial news.

Broadcasting
Radio: Extensive national and external services are available in Arabic, French, English, Spanish and Berber. The government controls Radio-Television Marocaine (RTM). The French language Medi-1 is a private radio station. The government has been encouraging more private radio stations to operate in Morocco since 2001.
Television: Local television stations broadcast for over 60 hours per week, with advertising in Arabic and French. The nationwide network is basically state-controlled, but a private cable channel is also in operation.

Economy

The economy has much to commend it with a well managed monetary policy that has achieved macroeconomic stability for over a decade. It has a current account surplus, low inflation at 1.0 per cent in 2005 and foreign exchange reserves which are strong. However, the weakness in the economy, from its slow growth of 1.8 per cent GDP, over-reliance on the agriculture sector and high unemployment and underemployment, mars what could be the economy of a mature industrialised state.
The service sector provides 56 per cent of GDP, agricultural accounts for 13 per cent and industry 31 per cent, of which manufacturing accounts for 17 per cent. Foreign remittances, of US$4.4 billion, provided around 9 per cent of GDP in 2005 when, for the first time, tourism revenue surpassed remittances as a share of GDP.
Agricultural production has been falling steadily since 1985, until in 2005 it registered negative growth of 15.2 per cent. Production is vulnerable to climatic shocks and droughts have a direct affect on the 50 per cent of the population that depend on the sector for their livelihood, which in turn correlates to rural poverty. To achieve long-term stability the economy has to be diversified with increased growth in secondary and tertiary industries.
State owned entities have been, or are in the process of being sold off, while trade liberalisation is ongoing. These measures will enhance Morocco's competitiveness, and maintain exports to its primary market, the EU, while reforms are being completed.
In 2004 the World Bank approved a US$37 million loan for the development of Morocco's rural roads, with a view to increasing road access to 80 per cent of the rural population by 2015. Another World Bank loan, of US$100 million, was approved to support the Moroccan government's efforts to improve public

resource management, a key step for accelerated growth and poverty reduction. Investment in social developments are medium-term budget objectives to improve access to education, healthcare, housing, basic infrastructure and rural development.
Morocco has implemented the regime the IMF has consistently argued should be adopted by developing countries with strong fiscal controls and a liberalised economy, it remains to be seen as to when Morocco reaps the benefits of its efforts.

External trade
In 2005 the Greater Arab Free Trade Area (Gafta) was ratified by 17 members, including Morocco, creating an Arab economic bloc. A customs union was established whereby tariffs within Gafta will be reduced by a percentage each year, until none remain. It is also a signatory of the Euro-Mediterranean Partnership agreement, which provides for the introduction of free trade between the EU and 10 Mediterranean countries by 2012.
Morocco belongs to the Arab Maghreb Union (AMU) with Algeria, Libya, Mauritania and Tunisia. However internal disputes have hampered the implementation of a free trade or customs union. In 2004, Morocco and the US concluded a free trade agreement.

Imports
Principal imports are crude oil, textiles, electronic and telecommunications equipment, wheat, gas and electricity, plastics.
Main sources: France (16.5 per cent total, 2006), Spain (11.6 per cent), Saudi Arabia (6.8 per cent).

Exports
Principal exports are clothing, fish, fruits and vegetables, inorganic chemicals, transistors, crude minerals, fertilisers (including phosphates) and petroleum products,
Main destinations: France (28.43 per cent total, 2006), Spain (20.8 per cent), UK (6.0 per cent).

Agriculture

Farming
The agricultural sector contributed 16.7 per cent to GDP on 2004, it typically employs 40 per cent of the workforce which can rise to 50 per cent during the harvest.
Grain harvests were bumper during 2003 and 2004, with production levels almost double the norm at eight million tonnes; levels returned to the usual four million tonnes in 2005.
Around 70 per cent of the 7.9 million hectares (ha) of arable land is cultivated, mainly by subsistent farmers.
Principal crops are wheat, barley, maize (grown in the rain-fed areas), citrus fruits, beans, chick peas and other pulses, tomatoes (mainly for export), potatoes, olives and oilseeds. Important agri-export crops are sugar cane, sugar beet (the production of which is being developed to cut down on sugar imports) and cotton.
Livestock productivity and crop yields have remained low and regular food imports of grain are necessary to meet domestic cereal requirements. Agricultural development has also been hampered by the small size of the majority of holdings and restricted access to EU markets. Many long-term government projects are under way, including irrigation schemes, development of new techniques and financial incentives to farmers.
As the increasing population puts pressure on available resources, access to water will become more difficult. The World Bank has estimated that Morocco will become a water deficit country by 2020.
Some 32,500 tonnes of cannabis is grown annually in the deprived north of Morocco for the European market. King Mohammed has made developing the north a priority in government policy in order to combat illicit crop cultivation.
Crop production in 2005 included: 4,448,430 tonnes (t) cereals in total, 3,043,000t wheat, 1,102,000t barley, *1,440,000t potatoes, 1,255,400t citrus fruit, *1,201,230t tomatoes, 257,440t pulses, *4,560,000t sugar beet, 137,571t oilcrops, *992,000t sugar cane, *267,000t grapes, *69,400t dates, 6,500t tobacco, 450,000t olives, *393,140t apples, 71,900t treenuts, 2,691,135t fruit in total, 4,889,890t vegetables in total. Estimated livestock production included: 599,500t meat in total, 148,000t beef, 33,000t game meat, 10,000t edible snails, 124,000t lamb and goat meat, 280,000t poultry, 230,000t eggs, 3,000t honey, 1,364,700t milk, 12,800t sheepskins.
* estimate

Fishing
The fishing sector offers considerable potential, although export markets for the main catch, sardines, are restricted by strong competition from Spain, Portugal and France. The total catch is estimated at around one million tonnes a year, of which 150,00 tonnes is shellfish and 930,000 tonnes is marine fish.
Morocco's fleet fishes in both Atlantic and Mediterranean waters and has an agreement to fish in the Gulf of Guinea. As well as its own ports, some of Morocco's catch is landed in Portugal. Fish frozen at sea is landed at Agadir and Tan-Tan.
The government is modernising the fishing fleet and ports to exploit the rich potential of local fishing grounds. The EU donated US$22.2 million to build four new fishing villages on Morocco's Mediterranean coast. A US$13 million expansion programme at Sidi Ifni fishing port, enabled catches in excess of 50,000 tonnes per annum.
After pursuing a policy of leasing fishing rights to foreign countries such as South Korea, Japan, the former Soviet Union, Spain and Portugal, the government is now encouraging national private enterprises in the sector.
Morocco has an agreement with Norway concerning co-operation on fishery issues, exchange of expertise and data and bilateral investment promotion.
In 2004, the total marine fish catch was 853,563 tonnes and the total crustacean catch was 9,530 tonnes.

Forestry
Only 9 per cent of land area is forested and most of Morocco's wood needs are imported. Timber imports in 2004 were US$510 million, while exports amounted to US$93 million.
Timber production in 2004 included 861,000 cubic metre (cum) roundwood, 563,000cum industrial roundwood, 83,000cum sawnwood, 185,000cum sawlogs and veneer logs, 378,000t pulpwood, 34,000cum wood-based panels, 298,000cum woodfuel; 96,965 tonnes (t) charcoal, 129,000t paper and paperboard, (including 2,000t newsprint), 34,000t printing and writing paper, 112,000t paper pulp.

Industry and manufacturing
The industrial sector accounts for 30–35 per cent of GDP and employs 37 per cent of the workforce. Most activity is concentrated in the Casablanca area.
The main industry is the processing of phosphates into phosphoric acid and fertilisers. Food processing is another major industry. Other significant industries include oil refining, steel, cement, chemicals, pharmaceuticals, toiletries, metallurgy, textiles, leather, paper and timber, metals, rubber, plastics and vehicle assembly. The textile and leather industries employ one quarter of the industrial workforce, and export successfully.
Industrial development has switched in recent years away from import substitution and towards encouraging the manufacture of goods for export, support for small- and medium-sized producers, devolution of spending powers to local authorities and investment in other areas of the country away from Casablanca.
Industrial production increased by 0.5 per cent in 2003.

Tourism
The tourism sector is active as a competitive destination for European tourists and is expected to contribute 9.5 per cent of GDP and 14.7 per cent of total employment in 2005. To further encourage

tourism, the prices of accommodation, restaurants and service charges have been reduced. Police checks on tourists have also been relaxed.
The private sector has pooled resources to set up a National Tourism Federation to plan renovation of hotels, development of infrastructure and coastal resorts. The continuing privatisation of state-owned hotels should contribute to the growth of the sector. Around 13 per cent of all capital investment in 2005 are planned to be in travel and tourism.
The government's tourist strategy is to attract 10 million visitors by 2010. Tenders were invited, in June 2005, for a new beach resort at Taghazout, this will be the fifth resort in a string of six, as contained in The Azur Plan.
The civil unrest that resulted in the 2003 Casablanca bombings appears to have been moderated and improved Morocco's international image. The government has launched a campaign to triple the number of Arab tourists visiting, at a time when Western destinations have been less welcoming to them.

Mining

Government policy has been to open up the mining sector to investments by both minor and major mining companies.
There are more than 90 mining companies producing 20 different mineral products. The sector contributes approximately 15 per cent to GDP and employs 4 per cent of the workforce.
Although phosphates account for 92 per cent of mineral production, smaller quantities of other minerals are produced, including 500,000 tonnes of anthracite. Morocco has large deposits of lead, zinc, copper, iron, fluorine, silver, manganese, cobalt, antimony, barytine, salt and other minerals.
Phosphate mining and the production of phosphoric acid are of vital importance to the Moroccan economy, although a large proportion of reserves is located in the disputed Western Sahara area occupied by Morocco since 1975. The sector is controlled by the state through the country's largest company, Office Chérifien des Phosphates (OCP). OCP is the world's largest exporter of phosphate rock. With reserves of approximately 110 billion tonnes, Morocco is estimated to contain three-quarters of the world's phosphate reserves.
Iron ore deposits in the northern Rif region, 25km from the port of Beni Eznar, include 18.2 million tonnes of magnetite ore, which could bring in 700,000–800,000 tonnes of ore per year. Silver, copper, zinc and lead are also mined.

Hydrocarbons

In 2004, Morocco had proven oil reserves of two million barrels producing 200 barrels per day (bpd) from its Sidi Rhelem oil field. With total consumption of around 150,000bpd, Morocco is heavily reliant on imported oil. Oil accounts for over 80 per cent of total energy requirements, mainly imported from Saudi Arabia. Exploration projects are under way onshore, mainly in the south-west and north-east, and offshore. By mid-2005 there were 15 foreign companies actively engaged in exploration.
Morocco has two oil refineries: Samir and Sidi Kacem with a combined capacity of 155 billion bpd. Samir was partly destroyed by fire in 2002; in June 2005 a US$628 million contract to modernise was let to Snamprogetti SpA (Italy) and Tekefen Company (Turkey). The upgrade is expected to by completed by 2008.
Morocco signed two controversial oil deals with TotalFinaElf of France and Kerr-McGee (US-based) to explore in the disputed Western Sahara in 2001. The Polisario Front, Western Sahara's independence movement, protested against the deals and invited companies to bid for 12 of its own offshore exploration rights. International protest campaigns have limited the involvement of all but Kerr-McGee in Western Sahara. The legality of these contracts can only be settled after the status of Western Sahara is internationally recognised.
Although Morocco contains only limited natural gas reserves at 1.2 billion cubic metres in 2004, the country is a major transit centre for Algerian gas exports to Europe. The Maghreb-Europe pipeline transports Algerian gas to Spain via Morocco and the Straits of Gibraltar. Ultimately it is planned to carry 20 billion cubic metres of gas per year to Europe, via Spain.
There is only one coal mine, at Jerada, with 91 million tonnes of reserves but with declining production most coal is imported from South Africa and Poland.

Energy

Morocco has a total installed electricity generating capacity of over 4GW, with plans to increase capacity to cater for its rapidly growing demand for electricity.
To avoid blackouts and government expenditure the private sector is increasing its market share of electricity generation.
The Office National de l'Electicité (One) is solely responsible for electricity transmission and distribution.
Morocco has completed 40 per cent of the construction of a nuclear reactor and is looking to other non-fossil fuel energy sources to provide 10 per cent its energy needs by 2011, including wind turbines and hydro- and solar power.
The country's goal is to supply 80 per cent of rural areas by 2008, and by 2005, 55 per cent of outlying villages had access to electricity.
The entire energy sector is expected to be liberalised by 2007.

Financial markets

Stock exchange

The Bourse de Casablanca (Casablanca Stock Exchange) (CSE) is a private company with stock held by brokers.
Despite an increase in foreign interest in the CSE, major foreign participation has yet to materialise. The limited size of the CSE is a disincentive to foreign investment. The daily volume of trade averages little more than US$10 million, too small for many international investors. Another obstacle to growth of the CSE is government regulation. In an attempt to curb the outflow of foreign exchange the government has legislated against Moroccans investing their funds abroad. As a consequence, insurance companies and mutual funds are competing intensively for the relatively few stocks available, inflating prices and making them comparatively unattractive to other investors.
The CFG25 index rose 26.0 per cent in 2007.

The CFG25, an index established by the Casablanca Finance Group to measure the stock exchange performance, rose 26.0%, or close to the average market increase of the past five years (27.3%). The CFG25 rose by an exceptional 57.4% in 2006. Most of the market gain in 2007 took place in the first four months of the year (31.6% up by May 8, 2007), driven by the anticipation of strong corporate annual results for the previous fiscal year, combined with an upbeat outlook for 2007. This report looks at the performance of the Casablanca Bourse and what analysts expect for 2008.

Banking and insurance

The Banque Marocaine du Commerce Extérieur (BMCE) was the first Moroccan bank and has grown steadily since 1995. It has broadened its international shareholder base and opened new branches throughout Morocco and abroad. At 8 per cent it has the largest capitalisations on the stock exchange, and around 25 per cent of that of the banking sector.
The Banque Commerciale du Maroc (BCM) holds the sector's best return on equity. It has a bad debt reduction strategy, and lower levels of bad debts than its competitors.
The Banque Centrale Populaire (BCP), the Banque Nationale pour le Développement Economique (BNDE) and the Crédit

Immobilier et Hôtelier (CIH) are scheduled for privatisation. They are criticised for being burdened with high levels of bad debt and may need radical restructuring if they are to survive and compete in an adverse economic climate.

Central bank
Bank al Maghrib

Main financial centre
Casablanca

Time
GMT

Geography
Morocco is situated in the extreme north-west of Africa. It has a long coastline on the shores of the Atlantic Ocean and, east of the Strait of Gibraltar, on the Mediterranean Sea, facing southern Spain. Morocco's eastern frontier is with Algeria, while to the south lies the disputed territory of Western Sahara.

There are four distinct geographical regions, from the low-lying arid Saharan desert in the south to the Rif mountains in the north. A wide, fertile, coastal plain runs in an arc along the western seaboard and around to the Mediterranean Coast, bounded by the Rif and Atlas mountains. The Atlas mountains bisect the country from south-west to north-east and contain the highest peak in North Africa, Jebel Toubkal (4,165 metres) in the main range called the Great Atlas. The two main rivers, the Moulouya flows into the Mediterranean sea and the Sebou flows into the Atlantic.

Western Sahara is typical semiarid Sahel (an Arab word to describe a border or margin) of savannah and scrubland with low hills in the north and south.

Hemisphere
Northern

Climate
Varies widely with area; while Mediterranean on the coast, it is hotter and drier inland and Alpine in the High Atlas, yet Saharan in the south. Summer is from May–October. It is dry and hot, with temperatures between 23–28 degrees Celsius (C) on the coast, 30–45 degrees C inland. Winter runs from November–April, with light rain on the coast, average temperature 15–21 degrees C, and dry inland with temperatures between 20–30 degrees C.

Dress codes
Lightweight suits are best for formal wear. Women should dress modestly. Some visitors adopt the traditional jellaba, which is more comfortable in both hot and cool weather and is usually worn by men. It can get cool quickly after dark, so a light overcoat or wrap is advised.

Entry requirements
Passports
Required by all. Passports must be valid for at least six months from the date of entry.

Visa
Required by all, except citizens of EU, North America and Australasia, for visits including business trips up to three months, for further exceptions and information see: www.maec.gov.ma and follow link from Consular to Formalities and procedures for international visitors.

Currency advice/regulations
The import and export of local currency is prohibited. The import and export of foreign currency is unlimited but all amounts over Dh15,000 must be declared.

Up to half (and a greater percentage for visits of less than 48 hours) of the Moroccan dirham purchased by a visitor may be re-exchanged for foreign currency, on the production of bank sales vouchers, when departing.

Travellers cheques are accepted in banks and to avoid additional exchange fees, cheques in US dollars and pounds sterling are best.

Prohibited imports
Import restrictions apply to firearms and ammunition, permits must be obtained before travelling.

Health (for visitors)
Mandatory precautions
Vaccinations against yellow fever are required if arriving from an infected area.

Advisable precautions
Typhoid, tetanus and polio vaccinations are recommended. Anti-malaria precautions should be taken. Water may be contaminated. Milk is unpasteurised and should be boiled.

Hotels
Inexpensive and widely available. Two main types: graded hotels (which are given a one- to five-star rating by the Tourist Board) and small (and usually old) unlisted hotels. A service charge and local tax is normally added to bill.

Credit cards
Major credit cards widely accepted. ATMs can be found in cities and large towns.

Public holidays (national)
Fixed dates
1 Jan (New Year's Day), 11 Jan (Independence Day), 1 May (Labour Day), 30 Jul (Feast of the Throne), 14 Aug (Oued Eddahab Allegiance Day), 20 Aug (The King and the People's Revolution Day), 21 Aug (King Mohammed's Birthday), 6 Nov (Anniversary of the Green March), 18 Nov (Independence Day).

Holidays that fall at the weekend are not transferred to another day.

Variable dates
Eid al Adha (two days), Islamic New Year, Birth of the Prophet (two days), Eid al Fitr (two days).

Islamic year – 1429 (10 Jan 2008–28 Dec 2008): The Islamic year contains 354 or 355 days, with the result that Muslim feasts advance by 10–12 days against the Gregorian calendar. Dates of feasts vary according to the sighting of the new moon, so cannot be forecast exactly.

Working hours
Banking
Mon–Thu: 0815–1215 and 1415–1715, Fri: 0815–1115 and 1430–1730; Sat 0900–1300. Ramadan: Mon–Fri: 0900–1530.

Business
Winter: Mon–Fri: 0800–1200 and 1400–1800/2000. Summer hours vary, some work Mon–Fri: 0800–1500/1600, others revert to winter hours. Ramadan: Mon–Fri: 0900–1500/1600.

Government
Winter: Mon–Fri: 0800–1200 and 1430–1800. Summer: Mon–Sat: 0800–1600. Ramadan: Mon–Sat: 0900–1500.

Shops
Shops are usually open between 0800 and 1800, often closing for a few hours in the middle of the day.

Telecommunications
Mobile/cell phones
GSM 900 services are available for most of Morocco and northern Western Sahara.

Electricity supply
220V AC, 50 cycles; sockets are typically the European two-pronged variety.

Social customs/useful tips
Business visits during the Muslim month of Ramadan are best avoided, as many businesses close during part or all of this period. During Ramadan, visitors should respect Muslim traditions and avoid drinking, eating and smoking in public during daylight hours.

Pork and alcohol are forbidden to Muslims at all times, so these should not be offered, although in practice alcohol is widely available and its consumption not considered an insult to Islam.

Business practices in most respects are similar to those in France and Spain.

Tipping is common for most services, including hotel porters, cinema usherettes, cloakroom attendants, railway porters, and so on. In hotels and restaurants a service charge is normally added to the bill. Taxi drivers (in grand taxis only) will expect a 10 per cent tip.

Security
Street crime is a problem, especially in the larger cities where petty theft is rife. Women may also encounter sexual harassment on the streets at any time, especially when walking alone.

Getting there
Air
National airline: Royal Air Maroc
International airport/s: Casablanca-Mohammed V (CMN), 30km south of the city, duty-free shops, restaurant, bank, post office, car hire and business centre. There are taxis to Casablanca and a rail link to Rabat.
Tangier-Boukhalef Souahel (TNG), 11km from city, with duty-free shops, restaurant, bank, post office, shops, car hire.
Other airport/s: Agadir-Inezgane (AGA), 6.5km south of city, bar, buffet, bank, car hire; Fez-Sais (FEZ), 10km from city; Rabat-Salé (RBA), 10km from city, restaurant, bank, car hire; Marrakesh (RAK), 6km from city.
Airport tax: None
Surface
Road: Road access is possible from Algeria via Oujda.
Rail: There are good rail connections to Tunisia, France and Spain (via rail-ferry link). The international rail link is via Oujda. In 2002, rail links to Algeria were suspended.
Water: Regular car ferry and hydrofoil services connect Spain, France and Gibraltar with Tangier and the Spanish administered ports of Ceuta and Melilla.
Main port/s: Agadir, Casablanca (major freight port), Jorf Lasfar, Kenitra, Mohammedia, Nador, Safi, Tangier (main passenger port).

Getting about
National transport
Air: Royal Air Maroc operates domestic services to main centres. Regional Airlines is another domestic carrrier.
Road: Morocco has approximately 30,000km of surfaced roads. The links between main centres are generally good. Some of the 30,000km country roads need care and/or local knowledge. The Atlas Mountains may be impassable in winter.
Buses: There are frequent, cheap services between towns. Long-distance services include: Tangier-Oujda, Fez-Marrakesh; Agadir-Casablanca and Tangier-Casablanca. It is advisable to book in advance.
Rail: A limited (1,893km) but efficient network is operated by Office National des Chemins de Fer (ONCF). Fares are cheap. Three classes are available. Air-conditioning, air-conditioned sleeping cars – couchettes and restaurant cars are available; supplements may be payable. Routes include:
Oujda-Fez-Rabat-Casablanca, Marrakesh-Casablanca-Rabat and Casablanca-Rabat-Tangier.
City transport
Taxis: The grand taxis (Moroccan bus-taxis), seating up to six persons, operate along specific routes and can be arranged at hotel receptions, or can be found outside bus and train stations and the airport. They are cheaper than a conventional taxi for long journeys and more comfortable and convenient than a bus. The petit taxis are metered and operate within cities. Fares vary considerably; drivers prefer to set fares in advance, rather than use the meter, so each journey is preceded by a negotiation. A 10 per cent tip is usual.
Buses, trams & metro: Agadir, Casablanca, Tangier and other main towns have good bus services. Tickets can be bought in advance of journeys. There is a shuttle bus service from the Casablanca rail station to the CTM Gare Routière (bus station) which takes at least 45 minutes, depending on traffic.
Trains: Train service every 30 minutes connects Casablanca's Mohammed V Airport with the city's main railway stations, Voyageurs and Port.
Car hire
Car hire is widely available but expensive. Major hire companies operate from Agadir, Casablanca and Tangier. National or international driving licences are accepted. Driving is on the right.

BUSINESS DIRECTORY

The addresses listed below are a selection only. While World of Information makes every endeavour to check these addresses, we cannot guarantee that changes have not been made, especially to telephone numbers and area codes. We would welcome any corrections.

Telephone area codes
The international dialling code (IDD) for Morocco is +212, followed by area code and subscriber's number:

Agadir	48	Mohammedia	232
Casablanca	22	Rabat	37
Fes	55	Tangier	39
Marrakech	44		

Chambers of Commerce
American Chamber of Commerce in Morocco, Hyatt Regency Casablanca, Place des Nations Unies, Casablanca (tel: 293-028; fax: 481-597; email: amcham@amcham-morocco.com).

British Chamber of Commerce for Morocco, 65 Avenue Hassan Seghir, Casablanca (tel: 448-860; fax: 448-868; email: britcham@casanet.net.ma).

Casablanca Chambre de Commerce, d'Industrie et des Services, 98 Boulevard Mohammed V,PO Box 423, Casablanca (tel: 264-327; fax: 268-436; email: ccisc@ccíscx.gov.ma).

Chambre de Commerce Internationale, Boulevard de Bordeaux, Casablanca (tel: 225-111; fax: 225-119; email: icc@casanet.net.ma).

French Chambre de Commerce et d'Industrie du Maroc,15 Avenue Mers Sultan, PO Box 15810, Casablanca (tel: 209-090; fax: 200-130; email: cfcim@cfcim.org).

Marrakech Chambre de Commerce, d'Industrie et de Services, Djnan El Harti Gueliz, Marrakech (tel: 431-951; fax: 430-950; email: ccismar@iam.net.ma).

Morocco Fédération des Chambres de Commerce et d'Industrie, 6 Rue Erfoud, Rabat (tel: 766-108; fax: 767-076; e-mail: fccjsm@maghrebnet.net.ma).

Rabat Chambre de Commerce, d'Industrie et de Services, 6 Rue Ghandi, PO Box 131, Rabat (tel: 703-185; fax: 703-166; email: ccisrs@ccisrs.org.ma).

Tangiers Chambre de Commerce, d'Industrie et de Services, Angle Rue Ibn Taymia et Rue El Hariri, Tangier (tel: 946-026; fax: 942-954; email: cciswtg@iam.net.ma).

Banking
ABN Amro Bank (Maroc) SA, PO Box 13478, 47 Rue Allal Ben Abellah, Casablanca 20000 (tel: 266-027; fax: 222-514).

Banque Centrale Populaire, 101 Boulevard Mohamed Zerktouni, Casablanca (tel: 222-589; fax: 222-699; e-mail: aslamti@cpm.co.ma).

Banque Commerciale du Maroc, 2 Boulevard Moulay Youssef, Casablanca (tel: 224-169; fax: 469-916).

Banque Marocaine du Commerce Extérieur SA, PO Box 13.425, 140 Avenue Hassan II, Casablanca 01 (tel: 220-0325, 220-0467; fax: 220-0005, 220-0060).

Crédit du Maroc SA, PO Box 13579, 48-58 Boulevard Mohammed V, Casablanca 20000 (tel: 477-000; fax: 277-127, 206-076/77).

Crédit Immobilier et Hôtelier, 187 Avenue Hassan II, Casablanca 20000 (tel: 222-7863; fax: 248-7537, 227-8631).

Groupement Professionel des Banques du Maroc (Moroccan Banking Association), 71 Avenue des Forces Armées Royales, Casablanca (tel: 311-624; fax: 311-911).

Société Marocaine de Dépôt et de Crédit, 79 Avenue Hassan II, Casablanca (tel: 224-114; fax: 271-590).

Wafabank, 163 Avenue Hassan II, Casablanca (tel: 220-0200, 227-1091, 226-5151, 222-4105; fax: 226-3621).

Central bank

Bank al Maghrib, PO Box 445, 277 Avenue Mohammed V, Rabat (tel: 702-626; fax:706-677).

Travel information

Casablana Airport, Office National des Aéroports, Casa-Oasis, BP 8101 Casablanca (tel: 539-040, 539-140; fax: 539-051, 539-901; internet: www.ondo.org.ma).

Office National des Chemins de Fer (ONCF) Tourist Office, 98 Boulevard Mohammed V, Casablanca (tel: 221-524).

Royal Air Maroc, 44 Avenue des Forces Armées Royales, Casablanca (tel: 311-122; fax: 442-409).

Ministry of tourism

Ministry of Economy, Finance and Tourism, Quartier Administratif, Chellah, Rabat (tel: 760-147; 760-509; fax: 761-575; e-mail: ministre@mfie.gov.ma; internet site: http://www.tourisme-marocain.com/frame/infos.htm).

National tourist organisation offices

Morocco National Tourist Board (ONMT), Rue Oued Fes, Angle Avenue Al Abtal, Agdal, Rabat (tel: 681-531; fax: 777-437; e-mail: visitemorocco@mbox.azure.net).

Ministries

Prime Minister's Office, Palais Royal, Le Méchouar, Rabat (tel: 762-709; fax: 769-995).

Ministry of Agriculture and Rural Development, Place Abdallah Chefchaouni, Quartier Administratif, Rabat (tel: 760-933; fax: 763-378).

Ministry of Communication, 10 Rue de Béni Mellal, Place de la Grande Poste, Avenue Mohammed V, Rabat (tel: 766-016; fax: 766-908; internet site: www.mincom.gov.ma).

Ministry of Economic Forecasts and Planning, Avenue Al Haj Cherkaoui, Agdal, Rabat (tel: 761-415; fax: 760-771).

Ministry of Economy, Finance and Tourism, Quartier Administratif, Chellah, Rabat (tel: 760-147; 760-509; fax: 761-575; email: ministre@mfie.gov.ma; internet site: www.finances.gov.ma).

Ministry of Education, Bab Rouah, Rabat (tel: 771-822; fax: 772-042).

Minister of Employment, Vocational Training, Social Development and Solidarity (tel: 760-695; fax: 766-633).

Ministry of Equipment, Quartier Administratif, Chellah, Rabat (tel: 762-811; fax: 765-505).

Ministry of Foreign Affairs and Co-operation, Avenue Roosevelt, Rabat (tel: 762-841; fax: 764-679; email: mail@maec.gov.ma; internet site: www.maec.gov.ma).

Minister of Habous and Islamic Affairs, Le Méchouar, Rabat (tel: 766-801; fax: 765-257; e-mail: webmaster@habous.gov.ma).

Ministry of Health, 335 Boulevard Mohammed V, Rabat (tel: 761-121; fax: 768-401; e-mail: webmaster@sante.gov.ma).

Ministry of Higher Education and Scientific Research, Charia Bouregreg, Rabat (tel: 707-496; fax: 737-236).

Ministry of Human Rights (tel: 673-131; fax: 671-967).

Ministry of Industry, Commerce, Energy, and Mines, Quartier Administratif, Chellah, Rabat (tel: 761-868; fax: 766-265; email: ministre@mcinet).

Ministry of Interior, Quartier Administratif, Rabat (tel: 761-861; fax: 762-056).

Ministry of Justice, Place Mamounia, Rabat (tel: 732-941; fax: 730-772).

Minister of Land Management, Urban Affairs, Housing and the Environment (tel: 763-539; fax: 763-510).

Ministry of Parliamentary Relations, Quartier Administratif, Agdal, Rabat (tel: 775-170; fax: 775-468).

Ministry of Public Service and Administrative Reform (770-894; fax: 775-690).

Ministry of Public Sector and Privatisation (internet site: www.minpriv.gov.ma).

Ministry of Sea Fisheries, Quartier Administratif, Rabat (tel: 770-154; fax: 778-540).

Ministry of Transport and Merchant Marine (tel: 774-266; fax: 779-525).

Ministry of Youth and Sport, Boulevard Ibn Sina, Agdal, Rabat, (tel: 680-045; fax: 680-916).

Other useful addresses

Bourse de Casablanca (Stock Exchange), Avenue de l'Armée Royale, Casablanca (tel: 452-626; fax: 452-625; email: contact@casablanca-bourse.com).

British Consulate-General, 43 Boulevard d'Anfa, Casablanca (tel: 221-653; fax: 265-779; email: british. consulate@casanet.net.ma).

British Embassy, 17 Boulevard de la Tour Hassan, Rabat (tel: 729-696; fax: 704-531; email: britemb@mtds.com).

Confédération Générale des Enterprises du Maroc (CGEM), Angle Avenue des Forces Armées Royales et Rue Mohamed Errachid, Casablanca (tel: 252-696; fax: 253-839).

Fédération des Industries Chimiques et Parachimiques (FICP), 36 Rue Chaouia, Casablanca (tel: 229-215; fax:225-613).

Fédération des Industries de la Conserve des Produits Agricoles du Maroc (FICOPAM), 77 Rue Mohamed Smiha, Casablanca (tel: 303-953; fax: 303-534).

Fédération des Industries Métallurgiques, Mécaniques, Electriques et Electroniques (FIMME), 147 Rue Mohamed Smiha, Casablanca (tel: 301-683; fax: 940-587).

Moroccan Centre for Export Promotion, 23 Rue Bnou Majed El Bahar, Casablanca (tel: 302-210; fax: 301-793).

Moroccan Embassy (USA), 1601 21st Street, NW, Washington DC 20009 (tel: (+1-202) 462-7979; fax: (+1-202) 265-0161; email: sifarausa@erols.com).

National Telecommunications Regulatory Agency (ANRT), Boulevard Ennakhil, Rabat (tel: 717-312; email: webmaster@anrt.net.ma).

Office pour le Développement Industriel (ODI), 10 Rue Ghandi, Rabat (tel: 708-460; fax: 707-695).

ONAREP (national oil company), 34 Avenue Al Fadila, Rabat (tel: 281-616; fax: 281-634; email: benkhadr@onarep.com).

United States Embassy, 2 Avenue de Mohamed El Fassi, Rabat (tel: 762-265; fax: 765-661).

Internet sites

Africa Business Network: www.ifc.org/abn

AllAfrica.com: http://allafrica.com

African Development Bank: www.afdb.org

Information on Morocco – historical events, cities, economy, culture and media: www.dsg.ki.se/maroc/

Mbendi AfroPaedia (information on companies, countries, industries and stock exchanges in Africa): http://mbendi.co.za

Menara Yellow Pages (in French): www.menara.co.ma/pagejauneHome.asp

Mozambique

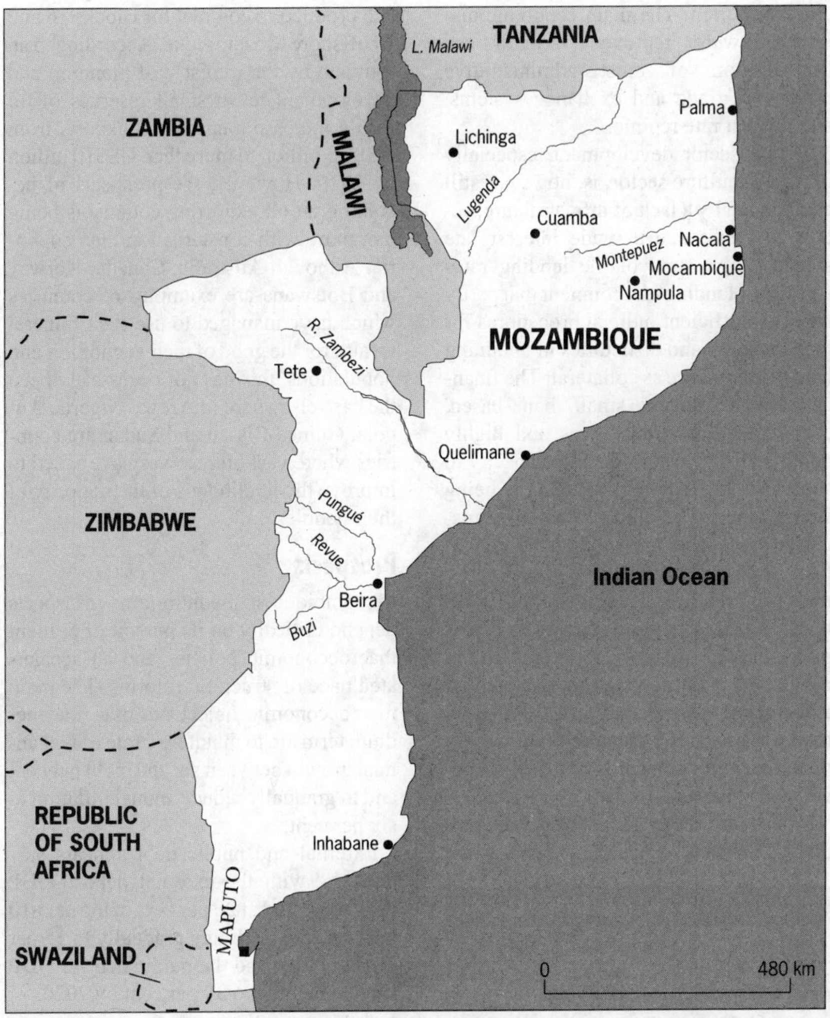

Mozambique's economy grew by 7.0 per cent in 2007 according to the Bank of Mozambique. But in July 2008 it announced that growth in the first quarter of 2008 had fallen to 3.5 per cent, largely due to poor performances in the industrial sector (-9.0 per cent) and the electricity and water sectors (-10.4 per cent). Exports from the Cahora Bassa dam on the Zambezi fell from US$64.9 million in the first quarter of 2007 to US$52.4 million in 2008; reason for this fall is partly due to the failure of Zimbabwe to pay its bills.

Macroeconomic success

Mozambique remains a successful example of post-conflict transition, with impressive economic growth averaging 8 per cent from 2000 to 2006, says the 2008 edition of *African Economic Outlook* (AEO). Growth in 2007 was down slightly on the 8 per cent of 2006, because of oil price increases and a downturn in tratitional exports. Growth has been driven by booming investment in mineral resources, industry, services and agro-industry, as well as the good performanceby the

KEY FACTS

Official name: República de Moçambique (Republic of Mozambique)

Head of State: President Armando Guebuza (Frelimo) (sworn in 2 Feb 2005)

Head of government: Prime Minister Luisa Diogo (from Feb 2004)

Ruling party: Frente de Libertação de Moçambique (Frelimo) (Front for the Liberation of Mozambique) (re-elected Dec 2004)

Area: 799,380 square km

Population: 20.50 million (2007)

Capital: Maputo

Official language: Portuguese

Currency: Metical (MT) = 100 centavos (New notes were issued in 2006 as part of a reform of the currency, which dropped three zeros).

Exchange rate: MT24.05 per US$ (Jul 2008)

GDP per capita: US$369 (2007)

GDP real growth: 7.00% (2007)

Labour force: 10.01 million (2004)

Inflation: 7.90% (2007)

Balance of trade: -US$487.10 million (2006)

construction sector as a result of donor-financed infrastructure projects. Overall, economic expansion is expected to be robust in the short term, with GDP growth expected to be 7 per cent in 2008 and 6.8 per cent in 2009.

After the shortages caused by lack of rain in the 2005/06 and 2006/07 agricultural seasons, the government forecasts growth of 7.5 per cent for the 2007/08 season. This growth will be partly because of increases in the area under cultivation and gains in productivity. Under the government's Green Revolution, output of grains is expected to increase by 9 per cent and beans and groundnuts by 12 per cent.

Mauritian and South African investments of about US$300 million in the rehabilitation and partial privatisation of four sugar-processing plants has made the country a net exporter of sugar. The industry employs some 26,000 and has promoted the development of the surrounding rural areas. The government is also considering a series of projects to produce bio-ethanol from the discarded sugar canes.

Reforms needed

After Mozambique's impressive performance over the past decade, the country needs a second wave of reforms to deepen and accelerate structural changes to sustain high and broadbased growth. Increased tax revenues, stronger public sector operations, reducing the costs of doing business, promotion of labour-intensive sectors, and the implementation of a rural development strategy are the key areas. The government is working with its Plano de Acção para Redução da Pobreza Absoluta (PARPA) for 2006–10, which was finalised in 2006.

The predominant role of the government in the economy has been diminished through an important privatisation programme, a sharp reduction in subsidies and military spending, and the elimination of the central bank financing of the government deficit. The main economic distortions were removed through the liberalisation of most administrative prices, the trade and exchange systems, and interest rate regime.

Private sector development, especially in the agriculture sector, is, however, still constrained by a lack of infrastructure, access to credit due to wide interest rate spreads, high and volatile lending rates and a poor lending environment that partly reflects inefficient judicial procedures for loan recovery and difficulties in obtaining land titles to serve as collateral. The financial system remains small, bank-based, concentrated in urban areas and highly dollarised. The central bank's capacity to supervise the banking system is being strengthened. The cumbersome administrative procedures and rigid labour regulations impose heavy costs on business. The relatively small and undiversified traditional export sector still cannot fully exploit market access opportunities in developed countries despite preferential agreements. This is due mainly to weak transportation infrastructure and inability to meet quality standards required by developed countries.

Mozambique has 2.5 Tcf of proven natural gas reserves located offshore in the Temane, Pande and Buzi-Divinhe fields. Sasol (of South Africa) has begun piping natural gas from the Temane and Pande fields through a 537 mile, US$1.2 million pipeline. To date this is Mozambique's only source of hydrocarbon production; however, exploration for additional natural gas reserves in the country continues. In June 2005, Sasol signed an exploration and production contract for Blocks 16 and 19 offshore Mozambique. According to an estimate by the ministry of planning and development, even small reserves of oil would increase total annual exports from US£6.5 billion to more than US$10 billion by 2010. However, the prospects of becoming an oil exporting country is being met more with consternation than euphoria. Although Australia, Canada, Norway and Botswana are examples of countries which have managed to use their mineral wealth for the good of their economies and populations, this has not necessarily been the case elsewhere in Africa. Nigeria, Angola, Guinea-Bissau and Sudan are countries where vast oil reserves have failed to improve the livelihoods of the majority of their peoples.

Prospects

Mozambique's medium-term prospects depend critically on its pursuit of prudent macroeconomic policies and an accelerated pace of structural reforms. The main macroeconomic objectives over the medium term are to maintain a rate of real annual growth between six and eight per cent and to gradually reduce annual inflation to six per cent.

External and public debt appears sustainable, with the external debt-to-GDP ratio projected at 20 per cent in the next 10 years before declining gradually to 15 per cent in 2025, and the public debt-to-GDP ratio to decline to 37 per cent by 2020.

Politics

President Armando Guebuza, from the ruling Frelimo party, succeeded Mozambique's long-time leader Joaquim Chissano, who stepped down after 18 years in power, in February 2005. The main opposition party, Resistencia Nacional de Moçambique (Renamo) (Mozambique National Resistance), disputed the outcome of the presidential poll and alleged that the election had been rigged. Monitors said irregularities were probably not sufficient to have changed the outcome.

Chissano had become president in 1986 after the death of founding president, Samora Machel, and oversaw a move

KEY INDICATORS — Mozambique

	Unit	2003	2004	2005	2006	2007
Population	m	18.44	18.58	19.59	20.04	20.50
Gross domestic product (GDP)	US$bn	4.30	5.90	6.64	6.78	7.56
GDP per capita	US$	239	292	339	338	369
GDP real growth	%	7.0	7.8	7.8	7.9	7.0
Inflation	%	10.8	12.6	6.4	13.2	7.9
Industrial output	% change	–	5.1	9.9	9.7	–
Agricultural output	% change	–	8.3	1.8	9.0	–
Exports (fob) (goods)	US$m	880.0	689.4	1,745.3	2,391.0	2,412.1
Imports (cif) (goods)	US$m	1,445.0	972.9	2,242.3	2,878.0	2,811.1
Balance of trade	US$m	-565.0	-283.5	-497.1	-487.0	-399.0
Current account	US$m	-730.0	-690.0	-730.0	1,335.0	-713.0
Total reserves minus gold	US$m	998.5	1,130.3	1,053.8	1,155.7	1,444.7
Foreign exchange	US$m	998.4	1,130.3	1,053.6	1,155.5	1,444.5
Exchange rate	per US$	23,347.75	22,581.00	25.83	25.83	24.19

away from Marxism and the introduction of a multi-party constitution.

Reducing corruption has become a centre-piece of President Guebuza's political programme. He appointed Augusto Paulino as attorney general in 2007, sending a strong signal to international donors about his intentions. Paulino had been the judge presiding at the Maputo city court that sentenced to long terms in prison the six men convicted of murdering investigative journalist, Carlos Cardoso.

Outlook

Mozambique is rich in resources and in labour. Although the macroeconomic picture looks passably rosy, the government will have to move to address the obstacles to economic and social reform if it is not to face a social backlash before long.

Mozambique's socio-economic progress since independence has been patchy. A variety of natural calamities have combined to leave thousands homeless and there has over the years been a steady exodus of skilled personnel. None the less, the Mozambique economy has continued to perform well despite the rises in petroleum prices, and a severe drought that left about 800,000 people in need of food aid in late 2005/early 2006. Looking ahead, the main challenge will be to maintain high and broad-based economic growth and make further progress in alleviating poverty.

Risk assessment

Politics	Fair
Economy	Fair
Regional stability	Fair

COUNTRY PROFILE

Historical profile

1498 Portuguese explorer Vasco da Gama landed on the shores of what is now Mozambique.

Portuguese settlements were quickly established, but full-scale colonisation did not begin until the seventeenth century. In the eighteenth and nineteenth centuries, Mozambique served as a major slave-trading centre.

1842 Portugal abolished the slave trade, although the practice continued.

1891 Mozambique's southern and western borders were defined by the British and Portuguese.

1932 Portugal broke up the companies which owned the land and controlled trade and imposed direct rule over Mozambique.

1962 The Frente de Libertação de Moçambique (Frelimo) (Front for the Liberation of Mozambique) was established and launched a military campaign for independence.

1975 Mozambique gained independence. A one-party system was implemented with Frelimo as the sole legal party. Mozambican support for the independence war in Rhodesia (Zimbabwe) and the African National Congress (ANC) in South Africa led to frequent reprisals from the governments of those countries. Independence was followed by 16 years of civil war against the rebels of the Resistencia Nacional de Moçambique (Renamo) (Mozambique National Resistance), a guerrilla army supported first by Rhodesia and later by South Africa and the US.

1977 Frelimo adopted Marxism-Leninism as its official doctrine.

1984 Frelimo reached a deal with South Africa in which it would halt its support for the ANC in return for an end to South Africa's aid to Renamo.

1986 President Machel was killed in an airplane crash; Joaquim Chissano became president.

1989 Frelimo formally abandoned Marxism-Leninism in favour of democratic socialism and a market economy. Renamo's support faltered as the civil war was already turning in the government's favour.

1990 A new consititution was promulgated to allow for a multi-party electoral system.

1992 A cease-fire was agreed, followed by a full peace agreement.

1994 In the first multi-party elections, Frelimo won an absolute parliamentary majority. Joaquim Chissano was re-elected president.

1995 Mozambique joined the Commonwealth, the only member not to have been a British colony.

1998 Low turnout for local elections, which were boycotted by the opposition, Renamo, due to flaws in voter registration prompted the government to overhaul the voting procedures for the national elections.

1999 Joaquim Chissano was re-elected president and Frelimo increased its parliamentary majority.

2000/01 Mozambique was devastated by a tropical cyclone and severe flooding. There was rioting over Renamo allegations that the 1999 elections were rigged; international observers claimed the elections were free and fair.

2003 Cyclones Delfina and Japhet caused extensive damage.

2004 Armando Guebuza (Frelimo) won the presidential elections and Frelimo was re-elected in parliamentary elections.

2005 Guebuza (Frelimo) became president. A new bridge spanning the Zambezi between Sofala and Zambezia provinces began construction.

2006 New bank notes were issued as part of a reform of the currency, which dropped three zeros. The range of notes bear the face of Samora Machel, independence leader and first president. The government announced a 13 per cent increase in the minimum wage for industry and services; the rate is now Mt1,443,170 (US$58) per month. The UK pledged £150 million (US$282 million) in aid (2006–16) to be spent on children's education.

2007 In January, severe flooding in the Zambezi valley, caused by 340mm of rain falling within 24 hours, displaced over 50,000 people and more than 3,500 people had to seek shelter in government accommodation centres in the provincial city of Quelimane, as parts of the city were submerged.

2008 Violence in South Africa towards foreign workers forced thousands of Mozambican workers to return home.2005 Armando Guebuza (Frelimo) was sworn in as president. A new bridge spanning the Zambezi between Sofala and Zambezia provinces began construction.

Political structure

Constitution

The 1975 independence constitution was replaced by the 1990 constitution, which provides for a multi-party system, direct elections and a free market economy.

Form of state

Unitary republic

The executive

The head of state is the president, directly elected for a five-year term, who can be re-elected on only two consecutive occasions, and who governs with his appointed prime minister and Council of Ministers.

National legislature

Legislative power is vested in the 250-seat unicameral Assembleia de la República (Assembly of the Republic), elected by direct universal adult suffrage every five years.

Legal system

Based on Portuguese/Roman law and the 1990 constitution. Since 1996, there has been a Law Reform Commission which has the responsibility for revising legislation.

Last elections

1–2 December 2004 (presidential and parliamentary)

Results: Presidential: Armando Guebuza of the ruling Frelimo won 63.7 per cent of the vote and Afonso Dhlakama of Renamo 31.7 per cent.

Parliamentary: Frelimo won 62 per cent of the vote (160 seats out of 250) and Renamo 29.7 per cent (90). Turnout was 36.3 per cent.

Next elections
2009 (presidential and parliamentary)

Political parties
Ruling party
Frente de Libertação de Moçambique (Frelimo) (Front for the Liberation of Mozambique) (re-elected Dec 2004)
Main opposition party
Resistencia Nacional de Moçambique (Renamo) (Mozambique National Resistance)

Population
20.50 million (2007)
Last census: August 1997: 16,099,246
Population density: 22 inhabitants per square km. Urban population: 38 per cent (1994–2000).
Annual growth rate: 2.4 per cent 1994–2004 (WHO 2006)
Ethnic make-up
Indigenous tribal groups, including Ronga, Shangaan, Chokwe, Manyika, Sena and Makua (99 per cent); European (1 per cent).
Religions
Some 300 registered religions, including traditional beliefs (50 per cent), Christianity (majority Roman Catholic) (30 per cent), Muslim (20 per cent).

Education
Primary education lasts until the aged 13. At this point students attend either a general or technical secondary school. The general school lasts for five years when students graduate for progression into higher education. Technical secondary school lasts for three years with a further two years for advanced courses.
The war devastated the education sector. However, by the end of the 1990s, the primary school network had recovered to levels seen in 1983. In 1999, there were 6,600 first-level primary schools (first to fifth years) attended by 2.1 million children. A third of primary school children attend schools that are so crowded that classes are oversubscribed by over 300 per cent. Educational provision is far worse in the second-level primary schools (sixth and seventh years), with only 440 operating in the entire country. The secondary school sector consists of 81 schools, with fewer than 64,000 students receiving basic secondary education.
There are around 7,000 students enrolled in Mozambique's six university-level institutions and 15,000 in vocational colleges.
Literacy rate: 47 per cent adult rate; 63 per cent youth rate (15–24) (Unesco 2005).
Compulsory years: 6 to 13
Enrolment rate: 60 per cent gross primary enrolment, 7 per cent gross secondary enrolment; of relevant age group (including repeaters) (World Bank).
Pupils per teacher: 58 in primary schools

Health
Per capita total expenditure on health (2003) was US$45; of which per capita government spending was US$28, at the international dollar rate, (WHO 2006).
With resources targetted at the growing problem of HIV/Aids, other healthcare needs are increasingly neglected. Moreover, the IMF forced the government to abandon its commitment to free healthcare provision and it is estimated that rural Mozambicans must walk an average of 46km to reach the nearest doctor. While modern health services reach around 40 per cent of the population the maternal mortality rate is high, and cholera has been rampant due to poor sanitation. However, mobile medical brigades have formed the backbone of the government's inoculation campaign, with polio virtually eradicated.
HIV/Aids
Mozambique has been one of the countries worst affected by the Aids pandemic which is sweeping Africa. Central provinces are more affected than southern and northern provinces with infection trends following the major transport routes and areas bordering Zimbabwe, Malawi and Zambia. In the cities of Chimoio and Tete, HIV seroprevalence in pregnant women is over 20 per cent.
HIV prevalence: 12.2 per cent aged 15–49 in 2003 (World Bank)
Life expectancy: 45 years, 2004 (WHO 2006)
Fertility rate/Maternal mortality rate: 5.4 births per woman, 2004 (WHO 2006); maternal mortality 1,100 per 100,000 live births (World Bank).
Birth rate/Death rate: 20 deaths and 40 births per 1,000 head of population (World Bank 2002).
Child (under 5 years) mortality rate (per 1,000): 101 per 1,000 live births (World Bank)
Head of population per physician: 0.03 physicians per 1,000 people, 2004 (WHO 2006)

Welfare
World Bank figures show 69 per cent of the population live in poverty.
Economic liberalisation, hailed as the driving force behind Mozambique's high growth levels, has also removed the safety nets that existed under the command economy. The minimum wage of US$30 per month is paltry and in many companies even the minimum is not paid and workers often receive their wages weeks or months late. There is no longer a basic ration of subsidised food, leaving many in the growing informal economy with little to eat.

Main cities
Maputo (capital, estimated population 1.1 million in 2004), Matola (464,669), Beira (503,874), Nampula (405,308), Chimoio (246,080), Nacala (212,650), Quelimane (173,100).

Languages spoken
Portuguese is spoken by less than 30 per cent of the population. English is widely spoken in business circles.
There are three main African language groups: Tsonga, Sena-Nyanja, Makua-Lomwe.
Official language/s
Portuguese

Media
Press
The 1990 constitution provides for press freedom. With the opening up of independent newspapers, the share of the civil war-era government newspapers has fallen. The most important media company to arise is the co-operative Mediacoop, which owns the successful Media Fax, faxed to hundreds of direct subscribers but read very widely, the periodical Mozambique Inview and the weekly Savana. Agencia de Informação de Moçambique (AIM) provides a daily bulletin in Portuguese and English and a monthly bulletin in French and English.
Dailies: The main privately owned publications are Media Fax, Imparcial and Demos. The government publishes Noticias de Moçambique.
Weeklies: Tempo (government), Savana (independent) and Domingo (government) are the main weeklies in circulation.
Business: Other fax newsletters targetted at businesses include Metical and Correio de Manha.
Periodicals: Mozambique Inview is an independent bi-monthly publication.
Broadcasting
Radio: Each province has its own broadcasting station which transmits programmes in Portuguese and local languages.
Radio Moçambique provides programmes in Portuguese, English and local languages. The programmes consist mainly of light entertainment, interspersed with news and political broadcasts. The only radio broadcaster with national coverage, it is owned by the government but operates independently of the information ministry.
Television: Maputo enjoys several local television stations. These are Radiotelevisão Klint, Radio Televisão de Portugal and the São Paulo, Brazil-based Miramar. Transmission coverage outside the region surrounding Maputo is poor,

but there are moves to improve the situation. The national television broadcaster is Televisão de Moçambique (TVM).

Economy

Mozambique has adhered to many of the macroeconomic recommendations for growth offered by international monetary agencies since the end of the civil war in 1992. From a low base, where it was one of the poorest countries in the world, Mozambique has recorded a remarkable growth that has resulted in sustained foreign aid, foreign direct investment (FDI) and significant poverty reduction.

After several years of economic reform when GDP growth was an average 8 per cent per annum and fiscal prudence kept deficits to a minimum, Mozambique's debts were either rescheduled or forgiven under the IMF Heavily Indebted Poor Countries (HIPC) and Paris Club of international creditors' initiatives. In December 2005, Mozambique's complete debt to the IMF, worth US$153 million, was cancelled.

Aqccording to the Bank of Mozambique the economy grew by 7 per cent in 2007, but growth in the first quarter of 2008, compared with the first quarter of 2007, was only 3.5 per cent

The service sector employs around 10 per cent of the population and consists mainly of the tourist industry, transport, communications and clerical work.

The main agricultural cash crops include sugar and cotton, although these products face problems competing on the international market. Cashew nut production has been hard hit by the closure of the country's only cashew nut processing plant, due to trade liberalisation.

The manufacturing sector employs up to 10 per cent of the population, mainly in food processing (maize and wheat flour, sugar and salt) and beverages. Light industry includes textiles, soap, batteries, radios and bicycles. Heavy industrial production includes megaprojects – those that attract large investment – such as the Mozal aluminium smelter, the 900km Sasol pipeline from Beira, the Maputo Corridor project (to develop infrastructure between southern Mozambique and South Africa) and the Chibuto heavy sand project, which attracted an estimated US$435 million in FDI in 2005 and prompted the government to introduce new fiscal and governance laws.

The currency was revised on 6 July 2006, so that the old metical bank notes lost three zeros and 1,000 old meticais became l metical.

The economy is diversifying rapidly and transport, metallurgy, manufacturing, energy, tourism, timber and fishing are all growth areas. Mozambique is being held up as a success story for sub-Saharan Africa and as per capita income slowly rises it has steadily achieved its Millennium Development Goals and provided an encouraging aspect for all.

External trade

Mozambique is also a member of the Southern African Development Community (SADC), the objectives of which include reducing trade barriers, achieving regional development and economic growth and evolving common systems and institutions.

Mozambique provides a major transit route for landlocked areas and countries in southern Africa transporting goods to ports and transfer services provide a significant amount of foreign earnings. A new aluminium smelter process local bauxite using domestically produced electricity.

Imports

Principal imports are capital machinery and equipment, vehicles, fuel, chemicals, metal products, foodstuffs and textiles.

Main sources: South Africa (37.4 per cent total, 2006), The Netherlands (15.8 per cent), India (4.6 per cent).

Exports

Principal exports are aluminium, minerals, fish and shellfish, cashews, sugar, citrus, cotton, timber and electricity.

Main destinations: The Netherlands (59.7 per cent total, 2006), South Africa (14.1 per cent), Zimbabwe (3.2 per cent).

Agriculture

Farming

The agricultural sector is the mainstay of the economy, employing 80 per cent of the workforce, mainly engaged in subsistence farming, and accounting for around a quarter of GDP. The main cash crops are cashew nuts, tea, sugar, sisal, cotton, copra, tobacco, oil seeds and some citrus fruits. Maize is the main subsistence crop, but cassava, millet, sorghum, groundnuts, beans and rice are also grown.

Some 45 per cent of the land area is considered suitable for agriculture, but only 4 per cent of that is under cultivation. Most production is carried out through rain-fed farming in the north, and much continues to be done by hand, with only 7 per cent of farmers using traction (animal or mechanical) and only 2 per cent using fertilisers and pesticides. The agricultural sector is dominated by peasant family smallholdings, which occupy 90 per cent of the total cultivated area. Only 5 per cent of cultivated land is used by commercial operations, which grow cash or export crops. There is significantly large potential for foreign investment in the agriculture sector due to the fertility and availability of unused cultivatable land.

Peace, good rains and an increase in the area under cultivation have resolved the chronic food deficit seen in the 1980s. However, food stocks are low and most families do not produce enough to build up a reserve of food and money that would see them through a bad harvest. Drought in 2003 and reduced rain in 2004 affected the grain harvest in central and southern Mozambique, but good rains in the 2005–06 growing season resulted in a bumper crop with the maize harvest up by 11 per cent and providing self-sufficiences for the country. Other crops and livestock production also rose. Nevertheless, the sector is in need of ongoing structural improvement particularly in the fragile marketing systems and poor infrastructure. The state marketing body intervenes in the market in order to pay farmers for crops they have been unable to sell, either due to low prices on the open market or because the transport infrastructure is too poor. However, with bank credit scarce and with a reluctance of international financial institutions to support marketing boards, the state has been unable to fulfil its role completely. This has encouraged the growth of unscrupulous middlemen who demand lower farm gate prices.

Estimated crop production for 2005 included: 2,015,100 tonnes (t) cereals in total, 1,450,000t maize, 6,150,000t cassava, 80,000t potatoes, 66,000t sweet potatoes, 314,000t sorghum, 201,000t rice, 205,000t pulses, 265,000t coconuts, 30,500t citrus fruit, 28,900t fibre crops, 58,000t treenuts, 87,500t oilcrops, 12,000t tobacco, 600t green coffee, 24,000t mangoes, 400,000t sugar cane, 10,500t tea, 43,000t papayas, 334,500t fruit in total, 116,700t vegetables in total.

Estimated livestock production included: meat in total, 90,000t meat in total, 38,100t beef, 12,840t pig meat, 2,712t lamb and goat meat, 36,348t poultry, 14,000t eggs, 68,765t milk, 390t honey, 5,080t cattle hides.

Fishing

Fishing is of increasing importance. Prawns have become one of the sector's main exports. Mozambique's sustainable fish catch is estimated at 500,000 tonnes, including 300,000 tonnes of anchovy. The sustainable catch of prawns is estimated at 14,000 tonnes. Inland fish farming, especially of prawns, expanded. Over-fishing, particularly in the shallow coastal waters, has left the majority small-scale fishermen, who do not have the boats or engines for deep-water fishing, without an income. The over-fishing is mostly caused by large international fishing boats.

In a meeting of African ministers in Namibia, held on 2 July, members discussed illegal and unregulated fishing, which is estimated to cost Africa US$1 billion per annum in lost revenue and the threat to stocks and local artisan fishing. In 2004, the total marine fish catch was 12,000 tonnes and the total crustacean catch was 13,731 tonnes.

Forestry

There is an important forestry sector, based on the exploitation of hardwoods from Zambezia, Sofala, Nampula, Manica and Niassa provinces. Almost 50 per cent of land is categorised as other wooded land. Wood fuel comprises almost 80 per cent of the country's energy needs. A wide variety of non-wood forest products includes grass, bamboo, medicinal plants and other wild edible plants.
Forestry resources are exploited on a more systematic basis than previously and the government compels timber concerns to initiate reforestation programmes.
Overall, Mozambique has an estimated one million hectares (ha) of productive woodland. The government-owned Industrias Florestais de Manica (Ifloma), which manages 20,000ha of forest, has established a sawmill and particle-board factory with Swedish government and Arab fund assistance.
Timber imports in 2004 were US$17.3 million, while exports amounted to US$38.1 million.
Timber production in 2004 included 18,043,000 cubic metre (cum) roundwood, 1,319,000cum industrial roundwood, 28,000cum sawnwood, 128,000cum sawlogs and veneer logs, 954,000t pulpwood, 3,400cum wood-based panels, 16,724,000cum woodfuel.

Industry and manufacturing

During the 1980s and 1990s, government policy emphasised the production of consumer goods, especially food, beverages and textiles, where supplies can be locally sourced, in an attempt to reduce import dependency and strengthen the market for peasant farmers producing cash crops. However, industry suffered from capital shortages, poor infrastructure and the high cost of credit. Manufacturers rely largely on internal funding from operating profits or owner savings. Recent metallurgical investments promise a dramatic departure from Mozambique's import substituting industrialisation strategy.
The greatest problems have occurred in the food processing industry, with cashew nut and sugar production particularly hit. Cashew nut prices have plummeted due to increased output in India, where production is more cost-effective and tree-planting has increased. India intends to become self-sufficient in cashew nuts, dealing a big blow to this important sector in Mozambique. The situation has been exacerbated by the damaging policy of trade liberalisation demanded by the World Bank, which had originally advised Mozambique to stop processing cashew nuts domestically, close down the processing factories and export unshelled nuts to India.
Sugar refining is another industry which was in the doldrums. Mozambican sugar mills were severely affected by the civil war, which virtually wiped out the industry. Foreign investment, mostly from South African companies such as Illovo, has been the driving force behind the rehabilitation of the sector.
By far the most important industrial project in Mozambique is the Mozal aluminium smelter. The plant is owned by BHP-Billiton (the leading shareholder), Mitsubishi, South Africa's Industrial Development Corporation (IDC) and the Mozambican government. The US$1.2 billion smelter is one of the largest industrial projects in sub-Saharan Africa and began production in June 2000, six months ahead of schedule. Mozal is already the world's cheapest producer of aluminium, and costs will fall as capacity is increased. The completion of the project will lead to around US$800 million in aluminium exports per year, increasing total exports by over 300 per cent of 2000 levels and adding up to 20 per cent to GDP. However, most of the profits from the smelter will be repatriated by its foreign investors and since it is highly capital intensive, it will not have a significant impact on employment. Although Mozal appears as a success story for Mozambique's development, it will have a limited long-term role in alleviating poverty and generating growth in other sectors.

Tourism

The sector has not played a significant role in the economy, due to the impact of the war. There is potential for the development of tourism in the south-eastern coastal region, where the beaches are attracting visitors as well as investment, especially from South Africa. The government is interested in developing high-value, low volume tourism and is rehabilitating the national parks. The first to reopen, the Maputo Elephant Park, is intended to with nature reserves and parks in neighbouring countries to form a trans-frontier conservation and tourism zone.

Environment

Unexpectedly high rainfall caused severe flooding in January 2008, forcing around 100,000 people living along the Zambezi River to be displaced. By February when waters had begun to receed the authorities for the Kariba Dam in Zambia announced that for safety reasons they had to release more water. The overflow was estimated to have displaced another 40,000 people as the water from the upper reaches of the river arrived downstream.

Mining

Mining is limited to gold in Manica province, pegmatites, ilmenite, zircon, rutile, monazite, tantalum, copper, marble and semi-precious stones. The sector is small and typically contributes to 1.4 per cent of exports and less than 0.25 per cent of GDP.
There are around 50,000 artisan miners who concentrate their operations on gold and gemstone extraction. Kenmare Resources has two gold licences in Niassa, with reserves of 200,000 ounces. Kenmare also has a licence for the titanium reserves at Congolone, which is considered one of the most valuable undeveloped titanium mines in the world. In mid-2003, the company announced it was investing US$200 million in developing the reserves to produce ilmenite, rutile and zircon by 2005. The titanium reserves near Xai-Xai, about 250km north of Maputo, have the potential to develop a second large mineral smelter project in the region. There are considerable secondary mineral resources, including iron, graphite, fluorites, mica, lime clays, tin, nickel and bauxite. There has been little foreign interest in developing these resources.

Hydrocarbons

There are no known reserves of oil in Mozambique. The government believes that there is oil in the Rovuma basin and elsewhere and in 2005 appealed to major petroleum companies to engage in exploration. Mozambique relies entirely on refined oil imports, mainly from South Africa, and consumes 8,200 barrels of oil per day.
There are substantial reserves of gas. There are three onshore gas fields: Pande, Temane and Buzi-Divinhe. Pande has reserves of 59 billion cubic metres (CUM); Temane has 28 billion cum; and Buzi-Divinhe has 281 million cum. Mozambique is likely to become a major gas producer in the region. An 865km pipeline to export gas to South Africa was opened in 2004.
Coal is mined at Moatize in Tete province. Proven coal reserves are approximately six billion tonnes.

Energy

Mozambique is one of the largest energy producers in the Southern African Development Community (SADC). A large proportion of the country's electricity supply is produced by one coal-fired power station. The Cahora Bassa dam produces electricity for export to South Africa. With considerable potential in hydroelectric power and gas-fired power stations, there is a distinct possibility that Mozambique will become an electricity exporter in years to come. However, with only 5 per cent of households connected to the electricity supply, there is room for improving domestic supply.

New generating plants are scheduled to begin operations by 2006. These include the Moatize thermal power station (1,000MW), the expansion of the Cahora Bassa hydroelectric plant (550MW) and the Mepanda Uncuna hydroelectric station (2,500MW). The construction of new dams is facing mounting domestic and international opposition. With flooding becoming a regular occurrence, many ecologists believe dams pose a significant threat to farming communities, particularly when dams release flood waters.

Financial markets

The listing of enterprises has seen slow and modest growth, although the privatisation programme will provide potential for growth.

Stock exchange

The Bolsa de Valores de Moçambique (BVM) (Mozambique Stock Exchange) opened in October 1999.

Banking and insurance

All banks in Mozambique are privately owned, with more foreign competition entering the sector with the completion of the bank privatisation process in January 2002 when Banco Austral was sold to Absa.

Central bank

Banco de Moçambique, with branches throughout the country.

Main financial centre

Maputo

Time

GMT plus two hours

Geography

Mozambique lies on the east coast of Africa, south of the equator. It is bordered by Tanzania to the north; Malawi, Zambia and Zimbabwe to the west; South Africa and Swaziland to the south and south-west; and by the Indian Ocean to the east (2,470km of coastline).

The country is divided into the coastal lowlands and plateaux (200–600 metres over most of the central region and north, reaching 1,000 metres in the north-west). The country is crossed by a large number of rivers, including the Zambezi (navigable for 460km), the Limpopo and the Save.

Hemisphere

Southern

Climate

Mozambique has two main seasons: a hot, normally wet season from October to March and a cooler, mostly dry season from April to September.

In the extreme south the mean annual temperature is around 23 degrees Celsius (C), with a difference of about 8 degrees C between the hottest and coldest months. In the north the mean annual temperature is about 25 degrees C. The temperature in Maputo is influenced by the direction of the wind and wide variations are experienced, especially during the cool season. Temperatures in Maputo can reach as high as 45 degrees C.

Most rain falls in the second half of the hot season. Northern regions receive 640–1,280mm and southern regions may receive 260–1,540mm. The average is 770mm.

Dress codes

During the hot wet season (October–March) light cotton clothes are advisable. During the temperate dry season (April–September) light or medium weight clothing should suffice. Warmer clothing is required for frequent cold spells.

Entry requirements

Passports

Required by all, valid for a minimum of six months beyond the intended date of departure.

Visa

Required by all. Business visas require a letter from the visitor's company and should include an itinerary.

Prohibited entry

Currency advice/regulations

The import and export of local currency is prohibited. Unlimited import of foreign currency is allowed, subject to declaration on arrival; export of foreign currency is limited to the amount declared on arrival.

It is advisable to take travellers cheques or currency in sterling, US dollars or South African rands. Travellers entering Mozambique have to fill out a statement detailing the amount of currency in bank notes, cheques and travellers cheques being brought into the country. The declaration is passed over to the Exchange Control Office at the point of entry.

A new 'family' of bank notes came into circulation on 1 July 2006. This was part of wider currency reforms which also dropped three zeros, making 50,000 old meticais 50 meticais. The new notes (1,000, 500, 200, 100, 50 and 20 meticais) all bear the face of Samora Machel, who was Mozambique's first president after independence.

Prohibited imports

Illegal drugs and pornography. A permit is required for firearms.

Health (for visitors)

Mandatory precautions

Yellow fever certificate if arriving from an infected area.

Advisable precautions

Typhoid, polio, tetanus and hepatitis A and B vaccinations are recommended. Malaria prophylaxis is essential as risk exists throughout the country, and cerebral malaria occurs in some places. There is a risk of rabies.

Water precautions are advisable, especially in the rural areas where bilharzia is present. Some milk is unpasteurised and should be boiled. Avoid dairy products and only eat well-cooked hot meat and fish. Vegetables must be cooked and fruit peeled.

Medical facilities are minimal and many medicines are not available. Basic medical supplies, medicines and sterile syringes should be carried. Full medical insurance is essential. Insurance cover which provides for medical evacuation by air to South Africa is advisable.

Hotels

Good accommodation is available in Maputo and Beira, but of lower quality elsewhere. Bills must be paid in hard currency, travellers cheques or credit cards.

Public holidays (national)

Fixed dates

1 Jan (New Year's Day), 3 Feb (Heroes' Day), 7 Apr (Women's Day), 1 May (Workers' Day), 25 Jun (Independence Day), 7 Sep (Victory Day), 25 Sep (Armed Forces' Day), 25 Dec (National Family/Christmas Day).

Working hours

Banking

Mon–Fri: 0745–1130.

Business

Mon–Thu: 0730–1230, 1400–1730; Fri: 0730–1230, 1400–1700.

Government

Mon–Thu: 0730–1230, 1400–1730; Fri: 0730–1230, 1400–1700.

Shops

Mon–Fri: 0800–1230; 1400–1800; Sat: 0800–1330.

Electricity supply

220 V AC, 50 cycles.

Social customs/useful tips

The courtesies and modes of address customary in Portugal and other Latin countries are still observed. Visitors are normally addressed as O Senhor. Occasionally camarada (comrade) is used, but this is not correct outside the circles of the ruling party, Frente de Libertaçao de Moçambique (Frelimo), and is discouraged.

Security

Street crime is an increasingly serious problem, with armed robbery prevalent in Maputo. Visitors should not carry or display cash or jewellery, and are advised not to venture outside well-lit, busy streets. Female visitors should not walk unaccompanied along any beaches in Mozambique.

Visitors should check conditions with the local authorities before travelling outside major urban areas and should be aware that Mozambique has a severe problem with landmines left over from the conflict between Frelimo and Renamo.

Identity documents should be carried at all times.

Getting there

Air

National airline: Linhas Aéreas de Moçambique (LAM) (Mozambique Airlines)

International airport/s: Mavalane International (MPM), 3km north of Maputo; bank, restaurant, bar, car hire and post office. Beira (BEW), 13km from the city; restaurant, shops, car hire and post office.

Airport tax: US$20 destinations outside Africa; US$10 destinations within Africa.

Surface

Road: Road access is possible from all neighbouring countries except Tanzania; there are good paved roads from South Africa and Zimbabwe. The condition of roads in Mozambique is poor and banditry along major highways threatens the safety of road travellers. Travel outside Maputo often requires four-wheel drive vehicles.

Rail: Rail services can be unreliable. A daily service runs from Johannesburg to the border at Komatipoort where there is a connection to Maputo. There is also an overnight train from Durban to Maputo. A service runs from Harare to Beira. There are connections from Malawi to Beira but the border has to be crossed on foot.

Water: There are no regular passenger services.

Main port/s: Beira, Maputo, Nacala and Quelimane.

Getting about

National transport

Air: Travel between cities within Mozambique is best by air. LAM and Air Corridor operate domestic service to main towns. Local and charter flights can also be arranged with companies with offices at Maputo Airport.

Road: There are around 30,000km of roads in Mozambique. Good roads connect Maputo to main centres. The majority of roads is unpaved and many are impassable in the rainy season (November–April).

Buses: There are services covering most parts of the country but are restricted by the state of the roads.

Rail: There are three separate networks: in the south (Maputo to Swaziland, South Africa and Zimbabwe), in the centre (Beira to Zimbabwe and Malawi) and in the north (Nacala to Malawi and to Lichinga). These lines are not connected, because the Portuguese did not build any north-south trunk lines. There is no link between Maputo and Beira. There are some branch lines (Xai-Xai to Manjacase; Inhambane to Inharrime; and Quelimane to Mocuba). Services are unreliable.

City transport

Taxis: Available in cities, taxis are metered but for long journeys fares should be negotiated. A 10 per cent tip is usual.

Car hire

Car rental is available at airports and hotels. Only hard currency will be accepted. International licence required. Traffic drives on the left. Driving after dark can be hazardous due to other vehicles travelling without headlights.

BUSINESS DIRECTORY

The addresses listed below are a selection only. While World of Information makes every endeavour to check these addresses, we cannot guarantee that changes have not been made, especially to telephone numbers and area codes. We would welcome any corrections.

Telephone area codes

The international dialling code (IDD) for Mozambique is +258 followed by the area code and subscriber's number. New area codes came into operation 1 August 2005.

Beira	23	Maputo	21
Chokwe	221	Nampula	26

Chambers of Commerce

American-Mozambique Chamber of Commerce, Rua Mateus Sansão Muthemba 452, Maputo (tel: 492-904; fax: 492-779; e-mail: mail@mail.ccmusa.co.mz).

Mozambique Camara de Comercio, Rua Mateus Sansão Muthemba 452, Maputo (tel: 491-970; fax: 492-211).

Portugal-Mozambique Chamber of Commerce, Hotel Rovuma Centro de Escritórios, Rua da Sé 114, Maputo (tel: 300-229; fax: 300-232; e-mail: ccpmoc@teledata.mz).

South Africa-Mozambique Chamber of Commerce, FACIM, Avenida 10 de Novembro, Maputo (tel/fax: 431-621).

Banking

Banco Comercial do Moçambique, PO Box 865, Av 25 de Setembro 1800, Maputo (tel: 307-533, 307-471, 307-532; fax: 307-564/557/543).

Banco Internacional de Moçambique SARL, Av Zedequias Manganhela 478, Maputo (tel: 429-390/3; fax: 429-389).

Banco Standard Totta de Moçambique SARL, PO Box 2086, Praça 25 de Junho Nr 1, Maputo (tel: 423-041/5, 424-405, 301-616; fax: 426-967, 423-029).

Banco de Fomento SARL; Av. Julius Nyerere 1016, Maputo (tel. 494-010/1; fax: 494-401).

Banco de Moçambique, PO Box 423, Av 25 de Setembro 1679, Maputo (tel: 428-150/9; fax: 429-721).

BIM Investimento SARL, Av Kim Il Sung 961, Maputo (tel: 490-085/7; fax: 490-212; e-mail: bimi@vircom.com).

BNP Nedbank (Mocambique) SARL, PO Box 1445, Prédio 33 Andares; Av 25 de Setembro 1230, Maputo (tel: 306-700; fax: 306-305; e-mail: bnpnebank@bnpnedbank.co.mz).

Novo Banco SARL, Av.do Trabalho, 750-Sede, Maputo (tel: 407-755/6, 408-209; fax: 407-755/6, 408-210; e-mail: novobanco@teledata.mz).

Uniao Comercial de Bancos (Moçambique) SARL, Av. Fredrich Engels 400, Maputo (tel: 499-900, 495-221-5 fax: 498-675; e-mail: banque_fc@teledata.mz).

Central bank

Banco de Moçambique, Avenida 25 de Setembro 1695, PO Box 423, Maputo (tel: 318-001; fax: 323-712; e-mail: cdi@bancomoc.mz).

The listing of enterprises has seen slow and modest growth, although the privatisation programme will provide potential for growth.

Travel information

Empresa Nacional de Turismo (ENT) (Mozambique National Tourism Company), PO Box 2446, Avenida 25 de Setembro 1203, Maputo (tel: 420-324; fax: 421-795).

Linhas Aereas de Moçambique, Avenida Karl Marx 220, PO Box 2060, Maputo (tel: 326-001; fax: 496-105; e-mail: commercial@lam.co.mz).

Ministry of tourism

Ministry of Tourism, Avenida 25 de Setembro 1018, PO Box 4101, Maputo (tel: 313-755; fax: 306-212; e-mail: info@turismo.imoz.com).

National tourist organisation offices

Fundo Nacional do Turismo-FUTURA, Avenida de 25 Setembro 1203, PO Box 4758, Maputo (tel: 307-320; fax: 307-324; e-mail: info@futur.org.mz).

Ministries

Ministry of Commerce, Industry and Tourism, Praça do 25 Junho 37, Maputo (tel: 426-091/7).

Ministry of Finance and Planning, Praça da Marinha Popular, CP 272, Maputo (tel: 420-648; fax: 425-240).

Ministry of Industry and Energy, Avenida 25 de Setembro, PO Box 2904, 1502 Maputo (tel: 420-963, 492-011).

Ministry of Trade, PO Box 1831, Maputo (tel: 426-091/7; fax: 421-305).

Other useful addresses

Agência de Informação de Moçambique (AIM), CP 896, Maputo (tel: 430-795).

Agência Nacional de Frete e Navegação (ANFRENA) (main national shipping agency), Rua Consiglieri Pedroson 366, CP 1430, Maputo (tel: 427-064, 428-111).

BP Mozambique, PO Box 854, Maputo (tel: 425-021/5; fax: 426-042).

British Council, Travessa da Catembe 21 (corner of Av Martires de Inhaminga 1421), CP 4178, Maputo (tel: 421-571; fax: 421-577).

British Embassy, Av Vladimir I Lenine 310, CP 55, Maputo (tel: 420-111/2/5/6/7; fax: 421-666).

Commonwealth Development Corporation, Maputo (tel: 421-325; fax: 422-150).

Direcção Nacional Portos e Caminhos de Ferro (railways), PO Box 276, Maputo (tel: 420-748, 424-133, 430-151).

Empresa Nacional de Minas, PO Box 1152, Maputo (tel: 423-933).

Empresa Nacional de Portos e Caminhos de Ferro de Moçambique, Maputo (tel: 427-173).

Empresa Nacional Petroleos de Moçambique (Petromoc), PO Box 417, Maputo (tel: 427-191/7).

FACIM, PO Box 1761, Maputo (tel: 423-713, 427-151/2; fax: 427-129) (annual international trade fair).

Hidroelectrica de Cabora Bassa (HCB) (operators of Cabora Bassa power complex), Head Office, CP 263, Songo, Tete (tel: 82-221/4; fax: 82-364); PO Box 4120, Maputo (tel: 400-551, 400-647, 491-346, 492-976).

Imprensa Nacional de Moçambique (publishes statistical bulletins, census information etc), PO Box 275, Maputo.

Maputo Development Corridor, Maputo (tel: 426-359; fax: 430-159).

Mozambique Embassy (USA), Suite 570, 1990 M Street, NW, Washington DC 20036 (tel: (+1-202)-293-7146; fax: (+1-202)-835-0245; e-mail: embamoc@aol.com).

Mozambique Institute of Export Promotion (IPEX) (Government agency for export promotion), Av 25 de Setembro 1008, PO Box 4487, Maputo (tel: 423-343).

Office for Foreign Investment Promotion (GPIE), Av 25 de Setembro 2049, 2 andar, PO Box 2049, Maputo (tel: 422-456/7; fax: 422-459).

Radio Moçambique, PO Box 2000, Maputo (tel: 434-041/5, 432-591; fax: 421-816).

Technical Unit for Enterprise Restructuring (UTRE) (information on company tenders for privatisation and investment opportunities), Ministry of Planning and Finance, Rua da Imprensa No 256, 7th Floor, Suites 704-708, PO Box 4350, Maputo (tel: 426-514/6; fax: 421-541).

Televisão de Moçambique, Av Julius Nyerere 942, PO Box 2675, Maputo (tel: 491-198).

World Bank, Maputo (tel: 492-841; fax: 492-893).

Internet sites

Africa Business Network: http://www.ifc.org/abn

AllAfrica.com: http://allafrica.com

African Development Bank: http://www.afdb.org

Africa Online: http://www.africaonline.com

Mbendi AfroPaedia (information on companies, countries, industries and stock exchanges in Africa): http://mbendi.co.za

Myanmar

KEY FACTS

Official name: Myanmar Naingngandaw (The Union of Myanmar)

Head of State: Chairman of the SPDC Senior General Than Shwe

Head of government: Prime Minister (acting) Lt General Thein Sein (since May 2007)

Ruling party: State Peace and Development Council (SPDC) (19-member military junta since 1997)

Area: 676,552 square km

Population: 57.64 million (2007)

Capital: Naypyidaw (Abode of Kings) (from November 2005)

Official language: Myanmar

Currency: Kyat (Kt) = 100 pyas

Exchange rate: Kt6.44 per US$ (Jul 2008)

GDP per capita: US$235 (2007)

GDP real growth: 5.50% (2007)*

Labour force: 27.46 million (2004)

Unemployment: 5.00% (2005)

Inflation: 34.40% (2007)

Balance of trade: US$383.00 million (2004)

* estimated figure

In May 2008 Myanmar hit the world's headlines for all the wrong reasons. Cyclone Nargis, which hit the country in May, created more problems than a largely corrupt and severely inefficient military regime could ever hope to deal with. The few foreign aid workers that managed to gain entry to the cyclone hit areas found that they faced not only bureaucratic hurdles erected by a xenophobic military government, but also an economy warped by years of misrule.

Some of the obstacles that needed to be overcome were simply absurd. Myanmar's military government limits the sale of mobile phones, bans satellite phones, restricts car imports and rations gasoline to a few litres a day. The main beneficiaries of this corrupt system are government employees and military officers, who have long profited by selling permits, gasoline and other items on the black market.

Aid workers from the United Nations and private NGOs and other relief agencies were only able to travel into the Irrawaddy Delta, the area hardest hit by the 2 May cyclone, after an agreement reached with the government. Richard Horsey, the spokesman for the United Nations relief effort, said the military was requiring aid workers to give 48 hours' notice before travelling into the delta. Official estimates reported that the cyclone left 134,000 people dead or missing. The United Nations estimated that 2.4 million survivors faced hunger and homelessness. To the outside world, the government's torpor in reacting to the cyclone appeared as callous indifference. But dysfunction was also a factor. One government official in Yangon observed that Myanmar didn't have the infrastructure for the kind of rescue needed in times of crisis. China, Sri Lanka, Indonesia and other countries struck in recent years by natural disasters also had varying degrees of political restrictions. But they all allowed something Myanmar lacked after 46 years of military rule: the right to do business. Myanmar's government controls many of the country's largest industries – including timber, gems and petroleum – and requires permits for the importation of the most basic items, including rice. The World Food Programme, which feared rice shortages later in 2008, had been denied permits to bring in foreign rice. Even in most parts of Yangon electricity was available just five or six hours a day.

Myanmar's constitution rings with impressive phrases establishing the equality of men, and women, before the law. One whole chapter is devoted to fundamental rights and duties. It guarantees that 'all citizens are equal before the law irrespective of race, status, official position, wealth, culture, birth, religion or sex.' The Achilles Heel of this weighty document is the one clause that tilts the government of Myanmar away from any kind of Western democracy. It (Article 11) says that 'The state shall adopt a single-party system'. So, whatever its constitution may say, for forty years Myanmar has been a military dictatorship, guilty of some of the most prolific human rights abuses, and ostracised by most of the international community. The US, which still uses the country's former name of Burma, named it as an 'outpost of tyranny' in 2005.

Aung San Suu Kyi

Myanmar's list of human rights abuses is one of the longest in the world. Aung San Suu Kyi, winner of the 1991 Nobel Prize for Peace, is undergoing her third stint of house arrest. She has now been detained for well over 19 years. Theoretically, she leads the National League for Democracy (NLD), which won an overwhelming 80 per cent of the votes in the 1990 elections. However, Suu Kyi is incommunicada and her party was prevented from taking office after their victory in the polls. The ruling *junta* forcibly prevents democratic practices such as the right to assemble and freedom of expression, and seeks to destroy the NLD.

The July 2005 meeting of Association of Southeast Asian Nations (Asean) had been dominated by calls for Suu Kyi's release. In June 2005 neighbouring nations applied pressure on the Myanmar authorities to force them to renounce floating leadership of Asean in mid-2006 on the grounds of the *junta*'s human rights abuses – which would prevent EU leaders

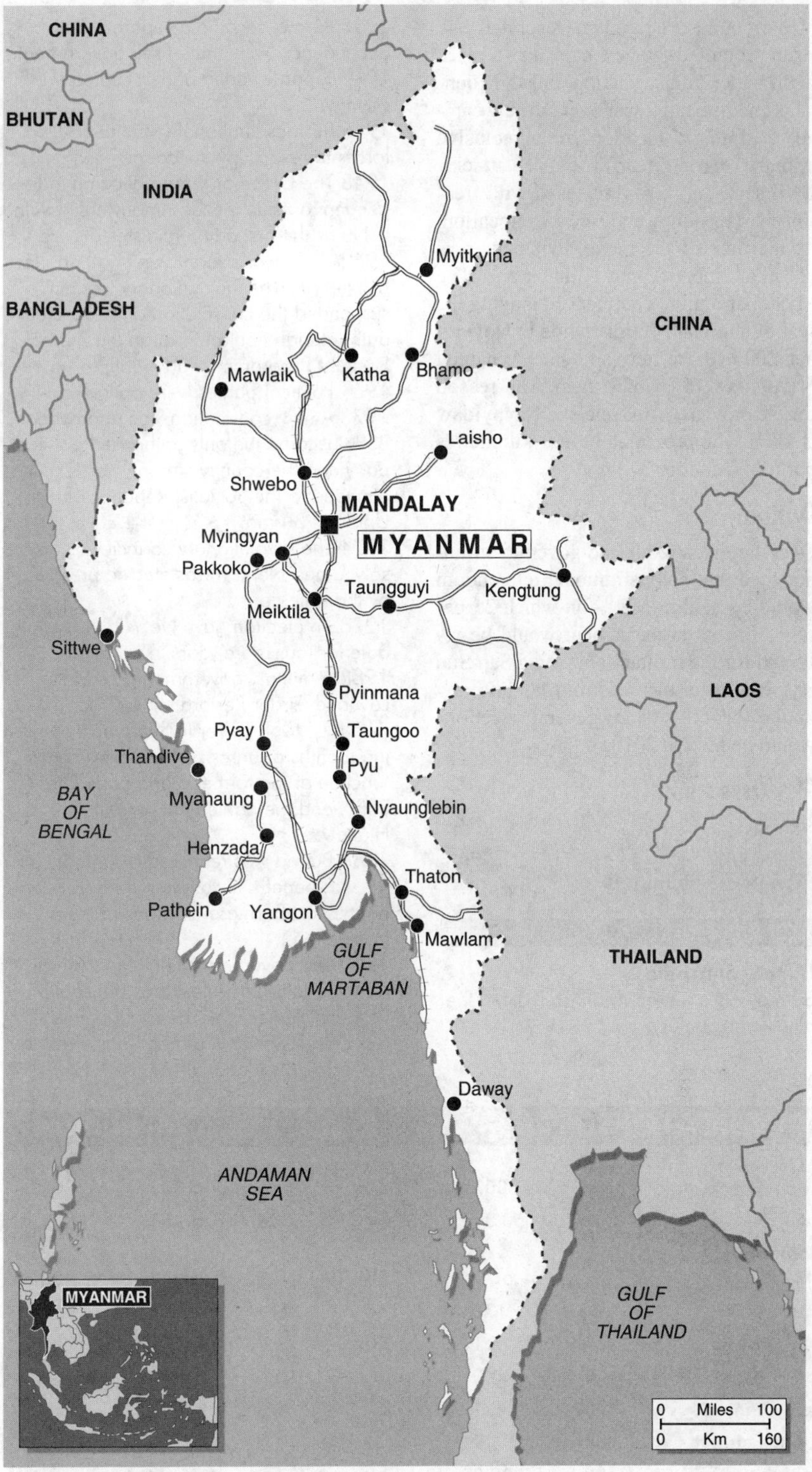

from participating in negotiations with Asean. The US and Japan declined to send their top-ranking representatives to the Asean security conference. Myanmar eventually conceded to pressure and ceded its proposed chairmanship, saying that the country needed to concentrate on internal law and order. By giving a platform to Myanmar the regional association would have risked its credibility. However the intervention does contradict the Asean agreement to not meddle in each other's domestic affairs.

America is one of the most vocal critics of the military regime. US secretary of state Condoleezza Rice lamented in July 2005 that 'there seems never to be progress' in the country's human rights arena and called on neighbouring south-east Asian countries to help press the need for peace and democracy. While America has tried to freeze Myanmar out of the international community and has imposed economic sanctions, Thailand has co-operated in the hope of facilitating an eventual adoption of democracy.

The EU has introduced some limits on investment in Myanmar but the NLD and other pro-democracy activists advocate the levying of more serious economic sanctions.

The *junta* has held the reins of power for over 40 years and is clinging to them tightly for fear of the imprisonment of its generals once it loosens its grip. The former prime minister of Malaysia has suggested that these commanders be granted judicial immunity to encourage them to allow the introduction of democracy.

Economy

GDP growth was 7.0 per cent in 2006 substantially up on the 5.0 per cent of 2005. While this is a respectable figure, future prospects are not good. Many countries are retreating from economic ties and investment with the country because of its poor human rights reputation. As a result many garment factories have closed.

China, however, has no such scruples and is likely to continue to be a large investor in coming years. Already 100 Chinese timber companies are involved in logging activities in Myanmar. There are estimates that 95 per cent of Myanmar timber shipments to China are illegal, meaning that the much-needed sum of US$250 million is sidelining the Myanmar fiscal system.

Half the budget is spent on the military, with very low rates of investment in social welfare. Inflation, which had dropped to 9.0 per cent in 2004 rose to an alarming 17.7, the highest rate since 2002 when it soared to 46.9 per cent. In June 2005 the ruling *junta* repossessed the commercial Myanmar Universal Bank and surrounded all branches with soldiers to prevent people withdrawing their savings. It was a sudden and unexplained takeover which seriously undermined the country's financial sector.

The new capital

In November 2005 the Myanmar military suddenly decided to relocate the national capital from Yangon to an isolated compound near Pyinmana, a town in the centre of the country. Brigadier General Kyaw Hsan promoted the new capital as a place with better transportation links. Mountains enclose and tower over the new capital, a strategic location for a reclusive military regime fearful of US attacks. Civil servants were threatened with treason charges if they opposed the relocation. At the time of the move, Pyinmana was not much more than a building site. The Myanmar regime commenced moving the seat of national administration in November 2005 to the new site since renamed Naypyidaw (Seat of Kings). The reason for the move remains unclear. Naypyidaw is located approximately 400 kilometres north of Yangon.

Outlook

On 9 February 2008 the government announced that a constitutional referendum would be held in May – in which 25 per cent of seats in parliament would be reserved for the military and Aung San Suu Kyi would be banned from holding any public office – and general elections would be held in 2010.

Risk assessment

Politics	Poor
Economy	Poor
Regional stability	Fair

COUNTRY PROFILE

Historical profile

Burma was annexed to British India in the nineteenth century.

1937 Burma became a separate British dependency, with limited self government.

1942 Japan invaded and occupied the country.

1945 Burmese nationalists helped Allied forces to re-occupy the country.

1948 The Union of Burma became independent outside the Commonwealth, with U Nu as the first prime minister.

1962 U Nu was overthrown in a coup led by Ne Win. The Revolutionary Council suspended the constitution and instituted authoritarian control through the Burma Socialist Programme Party (BSPP).

1964 Political parties were outlawed.

1973 A new constitution was approved. BSPP became the only authorised political party and the country's name was changed to the Socialist Republic of the Union of Burma.

1974 The revolutionary council was dissolved and Ne Win was elected president by the state council.

1978 An election gave Ne Win the mandate for four more years in power.

1988 A military government, the State Law and Order Restoration Council (SLORC), took power in September, ending months of unrest. It took over the function of the former ruling party, the BSPP, and the parliament, or Pyithu Hluttaw.

1989 Burma was renamed Myanmar, for the was benefit, it was claimed, for the minority, non-Burmese, sections of the population.

1990 The government fulfilled its promise to hold multi-party elections, but said a new constitution must be brought into effect before power could be transferred to the victorious National League for Democracy (NLD), led by Aung Sang Suu Kyi.

1996 The law and order situation deteriorated and open conflict erupted. SLORC closed the universities and detained protesters.

1997 Bomb attacks were aimed at leading SLORC figures. Several thousand Karen National Union (KNU) ethnic minority refugees were forced across the Thai border leading to international protests when refugees were killed by SLORC forces. The US imposed economic sanctions, banning investments by US companies. The Association of Southeast Asian Nations (Asean) admitted Myanmar as a full member of the Association. A governing military junta, formed by the top four SLORC leaders, was named the State Peace and Development Council (SPDC).

1998 The SPDC detained some 110 leading members of the NLD.

1999 Madame Aung Sang Suu Kyi was put under house arrest and isolated from the world. The authorities refused her dying husband a visa to come and visit her for the last time. The International Labour Organisation (ILO) banned Myanmar from its activities until it ceases using forced labour.

2001 The military junta approached Aung San Suu Kyi to arrange talks – the first contact in five years. President Jiang Zemin of China visited – the first Chinese head of state to visit since the military junta seized power in 1988.

2002 Aung San Suu Kyi (NLD) was released from house arrest.

2003 Aung San Suu Kyi, who was re-arrested and Japan suspended aid in protest. General Khin Nyunt was appointed prime minister.

2004 The government and the Karen National Union, the most significant ethnic insurgency group agreed to end hostilities. A constitutional convention began, despite a boycott by the NLD. General Khin Nyunt resigned and was replaced by Lt General Soe Win. An earthquake off the island of Sumatra caused a tsunami that damaged coastal areas, particularly in the Irrawaddy Delta. The final estimate for Myanmar was 61 dead or missing and 5,000 displaced.

2006 The military junta's renewed detention order of Aung San Suu Kyi. Her plight was the first case submitted to the newly established UN Human Rights Council. Thousands of ethnic Karens fled to Thailand in the face of construction of the new capital which had forced them from their homes. Pyinmana, the new capital, includes land clearance for new military facilities, luxury housing, industrial estates devoted to computer software and information technology, an upgraded airport

KEY INDICATORS — Myanmar

	Unit	2003	2004	2005	2006	2007
Population	m	50.89	52.81	55.39	56.51	*57.64
Gross domestic product (GDP)	US$bn	6.72	9.18	12.15	13.12	*13.53
GDP per capita	US$	132	167	219	232	*235
GDP real growth	%	5.1	5.0	13.2	12.8	*5.5
Inflation	%	40.0	9.0	10.1	25.7	34.4
Unemployment	%	5.1	5.2	5.0	–	–
Natural gas output	bn cum	6.9	7.4	13.0	13.4	14.7
Exports (fob) (goods)	US$m	2,600.0	2,137.0	3,787.8	4,554.7	–
Imports (cif) (goods)	US$m	1,900.0	1,754.0	1,759.4	2,343.4	–
Balance of trade	US$m	700.0	383.0	2,028.4	2,211.3	–
Current account	US$m	-11.9	111.5	587.7	802.0	541.0
Total reserves minus gold	US$m	550.2	672.1	770.7	1,235.6	–
Foreign exchange	US$m	550.1	672.1	770.5	1,235.4	–
Exchange rate	per US$	6.35	5.75	6.42	6.42	6.42

* estimated figure

and new infrastructure throughout the area.
2007 In May, Russia agreed to provide the technology and train technicians to build and operate a 10MW light-water nuclear reactor. In June, the International Committee of the Red Cross formally accused the government of abusing the rights of its citizens. In September, the government increased the price of domestic fuel by up to five times, sparking protests. Demonstrations against the ruling military Junta, led by Buddhist monks, called for a return to democratic rule. The government retaliated by arresting hundreds of monks and firing on protesters. Many monks were forced to flee from Yangoon during the bloody military crackdown. Government officials said 100 monks had been arrested; opposition said many more had been detained, as well as thousands of civilians including three prominent activists. Transparency International ranked Myanmar and Somalia as the two most corrupt countries in the world. A UN special envoy met the country's leader General Than Shwe in October, in an effort to stem the repression. An official announcement said 10 people had been killed (independent observers said the death toll was higher) since the civil disturbance began; internet and mobile telephone connections were cut by the authorities to prevent pictures and details of the demonstrations being sent to media outlets overseas. Following criticism from the UN the Junta agreed to appoint an official to liaise with Aung San Suu Kyi. In October Prime Minister Soe Win died. The government began to release detained protesters at the end of October, as monks again marched, although in fewer numbers.
2008 On 9 February the government announced that a constitutional referendum would be held in May – in which 25 per cent of seats in parliament would be reserved for the military and Aung San Suu Kyi would be banned from holding any public office – and general elections would be held in 2010. Cyclone Nargis struck the southern region of the Irriwaddy Delta on 2 May; relief efforts were hampered by the seeming indifference and obstruction of authorities to accept and distribute the huge international aid on offer to the country. Despite the disruption the constitutional referendum was held on 10 May and by 15 May the government claimed 92 per cent of voters had approved the constitutional changes. Aung San Suu Kyi's house arrest was extended for another year. Apart from the 24 June official estimate of 84,500 dead, hundreds of thousands of people more were at risk from disease, homelessness, lack of food and clean water following the disaster. UN President Ban Ki-moon criticised President General Than Shwe, who had refused to meet him to discuss the crisis. In July, it was estimated by the UN and Asean that relief and reconstruction work following Cyclone Nargis will cost over US$1 billion until 2011 for food, agricultural and housing needs. They also estimated was that as many as 134,000 had died during the cyclone.

Political structure

Constitution

From November 1997, the principal organs of power are the State Peace and Development Council (SPDC), headed by a chairman, and the 40-strong military-dominated cabinet.
Politically, Myanmar is spread over seven divisions where the ethnic Burmans are in the majority, and seven states where the non-Burmans, the ethnic minority groups, are in the majority.
On 17 May 2004, the government said it would reconvene the country's National Convention, in order to reopen negotiations on a constitution; this should result in a referendum on a new constitution and fresh elections. The National Convention was established in 1993, but it was adjourned in March 1996 following the withdrawal of the National League for Democracy (NLD), protesting against the undemocratic proceedings.

Last elections

27 May 1990 (parliamentary)
Results: Parliamentary: a Pyithu Hluttaw (People's Assembly) with 489 members elected on 27 May 1990 was not allowed to constitute itself.

Next elections

May 2008 (referendum on constitution); 2010 (general)

Political parties

Ruling party

State Peace and Development Council (SPDC) (19-member military junta since 1997)

Main opposition party

National League for Democracy (NLD)

Population

57.64 million (2007)
Last census: March 1983: 35,307,913
Population density: 73 inhabitants per square km. Urban population: 28 per cent (1995—2001). The urban population growth rate was estimated at 3.17 per cent in 2000.
Annual growth rate: 1.3 per cent 1994–2004 (WHO 2006)

Ethnic make-up

The indigenous population is Mongoloid. More than two-thirds are Burmans, racially akin to the Tibetans and the Chinese. There are also several indigenous minorities with their own language and culture – the Karen, Shan, Mon, Chin and Kachin; each group has its own state. The population includes immigrant minorities from India and China.

Religions

Theravada Buddhism (88 per cent), Christianity (7 per cent), Islam (3 per cent), Hinduism (0.5 per cent).

Education

Schooling begins in kindergarten for one year, then on to junior school for four years.
Secondary education is not compulsory and is divided into two phases: middle school, for four years, where all students undertake a general programme of learning; then upper secondary school where they elect to undertake either an academic course leading to higher education, or technical school, each lasting for two years. Technical education prepares students for admission to the government technical institutes or trade schools, or advancement on to university engineering courses.
All universities and colleges are financed by the state, although a nominal fee is charged for studies.
Literacy rate: 85 per cent adult rate; 91 per cent youth rate (15–24) (Unesco 2005).
Compulsory years: Five to 10.
Enrolment rate: 121 per cent gross primary enrolment of the relevant age group (including repetition rates); 30 per cent gross secondary enrolment (World Bank).
Pupils per teacher: 46 in primary schools.

Health

Per capita total expenditure on health (2003) was US$51; of which per capita government spending was US$10, at the international dollar rate, (WHO 2006).
Each year an estimated 150,000 children aged less than five die of malaria, acute respiratory infections and diarrhoea.
Access to clean drinking water is available to over 68 per cent of the population.
Malaria and Tuberculosis are widespread.

HIV/Aids

Stories of emigrant Burmese labour in Thailand uniformly infected with hepatitis and/or HIV/Aids are commonplace. Foreign estimates place some 2 per cent of the population as HIV positive. The proportion is many times higher in the army and areas crossed by the 'needle trail' of heroin exports into Manipur, India, and Yunnan, China, among others. This is a clear legacy of neglect of basic human development under the junta, in favour of internal and external security expenditures, and will be a dangerous and pressing cost to the Burmese economy over the long term, possibly on a sub-Saharan African level.

Without official statistics published, it can only be estimated by aid workers that there are over 660,000 people with HIV/Aids, making Myanmar the centre of one of south-east Asia's worst epidemics. In August 2005 the Global Fund to Fight Aids, Tuberculosis and Malaria announced that is was withdrawing from its US$98 million health programme due to government restrictions on health workers in the country. The HIV/Aids epidemic is one of the worst in Asia.

HIV prevalence: 1.2 per cent aged 15–49 in 2003 (World Bank)

Life expectancy: 59 years, 2004 (WHO 2006)

Fertility rate/Maternal mortality rate: 2.3 births per woman, 2004 (WHO 2006); maternal mortality 230 per 100,000 live births (World Bank).

Birth rate/Death rate: 10 deaths to 26 births per 1,000 people (World Bank).

Child (under 5 years) mortality rate (per 1,000): 76 per 1,000 live births (World Bank)

Head of population per physician: 0.36 physicians per 1,000 people, 2004 (WHO 2006)

Welfare

The department of social welfare (DSW) under the ministry of social welfare, relief and resettlement implements social welfare services in eight different areas of social needs by both direct and indirect means covering the aged, children, youths and women welfare services. There is provision for the rehabilitation of ex-drug addicts and the disabled. It provides grants-in-aids to voluntary organisations.

In Myanmar, all government servants retire at the age of 60, and are entitled to gratuity and pension.

There are approximately 45 homes for the aged throughout the country, which provide food, clothing, shelter and healthcare services to the aged. The traditional family structures also provide ample care for the aged. Several religious organisations donate large sums of money towards social welfare.

Main cities

Yangon (formerly Rangoon) (capital, estimated population 4.5 million in 2004), Mandalay (1.2 million), Mawla Myaing (formerly Moulmein, 395,900), Pathein (formerly Bassein, 212,600), Bago (198,000), Monywa (161,000), Sittwe (formerly Akyab, 159,200), Meiktila (157,900), Taung-gyi (149,600).

Languages spoken

English is used in business circles.

Official language/s

Myanmar

Media

Press

Dailies: In Yangon, The New Light of Myanmar, the multi-language official daily newspaper of the military junta was previously called The Working People's Daily. Other newspapers in Myanmar include Burma Daily, Loktha Pyithu Nesin, Kyemon (The Mirror), Myotaw (evening tabloid) and Yadanabon (Mandalay).

Periodicals: Burma Focus is a bi-monthly newsletter.

Broadcasting

Radio: Radio Myanmar broadcasts in English. Myanmar Broadcasting Service also broadcasts in Myanmar and other local languages. The Democratic Voice of Burma radio station (http://www.communique.no/dvb/) based in Oslo promotes free speech, democracy and human rights in Burma by non-violent means. Radio Free Burma is a weekly Burmese-Language radio programme from 2NBC Sydney, Australia.

Television: The first station opened in 1980.

Advertising

Advertising is available in the press, in cinemas and on poster sites, which are subject to government control. Direct mail advertising is available.

Economy

Myanmar is a secretive society that does not publish extensive details of its economy.

The economy is centralised with agriculture providing around 60 per cent of GDP, which grew by 13.6 per cent in 2004/05, through improved output in fisheries, manufacturing and forestry. There is a significant black market sector. The government is planning on food self-sufficiency by increasing production of rice as well as expanding output of pulses, cotton, sugar cane and oil seed. The industrial sector has been hampered by international trade and investment sanctions.

As the global price of oil rose in 2005 subsidies to state enterprises fell and the price of basic commodities grew. There is a thriving co-operative sector and private sector, which includes traders, farmers, small-scale industries and transport enterprises.

There are severe structural constraints, including shortages of power and foreign exchange and a widening budget deficit. Tourism has slumped due to international sanctions and boycotts called by Myanmar's opposition.

Foreign debt is equal to around three-quarters of GDP. Tax evasion is widespread and the government is limited in raising tax revenue by the size of the grey economy. Defence expenditure is high, while education and health expenditures have been cut to curb public sector deficits.

Although the long-term prospects for sustained growth may be good, the banking system needs to be strengthened and more investment applied to basic infrastructure, education, health and the reduction of poverty.

No multilateral or bilateral aid agency will openly help to ease Myanmar's financial problems until there is some evidence of progress on democracy, human rights and narcotic eradication. Myanmar is still a large producer of the opium poppy, and will therefore continue to face US sanctions. Myanmar has vowed to eradicate opium production by 2014, a date regarded as too distant by many in the international community.

External trade

Myanmar belongs to the Association of South East Asian (Asean) Free Trade Area (Afta) and maintains a list of goods that have preferential import duties between members and a programme of tariff reductions due to be introduced in the next few years.

There are a number of trade bans on Myanmar, led by the United Nations arms embargo (1990), however trade continues sub rosa.

Most import demands and exports originate with trade corporations and state boards. Trade is handled by the Myanmar Export Import Services using the Myanmar Five Star Line for shipping. The picture of external trade presented by official statistics does not reflect the considerable amount of smuggling and black market trading. Myanmar is a major centre for the production of illegal heroin, estimated at around 2,000 tonnes annually, and amphetamines. Heroin is by far the largest export commodity.

Imports

Principal imports textiles, crude oil and petroleum products, plastics, machinery, transport equipment, construction materials and foodstuffs.

Main sources: China (34.6 per cent total, 2006), Thailand (21.8 per cent), Singapore (16.2 per cent).

Exports

Principal exports are natural gas, timber, jade and precious stones, garments and agricultural produce including pulses, beans, fish and rice.

Main destinations: Thailand (49.0 per cent total, 2006), India (12.8 per cent), China (5.3 per cent).

Agriculture

Farming

Agriculture accounts for around 60 per cent of GDP and provides around 56 per

cent of employment. About 15 per cent of the total land area is cultivated.
Myanmar is usually self-sufficient in rice, although adverse weather conditions and an uninvested farming sector can cause shortages. Other main crops are sugar cane, wheat, maize, jute, cotton, beans, wheat and vegetables. Cattle, pigs, buffaloes, sheep, goats and poultry are raised for domestic consumption. Oil palm and rubber plantations are replacing forest in some areas.
Crop production in 2005 included: 25,637,000 tonnes (t) cereals in total, 24,500,000t rice, 6,370,000t sugar cane, 820,000t maize, 140,000t cassava, *400,000t potatoes, 602,000t plantains, 2,447,158t pulses, 100,000t garlic, *350,000t coconuts, 86,359t fibre crops, 700,600t oilcrops, 33,000t tobacco, 3,010t green coffee, 70,000t pimento, 40,000t natural rubber, 715,000t groundnuts in shells, 25,000t tea, 1,752,000t fruit in total, 3,841,000t vegetables in total. Livestock production included: 631,834t meat in total, 114,000t beef, 22,950t buffalo meat, 143,000t pig meat, 2,490t lamb, 9,080t goat meat, 340,314t poultry, 145,200t eggs, 667,200t milk, 300t honey, 23,997t cattle hides, 1,210t goatskins, 415t sheepskins, 450t greasy wool.
* estimate

Fishing

In 2004, the total marine fish catch was 1,091,740 tonnes and the total crustacean catch was 39,600 tonnes.

Forestry

Around 50 per cent of the land area is forest, containing about 75 per cent of world teak resources. Heavy logging is carried out, mostly of export hardwoods, bamboo and fuel, leading to fears of rapid deforestation.
Timber imports in 2004 were US$26.1 million, while exports amounted to US$339.7 million.
Timber production in 2004 included 41,755,900 cubic metre (cum) roundwood, 4,195,900cum industrial roundwood, 1,055,800cum sawnwood, 2,815,900cum sawlogs and veneer logs, 954,000t pulpwood, 117,600cum wood-based panels, 37,560,000cum woodfuel; 28,200 tonnes (t) charcoal, 42,900t paper and paperboard, (including 5,200t newsprint), 13,000t printing and writing paper, 15,200t paper pulp, 45,200t recovered paper.

Industry and manufacturing

The industrial sector accounts for around 7 per cent of GDP and employs around 9 per cent of the workforce.
Small enterprises predominate.
Manufacturing industries include food processing (sugar, tobacco, palm oil, rice), cement, textiles, beverages, cigarettes, aluminium products, paper and nails, steel, cotton yarn, soap, pharmaceuticals and fertilisers. Textile and jute production is being expanded.
There are 20 industrial zones. Foreign direct investment (FDI) is weak.

Tourism

Some liberalisation of the tourist industry has occurred. Tourists may now stay in licensed private hotels and travel on specially licensed buses from which they were previously prohibited. Tourism revenue is the second largest legal source of foreign exchange.

Mining

Mining accounts for around 4 per cent of GDP and employs around 3 per cent of the workforce.
Minerals mined include ores of zinc, lead, tin and copper, silver, gypsum, limestone and gems such as rubies, sapphires and jade.
In 2006 international sales of precious gems earned around US$300 million in foreign exchange. However the military crackdown of democracy demonstrations of 2007 prompted not only the French firm Cartier, US's Tiffany and Italy's Bulgari jewellers, but other Western jewellers as well, to halt purchases of rubies (prized for their rich red), jade and other gemstones. Myanmar supplies around 90 per cent of the world's rubies and 98 per cent of jade.

Hydrocarbons

Myanmar has proven oil reserves of around 50 million barrels and produces four million barrels of oil a year. Oil production does not meet demand and Myanmar relies on oil imports.
Myanmar has proven gas reserves of 353 billion cubic metres and produces eight billion cubic metres of gas a year. Around five billion cubic metres of gas is exported annually.
Myanmar produces a small quantity of coal for domestic consumption.

Energy

Myanmar is seeking to develop its considerable hydroelectric generating potential, but is constrained by the cost factor.
In many parts of the country severe shortages are the norm.

Financial markets

Stock exchange

The Myanmar Securities Exchange Centre opened in 1996.

Banking and insurance

Since 1995, the government has allowed foreign banks to operate in Myanmar which have opened representative offices, to set up joint ventures with private local banks.
Myanmar is on the Organisation for Economic Co-operation and Development (OECD) Financial Action Task Force (FATF) list of non-co-operative countries on money laundering.
In early 2003, there was trouble in the financial sector with the collapse of some private finance companies, which had taken deposits from the public. The problem spread to some private banks and large amounts of cash were withdrawn by depositors. A stronger regulatory framework for the banking system and a strategy to identify and resolve the problem banks are necessary to restore confidence in the sector.

Central bank

Central Bank of Myanmar

Offshore facilities

Time

GMT plus 6.5 hours

Geography

Myanmar lies in the north-west region of south-east Asia between the Tibetan plateau and the Malay peninsula. It is bordered by Bangladesh and India to the north-west, the People's Republic of China and Laos to the north-east and by Thailand to the south-east.
Myanmar covers an area of 676,552 square km. It is dominated by mountains, rivers and forests. The Irrawaddy river, which rises in Tibet, flows southwards through the country, dividing it in two, and opening out into a vast delta region. The system is extremely fertile. Other important rivers are the Chindwin and Sittaung. There are several high mountain ranges ringing the country and providing almost impassable barriers against neighbouring countries. These and other interior mountains make land travel difficult within Myanmar. The highest point in the country and in south-east Asia is Mount Hkakabo Razi, which reaches 5,881m. Much of the country is covered in thick, tropical forests.

Hemisphere

Northern

Climate

There are three seasons: the rainy season May/June–October with high humidity and monsoon rains; the hot season February/March–May with likely temperatures of 37 degrees Celsius (C) (coastal and delta areas) to 40 degrees C (central region); and the cool, dry season November–February with temperatures of 16 degrees C (central region) to 21 degrees C (coastal and delta areas). Average rainfall varies from 5,000mm (northern hills and coastal areas) to 2,500mm (delta areas) to 750mm (central region).

Dress codes
Revealing or sloppy clothing is not advisable on any occasion. There are no strict rules regarding business attire.

Entry requirements
Passports
Required by all, valid for six months beyond date of departure.
Visa
Required by all. Tourist and business visas, applied for well in advance of arrival, are valid for 28 days; they may be extended. For a business visa a letter of introduction and an invitation are required, with a full itinerary.
Currency advice/regulations
The import and export of local currency is not allowed. There are no restrictions on the import of foreign currency, subject to declaration; export is restricted to the amount declared on arrival. Exchange controls are strictly enforced and all foreign exchange receipts should be safeguarded.
Customs
Personal effects are allowed duty-free, but customs regulations are restrictive and it is best to travel light. Jewellery, cameras and electric goods must be declared on entry. Video cameras are not allowed into the country.

Health (for visitors)
Mandatory precautions
Yellow fever certificate if arriving from infected area.
Advisable precautions
It is advisable to be in date for polio (within 10 years), tetanus (within 10 years), hepatitis A and B, rabies (within one to three years, depending on exposure to risk), Japanese B encephalitis (within three years if travelling June to September), tuberculosis (children should be immunised at any age, although it is less important for adults), diphtheria (within 10 years). Dengue fever occurs intermittently, especially in the northern Mandalay division.
If travelling through the country it is advisable to be vaccinated against cholera.
Only Yangon (Rangoon) city and areas above 1,000m are malaria free; if in doubt, take malaria prophylaxis.
It is advisable to carry a pack of sterilised needles, and to take any medicines required – they can be in short supply.
Water should be boiled and filtered before drinking. It is advisable to drink bottled water.
There is a rabies risk.

Hotels
Accommodation has been described as 'decrepit almost to the extent of charm'. There is no official rating system. Main Yangon (Rangoon) hotels can arrange an interpreter or translation services if necessary. Some Yangon hotels require payment in foreign currency. A 10 per cent service charge and a 10 per cent government tax are included in the bill.

Credit cards
American Express, Diners Club, Master, Visa, JCB are accepted at airlines, major hotels and supermarkets.

Public holidays (national)
Fixed dates
4 Jan (Independence Day), 12 Feb (Union Day), 2 Mar (Peasants' Day), 27 Mar (Armed Forces Day), 13–16 Apr (Maha Thingyan/Water Festival), 17 Apr (Myanmar New Year), 1 May (May Day), 19 Jul (Martyrs' Day), 25 Dec (Christmas Day).
Variable dates
Eid al Adha, Full Moon of Tabaung (Feb/Mar), Full Moon of Kasone (Apr/May), Full Moon of Waso/Beginning of Buddhist Lent (Jul/Aug), Full Moon of Thadingyut/End of Buddhist Lent (Oct), Diwali/Deepavali (Oct/Nov), Tazaungdaing Full Moon Day (Nov), National Day (Dec), Kayin New Year (Dec).
In general, Hindu and Buddhist festivals are declared according to local astronomical observations.

Working hours
Banking
Mon–Fri: 1000–1400.
Business
Mon–Fri: 0930–1630.
Government
Mon–Fri: 0930–1630.
Shops
Mon–Sun: 0600–2200.

Electricity supply
230V AC, 50 cycles single-phase; five or 15 amp plugs with three round pins for power.

Weights and measures
Imperial system (the metric system and local units are also in use).

Social customs/useful tips
Shoes and socks must be removed before entering any religious building, and visitors should not wear shorts.
The title 'U' (pronounced 'oo') is the equivalent of 'Mr' in English. When addressing people always use the appropriate prefix and family name. Many people do not have a first name.
The head is considered the temple of the body and should not be touched by other people. It is also considered the ultimate in bad manners to put one's feet on the table or cross one's legs so that the sole of the shoe points at someone. This is because the feet are considered to be the least clean part of the body.
The code of standard behaviour is referred to as bamahsan chin. According to this mode of conduct, people are expected to respect elders, exhibit discretion in dealing with the opposite sex, be aware of Buddhist sayings and have an ability to recite some Buddhist verses. Additionally, one should maintain a reserved and indirect approach to another person and not be direct at all. This can lead to misunderstandings, especially in business dealings.

Getting there
Air
National airline: Myanmar Airways International .
International airport/s: Yangon International (RGN), 19km from city centre; duty-free shop, bar, restaurant, buffet, bank, post office and hotel reservations.
Mandalay International (MDL), 25km from city; post office, bank, duty-free shop, car rental.
Airport tax: US$10, payable in Foreign Exchange Certificates (FEC).
Surface
Road: There are overland entry points on the borders with China and Thailand. A border pass is required for entry.
Water: Cruise vessels stop at Yangon.
Main port/s: Yangon.

Getting about
Not all parts of the country are open to visitors, and some are subject to guerrilla or bandit activity.
National transport
Tourists are required to keep to officially designated tourist areas and all arrangements for internal travel must be made well in advance via Myanmar Travel and Tours. Travel outside Yangon (Rangoon) is difficult to arrange. No attempt should be made to travel to restricted areas.
Air: Flying is the best and generally only permitted method of traversing the country and visiting tourist destinations. Flight schedules are restricted and subject to change without warning.
Road: There is a large network of roads all over the country, which are being upgraded, and new roads are being built.
Buses: There are a number of privately-owned bus companies which operate air-conditioned coaches between main centres. The main routes are from Yangon to Meiktila, Pyay, Mandalay and Taunggyi.
Rail: There is an extensive rail network. Myanmar Railways operates services to main centres. The Yangon-Mandalay express service runs four trains daily, with a branch line to Shwenyaung and Taunggyi. A service from Yangon to Bagan runs every other day.There are services from Mandalay to Lashio, Monywa and Bagan. Standards of equipment, service and safety are not high.

Water: There is extensive river and coastal traffic. Trips can only be made as part of an organised tour.

City transport

Taxis: In Yangon the government operates blue taxis with standard fares; otherwise, fares are by negotiation. Taxis can be shared or hired on a time basis.

Buses, trams & metro: There are antiquated and overcrowded bus services in all cities; they are not recommended for visitors. Yangon has a circular rail system.

Car hire

Tourists are not permitted to drive. Cars are hired with driver.

BUSINESS DIRECTORY

The addresses listed below are a selection only. While World of Information makes every endeavour to check these addresses, we cannot guarantee that changes have not been made, especially to telephone numbers and area codes. We would welcome any corrections.

Telephone area codes

The international direct dialling (IDD) code for Myanmar is +95 followed by area code:

Bassein	42	Moulmein	32
Mandalay	2	Prome	53
Monywa	71	Yangon (Rangoon)	1

Useful telephone numbers

Ambulance: 192, 71-111
Red Cross: 295-133
Police (emergency): 199
(headquarters): 282-541, 284-764
Telephone enquiries: 100
Booking (inland): 101
Booking (overseas): 130, 131, 667-444, 667-555, 667-601/2
Airport Security: 662-677
Customs: 284-533
Immigration: 286-434

Chambers of Commerce

Myanmar Federation of Chambers of Commerce & Industry, 504 Merchant Street, Kyauktada Township, Yangon (tel: 243-150; fax: 248-177; e-mail: ird@umfcci.com.mm).

Banking

Asia Wealth Bank, Ahlone, River View Housing Project, Olympic Tower II, Yangon (tel: 212-701; fax: 212-704).

First Private Bank Ltd, 619-621 Merchant Street, Pabedan T/S, Yangon (tel: 251-748; fax: 242-320).

Innwa Bank Ltd; 554-556 Corner of Merchant Street & 35th Street, Yangon (tel: 254-641, 254-647; fax: 254-431).

Kanbawza Bank Ltd; 1st Floor, Lanmadaw Condo Centre, No. 02/06, 02/07 Lanmadaw Street, Latha T/S, Yangon (tel: 212-780; fax: 212-778).

Myanmar Agricultural Development Bank, No. 1/7 Corner of Latha St & Kanna Rd, Latha T/S, Yangon (tel: 253-180, 250-569; fax: 245-119).

Myanmar Economic Bank, 1-19 Sule Pagoda Rd, Pabedan T/S, Yangon (tel: 289-329; fax: 283-679).

Myanmar Foreign Trade Bank, PO Box 203, 80-86 Maha Bandoola Garden Street, Kyauktada T/S, Yangon (tel: 284-911; fax: 289-585, 254-585).

Myanmar Industrial Development Bank Ltd, 26/42 Pansodan Street, Kyauktada T/S, Yangon (tel: 249-536; fax: 249-529).

Myanmar Investment and Commercial Bank, 170/176 Bo Aung Kyaw Street, Botataung Township, Yangon (tel: 250-509; fax: 281-775).

Myanmar Livestock & Fisheries Development Bank Ltd, 654-666 Corner of Merchant Street & Shwe Bon Tha Street, Pabedan T/S, Yangon (tel: 249-620; fax: 243-240).

Myanmar Citizens Bank Ltd, 383 Maha Bandoola St, Kyauktada T/S, Yangon (tel: 283-209, 283-719; fax: 245-932).

Myanmar May Flower Bank Ltd, Yadana Housing Project, 9 Mile, Pyay Rd, Mayangon T/S, Yangon (tel: 661-261; fax: 661-262).

Myanmar Oriental Bank Ltd, 166-168 Pansodan Street, Yangon (tel: 246-596; fax: 251-831).

Myanmar Universal Bank Ltd, 81 Theinbyu Rd, Botataung T/S, Yangon (tel: 297-337; fax: 245-449).

Yoma Bank Ltd, 1 Kun Gyan Road, Mingalar Taung Nyunt Township, Yangon (tel: 703-493; fax: 246-548).

Central bank

Central Bank of Myanmar, PO Box 184, 26(A) Sethmin Road, Yankin Tsp, Yangon (tel: 543-751; fax: 543-621; e-mail: cbm.ygn@mptmail.net.mm).

Travel information

Myanmar Airways International , Sakura Toer, 339 Bogyoke Aung San Road, Yangon (tel: 255-260; fax: 255-305; e-mail: management@maiair.com).

Myanmar Tourism Promotion Board, Traders Hotel, 223 Sule Pagoda Road, Yangon (tel: 242-828; fax: 242-800; e-mail: mtpb@mptmail.net.mm).

Ministry of tourism

Ministry of Hotels and Tourism, 77-91 Sule Pagoda Road, Kyauktada Tsp, Yangon (tel: 285-689; fax: 289-588; e-mail: mtt.mht@mptmail.net).

National tourist organisation offices

Myanmar Travels and Tours, 77-91 Sule Pagoda Road, PO Box 559, Yangon (tel: 382-243; fax: 254-417; e-mail: mtt.mht@mptmail.net.mm).

Ministries

Ministry of Agriculture and Irrigation, Thiri Mingala Lane, Kaba Aye Pagoda Road, Yankin Tsp, Yangon (tel: 665-587; fax: 664-493).

Ministry of Commerce, 228-240 Strand Road, Pabedan Tsp, Yangon (tel: 289-660; fax: 289-578).

Ministry of Communications, Post and Telecommunications, 80 Corner of Merchant St & Theinbyu Street, Botahtaung Tsp, Yangon (tel: 292-019).

Ministry of Construction, 39 Nawaday Street, Botahtaung Tsp, Yangon (tel: 283-938).

Ministry of Co-operatives, 259-263 Bogyoke Aung San Street, Kyauktada Tsp, Yangon (tel: 277-096, 280-280; fax: 287-919).

Ministry of Culture, 26-42 Pansodan Street, Kyauktada Tsp, Yangon (tel: 243-235).

Ministry of Defence, Ahlanpya Phaya Street, Yangon (tel: 281-611).

Ministry of Education, Theinbyu Street, Botahtaung Tsp, Yangon (tel: 285-588).

Ministry of Energy, 23 Pyay Road, Yangon (tel: 221-060; fax: 222-964).

Ministry of Finance and Revenue, 26 Setmu Road, Kyauktada Tsp, Yangon (tel: 284-763).

Ministry of Foreign Affairs, Pyay Road, Dagon Tsp, Yangon (tel: 222-844; fax: 222-950).

Ministry of Forestry, Thirimingala Lane, Kabe Aye Pagoda Road, Mayangon Tsp, Yangon (tel: 289-184; fax: 664-459).

Ministry of Health, Theinbyu Street, Botahtaung Tsp, Yangon (tel: 277-334; fax: 282-834).

Ministry of Home Affairs, Corner of Saya San Street & No 1 Industrial Street, Yankin Tsp, Yangon (tel: 549-208).

Ministry of Immigration & Population, Theinbyu Street, Botahtaung Tsp, Yangon (tel: 249-215).

Ministry of Industry (I), 192 Kaba Aye Pagoda Road Yangon (tel: 566-066).

Ministry of Industry (II), 56 Kaba Aye Pagoda Road, Yangon (tel: 661-140; fax: 667-156).

Ministry of Information, 365-367 Bo Aung Kyaw Street, Kyauktada Tsp, Yangon (tel: 245-631; fax: 289-274).

Ministry of Labour, Theinbyu Street, Botahtaung Tsp, Yangon (tel: 278-320; fax: 256-185).

Ministry of Livestock Breeding and Fisheries, Theinbyu Street, Botahtaung Tsp, Yangon (tel: 280-398; fax: 289-711).

Ministry of Mines, 90 Kanbe Road, Yankin Tsp, Yangon (tel: 577-316).

Ministry of National Planning and Economic Development, Theinbyu Street, Botahtaung Tsp, Yangon (tel: 280-816; fax: 282-101).

Ministry of Development of Border Areas and National Races and Development Affairs, Theinbyu Street, Botahtaung Tsp, Yangon (tel: 280-032; fax: 285-257).

Ministry of Rail Transport, 88 Theinbyu Street, Botahtaung Tsp, Yangon (tel: 292-769).

Ministry of Religious Affairs, Kaba Aye Pagoda Precinct, Mayangon Tsp, Yangon (tel: 665-620; fax: 665-728).

Ministry of Science and Technology, 6 Kaba Aye Pagoda Road, Yangon (tel: 665-686).

Ministry of Social Welfare, Relief & Resettlement, Theinbyu Street, Botahtaung Tsp, Yangon (tel: 282-610).

Ministry of Sports, Office of the Ministrers, Yangon (tel: 553-958).

Ministry of Transport, 363/421 Merchant Street, Yangon (tel: 296-815; fax: 296-824).

Office of the Prime Minister, Minister's Office, Yangon (tel: 283-742).

Other useful addresses

ASEAN Investment Promotion Agency, 653/691 Merchant Street, Pabedan, Yangon (tel: 372-855; fax: 254-660; e-mail: dica.nped@mptmail.net.mm).

British Embassy, Commercial Section, 80 Strand Road, Box No 638, Yangon (tel: 281-700; fax: 289-566).

Central Statistical Organisation, New Secretariat, Yangon (tel: 270-578; e-mail: cso.stat@mptmail.net.mm).

Livestock Foodstuff & Milk Products Enterprise, Pyay Road, 10th Mile, Mayangon Tsp, Yangon (tel: 664-244; fax: 240-109).

Myanmar Embassy (US), 2300 S Street, NW, Washington DC 20008 (tel: (+1-202)-332-9044; fax: (+1-202)-332-9046; e-mail: thuriya@aol.com).

Myanmar Export and Import Services, 622-624 Merchant Street, Yangon (tel: 280-260; fax: 289-587).

Myanmar Fisheries Enterprise, 654 Merchant Street, Latha Tsp, Yangon (tel: 20-710; fax: 222-951).

Myanmar General Industries, 192 Kaba Aye Pagoda Road, Yankin Tsp, Yangon (tel: 660-521; fax: 56-066).

Myanmar Investment Commisssion, 653/691 Merchant Road, Yangon (tel: 272-912; fax: 282-101).

Myanmar Oil and Gas Enterprise, 604 Merchant Street, Pabedan Tsp, Yangon (tel: 282-121; fax: 222-964).

Myanmar Petrochemical Enterprise, 23 Pyay Road, Lanmadaw Tsp, Yangon (tel: 222-816; fax: 222-960).

Myanmar Ports Authority, 10 Pansodan Street, Yangon (tel: 283-122).

Myanmar Post & Telecommunications, 43 Bo Aung Gyaw Street, Kyauktada Tsp, Yangon (tel: 285-840; fax: 290-429).

Myanmar Railways, Bogyoke Aung San Street, Pabedan Tsp, Yangon (tel: 274-027; fax: 282-267).

Myanmar Textile Industries, 192 Kaba Aye Pagoda Road, Yankin Tsp, Yangon (tel: 566-320; fax: 566-053).

Post & Telecommunications Department, 125 Pansodan Street, Kyauktada Tsp, Yangon (tel: 283-737; fax: 286-365).

US Embassy, 581 Merchant Street, Yangon (tel: 282-055; fax: 280-409).

Internet sites

Myanmar Resources: http://www.myanmars.net

Official Website of Myanmar: http://www.myanmar.com

Myanmar Business Information: http://www.myanmarpyi.com

Radio Free Myanmar: http://users.imagiware.com/wtongue/dvb2.html

Namibia

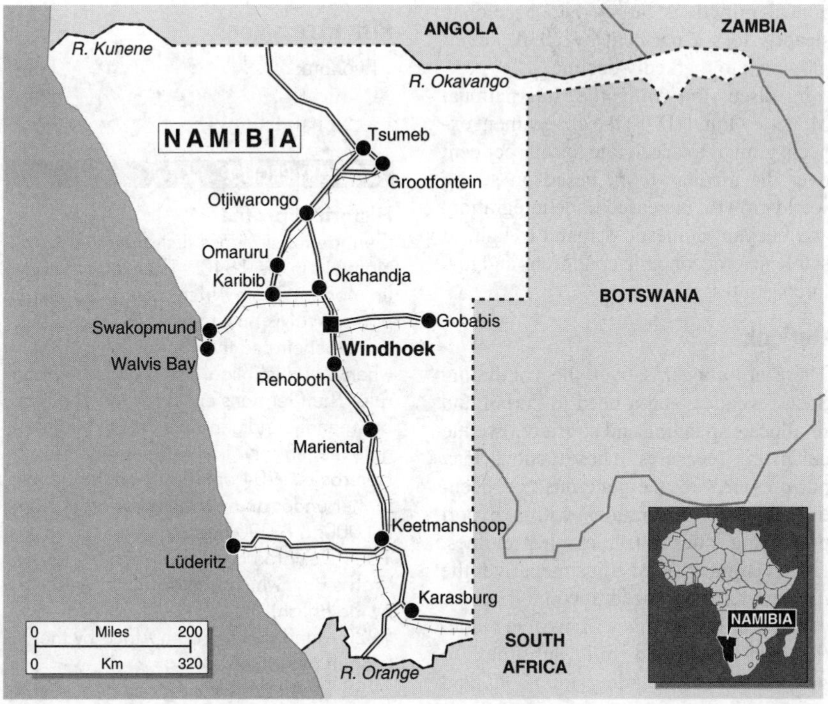

KEY FACTS

Official name: Republic of Namibia

Head of State: President Hifikepunye Pohamba (Swapo) (since 21 Mar 2005)

Head of government: Prime Minister Nahas Angula (appointed by the President 21 Mar 2005)

Ruling party: South West African People's Organisation (Swapo) (re-elected 16 Nov 2004)

Area: 824,269 square km

Population: 2.06 million (2007)*

Capital: Windhoek

Official language: English

Currency: Namibian dollar (N$) = 100 cents; at par with the South African commercial Rand

Exchange rate: N$7.55 per US$ (Jul 2008)

GDP per capita: US$3,584 (2007)*

GDP real growth: 4.40% (2007)*

Labour force: 820,000 (2005)*

Unemployment: 36.70% (2006)

Inflation: 6.70% (2007)

Balance of trade: US$984.00 million (2006)

Visitor numbers: 973,168 (2005)

* estimated figure

After 47 years as leader, Sam Nujoma stepped down from the presidency of the South West African People's Organisation (Swapo) in November 2007. He had been with the party since it was formed from the anti-contract labour movement in 1958.

During the forty years of German imperial conquest, the Namibian people were forcibly dispossessed of their land and cattle and 80,000 of them died as a result. South Africa then occupied the German colony of South-West Africa during the First World War and administered it as a mandate until after the Second World War, when it annexed the territory. In 1966 the Marxist South West Africa People's Organisation (Swapo) launched a war of independence for the area that was soon named Namibia, but it was not until 1988 that South Africa agreed to end its administration in accordance with a United Nations' peace plan for the entire region. Namibia won its independence in 1990 and has been governed by Swapo since.

Namibia is heavily dependent on the extraction and processing of minerals for export. Mining accounts for 20 per cent of GDP. It is a primary source for gem-quality diamonds, which are mined and marketed in partnership with De Beers. The capital intensive, highly mechanised mining sector employs only three per cent of the workforce. A high per capita GDP hides a great inequality of income distribution.

The government's single largest source of income is its receipts from the Southern African Customs Union (Sacu) which have contributed to significant external current account and fiscal surpluses. In 2007 official reserves had increased and it was expected that public debt would be reduced to less than 25 per cent of GDP by the end of the year.

In February 2008 the International Monetary Fund (IMF) reported that Namibia's real GDP was likely to remain robust for the immediate future. In 2007, it said, a modest strengthening of GDP had in part reflected buoyant diamond production. The external account surplus had risen to high levels in 2006 and 2007, reflecting strong diamond exports, high global prices of other mineral exports and large receipts from Sacu. Namibia's balance of payments position had accommodated a doubling of its international reserves since 2005.

Inflation pressures had intensified through the first half of 2007 as a result of increasing food prices. After rising 7.2 per cent in the year to July 2007, inflation declined to 6.6 per cent in the year through October. Consistent with Namibia's currency peg to the rand, the Bank of Namibia has, except for the rate increase in December 2007, matched interest rate increases by the South African Reserve Bank, with an increase of 350 basis points since early 2006.

Cattle and sheep breeding dominate agriculture, and Namibia has one of the richest potential fisheries in the world. Policies adopted since independence have aimed at sustaining economic growth, diversifying the country's productive base, and attracting foreign investors. Unemployment is estimated at over 30 per cent nationwide. This high rate is partly attributed to exports of unprocessed primary products and the low levels of education among the economically active population.

The country's long-term growth prospects are promising, provided that the government implements structural reforms. To strengthen private sector activity, these should include measures to privatise parastatals, raise labour skills, improve access to finance and capital, and strengthen the flexibility of the economy.

Namibia's *Vision 2030* is a long-term development planning framework to guide the policies and implementation strategies. It was developed through a participatory process, with technical advice by the United Nations' Development Programme. Its overarching economic objective is to transform Namibia into a diversified and industrialised country. Real annual growth is targeted to accelerate steadily to 9.5 per cent by 2030, unemployment to markedly decline.

In discussion with the International Monetary Fund (IMF) the government expects growth to accelerate to four per cent over the medium-term, based on strong world growth, increased trade integration, and buoyant domestic demand in light of stable macroeconomic conditions and low interest rates.

Outlook

There are concerns over the continuing Sacu revenues, and a need to curtail and re-allocate spending and consider revenue enhancing measures. These actions may put pressures on the generous tax incentives given to operations within export processing zones and under other regimes. However, most fiscal adjustment over the medium-term will need to come from the expenditure side. This will involve reductions in the wage bill, subsidies to parastatals, and spending for goods and services.

Jointly with its Southern African Development Community (SADC) partners, Namibia is creating a free trade area encompassing the 14 member states of the community in 2008. Namibia's simple average tariff has been reduced to 11.4 per cent, compared with 24 per cent in the late 1990s and the sub-Saharan average of 20 per cent. The biggest possible stumbling block to the continued expansion of the economy will be the agreement of white farmers to sell their land to the government.

KEY INDICATORS — Namibia

	Unit	2003	2004	2005	2006	2007
Population	m	1.88	1.97	2.03	*2.05	*2.06
Gross domestic product (GDP)	US$bn	3.00	5.70	6.06	6.94	*7.40
GDP per capita	US$	1,594	2,261	2,984	*3,389	*3,584
GDP real growth	%	4.0	4.4	4.2	4.0	*4.4
Inflation	%	9.0	5.5	2.4	5.1	6.7
Industrial output	% change	–	14.7	3.4	6.1	–
Agricultural output	% change	–	-2.9	3.5	0.6	–
Exports (fob) (goods)	US$m	1,210.0	1,356.0	1,402.0	1,503.0	–
Imports (cif) (goods)	US$m	1,380.0	1,473.0	1,980.0	2,090.0	–
Balance of trade	US$m	-170.0	-117.0	-578.0	984.0	–
Current account	US$m	170.0	586.0	434.0	1,106.0	*1,360.0
Total reserves minus gold	US$m	325.2	345.1	312.1	449.6	896.0
Foreign exchange	US$m	325.1	344.9	312.0	449.4	895.9
Exchange rate	per US$	7.56	6.46	7.23	7.23	6.83

* estimated figure

Risk assessment

Economic	Fair
Political	Fair
Regional stability	Fair

COUNTRY PROFILE

Historical profile

German missionaries first arrived in Namibia in the 1840s. The Cape Colony (in modern South Africa) controlled the port at Walvis Bay from 1878. The Germans penetrated the interior after 1884 when a Dr Nachtigal established German rule. The Germans exploited the conflicts between the indigenous tribes to subjugate the territory, finally defeating the Hereros in 1904 and reducing the people further under an extermination order from 80,000 to 8,000 people.

1884 Declared a German territory (except Walvis Bay, which was occupied in 1878 by the British).

1920 Mandated to South Africa by the League of Nations.

1958 The South West African People's Organisation (Swapo) was formed from the anti-contract labour movement.

1966 South Africa introduced apartheid laws, the UN terminated its mandate and Swapo launched an armed struggle for independence.

1973 The UN withdrew its mandate and recognised Swapo as the 'sole authentic representative of Namibian people'.

1985 South Africa established the Transitional Government (TG), an un-elected black majority government consisting of members of six different tribal parties, instructing it to draw up a constitution.

1988 South Africa turned down the TG's constitutional draft; independence was agreed by South Africa, Angola, Cuba, (the then) USSR and USA.

1989 Free and fair elections were held under the auspices of the UN. South Africa withdrew its forces. The Swapo leader, Sam Nujoma, formed a transitional ministerial team.

1990 Independence was granted and Nujoma became Namibia's first president.

1994 Walvis Bay and 12 offshore Penguin Islands were formally transferred from South African to Namibian sovereignty. In Namibia's first post independence presidential and National Assembly

elections in December, Swapo and Nujoma defeated the Democratic Turnhalle Alliance party of Mishake Muyongo.
1999 President Sam Nujoma and the ruling Swapo won the presidential and legislative elections.
2002 President Sam Nujoma dismissed his prime minister, Hage Geingob and replaced him with Theo-Ben Gurirab, the former foreign minister
2003 Flood waters from the Zambezi River affected 10,000 villagers in the eastern Caprivi.
2004 In January, Germany expressed regret for the colonial-era killing of tens of thousands of ethnic Hereros. Presidential and parliamentary elections took place on 15–16 November. President Nujoma was unable to run for another term in office although he will remain as leader of Swapo until at least 2007. Hifikepunye Lucas Pohamba was chosen by Swapo to run in the presidential election and won with 76.4 per cent of the vote. In National Assembly elections, Swapo won 76.1 per cent of the vote (55 out of 72 seats) and CoD 7.2 per cent (5).
2005 Hifikepunye Pohamba (Swapo) was elected president; he appointed Nahas Angula as prime minister. The ministry of lands and resettlement announced that it would cost N$ 3.7 billion (US$555 million) over 15 years to implement the land reforms proposed by the government. While 33 million hectares of communal land will be converted to small-scale farming, controversially one aspect of the reforms is the expropriation of white farmer-owned lands.
2007 A rich deposit of uranium was found in the Erongo region. Sam Nujoma resigned as president of Swapo in November; he had led the party for 47 years. A joint dam and hydroelectric power station project was agreed between Angola and Namibia in October. A new political party, the Rally for Democracy and Progress, was formed in November.
2008 On 1 May the location of a 500-year-old sunken treasure ship off the coast of Namibia was announced by the diamond company Namdeb during exploration operations. The finds included gold coins and tonnes of elephant tusks.

Political structure

Constitution
In 1999 the constitution was altered to allow President Nujoma to serve a third term.
Form of state
Multi-party republic
The executive
Executive power rests with the president, who is head of state, elected by universal suffrage for a five-year term, with the assistance of a cabinet headed by a prime minister appointed by the president.
National legislature
Legislative power is vested in a bicameral parliament comprising a directly elected, 72-member National Assembly with a five-year term, and an indirectly elected National Council (26 members, two members from each of Namibia's 13 regions), with a six-year term.
Last elections
15–16 November 2004 (National Assembly and presidential)
Results: Presidential: Samuel Daniel Shafiishuna Nujoma (Swapo) won 76.4 per cent of the vote, Ben Ulenga 7.28 per cent.
National Assembly: Swapo won 76.1 per cent of the vote (55 out of 72 seats), CoD 7.2 per cent (5), Democratic Turnhalle Alliance (DTA) 5.0 per cent (3), National Unity Democratic Organisation (NUDO), 4.1 per cent (3), United Democratic Front (UDF), 3.5 per cent (3); other parties one seat. Turnout was 84.8 per cent.
Next elections
November 2008 (presidential); November 2008 (parliamentary).

Political parties

Ruling party
South West African People's Organisation (Swapo) (re-elected 16 Nov 2004)
Main opposition party
Congress of Democrats (CoD)

Population

2.06 million (2007)*
Last census: August 2001: 1,830,330
Population density: Two inhabitants per square km. Urban population: 31 per cent (1995–2001).
Annual growth rate: 2.3 per cent 1994–2004 (WHO 2006)
Ethnic make-up
87.5 per cent black, 6.5 per cent mixed race (coloured) and 6.0 per cent white.
Religions
Christianity (approximately 80 per cent), traditional beliefs (20 per cent).

Education

Primary schooling is compulsory and lasts for seven years. Secondary education is divided into two stages, junior secondary between the ages of 12 and 15 and senior secondary level lasting for another two years. A final two-year school course may be undertaken for the pre-university certificate, until aged 19.
The country has a serious lack of secondary school teachers and because of the remoteness of villages many older children are unable to complete high school. Public expenditure on education amounts to approximately 4 per cent of annual GDP.
Literacy rate: 83 per cent adult rate; 92 per cent youth rate (15–24) (Unesco 2005).
Compulsory years: Five to 21
Enrolment rate: 131 per cent gross primary enrolment, 62 per cent gross secondary enrolment; of relevant age group (including repeaters) (World Bank).

Health

Per capita total expenditure on health (2003) was US$359; of which per capita government spending was US$252, (WHO 2006).
As a result of HIV/Aids, the annual cost of public healthcare has risen steadily.
Over 68 per cent of infants aged less than one year are immunised against measles. Access to clean drinking water is available to over 77 per cent of the population.
An outbreak of polio in June 2006 prompted three mass immunisation campaigns as, by July, 178 people were reported to have died of the disease. An international alert has increased vigilance in Namibia's border region with Botswana and Angola.
There were cases of polio reported to the World Health Organisation – Global Polio Eradication Initiative in 2006; the country had previously been free of the disease and its re-emergence was due to infected travellers.
HIV/Aids
Namibia has one of the highest rates of HIV infection in the world. If the trend continues, the number of individuals living with the disease will rise to 400,000 by 2006. Aids is the main single cause of death for all age groups. UNAIDS estimates that the annual loss to GDP per capita growth will be 1.5 per cent by 2010.
HIV prevalence: 21.3 per cent aged 15–49 in 2003 (World Bank)
Life expectancy: 54 years, 2004 (WHO 2006)
Fertility rate/Maternal mortality rate: 3.8 births per woman, 2004 (WHO 2006); maternal mortality 230 per 100,000 live births (World Bank).
Child (under 5 years) mortality rate (per 1,000): 48 per 1,000 live births (World Bank)
Head of population per physician: 0.3 physicians per 1,000 people, 2004 (WHO 2006)

Welfare

The social pension scheme (from 1949) has massive anti-poverty objectives. Surveys in Namibia have shown that pension-dependent households are better off than small farmers. The scheme offers a non-contributory social pension for its elderly citizens. Namibia's 85,000 social pensioners receive a much lower amount each month compared to South Africa and Botswana. The social pension also

supports unemployed adults, young grandchildren and other relatives. Increasingly, the pension is providing vital support to relatives of those suffering from HIV/Aids, with many elderly people fostering Aids orphans. The social pension costs the Namibian government an average of 4.8 per cent of total government expenditure.
Rape constitutes a massive problem in society. It is estimated that as many as 15,000 people a year could be victims of rape or attempted rape with only one in every 20 rapes being reported to the police.

Main cities
Windhoek (capital, estimated population 252,721 in 2005), Oshakati (53,736), Walvis Bay (49,656), Swakopmund (28,791), Otjiwarongo (26,334), Grootfontein (25,773), Rehoboth (21,899), Rundu (19,676).

Languages spoken
English is the first language of only 7 per cent of the population. All documents, notices and directional signs are in English. German and Afrikaans are widely used throughout the country.
There are six main African languages: Oshiwambo, Herero, Nama-Damara, Kwangali (Okavango region), Lozi (Caprivi region) and Tswana.
Official language/s
English

Media
Press
Dailies: Include Allgemeine Zeitung, Die Republikein, Namibian, Namibia News, National Mirror and Windhoek Advertiser.
Weeklies: Include New Era (published by the government since 1991), Tempo and Sunday Republikein. Namib Times (Walvis Bay) is a bi-weekly newspaper.
Business: Namibia Economist is a weekly publication covering financial and economic news.
Periodicals: Monitor is a monthly published from Windhoek.
Broadcasting
Radio: Local services in English, the principal African languages, Afrikaans, broadcast by state owned Namibian Broadcasting Corporation (NBC).
Television: The NBC broadcasts on one channel in English only; South Africa's M-net pay TV company also broadcasts. In October 2002, President Sam Nujoma (also information minister) ordered state television to stop showing western programmes.

Economy
GDP growth was 3.5 per cent in 2005 and was expected to be 4.6 per cent in 2006. The service sector provides 58 per cent of GDP, agriculture accounts for 10 per cent and industry 32 per cent, of which manufacturing is 14 per cent.
The economy has been typically dependent on the production and export of primary products, the most important of which are diamonds, uranium, fish and beef. Tourism has become a major industry since the mid 1990s, with the fastest growth of all sectors. There were almost one million visitors in 2005, an increase of 11.9 per cent from 2004, although this was less than the average 12 per cent growth for other countries in the region. Major investment in tourist facilities has been called for, to match that given to neighbouring tourist attractions.
The government is attempting to diversify economic activities. Namibia offers relatively low labour costs, and, at Walvis Bay, a strategic location for sea exports to the southern African region. The government is targetting manufacturing, transshipment and energy as the prime sectors for new business.
Unemployment continues to be a major problem at a rate in excess of 30 per cent, together with under-employment at 15 per cent. The government is attempting to address this issue by, among other actions, a land re-allocation programme. Much will depend on the training opportunities for native farmers who turn to subsistence farming for a living.
The rate of poverty has been falling, although it is still high at 28 per cent of total households. This figure has been exacerbated by the high rates of HIV/Aids (19.6 per cent of the adult population in 2005), which also undermines the potential for investment in human capital. The government has introduced measures to provide universal coverage of antiretroviral treatment by 2010.

External trade
Namibia is a member of the Southern African Customs Union (Sacu), with South Africa, Namibia, Swaziland and Botswana. Sacu sets customs duties for commodities passing between member states and members share the common pool of customs and excise revenue on all external trade. It is also a member of the Southern African Development Community (SADC), the objectives of which include reducing trade barriers, achieving regional development and economic growth and evolving common systems and institutions. The bulk of imports originate in South Africa.
In 2006, the Convention of International Trade in Endangered Species (Cites) approved the sale and export of 10 tonnes of ivory, by the government of Namibia.
Imports
Principal imports are foodstuffs, petroleum products and fuel, manufactured goods, machinery, equipment, chemicals and construction materials.
Main sources: South Africa (82.4 per cent total, 2006), China (3.5 per cent), Germany (2.2 per cent).
Exports
Principal exports are diamonds (typically 35 per cent), copper, gold, zinc, lead, uranium and agricultural produce including cattle, processed fish and sheep (karakul) skins and wool.
Main destinations: UK (25.6 per cent total, 2006), South Africa (24.6 per cent), Italy (7.2 per cent).

Agriculture
Farming
The agricultural sector contributes around 11 per cent to GDP and employs 39 per cent of the workforce. Only half the country is suitable for farming. In the north, yields remain low on average, due to overgrazing.
Farming supports directly or indirectly some 70 per cent of the population. There is wide disparity in land access between the 12,000, mainly white-owned, commercial farms and subsistence farmers, who number some 60 per cent of the population.
Commercial farming is dominated by livestock ranching – cattle in the north-central districts, sheep (karakul and mutton) and ostriches in the south – and accounts for 80 per cent of total agricultural output. Namibia normally produces some 40 per cent of its maize requirements from commercial farms and is generally self-sufficient in millet, the main food crop grown in the north by communal farmers. Beef is the most high-value product and exports go to the EU with an annual quota of 60,000 tonnes.
The government is pursuing a land reform programme to redistribute lands owned by white farmers. While initially the policy was to be implemented on a voluntary basis, expropriation orders began to be issued in 2005 against reluctant farmers.
Estimated crop production in 2005 included: 109,000 tonnes (t) cereals in total, 8,000t wheat, 33,000t maize, 6,000t sorghum, 9,000t pulses, 295,000t roots and tubers, 8,500t grapes, 621t oilcrops, 500t dates, 5,100t seed cotton, 1,683t cotton lint, 62,000t millet, 23,000t fruit in total, 18,000t vegetables in total. Estimated livestock production included: 108,960t meat in total, 77,253t beef, 577t pig meat, 14,040t lamb, 5,040t goat meat, 4,400t game meat, 7,650t poultry, 2,640t eggs, 109,000t milk, 8,250t cattle hides, 1,560t sheepskins, 2,200t greasy wool.

Fishing
The south-east Atlantic is a rich fishing ground, with sardines, hake and mackerel being the main species.
The government declared a 370km exclusive economic zone and banned unlicensed foreign trawlers after independence. A new fishing policy designed to maximise shore-based processing, and long-term concessions to 159 operators (including 54 new ones) were granted. Namibia has a 300-strong fishing fleet and foreign trawlers operate under charter. 60,000 tonnes of fish are caught annually, 90 per cent of which is exported. The industry employs 40,000 people and accounts for eight per cent of GDP.
In a meeting of African ministers in Namibia, held on 2 July, members discussed illegal and unregulated fishing, which is estimated to cost Africa US$1 billion per annum in lost revenue and the threat to stocks and local artisan fishing.
In 2004, the total marine fish catch was 564,819 tonnes and the total crustacean catch was 2,681 tonnes.

Industry and manufacturing
The industrial sector contributes around 25 per cent of GDP and employs 8 per cent of the workforce.
There is a small and highly specialised manufacturing sector, concentrated in Windhoek and Walvis Bay, with food processing (meat, agronomic products, fish) and beverages (beer and soft drinks) predominant. Other activities include structural metal products, non-metal mineral products, wood furniture, leather goods.
An export processing zone (EPZ) regime was established in 1995; it provides incentives to investors in manufacturing plants producing goods mainly for export, including a zero income tax liability for an unlimited period.

Tourism
Tourism is expected to contribute 5.6 per cent to GDP in 2005.

Mining
The mining sector is the traditional backbone of the economy, contributing around 20 per cent to GDP.
Around 7 per cent of government revenues and a third of the country's foreign exchange earnings come from diamonds.
Namdeb Diamond Corporation (50 per cent owned by De Beers and 50 per cent owned by the Namibian government) mines the world's richest source of high quality gem diamonds onshore north of Oranjemund, while offshore diamond recoveries by De Beers Marine have expanded significantly since commercial mining began in 1991.
The Skorpion zinc mining complex is one of the largest zinc producers in the world. Costs of extraction at Skorpion are low at around US$0.40 per kg, compared to the industry average of around US$0.70 per kg. This puts it in a good position to compete in tough markets.
Primary gold production started in 1989 and significant quantities of copper, lead, pyrite, salt and zinc are also produced while there are large unexploited deposits of base, precious and industrial minerals. Marble, granite and semi-precious stones such as rose quartz, tourmaline, amethyst and blue-lace agate are also mined; the government is seeking to promote local value by adding processing. Larger mines are mainly owned by foreign multinationals from South Africa and the UK.
Namibia is also a major uranium producer.

Hydrocarbons
Some exploration has taken place in Namibia with seven onshore wells and eleven offshore wells having been built. There is potential for oil production, however this would be a high risk venture for any companies interested. There is no refinery capacity and Namibia relies on refined oil imports. Dependence on South Africa for oil products has been reduced with supplies procured from Angola and overseas refineries.
Natural gas reserves total around 80 billion cubic metres. The Kudu offshore gas field in the south contains 36.8 billion cubic metres of natural gas. In 2004 the Namibian government announced the acquisition of a 10 per cent share in the Kudu fields.
Namibia does not produce coal. A small amount is imported from neighbouring countries to meet energy demands.

Energy
A new hydroelectric dam, to be located at Baynes, on the Kunene River, was agreed by the governments of Angola and Namibia in October 2007.
A power line from Victoria Falls in Zambia to Katima Mulilo in Namibia was commissioned by Presidents Mwanawasa and Pohamba in March 2008. The 231 kilometre line will allow Zambia to supply 220 kilovolts of power to Namibia; it will form part of the Zimbabwe-Zambia-Botswana-Namibia (ZIZABONA) agreement which will link the four country's power grids.

Financial markets
Stock exchange
The Namibian Stock Exchange (NSE) was launched in October 1992.

Banking and insurance
The banking sector is small, with four private commercial banks. The ratio of non-performing loans is relatively low, making the sector stable and financially sound.

Central bank
Bank of Namibia

Main financial centre
Windhoek

Time
GMT plus two hours

Geography
Namibia lies in south-western Africa, with South Africa to the south and south-east, Botswana to the east and Angola to the north. The country has a long coastline on the Atlantic Ocean. The narrow Caprivi Strip, between Angola and Botswana in the north-east, extends Namibia to the Zambezi river, giving it a border with Zambia. The arid Namib Desert stretches along the west coast, while the easternmost area is part of the Kalahari Desert.

Hemisphere
Southern

Climate
Namibia has one of the driest climates in the world. Sub-tropical, the hottest months are January–February (20–29 degrees Celsius (C)) and the coldest are June–July (6–18 degrees C).

Entry requirements
Passports
Required by all and must be valid for six months after intended departure date.

Visa
Required by all, except tourist visitors, for up to 90 days, from North America, Australasia, most of Europe, and some Asian countries, for a full list of exceptions see www.mfa.gov.na. Business visas require a letter of invitation or a full list and addresses of business contacts to be visited in Namibia. A certified copy of the return ticket should also be submitted. For a multiple entry visa, application should be made to the Ministry of Home Affairs on arrival in Windhoek.

Currency advice/regulations
The import and export of local currency is limited to N$50,000. The import of foreign currency is unrestricted but must be declared on arrival, and export is allowed up to declared amount.

Customs
Personal items are duty-free. Hunting rifles require a permit that can be issued by customs on arrival; handguns are prohibited.

Health (for visitors)
Mandatory precautions
Yellow fever vaccination certificate required if arriving from an infected area.

Advisable precautions
Visitors should take precautions against all tropical diseases. Vaccinations for

diphtheria, tetanus, hepatitis A and typhoid and polio are recommended. Hepatitis B vaccinations may be recommended. Malaria risk exists in most areas in the north. Water in all main towns is purified and safe to drink. There is a risk of rabies. To avoid the risk of bilharzia, only use well maintained, chlorinated swimming pools.
Tap water must be treated as unsafe unless boiled and filtered (bottled water is available in the main cities). Eat only well cooked meals, preferably served hot; vegetables should be cooked and fruit peeled. Dairy products are unpasteurised and should be avoided
A first aid kit that includes disposable syringes, is a reasonable precaution. Medical insurance is essential, including emergency evacuation, and an adequate supply of personal medicines is necessary.

Hotels
Classified from one to four stars. Accommodation in towns outside Windhoek is limited apart from Swakopmund so should always be booked well in advance. Luxury lodges or bungalow accommodation is available at Etosha and other national parks; there is also an expanding range of desert lodges and guest farms.

Credit cards
International cards are widely accepted throughout the country.

Public holidays (national)
Fixed dates
1 Jan (New Year's Day), 21 Mar (Independence Day), 1 May (Workers' Day), 4 May (Cassinga Day), 25 May (Africa Day), 26 Aug (Heroes' Day), 10 Dec (International Human Rights Day), 25 Dec (Christmas Day), 26 Dec (Family Day).
Variable dates
Good Friday, Easter Holiday (Mar/Apr), Ascension Day (Apr/May).

Working hours
Banking
Mon–Fri: 0900–1530; Sat: 0830–1100.
Business
Mon–Fri: 0800–1700.
Government
Mon–Fri: 0800–1700.
Shops
Mon–Sat 0800–1800.

Telecommunications
Mobile/cell phones
There are GSM 900/1800 networks that cover most populated areas.

Electricity supply
220 V AC

Getting there
Air
National airline: Air Namibia
International airport/s: Windhoek Airport (WDH), 40km from city. Facilities include restaurant, bars, duty-free shops, post office, bureau de change and car hire. Taxis, minivans and buses are available to the city.
Airport tax: None
Surface
Road: Tarred highways link the South African border via Keetmanshoop to Windhoek then Oshakati and the northern border with Angola, and between Windhoek and Swakopmund-Walvis Bay. The new Trans-Kalahari highway from Botswana via Ghanzi, along with the Trans-Caprivi tarred highway, provide direct road links between Walvis Bay and central Africa.
A road bridge across the River Zambezi, between the Caprivi Strip (Namibia) and Zambia, opened in 2004.
Rail: Main line runs from South African border via Keetmanshoop and Windhoek to Swakopmund, Walvis Bay, and via Otavi to Tsumeb and Grootfontein, the northern railheads.
Main port/s: Walvis Bay is a modern, deep-water harbour, Lüderitz is older and smaller.

Getting about
National transport
Air: Flying is the most efficient way of connecting with all main towns, either using the extensive scheduled services or charter flights.
Road: Roads are generally well maintained. There are 64,799km of road, of which 7,841km are tarred, while the rest are gravel and earth. The former Owambo region in the north of the country is inhabited by about 44 per cent of the population, yet is served by only 5 per cent of the total road network.
The Trans-Kalahari and Trans-Caprivi highway provide the backbone of a network serving rural areas as well as connecting landlocked countries with the coast.
Buses: A luxury bus service exists between Windhoek and all major towns.
Rail: The main rail routes in Namibia are Windhoek-Keetmanshoop-De Aar, Walvis Bay-Swakopmund-Windhoek-Tsumeb and Lüderitz-Keetmanshoop. First- and second-class carriages are available on these routes. Light refreshments are offered on some services. On overnight services, seats in first-class compartments convert to four couchettes and those in second-class to six couchettes.
City transport
Taxis: Available in main towns; 10 per cent tip is usual.
Buses, trams & metro: Bus services are not well developed and there is generally no transport except taxis.

Car hire
Available in Windhoek city centre, international airport, Walvis Bay.
Although roads between major towns are generally of a good standard, the distances involved can be prohibitive; four-wheel drive is advisable if going off the main routes.
International driving licence is required.
Traffic drives on the left. The general speed limit is 60kph in built-up areas and 120kph on open roads. Safety belts must be used at all times.

BUSINESS DIRECTORY
The addresses listed below are a selection only. While World of Information makes every endeavour to check these addresses, we cannot guarantee that changes have not been made, especially to telephone numbers and area codes. We would welcome any corrections.

Telephone area codes
The international dialling code (IDD) for Namibia is +264 followed by the area code and subscriber's number:

Keetmanshoop	631	Swakopmund	641
Luderitz	6331	Tsumeb	671
Mariental	661	Windhoek	61

Chambers of Commerce
Namibia Chamber of Commerce and Industry, 2 Jenner Street, PO Box 9355, Windhoek (tel/fax: 228-009; e-mail: nccihq@iwwn.com.na).

Windhoek Chamber of Commerce and Industries, 315 Swa Building, 7 Post Street Mall, PO Box 191, Windhoek (tel: 222-000; fax: 233-690; e-mail: whkchamber@namib.com).

Banking
Bank of Windhoek, 262 Independence Avenue, PO Box 15, Windhoek (tel: 299-1229; fax: 299-1285).

City Savings and Investment Bank, PO Box 63, FGI Building, Post St Mall, Windhoek (tel: 221-262; fax: 221-555).

Commercial Bank of Namibia, 12-20 Bulow Street, PO Box 1, Windhoek (tel: 295-9111, 295-2014; fax: 295-2046; e-mail: cbon@iwwn.com.na).

First National Bank Namibia, 209 Independence Avenue, PO Box 195, Windhoek (tel: 229-610; fax: 225-994).

Standard Bank Namibia, Mutual Platz Building, Post Street Mall, PO Box 3327, Windhoek (tel: 294-2283; fax: 294-2583).

Central bank
Bank of Namibia, PO Box 2882, 71 Robert Mugabe Avenue, Windhoek (tel: 283-5111; fax: 283-5067; e-mail: general.inquiries@bon.com.na).

Travel information

Air Namibia, PO Box 731, Transnamib Building, Bahnhofstreet, Windhoek 9000; (tel: 299-6000; fax: 299-6168); Town Office (tel: 229-6444; fax: 299-6168); internet: www.airnamibia.com.na).

Automobile Association, PO Box 61, Windhoek (tel: 224-201).

Etosha Northern Tourism and Publicity Association, PO Box 779, Tsumeb (tel: 220-728; fax: 220-916).

Lodge and Guest Farm Reservations, PO Box 21783, Windhoek (tel: 226-979; fax: 226-999).

Namibia Resorts International, PO Box 2862, Windhoek (tel: 233-145; fax: 234-512).

Southern Tourism Forum, Private Bag 2125, Keetmanshoop (tel: 2095; fax: 3818).

Tour and Safari Association of Namibia, PO Box 5144, Windhoek (tel: 232-748; fax: 228-461).

National tourist organisation offices

Namibia Tourism Board, Independence Avenue, Private Bag 13346, Windhoek (tel: 290-6000; fax: 254-848; email: tourism@mweb.com.na; internet: www.namibiatourism.com.na).

Ministries

Ministry of Agriculture, Water and Rural Development, Private Bag 13184, Windhoek (tel: 202-9111; fax: 229-961).

Ministry of Basic Education and Culture, Private Bag 13186, Windhoek (tel: 293-9411; fax: 224-277).

Ministry of the Environment and Tourism, Private Bag 13346, Swabour Building, Independence Avenue, Windhoek (tel: 284-2111; fax: 229-936).

Ministry of Finance, Private Bag 13295, Windhoek (tel: 209-9111; fax: 236-454).

Ministry of Fisheries and Marine Resources, Private Bag 13355, Windhoek (tel: 205-3911; fax: 233-286).

Ministry of Foreign Affairs, Private Bag 13347, Windhoek (tel: 282-9111; fax: 223-937).

Ministry of Higher Education, Vocational Training, Science & Technology, Private Bag 13391, Windhoek (tel: 253-670; fax: 253-671).

Ministry of Information and Broadcasting, Private Bag 13344, Windhoek (tel: 283-911; fax: 222-343).

Ministry of Mines and Energy, 1 Aviation Road, Private Bag 13297, Windhoek (tel: 284-8111; fax: 283-643; email: info@mme.gov.na).

Ministry of Trade and Industry, Private Bag 13340, Windhoek (tel: 283-7111; fax: 220-148).

Ministry of Works Transport and Communication, Private Bag 13341, Windhoek (tel: 208-9111; fax: 228-560).

President's Office, State House, Private Bag 13339, Windhoek (tel: 220-010; fax: 221-770).

Prime Minister's Office, Private Bag 13338, Windhoek (tel: 287-9111; fax: 226-189).

Other useful addresses

British High Commission, PO Box 22202, 116 Robert Mugabe Avenue, Windhoek (tel: 223-022; fax: 228-895; e-mail: bhc@iwwn.com.na).

Investment Centre, Private Bag 13340, Windhoek (tel: 283-7335; fax: 22-0278).

Meat Board of Namibia, PO Box 38, Windhoek (tel: 233-280; fax: 228-310).

Namibia Crafts Centre, 40 Talstreet, Windhoek (tel: 222-236).

Namibia Development Corporation, Private Bag 13252, Windhoek (tel: 206-9111; fax: 23-3943).

Namibia Power Corporation, PO Box 2864, Windhoek (tel: 205-4111; fax: 23-2805).

Namibian Embassy (USA), 1605 New Hampshire Avenue, NW, Washington DC 2009 (tel: (+1-202) 986-0540; fax: (+1-202) 986-0443; e-mail: embnamibia@aol.com).

Namibian Ports Authority, PO Box 361, Walvis Bay (tel: 20-8201; fax: 20-8242).

National Planning Commission (NPC), Office of the President, Private Bag 13356, Windhoek (tel: 222-549; fax: 226-501).

Offshore Development Company, Private Bag 13397, Windhoek (tel: 239-032; fax: 231-001).

Ombudsman's Office, Private Bag 13211, Windhoek (tel: 225-998; fax: 226-838).

Telecom Namibia, PO Box 297, Windhoek (tel: 201-2221; fax: 223-323).

TransNamib Ltd, Private Bag 13204, Windhoek (tel: 298-1111; fax: 298-2053).

UK High Commission, 116A Leutwein Street, PO Box 22202, Windhoek (tel: 223-022; fax: 228-895).

US Embassy, Private Bag 12029, 14 Lossen Street, Ausspannplatz, Windhoek (tel: 221-601; fax: 229-792).

Windhoek Show Society, PO Box 1733, Windhoek (tel: 224-748; fax: 227-707).

Internet sites

Africa Business Network: www.ifc.org/abn

AllAfrica.com: http://allafrica.com

African Development Bank: www.afdb.org

Africa Online: www.africaonline.com

Mbendi AfroPaedia (information on companies, countries, industries and stock exchanges in Africa): http://mbendi.co.za

Office of Prime Minister: http://opm.gov.na

Nauru

KEY FACTS

Official name: Republic of Nauru

Head of State: President Marcus Stephen (Dec 2007; re-elected 18 Apr 2008)

Head of government: President Marcus Stephens (re-elected 18 Apr 2008)

Ruling party: There is no formal party system; parliament is traditionally dominated by independents that form factions.

Area: 21 square km

Population: 13,287 (2006)*

Capital: Owing to its small size and absence of urban development, Nauru has no capital. Yaren is the main town.

Official language: Nauruan

Currency: Australian dollar (A$) = 100 cents

Exchange rate: A$1.03 per US$ (Jul 2008)

GDP per capita: US$2,739 (2005)*

Unemployment: 90.00% (2004)*

Inflation: 2.80% (2003)

Balance of trade: -US$19.10 million 2004

Foreign debt: US$33.30 million (2003)

* estimated figure

COUNTRY PROFILE

Historical profile

1798 Sighted by the British and named Pleasant Island.

1887 Nauru became a German protectorate.

1888 Became part of the (German) Marshall Islands.

1900 Phosphate was discovered.

1906 Mining began under an agreement signed by the Australian Pacific Phosphate Company and the German government.

1914 Nauru was captured by Australian forces.

1919 After Germany's defeat, the island was placed under the joint administration of the UK, Australia and New Zealand. The three countries formed the British Phosphate Commission in order to share phosphate-mining revenues.

1942 Nauru was invaded by the Japanese.

1945 At the end of the Second World War, Nauru was made a UN Trust Territory under Australian Administration.

1968 The adoption of the Nauru constitution established it as the world's smallest republic with a parliamentary system of government. Hammer DeRoburt was Nauru's first head of state.

1970 Nauru took control of its phosphate industry. Nauru's per capita income became one the world's highest.

1976 Parliament unseated DeRoburt after objections to his autocratic style.

1978 DeRoburt was re-elected.

1989 Bernard Dowiyogo was elected president, defeating DeRoburt by 10 votes.

1995 Lagumot Harris defeated Dowiyogo.

1996 Harris resigned and Dowiyogo returned to power. Dowiyogo was ousted in parliament and Kennan Adeang became president; he in turn was replaced by Reuben Kun.

1997 Kinza Clodumar won the presidential election, backed by Bernard Dowiyogo.

1998 Dowiyogo replaced Clodumar as president.

1999 Dowiyogo was defeated in parliament and René Harris, a former president of the Nauru Phosphate Corporation, was elected president.

2000 René Harris resigned and Dowiyogo was re-elected president.

2001 Nauru agreed to Australia's proposal to house its asylum-seekers, refugees and illegal immigrants in Nauru for a fee. Parliament ousted Dowiyogo and re-elected former President Harris. The Financial Action Task Force (FATF) on money laundering blacklisted Nauru for not implemented appropriate legislation to curb money laundering, especially by the Russian mafia.

2002 Over 400 asylum-seekers bound for Australia were rescued from a sinking ship in the Indian Ocean and 293 were sent to Nauru which housed around 1,000 in detention, awaiting processing.

2003 Bernard Dowiyogo ousted René Harris and became president. When Dowiyogo died of a heart attack Derog Gioura was appointed acting president. The US threatened to impose sanctions if Nauru did not halted the sale of passports and close down its banking sector, both allegedly used by the terrorist group al Qaeda. Ludwig Scotty won presidential elections. Scotty lost a no-confidence vote and was replaced by René Harris.

2004 Nauru defaulted on loan payments to Australia and had its assets seized when foreign debts were over US$165 million. Although René Harris organised a restructured loan Ludwig Scotty prevented the government finance bills and Harris lost his office as Scotty was re-appointed president. Australia installed officials in Nauru to handle state finances. Scotty declared a state of emergency and dissolved parliament after it failed to pass a reform budget. In parliamentary elections supporters of Scotty won.

2005 Ties were severed with China and links re-established with Taiwan. Nauru was removed from the FATF blacklist of countries lacking restrictions on international money laundering; the US also lifted its 2003sanctions.

2007 In parliamentary elections, supporters of Ludwig Scotty won 14 seats out of 18. Scotty was re-elected president on 28 August by 14 out of 18 votes, beating Marcus Stephen. On 19 December, President Scotty lost a vote of no confidence in parliament and Marcus Stephens was appointed in his place.

2008 The Australian offshore processing centre for asylum seekers was closed on 8 February when the remaining 21 Sri Lankans, who had been granted refugee status, were flown to Australia. This brought to an end the controversial 'Pacific Solution' that Australia had instituted in 2002. The centre is said to have contributed around 20 per cent of Nauru's GDP, and employed about 100 people. On 18 April President Stephen called a snap election after declaring a state of emergency, following political stalemate since he took office. In the elections, held on 26 April, President Stephen won most support with 12 members (out of 18) in his grouping elected; the remainder are either opposition or independent members. Former president, René Harris died on 5 July.

Political structure

Constitution
Republic
Voting is compulsory for all over the age of 20.

The executive
The president is head of state and head of government. The president, elected by parliament, governs for a three-year term, with the assistance of a cabinet of four or five ministers appointed from within parliament.

National legislature
Legislative power is vested in an18-member unicameral parliament, elected for a three-year term in multi-seat constituencies.

Last elections
25 August 2007 (parliamentary)
Results: Parliamentary: supporters of Marcus Stephens won 12 seats out of 18

Next elections
2010 (presidential and parliamentary).

Political parties

Informal alliances and personal links rather than formal, strong party discipline.

Ruling party
There is no formal party system; parliament is traditionally dominated by independents that form factions.

Political situation
Marcus Stephens rose from newly elected member of parliament in 2003 to president of his country in December 2007, and since then he has had a steep learning curve.
His administration has not only continued the process of constitutional revision (mainly proposing a directly election president), but also the inherited, unpopular austerity measures implemented by his predecessor Ludwig Scotty.
Within three month of Stephens taking office there was widespread unrest. In parliament the speaker accused him of degrading the rule of parliament when police refused to eject two government ministers. Instead of parliament sanctioning government business, executive powers and the personal rule of the president were taking precedence. The disagreement came to a head on 10 April when parliament attempted to suspend all supporters of Stephens. On the 18 April Stephens called a snap election and implemented a state of emergency, which was resolved when Stephens was re-elected with a solid majority.

Population
13,287 (2006)*
Last census: April 1992: 9,919
Population density: 592 per square km (2000); the highest in the Pacific.
Annual growth rate: 2.5 per cent 1994–2004 (WHO 2006)

Ethnic make-up
Nauruan (58 per cent), other Pacific islanders (26 per cent), Chinese (8 per cent), European (8 per cent). The indigenous population is of Micronesian descent.

Religions
Protestant (66 per cent), Roman Catholic (33 per cent).

Education

Schooling is provided free and is compulsory from aged 4–16. 10 per cent of schoolchildren are expected to complete secondary education.
Scholarships are available for higher education overseas.

Health

Per capita total expenditure on health (2003) was US$763; of which per capita government spending was US$675, at the international dollar rate, (WHO 2006).
The population's general health is not good; Nauru has a high rate of type two diabetes, with one-third of adults suffering from the disease due to the consumption of large amounts of processed food. In May 2004, a report ranked Nauruans as the most obese people in the world. A new diabetes centre has been set up as a focal point to provide multi-faceted treatment and education.
Life expectancy: 61 years, 2004 (WHO 2006)
Fertility rate/Maternal mortality rate: 3.8 births per woman, 2004 (WHO 2006)
Birth rate/Death rate: 26 births per 1,000 population; seven deaths per 1,000 population (2003).
Child (under 5 years) mortality rate (per 1,000): 10.3 per 1,000 live births (2003)

Main cities

Owing to its small size and absence of urban development, Nauru has no capital. Yaren is the main town (estimated population 4,900 in 2003).

Languages spoken

Nauruan and English, which is widely spoken and used for most government and commercial purposes.

Official language/s
Nauruan

Media

Other news agencies: ABC Pacific Beat: www.radioaustralia.net.au/pacbeat
Pacific Magazine: www.pacificmagazine.net

Press
The government-owned, weekly Nauru Bulletin, publishes in Nauruan and English. Other newspapers include the fortnightly Central Star News published on Saturdays and Nauru Chronicle.

Broadcasting
The Nauru Broadcasting Service operates public radio and TV.
Radio: Radio Nauru operated two services on AM and FM, in English and Nauruan, with imported material from Radio Australia and the BBC.
Television: Nauru Television (NTV) moved its operation to New Zealand in 1991 and broadcasts via satellite and on video-tapes.

Economy

The economy once relied almost solely on phosphate mining, giving the islanders in the 1960s the highest per capita income in the world. But eventually reserves ran out and the industry went into decline, so that by the 2000s Nauru's economy relies on foreign aid. Some benefit was achieved from income from earlier investment in the Philippine Phosphate Corporation, which paid a dividend of US$1.6 million in 2005, and is expected to pay out A$5 million (US$6.6 million) per annum, until around 2012.
The Australian company, Incitec Pivot, invested A$6 million (US$7.9 million) in a government backed revitalisation of the phosphate industry in 2006. Existing reserves are expected to last for 3–5 years.
Income from the Australian Offshore Processing Centre, for the housing of unregistered migrant workers, did not produce as much benefit as was expected when the project began, as the facility has been substantially reduced.
Inflation typically runs at around 3–4 per cent and the government often has difficulty in balancing the budget with poor agricultural productivity and little prospect for industrial expansion. International donors include Australia, Japan and Taiwan.

External trade

Nauru is a member of the South Pacific Regional Trade and Economic Co-operation Agreement (Sparteca) along with 12 other regional nations, which allows products duty free access by Pacific Island Forum members to Australian and New Zealand markets (subject to the country of origin restrictions).
The government announced it had set up a company to revive phosphate-mining operations in partnership with the Australian fertiliser company, Incitec Pivot in 2005. While Incitec Pivot's investment of US$4.4 million would revive the mine,

Nauru would fund the refurbishment of associated infrastructure.

Imports

Imports include food, fuel, consumer goods, building materials and machinery.

Main sources: Australia (63.0 per cent total, 2006), US (10.3 per cent), Germany (7.5 per cent).

Exports

Phosphates, besides financial services, are the sole export.

Main destinations: South Africa (56.7 per cent of total, 2006), India (15.4 per cent), Canada (5.9 per cent).

Agriculture

Arable land is confined to a strip 150–300 metres between the beach and the cliff, surrounding a vast crater caused by the phosphate mine.

Artisanal vessels (canoes and aluminium dinghies) supply fish for local consumption. Most food is imported.

There are long-term plans to rehabilitate former mining land into agricultural land with funds from the Australian government.

Estimated crop production in 2005 included: 1,600 tonnes (t) coconuts, 208t oilcrops, 450t vegetables in total and 275t fruit in total. Livestock production: 73t meat in total, 69t pig meat, 4t poultry, 16t eggs.

Fishing

The total fish catch is typically 400 tonnes per annum.

In 2004, the total marine fish catch was 18 tonnes.

Industry and manufacturing

Phosphate processing is the only industry.

Tourism

Nauru is not a tourist destination, but with the decline of phosphate reserves attempts have been made to develop it. There is a national tourism office. As well as being remote, the island's attractions are limited, diving and fishing being the main attractions. Infrastructure is weak. There are at present two hotels, both relatively expensive. The island is linked to Australia by Air Nauru.

Environment

Rehabilitation of the island is necessary after decades of phosphate mining.

Nauru was one of the first countries to sign the Framework Convention on Climate Change. Rising sea levels related to global warming mean that in the future habitable low-lying land areas will be at risk from tidal surges and flooding.

Mining

Nauru's phosphate reserves, the legacy of millennia of fossilised bird excreta, represented the highest-grade phosphate ore in the world. It is estimated that reserves will be exhausted by around 2008. There are plans to reach deeper sources via boring coral, in a more involved secondary mining process.

Hydrocarbons

Nauru does not produce any hydrocarbons and depends entirely on imports.

Banking and insurance

There are no reliable commercial banking services in Nauru. Setting up a viable domestic banking system will be a major task to be addressed in the government's economic reform programme.

Central bank

The Bank of Nauru is insolvent and operates on a very limited basis.

Offshore facilities

Nauru is in the process of closing down its offshore banking sector, and thereby closing off access of criminal monies to money laundering. The 2004/05 budget set aside funds for the establishment of a financial investigations unit to support the implementation process. The OECD's Financial Action Task Force on Money Laundering (FATF), proposed to withdrew counter-measures from Nauru in October 2004, but did not remove it immediately from the list of non-co-operative countries on money laundering.

Time

GMT plus 12 hours

Geography

Nauru is a small island in the central Pacific Ocean, lying about 40km (25 miles) south of the Equator and about 4,000km (2,500 miles) north-east of Sydney, Australia. Banaba (Ocean Island), in Kiribati, is about 300km (185 miles) to the east.

It is oval-shaped and was one of the Pacific's largest phosphate-rock islands (the phosphate has since been depleted), ringed by a wide coral reef that gives no natural harbour or anchorage. Sandy beaches fringe a fertile belt between the shore and a coral cliff that rises to a central plateau up to 60 metres above sea level. There are no rivers or large lakes and the populations' main source of fresh water is either the often brackish water of the 300 acre Buada lagoon, or rainwater; there is an underground lake in the south-east in the Moqua Cave.

Hemisphere

Southern

Climate

Tropical, tempered by sea breezes, but humid (80 per cent) with variable rainfall. Temperatures range from 24–34 degrees Celsius in the shade. Monsoon season from November–February; average annual rainfall is 2,060mm. Between May–October is the best time to visit.

Entry requirements

Passports

Required by all.

Visa

Required by all, except nationals of New Zealand for visits up to three months and South Korea for 14 days. Tourist visas, for up to 30 days, may be obtained on arrival by nationals of US, Canada, UK and Caribbean Commonwealth countries with proof of sufficient funds, accommodation and return/onward passage.

Business and visitors' visas from all other countries must be obtained in advance directly from the Department of Foreign Affairs in Nauru (details in Ministry Addresses).

Currency advice/regulations

The import of local and foreign currencies is unlimited but must be declared on arrival. Export of local currency is limited to the equivalent of A$2,500; amounts greater then this must be authorised by the Bank of Nauru. The export of foreign currency is unlimited.

Travellers cheques are readily accepted.

Customs

Personal property is duty-free.

Traditional artifacts of Nauru require an export licence.

Prohibited imports

Firearms, ammunition, pornography and illegal drugs.

Health (for visitors)

Mandatory precautions

Cholera vaccination certificate if arriving from or via an infected area within five days. Yellow fever vaccination certificate if arriving from an infected area.

Advisable precautions

Vaccination for diphtheria, tuberculosis, hepatitis A and B, polio, tetanus, typhoid. There is a rabies risk. Main water is chlorinated but may cause mild stomach upset. Local water may be contaminated. There are no medical specialists, and serious cases are sent to Australia so medical insurance, including emergency evacuation, is necessary.

Hotels

There are two hotels on the island the Menen and the Od-N-Aiwo.

Credit cards

All major credit and charge cards are accepted. ATMs are not available.

Public holidays (national)

Fixed dates

1 Jan (New Year's Day), 31 Jan (Independence Day), 17 May (Constitution Day), 25 Sep (Youth Day), 26 Oct (Angam Day), 25–26 Dec (Christmas).

Variable dates

Good Friday, Easter Monday and Tuesday.

Working hours
Banking
Mon–Thu: 0900–1600; Fri: 0900–1630.
Business
Mon–Fri: 0800–1200, 1330–1630.
Government
Mon–Fri: 0900–1700.
Shops
Mon–Fri 0800–1800. Some food shops are open for longer hours and at the weekend.

Telecommunications
There is an automatic island and international radio communications system in operation.
Telephone/fax
Postal services

Electricity supply
110/240V AC, 50Hz

Weights and measures
Metric system

Social customs/useful tips
In business an informal attitude prevails, shirts and smart trousers or skirts are acceptable and only on very special occasions is more formal wear advisable. It is customary to shake hands on meeting and taking leave.
Gratuities are not customary. The minimum drinking age is 21 years.

Getting there
Air
National airline: Our Airline (formerly Air Nauru), with limited services to Brisbane (Australia), Kiribati and the Marshall Islands.
International airport/s: Nauru Island International (INU), there are few facilities; buses run to Yaren after each arriving plane and there is a courtesy bus provided by the Menen Hotel.
Airport tax: Departures tax: A$25.
Surface
Water: The main sealinks are with Australia, New Zealand and Japan. Without a natural harbour most commercial vessels moor offshore, in what are reputedly some of the world's deepest permanent anchorages, and passengers and cargo have to be ferried ashore.

Getting about
National transport
Road: A main road (19.3km) circles the island, and all residential areas are linked by surfaced roads. A regular local bus service operates around the island. Buada and the former phosphate areas are linked by an inland road.
Car hire
Car hire can be arranged locally. Traffic drives on the left. A national driving licence should suffice.

BUSINESS DIRECTORY

The addresses listed below are a selection only. While World of Information makes every endeavour to check these addresses, we cannot guarantee that changes have not been made, especially to telephone numbers and area codes. We would welcome any corrections.

Telephone area codes
The international direct dialling (IDD) code for Nauru is +674 followed by subscriber's number.

Useful telephone numbers
Police: 110
Fire: 119
Ambulance: 118 or 117

Chambers of Commerce

Banking
Central bank
Bank of Nauru, PO Box 289, Civic Centre, Aiwo District (tel: 444-3238/3267; fax: 444-3203;
e-mail:bon@cenpac.net.nr).

Travel information
Air Nauru, Government Building, Yaren District (tel: 444-3141, 444-3418; fax: 444-3170).

Nauru International Airport, PO Box 40, Nauru Air Corporation (tel: 444-3754/3141; fax: 444-3282-3705).

Pacific Island Travel, Herengracht 495, 1017 BT Amsterdam, The Netherlands (tel: (+31) 020-626-1325; fax (+31) 020-623-0008; internet: www.pacificislandtravel.com).

National tourist organisation offices
National Tourist Office, c/o Special Project Officer (Culture and Tourism), Department of Island Development and Industry, Government Offices, Aiwo District (tel: 444-3191; fax: 444-3791).

Ministries
Address for all Government Offices: Government Offices, Yaren District.

Chief Secretary, Secretary to Cabinet, Public Service Commissioner and Registrar of Births, Deaths and Marriages (tel: 444-3133; fax: 444-3110).

Department of Foreign Affairs (tel: 444-3133; fax: 444-3105).

Secretary for Education (tel: 444-3130; fax: 444-3718).

Secretary for External Affairs (tel: 444-3191, 444-3701; fax: 444-3105).

Secretary for Finance (tel: 444-3285, 444-3287; fax: 444-3125).

Secretary for Health (tel: 444-3702; fax: 444-3106).

Secretary for Island Development and Industry (tel: 444-3281; fax: 444-3705) (economic development and privatisation and foreign investment).

Secretary for Justice (tel: 444-3747, 444-3160; fax: 444-3108).

Secretary for Works and Community Services (tel: 444-3703; fax: 444-3718).

Other useful addresses
Directorate of Telecommunications, Private Bag, Yaren (tel: 444-3132; fax: 444-3111).

Nauru Finance Corporation, PO Box 306, Yaren (tel: 3390; fax: 3345) (responsible for promoting economic diversification, including offshore banking).

Nauru Permanent Mission to the UN, 800 Second Ave, Suite 400D, New York, NY-10017 (tel: (+1-212) 937-0074; internet: www.un.int/nauru).

Other news agencies: ABC Pacific Beat: www.radioaustralia.net.au/pacbeat

Pacific Magazine:
www.pacificmagazine.net

Internet sites
Nauru International Airport:
www.airnauru.com.au

Nauru website: www.nauruwire.org

Nepal

KEY FACTS

Official name: Nepal Adhirajya (Kingdom of Nepal)

Head of State: President Ram Baran Yadav (Nepali Congress) (from 23 Jul 2008)

Head of government: Prime Minister Prachandra (formerly known as Pushpa Kamal Dahal) (Maoists) (from 15 Aug 2008)

Ruling party: Coalition of Maoists and the Seven Party Alliance (led by the Nepali Congress Party (Democratic)) (from Jan 2007)

Area: 147,181 square km

Population: 24.06 million (2007)*

Capital: Kathmandu

Official language: Nepali (Devnagari script)

Currency: Rupee (NRs) = 100 paisa (the NRs is pegged to the Indian rupee – NRs 160 = Rs100)

Exchange rate: NRs68.41 per US$ (Jul 2008)

GDP per capita: US$400 (2007)*

GDP real growth: 2.50% (2007)*

Labour force: 11.92 million (2003)

Unemployment: 47.00% (2003)

Inflation: 6.40% (2007)

Balance of trade: US$192.60 million (2006)

Foreign debt: US$3.29 billion (2005)

* estimated figure

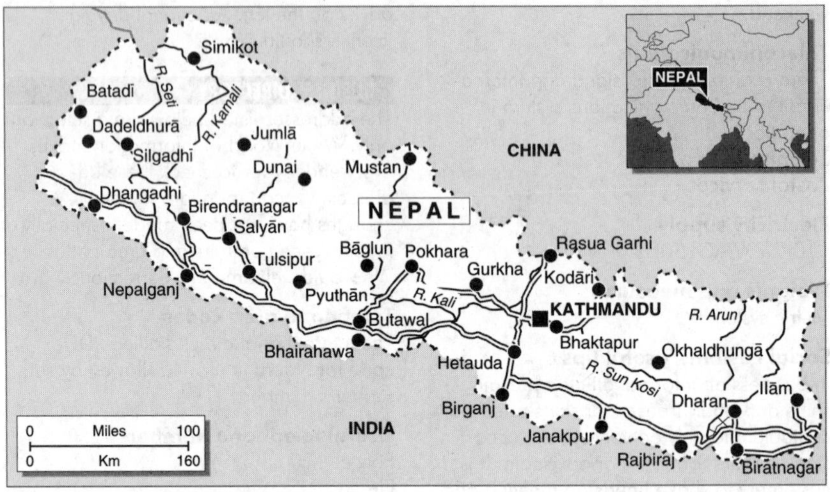

The results of the April 2008 general election in Nepal took most observers and analysts by surprise. They were won overwhelmingly by the Maoists – officially the Communist Party of Nepal (Maoist) – with 220 seats. Rather confusingly, two of the three main parties are communist of one hue or another: the winning Communist Party of Nepal (Maoist), the Nepali Congress Party (NCP) (second with 110 seats) and the Communist Party of Nepal (Unified Marxist-Leninist) (CPN (UML)) (103 seats). Most Nepalese had expected the former Maoist armed rebels to finish third, winning at best ten per cent of the 240 seats directly elected to the constituent assembly under Nepal's rather complex first-past-the-post system (335 of the remaining seats are elected under a proportional representation system). To complicate matters further there are also caste and gender quotas designed to give the new assembly a more representative appearance. The shock result appeared to reflect the Nepalese desire for change, a sentiment particularly apparent among the younger generation and the country's more marginalised elements.

The presidential election was won by Ram Baran Yadav of the Nepali Congress. He beat Ram Raja Prasad Singh (Maoist) in the second round of voting. Paramananda Jha (Madhesi Jana Adhikar Forum (MJF) (Madhesi People's Rights Forum)) was elected vice president.

No elections had taken place in Nepal since May 1999, a nine year interval, during which – as the election amply demonstrated – Nepal had changed completely. In the intervening years, the mountain kingdom had seen an armed rebellion and a new leftwing generation of political thinking emerge, as well as heightened ethnic consciousness and increased political aspirations. This time the ruling NCP machine failed to bring in the votes at election time. The CPN (UML) had been expected to do well because it deployed the best organisation and enjoyed the support of many among the small-business class. But it turned out to be the Maoists' efficient political machine and its ability, on the day, to turn out the voters, that was the biggest electoral surprise of all.

The vote represented the culmination of a political deal dating from 2006 in which Nepal's Maoist guerrillas agreed to a end their 10-year insurgency, which had claimed almost 14,000 lives, and instead to enter a UN-sponsored disarmament programme.

The monarchy goes

In simple terms, the people of Nepal declared that they no longer believed in the living god, the King. Lacking the popularity and personality of his predecessor

King Birendra, King Gyanendra Bir Bikram Shah Dev had tried to retain the monarchy and hold the country together. But when on 28 May 2008, the Constituent Assembly voted by 560–4 to declare the country a republic and depose King Gyanendra, he bowed to the inevitable and left the palace with his wife, Komal, on 11 June to take up temporary residence outside Kathmandu. He will now be known as Mr Shah. Within days the palace was turned into a museum, among the treasures housed are the royal throne and priceless crown and sceptre.

On 27 June, interim Prime Minister Koirala announced he would resign if the candidate he supported for president, Ram Raja Prasad Singh, was defeated. In the election held on 19 July, no candidate won the necessary 298 votes for victory and a second round had to be scheduled for 21 July, in which Ram Baran Yadav (Nepali Congress) won 308 votes, beating Ram Raja Prasad Singh (nominated by the Maoists). Baran was sworn in on 23 July as the first president of Nepal and Koirala tendered his resignation immediately after Baran took office. The Maoist leader, Prachandra (also known as Pushpa Kamal Dahal) was elected prime minister on 15 August, by 80 per cent of parliament, beating his only other rival for the office, Sher Bahadur Deuba. Prachandra took office on 18 August.

Poverty

Nepal's low level of growth (2.5 per cent in 2007) has been attributed to insurgency-related disruptions adversely affecting the industry and service sectors. Growth levels have for some time been well below the average 6 per cent per year required to begin making any impact on Nepal's high levels of poverty. Annual population growth over the past decade of over 2.0 per cent has not helped the situation. Nepal is one of the poorest countries in the world, with an estimated per capita income in 2007 of approximately US$400. Poverty and malnutrition are widespread and 20 per cent of the population is estimated to be without access to safe water. The incidence of disease is high and while health services have improved, most people do not have access to professional medical care. Average life expectancy is low at 60 years and the infant mortality rate of 540 per 100,000 births is high. The illiteracy rate for those over 15 is estimated at 55 per cent.

Over 80 per cent of the economically active population live in rural areas and support themselves through subsistence agriculture. Despite this, the contribution of agriculture to Nepal's GDP has declined from 72 per cent in 1974 to 39 per cent in 2003-04, owing to growth in public utilities, trade and tourism. Agricultural production is hampered by adverse climatic conditions, environmental degradation and structural deficiencies such as inadequate rural infrastructure and land ownership/tenancy problems.

The end of the World Trade Organisation (WTO) Multi-Fibre Agreement (MFA) production quotas, which had guaranteed Nepal a role in the global market was a severe blow. The Nepalese garment market was worth half the total national exports market and it will struggle to maintain this level in the face of increased competition. In the year after the industry shake-up, sales to the US alone plummeted 42 per cent.

Outlook

Hydroelectric power for export to India could be the saving of the Nepalese economy. Now that the 'guerrillas' are part of an elected government, it is hoped that international investors, and tourists, will return to Nepal. In a report published in mid-2008, the International Monetary Fund (IMF) noted that 'The ability to borrow from domestic financial markets remains a key constraint to next year's budget. Responsible fiscal management during the years of conflict has given Nepal a solid platform for economic growth. Protecting this asset will require a budget that recognises the economy's limited resources'.

Risk assessment

Politics	Improving
Economy	Improving
Regional stability	Fair

COUNTRY PROFILE

Historical profile

Modern Nepal began its formation in the second half of the eighteenth century, when the kingdom of Gorkha, led by Prithivi Narayan Shah, began to expand.
1769 Shah conquered Kathmandu and completed unification of what is today's Nepal, laying the foundation of a dynasty that was to last until 2008 after parliament voted on 28 December 2007 to abolish the monarchy.
1792 Nepal's expansion was halted by Chinese armies in Tibet.
1816 Nepal became a British protectorate after the Anglo-Nepalese war.
1846 Jang Bahadur Rana extracted a decree from the monarch that transferred sovereign powers to the family of Ranas, who ruled as hereditary prime ministers for 104 years.
1923 Nepal's independence was recognised by Britain, although it retained control of the country's foreign affairs.
1950–59 King Tribhuvan fled to India, intensifying the revolt led by the Nepali Congress Party (NCP) against the Ranas oligarchy. It ended with an agreement brokered by India which recognised the role of the monarch, legalised political parties and established a constitutional monarchy. In the eight years that followed, the King ruled the country while political parties took shape.

KEY INDICATORS — Nepal

	Unit	2003	2004	2005	2006	2007
Population	m	25.05	26.41	23.36	*23.59	*24.06
Gross domestic product (GDP)	US$bn	6.29	6.71	7.51	8.87	*9.63
GDP per capita	US$	251	239	322	*376	*400
GDP real growth	%	2.6	3.5	2.7	2.8	*2.5
Inflation	%	4.8	4.0	4.5	8.0	6.4
Industrial output	% change	–	1.0	1.4	3.5	–
Agricultural output	% change	–	3.9	3.0	1.7	–
Exports (fob) (goods)	US$m	720.0	740.0	902.9	865.0	924.9
Imports (cif) (goods)	US$m	1,600.0	1,890.0	2,276.5	2,011.0	2,935.6
Balance of trade	US$m	-880.0	-1,150.0	-1,373.6	-1,146.0	-2,007.6
Current account	US$m	119.9	-45.0	1.1	-10.4	-130.0
Foreign debt	US$bn	2.5	3.5	3.3	–	–
Total reserves minus gold	US$m	1,222.5	1,462.2	1,499.0	–	–
Foreign exchange	US$m	1,213.1	1,452.5	1,490.2	–	–
Exchange rate	per US$	74.75	73.67	71.08	71.08	62.95

* estimated figure

1959 The first election under a new constitution was won by the NCP.
1960 King Mahendra seized control and suspended parliament and politics.
1962 He introduced a new constitution establishing a party-less Panchayat system which banned political competition and parties. The King retained absolute powers.
1972 King Mahendra died in 1972 and was succeeded by his son, King Birendra, who continued his father's policies.
1979 After a series of protests against the Panchayat system, the King ordered a national referendum: the choice was between a 'reformed' panchayat or a multi-party democracy. A narrow majority voted in favour of the Panchayat, with reforms allowing direct elections – but still on a non-party basis.
1985 The NCP began a campaign of civil disobedience for the restoration of the multi-party system.
1986 Elections were boycotted by the NCP.
1990 Pro-democracy protests were staged by the NCP and leftist groups which resulted in killings and mass arrests by the police. The King bowed to pressure and agreed a new democratic constitution.
1991 The NCP won the elections and Girija Prasad Koirala became prime minister.
1994 Koirala's government was toppled due to party infighting. The Communist Party of Nepal-United Marxist-Leninist (CPN-UML) emerged as the largest single party in the elections and formed a minority government.
1995 The CPN-UML government was toppled, making way for a number of coalition and minority governments, until another round of elections was held in 1999.
1996 While the mainstream parties jostled for power in the centre, the Maoists launched their 'people's war'.
1998 The CPN-UML suffered a major blow when a faction of the party broke away.
1999 The NCP won the general elections; Krishna Prasad Bhattarai became prime minister.
2000 Bhattarai was forced him to step down due to party infighting. Koirala became prime minister again. The NCP remained effectively divided between the supporters of Koirala and Bhattarai.
2001 Crown Prince Dipendra killed his closest family members, including King Birendra and Queen Aishwarya, in a drunken shooting spree, before committing suicide. Gyanendra Bir Bikram Shah Deva became king. The Maoists increased their violent campaign of opposition. Koirala resigned and Sher Bahadur Deuba (NCP) became prime minister. In July a truce was agreed between the rebels and the government. In November the peace talks failed and the insurgency resumed as violence escalated
2002 Maoists rebel successfully staged a five-day general strike after more than 500 people were killed in clashes with government forces. King Gyanendra dissolved parliament and called for fresh general elections; the ruling NCP suspended Deuba from the party for advising the King to do so. King Gyanendra dismissed Deuba, abolished the Council of Ministers and assumed executive powers. The King appointed Lokendra Bahadur Chand as prime minister.
2003 On 1 February, Maoist rebels and the government agreed to a cease-fire. Prime Minister Chand resigned on 30 May. King Gyanendra appointed Surya Bahadur Thapa of the Rastriya Prajatantra Party (RPP) as prime minister. In August the Maoists ended the truce. Violence and political stalemate marked the end of the year.
2004 On 23 April, Nepal became the 147th member of the World Trade Organisation (WTO). Prime Minister Thapa resigned after weeks of civil protest. Former prime minister, Sher Bahadur Deuba, was re-appointed. In August, a blockade of Kathmandu by the Maoist rebels ended after one week.
2005 On 1 February, King Gyanendra dismissed Deuba and assumed absolute power, citing the imperative of defeating the Maoists. A royal anti-graft commission sentenced former prime minister Deuba to two years imprisonment for corruption. In September the rebels declared a unilateral cease-fire. Maoists and opposition parties agreed a strategy to restore democracy.
2006 Nepal, Bhutan, Bangladesh, India, Maldives, Pakistan and Sri Lanka signed the South Asia Free Trade Agreement (SAFTA), which came into effect on 1 January. In April, a seven-party alliance led by Girija Prasad Koirala (leader of NCP), in opposition to the King, called mass pro-democracy demonstrations. Riots broke out in the capital which left several police and demonstrators dead. International calls urged the King to negotiate with his opponents and in the face of so much opposition the King reinstated parliament and in May he was removed as head of the armed forces. On 10 June, parliament restricted the powers of the King as executive rule was passed to the Council of Ministers. On 21 November, a peace agreement was signed between the government and Maoist insurgents, formally ending 10 years of internal conflict and a six months cease-fire. Maoists rebels disarmed, monitored by the United Nations.
2007 On 15 January the two chambers of parliament were replaced by a unicameral interim legislature, with Maoists holding 83 out of 330 seats, under the terms of the temporary constitution agreed a week earlier. An interim multi-party cabinet, including five Maoists, was formed on 2 April to prepare the way for legislative elections in June (later postponed until November). The special assembly was charged with writing a new constitution, including deciding the future of the monarchy. In September, three bombs exploded in Kathmandu, the first terrorist attacks since the peace agreement in 2006. In September Maoist members of the interim government resigned in protest about the continued existence of the monarchy. A week later the Nepali Congress Party and the Nepali Congress Party (Democratic) reunited, forming a strong political bloc in time for the November elections. Rebel Maoists were accused of attacking a UN Food Programme convoy, which was providing humanitarian aid to southern Nepal. Deadlock between Maoist and ruling parties over the abotiltion of the monarchy and the adoption of proportional representation led to the postponing of general elections. On 28 December parliament voted to abolish the monarchy, thereby resolving the crisis. Five Maoists joined the cabinet in a number of key positions, including communication and information, which gave the Maoists control over the state-run media.
2008 In parliamentary elections held on 10 April the Communist Party of Nepal (Maoists), won 220 seats (out of 601), the Nepali Congress Party won 110 seats, the Communist Party of Nepal (Unified Marxist-Leninist) (CPN(UML)) won 103 seats, the Madhesi Jana Adhikar Forum won 52 seats, the Tarai-Madhesh Loktantrik Party won 20 seats; 20 other parties shared the remaining seats and none gained more than eight. On 28 May, the Constituent Assembly voted by 560–4 to declare the country a republic and depose King Gyanendra. Ex-King Gyanendra and his wife, Komal, left the palace on 11 June to take up temporary residence outside Kathmandu. He will be now be known as Mr Shah. Within days the palace was turned into a museum, among the treasures housed are the royal throne and priceless crown and sceptre. On 27 June, interim Prime Minister Koirala announced he would resign if the candidate he supported for president, Ram Raja Prasad Singh, was defeated. In the presidential election held on 19 July, no candidate won the necessary 298 votes for victory and a second round had to be scheduled for 21 July, in which Ram Baran Yadav (Nepali Congress) won 308 votes, beating Ram Raja Prasad Singh (nominated by the

Maoists). Baran was sworn in on 23 July as the first president of Nepal and Koirala tendered his resignation immediately after Baran took office. The Maoist leader, Prachandra (also known as Pushpa Kamal Dahal) was elected prime minister on 15 August, by 80 per cent of parliament, beating his only other rival for the office, Sher Bahadur Deuba. Prachandra took office on 18 August. Following the collapse of the Koshi dam, in August, in the south-east of Nepal severe flooding forced over 50,000 people to flee from their homes.

Political structure

Constitution

An interim constitution came into effect on 15 January 2007, the constitution for the State of Nepal replaced the previous constitution of the Kingdom of Nepal.

An amendment passed in March 2007 changed the country to a federal state from a unitary one. It also increased the number of constituencies in the south to 50 per cent of the seats in parliament.

Form of state

Federal democratic republic

The executive

The president is the Head of State. Under an amendment to the interim constitution (January 2007) the president, vice president, prime minister and constituent assembly chairman and vice chairman would be elected base on a 'political understanding' or failing that by a simple majority vote.

Members of the Nepalese Constituent Assembly (NCA) provide the executive which makes up the government. The 26 seats of the NCA are divided among nine political parties, proportional to the popular vote received.

National legislature

The Nepalese Constituent Assembly has 601 members, elected through either directly elected seats or by proportional representation. Under the interim Nepalese constitution a government cabinet is formed by 26 members, who provide the executive.

The assembly will re-write a constitution and govern the country until an elected government can be decided. The assembly has a mandate until 2010.

Legal system

Independent judiciary

Last elections

10 April 2008 (parliamentary); 19 and 21 July 2008 (presidential, first and second round).

Results: Parliamentary: the Communist Party of Nepal (Maoists), won 220 seats (out of 601), the Nepali Congress Party won 110 seats, the Communist Party of Nepal (Unified Marxist-Leninist) (CPN(UML)) won 103 seats, the Madhesi Jana Adhikar Forum won 52 seats, the Tarai-Madhesh Loktantrik Party won 20 seats; 20 other parties shared the remaining seats and none won more than eight. Presidential: (first round) Ram Baran Yadav (Nepali Congress) won 283 votes, Ram Raja Prasad Singh (Maoist) won 270. (Second round): Yadav won 308 votes beating Singh. Paramananda Jha (Madhesi Jana Adhikar Forum (MJF) (Madhesi People's Rights Forum)) was elected vice president with 305 votes; Shanta Shrestha (Maoist) won 243.

Next elections

2010 (parliamentary)

Political parties

Ruling party

Coalition of Maoists and the Seven Party Alliance (led by the Nepali Congress Party (Democratic)) (from Jan 2007)

Main opposition party

Population

24.06 million (2007)*

Last census: June 2001: 23,151,423

Population density: 160 inhabitants per square km. Urban population: 12 per cent (1995–2001).

Annual growth rate: 2.3 per cent 1994–2004 (WHO 2006)

Ethnic make-up

Nepal has a mixture of Indo-Caucasian and Tibeto-Mongoloid people and a number of Tibetan refugees. There are 61 different ethnic and caste groups and many have their own language and dialect.

Religions

Hinduism (90 per cent), Tibetan Buddhism (5.3 per cent), Islam (2.7 per cent). Nepal is a Hindu kingdom, but it allows other religions to practise their faiths. It is illegal to proselytise. The Kumari Devi is revered by both Hindus and Buddhists in Nepal as a 'living Goddess'.

Education

The education system is based on the Chinese model. A non-compulsory pre-school education can begin at aged three. Primary schooling lasts for five years at the end of which students are separated into academic and technical programmes.

The academic programme is divided into lower secondary, upper secondary and higher secondary schooling in a cycle of three, two and two years until the age of 18 when, if they have been successful, students may access higher education courses at university or other institutions.

The three-year lower secondary schools are of two types: general and Sanskrit. Upon completing the second stage, exams undertaken by students allows advancement to the higher secondary school or graduation with a school leaving certificate.

The Tribhuvan University, Mahendra Sanskrit University, Kathmandu University and Purbanchal University and B P Korala Institute of Health Science mainly provide higher education.

The technical programme is divided into cycles of either four and two, or four and four, years and students graduate with either a craftsman's certificate at age 16 or a technical certificate at aged 18.

Literacy rate: 44 per cent adult rate; 63 per cent youth rate (15–24) (Unesco 2005).

Compulsory years: Six to 16.

Enrolment rate: 113 per cent gross primary enrolment of the relevant age group (including repeaters); 42 per cent gross secondary enrolment (World Bank).

Pupils per teacher: 39 in primary schools.

Health

Per capita total expenditure on health (2003) was US$64; of which per capita government spending was US$18, (WHO 2006).

National morbidity patterns show ailments related to inadequate water and sanitation account for more than 70 per cent of all sickness reported. Furthermore, around 10,000 people die from cancer after a long-term exposure of arsenic compounds in drinking water.

There were cases of polio reported t the World Health Organisation – Global Polio Eradication Initiative in 2006; the country had previously been free of the disease and its re-emergence was due to infected travellers.

HIV/Aids

The UN estimated 60,000 people are living with HIV/Aids in 2003, which represents 0.25 per cent of the total population.

HIV prevalence: 0.5 per cent aged 15–49 in 2003 (World Bank)

Life expectancy: 61 years, 2004 (WHO 2006)

Fertility rate/Maternal mortality rate: 3.6 births per woman, 2004 (WHO 2006)

Child (under 5 years) mortality rate (per 1,000): 61.0 deaths per 1,000 live births; 48 per cent of children aged under five are malnourished (World Bank).

Head of population per physician: 0.21 physicians per 1,000 people, 2004 (WHO 2006)

Welfare

The government of Nepal and the Asian Development Bank (ADB) signed a partnership agreement aiming to reduce the incidence of poverty from over 40 per cent of the population to less than 10 per cent by 2017. The problems related to rural poverty are being tackled by improving access to impoverished areas. Several

non-government organisations have stepped up their aid to tackle poverty and disease in the country.
It is estimated that more than 10 out of 100 people in Nepal suffer from one or the other form of disability. The government does not have concrete programmes to address the problems facing the disabled.

Main cities
Kathmandu (capital, estimated population 812,026 in 2005), Biratnagar (185,000); Lalitpur (185,380); Pokhara (194,469); Birgañj (133,463), Dharan (110,475).

Languages spoken
Maithili, Bhojpuri, Hindi, Bengali and Newari are some other languages spoken. English is spoken, mainly in urban centres.

Official language/s
Nepali (Devnagari script)

Media
Press
Dailies: There are approximately 185 regular newspapers and magazines. The internet news portal, www.nepalnews.com, has its own breaking news as well as news from almost all major newspapers. Himal South Asian is a newsmagazine aimed at a South Asian readership.
Nepal has 10 broadsheet, daily newspapers published in Kathmandu. The state-run Gorkhapatra Corporation publishes two dailies. English-language dailies include Kathmandu Post and The Rising Nepal. Nepali dailies include Gorakhpatra, Kantipur, Mahanagar, Samacharpatra and Sandhya Times.
Weeklies: Most weeklies are published in the Nepali language. Local Nepali-language weeklies include Deshanter, Chalphal, Dristi, Budhabar, Jana Aastha and Sapthahik Bimarsha. English-language weeklies are Spotlight, Sunday Despatch, Sunday Post, Telegraph, Independent, People's Review and Nepali Times, which is the most widely read.
Business: Business publications include Business Age and New Business Age.
Periodicals: Monthly publications include Apsara, Kamana and On Time. There are many specialised publications catering for the tourism industry. These include Nepal Traveller and Nepal Travel Trade Reporter (both published monthly).
Himal Khabarpatrika and Nepal are the market leaders in fortnightly publications. Explore Nepal (local English newspaper) and Cyber Post are also published fortnightly.

Broadcasting
Radio: State-run Radio Nepal broadcasts on medium and short waves and has the largest coverage and reach. It leases FM time slots to private broadcasters. Nepal has licensed over 25 local, private FM stations, of which about 20 are operational. Kathmandu alone has eight private stations, which are largely commercial. Nepal also has a new genre of FM radio run by community groups, co-operatives and non-governmental organisations.
Television: State-run Nepal Television (NTV) dominates the airwaves with signals reaching about 55 per cent of the population. NTV began broadcasting via satellite in 2001. Nepal also has private cable operators. One of these runs Channel Nepal broadcasting via satellite from Thailand because unresolved licensing disputes have held up its permission to up-link from Nepal.

Economy
Nepal is an undeveloped country with a largely agrarian economy, which provides 40 per cent of GDP, and over 80 per cent of employment. The service sector accounts for 38 per cent of the economy and industry 21 per cent, of which manufacturing accounts for 8 per cent; the largest manufactured export was finished textiles. In 2005, GDP growth was 2.7 per cent and was expected to be 1.9 per cent in 2006.
Remittances from Nepalese workers abroad have grown into a major source of hard currency. Nepal also receives substantial amounts of external assistance from India, the UK, the US, Japan, Germany, the Scandinavian countries and several multilateral organisations.
An eleven-year insurgency, during which around 13,000 people died, when Maoists annexed large areas of the country and frequent popular demonstrations against the increasing loss of democracy led to King Gyanendra's absolute power being reduced to that of a purely ceremonial head of state in 2006.
An economy typically does not prosper during periods of insecurity and for Nepal GDP growth fell between 2000/01–2005/06 from 5 per cent to 2 per cent.
Despite the upheavals, macroeconomic stability was maintained; inflation was kept in single digits – the Nepalese rupee is pegged to the Indian rupee.
The poverty rate fell from 42 per cent in 1996 to 31 per cent in 2004. Nepal has abundant prospects for hydroelectricity production and plans to export surplus power. Its prospects depend largely on a stable government and improved infrastructure. Although tourism figures suffered during the insurgency, there is scope for the sector to become a healthy foreign exchange earner as well as employment provider.
A new government that brought together a broad spectrum of political ideas took office in April 2007 and the country's prospects will depend on their objectives to provide an environment for growth.

External trade
Nepal is a member of South Asia Association for Regional Co-operation, which operates a preferential trading arrangement (Sapta) that covers 6,000 products. In 2004 the South Asia Free Trade Area was agreed by Sapta, to be implemented between the member states (India, Pakistan, Bhutan, Nepal, Bangladesh, Sri Lanka and Maldives) by 2012.
Tourism and remittances represent major sources of foreign earnings since the WTO ruling (MFA in 2005) slashed garment exports to the US.
Valuable cashmere pashmina fabric is manufactured in Nepal and exported for couture clothing.

Imports
The principal imports petroleum, vehicles and manufactured goods.
Main sources: India (49.0 per cent total, 2006), China (12.4 per cent), UAE (11.7 per cent).

Exports
The principal exports are carpets, pashmina, and garments.
Main destinations: India (59.3 per cent total, 2006), US (14.0 per cent), Germany (5.9 per cent).

Agriculture
Farming
Agriculture accounts for around 40 per cent of GDP, providing most foreign exchange earnings and 80 per cent of employment. Only about 25 per cent of the total land area is cultivable; another 33 per cent is forested and most of the rest is mountainous. The lowland Terai region produces an agricultural surplus, part of which supplies the food-deficient hill areas.
Major food crops are rice, maize, wheat, barley and millet. The principal cash crops are sugar cane, soya beans, oilseeds, tobacco, potato and jute. Cattle, buffaloes, goats, sheep, pigs, yaks and poultry are also raised. River fish are an important source of protein.
Much of the agriculture is rain-fed and is carried out in the narrow strip of plains in the south along the border with India. Agricultural land is highly fragmented. Production is extremely vulnerable to adverse weather conditions, with little irrigation. Deforested plains and lower hilltops are terraced for rice production. Severe soil erosion is becoming a problem.
Nepal has removed all subsidies on fertilisers, which makes it difficult for Nepali produce to compete with highly subsidised Indian agro-products. There are some

transport subsidies for taking fertilisers to remote districts.

Crop production in 2005 included: 7,577,432 tonnes (t) cereals in total, 4,100,000t rice, 1,442,442t wheat, 1,716,042t maize, 1,738,840t potatoes, 289,838t millet, 265,655t pulses, 150,000t citrus fruit, 56,993t oilcrops, 3,016t tobacco, 17,661t jute, 94,000t ginger, 22.800 various herbs and spice, 2,376,103t sugar cane, 12,500t tea, 343t green coffee, 705,130t fruit in total, 1,891,238t vegetables in total. Livestock production included: 263,659t meat in total, 48,875t beef, 138,953t buffalo meat, 15,724t pig meat, 2,744t lamb, 41,698t goat meat, 15,665t poultry, 26,950t eggs, 1,352,428t milk, 4,680t cattle hides, 7,252t goatskins, 33,462t buffalo hides.

Forestry

Forests occupy around 33 per cent of Nepal's land area. The canopy cover in the mid-hills is growing thicker as a result of the government's successful policy of handing over forests to local communities. Deforestation is still high in the government-managed forests of the plains, coupled with timber that is smuggled into India.

Timber imports in 2004 were US$17.6 million, while exports amounted to US$9.5 million.

Timber production in 2004 included 13,961,765 cubic metre (cum) roundwood, 1,260,000cum industrial roundwood, 630,000cum sawnwood, 1,260,000cum sawlogs and veneer logs, 954,000t pulpwood, 30,000cum wood-based panels, 12,701,765cum woodfuel; 68,939t charcoal.

Industry and manufacturing

Industry accounts for around 21.7 per cent of GDP. The sector consists mainly of manufacturing low-end consumer goods – principally carpets, garments and handicrafts. The development of this sector is constrained by poor infrastructure, a small local market, high industrial factor costs and lack of access to the sea.

Nepal offers duty concessions on raw material imports and start-up tax holidays for new industry, but foreign direct investment flows have remained slow.

The end of the Multi-fibre Agreement in 2005 has had a devastating effect on the textile industry.

Tourism

Tourism is an important element in the economy, but has been badly affected in recent years by the global economic downturn, international terrorism, continuing civil war, the Sars outbreak and the tsunami of December 2004 (although Nepal was not directly affected, visitors to the whole region fell). In periods of calm, visitor numbers pick up, as shown in 2003 when arrivals increased by 23 per cent during a truce in the civil war and fell again after it ceased. The tsunami and continuing instability resulted in lower annual arrivals in 2005: 277,129 compared with 288,356 the previous year. Numbers were down in the earlier part of 2005, improving as the year wore on. Whereas there was a decline in tourists from the West, the number of Asian visitors increased.

Mount Everest is Nepal's greatest attraction.

Environment

The Sagarmatha (Mount Everest) Pollution Control Committee (SPCC), set up in 1991, spends US$15,000 cleaning up the Sagarmatha National Park every year. The government charges a minimum of US$50,000 for each expedition to Mount Everest, and ploughs back 30–40 per cent of this and other tourist fees to support the SPCC's work. Since the old trekking routes pose serious problems to the indigenous communities already, there are many opposing voices among the environmentalists in Kathmandu.

Mining

Mining and quarrying accounts for around 0.5 per cent of GDP.

Among the major known mineral reserves only limestone has been extracted for commercial use in considerable volumes. Nepal also has deposits of lead, zinc, marble, iron ore and magnesite.

Hydrocarbons

No economically extractable hydrocarbon reserves have been discovered in Nepal. The government has invited foreign companies to explore for oil. About 15,250 barrels per day of refined oil are imported.

Nepal does not import natural gas.

Nepal has a small coal industry with reserves of around two million tonnes. Annual output meets less than 5 per cent of domestic demand and about 531,000 tonnes of coal are imported

Energy

Nepal has an electricity generating capacity of 610MW, mostly supplied by hydropower, but around 10 per cent from thermal plants. Only one per cent of Nepal's energy needs is met by electricity. The hydropower potential is considerable, with estimated economically viable capacity of 43,000MW, which could supply a majority of the population, mostly rural, who lack access to lectricity. Annual demand for electricity continues to rise.

Wood fuel accounts for around 75 per cent of energy used, with agricultural waste providing most of the rest.

Banking and insurance

Central bank

Nepal Rastra Bank

Main financial centre

Kathmandu

Time

GMT plus five hours and forty-five minutes

Geography

Nepal is a landlocked, roughly rectangular country located south of the Himalayan mountain range. It is about 885km long (east to west) and an average non-uniform, north-south width of 193km. The country is divided into five development regions and 75 districts. Ecologically, Nepal is divided into three regions– mountain, hill and terai (plains). India borders Nepal in the east, south and west. China borders Nepal in the north. The topography is rugged and harsh and with a vertical distance of less than 200km, the altitude changes from sea level to the highest point on earth – the 8,848m Mount Everest.

Hemisphere

Northern

Climate

The climate is generally temperate but harsh and cold at high altitudes. The low-lying plains are hot in summer and warm during the winters. The high mountains are permanently covered with snow (above 4,800 metres). High temperatures range between 17–30 degrees Celsius (C) and lows are in the range of 0–17 C. May–September is the monsoon season; July is the wettest month and also the hottest.

Dress codes

If travelling outside Kathmandu, it is respectable and practical to wear casual trousers and full-sleeved shirts and jackets. Shorts may be acceptable only in urban centres.

Entry requirements

Passports

Required by all except nationals of India. Entry may be refused, and airlines may not carry passengers holding passports with less than six months validity.

Visa

Required by all, except nationals of India with a valid national ID card. Tourist visas are issued on arrival. Overnight visas are issued free of cost.

Business visas are only issued to those who have been officially recognised as either a) the official representative (of a commercial entity that has obtained a licence to invest in the Kingdom of Nepal in a business or industrial enterprise) or b) an individual who has obtained a licence to invest in Nepal in export trade. Applications for multiple-entry business visas (one or five years) need to be made in advance. Applications should be made to the Director General, Department of Immigration, Kathmandu (www.immi.gov.np). An authorisation from the relevant Nepalese ministry is needed, as are photocopies of the relevant pages of the visitor's passport. The applicant will be sent application forms which must be returned fully completed. If accepted, the visa will be stamped on the visitor's passport at Kathmandu airport.

The Nepal Tourism Board website (www.welcomenepal.com) provides updated information on changes in related policies and rules.

Currency advice/regulations
The import of local and Indian currency is prohibited. On arrival, all foreign currency must be declared, export is limited to the amount declared. Foreign currency exchange receipts must be retained as only 10 per cent of local currency will be reconverted on departure. Export of local currency is prohibited. Currency can be exchanged at banks or authorised foreign exchange dealers and at major hotels. Only Indian and Nepalese nationals may carry Indian currency; possession of Indian Rs500 bills is illegal in Nepal.

Travellers cheques are accepted in banks and large hotels.

Customs
Personal effects may be imported duty-free. Items such as cameras, laptop computers, portable music systems and 15 reels of film are permitted as long as they are re-exported.

Exports of antiques and religious artefacts must be certified and cleared by the Department of Archaeology. It is illegal to export goods which are over 100 years old, or endangered wildlife.

Prohibited imports
Narcotics, beef and beef products.

Firearms, ammunition and explosives, wireless radio transmitters and precious metals require special licences.

Health (for visitors)
Mandatory precautions
Vaccination certificate for yellow fever if travelling from an infected area.

Advisable precautions
Vaccinations that are necessary include: cholera, diphtheria, tetanus, hepatitis A, polio and typhoid. Vaccinations that may be advised include: hepatitis B, tuberculosis, Japanese B encephalitis and rabies.

Anti-malarial precautions should be taken; the use of mosquito nets and repellents and covering up the body after dark can help avoid malaria, hepatitis B and encephalitis.

Use only bottled or boiled water for drinks, washing teeth and making ice. Eat only well cooked meals, preferably served hot; vegetables should be cooked and fruit peeled; avoid dairy products. A first-aid kit, including disposable syringes, would be useful.

Full medical insurance including emergency repatriation is strongly recommended.

Hotels
Nepal has about 100 tourist-class hotels, ranging from up-market five-star deluxe to those with one-star ratings. Other accommodation includes over 750 non-star-rated, but affordable and safe, speciality establishments.

Hotels may be full during the tourist season and it is advisable to book in advance.

Payment is required in foreign currency.

Credit cards
All major credit and charge cards are accepted by banks, tourist hotels and shops. ATMs can be found in Kathmandu.

Public holidays (national)
Fixed dates
11 Jan (National Unity Day – cancelled in 2007), 29 Jan (Martyrs' Day), 19 Feb (National Democracy Day), 8 Mar (Women's Day), 14 Apr (Nepali New Year), 9 Nov (Constitution Day), 29 Dec (King Birendra's Birthday).

Variable dates
Vasant Panchami (Jan/Feb), Shivaratri (Feb/Mar), Ghode Jatra (Festival of Horses) (Mar), Holi (Mar), Chaite Dashain (Mar/Apr), Ram Nawami (Birthday of Lord Ram) (Mar/Apr), Lord Buddha's Birthday (Apr/May), Rakshya Bandhan (Janai Purnima) (Aug), Gai Jatra/Procession of Cows (Aug/Sep), Krishna Asthami (Birthday of Lord Krishna) (Aug/Sep), Teej (Festival of Women) (Sep), Dasain (Durga Puja Festival) (Oct), Diwali/Deepawali (Oct/Nov), Indra Jatra/Festival of Rain God (Oct/Nov).

In general, Hindu and Buddhist festivals are declared according to local astronomical observations.

Working hours
Banking
Sun–Thu: 1000–1500, Fri: 1000–1200; Kathmandu Valley, Mon–Fri: 0900–1530. Some banks open at weekends.

Business
Sun–Fri: 1000–1700; Kathmandu Valley, Mon–Fri: 0900–1700

Government
Mon–Fri: 0900–1700 (summer); Mon–Fri: 0900–1600 (winter, mid-Nov–mid-Feb).

Shops
Sun–Fri: 1000–1900 (some shops also open on Saturdays).

Telecommunications
Mobile/cell phones
GSM 900 and 1800 services are available in populated areas.

Weights and measures
Metric system (local measures are also used).

Social customs/useful tips
The traditional form of greeting is called namaste – performed by placing the palms together at chest height and bowing slightly; it means 'I celebrate the divinity in you'. Some Nepali women may prefer not to shake hands with a man. Always use the right hand to eat or pass anything on. Remove shoes before entering temples and homes.

Do not take photographs before asking permission.

Security
Internal terrorist activities have seen indiscriminate attacks in and around the capital as well as tourist areas, visitors are advised to exercise extra vigilance and also take care to respect any local curfews.

Getting there
Air
National airline: Royal Nepal Airlines (all flights must be paid for in hard currencies).

International airport/s: Kathmandu Tribhuwan International (KTM), 6km from the city. Facilities include bank, bureau de change, duty free, post office and tourist information.

Airport tax: Departure tax to regional neighbours (excluding China): NRs1,356; departure tax to all other destinations NRs1,695.

Surface
Road: There are many access routes from India and Tibet, however visitors must use official crossings, which are open 24 hours. Visitors driving their own vehicle must possess a international carnet.

Rail: There are two lines in India that run to the border of Nepal at Birgani/Sunauli and at Jaynagar, but neither cross the border.

Getting about
National transport
Air: The only way to reach many parts of Nepal is by air. Nepal has 44 domestic airports and 120 helicopter landing strips. Royal Nepal Airlines and private airline companies have flights to and from these airports. Special helicopter charters can also be arranged. Flights may be delayed during the rainy months; otherwise, they are an efficient means of getting around.

Road: There is a road network of over 13,000km. Kathmandu, Pokhara and Biratnagar are linked by surfaced road.

Transport is difficult outside main centres. The Mahendra Highway makes west Nepal accessible throughout the year. The mountainous nature of the country means that many of its roads are unusable, especially during the winter and the monsoon.
Buses: Long distance day or night bus services operate from Kathmandu to all cities of Nepal.
Rail: The only line serves Jaynagar to Janakpur and Bizalpura.

City transport

Taxis: Metered taxis can be hailed in Kathmandu. Private taxis are also available at the hotels, but they may cost more.
Buses, trams & metro: The airport bus to the city centre takes 35 minutes.

Car hire

Driving is on the left. An international driving permit is required. Local authorities also issue a local permit upon presentation of a national licence. Chauffeur-driven car hire is available.

BUSINESS DIRECTORY

The addresses listed below are a selection only. While World of Information makes every endeavour to check these addresses, we cannot guarantee that changes have not been made, especially to telephone numbers and area codes. We would welcome any corrections.

Telephone area codes

The international direct dialling (IDD) code for Nepal is +977, followed by area code and subscriber's number:

Bhairawa	71	Janakpur	41
Bhaktapur	1	Kathmandu	1
Birgunj	51	Nepalgunj	81
Biratnagar	21	Patan	1
Dhangadhi	91	Pokhara	61

Useful telephone numbers

Police: 100
Directory enquiries: 197

Chambers of Commerce

Federation of Nepalese Chambers of Commerce and Industry, Shahid Shukra FNCCI Milan Marg, Teku, Kathmandu (tel: 426-2061; fax: 426-2007; email: fncci@mos.com.np).

Nepal Britain Chamber of Commerce and Industry, British Embassy Premises, Lainchaur, PO Box 106, Kathmandu (tel: 441-0583; fax: 441-8137; email: info@nbcci.org).

Nepal Chamber of Commerce, Chamber Bhawan, Kantipath, PO Box 198, Kathmandu (tel: 422-2890; fax: 422-9998; email: chamber@wlink.com.np).

Nepal-US Chamber of Commerce and Industry, TNT Building, Tinkune, Koteshwor, PO Box 2769, Kathmandu (tel: 447-8020; fax: 447-4508; email: nusacci@vishnu.ccsl.com.np).

Banking

Agricultural Development Bank, Ramshahpath, Kathmandu (tel: 421-1744, 421-1802/3; fax: 422-5329).

Himalayan Bank Ltd, PO Box 20590, Karmachari Sanchaya Kosh Building, Tridevi Marg, Thamel, Kathmandu (tel: 422-7749, 425-0201; fax: 422-2800).

Nepal Arab Bank Ltd (Nabil Bank), PO Box 3729, Kantipath, Kathmandu (tel: 421-1784/6; fax: 422-6905).

Nepal Bangladesh Bank Ltd, PO Box 9062, Bijuli Bazar, Naya Baneshwor, Kathmandu (tel: 490-767/70; fax: 490-824, 493-259) .

Nepal Bank Ltd, Dharmapath, Kathmandu (tel: 422-1185, 422-4337; fax: 422-6905).

Nepal Grindlays Bank Ltd, PO Box 3990, Naya Baneswor, Kathmandu (tel: 421-2683/6; fax: 422-6762).

Nepal Indosuez Bank Ltd, PO BOx 3412, Durbar Marg, Kathmandu (tel: 422-8229; fax: 422-6349).

Rastriya Banijya Bank, Singha Durbar Plaza, Kathmandu (tel: 425-2595, 426-8409, 425-1982; fax: 425-2931).

Citibank, PO Box 2826, c/o Hotel Yak & Yeti, Durbar Marg, Kathmandu (tel: 422-8884; fax: 422-7884).

Standard Chartered Bank, PO Box 1526, Durbar, PO Box 1526, Durbar, Marg, Kathmandu (tel/fax: 422-0129).

Central bank

Nepal Rastra Bank, PO Box 73, Baluwatar, Kathmandu (tel: 422-1763; fax: 425-4170; e-mail: nrb@mos.com.np).

Travel information

Automobile Association of Nepal, c/o Traffic Police Office, Kathmandu (tel: 421-1093).

Everest Air, Durbar Marg, Kathmandu (tel: 422-4188; fax: 422-6795).

Himalayan Helicopters PVT Ltd, Durbar Marg, Kathmandu (tel: 421-7236; fax: 422-5150).

Kathmandu Tribhuvan International Airport, Air Traffic Controller, Gauchar (tel: 472-258 or 473-985, ext 486; fax: 474-180; e-mail: tiao@mod.com.mp).

Nepal Mountaineering Association, 16/53 Ramshah Path, PO Box 1435, Kathmandu (tel: 421-1596).

Royal Nepal Airlines, PO Box 401, RNAC Building, Kantipath, Kathmandu 711000 (tel: 421-4511; fax: 422-5348).

Tourist Information Centre, Basantpur, Kathmandu; Tribhuwan International Airport, Kathmandu (tel: 470-537).

Ministry of tourism

Ministry of Culture, Tourism and Civil Aviation, Bhrikutimandap, Kathmandu (tel: 425-6231/2, 425-6228; fax; 422-7281; email: tourism@mail.com.np).

National tourist organisation offices

Nepal Tourism Board, Tourist Service Centre, Bhrikutimandap, PO Bix 11018, Kathmandu (tel: 425-6909, 425-6229; fax: 425-6910; email: info@ntb.org.np; internet: www.welcomenepal.com).

Ministries

Ministry of Commerce, Babar Mahal, Kathmandu (tel: 223-489, 224-805; fax: 225-594).

Ministry of Finance, Hari Bhawan, Kathmandu (tel: 224-527, 227-367; fax: 227-529).

Ministry of Industry, Tripureshwor, Kathmandu (tel: 213-880, 213-838; fax: 226-112).

Ministry of Interior, Dept of Immigration, Bhrikutimandap, Kathmandu (tel: 422-3590, 422-1996; fax: 422-3127; email: deptimi@net.np; internet: www.immi.gov.np).

Office of the Prime Minister, Singh Durbar, Kathmandu (tel: 421-000; email: info@opmcm.gov.np).

Other useful addresses

British Embassy, Laimchaur, PO Box 106, Kathmandu (tel: 414-588, 410-583, 411-590, 411-281; fax: 411-789).

Department of Commerce, Kathmandu (tel: 422-7364, 422-7404).

Director General, Department of Immigration, Kathmandu (tel: 422-3681).

National Planning Commission, PO Box 1284, Singha Dubar, Kathmandu (tel: 421-5000).

Nepal Economic and Commerce Research Centre, PO Box 285, 7/358 Kohity Bahal, Kathmandu (tel: 421-5336).

Nepal Industrial Development Corporation (NIDC), NIDC Building, PO Box 10, Durba Marg, Kathmandu (tel: 411-211, 411-225).

Trade Promotion Centre, Kathmandu (tel: 524-771, 524-772; fax: 521-637).

Internet sites

Asian Sources Online: http://asiansources.com
Government of Nepal: www.nepalgov.np
Market information: www.feer.com
News portal: www.nepalnews.com
Nepalese tourism: www.visitnepal.com

The Netherlands

KEY FACTS

Official name: Koninkrijk der Nederlanden (The Kingdom of The Netherlands)

Head of State: Queen Beatrix (crowned 30 April 1980)

Head of government: Prime Minister Jan Peter Balkenende (CDA) (since 2002; re-elected Nov 2006)

Ruling party: Coalition government led by: Christen Democratisch Appèl (CDA) (Christian Democratic Appeal) Partij van de Arbeid (PvdA) (Labour Party) and ChristenUnie (CU) (Christian Union) (CDA since 2002; current coalition since 22 Nov 2006)

Area: 41,473 square km

Population: 16.62 million (2007)*

Capital: The Hague (seat of government); Amsterdam (legal and cultural)

Official language: Dutch and Frisian

Currency: Euro (eur) = 100 cents (from 1 Jan 2002; previous currency guilder, locked at f2.20 per euro)

Exchange rate: eur0.63 per US$ (Jul 2008)

GDP per capita: US$46,261 (2007)*

GDP real growth: 3.50% (2007)*

Labour force: 8.33 million (2004)

Unemployment: 3.20% (2007)*

Inflation: 1.60% (2005)

Balance of trade: US$46.95 billion (2005)

Foreign debt: US$1,699.39 billion (2004)

Visitor numbers: 10.74 million (2006)*

* estimated figure

In its extensive 2008 survey of the Dutch economy, the Paris based Organisation for Economic Co-operation and Development (OECD) noted that the recovery of the past years has been robust, helping to maintain Dutch GDP per capita in the OECD's top league. The very open Dutch economy has benefited from the supportive international environment and investors have continued to be attracted by its business-friendly environment. The country has also benefited from past structural reforms, notably reforms of pension systems, health care and disability benefits, which have contributed to putting public finances on a sounder footing and have encouraged labour market participation. Productivity growth, however, has remained sluggish, which may be partly due to the relatively high weight of traditional industries in the economy and a lack of innovation activity.

Labour utilisation has therefore contributed to growth more than in most other countries. So far, this has been made possible by the availability of under-utilised labour resources, but employers are running into increasing difficulties in hiring workers. This is largely because the working-age population has virtually stopped growing. Large groups of baby-boomers are reaching retirement age, a trend that will accelerate from 2010 onwards and persist for the following three decades. In addition, net migration flows have turned negative, as less foreign migrants are entering the country and more natives are leaving it, a rare occurrence in a high-income nation. Furthermore, the working week is getting shorter and there is a high incidence of part-time employment. If unaddressed, these hurdles will impose a constraint on growth in the medium-term. Hence, the present coalition government has decided to encourage labour market participation. The 2008 budget introduces several welcome measures in the tax-and-benefit system for this purpose. Nevertheless, more ambitious and broad-based reforms will be needed to keep growth on a strong trend in the medium-term.

The OECD survey goes on to note that the Dutch public finances are generally in a good condition. Following the breach of the 3 per cent limit in 2003, an impressive fiscal consolidation programme brought the budget successfully back into surplus in 2006. The fiscal stance was, however, eased somewhat in 2007 at a time when the economy was already running out of available capacity. The budget for 2008 showed an improvement in the structural balance, reflecting a projected rise in natural gas revenues. A gradual further improvement is planned for later years. Given the high uncertainty surrounding short-term prospects in the international economy, the authorities should be prepared to allow a flexible operation of automatic stabilisers. Over the medium-term, the challenge of ageing looms large, but less so than in other countries, thanks to the well-funded second pillar pension system. Since the last survey, the required consolidation for achieving fiscal sustainability has increased, reflecting both a re-assessment of future cost and revenue developments, and also an increase in life expectancy. A possible strategy to cope with the 'sustainability gap' would be to run large budgetary surpluses for a long period of time, but this is likely to prove politically challenging. An alternative strategy is the adoption of incentives to increase participation in the labour market, including at older ages, so as to widen the revenue basis. It would also be important to enact measures containing age-related spending.

According to the OECD, the Dutch labour market is functioning well, with employment and labour participation rates above OECD averages. Nevertheless, there are sizable pockets of under-activity, including social benefit recipients representing 17 per cent of the working-age population, which could be mobilised in order to address short-run labour shortages and the long-run ageing-related reductions in the labour supply. Reintegrating these benefit recipients would also help to reduce spending on labour market programmes, which is among the highest in the OECD. Policies should continue to tackle the high inactivity of these groups. For people on social assistance and older workers, job search requirements should be strengthened and the authorities should continue making the tax-benefit system more work-friendly. For women with low-earning capacities, existing work disincentives should be eliminated. For (partially) disabled people, it is important to envisage labour market re-integration at an early stage. For the long-term unemployed, policies should be further strengthened by adjusting the unemployment benefit and the employment protection systems, as well as further improving current profiling and training measures.

Immigration issues

A traditionally open and tolerant society known, among other things for keeping its curtains open at night so the neighbours could be impressed – and also for its 'coffee houses' selling hash and other recreational drugs – the country is now becoming increasingly illiberal. With the assassination of anti-immigration politician Pym Fortuyn in May 2002, and the murder of film-maker Theo van Gogh in late 2004, controversial political figures have started to watch their backs. The government is cracking down on immigration and the people are becoming more eurosceptic – they threw out the EU constitution in a referendum in June 2005.

Tolerance, rather than toleration has long been a part of the Dutch make-up. Since the Second World War The Netherlands has justifiably prided itself on its liberal, non-racist culture. However, as the economy flagged and jobs became harder to get, things changed. In February 2004 the Dutch parliament approved legislation providing for the expulsion of some 26,000 asylum seekers resident in The Netherlands. The move attracted a lot of popular support and just as much opposition from the asylum seekers – many of whom had been resident in The Netherlands for more than 5 years and in some cases for 10 years, while applying for residence. Under the legislation, all those asylum seekers who arrived before April 2001 were offered air tickets to their country of origin and given eight weeks in which to leave. Those who refused to leave risked facing a six-month jail sentence. By March 2005 nearly 5,000 refugees had left without being forced while 519 people had been deported. Opinion polls indicated more than 60 per cent support for an amnesty to be granted to all those asylum-seekers who have been living in The Netherlands for more than 5 years. Somewhat ironically, Dutch asylum applications have dropped by around 75 per cent since 2000. The anti-asylum legislation was something of a setback to The Netherlands' reputation for tolerance on social matters and risked establishing a pattern for the treatment of asylum seekers in other European countries.

KEY INDICATORS — The Netherlands

	Unit	2003	2004	2005	2006	2007
Population	m	16.20	16.36	16.31	16.35	*16.62
Gross domestic product (GDP)	US$bn	413.70	577.26	629.91	670.92	*768.70
GDP per capita	US$	31,883	35,416	38,618	41,046	*46,261
GDP real growth	%	-0.9	1.3	1.5	3.0	*3.5
Inflation	%	2.3	1.4	1.5	1.6	*1.6
Unemployment	%	3.7	4.8	4.7	3.9	*3.2
Natural gas output	bn cum	58.3	68.8	62.9	61.9	64.5
Exports (fob) (goods)	US$m	243,300.0	293,100.0	344,511.0	386,923.0	458,368.0
Imports (cif) (goods)	US$m	201,100.0	252,700.0	297,559.0	341,728.0	405,707.0
Balance of trade	US$m	42,200.0	40,400.0	46,952.0	45,195.0	52,679.0
Current account	US$m	15,120.0	19,400.0	39,986.0	55,874.0	50,931.0
Total reserves minus gold	US$m	11,012.0	10,102.0	9,124.0	10,802.0	10,270.0
Foreign exchange	US$m	7,180.0	6,657.0	1,192.0	9,327.0	8,749.0
Exchange rate	per US$	0.88	0.80	0.77	0.75	0.69

* estimated figure

Outlook

Having emerged from economic stagnation, things are improving for The Netherlands. The economy is highly dependent on a continued recovery in global trade and any sustained rise in the oil price will be bad news for The Netherlands.

Unemployment and the contentious immigration legislation both risk generating social unrest. Increasing participation in the workplace and increasing productivity and competitiveness are crucial tasks if economic growth is to be strong.

The Netherlands' most important trading partner is Germany. The Dutch economy was one of the few obvious beneficiaries of German unification in the early 1990s as Dutch exports to Germany increased dramatically. Over the years, its closeness to Germany and the importance of the German market has, to a degree, protected the Netherlands from the recessions which from time to time have beset the Anglo-Saxon economies. However, the reverse is also true and if the German economy falters, so will the Dutch.

Risk assessment

PoliticsGood

EconomyGood

Regional stabilityGood

COUNTRY PROFILE

Historical profile

1579 The Protestant majority in the Netherlands rebelled against the Catholic Habsburg Empire and declared independence, with William of Orange crowned Prince William I of Holland and Zeeland.

In the seventeenth century, the Netherlands became a powerful trading nation with an empire in the East Indies (modern day Indonesia) and the Caribbean. In the 1650s, the Dutch fought several wars against the English, mainly due to colonial rivalry.

1688 William of Orange (the grandson of William I) acceded to the English throne as William III, ending conflict between the two countries.

1704–06 The English army under John Churchill helped to defeat attempts by the combined armies of Austria and France to invade the Netherlands.

1804 The Netherlands was occupied by the French under Napoleon.

1812 The Netherlands was liberated by British and Prussian armies.

1815 A renewed invasion attempt by Napoleon was defeated at the Battle of Waterloo. Attempts to unify Catholic Belgium with the Netherlands at the Vienna Conference failed, and the two countries remained separate.

1914–18 The country remained neutral in the First World War.

1940–45 During the Second World War, the Netherlands was occupied by Germany despite its neutrality.

1949 The policy of neutrality was abandoned and the Netherlands became a founder member of NATO.

1958 The Netherlands was a founding member of the European Economic Community (EEC).

1980 Queen Juliana abdicated in favour of her eldest daughter Princess Beatrix. Prince Willem-Alexander became heir apparent.

1989 The Christen Democratisch Appèl (CDA) (Christian Democratic Appeal) and Volkspartij voor Vrijheid en Democratie (VVD) (People's Party for Freedom and Democracy) government fell in its second term when VVD refused to support Prime Minister Ruud Lubbers' proposal for a 20-year environmental protection programme. A centre-left cabinet was formed by CDA and the Partij van de Arbeid (PvdA) (Labour Party), with Lubbers still as leader.

1992–93 The government of Ruud Lubbers was discredited by a serious economic recession.

1994 Elections resulted in a three-party coalition, headed by Wim Kok (PvdA), and including VVD and Democraten 66 (D66) (Democrats 66). The CDA was frozen out of power for the first time since the First World War.

1998 The coalition government of PvdA, D66 and VVD, headed by Prime Minister Wim Kok, continued after winning an increased majority in elections.

1999 The Netherlands was a founder member of European Economic and Monetary Union (Emu). D66 threatened to leave the coalition after its proposals for constitutional reform were defeated in parliament, but a compromise was reached.

2000 Ruud Lubbers was chosen to head the UN High Commission on Refugees (UNHCR). After 25 years of debating, a bill to legalise euthanasia was approved.

2001 Prime Minister Wim Kok announced he would not seek re-election for a third term.

2002 The euro currency replaced the guilder. Pim Fortuyn, leader of the far-right, anti-immigration Lijst Pim Fortuyn (LPF) (List Pim Fortuyn) party, was shot dead during election campaigning. The CDA won parliamentary elections. Jan Peter Balkenende became prime minister, leading a fragile coalition government of CDA, LPF and VVD members. Two LPF ministers resigned and the cabinet collapsed; Balkenende resigned and a caretaker government took office. Prince Claus von Amsberg, husband of Queen Beatrix, died.

2003 After parliamentary elections, Prime Minister Balkenende was reinstated to head a coalition government, led by the CDA, and including the VVD and the D66.

2004 Former Queen Juliana (1948–80), died. Prominent filmmaker Theo van Gogh was murdered by an Islamist radical; tit-for-tat attacks on Dutch mosques and churches ensued.

2005 The Netherlands rejected the proposed constitution of the EU. Parliament introduced a test of the Dutch language and culture for would-be immigrants, while considering banning the wearing of the burqa in public.

2006 Prime Minister Balkenende resigned, following a row with D66 about immigration policies. Balkenende reformed its coalition government without the D66. In the Second Chamber parliamentary elections, the ruling CDA won 41 seats (out of 150). The SP increased its seats to 25. The new right-wing Partij voor de Vrijheid (PvdV) (Party for Freedom) won nine seats, while the LPF failed to win any.

2007 Negotiations began between Bonaire, Saba and St Eustatius and The Netherlands which will become city-states within the Kingdom of The Netherlands; the Netherlands Antilles will cease to exist as an entity. A coalition government was formed with the CDA, PvdV and Christen Unie (CU) (Christian Union), with Jan Peter Balkenende as prime minister. Relatives of victims of the Srebrenica massacre in Bosnia in 1995 filed a case against the UN and the Netherlands state, claiming negligence in allowing the massacre to take place; Bosnian-Serbs killed about 8,000 Muslims.

2008 A ban on tobacco smoking in public places was introduced on 1 July; no ban was introduced for smoking marijuana in designated coffee shops.

Political structure

Constitution

Under the constitution of 1983, The Netherlands is divided into 12 administrative provinces. Each province is run by a royal commissioner and an elected Provinciale Staten (regional parliamentary assembly). Each regional assembly elects its own governing executive (Gedeputeerde Staten) from among its members. Both council and executive are presided over by a royal commissioner, who is appointed by the crown.

The 672 municipalities, including the major cities, each have an elected council which in turn elects aldermen to sit on the municipal executive along with a mayor, who is appointed by the crown.

The constitution guarantees equality and freedom from discrimination on the

grounds of religion, political opinion, race, or sex. The constitution is unique in placing upon the government a duty to promote environmental protection both domestically and internationally.
Where there is no adult successor to the throne or the serving monarch is unable to exercise royal prerogative, the national legislature has the power to appoint a temporary regent.
The Kingdom of the Netherlands also includes overseas territories in the Caribbean – Aruba (which has been a separate entity since 1986) and the Netherlands Antilles (Bonaire and Curaçao). Aruba is unlikely to proceed to independence in the foreseeable future and will therefore remain a member of the Dutch Commonwealth.

Form of state
Parliamentary democratic monarchy

The executive
The monarch is the head of state but has few executive powers. However it does become actively involved in resolving political crises (for example, at times when no agreement could be reached on the formation of a cabinet). The monarch has the power to appoint the prime minister (on the recommendation of the national assembly), to dissolve the national assembly and call new elections.
The principle executive functions are carried out by the prime minister, who is selected by the national assembly and appoints a council of ministers from both inside and outside the assembly. State ministers are not allowed to continue to sit as members of parliament.

National legislature
Legislative power is vested in the Staten Generaal (States General), a bicameral national assembly.
The 150-member Tweede Kamer (Second Chamber or lower house), is directly elected by the d'Hondt system of proportional representation (a system invented in The Netherlands which takes account of the country's provincial units) for a four-year term. It is empowered to review the actions of the cabinet, debate bills and pass approved measures to the Eerste Kamer (First Chamber or upper house), for enactment.
The First Chamber has 75 members who are indirectly elected by the 12 provincial concils, for a period of four years. The First Chamber does not initiate legislation, but is responsible for approving or rejecting bills presented by the Second Chamber. The First Chamber cannot amend legislation directly, but acts which it rejects are likely to be amended in the Second Chamber and represented for approval.

Legal system
The Supreme Court is the highest legal body in the country and it hears appeals arising from cases previously heard in the lower courts. It also has the power of cassation over legislation deemed to conflict with the constitution.
There are five Appeal Courts at lower levels. Most cases are heard either at the 19 Provincial Courts of Justice or at the 62 Municipal Courts. Judges are nominated by the crown and serve for life.

Last elections
22 November 2006 (Second Chamber).
Results: Parliamentary (Second Chamber): the ruling CDA won 26.6 per cent of the vote (41 seats out of 150) the Partij van de Arbeid (PvdA) (Labour Party) 21.2 per cent (33); Socialistische Partij (SP) (Socialist Party) 16.6 per cent (25); Partij voor de Vrijheid (PvdV) (Party for Freedom) 5.9 per cent (nine); VVD14.6 per cent (22); Groen Links (GL) (Green Left) 4.6 per cent (seven); Christen Unie (CU) (Christian Union) 4 per cent (six); Democraten 66 (D66) (Democrats 66) 2 per cent (three). Turnout was 80.1 per cent.
First Chamber (membership is by appointment only): CDA (23 seats); PvdA (19 seats); VVD (15 seats); SP (four seats); LPF (one seat); GL (five seats); D66 (three seats); CU (two seats); SGP (two seats); Onafhankelijke Senaatsfractie-Fryske Nasjonale Partij (FNP) (Frisian National Party) (one seat).

Next elections
2007 (parliamentary)

Political parties

Ruling party
Coalition government led by: Christen Democratisch Appèl (CDA) (Christian Democratic Appeal) Partij van de Arbeid (PvdA) (Labour Party) and ChristenUnie (CU) (Christian Union) (CDA since 2002; current coalition since 22 Nov 2006)

Main opposition party
With multiply parties in parliament no one party is an official opposition party.

Population
16.62 million (2007)*
Last census: January 2002: 16,105,285
Population density: 469 inhabitants per square kilometre. Urban population: 90 per cent.
Annual growth rate: 0.5 per cent 1994–2004 (WHO 2006)

Ethnic make-up
Dutch (96 per cent); others, predominantly Afro-Caribbean (Surinamese), Indonesian, Moroccan and Turkish (4 per cent).

Religions
Catholic (34 per cent), Protestant (28 per cent), Muslim (3 per cent), Jewish (1 per cent).

Education
Primary schooling may begin at aged four, and continue until aged 12. At aged 12, pupils are channelled into secondary schools with courses designed for their aptitude. The length of time in these schools varies dependent on the courses undertaken; mixed general and vocational courses last for four years and pre-university courses last six years.
Schools are either publicly maintained by government, state or municipal authorities, (attended by 28 per cent of children), or private schools, mostly denominational (attended by 72 per cent of children).
Total public expenditure on education is equivalent to approximately 5 per cent of annual GNP.
Compulsory years: 5 to 16.
Enrolment rate: 109 per cent and 106 per cent, male and female gross enrolment rates respectively, of relevant age groups for primary schools, (including repeaters); 126 per cent and 122 per cent, male and female gross enrolment rates respectively, of relevant age groups for secondary schools, (including repeaters), 1997–2000 (Unicef 2004).
Pupils per teacher: 14 in primary schools.

Health
Per capita total expenditure on health (2003) was US$2,987; of which per capita government spending was US$1,863, at the international dollar rate, (WHO 2006).
The private sector is important in the supply of healthcare in the Netherlands and private health insurance is compulsory for most wage earners.

HIV/Aids
HIV prevalence: 0.2 per cent aged 15–49 in 2003 (World Bank)
Life expectancy: 79 years, 2004 (WHO 2006)
Fertility rate/Maternal mortality rate: 1.7 births per woman, 2004 (WHO 2006); maternal mortality 7 per 100,000 live births (World Bank).
Child (under 5 years) mortality rate (per 1,000): 4.8 deaths per 1,000 live births (World Bank)
Head of population per physician: 3.15 physicians per 1,000 people, 2003 (WHO 2006)

Welfare
The Netherlands provides generous income support linked to the minimum wage. However, following a government drive to limit the growth of social security spending, the criteria for eligibility for benefits has been narrowed and earnings-related benefits have been reduced from 80 to 70 per cent of previous income.
As in many EU countries, the ageing population is threatening to make the funding of state pensions an unsustainable burden on public finances over the next 30 years.

In 2000, expenditure on pensions was some 5.7 per cent of GDP, but this is projected to rise to the equivalent of 8.4 per cent by 2020 and 11.2 per cent by 2030.

Main cities

Amsterdam (cultural capital, estimated population 740,094 in 2005), Rotterdam (603,139), The Hague (seat of government, 471,677), Utrecht (269,853), Eindhoven (208,706), Tilburg (201,573), Groningen (179,048), Almere (185,622), Breda (167,354), Nijmegen (158,347).

Languages spoken

English, German and French are widely spoken. About 2.9 per cent of the population speak Frisian, mostly in the province of Friesland in the north-east. Turkish and Arabic are also spoken.

Official language/s

Dutch and Frisian

Media

Other news agencies: ANP (Netherlands National News Agency): www.anp.nl

Press

A free press is guaranteed under the constitution

Dailies: There are around 50 daily newspapers. Leading national dailies include De Telegraaf (www.telegraaf.nl), NRC Handelsblad (www.nrc.nl), Metro (www.metronieuws.nl) (tabloid), Nederlands Dagblad, Trouw (www.trouw.nl), Algemeen Dagblad (www.ad.nl), De Volkskrant (www.volkskrant.nl), Het Parool (www.parool.nl) (tabloid).

Weeklies: A number of daily newspapers publish weekend editions including De Telegraaf Weekeinde, NRC Handelsblad and De Volkskrant. Magazines include Vrij Nederland (www.vn.nl) for general news; in English a newsletter Dutch News (www.dutchnews.nl) is published online, with political and general news.

Business: In Dutch, (with some online English translations), publications include the daily Het Financieele Dagblad (www.fd.nl), periodicals include Intermediair (www.intermediair.nl), with the biggest circulation figure Management Team (www.mt.nl), (fortnightly) is a major publication, Elseviers Weekblad (www.elsevier.nl) (weekly), Bizz (www.bizz.nl) (monthly) and De Zaak (www.dezaak.nl) (fortnightly); Ondernemen (www.mkb.nl) (monthly) for entrepreneurs and Beleggers Belangen (www.beleggersbelangen.nl) for investors.

Periodicals: Official government publications are provided by Overheid (www.overheid.nl) the state-owned press.

Broadcasting

Domestic, public broadcasting allocates broadcasting time by proportional representation. Programmes can be made by any group, political, religious or civil and airtime is allocated based on the number of member they have.

The Netherlands has the largest take-up of cable television and consequently viewers have access to an ample range of domestic and foreign channels. The Netherlands Public Broadcasting (Omroep) operates three national TV channels and seven radio stations plus a website (http://portal.omroep.nl) with video access.

Radio: In addition to the seven national channels including an external service (Radio Netherlands, in several languages, www.radionetherlands.nl), and special interest radio, there are 10 regional stations and approximately 180 local channels. There are over 3,000 local and regional commercial radio stations catering for all styles of music and information, some of the largest include Sky Radio (www.skyradio.nl) with continuous music, Radio 538 (www.radio538.nl). BNR Nieuwsradio (www.bnr.nl) is a business radio station (in Dutch).

Television: All analogue TV broadcasting was discontinued in December 2006; broadcasts are now digital and by 2008 between 80–85 per cent of all transmissions will be in high definition (HD). Omroep operates channels Netherlands 1, 2 and 3 (Ned 1, 2, 3) and the children's channel ZapTV; each province has at least one local channel. BVN (www.bvn.nl) broadcasts an external service worldwide.

TV programmes are broadcast in their original languages – often English – with Dutch subtitles.

Advertising

The Ministry of Education, Culture and Science oversees all compliance with the Advertising Code. The Media Authority supervises compliance in the broadcast medium. Information and advice for advertisers are given online (www.aeforum.org).

Advertising is accepted in all forms of media, although TV and radio advertising is restricted to 12 minutes per hour.

Economy

In 2005 the Dutch economy improved with GDP growth at 1.5 and was estimated at 2.6 per cent in 2006 with private consumption and investment providing the drive. Inflation remained low at 1.5 per cent in 2005, due in large part to agreed wage restraint and is estimated to remain at this rate for 2006. Growth in exports slowed to an estimated 6.8 per cent in 2005, down from a rate of 9.8 per cent in 2004, but is expected to remain above 5 per cent through 2006–07.

The country's currency was converted to the euro in 2001 and the economy experienced a rough ride as the guilder, it was later realised, was undervalued when it was converted. With the low euro-zone exchange rate – set elsewhere and without regard for Dutch needs to curb spending – property speculation and rising inflation ensued. The economy began a cycle of boom and bust as unemployment jumped from 3.3 per cent in 2001 to 6.7 per cent by 2005 and the government was forced to introduce austerity measures to bring the economy back into solvency.

The Netherlands has a well-developed economy increasingly based on high technology industries and services, especially in international transport and shipping. The service sector accounts for over 70 per cent of GDP, and combined with its mercantile sector provides over 60 per cent of all exports. The industrial sector provides around 25 per cent of GDP, based largely on oil refining, chemical, and food processing and the steel industry. Agriculture and the fisheries sector provide around 2 per cent of GDP.

The Netherlands produces only a small quantity of crude oil, but is a relatively large producer and supplier of natural gas. Current gas production is about 75 billion cubic metres, around half of which is exported to other EU member countries.

External trade

As a member of the European Union, The Netherlands operates within a communitywide free trade union, with tariffs sets as a whole. Internationally, the EU has free trade agreements with a number of nations and trading blocs worldwide.

The economy it open to foreign trade with 60 per cent of agricultural produce exported, and the majority of foreign earnings provided by services including international transport and distribution, banking and insurance. Industrial production includes processed foods, petrochemicals and plastics, machinery and vehicle assembly.

Imports

Main imports include machinery and vehicles, chemicals, fuels, consumer goods, foodstuffs and clothing.

Main sources: Germany (18.1 per cent total, 2006), Belgium (10.3 per cent), US (8.8 per cent).

Exports

Major exports include petroleum and natural gas, organic chemicals, agricultural products and foodstuffs, machinery, electronics and vehicles.

Main destinations: Germany (24.2 per cent total, 2006), Belgium (11.9 per cent), UK (8.6 per cent).

Agriculture

Farming

The agricultural sector employs 4 per cent of the workforce and contributes 3 per cent to annual GDP, accounting for 25 per cent of total exports.

Despite high population density in the Netherlands, approximately 70 per cent of all land area is under cultivation. Population growth and wider commercial land use, combined with rising water levels, are placing considerable pressure on land resources.

Overall, Dutch farms tend to be larger than those in other EU member states, with only 25 per cent of farms smaller than five hectares, compared to an EU norm of 50 per cent. Productivity rates are consequently higher than the EU average, and the Netherlands is a net contributor to the EU's Common Agricultural Policy (CAP) budget.

Fundamental reform to the CAP was introduced throughout most of the EU on 1 January 2005. The subsidies paid on farm output, which tended to benefit large farms and encourage overproduction, were replaced by single farm payments not conditional on production. This is expected to reward farms that provide and maintain a healthy environment, food safety and animal welfare standards. The changes are also intended to encourage market conscious production and cut the cost of CAP to the EU taxpayer. The Netherlands is due to introduce this measure on 1 January 2006.

Dutch farmers are the world's most prolific consumers of pesticides, using 19,000 tonnes of active chemical ingredients per annum (an average 10 kilograms per hectare), with potatoes and flower bulbs the most intensively sprayed crops. Environmental legislation, which came into force in 2000, is designed to halve the level of chemical usage and some particularly damaging pesticides have been banned altogether.

Given the Netherlands' small surface area and high population density, farming is generally highly concentrated, specialised and efficient. Dairy farming is the most substantial activity, involving over a third of the country's farmers.

Traditional Dutch horticulture, in particular the production of flowers and bulbs, is the highest value-added sector. The Netherlands typically has over 24,000 hectares (ha) of land dedicated to open floriculture, and a further 7,000ha of floriculture under glass.

The crop production in 2005 included: 1,853,300 metric tonnes (t) cereals in total, 1,253,000t wheat, 6,835,985t potatoes, 337,800t barley, 215,000t maize, 18,500t pulses, 645,000t tomatoes, 6,750,000t sugar beets, 436,000t apples, 695,000t fruit in total, 3,831,000t vegetables in total. Livestock production included: 2,350,270t meat in total, 388,000t beef, 1,299,000t pig meat, 16,000t lamb, 646,000t poultry, 595,000t eggs, 10,531,800t milk, 41,500t cattle hides, 3,150t sheepskins, 2,700t greasy wool.

Fishing

The typical Dutch fish catch is over 500,000 tonnes per annum, of which approximately 450,000mt is seafood.

Around 20 per cent of the fish catch is exported, generating annual revenues of approximately US$250 million.

In 2004, the total marine fish catch was 500,755 tonnes and the total crustacean catch was 15,883 tonnes.

Forestry

Total forest area is 339,000 hectares (ha) or approximately 10 per cent of total land area. Almost all timber needs are imported, but The Netherlands is a major re-exporter of forest products.

Timber imports in 2004 were US$5.4 million, while exports amounted to US$3.4 million.

Timber production in 2004 included 1,026,000 cubic metre (cum) roundwood, 736,000cum industrial roundwood, 273,000cum sawnwood, 393,000cum sawlogs and veneer logs, 188,000t pulpwood, 8,000cum wood-based panels, 290,000cum woodfuel; 10,000 tonnes (t) charcoal, 3,459,000t paper and paperboard, (including 422,000t newsprint), 962,000t printing and writing paper, 119,000t paper pulp, 2,380,000t recovered paper.

Industry and manufacturing

The Netherlands has a broad industrial base. In 2004, manufacturing contributed 36 per cent to GDP and employ over 20 per cent of the labour force. Due to the small home market, Dutch industry is heavily dependent on foreign trade. It is also reliant upon imports of raw materials as industrial inputs.

As in most Western European countries, the industrial sector is increasingly focussed on high value-added manufacturing, where technological and skills advantages counteract the lower labour and production costs in emerging industrial economies. The Netherlands' lack of natural resources has increased its dependency on its manufacturing sector and imported materials.

Owing to rapid growth and the need for efficient land use, the construction industry is also significant and often pioneering in the field of space-saving design work.

Manufacturing accounts for 15.1 per cent of GDP and construction for a further 5.2 per cent.

Industrial production growth for the Netherlands was estimated at 0.8 per cent for 2004.

Tourism

The growing tourism sector was affected in 2001 by foot-and-mouth disease, which restricted movements to some extent, followed by the 11 September terrorist attacks in the US, as a result of which tourist arrivals began to decline. In 2002 and 2003, large areas were closed due to an outbreak of fowl pest, while the introduction of the euro led to increased prices. The Iraq war and the flu-like Sars outbreak added to the sector's woes. In addition to falling arrival numbers from the US and Japan, tourism from Germany, the largest market, also declined. In June 2004, the Dutch Tourism Board began an aggressive marketing campaign to revitalise the country's tourism sector.

Hydrocarbons

The hydrocarbons sector accounts for approximately 9 per cent of GDP and employs 4 per cent of the workforce.

Onshore deposits of oil were first discovered in the late 1930s near The Hague, but attention shifted in the 1940s to better deposits in the Schoonebeek region. It was in the nearby port of Rotterdam that the Dutch oil industry came to be based.

Offshore oil, by comparison, is a relatively recent discovery. The Netherlands produces around 28 per cent of its oil needs domestically, with almost 70 per cent of production coming from offshore deposits. However, average oil production in the Netherlands has fallen over recent years as a result of diminishing reserves in a number of oil fields in the Dutch sector of the North Sea. In 2003, total reserves stood at around 106 million barrels; consumption was 951,000 barrels per day (bpd) in 2002.

The largest onshore gas field is at Groningen, first discovered in the 1960s. This was the main source of gas until the discovery of offshore deposits. Natural gas reserves are around 1.77 trillion cubic metres (62.5 trillion cubic feet). Although it is expected that gas reserves will be depleted by 2030, the rate of new discoveries is sufficiently high that Dutch gas production is expected to continue beyond that time. Reserves were estimated to have dropped by 18 trillion cubic feet in 2002. Total natural gas production decreased by 2.9 per cent in 2002, with offshore production falling by 7.8 per cent. The Netherlands is a substantial net exporter of gas, importing only 8 per cent of total supplies and exporting approximately 48 per cent of domestic production.

The Netherlands has estimated coal reserves of 500 million tonnes, but poor deposit quality, high labour costs and falling demand made extraction unprofitable and the last coal pit was closed in 1970. Approximately 25 million short tonnes of coal are imported annually, of which over 90 per cent is consumed by Dutch thermal power stations.

Energy
The Netherlands has an electricity capacity of 20 million kilowatts (KW). Natural gas provides over 50 per cent of electric power needs and oil around 20 per cent. Nuclear power supplies around 4.5 per cent and the remainder by other material such as coal. The long-term emphases is on developing sustainable energy sources such as solar and wind power.
There is one nuclear power station in operation however development of nuclear power has been slow owing to popular opposition. Attempts to force the reactor to close early have been abandoned but the reactor is still anticipated to close at the end of its licensed period. There has been discussion about building a new reactor but without any determination in the near future.

Financial markets
Stock exchange
The Amsterdam Exchanges (AEX) are part of Euronext, an integrated cross-border single currency stock, derivatives and commodities market composed of the Brussels, Paris and Amsterdam exchanges. The merged exchange has four indices, Euronext 100 and Next 150, blue chip indices of the top 250 stocks, Next Economy, which lists high technology stocks, and M Prime, the largest index, which is for the remaining stocks in traditional sectors. These indices will not initially supplant Amsterdam's own AEX-25 blue-chip, Estar (high technology), Midkap (other stocks) and AAX (all-share) indices.
Euronext is the largest European exchange in terms of cash trading volume and is the second-largest exchange in Europe in terms of the number and total market capitalisation.

Banking and insurance
Banking supervision remains the responsibility of De Nederlandsche Bank (DNB). The oversight of currency transactions was in the hands of DNB until 2002, when it was assumed by the European Central Bank (ECB). Foreign banks operating in the Netherlands face no special restrictions.
The Dutch banking sector is dominated by three banking conglomerates, ABN Amro, ING Bank and Rabobank Nederland, which together control approximately 75 per cent of total domestic lending. Including Bank Nederlandse Gemeeten and the joint Belgian/Dutch banking group Fortis, these banks are estimated to hold almost 90 per cent of domestic banking assets, loans and deposits.
In 1995, ING bought Britain's Baring Bank for £1 when Baring was on the verge of collapse after the activities of employee and 'rogue trader' Nick Leeson. ING sold at a profit its remaining Baring division in November 2004.

Central bank
De Nederlandsche Bank (DNB); European Central Bank (ECB).

Main financial centre
Amsterdam

Time
GMT plus one hour (daylight saving, late March to late October, GMT plus two hours)

Geography
The Netherlands is situated in Western Europe, bordered to the east by Germany and to the south by Belgium. The North Sea lies to the north and west, giving the country a coastline of over 450km.
Except for small areas in the east of the country, the Netherlands' topography is dominated by river plains and flatlands which provide excellent growing conditions for agriculture. The major rivers are the Neder-Rijn and the Waal.
More than a third of the country is below sea level and made up of polder, land reclaimed from the sea by the construction of successive sea-walls over the years, but especially since the 1930s.
In the south-west of the country, the major cities of Amsterdam, Rotterdam, The Hague and Utrecht form a heavily urbanised area known as the Randstad or ring city. The flat character of the land, population density and intensive land use have heightened awareness of environmental issues such as air, soil and water pollution and the threat of rising sea levels caused by global warming.

Hemisphere
Northern

Climate
The country has an equitable north European climate, with warm though often damp summers and occasionally severe winters. Average temperatures peak in July and August at around 17 degrees Celsius (C), but manage barely 2 degrees C in January and February before picking up sharply in April and May. Rainfall is heaviest in March and April, when on average 76mm and 81mm respectively are recorded. July and August, by comparison, are the driest months with 41mm and 43mm of rainfall respectively.

Dress codes
Formal dress is usual for business; otherwise, no special restrictions apply. Warm clothing is recommended in winter, especially in coastal regions.

Entry requirements
Passports
Required by all, except nationals of countries which are signatories of the Schengen Accords, which includes most EU/EEA member states, who may visit on national IDs.

Visa
Required by all, except nationals of EU and Schengen Accord signatory countries; North America, Australasia and Japan. For further exceptions contact the nearest consulate. Schengen visas cover all entry needs; for business trips, an original invitation from a business contact in The Netherlands is necessary when applying. A Schengen visa application (offered in several languages) can be downloaded from http://europa.eu/abc/travel/ see 'documents you will need'.

Currency advice/regulations
There are no restrictions on the import or export of local and foreign currencies. Travellers' cheques are widely accepted.

Customs
Personal items are duty-free. There are no duties levied on alcohol and tobacco between EU member states, providing amounts imported are for personal consumption.

Prohibited imports
Illegal drugs and firearms

Health (for visitors)
Nationals of the European Economic Area (EEA) countries and Switzerland can access reduced cost and sometimes free medical treatment using a European Health Insurance Card (EHIC) while visiting the EEA. Exceptions include nationals of the 10 countries, which joined the EU in 2004, whose EHIC is not valid in Switzerland. Applications for the EHIC should be made before travelling.

Hotels
Classified from one- to five-star by Netherlands Board of Tourism, the Royal Dutch Touring Club and the Royal Netherlands Automobile Club. Accommodation may be booked through the Netherlands Reservation Centre in Leidschendam (tel: (070) 202-500). It is advisable to book well in advance during spring and summer. Foreign nationals must present passports before booking in, and are automatically registered with local police.

Credit cards
All major credit cards are accepted.

Public holidays (national)
Fixed dates
1 Jan (New Year's Day), 30 Apr (Queen's Day), 4 May (Remembrance Day), 5 May (Liberation Day), 25–26 Dec (Christmas). Holidays that fall on the weekend are not taken in lieu.

Variable dates
Easter Monday (Mar/Apr), Whitsun (May/Jun), Ascension Day (Aug).

Working hours
Banking
Mon–Fri: 0900–1600, some open Sat and on late shopping evenings.
Business
Mon–Fri: 0830–1730.
Government
Mon–Fri: 0830–1700.
Shops
0830/0900–1730/1800 (half-day closing usually Mon or Wed). Main shops open Sat and Thu/Fri evening.

Telecommunications
Mobile/cell phones
There is comprehensive GSM coverage throughout the country

Electricity supply
220V AC.

Social customs/useful tips
Appointments are necessary and business cards are exchanged, although the business climate is less formal than in some Western European countries and cordiality and consensus at business meetings are highly valued. The best months for business visits are considered to be March to May and September to November. When invited to a meal in a Dutch home it is usual to bring flowers or a small gift.

Security
There are no special problems with security in the Netherlands, although increased caution against petty theft is advised in the heavily populated areas of Rotterdam and Amsterdam.

Getting there
Air
National airline: KLM (Koninklijke Luchtvaart Maatschappij – Royal Dutch Airlines)
Air France acquired KLM in 2004.
International airport/s: Amsterdam Schiphol (AMS), 15km south-west of city; facilities include restaurants, duty-free shops, banks, showers, a business centre, conference rooms and car hire. There are regular, scheduled train and bus routes into the city, travel time 15–30 minutes. Taxis are numerous.
A direct, express train connects Schiphol with main cities in Holland, and some cities in Belgium.
A limited range of international flight destinations also originate from Eindhoven (EIN), 8km north of city; Maastricht (MST), 7km from city; Rotterdam (RTM), 8km north-west of city.
Airport tax: None
Surface
Road: Major routes from the rest of Europe are by a good network of motorways, well signposted with green 'E' symbols, indicating international highways.
Water: There are good connections between all major European ports. Boat trains operate to the Hook of Holland from many European countries.
The Netherlands is a leading international maritime shipper with extensive port facilities.
Main port/s: Ferries berth at Vlissingen, Rotterdam and Hook of Holland (Hoek van Holland).

Getting about
National transport
Air: Groningen (GRQ) in the north has connecting flights to the international airports. Den Helder (DHR), in the west is one of the largest heliports in Europe providing access to offshore oil and gas fields; charter planes are also available. Other internal services link Amsterdam, Eindhoven, Rotterdam and Maastricht.
Road: Roadways include high speed expressways, limited access motorways, dual highways and secondary roads. All roads are well signposted with red 'A's indicating national highways, and smaller routes indicated by yellow 'N's.
Buses: Most bus services run between 0600–2330. The Interliner is a service used for longer distances and has very few stops. The Connexxion bus company serves the major part of Holland including the provinces of Noord and Zuid Holland, Gelderland, Overijssel and Zeeland.
Rail: There is an hourly service, running 24 hours, between Utrecht, Amsterdam, Schiphol, The Hague and Rotterdam. The Netherlands Railways operate an Intercity (IC) network connecting large cities. IC trains only stop at the major stations. Local trains provide transportation to smaller cities. Tickets can be purchased from railway stations prior to travelling.
Water: There is an extensive network of inland waterways. Scheduled boat services operate from Enkhuizen to Urk and Staveren and between the mainland and the islands in the north.
City transport
The country is divided into zones with set tariffs. A strippenkaart, containing 15 strip tickets, is valid throughout the country for travel on buses, trams and subways, including trips within cities. To travel within one zone costs two strips. An extra strip is charged for each subsequent zone. A time limit, notated on the back of the card, allows interchange with other transport systems within the same zone.
Taxis: Taxis have blue licence plates with black letters and figures. Taxis can be booked in advance or, in some larger cities, hailed on the street. Prices may vary between regions and are sometimes open to negotiation.
A treintaxi (train-taxi) is a publicly shared taxi, offering shared costs.
Buses, trams & metro: Amsterdam has an intergrated public transport service that runs between 0600–0030 daily throughout the city; night buses run between 0030– 0730. Tickets (strippenkaart) can be purchased from a tobacconist, post office or railway station. They should be franked when boarding, for each trip. Elsewhere, city buses run within the boundaries of larger towns. A metro runs in Rotterdam, as well as trams, which also run in The Hague. They typically run between 0600–0000. The metro and trams are usually faster than city buses.
Trains: The train to the city centre from Schiphol is an efficient mode of transport. Inter-city train tickets are not interchangeable with local passenger services.
Ferry: There are ferries running on the canals of Amsterdam and Rotterdam, although these services are more for tourist purposes than for convenience.
Car hire
Car hire is widely available, the minimum age is dependent on insurance usually 21 years. An international driving license is necessary for all non-EU drivers. Traffic drives on the right. Speed limits: urban areas 50kph, normal roads 80kph, motorways 120kph. The wearing of seat belts is compulsory. It is illegal to use a handheld mobile phone while driving (including times when vehicle is stationary in traffic). Do not ignore parking fees as failure can result in a fine and if not paid within 24 hours, the car will be towed away when the cost of retrieval becomes very high.

BUSINESS DIRECTORY
The addresses listed below are a selection only. While World of Information makes every endeavour to check these addresses, we cannot guarantee that changes have not been made, especially to telephone numbers and area codes. We would welcome any corrections.

Telephone area codes
The international direct dialling (IDD) code for The Netherlands is +31, followed by area code and subscriber's number:

Amersfoort	33	The Hague	70
Amsterdam	20	Leiden	71
Breda	76	Rotterdam	10
Eindhoven	40	Tiel	344
Haarlem	23	Utrecht	30

Useful telephone numbers
Directory enquiries: 068-008 (national), 060-418 (international)
Operator: 060-410
Police/fire: 0611

National public transport information service: 0900-9292

Chambers of Commerce

American Chamber of Commerce in The Netherlands, 58 Scheveningseweg, 2517 KW The Hague (tel: 365-9808; fax: 364-6992; email: office@amcham.nl).

Amsterdam Chamber of Commerce, 5 De Ruyterkade, 1013AA Amsterdam (tel: 531-4000; fax: 531-4799; email: post@amsterdam.kvk.nl).

Arnhem Chamber of Commerce, 525 Kronenburginsel, 6800 KZ Arnhem (tel: 353-8888; fax: 353-8999; email: info@arnhem.kvk.nl).

British-Netherlands Chamber of Commerce, Oxford House, 328L Nieuwezijds Voorburgwal, 1012 RW Amsterdam (tel: 421-7040; fax: 421-7003; email: info@nbcc.co.uk).

Maastricht Chamber of Commerce, 5 Pierre de Coubertinweg, 6225 XT Maastricht (tel: 350-6666; fax; 350-6660; email: info@maastricht.kvk.nl).

Netherlands Federation of Chambers of Commerce, 1 Watermolenlaan, 3440 AG Woerden (tel: 426-911; fax: 426-216; email: site@vvk.kvk.nl).

Rotterdam Chamber of Commerce, 40 Blaak, 3000 AL Rotterdam (tel: 402-7777; fax: 414-5754; email: dvergeer@rotterdam.kvk.nl).

The Hague Chamber of Commerce, 30 Koningskade, 2502 LS The Hague (tel: 328-7100; fax: 326-2010; email: info@denhaag.kvk.nl).

Tilburg Chamber of Commerce, 1 Reitseplein, 5000 LG Tilburg, (tel: 594-4122; fax: 468-6215; email: info@tilburg.kvk.nl).

Utrecht Chamber of Commerce, 50 Kroonstraat, 3500 AA Utrecht (tel: 326-3211; fax: 231-2804; email: servicecenter@utrecht.kvk.nl).

Zwolle Chamber of Commerce, 1 Govert Flinckstrasse, 8021 ET Zwolle (tel: 455-3800; fax: 453-7424; email: info@zwolle.kvk.nl).

Banking

ABN Amro Bank, 10 Gustav Mahlerlaan, 1082 PP Amsterdam (tel: 628-9393; fax: 628-7637; e-mail: postbox@abnamro.com).

ASN Bank, 28 Alexanderstraat, 2514 JM The Hague (tel: 0800-0380; fax: 361-7948; e-mail: informatie@asnbank.nl).

NIB Capital Bank, 4 Carnegieplein, 2517 KJ The Hague (tel: 342-5425; fax: 363-5425).

ING Bank, De Amsterdamse Poort, 1102 MG Amsterdam (tel: 563-9111; fax: 563-5700; e-mail: info@ingbank.com).

Postbank NV, 506 Haarlemmerweg , 1014 BL Amsterdam (tel: 584-9111; fax: 584-6600; e-mail: postbank@postbank.nl).

Rabobank Nederland, 18 Croeselaan, 3521 CB Utrecht (tel: 216-0000; fax: 216-2672; e-mail: info@rabobank.nl).

Central bank

De Nederlandsche Bank, Head office, Postbus 98 1000 AB Amsterdam; 1 Westeinde, 1017 ZN Amsterdam (tel: 524-9111; fax: 524-2500; email: info@dnb.nl).

European Central Bank (ECB), Kaiserstrasse 29, D-60311 Frankfurt am Main, Germany (tel: (+49-69) 13-440; fax: (+49-69) 1344-6000; email: info@ecb.int).

Travel information

Algemene Nederlandse Vereniging van VVVs (ANVV) (association of tourist information offices), 25 Hogeweg, 3814 CC Amersfoort (tel: 33-756-060; fax: 33-723-146; e-mail: anvv@euronet.nl).

Amsterdam Schiphol Airport, 202 Evert van der Beekstraat, Schiphol-Centrum, Haarlemmermeer (tel: 601-9111; fax: 604-1475; e-mail: info@schiphol.nl).

Amsterdam Tourist Office (VVV), 10 Stationplein, 1012 AB Amsterdam (tel: 551-2512; fax: 625-2869; e-mail: info@amsterdamtourist.nl).

KLM Royal Dutch Airlines, 55 Amsterdamseweg, Schiphol Airport, 1182 GP Amstelveen (tel: 20-649-9123; fax: 20-649-300; e-mail: info@klm.nl).

Netherlands Reservation Centre, 1 Nieuwe Gouw, 1442 LE Purmerend (tel: 299-689-144; fax: 299-689-154; e-mail: info@hotelres.nl).

National tourist organisation offices

Netherlands Board of Tourism and Conventions, (head office) Postbus 458; Vlietweg 15, Leidschendam (tel: 370-5705; fax: 320-1654; email: info@holland.com; internet: www.nbtc.nl and www.holland.com).

Ministries

Ministry of Agriculture, Nature Management and Fisheries, 73 Bezuidenhoutseweg, 2594 AC The Hague (tel: 378-6868; fax: 378-6100; email: info@minlnv.nl).

Ministry of Defence, 38 Kalvermarkt, 2511 CB The Hague (tel: 318-8802; fax: 318-8320; email: defensie.voorlichting@co.dnet.mindef.nl).

Ministry of Economic Affairs, 30 Bezuidenhoutseweg, 2594 AV The Hague (tel: 308-1986; fax: 347-4081; email: ezinfo@postbus51.nl).

Ministry of Education, Culture and Science, 4 Europaweg, 2711 AH Zoetermeer (tel: 323-2323; fax: 323-2320; email: info@minocw.nl).

Ministry of Finance, 7 Korte Voorhout, 2511 CW The Hague (tel: 342-7540; fax: 342-7900; internet: www.minfin.nl).

Ministry of Foreign Affairs, 67 Bezuidenhoutseweg, 2594 AC The Hague (tel: 348-6486; fax: 348-4848; email: dvl-info@minbuza.nl).

Ministry of General Affairs, 20 Binnenhof, 2513 AA The Hague (tel: 356-4100; fax: 356-4683).

Ministry of Health, Welfare and Sport, 5 Parnassusplein, 2511 VX The Hague (tel: 340-7911; fax: 340-7890; email: info@minvws.nl).

Ministry of Housing, Spatial Planning and the Environment, Rijnstraat 8, 2515 XP The Hague (tel: 339-3939; fax: 339-1352; email: info@minvrom.nl).

Ministry of the Interior and Kingdom Relations, Schedeldoekshaven 200, 2511 EZ The Hague (tel: 426-6426; fax: 363-9153; email: info@minbzk.nl).

Ministry of Justice, Schedeldoekshaven 100, 2511 EX The Hague 9 (tel: 370-6850; fax: 370-7594; email: voorlichting@minjus.nl).

Ministry of Social Affairs and Employment, 4 Anna van Hannoverstraat, 2595 BJ The Hague (tel: 333-4444; fax: 333-4033; email: info@minszw.nl).

Ministry of Transport, Public Works and Water Management, 1-6 Plesmanweg, 2597 JG The Hague (tel: 351-6171; fax: 351-7895; email: info@minvenw.nl).

Other useful addresses

Algemeen Nederlands Persbureau (national news agency), 49 Handelskade, 2288 BA Rijswick (tel: 70-414-1414; fax: 70-414-1401; e-mail: nieuwsdienst@anp.nl).

American Embassy, 102 Lange Voorhout, 2514 EJ The Hague (tel: 310-9209; fax: 361-4688; email: usemb@usemb.nl).

British Embassy, 10 Lange Voorhout, 2514 ED The Hague (tel: 427-0427; fax: 427-0345).

Congrestolken (conference interpreters), 11 Jan van Goyenkade, 1075 HP Amsterdam (tel: 625-2535; fax: 626-5642; e-mail: interpreters@conferenceinterpreters.com).

Euronext Amsterdam (stock exchange), Beursplein 5, 1012 JW Amsterdam (tel: 550-4444; fax: 550-4900; email: info@euronext.nl).

Federation for Dutch Export (Fenedex), 14 Raamweg 2596 HL The Hague (tel: 330-5600; fax: 330-5656; email: info@fenedex.nl).

Netherlands Convention Bureau, 166 Amsteldijk, 1079 LH Amsterdam (tel: 646-2580; fax: 644-5935; email: info@nlcongress.nl).

Netherlands Council for Trade Promotions (NCH), 181 Bezuidenhoutseweg, 2594 AH The Hague (tel: 344-1544; fax: 385-3531; e-mail: info@nchnl.nl).

Netherlands Embassy (USA), 4200 Linnean Avenue, NW, Washington DC (tel: (+1-202) 244-5300; fax: (+1-202) 362-3430; email: webmaster@netherlands-embassy.org).

Netherlands Foreign Investment Agency (CBIN), 2 Bezuidenhoutseweg, 2594 AV The Hague (tel: 379-8818; fax: 379-6322; email: info@nfia.nl; internet: www.nfia.com).

Netherlands Foreign Trade Agency (EVD), 181 Bezuidenhoutseweg, 2594 AG The Hague (tel: 778-8888; fax: 778-8889; email: eic@info.evd.nl; internet: www2.holland.com/trade/).

Statistics Netherlands (CBS), 428 Prinses Beatrixlaan, 2273 XZ Voorburg (tel: 70-337-3800; fax: 70-387-7429; email: infoserve@cbs.nl; internet: (in Dutch): www.cbs.nl/enindex.htm).

Other news agencies: ANP (Netherlands National News Agency): www.anp.nl

Internet sites

Dutch Tourist Board: www.visitholland.com

Dutch yellow pages www.markt.nl./dyp/index-en.html

Netherlands web directory: www:nl-menu.nl

Tourist information: www:holland.com

Tourist information: www: nbt.nl

Hotel information: www:hotelsinholland.com

Statistics: www: cbs.nl:

Netherlands Embassy in the USA: www: netherlands-embassy.org

Dutch Railways: www: ns.nl

Ministry of Foreign Affairs: www: minbuza.nl

Dutch Parliament: www:parlement.nl

Ministry of Finance: www:minfin.nl

The Netherlands Antilles

KEY FACTS

Official name: Nederlandse Antillen (The Netherlands Antilles)

Head of State: Queen Beatrix of the Kingdom of The Netherlands (since 1980); represented by Governor General Frits Goedgedrag (since 2002)

Head of government: Prime Minister Emily de Jongh-Elhage (sworn in 26 Mar 2006)

Ruling party: Coalition government

Area: 800 square km

Population: 191,780 (2007)

Capital: Willemstad (on Curaçao)

Official language: Dutch, English and Papiamento

Currency: Netherlands Antilles guilder (Naf) = 100 cents

Exchange rate: Naf1.79 per US$ (Jul 2008); (official rate pegged to US$ since Jan 2000)

GDP per capita: US$17,270 (2005)

GDP real growth: 0.70% (2005)

Labour force: 101,000 (2004)

Unemployment: 16.30% (2005)

Inflation: 3.20% (2005)

Balance of trade: -US$2.31 billion (2004)

Foreign debt: US$1.35 billion (2003)

COUNTRY PROFILE

Historical profile

The islands of the Netherlands Antilles were first inhabited by Carib and Arawak Indians.
1493 Christopher Columbus was the first European to sight the islands.
1499 The Spanish explorer, Alonso de Ojedo, visited Curaçao but left without establishing a settlement.
1527 The islands were settled, mainly by Spanish and Portuguese Jews escaping persecution.
1634 The Dutch East India Company took over the islands, 'persuading' the settlers to depart, first in St Maarten and later from Aruba.
1642–46 Peter Stuyvesant was governor.
1816 After a number of changes in possession, the islands – Curaçao, Aruba and Bonaire (known as the Leeward Islands), St Eustatius, Saba and Sint Maarten (half of which is the French territory of St Martin) (which are known as the Windward Islands) – were confirmed as Dutch territory.
1863 Slavery was abolished.
1916 The first oil refinery was opened in Curaçao.
1954 Internal autonomy was granted as associated states within a federacy.
1986 Aruba separated from the other islands and became a self-governing member of the Kingdom of The Netherlands. The remaining islands became the Antilles of Five.
1998 The general election resulted in a six-party coalition government under Prime Minister Suzanne Camelia-Römer.
1999 The Partido Laboral Krusado Popular (PLKP) (Labour Party People's Crusade) left the coalition, to be replaced by the Partido Antiá Restrukturá (PAR) (Party for the Restructured Antilles), with Miguel Pourier becoming prime minister.
2000 In a referendum, St Maarten voted in favour of separate status within the Kingdom of The Netherlands and relinquishing membership of The Netherlands Antilles government.
2002 The ruling coalition was returned to power in the elections.
2004 The coalition government avoided collapse, caused by a corruption crisis, when support was offered by the Democratische Partij (DP) (Democratic Party) of Bonaire. However the collapse finally arrived when the National People's Party (PNP) withdrew citing its unwillingness to work with Justice Minster Ben Komproe. Prime Minister Louisa-Godett resigned and Etienne Ys became prime minister.
2005 The islanders of Curaçao voted to become an autonomous state within the Kingdom of The Netherlands and break with The Netherlands Antilles. The tiny neighbouring island, Sint Eustatius, decided to remain within the Antilles.
2006 Emily de Jongh-Elhage became prime minister, following parliamentary elections. The islands of Curaçao and St Maarten signed an agreement of independence with The Netherlands to become autonomous territories within the Kingdom of the Netherlands in December 2008. At the same time Bonaire, Saba and St Eustatius will become city-states of the Kingdom of the Netherlands. When these changes are enacted the Netherlands Antilles will cease to exist. A new terminal in the Curaçao International Airport was opened designed to accommodate around 1.6 million passengers per year. The growth in tourism on the island and in the region is seen as a major industry and a phase two expansion is planned for 2031.
2007 Negotiations for a change in their status began between Bonaire, Saba and St Eustatius and The Netherlands.
2008 The Netherlands Antilles failed to have its name removed from the blacklist of tax havens by the Tax Directorate of the European Commission, despite being named a co-operative country by the OECD, IMF and Egmont Group.

Political structure

Each island has a local administration, part of which is elected. Likewise, political parties are local and confined to each island.

Constitution

29 December 1954

Form of state

Overseas territory of The Netherlands

The executive

Executive power for external affairs and defence is exercised by the governor general (as the representative of the sovereign of The Netherlands), assisted by an advisory council of at least five members. The governor general is appointed by the monarch for a six-year term.

National legislature

Internal affairs are handled by the governor general and the council of ministers. The council of ministers is elected by, and responsible to, the legislature, the Staten (Estates), which has 22 members – Curaçao (14), Bonaire (three), St Maarten

(three), Saba (one), St Eustatius (one) – elected for a four-year term, by universal adult suffrage and proportional representation.
Following legislative elections, the leader of the majority party is usually elected prime minister by the Staten.

Legal system
The legal system is based on Dutch civil law, with some English common law. Judges are appointed by the monarch. Rights of appeal exist from The Netherlands Antilles Court of Appeals to the Supreme Court of The Netherlands, in The Hague.

Last elections
27 January 2006 (parliamentary)
Results: Parliamentary: On Curaçao the Partido Antiá Restrukturá (PAR) (Party for the Restructured Antilles) won five seats, the Movishon Antia Nobo (MAN) (New Antilles Movement) three seats, Frente Obrero Liberashon 30 Di Mei (FOL) (Workers' Liberation Front 30th of May) two seats, Partido Nashonal di Pueblo (PNP) (National People's Party) two seats, Forsa Kòrsou two seats.
On Sint Maarten the National Alliance won two seats and Democratishche Partij Sint Maarten (Democratic Party of Sint Maarten) one seat. On Bonaire the Union Patriotico Bonairano (UPB) (Bonaire Patriotic Union) won two seats, all other parties, one seat each.

Next elections

Political parties
Political parties are local and confined to each island.

Ruling party
Coalition government

Main opposition party
National Alliance of Sint Maarten; Democratische Partij Sint Maarten.

Population
191,780 (2007)
Last census: January 2001: 175,653
Population density: 268 inhabitants per square km. Urban population: 69 per cent (1995—2001).
Annual growth rate: 3 per cent (2003)

Ethnic make-up
African and mixed race (85 per cent), Carib Amerindian, white, East Asian.

Religions
Roman Catholic, Protestant, Jewish, Seventh-Day Adventist.

Education
Primary schooling lasts for six years (from age six to 12) and junior secondary school lasts four years (age 12 to 16). Following primary education, students have a choice of attending technical or vocational colleges in place of secondary school.
Higher education is provided by the Universiteit van de Nederlandse Antillen (University of the Netherlands Antilles). There is also a nursing school and a teacher training college in Curaçao.
Literacy rate: 97 per cent, adult rate (2003)

Health
Curaçao has two general hospitals and one surgical hospital and receives patients from the other islands of The Netherlands Antilles. Most health professionals receive training in The Netherlands.
It is estimated that around 30 per cent of the population of the Netherlands Antilles suffer from hypertension; psychological problems are also highly prevalent among adults. The general standard of health among the Antilleans is poor, with poor nutrition and little or no exercise undertaken by the adult population. The Dutch government has assigned priority to encouraging the population to develop healthier lifestyles.

HIV/Aids
In 2003 there were 432 confirmed cases of HIV infection. There is a national strategic action plan to halt the rapid spread of the disease. The drugs problem on the islands could prove to be a potent source of transmission.
Life expectancy: 76.3 years (estimate 2003)
Fertility rate/Maternal mortality rate: 2.1 births per woman (World Bank)
Birth rate/Death rate: 16 births per 1,000 population; 6.4 deaths per 1,000 population (2003).
Child (under 5 years) mortality rate (per 1,000): 11 per 1,000 live births (2003)

Welfare
A public insurance programme covers 100 per cent of health care costs for blue-collar workers. There is also an insurance fund for retired workers. Private companies also provide insurance plans for their employees. A social security fund covers employees of small private establishments.

Main cities
Willemstad (capital, on Curaçao, estimated population 49,885 in 2005). Kralendijk (Bonaire) and Philipsburg (St Maarten).

Languages spoken
English in St Maarten, St Eustatius and Saba.
Papiamento (a local patois mixture of Portuguese, Spanish, Dutch, English and French) in Curaçao and Bonaire.
Spanish is widely understood and spoken.

Official language/s
Dutch, English and Papiamento

Media

Press
Dailies: The only national daily newspaper is Amigoe (www.amigoe.com), other newspapers are local to the island of their publication including Antilliaans Dagblad (www.antilliaansdagblad.com), La Prensa (www.laprensacur.com), Vigilante (http://vigilante.nl) from Curacao; Bonaire Reporter (www.bonairereporter.com) and Daily Herald (www.thedailyherald.com) from Sint Maarten.
Weeklies: The Bonaire Reporter is the island's English language weekly.
Business: Business publications include in English Business Curaçao Directory (www.businesscuracao.com) and the annual Trade Statistics by Central Bureau of Statistics (www.cbs.an).

KEY INDICATORS — The Netherlands Antilles

	Unit	2003	2004	2005	2006	2007
Population	m	0.18	0.18	0.18	0.19	0.19
Gross domestic product (GDP)	US$bn	2.40	3.10	3.20	3.35	–0
GDP per capita	US$	11,400	17,164	17,270	17,750	0
GDP real growth	%	1.5	1.0	0.7	–	*4.0
Inflation	%	2.0	–	3.2	–	*3.0
Unemployment	%	15.1	16.1	18.2	15.1	*9.0
Exports (fob) (goods)	US$m	553.0	2,076.0	971.1	3,710.0	–
Imports (cif) (goods)	US$m	1,430.0	4,383.0	2,285.2	15,740.0	–
Balance of trade	US$m	-877.0	-2,307.0	-1,314.1	-12,030.0	–
Current account	US$m	-10.0	-90.0	-148.3	–	–
Total reserves minus gold	US$m	373.0	415.0	462.0	495.0	661.0
Foreign exchange	US$m	373.0	415.0	462.0	495.0	661.0

Broadcasting
There are several radio stations with the three based in Curacao, Radio Hoyer (www.radiohoyer.com), Easy FM and Dolfijn FM (www.dolfijnfm.com) and Radio Statia on Sint Eustasius, others include Voz di Bonaire (www.bonairenet.com), the Voice of St Maarten and Voice of Saba (ww.mannelli.com/saba). There are two commercial television channels operating, TeleCuracao is government owned and Leeward Broadcasting Corporation broadcasts in Sint Maarten.

Economy
The Netherlands Antilles economy, virtually devoid of natural resources, is heavily service-oriented, 84 per cent of GDP, and based largely on tourism with offshore financial services. Industry accounts for 15 per cent, primarily in oil-refining, transshipment, harbour and ship repair facilities. Agriculture only accounts for 1 per cent of GDP, producing aloes, sorghum, vegetables and tropical fruit. Dutch aid remains important to the economy.
The unemployment rate remains high, 16.3 per cent in 2005. The islands have a higher per capita income and a well-developed infrastructure, compared with other countries in the region.

External trade
Trade in the Netherlands Antilles is dominated by Curaçao's crude oil imports and the export of refined oil products.
Imports
Include crude petroleum, food and manufactures.
Main sources: Venezuela (52.3 per cent total, 2006), US (21.4 per cent), Italy (4.9 per cent), The Netherlands (4.6 per cent)
Exports
Main exports include petroleum products.
Main destinations: US (29.4 per cent total, 2005), Panama (14.4 per cent), Mexico (8.8 per cent), Haiti (5.6 per cent), Venezuela (4.9 per cent), Bahamas (4.5 per cent)
Re-exports
Curaçao re-exports petroleum and derived products.

Agriculture
The agricultural sector contributes 1 per cent to GDP and employs 5 per cent of the workforce.
About 8 per cent of total area is cultivated arable land. Soil is generally poor and rainfall inadequate for most crops.
Small amounts of fruit and vegetables are grown for local consumption.
Estimated livestock production in 2005 included: 579 tonnes (t) meat in total, 18t beef, 188t pig meat, 74t lamb and goat meat, 300t poultry, 510t eggs, 410t milk.
There is little commercial fishing except on St Maarten. The typical total annual fish catch is over 900t; shellfish, molluscs and cephalopods account for another 10t per annum.

Industry and manufacturing
The industrial sector contributes about 19 per cent to GDP and employs 20 per cent of the workforce. It is dominated by petroleum refining and transshipment.
Manufacturing is concentrated on food processing and import substitution (paints, paper, soap, beer, chemicals).
The emphasis is on diversification into light export-based industries such as electronics and pharmaceuticals.

Tourism
Tourism is the major industry on the islands of Curaçao and St Maarten, while there is increasing tourist activity in Bonaire. The majority of visitors are from the US (around 40 per cent of stay-over arrivals), followed by South America, the Netherlands, Canada and the Caribbean.

Mining
There are known deposits of pumice on St Eustatius. Salt production has decreased in recent years.

Hydrocarbons
The Netherlands Antilles has no hydrocarbon resources. The 1914 discovery of oil in Venezuela was the impetus for the island of Curaçao's choice as the location for one of the largest oil refineries in the world. Crude oil is imported mainly from Venezuela and Mexico under the San Jose Pact. Some of this is consumed domestically but the majority is refined and exported.
The Netherlands Antilles do not import natural gas or coal.

Banking and insurance
Under an EU tax directive introduced in July 2005 in a number of associate and dependent EU countries, the Netherlands Antilles imposes a withholding tax to be passed to the relevant EU country but retains the anonymity of the saver.
Withholding taxes began at 15 per cent and will rise to 35 per cent by 2011.
The Netherlands Antillies has also agreed to supply information on tax fraud, for criminal or civil trials, and notify EU member states about additional malpractices.
Central bank
Bank van de Nederlandse Antillen
Offshore facilities

Time
GMT minus four hours

Geography
The Netherlands Antilles (the Antilles of Five), located in the Caribbean Sea, comprises two island groups, the Netherlands Leeward and the Netherlands Windward islands, about 800km (500 miles) apart.
The former group (Curaçao and Bonaire) lies about 80km north of Venezuela; the latter group (St Eustatius, Saba and the southern half of St Maarten – the northern half of St Maarten is a dependency of Guadeloupe) lies about 260km east of Puerto Rico.
Curaçao consists of low hills. The southern part of Bonaire is flat and the northern end is hilly; the land is arid. Saba is a rugged island of volcanic origin; the highest point, Mount Scenery, rises to 887 metres. St Eustatius is hilly with a central flat plain; it is of volcanic origin. St Maarten is hilly, except for the western region, which forms a large lagoon.
Hemisphere
Northern

Climate
There are low levels of humidity and rainfall on Curaçao and Bonaire where temperatures average 29 degrees Celsus (C). Average annual rainfall on Curaçao is 550mm. Temperatures are cooler on St Maarten, Saba and St Eustatius, due to the north-east trade winds, averaging 26 degrees C. There are higher levels of rainfall from May–December.

Entry requirements
Passports
Required by all and must be valid for at least three months from date of departure.
Visa
Not required by nationals of countries which are signatories of the Schengen Accords, which includes most EU/EEA member states; North America and Australasia for visits up to three months. Lists of nationals that do and do not require a visa can be found on the website of the Dutch Ministry of Foreign affairs: www.mfa.nl/lon-en/homepage under visas.
All visitors must provide evidence of sufficient funds for their stay and a return/onward ticket.
Currency advice/regulations
There are no restrictions regarding the import and export of local or foreign currencies.
Travellers cheques are widely accepted; US dollar cheques will avoid additional exchange charges.

Health (for visitors)
Mandatory precautions
Yellow fever vaccination certificate required if arriving from an infected area.
Advisable precautions
Inoculations and boosters should be current for tetanus and hepatitis A. There may be a need for vaccinations for diphtheria, typhoid, tuberculosis and hepatitis B.

Hotels
There are numerous tourist hotels on St Maarten, Curaçao and Bonaire. Accommodation is very limited on Saba and St Eustatius. Government tax of 5 per cent and 10–15 per cent service charge is added to the bill.

Credit cards
All major credit and charge cards accepted. ATMs are available in major centres.

Public holidays (national)
Fixed dates
1 Jan (New Year's Day), 30 Apr (Queen's Birthday), 1 May (Labour Day), 2 Jul Curaçao Flag Day, 6 Sep Bonaire Day, 11 Nov St Maarten Day, 25–26 Dec (Christmas).
Variable dates
Carnival (Jan/Feb), Easter Monday (Mar/Apr) Ascension Day (Aug).

Working hours
Banking
Mon–Fri: 0830–1200, 1330–1630.
Business
Mon–Fri: 0800–1200, 1330–1630.
Government
Mon–Fri: 0800–1200, 1330–1630.
Shops
Mon–Sat: 0800–1200, 1400–1800. Gift shops open on Sundays and public holidays when cruise ships call.

Telecommunications
Mobile/cell phones
There are several 900, 900/1800 GSM services covering the islands.

Electricity supply
Variable: 120/127/220V AC at 50 cycles or 60 cycles.

Getting there
Air
National airline: There are three airlines based in The Netherlands Antilles, non provide more than short haul or feeder services for international carriers: AirStMaarten (AirSXM), Bonaire Express and Windward Island Airways (Winair).
International airport/s: Curaçao (CUR), 12km north of Willemstad; St Maarten-Queen Juliana (SXM), 15km from Philipsburg; Bonaire-Flamingo (BON), 3.5km south of Kralendlijk. All have duty-free shops, bar, restaurant, hotel reservations and car hire. Taxis are available, fares are standard and should be agreed in advance.
Airport tax: Departure tax: Naf36 (international); Naf10 inter-island.
Surface
Water: There is a weekly ferry to Curaçao from Venezuela.
Main port/s: Willemstad (Curaçao). A pier at Otrabanda, in the western part of Willemstad, handles large liners.

Getting about
National transport
Air: AirStMaarten (AirSXM), Bonaire Express and Windward Island Airways (Winair) provide limited services between the islands.
Road: The network on all islands is all-weather, though less extensive on Saba and St Eustatius.
Buses: Regular services operate in and around main centres. Car/jitney services and sightseeing tours are also available. There are no regular services on smaller islands.
City transport
Taxis: Taxis are usually identified by TX before the licence plate. Fares are standard and should be agreed before travelling. Tipping is discretionary.
Car hire
Car hire is widely available at reasonable prices. An international licence is required.

BUSINESS DIRECTORY
The addresses listed below are a selection only. While World of Information makes every endeavour to check these addresses, we cannot guarantee that changes have not been made, especially to telephone numbers and area codes. We would welcome any corrections.

Telephone area codes
The international dialling code (IDD) for The Nethelands Antilles is +599, followed by subscriber's number (preceded exceptionally by 9 for Curaçao).

Chambers of Commerce
Bonaire Chamber of Commerce and Industry, 53 Kaya Grandi, Kralendijk (tel: 717-5595; fax: 717-8995; e-mail: boncommerce@bonairelive.com).

Curaçao Chamber of Commerce and Industry, 1 Kaya Junior Salas, PO Box 10, Willemstad (tel: 9461-3918; fax: 9461-5652; e-mail: businessinfo@curacao-chamber.an).

St Maarten Chamber of Commerce & Industry, 11 CA Cannegieter Street, Philipsburg (tel: 542-3595; fax: 542-3512; e-mail: info@sintmaartenchamber.org).

Banking
Algemene Bank Nederland, Frontstraat, PO Box 295, Philipsburg, St Maarten (tel: 9542-7520).

Banco di Caribe, Schottegatweg Oost 205, PO Box 3785, Willemstad, Curaçao (tel: 9432-3410; internet: www.bancodicaribe.com).

Banco Industrial de Venezuela CA, Handelskade 12, PO Box 701, Willemstad, Curaçao (tel: 9461-1621; fax: 9461-6534).

Banco Mercantil Venezolano NV, A Mendez Chumaceiro Bvd; PO Box 565, Curaçao (tel: 9461-1566, 9461-2117; fax: 9461-1974; internet: www.bancomercantilcu.com).

Citco Bank Antilles NV, Schottegatweg Oost 44, Willemstad, Curaçao (tel: 9732-2322; fax: 9732-2330; email: curacao-bank@citco.com).

FirstCaribbean International Bank (Curacao) NV, De Ruyterkade 61, PO Box 3144, Willemstad (tel: 9433-8338; fax: 9433-8198; email: www.firstcaribbeanbank.an).

MCB Maduro & Curiel's Bank NV, Plaza Jojo Correa 2-4, PO Box 305, Willemstad, Curaçao (tel: 9466-1100; fax: 9466-1444; email: infor@mcb-bank.com).

MCB Maduro & Curiel's Bank, Schottegatweg Oost 130, Saliña, Curaçao (tel: 9466-1100; fax: 9466-1444; internet: mcb-bank.com).

Orco Bank N V, Dr H Fergusonweg 10, PO Box 3987, Curaçao (tel: 9737-2000; fax: 9737-6741).

Windward Islands Bank Ltd, Pondfill, Philipsburg, PO Box 220, St Maarten (tel: 542-2313; fax: 542-4761; internet: wib-bank.net).

Scotiabank, Backstreet 61, Philipsburg, PO Box 303, St Maarten (tel: 542-3317; fax: 542-2435; email: bns@stmaarten@scotiabank.com).

Central bank
Bank van de Nederlandse Antillen, 1 Simon Bolivar Plein, Willemstad, Curaçao (tel: 9434-5500; fax: 9461-5004; e-mail: info@centralbank.an).

Travel information
AirSXM, Tapaza, W G Buncamper Road 4, Unit 7, Emmaplein, Philipsburg, St. Maarten, (tel: 543-1023; fax: 543-1260; email: info@tapaza.com).

Bonaire Express airline, Airport Hato (tel: 717 0808; fax: 717 0880; email: reservations@flydae.com).

Winair, Princess Juliana International Airport, St Maarten (tel: 545-2568; fax: 545-4229; internet: www.fly-winair.com).

National tourist organisation offices
Tourism Corporation Bonaire, Kaya Grandi 2, (tel: 717-8322, 717-8649; fax: 717-8408; email: tcbinfo@tourismbonaire.com).

Curaçao Tourist Board, PO Box 3266; Pietermaai 19, Curaçao (tel: 9434-8200; fax: 9461-5017: internet: www.curacao-tourism.com).

St Maarten Tourist Bureau, Vineyard Office Park, WG Buncamper Rd 33, St Maarten (tel: 9542-2337; fax:

9542-2734; internet: www.st-maarten.com).

Ministries

Ministry of Finance, Pietermaai 4–4A, Willemstad, Curaçao (tel: 9461-2052).

Office of the Minister Plenipotentiary of the Netherlands Antilles, Badhuisweg 175, 2597 JP The Hague, The Netherlands (tel: (+31-70) 351-2811; fax: (+31-70) 351-2722).

Other useful addresses

British Consulate, PO Box 3803, Brombadiersweg z/n, Willemstad, Curaçao (tel: 9436-9366; fax: 9436-9533).

Curaçao Inc (for business information), International Trade Centre Bldg, Piscaderabay, PO Box 6112, Curaçao (tel: 9463-6250; fax: 9463-6485).

Curaçao Industry and International Trade Development Co (CURINDE), Emancipatie Boulevard 7, Curaçao (tel: 9437-6000; fax: 9437-1336).

Foreign Investment Agency Curaçao, Scharlooweg 174 Willemstad, Curaçao (tel: 9465-7044; fax: 9461-5788).

International Trade Centre, PO Box 6005, International Trade Centre Building, Piscadera Bay, Curaçao (tel: 9462-4433, 9463-6250; fax: 9462-4408, 9463-6485).

Island Government of Curaçao, Department of Economic Affairs, Hoogstraat 18, Curaçao (tel: 9462-4066; fax: 9462-6596).

New Caledonia

COUNTRY PROFILE

Historical profile

1766 Sighted by Europeans.
1774 Captain James Cook named the island after the Latin name for Scotland.
1853 New Caledonia became a French colony.
1863 Nickel deposits were discovered. The displacement of villages which stood on new mine sites and the encroachment of settlers' cattle on Kanak land provoked several rebellions, all of which were suppressed by the French authorities.
1864–97 The island became a penal colony.
1942 New Caledonia was transformed into a US military base during the Second World War.
1946 The colony became a French territory.
1988 Jean-Marie Tijbaou, leader of the Front de Libération Nationale Kanak et Socialiste (FLNKS) (Kanak and Socialist National Liberation Front), signed the Martignon Accord which divided New Caledonia into three distinct regions.
1989 Tijbaou was assassinated.
1998 A national referendum voted overwhelmingly in favour of the Nouméa Accord, giving increased autonomy and a referendum on independence in 15–20 years, by voters who have resided in New Caledonia since 1995.
1999 A three-party coalition government was formed, dominated by Rassemblement pour la Calédonie dans la République (RPCR) (Rally for Caledonia in the Republic). The Loi Organique (Organic Act) amended the constitution, changing the national assembly into a more autonomous congress and imposing requirements on voting rights.
2001 The territory's president, Jean Lèques, (RPCR), resigned. Pierre Frogier (RPCR) replaced him.
2002 Negotiations started on the future adoption of the euro. Land disputes caused ethnic clashes between native Kanaks and Wallisian immigrants.
2004 Parliamentary elections resulted in a four-party coalition government. Marie-Noëlle Thémereau (Avénir Ensemble (AE) (Future Together)) was elected president.
2005 Michel Mathieu was appointed High Commissioner.
2006 The French parliament voted on constitutional amendments to restrict the voting rights of settlers to long-term residents.
2007 Nicolas Sarkozy became head of state and president of the French Republic. Marie-Noëlle Thémereau resigned as the head of government in July. Harold Martin was elected President of the Congress in August. High Commissioner Mathieu resigned and his replacement Yves Dassonville took office in November.
2008 Despite scientific denial in June that the rich coral lagoon in Goro would be damaged from the release of liquid mining effluent, residents are not convinced and warned the authorities that they would keep a continued watch on the surrounding environment.

Political structure

Constitution

Under the Nouméa Accord of 1998, New Caledonia has a special status within the French constitution. The local government, elected by universal suffrage, has wider degrees of autonomy regarding legislative issues. Up until 2010, France will retain power only over justice, public order, currency, defence and foreign affairs outside the South Pacific region.
France is also obliged to conduct up to three referenda on independence between 2013–18. Until then, the High Commissioner has overall responsibility for the territory while the president of the Territorial Congress is the head of local government. New Caledonia is represented in the French parliament by two deputies and two senators
The territory is divided into three provinces, each with its own assembly and local executive. There is an economic and social committee, which has an advisory role, and a Custom Senate, which advises the government on matters affecting the indigenous Kanak community.

Form of state

Self-governing territory of France

The executive

Executive power is exercised by the High Commissioner, with delegated power, for local administration, from France. The president of Congress advises the High Commissioner on matters of local jurisdiction.
The Congress elects the president who represents the congress and directs administrative services aided by an 11-member executive council drawn from Congress members (with at least one member from all political parties represented).

KEY FACTS

Official name: Nouvelle Calédonie (New Caledonia)

Head of State: President of France President of France (Nicolas Sarkozy), represented by High Commissioner Yves Dassonville (from 9 Nov 2007)

Head of government: President of the Congress of New Caledonia, Harold Martin (from 7 Aug 2007)

Ruling party: Coalition led by Rassemblement pour la Calédonie dans la République (RPCR) (Rally for Caledonia in the Republic) with Avénir Ensemble (AE) (Future Together) (since 2004)

Area: 18,575 square km – Grande Terre island: 16,600 square km

Population: 244,600 (2007)*

Capital: Nouméa (on Grande Terre)

Official language: French

Currency: Comptoirs Français du Pacifique franc (CFPf) = 100 centimes

Exchange rate: CFPf92.21 per US$ (Jan 2007); (pegged CFPf119.25 per euro)*

GDP per capita: US$15,000 (2003)*

GDP real growth: 4.40% (2006)*

Labour force: 84,400 (2007)*

Unemployment: 16.30% (2004)

Inflation: 1.80% (2007)

Balance of trade: -US$600.00 million (2003)*

Foreign debt: US$79.00 million (2003)*

Visitor numbers: 103,363 (2007)

* estimated figure

National legislature
Under the Loi Organique (Organic Act, 1999) the Congress of New Caledonia has enhanced powers to elect the government and enact legislation, separately from France. It has 54-members elected by proportional representation from the provinces of New Caledonia (32 from the South Province, 15 from the Northern Province and 7 from the Province des Iles Loyauté). All members serve for five-year terms.
To be eligible to vote for congress members, voters must have been resident for 10 years and resident for 20 years to vote in referenda scheduled in 2015–20.
Last elections
9 May 2004 (parliamentary)
Results: Parliamentary: RPCR won 24.5 per cent of the vote (16 seats out of 54); Future Together won 22.8 per cent (16 seats); UNI-FLNKS 13.7 per cent (eight seats); UC 11.9 per cent (seven seats); four other parties shared the remaining seven seats. Turnout was 76.4 per cent.
Next elections
2010 (parliamentary)

Political parties
Ruling party
Coalition led by Rassemblement pour la Calédonie dans la République (RPCR) (Rally for Caledonia in the Republic) with Avénir Ensemble (AE) (Future Together) (since 2004)
Main opposition party
Front National (FN) (National Front)
Political situation
With one of the world's largest reserves of nickel, the community in New Caledonia has been trying to balance the need for foreign direct investment to boost the economy and the damage mining can do to tribal lands and the environment. The indigenous Kanak people are opposed to the Goro-Nickel mining operation and since a court in 2006 rejected its legal bid to halt the biggest industrial project in the South Pacific have taken direct actions in their attempt to halt production. An estimated US$10 million in damage was caused to heavy machinery and vehicles in the US$1.88 billion Goro-Nickel plant when a riot, inspired by the Rheebu Nuu Committee, broke out in April 2006. However, after police imposed rule, such action did not stop the project although the owner (Brazilian mining company CVRD) did review its investment and called for talks covering all aspects of local opposition, to reach a consensus. The plant was 70 per cent completed by 2008, after US$2.8 billion had been invested the expectation is that 4,500 tonnes per annum of cobalt will be produced by 2012. While mining output rose by 20 per cent in 2007, nickel production fell by 7 per cent, nevertheless world prices for commodities have given windfall bonuses.
In February 2007, for the first time in its history, the National Assembly in France had to amend the French Constitution specifically to allow New Caledonia to impose voting restrictions in local elections, in accordance with the 1998 Nouméa Accord. Only residents who have lived in New Caledonia for 20 years may vote in local elections and referenda, including those due to be held between 2015–2020 concerning New Caledonia's independence from France.

Population
244,600 (2007)*
Last census: August 2004: 230,789
Population density: 11 inhabitants per square km.
Annual growth rate: 1.8 per cent (2003)
Ethnic make-up
Of the total population, 45 per cent are Melanesian Kanaks, 34 per cent Europeans (mainly French), 20 per cent are Wallisians and the remainder are mainly Tahitian, Indonesian and Vietnamese.
The wealthy southern province is mainly inhabited by Europeans and the remainder of the country is mostly populated by the poorer ethnic Kanak community.

Education
Education is provided free for the compulsory years. Primary education covers ages six to 11 years and secondary education from aged 12 to a maximum of 18 years. There is a major shortage in the supply of trained secondary school teachers.
Public expenditure on education is typically 7 per cent of GNP. Nearly US$30 million was allocated, up to 2005, to implement the government's policy of equity funding for the early childhood education sector. The government also doubled funding for adult literacy, setting aside US$18 million to fund the Adult Literacy Strategy. More emphasis has been given to Mäori and Pacific children with special educational needs.
In October 2005 the government introduced a new primary school curriculum which places more emphasis on local culture and history and allows lessons to by taught in Kanak. The changes will come into force in early 2006.
Compulsory years: Six to 15
Enrolment rate: 101 per cent gross primary enrolment of the relevant age group (including repeaters) (World Bank 2003).
Pupils per teacher: 18 in primary schools.

Health
Life expectancy: 74 years (estimate 2003)
Fertility rate/Maternal mortality rate: 2.5 births per woman (World Bank)
Child (under 5 years) mortality rate (per 1,000): Seven deaths per 1,000 live births.

Main cities
Nouméa (capital, on Grande Terre, estimated population 89,207 in 2005) Le Mont Dore (26,180), Dumbea (26,290).

Languages spoken
Thirty Canaque languages are spoken. English is often understood.
Official language/s
French

Media
Other news agencies: ABC Pacific Beat: www.radioaustralia.net.au/pacbeat
Pacific Magazine:
www.pacificmagazine.net
Press
In French, the only dailies newspaper is Les Nouvelles Calédoniennes (www.info.lnc.nc), weeklies include Télé 7 Jours, Les Nouvelles Hebdo, L'Echo Calédonien, Dimanche Patinane and Femmes, which is a women's magazine.
Broadcasting
The French overseas broadcaster RFO (www.rfo.fr) provides locally produced radio and television news and imported French programmes, as well as internet TV services.
Radio: RFO operates Radio France Internationale (http://www.rfi.fr). Private local radio services operate 24 hours a day; stations include NRJ (www.nrj.nc) and Radio Djiido (www.radiodjiido.nc).
Television: From France, RFO Nouvelle-Calédonie
(http://nouvellecaledonie.rfo.fr) offers a fully range of programmes. Pay-to-view TV is also available.
Advertising
Advertising is available in the local press, on radio and TV and in cinemas.

Economy
There is a lack of economic diversity. The economy is almost entirely dependent on transfers from France, nickel extraction and processing and foreign aid. Infrastructure development has enjoyed a limited boost with the development of new mining and smelting enterprises, such as the development of the Koniambo deposit.
The territory's nickel production contributes around 12 per cent of global output and up to 10 per cent of GDP.
Although the French military presence in New Caledonia has been a source of internal tensions, it also makes a significant contribution to the local economy. France contributes around 25 per cent of GDP, 80 per cent of which covers healthcare, education and public sector wages. GDP

per capita is one of the highest in the region.
New Caledonia uses the euro-pegged Comptoirs Français du Pacifique franc (CFPf) as its currency. The government began negotiations in 2002 over the adoption of the euro, which would boost the territory's chances of attracting investment and tourism but has been unsuccessful in overcoming the objections of pro-independence groups.
The world's largest nickel development operation is underway in the southern Goro provinces. The consortium, headed by Inco Ltd (Canada) and including Sumitomo Metal Mining Co and Mitsui & Co of Japan, will be spending some US$1.88 billion in the Goro Nickel Development Project. Annual production is expected to be 60,000 tons of nickel oxide and up to 5,000 tons of cobalt carbonate. The project is scheduled to become operational in 2007.
The new and improved infrastructure made necessary by building the nickel plants will also benefit other sectors of the economy, such as tourism, education and health.
About US$26 million aid, spread over five years, was granted to New Caledonia by the EU in September 2004; the aid is to be used to train local professionals in skills necessary to meet the economy's needs in the territory's three northern provinces.

External trade

As a collectivité sui generic of France, New Caledonia is a Special Territories of the European Union and apply its rulings and trade agreements.

Imports

Main imports are machinery and equipment, fuels, chemicals and foodstuffs.
Main sources: France (31.9 per cent total, 2006), Singapore (14.4 per cent), Australia (9.5 per cent).

Exports

Main exports are processed ferro-nickels, nickel ore and fish
Main destinations: France (21.0 per cent total, 2006), Japan (18.4 per cent), China (11.3 per cent).

Agriculture

Farming

The agricultural sector typically accounts for as little as 2 per cent of GDP. Although the soil is fertile, only 10 per cent of the land area is cultivated. There is a ratio of around 50-50 for locally grown to imported foods. The number of farmers has fallen by almost 50 per cent since the early 1990s, with the greatest percentage loss in the northern province.
About one-third of the main island's land area is devoted to cattle raising, chiefly on the central and north-west coasts. Exports of coffee and copra crops have increased since the 1990s.
Estimated crop production in 2005 included: 16,000 tonnes (t) coconuts, 3,910 cereals in total, 3,800t maize, 2,000t potatoes, 3,000t sweet potatoes, 2,800t cassava, 2,300t taro, 11,000t yams, 2,080t oilcrops, 4,662t vegetables in total, 1,000t bananas, 4,368t fruit in total, 40t coffee. Livestock production included: 6,342t meat in total, 4,000t beef, 1,400t pig meat, 900t poultry, 42t sheep and goat meat, 1,680t eggs, 3,720t milk, 55t honey.

Fishing

Tropical shrimp farming has been developed, although the farms are fragile as there is always the risk of disease. Fishing is both for local consumption and for export, mainly to Japan.
Annual fish production typically includes 2,800t marine fish, 1,900t other seafood and 343,000 units of pearls and shells.
In 2004, the total marine fish catch was 2,973 tonnes and the total crustacean catch was 19 tonnes.

Forestry

Domestic forests supply about 35 per cent of timber demand, with some reforestation undertaken.

Industry and manufacturing

The industrial sector typically contributes 20 per cent to GDP. Main industries include nickel processing, domestic equipment, clothing, foodstuffs and beer.
There are three major nickel processing projects in the pipeline. New Caledonia's only existing nickel processing plant, owned by the Société le Nickel (SLN), is undergoing renovations to increase production from 60,000 tonnes to 75,000 tonnes annually. SLN will increase activity at one of its mines to supply enough ore for the plant's increased capacity. The project is expected to be completed in 2006.
Construction of a US$1.50 billion Koniambo nickel processing plant in the north, with production starting in 2008 is projected to output 60,000 tonnes of nickel a year.
Construction of a plant in the south, at Goro, is due to be completed by 2007. At an estimated capital cost of US$1.88 billion it is expected to produce 60,000 tonnes of nickel and 4,300–5,100 tonnes of cobalt annually, beginning in 2007.

Tourism

Tourism has been struggling since 2001 following the 11 September attacks in the US, the ongoing decline of the Japanese economy, French nuclear testing and the SARS epidemic. The high point in visitor numbers was 2000, when 109,587 arrivals were recorded.
Since then numbers have not shown any particular trend with arrivals at 99,203 in 2004, slightly down on the 101,983 in 2003. Cruise ship visits in early 2004 showed a healthy improvement, but still only account for 20,000 arrivals.
Stay-overs have not kept pace with hotel occupancies staying at around 55 per cent. A number of major tourist-related projects are currently under construction.
Japan and France are the main markets, followed by Australia and New Zealand.
In July 2008 New Caledonia's lagoons and reef ecosystems were added to Unesco's world heritage list

Mining

New Caledonia holds between 25–40 per cent of known world nickel deposits and is one of the world's largest producers.
There are several mines in New Caledonia, the principal ones are located at Koniambo, Tiebaghi, Thio, Kouaoua, Nepoui-Kopeto and Etoile du Nord.
The potential production capacity of the seven main nickel mining operators making up Société Le Nickel (SLN) has been estimated at 830,000 tonnes a year, with reserves expected to last until 2012. SLN is 60 per cent owned by France's Eramet and 30 per cent by the Société Minière de Sud Pacific (SMSP), which is owned by ethnic Kanak groups.
Nickel and ferronickel production accounts for up to 10 per cent of GDP and contributes 80 per cent of foreign earnings.
Chrome extraction is undertaken. There are also deposits of iron ore, copper, manganese, lead and zinc.
SLN is expanding its smelting plant in Nouméa, and in order to supply enough ore for the plant's increased capacity, it is increasing production at one of its mines from 250,000 tonnes to one million tonnes a year, creating around 200 new jobs. The project is to be completed in 2006.
In August 2004, a public enquiry on the future of the US$1.8 billion Goro nickel mining project in the Southern Province recommended the project go ahead, but precautions should be taken against environmental pollution.

Hydrocarbons

No significant oil, gas or coal reserves have been identified in New Caledonia. It relies on imports of hydrocarbons to meet domestic demand.

Energy

Around 80 per cent of electricity generation is produced by thermal generators. Renewable sources of energy, including hydroelectricity and wind generation, are growing in importance. The nickel extraction of smelting sectors consume around 75 per cent of electricity output.

Banking and insurance

Central bank

The Paris-based Institut d'Emission d'Outre-Mer (IEOM) provides all central banking services except foreign exchange reserves.

Main financial centre

Nouméa

Time

GMT plus 10 hours

Geography

New Caledonia comprises one large island and several smaller ones, situated in the south Pacific Ocean, about 1,500km (930 miles) east of Queensland, Australia. The main island is La Grand-Terre, it is long and narrow. Rugged mountains divide the west of the island from the east, and there is little flat land. The nearby Loyalty Islands and a third group of islands, the uninhabited Chesterfield Islands, lie about 400km north-west of the main island.

Hemisphere

Southern

Climate

Hot (average temperature 26 degrees Celsius (C)), with occasional tropical depressions and cyclones, from mid-November to mid-April; and cool (average temperature 23 degrees C), with moderate rains, from mid-May to mid-September. Rainfall is quite irregular and can be extremely heavy. The east coast (at about two metres per annum) has twice the rainfall of the west; the wettest months are January, February and March.

Entry requirements

Passports

Required by all, except certain French nationals; all passports must have at least six months validity from the date of visit.

Visa

Required by all, except citizens of EU, North America, Australasia and Japan, for stays up to one month; this includes business trips by representatives of foreign entities with an invitation from a local company or organisation. Proof of adequate funds for stay, an itinerary, a guarantee of repatriation if necessary and return/onward ticket are also required. For further exceptions, full details and a copy of the application form visit www.diplomatie.gouv.fr/thema/dossier.gb.asp and follow the path (going to France) to the database.

Currency advice/regulations

The import and export of local and foreign currencies are unristricted but amounts over CFPf 900,000 must be declared.

Customs

Personal effects are allowed entry duty-free. Duty is not payable on goods of EU origin, although all imported goods are subject to a general tax, and an increasing number of goods require import licences. Expensive items, such as laptop computers, may require proof of ownership when departing.

Prohibited imports

Parrots, parakeets, pigeons, turtle-doves and non-domestic mammals; plants and seeds require a health certificate.
Export of birds of paradise and objects of ethnographic interest are prohibited.

Health (for visitors)

Mandatory precautions

Vaccination certificate required for yellow fever if travelling from infected area.

Advisable precautions

Vaccination for diphtheria, tuberculosis, hepatitis A and B, polio, TB, tetanus, typhoid. There is a rabies risk.
There has been an increased risk of dengue fever, visitors are advised to use mosquito repellent, a mosquito net at night, and wear protective clothing at dawn and dusk, to reduce the risk.

Hotels

Tourist hotels are classified by category and size on the five-star system. Hotel tax is levied, the amount varying according to classification. Details of rural or tribal lodgings in some Melanesian villages and areas are available from tourist information offices. Upper-end bungalow accommodation is growing.

Credit cards

Most major credit cards are accepted.

Public holidays (national)

Fixed dates

1 Jan (New Year), 1 May (Labour Day), 8 May (1945 Victory Day), 14 Jul (Bastille Day), 15 Aug (Assumption Day), 24 Sep (New Caledonia Day), 1 Nov (All Saints' Day), 11 Nov (Armistice Day), 25 Dec (Christmas Day).

Variable dates

Easter Monday (Mar–Apr), Ascension Day (Apr–May).

Working hours

Banking

Mon–Fri: 0730–1545.

Business

Mon–Fri: 0730–1130, 1330–1730. Sat: 0730–1130.

Government

Mon–Fri: 0730–1130, 1215–1600.

Shops

Mon–Fri: 0730–1100, 1400–1800. Half-day Sat and Sun.

Telecommunications

Mobile/cell phones

There is a GSM 900 service that covers the coastal regions of Grand Terre and surrounding islands.

Electricity supply

220V AC, with two-pin plug fittings.

Weights and measures

Metric system

Social customs/useful tips

Tipping is not customary. Islanders find it offensive when women sunbathe topless.

Getting there

Air

National airline: Aircalin

International airport/s: Nouméa La Tontouta International (NOU), 48km from Nouméa; duty-free shop, bar, restaurant, bank, shops, car hire.

Airport tax: None

Surface

There are regular shipping services from Australasia, Europe, Japan and South East Asia.

Getting about

National transport

Air: Air Calédonie operates regular flights from Nouméa's domestic airport, Magenta, to the east and west coasts of Grande-Terre island and daily flights to the Ile des Pins, Maré, Tiga, Lifou and Ouvea. Charter and tour airplanes and helicopters are available.

Road: Grande-Terre, the main island, has a total road network of approximately 5,000km, about 71 per cent sealed in municipal areas and a considerable length of track suitable for four-wheel drive and similar vehicles. Exercise care driving along the west and east coasts, as some roads are not sealed. The Canala-Thio main road is one-way only, with direction of traffic changing at scheduled times.

Buses: Regular bus services operate on Grande-Terre.

Water: There is a high-speed catamaran link between Grande-Terre and Ile des Pins, and Loyalty Islands. Small trading vessels also sail to nearby islands.

City transport

Taxis: Taxis are available in the central square (Place des Cocotiers), with some operating 24 hours. Charges are for time and distance. There is a surcharge after 1900 and on Sundays.

Buses, trams & metro: Buses from the airport to city centre usually take about 60 minutes.

Car hire

Self-drive car hire is available in Nouméa. A current valid driving licence is required. Driving is on the right-hand side of the road.

BUSINESS DIRECTORY

The addresses listed below are a selection only. While World of Information makes every endeavour to check these addresses, we cannot guarantee that changes have not been made, especially to telephone numbers and area codes. We would welcome any corrections.

Telephone area codes
The international dialling code (IDD) for New Caledonia is +687 followed by subscriber's number.

Useful telephone numbers
Fire station: 18
Police: 17
Ambulance (Nouméa): 252-100

Banking
Bank of Hawaii-Nouvelle Calédonie, BP L3, 25 Avenue de la Victoire, Avenue Henri Lafleur, 98849 Nouméa Cedex (tel: 257-400; fax: 274-147).

Banque Calédonienne d'Investissement, BP K5, 50 Avenue de la Victore, 98849 Nouméa (tel: 256-565; fax: 274-035).

Banque Nationale de Paris Nouvelle Calédonie, BP K3, 37 Ave Henri Lafleur, 98800 Nouméa (tel: 258-400; fax: 258-459) .

Société Générale Calédonienne de Banque; 44 rue de l'Alma, Siége et Agence Principale, 98848 Nouméa (tel: 256-300; fax: 276-245).

Central bank
Institut d'Emission d'Outre-Mer (IEOM), 5 rue Roland Barthes, 75598 Paris Cedex 12, France (tel : (+33-1) 5344-4141; fax : (+33-1) 4347-5134; email: contact@ieom.fr).

European Central Bank, Kaiserstrasse 29, D-60311 Frankfurt am Main, Germany (tel: (+49-69) 13-440; fax: (+49-69) 1344-6000; e-mail: info@ecb.int).

Travel information
Air Caledonia, BP 98845 Nouméa (tel: 252-339; (bookings tel: 252-177); internet: www.air-caledonie.nc).

Aircalin, 8 rue Frederic Surleau, BP 3736, Nouméa (tel: 265-500; fax: 265-651; internet: www.aircalin.nc).

Destination Nouvelle Calédonie, 39-41 rue de Verdun, PO Box 688, Nouméa (tel: 272-632; fax: 274-623).

Nouméa La Tontouta International Airport, BP2, Tontouta 98840 (tel: 352-500; fax: 352-535; e-mail: ccita@cci.nc).

Nouméa Tourist Office, 24 rue Anotole France, BP 2828, Nouméa 98.800 (tel: 287-580; fax: 287-585).

National tourist organisation offices
New Caledonian Tourism Promotion Board (internet site: http://www.nouvelle-caledonie-tourisme.nc).

Other useful addresses
Institut Territorial de la Statistique et des Etudes Economiques, PO Box 823, 5 rue Gallieni, Nouméa (tel: 275-481, 283-156; fax: 288-148).

South Pacific Commission, PO Box D5 Cedex, Nouméa (tel: 262-000; fax: 261-844).

Other news agencies: ABC Pacific Beat: www.radioaustralia.net.au/pacbeat

Pacific Magazine: www.pacificmagazine.net

Internet sites
South Pacific Tourism Organisation: www.tcsp.com/new_caledonia/index.html

New Caledonia tourism: www.nctps.com/home.cfm

New Caledonia tourism: www.newcaledonia.com.au

New Caledonia website (in French): www.yahoue.com

Travel information: http://perso.wanadoo.fr/caledonie/indexe.htm

New Zealand

KEY FACTS

Official name: The Dominion of New Zealand

Head of State: Queen Elizabeth II, represented by Governor General Anand Satyanand (since 23 Aug 2006)

Head of government: Prime Minister Helen Clark (NZLP) (since 1999; re-elected 17 Sep 2005)

Ruling party: Coalition: New Zealand Labour Party (NZLP) and minor parties (since 1999; re-elected 2005)

Area: 268,676 square km: North Island (115,690 square km); South Island (152,356 square km)

Population: 4.24 million (2007)*

Capital: Wellington

Official language: English, Mäori

Currency: New Zealand dollar (NZ$) = 100 cents

Exchange rate: NZ$1.31 per US$ (Jul 2008)

GDP per capita: US$30,226 (2007)*

GDP real growth: 2.90% (2007)*

Labour force: 2.13 million (2005)*

Unemployment: 3.60% (2007)*

Inflation: 2.40% (2007)

Balance of trade: -US$2.36 billion (2005)

Foreign debt: US$36.76 billion (2004)

Visitor numbers: 2.41 million (2006)*

* estimated figure

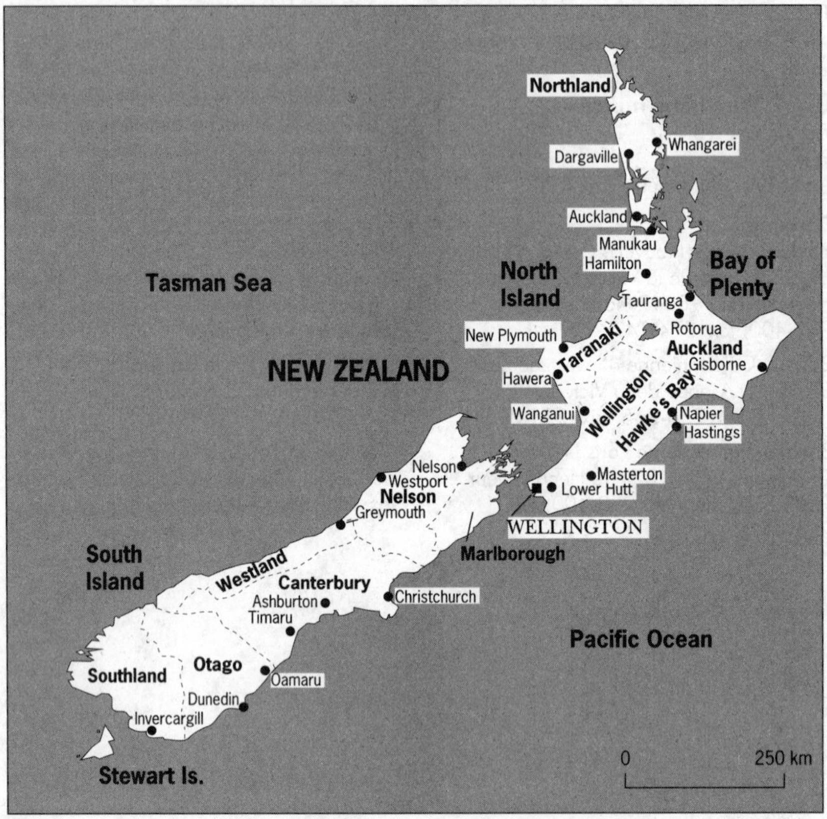

Reserve Bank of New Zealand (RBNZ) economists warned in mid-2008 that New Zealand was heading for a recession – or was already in one. A bank spokesman announced that the housing slump and global credit crunch had combined to form what he described as an almost 'perfect storm'.

Crunch?

The shortage of available credit continued to put upward pressure on interest rates at a time when householders were already struggling with rising mortgage rates. At the same time, New Zealand businesses were facing the prospect of rising debt servicing bills as the BNZ declared that the impact of the credit crunch was only just beginning to be felt. The statement came on a day that the share market dropped NZ$850 million, or 2 per cent, in value. A front-page article in March 2008 advised New Zealanders to 'Prepare for pain in the pocket'. In the article the *Dominion Post* expressed the view that householders should 'brace for prolonged pain as power and petrol prices rise, and with little relief in sight from punishingly high mortgage rates'.

On top of this grim economic news, the RBNZ announced that it would not consider a drop in interest rates until the second half of 2009 at the earliest, despite a housing slump and the deteriorating economy. It warned that, due to world events, higher interest rates were 'the new reality'. New Zealand already has the highest interest rates in the Organisation for Economic Co-operation and Development (OECD).

With higher interest rates than other developed countries and a small economy, New Zealand had attracted a flood of capital from offshore where rates were lower, pushing up the exchange rate. This had aggravated the inflation problem and the central bank then had to increase rates and start the whole cycle again.

For the best part of 100 years – even more – the New Zealand economy had the simple role of serving as a giant Antipoedean farm feeding the British industrial population. The entry of Great Britain into the European Community (EU) changed all that, causing New Zealand to search not only for new markets for its traditional products but also for a more diversified range of products to export. But old habits die hard: excitement is not normally associated with life in New Zealand, where mowing the lawn on the 'section' (house plot) constitutes an important Sunday activity. Across the Tasman Sea wages, productivity and living standards have all outstripped those of New Zealand. Gross domestic product (GDP) per capita figures for 2007 tell the tale – in Australia it was US$43,312 while New Zealand's was US$30,226.

Politics

Elections come round pretty quickly in New Zealand, every three years. The September 2005 elections almost rivalled the rugby in excitement. Although incumbent prime minister, Helen Clark became the first Labour prime minister to win three straight terms, she did so with a majority of only one seat, over the second placed National Party. Labour had lost one seat, down to 50, but the National Party, headed by former central bank governor Jim Brash, had gained 27. This gave the National Party an unprecedented 48 seats with a 39.6 per cent share of the vote, almost double its share in the 2002 elections. The National Party's gains, however, were largely at the expense of the smaller parties. The nail-biting result meant that neither of the two major parties held an outright majority. This left Labour leader Helen Clark seeking a deal to form a coalition government with one or more of the six minor parties represented in parliament.

After several weeks of horse trading, Mrs Clark announced the formation of a coalition government with the one seat Jim Anderton's Progressive Party, which was to be the only other party in the government. The coalition depended on the support of both the New Zealand First Party (seven seats) and the United Future New Zealand Party (three seats) in votes of confidence. In an unexpected and controversial move, Mrs Clark appointed the maverick New Zealand First Party leader, Winston Peters, as foreign minister. Although holding this important ministerial position, Mr Peters would not be a member of the cabinet.

Mr Peters resigned in August 2008, after being accused of mis-appriating political funds. He denies the accusations. Elections will be held on 8 November when Mrs Clark will attempt to lead her party to a fourth election victory. Analysts in New Zealand have said that the population is ready for a change, however, Mrs Clark is a hardened campaigner, and New Zealander are notorious for their reluctance to change.

Economy

New Zealand's economy grew strongly over the five years to 2004 but started to slow in 2005. However, real GDP growth was 2.9 per cent for the year 2007 after 1.3 per cent in 2006. The inflation rate rose to 3.4 per cent in 2006, falling back to 2.4 per cent in 2007. But by the second quarter of 2008 it had hit a two-year high of 4 per cent, leading the RBNZ to cut the interest rate by a 0.25 per cent in July and a further 0.5 per cent in September. New Zealand is currently experiencing labour shortages due to record low unemployment and high participation rates. The unemployment rate was 3.9 per cent in mid-2008. The New Zealand government has identified improving productivity as a key challenge for New Zealand's economy.

A number of factors lie at the heart of the imbalance within the New Zealand economy. House price inflation and consumer credit growth have both rocketed up at a rate of some 15 per cent annually. A tight labour market and increased public spending have fuelled the rise. In New Zealand's three year election cycle election promises play an exaggeratedly important role as an election is never far off. In the run-up to the 2005 elections, both the major political parties had included a commitment to increased government spending in their election proposals; the Labour Party's manifesto foresaw an increase of 5 per cent. The tight labour market, created in part by above average levels of youth emigration, has also meant increased inflationary pressures, with the annual rate topping the central bank's targeted 3 per cent mark.

The 2006 budget followed up on a number of the Labour Party's election pledges. Student loans ceased bearing interest from April 2006 and the so-called Working for Families package was extended to cover 350,000 families. In line with an agreement reached with the New Zealand First Party before the election, old-age pensions are now linked to the average national wage. The budget provided for NZ$1.9 billion (US$1.32 billion) of new capital expenditure over a two year period – NZ$780 million (US$542 million) in 2006/07, and NZ$540 million (US$375 million) in 2007/08.

Outlook

Mrs Clark is confident that the Labour Party will win the November elections. She has managed to maintain her support

KEY INDICATORS — New Zealand

	Unit	2003	2004	2005	2006	2007
Population	m	3.99	4.10	4.10	4,192.00	*4.24
Gross domestic product (GDP)	US$bn	76.30	99.69	108.42	105.34	*123.14
GDP per capita	US$	18,497	23,899	26,439	25,129	*30,226
GDP real growth	%	3.2	5.0	2.1	1.5	*2.9
Inflation	%	1.7	2.3	3.0	3.4	2.4
Unemployment	%	4.8	4.7	3.7	3.8	*3.6
Natural gas output	bn cum	4.1	3.6	3.7	3.9	4.0
Coal output	mtoe	3.2	3.0	3.2	3.6	1.7
Exports (fob) (goods)	US$m	16,505.0	20,456.0	22,210.0	22,574.0	27,350.0
Imports (cif) (goods)	US$m	18,559.0	21,889.0	24,570.0	24,573.0	29,057.0
Balance of trade	US$m	2,054.0	-1,433.0	-2,360.0	-1,999.0	-1,708.0
Current account	US$m	-3,280.0	-6,040.0	-9,770.0	-9,082.0	-10,378.0
Total reserves minus gold	US$m	4,907.0	5,294.0	8,893.0	14,068.0	17,247.0
Foreign exchange	US$m	4,235.0	4,786.0	8,694.0	13,916.0	17,124.0
Exchange rate	per US$	1.72	1.51	1.45	1.44	1.29

* estimated figure

within the party and tax cuts and the fall in interest rates should improve the party's image. However the polls are forecasting a win for the National Party under its comparatively young leader, John Kay.

Risk assessment

Politics	Good
Economy	Good
Regional stability	Good

COUNTRY PROFILE

Historical profile

Relations between the indigenous population and the descendants of Europeans were cemented in the Treaty of Waitangi in 1840, in what is generally considered the founding document of the nation.
New Zealand is a member of the Commonwealth and uses the British parliamentary system. However, links with Britain are tenuous at best and developing relations with Australia and South-East Asia are of more pressing priority.
Migrants from Polynesia arrived in New Zealand and colonised it between 800–1000AD.
1642 Dutch explorer Abel Tasman was the first European to sight New Zealand.
1769 and 1779 British explorer James Cook charted the islands of New Zealand. After his second voyage, British and other European settlers began to arrive.
1815 The first British missionaries arrived in New Zealand.
1840 European settlers and the Mäori tribes signed the Treaty of Waitangi, under which European settlers agreed to respect Mäori land rights in return for recognition of British rule.
1845–47 Mäoris revolted against land loss.
1852 New Zealand became a self-governing British colony.
1858 A series of major Mäori revolts began in response to encroachments by Europeans on to Mäori land.
1860–72 Mäoris revolted again. The conflict was resolved after the Europeans promised to abide by the Treaty of Waitangi.
1893 New Zealand became the first country to give women the right to vote.
1898 The government introduced old age pensions.
1907 New Zealand became an independent dominion within the British Empire.
1914–18 New Zealand fought alongside the UK during the First World War and suffered heavy casualties in the Gallipoli campaign in Turkey in 1915.
1931 The Westminster Declaration established the concept of a Commonwealth between the UK, New Zealand and several other former British colonies.
1939–45 New Zealand fought alongside the UK during the Second World War.
1947 Dominion status began to be phased out and replaced by the Commonwealth.
1951 New Zealand formed the ANZUS military pact with Australia and the US.
1963 New Zealand agreed to provide a military presence in Vietnam – initially with a military advisors.
1965 Under increasing US pressure for the commitment of troops in Vietnam, a non-combative engineering force was augmented by a field artillery battery of around 120 men.
1972 The last New Zealand troops were withdrawn from Vietnam.
1975 A legal tribunal ruled that there should be an investigation into whether Mäori land rights under the Treaty of Waitangi had been systematically ignored. This led to a vast number of lawsuits under which Maori tribes demanded financial reparations for the illegal confiscation of their lands.
1984 Prime Minister David Lange declared New Zealand a 'nuclear free zone' and forbade nuclear-powered vessels to dock at New Zealand ports.
1985 French secret agents bombed and destroyed the Greenpeace ship Rainbow Warrior in Auckland Harbour, killing one person.
1986 US suspended ANZUS obligations towards New Zealand.
1989 Lange resigned and was replaced by Geoffrey Palmer.
1990 The National Party (NP) won its first election victory for 10 years, with Jim Bolger becoming prime minister.
1993 The NP won elections. A referendum on electoral reform showed a majority in favour of proportional representation.
1996 New Zealand adopted a new parliamentary electoral system called Mixed Member Proportional (MMP), which was designed to give better representation for smaller parties and the Mäori community.
1997 Bolger resigned rather than face a leadership challenge from cabinet minister Jenny Shipley, who went on to become New Zealand's first woman prime minister.
1998 The NP-led coalition collapsed, leaving the NP as a minority government reliant on support from independent MPs.
1999 New Zealand sent troops to join UN peace-keeping forces in East Timor. In the general elections, the NP was defeated by the New Zealand Labour Party (NZLP) and Helen Clark became the country's first female prime minister and leader of the coalition government.
2001 The government re-nationalised Air New Zealand 12 years after it was privatised.
2002 A coalition governmen, led by NZLP, took office.
2004 Official contact with Israel was suspended after two Israelis were jailed for attempting to obtain New Zealand passports for Mossad agents. The convicted men were deported in September. A law was passed making all of the coastline public property; Mäori opposition claimed the law infringed the Treaty of Waitangi.
2005 Former prime minister, David Lange died. Prime Minister Helen Clark formed a coalition government following an indecisive general election.
2006 Anand Satyanand became Governor General. Te Arikinui Dame Te Atairangikaahu, the Great Chief of the Mäori population died, her eldest son Tuheitia Paki, became her successor.
2008 Edmund Hillary, the first mountaineer to climb Mount Everest successfully, died on 11 January.

Political structure

Constitution

New Zealand has no written constitution. Its constitutional history dates back to the signing of the Treaty of Waitangi in 1840, when the indigenous Mäori people ceded sovereignty over New Zealand to the British monarch. The Constitution Act 1986 brought together the most important constitutional provisions.
New Zealand is an independent parliamentary democracy and member of the Commonwealth. Government is based on the Westminster (United Kingdom) model.

Form of state

Constitutional monarchy

The executive

The head of state is the British sovereign, represented by a governor general who acts on the advice of the cabinet. The governor general is appointed by the sovereign on the advice of the New Zealand government.
The prime minister and cabinet are responsible to the legislature and are appointed by the governor general acting upon its advice. The prime minister and cabinet must be chosen from among elected members of parliament.
The Executive Council is a formal body made up of the cabinet and the governor general, who acts on the cabinet's advice. The cabinet consists of the prime minister and ministers, who must be chosen from among elected members of parliament.

National legislature

Legislative power is vested in a unicameral parliament (the House of Representatives). It has 120 members, elected for three-year terms through general elections at which all residents over 18 years of age are entitled to vote. Four seats are reserved for Mäori representatives.

Mixed Member Proportional (MMP) voting was introduced for the first time in the 1996 elections, replacing the first-past-the-post system. Under MMP, the single-chamber parliament was enlarged from 99 to 120 seats, with half representing specific electorates. The remainder are chosen from party lists. Parties must gain a minimum of 5 per cent of the vote before they can be represented in parliament.

Authority for raising revenue by taxation and for public expenditure must be granted by parliament. It also controls the government through its power to pass a resolution of no confidence.

Legal system

The law consists of common law, New Zealand statutes and some British statutes. The judiciary is independent from the executive. High Court judges, who also sit on the Court of Appeal, are appointed by the governor general and cannot be removed from office except by the sovereign or the governor general.

Last elections

17 September 2005 (parliamentary)

Results: NZLP won 41.1 per cent of the vote (50 seats out of 120); NP won 39.1 per cent (48 seats); New Zealand First Party (NZFP) 5.7 per cent (seven seats); Green Party of Aotearoa (GPA) 5.3 per cent (six seats); Maori Party 2.1 per cent (four seats); United Future New Zealand (UFNZ) 2.7 per cent (three seats); ACT New Zealand (ACT NZ) 1.5 per cent (two seats); and New Zealand Progressive Party (NZPP) 1.2 per cent (1 seat).

Next elections

15 November 2008 (parliamentary)

Political parties

Ruling party

Coalition: New Zealand Labour Party (NZLP) and minor parties

Main opposition party

New Zealand National Party (NP)

Population

4.24 million (2007)*

Last census: March 2001: 3,820,749

Population density: 14 inhabitants per square km. Urban population: 86 per cent (1995–2001).

Annual growth rate: 1.0 per cent 1994–2004 (WHO 2006)

Ethnic make-up

Approximately 77.3 per cent of the population is of European origin, with Mäoris representing another 14.5 per cent, Pacific Islanders 5.6 per cent and others 2.6 per cent. Pacific Islanders are attracted by job opportunities and a higher standard of living. However, socio-economic problems plague the Mäoris and Pacific Islanders.

Religions

Anglican (25 per cent), Presbyterian (18 per cent), Roman Catholic (15 per cent), Methodist (5 per cent), Baptist (2 per cent) and other Christian religions (34 per cent).

Education

Education is free and secondary admission is non-selective. Primary education covers ages five to 12 years and secondary education ages 13 to 16 years. A one-year sixth form follows and leads to a one-year pre-university course.

Public expenditure on education is typically 7 per cent of GNP. Nearly NZ$30 million (US$14.5 million) was allocated to implement the government's policy of equity funding for the early childhood education sector and funding for adult literacy was doubled, to NZ$18 million (US$8.7 million) as part of the Adult Literacy Strategy.

A campaign was launched that targets the Mäori community called Te Mana, with a specific objective of providing education from a Mäori perspective to youths, parents, life-long learners and teachers. It uses television, IT and a magazine, which has expanded to include study guides and a website, with relevent, current and contemporary tutoring.

Literacy rate: 99 per cent, adult rate

Compulsory years: Six to 17

Enrolment rate: 101 per cent gross primary enrolment of the relevant age group (including repeaters); 113 per cent gross secondary enrolment (World Bank).

Pupils per teacher: 18 in primary schools

Health

Per capita total expenditure on health (2003) was US$1,893; of which per capita government spending was US$1,483, at the international dollar rate, (WHO 2006).

The health system is made up of the public, private and voluntary sectors. The public sector provides free treatment at hospitals for immediate and major medical problems as well as chronic complaints, some continuing care and maternity and geriatric care. It also provides health benefits and subsidises pharmaceutical benefits and laboratory tests. The provision of mental health services is largely the responsibility of the public sector (with a small voluntary sector contribution) caring for both acute and chronic cases. It also provides free dental health treatment for school-age children. The public sector meets more than three-quarters of the total cost of healthcare and subsidises healthcare provided by general practitioners and specialists in private practice.

Private healthcare includes services provided by general practitioners, dentists, pharmacists and therapists in both public and private hospitals. The state subsidises many of these services although the main feature of this sector is the steady and rapid growth of private health and medical insurance.

HIV/Aids

HIV prevalence: 0.1 per cent aged 15–49 in 2003 (World Bank)

Life expectancy: 80 years, 2004 (WHO 2006)

Fertility rate/Maternal mortality rate: 2.0 births per woman, 2004 (WHO 2006); maternal mortality 15 per 100,000 live births (World Bank)

Birth rate/Death rate: 15 births and Seven deaths per 1,000 people (World Bank)

Child (under 5 years) mortality rate (per 1,000): 5.0 per 1,000 live births (World Bank)

Head of population per physician: 2.37 physicians per 1,000 people, 2001 (WHO 2006)

Welfare

New Zealand Superannuation (NZS), which is a universal, publicly provided pension, is at the core of its retirement income system provided to everyone over the age of 64 years and who meet certain residential qualifications. It is estimated that more than 92 per cent of older people receive NZS.

The government has tried to develop the welfare system, which actively works with beneficiaries to boost their skills. In 2002/03, a NZ$3 million (US$1.4 million) pilot programme was initiated to encourage sickness and invalids benefit recipients to participate in paid work and community-based activities.

Main cities

North Island: Wellington (capital, estimated population 184,257 in 2005); Auckland (426,457), Hamilton (155,698); Tauranga (108,756).

South Island: Christchurch (367,663), Dunedin (115,233), Nelson (59,587), Invercargill (48,371).

Languages spoken

Some Polynesian dialects are spoken and a variety of other languages, reflecting the diverse origins of New Zealand's immigrant population.

Official language/s

English, Mäori

Media

The media in New Zealand is independent and free from official restraint and censorship, operating within the constraints of libel laws and other statutes. Key players in the sector are merging with Internet service providers and telecommunications companies as part of the general convergence in the creation and distribution of information and entertainment.

Press

Dailies: There are several dailies in circulation. New Zealand Herald has the largest daily circulation and is published in Auckland. There are approximately nine morning and 23 evening papers which are published daily in the main towns. A few of the dailies published in main centres are distributed throughout the surrounding provinces. Other major dailies including the regional ones are Herald, Dominion, Evening Post, Waikato Times, Press and Otago Daily Times. On-line daily news service can be obtained from New Zealand News.net (www.newzealandnews.net/) and Aucklandlive News (www.aucklandlive.co.nz/news) that delivers up to date news covering local issues.

Weeklies: The two Sunday papers published in English from Auckland and Wellington are Sunday Star Times and Sunday News. Other major English-language weekly publications are Listener, TV Guide, Truth, New Zealand Women's Weekly and Women's Day New Zealand. Other regional language weeklies include Samoa Post and Samoana (Samoan), Taimi o Tonga and Lao & Hia (Tongan).

Business: The leading business journal is the weekly National Business Review. On-line business news is carried by National Business Review (www.nbr.co.nz/). Nieu Economic Review is an English-language monthly publication.

Periodicals: The majority of local magazines and community newsletters are published monthly. Some of these periodicals are The Lakesider (Upper Clutha), Aroha Nui Otara Community Newspaper and Fangufangumana in Tongan. Several local Maori-language monthly and quarterly publications in circulation are Te Karaka and Toi te Kupu (full colour tabloid). Bi-lingual publications in Māori and English are Pu Kaea, Kia Hiwa Ra, Pipiwharauroa and Mana. Cook Islands Sun is a bi-annual English-language publication. Pacific Network Newspaper published in English, Niuean, Tongan and Samoan provides news of the wider Pacific community.

Broadcasting

Radio: Radio New Zealand, a former service of the Broadcasting Corporation of New Zealand, was established as a fully commercial state-owned enterprise in 1988. With 35 commercial radio stations, three non-commercial radio networks (National Radio, Concert Programme and AM Network) and a shortwave service (Radio New Zealand International), it is one of the largest single radio operators in the world.

Television: There are three television stations, with about one-third of the programming produced in New Zealand. In addition, there are two pay-per-view vendors, Sky Television, offering a further five channels, and Telstra Saturn, with services in Wellington, Auckland and Christchurch. Television New Zealand (TVNZ) operates two of the three free channels, and claims to have 100 per cent coverage. The other channel, operated by TV3 Network Limited, has approximately 96 per cent coverage. Cable TV is a common means of accessing programmes. There are, in addition, local community stations.

Advertising

Advertising is available on commercial radio and TV, in the press, in cinemas and outdoors on buses and inside telephone booths. Direct mail advertising services are available. Various laws regulate the advertising of certain products, including drugs, cosmetics and medical instruments. Self-regulation is the responsibility of the Advertising Standards Authority and the Advertising Standards Complaint Board. The Broadcasting Standards Authority is responsible for radio and television advertising regulations.

Economy

New Zealand has been transformed from an agrarian society to an industrialised nation by the economic restructuring that took place after 1984. The economy was opened up to world markets and the government eliminated all domestic and export subsidies and most tariffs. New Zealand is reputed to be among the most open economies in the world, while inflation has consistently stayed within the government's 3 per cent target since the mid-1990s. Manufacturing has led growth, while traditional sectors have stagnated or shown only modest growth levels. Since 1992 New Zealand has recorded an average annual growth rate of 3.5 per cent, easily outperforming many other developed economies. To have maintained this during the global downturn of 2000–02 was a considerable achievement.

In opening itself up to international trade and investment, New Zealand became highly exposed to events in Asia. This was evident during the Asian crisis of 1998, which precipitated a collapse in the value of the New Zealand dollar. Even so, the country fared better than most in Asia and the Pacific due to its flexibility and its robust corporate and financial sectors and made a quick recovery.

Favourable terms of trade and a rise in farming output combined with a competitive exchange rate have boosted the economy. Although committed to monetary stability, both the IMF and the OECD have cautioned the government to maintain its track record on fiscal management as pressures to spend more on health and education grow.

In the long term, New Zealand will need to reduce its large current account deficit (its share of world trade is declining) and sustain the growth in productivity, particularly its quality of human capital. The perception of New Zealand as a safe haven, coupled with low levels of unemployment, have contributed to a relatively high level of net immigration. This development has eased skills shortages which were threatening to restrict economic growth. Even so, the key challenge is New Zealand's relatively low levels of labour productivity, underlying which are low levels of private sector research and development, skills shortages at management and employee level and relatively low investment in new technologies.

External trade

New Zealand (NZ) is a member of the South Pacific Regional Trade and Economic Co-operation Agreement (Sparteca) along with 13 regional nations, which allows products duty free access by Pacific Island Forum members to Australian and NZ markets (subject to the country of origin restrictions). Australia and NZ have a Closer Economic Relations (CER) agreement, which allows free trade in goods and many services. NZ has a number of bilateral free trade agreements, notably with Australia, China, and Malaysia. Exports contribute over 60 per cent of GDP, of which around 50 per cent is provided by agriculture produce. NZ supplies almost 40 per cent of mutton and lamb exports, worldwide.

Imports

Main imports include vehicles, machinery and equipment, vehicles and aircraft, petroleum, electronics, textiles and plastics.

Main sources: Australia (20.3 per cent total, 2006), US (12.3 per cent), China (12.1 per cent).

Exports

Main exports include mutton and lamb, dairy products, timber and fish and light manufacturing including machinery.

Main destinations: Australia (20.4 per cent total, 2006), US (13.1 per cent), Japan (10.3 per cent).

Agriculture

Farming

The New Zealand (NZ) agricultural sector is almost unique among its developed nation competitors in being virtually free of subsidies, with farming produce being forced to compete against that produced in countries that do provide subsidies and incentives to their farmers. With a level of

producer support estimate of 1 per cent (the OECD average is around 31 per cent) the agricultural industry still provides around 70 per cent of export earnings.
The removal of subsidies was both a burden and a boon to the NZ industry. Farmers contended with a fluctuating international market, which was dependent on the state of the general economy and specifically the value of the NZ dollar, while reorganising and diversifying. To compete, the industry shed obsolete equipment and old practices in favour of reinvestment and embracing market economies. The industry also adopted the latest research and development findings, applying biotechnology and information technology to improve productivity.
Beef and sheep farming have been the mainstay of the country's agricultural sector for over a century. Since subsidies were withdrawn in 1982, these sectors have been rationalised and have seen a fall in the number of farms and animals. Productivity in meat and wool has increased since 1994 with 14 per cent more lambs born to 32 per cent fewer ewes. Weight gain of the average lamb at slaughter and lamb meat production have increased.
Dairy farming, particularly in the South Island, has increased with the addition of 1,650 new farms since 1994; the number of dairy cows rose by 52 per cent to 5.24 million.
Exports of flowers and wines have steadily increased, with horticulture exports amounting to NZ$2.20 billion (US$1.46 billion) by 2004.
The agriculture, fishing and forestry sectors together account for approximately 7–8 per cent of GDP and provide employment for over 11 per cent of the workforce. Of the total land area, grazing accounts for almost 12 million hectares (ha), horticulture over 100,000ha and planted forests 1.9 million ha.
Deer farming has led to a rapid growth in venison exports, and goats are reared for mohair. Wheat production is sufficient to meet national demand, as do crops including barley, maize and fresh vegetables. Other products include apples, pears, stone and berry fruits, citrus and sub-tropical fruits.
Crop production in 2005 included: 893,700 tonnes (t) cereals in total, 277,000t wheat, 172,000t maize, 500,000t potatoes, 400,000t barley, 32,200t pulses, 29,800t citrus fruit, 170,000t grapes, 88,000t tomatoes, 280,000t kiwi fruit, 500,000t apples, 1,095,310t fruit in total, 1,002,580t vegetables in total. Livestock production included: 1,434,237t meat in total, 685,000t beef, 52,000t pig meat, 520,000t lamb, 32,000t game meat, 138,936t poultry, 53,382t eggs, 14,625,000t milk, 12,000t honey, 58,000t cattle hides, 140,000t sheepskins, 230,000t greasy wool.

Fishing

The seafood industry is one of New Zealand's top five export earners. The total fish catch is typically around 700,000 tonnes per annum, of which 80 per cent is produced through marine fishing. Annual export revenues from fishing amount to around US$150 million.
In 2004, the total marine fish catch was 443,562 tonnes and the total crustacean catch was 3,297 tonnes.

Forestry

Forests cover about 27 per cent (eight million ha) of New Zealand's land area. Of this, around 6.2 million ha are indigenous forest and 1.9 million ha are plantations. The majority of plantations, cultivating exotic species, are in the central region of North Island. Some 95 per cent of plantations grow exotic softwoods, of which 80 per cent are Pinus Radiata, 10 per cent Douglas Fir and 10 per cent other species. The state owns 55 per cent of the exotic resource, with forestry companies, Mäori incorporates, local authorities and individuals owning the remainder.
Chile is New Zealand's major competitor in the market for Pinus Radiata. The planting of exotic species began on a large scale in 1923; there was a second major planting in the 1960s and these trees are now reaching maturity, which will boost the supply of mature trees over the medium-term.
Timber imports in 2004 were US$447.6 million, while exports amounted to US$1.9 billion. In the long term a vibrant log processing industry, comparable to that of the southern US, could be developed.
Timber production in 2004 included 19,722,000 cubic metre (cum) roundwood, 19,722,000cum industrial roundwood, 4,369,000cum sawnwood, 9,174,000cum sawlogs and veneer logs, 3,336,000t pulpwood, 2,219,000cum wood-based panels, 920,000 tonnes (t) paper and paperboard, (including 380,000t newsprint), 1,596,000t paper pulp, 238,000t recovered paper.

Industry and manufacturing

The industrial sector typically accounts for under a fifth of GDP, employs just over a fifth of the workforce, and accounts for a similar proportion of export earnings.
The industrialisation that took place from the mid-1980s helped increase the added value of New Zealand's traditional sectors. Meat, dairy and fruit produce are processed in New Zealand for markets in Asia and Europe. Biotechnology, communications and information technology are also sectors growing in importance.

Tourism

Tourism is the principal earner of foreign exchange. The sector, which provides employment for around 10 per cent of the workforce, is expected to contribute 7.1 per cent to GDP in 2005. Visitor numbers continue to rise, having weathered the impact of recent external crises, including the Sars outbreak of 2003, which damaged many other countries' tourism industries, and demonstrating the strength of the sector. 2.1 million visitors were recorded in 2004, compared with 1.9 million in 2003.

Mining

The mining sector typically accounts for 2 per cent of GDP and employs 1.5 per cent of the workforce. Gold, silver, ironsand, clays, sand and aggregates are the main minerals mined. Ironsand is used to produce steel and is exported to Japan. Other metals include tungsten, manganese, copper, lead, zinc, tin, mercury (as cinnabar), platinum, titanium and aluminium (as bauxite). Non-metallic minerals include aggregates for roads; clays for ceramics and fillers; bentonite for bonding and drilling; limestone for agriculture and cement; and dolomite, serpentine, silica sand, sulphur, diatomite, mica, pumice and feldspar.

Hydrocarbons

New Zealand has around 190 million barrels of proven oil reserves and, in 2004, produced 7.6 million barrels per annum. Production has declined by around 50 per cent in recent years. Domestic consumption is rising. Without further investment, New Zealand's oil and gas reserves are expected to decline from about 2005.
New Zealand has around 84.9 billion cubic metres (cum) of natural gas reserves. Most of the gas is produced from the large offshore Taranaki Maui field, which is expected to be depleted by 2008. Small discoveries by Westech Energy and Orion Exploration were made in the largely unexplored East Coast Basin in 1998.
Fletcher Challenge's March 2000 discovery at its Pohokura well is expected to start producing gas in 2006; estimated reserves are 21million cum.
New Zealand has 8.6 billion tonnes of recoverable coal reserves and produces 3.2 million tonnes oil equivalent. Coal is New Zealand's largest energy resource. Coal production is increasing to meet domestic demand as oil and gas production falls, especially to supply steelworks and thermal power stations. Lignite makes up 82 per cent of recoverable coal resources,

with sub-bituminous coal comprising 14 per cent and bituminous coal comprising less than 4 per cent. A substantial proportion of coal is exported to markets in Japan, India, South Africa, South America, Europe and China.

Energy
New Zealand has installed electricity generating capacity of around 8.5GW. Hydro-power generated on numerous rivers and lakes provides around 70 per cent of all electricity generated, with another 5 per cent coming from geothermal sources. Most of the rest has been supplied by natural gas, but with the depletion of reserves and the need to expand capacity to meet the growing demand for electricity, coal, of which New Zealand has abundant reserves, is becoming increasingly important.

Financial markets
Stock exchange
New Zealand's stock exchanges are in Auckland, Christchurch, Dunedin and Wellington. The largest of the four is the New Zealand Stock Exchange (NZSE) in Auckland. On 30 May 2003, the NZSE re-named itself the NZX.

Banking and insurance
Banking has been opened up to international competition, but domestic demand for credit remains weak. All but one of New Zealand's 18 banks are foreign-owned.
Central bank
The Reserve Bank of New Zealand (RBNZ) formulates and implements monetary policy and is the supervisory authority for New Zealand's registered banks.
Main financial centre
Wellington

Time
GMT plus 13 hours October–March; GMT plus 12 hours March–October.

Geography
New Zealand is in the south-west Pacific, 1,600km south-east of Australia, separated from it by the Tasman Sea, and has no continental neighbours to the east before South America. Its combined length is over 1,600km and it is about 450km across at its widest point. Mount Cook in the Southern Alps is its highest point at 3,764 metres – one of more than 230 named peaks above 2,300 metres.
It consists of two main islands (North Island and South Island – usually referred to by locals as the mainland, as it is the larger of the two islands) and other outlying islands, the Stewart Island, off the southern tip of South Island and the Chatham Islands, 800km east of the South Island.
Geologically speaking, New Zealand is one of the youngest countries in the world, with a topography that is still being shaped by earthquakes, active volcanoes and glaciers.
The North Island has low-lying, rolling hills that rise to around 1,700 metres and form the heart of the area, with rich farmland on all sides. Lake Taupo, the largest in the North Island, is almost in the centre of the range, which is dominated by a volcanic plateau at Rotorua.
The South Island is much more rugged, with the Southern Alps that rise to over 3,000 metres running the length of the island. West of the Alps are rainforests and to the east farmland and the alluvial plains formed by rivers flowing down from the mountains. The Southern Alps contain glaciers, the largest of which is the Tasman glacier.
Stewart Island is largely low rolling hills which, unlike the two main islands, retains almost all of its native vegetation.
Hemisphere
Southern

Climate
New Zealand is a temperate country with a variable and unpredictable climate, generally drier and warmer on North Island than on South Island, particularly in winter. Rainfall averages 600–1,500mm annually and strong winds are common. On North Island, January temperatures average 18 degrees Celsius (C) and in winter 4 degrees C. It is 3 to 5 degrees C colder on South Island.

Dress codes
Visitors should take warm clothing during the winter months, from May to October. Even in the summer, from December to early March, a light sweater is an essential travelling item. Suits are worn for business meetings. For leisure, smart casual clothes are acceptable.

Entry requirements
Passports
Passports are required by all and must be valid for three months beyond the intended length of stay.
Visa
Required by all, except visitors from visa free countries. For a full list see www.immigration.govt.nz. Business visas may not be required for company representatives, a visitors visa is sufficient for stays up to three months. However proof of onward/return tickets and sufficient funds are required.
Currency advice/regulations
There are no restrictions on the import and export of local or foreign currencies.
Customs
Equipment used with animals, camping equipment, golf clubs and used bicycles must be declared.
Personal effects are allowed duty-free: 200 cigarettes, 4.5 litres of wine/beer, or goods up to the value of NZ$700 (or equivalent) are permitted.
Visitors arriving from countries suffering from certain diseases affecting livestock and plants may have items of clothing and produce disinfected.
Prohibited imports
Illegal drugs, plants or plant material, animals or by-products (these include any fruit, vegetables or meat – cooked or raw), biological specimens, artifacts made from endangered wildlife and weapons, such as flick knives, are prohibited. Firearms and ammunition require a permit.

Health (for visitors)
A reciprocal health agreement for urgent medical treatment exists with the United Kingdom. Some proof of UK residence will be required.
Mandatory precautions
There are no compulsory vaccinations.
Advisable precautions
Travellers are advised to have up-to-date tetanus and polio immunisations.

Hotels
Motel, serviced-unit accommodation is widespread. Neither a service charge nor tipping is customary. Advance booking is advisable for major hotels in urban centres.

Credit cards
All major credit cards are accepted.

Public holidays (national)
Fixed dates
1–2 Jan (New Year), 6 Feb (Waitangi Day), 25 Apr (Anzac Day), 25–26 Dec (Christmas).
Variable dates
Easter Holiday, Queen's Official Birthday (first Mon in Jun), Labour Day (Oct).

Working hours
Mid-December to mid-February is the summer holiday season during which the majority of New Zealanders take most of their annual leave.
Banking
Mon–Fri: 0900–1630.
Business
Mon–Fri: 0900–1700.
Government
Mon–Fri: 0800–1630.
Shops
Mon–Thu: 0900–1730; Fri: 0900–2100; Sat: 0900–1230. Some shops open on Sundays.

Telecommunications
Mobile/cell phones
GSM 900, 1800 and 3G services are available throughout most of the country.

Electricity supply
230/240V AC, 50 hertz, with three-pin flat plug fittings, most hotels supply 110V AC sockets for razors.

Weights and measures
Metric system

Social customs/useful tips
In general, be polite and patient. New Zealanders appreciate frankness and like prompt timekeeping for business meetings. Business can also be discussed over lunch and dinner. Late night life can be sparse. People tend to go to bed early and start work early.
Should a visitor be invited to a formal Mäori occasion the hongi (pressing of noses) is common.
Tipping is acceptable but is not particularly sought after and there is sometimes a built-in service charge at hotels and restaurants. There is a smoking ban in restaurants and pubs.

Security
The cities are safe, even at night.

Getting there
Air
National airline: Air New Zealand
International airport/s: Auckland International, Mangere (AKL), 22km south of Auckland; Christchurch International (CHC), 10km of the city; Wellington International (WLG), 8km south-east of the city; all with duty-free shop, bar, restaurant, bank, hotel reservations, post office, shops, car hire and office facilities. Taxi journeys from Auckland International Airport to the city centre take 35 minutes; from Christchurch Airport to city centre 15 minutes; from Wellington Airport to city centre 20 minutes.
Airport tax: Departures and security tax: up to NZ$30, depending on the airport; transit passengers up to 24 hours are exempt.
Surface
Water: Apart from cruise ships there are no regular passenger ships sailing to New Zealand. International shipping lines that maintain contacts with New Zealand may provide passenger services on cargo ships.
Main port/s: Auckland (containers), Dunedin, Lyttelton (containers), Tauranga, Wellington (containers), Port Chalmers (containers), Picton, Opua.

Getting about
National transport
Air: There are good regular air services between the four major cities (Wellington, Auckland, Christchurch and Dunedin) with links to smaller, regional towns and tourist centres. Internal air services serve around 30 airports.
Road: The road network includes over 11,000km of state highways. The main routes are surfaced, and roads are generally well-maintained.
Buses: Luxury coach services link the main centres. Advance booking for these is advisable, especially during the main holiday periods (December–February and Easter).
Rail: The rail network operates over 4,300km of track linking cities and main towns with express services that have buffet cars.
Water: Interisland Lines operates a regular ferry service between Wellington and Picton several times a day. Advance booking is advisable, especially during the main holiday periods.
City transport
Taxis: Taxis may be hired from ranks or by telephone 24 hours a day, although there is an extra charge for telephone booking. Fares are generally charged per km, but rates vary throughout the country and are generally higher at night and on weekends. Tipping is not customary.
Buses, trams & metro: Auckland's integrated transport system, in the city centre, is connected by the Britomart rail network that handles suburban and intercity trains, to buses and ferries. Wellington has a rail-metro with five lines terminating in the city centre. Christchurch has a comprehensive bus-metro.
There are good, privately operated, local buses in all urban areas.
Car hire
Car hire is available throughout the country; drivers must be over 21 years with either a national licence or international driving permit. It is advisable to book ahead at motels when touring. Driving is on the left-hand side of the road. Parking can be a problem in larger cities. Outside the major centres there is little traffic as country areas are sparsely populated.

BUSINESS DIRECTORY

The addresses listed below are a selection only. While World of Information makes every endeavour to check these addresses, we cannot guarantee that changes have not been made, especially to telephone numbers and area codes. We would welcome any corrections.

Telephone area codes
The international direct dialling code (IDD) for New Zealand is +64, followed by area code and subscriber's number:

Auckland	9	Nelson	3
Bay of Plenty	7	New Plymouth	6
Christchurch	3	Palmerston North	6
Dunedin	3	Rotorua	7

Gisborne	6	Tauranga	7
Hamilton	7	The South Island	3
Hastings	6	Timaru	3
Invercargil	3	Wanganui	6
Manawatu	6	Wellington	4
Napier	6	Whangarei	9

Useful telephone numbers
Emergency (all services): 111

Chambers of Commerce
American Chamber of Commerce in New Zealand, Affco House, 12-26 Swanson Street, PO Box 106002, Auckland Central 1001 (tel: 309-9140; fax: 309-1090; e-mail: amcham@amcham.co.nz).

Auckland Chamber of Commerce, 100 Mayoral Drive, PO Box 47, Auckland (tel: 309-6100; fax: 309-0081; e-mail: akl@chamber.co.nz).

British New Zealand Trade Council, PO Box 37162, Parnell, Auckland (tel/fax: 522-0526; e-mail: info@bnztc.co.nz).

Canterbury Employers Chamber of Commerce, 57 Kilmore Street, PO Box 359, Christchurch (tel: 366-5096; fax: 379-5454; e-mail: info@cecc.org.nz).

New Zealand Chambers of Commerce & Industry, 109 Featherston Street, PO Box 11043, Wellington (tel: 472-3376; fax: 471-1767).

Otago Chamber of Commerce & Industry, WestpacTrust Building, 106 George Street, Dunedin (tel: 479-0181; fax: 477-0341; e-mail: office@otagochamber.co.nz).

Wellington Regional Chamber of Commerce, 109 Featherston Street, PO Box 1590, Wellington 6015 (tel: 914-6500; fax: 914-6524; e-mail: info@wgtn-chamber.co.nz).

Banking
ANZ Banking Group (New Zealand) Limited, PO Box 1492, ANZ Tower, Level 9, 215-229 Lambton Quay, Wellington (tel: 496-6938; fax: 496-6934).

ASB Bank Ltd, 198-204 Lambton Quay, Wellington (tel: 499-0864; fax: 495-2102).

Bank of New Zealand, PO Box 2392, State Insurance Centre, 1 Willis Street, Wellington (tel: 474-6999; fax: 474-6861).

BNZ Finance Ltd; PO Box 401, Level 24, BNZ Centre, 1 Willis Street, Wellington (tel: 495-3630; fax: 495-3632).

National Bank of New Zealand Ltd, PO Box 1791, 1 Victoria Street, Wellington 6000 (tel: 498-6020; fax: 494-4023).

Reserve Bank of New Zealand, PO Box 2498, 2 The Terrace, Wellington (tel: 472-2029; fax: 473-8554).

Westpac Banking Corporation, PO Box 691, 157 Lambton Quay, Wellington (tel: 381-1430; fax: 470-8202).

Central bank

Reserve Bank of New Zealand, 2 The Terrace, PO Box 2498, Wellington (tel: 472-2029; fax: 473-8554; e-mail: rbnz-info@rbnz.govt.nz).

Travel information

Air New Zealand, Customer Support, Private Bag 92007, Auckland 1020 (tel: 255-8758; fax: 256-3531; internet site: www.airnz.co.nz/).

Intercity Coachlines (InterCity Group (NZ)), PO Box 26 601, Epsom, Auckland (tel: 623-1503; email: info@intercitygroup.co.nz; internet site: www.intercitycoach.co.nz).

Interislander (ferry service) (Ticket Office) PO Box 2085, Wellington (tel: 498-3302; fax: 498-3090; email: info@interislander.co.nz; internet site: www.interislander.co.nz).

Trains: tel (outside NZ): (+64-4) 495-0775; fax: (+64-4) 4728903; tel inside NZ: 0800-872-467; email: bookings@tranzscenic.co.nz; internet: www.transcenic.co.nz).

National tourist organisation offices

New Zealand Tourism Board, level 16, 80 The Terrace, PO Box 95, Wellington (tel: 917-5400; fax: 915-3817; internet: www.purenz.com).

Ministries

Ministry of Agriculture and Fisheries, PO Box 2526, Wellington (tel: 474-4100; fax: 474-4111).

Ministry of Civil Defence, PO Box 5010, Wellington (tel: 473-7363; fax: 473-7369).

Ministry of Commerce, PO Box 1473, Wellington (tel: 472-0030; fax: 473-4638).

Ministry of Consumer Affairs, PO Box 1473, Wellington (tel: 474-2750; fax: 473-9400).

Ministry of Defence, PO Box 5347, Wellington (tel: 496-0999; fax: 496-0859).

Ministry of Education, Private Bag 1666, Wellington (tel: 473-5544; fax: 499-1327).

Ministry for the Environment, PO Box 10362, Wellington (tel: 473-4090; fax: 471-0195).

Ministry of Foreign Affairs and Trade, Private Bag 18-901, Parliament Bldgs, Wellington (tel: 472-8877; fax: 472-9596).

Ministry of Forestry, PO Box 1610, Wellington (tel: 472-1569; fax: 472-2314).

Ministry of Health, PO Box 5013, Wellington (tel: 496-2000; fax: 496-2340).

Ministry of Mäori Development, PO Box 3943, Wellington (tel: 494-7100; fax: 494-7010).

Ministry of Pacific Island Affairs, PO Box 833, Wellington (tel: 473-4493; fax: 473-4301).

Ministry of Research, Science and Technology, PO Box 5336, Wellington (tel: 472-6400; fax: 471-1284).

Ministry of Transport, PO Box 3175, Wellington (tel: 472-1253; fax: 473-3697).

Ministry of Women's Affairs, PO Box 10049, Wellington (tel: 473-4112; fax: 472-0961).

Ministry of Youth Affairs, PO Box 10300, Wellington (tel: 471-2158; fax: 471-2233).

Prime Minister and Cabinet Department, Executive Wing, Parliament Bldgs, Wellington (tel: 471-9700; fax: 473-2508).

Other useful addresses

Airways Corporation of New Zealand, 44-48 Willis Street, PO Box 294, Wellington (tel: 471-1888; fax: 471-0395; internet: www.airways.co.nz/).

British High Commission, PO Box 1812, 44 Hill Street, Wellington 1 (tel: 472-6049; fax: 471-1974).

British/New Zealand Trade Council Inc, 22 Newton Road, Newton, Auckland (tel: 378-9066; fax: 378-0539).

Central Region Health Authority, PO Box 10097, 155 The Terrace, Wellington (tel: 472-7633; fax: 472-7639).

Coal Corporation of New Zealand Ltd, PO Box 439, Wellington (tel: 474-3600; fax: 474-3601).

Commerce Commission, PO Box 2351, Wellington (tel: 471-0180; fax: 471-0771).

Conservation Department, PO Box 10420, Wellington (tel: 471-0726; fax: 471-1082).

Customs Department, PO Box 2218, Whitmore Street, Wellington (tel: 473-6099; fax: 473-7370).

Earthquake Commission, PO Box 311, Wellington (tel: 499-0045; fax: 499-0046).

Electricity Corporation of New Zealand, PO Box 930, Wellington (tel: 472-3550; fax: 473-7091).

Hillary Commission for Sport, Fitness and Leisure, PO Box 2251, Wellington (tel: 472-8058; fax: 471-0813).

Housing Corporation of New Zealand, PO Box 5009, Wellington (tel: 495-1045; fax: 472-3152).

Human Rights Commission, PO Box 6751, Wellesley Street, Auckland (tel: 309-0874; fax: 377-3593).

Inland Revenue Department, PO Box 2198, Wellington (tel: 472-1032; fax: 499-0806).

Internal Affairs Department, PO Box 805, Wellington (tel: 495-7200; fax: 495-7222).

Justice Department, PO Box 180, Wellington (tel: 472-5980; fax: 499-2295).

Labour Department, PO Box 3705, Wellington (tel: 473-7800; fax: 495-4009).

Land Corporation Ltd, PO Box 5349, Wellington (tel: 471-0400; fax: 473-4966).

New Zealand Embassy (USA), 37 Observatory Circle, NW, Washington DC 20008 (tel: (+1-202) 328-4800; fax: (+1-202) 667-5227; e-mail: nz@nzemb.org).

New Zealand Manufacturers' Federation, 3–9 Church Street, PO Box 11543, Wellington (tel: 473-3000; fax: 473-3004).

New Zealand Minerals Industry Association, Druids Building, 188 Lambton Quay, PO Box 5039, Wellington (tel: 499-9871; fax: 499-9873; email: nzmia@xtra.co.nz).

New Zealand Stock Exchange, Caltex Tower, 286-292 Lambton Quay, PO Box 2959, Wellington (tel: 472-7599; fax: 473-1470).

New Zealand Trade Development Board (TRADENZ), Pastoral House, 25 The Terrace, PO Box 10341, Wellington (tel: 499-2244; fax: 473-3193).

Overseas Investment Commission, 2 The Terrace, PO Box 2498, Wellington (tel: 471-3838; fax: 471-3655).

Race Relations Office, PO Box 12411, Thorndon, Wellington (tel: 499-5885; fax: 499-5998).

Radio New Zealand, PO Box 2092, Wellington (tel: 474-1555; fax: 474-1712).

Statistics Department, 85 Molesworth Street, PO Box 2922, Wellington (tel: 495-4600; fax: 472-9135).

Survey and Land Information Department, Private Box 170, Charles Ferguson Building, Wellington (tel: 473-5022; fax: 472-2244).

Telecom New Zealand, PO Box 1473, Christchurch (tel: 374-0253; internet: www.telecom.co.nz).

Television New Zealand Ltd, PO Box 3819, Auckland (tel: 377-0630; fax: 375-0828).

Tranz Rail Ltd, Private Bag, Wellington (tel: 498-3095; fax: 498-3322).

Treasury Department, PO Box 3724, Wellington (tel: 472-2733; fax: 473-0982).

Works and Development Services Corporation Ltd, PO Box 12041, Wellington (tel: 496-1300; fax: 471-0224).

Internet sites

AA Travel: www.aatravel.co.nz

Air New Zealand: www:airnz.com

Asia Pacific Economic Co-operation (APEC): www.apecsec.org.sg

Auckland Airport: www:auckland-airport.co.nz

Destination New Zealand (gateway site): www.destinationnz.co.nz

Economic & Trade Development Agency: www:nzte.govt.nz

General Information: www:nz.com

Immigration: www:immigration.govt.nz

Ministry of Foreign Affairs and Trade: www:mft.govt.nz

New Zealand Government: www.govt.nz

New Zealand Herald newspaper: www:nzherald.co.nz

Parliament: www:parliament.govt.nz

Reserve Bank: www:rbnz.govt.nz

Statistics: www:stats.govt.nz

Stock exchange: www:nzse.co.nz

Treasury: www:treasury.govt.nz

Tourism: www:purenz.com

Nicaragua

KEY FACTS

Official name: República de Nicaragua (Republic of Nicaragua)

Head of State: President Enrique Daniel Ortega Saavedra (from 10 Jan 2007)

Head of government: President Enrique Daniel Ortega (FSLN)

Ruling party: Frente Sandinista de Liberación Nacional (FSLN) (Sandinista National Liberation Front) (from 10 Jan 2007)

Area: 147,950 square km

Population: 6.05 million (2007)*

Capital: Managua

Official language: Spanish

Currency: Córdoba de oro (gold córdoba) (C) = 100 centavos

Exchange rate: C19.41 per US$ (Jul 2008)

GDP per capita: US$945 (2007)*

GDP real growth: 3.70% (2007)

Labour force: 2.23 million (2004)

Unemployment: 5.60% (2005)* (official rate; 46.5% unofficial rate)

Inflation: 11.80% (2007)

Balance of trade: -US$1.96 billion (2006)

Foreign debt: US$5.14 billion (2004)

Visitor numbers: 773,000 (2006)*

* estimated figure

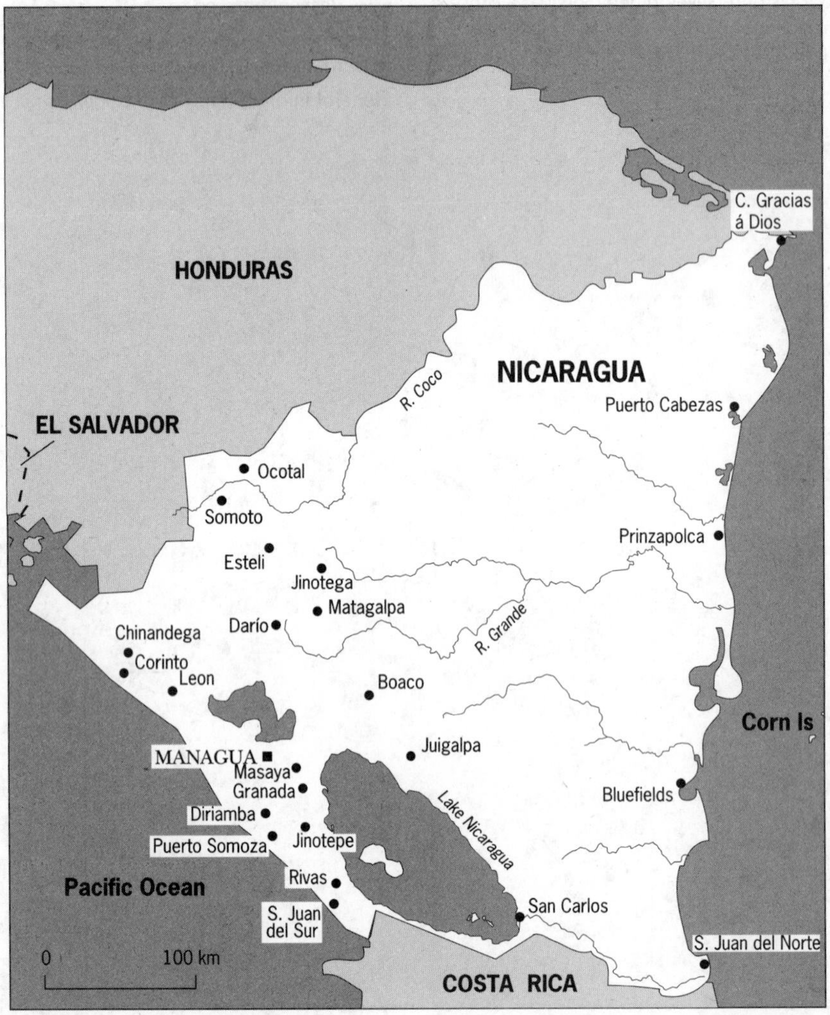

The Nicaraguan economy slowed down slightly in 2007. Gross domestic product grew by 3.0 per cent, but both consumption and private investment slowed. Under the continued stewardship of left-wing leader Daniel Ortega, unemployment edged up from 5.2 per cent in 2006 to 5.9 per cent in 2007.

Inflation concerns

The principal concern of the government, as well as Nicaragua's donors and investotors, was the apparently inexorable rise in the inflation rate, which went from 9.4 per cent in 2006 to 13.8 per cent, almost double the 7.3 per cent target set by Nicaragua's central bank. According to estimates prepared by the United Nations Economic Commission for Latin America and the Caribbean (ECLAC/CEPAL), growth in 2008 should be around 3.5 per cent and inflation should fall back to 8.5 per cent. Following the 2006 elections, in which the votes of Nicaragua's impoverished peasants proved critical, the government introduced a new economic programme, the main aim of which was to establish macroeconomic stability while providing enough fiscal leeway to reduce poverty. In October 2006 the government had signed a three year agreement with the International Monetary Fund (IMF) which resulted in an immediate payment of US$18.5 million. For the Ortega administration, achieving macroeconomic stability was seen as a means of reducing poverty rather than as an end itself.

2007 saw Nicaragua join the Bolivarian Alternative for Latin America and the Caribbean (ALBA – which in Spanish means 'dawn'). According to ECLAC, for Nicaragua membership of ALBA, which is an initiative of Venezuelan president Hugo Chávez, will mean co-operation in the energy sector, as well as increased resources for infrastructure, health, agricultural development and the construction of housing.

Nicaraguans went to the polls in November 2006 to elect a new president and 90 members of the national assembly, all of whom will serve five-year terms. Daniel Ortega of the Frente Sandinista de Liberación Nacional (FSLN) (Sandinista National Liberation Front) obtained just under 38 per cent of the vote, Eduardo Montealegre of the Alianza Liberal Nicaragüense (ALN) (Nicaraguan Liberal Alliance) come second with 28.30 per cent.

The previous presidency of Enrique José Bolaños Geyer had typified the self-indulgent brand of politics that had become inextricably linked with Nicaragua over the years. Political ambushes by the opposition and infighting within the president's own party were both been a feature of his administration, since it came to power in 2001. Bolaños, of mixed Spanish and Germanic ancestry, successfully opposed the governing Frente Sandinista de Liberación Nacional (FSLN) (Sandinista National Liberation Front) throughout the 1980s and was imprisoned for his efforts. He also saw his business interests shut down and eventually confiscated by the authorities as the Sandinistas attempted to remove him from the country's political arena.

The ultimate political streetfighter, Bolaños fought back and eventually climbed his way up the greasiest of greasy polls that is the Nicaraguan political system, to become former president Arnoldo Alemán's vice president. In 2001, Bolaños, running on the Partido Liberal Constitucionalista (PLC) (Constitutional Liberal Party) ticket, successfully saw off former president Daniel Ortega's FSLN challenge for the presidency. Ortega's day would come.

After being sworn in, Bolaños launched an anti-corruption drive that eventually led to the sentencing of his former boss, Alemán, to twenty years imprisonment on charges of money laundering and fraud, among other offences. However, his decision to go after Alemán by making him a symbolic figure of his clampdown on political practice, and his decision to break away from the PLC (to form the Alianza por la República (APRE) (Alliance for the Republic)), left him exposed to attacks from both ends of the political spectrum. In September and October both the PLC and the FSLN threatened to team up together in order to impeach the president. Though this initiative later tailed off, a reinvigoration of the impeachment drive remains a distinct future possibility.

Economy

The Nicaraguan economy has grown steadily since 2003 to reach growth of 3.7 per cent for 2007, although this was a dip from the 3.9 per cent of 2006. Inflation is rising alarmingly – to 11.8 per cent in 2007.

Nicaragua remains plagued by poverty; it is the second-poorest country in the Western Hemisphere after Haiti. Spending on education and health has taken a backseat to debt servicing. In terms of GDP, the country has one of the highest external debts in the world and was one of the first countries to qualify for the International Monetary Fund (IMF) Enhanced Heavily Indebted Poor Countrty (HIPC) initiative.

Although some of the government's failure to meet budgetary targets stem from its own corruption and incompetence, many of the problems are rooted in the ailing health of the economy, which has been blighted by a series of natural disasters and poor prices for its main commodity exports, particularly coffee. In January 2004, the country received some good news as the World Bank and the IMF wiped out 80 per cent of Nicaragua's debt by supporting US$4.5 billion of debt service relief. This gave the country the opportunity to address poverty as pressure from a rising national debt decreased.

According to the World Bank, with an estimated per capita GDP of US$945 in 2007, Nicaragua remained the second poorest country in the Latin America and Caribbean region after Haiti. Although overall poverty declined from 50 to 46 per cent in 1998–2001, and extreme poverty fell from 19 to 15 per cent in the same period, according to the Bank both poverty and extreme poverty continue to be staggeringly high in rural areas. Poverty changes between 1998 and 2001 varied substantially by region, with the greatest decline in poverty levels in the Central Rural Region. Despite these gains in poverty, nearly half of all Nicaragua's Poverty Reduction Strategy Paper (PRSP) and Millennium Development Goals (MDGs) targets look unlikely to be met by 2015.

Agriculture

Agriculture plays a very significant role in the economy of Nicaragua, contributing about a quarter of the country's total GDP. The sector also employs up to 30 per cent of the total workforce. The principal export crop is coffee, which represents approximately a fifth of total export earnings. The Nicaraguan government is actively engaged in the agricultural sector although it is estimated that upwards of 60

KEY INDICATORS **Nicaragua**

	Unit	2003	2004	2005	2006	2007
Population	m	5.67	5.58	5.77	*5.91	*6.05
Gross domestic product (GDP)	US$bn	4.10	4.50	4.90	5.29	5.72
GDP per capita	US$	495	788	850	*896	*945
GDP real growth	%	2.3	4.0	4.0	3.9	3.7
Inflation	%	5.2	8.2	9.6	9.1	11.8
Exports (fob) (goods)	US$m	596.0	750.0	1,551.5	1,027.0	2,313.2
Imports (cif) (goods)	US$m	1,624.0	2,020.0	2,865.2	2,988.0	4,078.0
Balance of trade	US$m	-1,028.0	1,270.0	-1,313.7	-1,961.0	-1,764.8
Current account	US$m	-810.0	-950.0	-697.0	-700.0	-989.0
Total reserves minus gold	US$m	502.1	668.2	727.8	921.9	1,103.3
Foreign exchange	US$m	502.0	667.7	727.5	921.5	1,103.2
Exchange rate	per US$	15.00	15.94	18.03	18.03	18.86

* estimated figure

per cent of cultivated land is in the hands of private smallholders. Despite continuous agrarian reform, food production has not kept up with demand owing mainly to poor weather, war damage and shortages of vital inputs.

During the 1980s, the national government of Nicaragua had launched an unsuccessful policy of industrial development, premised on the promotion of joint public and-private enterprises, in a bid to provide basic consumer goods at prices accessible to most people. Unfortunately, one unforeseen consequence of this policy was the lowering of economic efficiency as a result of subsidies on state-produced goods. By the end of the decade, many private producers had been forced to close their factories, sell out to the state or scale down activities.

However, there has since been significant growth in the non-traditional *maquiladora* (assembly line) sector, which has made use of the Free Trade Zones (FTZs). Concentrated mainly on textiles, particularly clothing, for the US market, the *maquiladora* sector has rapidly become a major sub-sector in Nicaraguan industry. Low labour costs and minimal labour regulation have made it both an attractive opportunity for foreign investors and a target for trade unions and labour rights activists.

Outlook

Daniel Ortega's election represents a remarkable comeback by this figure of the 1980s. The extent to which he can command respect from across the political spectrum, however, remains to be seen. Mr Ortega comes with a lot of political baggage.

Risk assessment

Politics	Fair
Economy	Fair
Regional stability	Good

COUNTRY PROFILE

Historical profile

1821 The Central American provinces (Costa Rica, Guatemala, Honduras, Nicaragua and El Salvador) declared independence from Spain.

1822 Central American confederation annexed itself to the Mexican Empire, under General Agustín de Iturbde, later Emporer Agustín I.

1823 Agustín I was overthrown and Mexico became a republic. The Central American states formed the United Provinces of Central America.

1825 Costa Rica, Guatemala, Honduras, Nicaragua and El Salvador formed the Central American Federation (CAF).

1838 The CAF was dissolved and Nicaragua became a fully independent republic.

1855—57 Nicaragua was ruled by a US buccaneer, William Walker, who proclaimed himself president after being invited by the Liberals. He was overthrown in 1857 following intervention by other Central American states. He attempted to take over Nicaragua for a second time, but was repelled by the British navy. He made another attempt to seize the country in 1860, but was captured by the British and executed.

1860 British ceded control over the Caribbean coast to Nicaragua.

1893 General José Santos Zelaya, a Liberal, seized power and established a dictatorship.

1909 Zelaya was driven from office following a US-backed coup. Nicaragua allowed the US to run its customs and excise (raising money to pay the foreign debt), the national bank and the railway.

1912—25 The US established a number of military bases.

1929—33 Guerrillas led by Augusto César Sandino campaigned against US military presence.

1934 Sandino was assassinated on the orders of the National Guard commander, General Anastasio 'Tacho' Somoza García. The US marines left with Somoza ruling as a puppet dicatator.

1956 General Somoza was assassinated and was succeeded as president by his son, Luis Somoza Debayle.

1961 The Frente Sandinista de Liberación Nacional (FSLN) (Sandinista National Liberation Front) was founded. The Central American Common Market (CACM) was formed, comprising Nicaragua, Costa Rica, El Salvador, Honduras and Guatemala.

1967 Anastasio Somoza Debayle was officially elected president, succeeding his brother Luis.

1969 CACM collapsed following the 'soccer war' between El Salvador and Honduras.

1978 Prominent opposition leader and editor of La Prensa newspaper, Pedro Joaquín Chamorro, was assassinated, leading to a general strike and consolidation within the opposition.

1979 The Somoza dynasty was overthrown by a cross-party junta led by the FSLN. The new government seized land and private businesses owned by Somoza and his allies who had fled the country.

1981 The US broke off diplomatic links with Nicaragua claiming it was part of the communist 'evil empire'. A number of opposition leaders fled to Costa Rica and Honduras where they established guerrilla groups known as 'counter-revolutionaries' or Contras.

1982 The US began the Contra war against Nicaragua, arming counter-revolutionaries allied to supporters of the former Somoza regime and using bases in Honduras.

1984 Daniel Ortega, leader of the nine ruling comandantes, was elected president (the only opposition candidate withdrew). The US mined Nicaragua's harbours. Nicaragua began legal action against the US in the World Court for violating international law.

1986 The Nicaraguan government closed La Prensa after it began receiving funds from the CIA. The US was found to have given aid to the Contras, funded with arms sales from the US to Iran in what became known as the Iran-Contra Affair. The World Court found the US guilty of violating international law and ordered reparations. The US ignored the judgement.

1988 The government and the Contras agreed a cease-fire.

1990 The US-backed Unión Nacional Opositora (UNO) assumed office after elections in which it defeated the FSLN. The presidential opposition candidate, Violeta Chamorro, publisher of La Prensa, won the presidential election.

1994 Following defections from the UNO coalition, the de facto ruling coalition became a centrist block in alliance with the FSLN.

1996 Arnoldo Alemán won the elections.

1997 President Alemán was inaugurated. His right-wing Alianza Liberal Nicaragüense (ALN) (Nicaraguan Liberal Alliance), dominated by the Partido Liberal Constitucionalista (PLC) (Constitutionalist Liberal Party), was the largest single group in the National Assembly.

1998 Hurricane Mitch devastated large parts of Nicaragua.

1999 The FSLN and the AL entered into a pact in order to force through controversial laws that worked against the emergence of a 'third force' in Nicaraguan politics.

2000 The FSLN made significant gains in the municipal elections, winning the major cities including the capital, Managua.

2001 PLC and Enrique Bolaños (PLC) were the winners of the elections.

2002 President Bolaños took office.

2003 The FSLN re-elected Daniel Ortega as party leader.

2004 Over 70 per cent of Nicaragua's debt to the World Bank was waived. An agreement was reached in July with Russia to cancel Nicaragua's huge debt, incurred with the former Soviet Union.

2005 Violent street protests erupted following fuel price rises. The government and an alliance of opposition parties in Congress began a power struggle over

constitutional reforms but later agreed to delay reforms.
2006 Daniel Ortega won the presidential elections and the FSLN won 38 of the 90 seats in the parliamentary elections. Tough laws that banned legal abortions, including those for mothers whose life was at risk, were approved.
2007 Ortega was inaugurated as president in January. In October after eight years of conflict, the International Court of Justice (ICJ) ruled on a new maritime boundary between Honduras and Nicaragua. The result gives both countries equal access to the rich fishing grounds and oil and gas exploration waters in the area.
2008 Nicaragua protested about alleged intimidation of its fishermen by Colombia in disputed waters. The ICJ had awarded three islands in the Caribbean Sea to Colombia in December 2007.

Political structure

In addition to their unicameral national parliaments, El Salvador, Guatemala, Honduras, Nicaragua, Panama and Dominican Republic also return directly-elected deputies to the supranational Central American Parliament.

Constitution

The National Assembly approved constitutional reforms in January 2000 which provide outgoing presidents and vice presidents with a lifelong seat in the legislature. Other constitutional reforms included a reduction of the percentage of votes required to elect a president without the need for a run-off election, from 45 per cent to 35 per cent of the total, and the restructuring of the judiciary, the electoral authorities and the comptroller general's office, giving the two main parties a bigger share of the posts.
The country comprises 16 departments which are divided into two zones: the Pacific zone and the Atlantic zone.
The minimum voting age is 16 years.

Form of state

Presidential democratic republic

The executive

Power is vested in the president who is head of state and commander-in-chief of the armed forces, elected for a period of five years by universal adult suffrage. The president appoints a cabinet of ministers.

National legislature

Legislative power is vested in the unicameral national assembly, consisting of 90 members elected by adult suffrage by proportional representation every five years. In addition, former presidents and vice presidents hold seats for life and occupied three seats following the 2001 elections.

Legal system

The Nicaraguan legal system comprises civil and military courts. The highest court is the Supreme Court, which administers the judicial system and nominates all appellate and lower court judges. The Supreme Court consists of 12 magistrates elected for seven-year terms by the National Assembly.

Last elections

5 November 2006 (presidential and parliamentary)
Results: Presidential: José Daniel Ortega Saavedra (FSLN) won 38 per cent of the vote; Eduardo Montealegre (Alianza Liberal Nicaragüense (ALN) (Nicaraguan Liberal Alliance) won 28.3 per cent; José Rizo Castellón (Partido Liberal Constitucionalista) (PLC) (Constitutional Liberal Party) 27.11 per cent; and Edmundo Jarquín Calderón (Movimiento de Renovación Sandinista (MRS) (Renewed Sandinista Moverment) 6.3 per cent.
Parliamentary: FSLN won 38 seats (out of 90); PLC won 25 seats; Alianza Liberal Nicaragüense-Partido Conservador (ALN-PC) (Nicaraguan Liberal Alliance-Conservative Party) 22 seats; and MRS five seats.

Next elections

2011 (presidential and parliamentary)

Political parties

Ruling party

Frente Sandinista de Liberación Nacional (FSLN) (Sandinista National Liberation Front) (from 10 Jan 2007)

Main opposition party

Partido Liberal Constitucionalista (PLC) (Liberal Constitutionalist Party)

Population

6.05 million (2007)*
Last census: April 1995: 4,357,099
Population density: 41 inhabitants per square km. Urban population: 57 per cent (1995—2001).
Annual growth rate: 2.1 per cent 1994–2004 (WHO 2006)

Ethnic make-up

Mestizo (mixed indigenous-European) (69 per cent), European (17 per cent), black (9 per cent) and indigenous people (5 per cent).
Creole and Indian peoples live in the eastern region of the country on the Atlantic coast. The Creoles number some 26,000, the Miskitos 182,000 and the Sumus 9,000. There are also two very small indigenous groups – the Ramas and the Garifunos.

Religions

The majority of the population is Catholic, although mainstream Protestant and evangelical groups make up 20 per cent of the population. The majority of the Atlantic coast population is Moravian. There is no official religion.

Education

Nicaragua has been slowly moving towards universal primary enrolment despite severe setbacks resulting from Hurricane Mitch in 1998.
Primary education is free for six years although a report issued by the Nicaraguan Office of the Advocate for Children and Youth revealed that 80 per cent of children in primary and secondary state schools were required to pay a minimum fee per month, including voluntary contributions to teachers' salaries and payments for examinations, in violation of the constitutional right to free education for children.
Secondary education runs in two cycles of three and two years and leads to higher education, or in a cycle of two and three years leading to a technical qualification.
There are both state universities and private universities. The Consejo Nacional de Universidades is responsible for all higher education planning. Nicaragua's major institutions of higher education are the Jesuit-run Central American University, Managua (UCA), the public National Autonomous Universities in Managua and León (Unan) and the private, Harvard-affiliated Central American Institute of Business Administration (Incae) outside Managua.
Spending on primary education amounts to less than US$10 per capita.
Literacy rate: 77 per cent adult rate; 86 per cent youth rate (15–24) (Unesco 2005).
Compulsory years: 6 to 12.
Enrolment rate: 102 per cent gross primary enrolment of the relevant age group (including repeaters); 55 per cent gross secondary enrolment (World Bank).
Pupils per teacher: 36 in primary schools.

Health

Per capita total expenditure on health (2003) was US$208; of which per capita government spending was US$101, at the international dollar rate, (WHO 2006).
Although public health improved during the 1990s, access to medical facilities continues to be uneven and many of the country's poor, particularly in rural areas and on the Atlantic coast, are experiencing inadequate healthcare due to government cutbacks in 2002/03. A growing market of private services exists, but the ministry of health continues to be the main provider of services for the Nicaraguan population as a whole.
Government spending emphasises primary healthcare with priority given to improving local healthcare systems, through national, departmental, regional and municipal co-ordination. The World Bank's International Development Association

(IDA) funded the rehabilitation of healthcare centres, nutrition centres for children, and schools for training nurses and other healthcare workers, and the provision of social services.

HIV/Aids

HIV prevalence: 0.2 per cent aged 15–49 in 2003 (World Bank)

Life expectancy: 69 years, 2004 (WHO 2006)

Fertility rate/Maternal mortality rate: 3.3 births per woman, 2004 (WHO 2006); maternal mortality 150 per 100,000 live births (World Bank).

Child (under 5 years) mortality rate (per 1,000): 30 per 1,000 live births; 12.2 per cent of children under aged five are malnourished (World Bank).

Head of population per physician: 0.37 physicians per 1,000 people, 2003 (WHO 2006)

Welfare

Under the presidency of Arnoldo Alemán (1997—2001), welfare expenditure was squeezed as a result of the government's IMF-dictated austerity measures and high levels of debt servicing. Funds for social protection remain decentralised and the responsibility for resource management lies with local authorities. There are no clear regulations about the amount of money that can be allocated or is necessary for the municipalities. An increasing number of self-employed people do not have access to social protection mechanisms.

Nicaragua's welfare programme combines a traditional cash transfer programme with financial incentives for families to obtain preventive healthcare and education and to participate in other government-sponsored welfare-related programmes.

In 2001, the government initiated a welfare reform programme under the auspices of a three-year Poverty Reduction and Growth Facility (PRGF) arrangement with the IMF. Pension reform is central to the structural adjustment programme. A pension system of privately managed individual accounts was introduced in the last quarter of 2001. Under the pension reform, the country changed from a pay-as-you-go pension system to a defined contribution system in which contributions are safeguarded. The reform was designed to contain the fiscal deficit created by the previous system, broaden the base of contributors and contribute to the development of domestic financial markets.

The Nicaraguan Institute for Social Security and Welfare (INSSBI) operates nursing homes for the elderly and rehabilitation centres for the physically and mentally handicapped, for prostitutes, drug addicts and alcoholics.

Main cities

Managua (capital, estimated population 926,883 in 2005), León (168,122), Chinandega (121,929), Masaya (123,164), Granada (101,229).

Languages spoken

Some business people speak English. In the Bluefields (Atlantic) region, English is particularly widely spoken.

Many names of towns, medicines, foods, flora and fauna are in the Nahuate language.

On the Atlantic Coast, Indian towns and ethnic communities still preserve their language and cultural traditions. Autonomous law guarantees bilingual education in the Miskito, Creole, English, Sumus, Ramas and Garifuna dialects.

Official language/s

Spanish

Media

There has been no censorship since 1988, the Interior Ministry is legally responsible for supervision of the media, including the imposition of fines and suspensions from publishing of up to four days for infractions.

Press

Dailies: The main daily newspapers are La Prensa, Bolsa de Noticias, Ciberdiario de Nicaragua, El Nuevo Diario, La Tribuna, Barricada, all based in Managua. Other dailies include El Centroamericano, Novedades, El Pueblo, Confidencial, Notifax, and Tiempos del Mundo.

Weeklies: An influential weekly paper is La Crónica.

Periodicals: Boletina La is a popular women's magazine.

Broadcasting

Radio: There are approximately 60 public and private radio stations. Among the most prominent are Radio Corporación and Radio Impacto.

Television: At the end of the 1980s the media law was repealed, making private TV stations possible. There are two TV stations, both of which are state-run and broadcast throughout the country, although Channel 6 carries a stronger signal than Channel 2.

Economy

Under the Sandinista government of the 1980s, the Nicaraguan economy went into reverse. A US trade embargo, the flight of many businessmen into exile, the civil war and the demise of the Soviet Union seriously undermined this predominantly agricultural economy. By the time the Sandinistas were defeated in the 1990 elections, Nicaragua was battling hyperinflation with interest rates soaring. Since the early 1990s, the government has won international backing for trade and financial sector reforms.

Despite the election in 1989 of a US-backed coalition government led by President Violeta Chamorro, it was years before the economy stabilised and recovered from war and diplomatic isolation.

Under President Arnoldo Alemán (1997–2001), GDP growth rose to record levels and inflation fell to single-digit figures, while non-traditional sectors boomed with high levels of investment in the new export processing zones (EPZs).

The impressive improvement in macroeconomic fundamentals was spurred on by a process of free-market liberalisation.

Although the figures look promising, Nicaragua remains plagued by poverty; it is the second-poorest country in the Western Hemisphere after Haiti. Spending on education and health has taken a backseat to debt servicing. In terms of GDP, the country has one of the highest external debts in the world and was one of the first countries to qualify for the IMF's Enhanced Heavily Indebted Poor Countries (HIPC) initiative.

Although some of the government's failure to meet budgetary targets stem from its own corruption and incompetence, many of the problems are rooted in the ailing health of the economy, which has been blighted by a series of natural disasters and poor prices for its main commodity exports, particularly coffee.

In January 2004, the World Bank and the IMF wiped out 80 per cent of Nicaragua's debt by supporting US$4.5 billion of debt service relief, alleviating the pressure of a rising national debt.

The Inter-American Development Bank estimated that in 2006 migrant workers, mostly in the US, sent some US$950 million to their families in Nicaragua.

External trade

Nicaragua is a member of the Central America Free Trade Agreement (DR-Cafta), which includes Dominican Republic Costa Rica, El Salvador, Guatemala and the US; it is working to remove all tariffs and barriers between members by 2024. It is also a member of the Central American Common Market (CACM), along with El Salvador, Guatemala, Honduras, which has removed duties on most products between members and unified external tariffs.

The US is Nicaragua's largest trading partner, accounting for a quarter of the country's imports and receiving some 60 per cent of its exports. As Nicaragua has developed its manufacturing base, imports of services, intermediate goods and capital goods have all risen while imports of consumer goods have slowed.

Imports
Principal imports include petroleum, consumer goods, machinery and equipment and raw materials.
Main sources: US (19.6 per cent total, 2005), Mexico (10.3 per cent), Venezuela (9.5 per cent), Costa Rica (8.5 per cent), Guatemala (6.7 per cent), El Salvador (4.5 per cent), South Korea (4.1 per cent)
Exports
Principal exports include coffee, tobacco, sugar and peanuts, beef, shrimp and lobster and gold.
Main destinations: US (60.7 per cent total, 2005), Mexico (8.6 per cent), El Salvador (6.2 per cent),

Agriculture

Farming
Agriculture plays a very significant role in the economy of Nicaragua, contributing about a quarter of the country's total GDP. The sector also employs up to 30 per cent of the total workforce.
The principal export crop is coffee which represents around a fifth of total export earnings. Meat, cotton, bananas and sugar are the other main agricultural exports. Maize, rice, beans and sorghum are also grown. Timber, tobacco, sugar cane and rubber are geared towards Nicaragua's agro-industrial sector.
The Nicaraguan government is actively engaged in the agricultural sector although it is estimated that upwards of 60 per cent of cultivated land is in the hands of private smallholders. Despite continuous agrarian reform, food production has not kept up with demand owing mainly to poor weather, war damage and shortages of vital inputs.
Crop production in 2005 included: 938,407 tonnes (t) cereals in total, 4,037,091t sugar cane, 268,531t rice, 578,114t maize, 31,000t potatoes, 90,762t sorghum, 64,909t bananas, 42,000t plantains, 72,000t citrus fruit, 119,362t cassava, 109,091t groundnuts in shell, 205,664t pulses, 60,000t oil palm fruit, 49,238t oilcrops, 5,400t fibre crops, 2,783t tobacco, 85,130t green coffee, 240,909t fruit in total, 35,200t vegetables in total. Livestock production included: 151,666t meat in total, 74,327t beef, 6,636t pig meat, 2,100t horsemeat, 54t lamb and goat meat, 68,549t poultry, 20,008t eggs, 612,945t milk, 400t honey, 8,650t cattle hides.

Fishing
Nicaragua's typical annual fish catch is over 28,000mt, 16,500mt of which is shellfish. The main seafood exports are shellfish, particularly shrimp and lobster. Offshore fishing consists mainly of tuna, bass and mackerel. The government follows an export subsidy policy, providing tax rebates on every kilogramme of trawled shrimp and farmed shrimp exported.
In 2004, the total marine fish catch was 10,471 tonnes and the total crustacean catch was 7,667 tonnes.

Forestry
Some 3.2 million hectares (ha) of Nicaragua is covered by forests and woodlands, amounting to 60 per cent of the country's total landmass. Nicaragua has some of the largest humid tropical rainforests concentrated in the north and east, in the Caribbean lowlands. Forest lands lie principally in the southern Atlantic coastal region. Species include pine, cedar and other hardwoods covering four million hectares. The government is keen to develop plans for self-sustaining exploitation of the forests. The Food and Agriculture Organisation (FAO) has estimated timber reserves at 33 million cubic metres.
The forestry industry thrives on sawnwood production, most of which is exported. Nicaragua imports moderate quantities of paper and wood-based panels. Most of the forest wood is used for fuel consumption.
Export of forest materials in 2004 amounted to US$15 million, while imports were US$30 million.
Timber production in 2004 included 5,999,111 million cubic metres (cum) roundwood, 45,000cum sawnwood, 93,000cum sawlogs and veneers, 5,906,111cum woodfuel, 23,528t charcoal.

Industry and manufacturing
Since the 1990s, there has been significant growth in the non-traditional maquiladora (in bond) sector, which has made use of the country's free trade zones (FTZs). Concentrated mainly on textiles, particularly clothing, for the US market, the maquiladora sector has rapidly become a major sub-sector in Nicaraguan industry. Low labour costs and minimal labour regulation have made it both an attractive opportunity for foreign investors and a target for trade unions and labour rights activists.
The most important projects undertaken since the mid-1990s have reflected a renewed priority placed on large-scale agro-industrial production, which had been neglected by the government in the early 1990s. The two biggest have been the Timal sugar refinery and the Sebaco food processing complex.
Investment in Nicaragua's fledgling manufacturing sector is crucial and reliant on structural reforms to make the sector more competitive and efficient. In the past, investment resources were often diverted to the defence sector, while factories closed as a result of non-availability of replacement parts and basic inputs.

Tourism
Nicaragua's tourism sector expanded significantly throughout 2005. The sector now accounts for 6.9 per cent of total GDP and 5.6 per cent of total employment. Visitor numbers grew until 2001, when the 11 September terrorist attacks in the US damaged the sector. 483,000 arrivals were recorded in 2001, a decline of 0.6 per cent on the previous year. A further fall to 472,000 visitors occurred in 2002, but 2003 showed a recovery of 7.65 per cent. Visitor numbers, as at end 2004, were 521,800. Capital investment in the sector has increased accordingly and now constitutes 7.1 per cent of total capital investment in the economy.
The development of Nicaragua's tourism sector, which has considerable potential, especially ecotourism, has been obstructed by residual negative perceptions about its stability and inadequate infrastructure. These difficulties are gradually being overcome. A generous incentive law was introduced in 1999 to encourage tourist-related investment, but, while improving, infrastructure is still patchy. Despite the disadvantages under which it has operated, tourism has become Nicaragua's main source of foreign exchange, earning around US$110 million per annum. The majority of visitors come from the other Central American countries, but about a fifth are from the USA.

Environment
The deforestation and cultivation of marginal lands in Nicaragua contributed to the mudslides after Hurricane Mitch hit the country in late 1998, while flooding was made worse due to a lack of watershed management.

Mining
Nicaragua is endowed with deposits of both gold and silver. The country also has mineral deposits, including copper, zinc, platinum, iron, magnesium, chrome, titanium, tungsten, lead, cadmium, bismuth, bentonite, marble, clay, masonry stone, limestone and gypsum.
Gold and silver are mined intensively in Siuna and Bonanza, inland from the northern Atlantic coast region. More modest mining activity takes place in Chontales and Nueva Segovia. Geological studies of the region identify the existence of a reserve of gold in the area of La Libertad, which could have a productive lifetime of 70 years. The reserves are estimated at 3.8 million ounces of gold and 4.9 million ounces of silver.
All natural resources are state property and exploitation rights are leased on a long-term basis. Since huge portions of the central areas of Nicaragua's mineral reserves have already been leased, the scope for investment remains limited. The

decline in global gold prices has affected the fortunes of foreign companies and the value of exports diminished.

The Toronto-based Black Hawk international mining and exploration company owns the El Limon mine through its 95 per cent-owned subsidiary Triton Minera SA. The mine, located 140km north of Managua, has been in continuous production for more than 50 years, gaining from both open pit and underground operations. Mill capacity is 1,000 tonnes per day and gold recoveries exceed 80 per cent.

Hydrocarbons

Nicaragua relies heavily on imports of fossil fuels to meet demand for energy consumption, as it has little known deposits of its own. The country imports approximately 84 per cent of its energy requirements, primarily from Mexico and Venezuela under the San José pact.

Legislation in July 2002 marked the opening of the country's hydrocarbon resources to foreign investors. Foreign companies are allowed oil exploration, which includes onshore concessions, as well as offshore blocks in the Atlantic and Pacific Oceans. One of the main problems for development is that both Colombia and Honduras claim the available 44,000 square miles of the Caribbean on offer as belonging to them.

There are no proven natural gas reserves and use of gas is negligible. A gas pipeline from Mexico to Guatemala, completed in 2004, could be extended to Nicaragua as part of a wider Central American gas pipeline network. There is also the possibility of pipeline construction from Colombia's northern offshore fields to Panama with connections to Nicaragua, but no plans have been formally agreed upon.

Coal is not imported or consumed in Nicaragua.

Energy

Nicaragua's demand for electricity is growing, driven by the country's recent economic growth and development. A major objective of the national government remains the electrification of rural areas. In 2003 the World Bank agreed terms on a US$12 million loan to finance off-grid rural areas. The loan is part of Nicaragua's National Rural Electrification Program, which aimed to bring electric power to 70 per cent of rural areas by 2005 and 90 per cent by 2012.

The government estimates that demand for electricity will grow by 6 per cent annually between 2000—20, requiring nearly US$2 billion in investment. Nicaragua currently has two 50MW hydroelectric plants, one 33MW geothermal plant, two diesel plants with combined output of 91MW and five thermoelectric plants which together generate a total of 220MW. The country will need up to 1,200MW of extra generating power by 2020 if it is to satisfy demand growth.

The government has attempted to attract foreign capital to the electricity sector through the privatisation of the Empresa Nicaragüense de Electricidad (Enel) (Nicaraguan Electricity Company).

Nicaragua is involved in plans for the Sistema de Interconexion Electrica para America Central (SIEPAC), an electricity grid that would connect Nicaragua to the national transmission grids of Guatemala, Honduras, El Salvador, Costa Rica and Panama. It is envisaged that SIEPAC will be completed by 2006.

Financial markets

Stock exchange

The Bolsa de Valores de Nicaragua was opened in January 1994. Government bonds dominate transactions on the stock market.

Banking and insurance

In recent years the banking and financial services sector of Nicaragua has undergone a degree of stabilisation, which in turn has resulted in increasing deposit levels. However, the sector still remains fragile and vocal critics have accused the regulatory authorities of failing to tackle the state banking system's overdue debt which has contributed to a feeling of pessimism in some quarters.

Moreover, the government's bail-out of the country's third largest bank – Interbank – in 2000 amid reports of widespread corruption did nothing to reassure foreign investors and donors of the legitimacy of the country's banking system. The failure of the Banco Nicaraguense de Industria y Comercio (Banic) to resolve its debt led to another government intervention in the banking sector in August 2001. Banic's assets and liabilities were subsequently auctioned off to Banpro, which had already absorbed Interbank in October 2000.

The chaos in the banking sector led to a shake-up of the regulatory system. In 2003, the government introduced a new, rigorous framework to bring the legal framework in line with the Basel Core Principles.

Although foreign banks were permitted to remain in Nicaragua when the banking system was nationalised in 1979, they were no longer permitted to accept local deposits. The branches of US, British and Canadian commercial banks continue to operate non-deposit business.

Central bank

Banco Central de Nicaragua (BCN)

Main financial centre

Managua

Time

GMT minus six hours

Geography

Nicaragua is in the central American isthmus, with the Pacific Ocean to the west and the Caribbean Sea to the east. Honduras is to the north and Costa Rica to the south. The Pacific plateau is noted for its rich lands, and is where the larger farms which grow crops for export are to be found, particularly in the northern area of Chinandega. The Atlantic plateau, occupying fully half of the national territory, is largely pasture savannah; small gold and silver mines are also found in this area. The lands along the Rio Coco (forming the border with Honduras) are a rich banana-growing area, and are worked largely by the Miskito Indians. Tropical rainforest predominates in the southern Atlantic coast adjacent to Costa Rica. Corn Island, in the Caribbean Sea, is home to a fishing community.

Hemisphere

Northern

Climate

Nicaragua has a semi-tropical climate; the hottest month is May (27–32 degrees Celsius (C) in Managua) and the coldest is January (23–30 degrees C in Managua). Temperatures may be up to 10 degrees C lower in the mountain range that runs the length of the country. The rainy season (May–December) is referred to as 'winter'; and the dry season (December–April) as 'summer'.

Dress codes

On the most formal of occasions Nicaraguan men traditionally wear the Caribbean-style guayabera, in white, although an increasing number of men today prefer to wear a suit and tie.

Entry requirements

Passports

Required by all and must be valid for at least six months from the date of entry, with onward/return tickets and proof of sufficient funds for length of stay.

Passports and entry cards must be carried at all times.

Visa

Most visitors may not need a visa; contact the nearest Nicaraguan consulate for details of requirements. Many visitors may visit with a tourist card that is issued on arrival, for a fee of US$10, paid in US dollars for either up to 30 or 90 days. A valid entry stamp is necessary to exit the country, therefore any extension must be applied for locally; failure to do so will result in a fine.

Visitors who are admitted using a tourist card for business trips must provide a letter of introduction from their employer or an invitation from a Nicaraguan company.

Currency advice/regulations
The import and export of local and foreign currency is unlimited, but amounts over the equivalent of US$10,000 must be declared.

Customs
Personal items, including cameras, personal music players and laptop computers to the value of US$500 are duty-free.

Prohibited imports
Fresh and canned meat and diary products. Firearms require a licence.
The export of archaeological artefacts and gold are prohibited.

Health (for visitors)

Mandatory precautions
Yellow fever vaccination certificate if arriving within six months from an infected area.

Advisable precautions
Inoculations and booster should be current for tetanus, hepatitis A and typhoid. There may be a need for vaccinations for diphtheria, tuberculosis, hepatitis B. Use malaria prophylaxis if travelling outside urban areas. Malaria, hepatitis B and dengue fever are caused by mosquitoes, precautions including mosquito repellents, nets and clothing covering the body after dark should be used. There is a risk of rabies in rural areas.
There is a shortage of routine medications and visitors should take all necessary medicines with them. A first aid kit that includes disposable syringes, is a reasonable precaution. Outside the main hoteld use only bottled or boiled water for drinks, washing teeth and making ice. Eat only well cooked meals, preferably served hot; vegetables should be cooked and fruit peeled. Dairy products are unpasteurised and should be avoided, unless cooked.
Healthcare is not to Western standards and medical insurance, including emergency evacuation, is necessary.

Hotels

Availability is limited but there are a few good hotels in Managua, the main coastal towns and along the Pan-American Highway. Bills are subject to 15 per cent sales tax, and must usually be paid in dollars. A 10 per cent tip is usual.

Credit cards

International credit and debit cards are accepted in banks in large towns.

Public holidays (national)

Fixed dates
1 Jan (New Year's Day), 1 May (Labour Day), 19 Jul (Liberation Day), 14 Sep (Battle of Jacinto), 15 Sep (Independence Day), 25 Dec (Christmas Day).

Variable dates
Maundy Thursday, Good Friday.

Working hours

Banking
Mon–Fri: 0830–1830; Sat: 0830–1230. Some banks close may close for an hour at lunch time.

Business
Mon–Fri: 0800–1700; Sat: 0800–1300.

Government
Mon–Fri: 0800–1700.

Telecommunications

Mobile/cell phones
There are GSM 1900 services available in most west-coast cities and a few east coast urban areas. A GSM 850 service is planned.

Electricity supply

110V AC, 60 cycles

Social customs/useful tips

It is helpful to know something of the political background and affiliations of those you are meeting.
Men and women shake hands in Nicaragua and social kisses on one cheek are also exchanged. The use of titles, such as Doctor, Arquitecto, Licenciado, Profesora, is widespread and it is courteous to learn and use the correct titles for both men and women.
Do not immediately launch into a business conversation. It is considered polite to first get to know the person to whom you are talking.
A small gift for the host or hostess is always appreciated.
Late-night parties, with dinner served at 2200 or 2300, are common. Guests need not plan to arrive on time for a large social gathering as being up to two hours late is acceptable. For smaller gatherings, arrival about 30 minutes later than the specified time is considered appropriate.

Security

Nicaragua had a low rate of violent crime compared to other Central American countries and armed groups involved in the civil war were demobilised however street crime is rising and visitors are advised not to walk alone at night.

Getting there

Air

National airline: Nicaragüenses de Aviación (Nica Airlines)

International airport/s:
Managua-Augusto César Sandino (MGA), 9km from city; duty-free shop, bar, restaurant, post office, shops (restricted hours in some instances), banks.

Airport tax: Departure tax: US$35 (may be included in the price of a ticket); excluding transit passengers.

Surface

Road: The Pan-American Highway is well maintained and runs from Honduras, through Managua, to Costa Rica.

Water: Shipping lines from North and South America and Europe regularly visit Nicaragua.

Main port/s: Bluefields, Corinto, Puerto Cabezas, Puerto Sandino, San Juan de Sur, Puerto Arlen Siu.

Getting about

National transport

Air: Nicaragüenses de Aviación (Nica Airlines) runs regional, passenger and cargo services.

Road: The western region is provided with most sealed roads connecting the more populated areas of the country. There is only one major road to the Caribbean side and this stops, before the coast, at Rama.

Buses: Services are regular and connect main towns served by the road system (eg Managua-Rama, Managua-León, Chinandega, Corinto), however they are not advised for foreign travellers.

Water: A boat service links Rama and Bluefields port on the Caribbean coast.

City transport

Taxis: Taxis are the best way to get around most cities; fares should be negotiated in advance of journeys and tipping is not necessary.

Buses, trams & metro: City buses are cheap but crowded.

Car hire
Foreign licences are acceptable for short stays (up to 30 days). Due to poor public transport, hired cars may often be the best way to get around in Managua. However roads are often in poor repair and need a skilled driver to avoid mishap. Drivers in accidents are always arrested even if they are insured and appear to be blameless. Licensed drivers can be hired, through local car rentals, who are familiar with local roads and conditions and, in the case of a traffic accident, will be taken into custody, in accordance with the law.

BUSINESS DIRECTORY

The addresses listed below are a selection only. While World of Information makes every endeavour to check these addresses, we cannot guarantee that changes have not been made, especially to telephone numbers and area codes. We would welcome any corrections.

Telephone area codes

The international dialling code (IDD) for Nicaragua is +505, followed by area code and subscriber's number:

León	311	Managua	2

Chambers of Commerce

American Chamber of Commerce of Nicaragua, Centro Finarca, PO Box 2720, Managua (tel: 67-3098; fax: 67-3099; e-mail: amcham@amchamnic.org.ni).

Nicaraguan Cámara de Comercio, Rotonda Gueguense, PO Box 135, Managua (tel: 68-3505; fax: 68-3600; e-mail: comercio@ibw.com.ni).

Banking

Banco de América Central (BAC), Apdo 2304 Managua (tel: 670-220; fax: 670-224).

Banco de Crédito Centroamericano (Bancentro), Edificio Bancentro, KM. 4-1/2 Carretera Masaya (tel: 782-777; fax: 786-001).

Banco de Exportación (Banexpo), Centro Comercial Metrocentro, Managua.

Banco de la Producción (Banpro), Plaza Libertad, Contiguo a Metrocentro, Apdo 2309, Managua (tel: 782-508/783-278/784-188; fax: 784-113).

Banco de Préstamos (Banpres), Esquina Opuesta Hotel Intercontinental, Managua (tel: 23-046/223-048; fax: 23-057).

Banco Europeo de Centro América SA (BECA), Apdo 188, Managua (fax: 783-827).

Banco Mercantil, Gerente General Oscar Martín Aguado A., Plaza Banco Mercantil, Managua (tel 668-228/668-231; fax: 668-024).

Banco Nacional de Desarrollo (Banades), Apdo 328-1447, Managua (tel: 671-334; fax: 670-869).

Central bank

Banco Central de Nicaragua, Km 7 carretera sur, PO Box 2252, Managua (tel: 65-0500; fax: 65-0561; e-mail: bcn@bcn.gob.ni).

Travel information

Aerolíneas Nicaragüenses (AERONICA), Contiguo Aeropuerto Internacional August C Sandino, Apdo 3688, Managua, JR (tel: 31-801).

Instituto Nicaragüense de Turismo, Avenida Bolivar Sur, Apdo 122, Managua (tel: 25-436; fax: 25-314).

Ministry of tourism

Ministry of Tourism, Residencial Bolonia, Hotel Intercontinental, 1c. al Oeste 1c. al Sur, Managua (tel: 226-610, 222-6617; fax: 226-618).

Ministries

Ministry of Agriculture and Livestock, Km 8 1/2, Carretera a Masaya, Managua (tel: 76-0200; fax: 76-0256).

Ministry of Construction and Transport, Frente Al Estadio Nacional, Managua (tel: 22-5111; fax: 22-6429).

Ministry of Economy and Development, Carretera a Masaya, Km 6 1/2 Frente a Centro Comercial Camino de Oriente, Managua (tel: 67-0161; fax: 78-4590).

Ministry of Education, Centro Cívico Camilo Ortega, Managua (tel: 65-0046; fax: 65-0715).

Ministry of the Environment and Natural Resources, Carretera Norte, Km 12 1/2, Managua (tel: 63-1343; fax: 63-2833).

Ministry of External Co-operation, Casa Ricardo Morales Aviles, Managua (tel: 28-5002; fax: 28-2026).

Ministry of Finance, Frente a la Asamblea Nacional, Managua (tel: 22-7231; fax: 78-5984).

Ministry of Foreign Affairs, Barrío Altagracia, Frente a Restaurante Los Ranchos, Managua (tel: 66-6222; fax: 66-2572).

Ministry of Health, Complejo Concepción Palacios, Managua (tel: 89-7554; fax: 89-7997).

Ministry of Industry and Commerce, Km 6, Carretera Masaya, Apdo 2412, Managua.

Ministry of the Interior, Barrio 19 de Julio, Edif Silvio Mayorga, Managua (tel: 85-005; fax: 627-910).

Ministry of Labour, Estadio Nacional, 300 vs. al Norte, Managua (tel: 28-1168; fax: 28-2028).

Ministry of the Presidency, Avenida Bolivar, Detrás de la Asamblea Nacional, Managua (tel: 78-5299; fax: 22-3448).

Ministry of Social Action, Pista de Resistencia ENEL Central, 150vs. al Sur, Managua (tel: 67-2907; fax: 67-0768).

Ministry of Tourism, Residencial Bolonia, Hotel Intercontinental, 1c. al Oeste 1c. al Sur, Managua (tel: 22-6610, 22-6617; fax: 22-6618).

Ministry of Transport and Construction, Frente al Estadio Nacional, Managua (tel: 283-698, 282-061, 225-954; fax: 282-161).

Ministry of Works, Estadio Nacional, 400 Metros Al Norte, Managua (tel: 226-002, 222-115, 226-677; fax: 622-103).

Other useful addresses

Association of Nicaraguan Producers and Exporters of Non-Traditional Products (APENN), Del Restaurante Terraza 1/2 C Al Norte (tel: 668-276, 668-279).

Bank of Central American Economic Intergration (BCIE), Edificio BCIE, 2do, piso, Plaza España, Managua (tel: 66-4120; fax: 66-4125).

British Embassy, El Reparto Los Robles 1, entrada principal de la Primera Etapa, Los Robles, Managua (tel: 780-014, 780-887, 674-050; fax: 784-085).

Central American Institute of Business Administration (INCAE), Carretera Sur Km 15 1/2, Managua.

Centre of Export and Investments, Hotel Intercontinental, 1c, abajo 3 1/2c al Sur, Managua (tel: 68-1063; fax: 66-4476; e-mail: cei@cei.Ibw.com.ni).

Development Bank (BID), Carretera a Masaya, Km 4 1/2, Managua (tel: 67-0831; fax: 67-3469).

Dirección General de Promoción de Exportaciones, Km 6, Carretera a Masaya, Apdo 2412, Managua, JR.

Empresa Nicaragüense de Promoción de Exportaciones, Apdo 1449, Managua.

Exports of the Handicraft Industry, S.A., Centro de Feria la Pinata (tel: 670-358; fax: 670-192).

Institute of Local Governments, Los Arcos, Entrada principal, 20 varas al Sur, Managua (tel: 66-6050; fax: 44-4567).

Institute of National Technology, Centro Cívico, Managua (tel: 65-0049; fax: 65-1976).

Institute of Nicaraguan Insurance and Reinsurance, Carretera Sur, Km 4 1/2, Managua (tel: 68-0239; fax: 68-0265).

Institute of Nicaraguan Social Security (NSS), Semáforos del Hotel Intercontinental, 2c abajo, 1c al lago, Contiguo a Policlínica Central, Managua (tel: 22-7445; fax: 22-7454).

Institute of Statistics and Censors, Frente Hospital Lenin Fonséca, Managua (tel: 66-7663; fax: 66-7872).

International Development Agency (AID), Semáforos Centroamérica, 400 mts al Oeste, Managua (tel: 67-3909; fax: 77-0210).

Nicaraguan Electricity, Frente Entrada a Colegio Rigoberto López, Pérez, Managua (tel: 77-4159; fax: 67-1700).

Nicaraguan Centre of Technological Information (CENIT), Sandy's 11/2 C. Arriba (tel: 675-325).

Nicaraguan Canals and Irrigation Authority, Carretera Sur Km 5, Managua (tel: 66-7863; fax: 66-7872).

Nicaraguan Development Fund, AP 2598, Managua (tel: 666-077, 666-066).

Nicaraguan Embassy (USA), 1627 New Hampshire Avenue, NW, Washington DC 20009 (tel: (+1-202) 939-6531; fax: (+1-202) 939-6532; ofemb@embanic.org).

Nicaraguan Institute for Economic and Social Investigations (INIES), del Hospital

Alejandro Davila Bolanas, 3 c. al Lago, Managua.

Nicaraguan Investment Fund (of Central Bank), Shell de Colonia Centroamericana, Media al Lago, Managua.

Nicaraguan Telephone Company, Residencial Villa Fontana, Edificio Ville Fontana, Managua (tel: 28-5280; fax: 28-4628).

Port Authority, Residencial Bolonia, Optica Nicaragüense, 1c al Lago, 1c abajo, Managua (tel: 66-3274; fax: 66-4622).

Superior Council of Private Enterprise (COSEP), del Restaurante Terraza, Media cuadra al lago, Managua.

UN High Commission for Relief (ACNUR), Residencial Bolonia, Contiguo a Viajes Atlantida, Managua (tel/fax: 68-0476).

US Embassy, Apdo 327, Managua (tel: 666-010).

World Bank, Plaza España, Edificio Málaga, Modulos No A 1/A 22, Managua (tel: 26-0562; fax: 661-000).

Internet sites

Banco Central de Nicaragua: www.bcn.gob.ni

Nicaraguan Centre for Exports and Investments (CEI): www.cei.org.ni

Organisation of American States: www.oas.org

Ministry of Foreign Affairs: www.cancilleria.gob.ni

Nicaraguan stock exchange: http://bolsanic.com

Nicaraguan Solidarity Campaign: www.nicaraguasc.org.uk

Nicaragua Network: www.nicanet.org

La Prensa: www.laprensa.com.ni

El Nuevo Diario: www.elnuevodiario.com.ni

La Noticia: www.lanoticia.com.ni

Niger

KEY FACTS

Official name: République du Niger (Republic of Niger)

Head of State: President Mamadou Tandja (MNSD) (since 1999; re-elected Dec 2004)

Head of government: Prime Minister Seyni Oumarou (since 7 Jun 2007)

Ruling party: Mouvement National de la Société de Développement (MNSD) (National Movement for a Developing Society) (since 1999; re-elected Dec 2004)

Area: 1,267,000 square km

Population: 13.70 million (2007, Institute for National Statistics)

Capital: Niamey

Official language: French; Hausa is the major lingua franca especially for trade

Currency: CFA franc (CFAf) = 100 centimes (Communauté Financière Africaine (African Financial Community) franc). New notes have been issued; old notes cease to be legal tender from Jan 2005.

Exchange rate: CFAf413.80 per US$ (Jul 2008); CFAf655.95 per euro (pegged from Jan 1999)

GDP per capita: US$313 (2007)*

GDP real growth: 3.20% (2007)*

Inflation: 0.10% (2007)*

Balance of trade: -US$392.00 million (2005)

* estimated figure

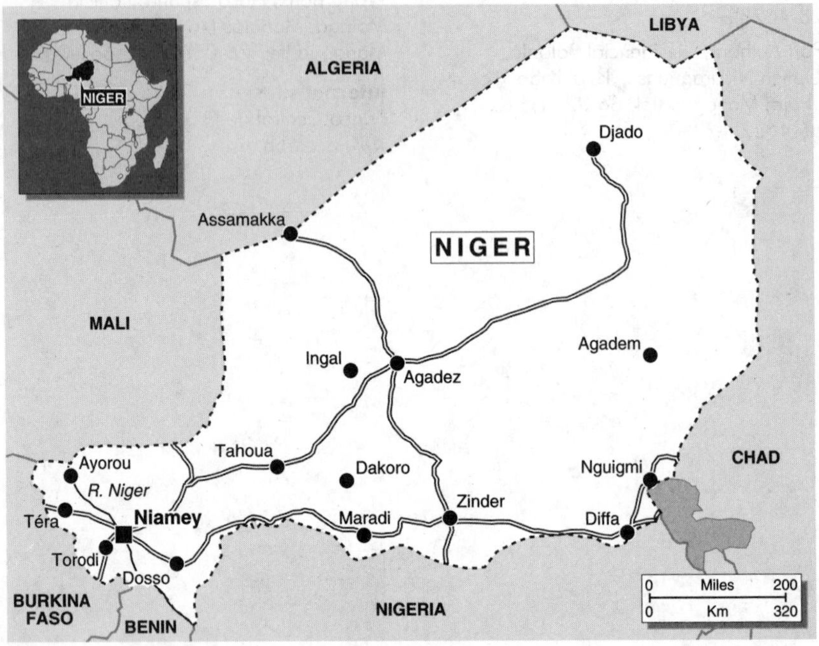

Niger, pronounced the French way and not to be confused with its larger and potentially wealthier neighbour to the south, Nigeria, is one of the largest but least populated countries in Africa. But it is one of the world's top five producers of uranium (Canada, Australia, Russia and Ukraine are the others). It is mining that drives the economy, along with agriculture.

At the beginning of the 1980s, some observers foresaw Niger having a rosy economic future. Its enormous potential as a uranium producer lead them to think that Niger would benefit as the developed world sought alternatives to oil. A quarter of a century later, not much of the hoped for boom has happened. Real gross domestic product (GDP) has grown at an average of only 3.6 per cent over the period 2003–06, only just above the population growth rate of 3.3 per cent.

Political stability for a while

Since 1999, following almost a decade of political instability, Niger has successfully transitioned to a democratically elected government, reformed the constitution and held presidential and parliamentary elections. Since then, a two-party coalition, consisting of the Mouvement Nigérien pour une Société de Développement (MNSD) (National Movement for a Developing Society) and Convention Démocratique Sociale (CDS) (Democratic and Social Convention), has run the country led by President Mamadou Tandja (MNSD). General elections were held in 2004 (presidential and legislative elections), resulting in the re-election of President Tandja. A new government was appointed in December 2004, with Mr Hama Amadou returning as prime minister and key ministers (finance, defense, foreign affairs and justice) retaining their positions.

There was a reorganisation of the government, which was dominated by a four party coalition consisting of the Mouvement National de la Société de Développement (MNSD) (National Movement for a Developing Society), the Rassemblement Social Démocratique (RSD) (Social Democratic Rally) and the Rassemblement pour la Démocratie et le Progrès (RDP) (Rally for Democracy and Progress) in March 2007. This was followed by parliamentary elections in June, which led to the removal of the government on the grounds of corruption and poor management of public affairs. Seyni Oumarou (MNSD) was appointed prime minister and he formed a new government the same month. NGOs have continued to complain about the mis-management of aid funds.

Getting there

According to the 2008 edition of African Development Bank's publication, *African Economic Outlook* (AEO) Niger's economic performance rebounded in 2005 and 2006 with growth of 7.2 per cent and 4.8 per cent respectively. In its broad growth strategy spelled out in the International Monetary Fund (IMF) Poverty Reduction Strategy Paper (PRSP), which was updated by end-April 2007, Niger's key macroeconomic objectives for 2007–09 are to achieve an annual real GDP growth rate of about 4.2 per cent.

Uranium, droughts and desertification

Niger is one of the poorest countries in the world with minimal government services and insufficient funds to develop its resource base. The largely agrarian and subsistence-based economy is frequently disrupted by extended droughts common to the Sahel region of Africa. Priorities include the implementation of a rural sector strategy, with emphasis on developing irrigation infrastructure and diversifying the economy including through the development of tourism.

Outlook

To ensure that revenue objectives for 2007–08 are met, the government has made some headway in implementing key revenue measures to expand the tax base and strengthen collection efforts. The government has put in place a presumptive tax of 0.25 per cent on transit/re-export of tobacco products and a property tax on land. Most importantly, it is focusing on strengthening tax and customs administration. Key actions are in the areas of streamlining customs clearance procedures, strengthening customs valuations, enhancing audits for major taxes and duties and closely monitoring the use of exemptions.

On the international front, a long running dispute with Benin over 25 islands in the River Niger was finally settled, mostly in Niger's favour. An International Court of Justice ruling in 2005 had awarded 16 of the islands, including the largest, Lete, to Niger and the remaining nine to Benin. In February 2007, after more bickering between the two countries, Niger took control of Lete.

Risk assessment

Politics	Fair
Economy	Poor
Regional stability	Poor

COUNTRY PROFILE

Historical profile

1800s The British were the first Europeans to explore the area.
1891–1911 France colonised the region, although it did not gain full control until much later and even then resistance movements continued.
1960 Niger gained independence from France under the presidency of Hamani Diori.
1974 Diori was overthrown and replaced by Lieutenant Colonel Seyni Kountche.
1987 Kountche died and was replaced by Brigadier Ali Saibou.
1989 Civilian rule was re-introduced with a new constitution, under a one-party system. Ali Saibou was re-elected president.
1990 The Tuareg people in the north began a rebellion.
1991 Saibou lost power to a transitional government led by Andre Salifou.
1992 A referendum overwhelming approved a new multi-party constitution
1993 Multi-party elections resulted in the Mahamane Ousmane being elected president; his coalition, the Alliance of the Forces of Change (AFC), won most seats in parliament.
1995 A peace accord was signed between the government and the Tuareg.
1996 Ousmane was toppled in a coup and replaced by Ibrahim Maïnassara Baré. A military-backed civilian government was formed. Maïnassara won the presidential election.
1997 A peace accord with the last Tuareg rebel group was signed.
1999 President Maïnassara was assassinated and Major Daouda Mallam Wanké assumed power. A new constitution was approved, which balanced the power between the president, prime minister and the National Assembly. Mamadou Tandja won the presidential election.
2000 Droughts caused widespread food shortages.
2001 After another poor harvest, food prices escalated and famine ensued.
2002 The EU granted US$319.5 million for Niger's poverty reduction effort.
2003 The US claimed Iraq had attempted to purchase uranium from Niger. A claim rejected by the government.
2004 The World Bank and the IMF supported a US$1.20 billion debt relief programme. Incumbent Tandja was re-elected president and the ruling MNSD won the parliamentary elections.
2005 Taxes were increased by 20 per cent and sparked widespread protests. The UN warned that three million faced starvation due to a severe drought after locusts had damaged crops.
2006 Seasonal rains caused widespread flooding, leaving thousands homeless and causing a cholera outbreak. The government began repatriating Mahamid Arab settlers to Chad.
2007 In February, Niger assumed control of the island of Lete and some other islands in the river Niger in accordance with an International Court of Justice ruling , settling the border dispute with Benin. On 1 June, following four parliament votes of no confidence, Prime Minister Hama Amadou and his government were voted

KEY INDICATORS — Niger

	Unit	2003	2004	2005	2006	2007
Population	m	12.13	12.67	12.56	*12.95	*13.70
Gross domestic product (GDP)	US$bn	2.55	3.10	3.40	3.58	*4.17
GDP per capita	US$	210	258	271	*276	*313
GDP real growth	%	4.0	0.9	6.8	5.1	*3.2
Inflation	%	-1.8	0.4	7.8	0.1	*0.1
Exports (fob) (goods)	US$m	293.0	393.0	438.0	–	–
Imports (cif) (goods)	US$m	368.0	705.0	830.0	–	–
Balance of trade	US$m	-75.0	-312.0	-392.0	–	–
Current account	US$m	-160.0	-190.0	-253.0	-307.0	*-321.0
Total reserves minus gold	US$m	114.1	67.6	249.5	370.9	593.0
Foreign exchange	US$m	98.7	53.4	236.9	357.8	579.3
Exchange rate	per US$	574.89	528.29	507.22	496.60	454.40

* estimated figure

out of office. Opponents accused the government of embezzling US$9 million from foreign donors funds for education, between 2002–06. The president appointed Seyni Oumarou as prime minister in June. 2008 New satellite images taken in June showed that extensive tree planting has transformed once deforested areas.

Political structure

Constitution
The 1989 constitution has been amended twice to introduce multiparty democracy and balanced power between the president, prime minister and National Assembly.
Voting: universal suffrage over 18 years. There are eight administrative regions, divided into 36 districts.

Form of state
Presidential, unitary, multiparty republic.

The executive
The directly elected president is the Head of State, elected for a five-year term, renewable only once.
The president, shares power with the prime minister but has final responsibility for co-ordinating the actions of the executive branch of government. The president names the prime minister, from a list of three candidates, who become head of government and is accountable to parliament.

National legislature
An elected 113-member Assemblée Nationale (National Assembly) with a maximum five-year term.

Legal system
Based on French civil law system and customary law.

Last elections
16 November/4 Decermber 2004 (presidential); 4 December 2004 (parliamentary).
Results: Presidential: Mamadou Tandja won 65.5 per cent of the vote; Mahamadou Issoufou 34.5 per cent. Turnout was 45 per cent.
Parliamentary: MNSD won 37.2 per cent of the votes (47 seats out of 113); PNDS won 21.3 per cent (25 seats); Convention Démocratique et Sociale (CDS) (Democratic and Social Convention) won 17.4 per cent (22 seats); Rassemblement Social Démocratique (RSD) (Social Democratic Rally) 7.1 per cent (seven seats); Rassemblement pour la Démocratie et le Progrès (RDP) (Rally for Democracy and Progress) 6.5 per cent (six seats); Alliance Nigérienne pour la Démocratie et le Progrès (ANDP) (Niger Alliance for Democracy and Progress) 5.4 per cent (five seats); and Parti pour le Socialisme et la Démocratie au Niger (PSDN) (Party for Socialism and Democracy in Niger) 1.3 per cent (one seat). Turnout was 44.7 per cent.

Next elections
2009 (presidential and parliamentary)

Political parties
Ruling party
Mouvement National de la Société de Développement (MNSD) (National Movement for a Developing Society) (since 1999; re-elected Dec 2004)
Main opposition party
Parti Nigerien pour la Démocratie et le Socialisme (PNDS) (Niger Party for Democracy and Socialism)

Population

13.70 million (2007, Institute for National Statistics)
Last census: May 2001: 10,790,352 (provisional)
Population density: Eight inhabitants per square km. Urban population: 21 per cent (1995–2001).
Annual growth rate: 3.3 per cent 2007 (INS)

Ethnic make-up
Hausa (56 per cent), Djerma (22 per cent), Tuareg (8 per cent).

Religions
Islam (85 per cent), traditional beliefs (14.5 per cent), Christianity (0.5 per cent).

Education

Public expenditure on education is around 2 per cent of GDP.
Primary education is free and compulsory and lasts until aged 12. Secondary schooling is divided, beginning with the first cycle secondary school from aged 12 to 16, then second cycle secondary school from aged 16 to 19, when students are expected to graduate with a Baccalauréat. Alternatively, at aged 16 students may elect to undertake a three year technical course. All education is conducted in French.
Literacy rate: 17 per cent adult rate; 25 per cent youth rate (15–24) (Unesco 2005).
Compulsory years: 6 to 12
Enrolment rate: 29 per cent gross primary enrolment, 7 per cent gross secondary enrolment; of relevant age groups (including repeaters) (World Bank).
Pupils per teacher: 41 in primary schools

Health

Per capita total expenditure on health (2003) was US$30; of which per capita government spending was US$16, at the international dollar rate, (WHO 2006).
Improved water sources are available to 59 per cent of the population.
A recurring drought and a devastating locust invation destroyed the 2004 harvest and in July 2005 the UN estimated a third of the population were short of food and that 150,000 children were 'severely malnourished'. The UN world food programme increased the number of people being fed by over one million through the Niger emergency operation.
There were cases of polio reported to the World Health Organisation – Global Polio Eradication Initiative in 2006; the country had previously been free of the disease and its re-emergence was due to infected travellers.

HIV/Aids
There are an estimated 64,000 people living with HIV/Aids, of which 36,000 are women. In addition there are 5,900 children (0–17) HIV positive and 24,000 orphans. In 2003 there were 4,800 deaths due to Aids, although Niger has so far escaped much of the African pandemic. However, with 25–35 per cent of sex workers testing positive, there is a chance that increased population mobility and a lack of condom use could make Niger vulnerable.
HIV prevalence: 1.2 per cent aged 15–49 in 2003 (World Bank)
Life expectancy: 41 years, 2004 (WHO 2006)
Fertility rate/Maternal mortality rate: 7.8 births per woman, 2004 (WHO 2006); maternal mortality 590 per 100,000 live births (World Bank).
Child (under 5 years) mortality rate (per 1,000): 154 per 1,000 live births; 40 per cent of children aged under five are malnourished (World Bank).
Head of population per physician: 0.03 physicians per 1,000 people, 2004 (WHO 2006)

Welfare

Around 61.4 per cent of the population live on less than US$1 per day and 85.3 per cent live on less than US$2 per day. The distribution of wealth is highly unequal with a Gini index of 50.5 and the richest 20 per cent of the population owning 53.3 per cent of the total wealth.

Main cities

Niamey (capital, estimated population 794,814 in 2005), Zinder (205,520), Maradi (179,040), Agadez (95,083), Tahoua (82,636), Arlit (90,669) (built for the uranium industry).

Languages spoken

The distribution of languages is dependent on the ethnic groups within Niger. The Hausa are the largest group and their language is recognised as a national language, as is Songhai-Zarma (Djerma) the next largest language group. Tamashek, which is spoken by the Tuareg, is related to Berber. Others languages in daily use include Fulani, Arabic, Kanauri, Courmantché and Toubou.

Official language/s
French; Hausa is the major lingua franca especially for trade

Media

Press

News bulletins include Le Sahel (daily), Sahel Hebdo (weekly) both in French, Anfani and Le Republicain covering issues of general interest. Alternative is a semi-monthly publication from Niamey.

Weeklies: Sahel Dimanche is a privately owned Sunday newspaper and is renowned for its objective reporting.

Broadcasting

Radio: The government operates La Voix du Sahel radio service in French and several Niger languages.

Television: Télé-Sahel broadcasts every day.

Economy

As one of the least developed countries in the world, Niger is heavily dependent on foreign aid and loans. Agriculture is the main source of income for most households and subsistence farming predominates.

Uranium exports provide the largest proportion of foreign exchange, although mining only employs a small percentage of the workforce and exports have declined since a worldwide slump in 1980. In the long-term, Niger hopes to move away from dependence on uranium with the exploitation of other mineral resources, such as gold and oil. The Samira gold mine opened in 2004 with expectations of total foreign exchange earnings of US$28 billion by 2010.

In April 2004, the World Bank and the IMF supported US$1.20 billion in debt relief under the enhanced Heavily Indebted Poor Countries (HIPC) initiative.

The IMF is also pushing, as part of Niger's three-year Poverty Reduction and Growth Facility (PRGF), programme to reduce budget deficits, strengthen revenue, keep wages down and reallocate government expenditure to increase measures for privatisation. However, problems with food security, negative trade growth and continued dependency on foreign aid restricts Niger's ability to meet IMF targets.

External trade

As a member of the Economic Community of West African States (Ecowas), Niger is also a member of the West African Economic and Monetary Union (WAEMU) using the common currency, the CFA franc. Ecowas was set up to promote economic integration among members.

Primary industries represent a major source of foreign exchange, include mining extraction of uranium (Niger has one of the world's largest deposits of uranium and was the third leading producer in 2005, and gold, as well as other reserves in coal, phosphate and salt. The price of uranium has risen from less than US$20 per pound in 2000 to over US$100lb in 2006, as worldwide demand has steadily grown. However, being landlocked with a poor infrastructure has hampered development, as all processing is undertaken abroad. Live animal exports, primarily to Nigeria, are also very important to the economy.

The lack of an industrial and manufacturing sector requires domestic needs to be met by imports.

Imports

Principal imports are foodstuffs, machinery, vehicles and parts, petroleum and cereals.

Main sources: France (14.5 per cent total, 2005), US (10.7 per cent), French Polynesia (7.5 per cent), Nigeria (7.4 per cent), Italy (6.7 per cent), Côte d'Ivoire (5.1 per cent), Belgium (4.6 per cent), Germany (4.5 per cent), China (4.5 per cent)

Exports

Principal exports are uranium ore, livestock, cow-peas and onions.

Main destinations: France (47.8 per cent total, 2005), Nigeria (21.4 per cent), US (20.3 per cent)

Agriculture

Farming

Subsistence farming and stock rearing contribute around 40 per cent to GDP and employ 70 per cent of the workforce. Less than 3 per cent of the total land area is cultivated.

Hides and skins and cotton account for around 20 per cent of export earnings.

The government is encouraging market gardening – galmi onions are an important cash crop.

Production of the two principal food crops, millet and sorghum, is generally insufficient to satisfy domestic needs, even in times of good rains, and is supplemented by food aid. Other food crops include rice, cowpeas and green beans.

Recurrent drought and desertification have had a serious impact on livestock rearing and have led to significant food shortages with disastrous consequences. The government is investing heavily in anti-desertification schemes and is encouraging animal husbandry.

In 2004 locust plagues attacked crops and damaged much of the harvest and exposed around 3.5 millions to food shortages. By October 2005 the UN World Food Programme had completed distributing food aid to 3 million people. Rains in mid-2005 were enough to bring about a good harvest but the country has inadequate food reserves.

Crop production for 2005 included: 2,645,100 tonnes (t) cereals in total, 2,100,000t millet, *100,000t cassava, *30,000t sweet potatoes, 500,000t sorghum, 39,300t rice, 572,270t pulses, *100,000t tomatoes, 42,940t oilcrops, 5,400t various spices, *220,000t sugar cane, *17,000t chillies and peppers, *1,500t pepper spice, *50,800t fruit in total, *644,900t vegetables in total.

* estimate

Estimated livestock production included: 133,027t meat in total, 37,000t beef, 1,418t pig meat, 15,200t lamb, 25,200t goat meat, 15,000t game meat, 7,800t camel meat, 28,960t poultry, 10,540t eggs, 315,400t milk, 5,600t cattle hides, 4,200t goatskins, 1,900t sheepskins.

Industry and manufacturing

The industrial sector is small-scale, contributing around 7 per cent to GDP and employing 5 per cent of the workforce.

Manufacturing is concentrated on the processing of agricultural commodities such as sugar refining, brewing, cotton ginning, tanning and flour/rice milling.

Other activities include small-scale production of cement and metals, textiles, plastics, soft drinks and construction materials.

Industrial development is handicapped by the shortage of capital and skilled labour and by the country's weak infrastructure.

Tourism

The tourist sector is expected to contribute 1.7 per cent of GDP and provide employment for 3.5 per cent of the workforce.

There is much room for expansion and travel and tourism is estimated to attract 9.1 per cent of all capital investment.

Mining

The mining sector accounts for around 11 per cent of GDP and employs 5 per cent of the workforce.

Niger is the third-largest exporter of uranium and has been the country's principal export since early 1970s. Proven reserves total 280,000 tonnes with extraction undertaken mainly at two opencast mines, at Arlit and Akouta. Production stagnated at 3,000–3,200 tonnes due to a world slump in the demand for uranium. Production has increased in recent years, but depressed prices on the world market have seen the value of uranium exports fall. The major export markets are France, Japan, Spain, Germany and Egypt.

Other minerals exploited are the tin-bearing ore cassiterite, phosphates, molybdenum, salt and coal. There are also known reserves of iron ore.

The Samira mine in Niamey, in the Koma Bangou concession in west Niger, produced its first, 15kg, gold bar in October 2004. The mine will produce 5,000 ounces of gold annually and, over its six-and-half-year life, is expected to produce three tonnes and earn US$28 billion. The government owns 20 per cent

and two Canadian mining companies the other 80 per cent of the mine. Gold prospecting agreements have been reached with three other Canadian companies for further research in the region.
Imperial Metals is drilling for diamonds on the M'Banga concession.

Hydrocarbons
Oil was discovered in the Termit Basin, east of Niamey, in 2005. A Chinese state oil company was given oil exploration rights by the government in June 2008, worth US$5 billion, in a deal local mining unions described as secretive and contemptuous of regulations and which was condemned by civil rights groups, who want how the funds will be spent to be scrutinised by parliament. Concern is centred on the benefit to the country from oil profits being either squandered or corruptly embezzled.
Niger is entirely dependent on the import of refined oil products, typically it imports around 5,000 bpd.
There are small coal reserves at Tchirozerine (1,000 km north of the capital). These reserves stand at around 780,000 tonnes. There is negligible domestic demand, although this is set to rise. There has been a further discovery of coal reserves in Takanamat, in central Niger.
Natural gas is neither produced nor consumed.

Energy
Domestic generation (mainly thermal) meets about 50 per cent of local needs, the deficit being imported from Nigeria. Niger and Nigeria signed a power supply agreement which guaranteed Niger 45MW of electricity in return for the uninterrupted flow of water along the Niger river. This means that Niger is unable to dam the river in its territory. Niger had an estimated hydroelectric potential of 250MW.

Banking and insurance
Central bank
Banque Centrale des Etats de l'Afrique de l'Ouest
Main financial centre
Niamey

Time
GMT plus one hour

Geography
Niger is a landlocked country in western Africa, with Algeria and Libya to the north, Nigeria and Benin to the south, Mali and Burkina Faso to the west and Chad to the east. It is 80 per cent desert, in the north, and 20 per cent savannah in the south. In the central north there is a volcanic mountain range, Aïr Massif, which includes Mount Gréboun, the tallest peak at a height of 1,944 metres. The Niger river flows from Mali to Nigeria through Niger in the south west for about 563km and a small portion of Lake Chad occupies the south-eastern corner of Niger.
Hemisphere
Northern

Climate
Niger is very hot with temperatures ranging from 28–44 degrees Celsius. There is rain mainly in the south from June–September. Frequent Sahara dust storms occur from November–January. The dry season is from October–May.

Entry requirements
Passports
Required by all and must have at least six month validity left; nationals of certain African countries may visit with national ID cards.
At each overnight stay passports must be presented to the police. As passports are stamped each time, they will require enough blank pages for the visit. Travel by any other route than that stamped in the passport by the police is forbidden.
Visa
Required by all, except citizens of some African countries close to Niger. Contact the nearest Niger embassy for further details and an application form. Visitors are required to supply proof of return/onward passage and funds, for living expenses of US$500. All documents require a French translation.
An exit permit will be required for all visitors that required an entry visa, from the Immigration Department in Niamey, before departure.
Currency advice/regulations
The import of local currency is unlimited; export is limited to CFAf25,000. Import and export of foreign currency is unlimited.
Travellers cheques are accepted in hotels and banks; to avoid extra exchange charges cheques in euros are recommended.

Health (for visitors)
Mandatory precautions
A yellow fever and cholera vaccination certificate is required if arriving from an infected area.
Advisable precautions
Inoculations and booster should be current for tetanus, hepatitis A, diphtheria, typhoid and yellow fever. There may be a need for vaccinations for tuberculosis, hepatitis B and meningitis and cholera.
Anti-mosquito measures including mosquito repellents, nets and clothing covering the body should be used for protection against hepatitis B and yellow fever. There is a risk of rabies.
There is a shortage of routine medications and visitors should take all necessary medicines with them. A first aid kit that includes disposable syringes is a reasonable precaution. Use only bottled or boiled water for drinks, washing teeth and making ice. Eat only well cooked meals, preferably served hot; vegetables should be cooked and fruit peeled. Dairy products are unpasteurised and should be avoided, unless cooked.
Medical insurance is essential, including emergency evacuation, and an adequate supply of personal medicines is necessary.

Hotels
There are good hotels in Niamey. A 5 per cent service charge is usually added to bills.

Credit cards
International credit and debit cards are accepted in a limited number of places.

Public holidays (national)
Fixed dates
1 Jan (New Year's Day), 24 Apr (National Concord Day), 1 May (Labour Day), 3 Aug (Independence Day), 18 Dec (Republic Day), 25 Dec (Christmas Day).
Variable dates
Islamic New Year (two days), Easter Monday (Mar/Apr), Eid al Adha (two days), Birth of the Prophet (two days), Eid al Fitr (four days).
Islamic year – 1429 (10 Jan 2008–28 Dec 2008): The Islamic year contains 354 or 355 days, with the result that Muslim feasts advance by 10–12 days against the Gregorian calendar. Dates of feasts vary according to the sighting of the new moon, so cannot be forecast exactly.

Working hours
Banking
Mon–Fri: 0800–1100 and 1600–1700.
Business
Winter: Mon–Fri: 0730–1230, 1500–1800; Sat: 0730–1230.
Summer: Mon–Fri: 0730–1230, 1530–1830; Sat: 0730–1230.
Government
Oct–Feb: Mon–Fri: 0730–1230 and 1500–1800; Mar–Sep: Mon–Fri: 0730–1230 and 1530–1830.
Shops
Mon–Fri: 0800–1200, 1600–1900; Sat: 0800–1200.

Telecommunications
Mobile/cell phones
There are 900 GSM services available in larger town in the south.

Electricity supply
220/380V AC, 50 cycles

Getting there
Air
International airport/s: Niamey International (NIM), 12km south-east of city; bar,

currency exchange, post office, shops, car hire, hotel courtesy coaches.

Airport tax: None

Surface

Road: There are road connections and border crossings with all neighbouring countries. Access from Algeria and Mali is difficult, but a surfaced road connects Benin with Niamey. Access from Chad may be restricted.

Water: Ferries on the Niger River coming from Mali are dependent on the water level.

Getting about

National transport

Air: Charter flights are available in Niamey.

Road: Main highways link Tillabery with N'guigmi, Tahoua and Arlit, however not all roads are open to visitors without a permit. Petrol is not always available. Best months for road travel December–March. Visitors must report to police on arrival at main centres.

Buses: Services operate from Niamey to Zinder, Agadez, and other towns.

City transport

Taxis: Fixed rates apply for long-distance and urban services. Taxis in Niamey are cheap and widely available. Tipping is optional.

Journey time from airport to city centre 10 minutes.

Car hire

Self-drive or chauffeur-driven cars are available in Niamey. Chauffeurs are compulsory outside the capital. International driving licence required. Petrol and spares are in short supply and there are no recovery services.

BUSINESS DIRECTORY

The addresses listed below are a selection only. While World of Information makes every endeavour to check these addresses, we cannot guarantee that changes have not been made, especially to telephone numbers and area codes. We would welcome any corrections.

Telephone area codes

The international direct dialling code (IDD) for Niger is +227, followed by subscriber's number.

Useful telephone numbers

Police: 17

Fire: 18

Chambers of Commerce

Maradi Chamber of Commerce and Agriculture, PO Box 79, Maradi (tel: 410-366; fax: 410-451).

Niger Chamber of Commerce, Agricul-ture, Industriy and Handicrafts, Place de la Concertation, PO Box 209, Niamey (tel: 732-210; fax: 734-668; e-mail: cham209n@intnet.ne).

Zinder Chambre of Commerce and Agriculture, PO Box 83, Zinder (tel: 510-087; fax: 510-217).

Banking

Bank of Africa (Niger, Head Office); BP 10 973, Immeuble Sonara II, Niamey (tel: 733-620, 733-621; fax: 733-818).

Banque Centrale des Etats de l'Afrique de l'Ouest (Agency); BP 487, Rond Point de la Poste, Niamey (tel: 722-491/92; fax: 734-743).

Banque Commerciale du Niger (Head Office); BP 11 363, Rond Point Maourey, Niamey (tel: 733-915, 733-331; fax: 732-163).

Banque Internationale pour l'Afrique au Niger (Head Office); BP 10350, Avenue de la Mairie, Niamey (tel: 733-101; fax: 733-595; e-mail: bia@intnet.ne).

Banque Islamique du Niger pour le Commerce et l'industrie (BINCI), BP 12754, Immeuble El-Nasr, Niamey (tel: 732-730, 732-740; fax: 734-735).

Caisse de Prêts aux Collectivités Territoriale, BP 730, Route Torodi, Rive droite, Niamey (tel: 723-412, 723-080).

Caisse Nationale d'Epargne, Avenue du Niger, BP 11778 Niamey (tel: 732-498, 732-499; fax: 735-812)

Crédit du Niger, BP 213, Blvd de la République, Niamey (tel: 722-701, 722-702; fax: 722-390).

Ecobank-Niger, BP 13804, Niamey (tel: 737-181, 901-052; fax: 737-204, 737-203).

Société Nigérienne de Banque, BP 891, Ave de la Mairie, Niamey (tel: 734-569, 734-643; fax: 734-693).

Central bank

Banque Centrale des Etats de l'Afrique de l'Ouest, Direction Nationale, Rue de l'Uranium, PO Box 487, Niamey (tel: 722-491; fax: 734-743).

Travel information

Niamey International Airport, ASECNA, BP 1096, Niamey (tel: 732-517/518/519, 732-381/382; fax: 735-512).

Ministry of tourism

Ministère du Tourisme et d'Artisanat BP 12710, Niamey, Niger (tel: 736 522; fax: 732 387).

National tourist organisation offices

Office du Tourisme du Niger, BP 612, Niamey.

Other useful addresses

Centre for Investment Promotion, BP 12129, Niamey (tel: 736-836; fax: 736-772).

Conseil National de Développement, c/o Ministry of Planning, Niamey (tel: 722-233).

Direction des Statistiques, c/o Ministry of Planning, Niamey (tel: 722-799).

Embassy of the Republic of Niger, 154 rue du Longchamp, 75116 Paris, France (tel: (+33-1) 4504 8060; fax: (+33-1) 4504 7973).

Niger Embassy (US), 2204 R Street, NW, Washington DC 20008 (tel: (+1-202) 483-4224; fax: (+1-202) 483-3169; e-mail: ambassadeniger@hotmail.com).

Office Nationale des Ressources Minières (Onarem), BP 210, Niamey (tel: 723-935).

Société Nationale de Commerce et de Production du Niger, BP 615, Niamey.

Société Nigérienne de Produits Pétroliers (Sonidep), BP 2735, Niamey (tel: 733-335).

Sonhotel (Société Nigerienne de Gestion des Hôtels de l'Etat) (tel: 732-387).

Syndicat des Commerçants, Importateurs et Exportateurs du Niger, BP 535, Niamey.

Internet sites

Africa Business Network: www.ifc.org/abn

AllAfrica.com: http://allafrica.com

African Development Bank: www.afdb.org

Africa Online: www.africaonline.com

Mbendi AfroPaedia (information on companies, countries, industries and stock exchanges in Africa): http://mbendi.co.za

Nigeria

KEY FACTS

Official name: Federal Republic of Nigeria

Head of State: President General Olusegun Obasanjo (PDP) (since 1999; re-elected May 2003) (President-elect Umaru Yar'Adua takes office 29 May 2007)

Head of government: President General Olusegun Obasanjo

Ruling party: People's Democratic Party (PDP) (since 1999; re-elected Apr 2003)

Area: 923,768 square km

Population: 143.85 million (2007)*

Capital: Abuja – federal capital since 1991; Lagos – commercial capital.

Official language: English

Currency: Naira (N) = 100 kobo

Exchange rate: N117.72 per US$ (Jul 2008)

GDP per capita: US$1,159 (2007)*

GDP real growth: 6.40% (2007)*

Labour force: 55.93 million (2004)

Unemployment: 2.60% (2004)

Inflation: 5.50% (2007)

Oil production: 2.36 million bpd (2007)

Balance of trade: US$27.50 billion (2006)

Foreign debt: US$35.00 billion (2004)

* estimated figure

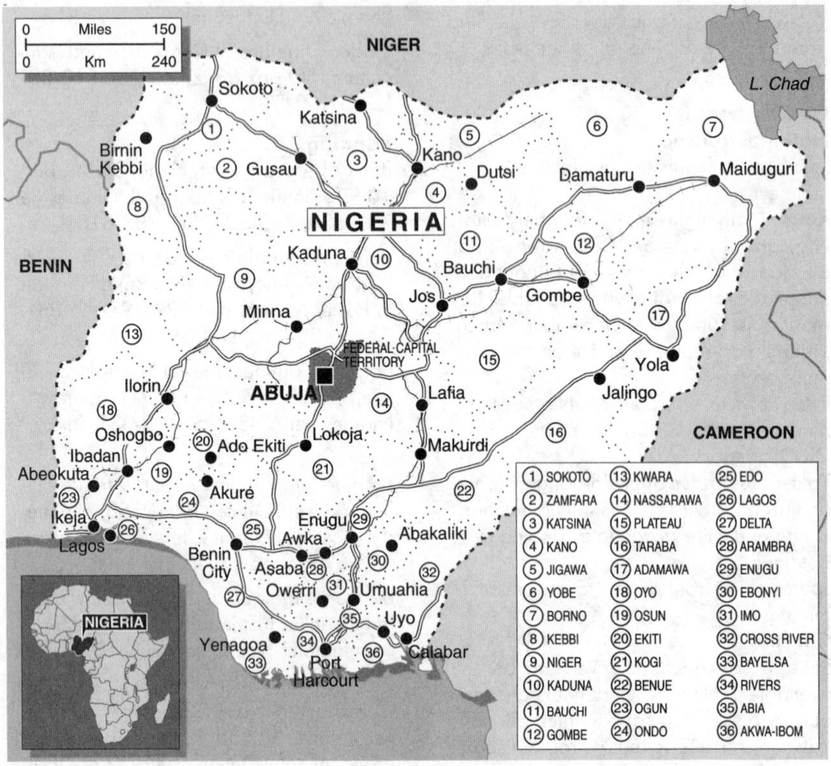

There is a saying in Nigeria that the country does not have 'elections' so much as 'selections', processes whereby one interest group decides who it will put forward for election against the chosen, or 'selected' of another interest group. In April 2003, Nigeria held its second consecutive national elections, further consolidating the transition from military to something resembling democratic rule that had begun in 1999. The elections in April 2007 were supposed to be the first time the presidency would be handed from one democratically elected leader to another. And indeed, this did happen, sort of. The elections themselves were marred by widespread allegations of fraud and intimidation, but President Umaru Yar'Adua, safely took office on 29 May. Tackling corruption is one of the new president's objectives, as it has been for all previous presidents.

Greater Lagos, Nigeria's commercial capital, is estimated to be the sixth-largest city in the world. By the year 2015 it is reckoned it will be the third largest, behind only Tokyo and Bombay, and with a population of twenty-three million. The city symbolises much that is wrong with Nigeria. A lack of planning means that growth just takes place where and when it can – not where it would be best. Resources are used as best they can be, but certainly not with any forethought and anticipation.

Oil drives the economy

High oil prices were the driving force behind Nigeria's economic growth in 2005 and 2006. Performance was mixed in 2007; GDP growth slowed to an estimated 3.2 per cent and inflation remained in single digits at 6.7 per cent. There was progress in the financial sector, debt management, foreign reserves management, exchange rate stability and the fight against corruption. Fiscal prudence was institutionalised through the National

Procurement and the Fiscal Responsibility Acts. Even so the Nigerian economy is still hampered by poor infrastructure, widespread insecurity, high levels of poverty and simmering political and ethnic tensions, especially in the oil producing areas.

Who NEEDS oil?

On the positive side, the National Economic Empowerment and Development Strategy (NEEDS to the acronym mad Nigerians), which is designed to accelerate economic growth and reduce poverty through the Millennium Development Goals (MDGs), has had some success in addressing structural and institutional weaknesses.

Oil was an estimated 33.1 per cent of GDP in 2007, less than the 36.7 per cent of 2006 as oil production contracted. With the relative stability of the Niger Delta following negotiations between the government and local militants, along with increased offshore investments, oil production is expected to expand in the short term. Consequently GDP is expected to grow by 6.2 per cent in 2008 and 6.1 per cent in 2009.

Even with the substantial oil wealth, Nigeria ranks as one of the poorest countries in the world, with less than US$800 per capita income and more than 70 per cent of the population living in poverty. In October 2005, the 15-member Paris Club announced that it would cancel 60 per cent of the debt owed by Nigeria. However, (here's the catch) Nigeria still needs to pay US$12.4 billion in arrears and meet other conditions. In March 2006, phase two of the Paris Club agreement included an additional 34 per cent debt cancellation, while Nigeria will be responsible for paying back any remaining eligible debts to the lending nations. The IMF praised the Nigerian government for adopting tighter fiscal policies, and is to be allowed to monitor Nigeria without having to disburse loans to the country.

Nigeria had 36.2 billion barrels of proven oil reserves at the end of 2007. The Nigerian government plans to expand its proven reserves to 40 billion barrels by 2010. The majority of reserves are found along the country's Niger River Delta, with the majority of oil located in approximately 250 small (i e, less than 50 million barrels each) fields. However, at least 200 other fields contain undisclosed reserves.

Nigeria had an estimated 5.3 trillion cubic metres (Tcm) of proven natural gas reserves as of the end of 2007, which makes Nigeria the seventh largest natural gas reserve holder in the world and the largest in Africa. The government plans to raise earnings from natural gas exports to 50 per cent of oil revenues by 2010. However, the Nigerian National Petroleum Corporation (NNPC) estimates that US$15 billion in private sector investments is necessary to meet its natural gas development goals by 2010.

In October 2005, the IMF approved an initial two years of support for Nigeria's national economic empowerment and development strategy. The new Policy Support Instrument (PSI) is designed for countries that may not need, or want, IMF financial assistance, but still seek IMF advice. The IMF said that Nigeria had made commendable progress in implementing its 'home grown' economic reform programme and the approval of a PSI programme signified IMF endorsement of Nigeria's plans. They were ambitious but realistic. Clear, measurable assessment criteria and benchmarks had been developed. Importantly the programme had been submitted to the National Assembly. This would greatly facilitate macroeconomic management by strengthening the co-ordination of fiscal policies in all tiers of government.

In the last five years, Nigeria has made important strides in economic reforms and the fight against corruption. Government efforts are beginning to bring results, as evidenced by Transparency International and other surveys. Streamlined due process procedures at the federal level are ensuring that public money cannot be disbursed for investment spending unless procurement procedures have been respected. The government is committed to and forcefully implementing the Nigeria Extractive Industry Transparency Initiative. Nigeria has also been removed from the Financial Action Task Force (FATF) on money laundering list of non-complying countries.

The medium-term outlook for Nigeria is broadly positive. The federal budget, for the first time in 2006, was prepared in the context of a medium-term expenditure framework; state budgets should strengthen macroeconomic performance and encourage economic growth and diversification. The government has also initiated a broad and ambitious structural reform programme aimed at improving public service delivery and the business environment. This includes measures to strengthen budgetary procedures, advance civil service reforms, restructure the banking system, unify the foreign exchange markets, rationalise the external tariff system, and improve governance and transparency.

Outlook

Poor infrastructure has been identified as the single most important constraint to development in Nigeria. The private sector cannot be expected to play the role of engine of growth without an improvement in infrastructure. It is estimated that an annual real GDP growth of eight per cent is needed and current estimates indicate a financing gap of about US$4 billion per annum

KEY INDICATORS — Nigeria

	Unit	2003	2004	2005	2006	2007
Population	m	138.00	141.59	146.22	*140.00	*143.85
Gross domestic product (GDP)	US$bn	58.40	72.11	98.56	146.89	*166.78
GDP per capita	US$	370	500	674	*1,049	*1,159
GDP real growth	%	3.2	3.5	7.2	6.2	*6.4
Inflation	%	14.0	15.0	17.8	8.3	5.5
Oil output	'000 bpd	2,185.0	2,508.0	2,580.0	2,460.0	2,356.0
Natural gas output	bn cum	19.2	20.6	21.8	28.2	35.0
Exports (fob) (goods)	US$m	27,416.0	33,990.0	53,100.0	61,600.0	–
Imports (cif) (goods)	US$m	18,692.0	17,140.0	27,588.0	34,096.0	–
Balance of trade	US$m	8,724.0	16,850.0	25,512.0	27,504.0	–
Current account	US$m	-2,080.0	2,020.0	9,104.0	13,891.0	*1,205.0
Total reserves minus gold	US$m	7,128.0	16,956.0	28,280.0	42,299.0	51,334.0
Foreign exchange	US$m	7,128.0	16,955.0	28,279.0	42,298.0	51,333.0
Exchange rate	per US$	134.98	132.89	128.16	128.16	118.04

* estimated figure

Yet, Nigeria has the lowest aid per capita among sub-Saharan countries, at about US$2 per capita, compared to the region's average of US$28.2. Nigeria has remained current on its debt service obligations to its multilateral and other creditors while maintaining dialogue and paying off its Paris Club creditors.

A key challenge going forward will be to maintain an appropriate stance and mix of fiscal and monetary policies, in view of the importance of reversing the upsurge in inflation. While the government is committed to containing spending the projected increase in spending is still large, and the resulting fiscal expansion will place more of the burden of controlling inflation on the central bank. The bank has taken strong measures to reduce money growth-including increased sales of foreign exchange, more aggressive open market operations, and a further increase in cash reserve requirements.

Risk assessment

Politics	Fair
Economy	Fair
Regional stability	Fair

COUNTRY PROFILE

Historical profile

Between the eleventh and fourteenth centuries, a number of Islamic Hausa kingdoms flourished in the area of modern-day Nigeria, while in the fourteenth and fifteeenth centuries the Yoruba empire developed into a regional power, and the Ibo (Igbo), with a diffuse political structure, lived in the east. The Yoruba first made contact with Europeans (Portuguese) in the fifteenth century, who, along with other European nations, began trading in slaves from West Africa.

1914 The territory that is now Nigeria was taken over by the British.

1922 A legislative council was set up. Much local power was left in the hands of traditional chiefs.

1947 A constitution established a federal system of government which attempted to take into account the interests of the three main regions of the colony – the northern and mainly Muslim Hausa and Fulanis, the predominantly Catholic Ibo in the east and the mixed Anglican and Muslim Yoruba in the west.

1960 Nigeria became independent.

1963 The Federal Republic of Nigeria was proclaimed.

1967–70 Three eastern states attempted to secede, as the Ibo people claimed their independence, resulting in the Biafran Civil War. Estimates for the death toll during the war range between 500,000 and two million.

1970s The Opec-led doubling of the price of oil in October 1973 and again in 1974, led to Nigeria becoming one of Africa's wealthiest states. Nigeria experienced a construction and consumer boom until the price of oil plummeted in the early 1980s.

1985 After 25 years of political turbulence, General Ibrahim Babangida seized power, he was widely supported by intellectuals, the press, some former politicians and the business community. The Genaral pledged to return Nigeria to civilian rule, but the hand-over date was repeatedly postponed.

1993 Elections were held, but were later annulled. Babangida stepped down from office. General Sani Abacha seized power in a coup d'état. He began to suppress all opposition.

1995 Ken Saro-Wiwa, Nigerian writer and advocate of the Ogoni people in eastern Nigeria, and eight other minority rights activists were executed. There was international outrage against both the government and Shell Oil Company, which had allegedly polluted Ogoni land. Nigeria was suspended from the Commonwealth and the EU imposed sanctions.

1998 Abacha died and General Abdulsalam Abubaker became Head of State.

1999 State legislative, National Assembly and presidential elections were held. Olusegun Obasanjo was declared president.

2000 Sharia (Islamic law) was adopted in several northern states despite opposition by the Christian minority. Religious and ethnic tensions grew and hundreds of deaths resulted from clashes between Muslims and Christians. Equatorial Guinea and Nigeria signed a treaty agreement about demarcation of their maritime border.

2001 The heads of Nigeria's army, navy and air force were asked to retire. President Obasanjo set up a National Security Commission in an attempt to halt the communal violence, sparked mainly by religious opposition, which had resulted in thousands of deaths.

2002 Nigeria rejected the International Court of Justice (ICJ) ruling that gave sovereignty of the oil-rich Bakassi peninsula to Cameroon.

2003 President Obasanjo of the People's Democratic Party (PDP) was re-elected and the PDP won large majorities in the Lower House and the Senate. EU observers said the elections were marred by 'serious irregularities'.

2004 The UN brokered talks between Nigeria and Cameroon about their disputed border and both countries agreed to start joint security patrols. Religious clashes in the central Plateau State resulted in a local state of emergency. Swiss authorities said that they would unfreeze most of the US$500 million deposited in Switzerland by the ex-dictator Sani Abacha.

2005 The opposition boycotted the national reform conference (NPRC), called to discuss constitutional reform, claiming it had too few powers.

2006 The Central Bank of Nigeria (CBN) announced that 13 banks faced liquidation for failing to meet the N25 billion capitalisation target. Nigeria ceded the Bakassi peninsula to Cameroon in accordance with the 2002 ICJ ruling.

2007 Umaru Yar'Adua was elected president in April. The Movement of the Emancipation of the Niger Delta (Mend) threatened to resume attacks on oil facilities and to abduct foreign workers in pursuit of their aims to gain more oil revenue for their region. Patricia Etteh resigned as Speaker of the House of Representatives in October; she was succeeded by Dimeji Bankole (PDP).

2008 Two leaders of Mend were extradited from Angola in January. Yar'Adua was confirmed as president following challenges to the elections were dismissed by a tribunal. Nigeria finally handed over the disputed maritime territory off the Bakassi Pensula to Cameroon in August. Over a dozen senior officials of the health ministry, including two former health ministers and the daughter of the former president Obasanjo were charged with embezzling around US$4 million of public funds in April. A series of strikes and attacks on oil pipelines caused intermittent oil production that helped keep world prices high.

Political structure

Constitution

The 1979 constitution was amended in 1999, when significant powers were devolved to the 36 states.

The political system is divided into three tiers: the federal or central level, the state level and local government.

Under a presidential system, the president, who is also the commander-in-chief of the armed forces, is vested with executive powers under the constitution of the federal republic. The president and his ministers form the federal executive council with the president as the chairman.

A similar structure exists in the states where the governor and his commissioners form the state executive councils. Each state has a legislature, executive and judiciary, although their legislative arm is unicameral.

Form of state

Federal republic comprising 36 states and the Federal Capital Territory (FCT, Abuja).

The executive
The Federal Executive Council is headed by an elected president who serves no more than two four-year terms.
The president is both Head of State and head of government, initiating the policies and programmes of the government and ensuring that they are implemented after they have been passed into law by the legislature. The success or failure of any government depends largely on the incumbent president who combines the roles of the chief executive with those of the ceremonial Head of State.
Despite his wide-ranging power, the president has restrictions, which include ratification of all his major appointments by the National Assembly. The president is excluded from membership of both houses of the National Assembly.
Although he is empowered to conduct foreign affairs, all treaties require the ratification of the Senate. Only the National Assembly can declare war and peace.
While he appoints members of the judiciary, he cannot remove them.
National legislature
The legislative powers of federal government are vested in a bicameral National Assembly. The Senate has 109 seats, three from each state and one from the FCT; members elected by popular vote to serve four-year terms and the House of Representatives 360 seats, with members elected by popular vote to serve four-year terms.
Each of the states of the federation has a unicameral legislature.
Legal system
Nigeria's legal system is based on English common law, Nigerian customs and tradition, and Sharia (Islamic law). Sharia predominates in the northern Islamic states.
Last elections
21 April 2007 (presidential and parliamentary).
Results: Presidential: Umaru Yar'Adua (PDP) won 24,784,227 votes; Muhammadu Buhari (ANPP) won 6,607,419 votes. Turnout was 57.5 per cent.
Senate: PDP won 53.69 per cent of the vote (76 seats out of 109); ANPP won 27.87 per cent (27 seats); and Alliance for Democracy (AD) 9.7 per cent (six seats). Turnout was 49.3 per cent.
House of Representatives: PDP won 54.49 per cent of the votes (223 seats out of 360); ANPP won 27.44 per cent (96 seats); AD won 9.28 per cent (34 seats). Turnout was 50 per cent.
Next elections
2011 (presidential and parliamentary)

Political parties
Ruling party
People's Democratic Party (PDP) (since 1999; re-elected Apr 2003)
Main opposition party
All Nigeria People's Party (ANPP)
Population
143.85 million (2007)*
Last census: March 2006: 140 million (men 71.7m, women 68.3m) (provisional results, Dec 2006). Previous census in 1991 showed a total of 88.5m.
Population density: 128 inhabitants per square km. Urban population: 45 per cent (1995—2001).
Annual growth rate: 2.4 per cent 1994–2004 (WHO 2006)
Internally Displaced Persons (IDP)
250,000 (UNHCR 2004)
Ethnic make-up
Hausas (21 per cent), Yorubas (20 per cent), Ibos (17 per cent) and Fulani (9 per cent) comprise the four major tribes.
Religions
Islam (about 50 per cent), Christianity (about 40 per cent), traditional beliefs (about 10 per cent).
Education
Primary schooling lasts for six years. Admittance to secondary schooling is through examination. Junior secondary school lasts for three years until age 15 with progress on to senior secondary school until age 18. Some students may undertake technical, vocational schooling from age 12 and can undertake academic and specialised subjects and graduate at age 18.
Around 7 per cent of the government's budget is allocated to education.
Literacy rate: 67 per cent adult rate; 89 per cent youth rate (15–24) (Unesco 2005).
Compulsory years: Six to 15
Enrolment rate: 98 per cent gross primary enrolment of relevant age group (including repeaters); 33 per cent gross secondary enrolment (World Bank).
Pupils per teacher: 34 in primary schools
Health
Per capita total expenditure on health (2003) was US$51; of which per capita government spending was US$13, (WHO 2006).
The Federal Ministry of Health (FMOH) provides policy and technical guidance to the 36 states and the federal capital territory (Abuja), co-ordinating state efforts towards the goals set by the national health policy. Annual health expenditure stands at around 3–4 per cent of GDP, of which government spending is approximately 23 per cent and foreign spending about 7 per cent.

The primary healthcare network has seriously declined with low level coverage of services such as immunisation and supply of essential drugs. The Health System Fund is a major project implemented by the state and federal ministries of health aimed at institutional development, training and an essential drug programme.
Nigeria has a growing problem of HIV/Aids as well as a significant rise of other non-communicable diseases, however, with 65 per cent of the population living below the poverty line, health measures can provide only short-term solutions to systemic problems.
Nigeria is one of only two countries that exports polio (the other is India), according to the World Health Organisation – Global Polio Eradication Initiative (WHO – Polio Eradication). In 2006, Nigeria accounted for 60 per cent of all global cases – five states in the north are the epicentre of over 50 per cent of all worldwide, and 80 per cent of Nigeria's, cases. There has been a history of mistrust by local people to immunisation and the WHO plans to target the population with more health benefits by combining the polio vaccinations with anti-malaria treatments and integrated healthcare.
Mass immunisation campaigns have been carried out in 22 countries spanning the Sahel region of Africa, from Senegal in the west, to Mali in the north and the Central African Republic in the east. For a population to be at only a minor risk of polio outbreaks 85 per cent must be vaccinated; it is estimated that, in many of the at risk countries, only 50 per cent were immunised.
Improved water sources are available to 39 per cent of the population.
HIV/Aids
An estimated 3.5 million adults and children are living with HIV/Aids and there are over one million orphans due to Aids. In March 2004 it was disclosed, by Dr Chindo Bissala, the co-ordinator of the State Action Committee against Aids (SACA), that 254,000 persons living in Niger State were confirmed as HIV positive. Dr Bissala was not optimistic that much was being done to check the spread of the disease and that generally people failed to recognise the problem.
In 2003, the government allocated US$157 million for prevention and control activities.
HIV prevalence: 5.4 per cent aged 15–49 in 2003 (World Bank)
Life expectancy: 46 years, 2004 (WHO 2006)
Fertility rate/Maternal mortality rate: 5.7 births per woman, 2004 (WHO 2006); maternal mortality 800 per 100,000 live births (World Bank).

Birth rate/Death rate: 39.6 births and 13.9 deaths per 1,000 people
Child (under 5 years) mortality rate (per 1,000): 98 per 1,000 live births; 28.7 per cent of children aged under five-years suffer malnutrition (World Bank).
Head of population per physician: 0.28 physicians per 1,000 people, 2003 (WHO 2006)

Welfare

The Nigerian public service schemes, the private sector self-administered and insured scheme, the National Provident Fund (NPF) and the Nigeria Social Insurance Trust Fund (NSITF) schemes, provide for old age, survivorship, invalidity and industrial injury benefits, gratuity and pension. The Workmen's Compensation Act provides for industrial injury benefits. Despite the existence of these bodies, the social security system is virtually non-existent in Nigeria.
The pensions fund management is divided into two categories: government schemes and occupational schemes. The government scheme provides basic social benefits that are not earnings-related, and earnings-related pension provisions. Such schemes are funded mainly through contributions from the government, with minimal contributions from the scheme members. The government policy allows individuals in self-employment to claim premiums paid to any insurance company, provided such premiums do not exceed 10 per cent of the individuals total income. This is in addition to any relief claimed in respect of life assurance policies. The occupational pension schemes consists of private companies' schemes, which are employment related and financed jointly by the employers and employees.

Main cities

Abuja (Federal Capital Territory in central Nigeria – estimated population 147,996 in 2005). Lagos (former capital – estimated population 8.7 million).
Capitals of the 36 states are: Kaduna (state of Kaduna) (1.4 million (m)), Kano (Kano) (3.0m), Jos (Plateau) (705,360), Sokoto (Sokoto) (455,642), Maiduguri (Borno) (854,613), Ilorin (Kogi – formerly Kwara) (735,478), Ibadan (Oyo) (2.5m), Port Harcourt (Rivers) (972,301), Calabar (Cross River) (439,656), Bauchi (Bauchi), Minna (Niger), Makurdi (Benue), Abeokuta (Ogun) (542,900), Akure (Ondo), Ikeja (Lagos), Owerri (Imo), Katsina (Katsina), Uyo (Akwa Ibom), Benin City (Edo) (1.0m), Enugu (Enugu) (563,619), Yola (Adamawa), Umuahia (Abia), Awka (Anambra), Asaba (Delta), Birnin Kebbi (Kebbi), Lokoja (Kogi), Yenogou (Bayelsa), Abakaliki (Ebonyi), Ado-Ekiti (Ekiti), Gombe (Gombe), Lafia (Nassarawa), Gusau (Zamfara), Osogbo (Osun), Jalingo (Taraba), Dutse (Jigawa), Damaturu (Yobe).

Languages spoken

English is used in business and public life. Hausa, Yoruba and Ibo are widely spoken.

Official language/s

English

Media

Press

The government controls the media through a media council, which has the power to discipline journalists and bar them from working. There are also strict laws of libel and an Official Secrets Act. However, the press is officially free and is often critical of the government. The News Agency of Nigeria (NAN), the country's only news agency, is government-owned but not official.
Dailies: At least 20 dailies circulate nationally. Three evening papers are published in Lagos and one in Ibadan. Principal dailies include Daily Times, National Concord, New Nigerian, The Guardian, Daily Sketch, The Punch, Vanguard, Daily Champion, Comet News, Post Express and The Tribune. Al Mizanr is published in the local language Hausa.
Weeklies: There are several weekly news magazines, notably Newswatch, African Concord, Abuja Mirror, Today and African Guardian.
Business: Policy is a business and investment magazine.

Broadcasting

Radio: The government-controlled Federal Radio Corporation of Nigeria (FRCN) operates Nigeria's radio network. It operates an external service but reception outside Lagos is poor. Four regional zonal services broadcast in English and appropriate local languages from stations based in Lagos, Ibadan, Kaduna and Enugu. External services broadcast in English, French, Hausa, Arabic, German, Swahili. In addition to the national service, each state runs its own commercial radio station. FRCN is divided into five zones:
Lagos (English speaking);
Enugu (English, Ibo, Izon, Efik and Tiv);
Ibadan (English, Yoruba, Edo, Urhobo and Igala);
Kaduna (English, Hausa, Kanuri, Fulfulde, and Nupe);
External Services (English, French, Hausa, Arabic, German and Swahili).
Television: The Nigerian Television Authority (NTA) has 25 stations nationwide and claims an audience of 30 million people for its main network news bulletin at 2100. Several states also run their own stations. There are 14 companies operating private television stations.

Economy

Despite its wealth of mineral and agricultural resources, Nigeria has since the 1980s become one of the world's poorest countries. Per capita income is lower than it was before independence in 1960 and around 60 per cent of the population lives in poverty. Nigeria's economic decline, due to incompetence and corruption, has been one of the most spectacular in Africa, aggravated by the venal dictatorship of General Sani Abacha (1993–98), who effectively looted the country's oil wealth, leaving Nigeria with a huge burden of foreign debt. Annual debt repayments have been a drain on the economy.
Since 2002, the economy has begun to recover. The civilian government of Olusegun Obasanjo has pursued a programme of reform, including fuel price deregulation, privatisation, infrastructural development, and improved fiscal and monetary management. At the same time, debt reduction has been prioritised, resulting in an agreement in 2005 by the Paris Club of international sovereign lenders to eliminate US$18 billion of Nigerian debt. Diversification is a major objective. The economy continues to be dominated by the oil and gas sector, which accounts for 20 per cent of GDP and contributes over 90 per cent of foreign exchange earnings and 65 per cent of government revenues, but the contribution of non-oil activities, such as agriculture and telecommunications, to GDP has increased. The role of the oil and gas sector has been impeded by continuing instability and damage to infrastructure. The contribution of non-oil activities is credited with driving the improvement in GDP growth in 2006.
The results of the Obasanjo government's measures met with international approval and improved Nigeria's standing, but the benefits have yet to be felt in the country. Poverty and corruption are still widespread. Food prices, rents and unemployment have risen. The power generation sector is on the verge of collapse, impacting adversely on business activity. Meanwhile, vested interests remain resistant to reform and the anti-corruption drive, while unrest and sabotage are on the rise, targeting power supplies and oil and gas installations, with a knock-on effect on export earnings and investment,

External trade

Nigeria is a member of the Economic Community of Western African States (Ecowas), which was set up to promote economic integration among members. It is a member of the Anglophone, West African Monetary Zone (WAMZ), which is due to introduce a common currency. WAMZ will eventually be merged with the Francophone-members' currency to

produce a single currency (the eco) for the region.
The oil sector is vital to the economy as it provides over 20 per cent of GDP, 95 per cent of foreign earnings and around 65 per cent of budget revenue.
As Africa's most populous nation, Nigeria is required to import food and goods.

Imports
Principal imports include fuel (Nigeria's oil refineries are inefficient), industrial raw materials, machinery, chemicals, vehicles, manufactured goods, food and live animals.
Main sources: China (10.6 per cent total, 2006), US (8.3 per cent), The Netherlands (6.1 per cent).

Exports
Principal exports are crude oil and petroleum products (typically 95 per cent of total), cocoa, rubber, timber and manufactured goods.
Main destinations: US (49.6 per cent total, 2006), Spain (8.1 per cent), Brazil (6.3 per cent).

Agriculture

Farming
Contribution to GDP by the agriculture sector fell to 16.6 per cent in 2004, down from the 26.4 per cent in 2003, even though annual growth has remained steady at 6.5 per cent. It contributes just 3 per cent to exports and receives much official encouragement.
The sector has suffered a relative decline because of the dominance of oil in the economy, but it is still the main area of employment, employing around half the workforce.
Land suitable for arable production has been put at 25 per cent of the total area, of which about 12 per cent is currently cultivated. The country suffers from soil degradation, deforestation and water pollution.
Key government policies include food self-sufficiency and boosting non-food crops to meet demand from the agri-processing sector. The sector is still dominated by unproductive smallholders raising subsistence crops such as sorghum, maize, cassava, yams, millet, rice and increasing quantities of wheat – up to 70 per cent of which is for private consumption. Nigeria is a leading world producer of cassava and the second largest producer of ginger.
Plantations, sometimes owned by, or in partnership with, multinational corporations, are gaining ground in producing raw materials for commercial use, for example grain for breweries. Irrigation schemes, higher producer prices, the expansion of credit and improvements in the rural infrastructure are beginning to show positive results.
Cash crops include cocoa, rubber (nearly all exported), coffee, cotton and palm kernels. Cocoa is Nigeria's largest foreign exchange earner after oil. The palm oil sector is being redeveloped. Livestock farming is important, while poultry farming is rapidly increasing.
Estimated crop production in 2005 included: 22,783,000 tonnes (t) cereals in total, 3,542,000t rice, 4,779,000t maize, 4,027,000t taro, 26,587,000t yams, 6,282,000t millet, 8,028,000t sorghum, 2,516,000t sweet potatoes, 38,179,000t cassava, 8,700,000t oil palm fruit, 657,000t potatoes, 2,103,000t plantains, 2,367,000t pulses, 140,900t fibre crops, 3,250,000t citrus fruit, 2,470,360t oilcrops, 2,937,000t groundnuts in shell, 366,000t cocoa beans, 3,520t green coffee, 142,000t natural rubber, 776,000t sugar cane, 9,127,000t fruit in total, 8,270,000t vegetables in total. Livestock production included: 1,066,947t meat in total, 280,000t beef, 208,231t pig meat, 100,650t lamb, 147,066t goat meat, 211,000t poultry, 102,000t game meat, 476,000t eggs, 432,000t milk, 43,080t cattle hides, 23,160t goatskins, 18,300t sheepskins.

Fishing
Over N30 billion (US$238 million) is spent annually on fish imports despite the country's large fishing potential.
There is extensive fishing in the Niger River network and along the south coast. In 2004, the total marine fish catch was 251,232 tonnes and the total crustacean catch was 28,552 tonnes.

Forestry
Nigeria has 15 per cent forest cover and an additional 54 per cent of other wooded land comprising mainly savannah. There are growing forestry operations in the tropical zones in southern Nigeria and north of Port Harcourt. The extensive network of national parks and reserves protect around 5 per cent of its forests.
Nigeria is one of the largest wood producers in Africa showing an annual harvest of more than 100 million cubic metres, most of which is used for fuel consumption. The large-scale industrial forestry sector produces sawn timber, plywood, particleboard and paper mostly to meet local demands.
Northern Nigeria is most threatened by deforestation and government concerns over desertification led to urgent action plans including a US$44.5 million National Tree Nursery Programme. However in 2008 the National Forest Conservation Council of Nigeria (NFCCN) reported that of the 50 million seedlings planted each year in the 11 northern states, 37.5 million died within two months. The remaining 12.5 million seedlings are insufficient to create a deforestation-reforestation equilibrium. An estimated 40.5 million tonnes is used as firewood in the north annually.
Timber imports in 2004 were US$241 million, while exports amounted to US$32.8 million.
Timber production in 2004 included 70,270,440 cubic metre (cum) roundwood, 9,418,000cum industrial roundwood, 2,000,000cum sawnwood, 7,100,000cum sawlogs and veneer logs, 39,000t pulpwood, 95,000cum wood-based panels, 60,852,440cum woodfuel; 3,420,800 tonnes charcoal.

Industry and manufacturing
Production costs in industry are considerably increased by a lack of basic infrastructure, which compels every factory to have its own standby electricity plant and sometimes a water borehole. Companies also find it difficult to source vital components from abroad with uncertain supplies of foreign exchange, although this situation is gradually improving thanks to the liberalisation of the economy.
The textile industry used to be one of Nigeria's more productive sectors. However, the Kano Textile Traders Association claims that imports of finished textile materials from China, Pakistan and India have resulted in the collapse of the textile industry. WTO agreements blocking advantageous exports to the US, and Ecowas tariff reductions allowing cheaper imports from neighbouring countries, have reduced the number of textile firms from a high of 250,000 to a current 50,000 with only 65 textile mills remaining. The number of job loses amounts to around 200,000.
Industrial production increased by 4.6 per cent in 2004.

Tourism
The tourism sector is expected to account for 1.5 per cent of GDP, or US$1 billion in 2005 and employ around 6.4 per cent of the working population. While travel and tourism is only expected to attract around US$340 million or 2.4 per cent of total capital investment in 2005, overall it should generate about US$4.7 billion in total tourist exports.
Nigeria has many diverse environments and attractions to offer the intrepid traveller, as well as marketing the country as a destination for eco-tourists it also emphasises it peoples and local customs.

Environment
Drilling operations in the Niger Delta region have created huge pollution problems from oil spills and explosions. Oil exploitation has been a fact of life for many people living in the Delta, particularly the Ogoni people.

Nigeria's pollution problems are exacerbated by the fact that the country does not have a pollution control policy. Analysts have reported that during oil production, Nigeria flares more natural gas than any other country in the world, contributing to global warming. The government hopes to end gas flaring by 2008.

Mining

Nigeria used to be one of the world's largest producers of tin, with production based around the highland district of Jos. It is now the smallest of the Association of Tin Producing Countries (ATPC). The country's only tin smelter is at Makeri. Tin reserves are estimated at 16,000 tonnes. Independent estimates place iron ore reserves at 800 million tonnes, averaging 37 per cent metal content.

Deposits of uranium, lead, zinc, tungsten and gold have not yet been exploited. There are 65 sites in Nigeria where gold has been located. The Iperindo gold project in Oshun State has a resource of some 400,000 ounces of gold.

Nigeria Mining Corp has taken up a number of projects including gold, tantalum and tin with the aim of attracting more capital in anticipation of increased private sector involvement.

Hydrocarbons

The petroleum sector is the mainstay of the economy, contributing 20 per cent to annual GDP and 75 per cent to government revenues. In 2004, Nigeria's proven oil reserves stood at 35.3 billion barrels, most of which is located in the Niger River Delta; production averaged 2.5 million barrels per day (bpd). Oil production dominates the Nigerian economy, accounting over 80 per cent of foreign earnings. At current production levels, reserves should last for approximately another 30 years. Nigeria hopes to increase production to four million bpd by 2010.

The Dutch/UK oil company Shell announced that the Bonga deepwater oil field had gone into production in 2005. It is expected to produce 225,000bpd and add 10 per cent to Nigeria's total production.

Multinational oil companies are in partnership with the Nigerian government for oil exploration and production. While the oil located is premium light and easily extractable, domestic political and managerial problems have led to Nigeria being discribled as 'one of the most difficult operating environments' in the world. Corruption has been blamed for much of the squandering of US$340 billion in oil revenue earned since 1965. So much so that of the 20 million people, in 3,000 communities living in the Niger River Delta, 70 per cent live on less than US$1 per day. Oil companies claim that government investment has not been forthcoming – down by US$1 billion in 2005 – so that key environmental plans, such as ending flaring of waste gas by 1 January 2008 will probably be missed.

Oil installations are frequently vandalised and company staff taken hostage, resulting in major disruptions to oil production. Some of the attacks are motivated by those who resent the development of the oil industry, the destruction of their environment and the uneven distribution of oil wealth to the federal rather than state governments. Illegal siphoning of fuel to supply the black market has resulted in a number of major explosions with hundreds of deaths each year. The government estimates that around 300,000bpd of oil is sold illegally on to the black market each year.

Nigeria has only four refineries producing 445,000bpd, about half their full capacity. All new exploration contracts require international oil companies to make a commitment to investing in new refining capacity.

Proven gas reserves stood at five trillion cubic metres in 2003, making Nigeria the second-largest African source of natural gas after Algeria. However there has been relatively little investment in projects to gather gas for commercial use, and Nigeria is considered to be the biggest burner of waste gas globally. Production was 20.6 billion cubic metres in 2004. At this production rate, reserves could last for several hundred years. Nigeria would like to provide gas as its principle source of domestic energy however capital investment in the necessary infrastructure is unavailable.

Nigeria, Ghana, Togo and Benin signed a deal for a US$500 million pipeline project to pump Nigerian natural gas across the region. Construction began in 2005 and will be ongoing for several years. Chevron Texaco will build and manage the pipeline.

Nigeria has plentiful coal reserves, although production supplies only a tiny percentage of domestic energy requirements. Coal exports are negligible, due to obsolete equipment and a lack of investment following years when the coal sector was a government monopoly.

In June 2008, the government announced that another oil exploration company would take over the operations of the global oil company Shell, which had suspended drilling operations in the Ogoniland oilfield of the Delta region in 1993, following local community protests and direct action. Large reserves of oil and gas remain to be exploited and the government was confident that negotiation for local agreement on sustainable development, environmental issues and community remunerations could resolve the issues. The Shell company halted production at its main offshore oilfield, 120km off the coast, when it was attacked by militants of the Movement for the Emancipation of the Niger Delta (Mend). The shutdown cut Nigeria's total output by 10 per cent.

Energy

Three hydroelectric stations and five thermal stations should provide around 5,900MW of installed electric generating capacity, although neglect and a lack of funding mean that actual capacity is only 2,000MW. The government's long-term objective is to increase capacity to 25,000MW.

It is estimated that only 10 per cent of rural households and 40 per cent of the total population have access to electricity. The government aims to increase total electricity coverage to 85 per cent by 2010 by building 16 new power plants and 15,000km of transmission lines. The development of hydroelectric power stations is hampered by persistent droughts and funding difficulties. As a result the government is turning to developing a solar energy system to serve rural communities not served by the national grid.

Transmission Company of Nigeria (TCN) said it was due to complete the 70 kilometre power transmission line to Benin in February 2007. The project is part of the West African Power Pool action plan and cost US$25 million.

Financial markets

Stock exchange

The Nigerian Stock Exchange (NSE) was established in 1960 as the Lagos Stock Exchange and became the NSE in 1977. The NSE conducts its business on six trading floors spread across the country. It has branches in Lagos, Kaduna and Port Harcourt, with the bulk of business conducted in Lagos. Most transactions are concentrated in the banking, conglomerates, breweries and food and drink sub-sectors. The banking sector, which offers high yields, is the most active sub-sector in the NSE, representing around 46 per cent of all transactions. On 3 January 2006, 22 banks were suspended from the trading floor following the withdrawal of their licences by the regulatory authorities.

Banking and insurance

Nigeria's banking sector is the second-largest in Africa behind South Africa, but it has experienced difficulties in recent years. Since the late 1990s, the Central Bank of Nigeria (CBN) has worked towards cleaning up the banking sector. The end of military rule in 1999 saw international banks return to Nigeria, although they concentrate their operations in Lagos and Abuja supplying services for big businesses and Nigerian expatriates. The CBN does not differentiate between licensing of commercial and merchant banks, which enables merchant banks to issue cheques and allows them to access the CBN's clearing house.

In 2005 the CBN began restructuring the banking sector by setting a minimum capital requirement that has forced banks into consolidation. The IMF is advising the CBN on the banking reform programme.

A persistent obstacle to the banking sector's development is Nigeria's culture of fraud; the CBN has been keen to address, the advance fee fraud scams, run by criminal gangs. A Financial Intelligence Unit monitors the banking environment to strengthen the anti-money laundering framework that is under way.

Other problems include the federal and state governments' borrowing from domestic banks, which has severely restricted liquidity in the banking sector.

It was announced in March 2005 that the introduction of the shared currency, the Eco, in Nigeria, Ghana, Guinea, Sierra Leone and The Gambia, which was due in July 2005, would be postponed. The currency was proposed to facilitate trade and growth with an ultimate plan to merge it with the CFA franc.

On 1 January 2006 the CBN announced that 13 banks faced liquidation for failing to meet its N25 billion capitalisation target.

Central bank

Central Bank of Nigeria (CBN)

Main financial centre

Lagos

Offshore facilities

Nigeria is on the Organisation for Economic Co-operation and Development (OECD) Financial Action Task Force (FATF) list of non-co-operative countries on money laundering.

Time

GMT plus one hour

Geography

Nigeria is bordered to the west by Benin, to the north by Niger, to the north-east by Chad, to the east by Cameroon and to the south by the Bight of Benin (Atlantic Ocean). The main rivers, the Niger and Benue, merge in the centre of the country, dividing it into three main regions of north, south and east. The north consists of dry savannah, the south of jungle, with mangrove swamps nearer the coast, and the east of a plateau leading into the country's only major mountain range along the Cameroon border.

Hemisphere

Northern

Climate

The climate varies from tropical on the coast to sub-tropical in the north. There are two main seasons, the rainy season from April to October and the dry season from November to March, which is characterised by a cool dust haze from the Sahara known as the harmattan.

Average temperatures remain fairly constant throughout the year at 29 degrees Celsius (C) in the south. The average daytime temperature in the north is 42 degrees C, but the temperature can drop to as low as 6 degrees C at night.

Humidity is high in the south, with a maximum varying from 100 per cent to 80 per cent. Rainfall is heavy on the coast, ranging from about 180cm a year in the south-west to 430cm in the south-east.

Near-temperate conditions are common on the central plateau and along the hilly north-eastern border with Cameroon.

Dress codes

Suits or traditional dress are worn for business meetings, but otherwise dress is informal. Women are advised to dress modestly, especially in the Islamic north. For social occasions, dress as for a business meeting.

Entry requirements

Passports

Required by all and must be valid for six months beyond the date of departure.

Visa

Required by all; some exceptions are made for citizens of countries located close to Nigeria. Visas should be obtained before arrival, contact the nearest consular office, or see www.nigeriabusinessinfo.com/visas.htm for details.

Business visitors will require a letter of invitation, from an organisation or individual, addressed to the Visa Section of the High Commission or Embassy. A declaration of full compliance of all entry requirements or proof of sufficient funds for expenses (such as traveller's cheques to be cashed in Nigeria), must be lodged.

Any individual inviting a visitor must attach photocopies of the first five pages of his/her own passport, while a resident must enclose a copy of his/her residence permit.

Currency advice/regulations

The import and export of local currency is limited to N20. The import of foreign currency is unlimited but must be declared, its export is limited to N100. Visitors are advised not to use unauthorised currency exchange methods, which are illegal.

Travellers cheques have limited use in cities and larger towns.

Customs

Laws against exporting Nigerian antiquities are strictly enforced.

Prohibited imports

Sparkling wines and beer, fruits and vegetables, eggs and cereals, precious metals and textiles including mosquito netting.

Health (for visitors)

Mandatory precautions

Yellow fever vaccination certificate required if coming from an infected area.

Advisable precautions

Inoculations and booster should be current for tetanus, polio, hepatitis A, diphtheria, typhoid and yellow fever. There may be a need for vaccinations for tuberculosis, hepatitis B and meningitis and cholera. Use malaria prophylaxis (which will also provide protection for hepatitis B and yellow fever) including mosquito repellents, nets and clothing that fully cover the body after dark. There is a risk of rabies.

Other diseases that require preventative measures are HIV/Aids, hepatitis C and E; to avoid bilharzia, use only well-maintained and chlorinated swimming pools.

Use only bottled or boiled water for drinks, washing teeth and making ice. Eat only well cooked meals, preferably served hot; vegetables should be cooked and fruit peeled. Dairy products are unpasteurised and should be avoided, unless cooked.

Walking in bare feet, or even open sandals, can attract parasites, notably jikkers.

Visitors should seek advice before accepting treatment involving hypodermic needles or blood transfusions. Medical insurance is essential, including emergency evacuation, and an adequate supply of personal medicines is necessary.

Hotels

There is a wide range of hotels available, though rooms are difficult to obtain and expensive in Lagos. Bills must be paid for in foreign currency and a high deposit in advance is required to cover the estimated length of stay. Most major hotels are air-conditioned.

Credit cards

Credit cards are not widely used.

Public holidays (national)

Fixed dates

1 Jan (New Year's Day), 1 May (Workers' Day), 29 May (Democracy Day), 1 Oct (National Day), 25–26 Dec (Christmas).

Variable dates

Easter (Mar/Apr), Eid al Adha, Birth of the Prophet, National Day (first Mon in Oct), Eid al Fitr.

Holidays that fall at the weekend may be taken on Monday.

Islamic year – 1429 (10 Jan 2008–28 Dec 2008): The Islamic year contains 354 or 355 days, with the result that Muslim feasts advance by 10–12 days against the Gregorian calendar. Dates of feasts vary according to the sighting of the new moon, so cannot be forecast exactly.

Working hours

Banking
Mon: 0800–1500; Tue–Fri: 0800–1330 (some banks work until 1600 or 1700); Sat, some banks only: 1000–1500.

Business
Mon–Fri: 0800–1230 and 1400–1630. Some offices also Sat: 0800–1200.

Government
Mon–Fri: 0730–1530, some states also Sat: 0800–1300.

Shops
Mon–Fri: 0800–1200 and 1430–1800; Sat: 0800–1300.

Telecommunications

Mobile/cell phones
There are GSM roaming facilities available, with coverage throughout most of the country.

Electricity supply

230V AC, 50 cycles

Social customs/useful tips

Because of the prodigious traffic jams, called 'go-slows', which often grip Lagos, it is hard to be punctual, so both Nigerians and expatriates are generally tolerant of latecomers.

Appointments with government officials should be made in advance. With business executives, a more informal attitude prevails. Business cards are exchanged after introduction and business is mostly conducted in English. Meetings can be long and they are less formal than in Europe. It is customary to shake hands on meeting and taking leave.

Confirm the business organisation's status with the Chamber of Commerce, Corporate Affairs Commission, Abuja and the Federal Ministry of Commerce and Tourism, Abuja, before entering into a firm contract.

Local customs and conventions should be adhered to, particularly in Muslim areas in the northern states. Women should not wear trousers.

Gifts are welcomed but not essential, unless hospitality extends to accommodation and/or meals, in which case gifts are expected on departure.

Gratuities are around 10 per cent. A service charge is usually added to restaurant and hotel bills. Tips are not expected by taxi drivers. Giving dash or gratuities for other commercial services is widespread, although officially discouraged .

Security

Security remains a serious problem in several Nigerian cities, but chiefly in Lagos. The biggest threat comes from armed robbers. They either attack houses at night or, more frequently, stop cars at gunpoint on urban or country expressways and order the driver to hand over the keys. Petty theft is also common; moneybelts are advisable.

During outbreaks of violence, the capital is likely to be dotted with checkpoints manned by armed police, where visitors should remain calm and courteous. It is not necessary to offer a bribe at these roadblocks.

Getting there

Air

International airport/s: Abuja Nnamdi Azikiwe (ABV), 35km from city; Kano-Mallam-Aminu Kano (KAN), 8km from city; Lagos-Murtala Muhammed (LOS), 22km from city. All airport facilities include duty-free shop, restaurant, bar, bank, post office, car hire.

It is advisable to be met at Lagos airport by someone you know, or someone who can prove their identity. Also make sure you do not give your passport to anyone but the immigration officer. Check in early for flights as overbooking is common.

Airport tax: None

Surface

Road: There are good roads linking Niger (Maradi, Zinder, Agadez, Niamey) to Kano, and from Benin; there are all-weather roads from Cameroon (Maroua, Mokolo) and Chad (N'Djamna). The southern road from Cameroon (Mamfe) to Enugu is not generally recommended.

Water: Nigeria has the biggest port facilities and international sailings in the region.

Main port/s: Apapa (Lagos), Port Harcourt, Calabar and the Delta Port complex including Warri, Sapele and Koko.

Getting about

National transport

Air: There is a number of local airlines providing intercity services. Routes and airlines frequently change.

Road: A national road network system of 113,000km links all main centres. Principal main roads connect Lagos and Port Harcourt in the south with Kano and Katsina in the north. The motorway running from Lagos-Ibadan is often congested. There are often long delays in major towns.

Some secondary roads can become impassable during rainy season.

Buses: Scheduled coach services include: Kaduna-Jos; Lagos-Umuahia.

Rail: There are some 3,500km of railway, mostly single track.

Rail travel is cheap, but slow. There are two classes. Some trains have restaurant cars and buffet facilities and some have air-conditioning.

There are two main rail lines: Lagos-Kano Express (via Ibadan and Minna) with branches to Baro, Kaura Namoda and Nguru, Plateau Express (Lagos-Jos); and Port Harcourt-Kano with branch to Jos and Maiduguri.

Water: There are over 8,575 km of waterways including the Niger and Benue rivers, with ferry services on these and along the southern coast.

City transport

Taxis: Taxis are widely available in Lagos and other main towns. The traditional taxis are usually yellow Peugeots in Lagos (these charge by distance), other colours elsewhere. Also numerous cars belonging to car hire companies. Taxi ranks are mainly found at the big hotels. Fare and tip should be agreed before starting journey. All drivers should have an Identity Card.

Journey time from Lagos Murtala Mohammed Airport to city centre is around 40 minutes, but can take several hours if the traffic is heavy.

Car hire

Available in most of the large towns through the main hotels. International driving licence and two passport-sized photographs required; chauffeur-driven services generally recommended.

Be aware that in Lagos the Lagos State Traffic Management Authority (Lastma) has wide powers and frequently stops and seizes vehicles for minor, alleged, offences. On the spot 'fines' are frequently suggested. Owners of vehicles that are impounded have to pay a daily charge to recover them.

BUSINESS DIRECTORY

The addresses listed below are a selection only. While World of Information makes every endeavour to check these addresses, we cannot guarantee that changes have not been made, especially to telephone numbers and area codes. We would welcome any corrections.

Telephone area codes

The international direct dialling code (IDD) for Nigeria is +234, followed by area code and subscriber's number:

Abuja	9	Katsina	65
Akure	34	Lagos	1
Bauchi	77	Maiduguri	76
Calabar	87	Makurdi	44
Enugu	42	Minna	66
Ibadan	22	Owerri	83
Ikeja	1	Oyo	38
Ilorin	31	Port Harcourt	84
Jos	73	Sokoto	60
Kaduna	62	Yola	75
Kano	64	Zaria	69

Useful telephone numbers

Police199
Fire and ambulance999

Chambers of Commerce

Abuja Chamber of Commerce and Industry, International Trade Fair Centre, Airport Road, PO Box 86, Abuja (tel: 523-0453; fax: 523-6231; e-mail: anmgbemere@hotmail.com).

British-Nigerian Chamber of Commerce, Ebani House, 149 Broad Street, Lagos (tel: 264-1266; fax: 266-0298; e-mail: hq@n-bcc.org).

Enugu Chamber of Commerce, Industry, Mines and Agriculture, International Trade Fair Complex, Abakaliki Road, PO Box 734, Enugu (tel: 250-575; fax: 252-186; e-mail: eccima@infoweb.abs.net).

Ibadan Chamber of Commerce and Industry, Commerce House, Ring Road, PO Box 5168, Ibadan (tel: 317-223; fax: 311-647; e-mail: icci@infoweb.abs.net).

Kaduna Chamber of Commerce, Industry, Mines and Agriculture, Kaduna-Zaria Road, Rigachikun, PO Box 728, Kaduna (tel: 318-794; fax: 318-795; e-mail: kadccima@inet-global.com).

Kano Chamber of Commerce and Industry, Trade Fair Complex, Zoo Road, PO Box 10, Kano (tel: 666-936; fax: 667-138; e-mail: kaccima@hotmail.com).

Lagos Chamber of Commerce and Industry, 1 Idowu Taylor Street, Victoria Island, PO Box 109, Lagos (tel: 774-6617; fax: 262-3665; e-mail: inform@lagoschamber.com).

National Association of Chambers of Commerce, Industry and Agriculture, 15A Ikorodu Road, Maryland, PO Box 12816, Lagos (tel: 496-4727, 496-4737; e-mail: naccima@pinet.com.ng).

Port Harcourt Chamber of Commerce, Industry, Mines and Agriculture, 169 Aba Road, PO Box 71, Port Harcourt (tel: 330-394; fax: 243-307; e-mail: phccima@hotmail.com).

Banking

Nigerian Industrial Development Bank Ltd (NIMB), PMB 205, 1st Floor, NIMB Building, 4th Avenue, Plot 207, Cadastral Zone AO, Off Herbert Macaulay Way, Central Business District, Abuja (tel: 234-6579; fax: 234-6578).

Commercial Bank (Crédit Lyonnais Nigeria) Ltd, PMB 12829, Plot 146B Ligali Ayorinde, Victoria Island Annex, Lagos (tel: 262-5700; fax: 262-5699).

Ecobank Nigeria plc, 2 Ajose Adeogun St, Victoria Island, Lagos (tel: 262-0910/4; fax: 261-6568, 262-0920).

Investment Banking & Trust Co Ltd (IBTC), PMB 71707, IBTC Place, Walter Carrington Crescent, Victoria Island, Lagos (tel: 262-6520/40; fax: 262-6541/2; e-mail: IBTC@IBTCLagos.com; internet site: http://www.IBTCLagos.com).

Lion Bank of Nigeria plc, PMB 12852, 121/125 Broad St, Lagos (tel: 266-914, 266-7735).

Nigerian Industrial Development Bank Ltd (NIDB), PMB 2357, NIDB House, 63/71 Broad St, Lagos (tel: 266-3495, 266-1545; fax: 266-7074, 266-6733).

Central bank

Central Bank of Nigeria, Central Business District, Cadastral Zone, PO Box 0187, Garki, Abuja (tel: 234-3191; fax: 234-3137; email: info@cenbank.org).

Travel information

ADC Airlines (tel: 271-4020; reservations: 496-1942; internet: www.adcairlines.com).

Virgin Nigeria, Head Office, 3rd Floor, Ark Towers, Plot 17, Ligali Ayorinde Street, Victoria Island Extension, Lagos (tel: 460-0505, 271-1111; internet: www.virginnigeria.com).

Ministry of tourism

Federal Ministry of Culture and Tourism, Area 1 Secretariat Complex, Garki, Abuja (tel: 234-2727).

National tourist organisation offices

Nigerian Tourism Developemnt Corporation, Old Secretariat, Area 1, Garki, PMB 167, Abuja (tel: 234-2764; fax: 234-2775; e-mail: information@nigeriatourism.net).

Ministries

Federal Ministry of Agriculture and Rural Development, Area 1 Secretariat Complex, Garki, Abuja (tel: 314-1185).

Federal Ministry of Aviation, New Federal Secretariat Complex, Shehu Shagari Way, Abuja (tel: 523-2112).

Federal Ministry of Commerce, Area 1 Secretariat Complex, Garki, Abuja (tel: 234-1884).

Federal Ministry of Communications, New Federal Secretariat Complex, Shehu Shagari Way, Abuja (tel: 523-7183).

Federal Ministry of Culture and Tourism, Area 1 Secretariat Complex, Garki, Abuja (tel: 234-2727).

Federal Ministry of Defence, Ship House, Central Area, Abuja (tel: 234-0534).

Federal Ministry of Education, New Federal Secretariat Complex, Shehu Shagari Way, Abuja (tel: 523-2800).

Federal Ministry for Federal Capital Territory, Area 11, Garki, Abuja (tel: 523-4014).

Federal Ministry of Finance, Garki, Abuja (tel: 234-4686).

Federal Ministry of Foreign Affairs, Maputo Street, Zone 3 Wuse District, Abuja (tel: 523-0576).

Federal Ministry of Health, New Federal Secretariat Complex, Shehu Shagari Way, Abuja, (tel: 523-0576).

Federal Ministry of Industries, Area 1 Secretariat Complex, Garki, Abuja (tel: 523-0576).

Federal Ministry of Information, Radio House, Herbert Macaulay Way, Garki, Abuja (tel: 234-6350).

Federal Ministry of Internal Affairs, Area 1 Secretariat Complex, Garki, Abuja (tel: 234-6884).

Federal Ministry of Justice, New Federal Secretariat Complex, Shehu Shagari Way, Abuja (tel: 523-5194).

Federal Ministry of Labour and Productivity, New Federal Secretariat Complex, Shehu Shagari Way, Abuja (tel: 523-5980).

Federal Ministry of Police Affairs, New Federal Secretariat Complex, Shehu Shagari Way, Abuja (tel: 523-0549).

Federal Ministry of Power and Steel, New Federal Secretariat Complex, Shehu Shagari Way, Abuja (tel: 523-7064).

Federal Ministry of Science and Technology, New Federal Secretariat Complex, Shehu Shagari Way, Abuja (tel: 523-3397).

Federal Ministry of Solid Minerals Development, New Federal Secretariat Complex, Shehu Shagari Way, Abuja (tel: 523-5830; fax: 523,6518; e-mail: minsolmindev@linkserve.com).

Federal Ministry of Sports and Social Development, New Federal Secretariat Complex, Shehu Shagari Way, Abuja (tel: 523-5905).

Federal Ministry of Transport, National Maritime Agency Building, Central Area, Abuja (tel: 523-7053).

Federal Ministry of Water Resources, Area 1 Secretariat Complex, Garki, Abuja (tel: 234-2376).

Federal Ministry of Women's Affairs and Youth Development, New Federal Secretariat Complex, Shehu Shegari Way, Abuja (tel: 523-7051).

Federal Ministry of Works and Housing, Mabushi Districti, Abuja (tel: 521-1622).

Other useful addresses

African Petroleum plc, AP House, 54-56 Broad Street, PO Box 512, Lagos (tel: 260-0050/9, 260-0145/9; fax: 263-5290).

Bureau of Public Enterprises, 1 Osun Crescent, Off Ibrahim Babangida Way,

Maitama, Abuja (tel: 413-4673; fax: 413-4674; internet: www.bpeng.org).

British High Commission, Dangote House, Aguyi Ironsi Street, Maitama District, Abuja (tel 413-4559–64 (6 lines); fax: 413-4565, 413-3888; email: visa.enquiries.abuja@fco.gov.uk).

Britain Nigeria Business Council, 2 Vincent Street, London, SW1P 4LD (tel: (+44-20) 7828-9661; fax: (+44-20) 7828-9779; email: bnbc-uk@btconnect.com)

Chevron Nigeria Ltd, 2 Chevron Drive, Lekki Peninsular, PMB 12825, Lagos.

Economic Community of West African States (Ecowas), 6 King George V Road, Lagos (tel: 260-0720/5).

Manufacturers' Association of Nigeria, 12th Floor, Unity House, 37 Marina, PO Box 3835, Lagos.

National Council on Privatisation, Secretariat, Bureau of Public Enterprises, 1 Osun Crescent, Off Ibrahim Babangida Way, Maitama District, PMB 442, Garki, Abuja (tel: 413-4660/4670/4673; fax: 413-4671/4672/4674; e-mail: bpegen@micro.com.ng).

National Maritime Authority, 4 Burma Road, Apapa, Lagos.

National Planning Commission, Federal Secretariat, Shehu Shagari Way, Abuja (tel: 523-6628; fax: 523-6625).

National Science & Technology Development Agency, PO Box 12695, Lagos.

Nigerian Communications Commission, 72 Ahmadu Bello Way, Benue Plaza, Abuja (tel: 234-2327, 234-4590/2; fax: 234-4593; email: ncc@cyberspace.net.ng; internet site: www.ncc.gov.ng).

Nigeria Export Processing Zone Authority, 4th Floor, Radio House, Herbert Macauley Way (South), PMB 037, Garki Abuja (tel: 234-3060; fax: 234-3061).

Nigerian Embassy (USA), 1333 16th Street, NW, Washington DC 20036 (tel: (+1-202) 986-8400; fax: (+1-202) 462-7124).

Nigeria-São Tomé and Príncipe Joint Development Authority, Plot 1101 Aminu Kano Crescent, Wuse II, Abuja (tel: 524-1069; fax: 524-1052; e-mail: enquiries@nigeriasaotomejda.com; internet site: www.nigeriasaotomejda.com).

Ports Sector Reforms, Bureau of Public Enterprises, 1 Osun Crescent, Off Ibrahim Babangida Way, Maitama, PMB 442, Garki, Abuja (tel: 413-4634/46; fax: 413-4671/2/4; email: husmanbpeng.org).

Internet sites

Portal site: www.nigerianation.com

Africa Business Network: http://www.ifc.org/abn

AllAfrica.com: http://allafrica.com

African Development Bank: http://www.afdb.org

Africa News Online: http://www.allafrica.com

Africa Online: http://www.africaonline.com

Mbendi AfroPaedia (information on companies, countries, industries and stock exchanges in Africa): http://mbendi.co.za

Movement for the Survival of the Ogoni People (MOSOP): http://www.mosopcanada.org/index1.html

Niue

COUNTRY PROFILE

Historical profile

The first inhabitants arrived from Tonga, Samoa and Fiji between AD600 and AD1000.

1774 Visited by Captain James Cook and given the name, Savage Island

1846 Conversion to Christianity commenced by the London Missionary Society.

1900 Niue became a British protectorate.

1901 Niue was formally annexed to New Zealand, as part of the Cook Islands.

1960 The first Niue Assembly was established.

1974 Niue was granted 'self-government in free association with New Zealand'. It became the smallest self-governing state with that status.

1982 Robert Rex was elected prime minister.

1992 Robert Rex died. He was succeeded by Young Vivian.

1993 Frank Lui won the election and became prime minister.

1996 Lui was re-elected.

1999 Sani Elia Lakatani of the Niue People's Party (NPP) was elected prime minister.

2001 The US imposed trading sanctions on Niue due its tax haven status. A census recorded 1,799 people.

2002 All 20 members of the Legislative Assembly were re-elected and Young Vivian of the NPP was elected prime minister.

2003 The NPP was dissolved, despite which the coalition government continued.

2004 A 300km per hour cyclone, Heta, devastated Niue; international aid was required to help with recovery and many Niueans living in New Zealand returned to help with the clean-up operation.

2005 A census recorded that the population figure was 1,600, a drop of almost 200 people, with the village of North Alofi losing 113 of its 256 residents. Prime Minister Young Vivian retained his parliamentary seat unopposed. He was re-elected prime minister by the Legislative Assembly by 17 votes to three for the independents' candidate, Mrs O'Love Jacobsen. Vivian proposed constitutional changes, whereby the parliamentary term would be extended from three years to five and the cabinet increased from four ministers to six.

2006 Niue had been suffering from frequent power failures when one of its generators was damaged in June causing further problems in pumping water from the reservoir. The island's electricity network was over 30 years old and due for upgrading; a new replacement five tonne generator was flown in from New Zealand at short notice. The government invited Malaysian loggers to re-start a furniture factory in an effort to increase the prospects for expanding the population.

2008 Parliamentary elections were held on 7 June. 20 independent members were elected (nine unopposed), including Young Vivian. The Legislative Assembly elected Toke Talagi as prime minister on 19 June; he won 14 votes to Vivian's five.

Political structure

Constitution

Under the 1974 constitution, New Zealand remains responsible for defence and foreign affairs and is ready to provide necessary economic and administrative assistance. Niueans are New Zealand citizens. The head of state, the British monarch, is represented in Niue by the Governor General of New Zealand. Village affairs are handled by 14 village councils of three to five members, elected to three-year terms in conjunction with the Community Affairs Office.

Form of state

Self-governing state, in free association with New Zealand.

The executive

The four-member executive cabinet is headed by a prime minister elected by the Legislative Assembly, who in turn appoints three ministers.

National legislature

The island is governed by a 20-member Legislative Assembly – 14 elected from village constituencies and six from the common roll – elected by popular vote for a three-year term.

Last elections

7 June 2008 (parliamentary)

Results: Parliamentary: 20 independent members were elected (nine unopposed). Young Vivian was re-elected.

Next elections

2011 (parliamentary)

Political parties

The Niue political system is not based on formal political

KEY FACTS

Official name: Republic of Niue

Head of State: Queen Elizabeth II, represented by the Governor General of New Zealand

Head of government: Prime Minister Toke Talagi (elected by the Legislative Assembly 18 Jun 2008)

Ruling party: There are no political parties; parliamentarians sit as independents

Area: 256 square km

Population: 1,600 (2005 – census figure); over 20,000 Niueans reside in New Zealand.

Capital: Alofi is the main town.

Official language: English, Niuean

Currency: New Zealand dollar (NZ$) = 100 cents

Exchange rate: NZ$1.31 per US$ (Jul 2008)

GDP per capita: US$7,070 (2003)

GDP real growth: 5.20% (2003)*

Inflation: 4.00% (2005)

Balance of trade: -US$8.84 million (2004)

Foreign debt: US$418,000 (2003)

Aid flow: US$2.60 million (annually)

Visitor numbers: 2,800 (2005)*

* estimated figure

organisations. Until 2003, two loose groupings existed: the Niue People's Party (NPP) and the Alliance of Independents. The NPP was dissolved in July 2003 and all candidates in the 2005 elections ran as independents.

Ruling party

There are no political parties; parliamentarians sit as independents

Main opposition party

Political situation

Population

1,600 (2005 – census figure); over 20,000 Niueans reside in New Zealand.

Last census: 30 April 2005: 1,600

Population density: 8 inhabitants per square km (2001).

Annual growth rate: -2.1 per cent 1994–2004 (WHO 2006)

Ethnic make-up

The population is mainly of Polynesian (Tongan) descent, with some New Zealand elements.

Religions

Predominantly Christian.

Education

The education system is modelled on New Zealand's with services provided free until aged 14. For the first four years teaching may be in either Niuean or English.

In 2004, the schools increased the content of Niuean language in the curriculum.

Compulsory years: Five to 14

Health

Per capita total expenditure on health (2003) was US$153; of which per capita government spending was US$150, at the international dollar rate, (WHO 2006).

Life expectancy: 71 years, 2004 (WHO 2006)

Fertility rate/Maternal mortality rate: 2.8 births per woman, 2004 (WHO 2006)

Main cities

Alofi (estimated population 404 in 2004).

Languages spoken

English is widely understood. The people who live in the north speak a Polynesian dialect which differs from the dialect of the people living on the rest of the island who speak a language closer to Tongan.

Official language/s

English, Niuean

Media

There is limited media availability.

Other news agencies: ABC Pacific Beat: www.radioaustralia.net.au/pacbeat

Pacific Magazine: www.pacificmagazine.net

Press

The weekly Niue Star is a private newspaper published in English and Niue. A fortnightly newspaper Niuean (www.niuean.com) is published in Australia. An online news round-up is Niue Business News (www.webpost.net/nb/nbn).

Broadcasting

The Broadcasting Corporation of Niue operates the only radio (Radio Sunshine) and television station, which broadcasts in English and Niue in the evenings only.

Radio: Radio Sunshine broadcasts are transmitted on AM594/FM91 six days/week during limited hours.

Television: Television Niue broadcasts in English and Niue in the evenings only, usually 1730–2200.

Economy

Niue is dependent on New Zealand's financial assistance (approximately 25 per cent of the Niue total government revenue) for its economic survival.

The economy is mainly agricultural, with the people earning wages on government work and raising vegetables, fruit, pigs and poultry for their own consumption. Industry is limited to agricultural production, although some small building and joinery operations have been started.

Sales of postage stamps and remittances from Niuean workers overseas are important sources of revenue.

Under the Niue Concerted Action Plan, New Zealand aid at around US$3.2 million per annum is designed to make the economy become self-sufficient. However, Niue has been hit in recent years by reductions of budgetary aid from New Zealand, as the aid programme has come under review. Many investors have left as the future looks uncertain.

In order to boost Niue's meagre income, the government leases international telephone codes for use by foreign companies and has built a quarantine station for alpaca – a wool-bearing llama-like South American mammal – en route to Australia. Marketing of the '.nu' Internet domain name has been a controversial income source.

The Niue government has been criticised for allowing the public sector to grow faster than the economy. However, privatisation of the telecommunications, forestry, power and water supplies are planned if buyers can be found for such assets.

The government is also hoping to gain revenue from investment partnerships in fishing and organic products and is seeking interest in developing tourism.

External trade

Niue is a member of the South Pacific Regional Trade and Economic Co-operation Agreement (Sparteca) along with 12 other regional nations, which allows products duty free access by Pacific Island Forum members to Australian and New Zealand markets (subject to the country of origin restrictions).

Imports

Main imports are food, live animals, manufactured goods, vehicles, fuels and medicines.

Main sources: Principally from New Zealand, Fiji, Japan, Samoa, Australia, US.

Exports

Agricultural products – copra, honey, vanilla, passion fruit, paw paws, root crops and limes, financial and telecommunication services.

Main destinations: Principally to New Zealand, Fiji, Cook Islands, Australia

Agriculture

Development of agriculture has been hindered by the limited amount of fertile or cultivable land, lack of surface water and susceptibility to drought conditions. Only 20 per cent of land can be used for agriculture. Cyclones are a major problem.

Alienation of land is forbidden, but leases may be granted for a maximum term of 66 years.

In March 2004, the UN provided US$700,000, together with four technical advisers, to help set up an irrigation system.

Limes and passion fruit are grown for export. Goats have been introduced on a trial basis.

Estimated production in 2005 included: 2,500 tonnes (t) coconuts, 3,200t taro, 250t sweet potatoes, 120t yams, 110t citrus fruit, 580t fruit in total, 325t oilcrops, 100t vegetables in total, 110t citrus. Livestock production included: 80t meat in total, 60t pig meat, 2t beef, 18t poultry, 12t eggs, 50t milk, 6t honey.

Annual fishing production typically includes 200t marine fish. A new fish plant opened in 2004 employing 30 people.

In 2004, the total marine fish catch was 200 tonnes.

About 20 per cent of the land area is forest with millable timber, and logging serves local demand.

Malaysian logging companies have approached the government to harvest timber from the small hardwood forests. Not everyone is in agreement with such production that could leave the island deforested and the terrain at more risk from cyclones.

Industry and manufacturing

The Office of Economic Affairs is responsible for planning and financing productive ventures relating to agriculture, tourism and industry. Niue Handicrafts handles production and marketing of objects plaited from pandanus and coconut palm leaves.

Small-scale industries include honey extraction and bottling, saw milling, joinery, furniture and handicrafts.

Investment has been made in the vanilla and forestry industries.

Tourism

Development of tourism is a priority, with emphasis on eco-tourism, but has been impeded by poor planning, uncertain air connections with New Zealand and nature in the form of seasonal cyclones. Visitor numbers have been small but rising; 2,758 arrivals were recorded in 2003. Additional Polynesian Airlines flights were announced in November 2002. The devastating Cyclone Heta in January 2004 damaged infrastructure and many of the island's scenic attractions. By June 2004 tourist services were back to normal and arrivals for the year totalled 2,558.

Hydrocarbons

Niue does not produce any hydrocarbons and relies on imports to meet domestic energy needs. Niue imports refined oil and imports around 20 barrels per day. Niue does not import gas or coal.

Banking and insurance

Central bank

Reserve Bank of New Zealand

Offshore facilities

In 2002, the introduction of US sanctions on banking activities was a major blow to Niue. The US accused Niue of having connections to Latin American tax haven operations.

Niue licensed six offshore banks operating in Australia, which the Organisation for Economic Co-operation and Development (OECD) wanted to close down. In June 2002, the Niue Legislative Assembly repealed the legislation which authorised the issuing of banking licences and Niue was removed from the OECD Financial Action Task Force (FATF) blacklist of places associated with money laundering.

Following the government's decision in 2004 not to renew four offshore banking licences, the international business company registry of Mossack Fonseca of Panama was informed that its operations would be shut down by the end of 2006.

Time

GMT minus eleven hours

Geography

Niue is a coral island in the Pacific Ocean about 480km (300 miles) east of Tonga and 930km (580 miles) west of the southern Cook Islands. It rises to only 65 metres, as an outcrop, from the sea, with a steep and jagged coastline. The land has many caves and fissures and although is has no rivers there are plenty of wells to keep the topsoil fertile.

Hemisphere

Southern

Climate

Subtropical and humid, with temperature 25–30 degrees Celsius and average rainfall of nearly 200cm per annum.

Entry requirements

Passports

Required by all.

Visa

Not required by tourist visitors staying less than 30 days. Visitors are required to have return/onward tickets and all necessary entry documentation for the next destination, as well as sufficient funds for length of stay and suitable accommodation. Visitors may extend their stay by applying to the Immigration officials upon arrival, an extension permit of three months (cost of NZ$30) is usually granted.

Visas are required by all visitors for stays of over 30 days. Further information may be obtained from the Immigration Department, PO Box 69, Alofi, Niue Island (email: immigrationniue@mail.gov.nu).

Currency advice/regulations

The import of local currency is unlimited; export is limited to NZ$10,000. The import of foreign currency must be declared; export is limited to the amount declared.

Customs

Personal items are duty free, only one personal electronic item, camera or binoculars are allowed.

The export of native artifacts, coral and rare shells is prohibited.

Prohibited imports

Firearms and ammunition require a permit from the Chief of Police in Alofi.

Health (for visitors)

Mandatory precautions

Vaccination certificates for yellow fever are required if travelling from infected area.

Advisable precautions

Vaccinations for diphtheria, TB, hepatitis A and B, polio, tetanus and typhoid are all recommended. There is a rabies risk. It is advisable to take water precautions.

Public holidays (national)

Fixed dates

1 Jan (New Year's Day), 4 Jan (Takai Commission Holiday), 6 Feb (Waitangi Day), 25 Apr (Anzac Day), 16–19 Oct (Constitution Celebrations), 17 Oct (Peniamina's Day), 25–26 Dec (Christmas).

Holidays that fall on the weekend are taken in lieu on the following Monday/Tuesday.

Variable dates

Good Friday (Mar/Apr), Easter Monday (Mar/Apr), Queen's Official Birthday (first Mon in Jun).

Working hours

Banking

Mon–Thur: 0900–1500; Fri: 0830–1500.

Business

Mon–Fri: 0730–1530.

Shops

Mon–Fri: 0830–1600; Sat: 0830–1500.

Telecommunications

Mobile/cell phones

The Harris Cellular Network provides fixed and mobile coverage.

Social customs/useful tips

It is customary to shake hands on meeting and taking leave. Gratuities are not encouraged.

Getting there

Air

There are limited connections from Auckland, New Zealand; Sydney, Australia; Samoa; Fiji and Los Angeles, US.

International airport/s: Hanan (IUE), 7km north of Alofi.

Airport tax: Departure tax: NZ$25

Surface

There are no port facilities. Ships anchor off Alofi and barges transfer cargo.

Getting about

National transport

Road: There are approximately 130km of all-weather road and 96km bush track negotiable by heavy trucks and four-wheel drive vehicles. A 60km road circles the island and roads link main centres.

Car hire

Visitors with an foreign driver's licence must obtain a local licence from the Niue police department before driving a hired vehicle. It is advisable to reserve hire vehicles before arrival.

Driving is on the left.

BUSINESS DIRECTORY

The addresses listed below are a selection only. While World of Information makes every endeavour to check these addresses, we cannot guarantee that changes have not been made, especially to telephone numbers and area codes. We would welcome any corrections.

Telephone area codes

The international direct dialling code (IDD) for Niue is +683 followed by subscriber's number.

Useful telephone numbers

Police, fire and ambulance:999/4000

Hospital:998.

Chambers of Commerce

Niue Chamber of Commerce and Industry, PO Box 160, Alofi (tel: 43-99; fax: 40-17; e-mail: chamber@sin.net.nu).

Banking

Westpac Banking Corporation, PO Box 76, Alofi (tel: 4221; fax: 4043).

Central bank
The Reserve Bank of New Zealand, PO Box 2498, Wellington, New Zealand (tel: (+64-4) 472-2029; fax: (+64-4) 473-8554).

Travel information
Air Nauru, Government Building, Yaren District, Republic of Nauru (tel: (+674) 3141, 3418; fax: (+674) 3170).

Matavai Resort (hotel), PO Box 133, Alofi (tel: 4360, email: matavai@niue.nu).

Niue International Airport (Hanan), PO Box 83, Alofi (tel: 4020, 4133, 4096; fax: 4010).

National tourist organisation offices

Niue Tourism Office, PO Box 42, Alofi (tel: 4224; fax: 4225; internet site: http://www.niueisland.com).

Other useful addresses
Broadcasting Corporation of Niue, PO Box 26, Alofi (tel: 4026; fax: 4217).

Business Advisory Service, Alofi (tel: 4228).

Department of Immigration, PO Box, Alofi (tel: 4349, 4333; fax: 4336; email: immigrationniue@mail.gov.nu).

Office of Economic Affairs, PO Box 42, Alofi (tel: 4126).

Office of the Prime Minister. PO Box 40, Alofi (tel: 4200; fax: 4206, 4232).

Office of the Secretary to Government, PO Box 67, Alofi (tel: 4017; fax: 4232).

Other news agencies: ABC Pacific Beat: www.radioaustralia.net.au/pacbeat

Pacific Magazine: www.pacificmagazine.net

Internet sites
Niue government website: http://www.gov.nu

Niue website: http://www.niueisland.nu

South Pacific Tourism Organisation: http://www.tcsp.com/niue/index.html

Norfolk Island

COUNTRY PROFILE

Historical profile

1774 First European sighting of Norfolk Island by Captain James Cook. He named the island in honour of the Ninth Duchess of Norfolk.
1788 Norfolk Island was occupied by the British.
1790 A settlement was established to supply the New South Wales penal colony.
1814 The settlement was abandoned.
1825 The island was re-settled as a penal colony.
1856 The British authorities moved the 193 descendants of the Bounty mutineers from Pitcairn Island to Norfolk Island.
1858 16 Pitcairners returned to Pitcairn Island after a dispute with the British about land ownership. Other Pitcairners followed.
1897 Norfolk Island became a dependency of New South Wales.
1914 Norfolk Island became a Territory under the authority of the Commonwealth of Australia.
1979 The Norfolk Island Act conferred a measure of self-government.
1992 Norfolk Islanders became entitled to vote in elections for the Australian parliament.
2000 Norfolk Islanders signed a deal with genetic researchers to study the population for genes that predispose people to high blood pressure or migraines.
2001 A census recorded a total population of 2,601 including 564 tourists and visitors.
2002 The killing of an Australian tourist, Janelle Patton, was first murder to take place since the 1850s.
2004 Deputy Chief Minister Ivens Buffett was shot dead. His son was later acquitted of his murder.
2006 A census taken on 8 August recorded a total population of 2,523 including 660 tourists and visitors. The Australian government published its Commonwealth Grants Commission report on the financial capacity of the Norfolk Island. A New Zealander, Glenn McNeill was arrested for the murder of Patton.
2007 A branch of the Australian Labor Party (ALP) was established to work to reform the political system. McNeill was convicted of the murder of Patton. In legislative assembly elections André Nobbs won most votes and was elected chief minister.

Political structure

Constitution

The Norfolk Island Act of 1979 provides for an administrator (appointed by the Governor General of Australia and responsible to the Australian government), a Legislative Assembly and Executive Council. The Act provides that proposed laws passed by the legislative assembly must be presented to the administrator for assent. Both the legislative assembly and Executive Council are presided over by the president of the legislative assembly.
Since 1992, Norfolk Islanders are entitled to vote in elections for the Australian parliament.

Form of state

Self-governing Territory of Australia

The executive

The Executive Council is made up of five members of the legislative assembly; each member holds the position of minister, with one or more portfolios. The Executive Council passes laws and devises governmental policy, which is agreed or not by the administrator.

National legislature

The legislative assembly has nine members, elected for a three-year term.

Legal system

The judicial system consists of a Supreme Court and a Court of Petty Sessions.

Last elections

March 2007 (parliamentary)

Results: Parliamentary: André Nobbs won most votes.

Next elections

2010 (parliamentary)

Political parties

There are no political parties in the legislative assembly; all members sit as independents.

Ruling party

None, legislative assembly members sit as independents

Political situation

The Norfolk Islanders are an independent people who consider their state to predate that of the Commonwealth of Australia, the country to which they were tied by a British administration in 1897. So when the Australian government proposed changes to the citizenship of Norfolk Islanders in February 2006 the reaction was not positive. The proposal was for Norfolk Island to drop its self-government, which does not necessarily adopt Australian law, and to become a territory of Australia, within its commonwealth and adopt Australian citizenship. Within weeks of the

KEY FACTS

Official name: Norfolk Island

Head of State: Queen Elizabeth II of Australia; represented by Administrator (appointed by Governor General of Australia) Owen Edward John Walsh (acting administrator) (from Oct 2007)

Head of government: Chief Minister André Nobbs (from Mar 2007)

Ruling party: None, legislative assembly members sit as independents

Area: 35 square km

Population: 1,863 (2006 – census figure 8 Aug)

Capital: Kingston

Official language: English

Currency: Australian dollar (A$) = 100 cents

Exchange rate: A$1.28 per US$ (Jan 2007)

Labour force: 1,345 (2005)*

Visitor numbers: 40,000 (annually)

* estimated figure

proposal a deputation was arguing before a constitutional, high court that locals didn't want Norfolk Island 'to be just another part of Australia' and that they had been voting in general elections since the 1800s without the benefit of Australian citizenship but these proposals would endanger their rights.
Both the Australian government and the island's Executive Council have had to go back into discussions to produce another, perhaps more acceptable, plan B.

Population
1,863 (2006 – census figure 8 Aug)
Last census: 8 August 2006: 2,523, including 660 tourists and visitors.
Population density: 50.2 inhabitants per sq km.
Annual growth rate: 1.3 per cent (2003)
Ethnic make-up
Approximately 37 per cent of the permanent population were born on Norfolk Island (of which 47 per cent are of Pitcairn descent), 31 per cent were born on the Australian mainland and 23 per cent were born in New Zealand.
Religions
Anglicans (40 per cent), Roman Catholics (12 per cent), Uniting Church of Australia (16 per cent) and Seventh-Day Adventist (5 per cent).

Education
Infant, primary and secondary schooling is provided by the Norfolk Island Government. Education is free until the age of 15.
Compulsory years: six to 15

Main cities
Burnt Pine, Kingston.

Languages spoken
English is spoken in business circles. Norfolk, a dialect derived from the language evolved by the Bounty mutineers and their Tahitian wives (a mixture of mainly English and Tahitian) and brought by settlers from Pitcairn Island in the nineteenth century, is also in use.
Official language/s
English

Media
Other news agencies: Norfolk Online: www.norfolkonline.nlk.nf
Press
There are two local weekly newspapers The Norfolk Islander and the Norfolk Window. National newspapers from Australia and New Zealand are available.
Broadcasting
Radio: The Norfolk Island Government Broadcasting Services operates the radio station. Radio Norfolk broadcasts on AM and FM for 10 hours per day during the week and for six to seven hours during the weekend.
Television: The privately owned TVN station broadcasts local material. Satellite services relay TV programmes from Australian. News agency

Economy
Norfolk Island's economy is based largely on its tourist industry, catering mainly to visitors from Australia and New Zealand. It receives no direct grants or aid from Australia although Australia has restored a number of historic buildings and provides certain technical services for public works on the island.
In addition to importing most of its requirements, Norfolk Island has developed a re-export industry geared to its tourist industry. Sales of re-export goods to tourists have, however, been inhibited by the imposition of an A$400 (US$250) duty-free limit by the Australian government.
Sales of Norfolk Island postage stamps contribute to the island's revenue. Australian income tax and other federal taxes, such as property tax or stamp duty, do not apply in Norfolk Island.

External trade
As a self-governing territory of Australia, Norfolk Island maintains strong links with the mainland but not an open market; taxes are levied on imports to provide government revenue. Exports to Australia are duty free, subject to the country of origin restrictions.
Imports
Main imports are petroleum, food, consumer goods, alcohol, building materials, footwear and clothing.
Main sources: Australia, New Zealand, neighbouring Pacific islands, Asia and EU
Exports
Main commodity exports are seeds from the Norfolk Island pine, gerbera and kentia palm, avocados and small quantities of timber, ceramics and local crafts and postage stamps.
Main destinations: Australia, neighbouring Pacific islands, New Zealand and the European Union.

Agriculture
Only 12 per cent of land is cultivatable so production is constrained by poor terrain, porous soil, a low water table and fragmented holdings. Many farms are run on a part-time basis. Crops tend to be seasonal, and provide cereals, vegetables and fruit. There is a successful commercial hydroponic vegetable garden. Livestock is limited to cattle and poultry and the island is self-sufficient in beef, poultry and eggs. The lack of a harbour restricts fisheries development, and catches serve local consumption only.
The Norfolk Island pine and kentia palm seeds are an important export and some hardwood afforestation is being undertaken.

Industry and manufacturing
The island produces its own handicrafts, chocolates, beers, liqueurs (including an 'aromatised whiskey' called Convict's Curse) and arabica coffee. Grapes are being planted for a wine industry.

Tourism
Since the mid-1960s, tourism has been the mainstay of the island's economy. The Norfolk Island Government Tourist Bureau promotes Norfolk Island in Australia and New Zealand, the island's primary markets. Approximately 30,000 tourists visit Norfolk Island each year.
It is a sub-tropical island with world-class scuba diving and fishing. There are areas of sub-tropical rainforest, much of it protected in national parks, with a network of tracks which is ideal for walking, birdwatching, cycling or horse riding.

Hydrocarbons
There are unexploited offshore oil and gas fields.

Energy
Norfolk Island Administration is the electricity supply authority. Electricity is expensive and in limited supply.

Banking and insurance
There are branches of the Commonwealth Bank of Australia (which has an ATM) and Westpac Banking Corporation on the island.

Time
GMT plus eleven and a half hours.

Geography
Norfolk Island lies off the eastern coast of Australia about 1,400km east of Brisbane, to the south of New Caledonia and 640km north of New Zealand. Norfolk Island is hilly and fertile, with a coastline of cliffs. It is about 8km long and 4.8km wide. The territory also includes uninhabited Phillip Island 7km south of the main island.
Hemisphere
Southern

Climate
The island has a sub-tropical climate. Temperatures can range from 11–27 degrees Celsius, with an average rainfall of 1,346mm per year. November tends to be the driest month and the wetter months are May to August. Most rain falls at night. Average morning humidity is around 80 per cent.

Dress codes
Clothing should be comfortable and casual to suit the subtropical climate. A

sweater is advisable on winter nights. A hat and sunscreen are necessary in summer.

Entry requirements
Passports
Required for all.
Visa
Required by all, except Australian and New Zealand citizens.
Any visitor who is in possession of an Australian visa may stay for up to 30 days, with travel insurance and confirmed accommodation obtained prior to arrival. Most citizens of EU and North America can apply for an Australian Electronic Travel Authority (ETA), issued by a travel agent or airline, or online. See www.eta.immi.gov.au for details of those eligible, and follow links to the application site. ETA-eligible business visitors may stay for up to three months without additional documentation.
Those not eligible for an ETA must apply using form 456, through the nearest embassy or mission. Business visas will require a letter of invitation from a local company or organisation, a business letter from an employer stating purpose of trip and details of employee's function, proof of sufficient funds, and a full itinerary. Further details and application form can be obtained at www.immi.gov.au/allforms.
Currency advice/regulations
There are no restrictions on import and export of local and foreign currency.
Customs
Some medications may be restricted and visitors should declare all prescription drugs.
Prohibited imports
Illicit drugs, dangerous weapons, fruit, vegetables, flowers and seeds; pork and poultry from New Zealand are also prohibited. Firearms require a permit.

Health (for visitors)
Mandatory precautions
Vaccination certificates required for yellow fever if travelling from an infected area.
Advisable precautions
Vaccination for diphtheria, TB, hepatitis A and B, polio, tetanus, typhoid. Rabies is a risk.

Public holidays (national)
Fixed dates
1 Jan (New Year's Day), 26 Jan (Australia Day), 6 Mar (Foundation Day), 25 Apr (Anzac Day), 8 Jun (Bounty Day), 25–26 Dec (Christmas).
If Christmas Day or New Year's Day falls on a Saturday, the next Monday is given as a holiday.
Variable dates
Good Friday and Easter Monday (Mar/Apr), Queen's Official Birthday (second Mon in Jun), Show Day, Thanksgiving Day (last Wed in Nov).

Working hours
Banking
Mon–Thu: 0930–1600; Fri: 0930–1700.
Business
Mon, Tue and Thu, Fri: 0900–1700; Wed and Sat: 0900–1200.
Government
Mon–Fri: 0800–1630.
Shops
Mon–Tues, Thu–Fri: 0900–1700; Wed/Sat: 0900–1230. Some shops open on Sun.
Supermarket, Mon–Sat: 0800–1800; Sun: 0900–1800.

Telecommunications
Mobile/cell phones
In 2002, the Norfolk Island residents voted against allowing a mobile phone service on the Island.

Electricity supply
Diesel generated 240V 50 cycles.

Social customs/useful tips
Tipping is not expected. It is customary to shake hands on meeting and taking leave. Punctuality on social occasions is appreciated.

Getting there
Air
The only air connections are provided by OzJet and Air New Zealand which fly from the east coast of Australia and New Zealand.
International airport/s: Norfolk (NLK).
Airport tax: A$30 for international departures, payable at the airport when leaving or at the Visitor Information Centre prior to departure.
Surface
Water: Ships anchor offshore.

Getting about
National transport
Road: The entire road network amounts to 200km.
Buses: There is no public transport system on the island, but tour buses are available for tourists.
City transport
Taxis: There is a limited taxi service.
Car hire
Arrangements may be made locally for hiring cars, motorcycles and bicycles.

BUSINESS DIRECTORY

The addresses listed below are a selection only. While World of Information makes every endeavour to check these addresses, we cannot guarantee that changes have not been made, especially to telephone numbers and area codes. We would welcome any corrections.

Telephone area codes
The international direct dialling (IDD) code for Norfolk Island is +672, followed by area code 3 and subscriber's number.

Useful telephone numbers
Police: 922
Fire: 955
Ambulance: 911
Telephone exchange: 22-244

Banking
Commonwealth Bank of Australia, Burnt Pine (tel: 22-144).

Westpac Banking Corporation, Burnt Pine (tel: 22-120).

Travel information
Norfolk Island Airport, P.O.Box 149, Norfolk Island (tel: 22-445; fax: 23-201; email (manager): grobinson@airport.gov.nf).

The Travel Centre, PO Box 172, Norfolk Island (tel: 22-502; fax: 23-205; email: travel@travelcentre.nf).

National tourist organisation offices
Norfolk Island Government Tourist Bureau, PO Box 211, Norfolk Island (tel: 22-147; fax: 23-109; email: info@norfolkisland.com.au).

Other useful addresses
Postal services for Norfolk Island have an Australian postal code – NSW 2899, Australia – to be added to the end of an address.

Customs House, Taylors Road, Norfolk Island (tel: 22-899; fax: 23-260; email customs@admin.gov.nf; internet: www.customs.gov.nf).

Legislative Assembly, Old Military Barracks, Quality Row, Kingston, Norfolk Island (tel:22-003; fax: 22-624; email: clerk@assembly.gov.nf).

Other news agencies: Norfolk Online: www.norfolkonline.nlk.nf

Internet sites
Australian Government (see territories of Australia): www.ag.gov.au

Norfolk Island website: www.norfolk.gov.nf

Northern Marianas

KEY FACTS

Official name: Commonwealth of the Northern Mariana Islands

Head of State: President George W Bush

Head of government: Governor Benigno R Fitial (Covenant) (took office Jan 2006)

Ruling party: Republican Party (since 3 Nov 2007)

Area: 471 square km (14 islands) – Saipan (122 square km); Tinian (101 square km)

Population: 82,459 (2006)*

Capital: Garapan (Saipan)

Official language: English

Currency: US dollar (US$) = 100 cents

GDP per capita: US$12,500 (2003)

Labour force: 6,010 (2003); (38,448, 2005, including foreign workers)

Inflation: 1.20% (2003)

* estimated figure

COUNTRY PROFILE

Historical profile

Ancestors of the native Chamorros settled on the islands in about 2000 BC.
1521 Magellan claimed the islands for Spain.
1698 The native population was transferred to Guam.
1899 The Germans bought the islands from the Spaniards.
1914 The Japanese seized the islands from the Germans.
1947 Northern Marianas was the first Japanese territory in the Western Pacific to be invaded by the US; it became a part of the Trust Territory of the Pacific Islands (TTPI), administered by the US, under a mandate granted by the UN.
1975 In a referendum islanders voted to become an unincorporated territory of the United States under a covenant.
1977 A new local constitution was adopted.
1978 The Commonwealth of Northern Mariana Islands (CNMI) was created, as the TTPI was dissolved.
1980s Tourism and clothing manufacture became major industries, leading to foreign contract workers outnumbering local residents.
1984 Many US civil and political rights were made available to the islands' residents.
1986 Following the end of the UN mandate, the islands, under the Covenant to Establish a Commonwealth of the Northern Mariana Islands (CNMI) in Political Union with the United States, acquired US Commonwealth status and residents were granted US citizenship
1990 The UN Security Council formally terminated the Trusteeship. Under the covenant, the US has responsibility for foreign affairs and defence but CNMI was omitted from customs and labour laws.
2001 The Republican Party was re-elected and Juan Babauta (Rep) was elected governor.
2003 The Covenant Party won the parliamentary elections.
2004 Anatahan's active volcano had a small eruption. Northern Marianas and Guam were struck by super-typhoon Chaba.
2005 Numerous (over 500) small earthquakes were recorded on three uninhabited islands. Anatahan volcano continued erupting, with the largest eruption sending ash up to a height of 15,000 metres. In gubernatorial elections, Benigno Fitial won 28.1 per cent and unseated the incumbent, Juan Babouta. The Covenant Party won 7 out of 18 seats in the House of Representatives and 3 out of the 9 seats in the Senate.
2006 The CNMI revised its agreement with the US for increased environmental protection on the US missile testing range on Kwajalein Atoll. Two extra seats were added to the House of Representatives through re-districting electoral areas.
2007 The US proposed taking the immigration system of the CNMI under US federal administration, due to the lack of funding provided by the CNMI government to resource and administer the service. In parliamentary election held on 3 November the Covenant party lost much of its support as the Republicans won 12 seats (out of 20), the Covenant Party four, Independents three and the Democrats one, in the House of Representatives. In the Senate, of the three seats in contention, Independents won two and the Covenant Party one.
2008 The Northern Mariana Islands Delegate Act (immigration, security and labour act) was agreed by the US Congress. The legislation will be presented to President Bush for ratification.

Political structure

Constitution

The 1978 constitution was fully effective until 1986. It provides for an executive governor and a bicameral legislature. It also obligates the people of the Northern Mariana Islands to adopt a Commonwealth Constitution providing for a republican form of government which contains a bill of rights.
CNMI citizens have US citizenship and have a degree of autonomy and are exempt from some US federal laws concerning employment and immigration. CNMI defers to the US for foreign policy and defence and CNMI citizens do not vote in US presidential elections. There is one resident representative present in the US Congress and federal government.

Form of state

Democratic, self-governing commonwealth

The executive

An executive governor and lieutenant governor are elected every four years by universal suffrage.

National legislature

A bicameral legislature consisting of a 20-member House of Representatives and a nine-member Senate (with staggered terms); all elected in single-seat constituencies for two-year terms.

Legal system

The system is based on US jurisprudence but is exempt from US laws for customs, wages, immigration and taxation.

Last elections

3 November 2007 (parliamentary); 5 November 2005 (gubernatorial).

Results: Parliamentary: (House of Representatives), the Republicans won 12 seats (out of 20), the Covenant Party four, Independents three and the Democrats one. Senate (three seats in contention), Independents won two and the Covenant Party one.

Gubernatorial: Benigno R Fitial (Covenant Party) won with 28.1 per cent of the vote, Heinz S Hofschneider (independent) 27.3 per cent, Juan Babauta (Republican) 26.6 per cent, Froilan C Tenorio (Democrat) 18 per cent.

Next elections

November 2009 (parliament and governor)

Political parties

Ruling party

Republican Party (since 3 Nov 2007)

Main opposition party

Covenant Party

Political situation

Elections held in November 2007 resulted in a change of ruling party as the Covenant party was swept from power, by losing five of its nine seats. Instead of an improved standard of living as promised in the 2005 elections, the rise in electricity prices and poor state of the economy left most voters disinclined to back the party again.

There was a split throughout the Commonwealth as an old proposal was resurrected. In 1979 a proposal to allow casino gambling was soundly defeated, but in 2007 the motion was backed by some of the smaller islands, which see the new licensing scheme as a way to draw in much needed revenue from tourist gamblers and alleviate the economic crisis fuelled by the collapse of the garment manufacturing industry and the general downturn in tourism. Opponents of the plan claim that gambling would increase prostitution, crime in general and fuel gambling addiction. In Saipan the initiative was defeated but on Rota it was approved.

The US Senate took a long hard look at the state of the CNMI Covenant Implementation Act, in 2007, and the Act's exemption from immigration and employment laws. The US federal government proposed a federalisation bill to bring the immigration system under its control. It has seen that CNMI authorities are unable to provide a fully comprehensive screening process for all visitors and migrant workers to the islands. US concerns regarding this did not only cover security – the CNMI is seen as a backdoor route to the US – but also problems of human trafficking, particularly of girls for the sex-trade and inappropriate migrant workers' visas. A federal minimum wage bill was also included in the federalisation bill.

Governor Fitial appealed to the US Senate not to impose a tightening of controls, as they would impact on the very areas of the economy most depressed in 2007. Failing that, local senators called for a postponement in February 2008.

Population

82,459 (2006)*

Last census: April 2000: 69,221

Population density: 143 inhabitants per square km.

Annual growth rate: 3.3 per cent (2003)

Ethnic make-up

There are tensions between the resident population and people from other countries – Philippines, Republic of Korea, Thailand and China. Approximately 75 per cent of the native population is Chamorro, the rest are Carolinian.

Religions

Roman Catholic and indigenous beliefs.

Education

Education is based on the US system. There are several private schools available to cater for the international community.

Literacy rate: 97 per cent, adult rate.

Compulsory years: Six to 16

Health

The major medical needs of the population are met by the Commonwealth Health Centre (CHC). The CHC operates inpatient and outpatient services. There is 24-hour emergency care available provided by a team of emergency nurses, emergency physicians and support staff. In addition to the CHC, there are several private health clinics. All medical services are required to meet US standards, although the cost of medical care is much cheaper than in the US.

Main cities

Garapan/Susupe (Saipan) (capital, population 4,105 in 2005), Kagman (8,012), San Antonio (6,001).

Main islands

Six islands, including the three largest (Saipan, Tinian and Rota) are inhabited.

Languages spoken

Chamorro and Carolinian are the native tongues and are widely spoken. Japanese and Korean are also spoken.

Official language/s

English

Media

Other news agencies: ABC Pacific Beat: www.radioaustralia.net.au/pacbeat

Pacific Magazine: www.pacificmagazine.net

Press

The daily newspaper Saipan Tribune (www.saipantribune.com) has the largest circulation, while Marianas Variety (www.mvariety.com) has news covering from other Micronesian islands.

Broadcasting

Radio: There are several radio stations including the public KRNM (www.krnm.org), commercial KRSI (www.pacificnewscenter.com), KPXP (www.radiopacific.com/p99) and KWAW (www.magic100radio.com). Religious stations include KFBS (www.febc.org) and KYOI.

Television: The TV station WSZE 10 transmits via cable and satellite.

Economy

The economy of the islands is small and has few natural resources. Bilateral aid from the US remains an important source of income, particularly aid directed towards improving the inadequate infrastructure. In 2006 an unfunded government liability of US$500 million in the Defined Pension Plan was identified and prompted new legislation in January 2007 for the introduction of a new pension system designed to be self-sustaining through employee's contributions.

Tourism and textiles, are the mainstays of the economy and both suffered setbacks in 2005. By July 2005 four major garment factories had closed with over 2,000, most non-residents, left without work. The factory closures were caused by the ending of the Multi-Fibre Agreement (MFA) under which Northern Mariana Islands had been allowed to export garments, principally to the US, without import levies.

Tourism is the leading foreign exchange earner, with Japanese tourists making up some 70–75 per cent of visitors. However, Japan Airlines (JAL) cut back flights to CNMI in 2005 and risked the jobs of over 2,500 related workers.

A Seattle-based fishing company has been reported to have secured the necessary permissions to begin long-line fishing for swordfish, tuna and other species.

External trade

As a self-governing territory of the US, CNMI has an open market with the US. Tourism is the main provider of foreign exchange earnings, with Japanese visitors accounting for around 70 per cent of total numbers. The textile sector provides the largest export commodities with the bulk of production going to the US.

Imports

Principal imports are food, construction equipment and materials, petroleum products and consumer goods.

Main sources: US, Japan

Exports

The principal export is garments; minor exports include livestock, tuna fish, fruit and vegetables.

Main destinations: Mainly to US

Agriculture

Farming

The agricultural sector contributes approximately 14 per cent to annual GDP. Cultivable land is rich and volcanic.
Vegetables such as coconuts, breadfruit, tomatoes, melons and cucumbers are widely grown on smallholdings. Livestock is reared for export. The copra industry is also important.

Fishing

The fishing sector has revived following a blanket ban in some areas, introduced in 2000, due to over-fishing. Stocks include black-tip sharks, tuna, emperor ship and bonito. Tuna is transshipped en route to the US via the canneries at Pago Pago (Fagatogo) in American Samoa.
In 2004, the total marine fish catch was 165 tonnes.

Industry and manufacturing

The industrial sector contributed approximately 19 per cent to annual GDP while the garment industry flourished under the Multi-Fibre Agreement (MFA). However, when this ended in 2004 exports to the US were threatened by even cheaper exports from China and a number of factories closed, putting some 2,000 workers out of their jobs.
Other industrial activity consists of construction, small-scale fish processing and handicrafts manufacture.

Tourism

Tourism is an important sector of the economy, though not as dominant as it was during the 1990s. Japan continues to provide the vast majority of visitors, followed by Korea and, to a lesser extent, the US. The industry's fortunes changed in response to Japan's 1997 economic recession. There had been 736,117 arrivals in 1996, which fell to 490,165 in 1998, although numbers rose thereafter they fell back to below 500,000 as a consequence of the 11 September 2001 terrorist attacks in the US. In 2004 visitor numbers were back over the half million mark, but the cancellation of JAL's twice weekly flights from Tokyo from October 2005 is expected to have a devasting affect unless Japan's second airline, ANA, can replace the flights. Japanese make up 70–75 per cent of visitors.
Direct tourism revenue in 2004 was US$367 million, with indirect revenue estimated at US$733 million. Without JAL's flights direct revenue could fall to as low as US$216 million.
Tourist arrivals in 2007 were 387,000, 12 per cent down on 2006, largely due to the cancellation of JAL's flights.
In 2008 as the cost of oil rose worldwide, many Pacific island tourism industries suffered a fall in tourist arrivals as Japan-based airlines charged passengers up to an additional US$150 per trip to their destinations on top of the regular airfare.

Hydrocarbons

Banking and insurance

Central bank

US Federal Reserve (Washington DC)

Time

GMT plus 10 hours

Geography

The Northern Marianas Islands comprises 16 islands across 640km of the western Pacific Ocean, about 5,300km (3,300 miles) west of Hawaii. The islands are part of the chain of Mariana Islands. The ones in the south are formed of limestone terraces, and those in the north are volcanic, several of which are still active. The largest volcano, Agrihan, is also the tallest peak in the islands at 965 metres. Saipan is a fertile island with lagoons and rolling hills. Rota has dense rain forests and is largely undeveloped.

Climate

The climate is tropical marine.

Entry requirements

Passports

Passports required by all except US citizens with proof of citizenship; (all US nationals require a passport for re-entry to the US from January 2007).

Visa

Required by all. There are a few exceptions for visits up to 30 days. See www.cnmiago.gov.mp or www.mymarianas.com for a full list and details or contact the Division of Immigration for further information. All applications must be made at least four weeks before intended departure.

Prohibited entry

See www.mymarianas.com for a full list and details, contact the Division of Immigration for further information.

Currency advice/regulations

The US dollar is the official currency.
There are no restrictions on import and export of local and foreign currency, however all amounts over US$10,000 (or foreign equivalent) must be declared.

Prohibited imports

Fruits, vegetables, plants and soils, meat and meat products, live animals and animal products.
Firearms and ammunition require a permit, obtained in advance. For more information see: www.cnmiago.gov.mp.

Health (for visitors)

Mandatory precautions

Vaccination certificate required for yellow fever if travelling from an infected area.

Advisable precautions

Vaccination for diphtheria, TB, hepatitis A and B, polio, tetanus, typhoid. Rabies risk.

Water from the mains is usually chlorinated and although safe to drink, may cause mild abdominal upsets. Drinking water outside the main cities and towns may be contaminated. Sterilisation by boiling is thus advisable.
Full medical facilities are available, although they are not free of charge. Health insurance is advisable.

Hotels

There is a 10 per cent hotel tax. A tip of 10–15 per cent is usual.

Credit cards

Major credit cards are accepted on Saipan and at car rental agencies on Rota.

Working hours

Banking

Mon–Thu: 0900–1500, Fri: 1000–1800.

Business

Mon–Fri: 0800–1200, 1300–1700.

Government

Mon–Fri: 0730–1130, 1230–1630.

Shops

Mon–Sat: 0800–2000, Sun: 0800–1800.

Telecommunications

Mobile/cell phones

A 1900 GSM service is available.

Electricity supply

220/240V, 50Hz

Weights and measures

Imperial

Getting there

Air

International airport/s: Saipan International (SPN), 13km south-east of Garapan, with duty-free shops, bar, restaurant, currency exchange, shops and car hire. Taxis are available to the centre of town.

Airport tax: None

Surface

Main port/s: Saipan, Tinian, Rota.

Getting about
National transport
Air: There are several daily flights between Saipan and Tinian and between Rota and Saipan.
Road: Roads are good on the main islands, particularly around the main centres. Driving is on the right-hand side.
Buses: There is no public bus system on Saipan, although shuttle buses run between the major towns.
Water: There are sea links between the islands.
City transport
Taxis: A taxi service is available on Saipan. Taxis are metered and privately owned.
Buses, trams & metro: Tour bus from airport to city centre, journey time is about 15 minutes.

BUSINESS DIRECTORY

The addresses listed below are a selection only. While World of Information makes every endeavour to check these addresses, we cannot guarantee that changes have not been made, especially to telephone numbers and area codes. We would welcome any corrections.

Telephone area codes
The international direct dialling (IDD) code for Northern Marianas is +1 670, followed by the subscriber's number.

Useful telephone numbers
Police, fire, ambulance: 911

Chambers of Commerce
Saipan Chamber of Commerce, PO Box 500806, Saipan MP 96950 (tel: 233-7150; fax: 233-7151; e-mail: saipanchamber@saipan.com).

Banking
Central bank
Bank of Saipan, PO Box 500690, Saipan MP 96950 (tel: 235-6260; fax: 235-1802; email: bankofsaipan@saipan.com).

Federal Reserve System, 20th Street and Constitution Avenue, NW, Washington DC 20551 (tel: (202) 452-3000; fax: (202) 452-3819).

Travel information
Continental Micronesia, PO Box 138CK, Saipan (tel: 234-8223; fax: 234-8358).

Pacific Island Travel, Herengracht 495, 1017 BT Amsterdam, The Netherlands (tel: (+31-20) 626-1325; fax (+31-20) 623-0008; internet: www.pacificislandtravel.com).

Saipan International Airport, PO Box 1055, Saipan (tel: 664-3500/01; fax: 234-5962; e-mail: cpa.admin@saipan.com).

Travel Bureau, PO Box 503 Rota (tel: 532-3561; fax: 532-3562).

National tourist organisation offices
Marianas Visitors Authority, P O Box 500861, Saipan, (tel: 664-3200/3201; fax: 664-3237; internet: www.mymarianas.com).

Other useful addresses
All Northern Marianas postal addresses have the US zip code: MP 96950, USA

Commonwealth of the Northern Mariana Islands, Caller Box 10,007, Saipan, (tel: 664-2200; internet: www.gov.mp).

Division of Immigration, Office of the Attorney General, Afetna Square Bld, San Antonio Village, PO Box 10007, Saipan (tel: 236-0922, 236-0923; fax: 664-3190; internet: www.cnmiago.gov.mp).

Other news agencies: ABC Pacific Beat: www.radioaustralia.net.au/pacbeat

Pacific Magazine: www.pacificmagazine.net

Internet sites
Commonwealth of the Northern Marianas General Information: www.gov.mp

Marianas Variety, newspaper: www.mvariety.com

Saipan Tribune: www.saipantribune.com

US Office of Insular affairs: www.doi.gov/oia

KEY FACTS

Official name: Kongeriket Norge (Kingdom of Norway)

Head of State: King Harald V (since 17 Jan 1991)

Head of government: Prime Minister Jens Stoltenberg (DNA) (elected 12 Sep 2005)

Ruling party: Coalition: Det Norske Arbeiderparti (DNA) (Norwegian Labour Party), Sosialistisk Venstreparti (SV) (Socialist Left Party) and Senterpartiet (SP) (Centre Party)

Area: 323,985 square km

Population: 4.67 million (2007)*

Capital: Oslo

Official language: Norwegian

Currency: Norwegian krone (Nkr) = 100 ore

Exchange rate: Nkr5.07 per US$ (Jul 2008)

GDP per capita: US$83,953 (2007)

GDP real growth: 3.50% (2007)

Labour force: 2.36 million (2004)

Unemployment: 2.50% (2007)

Inflation: 0.80% (2007)

Oil production: 2.56 million bpd (2007)

Balance of trade: US$50.14 billion (2005)

Foreign debt: US$292.43 billion (2004)

Visitor numbers: 3.94 million (2006)*

* estimated figure

Norway

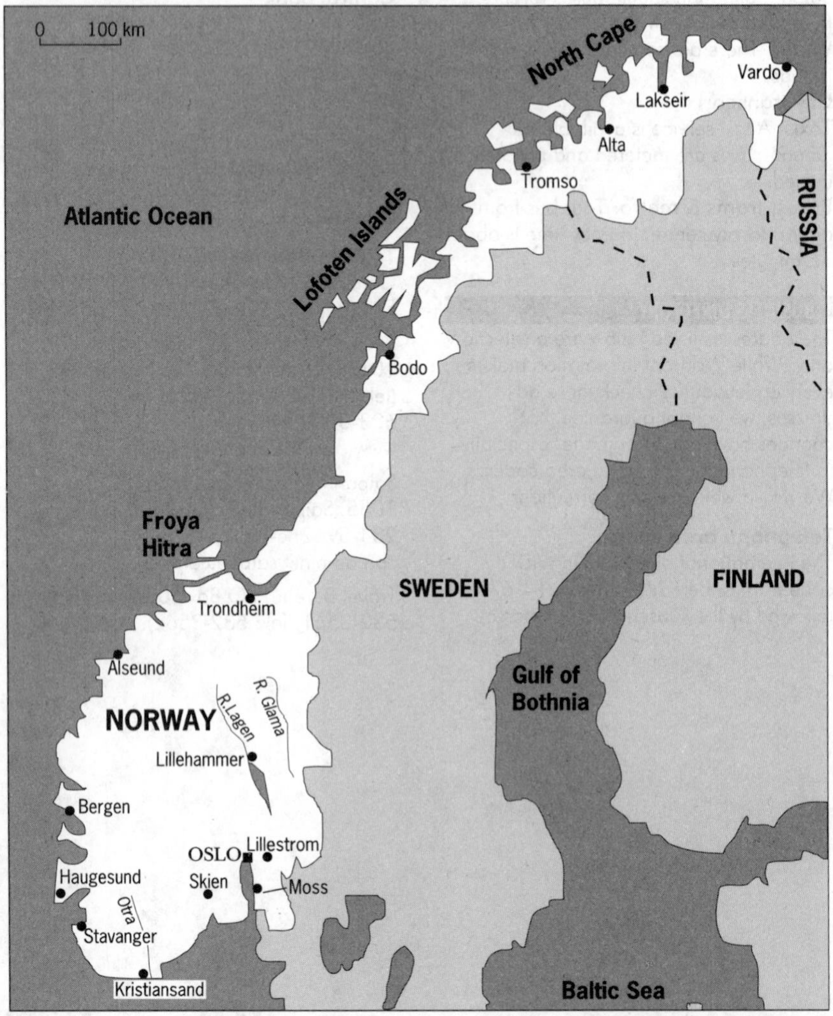

The boom in the Norwegian economy continued for the fourth continuous year into 2007, as both production and employment continued to increase markedly. While growth in domestic demand was expected to stay at a high level, a period of weaker demand from abroad was expected. Unemployment had fallen to a low level, and any further reductions will only be moderate.

Strong international growth, considerable growth in petroleum investments, fiscal stimuli, increased labour immigration and low interest rates have been important drivers behind the upturn in the Norwegian economy. The growth in petroleum investments is likely to continue, but the implementation of tighter monetary policy and cyclical developments internationally were expected to have a dampening effect on growth in Norway in future.

The archetypal stable European state, Norway is a constitutional monarchy complete with a parliamentary system of government. The King of Norway's power is almost exclusively ceremonial, with the majority of power being in the hands of the office of the prime minister. Jens Stoltenberg of the Det Norske

Arbeiderparti/Arbeiderpartiet (DNA /AP) (Norwegian Labour Party) has been prime minister since his party won the September 2005 elections. He is considered by most Norwegian and external political commentators to be on the right wing of the DNA, which is a broadly centre-left political party.

The telegenic 48-year old Stoltenberg has been leader of the DNA since 2002. On 12 September 2005 Stoltenberg led his party to electoral triumph and went on to form a broad coalition with the Sosialistisk Venstreparti (SV) Socialist Left Party and the Senterpartiet (SP) (Centre Party). The forming of the coalition government marked an historic moment in the country's political history, as DNA joined a coalition government for the first time. Other 'firsts' were that this was the first majority government in Norway for 20 years. The Labour Party (which in previous times ruled in its own right) had also never before taken part in a coalition, the Socialist Left Party had never been in government and the Centre Party was working for the first time with the political left. Altogether the coalition won 87 seats in the 169 member Storting (parliament). The Labour Party, which has dominated the political scene in Norway since the 1930s, continues to be the largest party in the Parliament with 36 per cent of the seats.

Economy

In terms of GDP per capita, Norway is one of the wealthiest countries in the world that has greatly benefited from the utilisation of its hydrocarbon resources. In 2007, Norway had a gross domestic product (GDP) of US$391.5 billion, and a 2006 per-capita GDP of US$83,923, which is one of the highest in the world. The economy is unique among Western European countries for its large and dominant offshore sector. Oil and gas extraction accounts for about 19 per cent of the country's GDP. Since the 1980s the economy has experienced a major structural change, becoming increasingly focussed on service industries, which account for about 37 per cent of GDP. Traditional primary sectors, like agriculture, forestry and fishing, have declined in terms of their contribution to GDP.

The Norwegian economy grew by 3.5 per cent in 2007. The buoyant energy sector has provided the country with strong fundamentals with which to ride out global shocks, and which present no long-term threat to growth. Income from oil exports is invested in the Petroleum Fund, some of which is used for the fiscal budget, but the main longer-term purpose is to prime the economy once oil reserves decline. In 2006, the value of Norway's Pension Fund (previously called the Petroleum Fund) stood at US$240 billion.

Norway had 8.2 billion barrels of proven oil reserves at the end of 2007, the largest in Western Europe. All of Norway's oil reserves are located offshore on the Norwegian Continental Shelf (NCS), which is divided into three sections: the North Sea, the Norwegian Sea and the Barents Sea. The bulk of Norway's oil production occurs in the North Sea, with smaller amounts in the Norwegian Sea. There is no current production and little exploration activity in the Barents Sea, but it is believed that the Barents Sea could contain sizable oil and gas reserves. Because Norway only consumed 221,000 barrels per day (bpd) in 2007, the country is able to export the vast majority of its oil production.

Norway had 2.96 trillion cubic metres (Tcm) of proven natural gas reserves as of end 2007. The North Sea holds the majority of these reserves, but there are also significant quantities in the Norwegian and Barents Seas. Norway is the eighth-largest natural gas producer in the world, producing 89.7 billion cubic metres (bcm) in 2007. However, because of the country's low domestic consumption, which totalled only 4.3bcm in 2007, Norway was the world's third-largest net exporter of natural gas in 2007, behind only Russia and Canada.

Outlook

Prime Minister Jens Stoltenberg's victory in the 2005 parliamentary elections has meant that his DNA party governs as part of a coalition government for the first time. The broad based nature of the coalition may cause some problems somewhere down the road, as competing interest groups battle for prominence within the governing elite. For the time being at least Stoltenberg should be able to govern successfully as a unifying, centrist figure. Norway's economy remains strong and the country should continue to record steady levels of growth.

Risk assessment

Politics	Good
Economy	Good
Regional stability	Good

COUNTRY PROFILE

Historical profile

1397 Under the Kalmar Union, the Kingdom of Norway ceased to exist as a separate nation and was ruled by Danish governors.
1720 Norway, a dominion of Denmark, was lost to Sweden following the Great Nordic War.
1814 An Act of Union with Sweden recognised Norway as an independent Kingdom with its own constitution and parliament.
1905 The Norwegian parliament dissolved the Act of Union with Sweden. A plebiscite voted for full independence and

KEY INDICATORS — Norway

	Unit	2003	2004	2005	2006	2007
Population	m	4.54	4.58	4.61	4.64	*4.67
Gross domestic product (GDP)	US$bn	221.60	250.21	301.74	337.43	391.50
GDP per capita	US$	48,672	54,521	65,509	72,768	*83,923
GDP real growth	%	0.4	2.9	2.7	2.5	3.5
Inflation	%	2.5	0.4	1.6	2.3	0.8
Unemployment	%	4.5	4.4	4.6	3.4	2.5
Oil output	'000 bpd	3,260.0	3,188.0	2,969.0	2,778.0	2,556.0
Natural gas output	bn cum	73.4	78.5	85.0	87.6	89.7
Exports (fob) (goods)	US$m	68,138.0	82,993.0	104,362.0	122,789.0	140,273.0
Imports (cif) (goods)	US$m	39,895.0	49,418.0	54,224.0	62,933.0	77,237.0
Balance of trade	US$m	28,243.0	33,576.0	50,138.0	59,856.0	63,036.0
Current account	US$m	28,320.0	34,360.0	46,714.0	58,278.0	63,657.0
Total reserves minus gold	US$m	37,220.0	44,307.5	46,985.9	56,841.6	60,839.6
Foreign exchange	US$m	35,890.2	43,078.2	46,377.4	56,181.4	60,294.1
Exchange rate	per US$	6.85	6.74	6.45	6.18	5.53

* estimated figure

a return to a monarchy. Denmark's Prince Frederick VIII became Norway's King Haakon VII.
1911 Norwegian Roald Amundsen was the first person to reach the South Pole, 35 days before Englishman Robert Scott.
1914–18 Norway adopted a policy of neutrality in the First World War.
1920 An international agreement on the Svalbard Arctic archipelago gave full sovereignty to Norway.
1940 Despite neutrality, Norway was invaded and occupied by the Germans in the Second World War. There was active resistance to the Nazi puppet government of Vidkun Quisling.
1945 Norway abandoned its policy of neutrality and lent troops to take part in the Allied war effort.
1949 Norway became a member of NATO.
1935–65 With the exception of the years of German occupation Det Norske Arbeiderparti (DNA) (Labour Party) held continuous office.
1952 Norway joined the Nordic Council, set up to promote co-operation between Nordic parliaments.
1959 Norway was a founding member of the European Free Trade Association (EFTA).
1957 King Olav V came to the throne.
1965 Centre-right coalition unseated the DNA government.
1960–80s From the late 1960s to early 1980s oil and gas were discovered in the Norwegian sector of the North Sea and within a decade their exploitation accounted for one-third of Norway's GDP.
1972 Norwegians rejected a proposal for membership of the European Community (EC).
1973–1981 Minority DNA government held power.
1981–86 The first majority conservative government since 1928 came to power. Following labour disputes, the government was defeated on its austerity programme.
1986 Minority DNA government was elected with Harlem Brundtland as Norway's first female prime minister.
1989 The election was won by a coalition of conservative, Christian democrat and centre parties.
1991 King Olav V died; he was succeeded by his son Harald V.
1992 Norway withdrew from the International Whaling Treaty, provoking international controversy.
1994 In a referendum, Norway rejects membership of the EU by 52.2 per cent (turnout 88.6 per cent).
1993 Norway brokered secret negotiations for a peace deal between Israel and the Palestinian Liberation Organisation that led to the Oslo Accords.
1997 The DNA failed to equal its 1993 performance in the general election. Kjell Magne Bondevik of the Kristelig Folkeparti (KrF) (Christian People's Party) set up a minority centrist coalition government.
2000 The government fell after Bondevik was defeated in a vote of no-confidence over controversial plans to build gas-fired power plants. A DNA-led government came to power under Jens Stoltenberg.
2001 In August, Norway and Australia became embroiled in a diplomatic row when a Norwegian-registered cargo ship attempted to set ashore, in Australia, Afghan refugees it had rescued at sea. In parliamentary elections in September, no party emerged with a majority. Stoltenberg and the DNA government resigned and Bondevik returned as prime minister, leading a centre-right coalition.
2003 Norway took the lead in trying to broker a peace deal in Sri Lanka.
2004 In June, the government intervened to end a strike by oil workers seeking better pension rights and job security.
2005 Parliamentary elections held on 12 September were won by a coalition of socialist parties led by DNA with the Sosialistisk Venstreparti (SV) and Senterpartiet (SP), winning between them 87 out of 169 parliament seats. Stoltenberg became prime minister for the second time. In November, Norway became embroiled in two diplomatic rows, one with Russia, the other with Spain, over fishing rights off the Norwegian island of Svalbard.
2006 In January, a law came into effect making it mandatory for all private companies to allocate 40 per cent of all board of director positions to women. In December, the Statoil and Norsk Hydro companies announced the merger of their offshore operations.
2007 The state-owned energy company, Statoil, posted annual net profits of US$6.5 billion in February.

Political structure

Constitution

The constitution dates from 1814. Norway is divided into 19 counties. There is universal direct suffrage for those aged 18 years and over.

Form of state

Parliamentary democratic monarchy

The executive

Executive power (nominally held by the monarch) is exercised by the Statsråd (Council of State), which is led by the prime minister, who is responsible to the Storting (parliament).
The Council of State is appointed by the monarch, with the approval of parliament. Following parliamentary elections, the leader of the majority party or the leader of the majority coalition is usually appointed prime minister by the monarch, with the approval of the parliament.

National legislature

Legislative power is vested in a unicameral Storting (parliament) comprising 165 members elected by a system of proportional representation (modified Sainte-Lague system) for four-year terms. The Storting is divided into a Lagtinget (upper house) and a Odelstinget (lower house) by internal election, although it sits as a single body except when discussing new legislation. There is no right of dissolution between elections.

Legal system

The legal system is a mixture of customary law, civil law, and common law traditions. The Hoyesterett (Supreme Court) renders advisory opinions to the legislature, when asked. Justices are appointed by the monarch. Norway accepts compulsory International Court of Justice (ICJ) jurisdiction, although with reservations.

Last elections

12 September 2005 (parliamentary)
Results: Parliamentary: DNA won 32.8 per cent of the vote (61 seats out of 169); FrP won 22.1 per cent (38 seats); Høyre (H) (Conservative Party) 14.1 per cent (23 seats); SV 8.8 per cent (15 seats); Kristelig Folkeparti (Krf) (Christian People's Party) 6.8 per cent (11 seats); SP 6.5 per cent (11 seats); and Venstre (V) (Liberal Party) 5.9 per cent (10 seats). Turnout was 76.6 per cent.

Next elections

September 2009 (parliamentary)

Political parties

Ruling party

Coalition: Det Norske Arbeiderparti (DNA) (Norwegian Labour Party), Sosialistisk Venstreparti (SV) (Socialist Left Party) and Senterpartiet (SP) (Centre Party)

Main opposition party

Fremskrittspartiet (FrP) (Progress Party)

Population

4.67 million (2007)*
Last census: November 2001: 4,520,947
Population density: 15 inhabitants per square km. Urban population: 75 per cent (1995—2001).
Annual growth rate: 0.6 per cent 1994–2004 (WHO 2006)

Ethnic make-up

Predominantly Norwegian. In addition, there are about 60,000 Sami (Lapps), mainly in the north of the country, although there are substantial Sami communities in larger cities.

Religions

More than 90 per cent of all Norwegians belong to the Church of Norway, an Evangelical Lutheran denomination. There are also small Roman Catholic, Jewish and Muslim communities.

Education
All public education in Norway is free. Primary education lasts for seven years; lower secondary education and upper secondary education, which is not compulsory, last for three years, from 13 to 16 and 16 to 19 respectively. On completion of a three-year course at an upper secondary school, students can apply to university. Alternatively, students may, at aged 16, undertake either technical training at vocational schools or practical training at apprenticeship schools; for three years.
Primary and lower secondary education is founded on the principle of every individual having a statutory right to primary, lower secondary and upper secondary education in a unified school system that provides equal education for all on the basis of a single national curriculum.
The right to upper secondary education has been in force since 2000, while the right to primary and lower secondary education was implemented from August 2002.
Higher education in Norway is mainly offered at state institutions, notably four universities, six university colleges, 26 state colleges and two art colleges. A degree candidate may combine studies from universities and colleges, as the courses offered are at the same academic level. The 26 colleges primarily offer shorter courses of a more vocational nature than those offered by the universities.
Compulsory years: Six to 16
Enrolment rate: 100 per cent gross primary enrolment of the relevant age group (including repeaters); 119 gross secondary enrolment (World Bank).
Pupils per teacher: Seven in primary schools

Health
Per capita total expenditure on health (2003) was US$3,809; of which per capita government spending was US$3,189, at the international dollar rate, (WHO 2006).
A national health insurance scheme covers medical treatment in hospitals and the reimbursement of costs for medical attention and medicines for certain chronic diseases. Sickness benefit is paid for short-term illness, while chronic or long-term illness is covered by a disability allowance. A small sum is charged for medicine and primary care. The majority of hospitals are state-run.
HIV/Aids
HIV prevalence: 0.1 per cent aged 15–49 in 2003 (World Bank)
Life expectancy: 80 years, 2004 (WHO 2006)
Fertility rate/Maternal mortality rate: 1.8 births per woman, 2004 (WHO 2006); maternal mortality 6 per 100,000 live births (World Bank).
Birth rate/Death rate: 13 births and 10 deaths per 1,000 population (World Bank).
Child (under 5 years) mortality rate (per 1,000): 3.4 per 1,000 live births (World Bank)
Head of population per physician: 3.13 physicians per 1,000 people, 2003 (WHO 2006)

Welfare
The extensive welfare system has greatly reduced the gap between rich and poor. Social security legislation stipulates that everyone has the right to employment, housing, education, welfare and healthcare. The main general social insurance schemes are the National Insurance Scheme (NIS) and the Family Allowance Scheme. The NIS is a compulsory insurance and pension system and covers pensions, unemployment pay and healthcare for all Norwegians.
A basic retirement pension, adjusted annually, is guaranteed for all Norwegians of 67 years and older regardless of assets or previous income.
Non-pensioners whose income falls below a certain minimum qualify for supplementary benefits. These may include loans or other financial assistance from the local municipality. All families with children under 16 receive a family allowance according to the number of children.
The government subsidises low-cost housing through loans with low rates of interest and easy repayment terms. Families living in housing financed by a state bank can receive an allowance for housing costs should they have difficulties meeting their living expenses.

Main cities
Oslo (capital, estimated population 526,090 in 2005), Bergen (239,329), Stavanger (112,983), Trondheim (155,248), Bærum (104,220), Fredrikstad (70,053), Kristiansand (76,167), Tromsø (62,200).

Languages spoken
Norwegian has two main dialects: Bokmål and Nynorsk. Finnish and Sámi are also spoken. English is widely understood and spoken, especially in urban areas.
Official language/s
Norwegian

Media
Press
There are over 210 newspapers, which reach almost 90 per cent of the adult population, and 1,100 magazines. Activity is concentrated in south-eastern Norway, especially around Oslo where the majority of papers are published. Local papers tend to dominate each particular region. Newspapers receive extensive support from the state.
Dailies: Major national and popular dailies include Verdens Gang (www.vg.no), Oppland Arbeiderblad, Nationen (mainly on agricultural and environmental issues), Aftenposten AM, Dagbladet, Adresseavisen, Bergens Tidende, Bergensavisen and Aftenposten PM. Stavanger Aftenblad provides daily news from one of Norway's regional newspapers. Norway Post is a online English edition (www.norwaypost.no).
Weeklies: These include Verdens Gang Sunday, Aftenposten Sunday, Dagbladet Sunday, Innherreds Folkeblad-Verdalingen, Klar Tale and Ranaposten. NorNewsNet (www.nornews.net) is a bi-weekly newsletter in English for Norwegians worldwide.
Business: A large number of business publications cover various aspects of Norwegian trade and industry, but most tend to have comparatively small and specialised readerships. The main publication is Dagens Naeringsliv. Others include Upstream, Finansavisen and two fortnightly publications Økonomisk Rapport and Kapital.
Periodicals: A large number of general and special interest magazines exist. Those aimed at women and the teens/twenties market have the largest circulations.
Broadcasting
The Norwegian Broadcasting Corporation's (NRK) monopoly was abolished in the mid-1980s. There are two national radio networks. Fifty-four per cent of national television programme time is devoted to Norwegian productions.
Radio: There are 383 radio stations, 158 commercial. Radio is divided into three groups: non-commercial national radio, commercial national radio and local radio stations. There are three main broadcasters: NRK, P4 and Radio 1. A growing number of local FM stations operate.
Television: There are seven TV stations, six commercial. Channel Scansat TV-3 broadcasts Scandinavian language programmes via cable. A commercially funded second channel, TV-2, broadcasts seven hours each evening.
More than a dozen different European channels are broadcast via satellite-cable, including several pan-Scandinavian channels.
Advertising
All usual media are available. The largest expenditure is on advertising cars, office equipment and travel. There is a ban on advertising for tobacco and all types of alcohol (except the very weakest kind of beer).

Economy

In terms of GDP per capita, Norway is one of the wealthiest countries in the world. The economy is unique among Western European countries for its large and dominant offshore sector. Oil and gas extraction accounts for about 25 per cent of GDP . Since the 1980s the economy has experienced a major structural change, becoming increasingly focussed on service industries, which account for about 37 per cent of GDP. Traditional primary sectors, like agriculture, forestry and fishing, have declined in terms of their contribution to GDP.

The buoyant energy sector has provided the country with strong fundamentals with which to ride out global shocks, most recently the global economic slowdown in 2001 and 2002, and which presented no long-term threat to growth. Income from oil exports is invested in the Government Pension Fund-Global (formerly the Petroleum Fund), some of which is used for the fiscal budget, but the main longer-term purpose is to prime the economy once oil reserves decline. In 2006, the value of the Fund stood at US$290 billion.

A key challenge for the government is the tight nature of its labour market, especially in the construction and health sectors. Norwegian firms have had to look abroad to fill vacancies as the unemployment rate is relatively low at around 4 per cent. Shortages in the labour market have caused high wage growth, leading to a loss of competitiveness in Norwegian exports.

External trade

Norway is a member of the European Economic Area (EEA) which maintains an internal market with, while not joining, the EU. The EU consults EEA members before making its decisions on community legislation. The EEA agreement allows freedom of movement of goods (excluding, to a significant degree, agriculture and fisheries), persons, services and capital.

Norway is the world's biggest producer of farmed salmon, 65 per cent of which is sold in the EU. Forests account for around 25 per cent of the productive land, almost 75 per cent is unproductive due to harsh conditions. Around 4 per cent of land is under cultivation and over 50 per cent of imports are food.

Norway is the third largest exporter of oil and gas, worldwide, and with shipping, provides the county's principal foreign exchange earnings.

Imports

Main imports include machinery and equipment, chemicals, metals and foodstuffs.

Main sources: Sweden (15.0 per cent total, 2006), Germany (13.5 per cent), Denmark (6.9 per cent).

Exports

Principal exports are crude oil and petroleum products, natural gas, machinery and equipment, metals, chemicals, ships and fish.

Main destinations: UK (26.0 per cent total, 2006), Germany (11.8 per cent), The Netherlands (10.1 per cent).

Agriculture

Farming

The agricultural sector typically accounts for 2 per cent of GDP and employs around 6 per cent of the workforce.

Grain and fodder are main lowland crops; mountain farms mainly raise livestock and grow fodder. Grain production is increasing, especially barley and oats, although wheat and rye are increasing in importance. The main grain-growing districts are in southern and central Norway. Coarse fodder, mostly hay and silage, can be cultivated at high altitudes and in the far north. Other crops include potatoes, other roots, berries and fruits. Crop yields per hectare have risen consistently over the last three decades. Some dairy produce is exported and there is self-sufficiency in meat, milk, cheese, butter, fish and potatoes.

Norway's agricultural policy has two main aims. The first is to promote a high degree of self-sufficiency in animal products and secondly to ensure an adequate livelihood for the country's 120,000 farmers and smallholders. In many regions, agriculture and related activities are the main source of income. Farm prices are set annually by agreement between the government and agricultural organisations. Almost all farmland is privately owned and farms tend to be small. Produce is bought and distributed by large co-operative purchasing and sales organisations.

The total cultivated area is just over 868,500 hectares (ha), only 3 per cent of the mainland area. Agricultural production is hampered by difficult topographical conditions and an unfavourable climate. However, Norwegian agriculture is generally efficient, with a high degree of mechanisation and emphasis on training and research.

Crop production in 2005 included: 1,316,700 tonnes (t) cereals in total, 375,000t wheat, 348,600t oats, 333,300t potatoes, 567,000t barley, 4,176t oilcrops, 11,232t apples, 23,203t fruit in total, 129,554t vegetables in total.

Livestock production included: 292,560t meat in total, 83,642t beef, 116,500t pig meat, 24,413t lamb, 3,000t game meat, 56,995t poultry, 51,344t eggs, 1,721,369t milk, 1,200t honey, 8,000t cattle hides, 7,436t sheepskins, 5,010t greasy wool.

Fishing

Fishing is a significant industry in the northern and western regions. Fish, including farmed fish, is Norway's second largest export group, accounting for 20 per cent of all exports. Mackerel, cod and capelin are the main species caught, but catches have been falling because of overfishing. The typical annual export value of fish is between Nkr 25–30 billion (US$3.3– 4 billion) and as a whole the fishing industry provides work for 23,000 people.

Whale hunting in 2004 produced 809 tonnes of meat, which was mainly sold in Norway as steaks. In 2003 Norway advised pregnant women and mothers who were breast-feeding infants to avoid whale meat due to the contamination, in wild caught whales, of traces of toxic mercury. Stocks of whale blubber, amounting to 363 tonnes, were turned into animal fodder, in 2004 when no other use could be found for them. Around 270 tonnes remain and Norway would like to sell it to Japan where the fat is considered a delicacy.

Fish farms produce mainly salmon and trout, although some are experimenting with other fish, such as halibut. Norway has the world's largest farmed salmon industry, producing about half the total supplies of Atlantic salmon. Demand for farmed salmon has increased by 20–30 per cent annually, but production normally exceeds demand. The emerging new markets in southern Europe are seen as a useful outlet for the surplus, even though salmon exports are in competition with EU production and the EU sets a minimum price requirement for sales from Norway. Salmon comprises 31 per cent of Norway's fish exports.

In February 2005 Norway challenged the EU imposed trade restrictions and import ceiling before the WTO. Norway's salmon sales account for 60 per cent of the EU market with exports valued at US1.29 billion. The UK and Ireland claimed salmon was being sold below production cost and that this was unfair competition. In April the EU imposed a 16 per cent duty on salmon while it investigated whether Norwegian exporters were 'dumping' salmon stocks on EU markets. This duty was replaced in June 2005 with a less punitive levy and a decision on whether or not the EU continues to penalise this sector is due by the end of January 2006.

Norway's relationship with Russia is complicated by a number of fishing-related disputes. In November 2005, Norway detained several Russian trawlers operating inside Norway's Svalbard protected zone. In December 2005, Russia announced a

ban on the import of Norwegian salmon, effective from 1 January 2006, on health grounds.
Also in November 2005, Norwegian authorities arrested Spanish trawlers operating off Svalbard and confiscated illegal halibut catches. In response, the Spanish government lodged an official protest with the EU.
In 2004, the total marine fish catch was 2,455,439 tonnes and the total crustacean catch was 65,343 tonnes.

Forestry

Forest cover is estimated at 8.8 million hectares (ha). In 1990–2000, forest cover increased by an annual average of 31,000ha. Some 22 per cent of the total land area is productive woodland. Most forests are situated in southern and central Norway. Spruce, used for making pulp and paper, makes up about 50 per cent of the forest. Pines account for about 30 per cent and broad-leafed trees for around 15 per cent. Mechanisation and automation have allowed logging in previously inaccessible forest land.
About 85 per cent of forest land is privately owned by farmers. The forestry sector has a well-developed co-operative sales apparatus. Forest-owner organisations have become more active in processing.
The forestry and the forest-products industry, contributes heavily to local economies. Norway exports nearly 90 per cent of the paper and paperboard production and nearly a quarter of the pulp production. Imports of roundwood and sawnwood, mainly from Sweden, have increased considerably. Per capita consumption of forest products is among the highest in Europe.
Export of forest materials in 2004 amounted to US$1.8 billion, while imports amounted to US$1.2 billion.
Timber production in 2004 included 8,780,000 cubic metre (cum) roundwood, 7,551,000cum industrial roundwood, 2,230,000cum sawnwood, 4,160,000cum sawlogs and veneer logs, 3,360,000t pulpwood, 493,000cum wood-based panels, 1,229,000cum woodfuel; 2,294,000 tonnes (t) paper and paperboard, (including 861,000t newsprint), 954,000t printing and writing paper, 2,389,000t paper pulp, 478,000t recovered paper.

Industry and manufacturing

The industrial sector typically accounts for around 32 per cent of GDP and employs 19 per cent of the workforce. Manufacturing accounts for barely 13 per cent of both GDP and employment (compared with around 22 per cent in 1970) and has developed more slowly than in most other industrial countries. The main industries include chemicals, fish processing, metals, timber and pulp and paper production.
The goals of industrial policy have traditionally been to maximise employment and the quality of production, maintain the rural population, promote a just and equitable distribution of wealth and income, and keep control over natural resources. Secondary goals have been to control inflation, protect the environment and achieve a balance between imports and exports.
The state channels financial resources to industry on concessionary terms through its Industry Fund and via state banks. Enterprises in depressed or uncompetitive markets are also given soft loans through the state-run District Development Fund.
The government aims for around 2 per cent of GDP to be invested in research and development (R&D). Priorities for R&D spending are biotechnology, communications, electronics, metallurgical technology and aquaculture.
Industrial production increased by an estimated 5.2 per cent in 2004.

Tourism

Over 3.5 million tourists visited Norway in 2004, a 7 per cent increase on the 2003 numbers. Discount airlines and direct flights were credited with providing the strong growth. Booking for cruise liners visiting Norway in 2005 passed 300,000 by the beginning of the year; the growth in cruising has risen fourfold in 20 years.

Environment

With the highest environmental standards in the world, sulphur emissions have plummeted by over 80 per cent since 1980. Pollution is kept low by the country's extensive hydroelectric production, although per capita nitrogen oxide emissions are among the highest in the world. In December 2001, environmentalists accused Norway December 2001of undermining the spirit of the Kyoto Protocol for announcing plans to triple coal production in Svalbard.

Mining

Norway has a highly skilled workforce, experienced in mining, quarrying and processing.
Activity is confined to small-scale mining of iron ore, copper, titanium, coal (on Spitsbergen), zinc, lead and pyrites. Most of these ores and concentrates are exported.
Mining continues to contract, causing many problems in areas where there is no alternative employment. However, the country's mining potential has yet to be fully explored and it is believed that Norway has the capacity to develop super-quarries.
On the south coast, near Lillesand, feldspars and quartz are found. Graphite, with differing carbon content and quality, is produced on the island of Senja and research is being carried out to upgrade the quality. Large dimension stones like granite, marbles and quartzites, are available in large quantities. Larvikite is one of the most predominant stones, there are also exclusive marbles, including Norwegian Rose, to be found in the north. From the quarries in northern and central Norway high quality quartzite and phullite-slate are processed. Rock aggregate is found along the coast, in both large sizes and quantities, making transportation very easy.

Hydrocarbons

Norway is the world's third largest net oil exporter after Saudi Arabia and Russia. Oil production doubled in the 1990s as improved recovery techniques were introduced and new wells came on stream. Reserves of 8.5 billion barrels (2005) ensure that production can carry on for many years to come. Oil production in 2004 was estimated at 3.31 million barrels per day (bpd). All of Norway's reserves are located offshore.
Between 2000–02, the oil sector underwent restructuring. The government reduced its 78.2 per cent stake in the state-owned oil company, Statoil, to 60 per cent. While the government resists foreign ownership of the oil sector, its restructuring plan is designed to maintain a competitive interest in the industry.
Natural gas reserves were 2.46 trillion cubic metres (cum) in 2003 with production of 73.4 billion cum. Norway is the seventh-largest gas producer in the world and is expected by 2005 to move into the top five. By 2005, Norway is expected to supply 30 per cent of the gas consumed in France and 40 per cent of that used in Germany.
Norway's coal comes from Spitsbergen, on the Svalbard Islands, off the country's northern coast, which also has the country's only coal-fired power plant. In 2002, 1.73 million tonnes of coal was produced 1.32 million tonnes and imported to meet domestic demand.

Energy

Norwegian electricity output exceeds demand, with some of the surplus being exported to Sweden and Denmark.
Hydro-electric plants supply 99 per cent of output. Plans for new gas-fired power plants in Kollsnes and Karst have failed in the face of strong opposition by environmentalists. Statoil, the forestry group Norske Skog and Elkem industrial group have extended the time scale on plans to build a 800MW gas-fired power station in

Skogn, to be fully operational by late 2006.

Financial markets

Stock exchange

In 1993, the Norwegian Stock Exchange, known as the Oslo Børs, joined Norex, an alliance that includes Sweden's Stockholmsbörsen, the Copenhagen Stock Exchange and the Icelandic Stock Exchange. The four members use the same trading system and follow similar rules and regulations.

Banking and insurance

Central bank

Norges Bank (Bank of Norway)

Main financial centre

Oslo

Time

GMT plus one hour (daylight saving, late March to late October, GMT plus two hours)

Geography

Norway lies on the west side of the Scandinavian peninsula, in north-west Europe. Its extended coastline faces the North Sea and the North Atlantic Ocean. It is the fifth-largest country in Europe and it has the third-lowest population density in Europe after Greenland and Iceland. The coastline measures 28,000km if fjords and inlets are included, 2,650km if they are not.

The capital, Oslo, in the south, lies on the same latitude as Greenland and Alaska, while Hammerfest on the northern tip of the Norwegian mainland, is the most northerly town in the world. The Svalbard Arctic archipelago is part of Norway, and sovereignty is also exercised over Jan Mayen island and the uninhabited island dependencies of Bouvet and Peter I. In Antartica, Queen Maud Land is a Norwegian dependency.

Norway shares a 1,619km land border with Sweden, and within the Arctic Circle, a 716km frontier with Finland and a 196km border with Russia.

The terrain mostly consists of high plateaux, deep fjords and mountains. More than 70 per cent of the mainland consists of mountains, glaciers, lakes, forest and moorland. The highest peak is Galdhoepiggen in the south which reaches 2,469 metres above sea level. Only 2.8 per cent of the land area is cultivable soil, while another 20 per cent is productive forest.

Hemisphere

Northern

Climate

Influenced by the Atlantic Gulf Stream and westerly winds, the climate is much warmer than that of other countries on the same latitude. The temperature varies little from north to south, but there is a big contrast between the inland and coastal regions. In winter, while the interior freezes hard, most fjords and harbours remain ice-free. The average annual temperature is 8 degrees Celsius (C) along the west coast, and minus 2 degrees C in the northernmost county, Finnmark. January and February are the coldest months, while July and August are the warmest. The average annual rainfall is 1,960mm in Bergen and 740mm in Oslo. Northern Norway is popularly known as the 'Land of the Midnight Sun'. In Finnmark the midnight sun is visible from mid-May to late-July, and the period of darkness lasts from mid-November to late-January.

Dress codes

Clothing to suit the climate is vital because of the extremes in weather; heavy coats, warm boots, gloves and ear protection are required in winter and light clothing in summer. Normal European business attire, otherwise dress is generally casual.

Entry requirements

Passports

Passports are required by all and must be valid for three months beyond the date of stay. Nationals of countries which are signatories of the Schengen Agreement may visit on national IDs.

Visa

Visas are not required by nationals of most European countries, US, Canada, Australasia, Japan or transit passengers. For further exceptions, contact the nearest embassy. AA Schengen visa application (offered in several languages) can be downloaded from http://europa.eu/abc/travel/ see 'documents you will need'.

Business visitors require a letter of invitation from a Norwegian entity, giving the nature and duration of the stay, with proof of accommodation.

Prohibited entry

Currency advice/regulations

The import and export of local currency is limited to Nkr25,000. The export of foreign currency is unlimited if proof of import or conversion from another currency can be produced.

Travellers cheque are widely accepted.

Customs

Personal effects duty-free, plus duty-free allowance. Imported products from certain countries such as Japan, South Korea and some East European countries require a licence. Imported cars are heavily taxed.

Prohibited imports

Illegal drugs, firearms.

Health (for visitors)

Nationals of the European Economic Area (EEA) countries and Switzerland can access reduced cost and sometimes free medical treatment using a European Health Insurance Card (EHIC) while visiting the EEA. Exceptions include nationals of the 10 countries which joined the EU in 2004 whose EHIC is not valid in Switzerland. Applications for the EHIC should be made before travelling.

Mandatory precautions

None

Advisable precautions

Hotels

There is a wide range of hotels available in most towns. There is no official rating system in operation. Private accommodation can be obtained through local tourist offices or accommodation offices in central railway stations. There is a service charge of 15 per cent included in the bill, but tipping is also expected.

Credit cards

Major credit and charge cards are accepted. ATMs are widely accepted.

Public holidays (national)

Fixed dates

31 Dec–1 Jan (New Year, from midday 31 Dec), 1 May (Labour Day), 17 May (Constitution Day), 24 Dec (Christmas Eve, afternoon only), 25–26 Dec (Christmas).

Variable dates

Maundy Thursday, Good Friday, Easter Monday, Ascension Day, Whit Monday.

Working hours

Banking

Mon–Thu: 0900–1600; Fri: 0900–1700; Sat: 0900–1200.

Business

Mon–Fri: 0900–1600.

Government

Mon–Fri: 0830–1600.

Shops

Mon–Wed: 0900–1700; Thu: 0900–1900; Sat: 0830–1300.

Many shops are increasingly introducing longer opening hours, and some are open on Sundays.

Telecommunications

Mobile/cell phones

GSM 3G, 900 and 1800 services are available in inhabited areas.

Electricity supply

220V AC

Social customs/useful tips

Punctuality is expected. Shake hands on meeting. Business lunches are rare. The main meal of the day is generally taken at home at 1700 hours, though people will expect to eat later if invited out.

Security

Serious crime is not a big problem. It is usually safe to walk at night in major cities, such as Oslo and Bergen, although some neighbourhoods are less safe than others. Car theft, on the other hand, is fairly common, especially in the major cities.

Getting there

Air

National airline: SAS Braathens
International airport/s: Oslo International Airport (OSL) (Gardermoen) 47km north of city. Facilities include duty-free shops, banks/bureaux de change, restaurants, car hire and dry cleaning. Business lounge including Internet facilities.
Other airport/s: Bergen (BGO), 19km from city; Stavanger (SVG), 14.5km south-west of city.
Airport tax: None

Surface

Road: The are several routes across the border from Sweden in the east and Finland in the north. These roads may be closed in winter.
Rail: There are daily train connections between Stockholm-Oslo-Trondheim. There are also train connections between Oslo-Gothenburg-Copenhagen-Helsingborg.
Water: There are frequent ferry services to Denmark, UK and Germany.
Main port/s: Oslo, Kristiansand, Bergen and Larvik.

Getting about

National transport

Air: Efficient services, operated by various carriers, link all major and many smaller towns. Charter sea and land planes are widely available.
Road: The road network is extensive; main highways are kept open although certain roads in the mountainous areas could be closed in winter and spring.
Buses: There is an extensive bus network. The main bus company is the Nor-Way Bussekspress with routes connecting every main city. Tickets can be purchased on the buses.
Rail: Norway has a good, though somewhat limited, national rail system. All railway lines are operated by the Norwegian State Railways (Norges Statsbaner or NSB). From Oslo, the main lines go to Stavanger, Bergen, Åndalsnes, Bodø and Sweden.
Water: There are regular and efficient motor ship services visiting all the major ports. There are also numerous local ferry, hydrofoil and catamaran services.

City transport

Taxis: Taxis are available in most cities. They can be obtained at ranks or by telephone (Oslo 388-090, Bergen 900-990, Stavanger 526-040). Telephone numbers of taxi stands are listed in the directory under Drosjer. Meters are compulsory. It is not expected that the tip will be more than small change.
In addition to regular taxis, there are airport taxis, cheaper taxis which must be ordered in advance by groups of up to three people, and wheelchair taxis.
Buses, trams & metro: There are eight tram lines and five metro lines in Oslo, plus numerous bus services. Public transport runs from 0530–2400 everyday. Tickets are best pre-purchased and self-cancelled, there is one hour's free transfer between any of the modes. (www.trafikanten.no can offer more information). Buses serving the airport take about 45 minutes and there is also a new regional bus station for services further afield.
Trains: A high-speed airport express train leaves every 10 minutes to and from Oslo's central station (20 minutes).
Ferry: Ferries from Oslo to Bygdøy leave from Rådhusbrygge, while ferries to the island in Oslofjord leave from Vippetangen.

Car hire

Available from airports and major towns. For travel between towns public transport tends to be quicker and much cheaper. Studded or winter tyres are recommended during winter. There are strict laws against drinking and driving and wearing seatbelts is compulsory. The speed limit in built-up areas is 50kph and 80kph on highways.

BUSINESS DIRECTORY

The addresses listed below are a selection only. While World of Information makes every endeavour to check these addresses, we cannot guarantee that changes have not been made, especially to telephone numbers and area codes. We would welcome any corrections.

Telephone area codes

The international direct dialling (IDD) code for Norway is +47, followed by subscriber's number.

Chambers of Commerce

American Chamber of Commerce in Norway, 20C Drammesveien, PO Box 2604 Solli, 0203 Oslo (tel: 2254-6040; fax: 2254-6720; fax: amcham@amcham.no).

Bergen Chamber of Commerce and Industry, 11 Olav Kyrresgt, 5014 Bergen (tel: 5555-3900; fax: 5555-3901; email: firmapost@bergen-chamber.no).

British-Norwegian Chamber of Commerce, 1 Dronning Maudsgate, 0250 Oslo (tel: 2311-1790; fax: 2283-4120; email: bncc@c21.net).

Kristiansand Chamber of Commerce, PO Box 269, 4663 Kristiansand (tel: 3812-3970; fax: 3812-3979; email: post@kristiansand-chamber.no).

Oslo Chamber of Commerce, 30 Drammensveien, PO Box 2874 Solli, 0230 Oslo (tel: 2212-9400; fax: 2212-9401; email: mail@chamber.no).

Stavanger Chamber of Commerce, 1 Rosenkildetorget, PO Box 182, 4001 Stavanger (tel: 5151-0880; fax: 5151-0881; email: post@stavanger-chamber.no).

Trondheim Chamber of Commerce, PO Box 778 Sentrum, 7408 Trondheim (tel: 7388-3110; fax: 7388-3111; email: firmapost@trondheim-chamber.no).

Tromsø Chamber of Commerce and Industry, 83 Grønnegata, PO Box 464, 9255 Tromsø (tel: 7766-5230; fax: 7766-5253; email: firmapost@tromso-chamber.no).

Banking

Christiania Bank og Kreditkasse, PO Box 1166, N-0107 Oslo (tel: 2248-5000; fax: 2248-4749).

Den norske Bank, Stranden 21, Aker Brygge, N-0021 Oslo (tel.: 2248-1050; fax: 2248-1870; internet: www.dnb.no; email: dnb@dnb.no).

Fokus Bank A/S, Vestre Rosten 77, PO Box 6090, N-7466 Trondheim (tel: 7288-2011; fax: 7288-2061).

Postbanken, Akersgata 68, N-0180 Oslo (tel: 2297-6000; fax: 2297-7665; internet: www.postbanken.no).

Central bank

Norges Bank, Bankplassen 2, PO Box 1179, Sentrum, 0107 Oslo (tel: 2231-6000; fax: 2241-3105; email: central.bank@norges-bank.no).

Travel information

Noges Automobilforbund (NAF), Storgata 2, N-0155 Oslo (tel: 2234-1400).

Nor-Way Bussekspress, Karl Johans gate 2; NO-0154 Oslo (tel: 8154-4444; fax: 2200-1631; email: administrasjon@nor-way.no; internet: www.nbe.no).

Road User Information Centre (tel: 2265-4040).

SAS Braathens, Oksenøyveien 3, Fornebu; PO Box 0080, Oslo (tel: 9150-54000; internet: www.sasbraathens.no).

National tourist organisation offices

Norwegian Tourist Board, Stortorvet 10, N-0155 Oslo; PO Box 722 Sentrum, N-0105 Oslo (tel: 2414-4600; fax: 2414-4601; e-mail: norway@ntr.no; internet: www.visitnorway.com).

Ministries

Department of Transport and Communications, Akersgaten 59, PO Box 8010 Dep, N-0030 Oslo (tel: 2224-9090; fax: 2224-9571).

Ministry of Agriculture, PO Box 8007 Dep, N-0032 Oslo (tel: 2224-9090; fax: 2224- 9555).

Ministry of Finance (Finansdepartementet), Akersgaten 40 (Blokk G), PO Box 8008 Dep, N-0030 Oslo (tel: 2224- 9090; fax: 2224-9510; internet: www.finans.dep.no).

Ministry of Foreign Affairs, 7 Juni-Plassen/Victoria Terrasse, PO Box 8114 Dep, N-0032 Oslo (tel: 2224-3600; fax: 2224-9580/81).

Ministry of Industry and Trade, Grubbegt 8, PO Box 8148 Dep, N-0033 Oslo (tel: 2224-9090; fax: 2224-9565).

Ministry of Petroleum and Energy, Einar Gerhardsens Plass 1, PO Box 8148 Dep, N-0033 Oslo (tel: 2224-6107; fax: 2224-9525).

Other useful addresses

Directorate of Immigration, PO Box 8108 Dep, N-0032 Oslo (tel: 2335-1500; fax: 2335-1504).

Næringslivets Hovedorganisasjon (Confederation of Norwegian Business and Industry), Middelthuns Gate 27, Pb 5250 Majorstua, N-0303 Oslo (tel: 2296-5000; fax: 2296-5593).

Norges Eksportrad (Export Council of Norway), Drammensveien 40, N-0243 Oslo (tel: 2292-6300: fax: 2292-6400).

Norges Varemesse (the Norwegian Trade Fair Foundation), PO Box 75, NO-2001 Lillestrøm (tel: 6693-9100: fax: 6693-9101; internet: www.messe.no).

Norinform, Norwegian Information Service, PO Box 241 Sentrum, N-0103 Oslo (tel: 2211-4685; fax: 2242-4887).

Norwegian Trade Council, N-0243 Oslo (tel: 2292-6300; fax: 2292-6400).

Oslo Bors (stock exchange), Tollbugaten 2, Box 460, Sentrum, 0105 Oslo (tel: 2234-1700; fax: 2234-1925; email: info@ose.no; internet: www.oslobors.no).

Royal Norwegian Embassy (US), 2729 34th Street, NW, Washington DC 20008 (tel: (+1-202) 333-6000; fax: (+1-202) 337-0870; email: emb.washington@mfa.no).

Statistics Norway, PO Box 8131 Dep, N-0033 Oslo 1 (tel: 2109-0000; fax: 2109-4973; internet: (English section) www.ssb.no//www-open/english/).

Internet sites

National bus company: www.nbe.no

National railway company: www.nsb.no

Nordic Pages: www.markovits.com/nordic

Yellow Pages: www.gulesider.no

Oman

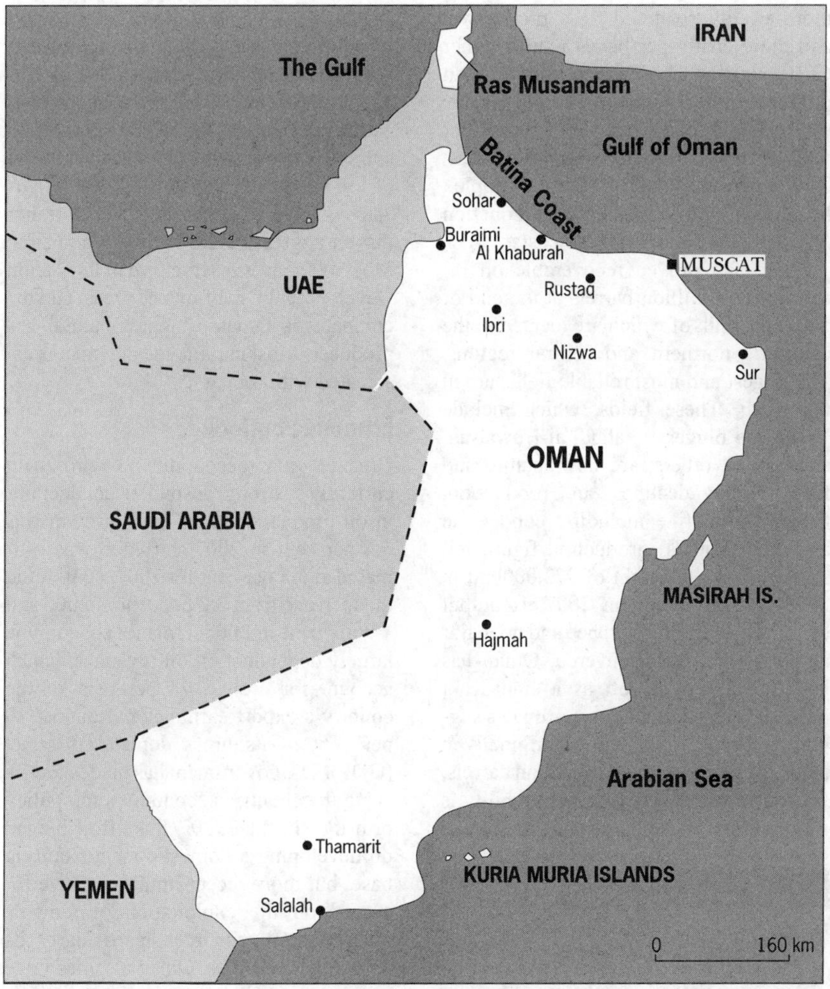

Oman's gross domestic product (GDP) saw a steady 8.3 per cent year-on-year increase at current prices during the period July to September 2007, matching the growth in the first half of the year, according to the ministry of national economy in its economic review for the third quarter.

According to the ministry's Directorate General of Statistics, the non-oil sectors were the engines of growth in the third quarter with year-on-year growth of 18.1 per cent, continuing a trend of consistently strong non-oil sector growth for the last nine quarters since the third quarter of 2005, when growth exceeded 12 per cent year-on-year. This contrasts with the negative growth of 2 per cent in the oil sector's value added in the same quarter. When added to the first six months of 2007, the cumulative oil sector growth for January to September stood at -0.2 per cent. This was despite the price of Oman crude rising to a new high of US$68.50 per barrel in the third quarter of 2007 and was mainly due to lower crude production in 2007. Domestic demand, according to the report, continued to act as a strong driver of growth in the second and third quarters of 2007.

Net imports in the second quarter of 2007 maintained the strong growth of the first quarter, exceeding the rate of growth of net imports throughout 2005 and 2006.

KEY FACTS

Official name: Sultanatu Oman (Saltanat Uman) (Sultanate of Oman)

Head of State: Sultan Qaboos bin Said (from 23 July 1970)

Head of government: Sultan Qaboos bin Said (from 1970)

Ruling party: Political parties are not permitted.

Area: 320,000 square km (including Kuria Muria Islands)

Population: 2.57 million (2007)*

Capital: Muscat (Masqat)

Official language: Arabic

Currency: Omani rial (RO) = 1,000 baiza

Exchange rate: RO0.38 per US$ (Jul 2008)

GDP per capita: US$15,584 (2007)*

GDP real growth: 6.40% (2007)*

Labour force: 782,000 (2004)

Unemployment: 15.00% (2004)

Inflation: 5.50% (2007)*

Oil production: 718,000 bpd (2007)

Balance of trade: US$10.66 billion (2005)

Foreign debt: US$4.81 billion (2004)

* estimated figure

The total number of new private sector jobs created in the first nine months of 2007 (103,959) exceeded the total created in 2006. This high private sector workforce growth has strengthened the demand side of the economy, creating buoyant demand for both local and imported goods. Increases in the Consumer Price Index (CPI) of 6.5 per cent in the third quarter were the highest year-on-year increases recorded in any quarter, representing a rapid acceleration of the rate of increase compared to the 4.7 per cent recorded in the first quarter of 2007 and the 4.8 per cent seen in the period April to June.

Oman's dynasty of sultans can be traced back to 1741, which is when the Ottoman invaders were expelled. Oman has a rich history, having been the only non-European colonial power in Africa. Oman also held the enclave of Gwadur (in Pakistan) until the 1960s. The right to vote was instituted in 2003 although democratisation has been limited. All power is concentrated in the hands of the Sultan, who also holds the top positions in the finance, defence, and foreign affairs ministries. Rules governing the succession to the throne were formalised in the 1996 Basic Law. There is no Omani legislative assembly, though there are two consultative bodies: the Majlis al-Dawla and the Majlis al-Shura. Together, the two chambers form the Council of Oman. The Majlis al-Dawla is appointed, while the Majlis al-Shura is elected. The last election was held in October 2003.

Oil extraction

In some respects, according to the US Energy Information Administration (EIA), Oman differs from other Gulf oil producers. Its petroleum deposits were not discovered until 1962, long after most of those of its neighbours. Additionally, Oman's oil fields are generally smaller, more widely scattered, less productive, and more costly per barrel than in other Gulf countries. The average well in Oman produces only around 400 barrels per day (bpd), about one-tenth the volume per well of those in neighbouring countries. To compensate, Oman uses more complex techniques. While these raise production levels, they also increase the cost.

Oman had proven recoverable oil reserves of 5.6 billion barrels at the end of 2007, the bulk of which are located in the country's northern and central regions. The largest and most reliable fields are in the north. These fields, which include Yibal (the biggest), Fahud, al-Huwaisah, and several others, are now mature and face future declines in production. Oman's total (i e including condensate and other liquids) production figure fell sharply from its height of 972,000bpd in 2000 to 718,000bpd in 2007. If output continues at the present pace and no major new reserves are discovered, Oman has less than 20 years left as a significant oil-exporting nation. Given estimates suggesting that the amount of oil originally in place in Oman is around 50 billion barrels, finding ways to increase recoverability is a top priority. In 2006 a new technology of steam recovery was applied to the reserves, heating and thinning the oil, which should increase the flow. This method, it is hoped, will significantly improve oil yield. If it is successful Oman will be able to turn the problem of inaccessible oil reserves and expensive extractive techniques into an advantage by exporting the new technology to other oil economies such as Kuwait.

Natural gas has become the chief focus of Oman's economic diversification strategy. Intense exploration has raised proven natural gas reserves from only 12.3 trillion cubic feet (Tcf) in 1992 to its current level of 29 Tcf, according to the *Oil and Gas Journal*. The government is also continuing its aggressive exploration campaign. Most of Oman's reserves are in Petroleum Development Oman-owned areas, and the company is Oman's biggest natural gas producer. Most natural gas in Oman is associated with oil

Economic outlook

Oman's macroeconomic environment currently is strong, despite recent declines in oil production. Real GDP growth was 6.4 per cent in 2007. Inflation was estimated at 5.5 per cent for 2007, continuing the increase from 3.2 per cent of 2006 and 1.9 per cent in 2005. Oman's economy is largely dependent on oil revenues, which account for around 75 per cent of the country's export earnings and almost 40 per cent of its gross domestic product (GDP). The government has made diversifying the country's economy a top policy priority. In the 1980s, this effort hinged on developing a domestic manufacturing base, but more recent initiatives have focussed on the exploitation of Oman's other natural resources, particularly its natural gas reserves. Oman also has large mineral and metal deposits, including silica, dolomite, copper, and gold.

Efforts to diversify the economy have included Omanisation, a programme conceived to increase the percentage of Omani citizens working in the private sector, at the expense of expatriate workers. The government also has continued to attempt to attract foreign investment, particularly in light industry, tourism, and electric power generation. Foreign investment incentives include a 5-year tax holiday for companies in certain industries, an income tax reduction for publicly held companies with at least 51 per cent Omani ownership, and soft loans to finance new and existing projects. The process of privatising some state-owned industries is to be accelerated under a decree issued in

KEY INDICATORS — **Oman**

	Unit	2003	2004	2005	2006	2007
Population	m	2.97	3.23	2.57	2.55	*2.57
Gross domestic product (GDP)	US$bn	21.70	24.30	30.84	35.73	*40.06
GDP per capita	US$	7,876	10,339	11,998	14,032	*15,584
GDP real growth	%	6.3	2.5	5.8	6.7	*6.4
Inflation	%	0.3	1.6	1.9	3.2	*5.5
Oil output	'000 bpd	823.0	785.0	780.0	743.0	718.0
Natural gas output	bn cum	16.5	17.6	17.5	25.1	24.1
Exports (fob) (goods)	US$m	12,055.0	13,140.0	18,692.0	21,586.0	–
Imports (cif) (goods)	US$m	7,653.0	6,373.0	8,029.0	9,896.0	–
Balance of trade	US$m	4,402.0	6,767.0	10,663.0	11,691.0	–
Current account	US$m	1,430.0	2,700.0	2,670.0	4,328.0	*3,996.0
Total reserves minus gold	US$m	3,593.5	3,597.3	4,358.1	5,014.0	9,523.5
Foreign exchange	US$m	3,466.6	3,484.5	4,308.7	4,970.2	9,485.1
Exchange rate	per US$	0.39	0.38	0.39	0.39	0.38

* estimated figure

July 2004, which will allow foreign ownership up to 100 per cent in power generation and water.

Outlook

Oman's location gives it obvious logistical advantages which it has yet to exploit to the full. The Co-operation Council for the Arab States of the Gulf (more commonly called the Gulf Co-operation Council (GCC)) established a common market at the beginning of 2007 and a single currency and central bank for the region by 2010.

Risk assessment

Economic	Good
Political	Fair
Regional Stability	Fair

COUNTRY PROFILE

Historical profile

Oman's history differs in many respects from that of its neighbours. It is, for example, the only non-European state to have held colonial possessions in Africa, ruling Zanzibar (now a part of Tanzania) and other East African enclaves for long periods. Omani navigators were acquainted not only with the coasts of India and the east Indies, but also reached as far as southern China. Oman's location also gave it strategic importance for European powers bent on eastward expansion and discovery. The Portuguese quickly appreciated this, occupying strategic locations in the sixteenth century and building numerous coastal forts, some of which can still be seen. For the British, Oman's principal importance was its location on the route to India, which led to a quasi-colonial relationship with the UK.

1507–1650 The Portuguese occupied Muscat and established a garrison there until they were expelled by Imam Sultan bin Saif.

1737–49 The Persians invaded and after they were driven out, the Al bin Said dynasty came to power, which still rules the country.

1798 The first treaty of friendship was signed between Oman and Britain.

1800s The Omani empire expanded to include Zanzibar and Mombasa and parts of the Indian subcontinent. When Sultan Said bin Sultan (known as Said the Great) died in 1856, his empire was divided: one son became Sultan of Zanzibar and the other the Sultan of Muscat and Oman.

1913 After an uprising against the Sultan, control of Oman split, with the interior being ruled by Ibadit imams and the coast by the Sultan.

1932 Said bin Taimur became Sultan.

1959 The Sultan regained control of the interior from the Ibadit imams.

1965–75 A rebellion in the southern region of Dhofar, led by the Popular Front for the Liberation of Oman (PFLO), was put down with the help of soldiers from India, Iran, Jordan, Pakistan, Saudi Arabia, the Trucial States and Britain.

1964 Oil was discovered.

1967 Extraction began.

1970 Qaboos bin Said, aged 30, overthrew his father, Said bin Taimur. Sultan Qaboos started to open up the country and, using money from oil, built roads, schools and hospitals and gave homes to people and boats to fishermen. He set in place strict environmental laws.

1971 Oman joined the Arab League.

1978 Sultan Qaboos was active in helping implement the Camp David Accords, signed by Israel and Egypt.

1981 Oman helped found the Gulf Co-operation Council (GCC).

1985 Oman established full diplomatic relations with the Soviet Union for the first time.

1991 During the Gulf War, Oman was used as a base for forces fighting Iraq. Sultan Qaboos established the Majlis Ash Shura (Consultative Council).

1996 Sultan Qaboos promulgated the 'Basic Statute of the State', or Basic Law, the Gulf's first written constitution.

1997 The Sultan issued a decree allowing women to stand for election to, and vote for, the Majlis Ash Shura, and two women were elected.

1999 Oman and the UAE signed a border agreement, which defined their disputed common frontier.

2000 Majlis Ash Shura elections involving just 25 per cent of the adult population and no parties were allowed, with candidates hand-picked by the Sultan. Oman joined the World Trade Organisation (WTO).

2001 Oman became an important base for international military operations against the Taliban government in Afghanistan.

2002 Voting rights were extended to all citizens over the age of 21.

2003 The 83-seat Majlis Ash Shura was freely elected for the first time.

2004 Sultan Qaboos appointed Oman's first female minister with portfolio.

2005 In May, a state security court convicted 31 people of plotting to overthrow the Sultan and install an Islamist government.

2006 In January, Oman signed a free trade agreement with the US, which entered into effect in September.2008 On 1 January, a common market was created by Bahrain, Kuwait, Oman, Qatar, Saudi Arabia and UAE, the six wealthiest Gulf states. Citizens of these countries are now allowed to travel between and live in any of the six states, where they may find employment, buy properties and businesses and use the educational and health facilities freely.

Political structure

Constitution

In November 1996, Sultan Qaboos bin Said promulgated the 'Basic Statute of the State', or Basic Law, the Gulf's first written constitution, that clarified the royal succession, provided for a legislature and guaranteed basic civil liberties for Omani citizens within a framework of Islamic and traditional law.

The country is divided into 59 wilayat (regions), each under the authority of a wali (governor). There are special governates for the cities of Muscat and Salalah, with Muscat consisting of six separate wilayat.

Form of state

Absolute monarchy

The executive

Executive and legislative power lies with Sultan Qaboos bin Said, who appoints the Council of Ministers and other officials and promulgates laws by decree.

National legislature

In 1991, Sultan Qaboos established a Majlis Ash Shura (Consultative Council), in which each of the 59 wilayat were represented.

In 1996, a draft law set up a bicameral parliament (Council of State), consisting of an upper chamber or Majlis Addawla (41 members appointed by the monarch) and a transformed lower chamber (Majlis Ash Shura), with 83 members elected by limited suffrage. The assembly meets with the Council of Ministers once a year at which Cabinet members present their departments' plans. Majlis power is limited to proposing and reviewing legislation and, although it can affect policy on minor issues, it remains relatively powerless.

In the September 2000 elections Sultan Qaboos had ultimate control over both the choice of candidate for each council seat and the eligibility to be a member of what is a very limited electorate. The elections involved just 25 per cent of the adult population with voters over 30 and vetted by the ministry of interior. The electorate included sheikhs, wise men, dignitaries, graduates and intellectuals; women can both vote and stand for election to the Majlis Ash Shura. Term of office is three years.

In November 2002, the Sultan announced the introduction of universal suffrage, with everyone over the age of 21 years eligible to vote for the 83-member Majlis Ash Shura.

Legal system

The legal system is mainly the preserve of Sharia courts, which apply Islamic law.

The local courts are administered by qadis (Islamic judges) appointed by the minister of justice. Appeals from local courts are heard at the Court of Appeal in Muscat.

Last elections

4 October 2003 (parliamentary)

Results: Non-party candidates were elected to the 83 seats in the Majlis al Shura (Consultative Assembly).

Next elections

October 2007 (parliamentary)

Political parties

Ruling party

Political parties are not permitted.

Main opposition party

There is no legal opposition.

Population

2.57 million (2007)*

Last census: December 2003: 2,340,815

Population density: 11 people per square km. Urban population: 76 per cent (1995–2001).

Annual growth rate: 1.8 per cent 1994–2004 (WHO 2006)

Ethnic make-up

Predominantly Arab, with non-Arab pockets in long-established Baluchi, Iranian and Gujarati communities. Many Omanis are of Zanzibari descendancy (prior to 1964, Zanzibar had been part of the Sultanate of Oman).

Religions

Islam is the official religion. The majority are Ibadi Muslims with about one-quarter being Sunnis. There is a small concentration of Shi'ite Muslims in Muscat.

Education

The government sponsors literacy centres in an attempt to improve the literacy rate. Primary education lasts from aged six to 12. Secondary education consists of two stages: first the preparatory school for three years then the secondary school for a further three years. Islamic Institute secondary schools accept students who have completed their preparatory study in a mosque. It teaches the same subjects as secondary schools but with an emphasis on Islam and the Arabic language.

Literacy rate: 74 per cent adult rate; 99 per cent youth rate (15–24) (Unesco 2005).

Compulsory years: None.

Enrolment rate: 76 per cent gross primary enrolment of relevant age group (including repeaters); 67 per cent gross secondary enrolment (World Bank).

Pupils per teacher: 26 in primary schools.

Health

Per capita total expenditure on health (2003) was US$419; of which per capita government spending was US$348, at the international dollar rate, (WHO 2006).

Free medical care is available throughout the Sultanate for all Omani citizens. In 2000, the WHO rated the Oman healthcare service in the top 10 worldwide, with first place in delivery efficiency and the untilisation of financial resources. Since 2001 the health development plan has been concentrating on the expansion of improved primary healthcare in villages and towns and providing additional specialist treatment centres.

HIV/Aids

HIV prevalence: 0.1 per cent aged 15–49 in 2003 (World Bank)

Life expectancy: 74 years, 2004 (WHO 2006)

Fertility rate/Maternal mortality rate: 3.6 births per woman, 2004 (WHO 2006); maternal mortality 19 per 100,000 live births (World Bank).

Birth rate/Death rate: 28 births and 3 deaths per 1,000 people respectively (World Bank).

Child (under 5 years) mortality rate (per 1,000): 10 per 1,000 live births (World Bank)

Head of population per physician: 1.32 physicians per 1,000 people, 2004 (WHO 2006)

Welfare

Most Omanis depend on the extended family for financial support. Since 1984 the Ministry of Social Affairs has run a scheme of monthly welfare payments for eight categories of Omani citizens, provided that they can prove indigence. The categories are: orphans, divorcees, people unable to work, refugees, widows, spinsters, people over 60 years of age and the families of prisoners.

The Sultanate of Oman has extended social security benefits for workers in the private sector. Since the issue of the Social Insurance law in 1992, the Public Authority for Social Insurance (PASI) has registered companies and establishments in the private sector including workers and their families, who are entitled to receive sickness, injury and disability benefits, pension and death compensation.

The Association for the Welfare of Handicapped Children, a charitable organisation, supplements the work of the ministry of social affairs, labour and vocational training with centres at Al-Khoudh, Quriyat and Bilad Banu Bu Hassan. The government has made donations towards women's training centres and nurseries for childcare. Special attention is given to the needs of the disabled, particularly young people who are encouraged to join the training centre at Al-Khoudh. The centre also cares for severely disabled children between 3—14 years of age. The ministry has developed sport facilities as part of the disabled welfare programme. The Oman Charitable Organisation (OCO), a non-governmental body, has co-operated with the ministry to build 45 shelters at a cost of RO58,500 (US$152,161) for the Bedu living in remote areas of the country and assisted with programmes for the disabled.

Main cities

Muscat (Masqat) (capital, estimated population 23,479 in 2005), Salalah (159,491), Sohar (105,585), Bawshar (154,878), Matrah (152,350), Ibri (99,142).

Media

National news agency: PO Box 3659, 112, Ruwi, Oman (tel: 2460-5659; email: editorarabic@omannews.com; internet: www.omannews.com).

Press

Government censorship is applied to political and cultural items and due to the law that requires all publications and journalists be licensed by the Ministry of Information, with stiff penalties for transgressions, has resulted in widespread journalistic self-censorship.

Dailies: In English, the Oman Daily Observer (www.omanobserver.com) is government-owned, while the Times of Oman (www.timesofoman.com) and Oman Tribune (www.omantribune.com), and Week (www.freetheweek.com) are independent. In Arabic, Oman Daily (www.omandaily.com), Al Shabiba (www.shabiba.com), Alquds Newspaper and the independent daily Al-Watan (www.alwatan.com).

Business: In English, Business Today, Zawya a business directory; multiply publications (by www.apexstuff.com) include Oman 2day and the free publication The Week.

Periodicals: In English, the monthly Oman Today (www.apexstuff.com) is a lifestyle publication.

Broadcasting

Radio: Radio Oman (www.oman-radio.gov.om/rdeng) is government-run, while Hala FM (www.ohigroup.com/ohigroup/news2.asp), which opened in May 2007, is privately owned. Presentations are in both English and Arabic.

Television: Oman has two government-run television channels (www.oman-tv.gov.om/tveng) and domestic satellite dishes allow programmes from Saudi Arabia, Yemen and the UAE to be received.

Advertising

With the rise of English-language media, in particular through satellite television, western advertisers are rapidly developing the industry in Oman. Apex Press has several English titles which take international advertising.

Economy

Since Sultan Qaboos came to power in 1970, Oman has been seen as one of the developing world's fastest growing economies. With a population of three million and a per capita income of over US$12,664 in 2005, Oman is a middle-income developing country. The country relies heavily on oil revenues, which account for around 40 per cent of GDP. Oman has only limited resources and although oil has been used as the motor for economic development, the government continues to diversify so as not to be too dependent on a single resource. The stated aim of economic diversification is to reduce oil's domination of the economy until it accounts for less than 20 per cent of GDP and to encourage private sector investment.

Oman has developed liquefied natural gas (LNG) production, a manufacturing sector, ports and telecommunications. Since the early 1990s, each of these sectors has registered major gains. While since the late 1990s, the economy has benefited from relatively high oil prices, diversification remains the top development priority. A US$2.4 billion aluminum smelter, to begin operations in 2008, could spearhead further diversification in the economy.

The government has set an economic development target, Vision 2020, to achieve a level of growth on a par with the Asian Tiger economies by 2020. Membership of the World Trade Organisation since 2000 has reduced barriers to entry in Oman and opened the country to foreign investment.

External trade

In 2005 the Greater Arab Free Trade Area (Gafta) was ratified by 17 members, including Oman creating an Arab economic bloc. A customs union was established whereby tariffs within Gafta will be reduced by a percentage each year, until none remain. In June 2007 a free trade agreement between the US and Oman was awaiting implementation.

Imports

Principal imports are machinery and transport equipment, manufactured goods, food, livestock and lubricants.

Main sources: UAE (25.9 per cent total, 2006), Japan (17.3 per cent), India (5.3 per cent).

Exports

Crude oil (typically 70 per cent of total exports), liquefied natural gas (LNG), fish, processed copper, textiles and dates.

Main destinations: South Korea (4.2 per cent total, 2006), UAE (1.9 per cent), Japan (0.9 per cent).

Agriculture

Farming

Agriculture accounts for around 3 per cent of GDP and employs around 200,000 people. Agriculture and fisheries account for an average 35 per cent per annum of Oman's main non-oil exports. Main crops include dates, alfalfa, lucerne, wheat, mangoes, limes and bananas, with market gardening of tomatoes, cabbages, aubergines, okra and cucumbers.

The shortage of water and pasture and the salinity of the soil are the main constraints on agricultural development. The emphasis of government investment in this sector has been on digging wells, repairing old irrigation systems and building dams to trap rainwater which previously ran off into the sea. Irrigation studies show potential arable land to be twice that under cultivation, but agriculture already uses over 90 per cent of the available water. Apart from a narrow coastal strip (the Batinah coastline), most of Oman is either mountain or desert.

A network of collection and distribution centres is run by the Public Authority for Marketing Agricultural Produce (Pamap). Pamap exports fruit and vegetables, particularly bananas, and operates a banana ripening and packing factory at Salalah and a handling centre at al Suwaiq.

Estimated crop production in 2005 included: 5,850 tonnes (t) cereals in total, 1,450t wheat, 2,515t papayas, 238,000t dates, 15,500t potatoes, 33,000t bananas, 3,000t sorghum, 7,500t citrus fruit, 11,000t mangoes, 43,000t tomatoes, 1,270t tobacco, 293,315t fruit in total, 186,500t vegetables in total.

Estimated livestock production in 2004 included: 41,102t meat in total, 4,160t beef, 10,800t lamb, 13,750t goat meat, 6,552t camel meat, 5,840t poultry, 8,600t eggs, 107,620t milk, 480t cattle hides, 1,375t goatskins.

Fishing

The fishing industry is well developed and has helped to diversify the economy. Stocks include between 15,000 and 27,000 tonnes of kingfish, 50,000 tonnes of tuna and 2,000 tonnes of shellfish. The total fish catch typically varies between 118,000 to 160,000 tonnes per annum. Fish and shellfish exports totaled $104.7 million in 2006.

Oman Fisheries Co SAOG is the largest fishing company in the country. It undertakes processing and marketing of fish and fishery products, which are approved for export to European countries. Exports include fresh fish, frozen fish and seafood (prawns, crabs and lobsters). The Gulf Co-operation Council (GCC) states are the destination for almost half of Omani fish exports.

In 2004, the total marine fish catch was 152,411 tonnes and the total crustacean catch was 729 tonnes.

Forestry

There is very little forest or woodland in Oman with forest cover estimated at 1,000 hectares, mainly composed of scattered areas of Juniperus forest in the Hajar Mountains. About 10 million date palms are grown along the northern Batinah coastal strip. Although some wood is used for domestic consumption, there is no significant commercial exploitation. Much of the demand for wood and paper products is met through imports.

Industry and manufacturing

The government is acutely aware that oil reserves are low and the population is growing significantly with a high proportion of young people. As a result, government policy aims to promote growth and employment through encouraging private sector investment in industry. This has been done by offering incentives such as tax exemptions, customs protection, soft or interest-free loans and by providing infrastructure, usually in the form of industrial estates. It favours small- to medium-sized industries which are import-substituting, use local raw materials, have a relative advantage in export markets or employ a high ratio of Omanis.

A series of five-year development plans, started in 1976, outline the government's main objectives of self-sufficiency, import substitution and the diversification of the economy to reduce reliance on oil. The five-year plans call for the manufacturing, trade and financial services sectors to contribute 80 per cent to annual GDP by 2020.

Industrial production increased by 4 per cent in 2003.

Tourism

As part of its programme of diversification, the government has introduced measures designed to promote private sector participation in the tourist industry. Tourism is believed to be capable of generating more foreign earnings and employment opportunities than heavy industry. The sector is expected to contribute 1.8 per cent to GDP in 2005. The government wants tourism to account for 5 per cent of GDP by 2020.

The sector, following World Trade Organisation advice, has targeted upmarket visitors, but more recently the example of Dubai has stimulated interest in the mass market. In June 2005, the construction of a huge, privately-financed resort called 'Blue City', costing US$15 billion, was announced. The project, covering 35 square kilometres along the al-Sawardi sea-front, will take 15 years to complete.

Mining

Mining typically contributes around 1 per cent to annual GDP and employs around 3 per cent of the workforce.

Oman has large resources of industrial rocks and minerals, some of which are already being exploited. They include silica sand, dolomite, limestone, gypsum, ornamental stone, clays, rockwool, iron oxides, heavy sands, wollastonite, celestite, asbestos, aggregate, laterite and barite. Mineral deposits of copper, manganese, lead, iron, zinc, chrome, phosphates, gold, silver and nickel exist, many of them in inaccessible areas.

Government policy is to exploit raw materials wherever commercially feasible and diversify the development of its mineral resources. As in other sectors of the economy, the government aims for self-sufficiency and the mineral-based industry is expected to contribute significantly to the growth of GDP in coming years. The indigenous mineral-based industries include cement, limestone, ceramics and construction and the production of processed marble, gold ore, chromite, industrial and edible salt and clays. The government has encouraged the processing of ores within Oman rather than exporting them untreated.

In the late 1990s, the Japan International Corporation discovered new gold and copper deposits at Ghuzayn and Daris, which led to the development of potential areas for copper and gold mineralisation. Copper and chromite are mined near Sohar by thegovernment-owned Oman Mining Company (OMCO). Saudi Arabia is the main market for cathode copper production. There are probable copper ore reserves of 15.2 million tonnes at Rakah and Hayl al Safil in the Willayat of Yanqul, about 275km from the smelter. Chromite reserves are put at two million tonnes and annual production is around 6,000 tonnes. Chromite is exported to Japan and China. Gold and silver are produced from the copper oxide deposits by the OMCO processing plant.

Hydrocarbons

Oil is the major sector of the economy, providing nearly 80 per cent of the country's export earnings and contributing 40 per cent to GDP. In 2004, proven oil reserves stood at 5.6 billion barrels. Production stood at 785,000 barrels per day (bpd), 4.4 per cent down on 2003. The reserves are located in the northern and central regions. Yibal, which produces around 180,000 bpd, is the largest oil field. Production has risen as new fields have been exploited – the Mukhaizina field (25,000bpd), the Burhaan field (24,000bpd) and the al-Noor field (9,400bpd). 263.6 million barrels were exported in 2004, compared with 278.5 million barrels in 2003. The decline in both production and exports of oil in recent years is offset by rising prices.

Proven natural gas reserves were one trillion cubic metres in 2004, but potential reserves are thought to be double that figure. Gas production stood at 17.6 billion cubic metres in 2004, an increase of 6.7 per cent on 2003 output. Oman is concentrating its efforts on developing liquefied natural gas (LNG) production. The existing natural gas pipeline network is being extended with the aid of foreign construction companies. The natural gas deposits in central Oman were linked by US$124 million and US$180 million pipelines to the coastal cities of Sohar and Salalah respectively in August 2002.

Coal deposits with reserves of over 22 million tonnes have been discovered in the Wadi Muswa and Wadi Fisaw areas of the Sharqiya near Sur. Coal from the Al Kamil field is of good quality, and could be used to provide the energy for a 300MW generator over a period of some 40 years, using 600,000 tonnes annually.

Energy

Installed electricity generating capacity is around 2.5 GW. Demand is growing rapidly at 5 per cent per annum. Natural gas is used to reduce domestic demand for oil, mainly by power plants, copper smelters and cement plants. Electricity reaches all populated areas except for some remote mountain villages. About 86 per cent of the country is fully supplied.

The 280MW Al Kamil power plant, built by International Power plc, the 430MW Barka power plant, owned by AES, the 240MW integrated power plant, owned by PSEG, to supply the Dhofar region, and the 140MW plant at Qarn Alam, owned by Bharat Heavy Electricals, all run on natural gas.

Financial markets

Stock exchange

The Muscat Securities Market (MSM) opened in 1989 with the purpose of attracting local savings and international capital. Modelled on the Amman (Jordan) exchange, the MSM has acquired a reputation for good management.

Banking and insurance

Oman has a robust banking sector both foreign and domestic with two specialised banks subsidised by the government – the Oman Housing Bank and the Oman Bank for Industrial Development. However, experts believe the sector is over-banked and have called for mergers to consolidate the sector.

Central bank

Central Bank of Oman

Main financial centre

Muttrah Business District

Time

GMT plus four hours

Geography

Oman lies at the south-eastern tip of the Arabian peninsula, bordering Yemen, Saudi Arabia and the United Arab Emirates (UAE). The Musandam Peninsula in the far north is separated from the rest of Oman by UAE territory. The coastline is 1,700km long.

There are two distinct areas of population, centred on the Hajar mountains, with a narrow, fertile strip along the coast, in the north and the Batinah plain and its hinterland in the south. Between them lies 800km of virtually uninhabited gravel plain.

Hemisphere

Northern

Climate

Most of the country is hot and arid, with noon temperatures in summer exceeding 40 degrees Celsius (C) and annual rainfall of around 100mm. There is a higher rainfall over the mountains. The southern region, however, has a tropical climate, with noon temperatures between 27 and 33 degrees C all year round and a rainy season from June to August.

Dress codes

Formal clothing is recommended for public places and in general the body should be fully covered. Businessmen should wear suits and ties to appointments, but the jacket can be carried. Shorts are not allowed, except for sports. Women are advised to dress modestly. Swimwear should be worn only at hotel pools and on the beach.

Entry requirements

Passports

Required by all, except citizens of some neighbouring countries. Passports must be valid for six months beyond the date of visit.

Visa

Required by all. Details for tourist or business visitors listed at www.destinationoman.com, follow link to Plan your trip, then Getting there. Visas may be obtained at a point of entry (all land and sea ports, but only at Seeb International airport if arriving by air).

Those who do not appear on the list of eligibility should contact the nearest Omani Embassy and apply for a visa as required. Oman has a joint visa agreement with the Emirate of Dubai – visitors with a visa for either country may cross to the other without a further visa, however the term of visit is a maximum of three weeks.

Prohibited entry
Holders of Israeli passports
Currency advice/regulations
The import and export of local and foreign currency is unlimited; Israeli currency is prohibited.
Travellers cheques are widely available.
Customs
Personal effects and one bottle of alcohol per non-muslim adult are duty-free.
Prohibited imports
Firearms, ammunition, narcotics and pornography. Certain food items and plant materials may be quarantined. Clothing bearing Koranic inscriptions is banned. Although goods of Israeli origin and imports from Israel are no longer illegal in Oman, goods produced by companies boycotted by the Arab League are prohibited.

Health (for visitors)
Mandatory precautions
Vaccination certificate against yellow fever if travelling from infected area.
Advisable precautions
Health facilities in the city are good but expensive for foreigners; health insurance is therefore recommended for visitors. All visitors should carry a list of their generic medication and if necessary their own hypodermic needles.
Inoculations and boosters should be current for tetanus, hepatitis A, and typhoid. There may be a need for vaccinations for tuberculosis, diphtheria, polio hepatitis B. Use malaria prophylaxis for visits to the far north of the country, including Musandam province, which will also provide protection for hepatitis B, these include mosquito repellents, nets and clothing that covers the body after dark. There is a risk of rabies. Avoid bathing in freshwater, use only well-maintained and chlorinated swimming pools.
Milk is unpasteurised and should be boiled or avoided. Meat, fish and vegetables should be served cooked and fruit peeled before consumption.
Between April and October the sun is very strong and sunscreens, protective clothing, sunglasses and hats are necessary.

Hotels
There are several five-star hotels in Muscat/Muttrah/Ruwi Capital Area. There is a lack of hotels in provincial towns, although a programme of expansion is underway.
A service charge of 10 per cent is included in all bills.
Dhofar coast beaches are the main tourist area.

Credit cards
Major credit cards are widely accepted. ATMs are available in largerly bank branches.

Public holidays (national)
Fixed dates
1 Jan (New Year's Day), 18 Nov (National Day), 19 Nov (Sultan's Birthday), 31 Dec (Bank Holiday).
Variable dates
Islamic New Year, Eid al Adha (four days), Eid Milad Nnabi (birth of prophet), Ascension of Mohammed, Eid al Fitr (three days), Birth of the Prophet (two days).
Islamic year – 1429 (10 Jan 2008–28 Dec 2008): The Islamic year has 354 or 355 days, with the result that Muslim feasts advance by 10–12 days against the Gregorian calendar each year. Dates of the Muslim feasts vary according to sightings of the new moon, so cannot be forecast exactly.

Working hours
Work hours are affected by Ramadan, the Muslim holy month of fasting during daylight hours.
Banking
Sat–Wed: 0800–1200.
Business
Sat–Wed: 0800–1300, 1400–1900; Thu: 0800–1300.
Government
Sat–Wed: 0730–1430.
Shops
Sat–Thu: 0900–1300, 1400–2100. Supermarkets and shopping malls: 0900–2200, with short lunch breaks.

Telecommunications
Mobile/cell phones
GSM 900 services are available in inhabited areas.

Electricity supply
220/240V AC, with two or three-pin round, or three-pin flat types, plug fittings.

Weights and measures
Metric.

Social customs/useful tips
Handshaking is the normal form of greeting and business cards are exchanged at business meetings. Appointments are required for business meetings.
It is discourteous to eat, drink or smoke in front of Muslims in daylight hours during Ramadan. It is polite to accept the refreshments customarily offered to visitors.
Alcohol is available in hotel bars and restaurants. Non-Muslims with liquor permits from the Omani police can buy alcoholic drinks at special stores for consumption at home.
The government regularly issues strong-worded ordinances designed to keep the country clean and tidy. It is an offence, for example, to drive a dirty car or hang out washing in view of main roads. Foreigners should take care to observe these regulations, although the police rarely enforce them.

Security
Visitors should keep in touch with developments in the Middle East as any increase in regional tension might affect travel advice. Oman is the most stable country in the Arabian peninsula. Even levels of petty crime are minimal.

Getting there
Air
National airline: Oman Air (regional airline); Oman is a shareholder of Gulf Air (international airline).
International airport/s: Seeb International Airport (MCT), 40km from Muscat, with duty-free shops and a restaurant; Salalah International Airport, near the southern city of Salalah.
Airport tax: None
Surface
Road: The Yemen border is not open to travellers, but there are road links with the United Arab Emirates, including regular bus services between Muscat and Dubai.
Water: There are some ferry services into Muscat from other Gulf States.

Getting about
National transport
Air: There are six civil airports. Oman Air operates scheduled flights to Salalah Airport, Fahud and Marmul. There are also flights to the Musandam Peninsula, Buraimi, Sur and the island of Masirah. All flights should be booked well in advance and confirmed on the day before travelling.
Road: An excellent asphalt road system links all the main centres. A 780km highway links Dhofar with the north and the national network.
There are over 9,000km of paved roads (550km of dual carriageway) and over 22,000km of unpaved track roads. Improvements and the widening of existing highways is on-going, as are linking roads between towns and villages of the interior.
Buses: The Oman National Transport Company (ONTC) operates national bus services and local services in the capital area.
Taxis: There is an excellent network of minibuses which operate as service taxis linking up the major centres of population.
Water: There are regular ferry services from Muscat to Khasab on the Musandam Peninsular.
City transport
Taxis: Taxis are expensive by Gulf standards; they should have a scale of charges, but it is advisable to negotiate fares in advance (there are no meters). Tipping is not usual. Some hotels offer a courtesy pick-up service; others offer the service but charge.
Buses, trams & metro: An urban bus service operates in Muscat, but is not recommended for visitors.

Car hire

It is necessary to hold an international driving licence when hiring a car in Oman. Check licence rules in advance. Speed limits are 120kph and driving is on the right-hand side of the road. Most hotels have self-drive car hire facilities.

BUSINESS DIRECTORY

The addresses listed below are a selection only. While World of Information makes every endeavour to check these addresses, we cannot guarantee that changes have not been made, especially to telephone numbers and area codes. We would welcome any corrections.

Telephone area codes

The international direct dialling (IDD) code for Oman is +968, followed by subscriber's number.

Useful telephone numbers

Capital area
Police: 560-099
Fire: 999
International operator: 195
International enquiries: 197
Directory enquiries: 198
Operator: 190

Chambers of Commerce

Oman Chamber of Commerce and Industry, PO Box 1400, Ruwi 112 (tel: 2470-7674; fax: 2470-8497; email: occi@chamberoman.com).

Banking

Bank Dhofar, PO Box 1507, Ruwi 112 (tel: 2479-0466; fax: 2479-7246; email: info@bankdhofar.com).

BankMuscat, PO Box 1708, 112 Ruwi (tel: 2445-6365; fax: 2445-6077; email: info@bankmuscat.com).

Industrial Bank of Oman, PO Box 2613, Ruwi 112 (tel: 2470-6786; fax: 2470-6986; email: indlbank@omantel.net.om).

Majan International Bank, PO Box 2717, Ruwi 112 (tel: 2478-0388; fax: 2478-0643; email: majanbk@omantel.net.om).

National Bank of Oman, PO Box 2613, 112 Ruwi (tel: 2470-6786 fax: 2470-6986; email: ask@nbo.om).

Oman Arab Bank, PO Box 2010, Ruwi 112 (tel: 2470-6265; fax: 2479-7736; email: mktoab@omantel.net.om).

Oman Development Bank, PO Box 309, Muscat 113 (tel: 2473-8021; fax: 2473-8026; email: odebe@omantel.net.om).

Oman Housing Bank, PO Box 2555, Muscat 112 (tel: 24704-444; email: i-ohb@i-ohb.com.om).

Oman International Bank, PO Box 1216, P C 112 Ruwi (tel: 2457-6039, 2457-6618; fax: 2457-6040; email: omintbnk@omantel.net.om).

Central bank

Central Bank of Oman, PO Box 1161, Ruwi 112 (tel: 2470-6175; fax: 2470-5961; email: markazi@omantel.net.com).

Travel information

Seeb International Airport, PO Box 58, Muscat 111 (tel: 2451-9285; fax: 2451-0805).

Gulf Air, PO Box 1444, Ruwi 112 (tel: 2470-3222; fax: 2479-3381).

Oman Air, PO Box 58, Seeb International Airport, Muscat 111 (tel: 2451-9953; fax: 2452-1075).

Oman Automobile Association, PO Box 2874, Muscat 111 (tel: 2451-0239; fax: 2451-0276; email: omanauto@omantel.net.om).

Oman Aviation Services, PO Box 58, Muscat 111 (tel: 2451-9237; fax: 2451-0805).

Oman National Transport Company, PO Box 620, Muscat 113 (tel: 2459-0046, 2459-0603; email: ontc01@omantel.net.om).

Ministry of tourism

Directorate General of Tourism, Ministry of Commerce and Industry, PO Box 550, Muscat 113 (tel: 2477-16527; fax: 2477-14213; e-mail: dgt@mocioman.org; internet: omantourism.gov.om).

Ministries

Ministry of Agriculture and Fisheries, PO Box 467, Muscat 113 (tel: 2469-6300; fax: 2460-5304).

Ministry of Awqaf and Religious Affairs, PO Box 3232, Ruwi 112 (tel: 2469-6870; fax: 2460-1109).

Ministry of Civil Service, PO Box 3994, Ruwi 112 (tel: 2469-6000; fax: 2460-1771).

Ministry of Commerce and Industry, PO Box 550, Muscat 113 (tel: 2477-13500; fax: 2477-17239).

Ministry of Defence, PO Box 113, Muscat 113 (tel: 2431-2605; fax: 2470-2521).

Ministry of Education, PO Box 3, Muscat 113 (tel: 2477-5209; fax: 2470-8485).

Ministry of Foreign Affairs, PO Box 252, Muscat 113 (tel: 2469-9500; fax: 2469-6641).

Ministry of Health, PO Box 393, Muscat 113 (tel: 2460-2177; fax: 2460-2647).

Ministry of Higher Education, PO Box 82, Ruwi 112 (tel: 24695330; fax: 2469-4481)

Ministry of Housing, Electricity & Water, PO Box 1491, Ruwi 112 (tel: 2460-3800; fax: 2469-9180).

Ministry of Information, PO Box 600, Muscat 113 (tel: 2460-3222; fax: 2460-1638; internet: www.omanet.com).

Ministry of Interior, PO Box 127, Ruwi 112 (tel: 2460-2244; fax: 2466-0644).

Ministry of Justice, PO Box 354, Ruwi 112 (tel: 2469-7699; fax: 2460-2725).

Ministry of Legal Affairs, PO Box 578, Ruwi 112 (tel: 2460-5802; fax: 2460-5697).

Ministry of National Economy, PO Box 506, Muscat 113 (tel: 2473-8201; fax: 2473-7068).

Ministry of National Heritage & Culture, PO Box 668, Muscat 113 (tel: 2460-2555; fax: 2469-7060).

Ministry of Oil and Gas, PO Box 551, Muscat 113 (tel: 2460-3333; fax: 2469-6972).

Ministry of Regional Municipalities, Environment and Water Resources, PO Box 323, Muscat 113 (tel: 2469-2550; fax: 2469-3995).

Ministry of Social Development, [PO Box 560, Muscat 113 (tel: 2460-2444; fax: 2469-9357).

Ministry of Transport and Telecommunications, PO Box 338, Ruwi 112 (tel: 2469-7888; fax: 24696817).

Other useful addresses

British Embassy, PO Box 300, 185 Mina al Fahral, Muscat 113 (tel: 2469-3086; fax: 2469-3088; email: becomu@omantel.net).

Capital Market Authority, PO Box 3265, Ruwi 112 (tel: 2482 3600; fax: 2481 6260).

Development Council, PO Box 881, Muscat 113 (tel: 2469-8900; fax: 2469-6285).

High Commitee for Conferences, PO Box 891, Muscat 113 (tel: 2469-8221; fax: 2460-7497).

Muscat Securities Market, PO Box 3265, Ruwi 112 (tel: 2482-3600; fax: 2481 5776).

Oman International Trade and Exhibitions (OITE), PO Box 112, Ruwi 112 (tel: 2456-4303; fax: 2456-5165; email: oitex@omantel.net.om).

Oman Oil Company, PO Box 261, Qurm 118 (tel: 2456-7392; fax: 2456-7386; email: oman-oil@omantel.net.om).

Omani Centre for Investment Promotion and Export Development, PO Box 25, Wadi Kabir 117 (tel: 2481-2344; fax: 2481-0890; email: info@ociped.com).

Omani Embassy (USA), 2535 Belmont Road NW, Washington DC 20008 (tel: (+1-202) 387-1980; fax: (+1-202) 745-4933; email: emboman@erols.com).

Petroleum Development Oman (PDO), PO Box 81, Muscat 113 (tel: 2467-8111; fax: 2467-7106).

Salalah Port Services Company, PO Box 105, Muscat 118 (tel: 2456-7188; fax: 2456-7166).

US Embassy, PO Box 202, Medinat Al Sultan Qaboos, Muscat 115 (tel: 2469-8989; fax: 2469-9189; email: aemctcns@gto.net).

National news agency: PO Box 3659, 112, Ruwi, Oman (tel: 2460-5659; email: editorarabic@omannews.com; internet: www.omannews.com).

Internet sites

Arab net: www.arab.net

Arabia on-line: www.arabia.com

Gulf business explorer: www.igulf.com

Official tourist site: www.destinationoman.com

Oman online archives of political, economic and business news: www.newsbriefsoman.info

Times of Oman: http://omantimes.com/

Pakistan

KEY FACTS

Official name: Islami Jamhuriya e Pakistan (Islamic Republic of Pakistan)

Head of State: President Asif Ali Zardari (from Sep 2008)

Head of government: Prime Minister Makhdoom Syed Yousaf Raza Gilani (PPP) (from 25 Mar 2008)

Ruling party: Coalition led by the Pakistan People's Party (PPP) with Pakistan Muslem League-Nawaz (PML-N), Pakistan Muslim League-Qaid e Azam (PML-QA), Awami National Party (ANP), Jamiat Ulema e Islam (JUI) (Assembly of Islamic Clergy) and Muttahida Qaumi Movement (MQM) (from 9 Mar 2008)

Area: 803,943 square km

Population: 152.53 million (2007)*

Capital: Islamabad

Official language: Urdu (national language) and English

Currency: Rupee (Rp) = 100 paisa

Exchange rate: Rp70.95 per US$ (Jul 2008)

GDP per capita: US$909 (2007)*

GDP real growth: 6.40% (2007)*

Labour force: 57,415 (2004)

Unemployment: 8.30% (2004) (plus additional underemployment)

Inflation: 7.70% (2007)

Balance of trade: -US$7.20 billion (2006)

Foreign debt: US$35.21 billion (2005)

Annual FDI: US$2.00 billion (2006)

* estimated figure

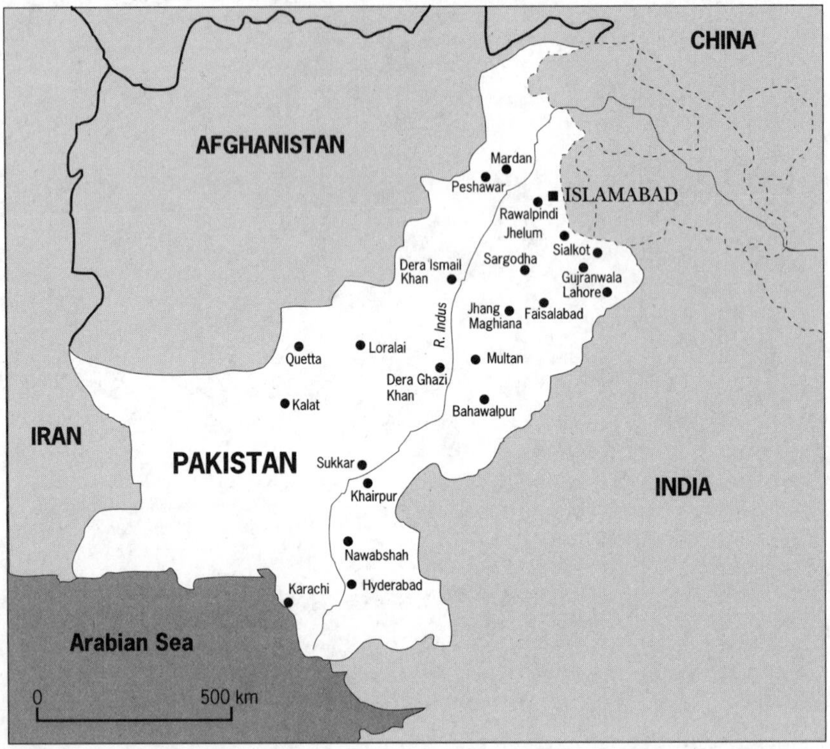

Asif Ali Zardari was sworn in as President of Pakistan in September 2008. Mr Zardari followed in the footsteps of his father-in-law, Zulfikar Ali Bhutto who was hanged for treason in 1979, and his wife, Benazir Bhutto who was murdered by an assassin at the beginning of 2008.

Uncertainties

President Zardari is by any reckoning a political novice, having at the age of 53 spent 10 years in jail following unproven allegations of corruption before which he was better known as a playboy than as a politician. Zardari had, however, demonstrated a degree of political resolve and cunning as he simultaneously orchestrated the resignation of Musharraf and the political sidelining of his principal rival Nawaz Sherif within the ruling coalition.

International concern over Pakistan's immediate future focussed on an increased threat from Afghanistan-based Taliban insurgents and a worsening economy that looked likely to need international assistance to avoid default. The US, Pakistan's principal supporter and bank-roller appeared to have taken heart from Zardari's appointment, strengthening its military presence in Pakistan. President Zardari had expressed his views on the ineffectual efforts of Pakistan's military against the Taliban although at the time of his election it was unclear exactly what he proposed to do to improve matters. Mr Zardari's party, the Pakistan People's Party founded by his hanged father-in-law has not managed its relations with Pakistan's army with much success. In the army, and more generally within Pakistan, Zardari's past is viewed with a combination of disapproval and suspicion. In the run up to the election, Zardari's approval rating never reached more than 26 per cent. His first challenge was to balance Pakistan's American support against a largely anti-American popular sentiment.

Pakistan is a complex country to understand. It is composed of four provinces – Baluchistan, the North West Frontier Province, Punjab and Sind: one of its greatest difficulties – and to a degree one of its successes – has been to try to weld the four into one Pakistan. The differences between the provinces are noticeable in every aspect: topographical, geographical, political and economic. Since independence in 1947 Pakistan has been dominated by the Punjab. Traditionally the Punjab provided the soldiers of the British Raj, a tradition which continued as Pakistan's army was very much a Punjab institution. Given the key role played by the army in Pakistani affairs, the Punjabi influence is significant.

India-Pakistan relations

The two countries have gone to war three times since partition and independence in 1947, twice over the border area of Kashmir. The disputed region of Kashmir has been the site of a 17-year violent uprising in which over 40,000 people have been killed. In early 2005 an election was held for the first time in nearly 30 years. Turnout was high despite widespread intimidation and five deaths. Pakistan has said that it wants a referendum to be held on the position of Kashmir, but India has resisted these calls.

India wants the line of control (LoC) that divides the Kashmir region to have the status of an international border whereas Pakistan will concede only to it being a 'soft border'. Previously then president Musharraf demanded that a deal on Kashmir be a prerequisite to normalising relations with India; in 2005, however, to the pleasure of US diplomats, he allowed the dispute to be put on the back burner while progress was made in other areas.

In August 2005 India and Pakistan reached a nuclear accord promising to give notice to the other before launching ballistic missile tests. The pact formalises an up-to-now informal notification system and tighten links between the two countries.

Earthquake after effects

The effects of the earthquake in October 2005 were still being felt in early 2008, mostly because of continuing allegations of corruption and misuse of aid funds. The earthquake, with a force of 7.6 on the Richter scale, hit Pakistan badly with a death toll of 73,000 and millions of people rendered homeless. It was the worst natural disaster the country has ever experienced. India's aid offerings were accepted, but not their search and rescue troops, on the basis of security concerns. Musharraf was roundly condemned for his rejection of what could have been crucial help in the immediate aftermath of the disaster. While Indian and Pakistani authorities were not immediately present, radical Islamic groups were, offering food and assistance and helping bolster their reputations among the Kashmiri population. Musharraf admitted that some extremist groups under official surveillance, Jamaat-ud-Dawa and Al-Rasheed Trust, were among the most active in relief efforts.

Economy

Musharraf and his government gained some credit for the fact that initially Pakistan's economy had recovered from years of sluggishness, caused primarily by droughts. GDP growth peaked at 8.0 per cent in 2005. Growth was principally seen in the agriculture, industry and service sectors. However, by the time Zardari took office in the third quarter of 2008, the economy had hit a down turn. Inflation had risen, reserves and inward investment were down and the rupee was down against the US dollar by almost 25 per cent.

Pakistan achieved gross domestic product (GDP) growth of 6.4 per cent in 2007, down on the 7.9 per cent of 2006. Inflation remained high at 7.7 per cent in 2007, but then reached a record 25 per cent in August 2008, the rise being attributed to escalating food and oil prices, higher housing rents and food item shortages. The International Monetary Fund (IMF), and the World Bank, both major donor organisations to Pakistan, have acknowledged the progress in Pakistan's structural reforms, but have stressed that even greater reforms are needed in the public institutions and the public energy sectors where progress has been slow.

The economy under Musharraf had also been boosted by high levels of inward investment, supporting the government's ambitious privatisation programme, and a busy large-scale manufacturing sector. FDI had doubled since 2000 to a current level of US$1 billion; in addition, US aid was around US$10 billion.

The demand for credit was very high partly due to a rise in imports of industrial machinery, and also due to activity in the textiles sector. Pakistan's credit bureau and the introduction of new safeguards are to be praised for this upturn. The budget deficit appeared to be under control at around 4 per cent of GDP, compared to figures of 7.5 per cent in the 1980s and 1990s. However, the 2005 earthquake is thought to have put inevitable pressure on the deficit figures, which are estimated to have risen to 4.1–4.3 per cent. The long-term reconstruction works continue

KEY INDICATORS Pakistan

	Unit	2003	2004	2005	2006	2007
Population	m	150.40	157.06	152.53	155.40	158.17
Gross domestic product (GDP)	US$bn	68.60	96.11	110.97	127.00	*143.77
GDP per capita	US$	470	550	728	817	*909
GDP real growth	%	5.1	6.5	8.0	6.9	*6.4
Inflation	%	3.2	6.7	9.3	7.9	7.7
Industrial output	% change	–	12.0	10.2	5.0	–
Agricultural output	% change	–	2.2	7.5	1.6	–
Natural gas output	bn cum	21.1	23.2	29.9	30.7	30.8
Coal output	mtoe	1.4	1.3	1.6	1.9	4.6
Exports (fob) (goods)	US$m	10,889.0	13,352.0	15,382.0	16,764.0	18,121.0
Imports (cif) (goods)	US$m	11,333.0	16,735.0	21,560.0	23,967.0	28,761.0
Balance of trade	US$m	-444.0	-3,382.0	-6,178.0	-7,203.0	-10,640.0
Current account	US$m	3,040.0	280.0	-1,534.0	-5,015.0	-7,105.0
Foreign debt	US$bn	32.3	35.7	35.2	–	–
Total reserves minus gold	US$m	10,941.0	9,799.0	10,033.0	11,543.0	14,044.0
Foreign exchange	US$m	10,693.0	9,554.0	9,817.0	11,328.0	13,829.0
Exchange rate	per US$	57.82	58.33	60.97	61.02	61.14

* estimated figure

to dent public finances despite foreign aid. Investor confidence was largely unaffected by the earthquake, demonstrated by the fact that the stock market passed the 9,000 points mark soon afterwards, demonstrating a general business confidence. The stock market later broke the 10,000 barrier, claiming to be the best performing exchange in the world.

Outlook

The economic fundamentals are robust and healthy – it is political events which threaten to upset the country's economy. Unrest, uprisings and extremism will all undermine performance. Rising global oil prices will undermine GDP growth and the credit sector. Mr Zardari will have his work cut out to meet the challenges of this vibrant but unruly country. Principal among these challenges will be how to deal with his one-time coalition partner, Nawaz Sharif, leader of the Pakistan Muslim League-Nawaz (PML-N). Unlike his predecessor, nor does Mr Zardari have cordial relations with the army, who have yet to state their intentions. Chief of staff, General Kiyani, has said that the army will stand back from politics, but that was while his former colleague, Pervez Musharraf, was running the show. Nor does the PPP have a clear majority in parliament. All in all the next six months will prove tricky for Mr Zardari.

Risk assessment

Politics	Poor
Economy	Fair
Regional stability	Poor

COUNTRY PROFILE

Historical profile

1906 The Muslim League was founded to promote Indian Muslim separatism.
1940 The Muslim League endorsed the idea of a separate nation for Indian Muslims.
1947 Pakistan, (including East Pakistan or what is now Bangladesh), was granted independence as a British Dominion following the partition of the British Indian Empire. The ruler of the Muslim-majority states of Jammu and Kashmir joined secular India rather than Islamic Pakistan. India and Pakistan have disputed Kashmir ever since.
1948 Muhammed Ali Jinnah, the first governor general of Pakistan, died. Pakistan and India fought over the disputed territory of Kashmir.
1951 Liaquat Ali Khan, Jinnah's successor, was assassinated.
1956 The Islamic Republic of Pakistan was proclaimed.
1958 Martial law was declared and General Ayub Khan took power.
1960 Ayub Khan became president.
1965 Pakistan and India fought over Kashmir.
1969 General Yahya Khan took control when Ayub Khan resigned.
1970 Tensions between East and West Pakistan escalated following the separatist Awami League's success in the general elections.
1971 A civil war broke out when East Pakistan attempted to secede. India intervened in support of East Pakistan, which broke away to become Bangladesh.
1972 The Simla peace agreement set a new LoC in Kashmir; India and Pakistan agreed to settle the dispute through peaceful and mutual means.
1973 Zulfiqar Ali Bhutto became prime minister.
1977 Allegations that Bhutto's party, Pakistan People's Party (PPP) won the general elections due to vote-rigging sparked widespread civil disturbances. General Zia ul Haq led a military coup d'état and deposed Bhutto.
1978 General Zia became president.
1979 The deposed prime minister Zulfiqar Ali Bhutto was hanged, having been convicted of murdering a political rival, (in a trial that was widely condemned as unfair).
1980 The US pledged military assistance to Pakistan in order to strengthen the Islamist opposition to the Soviet occupation in Afghanistan.
1985 After nearly eight years of martial law, parliamentary democracy with a civilian prime minister was reintroduced.
1986 Benazir Bhutto, (the daughter of former prime minister Bhutto), returned from exile to lead the PPP.
1988 Former military dictator and president, Zia ul Haq, remained pre-eminent until he died with the US ambassador and top Pakistani army officers in a mysterious air crash in August. Chaiman of the Senate, Ghulam Ishaq Khan, became Acting President. General elections on a party basis were finally allowed and were won by the PPP; Benazir Bhutto became Pakistan's first woman prime minister.
1990 President Ghulam Ishaq Khan dismissed Bhutto on charges of incompetence and corruption in August; Ghulam Mustafa Jatoi became caretaker prime minister until elections were held in October and Nawaz Sharif (Pakistan Muslim League (PML)) was elected prime minister in November.
1991 Sharif began a programme of economic liberalisation and incorporated Sharia (Islamic law) into the legal code.
1993 President Khan dismissed Prime Minister Sharif (for corruption) although the Supreme Court quashed the presidential order and Sharif was reinstated. However, both president and prime minister were forcedto resign in July. In the elections that followed, Farooq Ahmad Khan Leghari was elected president and Benazir Bhutto returned to power after winning the general elections and formed a government by allying with a number of smaller parties.
1996 President Leghari dismissed Bhutto's government for corruption.
1997 The Pakistan Muslim League (PML) won the elections and Sharif returned to power as prime minister.
1998 Muhammad Rafiq Tarar took office as president on 1 January. India and Pakistan conducted underground nuclear tests, leading to widespread international condemnation and US sanctions.
1999 Bhutto and her husband were convicted of corruption and given jail sentences in absentia; they remained in exile. Over 1,000 people died in clashes between Pakistani and Indian forces around Kargil in Kashmir. In October General Pervez Musharraf led a military coup that deposed Sharif. Pakistan was expelled from the Commonwealth.
2000 US President Bill Clinton visited and urged a return to democracy. Sharif was sentenced to life imprisonment on hijacking and terrorism charges, but was later pardoned and sent into exile in Saudi Arabia.
2001 General Musharraf assumed the presidency (dismissing the incumbent President Tarar) and dissolved parliament. Musharraf backed the US war on terrorism in Afghanistan, which led to the US lifting some of the sanctions imposed after the 1998 nuclear testing. Two Pakistan-backed Kashmir militant groups attacked India's parliament; India imposed sanctions.
2002 Musharraf took steps to curb religious extremism and banned two militant groups. He consolidated his power after a referendum, which was criticised as unconstitutional, approved his presidency for a further five years. Following the October general election, Mir Zafarullah Khan Jamali was elected prime minister. Tension between India and Pakistan increased and only intense diplomatic efforts prevented war.
2003 A cease-fire began across the LoC, dividing the disputed state of Kashmir and the Himalayan glacier Siachen – the first formal cease-fire since the insurgency began in 1989. After a two-year ban, Pakistan and India agreed to resume direct air links and allow over-flights. President Musharraf survived an assassination attempt.
2004 The Prime Minister of India, Atal Bihari Vajpayee, visited Pakistan for a meeting with President Musharraf.

Pakistan was re-admitted to the Commonwealth. On 26 June, Prime Minister Jamali resigned; Shaukat Aziz was elected by the National Assembly and sworn in as prime minister on 28 August.
2005 The first bus-link for 57 years between divided India- and Pakistan-held Kashmir commenced on 8 April. Not only did the Pakistani cricket team return victorious in May from its first tour of India in six years, but diplomatic relations were also boosted. Pakistan, Bhutan, Bangladesh, India, Maldives, Nepal and Sri Lanka signed the South Asia Free Trade Agreement (Safta), to come into effect on 1 January 2006.
2006 A third bus link between Pakistan and India was launched in January – the service (Lahore-Amritsar) became the first direct link across divided Punjab since partition in 1947. In July, the Muttahida Qaumi Movement (MQM), withdrew from the government coalition in protest at their party's exclusion from Sindh province's administration. Pakistan test-fired several nuclear-capable short-range ballistic missiles in November and December.
2007 On 12 March, President Musharraf suspended the chief justice, Iftikhar Chaudhary, on charges of misconduct and misuse of authority, leading to country-wide protests and a constitutional crisis. He was reinstated in July after a ruling by the Supreme Court of Pakistan on 20 July which reversed the president's suspension. On 24 July the leader of the Muttahida Majlis e Amal (MMA), Pakistan's biggest Islamic party, resigned his seat to protest against moves to allow President Musharraf to stand for a second term. Former president Nawaz Sharif's exile was lifted by the Supreme Court in August; however, when he attempted to return on 10 September he was accused of corruption and money laundering and sent back into exile in Saudi Arabia. Following the decision by the Supreme Court on 28 September that General Pervez Musharraf was eligible to stand in the presidential election, 86 opposition members of parliament resigned in protest. Federal parliament and provincial lawmakers (1,170 in total) re-elected Pervez Musharraf as president by 671 votes against 8 for Wajihuddin Ahmad; 6 votes were invalid. A state of emergency was declared on 14 November, allowing the President to purge the Supreme Court, which was believed to be on the verge of ruling against his re-election.
Mohammadmian Soomro was sworn in as interim prime minister on 16 November. On 21 November the reconstituted Supreme Court rejected the final legal challenge to President Musharraf's re-election. Commonwealth leaders suspended Pakistan's membership on 23 November, declaring that President Musharraf's emergency rule was 'unreasonable and unjustified'. On 26 November, Nawaz Sharif, returned from Saudi Arabia to participate in the presidential elections. He may however, boycott the elections, if calls for Musharraf to lift the state of emergency go unheeded. Musharraf stepped down as head of the armed forces on 28 November, as required by the Supreme Court, before taking up his second term as President. The state of emergency was lifted on 15 December. On 27 December, the former prime minister, Benazir Bhutto, was assassinated in a suicide attack. Following the reading of her will, her son Bilawal Bhutto Zardari was appointed as the leader of the PPP, although daily control will be held by her husband, Asif Ali Zardari. The Electoral Commission postponed parliamentary elections from January to 18 February.
2008 Investigators from Scotland Yard, London, concluded that Benazir Bhutto had not been shot by an assassin but had died from a head injury. The announcement, made on 8 February, was disputed by the PPP. In parliamentary elections held on 18 February the opposition parties PPP and PML-N together gained more seats (171 seats out of 342) than PML-QA (51 seats), which backed the president. On 9 March a coalition agreement between the PPP and PML-N to form a government was signed, others political parties including Awami National Party (ANP) and the PML-QA were also included. Parliament elected Makhdoom Syed Yousaf Raza Gilani as prime minister on 24 March; he took up his post the next day. Former prime minister Nawaz Sharif was banned by a court from standing in elections because he had been convicted of a crime.Unless the rulng is overturned he will not be able to become prime minister. President Musharraf resigned on 18 August, following parliamentary threats of impeachment. Mohammadmian Soomro became interim president for the 30 days until another presidential election was organised. Asif Zardari was nominated by the PPP. On 25 August the government banned the Taleban militant group, Tehreek e Taleban Pakistan (TPP). The group was said to have been behind a number of suicide attacks in the country. The ruling coalition collapsed on 25 August when the PML-N split over a dispute about reinstating the judges previously dismissed by Musharraf.

Political structure

Constitution

The federal constitution comprises four semi-autonomous provinces – Punjab, Sindh, North West Frontier Province (NWFP) and Baluchistan – as well as federally administered tribal areas (FATAs) and the federal capital area (FCA) of Islamabad. The constitution is an amended version of one promulgated in 1973.
In October 2002, parliament and regional assemblies were elected for the first time since they were suspended following the military take-over led by General Pervez Musharraf in October 1999.
Everyone over the age of 18 years and who is not deemed insane is allowed to vote. The president is chosen by the four provional election and the two chambers of parliament.

Form of state

Federal Islamic republic

The executive

Prior to the October 1999 military coup, executive power rested with the cabinet, responsible to parliament and headed by the prime minister.
On 15 October 1999, executive power was vested in General Pervez Musharraf, who took the title of chief executive, and replaced the cabinet with a National Security Council (NSC), composed of military officers. He subsequently made himself president on 20 June 2001. His rule was extended by five years after a referendum in April 2002 and he granted himself sweeping new powers, including the right to dismiss an elected parliament. A bill to allow President Pervez Musharraf to remain as army chief as well as president was signed into law in December 2004.

National legislature

The Majlis-i-Shura (parliament) has two chambers: the National Assembly and the Senate. The National Assembly has 342 members and is elected every five years, with 272 members elected in single-seat constituencies on a first-past-the-post basis, 60 female members chosen by the parties in accordance with their share of seats and 10 seats for minority groups, including religious minorities and the Quadiani and Lahori tribes. The National Assembly elects the prime minister from among its members.
The Senate has 100 members elected by the provincial assemblies. The four provinces are allocated 14 seats each, while the federally administered tribal areas (FATA) are assigned eight directly elected seats. The Federal Capital Area (FCA) is awarded two seats, distributed to parties on the basis of their support in the national assembly elections. Each province is also allocated four seats for technocrats and the Islamic clergy and four seats for women. A further two seats, one for technocrats and another for women, are allocated to the FCA.

Legal system
The Supreme Court is the highest court of justice. Each of the four provinces has a High Court. The Federal Sharia (Islamic) Court hears appeals against the decisions of lower courts under Islamic laws in force concurrently with ordinary laws, and its decisions can be appealed before a Sharia Appellate Bench of the Supreme Court.
Each province is divided into a number of districts, each of which is under the judicial jurisdiction, both civil and criminal, of a principal court presided over by a district or sessions judge. Subordinate civil judges and magistrates dispense justice at lower levels of the judicial hierarchy.
Following the coup of 12 October 1999, the army declined to adopt martial law. Therefore, the judicial system continues to operate.

Last elections
18 February 2008 (parliamentary); 6 October 2007 (presidential vote in parliamentary).
Results: Parliamentary: the PPP won 120 seats (out of 342) PML-N 90, PML-QA 51 and Muttahida Qaumi Movement (MQM) 25. (11 seats remain undecided in March 2008).
Presidential referendum: Pervez Musharraf won 671 votes; Wajihuddin Ahmad won six; six votes were invalid.

Next elections
February 2013 (parliamentary)

Political parties

Ruling party
Coalition led by the Pakistan People's Party (PPP) with Pakistan Muslem League-Nawaz (PML-N), Pakistan Muslim League-Qaid e Azam (PML-QA), Awami National Party (ANP), Jamiat Ulema e Islam (JUI) (Assembly of Islamic Clergy) and Muttahida Qaumi Movement (MQM) (from 9 Mar 2008)

Main opposition party

Population

152.53 million (2007)*
Last census: March 1998: 130,579,571
Population density: 189 inhabitants per square km (2003). Urban population: 33 per cent (1995–2001). Rural population density: 395 residents per square km.
Annual growth rate: 2.3 per cent 1994–2004 (WHO 2006)

Ethnic make-up
Punjabi, Sindhi, Pashtun, Baluchi and others including Mohajirs (Muslim emigrés from India). The populations are relatively homogeneous in Punjab, Baluchistan and North Western Frontier Province (NWFP) (predominantly Pashtun), but Sindh is more diverse, with many non-Sindhi communities in the cities of Karachi and Hyderbad. Precise ethnicity statistics are unobtainable, but a regional population breakdown can be used as an approximate estimate of ethnic proportions in the country as a whole. The most recent figures are as follows: Punjab (56 per cent), Sindh (23 per cent), NWFP (13 per cent) and Baluchistan (5 per cent).
Pakistan is home to millions of Afghan refugees and to one million illegal immigrants from Bangladesh, Sri Lanka, Iran, Iraq and India.

Religions
Islam 97 per cent, Christianity 1.5 per cent, Hinduism 1.5 per cent.

Education

More than 200,000 extra teachers have been recruited since 2001, most under US donor funding estimated at US$10 million.
The government proposes to establish an international centre of computer science in collaboration with the European Centre of Nuclear Physics. Free internet connections have been extended to public sector universities. A nationwide network of schools called the National Centres for the Rehabilitation of Child Labour (NCRCL) has been set up with 33 schools in areas where child labour is rampant.
Literacy rate: 42 per cent adult rate; 54 per cent youth rate (15–24) (Unesco 2005).
Compulsory years: Five to 15
Enrolment rate: 40 per cent in secondary schools.
Pupils per teacher: 40 in primary schools.

Health

Per capita total expenditure on health (2003) was US$48; of which per capita government spending was US$13, (WHO 2006).
Many in poorer rural areas have limited access to healthcare facilities. Although there have been improvements in provision, facilities remain relatively poor, and there are still fewer than 800 hospitals for the entire country, providing less than one hospital bed for every 1,000 people.
Pakistani authorities have made some efforts to provide increased preventive health care. Particular attention has been given to the provision of safe drinking water supplies, and the government claims that about 88 per cent of the Pakistani population have access to safe drinking water. The World Bank estimates that this is accurate for urban areas only, and the figure among the rural population is thought to be lower, with only about 50 per cent having access to proper sanitation.
The main objectives for the Ninth Five-Year Plan (1998–2003) were to increase the Contraceptive Prevalence Rate (CPR) from 24.4 per cent to 40.3 per cent by the end of 2003 and reduce the population growth from 2.4 per cent to 1.9 per cent for the same period. Latest estimates for 2003 puts the population growth at 2.1 per cent.
Some areas of the country's health services improved over the previous decade, including better access to immunisation and family planning services. Low government expenditure and the poor quality of private health care continue to be a problem. One quarter of the national budget is spent on the military, compared with less than 7 per cent on health.
Polio is endemic. In 2006, the number of cases rose slightly, however the World Health Organisation – Global Polio Eradication Initiative (WHO – Polio Eradication) said that improvements in vaccination programmes could only be successful when the central government and the Federally Administered Tribal Areas (FATA) region of North West Frontier Province (NWFP) in particular were fully engaged with the problem. Pakistan liaises with Afghanistan concerning the shared corridor of transmission in the NWFP and southern Afghanistan.

HIV/Aids
HIV prevalence: 0.1 per cent aged 15–49 in 2003 (World Bank)
Life expectancy: 62 years, 2004 (WHO 2006)
Fertility rate/Maternal mortality rate: 4.1 births per woman, 2004 (WHO 2006)
Birth rate/Death rate: 9.51 deaths to 32.11 births per 1,000 people (World Bank).
Child (under 5 years) mortality rate (per 1,000): 74 per 1,000 live births (2003); 38 per cent of children aged under five are malnourished (World Bank).
Head of population per physician: 0.74 physician per 1,000 people, 2004 (WHO 2006)

Welfare

A Poverty Alleviation Programme includes pension, death and marriage grants, and a policy formulated for the elimination of bonded and child labour. An estimated 40 per cent of the urban population lives in slums or other poor housing areas.

Main cities

Islamabad (capital, estimated population 955,629 in 2005), Karachi (12.2 million (m)), Lahore (6.4m), Lyallpur (2.5m), Faisalabad (2.5m), Rawalpindi (1.7m), Gujranwala (1.6m), Multan (1.5m), Hyderabad (1.3m), Peshawar (1.5m).

Media

National news agency: 18 Mauve Area, G-7/1, Islamabad (Tel: 220-3064–67; email: news@app.com.pk; internet: www.app.com.pk) (state run).

Press
Legislation gives the government powers to close media and Internet outlets. Foreign correspondents are allowed to move freely in Pakistan, but are barred from some border areas.
Dailies: There are over 100 national and regional daily newspapers representing all local languages with around 25 published either in English or as an English version of a local language.
In English, Dawn (www.dawn.com) is the leading newspaper; others include Daily Times (www.dailytimes.com.pk), Nation (www.nation.com.pk), Post (www.thepost.com.pk), Karachi News (www.kashmirnews.com), Daily Mail (http://dailymailnews.com), Statesman (www.statesman.com.pk) and Pakistan Observer (www.pakobserver.net).
In Urdu, the leading newspaper is Daily Jang (www.jang.com.pk), others include Daily Khabrain (www.khabrain.com), Daily Nawa i Waqt (www.nawaiwaqt.com.pk), Daily Al Akbar (www.alakhbar.com.pk), Daily Ausaf (www.dailyausaf.com), Daily Millat (www.millat.com) and Daily Asas (www.dailyasas.com.pk). In Sindh, the largest circulation is Daily Kawish (www.dailykawish.com) and the Daily Ibrat (www.dailyibrat.com).
Weeklies: In English, The Friday Times (www.thefridaytimes.com) is an independent newspaper; magazines include the Herald (www.dawn.com/herald), Newline (www.newsline.com.pk) and Weekly Cutting Edge (www.weeklycuttingedge.com). In Urdo, Akhbar e Jehan (www.akhbar-e-jehan.com).
Business: Two English publications include Pakistan and Gulf Economist (www.pakistaneconomist.com), (international magazine, HQ Karachi) and Business Recorder (www.brecorder.com), (daily newspaper also in Sindh).
Periodicals: Almost all major foreign magazines are available in Pakistan, although specific issues may be banned from time to time if they carry material deemed offensive to Islam or critical of Pakistan.
Broadcasting
The Pakistan Electronic Regulatory Authority (Pemra) (www.pemra.gov.pk) is the official organisation that regulates broadcast operations. There are state controlled and privately operated radio and television stations.
Only a Pakistani national or permanent resident may own and operate a broadcast company.
Radio: The state-run Pakistan Broadcasting Corporation (PBC) (www.radio.gov.pk) operates a nationwide service as well as regional and local services. It also operates a range of external services in 15 languages.
Television: The Pakistan Television Corporation (PTV) (www.ptv.com.pk) provides national as well as regional services. In 2002 the first private satellite TV station licenses were issued, by 2007, 20 had been granted and were operational. DawnNews is an English language news channel. ATV (terrestrial); Aaj TV, Indus TV and Ary Digital are satellite stations.
Films shown on television are censored to meet conservative Islamic standards of morality.
In June 2008 the authorities in UAE, asked Geo TV news channel to suspend transmission of two talk shows that were critical of President Musharraf. It is assumed that Pakistan put pressure on the UAE. Geo TV announced that rather than stop transmissions of 'objective and unbiased' information to millions of Urdu-speaking people worldwide it might move its operations to either the UK or Hong Kong.
Advertising
Advertising is available in the press, in cinemas and on commercial radio and television.

Economy
Pakistan's large population makes it a poor, under-developed country with high levels of poverty. Efforts to improve conditions have to keep pace with a huge and continuously growing population and the consequent pressures on land and water resources. Pakistan is able to meet much of its energy requirements from domestic coal, gas and hydro- electricity sources, but there is still a gap between supply and demand which inhibits manufacturing capacity and which has to be filled by the import of oil from the Middle East.
Since 2001, the economy has experienced strong growth, as the government of President Musharraf has pursued a programme of reform under IMF auspices. At the same time, foreign aid has increased, the national debt has been restructured and export markets for agricultural and manufactured goods have opened up. Expenditure on development projects has been increased over recent years, helping to reduce the poverty level by around 10 per cent.
The health of the economy is determined to some extent by the strength of the agricultural sector, which accounts for over 20 per cent of GDP and employs around 40 per cent of the work-force. The main crops are cotton, of which Pakistan is one the world's principal growers, wheat, tobacco, rice and sugar-cane. Other expanding sectors, especially large-scale manufacturing, telecommunications and financial services, are also significant contributors to Pakistan's growing economy.
The functioning of the economy in the provinces can be beyond the control of central government, especially in North West Frontier Province and Baluchistan. In the former, the distance from the capital and intense poverty, as well as its proximity to Afghanistan, have combined to create an area dominated by heroin processing and arms smuggling. In Baluchistan, an area rich in gas reserves (which the country needs, given declining reserves elsewhere), local tribesmen resent the arrival of foreign oil and gas exploration teams to the extent that the kidnapping and ransom of foreign workers is not uncommon.
The government announced in July 2007 that the annual FDI for 2006 was US$2 billion and was 25 per cent greater that the projected amount, due mainly to investment in banking, telecommunications, oil and gas.

External trade
Pakistan is a member of South Asia Association for Regional Co-operation, which operates a preferential trading arrangement that covers 6,000 products. In 2004 the South Asia Free Trade Area (Safta) was ratified, to be implemented between the seven member states (Bangladesh, Bhutan, India, Maldives, Nepal, Pakistan and Sri Lanka) by 2012.
Foreign exchange revenue is achieved from firstly textiles and garment production, then remittances and thirdly cotton (Pakistan is the fourth largest producer, worldwide), combined with shipping and industrial manufacturing foreign trade accounts for about 35 per cent of GDP.
Imports
Main imports include petroleum and derivatives, capital machinery, plastics, vehicles, edible oils, paper products, iron, steel and tea.
Main sources: UAE (11.9 per cent total, 2006), Saudi Arabia (10.5 per cent), China (9.5 per cent).
Exports
Main exports include textiles (garments, bed linen, cotton cloth, and yarn), cotton, rice, leather goods, sports goods, chemicals, carpets and rugs, oil, natural gas and fertilizers.
Main destinations: US (25.4 per cent total, 2006), UAE (8.2 per cent), Afghanistan (6.4 per cent).

Agriculture
Farming
Agriculture represents around a quarter of GDP and is the driver of the economy, supplying food and raw materials for the manufacturing sector. Sustainable economic development requires long-term growth in agriculture. Main food crops

include wheat, rice, maize, barley, millet, sorghum, sugar cane, tobacco, groundnuts, pulses, potatoes, onions, mangoes and citrus fruit. Cotton is the main cash crop and the largest foreign exchange earner, with productivity rising as greater use is made of insecticides. Rice is also an important export. Livestock production includes goats, sheep, cattle, buffaloes, pigs, donkeys, horses, mules, camels and poultry, and accounts for around 7.5 per cent of GDP, providing meat, eggs, dairy products, leather and wool, as well as draught power and fertiliser for cultivation. There are around 27 million hectares available for agriculture. Typically 26 per cent of agricultural land is given over to arable crops, while 6.25 per cent is permanent pasture. There are grazing difficulties in border regions, where Afghan refugees have brought about three million head of cattle with them.

The agricultural policies pursued by successive governments have traditionally been geared towards attaining self-sufficiency in the production of foodstuffs, increasing cash crop production and maximising foreign exchange earnings from the export of agricultural commodities such as cotton and rice. There was a record cotton crop harvested in 2004, which was attributed to an increase in area cultivated and productivity through the use of fertilisers.

In 2005, the government removed the 25 per cent import duty on imported raw and refined sugar. The removal was prompted by an expected shortfall of about a half a million tonnes in sugar. The sugar cane harvest was lower than expected as some farmers switched some land use over to cotton growing in expectation of higher profits, which resulted in local sugar prices rising sharply. Cane growers are critical of the poor condition of canals that provide an inadequate irrigation system, which currently hampers production. They are pressing for long-term investment to provide new dams and improve the canal network.

Owing to a shortage of unused cultivatable land, planners have concentratied on increased yields per hectare rather than an expansion of planted acreage. The government announced support for procurement prices for all major crops before sowing, and has encouraged farmers to adopt modern cultivation practices by providing them with subsidised inputs such as chemical fertilisers, pesticides and improved seed varieties. As the use of these inputs has become more popular and the government's budgetary constraints have become more pressing, these subsidies are gradually being phased out, but farmers are being compensated through rising crop prices.

The extended use of pesticides and fertilisers has been accompanied by a selective mechanisation of farm operations, facilitated by a liberal import policy for farm machinery and an expansion of domestic manufacturing capacity for the production of agricultural equipment. Mechanisation has become a routine operation for small farmers, who hire harvester's from richer farmers, and gain a higher yield in return. Farmers have called on the government to address the problems constraining the agricultural sector by allowing them a three-year remission period on their debts, deregulation, improving irrigation and water use and waiving tax and loan recovery in the areas worst hit by drought.

Special attention is being given to the problems of small farmers who suffer mainly from a lack of finance. To alleviate this problem, the government has traditionally adopted a liberal stance towards the provision of rural credit, which is disbursed by the state-run Agricultural Development Bank of Pakistan (ADBP), commercial banks and co-operatives.

In July 2004 the rupee was devalued and rice exports became more competitively priced at US$10 a tonne cheaper than regional competitors.

Crop production in 2005 included: 32,214,600 tonnes (t) cereals in total, 21,591,400t wheat, 7,351,000t rice, 2,797,000t maize, 2,024,300t potatoes, 47,244,100t sugar cane, 1,241,600t pulses, 1,673,900t mangoes, 1,670,000t citrus fruit, 171,936t various spices, 7,279,400t seed cotton, 2,426,500t cotton lint, 412,900t tomatoes, 84,400t tobacco, 43,500t treenuts in total, 1,159,747t oilcrops, 625,000t dates, 5,751,800t fruits in total, 5,071,639t vegetables in total. Livestock production included: 1,972,580t meat in total, 531,000t buffalo meat, 469,000t beef, 166,000t lamb, 370,000t goat meat, 420,680t poultry, 407,200t eggs, 29,474,000t milk, 1,500t honey, 96,000t cattle hides, 124,270t goatskins, 42,000t sheepskins, 40,000t greasy wool.

Fishing

Pakistan is largely self-sufficient in freshwater fish and seafood, with an active fishing fleet operating out of Karachi and on the Indus river. The typical annual fish catch is around 600,000 tonnes, of which 380,000 tonnes is through marine fishing. Around 87,000 tonnes of fish is exported, almost all of which is freshwater fish.

In 2004, the total marine fish catch was 347,945 tonnes and the total crustacean catch was 30,569 tonnes.

Forestry

Forests cover only 17,000 square kilometres, equivalent to 3 per cent of the country. A higher level of forestation is needed to improve the quality of the environment, reducing the severity of flooding and the impact of strong winds and sandstorms. The authorities have encouraged a growth in forests, with forest cover increasing by an average of 1.84 per cent per annum.

Around 90 per cent of Pakistan's wood production is used for fuel. Wood and wood-based products contribute little to external trade while timber imports in 2004 were US$325 million.

Timber production in 2004 included 28,277,952 cubic metre (cum) roundwood, 2,679,000cum industrial roundwood, 1,180,000cum sawnwood, 1,892,000cum sawlogs and veneer logs, 354,000cum wood-based panels, 25,598,952cum woodfuel; 61,294 tonnes (t) charcoal, 700,000t paper and paperboard, (including 138,000t newsprint), 160,000t printing and writing paper, 588,000t paper pulp, 670,000t recovered paper.

Industry and manufacturing

Industry contributes around 25 per cent to annual GDP, employing an estimated 17 per cent of the labour force.

Manufactured and semi-manufactured goods, mainly cotton textiles and garments, account for around 60 per cent of Pakistan's exports. The manufacturing sector depends on the agricultural sector for most of its raw materials: cotton for weaving, spinning and processing industries, leather and wool for handicrafts and carpet weaving. There is a growing emphasis on private sector development, with around 85 per cent of manufacturing output in private hands.

Tourism

Tourism has been slow to develop, hampered by lack of facilities and infrastructure as well as fears of terrorist attacks, hijackings and kidnappings which are endemic in some areas of the country. A large proportion of visitors tend to be overseas Pakistanis and their families. The sector collapsed in 2003, in the wake of the September 2001 terrorist attacks in the US and two major earthquakes in November 2002, but has seen a recovery in the following years. There were 648,000 arrivals in 2004, a 29.4 per cent increase on the previous year. The improvement of relations with India resulted in the opening of borders and easing of movement between the two countries and there was an increase in the number of visitors from other Asian countries.

Environment

In its efforts to improve living standards for its citizens Pakistan has compromised environmental standards in favour of economic development. Hazardous chemicals, including agricultural run-off, industrial activity and vehicle emissions all add to pollution in general and water contamination in particular.

Mining

Pakistan has deposits of a wide range of minerals, including uranium, rock phosphate, gypsum, iron ore, copper, gold, silver, magnesium, chromite, antimony, barite, rock salt, sulphur, porcelain, china clays and gemstones.

The government is seeking to enhance the role of the mining sector, which has historically played a negligible role in the Pakistan economy. In the past, priority has been given to the further development of rock phosphate mining at Kakul in the North West Frontier Province and the establishment of copper and iron ore mines at Saindak and Nokundi in Baluchistan. These projects have been delayed by insufficient investment, economic inviability and the poor quality of reserves.

Pakistan typically produces nine million tonnes of limestone, 800,000 tonnes of rock salt, 300,000 tonnes of argonite and marble, 30,000 tonnes of barytes, 30,000 tonnes of soap stone, 15,000 tonnes of sulphur, 2–3,000 tonnes of bauxite and 23 tonnes of uranium per annum.

Hydrocarbons

Pakistan had proven reserves of around 49 million cubic metres (cum) in 2004 and produced 60,000 barrels per day (bpd). There is no prospect of Pakistan becoming self-sufficient in oil. Domestic consumption stands at around 350,000 bpd. Pakistan is reliant on imports, which amount to around 18 million cum. Punjab and Sindh provinces produce all of Pakistan's oil output. The government wants to reduce dependency on imports and has encouraged foreign investment to boost production and raise domestic capacity. Exploration is taking place both onshore and offshore.

The state-owned Pakistan Petroleum is the largest exploration and production company as well as the largest gas production company; the government has plans to sell off 15 per cent of it to private investors.

Pakistan has a proven reserve of 75.8 billion cum of natural gas and produces 22.6 million cum per year, all of which is consumed domestically. Gas supplies around half of Pakistan's energy requirements. Consumption is growing and additional sources, including new fields in Pakistan and pipelines from Iran and Oman, are being explored. The most productive gas field is in Sui, producing 18.3 million cum per day.

Pakistan has estimated coal reserves of around 3,300 tonnes. Coal does not have a significant role in Pakistan's energy usage, but substantial new deposits of higher quality coal in the vicinity of Tharparkar should change its profile.

The government has set up the Gas Regulatory Authority (GRA) and Petroleum Regulatory Board (PRB) to separate out government functions from state-owned entities that are in the process of being privatised.

Energy

Pakistan has 18GW of electric generating capacity, with thermal plants making up 68 per cent, hydroelectricity making up 28 per cent and nuclear power contributing 2.6 per cent. Less than half the population is connected to the national grid and significant growth in demand is expected in the long-term.

Foreign investment has spurred rapid growth in the sector, helping to reduce the number of power cuts. Poor distribution infrastructure and electricity theft means that about 30 per cent of transmission is lost. Frequent droughts can also hamper electricity production.

Much of the energy sector is owned by the state and dominated by two parastatal utility companies: the Water and Power Development Authority (Wapda) and the Karachi Electricity Supply Company (KESC). Plans to privatise the two utility groups have made slow progress.

A number of independent power producers operate in Pakistan.

Financial markets

Stock exchange

Pakistan has three stock exchanges, located in Karachi, Lahore and Islamabad, of which the Karachi Stock Exchange (KSE) is the most important. Since the lifting of exchange controls in 1994, progress on the KSE has been disrupted by domestic and international upheaval.

Banking and insurance

The banking sector is dominated by state-owned banks: the United Bank Ltd (UBL), Habib Bank Ltd (HBL) and the National Bank of Pakistan (NBP).

In June 2002, the Islamic bench of Pakistan's Supreme Court reversed a decision made in 1999 to outlaw charging interest on bank transactions as un-Islamic. The move came less than a week ahead of a deadline by which all financial institutions had to conform to an Islamic system of banking, which prohibits fixed rates of interest. If the measures had gone ahead, Pakistan would have become the first country to adopt a pure Islamic system.

Banks had argued that full Islamicisation of the banking system would create chaos, leading to a possible collapse of the financial sector. Foreign banks were prepared to quit Pakistan if interest charging was abolished. International lenders were also wary of the changes, jeopardising Pakistan's ability to secure foreign loans.

Instead of converting to a fully Islamic financial system, Pakistan has effectively had to accept, at least in the medium-term, a dual system which allows Islamic and conventional banks to coexist.

The problem facing Pakistan is the high level of non-performing loans (NPLs) in the banking system caused mainly by economic mismanagement in the past.

The governor of the central bank, Ishrat Hussein, has indicated his desire to allow clients freedom of choice between Islamic and conventional banking.

Central bank

State Bank of Pakistan

Main financial centre

Karachi

Time

GMT plus five hours

Geography

Pakistan is a wedge-shaped country bordering India to the east, China to the north-east, Afghanistan to the north and Iran to the west. Its southern boundary is the shore of the Arabian Sea.

Pakistan has some of the hottest deserts and highest mountains in the world. The areas north of the capital Islamabad are mountainous, with a temperate climate. The world's second-highest mountain, K-2 (8,611 metres), also known as Mount Godwin Austen, is located in the Karakoram Range, where the Himalayas meet the Hindu Kush.

The plains of the Punjab and Sindh, irrigated by the Indus river and its tributaries, are the main agricultural areas. Apart from its temperate Makran coast on the Arabian Sea, Baluchistan is a vast and mostly empty area of deserts and low bare hills.

Hemisphere

Northern

Climate

The terrain ranges from mountainous to desert, and the climate varies accordingly. It is cool in the mountains and foothills, with rain in summer and snow in winter, and hot in summer and cool in winter in plateau regions, with some rain in winter. The Indus valley experiences year-round heat, with extreme heat and dry winds in summer. Temperatures vary from an average of 15 degrees Celsius (C) in January to an average of 37 degrees C in May–July. Summer temperatures can rise as high as 50 degrees C in northern Sindh and eastern Baluchistan. The monsoon season lasts from mid-July–September when the average monthly rainfall amounts to 16cm. The best time for tourists to visit is between October and April.

Dress codes
Pakistan is an Islamic country where modesty in dress is the rule. The widely worn national dress is the salwaar kameez, a unisex combination of baggy shirt and trousers completely covering the arms and legs. Western-style suits are seen only in big cities. Tourists are advised to dress modestly, especially when outside cities like Karachi, Lahore and Islamabad. Women are expected to dress soberly and act discreetly and a headscarf is essential when visiting holy places.

Entry requirements
Passports
Required by all and must be valid for six months beyond date of visit.
Visa
Required by all. Business travellers must provide, an invitation or sponsorship from a local company or organisation; a business letter of intention from an employer; a full itinerary; proof of financial guarantee of maintenance and emergency repatriation and proof of return/onward passage, with their application form. See www.mofa.gov.pk and follow link to consular services for full details and embassy locations worldwide.
Visitors staying over 30 days must register with the District Foreigners Registration Office within 30 days of arrival; over-staying the visa allowance can be treated as a criminal offence. Indian and Afghan visitors must register within 24 hours of arrival.
Prohibited entry
Israeli passport holders.
Currency advice/regulations
The import and export of local currency is limited to Rp100, in denominations up to Rp10 only. The import and export of foreign currency is unlimited; on departure, only amounts up to Rp500 may be reconverted into foreign currency and only with official exchange receipts.
Travellers cheques, in US dollars or pound sterling, are accepted in banks and major shops and hotels (all other currencies may attract higher exchange rates.
Customs
Personal effects are allowed duty-free. Visitors are not permitted to import alcohol. Motor vehicles may be imported duty-free for a period of up to three months. Export of certain antiques may require a permit.
Prohibited imports
Firearms and ammunition (without a permit), obscene and subversive publications. Fruit and plants may be destroyed to prevent agricultural diseases entering the country.

Health (for visitors)
Mandatory precautions
A vaccination certificate is required for yellow fever and cholera, if travelling from an infected area.
Advisable precautions
Inoculations and booster shots should be current for cholera, tetanus, hepatitis A, diphtheria, and typhoid. There may be a need for vaccinations for polio, tuberculosis, hepatitis B, Japanese B encephalitis and meningitis.
Use malaria prophylaxis (which will also provide protection for hepatitis B and encephalitis) including mosquito repellents, sleeping nets and clothing that cover the body after dark. There is a risk of rabies. Use only bottled or boiled water for drinks, washing teeth and making ice. Eat only well cooked meals, preferably served hot; vegetables should be cooked and fruit peeled. Avoid uncooked dairy products and salad, and food from street vendors. Healthcare facilities outside Islamabad and Karachi are limited, medical insurance is essential including emergency evacuation. A supply of any regular medicines required should be taken, with their prescription details and a full first-aid kit would be useful.

Hotels
There are modern hotels in major centres; price and quality can vary substantially and advanced booking is advised and a check of reservation before departure. A 17.5 per cent room tax is added to bills; further tipping optional.

Credit cards
Major credit cards are accepted in limited outlets. ATMs are found in city centres and at airports.

Public holidays (national)
Fixed dates
23 Mar (Pakistan Day), 1 May (May Day), 14 Aug (Independence Day), 9 Nov (Iqbal Day), 25 Dec (Birthday of Qaid-i-Azam/Christmas).
Variable dates
Eid al Adha (two days), Eid al Fitr (three days), Islamic New Year, Ashura (two days), Birth of the Prophet.
Islamic year – 1429 (10 Jan 2008–28 Dec 2008): The Islamic year contains 354 or 355 days, with the result that Muslim feasts advance by 10–12 days against the Gregorian calendar. Dates of feasts vary according to the sightings of the new moon, so cannot be forecast exactly.

Working hours
Banking
Mon–Thu and Sat: 0900–1330; Fri: 0900–1230.
Business
Mon–Thu and Sat: 0900–1700; Fri: 0900–1230, 1430–1700.
Government
Mon–Thu and Sat: 0900–1700; Fri: 0900–1230.
Shops
Sat–Thu: 0800/0900–1800/1900.

Electricity supply
220–240V AC, with two or three-pin round plug fittings.

Weights and measures
Metric system (local units are also in use).

Social customs/useful tips
It is customary to shake hands on meeting and taking leave; business cards are exchanged after introductions. Business appointments should be made in advance. The attitude to punctuality is variable. Visits during Ramadan should be avoided. Visitors should make themselves familiar with local customs and care should be taken to respect Muslim conventions. For instance, only use the right hand when shaking hands and passing or receiving anything.

Security
Visitors should keep in touch with regional conditions as any increase in political tensions might affect travel advice. Personal security arrangements should be thoroughly considered throughout a visit.
There is a risk from indiscriminate attacks and sectarian violence, including tribal killings, armed car-jacking, robbery, kidnap, murder and bombings in public places such as markets, offices and public transport. Although these may not be aimed at foreigners, there is always a risk of being caught up in such attacks.
Large-scale demonstrations that become violent can occur, throughout Pakistan, at short notice. Visitors should monitor local media and avoid any demonstrations announced or gatherings encountered.
There is also a threat of criminal violence, including theft, burglary and the kidnapping of businessmen, especially in Karachi. Visitors of visibly western origin should not linger in public places. In major towns, especially Karachi, visitors should confine themselves to business areas, and avoid the back streets and bazaars.
Avoid long road journeys (except between major cities), cross-country journeys, and non-essential travel to the border areas of Afghanistan and India (Kashmir province). If visitors must travel to these regions, contact with Pakistani authorities should be made in advance. Police protection may be arranged, as necessary; advice about a No Objection Certificate (issued by the Pakistani Ministry of Foreign Affairs) can also be obtained.

Getting there

Air

National airline: Pakistan International Airlines (PIA)

International airport/s: Karachi International (Jinnah International) Airport (KHI), 12km north-east of Karachi; duty-free and tax-free shops, bar, restaurant, buffet, bank, hotel reservations, post office, shops.

Other airport/s: Lahore (LHE), 3km south-east of Lahore; restaurant, bank, post office, shops, car hire; Peshawar (PEW), 4km from Peshawar; Islamabad International (ISB), 8km from Islamabad; restaurant, car hire, banks, post office.

Airport tax: Departure tax: Rp400–800 (cash only), amount depends on airport; transit passengers are exempt.

Surface

Road: Generally in poor condition. There is access via India (Amritsar-Lahore) and China (the 805km Karakoram Highway serving Sinkiang Province-Islamabad and Rawalpindi via the Khunjerab Pass), plus road connections to Iran. The route from China is open to foreigners, but not to most Pakistanis.

Routes from Afghanistan (via Qandhar-Chaman-Quetta or Kabul-Peshawar), are closed following the fighting in that country.

Rail: A line runs from Iran (Zahedan-Naukundi-Quetta).

The train service between Pakistan and India was restored in 2004 – one train a week between Lahore in Pakistan and Attari in India.

Water: There are some ferry services from Bombay, although these are not widely used.

Main port/s: Karachi and Bin Qasim (south-east of Karachi).

Getting about

National transport

Air: Four carriers operate daily flights to 37 cities, providing better access than other forms of travel.

Road: The 800km Karakoram Highway permits entry to northern areas. The only multi-lane road is a two-lane highway linking Karachi and Peshawar. Although a new network of highways has greatly facilitated inter-city road travel, it can still be long, hot and harrowing. Avoid travelling at night on mountain roads in northern areas.

Buses: The air-conditioned Flying Coach national buses running between main centres (hourly between Lahore and Rawalpindi) are recommended over the local buses, which are colourful but not very reliable. Seats should be booked in advance.

Rail: There is an extensive rail network with over 8,775km of track, but it is slow and somewhat dilapidated. It is not suited to the business traveller working to a tight timetable. The main route runs Karachi-Lahore-Rawalpindi-Peshawar, with three classes. Certain services include air-conditioning, restaurant cars, sleeping cars, ice containers and women only accommodation. Advance booking is generally advisable, and is essential for some services.

Water: Although the Indus is unnavigable in many places, there are some passenger boats operating on certain stretches, which are recommended more for tourism than commercial travel.

City transport

Business travellers are advised to avoid arriving in Karachi at night and to ensure they are met at the airport.

Taxis: Taxis can be hired at all big hotels, and provide the most practical way for visitors to travel in cities. It is advisable to keep the taxi for the return trip as taxis do not usually cruise looking for passengers and there are not many taxi stands. Waiting costs are low, especially when compared to the time and trouble the traveller would face in looking for another taxi. Hotel taxi drivers are more likely to speak at least some English than those from taxi stands. Metered taxis are painted black and yellow, although the meter may not be used. Tipping normally 10 per cent.

Car hire

Self-drive and chauffeur-driven car hire is available, and minibuses may be hired. Driving is on the left-hand side of the road. National licence and international driving permit required.

BUSINESS DIRECTORY

The addresses listed below are a selection only. While World of Information makes every endeavour to check these addresses, we cannot guarantee that changes have not been made, especially to telephone numbers and area codes. We would welcome any corrections.

Telephone area codes

The international direct dialling (IDD) code for Pakistan is +92 followed by area code and subscriber's number:

Faisalabad	41	Multan	61
Gujranwala	431	Peshawar	91
Hyderabad	221	Quetta	81
Islamabad	51	Rawalpindi	51
Karachi	21	Sialkot	432
Lahore	42	Sukkur	71

Useful telephone numbers

Karachi
Police: 222-222/224-400
Fire: 74-891
Ambulance: 73-259/70-600
International calls: 0102
Calls to India, Bangladesh, China: 102
To check on booked call: 0104

Islamabad
Police: 23-333
Fire: 27-222
International call: 109
To check on booked call: 103

All places
Directory enquiries: 17

Chambers of Commerce

American Business Council of Pakistan, NIC Building, PO Box 1322, Abbasi Shaheed Road, Karachi 74400 (tel: 567-6436; fax: 566-0135; email: abcpak@cyber.net.pk).

Federation of Pakistan Chambers of Commerce and Industries, Federation House, Sharea Firdousi, Main Clifton Road, Karachi 75600 (tel: 587-3691; fax: 587-4332; email: info@fpcci.com.pk).

Hyderabad Chamber of Commerce and Industry, PO Box 99, Aiwan-e-Tijarat, Saddar, Hyderabad (email: hcci@paknet3.ptc.pk).

Islamabad Chamber of Commerce and Industry, Aiwan-e-Sanat-o-Tijarat, Islamabad (tel: 225-0526; fax: 225-2950; email: icci@brain.net.pk).

Karachi Chamber of Commerce and Industry, PO Box 4158, Aiwan-e-Tijarat, Karachi 74000 (tel: 241-6091; fax: 241-6095; email: info@karachichamber.com).

Lahore Chamber of Commerce and Industry, 11 Sharah-e-Aiwan-eTijarat, Lahore (tel: 630-5538; fax: 636-8854; email: sect@lcci.org.pk).

Quetta Chamber of Commerce and Industry, PO Box 117, Zarghoon Road, Quetta (tel: 824-857; fax: 821-948; email: qcci@hotmail.com).

Rawalpindi Chamber of Commerce and Industry, Chamber House, 108 Adamjee Road, Rawalpindi (tel: 556-6238; fax: 558-6849; email: chamber@rcci.org.pk).

Overseas Investors Chamber of Commerce and Industry, Chamber of Commerce Building, Talpur Rd, Karachi (tel: 241-0814; fax: 242-7313; email: oicci@global.net.pk).

Banking

Allied Bank of Pakistan, Khayaban-e-Iqbal, Main Clifton Road, Bath Island, Karachi (tel: 567-8155; fax: 568-3312, 568-0134).

Federal Bank for Co-operative, 85-W, Rizwan Centre, Blue Area, PO Box 1218, Islamabad (tel: 81-2469).

Faysal Bank, PO Box 472, 11/13 Trade Centre, I. I. Chundrigar Road, Karachi (tel: 263-8011-20; fax: 263-7975).

Habib Bank, Habib Bank Plaza, 1.1 Chundrigar Road, Karachi (tel: 241-8000/8034; fax: 241-4191).

Industrial Development Bank of Pakistan, State Life Building 2, Off 1.1. Chundrigar Road, Wallace Road, Karachi (tel: 241-9160/9168; fax: 241-1990).

Metropolitan Bank, PO Box 1289, Spencer's Building, I.I. Chundrigar Road, Karachi (tel: 263-6740; fax: 263-0404/5).

Muslim Commercial Bank, Adamjee House, 1.1 Chundrigar Road, Karachi 74000 (tel: 241-4090/9, 241-4110/9; fax: 241-3116).

National Bank of Pakistan, 1.1 Chundrigar Rd, Karachi (tel: 241-6789; fax: 241-6769).

United Bank, 1.1 Chundrigar Road, PO Box 4306, Karachi (tel: 2417100; fax: 243-7068).

Central bank

State Bank of Pakistan, PO Box 4456, I.I Chundrigar Road, Karachi 74000 (tel: 111-727-111; fax: 921-2440; email: info@sbp.org.pk).

Travel information

Aero Asia, Karachi (tel: 778-3476, 778-3033).

Automobile Association of West Pakistan, 8 Multan Rd, PO Box 76, Lahore.

Karachi Automobile Association (KAA), Standard Insurance House, 1 Chundrigar Rd, Karachi 0226 (tel: 232-173).

Pakistan International Airlines (PIA), PIA Bldg, Quaid-e-Azam International Airport, Karachi 75200 (tel: 412-011; fax: 772-7727, 457-0419).

Ministry of tourism

Ministry of Culture and Tourism, 13-T/U, Comm Area, F-7/2, Islamabad (tel: 27-023).

National tourist organisation offices

Pakistan Tourism Development Corporation, House 2, St 61, F-7/4, PO Box 1465, Islamabad 44000 (tel: 811-001/2/3/4; fax: 824-173).

Ministries

Ministry of Commerce, Industry and Production, Block A, Pakistan Secretariat, Islamabad (tel: 921-0277; fax: 920-5241; email: mincom@meganet.com.pk).

Ministry of Communications and Railways, Block D, Pakistan Secretariat, Islamabad (tel: 920-1252; fax: 920-6171).

Ministry of Culture, Sports, Minority Affairs and Youth, College Road, Shalimar 7/2, Islamabad (tel: 921-3121; fax: 922-1863).

Ministry of Defence, Pakistan Secretariat No II, Rawalpindi 46000 (tel: 927-1114; fax: 927-1115).

Ministry of Education, Block D, Pakistan Secretariat, Islamabad (tel: 920-1401; fax: 920-2851; email: pak@yahoo.com).

Ministry of the Environment, Local Government, Rural Development, Labour, Manpower and Overseas Pakistanis, Islamabad (tel: 922-4579; fax: 920-2211; email: envir@isb.compol.com).

Ministry of Finance, Revenues, Economic Affairs, Planning and Development, and Statistics,Block Q, Pakistan Secretariat, Islamabad (tel:920-3687; fax: 921-3780; email: finance@isb.paknet.com.pk).

Ministry of Food, Agriculture & Livestock, Block B, Pakistan Secretariat, Islamabad (tel: 920-3307; fax: 922-1246).

Ministry of Foreign Affairs, Constitution Avenue, Islamabad (tel: 921-0335; fax: 920-4205; email: pak.fm@usa.net).

Ministry of Health, Block C, Pakistan Secretariat, Islamabad (tel: 921-1622; fax: 920-5481; email: sehat@apollo.net.pk).

Ministry of Information and Ministry Development, Cabinet Block, Pakistan Secretariat, Islamabad (tel: 920-7314; fax: 920-2448; email: dgep@isb.comsats.net.pk)

Ministry of the Interior, Block R, Pakistan Secretariat, Islamabad (tel: 921-0086; fax: 920-1472).

Ministry of Kashmir Affairs, Northern Affairs, States and Frontier Region, Housing and Works, Block R, Pakistan Secretariat, Islamabad (tel: 920-3032; fax: 920-2494; email: safron@isb.perd.net.pk).

Ministry of Law, Justice, Human Rights and Parliamentary Affairs, Islamabad (tel: 921-0062; fax: 920-2628; email: molaw@comsats.net.pk).

Ministry of Petroleum and Natural Resources, Block A, Pakistan Secretariat, Islamabad (tel: 921-1220; fax: 920-1770; email: info@mpnr.gov.pk).

Ministry of Religious Affairs, Zakat and Usher, Plot 20, Ramna-6, Islamabad (tel: 920-1909; fax: 920-1646; email: mara@paknet.ptc.pk).

Ministry of Science and Technology, Shaheed-e-Millat Secretariat, Islamabad (tel: 920-8026; fax: 920-2603; email: minister@most.gov.pk).

Office of the President, Constitution Avenue, Islamabad (tel: 922-0136; fax: 920-3938; email: psecyp@isb.paknet.com.pk).

Office of the Chief Executive, Islamabad (tel: 922-2666; fax: 920-4632).

Other useful addresses

All-Pakistan Textile Mills Association, 44-A Lalazar, Off MT Khan Rd, PO Box 5446, Karachi (tel: 552-296).

Asian Development Bank, Pakistan Resident Mission, Overseas Pakistani Foundation (OPF) Building, Sharah-e-Jamhuriyat, G-52, Islamabad (tel: 825-011; fax: 823-324; email: adbpim@mail.asiandevbank.org).

Board of Investment, Saudi Pak Tower, 61-A Jinnah Ave, PO BOx 3100, Islamabad (tel: 817-165/2, 218-267/6; fax: 217-665, 215-554, 263-9580).

British High Commission, Diplomatic Enclave, Ramna 5, PO Box 1122, Islamabad (tel: 822-131/5; fax: 826-217).

British Deputy High Commission, York Place, Clifton, Karachi 6 (tel: 532-041/6; fax: 587-4014).

British Trade Office, 65 Mozang Road, PO Box 1679, Lahore (tel: 631-6589/90; fax: 631-6591).

Export Promotion Bureau, Government of Pakistan, Block A, Finance & Trade Centre, Sharea Faisal, Karachi (tel: 566-0305/9; fax: 566-0300, 568-0422/4010).

Institute of Marketing Management, 68-B Block 2, PECHS, Karachi (tel: 455-8365).

Islamabad Stock Exchange (tel: 215-047/50).

Karachi Cotton Association, Cotton Exchange Bldg, 1.1 Chundrigar Rd, Karachi (tel: 241-0336/2570).

Karachi Stock Exchange (Guarantee) Ltd, Stock Exchange Bldg, Stock Exchange Rd, Karachi 2 (tel: 242-5501/2/3/4/5; fax: 241-0825).

Lahore Stock Exchange (tel: 636-8000, 636-8333).

Oil Companies Advisory Committee, 5th Floor, Karim Chambers, Mereweather Rd, Karachi (tel: 568-2246/8).

Pakistan Art Silk Fabrics & Garments Exporters Association, 204 Amber Estate, Shahrah-e-Faisal, Karachi (tel: 360-919, 368-488).

Pakistan Cotton Association, 5 Amber Court, Shaheed-e-Millat Rd, Karachi (tel: 438-461).

Pakistan Embassy (USA), 2315 Massachusetts Avenue, NW, Washington DC 20008 (tel: (+1-202) 939-6200; fax: (+1-202) 387-0484; email: parepwashington@erols.com).

Pakistan Fruit & Vegetables Exporters, Importers & Manufacturers Association, 8 New Onion & Potato Market, University Rd, Karachi (tel: 493-7126, 493-125).

Pakistan Handicrafts Manufacturers & Exporters Association, MA Jinnah Rd, Karachi (tel: 772-8121).

Pakistan Shipowners Association, Ralli Brothers Bldg, Talpur Rd, Karachi (tel: 242-7154).

Privatisation Commission, Government of Pakistan, 5A Constitution Avenue, EAC Building, Islamabad (tel: 920-5146; fax: 920-3076, 921-1692; email: info@privatisation.gov.pk).

Sindh Coal Authority, F-158/A-I, Block 5, Clifton, Karachi (tel: 583-3549, 583-3550; fax: 587-4708).

National news agency: 18 Mauve Area, G-7/1, Islamabad (Tel: 220-3064–67; email: news@app.com.pk; internet: www.app.com.pk) (state run).

Internet sites

Gateway site for official and media information: www.islamabad.net

Karachi Airport: www.karachiairport.com

Pakistan agricultural information: www.pakissan.com

Pakistan Government Homepage: www.pak.gov.pk

Pakistan Yellow pages: www.jamal.com

Trade index of Pakistan: www.PakistanBiz.com

UK trade export site: www.tradepartners.gov.uk

KEY FACTS

Official name: Belu'u era Belau (Republic of Palau)

Head of State: President Tommy Esang Remengesau (since 2000; re-elected Nov 2004)

Head of government: President Tommy Remengesau

Ruling party: Members of the national congress sit as independents

Area: 380 square km

Population: 20,802 (2004)

Capital: Melekeok, on Ngerekebesand Island, since 2006 (Koror: commercial centre)

Official language: English on all islands; there are four officially recognised dialects (Palauan, Sonsoralese, Tobi, Angaur – on Angaur, Japanese is also included as official)

Currency: US dollar (US$) = 100 cents

GDP per capita: US$6,925 (2005) (US$7,921 2006*)

GDP real growth: 2.50% (2007)

Labour force: 9,777 (2005)

Unemployment: 4.20% (2005)

Inflation: 2.70% (2005)

Balance of trade: -US$101.40 million (2004)

Aid flow: US$46.60 million (US Compact aid per annum, until 2009)

Visitor numbers: 82,397 (2006)

* estimated figure

Palau

COUNTRY PROFILE

Historical profile

1686 Spain claimed the Caroline Islands, including Palau.
1783 A British landing on Palau inaugurated a century of trading links.
1885 The Spanish claim to the Caroline Islands was upheld by the Pope.
1899 Spain sold the islands to Germany.
1914 Japan occupied the islands.
1947 Palau became part of the Trust Territory of the Pacific Islands, administered by the US under an UN trusteeship mandate.
1978 Palau voted against becoming a part of the Federated States of Micronesia.
1980 Palau adopted its own constitution in July.
1981 Palau became the Republic of Palau with Haruo Remeliik as its first president.
1982 A Compact of Free Association with the US (CFA) was signed.
1985 President Remeliik assassinated in June. Lazarus Salii elected president in September.
1987 Palau voted to amend its constitution to allow approval of the CFA by a simple majority.
1988 The Palau Supreme Court ruled the constitutional change invalid on procedural grounds. President Salii committed suicide in August. Ngiratkel Etpiison elected president in November.
1989 Agreements with the US provided aid in paying off foreign debt and funds for new development.
1992 Kuniwo Nakamura elected president in November.
1993 Palau voted in a referendum to adopt the CFA.
1994 Palau became an independent republic under the CFA.
1996 President Kuniwo Nakamura was re-elected.
2000 Tommy Remengesau won the presidential election in November.
2002 President Remengesau vetoed a gambling bill stating that he did not wish to encourage gambling.
2003 A new airport terminal, costing US$16 million, was completed.
2004 Incumbent Tommy Remengesau was re-elected president in November.
2006 On 7 October, the government began its relocation to the new capital of Palau, Melekeok, on Babeldaob Island; the new site has an area of 28 square km. Some departments such as the police, immigration and customs will remain on Koror, the former capital and still the largest settlement. The Pacific Savings Bank (PSB) collapsed. Following an independent investigation criminal charges were brought against all of the PSB's board of directors and senior managers. US$1.5 million was lost from pension deposits in the uninsured PSB.
2007 Palau and the US Peace Corps celebrated 40 years of partnership in regional development. Palau was elected as one of the 21 vice presidents of the United Nations. Convictions were achieved in Palau's first case of human trafficking.

Political structure

Constitution

The constitution was promulgated in January 1981.
Each state has a governor.
A council of chiefs advises the government on matters of traditional law and custom.
Voting: universal suffrage over 18 years.

Form of state

Republic, in free association with the US.

The executive

The president is head of state and head of government, elected for a four-year term by popular vote.

National legislature

The Olbiil Era Kelulau (OEK) (National Congress) has two chambers – a nine-seat Senate (upper chamber), elected by popular vote on a population basis for a four-year term, and a 16-member House of Delegates (lower chamber), elected by popular vote for a four-year term.

Legal system

The legal system is based on Trust Territory laws, acts of the legislature, municipal, common and customary laws.

Last elections

2 November 2004 (presidential and parliamentary)

Results: Presidential: incumbent Tommy Remengesau was re-elected with 64 per cent of the vote against Polycarp Basilius with 36 per cent.
Parliamentary: non-partisans were elected. No parties exist.

Next elections

November 2008 (presidential and parliamentary)

Political parties

There are no political parties.

Ruling party

Members of the National Congress sit as independents

Political situation
Palau's largest foreign earnings come from tourism, remittances and revenue from the Compact of Free Association (commonly referred to as the Compact) which Palau has with the US. And while the Compact brings in a regular income each year, it is capped and extra income from the other two are subject to the mercy of external pressures and vagaries. Added to which frequent disasters caused by hurricanes snap up any reserves that may be around. No matter how detailed Palau's economic plans are, they are always prone to external disruption and as such the government has poor a track record for steady fiscal management.
In 2007, the prospects for increased tourist numbers were enhanced by more flights from Asia but were limited by the lack of accommodation for the numbers forecast. President Remengesau had invited the US military to use remote, uninhabited islands for training excises but no decision was forthcoming.
Remittances provide a large part of Palau's economic activity, but the US dollar has fallen markedly since 2002, which, while it has resulted in greater value of remittances from workers outside US dollar regions, for those expatriates working largely in the US, their contributions have followed the fortunes of the dollar.
The government has had to turn to taxpayers to provide an unpopular increased share of its revenue. Tax reforms are being introduced at a time of falling revenue, which the IMF has stated is a problem of weak tax administration. The country's problems of a falling economy are coupled with uncertainties concerning the Compact negotiations and land laws that affect foreign investments. The government has the task of, not only being active in the economy but also pro-reactive when unwelcome external forces hit.

Population
20,802 (2004)
Last census: April 2000: 19,129
Population density: 41 inhabitants per square km.
Annual growth rate: 1.6 per cent 1994–2004 (WHO 2006)
Ethnic make-up
Palauan (Micronesian with Malayan and Melanesian mixtures) 70 per cent; Asian (Filipinos, Chinese, Taiwanese and Vietnamese) 28 per cent; white 2 per cent.
Religions
Predominantly Christian, although one third of the population practise an indigenous religion known as Modekngei.

Education
The school system of Palau follows that of the US. Education is compulsory until the age of 14. Palauian and English are taught in schools, but English has gradually become the main instruction medium. There were 22 elementary schools, one high school, seven private schools and one community college. Around 94 per cent of school-aged children attend school and 97 per cent complete elementary school. The completion rate for high school students is 78 per cent.

Health
Per capita total expenditure on health (2003) was US$798; of which per capita government spending was US$691, at the international dollar rate, (WHO 2006). Only around 75 per cent of the population have access to medical facilities.
Life expectancy: 68 years, 2004 (WHO 2006)
Fertility rate/Maternal mortality rate: 1.4 births per woman, 2004 (WHO 2006)
Child (under 5 years) mortality rate (per 1,000): 23 per 1,000 live births (World Bank)

Welfare
There is no social welfare system.

Main cities
Koror (capital, population 13,027 in 2005), Meyuns (1,210).

Languages spoken
Local languages and Japanese spoken in some states.
Official language/s
English on all islands; there are four officially recognised dialects (Palauan, Sonsoralese, Tobi, Angaur – on Angaur, Japanese is also included as official)

Media
Other news agencies: ABC Pacific Beat: www.radioaustralia.net.au/pacbeat
Pacific Magazine:
www.pacificmagazine.net
Press
The Government Media Office publishes the Palau Gazette monthly.
Dailies: In English Marianas Variety and the Independent published abroad but read in Palau. Regional online newspaper Pacific Magazine (www.pacificmagazine.net).
Weeklies: In English Tia Belau, Palau Horizon; in Palau Roureur Belau. These are independent local publications. Regional, online Inside Oceania (www.insideoceania.com)
Broadcasting
Radio: In Palau and English, Eco Paradise FM, is government-operated; T8AA radio station, WWFM and KRFM, and a Christian religious broadcaster (High Adventure Ministries), are independent.
Television: Over 90 per cent of households have cable television, there are no local or regional TV broadcasts. Island Cable Television ((www.palaunet.com/CableTV.asp) is the only cable provider.

Economy
Palau has one of the highest standards of living in the Pacific and is classified as a middle-income country.
Since the end of Japanese occupation in 1945, the US has retained control over defence and foreign policy matters in return for several hundred million dollars in aid over 15 years (1994—2009). Of the US$630 million guaranteed under the Compact of Free Association with the US, US$70 million was placed in an investment fund, to provide a US$5 million boost to the annual budget.
Palau is a member of the region's two main economic organisations, the South Pacific Forum and the South Pacific Commission.
The economy is based on agriculture, fishing and tourism. The tourism sector remained buoyant through the collapse of the Asian economies in the late 1990s and it is hoped that improved travel infrastructure in the region will bolster visitor numbers in the short term.
Foreign fishing vessels (mainly from Japan and Taiwan) pay royalties to fish in Palau's Exclusive Economic Zone. The government is investigating alleged use of the territory for money laundering activities.

KEY INDICATORS **Palau**

	Unit	2003	2004	2005	2006	2007
Population	m	0.02	0.02	0.02	–	–
Gross domestic product (GDP)	US$bn	0.17	*0.13	0.14	–	0.16
GDP per capita	US$	9,000	6,135	6,925	–	–
GDP real growth	%	2.0	2.0	–	3.7	6.5
Inflation	%	–	0.2	–	–	3.2
Tourist numbers	'000	59.9	830.4	–	–	–

* estimated figure

A two-lane highway, the Palau Compact Road, around the main island, Babeldaob, will be an important addition to Palau's infrastructure and basis for economic growth. With the road's completion in 2005–06, all Palau's major public infrastructure projects that started after the signing of the Compact in 1994, will have been constructed.

External trade

Palau is a member of the South Pacific Regional Trade and Economic Co-operation Agreement (Sparteca) along with 12 other regional nations, which allows products duty free access by Pacific Island Forum members to Australian and New Zealand markets (subject to the country of origin restrictions).

Commercial fishing licenses for foreign trawlers have become and important source of foreign earnings.

Imports

Principal imports are machinery and equipment, fuels, metals and foodstuffs.

Main sources: US, Singapore, Japan, South Korea

Exports

Main exports include shellfish, tuna, copra and garments, which have become a major export following investment by Chinese firms, eager to take advantage of Palau's access to the US market.

Main destinations: US, Japan, Singapore

Agriculture

Farming

Agriculture accounts for around 1 per cent of GDP, with farming accounting for around 0.5 per cent. Subsistence farming of taro, bananas, sweet potatoes, tapioca and vegetables, with pig and poultry raising, is the main occupation. Commercial farming is practised where climate and soils are favourable. Land is parcelled into an estimated 20,000 holdings; a Land Commission maintains a register to provide security of land tenure for Palauan citizens.

Fishing

Fishing supplies the principal source of protein and export revenues. Fishing revenue is valuable because of the sale of fishing licences to large foreign fleets, permitting them to fish within Palau's Exclusive Economic Zone.

In 2004, the total marine fish catch was 1,074 tonnes.

Industry and manufacturing

Small-scale industries include handicrafts, garments, fish processing, bottling, bakeries and boat building. Industry typically represents around 7–9 per cent of GDP, but has been boosted by on-going activity in the construction industry to around 15 per cent.

Tourism

Tourism is Palau's principal economic activity. It caters largely to the Asian market, most visitors coming from Taiwan and Japan. Arrivals, which had shown healthy growth in the mid-1990s, peaking at 73,719 in 1997, fell sharply from 1998 as a result of the economic recession, followed by the depreciation of the Japanese yen against the US dollar in 2000–02 and the 11 September 2001 terrorist attacks in the US. Despite the outbreaks of SARS in 2003 and dengue fever in 2004, the sector has recovered, recording 83,041 tourist arrivals in 2004.

Hydrocarbons

In June 2004 Palau approved oil exploration measures to be set up in the country. This would establish a framework for the possible development of reserves. Fossil fuel makes up for around 85 per cent of Palau's energy requirements. Currently, Palau relies on the import of hydrocarbons from the US to meet its requirements.

Banking and insurance

Palau has a well-developed banking sector with 12 commercial banks in operation and one development bank, several of which are representative offices of US or Asian corporations. US banks are dominant, holding around 80 per cent of deposits. The main banks are the Bank of Guam and the Bank of Hawaii.

Time

GMT plus ten hours

Geography

Palau consists of more than 200 islands in a chain about 650km (400 miles) long, lying about 7,150km (4,450 miles) south-west of Hawaii and about 1,160km (720 miles) south of Guam. Together with the Federated States of Micronesia, Palau forms the archipelago of the Caroline Islands.

Babeldaob is the largest island in Palau, and in the centre of its east coast is the new site for the capital, Melekeok, (relocation began on 7 October 2006) and is home to Lake Ngardok, the largest body of freshwater (5 square km) in Palau; Meyuns, the second largest settlement, is also located on the northern shore, and the international airport is in the south. Koror Island (still with the largest settlement, Koror) is connected to Malakal Island (location of Koror's port) by two land bridges and a man-made bridge to Babeldaob Island.

The islands are composed largely of volcanic and limestone rock with coral reefs encircling the inhabited islands. The tallest peaks are on Babeldaob and Koror, with elevations of 217 metres (m) and 628m, respectively.

Hemisphere

Northern

Climate

Warm and humid, with temperatures between 23–30 degrees Celsius and humidity around 80 per cent. Rainfall (variable, minimum 250 mm/year), can occur in downpours. Typhoons are possible.

Entry requirements

Passports

Required by all. US citizens may visit with photo ID, however all US nationals require a passport for re-entry to the US from January 2007).

Visa

Required by all and issued by travel agent or airline for visits up to 30 days with proof of return/onward passage and adequate funds for maintenance. Extended entry permits are issued on application to Chief of Immigration, Bureau of Legal Affairs, Ministry of Justice, PO Box 100, Koror, Palau 96940.

Special regulations may apply to some non-tourist destinations within the islands.

Currency advice/regulations

No restrictions on import and export of local and foreign currency. Foreign currency over US$5,000 must be declared.

Prohibited imports

Illegal drugs and weapons

Health (for visitors)

Mandatory precautions

Cholera and yellow fever immunisations are required for those arriving from infected areas.

Advisable precautions

Vaccination for diphtheria, TB, hepatitis A and B, polio, tetanus and typhoid are recommended. There is a rabies risk.

Hospitals often expect immediate cash payment for medical treatment.

Hotels

There are hotels and guest-houses in Melekeok, Koror, Peliliu and Angaur.

Credit cards

Major credit cards are widely accepted at main visitor facilities.

Public holidays (national)

Fixed dates

1 Jan (New Year's Day), 15 Mar (Youth Day), 5 May (Senior Citizens' Day), 1 Jun (President's Day), 9 Jul (Constitution Day), 1 Oct (Independence Day), 24 Oct (United Nations Day), 25 Dec (Christmas Day).

Variable dates

Labour Day (first Mon in Sep), Thanksgiving Day (last Thu in Nov).

Working hours

Banking

Mon–Thu: 1000–1500, Fri: 1000–1800.

Business
Mon–Fri: 0900–1700.
Government
Mon–Fri: 0900–1700.
Shops
Mon–Sat: 0800–2000; Sun 0800–1800.

Telecommunications
Telephone/fax
Palau National Communications Corporation provides all modern public and private telecommunications facilities, including phone cards, international calls and mobile phones.
Mobile/cell phones
There are 900/1800 GSM services available.

Electricity supply
115V AC 60Hz, with flat, two or three pin plugs.

Social customs/useful tips
An informal attitude prevails in business. Business cards are sometimes exchanged. Business is usually conducted in English. Visitors should familiarise themselves with local customs. Permission should be sought before photographing people. Gratuities are optional.

Getting there
Air
International airport/s: Koror Babeldaob (ROR), 19km north-east of Airai, on Babeldaob. Unmetered taxis, with fixed fares, are available, travel time to Koror 30 minutes. Hotel shuttle buses are available if requested when making bookings.
Airport tax: US$20
Surface
Water: Malakal Harbour is the main commercial port facility in Palau. Cargo ships that carry passengers visit occasionally.

Getting about
National transport
Road: Outside administrative areas, the road network may consist of tracks not passable to ordinary vehicles. Ngiwal, Melekeok and Ngaremlengui each have road systems which link up with the main hamlets.
Driving is on the right with 40km per hour as the maximum allowable speed. Passing is prohibited anywhere in Palau.
In July 2005, Japan awarded almost US$20 million in grants to improve Palau's roads.
Water: The islands of Peleliu and Anguar are served by municipal boats. Other inter-island services rely on privately operated boats.
City transport
Taxis: Although taxis are not metered all fares are fixed, enquire before travelling.

BUSINESS DIRECTORY

The addresses listed below are a selection only. While World of Information makes every endeavour to check these addresses, we cannot guarantee that changes have not been made, especially to telephone numbers and area codes. We would welcome any corrections.

Telephone area codes
The international direct dialling code (IDD) for Palau is +680, followed by subscriber's number.

Useful telephone numbers
Ambulance: 488-1411
Police: 911

Chambers of Commerce
Palau Chamber of Commerce, PO Box 1742, Koror 96940 (tel: 488-3400; fax: 488-3401; e-mail: pcoc@palaunet.com).

Banking
Bank of Guam, PO Box 338, Koror 96940 (tel: 488-1648/2696/2697; fax: 488-1384).

Bank of Hawaii, PO Box 340, Koror 96940 (tel: 488-2602/2428; fax: 488-2427).

Bank Pacific, PO Box 1000, Koror 96940 (tel: 488-5635; fax: 488-4752).

Pacific Savings Bank, PO Box 399, Koror 96940 (tel: 488-1859/1860; fax: 488-1858; email: bank@palaunet.com).

First Commercial Banking, PDC Building; PO Box 1605, Koror 96940 (tel: 488-6297/8/9; fax: 488-6295).

Central bank
National Bank of Palau, PO Box 816, Koror 96940 (tel: 488-2578; fax: 488-2579; internet: ndbp.com).

Travel information
Continental Micronesia, PO Box 138CK, Saipan MP 96950, Northern Mariana Islands (tel: (+1-670) 234-8223; fax: (+1-670) 234-8358).

National tourist organisation offices
Palau Visitors' Authority, PO Box 256, Koror, ROP 96940 (tel: 488-2793/1930; fax: 488-1453; internet site: http://www.visit-palau.com).

Ministries
Bureau of Commercial Development, PO Box 1471, Koror, 96940 (tel: 488-2502).

Bureau of Education, PO Box 189, Koror 96940 (tel: 488-1464; fax: 488-1465; email: moe@palaugov.net).

Bureau of National Treasure (tel: 488-2501; email: bnt@palaugov.net).

Other useful addresses
British High Commissioner (for information on Palau), Victoria House, 47 Gladstone Rd; PO Box 1355, Suva, Fiji (tel: (+679) 322-9100).

Office of the President, PO Box 100, Koror, ROP 96940 (tel: 488-2403/2828; fax: 488-2424/1662).

Palau Embassy (USA), Suite 400, 1700 Pennsylvania Ave, NW Washington, DC 20006 (tel (+1-202) 452-6814; fax (+1-202) 452-6281; internet: www.palauembassy.com).

Palau Liaison Office (Hawaii), 1441 Kapiolani Blvd, Suite 1120, Honolulu, Hawaii 96814 (tel: (+1-808) 941-0988/89; fax: (+1-808) 943-1689).

Palau Liaison Office (Guam) ITC Bldg, Suite 615, PO Box 9457, Tamuning, Guam 96911 (tel: (+1-671) 646-9281/81).

Other news agencies: ABC Pacific Beat: www.radioaustralia.net.au/pacbeat

Pacific Magazine: www.pacificmagazine.net

Internet sites
Government of Palau: www.palaugov.net

Destination Micronesia, Palau: www.destmic.com/palau.html

US Office of Insular affairs: www.doi.gov/oia

Yellow Pages: http://directory.palaunet.com/yellowpages

Palestine

KEY FACTS

Official name: Palestine

Head of State: President of the Palestinian Council Mahmoud Abbas (Fatah) (since 15 Jan 2005)

Head of government: Prime Minister Ismail Haniyeh (Hamas) (since 25 Jan 2006)

Ruling party: Coalition: Harakat al Muqawama al Islamia (Hamas) (Islamic Resistance Movement); Harak al Tahir al Falistin (Fatah) (Movement for the Liberation of Palestine); and independents (since 17 Mar 2007)

Area: 6,257 square km (West Bank 5,879 square km; Gaza Strip 378 square km)

Population: 4.00 million (2007)* (2.5 million (2007)* West Bank only)

Official language: Arabic

Currency: Israeli new shekel (NIS) and Jordanian dinar

Exchange rate: NIS4.22 per US$ and JD0.71 per US$ (Jan 2007)

GDP per capita: US$1,258 (2007)*

GDP real growth: -8.00% (2007)*

Labour force: 774,000 (2004)

Unemployment: 28.80% (2007) Gaza Strip (18.0% West Bank only)

Inflation: 6.90% (2007) (11.0% Sep 2007–Mar 2008)

Balance of trade: -US$1.30 billion (2003)

* estimated figure

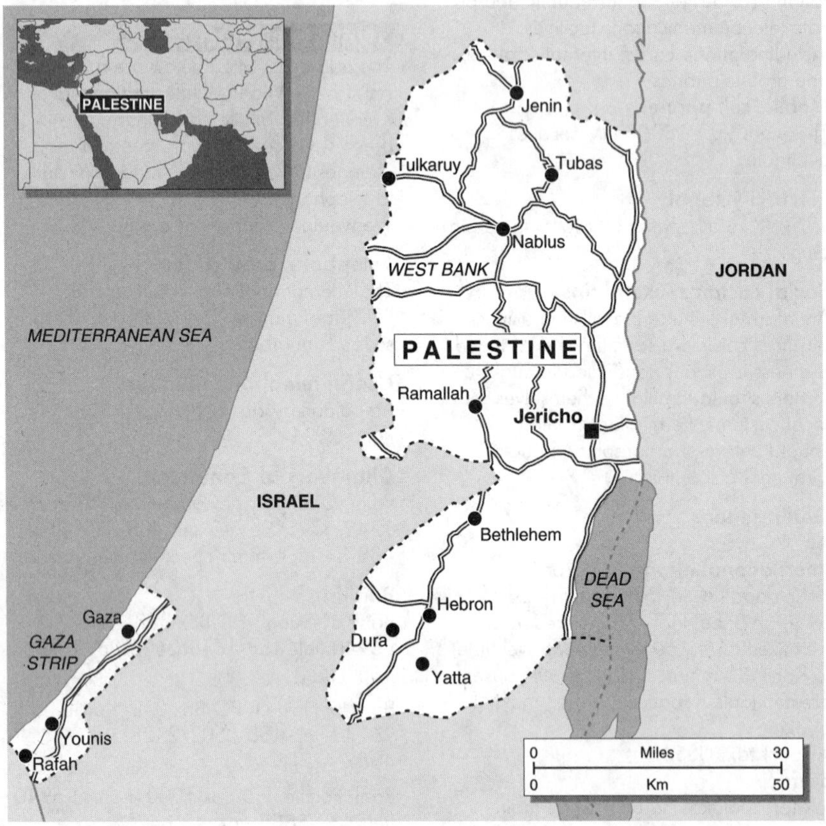

The Palestinian economy will inevitably be dependent on aid for some time to come, regardless of the December 2007 donor conference in Paris, a World Bank report released in December observed. 'Even under the most optimistic scenarios significant aid will continue to be required for the medium-term', the Bank reported. However, were donors to give the full amount the Palestinians requested – about US$5.6 billion over three years – and the Israeli blockade were to end, then the Palestinian economy has the potential to reach double digit growth 'and positively impact poverty levels'.

'Even with full funding but no relaxation in the closure regime, growth will be slightly negative... If the required aid also fails to materialise, incomes will decline even more, and the already high and growing poverty levels will rise dramatically' said the report, entitled *Investing in Palestinian Economic Reform and Development*. However, Israel claims it needs the checkpoints and closures for security reasons, at least until the Palestinian Authority (PA) is able to take full control over security in Palestine.

An IMF report, *Economic Performance and Reform Under Conflict Conditions* published in 2003 had noted that 'Before the *intifadah* between 1994 and 1999, the economy grew at a remarkable rate and was able to generate jobs and increase standards of living for its rapidly growing population. With the onset of the *intifadah*, the Palestinian economy went into a serious decline. At the time, the IMF chief of mission for West Bank-Gaza, had said that despite the difficulties, 'the economy has been much more resilient than one might have expected' and that the decline in the gross domestic product (GDP) had been in the region of 30 per cent instead of the 50 per cent often spoken about.

Expectations deferred

Any expectations held by the Palestinians that the 2006 war between Israel and the Lebanese based Hezbollah would bring about positive changes turned out to be mislaid. Ironically, world sympathy and support seemed to be diverted towards Lebanon, leaving Palestine languishing, impoverished and overlooked. Much of Palestine's problems stem from the fact that the Israelis, and to a lesser extent the rest of the world, simply no longer consider them to be serious negotiating partners.

The evacuation of Gaza in 2005 had been met with great public support both in Palestine and internationally. But the proposed follow through – the evacuation of a further 70,000 settlers (roughly a quarter of the total) from the West Bank appears to have stalled, maybe irrevocably. Israeli Prime Minister Ehud Olmert's Kadima party had been elected on a platform of unilateral disengagement. 'Unilateral' in this context meant that the settlers' repatriation was not negotiated with the Palestinians.

The PA president, Mahmoud Abbas, had urged Israel to co-ordinate the disengagement with his government and lobbied the US government to ensure that Israel would do so. Abbas feared that without such co-ordination, Harakat al Muqawama al Islamia (Hamas) (Islamic Resistance Movement), would simply claim credit for the withdrawal and cite it as the product of its own militancy. With several elections due in 2005 and early 2006, Abbas had been concerned that Hamas would threaten his own party, the Harak al Tahir al Falistin (Fatah) (Movement for the Liberation of Palestine)'s, stranglehold on Palestinian politics.

Israel eventually briefed the PA security services as to some of its disengagement plans and, in July, President Abbas moved to the Gaza Strip to personally oversee his forces.

Although President Abbas managed to insert a PA presence into the disengagement process, his bid to ensure that the PA could actually control events on the ground in the wake of the Israeli withdrawal was less successful. The disengagement only underscored the extent to which the Gaza Strip was beyond PA control. The 2006 war, by seriously weakening the Olmert administration, has conceivably further marginalised those Palestinians, largely Fatah members and supporters, who still advocate a negotiated, two-state solution to the Palestinian *impasse*.

The simple fact confronting Palestinians concerned with the agenda of the possible rather than that one apparently conceived in heaven, is that Fatah, not Hamas, is seen by most Israeli politicians, indeed by most Israelis who care to think it through, as their only possible negotiating partner.

Israelis remain

Although Palestinians took control of the Gaza Strip and four small sections of the northern West Bank in 2005, the Israeli occupation continued apace elsewhere. The Israeli government in 2005 had approved the building of yet more new housing units in Israeli settlements in the West Bank. The Israelis also stepped up efforts to complete the 'separation barrier' in the West Bank. Accordingly, up to 8 per cent of Palestinian land in the West Bank and tens of thousands of Palestinians were included on the Israeli side of the barrier. A confidential EU report, leaked in November, asserted that Israeli efforts to separate, through the building of the barrier, Arab East Jerusalem from the rest of the West Bank were particularly assiduous in 2005.

Checkpoints, both fixed and mobile, continue to choke Palestinian efforts to travel, and trade between their cities and villages. Most Palestinian population centres are effectively enclaves, surrounded by Israeli troops and settlers. This blockade was maintained, according the Israeli government, in order to prevent the movement of terrorists. The IDF also frequently raided Palestinian towns in search of suspected militants.

After Arafat

Palestinian politics had entered a new era in 2005, not least because of the death of PA President Yasser Arafat in November 2004. Mahmoud Abbas, Arafat's number two within the Palestine Liberation Organisation (PLO), was anointed by the ruling Fatah as Arafat's natural successor. Abbas had also previously served as PA prime minister in 2003. Abbas duly won presidential elections in January 2005. For the first time since 1969 the leadership of the Palestinians was not concentrated in the hands of one man – Arafat. While Abbas served as PA president and PLO chairman, the Fatah chair went to Farouk Kaddoumi.

As the Fatah-dominated PA attempted to renew itself in 2005, power was already slipping from its grasp. In the first Palestinian elections contested by Hamas, who had boycotted previous polls, Fatah emerged as the biggest vote-winner in all of these elections bar the December 2005 poll. However, starting from a base of zero, Hamas' gains were startling and only confirmed suspicions that a post-Arafat Fatah was no longer the monolithic entity it once was. In January, Hamas won majorities in 10 local councils in the Gaza Strip and in May, it took control of former Fatah strongholds in Qalqilya, Bethlehem and Rafah. After losing some momentum in September's elections, Hamas crushed Fatah in December elections, winning in three of the West Bank's biggest cities: Jenin, Nablus and al Bireh. Tellingly, after each election, the Fatah-led government attempted to delay future votes, fearing further losses to Hamas.

By far the most important development in Palestinian politics was Hamas'

KEY INDICATORS — Palestine

	Unit	2003	2004	2005	2006	2007
Population	m	3.49	3.52	3.76	3.70	*4.00
Gross domestic product (GDP)	US$bn	3.45	–	4.00	4.10	4.01
GDP per capita	US$	700	–	–	–	*1,258
GDP real growth	%	-18.5	-1.0	1.4	–	*-8.0
Inflation	%	–	–	–	–	6.9
Unemployment (West Bank only)	%	–	–	–	–	*18.0
Exports (fob) (goods)	US$m	–	–	433.0	–	–
Imports (cif) (goods)	US$m	–	–	1,866.0	–	–
Balance of trade	US$m	–	–	-1,433.0	–	–
Current account	US$m	–	–	0.0	-672.0	–
Exchange rate (NIS)	per US$	4.60	4.48	4.22	4.19	3.99

electoral triumphs as it expanded on to the national stage on 25 January 2006, when it won a landslide victory in elections to the Palestinian Legislative Council (PLC). The PLC is the legislature of the PA and its largest party generally makes up the PA government. There had been no elections to the PLC since 1996. Hamas won 76 out of the 132 seats, compared to Fatah's 43.

Unknown territory

With the Hamas landslide victory in January 2006, Palestinians had entered the unknown. Fatah had dominated Palestinian politics for nearly four decades and few predicted such a dramatic collapse. Israel, the US and many others in the international community have announced that they would refuse to deal with a PA headed by Hamas, unless Hamas renounces violence and recognises Israel. The US, one of the PA's single biggest donors, threatened to cut off all financial aid to the Palestinians if Hamas enter government without such changes. Hamas has thus far reiterated its position that it has the right to resist occupation through force of arms and that it will not recognise Israel.

Predictions that moderates within Hamas would move the party away from some of its more hard-line positions regarding Israel turned out to be well off the mark. Hopes that Hamas would eventually rehabilitate itself due to the necessity for gaining international recognition for its goal of an independent Palestinian state were simply misplaced. Some Hamas leaders have hinted at the possibility of some kind of accommodation with Israel but even these have not declared an end to their ambition to see an Islamic state established in all of Israel and the Palestinian Occupied Territories. Khaled Meshaal, Hamas' most senior leader, has indicated that Hamas will abide by all agreements made by the out-going government 'as long as it is in the interest of our people'.

In January 2007 rival Hamas and Fatah gunmen began a deadly power struggle in the Gaza Strip, killing over 20 people. The violence delayed talks on forming a government of unity until 14 March when a new government of unity was announced by President Abbas and prime minister since January 2006, Ismail Haniyeh of Hamas. A new cabinet was approved by the legislative council (83:3) and took office on 17 March. However, the US and EU continued to withhold recognition of the unity government until it recognised the state of Israel and renounced violence. Nevertheless, they have engaged with 'independent members' of the new government, although not Hamas ministers.

Collective punishment

Sanctions by Israel on fuel and energy supplies into Gaza were approved by the government of Israel on 25 October 2007, in retaliation for rockets fired into Israel. Palestinian leaders claimed this amounted to collective punishment. On 30 November the Israeli Supreme Court agreed that cutbacks in fuel were legal but that a cut-back in electricity supplies had to be delayed. On 17 December, a US$7 billion foreign aid package was agreed by foreign ministers to help underpin a viable Palestinian state and avoid bankruptcy. However, Hamas, which did not attend the conference, rejected the measures and although money was designated for Gaza the territory is unlikely to benefit from the aid. The World Bank warned that unless Israel lifted its system of restrictions on the movement of goods, finance and Palestinian people the measures will not rebuild the economy.

Following an Israeli army operation against Hamas forces in Gaza on 15 January 2008, 200 rockets were fired into Israel and in response, Israel imposed power cuts on Gaza. Petrol for vehicles and fuel for the Hamas-run power plant in the Gaza Strip was reduced on 20 January. Within days the UNHCR called the situation in Gaza desperate; adding that electricity provided by generators in hospitals was only able to power equipment and not provide the heating necessary during winter. Following international disquiet Israel eased the blockade of energy supplies while Palestinian militants exploded holes in the border wall near the Rafah crossing between Gaza and Egypt, on 22 January, allowing thousands of people to cross and stock up on essential supplies. Israel demanded that the border be closed to prevent the restocking of militant's armouries. Egypt rejected the demand, allowing access for humanitarian reasons.

Outlook

The continuing perception in the Arab world that the US is biased in favour of Israel was confirmed after a speech by US President Bush in May 2008. President Abbas again accused the US of bias towards Israel, after Bush said that the Arab world had to reform and the US was Israel's closest ally. Until and unless this perception is changed, the problem of Palestine and its effect on world issues will remain.

Risk assessment

Politics	Poor
Economy	Deteriorating
Regional stability	Poor

COUNTRY PROFILE

Historical profile

1916 The Sykes-Picot agreement.

1917 The Balfour Declaration.

1922 The Ottoman Arab territory of Palestine was mandated to Britain; it was divided into Palestine and Transjordan.

1929 Riots in Jerusalem between Arab Palestinians and Jews were sparked by a dispute over the use of the western wall of the Al Aqsa Mosque (the site is sacred to Muslims, and Jews claim it as part of their temple).

1936–39 The Arab Higher Committee opposed Jewish immigration to Palestine and the Peel Commission concluded that the mandate was unworkable. Legislation limiting the number of Jewish immigrants was introduced by the British government.

1945 Many of the Jews who had survived the Nazi German Holocaust arrived and Jewish extremists began to oppose Britain's immigration legislation.

1946 Transjordan became independent and was later re-named Jordan.

1947 Britain decided to leave. The UN adopted Resolution 181, which called for the establishment of both Jewish and Arab states within Palestine and a partition plan was drawn up, based solely on population, with Jerusalem as an international zone under UN jurisdiction. The Jews agreed to the partition; the Arabs did not.

1948 Conflict ensued between Arabs and Jews. Jewish leaders announced the formation of the State of Israel, open to the immigration of Jews from all countries. Egypt, Iraq, Lebanon, Syria and Jordan joined Palestinian and other Arab guerrillas and invaded Israel. The armistice agreements extended the territory under Israel's control beyond the UN partition boundaries. Many Arabs became refugees in the surrounding Arab countries, ending the Arab majority in the new Jewish state.

1957 Harak al Tahir al Falistin (Al Fatah) (Movement for the Liberation of Palestine) was formed by Arab students, including Yasser Arafat – an Egyptian Palestinian, who grew up in the Gaza Strip.

1964 The Palestine Liberation Organisation (PLO) was founded in Egypt as a Palestinian nationalist umbrella organisation dedicated to the establishment of an independent Palestinian state; later, it operated from Lebanon.

1967 Israel launched and won the Six Day War against Egypt, Jordan and Syria, taking control of the Sinai peninsular and the Gaza Strip, which had been Egyptian

territory, together with the Golan Heights, formerly claimed by Syria. Around 300,000 Palestinian Arabs fled to Jordan. After the Six-Day War, control of the PLO devolved to the leadership of the various fedayeen militia groups, the most dominant of which was Yasser Arafat's Al Fatah.
Israel's settlement policy started; it occupied the Sinai peninsular (returned to Egypt in 1982), the Golan Heights, the Gaza Strip and the West Bank, including East Jerusalem; the Jews transferred to these areas became known as settlers.
1969 Arafat was appointed chairman of the PLO's Executive Committee.
1970 Civil war (Black September) between the Jordanian army and Palestinians followed airplane hijackings by a Palestinian resistance group. The PLO was forcefully expelled from its bases in Jordan and moved to Lebanon.
1973 Lebanon was used by the Palestinians as a base for activities against Israel. In retaliation, Israeli commandos raided Beirut, killing three associates of Yasser Arafat. Arab states officially recognised the PLO as the representative of the Palestinians.
1981 Israel annexed East Jerusalem.
1982–85 Israel invaded Lebanon to prevent the PLO from carrying out armed resistance to its rule in the occupied territories of the Gaza Strip and the West Bank. A Western multinational force monitored the evacuation of the PLO; it relocated to Tunis, where it stayed until it moved to the Palestinian autonomous areas (Gaza and Jericho) in 1994.
1987 The Palestinians launched an intifida (uprising) against the Israelis. The Harakat al Muqawama al Islamia (Hamas) (Islamic Resistance Movement) was formed in the Gaza Strip, with two objectives: armed resistance to Israeli rule in the West Bank and the Gaza Strip and the establishment of a sovereign, independent state located in historic Palestine (present-day Israel, the West Bank, and the Gaza Strip). There was an upsurge in violence as large numbers of Jews from the Soviet Union began to settle in the West Bank and the Gaza Strip.
1988 The State of Palestine was declared, as outlined in the UN partition plan 181, the new state being recognised only by states that did not recognise Israel.
1993–95 The Oslo Peace Accords laid the basis for transfer of authority from the Israeli military administration to the PLO in the Gaza Strip and an undefined area around the town of Jericho in the West Bank. A follow-up treaty, Oslo II, was signed, which envisaged Palestinian autonomy with Israeli troop units withdrawing from the West Bank.
1996 Yasser Arafat was elected president of the Palestinian Legislative Council (PLC), the assembly of the Palestinian Authority (PA).
1998 The Wye peace agreement between the Israelis and the Palestinians, brokered by the US, ended 19 months of deadlock in the peace process.
2000 Israel agreed to allow the PA to control 39.8 per cent of the West Bank. However, after Israel's right-wing opposition leader, Ariel Sharon, visited the Temple Mount in Jerusalem and reiterated Israel's claims to Muslim holy places in the city, a second intifada was launched and a total blockade was imposed by Israel on the West Bank and Gaza.
2001 Israel declared the PA to be a terrorist-supporting organisation and launched Operation 'Defensive Shield', invading the PA-controlled West Bank and Gaza, attacking its institutions and besieging Arafat's headquarters. Deaths in Israel by Palestinian suicide bombers increased.
2002 Saudi Arabia proposed a peace initiative and a UN Security Council resolution endorsed a Palestinian state and called for the cessation of hostilities. Israel besieged Arafat's compound in Ramallah and reoccupied most of the West Bank. For five weeks the Israeli army surrounded militants and civilians taking sanctuary in the Church of the Nativity in Bethlehem; it ended when 13 militants were sent into exile. Israel began building a wall as a barrier between it and Gaza claiming it was the only way to control infiltration of militant terrorists.
2003 US President George W Bush unveiled the Road Map to Peace, with a cease-fire and end to Jewish settlements in the occupied territories and the creation of an independent Palestinian state by 2005. Ahmed Qureia became prime minister.
2004 In February, Sharon, declared he would remove all Jewish settlements in Gaza. President Yasser Arafat became ill and died in Paris on 11 November.
2005 On 9 January, Mahmoud Abbas (also known as Abu Mazen) was elected president of the Palestinian Authority, by an overwhelming majority. He persuaded Hamas and Islamic Jihad to an unofficial cease-fire. On 8 February, at the Sharm El Sheikh summit in Egypt, a truce was signed by Sharon and Abbas, ending four years of violence between Israel and Palestine. On 20 February, President Abbas and the Israeli cabinet approved the removal of Jewish settlers from Gaza and part of the West Bank.
2006 Mahmoud Abbas announced, in January, that he would not run for president again when his current term ends in 2009. Elections in January were won convincingly by Hamas with a majority of 74 seats. Turnout was 77.7 per cent. Ismail Haniya was appointed prime minister in February. In March, the new Hamas-dominated parliament revoked legislation passed by the previous Fateh-dominated parliament which had given increased powers to the president, including the right to allocate key administrative posts to Fateh members. The Hamas-led government was inaugurated on 29 March. Hamas refused to recognise Israel, give up violence and accept previous agreements made by Fatah and despite the democratic election, international sanctions, led by the US, were imposed on a Palestine administered by a government branded as a terrorist organisation. Sanctions caused financial hardship as government benefits and wages went unpaid and supplies to hospitals ran out. Hostilities broke out in October as members of the security forces (many belonging to Fatah) protested at the interruption in their pay. The president undertook negotiations with Israel and Hamas in an attempt to broker an accommodation and allow financial aid to resume.
2007 Rival Hamas and Fatah gunmen began a deadly power struggle in the Gaza Strip in January, killing over 20 people. The violence delayed talks on forming a government of unity. On 14 March, a new government of unity was announced by President Abbas and Prime Minister Haniya. A new cabinet was approved by the legislative council (83:3) and took office on 17 March. The US and EU continued to withhold recognition of the unity government until it recognised the state of Israel and renounced violence. The EU engaged with 'independent members' of the new government, although not Hamas ministers. In June, violence erupted again and a power struggle resulted in Hamas gaining control of Gaza while local Hamas leaders fled to Egypt. The president, based in the West Bank, dismissed Prime Minister Haniya and appointed Salam Fayyad while announcing that he would rule by presidential decrees; Hamas officials rejected this development. On 17 June the president swore in a new cabinet in Ramallah and outlawed a Hamas paramilitary force (the Executive Force) and other allied militia. However presidential rule cannot be enforced in Gaza. In June, the US signed an agreement to give the PA US$80 million towards reforming their security services. Israel imposed an economic embargo on Gaza, after Hamas gained control of the territory in June, and restricted the entry and exit of people to Gaza. The number of humanitarian convoys of supplies halved from 3,000 in July to 1,500 in September. Sanctions by Israel on fuel

and energy supplies into Gaza were approved on 25 October, in retaliation for rockets fired into Israel. Palestinian leaders claimed this amounted to collective punishment. On 30 November the Israeli Supreme Court agreed that cutbacks in fuel were legal but that a cut-back in electricity supplies had to be delayed. On 17 December, a US$7 billion foreign aid package was agreed by foreign ministers to help underpin a viable Palestinian state and avoid bankruptcy. However, Hamas, which did not attend the conference, rejected the measures and although money was designated for Gaza the territory is unlikely to benefit from the aid. The World Bank warned that unless Israel lifted its system of restrictions on the movement of goods, finance and Palestinian people the measures will not rebuild the economy.

2008 Following an Israeli army operation against Hamas forces in Gaza on 15 January, 200 rockets were fired into Israel and in response, Israel imposed power cuts on Gaza. Petrol for vehicles and fuel for the Hamas-run power plant in the Gaza Strip was reduced on 20 January. Within days the UNHCR called the situation in Gaza desperate; adding that electricity provided by generators in hospitals was only able to power equipment and not provide the heating necessary during winter. Following international disquiet Israel eased the blockade of energy supplies while Palestinian militants exploded holes in the border wall near the Rafah crossing between Gaza and Egypt, on 22 January, allowing thousands of people to cross and stock up on essential supplies. Israel demanded that the border be closed to prevent the restocking of militant's armouries. Egypt rejected the demand, allowing access for humanitarian reasons. George Habbash, founder of the radical Popular Front for the Liberation of Palestine (PFLP), died on 26 January. On 25 February the border was closed at 1500, but other openings elsewhere were made and hundreds more Palestinians continued to cross into Egypt. International support for President Abbas' proposal that his administration should take control of the border crossing failed when Hamas rejected his involvement. Meanwhile Hamas and Egyptian officials reached their own agreement, whereby all Palestinians would return to Gaza, except those finding medical treatment in Egypt and those travelling to a third country. On 3 February Egyptian forces closed the last breach in the border using razor-wire and metal barricades. Following a speech by US President Bush in May, President Abbas accused the US of bias towards Israel, as Bush said that the Arab world had to reform and the US was Israel's closest ally. Mahmoud Darwish, Palestine's respected poet and author of its 1988 declaration of independence, died on 9 August.

Political structure

Constitution

A provisional framework for the Palestinian state was approved by the Palestinian Legislative Council in a 1996 Draft Basic Law. This law will be fully endorsed when a permanent settlement is achieved.

Form of state

Parliamentary Democracy

The executive

Executive power is vested in the head of the Palestinian National Authority (PNA – also known as the Palestinian Authority (PA)), who is president, elected by direct universal suffrage for up to two five-year terms, and Head of State.

The president is head of armed and security forces, is responsible for initiating and proposing laws and foreign policy. The president appoints a prime minister, who forms a cabinet.

National legislature

The unicameral Palestinian Legislative Council (PLC) was established in 1994 and is composed of 132 members plus the president as an ex officio member. The PLC's members are elected in 16 multi-seat constituencies for 5-year terms.

Legal system

The Basic Law provides for an independent judiciary.

The High Judicial Council oversees the administration of a hierarchy of courts beginning with the magistrate courts, Courts of first Instance, Courts of Appeal and The Supreme Court.

Last elections

25 January 2006 (parliamentary); 9 January 2005 (presidential).

Results: Presidential: Mahmoud Abbas, also known as Abu Mazen, candidate of the mainstream Fatah, was elected president of the Palestinian council with 62.3 per cent of the vote against independent candidate, Mustafa Barghouti, 19.8 per cent. Turnout was 70 per cent.

Parliamentary: Hamas won 74 seats (out of 132); Fatah won 45 seats. The Popular Front for the Liberation of Palestine (PFLP) won 3 seats. Three groupings (The Alternative, Independent Palestine and Third Way) won 2 seats each. Independents won the 4 remaining seats. Turnout was 78.2 per cent.

Next elections

2010 (presidential)

Political parties

Ruling party

Coalition: Harakat al Muqawama al Islamia (Hamas) (Islamic Resistance Movement); Harak al Tahir al Falistin (Fatah) (Movement for the Liberation of Palestine); and independents (since 17 Mar 2007)

Main opposition party

Population

4.00 million (2007)* (2.5 million (2007)* West Bank only)

Last census: December 1997: 2,601,669

Population density: 489 inhabitants per square km. Urban population: 54 per cent (1994–2000).

Annual growth rate: 2.3 per cent (2003)

Ethnic make-up

Gaza: Palestinians and other Arabs (99.4 per cent), Israelis (0.6 per cent).

West Bank: Palestinians and other Arabs (83 per cent), Israelis (17 per cent).

Religions

The majority of the population is Muslim (mainly Sunni); also Jewish and Christian minorities.

Education

Formal basic education is provided to the majority of those who are of primary school age (94.7 per cent), although the quality of education does not correspond to the rising demand.

The education sector has suffered tremendous decline since the Israeli occupation. Most of the schools in the Gaza Strip are overcrowded and run two to three shifts per day. It is estimated that there are 1,175 schools of which 995 are in the West Bank and 180 in the Gaza Strip.

The education ministry in its five-year reform project (2000–05) is keen on developing a Palestinian curriculum emphasising studies in Palestinian identity and has invested in providing textbooks and improving the teaching methods in schools. It will also encourage the private sector to invest in vocational training, which otherwise concentrates on building and running cultural centres.

There are six universities in the West Bank and two in the Gaza Strip. West Bank Universities include Birzeit, Al Najah, Bethlehem, Al Quds University, Hebron University and Al Quds Open University.

Health

The Israeli occupation has almost paralysed the provision of healthcare to the civilian population. Most hospitals and clinics are unable to operate and as a result 73 per cent of Palestinians in rural areas are deprived of medical treatment. Vaccinations among children have been largely hindered spreading the fear of epidemics. Moreover, elderly people with chronic diseases suffer from acute shortages of medicine.

A hospital in Gaza, funded by the EU, is largely unworkable as staff, patients and

supplies are denied access by Israeli authorities during times of trouble.
Life expectancy: 73 years (estimate 2003)
Fertility rate/Maternal mortality rate: 4.9 births per woman (2003)
Birth rate/Death rate: 37.5 births per 1,000 population; 4.1 deaths per 1,000 population (2003).
Child (under 5 years) mortality rate (per 1,000): 22 per 1,000 live births (2003)

Welfare

The UN World Food Programme (WFP) aims to provide basic food support to 500,000 non-refugee Palestinians, in the West Bank and Gaza Strip. It targets those who have been classified as 'social hardship cases' (360,000 people according to latest estimates) and are eligible for welfare assistance from the PNA. In Jerusalem, an Emergency Food Crisis Group, chaired by WFP, has been established with the help of other UN agencies, non-governmental organisations and donors.

The Israeli occupation has forced the poverty level higher than ever before. While unemployment stands at 30 per cent, an estimated 40 per cent of Palestinian households have a monthly income that is less than US$200 per month. The percentage is 45 per cent in Gaza and 37 per cent in the West Bank.

Estimates show that 38 per cent of refugees live in the Palestinian territories; 15.8 per cent in the West Bank and 21.9 per cent in the Gaza Strip. The PNA along with other international non-government organisations have been struggling to rehabilitate the housing conditions of people in the refugee camps such as Jenin and Nablus. The Palestinian Housing Council has been active in providing low cost housing. More than 400,000 Palestinians are deprived of electricity and running water.

Main cities

Gaza Strip: Gaza (also called Gaza City) (estimated population 495,207 in 2005); Deir al Balah (61,581), became the first town to come under Palestinian self-rule in 1994, Rafah (130,621).

West Bank: East Jerusalem (261,043), Jericho (20,544), Ramallah (25,479), Nablus (135,253), Hebron (165,968).

Media

Press

A number of Palestinian newspapers are based in Nazareth, outside the PNA.
Dailies: In Arabic Al Quds, Al Hayat al Jadedah, Al Ayyam Daily Newspaper. In English, Palestine Times and Bethlehem News.
Weeklies: Weeklies include Kul-Alarab, Assabeel Weekly, Filsteen Almoslima and Akhbar Alnaqab.
Periodicals: In Arabic, Al Ayyam.

Broadcasting

The Palestinian Broadcasting Corporation broadcasts from Ramallah.
Radio: In Arabic, the Voice of Palestine, run by Hamas, and Gaza FM.
Television: The official Palestinian Broadcasting Corporation broadcasts televisions programmes from Ramallah as well as a satellite channel.

Economy

'We are obliged to mix politics with economics in Palestine' said Dr Hassan Adnan Yassin, the general manager of the Palestinian Stock Exchange. His words encapsulate Palestine's seemingly intractable problems. Analysts, World Bank officials, donor countries' representatives are all agreed that without the free passage for Gazan merchandise no amount of aid can sustain the territory. Israel, it seems, is equally certain that without its security being guaranteed – an assurance no country can claim in the current climate of international terrorism that uses suicide bombings – it will not relinquish its oppressive hold, by abrogating its customs union with Gaza, a measure which threatens to stifle Palestine's prospective economic viability.

International aid to Palestine amounts to US$1 billion per annum most of which has been soaked up, not by investing in people and infrastructure but by maintaining a community whose economy is shattered. Israel has targetted and destroyed the infrastructure, institutions and private property in the PA-controlled West Bank and Gaza Strip.

Since 1999 (the baseline) the economy has registered a fall of 11.5 per cent. Unemployment was around 27 per cent in 2005 with over 60 per cent of households lived below the poverty line. In the Gaza Strip the figure is higher as most workers crossing into Israel or working for Israelis in the now abandoned occupied territory have been unable to find alternative paid employment. The agriculture sector achieved a positive growth in 2006 of 6.8 per cent, as many went back to the land. The trade deficit – almost two-thirds with Israel – increased more rapidly than domestic production in 2004 and represented 65 per cent of GDP. Palestine has paid Israel the equivalent of all its international aid plus 50 per cent of the remittances of its workers in Israel for this deficit, since 2001. It will be another blow if Israel's proposal to withdraw work permits to Palestinian labourers in 2008 is carried out.

The embargo imposed by Israel on the Gaza Strip caused the industrial sector to collapse with no supplies coming in or goods going out and causing over 100,000 people to lose their jobs in the last six months of 2007. Politician and business leaders warn that the damaged caused by the embargo was irreparable. The food and beverages sector, which was never subject to the economic embargo as it was counted as humanitarian aid, managed to survive but without supplies of ancillary items such as wrappings those in operation may not be able to survive for long.

International proposals for US$3 billion in investment is predicated on Israel allowing free passage of people and goods to markets. The EU has proposed that it will back a loan guarantee for an investors fund, supply technical aid to Palestine to improve its customs security and US$30.5 million to construct a cargo terminal. However, it still wants to see more progress in the peace negotiations before such measures are implemented.

Public workers, who had been unpaid for months led protests and calls for a change in the makeup in the government in 2006. The factional violence that ensued finally moved the political impasse so that by early 2007, the Hamas led administration was restructured to include Fatah members, in an attempt to both appease US, European and Israeli objections to a 'terrorist organisation' (that will not declare Israels' right to exist), in power and gain access to much needed aid. The Palestinian Authority asked for US$1 billion in aid in April 2007, to fill the gap in its finances caused by its economic isolation. At the same time, the US congress agreed to provide US$60 million in funds to improve security, at the borders, for equipment and for President Abbas's security staff.

Over US$7 billion in foreign aid was agreed by foreign ministers to help underpin the economy of a viable Palestinian state and avoid the state's impending bankruptcy. Of the 68 states that made pledges, the European Union offered US$650 million, US US$555 million and Japan US$150 million; to be provided over three years, France offered US$300 million, Germany US$290, UK US$243 million and South Korea US$13 million. However, Hamas, which did not attend the conference and rejected the measures, although money was designated for Gaza, the territory is unlikely to benefit from the aid. The World Bank warned that unless Israel lifted its system of restrictions on the movement of goods, finance and Palestinian people the measures will not rebuild the economy.

External trade

Palestine has no operational ports or airports to ship goods directly to markets other than Israel. Since Hamas took control of the Gaza Strip in June 2007 and Israel closed the border, manufacturing has all but collapsed, as 80 per cent of businesses have closed in this region. Likewise raw materials and goods destined for Gaza began to pile up, stranded in Israel's Ashod port. The land border with Egyptian, at Rafah in southern Gaza was also closed by Israel.

Imports

Food, consumer goods and construction materials.

Main sources: Israel and Egypt

Exports

Citrus fruit, flowers, olives, fruit, vegetables, furniture and limestone.

Main destinations: Israel, Egypt, Jordan

Agriculture

The sector has been badly damaged by the Israeli-Palestinian conflict since 2000 when agriculture contributed 7 per cent to GDP and employed about 25 per cent of the workforce.

Before the second intifida and the Israeli invasion of the West Bank and Gaza, about a quarter of the land area was cultivated and smallholdings of five hectares (ha) or less dominated. Crops, including olives, grapes and almonds, took up 60 per cent of cultivated rain-fed areas and field crops (mainly cereals) about 30 per cent. Olive growing accounted for more than 50 per cent of cultivated land.

The Separation Barrier has led to confiscation and levelling of Palestinian lands and by mid-2004 around 260 square kilometres, or 15 per cent of agricultural land had been lost to production.

Crop production in 2005 included: 72,350 tonnes (t) cereals in total, 50,000t wheat, 21,000t barley, 45,000t potatoes, 140,000t olives, 206,000t tomatoes, 45,000t eggplants, 14,000t chillies and peppers, 9,200t bananas, 58,000t grapes, 7,300t figs, 5,000t dates, 6,460t pulses, 64,870t citrus fruit, 6,060t treenuts in total, 31,428t oilcrops, 182,440t fruits in total, 605,200t vegetables in total. Livestock production included: 97,050t meat in total, 6,548t beef, 9,940t lamb, 3,763t goat meat, 76,800t poultry, 40,260t eggs, 186,000t milk, 250t honey, 810t cattle hides, 1,050t sheepskins.

Fishing

In 2004, the total marine fish catch was 2,708 tonnes and the total crustacean catch was 128 tonnes.

Industry and manufacturing

There are proposals by a US-Led syndicate to invest US$500 million in industry and manufacturing after the withdrawal of Israeli troops from Gaza, but only if Israel allows free access of goods through its territory to overseas markets.

Tourism

Foreign investment has been sought to help develop tourism facilities throughout the West Bank; however, the fledging tourism sector has been devastated by the conflict with Israel.

Financial markets

Stock exchange

The Palestine Securities Exchange (PSE) in the West Bank town of Nablus started operating 1997. It was founded by the Palestinian Development Investment Company (Padco); PalTel – the telecommunications company – is the exchange's largest company trading.

Banking and insurance

Central bank

The Palestine Monetary Authority (PMA), was established in 1995, with responsibilty for licensing, supervising and inspecting banks; determining the liquidity requirements on all deposits held by banks operating in the self-rule areas; managing foreign exchange reserves and foreign currency transactions. The PMA also has the power to regulate and supervise capital activities in the self-rule areas including the licensing of capital market institutions, finance companies and investment funds.

Main financial centre

Ramallah

Time

GMT plus two hours (daylight saving GMT plus three hours)

Geography

Palestine consists of the Gaza Strip and the West Bank, which together measure 6,020 square km. The Gaza Strip is level, fertile, coastal land of only 5–12km wide and 45km long to the south-west of Israel and on the Mediterranean sea. It is almost entirely surrounded by Israel but has a short border with Egypt in the south.

The West Bank is 5,655 square km within the demarcation line set up in 1949. It is an area west of the Jordan River, including much of Jerusalem and areas north and south of the city, the borders of which have been in dispute since the 1967 Six Day War. Jordan lies to the east and in the south-east the border runs through the Dead Sea, the lowest lying land on earth at 399 metres below sea level.

The land is generally fertile, although arid.

Hemisphere

Northern

Climate

Summer (Apr–Oct): temperatures range from 23 degrees Celsius (C) to 31 degrees C; humidity 70–75 per cent. Winter (Nov–Mar): temperatures range from 15–20 degrees C. Rainfall: Nov–Mar in periodic downpours.

Entry requirements

Passports

Required by all. The only routes to the Palestinian territories are through Israel and visitors must comply with Israeli requirements before access is allowed to the West Bank or Gaza Strip. Israel imposes tight restrictions and passport holders are advised to contact Israeli authorities for written permission to cross into the Gaza Strip in advance of travelling. At the border crossing it can take at least five working days for the documentation to be verified.

The Israeli Ministry of the Interior insists that Palestinian citizens holding dual nationality must enter and leave Israel on a Palestinian passport; they are required to obtain travel documents to depart.

NB An Israeli stamp, or exit stamp from any of the neighbouring countries, will mean entry is barred to almost any other Arab country. It is possible to request that the passport should not be stamped and a separate form is stamped instead and attached to the passport; the form can be removed when exiting the country.

Visa

Egypt and Jordan have open borders with Palestine, access was via the Allenby bridge (West Bank-Jordan) or the border crossing at Rafah (Gaza-Egypt). However, since Israel commands these access points and limits admission, practical entry can only be gained through Israel. Israel has agreements with 65 countries for visa-free travel, including most citizens from Europe, the Americas, Australasia and some Asian countries (visa applications can be downloaded from: www.mfa.gov.il/mfa and follow link from About the ministry to Consular affairs, then Services for foreign nationals only). Travel within the West Bank and Gaza usually involves passing through multiple Israeli military checkpoints.

Currency advice/regulations

Most places accept US dollars, Israeli shekels and Jordanian dinars.

Customs

Video cameras and other electronic items must be declared to customs at Israeli points of entry.

Prohibited imports

Fresh meat and fruit and vegetables from Africa are prohibited by Israel.

Hotels

There is a lack of good hotels in the West Bank and Gaza.

Public holidays (national)

Fixed dates

14 Nov (National Day)

Variable dates
Eid al Adha, Islamic New Year, Birth of the Prophet, Ascent of the Prophet, Eid al Fitr.
Islamic year – 1429 (10 Jan 2008–28 Dec 2008): The Islamic year contains 354 or 355 days, with the result that Muslim feasts advance by 10–12 days against the Gregorian calendar. Dates of feasts vary according to the sighting of the new moon, so cannot be forecast exactly.

Working hours
The official weekend is Friday, and the working week varies, to accommodate Muslim, Christian or Jewish religious schedules.
Banking
Sat–Thu: 0800–1230. Some larger bank branches re-open Mon–Thu: 1500–1700.
Business
Sat–Thu: 0800–1430.
Government
Sat–Thu: 0800–1430.
Shops
Sat–Thu: 0800–1900. Christian owned shops open on Friday and close on Sunday.

Telecommunications
Mobile/cell phones
There is a 900 GSM service available throughout the territories.

Security
Foreign nationals are warned not to travel to the West Bank and Gaza Strip, which are subject to terrorist and military activity.

Getting there
Air
International airport/s: Dahaniya Gaza International Airport is not in operation. It is located south of Gaza City near the Egyptian border.
Surface
Gaza is accessible from the Rafah border with Egypt in the south. The Allenby Bridge crossing from the West Bank into Jordan is controlled by Israel.
Road: Private vehicles cannot cross from Israel into the Gaza Strip and may be stopped at checkpoints entering or leaving the West Bank.
Main port/s: An internationally funded port was opened in the late 1990s, with the aim of reducing the need for Palestinian trade to go through Israel before reaching the outside world. However, access to and from the port has become restricted due to the Israeli occupation of the West Bank and Gaza Strip in early 2002. All access to Gaza is via the port of Haifa.

Getting about
National transport
Road: Gaza Strip has a small, poorly developed road network. West Bank has 4,500km of roads, of which 2,700km are paved; Israel developed many highways to service their settlements.
Buses: Buses run from East Jerusalem to Nablus and between Tel Aviv and Ramallah.
Taxis: Collective taxis regularly commute between Gaza and Ramallah, Jerusalem or Hebron.
City transport
Taxis: Taxis operate in the main cities.
Car hire
Palestinian licence plates are either green or blue, whereas Israeli number plates are yellow. Visitors are advised not to drive vehicles with yellow licence plates in the West Bank or Gaza Strip.

BUSINESS DIRECTORY
The addresses listed below are a selection only. While World of Information makes every endeavour to check these addresses, we cannot guarantee that changes have not been made, especially to telephone numbers and area codes. We would welcome any corrections.

Telephone area codes
The international direct dialling code (IDD) for Palestine is +970, followed by area code and subscriber's number:

Bethlehem	2	Jericho	2
Gaza	7	Jerusalem	2
Hebron	2	Nablus	9
Jenin	6	Ramallah	2

Chambers of Commerce
Bethlehem Chamber of Commerce and Industry, PO Box 59, Bethlehem (tel: 274-2742; fax: 276-4402; e-mail: bcham@palnet.com).

European Palestinian Chamber of Commerce, 19 Nablus Road, PO Box 20185, Jerusalem (tel: 626-4883; fax: 626-4975; e-mail: epcc@palnet.com).

Federation of Palestinian Chambers of Commerce, Industry and Agriculture, Al-Rashid Street, PO Box 54107, Jerusalem (tel: 628-0727; fax: 628-0644; email: fpccia@palnet.com).

Gaza Palestinian Chamber of Commerce, PO Box 33, Gaza (tel: 282-1172; fax: 286-4588; e-mail: gazacham@palnet.com).

Hebron Chamber of Commerce and Industry, King Faisal Street, PO Box 272, Hebron, West Bank (tel: 222-8218; fax: 222-7490; e-mail: hebcham@hebronet.com).

Jenin Chamber of Commerce, Industry and Agriculture, City Centre, Jenin (tel: 250-1107; fax: 250-3388; e-mail: jencham@hally.net).

Jericho Commercial, Industrial and Agricultural Arab Chamber, PO Box 91, Jericho (tel: 232-3313; fax: 232-2394; e-mail: jercom@palnet.com).

Jerusalem Arab Chamber of Commerce, Al-Rashid Street, PO Box 19151, Jerusalem 91191 (tel: 628-2351; fax: 627-2615; e-mail: chamber@alqudsnet.com).

Nablus Chamber of Commerce and Industry, PO Box 35, Nablus (tel: 238-0335; fax: 237-7605; e-mail: nablus@palnet.com).

Qalqilya Chamber of Commerce, Industry and Agriculture, PO Box 13, Qalqilya (tel: 294-1473; fax: 294-0164; e-mail: chamberq@hally.net).

Ramallah and Albeireh Chamber of Commerce and Industry, PO Box 256, Ramallah (tel: 295-6043; fax: 298-4691; e-mail: ramcom@palnet.com).

Tulkarm Chamber of Commerce and Industry, PO Box 51, Tulkarm (tel: 267-1010; fax: 267-5623; e-mail: tulkarm@palnet.com).

Banking
Al-Ahli Jordan Bank, Al-Quds Street, PO Box 550, Ramallah (tel: 998-6370; fax: 998-6372).

Al-Ittihad Bank for Saving and Investment, Commercial Centre, Al-Barid Street, PO Box 1557, Ramallah (tel: 298-6412/5; fax: 298-6416).

ANZ Grindlays, PO Box 19390, East Jerusalem (tel: 626-3444; fax: 626-3311).

Arab Bank, Al-Harajeh, PO Box 1476, Ramallah (tel: 298-2456; fax: 298-2444).

Arab Land Bank, PO Box 565, Jerusalem/Ramallah Road, Ramallah (tel: 298-5958; fax: 295-8426/5).

Arab Palestinian Investment Bank, Regional Headquarters, Al-Harajeh Building, PO Box 1268, Ramallah (tel: 298-7126; fax: 298-7125).

Bank of Jordan, Al-Quds Street, PO Box 1328, Ramallah (tel: 295-2696; fax: 295-2705).

Bank of Palestine, Al-Rimal Quarter, Omar El-Mukhtar Street, PO Box 50, Gaza (tel: 286-5676; fax: 282-8974).

British Bank of the Middle East, PO Box 2067, Al-Quds Street, Ramallah (tel: 298-7802, 298-1551; fax: 298-7804).

Cairo Amman Bank, Wadi El-Tuffah Street, PO Box 665, Hebron (tel: 993-6768; fax: 993-6770).

Cairo Amman Bank, El-Hussein Circle, Nablus (tel: 238-1301; fax: 238-0188).

Commercial Bank of Palestine, Al-Awdah Street, PO Box 1799, Ramallah (tel: 295-4102; fax: 295-3888).

Jordan Gulf Bank, Al-Sa'ah Circle, Ramallah (tel: 998-7680; fax: 998-7682).

Jordan Housing Bank, Rukab Street, PO Box 1473, Ramallah (tel: 998-6255; fax: 998-6275).

Jordan Kuwait Bank, Commercial Centre, Sufian Street, PO Box 33, Nablus (tel: 237-7223; fax: 237-7181).

Palestinian Construction Bank, Al-Bireh, Al-Silwadi Building, Ramallah (tel: 995-4796; fax: 995-4797).

Palestinian International Bank, PO Box 1244, Gaza (tel: 282-7360; fax: 282-5269).

Palestinian Investment Bank, Midan Al-Nahda, Al-Hilal Street, PO Box 3675, Ramallah (tel: 998-7880; fax: 998-7881).

Palestinian Islamic Bank, PO Box 1244, Al-Rimal Quarter, Omar El-Mukhtar Street, Gaza (tel: 282-7360; fax: 282-5269).

Central bank

Palestine Monetary Authority, Nablus Road; PO Box 452,, Ramallah (tel: 240-9920/1; fax: 240-9922/24; e-mail: info@pma.gov.ps).

Travel information

The Higher Council for the Arab Tourist Industry, PO Box 19850, East Jerusalem (tel: 628-1805; fax: 628-7981).

Ministry of tourism

Ministry of Tourism and Antiquities, Manger Street; PO Box 534, Bethlehem (tel: 274-1581/2/3; fax: 274-3753; email: mota@pl.org; internet site: www.visit-palestine.com).

Ministries

Ministry of Agriculture, Abu Khadrah Building, Gaza (tel: 286-5990; fax: 286-3926).

Ministry of Economy and Trade, PO Box 1629, Ramallah, West Bank (tel: 298-1214/5; fax: 298-4011).

Ministry of Finance, Omer El-Mokhtar Street, Government Departments Complex, Gaza (tel: 282-4368; fax: 282-3356).

Ministry of Housing, PO Box 4034, Omer El-Mokhtar Street, Government Departments Complex, Gaza (tel: 282-2233/4; fax: 282-2235).

Ministry of Industry, PO Box 1629, Ramallah, West Bank (tel: 298-7641/2; fax: 298-7440).

Ministry of Planning and International Co-operation, PO Box 4017, Omer El-Mokhtar Street, Government Departments Complex, Gaza (tel: 282-9260; fax: 282-4090).

Ministry of Telecommunications, Gaza (tel: 282-5612; fax: 282-4555).

Other useful addresses

Arab Medical Professions College, Al-Bireh (tel: 995-5611).

Birzeit University, Ramallah (tel: 995-7650; fax: 995-7656).

College of Islamic Studies, PO Box 21402, Beit Hanina (tel: 585-3918).

Fine Arts Institute, Ramallah (tel: 995-5974).

Girls' Arts College, PO Box 19377, Jerusalem (tel: 627-3477; fax: 627-3477).

Hebron Polytechnic College, Hebron (tel: 992-8912; fax: 993-8912).

Hebron University, Hebron (tel: 992-0995).

Higher Council for the Arab Tourist Industry, PO Box 19850, East Jerusalem (tel: 628-1805; fax: 628-3981, 628-7981).

Ibrahimieh Community College PO Box 19014, Jerusalem (tel: 626-4216; fax: 628-2925).

Jerusalem Open University, PO Box 51800, Jerusalem (tel: 581-7237; fax: 581-6734).

Khaduri College, PO Box 7, Tulkarem (tel: 671-026; fax: 672-7733).

Palestine Agricultural Relief Committee (PARC), PO Box 25128, Jerusalem (tel: 583-1897, 583-3818; fax: 582-1898).

Palestinian Economic Council for Development and Reconstruction (PECDAR), PO Box 1629, Dahyet El-Bareed, West Bank (tel: 574-7040; fax: 574-9032).

Palestine Securities Exchange, PO Box 128, Nablus, West Bank (tel: 237-5946; fax: 237-5945).

Palestinian Standards Institute, PO Box 1648, Nablus, West Bank (tel: 238-5721; fax: 237-5745).

Palestine Telecommunications Company Ltd (Patel), PO Box 1570, Al-Adel Street, Nablus (tel: 237-6225; fax: 237-6227; e-mail: paltel@palnet.com).

Internet sites

Palestine and Holy Land Tourism Guide: www.palguide.com

Palestinian National Authority (links to other sites): www.palestine-net.com

Palestinian News Agency: http://english.wafa.ps

The Electronic Intifada: http://electronicintifada.net

Panama

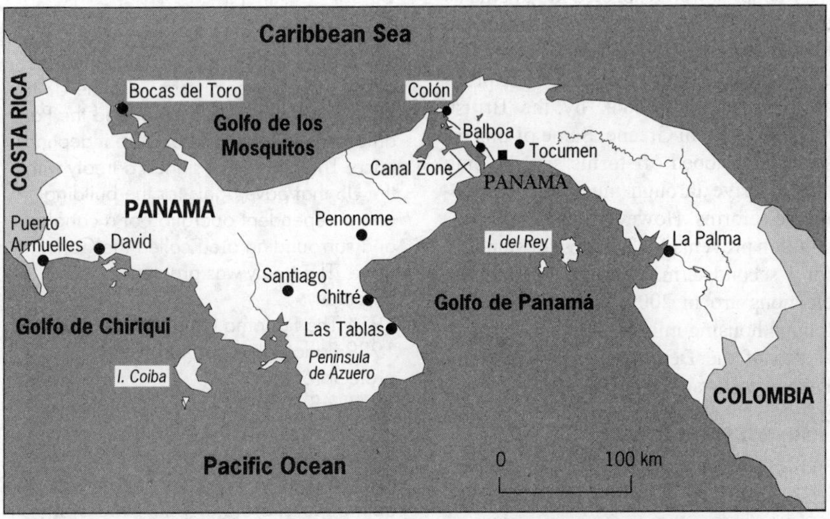

With its growth in real gross domestic product (GDP) averaging over 7.5 per cent from 2004–06, the World Bank estimates Panama to be among the fastest growing and best managed economies in Latin America. The decision to expand the Panama Canal, combined with the conclusion of a free trade agreement with the United States was eventually expected to boost and extend economic expansion. However, the World Bank noted that despite Panama's status as an upper-middle income nation, as reflected by its high GDP per capita, it is still a country of stark contrasts. Around one-third of Panama's population was living in poverty in 2007, over 10 per cent in extreme poverty.

The economy surges

In 2007, according to the United Nations Economic Commission for Latin America and the Caribbean (ECLAC), Panama's GDP grew by 9.5 per cent thanks to strong domestic and external demand. While the balance of payments current account deficit widened to the equivalent of 3.9 per cent of GDP (largely due to the increased imports needed by the fast-growing economy), on the fiscal front, the government of Martín Torrijos seemed to have the central deficit under control at 0.5 per cent of GDP. Inflationary tendencies became apparent as consumer prices climbed by an annual 5.8 per cent, more than double the rate of 2006 and the highest rate in over 20 years. Unsurprisingly, unemployment dropped significantly on the strength of high economic buoyancy. In 2008, government officials expected a comparable rate of economic growth to continue, albeit at the slower rate of 8.5 per cent. The public deficit was expected to remain below 1 per cent of GDP, reflecting the government's continued fiscal discipline.

Canal expands...

In the second half of 2007, work began on the US$5.25 billion project of extending the Panama Canal, with almost 25 per cent of GDP invested for the period 2007 to 2012. In 2007 tax revenues rose thanks to Panama's stronger economic growth, higher tax revenues resulting from the government's 2005 fiscal reform and improved efficiency in tax collection. The 23 per cent increase in tax collection exceeded expectations and was the result of higher receipts from direct and indirect taxes, especially tax on external trade. There was also a rise in transfers from decentralised enterprises (particularly the Panama Canal Authority) to the central government. According to ECLAC, Panama's public debt was estimated to represent US$10.4 billion by the end of the

KEY FACTS

Official name: República de Panamá (Republic of Panama)

Head of State: President Martín Erasto Torrijos Espino (PRD) (since Sep 2004)

Head of government: President Martín Erasto Torrijos Espino

Ruling party: Coalition: Partido Revolucionario Democrático (PRD) (Democratic Revolutionary Party) and Partido Popular (PP) (People's Party) (from May 2004)

Area: 77,082 square km

Population: 3.23 million (2007)*

Capital: Panama City

Official language: Spanish

Currency: Balboa (B and US$) and US dollar = 100 cents

Exchange rate: B and US$1.00 per US$ (fixed peg)

GDP per capita: US$5,904 (2007)*

GDP real growth: 11.20% (2007)

Labour force: 1.29 million (2004)

Unemployment: 12.60% (2004)

Inflation: 4.10% (2007)

Balance of trade: -US$3.14 billion (2006)

Visitor numbers: 843,000 (2006)*

* estimated figure

year, a reduction from 61 per cent of GDP to 54 per cent.

...free trade stalls

Although trade negotiations were completed with Nicaragua, the free trade agreement with the United States – already signed by President Bush – awaited approval by the United States Congress. At issue was the status of Mr Pedro Miguel González Pinzón, the president of Panama's National Assembly. Sr González was wanted by the USA for the murder of a US soldier in 1992 during the US invasion of Panama. The refusal of the PRD government to hand over Sr González, under pressure from the left wing of the party, had been met by opposition from business circles anxious to see the free trade agreement ratified. To complicate matters, the murdered soldier was from Puerto Rico, where the government had passed a resolution requesting the US Congress not to approve the free trade deal with Panama. Progress was also made in negotiations with Chile and Guatemala, as well as in joining the Central American integration scheme.

Although the level of transit and freight transported on vessels through the Panama Canal increased, the rise in revenues of 15 per cent was mostly a result of higher charges. Re-exports from the Colón Free Zone also grew, made up mainly by medicines, televisions, perfume and footwear driven by buoyant demand from Venezuela, Central America and Ecuador. Panama's high level of inflation, estimated at 5.8 per cent at the end of the year, pushed up the price of the basic basket reflecting higher prices for oil and other imports. The unemployment rate dropped to 4.6 per cent in August 2007.

Outlook

Sr Torrijos' father, General Omar Torrijos, who took power in 1968 in a military coup, is well respected in Panama as the dictator who recovered control of the Canal from the US. A contradictory figure, General Torrijos was also the improbable subject of a book by the British novelist Graham Greene. Some of this respect has rubbed off to his son, helping him to drive through much needed economic reforms. However, Panama's constitution prevents Mr Torrijos for standing for a second term. The next presidential elections are in 2009, when it looks as though housing minister, Balbina Herrera – also of the Democratic Revolutionary Party – will stand and win.

Risk assessment

Politics	Fair
Economy	Good
Regional stability	Good

KEY INDICATORS Panama

	Unit	2003	2004	2005	2006	2007
Population	m	3.00	3.24	3.23	*3.28	*3.34
Gross domestic product (GDP)	US$bn	12.90	14.09	15.48	17.13	19.74
GDP per capita	US$	3,870	4,524	4,799	5,217	5,904
GDP real growth	%	4.0	6.0	6.9	8.6	11.2
Inflation	%	1.7	0.5	2.9	2.5	4.1
Industrial output	% change	–	7.4	1.7	8.8	–
Agricultural output	% change	–	1.6	2.9	2.3	–
Exports (fob) (goods)	US$m	1,269.0	5,885.6	7,591.2	8,509.0	9,311.6
Imports (cif) (goods)	US$m	3,383.0	7,470.9	8,907.2	11,649.0	12,624.9
Balance of trade	US$m	-2,114.0	-1,585.3	-1,316.0	-3,140.0	-3,313.3
Current account	US$m	-410.0	-240.0	-780.0	-552.0	-1,579.0
Total reserves minus gold	US$m	1,011.0	630.6	1,210.5	1,335.0	1,935.1
Foreign exchange	US$m	992.5	611.4	1,192.5	1,315.9	1,915.4
Exchange rate	per US$	1.00	1.00	1.00	1.00	1.00

* estimated figure

COUNTRY PROFILE

Historical profile

1502 European explorers first visited Panama.
1519 Panama became part of the Vice-royalty of New Andalucia.
1821 Following independence from Spanish rule Panama joined the union of Central American provinces and became part of the confederacy of Gran Colombia. (Gran Colombia collapsed in 1830 and Panama became part of Colombia).
1846 The US signed a treaty with Colombia to build a railway across the isthmus.
1880 A canal, to link the Atlantic and Pacific oceans, was begun by Ferdinand de Lesseps, (who had previously built the Suez Canal), with French backing. Tropical disease killed thousands of workers; financial difficulties halted the project.
1903 After Colombian parliamentarians refused to endorse a treaty with the US to build a canal the US encouraged the Panamanians to rebel and declare independence. The new rulers signed a treaty with the US that gave rights for the building and independent operation of a canal and surrounding area called the Canal Zone. The treaty was granted in perpetuity.
1914 The Panama canal was completed.
1939 Panama ceased to be a US protectorate.
1941–68 Panama was mostly ruled by presidents representing the landowners, traders and building companies. Arnulfo Arias, ousted in 1941, was an unpredictable populist orator, much loved by the crowds. He was in and out of office between 1949–68.
1977 President Omar Torrijos and US president Jimmy Carter signed a treaty under which the US would hand back control of the canal to Panama and withdraw its troops by the end of 1999.
1981 Torrijos, president since 1968, died in a plane crash.
1983 General Manuel Antonio Noriega became commander of the National Guard. He increased his own power and that of the guard, which he renamed the Panama Defence Forces and assumed de facto rule of Panama.
1988 The US accused Noriega of drug trafficking. Noriega declared a state of emergency.
1989 The opposition, Alianza Democrática de Oposición Civilista (Civil Democratic Opposition Alliance) and its presidential canditate Guillermo Endara, won the elections. Noriega declared the results invalid. The US increased diplomatic pressure and threats until Noriega declared a 'state of war'. The US invaded and removed Noriega from power. He was taken to the US to stand trial on charges of drug smuggling. Endara became president.
1991 Constitutional changes adopted included the abolition of a standing army.
1992 Noriega was found guilty of drug offences and sentenced to 40 years in a US prison.
1994 Ernest Pérez Balladares won the presidential election.

1999 Mireya Elisa Moscoso Rodríguez of the Partido Arnulfista (PA) (Arnulfista Party) won the presidential elections, becoming Panama's first female president.
2000 Under the Torrijos-Carter treaty ownership and control of the Panama Zone was handed back to Panama on 1 January. President Moscoso set up a tribunal to investigate crimes and human rights abuses during the military control of 1968–89. The PA lost control of the National Assembly and an alliance led by the Partido Revolucionario Democrático (PRD) (Democratic Revolutionary Party) formed a majority.
2002 Panama signed a framework trade agreement with its five Central American neighbours to boost trade in the region. The PA gained from the defections of three members of the opposition PRD when they voted to approve Moscoso's appointees for the Supreme Court. The three deputies were accused by the PRD of accepting US$1 million in bribes. President Moscoso set up a commission to investigate corruption.
2003 A free trade agreement (FTA) with El Salvador, the first in Panama's history, came into effect in April.
2004 Martín Torrijos won presidential elections on 2 May. The PRD won most seats in the parliamentary elections, however a coalition government was formed by the PA, Movimiento de Renovación Nacional (Morena), Movimiento Liberal Republicano Nacionalista (Molirena) (Nationalist Republican Liberal Movement) and Partido Democrático (PD) (Democratic Party). On 1 September, Martín Torrijos was sworn in as president. In November it was announced that the Panama Canal had made record profits of US$1 billion during the financial year.
2005 From May to June, protesters took to the streets and strikes were called by unions after plans to increase pension contributions and raise the retirement age were announced.
2006 In July, parliament approved a US$5.25 billion programme to widen the Panama Canal. A referendum held on 22 October approved the project, which will begin in 2008 and is scheduled to be completed by 2014. On 7 November, Panama was elected as a non-permanent member of the UN Security Council.
2007 Panama took its seat on the UN Security Council on 1 January. Work began to widen the Panama Canal and build an additional series of locks, a project estimated to cost US$5.25 billion.

Political structure

In addition to their unicameral national parliaments, El Salvador, Guatemala, Honduras, Nicaragua, Panama and Dominican Republic also return directly-elected deputies to the supranational Central American Parliament.

Constitution
Panama's constitution dates from 1972 and was reformed in 1983 and 1994.

Form of state
Presidential democratic republic

The executive
The president is both head of state and head of government, elected for a period of five years by universal adult suffrage. The Cabinet is appointed by the president.

National legislature
The unicameral Asamblea Legislativa (National Assembly) has 78 seats. Members are elected by popular vote for a five-year term.

Legal system
The Corte Suprema de Justicia (Supreme Court of Justice) has nine judges appointed for 10-year terms. There are five superior courts and three courts of appeal.

Last elections
2 May 2004 (presidential and parliamentary)

Results: Presidential: Martín Torrijos won 47.44 per cent of the vote; Guillermo Endara Galimany won 30.86 per cent; José Miguel Alemán 16.39 per cent; and Ricardo Martinelli 5.31 per cent.
Parliamentary: PRD won 37.87 per cent of the votes (41 seats out of 78); Partido Arnulfista (Arnulfista Party) 19.25 per cent (17 seats); and Partido Solidaridad (Solidarity Party 15.67 per cent (nine seats).

Next elections
May 2009 (presidential and parliamentary)

Political parties

Ruling party
Coalition: Partido Revolucionario Democrático (PRD) (Democratic Revolutionary Party) and Partido Popular (PP) (People's Party) (from May 2004)

Main opposition party
Partido Panameñista (Panameñista Party) (formerly Partido Arnulfista - renamed 2005)

Population
3.23 million (2007)*

Last census: May 2000: 2,83177
Population density: 36 inhabitants per square km. Urban population: 56 per cent of the total (1994–2000).
Annual growth rate: 2.0 per cent 1994–2004 (WHO 2006)

Ethnic make-up
The population is predominantly mestizo, a mingling of indigenous Indian groups, Spanish and African (65 per cent), and Afro-Caribbean (14 per cent). Indians make up approximately 6 per cent of the total population. There are also descendants of North Americans, Chinese, French, Italians, Greeks and Asians (15 per cent).
The most numerous of Panama's indigenous groups are the Guaymi Indians who live primarily in the western provinces of Chiriqui, Bocas del Toro and Veraguas. The next most populous indigenous group is the Cuna, who live mainly in the San Blas Islands and along the nearby coast. The Choco is another indigenous group.

Religions
Traditionally the population is about 90 per cent Roman Catholic, with Protestants, Muslims, Baha'i and Hindus accounting for 5 per cent.

Education
Schooling lasts for 12 years, six years each in an elementary and a secondary school. Education is free up to university level. University education lasts for six years. There are three universities and nearly one in three of the relevant age group attends them.
Higher education is mainly provided by universities, schools and institutes. There are both public and private universities. State universities are autonomous. The University of Panama is responsible for establishing the guidelines relating to the universities in the country.

Literacy rate: 92 per cent adult rate; 97 per cent youth rate (15–24) (Unesco 2005).
Compulsory years: Six to 15
Enrolment rate: 106 per cent gross primary enrolment of relevant age group (including repeaters); 69 per cent gross secondary enrolment (World Bank).

Health
Per capita total expenditure on health (2003) was US$555; of which per capita government spending was US$368, at the international dollar rate, (WHO 2006).
Panama has both a free public health care system and a private system that are generally served by the same professionals. Panama's hospitals, clinics and insurance plans are scrambling to meet the healthcare needs of wealthier Panamanians, many of whom are retired US civil servants. The cost of healthcare in Panama is lower than in the US and is often of better quality. This is fuelling 'healthcare tourism', with US citizens visiting Panama for medical and surgical treatment.

HIV/Aids
HIV prevalence: 0.9 per cent aged 15–49 in 2003 (World Bank)
Life expectancy: 76 years, 2004 (WHO 2006)
Fertility rate/Maternal mortality rate: 2.7 births per woman, 2004 (WHO 2006)

Child (under 5 years) mortality rate (per 1,000): 18 per 1,000 live births (World Bank)

Welfare

There is a large difference between welfare levels in the cities and in the countryside in Panama. While the percentage of the population below the poverty line is 15 per cent in urban areas, it rises to 65 per cent in rural areas. The national average is 37 per cent.

Panama's social security system is financed through a 6.75 per cent contribution from individual incomes and a 2.75 per cent contribution from company payrolls. Retirement ages are 62 for men and 57 for women. Medical services are provided through the Social Insurance Fund. Sick workers can claim 70 per cent of their average earnings from the last two months for a maximum period of 52 weeks.

Main cities

Panama City (capital, estimated population 490,347 in 2005), San Miguelito (339,803), Tocumen (112,217), Arraiján (97,530), David (85,164), Colón (51,801).

Languages spoken

English is widely used, so much so that Panama should be considered bilingual. English is particularly spoken along the Caribbean coast and in the capital. Three distinct indigenous groups, the Cuna, Guaymi and Choco, also speak either Cuna, Movere or Embera.

Official language/s

Spanish

Media

Press

Dailies: In Spanish, La Prensa (www.prensa.com), El Heraldo (www.elheraldo.com.co), La Crítica Libre (www.critica.com.pa), La Estrella de Panamá (www.estrelladepanama.com) and El Siglo (www.elsiglo.com), and La República (evening). Online newspapers El Panama America (www.pa-digital.com.pa).

Weeklies: In English, The Panama News (www.thepanamanews.com) and The News Herald (www.newsherald.com) in Panama City.

Business: In Spanish, Revista Centro Financiero (www.asociacionbancaria.com) published by the central bank, FOB Zona Libre De Colón (www.colonfreezone.com) (trade directory) and Capital Financiero (www.capitalfinanciero.com).

Periodicals: There are some periodicals featuring travel and holiday news.

Broadcasting

The vast majority of television and radio broadcasting is in Spanish. There are 82 AM and 31 FM radio stations and six television stations.

Radio: In English, Panama FM (http://panamafm.com) regional station. In Spanish, RPC Radio (www.rpcradio.com), Meto 103.5 (www.meto103-5.com), Super Q (www.superqpanama.com), Omega Stereo (www.omegastereo.com) and KW Continente (http://kwcontinente.net). There are a number of local, commercial radio stations.

Television: Commercial stations, in Spanish, RPC TV (www.rpctv.com), Telemetro (www.telemetro.com) and Televisora Nacional (TVN) (www.tvn-2.com). FETV (www.fetv.org) is an educational channel.

Economy

Unlike other Central American countries, Panama does not rely on primary commodities for its wealth. As a result of its strategic position and especially the presence of the inter-oceanic canal, Panama has developed a strong service sector linked to international trade and banking. The services sector accounts for around 75 per cent of GDP. The canal, container ports and the Cólon Free Zone, which offers duty-free storage and redistribution to over 1,000 foreign companies, contribute around 20 per cent of GDP, with banking services, insurance, tourism and flagship registration also playing major roles. The prominence of the services sector in the economy helps to protect Panama from the consequences of adverse weather conditions on the agricultural sector and of low global commodity prices, which have affected neighbouring economies. In 2006, a decision was taken by referendum to expand the canal to take larger vessels.

Panama's is one of the fastest growing economies in Central America, with all the main sectors, especially tourism and financial services, showing improvements. GDP grew by 8.1 per cent in 2006, compared with 6.4 per cent in 2005. The conclusion in December 2006 of a free trade agreement with the US will encourage further growth in time.

Agriculture contributes less than 10 per cent of GDP (low by Latin American standards), industry makes up 12 per cent and construction an estimated 7 per cent.

Despite its economic strength, Panama has a highly unequal income distribution with 40 per cent of the country living below the poverty line and unemployment high. The Inter-American Development Bank estimated that in 2006 migrant workers sent some US$292 million to their families in Panama.

External trade

Panama does not belong to any regional trade or economic bloc; it has bilateral free trade agreements with El Salvador, Singapore and Taiwan.

Panama has the largest merchant fleet, with around 7,000 ships. In 2006 the Panama Canal provided 12 per cent of GDP with around 14,000 ships passing between the Pacific Ocean and the Caribbean Sea.

The Colón Free Zone (CFZ) provides the focus for foreign investment in a duty-free manufacturing zone, which is dominated by electronics, watches, pharmaceuticals, toiletries, clothing and jewellery, food processing, sugar refining and garment manufacturing.

Imports

Principal imports are capital goods, foodstuffs, consumer goods and chemicals.

Main sources: US (27.5 per cent total, 2005), The Netherlands Antilles (11.4 per cent), Costa Rica (4.7 per cent), Japan (4.0 per cent).

Main suppliers to the Colón Free Zone are Japan, (typically 20 per cent of total value), US (15 per cent), Taiwan (10 per cent) and Hong Kong (10 per cent).

Exports

Principal commodities are garments, bananas, shrimp, sugar and coffee.

Main destinations: US (44.9 per cent total, 2005), Spain (8.9 per cent), Sweden (5.6 per cent), The Netherlands (4.0 per cent)

Agriculture

Farming

Panama's principal cash crops include bananas, sugar cane and coffee. Approximately 60 per cent of the country's total landmass is in agricultural use. About 16 per cent is cultivated while the remainder is natural pasture and forest. Food production does not meet domestic demand and consequently food imports are supplied by the US in order to meet the shortfall.

As a result of its accession to the World Trade Organisation (WTO) in 1997, Panama's trading regime has been liberalised to reduce the average tariff level to 15 per cent for agricultural goods, regarded as one of the lowest in Latin America.

The agricultural sector is ailing and has experienced difficulties resulting both from metereological factors and poor demand for products. The strengthening of the agricultural sector is a government priority and includes upgrading irrigation systems and equipment. Problems include the decline in the price of coffee on international markets, which threatens to deepen rural poverty.

Crop production in 2005 included: 414,000t tonnes cereals in total, 1,680,000t sugar cane, 79,000t maize, 530,000t bananas, 125,000t plantains, 330,000t rice, 24,000t yams, 31,000t

cassava, 26,000t potatoes, 2,800t chillies and peppers, 23,500t tobacco, 17,018t oilcrops, 15,500t coconuts, 70,000t oil palm fruit, 23,500t tomatoes, 42,000t citrus fruit, 9,000t green coffee, 771,900t fruit in total, 176,450t vegetables in total.
Livestock production included: 169,154t meat in total, 63,470t beef, 20,584t pig meat, 85,100t poultry, 21,000t eggs, 187,000t milk, 6,960t cattle hides.

Fishing

The vast majority of Panama's annual fish catch is exported to the US- approximately 80 per cent- with the EU being the second biggest buyer of Panamanian fish.
Deep-sea shrimp fishing is the major activity in the sector and this type of fishing increased in increased in importance after the improvement to the port and fishing terminal at Vacamonte was completed in 1994.
Freshwater fishing and marine products have increased in production steadily since the 1990s. Lobster exports rose by 39 per cent and there were also increases in the sales of fresh and frozen fish. The exception was shrimp exports, which dropped by 50 per cent.
In 2004, the total marine fish catch was 184,119 tonnes and the total crustacean catch was 6,464 tonnes.

Forestry

The majority of Panama's forested area has semi-deciduous tropical moist vegetation, while plantation forest comprises mainly pine. Approximately 40 per cent of the country's total landmass is covered by forests.
Panama has a large network of protected forest areas. However, large-scale deforestation has led to an annual average loss of 1.65 per cent, the equivalent of 52,000ha of forest cover.
The forest industry produces modest quantity of industrial roundwood, which is used for manufacturing sawnwood and panels. Some amount of forest products particularly paper is imported. Timber imports in 2004 were US$83.5 million, while exports amounted to US$21.9 million.
Timber production in 2004 included 1,312,137 cubic metre (cum) roundwood, 93,000cum industrial roundwood, 30,000cum sawnwood, 954,000t pulpwood, 1,219,137cum woodfuel; 4,833t charcoal.

Industry and manufacturing

Panama's industrial sector remains relatively small scale, contributing around 12 per cent to total GDP and employing 16 per cent of the total workforce. The sector is predominantly geared toward domestic consumption.
The main industrial centres are Panama City and Colón, inclusive of food processing (about a third of the gross value of manufacturing output), textiles and clothing, footwear and leather goods, chemicals, plastics, paper, beverages, cigarettes, construction materials and petroleum products from the Las Minas refinery near Colón (capacity 100,000bpd).
The emphasis is on encouraging foreign investment in labour-intensive, light assembly, export-based industries.

Tourism

Tourism is now a very important industry in Panama. The sector has been actively developed by the national government as a key economic sector and now accounts for approximately 13.5 per cent of total GDP and 12.9 per cent of total employment in the country.
Still at an early stage of development, tourism offers considerable potential for growth. In addition to the Canal, there is a variety of inland and coastal destinations, particularly conducive to ecotourism, and heritage attractions.
There were 592,200 arrivals in 2004.
Cruise ship visits are being encouraged and account for a growing proportion of arrivals.

Environment

Deforestation continues at an alarming rate, even in National parks and the Canal watershed. About 80 per cent of Panama's coral reefs have been destroyed.
Soil erosion is becoming a serious problem in many areas, and Panama's desert in the province of Los Santos (the legacy of slash and burn ranching activities) is expanding.
Illegal gold mining by Colombian immigrants is also contaminating rivers and local water supplies in the Darien and Portobello National parks.
There is serious pollution in the Bay of Panama.

Mining

At present, the mining sector of the Panamanian economy contributes very little to GDP and accounts for a small section of the total labour force. Approximately 0.1 per cent of GDP is generated by the sector and 0.2 per cent of total employment is accounted for by it. However, the mining sector in Panama is, at present, severely underdeveloped. It is estimated that, if properly developed, the sector could grow to contribute as much as 15 per cent of total GDP and directly employ up to 4,000 people.
The government is keen on promoting exploration of gold and copper deposits.
Tax concessions and other benefits are available to foreign companies interested in developing the resources. However, proposals for new mines often face strong local opposition.
Copper reserves in Panama are considered to be relatively large with significant deposits in Cerro Colorado and Petaquilla, although the development of the mines has been slow. It is estimated that copper reserves at Cerro Colorado are one billion tonnes, making it one of the world's largest deposits. The Petaquilla studies show copper reserves of 1.1 billion tonnes and significant quantities of gold and molybdenum. The Cerro Quema mine has estimated gold reserves in the region of 300,000 ounces of microscopic gold.
There are also known reserves of manganese, and limited extraction of limestone, clays, gravel and sea salt. Cement is produced by Empresa Estatal de Cemento Bayano at a plant with a capacity of 300,000 tonnes per year (tpy).

Hydrocarbons

Owing to the fact that it does not possess substantial hydrocarbon reserves, Nicaragua is forced to export the vast majority of its energy needs, approximately 70 per cent. Some discoveries of oil and gas deposits have been made but not in commercially viable quantities. Therefore Panama continues to import all of the oil and coal it consumes.
There are coal deposits in provinces of Colón and Chiriquí. Panama has a refining capacity of around 60,000 barrels per day (bpd) and imports around 57,000bpd. Production of oil is very limited with production levels of around 1,000bpd.
The Panama Canal is a major transit centre, because of this Panama is very important to the hydrocarbon industry.
Petroleum products account for 14 per cent of total Canal shipments and is the largest commodity that passes through the canal. Around two-thirds of these petroleum products travel from the Atlantic to the Pacific. There are also plans to link North and South American gas and electricity grids, Panama would be essential to this idea.
Panama does not produce or import natural gas. However, it does import coal to meet consumption levels, around 69,000 tonnes.

Energy

The Plan Plan Puebla-Panama was signed in 2001. The document, which calls for an integration of electricity markets in the Central American region, includes Panama, Costa Rica, Honduras, Nicaragua, and El Salvador among its signatories.
There has been a rapid development of hydroelectric energy production in Nicaragua in recent years in, with the total potential estimated at 2,500MW. La Estrella, Los Valles and La Fortuna plants supply

around 70 per cent of the country's electricity requirements.

Financial markets

Stock exchange

There has been a stock exchange in Panama since 1960.

La Central Latinoamericana de Valores S.A. (LATIN CLEAR) began operations in May 1997, under the auspices of the Inter-American Development Bank (IDB) and the Asociación de Bolsas de Comercio de Centroamérica y Panamá (BOLCEN) (Stock Exchange Association for Central America and Panama). It serves as a regional central securities depository.

Banking and insurance

The banking and financial services sector is regulated by the Comisión Bancaria Nacional. The central bank carries out retail and commercial transactions and development banking, it is government-owned and operates as a depository of public funds. Only coins are minted locally, the notes in circulation being US dollars. Interest rates follow US dollar rates.

Panama banking was rated as top for tier one capital, among banks in Central America, as recently as 2004. The Panamanian banking sector is expected to benefit from growth in Central America rather than trying to compete against Brazil, Mexico or Argentina. Before the overall liberalisation of the banking sector in Latin America, banks had used Panama as a base to target markets in the rest of the region; those same banks can now target other Latin American markets directly.

Although it does not have the same size of assets in its banking sector, Panama has always seen its main competitors as the Cayman Islands and the Bahamas. Panama requests all banks to have a physical presence in the country.

Central bank

Banco Nacional de Panamá

Main financial centre

Panama City

Time

GMT minus five hours

Geography

Panama is a narrow country situated at the southern end of the isthmus separating North and South America. To the west is Costa Rica and to the east is Colombia in South America. The Caribbean Sea lies to the north and the Pacific Ocean to the south.

The eastern section of the country, adjoining Colombia, is thinly populated. The western section of the country, near the Costa Rican border, is the richest agricultural area.

Hemisphere

Northern

Climate

For its relatively small area, the geography of Panama's 'S'-shaped isthmus is quite varied and consists of three distinct areas. The largest, which accounts for approximately 85 per cent of the land area, is lowland coastal areas, with a tropical rainy climate. Here the temperature ranges from 21 degrees Centigrade (C) to 31 degrees C. The rainy season is approximately April–December, with the heaviest rains falling in November (about 570mm). Rainfall is significantly heavier on the Pacific coast than on the Caribbean. The driest season is January—April. About 10 per cent of the land area lies between 700 metres and 1,490 metres and has a temperate climate.

The remaining 5 per cent of the land is at an altitude of about 1,520 metres and is cold.

Dress codes

Like most of Central America, Panama remains fairly conservative and formal in respect of dress. Although Panama City is cosmopolitan, it is not considered proper for adults to wear shorts in the city, regardless of the heat. It is also considered inappropriate for women to wear shorts in public, either in the city or countryside. A certain amount of leniency is allowed to foreigners, who are thought not to know any better.

For business appointments, men should wear suits and women should wear dresses. A man may wear a panabrisa, a loose fitting, short sleeved shirt, which is not tucked into the trousers. However, these are not generally worn by top officials or businessmen during formal business meetings.

Entry requirements

Passports

Required by all, valid for six months.

Visa

Required by all, except nationals of EU/EEA and most Latin American countries, Israel, Singapore and North and South Korea. For latest information, see http://panama.embassy.uk.com.

Currency advice/regulations

There are no restrictions on the import and export of local or foreign currencies. Local currency exists only as coins and is interchangeable with US currency of the same denomination.

Health (for visitors)

Mandatory precautions

Cholera vaccination certificate if arriving from an infected area. Yellow fever vaccination certificate may be required for visits to certain regions.

Advisable precautions

A yellow fever vaccination certificate is required only for those who are going to visit the provinces of Bocas del Toro and Darien. Typhoid and polio vaccinations are advisable. Malaria risk exists in rural areas – prophylaxis recommended (in some places malaria is reported to be resistant to chloroquine). Water precautions should be taken, especially outside cities. Rabies is endemic.

Medical insurance is necessary as medical charges are high.

Hotels

There is a wide variety of hotels available. It is advisable to book in advance, particularly between December and May. There is a 10 per cent government surcharge on bills.

Credit cards

Major credit cards are accepted.

Public holidays (national)

Fixed dates

1 Jan (New Year), 9 Jan (Martyrs' Day), 1 May (Labour Day), 15 Aug (Panama City Day/Assumption Day), 3 Nov (Independence from Colombia Day), 4 Nov (Flag Day), 5 Nov (Colón City Independence Day, Colón City only), 10 Nov (First Call for Independence from Spain), 28 Nov (Independence from Spain Day,), 24 Dec (Christmas Eve), 25 Dec (Christmas Day), 31 Dec (New Year's Eve).

For public holidays falling on a Sunday, the following Monday is observed as a holiday.

Variable dates

Carnival (two days, Feb), Ash Wednesday, Maundy Thursday, Good Friday.

Working hours

Banking

Mon–Sat: 0800–1300.

Business

Mon–Fri: 0800–1200, 1400–1700; Sat: 0800–1200.

Government

Mon–Fri: 0900–1700.

Shops

Mon–Sat: 0800–1200, 1400–1800/1900.

Electricity supply

110V AC, 60 cycles (domestic), 220V AC (industrial).

Social customs/useful tips

The use of titles, such as Doctor, Arquitecto, Licenciado, Profesora, is widespread, and it is courteous to learn and use the correct titles for both men and women. Do not immediately launch into a business conversation. It is considered polite to first get to know the person to whom you are talking.

Men and women shake hands in Panama and social kisses on one cheek are also exchanged. At a large social gathering do not expect your host or hostess to introduce you to every individual. Feel free to circulate and introduce yourself. A small gift for the host or hostess is always appreciated.

Late night parties with dinner served at 2200 or 2300 are common. It is accepted to be up to two hours late for a large social gathering, 30 minutes for smaller gatherings.

Panama is an eclectic country, with a ready acceptance of immigrants from all over the world. Public celebrations therefore express the hybrid nature of its diverse cultures. Although once part of Colombia, Panamanian culture and traditions are uniquely its own and show Caribbean rather than South American influence. However, there is little interchange between different social and ethnic groups.

Do not take photos without permission, especially of Indians. Be prepared to pay for them if permission is given.

Security

Common street crime has always been prevalent in Panama City and Colón, but poverty as a result of the disrupted economy has worsened the situation. Visitors are warned specifically to avoid the San Miguelito squatter section of Panama City. The Judicial Technical Police (PTJ) is responsible for the struggle against the still prevalent narcotics traffic. The PTJ, which is supposed to work jointly with the Customs Service, is composed of former Panamanian Defence Force members and is widely reported to be corrupt.

Getting there

Air

National airline: Copa Airlines (Compañía Panameña de Aviación)

International airport/s: Panama City-Tocumen (PTY), 27km from city; duty-free shop, restaurant, buffet, bank, post office, car hire.

Airport tax: US$20.

Surface

Road: The Pan-American Highway is the main route into Panama from Costa Rica. The border with Colombia is forested and unsafe.

Rail: Panama has no rail connections with neighbouring countries.

Water: Cruise ships call at the ports of Colon on the Atlantic coast and Panama city on the Pacific coast.

Main port/s: Balboa (Pacific), Cristóbal (Atlantic).

Getting about

National transport

Air: Several domestic airlines link Panama City with all parts of the country.

Road: The road system is generally good, but sections can be unpassable in the rainy season (Apr–Dec). The Panama section of Pan-American Highway connects Chepo and Panama City with the Costa Rican border. The Trans-Isthmian Highway links Panama City and Colón.

Buses: Regional buses link most towns. Ticabus run modern air-conditioned service to main centres; it is advisable to book in advance.

Rail: The Panama Canal Railway Company operates trains daily (Mon–Fri) between Panama City and Colón.

City transport

Taxis: Travel by taxi is inexpensive. Taxis are readily available and can be ordered by telephone. Taxis are not metered, fares being regulated and fixed according to the number of zones traversed. The drivers carry a map of the zones for consultation. Fares should be agreed beforehand.

Car hire

Available in main towns and at the airport. International licence required. After 90 days a local permit is required.

BUSINESS DIRECTORY

The addresses listed below are a selection only. While World of Information makes every endeavour to check these addresses, we cannot guarantee that changes have not been made, especially to telephone numbers and area codes. We would welcome any corrections.

Telephone area codes

The international direct dialling (IDD) code for Panama is +507, followed by the customer's number.

Chambers of Commerce

American Chamber of Commerce and Industry of Panama, PO Box 168, Balboa Ancon, Panama (tel: 269-3881; fax: 223-3508; e-mail: amcham@panamcham.com).

Colón Cámara de Comercio, Agricutura e Industrias, Calle 6, Avenida Amador Guerrero 322, Colón (tel: 441-7223; fax: 441-7281; e-mail: camcolon@pananet.com).

Panama Cámara de Comercio, Industria y Agricultura, Avenidas Cuba y Ecuador 33A, PO Box 74, Zona 1, Panama (tel: 225-1233; fax: 227-4186; e-mail: infocciap@panacamara.com).

Panama Federacion de Cámaras de Comercio e Industria, Avenida Cuba, Zona 1, Panama (tel: 225-4615; fax: 227-4186).

Banking

Asociación Bancaria de Panamá, Apartado 4554, zona 5, Panama (tel: 263-7044).

Banco Comercial de Panamá SA (BANCOMER), PO Box 7659, Panama (tel: 263-6800; fax: 263-8033).

Banco Continental de Panamá SA, PO Box 135, Via España, Panama 9A (tel: 263-5955; fax: 263-7646).

Banco Disa, PO Box 7201, Panama 5 (tel: 263-5933; fax: 264-1084).

Banco de Latinoamérica SA (BANCOLAT), PO Box 4401, Panama 5 (tel: 264-0466; fax: 263-7368).

Banco del Istmo SA, PO Box 6-3823, El Dorado, Panama (tel: 269-5555; fax: 269-5168).

Banco del Pacífico SA, PO Box 6-3100, El Dorado, Panama (tel: 263-5833; fax: 263-7481).

Banco General SA, PO Box 4592, Panama 5 (tel: 227-3200; fax: 227-3427).

Banco Internacional de Costa Rica SA (BICSA), PO Box 600, Panama 1 (tel: 263-6822; fax: 263-6393).

Banco Internacional de Panamá SA (BIPAN), PO Box 11181, Panama 6 (tel: 263-9000; fax: 263-9514).

Banco Latinoamericano de Exportaciones SA (BLADEX), PO Box 6-1497, El Dorado, Panama (tel: 263-6766; fax: 269-6333).

Banco Nacional de Panamá, International Operations Department, PO Box 5220, Panama 5 (tel: 263-8292).

Banco Panamericano SA (PANABANK), PO Box 1828, Panama 1 (tel: 262-0881; fax: 269-1537).

Comisión Bancaria Nacional, Piso 12, Edificio de Boston, Viá Espana, Panama (tel: 223-2855; fax: 223-2864).

Central bank

Banco Nacional de Panamá, Via Espana 120, Torre Banco Nacional, PO Box 5220, Panama 5 (tel: 205-2000; fax: 205-2150; e-mail:mercador@banconal.com.pa).

Travel information

Copa Airlines, Avenida Justo Arosemena y Calle 39, Apartado 1572, Panama (tel: 227-5232; fax: 227-1952).

National tourist organisation offices

Instituto Panameño de Turismo, Centro de Convenciones Atlapa, PO Box 4421, Zona 5, Panama (tel: 226-7000; fax: 226-4002; e-mail: infotur@ns.ipat.gob.pa).

Ministries

Ministry of the Canal (tel: 263-4545; fax: 263-4355).

Ministry of Commerce and Industry, Edificio de la Loteria, Piso 21, Ave Cuba, Apartado 9658, Zona 4, Panama (tel: 227-4177; fax: 227-3927).

Ministry of Development and Agriculture, Edificio 576, Altos de Curundu, Avenida Frangipany, Panama (tel: 232-5041; fax: 232-5044).

Ministry of Education, Apartado 2440, Zona 3, Panama (tel: 262-2000; fax: 262-9087).

Ministry of Employment and Social Welfare, Apartado 2441, Zona 3, Panama (tel: 225-7503; fax: 225-4529).

Ministry of Finance and Treasury, Calle 35 y 36 entre Ave, Perú y Cuba, Apdo 5245, Zona 5, Panama (tel: 227-4879; fax: 227-2357).

Ministry of Foreign Affairs, Amador, Edificio, Panama 4 (tel: 228-2815; fax: 227-2716).

Ministry of Government and Justice, Calle 1 a, San Felipe, Apartado 1628, Zona 1, Panama (tel: 212-0287; fax: 212-0372).

Ministry of Health, Calle 36 y Ave Cuba, Apartado 2048, Zona 1, Panama (tel: 225-6080; fax: 227-5276).

Ministry of Housing, Ave Mexico y calle 12 de octubre, Apartado 5228, Zona 5, Panama (tel: 262-4358; fax: 262-9250).

Ministry of Labour and Social Welfare, Avenida Balboa, Edif de Diego, 7 Piso, Apdo 2441, Zona 3 (tel: 225-7503; fax: 225-4529).

Ministry of Planning and Economic Policy, Via Espana, Edif OGAWA, Apartado 2694, Zona 3, Panama (tel: 269-2810; fax: 264-7755).

Ministry of the President, Palacio Presidencial, San Felipe, Panama (tel: 227-9662; fax: 227-4119).

Ministry of Property and Finance, Calle 35 y 36, entre Ave Perú Ave Cuba, Pamana (tel: 227-3992; fax: 227-2357).

Ministry of Public Works, Curundu Edif 1019, Apartado 1632, Zona 1, Panama (tel: 232-5333; fax: 232-5776).

Other useful addresses

ARI Promotion and Marketing Department, PO Box 2097, Balboa Ancón, Panama (tel: 228-8037/5668; fax: 228-1698/7488; e-mail: ari@sinfo.net).

Asociación Panameña de Radiodifusión SA, Avenida 11 y Calle 28, Apdo 1795, Panama City (tel: 225-0160).

British Embassy, Commercial Section, Torre Swiss Bank, 4, Urb Marbella, Calle 53, Apdo 889, Panama 1 (tel: 269-0866; fax: 223-0730).

Central Post Office, Plaza Catedral, Calle 6, Panama City.

Colón Free Zone, Avenida Roosevelt, Apdo 1118, Colón (tel: 441-5794, 441-5114, 445-1033, 445-1559; fax: 445-2165).

Consejo Nacional de Inversiones (CNI), Edif Banco Nacional de Panamá, Apdo 2350, Panama (tel: 647-211).

Consular and Maritime Affairs, PO Box 5245, 50th Street and 69th Street, Plaza Guadalupe, San Francisco, Panama 5 (tel: 270-0166, 277-0326; fax: 270-0716).

Corporación Azucarera La Victoria, Apartado 1228,, zona 1, Panama (tel: 229-4797; fax: 229-4806).

Dirección Nacional de Medios de Comunicación Social (Panamanian Media Authority), Ministerio de Gobierno y Justicia, Apartado 1628, zona 1, Panama (tel: 262-3197/3166; fax: 262-1490).

Empleos y Servicios de Oficina SA (translator Service), Avenida 4, Panama City (tel: 225-0527).

Instituto de Recursos Hidráulicos y Electrificación (IRHE), Edif Poli, Avenida Justo Arosemanay 26 Este, Apdo 5285, Panama 5 (tel: 262-6272).

Instituto Panameño de Comercio Exterior, Avenida Manuel Icaza, Apdo 1897, El Dorado 6, Panama.

Panama Stock Exchange, Calle Elvira Mendez y Calle 52, Edificio Vallarino, Panama (tel: 269-1966; fax: 269-2457).

Panamanian Embassy (USA), 2862 McGill Terrace, NW, Washington DC 20008 (tel: (+1-202)-483-1407; fax: (+1-202)-483-8413: e-mail: panaemb@erols.com).

ProPrivat, Ave Perú y Calle 35, Apartado Postal 1464-Paitilla, Panama (tel: 225-0123/6172/4387/0630; fax: 227-4620).

Sindicato de Industriales de Panamá, Apdo 952, Panama City (tel: 230-0619).

US Embassy, Avenida Balboa entre Calle 37 y 38, Apdo 6959, Panama 5 (tel: 227-1777; fax: 203-9470).

Internet sites

Daily internet newspaper: El Siglo: http://www.elsiglo.com

General information on doing business in Panama: http://www.infonetsa.com/infonetsa/incorp/buss1.htm

Papua New Guinea

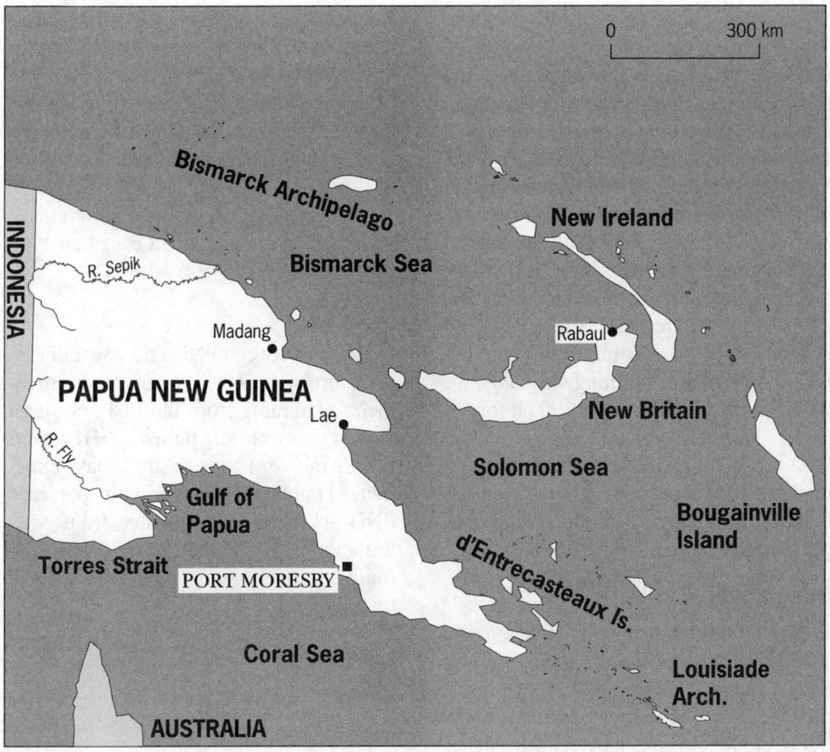

At the end of the Second World War Papua New Guinea (PNG) was just emerging from traditional modes of life. Educational facilities – whether supplied by government funds, aid or missionary donations – were limited. The indigenous population lived (and many still do) in small villages, clans and tribes, isolated from one another geographically and socially. This division has evolved into strong local and regional sentiments, and the central government has found it difficult to impose national cohesion.

Australian relations

Relations between PNG and Australia have long been complicated by the fact that PNG was once ruled as a colony by Australia. Accusations, from Port Moresby, of neo-colonialism and patronising behaviour are not uncommon. The Enhanced Co-operation Package (ECP) proved to be no exception. In December 2004, the PNG government was incensed by an Australian think-tank's report, which suggested that PNG was heading for social and economic meltdown. In May 2005, the PNG Supreme Court ruled that the deployment of 210 Australian police in PNG under the provisions of the ECP broke local laws. The Australian police were initially deployed to assist with law and order issues in the country and it had been stipulated in the ECP that they would be immune from local prosecution. Despite the ensuing chill in PNG-Australian relations, the Australian police units were allowed to return to PNG in August, although with a restricted mandate.

Relations between PNG and Australia also took another one of their periodical nosedives when PNG prime minister Sir Michael Somare was forced to remove his shoes during a brush with Australian airport security. Somare expressed his outrage and accused the Australian authorities of treating him like a suspected terrorist.

Prime Minister Somare, who led Papua New Guinea to independence, was its first prime minister. Twenty-five years later,

KEY FACTS

Official name: The Independent State of Papua New Guinea (PNG)

Head of State: Queen Elizabeth II; represented by Governor General Sir Paulias Matane (since 29 Jun 2004)

Head of government: Prime Minister Sir Michael Somare (NAP) (since 2002; re-elected 13 Aug 2007)

Ruling party: Coalition led by the National Alliance Party (NAP) (from Aug 2002)

Area: 462,840 square km

Population: 6.06 million (2007)*

Capital: Port Moresby

Official language: English, Tok Pisin, Motu

Currency: Kina (K) = 100 toea

Exchange rate: K2.57 per US$ (Jul 2008)

GDP per capita: US$991 (2007)*

GDP real growth: 6.20% (2007)*

Labour force: 3.40 million (2005)

Unemployment: 80.00% (In urban areas)

Inflation: 1.70% (2007)*

Balance of trade: US$1.48 billion (2006)

Foreign debt: US$2.80 billion (2003)

Visitor numbers: 102,400 (2007–08)

* estimated figure

after winning the national election in 2002, it was Somare who formed a ruling coalition involving 17 of the 18 political parties represented in parliament. Until May 2004, the only opposition party was the PNG Party lead by former prime minister, Sir Mekere Morauta. In May 2004, Sir Michael reshuffled his cabinet and governing coalition, bringing Sir Mekere's PNG Party into government and removing seven cabinet ministers, including Peter O'Neill and other members of the party he leads – the People's National Congress Party. As a result, Peter O'Neill became the Leader of the Opposition. 2006 saw a number of cabinet reshuffles, with Somare assuming the role of minister for foreign affairs and trade in addition to that of prime minister, and Don Polye appointed as deputy prime minister.

The 13 August 2007 elections saw the re-election of Prime Minister Sir Michael Somare with 86 votes to 21 for Sir Julius Chan.

A middling economy

After several years in the doldrums, the PNG economy continued to register steady growth of 6.5 per cent in 2007. In parliament in July 2008, PNG's treasurer, Patrick Pruaitch, delivered his state of the economy speech. 'The pick up in growth', he said, 'came mainly from the construction and communication sectors, a rebounding mining sector and more robust agriculture. Employment picked up by 10 per cent with particular strength in the retail, agriculture, building and construction, transport, storage, communication and the manufacturing sectors'. He expected growth in 2008 to be strong at 7.6 per cent.

The PNG economy is dependent on export earnings that are subject to price fluctuations in the external sector. Economic prospects from year to year are influenced significantly by international commodity prices, particularly those of gold, oil, copper, logs, coffee, copra oil and cocoa. Minerals, oil and agricultural products continue to account for the majority of PNG's exports. The contribution of the mining and petroleum sector to economic growth is uncertain in the longer term, with gains from new projects such as the PNG gas project and the Ramu nickel mine being offset to an extent by an expected long-term decline in oil production and closure of existing mines.

PNG has a dual, contrasting economy, comprising a formal, corporate-based economy and a large informal economy where subsistence farming accounts for the bulk of economic activity. The formal sector provides a narrow employment base, consisting of workers engaged in mineral production, a relatively small manufacturing sector, public sector employees and service industries.

Bougainville splits, sort of

In May 2005, the people of Bougainville voted in landmark elections for a president and parliament. According to the terms of the 2001 peace agreement, which had formally brought to an end nearly 14 years of separatist conflict, the island of Bougainville was to have its own autonomous president and parliament – the Bougainville Autonomous Government (BAG). This set it apart from PNG's 18 other provinces. Bougainville is also permitted to hold a referendum from 2011 on full independence from PNG. Many Bougainville inhabitants owe their tribal allegiance to the Solomon Islands. As a colony the island was ruled as part of the Solomon Islands by the UK, not by Australia. A former separatist leader, Sam Kabui, won the presidency in a landslide – taking more than 55 per cent of the vote in the first round. Kabui's party, the Peoples' Congress Party (PCP) emerged as the largest faction in the 40-seat parliament and proceeded to form a coalition government.

Joseph Kabui died in June 2008 and vice president John Tabinaman became acting president.

Outlook

Relations between PNG and Australia remain bruised from a series of disagreements stemming from the ECP, not least over the issue of policing. However, PNG's relations with Australia have experienced numerous peaks and troughs since PNG achieved independence from Australia in 1975. The fact remains that Australia is PNG's largest aid donor and trading partner.

With rises in world oil prices, PNG can expect a windfall from the export of its own domestic fields.

Risk assessment

Politics	Fair
Economy	Fair
Regional stability	Fair

KEY INDICATORS — Papua New Guinea

	Unit	2003	2004	2005	2006	2007
Population	m	5.45	5.50	5.94	*6.13	*6.32
Gross domestic product (GDP)	US$bn	3.40	4.29	4.01	5.58	*4.33
GDP per capita	US$	569	686	675	*708	*685
GDP real growth	%	2.0	2.5	3.3	3.7	*4.3
Inflation	%	11.8	7.4	1.7	3.5	*4.3
Natural gas output	bn cum	–	–	–	–	–
Exports (fob) (goods)	US$m	1,800.0	2,437.0	2,833.0	4,453.0	–
Imports (cif) (goods)	US$m	1,423.0	1,353.0	1,651.0	2,970.0	–
Balance of trade	US$m	377.0	1,084.0	1,182.0	1,483.0	–
Current account	US$m	380.0	640.0	152.0	*163.0	*259.0
Total reserves minus gold	US$m	494.2	632.6	718.1	1,400.7	2,053.7
Foreign exchange	US$m	489.9	631.2	717.5	1,400.0	2,052.9
Exchange rate	per US$	3.61	3.22	2.96	2.96	2.75

COUNTRY PROFILE

Historical profile

Papua New Guinea (PNG) was formed by the merger of the Territory of Papua, under Australian rule from 1906, with the Trust Territory of New Guinea, a former German possession which Australia administered from 1914, first under a military government, then under a League of Nations mandate, established in 1921, and later under a trusteeship agreement with the UN.

1942–45 Parts of both territories were occupied by Japanese forces during the Second World War.

1949 A joint administration for the two territories was established by Australia. The union was named the Territory of Papua and New Guinea.

1971 The territory was renamed Papua and New Guinea.

1975 Became independent as Papua New Guinea.

1988 Conflict on Bougainville Island began when a number of locals, unhappy with the level of royalties they were receiving from the Panguna copper mine and concerned about its environmental impact, began to protest. The islanders' opposition organised itself into the Bougainville Revolutionary Army (BRA) and full-scale war began.
1989 Panguna mine was closed down by protesters.
1997 Prime Minister Julius Chan attempted to hire UK-based mercenaries to quell the nine-year Bougainville uprising, prompting intervention by the Australian navy and the resignation of Chan. Bill Skate, a reformist, was elected prime minister in July. The government that took power with Skate was dominated by politicians from the previously ousted government.
1998 The government signed a truce with the secessionist group, the BRA, seeking to end the nine-year rebellion on the island of Bougainville, in which up to 20,000 are believed to have been killed. The People's Progress Party (PPP) left the ruling coalition, joining opposition parties and groups in an attempt to oust Skate's government. The prime minister announced the suspension of parliament.
1999 The interim Bougainville Reconciliation Government (BRG) held its first sitting. Skate resigned from the PNG premiership and was replaced by Sir Mekere Morauta of the People's Democratic Movement (PDM).
2000 Morauta was forced to adjourn parliament after a bid to limit inter-party defections threatened to trigger a vote of no confidence in his government. Local landowners brought a suit against Rio Tinto in the US courts, for environmental and social damage at Panguna.
2001 The Bougainville Peace Agreement was signed between the government of Papua New Guinea and leaders of Bougainville. Papua New Guinea accepted Australian aid for taking asylum-seekers who sought to settle in Australia.
2002 Elections were won by Sir Michael Somare's National Alliance Party (NAP); parliament elected Somare as prime minister and he formed a coalition government of 13 parties and 20 independent MPs, led by the NAP.
2003 A new heads of agreement was signed in July for the proposed US$6 billion PNG gas pipeline to Queensland, Australia. On 23 November, the Supreme Court ruled that the election of Sir Albert Kipalan as governor general was invalid. Parliament Speaker Bill Skate became acting governor general following the expiration of the term of Sir Silas Atopare. In December, Sir Pato Kakaraya was elected governor general, defeating Sir Albert Kipalan by 52 votes to 39.
In December, an agreement signed by Papua New Guinea and Australia introduced more Australian involvement in PNG in areas of law and order and public administration.
2004 On 31 March, the Supreme Court ruled the election of Sir Pato Kakaraya as governor general null and void and ordered a new election. On 18 May, Prime Minister Sir Michael Somare dismissed the People's National Congress (PNC) ministers from the cabinet.
In May, talks got under way to finalise the constitution for the autonomous government of Bougainville province.
Sir Paulias Matane was sworn in as governor general of PNG on 29 June.
2005 In elections held from 20 May to 2 June, Joseph Kabui of the Bougainville People's Congress was elected president of the Bougainville Autonomous Government. Rebel leader of the Bougainville secessionists, Francis Ona, died in July.
2006 Continuous, heavy rains early in the year caused destruction and food shortages in several provinces. The government declared a state of emergeny in Southern Highlands province in August.
2007 On 13 August, Prime Minister Sir Michael Somare was re-elected by parliament with 86 votes to 21 for Sir Julius Chan.
2008 On the 8 June, the president of Bougainville, Joseph Kabui died; vice president John Tabinaman became acting president.

Political structure

Constitution

The political structure is that of a unicameral parliamentary democracy. The present constitution came into effect in 1975 when the country became independent within the Commonwealth.
The 1975 constitution provided for the decentralisation of power to 20 provincial governments. Since then, Papua New Guinea (PNG) has been developing a system of local government.
An amendment to the constitution in 1977 led to the formation of 20 elected provincial governments which enjoy limited legislative and administrative powers and are funded mainly by central government.
Administrative divisions:

Bougainville	Milne Bay
Central	Morobe
Chimbu	National Capital
Eastern Highlands	New Ireland
East New Britain	Northern
East Sepik	Sandaun
Enga	Southern Highlands
Gulf	Western
Madang	Western Highlands
Manus	West New Britain

In May/June 2005, Bougainville elected an autonomous government to run the island, with PNG's federal government retaining control over defence and the economy.

Form of state

Sovereign independent state; it is a member of the Commonwealth.

The executive

The British monarch is the head of state and is represented by the governor general whose normal term of office is six years. Effective power resides with the prime minister and his cabinet, the National Executive Council. The governor general is appointed on the recommendation of the National Executive Council and on the basis of a simple majority vote in parliament. The prime minister is appointed by the head of state on the proposal of parliament.

National legislature

The National Parliament is a unicameral legislature, with 109 members, elected by universal adult suffrage. The normal term of office is five years. Eighty-nine of the parliamentary seats represent open constituencies and the remaining 20 seats represent the provincial constituencies. The speaker and deputy speaker, who may not hold ministerial posts, are elected by parliament.
The National Parliament was reconvened on 24 July 2001, having been adjourned in November 2000 by Prime Minister Sir Mekere Morauta to avoid a motion of no confidence.

Legal system

The legal system is based on English common law. The national judicial system comprises the Supreme Court, the national court and subsidiary courts. The Supreme Court is responsible for all matters concerning the interpretation of the constitution and is the final court of appeal. The Chief Justice is appointed by the head of state and the judiciary is formally independent of other branches of government.

Last elections

15–29 June 2002 (parliamentary)
Results: Parliamentary: NAP won 19 seats (out of 109); PDM won 13 seats; and the People's Progress Party (PPP) won eight.

Next elections

June 2007 (parliamentary)

Political parties

Papua New Guinea has no real party system and most members of parliament function as independents, although they have various party labels.

Ruling party

Coalition led by the National Alliance Party (NAP) (from Aug 2002)

Main opposition party
People's Democratic Movement (PDM)

Population
6.06 million (2007)*
Last census: July 2000: 5,190,786
Population density: 11 inhabitants per square km. Urban population: 18 per cent (1995—2001).
Annual growth rate: 2.4 per cent 1994–2004 (WHO 2006)

Ethnic make-up
Most of the population is Melanesian. There are numerous other ethnic groups in Papua New Guinea's 20 provinces, including those of Papuan, Polynesian and Micronesian descent. There is a sizeable minority of Australians, some Europeans and a small Chinese community in the country's limited commercial centre.

Religions
The indigenous population is mainly pantheistic, although a significant proportion has adopted Christianity. There are more than 10 different Christian religious groups in the country, including a substantial Roman Catholic congregation (22 per cent of the population) and various Protestant congregations (44 per cent). Indigenous beliefs account for 34 per cent of the population.

Education
Education standards before independence were poor, reflected in low literacy levels in the workforce. School fees have to be paid although these are subsidised by the government. Staff shortages remain an acute problem at secondary level. Lack of materials and up to date curricula are further burdens for the education system. Despite these disadvantages, there has been some development, made possible by help from the Australian government, through AusAid. AusAid has improved the condition of student housing and provided science laboratories in several schools.
In April 2004, Japan made a grant of US$2.6 million to the University of Goroka.
Literacy rate: 66 per cent, adult rates (2003).
Enrolment rate: 80 per cent gross primary enrolment of relevant age group (including repeaters); 47 per cent gross secondary enrolment (World Bank).
Pupils per teacher: 38 in primary schools.

Health
Per capita total expenditure on health (2003) was US$132; of which per capita government spending was US$118, at the international dollar rate, (WHO 2006).
The population suffers from poor health. The government provides hospitals and other health care facilities, and while hospital treatment is available in all major centres, they have varying levels of service and efficiency. A charge on the basis of ability to pay is levied for health services, although most people are treated free or make only a small contribution.
In May 2004, health authorities stated that the maternal death rate in PNG was greater than in any other Pacific island; over 1,000 women per annum, die of complications. A survey in late 2004 found that 1 per cent of expectant mothers were testing possitive for HIV and fears are that PNG has reached the trigger point for a widespread epidemic of Aids.
PNG is to receive US$20 million to fight malaria from the Global Fund, set up to fight malaria, Aids and tuberculosis; the money was allocated for a five-year period, with the first US$6 million forwarded in May 2004. Insecticide impregnated anti-malaria nets have been provided by the World Health Organistion and Australian aid, to increased numbers of children and reduced the incidence of the desease, acknowledged as the number one killer of children in PNG.
A measles inoculation programme to vaccinate over 120,000 children, mostly in the East Sepik Province, was undertaken in 2004.
An agreement of employment between the governments of PNG and Cuba in 2006, allowed 20 Cuban doctors to work in rural areas of PNG to overcome an acute shortage.

HIV/Aids
There is a serious AIDS epidemic in PNG, which has the largest number of HIV positive citizens in the Pacific region. While the prevalence rate is only 2 per cent, for those at most risk the rate is 16 per cent.
In 2002, 15,000 people had the disease, by August 2005 the reported number was over 40,000, however screening of 3000 A&E patients at the Port Moresby General Hospital found 18 per cent were HIV positive; other evidence indicates the current prevalence rate is doubling each year.
In August 2005 220 new HIV/Aids cases were being reported monthly, the overall number of HIV/Aids cases was 60,000. In 2006, the health minister reported that infection rates in some remote parts of the country was over 10 per cent and nationwide the rate was rising by 30 per cent per annum.
HIV prevalence: 2 per cent aged 15–49 in 2005
Life expectancy: 60 years, 2004 (WHO 2006)
Fertility rate/Maternal mortality rate: 3.9 births per woman, 2004 (WHO 2006)
Birth rate/Death rate: 31 births per 1,000 population; 7.6 deaths per 1,000 population (2003).
Child (under 5 years) mortality rate (per 1,000): 69 per 1,000 live births (2003)

Welfare
A number of defined-contribution provident funds provide limited social benefits. A National Provident Fund (NPF) provides social benefits for employees of private-sector companies with 20 or more personnel, while the Public Officers' Superannuation Fund (POSF) provides a similar facility for public servants.

Main cities
Port Moresby (capital, estimated population 299,396 in 2005), Lae (82,527), Kokopo (33,805), Arawa (40,266), Madang (29,015), Goroka (18,639).

Languages spoken
Tok Pisin or Pidgin is the lingua franca of the islands. It is derived from Melanesian Pidgin and includes German and English words. English is spoken by only 1–2 per cent of the population but is the language of government and business, however in parliamentary sessions, Pidgin is used. Motu is spoken by Motuan villagers and has been modified into Police Motu which is spoken widely in the southern region. There are 715 indigenous languages.

Official language/s
English, Tok Pisin, Motu

Media

Press
There are numerous newspapers and magazines published in English, Tok Pisin and vernacular languages.
Dailies: In English, the two main daily newspapers are The National (www.thenational.com.pg) and Papua New Guinea Post-Courier (www.postcourier.com.pg) published Monday to Friday.
Weeklies: Times of Papua New Guinea is a well-regarded weekly publication in English.

Broadcasting
Radio: The government-owned National Broadcasting Commission (NBC-PNG) (www.nbc.com.pg) operates two AM networks and a FM commercial station broadcasting in English, Tok Pisin and various other local languages. Two other independent, national commercial radio stations are in operation, Nau FM and Yumi FM; plus broadcasts are received from Australia.
Television: Fiji Television Limited owns PNG's only television station EMTV, which has an estimated 2.5 million audience and about 38 per cent of the advertising market. The Media council monitors the output for local content and community initiatives in broadcasting.

Economy

Papua New Guinea is a poor but potentially properous country, which is heavily reliant on international aid. It is well-endowed with natural resources, including gold, timber, hydrocarbons, fish and copper, but taking full advantage of them has been hampered by geography. Communications are poor, making minerals difficult and expensive to extract and transport. These sectors are exploited mainly by foreign interests. Minerals, including oil and gas, account for nearly three-quarters of exports and around 50 per cent of GDP.

The majority of the population live outside the narrow organised economic activity – 85 per cent of the population depend on subsistence farming for their livelihood. Over 40 per cent of the population survive on less than US$1 per day. Only around two per cent of the land is suitable for agriculture, mainly in coastal areas and upland plateaux. Some cash crops, such as coffee, palm oil and tea, are nevertheless grown and exported. The agricultural sector contributes around 30 per cent of GDP.

The Bank of Papua New Guinea has said that the fuel price per litre was around K2 (US$0.72) in 2007, compared with K5 ($1.82) in 2008. This has meant that throughout the country goods and services cost more, as the increase in the global fuel price is being passed on to businesses and consumers.

External trade

Papua New Guinea is a member of the South Pacific Regional Trade and Economic Co-operation Agreement (Sparteca) along with 12 other regional nations, which allows products duty free access by Pacific Island Forum members to Australian and New Zealand markets (subject to the country of origin restrictions). It is also a member of the Melanesian Spearhead Group (with Fiji, Solomon Islands and Vanuatu) as a sub-regional trade group, whereby customs tariffs have been harmonised and a free trade agreement is in negotiation.

Imports

Principal imports are machinery and transport equipment, manufactured goods, food, fuels and chemicals.

Main sources: Australia (52.3 per cent total, 2006), Singapore (12.6 per cent), China (5.9 per cent).

Exports

Principal exports are oil, gold, copper ore, timber, palm oil, coffee, cocoa and shellfish.

Main destinations: Australia (30.1 per cent total, 2006), Japan (8.1 per cent), China (5.7 per cent).

Agriculture

Farming

Agriculture accounts for around 27 per cent of GDP. More than 80 per cent of the population depend on agriculture for their livelihoods. Approximately 5 per cent of land area is cultivated arable, which is restricted by dense rain forests and mountainous terrain.

Coconuts, coffee, cocoa, palm oil, rubber and tea are grown as cash crops on plantations, emloying around one-third of those engaged in agriculture.

Processing, quality control and pricing for main crops are the concern of the Coffee Marketing Board and the Copra Marketing Board, which operate stabilisation funds for these products and for cocoa.

Smallholdings produce 70 per cent of all coffee for export, in addition to subsistence crops of yams, sago, cassava, bananas, pineapples, vegetables, sweet potatoes, tea, natural rubber, groundnuts, sorghum and rice, with some raising of pigs, goats and poultry.

A 2004 study showed that the population of PNG was eating less imported meat and rice. With the devaluation of the kina since the 1990s, it is thought that fewer people can afford the imported food and are returning to their native diets, which PNG farmers have been quick to provide. Food production has kept pace with the population growth.

Estimated crop production for 2005 included: 10,600 tonnes (t) cereals in total, 1,300,000t oil palm fruit, 260,000t taro, 520,000t sweet potatoes, 290,000t yams, 125,000t cassava, 5,600t treenuts, 870,000t bananas, 2,750t pulses, 9,000t tea, 650,000t coconuts, 477,640t oilcrops, 42,500t cocoa beans, 60,000t green coffee, 450,000t sugar cane, 4,000t natural rubber, 1,805,200t fruit in total, 500,720t vegetables in total. Livestock production included: 405,120t meat in total, 3,300t beef, 66,000t pig meat, 330,000t game meat, 5,697t poultry, 4,910t eggs, 160t honey.

Fishing

One considerable resource Papua New Guinea has yet to exploit is its fishing grounds, probably the world's richest. The total annual fish catch is over 300,000 tonnes, but the country's waters have been estimated to be capable of supplying up to one million tonnes of fish a year. PNG's waters are home to more than 1,800 different species of fish. Activity in the sector is largely centred on domestic fleets tapping the country's 2.3 million square kilometres exclusive fishing zone. Foreign fleets have been excluded from the zone. PNG has become one of the biggest players in the Western tuna fish industry. The growth of the industry has been encouraged by favourable government policies such as the removal of export duties on fisheries products.

Investment in a marine park was announced by the government in November 2007. The park of 860 acres at Vidar, outside Madang, with an estimated cost of US$36.3 million, will include a jetty for small boats and a wharf for large purse seiners, a fish market, cold rooms, ice-making and processing plants and other facilities including a township. PNG provides 10 per cent of the world's supply of tuna but its status as a primary industry does not return value-added revenue. The European Union, the biggest consumer of Pacific tuna, has negotiated with PNG to provide more favourable terms for importing its tuna.

In 2004, the total marine fish catch was 218,868 tonnes and the total crustacean catch was 1,708 tonnes.

Forestry

The economy benefits from huge exports of tropical logs, while the sawn timber industry caters to domestic demands. Forests and woodlands cover around 93 per cent of land area, but are subject to deforestation for tropical timber exports and to pollution from mining projects. The government is seeking to regain control of an industry which seems to have operated outside existing regulations and in which political corruption has played an important part. There has been little monitoring of commercial operations and reforestation is inadequate.PNG has a relatively small plantation estate.

PNG has an established presence in the Asian log market and exports around one million cubic metres of logs annually to South Korea, as well as around 400,000 cubic metres to Japan.

In 2004, forest exports amounted to US$225.8 million and imports amounted to US$9.5 million.

Timber production in 2004 included 7,241,000 cubic metre (cum) roundwood, 1,708,000cum industrial roundwood, 60,000cum sawnwood, 1,611,000cum sawlogs and veneer logs, 45,000cum wood-based panels, 5,533,000cum woodfuel.

Industry and manufacturing

The industrial sector, including mining, accounts for around 40 per cent of GDP and employs 10 per cent of the workforce. Manufacturing accounts for around 9 per cent of GDP.

Industry is focussed on mining (gold, silver, copper), crude oil and processing agricultural products. Copra crushing, palm and coconut oil processing, sugar processing, brewing, meat production, plywood production and wood chip production are prominent. Government policy, through the Industrial Centres

Development Corporation, aims to promote non-mining sectors, particularly import substitution and export-oriented industries such as manufacturing and downstream processing. Main activities include boat-building, steel fabrication and manufacture of cement, paper products, soap, matches, chemicals, paint, sawn timber, furniture, plywood, bottles and cigarettes.

Tourism

Tourism is at an early stage of development, but, with over 90 per cent of the land area still forested, there is enormous potential especially for adventure and eco-tourism. The sector is expected to contribute 5.8 per cent of GDP in 2005. The authorities recognise the economic value of tourism and have stepped up promotion and infrastructure development. A problem which was identified as a cause of a decline in visitor numbers in recent years was a perception of lawlessness in PNG. The decline was reversed by 2003, assisted by improved air connections, and continued into 2004, when 60,715 arrivals were recorded. Australia is the largest market, followed by Japan and other Asian countries. Around two-thirds of visits are for business purposes, but leisure tourism is an increasing proportion of the total, enhanced by cruise ship visits.
Unesco added the Kuk Early Agricultural Site to its World Heritage List in July 2008.

Environment

Papua New Guinea, Philippines, Indonesia, Australia and Solomon Islands are the countries with the most coral reef fish species.

Mining

Mining contributes around 8 per cent of GDP. Copper and gold are the most important export minerals. Most mineral resources are difficult and costly to extract.

Hydrocarbons

PNG has proven oil reserves of around 200 million barrels. Annual production, destined mostly for Asian and Australian markets, has declined significantly from its high of 140,000 barrels per day (bpd) in the 1990s to around 46,000 bpd. There is active exploration for oil both onshore and offshore. The challenge facing Papua New Guinea is to bring other discoveries online as older fields are depleted. PNG may have substantial untapped reserves of oil and gas, although the rugged terrain and the problems of inaccessibility are major obstacles to exploration and recovery costs are very high. There can also be problems in gaining permission to use land because of the land ownership system. InterOil Corporation completed the construction of Papua New Guinea's first oil refinery at Napa Napa in 2004. The refinery can process 32,500bpd at full capacity and supply the PNG domestic market, leaving 35 per cent of its output for foreign export.
PNG has natural gas reserves totalled 431 billion cubic metres, but as yet there is no extraction industry. A gas pipeline linking PNG to Queensland, Australia, is under construction. Although this pipeline remains a government priority, there is increasing emphasis on developing downstream gas processing facilities.
There are no known coal reserves or production in PNG. Negligible quantities of coal are imported.

Energy

Around 80 per cent of electricity supply is generated by hydro-power, most of the remainder by oil-fired thermal stations. The major hydroelectric schemes are located at Port Moresby, Ramu River and the Gazelle Peninsula.

Financial markets

Stock exchange

The Port Moresby Stock Exchange (POMsox) was established in 1999. It is one of the world's smallest exchanges, with only 13 listed companies in 2004. These include Credit Corporation (PNG) Limited and foreign companies: Durban Roodepoort Deep (DRD), Cue Energy Resources, Highlands Pacific, InterOil Corporation, Lihir Gold and Mosaic Oil.
Total turnover for week ending 20 August 2004 was K131,673.10.

Banking and insurance

Central bank

Bank of Papua New Guinea

Main financial centre

Port Moresby

Time

GMT plus 10 hours

Geography

Papua New Guinea (PNG) has only one land border with Indonesia, which lies at the west end of the island of New Guinea. PNG lies across the Torres Stait, north of the north-eastern extremity of Australia. Although the bulk of the country's land area is formed by the mainland, PNG includes many smaller islands, principally the Bismark Archipelago, which largely comprises New Britain, New Ireland and Manus, and the North Solomon Islands of which Bougainville and Buka are the largest. PNG has coastlines extending for a total of 5,152km; its highest point is Mount Wilhelm, at 4,509 metres.
The country is a land of great geographic diversity. The coast is low-lying swamp, the central core has a massive system of mountain ranges but there is also an extensive range of foothills as well as volcanoes (PNG forms a constituent part of the Pacific 'Rim of Fire' – a line of tectonic activity, which produces many volcanoes in a string that stretches from New Zealand in the south-east and circles the Pacific up to the Aleutian Islands and down along the US west coast). The country has substantial mineral wealth and good agricultural potential with fertile soil and abundant rainfall. There are large expanses of tropical forest and good fishery stocks.

Hemisphere

Southern

Climate

Papua New Guinea has a tropical climate with an average maximum temperature of 33 degrees Celsius (C) and an average minimum of 22 degrees C. Temperature and humidity are fairly constant throughout the year. The Highlands region has a more temperate climate than the rest of the country. Papua New Guinea also has seasonal monsoons, varying considerably between regions. Rainfall totals up to 4,600mm per year in some areas.

Dress codes

As Papua New Guinea is in the tropics, light clothes are worn at all times, although travellers to the Highlands may require sweaters for the evening. Business wear is usually lightweight trousers and a short sleeved shirt. The Australian sartorial influence can be seen in the wearing of shorts and long socks by males even in administrative positions. Jackets are not normally required but safari suits are often worn. Formal evening wear is seldom required but sometimes tropical formal wear is stipulated on invitations and this would mean a long sleeved shirt and tie for men and a cocktail dress for women.

Entry requirements

Passports

Required by all. Passports must be valid for 12 months from the date of entry.

Visa

Required by all. Contact the nearest PNG Consulate for visa details and application form.
All travellers should be in possession of sufficient funds for onward or return flight before the expiry date of their visa.
Visa conditions are liable to change and should be checked before travelling.

Currency advice/regulations

The import of local and foreign currency is unlimited. Export of local currency is limited to K200; foreign currency is limited to K10,000 (equivalent), amounts greater require approval from the Central Bank.
Travellers cheques are readily accepted; to avoid additional exchange charges

cheques should be in Australian or US dollars or pound sterling.

Customs

The export of items of ethnographic interest is banned.

Prohibited imports

Health (for visitors)

Mandatory precautions

Vaccination certificates for yellow fever if travelling from an infected area.

Advisable precautions

Vaccinations that are necessary include typhoid, tetanus, and hepatitis A. Vaccinations that may be advised include diphtheria, hepatitis B, tuberculosis, Japanese B encephalitis and rabies.

Anti-malarial precautions must be taken when visiting all but the central highlands; the use of mosquito nets and repellents and covering up the body after dark can help avoid malaria, hepatitis B, dengue fever and encephalitis (which is a risk in remote regions only). There is a very high prevalence of HIV/Aids.

Use only bottled or boiled water for drinks, washing teeth and making ice. Eat only well cooked meals, preferably served hot; vegetables should be cooked and fruit peeled. Eating grouper, snapper, amberjack, and barracuda reef fish can frequently result in ciguatera poisoning; the toxin remains active even when the fish is well cooked.

A full, first-aid kit would be useful. Visitors should seek advice before accepting treatment involving hypodermic needles or blood transfusions. Medical insurance is essential, including emergency evacuation, and an adequate supply of personal medicines is necessary.

Hotels

In addition to Western-style hotels, the Tourist Board operates a scheme of village-style guest-houses run by nationals. Tipping is not usual.

Public holidays (national)

Fixed dates

1 Jan (New Year's Day), 13 Jun (Queen's Birthday), 16 Sep (Independence Day), 25–26 Dec (Christmas).

Days in lieu are given for holidays that occur at the weekend, usually at the beginning of the following week.

Variable dates

Good Friday and Easter Monday (Mar/Apr), Anzac Remembrance Day.

Working hours

Banking

Mon–Thu: 0845–1500; Fri: 0845–1600.

Business

Mon–Fri: 0800–1630.

Government

Mon–Fri: 0800–1600.

Shops

Mon–Fri: 0900–1630/1700; Sat: 0900–1200. Markets open all daylight hours.

Telecommunications

Mobile/cell phones

There is a 900 GSM service available in the capital and six of the larger towns.

Electricity supply

240/415V AC, 50 cycles; plugs are three-pin Australian type.

Weights and measures

Metric system

Social customs/useful tips

The use of first names is common in business, reflecting the tendency (of Australian origin) towards informality. The Papua New Guineans have a relaxed attitude to punctuality and this can make it difficult for the foreign visitor to keep to a schedule of appointments or to make business arrangements.

The belief in magic and sorcery is still widespread. There is little interest in national issues but local group and tribal sympathies are strong. Pressure from the provinces has resulted in the formation of a separate and tribal level of provincial government.

The traditional (custom) land tenure system promotes social stability and equal access to land within clans. Land disputes are endemic.

Tipping is not practised or encouraged.

Security

It has been advised that visitors to Papua New Guinea (PNG) should take care and ensure their personal safety at all times. PNG is characterised by regionalism and tribalism, with widespread corruption and prevalent violent crime bordering on anarchy. Law and order remain very weak in Port Moresby and Lae, reflecting the rising level of unemployment in the urban areas and a breakdown in the customary lines of authority. Criminal gangs of so-called 'rascals' have become a serious problem, and particularly worrying is a growing tendency in some areas in the use of firearms. Robbery, vehicle hijacks, assaults and random shootings are all common. Violent incidents can occur without warning and while foreigners are not necessarily the target they are visible and can be engulfed by them. Outside urban areas the situation is better, although sporadic tribal fighting is common and areas where it is reported, such as the Southern Highlands Province, is a particularly dangerous area and should be avoided.

Getting there

Air

National airline: Air Niugini

International airport/s: Port Moresby Jacksons International (POM), 11km south of the city; duty-free shop, bar, bank, hotel reservations and car hire. Buses and taxis are available to the city, journey time 20–60 minutes.

Airport tax: Departure tax K30; transit passengers are exempt.

Surface

Water: Cruise ships call, and passenger accommodation is sometimes available on cargo ships from Australia, the Far East, Europe and the west coast of the US.

Main port/s: Port Moresby, Lae and Madang; Rabaul (on New Britain).

Getting about

National transport

Air: Domestic air services provide the only realistically efficient and speedy way of accessing all areas in PNG. Air Niugini, AirLink and Islands Nationair, operate scheduled and charter flights. Some flights may use light aircraft or helicopters to the hundreds of smaller air strips in remote locations.

Road: There are over 19,000km of roads; only around 5,000km are paved. The highland interior is still underdeveloped; most of the road systems form coastal networks with little connection between individual provinces.

Water: Inland waterways total 10,940km but there are no public transport systems using them. Ferries to other PNG islands and river transport may be available on an ad hoc basis.

City transport

Taxis: Metered taxi services are available in main centres, but are scarce and expensive. Negotiate fares wherever possible.

Buses, trams & metro: PMVs (public motor vehicles), usually light buses or covered trucks, operate within and between main centres from bus shelters in towns (or they can be hailed elsewhere).

Car hire

It is not recommended that visitors drive into the interior where the roads are rugged, unpredictable and without rescue service. A number of international car hire companies operate in the cities. A national driving licence is required.

BUSINESS DIRECTORY

The addresses listed below are a selection only. While World of Information makes every endeavour to check these addresses, we cannot guarantee that changes have not been made, especially to telephone numbers and area codes. We would welcome any corrections.

Telephone area codes

The international direct dialling (IDD) code for Papua New Guinea is +675 followed by subscriber's number.

Useful telephone numbers
Police, fire and ambulance: 000

Chambers of Commerce
Lae Chamber of Commerce and Industry, PO Box 265, Lae, Morobe Province (tel: 472-2340; fax: 472-6038; e-mail: lcci@global.net.pg.

Papua New Guinea Chamber of Commerce and Industry, PO Box 1621, Trukai Building, Lawes Road, Konebadu, Port Moresby, NCD (tel: 321-3057; fax: 321-0566; e-mail: pngcci@global.net.pg).

Port Moresby Chamber of Commerce and Industry, PO Box 1764, Monian Tower, Douglas Street, Port Moresby (tel: 321-3077; fax: 321-4203; e-mail: info@pomcci.org.pg).

Banking
ANZ Banking Group (PNG), 3rd Floor, Defens Haus, Cnr Champion Parade and Hunter St, Port Moresby (tel: 322-3333; fax: 322-3306).

Bank South Pacific Limited (BSP), PO Box 173, Douglas Street, Port Moresby 121 NCD (tel: 321-2444; fax: 321-7302).

Indosuez Niugini Bank Limited, PO Box 1390, Burns Haus, Champion Parade, Port Moresby (tel: 321-3533; fax: 321-3115).

Maybank (PNG) Limited, PO Box 882, Waigani Drive, Waigani (tel: 325-0101; fax: 325-6128).

Central bank
Bank of Papua New Guinea, PO Box 121, ToRobert Haus; Crn Douglas Street, Port Moresby 111 (tel: 322-7200; fax: 321-1617; e-mail: webmaster@bankpng.gov.pg).

Travel information
Air Niugini, PO Box 7186, Boroko 111 (tel: 325-9000; fax: 327-3482).

East New Britain Tourist Bureau, PO Box 385, Rabaul 611 (tel: 982-8697; fax: 982-8634).

Melanesian Tourist Services, PO Box 707, Madang 511 (tel: 854-1300; fax: 852-3543; internet: www.meltours.com).

National tourist organisation offices
PNG Tourism Promotion Authority, 2nd Floor, Pacific MMI Building, Champion Parade; PO Box 1291, Port Moresby 121 (tel: 320-0211; fax: 320-0223; internet: www.pngtourism.org.pg).

Ministries
Ministry of Agriculture and Livestock, PO Box 417, Konedobu NCD (tel: 325-9544; fax: 325-9722).

Ministry of Bougainville Affairs, House Tisa (2nd Floor), PO Box 343, Waigani NCD (tel: 325-2977; fax: 325-8038).

Ministry of Churches, Family Affairs, & NGO's, National Parliament, PO Parliament, Port Moresby NCD (tel: 327-7350; fax: 320-0903).

Ministry of Civil Aviation, PO Box 684, Boroko NCD (tel: 323-6185; fax: 325-1919).

Ministry of Commerce and Industry, PO Box 375, Waigani NCD (tel: 327-6621; fax: 323-3050).

Ministry of Defence, Murray Barracks, Free Mail Bag Service, Boroko NCD (tel: 327-346; fax: 327-7480).

Ministry of Education, Culture and Science, PSA Haus, PO Box 446, Waigani NCD (tel: 323-3944; fax: 327-7480).

Ministry of Employment and Youth, PO Box 5644, Boroko NCD (tel: 327-7578; fax: 327-7480).

Ministry of Environment, PO Box 6601, Boroko NCD (tel: 325-0174; fax: 325-0182).

Ministry of Finance and Internal Revenue, PO Box 777, Port Moresby NCD (tel: 322-6613; fax: 322-6856).

Ministry of Fisheries, Investment Haus (8th Floor), PO Box 2016, Port Moresby NCD (tel: 321-3443; fax: 320-3024).

Ministry of Foreign Affairs and Trade, PO Box 422, Waigani NCD (tel: 327-7545; fax: 325-4467).

Ministry of Forests, PO Box 1550, Boroko NCD (tel: 327-7591; fax: 327-7589).

Ministry of Health, Aopi Centre (5th Floor), PO Box 807, Boroko NCD (tel: 301-3605; fax: 301-3604).

Ministry of Justice, Po Box 591, Waigani NCD (tel: 323-0138; fax: 323-0241).

Ministry of Lands, Aopi Centre (4th Floor), PO Box 5665, Boroko NCD (tel: 301-3102; fax: 301-3205).

Ministry of Mining and Energy, NIC Building (1st Floor), Private Mail Bag, Port Moresby NCD (tel: 327-7350; fax: 320-0903).

Ministry of Petroleum and Gas, Parliament House, Waigani NCD (tel: 327-7752; fax: 327-7753).

Ministry of Provincial and Local level Government Affairs, PO Box 1287, Boroko NCD (tel: 301-1000; fax: 325-0553).

Ministry of Public Enterprises, Communications and Assisting Prime Minister on Infrastructure and Public Investment Program Matters, PO Parliament, Waigani NCD (tel: 327-7366; fax: 327-7387).

Ministry of Public Service, Morauta House, (2nd Floor, PO Box 519, Waigani NCD (tel: 327-6440; fax: 323-3050).

Ministry of Rural Development, PO Box 639, Waigani NCD (tel: 327-6767; fax: 327-6349).

Ministry of Transport, PO Box 1489, Port moresby NCD (tel: 321-1866; fax: 320-0556).

Ministry of Treasury and Corporate Affairs, Vulupindi Haus (4th Floor), PO Box 710, Waigani NCD (tel: 328-8460; fax: 328-8433).

Office of the Prime Minister, Parliament House (4th Floor), National Parliament, Waigan NCD (tel: 327-7489; fax: 327-7497).

Other useful addresses
Bureau of Customs, PO Box 932, Port Moresby NCD (tel: 321-2488; fax: 321-3004).

Department of Industrial Development, PO Box 5644, Goroko (tel: 327-2286).

Electricity Commission of PNG, PO Box 1105, Boroko NCD (tel: 324-3200; fax: 325-0072).

Forest Research Institute, PO Box 314, LAE, Morobe Province (tel: 342-4188; fax: 432-4357).

National Curltural Commission, PO Box 7144, Boroko NCD (tel: 325-3288; fax: 325-9119).

National Housing Corporation, PO Box 1550, Boroko NCD (tel: 324-7200; fax: 325-9918).

National Institute of Standards and Industrial Technology, PO Box 3042, Boroko NCD (tel: 327-2102; fax: 325-2403).

National Statistical Office, PO Wardstrip, Waigani NCD (tel: 327-1499; fax: 325-1869).

Papua New Guinea Investment Corporation, PO Box 155, Port Moresby (tel: 321-2855; fax: 321-1240).

Post and Telecommunication Corporation, PO Box 1349, Boroko NCD (tel: 300-4000; fax: 300-4098).

Small Business Development Corporation, PO Box 481, Port Moresby NCD (tel: 325-0100; fax: 325-3725).

US Embassy, PO Box 1492, Port Moresby (tel: 321-1455; fax: 321-3423).

Internet sites
Asian Development Bank: www.adb.org

Government departments: www.pngonline.gov.pg

Investment promotion authority: www.ipa.gov.pg

Tourism Council of the South Pacific: www.tcsp.com

Paraguay

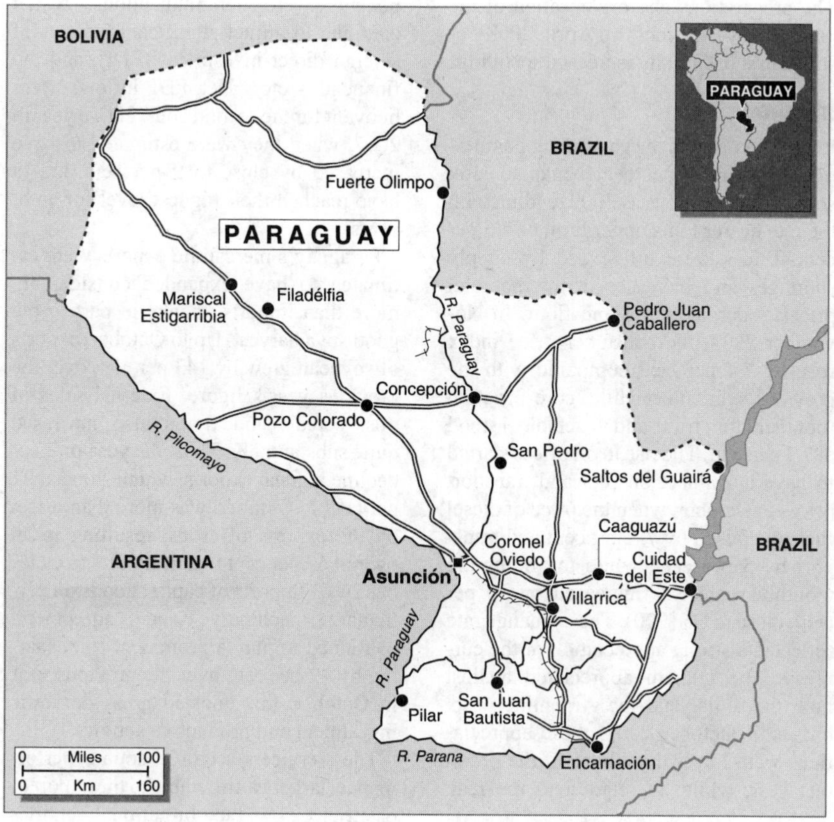

KEY FACTS

Official name: República del Paraguay (Republic of Paraguay)

Head of State: President Fernando Armindo Lugo Méndez (Partido Demócrata Cristiano (PDC) (Christian Democratic Party) (since 15 Aug 2008)

Head of government: President Fernando Armindo Lugo Méndez

Ruling party: Alianza Patriótica por el Cambio (APC) (Patriotic Alliance for Change) political alliance of eight parties led by the Partido Liberal Radical Auténtico (PLRA) (Authentic Radical Liberal Party) (from 15 Aug 2008)

Area: 406,752 square km

Population: 6.03 million (2007)*

Capital: Asunción

Official language: Spanish and Guaraní

Currency: Guaraní (G) = 100 pesos

Exchange rate: G3,927.50 per US$ (Jul 2008)

GDP per capita: US$1,802 (2007)*

GDP real growth: 6.40% (2007)*

Labour force: 2.24 million (2004)

Unemployment: 15.10% (2004)

Inflation: 8.10% (2007)

Balance of trade: -US$1.36 billion (2006)

* estimated figure

Paraguay's politics began to undergo something of a sea change in August 2008, when newly elected President Fernando Armindo Lugo Méndez of the Asociación Nacional Republicana-Partido Colorado (ANR) (National Republican Association-Red Party) took office. Mr Lugo's previous job was that of bishop of San Pedro, a largely agricultural and impoverished region of Paraguay. If nothing else, Sr Lugo represents something of a radical departure for Paraguayan politics.

El obispo de los pobres

Popularly known as *el Obispo de los pobres* (the bishop of the poor), Sr Lugo heads a coalition which includes Paraguay's Liberal Party and several lesser known left wing parties. Drawing inevitable comparisons with Brazil's President Lula, Sr Lugo's background is well on the left wing of Paraguayan politics. Lacking experience both in politics and government, Sr Lugo appears to have taken some cautious steps with his cabinet appointments. His finance minister, Dionisio Borda, got the administration off to a doubtful start by announcing the imposition of a 15 per cent tariff on soya production. Reacting to vociferous condemnation of the move by soya producers, Sr Lugo refused to meet with the soya producers, delegating the task to Sr Borda. Paraguay's outgoing president, Nicanor Duarte, had also attempted to impose a similar tax without success. In 2007 Paraguay harvested six million tons of soya. The 2008 crop is estimated at 8 million tons. Paraguay is South America's third largest soya producer, after Brazil and Argentina.

The IMF approves

According to the IMF, over the last five years Paraguay's GDP rose overall by about 25 per cent thanks to the pursuit of sound macro-economic policies and a favourable external environment. Impressively, Paraguay's public finances also remained in surplus throughout the period: consolidated public debt as a per cent of GDP was reduced by more than half to less than 30 per cent; the financial system strengthened considerably and no longer posed systemic risks; core inflation was reduced by about three-quarters to an annual rate of less than 5 per cent (although it has risen in 2008 mainly due to increased global food and fuel prices); international reserves have more than tripled, to about US$3.25 billion; Paraguay's currency, the guaraní strengthened against major currencies and per capita income more than doubled to over US$2,500.

Agricultural strength

Paraguay is a predominantly agricultural country. According to the United Nations Economic Commission for Latin America and the Caribbean (ECLAC/CEPAL), in 2007, the growth rate of the Paraguayan economy was in the 5.5 per cent range, driven by the extraordinary output in the crop-farming sector. Livestock farming, in contrast with the three preceding years, was affected by a decline in external demand and by drought in the second part of the year – and contracted, resulting in a fall in meat exports. Sales of soybean and cereals strengthened significantly and, together with services, contributed to the surplus on the current account. The guaraní continued to appreciate and, but at the same time, inflation remained high. The central government ended the year with its fiscal accounts in equilibrium and a primary balance estimated at 0.9 per cent of GDP. Growth in revenues was also forecast to be significant, exceeding the figure recorded in 2006. Yet again, the introduction of personal income tax was postponed, this time until January 2009. The preparations and organisation of the presidential elections in April 2008 resulted in substantially increased spending.

Inflation

ECLAC notes that the government's inflation target of 5 per cent began to look somewhat ambitious as 2007, ending with the rate nearer to its upper limit of 7.5 per cent. Prices were influenced by supply shortages and increases in international prices, such as wheat and flour. In November 2007, the consumer price index rose by 7.4 per cent compared with the previous year; meanwhile, core inflation (not including fruits and vegetables) stood at 7.3 per cent. The rise in oil prices started to have an impact on fuel and transport prices in October, when the price of diesel fuel was raised by 7.6 per cent and transport by 5 per cent, while the minimum monthly wage was increased by 10 per cent (close to US$270). The exchange rate reflected a strong appreciation of the currency. The guaraní appreciated against both the dollar and the Argentine peso, but, until October 2007, these appreciations were lower than those of the previous year, while, in relation to the real, from the middle of the year it registered a nominal and actual depreciation as a result of the substantial appreciation of the Brazilian currency against the dollar. The actual effective exchange rate showed an 8 per cent appreciation on average up to October, a result which did not affect the current account in any significant way.

In the services sector, the strongest components were communications, which continue to attract significant inflows of foreign direct investment (FDI), and the financial sector. Net FDI inflows were buoyant for the second consecutive year in 2007, when they were estimated to have increased by close to 9 per cent and to have reached their highest level for eight years.

Paraguay's mercantile exports were estimated to have expanded considerably more than imports, thanks in part to the good soya harvest. Up to October, exports of soybean grew by 143 per cent over the previous year's figure. External sales of oils, cereals and flours also increased quite substantially. Thus, the year-on-year decline in meat exports, which stood at 21 per cent in October, was more than offset by the exports of crops, resulting in an overall 67 per cent rise in exports to October 2007. Imports of capital goods, in particular machinery and equipment, continued to play a prominent role, soaring by 42 per cent over the previous year in October; this boosted gross domestic investment and productive activity.

The services sector's sound performance, largely attributable to the export of electricity by the bi-national entities (Brazil and Paraguay), was partially counterbalanced by a decrease in current transfers. The current account showed a surplus estimated at around 3.5 per cent of GDP. The capital and financial balances, including errors and omissions, showed a smaller surplus than in 2006 (1 per cent of GDP), owing to a slight outflow of financial capital.

KEY INDICATORS — Paraguay

	Unit	2003	2004	2005	2006	2007
Population	m	5.78	5.85	5.80	*5.92	*6.03
Gross domestic product (GDP)	US$bn	5.80	7.41	7.47	9.80	*10.87
GDP per capita	US$	921	1,155	1,289	*1,656	*1,802
GDP real growth	%	1.0	2.1	2.9	4.3	*6.4
Inflation	%	15.6	5.2	6.8	9.6	8.1
Industrial output	% change	–	4.0	3.2	3.5	–
Agricultural output	% change	–	3.0	3.2	3.5	–
Exports (fob) (goods)	US$m	2,451.0	2,936.0	2,647.0	4,026.0	–
Imports (cif) (goods)	US$m	2,666.0	3,330.0	2,472.0	5,383.0	–
Balance of trade	US$m	-215.0	-394.0	175.0	-1,357.0	–
Current account	US$m	15.0	90.0	-22.0	-118.0	*162.0
Total reserves minus gold	US$m	968.9	1,168.1	1,297.1	1,701.7	2,463.0
Foreign exchange	US$m	811.2	1,001.1	1,140.3	1,531.5	2,385.4
Exchange rate	per US$	6,695.00	5,974.60	2,500.00	2,500.00	4,685.00

* estimated figure

Risk assessment

Politics	Fair
Economy	Good
Regional stability	Good

COUNTRY PROFILE

Historical profile

1537 The Spanish began colonising the plains of Paraguay.

1811 Paraguay gained independence from Spain.

1864–70 A disastrous war against Argentina, Brazil and Uruguay was lost. It

halved Paraguay's population and stripped it of 155,400 square km of land.
1870 Occupation forces set up a provisional government with a liberal-democratic constitution, although the constitution was never put into practice.
1874 The Partido Colorado (PC) (Colorado Party) (also known as the Red Party), representing the land-owning elite, was formed.
1887 The Liberal party, who advocated a minimal state and representative government, was formed.
1883 A Colorado government began driving peasants off the land and selling it to foreign investors.
1904 After a revolution the Liberal party seized power and introduced political and economic changes.
1932–35 The Chaco War with Bolivia over disputed territory.
1936 The army, which held the government responsible for loosing the Chaco War, overthrew the government of President Eusobio Ayala (Liberal) in February and installed war hero Rafael Franco as president, an act that virtually destroyed the Liberals as a political force. The Partido Revolucionario Febrerista (PRF) (Febrerista Revolutionary Party) government was a mix of political ideologies, including Communists and Fascists. It implemented land re-distribution and workers rights. Franco's government had popular support but its policies were hastily devised and led to protests when Decree Law 152, promising a 'totalitarian transformation', was announced. The divergent political opinions within the government finally pulled it apart, although Franco continued to hold power with a new party, the Unión Nacional Revolucionaria (Revolutionary National Union). He was unable to provide more land to his peasant supporters and was undermined by Liberal party supporters in the army.
1937 Franco lost support of the army when he withdrew troops from the territories won in Chaco in 1935. The army revolted and returned the Liberal party to power.
1938 A treaty was signed between Bolivia and Paraguay following an international peace conference. It returned most of the disputed land to Bolivia.
1940 The military regime installed Higinio Morínigo, a follower of Nazi Germany's Adolf Hitler, as president.
1946 Following the defeat of Germany and Japan, Paraguay's chief trading partners, Morínigo legalised liberal, communist and Febrerista parties.
1947 Paraguay descended into civil war, following the emergence of political divisions within the army.
1948 The PC deposed Morínigo, leading to a series of coups and short-lived regimes.
1949 Federico Chaves became president.
1954 General Alfredo Stroessner led a coup d'état that deposed Chaves. Stroessner was re-elected seven times under the constitutional 'state-of-siege' provision. His dictatorship was ruthless against all opposition.
1967 A new constitution endorsed Stroessner's dictatorship. Paraguay was isolated within the world community.
1989 Stroessner was deposed in a bloodless coup by General Antonio Rodriguez who later won the presidential election. However the military-backed National Republican Association-PC won the parliamentary elections.
1993 Juan Carlos Wasmosy was elected president and the PC won a majority of parliamentary seats in the first free presidential and multi-party elections.
1998 Raúl Cubas Grau (PC) won the presidential election, despite allegations of fraud.
1999 Cubas resigned, following the assassination of his vice president, Luís Argaña. Luis González Macchi was appointed as interim president.
2000 Supporters of dissident Colorado leader, General Lino Oviedo, staged an unsuccessful coup. Oviedo fled and was found by Brazilian police at a Brazilian border hideout.
2001 Paraguay asked for, but was denied, Oviedo's extradition.
2002 President Macchi was accused of corruption. Violent street protestors demanded his resignation. He was impeached by congress.
2003 President Macchi survived his impeachment trial; the Senate voted 25–18 against him, short of the two-thirds majority (30 votes) necessary to remove him from power. Nicanor Duarte Frutos won presidential elections. Macchi was again charged with corruption and put on trial.
2004 Former military commander, General Oviedo, was arrested after returning from exile in Brazil. An estimated 464 shoppers were killed in a three storey supermarket fire, it was the worst fire in Latin American history. The daughter of former president, Raúl Cubas, was kidnapped.
2005 The body of Cecilia Cubas was found in a shallow grave. President Nicanor ordered a crackdown on organised crime, blamed for widespread kidnapping and murder. Plans to privatise the public utilities sector were defeated in the lower house of the legislature. Paraguay hosted the world's first conference of landlocked nations, which was attended by 30 states.
2006 A new leftist movement, Tekojoja (Equality), was launched to contest the 2008 presidential elections with the former Bishop Fernando Lugo as candidate.
2008 In the 20 April presidential elections, Fernando Armindo Lugo Méndez (Partido Demócrata Cristiano) (PDC) (Christian Democratic Party) won 41 per cent of the vote, ending the rule (since 1948) of the PC, and whose candidate Blanca Ovelar won 31 per cent, Lino Oviedo (Unión Nacional de Ciudadanos Éticos) (National Union of Ethical Citizens) (Unace) won 22 per cent. In elections for the Chamber of Deputies the ruling Colorado Party won 29 seats and the opposition Partido Liberal Radical Auténtico (PLRA) (Authentic Radical Liberal Party) won 26 seats, while the Unión Nacional de Ciudadanos Éticos (UNCE) (National Union of Ethical Citizens) won 16 seats; all other political parties won less than five seats. President Fernando Lugo was sworn into office on 15 August.

Political structure

Constitution

Paraguay became an independent republic in 1811. Under the dictatorship of Alfredo Stroessner (1954–89) a new constitution was introduced in 1967 which granted strong powers to the executive, entrenching political control in the hands of the ruling Partido Colorado (PC) (Colorado Party). In 1992, a new constitution was enacted.
There are 19 departments and 213 municipalities each with their own directly elected administration.
In 1990, a new electoral law was passed. Among its provisions were the introduction of proportional representation, provision for a second round in the event that no candidate secures an absolute majority in presidential elections, the prohibition of compulsory deductions from salaries of public-sector workers for political parties, the selection of party authorities by the direct vote of all members, a ban on party affiliation by members of the armed forces and the police and the lifting of a previous ban on electoral alliances by political parties.

Form of state

Presidential democratic republic

The executive

Under the constitution executive power is exercised by the president of the republic, who must be a Roman Catholic. The president is elected directly by popular vote for five years and formulates and enacts legislation. Executive power rests with the president who appoints a council of 11 ministers. The president has powers to rule by decree when congress is in recess. The president cannot be re-elected.

National legislature

The legislature is the bicameral National Congress, made up of the Senate (45 members) and the Chamber of Deputies (80 members). The term of both chambers is normally five years, coinciding with that of the presidency, and representation is decided by the vote in the presidential elections.

Legal system

At the apex of the judiciary is the Supreme Court which has the power to declare legislation unconstitutional. The five members of the Supreme Court are appointed by the president and their tenure of office coincides with that of the presidency. There are appeal courts and lower level criminal and civil courts.

Last elections

20 April 2008 (presidential and parliamentary)

Results: Presidential: Fernando Lugo (PDC) won 41 per cent, Blanca Ovelar (PC) won 31 per cent, Lino Oviedo (Unace) won 22 per cent.

Parliament (Chamber of Deputies): the Asociación Nacional Republicana-Partido Colorado (National Republican Association-Colorado Party) (Colorado Party) won 29 seats (out of 80), the Partido Liberal Radical Auténtico (PLRA) (Authentic Radical Liberal Party) won 26 seats, the Unión Nacional de Ciudadanos Éticos (UNCE) (National Union of Ethical Citizens) won 16 seats; all other political parties won less than five seats. (Senate) the Colorado Party won 15 seats (out of 45), the PLRA won 14 seats, the UNCE won 9 seats and the Movimiento Patria Querida (MPQ) (Beloved Fatherland Movement) won 4.

Next elections

2013 (parliamentary and presidential)

Political parties

Ruling party

Alianza Patriótica por el Cambio (APC) (Patriotic Alliance for Change) political alliance of eight parties led by the Partido Liberal Radical Auténtico (PLRA) (Authentic Radical Liberal Party) (from 15 Aug 2008)

Main opposition party

Asociación Nacional Republicana-Partido Colorado (National Republican Association-Colorado Party) (Colorado Party)

Population

6.03 million (2007)*

Last census: August 2002: 5,163,198

Population density: 12 inhabitants per square km. Urban population: 56 per cent (1994–2000).

Annual growth rate: 2.5 per cent 1994–2004 (WHO 2006)

Ethnic make-up

Over 95 per cent of the population is of Spanish-Guaraní origin. There are approximately 40,000 indigenous people in the country, most of whom live in the Chaco region.

In addition, there are large Korean, German and Japanese immigrant communities, along with small Italian and Polish communities, and some communities of people originating from Lebanon, Taiwan and Hong Kong.

Religions

Roman Catholicism is the state religion and is practised by 90 per cent of the population, the remainder are mostly Protestants.

Education

There are just over 4,300 primary schools and an estimated 92 per cent of the relevant age group attends primary school. Secondary education begins aged 13 years and comprises two cycles of three years each.

Paraguay has two universities – the National and the Catholic. The state-run Universidad Nacional de Asunción has a student enrolment of around 20,000. It comprises 11 faculties, law and social sciences, medicine, economics, chemistry, dentistry, philosophy, agriculture, veterinary science, fine arts, architecture and engineering. It also has six Institutes and six Higher Schools.

Literacy rate: 92 per cent adult rate; 96 per cent youth rate (15–24) (Unesco 2005).

Compulsory years: Seven to 13

Enrolment rate: 111 per cent gross primary enrolment of relevant age group (including repeaters); 47 per cent gross secondary enrolment (World Bank).

Pupils per teacher: 21 in primary schools

Health

Per capita total expenditure on health (2003) was US$301; of which per capita government spending was US$95, at the international dollar rate, (WHO 2006).

HIV/Aids

HIV prevalence: 0.5 per cent aged 15–49 in 2003 (World Bank)

Life expectancy: 72 years, 2004 (WHO 2006)

Fertility rate/Maternal mortality rate: 3.8 births per woman, 2004 (WHO 2006); maternal mortality 190 per 100,000 live births (World Bank).

Child (under 5 years) mortality rate (per 1,000): 25 per 1,000 live births (World Bank)

Head of population per physician: 1.11 physicians per 1,000 people, 2002 (WHO 2006)

Welfare

The Social Security Institute was formed by Decree Law 17071 in 1948, and is regulated by Decree Law 1860 of 1950. The laws refer to health, medical care and sickness benefits. Workers, their wives and children up to 16 have the right to receive medical, surgical and dental attention, medicine and hospitalisation, as well as cash subsidies for temporary illnesses, maternity and death. Old age pensions are paid to those who have made the necessary contributions. The social security system is in disarray and in 2001 the IMF urged the government to stop lending money to the system.

Women must not work for three weeks before or six weeks after childbirth. During these periods a woman receives a cash subsidy from the Social Security Institute. The worker has the right to receive an allowance equal to 5 per cent of the legal minimum wage for each child under 17 for whose maintenance and education he is responsible. This allowance is wholly the employer's expense and is discontinued once the worker's wage reaches 200 per cent more than the legal minimum.

Main cities

Asunción (capital, estimated population 520,722 in 2005), Cuidad del Este (266,366) (on the Brazilian border), Capiatá (236,725), Luque (212,359), Ñemby (105,492), Limpio (103,018), Fernando de la Mora (121,768), Encarnación (77,278) (on the Argentine border), Pedro Juan Caballero (68,349).

Languages spoken

Guaraní, the aboriginal Indian tongue is widely spoken. In some rural districts, the less educated speak little or no Spanish.

Official language/s

Spanish and Guaraní

Media

None are based in Paraguay but Mercopress (www.mercopress.com) specialises in news from Latin America countries within Mercosur and the Falkland Islands.

Press

Dailies: In Spanish, the main national dailies and Sunday newspapers are ABC Color (www.abc.com.py), Diario Popular (www.diariopopular.com.py), Ultima Hora (www.ultimahora.com), La Nacion (www.lanacion.com.py), and Viva Paraguay (www.vivaparaguay.com).

Weeklies: In Spanish, Paraguay Ahora (www.paraquayahora.com), La Síntesis Económic (http://kaavo.pol.com.py).

Periodicals: Itacom (www.itacom.com.py), Neike (www.neike.com.py), PPN (Portal Paraguayo de Noticias) (www.ppn.com.py), Paraguay Aldia (www.paraguayaldia.com), Paraguay News (www.paraguaynews.com.py), Zeta Revista (www.revistazeta.com.py), regional publications, International Action (www.accion.org), UnMundo Améruca Latina (www.un-mundo.org, in English: http://amlat.oneworld.net).

Broadcasting

Radio: The government-owned Radio Nacional del Paraguay (www.rnpy.com), broadcasts on AM and FM; there are several private radio stations. Radio Cardinal (www.cardinal.com.py), Radio Nanduti (www.nanduti.com.py), Radio Venus (www.venus.com.py), Radio Venus (www.fmradiocity.com), Radio Canal 100 (www.canal100.com.py).

Television: There are several television channels, all privately owned with broadcasts in Spanish – Sistema Nacional de Televisión (SNT, Canal 9) (www.snt.com.py), RED Guarani (Canal 2) (www.redguarani.com.py), Telefuturo (Canal 4) (www.telefuturo.com.py), Red Privada de Televisión (El Trece, Canal 13) (www.rpc.com.py), Paravision (Canal 5) (www.canal5paravision.com). These broadcasters syndicate their programmes around the country and on cable TV.

Economy

Paraguay is one of the poorest countries in South America. More than half of the population live in poverty and landlessness is increasing. With few mineral resources and little industry, the economy is dependent on agriculture for subsistence and exports. Agricultural produce makes up 90 per cent of the export market. Soybeans have replaced cotton as the main export crop, accounting for 10 per cent of GDP; other crops include tobacco, sugar-cane and coffee. Much of the large-scale farming sector is controlled by international companies.

Hard-wood timber is also exploited for export. After agriculture, Paraguay's most important export is hydroelectric power, which is generated far in excess of domestic requirements.

After a decade of stagnation, the economy has returned to growth since 2003, stimulated by government reforms and improvements in the exchange rate. Inflation has been brought down from the 2003 level of 15.6 per cent to single figures. The large informal sector, which is closely linked to contraband trade, suggests that official statistics underestimate the real size of the economy in general and foreign trade flows in particular.

Paraguay, the poorest member of Mercado Común del Sur (Mercosur) (Common Market of the South), is heavily reliant on trade with other members of the organisation, especially Brazil and Argentina. The health of Paraguay's economy is closely linked to the fortunes of those countries. The depreciation of the Brazilian real has created setbacks for Paraguayan trade since 1999 by increasing the value of its exports in the vital Brazilian market, while recession and economic crisis in Argentina also damaged the Paraguayan economy, with Argentine producers breaking quota agreements and dumping agricultural produce. The present improvement in the economy is conversely dependent on sustained growth in Brazil and Argentina.

The Inter-American Development Bank estimated that in 2006 migrant workers sent some US$650 million to their families in Paraguay.

External trade

As a member of Mercosur, the world's fourth largest free-trade zone, Paraguay (along with Argentina, Brazil and Uruguay), has access to a market of over 200 million consumers. The EU and Mercosur have been in negotiations to create a mutual free trade zone since 2004. Paraguay is also an associate member of the Andean Community (AC), when Mercosur negotiated a free trade area with AC.

Paraguay's economy is predominately agricultural which constitutes around 26 per cent of GDP and exports represent a large portion of this. The world's largest hydroelectric generating facility at the Itaipú Dam, is jointly owned and operated by Paraguay and Brazil.

Imports

Main imports include road vehicles, consumer goods, tobacco, petroleum products and electrical machinery.

Main sources: China (25.1 per cent total, 2006), Brazil (19.0 per cent), Argentina (13.0 per cent).

Exports

Main exports include cattle, cotton, grains, soya beans, sugar and timber, animal feed, cotton, meat, edible oils, leather, timber and electricity.

Main destinations: Uruguay (22.0 per cent total, 2006), Brazil (17.2 per cent), Russia (11.9 per cent).

Re-exports

The country re-exports significant amounts of US products to regional neighbours. There is evidence of trade through informal channels such as smuggling.

Agriculture

Farming

The agricultural sector remains important to the country's economy. The sector employs approximately 40 per cent of the labour force and contributes 29 per cent to total GDP.

Agricultural products account for more than 90 per cent of exports, of which cotton and soya beans together account for more than two-thirds of export earnings. Sawn timber, meat products and, to a lesser extent, fruit, vegetables and hides are also exported. Sugar cane, wheat, tobacco and various new specialist crops for industrial use are expanding as more land comes under cultivation. Paraguay has nearly achieved self-sufficiency in basic foodstuffs (rice, maize, wheat, beans).

Approximately 5 per cent of total land area is arable land or under permanent crops, pasture constitutes 35 per cent of the land and 50 per cent is woodland/forest. While the fertile eastern region is ideal for arable farming and cattle grazing the rich soil has been subject to erosion since the 1970s. There are extensive forests with a variety of timbers. The potential of the Chaco region to the west is still to be realised, dependent as it is upon the exploitation of its known groundwater resources for irrigated farming.

Agricultural production fluctuates from year to year owing to climatic conditions (both flooding and drought) and widespread smuggling (particularly livestock and soya beans).

Crop production in 2005 included: 1,604,040 tonnes (t) cereals in total, 630,000t wheat, 4,910,110t cassava, 3,513,000t soya beans, 3,820,020t sugar cane, 102,000t rice, 830,000t maize, 142,100t sweet potatoes, 42,040t sorghum, 15,600t tobacco, 2,920t green coffee, 724,190t oilcrops, 289,620t citrus fruit, 10,100t chillies and peppers, 198,000t seed cotton, 478,360t fruit in total, 305,350t vegetables in total. Livestock production included: 363,134t meat in total, 215,000t beef, 105,000t pig meat, 3,730t lamb and goat meat, 38,774t poultry, 100,820t eggs, 372,380t milk, 1,720t honey, 34,412t cattle hides.

Fishing

Despite its landlocked geographical status, Paraguay's annual fish catch amounts to approximately 10,000 tonnes. The illegal trade of fishery products remains a problem despite attempts by the authorities to bring it under control.

Forestry

Paraguay has a significant area of forested land, accounting for approximately 30 per cent of the country's total landmass. The majority of the forested areas are to the east of the Paraguay river. Historically, deforestation has been a problem in Paraguay. The country lost, on average 0.51 per cent of forest cover each year during the 1990-2000 period. This amounted to a decrease of 123,000 hectares year on year.

Local forest resources produce moderate volumes of sawn timber and panels, most of which is usually exported. Domestic demand for paper is usually met by imports. Consumption of wood fuel is significant. Timber imports in 2004 were US$64.2 million, while exports amounted to US$33.9 million.

Timber production in 2004 included 9,987,627 cubic metre (cum) roundwood, 4,044,000cum industrial roundwood, 550,000cum sawnwood, 3,515,000cum sawlogs and veneer logs, 954,000t pulpwood, 161,000cum wood-based panels, 5,943,627cum woodfuel; 187,456t charcoal.

Industry and manufacturing

In a typical year for the economy of Paraguay the industrial sector accounts for approximately a quarter of total GDP.

Though Paraguay is South America's least industrialised country, the sector does account for just under 20 per cent of the total workforce.

Manufacturing is small-scale and geared to the processing of primary products with agro-industry representing about 70 per cent of total industrial production. Construction contributes approximately 6 per cent of GDP. Manufacturing is centred on the processing of agricultural products, particularly textiles, cotton yarn, wood products, beef products, and industrial and edible oils. The country is self-sufficient in cement and there is an oil refinery (capacity 10,000 barrels per day (bpd)) and steel works (150,000 tonnes per year).

Contrasting with other Latin American countries, which have undergone a process of industrialisation based on import-substitution, development strategy in Paraguay has emphasised export-led growth. This involved minimal protection for domestic industry, whose growth problems have been compounded by the small size of the home market, high freight costs for imported products and the effects of extensive smuggling of a wide range of consumer goods from neighbouring countries.

Tourism

The tourism industry of Paraguay remains underdeveloped, with potential for greater economic productivity. The sector's contribution to total GDP has increased to 7.3 per cent and now accounts for 6.4 per cent of total employment.

In a typical year 211,400 people visit the country, with most arriving from Argentina and Brazil, often on day trips in search of bargains and duty-free goods.

Environment

In 2004, USAID reported that indiscriminate exploitation threatened the country's natural resources. In the eastern border region, which had been largely uncultivated until the 1970s, the rich topsoil was severely eroded and unmanaged use of land was jeopardising the largest underground water aquifer on the continent.

Mining

Paraguay's mining sector is negligible, contributing just 0.5 per cent to GDP in a typical year. The national government has attempted to introduce a programme of financial incentives in order to promote exploration for petroleum, lead and uranium. It has also encouraged mineral prospecting by granting tax concessions. However, few commercial reserves have been discovered and the sector employs just 0.3 per cent of the country's total workforce.

Studies commissioned by the Dirección General de Recursos Minerales (DGRM), with the support of the United Nations Development Programme (UNDP), have revealed that opportunities exist for the commercial extraction of marble, pyrophyllite, granite, slate, talc, gypsum and lignite.

Paraguay has limited proven mineral reserves and at present mining is concentrated on the extraction of salt, gypsum, limestone, kaolin and other clays. Prospecting has revealed the existence of uranium and bauxite, manganese, iron ore and copper. From the 1990s, none have been found in large enough quantities to overcome the high extraction costs involved.

Hydrocarbons

Paraguay has no proven reserves of crude oil, though the country uses oil for approximately 46 per cent of its total energy consumption. Therefore, Paraguay relies heavily on oil from abroad, importing 25,400 barrels per day (bpd) in 2005. Although oil exploration has failed to yield results in Paraguay, the discovery of oil deposits in the border regions of Formosa (Argentina) and Chaco (Bolivia) have raised hopes that Paraguay may also have oil. Currently however Paraguay relies entirely on imports to meet demand for its crude oil and petroleum products. A new refinery is due to come on stream at Villa Elisa with a capacity of 40,000 barrels per day (bpd). The refining capacity in 2003 was 7,500bpd. In early 2002, Paraguay's state oil company Petropar awarded six companies a one-year concession to transport oil and oil derivatives from Argentina to Paraguayan ports on the Paraguay River. Petropar expects to import some 800,000 cubic metres of petroleum products under this concession.

The country does not produce natural gas and consumption is negligible. However due to a possible discovery of commercially viable natural gas in the north-western Chaco region there may be more interest in exploration and possible production. There are discussions about building a 850km pipeline from south Bolivia to Asunción, Paraguay's capital. This would mean that demand for natural gas in Paraguay may increase along with the country becoming an important transit centre for Bolivian natural gas. It is predicted that this pipeline will be operational by late 2004.

Paraguay does not produce or import coal.

Energy

In a typical year Paraguay generates approximately 51.3 billion kilowatthours (kwh) of electricity and consumes just 3.5 billion kwh. Paraguay is the second largest net exporter of electricity in the world, trailing only France.

Paraguay's electricity supplies come mainly from the massive 12.6GW Itaipú hydroelectric plant on the River Paraná, the largest hydroelectric power plant in the world with Brazil as the co-owner, and the 3.2GW Yacyretá plant, with is co-owned by Argentina. Fifty per cent of the energy generated belongs to Paraguay, much of which is exported to Brazil.

Banking and insurance

Paraguay's banking and financial services sector has suffered from numerous crises and bad loans. The sector has undergone slow reform and the government has persisted in its policy of propping up ailing banking houses over recent years.

A new Bank of the South, with a headquarters in Venezuela, will be launched in 2008 to provide an alternative source of development funding for the participating countries. Assets of US$7 billion will underpin its operations.

Central bank

Banco Central del Paraguay.

Time

GMT minus four hours (daylight saving, Otober–March, GMT minus three hours)

Geography

Paraguay is a landlocked country in central South America. Bolivia lies to the north, Brazil to the east, and Argentina to the south and west. The River Paraguay effectively splits the country in two, with an area known as the Chaco to the west, which comprises 61 per cent (246,950 square km) of the country's land area, but only 3 per cent of the national population. In contrast, the eastern region is a much richer area in which most of the population is concentrated. This region is divided into two by a high ridge of hills. East of the hills lies the Paraná Plateau which is 300–600 metres high, and in the west lies a fertile, treeless pampas that floods once a year and stretches to the River Paraguay.

The Chaco is scrub forest used mostly for cattle. Much of the area is a national park, with jaguars, tapirs, puma and wild hog found here.

Hemisphere

Southern

Climate
The climate is subtropical with an average annual temperature of 23 degrees Celsius (C). The hot season is October–March and the average temperature rises to 32 degrees C. The temperate season is from April to September when the average temperature is 15 degrees C. The heaviest rains take place during this period, and the average annual rainfall is 1,500mm. In spring and autumn the arrival of cold fronts from the south can cause temperatures to fall suddenly by 10–20 degrees C within a few hours.

Dress codes
In the cities, businessmen wear European-style clothing; shorts are normally worn only for recreation.

Entry requirements
Passports
Required by all, except tourists from the Mercado Común del Sur (Mercosur) (Common Market of the South).
Visa
Required by all except citizens, visiting as tourists, from countries included on the list found at
www.paraguayembassy.co.uk/exemptlist.htm. All visits must commence within 90 days of visa issue. Business travellers should either contact the nearest consular section to request an application form. An invitation from a local company or organisation, provision of adequate funds for stay and proof of return/onward passage are necessary.
Currency advice/regulations
There are no restrictions on the import and export of foreign or local currency. Travellers cheques have limited acceptance.

Health (for visitors)
Mandatory precautions
Yellow fever vaccination certificates are required if arriving from an infected area.
Advisable precautions
Inoculations and booster should be current for tetanus, hepatitis A and typhoid. There may be a need for vaccinations for tuberculosis, diphtheria, yellow fever and hepatitis B. The use of malaria prophylaxis (including mosquito repellents, nets and clothing that cover the body after dark) will also provide protection for hepatitis B and yellow fever. There is a risk of rabies. Mains water is usually safe to drink in Asunción and other major towns. Elsewhere precautions should be taken. Bottled water is advisable for the first few weeks of any stay. Milk is unpasteurised and should be boiled. Dairy products likely to have been made from local milk should be avoided, and meat and fish should be well cooked.
Medical insurance is essential, including emergency evacuation; an adequate supply of personal medicines is necessary.

Credit cards
International credit cards are widely accepted. ATMs are found in most towns.

Public holidays (national)
Fixed dates
1 Jan (New Year's Day), 1 Mar (Heroes' Day), 1 May (Labour Day), 15 May (Independence Day), 12 Jun (Peace of Chaco), 15 Aug (Foundation of Asunción), 29 Sep (Battle of Boquerón), 8 Dec (Immaculate Conception), 25 Dec (Christmas Day).
Variable dates
Maundy Thursday, Good Friday.

Working hours
Banking
Mon–Fri: 0845–1500.
Business
Mon–Fri: 0800–1200 and 1430–1900; Sat: 0800–1200.
Government
Mon–Fri: 0700–1300.
Shops
Mon–Sat: 0900–2100. Some shops open 0730–2000.

Telecommunications
Mobile/cell phones
There are limited 850/1900 GSM services located in the capital and towns close by.

Electricity supply
220V AC, 50 cycles

Social customs/useful tips
Business people are punctual and expect appointments to be kept. Business cards are exchanged on visits and it is usual to shake hands when arriving or leaving an office or home. The best time to visit is between May and September
While most businessmen may speak English, it is advantageous to have some knowledge of Spanish. It is important to use the correct mode of address in writing or in speech.
Most businessmen do not wear a jacket and tie during office hours, but visitors, including businesswomen, are advised to wear lightweight business suits.
A 10–15 per cent tip is usually included on hotel and bar bills.

Security
Normal precautions apply. The level of street crime is much lower than other countries in Latin America.

Getting there
Air
National airline: Transportes Aéreo del Mercosur (TAM Mercusor).
International airport/s: Asunción-Silvio Pettirossi International Airport (ASU), 16km from city; bureau de change, duty-free shops, restaurants and car hire. Travel time to city centre by taxi or bus is 20 minutes.
Airport tax: International departures US$25; 24-hour transit passengers exempt.
Domestic departures from Asunción Pettirossi International Airport (ASU) US$4.
Surface
Road: There are paved roads from Brazil (Rio de Janeiro-Asunción; length 1,700km) and from Argentina (Buenos Aires-Asunción, length 1,450km) which are considered good, less so the access from Bolivia.
Rail: A regular service by means of a train-ferry runs from Concepión to Posadas (Argentina), where a connection can be made to Buenos Aires. Services are slow.
Water: There are ferry links with Argentina, Bolivia and Brazil. For journeys to Buenos Aires check the route chosen is the most direct. From Brazil, boats connect Corumba with Asunción.
Main port/s: Asunción (on River Paraguay) is approximately 1,500km from the sea; Concepción, in suitable conditions, is accessible by ocean-going ships.

Getting about
National transport
Air: There are six carriers operating scheduled services to most parts of the country. Planes can be chartered and seats booked on air taxis for many destinations. Flights are frequently affected by weather.
Road: Around 10 per cent of the total network is surfaced, those serving main centres are in good condition. The main route is triangular, linking Asunción, Encarnación and Ciudad del Este. The Trans-Chaco Highway runs to the Bolivian border, but is paved for only half the distance. Some unsurfaced roads are closed in bad weather; service stations etc may be widely spaced.
Buses: There are frequent express services linking major towns; for longer distances it is advisable to make advance bookings (eg Asunción-Encarnación; Asunción-Ciudad del Este).
Rail: The main route is Asunción-Villarrica-Encarnación but the service is slow.
Water: The river Paraná is a major access route from the Atlantic coast. Asunción-Concepción service is not frequent and takes 24 hours, Asunción-Pilar 20 hours, and Asunción-Encarnación nine hours.
City transport
Taxis: In Asunción metered taxis operate with a minimum fare system; they can be hired on a time basis; a 10 per cent tip is optional.

Buses, trams & metro: Private companies operate bus and minibus services in the capital. Two tram routes also operate.

Car hire

Foreign or international licences are acceptable. Chauffeur and self-drive cars are available at reasonable rates.

BUSINESS DIRECTORY

The addresses listed below are a selection only. While World of Information makes every endeavour to check these addresses, we cannot guarantee that changes have not been made, especially to telephone numbers and area codes. We would welcome any corrections.

Telephone area codes

The internatioanl direct dialling (IDD) code for Paraguay is +595, followed by area code:

Asunción	21	Encarnación	71
Ciudad Del Este	61	Pilar	86
Concepción	31	Villarrica	541
Coronel Oviedo	521		

Chambers of Commerce

American-Paraguayan Chamber of Commerce, General Diaz 521, Edificio El Faro Internacional, Piso 4, Asunción (tel: 442-136; fax: 442-135; e-mail: pamchamb@conexion.com.py).

British–Paraguayan Chamber of Commerce, Gral Diaz 521, Edificio Internacional Faro, Piso 2, Asunción (tel/fax: 498-274; e-mail:britcham@infonet.com.py).

Paraguay Cámara Nacional de Comercio y Servicios, Estrella 540-550, Asunción (tel: 493-321; fax: 440-817; e-mail: info@ccparaguay.com.py).

Banking

Private Banking Association (ABP), Juan O'Leary y Estrella, 30 Piso Asunción (tel: 491-450; fax: 491-450).

Banco Alemán Paraguayo, Estrella No 505 y 14 de mayo, Zona Postal 1428, Asunción (tel: 490-166/9, 444-714/6; fax: 447-645).

Banco Comercial Paraguayo, Av Mariscal López 780, Zona Postal 2350, Asunción (tel: 207-251/7, 440-504; fax: 207-259).

Banco Continental, Estrella No 621, Apartado postal 2260, Asunción (tel: 446-915/18; fax: 442-001, 441-377).

Banco de Asunción, Palma Esquina 14 de mayo, Asunción Central (tel: 493-191/8; fax: 493-190).

Banco de Inversiones del Paraguay, Palma No 202, Esquina Nuestra Señora de la Asunción, Apartado postal 702, Asunción (tel: 449-550, 498-593/94; fax: 443-749).

Banco de la Nación Argentina, Chile y Palma, Apartado postal 064, Asunción (tel: 447-433, 449-463; fax: 444-365).

Banco del Paraná, Yegros y 25 de mayo, Apartado postal 2298, Asunción (tel: 446-827, 446-691/5; fax: 498-909).

Banco do Brasil, Oliva y Nuestra Señora de la Asunción, Apartado postal 667, Asunción (tel: 90-121, 90-126; fax: 448-761).

Banco do Estado de Sâo Paulo, Ind Nacional, Esquina Fulgencio R Moreno, Apartado postal 2211, Asunción (tel: 494-981/3; fax: 494-985).

Banco Exterior, Yegros y 25 de mayo, Apartado postal 824, Asunción (tel: 492-072/9; fax: 448-103).

Banco Finamerica, Chile y Oliva, Apartado postal 824, Asunción (tel: 491-021/025; fax: 445-159, 445-604).

Banco General, Chile y Haedo, Apartado postal 3202, Asunción (tel: 496-815/9; fax: 496-822).

Banco Holandés Unido, E V Haedo 103, Esquina Independencia Nacional, Apartado postal 1180, Asunción (tel: 490-001; fax: 491-734).

Banco Nacional de Fomento, Independencia Nacional y Cerro Cora, Asunción (tel: 444-440/1/2/3; fax: 446-053).

Banco Paraguayo Oriental de Inversión y Fomento, Azara 197 Esquina Yegros, Apartado postal 1496, Asunción (tel: 444-212 al 16; fax: 446-820).

Banco Real del Paraguay, Calle Estrella y Alberdi, Apartado postal 1442, Asunción (tel: 493-171/80; fax: 443-664).

Banco Sudameris Paraguay, Independencia Nacional y Cerro Cora, Apartado postal 1433, Asunción (tel: 494-542/8, 444-172/3).

Citibank, Chile, Esquina Estrella, Apartado postal 1174, Asunción (tel: 494-951/9; fax: 444-820).

Inter-American Development Bank (IDB), Edif. Aurora 1-3 pisos, Caballero esq Eligio Ayala, Casilla 1209, Asunción (tel: 492-061; fax: 446-537).

Interbanco, 14 de mayo 339, Apartado postal 392, Asunción (tel: 494-992/5; fax: 448-587).

ING Bank (Internationale Nederlanden Bank), Av España y San Rafael, Apartado postal, 10007 Asunción (tel: 606-423; fax: 606-437).

Lloyds Bank, Palma Esq Juan E O'Leary, Casilla Postal 696, Asunción (tel: 443-580; fax: 443-569).

Central bank

Banco Central del Paraguay, Federación Rusa y Sargento Marecos, Asunción (tel: 619-2061; fax: 610-088; e-mail: ccs@bcp.gov.py).

Travel information

Dirección Nacional de Turismo, Palma 468, Alberdi/Oliva, Asunción (tel: 441-530; fax: 491-230).

Transportes Aéreo Marilia (TAM), Oliva 467, Asunción (tel: 91-041; fax: 96-484).

National tourist organisation offices

Secretaría Nacional de Turismo, Palma 468, Casi 14 de Mayo, Edificio Central, Asunción (tel: 494-110; internet: www.senatur.gov.py).

Ministries

Ministry of Agriculture and Livestock, Presidente Franco 479, Asunción (tel: 443-791, 449-614; fax: 441-036).

Ministry of Defence, Avenids Mcal López y Vice Pte Sánchez, Asunción (tel: 204-771; fax: 211-583).

Ministry of Education and Culture, Chile 898 c/ Humaitá, Asunción (tel: 443-078; fax: 443-919).

Ministry of Exterior Relations, Presidente Franco c/ O'Leary, Asunción (tel: 493-872; fax: 493-910).

Ministry of Finance, Chile 128 esq Palmas, Asunción (tel: 440-010; fax: 448-283).

Ministry of Foreign Affairs, Juan E O'Leary y Pte, Franco, Asunción (tel: 494-593, 493-872; fax: 493-910).

Ministry of Health and Public Welfare, Av Petirrossi y Brasil, Asunción (tel: 207-328; fax: 206-700).

Ministry of Housing, Chile 128 c/ Palma, Asunción (tel: 440-010; fax: 448-283).

Ministry of Industry and Commerce, Avenida España 323, Asunción (tel: 204-638; fax: 213-529; internet site: www.mic.gov.py).

Ministry of the Interior, Chile c/ Manduvirá, Asunción (tel: 493-661; fax: 448-446).

Ministry of Justice and Labour, Avda Dr Gaspar Rodriguez de Francia c/ EE UU, Asunción (tel: 447-196, 491-555; fax: 440-066).

Ministry of Public Health and Social Welfare, Av Pettirossi c/Brasil, Asunción (tel: 207-328; fax: 206-700).

Ministry of Public Works and Communications, Olivia c/ Alberdi, Asunción (tel: 444-411, 496-666; fax: 443-625).

Other useful addresses

Administración Nacional de Electricidad (ANDE) (National Electricity Board), España el Padre Caroloto 360, Asunción (tel: 22-713/719).

Administración Nacional de Telecom (Antelco – Telecommunications Authority),

Alberdi, esq General Diaz, Asunción (tel: 44-001).

Agencia Publicitaria Visión, 25 de Mayo, 966, Asunción (tel: 24-796).

Asociación Paraguaya de Cias de Seguros, 15 de Agosto esq Lugano, Casilla 1435, Asunción (tel: 446-474; fax: 444-343).

British Airways, Azara 192, Asunción (tel: 490-020).

British Embassy, Av. Boggiani 5848, C/R16 Boquerón, Casilla 404, Asunción (tel: 595-21 612 611; fax: 595-21 605 007).

Association of Cotton Ginners, CADELPA, Av Boggiani 4744, Asunción (tel: 595 21 609-272; fax: 595 21 600-739).

Customs Office, Colón c/ Plaza Isabel La Católica, Asunción (tel: 492-202, 495-086; fax: 445-085).

Dirección General de Estadísticas y Censos (National Statistics Office), Dr Miguel Torres, Asunción (tel: 610-331, 663-489).

Federation of Agroindustrial Exporters (FEDEXA), Brasilia 840 c/Sgto Gauto, Asunción (tel: 208-855, 205-749; fax: 213-971).

Federation of Industrial and Commercial Production (FEPRINCO), Palma 751 c/ Ayolas, Edif Unión Club, Piso 3, Asunción (tel: 444-963; fax: 446-638).

Importens Association (Centro de Importadores), Montevideo 671, Montevideo 671 c/ E V Haedo, Asunción (tel: 441-295, 490-291; fax: 441-295).

Industrial Union of Paraguay (UIP), Cerro Corá 1038 Casilla 782, Asunción (tel: 212-556; fax: 312-260).

Municipality of Asunción, Mariscal López y Cap. Villamayor Bloque A, 1er Piso Asunción (tel: 610-576, 610-577; fax: 610-578).

Paraguayan Embassy (USA), 2400 Massachusetts Avenue, NW, Washington DC 20008 (tel: (+1-202) 483-6960; fax: (+1-202) 234-4508; e-mail: embapar@erols.com).

Petróleos Paraguayos (Petropar), Oliva 299, 4er Piso, Casilla 571, Asunción (tel: 95-117).

Planning Office, Pdte Franco c/ Ayolas, Edif Ayfra, Piso 3, Asunción (tel: 491-159, 448-366; fax: 496-510).

Private Construction Association (CAPACO), Victor Hugo casi Cervantes, Asunción (tel: 295-424).

Pro Paraguay (Promotion of Exporters and Importers), Padre Cardozo 469 c/ España, Asunción (tel: 208-276, 208-641; fax: 200-425).

Rural Association of Paraguay (ARP), Ruta Transchaco Km 14, Mariano Roque Alonso (tel: 291-036, 291-061; fax: 291-061).

Siderurgia Paraguaya (Sidepar), Azara 197, 6er Piso, esq Yegros, Casilla 2441, Asunción (tel: 95-963).

Soybean Exporters Association (CAPECO), Av Brasilia 840, Asunción (tel: 208-855; fax: 595 21 213 971).

US Embassy, Avenida Mcal Lopez 1776, Casilla 402, Asunción (tel: 213-715; fax: 213-728).

Water Authority (Corporación de Obras Sanitarias Corposana), JoséBerges: e/Brasil y San José, Asunción (tel: 25-001/003).

Internet sites

ABC Color (newspaper): www.diarioabc.com.py

Noticias (newspaper): www.diarionoticias.com.py

Office of the President: www.presidencia.gov.py

The Congress of Paraguay: www.camdip.gov.py

Peru

KEY FACTS

Official name: República Peruana (Peruvian Republic)

Head of State: President Alan García Pérez (APRA) (since 28 Jul 2006)

Head of government: Prime Minister Jorge del Castillo Gálvez (APRA) (since 28 Jul 2006)

Ruling party: Coalition led by Partido Aprista Peruano (APRA) (Peruvian Aprista Party) (also known as Alianza Popular Revolucionaria Americana)

Area: 1,285,216 square km

Population: 28.07 million (2007)*

Capital: Lima

Official language: Spanish, Quechua and Aymara

Currency: Nuevo sol (S/) = 100 centimos

Exchange rate: S/2.85 per US$ (Jul 2008)

GDP per capita: US$3,886 (2007)*

GDP real growth: 9.00% (2007)

Labour force: 10.94 million (2004)

Unemployment: 8.80% (2004) (additional underemployment)

Inflation: 1.80% (2007)

Oil production: 114,000 bpd (2007)

Balance of trade: US$7.56 billion (2006)

Foreign debt: US$31.30 billion (2004)

Visitor numbers: 1.64 million (2006)*

Annual FDI: US$1.39 billion (2004)

* estimated figure

Peru maintained its impressive level of economic growth in 2007 as gross domestic product (GDP) expanded at an annual rate of 8.2 per cent. The United Nations Economic Commission for Latin America and the Caribbean (ECLAC) noted that domestic demand was a major contributor, rising by 10 per cent. Private investment rose dramatically, by 25 per cent, showing particular strength in the mining and construction sectors. Household consumption rose by over 7 per cent, reflecting strong levels of job creation and the continued expansion of credit. Despite the impressive level of economic growth and an increase of over 8 per cent in the number of formal jobs created, unemployment and underemployment levels remained high. Peru's central inflation target was lowered from 2.5 per cent to 2.0 per cent, but by October 2007 the inflation rate, fuelled by increased fuel and foodstuff prices, had risen above this level.

Following the 2006 election, Alan García had appeared at pains to avoid the mistakes made under his first premiership in the 1980s. One important dimension of the election was that a large proportion of the electorate had no experience of Mr Garcia as president. Over 45 per cent of the Peruvian electorate was aged between

18 and 34, although only 10 per cent appeared to have any direct involvement in politics. Criticisms raised against the candidates by representatives of the younger generation were that 'Lourdes Flores was supported by (what they referred to as) the mafia *fujimontesinista*', that Alan García was tainted by 'the corruption that characterised his government and his complicity in it' and Ollanta Humala by his improvisation and accusations of human rights abuses.

Peruvians chose from a total of 24 presidential candidates, the highest number in two decades, when they went to the polls on 9 April 2006. In many ways the political cycle in 2005 had been a prelude to the election, with various high profile public figures positioning themselves in anticipation of polling day. After a closely contested contest, Partido Aprista Peruano (formerly the Alianza Popular Revolucionaria Americana and still commonly known by the acronym APRA) (Peruvian Aprista Party) candidate and former president Alan García emerged as the winner. On the economic front, Peru's transformation from a politico-economic loose cannon in previous years, to macroeconomic stability is virtually complete.

APRA

The name Alianza Popular Revolucionaria Americana (Revolutionary Popular American Alliance) suggested it was a lot of things that it was not. Aprismo set out to be a continental movement as its name suggests, but never flourished outside Peru. Its early ideology (again as its name suggests) was anti-imperialist generally, and anti-US in particular. It advocated a resurgence of Indo-America rather than Spanish or Latino-America, proposing to return the land to the Indian communities by raising them above subsistence level farming. Despite its aspirations, it was among the emerging middle-classes that it found its support.

No change

The García administration that took office in mid-2006 was not expected to radically change Peru's macro-economic policy. The only apparent changes have been increases in public investment and more vigorous anti-poverty measures. Peru's official unemployment rate is above 10 per cent although analysts believe that the real unemployment rate is probably much higher. There is also widespread poverty in Peru, especially among the country's rural population. GDP per capita in 2007 was estimated at US$3,886 a figure which has not kept pace with Peru's economic growth over the past few years.

Peru had proven crude oil reserves at the end of 2007 of 1.1 thousand million barrels. Produced was 114,000 barrels per day (bpd) of oil (including crude oil and natural gas liquids) in 2007, a drop of 2,000bpd from the previous year. With the revival in oil exploration, Peru hope that new projects coming online will increase the country's oil production levels. However, oil consumption has grown dramatically over the past 20 years, reaching 145,000bpd in 2007. Peru has been a net importer of oil since 1992, with most imports coming from Ecuador and other South American countries.

Peru has proven natural gas reserves of 12.54 trillion cubic feet (Tcf), the fifth-largest amount in South America. However, once seismic work is complete on Block 56, Peru's proven reserves could well increase to 15-16 Tcf. In coming years, Peru hopes to become a net exporter of natural gas. To help mitigate Peru's high oil import bill, the Peruvian government is looking to implement a plan that will stimulate natural gas consumption in the country.

Over recent years Peru's economy has been successfully run by a tightly knit group of technocrats that has helped turn the country into a successful story of macroeconomic stabilisation, following years of branding as the politico-economic 'basket-case' of South America. Growth in real GDP has been consistent and looks set to remain within the 4.5-5.5 per cent range, according to the IMF's latest forecast. The rate of inflation has also remained firmly in check, currently standing at approximately 2 per cent. Total export revenues now stand at almost US$27 billion (2007). The export boom has been predominantly driven by the high price of minerals courtesy of growing China-led global demand. As a producer of gold, silver, zinc, and molybenum, Peru is uniquely placed to take advantage of such a boom.

Outlook

Alan García's first presidency ended in tears; disillusioned Apristas and angry Peruvians decided that they had had enough, even if they hadn't been told enough. Whether García has learnt his lesson, remains to be seen. The very fact that he has won a second term – albeit after twenty years or so – suggests a more pragmatic approach.

Risk assessment

Economy	Fair
Politics	Fair
Regional stability	Good

COUNTRY PROFILE

Historical profile

1500s The Inca empire stretched from the Pacific Ocean east to the sources of the Paraguay and Amazon rivers and from the

KEY INDICATORS — Peru

	Unit	2003	2004	2005	2006	2007
Population	m	26.73	27.55	27.22	27.64	*28.07
Gross domestic product (GDP)	US$bn	60.60	68.39	79.39	93.03	109.07
GDP per capita	US$	2,154	2,349	2,917	3,366	*3,886
GDP real growth	%	4.0	5.1	6.4	7.6	9.0
Inflation	%	2.5	3.7	1.6	2.0	1.8
Industrial output	% change	–	6.2	7.7	9.5	–
Agricultural output	% change	–	2.0	3.2	3.3	–
Oil output	'000 bpd	92.0	93.0	111.0	116.0	114.0
Natural gas output	bn cum	–	–	–	–	–
Exports (fob) (goods)	US$m	8,986.0	12,546.0	17,247.0	21,754.0	*27,679.5
Imports (cif) (goods)	US$m	8,255.0	9,818.0	12,084.0	14,197.0	*19,580.2
Balance of trade	US$m	731.0	2,728.0	5,163.0	7,557.0	*8,099.3
Current account	US$m	-1,061.0	-70.0	1,033.0	2,589.0	*1,750.0
Total reserves minus gold	US$m	9,776.8	12,176.4	13,599.4	16,733.3	26,856.5
Foreign exchange	US$m	9,776.4	12,176.1	13,598.9	16,732.4	26,852.7
Exchange rate	per US$	3.48	3.41	3.19	3.20	2.97

* estimated figure

region of modern Quito in Ecuador south to the Maule River in Chile.
1532 Francisco Pizarro of Spain led an armed expedition into the region. Weakened by a civil war over succession to the throne, the Inca empire was easily overturned by the Spanish.
1542 The vice-royalty of Peru was established with Lima as its capital.
1569 Francisco de Toledo was appointed by the Spanish crown to administer the colony. He established a harsh, repressive system of government that ensured political stability by co-opting indigenous people as low-level officials. The system of government lasted for almost 200 years.
1820 José de San Martín led an invasion army into Peru with the support of rebel Chilean troops in a regional war against Spanish imperial rule.
1821 Peru became independent from Spain after San Martín's forces captured Lima.
1824 Simón Bolívar (who later led Bolivia to independence) became head of state of a centralised state, which included a unicameral legislature.
1826 Bolívar left Peru, which was subsequently ruled by a series of military commanders.
1845 Ramón Castilla became president, ensuring a period of stability and economic development.
1860 Peru adopted a liberal constitution for the first time.
1864 Peru went to war with Spain over control of the guano-rich Chincha Islands. Aided by Ecuador, Bolivia and Chile, Peru defeated the Spanish.
1879–84 Peru backed Bolivia in the War of the Pacific with Chile, but Chile invaded Peru and occupied Lima.
1884 The Treaty of Ancón was signed with Chile. Peru's nitrate-rich province of Tarapacá was handed over to Chile, which also occupied the provinces of Tacna and Arica. The poor state of the nation's economy, weakened by war and the loss of resource-rich regions, undermined governments for the next 30 years.
1895 Civilian rule began, although it was tainted by corruption and economic mismanagement.
1919 President Augusto Leguía launched an autogolpe (self-coup), against his own government in order to abolish democratic rule and establish a dictatorship.
1924 The Alianza Popular Revolucionaria Americana (APRA) (American Revolutionary People's Alliance), the country's first mass-based political party, was formed and led by Haya de la Torre.
1930 Leguía was overthrown by a group, including the military, the ruling oligarchy and APRA. A tripartite system of government was formed between the three groups; APRA soon left the alliance to lead a series of popular uprisings. In the early 1930s, APRA was banned.
1933 Luis Miguel Sánchez Cerro, president since 1931 was assasinated. The Congress appointed General Benavides as president.
1939 Manuel Prado y Ugarteche (a moderate) was elected president; he relaxed the government's attitude to APRA.
1945 Free elections took place and José Luís Bustamente y Rivero won the presidency.
1948 General Manuel Odría, staged a coup d'état. His military junta banned the APRA.
1962 The APRA became the largest party in congress, but fell short of the one-third required to form a government, and entered a coalition with former military leader Manuel Odría, and his supporters. The military seized power and called new elections.
1963 The election of Fernando Belaúnde Terry as president marked the beginning of genuine democracy in Peru.
1968 Belaúnde nationalised Standard Oil's Peruvian subsidiary, the International Petroleum Company (IPC). General Juan Velasco Alvarado led a palace coup that removed Belaúnde from office. The military docenio (12-year rule) began.
1970s The Maoist Sendero Luminoso (Shining Path) terrorist group was formed by Abimael Guzman.
1975 Velasco was removed from office by General Franscisco Morales Bermúdez.
1978 A Constituent Assembly was elected, with leftist parties winning an unprecedented 36 per cent of the vote, although APRA won most of the seats.
1979 A new constitution was promulgated, which provided for free elections to be held every five years.
1981 Belaúnde returned to power under fresh elections enabled by the new constitution. The Peruvian economy was in a weak state, aggravated by the guerrilla group, Shining Path, which attacked rural areas and imposed its rule on villages. Military efforts to eliminate Shining Path were ineffectual. It is estimated that over 70,000 people were killed during the insurgency led by Shining Path. Debt repayment was suspended and Peru was denied further international loans.
1990 Alberto Fujimori won the presidential election. Under international pressure was he introduced a programme of sweeping economic reforms by removing state subsidies, privatising state-owned assets and reducing state involvement in virtually all aspects of the economy. These measures reduced inflation and increased growth.
1992 Guzman, the leader of the Shining Path, was captured. Fujimori instigated an autogolpe. He suspended the constitution, dismissed the National Assembly and assumed wide emergency powers, appointing ministers to a new, smaller, unicameral chamber. The economy had begun to recover but regional disparity had increased.
1993 The constitution was reinstated with some amendments.
1995 President Fujimori was elected for a second term. Several setbacks undermined his position including the collapse of foreign direct investment due to the worldwide effects of the Asian financial crisis, and the damage to agriculture from El Niño.
2000 Fujimori was sworn in for a third presidential term – after much-criticised elections – without a controlling majority in the National Congress. Fraud tainted his presidency and a bribery scandal prompted him to flee to Japan, from where he resigned. Valentin Paniagua became caretaker president.
2001 Alejandro Toledo won the presidential election and his party, Perú Posible (PP), won the congressional elections.
2002 Power was devolved when 25 regional presidents were elected. The centre-left APRA, led by former president Alan García, took 12 of the 25 regional presidencies.
2003 Toledo's presidency lost its popular support. He dismissed Beatriz Merino as prime minister and appointed Carlos Ferrero Costa.
2004 In February, President Toledo reshuffled his cabinet for the fifth time since coming to power. Prime Minister Ferrero survived a no-confidence vote in November.
2005 Prime Minister Carlos Ferrero resigned after the president appointed his close friend Fernando Olivera Vega as foreign minister. Pedro Pablo Kucznski became prime minister on 16 August. In November, former President Fujimori was arrested in Chile. Peru and the US signed a trade agreement in December. Also in December, the national government declared a state of emergency in six provinces following the suspected killing of eight police officers by Shining Path guerrillas.
2006 Alan García Pérez (Partido Aprista Peruano) (APRA) (Peruvian Aprista Party) won the presidential elections on 4 June. An APRA-led coalition government was formed in July. Abimael Guzman, leader of the Shining Path, was retried for terrorism and sentenced to life imprisonment in October. An earthquake struck on 15 August south of Lima, killing hundreds and demolishing many buildings along the coast near the epicentre.
2008 Controversial land laws designed to open up the Amazon to development, which had been approved by decree by

President Garcia, were repealed by congress by 66 votes to 29 in August. Indigenous rights campaigners welcomed the repeal.

Political structure

Constitution

Peru's constitution dates from 29 December 1993. The country is divided into 25 regions which each elect a president once every five years. Regions are divided into provinces, which in turn are divided into districts governed by mayors elected by direct popular vote every three years. The voting age is 18 years.

Form of state

Presidential democratic republic

The executive

Executive power is vested in the president, who is elected for a five-year term by universal adult suffrage. The president governs with the assistance of a prime minister and an appointed Council of Ministers. The prime minister is president of the Council of Ministers.

National legislature

Legislative authority is vested in a unicameral 120-member National Congress elected for a five-year term from a single national list.

Legal system

The judiciary consists of a 16-member Supreme Court, the ministry of justice and the nine-member Constitutional Court. By constitutional right the judiciary is entitled to at least 2 per cent of the central government budget. Members of the Supreme Court are appointed by the president. The posts are permanent, but members of the court must be aged over 50 and retire at 70.

Last elections

9 April 2006 (parliamentary); 9 April/4 June 2006 (presidential).

Results: Presidential: Alan García won 52.63 per cent of the vote; Ollanta Humala won 47.37 per cent.

Parliamentary: UP won 21.15 per cent of votes (45 seats out of 120); APRA won 20.58 per cent (36 seats); Unidad Nacional (UN) (National Unity) 15.33 per cent (17 seats); Alianza por el Futuro (AF) (Alliance for the Future) 13.09 per cent (13 seats) ;and Frente del Centro (FC) (Centre Front) seven per cent (five seats).

Next elections

2011 (presidential and parliamentary)

Political parties

Ruling party

Coalition led by Partido Aprista Peruano (APRA) (Peruvian Aprista Party) (also known as Alianza Popular Revolucionaria Americana)

Main opposition party

Unión por el Perú (UP) (Union for Peru)

Population

28.07 million (2007)*

Last census: July 2005: 26,152,265 (provisional)

Population density: 20 inhabitants per square km. Urban population: 73 per cent (1995–2001).

Annual growth rate: 1.6 per cent 1994–2004 (WHO 2006)

Ethnic make-up

45 per cent indigenous, 37 per cent mestizo, 15 per cent white, 3 per cent black, Asian or other.

Religions

Catholic (95 per cent), others (5 per cent).

Education

Adult literacy is relatively high in Peru. The 9 per cent difference in male and female litracy reflects the gender division in education provision.

The government provides free education for children up to the age of 15. Primary education lasts for six years, with secondary education divided into two stages of three and two years each. In rural areas, 40 per cent of the children traditionally help in the fields, with all but a few abandoning their schooling.

Literacy rate: 85 per cent adult rate; 97 per cent youth rate (15–24) (Unesco 2005).

Compulsory years: Six to 15

Enrolment rate: 123 per cent gross primary enrolment of the relevant age group (including repeaters); 73 per cent gross secondary enrolment (World Bank).

Pupils per teacher: 27 in primary schools

Health

Per capita total expenditure on health (2003) was US$233; of which per capita government spending was US$112, at the international dollar rate, (WHO 2006).

About three million people are in the pension and health schemes administered by the state-owned Peruvian Institute of Social Security (IPSS). Salaried workers are obliged to contribute to the scheme, which provides free health care.

The health ministry budget covers health care for those outside the IPSS system. A small charge is made for treatment under this service.

HIV/Aids

HIV prevalence: 0.5 per cent aged 15–49 in 2003 (World Bank)

Life expectancy: 71 years, 2004 (WHO 2006)

Fertility rate/Maternal mortality rate: 2.8 births per woman, 2004 (WHO 2006)

Child (under 5 years) mortality rate (per 1,000): 26 per 1,000 live births; 8 per cent of children aged under five are malnourished (World Bank).

Welfare

Peru reformed its pension system in 1993, allowing the investment of individual accounts in real assets and introducing private pension funds to replace state pensions. In addition, the system provides disability and survivors' benefits administered by insurance companies, and old-age pensions.

Employees are required to pay social security taxes equivalent to 13 per cent of their gross income into the public Oficina de Normalización Provisional (ONP) pension fund. Alternatively, employees may opt to pay 11.4 per cent of their salary into a private pension scheme. Workers are allowed to continue joining the old pay-as-you-go system, although the new system urges employers to pay more per worker into the private system than they were paying under the old system. One major challenge for the pension system in Peru is that as much as 51 per cent of the workforce is in the informal economy, covered by neither the old nor the new system.

Main cities

Lima (capital, estimated population 8.7 million in 2005), Arequipa (848,333), Trujillo (744,314), Chiclayo (567,675), Iquitos (426,464), Piura (356,637), Pucallpa (310,269), Sullana (200,661), Tacna (284,929).

Languages spoken

English is spoken in the main tourist regions.

Official language/s

Spanish, Quechua and Aymara

Media

Andina (Agencia Peruana de Noticias), Ave Alfonso Ugarte 873, Lima 1 (tel: 315-0400; email: andina@editoraperu.com.pe; internet: www.andina.com.pe).

Press

Dailies: Most national dailies and Sunday newspapers are published in Lima, in Spanish, including El Comercio (www.elcomercio.com.pe) El Mundo, Expreso (http://www.expreso.com.pe), La Tribuna (www.le-tribuna.org), Ojo (www.ojo.com.pe) – the largest selling newpaper, El Peruano (www.elperuano.com.pe) – the official State Gazette, Horas Libre (www.24horaslibre.com), La República (www.larepublica.com.pe) and Correo (www.correoperu.com.pe). There are also local publications for regional cities.

Weeklies: In Spanish Caretas (www.caretas.com.pe), Gatopardo (www.gatopardo.com), Sí (www.rcp.net.pe), Crónica Viva (www.cronicaviva.com.pe). In English, Peru Finance.

Online, in English, Lima Post (www.limapost.com) and Inside America-Peru (www.insideperu.com).
Business: In Spanish, Business (www.businessperu.com.pe), and Punto de Equilibrio (www.puntodeequilibrio.com.pe), Gestión (www.diariogestion.com.pe) and Nuevo Oiga (www.peru.com/revistas/oiga/index.asp).

Broadcasting

Radio: In Spanish, Radio Programas de Peru (RPP) (www.rpp.com.pe), Panamericana Radio (www.radiopanamericana.com), CPN Radio (www.cpnradio.com.pe), Radio Nacional (www.radionacional.com.pe) (government operated). Other regional and local radio stations, mainly commercial, broadcast in AM and FM throughout Peru.

Television: In Spanish, Panamericana Televisión (www.pantel.com.pe), Frecuencia Latina (www.frecuencialatina.com.pe), Andina de Radiodifusión (ATV) (www.atv.com.pe), América TV (www.americatv.com.pe), Uranio 15 (www.uranio15.com) and the state-owned Televisión Nacional de Pere, TVPeru (www.tvperu.gob.pe).

Economy

Since 2001, Peru has experienced a period of sustained growth, recording a 6.7 per cent increase in GDP in 2005. Although the economy had been in recession, a flexible exchange rate system and strong financial structure had been established during the preceding decade, giving the government of Alejandro Toledo a strong base from which to pursue economic recovery. A policy of fiscal responsibility has supported a stable currency and low inflation. The price of metals rose and with improved market access spurred GDP growth, which has been further stimulated by expanding exports and foreign investment attracted by the improving prospects. The main exports are minerals, textiles and agricultural produce. There has been strong growth in all sectors, especially in mining and hydrocarbons.
Peru is well-endowed with mineral resources and is an important exporter of gold, silver, copper and other metals. The growing mining sector is powering Peru's economic growth, but reliance on mining makes the economy potentially vulnerable to the volatility of world prices. Diversification, such as that promised by the growth of agricultural and other exports, is needed to minimise the adverse effects of this dependence. Nevertheless, the mining and hydrocarbon sectors continue to be particularly attractive to overseas investors.
Around half the economy is believed to operate informally, obscuring the true economic situation. The benefits of economic revival have yet to reach most of the population. Poverty is still widespread, with nearly 50 per cent surviving on the bare minimum. The government has adopted some social programmes and there has been some reduction in the numbers in poverty from 54.8 per cent in 2001 to 48 per cent in 2006.
The Inter-American Development Bank estimated that in 2006 migrant workers sent some US$2,869 million to their families in Peru.

External trade

Peru is a member of the Asia-Pacific Economic Co-operation (Apec) forum and the Andean Community which with Mercorsur formed the South American free trade area (SAfta).
Principal manufacturing includes textiles, consumer goods, processed food and fish products, and cement. Mining production includes silver (Peru is the world's second-largest producer), gold (it is the world's sixth-largest producer) and copper, with zinc and lead.

Imports

Principal imports are petroleum and petroleum products, plastics, machinery, vehicles, iron and steel, wheat and paper.
Main sources: US (16.4 per cent total, 2006), Brazil (10.5 per cent), China (10.3 per cent).

Exports

Main exports include minerals (typically 40 per cent of total), crude oil and petroleum products, and coffee.
Main destinations: US (23.5 per cent total, 2006), China (9.7 per cent), Switzerland (7.2 per cent).

Agriculture

Farming

The agricultural sector employs approximately 33 per cent of the population and contributes 9 per cent to GDP. Less than 3 per cent of Peru's land area is devoted to arable production and permanent crops. Subsistence farming predominates and productivity is low due to drainage and salinity problems, although productivity increased during the 1990s.
The government has given priority to farming as part of its programme to channel resources to the poorer regions and increase self-sufficiency. The highest priority sectors include rice, corn and wheat. By reviving traditional irrigation and terracing methods the government hopes to extend cultivation through the use of marginal land, while also promoting modern farming techniques.
Production has increasingly begun to focus on the winter export markets of the EU and the US. It is along the northern coast of Peru where export crops such as oranges, mangos, asparagus, passion fruit and limes are grown, together with cotton, rice and sugar for the domestic market.
Animal husbandry (sheep, poultry and cattle) is important in southern regions.
Coffee production is receiving considerable support from the US Agency for International Development (USAID), the United Nations Development Programme (UNDP) and GTZ, the German technical co-operation agency. Attempts to improve the production and marketing of Peruvian coffee, which has suffered since the left-wing military government of Juan Velasco effectively nationalised coffee marketing in the 1970s, have proved fruitful.
Crop production in 2005 included: 4,108,315 tonnes (t) cereals in total, 3,200,000t potatoes, 2,350,001t rice, 1,340,000t maize, 975,000t cassava, 210,000t sweet potatoes, 185,275t pulses, 7,100,000t sugar cane, 208,538t oil palm fruit, 42,198t olives, 200,000t seed cotton, 150,000t tomatoes, 155,000t green coffee, 28,500t cocoa beans, 4,500t tea, 18,050t various spices, 1,690,000t plantains, 760,100t citrus fruit, 268,000t mangoes, 12,500t tobacco, 3,798,935t fruit in total, 1,933,200t vegetables in total. Livestock production included: 967,786t meat in total, 152,000t beef, 90,000t pig meat, 33,640t lamb, 6,910t goat meat, 25,320t various indigenous meats, 650,000t poultry, 180,000t eggs, 1,311,000t milk, 1,200t honey, 21,400t cattle hides, 9,345t sheepskins, 11,100t greasy wool.

Fishing

The El Niño weather phenomenon of the late 1990s severely damaged the Peruvian fishing industry. The sector has now fully recovered and is performing well. One of the world's largest suppliers of fishmeal, Peru is also a major producer of canned, frozen and salted fish.
The shrimp industry has traditionally been a source of local employment, mainly in the northern coastal departments of Tumbes and Piura. Large quantities of shrimp are exported to the US, Canada, Spain and Taiwan. The shrimp industry is investing in improving the water quality of ponds and is also importing genetically treated baby shrimps to prevent white spot virus attacks in the future, which had caused production to decline.
In 2004, the total marine fish catch was 9,239,150 tonnes and the total crustacean catch was 9,060 tonnes.

Forestry

Timber imports in 2004 were US$273 million, while exports amounted to US$107 million. A little over half of the country's total landmass is covered by

forests, most of which are located in the montaña region.
The northern Pacific coast has areas of dry forests and savannas. The state owns all natural forests. There are significant numbers of privately-owned plantations, primarily consisting of eucalyptus. Estimates in 2002 showed that forest cover was about 65 million ha.
Peru produces a variety of woods including cedar, mahogany, dyewoods and other products, such as rubber and raw quinine from the Amazon Basin. Most production is geared towards sawn timber and panels with some quantities of bagasse pulp and solid wood products. Timber production in 2004 included 8,935,000 cubic metre (cum) roundwood, 1,635,000cum industrial roundwood, 671,000cum sawnwood, 1,318,000cum sawlogs and veneer logs, 954,000t pulpwood, 97,000cum wood-based panels, 7,300,000cum woodfuel; 493,692 tonnes (t) charcoal, 90,800t paper and paperboard.

Industry and manufacturing

The industrial sector of the Peruvian economy makes a significant contribution of approximately 37 per cent to total GDP. About 15 per cent of the country's total workforce is employed in industry.
Manufacturing activity, centred in Lima and Callao, includes food processing, beverages, fishmeal, chemicals, petrochemicals, rubber, plastics, basic metallurgy, metal products, cement, textiles, footwear, paper products, machinery and motor vehicle assembly. Large firms dominate the sector.
Traditionally, Peruvian governments have taken an interventionist and protectionist approach in order to support local industries and promote employment. By 2003, the Toledo administration had overseen the privatisation of all but a few of the state-owned industries not already sold by the previous Fujimori administration.

Tourism

The development of the tourist industry continued throughout 2005. Travel and tourism now accounts for 8.2 per cent of total GDP and employs 7.6 per cent of the country's workforce.
With its rich variety of environments and archaeological sites, Peru has much to offer and tourism is becoming an important contributor to the country's economic revival. More then a million visitors were recorded in 2000. Although numbers fell in late 2001, as a consequence of the earthquake in June and the 11 September terrorist attacks in the US, they picked up again during 2002, a trend which continued in 2003. An important agreement was reached with the US in 2002, allowing unlimited air traffic between the two countries. Some 927,400 people visited Peru in 2004.

Mining

Peru's mining sector contributes approximately 15 per cent to total GDP. The country remains one of the world's largest producers of silver, copper, zinc and lead. The mining sector as a whole accounts for around 8 per cent of total employment in Peru.
Copper dominates the economy, not only as the main export earner, but also as a major source of employment. Export revenue is set to rise as new investments come on stream. Southern Peru Copper Corporation, controlled by US-based Asarco, remains the largest copper producer with an annual output of around 340,000 tonnes of fine copper content from its mining operations at Toquepala and the open pit Cuajone mine. Minera Yanacocha gold mine is the largest private gold producer in Peru, producing 40 per cent of the country's gold production. Other important minerals include tin, iron and steel.
By 2002, the state's role in the sector was limited to supervising the commitments made by companies and administering new concessions. International companies such as Asarco, Avocet Ventures, Barrick Gold, BHP, Cyprus and Arequipa Resources generate much of Peru's mineral production.
Barrick Gold's Lagunas Norte gold deposit exploration during 2002 resulted in an increase in its estimated resource from 3.5 million to 7.3 million ounces of gold.
In 2004, after the President had promulgated a law to levy royalties of 1–3 per cent of sales on some mining companies, Anglo American pulled out of an auction to develop a large copper deposit. Violence directed against foreign mining interests in Peru has led the national government to attempt to clamp down on activists.

Hydrocarbons

Peru's proven oil reserves stand at approximately 253 million barrels. Production of oil in Peru has slowed considerably over the past two decades as no new deposits have been unearthed and oil fields have matured.
With oil consumption at nearly 163,000bpd, Peru needs to import oil, mainly from Colombia, Ecuador and Venezuela.
The government hoped for more interest in exploration in 2003 and 2004 after it reduced royalties on oil and gas exploration and production in 2002.
Peru's natural gas reserves totalled 246.21 billion cubic metres (cum) in 2004. Annual production is estimated at 438 million cum, all of which is consumed domestically. The largest gas reserves are located in the Amazon region. Peru's main natural gas field is located at Camisea, with proven gas reserves the equivalent of 2.2 million barrels of oil.
Peru produces a small amount of coal, however it is almost entirely reliant on imports to meet domestic consumption levels. In a typical year, Peru produces 20,350 tons, and imports 1,210,000 tons, of coal.

Energy

Approximately half of Peru's 6,100MW of instilled generating capacity is powered by hydroelectric power. The remainder is generated using traditional thermal sources.
Much of Peru's electric sector remains in the hands of the government, including the electric tariff commission (CTE). Many utilities are fully or partly state-owned, including ElectroPeru (the largest generator), Edegel, Egenor, Egasa and Egesur. The privatisation of Egasa and Egesur was abandoned in 2002 following large-scale protests.
Three Colombian companies, Interconexion Electrica (ISA), Trascelca and Empresa de Energia de Bogatá (EEB), took control of Peru's electricity network and set up Red de Energia del Peru to manage the system.

Financial markets

Stock exchange

The Lima Stock Exchange (LSE) opened in 1971.

Banking and insurance

Peru's banking and financial services sector has suffered a series of external shocks in recent years, with the Asian crisis, El Niño and turmoil in Brazil and Russia affecting confidence in emerging markets. Restoring confidence in Peru is widely considered to be just a matter of time, with the country's regulatory system among the most effective in the region. Moreover, the presence of foreign competition (foreign banks account for four of the country's top five banks), a tough provisioning system and a federal programme to facilitate commercial debt restructuring, meant that in 2002 the Peruvian banking sector was less affected by external crises than many in the region.
Peru's banking sector includes over 25 commercial banks and a number of local savings banks, with the four largest groups accounting for over 60 per cent of the systems assets, loans and deposits.

Central bank

Banco Central de Reserva del Perú

Main financial centre

Lima

Time

GMT minus five hours

Geography
The geography of Peru, the third-largest country in South America, ranges from Andean peaks almost 7,000 metres high to tropical Amazonian rain forests and burning coastal deserts.
Peru is bordered by Ecuador and Colombia to the north, Brazil and Bolivia to the east, Chile to the south and the Pacific Ocean to the west.
Almost half the population lives in a narrow coastal strip which covers about 10 per cent of the country's total area. The coastal zone, running 3,079km from Ecuador to Chile, is a desert cut by rivers and oases which are fed by melting snow from the Andes.
The Andes cover around 30 per cent of Peru and form a plateau averaging 3,000 metres high studded with towering peaks. The highest summit is Huascaran at 6,768 metres. In the Andes there are many fertile valleys, such as those of Cuzco and Cajamarca. Lake Titicaca in the south, at an altitude of 3,815 metres, is the highest navigable lake in the world.
East of the Andes, around 60 per cent of Peru's area is covered by the jungle of the Amazon basin. Ecuador claims a large section of the northern Amazonian territory. The area is flat and very low. Iquitos, the main town in the area, is about 4,000km from the mouth of the Amazon but only 106 metres above sea level.
Hemisphere
Southern

Climate
Although Peru lies between the equator and the tropic of Capricorn, only the Amazonian jungle has a typically tropical climate, with high rainfall and humidity and little seasonal change in temperatures.
The effects of altitude in the Andes and the cold Humboldt current flowing up from the south moderates the climate in the central and coastal sections.
Temperatures in the capital, Lima, vary only slightly throughout the year due to the cold Humboldt current. They rarely rise above 28 degrees Celsius (C) in summer or dip below 12C in winter. Although Lima is set in a coastal desert, with annual rainfall around 48mm, the sky is overcast with a thick sea mist from June to September. This can be so dense as to resemble light drizzle and requires the use of a raincoat. In the Andes, the rainy season lasts from December to March and makes some road travel hazardous. About three-quarters of Cuzco's average annual rainfall of 80cm falls in this period.

Dress codes
Peruvians dress relatively informally, especially in the summer months from January to March when many government officials and other professionals go to work in casual loose-fitting clothes. In winter, jackets and ties for men and skirts for women are more common.

Entry requirements
Passports
Required by all.
Visa
Tourist visas are not required by nationals of EU/EEA countries, the Americas, Australasia and the Pacific, Asia and South Africa, for visits of up to 90 days.
Business visas, valid for 90 days, are required by nationals of all countries. Applications must include a letter of introduction from the employer or, where self-employed, the local chamber of commerce, detailing the purpose of the visit and length of stay, together with proof of adequate funds and return/onward passage.
For further information see http://peru.embassyhomepage.com.
Currency advice/regulations
There are no restrictions on the import and export of local currency or on the import of foreign currency, the export of which is restricted to the amount imported.

Health (for visitors)
Mandatory precautions
A yellow fever vaccination certificate is required if arriving from an infected area.
Advisable precautions
Yellow fever vaccination is recommended (essential for visits to some rural areas). Diphtheria, TB, typhoid, polio, tetanus and hepatitis A and B vaccinations are also advisable.
Malaria risk exists in some rural areas – prophylaxis is recommended.
Water precautions should be taken – it is advisable to drink only bottled water.

Hotels
In main centres hotels are classified by stars (maximum five) according to available facilities. In smaller towns, the best accommodation is often the government-run Hoteles Turistas. Hotel bills include a 10 per cent service charge; for stays of less than 60 days, foreign visitors are exempted from the 19 per cent government sales tax on presentation of travel documents.
Visitors arriving in Lima are well advised to inform their hotel of their arrival flight number and time. Most major hotels operate a free courtesy coach service to Jorge Chávez airport and will meet arriving guests.

Public holidays (national)
Fixed dates
1 Jan (New Year's Day), 1 May (Labour Day), 24 Jun (Inti Raymi), 29 Jun (St Peter and St Paul's Day), 28–29 Jul (Independence Day Celebrations), 30 Aug (St Rose of Lima Day), 8 Oct (Battle of Angamos Day), 1 Nov (All Saints' Day), 8 Dec (Immaculate Conception), 24–25 Dec (Christmas).
Variable dates
Maundy Thursday, Good Friday.

Working hours
Banking
Mon–Fri, Jan–Mar: 0815–1130.
Mon—Fri, Apr–Dec: 0915–1245. Some banks may open afternooons.
Business
Mon–Fri: 0900–1300 and 1430–1630.
Government
Mon–Fri: 0900–1300 and 1430–1630.
Shops
Mon–Sat: 1000–1300 and 1600–1900.

Telecommunications
Mobile/cell phones
GSM 1900 service available around the largest cities and towns.

Electricity supply
Generally 220V AC, 60 cycles. Exceptions include Arequipa (220V AC, 50 cycles) and Iquitos (110V AC, 60 cycles).

Social customs/useful tips
It is customary to shake hands on meeting and taking leave. Professional titles should be used and although most people have two family names, only the first is used.
The style of business is generally relaxed and the informal tu form is commonly used with younger Spanish-speaking business visitors. Meetings should be arranged in advance and reconfirmed. Visiting cards are used. While Peruvians are sometimes inclined to be late for appointments, visitors are expected to be punctual.
Never point the soles of your feet at anyone; it is considered highly insulting.

Security
Internal terrorist groups no longer pose a threat to security in most regions, but Sendero Luminoso (Shining Path) terrorists are still active in the remoter areas of central Peru Apurimac. There is a risk of armed robbery and hijacking of buses and cars on the road between Lima and Cuzco.
It is not considered safe to walk around the centre of Lima at night. There is a high level of street crime particularly in the city centre. Extreme caution should be taken on all streets, especially in pedestrian precincts. Visitors should be careful not to display valuables – especially at bus stations, railways and airports. Travellers should never journey outside the principal cities after dark and as a general rule are advised to use air travel wherever possible.
If you are robbed, report immediately to the nearest police station and ensure you

receive a certified copy of the official statement.

Getting there

Air

National airline: LAN Perú.

International airport/s: Lima, Jorge Chávez International (LIM), 16km west of city; duty-free shop, bar, restaurant, bank, post office, shops, car hire.

Airport tax: US$30.25.

Surface

Road: There is road access and bus services from neighbouring countries.The Pan-American Highway passes through Peru, from Ecuador in the north to Chile in the south.

Main port/s: Callao, San Martin, Matarani.

Getting about

National transport

Visitors are advised to contact the tourist police or the South American Explorers' Club in Lima for up-to-date information on travel to the interior of the country.

Air: There are regular services between Lima and all main towns, provided by several operators, including Aerocóndor Perú, LAN Perú, Star Perú and Taca Perú. There are 19 airports which receive domestic flights; another 22 airports operate charter and support services.

Due to weather conditions flights may be delayed or cancelled. It is essential to reconfirm bookings as flights are often overbooked.

Road: The Pan-American Highway, paved over most of the distance, runs north to south along the coast from the Ecuador border to the Chilean border (with a north-east arm into the Sierra, through Arequipa and on to the Bolivian frontier). The Trans-Andean Highway runs from Lima to Pucallpa, via La Oroya and Huanuco. The Central Highway connects Lima with La Oroya, Huancayo, Huancavelica, Ayacucho, Cuzco and Puno (linking with the Pan-American Highway spur from Arequipa).

In the rainy season (Dec–Apr) landslides are frequent, causing blockages and delays.

Buses: Cheap but fairly uncomfortable services are available on the Pan-American Highway north to Ecuador, south to Chile and on the highway to Callejon de Huaylas in northern Andes. Yellow city buses and mini-buses connect Lima with Callao and the residential suburbs.

Rail: There are regular rail services between Lima and La Oroya with branches to Cerro de Pasco, Huancayo and Huancavelica. The Southern Railway of Peru operates between Arequipa and Puno (on Lake Titicaca) with one weekly connection (Wed) by steamer across the lake to Bolivia. Also regular rail connections from Puno to Cuzco. A short line runs from Tacna to Arica in Chile. Railways have separate summer and winter schedules.

City transport

Taxis: Taxis are the best means of travel in the main cities. For safety reasons, radio-controlled taxis and, in Lima, yellow registered taxis should be used rather than unlicensed or cruising taxis. The passenger should avoid taxis containing anyone other than the driver and always lock the rear doors and close the rear windows if possible.

Recognised taxi ranks (estaciones) are found at hotels and airports. Taxis are not metered and fares should be agreed in advance.

Car hire

Major international companies operate in Lima and other main centres. Chauffeur and self-drive cars available. International licence preferred and credit cards essential. Cost includes basic insurance cover. Traffic is congested in Lima.

BUSINESS DIRECTORY

The addresses listed below are a selection only. While World of Information makes every endeavour to check these addresses, we cannot guarantee that changes have not been made, especially to telephone numbers and area codes. We would welcome any corrections.

Telephone area codes

The international dialling code (IDD) for Peru is +51 followed by area code and subscriber's number:

Amazonas	41	Junin	64
Ayacucho	66	Lima	1
Cajamarca	76	Loreto	65
Cuzco	84	San Martin	42

Useful telephone numbers

Police: 105

Fire: 116

Ambulance: 117

Chambers of Commerce

American Chamber of Commerce of Peru, Avenida Ricardo Palma 836, Lima 18 (tel: 241-0708; fax: 241-0709; e-mail: amcham@amcham.org.pe).

British-Peruvian Chamber of Commerce, Avenida José Larco 1301, Lima 18 (tel: 617-3090; fax: 617-3095; e-mail: bpcc@bpcc.org.pe).

Lima Cámara de Comercio, Avenida Gregorio Escobedo 398, Lima 11 (tel: 463-8080; fax: 463-2837; e-mail: presidencia@camaralima.org.pe).

Trujillo Cámara de Comercio y Producción de la Libertad, Jirón Junín 454, PO Box 729m Trujillo (tel: 231-114; fax 242-888; e-mail: camara@camaratru.org.pe).

Banking

Banco Banex, Av República de Panamá 3680, San Isidro, Lima 27 (tel: 210-0071; fax: 440-3298).

Banco do Brasil SA, Avenue Camino Real 348, Torre el Pilar Piso 9, San Isidro, Lima 27 (tel: 221-2258; fax: 442-4208).

Banco Continental, Av República de Panamá 3073, 27 Lima (tel: 421-7272; fax: 441-8922).

Banco de Comercio, Jr Lampa 560, Piso 2, Lima 1 (tel: 428-9400; fax: 426-8454).

Banco de Crédito del Perú, Av Huarochiri y Calle Centenario, 156 URB Las Ladera de Melgarejo, Lima 12 (tel: 349-0304; fax: 349-0548).

Banco de Desarrollo, Jr Camaná 700, Lima 1 (tel: 428-6360; fax: 427-7665).

Banco Exterior de Los Andes y de España, Extebandes, Av Canaval Y Moreyra 454, Lima 27 (tel: 442-2121; fax: 440-4572).

Banco Financiero Del Perú, Avenue Ricardo Palma 229, Lima 18 (tel: 241-0324; fax: 447-8766).

Banco Interamericano de Desarrollo, Paseo de la República 3245, 14th Floor, PO Box 270154, San Isidro, Lima 27 (tel: 442-3400).

Banco Interamericano de Finanzas (BIF), Ricardo Rivera Navarrete 543, Lima 27 (tel: 221-2888; fax: 221-2489).

Banco Interandino Saema, Augusto Tamayo 120, Lima 27 (tel: 471-7777; fax: 441-1404).

Banco Internacional Del Perú (Interbanc), Jr De La Unión 600, Lima 1 (tel: 427-2000; fax: 426-2630).

Banco Latino, Av Paseo de la República 3505, Lima 27 (tel: 422-1290; fax: 442-6200).

Banco del Libertador, Av P De la República 3245, San Isidro, Lima 27 (tel: 442-1661; fax: 441-4908).

Banco de Lima, Esquina Puno y Carabaya 698, Lima 1 (tel: 426-8676; fax: 426-2356).

Banco Mercantil del Peru SA, Av Rivera Navarrete 641, Lima 27 (tel: 442-1290; fax: 442-5277).

Banco de la Nación (national bank), Av Nicolas de Piérola, Lima 1 (tel: 426-2000; fax: 426-1133).

Banco del Nuevo Mundo, Av Paseo de la República 3033, 27 Lima (tel: 472-5121; fax: 440-2940).

Banco del Progreso - Probank, Av Javier Prado Este 595, 27 Lima (tel: 421-2800; fax: 441-1058).

Banco Regional del Norte (Norbank), Av Emancipación 199, Lima 1 (tel: 422-3589; fax: 442-2703).

Banco República, Jr Camaná 700, Lima 1 (tel: 444-3214; fax: 444-3774).

Banco Santander, A Tamayo 120, San Isidro, Lima 27 (tel: 221-5000; fax: 221-5001).

Banco Solventa, Av Aviación 2401, Piso 11, San Borja (tel: 225-0505; fax: 225-0505).

Banco Sudamericano SA, Av Camino Real 815, Lima 27 (tel: 221-1111; fax: 442-3392).

Banco del Sur del Perú (Bancosur), Chinchón 986, San Isidro, Lima 27 (tel: 442-1170; fax: 442-1178).

Banco del Trabajo, Av Paseo de La República 3587, San Isidro, Lima 27 (tel: 421-9000; fax: 421-2521).

Banco Wiese Ltdo, Jr Cuzco 245, Lima 1 (tel: 428-6000; fax: 426-3977).

Citibank NA, Av Camino Real 456, Torre Real, Piso 5TO, Lima 27 (tel: 421-400; fax: 440-9044).

Central bank

Banco Central de Reserva del Perú, Miroquesada 441, Lima (tel: 613-2000; fax: 427-5880; e-mail: webmaster@bcrp.gob.pe).

Travel information

South American Explorers Club, Cale Piura 135, Miraflores, Lima (tel: 445-3306; e-mail: limaclub@saexplorers.org).

Tourist Bureau of Complaints, PO Box 1596, Lima (tel: 224-7888; e-mail: postmaster@indecopi.gob.pe).

Tourist Police (speak several languages; wear white belts over their green dress uniforms), Lima (tel: 225-8698; fax: 476-7708); toll-free number for tourists outside Lima: 0800-42579).

Ministry of tourism

Ministry of International Trade and Tourism, Calle 1 Oeste No 50, Urbani Córpac, Edificio Mincetur, San Isidro, Lima (tel: 224-3347; fax: 224-3264; e-mail: informa@mincetur.gob.pe).

National tourist organisation offices

PromPeru, Calle 1 Oeste No 50, Urbanización Córpac, Edificio Mincetur, San Isidro, Lima (tel: 224-3131; Fax: 224-7134; e-mail: postmaster@promperu.gob.pe).

Ministries

Ministry of Agriculture, Avenida Salaverry s/n, Jesús Maria, Lima (tel: 433-3034; fax: 432-9098).

Ministry of Defence, Avenida Arequipa 291, Lince, Lima (tel: 435-9567; fax: 433-5150).

Ministry of Economy and Finance, Jr Junín 339, Lima (tel: 427-3930; fax: 431-7836).

Ministry of Education, Avenida San Develde 160, San Borja, Lima (tel: 436-1240; fax: 433-0230).

Ministry of Energy and Mines, Avenida Las Artes s/n, San Borja, Lima (tel: 475-0206; fax: 475-0689).

Ministry of Fisheries, Calle Uno Oeste s/n, Urbanización Corpac, San Isidro, Lima (tel: 224-3336; fax: 224-3233).

Ministry of Foreign Affairs, Palacio de Torre Tagle, Jr. Ucayali 363, Lima (tel: 427-3860; fax: 426-3266).

Ministry of Health, Avenida Salaverry Cdra 8, Jesús María, Lima (tel: 432-3535; fax: 431-3671).

Ministry of the Interior, Plaza 30 de Agosto 150, San Isidro, Lima (tel: 475-2995; fax: 441-5128).

Ministry of Justice, Scipión e Llona 350, Miraflores, Lima (tel: 441-7320; fax: 440-4407).

Ministry of Labour and Social Promotion, Avenida Salaverry 655, Jesús Maria, Lima (tel: 433-2512; fax: 433-8126).

Ministry of the Presidency, Avenida Paseo de la República 4297, Lima (tel: 446-5886; fax: 447-0379).

Ministry of Transport, Communications, Housing and Construction, Avenida 28 de Julio 800, Lima 1 (tel: 433-1212; fax: 433-9378).

Ministry for Women's Promotion and Human Development, Avenida Emancipación 235 o Esquina Jr Camaná 616, Lima 1 (tel: 426-4336).

Other useful addresses

Adex (export association), Javier Prado Este No 2875, San Borja, Lima (tel: 346-2530; fax: 346-1879; e-mail: postmast@adex.org.pe).

Andean Group, Avda Paseo de la República, Casilla Postal 3237, Lima.

Asociación de Bancos del Perú (Bank Association), Av Antonio Miro Quesada 247 of 409, Lima 1 (tel: 428-8850, 427-6378, 428-5136).

Centromin (Empresa Minera del Centro del Perú SA), Avda Javier Prado Este 2175, San Borja, Apdo 2412, Lima 34 (tel: 365-924; fax: 358-782).

Cepri (Electroperú Privatisation), Avda Pedro Miotta s/n, Lima 29 (tel: 661-844; fax: 661-899).

Cofide (Corporación Financiera de Desarrollo), Camino Real 390, San Isidro, Lima 27 (tel: 422-550; fax: 423-384).

Conaco (Confederación Nacional de Comerciantes) (National Federation of Commerce), Avenida Abancay 210, Lima (tel: 273-528, 286-026).

Conite (National Commission for Investments and Foreign Technology), Avenida Abancay 500, Piso 6 (MEF), Lima 1.

Copri (Private Investment Promotion Committee), Comité Especial de Minero Perú SA, Bernardo Monteagudo No 222, Piso 12, Lima 17 (tel: 461-4300; fax: 462-7049).

Corpac (Corporación Peruana de Aeropuertos y Aviación Comercial), Aeropuerto Internacional Jorge Chávez, Avenida Faucett s/n, Callao (tel: 529-570).

Electroperú, Centro Cívico, Paseo de la República 144, Lima 1 (tel: 310-664).

Empresa Nacional de Ferrocarriles del Perú, Ancash 207, Apdo 1379, Lima (tel: 289-440).

Hierroperú(State Iron Company of Peru), Avenida Paseo de la República 3587, Lima (tel: 410-636).

Lima Stock Exchange, Pasaje Acuna 191, Lima (tel: 286-280; fax: 337-650).

Mineroperú (State Mining Company of Peru), Avenida Bernardo Monteagudo Orrantia 222, Magdalena del Mar, Lima (tel: 620-740; fax: 627-049).

Peruvian Embassy (USA), 1700 Massachusetts Avenue, NW, Washington DC (tel: (+1-202) 833-9860; fax: (+1-202) 659-8124; e-mail: peru@peruemb.org).

PetroPerú (State Petroleum Company), Paseo de la República 3361, San Isidro, Lima 27 (tel: 411-919).

PromPerú, Comisión de Promoción del Perú (investment promotion), Edificio Mitinci, Piso 13, calle 1 Oeste S/N, Lima 27 (tel: 224-3125/3271/3279; fax: 224-3323; e-mail: perunet@promperu.gob.pe).

Sociedad de Industrias (Society of Industries), Los Laureles 365, San Isidro, Lima 27 (tel: 408-700).

Internet sites

PromPerú, Comisión de Promoción del Perú (for general information on Peru and daily updates): http://www.rcp.net.pe/perunet

ADEX, Asociacion de Exportadores: http://www.adexperu.org.pe

Philippines

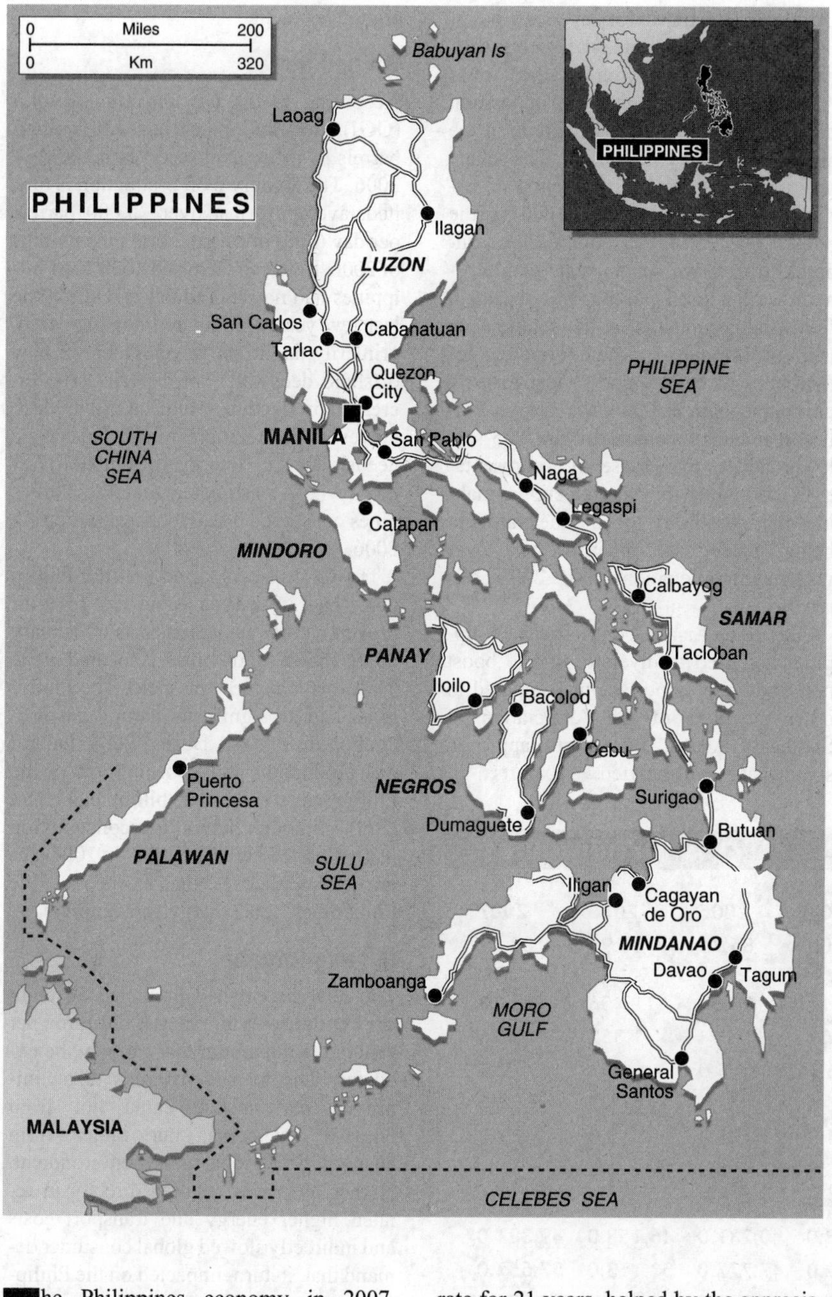

KEY FACTS

Official name: Republika ng Pilipinas (Republic of the Philippines)

Head of State: President Gloria Macapagal Arroyo (since 2001; elected May 2004)

Head of government: President Gloria Macapagal Arroyo

Ruling party: Coalition government, Team (Together Everyone Achieves More) Unity, led by Kabalikat ng Malayang Pilipino (Kampi) (Partner of the Free Filipino) with Lakas ng Edsa (Lakas-Christian Muslim Democrats Party) (Lakas-CMD), Koalisyon ng mga Pulitikong na Maka-Administrasyon (Coalition of Administrative Political Party) (CAPP), Laban ng Demokratikong Pilipino (LDP) (Struggle of Democratic Filipinos) and Partido Demokratiko-Sosyalista ng Pilipinas (PDSP) (Philippines Democratic Socialist Party) (since 2001; re-elected 2007)

Area: 300,439 square km (7,107 islands)

Population: 82.81 million (2005)

Capital: Manila (on Luzon)

Official language: Filipino (based on Tagalog)

Currency: Peso (P) = 100 centavos

Exchange rate: P44.45 per US$ (Jul 2008)

GDP per capita: US$1,625 (2007)

GDP real growth: 7.30% (2007)*

Unemployment: 11.80% (2004)

Inflation: 2.80% (2007); 11.4% (June 2008

Balance of trade: -US$6.96 billion (2006)

Foreign debt: US$60.55 billion (2004)

Visitor numbers: 2.84 million (2006)*

* estimated figure

The Philippines economy in 2007 achieved its highest growth rate in some thirty years, registering an annual increase in gross domestic product (GDP) of 7.3 per cent, well up on the 5.2 per cent averaged for the previous 5 years. Not only this, but the republic's inflation rate dropped to 2.8 per cent, the lowest rate for 21 years, helped by the appreciation of the Philippine peso against the dollar.

The economic edge

According to the Asian Development Bank (ADB) in its *Asian Development Outlook* for 2008, private consumption rose by 6.3 per cent. The services sector, which represents about half the economy, was the main contributor to GDP growth, increasing by an impressive 8.7 per cent. Industry showed more muted growth, at 6.6 per cent with manufacturing under-performing and not creating as many jobs as expected. Lower export demand meant that there was a 5.6 per cent drop in the production of electrical machinery. None the less, unemployment dropped from the 8.0 per cent registered in 2006 to 7.3 per cent in 2007. Low levels of investment in manufacturing and lower foreign direct investment (FDI) in comparison to other Association of Southeast Asian Nations (Asean) countries such as Malaysia and Thailand looked like leading to a lower rate of economic expansion in 2008, which the ADB put at 6.0 per cent, edging up again in 2009.

Electoral violence

The Philippines May 2007 elections in which approximately 17,263 positions at national, provincial and local level were contested by some 79,000 candidates, were held despite the scale of violence in the country overall, which was horrific. There were 128 election-related killings and over 200 other incidents of violence throughout the campaign period, which officially began on 14 January, including ten killed on election day. Killings included candidates, their family members and supporters, and teachers working as poll officials. Electoral fraud in the Philippines is endemic and widespread and includes blatant vote buying (prices vary from a few cents to hundreds of dollars), pre-filled ballots, manipulation of registered voter lists, vote 'shaving and padding' where votes are lost or gained in the lengthy manual counting process.

Opponents of President Gloria Arroyo's administration won a resounding victory in the election contest for key senate posts. Of ten of the 12 senate seats being contested only two were won by allies of Ms Arroyo. This means that the opposition has a majority in the senate, giving it the ability to veto key legislation. The senate positions were among thousands of national and local seats contested in the polls. The election commission announced that two senate seats would remain vacant until polling was repeated, following complaints on the southern island of Mindanao, where hundreds of thousands of ballot papers went missing during the main election. Ms Arroyo's allies maintained control of the 275-seat lower house, the House of Representatives, following the May elections, making the possibility of another attempt being made to impeach her over vote-rigging allegations in the 2004 polls remote.

Like other Asian countries, the Philippines has tried to diversify and to boost non-traditional exports. But compared to other members of the Association of Southeast Asean, its efforts appeared somewhat half-hearted. Exports of non-traditional products have certainly increased, but generally in highly competitive – and therefore highly vulnerable – sectors.

Nevertheless, under the leadership of President Gloria Macapagal Arroyo, the Philippines has undergone an economic transformation, deregulating its energy sector and offering new incentives for foreign investment.

Oil and gas

According to the *Oil and Gas Journal* (OGJ), the Philippines had 138 million barrels of proven oil reserves in January 2006. The country's oil production is limited, averaging just over 25,000 barrels per day (bpd) during the first nine months of 2006. Between 1996 and 2000, the Philippines had no oil production. During the last few years, production has increased, primarily due to the development of new offshore deepwater oil deposits. The increased production volume is still modest, however, in relation to the country's needs. The US Energy Information Authority (EIA) estimated that the Philippines consumed 349,000bpd of oil during 2006.

The OGJ also reported that the Philippines had 3.9 trillion cubic feet (Tcf) of proven natural gas reserves as of January 2006, almost all of which is located in the Malampaya natural gas field. The Philippines had no significant natural gas production until 2001. During 2004, natural gas production and consumption in the Philippines stood at 102 billion cubic feet (Bcf). Although natural gas consumption has ballooned in recent years, in 2004 natural gas supplied less than 8 per cent of the Philippines' total energy consumption.

Missing targets

The government had predicted an eight per cent growth in exports, but three per cent is the maximum that can now be expected. The main constraints to an improved performance came not from domestic concerns, but rather from changes in the global market environment. Higher oil prices resulted directly in related higher energy and transport costs and indirectly slowed global consumer demand that, in turn, impacted on the Philippines export performance.

Owing predominantly to the oil shock, throughout 2005 and 2006 the Philippines experienced annual inflation of 7.6 per cent and 6.2 per cent respectively, however inflation fell sharply in 2007 to 2.8 per cent. The Philippines' consistently large budget deficit has produced a high

KEY INDICATORS — Philippines

	Unit	2003	2004	2005	2006	2007
Population	m	81.65	82.00	85.26	86.97	*88.71
Gross domestic product (GDP)	US$bn	80.60	90.11	98.37	117.56	144.13
GDP per capita	US$	1,010	1,014	1,154	1,352	*1,625
GDP real growth	%	4.0	6.1	5.0	5.4	7.3
Inflation	%	3.0	5.5	7.6	6.2	2.8
Unemployment	%	11.4	11.8	11.4	8.0	7.3
Industrial output	% change	–	5.2	5.3	4.5	–
Agricultural output	% change	–	4.9	2.0	3.8	–
Exports (fob) (goods)	US$m	35,414.0	38,728.0	40,231.0	46,158.0	49,321.0
Imports (cif) (goods)	US$m	36,972.0	45,109.0	47,777.0	53,113.0	57,557.0
Balance of trade	US$m	-1,558.0	-6,381.0	-7,546.0	-6,955.0	-8,236.0
Current account	US$m	3,350.0	3,890.0	1,955.0	5,347.0	6,351.0
Total reserves minus gold	US$m	13,655.0	13,116.0	15,926.0	20,025.0	30,211.0
Foreign exchange	US$m	13,523.0	12,980.0	15,800.0	19,891.0	30,071.0
Exchange rate	per US$	54.50	56.05	49.00	49.45	41.21

* estimated figure

debt level. This has forced Manila to spend a large portion of the national government budget on debt service. Large, unprofitable public enterprises, especially in the energy sector, contribute to government debt because of slow progress on privatisation. Credit rating agencies have expressed concern about the Philippines' ability to service its debt, which will further influence the imposition of new revenue measures.

It is estimated that US$2.5 billion was generated from the influx of 2.6 million foreign tourists in 2005, up from US$2 billion and 2.3 million tourists in 2004. The growth of revenue from tourism is expected to have accelerated in 2006 and 2007, despite the increase in the cost of flying.

Outlook

As in so many developing economies throughout the world, the politico-economic dynamic is of huge importance to the Philippines. The continued presence of political stability and predictability is vitally important, as foreign investors are unlikely to plough their hard earned money into dysfunctional democracies. This problem is one that the Philippines will most likely continue to deal with throughout 2008. Civil-military relations remain in a state of flux in the Philippines and it looks highly likely that the incumbent president will see her authority challenged again.

Risk assessment

Politics	Fair
Economy	Good
Regional stability	Good

COUNTRY PROFILE

Historical profile

The Philippines became a Spanish colony during the sixteenth century; they were ceded to the US in 1898 following the Spanish-American War. In 1935 the Philippines became a self-governing commonweaflth. Manuel Quezon was elected president and tasked with preparing the country for independence after a 10-year transition. In 1942, during the Second World War, the islands fell under Japanese occupation and US and Filipino soldiers fought together during 1944—45 to retake them. On 4 July 1946 the Philippines attained independence under Ferdinand Marcos. His 21-year rule ended in 1986 when a widespread popular rebellion forced him into exile and installed Corazon Aquino as president. Her presidency was hampered by several coup attempts, which prevented a return to full political stability and economic development.

1898 During the Spanish-American War, the independence of the Philippines was declared by General Emilio Aguinaldo, leader of the revolutionary movement, with the support of the US. By the Treaty of Paris, Spain ceded the islands to the US.

1935 A constitution was ratified by plebiscite, giving the Philippines internal self-government and providing independence after 10 years.

1946 The islands were occupied by Japanese forces from 1942–45. US rule was restored at the end of the Second World War, and the Philippines became an independent republic with Manuel Roxas as its first president.

1965 After a succession of presidents, under the control of US economic interests and the Filipino land-owning class, Ferdinand Marcos won elections.

1972 Martial law was imposed by the President, in order to deal with subversive activity and to introduce drastic reforms.

1973 A new constitution was ratified by President Marcos. Transitional provisions gave the president the combined authority of the presidency and the premiership without any fixed term of office.

1981 Martial law was lifted.

1986 Ferdinand Marcos claimed to have defeated his challenger, Corazon Aquino, in the general election. However, it was so blatantly rigged that the result triggered a popular revolt. Marcos and associates fled the country and Aquino took over.

1987 A plebiscite ratified a new constitution with Aquino as president. Congressional elections confirmed her popular support.

1992 In the presidential and legislative elections, Aquino's chosen successor, Fidel Ramos, succeeded her as president, although his supporters failed to achieve an overall majority in the legislature.

1994 President Ramos' Lakas ng Edsa (Lakas-NUCD) (National Union of Christian Democrats) party formed an electoral pact with the Laban ng Makabayang Masang Pilipino (LaMMP) (Struggle of the Nationalist Filipino Masses).

1995 Candidates representing the Lakas-NUCD/LDP alliance secured the bulk of the seats contested in the mid-term elections.

1996 A peace agreement was reached with Mindanao's Muslim rebels, the Moro Islamic Liberation Front (MILF).

1998 Joseph Estrada easily won the presidential elections. Estrada replaced Ramos, who during his six years in power had built up a reputation for ensuring the political stability and economic growth urgently required after the Marcos era.

2000 President Estrada was impeached by the lower house of the legislature after allegations that he had accepted bribes and diverted taxes for personal use.

2001 Estrada was stripped of his powers by a Supreme Court ruling, paving the way for the inauguration of Vice President Gloria Macapagal Arroyo as president. Supporters of President Arroyo won control of the Senate in the legislative elections. The government's offer of enhanced autonomy to Mindanao, instead of independence, was turned down by the MILF.

2002 Filipino and US military forces launched joint exercises near to the stronghold of Abu Sayyaf, the high-profile Muslim rebel whose group was believed to have links with the al Qaeda terrorist group. Tensions in southern Philippines increased following a declaration made by exiled Filipino Muslim leader Nur Misuari for an independent Muslim state. Indonesia, Malaysia and the Philippines signed a pact to counter terrorism and to stop a network that is believed to be bent on turning all three into a single Islamic state.

2003 The army intelligence chief, Brigadier General Victor Corpus, resigned in August after a mutiny led by young army officers, calling for the resignation of the government, was quelled without bloodshed.

2004 Gloria Arroyo was elected president for a six-year term with 40 per cent of the vote, defeating her nearest rival, actor Fernando Poe, with 36.51 per cent. The opposition claimed that there were irregularities in the poll. A typhoon and powerful storms caused major floods and mudslides that killed hundreds of people.

2005 The two-year ceasefire was broken when heavy fighting broke out between government troops and the MILF in July. In September, the opposition failed in its attempt to impeach President Arroyo for election fraud in 2004.

2006 A law abolishing the death penalty that had been reintroduced was signed by President Arroyo in June. In August President Arroyo survived an impeachment ruling over allegations of human rights abuses, corruption and election fraud.

2007 The body of Khaddafy Janjalani, leader of Abu Sayyaf was found; the army stated he had been killed during fighting in 2006. Elections were held in May. On 12 September former president, Joseph Estada, was found guilty of corruption and embezzlement of an estimated US$84 million; he was sentenced to life imprisonment. In November an agreement was reached between the government and the Moro Islamic Liberation Front (MILF), the main separatist group, on a boundary for a Muslim homeland in the southern region of Mindanao.

2008 Jose de Venecia, speaker of the parliament, was ousted by House of Representatives vote on 4 February; he had accused President Arroyo of corruption.
An official announcement, on 28 July, stated that a negotiated settlement between the government and the Moro Islamic Liberation Front (MILF), had agreed to an enlarged autonomous region in the south of the country for the Muslim rebel separatist group. Critics said the deal effectively established an independent state within the Philippines, contrary to the constitution. The Supreme Court blocked the territorial deal on 4 August, forcing the government to break the deal on 21 August. Fierce fighting broke out as militants, led by the MILF, attacked towns and villages in the previously designated border area. The government estimated 100,000 people had been killed and hundreds of thousands had been displaced since the insurrection began in the 1970s.

Political structure

Constitution

Between January 1987 and February 1988, the Philippines adopted a new constitution, elected a newly created two-tier congress, and voted in provincial governors, and town and city councils around the country. The written constitution provides for a presidential system of government with separation of powers and was ratified by national referendum in February 1987. The drafting of the constitution was designed to prevent the emergence of another dictator.
Its principal provisions are that sovereignty resides in the people, and all government authority emanates from them; war is renounced as an instrument of national policy; and civilian authority is supreme over military authority. It has wide powers to check the presidency, including presidential impeachment, the right to lift any imposition of martial law, veto of presidential appointments and human rights protection. These steps completed the rebuilding of democratic structures after two decades of martial law and dictatorial rule by Ferdinand Marcos, whose presidency was ended in the near-bloodless revolution of February 1986.
Suffrage is granted to all citizens over 18 years of age who have resided for at least one year previously in the Philippines, and for at least six months in their voting district. Voting is by secret ballot.
Local government is vested in 13 regions, with provincial, city and municipal councils.

Form of state

Republic

The executive

Executive power is vested in the directly elected president and an appointed cabinet.
The constitution allows the president a single six-year term and prevents any vice president from serving for more than two successive terms.
The president is head of state, chief executive of the republic and commander-in-chief of the armed forces. The vice president is elected on a separate ticket and may represent a different political party.

National legislature

The 1987–88 constitution established a bicameral legislature. It has wide powers to check the presidency, including presidential impeachment, the right to lift any imposition of martial law, veto of presidential appointments and human rights protection.
The Senado (Senate) (upper chamber) has 24 members elected by proportional representation; the 12 senators receiving the largest share of the popular vote serve six-year terms, while the rest serve three-year terms.
The Kapulungan Mga Kinatawan (House of Representatives) (lower chamber) has 260 members, 52 allocated via proportional representation from party lists and 208 elected in single-seat constituencies. House of Representatives members serve terms of three years.

Legal system

Based on Spanish and Anglo-American law.
There is a formal separation of powers between legislative, executive and judiciary. There are also the following courts: the Supreme Court, the court of appeals (formerly the intermediate apellate court), regional trial courts, metropolitan trial courts, municipal trial courts and municipal circuit trial courts. Other laws have created special courts such as the Sandiganbayan (with an anti-corruption brief), and the Sharia courts (for matters involving Muslims). The Supreme Court comprises a chief justice and 14 associate judges, 10 of whom are required to declare on constitutional matters.

Last elections

14 May 2007 (parliamentary); 10 May 2004 (presidential)
Results: Presidential: Gloria Arroyo was elected for a six-year term, defeating her nearest rival, actor Fernando Poe, by more than a million votes.
House of representative: the Lakas ng Edsa (Lakas-CMD) (Lakas-Christian Muslim Democrats Party) won 70 seats (out of 235); the Kabalikat ng Mamamayang Pilipino (Kampi) 47; the Nationalist People's Coalition (NPC) 26; Partido Liberal ng Pilipinas (Liberal Party) (LP) 16; the Nacionalista Party (NP) (National Party) 6; Partido Demokratikong Pilipino-Lakas ng Bayan (PDP-Laban) (Philippines Democratic Party-National Struggle) 4; all other seats were allocated via party lists up to a maximum of three seats.
Senate: (only 12 seats, out of 24, were in election), a coalition Genuine Opposition (Kampi, LP, NP and PDP-Laban) won 7 seats, Lakas-CMD 3 and independents 2.

Next elections

2010 (presidential and parliamentary).

Political parties

Ruling party

Coalition government, Team (Together Everyone Achieves More) Unity, led by Kabalikat ng Malayang Pilipino (Kampi) (Partner of the Free Filipino) with Lakas ng Edsa (Lakas-Christian Muslim Democrats Party) (Lakas-CMD), Koalisyon ng mga Pulitikong na Maka-Administrasyon (Coalition of Administrative Political Party) (CAPP), Laban ng Demokratikong Pilipino (LDP) (Struggle of Democratic Filipinos) and Partido Demokratiko-Sosyalista ng Pilipinas (PDSP) (Philippines Democratic Socialist Party) (since 2001; re-elected 2007)

Main opposition party

Coalition called Genuine opposition (GO) (formed on 15 February 2007) comprising Aksyon Demokratiko (Democratic Action), Kilusang Bagong Lipunan (KBL) (New Society Movement), Partido Liberal (Liberal Party), Nacionalista Party (NP) (National Party), Nationalist People's Coalition (NPC), Partido Demokratikong Pilipino-Lakas ng Bayan (PDP-Laban) (Philippines Democratic Party-National Struggle) and Pwersa ng Masang Pilipino (Force of the Filipino Masses).

Population

82.81 million (2005)
Last census: May 2000: 76,504,077
Population density: 263 inhabitants per square km. Urban population: 59 per cent (1995—2001).
Annual growth rate: 2.0 per cent 1994–2004 (WHO 2006)

Ethnic make-up

Filipinos are of Malayan descent with Chinese and Spanish ancestries. There are around six million tribal Filipinos – 60 ethnological groups – comprising approximately 8 per cent of the total population, mainly around North Luzon, central Luzon and western Mindanao and the Sulu Islands.

Religions

The Philippines is the only country in Asia with a Christian majority. About 85 per cent of the population are baptised Roman Catholics; a sect, the Philippine Independent Church which, since 1902, has not recognised the authority of the Holy See, (4 per cent). There is a strong Muslim presence (5 per cent) especially on Mindanao and a Protestant minority (4 per cent). Buddhism and other beliefs (2 per cent) account for the remainder.

Education
Primary education lasts for four years followed by two years of intermediate and four years of secondary education. Instruction is in both English and Filipino at elementary level, while English is the usual language at secondary level and beyond. However, a curriculum for secondary schools, introduced in 1989, made Filipino (Tagalog) the language of instruction for all subjects except mathematics and the sciences.
Both public and private universities offer higher education. Estimates in 2001 showed that 72 per cent of all students were enrolled in private higher education institutions. Public expenditure on education typically amounted to 3.4 per cent of annual gross national income between 1994–1997.
Literacy rate: 93 per cent adult rate; 95 per cent youth rate (15–24) (Unesco 2005).
Compulsory years: 6 to 12
Enrolment rate: 117 per cent gross primary enrolment of relevant age group (including repeaters); 78 per cent gross secondary enrolment (World Bank).
Pupils per teacher: 35 in primary schools

Health
Per capita total expenditure on health (2003) was US$174; of which per capita government spending was US$76, at the international dollar rate, (WHO 2006).
HIV/Aids
HIV prevalence: 0.1 per cent aged 15–49 in 2003 (World Bank)
Life expectancy: 68 years, 2004 (WHO 2006)
Fertility rate/Maternal mortality rate: 3.1 births per woman, 2004 (WHO 2006); maternal mortality 170 per 100,000 live births (World Bank).
Child (under 5 years) mortality rate (per 1,000): 27 per 1,000 live births; 32 per cent of children aged under five are malnourished (World Bank).

Welfare
The government runs a comprehensive social security scheme, providing a retirement fund, hospital coverage, funeral grants, sickness and disability leave and maternity benefits. Three separate and complementary social security programmes are operated by the state. The first is the basic scheme, providing a pension plan and illness, disability and maternity leave. The second is employee compensation covering disability or work related death and the third is medical care, providing for hospital coverage.
Despite government intentions, only a small proportion of the population benefit from these schemes. Income disparities are extreme, with approximately one out of every four residents in Manila a squatter. Two-thirds of the population live below the national poverty line, with the richest 20 per cent typically receiving more than half of the country's income. At least five million families are estimated to be in extreme poverty or severely malnourished.

Main cities
Manila (on Luzon) (capital, estimated population – excluding urban areas – 1.6 million (m) in 2005). Quezon City (2.6m), Caloocan (1.4m), Cebu, on Visayas (776,140), is competing with Manila as the country's business capital; Davao, on Mindanao (804,074); Tagig (605,875), Las Piñas (584,813), Pasig (563,498), Parañaque (535,833), Iloilo, on Panay (395,809).

Languages spoken
English is widely understood and generally used in government and commerce. There are altogether 11 long-established cultural and racial groups, each with their own language. The major linguistic groups are Tagalog, Ilocano, Cebuano, Hiligaynon, Bicolana, Waray, Pampanago and Pangasinense. Other languages include Leytenhon-Samarnon, Maranao, Tausog and highland ethnic languages. Based on a survey by the national census and statistics office, a representative population of 8.6 million Filipinos showed that 2.5 million speak Tagalog as a mother language and 2.1 million speak Cebuano. The rest of the surveyed population speak one of the more than 80 other dialects in the country. Arabic and Chinese dialects are spoken by a minority of the population.
Official language/s
Filipino (based on Tagalog)

Media
Press
Dailies: Others are The Daily Tribune (www.tribune.net.ph), Malaya (www.malaya.com.ph), Manila Standard (online: www.manilastandardtoday.com) The Manila Times (www.manilatimes.net) and the Manila Bulletin (www.mb.com.ph) with a large circulation, Philippines Daily Inquirer (www.inquirer.net). Major regional dailies, in English, include Sun Star Sebu (www.sunstar.com.ph/cebu), Mindanao Times (www.mindanaotimes.com.ph), Davao Today (www.davaotoday.com) and Minda News (www.mindanews.com). In Tagalog, Abante (www.abante.com.ph), Ang Pilipino Star Ngayon (www.philstar.com) and Taliba (www.journal.com.ph).
English language newspapers with Online editions updated regularly include the Philippine Star (www.philstar.com) and Philippine Daily Inquirer and Philippines News.Net (www.philippinesnews.net).
English language newspapers with Online editions updated regularly include the Philippine Star (www.philstar.com) and Philippine Daily Inquirer and Philippines News.Net (www.philippinesnews.net)
Weeklies: The leading magazines, in English, are Cosmopolitan Philippines (www.cosmomagazine.com.ph) for women, Candy (www.candymag.com) for teenagers, FHM Philippines (www.fhm.com.ph) for men and Bayani Magazine (http://bayanimagazine.com) on general interest. In Tagalog, Pinoy Weekly (www.pinoyweekly.org).
Business: In English, national and Manila based Business World (www.bworldonline.com), Business Mirror (www.businessmirror.com.ph). Agricultural and agribusiness publications are issued by the Philippine Council for Agriculture, Forestry and Natural Resources Research and Development.
Periodicals: Periodicals include the women's quarterly Attitude.
Broadcasting
Radio: There are 350 local radio stations, of which around 10 per cent are either government-owned, non-commercial religious or educational stations, the remaining 90 per cent are commercial broadcasters. National radio networks include Bombo Radyo (www.bomboradyo.com), FEBC (Far East Broadcasting Company) (www.febc.org), MBC Radio (www.mbcradio.net), Radio Philippines (www.radiophilippines.com). and the state-owned PBS (Philippine Broadcasting Service). In Tagalog, RMN Networks (www.rmn.com.ph).
Television: In English, ABS-CBN (www.abs-cbnnews.com), GMA Network (www.gmanews.tv). Online television services in English and Tagalog, iGMA TV (www.igma.tv) and Filamvision TV (www.filamvision.tv).
There are over 50 originating television stations around the country, five of them in Manila, and about 30 relay stations.
Advertising
Advertising is available in the press, radio, television, cinemas and via direct mail.

Economy
Under Ferdinand Marcos's 20-year tenure, the economy suffered serious stagnation, when compared to its regional neighbours (annual GDP growth 1976–86 was a meagre 1.8 per cent). His policy of granting monopoly privileges to cronies while systematically robbing the

country eliminated domestic and foreign investment and increased the trade gap as export competitiveness declined precipitously. During this period income inequality also widened considerably as wealth became concentrated in the hands of the operators of large conglomerates, which still wield considerable influence over the economy. The key problem in the post-Marcos era has been how to open up the economy without creating a backlash from big business.

The liberalisation process began in earnest after Fidel Ramos became president in 1992. The government adopted an IMF structural adjustment plan and legislative and institutional reforms combined with fiscal and monetary stability became key tenets of the government's economic policy.

Despite these positive developments under the programme, the Philippine economy continues to be beset by deep-rooted structural flaws. Concentration of ownership in the hands of a few large companies has slowed the pace of economic liberalisation in the past and will continue to do so. Inadequate and poorly maintained infrastructure, particularly transport, water and sewage services, will hamper economic growth for many years and the state remains unable to provide improved health and education for the massive underclass. Further, despite the concentration of agriculture in Mindanao, the inability of recent governments to achieve peaceful co-existence with the Muslim rebels discourages much-needed investment on the island. As a result, the governement has found it difficult to maintain the momentum of economic reform.

The Philippines is highly dependent on the economic state of America and Japan, its two major export destinations, and on natural conditions. In 2003, the Philippines suffered from drought and the service sector declined after an outbreak of Severe Acute Respiratory Syndrome (Sars). The effects of global economic slowdown were offset to some extent by falling interest rates, which pushed up consumer spending. In 2004, better weather and the improvement in the world economic situation worked to the Philippines' advantage; agricultural and manufacturing output increased and growth exceeded expectations. The upward growth rate was not sustained in 2005, when a decline in the global electronics market affected exports and bad weather hit agriculture. Since 2004, rising exports, especially of electronic goods, together with buoyant consumer spending, have kept GDP growth to five to six per cent annually, compared with four per cent in 2003. High private consumption has been a vital component of the Philippine economy, but is founded on remittances from the huge migrant population. Around eight million Filopinos work overseas and in 2006 sent home US$12 billion. Against the benefits of this source of revenue must be offset the structural consequences of the continuing loss of both professional and unskilled workers to the economy.

External trade

The Philippines is a member of Association of Southeast Asian Nations (ASEAN) Free Trade Area (Afta) and maintains a list of goods that have preferential import duties between members and a programme of tariff reductions due to be introduced in the next few years.

The country has some of the world's highest levels of mineral reserves, including copper, gold, and zinc; most deposits have yet to be exploited. There is an extensive heavy industrial sector as well as a manufacturing sector with commodities dominated by electronics goods which represent around 60 per cent exports.

Foreign trade accounts for 95 per cent of GDP and remittances, totalling an average of US$2.9 billion per annum, have ensured the current account has been in surplus since 2003.

Imports

Principal imports are petroleum and oil products, transport equipment, capital machinery, plastics, ores and scrap metal, telecommunication equipment, consumer goods, foodstuff, garments and textiles.

Main sources: US (16.3 per cent total, 2006), Japan (13.6 per cent), Singapore (8.5 per cent).

Exports

Principal exports are semiconductors, electrical and electronic equipment, vehicles, garments, optical and medical instruments, petroleum products, gold, copper concentrates and chemicals, processed foods, fruits and nuts.

Main destinations: US (18.2 per cent total, 2006), Japan (16.5 per cent), The Netherlands (10.1 per cent).

Agriculture

Farming

Agriculture, once the main contributor to GDP, has lost its position to the services sector. It accounts for around 14 per cent of GDP and employs about 41 per cent of the labour force.

Some 35 per cent of the total land area is used to cultivate food crops, mostly on smallholdings.

About one-third of the population depends on coconuts, the major export crop. Other commercial crops include sugar cane, hemp, bananas, coffee, tobacco, peanuts and various fruits. Rice and maize production is sufficient to meet domestic demand and other crops include sweet potatoes, cassava, plantains, pineapples, mangoes and cocoa.

The Asian Development Bank has highlighted the need for further reforms to stimulate rural development, to improve irrigation systems, which cover only 42 per cent of irrigatable areas, and to improve the yield and production of paddy rice.

Livestock reared for local consumption include cattle, goats, pigs and poultry.

Estimated crop production in 2005 included: 20,000,000 tonnes (t) cereals in total, 14,800,000t rice, 5,200,000t maize, 1,630,000t cassava, 545,000t sweet potatoes, 31,000,000t sugar cane, 14,500,000t coconuts, 233,000t oil palm fruit, 168,000t tomatoes, 100,911t green coffee, 5,650t cocoa beans, 5,800,000t bananas, 950,000t mangoes, 1,800,000t pineapples, 69,650t Manila hemp, 47,800t tobacco, 176,500t citrus fruit, 1,967,570t oilcrops, 96,000t natural rubber, 12,452,620t fruit in total, 5,309,560t vegetables in total.

Livestock production included: 2,073,185t meat in total, 79,000t buffalo meat, 179,000t beef, 1,100,000t pig meat, 35,400t goat meat, 669,975t poultry, 545,000t eggs, 13,000t milk, 15,060t cattle hides, 9,923t goatskins.

Fishing

The fishing industry is a big export earner for the Philippines. During the mid-1990s, the annual net trade surplus in fish products amounted to almost US$100 million. In recent years, thousands of hectares, estimated at 40 per cent of former sugar lands, have been converted into shrimp aquaculture ponds. The southern Philippines have traditionally been bountiful for tuna fishermen, but the tuna catch decreased during the 1990s. There is massive overcapacity at Philippine canneries and fishing companies blame years of unrestrained plunder, rising imports and the destruction of the habitat for the slump in the annual catch.

Since the government initiated a reef development plan to create artificial fish spawning grounds, production of fish has increased dramatically, and the Philippines now boasts the largest area of developed estuarine fishponds in south-east Asia.

In 2004, the total marine fish catch was 1,928,428 tonnes and the total crustacean catch was 87,008 tonnes.

Forestry

Woodland and forests cover 51 per cent of the land area and contain an estimated 1.45 billion cubic metres of hardwood. Exports of logs were phased out to assist the local timber processing industries. The reafforestation programme is markedly behind schedule, but is being accelerated.

Timber imports in 2004 were US$573.9 million, while exports amounted to US$147.9 million.
Timber production in 2004 included 16,044,590 cubic metre (cum) roundwood, 2,975,000cum industrial roundwood, 339,000cum sawnwood, 325,000cum sawlogs and veneer logs, 355,000t pulpwood, 777,000cum wood-based panels, 13,069,590cum woodfuel; 128,000 tonnes (t) charcoal, 1,056,000t paper and paperboard, (including 258,000t newsprint), 296,000t printing and writing paper, 202,000t paper pulp, 326,000t recovered paper.

Industry and manufacturing
The industrial sector accounts for around a third of GDP and employs 16 per cent of the workforce.
Food and beverage processing is the main manufacturing activity, including sugar, meat, fruit and vegetables, fish and shrimp processing, soft drinks and alcoholic beverages. Electronics (semiconductors, circuit boards etc) has been the fastest growing sector of the economy. Production of computers and computer parts is principally carried out by Japanese, US, South Korean and Taiwanese companies. Other major industries include petroleum and coal products, chemicals and chemical products. Main light industrial products, which are often produced from imported materials or components, are cotton and textiles, vehicles, chemicals, machine tools and electrical and consumer goods such as refrigerators, radios, TVs, freezers, air-conditioning equipment, sewing machines and watches.

Tourism
Tourism is under-developed, despite recognition of its economic potential and the attractiveness of the Philippines as a destination. Although visitor numbers are rising, at around two million visitors a year, the Philippines compares badly with its regional rivals. The sector contributes less than three per cent to GDP, being expected to account for 2.7 per cent in 2005. The Philippines lacks adequate tourist infrastructure and accommodation away from the resort areas. There are few international airports outside Manila to allow growth in tourism from North America and Europe and terrorism fears are a deterrent. The Philippines did not even benefit much from the impact of the December 2004 tsunami on rival destinations. 2004 saw an increase in the number of arrivals from Asian countries, who made up around 50 per cent of the total of 2.29 million visitors. The US remains the largest market with around 21 per cent of visitors in 2004. The government is seeking to promote the Philippines as a tourist destination, although not with the vigour of even its smallestr rivals. The government's aim is to attract five million visitors by 2010.

Environment
Tree felling in the 1980s caused erosion and soil degradation, and in 1989 deforestation was prohibited by law.
New mining regulations introduced after copper leakages into river systems in the mid-1990s, stipulate that companies must allocate 10 per cent of initial costs for environmental improvements, and set aside a further 3–5 per cent of mining and milling costs for an environmental protection programme, to be audited annually.
Fishing methods using dynamite and cyanide to stun tropical fish in the coral reefs have poisoned the reef and killed other sea creatures living there.
Philippines, Indonesia, Australia, Papua New Guinea and Solomon Islands are the countries with the most coral reef fish species.

Mining
The mining sector accounts for 2 per cent of GDP and a similar proportion of the workforce.
The Philippines is the second largest gold producer in Asia (after Indonesia) and one of the top 20 producers in the world. It also produces large quantities of silver. There are copper reserves estimated at 3.6 billion tonnes.
Nickel (fourth-largest reserves in the world after Cuba, New Caledonia and Indonesia), chromium, manganese, zinc, mercury, sand, gravel and rock asphalt are also mined. Other metal and mineral resources include iron ore (reserves, mainly laterite, 1.3 billion tonnes), molybdenum, lead, platinum, palladium, cadmium, cobalt, uranium, phosphate, guano, sulphur, pyrites, limestone, shale, gypsum, clay, kaolin, feldspar and silica sand. Large mineral resources, scattered throughout the archipelago, remain unmeasured and untouched.

Hydrocarbons
The Philippines has proven oil reserves of 152 million barrels and produces around 25,000 barrels per day (bpd). With consumption at 333,000 bpd in 2004, the Philippines is still heavily reliant on imports of crude oil and petroleum produsts, which amounted to 307,000 bpd in 2004.
The Philippines has natural gas reserves of 133 billion cubic metres (cum). Natural gas is being used to replace oil for electricity generation. The US$4.5 billion development of the Malampaya offshore field, containing up to 73.2 billion cum of gas, is one of the largest investments the Philippines has ever seen. The field is being developed by an international consortium, including operator Shell Philippines Exploration (SPEX) (45 per cent), Texaco (45 per cent) and the Philippine National Oil Company (PNOC) (10 per cent).
The Philippines has around 300 million tonnes of recoverable coal reserves and produces around two million tonnes per year (tpy), which satisfies around 25 per cent of annual domestic consumption. The remaining 75 per cent is imported, primarily from Indonesia, China and Australia. The sector has been affected by the increasing use of natural gas since 2001.

Energy
The Philippines has installed electricity generation of 12GW, 65 per cent of which is thermal, 19 per cent hydroelectric and 16 per cent geothermal.
The country is spearheading the development of environmentally friendly electricity generation. The Philippines is the largest user of geothermal power in the world. The government estimates that geothermal energy has saved the country US$2.5 billion in oil imports since the industry was launched in 1971 and has prevented the emission of thousands of tonnes of hydrocarbon gases – although the coal sector continues to expand. By 2020, almost 50 per cent of the country's power generation, currently dependent on imported oil, will come from gas-driven plants fed from the country's gas fields.
The government also plans to complete the restructuring process that involves full electrification of the archipelago. Private investment in the energy sector will also be encouraged.

Financial markets
Stock exchange
The Philippine Stock Exchange (PSE) was created in 2000 after the merger of the Manila and the Makati Stock Exchanges.

Banking and insurance
The government made its first step to liberalise the banking sector in 2000 when it introduced a general banking law, allowing foreign banks to gradually take over domestic banks. However, the government continues to intervene in the sector, bailing out banks that experience difficulties.
Philippines was removed from the OECD Financial Action Task Force (FATF) list of non-co-operative countries on money laundering in 2005.

Central bank
Bangko Sentral ngPilipinas (Central Bank of the Philippines).

Main financial centre
Manila, Makati

Offshore facilities

Time

GMT plus eight hours

Geography

The Philippines is an archipelago of 7,107 islands, some large and some only islets, stretching more than 1,700km north to south. Fewer than 5,000 of the islands have names, and less than 2,000 are inhabited.

The nearest neighbours are Indonesia and parts of Malaysia to the south and Taiwan to the north. To the west, across the South China Sea, are Vietnam and peninsular Malaysia. The Pacific Ocean is to the east. The Philippines is situated in the centre of the Asia Pacific region – Japan, South Korea, Hong Kong, Thailand, Malaysia, Singapore and Indonesia can all be reached within two to four hours flying time.

Nearly 95 per cent of the population live on the 11 largest islands. These are mostly mountainous, except for coastal areas and the central plain on Luzon, the largest island (104,683 square km). The second largest island is Mindanao (94,596 square km) in the south, followed by Palawan (14,896 square km), Panay (12,327 square km) and Mindoro (10,245 square km).

There are some 40 active volcanoes (including Balusan and Mayon, both of which erupted in 2006) scattered across the country, and 21 less active ones.

Hemisphere

Northern

Climate

The climate is tropical, with an average temperature of 27 degrees Celsius. Tropical storms and typhoons are common between July–October and they can hit any part of the country. The Philippines is vulnerable to the El Niño phenomenon, which has severely affected agricultural output. The climate is drier and more comfortable between October–February, and can be very pleasant at the higher elevations.

Dress codes

National dress, often worn by men in the office or at any formal occasion, is the barong or embroidered native shirt worn outside the trousers. Reflecting US influence, business suits are almost as prevalent. National dress for women, a scoop-necked dress with ballooning short sleeves, is worn at formal social occasions, not for work. Leisure wear tends to be 'smart casual'.

Entry requirements

Passports

Required by all, valid for six months beyond date of departure.

Visa

Visas are not required by nationals of most countries, including business travellers, for visits of up to 21 days, with valid passports and proof of return/onward passage. For details see www.gov.ph/faqs/visa.asp.

Currency advice/regulations

Import and export of local currency up to P10,000 is allowed; amounts exceeding this figure require authorisation from the Central Bank of the Philippines. There are no restrictions on the import and export of foreign currency, subject to declaration of amounts over P10,000.

Travellers cheques and major foreign currencies may be cashed in large commercial banks and by central bank dealers in Manila, and they are also accepted in most hotels, restaurants and shops. Always use authorised money changers or banks. Outside the capital, it is advisable to carry a sufficient amount of local currency when travelling to provinces, as there is a shortage of exchange facilities.

Customs

Personal effects are allowed duty-free. Visitors may import motorcycles and boats duty-free for stays of up to one month; longer stays require a bond guaranteeing re-export.

Health (for visitors)

Mandatory precautions

Vaccination certificate required for yellow fever if travelling from an infected area.

Advisable precautions

Vaccinations for diphtheria, tuberculosis, hepatitis A and B, Japanese B encephalitis, polio, tetanus and typhoid are advisable. Anti-malaria precautions should be taken if travelling outside urban areas. There is a rabies risk. Tap water is generally clean and safe to drink in the towns.

Hotels

A service charge of 13 per cent and a government tax of 10 per cent are usually added to hotel bills, and gratuities are not necessary, although it is customary to leave small change.

Credit cards

International credit cards are widely accepted in major establishments throughout big cities.

Public holidays (national)

Fixed dates

1 Jan (New Year), 9 Apr (Bataan and Corregidor Heroes Day), 1 May (Labour Day), 12 Jun (Independence Day), 1 Nov (All Saints' Day), 30 Nov (Bonifacio Day), 25 Dec (Christmas Day), 30 Dec (Rizal Day), 31 Dec (New Year's Eve).

Variable dates

Easter, National Heroes Day (last Sun in Aug), Eid al Fitr.

Easter is a major holiday in the Philippines and travel may be disrupted.

Working hours

Working hours vary. Some banks and offices open for a half day on Saturday and, in the Manila area, many shops open for a half day on Sunday.

Banking

Mon–Fri: 0900–1600. Automated banking systems exist (24 hours).

Business

Mon–Fri: 0800–1200/1300, 1300/1400–1700; Sat: 0830–1200.

Government

Mon–Fri: 0730–1130, 1230–1630 or 0800–1200, 1300–1700.

Shops

Mon–Sat: 0930–2030. Most tourist shops open on Sundays.

Electricity supply

220 or 110V AC, 60 cycles with flat and round two-pin plug fittings.

Weights and measures

Metric system, with some local units still in use.

Social customs/useful tips

It is customary to shake hands on meeting and taking leave. If people have an academic or professional title (eg doctor, director) they should be addressed by their title. Senior citizens should be treated with particular respect. Shoes should be removed before entering someone's home.

Central to Filipino values is the concept of maintaining 'face'. Anything which appears to constitute a slight to a Filipino can have serious consequences. Criticism, however mild, of anyone present is to be avoided. New ideas need to be carefully introduced. A strong personal element to relationships, including those of business and state, makes refusal of frequently proffered hospitality offensive. It can be common to receive a positive answer to a question when the appropriate answer is negative. Reciprocity of hospitality is also required. Despite the appearance of extensive westernisation, conservative values usually apply.

Religious matters are taken seriously, but so is superstition to the extent that no building displays a thirteenth floor. Belief in witches happily co-exists alongside more mainstream religions.

Punctuality is aimed at, but not always achieved. Tips of about 10 per cent for most services are considered standard.

Gift-giving, on the smallest pretext, is widely practised, although the gift itself may be inexpensive.

Old-style chivalry towards women reigns supreme, disguising the extent to which women's dominance at home translates into effective control of the Filipino male. Male visitors will be offered companions as a matter of course, but should not extend this apparent availability into loose behaviour with women outside the bounds of the sex industry.

The most important tradition is that of utang na loob, or a lifelong debt of gratitude. This is not just a matter of mutual back-scratching. It is a deeply felt belief that even small favours can never be fully repaid, so that complex networks of loyalties develop, providing a hidden structure to relationships.

Another important tradition is that of pakikisama, or co-operating with the team view. Group identification is all-important, reaching back to one's class at school, or to one's village of origin. Approval of the group is often needed before any serious decision is reached. In this context, the supreme importance of family links can be seen, and the paramount significance of family honour understood.

Security

Widespread poverty makes robbery the most common crime. Changing money at a black-market operator will probably deliver you into the hands of pickpockets outside. Foreigners are rarely targetted for more violent crimes.

Getting there

Air

National airline: Philippine Airlines (PAL)

International airport/s: Ninoy Aquino International Airport (MNL) is 12km south of Manila; facilities include bank, duty-free shop, restaraunts, post office and car hire. Mactan-Cebu International Airport (CEB), on Mactan Island, is 9km from Cebu City and 45km from Manila.

Airport tax: P550.

Surface

Water: It may be possible to find a freight ship which will carry passengers from nearby Malaysian or Indonesian ports, but schedules are unreliable. Cruise ships stop in Manila Bay. There is danger from smugglers and pirates operating between Borneo and Mindanao.

Main port/s: Manila, Batangas City, Cebu, Davao, Iloilo, Zamboanga, Cagayan de Oro, Subic Bay Freeport.

Getting about

National transport

Air: Philippine Airlines (PAL), Cebu Pacific Air, and Air Philippines are the main operators of relatively inexpensive domestic flights.

Road: The network of highways is mainly confined to coastal areas. The Maharlika Highway runs from Luzon to Mindanao, with connecting ferry services.

Buses: There are bus services between Manila and the rest of the country.

Air-conditioned buses are available. There is no central bus terminal in Manila, each company having its own terminal.

Rail: The only railway line is on Luzon island, running south from Manila to Legazpi. A line from Manila to San Fernando and San Jose in the north is not open. Both lines are single track and narrow gauge. Train services are slow; some have restaurant cars and air-conditioning.

Water: Inter-island services are operated by several companies, some with air-conditioned cabins and dining rooms. There are numerous public and private ports, many serving coastal shipping traffic.

City transport

If travelling by road, allow extra travel time between appointments – there are many traffic jams. Tricycles (motorbikes with sidecars) and trishaws are a cheap alternative for shorter distances around towns.

Taxis: Taxis are plentiful and cheap, but not easy to hail. Because traffic is heavy, drivers will often refuse to go beyond the local district. It may be worthwhile retaining a driver for the day. Taxis are metered, but passengers need to ensure that the drivers switch them on; if they make excuses, they should not be engaged. Tipping taxi drivers is not customary.

Buses, trams & metro: Numerous inexpensive bus services operate in and around main centres, but they can be crowded, and knowledge of the area is recommended before travelling by bus. Jeepneys are shared taxis, which ply regular routes and are cheap.

The Metrorail Light Rail Transit (LRT) is an overhead railway which runs from north to south Manila.

Car hire

Self-drive and chauffeur-driven car hire is available. It is advisable to hire a car and driver. Local driving habits make traffic conditions extremely difficult. International driving licences are acceptable. Driving is on the right-hand side of the road.

BUSINESS DIRECTORY

The addresses listed below are a selection only. While World of Information makes every endeavour to check these addresses, we cannot guarantee that changes have not been made, especially to telephone numbers and area codes. We would welcome any corrections.

Telephone area codes

The international dialling code (IDD) for the Philippines is +63, followed by the area code and subscriber's number:

Bacolod	34	Iloilo	33
Cebu	32	Manila	2
Dagupan	75	San Pablo	49
Davao	82		

Useful telephone numbers

Manila

Police: 599-011

Fire: 581-176

Chambers of Commerce

American Chamber of Commerce of the Philippines, Corinthian Plaza, Paseo de Roxas, Legazpi Village, PO Box 2562, Makati, Manila (tel: 818-7911; fax: 811-3081; e-mail: info@amchamphilippines.com).

British Chamber of Commerce of the Philippines, c/o British Embassy, 6752 Ayala Avenue corner Makati Avenue, Makati, Manila (tel: 580-8359; fax: 893-9073; e-mail: administrator@bccphil.com).

Cebu Chamber of Commerce and Industry, CCCI Center, Corner 11th and 13th Avenues, North Reclamation Area, Cebu City (tel: 232-1421; fax: 232-1422; e-mail: ccci@gsilink.com).

Davao City Chamber of Commerce and Industry, DCCII Building, JP Laurel Avenue, Davao City (tel: 221-4148; fax: 226-4433; e-mail: dccii@skynet.net).

European Chamber of Commerce of the Philippines, Axa Life Center, Sen Gil Puyat Avenue corner Tindalo Street, Makati, Manila (tel: 845-1324; fax: 845-1395; e-mail: info@eccp.com).

Philippine Chamber of Commerce and Industry, Salcedo Towers, 169 HV dela Costa Street, Salcedo Village, Makati, Manila (tel: 844-5713; fax: 843-4102; e-mail: pcci@philcham.com).

Banking

Allied Banking Corp, Allied Bank Centre, 6754 Ayala Avenue corner Legaspi Street, Makati, Manila (tel: 816-331; fax: 816-0921).

Bank of the Philippine Islands, PO Box 1827 MCC, BPI Bldg, Ayala Avenue, corner Paseo de Roxas, Makati City (tel: 818-5541; fax: 815-9434).

Development Bank of the Philippines, DBP Building, Makati Avenue corner Sen Gil Puyat Avenue, Makati, Manila (tel: 818-9511; fax: 818-6699).

Equitable PCI Bank, Equitable PCI Bank Tower 1, Makati Avenue corner HV Dela Costa Street, Makati, Manila (tel: 817-7330; fax: 817-6984).

Land Bank of the Philippines, 319 Sen Gil Puyat Avenue, Makati, Manila (tel/fax: 814-0179).

Metrobank, Metrobank Plaza Building, Sen Gil Puyat Avenue, Makati, Manila (tel: 810-3311; fax: 817-6248; e-mail: metrobank@metrobank.com.ph).

Philippine National Bank, Cacho-Gonzales Bldg, cor Aguirre & Transierra Sts, Legaspi Village, Makati

City 1229 (tel: 892-8780; fax: 840-3039).

Rizal Commercial Banking Corporation, RCBC Building, 333 Sen Gil Puyat Avenue, Makati, Manila (tel: 819-3061; fax: 891-0775).

Security Bank Corporation, SBTC Building, 6776 Ayala Avenue, Makati, Manila (tel: 888-7340; fax: 893-2563; e-mail: inquiry@securitybank.com.ph).

Union Bank of the Philippines, SSS (Makati) Building, Ayala Avenue corner Herrera Street, Makati, Manila (tel: 892-0011; fax: 840-0168).

Central bank

Bangko Sentral ng Pilipinas, A Mabini Street, Corner Pablo Ocampo Street, Malate, Manila 1004 (tel: 524-7011; fax: 523-6210; e-mail: bspmail@bsp.gov.ph).

Travel information

Automobile Association Philippines, PO Box 999, 683 Aurora Boulevard, Quezon, Manila (tel: 723-0808; fax: 726-5878; e-mail: aaphils@greendot.com.ph).

Cebu Pacific Air, Robinsons Equitable Building, Ortigas Centre, Pasig, Manila (tel: 702-0888; fax: 637-9170; e-mail: feedback@cebupacificair.com).

Hotel and Restaurant Association of the Philippines, Regina Building, Legazpi Village, Makati, Manila (tel: 815-4659; fax: 815-4663; e-mail: hrap@mnl.sequelnet).

Manila Ninoy Aquino International Airport, NAIA Complex, Pascay, Manila (tel: 877-1109; fax: 833-1180; e-mail: info@miaa.gov.ph).

Philippine Airlines (PAL), PO Box 954, Philippine Airlines Centre, Legazpi Street, Makati, Manila (tel: 818-0111; fax: 818-3298; e-mail: webmgr@pal.com.ph).

Philippine Travel and Tourism Council, 1102 City and Land Mega Plaza, Ortigas Centre, Pasig, Manila (tel: 687-4812; fax: 931-8307; e-mail: info@philppinetourism.org).

Ministry of tourism

Department of Tourism, Kalaw Street, Rizal Park, Manila (tel:525-2000; fax: 521-7374; e-mail: webmaster@tourism.gov.ph).

National tourist organisation offices

Philippine Tourism Authority, Kalaw Street, Ermita, PO Box 1813, Manila (tel: 524-7141; fax: 521-8113; e-mail: info@philtourism.gov.ph).

Ministries

Office of the President, Malacanang Palace , JP Laurel Street, San Miguel, Manila (tel: 564-1451; fax: 742-1641).

Department of Agrarian Reform, Elliptical Road, Diliman, Quezon City (tel: 928-3979; fax: 929-3088).

Department of Agriculture, Elliptical Road, Diliman, Quezon City (tel: 920-4358; fax: 920-3986).

Department of Budget and Mangement, General Solano Street, San Miguel, Manila (tel: 735-4929; fax: 735-4927).

Department of Defence, Camp Aguinaldo, Quezon City (tel: 911-6193; fax: 911-6213).

Department of Education, Culture and Sports, Meralco Avenue, Pasig, Manila (tel: 634-2925; fax: 636-4876).

Department of Energy, PNCP Complex, Meritt Road, Fort Bonifacio, Makati, Manila (tel: 844-2850; fax: 817-8603).

Department of Environment and Natural Resources, Visayas Avenue, Diliman, Quezon City (tel: 929-6633; fax: 920-4352).

Department of Finance, Vito Cruz corner Mabini Street, Malate, Manila (tel: 523-4255; fax: 521-9495).

Department of Foreign Affairs, 2330 Roxas Boulevard, Pasay, Manila (tel: 831-8955; fax: 832-1597).

Department of Health, Rizal Avenue, Santa Cruz, Manila (tel: 743-8301; fax: 711-6055).

Department of the Interior and Local Government, EDSA corner Reliance Street, Mandaluyong, Manila (tel: 631-8777; fax: 631-8831).

Department of Justice, Padre Faura Street, Ermita, Manila (tel: 521-8344; fax: 521-1614).

Department of Labour and Employment, San Jose Street, Intramuros, Manila (tel: 527-2118; fax: 527-3499).

Department of Public Works and Highways, Bonifacio Drive, Port Area, Manila (tel: 527-4111; fax: 527-5635).

Department of Science and Technology, General Santos Avenue, Bicutan, Taguig, Manila (tel: 837-2939; fax: 837-2937).

Department of Social Welfare and Development, Constitution Hills, Quezon City, Manila (tel: 931-8101; fax: 931-8191).

Department of Tourism, Kalaw Street, Rizal Park, Manila (tel:524-1751; fax: 521-7374).

Department of Trade and Industry, 385 Sen Gil Puyat Avenue, Makati, Manila (tel: 895-3515; fax: 896-1166).

Department of Transportation and Communications, Ortigas Avenue, Pasig, Manila (tel: 726-7106; fax: 632-9985).

National Economic and Development Authority, Amber Avenue, Pasig, Manila (tel: 631-3716; fax: 631-3747).

Other useful addresses

ASEAN Investment Promotion Agency, Board of Investments (BOI), Industry and Investments Building, 385 Sen Gil J Puyat Avenue, Makati, Manila (tel: 890-1332; fax: 895-3512).

ASEAN Secretariat, 70 Jl Sisingamangaraja, Jakarta 12110, Indonesia (tel: 62 (21) 726-2991; fax: 739-8234; e-mail: termsak@asean.or.id).

Asian Development Bank, 6 ADB Avenue, Mandaluyong, Manila (tel: 632-4444; fax: 636-2444; e-mail: information@adb.org).

Board of Investments, Industry and Investments Building, 385 Sen Gil Puyat Avenue, Makati, Manila (tel: 897-6682; fax: 895-3521; e-mail: mis@boi.gov.ph).

British Embassy, L V Locsin Building, 6752 Ayala Avenue corner Makati Avenue, Makati, Manila (tel: 816-7116; fax: 819-7206).

Bureau of Export Trade Promotion, New Solid Building, 357 Sen Gil Puyat Avenue, Makati, Manila (tel: 899-0133; fax: 890-4707; e-mail: betpod@dti.gov.ph).

National Economic Development Authority, NEDA Building, Blessed Joseph Maria Escriva Drive, Pasig, Manila (tel: 631-0945; fax: 633-6011; internet site: http://www.neda.gov.ph).

Petroleum Association of the Philippines, c/o 7/F Basic Petroleum Building, C. Palanca Jr Street, Legaspi Village, Makati, Manila (tel: 817-3329; fax: 817-0191).

Philippine Convention and Visitors Corporation, Legazpi Towers, 300 Roxas Boulevard, Pasay City, Manila (tel: 525-9318; fax: 521-6165; e-mail: pcvcnet@info.com.ph).

Philippine Electronics & Telecommunications Federation, 7/F PS Bank Building, Tindalo Street corner Sen.Gil Puyat Avenue, Makati, Manila (tel/fax: 813-6397).

Philippine Exporters Confederation, Roxas Boulevard corner Sen Gil Puyat Avenue, Pasay City, Manila (tel: 833-2531; fax: 831-2132; e-mail: philxprt@l-next.net; internet site: http://www.philexport.org/launch/index.htm).

Philippines Embassy (US), 1600 Massachusetts Avenue, NW, Washington DC 20036 (tel: (+1-202)-467-9300; fax: (+1-202)-467-9417; e-mail: uswashpe@aol.com).

Philippines Food Processors and Exporters Organisation, Suite 304, JS Contractor Building, 423 Magallanes Street,

Intramuros, Manila (tel: 527-5540; fax: 527-5539).

Philippine Information Agency, PIA Building, 1100 Visayas Avenue, Quezon City, Manila (tel: 921-7941; fax: 920-4394; e-mail: odg@pia.gov.ph).

Philippine Iron and Steel Traders Association, 700 Aurora Boulevard, Quezon City, Manila (tel: 722-0536; fax: 721-3599).

Philippine International Trading Corporation, Philippines International Centre, 46 Sen Gil Puyat Avenue, Makati, Manila (tel: 845-4376; fax: 845-4363; e-mail: pitc@info.com.ph).

Philippine Stock Exchange, Exchange Road, Ortigas Centre, Pasig, Manila (tel: 636-0122; fax: 634-5920; e-mail: write@pse.org.ph).

Subic Bay Metropolitan Authority, Building 229, Waterfront Road, Subic Bay Freeport Zone, Olongapo City (tel: 252-4365; fax: 252-3014; e-mail: bgroup@sbma.com).

Textile Producers Association of the Philippines, Room 513, Downtown Center Building, 516 Quintin Paredes Street, Binondo, Manila (tel: 241-1144; fax: 241-1162).

US Embassy, 1201 Roxas Boulevard, Ermita, Manila (tel: 523-1001; fax: 522-4361).

Internet sites

Philippine Consulate General Toronto (gateway site): http://www.philcongen-toronto.com/links.htm

Philippine National Statistics Offices: http://www.census.gov.ph/

Tanikalang Ginto (small gateway site): http://www.filipinolinks.com/business/businformation.html

Pitcairn Island

KEY FACTS

Official name: Pitcairn, Henderson, Ducie and Oeno Islands (Pitcairn Island)

Head of State: Queen Elizabeth II, represented by UK High Commissioner to New Zealand and Governor (non-resident) of the Pitcairn Islands George Fergusson (since 2 May 2006)

Head of government: Commissioner of Pitcairn (based in New Zealand), Leslie Jaques

Area: 27 square km (four islands)

Population: 46 (2008) (all on Pitcairn Island)

Capital: Adamstown

Official language: English

Currency: Pound sterling (£) (£=100 pence); New Zealand dollar (NZ$=100 cents)

Exchange rate: £0.50 per US$ (Jul 2008); NZ$1.31 per US$ (Jul 2008)

COUNTRY PROFILE

Historical profile

1767 Pitcairn's island (as it was originally called, after the young seaman on the Swallow who first spotted it) was sighted and its position recorded, although the longitude was incorrect. The island was uninhabited.

1790 Pitcairn's inaccessibility made it a perfect hideaway for the survivors of the mutinous crew of the British HMS Bounty, led by the Master's Mate, Fletcher Christian, and their Tahitian consorts when they arrived in January. Because the island's longitude had been incorrectly recorded in 1767 (it was in fact some 200 miles from its recorded position), it was 18 years before an American whaler, the Topaz next found the island.

1808 The community of descendants of Christian's original 27-strong group of settlers was discovered by a group of American whalers.

1838 Pitcairn Island was constituted a British colony when Captain R Elliot of HMS Fly gave the Pitcairners formal authority to elect 'a magistrate or elder to be periodically chosen among themselves and answerable for their proceedings to Her Majesty's government'.

1855 The prison on Norfolk Island was decreed to be shut down, but because of increased whaling activity and other traffic in the South Pacific it was considered by the British government to be prudent to colonise the island on a permanent basis. As the resources of Pitcairn Island were by now deemed to be insufficient for the islanders it was suggested that the Pitcairners might relocate to Norfolk Island, a similarly isolated island.

1856 The British offer of Norfolk Island was accepted and all 193 islanders were moved on the Morayshire, with their material possessions, including animals, tools, relics and documents, arriving on 8 June.

1858 16 of the original Pitcairners left Norfolk Island and returned to Pitcairn Island after a land ownership dispute; the second Pitcairn settlement was established. They were followed by other disenchanted groups over the next decade.

1998 Pitcairn became a member of the Secretariat of the Pacific Community.

1999 British economic aid to the island was withdrawn.

2000 British police began investigating allegations of child molestation by islanders.

2003 A scientific diving expedition began studying marine life surrounding the islands. In April 13 men went on trial accused of sex crimes. Islanders warned that if the men were jailed their society would collapse through lack of manpower. The UK dismissed Pitcairn Island commissioner, Leon Salt, amid claims that he had obstructed the pursuit of the alleged child rapists. The first child to be born since 1986 was born in September.

2004 The Supreme Court of Pitcairn Island (sitting in New Zealand) found six men, including the mayor Steve Christian, guilty of sex crimes; four were sentenced to between two and six years in prison and two to community service. On 15 December, Jay Warren, who had been cleared of indecent assault, was elected mayor. Leslie Jacques was appointed Commissioner of Pitcairn by the British government. A UK fund of US$15.3 million was set up to aid development on the island.

2005 In May the Supreme Court rejected the appeal of the men convicted of sexual assault, and confirmed Britain's sovereignty and jurisdiction over the islands.

2006 By September every home on the island had a telephone line, with broadband internet access and live television broadcasts. In October the UK Privy Council turned down the last appeal by the defendants convicted of sex offences. In November the first full-time policeman was appointed.

2007 A new silver, enamelled coin was issued, with an engraving of a rat to coincide with the Chinese year of the rat. Although the face value has NZ$2 the coins retail for NZ$79 (US$70). A second child, to be born since 1986, was born in March.

Political structure

Constitution

The Pitcairn Order of 1970 and the Pitcairn Royal Instructions provide for the constitution. It established the office of governor, who is appointed by the British monarch.

The governor has full legislative authority and has the power to create laws, subject to approval by the monarch. The UK government has the power to legislate directly for Pitcairn Island.

Form of state

British dependent territory

The executive

The UK High Commissioner to New Zealand is also the governor of Pitcairn Island. He is represented on the island by the governor's representative.

The non-resident commissioner of Pitcairn serves as liaison between the governor and the Island Council.

National legislature

The Island Council is a unicameral 10-member Island Council, which deals with internal matters. Council-members are part nominated and part elected: six elected by popular vote, one appointed by the six elected members, two appointed by the governor and one seat for the Island Secretary; members serve one-year terms and are elected on 24 December every year. Decisions made are implemented by an Internal Committee.

Legal system

The Island Court is presided over by the Island Magistrate elected every three years.

Last elections

December 2004

Results: Jay Warren was elected mayor for a three-year term. Mike Warren was elected to the Chairmanship of the Council. The chairman and councillors are elected in December each year.

Next elections

December 2007 (parliamentary)

Political parties

There are no political parties.

Ruling party

Political situation

The community has begun to rebuild both physically and metaphorically since the convictions of six men for sex offences in 2004. With the celebration of Bounty Day on 20 January 2008, which included families re-united and the women verses men tug-of-war (the women won), plus the UK government funded development to give the islanders more contact with the outside world with the construction of a slipway to allow boats to land, for which a scheduled boat services is planned, running from Mangareva in French Polynesia, six time per year, it is intended that the island's unhealthy isolation will be ended.

Population

46 (2008) (all on Pitcairn Island)

Last census: December 1991: 66

Annual growth rate: Declined by 1.32 per cent in 2002.

Ethnic make-up

The inhabitants are mostly descendants of mutineers from the Bounty, and Tahitian women, who settled in Pitcairn in 1790.

Religions

Christian (Seventh-day Adventist).

Education

Island children go to school in New Zealand when they are 16 and few return.

Languages spoken

Pitkern (Pitcairn dialect – a mixture of English and Polynesian) uses many eighteenth century expressions.

Official language/s

English

Media

Press

The Pitcairn Islands Study Centre (PISC) publishes Pitcairn Log and the Online Pitcairn News Page (http://library.puc.edu/pitcairn/index.shtml), covering key news stories. The Pitcairn Islands Study Group (PISG) publishes a UK Log newsletter. With an English edition, the German Mare magazine publishes regular columns including items about Pitcairn.

Periodicals: The Pitcairn Miscellany (www.miscellany.pn), started in 1959, publishes monthly, with a circulation of over 3,000 sent to subscribers worldwide. The Pitcairn Postcard Magazine is an occasional publication illustrating Pitcairn Island postcards, for collectors and people interested in Pitcairn.

Economy

The major sources of public revenue are the sale of postage stamps, which were first introduced in 1940, to collectors, the sale of handicrafts to passing ships and interest on some investments. There is no retail trading except from a small co-operative store which was established on the island in 1967. Bartering is an important part of the economy.

Except for minor licences, there is no formal taxation – every person between the age of 15–65 is required to perform public work each month, in lieu of taxation. Allowances and wages are paid to members of the community who participate in local government activities and who perform communal services. Local expenditure is estimated and controlled by the Island Council. The financial administration for Pitcairn Island is vested in the governor.

There is no price index maintained on the island and there are no statistics relating to external trade, GDP, trade balance etc. Pitcairn Island licensed its internet suffix '.pn', which generated around US$100,000 in 2000, however revenue has since fallen.

The internet provides the islanders with a small international market. A limited amount of honey is exported, generating around US$15,000 per annum. Pitcairn's isolation means that the honey produced is pure and disease free. The islanders have set up the Pitcairn Island Producer's Co-operative (PIPCO) to promote honey production. In 2003, PIPCO temporarily suspended the sale of honey after supply failed to keep up with demand and a backlog of orders developed.

The Pitcairn Investment Fund (PIF) provides financial subsidies for transportation and costs of island living. To extend the life of the Investment Fund, the islanders modified the subsidy plan to allow the PIF to remain solvent until 2010, extending it at least five years beyond earlier projections.

Modest and simple banking facilities are proposed to allow islanders access to funds through the treasurer's office and made available for purchases in New Zealand.

The island costs around US$1 million a year to run, but brings in just half that in revenue. In August 2004, the Pitcairn Island economy received US$6.5 million from the UK government and the EU to save it from bankruptcy.

A US$6 million upgrade of the island's infrastructure began in February 2005, with the start of upgrades for roads and slipway, and construction of the new jetty. By improving facilities and offering jobs in tourism, agriculture and fisheries, the British government is hoping that the population can be doubled to a more sustainable level.

External trade

Sales of postage stamps no longer have pre-eminence since a turndown in the market. All export goods are marketed by mail order through the Internet.

Imports

The principal imports are fuel oil, machinery, building materials, textiles, flour, sugar and other foodstuffs.

Exports

The main exports are handicrafts, wood carvings, basketry and stamps. Fruit and vegetables are sold to visiting ships.

Agriculture

Farming

The island has highly fertile volcanic soil and rainfall is adequate. Main crops include a wide variety of fruits and vegetables, including citrus, sugar cane, watermelons, bananas, yams, beans and honey. Taro and coconuts are also grown. There is some goat and poultry rearing.

In 2005 the development of a new, US$14,000, nursery began. The potential for exporting Pitcairn plants will be investigated.

Fishing

Fish is caught for the islanders' own consumption.

Industry and manufacturing

Production is limited to handcrafted miro-wood carvings, basketry, Pitcairn Island flags and postage stamps.

Tourism

There are no beaches on Pitcairn and landing on Pitcairn is tricky. The construction of a new jetty began in February 2005.

The UK government has made US$6.6 million available to improve roads, a slipway and the jetty, in anticipartion of attracting tourists.
There will be no more than 30 visitors at any one time and the emphasis will be on ecotourism. The improvements began in February 2005.

Environment
Deforestation is a problem, caused by historic slash-and-burn agriculture and settlement.

Mining
Manganese, iron, copper, gold, silver, and zinc have been discovered offshore.

Hydrocarbons
There are no known hydrocarbon resources, all fuels are imported.

Energy
Electricity is produced by diesel generators. Two small windmills will be build to gauge the viability of supplying electricity through windpower.

Time
GMT minus nine hours

Geography
The islands consist of Pitcairn Island and three uninhabited islands, Henderson, Ducie and Oeno. Pitcairn is situated about midway between Peru and New Zealand. The island is volcanic in formation and has a rocky coastline with cliffs. Pawala Valley Ridge, 347 metres, is the highest point.

Hemisphere
Southern

Climate
Subtropical and humid, with temperatures ranging from 13–30 degrees Celsius (C), averaging 18 degrees C in August and 24 degrees C in February. There are south-east trade winds. The rainy season runs from November to March with a possibility of typhoons. Rainfall varies, but can exceed 2,000mm per year.

Entry requirements

Passports
Required by all, valid for six months beyond the intended length of stay.

Visa
Required by all; referred to as a Licence to Land and Reside. This should be applied for, from the governor (Pitcairn Island Administration Office in Auckland), for visits up to six months. The application must include a certificate of good health, proof of return/onward passage, US$300 per week for maintenance and health insurance (including emergency repatriation). See http://www.government.pn/noticapp.htm for the full list of requirements.

Health (for visitors)

Mandatory precautions
Vaccination certificates are required for yellow fever if travelling from an infected area.

Advisable precautions
Vaccination is recommended for diphtheria, tuberculosis, hepatitis A and B, polio, tetanus and typhoid. There is a risk of rabies.

Public holidays (national)

Fixed dates
New Year's Day (1 Jan), Bounty Day (28 Apr), Christmas Day (25 Dec), Family Day (26 Dec).

Variable dates
Good Friday, Easter Monday, Early May Bank Holiday, Queen's Birthday (second Sat in Jun).

Telecommunications
External contacts used to be by SSB, wireless telegraphy, radio telephone and one satellite phone; some islanders are amateur radio enthusiasts. Since 2006 however, every home on the island has a telephone with broadband internet access, and live television broadcasts..

Telephone/fax

Internet/e-mail

Getting there

Air
Pitcairn Island is not accessible by air. The nearest airstrip is on Mangareva, in French Polynesia, which is served weekly by Air Tahiti. Boats may be chartered to sail to Pitcairn.

Surface
Water: Cruise ships make brief stopovers and yachts may be chartered from Mangareva and Tahiti. Otherwise, the only shipping services are occasional supply and mail ships from New Zealand, which will accept passengers for Pitcairn. As there are no port facilities for large vessels, longboats are used to pick up mail, passengers, etc, and, consequently, contact and therefore landing may be prevented by adverse weather conditions.

Getting about

National transport
Road: There is only one paved road. The Hill of Difficulty from the Botany Bay jetty to Adamstown was formerly a dirt track, which became impassable in bad weather. It was surfaced in 2005. Other routes are still dirt tracks. Walking and all-terrain bikes are the principal means of getting about.
Water: In Bounty Bay, on the north side of the island, there is a slip for launching the islanders' longboats.

BUSINESS DIRECTORY

The addresses listed below are a selection only. While World of Information makes every endeavour to check these addresses, we cannot guarantee that changes have not been made, especially to telephone numbers and area codes. We would welcome any corrections.

Telephone area codes
The international direct dialling (IDD) code for Pitcairn Island is +124 followed by the subscriber's number.

Ministries
Pitcairn Islands Administration, PO Box 105-696, Auckland, New Zealand (tel: (+64-9)-366-0186; fax: (+64-9)-366-0187; e-mail: admin@pitcairn.gov.pn).

Other useful addresses
Pitcairn Islands Philatelic Bureau, PO Box 17184, Karori, Wellington, New Zealand (tel: (+64-4) 476-9507; fax: (+64-4) 476-9506; e-mail: stamps@pitcairn.gov.pn).

Pitcairn Island Producers Co-operative (PIPCO), PO Box 69, Adamstown, Pitcairn Island (Fax: (+872) 7612-24116).

Pitcairn Island Study Center, Pacific Union College, 1 Angwin Avenue, Angwin, CA 94508, USA (tel: (+1-202) 707-965-6625; fax: (+1-202) 707-965-6504; e-mail: hford@puc.edu).

Pitcairn Log, Editor Dr Everett L Parker, 719 Moosehead Lake Road, Greenville, ME 04441 9727, USA (e-mail: eparker@midmaine.com).

Internet sites
Pitcairn Island Study Centre: http://library.puc.edu/pitcairn/index.shtml

Pitcairn Island Web Site: http://www.lareau.org/pitc.html

Pitcairn Islands Office: http://www.pitcairn.pn

Pitcairn Islands Study Group: http://www.pisg.org

Pitcairn Miscellany: http://www.miscellany.pn

Pitcairn News: http://www.pitcairnnews.co.nz

Poland

According to the US based Heritage Foundation, in 2008 Poland's economy was 59.5 per cent free, making it the world's 83rd freest economy. Poland is ranked 35th out of 41 countries in the European region, and its overall score is lower than the regional average. Poland scores moderately above average in half of the areas measured by the foundation: trade freedom, monetary freedom, investment freedom, financial freedom, and property rights. The average tariff rate is low, although non-tariff barriers include distorting EU subsidies of agricultural and other goods. Poland's inflation is also low. Like many of its former communist neighbours, Poland faces several economic challenges. It remains weak in government size, freedom from corruption, and labour freedom. The court system, though fairly reliable, is prone to inefficiency and sudden changes in laws or regulations. Foreign investment is generally welcome, but foreign ownership of companies in certain industries is limited. The financial sector is still subject to government interference but is well regarded overall.

Following its accession to the European Union in 2004 Poland had witnessed a colossal emigration of its educated and more ambitious youth. They left in their thousands in search of work, pay and prospects to a number of countries – the UK, Ireland and Sweden initially appearing to be the most popular. The jokes about 'Polish plumbers' in London were meant to be taken in good spirit – and generally they were. In a very short time Polish workers

KEY FACTS

Official name: Rzeczpospolita Polska (Republic of Poland)

Head of State: President Lech Aleksander Kaczynski (PiS) (took office 23 Dec 2005)

Head of government: Prime Minister Donald Tusk (PO) (appointed 9 Nov 2007, sworn in 16 Nov)

Ruling party: Coalition government led by The Platforma Obywatelska (PO) (Civic Platform)

Area: 312,683 square km

Population: 38.14 million (2007)

Capital: Warsaw

Official language: Polish

Currency: Zloty (Zl) = 100 groszy

Exchange rate: Zl2.02 per US$ (Jul 2008)

GDP per capita: US$11,041 (2007)*

GDP real growth: 6.50% (2007)

Labour force: 16.95 million (2004)

Unemployment: 17.70% (2005)

Inflation: 2.50% (2005)

Balance of trade: -US$15.68 billion (2006)

Foreign debt: US$99.19 billion (2004)

Visitor numbers: 15.67 million (2006)*

Annual FDI: US$7.90 billion (2004)

* estimated figure

established a reputation for hard work, reliability and honesty.

Formed over 1,000 years ago, but subject to wrangling ever since, Poland is the third largest country of the former central European bloc. It is easy to see why the country has always been a strategic territory, or buffer zone between East and West: to the west is Germany, at the southern border are the Czech Republic and Slovakia, Ukraine and Belarus are to the east, and the Baltic Sea, Lithuania, and Russia (the Kaliningrad Oblast exclave) to the north. In 1990 Poland embarked on the road to capitalism and democracy without much of a map to steer by.

Today however, Poland is no longer the battleground it once was. The country is a proud member of the EU and has increased its economic output significantly in recent years, from US$158.5 billion GDP in 2000 to an estimated US$303.2 billion GDP by 2005.

Parliamentary elections

The parliamentary elections that took place in 2005 had resulted in the replacement of the Sojusz Lewicy Demokratycznej (SLD) (Democratic Left Alliance) by the centre-right Kaczynski's Prawo i Sprawiedliwosc (PiS) (Law and Justice Party) (156 of the 460 seats in the Sejm). It was generally expected that the PiS would form a coalition government with the Tusk's Platforma Obywatelska (PO) (Civic Platform) but negotiations had broken down, leaving the government to rule as a minority government until early 2006

Between May and September 2006, the PiS managed to govern Poland through an improbable majority coalition with the rather extreme right-wing Samoobrona Rzeczypospolitej Polskiej (SRP) (Self-Defence of the Polish Republic) and Liga Polskich Rodzin (LPR) (League of Polish Families) parties. In September, the leader of the SRP, Andrzej Lepper, was dismissed from the posts of deputy prime minister and agricultural minister due to his repeated threats to vote against the coalition's budget. This was thought to have effectively ended the three party governing coalition. However, on 16 October 2006 a new coalition agreement was signed and, somewhat surprisingly, Andrzej Lepper was sworn in again as deputy prime minister and minister of agriculture. As luck would have it, the unexpected resignation of an SRP MP only hours before the signing of the agreement left the coalition still one seat short of a majority in the Polish parliament.

The inevitable perils of minority government – split loyalties and endless horse-trading – enveloped the coalition members. Polish politics had earlier taken a further turn to the right when, on 23 December 2005, Lech Aleksander Kaczynski took office as president. Kaczynski, a 56 year old lawyer, former major of Warsaw and one time anti-communist activist comes from a politically active family. Along with his identical-twin brother, Jaroslaw Kaczynski, he had established PiS in 2001. The party's personnel are predominantly former members of the Ruch Odbudowy Polski (ROC) (Movement for the Reconstruction of Poland) or Akcja Wyborcza Solidarnosc (AWS) (Solidarity Electoral Action). The party's politics are broadly of the centre right and PiS's eurosceptic attitude toward Europe initially alarmed many within the European political establishment in Brussels, Paris and Berlin.

The coalition government finally broke up on 13 August 2007 and a minority government remained in power. In snap parliamentary elections held on 21 October the opposition PO won 41.5 per cent of the vote (209 seats out of 460), the ruling PiS won 32.1 per cent (166). Turnout was 53.9 per cent, the highest since 1991. The PO immediately began talks to form a coalition. On 9 November, the president nominated Donald Tusk as prime minister; he took office on 16 November.

Economy strengthens

From 2007, the Polish government, headed by Donald Tusk, presided over a booming economy and faced no serious opposition. Mr Tusk's PO had defeated its centre-right rival, PiS, in a tight election in October 2007. The outgoing had government appeared to many observers determined to make a nonsense of Poland's foreign policy, arguing with Poland's neighbours, not least Germany. Its efforts to fight corruption and reform the judicial system led to abuses of power, not cleaner government. It failed to reform public services or modernise creaking infrastructure.

Privatisation

The privatisation of small- and medium-sized state-owned companies and a liberal law on establishing new firms has encouraged the development of the private business sector in Poland, but legal and bureaucratic obstacles alongside persistent corruption are still hamper its further development. The restructuring and privatisation of 'sensitive sectors' (coal, steel, railroads, and energy) is largely on hold. Reforms in health care, education, the pension system and state administration have resulted in larger-than-expected fiscal pressures. Further progress in public finance depends mainly on reducing losses in state enterprises and overhauling

KEY INDICATORS — Poland

	Unit	2003	2004	2005	2006	2007
Population	m	38.20	37.19	38.16	0.04	*38.14
Gross domestic product (GDP)	US$bn	209.60	252.40	303.16	341.72	420.28
GDP per capita	US$	5,507	6,227	7,943	8,959	*11,041
GDP real growth	%	3.3	5.3	3.5	5.8	6.5
Inflation	%	0.8	3.5	2.1	1.0	2.5
Unemployment	%	19.3	19.5	17.7	13.9	12.7
Industrial output	% change	–	6.0	4.4	9.1	–
Agricultural output	% change	–	9.9	-0.6	6.7	–
Natural gas output	bn cum	4.0	4.4	43.0	4.3	4.3
Coal output	mtoe	70.8	69.8	68.7	67.0	57.1
Exports (fob) (goods)	US$m	61,000	81,596	95,846	110,33	144,609
Imports (cif) (goods)	US$m	66,700	87,180	-98,540	126,013	160,162
Balance of trade	US$m	-5,700	5,584	-2,694	-15,683	-15,553
Current account	US$m	-4,080	-3,640	-5,105	-11,084	-15,479
Total reserves minus gold	US$m	32,579.1	35,323.9	40,863.7	46,371.1	62,966.8
Foreign exchange	US$m	31,724.9	34,552.8	40,486.9	46,107.0	62,720.3
Exchange rate	per US$	3.79	3.65	2.99	2.88	2.49

* estimated figure

the tax code to incorporate the growing grey economy, and farmers, the majority of whom pay no tax at all.

World Bank: a helping hand

Poland was one of the founding members of the World Bank, participating in the UN Monetary Conference at Bretton Woods. After resigning from its membership in the 1950s, it rejoined in June 1986. The World Bank's office in Poland was opened in 1990 when it made its first loan to Poland. Since then, the World Bank has supported the country's economic transformation through lending, advice and technical assistance.

The bank is currently helping Poland to maximise the benefits of EU membership. It is assisting the government's efforts to enhance its transport infrastructure by using EU Structural Funds. The government's infrastructure drive is intended to bring improvements to economically depressed and socially deprived areas and to narrow the differences in income between the 'new' and 'old' EU members as fast as possible.

World Bank commitments to the country amount to US$5.7 billion for a total of 40 separate operations. Thirteen on-going projects are mainly focused on upgrading the infrastructure and energy sectors, protecting the environment, and promoting rural development. The bank has a strong programme to assist Poland in combating corruption. It has also provided advice and analysis on promoting corporate social responsibility and improving the education system.

A real European

A great deal was made in the corridors of power in Brussels of the victory of the Polish right in 2005. The rise and eventual triumph of the PiS was seen as something of a threat to Poland's hitherto accelerated drive to be at the heart of everything European. PiS's euroscepticism and in particular its pledge to delay full membership of the single currency was taken in certain quarters to represent the beginnings of fully fledged hostility toward the supra-national institutions of Brussels.

However, such fears appeared to be wide of the mark when top Polish officials pledged their country's continued commitment to the EU.

Poland has also been in the process of fostering a new relationship with Russia. President Lech Kaczynski has described Russia as a country of exceptional importance to Poland and 'a state with which we would like to have the best relationship possible'. Russia has subsequently invited Polish companies to invest, modernise old factories and move their assembly lines to Russia, where, it says, companies are unable to satisfy their domestic markets, forcing the country to import almost 50 per cent of its food. The government intends to create a special industrial zone to offer better investment conditions.

Outlook

The most serious economic problem in Poland is chronic unemployment, which is behind much of the country's youth emigration to other EU countries. In 2006, unemployment was around 16 per cent in December, the modest improvement helped by both continuing rapid economic growth and the larger number of Poles travelling to other EU countries (mainly UK, Ireland and Germany) for work. However, some regional areas still have a higher rate of unemployment (around 23 per cent), particularly among the young. The exceptionally high level of unemployment is the result of deep restructuring of heavy industry and the chronic lack of commercial activity in rural areas. In 2006, the budget deficit was 3.4 per cent of GDP. The Polish government is not pushing for early entry into the eurozone and is it is unlikely that Poland will join the eurozone before 2013.

The relative level of growth in the Polish economy will depend on the flow of investment from external sources. Private consumption should accelerate while exports continue to benefit from good export market growth and improvements in competitiveness over the past few years. The current account deficit remains within safe limits but investment is the major uncertainty. With indecisive policy signals, investment could remain sluggish. If investor concerns about future policies and the business environment were addressed however, it could pick up significantly. Though there will undoubtedly be trials and tribulations for the new coalition government, as is always the case with such constitutional settlements.

Risk assessment

Politics	Fair
Economy	Good
Regional stability	Fair

COUNTRY PROFILE

Historical profile

Poland's geographical position between east and west Europe has put it at the mercy of the great European powers.

1918 An independent republic was declared at the end of the First World War.
1919–21 The Polish-Russian War broke out in February 1919. After the Poles defeated the Russians during the Battle of Warsaw in August 1920, a peace treaty was eventually signed in April 1921.
1939 The Second World War began as Germany, with military assistance from the Soviet Union, invaded Poland. German forces occupied Poland until 1945, when the Soviet Union, now on the side of the Allies, liberated the country.
1945 After the end of the Second World War, Poland came under the Soviet Union's sphere of influence and it annexed Poland's eastern provinces. The Soviet Union established a puppet government in Poland, comprised mostly of communists of the Polskiej Partii Robotniczej (PPR) (Polish Workers' Party) and Polskiej Partii Socjalistycznej (PPS) (Polish Socialist Party). Communist rule did not end until 1989.
1948 The PPR and PPS merged to form the Polska Zjednoczona Partia Robotnicza (PZPR) (Polish United Workers' Party) to cement Poland's one-party political system.
1956 Riots due to food shortages resulted in the reinstatement of Wladyslaw Gomulka as the first secretary of the PZRP. Gomulka had been distrusted as too liberal in 1948. Liberalisation and some economic reform ensued.
1970 Food price strikes brought about the resignation of Gomulka, who was succeeded by Edward Gierek.
1980–82 The rise of the trade union, Solidarnosc (Solidarity), under Lech Walesa, followed strikes at the Gdansk, Gdynia and Szczecin shipyards. The right to form independent unions was recognised by the government. General Wojcieck Jaruzelski succeeded Gierek as PZPR leader. Serious unrest continued during the 1980s, including a period of martial law, the imprisonment of Solidarnosc leaders and the abolition of independent unions.
1987 Government plans for rapid economic reform necessitating further hardship were rejected in a referendum, but political reform was approved.
1988 A series of politically motivated strikes kept up pressure on the government for change.
1989 The rule of communism ebbed as semi-free elections for the national assembly were held in April. Seats for the Sejm were allocated one-third to communists, one-third to existing communist coalition partners; one-third and all Senate seats were free-to-vote, the majority of which were won by supporters of Solidarnosc.
1990 Lech Walesa became Poland's first democratically-elected president.

1991 The first completely free parliamentary elections were held, resulting in the election of a new centre-right government under Prime Minister Jan Olszewski. He was succeeded by Waldemar Pawlak, who was unable to form a government.
1992 Hanna Suchocka became prime minister (Poland's fifth prime minister since the end of communist rule in 1989).
1993 Suchocka resigned in March and in September, elections under the new 5 per cent threshold rule (parties not reaching this level are not eligible for parliamentary representation) reduced the number of parties in parliament. Voters opted for a slowdown in the pace of market-led economic reforms by bringing back the former communists – the Sojusz Lewicy Demokratycznej (SLD) (Democratic Left Alliance). A coalition government of the SLD and the Polskie Stronnictwo Ludowe (PSL) (Polish People's Party) was formed. Waldemar Pawlak of the PSL became prime minister.
1995 Aleksander Kwasniewski (SLD) was elected president.
1996 Poland became a member of the Organisation for Economic Co-operation and Development (OECD). A political wing of Solidarnosc was founded as the Akcja Wyborcza Solidarnosc (AWS) (Solidarity Electoral Action)
1997 A new constitution strengthened the powers of parliament. The AWS formed a centre-right coalition government with Unia Wolnosci (UW) (Freedom Union) after the election.
1999 Poland joined NATO.
2000 UW withdrew from the coalition government in order to slow pace of reform. Kwasniewski was re-elected president.
2001 After parliamentary elections, Leszek Miller, leader of the centre-left SLD, formed a left-wing coalition government with the Unia Pracy (UP) (Labour Union) and the PSL.
2003 The coalition split when the PSL was ejected from government after it refused to vote in favour of government legalisation. The SLD and UP carried on as a minority government.
2004 Poland entered the EU on 1 May.
2005 The referendum on the EU constitution, expected in 2005, was postponed indefinitely. There was a swing to the right in the general elections, the Prawo i Sprawiedliwosc (PiS) (Law and Justice) party won 28 per cent of the vote. Lech Kaczynski was elected president and a new PiS minority government was formed with eight non-partisan members of parliament providing support; Kazimierz Marcinkiewicz became prime minister.
2006 The PiS party established a new ruling coalition with Samoobrona Rzeczypospolitej Polskiej (SRP) (Self-Defence of the Polish Republic) and Liga Polskich Rodzin (LPR) (League of Polish Families). Kazimierz Marcinkiewicz resigned as prime minister and was replaced by the president's twin brother, Jaroslaw Kaczynski. A new lustration law was introduced in August designed to purge ex-communist and communist collaborators from current positions of power.
2007 The Bishop of Warsaw resigned as Archbishop hours after being appointed, following revelations that he had collaborated with the Polish communist secret police. The coalition government broke up on 13 August; a minority government remained in power. In snap parliamentary elections held on 21 October the opposition Platforma Obywatelska (PO) (Civic Platform) won 41.5 per cent of the vote (209 seats out of 460), the ruling PiS won 32.1 per cent (166). Turnout was 53.9 per cent, the highest since 1991. The PO immediately began talks to form a coalition. On 9 November, the president nominated Donald Tusk as prime minister; he took office on 16 November. On 20 December Poland became a member of the European Union Schengen area whereby all travellers may cross borders without a passport or visa.

Political structure

Constitution

The 1952 constitution was amended in 1989 and 1990. Poland is divided into 49 regional vovoids (administrations).

Form of state

Parliamentary democratic republic

The executive

The president is head of state, directly elected by universal suffrage for a five-year term. The president has the power to dissolve parliament and nominates the prime minister. Supreme executive power is vested in the Council of Ministers, headed by the prime minister, responsible to the Sejm.

National legislature

The legislative is the bicameral parliament, which has 460 members in the Sejm (lower house), and 100 members in the Senat (Senate, upper house), who are directly elected for four years.

Legal system

The apex of the legal structure is the Supreme Court, whose judges are elected by the State Council for five years. The Council also appoints a prosecutor general. Below the Supreme Court are district and special courts. Family courts deal with cases involving divorce and domestic relations.

Last elections

14 October 2007 (parliamentary); 8 October 2005 (presidential)

Results: Parliamentary: The Platforma Obywatelska (PO) (Civic Platform) won 41.5 per cent of the vote (209 seats out of 460), Prawo i Sprawiedliwosc (PiS) (Law and Justice) 32.1 per cent (166), the Lewica i Demokraci (LiD) (Left and Democrats) 13.2 per cent (53), and the Polskie Stronnictwo Ludowe (PSL) (Polish Peasant Party) 8.9 per cent (31). Turnout is 53.9 per cent.
Presidential: Lech Aleksander Kacznski won with 54.04 per cent of the vote; his opponent, Donald Tusk won 45.9 per cent. Turnout was 50.99 per cent.

Next elections

September 2009 (parliamentary); October 2010 (presidential)

Political parties

Ruling party

Coalition government led by The Platforma Obywatelska (PO) (Civic Platform)

Main opposition party

The left-wing Sojusz Lewicy Demokratycznej (SLD) (Alliance of Democratic Left) gained third place.

Population

38.14 million (2007)
Last census: May 2002: 38,230,080
Population density: 127 inhabitants per square km. Urban population: 62 per cent (1995–2001).
Annual growth rate: 0.0 per cent 1994–2004 (WHO 2006)

Ethnic make-up

Poland is one of the most ethnically uniform countries in Europe. The non-Polish population, including Ukrainians, Germans and Russians, accounts for only 1.3 per cent of the total population.

Religions

The population is predominantly Roman Catholic. There are small communities of Protestants, Orthodox Christians and Jews.

Education

Public expenditure on education is typically equivalent to 7.5 per cent of annual GNP, including subsidies to private education at the primary, secondary and tertiary levels.
Education is provided free of charge; primary schooling lasts for eight years followed by secondary, academic and technical or vocational qualifications.
Under the former communist state, technical education was biased towards heavy industries and the decline of these industries has left large sections of the mature workforce in need of retraining. Current government aims are to improve education and information technology skills as part of its long-term growth programme. Students attending Poland's most prestigious universities must pass a tough

entrance exam. Since 1990, over 280 private universities have opened, providing an extra 50,000 graduates for the employment market. Typical fees for private universities can vary from US$530 (the average monthly wage), up to US$1,855 per annum, for high cost subjects like medicine.

Compulsory years: 7 to 14

Enrolment rate: 96 per cent gross primary enrolment,98 per cent gross secondary enrolment, of relevant age groups (including repeaters) (World Bank).

Pupils per teacher: 15 in primary schools.

Health

Per capita total expenditure on health (2003) was US$745; of which per capita government spending was US$521, at the international dollar rate, (WHO 2006).

Primary healthcare is provided by a network of healthcare centres and specialist physicians. Initial reforms during the 1990s started with the decentralisation of healthcare (mostly primary care) and the introduction of new payment mechanisms to doctors. This led to a range of publicly subsidised private providers.

The concept of primary healthcare is now based on family medicine. Clinics are run by family practitioners who provide a wide range of healthcare services, or make referals to contracted specialists. Development according to this model has signalled movement towards the privatisation of state-owned primary healthcare. Private healthcare services are provided to eligible individuals via contracts with sickness funds.

A common form of mobile healthcare delivery is the non-public clinic (npzoz), which typically employs two or more doctors. The high investment cost has limited the number of private hospitals to gynaecological and surgical clinics.

HIV/Aids

HIV prevalence: 0.1 per cent aged 15–49 in 2003 (World Bank)

Life expectancy: 75 years, 2004 (WHO 2006)

Fertility rate/Maternal mortality rate: 1.2 births per woman, 2004 (WHO 2006); maternal mortality 8 per 100,000 live births (World Bank).

Child (under 5 years) mortality rate (per 1,000): 6.0 per 1,000 live births (World Bank)

Head of population per physician: 2.47 physicians per 1,000 people, 2003 (WHO 2006)

Welfare

Poland has operated a dual state-run social insurance system and a mandatory private insurance system since 1999. The system, for those under the age of 30, who are obliged to join, consists of a modified social insurance and individual accounts.

Social insurance covers employees, members of co-operatives, self-employed artisans, homeworkers, lawyers and clergy. Special systems exist for independent farmers.

Poland is unique among the former Soviet bloc countries in creating Kasa Rolniczego Ubezpiecznia Spolecznego (KRUS) (Office of Rural Social Insurance), a farmers' social security system, distinct and separate from the workers' system.

Main cities

Warsaw (capital, estimated population 1.7 million in 2005), Lodz (783,022), Krakow (763,826), Wroclaw (642,889), Poznan (581,698), Gdansk (461,818), Szczecin (418,401), Bydgoszcz (376,407), Lublin (363,607)

Languages spoken

There is a small German-speaking community and German is widely understood and spoken. Kashubian, Ukrainian and Belarusian are also spoken. English and French are used in business circles.

Official language/s

Polish

Media

Press

Dailies: In Polish, the leading newspapers are Rzeczpospolita (www.rzeczpospolita.pl), Gazetta Wyborcza (www.gazetawyborcza.pl), with English online version and Trybuna Slaska (www.trybuna.com.pl). Other, mainly tabloids, include Super Express, (www.se.com.pl), Dziennik (www.dziennik.pl), Fakt (http://efakt.pl) and regional newspapers including Gazeta Krakowie (www.gk.pl) Krokaw, Glos Wielkopolski (www.glos.com) Pozan, Kurier Szczecinski (www.kurier.szczecin.pl) Szczecin, Dziennik Baltycki (www.dziennikbaltycki.pl) Gdansk, and Zycie Warszawy (Life) (www.zw.com.pl) Warsaw.

Weeklies: In Polish, the most influential weeklies are Polityka (polityka.onet.pl), Wprost (News) (www.wprost.pl), Gazeta Polska (www.gazetapolska.pl) and Newsweek Polska (www.newsweek.pl). Others include Nie (satirical), Przyjaciolka (womens' magazine), Poradnik Domowy (home ideas). Sports magazines, TV/radio guides and youth magazines are also widely available.

Business: In Polish, newspapers include Parkiet (www.parkiet.com) and Puls Biznesu (www.pb.pl). The most influential periodicals are Gazeta Bankowa (Bankers' Weekly) (www.gazetabankowa.pl), Zycie Gospodarcze (www.nzq.pl) (economic weekly), Rynki Zagraniczne (www.rynkizagraniczne.pl) (three per week; foreign trade), Gazeta Prawna (Legal Gazette) and Handel Zagraniczny (Foreign Trade). In English, The Warsaw Voice (www.warsawvoice.pl) and Warsaw Business Journal (www.wbj.pl).

Broadcasting

Radio: There are many public and commercial radio stations. The public broadcaster, Polskie Radio, operates six nationally channels including an external service broadcasting in several languages including English (www.polskieradio.pl/zagranica/gb). There are around six commercial radio networks broadcasting locally and nationally in FM and AM.

Television: The national broadcasting corporation is Telewizja Polska Spólka Akcyjna (TVP SA, known as PTV), with three commercial channels, broadcasting general programmes with an additional four speciality channels. International, satellite and pay-for-TV networks are also available.

Advertising

Print advertising is on the increase, due mainly to many new titles plus improved availability of raw materials. A number of privately owned or co-operative advertising and business consultancies have appeared. TV and radio are popular advertising media.

Economy

After a decade of high import-led growth in the 1970s, economic performance was undermined in the 1980s by high levels of inflation, a heavy debt burden, labour unrest and contraction in export demand.

The first democratically elected government in 1991 instituted a shock restructuring policy, allowing prices to be set by the market and leaving firms to sink or swim in a climate dictated by market forces. Although heavy industry bore the brunt of economic changes, the early 1990s were also difficult for other sectors, such as light industry.

Economic reforms were continued but, by 2005, the strong economic performance that had been predicted was absent. Governments of the day had ignored or delayed difficult reforms in sectors such as agriculture and social welfare, improving infrastructure and opening up trade, while a second wave of enterprise restructuring took place. The high levels of unemployment seen in 2003 and rising inequality for nearly a decade resulted in many wanting to return to the command economy of Poland's Communist past.

Since then a change in government and membership of the European Union (EU) has changed Poland's prospects.

Inward EU investment (second only to Germany in attractiveness), the earlier business restructuring and the ability of its migrants to gain employment elsewhere in the community (albeit in only three countries to begin with), which accounted for 2.5 per cent of GDP in 2006 in remittances, was marked by GDP growth in 2005 of 3.2 per cent, with an estimated 4.9 per cent for 2006. Inflation was 3.5 per cent in 2004 and 2.1 per cent in 2005 and is expected to fall to 0.8 per cent in 2006.

Public debt is still a concern, with continued high unemployment of 17.7 per cent in 2005 and an estimated 15.9 per cent in 2006. Fiscal deficits have continued to widen with revenues achieving 39.2 per cent of GDP, while expenditures accounted 43.1 per cent; overall, public debt was 47.7 per cent of GDP in 2005. The situation does not appear to be healthy for adoption of the euro in 2008–09. Although the government proposes to cap state budgets and reduce tax rates to achieve stability.

The service sector provides 65 per cent of GDP, agriculture 5 per cent and industry 30 per cent, of which manufacturing accounts for 18 per cent. Processed foods are a major export, including meat, dairy, fruit, vegetables and confectioneries. However, over 50 per cent of all farms only produce foods for their own consumption and have virtually no commercial sales forcing food processors to import their raw materials.

Poland has a long tradition of heavy industry in coal, iron and steel, chemical and petrochemicals, machinery and textiles, although many have been restructured some large state-owned enterprises remain outmoded and resistant to an open market economy.

External trade

As a member of the European Union, Poland operates within a communitywide free trade union, with tariffs sets as a whole. Internationally, the EU has free trade agreements with a number of nations and trading blocs worldwide.

Manufacturing represents 30 per cent of GDP, of which almost 75 per cent is foreign trade. Imports recently have been predominately capital goods for industrial retooling. Poland's industrial sector produces vehicles, machinery, telecommunications, building supplies and processed food.

Imports

Main imports include machinery and transport equipment (over 35 per cent), petroleum and lubricants, intermediate manufactured goods and raw materials, chemicals, minerals and related materials.

Main sources: Germany (24.0 per cent total, 2006), Russia (9.7 per cent), Italy (6.8 per cent).

Exports

Principal exports are semiconductors and electronic equipment (over 35 per cent), machinery and transport intermediate manufactured goods, miscellaneous manufactured goods, processed food and live animals.

Main destinations: Germany (27.1 per cent total, 2006), Italy (6.5 per cent), France (6.2 per cent).

Agriculture

Farming

Poland's large agricultural sector remains handicapped by structural problems, surplus labour, small farms and a lack of investment. There are about 2 million small private farms averaging eight hectares in size. Production is concentrated in livestock farming (dairy and pigs), cereals, potatoes, sugar beet and oilseed. Pork and poultry output have increased considerably. The agricultural sector contributes around 3 per cent to GDP and employs around a quarter of the workforce.

The government's agricultural policy is largely dictated by the need to join the EU Common Agricultural Policy (CAP) over a 10-year transition period. Poland is a net importer of food and its membership of the CAP is likely to have a positive impact on EU finances.

Between 2004 and 2006, the EU will spend eur7.6 billion (US$8 billion) on Polish agriculture in the form of direct subsidies, export subsidies and funds to allow intervention in the market. In the period 2004–06, the government has the opportunity to top-up EU funding, up to 55 per cent in 2004, 60 per cent in 2005, and 65 per cent in 2006, of the levels enjoyed by other member states.

During its transitional entry stage Poland has decided to implement the reform of the CAP on 1 January 2009. The reform was introduced throughout most of the EU on 1 January 2005, when subsidies on farm output, which tended to benefit large farms and encourage overproduction, were replaced by single farm payments, not conditional on production. The change is expected to reward farms that provide and maintain a healthy environment, food safety and animal welfare standards. The changes are also intended to encourage market conscious production and cut the cost of CAP to the EU taxpayer.

Crop production in 2005 included: 26,274,422 tonnes (t) cereals in total, 8,556,248t wheat, 3,460,713t barley, 1,917,388t maize, 3,359,452t rye, 1,311,378t oats, 11,009,392t potatoes, 10,972,027t sugar beets, 1,434,032t rapeseed (canola), 550,165t oilcrops, 26,756t tobacco, 2,050,000t apples, 2,846,000t fruit in total, 5,335,000t vegetables in total. Livestock production included: 3,234,634t meat in total, 304,000t beef, 1,923,484t pig meat, 1,650t lamb, 984,500t poultry, 520,000t eggs, 12,401,145t milk, 12,500t honey, 39,000t cattle hides.

Fishing

Poland has no immediate access to oceanic fishing grounds, but it has its own deep-sea fleet, which has been granted an EU export licence. It has about 44 fish processing plants regulated by EU requirements.

While annual fish consumption has remained stable – at around 215,000 tonnes – Poland's fishing industry is in decline, with the local catch representing an estimated 41.7 per cent of domestic consumption.

In 2004, the total marine fish catch was 157,013 tonnes and the total crustacean catch was 10,533 tonnes.

Forestry

Forests account for less than 33 per cent of Poland's land area. Over 90 per cent of forested land is available for wood supply and the most common species are coniferous, mostly Scots pine. Pollution and insect infestation have degraded much of the forestry resources, although the government has attempted to repair the damage by placing most of the forests under protection. Only the Bialowieza primeval forest is excluded from harvesting.

Export of forest products in 2004 amounted to US$2.5 billion, while imports amounted to US$2.0 billion.

Timber production in 2004 included 32,733,000 cubic metre (cum) roundwood, 29,337,000cum industrial roundwood, 3,743,000cum sawnwood, 13,076,000cum sawlogs and veneer logs,13,960,000cum pulpwood, 6,491,000cum wood-based panels, 3,396,000cum woodfuel; 82,000 tonnes (t) charcoal, 2,634,700t paper and paperboard, (including 217,000t newsprint), 733,000t printing and writing paper, 1,029,000t paper pulp, 1,100,000t recovered paper.

Industry and manufacturing

The industrial and manufacturing sectors form the mainstay of the economy, accounting for around a third of GDP. Heavy export-based industries, such as shipbuilding, metallurgy (particularly steel), chemicals, motor vehicles and cement, dominate. The 1990s saw growth in sectors such as electronics and light industries, while food processing, glass, beverages, textile and forestry industries are also significant. The Polish car market is the sixth largest in Europe behind Germany, Italy, France, UK and Spain. The best investment opportunities are

considered to be in food, textiles, timber, paper, mechanical engineering and furniture.
The steel sector was the focus of early restructuring plans in preparation for entry into the EU. Progress has been slow due to opposition from trade unions.

Tourism
Poland is a popular destination, which is recovering from the effects of the general slump in world tourism from 2000. Whereas there were around 20 million tourist arrivals in 1995, by 2003 numbers had fallen to 13.7 million. In 2004, there was an improvement, when 14.3 million arrivals were recorded. The expansion of budget airlines is seen as an important component in the enhanced tourist figures. The sector, which employs 7.9 per cent of the workforce, is expected to account for 1.6 per cent of GDP in 2005. Most visitors are from neighbouring countries, in particular Germany.
The sector is dominated by the formerly state-owned Orbis SA company, a holding company for Orbis Travel, Orbis Transport and Orbis Hotels.
Poland is seen as having the potential for much greater development since accession to the EU. It is thought that Poland could have over US$23 billion in tourism receipts and 1.5 million jobs if the focus on travel and tourism were fully met.

Environment
Cutting pollution was a condition for Poland's entry into the EU.
While industry has tackled its pollution domestic consumers burn coal in boilers and fires, and more people are buying cars to add to the growing traffic jams on Poland's roads (motor vehicle population is expanding at 30 per cent a year).

Mining
Rich mineral resources include the largest deposits of copper ore in Europe and substantial deposits of coal, zinc-lead ores, sulphur and salt. Lesser deposits include nickel and precious metals such as silver.

Hydrocarbons
Poland has oil reserves of around 96 million barrels. Oil production of around 16,800 barrels per day (bpd) is well below the national oil demand. Poland relies on crude oil imports for some 98 per cent of domestic demand, mostly from Russia. Domestic refining does not meet demand; around 20 per cent of refined liquid fuels are imported. The oil industry contributes 8.5 per cent to GDP.
Poland has gas reserves of 170 billion cubic metres (cum). Gas production meets around 50 per cent of local needs. Polskie Górnictwo Naftowe i Gazownictwo (PGNiG), the Polish oil and gas company, plans to increase its gas distribution network by 2010.
Poland has coal reserves of 22.2 billion tonnes. Coal makes a significant contribution to Poland's energy needs, meeting 95 per cent of the country's primary energy production and 65 per cent of electricity generation. Polish coal exports, mostly to Europe, are a major source of foreign exchange. Coal accounts for two per cent of GDP.

Energy
Poland has installed electricity capacity of around 35 GW, most of which is generated by coal-fired power plants. Polskie Sieci Elektroenergetyczne runs the electricity network. Poland has one of the largest power generation sectors in central and eastern Europe.

Financial markets
Stock exchange
The Gielda Papierow Wartosciowych (GPW) (Warsaw Stock Exchange) was re-established in 1991. A relatively small number of listings dominate, with banks and the copper company KGHM Polska Miedz accounting for a quarter of the market capitalisation. There are over 200 companies listed on the GPW.

Banking and insurance
Banks are moving into new areas, such as investment banking, retail banking and asset management. Foreign banks have increased their involvement in the sector – over 70 per cent of Polish banking assets are administered by foreign companies. In the period 2000–05 the banking sector expanded by 14 per cent per annum as foreign competition increased and banking services attracted more customers.
Central bank
Narodowy Bank Polski (NBP) (National Bank of Poland)
Main financial centre
Warsaw

Time
GMT plus one hour (daylight saving, late March to late October, GMT plus two hours)

Geography
Poland is situated to the north of Central Europe, with Germany to the west, the Czech Republic to the south-west, Slovakia to the south and the Russian Federation enclave around Kaliningrad on the Baltic coast to the north. There is a short border with Lithuania to the north-east and Belarus lies beyond the northern part of the eastern border and Ukraine the southern. Poland has a 520km coastline along the Baltic Sea to the north-west. The country's borders are marked by the Odra and Neisse rivers in the west, the River Bug in the east, the Sudetic Mountains in the south-west and the Carpathian range of mountains in the south-east.
The highest point in the country is 2,499 metres at Rysy on the border with Slovakia. The two major rivers are the Odra and the Vistula which rise in the Sudetic and Carpathian mountains respectively, along the southern borders, and flow into the Baltic Sea.
Hemisphere
Northern

Climate
Poland has a continental climate with cold winters and warm summers. The mountainous regions of the south have a long, cold winter and a relatively short summer. Areas around the Baltic are warmer, with an average temperature of minus one degree Celsius (C) in January and 18 degrees C in July. Southern Poland has annual rainfall of more than 1,500mm, while the rest of the country experiences moderate rainfall of 500–650mm per year. The Vistula and Odra rivers are usually frozen for about two months each year.

Dress codes
Dress codes are generally similar to western European. Lightweight clothing is required from June to August, medium to heavyweight for the rest of year, plus a heavy topcoat in winter.

Entry requirements
Visitors are required to possess sufficient funds for stay, Zl100 per day (or foreign equivalent) and Zl300 per day for medical expenses (or valid insurance).
Passports
Required by all, except members of the EU, EEA and Switzerland who may use a valid national ID card. Passports must be valid for at least three months from date of arrival.
Visa
Required by all, except nationals of EU and Schengen area signatory countries, North America, Australasia and Japan. For further exceptions contact the nearest embassy. A Schengen visa application (offered in several languages) can be downloaded from http://europa.eu/abc/travel/ see 'documents you will need'. For details of those who must apply for a visa see www.polandembassy.org and follow link from consular services to visas for Poland. Contact the nearest embassy consular section for further information and application form.
Those business people who require a visa should have a formal invitation from a local company or organisation giving specific details regarding the purpose and duration of the intended trip. Also required are a company letter from the

applicant's employer regarding his/her status, proof of financial means and receipt of payment for full board accommodation, and return/onward passage.

Currency advice/regulations

The import or export of local currency is limited to the equivalent of eur10,000.

The import and export of foreign currency is unlimited, although all amounts must be declared on entry.

Travellers cheques are accepted in larger bank branches only.

Customs

Personal items, including one example of electronic items, are duty-free. There are no duties levied on alcohol and tobacco between EU member states, providing amounts imported are for personal consumption.

Artistic items dated before 1945 should have customs clearance before export.

Prohibited imports

Illegal drugs, poisons and explosives.

Plants and animals are restricted. Firearms and ammunition require a permit.

Health (for visitors)

Nationals of the European Economic Area (EEA) countries and Switzerland can access reduced cost and sometimes free medical treatment using a European Health Insurance Card (EHIC) while visiting the EEA. Exceptions include nationals of the 10 countries, which joined the EU in 2004, whose EHIC is not valid in Switzerland. Applications for the EHIC should be made before travelling.

Mandatory precautions

None.

Advisable precautions

Hepatitis A, tetanus and polio immunisations. Rabies is a health risk.

Hotels

Most locally run hotels belong to the Orbis hotel chain and are classified one- to four-star. Internationally run chains include the Intercontinental, Holiday Inn and Novotel. Accommodation can be scarce in all main towns, so it is advisable to book well in advance. In an emergency a large travel agency or airline may be able to provide a hotel room. Bills include a 10 per cent service charge; tipping around 10 per cent is customary.

Credit cards

International credit cards are accepted where displayed signs are shown.

Public holidays (national)

Fixed dates

1 Jan (New Year's Day), 1 May (Labour Day), 3 May (National Day), 15 Aug (Assumption Day), 1 Nov (All Saints' Day), 11 Nov (Independence Day), 25–26 Dec (Christmas).

Variable dates

Easter Monday (Mar/Apr), Corpus Christi (May/Jun).

Working hours

Banking

Mon–Fri: 0800–1800.

Polski Bank Kredytowy, Warsaw Okecie airport Mon–Fri: 0730–1700, Sat: 0730–1130. Banks at Katowice Pyrzowice airport Mon–Fri: 0830–1500.

Business

Mon–Fri: 0800–1600.

Government

Mon–Fri: 0800/0900–1500/1600.

Post Offices, Mon–Fri: 0800–2000.

Shops

Mon–Fri: 1100–1900; Sat: 1000–1500, general shops.

Mon–Fri: 0600/0700–1800/1900, food shops.

Commercial companies and shops, other than food shops, close on 'Free Saturdays' which vary between businesses, but usually three per month (one for shops).

Telecommunications

Mobile/cell phones

There are GSM 900/1800 and a 3G services available throughout country with more 3G services planned.

Electricity supply

Domestic 220V AC, 50 cycles; adaptor need for continental-type, round two-pin sockets.

Weights and measures

Metric system

Social customs/useful tips

Organisations do not stop for lunch in the middle of the day. The main meal obiad is taken from 1500. Formal address in the Polish language is expected. Polite small talk is appreciated as a prelude to talking business.

Security

Poland has no particular problem with security and street crime, although since the collapse of communism, street crime has increased. Normal precautions should be followed.

Getting there

Air

National airline: LOT Airlines (Polskie Linie Lotnicze)

International airport/s: Warsaw-Okecie (WAW), 10km south-west of the city (20–40 minutes by bus; 20–30 minutes by taxi); duty-free shops, post office, banks and bureaux de change, bars and restaurants, left-luggage, tourist information and car hire.

Other airport/s: Kraków-Balice (John Paul II International) (KRK), 11km from the city. Wroclaw-Strachowice (WRO), 10 km from the city. Katowice International (KTW), 34km from the city.

Gdansk-Trojmaaaiasto (GDN), 10km from the city.

Airport tax: None

Surface

Road: Access is best through Germany and the Czech Republic. All vehicle documentation should include car registration, driver's national driving licence and valid Green Card motor insurance. An International Driving Permit is also required.

Rail: EuroCity rail services from Western Europe pass through Germany (from Berlin, travelling time is approximately 80 minutes), the Czech Republic or the Slovia Republic. Main lines also link Warsaw with Cologne, Vienna, Budapest and Prague. There are car-sleeper services from the Hook of Holland to Poznan/Warsaw.

Water: Pol Ferries operates between Poland and Sweden, Denmark and Finland.

Getting about

National transport

Air: LOT operates regular services connecting all major cities.

Road: Approximately 154,000km surfaced roads, of which 80 per cent are main roads.

The motorways include a north-south expressway, the Polish section of the Helsinki-Warsaw highway, known as the Via Baltica, and an expressway from Golonice to Opole.

Buses: Extensive bus and coach services are operated by Polish Motor Communications (PKS) and Polski Express.

Rail: There are approximately 30,000km of track. Some lines are narrow-gauge, and some are steam-hauled. Diesel is typical with only 33 per cent of the lines electrified. Regular services are operated by Polskie Koleje Panstwowe (PKP) (Polish State Railways), connecting major towns. Intercity express trains are inexpensive and reliable.

Polrailpass tickets valid for between 8–30 days are available from travel agents and railway offices, both locally and internationally. For an additional sum tickets for sleeping berths are available.

Water: About 4,000km of navigable inland waterways, including about 400km of canals. Ferries and hydrofoils link Baltic resorts in summer.

City transport

Taxis: Metered taxis are available in all main towns; they can be hired from ranks or ordered by phone. Payment in hard currency may be required; tipping is usual. A surcharge is imposed for journies between 2300–0500, out of town, and at weekends.

Buses, trams & metro: Regular public transport operates 0530–2300. Good bus services in all towns, also trams in some. Tickets for Warsaw can be bought at RUCH kiosks and used indiscriminately. In Warsaw seven-day tram tourist tickets can be bought at 37 Senatorska Street (entrance E) (Mon–Wed: 0730–1700, Thu–Fri: 0730–1400).

A metro is in operation in Warsaw.

Car hire

A hirer must be over 21 and have held a full licence for a year. Rental firms are available in all main towns through Orbis. International driving licence and insurance cover recommended. Minimum renting period is 24 hours. Payment is by cash or credit card. Speed limits: built-up areas 60kph, normal roads 90kph, motorways 100kph.

BUSINESS DIRECTORY

The addresses listed below are a selection only. While World of Information makes every endeavour to check these addresses, we cannot guarantee that changes have not been made, especially to telephone numbers and area codes. We would welcome any corrections.

Telephone area codes

The international direct dialling code (IDD) for Poland is +48, followed by area code and subscriber's number:

Bialystok	85	Lódz	42
Bydgoszcz	52	Lublin	81
Gdansk	58	Poznan	61
Katowice	32	Szczecin	91
Kraków	12	Warsaw	22
Leszno	65	Wroclaw	71

Useful telephone numbers

Ambulance: 999
Police emergency service: 997
Fire Brigade: 998
Customs information: 694-5596
Central Tourist Information Office: 270-000
Intercity directory assistance: 912
Local directory assistance: 911/913
Radiotaxi: 919 (complaints 224-444)

Chambers of Commerce

American Chamber of Commerce in Poland, Warsaw Financial Centre, 53 ulica Emilii Plater, 00-113 Warsaw (tel: 520-5999; fax: 520-5998; e-mail: office@amcham.com.pl).

British-Polish Chamber of Commerce, 2 ulica Zimna, 100-138 Warsaw (tel: 654-5971; fax: 621-1937; e-mail: bpcc@bpcc.org.pl).

Banking

AmerBank, Marszalkowska 115, 00-102 Warsaw.

American Express Bank, ul Krakowskie Przedmiescie 11, 00-068 Warsaw.

Bank Gospodarki Zywnosciowej (commercial bank), ul Grzybowska 4, 00-131 Warsaw.

Bank Polska Kasa Opieki SA (Grupa Pekao), Grzybowska 53/57, PO Box 1008, 00-950 Warsaw (tel: 656-0000; fax: 656-0004; e-mail: info@pekao.com.pl).

Bank Przemyslowo-Handlowy (Bank BPH), ul Na Zjezdzie 11, 30-527 Krakow.

Bank Rozwoju Eksportu SA (export development bank), PO Box 728, Bankowy 2, 00-950 Warsaw (tel: 829-0000; fax: 829-0081).

Bank Zachodni we Wroclawiu (Western Bank in Wroclaw), 41–43 Ofiar Oswiecimskich St, 50-850 Wroclaw.

Bre Bank SA, ul Senatorska 18, PO Box 728, PL 00-950 Warsaw (tel: 829-0000; fax: 829-0033).

Citibank, ul. Senatorska 12, 00-082 Warsaw (tel: 657-7200).

Creditanstalt, ul Prosta 69, 00-838 Warsaw (tel: 637-9000; fax: 637-9099).

ING Bank, ul. Emilii Plater 28 pietro 7, 00-950 Warsaw (tel: 630-5695).

Lodzi Bank Rozwoju SA, PO Box 465, ul Piotrkowska 173, 90-950 Lodz.

National Credit Bank, Nowy Swiat 6–12, 00-950 Warsaw (tel: 210-321; fax: 296-988).

Polski Bank Rozwoju SA (Polish development bank), ul Zurawia 47–49, 00-680 Warsaw (tel: 628-0490, 628-0790; fax: 628-6164; (Saturday 2120-828); satellite phone and fax: (39) 120-828, 120-844).

Powszechny Bank Gospodarczy w Lodzi, Pilsudskieo 12, 90-950 Lodz (tel: 361-470, 362-886; fax: 362-870).

Powszechna Kasa Oszczednosci Bank Panstwowy (state savings bank), ul Swietokrzyska 11–21, 00-950 Warsaw (tel: 220-0321, 226-3839; fax: 226-3863).

WBK (Wielkopolski Bank Kredytowy SA), 60-967 Posnan Place, Wolnosci 16 (tel: 56-4900; fax: 52-1113).

Central bank

Narodowy Bank Polski, ul Swietokrzyska 11/21; PO Box 1011, 00-919 Warsaw (tel: 653-1000; fax: 620-8518; e-mail: nbp@nbp.pl).

Travel information

Central Bus Station, Warszawa Zachodnia Aleje Jerozolimskie 144 (tel: 236-394/6).

Central Railway Station, Warszawa Centralna 54 Aleje Jerozolimskie (tel: 255-001, 255-000).

Foundation for Tourism Development, Ul Mazowiecka 7, 00059 Warsaw (tel: 269-238; fax: 269-695).

International train connections – information (tel: 204512); local train connections – information (tel: 200-361).

LOT, Aleje Jerozolmskie 6579, 00-697 Warsaw (reservations in Poland, tel: 0801-703-703; fax: 630-5229); airport information in Warsaw (tel: 650-4220); internet: www.lot.com).

Lufthansa Warsaw Airport Office (tel: 650-4510); town office, Al Jerozolimskie 56c, Warsaw (tel: 630-2555; fax: 630-2535); Katowice Airport Office (tel: 184-5045); town office Al Korfantego 51, Katowice (tel: 106-2443; fax: 106-2444).

Orbis, 16 Bracka Street, 00-028 Warsaw (tel: 829-3939; fax: 827-3301).

State Sports and Tourism Administration, Swietokrzyska 12, 00916 Warsaw (fax: 694-5176).

Warsavawfie Centrum Informacji Gurwstycznej (Warsaw Tourist Information Centre), Zankowy Square 1/13, 00-262 Warsaw (tel: 635-1881).

Ministry of tourism

National Administration of Tourism and Physical Culture, ul. Swietokrzyska 12, 00-916 Warsaw (tel: 694-5555; fax: 826-2172).

Ministries

Ministry of Agriculture and Rural Development, ul Wspólna 30, 00-930 Warsaw (tel: 623-1000; fax: 623-2750; e-mail: kancelaria@minrol.gov.pl).

Ministry of Culture and National Heritage, Ul Krakowskie Przedmiescie 15/17, 00-071 Warsaw (tel: 620-0231; fax: 826-7533).

Ministry of Defence, ul Klonowa 1, 00-909 Warsaw (tel: 845-0441; e-mail: bpimon@wp.mil.pl).

Ministry of Education, Al Szucha 25, 00-918 Warsaw (tel: 628-0461; fax: 628-0461; e-mail: minister@men.waw.pl).

Ministry of the Environment, ul Wawelska 52/54, 02-922 Warsaw (tel: 825-0001; fax: 253-332; e-mail: info@mos.gov.pl).

Ministry of Foreign Affairs, Al Szucha 23, 00-580 Warsaw (tel: 523-9000; fax: 629-0287; e-mail: poland@mfa.gov.pl; internet: www.msz.gov.pl).

Ministry of Health, ul Miodowa 15, 00-923 Warsaw (tel: 831-3441; fax: 831-1553; e-mail: rzecznik@mzios.gov.pl).

Ministry of Internal Affairs and Administration, ul Batorego 5, 02-514 Warsaw (tel: 621-0251; fax: 628-9983; e-mail: wp@mswia.gov.pl).

Ministry of Justice, Al Ujazdowskie 11, 00-950 Warsaw (tel: 521-2808; fax: 628-1692; nagorska@ms.gov.pl).

Ministry of Labour and Social Policy, ul Nowogrodzka 1/3/5, 00-513 Warsaw (tel: 661-0100; fax: 628-4048; e-mail: bip@mpips.gov.pl).

Ministry of Post and Telecommunications, pl Malachowskiego 2, 00-940 Warsaw (tel: 656-5000; fax: 826-4840; e-mail: rzecznik@ml.gov.pl).

Ministry of Transport and Maritime Economy, ul Chalubinskiego 4/6, 00-928 Warsaw (tel: 624-4000; fax: 628-5365).

Ministry of the Treasury, ul Krucza 36, 00-522 Warsaw (tel: 695-9000; fax: 625-1114; e-mail: minister@mst.gov.pl).

President's Office, ul Wiejska 10, 00-902 Warsaw (tel: 695-2900; fax: 695-3819; e-mail: listy@prezydent.pl).

Prime Minister's Office, Al Ujazdowskie 1/3, 00-583 Warsaw (tel: 694-66983; fax: 625-2637; e-mail: cirinfo@kprm.gov.pol).

Other useful addresses

British Consul (Szczecin), Ul Starego Wiarusa 32, 71-206 Szczecin (tel: 487-0302; fax: 487-3697).

British Embassy, Corporate Centre, 2nd Floor, Emilii Plater 28, Warsaw 00-688 (tel: 625-3030; fax: 625-3472); Aleja Roz 1, 00-556 Warsaw (tel: 628-1001/5; fax: 621-7161).

Central Board of Customs, Swietokrzyska 12, 00-916 Warsaw (tel: 694-5555). Press Office (tel: 694-5882; fax: 827-3427).

Central Statistical Office, International Co-operation Division, Al Niepodleglosci 208, 00-925 Warsaw (tel: 608-3113; fax: 608-3870; e-mail: j.szczerbinska@gus.stsp.gov.pl).

Co-operation Fund, Ul Zurawia 4a, 00-503 Warsaw (tel: 693-5165/827/868; fax: 693-5815/365).

Energy Restructuring Group, Ministry of Industry and Trade, 2 Mysia Street, 00926 Warsaw 63 (tel: 625-6280; fax: 625-6305, 628-0970).

Euro Information Centre Network/Correspondence Centre, Ul Zurawia 6/12, 00-503 Warsaw (tel: 625-1319; fax: 625-1290).

European Integration Committee, Aleje Ujazdowskie 9, 00-583 Warsaw (tel: 694-7354; fax: 629-4888).

Foreign Trade Research Institute Market Information Center of Foreign Trade, Krucza 38/42, 00-512 Warsaw (tel: 629-1222; fax: 628-8680).

Foundation for Privatisation, 36 Ul Krucza, 00525 Warsaw (tel: 628-2198/99; fax: 625-1114); external department (tel: 693-5419, 693-5818; fax: 693-5300).

Government Centre for Strategic Studies, Wspolna 4, 00-926 Warsaw (tel: 661-8111); Press Office (tel: 661-8664; fax: 629-1619).

Government Information Department, Ul. Wiejska 4/6, 00-902 Warsaw (tel: 694-2500; fax: 694-1911).

Housing and Urban Development Office, ul. Wspolna 2, 00-926 Warsaw (tel: 661-8111; fax: 628-5887).

Industrial Development Agency, ul Wspolna 4, 00-930 Warsaw (tel: 628-7954, 628-0934; fax: 628-2363).

Main Post Office (open 24 hours), 31–33 Swietokrzyska Street, Warsaw.

National Administration of Tourism and Physical Culture, ul. Swietokrzyska 12, 00-916 Warsaw (tel: 694-5555; fax: 826-2172).

Parliament, Sajm RP, ul. Wiejska 4/6/8, 00-902 Warsaw (tel: 694-2500; fax: 694-2215).

Polcargo (cargo experts and supervisors), Zeromskiego 32, Box 223, 81963 Gdynia (tel: 213-921/957).

Polish Agency for Foreign Investment (PAIZ), Al Roz 2, 00-556 Warsaw (tel: 621-6261; fax: 621-8427).

Polish Chartering Agents (Polfracht), Ul Pulaskiego 8, Box 206, 81368 Gdynia (tel: 214-991).

Polish Corporation of Trade Fairs and Economic Exhibition Organisers, Ul Glogowska 26, 60-734 Poznan (tel: 661-532, 692-245; fax: 661-053; e-mail: korptarg@soho-online.com).

Polish Embassy (USA), 2640 16th Street, NW, Washington DC 20009 (tel: (+1-202) 234-3800; fax: (+1-202) 328-6271; e-mail: information@ioip.com).

Polish Foundation for Promotion and Development of SMEs, Ul Zurawia 4a, 00-503 Warsaw (tel: 693-5868/18/27; fax: 693-5815/365).

Polish State Railways (PKP), Ul Chalubinskiego 4/6, 00-928 Warsaw (tel: 628-4909, 293-596; fax: 244-039, 621-9557, 244-870).

Polska Agencja Interpress (Polish information agency), Ul Bagatela 12, 00-585 Warsaw (tel: 628-2221; fax: 628-4651).

Polska Agencja Prasowa (Polish press agency), Ul Jerozolimskie 7, 00-950 Warsaw (tel: 628-0001).

Polskie Linie Oceaniczne (Polish Ocean Lines), Ul 10 Lutego 24, 81-364 Gdynia (tel: 201-901).

Poznan International Fair Co Ltd, Ul Glogowska 14, 60-734 Poznan (tel: 869-2000; fax: 866-5827; e-mail: info@mtp.com.pl); Department of Services (tel: 668-320, 692-547; fax: 660-642); Department of Employment (contracts out exhibition stall personnel) (tel: 666-721, 692-250; fax: 665-827).

State Committee of Science and Technology, ul, Wspolna 1/3, 00-529 Warsaw (tel: 628-4071; fax: 628-0922).

Technology Agency, Krucza 38/42, 00-512 Warsaw (tel: 661-8610; fax: 628-3611).

Telekomunikacja Polska SA, Special Projects Department, Ul Obrzezna 7, 02-691 Warsaw (tel: 275-037; fax: 276-789); External Department, Telephony Polskie Fundacja (Polish Telephone Foundation), Al Stanow Zjednoczonych 24, 03-964 Warsaw (tel/fax: 136-833; fax: 120-544).

Universal SA (foreign trading company), Al Jerozolimskie 44, 00-950 Warsaw (tel: 8144-3135, 693-6091/92; fax: 278-312).

Internet sites

Official Website of Poland: http://poland.pl

Business Directory: www.polish-bus.com/anghome.html

Business Polska: www.polska.net

Polish company directory: www.teleadreson.com.pl

Polish Embassy, London: http://home.btclick.com/polishembassy

Polish Tourism: www.poland-tourism.pl

Warsaw Business Journal: www.wbj.pl

Portugal

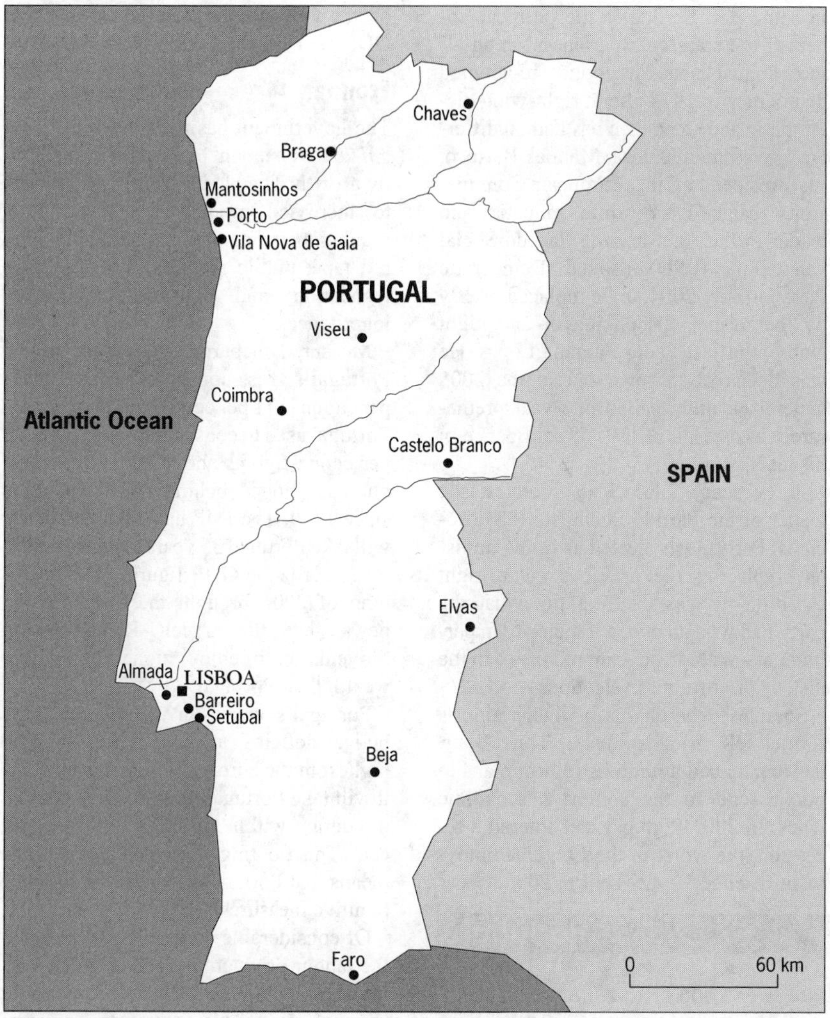

Portugal acquired, in 2007, the dubious distinction of being Europe's slowest growing nation. In its 2008 *Economic Survey* of Portugal, the Paris based Organisation for Economic Co-operation and Development (OECD) reported that Portugal's fiscal deficit fell substantially in 2006 and 2007, with a wide-ranging consolidation programme, including shorter-term measures and deeper reforms to address problems in spending control. In particular, the comprehensive reforms to the public administration and the pension schemes tackle some of the main underlying drivers of spending growth and are likely to continue paying dividends in the medium-term. The main fiscal challenge for Portugal is to secure the results achieved in fiscal consolidation and reduce the deficit further. The focus should be on the implementation of the public administration reform, continuing the health care reform, improving the performance and efficiency of state-owned enterprises, ensuring the sustainability of the contributory pension scheme, which may require that additional measures be taken, and dealing with ageing pressures on the health budget. Further improvements should also be made in

KEY FACTS

Official name: República Portuguesa (Portuguese Republic)

Head of State: President Aníbal Cavaco Silva (PSD) won the 22 Jan 2006 election and took office 9 March.

Head of government: Prime Minister José Sócrates (PS) (from 12 Mar 2005)

Ruling party: Partido Socialista (PS) (Socialist Party) (elected 20 Feb 2005)

Area: 92,072 square km

Population: 10.62 million (2007)*

Capital: Lisbon

Official language: Portuguese

Currency: Euro (eur) = 100 cents (from 1 Jan 2002; previous currency escudo, locked at esc200.48 per euro)

Exchange rate: eur0.63 per US$ (Jul 2008)

GDP per capita: US$21,019 (2007)

GDP real growth: 1.90% (2007)

Labour force: 5.43 million (2004)

Unemployment: 7.70% (2005)

Inflation: 2.40% (2005)

Balance of trade: -US$20.86 billion (2005)

Foreign debt: US$309.68 billion (2004)

Visitor numbers: 11.28 million (2006)*

* estimated figure

strengthening the medium-term fiscal framework and enhancing the efficiency of public finances.

Openness has contributed to Portugal's growth performance in the past. However, according to the OECD export performance has been disappointing over the past decade. Portugal has the potential to benefit more from globalisation. There are encouraging signs of the economy's capacity to seize this opportunity, including growing product and market diversification and recent large foreign direct investment (FDI) inflows. The government has already made significant progress in enhancing the business environment. Portugal also needs to strengthen competition and improve regulations in key infrastructure sectors such as telecommunications, electricity and transportation, to enhance the quality, efficiency and quantity of the services they provide. This would help the cost-competitiveness of companies based in Portugal, facilitate trade flows and make Portugal a more attractive destination for FDI.

It is perhaps a sad reflection on a country's national standing when its best known inhabitant is a football player. Cristiano Ronaldo , who in April 2007 signed a US$250,000 per week contract with the UK's Manchester United has, for the time being, left the Portuguese island of Madeira for the less sun-drenched shore of the River Irwell. Not only is he Portugal's best known national, he is almost certainly its best paid. Not that that has become too difficult: with a recent recession and a staggering budget deficit, Portuguese wealth per head is falling behind that even of some of its eastern European fellow European Union (EU) members. Disillusion with EU membership has grown – even among the middle classes who not that long ago were enjoying a 'never had it so good' period.

General election

Portugal's weak economic status – it is the poorest country in Western Europe – must in some part be due to the political upheaval the country experiences on an almost annual basis. The country re-adopted democracy in 1974 after a right-wing dictatorship and since then has had 16 different governments. José Manuel Barroso, the president of the European Commission, resigned as prime minister and leader of the right-leaning Partido Social Democrata (PSD) (Social Democratic Party) in July 2004, to be replaced briefly by the former Lisbon mayor and night club enthusiast Pedro Santana Lopes. He was decisively thrown out in the 2005 general election, called one year prematurely as a result of lack of confidence in his leadership.

In February 2005 José Sócrates, the leader of the Partido Socialista (PS) (Socialist Party), was elected as prime minister, replacing the previous centre-right coalition. It was the first time that the party had won an outright majority in parliament – with 45 per cent of votes – in the history of Portuguese elections.

Sócrates, who claims his inspiration is former UK prime minister, Tony Blair, has announced ambitious reform plans to put an end to the country's economic woes. In 2003 Portugal had entered a recession, the worst in the EU. Unemployment reached 7.6 per cent in 2005. Gross domestic product (GDP) growth in 2009 was 1.9 per cent, which Socrates aims to treble in coming years. It is not altogether clear how he plans to do this. His ambitious (some would say unrealistic) proposals include a huge boost to state investment in research and development and the creation of 150,000 jobs. The 2007 growth rate was at least an improvement on the 0.6 per cent marked up in 2006. GDP per capita in 2007 was US$21,019

Economy

The government has formulated a *Portugal 2010* document to speed up productivity growth. The plan identifies six barriers to increased productivity: informality, regulation and competition, land planning red tape, public services, labour market legislation and Portugal's industrial inheritance.

Measured in purchasing power parity, Portugal's gross domestic product (GDP) per capita is 71 per cent of the EU average. Portugal used to consistently register GDP per capita figures above the EU average, but has slipped behind its EU partners since 1999. The IMF has predicted that it will take Portugal 35 years to reach the average eurozone GDP figures. The beginning of 2006 brought the disheartening news that the Czech Republic and Slovenia both enjoy higher per capita wealth than Portugal.

Portugal's worst sin in EU eyes is its budget deficit – at 6.2 per cent it is the highest in the eurozone. Sócrates believes it will take Portugal three years to contain the deficit within the EU's limit of 3 per cent. This flouting of financial regulations means that Portugal has been the focus of punitive measures.

Of considerable concern is the fact that the labour productivity gap between Portugal and the EU as a whole appears to have widened. This represents a reversal of the trend in the period 1995–99 when productivity growth in Portugal exceeded that of the EU average. Lower levels of productivity growth, combined with excessive wage increases have resulted in the erosion of Portugal's cost competitiveness and a cumulative loss of export market share. The government halted all civil service promotions and the recruiting of new staff until the end of 2006. Pension schemes were reformed and career and wage scales re-addressed.

A significant contributory factor to the budget deficit is Portugal's traditionally low ratio of tax revenues. Tax breaks have largely been phased out, tax evasion and fraud tackled, and the upper level of

KEY INDICATORS — Portugal

	Unit	2003	2004	2005	2006	2007
Population	m	10.45	10.40	10.55	10.59	10.62
Gross domestic product (GDP)	US$bn	149.30	168.28	185.64	194.97	223.30
GDP per capita	US$	14,799	16,375	17,498	18,418	21,019
GDP real growth	%	-1.2	1.0	0.5	1.3	1.9
Inflation	%	3.3	2.5	2.1	3.0	2.4
Unemployment	%	6.4	7.6	7.6	7.7	7.7
Exports (fob) (goods)	US$m	31,172.0	38,110.0	38,167.0	43,259.0	–
Imports (cif) (goods)	US$m	44,821.0	55,999.0	59,022.0	64,451.0	–
Balance of trade	US$m	-13,649.0	-17,888.0	-20,855.0	-20,872.0	–
Current account	US$m	-8,020.0	-13,270.0	-18,030.0	-18,283.0	-20,887.0
Total reserves minus gold	US$m	5,174.0	6,582.0	3,479.0	2,064.0	1,258.0
Foreign exchange	US$m	4,631.0	5,993.0	3,173.0	1,835.0	1,044.0
Exchange rate	per US$	0.88	0.80	0.77	0.75	0.69

income tax lifted to 42 per cent. The VAT rate has been raised from 19 to 21 per cent and tax margins on cigarettes and petrol increased, in efforts to boost taxation revenues. The austerity measures and tax increases were greeted with a series of protests from public workers and trade unions.

EU funding runs out

Portugal's main foreign policy concern is its relations with the EU. Unlike France or Germany, which also have high budget deficits, Portugal was forced to respond to EU pressure to reduce or balance its budget deficit when the EU threatened to stop providing Portugal with cohesion funding. Between 2000–06, Portugal received US$25 billion from the EU to fund the development and modernisation of the transport network. As more of the cohesion funds are now going to the EU accession countries, Portugal is receiving a reduced amount of funding. It is also feared that the EU's reform of the Common Agricultural Policy (CAP) will adversely affect Portugal. The main aim of CAP reform is to reduce EU spending on agricultural subsidies (approximately eur40 billion (US$43.4 billion) per year) due to the extra costs of EU enlargement from 2004. Portugal received eur2 billion (US$2.1 billion) annually in farming subsidies, but this has fallen the CAP reforms were implemented.

Outlook

The government's sweeping cuts on public spending and workplace reforms should eventually begin to bear fruit. But as FDI drops and Portuguese companies face more and more international competition, it remains doubtful if Prime Minister Socrates' economic reforms will arrive in time. The prospects are not good for Portugal in the short term.

Risk assessment

Politics	Good
Economy	Fair
Regional stability	Good

COUNTRY PROFILE

Historical profile

Until the twelfth century, the Atlantic coastal regions of the Iberian peninsula were occupied by the Phoenicians, Greeks, Romans, Visigoths and the Moors. Following internal struggles and an end to the Moors' rule, Afonso Henriques declared himself king and founded an independent Portugal in the late 1100s.

1383 The seventh Portuguese King, Fernando I, died. The Spanish Castillians invaded Portugal in an attempt to claim the country's throne.

1385 João I of Avis defeated the Castillians and became King.

1400s Portugal expanded its trading routes by colonising parts of Africa, Asia and the Americas.

1558 Portugal tried to colonise Morocco. After Portugal was defeated, the country went into economic and imperial decline.

1580 King Phillip II of Spain invaded Portugal. It remained under Spanish rule until a revolt in 1640.

1600s Portugal colonised Brazil and became a major gold exporter. Portugal became a major trading partner to Britain.

1793–1801 Portuguese and Spanish troops invaded France, but were defeated. Portugal was forced to temporarily break relations with Britain as part of a peace settlement with France.

1807–10 Portugal re-established relations with Britain and declared its neutrality. France and Spain invaded Portugal three times after it had refused to break relations with Britain. A joint Anglo-Portuguese Army eventually expelled the occupation forces.

1822–24 Brazil declared its independence in 1822. An attempt to introduce a new constitution in Portugal failed. Royalists refused to accept the constitution, which would have separated the powers of the monarchy, government and judiciary, and launched uprisings against the government. Power remained in the hands of the monarchy.

1828–51 Liberals rebelled against the Royalist government. Despite splitting into moderate and radical elements, the Liberals eventually gained control of the government.

1907–08 The Republicans, who were gaining support among the population, failed in an attempt to overthrow the government of João Franco.

1908, Republican extremists assassinated King Carlos I. His son, Manuel II succeeded him as Portugal's last king.

1910 The army overthrew the monarchy forcing the King to abdicated. A Republican government was installed and Portugal was declared a republic. Teófilo Braga was appointed as Portugal's first president.

1911 A new constitution was introduced confirming Portugal's republican status and introducing a bicameral legislature.

1914–18 Portugal fought alongside Britain and France in the First World War.

1926 A military coup d'état overthrew the government and replaced it with a junta. The coup leader, General Gomes da Costa, was temporarily appointed head of the junta before General Óscar Fragoso Carmona replaced him.

1928 General Carmona was appointed president and Colonel José Vicente de Freitas became prime minister.

1932 A civilian academic, António de Oliveira Salazar, was appointed prime minister. Salazar introduced a new constitution consolidating authoritarian government.

1939–45 Portugal was neutral during the Second World War, but allowed the Allies to establish military bases in the Azores.

1955 After initially being blocked by the Soviet Union, Portugal was allowed to join the UN.

1968 Marcello José das Neves Caetano succeeded Salazar who had suffered a stroke and coma.

1970 Salazar died.

1974 A group of army officers of the Movimento das Forças Armadasa (MFA) (Armed Forces Movement), and led by General António de Spínola staged a coup d'état and overthrew Caetano's government. A provisionary coalition government restored civil liberties and freedom of the press, abolished the secret police and freed political prisoners.

1975 Portugal granted independence to its African territories, where wars against nationalist forces had long been a drain on the economy; military spending had absorbed about 40 per cent of GDP per annum. Portugal also withdrew from East Timor. Many expatriates return from former colonies. The first free parliamentary elections were held, with victory for the Partido Socialista (PS) (Socialist Party). Mário Lopes Soares becomes prime minister and General Antonio Ramalho Eanes won the presidency. Banks and many industries were nationalised.

1976 A new constitution was introduced, officially establishing Portugal as a parliamentary democracy.
The constitution was later amended in 1982, 1989, 1992 and 1997.

1977–86 A period of political instability with 17 left-wing coalition governments in power.

1986 Portugal joined the forerunner of the EU, the European Community (EC). Former prime minister Mário Soares became the first civilian president for 60 years.

1987 In the general election, Partido Social Democrata (PSD) (Social Democratic Party) became the first majority party in parliament since the 1974 revolution. Anibal Cavaco Silva was elected prime minister.

1991 Mário Soares was re-elected president and PSD won re-election. Portugal took Australia to the International Court of Justice (ICJ), on behalf of its former colony, alleging Australia had failed to

observe the rights of the Timorese to national self-determination, when it recognised Indonesia's occupation of Timor-Leste. in 1975.
1995 PSD lost to the PS in the general election. António Guterres became prime minister. The ICJ ruled it did not have jurisdiction in the matter of Australia actions concerning Timor-Leste.
1996 The presidential election was won by the PS's Jorge Sampaio.
1998 Portuguese voters narrowly rejected in a referendum a proposal to legalise abortion.
1999 António Guterres and the PS were re-elected. Macau, Portugal's last colonial territory, was returned to China. Portugal joined the EU single currency unit.
2001 Jorge Sampaio was re-elected as president for a second five-year term. Guterres resigned as prime minister after the PS was defeated in local elections.
2002 Euro currency replaced the escudos. After parliamentary elections in which the PS government was unseated, the PSD leader, José Manuel Durão Barroso, formed a coalition government, comprising PSD and Partido Popular (PP) (Popular Party).
2003 The last extension on the Via Infante motorway Lisbon-Algarve-Spain (known as the A22) was opened.
2004 Prime Minister Barroso resigned on 5 July; he assumed the presidency of the European Commission.
2005 The opposition PS won the 20 February parliamentary elections and José Sócrates (PS) became prime minister. In October, Portugal's constitutional court ruled against the government's decision to hold a referendum on relaxing the country's abortion laws. In June the country's economic rating was downgraded, by Standard and Poor's, from AA to -AA, as a result of deterioration in public finances and the lack of fiscal reforms necessary to boost fiscal dynamics. In October the government introduced a radical budget designed to cut public spending in an attempt to revive the economy and cut a deficit that was twice the permitted level, under EU monetary rules.
2006 Aníbal Cavaco Silva won the presidential election on 22 January; he took office on 9 March. The government forecast that public spending would be cut by 1 per cent of GDP in 2005/06, as value added tax (VAT) was raised and reforms to social security and public administration were introduced, as well as capping regional state spending. Public workers protested but opinion polls showed agreement with government's policies.

Political structure

Constitution
The constitution was promulgated in 1976 and amended in 1982, 1989, 1992 and 1997. Voting is by direct universal suffrage. Voting age: 18 years.

Form of state
Parliamentary democratic republic

The executive
The president, who is directly elected for a maximum of two consecutive terms of five years, appoints a prime minister, and, on his recommendation, the rest of the government.
The principal organ of executive power within the government is the Council of Ministers which is responsible to parliament.

National legislature
Legislative power is vested in the president, the unicameral Assembléia da República (parliament) and the government.
The Assembléia da República comprises 230 members elected for four-year terms by proportional representation in 20 multi-seat constituencies.
The president can dissolve parliament, call elections and is supreme commander of the armed forces.

Legal system
The legal system is based on the 1976 constitution.

Last elections
22 January 2006 (presidential); 20 February 2005 (parliamentary).
Results: Parliamentary: The PS won 45.1 per cent of the vote (121 seats out of 230), the PSD 28.7 per cent (75), the Coligação Democrática Unitária (CDU) (United Democratic Coalition), comprising Partido Comunista Português and Partido Ecologista Os Verdes (PCP and OV) (Portuguese Communist Party and Ecologist Party The Greens) 7.6 per cent (14), the rightist Partido Popular (PP) (Popular Party) 7.3 per cent (12) and the Bloco de Esquerda (BE) (Left Bloc) 6.4 per cent (eight). Turnout was 65 per cent.
Presidential: Aníbal António Cavaco Silva (SDP) won 50.6 per cent of the vote; Manuel Alegre Duarte won 20.7 per cent. Turnout is 61.5 per cent.

Next elections
2011 (presidential); 2009 (parliamentary).

Political parties

Ruling party
Partido Socialista (PS) (Socialist Party) (elected 20 Feb 2005)

Main opposition party
Partido Social Democrata (PSD) (Social Democratic Party)

Population

10.62 million (2007)*

Last census: March 2001: 10,148,259 (provisional; includes the Azores and Medeira Islands)
Population density: 109 inhabitants per square km. Urban population: 66 per cent of the total (1995–2001).
Annual growth rate: 0.4 per cent 1994–2004 (WHO 2006)

Ethnic make-up
Predominantly Portuguese. There are immigrant groups from former African colonies – Cape Verde, Mozambique, Angola, Guinea-Bissau and São Tomé. Also from East Timor and Chinese from Macao. There were 200,000 members of ethnic minorities in Portugal in 2000 (1.8 per cent of the total population).

Religions
Roman Catholic (97 per cent), Protestant denominations (1 per cent).

Education

Basic education is undertaken between the ages of six and 15. Secondary education is optional and is undertaken over three years. Higher education is divided into two sub-systems: university education and non-university higher education and it is provided in autonomous public universities, private universities, polytechnic institutions and private higher education institutions of other types. The two systems of higher education are linked and it is possible to transfer from one to the other. It is also possible to transfer from a public institution to a private one and vice versa.
Literacy rate: 94 per cent male, 89 per cent female; adult rates (World Bank).
Enrolment rate: 128 per cent gross primary enrolment of the relevant age group (including repeaters); 98 per cent gross secondary enrolment (World Bank).
Pupils per teacher: 12 in primary schools.

Health

Per capita total expenditure on health (2003) was US$1,791; of which per capita government spending was US$1,249, at the international dollar rate, (WHO 2006).
Health care is delivered under a national health service, which is accessible to all Portuguese citizens and to citizens of member states of the EU.

HIV/Aids
HIV prevalence: 0.4 per cent aged 15–49 in 2003 (World Bank)
Life expectancy: 78 years, 2004 (WHO 2006)
Fertility rate/Maternal mortality rate: 1.5 births per woman, 2004 (WHO 2006); maternal mortality 8.0 per 100,000 live births (World Bank).
Birth rate/Death rate: 11 deaths to 12 births per 1,000 people (World Bank).

Child (under 5 years) mortality rate (per 1,000): 4.0 per 1,000 live births (World Bank).
Head of population per physician: 3.42 physicians per 1,000 people, 2003 (WHO 2006)

Welfare
Portugal's social security system is characterised by a general contributory scheme covering all workers and their families, with special arrangements for self-employed persons and a non-contributory protection scheme for people facing social or economic problems. Benefits available under the general scheme include sickness (cash benefits), birth/adoption, accidents at work and occupational diseases, invalidity, old age and death, unemployment and dependants.
Self-employed persons are entitled to a compulsory insurance scheme and there is an opt-in extended benefits scheme relating to sickness, occupational diseases and dependants. Membership of the general scheme is compulsory. In addition, there is a voluntary social security scheme for those not in work or who are in work but are not covered by the general scheme.
As a rule, the employer pays the contributions and deducts the employee's social security contribution from his or her pay. Employers are also responsible for full financing of the protection of employees against accidents at work and occupational diseases.

Main cities
Lisbon (capital, estimated population 530,321 in 2005), Oporto (249,260), Amadora (163,335), Braga (121,487), Coimbra (107,490).

Languages spoken
Business languages include English, Spanish and French.
Official language/s
Portuguese

Media
National news agency: Lusa News Press Agency
Other news agencies: Photonews (Agência Noticiosa) (www.photonews.com.pt)
Press
Dailies: In Portugese, Jornal de Noticias (http://dn.sapo.pt) is the largest daily.. Others include Diario de Noticias (http://dn.sapo.pt), Record, Correio da Manha and Público (ww2.publico.clix.pt), Destak (www.destak.pt), government announcements and politics in Diário da República (www.dre.pt), and Correio da Manha (www.correiomanha.pt). On Madeira Diário de Notícias (www.dnoticias.pt), the Tribuna da Madeira (www.tribunadamadeira.pt) and Jornal da Madeira (www.jornaldamadeira.pt); in English, The Madeira Times (www.themadeiratimes.com), In the Azores, O Açoriano Oriental (http://acorianooriental.sapo.pt) and Diario Insular (www.diarioinsular.com).
Weeklies: Major weeklies are published in Lisbon. The most widely circulated is Expresso (http://expresso.clix.pt), others include O Independente (www.oindependente.pt) and Sol (http://sol.sapo.pt/). Political and news publications include Courrier Internacional (http://clix.courrierinternacional.com.pt), Focus (http://html.impala.pt) and Sábado (www.sabado.xl.pt). Women's magazines include Mulher Moderna (www.mulhermoderna.com), Exame and Activa are both imprints of (www.edipresse.com).Máxima (www.maxima.xl.pt), Guia, Maria and Marie Claire are also popular. Sojornal is a general interest weekly. The News is Portugal's national weekend newspaper. Visão (http://aeiou.visao.pt). In English, with news and current affairs are The Portugal News (www.the-news.net), The Resident (www.portugalresident.com) and Euro Weekly News (www.euroweeklynews.com).
Business: In Portuguese, the most influential business newspapers are Diário Económico (http://diarioeconomico.sapo.pt), Jornal de Negócios (www.jornaldenegocios.pt), Oje (www.oje.pt), and Vida Económica (weekly) (www.centroatl.pt). Many newspapers have economic sections.
Broadcasting
The national public broadcaster is Radio e Televisão de Portugal (RTP) (www.rtp.pt), which runs television, radio, teletext and online, transmits national and regional programmes including services to the Madeira Islands and the Azores.
Radio: There are over 280 radio stations, almost all of which are commercial, RTP runs Antena 1–3, and an external service broadcasting to Africa. The Roman Catholic Church operates Radio Renascença, the only private national radio station. The major commercial stations are Radio Comercial (radiocomercial.clix.pt), TSF (http://tsf.sapo.pt) and Radio Clube Portugues (http://radioclube.clix.pt)
Television: RTP operates two channels on the mainline and regional services to the Azores and Madeira and the external services RTP Africa and RTP Internacional. SIC (http://sic.sapo.pt) and TVI (www.tvi.iol.pt), which has close ties with the Roman Catholic church in Portugal, are private stations. There are satellite TV broadcasts from several international sources.

Advertising
Television is the most popular medium, taking about 45 per cent of total advertising, followed by radio, newspaper and magazine advertisements. Other methods used are cinema shorts, posters, direct mail and door-to-door canvassing. There are about 50 advertising agencies, mainly specialising in radio and TV work and newspapers

Economy
Portugal has a small mixed economy with a heavy dependence on foreign trade and few natural resources. The tourist sector and an export-oriented manufacturing sector, including a globally recognised die and mould making industry for automobile assembly, are of major importance. Portugal, which had the lowest per capita income in the euro-zone, continues to be one of the EU's poorer members.
Whereas it could achieve a competitive edge through relatively low labour costs, new EU members in eastern Europe have negated this advantage. The government has an economic development plan to move from a public consumption and investment economy to one driven by exports and private investment and development in the hi-tech sector.
The economy benefited from EU membership, in 1986, since when a high inflow of EU funding has resulted in much development and structural reforms. However when Portugal prepared for membership of the European Monetary Union (EMU) and adopted the euro, the economy was in recession and suffering from excessive private debt, which pushed the fiscal deficit beyond the limit of 3 per cent set by the European Central Bank (ECB) in 2003. Following a rebuke from the ECB the government undertook an austerity programme. The situation began to improve slowly, GDP growth was only 0.4 per cent in 2005 and the IMF has claimed that 'a mild recovery is underway', with GDP growth estimated to be 1.2 per cent in 2006 and projected to be 1.5 per cent in 2007. Nevertheless, it has also warned that with an unemployment rate that has doubled since 2000 to 7.6 per cent in 2005 there needs to be more structural reforms in employment laws to increase flexibility and competitiveness.
The economy is typically based on 60 per cent service sector, agriculture 6 per cent and the remainder industry, which includes textiles, clothing and footwear, cork and wood products, wine and port, porcelain and glass.

External trade
As a member of the European Union, Portugal operates within a communitywide free trade union, with tariffs sets as a whole. Internationally, the EU has free

trade agreements with a number of nations and trading blocs worldwide.

Around 70 per cent of GDP is provided through foreign trade, of which 80 per cent is with other EU members. The modern manufacturing sector provides a major input of mould-making items for Europe's automotive industry. Important export products include marble, wine, especially port, and cork as well as minerals ores.

Imports

Main imports are machinery and transport equipment, chemicals, petroleum, textiles and agricultural products.

Main sources: Spain (28.9 per cent total, 2006), Germany (13.1 per cent), France (8.1 per cent).

Exports

Main exports include clothing and footwear, machinery, chemicals, cork and paper products and hides.

Main destinations: Spain (26.5 per cent total, 2006), Germany (12.8 per cent), France (11.9 per cent).

Agriculture

Farming

About 34 per cent of the land area is arable, 9 per cent is under pasture and 32 per cent is used for forestry or is woodland. Farming is the most backward sector of the economy and crop yields and animal productivity are well below the EU average due to a legacy of low agricultural investment, minimal machinery, little use of fertiliser, poor soil quality and a fragmented land tenure system.

The EU's Common Agricultural Policy (CAP) is the basis for agricultural development in Portugal. Investment and productivity have risen under the CAP, but Portuguese agriculture remains backward by EU standards. The CAP is based on three broad principles:

the EU is treated as a single market for agricultural produce

EU farmers are given preference over outside suppliers

the cost of the CAP is met by EU member governments.

Fundamental reform to the CAP was introduced on 1 January 2005 in Portugal. Portugal was the only EU member state to vote against the reform package when it was finalised in June 2003. As of January 2005, the subsidies paid on farm output, which tended to benefit large farms and encourage overproduction, were replaced by single farm payments not conditional on production. This is expected to reward farms that provide and maintain a healthy environment, food safety and animal welfare standards. The changes are also intended to encourage market conscious production and cut the cost of CAP to the EU taxpayer.

Portugal is the world's largest exporter of tomato paste and a leading exporter of wine. Its principal agricultural imports are wheat and meat.

The main crops grown in Portugal are cereals (wheat, barley, corn and rice), potatoes, grapes, olives and tomatoes.

Crop production in 2005 included: 1,190,000 tonnes (t) cereals in total, *1,250,000t potatoes, 251,000t wheat, *700,000t maize, 246,000t apples, 16,500t cherries, *14,000t figs, 19,210t pulses, 64,830t treenuts, 330,200t citrus fruit, *1,000,000t grapes, 1,175,000t tomatoes, 67,428t oilcrops, *270,000t olives, 485,000t sugar beet, 1,900,031t fruit in total, 2,403,700t vegetables in total. Livestock production included: 710,200t meat in total, 119,500t beef, 321,000t pig-meat, 22,100t lamb, 242,000t poultry, 132,450t eggs, 2,076,600t milk, 6,700t honey, 12,659t cattle hides, 4,200t sheepskins, 7,600t greasy wool.

* estimate

Fishing

The waters around Portugal are rich fishing grounds. Sardines, anchovies and tuna are caught near the coast and species such as cod are caught by deep sea trawlers in the North Atlantic.

Portugal's territorial waters were ceded to the EU on its accession. This stimulated investment of the fishing sector and helped modernise the industry.

In 2004, the total marine fish catch was 199,303 tonnes and the total crustacean catch was 2,533 tonnes.

Forestry

Portugal's forests are a major natural resource. More than one-third of the country's total continental territory (3.1 million hectares out of a total of 8.9 million hectares) is forested, notably with pine, cork oak and eucalyptus. More than 90 per cent of forested land is privately owned, the highest proportion in the EU.

Portugal's cork production supplies around 52 per cent of the world market. Cork forests are declining and being replaced by eucalyptus plantations as plastic corks become more popular in wine bottles. Eucalyptus trees are contributing to desertification as they require large amounts of water to grow.

Exports of forest material in 2004 amounted to US$1.7 billion, while imports amounted to US$1.1 billion.

The summers of 2003 and 2005 saw large-scale devastation of Portugal's forests through fire, particularly in the north and centre of the country. In 2003 alone, 215,000 hectares, an area approximately the size of Luxembourg, were destroyed.

Timber production in 2004 included 11,553,000 cubic metre (cum) roundwood, 10,953,000cum industrial roundwood, 1,100,000cum sawnwood, 1,890,000cum sawlogs and veneer logs, 8,883,000cum pulpwood, 1,316,000cum wood-based panels, 600,000cum woodfuel; 20,000 tonnes (t) charcoal, 1,674,000t paper and paperboard, 1,093,000t printing and writing paper, 1,949,000t paper pulp, 296,000t recovered paper.

Industry and manufacturing

Although it contributes around 38 per cent to GDP and employs 32 per cent of the workforce, industry remains relatively underdeveloped and dependent on imported energy and materials.

Portugal faces a difficult transition from traditional industries – clothing, textiles and footwear – afflicted by low value-added products, inefficient management and outmoded technology, to a diversified industrial base.

Important industries include processed cork, paper, cement, fertilisers, steel and glassware. High-growth sectors include vehicle manufacture, semiconductors, electronics, plastics, food processing and franchising.

Industrial production increased by 1.5 per cent in 2003 and an estimated 1.1 per cent in 2004.

Tourism

The sector earns as much as a quarter of total export earnings, and employs 8 per cent of the labour force.

The tourism ministry has encouraged investors to modernise and re-equip existing units, construct additional facilities such as golf courses and conference centres and diversify from beach holidays into sports and cultural tourism.

The Algarve is estimated to account for 50 to 60 per cent of the Portuguese tourist business. New destinations, such as the Douro valley, are being developed.

The UK, Germany, Spain and France account for 75 per cent of all tourism to Portugal, although efforts have been made to tap new tourist sources, such as Japan.

Recovering from the slump of 2002–03 when tourist numbers fell due to the Sars outbreak and the Iraq War, tourist receipts for 2003–04 were boosted by the Euro 2004 football competition

Portugal has invested in major infrastucture, aiding the tourism industry, with the addition of several new motorways and airport extensions. Cultural sites also received government investment as they attacted more visitors.

Tourist arrivals increased by 4.20 per cent in 2003, compared to 2002.

Mining

The mining sector contributes around 1 per cent of GDP and employs a similar fraction of the workforce. Although there is considerable mineral wealth, deposits are scattered and not easily exploitable on a large scale. The most important mineral resources include non-metallic ores such as rock salt, pyrites (the reserves in the Alentejo region make up nearly 23 per cent of total worldwide reserves) and excellent quality marble. Large reserves of uranium are also available. Small-scale mining of tin, copper, tungsten concentrates, marble, stone and iron pyrites takes place.

Hydrocarbons

Portugal imports around 90 per cent of its total energy demands and all of its oil demands. Over 25 per cent of the oil is used for electricity generation. Petrogal operates two oil refineries in Portugal with a joint refining capacity of 304,174 bpd, accounting for around two-thirds of the country's oil product sales. Despite exploration efforts Portugal has no proven commercially viable oil reserves. In September 2005, Portugal agreed to lend 2 per cent of its oil stockpile to the US in order to alleviate the damage inflicted by Hurricane Katrina.

In the past few years natural gas consumption has increased considerably. A liquid natural gas (LNG) terminal has been built at the port of Setubal, south of Lisbon, connected by a pipeline extended along the Atlantic coast to the northern town of Braga. The pipeline is linked to the European natural gas network via Spain, providing an alternative source of supply for Europe.

Coal is scarce and of poor quality and production ceased when the last coal mine closed in 1994. Portugal imports small quantities of coal, which is used entirely for electricity production. Demand is declining due to the development of other means of producing electricity.

Energy

Portugal is heavily dependent on imported fuels, particularly oil (70 per cent). Hydroelectricity contributes around 50 per cent of electricity generated.

Portugal and Spain's electricity grids are connected. Electricidade de Portugal (EdP) is the national power utility.

Financial markets

Stock exchange

In January 2002, shareholders of the Bolsa de Valores de Lisboa e Porto (BVLP) (Lisbon and Oporto Stock Exchange), which was formed by the union of the two cities' exchanges in 1999, agreed to the acquisition of BVLP by Euronext, the pan-European exchange created in September 2000. The bourse was renamed Euronext Lisbon.

Banking and insurance

The booming economy has benefited banks. Although there has been some political resistance, the arrival of the euro will continue to bring about takeovers in the banking sector as Portugal's leading banks are far behind the size of those in other euro-zone countries. Banco Santander Central Hispanico, Spain's largest bank, has been attracted to the sector.

In October 2005, a number of Portugal's major banks were the subject of police investigations centred on allegations of money-laundering and tax evasion. Those involved include the Banco Espirito Santo and Millenium-bcp.

Central bank

Banco de Portugal (Bank of Portugal); European Central Bank (ECB).

Main financial centre

Lisbon

Time

GMT (daylight saving, late March to late October, GMT plus one hour)

Geography

Mainland Portugal lies on the west side of the Iberian peninsula with the furthermost point of western Europe jutting into the Atlantic Ocean. The 837km coastline runs down along the west and south coast. Spain borders Portugal in the north and east. There are two archipelagos in the Atlantic Ocean – the Azores and the Madeira Islands.

All inclusive, Portugal is 92,080 square km in size. There are six major rivers, three of which rise in Spain and flow into the Atlantic Ocean. The Duoro in the mountainous north runs east-west across the country and used to provide an important shipping route. It flows through the city of Oporto. The longest river, the Tagus, has a large estuary, on which the capital, Lisbon, sits and is navigable for over 100km by seagoing ships. The Guadiana in the south, forms part of the border with Spain. The tallest peaks at 1,991 meters (m) are in the Serra da Estrela, in central Portugal. In the south the land is rolling hills and plains.

Lying south-west of the European mainland, the Azores consist of three scattered groups of nine inhabited islands and several uninhabitable ones, and include 12 active volcanoes. The Madeira archipelago is west of North Africa and has only two inhabited islands. The Azores and Madeira are volcanic in origin with steep topographies, the tallest – and youngest due to the continued lava flows that add to its mass – is located on Pico (Azores), at 2,321m high.

Hemisphere

Northern

Climate

Situated in the middle of the northern hemisphere, Portugal has a mild welcoming climate. However, the difference between the north/south and coast/inland weather is marked. Inland areas have more variable weather than coastal regions. To the south of the Tagus river the Mediterranean influences are clear. Long, hot, humid summers and dry, short, relatively mild winters. May–October dry and warm, November–April cool with rain in north, mild in south (though often wet and windy January–March). Temperatures vary between 8–28 Celsius.

Dress codes

Business people dress conservatively in dark blue or grey suits and ties.

Entry requirements

Passports

Required by all, except members of the EU, EEA and Switzerland who may use a valid national ID card. Passports must be valid for at least three months from date of arrival.

Visa

Required by all, except nationals of EU and Schengen Accord signatory countries, North America, Australasia and Japan. For further exceptions contact the nearest Portuguese consulate or a travel agent. Schengen visas cover all entry needs..For business trips, an original invitation from a business contact in Portugal is necessary, plus proof of accommodation booking and a letter from an employer giving the purpose and duration of the visit, when applying. A Schengen visa application (offered in several languages) can be downloaded from http://europa.eu/abc/travel/ see 'documents you will need'.

Currency advice/regulations

The import of local and foreign currency is unlimited but amounts over eur5,000 should be declared on entry. Export of local currency is limited to eur5,000 and an equivalent amount in foreign currency may require currency exchange receipts to be produced.

Travellers cheques are readily accepted.

Customs

Personal items are duty-free. There are no duties levied on alcohol and tobacco between EU member states, providing amounts imported are for personal consumption only. The export of luxury goods, such as gold, silver and jewellery, is limited to the value of eur150, without special permission.

Health (for visitors)

Nationals of the European Economic Area (EEA) countries and Switzerland can access reduced cost and sometimes free medical treatment using a European Health Insurance Card (EHIC) while visiting the EEA. Exceptions include nationals of the 10 countries, which joined the EU in 2004, whose EHIC is not valid in Switzerland. Applications for the EHIC should be made before travelling.

Mandatory precautions

Yellow fever vaccination certificate required for Azores and Madeira only if arriving from infected areas.

Advisable precautions

Immunisations that may be recommended is for hepatitis A and tuberculosis (although not for a short duration stay).

Hotels

A full range of hotels are available throughout the country, and are classified from one- to five-star. There is a 10 per cent service charge but a tip is also expected.

Credit cards

All usual credit cards are widely accepted. ATMs are readily available.

Public holidays (national)

Fixed dates

1 Jan (New Year's Day), 25 Apr (Liberty Day), 1 May (Labour Day), 10 Jun (Portugal Day), 15 Aug (Assumption Day), 5 Oct (Republic Day), 1 Nov (All Saints' Day), 1 Dec (Restoration of Independence Day), 8 Dec (Immaculate Conception), 25 Dec (Christmas).

Variable dates

Carnival (Feb), Good Friday (Mar/Apr), Corpus Christi (May/Jun).

Working hours

Banking

Mon–Fri: 0830–1500. Some banks in Lisbon open until 1800.

Business

Mon–Fri: 0900–1300 and 1500–1900.

Government

Mon–Fri: 0930–1200 and 1430–1800, closed 1730 on Mon and Tue.

Shops

Mon–Fri: 0900–1300, 1500–1900; Sat: 0900/1000–1300 general shops.
Mon–Sun: 1000–2300/2400 shopping centres/malls.

Telecommunications

Mobile/cell phones

There are 900/1800 and 3G GSM services available throughout the country.

Electricity supply

220V AC, with two round-pin plugs.

Social customs/useful tips

The Portuguese like to entertain. Lunch usually takes place between 1200 and 1400, dinner between 1900 and 2200. The Portuguese are extremely courteous, helpful and open to foreigners. Men always shake hands when they meet strangers or male friends. Women often kiss each other or their male friends once on each cheek.
It is impolite to refuse an offer of coffee.
Tips should be given to anyone who carries out a service for you. There is no set rule on how much to tip.

Getting there

Air

National airline: TAP-Air Portugal.
International airport/s: Lisbon (LIS), 7km north of capital. Facilities include 24-hour bureau de change, banks, tourist information, post office, duty-free shops and car hire.
A special aerobus departs for the city centre every 20 minutes. Other express buses run to the railway station and other destinations around the country. Taxis are available, with a surcharge after 2200hrs.
Other airport/s: Oporto (OPO), 11km from city, Faro (FAO), 4km from city; Funchal (FNC) on Maderia; and Santa Maria (SMA) in the Azores, 3.2km from Vila do Porto.
Airport tax: None

Surface

Road: There are only road connections with Spain, of which the principle are motorways (with tolls), these in turn connect to the trans-European road network. Smaller cross-border roads maintain traditional routes.
Rail: There are four cross-border railway lines from Spain via either Salamanca, Santiago de Compostela, Badajoz or Madrid, which is the hub for lines to France.
Water: There are car ferry services from Plymouth or Portsmouth (UK) to Santander or Bilbao (northern Spain) respectively, from March–December.
The islands of Madeira and Azores have regular ferry services to the mainland of Spain and Portugal as well as to Grand Canary and Cape Verde.
Main port/s: The three most important ports are Lisbon, Leixes (Oporto) and Sines (south of Lisbon).

Getting about

National transport

Air: TAP and domestic charter airlines operate scheduled flights between most major cities, Madeira and the Azores.
Road: The Lisbon-Oporto, Lisbon-Algarve and Lisbon-Badajoz roads are national highway, toll roads. The road network has been upgraded in recent years and while local roads can often be narrow they link all rural communities with provincial roads.
Buses: Regular coach services, Expresso are inter-city and Rápidas link major regional towns, they can provide a quicker alternative service than by rail, although with a relatively higher priced ticket.
Rail: Caminhos de Ferro Portugueses (CP) operates about 3,600km of track, of which 500km are electrified. The Alfa Pendular provides a high-speed service between Oporto-Faro via Lisbon (journey time around six hours) reservations must be made and bookings can be made online. Regional services are available between cities and main towns.
Water: The 800km of inland waterways are only rarely used. Some coastal shipping operates, including services to Madeira and the Azores.

City transport

Taxis: Lisbon taxis are green and black. They are relatively cheap and offer an efficient service. A tip of 15 per cent is expected. Taxis may be scarce during rush-hours.
Buses, trams & metro: Lisbon has some steep climbs and there are three elevadors (funiculars – cable cars) from Baixa to the Bairro Alto neighbourhood and the Santa Justa. Buses run throughout the city.
The metro (from 0630–0100) provides four lines within the city and links to five suburban lines. the remaining services for the city.
Other cities and towns have public bus services.
Ferry: There are two ferry companies operating in Lisbon on the river Tagus. CP provides links from the city centre to Barreiro, on the south shore, which connects with the railway line to the Algarve. Transtejo provides services to Montijo, Seixal and Cacilhas.

Car hire

Self-drive and chauffeur-driven cars are available throughout the country.
An international driving licence or full national licence is required, as well as an international insurance Green Card. The wearing of seat belts is compulsory and all vehicles must carry a warning red triangle and warning waistcoats (fluorescent jackets) when leaving a vehicle during a breakdown or emergency.
Detailed motoring information is available from Automovel Clube de Portugal in Lisbon.
Driving in Portugal can be hazardous. In proportion to the number of vehicles, the country has one of the highest death and accident rates in Europe.

BUSINESS DIRECTORY

The addresses listed below are a selection only. While World of Information makes every endeavour to check these addresses, we cannot guarantee that changes have not been made, especially to telephone numbers and area codes. We would welcome any corrections.

Telephone area codes

The international dialling code (IDD) for Portugal is +351, followed by area code and subscriber's number:

Beja	284	Faro	289
Braga	253	Lisbon	21
Braganca	273	Madeira	291
Coimbra	239	Oporto	22
Covilha	275	Ponta Delgado	296

Chambers of Commerce

American Chamber of Commerce in Portugal, 155 Rua D Estefânia, 1000-154 Lisbon (tel: 357-2561; fax: 357-2580; e-mail: nop37676@mail.telepac.pt).

British-Portuguese Chamber of Commerce, 8 Rua da Estrela, 1200-669 Lisbon (tel: 394-2020; fax: 394-2029; e-mail: info@bpcc.pt).

Coimbra Chamber of Commerce and Industry, Rua Coronel Júlio Veiga Simão, Edificio Novotecna, 3020-260 Coimbra (tel: 497-160; fax: 494-066; e-mail: geral@cec.org.pt).

Madeira Chamber of Commerce and Industry, 41 Avenida Arriaga, 9004-507 Funchal (tel: 206-800; fax: 206-868; e-mail: geral@acif-ccim.pt).

Oporto Chamber of Commerce and Industry, Rua Ferreira Borges, Palácio da Bolsa, 4050-253 Oporto (tel: 399-000; fax: 399-090; e-mail: cciporto@mail.telepac.pt).

Ponta Delgada Chamber of Commerce and Industry, 13 Rua Ernsto do Canto, 9504-531 Ponta Delgada, Azores (tel: 305-000; fax: 305-050; e-mail: ccipd@ccipd.pt).

Portuguese Chamber of Commerce and Industry, 89 Rua das Portas de Santo Antão, 1169-022 Lisbon (tel: 322-4050; fax: 322-4051; e-mail: geral@port-chambers.com).

Banking

ABN AMRO Bank NV, Av da Liberdade 131, 5, Lisbon (tel: 321-1800; fax: 321-1900).

Associação Portuguesa de Bancos (Portuguese Bankers' Association), 35 Avenida da República, Lisbon (tel: 357-9804; fax: 357-9533, 352-9682).

Banco BPI SA, Rua do Comércio 132, Lisbon (tel: 887-4801, 887-3161, 311-1000; fax: 346-7308).

Banco Comercial Português SA, International Division, Rua Augusta 62—74, Lisbon (tel: 321-1780, 312-5936; fax: 321-1789; e-mail: dint@bcp.pt); Investor Relations Division (tel: 321-1080; e-mail: investors@bcp.pt).

Banco Espírito Santo e Com de Lisbon, Avenida da Liberdade 195, Lisbon (tel: 315-8331; fax: 353-2931, 350-8977).

Banco Internacional de Crédito, Avenida Fontes Pereira de Melo 27, Lisbon (tel/fax: 315-7135).

Banco Mello, Av José Malhoa, Lote 1682, Lisbon (tel: 720-1500; fax: 720-1766, 720-1599; e-mail: investor@bancomello.pt).

Banco Nacional Ultramarino (commercial bank), Av 5 de Outubro 175, Lisbon (tel: 793-3223, 793-0112; fax: (International Department) 793-8952).

Banco Pinto e Sotto Mayor (commercial bank), Rua do Ouro 28, Lisbon (tel: 340-3000, 347-6261; fax: (International Department) 357-3973).

Banco Português do Atlântico SA, Tagus Park, Edif Serv 1, Piso 2, Oeiras (tel: 422-4000; fax: 422-4489).

Banco Santander Portugal SA, Praça Marquês de Pombal 2, Lisbon (tel: 310-7000; fax: 315-4963).

Banco Totta & Açores SA (commercial bank), Rua do Ouro 88, Lisbon (tel: 321-3000; fax: 321-1582).

Caixa Geral de Depósitos (savings bank), International Department, Largo do Calhariz, Lisbon (tel: 790-5018; fax: 790-5068).

Central Banco de Investimento SA, Rua Castilho 233-4, Lisbon (tel: 386-4097; fax: 387-3208).

Credito Predial Português, Rua Augusta 237, Lisbon (tel: 321-4200; fax: (International Department) 313-7438).

Finibanco, Av de Berna, 10-1064, Lisbon (tel: 790-2800; fax: 790-2801).

Central bank

Banco de Portugal, 27 Rua do Ouro 1100-150 Lisbon (tel: 321-3200; fax: 346-4843; email: info@bportugal.pt).

European Central Bank (ECB), Kaiserstrasse 29, D-60311 Frankfurt am Main, Germany (tel: (+49-69) 13-440; fax: (+49-69) 1344-6000; email: info@ecb.int).

Travel information

Comissão Municipal de Turismo de Lisboa, Pavilhao Carlos Lopes, Parque Eduardo VII, 1070 Lisbon (tel: 315-1915/6/7/8; fax: 352-1472).

Comissão Municipal de Turismo do Oporto, Rua Clube dos Fenianos 25, 4000 Oporto (tel: 323-303, 312-543; fax: 208-4548).

Costa Verde Tourism Office, Praça D Joao I 43, 4000 Oporto (tel: 317-514).

Lisbon Airport Tourism Office, 1700 Lisbon (tel: 849-4323/3689; fax: 848-5974).

Lisbon Tourist Office, Palácio Foz, Praça dos Restauradores, 1200 Lisbon (tel: 346-3314/3643; fax: 346-8772).

Madeira Tourism Office, Avenida Arriaga 18, 9000 Funchal (tel: (+091) 229-057, 225-658; fax: (+091) 232-151; internet: www.madeiraguide.com).

Pousadas of Portugal, Rua Soares de Passos, 3 Alto de Santo Amaro, 1300-314 Lisbon (tel: 844-2001; fax: 844-2085; internet: www.pousadas.pt).

Regiao de Turismo da Planicie Dourada, Praca da Republica 12, 7800 Beja (tel: 321-369; fax: 326-332).

Ministry of tourism

National tourist organisation offices

Portuguese Tourism Board (ITP), Rua Ivone Silva, Lote 6, 1050-124 Lisbon (tel: 781-0000; fax: 793-7537; email: info@iturismo.pt; internet: www.iturismo.pt).

Ministries

Ministry of Agriculture, Food and Fisheries, Praça do Comércio, 1149-010 Lisbon (tel: 346-3151; fax: 347-7890).

Ministry of Culture, Palácio Nacional da Ajuda, 1349-003 Lisbon (tel: 361-4500; fax: 364-9999).

Ministry of Defence, Avenida Ilha da Madeira, 1400-204 Lisbon (tel: 303-4500; fax: 303-4525).

Ministry of Economy, Rua da Horta Seca 15, 1200-221 Lisbon (tel: 322-8600; fax: 322-8741).

Ministry of Education, Avenida 5 de Outubro 107-13, 1069-018 Lisbon (tel: 795-0330; fax: 793-3618).

Ministry for Employment, Praça de Londres 2-14, 1049-056 Lisbon (tel: 844-1700; fax: 847-0027).

Ministry of the Environment, Rua do Século 51-2, 1200-433 Lisbon (tel: 3223-2500; fax: 323-2531).

Ministry of Finance, Avenida Infante D Henriques 5, 1149-009 Lisbon (tel: 888-4675; fax: 886-0032).

Ministry of Foreign Affairs, Largo do Rilvas, 11399-030 Lisbon (tel: 394-6000; fax: 390-9708).

Ministry of Health, Avenida João Crisóstomo 9-6, 1049-062 Lisbon (tel: 354-4560; fax: 354-0302).

Ministry of Home Affairs, Praça do Comércio, 1149-015 Lisbon (tel: 323-3000; fax: 342-7372).

Ministry of Industry and Energy, Rua da Horta Seca 15, 1200 Lisbon (tel: 346-3091/6091; fax: 347-5901).

Ministry of Justice, Praça do Comércio, 1149-019 Lisbon (322-2300; fax: 347-9208).

Ministry of Planning, Public Works and Territorial Administration, Palacio Penafiel, Rua de S Mamede ao Caldas 21, 1149-050 Lisbon (tel: 886-1119; fax: 886-3827).

Ministry of Science and Technology, Praça do Comércio - Ala Oriental, 1149-003 Lisbon (tel: 881-2000; fax: 888-2434).

Ministry of Social Security, Rua Rosa Araújo 43, 1250-194 Lisbon (tel: 353-0049; fax: 353-0074).

Prime Minister's Office, Rua da Imprensa a Estrela 2, 1200 Lisbon (tel: 397-4091; fax: 395-1616).

Other useful addresses

Agencia de Informação LUSA (news agency), Rua Dr João Couto, Lote C, Lisbon (tel: 714-4099).

Associação Industrial Portuguesa, Apt 5200, Praça das Indústrias, 1301 Lisbon (tel: 360-1500).

Associação Industrial Portuense, Avenida da Boavista 2671, Oporto (tel: 615-8500; fax: 617-6840).

Bolsa de Valores de Lisboa (Lisbon Stock Exchange), Edificio da Bolsa, Rua Soeiro Pereira Gomes, Lisbon (tel: 790-0000; fax: 795-2021; e-mail: Infomktg@bvl.pt; internet site: www.bvl.pt/).

Comissão Co-ordenação Regiao (CCR) Norte, Rua Rainha D Estefania 251, Oporto (tel: 695-236/7/8/9/0; fax: 600-2040).

CCR Algarve, Praça da Liberdade 2, Faro (tel: 802-401; fax: 803-591).

CCR Lisboa e Vale do Tejo, Rua Artilharia Um 33, Lisbon (tel: 387-5541; fax: 691-292).

Instituto de Apoio às Pequenas e Médias Empresas Industriais (IAPMEI), Rua Rodrigo da Fonseca 73, Lisbon (tel: 562-211).

Instituto Nacional de Estatistica (INE), Av António José de Almeida 2, Lisbon (tel: 847-0050; fax: 848-9480; internet site: www.ine.pt).

Investimentos Comércio e Turismo de Portugal (ICEP), (e-mail: icepdiesnar@mail.telepac.pt; internet: www.icep.pt).

Portugal Telecom (PT), Investor Relations, Lisbon (tel: 500-1701, 500-8739; e-mail: manuel.j.castela@telecom.pt).

Portuguese Embassy (USA), 2125 Kalorama Road, NW, Washington DC 20008 (tel: (+1-202) 328-8610; fax: (+1-202) 462-3726; e-mail: embportwash@mindspring.com).

Privatisation Office, c/o Ministério das Finanças – Commissão de Acompanhamento das Privatizacöes (c/o Ministry of Finance – Commission for the Accompaniment of Privatisations), Av Infante D Henrique 5, Lisbon (tel: 618-0057).

Radiotelevisão Portuguesa – RTP (Portugal's radio/television broadcaster), 197 Avenida 5 de Outubro, Lisbon (tel: 793-1774; fax: 796-6227).

Sociedade de Desenvolvimento da Madeira SA (SDM), 1st Floor, 9 Rua da Mouraria; PO Box 4164, Funchal, Madeira (tel: (351-291) 201-333; fax: (351-291) 201-399; email: sdm@sdm.pt; internet site: www.sdmadeira.pt).

Sociedade Independente de Comunicação – SIC (independent broadcasting company), 119 Estrada da Outurela, Carnaxide, Linda a Velha (tel: 417-3138; fax: 417-3118).

Televisão Independente – TVI (independent television broadcasting), Pt16-s 603-B Rua 3, Matinha, Lisbon (tel: 858-7968; fax: 858-2319).

National news agency: Lusa News Press Agency

Other news agencies: Photonews (Agência Noticiosa) (www.photonews.com.pt)

Internet sites

Guide to business: www.portugaloffer.pt

Icep Portugal (business promotion): www.portugalinbusiness.com

Portugal portal: www.portugal.org

Lisbon Airport: www.ana-aeroportos.pt

Tourist portal: www.portugalvisitor.com

Yellow Pages: www.paginasamarelas.pt

Puerto Rico

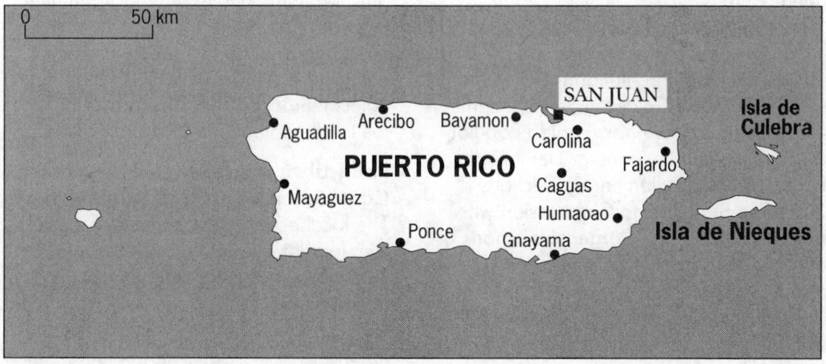

In June 2008 Governor Governor Aníbal Acevedo Vilá called on the United Nations (UN) to back Puerto Rico's bid for self-determination. Mr Acevedo's party, the Partido Popular Democrático (PPD) (Popular Democratic Party), had previously supported the island's commonwealth status, while opposition Partido Nuevo Progresista (PNP) (New Progressive Party) favours full integration with the United States as the 51st state. The UN committee voted to support a motion calling on the US to grant Puerto Rico the right to determine its own status. The people of Puerto Rico have already voted to reject independence three times – first in a plebiscite in 1967, a referendum in 1993 and a second referendum in 1998, which was lost by a much narrower margin.

If Puerto Rico had outshone most of its Caribbean neighbours in 2005, in terms of main economic indicators that ceased to be the case in 2006. The island's gross national product (GNP) grew by a measly 0.8 per cent (compared to 2.2 per cent in 2005), inflation rose to an annual rate of 15.1 per cent, its highest rate for years. Puerto Rico was beginning to realise that what had been its economic success, relative to the rest of the region, its company taxation policy, was not enough on which to build a modern economy. Firms from the US mainland have flocked to Puerto Rico in recent years to set up office in the island's tax free environment. Towns like Barceloneta, population 20,000, now host dozens of pharmaceutical companies. Called 'Viagra town' by some due to the amount of the drug produced there, Barceloneta is almost totally dependent upon pharmaceutical companies for its employment and revenue needs. Some analysts argue that this arrangement is unsustainable and dangerously exposes the population to shifts in global taxation regimes.

Constitutional status

In 2005, Puerto Ricans had voted in a referendum to abolish the Commonwealth's bicameral parliamentary system. A unicameral system was subsequently adopted.

In September, the issue of Puerto Rico's constitutional status was again thrust into the spotlight when FBI agents killed the fugitive Filiberto Ojeda Rios in a shoot-out near the Puerto Rican town of Hormigueros. Ojeda Rios was wanted on the US mainland for a bank robbery committed in 1983. He was also the leader of the *Macheteros* (the Cane Cutters), the main Puerto Rican independence movement. Hundreds protested as the news of Ojeda Rios' death broke. Although support for independence in Puerto Rico rarely moves above 3 per cent support in opinion polls, many Puerto Ricans regarded Rios as an eccentric hero, fighting against overwhelming odds. His death at the hands of the FBI also sparked accusations that US mainland officials operate in Puerto Rico as if they have impunity.

KEY FACTS

Official name: Estado Libre Asociado de Puerto Rico (Commonwealth of Puerto Rico)

Head of State: US President George W Bush

Head of government: Governor Aníbal Acevedo Vilá (PPD) (from 2 Jan 2005)

Ruling party: Partido Popular Democrático (PPD) (Popular Democratic Party)

Area: 8,897 square km (Puerto Rico comprises the main island plus two smaller islands (Vieques and Culebra) and numerous smaller islets.)

Population: 3.96 million (2007)*

Capital: San Juan

Official language: Spanish, English

Currency: US dollar (US$) = 100 cents

GDP per capita: US$19,600 (2007)*

GDP real growth: 1.20% (2007)*

GNP growth: 1.20% (2007)*

Labour force: 1.52 million (2004)

Unemployment: 12.00% (2004)

Inflation: 12.40% (2007)*

Balance of trade: US$15.28 billion (2007)

Visitor numbers: 3.72 million (2006)*

* estimated figure

In late 2005, a special US presidential taskforce handed down its findings on the future status of Puerto Rico. The report advocated holding a referendum on whether or not Puerto Ricans wanted a change in status. In the case of a 'yes' vote, a second referendum on whether the island's people wanted outright independence or to become the 51st state of the USA would be held. In March 2006 the US Supreme Court turned down an appeal to give Puerto Ricans voting rights in presidential elections.

Outlook

Despite Puerto Rico's privileged economic position relative to its insular neighbours, its own economy remains dangerously exposed to downward swings in the US economy. Moreover, as it is almost totally dependent upon imports, continued high oil prices may trigger high inflation.

Risk assessment

Politics	Stable
Economy	Fragile
Regional stability	Stable

COUNTRY PROFILE

Historical profile

1493 The island was inhabited by some 100,000 Taíno Indians (an Arawak culture that also occupied most of Hispaniola and part of Cuba) at the time of the first European sighting by Columbus.
1508 Juan Ponce de Léon landed from Hispaniola and took control of the island. He named it San Juan.
1898 The island was ceded to the US by Spain at the end of the Spanish-American war. The US ruled it as an unincorporated territory.
1917 The inhabitants became citizens of the US.
1948 Puerto Rico elected Luis Muñoz Marín as its first governor.
1952 A new constitution designated Puerto Rico a self-governing commonwealth within the US.
1967 A plebiscite rejected the option of becoming a state of the US.
1993 The statehood option was rejected for a second time in a national referendum.
1998 Puerto Ricans again narrowly rejected the option of statehood in favour of maintaining the constitutional status quo.
2000 Sila Maria Calderón Serra became the first female governor. Partido Popular Democrático (PPD) (Popular Democratic Party) won the parliamentary elections.
2001 The Blue Riband Commission was empanelled to review large transactions made by the previous (Rosselló) administration.
2002 Puerto Rico failed to get an injunction stopping US naval training on the island of Vieques.
2003 The closure of the US navy base on Vieques will lose Puerto Rico an estimated US$300 million per year in revenues.
2004 In gubernatorial elections on 2 November, Aníbal Acevedo Vilá and former governor Pedro Rosselló won about 48 per cent each. In December, the election was given to Acevedo Vilá.
2005 On 2 January, Aníbal Acevedo Vilá became governor. A referendum agreed that the Senate and House of Representatives should be replaced by a unicameral legislature. In December, a US presidential task force recommended that a referendum should be called to decide whether the islanders wanted a change in status.
2006 In March, the US Supreme Court turned down an appeal to give Puerto Ricans voting rights in presidential elections. A budget crisis led to the closure of government offices and schools in May, resulting in mass demonstartions.
2008 In June, the governor, Anibal Acevedo, called on the UN to back Puerto Rico's right of self-determination. The UN voted to call on the US to grant Puerto Rico the right to determine its own status. Acevedo claimed that the US had failed to build on the sovereignty promised in 1952 when the US granted greater autonomy to Puerto Rico in return for remaining in a commonwealth with the US. The governing political party had favoured the commonwealth status but a change may reflect the opposition party proposal for full integration as the 51st state of the US.

Political structure

Constitution

The local government consists of executive, legislative and judicial branches. Puerto Rico has 78 municipal governments.
Detailed laws governing the status and relationship of the Commonwealth of Puerto Rico with the US cover, among other aspects: military conscription, tax and trade, social security, citizenship, constitutional changes and internal autonomy.
There is universal suffrage from aged 18 years.

Form of state

Puerto Rico is an overseas commonwealth territory and freely associated state of the US.
Both the constitution of Puerto Rico and the US constitution are applicable. Puerto Rican nationals are US citizens but do not vote in US presidential elections.

The executive

The Head of State is the president of the US.
Executive power is exercised by the governor, elected by popular vote every four years, who leads a cabinet of 15 ministers.

National legislature

The Asamblea Legislativa (Legislative Assembly) has two chambers.
The Cámara de Representantes (Chamber of Representatives) has 51 members, elected for a four-year term, 40 elected in single-seat constituencies — 11 at large by proportional representation. Up to an additional three seats can be allocated to allow the opposition to have one-third of the seats.
The Senado (Senate) has 28 members, elected for a four-year term – 16 members elected in two-seat constituencies and 11 at large by proportional representation and one additional seat to allow the opposition to have one-third of the seats.
In 2005 the vote in a national referendum favoured replacing the Senate and House

KEY INDICATORS — Puerto Rico

	Unit	2003	2004	2005	2006	2007
Population	m	3.97	3.98	3.90	3.93	*3.96
Gross domestic product (GDP)	US$bn	45.66	68.95	53.40	*75.82	*77.41
GDP per capita	US$	11,500	12,659	13,622	*19,300	*19,600
GDP real growth	%	2.0	2.8	2.2	0.5	*1.2
Inflation	%	8.1	8.9	13.5	15.1	*12.4
Unemployment	%	12.0	10.5	10.4	10.4	10.9
Exports (fob) (goods)	US$m	55,175.0	55,080.0	56,543.0	60,119.0	61,321.0
Imports (cif) (goods)	US$m	33,750.0	38,898.0	38,905.0	42,630.0	46,041.0
Balance of trade	US$m	21,425.0	16,182.0	17,638.0	17,489.0	15,280.0
Exchange rate	per US$	1.00	1.00	1.00	1.00	1.00

* estimated figure

of Representatives with a unicameral legislature.

Legal system

The civil and commercial codes; penal, procedural, public (including constitutional) laws are fashioned after US models.

Last elections

2 November 2004 (gubernatorial and parliamentary).

Results: Gubernatorial: Aníbal Acevedo Vilá won 48.40 per cent; Pedro Rosselló won 48.22 per cent; and Rubén Berríos Martínez 2.74 per cent.

Senate: PNG won 17 seats (out of 27); PPD won nine seats; and Partido Independentista Puertorriqueño (PIP) (Puerto Rican Independence Party) one seat.

House of Representatives: PNG won 32 seats (out of 51); PPD won 18 seats; and PIP one seat.

Next elections

November 2008 (gubernatorial and parliamentary)

Political parties

Ruling party

Partido Popular Democrático (PPD) (Popular Democratic Party)

Main opposition party

Partido Nuevo Progresista (PNP) (New Progressive Party)

Population

3.96 million (2007)*

Last census: April 2000: 3,808,610

Population density: 436 inhabitants per square km. Urban population: 76 per cent (World Bank 2002).

Annual growth rate: 0.9 per cent (2003); projected 0.7 per cent 2002–15.

Ethnic make-up

There is a fusion of three main cultures: native Indian, European and African.

The Spanish conquistadores initially came to the New World without wives or family and married into the native population, producing the mestizo (Spanish and Taío) and the mulatto (Spanish and African) groups.

The Spanish settlers brought in African slaves to work in the sugar cane plantations. When migration restrictions were relaxed, more Spanish came, together with a large contingent of Corsicans and a small number of Irish.

Thousands of mainland Americans have established themselves in Puerto Rico and migrants have also come from the Dominican Republic, Canada, Europe, Asia, Cuba and South and Central America.

Religions

99 per cent of the population are Christians (85 per cent Roman Catholic). Religion has traditionally played an important role in the island's history. The religious groups have been instrumental in fostering community co-operation and providing health and educational services.

Education

Six years of elementary (primary) school are followed by three years of junior high school and three years of senior high school. All teaching is conducted in Spanish, although English is a compulsory subject at all levels. There are 34 post-school educational institutions, both government and private. The State University has three main campuses and six colleges. Special training programmes are provided in technical and vocational schools, as well as on-the-job training for labour skills for which a workforce does not exist.

Literacy rate: 93.7 per cent male, 94 per cent female; adult rates (World Bank).

Compulsory years: Six to 16

Health

HIV/Aids

It is estimated that there are 7,397 people living with HIV/Aids.

Life expectancy: 79 (estimate 2005)

Fertility rate/Maternal mortality rate: 1.75 per woman (2005)

Birth rate/Death rate: 12.88 births and 7.54 deaths per 1,000 population (2005)

Child (under 5 years) mortality rate (per 1,000): 9.28 per 1,000 live births (2005)

Welfare

The US social security system is in operation, together with Puerto Rico's own health, unemployment, and workers' compensation schemes. Employer contributions to the unemployment and social security funds are compulsory. Despite a high per capita national income, about 60 per cent of the population were recorded as living below the official US poverty line, and 45 per cent of the population received federal food stamps. Federal medical aid is also provided. These provide an important cushion against the effects of unemployment, to which a further safety valve is supplied by emigration. There are more Puerto Ricans living in New York than in San Juan.

Main cities

San Juan (capital, population estimated at 421,356 in 2005), Bayamón (208,138), Ponce (153,496), Carolina (173,386).

Languages spoken

Spanish is the primary language of the vast majority of Puerto Ricans. English as an important second language is taught in public and private schools from first grade through to tertiary institutions. Government affairs are conducted in Spanish while English is the language of commerce.

Official language/s

Spanish, English

Media

Press

Dailies: The three main dailies widely circulated include El Vocero de Puerto Rico (www.vocero.com), El Nuevo Día (www.elnuevodia.com) and Primera Hora (www.primerahora.com). Other regional dailies and those published from San Juan are El Impacto (www.elimpacto.com) and El Vocero (www.vocero.com).

In English San Juan Star (www.thesanjuanstar.com) Puerto Rico Herald (www.puertorico-herald.org) (published by the statehood campaign) and Caribbean Business (http://pal.prwow.com).

Weeklies: Caribbean Business.

Business: A multilingual, regional publication América Economía (www.americaeconomia.com) is the leading magazine.

Periodicals: In Spanish La Estrella de Puerto Rico (www.periodicolaestrella.com), El Expresso (www.elexpresso.com), La Esquina (www.laesquina.com), El Periódico (www.elperiodico.com), Bilingual (Spanish and English) publications include El Boricua (www.elboricua.com) featuring people and culture, An(with a wavy line ontop)il (www.plazaboricua.com).

Broadcasting

Radio: There are over 20 public and commercial radio stations, broadcasting news, music and special interest programmes. Spanish is the typical broadcast language including Radio Puerto Rico (www.radiopr740.com) and Sistema102 (www.sistema102.com); there is one local radio station broadcasting in English, WOSO (www.woso.com).

Television: The public broadcast service TUTV (www.tutv.puertorico.pr) transmits educational and international material. Other, commercial stations, Telemundo (http://tv.telemundo.yahoo.com), Televincento (www.wapa.tv) and Univision (http://univision.centennialpr.net) broadcast a wide variety of programmes in Spanish.

Around 115 national commercial radio stations and nine television stations broadcast. There are satellite TV broadcasts from several international sources.

Economy

Puerto Rico has few natural resources and is heavily dependent on federal aid from the US government. Major improvements to Puerto Rico's business environment have been made in recent years with diversification away from tourism to the high-tech and manufacturing industries being a primary aim. Changes include the slashing of capital gains taxes and lowering operating costs for manufacturing plants. There still exists a high degree of red tape and Puerto Rico has yet to adopt a private sector mentality.

The weaknesses in Puerto Rico's manufacturing sector, which accounts for 42 per cent of GDP, are being addressed – essential if exports are to remain steady and economic growth sustained. Regional agreements such as the North American Free Trade Agreement (Nafta) have made countries such as Mexico attractive low wage, tariff free alternatives to Puerto Rico.

The government has lobbied for permanent tax exemption status, saying this would be the best way to secure the Commonwealth's fiscal autonomy from federal government. With approximately 50 per cent of the economy supported by special exemptions for foreign firms, the repeal of tax incentives would severely undermine Puerto Rico's ability to compete with its Caribbean neighbours, prompting concern that the economy could collapse.

Susceptible to external shocks due to the reliance on imports, the recent high prices of oil have had a detrimental effect on the economy, raising inflation.

The withdrawal of the US Navy in 2003 has had some impact on the economy. The Navy injected around US$300 million into the economy each year and was one of the nation's largest employers. Its departure increased unemployment and reduced government revenues.

External trade

As an overseas commonwealth territory of the United States, the US has authority over interstate trade, commerce and customs administration. Puerto Rico is part of the North American free trade agreement (Nafta).

Since Nafta was signed, the level of exported manufactured goods has fallen as Mexico, with its lower unit costs, has become a major supplier to the US and Canada. However, while low paid jobs were lost to Mexico there was an increase in pharmaceutical and hi-tech manufacturing in Puerto Rico.

The US accounts for over 75 per cent of imports and exports. Most trade is intra-company shipments, as parts from US companies are imported and finished goods are exported in return. This flow of materials and products creates profits for private companies and jobs for workers in Puerto Rico and the US.

Without many natural resources the balance of payments is still reliant on US federal aid and tax incentives.

Imports

Principal imports include petroleum and derivatives, chemicals, capital machinery and electronic components, textiles and yarns, raw and processed foodstuff, building material and manufacturing raw materials.

Main sources: US (41.2 per cent total, 2006), Ireland (16.6 per cent), Japan (3.3 per cent).

Exports

Principal exports include chemicals, pharmaceuticals and medical products, finished goods, clothing, tuna and other fish products, beverages, tropical fruit, dairy and meat.

Main destinations: US (77.7 per cent total, 2006), The Netherlands (3.0 per cent), Belgium (2.2 per cent)

Agriculture

Farming

The agricultural sector is small-scale and only contributes 0.3 per cent to GDP while employing 2 per cent of the workforce. Only 10 per cent of land is suitable for agriculture. An additional 25 per cent of the island is composed of uplands, partially suited for agricultural purposes. Dairy and livestock farming is of increasing importance.

Farming on the island has changed considerably since the 1940s and 1950s, when traditional small-scale farming methods prevailed and sugar cane, coffee and tobacco were the dominant crops. Of these, only coffee has survived, but it lags behind milk and poultry production. Milk production accounts for 34 per cent of total gross farm income. Changes in consumer preferences are slowly taking place as the population ages.

Around 90 per cent of food requirements are met by imports. Almost all of Puerto Rico's farm output is consumed locally, although small quantities of coffee are exported to Europe and Japan. Some fruit and vegetables, mangoes, tomatoes and onions also go to Europe.

Agriculture has been traditionally based on sugar, coffee, pineapples, plantains, bananas, livestock products and poultry. Sugar production declined during the 1980s, partly due to the closure of the Central Cambalache sugar mill in 1982. Coffee production meets only three-quarters of local demand but half of production is exported. Livestock production has not displayed the same rate of decline as arable agriculture, but is still insufficient to meet local demand. The cost of imported feed represents a major constraint on development.

Crop production for 2005 included: *450 tonnes (t) maize, 3,300t sweet potatoes, 540t cassava, 3,600t yams, 1,088t pulses, 20,120t citrus fruit, 52,400t bananas, 105,000t plantains, 12,150t mangoes, 20,000t tomatoes, 5,250t coconuts, *10,000t green coffee, 4,290t chillies and peppers, 19,100t pineapples, 219,270t fruit in total, 42,140t vegetables in total. Livestock production included: 71,565t meat in total, *10,000t beef, 11,500t pig meat, 65t lamb and goat meat *50,000t poultry, 11,894t eggs, 370,000t milk, 40t honey, *1,100t cattle hides.

* estimate

Fishing

Although fishing is conducted on a relatively small scale, it is nevertheless important. Puerto Rico used to be a major tuna supplier to the USA but in recent times has faced a number of problems such as increased competition from south-east Asia. The annual production of processed fish is around 4,000 tonnes.

In 2004, the total marine fish catch was 1,047 tonnes and the total crustacean catch was 159 tonnes.

Industry and manufacturing

The industrial sector forms the mainstay of the economy, contributing approximately 42 per cent to GDP and employing 11 per cent of the workforce. Financial services produce 17 per cent of GDP and trade accounts for 11.6 per cent, other industries produce less than 10 per cent of GDP. Most of the island's manufacturing output is shipped to mainland US.

Industrialisation has been the focus of government economic policy since the late 1940s when a programme known as 'Operation Bootstrap' was launched. In 1950, there were 82 industrial plants in Puerto Rico, but by 1965 there were around 1,000. Since then industrial development has tended to be more capital intensive and dependent upon highly skilled labour.

Production is centred on food processing, textiles, petrochemicals, rum distilling, pharmaceuticals, metal fabrication and assembly of electrical/electronic components.

Most of the assembly industries are US-owned and are heavily dependent on the US market. Manufacturers exporting goods to the US benefit from being within the US Customs zone, with the US dollar as the local currency, and US legal protection of intellectual property – particularly useful for IT industries.

The US Commerce Department's Foreign Trade Zones Board has approved the conversion of all the island's industrial parks into free trade zones (FTZs). This, together with Puerto Rico's generous incentives package and skilled workforce has in the past made the island a prime destination for companies looking to expand or relocate. However, competition, from Mexico in particular, has had an adverse effect.

The island's agricultural industry makes an important contribution to the economy

through the food industry services of prepared food and retail sales.
The pharmaceutical industry is crucial to Puerto Rico; 16 of the top 20 pharmaceutical drugs in the US are manufactured in Puerto Rico and all the leading US manufacturers are represented, some with major investments. There is heavy investment by US computer and electronics companies, footwear and rubber goods manufacturers. The K-Mart Corporation, the US retailing group, is well represented in Puerto Rico.

Tourism
Tourism is an important source of revenue and Puerto Rico benefits from its connection with the US, from where 80 per cent of visitors come. Although it is a major player in the region, the sector accounts for only around 7 per cent of GDP, a much lower share than other major destinations in the Caribbean. Over five million arrivals were recorded in 2003, a quarter of them being cruise passengers. In January 2004 Disney Cruise Line announced that San Juan would be included in it scheduled ports of call; passenger arrivals recorded between January–October 2004 reached 1,065,215 an increased of 13.5 per cent over 2003.
To meet the growing pressure of competition from its neighbours, Puerto Rico has embarked on a vigorous programme of promotion and infrastructure development, with particular attention on the US and European markets. A new self-contained, all-inclusive resort – Paradisus Puerto Rico, owned by Spain's Sol-Melia – was opened in 2004. It comprises a 500 room hotel and individual accommodation, with sports, entertainment and convention centre. In 113 acres of the Puerto Rico Convention District, on the peninsula of Isla Grande, the US$415 million Convention Centre opened in mid-2005; with over 175,000 square metres, it will be the largest such facility in the Caribbean. Previously unexploited parts of the island are being marketed.

Mining
Activity in this area is extremely small – production is centred on non-metals such as stone, sand, salt and clay.
There are small unquantified reserves of copper, nickel, cobalt, iron, chromium, lead, gold and silver.

Hydrocarbons
Puerto Rico has no hydrocarbon reserves and relies entirely on imports of fuels. Imported oil accounts for just over 90 per cent of Puerto Rico's total primary energy consumption. Puerto Rico typically consumes over 225,000 barrels per day (bpd), all of which is imported. There are two refineries, one located at the Bayamon refinery owned by the Caribbean Petroleum Corporation and the other owned by Royal Dutch/Shell and located at Yabucoa.
Puerto Rico started importing liquid natural gas (LNG) in 2000, to supply the new gas fuelled power plant EcoEléctrica. Most LNG is imported, mainly from Trinidad and Tobago.
All coal products are imported, and since the completion in 2002 of a coal-fired plant in Guayama, demand for coal is slowly increasing.

Energy
Puerto Rico depends on imported energy fuels, mainly from Trinidad and Tobago, Venezuela and the Netherlands Antilles.
The Puerto Rico Electric Power Authority (Prepa) is the second-largest municipally-owned US utility. Demand for power is growing at 3.5 per cent a year; in 2003 electicity consumption was 23.7 billion kWh. Additional capacity is also being provided through the refurbishing of some Prepa power stations and the opening of new plants. This will add significantly to Prepa's capacity. Prepa spent US$1.9 billion during the period 2000–03 to improve generating, transmission and distribution infrastructure. Many companies still maintain their own generators as essential back-up.

Banking and insurance
The Puerto Rican commercial banking system comprises about 17 banks with around 300 branches. Financial deregulation and consolidation in the industry have improved operating conditions. Major US banks include Citibank, Chase Manhattan and First National Bank of Boston. Foreign banks include Royal Bank of Canada, Bank of Nova Scotia, Banco Central de Madrid, Banco Bilbao Vizcaya and Banco de Santander.
Banco Popular de Puerto Rico, Puerto Rico's largest bank, continues to expand into US Hispanic markets.

Central bank
There is no central bank.
Such functions as fiscal agent for the Commonwealth of Puerto Rico and its public entities, and the provision of development loans to the public as well as the private sector, are undertaken by the Government Development Bank for Puerto Rico (GDB).

Time
GMT minus four hours

Geography
Puerto Rico comprises the main island, together with the small offshore islands of Vieques and Culebra and many other smaller islets, lying about 80km (50 miles) east of Hispaniola (Haiti and the Dominican Republic) in the Caribbean Sea.
Roughly 160km long by 48km wide, Puerto Rico is the smallest and most westerly of the Greater Antilles. The centre of the island is composed of dead volcanoes, the highest of which, the Cordillera Central, has an elevation of 1,325 metres. To the north of the mountains lies a belt of broken limestone country, and then a fertile coastal plain. The whole island is well supplied with rivers. Only about 1 per cent of the country remains forested and is largely reserved.

Hemisphere
Northern

Climate
Tropical with extremes of heat tempered by constant sea winds. Temperatures are 28–30 degrees Celsius (C) in summer, and 21–26 degrees C in winter. Rainfall is heaviest in the second half of the year, especially June–October. Puerto Rico lies in the 'hurricane belt'.

Dress codes
Suits and ties are customary for businessmen since almost all offices are air conditioned. A jacket and tie may be required in first class restaurants. The Hispanic Caribbean guayabera, a long decorated shirt, is worn increasingly commonly.

Entry requirements
US entry requirements apply.

Passports
Required by all, valid for six months from date of entry.

Visa
Required by all, except nationals of Canada and Visa Waiver Scheme countries in possession of machine-readable passports; otherwise, visas must be applied for. Visits, for both tourism and business, and visas are valid for up to 90 days. A return/onward ticket is also required. Further information can be found at http://travel.state.gov.

Currency advice/regulations
There are no restrictions on the import or export of local and foreign currencies, subject to declaration of amounts in excess of US$10,000.

Health (for visitors)
The standard of health care in both government and private hospitals is high, but expensive.

Mandatory precautions
None

Advisable precautions
Hepatitis A occurs in the northern Caribbean. There is also a risk of rabies. Travellers should consider vaccination before travelling. Dengue fever, transmitted by mosquitoes, is endemic in rural areas. Its initial symptoms may be similar to influenza. Bilharzia parasites may be present in rivers.

No special precautions are necessary for food and drink.

Hotels
There are several modern business hotels in San Juan. There are also paradores, government-owned inns, that are of a reasonable standard. Fifteen per cent tip usual.

Public holidays (national)
Fixed dates
1 Jan (New Year's Day), 6 Jan (Epiphany), 10 Jan (Eugenio Maria De Hostos' Birthday), 22 Mar (Emancipation Day), 4 Jul (US Independence Day), 25 Jul (Constitution Day), 26 Jul (José Celso Barbosa's Birthday), 11 Nov (Veterans' Day), 19 Nov (Discovery of Puerty Rico Day), 25 Dec (Christmas Day).
Each town celebrates a festival or fiesta in honour of a local patron saint. These can last up to 10 days.
Variable dates
Eugenio Maria de Hostos' Birthday (second Mon in Jan), Martin Luther King's Birthday (third Mon in Jan), Washington's Birthday (third Mon in Feb), Good Friday, José de Diego Day (Apr), Memorial Day (last Mon in May), Luis Muñoz Rivera's Day (Jul), Labour Day (first Mon in Sep), Columbus Day (second Mon in Oct), Thanksgiving Day (fourth Thu in Nov).

Working hours
Banking
Mon–Fri: 0830–1430. (Some banks 0830–1700; some banks open Sat.)
Business
Mon–Fri: 0800–1700.
Government
Mon–Fri: 0800–1630.

Telecommunications
Puerto Rico's telecommunications system is fully integrated with that of the US.
Telephone/fax
Direct dialling and fax facilities are available at all main hotels.
Mobile/cell phones
The main providers of mobile phone services are Centennial, Cingular, MoviStar, Suncom, Verizon and Sprint PCS.

Electricity supply
120V AC

Social customs/useful tips
Despite links with the US and the almost universal ability in the business community to understand English, the use of Spanish by the visitor is appreciated.
Hotel and restaurant staff, and taxi drivers, may expect tips of 15–20 per cent. Service charges are rarely included in restaurant bills.
Puerto Rico combines the lifestyle and social customs of the modern US and the traditional Spanish-speaking Caribbean.

Security
Poverty and unemployment have helped to contribute to a growing crime rate, particularly in San Juan. As in all cities, it is unwise to leave articles unattended in parked cars or hotel rooms.

Getting there
Air
There are direct flights from Europe. Latin American countries are connected via Miami. There are also numerous other connections via New York. Other US cities are also well connected to Puerto Rico.
International airport/s: Luis Muñoz Marín (SJU), 14km east of San Juan; duty-free shop, restaurants, bank, post office, shops, car hire.
Airport tax: None
Surface
Main port/s: San Juan, Ponce and Mayagüez.

Getting about
National transport
Air: Several local airlines operate flights within Puerto Rico, as well as island-hopping trips. Charter services are available.
Road: An extensive network of modern roads and highways link all main centres.
Buses: Regular bus (guagua) services operates in San Juan from central terminal at Plaza Colón.
Buses are scarce after 2100.
Taxis: Officially regulated, independently owned públicos (publicly shared) taxis have 'P' or 'PD' at the of end a licence plate and run regular routes from established points, picking up and dropping off passengers along the way. They are an inexpensive way of reaching urban areas and provincial towns less accessible by public transport.
Water: There is a ferry service linking the islands of Culebra and Vieques to the port of Fajardo, on the east coast of Puerto Rico.
City transport
Taxis: Special tourist taxis (Taxi Turístico) operate between the airport and main tourist areas around San Juan. They operate on a zonal basis and charge set fares. Commercial taxis are metered and can be hired by the hour.
Buses, trams & metro: There are good bus services (guaguas) in San Juan. Services outside the capital are less reliable. A metro system Tren Urbano (Urban Train) provides regular services running through the San Juan metropolitan area.
Car hire
The major car hire companies are represented. Parking is in short supply.

BUSINESS DIRECTORY

The addresses listed below are a selection only. While World of Information makes every endeavour to check these addresses, we cannot guarantee that changes have not been made, especially to telephone numbers and area codes. We would welcome any corrections.

Telephone area codes
The international dialling code (IDD) for Puerto Rico is +1, followed by area code (787) and subscriber's number.

Chambers of Commerce
Puerto Rico Chamber of Commerce, PO Box 9024033, San Juan 00902 (tel: 721-6060; fax: 723-1891; e-mail: camarapr@camarapr.net).

West of Puerto Rico Chamber of Commerce, PO Box 9, Mayagüez 00681 (tel: 832-3749; fax: 832-4287).

Banking
Banco Comercial de Mayagüez, Mayagüez 00708 (tel: 834-3717).

Banco de Ponce, Plaza Degetau, Ponce 00731 (tel: 842-8000).

Banco Popular, M. Rivera Avenue and Bolivia Street, Hato Rey, San Juan (tel: 765-9800; fax: 764-1706).

Banco Santander de Puerto Rico, 207 Ponce de León Avenue, Hato Rey, San Juan (tel: 759-7070; fax: 751-3639).

Government Development Bank for Puerto Rico, PO Box 42001, San Juan 00940-2001 (tel: 726-2525).

Central bank
Government Development Bank for Puerto Rico, PO Box 42001, San Juan 00940-2001 (tel: 722-2525; fax: 721-5496; e-mail: gdbcomm@bgf.gobierno.pr).

Federal Reserve System, 20th Street and Constitution Avenue, NW, Washington DC 20551 (tel: (+1-202) 452-3000; fax: (+1-202) 452-3819).

Travel information
National tourist organisation offices

Puerto Rico Tourism Company, La Princesa Building, 2 Paseo La Princesa, PO Box 902-3060, Old San Juan 00902 (tel: 721-2400; fax: 725-4417).

Ministries
Department of Agriculture, PO Box 10163, San Juan (tel: 721-2120; fax: 723-9747).

Department of Economic Development and Commerce, F.D. Roosevelt Ave 355, 4th Floor, Hato Rey, 00918 (tel: 764-1175 fax: 765-7709).

Department of Education, PO Box 190759, 00919 (tel: 758-4949; fax: 250-0275).

Department of Justice, PO Box 191, 00912 (tel: 721-2900; fax: 724-4770).

Department of Labour and Human Resources, 505 Munoz Rivera Avenue, 00918 (tel: 754-5353; fax: 753-9550).

Department of Natural and Environmental Resources, PO Box 5887, 00906 (tel: 724-8774; fax: 723-4255).

Department of the State, PO Box 3271, 00902 (tel: 722-2121; fax: 725-7303).

Department of the Treasury, PO Box 4515, 00902 (tel: 721-2020; fax: 723-6213).

Department of Transportation and Public works, PO Box 41269, 00940 (tel: 722-2929; fax: 728-8963).

Government of Puerto Rico Economic Development Administration, PO Box 362350, San Juan 00936 (tel: 758-4747; fax: 764-1415).

Office of the Governor, La Fortaleza, 00901 (tel: 721-7000; fax: 721-7483).

Other useful addresses

Caribbean Development Programme, Puerto Rico Department of State, PO Box 3271, San Juan, 00912 (tel: 721-1751; fax: 723-3304).

Legislative Assembly, Capitol Building, 00901 (tel: 724-5200; fax: 724-2428).

Puerto Rico Bankers' Association, 820 Banco Popular Center, San Juan, 00918 (tel: 753-8630; fax: 754-6077).

Puerto Rico Industrial Development Company (FOMENTO), FD Roosevelt Ave, Hato Rey, San Juan, 00918; PO Box 362350, San Juan, PR 00936-2350 (tel: 758-4747; fax: 754-9640; internet site: http://www.pridco.com).

Puerto Rico Manufacturers' Association, PO Box 192410, San Juan, 00919 (tel: 759-9445; fax: 756-7670).

Puerto Rico Ports Authority, PO Box 362829, San Juan (tel: 723-2260; fax: 724-6444).

San Juan Convention Bureau, Ashford Avenue 1110, San Turce, 00907 (tel: 725-2110).

Supreme Court, Supreme Court Building, 00901 (tel: 723-6033; fax: 725-4910).

Internet sites

Puerto Rico Tourism Company: http://www.gotopuertorico.com

Urban transit: http://www.urbanrail.net

Welcome to Puerto Rico: http://www.topuertorico.com

Yellow and White Pages: http://www.escapetopuertorico.com/ypages

Qatar

KEY FACTS

Official name: Dawlat Qatar (State of Qatar)

Head of State: Emir Sheikh Hamad bin Khalifa al Thani (since Jun 1995)

Head of government: Prime Minister Sheikh Hamad bin Jassem (appointed 3 Apr 2007)

Area: 11,437 square km

Population: 930,000 (2007)*

Capital: Doha

Official language: Arabic

Currency: Rial (QR) = 100 dirhams

Exchange rate: QR3.64 per US$ (fixed)

GDP per capita: US$72,849 (2007)*

GDP real growth: 14.20% (2007)

Labour force: 508,000 (2006)*

Unemployment: 3.20% (2006)*

Inflation: 13.80% (2007)*

Oil production: 1.20 million bpd (2007)

Balance of trade: US$18.19 billion (2005)

Foreign debt: US$18.62 billion (2004)

Visitor numbers: 962,000 (2006)*

* estimated figure

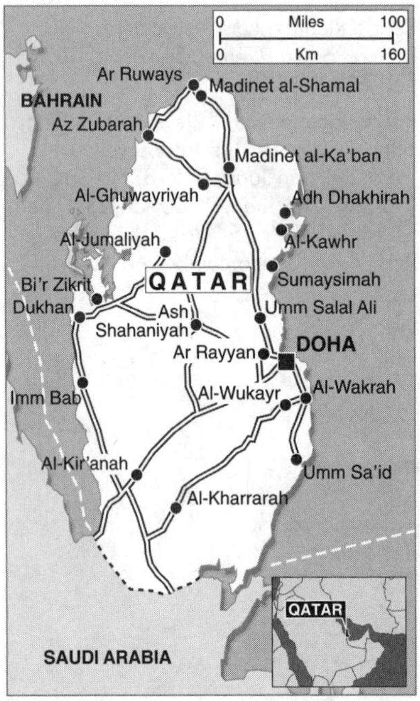

In its report on economic and financial developments in Qatar, the International Bank of Qatar (IBQ) expects the size of the economy to double by 2012. Nominal gross domestic product (GDP) expanded by an impressive 24 per cent in 2006, after averaging 30 per cent per annum for the previous three years. Real growth was supported by solid gains in hydrocarbon output and massive investment flows. The IBQ report, prepared in conjunction with the economic research team of its partner, the National Bank of Kuwait, pointed out however, that price pressures continued to mount, with consumer price inflation reaching 11.8 per cent in 2006, fuelled by soaring rents.

Risk of inflation

Expansionary fiscal policy and resource constraints contributed as well to the acceleration in inflation. There were also some seeds of a wage-price-inflation spiral. Unless structural adjustments in the housing market stabilise rents, the risk of accelerating inflation is not expected to abate. With monetary policy remaining largely accommodative, high inflation may well become entrenched in the economy with long-lasting negative repercussions on the real economy, the report said. The government is investing in its capacity to manage the pace of growth and to reduce inflationary pressures symptomatic of such a high pace. It is also increasing spending to address infrastructure bottlenecks and improve education and health care.

In the next five years, the government is leading a massive investment programme estimated to be worth US$130 billion to develop energy, infrastructure, industries, utilities and aviation.

The fast pace at which Qatar is progressing naturally carries some costs, including testing the country's absorptive capacity and possibly incurring a higher bill. This is largely a timing issue, given future flows anticipated from natural gas. As long as the investment programme continues to be managed prudently, the prospects are positive. The government is also committed to creating a vibrant and active private sector. This in turn is expected to create job opportunities for the national work force, which has traditionally been absorbed by the public sector. Efforts in this area include the government's push to position Qatar as a hub for major sports and energy events, thus laying the foundation for significant private sector investments in the tourism industry.

Oil and gas rule

At the end of 2007 Qatar's oil reserves were 27.4 thousand million barrels and production was 1.2 million barrels per day (bpd). Gas reserves were 25.6 trillion cubic metres (tcm) and production 59.8 billion cubic metres (bcm). Qatar exported 25 million tons of liquefied natural gas (LNG) in 2006 double that of 2002, making it the fourth-largest exporter of LNG in the world. Dry gas, which so far has mainly fed local industry, is also emerging as a new foreign exchange earner as the first shipments make their way to the United Arab Emirates (UAE) through the Dolphin pipeline. Gas production through the gas-to-liquids (GTL) process is also expected to take off in 2007–08, providing an option to convert gas into environment-friendly, high-value fuels at higher returns. Crude oil remains the backbone of the economy, earning 60 per cent of total export receipts. In 2006, oil and gas revenues continued to rise, reaching over US$20 billion, although tempered by slower growth in output and prices in the second half of the year.

By the end of 2006, net foreign assets held by the Qatar Central Bank (QCB) had reached US$5.4 billion, while accumulated surpluses in the current and fiscal accounts over the last five years are estimated to have surpassed US$30 billion and US$10 billion respectively. Unofficial estimates put the size of Qatar's foreign assets at US$70 billion. Meanwhile, the country's external debt has been dropping relative to GDP, from 58.3 per cent in 2003 to 40.8 per cent in 2006 according to World Bank estimates. The country's improved external position continues to enhance its international credibility. Moody's, the credit rating agency, has upgraded Qatar's sovereign long-term rating to Aa3, and Standard and Poor's to AA-/A-1+.

Downside risks clearly exist from a sharp decline in oil prices. The economy remains highly reliant on hydrocarbon exports, although the fiscal and external current accounts are less sensitive to a downturn in energy prices than those of other hydrocarbon exporting countries, mainly due to the long-term nature of gas export contracts.

The al Thani family have ruled Qatar since independence in 1971. There have been peaceful transfers of power within the family based on collective decisions. Traditionally Qatar has maintained close connections with Dubai, to the extent of sharing a common currency – the riyal – for some years. It was the then ruler of Qatar, Sheikh Khalifa who in 1973 first proposed the establishment of the common market with a common currency which came into being on 1 January 2008. Citizens of the six states – Bahrain, Kuwait, Oman, Qatar, Saudi Arabia and UAE – are now allowed to travel between and live in any of the six states, where they may find employment, buy properties and businesses and use the educational and health facilities freely.

Economic diversification

Qatar's gross domestic product (GDP) increased by 12.5 per cent in 2007, after growth of 6.7 per cent in 2006. Inflation in Qatar has accelerated somewhat in recent years, rising to 13.7 per cent in 2007 (in 2006 it was 9.0 per cent), driven in large part by rapid increases in rental values for housing and commercial property. Qatar's GDP per capita in 2007 was US$75,900.

Qatar's enlightened policy of economic diversification has led to the growth in the number of projects related to the export of liquid natural gas (LNG) and petrochemicals. Seeking to add value to its natural resources, the government expects that it will be able to earn more per barrel of crude oil produced if it can export refined products and petrochemicals, as well as create private sector jobs. Qatar has traditionally been dependent on government ministries to provide employment, or rather under-employment, for its population.

Qatar has a relatively large foreign debt which is being rapidly paid off as oil and LNG export revenues rise. Qatar accumulated this debt largely for infrastructure investment to expand oil production capacity, build LNG export terminals, and build additional petrochemical plants.

For three decades oil has been Qatar's main source of income. Qatar began its rapid course of development with the first commercial exports of oil in 1949. This first crude shipment was from the onshore Dukhan field operated by the Qatar Petroleum Company (once an affiliate of the Iraq Petroleum Company) which operated the onshore concession. Shell Qatar, which operates offshore, started producing in 1964. The Dukhan field, located along the west coast of the peninsula, is the largest producing oilfield. Qatar also has six offshore fields – Bul Hanine, Maydan Mahzam, Id al Shargi North Dome, al Shaheen, al Rayyan, and al Khalij. Despite the country's oil production and reserves, oil now accounts for less than 15 per cent of domestic energy consumption.

And the gas

Qatar has for some time looked set to become one of the biggest exporters of natural gas in the world. Qatar has signed several multi-billion dollar (US) deals aimed at exploiting the country's LNG reserves. ExxonMobil and Royal Dutch-Shell have signed extraction and export agreements worth US$12.8 billion and US$6 billion respectively. In November 2005, Qatar launched a US$14 billion project with the US government that will build the world's largest LNG plant.

Most of Qatar's natural gas is located in the offshore North Field, which is the largest known non-associated natural gas field in the world.

The constitution…

In 2005 Qatar's first written constitution came into force. The constitution had been approved at a referendum in April 2003 and provides for a partially elected legislative body. The devolution of legislative powers was unprecedented in the emirate's history. The constitution also guarantees expression, assembly and religious freedom. The first election to the new parliament will be in 2007. In 2007 Sheikh Abdullah bin Khalifa resigned as prime minister on April 3 and was replaced by Sheikh Hamad bin Jassem.

Outlook

As more hydrocarbon, and in particular LNG, fields come online, Qatar can

KEY INDICATORS — **Qatar**

	Unit	2003	2004	2005	2006	2007
Population	m	0.62	0.64	0.80	0.84	*0.93
Gross domestic product (GDP)	US$bn	20.43	28.50	42.46	52.72	*67.76
GDP per capita	US$	30,438	37,610	53,333	62,914	*72,849
GDP real growth	%	8.5	9.9	6.1	*10.3	*14.2
Inflation	%	2.0	7.5	8.8	11.8	*13.8
Oil output	'000 bpd	917.0	990.0	1,097.0	1,133.0	1,197.0
Natural gas output	bn cum	30.8	39.2	43.5	49.5	59.8
Exports (fob) (goods)	US$m	10,900.0	15,000.0	24,900.0	–	–
Imports (cif) (goods)	US$m	3,900.0	6,150.0	6,706.0	–	–
Balance of trade	US$m	7,000.0	8,850.0	18,194.0	–	–
Current account	US$m	6,840.0	11,960.0	10,713.0	*16,113.0	*23,423.0
Total reserves minus gold	US$m	2,944.2	3,395.9	4,542.4	5,382.7	9,416.4
Foreign exchange	US$m	2,758.1	3,225.4	4,456.5	5,307.1	9,345.0
Exchange rate	per US$	3.64	3.64	3.64	3.64	3.64

expect further multi-billion dollar budget surpluses. To date Qatar's economic diversification policy has been one of diversification away from oil and into gas. Real economic growth is expected to be 11.7 per cent in 2008, then peak at 13.3 per cent in 2009 as the LNG programme expansion reaches its high mark, according to *Qatar Economic and Financial Review* published by the National Bank of Kuwait April 2008.

Risk assessment

Politics	Fair
Economy	Good
Regional stability	Good

COUNTRY PROFILE

Historical profile

The Al Khalifa family of Bahrain occupied the northern part of Qatar until 1868. That year, at the request of Qatari nobles, the British negotiated the termination of the Khalifa claim to Qatar, except for the payment of tribute. The tribute ended with the occupation of Qatar by the Ottoman Turks in 1872, when the Khalifa family moved to Bahrain.

The Al Thani family gained control of Doha in the middle of the nineteenth century. After being part of the Turkish Ottoman empire, the country became a British protectorate from 1916 until 1971, when it declared its independence. Originally one of the poorest of the Gulf states with its income based on pearling, fishing and trading, Qatar has developed, with the exploitation of large oil and gas fields, into one of the richest Gulf states, with one of the highest per capita incomes in the world.

632 Advent of Islam.
1700s Mining and pearl fishing settlements were established along the coast.
1868 Qatar's first Al Thani Emir, Sheikh Mohammed bin Thani, signed a treaty with Britain.
1871–1916 A treaty with the Turks allowed them to place a garrison in Doha. After Turkey entered the First World War on the side of Germany, the Turkish forces were expelled by the British.
1916 Qatar became a British protectorate with Sheikh Abdullah bin Jassim al Thani as ruler.
1930 The collapse of the pearl trade devastated the economy.
1939 Oil was discovered, but the Second World War delayed exploitation.
1949 Qatar began exporting oil.
1950s Qatar's infrastructure was modernised and extended, using oil revenues.
1968 Britain announced its intention to withdraw from the Gulf by 1971.
1971 Qatar became independent. Land disputes with Bahrain ensued.
1972 Sheikh Khalifa bin Hamad al Thani became Emir after deposing his uncle.
1980s and 1990s Qatar had territorial disputes with Bahrain and Saudi Arabia.
1990 After Iraq invaded Kuwait, Qatar allowed foreign forces into the country and Qatari troops took part in the liberation of Kuwait.
1995 In a bloodless coup, Sheikh Hamad bin Khalifa al Thani, replaced his father Sheikh Khalifa.
1996 Qatar began exporting liquefied natural gas. Based in Qatar and funded by the Emir, the pan-Arab Al Jazeera satellite TV station was launched.
1999 A democratisation programme began when male citizens over the age of 18 were allowed to vote in municipal council elections. Only half the 40,000 eligible to vote actually registered.
2000 The Emir's cousin and 32 others were jailed for life for planning a coup, in 1996, which was foiled.
2001 The International Court of Justice settled a land dispute with Bahrain, awarding Zubarah town and the shallows surrounding the islet of Fasht el Dibal to Qatar. A border dispute with Saudi Arabia was also settled. WTO trade talks, held in Doha, called for the US, EU and Japan to open their markets and remove agricultural export subsidies.
2002 The Al Udeid air base was redeveloped in preparation for the Iraq War when it became the HQ for the US Central Command.
2003 A referendum approved a new constitution, which guarantees equal rights and a 45-member parliament. The Emir named his younger son, Prince Tamim, as crown prince, replacing his elder son Prince Jassim.
2004 The exiled former Chechen president, Zelimkhan Yanderbiyev, was assassinated in Doha; two Russian agents were convicted of the murder. Around six thousand members of the Al Ghfran clan, a sub-set of one of Qatar's largest tribes, had their citizenship revoked on the grounds that they held dual nationality with Saudi Arabia.
2005 A suicide bombing in Doha on 19 March injured 12 and killed one Briton; it was the first major terrorist attack in Qatar. The new constitution was implemented in June.
2006 The 15th Asian Games were held in Qatar in December.
2007 Sheikh Abdullah bin Khalifa resigned as prime minister on April 3 and was replaced by Sheikh Hamad bin Jassem.
2008 On 1 January, a common market was created by Bahrain, Kuwait, Oman, Qatar, Saudi Arabia and UAE, the six wealthiest Gulf states. Citizens of these countries are now allowed to travel between and live in any of the six states, where they may find employment, buy properties and businesses and use the educational and health facilities freely.

Political structure

Constitution

A new, written constitution came into effect on 8 June 2005. It provides for the hereditary rule of the al Thani family. A new unicamal, legislative authority was inaugurated.

Form of state

Constitutional Emirate

The executive

Executive power is vested in the Emir, who is the Head of State. He appoints a prime minister and ministers. He also appoints 15 members of the Majlis al Shura. The Emir is the supreme commander of the armed and security forces.

National legislature

The unicameral Majlis al Shura (Advisory Council) has 45 seats – 30 directly elected and 15 appointed by the Emir. The council has legislative authority, approves the budget and monitors the executive authority. Its 45 members serve four-year terms. Sessions of the council are public, although they may be held in camera by request of a third of its members or by a request from the cabinet.

No law can be issued unless endorsed by the Emir, who has the right to dissolve the council by decree.

Legal system

Two former court systems – civil and Sharia (Islamic law) – were merged under a higher court, the Court of Cassation, established for appeals, under a new judiciary law issued in 2003.

Last elections

None.

Next elections

March 2007

Political parties

Ruling party

Political parties are not permitted.

Population

930,000 (2007)*

Last census: March 2004: 744,029

Population density: 51 inhabitants per sq km. Urban population: 92.3 per cent (2001).

Annual growth rate: 4.2 per cent 1994–2004 (WHO 2006)

Ethnic make-up

Arab (40 per cent), Pakistani (18 per cent), Indian (18 per cent), Iranian (10 per cent), others (14 per cent).

Expatriates comprise about 80 per cent of the total population. Some foreign nationals have been resident in Qatar for many years and come largely from the Indian sub-continent, other Arab countries and south-east Asia. The number of non-national children is high, indicating a trend among non-nationals to settle in the country.

Religions

Islam is the state religion. Most Qataris (95 per cent) are Sunni Muslims of the strict Wahhabi sect, known as muwahhidun (unitarians); they shun the veneration of saints and shrines. The small Hindu and Christian communities do not have formal places of worship.

Education

Primary education begins at aged six and lasts until aged 12. From aged 12 to 15 students attend a preparatory school and if they pass their promotional examination go forward to secondary school. There are three different types of secondary schools: academic, commercial and technical, and each offer three-year courses. However, girls are only allowed to attend the academic secondary schools.

In 2004, Qatar announced that it would spend US$900 million on a huge new medical teaching hospital to be built on the outskirts of Doha; it is expected to be completed by 2008. An endowment of US$8 billion will also be provided to carry out research. The hospital's teaching programme will be run in partnership with the US Cornell University, and have US$200 million per annum to spend on research, initially concentrating on women's health and paediatric medicine. The emphasis on research is a new direction for medical facilities in the region.

Literacy rate: 83 per cent, adult rate (2003)

Compulsory years: None.

Health

Per capita total expenditure on health (2003) was US$685; of which per capita government spending was US$506, at the international dollar rate, (WHO 2006).

All residents have access to free medical services.

Life expectancy: 76 years, 2004 (WHO 2006)

Fertility rate/Maternal mortality rate: 2.9 births per woman, 2004 (WHO 2006)

Birth rate/Death rate: 16 births per 1,000 population; 4.4 deaths per 1,000 population (2003).

Child (under 5 years) mortality rate (per 1,000): 11 per 1,000 live births (2003)

Head of population per physician: 2.22 physicians per 1,000 people, 2001 (WHO 2006)

Welfare

The state provides generous welfare services for indigenous Qataris.

Main cities

Doha (capital, estimated population 339,847 in 2004), ar Rayyan (251,437), al Wakrah (27,462).

Media

National news agency: Qatar News Agency

Press

The government formally lifted censorship of the media in 1995 and since then government interference has remained limited although censorship is implicit and self-censorship by editors common.

Dailies: The main daily newspapers in Arabic are al Sharq (The East) (www.al-sharq.com), al Raya (The Banner) (www.raya.com), al Watan (The Homeland) (www.al-watan.com) and the regional publication al Arab (www.alarabonline.org) of political matters.

In English, Qatar Post (www.qatarpost.com), Qatar Journal (www.qatarjournal.com) and The Peninsula (www.thepeninsulaqatar.com) is the leading English newspaper. A regional publication is The Gulf Times (www.gulf-times.com).

Weeklies: The Gulf Times is published in English.

Periodicals: In Arabic, the monthly al Sehah Magazine publishes items on health. In English, This is Qatar is a tourist magazine, Qatar Falcon (http://www.qatar-falcon.com) is a lifestyle publication aimed at male readers, while Zawya (www.zawya.com) is an online business magazine, with news and features.

Broadcasting

Isreal began a boycott of al Jazeera on 12 March 2008 in reaction to what it claimed was al Jazeera's bias when it reported on the conflict in Gaza – Israeli action in bombing the territory was not matched by reports of missiles fired on the city of Ashkelon.

Radio: Radio broadcasts are in Arabic, with other services in English, French and Urdu also available. The government run, Qatar Broadcasting Service broadcasts nationally. A few local radio stations also broadcast in FM and AM.

Television: Although privately funded, al Jazeera (www.aljazeera.com) has grown in size and reputation from a regional TV Channel, to an international broadcaster with an English language service that was launched in 2006 and video streaming supplied over the Internet. The state television runs three channels, including one for the Koran channel and two others in Arabic and English channel. Cable satellite TV is also available throughout Qatar and offers some 20 channels.

Advertising

Advertising is available in the press, on commercial TV and in cinemas.

Economy

Since the discovery of oil in 1939, Qatar's economic development has been largely based on the hydrocarbons sector and has resulted in its citizens being in the world's top 10 highest per capita income bracket. As a relatively small oil producer, the country is vulnerable to shifts in the international oil market, however record prices have given it large windfall payments since 2004. Hydrocarbon earnings contribute over 60 per cent of GDP, making the country's economy reliant on the continuation of the oil and gas industry. Record gas exports and oil prices have driven export revenue resulting in significant trade surpluses and foreign reserves.

The economy, which grew by 5.5 per cent in 2005 and GDP growth is estimated to be 7.1 per cent in 2006. Inflation has been climbing since 2003 and was 8.8 per cent in 2005, but is estimated to have fallen to 7.8 per cent in 2006.

Industrial production accounts for 77 per cent of GDP, of which manufacturing was only 8 per cent while services contributes 23 per cent.

Contracts to build a US$5 billion airport were signed in 2004 and phase one of the airport construction is due for completion in 2009. This large investment will be an impetus for growth and possibly assist the country's diversification strategy by encouraging tourism.

A US$6 billion project to build a liquefied natural gas plant in Qatar will boost the country's gas earnings even further. Investments in refining and petrochemical development have been agreed between Qatar Petroleum and US ExxonMobil, with the signing of an agreement in 2005, to build the world's largest petrochemical plant. The US$2 billion plant is expected to produce around 1.6 million tonnes of ethylene per annum and to be completed in 2010.

To improve the country's long-term prospects, the government has introduced incentives to encourage diversification towards the non-oil sector, in particular light industry. It has also relaxed its restrictive policies on foreign investment and encouraged stronger private investment.

Although key personnel involved in all projects must be Qatari, the foreign investment law implemented in 2000 allows 100 per cent foreign equity in most commercial sectors, including agriculture, manufacturing, healthcare, education, tourism, power and water plants and mining.

External trade

In 2005 the Greater Arab Free Trade Area (Gafta) was ratified by 17 members, including Qatar, creating an Arab economic bloc. A customs union was established whereby tariffs within Gafta will be reduced by a percentage each year, until none remain.

Qatar has the world's largest liquefied natural gas (LNG) processing facility which exports over 31 million tonnes per annum. It has other heavy industrial processing sites producing fertilizers and petrochemicals and a steel plant.

Imports

Principal imports are machinery and vehicles, manufactured goods and building materials, foodstuffs and live animals, (virtually everything – except concrete and steel bars – has to be imported).

Main sources: France (13.3 per cent total, 2006), Japan (10.1 per cent), US (9.3 per cent).

Exports

Exports are dominated by LNG, crude oil, petroleum products, fertilisers and steel.

Main destinations: Japan (39.8 per cent total, 2006), South Korea (18.6 per cent), Singapore (6.4 per cent).

Agriculture

Farming

The agricultural sector in 2004 only contributed 0.2 per cent to GDP; it employs 1 per cent of the workforce. The country is 70 per cent self-sufficient in summer vegetables and 40 per cent in winter vegetables; 25 per cent in dairy produce and 10 per cent in cereals. Other crops include fruit, dates, fodder crops and cereals.

All agricultural land in Qatar is owned by the government, which is keen to support and encourage agricultural production. However, this is limited by the scarcity of water and the unfavourable terrain. In 2005 a new industrial project was begun in Ras Laffan, it will provide a desalination plant as part of the plan and may be used in irrigation. Only about 8,000 hectares of the estimated 65,000 hectares of cultivable land (5.7 per cent of the total land area) is farmed.

Major emphasis is placed on educating the population in agricultural techniques, experimenting with new methods of cultivation and developing better marketing structures.

One project considered vital to long-term productivity is experimental cultivation of crops on sand using solar energy and sea water. In April 2003, the Islamic Development Bank approved a US$24 million loan to Qatar to finance a soya bean scheme.

Crop production for 2005 included: 6,785 tonnes (t) cereals in total, 5,250t barley, 1,500t maize, *800t citrus fruit, 30t grapes, *3,500t eggplants, 260t chilies and peppers, 5,000t tomatoes, *17,000t dates, *200t figs, 18,380t fruit in total, 38,390t vegetables in total. Livestock production included: 12,822t meat in total, 1,090t camel meat, *324t beef, 5,850t lamb, 658t goat meat, 4,900t poultry, *5,000t eggs, 31,850t milk, 780t sheepskins.

* estimate

Fishing

Fish catches meet 70 per cent of demand. Fish stocks have declined as a result of water pollution.

In 2004, the total marine fish catch was 11,036 tonnes and the total crustacean catch was 77 tonnes.

Industry and manufacturing

The industrial sector contributes 7.6 per cent of GDP; it employs around 25 per cent of the working population.

Non-oil, heavy industry, often developed as state-owned joint ventures, received the bulk of government investment in industry and now contributes about 9 per cent of national revenues. The government offers incentives to encourage private sector development of light industry. Industries include the production of intermediate building materials (cement, concrete, moulded aluminium, marble tiles and paving stone), food processing, freezing and packaging, paper products, batteries, paint, plastics, detergents, lubricants, household utensils and furniture. The government has pledged to spend US$110 million in industrial plant development, most of which is concentrated in the industrial city of Messaieed.

Tourism

Tourism is being developed as part of the government's programme of economic diversification. Qatar is promoted as an up-market destination, with the emphasis on resorts, festivals, shopping, conferencing, culture and sport. A master plan, announced in May 2004, will channel massive investment into the creation of the facilities and infrastructure, with the aim of increasing visitor numbers from around 400,000 to 1 million by 2010. Several luxury hotels have been opened since 2000. Construction work in connection with the Asian Games, which Qatar will host in 2006 has already boosted the sector. A new international airport at Doha, scheduled for completion by 2015, is envisaged as a regional gateway.

Travel and tourism is expected to contribute US$1 billion in 2005, or 4.2 per cent, to GDP and employ 21.8 per cent of all workers. The sector is estimated to have attracted 11.1 per cent of total capital investment in 2005, of US$633 million. Tourism generates around 18 per cent of total export revenue and is a growth industry.

Environment

Among the proposals to meet the country's water shortage are the construction of a 700km pipeline from the Karun River in northern Iran to Qatar, as well as the development of more desalination plants.

Hydrocarbons

The hydrocarbons sector contributes around 55 per cent to GDP. Oil reserves stood at 15.2 billion barrels in 2004 and are expected to last until 2030 at the latest. The largest reserves of crude oil are found onshore, particularly at the Dukhan oil field, which produces around half of Qatar's total oil output. Production stood at 785,000 barrels per day (bpd) in 2004. All oil operations are nationalised under the Qatar General Petroleum Company (QGPC). About 80 per cent of crude output is exported under contract to Japan.

The government entered into a number of production sharing agreements (PSAs) with companies such as Chevron and BP Amoco after the oil sector was opened up to foreign investment in 1995.

Proven natural gas reserves stood at around 25.8 trillion cubic metres in 2004, with annual natural gas production at 39.2 billion cubic metres. Qatar possesses nearly 6 per cent of the world's proven gas reserves, concentrated largely in the massive North Field, off the north-east coast, which is the largest known non-associated gas field in the world.

In 2003, Qatar Petroleum opened its fourth liquid natural gas (LNG) plant, which has a capacity of 2,900 tonnes per day (tpd) of ethane, 2,700tpd of propane, 1,900tpd of butane and 708tpd of natural gas liquid condensates. According to the government, the opening of the plant doubled the output of its gas-related products. Two other LNG plants are run by Qatar LNG Company (QatarGas) and Ras Laffan LNG Company with long-term contracts supplying LNG to Japan, South Korea, and Spain. Contracts for other destinations are in negotiation.

Qatar does not produce or import coal.

Energy

Qatar has an electricity generation capacity of 1,880MW. As a result of rapidly rising demand, the government has embarked on a process of restructuring the electricity sector with an emphasis on attracting foreign investment. It has also sought to prevent rampant electricity demand by limiting free residential electricity and charging for electricity consumption exceeding a certain predetermined level.

The Ras Abu Fontas power station has been re-furbished with increased generating capacity of 1,030MW. A new power plant in the Ras Laffan industrial complex began operations in May 2004 with a generating capacity of 750MW. Independent power projects (IPPs) are likely to increase in number as the government seeks to inject foreign investment into the electricity sector.
The Qatar General Electricity and Water Company (QEWC) is part-privatised and is 43 per cent owned by the state with the rest owned by Qatari investors.
Solar energy is being developed in conjunction with desalination.

Financial markets
In 2005 government plans to develop a regional financial services centre were agreed. Initially the centre will provide Qatar-based project financing, bond insurance and asset management to financial institutions and allow them to enter the liquefied natural gas markets. A regulator was appointed to the post of head of the financial services centre in March 2005.

Stock exchange
The Doha Securities Market became operational in 1996 and the stock exchange was opened in 1997; foreigners were allowed to trade in 2000. The market is dominated by banks, which account for around 50 per cent of trading activity. Services account for around 40 per cent of trading.

Banking and insurance
The banking sector consists of 15 commercial banks, including seven locally owned banks. There are 12 insurance companies, the majority of which are foreign-owned; the largest is the locally-owned Qatar Insurance Company.

Central bank
The Qatar Central Bank (QCB)

Main financial centre
Doha

Time
GMT plus three hours

Geography
Qatar occupies a peninsula, projecting northwards from the Arabian mainland, on the west coast of the Gulf. It is bordered, to the south by Saudi Arabia and the United Arab Emirates. The archipelago of Bahrain lies to the north-west. On the opposite side of the Gulf lies Iran.
The terrain consists primarily of sand dunes laid over flat rocky areas or salt flats, with some limestone outcrops, particularly in the west around Dukhan and in the north around Fuwairit.

Hemisphere
Northern

Climate
Desert climate with extremely hot and humid summers, when temperatures can reach 44 degrees Celsius from July–September, and mild winters with occasional rainfall.

Entry requirements

Passports
Required by all.

Visa
Required by all; except nationals of neighbouring countries.
For all others, requirements are subject to change and it is advisable to contact an embassy of Qatar for up-to-date information. Business and tourist visas (valid for 21 days) may be obtained on arrival. However, obtaining a visa in advance will save time.

Prohibited entry
Holders of passports issued by Israel.

Currency advice/regulations
There are no exchange restrictions. Israeli currency is prohibited.

Customs
Personal effects are duty-free. Certain goods (firearms, ammunition, drugs and alcohol) may only be imported under licence.
Import of pork and pork products, cultured pearls, and obscene or seditious literature is forbidden.
Importers must register with the Controller of Companies and appear on the Chamber of Commerce's register of importers. All foodstuffs must be labelled in Arabic.

Prohibited imports
Alcohol, even for personal consumption.

Health (for visitors)

Mandatory precautions
Vaccination certificate against yellow fever if travelling from infected area.

Advisable precautions
Inoculations and boosters should be current for tetanus, polio, typhoid and hepatitis A. There may be a need for vaccinations for tuberculosis, diphtheria and hepatitis B. In border areas with Saudi Arabia rabies is considered high risk and therefore any animal or bat bites should be assessed carefully.
A supply of any regular medicines required should be taken, with their prescription details; medical insurance, which includes emergency evacuation, is recommended.

Hotels
There is a large selection of first-class hotels. Tax of 15 per cent is added to the bill.

Credit cards
Major credit cards are accepted.

Public holidays (national)

Fixed dates
27 Jun (Accession of the Emir), 3 Sep (Independence Day), 31 Dec (banks only).

Variable dates
Eid al Adha (five days), Islamic New Year, Eid al Fitr (four days),
Islamic year – 1429 (10 Jan 2008–28 Dec 2008): The Islamic year has 354 or 355 days, with the result that Muslim feasts advance by 10–12 days against the Gregorian calendar each year. Dates of the Muslim feasts vary according to sightings of the new moon, so cannot be forecast exactly.

Working hours
Friday is the official weekend holiday. During Ramadan, the Muslim holy month of fasting during daylight hours, most officials work 0900–1300.

Banking
Sat–Wed: 0730–1330.

Business
Sat–Thu: 0800–1200, 1600–1900.

Government
Sat–Thu: 0700–1400.

Shops
Sat–Thu: 0830–1230, 1630–2030; Fri: most shops are closed, although some supermarkets are open.

Telecommunicationses
There is a 900/1800 GSM service available throughout the country.

Electricity supply
220/240V AC, with three-pin flat plug fittings most common.

Weights and measures
Metric system; other weights are still in use, however.

Social customs/useful tips
Correspondence and technical literature is acceptable in English.
At business meetings it is not uncommon for several people to be present. While in negotiations be careful about committing yourself orally. In a traditional Muslim Sharia Court, oral evidence carries far more weight than written. You should also be aware that you will be held to the letter of any agreement.
Keep contracts as simple as possible; the main part should be couched in easily translated terms with detailed ramifications of the deal relegated to annexes. Amendments should be avoided as they are considered dishonourable. Increasingly, be prepared to consider contracts under local law – with the provision of neutral (ie Swiss, Dutch) arbitration.
In public places, women should dress modestly.
Refrain from taking photographs without permission.

Pork should not be eaten in the presence of Muslims. It is polite to avoid eating, drinking or smoking in front of Muslims, during daylight hours in the month of Ramadan (when such consumption in public is illegal).

The purchase of alcohol is restricted to expatriate residents with a special liquor permit (not available to Muslims) and its consumption is confined to their private homes. Alcohol is a particularly sensitive subject in Qatar and the utmost discretion must be shown at all times by those permitted to consume it.

Getting there

Air

National airline: Qatar Airways

International airport/s: Doha International (DOH), 8km from city, with restaurant, bank, hotel reservations, shops, car hire.

A taxi from the airport to the city centre takes about 15 minutes. The larger hotels will send transport to the airport to collect their guests.

Airport tax: None

Surface

Road: Tarmac roads link all towns and villages in Qatar with Saudi Arabia. It is also possible to enter by good roads from the UAE.

Main port/s: Passenger services through Mina Salman, Mina Manama and Mina Muharroq, with ferries to Iran and Bahrain.

Getting about

National transport

Road: There are more than 1,000km of good roads (some dual carriageway), with a ring road system around Doha.

The Trans-Arabian Highway which links Doha with Saudi Arabia provides a continuous land connection between Qatar and Europe. Another highway which was build in conjunction with the UAE, links Qatar with the Gulf countries' network.

Buses: Doha's public bus service provides transport to and from the neighbouring towns. There is no public transport within the city.

City transport

Taxis: Taxis are orange and white and have black-on-yellow number plates, with metered fares.

Two-tier (day and night) fare system applies within the Doha city limits. They can be hired on a time basis, with a set hourly rate.

Some hotels offer a courtesy pick-up service; others offer the service but charge. A limousine can be booked through the hotel.

Car hire

If hiring for more than seven days, it is necessary to obtain a 30-day local licence – international or foreign licences are not acceptable. For this, a foreign or international licence, a letter from a local sponsor and passport must be produced within a week of arrival, and a test on road signs may be required. Third-party insurance is compulsory.

Speed limits are 60kph in cities and 100kph on highways. Traffic drives on the right.

Air-conditioned cars are available for hire, with a driver, and can be delivered to the airport or hotel.

BUSINESS DIRECTORY

The addresses listed below are a selection only. While World of Information makes every endeavour to check these addresses, we cannot guarantee that changes have not been made, especially to telephone numbers and area codes. We would welcome any corrections.

Telephone area codes

The international dialling code (IDD) for Qatar is +974, followed by subscriber's number.

Useful telephone numbers

Emergency (all services): 999
International operator: 150
Directory enquiries: 180
International enquiries: 190
Telegram service: 130
Speaking clock (English): 140
Ship to shore: 864-444

Chambers of Commerce

Qatar Chamber of Commerce and Industry, PO Box 402, Doha, (tel: 455-9111; fax: 466-1693; email: infor@qcci.org; internet: www.qcci.org).

Banking

Al Ahli Bank of Qatar, PO Box 2309, Doha (tel: 4326-611; fax: 4444-652).

Al Mashriq, PO Box 173, Doha (tel: 4413-213; fax: 4413-880).

Arab Bank Ltd., PO Box 172, Doha (tel: 4437-979; fax: 4410-774).

Bank Saderat Iran, PO Box 2256, Doha (tel: 4414-646; fax: 4428-077).

Banque Paribas, PO Box 2636, Doha (tel: 4433-844; fax: 4410-861).

Bank Sederat Iran, PO Box 2256, Doha (tel: 4414-646; fax: 4430-121).

Bank of Oman Ltd., PO Box 173, Doha (tel: 4413-213; fax: 4413-800).

Commercial Bank of Qatar Ltd, PO Box 3232, Doha (tel: 4490-222; fax: 4438-182).

Doha Bank, PO Box 3818, Doha (tel: 4456-660; fax: 4416-631).

Grindlays Qatar Bank, PO Box 2001, Doha (tel: 4425-466; fax: 4428-077).

HSBC Bank of the Middle East, PO Box 57, 810 Abdulla bin Jassim Street, Doha (tel: 4438-2100; fax: 4416-353).

Qatar Industrial Development Bank, PO Box 22789, Doha (tel: 4421-600; fax: 4416-631).

Qatar International Islamic Bank, PO Box 664, Doha (tel: 4409-409; fax: 4444-101).

Qatar Islamic Bank, PO Box 559, Doha (tel: 4438-000; fax: 4412-700).

Qatar National Bank, PO Box 1000, Doha (tel: 4407-407; fax: 4413-753; e-mail: webmaster@qatarbank.com).

Standard Chartered Bank, PO Box 29, Doha (tel: 4414-252; fax: 4413-739).

United Bank Ltd, PO Box 242, Doha (tel: 4438-666; fax: 4424-600).

Central bank

Qatar Central Bank, Corniche Street; PO Box 1234, Doha (tel: 445-6456; email: webmaster@qcb.gov.qa; internet: www.qcb.gov.qa).

Travel information

Doha International Airport information (tel: 4438-111).

Gulf Air, PO Box 138, Manama, Bahrain (tel: (+973) 322-200; fax: (+973) 440-466).

Qatar Airways, Almana Tower, PO Box 22550, Doha (tel: 4430-707; fax: 4352-433).

Qatar National Hotels Co, PO Box 2977, Doha (tel: 4426-414; fax: 4431-223).

Ministry of tourism

National tourist organisation offices

Qatar Tourism Authority, P.O. Box 24624, Doha (tel: 441-1555; fax: 437-2993; email: info@experienceqatar.com; internet: http://experienceqatar.com)

Ministries

Ministry of Amiri Diwan Affairs, PO Box 923, Doha (tel: 4468-333; fax: 4412-617).

Ministry of Communications and Transport, PO Box 3416, Doha (tel: 4464-000; fax: 4413-886).

Ministry of Defence, PO Box 37, Doha (tel: 4604-111; fax: 4608-366).

Ministry of Education, PO Box 80, Doha (tel: 4333-444; fax: 4413-954).

Ministry of Electricity and Water, Department of Electricity, PO Box 41, Doha (tel: 4326-622; fax: 4426-608).

Ministry of Endowments and Islamic Affairs, PO Box 232, Doha (tel: 4452-222).

Ministry of Finance, PO Box 83, Doha (tel: 446-1444; fax: 441-3617).

Ministry of Foreign Affairs, PO Box 250, Doha (tel: 4334-334; fax: 4442-777).

Ministry of Information and Culture, PO Box 1836, Doha (tel: 4831-333; fax: 4831-518).

Ministry of Interior, PO Box 920, Doha (tel: 4430-000; fax: 44330-168); Passport and Immigration Division, PO Box 122, Doha (tel: 4443-300); Police Headquarters, PO Box 920, Doha (tel: 4330-000); Police Traffic Division, PO Box 8989, Doha (tel: 4868-000; fax: 4872-624); Residence Permits, PO Box 122, Doha (tel: 4325-588); Visa Section, PO Box 122, Doha (tel: 4328-129).

Ministry of Justice, PO Box 2377, Doha (tel: 4435-777; fax: 4832-868).

Ministry of Labour, Social Affairs and Housing, PO Box 201, Doha (tel: 4321-955; fax: 4432-929).

Ministry of Municipal and Agricultural Affairs, PO Box 2727, Doha (tel: 4336-336; fax: 4430-239).

Ministry of Public Health, PO Box 42, Doha (tel: 4441-555; fax: 4429-565).

National Oil Distribution Company (NODCO), PO Box 50033, Mesaieed (tel: 4776-555; fax: 4771-232).

Other useful addresses

Broadcasting and Television Corporation, PO Box 1836, Doha (tel: 4831-333; fax: 4831-518).

Central Tenders Committee, PO Box 1968, Doha (tel: 4413-089; fax: 4439-360).

Department of Civil Aviation, PO Box 3000, Doha (tel: 4426-262; fax: 4429-070).

Department of Commercial Affairs, PO Box 22355, Doha (tel: 4432-103; fax: 4431-412).

Department of Customs, PO Box 81, Doha (tel: 4457-457; fax: 4414-959).

Department of Economic Affairs, PO Box 1968, Doha (tel: 4416-234; fax: 4415-731).

Department of Environmental Affairs, PO Box 7634, Doha (tel: 4320-825; fax: 4415-246).

Department of Financial Affairs, PO Box 83, Doha (tel: 4461-444; fax: 4413-617).

Department of Industrial Development, PO Box 2599, Doha (tel: 4832-121; fax: 4832-024).

Department of Museum and Antiquities, PO Box 2777, Doha (tel: 4438-123).

Department of Post, PO Box 713, Doha (tel: 4835-555; fax: 4837-777).

Department of Safety, Quality and Environment, PO Box 47, Doha (tel: 4402-538; fax: 4402-207).

Department of Water, PO Box 162, Doha (tel: 4494-444).

Doha Securities Market, PO Box 22114, Doha (tel: 4328-025; fax: 4326-497).

Exhibitions Department, PO Box 1968, Doha (tel: 4834-450; fax: 4834-480).

Exploration and Development of New Ventures Department, PO Box 3212, Doha (tel: 4491-288; fax: 4831-850).

Government House, ¡PO Box 83, Doha (tel: 4461-444).

HH the Emir's Doha Palace, PO Box 923 (tel: 4415-888).

Information and Computer Services Department, PO Box 47, Doha (tel: 4402-240; fax: 4413-629).

Al Jazeera Satellite Channel, PO Box 23123, Doha (tel: 4890-890; fax: 4885-333).

Legal Affairs and Contracts Department, PO Box 3212, Doha (tel: 4491-467; fax: 4831-752).

Materials Department, PO Box 47, Doha (tel: 4332-222; fax: 4343-458).

Petroleum Engineering Department, PO Box 47, Doha (tel: 4402-440; fax: 4402-215).

Pharmaceuticals and Medicines Control Department, PO Box 1919, Doha (tel: 4447-828; fax: 4425-399).

Qatar Broadcasting Services, PO Box 3939, Doha (tel: 4894-4444; fax: 4894-202).

Qatari Business Association, PO Box 24475, Doha (435-3120; fax:435-3834).

Qatar Clean Energy Company (QACENCO), PO Box 22074, Doha (tel: 4415-556; fax: 4415-640).

Qatar Embassy (USA), 4200 Wisconsin Avenue, NW, Washington DC 20016 (tel: (+1-202) 274-1603; fax: (+1-202) 237-0061; email: washington@mofa.gov.qa).

Qatar Fertiliser Company (QAFCO), PO Box 50001, Doha (tel: 4770-252; fax: 4771-655).

Qatar Fuel Additives Company (QAFAC), PO Box 22700, Doha (tel: 4433-700; fax: 4433-766).

Qatar General Petroleum Corporation, Headquarters: PO Box 3212, Doha (tel: 4491-491; fax: 4836-999; internet: www.qgpc.com.qa); Oil and Gas Operations: PO Box 47, Doha (tel: 4402-000).

Qatar Liquefied Gas Company (QATARGAS), PO Box 22666, Doha (tel: 4739-400; fax: 4739-423).

Qatar National Cement Company, PO Box 1333, Doha (tel: 4350-800).

Qatar Petrochemical Company (QAPCO), PO Box 756, Doha (tel: 4321-105; fax: 4324-700).

Qatar Public Telecommunications Corp, PO Box 217, Doha (tel: 4400-333; fax: 4413-904).

Qatar Steel Company Ltd, PO Box 50090, Doha (tel: 4770-011; fax: 4771-424).

Qatar Television, PO Box 1944, Doha (tel: 4894-444; fax: 4438-316).

Ras Laffan Liquefied Natural Gas Company, PO Box 2400, Doha (tel: 4859-400; fax: 4833-855).

State Audit Bureau, PO Box 2466, Doha (tel: 4441-000; fax: 4412-101).

Qatar Financial Centre, PO Box 23245, Doha (tel: 4945-508; fax: 4830-928; email: info@qfc.com.qa, website: www.qfc.com.qa).

Qatar Financial Centre Regulatory Authority, PO Box 22989, Doha (tel: 4945-433; fax: 4835-031; email: info@qfcra.com.qa, website: www.qfcra.com.qa).

National news agency: Qatar News Agency

Internet sites

Arab net: www.arab.net/welcome.html

Arabia on line: www.arabia.com

Gulf business explorer: www.igulf.com/main.htm

Qatar Investment Promotion Department: www.investinqatar.com.qa

Qatar website: www.dib-qatar.com

Qatar yellow pages: www.qatar-yellowpages.com

Réunion

KEY FACTS

Official name: La Réunion

Head of State: President of France Nicolas Sarkozy represented by Préfet Pierre-Henry Maccioni (from Aug 2006)

Head of government: President of the Conseil Général Nassimah Dindar (since 2004; re-elected March 2008); President of the Conseil Régional Paul Vergès (since Mar 1998)

Ruling party: Coalition led by Mouvement Démocrate (MoDem) (Democratic Movement), with Parti Socialiste (PS) (Socialist Party), Parti Communiste de Réunion (PCR) (Réunion Communist Party), Union pour un Mouvement Populaire (UMP) (Popular Movement Union) (from 24 Mar 2008)

Area: 2,512 square km

Population: 787,400 (2005)*

Capital: Saint Denis

Official language: French

Currency: Euro (eur) = 100 cents

Exchange rate: eur0.63 per US$ (Jul 2008)

GDP per capita: US$6,200 PPP (2005)

GDP real growth: 2.50% (2005)

Labour force: 309,900 (2003)

Unemployment: 36.00% (2003)

Balance of trade: -US$2.29 billion (2003)

Visitor numbers: 279,000 (2006)*

* estimated figure

COUNTRY PROFILE

Historical profile

The island was uninhabited until the beginning of the seventeenth century when Arab explorers called it Diva Margabin. The Portuguese renamed it Ilha Santa Apolonia and the French settlers called it l'Île Bourbon. After the French Revolution it was given its current name, La Réunion.

1642 The island was first occupied by France and was ruled as a colony.

1946 La Réunion became a French Département d'Outre-Mer (DOM) (Overseas Department).

1973 The headquarters of French military forces in the Indian Ocean was established on the island.

1974 La Réunion was further incorporated into the French political system and granted the status of region of France.

1983 France granted autonomy in the administration of La Réunion through devolution, establishing a Regional Council.

1992 A contentious newcomer to local politics, Camille Sudre, the owner of a pirate television station, created the Free-DOM party, which won the largest block of seats in the Regional Council. The result was annulled when Sudre's TV broadcasts for his party were deemed political propaganda.

1993 The Free-DOM party led by Camille Sudre's wife, Marguerite, won the elections with a reduced majority.

1996 Unemployment reached 40 per cent.

1998 Paul Vergés was elected head of the regional council.

2001 Gonthier Friederici became préfet.

2002 La Réunion adopted the euro as its official currency.

2004 There was volcanic activity at Piton de la Fournaise on 9 January. On 16 August, Dominique Vian took office as préfet.

2005 Laurent Cayrel was appointed préfet on 29 June.

2006 On 19 June, Pierre-Henry Maccioni was appointed préfet. The mosquito-borne chikungunya disease, which broke out in 2005, afflicted an estimated one-third of the population and killed several hundred by 2006; the tourist industry suffered a sharp downturn and the French army sanitisation crews were drafted in to spray insecticide.

2007 On 16 May, Nicolas Sarkozy became head of state and president of the French Republic.

2008 In March local elections Nassimah Dindar was re-elected Conseil Général. She organised a broad spectrum political coalition including the Mouvement Démocrate (MoDem) (Democratic Movement) with Parti Socialiste (PS) (Socialist Party), Parti Communiste de Réunion (PCR) (Réunion Communist Party), Union pour un Mouvement Populaire (UMP) (Popular Movement Union) and other various small, right-wing groupings.

Political structure

Constitution

28 September 1958 (French Fifth Republic)

Under the 1946 constitution of the French Fourth Republic, La Réunion became a Département d'Outre-Mer (DOM) (Overseas Department) of France. In 1974, it was granted additional status as a region of France.

La Réunion is represented in the French National Assembly in Paris by five directly elected deputies and in the Senate by three indirectly elected senators.

Since 1983, following the French government's policy of decentralisation, regional councils have been elected with powers similar to those of the regions.

Administration is by a préfét appointed by the government in Paris.

The local government comprises a Conseil Général (General Council) of 44 members and a 45-member Conseil Régional (Regional Council), both directly elected for six-year terms.

There are five arrondisements.

Form of state

Democratic, presidential republic Département d'Outre-Mer (DOM) (Overseas Department) of France, with additional status as a région (region) of France.

The executive

A préfet, appointed from Paris, governs the locally elected Conseil Général (General Council).

National legislature

La Réunion is represented in the French National Assembly by five directly elected deputies, for five-year terms and in the Senate by three indirectly elected senators for three-year terms.

Since 1983, the local regional Conseil Général (General Council) has been elected with powers similar to those of mainland regions of France.

The local government comprises a Conseil Régional (regional council) with

45 members, elected for four-year terms by proportional representation.

Legal system
French legal system

Last elections
March 2004 (Conseil Général and Conseil Régional)

Next elections
2010 (Conseil Général and Conseil Régional)

Political parties
Free-DOM (right-wing group); Parti Communiste de Réunion (PCR) (Réunion Communist Party); Rassemblement pour la République (RPR) (Gaullist Rally for the Republic); two factions of the Parti Socialiste (PS) (Socialist Party); Union pour la France (UPF) (Union for France); Union pour la Démocratie Française-Centre Démocratique Sociale (UDF-CDS) (Union for French Democracy-Social Democratic Centre).

Ruling party
Coalition led by Mouvement Démocrate (MoDem) (Democratic Movement), with Parti Socialiste (PS) (Socialist Party), Parti Communiste de Réunion (PCR) (Réunion Communist Party), Union pour un Mouvement Populaire (UMP) (Popular Movement Union) (from 24 Mar 2008)

Population
787,400 (2005)*
Last census: March 1999: 706,180
Population density: 262 inhabitants per square km. Urban population: 69 per cent.
Annual growth rate: 1.8 per cent (2003)

Ethnic make-up
African (64 per cent), Indian (28 per cent), European (2.2 per cent) and Chinese (2.2 per cent) descent.

Religions
The majority of the population is Roman Catholic (86 per cent); there are also groups of Hindus, Muslims and Buddhists.

Education
Literacy rate: 89 per cent, adult rate (2003)

Health
Health services comply with French standards, there are some 1,270 doctors, 275 pharmacies and 17 hospitals, including clinics.
Life expectancy: 73.4 years (estimate 2003)
Fertility rate/Maternal mortality rate: 2.5 births per woman (2003)
Birth rate/Death rate: 20 births per 1,000 population; 5.5 deaths per 1,000 population (2003).
Child (under 5 years) mortality rate (per 1,000): Eight per 1,000 live births (2003)

Main cities
Saint Denis (capital, estimated population 140,415 in 2005), Saint Paul (100,849), Saint Pierre (76,900), Le Tampon (69,043), Saint Louis, Le Port, Saint André.

Languages spoken
As well as French, Creole is commonly spoken.

Official language/s
French

Media
Other news agencies: Imaz Press Réunion, (tel: 200-656; email: fax: 200-549; email: ipr@ipreunion.com; internet: www.ipreunion.com).

Press
In French, Le Journal de L'Ile (www.clicanoo.com) and Temoignages (www.temoignages.re) are published daily in St Denis. Regional publications, in English, include APA (www.apanews.net) and Panapress (www.panapress.com).

Broadcasting
RFO Réunion (http://reunion.rfo.fr) is the pubic broadcasting network providing radio and television programmes originating from France. The private TV station Antenne Réunion Télévision (www.antennereunion.fr) provides a range of local news and international programmes. All broadcasts are in French.

News agencies
Other news agencies: Imaz Press Réunion, (tel: 200-656; email: fax: 200-549; email: ipr@ipreunion.com; internet: www.ipreunion.com).

Economy
La Réunion is dependent on France for 75 per cent of its GNP.
Sugar cane used to dominate the economy, accounting for up to 85 per cent of export earnings, but the dependence on agriculture made the country vulnerable to external price fluctuations, and adverse climatic conditions. The government has been looking at ways to diversify the economy, focussing on tourism.
The service sector has grown considerably and provides around three quarters of GDP, with agriculture shrinking and providing only 8 per cent of total GDP.
In December 2003, the EU approved French air transport subsidies for Réunion, which should help boost tourist numbers.
GDP growth was 2.5 per cent in 2004, less than the 3.8 per cent in 2003. Although social indicators are good, unemployment is a pressing problem affecting almost 40 per cent of the labour force.
There is a great income and social divide between the majority of the population, which is impoverished and black, and the rich minority, which is white or Indian.

External trade
As a département d'outre-mer (DOM) of France, Réunion is integrated as an outermost region of the European Union and adopts all EU trade agreements.

Imports
The main imports are manufactured goods, food, beverages, tobacco, machinery and transportation equipment, raw materials, and petroleum products.
Main sources: France (64 per cent), Bahrain (3.0 per cent), Germany (3.0 per cent), Italy (3.0 per cent)

Exports
The main export is sugar (over 60 per cent), rum and molasses, perfume essences and lobster.
Main destinations: France (74 per cent), Japan (6.0 per cent), Comoros (4.0 per cent)

Agriculture
Farming
Sugar cane, the main crop, is grown on 30,900 hectares. Cash crops include tea and tobacco. Ylang-ylang, vetiver and geraniums are used as components of aromatic essences.
The agriculture sector contributes about 8 per cent to GDP and employs approximately 13 per cent of the workforce.
Around 22 per cent of the land is cultivated. Much of the island's food supply is imported.
Estimated crop production in 2005 included: 17,000 tonnes (t) maize, 3,700t potatoes, 600t cassava, 1,800t bananas, 2,000,000t sugar cane, 5,350t citrus fruit, 1,100t pulses, 4,000t tomatoes, 6,150t roots and tubers, 10,000t pineapples, 1,035t various spices, 42,460t fruit in total, 51,020t vegetables in total. Estimated livestock production included: 35,100t meat in total, 1,750t beef, 94t lamb and goat meat, 12,000t pig meat, 2,016t rabbit meat, 19,227t poultry, 5,700t eggs, 23,300t milk, 100t honey.

Fishing
Typical annual fish catches are over 4,000mt and crustacea catches are over 15mt.
In 2004, the total marine fish catch was 3,101 tonnes and the total crustacean catch was 12 tonnes.

Industry and manufacturing
The industrial sector contributes about 19 per cent to GDP and employs some 12 per cent of the workforce.
The production of processed sugar and rum accounts for most industrial activity. The Ecopipe steel pipe mill (funded by the French government and South African private capital) started operations in 1997 at Le Port, on the west coast of Réunion. It has the capacity to produce 15,000 tonnes a year and employs 80 people.

Tourism
Tourism is now the principal economic activity. As a département of France, the majority of visitors tend to be French. Numbers fell as a consequence of the 11 September 2001 terrorist attacks in the US, when worldwide travel dropped. In 2003 recovery was under way with 432,000 tourist arrivals recorded. La Réunion's link with France gives its tourism sector an edge, in the European market, over its local rivals.
Air Austral is able to offer the cheapest flights from Europe to the region, while the island's currency is the euro.

Mining
There are no significant mineral resources.

Hydrocarbons
There are no hydrocarbon reserves and Réunion relies entirely on the import of refined oil, including gasoline, jet fuel and distillate. Import costs are generally high as they come from France.
Distribution and marketing of fuel products is carried out by Esso, Total, Caltex, SRPP, Shell and Elf.

Energy
Approximately 60 per cent of the power is hydroelectric. Réunion has one thermal power plant that runs on imported coal. This produces around 39 per cent of Réunion's electricity needs. Réunion does not import or consume natural gas.

Banking and insurance
Central bank
Banque de France; European Central Bank (ECB).

Time
GMT plus four hours

Geography
Réunion is an island in the Indian Ocean, lying about 800km (500 miles) east of Madagascar. It is a volcanic, mountainous island.
Hemisphere
Southern

Climate
The climate varies greatly according to altitude: at sea-level, it is tropical, with average temperatures between 20 and 28 degrees Celsius (C); in the uplands, it is much cooler, with average temperatures between 8 and 19 degrees C. From July to November, the temperature in high altitude places can drop to 10 degrees C during the day and to 6 degrees C at night.
Rainfall is abundant; the cyclone season lasts from December to April.
Summer runs from November to April with an average temperature of 27 degrees C. Winter stretches from May to October with an average temperature of 23 degrees C.

Dress codes
Generally light summer clothes are required, with some woollen garments for chilly evenings.

Entry requirements
Passports
Required by all, except nationals of EU/EEA countries, Monaco, Switzerland with national identity cards; passports must be valid for three months beyond date of departure,
Visa
Required by all, except nationals of EU/EEA countries, North America, Australasia, Japan, Israel and some other countries for stays up to three months. Nationals of the US, Canada and several other countries need a visa if they receive a salary. Nationals of EU/EEA countries, the Vatican, Liechtenstein and Monaco do not require long-term visas issued for stays in excess of three months. Proof of adequate funds for stay, an itinerary, a guarantee of repatriation if necessary, return/onward ticket and, for business travellers, an invitation from a local company or organisation are also required. .
Currency advice/regulations
There are no restrictions on the import or export of local and foreign currenc, subject to declaration of amounts over eur7,600.

Health (for visitors)
There are no compulsory vaccinations. Passengers from endemic countries should be inoculated against yellow fever.
Advisable precautions
Vaccinations for diphtheria, tetanus, typhoid fever, hepatitis A and tuberculosis are advisable, and precautions should be taken against malaria. Malaria and chikungunya are caused by mosquitoes, precautions including mosquito repellents, nets and clothing covering the body should be used.

Credit cards
Major credit cards are accepted.

Public holidays (national)
Fixed dates
1 Jan (New Year's Day), 1 May (Labour Day), 8 May (1945 Victory Day), 14 Jul (Bastille Day), 15 Aug (Assumption Day), 1 Nov (All Saints' Day), 11 Nov (Armistice Day), 20 Dec (Abolition of Slavery Day), 25 Dec (Christmas Day).
Variable dates
Good Friday, Easter Monday, Ascension Day, Whit Monday.

Working hours
Banking
Mon–Fri: 0800–1600.
Business
Mon–Fri: 0800–1200; 1400–1800.
Government
Mon–Fri: 0800–1900; Sat: 0900–1400.
Shops
Mon–Sat: 0830–1200; 1430–1800.
Some food stores are open on Sunday.

Telecommunications
Telephone/fax
The telephone network is entirely automatic and is linked to metropolitan France and the rest of the world via satellite.
Mobile/cell phones
There are GSM 900 and 1800 services available.

Electricity supply
220V

Weights and measures
The metric system is in use.

Getting there
Air
National airline: Air Austral.
International airport/s: Roland-Garros Airport (RUN), 8km from Saint Denis; post office, restaraunts, duty free shop, car hire.
Other airport/s: Pierrefonds Airport (ZSE), 5km from Saint Pierre.
Airport tax: None..
Surface
Water: There are limited passenger services to Réunion. A cruise liner from Mauritius visits regularly.
Main port/s: Port Réunion.

Getting about
National transport
Road: A route nationale circles the island, following the coast and linking all the main towns, and another crosses the island from south-west to north-east linking Saint Pierre and Saint Benoît. There are 370km of main roads, 754km of secondary roads and nearly 1,600km of smaller secondary roads, all in good condition.
Buses: A comfortable bus service (cars jaunes), links most towns.
Car hire
A French or international driver's licence is required. The highway code is the same as for France. Driving is on the right.

BUSINESS DIRECTORY
The addresses listed below are a selection only. While World of Information makes every endeavour to check these addresses, we cannot guarantee that changes have not been made, especially to telephone numbers and area codes. We would welcome any corrections.

Telephone area codes
The international dialling code (IDD) for Réunion is +262; this is followed by another 262 and then the subscriber's number.

Useful telephone numbers
Available services for visiting cell phone users:
Emergency calls: (free)112
Telephone enquiries: (call SFR for information)222
Suberscriber services: (local rate)900

Chambers of Commerce
Réunion Chamber of Commerce Industry, 13 Rue Pasteur, PO Box 120, 97463 Saint-Denis cedex (tel: 942-100; fax: 942-290; e-mail: sg.dir@reunion.cci.fr).

Banking
Banque de la Réunion, 27 rue Jean Chatel, 97711 Saint Denis, Cedex 9 (tel: 400-157; fax: 400-060).

Banque Nationale de Paris Intercontinentale (BNPI), 67 rue Juliette-Dodu, Saint Denis (tel: 403-030).

Banque Régionale d'Escompte et de Depot (BRED), 33 rue Victor-Mac-Auliffe, Saint Denis (tel: 901-560).

Caisse d'Epargne Ecureuil, 55 rue de Paris, Saint Denis (tel: 948-000).

Crédit Agricole, 18 rue Félix-Guyon, Saint Denis (tel: 909-100).

Banque Française Commerciale (BFC'OI'), 60 rue Alexis-de-Villeneuve, Saint Denis (tel: 405-555).

Central bank
Banque de France, 1 rue la Vrillière, 75001 Paris, Dept 75, France (tel: (+33-1) 4292-4292; fax: (+33-1) 4292-4500)
European Central Bank (ECB), Kaiserstrasse 29, D-60311 Frankfurt am Main, Germany (tel: (+49-69) 13-440; fax: (+49-69) 1344-6000).

Travel information
Air Austral, PO Box 611, 4 Rue de Nice, 97473 Saint Denis Cedex (tel: 909-090; fax: 909-09; e-mail: reservation@air-austral.com).

Air France, PO Box 845, 7 Avenue de la Victoire, 97477 Saint Denis Cedex (tel: 403-800; fax: 403-840; e-mail: mail.runsh@airfrance.fr).

Fédération Réunionnaise du Tourisme, Résidence Sainte Anne, 18 rue Sainte Anne, 97400 Saint Denis (tel : 413-967; fax : 943-180; e-mail: fr-pat@wanadoo.fr).

Maison de la Montagne, 5 rue Rontaunay, 97400 Saint-Denis (tel: 907-878; fax : 418-429; e-mail : resa@reunion-nature.com).

Ministry of tourism
Delegation Régionale au Commerce, à l'Artisanat et Tourisme, Préfecture de la Réunion, 31 rue de Paris, 97400 Saint-Denis

(tel: 319-999; fax: 316-666; e-mail: DRT974@tourisme.gouv.fr).

National tourist organisation offices
Comité du Tourisme de la Réunion, PO Box 615, Place du 20 Décembre 1848, 97472 Saint Denis Cedex (tel: 210-041; fax: 210-021; e-mail: ctr@la-reunion-tourisme.com).

Ministries
Direction Départementale des Affaires Sanitaires et Sociales, Rue Georges Brassens, BP 199, 97490 Sainte-Clothilde (tel: 486-060; fax: 486-008).

Direction Départementale du Travail et de l'Emploi, 24 Rue Maréchal Leclerc, 97488 Saint Denis Cedex (tel: 486-600; fax: 486-666).

Direction Régionale des Affaires Culturelles, 31 Rue Amiral Lacaze 97400 Saint Denis (tel: 219-171; fax: 416-193).

Direction Régionale de la Jeunesse et des Sports, 14 Allée des Saphirs, BP 297, 97487 Saint Denis Cedex (tel: 901-616; fax: 213-864).

Other useful addresses
Agence Nationale pour l'Emploi 10 Rue Champ Fleury, 97490 Sainte Clothilde (tel: 219-236; fax: 417-383).

Association pour le Développement Industriel de la Réunion, 18 Rue Milius, 97468 Saint Denis Cedex (tel: 214-269; fax: 203-757).

British Consul, 94b Avenue Leconte Delisle, 97490 Sainte Clotilde (tel: 291-491; fax: 293-991).

Civil Aviation Management, 11 Avenue de la Victoire, 97489 Saint Denis Cedex (tel: 930-000; fax: 211-331).

Compagnie Générale Maritime (CGM), 2 Rue de l'Est, BP 2010, 97822 Le Port Cedex (tel: 420-088; fax: 432-304).

Conseil Economique et Social de la Réunion, PO Box 7191, 10 Rue du Béarn, 97719 Saint Denis (tel: 979-630; fax: 979-631; e-mail: webmaster@cesr-reunion.fr).

Conseil Général, Hôtel du Département, 2 Rue Source, 97400 Saint Denis (tel: 903-030; fax: 903-999).

Conseil Régional, Hôtel de la Région, Avenue René Cassin, Le Moufia, 97494 Sainte Clothilde Cedex (tel: 487-000; fax: 487-071).

Institut National de la Statistique et des Etudes Economiques, Service Régional de la Réunion, 15 Rue de l'Ecole, 97490 Sainte Clotilde (tel: 295-157).

Palais du Justice, 166 Rue Juliette Dodu, 97488 Saint Denis (tel: 405-858; fax: 219-532).

Rectorat de la Réunion, 24 Avenue Georges, Brassens, 97702 Saint Denis, Messagerie Cedex 9 (tel: 481-010; fax: 481-366).

Société de Développement Economique de la Réunion (SODERE), 26 Rue Labourdonnais, 97469 Saint Denis (tel: 200-168; fax: 200-507).

Internet sites
Africa Business Network: http://www.ifc.org/abn

African Development Bank: http://www.afdb.org

Mbendi AfroPaedia (information on companies, countries, industries and stock exchanges in Africa): http://mbendi.co.za

Romania

KEY FACTS

Official name: Romania

Head of State: President Traian Basescu (PD) (elected 12 Dec 2004)

Head of government: Prime Minister Calin Popescu Tariceanu (PNL) (since Dec 2004)

Ruling party: Coalition (known as Da PNL-PD): Alianta Dreptate si Adevar (DA) (Justice and Truth Alliance) led by Partidul National Liberal (PNL) (National Liberal Party), Partidul Democrat (PD) (Democratic Party), Uniunea Democratica Maghiara din Romania (UDMR) (Hungarian Democratic Alliance of Romania), Partidul Conservator (PC) (Conservative Party) (since 2004)

Area: 237,500 square km

Population: 21.56 million (2007)

Capital: Bucharest

Official language: Romanian

Currency: New leu (plural lei) (Nleu) = 100 ban (New leu introduced 1 Jul 2005; four zeroes removed from old leu; Nleu1 = 10,000 old lei)

Exchange rate: Nleu2.24 per US$ (Jul 2008)

GDP per capita: US$7,697 (2007)*

GDP real growth: 6.00% (2007)*

Labour force: 10.48 million (2004)

Unemployment: 5.60% (2005)

Inflation: 4.80% (2007)

Oil production: 105,000 bpd (2007)

Balance of trade: -US$5.65 billion (2006)

Foreign debt: US$13.70 billion (2003)

* estimated figure

When Romania joined the European Union in January 2007, it was expected to pass EU-mandated anti-graft reforms. Political manoeuvrings, had, however, by mid-2008 prevented the legislation from passing and Romania was better known in the rest of the EU for its corruption than its economic progress. If Romania doesn't bring itself into line, it may face EU penalties, including the withholding of aid payments.

Romania posted a 0.3 per cent budget surplus for the first quarter of 2007, with the economy expected to grow at about 7 per cent for the year, exceeding forecasts, according to the finance minister, Varujan Vosganian. The government had initially forecast a deficit of 1.8 per cent of gross domestic product (GDP), announcing that Romania would not exceed the 3 per cent deficit European Union (EU) target guideline for member states. The EU Economic and Monetary Affairs Commissioner Joaquin Almunia expressed the view that Romania needed to rein in public spending and adhere to stricter fiscal policies, following EU estimates that Romania's budget deficit could reach 3.2 per cent for 2007. In 2007 Romania's economy grew by 6.0 per cent, down on the 7.7 per cent of 2006 when it recorded a budget deficit of 1.9 per cent, compared to 1.4 per cent in 2005.

A Romanian ministry of finance report addressing the country's macroeconomic situation for 2007–10 forecast that Romania's GDP would continue to post a growth rate of more than 5 per cent, but that the trend was expected to be a downward one. After the initial economic growth of 6.4 per cent expected for 2008, the GDP growth rate would decrease to 5.6 per cent in 2010. In the period 2008–10, GDP average growth would be 5.9 per cent, against a background of improved internal and external economic competitiveness, which should result in improved exports. In 2007, the current account deficit was expected to show a decrease to 8.6 per cent, and in 2008 and in 2009 this was expected to return to 8.7 per cent.

When Romania, along with Bulgaria, became a member of the EU it showed it had come a long way since the collapse of the Ceaucescu regime in 1990. Unlike its neighbours to the north, Romania had been ill-prepared for any form of democracy. Such was the oppressiveness of the regime that all intellectual and political activity was effectively stifled. This long-awaited event heralded a future of economic and social modernisation, development, security and integration for the once-communist, still impoverished country. January 2007 is certain to go down in Romanian history as an all-important date.

Politics

The parliamentary and presidential elections in 2004 had resulted in the ruling Partidul Democratiei Sociale din Romania (PDSR) (Democratic Social Party of Romania) winning the greatest proportion of votes in the house of representatives (114 seats), against the opposition coalition (PNL-PD) of the Partidul National Liberal (PNL) (National Liberal Party) and the Partidul Democrat (PD) (Democratic Party) (112 seats) – but neither had won more than the 167 seats needed for an absolute majority. The Partidul România Mare (PRM) (Greater Romania Party) and the Hungarian Democratic Union (HDU) won 48 and 22 seats respectively, and the Partidul Umanist din Romania (PUR) (Humanist Party of Romania) came in with 18 seats. After the election results were announced, the PNL-PD formed a fragmented coalition with the PUR and HDU and minority representatives.

The new coalition government holds a majority in the 136 seat Senate. Presidential elections went to a second round on 12 December, with the PNL-PD candidate Traian Basescu (former Mayor of Bucharest) elected with over 51 per cent of the vote, defeating outgoing prime minister Adrian Nastase. Traian Basescu was sworn in as President of Romania on 20 December 2004. President Basescu selected Mr Calin Popescu-Tariceanu as Prime Minister, who was sworn in along with the new cabinet on 29 December 2004. Prime Minister Tariceanu later resigned, with the announcement 'this is an irrevocable decision'. Less than two weeks later he revoked it. Tariceanu claimed to be re-instating himself in response to the country's heavy flooding. He declared that the country needed stable leadership at this time and promised to rebuild damaged infrastructure.

Oil and gas

Until the development of the North Sea oilfields, Romania was virtually alone as a European oil producer. The exploitation of its oilfields has enabled Romania to develop homegrown skills in petroleum and gas engineering which stand it in good stead. Romanian oil reserves were estimated at 500,000 million barrels at the end on 2007. In 2005, the country domestically produced roughly 115,000 barrels per day (bpd) of its 241,000bpd of consumption; by 2007 production had fallen to 105,000bpd. Romania continues to dominate south-eastern Europe's downstream petroleum industry, with ten of the region's eleven refineries. Because its refining capacity exceeds domestic demand, Romania exports a wide range of oil products and petrochemicals. Romania has privatised several refineries, including Petrotel (majority owned by Russia's LUKoil) and Petromidia (controlled by Dutch Rompetrol Group). LUKoil restarted the 104,000bpd Petrotel refinery in 2004, after two years of necessary upgrades to meet EU fuel standards. In 2006, Romanian oil company Rompetrol announced that it will invest more than US$140 million in its Petromidia refinery over the 2006–08 period in order to increase its capacity

Romania had proven natural gas reserves of some 22.18 trillion cubic feet (Tcf) at the end of 2007. Although it is central and eastern Europe's largest producer of natural gas (11.6 billion cubic metres (Bcf) in 2007), Romania's production has fallen significantly in recent years, making it a net natural gas importer, with supplies coming from Russia along the southbound Progress pipeline. Romania imports about a quarter of its domestic requirements from the Russian company Gazprom, with state-owned company Romgaz supplying over half of the national output.

Currency reform

With optimistic eyes on the eventual adoption of the single currency, the government re-launched the national currency in 2005. The system was streamlined with the removal of four digits. This move should preclude any repeat of the 300 per cent hyperinflation of 1993, after the disintegration of the Soviet Union. The second major financial reform carried out in 2005 was the slashing of taxes. Paradoxically, this move was hoped to generate greater revenue from taxation, as it lessens the incentive for fraud. The black market in Romania was estimated to account for a staggering half of GDP in 2005. In January the government instituted a new uniform income tax rate of 16 per cent, down from 20–40 per cent. With the possible exception of Ireland, no Western country has standardised taxation rates in this way but it is becoming a common practice in ex-communist countries. Estonia, Russia, Georgia, Latvia and Serbia all have a

KEY INDICATORS — Romania

	Unit	2003	2004	2005	2006	2007
Population	m	21.57	21.48	21.71	21.64	21.56
Gross domestic product (GDP)	US$bn	57.37	75.50	98.57	122.65	*165.98
GDP per capita	US$	2,660	3,207	4,539	5,668	*7,697
GDP real growth	%	4.5	8.3	4.1	7.9	*6.0
Inflation	%	15.0	11.9	9.0	6.5	4.8
Unemployment	%	8.9	6.8	5.6	5.5	4.1
Industrial output	% change	–	6.2	4.4	6.0	–
Agricultural output	% change	–	22.2	3.5	3.0	–
Oil output	'000 bpd	123.0	119.0	114.0	105.0	105.0
Natural gas output	bn cum	12.6	13.2	12.9	12.1	11.6
Coal output	mtoe	7.1	6.9	6.5	7.4	9.0
Exports (fob) (goods)	US$m	17,618.0	23,540.0	27,730.0	30,206.0	40,349.0
Imports (cif) (goods)	US$m	23,983.0	28,430.0	37,348.0	35,859.0	64,689.0
Balance of trade	US$m	-6,365.0	-4,890.0	-9,618.0	-5,653.0	-24,340.0
Current account	US$m	-3,900.0	-5,370.0	-8,575.0	-12,748.0	-23,125.0
Total reserves minus gold	US$m	8,040.0	14,616.0	19,872.0	28,066.0	37,194.0
Foreign exchange	US$m	8,040.0	14,616.0	19,872.0	28,066.0	37,194.0
Exchange rate	per US$	33,952.00	32,526.60	2.63	2.58	2.45

* estimated figure

homogenous tax rate. Although the tax generates better rates of compliance, it does also severely restrict opportunities for wealth redistribution.

Outlook

The EU has criticised both Bulgaria and Romania for making insufficient efforts to root out corruption. In July 2008 a tough report commented that 'Romania has started to move in the right direction. The new institutions and processes need time to prove their effectiveness and should be allowed to continue on a steady course'. The report made clear that the European Commission was not threatening to suspend around US$32 billion of aid earmarked from the EU budget for Romania in the EU's 2007–13 budget cycle.

Risk assessment

Politics	Fair
Economy	Good
Regional stability	Fair

COUNTRY PROFILE

Historical profile

1881 After surviving numerous invasions and regional upheavals, Romania became an independent country headed by a monarchy.
1918 Romania supported the Allies during the First World War and gained territory close to its borders.
1919 Hungary attacked Romania in retaliation for lost territory. The Romanians quickly defeated Hungary and briefly occupied parts of the country.
1920 Romania gained further parts of Hungarian territory through the Treaty of Trianon.
1929—34 Romania's agricultural sector was severely affected by a collapse in international grain prices. With the country in recession, the fascist and German-funded Iron Guard movement increased in popularity. In 1933, the organisation assassinated the prime minister, Ion Duca.
1938 King Carol, the head of state, declared Romania a royalist dictatorship and appointed a right-wing government. Carol ordered the arrest and execution of members of the Iron Guard.
1940 Military officers, helped by the Iron Guard, seized power. General Ion Antonescu forced Carol to abdicate. Carol's son, Michel V, replaced him as King. German troops were deployed in Romania and the country joined the Axis powers.
1941 The Iron Guard attempted to rebel against the Romanian government after they were ordered to disarm. A joint Romanian and German operation crushed the Iron Guard's rebellion.
1943 The Soviet Union invaded Romania.
1944 Antonescu's government was overthrown and replaced by a Communist coalition government.
1947—48 The monarchy was deposed and the Communist government declared the Romanian People's Republic.
1965 Nicolae Ceausescu took the position of first secretary of the Partidul Comunist Roman (RCP) (Romanian Communist Party).
1974 Ceausescu became president.
1989 Riots in the city of Timisoara ignited a nationwide revolt. Parts of the army joined the revolutionaries, forming the Frontul Salvarii Nationale (FSN) (National Salvation Front). Ceausescu and his wife, Elena, were summarily executed by a military tribunal and nearly 45 years of Communist dictatorship came to an abrupt and bloody end.
1990 Ion Iliescu was elected president, winning 85 per cent of the vote as the FSN candidate. Petre Roman formed a new government.
1991 Roman resigned as prime minister and was replaced by Teodro Stolojan after his reform programme led to civil unrest. Stolojan successfully guided Romania's new constitution through a referendum and a parliamentary vote.
1992 Presidential elections were again won by Iliescu, who had formed his own political party, the Frontul Democrat al Salvarii Nationale (FDSN) (Democratic National Salvation Front), following a split within the FSN.
1996 Iliescu stood again for the presidency and was defeated by Emil Constantinescu of the Conventia Democrata Romana (CDR) (Romanian Democratic Convention) coalition. The FSN re-named itself the Partidul Democratiei Sociale din Romania (PDSR) (Democratic Social Party of Romania).
1998 After becoming prime minister in 1996, Victor Ciorbea (of the ruling CDR coalition) resigned and was replaced by Radu Vasile.
1999 After relations with his cabinet collapsed, Vasile was replaced as prime minister by Mugur Isarescu.
2000 Cyanide leaked from a mine in northern Romania and polluted rivers in Hungary and Yugoslavia. Ion Iliescu won the presidency in the second round of voting. After parliamentary elections Adrian Nastase became prime minister, heading a coalition government, comprising the PDSR, Partidul Social Democrat Romania (PSDR) (Romanian Social Democratic Party) and the Partidul Umanist din Romania (PUR) (Humanist Party of Romania).
2001 Iliescu's PDSR merged with the PSDR to become the Partidul Social Democrat (PSD) (Social Democratic Party).
2003 A 5 per cent reduction in payroll taxes was implemented in January to cut labour costs, improve the business environment and reduce the rate of unemployment. In a referendum, 90 per cent of voters approved constitutional amendments to bring Romania law in line with EU law.
2004 Romania joined Nato on 2 April. An alliance of four reformist liberal and democrats won the general elections. Bucharest mayor, Traian Basescu of the opposition (Partidul Democrat (PD) Democratic Party – he later resigned as required by the constitution), won the run-off presidential election with 51.2 per cent of the votes against 48.8 per cent for Adrian Nastase (PSD). Basescu appointed Calin Popescu Tariceanu (PNL) as prime minister.
2005 Romania approved the EU accession treaty. The currency was re-valued at the rate of 10,000 old lei to one new leu. Prime Minister Tariceanu and his cabinet resigned. After severe floods killed 20 people, he retracted his resignation in order to focus on the reconstruction of the country.
2006 In September, the EU officially agreed to Romania's membership from 1 January 2007. Curbs on organised crime and corruption and the use of EU funds were among the stipulations imposed and were stronger than those placed on previous accession countries.
2007 On 1 January, Romania joined the EU. On 19 April, President Basescu was suspended by parliament after months of dispute between the president and prime minister, which culminated in supporters of the president within the cabinet being sacked and the prime minister relying on the support of the opposition to govern. Nicolae Vacaroiu was appointed acting president. The EU expressed its concern as President Basescu was seen as a prime opponent of organised crime. On 19 May, in a referendum the motion to impeach President Basescu was defeated by 74.4 per cent of the vote. The Constitutional Court reinstated his presidency on 23 May.

Political structure

Constitution

The 1991 constitution proclaimed a democratic, pluralist system of government in which citizens' freedom and rights are guaranteed, although there are no specific measures protecting minority rights. It also stipulated the separation of the three public authorities – legislative, executive and judicial.

Both parliament and the president are elected by universal vote every four years. The president may not remain a member of any political party, and is limited to a maximum two terms in office.
Members of the Chamber of Deputies are required to be of a minimum age of 23 years while members of the Senate and the president are required to be over 35 years of age.
Romania is divided into 40 administrative counties, with Bucharest divided into administrative sectors. Each county, town and village has its own local authority headed by an elected, executive mayor and an elected council. Local government is based on the principle of local autonomy and decentralisation of public services, with locally elected mayors, city and county councils. A prefect for each county is appointed by central government as the ultimate authority for that region.
The minimum voting age is 18 years.
On 19 October 2003, 90 per cent of voters approved changing the constitution to bring it closer to EU law. Under the constitutional changes, private property is guaranteed, the police is demilitarised and the justice system is independent; ethnic minorities may use their mother tongue when dealing with the state and foreigners are permitted to buy land in Romania.

Form of state

Parliamentary democratic republic

The executive

The president nominates the prime minister and the government on the basis of a vote of confidence from parliament and is the commander-in-chief of the armed forces. The president's term of office is four years, renewable once only.

National legislature

The two-chamber Parlamentul Romaniei (Romanian Parliament) consists of Camera Deputatilor (Chamber of Deputies) (327seats) and a Senatul (Senate) (143 seats) and is the supreme representative body and sole law-making authority. The parliament is elected for a four-year term.

Legal system

The legal system is based on the Napolenic Code and the 1991 constitution. There is an independent judiciary, although judges are appointed by the president and parliament. The Supreme Court comprises judges appointed by the president for a term of six years. It administers law, but cannot undertake judicial review. This is undertaken by the Constitutional Court, which comprises nine judges appointed by the president and parliament for a period of nine years.

Last elections

28 November/12 December 2004 (presidential); 28 November 2004 (parliamentary).

Results: Parliamentary: chamber of deputies, the PSD won 36.6 per cent of the vote (132 of 332 seats); the Alianta Dreptate si Adevar (DA) (Justice and Truth Alliance) (consisting of PNL and DP) won 30.5 per cent (101); independent won 10.2 per cent (30); UDMR won 6.6 per cent (22); Partidul Conservator (PC) (Conservative Party) won 5.7 per cent (19); minority parties 5.4 per cent (18).
Senate: PSD won 43 seats; Da PNL-DP 50; România Mare (PRM) (Greater Romania Party) 18; PC 11; UDMR 10; independent 5.
Presidential: Traian Basescu (PNL) won 51.2 per cent of the vote; Adrian Nastase (PSD) won 48.8 per cent.

Next elections

25 November 2007 (EU parliamentary); 2008 (parliamentary); 2009 (presidential).

Political parties

Ruling party

Coalition (known as Da PNL-PD): Alianta Dreptate si Adevar (DA) (Justice and Truth Alliance) led by Partidul National Liberal (PNL) (National Liberal Party), Partidul Democrat (PD) (Democratic Party), Uniunea Democratica Maghiara din Romania (UDMR) (Hungarian Democratic Alliance of Romania), Partidul Conservator (PC) (Conservative Party) (since 2004)

Main opposition party

Partidul Social Democrat (PSD)

Population

21.56 million (2007)
Last census: March 2002: 21,680,974
Population density: 98 inhabitants per square km. Urban population: 55 per cent (1995–2001).
Annual growth rate: -0.5 per cent 1994–2004 (WHO 2006)

Ethnic make-up

Romanian (89 per cent), Hungarian (9 per cent), German (0.4 per cent), Ukrainian, Serb, Croat, Russian Turk and Gypsy (1.6 per cent). The Hungarian minority live principally in the Transylvania region. Around half of the then resident ethnic Germans returned to Germany in 1990 and many of the remainder have followed in recent years. Other small ethnic groups include Jews and a number of Greeks and Armenians.

Religions

Romanian Orthodox (70 per cent), Roman Catholic (6 per cent, of which 3 per cent are Uniate), Protestant (6 per cent), and unaffiliated (18 per cent). Since the revolution of 1989 there has been complete religious freedom. The dominant religion is Romanian Orthodox, with over 18 million believers, headed by a Patriarch based in Bucharest. The Roman Catholic Church has approximately 1.35 million members, and includes adherents of the Armenian, Latin and Romanian (Byzantine) rites. The Hungarian and German minorities are predominantly Protestant, and there are communities of the Old-Rite Christian Church (an Orthodox sect) and the Armenian-Gregorian Church. Despite emigration there is still a small Jewish community.

Education

Romania's transition to a market economy made a comprehensive reform of the education sector necessary. The World Bank has supported three reform projects with loan contributions amounting to US$170 million. The centralised education system, with a standard curriculum and ineffective student evaluation system, has been replaced by a flexible curriculum framework, alternative textbooks and a modern evaluation system. Improvements in teacher training, financing and management are under way.
Primary education begins at age seven and lasts until age 11. Lower secondary education lasts for four years until age 15. Upper secondary courses take another four years to complete. Romania's five types of secondary schools specialise in different areas of education, including general secondary schools, vocational and art schools, those specialising in physical education and teacher training. Minority language schooling is available, mainly in Hungarian and German. Higher education is offered in both public and private institutions.
Public expenditure on education typically amounts to 3.6 per cent of annual gross national income.
Literacy rate: 97 per cent adult rate; 98 per cent youth rate (15–24) (Unesco 2005).
Compulsory years: Seven to 15.
Enrolment rate: 104 per cent gross primary enrolment of relevant age group (including repeaters); 78 per cent gross secondary enrolment (World Bank).
Pupils per teacher: 20 in primary schools.

Health

Per capita total expenditure on health (2003) was US$540; of which per capita government spending was US$340, at the international dollar rate, (WHO 2006).
As primary healthcare units suffer due to financial shortage, there is over-concentration of already scarce resources on hospitals. Outbreaks of infectious diseases, often contracted in hospitals, are common.

HIV/Aids

HIV prevalence: 0.1 per cent aged 15–49 in 2003 (World Bank)
Life expectancy: 72 years, 2004 (WHO 2006)

Fertility rate/Maternal mortality rate: 1.3 births per woman, 2004 (WHO 2006)
Birth rate/Death rate: 10.8 births per 1,000 population; 12.3 deaths per 1,000 population (2003).
Child (under 5 years) mortality rate (per 1,000): 18 per 1,000 live births (2003)
Head of population per physician: 1.9 physicians per 1,000 people, 2003 (WHO 2006)

Welfare

The comprehensive state insurance scheme, with premiums paid by enterprises and institutions on behalf of employees, provides free health care and benefits for all Romanian citizens. An unemployment allowance was created in 1991 and there are also funds allocated to sickness benefits, children's allowance and pensions. Employers make social security contributions of 28—38 per cent, unemployment fund contributions of 5 per cent and disabled fund contributions of 1 per cent on gross salaries. Employees pay 3 per cent of gross salaries to the supplementary pension fund and 1 per cent to the unemployment insurance fund.
There is high unemployment in Romania and there has been a 40 per cent fall in real wages since 1989. Survival is partly due to the fact that most Romanians do not pay rent or have a mortgage, since over 90 per cent were able to buy their homes for the equivalent of a few months rent after the revolution. Many also have small plots of farm land for subsistence farming. It is expected that there will be a housing crisis for future generations, with many houses too small to be occupied by more than one family. Mortgages to buy houses are very expensive and are almost impossible to obtain. The government's housing programme aims to complete the tower blocks and apartments that were left unfinished after the revolution, and then allocate funds to social housing.
There is wide variation between urban and rural infrastructure, with less than 10 per cent of country dwellers living in houses with running water and sewerage.

Main cities

Bucharest (capital, estimated population 1.9 million in 2005), Iasi (326,502), Constanta (314,490), Cluj-Napoca (316,400), Timisoara (321,930), Ploiesti (234,920),

Languages spoken

The most significant minority language is Hungarian. German and English are spoken in tourist regions. Romanian, although a Romance language developed from Latin, has influences from Slavic languages as well as Hungarian, French and Turkish.

Official language/s
Romanian

Media

National news agency: Rompres
Other news agencies: Mediafax (www.mediafax.ro)

Press
The press is highly regionalised and includes publications in minority languages such as Hungarian, German and Serbian. Over 60 per cent of the population read one or more newspapers a day. There are around 10 national dailies, as well as dailies and weeklies published in the main cities. Newspapers tend to be independent, governmental or published by a political party.
Dailies: The most important independent national dailies in Romanian are Evenimental Zilei (www.evz.ro) is a mass-market newspaper, Adevarul (www.adevarul.ro), Cronica Romana (www.cronicaromana.ro), Curierul National (www.curierulnational.ro), Libertatea (www.libertatea.ro) and Romania Libera (www.romanialibera.ro).
In English, Nine O'Clock (www.nineoclock.ro), Jurnalul National (www.jurnalul.ro) and Evenimentul (www.evenimentul.ro) have English online editions. In German, Allgemeine Zeitung für Rumanien is published five times a week and Hermannstadter Zeitung (www.hermannstaedter.ro); in Turkish Zaman (www.zaman.ro) and in Hungarian, Uj Magyar Szo (www.maszol.ro) Háromszék (www.3szek.ro) and Krónika (www.kronika.ro).
Regional dailies include Azi (www.azi.ro/) Gardianul (www.gardianul.ro), Ieseanul (www.ieseanul.ro) and Observator de Constanta (www.observator.ro).
Weeklies: The Sunday newspapers include Adevarul, Cronica Romana, Curierul National, Nine O'Clock (English) and Azi.
Business: In Romanian, Bursa (www.bursa.ro) reports on the stock exchange, Capital (www.capital.ro), Sàptàmàna Financiarà (www.sfin.ro) and Ziarul Financiar (www.zf.ro) deal with financial news. In English, Bucharest Business Week (www.bbw.ro) and The Diplomat (www.thediplomat.ro) is publish weekly.
Periodicals: Many special interest and business publications are published, mostly by independent companies.

Broadcasting
Radio: There are several domestic stations with the state-owned Radio Romania (www.srr.ro) providing four nationwide networks, featuring news, music and cultural shows, plus an international channel in English and 11 other languages. Commercial radio stations include Europa FM (www.europafm.ro), Kiss FM (www.mykiss.ro), Pro FM (www.profm.ro) and Radio 21 (www.radio21.ro).
Television: The state-owned television, Televiziunea Romana (TVR) (www.tvr.ro) operates two channels – Romania 1 and TVR2. Commercial networks include Antena 1 (www.antena1.ro), Prima TV (www.primatv.ro), Acasa TV (www.acasatv.ro) and Realitatea TV (www.realitatea.net) showing domestic and international programmes.

Advertising
Advertising agencies, some in joint ventures with Western firms (UK-based Saatchi & Saatchi and Lintas Worldwide) operate throughout the country. As well as advertising through television and radio, cinema advertising is increasingly popular with billboard locations growing and advertising on public transport vehicles common.

Economy

Romania is one of the fastest growing economies in Europe. Several years of radical restructuring and reform measures, along with a period of recession, was followed by steady growth starting in 2001. GDP growth has been around 5 per cent a year, although 8.3 per cent was achieved in 2004. Inflation has been brought down from over 40 per cent in 2000 to around 8 per cent in 2006. Exports are thriving, with annual growth of over 10 per cent. Productivity has been strengthened significantly and contributions to social security have been cut. These developments have benefited competitiveness.
A significant factor in Romania's success is the infusion of foreign investment, attracted by a favourable corporate tax regime, low wages and a stable and strengthening currency. Romania received US$12 billion in foreign investment in 2006, in the run-up to EU accession on 1 January 2007. The main sources of foreign investment have been The Netherlands, Germany and France.
The EU has urged Romania to fight corruption, speed up economic reforms and tackle judicial reforms as well as public administration reforms. Romania has carried out the majority of necessary structural reform, but needs now to concentrate on corporate governance. Membership of the EU, bringing with it funds as well as more investment, should further strengthen the economy.
An important source of consumer revenue is the remittances sent by migrant workers living abroad. The negative side of the departure of large numbers of workers to countries offering higher wages, which

was accelerated with entry into the EU, is that it is leaving Romania with a labour shortage, which could impede economic expansion. It has also been predicted that by 2050 the population could decrease by 29 per cent.

External trade

As a member of the European Union, Romania operates within a communitywide free trade union, with tariffs sets as a whole. Internationally, the EU has free trade agreements with a number of nations and trading blocs worldwide.

Foreign trade represented 85 per cent of GDP and is expected to rise further since entry to the EU. Over 30 per cent of trade is with the EU, Russia supplies the majority of Romania's energy imports.

Imports

Main imports include machinery and equipment, fuels and minerals, chemicals, textile and products, basic metals and agricultural products.

Main sources: Germany (15.2 per cent total, 2006), Italy (14.6 per cent), Russia (7.9 per cent).

Exports

Main exports include clothing and footwear, metals and metal products, machinery and equipment, minerals and fuels, chemicals and agricultural products.

Main destinations: Italy (18.1 per cent total, 2006), Germany (15.7 per cent), Turkey (7.7 per cent).

Agriculture

Farming

The agricultural sector accounts for 12.8 per cent of GDP and employs 25 per cent of the workforce.

The total agricultural area is 147,900 sq km, of which 94,100 sq km is arable. Arable land, pastures and hayfields cover 59.5 per cent of Romania, forests 26.7 per cent and vineyards 2.5 per cent.

Romania is Central Europe's most important agricultural producer after Poland. Important agricultural produce includes grapes (the leading European producer), corn, wheat, maize, rye, sugar beet, oilseed, potatoes, plums, apples and meat.

Although there has been progress in restructuring the sector, it has been slower than international financial institutions would like. Moreover, concerns have also been expressed at the re-introduction of import barriers and subsidies to protect the sector from Hungarian wheat and flour exports.

The restitution and privatisation of land has – in comparison with enterprise privatisation – advanced at a rapid pace, with over 85 per cent of agricultural land in private ownership by 2002. Land restitution was highly politicised, with arguments surrounding the amount of land that was returned to claimants. Claims exceeded by a third the amount of land held in state hands, and delays in the process held up investment in the sector. Although land restitution was a major step forward, problems facing the sector include the small size of farms, no functioning land market, very few rural credit and investment schemes, and an extremely limited distribution and marketing infrastructure.

There may be a trend towards protectionism in Romanian agricultural policy as the government considers shielding the domestic sector from competitive producers within the EU, which Romania is theoretically in line to join in 2007.

In October 2005 Romanian officials discovered bird flu in three ducks near the Danube. Thousands of birds were killed and quarantine imposed on others. The authorities began testing humans for the disease.

Crop production for 2005 included: 18,605,000 tonnes (t) cereals in total, 7,027,000t wheat, 9,965,000t maize, 3,985,000t potatoes, 1,135,000t barley, 1,027,606 grapes, 1,257,000t sunflower seeds, 821,451t tomatoes, 625,819t oilcrops, 694,000t sugar beets, 237,000t chillies and peppers, 254,000t soya beans, 478,099t apples, 409,286t plums, 2,099,336t fruit in total, 4,025,364t vegetables in total. Livestock production included: 781,380t meat in total, 162,200t beef, 375,000t pig meat, 66,800t lamb, 154,000t poultry, 405,600t eggs, 5,064,000t milk, 19,200t honey, 22,440t cattle hides, 15,600t sheepskins, 17,600t greasy wool, 1,000t cocoons, silk.

Fishing

Romania's fishing sector has declined in the past decade, making little contribution to GDP. National consumption is falling too. Fisheries in the Black Sea have been spoilt by eutrophication and overfishing. Carp, mackerel and sardines are the principal catches. European spratt and anchovy are also plentiful. There are an estimated 10,000 persons working in the fishing industry.

Fish farming, including primary processing, packaging and trade will be improved through major investment projects. In 2004, the total marine fish catch was 1,802 tonnes.

Forestry

Forest and other wooded land accounts for less than one-third of the land area, with forest cover estimated at 6.4 million hectares (ha). Most of the forest area is located in the Carpathian mountainous region in the centre and west of the country. About nine-tenths of the forest is available for wood supply and is largely semi-natural. The growing stock consists of Norway spruce as the principal coniferous species, with beech and oak the main deciduous varieties. Although most of the forest is owned by the state, claims for restitution have increased private ownership.

Forests provide sufficient raw materials for the domestic industry to meet internal demands and also product for exports. Romania has a well developed timber and wood processing industry, concentrated in the northern regions of Moldavia and Transylvania. Substantial investments have been made to modernise older mills so as to improve its existing export base. Over half of the sawnwood production is exported, while more value-added products such as parquet, solid wood panels and furniture are obtained from hardwoods. Most of the paper demand is met by imports.

Export of forest material in 2004 amounted to US$898.4 million, while imports amounted to US$526.0 million.

Timber production in 2004 included 15,777,000 cubic metre (cum) roundwood, 12,762,000cum industrial roundwood, 4,588,000cum sawnwood, 8,166,000cum sawlogs and veneer logs, 2,500,000cum pulpwood, 951,000cum wood-based panels, 3,015,000cum woodfuel; 26,000 tonnes (t) charcoal, 462,000t paper and paperboard (including 44,000t newsprint), 35,000t printing and writing paper, 262,000t paper pulp, 262,000t recovered paper.

Industry and manufacturing

The industrial sector accounts for 36.3 per cent of GDP with manufacturing accounting for 27 per cent of GDP.

Industrial production increased by an estimated 4 per cent in 2004.

The main industries are textiles and footwear, light machinery and auto assembly. Mining, timber, construction materials, chemicals, food processing and petroleum refining are all also significant sectors.

Tourism

The tourism sector declined following the collapse of Communism, despite the wealth of attractions. Poor infrastructure, including existing but deteriorating facilities, and inadequate marketing, as well as competition from neighbouring destinations, have contributed to the malaise.

The sector contributes only 1.3 per cent to GDP. The industry supplies 115,000 jobs, which amounts to 1.2 per cent of the workforce.

3.4 million arrivals were recorded in 2004, an improvement on previous years. State-owned tourist resources have been privatised and the Ministry of European Integration is allocating financial assistance to the sector.

Mining

Taken together, the mining and hydrocarbons sectors account for around 13 per cent of GDP and employ 8 per cent of the workforce. Output dramatically declined in the 1990s, reflecting prolonged restructuring. Romania's mining industry is well developed, although it suffers from outdated technology and a lack of investment.

Mineral deposits include salt, lignite, iron ore, bauxite, manganese and small quantities of gold, zinc, uranium, tin and copper.

Romania aims to exploit domestic resources instead of relying on imports, even if the initial cost is high. Annual zinc output is around 28,000 tonnes, aluminium output around 150,000 tonnes and copper output around 30,000 tonnes. Minvest, privatised in 1999, accounts for 60 per cent of Romania's copper production.

The government opened the gold mining sector to foreign exploration in 1999. Gabriel Resources, a Canadian company, are behind a US $400 million project to create Europe's largest open-pit gold mine in the Rosia Montana valley. The International Finance Corporation (IFC) have refused financial backing to the proposal, which would displace 2,000 residents and produce high levels of hazardous cyanide.

Hydrocarbons

Oil reserves stood at 0.5 billion barrels in 2004. Production has fallen from 294,000 barrels per day (bpd) in 1976 to 119,000bpd in 2004, while consumption is 212,000bpd. Although production covers under half of total consumption, Romania has the potential to become self-sufficient in oil and could become an important oil producer. Idle oil wells are being re-opened following the liberalisation of state prices and rising world prices. Foreign investors began to show an interest in Romania in the late 1990s, including TotalFinaElf and Sterling Resources (Canada), who were given a five-year licence to explore around 700,000 hectares near Craiova, southern Romania.

Russia's LUKOIL is a major player in the downstream sector, with a majority stake in the third-largest refinery in Romania, the Petrotel refinery. It has an annual capacity of 4.2 million tonnes, three million tonnes of which comes from LUKOIL's own fields and the rest from Romanian fields. Other refineries have also sought external links, although the Romanian government is in general wary of Russian interests expanding into the domestic industry.

Natural gas reserves stood at 0.3 trillion cubic metres in 2004. Even though Romania is central and eastern Europe's largest natural gas producer, in 2004, production has fallen. In 1994 production stood at 18.7 billion cubic metres and in 2004 this figure was 13.2 billion. Gas is imported by pipeline through Ukraine. Russia is Romania's sole gas provider, although the Romanian government is seeking to diversify its foreign sources of gas. Ukraine, Moldova, Italy and Norway have been identified as potential sources. Romgaz operates the national gas distribution system and is entirely owned by the state.

Coal reserves stood at 494 million tonnes at end-2004. Production totalled 6.9 million tonnes oil equivalent (toe) in 2004, down slightly from the previous year.

Energy

There is significant domestic production of oil, gas and coal. Although dependent on Russian imports to satisfy domestic oil needs, Romania houses ten of south-eastern Europe's eleven oil refineries. The Petrotel refinery was upgraded in October 2004 to conform to EU standards. The company was privatised together with Petromidia.

In 2005 construction began on a new oil refinery near Bucharest. The project is a joint venture between South Korean LG International and Petrom, the national oil company. At the end of 2005 construction of a crude oil pipeline, the South East European Line (SEEL), commenced. It will connect Romania to Italy, via Serbia and Bosnia. By 2007 inflows through this line are projected to reach 480,000 bpd.

Gas is the most important domestic fuel resource, and Romania is the region's biggest producer. However, output is declining significantly. In 2004 two more gas companies were privatised, taking the total percentage of private gas providers to 40 per cent. By 2007 the government intends to have opened up the gas market in its entirety to conform to EU regulations. Seventy per cent of electricity production in Romania is produced in thermal power plants, 20 per cent in hydroelectric power plants and 10 per cent in the Cernavoda Unit I nuclear reactor.

In December 2002, Canada announced that it would guarantee up to US$207 million in loans towards the construction of a new nuclear reactor, the 'Cernavoda II'. The project is being managed by the Atomic Energy of Canada and is expected to be completed by the end of 2006. There is a lot of public opposition to the reactor, not least because the country already has a surplus of generational capacity.

Financial markets

Stock exchange

After a 50-year gap, the Bucharest Stock Exchange (BSE) was re-opened in 1995.

Banking and insurance

Since the early 1990s, the banking sector has undergone major restructuring and privatisation, although some areas of the banking, insurance, legal and financial sectors require upgrading. About 55 per cent of the banking system is foreign owned. Privatisation of Romania's largest bank, Banca Comerciala Romana (BCR), is scheduled for completion in 2006. When both BCR and Casa de Economii si Consemnatiuni (CEC) are privatised, the banking sector will be 90 per cent foreign owned and highly competitive.

Central bank

Banca Nationala a Romaniei (BNR) (National Bank of Romania)

Main financial centre

Bucharest

Time

GMT plus two hours (daylight saving, late March to late October, GMT plus three hours)

Geography

Romania is situated in south-eastern Europe in the lower Danube basin bordering the Black Sea to the south-west (250km of coastline). Much of the country forms part of the Balkan Peninsula. Romania is the largest of the Balkan states. Ukraine is to the north, Moldova to the north-east, Hungary to the north-west, Serbia and Montenegro and Macedonia to the south-west and Bulgaria to the south.

Romania is divided into four geographical areas. Moldavia and Transylvania (forest and mountains) make up the northern half, which is divided by the Carpathian Mountains. South of the Carpathians is the Danube plain of Walachia (including Bucharest), with the lower Danube marking the border with Bulgaria. Romania's Black Sea coastline incorporates the Danube delta and the port of Constanta.

Hemisphere

Northern

Climate

Romania has a moderate, continental temperate climate with long hot summers and cold winters. Snow falls throughout the country, although winters are coldest in the Carpathian mountains with snow between December and April, and mildest on the Black Sea coast. Mean temperatures in Bucharest are minus 2 degrees Celsius (C) in January and 23 degrees C in July. The coldest month is January with a mean temperature of minus 7 degrees C, rising to a peak of 30 degrees C in July. Temperatures can differ by 5–10 degrees C from the plains to the mountains.

The wettest month is June with approximately 85mm of rain; the driest September with 30mm. The Black Sea water temperatures are 20-28 degrees C in July and August.

Dress codes

The business dress code is usually informal, with ties, sports jackets or blazers acceptable for meetings.

Clothing should be medium-weight, plus a heavy topcoat and overshoes for winter. Lightweight clothing and a light raincoat are advisable for summer.

Entry requirements

Passports

Required by all, valid for six months from date of arrival.

Visa

Required by all, except nationals of EU/EEA countries, USA, Canada, Japan, Israel and some other countries. Transit visas are required by nationals of some countries. For full details of countries affected by all visa requirements, see www.roembus.org. An application form can also be downloaded. Business visitors, when required to apply for visas, should provide an employer's letter certifying purpose of visit, an invitation from a local company, proof of sufficient funds, travel insurance and return/onward passage.

Currency advice/regulations

The import and export of local currency is prohibited. There are no restrictions on the import of foreign currency, subject to declaration over eur10,000 (or foreign equivalent); export of foreign currency is limited to the unused amount, subject to presentation of exchange receipts.

Changing money at private exchange offices is often better than at banks. Kiosks are required to advertise an official rate, but ask if they can offer a better deal.

Romania is largely a cash-only economy. In Bucharest and main centres, major credit cards may be accepted at large hotels, car hire firms and stores; travellers cheques can be changed at banks and hotels. US dollars are the preferred hard currency.

Customs

Personal effects, 200 cigarettes and two litres of alcoholic beverages and small gifts are permitted duty-free. Banned imports include ammunition, explosives, narcotics and pornography.

Health (for visitors)

Hospital emergency rooms provide free first aid, but charge for all other medical services.

Mandatory precautions

There are no special requirements.

Advisable precautions

Typhoid, diphtheria and both hepatitis A and B inoculations are recommended, as well as inoculation against tick-borne encephalitis. It is advisable to boil water or drink bottled water where possible, although water in mountainous regions is supplied from local springs and is safe.

Rabies is a health risk.

Basic medical supplies are limited, especially outside major cities, so always travel with sufficient medication.

Hotels

Classified as de luxe, A and B. Accommodation outside Bucharest is generally cheaper. Advisable to purchase pre-paid vouchers for accommodation through travel agents, as a confirmed reservation, if not pre-paid, is not a guarantee of accommodation.

Credit cards

Credit cards are not widely used but are accepted in most major hotels. American Express, Visa and Eurocard are preferred. Credit card transactions are charged at a worse rate than that offered by exchange bureaux

Public holidays (national)

Fixed dates

1–2 Jan (New Year's Day), 1 May (Labour Day), 1 Dec (National Day), 25–26 Dec (Christmas).

Variable dates

Orthodox Easter Sunday, Orthodox Easter Monday

Working hours

Banking

Mon–Fri: 0900–1200 and 1300–1500. Creditbank, Bucharest Otopeni airport, open 1000–1800 daily.

Business

Mon–Fri: 0800–1700, lunch usually 1230–1300. Business hours can be haphazard with many offices closing on Friday afternoons.

Government

Mon–Fri: 0800–1700, lunch usually 1230–1300.

Shops

Mon–Fri: 0900–1800; Sat: 0900–1400.

Telecommunications

Telephone/fax

There are only basic telephone services.

Mobile/cell phones

There is widespread coverage, particularly in the major cities.

Social customs/useful tips

Traditional Central European courtesies with a measure of Latin informality are expected. Punctuality is observed to a degree. Shaking hands is the traditional form of greeting. Accepting hospitality from and giving social invitations to officials is normal, usually taking place in restaurants or hotels.

Smoking is prohibited on public transport and in cinemas and theatres, although many Romanians smoke and Western cigarettes are greatly appreciated.

Tips are expected by porters, chambermaids and taxi drivers.

Anyone photographing demonstrations risks arrest.

It is advisable to avoid the many stray dogs in and around Bucharest.

Security

Crimes against tourists are a growing problem in Romania. Money exchange schemes targetting travellers are becoming increasingly common. Bogus policemen are an increasing hazard for the unwary business traveller. Their technique is to demand to see proof of identification, and then make off with a visitor's wallet. Keep passports separate from other valuables.

Extreme caution must be taken with unofficial change vendors: they are illegal and often fraudulent.

Getting there

Air

National airline: Tarom (Transporturile Aeriene Romane) (Romanian Air Transport)

International airport/s: Henry Coanda International Airport (OTP), 16km north of Bucharest; bank, post office, duty-free shop, car hire

Airport tax: None

Surface

Road: International roads connect Romania with Hungary. The E64 from Budapest goes through Arad, Brasov, Campina and Ploiesti to Bucharest. From Germany, the E60 goes via northern Hungary before going through Oradea. The route from Bucharest to Ukraine goes north through Bacau and to Chernovtsy in southern Ukraine. From Moldova, take the road from the border to the town of Husi. The better road links are via Germany, Austria and Hungary.

Rail: There are good rail connections with all neighbouring countries.

Water: Ships provide regular passenger services and cruises on the Danube, starting at Passau in Germany, through Austria, Slovakia, Hungary, Serbia, to Giurgiu (48km from Bucharest), and finally Constanta on the Black Sea.

Main port/s: Black Sea ports: Constanta, Mangalia and Sulina.

Danube ports: Orsova, Drobeta-Turnu Severin, Turnu Magurele, Giurgiu, Oltenita, Calaras, Cernavoda. Braila, Galati and Tulcea are both river and sea ports. The Danube is used heavily for freight transport since the opening of the canal link with the Black Sea.

Getting about

National transport

Air: Tarom and Carpatair operate regular internal services to main centres in Romania.

Road: Romania has around 78,000km of roads, of which 14,500km are national roads; 4,680km of the national roads are included within the European Road Network ('E' roads).

Buses: There are regular inter-city connections and local services to most towns and villages.

Rail: There is an extensive rail network. Efficient and cheap services operate between all main cities and towns. In addition to slower local services, there are express and inter-city services with dining and sleeping cars. Bucharest's principal station is the Gara de Nord.

Water: The principal navigable waterway is the Danube, on which cruises are available.

City transport

Taxis: Taxis are readily available in main centres and are inexpensive. Authorised taxis are identified by a 'Taxi' sign on the roof. Metered taxis should be used, although drivers may need to be reminded to switch them on. While a taxi may be hailed in the street, it is advisable to arrange a taxi by telephone, preferably from a company. A 10 per cent tip is normal. Informal operators at the main hotels and the airport overcharge and should be avoided.

Buses, trams & metro: It is easy to get around by bus, both within towns and cities and cross-country, but they are often slow, over-crowded and uncomfortable. Trams and trollies also run in many centres. Tickets are purchased from booths and in some hotels; they should be punched immediately upon entering the vehicle. There is a metro system in Bucharest.

Car hire

Self-drive and chauffeur-driven cars are available from international and local companies in the main cities and airports. International or national driving licences are required. Traffic drives on the right, although Romanian driving can be very unpredictable. Speed limits are 120km per hour on highways, 90km per hour on other roads and 50km per hour in built-up areas.

BUSINESS DIRECTORY

The addresses listed below are a selection only. While World of Information makes every endeavour to check these addresses, we cannot guarantee that changes have not been made, especially to telephone numbers and area codes. We would welcome any corrections.

Telephone area codes

The international dialling code (IDD) for Romania is +40, followed by area code and subscriber's number:

Braila	239	Gaesti	245
Brasov	268	Oradea	259
Bucharest	21	Ploiesti	244
Cluj-Napoca	264	Sibiu	269
Constanta	241	Timisoara	256

Useful telephone numbers

Fire brigade: 981
Police: 955
Ambulance: 961
Special ambulance service (pregnant women or women with small children): 969
Emergency hospital: 679-4310
Special information: 951
Time: 958
Railway information: 952
Weather report: 959
Enquiries: 930, 931, 932

Chambers of Commerce

American Chamber of Commerce in Romania, Union International Centre, 11 Ion Cimpineanu Street, Sector 1, 78664 Bucharest (tel: 315-8694; fax: 312-4851; e-mail: amcham@amcham.ro).

Brasov Chamber of Commerce and Industry, 18-20 M Kogalniceanu Street, 2200 Brasov (tel: 412-357; fax: 477-333; e-mail: ccibv@ccibv.ro).

Constanta Chamber of Commerce, Industry, Shipping and Agriculture, 84 Mircea cel Batran Street, bl MF1, Constanta tel: 619-854; fax: 619-454; e-mail: office@ccina.ro)

Prahova Chamber of Commerce and Industry, 8 Cuza Voda Street, Ploiesti (tel: 513-122; fax: 516-666; e-mail: office@cciph.ro).

Romania and Bucharest Chamber of Commerce and Industry, 2 Octavian Goga Boulevard, Sector 3, Bucharest (tel: 322-9535; fax: 322-9542; e-mail: ccir@ccir.ro).

Sibiu Chamber of Commerce, Industry and Agriculture, 1 Telefoanelor Street, 2400 Sibiu (tel: 210-503; fax: 211-831; e-mail: cciasb@cciasb.ro).

Timisoara Chamber of Commerce, Industry and Agriculture, 3 Piata Victoriei, 300030 Timisoara (tel: 490-766; fax: 490-311; e-mail: cciat@cciat.ro).

Banking

Banca Agricola, B-dul Voda, Sector 3, Bucharest (tel/fax: 323-6027).

Banco Comerciala Romana, B-dul Regina Elisabeta 5, Sector 3, Bucharest (tel: 312-6185; fax: 312-0056).

Bankco-op, 13 Ion Ghica St, Bucharest (614-3900; fax: 312-0037).

Romanian Bank for Development, 4 Doamnei St, Bucharest (tel: 613-3200, 615-9600; fax: 615-7603).

Romanian Commercial Bank, 14 Republicii Ave, Bucharest (tel: 614-5680, 615-7560; fax: 614-3213).

Central bank

National Bank of Romania, 25 Lipscani Street, Bucharest (tel: 313-0410; fax: 312-3831; e-mail: bnr@bnro.ro).

Travel information

Association of Ecotourism in Romania, Gabroveni Street 2, Sector 3, Bucharest (tel: 319-742; fax: 828-721; e-mail: roving@deltanet.ro).

Henri Coanda International Airport, 224E Bucharest Road, Otopeni (tel: 204-1200; fax:201-4990; e-mail: otp@otp-airport.ro).

Romanian Automobile Club (Automobil Clubul Roman), 27 Tache Ionescu Street, 010353 Bucharest (tel: 317-8253; fax: 317-3964; e-mail: acr@acr.ro).

Tarom (Airline), Victoria Sq., 59 Buzesti Street, Bucharest (tel: 204-6464; fax: 204-6427; e-mail: agvictoria@tarom.ro).

Ministry of tourism

Ministry of Transport, Construction and Tourism, Bulevardul Dinicu Golescu 38, 010873 Bucharest 1 (tel: 319-6112; fax: 319-6204; e-mail: relpub@mt.ro).

National tourist organisation offices

Autoritatea Nationala Pentru Turism, Bulevardul Dinicu Golescu 38, 010873 Bucharest 1 (tel: 314-9957 fax: 314-9964; ie-mail: promovare@mturism.ro).

Ministries

Ministry of Agriculture, Blvd Carol I 24, 70312 Bucharest (tel: 614-4020; fax: 312-4410).

Ministry of Communications and Information Technology, 14 Libertatii Blvd, 76106 Bucharest 5 (tel: 400-1100, 312-0017; fax: 400-1329; internet site: http://www.mcti.ro).

Ministry of Culture, Piata Presei 1, Bucharest 71341 (tel: 223-1516; fax: 223-4951).

Ministry of Defence, Str Izvor 1-3, 70642 Bucharest (tel: 410-4040; fax: 312-0863).

Ministry of Foreign Affairs, Aleea Modrogan 14, 71274 Bucharest (tel: 212-2160; fax: 230-7489).

Ministry of Health, Str Ministerului 1-3, 70109 Bucharest (tel: 222-3850; fax: 312-4916).

Ministry of the Interior, Str Mihai Voda 3-5, 070622 Bucharest (tel: 311-2021; fax: 614-0909).

Ministry of Justice, Bd Mihail Kogalniceanu 33, 70602 Bucharest (tel: 614-4400; fax: 323-6179).

Ministry of Labour and Social Protection, Str Dem I Dobrescu 2, 70119 Bucharest (tel: 222-3850; fax: 312-2768).

Ministry of National Education, Str Gen Berthelot 28-30, 70749 Bucharest (tel: 614-4588; fax: 312-4719).

Ministry of Privatisation, Str Ministerului 2-4, 70109 Bucharest (tel: 222-3850; fax: 312-0809).

Ministry of Public Finance, Str Apolodor 17, 70663 Bucharest (tel: 410-3400; fax: 312-2077).

Ministry of Public Works and Land Use Planning, Str Apollodor 15-17, Sector 6, 70663 Bucharest (tel: 410-1933; fax: 411-1138).

Ministry of Youth and Sports, Str Vasile Conta 16, 70139 Bucharest (tel: 211-5550; fax: 211-1710).

Office of the Prime Minister, Piata Victoriei 1, 71201 Bucharest (tel: 212-1660; fax: 222-5814).

Presidency of Republic, Building Geniului 1 Cotroceni Palace, Bucharest 76238 (tel: 410-0581; fax: 312-1247).

Other useful addresses

Administration of Sulina Free Trade Zone, Dr Marcovici Str 2, Ground Floor, Bucharest (tel: 613-8733).

Agency for Restructuring, 152 Calea Victoriei, Sector 1, Bucharest (tel: 212-2424; fax: 212-1176).

Asigurara Romaneasca SA (Asirom), Str Smirdan 5, 70406 Bucharest (tel: 312-5020; fax: 312-4819).

British Embassy, Str Jules Michelot 24, 70154 Bucharest (tel: 312-0303; fax: 312-9741).

Centrul Roman pentru Dezvoltarea Intreprinderilor Mici si Mijlocii (Crimm)-PMU, 20 Ion Campineanu Str, Sector 1, 70709 Bucharest (tel: 311-1995/6/7; fax: 312-6966).

Chamber of Deputies, 1 Parlamentului Str, Bucharest (tel: 335-0111; fax: 312-0827).

Constanta South Free Zone Administration, Ferry Boat Terminal Building Agigea, code 8711, Jud Constanta (tel: 741-378, 618-718, 619-100 (ext 2118, 2162); fax: 639-000, 619-729, 693-913).

Council for Reform, Piata Victoriei 1, 71201 Bucharest (tel: 222-3687; fax: 222-4686).

Council for Economic Co-ordination, Strategy and Reform, Piaja Victorei 1, 71201 Bucharest (tel: 222-3687, 312-4767; fax: 222-4686).

Department for European Integration (tel: 312-6928; fax: 312-6929).

Department of Public Information (tel: 222-3619; fax: 222-6088).

Department for Selective Restructuring of the State Ownership Fund, 6-10, Callea Grivitei, Sector 1, Bucharest (tel: 650-4822; 659-7693).

Economic Reform and Strategy and Co-ordination Council, 1 Victoriei Sq, Bucharest (tel: 617-7977; fax: 312-4686).

Fiman Fund PMU, 6-8 Povernei Str, Bucharest (tel: 212-2912; fax: 211-1937).

Insurance and Reinsurance Company SA (Aatra), Str Smirdan 5, 79118 Bucharest (tel: 150-986; fax: 139-306).

Land Reclamation Agriculture Department, Sos Oltenitei 35-37, 75501 Bucharest (tel: 634-5020; fax: 312-3712).

Lignite Public Authority, Str Tudor Vladimirescu 2, 1400 Târgu-Jiu (tel: 321-2513; fax: 321-664).

National Administration of Roads, Blvd Dinicu Golescu 38, 77113 Bucharest (tel: 312-8496).

National Agency for Privatisation, Str Ministerulei 2-4, 4th Floor, Bucharest sector 1 (tel: 615-8558, 614-9495, 312-3030, 614-7854; fax: 312-0809/3030, 613-6136).

National Committee for Statistics, 16 Libertatii Str, Sector 5, Bucharest (tel: 312-4875; fax: 312-4873).

National Council for Environmental Protection, Piata Victorei 1, Bucharest (tel: 143-400).

Nord-Est Press (Independent news agency), Str Smirdan 5, 6600 Iasi (tel/fax: 144-776).

Petrotel SA, Str Mihai Bravu 235, Jud Prahova, 2000 Ploiesti (tel: 146-671; fax: 142-408).

Project Implementation Unit within the Authority for Privatisation and Management of the State Ownership, Bucharest (tel: 303-6417; fax: 303-6416).

Radiodifuziuna Romana, Str Gral Berthelot 61-62, PO Box 63-1200, Bucharest (tel: 633-4710; fax: 312-3640).

Radioteleviziuna Romana (Romanian Radio and Television), Calea Dorobantilor 191, PO Box 63-1200, Bucharest (tel: 334-710; fax: 337-544).

Radio Nord-Est, Str Smirdan 5, 6600 Iasi (tel: 145-530; fax: 146-363).

Research Institute for Foreign Trade, Str Apollodor 17, 5 Bucharest (tel: 312-3652, 631-1293; fax: 312-5652).

Romanian Agency for Energy Conservation, Splaiul Independentei 202A, 77208 Bucharest (tel: 650-6470; fax: 312-3197).

Romanian Commodity Exchange, 71341 Bucharest 1, Presei Libere Sq, Bucharest (tel: 01-617-2231; fax: 01-312-2167).

Romanian Development Agency (RDA), Boulevard Magheru 7, Bucharest 1 (tel: 615-6686, 312-3311; fax: 613-2415).

Romanian Embassy (USA), 1607 23rd Street, Washington DC 20008 (tel: (+1-202)-332-4846; fax: (+1-202)-232-4748; e-mail: info@roembus.org).

Romanian Government, 1 Victoriei Sq, Bucharest (tel: 222-3677; fax: 222-6088).

Romanian Parliament, Calea 13, Septembrie 1, 76117 Bucharest (tel: 335-0111).

Romanian Post Office, 14 Libertatii Avenue, 70106 Bucharest 5 (tel: 400-1102; fax: 400-1515).

Romanian State Railways (SNCFR), Blvd 38 Dinicu Golescu, Sector 1-Cod 78123 Bucharest (tel: 617-0148).

Secretariat for the Privatisation and Restructuring Programmes within the Council for Co-ordination, Strategy and Economic Reform, 1 Piata Victoriei, Sector 1, Bucharest (tel: 312-8445, 222-8335; fax: 312-6932).

Senate of Romania, 1 Revolutiei Sq, Bucharest (tel: 615-0200, 617-0160; fax: 312-1752).

Societatea Nationala a Cailor Ferate, State Ownership Fund, CA Rosetti Str 21, Bucharest (tel: 611-4943).

Supreme Court of Justice, 4 Rahovei Str, Bucharest (312-0920; fax: 613-0882).

Prosecutor General's under the Supreme Court of Justice, 2-4 Unirii Ave, Bucharest (tel: 631-1750, 781-3065; fax: 781-6210).

Televiziuna Romana – Telecentrul Bucuresti, Calea Dorobantilor 191, PO Box 63-1200, Bucharest (tel: 633-4710; fax: 633-7544).

USA Embassy, Str Tudor Arghezi 7-9, Bucharest (tel: 312-4042; fax: 312-0395).

National news agency: Rompres, Piata Presei Libere I, 71341 Bucharest (tel: 618-2878; fax: 617-0487).

Other news agencies: Mediafax (www.mediafax.ro)

Internet sites

Association of Ecotourism in Romania: http://www.eco-romania.ro

Romanian Home Page: http://www.ici.ro/romania

Romanian National Tourist Office: http://www.romaniantourism.com

Russia

KEY FACTS

Official name: Rossiiskaya Federatsiya (Russian Federation)

Head of State: President Dmitry Medvedev (from 7 May 2008)

Head of government: Prime Minister Vladimir Putin (appointed 8 May 2008)

Ruling party: Yedinaya Rossiya (YR) (United Russia) (elected 2003; re-elected 2 Dec 2007)

Area: 17,075,000 square km

Population: 142.10 million (2007)*

Capital: Moscow

Official language: Russian

Currency: Rouble (R) = 100 kopeks

Exchange rate: R23.21 per US$ (Jul 2008)

GDP per capita: US$9,075 (2007)*

GDP real growth: 8.10% (2007)

Labour force: 73.88 million (2006)*

Unemployment: 6.60% (2006) (with additional underemployment)

Inflation: 9.00% (2007)

Oil production: 9.98 million bpd (2007)

Balance of trade: US$144.09 billion (2006)

Visitor numbers: 20.20 million (2006)*

Annual FDI: US$31.00 billion (2006)*

* estimated figure

In early 2008 Moscow the average monthly wage or salary was some $1,000. Nationally the figure was lower, ranging between US$300–500. Compared to Western Europe, Russian disposable incomes are relatively high, as many purchased their houses outright, and cheaply, during the 1990s sell-offs. Russia's population continues to shrink at an alarming rate and growth in the working population remains negligible.

Simply rich

Russia has, in many ways 'arrived', or at least returned to the international stage. At the end of 2007 Russia had the third largest currency reserves in the world – estimated at some US$400 billion; it produces more oil than any country in the world except Saudi Arabia and has amassed US$50 billion in its so-called stabilisation fund. According to the World Bank's June 2008 *Russian Economic report*, Russia's GDP growth, which had reached an annual rate of 7.4 per cent in 2006 increased to 8.1 per cent in 2007, well above the long-term trend of 7 per cent. Early data for 2008 showed growth running at more than 8 per -cent. This is also well above International Monetary Fund (IMF) estimates, putting Russia's long-term annual growth potential at about 6 per cent. Such levels of growth suggest that the economy is straining its productive capacity; capacity use is up from 69 per cent in 2001 to 81 per cent in March 2008, with two of every five firms surveyed reporting levels of more than 90 per cent. The World Bank also notes that unemployment, which was down to 6.1 per cent at the end of 2007, was at its lowest level since 1994

Inflation nags

According to Russia's Federal State Statistics Service (Rosstat), consumer prices rose 11.9 per cent in 2007, an increase of 2.9 percentage points on 2006. They gained 3.4 per cent in the first quarter, 2.2 per cent in the second, 1.8 per cent in the third and 4.1 per cent in the fourth. The acceleration of inflation was due to core inflation, which stood at 4 per cent in the fourth quarter as against 1.7 per cent in the first, 1.2 per cent in the second and 3.7 per cent in the third. Core inflation accelerated to 11 per cent in 2007 as against 7.8 per cent in 2006. It is estimated that growth in the prices of goods and services included in the calculation of the core consumer price index in 2007 accounted for 8.7 percentage points, or 72.8 per cent, of overall consumer price growth (as against 6.1 percentage points, or 67.1 per cent, in 2006).Significant growth in food prices, excluding vegetable and fruit prices, made the principal contribution to the acceleration of inflation. These prices gained 14.9 per cent in 2007 year on year (in 2006 they rose 8.5 per cent). According to estimates, growth in these prices accounted for 5.4 percentage points, or 45.6 per cent, of overall consumer price growth in 2007. At the same time, growth in bread and bakery product prices and milk and dairy product prices accounted for about 1.3 percentage points, or 11.0 per cent. In 2006, this group of products accounted for 0.5 percentage points, or 5.8 per cent, of overall consumer price growth. Industrial producer prices rose 25.1 per cent in 2007 as against 10.4 per cent in 2006.

The acceleration of growth in producer prices was due to the fact that prices in the mining sector soared 52.3 per cent as compared with 1.6 per cent in 2006. Fuel and energy producer prices jumped 58.1 per cent, whereas in 2006 they fell 3.6 per cent. Metal ore producer prices increased 11.5 per cent as against 49.4 per cent in 2006. It has been estimated that the change in producer prices in the mining sector in 2007 accounted for 11.7 percentage points, or 46.8 per cent, of overall growth in industrial producer prices. In 2006, it accounted for 0.4 percentage points, or 3.5 per cent. Rapid growth in industrial producer prices increased costs and this stimulated inflation. In 2007, price growth in the manufacturing sector stood at 17.9 per cent as against 13.3 per cent in 2006.

Budget surplus

In 2007 the federal budget surplus stood at 5.5 per cent of GDP. This represents a decrease of 1.9 percentage points from 2006, caused by significant growth in budget expenditures. Federal budget revenues in

2007 increased by 0.3 percentage points year on year and stood at 23.6 per cent of GDP. This was due to the acceleration of economic growth and additional revenues from the sale of Yukos Oil Company assets. Meanwhile, oil revenues fell by 1.5 percentage points as compared with 2006, to 6.6 per cent of GDP, largely as a result of the rouble's appreciation against the US dollar. Federal budget expenditures rose to 18.1 per cent of GDP in 2007 (as against 15.9 per cent in 2006). Non-interest expenditures made up 17.7 per cent of GDP (as against 15.3 per cent in 2006), the highest ratio since 2000. Expenditures on development institutions, such as the Municipal Infrastructure Reform Fund, the Russian Nanotechnology Corporation, the Development Bank and the Investment Fund accounted for most of the growth in expenditures. Meanwhile, the federal budget expenditure in 2007 was just 91.6 per cent of the level stipulated in the federal budget law (96.3 per cent in 2006) due to the under-financing of expenditures on general government programmes, healthcare and sports and social programmes.

There was a significant increase in investment activity in 2007: fixed capital investment grew 21.1 per cent (as against 13.7 per cent in 2006). The largest sums were invested in the mining sector, transport and communications. Investments in machinery, equipment and transport vehicles accounted for more than a third of total investments. One fifth was used to acquire imported equipment. Imports of machinery, equipment and transport vehicles increased 57.6 per cent in the period January to November 2007 (as against 49.5 per cent in the same period of 2006). This growth was partly the result of the strengthening of the rouble in real terms. Fixed capital investments were largely financed (57.2 per cent) by raising funds in the period. As imports grew considerably faster than exports, net exports of goods and services decreased by 30.7 per cent in 2007.As a result, on the one hand, high investment activity and growth in household incomes stimulated economic growth; on the other hand, these processes caused production to exceed its natural (potential) level and, consequently, contributed to the acceleration of price growth on the consumer goods market.

They're changing the guard?

By mid-2008 few Russians had doubts about who was running the Kremlin. The question remained as to whether, following Mr Medvedev's election as president, a deal had been made between Messrs Putin and Medvedev which envisaged Mr Putin's return to power after a two year grace period, or whether the two year period was there to allow Mr Medvedev to get his feet under the desk. If the latter, then Mr Putin had adopted a strange approach to helping Mr Medvedev. Following the election, the government was quickly filled with Putin loyalists, suggesting that the protection of the Putin 'empire' had prevailed over any Medvedev independence. In the role of cabinet secretary – head of Mr Medvedev's administration – was Putin loyalist Sergei Naryshkin, once thought likely to be Putin's successor as president. Mr Naryshkin is a former KGB agent who worked alongside Mr Putin in St Petersburg. In a game of musical chairs, Mr Medvedev's electoral 'campaign' manager, Sergei Sobyanin, was appointed the deputy premier responsible for government administration. Alongside these two sat Mr Putin's former press secretary, Alexi Gromov, appointed deputy premier of the presidential administration. Mr Putin's economic adviser Igor Shuvalov was appointed first deputy prime minister with the role of deputising for Mr Putin in his absence abroad. Mr Putin appeared reluctant to release his grip on Russia's foreign affairs, even though the Russian constitution clearly makes this the responsibility of the president. Former ambassador to the US Yuri Ushakov was named cabinet co-ordinator for Mr Putin's foreign policy.

To gild the lily, Mr Putin also created a new praesidium, a mini-cabinet chaired by Mr Putin himself and comprising his seven deputy prime ministers and an additional seven ministers. This was no lightweight body; it included ministers holding the foreign, interior and defence portfolios – who in principle reported directly to the president rather than the prime minister. How Mr Medvedev was to relate to the praesidium remained an open question. But what was clear was that Mr Putin had not gathered around him this immensely powerful grouping of *siloviki* ministers for nothing. Some observers considered that Mr Putin's principal concern was to protect his allegedly extensive business interests. Some press reports put his personal wealth at around US$40 billion. Although the Kremlin's offices may still have the down at heel feel of Soviet days, Russia's government machine has been simplified: Mr Putin gives the orders – either directly or via Mr Medvedev – and everyone else obeys. In this *upravlyaayemaya demokratiya* (managed democracy) the opposition has been neutered and the Duma reduced to a rubber stamping operation. The overall objective is a *ukrepleniye gosudarstva* (strengthening of the state) which just happens to coincide with the dramatic enrichment of the *siloviki* clique. Not that the Russian population seemed to object to Mr Putin's rumoured wealth. His pursuit of personal enrichment is shared by a vast majority of the population. During the Putin presidency Russians saw the stabilisation of the economy and the strengthening of the state. In the process, and unsurprisingly in view of Mr Putin's KGB background, genuine democracy and what the West would accept to be basic freedoms were sacrificed, to be replaced by purely material objectives.

Kreminologists were at pains to judge Mr Putin's real objectives. What was certain was that Mr Putin kept his cards close to his chest. Despite the contradictory, often authoritarian image he presents to the west, at home for the most part the Russian electorate considered him to be hugely successful. For them, Putin was the man who has allowed them to hold their heads high following the humiliations and destitution of the immediate post-Communist years. In 2007 most Russians lived in a relatively free society, with a lively press, unrestricted internet access and free international movement.

Litvinenko

The freedoms enjoyed by average Russians did not, however, apply to those who chose to criticise the government. The streets of the run of the mill north London suburb of Muswell Hill are not normally the scenario for international political murder plots. But the December 2006 murder of Russian exile Alexander Litvinenko, appeared to bear the hall-mark of a state, rather than a private, assassination. It can be no accident that all over the world, both inside and outside Russia, opponents of Mr Putin have been falling like flies. Some jailed, some exiled, some killed. It is unlikely that Mr Litvinenko's murder will be traced directly to the unsmiling ex-KGB officer in the Kremlin, no matter how persistent the British police investigation. State-sponsored assassinations are rarely traceable to the source.

But Alexander Litvinenko's death fell into a particular, rather sinister pattern. And Russia does have a long and distinguished history of state-sponsored assassination. Litvinenko's polonium-210 murder combines the old with the new. Nor did it appear to have been accomplished with much skill, leaving a trail across London of contaminated hotel bars and bedrooms, restaurants, even five British Airways aircraft were contaminated. Subtle it was not, with 30,000 people alerted: effective it certainly was. Alexander Litvinenko's death followed soon on the shooting, in her apartment lift, of Moscow journalist Anna Politkovskaya. Miss Politkovskaya was well known in Russia, and internationally, as a critic of Mr Putin; Mr Litvinenko was allegedly investigating her death. The repercussions of Litvinenko's death stretched well into 2008 when the UK asked for the extradition of prime suspect, Andrei Lugovoi. Russia refused, and continued to push for the expulsion of Chechen separatist emissary Akhmad Zakayev and business tycoon Boris Berezovsky, both of whom were in London. Russia-UK relations sunk to the lowest since the Cold War years.

Energy rules – OK?

In a letter to the London *Financial Times* in November 2007, Russia's energy minister, Viktor Khristenko, explained that 'Russia stretches across more than one geographical region and we can diversify our industrial and energy co-operation by turning to Asian and Pacific countries. Incidentally, the eastern vector has an important economic dimension – such co-operation will help us develop eastern Siberia and East Asia'. This veiled threat to the European countries that had come to depend not only on one country, but for the most part one company – Russia's Gazprom – for their energy requirements. Russia has the largest potential gas reserves in the world; one quarter of Europe's total gas reserves are supplied by Russia. The strategic development of Russia's gas reserves reflects Russia's awareness that national security and energy security are closely related. By 2015, Germany – Western Europe's largest economy – will be dependent on Russia for 80 per cent of its gas.

The Kremlin's concerted drive to gain – and maintain – control of Russia's energy

KEY INDICATORS — Russia

	Unit	2003	2004	2005	2006	2007
Population	m	145.51	146.74	143.50	142.80	*142.10
Gross domestic product (GDP)	US$bn	435.35	590.39	763.88	988.67	1,289.58
GDP per capita	US$	2,992	4,093	5,323	6,923	*9,075
GDP real growth	%	6.3	7.1	6.4	7.4	8.1
Inflation	%	13.0	10.9	12.7	9.7	9.0
Unemployment	%	8.3	8.1	7.6	7.2	0.0
Industrial output	% change	0.0	6.9	4.1	5.3	0.0
Agricultural output	% change	0.0	2.9	1.1	1.7	0.0
Oil output	'000 bpd	8,543.0	9,285.0	9,551.0	9,769.0	9,978.0
Natural gas output	bn cum	578.6	589.1	598.0	6,121.0	607.4
Coal output	mtoe	124.9	127.6	137.0	144.5	94.5
Exports (fob) (goods)	US$m	135,929	183,452	243,569	303,926	355,465
Imports (cif) (goods)	US$m	78,539	96,307	125,303	159,838	223,421
Balance of trade	US$m	57,390	87,145	118,266	144,088	132,043
Current account	US$m	35,410.	59,610	83,348	94,257	76,600
Foreign debt	US$bn	153.5	213.5	197.3	257.2	310.0
Total reserves minus gold	US$m	73,174.	120,808	175,891	295,567	464,379
Foreign exchange	US$m	73,172	120,805	175,689	295,277	464,004
Exchange rate	per US$	30.56	28.81	26.57	26.29	24.68

* estimated figure

reserves continued into 2008. This time the target was the TNK-BP joint venture between the Alfa-Access-Renova (AAR) group and the UK's British Petroleum (BP). The Russian strategy in gaining control was crude in the extreme, consisting of preventing TNK-BP's chief executive from entering Russia. This was followed by a summons, which enabled the authorities to claim that his failure to present himself in court made him liable to suspension as a Russian company director. BP alleged governmental involvement in the process, claiming that there was obvious collusion between government officials and AAR.

Military might?

As Russia's energy economy expanded daily, its defence budget remained less than 5 per cent that of the US. That still represented a huge increase: in 2001 the defence budget was 140 billion roubles. By the beginning of 2007 it had risen to 870 billion roubles (US$32 billion). In 2006 six new intercontinental missiles were added to the arsenal, not to mention 12 launch vehicles, 31 battle tanks and seven Mi-28N night attack helicopters. Small beer, perhaps by US or Nato standards, but still strategically important. The new Topol-M missile has multiple warheads which reportedly splinter so that they cannot be shot out of the sky. In January 2007 it was rumoured that Russia's military hierarchy sought to re-direct the country's military policy, reportedly identifying the Nato alliance and the US as Russia's *glavny protivnik* – primary enemies. In March 2007 the Russian Security Council announced that it no longer considered terrorism (ie Chechnya) to be the greatest threat. In its place came a strategy based on 'geopolitical realities'.

The Western European response was largely one of surprise. Russia's paranoia is that of a former world power that has lost its empire and is seeking to re-establish itself. In many respects, following the collapse of communism, the Western powers had tended to treat Russia like a defeated enemy, unwittingly creating serious resentment. This feeling probably accounts for Russia's apparent ability to see enemies where none exist. Nowhere has this been more apparent than over the proposed US plan to locate a missile defence radar system in Poland, a former Russian satellite country. This rubs salt in the wound of Russia's reduced status and encourages Russia's military to seek to restore some sort of hegemony. Not one to miss an opportunity, Mr Putin's overt response verged on the incendiary. In June 2007 he declared that 'we disclaim responsibility for our retaliatory steps, because it is not we who are the initiators of the new arms race which is undoubtedly brewing in Europe'.

Risk assessment

Politics	Poor
Economy	Improving
Regional stability	Fair

COUNTRY PROFILE

Historical profile

The first monarchic dynasty ruled from the ninth century and built Kiev as its capital. It was overthrown by the Mongol invasion in the thirteenth century.

In the fifteenth century, the Grand Prince of Moscow, Ivan III, annexed the rival principalities of Russia and became its first national sovereign.

Ivan IV (Ivan the Terrible) further expanded Russia's frontiers and became the first holder of the title of Tsar.

Peter the Great (1682–1725) and Catherine the Great (1762–96) consolidated the regime.

1812 The French invasion of Russia ended when France was driven out.

In the mid-nineteenth century, most of Siberia was annexed and expansion to the south and east continued until 1905.

1914–16 After initial success in the First Would War against Germany and Austria, later military defeats weakened the position of the Tsar as personal head of the army and increased political and economy tensions.

1917 In February Tsar Nicholas II was forced to abdicate. The liberal government was overthrown in a Bolshevik coup, under the leadership of Lenin.

1918–20 A civil war raged between the communist Bolsheviks and anti-Bolsheviks, the right-wing white army. The Tsar and his family, captives of the Bolsheviks, were executed by their jailers on 17 July 1918, to prevent them from being liberated by Tsarist forces. The civil war ended in defeat for the white army, despite assistance from the UK, France, Japan and the US.

1922 The Union of Soviet Socialist Republics (USSR) was formed by Russia, Ukraine, Belarus and the Transcaucasus region.

1924 Following Lenin's death, Josef Stalin took over the leadership of the USSR as the general secretary of the Communist Party of the Soviet Union (CPSU) and a period of industrialisation, collectivisation of agriculture and purges of Stalin's opponents began. Key leadership rival Leon Trotsky was exiled in 1927 and assassinated in 1940.

1939 The USSR signed a non-aggression pact, the Molotov-Ribbentrop Treaty, with Nazi Germany. Soviet forces assisted the German invasion of Poland. The USSR also invaded Finland but was forced to respect Finnish independence in a 1940 peace agreement. Stalin ordered the execution of around 8,000 captured polish army officers at Katyn, near Smolensk in Russia.

1941 After the USSR was invaded by Germany, it joined the Allies and declared war on the Axis powers.

1944–45 The USSR liberated parts of Eastern Europe and Eastern Germany, these being pulled into its sphere of influence after the Second World War. Western Europe, meanwhile, fell under the sphere of influence of the US, marking the start of the Cold War.

1949 The USSR became the world's second nuclear power (after the US), when it exploded its first atomic bomb.

1953 Following Stalin's death, Nikita Krushchev took over the leadership of the USSR.

1955 The Warsaw Pact was established by the USSR and its satellite eastern European states as a security apparatus to defend the region against NATO.

1962 The USSR's deployment of nuclear missiles in Cuba, within striking distance of the US, led to the 14-day missile crisis between the US and the USSR.

1964 After Krushchev's fall from power, the USSR was led by Leonid Brezhnev.

1979 Soviet forces invaded Afghanistan to prop up the communist Afghan government.

1982 After Brezhnev's death, Yuri Andropov became leader of the USSR.

1984 Konstantin Chernenko replaced Andropov, following his death.

1985 Chernenko died. His successor, Mikhail Gorbachev, instigated a programme of social, political and economic reforms, centred on two slogan concepts: perestroika (restructuring) and glasnost (openness).

1989 The USSR withdrew from Afghanistan. Communist rule ended in most of eastern and central Europe.

1991 Gorbachev survived a coup attempted by communist hard-liners, in August, but lost power; he dissolved the CPSU, the communist central committee. In the ensuing power vacuum Boris Yeltsin emerged as a leader when he prevented a military takeover in Moscow. He was elected Russia's president. The USSR ceased to exist on 31 December and the Commonwealth of Independent States (CIS) was formed by 11 of the former USSR republics, including Russia. In December, Dzhokhar Dudayev won presidential elections in Chechnya and proclaimed independence from Russia. The remains of the last Tsar and his

family, found in 1989, were identified after two years of forensic and DNA tests.
1992 In June, Yeltsin appointed Yegor Gaidar acting prime minister. In December, Yeltsin appointed Viktor Chernomyrdin prime minister.
1993 Yeltsin ordered the army to crush an anti-government uprising in Moscow and end a parliamentary sit-in, in October. The Federal Assembly, comprising the State Duma and the Federation Council replaced the Supreme Soviet. In December a referendum approved a new constitution that gave the president sweeping powers.
1994 In December, Russian troops invaded Chechnya, which is de facto independent, but de jure part of Russia. Uzbekistan and Russia signed an economic integration treaty.
1995 In the Duma elections, the reformed Kommunisticheskaya Partiya Rossiiskoi Federatsii (KPRF) (Communist Party of the Russian Federation) won the largest vote. In June, Chechen rebels seized hundreds of hostages during a raid on the southern Russian town of Budennovsk. More than 100 are killed in the ensuing violence.
1996 In July Yeltsin was re-elected president. Russia joined in G7 discussions on nuclear security.
In Chechnya: in January, Chechen rebels seize thousands of hostages in the Russian town of Kizlyar. In April, President Dudayev was killed by the Russian airforce; he was succeeded by Zelimkhan Yandarbiyev. In May, a peace treaty was signed between Russia and Chechen separatists, temporarily ending the conflict. In August, Chechen forces drove the Russian army out of Grozny.
1997 Yeltsin and the Belarussian president, Aleksander Lukashenko, signed the Treaty on the Union of Belarus and Russia. The treaty aimed at increasing political and economic co-operation between the two states. In May, Yeltsin and the new Chechen president Aslan Maskhadov signed a formal peace agreement.
1998 The Russian rouble collapsed, sending Russia into temporary economic crisis as it defaulted on foreign debts. The rouble was revalued (one new rouble = 1,000 old roubles). Yeltsin appointed Sergei Kiriyenko as prime minister but this was opposed by the Duma, as was his second choice Vikto Chernomyrdin. In September, Yeltsin appointed Yevgeny Primakov prime minister. The bodies of the last Russian Tsar and his family was interred in the Cathedral of Saints Peter and Paul, in St Petersburg.
1999 An Islamist separatist group declared the Russian republic of Dagestan to be independent. Chechen fighters under the command of the former prime minister of Chechnya, Shamil Basayev, invaded Dagestan in support of the separatists. Yeltsin sacked Primakov and appointed Vladimir Putin as prime minister. In September, a series of bomb explosions in Russian cities were blamed on Chechen separatists and Russia launched a second invasion of Chechnya. On 31 December, Yeltsin resigned before the official end of his term. Putin became acting president.
2000 Vladimir Putin was elected president with 52.9 per cent of the vote. The presidents of Belarus, Kazakhstan, Kyrgyzstan, Russia and Tajikistan (formerly the Customs Five) established the Eurasian Economic Community (EEC).
2001 The Russian army started a gradual withdrawal of troops from Chechnya. The Federation Council approved a monetary union with Belarus. A joint action plan included the introduction of the new rouble on 1 January 2005, in preparation for introducing a new single currency in Russia and Belarus by 2008. The main pro-Putin parties created the Yedinaya Rossiya (YR) (United Russia) party by merging the ruling Mezhregional'noye Dvishenie Yedinstvo (Medved) (Inter-Regional Movement Unity) and the Otechestvo-Vsya Rossiya (OVR) (Fatherland-All Russia). Tajikistan, China, Russia, Kazakhstan, Kyrgyzstan and Uzbekistan formed the Shanghai Co-operation Organisation (SCO) and agreed to fight ethnic and religious militancy, while promoting investment and trade.
2002 The US and Russia agreed to cut 70 per cent of their nuclear arsenals. Chechen Prime Minister Stanislav Ilyasov resigned and was appointed by President Putin as Russia's federal minister of Chechnya affairs. Akhmed Kadyrov, appointed Mikhail Babich as prime minister of Chechnya. Chechnya's leading rebel warlord, Shamil Basayev, claimed responsibility for the Moscow theatre siege in which 119 hostages died.
2003 In February, Kadyrov dismissed Babich as Chechen prime minister and appointed Anatoly Popov in his place. In September, Russia, Ukraine, Kazakhstan and Belarus signed an economic union treaty. The YR won the December parliamentary elections.
2004 President Putin dismissed Prime Minister Kasyanov's and appointed Mikhail Fradkov, in his place. Incumbent Vladimir Putin won the 14 March presidential elections.
In Chechnya: Sergei Abramov was confirmed as prime minister of a pro-Moscow government. The president, Akhmad Kadyrov, was killed in an explosion and Abramov became acting president. On 29 August, Alu Alkhanov won the Chechnya presidential elections. In September, at least 330 people died in the Beslan school massacre when Russian troops stormed the school held by Chechen terrorists, in an attempt to free the hostage schoolchildren and teachers.
2005 In Chechnya Russian special forces killed the Chechen rebel leader, Maskhadov in March. Russia gave asylum to President Askar Akayev of Tajikistan, who was facing widespread demonstrations against his rule. In May, the former 'oligarch' and head of the oil company, Yukos, Mikhail Khodorkovsky, was jailed for tax evasion and fraud. On 13 November, a blast at a chemical factory in Jilin, north-east China caused a spillage of highly toxic benzene and nitrobenzene into the Songhua river, which is a tributary of the Amur river from which cities in south-east Russia draw their water supplies. President Putin restricted the operations of NGOs in December; they were accused of being foreign-funded and directed and fronts for intelligence gathering activities. State control over the media and electoral laws were also tightened. In December, a diplomatic row developed when Ukraine refused to pay a four-fold increase in the price of gas and Gazprom cut off supplies. The row escalated and antagonised the EU when supplies to some of its member states were also cut, by default. Germany and Russia signed an agreement to build a gas pipeline beneath the Baltic Sea and secure Russian natural gas to western Europe.
2006 The dispute with Ukraine was resolved on 6 January and a similar dispute with Bulgaria was resolved in February. President Putin announced the rouble would be fully convertible and float freely against foreign currencies by 2007. On 17 June, Abdul-Khalim Sadulayev, the president of separatist Chechnya was killed by Russian forces. In November, Russia denied it was responsible for the death of outspoken critic of Putin's regime and former security service officer, Aleksandr Litvinenko, by radioactive poison. In December, Belarus became the latest former Soviet-satellite country to be given an ultimatum of paying the market price for Russian gas or being denied supplies. Belarus agreed to the new contract whereby it would pay over double its current price and phase in further increases by 2010.
2007 The oil pipeline through Belarus was shutdown in January as Belarus attempted to impose a transit tax on the oil; Russia accused Belarus of siphoning off oil. The row was resolved as both countries cancelled their respective tax and export duty. On 15 February, President Putin dismissed Chechen president, Alu Alkhanov and appointed Ramzan Kadyrov in his place. The Russians planted their flag below the North Pole on 4 August using two mini-submarines in an action

laying claim to the potential oil and minerals below the seabed. The US and Canada criticised both the claim and exploit; countries with territories bordering the Arctic launched competing claims. In 2007, the North Pole (administered by the International Seabed Authority) was regarded as not subject to any one country's claim. The remains of the last two missing children of Tsar Nicholas II, including his son Alexei, were found near Ekaterinburg in July and confirmed in September. The bodies had not been found with the remains of the rest of the family, discovered in 1991. On 12 September, the government, led by Prime Minister Mikhail Fradkov, was dissolved by President Putin, who nominated Viktor Zubkov as prime minister. The Duma confirmed Zubkov's appointment on 14 September. On 1 October, Vladimir Putin declared that he would accept the post of prime minister on behalf of the ruling YR party when he steps down as president in 2008. On 7 November the Duma unanimously voted to abandon temporarily the 1990 Conventional Forces in Europe (CFE) treaty, which, in view of NATO expansion, it considered 'no longer responds to the security interest of the Russian Federation'. President Putin accused the US of orchestrating a plot by Western observers to boycott and discredit the 3 December presidential elections. The Organisation for Security and Co-operation in Europe (OSCE) announced that it was withdrawing its observer team due to 'unprecedented' curbs imposed by Russian authorities and the lack of visas for all its team members. In the 2 December parliamentary elections Presidential Putin's YR won over 64.3 per cent of the vote (315 seats out of 450); the KPRF party 11.6 per cent (57). Only parties that won votes to pass the 7 per cent voting threshold gained seats in the Duma. There were reports of voting irregularities by opposition leaders and although confirmed by YR the electoral commission said there were no significant violations. Observers from the Council of Europe and the OSCE declared the election was 'not fair and failed to meet many... commitments and standards for democratic elections'. President Putin claimed the election was legitimate and a public vote of trust in him. Russia suspended its participation in the Conventional Forces in Europe treaty on 12 December. The treaty is considered the cornerstone of European security and was negotiated between Nato and the ex-Warsaw Pact states in 1990. It limits the amount of military equipment in designated areas.

2008 In the presidential election on 2 March, Dmitry Medvedev won the presidential election with 70.3 per cent of the vote, his nearest rival, Gennady Zyuganov won 17.7 per cent; turnout was 69.8 per cent. International observers criticised the election campaign stating candidates did not have equal access to the media. Vladimir Putin accepted the offer of chairmanship of the ruling Yedinaya Rossiya (YR) (United Russia) party and will become prime minister in May. President Medvedev was sworn into office on 7 May. Vladimir Putin accepted the offer of chairmanship of the ruling Yedinaya Rossiya (YR) (United Russia) party and became prime minister on 8 May. Winner of the Nobel Prize for Literature in 1970, Alexander Solzhenitsyn, died on 4 August.

Political structure

Constitution

The constitution was adopted in December 1993. The Russian Federation consists of 89 republics and regions, including the federal cities of Moscow and St Petersburg.

If the ruling party has over two thirds of the Duma seats it has enough power to amend the constitution unchallenged.

Electoral system: universal direct suffrage over the age of 18.

Form of state

Federal state with a republican form of government

The executive

Executive power is held by the president, who has the right to veto parliamentary legislation, while issuing decrees on which the Federal Assembly may advise but not veto. The president is elected for a four-year term.

The cabinet is appointed by the prime minister, who is appointed by the president.

The State Council of the Russian Federation, which has consultative functions only, was formed in 2000. It advises the president on issues concerning the relationship between the central administration and the regions.

National legislature

The 1993 constitution created a bicameral Federalnoe Sobranie (Federal Assembly), comprising the Gosudarstvennaya Duma (State Duma, lower house) with 450 seat and the Sovet Federatsii (Federation Council, upper house) with 178-seat and include two deputies from each of Russia's 89 republics and regions (representatives of regional executives and legislative bodies); all serving for four-year terms.

Half of the State Duma members are elected by proportional representation from party lists and half in a simple majority contest from territorial constituencies. A party failing to gain at least 5 per cent of the total vote cannot win parliamentary seats.

Legal system

The legal system is based on civil law. There is judicial review of legislative acts. The top levels of the judicial branch consist of: the Constitutional Court, which reviews the constitutionality of federal legislation; the Supreme Court, which is the highest civil and criminal judiciary body; and the Supreme Arbitration Court, which resolves economic disputes between subjects of the Federation. The Supreme Court and Supreme Arbitration Court preside over a federal system of lower criminal and civil courts.

Last elections

2 March 2008 (presidential); 2 December 2007 (parliamentary).

Results: Presidential: Dmitry Medvedev won 70.3 per cent of the vote, Gennady Zyuganov won 17.7 per cent, Vladimir Zhirinovsky won 9.3 per cent; turnout was 69.8 per cent.

Parliamentary: YR won over 64.3 per cent of the vote (315 seats out of 450); the KPRF party 11.6 per cent (57); the Liberal'no-Demokraticheskaya partiya Rossii 8.2 per cent (40) and Spravedlivaya Rossiya (Fair Russia) 7.8 per cent (38).

Next elections

December 2011 (parliamentary); March 2012 (presidential).

Political parties

Ruling party

Yedinaya Rossiya (YR) (United Russia) (elected 2003; re-elected 2 Dec 2007)

Main opposition party

Kommunisticheskaya Partiya Rossiiskoi Federatsii (KPRF) (Communist Party of the Russian Federation)

FT clipping - Opposition Other Russia coalition splits

Population

142.10 million (2007)*

Last census: March 2002: 145,537,200 (provisional)

Population density: Nine inhabitants per square km. Urban population: 73 per cent (1995—2001).

Annual growth rate: -0.3 per cent 1994–2004 (WHO 2006)

Internally Displaced Persons (IDP)
330,000 (UNHCR 2004)

Ethnic make-up

Russian (82 per cent), Tatars (4 per cent) and Ukrainians (3 per cent).

Religions

The majority of the population is Christian, mainly Russian Orthodox. Religion, while not actually forbidden under communism, was officially discouraged. Religious observance and interest is growing steeply with the relaxation of state restrictions. Russian Orthodox Christmas was made an official holiday for the first time in 1991.

Russia also has sizeable Muslim (12 million) and Jewish (700,000) minorities.

Education

After compulsory education at age 15, secondary (complete) general education begins. Students may also enter vocational schools or non-university level higher education institutions. Initial vocational schools offer one-and-a-half to two years of vocational education. Secondary (complete) general education continues for two years and ends when students are aged 17–18 years.

Higher education is provided by 553 public and 260 non-public accredited higher education institutions. Education in public higher education is free of charge. There are three levels of higher educational institutions including those lasting between two to four years and an advanced level lasting between five and six years. The government aims to diversify higher education courses and boost the private sector. In addition to universities in the public and private sector, there are 3,000 non-university institutions in Russia.

Literacy rate: 100 per cent adult rate; 100 per cent youth rate (15–24) (Unesco 2005).

Compulsory years: Six to 15 years.

Enrolment rate: 107 per cent total primary enrolment of the relevant age group (including repeaters) (World Bank).

Pupils per teacher: 20 in primary schools.

Health

Per capita total expenditure on health (2003) was US$551; of which per capita government spending was US$325, at the international dollar rate, (WHO 2006).

In May 2006 President Putin announced government sponsored health measures to reduce the falling birth rate, low life expectancy and unusually high male mortality rate. Russia is investing US$7 billion in four 'national projects', one of which is healthcare. Child benefits are being increased and one-off payments made to mothers to encourage fertility. Nevertheless, Russia has one of the highest rates of abortion in the world, with 66 terminations for every 100 pregnancies. Fertility rates fell from 2.19 births per woman in 1986–87 to 1.34 in 2003 and is still below the 2.1 births necessary to sustain population growth.

In every hour they is only one birth for 77 deaths and Russia has been warned that its population could crash by 2050 if the trend is not reversed. Mortality rates have ballooned for a wide number of reasons including poor diet, disease, alcoholism and risky activities – Russia has twice as many road accident fatalities as any other G8 country.

HIV/Aids

HIV/Aids has spread in Russia at a time when infection rates have been steady and declining for a number of years in Europe and North America. Few Russians can afford the expensive new treatments that have been discovered in the past few years. HIV/Aids cases have more than trebled since 2000. Russian health officials blame the high number of HIV/Aids cases on intravenous drug use rather than sexual activity.

HIV prevalence: 1.1 per cent aged 15–49 in 2003 (World Bank)

Life expectancy: 65 years, 2004 (WHO 2006)

Fertility rate/Maternal mortality rate: 1.3 births per woman, 2004 (WHO 2006)

Birth rate/Death rate: 10 births per 1,000 population; 14 deaths per 1,000 population (2003).

Child (under 5 years) mortality rate (per 1,000): 16 per 1,000 live births (World Bank)

Head of population per physician: 4.25 physicians per 1,000 people, 2003 (WHO 2006)

Welfare

In January 2005, widespread demonstrations forced Vladimir Putin to amend newly instigated reforms to the benefits system after they were introduced. The plan to offer cash payments in exchange for what had been free services such as medicines, transport and subsidised housing continued but the amounts were increased and pension payments brought by a month. About 34 million pensioners, infirm and war veterans are estimated to be affected by the changes, with the lowest payments at just US$7.5 per month.

Critics said that the implimentation of the change was mishandled and the calculations sloppy, whereas the government believes that 'monetising' benefits was the only option to streamline social benefits and generate considerable cost savings. This set-back is thought, by some, to risk Putin's reform agenda.

Given budgetary constraints, reforms are targetted at increasing the transparency and efficiency of Russia's main social funds and eliminating unproductive social programmes. There have been massive increases in health service funding, especially to reduce infant mortality rates and bring healthcare up to world standards. Maternity benefits are being enhanced in order to induce women to stay at home for two or three years.

The tax code has been used to unify and reduce the different social security contributions but, despite recent tax cuts, average real incomes remain low.

Unemployment benefits based on past earnings remain very low due to high inflation. Income inequality levels have consequently been increasing and it is estimated that about 20.4 per cent of the population live below the minimum subsistence level laid down by the state.

Main cities

Moscow (capital of the Russian Federation, estimated population 10.4 million (m) in 2005); St Petersburg (formerly Leningrad) (4.2m); Novosibirsk (1.4m); Nizhny Novgorod (formerly Gorki, 1.3m); Yekaterinburg (formerly Sverdlovsk) (1.3m); Samara (formerly Kuybyshev) (1.2m); Rostov-on-Don (1.0m); Omsk (1.1m); Kazan (capital of the sovereign republic Tatarstan) (1.1m); Cheljabinsk (1.1m); Volgograd (1.0m), Ufa (1.1m); Vladivostok (601,161); Irkutsk (599,718); Krasnodar (655,736).

Languages spoken

There are as many as 100 local ethnic languages, some of the larger groupings include Baskin, Chuvash Tatar and Yakut. Russian is spoken throughout the country. Russian and most local languages are written in variants of the Cyrillic alphabet, which was devised by the ninth century saints, Cyril and Methodius. In September 2000, the Tatarstan republic (population four million, a large minority of whom are Russian) began a 10-year transition period for the switch in schools from Cyrillic to the Latin alphabet for the local Turkic language. Russian is the second language spoken in Tatarstan. However, Russian MPs voted in June 2002 to make the use of the Cyrillic alphabet mandatory throughout the country.

On 5 Feb 2003, the State Duma passed a law making Russian the official state language, prohibiting the use in public documents of foreign words or expressions that have Russian-language equivalents).

Ukrainian, Mordvin and Chechen are also spoken.

Official language/s

Russian

Media

In February 2008 the worldwide human right's campaigning organisation, Amnesty International, stated that freedom of speech was 'shrinking alarmingly' with intimidation and arbitrary laws to curb outspoken media outlets and NGOs, while others alleged the extrajudicial killing of journalists.

National news agency: Itar-Tass News Agency

Other news agencies: RIA Novosti, 4 Zubovsky Blvd, Moscow 119031 (tel: 637-2424; internet: http://en.rian.ru).

Interfax, 2 Pervaya Tverskaya-Yamskaya Ul, Building 1, Moscow 127006 (tel: 250-9840; fax: 250-9727; internet: www.interfax.ru).

Press

Dailies: There are many national and regional newspapers, most of which publish in Russian with a few in minority languages, as well as English. Some regional news is published over the Internet only while others are published (see www.wps.ru, monitoring – regional press). Major nationals in Russian are Izvestia (www.izvestia.ru) owned by Gazprom and Rossiyskaya Gazeta (www.rg.ru) is government owned. The Komsomolskaya Pravda (www.kp.ru) is a mass-circulation paper while Nezavisimaya Gazeta is an influential privately owned daily. Kommersant (www.kommersant.ru) is business orientated while Trud (www.trud.ru), is a socialist minded paper.

In English, The Moscow Times (www.themoscowtimes.com) and its companion newspaper the St Petersburg Times (ww.sptimes.ru) report, among other things, on politics and business.

Weeklies: In Russian, the most popular publication is Argumenty i Facty (Arguments & Facts) (www.aif.ru) containing in-depth analysis of political and economic events. Others include Itogi (www.itogi.ru), Ogonyok (www.ogoniok.com) and Profil (www.profile.ru) and the Moskovskie Novosti (www.mn.ru) is a weekly international socio-political newspaper. In English, Russia Profile (www.russiaprofile.org) is published 10 times per year, the Moscow News Weekly (www.mnweekly.ru) and The Russia Journal (www.russiajournal.com) contain weekly news, analysis, and political opinion.

Business: Moscow Times is an English-language business publication.

Periodicals: In English, Russia Profile (www.russiaprofile.org) is published 10 times per year, and Vladivostok News (http://vn.vladnews.ru) both cover political and business information.

Broadcasting

Russian authorities pressured all radio stations to stopped broadcasting the BBC's Russian services in 2007.

Radio: There are two national state-run radio networks, Radio Russia (www.radiorus.ru) and Radio Mayak (www.radiomayak.ru). There are many commercial radio stations broadcasting in regional markets, Russkoye Radio (www.rusradio.ru) and Moscow Echo (www.echo.msk.ru) are the two most important.

The Voice of Russia (http://ruvr.ru) broadcasts programmes in 33 languages to 160 countries worldwide.

Television: Since 2001 the independence of Russian television has been circumscribed by government regulations that restricted majority foreign ownership and banned some stations, particularly those critical of the government.

The state-run Russia TV Channel (www.rutv.ru) network, the state part-owned Channel One (www.1tv.ru) and the Gazprom-owned NTV (www.ntv.ru), broadcast nationally. Fully commercial stations include Centre TV (www.tvc.ru) and Ren TV (www.ren-tv.com). Russia Today (www.russiatoday.ru) with news programming is state-funded and broadcasts in English, by satellite and cable.

Advertising

Commercial advertising is widely available. Limited television and radio advertising is available to Western companies; billboards and illuminated signs can be bought in most major cities.

Economy

The difference between a banana republic and Russia's one-industry driven economy is that the rest of the world can take or leave bananas, but natural gas, which Russia has in great quantity (16 per cent of total global reserves and 20 per cent of world production), is a necessity that cannot be dismissed.

The state-owned energy company has become not an instrument of state policy but rather the opposite, a company which policies are, if not those of the state, at least wholly state sanctioned. Gazprom has the commercial objective of producing a profit at the end of the year, but it also has a political element, as it increasingly becomes a weapon of foreign policy: what's good for Gazprom is good for Russia.

Russia does not wish to be just a supplier of gas and oil, it wants to be a producer, which brings a value-added price to the commodity. When its hydrocarbon reserves are finally depleted, it plans to have diversified into enough external markets for the shock to be minimal. To do this it has two strategies: for existing facilities the option to pipeline owners is either 'let us buy a share of the operation or you risk losing the supply of gas'; the option for new gas and oil pipelines under construction has been through joint partnerships from the outset. The Russian parliament reinforced Gazprom's monopoly by reserving its 'right to export gas', in the face of European opposition and the Energy Charter Treaty, (signed in 1991), which should give open access to pipelines and investment in new markets, but does not. The old adversary, the US, has used Gazprom's aggressive and expansionist policies which precluded foreign ownership as evidence that Russia was not ready to join the World Trade Organisation (WTO), as it saw the erstwhile hand of the Kremlin and the progressively more magisterial President Putin behind the strategy of aggressive takeovers.

Russia fell from its ranking as one of only two world superpowers in 1991 and is currently regarded as an 'upper middle-income' economy, equal in status with Brazil, India and China (referred to collectively as the BRICs) and has been attempting to reclaim its former glory. Its industrial base is in places still old, outmoded and unproductive, its people, while generally well educated, were unused to the capitalistic ethos of work smart and earn more, embrace change and survive. At a time when Russia's GDP growth was 6.4 per cent, in 2005, and expected to be 6.5 per cent in 2006, its population has been falling, along with life expectancy, with the highest rates of HIV/Aids in the European region. International observers have warned that the population is declining at an unprecedented rate for an industrialised country – 700,000 per year and that health and welfare provisions should be increased and improved. In the meantime, the labour force is dropping worrying, which will possibly have an adverse effecton GDP growth.

President Putin gave the economy an environment in which to expand. Foreign companies, particularly global brand names are well represented, but there is still an air of lawlessness, with old scores settled by extreme measures and corruption and favouritism by officials (a throwback to the Soviet era of business) which still taints the market place.

Russia changed to a three-year budget system in 2007, in an attempt to hold budget spending as oil prices rose sharply. Large increases in public sector wages and pensions before the elections in 2007 contributed to high inflation rates in 2008 (over 15 per cent, well above the government target of 10.5 per cent). In June 2008 President Medvedev said that the 2009/11 budget would focuss on inflation and pensions

In June 2008 President Medvedev

The Russian economy is as large and diverse as its people and lands, it is attempting to find its place in the world by using the only assets it has, it may be unsubtle and aggressive but it is at least going in the right direction.

External trade

Following the break-up of the Soviet Union, trade was formalised with former republics through the Commonwealth of Independent States (CIS), however a free trade zone between members had not, by 2007, been implemented, due to

differences in economic objectives, degrees of reforms and economic development.
Russia has immense mineral deposits in diamonds, precious metals and coal as well as timber and is a leading world supplier of oil and natural gas, which represents around 80 per cent of its exports.
Foreign trade provides over 55 per cent of GDP and with high world oil and gas prices will remain a dominant component.
Investment in industry, manufacturing and infrastructure has been low and hampers progress.
Russia inherited the majority of the Soviet Union's military industrial base and weapons are the largest manufactured items exported.

Imports
The principal imports include vehicles, consumer goods, medicines, meat, sugar, machinery and equipment, and semi-finished metal products.
Main sources: Germany (13.4 per cent total, 2006), China (9.4 per cent), Ukraine (6.7 per cent).

Exports
The principal exports include petroleum and derivatives, natural gas, timber, metals, chemicals, and a wide variety of civilian and military manufactures.
Main destinations: The Netherlands (11.9 per cent total, 2006), Italy (8.3 per cent), Germany (8.1 per cent).

Agriculture

Farming
Production in the agricultural sector in Russia has fallen since reforms began in 1992, following the substantial reduction in large state subsidies. The livestock sector contracted by about half. Progress has been particularly slow in land reform, and Russia still lacks a free market in agricultural land. Agricultural production contributes only 7 per cent of GDP, with 133 million hectares (ha) of arable land, and a large agrarian workforce constituting nearly 14 per cent of the total.
The sector has suffered due to incomplete agriculture-specific and economy-wide institutional reform, such as price and trade reform, as well as privatisation. Russia has the potential to increase grain exports significantly if such reforms are implemented and the situation seems to be improving.
Wheat and barley are the most significant crops produced in Russia that are widely traded on world markets.
Crop production ('000) in 2005 included: 76,420 tonnes (t) cereals in total, 47,608t wheat, 17,773t barley, 3,179t maize, 3,630t rye, 4,569t oats, 36,400t potatoes, 21,520t sugar beets, 3,985t cabbages, 1,628t pulses, 325t grapes, 6,280t sunflower seed, 2,839t oilcrops, 1,980 tomatoes, 2,050t apples, 217t strawberries, 4,019t fruit in total, 15,201t vegetables in total. Livestock production included: 4,885t meat in total, 1,915t beef, 1,610t pig meat, 141t lamb and goat meat, 1,130t poultry, 2,067t eggs, 30,859t milk, 53t honey, 220t cattle hides, 13t sheepskins, 46t greasy wool.

Fishing
There has been a very noticeable drop in recorded fish production in Russia, since the end of the Soviet era. Production shortfalls have resulted in rising prices and steadily increasing imports of fish and fishery products.
Russia's lucrative caviar industry, based on the Caspian Sea and long stymied by dwindling stocks, was effectively shut down in 2001–02 by an international ban on the export of caviar products, imposed by the Convention on International Trade in Endangered Species (Cites). The US government unilaterally introduced its own ban in 2002 and Cites reimposed an international ban in January 2006.
In addition to the consequences of major economic and political changes, aquaculture and inland capture fisheries continue to face problems from environmental impacts on water resources affecting living aquatic resources. The environmental degradation of inland waters through industrial, urban and agrochemical pollution, and the damming of major rivers has had significant local impacts on fish stocks. As a result of the large-scale uptake of water for irrigation, the original fish fauna of Russia has been significantly modified.
Production from subsistence and recreational fisheries is seldom accurately reflected in the official statistics, and it is likely that production from these sectors plays an important role for food supply in the country. However, capture fisheries in many inland waters of the region, including, in particular, reservoirs and lakes, continue to depend heavily on stocking of fry and fingerlings produced in hatcheries, lake farms and artificial spawning grounds, or by other types of enhancement measures.
Improved stocking and fisheries management measures provide the potential for significant increases in fish production from reservoirs and lakes in Russia. It is estimated that fisheries production from reservoirs could be increased between four and six-fold by improved stocking; inland fish production could realistically be doubled by 2010. It is expected that recreational fisheries, often contributing significantly to household food supply, will gain increasing importance.
The annual total fish catch is approximately five million tonnes (t). Russia imports some 6,000t of sea products while it exports around 117,000t annually.
In 2004, the total marine fish catch was 2,504,682 tonnes and the total crustacean catch was 48,018 tonnes.

Forestry
Russia has by far the largest forested area of any country in the world with forest and other wooded land constituting more than half of its land area estimated at 851.3 million hectares (ha) or almost 55 per cent of the total land area. Russia accounts for more than 20 per cent of global forest resources, more than 35 per cent of temperate/boreal forests in terms of area and 45 per cent in terms of growing stock. The area of forest is fairly stable, showing a marginal average annual increase of 0.02 per cent, or the equivalent of 135,000ha of forest cover. The importance of Russia's forests as a regulator of the global carbon balance, and mitigation of climate change, is difficult to overestimate.
The predominant coniferous species are larch and spruce. The deciduous species are represented mainly by birch, aspen and oaks (either European or Mongolian), and hornbeam, ash, maple and elm to a lesser degree. Mature and over-mature stands, situated mainly in the Asian part of Russia, prevail and about two-thirds of the forest is available for wood supply.
Russia is one of the largest producers and exporters of industrial roundwood in the world market. Significant volumes of sawn wood, plywood and pulp and paper are exported. The forest industry is almost completely privatised, although the forests and the roundwood production remain under state control.
Export of forest material in 2004 amounted to US$6.4 billion, while imports amounted to US$1.1 billion.
Timber production ('000) in 2004 included 182,000cum cubic metre (cum) roundwood, 134,000cum industrial roundwood, 21,500cum sawnwood, 58,758cum sawlogs and veneer logs, 54,171cum pulpwood, 7,159cum wood-based panels, 48,000cum woodfuel; 60,000 tonnes (t) charcoal, 6,789,000t paper and paperboard, 601,000t printing and writing paper (including 1,979,000t newsprint), 6,725,000t paper pulp, 1,900,000t recovered paper.

Industry and manufacturing
The industrial sector accounts for 30 per cent of GDP and provides employment for a third of the working population.
Factors that continue to dog efficiency include wasteful consumption of fuel and raw materials, antiquated machinery, poor technology and management and overstaffing. Early on in the reform process emphasis was placed on individual enterprise and factory production

decisions, resulting in anarchic management practices.
Major production bottlenecks in the 1990s included steel, construction inputs (such as cement) and consumer and light industry products (such as television sets, robots and computers).
Emphasis during the 1990s was on light industry, modernisation and computerisation. Towards the end of the 1990s, there were attempts by major industrial and manufacturing companies to consolidate their activities, with many mergers. The sector remains reliant on large- and medium-sized firms to increase production and stimulate growth, particularly in engineering and metallurgy working.
Industrial production increased by 3.7 per cent in 2003 and an estimated 6.4 per cent in 2004.

Tourism

Russia is an increasingly important tourist destination with considerable potential, but it only accounts for 1.7 per cent of GDP. It attracts around 8 million holiday visitors. However, foreign exchange earnings are offset by the larger outflow of Russian tourists. The sector remains relatively undeveloped. Infrastructure is inadequate. Expansion is hindered by a shortage of tourist-oriented accommodation, not only in the provinces, but also in Moscow and other major cities, where luxury hotels have been the norm. Investment is being directed towards increasing the availability of two- and three-star hotels. Other problems include visa regulations and the lack of a structured national tourism organisation. In July 2004, the St Petersburg region secured EU funding support for an initiative to develop its tourism industry.

Mining

Russia is the world's largest producer of iron ore, asbestos, manganese ore, nickel, chromite, platinum group metals and potassium salts, and the second-largest producer of gold, lead and phosphate ores. There are vast reserves, but extraction has been held back due to rising production costs, labour shortages and a shortage of technology.
Major foreign exchange earners include gold and diamonds. Estimated annual production of diamonds is 12,000 tonnes. Russia is estimated to have 30 per cent of world iron ore reserves and 20 per cent of many other minerals. Significant quantities of iron ore, chromium, nickel, asbestos and fertiliser materials are exported.
There are large deposits of antimony, beryllium, cadmium, mercury, molybdenum, tin and vanadium plus workable deposits of all rare earth metals.
Large-scale investment in the sector is improving extraction and processing techniques, while reducing wastage and controlling production costs. Gold production in 2005 totalled 157.6 tonnes, much of which originates in Russia's Sakha Republic (formerly Yakutia). This represents a decline in production of nearly 7 per cent since 2004.

Hydrocarbons

Russia had 69.1 billion barrels of proven oil reserves in 2003. Crude oil production increased by 11 per cent in 2003 to 8.54 million barrels per day (bpd) and increased again in 2004 to 9.27 million bpd, making it the second largest producer in the world after Saudia Arabia. Russia is also the second largest oil exporter in the world, again after Saudia Arabia, exporting 6.67 million bpd. Its production increases have been far higher than any other non-member of the Organisation of the Petroleum Exporting Countries (OPEC). Russia has 42 refineries with a total capacity of 5.51 million bpd, which require further development and investment due to their inefficiency and ageing. Recovery of the estimated 139 million tonnes of crude oil from western Siberia began in 1998 and production is expected to reach six million tonnes per annum by the end of 2004. The government is at present promoting extensive oil exploration and extraction in eastern Siberia, particularly in the Sakha Republic (formerly Yakutia). In 2004, based on proven oil reserves, the International Energy Agency estimated that production in Russia would continue to expand for another two to three years before entering a period of decline.
Proven gas reserves of 47 trillion cubic metres (cum) (2003) account for around 26.7 per cent of world reserves. Russia has the world's largest reserves and is the world's largest producer of natural gas, with production totalling 578.6 billion cum in 2003. Gas meets nearly 55 per cent of the country's energy needs, a ratio forecast to reach 60 per cent by 2010, with production anticipated to double from the current level. Construction of the 1,213km Blue Stream pipeline was completed in 2002 and transit began in 2003. It will supply Turkey with 15.9 billion cum of natural gas, more than 60 per cent of its domestic needs. In December 2005, work began on a trans-Baltic Sea gas pipeline linking the Russian town of Vyborg with the German town of Greifswald. Gazprom hold a 51 per cent stake in the venture and has recruited former German chancellor Gerhard Schröder to chair the project. New gas and fields off the coast of Sakhalin Island, in Russia's far east, have been in development since 2003 but these face criticism from environmentalists concerned with the impact on local marine life.
Coal reserves totalled 157.0 billion tonnes oil equivalent (toe) in 2003. Russia produced 124.9 million toe, an increase of 8.8 per cent on 2002 production levels. The government had hoped to expand coal production to 335 million tonnes in 2010 and 430 million tonnes by 2020.
Russia's hydrocarbon sector is dominated by state-owned enterprises, foremost of which are Gazprom (gas) and Rosneft (oil). This is the product of a government policy, particularly since 2004, to regain control of key resources in the wake of chaotic liberalisation in the early 1990s and has at times involved questionable methods. In December 2004, President Putin backed a move to strip the privately owned Yukos oil company of its main production arm, Yuganskneftegas, and subsequently permitted its purchase by the state-owned oil company Rosneft. This left Rosneft in control of some 16 per cent of Russia's total crude oil output . In the process, Yukos chairman Mikhail Khodorkovsky, who resisted the takeover, was jailed for fraud. In June 2005, the government increased its stake in Gazprom from 38 to 51 per cent.
Gazprom currently controls 20 per cent of the world's natural gas reserves. In October 2005, Gazprom bought the Sibneft oil company from Roman Abramovich, giving the Kremlin (via Gazprom and Rosneft) control of over one third of Russia's total oil output. In December 2005, the Russian parliament voted to lift the ceiling on foreign ownership of Gazprom shares above 20 per cent but the government's 51 per cent stake remains in place.

Energy

Russia is the second-largest generator of electricity in the world with installed capacity of 206GW and an output of about 860 billion kWh (2004 estimate), of which about 63 per cent is produced thermally, 21 per cent by hydroelectricity and 16 per cent nuclear. The sector is in a poor state and requires investment of up to US$11 billion annually between 2002–05 to expand and maintain existing electricity generation. The Russian government has only allocated US$1 billion per annum and it is unlikely that the sector will attract significant foreign capital. As a result, the country faces an energy crisis that could dampen industrial development and therefore hinder economic growth.
Russia's 31 nuclear power plants are being assessed. By 2001, four plants had come to the end of their 30-year prescribed service life and 16 of its reactors are of the same design as the one in Chernobyl, Ukraine. By 2010, another 10 reactors will be due for closure.

The government has prioritised the need to extend the working life of these plants. In January 2001, Russia announced it will build 40 nuclear reactors by 2020 to prevent an energy crisis. The 1,000MW Rostov-1 reactor began operating in March 2001. Russia commissioned five new nuclear power plants in 2001, increasing the country's generating capacity by a further 3,000MW by 2005.

In March 2004, the Putin government began to reform the electricity sector, with the intent of introducing greater competition and partial privatisation. Gazprom, the state-controlled gas company, has begun to buy into electricity sector.

Russia exports electricity to most countries of the former USSR and also to China, Poland, Turkey and Finland. In October 2003, Russia and the EU agreed to fully integrate their respective power grids by 2007.

Financial markets

Stock exchange

The main exchange markets are the Russian Exchange and the St Petersburg Stock Exchange.

Enthusiasm for Moscow stocks diminished following the collapse of the rouble in 1998. The fall partly reflected continued uncertainty about investing in the country, as well as international downward pressure driven by scepticism about the fast-growing 'new economy'. Stability of the rouble's exchange rate in 2002 encouraged financial market participants to invest in government securities.

Banking and insurance

Most major banks are located in Moscow. The majority of Russian banks suffer from being undercapitalised and the high rate of inflation has constantly eroded their reserves. This is not surprising given the high degree of fragmentation in the sector. The system has been criticised for having too many owner-operators; this is a situation with potential for abuse. The retail banking sector is still in its infancy and branch networking is not particularly common.

Foreign banks are not permitted to open their own branches in Russia and instead must rely upon subsidiaries, which drives up their costs. President Putin reiterated his opposition to direct foreign entry in December 2005. The US has protested this decision and has pointed out that Russia's desire to join the WTO will require banking liberalisation.

In June 2003, Russia was removed from the Organisation for Economic Co-operation and Development (OECD) black list of havens for money laundering.

Beginning 29 July 2004, the Central Bank revoked the licences for operations of three Moscow banks: the Commercial Bank of Savings, the Industrial Export-Import Bank and the Investment and Commercial Moscow Housing Construction Bank.

Central bank

Central Bank of the Russian Federation

Main financial centre

Moscow

Time

The Russian Federation covers 11 time zones, from GMT plus two hours in the Russian enclave of Kaliningrad Oblast (between Poland and Lithuania), to the eastern, Siberian city of Andyr at GMT plus 12 hours.

Moscow (daylight saving GMT plus four hours) – GMT plus three hours

Tomsk (daylight saving GMT plus eight hours) – GMT plus seven hours

Yakutsk (daylight saving GMT plus 10 hours) – GMT plus nine hours

Magadan (daylight saving GMT plus 12 hours) – GMT plus 11 hours

Petropavlovsk-Kamchatsky (daylight saving GMT plus 13 hours) – GMT plus 12 hours

Geography

The Russian Federation is the largest country in the world at 17.07 million square km. Even European Russia (west of the Ural Mountains), which is only a quarter of the total landmass, dwarfs all other European countries. Major cities and towns are concentrated in western Russia, with the population thinning out to the far north and east.

Norway lies to the far north-west of Russia, with Finland, Estonia, and Latvia to the north. Belarus and Ukraine lie to the south-west of European Russia, the southern borders of which are with the Trans-Caucasian states of Georgia and Azerbaijan, and with Kazakhstan. In the north-west, near St Petersburg, there is a short coastline where there is access to the Baltic Sea via the gulf of Finland. Towards the south, European Russia has a coastline on the Black Sea in the south-west, with the Caspian Sea to the east. Beyond the Ural Mountains, the Siberian and Far Eastern regions have southern frontiers with the People's Republic of China, Mongolia, and in the south-east, North Korea. The eastern coastline is on the Sea of Japan, the Sea of Okhotsk, the Pacific Ocean and the Barents Sea. The northern coastline is on the Arctic Ocean. The region around Kaliningrad on the Baltic Sea is separated from the rest of the Russian Federation by Lithuania to the north and east, and has a coastline on the Baltic Sea.

The territory includes a wide variety of physical features. European Russia and western Siberia form a vast plain. Between the Black and Caspian Seas in the south, the land is more undulating, until it reaches the foothills of the Caucasus mountain range in the far south. The northern regions of both Asian and European Russia are inhospitable areas, much of the territory being covered by permafrost.

Europe's highest mountain, Elbrus (at 5,642 metres), is just on the Russian side of the Georgian border. Russia has Europe's longest river, the 3,690km Volga which rises north-west of Moscow and flows east before turning south to the Caspian Sea. The two largest lakes in Europe are also in Russia. Lake Ladoga (18,390 square km) and Lake Onega (9,600 square km) are both north-east of St Petersburg. Lake Baikal, located in the south-east in Siberia, at over 31,000 square km is the world's deepest and largest (by volume) freshwater lake, containing 20 per cent of the planet's liquid freshwater.

Hemisphere

Northern

Climate

The climate in Russia is extremely varied. The north is arctic, with an extensive zone of permafrost, but there are a few subtropical zones in the southern region of the country. The majority of the land mass is continental or moderate continental.

The Russian winter is deservedly famous: winter snow cover lasts as long as 160 days in St Petersburg.

Moscow has a warm spring with an average temperature of 18 degrees Celsius (C) in the period April to May. It is often hot in summer (June to August 20–30 degrees C), mild in autumn (September to October 10–15 degrees C) and freezing (down to minus 30 degrees C) for the rest of the year. Average annual rainfall is 575mm.

Average temperatures in the southern Siberian town of Irkutsk range from minus 21 degrees C in January to 18 degrees C in July. Average annual rainfall is 458mm, most of which falls in the summer. In the far north of Siberia, the average January temperature is minus 47 degrees C.

The far eastern region combines the extreme temperatures of Siberia with monsoon-type conditions common elsewhere in Asia. The mean temperature in January in the eastern port of Vladivostok is minus 14 degrees C; in August the average is 21 degrees C.

In the more moderate western portion of Russia, the average January temperature is slightly below zero. Summer is very hot in some areas. The snow in European Russia begins to melt in March and the muddy transition period demands waterproof footwear.

Dress codes
Dress well as business people are judged by their attire. Warm outer clothes, hats, gloves and footwear are essential in winter, although interiors are well heated. The most important factor is neatness. Shoes should be polished and clothes pressed. Russians themselves do not always wear a suit and tie at business meetings, but it is wise to err on the safe side. Dark suits, white shirts and conservative ties are the norm, with business suits for women. Formal evening wear is not normally necessary. Summer dress is modest.

Entry requirements
Passports
Required by all.
Visa
Required by all. See www.rusemblon.org/ and follow link to application forms to download a visa form. US citizens should see www.russianembassy.org for further information. All travellers should check the general information links to see if the additional requirements affect them. All applications should be submitted to the closest Russian consulate.
Visitors must register their visas within three working days of arrival in Russia with the local branch of the ministry of the interior. Most major hotels will do this for their guests automatically. All visas are issued with an exit visa included.
Business travellers must include, with their application, a letter of invitation from the Russian foreign ministry or its regional representatives or ministry of the interior or its local offices. The letter must contain the official seal and legal address of the agency, a document registration number, date of registration, the signature and name of official authorised to issue invitations, and a travel itinerary with dates of stay and names of persons involved. A letter from an employer (or own letter if self-employed) giving personal details, a full itinerary, purpose of visit and a guarantee accepting full responsibility for any expenses incurred must also to be included. The right to request the submission of all original documents is reserved by the embassy, and multiple entry visas require original letters of invitation in all cases.
Currency advice/regulations
The import and export of local currency is prohibited. The import of foreign currency is unlimited up to US$10,000 (or equivalent), but amounts over US$3,000 must be declared. Export of foreign currency is limited to the amount declared on arrival. It is illegal to exchange money anywhere except official exchange facilities; shops, hotels and restaurants may advertise dollar prices, but bills must be paid in roubles. It is advisable to retain all exchange receipts.
Travellers cheques have limited acceptance. Unmarked US dollar bills in good condition should be used for travel to more remote regions.
Customs
The customs declaration made on entry must be retained for exit, this allows for personal items, such as jewellery, cameras, computers and musical instruments to remain duty-free.
Retain all shop receipts and certificates of money exchange for customs formalities on exit.
In 2006, 250g caviar per person was allowed for export, with proof of purchase from licensed purveyors.
Prohibited imports
Firearms, ammunition, illegal drugs, precious metals and furs, radio, electrical items, fruit and vegetables, sturgeon and sturgeon products and photographic and printed material that vilifies the Russian Federation.
Live animals, antiques and works of art require permits.

Health (for visitors)
Mandatory precautions
Advisable precautions
Inoculations and boosters should be current for tetanus, hepatitis A and diphtheria. There may be a need for vaccinations for typhoid, tuberculosis, hepatitis B and meningitis (Moscow only). Visitors to Asian and far-eastern provinces may need vaccinations for Japanese B encephalitis and cholera. There is a risk of rabies.
Water precautions outside main cities are recommended (purification tablets may be useful or use bottled or boiled water for drinks, washing teeth and making ice – especially in St Petersburg, where the water supply may be infected by giardia).
Mosquito repellents and long clothing will help avoid hepatitis B and Japanese B encephalitis; there is a risk of HIV/Aids.
Russian medical care is not up to Western standards and medical insurance, including emergency evacuation, is necessary. A travel kit including a disposable syringe is a reasonable precaution. A supply of any regular medicines required should be taken, with their prescription details and it could be wise to have precautionary antibiotics if going outside major urban centres.

Hotels
Moscow has an increasing number of Western-run hotels. Accommodation is difficult to obtain in Moscow at short notice. It is crucial to make bookings in advance as hotels refuse to check in a guest without a reservation. First-class and tourist class are available, with all prices fixed by Intourist. Main hotels have foreign currency restaurants and bars. Tipping is increasingly common, typically 10 per cent.

Credit cards
Credit cards are not widely accepted outside Moscow and St Petersburg. ATMs are widely available.

Public holidays (national)
Fixed dates
1–10 Jan (New Year Holidays), 23 Feb (Defender's Day), 8 Mar (Women's Day), 1 May (Labour Day), 9 May (Victory Day), 12 Jun (Russia Day), 4 Nov (National Unity Day).
Days in lieu are given for holidays that occur at the weekend, usually at the beginning of the following week.
Variable dates
Russian Orthodox Christmas

Working hours
Banking
Mon–Fri: 0930–1730.
Business
Mon–Fri: 0900–1800 (appointments best between 0900–1000).
Shops
Mon–Sat: 0900–1900.

Telecommunications
Mobile/cell phones
There are limited 900, 1800, 900/1800 GSM services available in Moscow, St Petersburg and other major cities.

Electricity supply
220V AC

Social customs/useful tips
A firm handshake is important as is negotiating an agenda at the beginning of the meeting. Smoking in meetings is very common. Ask permission before lighting a cigarette and offer cigarettes generously.
Written communications are particularly important with large bureaucracies. Address the recipient formally and keep a copy of everything.
It is customary to take a small gift on a business or social visit. Offering basic food is considered insulting. Offer little luxuries.
It is impolite to take along people who are not invited to a social function. If you are offered a second helping of caviar, resist the temptation and refuse. The offer will be made again, but it is polite to refuse the first time.
Many Russians take certain superstitions somewhat seriously. Do not give an even number of flowers, for example, as this is for funerals only; do not greet people in a doorway – it is considered unlucky.

Security
The normal precautions should be taken when visiting Russia – avoid showing large amounts of cash or expensive personal

belongings. Avoid travelling alone at night in Moscow and St Petersburg, particularly on the metro.

Getting there

Air

National airline: Aeroflot – Russian Airlines

International airport/s: Moscow-Sheremetyevo International (SVO), 29km north-west of city centre; St Petersburg-Pulkovo (LED), 17km from city. Both airports have duty-free shops, banks, bureau de change, restaurants.

Taxis, to Moscow city centre (journey time 30–40 minutes) and fixed route and buses are available. There are scheduled express coaches and trains to other destinations.

There are taxis to St Petersburg (journey time 10 minutes) as well as buses.

Airport tax: None

Surface

Road: Major European highways connect Moscow via Kiev (Ukraine), Minsk (Belarus), Riga (Latvia), Warsaw (Poland) and Scandinavia to St Petersburg via Helsinki (Finland).

Rail: The Russian/CIS rail network (around 87,079km) extends to all Russian Federation countries. The main European rail services are through Germany including a sleeper service from Cologne to Moscow and the Mockva Express via Berlin-Warsaw-Moscow.

Through-trains are also available from other Western and Eastern European cities and from Turkey, Iran, and the Trans-Siberian Express from Mongolia and China.

Water: There are sea links from Finland, Norway, Sweden and Germany and from the Ukraine in the west. In the east, a weekly ferry runs between Vladivostok and Niigata-Fushiki in Japan.

Main port/s: Vladivostok, Magadan, Nakhodka, St Petersburg and Kaliningrad. Links to the Atlantic are provided by the Murmansk (Arctic Ocean) and Archangelisk ports (during summer months only).

Getting about

National transport

Air: There is an extensive internal air service which provides the only viable option for travelling between cities. Domestic services are operated by Aeroflot and Transaero (due to a small fleet, flights are more often delayed than those of Aeroflot). Sky Express, a budget airline, began operations in early 2007. It will initially fly between Moscow and Sochi on the Black Sea, charging US$19, compared to Aeroflot's rate of US$120.

The internal air network centres around Moscow. Domestic airports include Vnukovo (VKO), 29km south-west of city; Domodedovo (DME), 40km south-east of city and Irkutsk (IRK), 7km from city.

Road: Distances between major cities are extensive: Moscow to St Petersburg 692km (432 miles); Moscow to Odessa 1,347km (837 miles). Approximately 60 per cent of the road network needs to be rehabilitated or upgraded. In general the few roads connecting with Siberia are impassable during winter. Secondary roads are often untarred.

Buses: Long-distance coach services operate.

Rail: Rail is the major means of transport. There is a cheap and efficient service to all major towns. There is an extensive network of commuter and inter-city services, most offering first and second class seats or accommodation.

The rolling stock needs modernising and trains are typically over-crowded and over-booked. Food is often available on inter-city services but, because of the generally poor quality, most passengers bring their own. Many carriages have a samovar which produces hot water for drinks. Security can be a problem, especially on overnight services. The famous Trans-Siberian railway stretches from Moscow to Vladivostok.

The railways are wide gauge. Almost all the rail network is electrified. Sleepers should be booked well in advance.

Water: Rivers play an important role in transport; in summer it is possible to travel great distances either by cruises or river passenger boats. Routes include: St Petersberg-Astrakhan on the Caspian sea, and St Petersberg-Rostov-on-Don on the Black Sea. These routes may include detours via Moscow.

The largest inland waterway is the River Volga. There are a number of inland ports and canals.

City transport

Taxis: Use only officially marked taxis and do not share them with strangers. Taxis are yellow with a checkerboard stripe and a green light at the top right hand corner of the windscreen indicating availability; they can be hired at taxi ranks or by booking in advance. Beware of illegal taxi touts operating at both the airport and city centre.

Tariffs for foreigners are often subject to negotiation and may be charged in hard currency.

It is possible to find a reliable taxi firm in the airport arrivals section at Moscow airport. Payment is by credit card though fares may have to be negotiated with the driver as the fare shown on the meter may not correspond with the fare asked. Arrangements to be met at the airport in advance can be made by contacting Intourist, or telephoning Moscow Taxi (tel: 238-1001).

Buses, trams & metro: Cheap and reliable, though often crowded, available from 0600–0100. Bus services 5817 and 551 from Moscow airport to the city centre operate between 0500–2359 every 10 minutes, with a journey time of 30–45 minutes. Long distance coach services operate.

Trains: An express train service from Moscow airport to the city centre operates every 30 minutes.

Car hire

Available in major towns. International driving licence required with Russian translation of details. Notification of route to be taken should be given if travelling outside main cities.

Visitors travelling in private cars should be in possession of their passport and visa, and an itinerary card complete with visitor's name and citizenship and car registration number.

Traffic drives on the right. Speeds are limited to 60kph (37mph) in built-up areas and 90kph (55mph) elsewhere. Cars are required to display registration plates and stickers denoting the country of registration.

BUSINESS DIRECTORY

The addresses listed below are a selection only. While World of Information makes every endeavour to check these addresses, we cannot guarantee that changes have not been made, especially to telephone numbers and area codes. We would welcome any corrections.

Telephone area codes

The international direct dialling code (IDD) for Russia is +7, followed by the area code and subscriber's number:

Chelyabinsk	3512	St Petersburg	812
Ekaterinberg	3432	Smolensk	481
Kaliningrad	401	Tula	487
Moscow	495	Vladivostok	4232
Nizhny Novgorod	8312	Yakutsk	41122

Useful telephone numbers

International operator: (English-speaking operator): 8196

General enquiries (Moscow area): 09

Police: 02

Fire: 01

Ambulance: 03

Chambers of Commerce

American Chamber of Commerce in Russia, 7 Dolgorukovskaya Street, Moscow 127006 (tel: 961-2141; fax: 961-2142; e-mail: info@amcham.ru).

Moscow Chamber of Commerce and Industry, 22 Akademika Pilyugina Street, Moscow 117393 (tel: 132-7510; fax: 132-0547; e-mail: mtpp@mtpp.org).

Nizhny Novgorod Region Chamber of Commerce and Industry, 1 Oktyabrskaya

Square, Nizhny Novgorod 603005 (tel: 194-210; fax:194-009; e-mail: tpp@rda.nnov.ru).

Russian Federation Chamber of Commerce and Industry, 6 Ilyinka Street, Moscow 109012 (tel: 929-0009; fax: 929-0360; e-mail: tpprf@tpprf.ru).

St Petersburg Chamber of Commerce and Industry, 46-48 Chaikovsky Street, St Petersburg 191194 (tel: 279-2833; fax: 272-6406; e-mail: spbcci@spbcci.ru).

South Ural Chamber of Commerce and Industrym 63 Vasenko Street, Chelyabinsk 454080 (tel: 661-816; fax: 665-223; e-mail: mail@tpp.chelreg.ru).

Smolensk Chamber of Commerce and Industry, 12 Karl Marx Street, Smolensk 214000 (tel: 554-142; fax: 237-450; e-mail: smolcci@keytown.com).

Tula Chamber of Commerce and Industry, 25 Krasnoarmeisky Prospekt, Tula 300600 (tel: 364-517; fax: 360-216; e-mail: tulacci@tula.net).

Banking

Agropromstraybank, Krasina Per, 123056 Moscow (tel: 254-4263; fax: 254-7081).

Gazprombank, Nametkina Str 16B, 117420 Moscow (tel: 719-1697/17; fax; 719-1763).

ING Bank Eurasia, ul Krasnaya Presnya 31, 125178 Moscow (tel: 755-5400; fax: 755-5459; fax: 755-5499).

Sberbank (savings bank), Vavilova Str 18, 117817 Moscow (tel: 971-4981, 957-5690, 957-5862; fax: 957-5731; internet site: http://www.sbrf.ru).

SDM Bank, 73 Volokolamskoe Shosse, 123424 Moscow (tel: 490-1545, 491-7572, 490-0703; fax: 490-6509).

United Export Import Bank (UNEXIM), 11 Masha Paryvaeva Street, PO Box 207, 107078 Moscow (tel: 232-3727; fax: 975-2205; e-mail: mailbox@mail.unexim.ru).

Vnesheconombank (Bank for Foreign Economic Affairs), Akademika Sakharova Prospekt 9, 107996 Moscow (tel: 207-1037).

Vneshtorgbank (Bank for Foreign Trade), Kuznetskiy Most Str 16, 103031 Moscow (tel: 929-8900; fax: 956-3727).

Central bank

Central Bank of the Russian Federation, 12 Neglinnaya Sreet, 107016 Moscow (tel: 771-9100; fax: 921-6465; e-mail: webmaster@www.cbr.ru).

Travel information

Aeroflot, 37/9 Leningradsky Prospect, Moscow 125836 (tickets and enquiries, tel: 223-5555; fax: 186-2092; internet: www.aeroflot.ru/eng/).

Intourist, 150, Prospect Mira, Moscow 129366 (tel: 956-4207; fax: 730-1957; email: info@intourist.ru; internet: www.intourist.com/ENG/).

Russian National Group, Suite 214, 5/10 Chistoprudni Blvd, Moscow (tel: 980-8440; 980-8441; internet: www.russia-travel.com).

JSC Russian Railways (JSCo RZD), Novaya Basmannaya 2, 107174 Moscow (tel: 262-9901; email: info@rzd.ru; internet: www.eng.rzd.ru).

Ministries

Ministry of Agriculture and Food, 1-11 Orlikov Lane, Moscow 107139 (tel: 207-8000; fax: 207-8362, 288-9580).

Ministry of Atomic Energy, 24-26 Bolshaya Ordynka Str, Moscow 101100 (tel: 239-4753; fax: 233-4679).

Ministry for Civil Defence, Emergencies and Disaster Resources, 3 Teatralniy Pr-D, Moscow 103012 (tel: 926-3901; fax: 924-5683).

Ministry for Communications, 7 Tverskaya Str, Moscow 119332 (tel: 229-6966, 292-7070; fax: 292-7128).

Ministry of Construction, Comp 2, 8 Stroitelei Str, Moscow 117987 (tel: 930-1755; fax: 938-2202).

Ministry for Co-operation Between CIS Member Countries, 7 Varvarka Str, Moscow 103073 (tel: 206-1365; fax: 206-1084).

Ministry of Culture, 7 Kitaiskiy Pr-D, Moscow 103693 (tel: 925-1195; fax: 928-1791).

Ministry of Economics, 19 Noviy Arbat Str, Moscow 103025 (tel: 203-7534; fax: 203-7482).

Ministry of Education, 6 Chistoprudniy B-R, Moscow 101856 (tel: 927-0568; fax: 924-6989).

Ministry for Environmental Protection and Natural Resources, 4-6 B Gruzinskaya Str, Moscow 123812 (tel: 254-7683; fax: 254-8283).

Ministry of Finance, 9 Ilyinka str, Moscow 103097 (tel: 298-9101, 923-0967; fax: 925-0889).

Ministry of Foreign Affairs, 32-34 Smolenskaya-Sennaya Sq, Moscow 121200 (tel: 244-1606; fax: 230-2130).

Ministry for Foreign Economic Relations, 32-34 Smolenskaya-Sennaya Sq, Moscow 121200 (tel: 244-2450; fax: 244-3068/3981).

Ministry for Fuel and Power Development, 7 Kitaiskiy Pr, Moscow 103074 (tel: 220-5500; fax: 220-4818).

Ministry of the Interior, 16 Zhitnaya Str, Moscow 117049 (tel: 237-7585, 924-6572, 222-6669; fax: 925-2098).

Ministry of Justice, 4 Vorontsovo Pole Str, Moscow 109830 (tel: 209-6009/98; fax: 916-2903).

Ministry of Labour, 1 Birzhevaya Sq, Moscow 103706 (tel: 261-2030, 928-8208; fax: 230-2407).

Ministry for Nationalities and Regional Policy, 19 Trubnikovskiy Lane, Moscow 121819 (tel: 248-8635; fax: 202-4490).

Ministry of Public Health, 3 Rakhmanovskiy Lane, Moscow 103051 (tel: 928-4478; fax: 921-0128).

Ministry for Railways, 2 Novo-Basmannaya Str, Moscow 107174 (tel: 262-9901; fax: 262-9095).

Ministry for Science and Technology, 11 Tverskaya Str, Moscow 103905 (tel: 229-1192; fax: 230-2823).

Ministry for Social Protection, Bld 1, 4 Slavianskaya Sq, Moscow 103715 (tel: 220-9511/9384; fax: 924-3690).

Ministry of Transport, 10 Sadovo-Samotyochnaya Str, Moscow 101433 (tel: 200-0809; fax: 200-3356).

Other useful addresses

British Consulate, Sfoskaya Nberezhnaya 14, Moscow (tel: 956-7420; fax: 956-7420).

British Consulate, St Petersburg, Pl Proletarsky, Dikatury 5, 193124 St Petersburg (tel: 325-6036; fax: 325-6037; e-mail: uk.stpet@vmail.sprint.com).

British Consulate for Southern Russia, Petrak, 3a Fabrichnaya Street, Novorossisk (tel: 93-319; fax: 34-959).

British Embassy, Kutuzovsky Prospekt 7/4, Moscow 121248 (tel: 956-7200, 956-7477; fax: 956-7480, 956-7420; e-mail: uk.moscw@vmail.sprint.com).

British Trade Office, 4th Floor, 15a Gogol Street, Ekaterinburg 620151 (tel: 564-931; fax: 592-901; e-mail: uk.ekate@vmail.sprint.com).

BSCC British-Russian Business Centre, 42 Southwark Street, London SE1 1UN (tel: (+44-(0)171) 403-1706; fax: (+44-(0)171) 403-1245); 22/25 Bolshoi Strochenovskiy Pereulok, Moscow 113054 (tel: 230-6120; fax: 230-6124).

Delegation of the European Union (Office of), 2/10 Astakhovsky Pereulok, Moscow 109208 (tel: 956-3600; fax: 956-3615).

Expocentr, 1a Sokolnicheskiy val, Moscow 107113 (tel: 268-7083) (responsibility for organising, on a commercial basis, international and foreign exhibitions and symposia).

Foreign Investment Promotion Centre (FIPC), Ul Novy Arbat 19, 119898 Moscow (tel: 203-4863; internet site: www.fipc.ru/fipc/).

Foreign Trade Arbitration Commission, Moscow (tel: 205-6855).

Government of St. Petersburg, Smolny, 193060 St Petersburg (tel 576-4501; fax: 576-7827; internet: http://eng.gov.spb.ru).

Interstate Statistical Committee of the Commonwealth of Independent States, 39 Myasnitskaya Str, Moscow 103450 (tel: 207-4237/4802/4567; fax: 207-4592; e-mail: Statpro@Sovam.com).

Russian Federation Embassy (USA), 2650 Wisconsin Avenue, NW, Washington DC 2007 (tel: (+1-202) 298-5700; fax: (+1-202) 298-5735; e-mail: russ-amb@cerfnet.com).

Russian Federation Foreign Trade Organisation, Barrikabnaya Str Bld 8-5, 123242 Moscow (tel: 254-8090; fax: 253-9675).

Russian Information Telegraph Agency (ITAR-TASS) (news agency), Tverskoy bul 10, Moscow (tel: 3229-8053).

Russian Television and Radio, Corolov St 12, Moscow (tel: 217-7898; fax: 288-9508).

State Committee for Statistics, 39 Myasnitskaya Street, Moscow 103450 (tel: 207-4902; fax: 207-4640).

TACIS Technical Assistance Centre, 165 Nemirovicha-Danchenko, Novosibirsk 630087 (tel: 465-395, 464-836; fax: 464-426; e-mail: centre@tac.sib.ru).

US Consulate, St Petersburg (tel: 275-1701).

National news agency: Itar-Tass News Agency

Other news agencies: RIA Novosti, 4 Zubovsky Blvd, Moscow 119031 (tel: 637-2424; internet: http://en.rian.ru).

Interfax, 2 Pervaya Tverskaya-Yamskaya Ul, Building 1, Moscow 127006 (tel: 250-9840; fax: 250-9727; internet: www.interfax.ru).

Internet sites

Moscow Guide: www.moscow-guide.ru

Rusline (government information, company directories): www.rusline.com

Russian tourism: www.visitrussia.com

Russian travel: www.realrussia.com

Russian web portal: www.ru

Rwanda

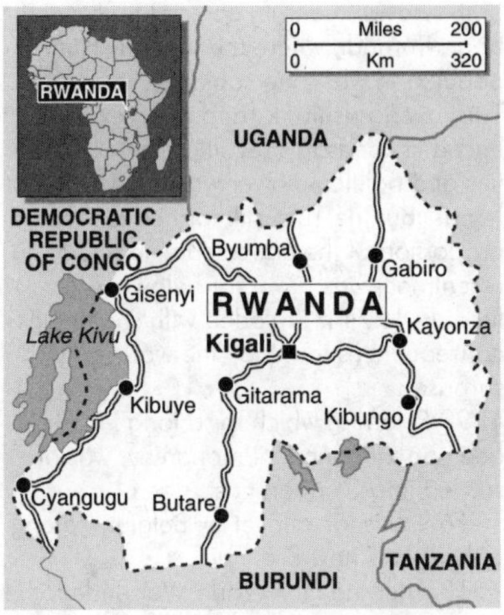

In African terms, Rwanda is a comparatively small (26,300 square kilometres) and densely populated (357 people per square kilometre) country, and this pressure for land has been the root cause of Rwanda's poverty. Over 90 per cent of the population live scattered on the rolling hillsides in separate little family compounds. A large number – as high as 10 per cent – of hospital deaths are caused by sicknesses related to malnutrition. The need is to increase crop production by raising the yields on the present farm structures without disturbing the agricultural pattern of peasant small-holdings.

Reconciliation moves

To encourage the process of healing and reconciliation after the genocide of 1990s the government passed a bill in June 2007 repealing the use of the death penalty; the *Gacaca* courts, the traditional courts trying genocide suspects, had their mandate continue to operate extended. In April, President Kagame had pardoned former president Pasteur Bizimungu and he was released from prison. In the wider sphere, tensions in the Great Lakes region continue to impact on Rwanda and are being closely monitored. In April 2007 the Communaute Economique des Pays des Grands Lacs (CEPGL) (Great Lakes Countries Economic Community) was re-launched by Burundi, Democratic Republic of Congo and Rwanda. CEPGL is intended to promote regional economic co-operation and integration.

Economy

Rwanda is a poor country with about 90 per cent of the population engaged in mainly subsistence agriculture. The country is striving to rebuild its economy, with coffee and tea production being among its main sources of foreign exchange, after the 1994 genocide decimated this fragile economic base. Nearly two thirds of the population lives below the poverty line. Rwanda has made substantial progress in rehabilitating its economy to pre-1994 levels. It continues to receive substantial aid money and received IMF\World Bank Heavily Indebted Poor Country (HIPC) debt relief in 2005. An energy shortage and instability in neighboring states slowed growth in 2006, while the lack of adequate transportation linkages to other countries continues to handicap export growth.

At first glance, Rwanda's economy looks to be performing well. In 2006 gross domestic product (GDP) registered growth of 5.5 per cent, and this continued in 2007 with 6.0 per cent. With Rwanda's economic policy implementation broadly on track, indications are that growth will be at the upper end of the 4–5 per cent range, reflecting mostly an expected recovery in agricultural production due to good weather conditions. Inflation dropped to 8.8 per cent in 2006, but was up again to 9.4 per cent in 2007. But the disappointing feature of the Rwandan economy is an inability to improve GDP per capita, which was still only US$353 in 2007.

The government launched a poverty reduction reform strategy in 2007. The boldly named *Rwanda's Economic Development and Poverty Reduction Strategy* (EDPRS) sets out the country's objectives, priorities and major policies for the 2008–12 five year period. The strategy provides a medium-term framework for achieving long-term development goals.

The strategy redefines growth and development priorities to emphasise accelerating growth of GDP and exports to create employment. It also aims to consolidate

KEY FACTS

Official name: Republika y'u Rwanda (Republic of Rwanda)

Head of State: President Paul Kagame (FPR) (elected 2000; re-elected Aug 2003)

Head of government: Prime Minister Bernard Makuza (since 2000; re-appointed 2003)

Ruling party: Front Patriotique Rwandais (FPR) (Rwanda Patriotic Front) (Tutsi-dominated) (elected Sep 2003)

Area: 26,338 square km

Population: 9.39 million (2007)

Capital: Kigali

Official language: Kinyarwanda, French and English.

Currency: Rwanda franc (Rwf)

Exchange rate: Rwf543.67 per US$ (Jul 2008)

GDP per capita: US$353 (2007)*

GDP real growth: 6.00% (2007)*

Labour force: 4.57 million (2003)

Inflation: 9.40% (2007)

Balance of trade: -US$296.00 million (2006)

Foreign debt: US$1.66 billion (2004)

* estimated figure

the decentralisation of public spending and to institute accountability mechanisms. It recognises the key role of the private sector in improving growth and reducing poverty.

Rwanda's financial system is shallow and dominated by the commercial banking system. Banking services are basic, while credit to the private sector is concentrated in few sectors and mostly short term. Banks compete for deposits and loans of a group of only about 50 corporate customers. While about one-third of households have an account in financial institutions, insurance penetration is low, pensions are largely restricted to a public system, and the capital market is limited to treasury bills. Parts of the legal and regulatory frameworks governing the financial and commercial sectors are dated, including in accounting, auditing, insolvency, leasing, and anti-money laundering. As financial institutions are too small to achieve economies of scale and adequate risk diversification, Rwanda will need to strive for greater harmonisation of policies and establishment of a more open market in financial services.

Politics

In August 2003 Paul Kagame – who had been selected as candidate by MPs in 2000 – claimed a landslide victory in the first presidential elections since the 1994 genocide. Born a Tutsi in western Rwanda in 1957, Kagame grew up in Uganda, where his parents fled to escape Hutu violence. He joined Yoweri Museveni – now Uganda's president – and became his intelligence chief. He established the Rwandan Patriotic Front (RPF), which ended the 1994 genocide.

In January 2006 the country's 12 administrative provinces were replaced by a larger number of ethnically-diverse districts. Rwanda was admitted to membership of the East African Community (EAC) on 30 November. Relations with France deteriorated as a French judge investigating the shooting down of President Juvénal Habyarimana's plane in 1994 and the killing of its French crew, accused President Kagame and nine top officials with involvement in the assassination. The president has immunity from prosecution as head of state and he strenuously denied the RPF were responsible for the death of the former president. A counter claim by Rwandan officials accused French authorities of attempting to divert international attention away from French collaboration in the Hutu regime responsible for the genocide.

Rwanda has experienced relative stability under Kagame, who reportedly tolerates no criticism or challenge to his authority. He is an incorruptible teetotaler who downplays any ethnic agenda in Rwanda, presenting himself as a Rwandan and not a Tutsi.

Risk assessment

Politics	Poor
Economy	Poor
Regional stability	Poor

KEY INDICATORS — Rwanda

	Unit	2003	2004	2005	2006	2007
Population	m	8.32	8.59	9.04	9.20	*9.39
Gross domestic product (GDP)	US$bn	1.68	1.85	2.15	2.87	*3.32
GDP per capita	US$	242	215	238	312	*353
GDP real growth	%	3.2	4.0	6.0	5.5	*6.0
Inflation	%	7.4	12.0	9.2	8.8	9.4
Industrial output	% change	–	2.2	4.2	12.5	–
Agricultural output	% change	–	*0.1	4.5	0.1	–
Exports (fob) (goods)	US$m	68.0	69.8	125.0	142.0	184.0
Imports (cif) (goods)	US$m	253.0	260.0	354.0	438.0	637.0
Balance of trade	US$m	-185.0	-190.2	-229.0	-296.0	-452.0
Current account	US$m	-130.0	-50.0	-70.0	-186.0	*-161.0
Foreign debt	US$bn	1.3	1.6	1.7	–	–
Total reserves minus gold	US$m	214.7	314.6	405.8	439.7	552.8
Foreign exchange	US$m	184.9	284.4	379.9	416.8	528.7
Exchange rate	per US$	528.28	574.62	549.20	549.20	545.10

* estimated figure

COUNTRY PROFILE

Historical profile

Once known as the land of a thousand hills, Rwanda became synonymous with genocide and massacre in the 1990s as members of the Hutu tribe went on the rampage. Their target consisted primarily of members of the minority Tutsi tribe, but also included moderate Hutus and critics of the government. In contrast to its neighbour, Burundi, where the majority Hutu population was long subjected to minority Tutsi overlordship, Rwanda had experienced its 'peasants revolt' in the early sixties and political power was firmly in Hutu hands. But the Tutsi still formed a sizeable proportion of the educated élite and Hutu resentment was never far below the surface. In 1994 it exploded with shattering consequences that took the world by surprise.

1899 Rwanda, which for a long time had been an independent monarchy, was absorbed into German East Africa.

1916 It was taken over by Belgium, along with what is now Burundi.

1918 After the First World War ended, the two became Ruanda-Urundi, a Belgian-administered trust territory of the League of Nations (and later, the UN).

1950s Belgian missionaries encouraged the formation of a modern Hutu identity.

1961 Rwanda's monarchy was abolished and a republic was proclaimed.

1962 Independence was granted.

1963 A massacre killed about 20,000 people, mostly Tutsis, causing many to flee to Uganda.

1973 President Gregoire Kayibanda, was overthrown by Major General Juvenal Habyarimana.

1990 Some 10,000 rebel Tutsi guerrillas invaded Rwanda from Uganda and occupied several towns.

1993 President Habyarimana signed a power-sharing agreement with the Tutsis. A UN mission was sent to monitor the agreement.

1994 The death of Habyarimana in a plane crash in April (which also killed the president of Burundi), triggered the breakdown of civil society. Extremist Hutu militia began the systematic murder of Tutsis. Within four months an estimated 800,000 Tutsis and moderate Hutus were killed. The Tutsis Front Patriotique Rwandais (Rwandan Patriotic Forces) (RPF) forced the militia to flee, taking with them around two million Hutu refugees, who fled in fear of reprisal for the genocide, into neighbouring Democratic Republic of Congo (DRC), Tanzania and Burundi.

1995 The militia responsible for the genocide were able to take control of the refugee camps and deter people from returning to Rwanda on pain of death.

Mass repatriation efforts were complicated by screening operations, which were needed to identify genocide rebels from genuine refugees. President Pasteur Bizimungu and a transitional coalition government were sworn in.
1998 The United Nations Human Rights Field Office in Rwanda (HRFOR) was withdrawn when its mandate was not renewed.
1999 An extension of the transitional government's term of office was approved.
2000 Pasteur Bizimungu resigned and Paul Kagame was officially elected president (the first Tutsi to hold presidential office since Rwanda's independence in 1961) in a joint vote of the Rwandan legislature and cabinet.
2001 A peace agreement was signed between Rwanda and Uganda. A new national flag, emblem and anthem were unveiled.
2002 Rwanda and the Democratic Republic of Congo (DRC) signed a peace agreement.
2003 In a referendum, voters approved a new, more democratic constitution. Incumbent Paul Kagame won the August presidential elections and the ruling party, FPR, won the parliamentary elections with 223 out of 360 seats.
2004 Kagame denied he ordered the attack on the president's plane in 1994 which had sparked the genocide. Former president Bizimungu was sentenced to 15 years imprisonment for embezzlement and inciting violence.
2005 The Forces Democratiques de Liberation du Rwanda (FDLR) (Democratic Liberation Forces of Rwanda) declared a cease-fire. A mass release of 36,000 prisoners took place as part of the process of reconciliation; many had confessed to acts of genocide.
2006 The country's 12 administrative provinces were replaced by a larger number of ethnically-diverse districts. Rwanda was admitted to membership of the East African Community (EAC). The Roman Catholic priest, Fr Athanase Seromba, was convicted of involvement in the genocide, by the International Tribunal and sentenced to 15 years imprisonment. Relations with France deteriorated as a French judge investigating the shooting down of President Juvénal Habyarimana's plane in 1994 and the killing of its French crew, accused President Kagame and nine top officials with involvement in the assassination. The president has immunity from prosecution as head of state and he strenuously denied the RPF were responsible for the death of the former president. A counter claim by Rwandan officials accused French authorities of attempting to divert international attention away from French collaboration in the Hutu regime responsible for the genocide.
2007 In April the Communaute Economique des Pays des Grands Lacs (CEPGL) (Great Lakes Countries Economic Community) was re-launched by Burundi, Democratic Republic of Congo and Rwanda. CEPGL is intended to promote regional economic co-operation and integration. President Kagame pardoned former president Pasteur Bizimungu and he was released from prison in April. Use of the death penalty was repealed in June. The Gacaca courts, the traditional courts trying genocide suspects, had their mandate extended into 2007.

Political structure

Constitution

A new 2003 constitution prevents a one-party dominance of the political system and bans incitement to racial hatred. It stipulates that no party can hold more than 50 per cent of the seats in cabinet, even if it secures an absolute majority in parliamentary elections.
The president, prime minister and president of the lower house cannot belong to the same party.

Form of state

Republic

The executive

The president is eligible for election for two seven-year terms.

National legislature

Under the new constitution, there is a two-tier parliament, with members serving five-year terms.
The Chamber of Deputies is composed of 80 members, including 53 members from political organisations and independent members, 24 women representatives (at least two from each province), two representing the youth and one representing the disabled groups.
The Senate is composed of 26 members elected as follows: 12 members (at least two from each province), eight appointed by the president, four from the forum of political parties and two each from the universities.

Last elections

29–30 September and 2 October 2003 (parliamentary); 25 August 2003 (presidential).
Results: Parliamentary: the first legislative elections since the 1994 genocide were won by the ruling party, the FPR, with 73.8 per cent of the vote, followed by the SDP with 12.3 per cent and the Liberal Party with 10.6 per cent; turnout was 99.5 per cent.
Presidential: President Paul Kagame won with 95.1 per cent of the vote. The scale of the victory indicated he had the support of a majority of both Tutsis and Hutus.

Next elections

2008 (parliamentary); 2010 (presidential).

Political parties

Ruling party

Front Patriotique Rwandais (FPR) (Rwanda Patriotic Front) (Tutsi-dominated) (elected Sep 2003)

Main opposition party

Social Democratic Party (SDP)

Population

9.39 million (2007)
Last census: August 1999: 8,128,553
Population density: 300 per square km.
Urban population: 10 per cent.
Annual growth rate: 4.9 per cent 1994–2004 (WHO 2006)

Ethnic make-up

There are three ethnic groups: the Hutu (90 per cent), the Tutsi (9 per cent) and the Twa (1 per cent).

Religions

Roman Catholic (56 per cent), Protestant (26 per cent), Adventist (11.1 per cent), Islam (4.6 per cent), indigenous beliefs (0.1 per cent).

Education

On completion of primary education, a competitive entrance examination allows students to progress to the first cycle secondary school for general education, from age 13 to 16. The second cycle secondary school covers either modern or classical humanities, from age 16 to 19.
Technical education is provided for students who have completed two to three years general secondary education, although some may begin straight from primary education joining four-year courses.
Education suffered badly as communities and the social infrastructure were devastated by the internal conflict of the early 1990s. This included the destruction of schools and educational institutions, as well as the loss of trained teachers. By 1998 it was estimated that approximately one-third of school-age children were not in school (having died or become refugees) and two-thirds of teachers were secondary school graduates with no teacher training (VSO 2003).
Literacy rate: 69 per cent adult rate; 85 per cent youth rate (15–24) (Unesco 2005).
Compulsory years: Seven to 13.
Enrolment rate: 95.5 per cent net primary (World Bank).

Health

Per capita total expenditure on health (2003) was US$32; of which per capita government spending was US$14, at the international dollar rate, (WHO 2006).

HIV/Aids

The average life expectancy of Rwandan citizens has reduced to under 40 due to the Aids epidemic. In 2003 there were

230,000 people HIV positive, of which 130,000 were women. There were also 22,000 children (0–17 years) with HIV/Aids and 160,000 orphans created by Aids. There has been evidence that national adult prevalence has fallen in Rwanda since reaching a peak in the mid-1990s (UNAID 2003).

HIV prevalence: 5.1 per cent aged 15–49 in 2003 (World Bank)

Life expectancy: 46 years, 2004 (WHO 2006)

Fertility rate/Maternal mortality rate: 5.6 births per woman, 2004 (WHO 2006)

Birth rate/Death rate: 40 births per 1,000 population; 21.7 deaths per 1000 population (2003).

Child (under 5 years) mortality rate (per 1,000): 118.0 per 1,000 live births (World Bank)

Head of population per physician: 0.05 physicians per 1,000 people, 2004 (WHO 2006)

Welfare

More than half the population live below the national poverty line. According to the 2002 UN Development Report, 84.6 per cent of the population exist on less than US$2 per day and 35.7 per cent on less than US$1 per day.

Main cities

Kigali (capital, estimated population 718,414 in 2005),Gitarama (108,760), Ruhengeri (81,960), Butare (88,585), Byumba (70,781), Gisenyi (79,959), Cyangugu (75,085).

Languages spoken

KiSwahili is also used among traders.

Official language/s

Kinyarwanda, French and English.

Media

Other news agencies: This is no national news agency but the African Press Agency (APA) (www.africanewsagency.org) and Panapress (www.panapress.com) report on news from Rwanda.

Press

There are only two domestically published newspapers, La Nouvelle Relève (www.orinfor.gov.rw), is government owned and printed in French, The New Times (www.newtimes.co.rw) is privately owned and printed in English.

A magazine, published regionally in French Jeune Afrique (www.jeuneafrique.com) covers news and interviews. Internet outlets in English include Inside Rwanda (www.insideworld.com/rwanda), and Rwanda Information Exchange (www.rwanda.net), and in French, Observatoire de l'Afrique Centrale (www.obsac.com).

Broadcasting

Radio: Most residents of Rwanda receive their news from radio broadcasts and the most listened to radio station is the government-owned, commercial Radio Rwanda (www.orinfor.gov.rw) broadcasting in KiSwahili, Kinyarwanda, French and English. There are six other private radio stations, including Radio Maria with religious programmes.

Television: Television Rwandaise (TVR) is the only television broadcasting company in the country.

News agencies

Other news agencies: This is no national news agency but the African Press Agency (APA) (www.africanewsagency.org) and Panapress (www.panapress.com) report on news from Rwanda.

Economy

Rwanda has pushed forward with national rehabilitation since the genocide in 1994. Output has recovered through debt relief and aid, but there is still much to be achieved if poverty rates are it to be reduced significantly. The infrastructure remains severely dilapidated and agricultural yields are low. Without social and structural reforms poverty will stay pervasive – 60 per cent of the population live below the poverty line.

Aid is expected to increase in 2007, including relief of US$13.9 million (around 0.6 per cent of GDP). The IMF has cautioned that Rwanda must preserve macroeconomic stability, manage fiscal policies and control domestic demand to gain maximum benefit. The central bank has made a commitment to closely monitor credit and inflationary pressures and tighten the monetary position if necessary. The government is implementing measures to improve tax procedures, reform the public service, strengthen financial institutions and privatise publicly owned commercial enterprises.

In 2005, GDP growth was 5.0 per cent and was expected to be 4.2 per cent in 2006. Inflation was 9.2 per cent in 2005 but grew to over 11 per cent year-on-year by November and remains a problem to be redressed by fiscal policies.

The economy is composed of services at 38 per cent of GDP, industry 20 per cent (of which manufacturing is 10 per cent), and the greater proportion of 42 per cent from agriculture. Land reforms are underway to give secure tenure and user rights. Tea provides 60 per cent of export earnings, with coffee and pyrethrum,a plant extract used in insect repellent, providing much of the rest.

External trade

Rwanda is a member of the Common Market for Eastern and Southern Africa (Comesa), and operates within a free trade zone with 13 of the 19 member states.

As a landlocked country, the infrastructure must be maintained to move any imports and exports from neighbouring countries, which increases shipping costs; there is no railway linking Rwanda to the Tanzanian rail system. Rwanda has few natural resources and imports its energy (beyond bio-fuels) as well as capital goods. Exports are limited to cash crops – tea represents 60 per cent – and pyrethrum, the extract of which is used in insect repellent.

Imports

Principal imports include foodstuffs, machinery and equipment, steel, petroleum products, cement and construction material.

Main sources: Kenya (19.7 per cent total, 2006), Germany (7.3 per cent) Uganda (6.9 per cent).

Exports

Principal exports are tea, coffee, pyrethrum, animal hides and tin ore.

Main destinations: China (10.3 per cent total, 2006), Germany (9.7 per cent), US (4.3 per cent).

Agriculture

Farming

The agricultural sector contributes about 40 per cent to GDP and employs 90 per cent of the labour force. Approximately 30 per cent of the land area is cultivated arable land, 31 per cent pasture and 9 per cent forest; tree planting programmes are under way to combat deforestation.

The main food crops are beans (17 per cent of cultivated land), sweet potatoes (14 per cent), sorghum (7 per cent), plantains, bananas, potatoes, cassava and maize. Crop yields fluctuate due to drought, soil erosion and underinvestment.

The coffee industry is scheduled for privatisation although little progress has been made. Coffee production fell so the government is encouraging the growth of speciality coffees that receive higher prices on the international market. If this move is successful, export revenues could be boosted, but if not, it is unlikely the failing coffee industry will recover swiftly.

Tea overtook coffee as the country's main export.

Food production was boosted in early 2008 when high-yielding seed varieties provided by under the Crop Intensification Project proved successful.

Crop production for 2005 included: 365,042 tonnes (t) cereals in total, 781,639t cassava, 1,314,050t potatoes, 885,648t sweet potatoes, 3,122,232t roots and tubers, 2,593,080t plantains, 222,927t sorghum, 218,502t pulses, 7,296t oilcrops, 3,800t tobacco, 22,500t green coffee, 15,000t tea, 70,000t sugar cane, 23,703t soya beans, 2,670,080t fruit in total, 267,000t vegetables in total. Livestock production included: 50,811t meat in total, 23,088t beef, 11,000t game meat, 6,384t pig meat, 4,675t goat meat, 2,250t poultry, 2,300t eggs, 145,900t milk, 30t honey, 3,330t cattle hides, 1,063t goatskins.

Forestry

Timber imports in 2004 were US$3 million, while exports only amounted to US$340,000.

Timber production in 2004 included 5,495,000 cubic metre (cum) roundwood, 495,000cum industrial roundwood, 79,000cum sawnwood, 245,000cum sawlogs and veneer logs, 2,500,000cum pulpwood, wood-based panels, 5,000,000cum woodfuel; 48,000t charcoal.

Industry and manufacturing

The industrial sector contributed 21.5 per cent to GDP in 2004 and typically employs 6 per cent of the workforce.

Industries include brewing, food processing, cigarette production, soaps, plastics, tin smelting and textiles. Growth of the sector is limited by the small domestic market, transport difficulties and irregular supply of imported fuels and raw materials which comprise 77 per cent of inputs.

Industrial production increased by 4–5 per cent in 2004.

Tourism

Rwanda receives around 16,000 tourists annually and is aiming to become Africa's newest eco-tourism destination. It plans to raise the number of visitors to 70,000 by 2010 and boost tourism income to US$99 million a year.

In February 2008 the governments of Democratic Republic of Congo, Rwanda and Uganda agreed to joint measures to protect the mountain gorillas found within their shared border regions. Tourists visiting the area to view the endangered great apes raise a combined US$5 million for the countries concerned.

Environment

In February 2008 the governments of Democratic Republic of Congo, Rwanda and Uganda agreed to joint measures to protect the mountain gorillas found within their shared border regions. Tourists visiting the area to view the endangered great apes raise a combined US$5 million for the countries concerned. However, poaching and civil strife have dropped the numbers of gorillas to critically endangered levels, so that a 10-year conservation project which focuses of security and encouraging local people to preserve the animals and habitat is seen as the only hope for the gorilla's survival

Mining

The mining sector contributes 7 per cent to GDP and employs 1 per cent of the workforce.

Extraction of cassiterite (known reserves 90,000 tonnes) has been carried out since 1985, on an artisanal scale only.

Hydrocarbons

Rwanda has no upstream oil industry or refining plants and imports all its refined petroleum products from Kenya and Tanzania. The proposed Kenya-Uganda 320 km oil pipeline will benefit Rwanda through the lower costs of transportation of imported oil.

There are around 70 billion cubic metres of methane gas in Lake Kivu, with a regenerative capacity of around 250 million cubic metres per annum. Rwanda has been looking to exploit this resource since 1998. In 2005, an agreement was signed with a private operator to develop and gather commercial quantities of gas for use in electricity production.

Rwanda does not import or consume natural gas nor does it have significant coal reserves.

Energy

The subsistence farming sector currently relies on wood and charcoal.

Electrogaz, Rwanda's privatised national electricity generating company, has a power generating capacity of 10MW. In March 2005 an agreement was signed with the UK company Dane Associates to build a 35MW power station at Kibuye by March 2007, with all electricity supplied to Electrogaz.

Urban areas and industry energy requirements are met by hydroelectricity generated by the Ntaruka, Mukungwa and Sebeya stations. The Rusizi power station has been developed with Burundi and DRC and generates more than 40 per cent of the energy used in Rwanda.

In mid-2002, the Israeli Electric Company announced that it was conducting a preliminary study on the construction of a 25MW power station, using gas from Lake Kivu. The Gisenyi Electric and Gas Company also hopes to construct a plant that would have an initial capacity of 2.5MW, eventually expanding to 10MW. Analysts believe that Lake Kivu has enough natural gas to produce 200MW of electricity.

Financial markets

Stock exchange

A new securities exchange, the Rwanda Capital Market, was set up by the Central Bank of Rwanda in Kigali in January 2008. To begin with it will deal in domestic corporate and treasury bonds, although other products such as shares will be included as the operation develops.

The exchange is seen as an alternative market for cheaper financing than that offered by commercial banks.

Banking and insurance

Central bank

Banque Nationale du Rwanda

Main financial centre

Kigali

Time

GMT plus two hours

Geography

Rwanda is a landlocked country in central Africa, just south of the Equator, bounded by the Democratic Republic of Congo to the west, where Lake Kivu (one of the Great Lakes) provides the border; Uganda is to the north, Tanzania to the east and Burundi in the south.

Rwanda has rolling hill terrain for most of its eastern region. However, a chain of rugged, volcanic mountains runs from the north-west south to the border with Burundi in the south-west. The highest peak is Mount Karisimbi (4,532 metres). To the west of the mountain range Lake Kivu flows into the Congo River basin through the Ruzizi River valley, a section of Africa's Great Rift Valley. The south is swamp and savannah, which, in the south-east, peters out into desert.

Hemisphere

Southern

Climate

Warm, tempered by altitude. Rainfall is low and is concentrated in two seasons from mid-January to mid-May, and mid-October to mid-December. Temperatures in Kigali range from 12–14 degrees Celsius (C) at night to 28–32 degrees C during the day. Cooler in the highland areas.

Entry requirements

Passports

Required by all. Passports must be valid for six months from date of visit.

Visa

Are required by all, except nationals of US, Germany, Canada, Uganda, Tanzania, Kenya, Burundi and the DRC for visits up to 90 days; entry permits are issued on arrival, when visitors must provide evidence of sufficient funds for stay and return/onward passage.

Business travellers or tourists staying for longer must apply for a visa. A business visa requires a letter of introduction by an employer stating purpose of visit. Contact the nearest Rwanda Consulate for further details.

Currency advice/regulations

Import and export of local currency is limited to a maximum Rwf5,000. Import of foreign currency is unlimited, but amounts

should be declared; export is only allowed up to the amount declared.
Travellers cheques are not readily accepted.

Customs
Personal possessions are duty-free.
Export of game trophies require agreement from the relevant authority.

Health (for visitors)
Mandatory precautions
Yellow fever vaccination certificate is required by all.

Advisable precautions
Hepatitis A, tetanus, typhoid and polio vaccinations. Malaria prophylaxis is recommended. Water precautions should be taken. Aids is prevalent. There is a rabies risk.

Hotels
Tend to be expensive in Kigali; cheaper in Butare, Gisenyi and Ruhengeri. Advisable to book in advance.

Public holidays (national)
Fixed dates
1 Jan (New Year's Day), 28 Jan (Democracy Day), 7 Apr (Genocide Memorial Day), 1 May (Labour Day), 1 Jul (Independence Day), 4 Jul (Liberation Day), 15 Aug (Assumption Day), 25 Sep (Republic Day), 1 Nov (All Saints Day), 25–26 Dec (Christmas).

Variable dates
Good Friday and Easter Monday (Mar/Apr).

Working hours
Banking
Mon–Fri: 0800–1200, 1400–1800; Sat: 0800–1300.

Business
Mon–Fri: 0800–1230, 1330–1700.

Government
Mon–Fri: 0800–1230, 1330–1700.

Shops
Dawn to dusk.

Telecommunications
Telephone/fax

Mobile/cell phones
A GSM900 coverage exists.

Internet/e-mail

Electricity supply
220V AC

Security
The threat of attack from rebel groups continues and despite the cease-fire and elections in neighbouring DRC, the border regions are volatile. Local advice should be sought by those proposing to visit such areas; a military escort may be necessary. Kigali and major towns in the east, such as Butare and Gitarma, can be visited, but precautions need to be taken. Cars should not be left unattended in the centre of town and walking after dark or carrying large amounts of money or valuables is ill-advised.

Getting there
Air
National airline: Rwandair Express
International airport/s: Kigali-Kanombe (KGL), 12km east of city; duty-free shop, bar, currency exchange, post office, shops, coach, taxi service.
Airport tax: None

Surface
Road: Roads from Uganda,Tanzania and Burundi are well-surfaced.
Water: Although landlocked there is a link on Lake Kivu, between the north and south.
Main port/s: Gisenyi, Cyangugu.

Getting about
National transport
Air: Rwandair Express operates a limited internal service.
Road: All cities are linked to Kigali by paved roads, and the roads Ruhengeri-Cyanika and Kayonza-Kagitumba are paved. Other roads are poor with many being impassable in bad weather.
Buses: Reliable regular bus services are available from Kigali to the main cities and between some cities themselves. Private minibuses (belonging to an association called ATRACO) also operate between Kigali and other cities.
Water: Services run between Gisenyi and Cyangugu, on Lake Kivu.

City transport
Taxis: They can be found in large towns; fares should be agreed at the start of journey and tipping is not necessary.

Car hire
Limited service is available in Kigali. International driving licence is required. All-weather roads are sparse and in poor condition.

BUSINESS DIRECTORY
The addresses listed below are a selection only. While World of Information makes every endeavour to check these addresses, we cannot guarantee that changes have not been made, especially to telephone numbers and area codes. We would welcome any corrections.

Telephone area codes
The international dialling code (IDD) for Rwanda is +250, followed by subscriber's number.

Chambers of Commerce
Fédération Rwandaise du Secteur Privé, PO Box 319, Kigali (tel: 583-538/41; fax: 583-532; e-mail: frsp@rwanda1.com).

Banking
Banque à la Confiance d'Or, BP 2059, Kigali (tel: 575-780, 75-763; fax: 575-761).

Banque Commerciale du Rwanda, BP 354, Boulevard de la Revolution, Kigali (tel: 575-591, 576-117; fax: 573-395).

Banque Continentale Africaine (Rwanda) SA, BP 331, 20 Kigali, Boulevard de la Revolution, Kigali (tel: 574-456/7/8; fax: 573-486).

Banque de Commerce, de Developpement et d'Industrie, BP 3268, Kigali (tel: 574-143, 574-132, 74-427; fax: 573-790, 74-479).

Banque de Kigali, BP 175, 63 Avenue du Commerce, Kigali (tel: 576-931/2/3/4; fax: 573-461, 75-504).

Banque Nationale du Rwanda, BP 531, Kigali (tel: 574-282, 575-249; fax: 572-551).

Banque Rwandaise de Developpment, BP 1341, Kigali (tel: 575-079, 575-080; fax: 573-569).

Campagne Generale de Banque, BP 5230, Kigali (tel: 586-875; fax: 586-876).

Union des Banques Populaires du Rwanda, BP 1348, Kigali (tel: 573-564; fax: 573-579).

Central bank
Banque Nationale du Rwanda, Avenue Paul VI, BP 531, Kigali (tel: 574-282; fax: 572-551; e-mail: webmaster@bnr.rw).

Travel information
Air France, BP 411, Kigali (tel: 575-566).
Rwandair Express, Ground & 2nd floor, Centenary House, Av de Revolution; BP 7275 Kigali (575-757, 503-687; fax: 503-686; internet: www.rwanda.com).

Office Rwandais du Tourisme et des Parcs Nationaux, BP 905, Kigali (tel: 576-514/5, 573-396; fax: 576-512; e-mail: Ortpn@rwandatel1.rwanda1.com).

Rwanda Travel Service, BP 140, Kigali (tel: 572-210).

Rwanda Explorations, BP 1514, Kigali (tel: 573-284).

Ministries
Ministry of Agriculture and Animal Resources, PO Box 621, Kigali (tel: 586-104; fax: 587-038; internet: www.minagri.gov.rw).

Ministry of Comerce, Industry, Investment, Promotion, Tourism and Co-operatives (tel: 574-725, 574-734; fax: 575-465; email: jnsengiyumva@minicom.gov.rw: internet: www.minicom.gov.rw).

Ministry of Education, Science, Technology and Scientific Research, BP 622 Kigali (tel: 583-051; fax: 582-161; email: info@mineduc.gov.rw).

Office of the Prime Minister, Kigali (tel: 585-444/5, 584-648; fax: 583-714; internet: www.primature.gov.rw).

Other useful addresses

Agence Rwandaise de Presse (ARP), 27 avenue du Commerce, BP 83, Kigali (tel: 575-665).

Economat Général (tobacco exports), BP 45, Ruhengeri.

L'Institut des Sciences Agronomiques du Rwanda, BP 138, Butare.

Office des Cafés, BP 104, Kigali (tel: 575-277).

Office du Pyrèthre au Rwanda, BP 79, Ruhengeri.

Office du Thé, BP 1344, Kigali (tel: 572-416).

Rwandan Embassy (USA), 1714 New Hampshire Avenue, NW, Washington DC 20009 (tel: (+1-202) 232-2882; fax: (+1-202) 232-4544; email: rwandemb@rwandemb.org).

Internet sites

General information: www.rwanda.net

Africa Business Network: www.ifc.org/abn

African Development Bank: www.afdb.org

Africa Online: www.africaonline.com

AllAfrica.com: http://allafrica.com

Mbendi AfroPaedia (information on companies, countries, industries and stock exchanges in Africa): http://mbendi.co.za

Official website of government of Rwanda: www.gov.rw

St Helena

KEY FACTS

Official name: St Helena Colony with Dependencies

Head of State: Queen Elizabeth II, represented by Governor and Commander-in-Chief Andrew Gurr (since Nov 2007)

Ruling party: All members of the legislative council stand as independents

Area: 122 square km

Population: 7,502 (2006)*

Capital: Jamestown

Official language: English

Currency: St Helena pound (StH£) = 100 pence

Exchange rate: StH£0.50 per US$ (Jul 2008); (pegged to pound sterling)

GDP per capita: US$2,500 (2003)

Labour force: 3,500 (2003)

Unemployment: 14.00% (2003)

Inflation: 3.20% (2003)

Balance of trade: -US$14.43 million (2003)

* estimated figure

COUNTRY PROFILE

Historical profile

1502 St Helena was sighted by Portuguese mariners on 21 May (St Helena's Day).
1513 The island was first settled.
1633 The Dutch claimed possession.
1659 The East India Company took possession of the uninhabited island.
1673 The island was briefly captured by the Dutch, before being regained by the East India Company.
1815 Napoleon Bonaparte was exiled to the island, where he died in 1821; his body was returned to France in 1840.
1834 The island passed under British control.
1981 The Nationality Act ended the islanders' British citizenship and right of abode, which they had held since 1673.
1992 The islanders established a Citizenship Commission, which began its case for full British citizenship.
2002 Full British citizenship was restored to the islanders.
2004 Michael Clancy became Governor and Commander-in-Chief on 15 October.
2005 Elections were held 31 August. An environmental team from the UK conducted the first stage of investigations required to carry out an Environmental Impact Assessment (EIA) for the proposed new airport on Prosperous Bay Plain in October and November.
2007 HMS Nottingham, a destroyer class ship, became the South Atlantic patrol ship to maintain a British maritime presence in the South Atlantic around Ascension Island, St Helena, Tristan da Cunha, South Georgia, the South Sandwich Islands and the Falkland Islands. The new governor, Andrew Gurr, was inaugurated on 11 November.

Political structure

St Helena has an appointed governor assisted by an Executive Council (the chief secretary, the financial secretary, attorney general and committee chairmen) and also by a Legislative Council (made up of the same ex-officio members and 12 elected members). Restoration for the islanders of full British citizenship was granted in May 2002.

The creation of a new overseas territories minister within the Foreign and Commonwealth Office (FCO) and the establishment of an Overseas Territories Consultative Council were both implemented in 1999, but responsibility for the British Overseas Territories, including St Helena, remains divided between the FCO and the Department for International Development.

Constitution

The St Helena Constitution Order came into force in February 1989. It sets out the separation of powers and the responsibilities of the executive, legislature and judiciary.

Form of state

As a British Overseas Territory, St Helena is a dependency of St Helena.

The executive

As a British Overseas Territory, St Helena has an appointed governor assisted by an Executive Council with three ex-officio appointments (the chief secretary, the financial secretary, attorney general and committee chairmen) and five elected members of the Legislative Council.

The creation of a new overseas territories minister within the Foreign and Commonwealth Office (FCO) and the establishment of an Overseas Territories Consultative Council were both implemented in 1999, but responsibility for the British Overseas Territories, including St Helena, remains divided between the FCO and the Department for International Development.

National legislature

The unicameral legislative assembly has 12 members elected for four-year terms. There are also three ex-officio appointments including the chief secretary, the financial secretary and the attorney general.

Last elections

August 2005 (parliamentary)

Results: Parliamentary: only non-partisans were elected; turnout was 47 per cent.

Next elections

2009 (parliamentary)

Political parties

No parties exist.

Ruling party

All members of the legislative council stand as independents

Political situation

Governor Gurr spelt out two major problems for the residents of St Helena, in his inaugural speech – depopulation and dependency. As experienced by so many small communities, St Helena is losing too many of its young and potentially most valuable members to the outside world, even though families welcome the immediate value of remittances. Self-sufficiency is a goal the UK government is keen for all its dependencies to achieve and a Sustainable Development Plan was proposed by the island's executive council which outlined six objectives necessary for future sustainability: improved access – there is no air access and sea connections are slow and costly; improved standard of education; development of a sustainable and vibrant economy; and promote and develop a sustainable workforce; develop a healthy community in a safe environment and establish the democratic and human rights and self-determination of the people of St Helena.

An airport is costly and while the UK government is funding the project the island's long term viability will ultimately be dependent on commercial projects such as tourism, but as the island has little to offer this would also need great investment – which the UK government has not indicated it is prepared to make. Better education is a long term objective and in the meantime newly qualified students are leaving and depriving any nascent business of its workforce.

Population

7,502 (2006)*

Last census: March 1998: 6,054

Population density: 43.8 inhabitants per square km.

Annual growth rate: 0.5 per cent (2003)

Ethnic make-up

Black African (50 per cent), white (25 per cent), Chinese (25 per cent).

Religions

Anglican (majority), Baptist, Seventh-Day Adventist, Roman Catholic.

Health

Life expectancy: 74.5 years (estimate 2003)

Fertility rate/Maternal mortality rate: 1.5 births per woman (2003)

Birth rate/Death rate: 13 births per 1,000 population; 6.3 deaths per 1,000 population (2003).

Child (under 5 years) mortality rate (per 1,000): 21 per 1,000 live births (2003)

Main cities

Jamestown (capital, estimated population 1,500 in 2003).

Languages spoken

Official language/s

English

Media

Press

Weeklies: The St Helena Herald (www.news.co.sh) is government funded while The St Helena Independent (www.saint.fm/Independent/) is independent.

Business: A publication, giving sailing, details of the Royal Mail Service (RMS) ship St Helena (www.albionshipping.co.uk), which has a regular service to the island from UK and Cape Town. The Gulf and South Atlantic Fisheries Foundation publishes a newsletter concerning fishery matters (www.gulfsouthfoundation.org/newsletters).

Periodicals: The St Helena News Bureau publishes the periodical St Helena and South Atlantic News Review and the monthly The St Helena Catalogue.

Broadcasting

Radio: The government-funded Radio St Helena (www.news.co.sh) operates on short wave (AM) daily, with relays of a number of BBC World Service programmes. Saint FM (www.saint.fm) features music, local events and information.

Television: There is no locally made television service. Cable & Wireless provides a two channel television service relaying selected programmes from BBC World, CNN, Supersport, Discovery Channel and MNET, a South African commercial service.

Economy

St Helena was developed as a re-victualling post for East India Company ships returning from the east. With the decline of sail from the 1870s, the island has struggled to find a basis for its economy. The production of New Zealand flax was started in 1874 and had some success during times of high world prices. However, St Helena's terrain is not suited to plantation cropping and the industry, heavily subsidised for most of its history, finally collapsed in 1966.

St Helena depends on aid from the UK for between 20–25 per cent of its recurrent public sector budget of approximately StH£10 million (US$14.2 million). Fishing licence sales earn StH£0.75 million (US$1 million) in revenue per annum. Local catches, philatelic sales, livestock and timber additionally provide the main sources of revenue, together with remittances from offshore workers which are estimated to be worth StH£2–3 million (US$2.8–4.2 million) per year.

Andrew Weir Shipping Ltd took over the management of the RMS St Helena from Curnow Shipping in 2001. Plans to build an airstrip were approved by a referendum held in 2002. There is also a privately funded proposal by Shelco for an airport/golf course/airline scheme.

A new mail ship schedule, which started a one-year trial in September 2004, will provide a more regular service, which it is hoped will also benefit the tourism sector.

External trade

As a UK Overseas Territories St Helena is a part of the European Union's Association of Overseas Countries and Territories (OCT Association), and some EU laws apply.

The small quantity of coffee exported, three tonnes per year, produces one of the world's most expensive beverages. Fishing licences and frozen and canned tuna provide most foreign earnings.

Imports

Principal imports are foodstuffs, tobacco, petroleum, animal feed, building materials, vehicles and parts, machinery and parts.

Main sources: UK (53.5 per cent total, 2006), South Africa (14.3 per cent), Spain (10.3 per cent).

Exports

Principal exports are fish (frozen, canned, and salt-dried skipjack, tuna), coffee and handicrafts.

Main destinations: Tanzania 37.7 per cent (of total, 2006), US 17.4 per cent, Japan 15.2 per cent.

Agriculture

Farming

St Helena's volcanic origins, hills and deep valleys dominate the landscape. Semi-desert gives way to upland grasslands and lush valleys over a very short distance.

Arable and garden land is about 3 per cent of the total area, forest and woodland 5 per cent, pasture 11 per cent, barren and badland 53 per cent. New Zealand flax (hemp) was grown until the 1960s, but much of this land is now planted with trees. Principal crops include potatoes, coffee, bananas, vegetables, sweet potatoes.

Livestock raising is a main activity but there is no dairy production and all dairy products are imported.

Agricultural production does not meet demand. Seed potatoes, onions and eggs are all imported in quantity.

Fishing

In the past, the government of St Helena earned StH£1.0 million (US$1.4 million) per annum from fishing licence revenue, but fish stocks have declined.

There is a local fishery run by the St Helena Fisheries Corporation, which buys the fish from the local fishermen.

The fishing boats range from eight to 13 metres in size and fish on a daily basis. They meet EU standards and carry ice with them. All of the catch is landed within 12 hours.

St Helena has satellite surveillance, but no patrol boat to stop unlicensed boats fishing the waters.

Industry and manufacturing
Local fishermen sell their catch to the St Helena Fisheries Corporation (a government parastatal). St Helena Fisheries Corporation sells its product in frozen and smoked form primarily to the UK and South Africa and supplies the domestic market.
Working in partnership with the St Helena Fisheries Corporation, Argos Helena Ltd, a joint UK-Spanish owned company, runs a blast freezer and fish processing/canning facility. Locally caught high-quality tuna is processed for export to the European Union and the Far East. The Corporation's fish products have organic certification from the Soil Association in the UK.

Tourism
St Helena has few resources and a declining population. Tourism is seen as a means of rescuing the island's economy and future. However, until the new airport is ready, access is restricted. Heavy seas make yachting anchorage unsafe.
The only means of reaching the island at the moment is by the RMS St Helena, which carries only 128 passengers on a round trip from UK (Portland) twice a year, and monthly from Cape Town to Walvis Bay (Namibia), St Helena and Ascension Island.
Although the rugged nature of the island has precluded air access, the possibility of constructing an airstrip is being investigated.
Tourism is currently worth about StH£250,000 per annum and employs around 50 people. Projections suggest that it could support 200 jobs and generate a value of StH£1 million (US$1.4 million) if transport links are improved.

Hydrocarbons
St Helena does not have any hydrocarbon reserves and relies entirely on the import of refined oil products to meet energy needs. St Helena does not import natural gas or coal.

Time
GMT

Geography
St Helena is situated in the South Atlantic Ocean and is 1,950km (1,200 miles) due west from the south-west coast of Africa and 2,900km (1,800 miles) east of South America. The nearest land is one of its dependencies, Ascension Island, 1,130km (700 miles) to the north-west.
The island is of volcanic in origin. It is mountainous, presenting an almost continuous line of high, sheer cliffs, cut only by a few narrow and steep-sided valleys around its coastline. It is criss-crossed by deep valleys and slopes steeply from the central ridges to the sea. The highest point is Diana's Peak (820 metres above sea-level).

Hemisphere
Southern

Climate
Summer temperatures range from 21–29 degrees Celsius (C); winter 18–24 degrees C on coasts; inland temperatures may be five degrees lower; annual average rainfall in Jamestown is around 200mm, inland up to 950mm.

Entry requirements
Passports
Required by all.
Visa
All visitors must have the Administrator's written permission to land, before travelling. An Ascension Island Entry Permit form (valid for St Helena), to be completed, can be downloaded from www.ascension-island.gov.ac/visitors.htm. Entry is only granted with evidence of visitors full medical insurance policy, covering medical evacuation by air, when necessary.
Currency advice/regulations
Travllers cheques are accepted in the bank.
Customs
Prohibited imports
Obscene or pornographic materials are prohibited.
Firearms, ammunition, fruit, vegetables and plant materials require an import permit.

Health (for visitors)
There is one general hospital based in Jamestown and six health clinics on the island. The health service is not free and all St Helenians have to pay fees for medical treatment. UK Passport holders visiting the island pay local rates for medical treatment, while non-UK residents have to pay higher fees.
Mandatory precautions
None.

Hotels
There are three hotels on the island, reservations are necessary from December–March.

Credit cards
Major credit cards are accepted in a few locations.

Public holidays (national)
Fixed dates
1 Jan (New Year's Day), 21 May (St Helena Day), 25–26 Dec (Christmas).
Variable dates
Good Friday and Easter Monday (Mar/Apr), Pentecost (May/Jun), August Bank Holiday (last Mon in Aug).

Working hours
Banking
Mon–Sat: 0845/0900–1500/1600; except Thu: 0845–1200. Opening hours may be varied when a cruise ship is visiting.
Business
Mon–Fri: 0830–1230 and 1300–1600.
Government
Mon–Fri: 0830–1230, 1300–1600.
Shops
Mon–Sat: generally 0900–1700.

Getting there
Air
St Helena has no airport and can only be reached by sea. Wideawake Airfield on Ascension Island is the nearest airfield. It is a US military base, and will allow private air-charter access to Wakefield in 2007–08. Passengers for St Helena will need to transfer to a boat to reach the island.
Surface
Water: The RMS St Helena operates twice a year from the UK (Portland) and monthly from Cape Town to Walvis Bay (Namibia), St Helena and Ascension Island. The ship is operated under contract by Passenger Services Department, Andrew Weir Shipping Ltd (see travel information addresses).
Air connections can be made with the ship either through Cape Town, via commercial flights, or via military flights from Royal Air Force Brize Norton in Oxfordshire, UK to Ascension Island.
Main port/s: Jamestown

Getting about
National transport
Road: Road network of 80–85km classified as all-weather; at least further 60km surfaced and 25–30km suitable for dry-weather travel only. Roads are best described as steep and tortuous. Because most roads are single lane, motoring etiquette requires the driver coming down to make way for upcoming traffic.

BUSINESS DIRECTORY
The addresses listed below are a selection only. While World of Information makes every endeavour to check these addresses, we cannot guarantee that changes have not been made, especially to telephone numbers and area codes. We would welcome any corrections.

Telephone area codes
The international dialling code (IDD) for St Helena is +290 followed by subscriber's number.

Chambers of Commerce
St Helena Chamber of Commerce, c/o The Castle, Jamestown. (fax: tel: 22-58; fax: 25-98).

Banking
Bank of St. Helena, Post Office Building, Main Street, Jamestown STHL 1ZZ (tel: 2390; fax: 2553; internet: www.SaintHelenaBank.com).

Travel information
For air travel and bookings on the RMS St Helena:

Passenger Services Department, Andrew Weir Shipping Ltd, Dexter House, 2 Royal Mint Court, London EC N4XX, UK (tel: (+44-20) 575-6480; fax: (+44-20) 575-6200; e-mail: reservations@aws.co.uk).

St Helena Line, Andrew Weir Shipping (SA) Pty Ltd, 3rd Floor, BP Centre, Thibault Square, Cape Town, South Africa (tel: (+27-21) 425-1165; fax: (+27-21) 421-7485; e-mail: sthelenaline@mweb.co.za; internet site: www.aws.co.uk).

Miss Kerry Yon, Solomon and Co plc, Jamestown (tel: 2523; fax: 2423; e-mail: solco.shipping@helanta.sh).

National tourist organisation offices
St Helena Tourism, Jamestown (tel: 2158; fax: 2159; email: StHelena.Tourism@helanta.sh; internet: www.sthelenatourism.com).

Ministries
Governor's Office, The Castle, Jamestown (tel: 2555; fax: 2598; e-mail: OCS@helanta.sh).

Other useful addresses
Argos Atlantic Cold Stores, PO Box 151, Jamestown (tel: 2333; fax: 2334; e-mail: argos@argonaut.co.sh).

Cable & Wireless Fax Bureau, The Briars, Jamestown.

Director of Inward Investment, Office of the Chief Secretary, Government of St Helena, Jamestown (tel: 2470; fax: 2598; e-mail: DEPD@atlantis.co.ac).

Information Office, Broadway House, Jamestown (tel: 2612; fax: 2159; email: StHelena.Tourism@atlantis.co.ac).

Miles Apart (books, maps, videos on South Atlantic Islands), 5 Harraton House, Exning, Newmarket, Suffolk CB8 7HF, UK (tel: (+44-1638) 577-627: fax: (+44-1638) 577-874); 5929 Avon Drive, Bethesda, Maryland 20814, USA (tel/fax: (+1-301) 571-8942; e-mail: familycarter@msn.com).

The Postmistress, The Philatelic Bureau, The Post Office, Jamestown (fax: 2242).

St Helena Commercial Representative, Mr Wes Huxtable, 1 The Stables, Great Hyde Hall, Sawbridgeworth, Herts CM21 9JA, UK (tel: (+44-1279) 725-833; fax: (+44-1279) 724-894; e-mail: weston@huxtable.freeserve.co.uk).

St Helena Desk Officer, Foreign and Commonwealth Office, King Charles Street, London SW1A 2AH, UK (tel: (+44-20) 270-2695).

St Helena Development Agency, No 2 Main St, Jamestown (tel: 2920, fax: 2166, e-mail: shda@atlantis.co.uk).

The St Helena Link (cultural information), Trevor Hearl, 49 Noverton Lane, Prestbury, Cheltenham, Glos GL52 5DD, UK (tel/fax: +44 (0)1242-244-430).

Internet sites
East India Company (coffee): www.theeastindiacompany.com

St Helena Development Agency: www.shda.helanta.sh/

St Helena government: www.sainthelena.gov.sh

St Helena News: www.news.co.sh

St Helena web portal: www.sthelenaonline.com

KEY FACTS

Official name: Federation of St Christopher and Nevis

Head of State: Queen Elizabeth II; represented by Governor General Sir Cuthbert Montroville-Sebastian (since 1996)

Head of government: Prime Minister Denzil Douglas (SKNLP) (since 1995; re-elected 2004)

Ruling party: St Kitts and Nevis Labour Party (SKNLP) (since 1995; re-elected 2004)

Area: 269 square km

Population: 49,600 (2007)*

Capital: Basseterre (St Kitts)

Official language: English

Currency: East Caribbean dollar (EC$) = 100 cents

Exchange rate: EC$2.70 per US$ (fixed)

GDP per capita: US$10,143 (2007)*

GDP real growth: 3.30% (2007)*

Labour force: 18,172 (2004)

Unemployment: 5.10% (2006)

Inflation: 4.50% (2007)*

Balance of trade: -US$98.00 million (2005)

Foreign debt: US$301.20 million (2005)

* estimated figure

St Kitts and Nevis

COUNTRY PROFILE

Historical profile

1623 Britain settled St Christopher (known as St Kitts), which became the first British colony in the West Indies.
1628 Nevis was settled by the British.
1816 Anguilla was joined to the territory.
1932 The St Kitts and Nevis Labour Party (SKNLP) was formed and campaigned for independence for the islands.
1958 St Christopher-Nevis-Anguilla became a member of the attempted West Indies Federation.
1962 The West Indies Federation was dissolved after the departure of Jamaica.
1967 St Christopher-Nevis-Anguilla, became a self-governing state in association with the UK. A House of Assembly replaced the Legislative Council, the administrator became governor and the chief minister became the state's first premier. The pro-independence SKNLP, became the ruling political party. The UK retained responsibility for defence and foreign relations.
1971 Anguilla reverted to being a British Dependent Territory after renouncing the rule of St Kitts.
1980 The SKNLP lost power to a coalition of the People's Action Movement (PAM) and the Nevis Reformation Party (NRP).
1983 Independence from Britain was attained.
1995 The SKNLP returned to power.
1997 The Nevis Island Assembly elections were won by the Concerned Citizens' Movement (CCM) with three seats. The opposition Nevis Reformation Party (NRP) secured the remaining two seats.
1998 A referendum on independence for Nevis failed to achieve the two-thirds majority required for approval.
2000 The ruling SKNLP was re-elected and Denzil Douglas began a second term as prime minister.
2001 The Nevis ruling party, the CCM , won four seats in the elections to the five-seat Nevis Island Assembly (NIA).
2003 The largest hotel complex in the eastern Caribbean region opened at Frigate Bay.
2004 The NaturalSweet Corporation invested US$90 million for the cultivation and commercial development of stevia, a natural herbal plant. The ruling SKNLP won the parliamentary elections.
2005 The last harvest of sugar cane was delivered to the only remaining refinery, which ceased operations after the last run was made, and ended a centuries old industry.
2006 In the NIA elections, the NRP won 3 (out of 5 seats) beating the CCM with 2; Joseph Parry was sworn in as prime minister of Nevis.
2007 Cotton lint for export has been added to the agricultural products of Nevis, with a crop of sea island cotton, forecast at over 45,000kg, expected to be harvested in mid-2008.

Political structure

Constitution
The constitution of 1983 gives the island of Nevis considerable autonomy within a federal framework.

Form of state
Independent parliamentary democratic state; it is a member of the Commonwealth with the British monarch as head of state, represented by a governor general, who exercises executive power.
Nevis has limited self-government.

National legislature
The legislature is the National Assembly comprising 11 members elected for a five-year term (eight from St Kitts, three from Nevis) plus three appointed members.
The cabinet headed by a prime minister is collectively responsible to the National Assembly.

Legal system
The legal system is based upon English common law. Appeals go to the Eastern Caribbean Supreme Court based on Saint Lucia. The final court of appeal is the Privy Council in the UK.

Last elections
25 October 2004 (National Assembly); 10 July 2006 (Nevis Island Assembly (NIA).
Results: Parliamentary: the ruling Labour Party (LP) won seven seats out of 11, the Concerned Citizens' Movement (CCM) two, the People's Action Movement (PAM) one, and the Nevis Reformation Party (NRP) one.
NIA: the NRP won 3 out of 5 seats, beating the CCM with 2.

Next elections
2009 (National Assembly)

Political parties

Ruling party
St Kitts and Nevis Labour Party (SKNLP) (since 1995; re-elected 2004)

Political situation
In May 2008, front of supporters and representatives of the business and diplomatic community, the Prime Minister

Denzil Douglas was keen to announce that his strategy for the economy had shown marked success. In 2005 the government decided to close down the 300-year old sugar industry that was haemorrhaging millions of dollars a year. Instead the government invested in and supported projects in high-end tourist facilities and modernised infrastructures that attracted not only foreign direct investment but also local ownership.

The IMF supported this assertion in its review of the economy in 2007, saying the economy 'remained strong' driven by tourism construction and communication although high public debt was still a worrying concern.

Population
49,600 (2007)*
Last census: May 2001: 45,841
Population density: 114 inhabitants per square km. Urban population: 34 per cent (1995–2001).
Annual growth rate: 0.5 per cent 1994–2004 (WHO 2006)

Ethnic make-up
Black African (91 per cent), mixed race (5 per cent), Asian (3 per cent), British, Portuguese and Lebanese descent (1 per cent).

Religions
Anglican (25 per cent), Methodist (25 per cent), Pentecostal (8 per cent), Moravian (7 per cent), other Protestant (12 per cent), Roman Catholic (7 per cent), Hindu (1 per cent).

Education
Compulsory years: Five to 17
Enrolment rate: 101 per cent boys, 94 per cent girls gross primary enrolment of relevant age group (including repeaters) (Unicef 2004).

Health
Per capita total expenditure on health (2003) was US$670; of which per capita government spending was US$427, at the international dollar rate, (WHO 2006).
Life expectancy: 71 years, 2004 (WHO 2006)
Fertility rate/Maternal mortality rate: 2.4 births per woman, 2004 (WHO 2006)
Birth rate/Death rate: 18.5 births per 1,000 population; nine deaths per 1,000 population (2003).
Child (under 5 years) mortality rate (per 1,000): 19 per 1,000 live births (World Bank)

Main cities
Basseterre (capital of St Kitts, estimated population 13,043 in 2005), Charlestown (capital of Nevis, 1,944).

Languages spoken
Official language/s
English

Media
Press
There are no daily newspapers. Weekly publications include The Democrat (www.pamdemocrat.org), The Leewards Times (www.leewardstimes.com), Sun St Kitts Nevis (http://sunstkitts.com), The St Kitts and Nevis Observer and the bi-weekly Labour Spokesman (www.labourworksforme.com).
A regional online publication Caribbean Net News (www.caribbeannetnews.com) covers news from St Kitts and Nevis.
Broadcasting
The government-owned commercial radio and television station is ZIZ (www.zizonline.com).
Radio: There are ten radio stations, including two government-owned ZIZ and Big Wave. Commercial stations on St Kitts include Sugar City Rock (www.sugarcityrock.com) Kyss FM (kyssonline.com) and on Nevis, Voice of Nevis (VON) (www.vonradio.com), Choice FM (http://choicefm1053.com) and Radio Paradise in Nevis.
Television: There is ZIZ Television which airs on two free cable channels and Winn FM (www.winnfm.com).

Economy
The Eastern Caribbean Central Bank shows that economic activity in St Kitts Nevis expanded in the first half of 2006 relative to the same period in 2005. This was partly down to increased construction activity in preparation for the Cricket World Cup 2007, which will increase in the second half of the year as preparations intensify. Projects included up-grading the Warner Park Stadium and expanding the airport on St Kitts.
Performance in the tourism sector was mixed, while agricultural output fell in the wake of the sugar industry's closure in 2005.

External trade
As a member of the Caribbean Community and Common Market (Caricom), St Kitts and Nevis operates within the single market (Caribbean Single Market and Economy (CSME)), which became operational on 1 January 2006. Goods, services, businesses and money are free to move within CSME without barriers and tariffs. It is also a member of the Eastern Caribbean Currency Union (ECCU) using the East Caribbean Dollar.
Since the closure of the sugar industry exports have fallen sharply so that light manufacturing and tourism provides foreign earnings. The islands have a large budget deficit and public debt that represents over 180 per cent of GDP. By 2006 St Kitts and Nevis was the second highest indebted country in the world.
The manufacture of cotton lint was re-introduced in 2008, after a gap of four years, when a valuable contracts for over 3,200kg of cotton lint for export to Japan were agreed.
Imports
Main imports are food, machinery, manufactured goods, petroleum and derivatives.
Main sources: US (46.9 per cent total, 2005), Trinidad and Tobago (13.7 per cent), UK (5.4 per cent), France (4.5 per cent), Japan (4.2 per cent)
Exports
Main exports are electrical appliances, electronic items and instrumentation, plastics, food and beverages.

KEY INDICATORS St Kitts and Nevis

	Unit	2003	2004	2005	2006	2007
Population	m	0.05	0.05	0.04	0.05	*0.05
Gross domestic product (GDP)	US$bn	0.34	0.40	0.44	0.50	*0.53
GDP per capita	US$	8,800	10,351	10,637	9,723	*10,143
GDP real growth	%	1.2	5.1	4.1	6.4	*3.3
Inflation	%	2.0	2.4	3.6	8.5	*4.5
Exports (fob) (goods)	US$m	47.0	60.1	62.0	–	–
Imports (cif) (goods)	US$m	152.0	183.3	180.0	–	–
Balance of trade	US$m	-105.0	-123.2	-98.0	–	–
Current account	US$m	-110.0	-100.0	-113.0	-144.0	*-163.0
Total reserves minus gold	US$m	64.8	78.5	71.6	88.7	95.8
Foreign exchange	US$m	64.7	78.3	71.5	88.6	95.7
Exchange rate	per US$	2.70	2.70	2.70	2.70	2.70

* estimated figure

Main destinations: US (63.5 per cent total, 2005), Canada (8.4 per cent), UK (5.8 per cent)

Agriculture

Farming

The agricultural sector contributes around 3 per cent to GDP.

Historically, the most important crop had been sugar. About 80 per cent of available arable land on St Kitts had been given over to sugar growing, with around 30 per cent of the labour force being employed in the industry. In 2005 the government decided that the industry was unsustainable and the last harvest of sugar cane was delivered to the only remaining refinery, which then ceased operations after the last run was made, and ended a centuries old industry. International competition, a lack of cane cutters and the change of policy by the EU to reduce guaranteed prices for sugar led to the demise of the national sugar manufacturing corporation with debts of over US$150 million.

Diversification into food crops has been encouraged to reduce dependence on imports.

The manufacture of cotton lint was re-introduced in 2008, after a gap of four years, when a valuable contracts for over 3,200kg of cotton lint for export to Japan were agreed. Old, retired ginnery equipment was renovated with new parts before the work could begin; when the operation is fully functioning the machinery will be able to gin 900kg per day. Processing raw cotton began in May 2008, however the only supply available came from government owned farms, after the first year of cotton cultivation, but supplies from private sources are expected to maintain the volume of production in future.

Estimated crop production in 2005 included: 150 tonnes (t) potatoes, 155t sweet potatoes, 100,000t sugar cane, 1,000t coconuts, 1,300t fruit in total, 210t pulses, 98t tomatoes, 140t oilcrops, 683t vegetables in total. Livestock production included: 428t meat in total, 93t beef, 132t pig meat, 47t lamb and goat meat, 156t poultry, 220t eggs.

Fishing

Inshore fishing is a traditional occupation and a significant source of protein.

The fisheries management unit introduced new fishing methods resulting in a fish catch that increased over 40 per cent during the first year. Other improvements include a new fisheries complex, opened in 2003, housing commercial storage and a fish market, constructed in Basseterre on St Kitts, while on Nevis the largest fishing facility includes a fish processing plant, walk-in freezers and market, is sited in Charlestown.

In 2004, the total marine fish catch was 336 tonnes and the total crustacean catch was 40 tonnes.

Industry and manufacturing

The industrial sector contributes around 24 per cent to GDP, with manufacturing contributing around 10 per cent.

Manufacturing activities have declined, with contraction in electrical and electronic components, due to poor US demand. The recession also led to a decline in domestic demand for locally produced manufactured goods.

In March 2004, the government approved a US$90 million investment plan by NaturalSweet Corporation to proceed with the cultivation and commercial development of stevia, a natural herbal plant, and construction of a plant to produce a dietary supplement.

Tourism

The tourism sector was badly affected by hurricane damage to the islands' tourism infrastructure in 1999 and 2000 and the terrorist attack in the US in 2001. The sector has recovered with improved marketing, government investment in port facilities at Basseterre, the construction of new hotels and improved air connections with other Caribbean islands and the US. The completion of a cruise ship pier at Porte Zante in late 2002 helped the tourist industry to eclipse sugar as the prime source of foreign exchange earnings. The improved international economic climate, especially in the US, has consolidated the sector's strong growth since 2002. Tourism is estimated to have contributed 7.8 per cent to GDP in 2005.

Estimates of stay-over arrivals indicate a 2 per cent increase in the first half of 2006, partly due to preparations for the Cricket World Cup 2007, and the annual meeting of the International Whaling Commission. However, cruise ship passengers fell by 6.1 per cent, despite an increase in cruise ship calls. Tourism provides work for 8.9 per cent of the labour force.

Hydrocarbons

St Kitts and Nevis does not have any hydrocarbon reserves and relies on imports of refined oil products. In 2001 it imported 710 barrels per day (bpd) to meet domestic demand. Gas and coal are not imported. The planned natural gas pipeline from Trinidad and Tobago linking the Caribbean islands could mean St Kitts and Nevis will import natural gas in the future.

Energy

St. Kitts and Nevis is planning the commercial development of geothermally-fuelled electric power plants.

Financial markets

Stock exchange

The St Kitts-based Eastern Caribbean Securities Exchange (ECSE) was launched by the Eastern Caribbean Central Bank (ECCB) in October 2001. The Bank of Nevis Ltd, based in St Kitts and Nevis, was one of only two securities listed on the ECSE at the start of trading activity.

Banking and insurance

The state-owned Development Bank provides credit to finance agriculture, industry, education and mortgages.

The seven members of the Organisation of Eastern Caribbean States (OECS), Antigua and Barbuda, Dominica, Grenada, Montserrat, St Kitts and Nevis, St Lucia and St Vincent and the Grenadines, share a common currency and central bank. The British Virgin Islands and Anguilla are associate members.

Central bank

East Caribbean Central Bank (ECCB)

Main financial centre

Basseterre

Offshore facilities

After St Kitts and Nevis was listed by the OECD as a tax haven which was unco-operative in fighting money laundering, the government passed the Money Laundering (Prevention) Bill, the Financial Services Intelligence Unit Bill and the Financial Services Commission Bill. The latter Bill established the Financial Services Commission as the main regulatory body for the offshore sector.

In 2002, St Kitts and Nevis was removed from the blacklist drawn up by the OECD.

Time

GMT minus four hours

Geography

St Kitts and Nevis is situated at the northern end of the Leeward Islands chain of the West Indies, with Saba and St Eustatius (both in the Netherlands Antilles) to the north-west, Barbuda to the north-east and Antigua to the south-east. Nevis lies about 3km (2 miles) to the south-east of St Kitts, separated by a narrow strait.

They are rugged volcanic islands covered with either original rich tropical rainforests or cultivated sugar cane plantations. St Kitts has a large crater, Mount Liamuiga, of 1,200 metres (m) high. In the south-east a peninsula stretches into the Caribbean Sea. Nevis is a circular island with a range of mountains. The highest peak, Mount Nevis, is 985m high.

Hemisphere

Northern

Climate

Tropical, tempered by trade winds, with an annual mean temperature of 27 degrees Celsius. December–April are the driest months. Rain can occur throughout the year, although generally wetter from May–October.

Entry requirements

Passports

Required by all except Canadian or US nationals with proof of identity (all US and Canadian nationals require a passport for re-entry to their country from January 2007). Passports must be valid for at least six months after date of entry.

Visa

Required by all with some exceptions; see www.gov.kn and follow link to Information for non-citizens, to view a list of those who require a visa and to download an application form.

Further information should be obtained from the nearest consulate.

Currency advice/regulations

The import of local and foreign currency is unlimited but must be declared; export of either is limited to the amount declared on arrival.

Travellers cheques in major currencies are widely accepted.

Health (for visitors)

Mandatory precautions

Vaccination certificates for yellow fever and cholera required when travelling from infected areas.

Advisable precautions

Typhoid, polio vaccinations. Water precautions.

Hotels

Advisable to book in advance. A 9 per cent room tax is added to bills and 10 per cent service charge usual.

Credit cards

Major credit and charge cards are widely accepted. ATMs are widely available.

Public holidays (national)

Fixed dates

1 Jan (New Year's Day), 2 Jan (Carnival Day), 1 May (Labour Day), 12 Jun (Queen's Birthday), 19 Sep (Independence Day), 25–26 Dec (Christmas).

Variable dates

Good Friday and Easter Monday (Mar/Apr), Whit Monday (May/June), Queen's Official Birthday (second Sat in Jun), August Monday (first Mon in Aug).

Working hours

Banking

Mon–Thu: 0800–1400; Fri: 0800–1600; Sat: 0830–1100.

Business

Mon–Fri: 0800–1200, 1300–1600/1630. Businesses generally close Thu afternoons and open Sat: 0800–1600.

Government

Mon–Fri: 0800–1200, 1300–1600/1630.

Telecommunications

Telephone/fax

Mobile/cell phones

There are 850/1900 and 900/1800 GSM services in operation.

Internet/e-mail

Electricity supply

220V AC, 60 cycles. (Some hotel supplies are at 110V AC.)

Electricity is supplied from diesel engine generators and is available island-wide.

Getting there

Air

There are no direct intercontinental flights, only flights from regional hubs land in St Kitts or Nevis.

International airport/s: Robert Llewellyn Bradshaw International Airport (RLB), 3.2km from Basseterre, duty-free shop, restaurant, hotel reservations.

Taxis from the airport have regulated fares.

Other airport/s: Newcastle Airfield (NEV), 11km from Charlestown on Nevis.

Airport tax: Departure tax: EC$60

Surface

Water: There are regular ferry services between St Maarten and St Kitts. Cruise ships visit.

Main port/s: Basseterre (St Kitts) has a deep-water harbour, Charlestown (Nevis).

Getting about

National transport

Road: There is a 300km road network. Main routes cover perimeters of both islands.

In 2004, the Caribbean Development Bank (CDB) provided a loan of US$7.56 million to finance the construction of a new by-pass to reduce traffic congestion in Basseterre. It was opened on 17 October 2006.

Buses: Privately operated buses provide a regular but unscheduled service.

Water: There are regular daily ferry services between the islands of St Kitts and Nevis.

City transport

Taxis: Serve both islands with set fare systems; 10 per cent tip usual.

Car hire

It is advisable to reserve a hire car well in advance. National licence required in order to obtain visitor's temporary licence. Traffic drives on the left.

BUSINESS DIRECTORY

The addresses listed below are a selection only. While World of Information makes every endeavour to check these addresses, we cannot guarantee that changes have not been made, especially to telephone numbers and area codes. We would welcome any corrections.

Telephone area codes

The international direct dialling code (IDD) for St Kitts and Nevis is +1 869, followed by subscriber's number.

Useful telephone numbers

Emergency	911
Fire	333
Air Ambulance	465-2801
JNF General Hospital	465-2551

Chambers of Commerce

St Kitts/Nevis Chamber of Industry and Commerce, South Independence Square, PO Box 332, Basseterre (tel: 465-2980; fax: 465-4490; e-mail: skchamber@caribsurf.com).

Banking

Bank of Nevis, The Main Street, Box 450, Charlestown, Nevis (tel: 469-5564/5796; fax: 469-5798).

Bank of Nova Scotia, Fort Street, Box 433, Basseterre, St Kitts (tel: 465-4141; fax: 465-8600).

Barclays Bank, The Circus, Box 42, Basseterre, St Kitts (tel: 465-2519/10/2449/1081/2264; fax: 465-1041).

Development Bank of St. Kitts & Nevis, Church Street, Box 249, Basseterre, St. Kitts (tel: 465-2288/2964/4041; fax: 465-4016).

National Bank, Central Street, Box 343, Basseterre, St Kitts (tel: 465-2204; fax: 465-1050).

Nevis Co-Op Banking Company, Chapel Street, Box 60, Charlestown, Nevis (tel: 469-5277/0113/4; fax: 469-1493).

Royal Bank of Canada, Cnr Bay Road & Fort Street, Box 91, Basseterre, St Kitts (tel: 465-2259/2409/2389/4374; fax: 465-1040).

Central bank

Eastern Caribbean Central Bank, Bird Rock Road, PO Box 89, Basseterre (tel: 465-2537; fax: 465-5615; email: info@eccb-centralbank.org).

Travel information

Nevis Tourism Bureau, Charlestown, Nevis (tel: 469-1042; fax: 469-1066).

St Kitts-Nevis Hotel and Tourism Association, PO Box 438, Basseterre, St Kitts (tel: 465-5304; fax: 465-7746).

Ministry of tourism

Ministry of Trade, Industry and Tourism (National Development Corporation), Government Headquarters, Basseterre (tel: 465-2521, 465-4106; fax: 465-5202, 465-1778).

National tourist organisation offices

St Kitts-Nevis Department of Tourism, Pelican Mall, PO Box 132, Basseterre, St Kitts (tel: 465-2620; fax: 465-4040).

Ministries

Ministry of Agriculture, Lands, Housing and Development, Education, Youth and Community Affairs, Government Headquarters, PO Box 186, Basseterre (tel: 465-2521; fax: 465-9069).

Ministry of Finance, Marketing and Development Department, Rams Building, Liverpool Row, Basseterre, St Kitts (tel: 465-1153; fax: 465-1154).

Ministry of Health, Labour and Women's Affairs, Government Headquarters, Basseterre (tel: 465-2521; fax: 456-1316).

Office of The Prime Minister, Government Headquarters, PO Box 186, Basseterre (tel: 465-2103; fax: 465-1001).

Other useful addresses

Attorney General's Office, Government Headquarters, Basseterre (tel: 465-2521; fax: 465-5202).

Eastern Caribbean Securities Exchange, PO Box 94, Bird Rock, Basseterre (tel: 466-7192; fax: 465-3798; email: Info@ECSEonline.com).

Financial Services Department, PO Box 186, Basseterre (tel: 466-5048; fax: 466-5317; internet: www.fsd.gov.kn).

Government Offices, Administration Building, Charlestown (465-5521; fax: 465-5202).

Investment Promotion Agency, Bay Road, Basseterre (tel: 465-4106).

Embassy of St Kitts and Nevis (USA), OECS Bldg, 3216 New Mexico Ave, NW Washington DC 20016 (tel: (+1-202) 686-2636; fax: (+1-202) 686-5740).

St Kitts-Nevis Information Service, Government Headquarters, Church Street, Basseterre (tel: 465-2521; fax: 466-4504; email: skninfo@caribsurf.com; internet: www.gov.kn).

St Kitts-Nevis Manufacturers' Association, PO Box 392, Basseterre (tel: 465-6226).

Internet sites

Caribbean Export Development Agency: www.cartis.com/

Government website: www.gov.kn

Organisation of American States: www.oas.org

St Lucia

COUNTRY PROFILE

Historical profile

1605 Britain made an unsuccessful attempt to colonise the islands which were populated by a Carib people.
1642 France claimed sovereignty.
1814 After changing hands 14 times during the seventeenth and eighteenth centuries, St Lucia became a British colony. It formed part of the Windward Islands.
1924 A representative government was introduced.
1936 A constitution was provided with a legislative council of elected representatives.
1951 The first elections, under universal adult suffrage, were won by the St Lucia Labour Party (SLP).
1958 St Lucia joined the UK-sponsored West Indies Federation.
1962 The West Indies Federation was dissolved.
1964 Sugar cane production was abandoned.
1967 St Lucia became a self-governing associated state, with full autonomy over internal affairs. The UK retained, control of foreign affairs and defence.
1979 St Lucia gained independence within the Commonwealth.
2002 Hurricane Lili destroyed around half of the annual banana crop.
2003 An amended constitution replaced the oath of allegiance to the British monarch with a pledge of loyalty to St Lucia. Julian Hunte, St Lucia's foreign minister, was elected president of the UN General Assembly June session, the smallest country ever to lead the 191-member world body.
2004 The Caribbean Development Bank (CDB) approved a loan to help St Lucia build infrastructure against flooding in coastal cities.
2006 Air Jamaica introduced non-stop flights from New York. The opposition UWP won 11 seats (out of 17), in parliamentary elections, the incumbent SLP won six. Sir John Compton became prime minister. St Lucia was voted the year's top Caribbean destination.
2007 Diplomatic relations with Taiwan was re-established, after a 10-year break. Prime Minister Sir John Compton died on 7 September. Stephenson King was elected prime minister by the UMP.

Political structure

Form of state
Parliamentary democracy

The executive
The British monarch is Head of State and represented by the governor general. The prime minister exercises executive power.

National legislature
The bicameral parliament has a House of Assembly with 17 members directly elected in single-member constituencies, for five-year terms. The Senate has 11 nominated members, six appointed by the prime minister, three by the leader of the opposition and two chosen by the governor general.
Universal age of suffrage 18.

Legal system
The legal system is a hybrid of English common law with a strong influence of French civil law.
Appeals are heard by the Eastern Caribbean Supreme Court. The final court of appeal is the Judicial Council of the Privy Council in the UK.

Last elections
December 2006 (parliamentary)
Results: Parliamentary: the United Workers Party (UWP) won 11 out of the 17 seats total, and the St Lucia Labour Party (SLP) won six.

Next elections
December 2011 (parliamentary)

Political parties

Ruling party
United Workers Party (UWP) (elected Dec 2006)

Main opposition party
St Lucia Labour Party (SLP)

Political situation

Population

168,000 (2007)*
Last census: May 2000: 157,164
Population density: 253 inhabitants per square km. Urban population: 38 per cent (1995—2001).
Annual growth rate: 0.9 per cent 1994–2004 (WHO 2006)

Ethnic make-up
Black African (90 per cent), mixed race (6 per cent), East Indian (3 per cent).

Religions
Roman Catholic (90 per cent), Anglican (3 per cent) other Protestant (7 per cent).

Education

The education system is in great need of reform. Hampering the development of the island's education is the instructor-led method of learning but there has been little attempt to progress to a more learner-orientated approach.

KEY FACTS

Official name: St Lucia

Head of State: Queen Elizabeth II; Governor General Dame Calliopa Pearlette Louisy (since 1997)

Head of government: Prime Minister Prime Minister Stephenson King (UWP) (from Sep 2007)

Ruling party: United Workers Party (UWP) (elected Dec 2006)

Area: 616 square km

Population: 168,000 (2007)*

Capital: Castries

Official language: English

Currency: East Caribbean dollar (EC$) = 100 cents

Exchange rate: EC$2.70 per US$ (fixed)

GDP per capita: US$5,689 (2007)*

GDP real growth: 5.00% (2007)*

Labour force: 80,000 (2006)

Unemployment: 15.70% (2006)

Inflation: 1.90% (2007)*

Balance of trade: -US$298.00 million (2006)

Foreign debt: US$339.80 million (2004)

Visitor numbers: 813,681 (2004)

* estimated figure

The secondary education system will benefit from the construction of two new schools, with allocated funds of US$23 million, in 2005/06. The new facilities, one geared to the arts and the other towards agriculture and science will provide places for over 700 students. The government is aiming to achieve universal secondary education and has been aided by the World Bank Education Development Plan.

Compulsory years: 4 to 16.

Enrolment rate: 101 per cent primary and 85 per cent secondary enrolment; 111 per cent and 104 per cent enrolment respectively of boys and girls of relevant age group (including repeaters) (Unicef 2004).

Health

Per capita total expenditure on health (2003) was US$294; of which per capita government spending was US$200, at the international dollar rate, (WHO 2006).

The provision of healthcare will be changed within 2005/06 when the environment levy will be replaced with a fixed tax on consumer goods of between 3.5–4 per cent and will be called the health and environment levy. It is expected to raise US$11 million to fund services for most of the population.

The government is concerned about the loss of medical personnel. Nurse migration, due to low pay, lack of opportunities and poor working conditions, has left Victoria Hospital the principal hospital facility chronically understaffed.

The European Commission has granted US$23 million in 2005 for a new hospital to replace Victoria Hospital, to be built on a new site. Construction is scheduled to begin in early 2006.

HIV/Aids

The Caribbean has the second highest rate of HIV/aids infection, after sub-Saharan Africa and the impact on the economy is already being felt with St Lucia losing around US$74 million since the mid-1980s. In February 2005 the Global Fund to Fight Aids approved a grant of US$10.1 million, over 2005–10, to help St Lucia fight the epidemic. The programme is targetting a 50 per cent reduction in HIV patients and HIV/Aids deaths as well as mother-to-infant transmission reduced from 30 per cent to less than 10 per cent.

Life expectancy: 74 years, 2004 (WHO 2006)

Fertility rate/Maternal mortality rate: 2.2 births per woman, 2004 (WHO 2006)

Birth rate/Death rate: 21 births per 1,000 population; five deaths per 1,000 population (2003).

Child (under 5 years) mortality rate (per 1,000): 16 per 1,000 live births (World Bank)

Welfare

The social welfare system in St Lucia has been described as unfair, partial and out of touch with social realities and legislation is out of date. The Catholic Church run homes for the elderly and assistance is provided to the needy. There is no law protecting children born outside of marriage with regard to their property rights and no laws against sexual harassment.

Main cities

Castries (capital, estimated population 12,196 in 2005).

Languages spoken

English and French patois.

KEY INDICATORS — St Lucia

	Unit	2003	2004	2005	2006	2007
Population	m	0.16	0.16	0.17	0.17	*0.17
Gross domestic product (GDP)	US$bn	0.87	0.73	0.88	0.93	*0.96
GDP per capita	US$	5,400	4,021	5,355	5,546	*5,689
GDP real growth	%	1.5	2.0	5.8	5.0	*5.0
Inflation	%	1.0	0.7	3.9	3.6	*1.9
Exports (fob) (goods)	US$m	68.3	77.5	106.0	116.0	–
Imports (cif) (goods)	US$m	319.4	381.4	449.0	524.0	–
Balance of trade	US$m	-251.1	-303.8	-343.0	-408.0	–
Current account	US$m	-13.0	-70.0	-206.0	-298.0	*-199.0
Total reserves minus gold	US$m	106.9	132.5	116.4	134.5	153.7
Foreign exchange	US$m	104.7	130.2	114.2	132.2	151.2
Exchange rate	per US$	2.70	2.70	2.70	2.70	2.70

* estimated figure

Official language/s

English

Media

Press

Weeklies: There are no daily newspapers, weeklies include The Vanguard, The Voice of St Lucia published on Wednesday and The Crusader and The Star (www.stluciastar.com), appear on Saturday. Online publications Saint Lucia One Stop (www.sluonestop.com) a local news service covering local news and business and St Lucia Mirror (www.stluciamirroronline.com) and One Caribbean (www.onecaribbeanmedia.net), based in Trinidad. Another regional online publication is Caribbean Net News (www.caribbeannetnews.com), which reports news from St Lucia.

The Saint Lucia Nationwide(www.stlucia.gov.lc – follow link from NTN) is published weekly by the Department of Information Services concerning government news and notices.

Broadcasting

Radio: In 2004 a radio service – Radio Caricom, the Voice of the Caribbean Community – was launched with St Lucia being one of the 'pilot states' in the project, which eventually will be available to all Caricom member states.

Commercial radio stations includes Radio Saint Lucia (RSL) (www.rslonline.com) is government-owned, Radio 100 (www.htsstlucia.com), affiliated to HTS, and Hot FM (www.caribbeanhotfm.com)

Television: The three networks are private, Daher Broadcasting service (DBS), Catholic Broadcasting (CBTN) and the commercial Helen Television Systems (HTS) (www.htsstlucia.com), which also runs a radio station. For a fee, there is cable television providing 40 channels of international and local viewing.

Economy

According to the Eastern Caribbean Central Bank, the economy of St Lucia is estimated to have expanded in the first half of 2006 compared to 2005. This was fueled largely by the Cricket World Cup (CWC) 2007-effect and developments in the construction sector as authorities undertook infrastructural upgrading as one of the hosts of the CWC. Output in the agricultural sector is estimated to have expanded based on an increase in banana production, while tourism activity declined.

The economy has made a good recovery since hurricane Lili devastated the island in late 2002, with infrastructure repaired and crop production back to pre-hurricane levels. However, the economy is always vulnerable to natural disasters. Manmade problems range from rising international oil prices to the threat to exports of St Lucia's principal crop, bananas. There has been an international wrangle between several Central and South American banana producers and the European Union since 1999 over import duties. In 2005 the World Trade Organisation (WTO) ruled that the EU's preferential import duties for Caribbean countries contravened the WTO agreement for free trade and that the EU would have to accept Latin American bananas on the same terms as Caribbean bananas.

Tourism has overtaken all other sectors, producing the lion's share of GDP. The government struggles to maintain fiscal discipline to reduce public debt.

To minimise the effect of adverse external forces economic diversification is a priority for the government, with farmers encouraged to grow various cash crops such as mangoes and avocados; a lucrative deal was signed in 2005 to supply over 25 tonnes of cocoa beans to a leading US chocolate manufacturer. Other development projects focus on computer-driven information technology.

External trade

As a member of the Caribbean Community and Common Market (Caricom), St Lucia operates within the single market (Caribbean Single Market and Economy (CSME)), which became operational on 1 January 2006. Goods, services, businesses and money are free to move within CSME without barriers and tariffs. It is also a member of the Eastern Caribbean Currency Union (ECCU) using the East Caribbean Dollar.

Foreign earnings are principally generated by tourism, as Saint Lucia is a prime yachting centre and cruise destination, and remittances. The small manufacturing sector is diverse producing clothing, processed coconuts, electronic components and beverages.

Imports

Main imports are food, manufactured goods, machinery and transport equipment, chemicals and fuels.

Main sources: US (19.6 per cent total, 2006), Trinidad and Tobago (13.9 per cent), Italy (11.5 per cent).

Exports

Main exports bananas (over 40 per cent of total), clothing, cocoa, vegetables, fruits and coconut oil.

Main destinations: France (69.2 per cent total, 2006), US (10.1 per cent), UK (8.7 per cent).

Agriculture

Farming

The agricultural sector used to be the mainstay of the economy, but has been overtaken by tourism. Over 50 per cent of the total area is cultivated arable land. In the first six months of 2006 agricultural output is estimated to have increased, largely because of developments in the banana industry. Banana production rose by 1.5 per cent to 8,151 tonnes, in contrast to a 35.8 per cent fall in the corresponding period of 2005. The rebound in output is attributed to favourable weather conditions and the containment of the leaf spot disease which affected production in 2005.

The main export crop is bananas and St Lucia continues to be the leading Windward Island banana producer. Under a 2005 ruling by the WTO, exports to the EU no longer receive preferential treatment and St Lucia will have to work hard to maintain export levels in the face of stiff competition from larger Central and South American plantations.

Diversification into other cash crops has been encouraged. In August 2005, a multi-million dollar deal was signed between St Lucia and the World's Finest Chocolate Inc to supply 256,800 kilogrammes of cocoa beans a year.

There has been an increase in non-banana agriculture production, in particular in copra cultivation, which has resulted in increased exports of coconut oil to Jamaica. Also grown are traditional fruits and vegetables for the domestic and regional markets, and tree crops, such as mangoes and avocados.

Estimated crop production in 2005 included: 850 tonnes (t) sweet potatoes, 1,000t cassava, 4,500t yams, 14,000t coconuts, 120,000t bananas, 1,300t plantains, 3,878t citrus, 28,000t mangoes, 30t cocoa beans, 250t pepper spice, 215t other spices, 1,820t oilcrops, 157,923t fruit in total, 1,000t vegetables in total. Livestock production included: 2,282t meat in total, 528t beef, 713t pig meat, 142t lamb and goat meat, 900t poultry meat, 1,000t milk, 482t eggs.

Fishing

The typical total annual fish catch is over 2,000t, shellfish, molluscs and cephalopods account for another 77t per annum. In 2004, the total marine fish catch was 1,451 tonnes and the total crustacean catch was 11 tonnes.

Industry and manufacturing

The manufacturing sector is negligible and manufacturing activity is dominated by food and drinks production, electrical products and corrigated paper production.

Tourism

Tourism has become the most important sector generating most activity in St Lucia's economy. Travel and tourism represented 42.8 per cent of the country's economy in 2004, generating US$348.6 million in business transactions. The tourist industry earned US$121.8 million in 2004 or 15 per cent of total GDP. Capital investment in tourism amounted to 40.2 per cent overall or US$72.2 million. The tourist industry employed 11,000 people or 15.9 per cent of total employment. Visitor numbers in the first half of 2006 were down by 8.5 per cent on 2005 to 400,719. This was attributed mainly to reductions in stay-over visitors and cruise ship passengers.

The Cricket World Cup will be held on the island in 2007, and several projects are designed to be completed to accommodate sports fans. Three new developments will add greatly to St Lucia's capacity for tourism. A multi-use resort was begun in May 2005, with plans for 3,000 rooms with multiple amenities. The development is located on 130 acres and estimated at US$380 million with partial completion by 2007.

A major hotel with 124 apartments overlooking the bay of Marigot is expected to be completed by 2006. Eco-tourism will benefit from a new aerial tram project that will provide a raised, suspended ride through the rain-forest canopy in the Babonneau forest.

In 2005 the International Bank for Reconstruction and Development agreed a loan of US$3.7 million, while the International Development Association granted US$3.8 million to go towards the cost of coastal and flood protection works protecting the town of Dennery. These amounts are in addition to the US$80 million loan approved by the Caribbean Development Bank (CDB) in March 2004, also to help St Lucia protect itself against flooding in coastal regions.

Hydrocarbons

Saint Lucia does not have any hydrocarbon reserves, it relies entirely on imported refined oil products.

Energy

Attempts to reduce dependence on imported fuel include the construction of a dam in Roseau and a geothermal project in Soufrière. The main power station is Cul de Sac, south of Castries.

In 2004, St Kitts and Nevis, along with Dominica and St Lucia, one planning the commercial development of geothermal electric power plants.

Banking and insurance

The seven members of the Organisation of Eastern Caribbean States (OECS), Antigua and Barbuda, Dominica, Grenada, Montserrat, St Kitts and Nevis, St Lucia and St Vincent and the Grenadines, share a common currency and central bank. The British Virgin Islands and Anguilla are associate members.

Central bank
Eastern Caribbean Central Bank, St Kitts and Nevis

Offshore facilities
St Lucia is a relatively new entrant to the offshore financial sector. The Organisation for Economic Co-operation and Development (OECD) removed St Lucia from its blacklist of non-complainant government implementing anti-money laundering legislation after St Lucia introduced measures consistent with the OECD's call for transparency in the banking sector.

Time
GMT minus four hours

Geography
St Lucia is in the Windward Islands group of the West Indies, 40km (25 miles) to the south of Martinique and 32km (20 miles) to the north-east of St Vincent, in the Caribbean Sea. The island is volcanic, with spectacular mountain scenery.

Hemisphere
Northern

Climate
The mean annual temperature is 26 degrees Celsius. The island is cooled by the north-east trade winds. The weather is driest from January–April. The rainy season is from July–October.

Entry requirements

Passports
Required by all, except US, Canadian, French and UK citizens who possess valid identification, return tickets and are staying for less than eight days (all US and Canadian nationals require a passport for re-entry to their country from January 2007).

Visa
Requirements vary for citizens, country by country. See www.stlucia.gov.lc under FAQ, see Do I need a Visa? for a full list and procedures, plus an application form to be downloaded.

Currency advice/regulations
The import and export of local and foreign currency is unrestricted.
Travellers cheques, in US dollars, are widely accepted.

Health (for visitors)

Mandatory precautions
Yellow fever vaccination certificate required if arriving from an infected area.

Advisable precautions
Typhoid, polio vaccination. Medical services are limited. Travel insurance is essential, including cover for repatriation. Hospitalisation is costly and doctors often expect immediate cash payment before treatment begins.

Hotels
Bills include 8 per cent tax and usually a 10 per cent service charge.

Credit cards
Major credit and charge cards are accepted in large shopping areas. ATMs are widely available.

Public holidays (national)

Fixed dates
1–2 Jan (New Year), 22 Feb (Independence Day), 1 May (Labour Day), 1 Aug (Emancipation Day), 13 Dec (St Lucia Day), 25–26 Dec (Christmas).

Variable dates
Good Friday, Easter Monday, Whit Monday, Corpus Christi (May/Jun), Thanksgiving Day (first Mon in Oct).

Working hours

Banking
Mon–Thu: 0800–1400, Fri: 0800–1700. Banks are closed on weekends and public holidays. The Bank of Saint Lucia and First National Bank open Sat 0800–1200 at sub-branches in and around Rodney Bay.

Business
Mon–Fri: 0800–1230, 1330–1630.

Government
Mon–Fri: 0800–1230, 1330–1630.

Shops
In Castries (some shops may vary), Mon–Fri: 0830–1630, Sat: 0800–1230. In Sunny Acres, Mon–Sat: 0900–1900. In Rodney Bay, Mon–Thu: 0900–1900, Fri–Sat: 0900–2000. All shops, except supermarkets, close Sunday.

Telecommunications

Mobile/cell phones
There are 850/900/1800/1900 GSM services operating throughout most of the territory.

Electricity supply
220V AC, 50 cycles; UK standard 3-pin plugs.

Weights and measures
The metric system was introduced in 2005 however the imperial system is still used unofficially.

Getting there

Air
National airline: LIAT (St Lucia is a major shareholder in this regional airline).
International airport/s: Hewanorra International Airport (UVF), 67km south of Castries, duty-free shop, bar, restaurant, shops, car hire, VIP business lounges. Caters for intercontinental flights. Transport from the airport includes taxis, buses and helicopter (by reservation).
Vigie (SLU), 3km from Castries, bar, restaurant, car hire. Caters for regional flights only.
Airport tax: Departure tax: EC$54

Surface
Main port/s: Castries, Vieux Fort, Soufrière.

Getting about

National transport
Road: All centres are served by a well maintained road network. Main roads constitute over half of 800km network.
Buses: Unscheduled local basic services are offered by independent drivers.
Water: Boats ply to various destinations.

City transport
Taxis: Taxis are relatively cheap and widely available. A fixed rate system operates but it is advisable to negotiate fares in advance, especially for long journeys. Tips are not expected.

Car hire
Available in Castries, Vieux Fort and Soufrière and through hotels. A national or international licence is acceptable. Traffic drives on the left.

BUSINESS DIRECTORY

The addresses listed below are a selection only. While World of Information makes every endeavour to check these addresses, we cannot guarantee that changes have not been made, especially to telephone numbers and area codes. We would welcome any corrections.

Telephone area codes
The international direct dialling code (IDD) for St Lucia is +1 758, followed by subscriber's number.

Useful telephone numbers

Emergencies	911
Tourist Board	452-5968, 453-0053

Chambers of Commerce
St Lucia Chamber of Commerce, Industry and Agriculture, Vide Bouteille, PO Box 482, Castries (tel: 452-3165; fax: 453-6907; e-mail: info@stluciachamber.org).

Banking
Bank of Nova Scotia, 6 Wm Peter Blvd, Box 301, Castries (tel: 452-2292, fax: 453-1051; e-mail: bns@candw.lc).

Barclays Bank, Bridge Street, Box 335, Castries (tel: 452-3306; fax: 452-6860).

CIBC Caribbean, Wm Peter Blvd, Box 350, Castries (tel: 452-3751; fax: 452-3735).

Caribbean Banking Corporation, Micoud Street, Box 1531, Castries (tel: 452-2265; fax: 452-1668, 451-7484).

First National Bank of St Lucia Ltd, 21 Bridge Street, Box 168, Castries (tel: 450-7000; fax: 453-1630).

National Commercial Bank of St Lucia, Waterfront Branch, Box 1031, Castries (tel: 452-2103/3562; fax: 453-1604, 451-7106; e-mail: ncbslu@candw.lc).

Royal Bank of Canada, Wm Peter Blvd, Box 280, Castries (tel: 452-2245, 451-6537; fax: 452-7855).

St Lucia Development Bank, National Insurance Bldg Block A, Waterfront, Box 368, Castries (tel: 452-3561/1493, 453-0236; fax: 453-6720).

Central bank
Eastern Caribbean Central Bank, Agency Office, PO Box 295; Ground Floor, Michael Chastnet's Colony House, John Compton Highway Castries (tel: 452-7449; fax: 453-6022; email: eccbslu@candw.lc).

Travel information
St Lucia Helicopters, PO Box 2047, Gros Islet (tel: 453-6950; fax: 425-1553; internet: www.stluciahelicopters.com).

St Lucia Hotel and Tourism Association, Pointe Seraphine, PO Box 545, Castries (tel: 452-5978).

Ministry of tourism
Ministry of Commerce, Tourism, Investment and Consumer Affairs, 4th Floor, Heraldine Rock Building, Waterfront, Castries (tel: 468-4202, 468-4204; fax: 451-6986; email: mitandt@candw.lc).

National tourist organisation offices
St Lucia Tourist Board, PO Box 221; Sureline Building, Vide Boutielle, Castries (tel: 452-4094; fax: 453-1121; email: slutour@candw.lc; internet: www.stlucia.org).

Ministries
Ministry of Agriculture, Fisheries and Forestry, Stanislaus James Building, Waterfront, Castries (tel: 468-4210; fax: 453-6314; internet: www.slumaffe.org).

Ministry of Commerce, Tourism, Investment and Consumer Affairs, 4th Floor, Heraldine Rock Building, Waterfront, Castries (tel: 468-4202, 468-4204; fax: 451-6986; email: mitandt@candw.lc).

Ministry of Communications, works, Transport and Public Utilities, Union, Castries (tel: 468-4300; email: min_com@candw.lc).

Ministry of Education, Human Resources Development, Youth and Sorts, Francis Compton Building Waterfront, Castries (tel: 486-5203; fax: 453-2299; internet: www.education.gov.lc).

Ministry of External Affairs, International Trade and Civil Aviation, Conway Business Centre, Waterfront, Castries (tel: 468-4501/2; fax: 452-7427; email: foreign@candw.lc).

Ministry of Finance, International Financial Services and Economic Affairs, 2nd Floor, Bridge Street, Castries (tel: 468-5520; fax: 451-9231; email: minfin@gosl.gov.lc).

Ministry of Health, Human Services, Family Affairs and Gender Relations, Chaussee Road, Castries (tel: 452-2859; fax: 452-5655; email: health@candw.lc).

Ministry of Home Affairs and Internal Security, Erdistron's Place, Manoel Street, Castries (tel: 452-3772; fax: 453-6315).

Ministry of Labour, Public Service and Co-operatives, 2nd Floor, Greaham Louisy Administrative Building, Waterfront, Castries (tel: 468-2202, 468-2205; fax: 453-1305; email: minpet@candw.lc).

Ministry of Physical Development, Housing and Environment, 3rd Floor, Greaham Louisy Administrative Building, Waterfront, Castries (tel: 568-4402; fax: 452-2506; email: econdept@candw.lc).

Ministry of Social Transformation, Culture and Local Government, 4th Floor, Greaham Louisy Administrative Building, Waterfront, Castries (tel: 468-5101, 468-5108; fax: 453-7921).

Other useful addresses
British High Commission, 24 Micoud St, Castries (tel: 452-2484; email: britishhc@candw.lc).

Cable & Wireless Public Telex Booth, Bridge Street, Castries (tel: 452-3301; fax: 452-2363).

Embassy of St Lucia 3216 New Mexico Avenue, NW, Washington, DC 20016, USA (tel: (+1-202) 364-6792, fax: (+1-202) 364-6723; email: eofsaintlu@aol.com; internet: www.sluonestop.com).

Financial Centre Corporation, NIS Building, Ground Floor, The Waterfront, Castries (tel: 455-7700; fax: 455-7701; email: fcc@stluciaoffshore.com; internet: www.pinnaclestlucia.com).

National Development Corporation (NDC), PO Box 495, Monplaisir Building, Brazil Street, Castries (tel: 452-3614; fax: 452-1814; email: devcorp@candw.lc; internet: www.stluciandc.com).

National Research & Development Foundation (NTDF), PO Box 3067, La Clergy, Castries (tel: 452-4253; fax: 453-6389; email: ntdf@candw.lc).

Organisation of Eastern Caribbean States Natural Resources Management Unit (OECS NRMU), PO Box 1383, Morne Fortune, Castries.

Police Headquarters, Bridge Street, Castries (tel: 452-3854/5).

St Lucia Air and Sea Ports Authority, Micoud St, PO Box 651, Castries (tel: 452-2893; fax: 452-2062).

St Lucia Yacht Services Ltd, PO Box 188, Castries (tel: 452-5057).

Windward Islands Banana Growers' Association (WINBAN), Box 115, Compton Building, William Peter Boulevard, Castries (tel: 452-3975).

Internet sites
Government of St Lucia: www.stlucia.gov.lc

The Star Newspaper: www.stluciaStar.com

St Lucia Search Engine: www.stlucia.com

St Vincent and the Grenadines

KEY FACTS

Official name: Commonwealth of St Vincent and the Grenadines

Head of State: Queen Elizabeth II; Governor General Sir Frederick Ballantyne (from 2002)

Head of government: Prime Minister Ralph Gonsalves (ULP) (since 2001; re-elected 2005)

Ruling party: Unity Labour Party (ULP) (since 2001; re-elected 2005)

Area: 388 square km

Population: 117,848 (2007)*

Capital: Kingstown

Official language: English

Currency: East Caribbean dollar (EC$) = 100 cents

Exchange rate: EC$2.70 per US$ (fixed)

GDP per capita: US$3,950 (2005)

GDP real growth: 2.20% (2005)

Labour force: 55,431 (2004)

Unemployment: 14.00% (2004)

Inflation: 3.70% (2005)

Balance of trade: -US$188.00 million (2004)

Foreign debt: US$167.20 million (2003)

* estimated figure

COUNTRY PROFILE

Historical profile

The country's first known inhabitants were Arawak Indians, who were later driven out by Carib Indians.

1498 The principal island was sighted by Columbus. No immediate European immigration followed this discovery.

1779 France occupied the island.

1783 Possession of the islands, as part of the Windward Islands, was passed from France to Britain under the Treaty of Versailles.

1795 Thousands of Carib Indians were deported to Belize, following an uprising.

1812 The volcano, La Soufrière, erupted and destroyed most of the island of St Vincent.

1834 After the emancipation of slaves by Britain, indentured labour from the East Indies and Portugal was brought in to remedy the labour shortage.

1958 St Vincent and the Grenadines became part of the UK-sponsored West Indies Federation.

1962 Dissolution of the West Indies Federation.

1969 The territory gained internal self-government, the UK retained responsibility for foreign affairs and defence.

1979 St Vincent and the Grenadines gained independence, within the Commonwealth.

1998 The New Democratic Party (NDP), led by Prime Minister James Mitchell, was re-elected.

2000 Prime Minister Mitchell stepped down and Arnhim Eustace became prime minister. Anti-government demonstrations forced the government to hold early elections.

2001 The Unity Labour Party (ULP) won early elections and Ralph Gonsalves became prime minister.

2002 Sir Charles James Antrobus, governor general from 1996 died; Sir Frederick Ballantyne became the governor general.

2003 The leaders of the Organisation of the Eastern Caribbean States (OECS) agreed to an economic union and introduced a common passport for nationals of the member countries.

2005 Parliamentary elections were won by the ULP.

2006 Taiwan gave a grant of US$15 million and provided a loan of US$10 million, to assist in the construction of an international airport on St Vincent. Taiwan and St Vincent celebrated 25 years of diplomatic relations.

2008 Prime Minister Gonsalves sued the local radio station, Cross Country, for defamation, concerning accusations of sexual assault perpetrated by Gonsalves in 2004.

Political structure

Constitution

The 1979 constitution is being reviewed by the Constitutional Review Commission (CRC); the first interim report was made in 2004.

Form of state

Parliamentary democracy, within the Commonwealth.

The executive

The British monarch is Head of State and represented by a governor general, but both are largely ceremonial functions. Executive power is exercise by the prime minister and the cabinet.

The governor general appoints senators for the House of Assembly, four on the advice of the prime minister and two on the advice on the leader of the opposition.

National legislature

The unicameral, House of Assembly, with 21 members, six of which are appointed by the governor general and 15 directly elected. The parliamentary term of office is five years, although the prime minister may call elections earlier.

Legal system

The legal system is based on English common law with variations. Magisterial district courts exercise both civil and criminal jurisdiction up to a certain limit. The primary court of first instance is the High Court of Justice, from which appeal is made to the Eastern Caribbean Court of Appeal. Final appeals go to the Privy Council in the UK.

Last elections

4 December 2005 (parliamentary)

Results: Parliamentary: Unity Labour Party (ULP) 55.3 per cent (12 out of 15 elected seats), New Democratic Party (NDP) 44.7 per cent (3 seats). Turnout was 63.7 per cent.

Next elections

2010

Political parties

Ruling party

Unity Labour Party (ULP) (since 2001; re-elected 2005)

Main opposition party

New Democratic Party (NDP)

Population

117,848 (2007)*

Last census: May 2001:109,202 (provisional)
Population density: 293 inhabitants per square km. Urban population: 56 per cent (1995—2001).
Annual growth rate: 0.5 per cent 1994–2004 (WHO 2006)
Ethnic make-up
Most of the population are the descendants of African slaves brought to the island to work on plantations. There are also a few white descendants of English colonists, as well as some East Indians, Carib Indians and a minority of mixed race.
Religions
Anglican (32 per cent), Methodist (18 per cent), Roman Catholic (10 per cent), Seventh-Day Adventist, Hindu, other Protestant (40 per cent).

Education
Education is not compulsory, but children are expected to attend school between the ages of five and 15. Public schooling is provided free of charge up to age 15, although books and equipment have to be supplied by parents. An estimated 95 per cent of the population attend school, but attendance may drop when family needs are pressing. There are 65 primary schools and 23 secondary schools.
Around 10 per cent of the population have no formal education and are illiterate.
The emphasis on academic subjects in secondary schools has shifted to include more practical courses like carpentry and agricultural studies.

Health
Per capita total expenditure on health (2003) was US$384; of which per capita government spending was US$259, at the international dollar rate, (WHO 2006).
Health care is free until the age of 17.
There are six public hospitals in Kingstown and five other hospitals in rural areas. There is also a mental health institution and an old people's residence.
A national family planning policy has been in place since 1974 and as a result the fertility rate has dropped considerably.
Life expectancy: 69 years, 2004 (WHO 2006)
Fertility rate/Maternal mortality rate: 2.2 births per woman, 2004 (WHO 2006)
Birth rate/Death rate: 17 births per 1,000 population; six deaths per 1,000 population (2003).
Child (under 5 years) mortality rate (per 1,000): 23 per 1,000 live births (World Bank)

Welfare
The social welfare system is weak. There is no national health insurance, nor any pension allowance for the elderly. The infant mortality rate is high.
There is a limited framework for the protection of children and the number of child abuse cases that are reported is high.
The situation is generally difficult for disabled people, who seldom leave their homes. There is one institution that offers care and support to the elderly.

Main cities
Kingstown (capital, estimated population 16,031 in 2005), Barrouallie (1,318), Layou (1,164), George Town (1,117).

Languages spoken
English, Vincentian Creole
Official language/s
English

Media
Press
Dailies: The Daily Herald was the first international daily newspaper published from Kingstown. A regional online publication Caribbean Net News (www.caribbeannetnews.com) covers news from the islands.
Weeklies: Publications include The News, The Vincentian (www.thevincentian.com) and Searchlight (www.searchlight.vc).
Broadcasting
Radio: There are five radio stations; the National Broadcasting Corporation (NBC) (www.nbcsvg.com) is the oldest and part government-owned network. Hitz FM (www.svgbc.com) is affiliated to SVGTV, We-FM (www.999wefm.com) is a private commercial service; Praise FM (www.praisefmsvg.com) is a Christian station; First FM and Hot 97 are local stations without internet access.
Television: The government-owned free-to-air SVGTV (www.svgbc.com) has six channels covering news, entertainment and sport. Cable TV provides US programmes for paying customers.

Economy
Tourism and agriculture are the principal sectors of the economy. According to the Eastern Caribbean Central Bank, the economy of St Vincent and the Grenadines is estimated to have expanded in the first half of 2006 compared to 2005. This was largely influenced by buoyant activity in construction and an increase in manufacturing output. Tourism improved, although agriculture contracted. Inflation rose by 1.9 per cent (compared to 3.7 per cent for the whole of 2005).
St Vincent benefited from the Cricket World Cup 2007-effect as the Arnos Vale Playing Field was upgraded and various other construction projects, particularly tourism-related, were underway. Performance in the manufacturing sector improved, reflecting growth in the production of some major commodities; in particular, beer production grew by 23.2 per cent, attributable to an increase in domestic demand. There were also increases in rice output (20.2 per cent) and feed (10.4 per cent) as a result of the establishment in 2005 of a direct distribution operation for these commodities in St Kitts Nevis.
Rising international oil prices led to higher costs of petroleum products and electricity services, which contributed to increases in the fuel and light (16.6 per cent) and transport and communications (6.5 per cent) sub-indices.

External trade
As a member of the Caribbean Community and Common Market (Caricom), St

KEY INDICATORS — St Vincent and the Grenadines

	Unit	2003	2004	2005	2006	2007
Population	m	0.12	0.12	0.11	0.11	*0.12
Gross domestic product (GDP)	US$bn	0.34	0.40	0.43	0.50	0.56
GDP per capita	US$	2,900	3,512	4,032	*4,695	*5,229
GDP real growth	%	2.2	2.8	2.2	6.9	*6.6
Inflation	%	0.3	2.0	3.7	3.0	*6.1
Exports (fob) (goods)	US$m	53.7	37.0	41.5	*48.5	–
Imports (cif) (goods)	US$m	185.6	225.0	203.3	*223.0	–
Balance of trade	US$m	-131.9	-188.0	-161.8	*-174.4	–
Current account	US$m	-50.0	-50.0	-103.0	-120.0	*-149.0
Total reserves minus gold	US$m	51.2	75.0	69.5	78.7	87.0
Foreign exchange	US$m	50.4	74.2	68.8	77.9	86.2
Exchange rate	per US$	2.70	2.70	2.70	2.70	2.70

* estimated figure

Vincent and the Grenadines operates within the single market (Caribbean Single Market and Economy (CSME)), which became operational on 1 January 2006. Goods, services, businesses and money are free to move within CSME without barriers and tariffs. It is also a member of the Eastern Caribbean Currency Union (ECCU) using the East Caribbean Dollar. Although the export of bananas produces around 50 per cent of all commodity sales, tourism is the principal foreign exchange earner and St Vincent and the Grenadines is a popular high-end tourist destination.

Imports

Main imports are machinery and telecommunication equipment and manufactured goods, foodstuffs, fertilisers and fuels.

Main sources: US (32.6 per cent total, 2006), Trinidad and Tobago (25.9 per cent), UK (7.1 per cent).

Exports

Main exports are bananas, taro and arrowroot starch.

Main destinations: UK (25.4 per cent total, 2006), Trinidad and Tobago (14.7 per cent), Barbados (13.9 per cent).

Agriculture

Farming

The agricultural sector is traditionally the mainstay of the economy, but its contribution to GDP, which stood at 40 per cent in 1960, has fallen to around nine per cent. Half of the total land area is arable with only a small proportion unused. St Vincent is the world's leading producer of arrowroot and an exporter of coconut oil. Carrots and plantains are also cash crops. The main food crops are sweet potatoes, tannias, yams, vegetables, and various fruits.

Bananas (grown mainly on small farms under the auspices of St Vincent Banana Growers Association) are the main export crop. The production of bananas, and earnings from their export, have declined in recent years. Unfavourable weather conditions, a sharp fall in the average domestic currency price received for fruit, and a reduction in the average green wholesale price of fruit have weakened the industry. An estimated 25 per cent of the 2004 crop was lost as a result of Hurricane Ivan in September

The EU phased out preferential treatment for banana producers from former colonies in 2006. The liberalisation of the banana trade has made it difficult for family-run businesses in St Vincent to compete.

Estimated crop production in 2005 included: 1,225 tonnes (t) sweet potatoes, 2,200t yams, 50,000t bananas, 3,500t plantains, 650t maize, 3,225t citrus fruit, 720t cassava, 20,000t sugar cane, 2,560t coconuts, 1,500t mangoes, 170t coffee beans, 175t cocoa beans, 150t nutmeg, 500t other spices, 427t oilcrops, 59,816t fruit in total, 13,945t roots and tubers, 4,315t vegetables in total. Livestock production included: 1,065t meat in total, 182t beef, 550t pig meat, 82t lamb and goat meat, 250t poultry, 625t eggs, 1,200t milk.

Fishing

The typical total annual fish catch is over 45,800t. Shellfish, molluscs and cephalopods account for another 1,800t per annum.

In 2004, the total marine fish catch was 8,609 tonnes.

Industry and manufacturing

The industrial sector employs around 8 per cent of the workforce and contributes 10 per cent to GDP.

Activity is primarily based on agricultural processing. Units in operation include those producing cigarettes, tobacco products, coconut oil, textiles and clothing, soft drinks, fruit juices, milk, beer, rum, furniture, arrowroot starch, tyre retreading, concrete blocks and quarry products. A flour mill, serving all the Windward Islands, a box factory and a yacht building yard are the main export industries.

The sector has continued to contract since 1999, although in 2004 the brewery, the second largest manufacturer, reported its best year since then.

Tourism

Tourism is a vital part of the islands' economy. The percentage of GDP in 2005 was 10.3 per cent (and 10 per cent of GDP growth for the year) while the sector employs 9.6 per cent of the work force.

St Vincent is a volcanic island and has only one white sand beach; the industry is thus limited, and there is only minimal scope for further expansion. The Grenadines have more white sand beaches, and the government has stepped up promotional work in the sector's main markets of the US, the UK, Canada and the Caribbean. Infrastructure is being gradually upgraded. Particular attention has been paid to encouraging the cruise ship market. Visitor numbers increased in the first half of 2006 by 31 per cent to 176,122, compared to a fall of 12.4 per cent in the corresponding period for 2005. The turnaround was largely attributable to growth of 84 per cent in cruise ship passengers.

Hydrocarbons

St Vincent and the Grenadines has no hydrocarbon resources. It relies entirely on imports of refined oil. Natural gas and coal are not imported.

Energy

Hydroelectric power generates 44 per cent of energy requirements. The government is exploring ways to tap the active volcano, La Sourière, for geothermal energy. Many people have private generators.

Banking and insurance

The banking sector contributes around 6 per cent of GDP.

The seven members of the Organisation of Eastern Caribbean States (OECS) (Antigua and Barbuda, Dominica, Grenada, Montserrat, St Kitts and Nevis, St Lucia and St Vincent and the Grenadines), share a common currency and central bank. The British Virgin Islands and Anguilla are associate members.

Central bank

Eastern Caribbean Central Bank, St Kitts and Nevis.

Offshore facilities

The offshore financial centre is an important element of the economy. The Exchange of Information Act, passed in 2002, attempts to increase financial transparency and accountability. An International Banks Act was also passed in 2002 that aims to strengthen the supervision of banking activities.

St Vincent and the Grenadines was removed from the OECD Financial Action Task Force (FATF) list of non-co-operative countries on money laundering in June 2003, after reforms had been implemented. The government, recognising the sector's importance to its diversification policy, responded by strengthening the regulatory and supervisory framework in line with international best practice. At end-2003, the former Offshore Finance Authority (OFA) was renamed the International Financial Services Authority of St Vincent and the Grenadines (IFSA).

In April 2004, the IFSA reported that in real terms 2004 had seen a growth in the registration of international business companies of 84 per cent over the same period in 2003.

Time

GMT minus four hours

Geography

St Vincent and the Grenadines is an archipelago of islands and cays (low-lying coral islets) in the Caribbean located in the Windward Islands group, approximately 160km west of Barbados in the West Indies. St Lucia is 34km to the north-east and Grenada is to the south. St Vincent, is a volcanic island, is 29km long and 18km wide and the most northerly of the chain. Of the Grenadines there are 32 islands and cays (not all inhabited) of which the principal islands of the group are Bequia, Canouan, Mustique, Mayreau, Isle D'Quatre and Union Island. St. Vincent has a mountainous centre with an inactive (since 1979) volcano, La Soufrière (1,220 metres (m)) at the north end of the island. The mountains are covered in rich rainforests with a 21m waterfall at Baleine.

Hemisphere
Northern

Climate
Tropical, tempered by trade winds, with temperature range 18–32 degrees Celsius. High levels of rainfall from May–November, especially in the north.

Entry requirements
Passports
Required by all. All visitors must have proof of a return/onward passage and enough funds for their stay.
Visa
Not required, except for nationals of the Dominican Republic, Jordan, Syria, Iran, Iraq, Lebanon and Nigeria who must apply to the Ministry of National Security in Kingstown (details in Addresses following).
Currency advice/regulations
The import of local and foreign currency is unlimited; export is limited to the amount declared on arrival.
Travellers cheques (in US dollars) are widely accepted.

Health (for visitors)
Mandatory precautions
Yellow fever vaccination certificate required if arriving from an infected area.
Advisable precautions
Typhoid, polio vaccination.

Hotels
Wide range of good hotels available at reasonable prices, except on the privately owned islands of Palm, Mustique and Petit St Vincent, where rates are higher. Seven per cent tax is added to room rates; 10 per cent tip is usual if service charge not included on bill.

Public holidays (national)
Fixed dates
1 Jan (New Year's Day), 14 Mar (National Heroes' Day), 1 May (Labour Day), 1 Aug (Emancipation Day), 27 Oct (Independence Day), 25–26 Dec (Christmas).
If a holiday falls on a Sunday, the following Monday is taken as a public holiday.
Variable dates
Good Friday, Easter Monday, Whit Monday, Carnival Monday (first Mon in Jul), Carnival Tuesday (first Tue in Jul).

Working hours
Banking
Mon–Fri: 0800–1300; also Fri: 1500–1700.
Business
Mon–Fri: 0800–1200, 1300–1600; Sat: 0800–1200.
Government
Mon–Fri: 0800–1615.
Shops
Mon–Fri: 0800–1200, 1300–1600; Sat: 0800–1200.

Telecommunications
Mobile/cell phones
There are 850, 900/1800, 900/1900 GSM services available throughout most of the territories.

Electricity supply
220/240V AC, 50 cycles with flat three-pin plugs.

Getting there
Air
National airline: LIAT (Leeward Islands Air Transport)
International airport/s: ET Joshua Airport (SVD) on St Vincent, 3km from Kingstown. Flights arrive from surrounding Caribbean islands only. Facilities include duty-free shops, restaurant and car hire.
Airport tax: Departure tax: EC$40.
Surface
Water: Cruise ships make regular stops. International shipping lines that maintain contacts with St Vincent may provide passenger services on cargo ships.
Main port/s: Kingstown (only deep-water harbour in country).

Getting about
National transport
Air: There are four local airports on Bequia, Mustique, Canouan and Union Island suitable for light aircraft only. LIAT, SVG Air, Mustique Airways provide scheduled services between Kingstown and most domestic islands.
Road: There is almost 600km of paved roads with the Leeward and Windward highways circling St Vincent. Interior roads are narrow with steep inclines.
Buses: Buses are fairly widespread. Stopping is on demand rather than at pre-specified points.
Water: There are regular, scheduled inter-island ferry services providing round trips between the large inhabited islands.
City transport
Taxis: The rate of fares are set by the government but taxis are unmetered and fares should be agreed at the start of a journey. Prices increase from late at night to early morning. Tipping is up to 10 per cent.
Car hire
Either an International Driving Permit must be stamped at the central police station, or a temporary driving licence can be obtained (for a fee) from the police station on Bay Street, or the Licensing Authority on Halifax Street (Kingstown, St Vincent), with the presentation of a valid overseas driving licence, is necessary.
Driving is on the left, road signs are limited and it is recommended drives should use the horn on sharp curves and turns.

BUSINESS DIRECTORY

The addresses listed below are a selection only. While World of Information makes every endeavour to check these addresses, we cannot guarantee that changes have not been made, especially to telephone numbers and area codes. We would welcome any corrections.

Telephone area codes
The international direct dialling code (IDD) for St Vincent is +1-784, followed by subscriber's number.

Useful telephone numbers
Local information: 118.
International information: 115.
Police: 457-1211.
Kingstown General Hospital: 456-1185.

Chambers of Commerce
St Vincent Chamber of Commerce and Industry, Corea's Building, Halifax Street, PO Box 134, Kingstown (tel: 457-1464; fax: 456-2994; e-mail: svgcic@caribsurf.com).

Banking
Bank of Nova Scotia, 76 Halifax Street, Box 237, Kingstown (tel: 457-1601; fax: 457-2623).

Barclays Bank, Halifax Street, PO Box 604, Kingstown (tel: 456-1706; fax: 457-2985).

CIBC Caribbean, Halifax Street, Box 212, Kingstown (tel: 457-1587; fax: 457-2873).

Canadian Imperial Bank of Commerce, Halifax Street, Box 212, Kingstown (tel: 457-1587/2873; fax: 457-2873).

Caribbean Banking Corporation, 81 South River Road, Box 118, Kingstown (tel: 456-1501; fax: 456-2141).

Development Corporation, Sharpe Street, Box 841, Kingstown (tel: 457-1358; 457-2838).

First St Vincent Bank, Lot 112 Granby Street, Box 154, Kingstown (tel: 456-1873; fax: 457-2675).

National Commercial Bank, Bedford Street, Box 880, Kingstown (tel: 457-1844; fax: 457-2612).

New Bank, Blue Caribbean Bldg Bay Street, Box 1628, Kingstown (tel: 457-1411, 456-2453; fax: 457-1357).

Owens Bank, Box 1045, Kingstown (tel: 457-1230; fax: 457-2610).

St. Vincent Co-operative Bank, Corner Long Lane Upper & South River Road, Box 886, Kingstown (tel: 456-1894).

Central bank
Eastern Caribbean Central Bank, Agency Office, PO Box 839, Granby Street, Kingstown (tel: 456-1413; fax: 456-1412).

Travel information
Air Martinique (tel: 458-4528; fax: 458-4187).

LIAT Ltd, VC Bird International Airport, PO Box 819; Coolidge, Antigua (tel: (+1-268) 480-5634; fax: (+1-268) 480-5635; email: customerrelations@liatairline.com).

Mustique Airways, PO Box 1232, Arnos Vale (tel: 458-4380; fax: 456-4586).

St Vincent and The Grenadines Hotel and Tourism Association, PO Box 834, E T Joshua Int'l Airport, Kingstown, St Vincent (tel: 458-4379; fax: 456-4456; email: svghotels@caribsurf.com or office@svghotels.com; internet: www.svghotels.com).

SVG (airline), Arnos Vale (tel: 457-5124; fax: 457-5077; internet: www.svgair.com).

Ministry of tourism
Ministry of Tourism, Youth and Sports, Cruise Ship Terminal, Harbour Quay, St. Vincent (tel: 457-1502; fax: 451-2425).

National tourist organisation offices
Department of Tourism, Bay Street, PO Box 834, Kingstown (tel: 457-1502; fax: 451-2425; email: tourism@caribsurf.com; internet: www.svgtourism.com).

Ministries
Ministry of Agriculture and Labour, Administrative Building, Kingstown (tel: 456-1410; fax: 457-1688).

Ministry of Communications and Works, Administrative Building, Kingstown (tel: 456-1111; fax: 456-2168).

Ministry of Education, Youth and Women's Affairs, Administrative Building, Kingstown (tel: 457-2282; fax: 457-1114).

Ministry of Foreign Affairs and Tourism, Administrative Building, Kingstown (tel: 456-1111; fax: 456-2610).

Ministry of Health and the Environment, Administrative Building, Kingstown (tel: 457-1729; fax: 456-2610).

Ministry of Housing, Local Government and Community Development and Sports, Administrative Building, Kingstown (tel: 456-1111; fax: 456-2610).

Ministry of Legal Affairs and Information, Administrative Building, Kingstown (tel: 456-1111; fax: 457-2898).

Ministry of National Security, Halifax Street, Kingstown, St Vincent (tel: 451-2707; fax: 451-2820; email: office.natsec@mail.gov.vc).

Ministry of Trade, Industry and Consumer Affairs, Administrative Building, Kingstown (tel: 457-1223; fax: 457-2880).

Office of The Prime Minister, Administrative Building, Kingstown (tel: 456-1703; fax: 457-2152).

Other useful addresses
British High Commission PO Box 132, Granby Street, Kingstown (tel: 457 1701; fax: 456 2750; email: bhcsvg@caribsurf.com).

National Broadcasting Corporation, PO Box 705, Kingstown (tel: 457-1111).

Offshore Finance Authority, Kingstown (tel: 456-2577; fax: 457-2568; email: info@stvincentoffshore.com; internet: www.stvincentoffshore.com).

Radio St Vincent and the Grenadines, PO Box 705, Kingstown (tel: 456-1516).

Statistical Office, Central Planning Division, Ministry of Finance and Planning, Kingstown (fax: 457-2943).

St Vincent and the Grenadines Embassy (US), Suite 102, 1717 Massachusetts Avenue, Washington DC 20036 (tel: (+1-202) 462-7806).

St Vincent Development Corporation (DEVCO), PO Box 841, Granby Street, Kingstown (tel: 457-1358; fax: 457-2838).

Internet sites
Caribbean newspaper online: http://caribbeannetnews.com

Official government website: www.gov.vc

Samoa

COUNTRY PROFILE

Historical profile

The first Polynesians settled in the islands around 600BC. A former German protectorate, Samoa was governed by New Zealand from 1914 until its citizens voted for independence in 1961. The Independent State of Samoa was known as Western Samoa until 1997.

1722 The Dutch navigator, Jacob Roggeveen, was the first European to sight the islands.

1831 The London Missionary Society arrived in Samoa to convert native Samoans, establishing a British presence.

1889 The Treaty of Berlin between Britain, the US and Germany promised an independent Samoan government.

1899 The Berlin treaty was annulled by the Tripartite Treaty, which granted the US rights to all eastern islands of the Samoan group and giving Germany the remainder. In exchange for withdrawing its claim to Samoa, Britain gained control of Germany's rights in Tonga, Niue, and the Solomon Islands (excluding Bougainville).

1914 New Zealand occupied Western Samoa during the First World War and continued to administer it after the War under a League of Nations' mandate.

1929 Eleven members of the passive Mau independence movement were killed by New Zealand authorities.

1946 After the Second World War, Western Samoa was administered as a UN Trust Territory by New Zealand.

1961 In a UN-supervised plebiscite the majority voted for independence.

1962 Western Samoa became the first Pacific island to declare independence.

1970 Western Samoa became a member of the Commonwealth.

1990 Voters approved universal suffrage and increased the legislature's term from three to five years.

1991 The general election employed universal suffrage for all those over 21.

1997 The constitution was amended and Western Samoa was re-named Samoa.

1998 The government imposed restrictions on media freedom.

2000 Samoa was one of the first to sign the Pacific Island Countries (free) Trade Agreement. Two former cabinet ministers, sentenced to death for a murder attempt on a fellow politician who could have exposed them for corruption, had their death sentences commuted to life imprisonment.

2001 In parliamentary elections incumbent prime minister, Tuiaepa Sailele Malielegaoi, Human Rights' Protection Party (HRPP) won a closely run election and retained control of the legislative assembly (Fono) with the support of independent members.

2002 New Zealand formally apologised for its poor treatment of Samoan citizens in colonial times.

2004 The death penalty, which had not been used since the 1930s, was abolished.

2005 Samoa was awarded the 2007 South Pacific Games.

2006 HRPP was re-elected in elections on 31 March, winning 36 of the 49 parliamentary seats.

2007 Susuga Malietoa Tanumafili II died on 11 May, aged 94. On 16 June Tupua Tamasese Tupuola Tufuga Efi (known as Tuiatua Tupua Tamasese Efi) was appointed by parliament as O le Ao o le Malo (traditional head of state) Tupuola Efi.

2008 In February, the government announced that road code would change to introduce right-hand driving. The change will take place on 6 September 2009, at the beginning of the school holidays.

Political structure

Constitution

The O le Ao O le Malo (Head of State) acts as a constitutional monarch with the power to dissolve the Fono (legislative assembly) and to appoint a prime minister with its recommendation.

The executive

Executive power rests with the prime minister who selects a 12-member cabinet. The Head of State (O le Ao o le Malo) does not play an active role in government. He appoints the prime minister on the Fono's recommendation and approves the laws passed by the Fono. The Head of State is elected for a five-year term.

National legislature

The unicameral 49-member Fono is elected, by universal suffrage, for a period of up to five years. Only those members of the Matai (elected clan leaders), are eligible to stand for election to the assembly.

Last elections

31 March 2006 (parliamentary)

Results: Parliamentary: HRPP won 36 seats (out of 49 seats); SDUP won seven seats; and independents six seats.

KEY FACTS

Official name: Malotuto'atasi o Samoa (Independent State of Samoa) (dropped 'Western' 1997)

Head of State: O le Ao o le Malo, Tupuola Efi (from 11 June 2007)

Head of government: Prime Minister Tuila'epa Sailele Malielegaoi (HRPP) (since Nov 1998; re-elected Mar 2006)

Ruling party: Human Rights Protection Party (HRPP) (since 1982; re-elected Mar 2006)

Area: 2,840 square km (nine islands): Savai'i (1,708); Upolu (1,118)

Population: 189,000 (2007)*

Capital: Apia (on Upolu)

Official language: Samoan

Currency: Tala or Samoan dollar (S$) = 100 senes, or cents

Exchange rate: S$2.50 per US$ (Jul 2008)

GDP per capita: US$2,101 (2007)

GDP real growth: 6.00% (2007)*

Labour force: 17,630 (2007)

Inflation: 6.00% (2007)*

Balance of trade: -US$188.00 million (2006)

Foreign debt: US$177.00 million (2004)

Visitor numbers: 98,000 (2004)

* estimated figure

Next elections
2011 (parliamentary)

Political parties
Ruling party
Human Rights Protection Party (HRPP) (since 1982; re-elected Mar 2006)
Main opposition party
Samoan Democratic United Party (SDUP)
Political situation

Population
189,000 (2007)*
Last census: November 2001: 176,710
Population density: 60 inhabitants per square km. Urban population: 22 per cent (1995—2001).
Annual growth rate: 1.0 per cent 1994–2004 (WHO 2006)
Ethnic make-up
Samoan (92.6 per cent); European and Polynesian mixed race (7 per cent); Europeans (0.4 per cent).
Religions
Christian

Education
The introduction of the bilingual, single curriculum in primary and secondary schools has increased the number of students successfully completing schooling. Teaching methods and teacher's tools, including dictionaries, grammars and workbooks for teachers, were re-oriented so that the focus became localised and seen as more relevant to the student's lives. The dual streaming of academic and non-academic students in secondary schools was discontinued and has improved the educational outcome of more students.
Literacy rate: 98.9 per cent, adult male rate; 98.4 per cent adult female rate (World Bank).
Compulsory years: Five to 13
Enrolment rate: 91.9 per cent net primary enrolment; 67.4 per cent net seconday enrolment (World Bank).

Health
Per capita total expenditure on health (2003) was US$209; of which per capita government spending was US$165, at the international dollar rate, (WHO 2006).
Life expectancy: 68 years, 2004 (WHO 2006)
Fertility rate/Maternal mortality rate: 4.3 births per woman, 2004 (WHO 2006)
Birth rate/Death rate: 15 births per 1,000 population; six deaths per 1,000 population (2003).
Child (under 5 years) mortality rate (per 1,000): 19 per 1,000 live births (World Bank)

Main cities
Apia, on Upolu (capital, estimated population 39,813 in 2005).

Languages spoken
English is widely spoken. The Samoan language has an equal status with English in schools.
Official language/s
Samoan

Media
Other news agencies: ABC Pacific Beat: www.radioaustralia.net.au/pacbeat
Pacific Magazine:
www.pacificmagazine.net
Press
Publications are typically printed in both English and Samoan. Locally published newspapers include the Samoa Observer, a leading daily and Samoa News (www.samoalive.com) publishes every weekday. Samoa Weekly and Talamua Magazine are privately owned and Savali is a government-owned periodical.

KEY INDICATORS **Samoa**

	Unit	2003	2004	2005	2006	2007
Population	m	0.17	0.17	0.18	*0.19	*0.19
Gross domestic product (GDP)	US$bn	0.28	0.36	0.34	0.37	*0.40
GDP per capita	US$	1,672	1,750	1,853	1,990	2,101
GDP real growth	%	3.5	2.3	5.4	1.8	*6.0
Inflation	%	4.2	16.0	7.8	3.8	*2.6
Exports (fob) (goods)	US$m	14.3	33.1	32.5	11.0	–
Imports (cif) (goods)	US$m	381.8	431.6	507.7	199.0	–
Balance of trade	US$m	-337.5	-398.5	-475.2	-188.0	–
Current account	US$m	-10.0	1.0	-8.0	-23.0	*-24.0
Total reserves minus gold	US$m	83.9	95.5	92.2	80.7	95.3
Foreign exchange	US$m	79.3	90.7	87.7	75.9	90.2
Exchange rate	per US$	2.99	2.78	2.75	2.70	2.54

* estimated figure

Online news networks include Pacific Islands Report (www.eastwestcenter.org) and Samoa Live (www.samoalive.com). Several Samoan (and English) language publications are printed in New Zealand, including Samoana Samoa Star and Samoa Sun.
Dailies: The Samoa Observer is a leading daily. Samoa Live (www.samoalive.com/samoanews.htm) is the leading local on-line network with regional Asia Pacific and international news links. Other regular publications include the Samoa Times and South Seas Star.
Weeklies: Local weekly publications include Newsline, Le Samoa, Samoa Post and Samoa Weekly.
Business: Talanei News (www.samoana.org/talanei) covers business news.
Periodicals: Periodicals include Savali and Samoa Sports Monthly.
Broadcasting
It is possible to pick up television and radio broadcasts from American Samoa.
Radio: There are three commercial FM stations and the Samoa Broadcasting Corporation operates commercial AM and FM radio stations.
Television: There are four TV stations the state-run SBC, and the private O Lau TV broadcasting 24 hours, TV3 broadcasting for 12 hours, and CCTV relays programmes from the Chinese state-run broadcaster.
Advertising
All radio stations and most weekly newspapers accept advertising and there are a few opportunities for billboards however cinemas do not offer advertising.

Economy
The management of the economy has attracted praise from the IMF for its solid performance since 1995. It has registered solid growth, low inflation with improved public finances and international reserve levels that have outperformed comparable countries within the Pacific Island region. Nevertheless, since 2003, the performance has lacked the previous momentum. GDP growth was 5.6 per cent in 2005 but was only estimated to have been 3.0 per cent in 2006. The narrow export base of fish, tourism and automotive parts restrains growth and while the economic reforms undertaken in the 1990s have led to tangible benefits they did not sustain higher growth nor diversify the economy or reduce its vulnerability to external shocks and natural disasters. The economy is sustained by tourism, overseas remittances, manufacturing, agriculture and foreign aid. Remittances account for around 25 per cent of GDP, but are subject to the economic performance of their host countries. The IMF

recommends that remittances should be encouraged to flow through formal financial sector channels, to provide investment, by reducing transaction costs.
The service sector, and tourism in particular, employs about 30 per cent of workers and generates over 50 per cent of GDP. Samoa will host of the 2007 South Pacific Games, which will give a boost to both tourism and construction. The government has begun improvements in tourist infrastructures by upgrading roads and bridges and there are four new hotels and two resorts in various states of completion. One resort planned will include a 5 star hotel, built for the growing ecotourism market.
Construction has led growth in the industry sector, which accounts for just over 25 per cent of GDP although it only employs around 6 per cent of workers. The largest manufacturing entity is a Japanese-owned automotive components factory that exports parts to Australia under a market-access concession arrangement.
Agriculture (including fishing) accounts for around 17 per cent of GDP and employs about 64 per cent of the workforce.
Samoa is a stable democratic country that has taken measures to liberalise its economy in an attempt to attract foreign direct investment (FDI).

External trade

Samoa is a member of the South Pacific Regional Trade and Economic Co-operation Agreement (Sparteca) along with 12 other regional nations, which allows products duty free access by Pacific Island Forum members to Australian and New Zealand markets (subject to the country of origin restrictions).
Foreign trade underpins the economy in three major fields, agricultural produce, manufacturing and capital flows. Tourism, particularly by expatriates, and remittances (over 20 per cent of GDP) has covered Samoa's persistently large trade deficit for a number of years. Manufacturing is largely based in automotive components that are shipped to Australia. Agricultural products are mostly exported for processing except coconuts and their derivates. Around 15 per cent of all exports are bound for European markets.

Imports

Principal imports are machinery and equipment, industrial supplies and foodstuffs.
Main sources: New Zealand (21.3 per cent total, 2006), Fiji (14.6 per cent), Singapore (13.1 per cent), Australia (8.6 per cent).

Exports

Commodity exports include coconut products, such as coconut oil and cream providing over 40 per cent of export earnings. Fish, automotive parts, garments and beer.
Main destinations: Australia (42.8 per cent total, 2006), American Samoa (29.1 per cent), US (3.3 per cent)

Agriculture

Farming

Agriculture, including fishing, typically accounts for 17 per cent of GDP and employs over 60 per cent of the workforce with smallholdings producing surpluses in Samoa's fertile volcanic soil, enough for healthy export sales.
A devastating blight of the taro in 1994, which almost wiped out the entire stock, led to a diversification that is benifitting the economy in 2005. Export of nonu juice in 2004 earned US$632,000 and replaced fresh fish as Samoa's principle foreign exchange earner. Other produce under development include macadamia nuts, annatto (dye), timber and cattle.
In August 2004 a shipment of sheep arrived from Fiji where they had been specially bread to have a high meat content and to be suitable for tropical climates.
Production of subsistence crops include cassava, breadfruit maize and taro.
Agriculture was hit hard by Cyclone Heta in early 2004, disrupting the food supply and pushing up prices.
Estimated crop production in 2005 included: 17,000 tonnes (t) taro, 2,600t yams, 140,000t coconuts, 21,500t bananas, 18,230t oilcrops, 4,000t mangoes, 3,600t papayas, 3,000t plantains, 500t cocoa beans, 140t tobacco, 100t spices, 2,600t yams, 18,230t oilcrops, 130t vanilla, 44,350t fruit in total, 1,020t vegetables in total. Estimated livestock production included: 5,140t meat in total, 1,000t beef, 3,800t pig meat, 340t poultry, 260t eggs, 1,500t milk, 400t honey.

Fishing

Fishing is one of Samoa's major export earners. The typical annual fish catch is around 11,000t (an increase from 7,500t in 1998); there are concerns that overfishing is depleting fish stocks.
In 2004, the total marine fish catch was 3,065 tonnes and the total crustacean catch was 208 tonnes.

Forestry

In 2003 forest exports amounted to US$972,000 and imports amounted to US$5.6 million. Production in 2003 included 131,000 cubic metres (cum) roundwood, 61,000cum industrial roundwood, 21,000cum sawnwood, 58,000cum sawlogs & veneer logs, 70,000cum wood fuel.

Industry and manufacturing

The industrial sector typically accounts for over 25 per cent of GDP and employs approximately 6 per cent of the workforce.
Small-scale manufacturing and industry has expanded. The government's industrial area of Vaitele (on Upolu) houses a brewery, a cigarette factory and a match factory.
Other industries include copra processing, food processing, light engineering, woodworking and manufacture of coconut oil, paint, concrete and construction materials, bottled gases, plastic bags, corned beef and garments. US food processors have expressed interest in investing in fish-processing capacity.
Output of automotive wiring harnesses for export increased following the extension of the Yazaki Samoa plant, the largest employer. However production fell in 2004. Garment exports also declined when production was interupted by a move to new premises.
Industrial production grew in 2004 by 2.6 per cent, led by construction both private and public. The construction sector, following the damage from Cyclone Heta in January 2004, sparked a boom and coupled with major building projects in offices, schools, the National University of Samoa and the facilities for the South pacific Games, have more than bolstered the declines seen in other areas of the economy.

Tourism

Tourism is the main economic activity and the largest foreign exchange earner. The number of visitors continues to rise by about 20 per cent. Visitor numbers in 2003 totalled 93,000, and increased to 97,000 in 2004 – partly due to Samoa hosting the Pacific Forum meetings. The main markets are American Samoa and New Zealand.
There is still competition between tourists and business travellers for limited accommodation; however this should ease when the new hotels and resorts are finally completed by 2007.

Hydrocarbons

As there are no hydrocarbon reserves, Samoa relies entirely on the import of refined oil that makes up around 58 per cent of Samoa's energy consumption. Imports come from New Zealand, Australia, Fiji and the US. Samoa does not import natural gas or coal.

Energy

The Electric Power Corporation operates a wood-fuel power station. There are four hydroelectric plants. Growth in demand is running at about 7 per cent per year.

Banking and insurance

The government has increased its deposits in the banking system over the last few years, enabling commercial banks to lend and boosting private sector credit growth.

Banks are strongly capitalised and earn good profits.
Central bank
Central Bank of Samoa

Time
GMT minus 11 hours

Geography
Samoa lies in the southern Pacific Ocean about 2,400km north-east of New Zealand and about 450km west of American Samoa. Samoa comprises two large islands – Savii and Upolu, separated by a 13km ocean channel – and seven small, mostly uninhabited islands. The total land area is 2,934 square km. Savii and Upolu are coral fringed, rugged volcanic mountains rising to 1,856 metres (m) and 1,115m respectively.
Hemisphere
Southern

Climate
Temperatures 24–30 degrees Celsius (hottest in March) and high humidity. Rainy season November–April, rainfall at least 5,000 mm/year, heaviest in January.

Entry requirements
Passports
Required by all and valid for six months beyond the date of departure. Proof of onward/return passage and visa documentation for following destination, booked accommodation and sufficient funds for stay are required.
Visa
Not required by tourists for a period not exceeding 60 days. American Samoan and US citizens resident in American Samoa may visit with a 14–30 days visitor permit.
Business visitors should apply for a temporary resident permit from the Samoan Immigrations Department. Requirements and application form can be found at www.samoaimmigration.gov.ws under Permit Services.
Currency advice/regulations
The import of local and foreign currency is unlimited. Export of local currency is prohibited and foreign currency is limited to the amount imported.
Travellers cheques are accepted in banks and larger hotels.
Customs
Personal effects allowed duty-free.
Prohibited imports
Firearms, ammunition, explosives, illegal drugs and pornography. Plants, seeds, soil and animals may be imported subject to approval from the Department of Agriculture.

Health (for visitors)
Mandatory precautions
Vaccination certificate for yellow fever if travelling from an infected area.
Advisable precautions
Vaccinations for diphtheria, tuberculosis, hepatitis A and B, polio, tetanus, typhoid. There is a rabies risk.

Hotels
Most hotels are located close to the capital. There are five standards available from deluxe and superior to budget.

Credit cards
Major credit cards are accepted; ATMs are available.

Public holidays (national)
Fixed dates
1–2 Jan (New Year), 25 Apr (Anzac Day), 10 May (Mothers-of-Samoa Day), 1 Jun (Independence Day), 3 Nov (Arbor Day), 25–26 Dec (Christmas).
Variable dates
Good Friday, Easter Monday, Labour Day (first Mon in Aug), Lotu-a-Tamaiti (second Mon in Oct, the day after White Sunday).

Working hours
Banking
Mon–Fri: 0900–1500. Larger branches are open Sat: 0900–1200.
Business
Mon–Fri: 0800–1200, 1300–1630.
Government
Mon–Fri: 0800–1200, 1300–1630.
Shops
Mon–Fri: 0800–1200, 1330–1630; Sat: 0800–1230.

Telecommunications
Samoa uses satellite communications and some domestic transmissions are conducted over microwave, generally in less densely populated areas, and between the islands of Upolu and Savaii. All can be adversely affected by bad weather.
Mobile/cell phones
A GSM 900 service is expected to be inaugurated in 2007.

Electricity supply
240V AC, with flat, three-pin plugs (Australian style).

Weights and measures
Imperial system, with metric systems in use.

Social customs/useful tips
Appointments should be made in advance. Ties need only be worn for formal meetings. English is used for business and commerce. Care should be taken to respect local customs and practices. Samoans do not like to disagree with someone in authority, or not give the anticipated reply, which can lead to misunderstandings by foreign visitors (a 'yes' can mean 'no'). Gratuities are optional and gifts for excellent service are appreciated. The minimum drinking age is 18 years.

Getting there
Air
National airline: Polynesian Airlines
International airport/s: Faleolo International (APW), 34km west of Apia, with banks, post office, duty-free and car hire. There are taxis and buses to the city.
Airport tax: Departures tax: S$40
Surface
Water: Ferry services operate from American Samoa; cargo ships also carry passengers from New Zealand, Australia, Japan and other Pacific islands, as well as Europe and the US.
Main port/s: Apia and Asau

Getting about
National transport
Air: Polynesian Airlines operates regular services between Faleolo (Upolu) and Maota (south-east Savii).
Buses: Scheduled bus services operate in and around Apia and Salelologa (Savai'i).
Water: Daily ferry services operate between Salelologa (Savai'i) and Mulianua (Upolu).
City transport
Taxis: Taxi service is available in Apia.
Car hire
International or national driving licence required. Traffic drives on the left, until 6 September 2009 when it will change to the right.

BUSINESS DIRECTORY

The addresses listed below are a selection only. While World of Information makes every endeavour to check these addresses, we cannot guarantee that changes have not been made, especially to telephone numbers and area codes. We would welcome any corrections.

Telephone area codes
The international direct dialling (IDD) code for Samoa is +685 followed by subscriber's number.

Useful telephone numbers
Police, fire and ambulance: 999.

Chambers of Commerce
Samoa Chamber of Commerce and Industry, PO Box 2014, Lotemau Centre, Vaea Street, Apia (tel: 21-237; fax: 21-578; email: info@samoachamber.com).

Banking
ANZ Bank (Samoa) Ltd, PO Box L1855, Beach Road, Apia (tel: 22-422; fax: 24-595, 23-807).

Australia and New Zealand Banking Group Ltd, PO Box L1855, Apia (tel: 22-422; fax: 24-595).

Development Bank of Samoa, PO Box 1232, Apia (tel: 22-861; fax: 23-888).

International Business Bank Corp Ltd; Level 2, Chandra Hse, Convent St, Apia (tel: 22-393; fax: 23-253).

National Bank of Samoa Limited; PO Box L3047, Apia (tel: 23-077; fax: 23-085).

Pacific Commercial Bank Ltd, PO Box 1860, Beach Road, Apia (tel: 20-000; fax: 22-848).

Central bank
Central Bank of Samoa, Central Bank Building, Private Bag, Apia (tel: 34-100; fax: 20-293; e-mail: cbs@samoa.net; internet: www.cbs.gov.ws).

Travel information
Faleolo International Airport, Private Bag, Apia (tel: 23-201, 23-202, 42-050; fax; 24-281; e-mail: etuale@samoa.net).

Mulifanua Ferry Terminal Pier, PO Box 3267, Apia.

Polynesian Airlines, PO Box 599, Beech Road, Apia (tel: 21-261; fax: 20-023).

Samoa Shipping Corp, Shipping House, Matautu-tai; PO Bag, Apia (tel: 20-935/6; fax: 22-352; email: info@samoashipping.com).

Ministry of tourism
Samoa Tourism Authority, PO Box 2272, Apia (tel: 63-500; fax:20-886; email: info@visitsamoa.ws).

National tourist organisation offices
Samoa Visitors' Bureau, PO Box 862, Apia (tel: 20-878; fax: 20-886; e-mail: samoawsvb@pactok.peg.apc.org; internet site: http://www.visitsamoa.ws).

Ministries
Ministry of Agriculture, Quarantine Division, P O Box 1874, Apia (tel: 22-561; fax: 24-576; internet: www.samoaquarantine.gov.ws).

Ministry of Commerce, Industry and Labour, Level 4, ACB Building, Apia (tel: 20-441/2; internet: www.mcilsamoa.ws).

Ministry of Finance, Central Bank Bld, Matafele; Private Bag, Government of Samoa, Apia (tel: 34-333; fax: 21-321; internet: www.mof.gov.ws).

Ministry of Prime Minister and Cabinet, Samoa Immigration, Lever 2, Lober Bld; PO Box L1861, Apia (tel: 20-291/2; fax: 22-243; internet: www.samoaimmigration.gov.ws).

Other useful addresses
Asian Development Bank (ADB), South Pacific Regional Mission, La Casa di Andrea, Fr. Dr. W. H. Lini Highway; PO Box 127, Port Vila, Vanuatu (tel: (+678-2) 23-300; fax: (+678-2) 23-183; email: adbsprm@adb.org; internet: www.adb.org/SPRM).

Department of Statistics, PO Box 1151, Apia.

Department of Trade, Commerce and Industry, Chandra House, Trade Information Centre, PO Box 862, Apia (tel: 20-471; fax: 21-504; email: IPU@tci.gov.ws; internet: www.tradeinvestsamoa.ws).

Government of Samoa, PO Box L 1864, Apia (tel: 24-799, 63-115; fax: 21-742, 26-396; e-mail: contact@govt.ws).

Samoa Mission to the United Nations, 800 Second Avenue, Suite 400J, New York, NY 10017 (tel: (+1-212) 599 6196; fax: (+1-212) 599 0797).

Other news agencies: ABC Pacific Beat: www.radioaustralia.net.au/pacbeat

Pacific Magazine: www.pacificmagazine.net

Internet sites
Samoan Government site: www.govt.ws

South Pacific Tourism Organisation: www.tcsp.com

San Marino

KEY FACTS

Official name: Serenissima Repubblica di San Marino (Most Serene Republic of San Marino)

Head of State: Two Capitani-Reggenti (Captains-Regent), elected for six month terms: Rosa Zafferani (PDCS) and Federico Pedini Amati (PSD) (from 1 Apr 2008)

Head of government: Secretary of State for Foreign and Political Affairs Fiorenzo Stolfi (PSD) (from 27 Jul 2006)

Ruling party: Coalition led by Partito dei Socialisti e dei Democratici (PSD) (Party of Socialists and Democrats) with Alleanza Populare (AP) (Popular Alliance) and Sinistra Unita (SU) (United Left) (since Jul 2006)

Area: 61 square km

Population: 29,251 (2006)*

Capital: San Marino

Official language: Italian

Currency: Euro (eur) = 100 cents

Exchange rate: eur0.63 per US$ (Jul 2008)

GDP per capita: US$34,600 (2003)

GDP real growth: 7.50% (2003)

Labour force: 18,500 (2003)

Unemployment: 2.60% (2003)

Inflation: 3.30% (2003)

Visitor numbers: 3.00 million (2003)*

* estimated figure

COUNTRY PROFILE

Historical profile

San Marino is completely surrounded by Italy. It is the oldest surviving republic in the world, having been an independent republic since the year 301 AD.

1600 The constitution was ratified on 8 October.

1926 An additional electoral law was passed, which serves some of the functions of a constitution.

1988 San Marino joined the Council of Europe.

1990–92 A coalition of Partito Democratico Progressista (PDP) (Progressive Democratic Party), (ex-communists) and Partito Democratico Cristiano Sammarinese (PDCS) (San Marino Christian Democratic Party) took office.

1992 PDCS formed a coalition with the Partito Socialista Sammarinese (PSS) (San Marino Socialist Party). San Marino became a member of the UN.

1993 In the general election, the PDCS won 26 seats and the PSS, 14 seats; the coalition continued.

1998 After general elections, the PDCS/PSS coalition continued.

2001 Differences within the PDCS/PSS coalition government led to early parliamentary elections (they were originally scheduled for 2003), which resulted in a continuation of the coalition government.

2002 San Marino, in line with Italy, replaced the lira with the euro currency.

2005 San Marino and the Kingdom of Nepal established diplomatic relations. The Partito dei Socialisti e dei Democratici (PSD) (Party of Socialists and Democrats) was formed from the amalgamation of PSS and the Partito dei Democratici (PD) (Democratic Party).

2006 In parliamentary elections on 4 June the PDCS won 21 seats. In July, the PSD, which had won 20 seats in the election, formed a coalition government with two other parties.

2007 Alessandro Mancini (PSD) and Alessandro Rossi (SU) took office as captains-regent on 1 April. Mirko Tomassoni (PSD) and Alberto Selva (AP) took office as Captains-Regent on 1 October.

2008 Rosa Zafferani (PDCS) and Federico Pedini Amati (PSD) took office as captains-regent on 1 April.

Political structure

Constitution

The constitution was ratified on 8 October 1600. An additional electoral law was passed in 1926, which serves some of the functions of a constitution.

The country is divided into nine castelli (municipalities), each governed by a Captain.

The executive

The Consiglio Grande e Generale (CGeG) (the Great and General Council) elects two members every six months to act as captains-regent, who functions jointly as heads of state and, together with a 10-member Congress of State (cabinet), exercise executive power. The secretary of state for foreign affairs has come to assume many of the prerogatives of a prime minister.

The Congress of State is elected by the CGeG for a five-year term.

National legislature

Legislative power is vested in the unicameral Consiglio Grande e Generale (CGeG) (Great and General Council), with 60 members elected by universal adult suffrage for five-year terms.

Legal system

Last elections

4 June 2006 (parliamentary)

Results: Parliamentary: PDCS won 32.92 per cent of the vote (21 seats out of 60); Partito dei Socialisti e dei Democratici (PSD) (Party of Socialists and Democrats) 31.83 per cent (20 seats); Alleanza Popolare (Popular Alliance) 12.05 per cent (seven seats); Sinistra Unita (SU) (United Left) 8.67 per cent (five seats); Nuovo Partito Socialista (NPS) (New Socialist Party) 5.42per cent (three seats); other parties one seat each. Turnout was 71.8 per cent.

Next elections

2011 (parliamentary)

Political parties

Ruling party

Coalition led by Partito dei Socialisti e dei Democratici (PSD) (Party of Socialists and Democrats) with Alleanza Populare (AP) (Popular Alliance) and Sinistra Unita (SU) (United Left) (since Jul 2006)

Main opposition party

Partito Democratico Cristiano Sammarinese (PDCS) (San Marino Christian Democratic Party)

Population

29,251 (2006)*

Last census: July 2000: 26,941

Population density: 433 inhabitants per sq km.

Annual growth rate: 0.9 per cent 1994–2004 (WHO 2006)

Ethnic make-up
The population includes Sammarinese and Italians.

Religions
Roman Catholic

Education
Schooling is free of charge and until aged 16. Primary schooling lasts until aged 11, then on to lower secondary education for three years, from ages 11 to 14, of general education, then the last two years of either technical or specialised academic study.
Higher secondary schools, from aged 16 to 19, provide two-year courses in preparation for higher education.
Higher education is provided by the Università degli Studi della Repùbblica di San Marino, and its Istituto di Cibernetica.
Compulsory years: 6 to 15.

Health
Per capita total expenditure on health (2003) was US$3,133; of which per capita government spending was US$2,467, at the international dollar rate, (WHO 2006).
The age of the population has risen, reflecting a general trend in Western Europe; those aged over 60 increased from 21.5 per cent of the population in 1991 to 24.3 per cent, in 2001.
Life expectancy: 82 years, 2004 (WHO 2006)
Fertility rate/Maternal mortality rate: 1.2 births per woman, 2004 (WHO 2006)
Birth rate/Death rate: 10.5 births per 1,000 population; eight deaths per 1,000 population (2003).
Child (under 5 years) mortality rate (per 1,000): 4.0 per 1,000 live births (World Bank)

Main cities
San Marino (capital, estimated population 2,276 in 2005); Serravalle/Dogano (4,813); Borgo Maggiore (2,442), Murata (1,580).

Languages spoken
Italian

Official language/s
Italian

Media
Press
In Italian, the two dailies published are La Tribuna Sammarinese (www.latribunasammarinese.net) and San Marino Oggi, with periodicals San Marino and La Sportivo. In Italian, L'Informazione di San Marino (www.libertas.sm) and San Marino Notizie (www.sanmarinonotizie.com) are online news outlets, while Italica (www.italica.sm) is in English.

Broadcasting
Radio: The government-controlled San Marino RTV (www.sanmarinortv.sm) broadcasts over several wavebands in FM. Some regional Italian stations can also be received.
Television: RTV operates the television station while some regional Italian broadcasts can also be received.

Economy
The economy is closely linked with that of Italy, which surrounds it geographically. The Sammarinese budgetary position has generally been stronger than the Italian one. Enjoying good economic health, thanks to the banking sector and foreign direct investment (FDI) (mainly from Italy) and trade with Italy and some further-flung economies, San Marino registers a year-on-year surplus on its balance of payments.
The economy is impressive in its diversity, a characteristic which has contributed to economic stability. The main source of revenue is tourism. The traditional industry of quarrying for building stone is also important. Emphasis is being placed on light manufacturing industries. Sales of postage stamps and coins to collectors provide 10 per cent of the government's income.
San Marino adopted the euro in 2002, which has enhanced the republic's economic prospects by reducing costs and risks associated with exchange rates. However, given that the majority of San Marino's trade is conducted with neighbouring Italy, whose economy is not as robust, the strength of the euro does not benefit San Marino as it exports to other countries.

External trade
San Marino does not belong to the European Union but as it maintains a customs and currency union with Italy and using the euro it has de facto ties with the EU. Italy accounts for 87 per cent of all external trade.

Imports
Imports predominantly consist of food and manufactured goods.

Exports
Important exports include building stone, lime, timber, hides and ceramics; foodstuffs, chestnuts, wheat, wine and baked goods,

Agriculture
Farming
The republic was formerly dependent on agriculture and forestry. The agricultural sector employs around 1 per cent of the workforce. Approximately 17 per cent of the land is arable. Principal crops include olives, grapes, wheat and corn.

Industry and manufacturing
Quarrying for building stone is a traditional industry.
Manufacturing employs 41 per cent of the workforce, construction 11 per cent, and services, transport and communications 19 per cent.

Tourism
Tourist numbers in 2004 amounted to 2.6 million, down from the 2.8 million in 2003, this was the second year of negative growth. Only in 2002 was growth possitive at 2.2 per cent. Tourism has been depressed by the downturn in the Italian economy, and less Italian visitors arrive.

Banking and insurance
The banking sector is of strategic importance to San Marino's economy, making a sizeable contribution to the state revenue; its banks are profitable, well-provisioned and cost efficient. The Istituto di Credito Sammarinese (ICS) operates as a central bank, although it does not have an independent monetary policy.
San Marino is a signatory of a new EU tax agreement with non-EU countries. San

KEY INDICATORS **San Marino**

	Unit	2003	2004	2005	2006	2007
Population	m	0.03	0.03	0.03	0.03	0.03
Gross domestic product (GDP)	US$bn	0.88	–	–	–	–
GNP real growth	%	–	*2.0	–	–	–
Inflation	%	2.5	2.1	–	–	–
Unemployment	%	4.5	2.9	–	–	–
Total reserves minus gold	US$m	252.7	355.6	354.0	–	–
Foreign exchange	US$m	245.9	348.3	347.2	–	–
Tourist numbers	'000	2,800.0	2,600.0	–	–	–
Exchange rate	per US$	0.88	0.80	0.77	0.75	0.69

* estimated figure

Marino will impose a withholding tax, up to 35 per cent, to be passed to the tax department of an EU citizen's country, but retaining the anonymity of the saver.
San Marino has also agreed to supply information on tax fraud, for criminal or civil trials, and notify EU member states about additional malpractices.

Central bank

Banca Centrale della Repubblica di San Marino (Central Bank of the Republic of San Marino); European Central Bank (ECB).

Time

GMT plus one hour (daylight saving, late March to late October, GMT plus two hours)

Geography

San Marino is a landlocked country of 61.2 square kilometres, entirely surrounded by and located in central Italy. The Italian region of Emilia-Romagna borders to the north and east and the Marche to the south and west. The capital, also called San Marino has eight satellite villages. The geography is mountainous dominated by Mount Titano, the highest peak.

Hemisphere

Northern

Climate

San Marino enjoys a Mediterranean climate with warm summers and dry, cold winters. Temperatures can range between 0–30 degrees Celsius.

Dress codes

Lightweight clothing for summer, medium-weight and topcoat for winter.

Entry requirements

As per Italy

Passports

Required by all and passports must be valid for three months from arrival. Nationals of countries which are signatories of the Schengen Accords, which includes most EU/EEA member states, San Marino and Croatia, may visit on national IDs.

Visa

No visa requirements for citizens of most of Europe, the Americas, Australasia and some Asian countries, visiting for up to 90 days. For a full list, and further information for those citizens not included on the list of visa-free travel, visit www.ambwashingtondc.esteri.it and see consular services. A Schengen visa application (offered in several languages) can be downloaded from www.eurovisa.info/ApplicationForm.htm.
Business travellers who do not have visa-free arrangements must provide a letter from their employer guaranteeing travel expenses, including full itinerary and purpose of the trip. Letters of invitation from all Italian companies to be visited, and a current (not over 90 days) Visura Camerale issued by the Italian Chamber of Commerce should be attached; a return/onward ticket must be produced before collection of the passport and visa from the issuing consulate, which may request any additional documents at its discretion.
Within eight days of arrival in San Marion the visa traveller must appear before local police authorities to receive a Residency Permit and will also need to show proof of health insurance.

Prohibited entry

Visitors may be refused entry for public security or health reasons, or if not holding visible means of support and onward/return tickets and documents for their next destination.

Currency advice/regulations

The import and export of local or foreign currency up to eur10,300 is allowed. Any amount over this must be declared on Form V2 at customs on arrival.

Health (for visitors)

Mandatory precautions

None

Advisable precautions

Up-to-date tetanus and polio immunisations are recommended. Long-term visitors should consider hepatitis A immunisation.

Public holidays (national)

Fixed dates

31 Dec–1 Jan (New Year), 6 Jan (Epiphany), 5 Feb (Liberation Day), 25 Mar (Arengo Day), 1 Apr (Captains Regent Investiture Day), 1 May (Labour Day), 28 Jul (Fall of Fascism Anniversary), 15 Aug (Assumption Day), 3 Sep (Republic Day), 1 Oct (Captains Regent Investiture Day), 1 Nov (All Saints' Day), 2 Nov (All Souls' Day), 8 Dec (Immaculate Conception), 24–26 Dec (Christmas).
Holidays which falls on a Sunday are observed on Monday.

Variable dates

Good Friday, Easter Monday, Corpus Christi (May/Jun).

Working hours

Banking

Mon–Fri: 0830–1330, 1530–1630.

Shops

Mon–Sat: 0830–1300, 1530–1930.

Telecommunications

Mobile/cell phones

Networks 900/1800 GSM are in operation.

Electricity supply

220V AC 50Hz

Getting there

Air

Closest international airports: Rimini (RMI) (Italy) 27km, or Bologna (BLQ) (Italy) 135km.

Surface

There are regular bus services, by highways, from Rimini or Bologna, Italy. The nearest railhead is at Rimini.

Getting about

National transport

The roads are good. A funicular (cable car) operates between Borgo Maggiore and the capital.

BUSINESS DIRECTORY

Telephone area codes

The international direct dialling (IDD) code for San Marino is +378 followed by 0549 and subscriber's number.

Chambers of Commerce

Agency for Promotion and Development of the Economy, 33 Via G Giacomini, 47890 San Marino (tel: 914-001; fax: 913-473; e-mail: info@apse.sm).

Banking

Central bank

Banca Centrale della Repubblica di San Marino (Central Bank of the Republic of San Marino), 120 Via del Voltone, 47890 San Marino (tel: (+378) (0)549 882-325; fax: (+378) (0)549 882-328).

European Central Bank (ECB), Kaiserstrasse 29, D-60311 Frankfurt am Main, Germany (tel: (+49-69) 13-440; fax: (+49-69) 1344-6000).

Travel information

National tourist organisation offices

Ufficio di Stato per il Turismo (state tourist office), Contrada Omagnano 20, 47031, San Marino (tel: 882-998).

Other useful addresses

Azienda Autonoma di Stato Filatelica e Numismatica (AASFN) (stamps and coins), 5 Piazza Garibaldi, 47031 San Marino (tel: 882-370; fax: 882-363; e-mail: aasfn@omniway.sm).

Notizie de San Marino, Radiotelevisione Italiana, 14 Viale Mazzini, 1-00195 Rome, Italy (fax: (+39-06) 372-5680).

Office for Industry, Handicrafts and Trade, Palazzo Mercuri, San Marino (tel: 992-745, 991-385).

Secretariat of State for Finance and the Budget, Palazzo Begni, San Marino (tel: 992-345).

Internet sites

San Marino tourism authority: www.visitsanmarino.com

Web portal for trade: www.tradecenter.sm/index_e.htm

São Tomé and Príncipe

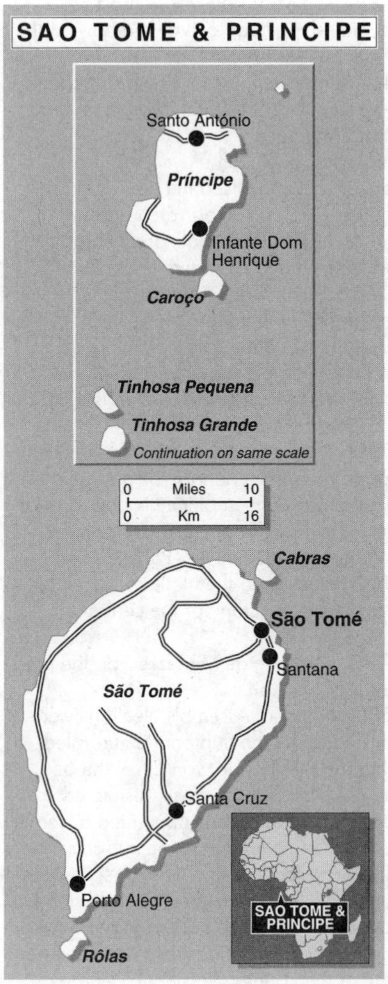

Legislative elections took place in March 2006. The election process was deemed fair by the international observers present, but has nonetheless been tainted with controversy and accusations of vote buying by the political parties. The result was a win for a coalition led by Movimento de Libertação de São Tomé e Príncipe-Partido Social Democrata (MLSTP/PSD) (Movement for the Liberation of São Tomé and Príncipe-Social Democratic Party). The July 2006 presidential elections led to the re-election of wealthy cocoa exporter Mr Fradique de Menezes for a second and last five-year term. De Menezes is the country's third president, after Miguel Trovoada, who served two five-year terms, the maximum permitted by the constitution (1990–2001) and Pinto da Costa (1975–91). Local elections took place in late August 2006. In June 2008 Joaquim Rafael Branco (MLSTP/PSD) was appointed prime minister.

Fragile economy

São Tomé and Príncipe's economy is fragile, having been burdened by a high debt per capita ratio of over 600 per cent. São Tomé and Príncipe is trying to shake off its dependence on agriculture, primarily the export of cocoa. Falls in production and prices have left the island state heavily reliant on foreign aid. Additional economic activities include modest fishing, and small but growing construction and tourism sub-sectors.

São Tomé is optimistic about the development of petroleum resources in its territorial waters in the oil-rich Gulf of Guinea that are being jointly developed in a 60–40 split with Nigeria. The first production licences were sold in 2004, though a dispute over licensing with Nigeria delayed São Tomé's receipt of more than US$20 million in signing bonuses for almost a year. Oil production is expected to start no earlier than 2010. However, so far, a first exploratory well in Block 1 in early 2006 has been deemed commercially non-viable. Other blocks (2, 3 and 4) have also been contracted recently. Negotiations on two additional blocks (5 and 6) are suspended until further notice.

In a report published in July 2008 the International Monetary Fund (IMF) reported that GDP had grown at an estimated 6 per cent in 2007, led by construction and services sectors, financed by an inflow of foreign direct investment (FDI). However, because so much needs to be imported, the benefits were less than might have been expected. Inflation rocked to 28 per cent by the end of the year, reflecting an increase in food and oil prices.

Tourism

There is also potential for a more developed tourist industry. Promoters say the

KEY FACTS

Official name: República Democrática de São Tomé e Príncipe (Democratic Republic of São Tomé and Príncipe)

Head of State: President Fradique Bandeira Melo de Menezes (MDFM-PSD) (since 2001; re-elected 30 Jul 2006)

Head of government: Prime Minister Joaquim Rafael Branco (MLSTP/PSD) (appointed 22 Jun 2008)

Ruling party: Coalition led by Movimento de Libertação de São Tomé e Príncipe-Partido Social Democrata (MLSTP/PSD) (Movement for the Liberation of São Tomé and Príncipe-Social Democratic Party) (elected 26 Mar 2006)

Area: 964 square km

Population: 164,000 (2007)*

Capital: São Tomé

Official language: Portuguese

Currency: Dobra (Db) = 100 centavos

Exchange rate: Db14,385.00 per US$ (Jul 2008)

GDP per capita: US$880 (2007)*

GDP real growth: 6.00% (2007)*

Inflation: 19.90% (2007)

Balance of trade: -US$56.00 million (2006)

Foreign debt: US$362.00 million (2004)

* estimated figure

islands have plenty for visitors to see, but hurdles include ignorance about the country and the difficulties of getting there. Exports of tourism and cocoa are equivalent to a third of GDP of US$60 million.

Outlook

Fiscal consolidation, which will require reining in expectations fuelled by the prospect of oil riches, while protecting pro-poor spending, remains an essential element of macroeconomic stabilisation. The continuous large increases in the civil service wage bill are a matter of concern.

Risk assessment

Politics	Poor
Economy	Poor
Regional stability	Fair

COUNTRY PROFILE

Historical profile

1469–72 The islands were first sighted by Portuguese sailors.
1485 The town of São Tomé was founded; Príncipe was not settled until 15 years later. The islands quickly became the largest sugar producing area in the world and used slave labour.
1700–1800 Coffee and cocoa plantations were also set up using slave labour.
1875 Slavery was abolished, only to be replaced by a system of forced labour. The labour force consisted mainly of workers brought by the Portuguese from Angola, Mozambique and Cape Verde. On several occasions they launched rebellions against their colonial rulers which were brutally suppressed.
1951 The islands became an overseas province of Portugal.
1974 The end of fascist rule in Portugal marked the beginning of independence for its overseas colonies. A transitional government was established.
1975 The Democratic Republic of São Tomé and Príncipe gained independence from Portugal. Manuel Pinto da Costa, the leader of the Movimiento de Libertação de São Tomé e Principe (MLSTP) (Movement for the Liberation of São Tomé), made a clean sweep in the general elections and became the first president and the Marxist MLSTP was the only legal party allowed. The economy was hard-hit when Portugal withdrew support, then when most plantations were quickly nationalised foreign investors and workers left; the islands developed strong links with Cuba.
Under colonial administration there had been little investment in education or healthcare systems for the local population; at independence the literacy rate was 10 per cent and there was only one doctor in the entire country.
1980s A severe drought and a drop in world prices for cocoa crippled the economy. Pinto da Costa began a process of releasing economic ties with the Eastern Bloc in favour of a capitalist, market economy.
1989 Changes within MLSTP began; multi-party democracy was introduce as an objective.
1990 The MLSTP changed its name and adopted MLSTP-PSD (Social Democratic Party) to fight the next election. A multi-party constitution was approved by referendum, allowing direct and free elections for the presidency and legislature.
1991 The ruling MLSTP-PSD lost the country's first election, defeated by the Partido da Convergencia Democrática-Grupo de Reflexão (PCD-GR) (Democratic Convergence Party-Reflection Group). Miguel Trovoada, an independent candidate supported by the PCD-GR, was elected president. The currency was devalued by 40 per cent as part of stringent austerity measures, imposed by the IMF and the World Bank in exchange for economic assistance.
1994 The MLSTP-PSD won most seats, but fell short of an overall majority, in the National Assembly.
1995 In April, Príncipe was granted autonomy; the MLSTP-PSD won most seats in its assembly.
Strikes by public employees for promised pay rises destabilised the president and government. An abortive coup resulted in the formation of a coalition government which included members of the Ação Democrática Independente (ADI) (Independent Democratic Action), the Coligação Democrático da Oposição (CDO) (Democratic Opposition Coalition) and the Frente Democrática Crista (FDC) (Christian Democratic Front).
1996 Trovoada was re-elected president. Prime Minister Armindo Vaz d'Almeida was removed from office his position was taken by Raw Wagner da Conceiçao Bragança Neto (MLSTP-PSD).
1998 Election to the National Assembly resulted in a victory for the centre-left MLSTP-PSD.
2001 Fradique de Menezes won the presidential election.
2002 National Assembly elections were misread until the Supreme Court ruled that the MLSTP had won 24 of the 55 seats. After Gabriel Costa dismissed, Maria das Neves was appointed as the country's first female prime minister.
2003 The constitution was revised in January. On 16 July, a military coup staged by Major Fernando Pereira toppled the government while President Menezes was out of the country. President Menezes signed an accord with the coup leaders, which restored democratic rule and included an amnesty for the insurgents. On 1 August, Prime Minister das Neves resigned but was reappointed several days later. In October, bidding began for offshore oil blocs controlled by São Tomé and Príncipe and Nigeria.
2004 The president and prime minister clashed over control of oil deals. Maria das Neves was dismissed as prime minister after a series of corruption scandals. Damião Vaz d'Almeida became prime minister.
2005 Maria do Carmo Silveira was nominated prime minister after Vaz d'Almeida's resigned.
2006 In parliamentary elections, the ruling MLSTP was defeated by a coalition led by the president's Movimento de

KEY INDICATORS São Tomé and Príncipe

	Unit	2003	2004	2005	2006	2007
Population	m	0.16	0.16	0.16	*0.17	*0.17
Gross domestic product (GDP)	US$bn	0.05	0.06	0.07	0.12	*0.14
GDP per capita	US$	300	402	439	*769	*880
GDP real growth	%	5.0	6.0	6.0	*6.7	*7.0
Inflation	%	9.0	12.8	16.3	23.1	18.6
Exports (fob) (goods)	US$m	5.5	6.7	7.0	3.0	6.8
Imports (cif) (goods)	US$m	24.8	41.0	38.0	59.0	64.9
Balance of trade	US$m	-19.3	-34.3	-31.0	-56.0	-58.1
Current account	US$m	-10.0	-20.0	-22.0	-49.0	-66.8
Total reserves minus gold	US$m	25.5	19.8	26.7	34.2	–
Foreign exchange	US$m	25.4	19.8	26.7	34.1	–
Exchange rate	per US$	8,859.85	9,900.40	6,780.00	6,780.00	14,101.00

* estimated figure

Libertação de São Tomé e Príncipe-Partido Social Democrata (MLSTP-PSD) (Movement for the Liberation of São Tomé and Príncipe-Social Democratic Party). Tomé Vera Cruz became prime minister. Fradique de Menezes was re-elected president in July.
2008 Prime Minister Tomé Vera Cruz resigned on 7 February, having failed in parliament to get the 2008 budget passed; Patrice Trovoada (ADI) was appointed as prime minister. Prime Minister Trovoada's government lost in a censure motion (30-23) on 20 May. The president appointed Joaquim Rafael Branco (MLSTP/PSD) as prime minister on 22 June and requested that he form a coalition government.

Political structure

Constitution
The 5 November 1975 constitution was revised in September 1990, following a national referendum, which approved a multi-party constitution, allowing direct and free elections for the presidency and legislature. The constitution was revised again in January 2003.
The island of Príncipe was granted political and administrative autonomy in April 1995.

Form of state
Sovereign, unitary and democratic state.

The executive
The president is elected for a maximum of two five-year terms of office.

National legislature
Legislative power is vested in the Assembleia Popular Nacional (National People's Assembly), which has 55 members serving a four-year term and holds two sessions a year. The members are elected by party list vote from 12 multi-seat constituencies.
There are six district assemblies on Sao Tomé .
The island of Príncipe has a seven-member Regional Assembly.

Legal system
Portuguese legal system. The Supreme Court is appointed by the National Assembly.

Last elections
26 March 2006 (parliamentary); 30 July 2006 (presidential).
Results: Parliamentary: MDFM-PL and PCD-GR coalition won 36.79 per cent (23 seats); MLSTP 29.47 per cent (20 seats); ADI 20 per cent (11 seats); MNR 4.7 per cent (one seat). Turnout was 66.9 per cent.
Presidential: Fradique de Menezes won 60.58 per cent of the vote; Patrice Trovoada won 38.82 per cent. Turnout was 64.9 per cent.

Next elections
2010 (parliamentary and presidential)

Political parties

Ruling party
Coalition led by Movimento de Libertação de São Tomé e Príncipe-Partido Social Democrata (MLSTP/PSD) (Movement for the Liberation of São Tomé and Príncipe-Social Democratic Party) (elected 26 Mar 2006)

Main opposition party
Movimiento de Libertaçao de São Tomé e Príncipe (MLSTP) (Movement for the Liberation of São Tomé and Príncipe).

Population
164,000 (2007)*
Last census: August 2001: 137,599
Population density: 151 inhabitants per square km. Urban population: 48 per cent.
Annual growth rate: 2.0 per cent 1994–2004 (WHO 2006)

Ethnic make-up
There are five groups among the islands' inhabitants: the Filhos da Terra are the descendants of imported slaves and Europeans (mostly Portuguese); the Angolares are descendants of former castaway slaves from Angola, now primarily fishermen; the Forros are descendants of slaves freed when slavery was abolished in 1875; the Servicais are migrant labourers from Angola, Mozambique and Cape Verde, and the Tongas are their children, born on the islands.

Religions
Eighty per cent of the population are Roman Catholic, Evangelical Protestant or Seventh-Day Adventist.

Education
The literacy rate for the period 1995—2001 was estimated at 63 per cent.

Health
Per capita total expenditure on health (2003) was US$93; of which per capita government spending was US$78, at the international dollar rate, (WHO 2006).
Life expectancy: 59 years, 2004 (WHO 2006)
Fertility rate/Maternal mortality rate: 3.9 births per woman, 2004 (WHO 2006)
Birth rate/Death rate: 42 births per 1,000 population; seven deaths per 1,000 population (2003).
Child (under 5 years) mortality rate (per 1,000): 75 per 1,000 live births (World Bank)
Head of population per physician: 0.49 physicians per 1,000 people, 2004 (WHO 2006)

Main cities
São Tomé (capital, estimated population 56,166 in 2005) Trinidade (6,636), Santo Amaro (8,411).

Languages spoken
Portuguese is spoken by 95 per cent of the population; Lungwa Santomé is the main national dialect and Fôrro and Crioulo are also spoken.

Official language/s
Portuguese

Media

Press
In Portuguese, there are two weekly newspapers, Diário da República (www.cstome.net) and the official organ of Ministry of Information Revolução. The weekend newspaper and magazine is Povo and the sole independent periodical is O Parvo.
Jornal de São Tomé and Príncipe (www.jornal.st) is an online news outlet, in Portuguese.

Broadcasting
Radio: Radio Nacional de São Tomé e Príncipe broadcasts two FM services in Portuguese from Lisbon, Portugal. The French radio station RFI (www.rfi.fr), from neighbouring Cameroon, can also be picked up along with Voice of America (VoA).
Television: The state-run television service is Televisao Saotomense (TVS).

Economy
The country has one of the lowest per capita incomes and one of the highest debt ratios in the world and is primarily dependent on foreign aid and cocoa exports. The economy has suffered from dependence on cocoa, the country's principal commodity export, which is susceptible to fluctuations in world prices and other factors. In 2005, São Tomé and Príncipe received its first signature bonus from successful oil exploration, undertaken offshore since 2004. GDP growth was 3.8 per cent and inflation 16.2 per cent in 2005.
Oil production is unlikely to come on-stream until 2010, when the enormous impact of oil receipts will be managed by an oil revenue management law and a percentage of the profits channelled into a trust fund for future generations. Revenue from oil is expected to pay debts and provide more government spending, particularly on poverty reduction schemes. There are already some benefits as construction and other activities increase to cater to the industry. Nigeria and São Tomé have a contract whereby joint development will result in 60 per cent of proceeds going to Nigeria and the remainder to São Tomé. The net value of total outstanding external debt has fallen in recent years, largely due to the efforts made at debt reduction under the IMF and World Bank's enhanced Heavily Indebted Poor Countries (HIPC) initiative. Debt relief under HIPC is

projected at 9 per cent of GDP between 2001–07.
Althouth the dominant crop on São Tomé is cocoa, representing about 95 per cent of exports, other export crops include copra, palm kernels, and coffee. Domestically, fishing and a small industrial sector processing local agricultural products and producing a few basic consumer goods provide an inadequate employment environment. However, the islands have potential for tourism, and the government is attempting to improve the undeveloped tourist infrastructure.

External trade
São Tomé and Príncipe is a member of the Common Market for Eastern and Southern Africa (Comesa), and operates within a free trade zone with 13 of the 19 member states.
It is a mono-exporter with around 95 per cent of all exports being cocoa that is shipped mainly to Europe. World prices of cocoa have a direct influence on GDP as it represents 40 per cent of the whole, such exports cannot maintain a balance of payments.
New found oil deposits are not expected to be in production until 2010, when it will radically favour foreign earnings.
Imports
Principal imports are machinery and electrical equipment, food products and petroleum products.
Main sources: Portugal (43.0 per cent total, 2005), UK (33.4 per cent), France (16.0 per cent), The Netherlands (4.5 per cent)
Exports
Principal exports are cocoa, copra, coffee, palm oil.
Main destinations: The Netherlands (61.1 per cent total, 2005), Belgium (9.2 per cent), Turkey (5.5 per cent), South Korea (4.0 per cent)

Agriculture
Farming
Plantation agriculture forms the basis of the economy, but growth is slowing. It accounted for 17 per cent of GDP in 2004, which represents a decline in the sector's contribution. Cocoa is the main crop, accounting for around 90 per cent of exports. Cocoa production, once the biggest in the world, has fallen over the years and now totals about 4,000 tonnes a year.
The plantations were nationalised after independence to their detriment, but have since been privatised.
The second-largest export crop is coffee; other cash crops are copra, palm kernels, cinnamon, pepper and breadfruit. Priority is being given to the diversification of food crops in an effort to reduce the large food import bill.
The estimated crop production for 2005 included: 2,700 tonnes (t) maize, 5,800t cassava, 28,000t taro, 1,500t yams, 27,000t bananas, 37,500t roots and tubers, 28,500t coconuts, 40,000t oil palm fruit, 7,775t oilcrops, 3,500t cocoa beans, 30t cinnamon, 29,900t fruit in total, 6,500t vegetables in total. Estimated livestock production included: 875t meat in total, 122t beef, 92t pig meat, 25t lamb and goat meat, 636t poultry, 385t eggs, 145t milk, 21t cattle hides.
Fishing
Fishing remains small-scale, but is being encouraged for local consumption and possible future export.
In 2004, the total marine fish catch was 4,127 tonnes.

Industry and manufacturing
The industrial sector is limited to small-scale manufacturing concerns such as soap, soft drinks, timber processing, palm oil, bricks and textiles. The development of oil fields in the Gulf of Guinea is likely to increase industrial activity associated with the sector, particularly construction. In 2002, the government announced it was developing a number of export processing zones (EPZs) in order to exploit the country's position as a regional trading platform. These will give incentives to investors, with tax breaks and free movement of goods.

Tourism
Tourism is under-developed. It has tended towards the luxury market, catering mainly to Portuguese and French visitors. The sector has potential and infrastructure is being expanded. Tourism is expected to contribute 14.4 per cent to GDP in 2005.

Mining
São Tomé and Príncipe has no mineral resources.

Hydrocarbons
São Tomé and Príncipe is dependent on imported refined oil products. Oil-derived products supply 96 per cent of commercial energy requirements. Distribution and marketing of fuels is carried out by the state-owned oil company, Empresa Nacional de Combustiveis e Oleos (Enco).
São Tomé and Príncipe has established with Nigeria a joint authority to manage offshore oil exploration in the oil-rich Gulf of Guinea. Under the accord, Nigeria will receive 60 per cent of revenues and São Tomé and Príncipe 40 per cent. Several blocks in the joint development zone were awarded in 2004 and 2005. The first exploration and production contract was signed in February 2005. Preliminary indications suggest that there may be substantial commercial reserves of oil in the area. If confirmed, production is expected to commence some time after 2010.
São Tomé and Príncipe does not produce or import gas or coal.

Energy
Installed electricity generating capacity is around 9MW. Blackouts are frequent.

Banking and insurance
Main financial centre
São Tomé.

Time
GMT.

Geography
The islands of the Republic of São Tomé and Príncipe, are located in the equatorial Atlantic Ocean, about 300–250km off the coast of Gabon, in the Gulf of Guinea. Both islands are remnants of an extinct volcanic mountain range. The tallest mountain is São Tomé Peak (2,024 metres) on the island of São Tomé. Príncipe's mountains have lush forests with swift streams flowing down to the sea. The country also includes the rocky islets of Caroço, Pedras and Tinhosas, off Príncipe, and Rôlas, off São Tomé.
Hemisphere
Northern

Climate
Equatorial with high temperatures and humidity. Average temperatures remain fairly constant throughout the year with a daily range from 20–32 degrees Celsius (C). Driest month July, wettest March.

Entry requirements
Passports
Required by all.
Visa
Required by all; apply well in advance. European visitors should contact the São Tomé e Príncipe consulate in Brussels; US visitors should contact the consulate in either New York or Atlanta; visitors from Canada and Australia should contact the Canadian embassy in Libreville in Gabon (See: Other useful addresses, for further information).
Currency advice/regulations
There are no restrictions on the import of local or foreign currency. Export is allowed up to the amount declared on entry.
Travellers cheques are not widely accepted. US dollars and euro are easily converted, other currencies may attract higher exchange fees.

Health (for visitors)
Mandatory precautions
Yellow fever vaccination certificate is required by all.
Advisable precautions
Inoculations and boosters should be current for cholera, tetanus, yellow fever,

hepatitis A, diphtheria, typhoid and polio. There may be a need for vaccinations for tuberculosis, hepatitis B and meningitis. Use malaria prophylaxis (which will also provide protection against yellow fever, dengue fever, hepatitis B and encephalitis) including mosquito repellents, sleeping nets and clothing that cover the body after dark. To avoid bilharzia, avoid exposure to fresh water and use only well-maintained, chlorinated swimming pools. There is a risk of rabies.
Use only bottled or boiled water for drinks, washing teeth and making ice. Eat only well cooked meals, preferably served hot; vegetables should be cooked and fruit peeled. Dairy products are unpasteurised and should be avoided, unless cooked. There is a shortage of routine medications, including sun-screens, and visitors should take all necessary medicines with them. A first aid kit that includes disposable syringes, is a reasonable precaution.
Healthcare is not to Western standards and medical insurance, including emergency evacuation, is necessary.

Hotels
There is a limited number of reasonable hotels.

Public holidays (national)
Fixed dates
1 Jan (New Year's Day), 3 Feb (Heroes' Day), 1 May (Labour Day), 12 Jul (Independence Day), 6 Sep (Armed Forces Day), 30 Sep (Agricultural Reform Day), 26 Nov (Argel Accord Day), 21 Dec (São Tomé Day, Catholic), 25 Dec (Christmas Day).
Variable dates
Ash Wednesday, Good Friday.

Working hours
Banking
Mon–Fri: 0730–1130, 1430–1630.
Business
Mon–Fri: 0730–1200, 1430–1800.
Government
Mon–Fri: 0800–1200, 1500–1800; Sat: 0800–1300.
Shops
Mon–Sat: 0800–1200, 1500–1900.

Telecommunications
Mobile/cell phones
A 900 GSM service is available over most of the islands of São Tomé and Príncipe.

Electricity supply
220V AC

Weights and measures
Metric

Social customs/useful tips
Business is conducted in Portuguese. Many executives speak French, and some speak English.

Getting there
Air
The national airlines of Portugal (TAP) and Angola (TAAG), fly services to São Tomé.
National airline: Air São Tomé e Príncipe (KY), flies to Gabon only.
International airport/s: São Tomé (TMS), 5.5km from town. A minibus, taxi and buses provide transport to the centre of town.
Airport tax: Departure tax: US$21 or eur24, in cash.
Surface
Main port/s: São Tomé, this is not a deep-water harbour so few international ships visit.

Getting about
National transport
Air: Restricted services link the two islands. Travellers should book their seats well in advance, to avoid being stranded.
Road: There are only about 300km of roads, of which about two-thirds are asphalted, but the network is being improved.
Buses: Frequent, efficient service on São Tomé. Limited bus service on Príncipe.
City transport
Taxis: On São Tomé a minivan or collectivo shared taxi can be taken to anywhere on the island. There are no fixed schedules and they leave only when they are full; this is no other public transport available.

BUSINESS DIRECTORY

Telephone area codes
The international dialling code (IDD) for São Tomé and Príncipe is +239, followed by subscriber's number.

Chambers of Commerce
Camara de Comircio, Industria, Agricultura e Servicios, Avenida Marginal 12 de Julho, PO Box 527, Saõ Tomé (tel: 22-2723; fax: 22-1409; e-mail: ccias@cstome.net).

Banking
Banco Comercial do Equador, CP 361, Rua de Moçambique, São Tomé (tel: 22-3829; fax: 22-1989).

Banco Internacional de S Tomé e Príncipe, CP 536, Praça da Independência 3, São Tomé (tel: 22-1445; 22-5821; fax: 22-2427, 22-3462).

Central bank
Banco Central de São Tomé e Príncipe, CP 13, Praça da Independencia, São Tomé (tel: 22-1269, 22-1300; fax: 22-501, 22-2777; email: bcentral@cstome.net; internet: www.bcstp.st).

Travel information
TAP (Air Portugal), CP 414; Avenida Marginal 12 de Julho, São Tomé (tel: 22-2307, 22-1528).

National tourist organisation offices
Tourism Office, CP40, Avenue Marginal, 12 de Julho, São Tomé (tel: 221-542).

Ministries
Ministry of Commerce, Industry and Tourism, Largo das Alfândegas São Tomé; CP 201, São Tomé e Príncipe (tel: 22-4657, 22-4872, 22-4975).

Ministry of Foreign Affairs, Avenida 12 de Julho, São Tomé (tel: 22-2309; fax: 22-3237; email: popgender@sctome.net).

Ministry of Planning and Finance, Largo das Alfândegas São Tomé (tel: 22-4172/3; fax: 22-2182; email: fpublica@cstome.net).

Office of the President, Avenida da Independência, São Tomé (tel: 22-1143; fax: 22-1226).
Office of the Prime Minister, Rua do Município, São Tomé (tel: 22-3596, 22-4189; fax: 22-1670).
National Assembly, Palácio dos Congressos, São Tomé (tel: 22-1899, 22-2986; fax: 22-2835).

Other useful addresses
Directorate of Finance, Praça da Independência, São Tomé; CP 168, São Tomé and Príncipe (tel: 22-2372, 22-1484; fax: 22-1182; email: financas@cstome.net).

Nigeria-São Tomé and Príncipe Joint Development Authority, Plot 1101 Aminu Kano Crescent, Wuse II, Abuja, Nigeria (tel: (+234-9) 524-1069; fax: (234-9) 524-1052; e-mail: enquiries@nigeriasaotomejda.com; internet: www.nigeriasaotomejda.com).

STP-Press, c/o Rádio Nacional de São Tomé e Príncipe, Avenida Marginal de 12 de Julho, CP 44, São Tomé (tel: 22-217).

São Tomé and Príncipe Telecom (CST), Av Marginal 12 de Julho, São Tomé; CP 141, São Tomé and Príncipe (tel: 22-2273; internt: www.cst.st).

Internet sites
AllAfrica information: http://allafrica.com/saotomeandprincipe

National Assembly (in Portuguese): www.parlamento.st

São Toméand Príncipe tourist site: www.saotome.st

São Tomé and Príncipe website: www.sao-tome.com

Saudi Arabia

KEY FACTS

Official name: Mamlaka al Arabiya as Sa'udiya (The Kingdom of Saudi Arabia)

Head of State: Custodian of the Two Mosques King Abdullah bin Abdul Aziz al Sa'ud (from 1 Aug 2005)

Head of government: King Abdullah bin Abdul Aziz al Sa'ud

Ruling party: None

Area: 2,149,690 square km (approximately)

Population: 24.29 million (2007)*

Capital: Riyadh

Official language: Arabic

Currency: Saudi riyal (SR) = 100 halalas

Exchange rate: SR3.75 per US$ (fixed)

GDP per capita: US$15,481 (2007)*

GDP real growth: 4.10% (2007)*

Labour force: 7.17 million (2004)

Unemployment: 13.00% (2005; Saudi males only), (25.00% unofficial total)

Inflation: 4.10% (2007)*

Oil production: 10.41 million bpd (2007)

Balance of trade: US$143.60 billion (2006)

Visitor numbers: 8.62 million (2006)*

* estimated figure

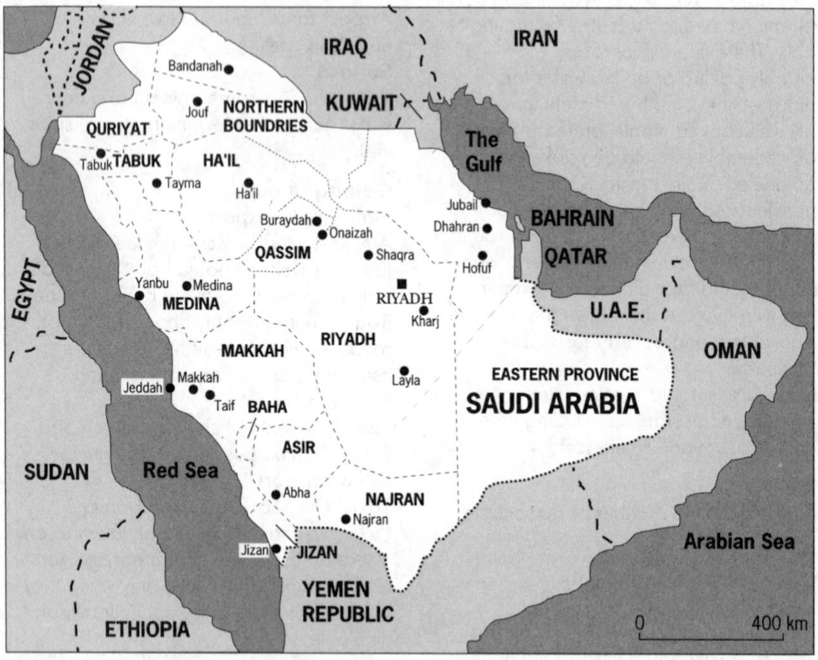

In the view of most analysts, Saudi Arabia's economic fundamentals have rarely been sounder. The kingdom's oil revenues reached US$194 billion in 2006 and as a result, Saudi Arabian Monetary Agency (SAMA), the country's central bank, estimated that the Kingdom's trade balance was 17.5 per cent up on the previous year at SR553.4 billion (US$148 billion). SAMA increased its foreign assets by US$63 billion to US$216 billion in 2006, almost equal to the total assets held by the domestic banking sector. This means that in the last four years the Kingdom's foreign assets have risen fourfold. This wealth is sustaining high project expenditure but also represents three years of import cover, a massive cushion against any weakening in oil prices. Growing confidence is illustrated by the country's national budget for 2007, the largest in the Kingdom's history.

Increased spending

Spending allocated for new development projects was planned to nearly double to US$37 billion, with a big emphasis on programmes for educational facilities and hospitals as well as the country's ambitious new economic cities. The latter are a key part of the Kingdom's eighth five-year development plan. Economy and planning minister, Khaled Al Gosaibi, announced that the budget aimed to improve living standards, create job opportunities as well as expand educational, health and other social facilities and develop infrastructure.

Some US$26 billion alone has been allocated for education and manpower development including the building of 2,000 new schools as well as universities in Tabuk, Najran, Al Baha and one in Riyadh uniquely dedicated to women's higher education. Nearly 400 primary health care centres and 13 new hospitals are planned in addition to more than 60 other hospitals in various stages of development. These are aimed to provide almost 10,000 new beds for the health service. Road construction is another big winner with 8,000 kilometres of new highway planned in addition to 16,000 kilometres already under construction.

No more delays

King Abdullah has stressed that meeting project deadlines is essential. A special ministerial committee has been formed to look at the obstacles to implementing development programmes that have caused delays in the past. Significantly, the government is also to cut public debt to SR310 billion (US$83 billion) from SR366 billion (US$98 billion), a fall from 28 per cent of GDP to 24 per cent. The debt is held by local state institutions including domestic banks, social and pension funds. Observers believe the expansionary budget is prudent and appears hugely to underestimate potential revenues with an implied price of US$35 per barrel of oil compared to an average of US$55 in 2006. Prospects for the economy continue to look good. While Saudi real GDP growth in 2007 is estimated at 4.1 per cent compared to 4.3 per cent in 2006, the Kingdom is still expected to record a surplus albeit a much smaller one in 2007 while maintaining its high levels of development spending.

Saudi Arabia remains one of the most conservative and traditional of the major Arab states. Resistance to pressures for modernisation and democratisation has, if anything, increased those pressures. This, combined with the threat from al Qaeda, has placed the Saudi government between a rock and a very hard place. Much of the populace, and the government (for which read the royal family) retain a strong streak of Wahhabite Puritanism. The Sharia is officially Saudi Arabia's constitution and for decades Saudi Arabia was the citadel of the more traditionalist camp in Arab politics. Saudi Arabia has, more recently, seen fit to loosen its conservative approach, while the more modernist, liberal Arab states have succumbed to Saudi generosity, particularly in times of conflict.

Developing democracy

Saudi Arabia began to flirt with democracy in 2005, the first such experience in the history of the kingdom. In January, the government announced plans to expand the Majlis al Shura (Consultative Council), a consultative body appointed by the King. The government also stated that it would increase the powers of the Majlis, which at present can challenge but not propose or amend legislation.

The democratic experiment gathered pace February–April, when Saudi men over the age of 21 were allowed to vote in elections for newly formed local councils. Conservative Islamist candidates won in the Riyadh area and candidates identifying themselves as political and religious moderates won the most seats in councils in Jeddah, Mecca and Medina. Turnout was particularly high in Ash Sharqiyah (Eastern Province), home to most of Saudi Arabia's traditionally oppressed Shi'a population. Council members will only be allowed to advise on local affairs. The councils were formally constituted in December 2005.

In November, Saudi women were allowed to vote and stand in elections for the first time. The election was to the Jeddah Chamber of Commerce and Industry. Two women won seats.

The economy

Despite the government's efforts, and investments in diversification programmes, Saudi Arabia remains heavily dependent on its oil industry. The International Monetary Fund (IMF) reported that oil export revenues account for around 90 per cent of total Saudi export earnings, 70–80 per cent of state revenues, and 44 per cent of the country's gross domestic product (GDP).

Oil reserves at the end of 2007 were 264.2 thousand million barrels, or around one-fifth of proven, conventional world oil reserves. Around two-thirds of Saudi reserves are considered light or extra light grades of oil, with the rest either medium or heavy. Although Saudi Arabia has over 100 oil and gas fields (and more than 1,500 wells), over half of its oil reserves are contained in only eight fields. Saudi Arabia also maintains the world's largest crude oil production capacity, estimated to be around 10.5–11.0 million bpd. In May 2006, Saudi Aramco announced the details of an US$18 billion plan to increase capacity to 12.5 million bpd by 2009 and 15 million by 2020. Production in 2007 was 10.4 million bpd.

At the same time gas reserves were 7.17 trillion cubic metres (tcm), and production 75.9 billion cubic metres. Saudi Arabia has the fourth largest proven natural gas reserves in the world. Over the last decade, Saudi Aramco has added 72 trillion cubic feet (Tcf) of non-associated reserves, including the fields Mazalij, Manjura, Shaden, Niban, Tinat, Al-Waar, and Fazran in the deep Khuff, Unaizah and Jauf reservoirs. However, around 57 per cent of Saudi Arabia's proven natural gas reserves consist of associated gas at the giant onshore Ghawar field and the offshore Safaniya and Zuluf fields. The Ghawar oil field alone accounts for approximately one-third of the country's proven natural gas reserves. Both associated and non-associated natural gas has also been discovered in the country's extreme north-west, at Midyan, and in the Empty Quarter (Rub al Khali) in the country's south-eastern desert. The Rub al Khali alone is believed to potentially contain natural gas reserves as high as 300 Tcf, although these are not proven.

Saudi Arabia's accession to the World Trade Organisation (WTO) at the end of 2005 reflected the government's efforts at economic reform, although the WTO appeared to turn a blind eye to some of the government's shortcomings.

KEY INDICATORS — Saudi Arabia

	Unit	2003	2004	2005	2006	2007
Population	m	22.66	24.60	23.11	23.70	*24.29
Gross domestic product (GDP)	US$bn	214.70	250.34	309.94	349.14	*376.03
GDP per capita	US$	8,879	9,972	13,410	*14,733	*15,481
GDP real growth	%	2.9	5.3	6.6	4.3	*4.1
Inflation	%	0.7	0.2	0.7	2.3	*4.1
Oil output	'000 bpd	9,817.0	10,584.0	11,035.0	10,859.0	10,413.0
Natural gas output	bn cum	61.0	64.0	69.5	73.7	75.9
Exports (fob) (goods)	US$m	84,076	126,063	174,635	211,305	–
Imports (cif) (goods)	US$m	33,928	40,841	51,327	63,914	–
Balance of trade	US$m	50,148	85,222	123,308	147,391	–
Current account	US$m	29,702	49,280	90,785	99,066	*100,767
Total reserves minus gold	US$m	22,620.0	27,291.0	26,530.0	27,523.0	33,760.0
Foreign exchange	US$m	17,662.0	23,273.0	24,074.0	25,971.0	32,308.0
Exchange rate	per US$	3.75	3.75	3.75	3.75	3.74

* estimated figure

Large state-owned corporations still control the Saudi economy, not least Saudi Aramco, which has a monopoly on Saudi upstream oil development and controls 98 per cent of the country's oil reserves, and the Saudi Basic Industries Corporation (Sabic) one of the world's largest petrochemicals producers and the largest non-oil company in the Middle East. To date, there has not been a complete sale of state assets to private control, and Saudi privatisation has been limited to allowing private firms to take on service functions or offering limited partnerships, particularly foreign investors.

Outlook

King Abdullah, is widely regarded, both inside the country and outside, as an experienced operator. He will no doubt continue to prosecute the war against al Qaeda in his country and continue implementing the gradual democratic reforms that he has championed for so long. Although Abdullah is regarded as being in good health, he turned 83 in 2007. Abdullah's heir apparent, Prince Sultan, also in his 80s, is in relatively poor health and has in the past criticised the democratic reform process. In October 2006 a committee of princes was created under the Allegiance Institution Law to ensure the orderly succession to the throne.

Risk assessment

Politics	Stable
Economy	Good
Regional stability	Fair

COUNTRY PROFILE

Historical profile

The Arabian peninsula, including modern-day Saudi Arabia, became part of the Turkish Ottoman empire in the sixteenth century. Although under the overall rule of the Ottoman Sultan, local leaders developed varying degrees of autonomy.

The espousal of a strict interpretation of Sunni Islam, known as Wahhabism, by the al Sa'ud ruling family led the country to develop a strongly religious self-identity. Al Sa'ud dynasty's monopoly of power meant that during the twentieth century, successive kings were able to concentrate on modernisation and developing the country's role as a regional power, and due to its vast oil resources, Saudi Arabia has become one of the wealthiest nations in the Middle East. The ruling family has tried to preserve stability by clamping down on extremist elements, but it is possible that its refusal to tolerate any kind of opposition may have encouraged the growth of various terrorist groups, including Osama bin Laden's al Qaeda, supported by those who resent the US's role in the Middle East.

1871 The Ottomans took the province of Al Ahsa.

1891 The Rashidi family seized control of Riyadh from the Sa'ud family, which was exiled to Kuwait.

1902 Abd al Aziz and other members of the deposed Sa'ud family regained control of Riyadh, expelling the Rashidis.

1913 Al Ahsa was taken back from the Ottomans by Abd al Aziz. The Anglo-Ottoman Convention established the 'Blue Line' as the eastern Arabian boundary between the Ottoman and British empires.

1914 Abd al Aziz signed a treaty with the Ottomans.

1915 The first Anglo-Saudi treaty provided recognition of Abd al Aziz.

1919–26 Between 1919 and 1925, Abd al Aziz defeated the four Arabian states of Hejaz, Asir, Ha'il and Jauf and incorporated them. Abd al Aziz took Makkah (Mecca) from King Ali of al Hejaz. In 1925, Medina, Yanbu and Jeddah surrendered to Abd al Aziz, and in 1926, Abd al Aziz was proclaimed King of Al Hejaz and Sultan of Najd and its dependencies.

1927 In the second Anglo-Saudi treaty, the British recognised the full independence of Abd al Aziz, while the Saudi leader acknowledged the British treaty relationships with the sheikhdoms of the Gulf.

1932 The Kingdom of Saudi Arabia was established when the two monarchies of Najd and Al Hejaz merged, with Abd al Aziz as King.

1933 His eldest son, Sa'ud, was named crown prince.

1938 Oil was discovered and production started under California Arabian Standard Oil Company (CASOC).

1944 CASOC changed its name to Arabian American Oil Company (Aramco).

1945 Oil exploration and exploitation increased after the Second World War and the country's infrastructure was modernised and developed with the growing oil revenues.

1953 King Abd al Aziz died and was succeeded by Crown Prince Sa'ud ibn Abdul Aziz al Sa'ud.

1960 Saudi Arabia was a founding member of OPEC (Organisation of Petroleum Exporting Countries).

1964 King Sa'ud was deposedby his brother, Faisal ibn Abdul Aziz al Sa'ud, previously the crown prince and prime minister.

1972 Saudi Arabia gained controlled of 20 per cent of Aramco.

1973 An oil boycott was led by Saudi Arabia against Western countries that supported Israel in the 6 October War against Egypt and Syria. Oil prices subsequently quadrupled and world economy went into depression.

1975 King Faisal was assassinated by one of his nephews and was succeeded by Khalid ibn Abdul Aziz al Sa'ud.

1979 Saudi Arabia cut off diplomatic relations with Egypt after the Egyptian-Israeli Peace Treaty was signed. The Grand Mosque of Makkah was seized by extemists; the government regained control and executed those captured.

1980 Saudi Arabia took over full control of Aramco.

1981 Saudi Arabia was a founder member of the GCC (Gulf Co-operation Council).

1982 King Khalid died and Fahd ibn Abdul Aziz al Sa'ud, his brother, became King.

1986 The King Fahd Causeway between Bahrain and Saudi Arabia opened.

1987 Diplomatic relations with Egypt were resumed.

1991 Saudi Arabia was the launch pad for a US-led military operation, which ejected Iraqi forces occupying Kuwait.

1992 King Fahd announced the country's Basic Law, which declares that the Quran is the country's constitution, and he proposed setting up a Majlis al Shura (Consultative Council).

1993 The Majlis al Shura was inaugurated.

1994 Osama bin Laden, who was later to become notorious as the leader of al Qaeda, a terrorist organisation, reportedly responsible for flying two aircraft into the World Trade Centre in New York in September 2001, was stripped of his Saudi nationality.

1995 King Fahd suffered a debilitating stroke and handed over de facto power to Crown Prince Abdullah.

1996 A bomb exploded at the US military complex near Dhahran.

1997 The Majlis al Shura membership was increased from 60 to 90.

1999 Women were allowed to attend a session of the Majlis al Shura for the first time.

2000 Yemen and Saudi Arabia signed a treaty resolving 65 years of dispute over land and sea boundaries.

2001 Saudi Arabia and Iran signed a security accord to combat terrorism, drug trafficking and organised crime. Out of 19 hijackers involved in the 11 September attacks in the US, 15 were Saudi nationals. King Fahd said that terrorism should be eradicated and that it is prohibited by Islam. Identity cards were issued to women for the first time.

2002 New criminal rights came into force banning torture and giving suspects legal representation. Crown Prince Abdullah

proposed a peace initiative for Israel and Palestine, at the Beirut Summit of the Arab League. He suggested a settlement between Israel and the whole Arab world if Israel withdrew from all Palestinian territories it had occupied since 1967.
2003 Saudi Arabia denied US air bases and troops access to Iraq through its territory during the second invasion of Iraq. More than 300 Saudi intellectuals, including women, signed a petition calling for far-reaching political reforms and around 270 people were arrested when attending a rally in Riyadh, also calling for political reform. King Fahd granted wider powers to the Majlis al Shura, enabling it to initiate legislation without first seeking his permission.
2004 There was a stampede at the Haj pilgrimage in February, in which 251 people died. Security forces killed local al Qaeda leader, Abdul Aziz al Muqrin.
2005 In February, male Saudis voted in the first-ever nationwide municipal elections. King Fahd died on 1 August and was succeeded by his half-brother, Crown Prince Abdullah bin Abdul Aziz. Saudi Arabia became a member of the World Trade Organisation on 11 December.
2006 On 20 October, a committee of princes was created under the Allegiance Institution Law to ensure the orderly succession to the throne.
2008 On 1 January, a common market was created by Bahrain, Kuwait, Oman, Qatar, Saudi Arabia and UAE, the six wealthiest Gulf states. Citizens of these countries are now allowed to travel between and live in any of the six states, where they may find employment, buy properties and businesses and use the educational and health facilities freely.

Political structure

Political parties are not allowed and legislative elections are not held. The Council of Ministers is appointed by and answerable to the king.

Constitution

Saudi Arabia is an absolute monarchy. The country's 1992 Basic Law declares that the Quran is the country's constitution.
A system of provincial government was introduced in 1993. Thirteen regional authorities, subdivided into 103 governorates, provide provincial services alongside district councils and tribal and village councils. The 13 provinces are governed by princes or close relatives of the royal family and governors are appointed by the King.

Form of state

Absolute monarchy

The executive

The Custodian of the Two Holy Mosques, King Fahd ibn Abdul Aziz al Sa'ud, heads the government as prime minister and general commander of the armed forces. Crown Prince Abdullah ibn Abdul Aziz al Sa'ud is first deputy prime minister and commander of the National Guard.
The 25-member Council of Ministers, an executive body appointed for a four-year term by the King, serves as an instrument of royal authority, passing legislation that becomes law once ratified by royal decree. The majority of the Council is comprised of members of the royal family, with the King as Council leader.

National legislature

There is no elected legislature. A Majlis al Shura (Consultative Council) was formed in 1993; it provides a forum for debate. Membership was increased from 60 to 90 in 1997, serving a four-year term. Members are appointed by the King. On 30 November 2003, King Fahd granted wider powers to the Majlis al Shura, enabling it to initiate legislation without first seeking his permission.

Legal system

Saudi Arabia has judicial-Islamic courts of first instance and appeals based on Sharia (Islamic law) and the Sunna (practices or mode of life) of the Prophet Mohammed. Judges are appointed by the King on the recommendation of the Supreme Judicial Council, comprised of 12 senior jurists. Royal decrees and ministerial resolutions have been used to complement Sharia in modern Saudi Arabia and a dual system has developed. Sharia judgements generally override the judgements of non-Sharia tribunals. The King is the final court of appeal and has the power of sentencing or pardoning those found guilty of breaking the law.
In 2002, a new criminal justice system came into force, which included a ban on torture and the right of suspects to legal representation.

Last elections

None

Next elections

Legislative elections are not held. Elections at municipal level were held for the first time in 2005.

Political parties

Ruling party

None

Population

24.29 million (2007)*

Last census: September 2004: 22,678,262

Population density: Urban population: 85 per cent (1995–2001).

Annual growth rate: 2.8 per cent 1994–2004 (WHO 2006)

Ethnic make-up

The majority of Saudis originate in the peninsula and are of Arab extraction, but there is a sizeable minority of the population which has migrated mainly from central Asia and China. One-third of the population is non-Saudi. Most of these are from Yemen, Pakistan, Thailand and the Philippines as well as a significant number from Western Europe and North America.

Religions

The majority of the population is Sunni (Wahhabi) Muslim, with around 8 per cent Shi'a Muslim, the latter being mainly located in the Hasa (Eastern) Province. Sufism is practised throughout the Hejaz, and there is a Sunni Salafi opposition movement which, in particular, opposes the authoritarian rule of the clergy.
Islam's two holiest cities of Makkah (Mecca) and Medina are both in Saudi Arabia.
Despite Islam's recognition of Christians and Jews as People of the Book, public adherence to other faiths is forbidden in the Kingdom.

Education

Although education at all levels is free, it is not compulsory. Both primary and secondary education last for six years and begin at the ages of six and 12 years respectively. On average, boys receive an extra year of schooling (nine years) compared to girls and their education is completely segregated.
The educational system is geared to a future of high technology with computer science taught as a basic subject in secondary schools. However, the education system is widely recognised as being outdated and inefficient. There are over 22,700 schools and colleges, which are attended by about five million students.

Literacy rate: 78 per cent adult rate; 97 per cent youth rate (15–24) (Unesco 2005).

Enrolment rate: 77 per cent boys; 75 per cent girls, total primary enrolment (including repetition rates) of the relevant age group between 1994–2000 (World Bank).

Pupils per teacher: 13 in primary schools.

Health

Per capita total expenditure on health (2003) was US$578; of which per capita government spending was US$439, at the international dollar rate, (WHO 2006).
All medical care, including the cost of medicines, is provided free for Saudi citizens.
Saudi Arabia provides a two-tier health service plan. The first tier comprises a network of over 3,500 primary healthcare centres and clinics established throughout the country. These centres are supplemented by a fleet of mobile clinics that routinely visit the more remote villages and provide basic medical services. A

network of over 300 advanced hospitals and specialised clinics spanning the urban areas constitute the second tier of health services with a capacity of almost 45,000 beds. The King Fahd Medical City in Riyadh is probably the largest medical facility in the Middle East.

Life expectancy: 71 years, 2004 (WHO 2006)

Fertility rate/Maternal mortality rate: 3.9 births per woman, 2004 (WHO 2006)

Birth rate/Death rate: 37 births per 1,000 population; six deaths per 1,000 population (2003).

Child (under 5 years) mortality rate (per 1,000): 46 deaths per 1,000 live births (2004)

Head of population per physician: 1.37 physicians per 1,000 people, 2004 (WHO 2006)

Welfare

The General Organisation for Social Insurance (GOSI) administers programmes that support workers or their families in cases of disability, retirement and death and also covers occupational hazards for employees. Another major programme provides social security pensions, benefits and relief assistance to the disabled, the elderly, orphans and widows without income. The seventh Development Plan (2000—04) aims to expand national programmes for the rehabilitation and welfare of the handicapped, and immunisation of all children against infectious diseases.

Out of the 60 centres around the country that care for those with social, economic and physical problems, six specialise in rehabilitation of juvenile delinquents, nine in assisting the elderly and 14 in caring for orphans. A particularly important government policy has been to provide interest-free, easy-term loans towards low cost home construction for students and low-income employees.

Main cities

Riyadh (capital, estimated population 7.3 million (m) in 2005), Jeddah (4.9m), Makkah (Mecca) (1.8m), Dammam (1.1m), Medina (al Madinah) (1.3m).

Media

National news agency: Saudi Press Agency (SPA)

Press

The press is closely monitored and subject to legal restrictions affecting freedom of expression, censorship is strict and criticism of the government is rare. Most newspapers are privately owned. There was a slight increase in press freedom after the accession of King Abdullah in 2005 although in August 2007 al Hayat was banned for a number of days after it had 'crossed a red line' by criticising the ministry of agriculture's handling of the death of over 2,000 camels from poisoning.

Dailies: Leading newspapers are regionally based. In Arabic, from Dammam al Yaum Newspaper (www.alyaum.com), from Riyadh al Watan (www.alwatan.com.sa), al Jazirah (www.al-jazirah.com), al Sharq al Awsat (www.asharqalawsat.com) and al Riyadh (www.alriyadh.com). From Jeddah, Okaz (www.okaz.com.sa) and al Hayat (www.daralhayat.com), also published in English as well as Arab News (www.arabnews.com) and The Saudi Gazette (www.saudigazette.com.sa). Many foreign publications can be found in the Kingdom.

Weeklies: There are a number of magazines and periodicals, including al Yamama and Igraa. Um al Qura is the official weekly newspaper issued by the Saudi government.

Business: The leading business journal is the Saudi Economic Survey (weekly in English).

Periodicals: Alnafetha

Broadcasting

The Broadcasting Service of the Kingdom of Saudi Arabia (BSKSA) is responsible for all transmissions and no private radio or television networks are allowed to broadcast in Saudi Arabia but may operate from neighbouring countries.

Radio: Saudi Radio (www.saudiradio.net) is state-run, with regional programming and broadcasts in Arabic and English. It runs overseas services in Urdu, Indonesian, Persian, French, Somali and Swahili. Aramco Radio is a private amateur radio station from Dhahran broadcasting in English. Voice of America (VoA) can be received.

Television: BSKSA operates four TV networks including al Ikhbariya a news channel. The private and independent satellite broadcaster Arab Radio and Television Network (known as ART) (www.art-tv.net), based in Jeddah, operates 10 domestic and five international channels, by subscription. There are many satellite and cable TV stations operating from outside Saudi Arabia.

Advertising

Saudi Arabia is the largest advertising market in the Gulf, with total advertising expenditure typically reaching US$300 million per annum. Newspaper advertising is the most popular form, representing over 60 per cent of total spending. All advertising is subject to review of content and image.

Economy

With the world's largest reserves of oil and as leading member of the Organisation of Petroleum Exporting Countries (Opec), Saudi Arabia's economy is dominated by oil and gas, which provides 95 per cent of GDP. The government has a fairly unusual problem, in a world where most administrations are borrowing to pay for spending, Saudi Arabia has to manage an economy with a large surplus (over US$30 billion in windfall amounts in 2005 alone), which is typically ready to pump up inflation. Oil prices rose sharply in 2005 and the balance of trade increased dramatically with an estimated US$90.8 billion, which is forecast to increase to US$98.1 billion in 2006. The external current account was projected to reach 31.3 per cent of GDP in 2006. However, inflation remained low at 0.4 per cent in 2005, as much of the surplus was used to reduce government debt.

Structural reforms and an expansion of the non-oil economy have increased employment rates; the government's target is to create 800,000 new jobs a year for Saudi nationals. Further investment in private sector growth through increased spending, in places where social and private returns are judged to be best, are underway, including infrastructure development.

Ultimately, the economy is underpinned by its vast oil reserves, which will last another century at current rates of production. Diversification is needed to strengthen the economy, but reliance on oil continues.

The slow pace of economic reforms and a lack of accountability in government is being questioned by the public who want an explanation as to how the oil money is spent, particularly with unexplained persistent budget deficits and a lack of transparency.

As a member of the WTO since 2005, Saudi Arabia has undertaken to liberalise its trade regime and accelerate its integration into the world economy.

External trade

In 2005 the Greater Arab Free Trade Area (Gafta) was ratified by 17 members, including Saudi Arabia, creating an Arab economic bloc. A customs union was established whereby tariffs within Gafta will be reduced by a percentage each year, until none remain.

Saudi Arabia was a founder member of the Organization of the Petroleum Exporting Countries (Opec) which organises oil production policies of 13 members countries.

Pocessing one-quarter of the world total reserves of oil, around 95 per cent of GDP is provided by oil and export trade provides almost 87 per cent of GDP.

Imports
Main imports are vehicles, machinery and equipment, industrial raw materials and foodstuffs.
Main sources: US (13.0 per cent total, 2005), Germany (9.5 per cent), Japan (7.9 per cent), China (7.3 per cent), France (4.7 per cent), Italy (4.2 per cent)

Exports
The principal export is petroleum; minor exports include petrochemical, construction material and agricultural products.
Main destinations: US (16.4 per cent total, 2005), Japan (16.1 per cent), South Korea (9.1 per cent), China (6.9 per cent), Singapore (5.1 per cent), Taiwan (4.2 per cent)

Agriculture

Farming

The sector contributes around 5 per cent to GDP and employs 4 per cent of the labour force. Agricultural produce accounts for only around 5 per cent of non-oil exports.

Agricultural development projects have helped Saudi Arabia achieve self-sufficiency in wheat, eggs, some dairy products and vegetables. The development of water desalination plants is crucial to future development.

The role of agriculture in the overall economy is being re-evaluated. Subsidies have created large surpluses of wheat, while agricultural production has depleted scarce water supplies.

The agricultural sector is heavily subsidised and accounts for 90 per cent of Saudi Arabia's 14–16 billion cubic metres of annual water consumption. The policy of agricultural expansion has come under heavy criticism, as some 3,000 tonnes of water is required to produce one tonne of wheat, most of which is then exported. At present rates of depletion, fossil water sources are not expected to last more than 20 years. The importance of conservation and subsidy reduction to slow water demand is clear, but this needs to be balanced against the need to expand Saudi Arabia's agricultural output.

Most agricultural activity is north of Riyadh in Qasim, Hail and Al-Jauf areas and on a smaller scale in Wadi Dawasir and Abha. Despite significant growth in agricultural production, Saudi Arabia increasingly relies on imports to meet the demands of a rapidly growing population.

Estimated crop production in 2005 included: 2,834,199 tonnes (t) cereals in total, 2,400,000t wheat, 138,432t barley, 43,697t maize, 243,746t sorghum, 320,897t potatoes, 2,151t oilcrops, 900,540t dates, 440,033t tomatoes, 101,653t grapes, 73,204t eggplants, 140,000t citrus fruit, 1,322,193t fruit in total, 1,949,897t vegetables in total.

Livestock production included: 658,300t meat in total, 22,800t beef, 76,000t lamb, 22,500t goat meat, 495,700t poultry, 143,000t eggs, 1,149,000t milk, 174t honey, 41,300t camel meat, 32,000t sheepskins.

Fishing

Saudi Arabia has a small and developing fishing industry. The Saudi Fisheries Company (SFC) operates the fishing fleet, comprising 49 vessels. SFC operates four processing plants in Dammam, Jazan, Jeddah and Riyadh. Annual catch includes bream, barracuda, mackerel, sardine and tuna.

In 2004, the total marine fish catch was 44,867 tonnes and the total crustacean catch was 9,053 tonnes.

Forestry

Forest and wooded land accounts only for 1 per cent of Saudi Arabia's total land area. Most wood products are imported; timber imports in 2004 amounted to US$828.1 million, while exports were US$18.1 million.

Industry and manufacturing

Saudi Arabia's economy is dominated by the oil industry, with the majority of manufactured goods imported and the services sector largely supporting the hydrocarbon sector. The industrial sector accounts for around 55 per cent of GDP, while manufacturing accounts for only 10 per cent.

The government has played a major role in the economy since an industrialisation programme was launched in the 1960s. Despite attempts to develop the private sector and withdraw the state from the economy, such attempts have not progressed very far. The main sector, oil, is dominated by the largest domestic oil company – the 100 per cent state-owned Saudi Arabian Oil Company (Saudi Aramco). Upstream oil exploration and development, the country's most lucrative industry, is closed to foreign investment, with all activities undertaken by Saudi Aramco.

The state also intervenes in the price of domestic goods, with significant subsidies provided on a wide range of agricultural, utility and industrial products. As a result, the domestic economy rarely reflects international market prices.

Tourism

Little effort has been made to attract non-Arab tourists. The annual pilgrimage (haj) brings some two million Muslim visitors each year to the holy cities, Makkah and Medina. Other principal destinations are the capital, Riyadh, and the commercial centre, Jeddah.

The government has established a commission for tourism to develop the sector as part of its diversification policy. Facilities are being expanded to encourage the domestic population to spend their holidays in the country (an estimated US$6 billion is spent on overseas vacations each year) and pilgrims on haj to extend their visits. With the basic infrastructure already developed, resources are going into accommodation and recreational facilities, including resort cities and amusement parks.

The commission has also been charged with developing plans to promote the country to non-Muslim visitors. Around 6,000 such tourists visit each year, mainly in groups organised by Saudi Arabian Airlines. The development of Saudi holiday destinations for western tourists may prove to be difficult to achieve, as local conditions clash with tourist expectations. Not all historic sites are open to non-Muslims, while hotel resorts must conform to Islamic traditions of modest dress, temperance and the social separation of men and single women.

Tourism is expected to contribute around two per cent to GDP in 2005.

Mining

The exploitation of mineral resources other than oil is the responsibility of the petroleum and minerals resources ministry.

The principal minerals are gold, silver, copper, zinc, lead, iron, magnesite, bauxite, phosphates, beryl, fluorite, magnesium, salt and sulphur and certain radioactive minerals. Other sought-after minerals are those used for making cement and plaster such as granite, sandstone, coral stone and marble. Saudi Arabia is self-sufficient in these materials. Industrial minerals produced include limestone, gypsum, sulphur, marble, clay and salt. Much of the mineral deposits can be extracted by surface mining or quarrying. A new mining code passed in January 2005 seeks to attract more foreign companies, mainly by giving them greater freedom to invest as they see fit. Gold exploration has been opened up to foreign companies for the first time.

Hydrocarbons

Saudi Arabia is the world's largest producer and exporter of oil, with proven reserves of 262.7 billion barrels. Output stood at 10.6 million barrels per day (bpd) in 2004. Oil exports make up over 90 per cent of total export revenues and around 40 per cent of GDP. The United States is one of Saudi Arabia's largest customers, but following the war in Iraq more emphasis is placed on exporting to Europe, China and Russia.

Saudi Arabia has eight refineries with a total capacity of 2.06 million bpd in 2004, an increase of 7.8 per cent over 2003. While there are approximately 80 oil and gas fields in Saudi Arabia, over half of the country's reserves are located in eight fields. Of these, the most significant is Ghawar (the world's largest onshore oil field), Abqaiq, Safaniya (the world's largest offshore field), and Berri. Natural gas reserves amounted to 6.75 trillion cubic metres in 2004. Total gas production in 2004 was 64 billion cubic metres, an increase of 6.6 per cent over the previous year. This is all consumed domestically. Future exploration by Saudi Aramco is to be focused on pure natural gas in order to meet domestic demand, which is growing at about 8 per cent a year. Previously, all the gas produced was a by-product of oil production. A number of new gas fields have been discovered in recent years.

With record prices and a high demand for oil, the government agreed to increase the production of oil by 200,000bpd, from July 2008, which when coupled with the extra production in May, brings the total to 500,000bpd over the typical daily amount. The oil minister considered world oil price, which reached US$139 per barrels on 6 June 2008, was abnormal and unjustified and caused by speculators and not by any shortage in crude oil.

Energy

Generating capacity is estimated at 25GW. Power demand is growing at a rate of 4.5 per cent per annum; Saudi Arabia has the world's highest per capita consumption. It is estimated that 66GW will be needed by 2020, calling for investment of US$2 billion per annum, mainly from the private sector and most of which will be spent on gas-fired power stations. The sector is monopoly-conytrolled by the Saudi Electricity Company (SEC), which was established in April 2000 as a joint-stock company, 50 per cent owned by the Saudi government.

Financial markets

Stock exchange

The Saudi stock exchange was opened to foreign investment in 1997. Saudi Arabia's stock market is around twice the size of the Egyptian stock market, the second largest in the Middle East and North Africa region. The market is led by the banking sector. In October 2001, the Saudi Arabian Monetary Agency (SAMA) created a new stock market, Tadawul, which offers high-tech trading and real-time transactions. It is envisaged that Tadawul will become part of a regional market network. From 25 March 2006 foreign residents have been allowed to invest directly in the stock market, although not able to participate in initial public offerings (IPOs).

Banking and insurance

Islamic banking rules are in force. The sector comprises 10 domestically-owned banks. Foreigners cannot own more than 49 per cent of domestic banks and foreign participation is mostly in the form of joint-ventures.

Central bank

Saudi Arabian Monetary Agency (SAMA)

Main financial centre

Riyadh

Time

GMT plus three hours

Geography

Saudi Arabia is bordered to the north by Egypt (the Sinai Peninsula), Jordan, Iraq and Kuwait; to the south by Yemen, Oman, the United Arab Emirates, Qatar and Bahrain (connected by a causeway); to the west by the Red Sea; and to the east by the Persian Gulf.

Saudi Arabia is a mainly barren land covering an area of 2.24 million square km. On the western coast is the Tihama plain, a hot region almost devoid of rainfall but with a humid coast. Inland from the Tihama rises a steep escarpment. In the centre of the Kingdom lies the Najd region and the Rub al-Khali (Empty Quarter) lies in the south-east. The eastern province, containing the oil fields, has an undulating topography with rocky outcrops.

Hemisphere

Northern

Climate

Average maximum temperatures are 38 degrees Celsius (C) in summer and the winter minimum is 13 degrees C. The summers are generally hot and dry (although humidity in some areas may reach 90 per cent) and the winters are cold. The coastal towns tend to be hot and humid all year. Rainfall in the Kingdom rarely exceeds 250mm a year, except in the extreme south-west.

Dress codes

A lightweight suit or jacket and trousers are advised. A tie and a long sleeved shirt should be worn at business meetings, but a jacket is not essential. Women should dress modestly, covering their arms and knees. Expatriate women often find it convenient to wear an abaya, a wrap-around shoulder cloak.

Entry requirements

Passports

Required by all, valid for six months from date of entry, except pilgrims with passes.

Visa

Required by all. Pilgrims should apply for visas through a visa agency accredited to an embassy of Saudi Arabia. During Haj and Umrah, pilgrims and visitors must have a valid certificate of vaccination against the ACWY strains of meningitis.

For business visas a letter of invitation from a Saudi company, endorsed by a Saudi Chamber of Commerce and Industry, must be faxed directly by the sponsor company to the Consulate to which the application is submitted. The original or copy of this invitation, together with an introductory letter from the employee's company addressed to the Embassy, should be submitted with the application form.

Women visitors are required to be met by their sponsor upon arrival. Women travelling alone, who are not met by sponsors, may experience delays before being allowed to enter or, if in transit, to continue their journey.

Prohibited entry

Travellers who arrive obviously inebriated are liable to arrest or deportation. Israeli nationals are barred from entering the Kingdom and an Israeli visa or stamp in a visitor's passport is likely to result in a ban on entry. Consultation with Saudi officials prior to departure is strongly recommended.

Currency advice/regulations

There are no restrictions on the import or export of local and foreign, except Israeli, currencies.

Customs

Personal effects are allowed duty-free. Duty is chargeable on many imported items, starting at 12 per cent but rising to 20 per cent for goods normally manufactured in the Kingdom; no duty on samples of low value.

Prohibited imports

The penalty for smuggling, promoting or circulating illegal drugs is capital punishment.

Other prohibitions include anything with an alcoholic content, certain foodstuffs (such as pork), pornography and censored literature. Prescription drugs should be carried only in small quantities in original containers. Dogs are banned, with the exception of guard dogs, hunting dogs and guide dogs.

Health (for visitors)

Mandatory precautions

A certificate of vaccination against yellow fever is required if travelling from an infected area.

During Haj and Umrah, pilgrims and visitors must have a valid certificate of vaccination against the ACWY strains of meningitis.

Advisable precautions

Vaccinations against cholera, typhoid and polio are recommended. Medical facilities in the Kingdom are excellent and there are few obvious health hazards.

Saudi Arabia is considered a high risk area for rabies, any animal or bat bites should be assessed carefully.

Hotels
There are many good hotels in the Kingdom. Alcoholic drinks are strictly prohibited.

Credit cards
All major credit cards are accepted.

Public holidays (national)
The Islamic year contains 354 or 355 days, with the result that Muslim feasts advance by 10–12 days against the Gregorian calendar. Dates of feasts vary according to the sighting of the new moon, so cannot be forecast exactly. During the Haj, which immediately precedes Eid al Adha, government offices and some businesses close for 10 days. Work schedules may be seriously disrupted during the month of Ramadan, and businesses may take time off for other Islamic holidays.
Fixed dates
23 Sep (Saudi National Day)
For civil purposes, Saudi Arabia uses the Umm-ul-Qura calendar.
Variable dates
Eid al Adha (five days), Eid al Fitr (three days).

Working hours
Banking
Sat–Wed: 0830–1200 and 1700–1900; Thu: 0830–1130; 1000–1330 during Ramadan.
Business
Sat–Wed: 0800–1200, 1630–2000 in Riyadh; 0900—1330, 1630–2000 in Jeddah; 0730–1200, 1430–1730 in Eastern Province (closed Thu afternoon and Fri).
Private business offices in other areas: 0800–1200; 1500–1800.
Government
0730–1430 (Sat–Wed); 1000–1430 during Ramadan.
Shops
0800/0830–1200 and 1600–2100/2200; closed Thursday and Friday and four times a day for prayer for up to half an hour.

Telecommunications
Telephone/fax
The Saudi telephone system is highly modernised and direct dialling is available to most of the world. The telephone, telex, telegraph and fax systems are operated by the Ministry of Posts, Telegraphs and Telecommunications (MOPTT).
The country's massive demand for telephone and fax connections has put the Kingdom's 2.3 million line capacity system under pressure. The telephone network is serviced by satellite and microwave systems as well as underground cables. The government, in a partnership with AT&T of the US, is embarking on a large scale telecommunications upgrade programme, Telephone Expansion Project 7 (TEP7), which will provide an additional four million lines by 2002.

Electricity supply
127V or 220V AC, 60 cycles, with two-pin European-type plugs and both bayonet and screw light fittings in use. 380V AC, 60 cycles is used by industry.

Social customs/useful tips
Punctuality is not always a Saudi virtue. While the foreign businessman will be expected to arrive at a meeting punctually, his Saudi counterpart may think nothing of being late or even of not showing up at all. Always shake hands (with your right hand) on meeting and leaving.
Take account of business hours and prayer times when making appointments; Saturday to Thursday is working week in Saudi Arabia.
Hospitality to the stranger lies at the heart of Arabian life. It is polite to accept at least one cup of tea or coffee when it is offered: oscillate the coffee cup when you do not want any more, otherwise the server will continue to fill it. Do not eat or drink with the left hand, as it is considered unclean; do not point the sole of your shoe at a Saudi at any time. You may ask after a man's children but not after his wife.
Saudi women are generally barred from public life. They do not drive and schools and universities are segregated.
The possession of alcohol is illegal. Although it is discreetly available it should not, in general, be offered to Saudis.

Security
Visitors should keep in touch with developments in the Middle East as any increase in regional tension might affect travel advice.
The level of street crime has traditionally been far lower than in the west however, the influx of immigrant workers since the early 1970s has encouraged incidents of theft, although murder and violent crimes such as mugging and rape remain relatively rare.

Getting there
Air
National airline: Saudi Arabian Airlines (Saudia).
International airport/s: Jeddah-King Abdul Aziz International (JED), 18km north of city;, restaurant, bank, post office, shops, car hire and special pilgrimage facilities (during the annual pilgimages, the number of passengers using Jeddah airport can swell by 1.5m adding considerable delays to passport and visa controls); Riyadh-King Khaled International (RUH), 35km from the city; mosque, post office, bank, restaurant, shops, car hire.
Airport tax: SR50; not applicable to pilgrims.
Surface
Road: There are links to all countries sharing a common border with Saudi Arabia, as well as Bahrain via the causeway.
Main port/s: Dammam, Jeddah, Jizan, Jubail, Ras Tanura and Yanbu.

Getting about
National transport
Non-Muslims may not travel to the holy cities of Medina and Makkah (Mecca).
Air: Air travel is the most convenient way of getting around Saudi Arabia; there are numerous airports. Saudi Arabian Airlines operates a comprehensive schedule of domestic flights between Jeddah and Riyadh and other major centres. Always confirm flight bookings 24-hours before take-off, especially during the annual pilgrimage (Haj).
Road: The total length of the Saudi road network is over 156,000km, of which around 50,000km is asphalted and the remainder earth-surfaced. The main centres are linked by the Trans-Arabian Highway. Much of the network is of a high standard and undergoes regular maintenance and improvement.
Buses: Saudi Arabian Public Transport Company (SAPTCO) operates frequent bus services throughout the country on numerous local and national routes. Travel by bus is comparatively cheap and an increasingly favoured means of seeing the country.
Rail: Daily rail service links Riyadh and Damman, with refreshments and air-conditioning available.
City transport
Taxis: Taxis are yellow and should have a visible meter and taxi number in addition to normal registration. If using a taxi, it is adviable to agree the fare in advance. Taxi drivers do not expect a tip.
White limousines are operated by a number of companies within the cities and especially to and from airports. Fixed fares for specific journeys are prominently displayed at airports and available from drivers.
Car hire
Available at airports and main hotels. Driving licence required. Valid licences from most countries will be accepted by car hire companies. Women are not allowed to drive (although in 2008 two Saudi Scholars said that there is nothing in Islamic law that forbids women drivers). Driving is on the right-hand side of road at maximum 110kph on motorways and 40kph in cities. Insurance claims are not legally enforceable unless a police certification of the damage is obtained. Chauffeur-driven service is usually recommended.

BUSINESS DIRECTORY

The addresses listed below are a selection only. While World of Information makes every endeavour to check these addresses, we cannot guarantee that changes have not been made, especially to telephone numbers and area codes. We would welcome any corrections.

Telephone area codes

The international direct dialling (IDD) code for Saudi Arabia is +966, followed by area code and subscriber's number:

Jeddah	2	Medina	4
Hofuf	3	Qatif	3
Makkah	2	Riyadh	1

Useful telephone numbers

Emergency police: 999
Ambulance: 997
Traffic accidents: 993
Fire: 998
Directory enquiries: 905

Chambers of Commerce

Abha Chamber of Commerce & Industry, PO Box 722, Abha (tel: 227-1818; fax: 227-1919).

Al-Baha Chamber of Commerce & Industry, PO Box 311, Al-Baha (tel: 725-0476; fax: 727-0146).

American Business Association - Eastern Province, PO Box 1868, Al-Khobar 31952 (tel: 882-5288 ext 1253; fax: 882-5288 ext 1497; e-mail: abaep@al-bustinet.com).

American Businessmen's Group of Riyadh, PO Box 8273, 11482 Riyadh (tel: 478-2738; fax: 476-4363).

British Businessmen's Group - Jeddah, PO Box 393, Jeddah (tel: 622-5550; fax: 622-6249; e-mail: bbj@tri.net,sa).

Eastern Province Chamber of Commerce and Industry, PO Box 719, Dammam 31421 (tel: 857-1111; fax: 857-0607).

Jeddah Chamber of Commerce and Industry, PO Box 1264, Jeddah 21431 (tel: 651-5111; fax: 651-7373; e-mail: info@jcci.org.sa; website: www.jcci.org.sa).

Jizan Chamber of Commerce & Industry, PO Box 201, Jizan (tel: 322-5155; fax: 322-3635).

Makkah Chamber of Commerce and Industry, PO Box 1086, Makkah (tel: 534-3838; fax: 534-2904).

Medina Chamber of Commerce and Industry, PO Box 443, Medina (tel: 826-8961; fax: 826-8965).

Najran Chamber of Commerce & Industry, PO Box 1138, Najran (tel: 522-2216; fax: 522-3926).

Riyadh Chamber of Commerce and Industry, PO Box 596, Riyadh 11421 (tel: 404-0044; fax: 402-1103; website: www.riyadhchamber.com).

Tabuk Chamber of Commerce & Industry, PO Box 567, Tabuk (tel: 422-0464; fax: 422-7387).

Taif Chamber of Commerce and Industry, PO Box 1005, Taif (tel: 736-6800; Fax: 738-0040).

Yanbu Chamber of Commerce & Industry, PO Box 58, Yanbu (tel: 322-7722; fax: 322-6800).

Banking

Arab National Bank, PO Box 56921, Riyadh 11411 (tel: 402-9000; fax: 403-0052).

Al Bank al Saudi al Fransi, PO Box 56006, Riyadh 11421 (tel: 477-4770; fax: 404-2311).

Al Rajhi Banking & Investment Corporation, PO Box 28, Riyadh 11411 (tel: 405-4244; fax: 403-2969).

Bank al Jazira, PO Box 6277, Jeddah 21442 (tel: 660-8820; fax: 661-3044).

National Commercial Bank, PO Box 3555, Jeddah 21421 (tel: 644-6644; fax: 643-7670; internet site: http://www.alahli.com/islamic_banking).

Riyad Bank, PO Box 22622, Riyadh 11411 (tel: 401-0908; fax: 404-0090).

Saudi American Bank, PO Box 833, Riyadh 11421 (tel: 477-4770).

Saudi British Bank, PO Box 9084, Riyadh 11413 (tel: 405-0677; fax: 405-0660).

Saudi Hollandi Bank, PO Box 1467, Riyadh (tel: 406-7888; fax: 401-0968).

Saudi Investment Bank, PO Box 3533, Riyadh (tel: 477-8433; fax: 478-1557).

Central bank

Saudi Arabian Monetary Agency, PO Box 2992, Riyadh 11169 (tel: 463-3000; fax: 466-2936; e-mail: info@sama.gov.sa).

Travel information

Saudi Arabian Airlines, PO Box 620, Jeddah 21231 (tel: 684-2000; fax: 686-4552; e-mail: webmaster@saudiairlines.com.sa).

National tourist organisation offices

Supreme Commission for Tourism, Kindi Center, PO Box 66680, Riyadh 11586 (tel: 480-8855; fax: 480-8844; e-mail: info@sctsaudi.com).

Ministries

Ministry of Agriculture & Water, PO Box 2639, Airport Road, Riyadh 11195 (tel: 401-6666; fax: 403-1415).

Ministry of Communication, PO Box 3813, Airport Road, Riyadh 11178 (tel: 404-3000; fax: 403-1401).

Ministry of Defence and Aviation, Airport Road, Riyadh 11165 (tel: 478-5900; fax: 401-1336).

Ministry of Education, Airport Road, Riyadh 11148 (tel: 404-2888; fax: 401-2365).

Ministry of Foreign Affairs, Nesseriya St. Riyadh 11124 (tel: 406-7777; fax: 403-0159; internet site: http://www.mofa.gov.sa).

Ministry of Health, PO Box 21217, Airport Road, Riyadh 11176 (tel: 401-2220; fax 402-9876).

Ministry of Higher Education, PO Box 1683, Riyadh 11153 (tel: 464-4444; fax: 441-9004).

Ministry of Information, PO Box 843, Nasseriya Street, Riyadh 11161 (tel: 401-4440; fax: 402-3570).

Ministry of Interior, PO Box 2933, Airport Road, Riyadh 11134 (tel: 401-1944; fax: 403-1185).

Ministry of Islamic Affairs, Endowments, Call and Guidance, Riyadh 11232 (tel: 473-0401).

Ministry of Labour & Social Affairs, PO Box 1182, Omar Ibn Al-Khatab Street, Riyadh 11157 (tel: 477-1480; fax: 477-7336).

Ministry of Justice, University Street, Riyadh 11137 (tel: 405-7777).

Ministry of Municipal and Rural Affairs, PO Box 5736, Nasseriya Street, Riyadh 11136 (tel: 441-5434; fax: 456-3196).

Ministry of Petroleum/Mineral Resources, PO Box 757, Airport Road, Riyadh 11189 (tel: 478-1661; fax: 479-3596).

Ministry of Pilgrimage, Omar Ibn Al-Khatab Street, Riyadh 11183 (tel:402-2200; fax: 402-2555).

Ministry of Post, Telegraphs & Telephones, Intercontinental Road, Riyadh 11112 (tel: 463-7225; fax: 405-2310).

Ministry of Public Works & Housing, Weshem Street, PO Box 56059, Riyadh 11151 (tel: 402-2268; fax: 402-2723 (public works), 406-7376 (housing)).

Other useful addresses

Arabian Oil Company, PO Box 256, Khafji 31971 (tel: 766-0555; fax: 766-2001).

Arab Petroleum Investments Corporation, PO Box 448, Dhahran Airport 31932 (tel: 864-7400; fax: 894-5076).

Arab Satellite Communiction Organisation, PO Box 1038, Riyadh 11431 (tel: 464-6666; fax: 465-6983).

Central Department of Statistics, PO Box 3735, Off Airport Road, Riyadh 11187 (tel:405-9638; fax: 405-9493).

Central Planning Organisation, Ministry of Planning, Riyadh.

Civil Defence, Airport Road, Riyadh 11174 (tel: 479-2828; fax: 478-0846).

Civil Service Commission, Washem Street, PO Box 18367, Riyadh 11114 (tel: 402-6900; fax: 403-4998).

Customs Department, PO Box 3483, Riyadh 11471 (tel: 401-3334; fax: 404-3412).

Dammam Seaport (King Abdul Aziz Sea Port) PO Box 28062, Dammam 31188 (tel: 833-2500; fax: 857-9223).

Dhahran International Expo, PO Box 7519, Dammam 31742 (tel: 833-7900; fax: 833-8010).

Director-General of Mineral Resources, PO Box 2880, Jeddah 21461 (tel: 631-0355; fax: 631-0357).

Directorate General of Zakat and Income Tax, Off Airport Road, Riyadh 11187 (tel: 404-1537; fax: 404-1495).

Federation of GCC Chambers, PO Box 2198, Dammam 31451 (tel: 826-5943; fax: 826-6794).

General Electricity Corp. (ELECTRICO), PO Box 1185, Riyadh 11431 (tel: 477-2772; fax: 477-5322).

General Organisation for Petroleum & Minerals (PETROMIN), PO Box 757, Riyadh 11189 (tel: 498-0995).

General Organisation for Social Insurance (GOSI), PO Box 2963, Riyadh 11461 (tel: 477-7735; fax: 477-9958).

General Organistion for Technical Education and Vocational Training, PO Box 7823, Riyadh 11472 (tel: 405-2770; fax: 406-5876).

General Ports Authority, PO Box 5162, Riyadh 11422 (tel: 476-0600).

General Presidency for Girls' Education, Television Street, Riyadh 11192 (tel: 402-9877; fax: 403-9570).

Grievances Court (Diwan-Al-Mazalem) Morabba-Nasseria Street, Riyadh 11138 (tel: 402-1724; fax: 403-4296).

Institute of Public Administration (IPA), PO Box 205, Riyadh 11411 (tel: 476-1600; fax: 479-2136).

International Airports Projects, PO Box 6326, Jeddah 21174 (tel: 685-4200).

Irish Embassy, Diplomatic Quarter, PO Box 94349, Riyadh 11693 (tel: 488-2300; fax: 488-0927; e-mail: irishembassy@awalnet,net.sa).

Jeddah Broadcasting Service, Broadcasting Station, Jeddah.

Jeddah Seaport, (Jeddah Islamic Port) PO Box 9285, Jeddah 21188 (tel: 643-2552).

King Abdul Aziz City for Science and Technology, PO Box 6068, Riyadh 11442 (tel: 478-8000; fax: 488-13756).

Meteorology and Environment Protection Agency, PO Box 1358, Jeddah 21431 (tel: 651-8887).

National Guard, PO Box 9799, Riyadh 11423 (tel: 491-2400; fax: 491-2824).

Presidency of Civil Aviation, Off Palestine Road East, PO Box 887, Jeddah 21421 (tel: 667-9000).

Real Estate Development Fund, PO Box 5591, Riyadh 11433 (tel: 477-5120; fax: 479-0148).

Royal Commission for Jubail and Yanbu, PO Box 5864, Riyadh 11432 (tel: 479-4444; fax: 477-5404).

Saline Water Conversion Corporation (SWCC), PO Box 5968, Riyadh 11432 (tel: 463-0501; fax: 463-1952).

Saudi Arabian Airlines Corporation, PO Box 620, Jeddah 21421 (tel: 684-2000; fax: 686-4552).

Saudi Arabian Embassy (USA), 601 New Hampshire Avenue, NW, Washington DC 20037 (tel: (+1-202 -342-3800; fax: (+1-202) 944-3140; e-mail: info@saudiembassy.net).

Saudi Arabian Oil Company (Saudi Aramco), PO Box 5000, Dhahran Airport 31311 (tel: 875-5229; fax: 876-6520).

Saudi Arabian Standards Organisation, PO Box 3437, Riyadh 11471 (tel: 479-3332; fax: 479-3063).

Saudi Aramco (Saudi Arabian Oil Company), PO Box 5000, Dhahran 31311 (tel: 875-4915; fax: 873-8490).

Saudi Basic Industries Corporation (SABIC), PO Box 5105, Riyadh 11422 (tel: 401-2033; fax: 401-2045).

Saudi Export Development Centre, PO Box 16683, Riyadh 11474 (tel: 405-3200; fax: 402-4747).

Saudi Fund for Development, PO Box 50483, Riyadh 11523 (tel: 464-0292; fax: 464-7450; e-mail: info@sfd.gov.sa; website: www.sfd.gov.sa).

Saudi National Shipping Company, Po Box 8931, Riyadh 11492 (tel: 478-5454; fax: 477-8036).

Saudi Ports Authority, Riyadh 11188 (tel: 405-0005; fax: 405-9974).

Saudi Public Transport Co, PO box 10667, Riyadh 11443 (tel: 454-5000; fax: 454-2100).

Saudi Railroad Organisation, PO Box 92, Dammam 31411 (tel: 871-2222; fax: 827-1130).

Saudi Red Crescent Association, al Dhabab Road, Riyadh 11129 (tel: 406-9072; fax: 405-1566).

Youth Welfare Organisation, PO Box 965, Riyadh 11421 (tel: 401-4576; fax: 401-0376).

National news agency: Saudi Press Agency (SPA)

Internet sites

Arab net: www.arab.net/welcome.html

Arabia on line: www.arabia.com

Saudi Arabia Information Resourse (in London): wwwsaudinf.com

Saudi Embassy, UK, with web links to other Saudi enterprises: www.saudiembassy.org.uk/index2.htm

Saudi Times: www.sauditimes.com

KEY FACTS

Official name: République du Sénégal (Republic of Senegal)

Head of State: President Abdoulaye Wade (PDS) (since 2000; re-elected 25 Feb 2007)

Head of government: Prime Minister Macky Sall (PDS) (appointed 21 Apr 2004)

Ruling party: Coalition: Sopi (Change) alliance led by Parti Démocratique Sénégalais (PDS) (Senegalese Democratic Party) and Ligue Démocratique-Mouvement pour le Parti du Travial (LD-MPT) (Democratic League - Movement for the Labour Party) (since 2001; re-elected 3 Jun 2007)

Area: 196,192 square km

Population: 12.23 million (2007)

Capital: Dakar

Official language: French

Currency: CFA franc (CFAf) = 100 centimes (Communauté Financière Africaine (African Financial Community) franc). New notes are in circulation; old notes cease to be legal tender in 2005.

Exchange rate: CFAf413.80 per US$ (Jul 2008); CFAf655.95 per euro (pegged from Jan 1999)

GDP per capita: US$910 (2007)

GDP real growth: 5.00% (2007)

Labour force: 4.67 million (2004)

Unemployment: 48.00% (2005)*

Inflation: 5.90% (2007)

Balance of trade: -US$1.92 billion (2006)

Foreign debt: US$3.94 billion (2004)

* estimated figure

Senegal

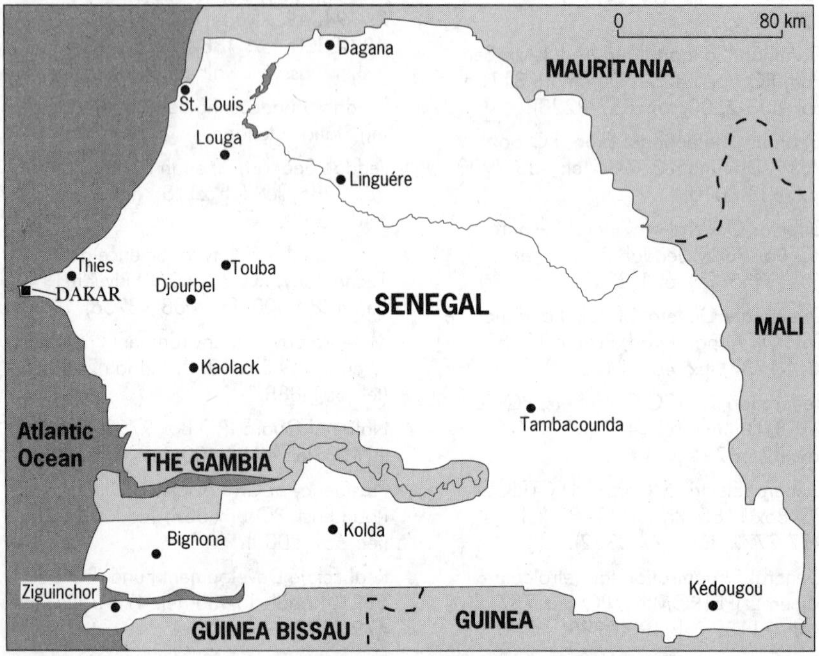

Parliamentary elections, scheduled to be held on the same day as presidential elections on 25 February 2007, were postponed until June by a court order, due to a legal challenge to the organisation of the polls and a charge of gerrymandering of certain constituencies, by the president.

As it happened Abdoulaye Wade won the presidential election comfortably, beating four other candidates. On 3 June in the general elections the ruling Sopi (Change) alliance led by Parti Démocratique Sénégalais (PDS) (Senegalese Democratic Party) and Ligue Démocratique-Mouvement pour le Parti du Travial (LD-MPT) (Democratic League - Movement for the Labour Party) won 69.2 per cent of the vote (131 seats, out of 150). Turnout was 34.8 per cent. The opposition boycotted the election claiming there was a need for an independent electoral commission and a new, transparent voter list. In August the Senate (upper house) was reinstated, with elections for one-third of its members, while the president appointed the remaining two-thirds, for five-year terms.

Unlike the British, whose chief imperial pre-occupations were the maintenance of peace so that trade could flourish, the French had a vision of their imperial purpose and destiny which was much more grandiose. Confident that French civilisation was the pinnacle of man's earthly achievements they sought to pass it on to the people they ruled. Nowhere was this more apparent than in Senegal, a country in which the arts and culture of France have continued to enjoy greater importance than almost anywhere else on the African continent.

Economy

Key components of Senegal's economic and financial plan for the years ahead are that the government is seeking to improve quality and expand availability of basic social services; it is continuing its infrastructure investment programme and strategy to promote the growth of private investment. An investment code and new corporate tax legislation have been simplified.

The improvement in access to credit for the establishment and growth of enterprises, in particular small and medium-sized enterprises, is a priority. The government wants the central bank, banks and financial institutions, microfinance institutions, and the regional stock market to foster the contribution of the financial sector to the development of economic activity.

Initiatives at regional level have been to increase bank financing to the economy, promote the regional financial market, and enhance the soundness of the financial sector.

The International Monetary Fund (IMF), in a report published in June 2008 noted that over the last decade Senegal had achieved macroeconomic stability and recorded economic growth above that of other West African Economic and Monetary Union (WAEMU) countries. Buoyant activity in the services and construction sectors helped to increase GDP growth for 2007 to 5.0 per cent. A satisfactory increase over the 2.1 per cent of 2006. However, agriculture experience a second year output drop, and inflation was a record 5.9 per cent.

Rising energy and food prices had contributed to the rise in inflation. As a result, in mid-2007, the government suspended the implementation of value added tax (VAT) and customs duties on some food items. This settled inflation at a lower rate, but the budgetary costs were adverse at 1.5 per cent of GDP.

Senegal's macroeconomic polices are being carried out under an economic programme supported an IMF Policy Support Instrument (PIS), which includes safeguarding debt sustainability, improving fiscal governance and transparency, encouraging the private sector and raising the financial sector's contribution to the economy.

Outlook

Senegal remains one of the most stable democracies in Africa. It has an established multi-party system and a tradition of civilian rule and peaceful transfers of power over its 45 years of independence from France. It has a long history of participation in international peacekeeping. Although poverty is widespread and unemployment is high, the country has one of the region's more stable economies. Wade supports stronger ties with the United States and greater regional integration with a unified external tariff and a more stable monetary policy.

President Wade is a supporter of the New Partnership for Africa's Development (Nepad) and plays an active role in encouraging conflict resolution in West Africa. President Wade is a lawyer and a veteran politician. He has been exiled and imprisoned several times. He founded the Parti Démocratique Sénegalais (PDS) (Senegalese Democratic Party) and has run in five presidential races.

Risk assessment

Politics	Good
Economy	Good
Regional stability	Fair

COUNTRY PROFILE

Historical profile

1960 Senegal gained independence from France as part of the Federation of Mali, which almost immediately collapsed due to conflicts between the political leaders of the two territories (former French Soudan and Senegal). An independent Senegal was proclaimed under President Leopold Senghor.

1978 The first multi-party elections were held.

1980 President Senghor resigned.

1981 Abdou Diouf became president.

1982 Fighting began in Casamance between the Movement des Forces Démocratiques de Casamance (MFDC) (Democratic Forces of Casamance Movement), a separatist movement, and Senegalese government troops.

1983 The ruling Parti Socialiste Sénégalais (PS) (Senegal Socialist Party) returned to power with an overwhelming majority.

1993 Diouf was re-elected.

1994 The CFA Franc was devalued in January.

1998 Parliamentary elections were won by the PS. The constitution was amended to include a second legislative chamber, the Senate, with the president appointing 20 per cent of the delgates and most of the rest chosen by an electoral college. The opposition boycotted the Senate elections and the PS won all the seats, later winning a majority in the elections for the expanded National Assembly.

1999 The government entered into a peace initiative with the secessionist MFDC, which resulted in a cease-fire later in the year.

2000 Presidential elections were won by Abdoulaye Wade, of the Parti Démocratique Sénégalais (PDS) (Democratic Party of Senegal). President Wade dissolved the Senate which removed the Senate leader who, under the constitution, would assume the presidency in the event the incumbent was incapacitated.

2001 A 90 per cent vote favoured the proposed new constitution that limited presidential power. President Wade's coalition won the parliamentary elections.

2002 The EU paid Senegal US$63 million for fishing rights to exploit Senegalese waters until 2006. When the Senegalese ferry, Joola, sank off the Gambian coast 1,863 passengers were killed.

2003 The MFDC declared the Casamance secessionist war was over. President Wade and King Mohammed VI of Morocco agreed a mutual political and economic accord.

2004 The president and Father Diamacoune Senghore, leader of the MFDC, signed a peace deal.

2005 Travel between Senegal and The Gambia was blockaded in a dispute, which broke out over border ferry tariffs.

2006 Agreement was reached with Spain to promote a legal migration policy. Salif Sadio, leader of a breakaway faction of

KEY INDICATORS — Senegal

	Unit	2003	2004	2005	2006	2007
Population	m	10.35	10.63	11.66	11.94	12.23
Gross domestic product (GDP)	US$bn	6.50	7.67	8.62	9.16	11.12
GDP per capita	US$	530	733	739	768	910
GDP real growth	%	6.3	6.0	5.5	2.1	5.0
Inflation	%	0.2	0.5	1.7	2.1	5.9
Agricultural output	% change	–	4.3	7.5	-2.9	–
Exports (fob) (goods)	US$m	1,332.0	1,374.0	1,593.0	1,519.0	–
Imports (cif) (goods)	US$m	2,247.0	2,128.0	2,946.0	3,437.0	–
Balance of trade	US$m	-91.5	-754.0	-1,353.0	-1,918.0	–
Current account	US$m	-420.0	-470.0	-694.0	-895.0	-906.0
Total reserves minus gold	US$m	794.5	998.8	1,191.0	1,334.2	1,660.0
Foreign exchange	US$m	781.8	989.1	1,187.4	1,331.8	1,657.3
Exchange rate	per US$	574.89	528.29	507.22	496.60	454.40

the MFDC refused to accept the 2004 peace agreement.
2007 Parliamentary elections, scheduled to be held on the same day as presidential elections on 25 February, were postponed until June by a court order, due to a legal challenge to the organisation of the polls and a charge of gerrymandering of certain constituencies, by the president. Abdoulaye Wade won the presidential election beating four other candidates. On 3 June in the general elections the ruling Sopi alliance won 69.2 per cent of the vote (131 seats, out of 150). Turnout was 34.8 per cent. The opposition had boycotted the election claiming there was a need for an independent electoral commission and a new, transparent voter list. In August the Senate was reinstated, with elections for one-third of its members, while the president appointed the remaining two-thirds, for five-year terms. Ahead of the Organisation of Islamic Conference (OIC) summit to be held in 2008, the buildings in the capital were given a refurbishment and the estimated 1,500 unlicensed street vendors were forced to close down, sparking protest riots in November. To halt two days of violence, the authorities reversed their policy and allowed market stalls back providing they did not obstruct traffic.

Political structure

Constitution

The 2001 constitution allows for the formation of opposition parties, gives enhanced status to the prime minister and sets the length of the president's term of office at five years. It also gives the president power to dissolve the National Assembly after it has served for two years and call fresh parliamentary elections.

Form of state

Unitary republic

The executive

Executive power is vested in the president who is head of state and commander-in-chief of the armed forces. The president is directly elected by universal adult suffrage, for a five-year term, renewable once.
In the event of the presidency falling vacant, the president of the National Assembly automatically becomes head of state.

National legislature

Legislative power is held by the 120-member National Assembly. The prime minister is appointed by the president and the Council of Ministers is appointed by the prime minister in consultation with the president.

Legal system

The members of the Supreme Court of Justice are appointed by the president, on the advice of the Superior Court of Magistrates, which determines the constitutionality of laws. The High Court of Justice is appointed by the National Assembly from its members; it has the power to impeach the president or members of the government.

Last elections

25 February 2007 (presidential); 3 June 2007 (parliamentary).
Results: Presidential: Abdoulaye Wade won 55.9 per cent of the vote, the next candidate, Idrissa Seck, won 14.9 per cent. Turnout was 70.5 per cent. Parliamentary: Sopi alliance won 69.2 per cent of the vote (131 seats out of 150); Takku Defaraat Sénégal (TDS) 5 per cent (three); Defar Senegal 4.9 per cent (three); Waar Wi coalition 4.4 per cent (three); ten other political parties won one seat each. Turnout was 34.75 per cent.

Next elections

25 February 2007 (presidential); 2007 (parliamentary).

Political parties

Ruling party

Coalition: Sopi (Change) alliance led by Parti Démocratique Sénégalais (PDS) (Senegalese Democratic Party) and Ligue Démocratique-Mouvement pour le Parti du Travial (LD-MPT) (Democratic League - Movement for the Labour Party) (since 2001; re-elected 3 Jun 2007)

Main opposition party

Parti Socialiste Sénégalais (PS) (Socialist Party) (boycotted 2007 elections).

Population

12.23 million (2007)
Last census: December 2002: 9,956,202 (provisional)
Population density: 45 inhabitants per square km. Urban population: 48 per cent (1995–2001).
Annual growth rate: 2.5 per cent 1994–2004 (WHO 2006)
Internally Displaced Persons (IDP) 5,000 (UNHCR 2004)

Ethnic make-up

Wolof (43 per cent), Pular (24 per cent), Serer (15 per cent), Jola (4 per cent), Mandinka (3 per cent), Soninke 1 per cent), European and Lebanese (1 per cent).

Religions

Islam (94 per cent), Christian (mainly Roman Catholic) (5 per cent), indigenous beliefs (1 per cent).

Education

The investment in education amounts to 3.2 per cent of GDP. The government is pursuing a broad based programme to eliminate illiteracy by 2010.
Primary education is provided free of charge and is officially compulsory. However, attendance is low and on average approximately half the relevant age groups do not attend. School attendance rates in urban areas can be as high as 80 per cent, while those of rural areas can be as low as 30 per cent.
Secondary school lasts for seven years and is divided into two cycles of four- and three-years. The first cycle is middle school when all students undertake general education. At the age of 16, all those that pass an exam can choose between a general; short or long term technical; vocational or professional, upper secondary school. Only the general and professional schools culminate in a baccalauréat (at age 18) and students can continue to Dakar University or the smaller university at Sanar near Saint Louis. Vocational and technical secondary schools concentrate on applied subjects, particularly agriculture.
Literacy rate: 39 per cent adult rate; 53 per cent youth rate (15–24) (Unesco 2005).
Compulsory years: Six to 12.
Enrolment rate: 71 per cent gross primary enrolment of relevant age group (including repeaters); 16 per cent gross secondary enrolment (World Bank).
Pupils per teacher: 58 in primary schools.

Health

Per capita total expenditure on health (2003) was US$58; of which per capita government spending was US$24, at the international dollar rate, (WHO 2006).
In April 2008 pharmacists in a nationwide general strike protested at the illegal sale of fake drugs, worth an estimated US$23.7 million per year and centred openly in a compound in the capital, Dakar. There has been a rise in 'unknown' and 'inexplicable' medical cases which are being linked to the use of medicines brought from street vendors.

HIV/Aids

HIV prevalence: 0.8 per cent aged 15–49 in 2003 (World Bank)
Life expectancy: 55 years, 2004 (WHO 2006)
Fertility rate/Maternal mortality rate: 4.9 births per woman, 2004 (WHO 2006)
Birth rate/Death rate: 36 births per 1,000 population; 11 deaths per 1,000 population (2003).
Child (under 5 years) mortality rate (per 1,000): 78 per 1,000 live births (World Bank)
Head of population per physician: 0.06 physicians per 1,000 people, 2004 (WHO 2006)

Welfare

Most Senegalese are heavily indebted and poverty stricken. According to the World Bank, around 26 per cent of the population live below US$1 a day and around 68 per cent live on less than US$2 a day.

There is a state medical service and workers receive some maternity and family benefits, but the welfare system is unable to provide sufficient economic security for Senegal's poor.

Main cities

Dakar (capital, estimated population 2.0 million in 2005), Touba (428,059), Thiès (240,152), Rufisque (187,203), Kaolack (173,782), Mbour (170,699), Ziguinchor (162,436), St Louis (130,750).

Languages spoken

The main national languages are Jola-Fogny, Malinke, Mandinka, Pulaar, Serere-Sine, Soninke and Wolof. There are 36 spoken living languages. In business, it is essential to speak French. Very few executives speak English.

Official language/s

French

Media

National news agency: Agence de Presse Senegalaise (APS)

Press

The press is subject to a Code de la Presse, adopted in March 1979, which stipulates that owners of national newspapers and magazines must be Senegalese. The same Code de la Presse provides for regulation and authorisation of journalists working in the national press, although there are no restrictions on the publication and distribution of the papers and magazines themselves. cannot verify this, EM Nov 2007

Dailies: In French national newspaper include Le Soleil (www.lesoleil.sn) is government-controlled, privately owned are Sud quotidien (www.sudonline.sn), Le Quotidien (www.lequotidien.sn) Wal Fadjri L'Aurore (www.walf.sn) and L'Actuel (www.lactuel.info), Il est Midi (www.ilestmidi.net), Le Messager (www.lemessager.sn), L'Observateur (www.lobservateur.sn), L'Office (www.loffice.sn) and L'AS (www.las.sn).

Periodicals: Various political parties and independent owners publish journals, mostly available in French. There are several satirical journals including Le Cafard Libéré and Vive la République (weeklies) and Le Politicien (fortnightly). Other monthly publications include Afrique Tribune, Démocratie and Le Tournant; Le Journal de l'Economie is a business magazine.

Broadcasting

Radiodiffusion-Télévision du Sénégal (ORTS) is the state-run broadcaster.

Radio: For most people radio is the main medium for news and information. ORTS operates regional, national, and international networks and an FM station in Dakar, broadcasting in French, Portuguese, Arabic, English and six African languages.

There are four private radio stations located mainly in Dakar, Sud FM (www.sudonline.sn) operated by the telecommunications company Groupe Sud, Sept FM, Walf FM (www.walf.sn) operated by Groupe Wal Fadjri, Radio Dunyaa and Radio Future Medias. The online portal www.seneweb.com provides access to several radio broadcasts and newspaper publications.

Television: ORTS has two television channel. Commercial satellite and cable TV are also available. There are many production companies operating out of Senegal for the West African market.

News agencies

National news agency: Agence de Presse Senegalaise (APS)

Economy

In 2000, Senegal received US$800 million from the IMF and World Bank in debt service relief under the enhanced Highly Indebted Poor Country (HIPC) initiative. Since then, the authorities have adopted the necessary policies to reduce external debt, which by 2005 had been brought down to a manageable, domestic, 6 per cent and, external, 48 per cent of GDP. Barring unforeseen external shocks debt sustainability is expected to be preserved in the medium term.

GDP growth was 6.2 per cent in 2005 and expected to be 5.2 per cent in 2006, with inflation low at 1.8 per cent and 2.0 per cent in 2005 and 2006 respectively. The economy is typically made up by 63 per cent services, 17 per cent agriculture and 20 per cent industry, of which manufacturing is 12 per cent. In terms of economic diversification, Senegal is better placed than other West African countries. It has a relatively advanced industrial sector that employs over 17 per cent of the population. However, the likelihood that Senegal can forge an independent development programme without significant development aid is doubtful over the medium-term.

A major export earner is groundnuts and the state-owned enterprise is in the process of being privatised, along with other state enterprises such a energy producers and telecommunications.

Civil unrest resulted in a decline of tourist revenues in 2003, which have since recovered, especially in ecotourism.

Unemployment remains one of Senegal's most prominent problems with just under half the population jobless, the majority being urban youth. High unemployment rates hinder the reduction of poverty with around 54 per cent of the population living below the poverty line.

External trade

As a member of the Economic Community of West African States (Ecowas), which was set up to promote economic integration among members, Senegal is also a member of the West African Economic and Monetary Union using the common currency, the CFA franc.

Foreign trade provides around 70 per cent of GDP. Industrial production is limited to food processing of domestic agricultural products and extracting minerals. Manufacturing includes foreign-owned assembly production of vehicles and other consumer goods.

Imports

Principal imports are food and beverages, petroleum, capital goods and fuels semi-manufactured goods.

Main sources: France (24.4 per cent total, 2006), UK (6.0 per cent), China (4.3 per cent).

Exports

Principal exports are processed fish and groundnuts (peanuts), petroleum products, limestone, iron ore, gold and phosphates, cotton and textiles.

Main destinations: Mali (20.2 per cent total, 2006), France (7.6 per cent), The Gambia (5.6 per cent).

Agriculture

Farming

Agriculture contributes around 17 per cent to GDP and employs 70 per cent of the working population. Farming is carried out almost exclusively on smallholdings and is relatively inefficient. Agricultural development has been hindered by poor transport infrastructure. Since 1984, Senegal has liberalised the sector by reducing state intervention. As a result, the distribution of fertilisers has ceased to be a state monopoly and is now handled by the private sector. The government phased out subsidised credit for agricultural supplies but also established an agricultural development bank, the Caisse Nationale de Crédit Agricole. Marketing co-operatives were replaced by village co-operatives which enjoyed greater autonomy. In 2002, the UN Food and Agricultural Organisation (FAO) initiated a six-year small-scale agricultural project in several villages, introducing simple technologies useful for raising yields in rice and vegetables.

The main subsistence crops are sorghum and millet, although production of rice is increasing. Horticultural output is also rising, supplying the domestic market and providing exports of out-of-season fruit and vegetables to European markets.

Cash crops include groundnuts, cotton and sugar. Groundnut farming is crucial to the economy and employs a large percentage of the rural population. The

Société National de Commercialisation des Oléagineux de Sénégal (Sonacos), the national groundnut company, was privatised in December 2004.

Sugar cane is the only sector with large plantations, which are operated by Compagnie Sucrière du Sénégal (CSS).

Both groundnut and cotton output have been affected by the lack of farm credit and high levels of debt.

Cattle, sheep and goats are widely kept for domestic use. Poultry numbers are showing a long-term increase and there has been a marked increase in the sheep population since the mid-1980s.

Crop production in 2005 included: 1,504,719 tonnes (t) cereals in total, 412,756t maize, 401,448t cassava, 388,946t millet, 150,739t sorghum, 251,027t rice, 20,300t pulses, 269,132t oilcrops, 820,000t groundnuts in shell, *850,000t sugar cane, 46,580t seed cotton, *139,500t fruit in total, 411,673t vegetables in total. Livestock production included: 169,795t meat in total, 47,200t beef, 10,600t pig meat, 16,150t lamb, 16,855t goat meat, 7,100t horsemeat, 65,300t poultry, 34,000t eggs, 129,068t milk, 550t honey, 9,440t cattle hides, 3,511t goatskins, 3,345t sheepskins.

* estimate

Fishing

Fishing is important for the export revenues from the fish processing and canning industries, as well as licence revenues from foreign ships operating in Senegalese waters. Fish and fish products are typically the largest single item in export earnings. The fisheries sector is targetted for expansion, with assistance being given to artisan fishermen, and the development of producer groups. Finance for this programme is partly derived from the foreign fishing licence revenues. The Senegalese government is supporting the development of marine fish farming (tuna, oysters, prawns and lobsters).

In January 2002, Senegal refused to extend a fishing rights accord which had allowed EU vessels to fish in Senegalese waters since 1997. The EU and Senegal clashed over which areas should be fished and the length of the rest periods, which are essential for fish stock recovery. The Senegalese authorities raised the problem of overfishing and illegal methods employed by EU trawlers, which is causing fish stocks to plummet and has put Senegalese fishermen's livelihoods at risk; around 500,000 people in Senegal depend on the fishing industry for an income. In June 2002, the EU agreed to pay Senegal eur64 million (US$62 million) for the right to exploit its fishing grounds until 2006. The deal bans pelagic fishing, in which a net is dragged by two trawlers which results in significant wastage, and imposes a two-month rest period. Conservationists dismissed the deal, claiming it would continue to seriously undermine fish stocks and local livelihoods.

In 2004, the total marine fish catch was 374,245 tonnes and the total crustacean catch was 1,985 tonnes.

Forestry

Forest resources in Senegal are modest, although the country is well forested with 38 per cent forest cover estimated at 6.2 million hectares (ha) and an additional 30 per cent of other wooded land. Deforestation occurs at an average rate of 0.7 per cent per year. Desertification continues to be a major environmental problem in northern Senegal. The country has established significant areas of plantation forest to meet fuel and fodder needs. A programme of reforestation now under way aims to include the revival of gum arabic production.

Wood is mostly used for fuel consumption, while production of sawn timber and industrial roundwood caters to the domestic market. Some amount of wood and paper is also imported. In 2004, total imports of forest products amounted to US$52.5 million, while exports amounted to US$2.1 million.

Timber production in 2004 included 6,039,939 cubic metre (cum) roundwood, 794,000cum industrial roundwood, 23,000cum sawnwood, 40,000cum sawlogs and veneer logs, 2,500,000cum pulpwood, 951,000cum wood-based panels, 5,242,939cum woodfuel; 110,208t charcoal.

Industry and manufacturing

The industrial sector contributes around 25 per cent to GDP, with the manufacturing sector contributing 17 per cent of GDP. Most industry is located inside the Dakar area of the Cap Vert peninsula.

The only heavy export industries are an oil refinery at Dakar-Mbao, a sulphuric/phosphoric acid plant at Darou Khoudou and a fertiliser complex at Mbao.

The main industrial activity is light industry, processing locally-produced primary commodities for export and manufacturing import substitution goods to meet local demand. The government's industrial policy aims to make the economy more market-responsive and less centrally controlled. This entails a reduction in government participation in industry, price liberalisation and the encouragement of foreign investment (through a more favourable tax regime) and small businesses (through special incentives). It gives priority to high-value and export industries, especially chemicals, textiles, food processing and leather goods. The food-processing sector and, to a lesser extent, textile manufacturing, are influenced heavily by agricultural performance, as they rely mainly on locally produced inputs. Therefore, industrial performance is affected by climatic conditions in a similar way to the agricultural sector.

Light industry is mostly privately-owned and relies heavily on foreign capital and management skills. Lack of adequate infrastructure has curtailed industrial development outside the capital.

Tourism

The state tourism agency is involved both in promoting the country in Europe (particularly in Italy and the UK), and in encouraging foreign investment in the development of further tourist facilities. The government sees tourism as a key foreign currency earner. Tourism is expected to contribute 3.5 per cent to GDP in 2005.

Mining

The mining sector contributes around 7 per cent to GDP and employs 3 per cent of the workforce.

Extraction of calcium and phosphates from open mines near Thiès are the most important mining activities. Workable deposits are estimated at around 130 million tonnes. Production (around 1.5 million tonnes per annum) is mainly for export, although it is also an important source of supply for the fertiliser complex at Mbao. Phosphates represent around 17 per cent of export earnings, although production declined by 30 per cent over the 1990s. The phosphate mine in the Matam area holds deposits of around 40.5 million tonnes.

Titanium, zircon and rutile are mined along the south coast of Cap Vert. The total available iron ore reserves at the Faleme iron ore project near the Mali border are estimated at 391 million tonnes, enough to sustain mining activities for over 30 years at the planned production rate of 12 million tonnes of marketable products per year. The Farangalia and Goto deposits hold estimated reserves of 250 million tonnes.

Hydrocarbons

Senegal's oil requirements are met by imports. Downstream, the Société Africaine de Raffinage (SAR) refinery has a nominal capacity of 17,000 barrels per day (bpd). The government is actively promoting increased offshore petroleum exploration along with its neighbouring countries.

Gas reserves are estimated at three billion cubic metres and are primarily located offshore. Annual gas production is around 1.4 billion cubic metres. Gas currently produced on the Diam Niadio East concession is supplied to Société Nationale d'Electricité (Senelec). All of this is consumed domestically. No natural gas is imported. There is a small natural gas field at Diam-Niadio, which has been used to fire a generator. The market for butane has increased more than 15-fold since 1974, and further expansion is forecast. The government has been encouraging its use, as an alternative to firewood. Senegal does not produce or import coal.

Energy

Electric power is supplied from six thermal stations, with a total installed capacity of 422MW. Virtually all commercial energy requirements are imported.
Only one in three people in Senegal has access to electricity. In rural areas, wood provides most fuel requirements, with consequent serious deforestation. A programme of reforestration is under way. The government's 10-year energy plan aims to substitute 50 per cent of imported oil by local products, including oil/gas from the Dome Flore offshore field, peat deposits from Niayés and the expansion of hydropower from the Senegal and Gambia Rivers.
The government has failed to divest the Société Nationale d'Electricité (Senelec), the state-owned electricity company, despite two attempts at privatisation.

Banking and insurance

Eight commercial banks operate in Senegal, with the three largest banks holding approximately two-thirds of total deposits. The largest bank in Senegal is the Société Générale de Banques au Sénégal (SGBS). The SGBS faces strong competition from its main rival, the Banque International pour le Commerce et l'Industrie du Sénégal (BICIS).
The banking sector is overseen by the Banque Centrale des Etas de l'Afrique de l'Ouest (BCEAO), which sets policy throughout the Union Economique et Monetaire Ouest Africaine (UEMOA) (West African Economic and Monetary Union).

Central bank

Banque Centrale des Etats de l'Afrique de l'Ouest (BCEAO)

Main financial centre

Dakar

Time

GMT

Geography

Senegal lies on the west coast of Africa, bordered to the north by Mauritania, to the east by Mali, and to the south by Guinea and Guinea-Bissau. Senegal surrounds the small state of The Gambia, which straddles the River Gambia in the south-west of Senegal, and forms a narrow enclave extending some 320 kilometres (200 miles) inland.
The country is low-lying and flat, and is situated in the savannah grasslands. Apart from the River Gambia and the Senegal River, which forms the northern boundary, most rivers are seasonal and dry up in the arid winter months.

Hemisphere

Northern

Climate

The climate is tropical in the south (Casamance) and more temperate in the north.
The best time to visit is October—June, when it is cool and dry. The safest time to avoid the rain is mid November—April, but it is hot and humid during the day (cooler at night). During the rainy season, July—September, the humidity gets very high and the days very hot. In the southern part of the country, the rainy season can extend through October.

Dress codes

There is no restriction on clothing, although women are advised to dress modestly. In the dry season lightweight European clothing is suitable, and many government ministers wear lounge suits. Businessmen and other officials wear local dress – the boubou. Tropical clothing (not white) is necessary in the wet season.

Entry requirements

Passports

Required by all.

Visa

Required by all; except nationals of the EU, North America, Japan and many countries in the region for visits up to 90 days (for a full list of exceptions see www.senegalembassy.co.uk). Visitors should contact the nearest consulate to obtain an application form. Proof of return/onward passage is necessary.
Business travellers should include a letter of invitation, from a local company or organisation, and a business letter of intent, with their application form.

Currency advice/regulations

The import of local and foreign currency is unlimited. Export of local currency is only allowed to other African Financial Community countries and only up to CFAf20,000; export of foreign currency is limited to the equivalent of CFAf50,000. All foreign currency must be declared on arrival and departure.
Travellers cheques should be euro or US dollars to avoid additional exchange fees.

Customs

Alcoholic spirits are not duty-free.

Health (for visitors)

Mandatory precautions

A yellow fever certificate is required if arriving from an endemic area.

Advisable precautions

Inoculations and boosters should be current for tetanus, hepatitis A, diphtheria, typhoid and yellow fever. There may be a need for vaccinations for tuberculosis, hepatitis B and meningitis and cholera. Anti-mosquito measures including mosquito repellents, nets and clothing covering the body should be used for protection against hepatitis B and yellow fever. Rabies is a risk. Bilharzia is present, visitors should avoid wadding in fresh water, only use well maintained, chlorinated swimming pools.
There is a shortage of routine medications and visitors should take all necessary medicines with them. A first aid kit that includes disposable syringes is a reasonable precaution. Use only bottled or boiled water for drinks, washing teeth and making ice. Eat only well cooked meals, preferably served hot; vegetables should be cooked and fruit peeled. Dairy products are unpasteurised and should be avoided, unless cooked.
Healthcare is not to Western standards and medical insurance, including emergency evacuation, is necessary.

Hotels

Air-conditioned hotels are available in Dakar, although they can be expensive. Hotel bills usually include service charges and local tax. Tipping is therefore optional.

Credit cards

Major credit cards are accepted; charge cards are not accepted. There are ATMs in Dakar.

Public holidays (national)

Fixed dates

1 Jan (New Year's Day), 4 Apr (Independence Day), 1 May (Labour Day), 15 Aug (Assumption Day), 1 Nov (All Saints' Day), 25 Dec (Christmas Day).

Variable dates

Eid al Adha, Islamic New Year, Birth of the Prophet, Easter Monday (Mar/Apr), Ascension Day, Whit Monday, Eid al Fitr.
Islamic year – 1429 (10 Jan 2008–28 Dec 2008): The Islamic year contains 354 or 355 days, with the result that Muslim feasts advance by 10–12 days against the Gregorian calendar. Dates of feasts vary according to the sighting of the new moon, so cannot be forecast exactly.

Working hours

Banking

Mon–Thu: 0730–1300, 1400–1630; Fri: 0730–1300, 1530–1730.

Business

Mon–Fri: 0800–1230, 1300–1600.

Government

Mon–Fri: 0800/ 0900–1200, 1500–1800; Sat: 0800/0900–1200.

Shops
Mon–Sat: 0800–1200, 1430–1800.

Telecommunications
Mobile/cell phones
There are GSM 900 services available over half of the country.

Electricity supply
127/220V AC, 50 cycles, with mainly round two-pin plugs.

Social customs/useful tips
Visitors should be punctual for appointments and visiting cards should be presented at business meetings. French-style formalities are observed. These include shaking hands when greeting and before departing.
Use the right hand when shaking hands and passing or receiving anything.
A service charge is normally added to the bill. Gratuities are not customary for taxis.
The minimum drinking age is 20 years.
Smoking is banned in some public places, including mosques.

Security
Purse snatching and pickpocketing is on the increase, particularly in the downtown area of Dakar. Avoid political gatherings and street demonstrations and maintain security awareness at all times.
The permission of the Senegalese authorities is required for travel to certain areas of the Casamance region where attacks from armed separatist rebels and bandits occur.

Getting there
Air
National airline: Air Sénégal
International airport/s: Dakar-Léopold Sédar Senghor (DKR), 17km north west of city; duty-free shop, bar, restaurant, bank, post office, car hire and taxis.
In March 2006 the ministry of tourism announced plans for a new international airport at Diass, 45km from Dakar. It will replace the existing Dakar airport and be named Aéroport International Blaise Diagne. The plans are for an initial capacity of three million passengers; it is anticipated it will relieve congestion around Dakar and encourage the creation of an economic development zone.
Airport tax: None
Surface
Road: Principal road routes are from the Gambia, Mali, Mauritania – those from Guinea are not generally recommended.
A 720 metre bridge over the Mansoa river has improved the traffic flow on the trans-African coastal road between Bissau, Guinea-Bissau, and Senegal.
Rail: A rail service operates between Dakar and Bamako (Mali) via Kaolack and Tambacounda.
Water: Cargo ships carrying passengers have services from Spain, France, Morocco and the Canary Islands.
Main port/s: Dakar is the second-largest port in West Africa and serves Senegal, Mauritania and the Gambia. The port has extensive facilities for fishing vessels and fish processing.

Getting about
National transport
Air: Air Sénégal links Dakar with all the main towns. Small aircraft can be chartered from Amana Air Charters.
Road: Tarred roads are mainly near the coast; inland areas are served by roads of variable quality. Main highways: Dakar to St Louis, Rosso, Djourbel, Joal, Koalack and Ziguinchor.
Buses: Coach services Dakar-Ziguinchor; Tambacounda-Ziguinchor; Tambacounda-Gaoual are operated subject to demand.
Rail: The railway links Dakar with Tambacounda to the east, and with St Louis and Linguère to the north-east.
Water: The Senegal river in the north is only navigable for parts of the year: for three months as far as Kayes (Mali); for six months as far as Kaedi (Mauritania); and all year as far as Rosso and Podor. Other rivers include the Saloun and the Casamance.
City transport
Taxis: Taxis are plentiful in Dakar, all are fitted with meters. Rates are greater after midnight. Tipping is not customary.
Buses, trams & metro: Large green and yellow public buses operate a regular flat-fare service.
Car hire
An international or national driving licence, insurance and car registration document (Carte Grise) are required. Vehicles coming from the right always have right of way.

BUSINESS DIRECTORY

The addresses listed below are a selection only. While World of Information makes every endeavour to check these addresses, we cannot guarantee that changes have not been made, especially to telephone numbers and area codes. We would welcome any corrections.

Telephone area codes
The international dialling code (IDD) for Senegal is +221, followed by subscriber's number.

Useful telephone numbers
Police: 823-7149, 823-2529, 823-8383.

Chambers of Commerce
Union des Chambres de Commerce, d'Industrie et d'Agriculture de Senegal, 1 Place de l'Independence, PO Box 118, Dakar (tel: 823-7189; fax: 823-9363; e-mail: cciad@telecomplus-sn).

Dakar Chambre de Commerce, d'Industrie et d'Agriculture, 1 Place de l'Indépendance, PO Box 118, Dakar (tel: 823-7189; fax: 823-9363; e-mail: ccaid@telecomplus.sn).

Diourbel Chambre de Commerce, d'Industrie et d'Agriculture, PO Box 7, Diourbel (tel/fax: 971-1203; e-mail: ccdiour@cyg.sn).

Fatick Chambre de Commerce, d'Industrie et d'Agriculture, PO Box 66, Fatick (tel/fax: 949-1425).

Kaolack Chambre de Commerce, d'Industrie et d'Agriculture, Rue Noirot, PO Box 203, Kaolack (tel: 941-2050; fax: 941-2291; e-mail: cciak@visto.com).

Kolda Chambre de Commerce, d'Industrie et d'Agriculture, Quartier Escale, PO Box 23, Kolda (tel: 996-1230; fax: 996-1068; e-mail:cciakd@sentoo.sn).

Louga Chambre de Commerce, d'Industrie et d'Agriculture, 2 Rue Glozel, Quartier Thiokhma, PO Box 26 Louga (tel: 967-1114; fax: 967-4658; e-mail: ccial@sentoo.sn).

Saint Louis Chambre de Commerce, d'Industrie et d'Agriculture, 10 Rue Blanchot, PO Box 19, Saint Louis (tel: 961-1088; fax: 961-2980; e-mail: cciasl@tpsnet.sn).

Tambacounda Chambre de Commerce, d'Industrie et d'Agriculture, PO Box 27, Tambacounda (tel: 981-1014; fax: 981-2995).

Thies Chambre de Commerce, d'Industrie et d'Agriculture, 96 Avenue Lamine Gueye, PO Box 3020 Thies (tel: 951-1002; fax: 951-1397; e-mail: cciath@tpsnet.sn).

Ziguinchor Chambre de Commerce, d'Industrie et d'Agriculture, Rue de Général de Gaulle, PO Box 26, Ziguinchor (tel: 991-1310; fax: 991-2163).

Banking
Banque de l'Habitat du Sénégal, PO Box 229, 69 Boulevard Général de Gaulle, Dakar (tel: 8231-004; fax: 8238-043).

Banque Internationale pour le Commerce et l'Industrie du Sénégal SA, PO Box 392, 2 Avenue du Président L Senghor, Dakar (tel: 8390-390; fax: 8233-707).

Banque Islamique du Sénégal, PO Box 3381, Immeuble Abdallah Fayçal, Dakar (tel: 8496-262; fax: 8224-948) .

Banque Senegalo-Tunisienne (BST), PO Box 4111, Immeuble Kebe, 97 Avenue André Peytavin, Dakar (tel: 8237-576; fax: 8238-238).

Caisse Nationale de Crédit Agricole du Sénégal, PO Box 3890, 45 Avenue Albert Sarraut, Dakar (tel: 8222-300; fax: 8212-606).

Compagnie Bancaire de l'Afrique Occidentale, PO Box 129, 2 Place de l'Indépendance, Dakar (tel: 8231-000; fax: 8232-005).

Crédit Lyonnais Sénégal, PO Box 56, Boulevard El Hadji Djily Mbaye, Angle Rue Huart, Dakar (tel: 8231-008; fax: 8238-430).

Société Générale de Banques au Sénégal SA, PO Box 323, 19 Avenue du Président L Senghor, Dakar (tel: 8395-500; fax: 8219-119).

Central bank
Banque Centrale des Etats de l'Afrique de l'Ouest, Boulevard du Général de Gaulle, Angle Rue 11; PO Box 3159, Dakar (tel: 889-4545; fax: 823-5757).

Travel information
Air Sénégal International, 45 Albert Sarraut Ave, Dakar (tel: 842-4100, 823-4970; internet: www.air-senegal-international.com).

Amana Air Charters, 2 Rue Galandou Diouf, Dakar (tel: 842-2911/2933

Ministry of tourism
Ministry of Tourism and Air Transport, 23 Rue Calmette, BP 4049, Dakar (tel: 8229-226; fax: 8229-413; email: mtta@primature.sn; internet: www.tourisme.gouv.sn).

National tourist organisation offices
National Tourist Office, 23 Rue Calmette, PO Box 4049, Dakar (tel: 8229-226; fax: 8229-413).

Ministries
Ministry of Armed Forces, Batîment Administratif, Avenue Roume, Dakar (tel: 8231-216; fax: 8236-338).

Ministry of Commerce, Batîment Administratif, Avenue Roume, Dakar (tel: 8229-542; fax: 8219-132).

Ministry of the Habitat, Ex-Camp Lat-Dior, Dakar (tel: 8233-278; fax: 8236-245).

Ministry of the Interior, Place Washington, Dakar (tel: 8234-151; fax: 8210-542).

Ministry of Justice, Batîment Administratif, Avenue Roume, Dakar (tel: 8238-042; fax: 8232-727).

Ministry of Modernisation of the State, Rue Emile Zola, Dakar (tel: 8232-922; fax: 8229-764).

Ministry of National Education, Rue Calmette, Dakar (tel: 8224-123; fax: 8218-930).

Ministry of Tourism and Environment, 23 Rue Calmette, BP 4049, Dakar (tel: 8211-126; fax: 8229-413).

Ministry of Women, Children and the Family, Rue Beranger Ferraud, Dakar (tel: 8236-919; fax: 8236-673).

Prime Minister's Office, Batîment Administratif, Avenue Roume, Dakar (tel: 8224-917; fax: 8225-578).

Other useful addresses
British Embassy, 20 rue du Docteur Guillet, PO Box 6025, Dakar (tel: 8237-392, 8239-971; fax: 8232-766).

Direction de la Statistique, BP 116, Dakar (tel: 8230-881).

Foire Internationale de Dakar, route de l'Aéroport, BP 3329, Dakar (tel: 8231-011).

Port Autonome de Dakar, 35 boulevard de la Libération, Dakar (tel: 8224-545, 8227-421).

Senegalese Embassy (UK) 39 Marloes Road, London W8 6LA (tel: (+44-(0)20) 7937-7237, 7938-4048; fax: (+44-(0)20) 7938-2546; internet: www.senegalembassy.co.uk).

Senegalese Embassy (US), 2112 Wyoming Avenue, NW, Washington DC 20008 (tel: (+1-202) 234-0540; fax: (+1-202) 352-6315).

Société de Développement Agricole et Industriel du Sénégal, 23 avenue Roume, PO Box 222, Dakar (tel: 8251-818).

Société Nationale d'Etudes et de Promotion Industrielle, BP 100, derrière Residence Seydou Nourou Tall, Dakar (tel: 8252-130).

Société Nationale des Télécommunications du Sénégal (SONATEL), 6 rue Wagane Diouf, BP 62, Dakar (tel: 8231-023, 8214-242).

Société Nouvelle des Etudes de Développement en Afrique, 36 rue Calmette, PO Box 2084, Dakar (tel: 8234-231).

Syndicat des Commerçants, Importateurs et Exportateurs de l'Ouest Africaine (Scimpex), angle rue Parent et avenue Abdoulaye Fadiga, PO Box 806, Dakar (tel: 8213-662).

US Embassy, avenue Jean XXIII, PO Box 49, Dakar (tel: 8234-296; fax: 8222-991).

National news agency: Agence de Presse Senegalaise (APS)
Address: 58 Bld de la République; BP 117, Dakar (tel: 821-1427; fax: 822-0767; email: aps@aps.sn; internet: www.aps.sn).

Internet sites
Africa Business Network: www.ifc.org/abn

AllAfrica.com: http://allafrica.com

African Development Bank: www.afdb.org

Press agency (in French): www.aps.sn/

Web portal: www.au-senegal.com/

Serbia

KEY FACTS

Official name: Republika Srbije (Republic of Serbia) (ROS)

Head of State: President Boris Tadic (since Jul 2004, re-elected 3 Feb 2008)

Head of government: Prime Minister Mirko Cvetkovic (took office 7 Jul 2008)

Ruling party: The coalition For a European Serbia, formed from Socialist Party of Serbia, the Party of United Pensioners of Serbia, the United Serbia coalition, the For a European Sandzak coalition and the Alliance of Vojvodina Hungarians. (since Jun 2008)

Area: 102,173 square km

Population: 7.45 million (2007) (excluding Kosovo)

Capital: Belgrade

Official language: Serbian

Currency: Dinar (D) = 100 paras

Exchange rate: D49.72 per US$ (Jul 2008)

GDP per capita: US$2,880 (2005)

GDP real growth: 6.30% (2005)

Labour force: 3.93 million (2004)*

Unemployment: 28.05% (2005)*; 50.00% (Kosovo, 2004)*

Inflation: 17.30% (2005)

Balance of trade: -US$6.03 billion (2005) (excluding Kosovo)

Foreign debt: US$9.20 billion (2003)*

Visitor numbers: 283,000 (1998)

* estimated figure

In September 2008 Serbia ratified a pre-membership agreement with the European Union (EU) that neatly coincided with a comprehensive oil and gas deal with Russia. Both agreements had been signed earlier in 2008, but required parliamentary approval before they could be implemented.

The ratification of the agreement with the EU was seen by those members of the government better disposed towards greater co-operation with Europe as a big step towards integration into the EU. The nationalist opposition rejected the agreement on the basis that virtually all the EU states had supported the independence of Kosovo. Agreement with the EU had been blocked for years as Serbia proved unable or unwilling to arrest alleged war criminals. The capture in July 2008 of the high profile Bosnian Serb leader Radovan Karadic represented a positive catalyst towards Serbian EU membership.

Serbia's agreement with Russia was seen as something of a balancing exercise, providing as it did for a pan-European pipeline running through Serbia and the sale of Naftna Industrija Srbije (NIS), Serbia's state-owned oil monopoly to Russia.

For a short time (2003–06) Serbia and Montenegro consisted of two republics,

Montenegro and Serbia. Serbia in turn contained two autonomous provinces – largely Albanian Kosovo (and Metohija, although the Serbian government is the only entity to include this in the province's name), and Vojvodina. The union was a last ditch effort to retain some sort of collective power base, but the two republics had long turned their backs on each other in an unhappy, unconsummated marriage. Serbia's larger population made it a more powerful entity than the sum of the federation's parts.

The Montenegro parliament declared independence on 3 June 2006, after a referendum on 21 May had been in favour of independence, followed two days later by the Serbian parliament which declared Serbia the successor state to the union of Serbia and Montenegro. The international community recognised the independent state of the Republic of Montenegro on 27 June 2006.

Thus concluded the long process of the disintegration of the old Republic of Yugoslavia, a process begun in 1990 when Slovenia first sought to separate. What in 1989 had seemed an impossibility, with the separation of Serbia from Montenegro was concluded peacefully. Serbia, once the hub of a federal republic of 23 million people found itself alone, and well behind its neighbours in the process of European integration.

The old Federal Republic of Yugoslavia had very much been a Serbian dominated arrangement. Thus the Montenegrans had found themselves tarred with the Serbian brush. Negative international responses to Serbia's perceived responsibility for, and involvement, in the civil wars that had followed the fall of communism had resulted in wide ranging UN sanctions and an EU trade embargo. Initially these sanctions had halved the republic's exports and doubled it's foreign trade deficit.

Another chapter also concluded in 2006 when former president Slobodan Milosevic died in prison in the Hague in March. This ended his trial for war crimes, and removed a possible tricky situation had he been convicted.

Economy

Serbia continues to grow strongly. GDP in 2007 was 7.3 per cent and inflation was half the over 12 per cent rate for 2006. The International Monetary Fund (IMF) was pleased to note in early 2008 that as a result of the hundreds of companies that had been privatised the corporate sector was able to show aggregate profits for the f irst time in years.

However, the IMF went on to say that sustaining the reform momentum had been a challenge and weaknesses in the corporate sector did persist. Structural reforms had stalled in 2006–07 and progress and growth had only been achieved in a few sectors. State- and socially-owned enterprises continued to drain domestic savings while fixed investment remained low. With slow job creation, employment continued declining and unemployment remained high at 21 per cent.

Elections

In parliamentary elections held on 21 January 2007 the Srpska Radikalna Stranka (SRS) (Serb Radical Party) won 28.7 per cent of the vote (81 out of 250 seats) and became the largest single bloc. However, it was deemed unlikely to form a government as the Demokratska Stranka (DS) (Democratic Party – led by President Tadic) and the DSS (led by the prime minister), which won 22.9 per cent (65 seats) and 47 per cent (47 seats) respectively are expected to form a coalition. Nevertheless, the result was seen as an impediment to Serbia's EU membership aspirations, as such a large proportion of the electorate supporting a staunch nationalist agenda was viewed as a challenge to the UN and EU's declared aims in maintaining peace in Kosovo and allowing the region a degree of self-government.

Presidential elections on 3 February 2008 were won by President Boris Tadic with 51.61 per cent of the vote. In snap parliamentary elections called for 11 May the coalition For a European Serbia, led by Kostunica, won 38.7 per cent of the vote (103 seats of 250), the Serbian Radical Party 29.1 per cent (77), the Democratic Party of Serbia-New Serbia coalition 11.3 per cent (30), the coalition led by the Socialist Party of Serbia 7.9 per cent (20), and the Liberal Democratic Party 5.2 per cent (13). Kostunica became prime minister until he resigned in mid-2008 and President Kostunica appointed Mirko Cvetkovic as prime minister, taking office with his government on 7 July 2008.

Outlook

With Kosovo's declaration of independence in 2008, the Balkans witnessed the emergence of three new independent states, Serbia, Montenegro and Kosovo. Of the three, Kosovo will face the most profound economic challenges. Serbia will again face pressure to apprehend war crimes suspects, possibly to the detriment of its EU membership hopes. But with its energetic peoples is likely to end the year in a stronger position.

Risk assessment

Economic	Poor
Political	Poor
Regional stability	Poor

COUNTRY PROFILE

Historical profile

The Serbs are believed to be an ethnic Slavic clan that settled in the Balkans by

KEY INDICATORS — Serbia

	Unit	2003	2004	2005	2006	2007
Population	m	11.02	11.03	*7.47	7.45	*7.45
Gross domestic product (GDP)	US$bn	18.08	24.40	26.23	31.78	41.68
GDP per capita	US$	1,641	2,893	*3,551	4,271	*5,596
GDP real growth	%	–	7.0	6.2	5.7	7.3
Inflation	%	11.0	10.0	17.3	12.7	6.8
Unemployment	%	30.0	30.0	–	–	–
Industrial output	% change	–	7.5	3.5	–	–
Agricultural output	% change	–	18.2	2.0	–	–
Exports (fob) (goods)	US$m	–	–	4,553.0	6,487.0	–
Imports (cif) (goods)	US$m	–	–	10,580.0	13,119.0	–
Balance of trade	US$m	–	–	-6,027.0	-6,632.0	–
Current account	US$m	–		-2.5	-3,966.0	–
Total reserves minus gold	US$m	3,410.8	4,095.8	5,627.9	11,647.7	13,892.6
Foreign exchange	US$m	3,410.4	4,095.8	5,597.7	11,638.9	13,891.8
Exchange rate	per US$	0.00	65.00	61.46	61.46	54.20

* estimated figure

the eleventh century. A Serbian state was established in the twelfth century.
1389 The Turks defeated the Serbs at the Battle of Kosovo, and Serbia become an Ottoman subject state.
1860 Turkish troops left. Serbia signed a series of alliances with Montenegro, Romania and Greece. The Serbia-Greece pact assigned ownership of Bosnia and Hercegovina (BiH) to Serbia, with Thessaly and Epirus going to the Greeks.
1876 Serbia was again defeated by Turkey, although Austrian protection prevented the Serbs from falling under Turkish rule.
1878 Austria invaded Serbia. The Treaty of Berlin settled Serbian independence. Montenegro was also recognised as an independent state and doubled in size.
1913 The London Conference reduced the territory claimed by Albania after recognising its independence. Kosovo was granted to Serbia and Cameria (Chamouria) to Greece.
1914 Growing hostility in relations between the Serbs and the Habsburgs of Austro-Hungary came to a head with the assassination of the Austrian Archduke Frans Ferdinand by a Serbian nationalist, Gavrilo Princip. Austria and Germany declared war on Serbia, resulting in the First World War.
1918 The defeat of the Austro-Hungarian empire during the World War One saw the creation of the Kingdom of the Serbs, Croats and Slovenes, encompassing Bosnia and Hercegovina (BiH), Croatia, parts of Dalmatia and Macedonia, Montenegro, Serbia, Slavonia and Slovenia.
1921 Prince Alexander, Regent of Serbia, became King.
1929 Following disputes between Serbs and Croats, King Alexander assumed dictatorial powers and the country was renamed Yugoslavia.
1934 King Alexander was assassinated in Marseilles, while on a state visit to France.
1941 Parts of Yugoslavia were occupied by the Germans, Italians, Hungarians and Bulgarians.
1945–46 Following the end of the Second World War, Serbia and Montenegro became two of the constituent republics of the Federal People's Republic of Yugoslavia.
1948 Yugoslavia was expelled from the Communist Information Bureau (Cominform), responsible for co-ordinating Communist activities throughout the world.
1953 Tito was elected president in January.
Constitutions adopted in 1953, 1963 and 1974 increased the autonomy extended to the country's constituent republics.
1955 After building a relationship with the West, Yugoslavia restored relations with the Soviet Union.
1960–70s To keep Yugoslavia out of the Cold War, President Tito pursued a policy of non-alignment and the country became one of the founder members of the Non-Alignment Movement (NAM). In 1963 the official name was changed to the Socialist Federal Republic of Yugoslavia.
1980 Tito died. A system of a collective (rotating) presidency was adopted.
1989 Differences and friction between the wealthier republics, Slovenia and Croatia, and the different ethnic groups intensified. Serbian and Montenegrin constitutions were inaugurated.
1990 Multi-party elections brought into power a government in Croatia which supported outright independence.
1991–92 The secession of Croatia, Slovenia and BiH led to invasions of these republics by the Jugoslovenska Narodna Armija (JNA) (Yugoslav National Army). In Slovenia, the JNA was promptly defeated. JNA units were eventually incorporated into the ethnic Serb armies in BiH and the Krajina region in Croatia. The reduced Yugoslav state, renamed the Federal Republic of Yugoslavia (FRY), comprised Serbia, Montenegro, Vojvodina and Kosovo and was not internationally recognised and deprived of its UN seat.
1993 Zoran Lilic was elected FRY president, replacing Dobrica Cosic, who had criticised the president of Serbia, Slobodan Milosevic.
1995 Milosevic was one of the signatories of the Dayton Peace Agreement, which ended the civil war in BiH.
1996 FRY and Croatia signed an agreement of mutual recognition, formally ending five years of hostility.
1997 Milosevic, for 10 years the president of Serbia, took over as the FRY president. A coalition government, led by Milosevic's Socialisticka Partija Srbije (SPS) (Socialist Party of Serbia), remained in power in Serbia, despite losing its parliamentary majority in elections. The first election for the presidency of Serbia was invalidated because less than half the electorate voted; Milan Milutinovic was elected president of Serbia at the end of the year.
1998 Since the 1980s, the Milosevic regime had been gradually reducing the civil rights of the ethnic Albanians in Kosovo. Opposition to this gathered momentum during the 1990s as the Ushtria Çlirimtare e Kosovës (UÇK) (Kosovo Liberation Army) began to carry out armed offensives and bombings against the Yugoslav authorities. By the beginning of the year, the UÇK controlled approximately half of the province of Kosovo. FRY security forces launched a counter-offensive against the UÇK, destroying villages and displacing many thousands of Kosovans. Mirko Marjanovic (Montenegrin prime minister since 1994) was re-appointed to form a government in Montenegro.
1999 Vuk Draskovic resigned from the FRY government and took his party out of the coalition. After unsuccessful mediation and increased violence in Kosovo, NATO launched air strikes in March against FRY targets, centred primarily on Belgrade. In June, FRY forces withdrew entirely from Kosovo. NATO deployed peace-keeping troops in Kosovo, which became an international protectorate under UN control.
2000 Milosevic called early elections for the FRY presidency. Vojislav Kostunica of the Demokratska Opozicija Srbije (DOS) (Democratic Opposition of Serbia; a coalition formed to challenge Milosevic's rule) won the election but Milosevic remained in power (officially his term in office was to end in 2001). Street protests and workers strikes ensued until 5 October when the Radio Televizije Srbije (RTS) (Radio Television Serbia) broadcast offices were stormed and Milosevic was toppled. Kostunica became president of FRY. The DOS won FRY parliamentary elections, held in December. Local elections, held in Kosovo, were won by the Lidhja Demokratike e Kosovës (LDK) (Democratic League of Kosovo), led by Ibrahim Rugova. The Federal Republic of Yugoslavia (FRY) was allowed back into the UN after eight years of exclusion.
2001 Milo Djukanovic's Pobjeda je Crne Goru (PjCG) (Victory for Montenegro) coalition won the Montenegrin parliamentary elections. Slobodan Milosevic was extradited to stand trial at the International Criminal Tribunal for the former Yugoslavia (ICTY) in The Hague. The UN mission in Kosovo set up the Provisional Institutions of Self-Government (PISG), in May and included an assembly, mandated to elect a president and president of the territory. The LDK won 46 per cent of the vote in the Assembly of Kosovo elections, but failed to get a majority.
2002 The Kosovo assembly elected Ibrahim Rugova as president; Bajram Rexhapi of the Partia Demokratike e Kosovës (PDK) (Democratic Party of Kosovo) was elected as prime minister of a power-sharing 10-member cabinet. Montenegrin President Milo Djukanovic's Demokratska Lista za Evropsku Crnu Goru (DLECG) (Democratic List for a European Montenegro) alliance won the Montenegro parliamentary elections. Parliamentary Speaker Natasa Micic was appointed Serbia's acting president after the results of three separate presidential elections were declared invalid due to insufficient voter turnout.

2003 The FRY state was reconstituted and renamed the State Union of Serbia and Montenegro; a looser federation of its two member states, Serbia and Montenegro and two autonomous provinces of Vojvodina (within Serbia) and Kosovo and Metohia (under UN administration). FRY President Kostunica stepped down and was replaced as head of state of Serbia and Montenegro by Svetozar Marovic, a Montenegrin. Serbian prime minister, Zoran Djindjic, was assassinated. In parliamentary elections an alliance of three political blocs led by the Demokratska Stranka Srbije (DSS) (Democratic Party of Serbia), led by Zoran Zivkovic won. Later, the Srbije Demokratska Stranka (SDS) (Serbian Democratic Party) and the Narodna Demokratska Stranka (NDS) (People's Democratic Party) merged with the DSS.

2004 Boris Tadic, a pro-West liberal, was elected president of Serbia. Vojislav Kostunica replaced Zivkovic as leader of the DSS and became prime minister. In Kosovo, parliamentary and presidential elections took place; the LDK won the parliamentary elections and Ramush Haradinaj became prime minister. Incumbent President Ibrahim Rugova was re-elected

2005 The Kosovo prime minister Haradinaj resigned and Adem Salihaj replaced him. The US resumed aid to Serbia as a reward for improved co-operation with the ICTY. The EU agreed to open talks with Serbia and Montenegro on a stabilisation and association agreement that could lead to EU membership. Five former Serbian policemen accused of taking part in the 1995 Srebrenica massacre went on trial in Belgrade.

2006 Kosovo president, Ibrahim Rugova, died; he was considered a moderate Kosovo-Albanian leader and his death just as negotiations on the future of Kosovo were about to start, was considered a setback. He was succeeded by Fatmir Sejdiu. Agim Çeku became prime minister of Kosovo. Slobodan Milosevic was found dead of a heart attack, in his cell in The Hague. The EU broke off membership talks with Serbia and Montenegro, citing failure by the authorities to arrest war crimes suspect Ratko Mladic and deliver him to the ICTY. Montenegro formally declared independence from Serbia; Serbia declared itself the union's legal successor. Joachim Rucker took office as the head of the UN Interim Administration Mission, in Kosovo. In a referendum it was agreed by 51.5 per cent of the electorate (excluding ethnic Albanians from Kosovo) to constitutional changes. Among the articles promulgated was a ban on capital punishment and human cloning, guaranteed human rights and a degree of autonomy for the province of Vojvodina. Controversially, however, other articles claimed sovereignty over the UN-administered province of Kosovo and enshrined the Cyrillic alphabet (unused by ethnic minorities) as the official script.

2007 In parliamentary elections held in January the Srpska Radikalna Stranka (SRS) (Serb Radical Party) won 28.7 per cent of the vote (81 out of 250 seats) and became the largest single bloc. However, a coalition was formed by the Demokratska Stranka (DS) (Democratic Party – led by President Tadic) and the DSS (led by the prime minister), which won 22.9 per cent (65 seats) and 47 per cent (47 seats) respectively. Nevertheless, the result was seen as an impediment to Serbia's EU membership aspirations, as such a large proportion of the electorate supporting a staunch nationalist agenda. Serbia rejected the UN plan for Kosovo that proposed a form of self-rule, although not independence. In July provisional prime minister of the UN protectorate of Kosova, Agim Ceku, said that no unilateral declaration of independence would be made (by the ethnic Albanian leaders) without the support of the EU and US. During the first round of talks in September, concerning the future of Kosovo, no agreement was reached: Serbian authorities offered broad autonomy and the province's ethnic Albanians demanded full independence. The Kosovo parliamentary elections held in November were won by the Democratic Party, led by Hashim Thaçi, former leader of the Kosovo Liberation Army. After a number of talks on the future sovereignty of Kosovo had failed, a multinational tribunal was called by the UN, including representatives from the European Union, the US, Russia and Serbian and Albanian Kosovas. Two camps developed with the US and Albanian Kosovas advocating a fully independent Kosovo, while Serbia and Russia are staunchly opposed to it. In November, Albanian Kosovas threatened to declare a unilateral declaration of independence if the 10 December talks fail to find a negotiated peace. In December, Hashim Thaçi, became prime minister of the Assembly of Kosovo, as leader of a coalition led by the Partia Demokratike e Kosovës (PDK) (Democratic Party of Kosovo) and Lidhja Demokratike e Kosovës, (LDK) (Democratic League of Kosovo).

2008 In presidential elections for the Republic of Serbia, held in two rounds on 20 January and 3 February, Boris Tadic won 51.61 per cent of the vote, his opponent Tomislav Nikolic won 47.69 per cent. Thaçi, a pro-independence leader, was sworn into office in Kosovo on 9 January. Kosovo declared its independence on 14 February in the face of Serbian objections. A riot broke out in Belgrade as many countries immediately recognised the newly independent Kosovo. Russia pledged its support for Serbia, while some EU countries with unresolved independence situations or historic sensibilities (Cyprus, Romania, Slovakia) also said they would not recognise the new state. On 22 February mobs attacked foreign embassies, targeting the US embassy in particular until the EU threatened to suspend entry negotiation talks if the violence did not stop. Prime Minister Kostunica resigned following his inability to get his cabinet to reject closer ties to the EU in protest at the EU's backing of Kosovo's independence. President Tadic called a snap general election. Serbia took control of the 50km railway line from Lesak-Zvecan in the ethnic Serb dominated northern region of Kosovo on 3 March. In parliamentary elections held on 11 May the coalition For a European Serbia, led by Kostunica, won 38.7 per cent of the vote (103 seats of 250), the Serbian Radical Party 29.1 per cent (77), the Democratic Party of Serbia-New Serbia coalition 11.3 per cent (30), the coalition led by the Socialist Party of Serbia 7.9 per cent (20), and the Liberal Democratic Party 5.2 per cent (13). Turnout was 60.7 per cent. As a last act of the outgoing government in Serbia the Serbian minister for Kosovo set up a new parliament in the divided city of Mitrovica (in Kosovo) for minority Serbs. Ethnic Serbs insist that the new Kosovan constitution does not apply to them. The new Kosovan Serb Assembly may challenge the legitimacy of the Kosovan Assembly and entrench de facto partition of Kosovo. President Tadic nominated Mirko Cvetkovic as prime minister; parliament approved the choice and Cvetkovic and his government took office on 7 July. The former Bosnian Serb leader Radovan Karadzic was arrested on 22 July in Belgrade. He had been in hiding since 1995. On 30 July he was extradited to the UN War Crimes Tribunal in The Hague on charges of genocide. Karadzic elected to defend himself. After months of obstruction parliament ratified the pre-accession Stabilisation and Association Agreement with the EU on 9 September. The agreement is subject to the arrest of the remaining two Serb war crimes suspects but is seen as the first step towards EU membership.

Political structure

Constitution

The constitution was promulgated in 1990 and has articles that covers the soveignty of state, the legal system and executive. A referendum on constitutional amendments was held in October 2006 with over 100 new or amended articles agreed.

Form of state

Democratic republic

The executive

The president is the head of state, directly elected for a term of five years; for two-terms only. The president nominates a prime minister, after conferring with the largest political party in the national assembly. Other powers include dissolving parliament, calling elections and vetoing legislature until it has been reconsidered. The government is comprised of the prime minister and cabinet ministers approved by the national assembly.

Kosovo has its own president and government which are responsible for the economy, education, health, agriculture and tourism, but requires UN approval to introduce or change any new legislation in these areas. The UNMIK representive also has the power to dissolve the Kosovo assembly and call new elections. The president is appointed by the Kosovan assembly for a period of three years.

National legislature

The national assembly (narodna skupstina) is unicameral, with 250 members, elected for four-year terms, by general election.

It is the highest law making body in the country with the power to elect and dismiss the president, vice president, prime minister and any other person in a constitutionally mandated post.

Serbia has de jure sovereignty of Kosovo, however de facto government of the province is under the auspices of the UN Mission in Kosovo (UNMIK) and local Provisional Institutions of Self-Government (PISG).

Legal system

The legal system is based on the written constitution which states basic provisions and guarantees for a range of individual and collective rights, including civil laws. The court system is governed by the Supreme Court, the highest civil and criminal court in Serbia. The constitutional charter of Serbia was ratified in February 2003.

The Constitutional Court, which deals with the law and the constitution, comprises judges elected for a period of six years by the national assembly upon the recommendation of the Council of Ministers.

Last elections

11 May 2008 (parliamentary); 20 January and 3 February 2008 (presidential, two rounds).

Results: Parliament: Za Evropsku Srbiju (ZES) (For a European Serbia) coalition won 38.7 per cent of the vote (102 seats of 250), the Srpska Radikalna Stranka (SRS) (Serbian Radical Party) 29.1 per cent (78), the Demokratska Stranka (DS) (Democratic Party of Serbia)- Nova Srbija (New Serbia) coalition 11.3 per cent (30), the Socijalisticka Partija Srbije (SPS) (Socialist Party of Serbia) coalition 7.9 per cent (20), and the Liberalno-Demokratska Partija (LDP) Liberal Democratic Party 5.2 per cent (13). Turnout was 60.7 per cent. Presidential: first round Boris Tadic (DSS) won 35.39 per cent of the vote, Tomislav Nikolic (SRS) won 39.99 per cent; no other candidate won more than 8 per cent. Second round, Boris Tadic won 51.61 per cent of the vote, Tomislav Nikolic won 47.69 per cent.

Next elections

11 May 2008 (parliamentary); 2012 (presidential).

Political parties

Ruling party

The coalition For a European Serbia, formed from Socialist Party of Serbia, the Party of United Pensioners of Serbia, the United Serbia coalition, the For a European Sandzak coalition and the Alliance of Vojvodina Hungarians. (since Jun 2008)

Main opposition party

Socijalisticka Partija Srbije (SPS) (Serb Socialist Party)

Population

7.45 million (2007) (excluding Kosovo)

Last census: March 2002: 7,445,531 (exludes Kosovo and Metohia).

Population density: 104 inhabitants per square km. Urban population: 52 per cent (1995–2001).

Annual growth rate: 0.0 per cent 1994–2004 (WHO 2006)

Ethnic make-up

Serbian (63 per cent), Albanian (14 per cent), Montenegrin (6 per cent) and Hungarian (4 per cent).

Religions

Serbian Orthodox (65 per cent), Islam, Roman Catholic and Protestant

Education

With less developed education systems than Slovenia and Croatia during the Tito period, Serbia had an adult illiteracy rate of 10 per cent in 1990 (in Kosovo, the figure was then 17 per cent).

Primary education lasts for eight years from aged seven. Secondary education is provided in grammar, vocational and art schools with courses lasting up to four years. Higher education is provided in universities and colleges.

There are four universities in Serbia (Belgrade, Novi Sad, Nis and Kragujevac) and one in Kosovo (Pristina). However, graduate unemployment is high.

There was a major exodus of younger and more educated people abroad during the 1990s. In 1994 alone, around 100,000 people, or around 1 per cent of the population, may have emigrated.

During the lead-up to the conflict in Kosovo, education was a very controversial issue, with the majority Albanian population refusing to be taught in the Serbian language. Alternative or Albanian language education thus emerged in Kosovo.

Literacy rate: 99 per cent total; 97 per cent female; adult rates (Unicef 2004).

Compulsory years: 7 to 15

Enrolment rate: 66 per cent gross primary enrolment, 59 per cent gross secondary enrolment; of relevant age group (including repeaters) (Unesco).

Pupils per teacher: 20 primary; 14 secondary, (Unesco 2002)

Health

Per capita total expenditure on health (2003) was US$373; of which per capita government spending was US$282 (WHO 2006).

Since 1992, the extent and quality of healthcare provision has sharply deteriorated. However, a well-developed private healthcare system has emerged for the better-off. Largely free at the point of delivery and funded by a universal social insurance tax levied on all employees and employers, public healthcare provision now require all kinds of charges, most notably for imported medications.

HIV/Aids

HIV prevalence: 0.2 per cent aged 15–49 in 2003 (World Bank)

Life expectancy: 73 years, 2004 (WHO 2006)

Fertility rate/Maternal mortality rate: 1.6 births per woman, 2004 (WHO 2006)

Birth rate/Death rate: 12.7 births and 10.6 deaths per 1,000 population (2003)

Child (under 5 years) mortality rate (per 1,000): 12 per 1,000 live births (World Bank)

Head of population per physician: 2.06 physicians per 1,000 people, 2002 (WHO 2006)

Welfare

Welfare provision in Serbia was relatively generous during the Tito period, when retirement pensions were around 80 per cent of average monthly incomes. Since 2000, the World Bank has helped fund pensions and social benefits. A three-year Country Assistance Stratergy (CAS) includes reducing poverty levels through improved social protection.

Main cities

Belgrade (capital, estimated population 1.1 million in 2005), Novi Sad (194,374), Niš (175,477), Kragujevac (157,166); (169,354), Prizren (110,482).

Languages spoken
Croatian, Bosnian, Hungarian, Slovak, Albanian (principally in Kosovo), Macedonian and Slovenian are all spoken.
English is the most commonly used foreign business language. Other languages include German, Russian and Italian.
Official language/s
Serbian
Media
National news agency: Tanjug
Other news agencies: Beta News Agency (www2.beta.co.yu); FoNet (www.fonet.co.yu), Tiker (www.tiker.co.yu).
Press
Dailies: National publications in Serbian, include Danas (www.danas.co.yu), Vecernje Novosti (www.novosti.co.yu), Politika (www.politika.co.yu), Glas Javnosti (www.glas-javnosti.co.yu) and Borba (www.borba.co.yu). Regional papers in Serbian include Dnevnik (www.dnevnik.co.yu) from Novi Sad, 24 Sata (www.24sata.co.yu) and Kurir (www.kurir-info.co.yu) are tabloids from Belgrade. In English Blic (www.blic.co.yu), Balkan Web (www.balkanweb.com/maineng.htm), Kosovo Daily (www.kosovodaily.com) and Belgrade Newswww.belgradenews.com.
Weeklies: In Serbian, Nedeljne Telegraf (www.nedeljnitelegraf.co.yu) is the largest weekly tabloid newspaper. Vojvodina (www.vojvodina.com) is an independent, open weekly newspaper about cultural, political, economic, agriculture and sports. Other significant weeklies are NIN (www.nin.co.yu), Standard (www.standardmagazin.com) and Vreme (www.vreme.com).
Business: The main magazine, in English, is Ekonomist (www.ekonomist.co.yu/eng).
Broadcasting
The Broadcasting Agency Council (BAC) oversees radio and television output and licenses operators.
Radio Televizije Srbije (RTS) (Radio Television Serbia) (www.rts.co.yu) is the national, public, state broadcaster, with two television channels and three radio stations with internet access and podcasts.
Radio: There are many private radio stations. B92 (www.b92.net) has a youthful audience; Medunarodni Radio Serbija (www.radioyu.org); Radio Index (www.indexradio.com) and Radio Pink (www.rtvpink.com). International radio stations from US, UK, France and Germany can be received.
Television: Independent networks include TV Pink (www.rtvpink.com) and TV-Avala (www.tv-avala.com) showing popular international programmes and local content shows.

Advertising
All principal media are available through advertising agencies or directly. There are Western agencies operating in Belgrade. Tobacco and alcohol advertising is banned on television.

Economy
By 1990, the last year of comparative economic normality, the republics of Serbia and Montenegro together accounted for around 35 per cent of the combined GDP of the former Yugoslav state. Relative to population (around 40 per cent of the Yugoslav total in 1990), Serbia's share of all Yugoslav GDP, foreign exchange-denominated exports and service income was below that of Slovenia and Croatia. On the other hand, Serbia's share of imports payable in foreign exchange was then relatively large, with the resultant trade deficit (US$1.3 billion in 1990) financed by foreign exchange and other transfers from elsewhere in Yugoslavia. These transfers were also central to the servicing of Serbia's large foreign debt.
Serbia's orientation towards non-foreign exchange denominated markets elsewhere in Yugoslavia and beyond was far greater than that of Slovenia and, to a lesser extent, Croatia. Structurally, Serbia's economy in the 1990s had many of the characteristics of relative underdevelopment, including an emphasis on the domestic export of low value raw materials and semi-processed goods and a barter-based form of foreign trade in predominantly non-Western markets. At the federal level of government, Serbia then also benefited from internal economic transfers, although these were mainly directed to Kosovo during the post-war period. Serbia is breaking out of its state-controlled siege economy following the fall of Slobodan Milosevic. The economy of Kosovo is being rebuilt with substantial international assistance.
Serbia has begun privatising state assets, but a number of major assets remain to be sold off. This process is an important source of revenue, but political uncertainty in early 2007 has threatened to delay further sales, which could affect the prospects of a budgetar surplus.
Serbia has had financial assistance, including World Bank and IMF loans, but has repaid some of these and reduced its debt burden to 37 per cent of GDP. Foreign direct investment (FDI) has been deterred in the past by Serbia's poor record of corruption and crime, although recent reforms aim to improve conditions for investment and there is growing interest. FDI has increased from US$950 million in 2004 to US$5.56 billion in 2006. Serbia's continued failure to surrender Ratko Mladic resulted in the freezing of negotiations with the EU for a Stabilisation and Association Agreement in 2006. The absence of a relationship with an institution which might demand discipline from Serbia could damage market confidence.
GDP grew by 7.2 per cent in 2004, largely due to successes in structural reform, but fell to 6.3 in 2005. Inflation, although still high at 17.3 per cent in 2005, has dropped from 113.5 per cent in 2000. Serbia needs steady growth to address its low standard of living with around a third of the population living close to the poverty line. Unemployment is a constant problem, rising to 31.6 per cent in 2005.

External trade
Serbia is a member of the Central European free trade agreement (Cefra) which, by 2007, following the loss of those countries that had joined the European Union, has left eight countries all located in the Balkans (except Moldova), provides a budget surplus with other members.
Foreign trade is underdeveloped and imports sustain a distorted balance of payments. Serbia has large deposits of minerals (coal, lead, zinc, copper and gold) but lack of investment has hampered development, which in turn hinders growth in the economy. Manufacturing includes foodstuffs, furniture and base metals.
Imports
Main imports include machinery and vehicles, fuels and lubricants, consumer goods, chemicals, food and live animals and raw materials.
Main sources: (Figures include Montenegro) Russia (20.2 per cent total, 2006), Germany (5.1 per cent), Italy (18.1 per cent).
Exports
Principal exports include manufactured goods, food and live animals, electrical machinery and appliances.
Main destinations: (Figures include Montenegro) Italy (14.4 per cent total, 2006), Bosnia and Hercegovina (11.7 per cent), Germany (9.9 per cent).

Agriculture
Farming
Agriculture is the mainstay of the economy, accounting for up to 70 per cent of GDP. The main crops are wheat, maize, sugar beet and tobacco. There are extensive orchards and livestock is reared. Agricultural exports and imports are important for the whole economy. Animal husbandry is still developing and is of minor importance.
About 80 per cent of the total agricultural area, which is the equivalent of 4.96 million hectares, is under mixed farming systems with elements of ecological farming.

Most of the highly productive soil, located in the lowlands, receives small quantities of rainfall.
The agricultural sector in Serbia is hampered by shortages of industrial goods such as fertiliser, with an estimated US$44 million investment needed to ensure sufficient supplies of agri-chemicals annually.
The country also suffers periodically from droughts which reduce agriculture production and economic growth.
Crop production in 2005 included: 9,557,250 tonnes (t) cereals in total, 2,700,000t wheat, 6,300,000t maize, 125,000t oats, 1,100,000t potatoes, 2,700,000t sugar beets, 332,000t soya beans, 141,000t pulses, 475,000t grapes, 225,000t tomatoes, 248,723t oilcrops, 13,500t tobacco, 188,000t apples, 580,000t plums, 175,000t chillies and peppers, 1,699,450t fruit in total, 1,370,200t vegetables in total. Livestock production included: 848,240 meat in total, 175,000t beef, 560,000t pig meat, 22,000t lamb, 88,400t poultry, 88,400t eggs, 1,852,000t milk, 4,000t honey, 17,850t cattle hides, 4,290t sheepskins, 2,700t greasy wool.

Fishing

In 2004, the total marine fish catch was 433 tonnes and the total crustacean catch was 14 tonnes.

Forestry

Forestry has experienced only slight falls in output, mainly because at times shortages of other fuels increase the demand for firewood locally.
Exports of forest material in 2004 amounted to US$139.1 million, while imports amounted to US$352.8 million.
Timber production in 2004 included 3,520,000 cubic metre (cum) roundwood, 1,423,000cum industrial roundwood, 575,000cum sawnwood, 1,138,000cum sawlogs and veneer logs, 196,000cum pulpwood, 77,000cum wood-based panels, 2,097,000cum woodfuel; 159,000 tonnes (t) paper and paperboard (including 49,000t newsprint), 22,000t paper pulp.

Industry and manufacturing

Prior to the 1999 Kosovo War, Serbia and Montenegro had a diversified industrial base with major industries including metal processing, food production, textile and other manufacturing. The industrial sector accounted for almost US$1 billion of former Yugoslavia's exports. Much of the energy-dependent industry, including chemicals and iron and steel, collapsed because of shortages of energy and raw materials following the imposition of UN sanctions in 1999.
The damage done by the Nato bombing campaign to manufacturing was second only to the destruction to hydrocarbons and energy production. Total industrial production is thought to have fallen by 60 per cent, with whole sectors being wiped out. The sector's share of GDP dropped from 45 per cent to 15–20 per cent. Previously, over 40 per cent of the labour force were employed in industry, but more than 100,000 jobs were lost immediately as a result of industrial destruction. Financial aid and FDI have been crucial to rebuilding Serbia industrial base.

Tourism

The revival of the tourist sector is seen as central to the reconstruction of the economy of Serbia after the upheavals of recent years. It had serious war-damage, but has gradually recovered. Considerable investment in renovation and expansion of infrastructure is required to sustain continued growth.

Mining

Serbia has a significant mining sector. Lead and zinc are produced in substantial quantities. There is a large gold and silver mine at Bor in eastern Serbia. The fact that many of the most valuable non-ferrous metal mineral deposits are in Kosovo makes the area of great economic importance. In the longer-term, there is likely to be considerable foreign investor interest in Serbia's non-ferrous metal mineral ore resources, particularly copper and gold.

Hydrocarbons

Serbia has oil reserves of around 78 million barrels. Most oil production is undertaken in the autonomous province of Vojvodina. Production is not sufficient to meet domestic consumption and 53,000bpd are imported yearly.
Serbia has natural gas reserves of 48 billion cubic metres, about 60 per cent of the Balkan region's total reserves. Russia supplies over 60 per cent of Serbia's gas needs. A small amount of natural gas is produced domestically in Vojvodina.
The province of Kosovo has extensive coal reserves, comprising a large proportion of the estimated total of 18.2 billion tonnes. Coal is also extracted in the Kolubara and Kostolac basins in central Serbia.

Energy

Serbia depends on imports of oil and gas for about 40 per cent of its energy despite increased utilisation of local resources of coal and water power. Hydroelectric power accounts for nearly 60 per cent of electricity generation and thermal for 40 per cent.
Much of Serbia's energy sector was damaged by neglect, lack of investment and war damage. However, there are plans to harness more water courses in the Drina and Morava River catchment areas for hydroelectric plants, producing up to 10MW each.

Financial markets

Stock exchange

Opened in 1990, the Beogradska Berza (BB) (Belgrade Stock Exchange) was not an important financial intermediary in Serbia but with more privatisation being undertaken and improved relations with the West, the prospects for Serbian financial markets has improved.

Banking and insurance

Begradska Banka, Jugobanka, Investbanka and Beobanka, four of the country's old banking giants, were closed down in 2002. By 2006 Beobanka was merged with the Greek, Alpha Bank and the Hungarian OTP Bank bought almost 90 per cent of the provincial Niska Bank.

Central bank

Narodna Banka Srbije (NBS) (National Bank of Serbia).

Main financial centre

Belgrade

Time

GMT plus one hour (daylight saving, late March to late October, GMT plus two hours)

Geography

Landlocked and situated in the central Balkan Peninsula in south-eastern Europe, Serbia consists of two parts: the Great Danubian Plains of Vojvodina to the north, where the two main rivers are the Sava and the Danube, which meet at Belgrade; and the hilly and forested areas of inner (central) and southern Serbia, where the main rivers are the Drina, Morava and Vardar.
Serbia is bordered by Hungary to the north; Croatia, Bosnia and Hercegovina (BiH) and Montenegro to the west and south-west; Albania and Macedonia to the south and south-east; and Bulgaria and Romania to the east. Serbia has borders with Croatia and Romania along the River Danube. The River Drina marks the border between Serbia and BiH.

Hemisphere

Northern

Climate

The climate is largely continental. The summers are very hot and the winters bitterly cold. The average summer temperature in Belgrade is 22 degrees Celsius (C) and in winter the average temperature is zero degrees C. Precipitation is generally constant, with average annual rainfall in Belgrade of around 635mm. Snowfall is extensive in winter.

Entry requirements

Passports

Required by all.

Visa
Required by all, with the exception of nationals of most European countries, North America, Australasia and a number of other countries. A full list of exceptions and lengths of stay permitted will be found at www.mfa.gov.yu/Visas/f_without_visa.htm.

Currency advice/regulations
There are no restrictions on the import of local or foreign currencies. Local currency in excess of D120,000 must be declared and shown to have been acquired abroad. Foreign currency may be declared against a receipt which will allow re-export.

Customs
Various personal articles and goods are allowed duty-free.

Health (for visitors)

Mandatory precautions
None required

Advisable precautions
Hepatitis A and B, diphtheria, polio, TB, typhoid, tetanus vaccinations are recommended. There is a rabies risk.

Hotels
Hotels are classified into five categories: L (extra), A, B, C and D; boarding houses into three, I, II and III. There is a 10–20 per cent service charge. Visitors must also pay a residential tax, which varies between regions.

Credit cards
International credit cards are accepted in large hotels and businesses in Serbia.

Public holidays (national)

Fixed dates
1 Jan (New Year's Day), 7 Jan (Orthodox Christmas Day), 15 Feb (Serbia National day), 1–2 May (Labour Days), 9 May (Victory Day).

Variable dates
Orthodox Good Friday, Orthodox Easter Monday.

Working hours

Banking
Mon–Fri: 0700–1500; Sat: 0800–1400. Belgrade airport 0800–2000.

Business
Mon–Fri: 0800–1500.

Government
Mon–Fri: 0730–1530.

Shops
Mon–Fri: generally in larger towns: 0800–2000 (some shops closing between 1200 and 1700); Sat: 0800–1500.

Telecommunications

Mobile/cell phones
There are GSM 900/1800 services available throughout most of the country.

Electricity supply
220V, 50Hz with European flat and round, two-pin plugs.

Social customs/useful tips
Punctuality depends on the ethnic region: it is important in some, more casual in others. As elsewhere, it is customary to shake hands on meeting and taking leave. Do carry some form of identity at all times. Appointments must be made in advance. Business cards should indicate academic/professional titles and are exchanged after introduction. Many executives speak a second language, including German, English, Italian or Russian. There are some restrictions on photography.

Security
Visitors are advised to avoid Kosovo unless absolutely necessary and should remain vigil if required. Armed conflict continues in parts of Kosovo, and the crime rate (including violent crime) is high. Any travel into these areas should only take place in organised groups after seeking advice from the local authorities before the journey is made.

Getting there

Air

National airline: JAT Airways

International airport/s: Belgrade Nikola Tesla Airport (LYBE), 18km west of Belgrade.

Airport tax: Around D1,200, but may be included in ticket price.

Surface

Road: There are border crossings from Hungary, Romania, Bulgaria, and Albania, Bosnia and Hercegovina, Croatia, Macedonia and Montenegro.

The E5 highway, part of the pan-European 'Corridor 10' road and rail project linking Germany to Greece, will traverse Serbia from the Hungarian to the Macedonian borders when completed. Construction of the southern part of the Serbian section of the highway has been held up due to lack of funding.

Rail: There are rail links with neighbouring countries. It is possible to travel to Belgrade via Budapest.

Water: Ships provide regular passenger services and cruises on the Danube from Germany, passing through Serbia. There are also links with the rivers Rhine and Main and the Black Sea.

Getting about

National transport

Air: JAT Airways flies several domestic routes and provides a charter service.

Road: There are some 48,423km of roads, including 374km of motorways. The main route links Belgrade with Subotica (via Novi Sad), Kragujevac and Nis. Road maintenance is often inadequate.

Buses: An extensive network of express buses links Serbia's cities, although fuel shortages can often restrict services. Multi-journey tickets are available and sold through tobacconists. In general, fares paid to the driver are usually double the price of pre-purchase tickets.

Rail: There are around 4,000km of track, of which over a quarter is electrified. Maintenance of track and stock has deteriorated in recent years. The services are often overcrowded, unpunctual and slow. International express trains link Belgrade with Subotica, Novi Sad, Kragujevac, Nis and Pristina.

Water: There is a well established inland waterways system, based on the Danube, Sava, Tizsa and Begej rivers.

City transport

Taxis: Good services operate in most large cities and towns. All taxis are metered. There are taxi stands in central locations, but they can also be hailed in the street. Taxis are cheaper in Belgrade if arranged by telephone.

Buses, trams & metro: All cities and towns are served by buses; trams only in the centre of Belgrade and in Subotica. The service is generally regular.

Car hire
Cars can be hired in most main towns through travel agencies. There is a speed limit of 120kph on motorways and 60kph in built-up areas. Drive on the right and give way to traffic from the right unless clearly marked otherwise. Seat belts are compulsory in front seats.
To be on the safe side, carry an international driver's licence as well as a national licence.

BUSINESS DIRECTORY

The addresses listed below are a selection only. While World of Information makes every endeavour to check these addresses, we cannot guarantee that changes have not been made, especially to telephone numbers and area codes. We would welcome any corrections.

Telephone area codes
The international direct dialling (IDD) code is +381, followed by area code and subscriber's number:

Belgrade	11	Pec	39
Kragujevac	34	Podgorica	81
Krusevac	37	Pristina	38
Leskovac	16	Uzice	31
Novi Sad	21		

Useful telephone numbers
Police: 92
Fire: 93
Ambulance: 94

Chambers of Commerce

American Chamber of Commerce in Serbia, 30 Vlajkoviceva, 11000 Belgrade (tel: 334-5961; fax: 324-7771; e-mail: info@amcham.yu).

Belgrade Chamber of Economy , 12 Kneza Milosa, 11001 Belgrade (tel:264-1355; fax: 264-2029; e-mail: mmj@komberg.org.yu).

Kragujevac Chamber of Commerce and Industry, 10 Mose Pijade, 34000 Kragujevac (tel: 335-805; fax: 334-049; e-mail: rpkkg@eunet.yu).

Serbian Chamber of Commerce and Industry, 13-15 Resavska, 11000 Belgrade (tel: 324-0611; fax: 323-0949; e-mail: centar@pks.co.yu).

Uzice Regional Chamber of Commerce, 52 Dimirija Tucovica, 31000 Uzice (tel: 513-483; fax: 514-184; e-mail: office@rpk-uzice.co.yu).

Banking

Association of Serbian Banks (Udruzenje Banaka Srbije), Bulevar Kralja Aleksandra 86, 11000 Belgrade (tel: 302-0760; fax: 337-0179).

JIK Banka, Knez Mihailova 42, Belgrade (tel: 632-822; fax: 183-198).

JUBMES Banka, Bulevar Avnoja 121, 11070 Belgrade (tel: 220-5500; fax: 311-0217; e-mail: jubmes@jubmes.co.yu).

Kreditna Banka Beograd, Lenjinov Bulevar 111, Belgrade (tel: 222-4428; fax: 144-923).

Panonska Banka, Bulevar Oslobodenja 76, Novi Sad (tel: 488-7100; e-mail: office@panban.co.yu).

PKB Banka, 29 Novembra 68a, Belgrade (tel: 753-366; fax: 750-932).

Privredna Banka, Brace Jugovica 17, Belgrade (tel: 623-272; fax: 627-247).

Vojvodjanska Banka, Trg Slobode 7, 21000 Novi Sad (tel: 621-277; fax: 021-624-940).

Central bank

Narodna Banka Srbije (NBS) (National Bank of Serbia), 12 Kralja Petra Street, 11000 Belgrade, (tel: 302-7100; fax: 302-7381; e-mail: gen.sec@nbs.yu).

Travel information

AutomobileAssociation of Serbia (AMSS), Kneginje Zorke 58, Belgrade (tel: 333-1100; fax: 245-1078; e-mail: info@amss.org.yu).

JAT Airways, Bulevar Umetnosti 16, 11070 Belgrade (tel: 311-4222; fax: 311-1082; e-mail: jatairways@jat.com).

Ministry of tourism

Ministry of Trade, Tourism and Services, Nemanjina Street 22-26, Belgrade (tel: 361-0579; fax: 361-0258; e-mail: kabinet@minttu.sr.gov.yu).

National tourist organisation offices

National Tourism Organization of Serbia, Decanska 8, 11000 Belgrade (tel: 323-0566; fax: 322-1068; e-mail: ntos@yubc.net).

Ministries

Ministry of Agriculture, Forestry and Water Management, 22-26 Nemanjina Street, Belgrade (tel: 306-5038; fax: 361-6272; e-mail: office@minpolj.sr.gov.yu).

Ministry of Capital Investment, 22-26 Nemanjina Street, Belgrade (tel: 361-6426; fax: 361-7486; e-mail: cabinet@mki.sr.gov.yu).

Ministry of Culture, 3 Vlajkoviceva Street, Belgrade (tel: 339-8404; fax: 339-8936; e-mail: kabinet@min-cul.sr.gov.yu).

Ministry of Diaspora, 42 Svetozara Markovica, Belgrade (tel: 263-8033; fax: 263-7624; e-mail: info@mzd.sr.gov.yu).

Ministry of Economy, 16 Kralja Milana Street, Belgrade (tel: 361-7599; fax: 361-7640; e-mail: officempriv@mpriv.sr.gov.yu).

Ministry of Education and Sport, 22-26 Nemanjina Street, Belgrade (tel: 361-6357; fax: 361-6491; e-mail: webmaster@mps.sr.gov.yu).

Ministry of Energy and Mining, 22-26 Nemanjina Street, Belgrade (tel: 334-6755; fax: 361- 6603; e-mail: kabinet@mem.sr.gov.yu).

Ministry of Finance, 20 Kneza Milosa Street, Belgrade (tel: 361-4972; fax: 361-8914; e-mail: informacije@mfin.sr.gov.yu).

Ministry of Foreign Affairs, 24-26 Kneza Milosa Street, Belgrade (tel: 361-6333; fax: 361-8366; e-mail: mfa@smip.sv.gov.yu).

Ministry of Health, 22-26 Nemanjina Street, Belgrade (tel: 361-6251; fax: 656-548; e-mail: kabinet.zdravlje@zdravlje.sr.gov.yu).

Ministry of the Interior, 101 Kneza Milosa Street, Belgrade (tel: 306-2000; fax: 361-7814; e-mail: muprs@mup.sr.gov.yu).

Ministry of International Economic Relations, 10 Vlajkoviceva Street, Belgrade (tel: 361-7583; fax: 363-3142; e-mail: cabinet@mier.sr.gov.yu).

Ministry of Justice, 22-26 Nimanjina Street, Belgrade (tel: 361-6548; fax: 361-6419; e-mail: kabinet@mpravde.sr.gov.yu).

Ministry of Labour, Employment and Social Affairs, 22-26 Nemanjina Street, Belgrade (tel: 361-3734; fax: 363-1792; e-mail: kabinet@minrzs.sr.gov.yu).

Ministry of Public Administration and Local Self-Government, 6 Bircaninova Street, Belgrade (tel: 268-5387; fax: 268-5315; e-mail: info.mpalsg@mpalsg.sr.gov.yu).

Ministry of Religion, 11 Nemanjina Street, Belgrade (tel: 306-5960; fax: 363-3446; e-mail: kabinet.mv@mv.sr.gov.yu).

Ministry of Science and Environmental Protection, 22-26 Nemajina Street, Belgrade (tel: 268-8047; fax: 361-6516; e-mail: info@mntr.sr.gov.yu).

Ministry of Trade, Tourism and Services, Nemanjina Street 22-26, Belgrade (tel: 361-0579; fax: 361-0258; e-mail: kabinet@minttu.sr.gov.yu).

Other useful addresses

British Embassy, Resavska 46, 11000 Belgrade (tel: 264-5055; fax:265-9651; e-mail: belgrade.man@fco.gov.uk).

Kosovo Trust Agency, Ilir Konushevi 8, Pristina, Kosovo (tel: 500-400; fax: 248-076; e-mail: kta@eumik.org).

Novinska Agencija Tanjug (news agency), Obilicev Venac 2, Box 439, Belgrade 11001 (tel: 332-221).

Roads Directorate of the Republic of Serbia, Ljube Cupe 5, 11000 Belgrade (tel: 454-779; fax: 444-5557; e-mail: dzpnapl@eunet.yu).

Statistical Office of the Republic of Serbia, Milana Rakica 5, 11000 Belgrade (tel: 241-2922; fax: 240-1284; e-mail: stat@statserb.sr.gov.yu).

US Embassy, Kneza Milosa 50, 11000 Belgrade (tel: 361-9344; fax: 361-5489; e-mail: belgradeacs@state.gov).

National news agency: Tanjug

Other news agencies: Beta News Agency (www2.beta.co.yu); FoNet (www.fonet.co.yu), Tiker (www.tiker.co.yu).

Internet sites

Assembly of Kosovo: www.assembly-kosova.org

Belgrade News: www.belgradenews.com

B92 independent broadcasting station: www.b92.net

European Commission/World Bank, Balkans reconstruction web site: www.seerecon.org

Pink International (TV): www.rtvpink.com

Seychelles

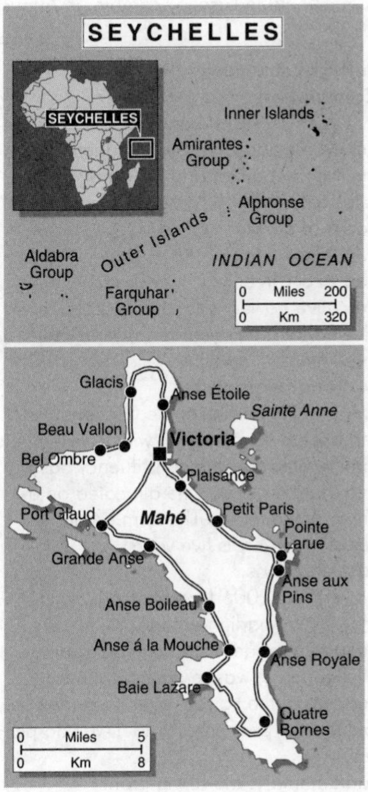

The Seychelles is comprised of approximately 115 islands spread over a large area of the western Indian Ocean. The largest of the islands, Mahe, on which is the country's capital, Victoria, is 153 sq km in area. The country declared independence from Britain in 1976, it is a republic and member of the Commonwealth.

'Strategy 2017'

in January 2008 the International Monetary Fund (IMF) reported that economic growth had continued to be robust in 2007. GDP had been over 5 per cent, supported by strong foreign direct investment (FDI), mainly in the tourism sector. Unemployment was low, while inflation rose in response to the gradual realignment of the rupee, which is aimed at increasing Seychelles' international competitiveness. The current account deficit increased, partly as a result of increased imports related to record inflows of new FDI and the purchase of another oil tanker.

A range of structural reforms include increases of utility prices, removal of price controls on imports, and foreign exchange market liberalisation measures. The aim of these reforms in to reduce subsidies to public enterprises, limit budgetary pressures and improve market signals.

Citizens of the Indian Ocean archipelago enjoy a relatively high per capita income, good health care and education. Although the economy is based largely on tourism, tuna canning and fishing make significant contributions. The government encourages foreign investment in the tourism industry, and also tries to reduce dependence on tourism by promoting the development of farming, fishing, and small-scale manufacturing.

Politics

The last presidential elections took place in July 2006. As expected, the contest was close, and incumbent President Michel was elected by 54 per cent of the vote. In late May 2006, Seychelles National Party (SNP) leader Mr Ramkalawan proposed a motion for the dissolution of the National Assembly, allowing for parliamentary elections to be held simultaneously with the presidential elections. However, the motion was unsuccessful. The parliamentary elections were therefore held in 2007 as originally scheduled. The Seychelles People's Progressive Front won 56.16 per cent of the vote held on 10-12 May; the Seychelles National Party won 43.84 per cent. Seychelles was re-admitted to the Southern African Development Community (SADC) at the its summit held in Lusaka, Zambia, in August 2007.

Outlook

The IMF has recommended that the government continue to broaden its reforms to reduce the vulnerability of the economy and contribute to long-term improvements in living standards.

Risk assessment

Economic	Improving
Political	Fair
Regional stability	Good

KEY FACTS

Official name: Republic of Seychelles

Head of State: President James Michel (appointed 2004; elected 30 Jul 2006)

Head of government: President James Michel

Ruling party: Front Progressiste du Peuple Seychellois (FPPS) (Seychelles People's Progressive Front) (since 1993; re-elected May 2007)

Area: 453 square km

Population: 90,000 (2007)*

Capital: Victoria

Official language: Creole, French and English

Currency: Seychelle rupee (SR) = 100 cents

Exchange rate: SR7.99 per US$ (Jul 2008)

GDP per capita: US$8,581 (2007)

GDP real growth: 5.20% (2007)

Inflation: 5.70% (2007)*

Balance of trade: US$264.60 million (2005)

Foreign debt: US$650.00 million (2005)

Visitor numbers: 140,627 (2006)

* estimated figure

COUNTRY PROFILE

Historical profile

The Seychelles, a cluster of 89 granite and coral islands in the Indian ocean some 1,000 miles from the African coast, won independence from the United Kingdom in 1976, after two centuries of colonial rule. The islands had been uninhabited until they were occupied in the 18th century by the French, who explored the islands in the 1740s and later settled there with their African slaves, in the 1770s. During the Napoleonic wars, the British blockaded the islands and the Seychelles changed hands several times between 1796 and 1810. British sovereignty was finally confirmed in the Treaty of Paris in 1814. Administered as a dependency of Mauritius for nearly a century, the Seychelles became a Crown Colony in 1903.

The uninhabited islands were sighted by the Portuguese explorer Vasco da Gama in the early sixteenth century, but it was not until the 1770s that any attempt to settle them was made when French farmers landed and introduced cinnamon, clove and nutmeg plantations (worked by slaves).

1794 The islands were taken over by the British and administered from Mauritius.

1903 Seychelles became a separate colony.

1948 The first elections to the legislative assembly took place.

1964 The Seychelles' first political organisations were established – the Seychelles Democratic Party (SDP) led by James Mancham and the Front Progressiste du Peuple Seychellois (FPPS) (Seychelles People's Progressive Front) (formerly the SPUP) of France-Albert René.

1975 The Seychelles was granted internal self-government; the SDP and the FPPS formed a coalition government under the premiership of Mancham.

1976 Became an independent republic. James Mancham became president and René became prime minister.

1977 René seized power in an armed coup and established a one-party state with the FPPS as the sole legal party.

1982 A mutiny in the army was put down by pro-government troops.

1991 René re-established a multi-party democracy.

1993 Multi-party presidential and legislative elections resulted in a landslide victory for both President René and the FPPS.

1998 Presidential and legislative elections were won by President René and the FPPS.

2001 Presidential elections resulted in a victory for President René (54.2 per cent of the vote).

2002 The FPPS won the parliamentary elections.

2004 On 14 April, President René, who came to power in a bloodless coup in 1977, retired and Vice President James Michel was sworn in as president. On 26 December, the Indian Ocean tsunami caused structural damage, but little loss of life.

2006 In 30 July presidential elections, incumbant James Michel (FPPS) was re-elected with 53.7 per cent of the vote, Wavel Ramkalawan (SNP) won 45.7 per cent and independent candidate, Philippe Boulle 0.5 per cent. Turnout was 86 per cent. There was a record annual number of 140,627 visitors. The government has stated that it does not want numbers to exceed 200,000 in future citing environmental degradation as a risk of mass tourism. The tourist industry intends to promote its attractions to visitors from the high-end of the market.

2007 The Seychelles People's Progressive Front won 56.16 per cent of the vote in parliamentary elections were held on 10-12 May; the Seychelles National Party won 43.84 per cent. Seychelles was re-admitted to the Southern African Development Community (SADC) at the its summit held in Lusaka, Zambia, in August 2007.

Political structure

Constitution

In a June 1993 referendum, a new constitution was approved, institutionalising multi-party politics and providing for the establishment of a National Assembly.

Form of state

Republic

The executive

Executive power rests with the president, elected for a five-year term; renewable three times.

National legislature

The Assemblée Nationale (National Assembly) of 34 members, with 25 members directly elected on a constituency basis and the remaining nine allocated on a proportional basis. The term of the National Assembly is five years.

Last elections

28–30 July 2006 (presidential); 10–12 May 2007 (parliamentary).

Results: Presidential: Incumbent James Michel (FPPS) was re-elected with 53.7 per cent of the vote, Wavel Ramkalawan (SNP) 45.7 per cent. Turnout was 86 per cent.

Parliamentary: the ruling Front Progressiste du Peuple Seychellois (FPPS) (Seychelles People's Progressive Front) was re-elected with 56.16 per cent of the vote (23 seats out of 34) and the Seychelles National Party (SNP) 43.84 per cent (11); turnout was 85.9 per cent.

Next elections

2011 (presidential); 2012 (parliamentary)

Political parties

Ruling party

Front Progressiste du Peuple Seychellois (FPPS) (Seychelles People's Progressive Front) (since 1993; re-elected May 2007)

Main opposition party

Seychelles National Party (SNP)

Population

90,000 (2007)*

Last census: August 2002: 81,755

Population density: 178 inhabitants per square km. Urban population: 65 per cent (1995–2001).

Annual growth rate: 0.7 per cent 1994–2004 (WHO 2006)

KEY INDICATORS — Seychelles

	Unit	2003	2004	2005	2006	2007
Population	m	0.08	0.08	0.08	0.08	*0.09
Gross domestic product (GDP)	US$bn	0.63	0.70	0.72	0.78	*0.71
GDP per capita	US$	7,625	8,499	8,899	9,366	*8,581
GDP real growth	%	-5.1	-2.0	1.2	5.3	*5.2
Inflation	%	7.0	4.0	1.0	-1.4	*5.7
Exports (fob) (goods)	US$m	235.0	256.2	355.8	427.0	–
Imports (cif) (goods)	US$m	380.0	393.4	620.4	579.0	–
Balance of trade	US$m	-145.0	-137.2	-264.6	-152.0	–
Current account	US$m	-12.4	-63.7	-209.5	-175.5	–
Total reserves minus gold	US$m	67.4	34.6	56.2	112.9	40.8
Foreign exchange	US$m	67.4	34.6	56.2	112.9	40.8
Exchange rate	per US$	5.56	5.50	5.49	5.49	8.02

* estimated figure

Ethnic make-up
The islanders have a variety of ethnic origins – African, French, Indian, Chinese and Arab.
Religions
Practically the whole population is Christian, with 87 per cent belonging to the Roman Catholic faith.

Education
The government provides free education. The school-going age population is largely concentrated on Mahe, the main island where most of the economic activities are concentrated. There are only two private schools as well as public schools. Total expenditure in public education has grown in real terms. The pupil per capita cost in (public) primary schools is typically US$910.
Literacy rate: 90 per cent (plus)
Compulsory years: 6 to 15
Pupils per teacher: 15 in primary schools (Unesco)

Health
Per capita total expenditure on health (2003) was US$599; of which per capita government spending was US$439, at the international dollar rate, (WHO 2006).
The Victoria Hospital has about 445 beds and there are 56 in-patient admissions per bed per year. Health care is provided free of charge.
Life expectancy: 72 years, 2004 (WHO 2006)
Fertility rate/Maternal mortality rate: 2.1 births per woman, 2004 (WHO 2006)
Birth rate/Death rate: 17 births per 1,000 population; 6.5 deaths per 1,000 population (2003).
Child (under 5 years) mortality rate (per 1,000): 11 per 1,000 live births (World Bank)
Head of population per physician: 1.15 physicians per 1,000 people, 2004 (WHO 2006)
Welfare
The social security law requires employers and employees to contribute to a national pension programme that gives retirees a modest pension. Self-employed persons contribute by paying 15 per cent of gross earnings. The government also provides low-cost housing and housing loans.
There is welfare provision for children and the disabled.

Main cities
Victoria, on Mahé island (capital, estimated population 29,298 in 2007).

Languages spoken
Creole is the local language, but English is used in business and government circles. French is also widely spoken.

Official language/s
Creole, French and English

Media
Freedom of speech has been improved since 1993 however tough libel laws are used by the government to contain opposition opinion.
Press
Dailies: The government-owned newspaper Seychelles Nation (www.nation.sc) is published from Monday to Saturday.
Weeklies: The People (www.thepeople.sc) is published by the FPPS political party, while Le Nouveau Seychelles Weekly (www.seychellesweekly.com), and Regar are FPPS-opposition.
Periodicals: The People is a monthly publication. A few periodicals are also published in English, French and Creole.
Broadcasting
The state-run, Seychelles Broadcasting Corporation (www.sbc.sc) (formerly known as Radio Television Seychelles) operates the only television network along with its radio services in Creole, English and French. Both mediums carry advertising. Reception is good on Mahé and the other main islands.
Radio: Along with Paradise FM, the SBC service, international broadcast from, RFI, BBC and VOA may be picked up on shortwave radios.
News agencies
The African Press Agency (ww.apanews.net) and Panapress (www.panapress.com) provide information from the Seychelles.

Economy
The Seychelles has the highest standard of living in Africa. The economy is reliant on tourism and fishing and suffers a foreign exchange shortage, partly due to government spending and high imports of food and equipment. The fishing industry is a major foreign currency earner, which the government is seeking to develop further. Beyond fishing and tourism, the country is looking to develop in areas such as telecommunications, financial services, light industry and international conferencing. This will require considerable foreign investment and the government will need to institute policies and adopt attitudes more compliant to investors.
External shock, high government spending and lower revenues have caused negative GDP growth for several years, but there was some indications of improvement for 2006. In December 2004, the tsunami caused by an earthquake off the coast of Sumatra, Indonesia, reached the Seychelles, causing widespread damage to infrastructure and adding to concerns about the longer-term stability of the economy, dependent as it is on fishing and tourism.

External trade
The Seychelles is a member of the Common Market for Eastern and Southern Africa (Comesa), and operates within a free trade zone with 13 of the 19 member states.
The visible trade deficit is partially offset by earnings from tourism which is the main foreign exchange earner, plus foreign aid and investment, rental from a US satellite tracking station and a BBC relay station.
Preferential import tariffs are granted to goods from Indian Ocean Commission (IOC) member countries – Mauritius, Comoros, Madagascar, Réunion. In return, Seychelles receives preferential import tariffs from IOC countries.
Imports
Principal imports are machinery and equipment, foodstuffs, petroleum products and chemicals.
Main sources: Saudi Arabia (26.4 per cent total, 2006), Singapore (11.3 per cent), France (8.1 per cent).
Exports
Principal exports are canned tuna, fresh/frozen fish, copra and various herbs and spices including vanilla, cinnamon, nutmeg and mace.
Main destinations: Saudi Arabia (42.1 per cent total, 2006), UK (23.9 per cent), France (15.4 per cent).
Re-exports
Petroleum products.

Agriculture
Farming
With the expansion of the tourist industry, the overall importance of agriculture to the economy has declined, although it is still important as a source of foreign exchange and employment. In 2004, the sector accounted for 2.6 per cent of GDP.
There is a shortage of cultivable land and fertile soil. Approximately 4 per cent of the total land area is agricultural, much of which is given over to copra and cinnamon, which are the major export crops.
Farming is traditionally organic and eco-friendly.
Small quantities of coconuts, vanilla, tea and limes are exported. Crops grown for local consumption include tropical fruits, cassava, sweet potatoes, yams, sugar cane, bananas, tea and vegetables; rice, the staple food crop, has to be imported.
Seychelles is self-sufficient in pork, chicken, fish and some vegetables.
There are a number of large farms, 650 small farms and thousands of smallholdings, which the government hopes will reduce dependence on imported foods.
Government reforms include privatisation of state farms, while setting up smaller co-operatives, new marketing structures,

upgrading infrastructure and irrigation facilities for farms. An animal feed factory has been established by the Seychelles Marketing Board (SMB) to support production of meat and eggs. About 98 per cent of milk is imported. The government is encouraging the production of bananas and mangoes.

The estimated crop production for 2005 included: 150 tonnes (t) cassava, 1,970t bananas, 3,200t coconuts, 190t tomatoes, 160t pineapples, 416t oilcrops, 30t mangoes, 200t cinnamon, 213t tea, 2,475t fruit in total, 1,940t vegetables in total. Estimated livestock production included: 1,162t meat in total, 30t beef, 1,105t pig meat, 20t goat meat, 1,007t poultry, 2,182t eggs, 310t milk.

Fishing

The fishing industry is an important source of income and foreign exchange, accounting for around 85 per cent of domestically-produces exports. It is being expanded as part of the government policy of economic diversification, with foreign companies being encouraged to become involved. HJ Heinz acquired a 60 per cent majority stake in the government-owned Indian Ocean Tuna processing factory. Heinz has invested nearly US$8 million in the plant, which operates in the country's International Trade Zone. France and Italy are the main importers of Seychelles tuna.

The fishing infrastructure sustained damage from the tsunami in December 2004. The Seychelles sells fishing licences in its exclusive 1.3 million square km economic zone. Despite the desire for a growth in capacity and productivity through the development of commercial fishing operations, small-scale artisanal fishing still represents about one-third of fishing exports.

In a meeting of African ministers in Namibia, held on 2 July, members discussed illegal and unregulated fishing, which is estimated to cost Africa US$1 billion per annum in lost revenue and the threat to stocks and local artisan fishing. In 2004, the total marine fish catch was 93,683 tonnes and the total crustacean catch was 23 tonnes.

Industry and manufacturing

The industrial sector, including mining, manufacturing, construction and power, accounted for 27.5 per cent of GDP in 2004.

There is a small-scale manufacturing sector. The main activities include the production of canned tuna, soft drinks, juices, jams, beer, cigarettes, paints, assembling of television sets and processing of cinnamon and coconuts.

Emphasis is on private-sector investment. The government aims to expand light industry in other areas such as artisanal products, packaging, assembly and services.

Tourism

Tourism is the country's main economic sector, accounting for 70 per cent of foreign exchange earnings and around 40 per cent of employment. Tourism is expected to contribute 33 per cent of GDP in 2005. Seychelles is marketed as an exclusive destination. There are tight building controls limiting accommodation and favouring luxury hotels. The high cost of holidaying in Seychelles had resulted in a slight decline in visitor numbers in 2003, while at the same increasing receipts. Most visitors come from European and African countries. The Indian Ocean tsunami in December 2004 caused some damage to infrastructure.

Mining

Some granite is quarried. Offshore surveys have indicated the presence of certain metals on the seabed.

Hydrocarbons

The downstream oil industry is highly important, accounting for 25 per cent of imports and supplying 95 per cent of energy needs. There are no refineries in the Seychelles. Downstream activities are directed by the state-run Seychelles Petroleum Company.

The Seychelles does not produce oil, but there are indications of exploitable offshore reserves. The Seychelles National Oil Company co-ordinates the search for hydrocarbons, but there has been no activity in recent years. The government has revised legal and fiscal regimes to encourage exploration. An agreement was concluded in January 2005 with PetroQuest International to explore the southern shelf The Seychelles do not produce or import natural gas. Some gas reserves have been found offshore, but they have not been exploited.

The Seychelles does not produce or import coal.

Energy

Electricity is provided from petroleum and gas turbines. Annual generation of electricity amounts to around 83GW.

Banking and insurance

Central bank

Central Bank of Seychelles

Time

GMT plus four hours

Geography

There are around 115 islands and islets comprising the Seychelles, which cover more than 1.3 million square km in the Indian Ocean, North of Madagascar and over 1,500km from the coast of Kenya. The major islands are a compact group of 41 granite islands, the largest of which includes Mahé, Praslin and La Digue. These islands have high central granite ridges, the highest of which is Morne Seychellois (905 metres) on Mahé. Other islands are composed of coral and are low-lying; many are sparcely populated and four are uninhabited bird sanctuaries. All major islands are lush with vegetation dependent on the surface composition – forests cover the granite islands and coconut palms the coral islands.

Hemisphere

Southern

Climate

Tropical and humid. Average daily temperature are 24–32 degrees Celsius throughout the year. Hottest months are December–May; the wettest are from December–March and cooler from June–November. The islands lie outside the cyclone belt.

Entry requirements

Passports

Required by all and must be valid for at least six months beyond length of stay.

Visa

Are not required. A Visitor's Permit is issued on arrival, valid for four weeks (extensions are possible for three-month periods). All visitors must have confirmed accommodation and sufficient funds for the intended length of stay and hold onward/return tickets or pay a deposit equivalent to the value of a return ticket to the country of origin.

Currency advice/regulations

Unlimited import/export of foreign currency is permitted. Only legal to exchange foreign currencies for Seychelles Rupees through a bank.

Travellers may take or send out of Seychelles up to SR100 of domestic currency.

Customs

Personal items, including one video and one single frame camera, a musical instrument, an item of portable electronic equipment and personal music player. Video tapes must be declared. Animals and agricultural products require an entry permit.

Prohibited imports

Firearms, illegal drugs and spear-fishing equipment.

Health (for visitors)

Mandatory precautions

Yellow fever certificate if arriving from infected area.

Advisable precautions

Inoculations and boosters should be current for tetanus, hepatitis A and diphtheria. There may be a need for vaccinations for typhoid, tuberculosis, hepatitis B and cholera. Anti-mosquito measures including mosquito repellents, nets and clothing covering the body should be used for protection against dengue fever, hepatitis B and chikungunya fever, which include mosquito repellents and nets and clothing that covers the body after dark. There is a risk of rabies.

There is a shortage of routine medications and visitors should take all necessary medicines with them. A first aid kit that includes disposable syringe, is a reasonable precaution. Use only bottled or boiled water for drinks, washing teeth and making ice. Eat only well cooked meals, preferably served hot; vegetables should be cooked and fruit peeled. Dairy products are unpasteurised and should be avoided, unless cooked.

Healthcare is not to Western standards and medical insurance, including emergency evacuation, is necessary.

Hotels
Good standard and widely available. All the large hotels in Mahé are on the beach. Advisable to book and confirm reservation in advance, particularly at Christmas and during August. Government trades tax of 5 per cent is added to bill, and usually also a service charge. Tipping optional.

Credit cards
Major credit cards widely accepted.

Public holidays (national)
Fixed dates

1–2 Jan (New Year), 1 May (Labour Day), 5 Jun (Liberation Day), 18 Jun (National Day), 15 Aug (Assumption Day/La Digue Festival), 1 Nov (All Saints' Day), 8 Dec (Immaculate Conception), 25 Dec (Christmas Day).

Variable dates

Good Friday (Mar/Apr), Corpus Christi (May/Jun).

Working hours
Banking

Mon–Fri: 0830–1300; Sat: 0800–1200.

Business

Mon–Fri: 0800–1200, 1300–1600.

Government

Mon–Fri: 0800–1200, 1300–1600.

Shops

Mon–Fri: 0800–1200, 1330–1700; Sat: 0800–1200; some open Sun morning.

Telecommunications
Telephone/fax

Mobile/cell phones

There are 900 and 1800 GSM services available throughout Mahé and surrounding islands.

Electricity supply
240V AC, 50 cycles. Plugs are three-pin bayonet.

Getting there
Air

National airline: Air Seychelles

International airport/s: Seychelles International (SEZ), on Mahé Island, 10km from Victoria; duty-free shop, bar, restaurant, bank and car hire.

Airport tax: Included in ticket price

Surface

Water: International shipping lines that maintain contacts with Seychelles may provide passenger services on cargo ships.

Main port/s: Victoria, on Mahé island.

Getting about
National transport

Air: Air Seychelles operates regular services from Mahé to Praslin, Desroches, Fregate, Bird and Dennis islands.

Aircraft charters are available to Assumption, Farquhar and Poivre. Helicopter Seychelles provides services and charters from Mahé.

Road: Only three islands have metalled road, Mahé, La Digue and Praslin; all other roads are unpaved tracks.

Buses: The Seychelles Public Transport Corporation (SPTC) operate regular services on Mahé from Victoria and Praslin, between 0520–2130.

Water: There are regular ferry services; a catamaran, Cat Cocos, links Mahé-Praslin, traditional schooners link Praslin-La Digue and La Digue-Mahé.

City transport

Taxis: Taxis are available on Mahé and Praslin, they are privately operated, but with government controlled rates. On Praslin a surcharge is levied between 2200–0600.

Car hire

There are a limited number of hire cars available on Mahé and Praslin; reservations during peak seasons should be made well in advance. A foreign or international driving licence is required. Driving is on the left, the speed limit outside urban areas is 65kph and 40kph in towns.

BUSINESS DIRECTORY
The addresses listed below are a selection only. While World of Information makes every endeavour to check these addresses, we cannot guarantee that changes have not been made, especially to telephone numbers and area codes. We would welcome any corrections.

Telephone area codes
The international dialling code (IDD) for Seychelles is +248, followed by subscriber's number.

Chambers of Commerce
Seychelles Chamber of Commerce & Industry, Ebrahim Building, PO Box 1399, Victoria, Mahé (tel: 323-812; fax: 321-422; e-mail: scci@seychelles.net).

Banking
Barclays Bank (Seychelles), PO Box 167, Victoria (tel: 383-838; email: barclays@seychelles.net).

Bank of Baroda, PO Box 124, Victoria, (tel: 323-037/8; email: baroda@seychelles.net).

Habib Bank, PO Box 702, Victoria (tel: 224-371/2; email: habibsez@seychelles.net).

Mauritius Commercial Bank (Seychelles), PO Box 122, Victoria (tel: 284-555; email: contact@mcbseychelles.com).

Nouvobanq (Seychelles International Mercantile Banking Corporation), PO Box 241, Ground Floor, Victoria House, State House Avenue, Victoria (tel: 293-000; fax: 224-670; email: nvb@nouvobanqu.sc).

Seychelles Savings Bank Limited; PO Box 531, Independence Ave, Victoria (tel: 293-000; fax: 224-713; email: ssb.savingsbank.sc).

Central bank
Central Bank of Seychelles, Independence Avenue, PO Box 701, Victoria, Mahé (tel: 225-200; fax: 224-958; e-mail: cbs@seychelles.sc).

Travel information
Air Seychelles, Victoria House, PO Box 386, Victoria (tel: 225-300; fax: 225-159; internet: www.airseychelles.com).

Helicopter Seychelles, Providence Industrial Estate; PO Box 595, Victoria (tel: 385-858; fax: 373-055; internet: www.helicopterseychelles.com).

Island Development Co (charter flights), New Port; PO Box 638, Mahé (tel: 224-640; fax: 224-467; email: idc@seychelles.sc).

National Travel Agency, Kingsgate House, PO Box 611, Victoria (tel: 224-900; fax: 225-111).

Seychelles Tourist Office–La Digue, La Passes, La Digue (tel/fax: 234-393; email: stbladigue@seychelles.sc).

Seychelles Tourist Office–Praslin, Iles des Palmes Airport, Grand Anse, Praslin (tel: 233-346; fax: 233-571; email: praslin@seychelles.sc).

Travel Services (Seychelles) Ltd., Victoria House, PO Box 356, Victoria (tel: 322-414; fax: 325-010).

Ministry of tourism
Ministry of Tourism and Transport, Independence House, PO Box 92, Victoria (tel: 225-313; fax: 225-131).

National tourist organisation offices
Seychelles Tourist Board, Bel Ombre; PO Box 1262, Victoria, Mahé (tel: 671-300, fax: 620-620; internet: www.seychelles.com).

Ministries
Investment Development Advisory Services (IDEAS), c/o Ministry of Finance and Communication, 3rd Floor, Central Bank Building, Box 313, Victoria (tel: 225-252; fax: 225-265).

Ministry of Administration and Manpower, National House, PO Box 56, Victoria (tel: 383-000; fax: 224-936).

Ministry of Agriculture and Marine Resources, Independence House, PO Box 166, Victoria (tel: 224-030; fax: 225-245).

Ministry of Community Development, Independence House, PO Box 199, Victoria (tel: 224-030; fax: 225-287).

Ministry of Education and Culture, Mont Fleuri (tel: 224-777; fax: 224-859).

Ministry of Finance and Communication, 3rd Floor, Central Bank Building, PO Box 313, Victoria (tel: 225-252; fax: 225-265).

Ministry of Foreign Affairs, Planning and Environment, Mont Fleuri (tel: 224-688; fax: 224-845).

Ministry of Health, PO Box 52, Mont Fleuri (tel: 388-000; fax: 224-792).

Ministry of Industry, Maison du People, Victoria (tel: 224-030; fax: 225-086).

Ministry of Local Government Youth and Sports, Oceangate House, Victoria (tel: 225-477; fax: 225-262).

Other useful addresses
Island Development Company (IDC), PO Box 638, New Port, Victoria (tel: 224-640; fax: 224-467).

Public Utilities Corporation (PUC) (Electricity), PO Box 174, Victoria (tel: 322-444; fax: 321-020). (Water) Unity House, PO Box 34, Victoria (tel: 322-444; fax: 322-127).

RTS Radio, PO Box 321, Union Vale, Victoria (tel: 224-161).

RTS TV, PO Box 321, Hermitage, Mahé (tel: 224-161).

Seychelles Agricultural Development Company Ltd., PO Box 172, Victoria (tel: 276-618).

Seychelles Broadcasting Corporation, Hermitage, PO Box 321, Victoria (tel: 224-161; fax: 224-641).

Seychelles Embassy (USA), Suite 400C, 800 Second Avenue, New York, NW, 10017 (tel: (+1-202) 972-1785; fax: (+1-202) 972-1786; e-mail: seychelles@un.int).

Seychelles Fishing Authority (SFA), PO Box 449, Victoria (tel: 224-521; fax: 224-508).

Seychelles Industrial Development Corporation (SIDEC), PO Box 537, Victoria (tel: 224-941; fax: 225-121).

Seychelles International Business Authority (SIBA), PO Box 991, Central Bank Building, Victoria (tel: 225-402; fax: 225-851).

Seychelles Licensing Authority, PO Box 3, Francis Rachel Street, Victoria (tel: 224-314; fax: 224-256).

Seychelles Marketing Board, PO Box 516, Victoria (tel: 224-444).

Seychelles National Statistics Bureau, PO Box 206, Victoria, (internet: www.seychelles.net/misdstat).

Seychelles Timber Company, Grand Anse, Mahe (tel: 278-343).

State Assurance Corporation ofSeychelles, Pirate's Arms Building, PO Box 636, Victoria (tel: 225-000; fax: 224-495).

Internet sites
Africa Business Network: www.ifc.org/abn

AllAfrica.com: http://allafrica.com

African Development Bank: www.afdb.org

Africa Online: www.africaonline.com

Mbendi AfroPaedia (information on companies, countries, industries and stock exchanges in Africa): http://mbendi.co.za

Seychelles Nation online: www.nation.sc

Sierra Leone

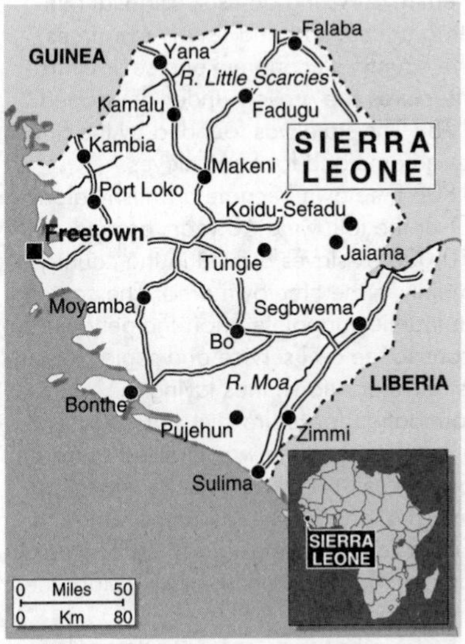

The September 2007 elections were deemed by observers to be largely peaceful and fair. Former opposition leader Ernest Bai Koroma of the All Peoples Congress (APC) defeated former ruling party candidate Solomon Berewa of the Sierra Leone People's Party (SLPP) and was sworn in as president on 17 September. In his inaugural speech he told Sierra Leoneans that 'You have suffered for too long'. Sierra Leone, six years after the bitter civil war ended was still one of the poorest countries in the world, with low life expectancy, few basic human services and widespread corruption.

One of President Koroma's first acts was to commission an inquiry into the widespread corruption and mismanagement which is endemic throughout the country. The report details unauthorised loans, aid that did not reach the intended recipients, financial accounts missing from ministries, and 'almost zero productivity' at the lower levels of employment at the ministry of agriculture.

Economy

Sierra Leone used to earn its foreign exchange from the export of agricultural products such as cocoa, coffee, rubber and palm kernel. While President Koroma has said that the government will encourage a shift from subsistence farming to commercial farming, some 75 per cent of the population depend on small scale farming for their livelihoods. Minerals, in particular diamonds, were also once an important revenue earner. The government has set up a task force to reassess the mining law, under which 3 per cent of export revenue is paid to the government as a royalty. Activists say this is not enough to compensate the mining communities who get barely 0.75 per cent royalties for infrastructure and community developments.

The International Monetary Fund (IMF) has said that Sierra Leone has made significant progress towards macroeconomic stability in recent years. The first Poverty Reduction and Growth Facility (PRGF 1) for the period, 2001–05, immediately after the fighting ceased was successfully completed and a second PRGF approved in May 2006. However, there were fiscal slippages in the second half of 2006 and into 2007, exacerbated by delays and non-disbursement of some programmed budget support. The government switched to a cash-budget management system in April 2007 and by the end of the year the PRGF was back on track.

Real GDP growth has been strong since the end of the conflict and is forecast to continue. Economic growth was driven mainly be buoyant activities in agriculture, mining, construction and services sectors.

Sierra Leone is rich in diamonds. Illicit trade in them funded the war and gave rise to the term 'blood diamonds'. NGO posters showed dying children and glittering diamonds and urged consumers to stop buying the gems. The international diamond industry, including several African countries, managed to avoid a consumer boycott by banding together and against stringent international checks, certifying their diamonds as Diamonds for Development. Diamond marketing organisations would buy only such certified stones. Cross-border diamond trafficking still exists.

Iron ore and gold production should benefit from the presence of two new mining companies in 2007. These British owned companies are the Sierra Leone Diamond Company (SLDC) and the London Mining

KEY FACTS

Official name: Republic of Sierra Leone

Head of State: President Ernest Bai Koroma (APC) (elected 8 Sep 2007)

Head of government: President Ernest Bai Koroma

Ruling party: All People's Congress (APC) (elected 11 Aug 2007)

Area: 72,325 square km

Population: 5.74 million (2007)*

Capital: Freetown

Official language: English

Currency: Leone (Le) = 100 cents

Exchange rate: Le2,968.26 per US$ (Jul 2008)

GDP per capita: US$290 (2007)*

GDP real growth: 6.90% (2007)*

Inflation: 11.70% (2007)*

Balance of trade: -US$119.00 million (2006)

Foreign debt: US$1.72 billion (2004)

* estimated figure

Company. The authorities indicated that given the post conflict stigma still affecting investors' perception of Sierra Leone, they are considering providing tax incentives to attract foreign direct investments. In addition, the Foreign Investment Advisory Service (of the World Bank), and the UK Department for International Development (DfID) are assisting the government to strengthen the legal framework through revision of the Bankruptcy Act, preparation of a Securities Act, and a new Companies Act. Fiscal policy will aim at strengthening domestic revenue mobilisation while redirecting resources from current toward capital expenditures. Steps will be taken to protect poverty-related spending consistent with the framework developed with the World Bank. Capital expenditures increased from 5 per cent of GDP in 2006 to 8.6 per cent in 2007, in line with the authorities' decision to give priority to infrastructure projects.

Sierra Leone is rich in diamonds. Illicit trade in them funded the war and gave rise to the term 'blood diamonds'. NGO posters showed dying children and glittering diamonds and urged consumers to stop buying the gems. The international diamond industry, including several African countries, managed to avoid a consumer boycott by banding together and against stringent international checks, certifying their diamonds as Diamonds for Development. Diamond marketing organisations would buy only such certified stones. Cross-border diamond trafficking still exists.

Outlook

The short- to medium-term fate of the economy depends upon the maintenance of domestic peace and the continued receipt of substantial aid. The government is slowly re-establishing its authority after the 1991–2002 civil war that resulted in tens of thousands of deaths and the displacement of more than two million people (about one-third of the population). The last UN peace-keepers withdrew in December 2005, leaving full responsibility for security with domestic forces. A new civilian UN office remains to support the government. Mounting tensions are likely as the 2007 elections approach. Deteriorating political and economic conditions in Guinea and the tenuous security situation in neighbouring Liberia may also present challenges to continuing stability in Sierra Leone.

Risk assessment

Politics	Fair
Economy	Improving
Regional stability	Fair

COUNTRY PROFILE

Historical profile

The English translation of Sierra Leone means Lion Mountains. In fact, its educated élite would jokingly refer to it as the Athens of Africa, when the country became known – in West Africa at least, as a centre of education. It was in Freetown, the settlement established by the British in 1787 to provide a home for freed slaves (later mainly captives freed from slave ships who had never left African waters) that, in 1827, established the institution that was to become Fourah Bay College. There, in the late 19th century, University education began in West Africa. Many future African leaders and politicians attended the college.

By 1876 Freetown was already well-endowed with educational establishments. But it was not until 1896 that the greater part of modern Sierra Leone, called until independence the Protectorate was added to the original British colony. Emerging from a lengthy civil war, Sierra Leone is an extremely poor African country with a highly unequal distribution of wealth. Surviving on its substantial mineral, agricultural and fishery resources, the country's economic and social infrastructures are gravely under-developed.

1787 The state was founded by the British as a homeland for freed slaves.

1808 Freetown became a British colony. Over the following 60 years around 70,000 ex-slaves arrived in the country, mainly in the Freetown area. The colonial authorities appointed non-indigenous Africans to the civil service and senior administrative positions, thus laying the foundation for future civil strife.

1954 Sierra Leone was allowed some degree of self-rule through a new local administration. Sir Milton Margai of the Sierra Leone People's Party (SLPP) was appointed the head of the newly-established administration.

1961 Sierra Leone gained independence from Britain in April, but remained part of the Commonwealth. Sir Milton Margai became the country's first prime minister.

1964 Following Sir Milton's death, his half-brother, Sir Albert Margai, was appointed prime minister.

1967 The All Peoples Congress (APC) won the parliamentary election, its leader, Siaka Stevens, was appointed prime minister. Sierra Leonean military officers staged a coup.

1968 After an army revolt, Stevens and the APC returned to government.

1971 Sierra Leone became a republic. Stevens was appointed as the country's first president.

1978 A new constitution established one-party rule with the APC as the only legal party.

1985 Stevens retired, Major General Joseph Momoh became president.

1991 Rebels opposed to the Momoh government – principally the Revolutionary United Front (RUF) led by Foday Sankoh – launched a series of attacks, which took much of the eastern part of the country. They were backed by Liberia.

1992 A coup brought Captain Valentine Strasser to power. He presided over a military government, which suspended the constitution and ruled by decree.

1996 Strasser was deposed by Brigadier Julius Bio. Multi-party elections ended four years of military rule. Ahmed Tejan Kabbah (SLPP) became president.

1997 Major Johnny-Paul Koroma led a coup and ousted Kabbah, who went into

KEY INDICATORS — Sierra Leone

	Unit	2003	2004	2005	2006	2007
Population	m	4.80	4.85	5.45	*5.59	*5.74
Gross domestic product (GDP)	US$bn	0.81	1.10	1.22	1.42	*1.66
GDP per capita	US$	169	201	223	254	*290
GDP real growth	%	6.5	7.4	7.3	7.4	*6.9
Inflation	%	8.2	13.7	12.1	9.5	*11.7
Exports (fob) (goods)	US$m	35.0	174.0	192.0	244.0	–
Imports (cif) (goods)	US$m	190.0	319.0	340.0	363.0	–
Balance of trade	US$m	-155.0	-145.0	-148.0	-119.0	–
Current account	US$m	-80.0	-100.0	-93.0	-51.0	*-63.0
Total reserves minus gold	US$m	66.6	125.1	170.5	183.9	216.6
Foreign exchange	US$m	32.1	74.1	137.7	154.7	185.8
Exchange rate	per US$	2,230.00	2,701.30	2,970.11	2,970.11	2,989.20

* estimated figure

exile. The Armed Forces Revolutionary Council (ARFC) was installed, backed by the RUF. International sanctions were imposed. The Economic Community of West African States (Ecowas) dispatched a peace-keeping force, the Ecowas Monitoring Group (Ecomog) in order to reinstate the government of President Kabbah. A peace accord was reached in October.
1998 Ecomog launched a military offensive against the AFRC after Koroma showed no sign of implementing the 1997 agreement and steppin down from power. Ecomog ejected the AFRC from Freetown and Kabbah returned to Sierra Leone. The RUF remained in control of large areas outside the capital. The civilian population in rebel held territories were subjected to brutal treatment, with limb amputations meted out to victims of all ages.
1999 RUF rebels counter-attacked the capital and were finally driven off after weeks of fierce fighting. Liberia was accused of supporting the rebels and trading weapons for diamonds, mined in rebel territories. The government and the FUC signed a peace agreement, allowing for the deployment of UN peace-keeping forces.
2000 Foday Sankoh condemned the presence of UN forces in the country. The UN reported that civilians continued to be mutilated, raped and abducted in rebel held areas. RUF rebels clashed with UN troops when they were required to disarm. Over 13,000 UN troops held a limited peace in the south while British paratroopers trained government forces. Under a UK plan, thousands of British troops arrived to stabilise President Kabbah's regime. Sankoh was captured in Freetown where he had been hiding for weeks. Within two months, Britain withdrew most of its forces leaving a contingent to continue training local government forces.
2001 Military operations continued to push into lawless regions of the country and restore civil society. Legislative and presidential elections were postponed because of the unstable security situation in the country.
2002 In January the 11-year civil war was officially declared ended and state of emergency measures were lifted. Ahmad Tejan Kabbah (SLPP) won a landslide victory as president. The SLPP won the parliamentary elections.
2003 Agriculture production recovered to pre-war levels, as many people displaced during the civil war returned to their homes. In July, rebel leader Foday Sankoh died of natural causes while awaiting trial for war crimes.
2004 The first local elections in more than three decades were held in May. A war crimes court, staffed by senior US legal personnel, began taking evidence for a court mandated for three years and empowered to 'arrest, try and convict' those accused of war crimes.
2005 In November the UN agreed that former Liberian leader Charles Taylor should be handed over to Sierra Leone to stand trial for war crimes perpetrated by Sierre Leone insurgents he had supported while he was Liberian president. The last UN-troops withdrew in December.
2006 In March former president Charles Taylor was flown from Nigeria, where he had been living, to Freetown, where he was wanted for war crimes and his alleged role in Sierra Leone's civil war. In June, Taylor was transferred to stand before the International Criminal Court in The Hague (The Netherlands). The transfer was made possible after the UK agreed to provide detention facilities if Taylor was convicted. In a deal with creditors, announced in December, around 90 per cent of Sierra Leone's debt, worth about US$1.64 billion, will be written off following measures taken to stabilise the economy, tackle poverty and improve governance, with reforms undertaken in the economy, health, education and government administration. External debt has been reduced to around US$110 million.
2007 In January, the Paris Club of creditors forgave a further US$218 million of Sierra Leone's debt. The World Bank advised that the money which would have been spent on debt servicing should be spent on 'legitimate things for the people'. The vital Mano River bridge connecting Sierre Leone with Liberia was officially reopened in June. In general elections held on 11 August the opposition APC won 59 seats (out of 112), the SLPP 43, the People's Movement for Democratic Change (PMDC) 10. After two rounds in the presidential election, Ernest Bai Koroma (APC) won 54.6 per cent, Solomon Berewa (SLPP) won 45.5 per cent.

Political structure

Constitution
The 1991 referendum, adopting a multi-party parliamentary system, based on the US model, was amended in 2002, and introduced the District Block System (DBS) for voting.
Form of state
Unitary republic
The executive
Executive power is vested in the president, who is both Head of State and head of government. The president is directly elected for up to two, five-year terms. The president appoints ministers, approved by parliament. The cabinet is composed of ministers who are answerable to the president.
National legislature
The national legislature is the 124-member House of Representatives. Under the District Block System (DBS), eight representatives are elected from each of the 14 districts, elected by proportional representation. The remaining 12 seats are reserved for paramount chiefs who are indirectly elected. All members serve for five-year terms.
Legal system
It is based on English law and is composed of a Supreme Court, Appeals Court and a High Court.
A special war crimes court, operating under Sierra Leonean law, was set up in 2004 to try those accused of heinous war crimes.
Last elections
11 August 2007 (parliamentary); 11 August/8 September 2007 (presidential)
Results: Presidential: (first round) Ernest Bai Koroma (APC) won 44.3 per cent of the vote; Solomon E Berewa (SLPP) 38.3 per cent; Charles F Margai (People's Movement for Democratic Change (PMDC)) 13.9 per cent. In second round, Koroma won 54.6 per cent of the vote, Berewa won 45.5 per cent. Turnout 68.1 per cent.
Parliamentary: the APC won 59 seats (out of 112), the SLPP 43, the People's Movement for Democratic Change (PMDC) 10.
Next elections
2012 (presidential and legislative); 5 July 2008 (local government).

Political parties

Ruling party
All People's Congress (APC) (elected 11 Aug 2007)
Main opposition party
Sierra Leone People's Party (SLPP)

Population

5.74 million (2007)*
Last census: December 2004: 4,963,298 (provisional)
Population density: 66 inhabitants per square km. Urban population: 37 per cent (1995–2001).
Annual growth rate: 2.6 per cent 1994–2004 (WHO 2006)
Ethnic make-up
African groups: Temne (30 per cent), Mende (30 per cent), others (20 per cent)); Creole (Krio) (descendants of freed Jamaican slaves settled in the Freetown area in the late-18th century) (10 per cent); refugees from Liberia's civil war and small numbers of Europeans, Lebanese, Pakistanis and Indians.
Religions
Islam (60 per cent), indigenous beliefs (30 per cent), Christian (10 per cent).

Education

Government plans to increase primary school enrolment and to reduce the gender gap in education has only been under way since 2001 and while enrolment levels are rising the gender gap has also widened. The civil conflict has left about 50 per cent of primary schools functioning in inadequate accommodation. Unicef is assisting in the provision of teaching and learning materials and teacher training, it is also funding the Complementary Rapid Education for Primary Schools (CREPS) programme, designed to enable over-aged children to complete the primary school programme.

Primary education begins at aged six and lasts for six years. Junior secondary school lasts for three years. Students who are successfully may progress to the senior secondary school for a further three years and then onto university.

The University of Sierra Leone is the only institute of higher learning.

Literacy rate: 36 per cent (2004)

Compulsory years: Six to 12.

Enrolment rate: 39 per cent, boys; 34 per cent, girls; primary enrolment (Unicef).

Health

Per capita total expenditure on health (2003) was US$34; of which per capita government spending was US$20, at the international dollar rate, (WHO 2006).

UN programmes aid the healthcare system to improve the country's ranking in the Human Development Index which is only one higher than Niger which, in 2005, is the lowest ranking. Around 70 per cent of the population lives below the poverty line.

Technical aid, rehabilitation and funding will be provided through a four-year programme (2004–07), including measures to improve water sources and sanitation and HIV/Aids education and prevention.

Donor support will have to be sustained over the long-term to cope with the ongoing rehabilitating of civil war amputees.

HIV/Aids

Aids has killed between two to three times more people than during the civil war, yet has received relatively little attention.

Around 68,000 people are infected with HIV/Aids, 3,300 of them are under 15-years-old. Since the beginning of the epidemic, over 56,000 children have lost their mother or both parents. The spread of the disease is due to a low prevelance of condom use.

HIV prevalence: 0.9 per cent adult population (government statistic)

The Global Fund to Fight HIV/Aids, Tuberculosis and Malaria states government statistic significantly underestimates the prevalence rate and puts the figure closer to 3.4 per cent generally, and 5 per cent in Freetown. An international medical charity that undertook a study in Freetown in 2004 found a prevalence rate of 4.6 per cent among prenatal women, a typically non-risk group, which suggests the prevalence rate could be higher even than the Global Funds' estimation.

In February 2005 the government announced that it would undertake a nationwide survey to provide 'baseline information' about HIV/Aids in Sierra Leone.

Life expectancy: 39 years, 2004 (WHO 2006)

Fertility rate/Maternal mortality rate: 6.5 births per woman, 2004 (WHO 2006); maternal mortality, 1,800 per 100,000 live births (Unicef 2004).

Birth rate/Death rate: 44 births per 1,000 population; 20.7 deaths per 1,000 population (2003).

Child (under 5 years) mortality rate (per 1,000): 166 per 1,000 live births (World Bank)

Head of population per physician: 0.03 physicians per 1,000 people, 2004 (WHO 2006)

Main cities

Freetown (capital, estimated population 1.1 million in 2004), Koidu (113,700), Makeni (110,700), Bo (82,400).

Languages spoken

English is the main medium for business. Mende is spoken principally in the south, Temne in the north and Krio (English-based Creole) is spoken by 10 per cent of the population and understood by 95 per cent.

Official language/s

English

Media

Press

Dailies: In English, main newspapers are Concord Times (www.concordtimessl.com), Standard Times Press (http://standardtimespress.net) and Awoko (www.awoko.org), Awareness Times (http://awarenesstimes.com) and Christian Monitor (www.christian-monitor.org).

Weeklies: Weeklies include New Sierra Leonean, Vision and Weekend Spark.

Business: The Ministry of Information and Broadcasting publishes the quarterly Sierra Leone Trade Journal.

Broadcasting

Radio: The government-owned Sierra Leone Broadcasting Service (SLBS) broadcasts in English, French and local languages. There are several private stations operating in the Freetown area, including Sky FM, Kiss Fm, Radio Democracy (run by the UN) and Voice of the Handicapped (set up for the disabled, injured during the civil war, but attracting a wider audience). International broadcast from RFI and BBC can be received.

Television: There are two commercial TV stations (mainly received in Freetown area) operated by SLBS and ABC TV.

News agencies

The African Press Agency (ww.apanews.net) and Panapress (www.panapress.com) provide information from Sierra Leone.

Economy

Despite its extensive mineral resources, which include large quantities of alluvial diamonds, Sierra Leone is an impoverished country. The brutal 11-year civil war which ended in 2002 was funded by diamonds mined by itinerant diggers attached to rebel forces.

Sierra Leone was granted, by the World Bank and IMF, a debt reduction package under the Heavily Indebted Poor Countries (HIPC) initiative, in 2002. This package was estimated to be worth US$950 million in debt servicing obligations. For its part the Sierra Leonean government has introduced wide-ranging structural reforms and pursued practical macroeconomic policies to enhance the country's potential recovery.

To promote growth and reduce poverty the government has focussed on six key targets: state security, a sustainable fiscal position, raising domestic savings and investment, increasing infrastructure, agricultural and rural development and promoting the private sector.

While agriculture provides one of the largest elements of GDP at around 40 per cent, diamonds provide the most foreign revenue. Since diamond certification was introduced in 2000, revenues have almost doubled year-on-year and earned US$126 million in 2004. A quarter of diamond taxes are reinvested in mining communities to provide social assets such as schools and roads, as well as co-operatives to help miners market their finds.

The economy is beginning to recover with improved business confidence. Annual GDP growth was 7.2 per cent in 2005.

Inflation is high due to high fuel costs, the expansionary monetary policy and a depreciating currency; it reached around 14 per cent in 2004, falling to 12.5 per cent in 2005.

The economy is broadly open and the government is attempting to attract direct foreign investment through the sale of state-owned financial, utilities, commercial and transport entities. Because outright sale of national assets might be unpalatable to the majority of Sierra Leoneans, the government proposed

incremental privatisation, with management contracts offered along with public/private partnerships.
Sierra Leone has one of the worst rates of gross domestic savings in Africa and much needs to be done to encourage a reversal in this pattern.

External trade
Sierra Leone is a member of the Economic Community of Western African States (Ecowas), which was set up to promote economic integration among members.
Mining natural resources provides the majority of export earnings with gem-quality diamonds being paramount. Diamond exports, up to July 2007, were official reported to be a record breaking 449,988 carats, worth US$102 million, with an estimated US$175 million due for the year.
Exports of rutile (titanium dioxide used as a paint pigment) and bauxite resumed in 2005. Cash crops, coffee and cocoa, are exported to Europe.

Imports
Principal imports are foodstuffs (typically over 30 per cent of total value), machinery and vehicles, manufactured goods, fuels and lubricants, building materials, cloths and textiles.
Main sources: Côte d'Ivoire (9.7 per cent total, 2006), US (8.1 per cent), China (8.0 per cent).

Exports
Commodity exports are diamonds, rutile, bauxite, cocoa, coffee and fish.
Main destinations: Belgium (51.9 per cent total, 2006), US (19.0 per cent), The Netherlands (6.8 per cent).

Agriculture
The civil war seriously disrupted agricultural activity, destroying the homes and livelihood of many farming families. This will impact on food security for a number of years to come.
The agricultural sector contributes around 50 per cent to GDP and employs 65–75 per cent of labour force. Many young people have left rural areas since 2002 to find work in the cities.
Area under cultivation is approximately 25 per cent of the total land area. It is limited by a traditional land tenure system and is mostly in the hands of smallholders engaged in subsistence farming.
Major cash export crops are cocoa, coffee, palm kernels and ginger. Despite government efforts towards self-sufficiency, rice imports have risen.
Other food crops include maize, cassava, sweet potatoes and sorghum.
Production has been hampered by poor infrastructure, a lack of incentives and a poor marketing and distribution system.
The estimated crop production for 2005 included: 309,400 tonnes (t) cereals in total, 265,000t rice, 390,000t cassava, 26,000t sweet potatoes, 21,000t sorghum, 33,000t plantains, 58,700t pulses, 16,000t groundnuts in shell, 195,000t oil palm fruit, 85,000t citrus fruit, 56,211t oilcrops, 11,000t cocoa beans, 18,000t green coffee, 70,000t sugar cane, 184,500t fruit in total, 235,000t vegetables in total. Estimated livestock production included: 23,259t meat in total, 5,400t beef, 2,320t pig meat, 1,705t lamb and goat meat, 11,334t poultry, 8,290t eggs, 21,250t milk, 500t honey, 1,290t cattle hides, 220t sheepskins.

Fishing
The fishing sector has two distinct patterns. Coastal fishing, undertaken by men, is commercially driven with catches either sold fresh or preserved for transport inland. Inland fishing is performed by women and largely for private consumption.
Coastal fishing fleets have contracted since 2001, however production has risen.
The majority of vessels harvest shrimps. In 2004, the total marine fish catch was 112,477 tonnes and the total crustacean catch was 2,205 tonnes.

Forestry
The majority of timber production is used as domestic fuel. Timber imports in 2004 were US$4.5 million, while exports amounted to US$1.3 million.
In December 2007 the Gola Forest Reserve, on the eastern border with Liberia, was designated as a national park. In January 2008, the government re-imposed an export ban on timber. It accused foreign companies, in particular Chinese loggers, of plundering the country's timber assets and causing serious soil erosion. The ban will be lifted when a policy that benefits local communities and re-planting has been achieved.
Timber production in 2004 included 5,526,720 cubic metre (cum) roundwood, 123,600cum industrial roundwood, 5,300cum sawnwood, 5,403,120cum woodfuel; 328,170t charcoal.

Industry and manufacturing
The industrial sector accounts for around 30 per cent of GDP and employs 5 per cent of the workforce.
The sector is mainly limited to food processing and light manufacturing of consumer goods such as cigarettes, alcoholic beverages, plastic footwear, nails, paint and confectionery. Emphasis is placed on import substitution industries, but attempts to establish heavy industry have met with only limited success and have been undermined by political instability.
Expansion is limited by weak local demand, power shortages, foreign exchange shortages and low investment.

Tourism
The tourist sector is expected to contribute US$27 million or 2.9 per cent of GDP, while employing over 47 thousand people and should attract 3.4 per cent of all capital investment in 2005.
The country has much to offer with a diverse landscape and friendly people although continued peace is paramount.
The main foreign investors in Sierra Leone's tourist sector are Chinese companies who see the opportunities for refurbished and new tourist attractions as sound investments. A US$266 million ocean-front tourism complex with holiday homes, golf course and five-star hotel, was signed in 2004 and is due to be opened in 2006. Another US$270 million invested in various hotels developments is expected to help set off a tourism boom.

Mining
The mining sector contributes around 35 per cent to GDP and employs 10 per cent of the workforce.
Diamonds play an essential part in the economy. In 2004, US$126.7 million gem-quality diamonds were exported and revenue earned was US$4.2 million. The government, in an effort to bring artisanal mining into legal and regulated operation and minimise smuggling, has introduced a certification system for exporting diamonds and created a mining community development fund to return a percentage of the taxes back to the local population.
Sierra Leone has one of the world's largest deposits of rutile (a titanium ore). The Sierra Rutile mining operation was closed and damaged during the civil war. In March 2005 a re-start operation was undertaken and the facility is expected to begin production in early 2006.
Bauxite mining is also an important sector with large reserves at Sieromco and Port Loko. Production was suspended due to the civil war. Foreign investment is necessary to begin a re-start operation.

Hydrocarbons
Sierra Leone imports all its oil requirements.
There are large deposits offshore within the West African region, which it is not economically viable to extract currently.
Sierra Leone does not produce or import natural gas or coal.

Energy
The Sierra Leone Electricity Company (SLEC) oversees electricity generation and supply.
Installed generating capacity is approximately 100MW (mostly oil-fired thermal power stations). However, the supply is is insufficient and undependable.
A US$300 million hydroelectric project under construction on the Seli River at

Bumbuna with a capacity of 53MW, will supply power to Freetown and northern provinces by mid-2006.
The serious energy shortage has forced many citizens to buy personal diesel generators; more than 86 per cent of the population uses bio-mass (wood fuel, kerosene charcoal) for energy.

Banking and insurance
The banking sector has been weakened by war. However, the government has given the central bank power to tighten fiscal controls and prepare some for sale. The IMF is wary of donor funds that are distributed through local banks, bypassing the close scutiny and anti-corruption measures instituted by the central bank.
It was announced in March 2005 that the introduction of the shared currency, the eco, in Sierra Leone, Ghana, Guinea, Nigeria and The Gambia, which was due in July 2005, would be postponed. The currency was proposed to facilitate trade and growth with an ultimate plan to merge it with the CFA franc.

Central bank
Bank of Sierra Leone

Main financial centre
Freetown

Time
GMT

Geography
Sierra Leone – lion mountains, as named by an early Portuguese explorer – lies on the west coast of Africa; Guinea encircles it from the north-west around to the east and Liberia borders it to the south. There is a 400km Atlantic coastline in the west. The Guinea highlands cross the country from the south-east to the north. The tallest peak is Bintimani (1,948 metres) in the Loma Mountains of central Sierra Leone. There are a number of rivers, two of which have estuaries navigable by ocean-going ships, the Jong and the Rokel. The Freetown peninsular is heavily forested, mangrove swamps line the coast with savannah stretching to the once thickly forested central inland that has been largely cleared for agriculture.

Hemisphere
Northern

Climate
Is tropical, with high humidity and rainfall; the dry season is November–April. It is wet for the rest of year. The daily temperature range is 21–32 degrees Celsius, which remains fairly constant throughout the year.

Entry requirements

Passports
Required by all and must be valid for six months beyond date of entry.
Requirements may be subject to change at short notice; contact an embassy or consulate before departure.

Visa
Required by all, and must be obtained in advance. Citizens of Ecowas countries are exempt. Contact the nearest embassy for an application form. All visas require evidence of return/onward passage; tourists must provide evidence of hotel reservations.
Business visitors should include a letter of invitation from a local contact and a letter of introductory from their employer outlining the purpose of the trip, the nature of business and contacts in Sierra Leone. For new business, an applicant must provide evidence of commercial veracity and financial standing.

Prohibited entry

Currency advice/regulations
The import and export of local currency is limited to Le50,000. Import of foreign currency is unlimited however it must be declared and cash must not exceed US$5,000 (or equivalent); export is limited to the amount declared on arrival.
It is illegal to exchange money anywhere except official exchange facilities at banks and bureau de change.
Travellers cheques have very limited use.

Customs
All visitors must complete a customs declaration form on entering the country.
All gem stones require an export licence.

Prohibited imports
Illegal drugs, firearms and explosives, pornography and live animals.
It is illegal to export gold and historical artefacts, live animals, firearms and explosives.

Health (for visitors)

Mandatory precautions
Yellow fever, malaria and cholera vaccination certificates are required.

Advisable precautions
Hepatitis A, tetanus, polio, and typhoid vaccinations. Malaria prophylaxis should be taken. HIV/Aids is prevalent. Water precautions should be taken. There is a rabies risk. Use only well maintained, chlorinated swimming pools to avoid bilharzia. Lassa fever can be contracted in Kenema and the east; seek urgent medical advice for any fever not positively identified as malaria.
Visitors should carry basic medical supplies and any prescription medication necessary. Medical and emergency insurance (to include repatriation) is strongly recommended.

Hotels
Available in Freetown, especially at Lumley Beach, within easy taxi access of the centre of Freetown. Limited availability outside capital. Credit cards accepted only in major hotels and payment required in US dollars. A service charge is usually included in bill.

Credit cards
Not accepted. The government tourist organisation operates an international hotel reservation service that allows pre-payment of hotel accommodation by credit card (see: www.visitsierraleone.org/hotel-reservation.asp).

Public holidays (national)

Fixed dates
1 Jan (New Year's Day), 27 Apr (Independence Day), 25–26 Dec (Christmas).

Variable dates
Eid al Adha (Tabaski), Birth of the Prophet, Good Friday and Easter Monday (Mar/Apr), Eid al Fitr (Korité).
Islamic year – 1429 (10 Jan 2008–28 Dec 2008): The Islamic year contains 354 or 355 days, with the result that Muslim feasts advance by 10–12 days against the Gregorian calendar. Dates of feasts vary according to the sighting of the new moon, so cannot be forecast exactly.

Working hours

Banking
Mon–Thu: 0800–1330; Fri: 0800–1400.

Business
Mon–Fri: 0800–1200, 1400–1630.

Government
Mon–Fri: 0800–1230, 1330–1645; close 1500 on Fri.

Shops
Mon–Fri: 0800–1200, 1400–1630; shops open Sat.

Telecommunications

Mobile/cell phones
There are several GSM 900 and 900/1800 services available throughout most of the country.

Electricity supply
230/240V AC, 50 cycles. Voltage fluctuation and power cuts occur.

Social customs/useful tips
Carry some form of identification at all times.
Punctually and business cards are expected.

Security
Sierra Leone has begun to emerge from a brutal civil war and the security situation is improving. Visitors should take care travelling outside the capital at night, as much for the poor state of the roads as any criminal intent.

Getting there

Air
International airport/s: Freetown-Lungi International (FNA), 20km north of city; bar, currency exchange, post office, shops. The airport is on the opposite bank

of the Sierra Leone River from Freetown which must be crossed either by helicopter, hovercraft or ferry.

Airport tax: Departure tax US$20, payable in hard currency; transit passengers are exempt.

Surface

Road: There are routes from Conaky (Guinea Republic). Access to Liberia requires a special permit to transit the border region in a private vehicle. The vital Mano River bridge connecting Sierre Leone with Liberia was officially reopened in June.

Water: Regional services run from Guinea and Liberia. International shipping lines that maintain contacts with Sierra Leone may provide passenger services on cargo ships.

Main port/s: Freetown

Getting about

National transport

Public transport is neither reliable nor safe. The heavy rainy season, which lasts for several months between May and November makes travel to outlying areas both difficult and hazardous.

Air: Internal air services were begun in 2006 by Eagle Air, which operates a 17 seat aircraft to Bo, Kenema and Yengema. Information is limited and visitors should contact local travel agents for further details.

Road: Most main roads in Freetown are paved but have potholes; unpaved side streets are generally poor. A major road resurfacing and repair programme in Freetown is slowly improving the quality of roads in the city. Most roads outside Freetown are unpaved. All roads are unlit and many in need of repair.

Buses: Buses in Freetown tend to be overcrowded and unreliable. Regular service Freetown-Kambia, Freetown-Pendembu, Freetown-Makeni-Kabala.

City transport

Public transport, when it exists, is unreliable.

Taxis: Available at the airport and in main towns; fares by negotiation; tipping is not usual. It is considered safer to use taxis that work in conjunction with an hotel.

Buses, trams & metro: There are buses from the airport to the city centre, but the services can be erratic.

Helicopter: Services operate between Freetown and Lungi airport – flight time five minutes.

Ferry: Links Lungi Airport with central Freetown and Lumley Beach area.

Car hire

Car hire is available at relatively high rates. International driving licence required.

BUSINESS DIRECTORY

The addresses listed below are a selection only. While World of Information makes every endeavour to check these addresses, we cannot guarantee that changes have not been made, especially to telephone numbers and area codes. We would welcome any corrections.

Telephone area codes

The international direct dialling code (IDD) for Sierra Leone is +232, followed by area code and subscriber's number:

Freetown	22	Kenema	32

Chambers of Commerce

Sierra Leone Chamber of Commerce, Guma Building, Lamina Sankoh Street, (tel: 226-305; fax: 220-696; e-mail: cocsl@sierratel.sl).

Banking

Bank of Sierra Leone, PO Box 30, Siaka Stevens Street, Freetown (tel: 226-501; fax: 224-764).

First Merchant Bank of Sierra Leone Ltd, Sparta Building, 12 Wilberforce Street, Freetown (tel: 228-493; fax: 228-318).

National Development Bank Ltd, 21/23 Siaka Stevens Street, Freetown (tel: 226-791/2; fax: 224-468).

Sierra Leone Commerical Bank Ltd, 29-31 Siaka Stevens Street, Freetown (tel: 225-264; fax: 225-292).

Standard Chartered Bank Sierra Leone Ltd, PO Box 1155, 9 -11 Lightfoot Boston Street, Freetown (tel: 226-220, 225-021; fax: 225-760).

Union Trust Bank Ltd, 2 Howe Street, Freetown (tel: 222-792, 226-954; fax: 226-214).

Central bank

Bank of Sierra Leone, Siaka Stevens Street, Freetown (tel: 226-501; fax: 224- 764; e-mail: info@bankofsierraleone.org).

Travel information

Astraeus (charter flights) Astraeus House, Faraday Court, Faraday Road, Crawley, West Sussex, RH10 9PU (tel: (+44) 1293-819800; fax: (+4 4) 1293-819832; internet: www.flyastraeus.com).

BMED (airline), Hetherington House, Bedfont Road, Heathrow Airport, Middlesex TW19 7NL (tel: (+44-20) 8630-4212; fax: (+44-20) 8630-4007; internet: www.flybmed.com).

Freetown International Airport, 15 Rawdon Street, Freetown (tel: 223-881; fax: 224-653; internet: www.freetownairport.org).

Ministry of tourism

Ministry of Tourism and Culture, Stadium Hostel, Syke Street, Freetown (tel: 241-256).

National tourist organisation offices

National Tourist Board of Sierra Leone, Room 100, Cape Sierra Hotel, Aberdeen; PO Box 1435

Freetown (tel: 236-620; fax: 236-621; email: info@welcometosierraleone.org or mailto:ntbslinfo@yahoo.com; internet: www.welcometosierraleone.org).

Ministries

Department of Finance, Secretariat Building, George Street, Freetown (tel: 26-911, 22-211; fax: 28-355).

Ministry of Information and Broadcasting, Youyi Building, Brookfields, Freetown.

Ministry of Tourism and Culture, Wallace Johnson Street, Freetown (tel: 26-345, 24-776).

Ministry of Trade and Industry, Ministerial Building, George Street, Freetown (tel: 26-045, 22-755, 22-706; fax: 28-373).

Other useful addresses

Central Statistics Office, Tower Hill, Freetown (tel: 223-897, 224-267).

National Trading Co, Howe Street, Freetown (tel: 223-986, 226-179).

Sierra Leone Embassy (USA), 1701 19th Street, NW, Washington DC 20009 (tel: (+1-202) 939-9261; fax: (+1-202) 483-1793; e-mail: fsec@embassyofsierraleone.org; internet: www.sierra-leone.org).

Sierra Leone Export Development and Investment Corp, 18/20 Walpole Street; Private Mail Bag 6, Freetown (tel: 229-760, 227-604; fax: 229-097; email: info@sledic-sl.org; internet: sledic-sl.org).

SierraTel, Wallace Johnson Street, Freetown (tel: 222-801, 224-591).

Sierra Leone High Commission (UK), 245 Oxford Street, London W1D 2LX (tel: (+44-20) 7287-9884; fax: (+44-20) 7734-3822; e-mail: info@slhc-uk.org.uk; internet: www.slhc-uk.org.uk).

Sierra Leone Ports Authority, PO Box 386, Freetown.

The Chief Immigration Officer, Rawdon Street, Freetown (tel 227-174; fax: 224-761).

Internet sites

Africa Business Network: www.ifc.org/abn

African Development Bank: www.afdb.org

AllAfrica.com: http://allafrica.com

Africa Online: www.africaonline.com

Mbendi AfroPaedia (information on companies, countries, industries and stock exchanges in Africa): http://mbendi.co.za

Sierra Leone: www.sierra-leone.org

Sierra Leone government: www.sierraleone.gov.sl

Singapore

KEY FACTS

Official name: Repablik Singapura, Xinjiapo Gongheguo, Singapur Kutiyarasu, Republic of Singapore

Head of State: President Sellapan Ramanathan (S R Nathan) (since 1999, re-elected Aug 2005)

Head of government: Prime Minister Lee Hsien Loong (appointed 12 Aug 2004)

Ruling party: People's Action Party (PAP) (since 1965; re-elected 6 May 2006)

Area: 636 square km

Population: 4.59 million (2007)*

Official language: English, Mandarin Chinese, Malay, Tamil.

Currency: Singapore dollar (S$) = 100 cents

Exchange rate: S$1.35 per US$ (Jul 2008)

GDP per capita: US$35,163 (2007)*

GDP real growth: 7.70% (2007)

Labour force: 2.15 million (2004)

Unemployment: 2.10% (2007)

Inflation: 2.10% (2007)

Balance of trade: US$16.50 billion (2005)

Foreign debt: US$23.80 billion (2005)

Visitor numbers: 7.59 million (2006)*

* estimated figure

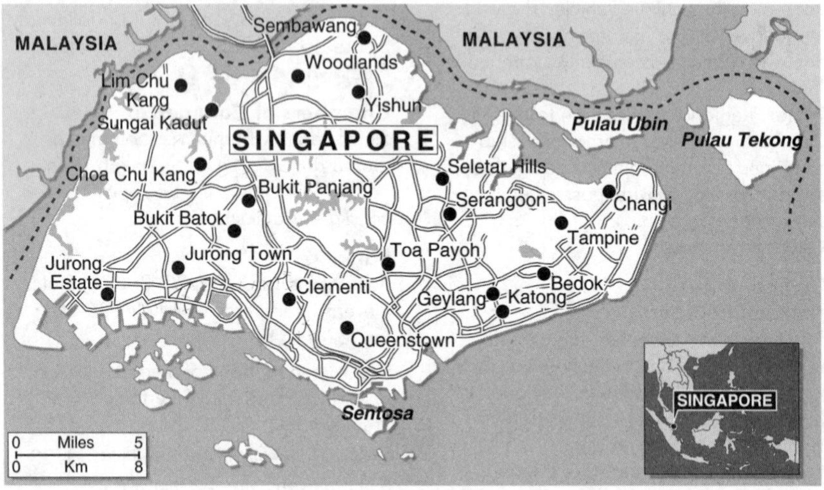

Singapore's growth in 2007 was 7.7 per cent, much in keeping with the solid growth registered over the previous four years. The fastest growing sectors were construction and financial services. The government continues to upgrade and restructure the economy. In the 2008 budget, the government announced a number of measures for households and individuals, including a substantial personal income tax rebate of 20 per cent. Key business outcomes built on initiatives announced in the 2007 budget included measures in support of R&D activities, tax incentives to enhance business competitiveness and further measures to promote Singapore's financial services and maritime sectors. The Singapore government's economic outlook is good, with continued strong growth.

Growth

Economic growth is forecast to be between 4 and 6 per cent in 2008. However, there are some downside risks in 2008 if the US economy slips into recession. Manufacturing growth dropped by half, from 11.9 per cent in 2006 to 5.8 per cent in 2007. Inflation accelerated from 0.5 per cent in the first quarter of 2007 to a dramatic (by Singapore standards) 4.1 per cent in the fourth quarter. For the year as a whole the consumer price index rose by 2.1 per cent, double the rate recorded in 2006. Given global trading patterns, it was inevitable that the expansion was due to slow down. However, in the view of the Asian Development Bank (ADB) strong job creation, large inflows of foreign workers and relatively low interest rates would continue to provide a strong economic stimulus in 2008.

Once described as a 'Smart Chinese minnow in a Malay sea' the Asian city-state of Singapore has greater GDP wealth per capita (US$35,163 in 2007) than the European average, a developed concrete island nation tucked away between Malaysia and Indonesia. It has one of the highest densities worldwide of shopping malls and restaurants, which reflects the favoured pastimes of the mainly Chinese, but also Malay, Muslim and ethnic Indian population. The 'trafficking' of chewing gum into this country incurs a 12 month jail sentence and a hefty cash fine.

The economy

Singapore has been one of Asia's fastest growing economies in recent years although not aspiring to Chinese rates of growth. In 2007 gross domestic product (GDP) growth was 7.7 per cent, following 8.1 per cent growth in 2006; but still respectable. This growth was led by the manufacturing sector and the services sector. The Singaporean government continues to upgrade and restructure its economy. In the

2006 budget, it had sought to do this in five ways by: becoming a knowledge hub; promoting existing and new manufacturing and service industries; supporting entrepreneurship; growing human capital; and maintaining a competitive tax environment. Research and development (R&D) has become a declared national priority. In the 2006 budget, Prime Minister Lee announced S$500 million (US$250 million) would be spent on R&D with the objective of spending S$5billion (US$2.5 billion) over five years.

The Singapore government's economic outlook is good. The manufacturing and wholesale and retail trade sectors, together with strong external demand, are contributing to strong growth. Economic growth from Singapore's major trading partners is expected to be moderate and firms in the manufacturing and services sectors are optimistic about business conditions. Risks include a sharp correction in the housing market which could adversely affect external demand, a possible slowdown in growth of the semiconductor industry and persistently high oil prices

Manufacturing is an important source of Singaporean wealth – it is the hard disk drive capital of the world, responsible for one-third of the world's output. Six of the top ten world pharmaceutical firms manufacture in Singapore although in 2007 there was some concern in this unpredictable sector.

Tourism also helped boost revenues in 2007. In order to encourage even more foreign arrivals, the Lee government passed a bill to legalise gambling in April 2005, paving the way for the proposed construction of two large casinos.

Singapore is one of the major petroleum refining centres of Asia, and the third biggest in the world, with total crude oil refining capacity of 1.255 million barrels per day (bpd) in 2007. ExxonMobil said in early 2005 that it would be expanding its petrochemical complex, developing a new ethylene cracker. The extension was finished during 2006, and increased output from 75,000 tonnes per year to more than 900,000. Royal Dutch/Shell will also invest in a new naphtha cracker in its Jurong Island plant.

Policy issues

After physical security, the Singapore government's overriding concern remains the maintenance of the economy's competitiveness. The old capital-intensive oil- and chemical-based heavy industries will not provide long-term economic security for Singapore when wages in neighbouring Indonesia and Malaysia are a fraction of those in Singapore. The government sees the economy's future being tied to developing value-added services and developing its impressive human resources further with the aim of maintaining Singapore as a globally competitive, knowledge-intensive city, especially in financial services, telecommunications and energy.

The government continues to encourage the development of a more competitive and sophisticated labour force as well as biotechnology and the information and communications technology industries.

Financial markets

Financial markets tend to run in cycles since they are driven by a combination of the fluctuations of the underlying economic realities and investors' perceptions of these realities, especially their emotional and psychological reactions. Some commentators refer to this as the fear and greed symptoms. The last time investors became enthusiastic about emerging markets was in 1993/94 when some of the great and good in Wall Street briefly discovered that there were stock markets outside North America. Asia received the full blast of those walls of money and markets were driven to peaks from which they first declined gently and then crashed after the Asian crisis of 1997/98. They have been recuperating since then.

The Singapore market is well regulated and corporate governance standards are the highest in the region, according to the regional stockbroker Credit Lyonnais Securities Asia (CLSA). Singapore is uniquely exposed to the global trading environment and like the rest of the region is tied to US economic developments. However, beyond its own attractions, Singapore is seen as especially attractive for US companies to invest in order to give them an additional leg up into Asean and even EU markets.

Lee Kwan Yew passed the baton to his relatively colourless deputy Goh Chok Tong in 1990. Goh performed well as the head of a meritocratic government and his interregnum had extended to 13 years when he announced on 17 August 2003, at a National Day celebration, that he was stepping down before 2005 and allowing Lee's son, BG (short for Brigadier General) Lee Hsien Loong, to fill the position of prime minister. BG Lee is Harvard and Cambridge educated and is following a noticeably more authoritarian agenda than his predecessor.

Freedoms and rights

Singapore Prime Minister Lee Hsien Loong said in October 2005 that he did not believe an 'idealised form' of democracy was the right framework for Singapore. Neither, he said, were gay pride marches appropriate in a country where homosexuality is still viewed by some as sinful and taboo.

On his departure from the post in October 2005, US ambassador, Frank Lavin condemned Singapore's record on free speech, forecasting that the government 'will pay an increasing price for not allowing full participation of its citizens'. Lavin

KEY INDICATORS — Singapore

	Unit	2003	2004	2005	2006	2007
Population	m	4.19	4.22	4.34	4.40	*4.59
Gross domestic product (GDP)	US$bn	91.34	106.82	116.70	136.57	161.35
GDP per capita	US$	21,821	24,740	26,879	31,028	*35,163
GDP real growth	%	0.5	8.4	6.6	8.1	7.7
Inflation	%	0.6	1.7	0.5	0.9	2.1
Unemployment	%	4.9	3.7	3.1	2.6	2.1
Exports (fob) (goods)	US$m	144,134	174,000	204,800	274,980	–
Imports (cif) (goods)	US$m	127,898	155,200	188,300	230,233	–
Balance of trade	US$m	16,236	18,800	16,500	44,747	–
Current account	US$m	26,950	27,880	28,609	29,765	39,157.0
Total reserves minus gold	US$m	95,746	112,232	115,794	136,260	162,957
Foreign exchange	US$m	81,367	111,498	115,334	135,814	162,517
Exchange rate	per US$	1.72	1.69	1.54	1.54	1.45

* estimated figure

conceded to the strengths of an essentially one party state but also criticised the resultant lack of debate and discussion.

International organisations are unanimous in praise for Singapore's legal and political progress – and unanimous in condemnation of its civil liberties laws. The Singaporean authorities claim that such a tight control on expression is necessary to ensure order in a country with a potentially volatile mix of ethnicities and religions.

Singapore earned an unprecedented rebuke for seeking to prevent accredited activists from attending the IMF and World Bank annual meeting in Singapore in September 2006 and was obliged to abide by its obligations as host nation.

Outlook

Singapore worries about its population, mostly because it is not big enough. There are tax incentives for larger families, and night classes for those, mostly men, who are looking for a spouse. A larger population would encourage more manufacturers because there would be a better economy of scale, and it would enable manufacturers to build domestic demand to help balance fluctuations in external demand. And export oriented services that targeted for expansion, such as tourism, health care, entertainment and education would benefit from a larger domestic market that would help increase scale and therefore keep costs low.

For the meantime, Singapore has to rely on foreign workers as the labour market tightens as total employment expanded by over 9 per cent in 2007. The unemployment rate was 2.1 per cent.

Risk assessment

Politics	Good
Economy	Good
Regional stability	Good

COUNTRY PROFILE

Historical profile

The Republic of Singapore consists of Singapore Island, where Singapore City is located, and 57 smaller islands. One of these, Pedra Branca (Batu Putih), is claimed by Malaysia.

1819 Sir Stamford Raffles established a trading station in Singapore for the British East India Company. Singapore's free trade policy with no taxation attracted merchants from the entire region. The port captured much of the entrepôt trade of the East Indies. During the nineteenth century thousands of immigrant Chinese, Indians, Indonesians and Malays emigrated there.

1824 The Sultan of Johore allowed the British East India Company full control of the territory.

1826 Singapore, Malacca and Penang were incorporated into the Straits Settlements, part of the British East India Company.

1867 The Straits Settlements became a crown colony.

1942 During the Second World War, the island was captured and controlled by the Japanese.

1945 The British regained control of Singapore.

1946 The Straits Settlement dissolved. Penang and Malacca became part of Malaya while Singapore was made into a British Crown Colony.

1954 Lee Kuan Yew founded the People's Action Party (PAP). It attracted a strong following among the poor and the non-English speaking population.

1959 Singapore achieved internal self-government. The PAP won the election and Lee Kuan Yew became the first prime minister. Under Lee Kuan Yew, government opposition was suppressed. Lee's government attracted much international critisism for its authoritarian approach. Under Lee's leadership however, Singapore became a financial and industrial powerhouse.

1963 Singapore became a state of the Federation of Malaysia.

1965 The Republic of Singapore was legally declared an independent, sovereign state.

1967 Singapore was a founder member of the Association of Southeast Asian nations (Asean).

1971 The last British troops were withdrawn from Singapore.

1984 For the first time in Singapore's political history, two opposition MPs were elected to parliament.

1990 Goh Chok Tong took over from Lee Kuan Yew as prime minister.

1993 In the first direct presidential election, the PAP candidate, Ong Teng Cheong, secured the post.

1997 The PAP was re-elected in parliamentary elections.

1999 Sellapan Ramanathan (S R Nathan) was declared president in August.

2001 A political rally by parliamentarian J B Jeyaretnam of the Workers' Party of Singapore (WPS) was allowed by the government to take place — the first permitted outside an election period. The PAP was re-elected in parliamentary elections on 3 November.

2003 The Sars virus affected Singapore early in the year, infecting 206 people and killing 31. By the end of May, the World Health Organisation (WHO) declared that Singapore was free of Sars. A free trade agreement with the US came into effect.

2004 Prime Minister Goh Chok Tong stood down and Lee Hsien Loong was sworn in as prime minister on 12 August.

2005 President S R Nathan was appointed to a second term on 17 August after rivals were disqualified.

2006 The PAP was re-elected in parliamentary elections on 6 May. The IMF and World Bank held their annual meeting in Singapore in September; Singapore earned an unprecedented rebuke for seeking to prevent accredited activists from attending the meeting and was obliged to abide by its obligations as host nation.

Political structure

Constitution

The 1959 constitution was amended in 1965, 1988, 1991 and 1996. Consequently, there are now 15 Group Representation Constituencies (GRCs) which elect teams of up to six members of parliament. At least one member of each team has to be of minority (non-Chinese) ethnic origin. The number of single member constituencies has been reduced from 21 to eight.

In the 1991 amendment, the position of president was modified to become a directly elected post with a six-year term. The responsibilities of the office were extended to include the safeguarding of Singapore's financial reserves, and the right to veto senior civil service and judicial appointments. Only those who have served as cabinet ministers, chief justice, senior civil servants or have headed a large company are eligible as presidential candidates.

Elections must be held within three months of the dissolution of parliament.

There is full adult suffrage; voting is compulsory for all citizens aged 21 years and over.

Form of state

Republic

The executive

Executive power is vested in the cabinet, which is presided over by the prime minister and responsible to the unicameral parliament. The political hegemony of the People's Action Party (PAP) is absolute and parliamentary oversight of executive power is virtually non-existent. In 1995, a three-judge tribunal ruled that the president had no power to veto any bill that sought to restrict his existing powers.

National legislature

The unicameral parliament has 90 members. Seven are appointed by the president and 83 are elected for a five-year term in single and multi-seat constituencies.

Parliament can include in its membership up to nine nominated members of parliament (NMPs).

Legal system

Singaporean law is based on English common law.

The independence of the judiciary is safeguarded by the constitution. Judicial power is vested in Singapore's Supreme Court and in the Subordinate Courts. The Supreme Court consists of the High Court, the Court of Appeal and the Court of Criminal Appeal. The chief justice is appointed by the president, acting on the advice of the prime minister.

The Subordinate Courts consist of District Courts, Magistrates' Courts, Juvenile Courts, Coroners' Courts and Small Claims Tribunals. District judges, magistrates and coroners are appointed on the recommendation of the chief justice.

Although the constitution stipulates that the judiciary should act independently of government, it rarely does so in practice. Judges and judicial officials are appointed and dismissed by the president and judicial redress against abuses of executive power is therefore limited.

Sharia is the religious court with jurisdiction over Muslim law and domestic proceedings between Muslim parties.

Last elections

6 May 2006 (parliamentary); 27 August 2005 (presidential).

Results: Parliamentary: PAP won 66.60 per cent of the vote (82 seats out of 84); the WP won 16.34 per cent (one seat); and SDP 12.99 per cent (one seat).

Presidential: Sellapan Ramanathan (S R Nathan) was the only candidate declared eligible by the Presidential Elections Committee and retained the presidency without an election.

Next elections

May 2011 (presidential and parliamentary)

Political parties

Ruling party

People's Action Party (PAP) (since 1965; re-elected 6 May 2006)

Main opposition party

Workers' Party (WP); Singapore Democratic Party (SDP).

Population

4.59 million (2007)*

Last census: June 2000: 4,017,700

Population density: 6,590 inhabitants per square km; one of the world's highest population densities.

Annual growth rate: 2.4 per cent 1994–2004 (WHO 2006)

Ethnic make-up

Singapore is a multi-racial society. There are approximately 950,000 non-nationals. Chinese make up the majority of the population (77 per cent), and Malays (14 per cent), Indians (8 per cent), and other ethnic groups (1 per cent) make up the remainder.

Religions

Buddhism (32 per cent), Taoism (22 per cent), Islam (Sunni) (15 per cent), Christianity (13 per cent) and Hinduism (3 per cent) are the main religions. Other religions include Zoroastrianism (0.6 per cent) and Judaism. The constitution provides for freedom of worship.

Education

Primary school lasts for six years between the ages six and 12. Lower secondary education last for four years and students must attain good exam results to progress on to higher secondary school for a further three years, before advancing to higher education. There are three kinds of tertiary institutions: universities, polytechnics, and other centres of public and private training. The government almost wholly finances the National University of Singapore and the Nanyang Technological University. Many Singaporean students go abroad for their university education, increasingly to the US.

In October 2005, the UK's Warwick University pulled out of plans to set up a campus in Singapore, citing likely restrictions on academic freedom and reservations about the limitations on freedom of speech and assembly. Singapore probably was not too worried: already established are the campuses of many US universities – the University of Chicago, the Johns Hopkins University, the University of California and the Cornell and Stanford universities to name a few. In 2005 the prestigious Indian Institute of Management-Bangalore (IIM-B) opened a campus in the country and will initially offer a part-time course taught online.

Public expenditure on education typically amounts to 3 per cent of annual gross national income. In 2001 S$6,577 million was spent on education (Asian Development Bank 2004).

Literacy rate: 93 per cent adult rate; 100 per cent youth rate (15–24) (Unesco 2005).

Compulsory years: 6 to 12

Enrolment rate: 94 per cent gross primary enrolment of relevant age group (including repeaters); 74 per cent gross secondary enrolment (World Bank).

Pupils per teacher: 25 in primary schools

Health

Per capita total expenditure on health (2003) was US$1,156; of which per capita government spending was US$417, at the international dollar rate, (WHO 2006).

Singapore has managed to create a developed country healthcare system at relatively little cost. The health care system has a mixture of private and public provision and shows radically improved healthcare indices.

The private sector provides over 60 per cent of primary healthcare through doctors in private practice. Hospital healthcare is mostly public sector, with only 20 per cent of beds in the private sector. The government provides public subsidies through a ward system in public hospitals. Basic healthcare is financed through Central Provident Fund (CPF) Medisave accounts. Between 6 and 8 per cent of a worker's monthly contribution to the CPF, depending on age, is set aside for Medisave, a mandatory national health programme which encourages individuals to pay for their own healthcare. An additional endowment fund, Medifund, is targetted at poor and indigent Singaporeans.

Government officials have warned that if Singapore's predominantly Chinese population age too quickly, this could lead to expensive healthcare problems. Official statistics show that the number of Singaporeans aged 64 and above will rise fourfold to make up 20 per cent of the total population by the year 2030, when the population is projected to decline after it has reached a 7.9 million peak.

HIV/Aids

HIV prevalence: 0.2 per cent aged 15–49 in 2003 (World Bank)

Life expectancy: 80 years, 2004 (WHO 2006)

Fertility rate/Maternal mortality rate: 1.3 births per woman, 2004 (WHO 2006)

Birth rate/Death rate: 12.8 births per 1,000 population; 4.3 deaths per 1,000 population (2003).

Child (under 5 years) mortality rate (per 1,000): 3.6 per 1,000 live births (2003)

Head of population per physician: 1.4 physicians per 1,000 people, 2001 (WHO 2006)

Welfare

The government discourages dependence on the state for social security; rather, all workers and employers contribute to the compulsory savings scheme, the CPF. The CPF has developed into a wide-ranging social security scheme covering retirement, home ownership and health needs. Members can withdraw their savings upon reaching 55 but must set aside a minimum amount to ensure they have enough money for their retirement. The minimum amount to be saved every year was capped at S$80,000 (US$43,618) in 2003. Employment assistance is provided free of charge by the Ministry of Manpower.

Some 85 per cent of the population is housed in accommodation built and developed by the Housing and Development Board (HDB), set up in 1960 as a statutory board of the Ministry of National Development to provide low-cost public housing.

Main cities

Singapore is a city-state (estimated population 4.4 million in 2005).

Languages spoken

English is the main administrative language and is almost universally understood. In parliamentary debates, members may speak in English, Malay, Mandarin Chinese or Tamil, and simultaneous translations are provided. Other dialects of Chinese, mostly Hokkien (Fukienese) and Cantonese, are also spoken.

Most Singaporeans are bi- or tri-lingual.

Official language/s

English, Mandarin Chinese, Malay, Tamil.

Media

Press

Newspapers and magazines are published only under government licence in a highly regulated market. The government has a reputation of litigation for defamation, which has led to widespread self-censorship.

Singapore Press Holdings (SPH) is one of the largest companies listed on the Singapore Exchange, controlling 15 newspapers, a number of regional magazines and a book distribution network.

Dailies: The two main Chinese-language dailies are Lian He Zao Bao (United Morning News) and Lian He Wan Bao (United Evening News). The major English-language dailes are The Straits Times and Business Times. Berita Harian (in Malay) and Tamil Murasu (in Tamil) have smaller circulations. International editions of foreign newspapers are also available.

Weeklies: Most daily newspapers have a Sunday edition with extended features.

Business: In Chinese, the highest circulation papers are Lianhe Zaobao (United Morning News) (www.zaobao.com) a major regional and international news gathering organ and Lianhe Wanbao (United Evening News). In English, The Straits Times (www.straitstimes.com), Business Times (www.businesstimes.com.sg), The New Paper (http://newpaper.asia1.com.sg) a tabloid and Today is a free issue. In Malay Berita Harian (http://cyberita.asia1.com.sg) and in Tamil, Tamil Murasu (http://tamilmurasu.tamil.sg) is a broadsheet.

Periodicals: In English, The Executive (www.executive.sg) is published monthly. The Singapore International Chamber of Commerce publishes a quarterly, Business Minds (www.sicc.com.sg) with business, corporate and personnel news. There are also numerous interest and trade publications, including Singapore Business Federation (www.sbf.org.sg).

Broadcasting

The government-owned MediaCorp operates the national television and radio stations.

Radio: MediaCorp operates 14 radio stations broadcasting in English, Mandarin, Malay and Tamil. There are a number of private, commercial stations.

Television: MediaCorp has a monopoly with six free-to-air TV channels, broadcasting in the four official languages. Private satellite dishes are banned however foreign broadcasts are available through cable TV.

Advertising

Advertising is available in the press, on commercial radio, television, cinemas and via direct mail and house-to-house distribution of samples. Outdoor advertising, especially posters used for short-term advertising campaigns are widely used. Expenditure on advertising is typically around 1 per cent of GDP. There are also numerous trade magazines and trade fairs for business-to-business marketing.

Economy

The Singaporean economy has perhaps been the best managed in the Asia-Pacific region. Despite unorthodox economic policies, such as artificially increasing wages in order to move the economy towards greater capital intensity, sustained economic growth and low inflation have transformed Singapore into one of the richest countries in the world, with a GDP per capita which is the envy of many industrialised nations. Lacking in any natural resources, it has capitalised upon its human capital and fortunate location on the Straits of Malacca, closure of which would affect half of the world's shipping.

Strong economic growth for the past few decades has been achieved by a combination of economic liberalism, government investment in selected sectors and an efficient bureaucracy.

Singapore's traditional strengths are in trade and in its substantial value-added high-technology electronics manufacturing sector. Life sciences and petrochemicals are also significant. However, Singapore's economic planners are realising that its future lies in its historically more sluggish service sectors, if it is to maintain its competitive edge. Manufacturing now makes up only a quarter of GDP, and the small size of the economy is putting upward pressure on land and labour costs. Singapore has accordingly become keen to promote itself not just as Asia's premier banking centre, but as a world-class provider of financial services. The goal is clearly to limit dependence on less mature regional economies and vulnerability to their financial and political difficulties.

Wage reforms have been instituted to increase Singapore's competitiveness against emerging economies, such as China; they are designed to produce wages linked to performance as opposed to seniority, thus increasing efficiency.

External trade

Singapore belongs to the Association of South East Asian (Asean) Free Trade Area (Afta) and maintains a list of goods that have preferential import duties between members and a programme of tariff reductions due to be introduced in the next few years. It is also a member of the Asia-Pacific Economic Co-operation (Apec) forum, which is a group of 21 countries that border the Pacific. The objective of Apec is to facilitate trade, economic growth and investment in the region.

Foreign trade is a major function of the economy equalling over 300 per cent of GDP and many multinational corporations have based manufacturing (which accounts for 65 per cent of total output) and direct export sales operations in Singapore. Of the major economic sectors, electronics represents 40 per cent of industrial production with petrochemicals 20 per cent. Singapore is a regional trading hub and leading entrepôt, ranked second as the world's busiest container transhipment port (after Hong Kong). Almost 50 per cent of exports are re-exports and due to the lack of land for agricultural purposes most foodstuffs have to be imported.

Imports

Principal imports are machinery and equipment, mineral fuels, chemicals and foodstuffs.

Main sources: Malaysia (13.1 per cent total, 2006), US (12.5 per cent), China (11.4 per cent).

Exports

Principal exports are machinery and equipment (including electronics), consumer goods, chemicals and fuels.

Main destinations: Malaysia (13.1 per cent total, 2006), Hong Kong (10.0 per cent), US (9.9 per cent).

Agriculture

Farming

Only 3 per cent of Singapore's land area is used for agriculture. Singapore has some 2,000 licensed farms producing poultry, eggs, vegetables, fruit, orchids (both for domestic demand and export) and ornamental plants. Less than 6 per

cent of fresh vegetables is produced locally, with the rest imported from Malaysia, Indonesia, China and Australia.
Although agriculture plays only a minor role in Singapore's economy, the Primary Production Department promotes intensive farming methods. Agri-technology parks have been developed on 554 hectares of land in Murai, Sungai Tengah, Nee Soon and Loyang.
The effect of bird flu on the consumption of poultry showed a drop in production from the low 72,578 tonnes in 2004, rising to 83,861 tonnes in 2005, from the average 92,000 tonnes per annum before the outbreaks became public in 2003. The consumption of eggs was unaffected.
Estimated crop production in 2005 included: 130 tonnes (t) coconuts, 17t oilcrops, 10t roots and tubers, 10t fruit in total, 5,801t vegetables in total. Livestock production included: 104,934t meat in total, 35t beef, 21,000t pig meat, 27t lamb, 11t goat meat, 83,861t poultry, 22,000t eggs.

Fishing

With limited agricultural and water resources, there is little scope for the development of Singapore's fisheries, although fish is an important component of the Singaporean diet. Singapore relies mainly on imports for domestic consumption. The government's priority is to increase imports through trade relations. The quality of Singapore's own catch is often decsribed as poor. Rapid urbanisation and development have damaged natural habitats and caused the quality of inshore fish to deteriorate.
In 2004, the total marine fish catch was 1,533 tonnes and the total crustacean catch was 366 tonnes.
Forests constitute only 7 per cent of the total land area of Singapore. There are three major forest reserves – Bukit Timah , Palau Ubin and Sungei Buloh. Singapore produces plywood and veneer and imports pulp and paper. Timber imports in 2004 were US$533.1 million, while exports amounted to US$451.3 million. Timber production in 2004 included 355,000cum wood-based panels, including 280,000cum plywood and 65,000cum veneer sheets.

Industry and manufacturing

The industrial sector accounts for around 35 per cent of GDP. Manufacturing employs around 19 per cent of the workforce and construction employs a further seven per cent. Electronics is the largest industry and typically contributes about 14 per cent to GDP, accounting for 70 per cent of non-oil exports. The second largest industry group encompasses life sciences, chemicals and petroleum refining. Other major industries include transport equipment, especially shipbuilding, and related repair and conversion activities.

Tourism

Tourism contributes around three per cent of GDP. Government policy is to build on the sector's success and increase its role in the economy as a means of diversification. To this end, two huge casino resorts are being planned.
8.94 million arrivals were recorded in 2005, a seven per cent increase on 2004. Singapore's major markets are Indonesia, China, Malaysia, Japan, Australia, UK, India, US, South Korea and Thailand.

Environment

The Singapore Green Plan (SGP), released in 1992, called for 5 per cent of the country's land to be classified as protected areas. Around S$3 billion (US$1.7 billion) was allocated towards the upgrade of sewage treatment, a refuse incineration plant and improvements to water sources in 2002.

Hydrocarbons

Singapore does not have any oil or natural gas reserves and is entirely reliant on imports. Singapore is one of Asia's principal oil refining centres, with 11 refineries and total oil refining capacity of around 1.3 million barrels per day (bpd). The refining industry was hit hard by the Asian Economic Crisis of 1997/98. The establishment of refineries in Singapore's major export markets has also had a negative effect. New refineries in India significantly reduced Indian demand for oil from Singapore, while a new plant in Melaka, Malaysia, has increased competition. With Singapore's large refining industry there has been rapid growth of the petrochemical industry.
Demand for natural gas in Singapore is rising, due to the government's policy on cutting carbon emissions in power generation and the growing petrochemical industry. Singapore depends on Malaysia and Indonesia for a steady supply of natural gas for power generation. This includes the 155 million cubic feet provided by Malaysia through a transnational pipeline, the first of its kind in Asia. Singapore's policy is to avoid over-dependence on one country for its gas supply. A gas pipeline connecting Singapore to Indonesia was inaugurated in 2003.
Singapore does not produce or import coal.

Energy

Singapore has an electricity-generating capacity of around 9.0GW. The electricity is supplied by four thermal power stations, fuelled mainly by natural gas.

Financial markets

Stock exchange

Banking and insurance

Full liberalisation is expected by 2007, including the freeing up of retail banking, The government is also looking at plans to privatise the central provident fund (CPF), a compulsory savings mechanism which forces employers and employees to contribute. Access to CPF funds would allow banks to hold more of the country's savings.

Central bank

Monetary Authority of Singapore

Main financial centre

Singapore

Time

GMT plus eight hours

Geography

Singapore consists of the main island of Singapore and 58 smaller islands, more than 20 of them inhabited. Lying 137km north of the equator, it is linked to peninsular Malaysia in the north by a causeway carrying a road, railway and water pipeline across the narrow Straits of Johor, and separated from Indonesia to the south by the Straits of Singapore.
The island of Singapore itself is 42km long and 23km wide, with a coastline measuring 138km. It can be divided into three broad regions: a central hilly region, an area of hills and valleys in the west, and a relatively flat eastern region.

Hemisphere

Northern

Climate

The climate is equatorial, with uniformly high temperatures, high humidity and mean annual rainfall of 2,463mm with no defined wet or dry season. Mean daily temperatures range from a minimum 24 degrees Celsius (C) to a maximum 31 degrees C. The hottest month is May. The driest month is July, with an average rainfall of 70mm. November to January are generally the cooler and wetter months. Sometimes it rains for several days continuously and there may be serious flooding. Between monsoons, from April to November, there are regular pre-dawn thunderstorms, known as Sumatras. Singapore has an average of 180 lightning days a year.

Dress codes

Dress is generally informal, with light summer clothing the norm. A shirt and tie, or a safari suit, is the usual office dress for men, although jackets may be required in some restaurants for dinner; women should also dress smartly for business. Singapore's predominantly Chinese population follows Western fashion; a small section among the minority Indian and Malay communities wear traditional dress.

Entry requirements

Passports

Required by all, valid for six months beyond date of departure.

Visa

Visas are not required by nationals of most countries; a list of the countries whose nationals require visas is given on app.ica.gov.sg/travellers/entry/visa_requirements.asp. Social visit passes are issued on arrival to all other visitors by Immigration Officers, who determine the length of visit and grant social visit passes on the basis of sufficient funds for maintenance during the expected stay and confirmed return/onwards passage (including relevant visas for further destinations).

Prohibited entry

Singapore has tough laws against drug trafficking. The death penalty is mandatory for trafficking above certain prescribed levels.

Currency advice/regulations

There are no restrictions on the import or export of local or foreign currencies. Credit cards and travellers cheques are widely accepted.

Customs

1 litre each of spirits, wine and beer. Tobacco products are not duty-free and must be declared.

Prohibited imports

Include chewing gum, chewing tobacco and imitation tobacco products, cigarette lighters of pistol or revolver shape, controlled drugs and psychotropic substances, endangered species and by-products, firecrackers, obscene articles, publications, video tapes and software, reproduction of copyright publications, video tapes or disks, records or cassettes, or seditious and treasonable materials.

Health (for visitors)

Mandatory precautions

Yellow fever vaccination certificates for anyone who, within the preceding six days, has been to an infected area.

Advisable precautions

Vaccinations for diphtheria, tuberculosis, hepatitis A and B, polio, tetanus and typhoid are advisable. Tap water is safe. All necessary medicines (especially sleeping pills, depressants, stimulants, etc) must have a physician's certification declaring their prescribed use.

The Singapore Medical Centre, on the sixth floor of Tanglin shopping centre, houses a large community of specialist doctors.

Hotels

There are numerous five-star international-class hotels with shopping arcades, bars and swimming pools. Tipping is discouraged. A 4 per cent tax and a 10 per cent service charge are generally added to the hotel bill.

Credit cards

All major credit cards are widely accepted.

Public holidays (national)

Owing to its multi-ethnic composition, Singapore celebrates a wide range of religious festivals and holidays in addition to those listed. Many festivals are based on a lunar calendar, while the dates of some are only finalised at the last minute. Check with the Singapore Tourist Promotion Board for exact dates and locations affected.

Fixed dates

1 Jan (New Year's Day), 1 May (Labour Day), 9 Aug (National Day), 25 Dec (Christmas Day).

Variable dates

Chinese New Year (Jan/Feb), Good Friday, Vesak Day, Diwali (Oct/Nov), Eid al Adha, Eid al Fitr.

Working hours

During the Lunar New Year, many Chinese firms close for the whole week.

Banking

Mon–Fri: 1930–1500; Sat: 0930–1200; 0900–1500 (selected banks only).

Business

Mon–Fri: 0900–1300, 1400–1700.

Government

Mon–Fri: 0800–1300, 1400–1700.

Shops

Mon–Sat: 1930–2100. Some shops, particularly in tourist areas, open on Sundays.

Electricity supply

220—240V, 50 Hz, with three-pin (square) plug fittings.

Weights and measures

Metric system, with local variations.

Social customs/useful tips

Singaporeans are highly 'face' conscious and try to avoid self-embarrassment at all time.

Observe local etiquette – suit jackets remain off only as a concession to the climate, otherwise Western-style business formalities are in place.

Visiting cards are essential (although government officials do not use them). The cards should be presented with both hands. As a courtesy, it is a good idea to have cards printed in both Chinese and English. Cards should never be written on, put away before the meeting is over, or left behind.

When addressing Chinese persons, family or surname is mentioned first. When addressing Malay persons, the first of their two family names is used. Singaporean Indians use many different conventions.

Men and women should not touch each other. The heads of children should not be patted.

Tipping is not customary; it is not illegal, but is officially discouraged. In hotels and restaurants a 10 per cent service charge is included in the bill.

On-the-spot fines can be imposed for some offences. Smoking is not permitted in public buildings and restaurants, and is restricted in other public places.

Singapore celebrates the religious and cultural festivals of its four major communities, and therefore the year is punctuated by a series of colourful festivals. Celebration of the Chinese New Year, the main event in the Chinese calendar, centres on traditional reunion dinners and visits to friends and relations. Business people should avoid visiting at Christmas, Easter, Chinese New Year, Islamic and Hindu religious holiday periods.

Security

Tourists can walk the streets without fear of being robbed or attacked.

Getting there

Air

National airline: Singapore Airlines.

International airport/s: Singapore-Changi International Airport (SIN), 20km north-east of city; bank, bureau de change, duty-free shop, post office, restaurants, shops, car rental. A third terminal is scheduled to open in 2008.

Airport tax: The departure tax of S$21 is usually included in the price of the air ticket.

Surface

Road: Road transport arrives via two causeways from Malaysia, with express bus services from Kuala Lumpur and Johor Bahru.

Rail: There are rail services to Kuala Lumpur and Bangkok.

Water: There are excellent sea links with other countries.

Getting about

National transport

Road: The road network comprises some 2,900km of roads, including about 100km of expressways. Vehicular access to the Central Business District (CBD) is restricted and there are charges for vehicles entering the area at certain times.

Buses: Timetables for the extensive and inexpensive bus network are widely available at news-stands. Fares to various destinations are displayed on a signboard on the front of the bus stop.

Rail: The light overland railway network reaches all districts of Singapore Island.

Water: Regular ferry services from the World Trade Centre operate to some of the islands; others may be reached by charter boats.

City transport

Taxis: Metered, air-conditioned taxis are widely available from taxi pick-up points and can be hailed in the street. Taxi companies are allowed to set their own fares. The basic meter fare is displayed on the window of the rear door and details of surcharges are displayed on the fare card in all taxis.Taxis can also be hired by the hour.

Buses, trams & metro: The easy-to-use bus service is extensive.

The Mass Rapid Transit system (MRT) is fast, clean and efficient. It comprises three lines running north/south, east/west and north/east with around 70 underground and elevated stations.

Car hire

An international driving licence is required for car hire. Driving is on the left. Coupons for use of the public car parks managed by the Urban Redevelopment Authority (URA) or Housing & Development Board (HBD) can be purchased at post offices, URA parking kiosks and some gas/petrol stations. Car hire companies are listed in the Yellow Pages of the telephone directory.

BUSINESS DIRECTORY

The addresses listed below are a selection only. While World of Information makes every endeavour to check these addresses, we cannot guarantee that changes have not been made, especially to telephone numbers and area codes. We would welcome any corrections.

Telephone area codes

The international direct dialling (IDD) code for Singapore is +65, followed by subscriber's number.

Useful telephone numbers

Police: 999
Fire/ambulance: 995
Directory enquiries: 103
International calls: 104
International enquiries: 162
Trunk calls to Malaysia: 109
Time of Day: 1711
Flight information: 6542-1234
Bus information: 6287-2727
AA road service (24 hrs): 6748-9911
Post Office information: 6533-0234, 6532-4536
Immigration Department: 6532-2877
Telecoms Customer Services Centres: 6734-3344, 6534-3111

Chambers of Commerce

American Chamber of Commerce in Singapore, Shaw Centre, 1 Scotts Road, Singapore 228208 (tel: 6235-0077; fax: 6732-5917; e-mail: info@amcham.org.sg).

British Chamber of Commerce Singapore, Cecil Court, 138 Cecil Street, Singapore 069538 (tel: 6222-3552; fax: 6222-3556; e-mail: info@britcham.org.sg).

Singapore Chinese Chamber of Commerce & Industry, SCCCI Building, 47 Hill Street, Singapore 179365 (tel: 6337-8381; fax: 6339-0605; e-mail: corporate@sccci.org.sg).

Singapore Indian Chamber of Commerce and Industry, Tong Eng Building, 101 Cecil Street, Singapore069533 (tel: 6222-2855; fax: 6223-1707; e-mail: sicci@sicci.com).

Singapore International Chamber of Commerce, John Hancock Tower, 6 Raffles Quay, Singapore 048580 (tel: 6224-1255; fax: 6224-2785; e-mail: general@sicc.com.sg).

Singapore Malay Chamber of Commerce, 72A Bussorah Street, Singapore 199485 (tel: 6297-9296; fax: 6392-4527; e-mail: smcci@singnet.com.sg).

Banking

ABN Amro Bank NV, 63 Chulia Street (tel: 6231-8888; fax: 6532-3108).
ABSA Bank Ltd, 7 Temasek Boulevard, Suntec Tower One (tel: 6333-1033; fax: 6333-1066).

Agricultural Bank of China, 80 Raffles Place, UOB Plaza 2 (tel: 6535-5255; fax: 6538-7960).

American Express Bank Ltd, 16 Collyer Quay, Hitachi Tower (tel: 6538-4833; fax: 6534-3022).

Arab Bank plc, 80 Raffles Place, UOB Plaza 2 (tel: 6533-0055; fax: 6532-2150).

Arab Banking Corporation (BSC), 35-01 Republic Plaza Singapore, 9 Raffles Place, 048619 (tel: 6535-9339; fax: 6532-6288).

Bangkok Bank plc, 180 Cecil Street (tel: 6221-9400; fax: 6225-5852).

Bank of America, National Association, 9 Raffles Place, Republic Plaza Tower 1 (tel: 6239-3888; fax: 6239-3068).

Bank of China, 4 Battery Road, Bank of China Building (tel: 6535-2411; fax: 6534-3401).

Bank of East Asia Ltd, 137 Market Street, Bank of East Asia Building (tel: 6224-1334; fax: 6225-1805).

Bank of India, 138 Robinson Road, Hong Leong Centre (tel: 6222-0011; fax: 6225-4407).

Bank of Montreal, 150 Beach Road, Gateway West (tel: 6296-3233; fax: 6296-5044).

Bank of New York, 1 Temasek Avenue, Millenia Tower (tel: 6432-0222; fax: 6337-4302).

Bank of Nova Scotia, 10 Collyer Quay, Ocean Building (tel: 6535-8688; fax: 6532-2440).

Bank of Singapore, Tong Eng Building, 101 Cecil Street 01-02, 0106 (tel: 6223-9266).

Bank of Tokyo-Mitsubishi Ltd, 9 Raffles Place, Republic Plaza (tel: 6538-3388; fax: 6538-8083).

Chase Manhattan Bank, Shell Tower, 50 Raffles Place, 048623 (tel: 6530-4135, 6224-2888; fax: 6530-4331).

Far Eastern Bank, 156 Cecil Street, Far Eastern Bank Building, PO Box 2950, 0106 (tel: 6221-9055).

Hongkong & Shanghai Banking Corp Ltd, 21 Collyer Quay, 19-00 Hongkong Bank Building (tel: 6530-5412; fax: 6225-0663).

Indian Overseas Bank, 64 Cecil Street, IOB Building (tel: 6225-1100; fax: 6224-4490).

Industrial and Commercial Bank, ICB Building, 2 Shenton Way, 0106 (tel: 6221-1711).

Overseas Chinese Banking Corporation, OCBC Centre, 65 Chulia Street, 0104 (tel: 6535-7222; fax: 6533-7891).

Overseas Union Bank, OUB Centre, 1 Raffles Place, 0104 (tel: 6533-8686; fax: 6533-2293).

Standard Chartered Bank, 6 Battery Road (tel: 6225-8888; fax: 6225-9136).

United Overseas Bank, UOB Plaza, 80 Raffles Place, 048624 (tel: 6533-9898; fax: 6534-2334).

Central bank

Monetary Authority of Singapore, MAS Building, 10 Shenton Way, Singapore 079117 (tel: 6225-5577; fax: 6229-9229; e-mail: webmaster@mas.gov.sg).

Travel information

Automobile Association of Singapore, 336 River Valley Road, AA Centre, Singapore (tel: 6333-8811; fax: 6733-50944; e-mail: aasmail@aas.com.sg).

Singapore Airlines, Airline House, 25 Airline Road, Singapore 819829 (tel: 6541-4855; fax: 6542-3002).

Ministry of tourism

Ministry of Trade and Industry, 100 High Street, 09-01 The Treasury, Singapore 179434 (tel: 6225-9911; fax: 6332-7260; e-mail: mti_email@mti.gov.sg).

National tourist organisation offices

Singapore Tourism Board, Tourism Court, 1 Orchard Spring Lane, Singapore 247729 (tel: 6736-6622; fax: 6736-9423; e-mail: ms@stb.com.sg).

Ministries

Ministry of Communications, 39th Storey PSA Building, 460 Alexandra Road, Singapore 119963 (tel: 6270-7988; fax: 6279-9734).

Ministry of Defence, Gombak Drive (off Upper Bukit Timah Road), Mindef Building, Singapore 2366 (tel: 6760-8188; fax: 6762-0112).

Ministry of Development, c/o Meeting Planners Pte Ltd, 2nd Floor, Pico Centre, 20 Kallang Avenue, Singapore 1233 (tel: 6297-2822; fax: 6296-2670, 6292-7577).

Ministry of Environment, Sewerage Department, 14-00 Environmental Building, 40 Scotts Road, Singapore 228231 (tel: 6732-7733; fax: 6731-9699 (sewerage dept), 6731-9456 (general).

Ministry of Finance, 8 Shenton Way, 43rd, 45th, 46th and 50th Storey, Treasury Building, Singapore 0106 (tel: 6225-9911; fax: 6320-9435 (budget), 6320-9932 (PSD), 6224-6847 (revenue)).

Ministry of Foreign Affairs, 250 North Bridge Road, 07-00 Raffles City Tower, Singapore 0617 (tel: 6336-1177, 6330-5795 (after hours); fax: 6339-4330).

Ministry of Information, Communications and the Arts, Public Relations Department, 460 Alexandra Road 36-00, PSA Building, Singapore 0511 (tel: 6270-7988; fax: 6279-9765); Media Division, MITA Building, 140 Hill Street, 2nd Storey, Singapore 179369 (tel: 6837-9666).

Ministry of Manpower, 18 Havelock Road, Singapore 059764 (tel: 6438-5122; fax: 6534-4840; internet: www.mom.gov.sg).

Ministry of National Development, National Development Building, Maxwell Road, Singapore 0106 (tel: 6222-1211; fax: 6322-6254).

Ministry of Trade and Industry, 100 High Street, 09-01 The Treasury, Singapore 179434 (tel: 6225-9911; fax: 6332-7260; e-mail: mti_email@mti.gov.sg).

Other useful addresses

ASEAN Investment Promotion Agency, Economic Development Board, 250 North Bridge Road, 24-00 Raffles City Tower, Singapore 0617 (tel: 6336-2288; 6338-8265).

ASEAN Secretariat, 70 A J1 Sisingamangaraja, Jakarta 12110, Indonesia (tel: (+62-21) 726-2991,) (+62-21) 724-3372; fax: (+62-21) 724-3504, (+62-21) 739-8234; e-mail: asean.or.id).

The Association of Banks in Singapore, 12-08 MAS Building, 10 Shenton Way, Singapore 0207 (tel: 6224-4300; fax: 6224-1785).

The Association of Small & Medium Enterprises, Blk 139 Kim Tain Road, Singapore 0316 (tel: 6271-2566; fax: 6271-1257).

Civil Aviation Authority of Singapore, Singapore Airtropolis, Changi Airport (tel: 6542-1122; fax: 6545-6222).

Construction Industry Development Board, Annexe A, 3rd Storey, National Development Building, 9 Maxwell Road, Singapore 0106 (tel: 6225-6711; fax: 6225-7307).

Controller of Immigration, 95 South Bridge Road, Pidemco Centre, Singapore (tel: 6532-2877; fax: 6530-1840).

Customs & Excise Department, 03-01 & 10-01 World Trade Centre, 1 Maritime Square, Singapore 099253 (tel: 6272-8222; fax: 6375-2090).

Economic Development Board, 24-00 Raffles City Tower, 250 North Bridge Road, Singapore 0617 (tel: 6336-2288; fax: 6339-6077).

Housing and Development Board, 3451 Jalan Bukit Merah, HDB Centre, Singapore 0315 (tel: 6273-9090).

Immigration Department, 7th & 8th Storey, 08-26 Pidemco Centre, 95 South Bridge Road, Singapore 0105 (tel: 6532-2877; fax: 6530-1840).

Inland Revenue Authority of Singapore, Fullerton Building, B1-00 Fullerton Square, Singapore 049178 (tel: 6535-4244; fax: 6535-5393).

Jurong Town Corporation, Jurong Town Hall, 301 Jurong Town Hall Road, Singapore 609431 (tel: 6560-0056; fax: 6565-5301).

National Arts Council, Arts Division, MCD Building, 512 Thomson Road, Singapore 1129 (tel: 6258-9595; fax: 6350-6118).

National Productivity Board, 2 Bukit Merah, Central NPB Building, Singapore 0315 (tel: 6734-5534).

Port of Singapore Authority (PSA), PSA Building, 460 Alexandra Road, Singapore 119963 (tel: 6274-7111; fax: 6274-4677).

Public Utilities Board, PUB Building, 111 Somerset Way, Singapore 0207 (tel: 6235-8888; fax: 6731-3020).

Registry of Trade and Businesses, 05-01/15 International Plaza, 10 Anson Road, Singapore 0207 (tel: 6227-8551; fax: 6225-1676).

Singapore Confederation of Industries (formerly Singapore Manufacturers' Association), SMA House, 20 Orchard Road, Singapore 238830 (tel: 6338-8787; fax: 6339-3340).

Singapore Embassy (US), 3501 International Place, NW, Washington DC 20008 (tel: (+1-202)-537-3100; fax: (1-202)-537-0876; e-mail: singemb.dc@verizon.net).

Singapore Hotel Association, 11 Mount Sophia, Singapore 228461 (tel: 6339-9918; fax: 6339-3795).

Singapore Importers and Exporters Association, 2nd Floor, 76-C Robinson Road, Singapore 0106 (tel: 6222-3451).

Singapore Institute of Standards and Industrial Research (SISIR), 1 Science Park Drive, Singapore 0511 (tel: 6778-7777; fax: 6778-0086).

Singapore International Monetary Exchange (SIMEX), Square, 07-00 OUB Centre, Singapore 0104 (tel: 6535-7282; fax: 6535-7382).

Stock Exchange of Singapore, 26-01/08 The Exchange, 20 Cecil Street, Singapore 049705 (tel: 6535-3788; fax: 6535-0775).

Telecommunication Authority of Singapore, TAS Building, 35 Robinson Road, Singapore 068876 (tel: 6738-7788; fax: 6733-0073).

Trade Development Board, 07-00 Bugis Junction Office Tower, 230 Victoria Street, Singapore 188024 (tel: 6271-9388; fax: 6274-0770).

US Embassy, 30 Hill Street, Singapore 0617 (tel: 6338-0251; fax: 6338-8472).

Work Permit and Employment Department, Ministry of Labour, 18 Havelock Road, Singapore 059764 (tel: 6534-1511; fax: 6539-5344/5).

Internet sites

Singapore Connect: http://sgconnect.asia1.com.sg

Singapore Government: http://www.gov.sg

Singapore Statistical Office: http://www.singstat.gov.sg

Singapore Yellow Pages: http://www.yellowpages.com.sg

Slovakia

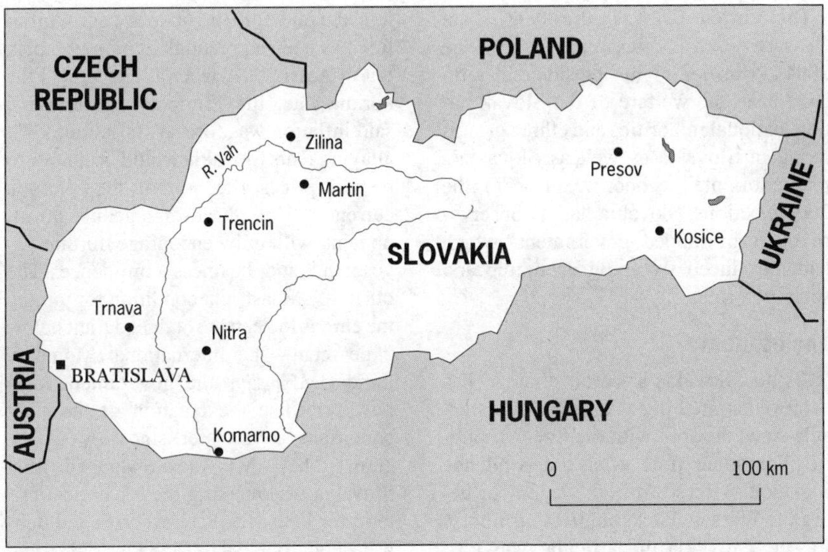

According to the Organisation for Economic Co-operation and Development (OECD) Slovakia's economy remained on course for further growth and was expected to meet adoption criteria for the euro in early 2009. In its annual report on Slovakia, the OECD noted that the euro membership criteria for the public deficit, debt and inflation all appeared to be within Slovakia's reach.

Slovakia's record breaking 8.3 per cent gross domestic product (GDP) growth in 2006 was estimated to have continued at 7.5 per cent in 2007 and was forecast to reach 8.0 per cent in 2008. The upbeat report nonetheless contained some warnings for Slovakia's left-wing coalition government. One of these focussed on the increase of the minimum wage by 10.1 per cent in October 2007. Despite efforts to reduce the jobless total in 2007, long-term unemployment at around 10.0 per cent remained the highest in the OECD.

Slovakia's impressively high productivity gains have been based on the introduction and acceptance of new technology and know-how. Despite this, Slovakia's overall education level lags behind the OECD average, as is also the case in the neighbouring Czech Republic. The education of Slovakia's large Roma minority, which accounts for around seven per cent of the population, is particularly poor. Official figures suggest that at most 75 per cent of the Roma children receive a primary school education.

Obstacles to business development, such as high administration costs and weak competition in some areas of the economy (such as retailing and energy) also need to be addressed. Privatisation efforts need to be re-launched in some areas where competition is lacking, such as the energy and telecommunications sectors, the OECD report recommends, a veiled criticism of prime minister Robert Fico's government, which has effectively put a brake on the sale of state assets. Adoption of the single currency will in all likelihood produce a sharp fall in interest rates, in turn sparking an economic boom which risks triggering a boom and bust cycle the OECD report warned. It was hoped that the government's long-term budget reform measures, due to continue into 2010, would give it room to take measures to boost or suppress growth.

For a long time in the shadow of its neighbour and former co-federation member the Czech Republic, the Slovak Republic now stands proudly on its own two feet, in terms of deciding its own political, economic and strategic direction. For a country that has been part of Greater

KEY FACTS

Official name: Slovenská Republika (Slovak Republic)

Head of State: President Ivan Gasparovic (formerly HZD) (from 15 Jun 2004)

Head of government: Prime Minister Robert Fico (Smer) (took office 4 Jul 2006)

Ruling party: Coalition led by: Smer-Sociálna Demokracia (Smer) (Direction party-Social Democracy), with the Ludová Strana-Hnutie Za Demokratické Slovensko (LS-HZDS) (People's Party-Movement for a Democratic Slovakia), and the Slovenská Národná Strana (SNS) (Slovak National Party) (from 2 July 2006)

Area: 49,035 square km

Population: 5.40 million (2007)

Capital: Bratislava

Official language: Slovak

Currency: Slovak koruna (Sk) = 100 haléru

Exchange rate: Sk19.14 per US$ (Jul 2008); Slovakia entered ERMII in Nov 2005 when the rate was set at SK38.4550 to the euro.

GDP per capita: US$13,857 (2007)

GDP real growth: 10.40% (2007); 7.5% (2008) (official forecast)

Labour force: 2.62 million (2004)

Unemployment: 14.30% (2004)

Inflation: 2.80% (2007)

Balance of trade: -US$3.08 billion (2006)

Foreign debt: US$22.07 billion (2004)

Annual FDI: US$1.10 billion (2004)

Hungary, then ruled by the Soviet Empire, then half of Czechoslovakia, this is no mean feat. The country has been independent since 1993 when it broke away from the Czech Republic. Slovakia joined Nato and the European Union (EU) in the spring of 2004 and entered the Exchange Rate Mechanism (which is for EU countries not taking part in the monetary union, but which helps to enable a smooth transition to euro adoption later) in 2005.

Politics

Since October 1998, the Slovenská Demokratická a Krestanská Únia (SDKÚ) (Slovak Democratic and Christian Union) has led a coalition government that includes the Krest'ansko-Demokratické Hnutie (KDH) (Christian Democratic Movement), the Strana Madarskej Koalície-Magyar Koalíció Pártja (SMK) (Hungarian Coalition Party) and the Aliancia Nového Obcana (ANO) (New Citizen Alliance).

Mikulas Dzurinda, of the SDKU, had won a second term as prime minister in September 2002. He endeavoured to become a significant figure on the world stage, despite being domestically unpopular. The Slovak population were not sufficiently impressed however. In the 2006 general elections, the left-leaning Smer-Sociálna Demokracia (Smer) (Direction party-Social Democracy) won most votes with 29.14 per cent (50 seats out of 150) but without enough to gain a majority; the prime minister's SDKÚ won 18.36 per cent (31). Turnout was 54.7 per cent. On 2 July 2006 an agreement between Smer, the Ludová Strana-Hnutie Za Demokratické Slovensko (LS-HZDS) (People's Party-Movement for a Democratic Slovakia), and the Slovenská Národná Strana (SNS) (Slovak National Party), created a coalition government. Robert Fico (leader of Smer) took office as prime minister on 4 July 2006.

The current Slovak President, Ivan Gasparovic, was sworn in on 15 June 2004. Priorities of his presidential term have been the welfare of the Slovak nation, national minorities and ethnic groups living in Slovakia as well as Slovakia's market-oriented economy. Prior to the 2006 elections, Slovakia had a conservative reform-minded government, which had introduced sweeping economic and social reforms.

The economy

It is to Slovakia's credit that it has achieved something of an economic miracle since the split with the Czech republic. For some time after independence Slovakia suffered from the legacy of being the Warsaw Pact countries' armoury. Eastern Slovakia in particular was also devastated by the then (Czech) president Vaclav Havel's declaration in1990 that Czechoslovakia would cease the production and export of arms. Military production contracted by an estimated 91 per cent, turning Slovak cities such as Martin into unemployment blackspots. This unappealing export profile, and the poor foreign investment record that went with it held Slovakia back for a number of years.

Toward the euro

Slovakia's entry into the Exchange Rate Mechanism, the 'waiting room' for adoption of the euro, was seven months earlier than expected. The country will remain in the ERM until January 2009 when it will join at a rate of K30.160 to the euro. Inflation has been a potential stumbling block, but in April 2008, when it announced the koruna rate, the European Commission said inflation was forecast to fall in 2009, allaying fears Slovakia would be unable to restrain prices after joining the common currency. This ahead-of-schedule development will only encourage further investment and business confidence. The other key Maastricht condition for joining the euro is to keep the budget deficit below 3 per cent. The International Monetary Fund (IMF) says the government must now prioritise the creation of the right conditions to transfer smoothly to the euro. The IMF acknowledged that Slovakia was meeting the Maastricht criteria for long-term interest rates and public debt, but said several risks and challenges remained. The government intended to ratify the EU reform treaty in 2008 but was thwarted by the opposition.

Risk assessment

Politics	Good
Economy	Good
Regional stability	Good

KEY INDICATORS Slovakia

	Unit	2003	2004	2005	2006	2007
Population	m	5.11	5.20	5.41	5.41	5.40
Gross domestic product (GDP)	US$bn	32.50	41.10	47.43	56.05	74.99
GDP per capita	US$	6,010	7,603	8,769	10,357	13,857
GDP real growth	%	4.2	5.5	6.0	8.5	10.4
Inflation	%	8.6	7.5	2.8	4.4	2.8
Unemployment	%	17.6	14.3	11.7	10.4	–
Industrial output	% change	–	11.5	9.5	10.5	–
Agricultural output	% change	–	9.6	7.9	2.6	–
Exports (fob) (goods)	US$m	21,838.0	29,240.0	32,026.0	41,696.0	57,806.0
Imports (cif) (goods)	US$m	22,479.0	29,670.0	34,476.0	44,778.0	58,715.0
Balance of trade	US$m	-641.0	-430.0	-2,450.0	-3,082.0	-909.0
Current account	US$m	-280.0	-1,390.0	-4,090.0	-3,963.0	-3,998.0
Total reserves minus gold	US$m	11,678.0	14,417.0	14,901.0	12,647.0	18,032.0
Foreign exchange	US$m	11,677.0	14,416.0	14,899.0	12,645.0	18,026.0
Exchange rate	per US$	36.14	32.22	26.95	26.45	23.23

COUNTRY PROFILE

Historical profile

Slovakia, called Oberungarn (Upper Hungary) in some older maps, had politically been a part of the Hungarian kingdom for centuries, ever since the Moravian Kingdom had been destroyed in 902.

1536–1783 Bratislava, formerly Pressburg, was the capital of Hungary.

1867–1917 The Habsburg domains in central Europe were reconstituted as the dual monarchy of Austria-Hungary. Slovakia's struggle for independence suffered a setback when Hungary's parliament gained a large degree of political autonomy from the Austrian administration in Vienna. The policy of Magyarisation that the Hungarian administration strove to achieve – Hungarian was to be the exclusive language of administration, jurisdiction and education – was most disturbing to Slovakia.

1918 At the end of the First World War, Slovakia announced its independence from the Austro-Hungarian empire and incorporation into the new Republic of

Czechoslovakia with Thomas Masaryk as the country's first president.
1938 Czechoslovakia ceded its German-speaking areas of Sudetenland to Germany.
1939–45 The country fell under German control until the end of the Second World War.
1946 The Czechoslovak Communist Party (CPCz) formed a power-sharing government following national elections.
1948 After mass protests and strikes orchestrated by the Communists, a government crisis left the CPCz with a majority in government.
1949–67 Stalinist-style rule, complete with party purges.
1968 Alexander Dubcek, the CPCz leader, introduced the policy of 'socialism with a human face', which ended with the crushing of the reformist movement by the Soviet army.
1969–88 There were on-going protests at occupation by the Soviet troops. Václav Havel and a group of dissidents called for the restoration of civil and political rights. Mass demonstrations in 1988 marked the anniversary of the 1968 invasion.
1989 The new spirit of glasnost was met with scepticism as the government initially resisted political and economic change. However, large public demonstrations in the major cities, the 'Velvet Revolution', led to the resignation of the Communist Party leadership. Václav Havel was elected president and a pluralistic political system and market economy were introduced.
1990 The country was renamed the Czech and Slovak Federative Republic. The first free elections since 1946 led to the establishment of a coalition government involving all major parties, with the exception of the CPCz, and Havel was re-elected president.
1991 The Soviet forces completed their withdrawal.
1992 In elections, the Czech voters backed the centre-right, while the Slovaks supported Slovak separatists and left-wing parties. Vladimir Meciar (a supporter of Slovak separatism) became Slovak prime minister. He opposed the rapid privatisation of the public sector proposed by the Czech prime minister, Václav Klaus. Neither was prepared to compromise and agreed to the separation of Slovakia, despite President Havel's objections.
1993 Czechoslovakia divided into two independent countries, the Czech Republic (comprising the regions of Bohemia and Moravia) and the Slovak Republic (Slovakia). Michal Kovac became president of the Slovak Republic, with Vladimir Meciar continuing as prime minister.
1994 Meciar was voted out of office in March and was replaced by Jozef Moravcik. Moravcik lasted until the National Council elections in December when Meciar was returned to power with a new coalition government.
1997 A referendum to debate electoral change became a farce when the central question was withdrawn and the majority of voters stayed away.
1998 Kovac's presidential term expired and Prime Minister Meciar assumed some presidential powers. Mikulas Dzurinda became prime minister as opposition parties refused to co-operate with Meciar, despite his party, Hnutie Za Demokratické Slovensko (HZDS) (Movement for Democratic Slovakia), gaining most seats in the general elections.
1999 Rudolf Schuster was elected president.
2000 The Slovenská Demokratiká Koalícia (SDK) (Slovak Democratic Coalition), was replaced by the Slovenská Demokratická a Krestanská Únia (SDKÚ) (Social Democratic Christian Union), and gave Dzurinda an electoral platform to contest the 2002 elections.
2002 The parliamentary elections were won by the SDKÚ. Prime Minister Dzurinda formed a centre-right coalition government with the Hungarian Coalition Party (SMK), the Christian Democratic Movement (KDH) and the New Citizen Alliance (ANO). NATO invited Slovakia to join the alliance by 2004.
2003 Voters in the May referendum approved EU membership.
2004 Ivan Gasparovic won the presidential election on 17 April with 59.9 per cent of the vote. Slovakia entered the EU on 1 May. Ivan Gasparovic took office on 15 June.
2005 Slovakia entered the European Exchange Rate Mechanism (ERM II) in November.
2006 In general elections, the left-leaning Smer-Sociálna Demokracia (Smer) (Direction party-Social Democracy) won most votes with 29.14 per cent (50 seats out of 150) but without enough to gain a majority; the prime minister's SDKÚ won 18.36 per cent (31). Turnout was 54.7 per cent. On 2 July 2006 an agreement between Smer, the Ludová Strana-Hnutie Za Demokratické Slovensko (LS-HZDS) (People's Party-Movement for a Democratic Slovakia), and the Slovenská Národná Strana (SNS) (Slovak National Party), created a coalition government. Robert Fico (leader of Smer) took office as prime minister on 4 July 2006.
2007 On 20 December Slovakia became a member of the European Union Schengen area whereby all travellers may cross borders without a passport or visa.
2008 An agreement for visa-free visits of citizens to the US was signed on 14 March 2008. The government intended to ratify the EU reform treaty but was thwarted by the opposition. When Slovakia formally adopts the euro on 1 January 2009, the official rate exchange for the korunas will be set at K30.1260 per euro. It will be the sixteenth member country to adopt the euro.

Political structure

Constitution

The constitution was ratified in 1992. No new government can be formed until the president has accepted the resignation of the former one. Further amendments in January and February 2001 created an independent council, increasing the powers of the constitutional court, and paved the way for reform of the public administration.
With reference to accession to EU and NATO, an amendment to the constitution was approved on 1 July 2001, which reclassified the relationship between national and international law, introduced judicial regulations and allowed for the creation of a second tier of self-administrative government in the regions.
Electoral system: Universal direct suffrage for party lists. All electoral coalitions have to win 5 per cent of the vote for every party they contain.

Form of state

Parliamentary democratic republic

The executive

Executive power lies with the prime minister and ministers, the former being appointed by the president.
The head of state is the president, elected by the National Council of the Slovak Republic by secret ballot for a period of five years. A majority of three-fifths of all deputies' votes is required for the president to be elected.

National legislature

Legislative authority is vested in the 150-member Národná Rada Slovenskej Republiky (National Council of the Slovak Republic) which is directly elected for a four-year term.

Legal system

Slovakia's legal system is partly based on the Czechslovakian system introduced before independence in 1993. The judiciary is independent of the government, although the president appoints judges to both the Constitutional Court and Supreme Court. The Constitutional Court is responsible for ensuring that legislation adheres to the constitution and 13 judges are appointed for a period of 12 years. Judges of the Supreme Court are appointed for an unlimited time period.

As part of the process toward accession to the EU, Slovakia has been attempting to harmonise its existing and new legislation with that of the organisation.

Last elections
18 June 2006 (parliamentary); 3/17 April 2004 (presidential).

Results: Parliamentary: the Strana Smer-Tretia Cesta (Smer) (Direction Party) won 29.14 per cent (50 seats out of 150), the SDKÚ 18.36 per cent (31), SNS 11.73 per cent (20), SMK 11.69 per cent (20), LS-HZDS 8.8 per cent (15), KDH 8.31 per cent (14). Turnout was 54.7 per cent.
Presidential: Ivan Gasparovic (Hnutie za Demokraciu (HZD) (Movement for Democracy)) won with 59.9 per cent of the vote against Vladimír Meciar (LS-HZDS) 40.1 per cent; turnout was 43.5 per cent.

Next elections
2009 (presidential); 2010 (parliamentary)

Political parties

Ruling party
Coalition led by: Smer-Sociálna Demokracia (Smer) (Direction party-Social Democracy), with the Ludová Strana-Hnutie Za Demokratické Slovensko (LS-HZDS) (People's Party-Movement for a Democratic Slovakia), and the Slovenská Národná Strana (SNS) (Slovak National Party) (from 2 July 2006)

Main opposition party
Coalition government led by Slovenská Demokratická a Krestanská Únia (SDKÚ) (Slovak Democratic and Christian Union) and including Strana Madarskej Koalície-Magyar Koalíció Pártja (SMK) (Hungarian Coalition Party), Krest'ansko-Demokratické Hnutie (KDH) (Christian Democratic Movement) and Aliancia Nového Obcana (ANO) (New Citizen Alliance)

Population

5.40 million (2007)

Last census: May 2001: 5,379,455

Population density: 110.4 inhabitants per square km. Urban population: 58 per cent (1995–2001).

Annual growth rate: 0.1 per cent 1994–2004 (WHO 2006)

Ethnic make-up
The chief non-Roma minorities are Hungarians (10.8 per cent of the population), Czechs (3 per cent), Ruthenians, Ukrainians, Germans and Poles. Roma, although making up only 1.5 per cent of the overall population, make up a significant minority in some areas, and are growing faster than the national average.

Religions
Roman Catholic (60.3 per cent), Protestant (8.4 per cent), Orthodox (4.1 per cent).

Education

Slovakia has universal literacy and offers free education to all. Enrolment at all levels is high and there is no noticeable gender disparity. Languages of instruction are English and Slovak, although Hungarians may be taught in their own language.
In June 2004 the government failed, in a vote in parliament, to introduce student loans for teriary education.

Literacy rate: 100 per cent adult rate; 100 per cent youth rate (15–24) (Unesco 2005).

Compulsory years: 6 to 15

Enrolment rate: 102 per cent total primary enrolment, 94 per cent gross secondary enrolment; of the relevant age groups (including repeaters); (World Bank).

Pupils per teacher: 20 in primary schools

Health

Per capita total expenditure on health (2003) was US$777; of which per capita government spending was US$687, at the international dollar rate, (WHO 2006).
There is a significant disparity between male and female life expectancy (9 years), partly due to the unbalanced diet and high cigarette and beer consumption by men, which the government is attempting to reduce.

HIV/Aids

HIV prevalence: 0.1 per cent aged 15–49 in 2003 (World Bank)

Life expectancy: 74 years, 2004 (WHO 2006)

Fertility rate/Maternal mortality rate: 1.2 births per woman, 2004 (WHO 2006)

Birth rate/Death rate: 10 births per and nine deaths per 1,000 population (2003).

Child (under 5 years) mortality rate (per 1,000): 7.0 per 1,000 live births (World Bank)

Head of population per physician: 3.18 physicians per 1,000 people, 2003 (WHO 2006)

Welfare

Slovakia has a 42.5 hour working week with a minimum wage set by the government. It has a well-developed social security system, including health, unemployment and pension benefits. Employees contribute 12 per cent of their wages to social security schemes and employers an additional 38 per cent.

Main cities

Bratislava (capital, estimated population 424,207 in 2005), Košice (236,519), Presov (94,639), Nitra (86,407), Zilina (85,956).

Languages spoken

The Czech and Slovak languages are mutually comprehensible. Hungarian is widely spoken, especially in the south and east.
A large proportion of the population, particularly those engaged in industry and foreign trade, speaks German. Russian is also spoken by some executives. English is increasing, especially among the younger generation.

Official language/s
Slovak

Media

Press

Dailies: There are national and regional dailies, most published in Slovakian, including Pravda (www.pravda.sk), Praca (www.praca.sk), Novy CAS (www.bleskovky.sk),SME (www.sme.sk). In Hungarian, Új Szó (www.ujszo.com) and in English Slovak Spectator (www.slovakspectator.sk).
Regional publications in Slovakian includes, Korzár (www.cassovia.sk/korzar) from Kosice, Presovsky Vecernik (www.slovanet.sk/vecernik/pv) from Presov and Nitrianske Noviny (www.mynoviny.sk) from Nitra.

Weeklies: Magazines in Slovakian include Plus 7 Dni (www.plus7dni.sk), Tyzden (www.tyzden.sk) and in Hungarian Vasárnap (www.vasarnap.com).

Business: Magazines, in Slovakian, include Profit (http://profit.etrend.sk) and in English Trend (http://english.etrend.sk). Newspapers in Slovakian Hospodarske Noviny (www.hnonline.sk) and Profini (www.profini.sk).
Many dailies include sections on business news.

Periodicals: Slovak Spectator, an English-language newspaper, is published every second Wednesday.

Broadcasting

Radio: There are over 20 private, commercial radio stations. The public Slovensky Rozhlas (Slovak Radio) broadcasts nationwide as well as international programmes. Other major radio stations includes Radio Expres (www.expres.sk), Radio Viva (www.radioviva.sk), Radio Okey (www.okey.sk) and Fun Radio (www.funradio.sk).
Other European radio stations are available.

Television: There are several networks available including, TV Markiza (www.markiza.sk) which has the largest audience, Slovenská televízia (Slovak TV) (www.stv.sk) is the public channel, Joj TV (www.joj.sk) and the news channel TA3 (www.ta3.com), which broadcasts regional programmes via cable.
Reception of broadcasts from neighbouring countries allows greater variety.

Advertising
There are a number of foreign and domestic advertising agencies. The most

commonly used media include newspapers, radio and television. Billboards and posters are widely used.

Economy

Although Slovakia was politically isolated during the 1990s, its economy has shown signs of vibrancy. Growth has been strongly positive since the mid-1990s and inflation has remained at a respectable level. Despite the appearance of growing prosperity, structural change is badly needed. The experience of Slovakia since the end of the Cold War reflects its use within Czechoslovakia as a command military-industrial economy which had built up very rapidly on a relatively fragile base – until Czechoslovakia was formed out of the ashes of the Austro-Hungarian Empire in 1918, Slovakia was considered to be a backward agricultural society.

Since 2002, the government has been committed to curbing fiscal deficits on a sustained basis, thereby alleviating the burden of economic stabilisation on monetary policy. Unemployment remains high, but the government is reforming the over-generous welfare system and stimulating labour supply and demand. Welfare benefits are being reduced, the retirement age increased and pension benefits made dependent on work and contribution history. Labour code reforms make both permanent and temporary job creation less costly and targeted employment subsidies are being introduced for the long-term unemployed. Incentives for small businesses and the self-employed have been increased.

The favourable operating environment has attracted more foreign direct investment (FDI) and the economy is growing. Labour costs are the second lowest in OECD countries.

Domestic demand, which began to expand in the first half of 2004, has remained strong and annual GDP growth, which was expected to remain at around 4.75–6.0 per cent for the foreseeable future, exceeded 6 per cent in 2006 and is continuing to rise. Employment rates have not maintained such a healthy level, but in 2005 fell below 16 per cent for the first time. Unemployment is regionally based, however, and Bratislava and Trenciansky have unemployment rates of less than 10 per cent.

Fiscal policy outcomes have been good but, to remain on target to join the European Monetary Union (EMU) in 2009, strict adherence to planned expenditure cuts is needed. Tighter fiscal policies will have to be implemented if there are any signs of economic overheating or renewed exchange rate appreciation.

The rate at which korunas will be exchanged for euros when Slovakia adopts the euro on 1 January 2009 has been set at 30.1260 korunas to the euro.

External trade

As a member of the European Union, Slovakia operates within a communitywide free trade union, with tariffs sets as a whole. Internationally, the EU has free trade agreements with a number of nations and trading blocs worldwide.

Foreign trade represents over 160 per cent of GDP, of which the greater part is automobile assembly – in 2006 Slovakia produced more cars per head than any other worldwide. Traditional heavy industry is being replaced in importance by manufacturing of consumer goods, electronics and engineering and the petrochemical industry.

Natural resources, geared to exports include mineral extraction (high-grade iron ore, copper, lead, and zinc) and forestry products.

Imports

Principal imports include capital machinery and transport equipment (over 40 per cent), intermediate and other manufactured goods, fuels and chemicals.

Main sources: Germany (25.1 per cent total, 2005), Czech Republic (19.3 per cent), Russia (10.5 per cent), Austria (6.1 per cent), Poland (4.7 per cent), Hungary (4.6 per cent), Italy (4.5 per cent)

Exports

Principal exports include vehicles (around 30 per cent), machinery and electrical equipment, base metals, minerals, chemicals, plastics and timber.

Main destinations: Germany (26.2 per cent total, 2005), Czech Republic (14.1 per cent), Austria (7.1 per cent), Italy (6.7 per cent), Poland (6.3 per cent), Hungary (5.7 per cent)

Agriculture

Farming

The agricultural sector suffered from under-investment during the communist era. In an attempt to increase productivity, a land restitution act was adopted in 1990, under which all agricultural land taken by the state between 1948–55 was returned to its original owners.

Agriculture contributes around 3.5 per cent to GDP.

Wheat, maize and barley are exported. Only 10 per cent of potato requirements are imported, and about 20 per cent of raw sugar requirements. Slovakia is a net importer of oil crops, although the margin is very small, with equal amounts of rape and mustard seed imported and exported. Slovakia is mostly self sufficient in meat, eggs and milk.

During its EU transitional entry stage, Slovakia has decided to implement the reform of the Common Agricultural Policy (CAP) on 1 January 2009. The reform was introduced throughout most of the EU on 1 January 2005, when subsidies on farm output, which tended to benefit large farms and encourage overproduction, were replaced by single farm payments, not conditional on production. The change is expected to reward farms that provide and maintain a healthy environment, food safety and animal welfare standards. The changes are also intended to encourage market conscious production and cut the cost of CAP to the EU taxpayer.

Crop production in 2005 included: 3,625,400 tonnes (t) cereals in total, 1,700,000t wheat, 943,000t maize, *381,891t potatoes, 799,000t barley, *54,469t pulses, 56,500t grapes, 62,000t tomatoes, 184,682t oilcrops, *1,298t tobacco, *1,598,773t sugar beets, 250,000t rapeseed (canola), 192,193t fruit in total, 329,537t vegetables in total. Livestock production included: 314,295t meat in total, 43,000t beef, 137,000t pig meat, 2,300t lamb, *127,300t poultry, 68,000t eggs, 1,152,900t milk, 2,600t honey.

* estimate

Fishing

The fishing sector, based on inland fisheries and imported sea-fish, is not significant, producing around 2,500 tonnes a year.

Forestry

Forest and other wooded land accounts for over two-fifths of the land area, with forest cover estimated at 2.1 million hectares (ha). More than 80 per cent of the forest is available for wood supply and the rest is preserved. The ownership structure of forest areas has changed considerably since 1990 as a result of privatisation and restitution. Half of the forested area is state-owned.

Consumption of forest products per capita is below the European average. Nearly all of the roundwood is processed in the country, using much of the hardwood and softwood species. Slovakia is a net exporter of forestry products and although the industry is in need of modernisation, it is a significant earner of foreign exchange. Over three-quarters of sawnwood produced is exported, mostly to Hungary. The pulp industry utilises half of the hardwood production, recovered paper and some non-wood fibre pulp. The bulk of exports also constitute paper and pulpboard.

Timber imports in 2004 were US$540.4 million, while exports amounted to US$872.3 million.

Production in 2004 included 7,240,000 cubic metres (cum) roundwood, 6,936,000cum industrial roundwood, 1,837,000cum sawnwood, 3,119,000cum sawlogs and veneers,

3,397,000cum pulpwood, 508,000cum wood-based panels, 304,000cum woodfuel; 798,000 tonnes (t) paper and paperboard, 371,000t printing and writing paper, 520,000t paper pulp, 204,000t recovered paper.

Industry and manufacturing
Industry accounts for around 30 per cent of GDP and 30 per cent of employment. Industrial production fell by approximately 20 per cent after the end of the Communist regime and privatisation has been unable to inject the necessary cash required for investment. Compared to neighbouring Hungary and Czech Republic, Slovak industry is marked by inefficiency, hidden bankruptcies and government subsidies.
The principal industries are the manufacture of machinery, chemicals and rubber, food and beverages, and iron metallurgy.
Slovakian industry remains more vulnerable to the instability of Eastern European markets than its Czech neighbour. The long-term prospects for the sector depend on how successfully the country can recover from the dislocation of its traditional markets and find new ones for such key industries as steel. Half of all foreign direct investment (FDI) in Slovakia goes to the manufacturing sector.

Tourism
Tourism has been slow to develop, the government providing little incentive. EU accession boosted the number of visitors to Slovakia in 2004 to over a million, but many were for short periods of a few days. The government is seeking to encourage more domestic tourism. The sector is expected to contribute 1.9 per cent in 2005.

Mining
Slovakia has workable deposits of antimony ore, mercury, iron ore, copper, lead, zinc, precious metals, limestone, dolomite, gravel, brick loam, ceramic materials and stone salt. In each case, except iron ores, only small quantities are actually mined.

Hydrocarbons
Slovakia has oil reserves of nine million barrels and produces about 1,000 barrels per day (bpd) of oil. Production does not meet consumption levels, over 98 per cent of all oil consumed having to be imported. Oil imports come from Russia through two pipelines, which transports around 187,000bpd, 57 per cent going to the Slovnaft refinery in Bratislava and the rest to the Czech Republic.
Slovakia has natural gas reserves of 15 billion cubic metres. Slovakia relies on the import of natural gas to meet demand. Around 7 billion cubic metres are consumed annually, nearly all of this was imported from Russia. Slovakia is as an important transit route for gas and around a quarter of gas consumed in Western Europe and 70 per cent of Russia's total gas exports to the west transits through Slovakia.
Coal is mined on a large scale. Reserves could last more than 40 years. Most is low quality brown coal (lignite) and looks likely to diminish as a key energy source due to the amount of pollution it causes. Coal consumption has fallen since 1993 due to the decreasing domestic output, largely through the closing of inefficient mines, restructuring and the need to cut greenhouse gas emissions in compliance with EU standards.

Energy
Slovakia has installed electricity generating capacity of 7.8 million kW. Most of the electrical capacity is from thermal sources, the rest coming from hydroelectric and nuclear stations. Emphasis is placed on the commissioning of new nuclear power stations and the upgrading of Chernobyl-style reactors. Slovakia is a net exporter of electricity.

Financial markets
Stock exchange
The Bratislava Stock Exchange (BSE) is the country's main bourse. The equity-based SAX is the main index and its base of 100 was set in the third quarter of 1998. There is also a bond-based SDX index.
Until recently, foreign interest in the bourse was low due to poor perceptions of Slovakia engendered by the Meciar government. However, as Slovakia geared up for accession to the EU, investor attitudes experienced something of a turnaround. International financial investors made a series of purchases of koruna-denominated debt.
The growth of the local bourse continues to face foreign investor wariness due to low levels of capitalisation, illiquidity and a lack of transparency as well as few exciting rich pickings. This has been compounded by the lack of initial public offerings (IPOs) and the government's failure to float shares in its privatisation programme.

Banking and insurance
Slovakia's banking system has been reformed, although the sector has been plagued by bad debts coupled with massive losses affecting a third of banks. As a result, economic structuring has been essential to both macroeconomic stability and the integrity of the banking sector.
Many of the country's larger banks have been privatised. In early 2002, a 66.7 stake in Slovenska Poistovna (Slovak Insurance Bank) was sold to Germany's Allianz AG for US$142 million. Smaller banks have closed as the central bank has imposed a tough regulatory framework on commerce, with greater power given to creditors.

Central bank
Narodna Banka Slovenska (NBS) (National Bank of Slovakia)

Main financial centre
Bratislava

Time
GMT plus one hour (daylight saving, late March to late October, GMT plus two hours)

Geography
Slovakia is a landlocked, hilly country in the heart of Europe. Around 80 per cent of the country has an altitude of over 750 metres above sea level. The High Tatra Mountains in the north give way to large lowlands, broad valleys and meadows in the south.
Slovakia is bordered by the Czech Republic to the west (the border is 215km long), by Poland to the north (444km), Ukraine to the east (90km), Hungary to the south (515km) and Austria to the south-west (the border with Austria is only 15km from the capital, Bratislava).
The High Tatra Mountains are on the northern Polish border and the Low Tatras are in the centre and east of the country. The highest peak is Gerlach in the High Tatras (2,655 metres), with the lowest point the Bodrog river near Streda and Bodrogom (95 metres).
There are numerous rivers flowing south to the lowland areas, including the Váh, Nitra, Hron and Hornád. The River Danube marks part of the southern border. The lowland areas are in the south-west and south-east of the country.

Hemisphere
Northern

Climate
Slovakia has a continental climate (warm summers and cold winters). Summer maximum temperatures are 32 degrees Celsius (C) to 35 degrees C; July is the hottest month (average 30 degrees C). Minimum temperatures are minus 12 degrees C to minus 20 degrees C. January is the coldest month (average minus 8 degrees C). Long-term average rainfall is approximately 490mm.

Dress codes
Most people dress in standard casual wear. For winter, mediumweight clothing is required with a heavy coat. For summer, lightweight clothing is suitable. For business meetings, men should wear a suit and tie.

Entry requirements
Passports
Required by all. Passport must be valid for eight months from the date of issue of the visa.

Visa
Required by all, except nationals of EU and Schengen area signatory countries, North America, Australasia and Japan. For further exceptions contact the nearest embassy or see www.foreign.gov.sk (or www.slovakia.org and follow link through tourism to visa information). A Schengen visa application (offered in several languages) can be downloaded from http://europa.eu/abc/travel/ see 'documents you will need'.
Visitors are required to have onward/return passage.

Currency advice/regulations
Import of local currency is prohibited. There are no restrictions on import of foreign currency, but it must be declared on arrival.
Local currency up to Sk100 can be exported, and foreign currency up to the amount declared on entry.

Customs
Personal items are duty-free. There are no duties levied on alcohol and tobacco between EU member states, providing amounts imported are for personal consumption.
Items of value, such as cameras, should be declared.

Health (for visitors)
Nationals of the European Economic Area (EEA) countries and Switzerland can access reduced cost and sometimes free medical treatment using a European Health Insurance Card (EHIC) while visiting the EEA. Exceptions include nationals of the 10 countries, which joined the EU in 2004, whose EHIC is not valid in Switzerland. Applications for the EHIC should be made before travelling.

Mandatory precautions
Full medical insurance, covering the whole territory of the Slovak Republic, is required. Random checks at Slovak points of entry are carried out and entry can be refused if no medical insurance for the whole country can be produced.

Advisable precautions

Credit cards
Credit cards are generally accepted by major hotels and restaurants.

Public holidays (national)
Fixed dates
1 Jan (New Year's Day/Independence Day), 6 Jan (Epiphany), 1 May (Labour Day), 8 May (Liberation of the Republic), 5 Jul (Ss Cyril and Methodius Day), 29 Aug (Slovak National Uprising Day), 1 Sep (Constitution Day), 15 Sep (Our Lady of the Seven Sorrows Day), 1 Nov (All Saints' Day), 17 Nov (Freedom and Democracy Day), 24–26 Dec (Christmas).

Variable dates
Good Friday, Easter Monday.

Working hours
Banking
Mon–Fri: 0800–1700. There are also exchange offices in the main city centres, which operate seven days a week until 1900.

Business
Mon–Fri: 0800–1600.

Government
Mon–Fri: 0900–1700.

Shops
Mon–Fri: 0900–1800; Sat: 0900–1200; some shops remain open late on Thursday evenings.

Electricity supply
220V, 50 cycles AC

Weights and measures
Metric system. In addition, the following measures are used: quintal or metric hundredweight = 100 kg. Food is usually purchased by the decagramme and kilogram.

Social customs/useful tips
Appointments should be made in advance and punctuality is important. Shaking hands is customary when meeting people and on parting. Business is conducted in Slovak; many executives speak a second language – German, Russian or English. When drinks are served, it is considered polite to wait for everyone to be served and then wish each person Nazdravi ('to your health'). At meals it is usual to wait for everyone to be served before starting and to wish everyone bon appetit or dobrou chut just before eating. The terms Pan (Mr), Pani (Mrs) and Slecna (Miss) are used. Slecna is used for single women under 30 only; single women over 30 will usually be addressed as Pani.
Gratuities are between 5 and 10 per cent. The minimum drinking age is 18 years. When visiting private homes it is customary to take flowers for the hosts. Visitors also generally leave their shoes in the hallway, partly as a mark of respect and partly because of pollution in the streets. Men always take off their hats indoors. Illegally parked cars tend to be towed away by the police and it is advisable to park at attended car parks where the cost is relatively low.

Security
Street crime, especially in the towns, has become a problem since the 1989 revolution because the police tend to keep a low profile. Although the situation has improved, it is still advisable to carry as little in the way of valuables and cash as possible. Car vandalism and theft are also problems.

Getting there
Air
National airline: Slovak Airlines
International airport/s: MR Stefanik Airport (BTS), 9km from Bratislava; post office, bank, bureau de change, restaurants, duty free shop, car hire.
Airport tax: None

Surface
Slovakia is included in the Pan-European Corridor 5 scheme. The project has some 3,270km of railways, linking Kiev in the Ukraine with western Europe via Italy, and 2,850 of new and upgraded roads.
Road: There is ample road access from Czech Republic, Poland, Ukraine, Hungary and Austria. There is a motorway from Bratislava to Prague.
Rail: Slovakia has rail connections with Vienna, Hamburg, Berlin, Warsaw, Budapest, Moscow and St Petersburg.
Water: Ships provide regular passenger service and cruises on the Danube, from Passau and Regensburg (Germany) via Vienna (Austria). There are also links with the Rhine and Main rivers and the Black Sea.

Getting about
National transport
Air: There are internal connections provided by Slovak Airlines, SkyEurope Airlines and Air Slovakia.
Road: The road network is extensive and in good condition. The major route is from Bratislava to Presov and Kosice.
Buses: There is an extensive coach network.
Rail: Slovakia has a rail network of 3,665km, of which around 1,590km are electrified. There are frequent express services between Bratislava and the main centres and tourist destinations.
Water: The principal navigable waterway is the Danube, on which cruises are available.

City transport
Taxis: Taxis are available in all main towns and are relatively cheap. They are metered, but passengers should ensure that the driver switches them on before starting off.
Buses, trams & metro: Bratislava and other cities are well served by trams, trolley-buses and buses. Tickets can be purchased at news-stands or from dispensers at the queues.

Car hire
Car hire is available in major towns. Traffic drives on the right. There is an extensive network of roadside restaurants and petrol stations. Emergency telephones are located at half mile intervals on motorways and the emergency system is generally quick and reliable.

BUSINESS DIRECTORY
The addresses listed below are a selection only. While World of Information makes every endeavour to check these addresses, we cannot guarantee that

changes have not been made, especially to telephone numbers and area codes. We would welcome any corrections.

Telephone area codes

The international direct dialling code (IDD) for Slovakia is +421, followed by area code and subscriber's number:

Banska Bystricá	48	Nitra	37
Bratislava	2	Presov	51
Kosice	55	Zilina	41
Liptoský Mikuláš	44		

Useful telephone numbers

Police: 158
Ambulance: 155
Fire: 150
Directory enquiries: 154

Chambers of Commerce

American Chamber of Commerce in the Slovak Republic, Hotel Danube, 1 Rybne namestie, 81338 Bratislava (tel: 5934-0508; fax: 5934-0556; e-mail: director@amcham.sk).

Banska Bystrica Regional Chamber of Commerce and Industry, 4 namestie S Moysesa, 97401 Banska Bystrica (tel: 412-5643; fax: 412-5636; e-mail: sopkrkbb@sopk.sk).

Bratislava Regional Chamber of Commerce and Industry, 6 Jasikova, 82673 Bratislava (tel: 4829-1257; fax: 4829-1260; e-mail: sopkrkbl@scci.sk).

British Chamber of Commerce in the Slovak Republic, 14 Cukrova, 81339 Bratislava (tel/fax: 5292-0371; e-mail: director@britcham.sk).

Kosice Regional Chamber of Commerce and Industry, 48/A Trieda SNP, 04011 Kosice (tel: 641-9477; fax: 641-9470; e-mail: sopkrkke@scci.sk).

Lucenec Regional Chamber of Commerce and Industry, 2 Vajanskeho, 98401 Lucenec (tel: 433-3939; fax: 433-3937; e-mail: sopkrklc@scci.sk).

Nitra Regional Chamber of Commerce and Industry, 4 Akademicka, 94901 Nitra (tel: 653-5466; fax: 733-6739; e-mail: sopkrknr@scci.sk).

Presov Regional Chamber of Commerce and Industry, 22 Masarykova, 08001 Presov (tel: 773-2818; fax: 773-2413; e-mail: sopkrkpo@scci.sk).

Slovak Chamber of Commerce and Industry, 9 Gorkeho, 81603 Bratislava (tel: 5443-3291; fax: 5413-1159; e-mail: sopkurad@sopk.sk).

Trencin Regional Chamber of Commerce and Industry, 2 Jilemnickeho, 91101 Trencin (tel: 652-3834; fax: 652-1023; e-mail: sopkrktn@scci.sk).

Trnava Regional Chamber of Commerce and Industry, 2 Trhova, 91701 Trnava (tel: 551-2588; fax: 551-2603; e-mail: sopkrktt@sopk.sk).

Zilina Regional Chamber of Commerce and Industry, 31 Halkova, 01001 Zilina (tel: 723-5101; fax: 723-5102; e-mail: sekrza@za.scci.sk).

Banking

Citibank (Slovakia),Mlynské nivy 43, 82501 Bratislava (tel: 5823-0224; fax: 5823-0211).

Consolidation Bank SFI, Cintorisíka 21, 81499 Bratislava (tel: 368-011; fax: 321-353).

Crédit Lyonnais Bank Slovakia, Medena 22, 811 02 Bratislava (tel: 325-320).

Deí1n Banka as, Frantiskánske nám 8, 81310 Bratislava (tel: 333-376; fax: 330-376).

General Credit Bank, Námestie SNP 19, 81856 Bratislava (tel: 531-7283; fax: 531-7020/05).

ING Bank, Kolarska 6, 811 06 Bratislava PO Box 123 (tel: 5346-111).

Investment and Development Bank, Stúrova 5, 81855 Bratislava (tel: 326-121; fax: 321-433).

Istrobanka as, Laurinská 1, 81101 Bratislava (tel: 539-7524; fax: 533-1744).

Konsolidacna Banka Bratislava, Cintorinska 21, 814 99 Bratislava (tel: 321-387; fax: 321-353).

Polnobanka as, Vajnorská 21, 83265 Bratislava (tel: 273-964; fax: 259-024).

Post Bank, PO Box 149, Gorkého 3, 81499 Bratislava (tel: 329-253; fax: 211-204).

Slovak Savings Bank, Námestie SNP 18, 81607 Bratislava (tel: 560-6580; fax: 560-6220).

TATRA Bank, Vajanského nábrezie 5, 81006 Bratislava (tel: 210-3519; fax: 324-760).

Volksbank, Námestie SNP 15, 81000 Bratislava (tel: 381-1140; fax: 364-847).

Central bank

Narodna banka Slovenska (National Bank of Slovakia), Imricha Karvasa 1, 81325 Bratislava (tel: 5787-1111; fax: 5787-1100; e-mail: webmaster@nbs.sk).

Travel information

Air Slovakia BWJ, Pestovatelská ul c 2, 821 04 Bratislava (tel: 4342 2744; fax: 4342 2742; e-mail:

Association of Slovak Information Centres, Námestie Mieru 1, 03101 Liptoský Mikuláš (tel: 551-4541; fax: 551-4448; e-mail: info@airslovakia.sk)

Slovak Airlines, Ivanka Airport, Bratislava (tel: 4857-5170/1).

Slovak Association of Travel Agents, Bajkalská 2, 821 01 Bratislava 2, (tel: 5823-3385; fax: 5341-9058; email:sacka@ba.sknet.sk).

Slovak Republik Automobile Association (Autoklub SR), Údernicka 14, 85101 Bratislava (tel: 6383-4567; fax: 6383-4678; e-mail: autoklub@autoklubsr.sk).

Slovak Tourist Board (Bratislava branch), PO Box 97, Záhradnícka 153, 82005 Bratislava 25, (tel: 5070-0801; fax: 5557-1649; email: sacrba@sacr.sk).

Ministry of tourism

Ministry of Economy, Tourism Department, Mierova 19, 82715 Bratislava (tel: 4854-2315; fax: 4854-3321; e-mail: info@economy.gov.sk).

National tourist organisation offices

Slovak Tourist Board, Námestie L Štúra 1, PO Box 35, 974 05 Banská Bystrica, (tel: 413-6146-8; fax: 413-6149; email: sacr@sacr.sk).

Ministries

Ministry of Administration and Privatisation of National Property, Drienova 24, 82009 Bratislava (tel: 230-678; fax: 233-335).

Ministry of Agriculture, Dobrovicova 12, 81266 Bratislava (tel: 368-561, 456-111; fax: 3066-294).

Ministry of Construction and Public Works, Spitalska 8, 81644 Bratislava (tel: 536-1111; fax; 536-1203).

Ministry of Culture of the Slovak Republic, Dobrovicova 12, 81331 Bratislava (tel: 323-295; fax: 368-140).

Ministry of Defence, Kutuzovova 7, 83247 Bratislava (tel: 250-320; fax: 258-907).

Ministry of Economy of the Slovak Republic, Mierová 19, 82715 Bratislava (tel: 574-1407; fax: 237-827).

Ministry of Education and Sciences, Stromova 1, 81330 Bratislava (tel: 370-4111; fax: 370-4333).

Ministry of the Environment of the Slovak Republic, Namestie L Stura 1,, 81235 Bratislava (tel: 516-2458; fax: 516-2457).

Ministry of Finance of the Slovak Republic, Stefanovicova 5, 81308 Bratislava (tel: 518-2562; fax: 396-146).

Ministry of Foreign Affairs, Hlboka Cesta 3, 83336 Bratislava (tel: 438-1111; fax: 438-2005; internet: http://www.foreign.gov.sk).

Ministry of Health, Limbova 2, 83105 Bratislava (tel: 377-940; fax: 377-659).

Ministry of the Interior, Pribinova 2, 81272 Bratislava (tel: 546-1111; fax: 368-835).

Ministry of Justice, Zupné námestie 13, 81311 Bratislava (tel: 535-3111; fax: 531-5952).

Ministry of Labour, Social Welfare and Family of the Slovak Republic, Spitálska 4, 81643 Bratislava (tel: 338-2414; fax: 362-150).

Ministry of Transport and Communications, Nam Slobody 6, 81005 Bratislava (tel: 395-251; fax: 256-414).

Office of the Government, Nam Slobody 1, 84218 Bratislava (tel: 359-5111; fax: 397-595).

Office of the President, Stefanikova ul 1, 81104 Bratislava (tel: 531-7567; fax: 531-7065).

Other useful addresses

Bratislava International Commodity Exchange, Ruzinovská 1, 82102 Bratislava (tel: 522-6311; fax: 522-6318).

Bratislava Stock Exchange, Vysoká 17, 81499 Bratislava (tel: 386-121; fax: 386-103).

British Embassy, Panskà 16, 81101 Bratislava (tel: 5441-9632; fax: 5441-0002; e-mail: bebra@internet.sk).

Federation of Employers' Unions and Associations of Slovak Republic, Information and Consulting Centre, Drienová 24, 82603 Bratislava (tel: 235-024; fax: 233-542).

National Agency for Development of Small and Medium Enterprises, Nevädzová 5, 82101 Bratislava (tel: 237-472/563, 231-873; fax: 522-2434); External Advisors (tel: 237-472; fax: 522-2434); BIC (Business Innovation Centre) (tel: 290-7417; fax: 522-2434, 290-7217).

National Property Fund PARP PMU, Drienova 27, 82656 Bratislava (tel: 561-1258, 561-1230, 561-1447, 235-280, 231-300, 231-531; fax: 561-1446, 235-280); external department (tel: 250-248; fax: 259-208).

Slovak National Agency for Foreign Investment and Development (SNAFID), Sládkovicova 7, 81106 Bratislava (tel: 533-5175; fax: 533-5022); Slovenska polnohospodarska a potravinarska komora, Krizna 52, 82108 Bratislava (tel: 566-2657, 526-1778; fax: 526-7336, 211-251).

Slovak Republic Embassy (USA), 3523 International Court, NW, Washington DC 20008 (tel: (+1-202) 237-1054; fax: (+1-202) 237-6438; e-mail: info@slovakembassy-us.org).

Statistical Office of the Slovak Republic, Mileticova 3, 82467 Bratislava (tel: 215-802; fax: 214-587).

Transport Department, Dept of European Integration, Namestie Slobody 6, 81370 Bratislava (tel: 499-766, 498-156 Ext. 331, 498-841, 495-251; fax: 499-761).

Internet sites

Slovakia Daily Surveyor: http://www.slovensko.com

Slovaks and Slovakia: http://www.slovak.com

Slovak Republic Government: http://www.government.gov.sk

Slovak Tourist Board: http://www.slovakiatourism.sk

Slovenia

KEY FACTS

Official name: Republika Slovenija (Republic of Slovenia)

Head of State: President Danilo Tuerk (from 22 Dec 2007)

Head of government: Prime Minister Janez Jansa (SDS) (since 9 Nov 2004)

Ruling party: Coalition: Slovenská Demokratska Stranka (SDS) (Slovenian Democratic Party); Nova Slovenija Krsanski Ljudska Stranka (Nsi) (New Slovenia Christian People's Party); Slovenska Ljudska Stranka (SLS) (Slovenian People's Party); and Demokratina Stranka Upokojencev Slovenije (DeSUS) (Democratic Party of Pensioners of Slovenia) (since Nov 2004)

Area: 20,251 square km

Population: 2.03 million (2007)

Capital: Ljubljana

Official language: Slovene

Currency: Euro (eur) = 100 cents (from 1 Jan 2007; previous currency tolar, locked at T239.64 per euro)

Exchange rate: eur0.63 per US$ (Jul 2008)

GDP per capita: US$22,933 (2007)

GDP real growth: 6.00% (2007)

Labour force: 857,400 (2003)

Unemployment: 4.80% (2007)

Inflation: 3.60% (2007)

Balance of trade: -US$1.27 billion (2005)

Annual FDI: US$5.16 billion (2005)

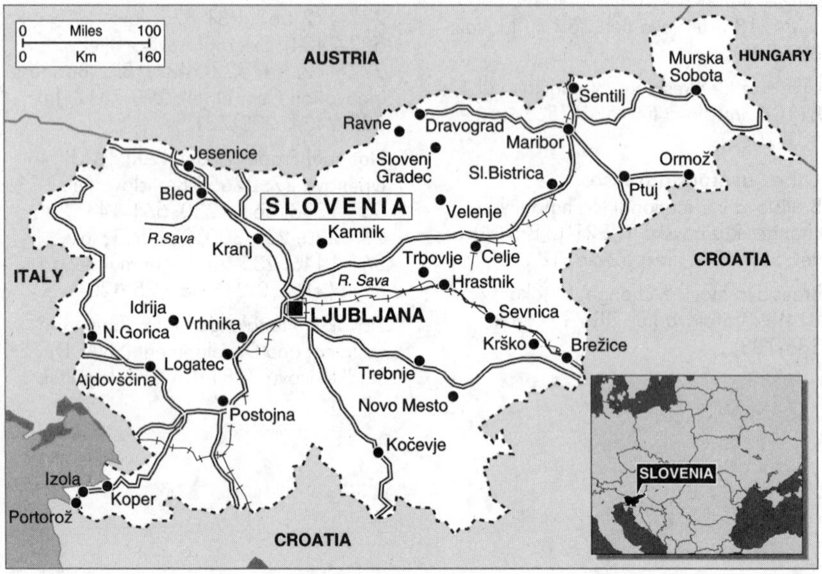

In January 2007, Slovenia became the first EU member from Eastern Europe to adopt the euro as its currency. However, political events in 2007 were dominated by the presidential election held on 21 October 2007. Outgoing President Janez Drnovšek was not a candidate for re-election, but there were seven candidates for the largely ceremonial office.

Preliminary first round results left no doubt that there would be a run-off election, and that Lojze Peterle would be one of two candidates taking part in that vote, but it was initially unclear who his opponent would be, as less than 0.4 per cent of the vote separated second- and third-place contenders, Danilo Türk and Mitja Gaspari. Final results confirmed preliminary figures which placed Danilo Türk in second place by just 3,717 votes over Mitja Gaspari. Despite his second-place finish in the first round of voting, Dr Türk went on to win the November election by a landslide victory, a result that had been accurately predicted by opinion polls that gave Dr Turk a lead of more than two-to-one over former prime minister Lojze Peterle.

President elected, economy booms

Slovenia is one the best economic performers in central and eastern Europe, with a GDP per capita in 2007 of US$22,933. Slovenia has had strong growth figures for the past eighth years, averaging over 4.0 per cent annual GDP growth. Although the European economic slowdown reduced growth levels after 2000, Slovenia's GDP grew by 6.0 per cent in 2007. Some 60 per cent of Slovenia's trade is with the EU. The services sector contributed the most to national output in 2007, accounting for 63.5 per cent of total GDP. Industry and construction made up 34.4 per cent of GDP, with agriculture, forestry, and fishing accounting for a lowly 2 per cent.

Slovakia's 2008 budget aims to keep the public deficit to 0.9 per cent of GDP, well within the Maastricht guidelines. In 2007, the current account balance showed a deficit of US$2.222 billion. Following the adoption of the euro, controlling inflation has become a government priority. Slovenia's ability to meet its growth rate objectives will largely depend on the state of the world economy, particularly since export demand in Slovenia's primary market has stalled. Foreign direct investment (FDI) will take up the slack to some extent, as analysts forecast FDI levels will continue to increase with the further privatisation of state assets, including the telecommunications, financial and energy sectors. In many cases under the Slovenian brand of privatisation, managers and workers in formerly state-owned enterprises have become the majority shareholders, perpetuating the monopoly practices that were the hallmark of the Yugoslav brand of socialism. However, the problems associated with that form of privatisation are expected to decrease under competitive pressures, as shares in these firms change hands, and as European inspired reforms introduce more Western-oriented practices.

In 2007, Slovenia saw its European aspirations fulfilled with membership of the so-called eurozone, the countries that have been allowed to adopt the euro as their currency. It was the first of the 13 new members to do so, and the thirteenth country to adopt the euro as its currency. However, despite having traded for years on its image as a Central European as opposed to a Balkan state, ironically it was the Balkans that set Slovenia's regional agenda.

High praise for the economy

Long before the break-up of the former Yugoslavia, the Slovenian economy was more oriented to the West than those of the other former Yugoslav Republics, with over 40 per cent of its trade conducted with Germany and Italy. According to the IMF the economy has performed strongly since the entry into the Exchange Rate Mechanism in 2004. Growth has been driven by a large increase in the contribution of net foreign demand, while domestic demand growth has maintained its momentum. Whilst private consumption has strengthed and exports risen, investment growth has slowed and Slovenia's total external debt has grown sharply as banks have recourse to external financing. Stable domestic demand and export activity has underpinned growth in Slovenia. Inflation in 2007 at 7 per cent was up on the 2.5 per cent in 2006.

An original tax reform package of the government including the introduction of a flat tax on all incomes in 2007 was scrapped in the face of trade union opposition. Instead, the government proposed to reduce the number of tax brackets, and to alleviate the tax burden on businesses. The proposal, which entered into force in 2007, also provides for a reduction of corporate income tax from 25 per cent to 23 per cent in 2007 and to 20 per cent by 2010. Despite trade union resistance, the government seeks to relax collective wage bargaining regulations and is also striving at reducing employment protection in the public sector.

Slovenia and the EU

Unlike in some new member-states, the EU has retained popular affection in Slovenia. In February 2005, the Slovene parliament had comfortably ratified the (now moribund) EU Constitution. A poll in September also revealed that the vast majority of Slovenes believed that entry into the EU had benefited the country and that future enlargement was a good thing. However, during negotiations in Brussels for the 2007–13 EU budget, the government of Prime Minister Janez Jansa insisted that Slovenia would not be a net contributor.

Slovenia also found itself embroiled in a dispute with Serbia over the future status of Kosovo. In October, President Drnovšek suggested that Kosovo be allowed independence, prompting Serbia to cancel Drnovšek's planned state visit to Belgrade. Compounding this problem was the suspicion in Belgrade that Ljubljana also favoured independence for Serbia's the sister republic, Montenegro, which did itself become independent in mid-2006.

Outlook

After being the first former Communist state to join the euro on 1 January 2007, on 1 January 2008, Slovenia became the first to take its turn as president of the EU for six months. The declining popularity of the Jansa government and President Drnovšek's tendency to pre-empt government policy may cause some jitters in the governing coalition. However, with elections not due until 2008, there is plenty of scope for Prime Minister Jansa to consolidate his grip.

Risk assessment

Economic	Good
Political	Stable
Regional stability	Satisfactory

COUNTRY PROFILE

Historical profile

In the thirteenth century, Slovenia became a hereditary possession of the House of Habsburg.
1867 The Slovenes fell under the jurisdiction of the Austrian Crown.
1918 After the downfall of the Austro-Hungarian Empire, Slovenia became a part of the new 'Kingdom of Serbs, Croats and Slovenes' (re-named Yugoslavia in 1929).
1941 Yugoslavia was divided between Germany, Italy, Hungary and Bulgaria.
1945 Following the end of the Second World War, Slovenia became a constituent republic of the Yugoslav Federation. Josip Broz Tito assumed power, and a Soviet-style constitution was adopted. The other republics were: Bosnia and Hercegovina (BiH), Croatia, Macedonia, Montenegro and Serbia, and the two autonomous regions of Vojvodina and Kosovo.
1950-80s Constitutions adopted in 1953, 1963 and 1974 increased autonomy extended to the constituent republics.
The ruling Slovene Communists supported the Croats' demand for a confederal

KEY INDICATORS — Slovenia

	Unit	2003	2004	2005	2006	2007
Population	m	2.00	2.00	2.00	2.01	2.03
Gross domestic product (GDP)	US$bn	26.30	32.18	34.41	38.24	46.08
GDP per capita	US$	14,084	16,447	17,175	19,021	22,933
GDP real growth	%	3.1	4.4	4.0	5.7	6.0
Inflation	%	5.6	3.6	2.5	2.5	3.6
Unemployment	%	11.3	10.3	6.5	5.9	4.8
Exports (fob) (goods)	US$m	12,738.0	15,817.8	18,043.0	21,397.0	27,123.0
Imports (cif) (goods)	US$m	13,812.0	16,862.1	19,312.9	22,856.0	29,432.0
Balance of trade	US$m	-1,074.0	-1,044.3	-1,269.9	-1,458.0	-2,310.0
Current account	US$m	-216.0	-893.0	-682.0	-1,076.0	-2,222.0
Total reserves minus gold	US$m	8,496.9	8,793.4	8,076.4	7,036.1	979.8
Foreign exchange	US$m	8,343.1	8,662.3	8,013.1	6,987.1	942.0
Exchange rate	per US$	204.43	192.36	159.91	190.61	0.69

Yugoslavia during the 1960s and 1970s, although never to the point of provoking repression.
1980 Tito died. A system of a collective (rotating) presidency was adopted.
1986 Milan Kucan became the leader of the Slovene Communists.
1990 Kucan guided Slovenia towards independence following multi-party general elections, resulting in a six-party centre-right coalition, the Demokratska Opozicija Slovenije (DeMOS) (Democratic Opposition of Slovenia), under the leadership of Lozle Peterle.
1991 After a 10-day war against the Yugoslav army, Slovenia won independence.
1992 Slovenia was admitted to the UN. Following the collapse of the DeMOS government, Janez Drnovšek took over as interim prime minister. In the parliamentary elections, the Liberal Democrats emerged as the largest party and Janez Drnovšek became prime minister at the head of a five-party coalition. Milan Kucan was elected president.
1994 The Liberal Democrats merged with the Democratic Party and the Ecologists to create the Liberalna Demokracija Slovenije (LDS) (Liberal Democrats of Slovenia).
1996 After the general elections, the LDS and its former opponent, Slovenska Ljudska Stranka (SLS) (Slovenian People's Party) formed a coalition with the Demokratièna Stranka Upokojencev Slovenije (DeSUS) (Democratic Party of Slovenian Pensioners). Drnovšek was re-elected prime minister.
1997 Kucan was re-elected president for a second and last consecutive five-year term.
2000 Withdrawal of the SLS from the government coalition prompted its collapse. A centre-right government, composed of the SLS and Slovenski Krsèanski Demokrati (SKD) (Slovenian Christian Democratic Party), together with the Socialdemokratska Stranka Slovenije (SDSS) (Social Democratic Party of Slovenia) was formed. The general election was won by the LDS, led by the former prime minister, Janez Drnovšek, who formed a coalition government.
2002 NATO invited Slovenia to join the alliance and the EU confirmed Slovenia's accession. Prime Minister Janez Drnovšek won the presidential run-off. Anton Rop of the LDS, the senior coalition party, was elected prime minister with 63 votes for and 24 votes against (to be elected, Rop needed 46 votes from the members of parliament).
2003 In a referendum, 89.6 per cent of Slovenes voted to join the EU and 66 per cent voted to join NATO.
2004 Slovenia joined NATO and the EU. Slovenska Demokratska Stranka (SDS) (Slovenian Democratic Party) won the parliamentary elections and Janez Jansa was elected prime minister by parliament.
2005 Parliament ratified the EU constitution in February.
2006 EU finance ministers gave final approval to Slovenia's application to adopt the euro currency.
2007 Slovenia joined the European Economic and Monetary Union (EMU) on 1 January and introduced the euro as the official currency. On 11 November after the second round of presidential elections, Danilo Türk won with 68.3 per cent of the votes; his rival, Lojze Peterle, won 31.7 per cent. Turnout was 57.8 per cent. Türk's inauguration took place on 22 December. On 20 December Slovenia became a member of the European Union Schengen area whereby all travellers may cross borders without a passport or visa.
2008 Former president and prime minister, Janez Drnovšek died on 23 February.

Political structure

Constitution
The Slovenian constitution was adopted in December 1991 and amended in 1997 and 2000.

Form of state
Parliamentary democratic republic

The executive
The president, who is elected for a five-year term, by universal adult suffrage, is head of state and commander-in-chief of the armed forces.
The president proposes a candidate for prime minister to the Skupšcina Slovenije (Assembly of Slovenia) after consultation with parliamentary groups. The assembly has the final power of appointment of the prime minister and the government.

National legislature
The Assembly of Slovenia is a bicameral legislature and consists of the Drzavni Zbor (National Assembly) and the Drzavni Svet (National Council).
The National Assembly is the principal legislative body and consists of 90 members elected for a four-year term. Through proportional representation, 88 members are elected, with two non-elected representatives of the country's Hungarian and Italian minorities.
The government is made up of members of the National Assembly, and it is answerable to that body.
The 40 members of the National Council sit for a five-year term. Twenty-two are directly elected and 18 appointed by an electoral college to represent various groups. The Council fulfils a mainly advisory role, but may veto decisions of the National Assembly and must approve the composition of any government.

Legal system
The legal system is based on the 1991 constitution.
The judiciary is structurally independent from the government, with the Constitutional Court empowered to determine the conformity of national legislation with the constitution. All civil and criminal cases are dealt with by eight basic and four higher courts, and the Supreme Court is the final court of appeal. Prosecutions are the responsibility of the Public Prosecutor and to safeguard defendants rights there is also a Public Attorney. The Justice Ministry is the administrative authority of the Slovenian judiciary.

Last elections
3 October 2004 (parliamentary); 21 October/11 November 2007 (presidential).
Results: Parliamentary: SDS won 29.1 per cent of the vote (29 seats out of 90); LDS 22.8 per cent (23 seats); Zdruzena Lista Socialnih Demokratov (ZLSD) (United List of Social-Democrats) 10.2 per cent (10 seats); Nsi 9.0 per cent (nine seats); SLS 6.8 per cent (seven seats); Slovenska Nacionalna Stranka (SNS) (Slovenian National Party) 6.3 per cent (six seats); DeSUS 4.0 per cent (four seats).
Presidential: (first round) Lojze Peterle won 28.5 per cent of the vote, Danilo Türk 24.5 per cent, Mitja Gaspari 24.1 per cent, and Zmago Jelincic 19.3 per cent.

Next elections
November 2012 (presidential); October 2008 (parliamentary).

Political parties

Ruling party
Coalition: Slovenská Demokratska Stranka (SDS) (Slovenian Democratic Party); Nova Slovenija Krsanski Ljudska Stranka (Nsi) (New Slovenia Christian People's Party); Slovenska Ljudska Stranka (SLS) (Slovenian People's Party); and Demokratina Stranka Upokojencev Slovenije (DeSUS) (Democratic Party of Pensioners of Slovenia) (since Nov 2004)

Main opposition party
Liberalna Demokracija Slovenije (LDS) (Liberal Democracy of Slovenia)

Population
2.03 million (2007)
Last census: March 2002: 1,964,036 (provisional)
Population density: 99 inhabitants per square km. Urban population: 51 per cent (1995–2001).
Annual growth rate: 0.0 per cent 1994–2004 (WHO 2006)

Ethnic make-up
Around 88 per cent of the population are Slovenes, with small numbers of ethnic Serbs, Croats, Muslims, Albanians, Hungarians, Italians and Germans. Only the Italian and Hungarian communities are officially recognised minorities.

Religions
Roman Catholic (71 per cent), Lutheran (1 per cent), Islam (1 per cent).

Education
Unlike other parts of the former Yugoslavia, where adult illiteracy remains a major socioeconomic problem, Slovenia has always had a relatively highly educated society. Adult illiteracy is therefore virtually non-existent.

Primary and initial secondary schooling are combined in one school for nine-years. At aged 15 students are channelled onto one of three paths, general, technical or vocational. General and technical education lasts for four years, while vocational courses last for either two or three years.

As a critical determinant of future socioeconomic development, higher education experienced significant growth during the 1990s. Unesco estimates total gross enrolment rates for tertiary education at over 60 per cent. Law, business and economics remain popular courses, while further education institutions find it difficult to attract students to technical courses, resulting in a lack of skills in certain sectors of the workforce.

Literacy rate: 100 per cent adult rate; 100 per cent youth rate (15–24) (Unesco 2005).

Compulsory years: 6 to 15

Enrolment rate: 98 per cent gross primary enrolment, 92 per cent gross secondary enrolment; of relevant age groups (including repeaters) (World Bank).

Pupils per teacher: 12 in primary schools.

Health
Per capita total expenditure on health (2003) was US$1,669; of which per capita government spending was US$1,274, at the international dollar rate, (WHO 2006).

Formerly entirely state controlled and funded, healthcare is now a growing private sector activity so that Slovenia is comparable with the EU for healthcare provision. In the long-term though, more funds will have to be directed towards it due to its ageing population. Healthcare provisions also includes a well-developed network of medicinal spas for all types of ailments. Lower healthcare charges attract paying customers from neighbouring countries.

Private health insurance is increasing rapidly and the government has encouraged additional forms of health insurance, and the preparation of national preventative programmes, that should reduce dependency on the state and bolster private sector provision.

HIV/Aids
HIV prevalence: 0.1 per cent aged 15–49 in 2003 (World Bank)

Life expectancy: 77 years, 2004 (WHO 2006)

Fertility rate/Maternal mortality rate: 1.2 births per woman, 2004 (WHO 2006)

Birth rate/Death rate: Nine births per 1,000 population; 10 deaths per 1,000 population (2003).

Child (under 5 years) mortality rate (per 1,000): 4.0 per 1,000 live births (World Bank)

Head of population per physician: 2.25 physicians per 1,000 people, 2002 (WHO 2006)

Welfare
The Pension and Disability Act, which significantly reformed the pension system, became effective from 2000 and consists of a reformed pay-as-you-go scheme, with a supplementary fund as part of waged contracts. The minimum age of retirement for women has gradually risen and the amount of full pensions reduced relative to the wage rate.

The government ensured better legal protection for workers by defining their rights at the minimum level, and strengthened investment in the area of labour, family and social welfare.

Main cities
Ljubljana (capital, estimated population 264,265 in 2005), Maribor (92,443), Celje (38,601), Kranj (35,907).

Languages spoken
The main minority languages are Albanian, Hungarian and Italian, but Hungarian and Italian are officially recognised. Serbian, Croatian, German, English and French are also spoken.

Regional identities and dialects remain very strong.

Official language/s

Slovene

Media
Press

Dailies: A major publishing organisation Delo (www.delo.si) (with an English online edition) produces two dailies (including Slovenske Novice and Ne Delo), four magazines (including a free monthly magazine, Delnicar, with the highest circulation) and has three internet portals. Other national publications include Dnevnik (www.dnevnik.si), Vecer (www.vecer.si) and Zurnal (www.zurnal24.si). Major regional newspapers include Direkt (www.direkt.si) and Ekipa-sport.so both tabloids, from Ljubljana as does the Slovenia Time (www.sloveniatimes.com) published in English. From Celje Novi Tednik (www.novitednik.com) in Slovene, Nepujsag (www.nepujsag.net) is published in Hungarian in Lendava.

Weeklies: In Solvene, the variety includes Demokracija (www.demokracija.si) and Dolenjski List (www.dol-list.si), Gorenjski Glas (www.g-glas.si), Jana, Kmecki Glas (www.czd-kmeckiglas.si), Mariborcan (www.revijakapital.com/mariborcan), Mladina (www.mladina.si), Primorske Novice (www.primorske.si), and Vestnik Murska Sobota (www.p-inf.si) provide general information and local news. Druzina (www.druzina.si) is a Roman Catholic publication,

Based abroad, TOL reports on central European issues. The government publication Sinfo covering politics, business, culture can be accessed online (www.ukom.gov.si).

Business: In Slovene, the national publication Podjetnik (www.podjetnik.com) and the regional Kapital (www.revijakapital.com) are magazines, Finance (www.finance.si) is a regional newspaper. In English, Slovenian Business Report (www.sbr.si).

Periodicals: The free monthly newspaper, Delnicar, has the highest circulation.

Broadcasting

Radio: There are many commercial radio stations. RTV Slovenija (www.rtvslo.si) is the state-owned radio station which is the market leader with three national channels, of which one broadcasts in Italian, one in Hungarian and one in Slovene. During the tourist season, there are broadcasts in German and English each day covering: news, traffic news, local weather and tourist directions. Other major radio stations include Radio Hit (www.r-hit.si) and Radio City (www.radiocity.si).

Television: The state-owned Radio Televizija Slovenija (RTV) (www.rtvslo.si), broadcast in Slovene, Italian and Hungarian. The privately owned commerical TV stations Pop Tv (http://24ur.com) broadcasts foreign programmes. Both TV stations offer programmes online. Satellite and cable TV is also available, including TV Si21 (http://tv.si21.com).

Advertising

Advertising outlets are available on TV, radio, billboards and in newsprint.

Economy
Slovenia was by far the most economically advanced and developed of the six Yugoslav republics and has continued to experience economic growth since 1993. GDP has increased by around four per cent annually since 2004. Privatisation of the economy and structural reforms have improved the business environment and allowed for greater foreign participation, which is gradually helping to reduce unemployment. Inflation is low, having fallen

to 2.5 per cent in 2005 and remaining steady in 2006.

In March 2004, shortly before EU accession, Slovenia became a donor partner at the World Bank. Further recognition of Slovenia's economic strength came in January 2007 with the adoption of the euro as its currency. Nevertheless, Slovenia needs to attract more foreign investment. Towards this end the government is planning to cut back state control of infrastructer, make the work-force more flexible and reform taxes.

External trade

As a member of the European Union, Slovenia operates within a communitywide free trade union, with tariffs sets as a whole. Internationally, the EU has free trade agreements with a number of nations and trading blocs worldwide.

Foreign trade represents over 130 per cent of GDP, of which over 60 per cent is with the EU. The manufacturing sector is diversified with food processing, electrical equipment and electronics, textiles and timber products. Wine and animal husbandry are important agricultural exports, while industrial and mineral extraction represents around 30 per cent of GDP.

Imports

Main Imports are vehicles, machinery, manufactured goods, chemicals, petroleum and derivatives and foodstuffs.

Main sources: Germany (19.9 per cent total, 2005), Italy (12.7 per cent), Croatia (9.4 per cent), Austria (8.1 per cent), France (8.1 per cent)

Exports

The principal exports are manufactured goods, machinery and transport equipment, chemicals and food.

Main destinations: Germany (19.9 per cent total, 2005), Italy (12.7 per cent), Croatia (9.4 per cent), Austria (8.1 per cent), France (8.1 per cent)

Agriculture

Farming

Agriculture accounts for around 2.5 per cent of GDP and employs six per cent of the workforce.

Farming is generally carried out on smallholdings of less than 25 hectares (ha). There are also a number of large farms and co-operatives which produce most food exports as well as food consumed domestically. Agricultural production fell substantially after independence, but recovered quickly and is above pre-independence levels.

The restoration of farming land and forests to claimants continues, although agricultural development is still being held up. Several issues pertaining to rural development, including aid to underdeveloped regions and environmental programmes, are on the political agenda. When Slovenia joined the EU in 2004, it became eligible for EU subsidies and rural development funds through the Common Agricultural Policy (CAP), but, like the other new accession countries, Slovenia will only get the full amount by 2013. This follows the EU decision to introduce CAP support funds gradually over a 10-year period.

During its transitional entry stage, Slovenia has decided to implement the reform of the CAP on 1 January 2007. The reform was introduced throughout most of the EU on 1 January 2005, when subsidies on farm output, which tended to benefit large farms and encourage overproduction, were replaced by single farm payments, not conditional on production. The change is expected to reward farmers that provide and maintain a healthy environment, food safety and animal welfare standards. The changes are also intended to encourage market conscious production and cut the cost of CAP to the EU taxpayer. Slovenia's introduction of the new CAP before its fellow accession countries will align it with most of Europe and lessen disruption during the transition period imposed as part of the EU entry requirements.

Crop production in 2005 included: 566,116 tonnes (t) cereals in total, 141,293t wheat, 339,657t maize, 153,300t potatoes, 3,733t treenuts, 120,000t grapes, 227,004t sugar beets, 225,000t apples, 5,900t chillies and peppers, 390,824t fruit in total, 56,020t vegetables in total. Livestock production included: 181,082t meat in total, 45,500t beef, 70,000t pig meat, 1,100t lamb, 64,000t poultry, 20,000t eggs, 654,000t milk, 2,500t honey, 5,643t cattle hides.

Fishing

The annual commercial catch of fish amounts to between 1,815 and 2,270 tonnes. This excludes the catches of private fishermen estimated between 182 and 272 tonnes. Another 136 tonnes of fish is obtained by mariculture. About 454 tonnes of freshwater fish is bred on fish farms. Slovenia imports about 7,258 tonnes of fish annually.

Slovenia's legislation on fisheries is largely oriented towards Europe, although more resources will be necessary to meet the requirements of the EU's Common Fisheries Policy (CFP). Slovenia has a fisheries agreement with Croatia and is also a member of the General Fisheries Commission for the Mediterranean.

In 2004, the total marine fish catch was 748 tonnes.

Forestry

Slovenia has a significant forestry sector. Forest cover is estimated at 1.1 million hectares (ha). The sector has a long tradition of sustainable management and less than a third of the forest area is publicly owned. Only a small area of forest is available for wood supply. Forestry forms the basis of a number of key industrial sectors, notably furniture making, paper, pulp and construction materials. The industry includes both large and small saw mills, which rely on the domestic supply of raw materials. Paper is mainly exported to European countries. Per capita consumption of forest products remains around the European average.

Exports of forest material in 2004 amounted to US$624.0 million, while imports amounted to US$540.0 million. Production in 2004 included 2,551,000 cubic metres (cum) roundwood, 1,826,000cum industrial roundwood, 461,000cum sawnwood, 1,372,000cum sawlogs and veneers, 283,000cum pulpwood, 474,000cum wood-based panels, 725,000cum woodfuel; 557,600t paper and paperboard (including 31,000t newsprint), 204,900t printing and writing paper, 153,000t paper pulp.

Industry and manufacturing

Manufacturing accounts for 24 per cent of GDP and industry overall for 32 per cent. The manufacture of capital goods has traditionally been the mainstay of Slovenia's industry, with iron and steel, metal working and machine-building accounting for a third of total manufactured added value. With intermediate goods accounting for 15 per cent and consumer goods for 55 per cent of manufactured added value, Slovenia has all the characteristics of an advanced industrial economy.

Slovenia is anxious to boost its exports to the EU. This strategic redirection of its industrial exports will require a complete restructuring of its entire industrial sector. The major structural problems are low levels of new investment, over-manning, technological backwardness and too many industrial enterprises for what is now a small domestic market with limited export potential. The newer and rising consumer goods industries, such as electrical products, are expected to become more capital intensive in order to compete internationally. High-technology industries based on computing and high added-value have yet to make a significant appearance.

Tourism

Tourism is a major industry, offering coastal holidays, skiing, golf and other sports, spa treatment and river trips. It employs some 16,000 people. Slovenia can provide around 80,000 beds in various accommodation facilities (hotels, motels, tourist villages, health-resorts, boarding-houses) all over the country. In 2004, the sector recorded its best year since before independence in 1991. There were

2,341,281 arrivals, an increase of 4.28 per cent over 2003, and an increasing number of overnight stays. Tourism is expected to contribute 2.9 per cent to GDP in 2005.

Hydrocarbons

Slovenia has oil reserves of less than 50 million barrels, with production being less than 500 barrels per day (bpd). Slovenia relies almost entirely on imports of refined oil to meet consumption levels. The sole refinery was closed in 1999 as it became uneconomical to operate. Downstream operations dominate the sector.

Slovenia has negligible reserves of natural gas and relies entirely on imports of around 1 billion cubic metres annually. Algeria and Russia are the sole suppliers of natural gas to Slovenia. Gazprom, the Russian gas company, provides 60 per cent of Slovenia's imports. The state-owned natural gas company, Geoplin, is responsible for the sale of gas within the country as well as transit to Croatia. Natural gas provides for around 12 per cent of the country's total energy needs.

Slovenia has proven coal reserves, mainly lignite found in the Saleška Valley near Velenje, and sub-bituminous coal in several other parts of the country. Exploitable reserves at Velenje amount to 227 million tonnes, and production could be sustained for 60 years. The sub-bituminous reserves are of low quality with high ash and sulphur content. Coal provides for one-quarter of the country's energy needs.

Energy

Slovenia has installed electricity capacity of 2.65GW, generated by thermal, hydropower and nuclear stations. The sole nuclear plant, sited at Krško, is jointly-owned with Croatia. Slovenia is a net exporter of electricity.

Financial markets

Stock exchange

The Ljubljanska Borza (LJSE) (Ljubljana Stock Exchange) opened in 1989.

The main LJSE index, the SB120, is dominated by Krka and Lek, the country's two large pharmaceutical firms.

Banking and insurance

Slovenia has a well-developed banking sector. The central bank and the finance ministry are responsible for implementing EU banking directives.

Nova Ljubljanska Banka (NLB) and Nova Kreditna Banka Maribor, both state-owned, dominate the sector, together holding some 40 per cent of banking assets. The merger of the Abanka and Banka Vipa in December 2002 created a new bank, Abanka Vipa, which now has a major slice of the Slovenian banking sector.

Foreign banks own around 30 per cent of the banking sector. Approximately 96 per cent of SKB Banka was sold to France's Société Générale and a 34 per cent stake in NLB was sold to Belgium's KBC Bank.

Central bank

Banka Slovenije (BSI) (Bank of Slovenia)

Main financial centre

Ljubljana

Time

GMT plus one hour (daylight saving, late March to late October, GMT plus two hours)

Geography

Slovenia is bordered by Italy to the west, Austria to the north, Hungary to the east and Croatia to the south. There is a 46km coastal strip on the Gulf of Trieste in the Adriatic Sea, around the Istrian port of Koper.

An Alpine terrain covers over half Slovenia's area, stretching down from the north. This region is dominated by the Julian Alps in the north-west, where Mount Triglav (2,864 metres), the tallest peak, is located. The Slovene Alps are covered in forests, including some remnants of primeval forests, particularly around Kocevje in the south, and producing scores of rivers. The river Sava rises from two headstreams in the Julian Alps and flows down for 933km to the river Danube in Serbia.

The other half of the country is Mediterranean, one part of which, around the region of Karst, has a limestone landscape. A geological phenomenon where water has eaten into the rock has produced numerous sinkholes and cave networks and has given its name to a branch of science – karstology. The large Pannonian plain, in the east (around 20 per cent of the country) is fertile farmland and the source of thermal and mineral water springs.

Hemisphere

Northern

Climate

Ljubljana has an average summer temperature of 25 degrees Celsius (C) and in winter –3 degrees C. Precipitation is heavy, with an annual average rainfall of 1,407mm. Air pollution has had an adverse effect on the weather, notably in the Ljubljana Basin.

The north has an alpine climate with warm summers and cold winters, the west has Mediterranean weather with hot summers and mild winters and the east has a continental climate with hot summers and cold winters.

Dress codes

Formal dress is the norm for business and social meetings in Slovenia. Business visitors should be smartly dressed.

Entry requirements

Passports

Required by all except nationals of countries which are signatories of the Schengen Accords, which includes most EU/EEA member states, who may visit on national IDs. Passports must be valid for three months beyond the visit.

Visa

Required by all, except nationals of EU and Schengen area signatory countries, North America, Australasia and Japan. See www.mzz.gov.si and follow path to Embassies, Diplomatic Missions and Consulates for a list of Slovene consulates and further information for other visitors regarding necessary documentation. A Schengen visa application (offered in several languages) can be downloaded from http://europa.eu/abc/travel/ see 'documents you will need'.

Currency advice/regulations

The import and export of local currency is unlimited, however amounts over T3 million (or foreign equivalent) must be declared. Slovenia will join the European Monetary Union on 1 January 2007 when the euro will become legal tender along side the tolar, which will be withdrawn after 14 days.

Travellers cheques are widely accepted.

Customs

Personal items are duty-free. There are no duties levied on alcohol and tobacco between EU member states, providing amounts imported are for personal consumption.

All items of cultural value, including artistic, archaeological, ethnographic, scientific and antiques over 100 years are prohibited from being exported.

Health (for visitors)

Nationals of the European Economic Area (EEA) countries and Switzerland can access reduced cost and sometimes free medical treatment using a European Health Insurance Card (EHIC) while visiting the EEA. Exceptions include nationals of the 10 countries which joined the EU in 2004 whose EHIC is not valid in Switzerland. Applications for the EHIC should be made before travelling.

Credit cards

International credit and charge cards are widely accepted. Credit cards can be used to get cash advances from banks.

Public holidays (national)

Fixed dates

1–2 Jan (New Year), 8 Feb (Preseren/Culture Day), 27 Apr (Resistance Day), 1–2 May (Labour Day), 25 Jun (National Day), 15 Aug (Assumption Day), 31 Oct (Reformation Day), 1 Nov (All Saints' Day), 25 Dec (Christmas Day), 26 Dec (Independence Day).

Holidays that fall at the weekend are not replaced.
Variable dates
Easter Monday

Working hours
Banking
Mon–Fri: 0730–1800; Sat: 0730–1200.
Business
Mon—Fri: 0800—1600.
Government
Mon–Fri: 0800–1600.
Shops
Mon–Fri: 0700–1900 or 0800–2000; some shops also open Sat: 0800–1300/1500, Sun: 0800–1200.

Telecommunications
Mobile/cell phones
GSM 900 and 1800 services available throughout most of the country.

Electricity supply
220V AC, with round two-pin plugs.

Weights and measures
Metric system

Social customs/useful tips
For business meetings, when appointments are made, visitors should be punctual. Business cards are essential. Slovenia has a reputation for being efficient and reliable. Executives will generally have a good knowledge of German, English and sometimes Italian. There is a well-developed network of local agents, advisers, consultants and lawyers willing to act for foreign companies.
Slovenians are a rather reserved people with a tendency towards formality. As in Austria and Germany, titles are widely used. Informality on the part of a foreigner is not considered acceptable. It is not unusual for Slovenians to prefer to hold business discussions over lunch.
Athough smoking is generally accepted, it is restricted in many public places and buildings.
Visitors should carry some form of identity at all times.

Security
Slovenia has a low crime rate. Sometimes tourists are the targets of pickpockets and purse-snatchers, especially on the trains.

Getting there
Air
National airline: Adria Airways
International airport/s: Ljubljana (LJU), 27km from city centre, facilities include duty-free shops, bank, post office, restaurant, internet access and car hire. Buses provide access to Ljubljana (travel time 45 minutes). Taxis are available.
Other airport/s: Maribor (MBX) and Portoroz (POW) have European connections. They are open only during daylight hours.
Airport tax: None
Surface
Slovenia is included in the Pan-European Corridor 5 scheme. The project has some 3,270km of railways, linking Kiev in the Ukraine with western Europe via Italy, and 2,850km of new and upgraded roads.
Road: Most frontier posts are open for road traffic from Italy, Austria, Hungary and Croatia; almost all border crossings are open 24 hours.
Rail: Connections are available from major European cities. The Eurocity Mimara train connects Zagreb, Ljubljana, Munich and Leipzig. Direct trains to Slovenia are available from Italy (Rome, Milan, Venice and Trieste), Austria (Vienna and Villach) and Hungary (Budapest). Transport for cars may be available on some routes.
Water: A catamaran runs regular scheduled trips between Venice-Portoroz and Piran, between March–October.
Main port/s: Koper, Izola, Piran and Portoroz.

Getting about
National transport
Air: Domestic airports are situated at Maribor (MBX) in eastern Slovenia, with Potoroz (POW) on the Adriatic coast. There are regular services from the capital, Ljubljana.
Road: There is an extensive network of roads in Slovenia, many of which are in good condition. The main arterial road running south-west to north-east is a stretch of the Pan-European Corridor 5. The roads can be congested particularly during peak periods but have clear signposts, with rest and food facilities.
The following are toll motorways: Ljubljana-Razdrto, Arja vas-Hoce and Ljubljana-Kranj.
Buses: Good nationwide services operated by a number of companies.
Rail: There are good rail connections and rail travel is inexpensive. A high-speed train links Ljubljana-Maribor throughout the year and Ljubljana-Koper during the summer only. Intercity and Urban trains run to most regions
City transport
Taxis: Metered taxis are available in Ljubljana and other major towns. A tip of 10 per cent is expected.
Buses, trams & metro: Most city centres are served by trams, and the suburbs by buses. Service is inexpensive and regular, but radically reduced at night. Exact fares are required on the bus or tram, or tokens can be purchased from kiosks, post offices and in supermarkets beforehand.
Car hire
Many major car hire companies operate from the airport and capital. A full national driving licence and third party insurance for foreigners is compulsory. Speed limits are 130kph on motorways, 100kph on open highways, 90kph on urban roads outside residential areas and 50kph in cities and towns. Safety belts are compulsory and school buses must not be overtaken. The AMZS (Automobile Association of Slovenia) provides a good emergency roadside service.
Much of the centre of Ljubljana has been pedestrianised and traffic is very congested. Finding parking spaces can be very difficult; use of a car in the city on weekdays is not advisable.

BUSINESS DIRECTORY

Telephone area codes
The international direct dialling code (IDD) for Slovenia is +386, followed by area code and subscriber's number:

Celje	3	Murska Sobota	02
Koper	5	Nova Gorica	5
Kranj	4	Novo Mesto	7
Krsko	7	Postojna	5
Ljubljana	1	Ravne	2
Maribor	2	Trbovlje	3

Useful telephone numbers
Emergency112

Chambers of Commerce
American Chamber of Commerce in Slovenia, 55 Pod Hribom, 1000 Ljubljana (tel: 581-6285; fax: 581-6111; e-mail: office@am-cham.si).

Koper Chamber of Commerce and Industry, 2 Ferrarska, 6000 Koper (tel: 639-5311; fax: 639-5316; e-mail: kozlovic@hg.gzs.si).

Ljubljana Chamber of Commerce and Industry, 9 Dimiceva, 1504 Ljubljana (tel: 230-1133; fax: 431-3040; e-mail: samardzija@hg.gzs.si).

Maribor Chamber of Commerce and Industry, 24 Talcev, 2000 Maribor (tel: 220-8700; fax: 252-2283; e-mail: breznik@hg.gzs.si).

Northern Primorska Chamber of Commerce and Industry, 3 Trg Edvarda Kardelja, 5000 Nova Gorica (tel: 330-6030; fax: 330-6031; e-mail: velikonja@hg.gzs.si).

Novo Mesto Chamber of Commerce and Industry, 5 Novi Trg, 8000 Novo Mesto (tel: 332-2182; fax: 332-2187; e-mail: goles@hg.gzs.si).

Postojna Chamber of Commerce and Industry, Cankarjeva 6, 6230 Postojna (tel: 720-0111; fax: 726-5344; e-mail: tiselj@hg.gzs.si).

Slovenia Chamber of Commerce and Industry, 13 Dimiceva, 1504 Ljubljana (tel: 589-8000; fax: 589-8100; e-mail: infolink@gzs.si).

Banking

Abanka Vipa dd, Slovenska 58, 1517 Ljubljana (tel: 471-8100; fax: 432-5165; email: info@abanka.si; internet site: www.abanka.si).

Bank Austria dd, Smartinska 140, 1000 Ljubljana (tel: 587-6600; fax: 587-6684; email: info@si.bacai.com).

Banka Celje dd, Vodnikova 2, 3000 Celje (tel: 543-1000 fax: 548-3511; email: info@banka-celje.si).

Banka Koper, Pristaniska 14, 6502 Koper (tel: 665-1100; fax: 639-7842; email: infor@banka-koper.si; internet site: www.banka-koper.si).

Factor Banka dd, Tivolska 48, 1000 Ljubljana (tel: 230-6600; fax: 230-7760; email: info@factorb.si).

Gorenjska Banka dd, Bleiweisova 1, 4000 Kranj (tel: 208-4000; fax: 202-1503; email: info@gbkr.si).

Hypo-Alpe-Adria Bank dd, Trv Osvobodine fronte 12, 1000 Ljubljana (tel: 300-4400; fax: 300-4401; email: hypo-banka@hypo.si).

Koroska Banka dd, Glavni trg 30, 2380 Slovenj Gradec (tel: 884-9111; fax: 884-2382).

Krekova Banka, Slomskov trg 18, 2000 Maribor (tel: 229-3100; fax: 252-2261; email: info@krekova-banka.si).

Nova Kreditna Banka Maribor, Vita Kraigherja 4, 2505 Maribor (tel: 229-2290; fax: 252-4333, 252-4371; email: info@nkbm.si).

Nova Ljubljanska Banka dd, Trg Republike 2, 1520 Ljubljana (tel: 425-0155; fax: 252-2422; email: info@nlb.si).

Postna Banka Slovenije dd, Vita Kraigherja 5, 2000 Maribor (tel: 228-8200; fax: 228-8210; email: info@pbs.si).

Probanka dd, Gosposka Ulica 23, 2000 Maribor (tel: 252-0500; fax: 252-5882; email: info@probanka.si).

SKB Banka dd, Ajdovscina 4, 1513 Ljubljana (tel: 433-213; fax: 231-4549: email: info@skb.si).

Slovenska Investicijska Banka dd, Copova 38, 1000 Ljubljana (tel: 242-0300; fax: 242-0521; email: sib@si-banka.si).

Slovenska Zadruzna Kmetijska Banka dd, Kolodvorska 9, 1000 Ljubljana (tel: 472-7100; fax: 472-7405); email: info@szkbanka.si).

Volksbank-Ljudska Banka dd, Dunajska 128a, 1101 Ljubljana (tel: 530-7400; fax: 520-7555; email: banka@volksbank.si).

Central bank

Banka Slovenije, Slovenska 35, 1505 Ljubljana (tel: 471-9000; fax: 251-5516; email: bsl@bsi.si; internet: www.bsi.si/en).

Travel information

Adria Airways, Kuzmiceva 7, 1000 Ljubljana (tel: 369-1000; fax: 230-1325; internet: www.adria.si).

Automobile Association of Slovenia, Dunajska 128a, SI-1000 Ljubljana (breakdown assistance tel: 530-5353; internet: www.amzs.si).

Ljubljana Airport, Zg Brnik 130a, 4210 Brnik (tel: 4-206-1981; fax: 4-202-1220; email: info@lju-airport.si; internet: www.lju-airport.si).

Slovenian Tourist Information Centre, Krekov trg 10, 1000 Ljubljana (tel: 306-4575/6; fax: 306-4580; email: stic@ljubljana-tourism.si; internet: www.ljubljana-tourism.si).

National tourist organisation offices

Slovenska Turisticna Organizacija (Slovenian Tourist Organisation), WTC, Dunajska 156, 1001 Ljubljana (tel: 589-1840; fax: 589-1841; e-mail: info@slovenia-tourism.si; internet: www.slovenia-tourism.si).

Ministries

Ministry of Agriculture, Forestry and Food, Dunajska 52, 1000 Ljubljana (tel: 478-9000; fax: 478-9021; email: janez.vertacnik@gov.si).

Ministry of Culture, Cankarjeva 5, 1000 Ljubljana (tel: 478-5900; fax: 478-5901; email: mkinfo@gov.si).

Ministry of Defence, Kardeljeva ploscad 25, 1000 Ljubljana (tel:471-2211; fax: 131-8164; email: darko.lubi@pub.mo-rs.si).

Ministry of the Economy, Kotnikova 5, 1000 Ljubljana (tel: 478-3600; fax: 478-3522; email: tatjana.zabasu@gov.si).

Ministry of Education, Science and Sport, Zupanèièeva 6, 1000 Ljubljana (tel: 478-5437; fax: 478-5669; email: info@mss.edus.si).

Ministry of Environment and Spatial Planning, Dunajska 48, 1000 Ljubljana (tel: 478-7400; fax: 478-7422; email: info.mop@gov.si).

Ministry of Finance, Zupanèièeva 3, 1502 Ljubljana (tel: 478-5211; fax: 478-5655; email: tilen.majnardi@mf-rs.si).

Ministry of Foreign Affairs, Presernova 25, 1000 Ljubljana (tel: 478-2000; fax: 478-2340; email: info.mzz@gov.si).

Ministry of Health, Stefanova 5, 1000 Ljubljana (tel: 478-6001; fax: 478-6058; email: ministrstvo.zdravsto@gov.si).

Ministry of the Information Society, Langusova 4, 1000 Ljubljana (tel: 478-8223; fax: 478-8142; email: mid@gov.si).

Ministry of the Interior, Stefanova 2, 1000 Ljubljana (tel: 472-5111; fax: 251-4330;email: jelka.smreka@mnz.si).

Ministry of Justice, Zupanèièeva 3, 1000 Ljubljana (tel: 478-5211; fax: 251-0200; email: stojan.klancar@gov.si).

Ministry of Labour, Family and Social Affairs, Kotnikova 5, 1000 Ljubljana (tel: 478-3450; fax: 478-3456; email: zmaga.grah@gov.si).

Ministry of Transport, Langusova 4, 1000 Ljubljana (tel: 478-8000; fax: 478-8139; email: mpz.info@gov.si).

Office for European Affairs, Subièeva 11, 1000 Ljubljana (tel: 478-24-47; fax: 478-2310; email: svez@gov.si).

President's Office, Erjavceva 17, 1000 Ljubljana (tel: 478-1205; fax: 478-1357).

Prime Minister's Office, Gregorèièeva 20, 1000 Ljubljana (tel: 478-1000; fax: 478-1607).

Other useful addresses

Agency of the Republic of Slovenia for Restructuring and Privatisation, Kotnikova Ulica 28, 1000 Ljubljana (tel: 131-2122; fax: 131-6011).

British Embassy, Fourth Floor, Trg Republike 3, 1000 Ljubljana (tel: 200-3910; fax: 425-0174; email: info@british-embassy.si).

Government Office for European Affairs, Subiceva 11, 1000 Ljubljana (tel: 478-2228; fax: 478-2310).

Government of the Republic of Slovenia, Gregorciceva 20, 1000 Ljubljana (tel: 478-1100; fax: 478-1607).

Government PR and Media Office, Slovenska 29, 1000 Ljubljana (tel: 478-2629; fax: 251-2312; internet: www.uvi.gov.si/eng).

Ljubljana Stock Exchange, Trg Republike 3, 1000 Ljubljana (tel: 477-5500; fax: 477-5507, 477-5508).

Small Business Development Centre, Dunajska 156, 1001 Ljubljana (tel: 189-1870; fax: 188-1178).

Trade and Investment Promotion Office (TIPO), Kotnikova 28, 1000 Ljubljana (tel: 478-3557; fax: 478-3599; email: tipo@gov.si; internet site: www.investslovenia.org).

Internet sites

Republic of Slovenia website: www.sigov.si

Slovenske Zeleznice (Slovenian Railways): www.slo-zeleznice.si/en/home

Solomon Islands

KEY FACTS

Official name: Solomon Islands

Head of State: Queen Elizabeth II, represented by Governor General Nathaniel Waena (since 7 Jul 2004)

Head of government: Prime Minister Derek Sikua (SILP) (since 20 Dec 2007)

Ruling party: The Solomon Islands Alliance for Change; a coalition of independents and four political parties including the National Party, Solomon Islands Liberal Party (SILP), Solomon Islands Social Credit Party (Socreds) and Rural Advancement Party (RAP), (since 2006)

Area: 27,556 square km – Guadalcanal: 5,302 square km

Population: 495,026 (2007)

Capital: Honiara (on Guadalcanal)

Official language: English

Currency: Solomon Islands dollar (SI$) = 100 cents

Exchange rate: SI$7.66 per US$ (Jul 2008)

GDP per capita: US$704 (2007)*

GDP real growth: 10.30% (2007)

Labour force: 200,000 (2006)

Inflation: 6.30% (2007)

Balance of trade: US$23.90 million (2007)

Foreign debt: US$137.00 million (2003)

Visitor numbers: 13,748 (2007)

* estimated figure

COUNTRY PROFILE

Historical profile

The Solomon Islands were settled between 2,000–3,000 BC by Austronesians, Neolithic people from south-east Asia.

1568 The Spanish explorer, Álvaro de Mendaña, first visited the islands. The islands were named after King Solomon as Mendana hoped that the islands were rich with gold.

The islands were left alone until the mid-nineteenth century when whaling ships stopped off for supplies.

1893 The central islands became a British protectorate.

1899 In the Tripartite Treaty; Britain gained control of the whole of the Solomon Islands in exchange for withdrawing its claim to Samoa.

1942–45 During the Second World War, Japanese occupied the islands and US troops fought one of the fiercest battles on Guadalcanal.

1945 Britain resumed the administration of the islands.

1946 An independence movement was founded to resist British rule.

1976 Self-government was granted.

1978 The Solomon Islands became fully independent.

1997 In the general election Bartholomew Ulufa'alu (Liberal Party) (a Mataita) won.

1999 Ethnic violence broke out on Guadalcanal as a native's militia, the Isatabu Freedom Movement (IFM), tried to evict thousands of immigrant Mataitan. The Malaita Eagles Force (MEF) militia seized control of the capital, Honiara, claiming it was protecting Malaitan interests.

2000 Fighting broke out between the IFM and MEF. The MEF seized the parliament and forced Prime Minister Ulufa'alu to resign. The violence resulted in the breakdown in civil order with security and police forces often siding with one faction or another. The IFM and MEF signed The Townsville Peace Agreement in Australia. Unarmed peace-keepers were deployed.

2001 The IFM rebel leader, Selwyn Sake, was murdered. Sir Allan Kemakeza, (People's Alliance Party (PAP)), was elected prime minister by the new 50-member parliament.

2002 The economy began to collapse, as the government was unable to pay wages and fund services. Law and order began to disintegrate.

2003 A formal request for international assistance to avert a spiral of anarchy led to the deployment of the Regional Assistance Mission of the Solomon Islands (Ramsi), including 300 police officers, which began to restore order and disarm militant groups. Infamous rebel leader, Harold Keke, viewed by many as a bandit warlord, particularly after he ordered the razing of two villages, surrendered to Ramsi forces. With peace restored RAMSI was scaled down.

2004 Nathaniel Waena became governor general. A constitution for a new federal system of government was drafted.

2005 The EU signed an agreement to provide US$13 million in aid. Keke was sentenced to life imprisonment for murder. The political party Solomon Islands Social Credit Party (Socreds) was founded. It advocated domestic control of the economy and full monetary and financial reform along social credit ideology.

2006 In general elections Snyder Rini (Association of Independent Members (AIM)) was elected prime minister, but rioting broke out following the announcement and he was forced to stand down within eight days. Manasseh Sogavare (Socreds) was elected prime minister, leading the Solomon Islands Alliance for Change coalition, including the National Party, the Solomon Islands Liberal Party (SILP), (Socreds), the Rural Advancement Party and independents. Julian Moti fled from Papua New Guinea, wanted by the Australian Federal Police on charges of sex tourism crimes.

2007 Prime Minister Sogavare questioned when the Ramsi mission would end, calling for 'an exit strategy'. The speech, to the Pacific Islands Forum, said the regional character should not be 'Australia dictated' and underlined the tensions between the Solomon Islands and Australia. Sogavare appointed Julian Moti as the attorney general. Australian soldiers raided the prime minister's office in a search of Moti. On 12 December, the Sogavare government was removed following a vote of no confidence in parliament. Derek Sikua was elected prime minister by 32 to 15 votes for Patterson Oti, on 20 December. Moti was extradited to Australia on 27 December.

Political structure

Constitution

The constitution of May 1978 delegates authority from the British monarch, through the governor general appointed on the recommendation of parliament.

There are nine administrative areas each governed by elected provincial assemblies, and the tenth, Honiara, is administered by a town council.
A draft constitution for a new federal system of government is expected to be ready by July 2009.

Form of state
Independent democracy, with British monarch as Head of State

The executive
The Head of State is the British Monarch, who is represented by the Governor General, who is chosen by the National Parliament, for a term of five years.
Executive power rests with the prime minister as head of government.

National legislature
The unicameral, National Parliament has 50 members, elected in single-seat constituencies for four-year terms. A parliament may be dissolved by a majority of its members before the term expires. Parliament elects the prime minister from its membership; the prime minister appoints a cabinet of 18 ministers.

Last elections
5 April 2006 (parliamentary)
Results: Parliamentary: Independents won 60.3 per cent (30 seats out of 50); National Party won 6.9 per cent (four seats); Rural Advancement Party (RAP) 6.3 per cent (four seats); PAP 6.3 per cent (three seats); Solomon Islands Liberal Party (SILP) 5.0 per cent (two seats); Democratic Party 4.9 per cent (three seats); Socred 4.3 per cent (two seats); Lafari Party 2.8 per cent (two seats).

Next elections
2009 (governor general – chosen by parliament); 2010 (parliamentary).

Political parties

Ruling party
The Solomon Islands Alliance for Change; a coalition of independents and four political parties including the National Party, Solomon Islands Liberal Party (SILP), Solomon Islands Social Credit Party (Socreds) and Rural Advancement Party (RAP), (since 2006)

Main opposition party
Non specifically

Political situation
As the political situation stabilised following the intervention of the Regional Assistance Mission of the Solomon Islands (Ramsi), lead by Australia, in 2003, the Solomon Islands has been reasserting not only its internal authority but also its sovereign rights. Inter-ethnic violence, as thousands of outer-islanders relocated to central island looking for work, caused much death, destruction and mayhem. The economy was left in tatters and it took the concerted efforts of regional powers to bring the failing state back into viability. As the country became calm the government, lead by Manasseh Sogavare, was impatient to reclaim its control and began to agitate for the Ramsi training wheels to be removed. However the issue that strained and almost caused a meltdown in relations with Australia was the extradition of Julian Moti for alleged criminal charges of child abuse in Vanuatu.
Moti, a naturalised Australian, had first fled to Papua New Guinea for sanctuary but when, in 2006 it seemed his save haven was ending he escaped to the Solomon Islands, while on bail. However he was arrested by Ramsi when he arrived in the Solomon Islands, which enraged Prime Minister Sogavare who said Ramsi had violated the Solomon Islands' national sovereignty. In 2007 Sogavare appointed Moti as the Solomon Islands' Attorney General, but in December 2007 Sogavare's government fell and Moti was extradited to Australia.
The diplomatic crisis this caused between three regional governments may have lingering consequences but with the replacement of two of those governments pragmatism may prevail.

Population
495,026 (2007)
Last census: November 1999: 409,042
Population density: 16 inhabitants per square km. Urban population: 20 per cent (1995–2001).
Annual growth rate: 2.8 per cent 1994–2004 (WHO 2006)

Ethnic make-up
About 93 per cent Melanesian, 4 per cent Polynesian, 1.5 per cent Micronesian, European, Chinese and others. Many of the inhabitants of Western and Choiseul Provinces in Malaita are from Papua New Guinea. Ethnic disputes have simmered since the end of the Second World War, as Malaitans have migrated to Guadalcanal for work.

Religions
Anglican (45 per cent), Roman Catholic (18 per cent), other Protestants (33 per cent). There are some native religions, especially on Malaita.

Education
Primary education last for six years. Lower secondary schooling lasts for three years and finishes at aged 15. Upper secondary school lasts for two years and is completed in a one-year sixth form. Students who have completed these years may attend a one-year's foundation programme to enter the University of the South Pacific; or enrol in a college of higher education.
The Solomon Islands has one of the lowest literacy rates in the world and the government intends to tackle this with the aid that has been forthcoming since 2003 so that by January 2005 free education was offered to all primary school aged children.
Literacy rate: 64 per cent, adult rate (2003).
Compulsory years: Six to 15
Enrolment rate: 104 per cent boys, 90 per cent girls: gross primary enrolment (including repeaters); 21 per cent boys, 1 per cent girls: gross secondary enrolment (Unicef 2004).

Health
Per capita total expenditure on health (2003) was US$87; of which per capita government spending was US$81, at the international dollar rate, (WHO 2006).
The Solomon Islands suffer from one of the highest malaria incidence rates in the world. It varies across the country with

KEY INDICATORS **Solomon Islands**

	Unit	2003	2004	2005	2006	2007
Population	m	0.47	0.49	0.48	*0.50	*0.51
Gross domestic product (GDP)	US$bn	0.23	0.26	0.29	0.33	*0.36
GDP per capita	US$	497	554	611	*661	*704
GDP real growth	%	5.0	6.0	5.0	6.1	*5.4
Inflation	%	10.1	6.8	7.3	8.1	6.3
Exports (fob) (goods)	US$m	74.2	*83.0	103.0	120.0	167.9
Imports (cif) (goods)	US$m	82.0	*-102.0	185.0	251.0	191.8
Balance of trade	US$m	-7.8	-19.0	-82.0	-131.0	-23.9
Current account	US$m	0.1	20.0	-71.0	-87.0	*-143.0
Total reserves minus gold	US$m	37.2	80.6	95.4	104.4	119.1
Foreign exchange	US$m	36.4	79.7	94.6	103.6	118.2
Exchange rate	per US$	7.49	7.48	7.42	7.42	7.11

* estimated figure

Honiara, Western Province and Choiseul Province the worst affected. Population growth and the mortality of mothers and children are one of the highest in the South Pacific due to endemic infectious diseases and low quality of rural health care.
Hospitals and pharmacies are limited, there are eight hospitals, the largest is the Central Hospital in Honiara. Church missions provide medical facilities on outlying islands. Serious health conditions usually require immediate medical evacuation to the nearest reliable medical facilities which are in Australia or New Zealand.
Life expectancy: 68 years, 2004 (WHO 2006)
Fertility rate/Maternal mortality rate: 4.2 births per woman, 2004 (WHO 2006)
Birth rate/Death rate: 32.5 births per 1,000 population; four deaths per 1,000 population (2003).
Child (under 5 years) mortality rate (per 1,000): 19 per 1,000 live births (World Bank)

Welfare
Political instability and fighting have caused extensive damage requiring emergency rehabilitation of critical infrastructure. The Post-Conflict Emergency Rehabilitation Project entails restoration of government offices, roads, bridges, water supply and sanitation facilities, schools, and health facilities. The cost of restoration work on Guadalcanal and nearby provinces has been estimated at between US$30–35 million.

Main cities
Honiara, on Guadalcanal (capital, estimated population 59,288 in 2005), Gizo (on Gizo Island) (3,408), Auki (on Malaita) (1,745), Noro (3,720), Tulagi (1,234)

Languages spoken
There is no main native language although nearly all the languages are distantly related to the Oceanic Austronesian language group. There are at least 12 different language groups containing 87 various languages and dialects. Melanesian pidgin is the lingua franca. It has evolved since the time of the first traders, whalers, missionaries and labour recruiters. The vocabulary is derived from English with Melanesian syntax and uses different intonations. English, as a first language, is spoken by 1–2 per cent of the population.

Official language/s
English

Media
Other news agencies: ABC Pacific Beat: www.radioaustralia.net.au/pacbeat
Pacific Magazine: www.pacificmagazine.net

Press
Dailies: In English, Solomon Star (www.solomonstarnews.com) is the only domestic newspaper. Online news is published by Solomon Times Online (www.solomontimes.com) and People First (www.peoplefirst.net.sb). Published abroad, other internet news outlets report on the Solomon Islands Event Polynesia (www.eventpolynesia.com), Pacific Islands Report (http://pidp.eastwestcenter.org) and Pacific Beat (www.radioaustralia.net.au/pacbeat) from Australia.
Periodicals: There are a number of publications, Link and Solomon Nius are government-owned, private monthlies include Agrikalsa Nius and Citizen's Press; Mere Save is a women's magazine.

Broadcasting
Radio: The public service broadcaster is SIBC (the Solomon Islands Broadcasting Corporation) (www.sibconline.com.sb), which produces radio programmes in English and Pidgin, transmitting on medium and short waves, plus FM, to local and overseas populations from Honiara, Gizo (in Western Province) and Lata.
Television: Terrestrial television services are not available, although satellite transmissions can be received.

Advertising
Newspapers, radio and cinemas accept advertising.

Economy
The economy is based on agriculture, with 90 per cent of the population living in rural areas. Much real national income is derived from non-market, subsistence production of food crops, fish, meat, fuel and services. Primary products, mainly timber and fish, led to a 6 per cent growth rate in 2004, with inflation down to 6.8 per cent. Foreign investment is leading to a slow recovery. A memorandum of understanding has been signed with a Papua New Guinea-based palm oil company that proposes to reconstruct the palm oil operation on Guadalcanal. Some interest is being shown in mineral exploration although the Gold Ridge gold mine is yet to reopen. Logging remains a high foreign income earner, although it is being operated at an unsustainable level and government plans to curb production is expected to reduce revenue from the industry by 2007.
Overall, the economy suffers from the high cost of imported fuel and low worldwide prices for its agricultural products. The government's National Economic Recovery, Reform and Development Plan, 2003–06, includes public sector reform. Services contributed 24 per cent to the 2004 growth rate. The payment of wage arrears to public service workers also fuelled consumption and helped government accounts as funds came back in better than expected revenue collection. The 2004 budget followed the settlement of Solomon Island arrears to the Asian Development Bank (ADB) and World Bank, and tightened expenditure controls as its central plank. International aid also targetted comprehensive reforms and good governance.
The budget provided for a balanced cash position, with budget support from Australia and New Zealand amounting to almost 25 per cent of total revenues. New Zealand's contribution was set aside for education.
In an effort to stamp out corruption, Solomon Islands is in the process of revising its foreign investment laws, which are time-consuming and costly. The system under discussion aims to create a single registration process, after which foreign companies will be treated in the same way as local companies.
The medium-term outlook is for faster economic growth, led by exports and externally funded government spending.
In September 2004, the ADB announced grants worth US$3 million for transport and for the development of private businesses, and in July 2005, the Solomon Islands signed agreements to US$13 million in EU funding for development programmes.

External trade
The Solomon Islands is a member of the South Pacific Regional Trade and Economic Co-operation Agreement (Sparteca) along with 12 other regional nations, which allows products duty free access by Pacific Island Forum members to Australian and New Zealand markets (subject to the country of origin restrictions). It is also a member of the Melanesian Spearhead Group (with Fiji, Papua New Guinea and Vanuatu), which is a sub-regional trade group, whereby customs tariffs have been harmonised and a free trade agreement is in negotiation.
There are traditional industries in timber, copra and palm oil and gold extraction. However the ethnic violence from 1998 badly affected exports and by 2007 production had not fully recovered.

Imports
Principal imports are food, plant and equipment, manufactured goods, fuels and chemicals.
Main sources: Australia (25.3 per cent total, 2006), Singapore (23.4 per cent), Japan (7.8 per cent).

Exports
Principal exports are timber (around 50 per cent of total), fish, copra, palm oil and cocoa.
Main destinations: China (45.6 per cent total, 2006), South Korea (14.0 per cent), Japan (8.5 per cent).

Agriculture
Farming
Agriculture typically accounts for over 60 per cent of GDP and almost three-quarters of the workforce. About 25–30 per cent of total land area is suitable for intensive, non-traditional agriculture, mainly on Guadalcanal. Over 85 per cent of land is communally owned, which deters investment.
The islands are self-sufficient in beef and vegetables. Copra and cocoa are produced for market on smallholdings and private plantations.
The Government Shareholding Agency, in association with major plantations, has been encouraging new coconut and cocoa planting and extension of the palm oil plantations.
Estimated crop production in 2005 included: 5,500 tonnes (t) rice, 276,000t coconuts, 155,000t oil palm fruit, 86,000t sweet potatoes, 40,000t taro, 74,360t oilcrops, 29,000t yams, 5,000t cocoa beans, 19,330t fruit in total, 8,200t vegetables in total. Estimated livestock production included: 3,340t meat in total, 740t beef, 2,320t pig meat, 280t poultry, 480t eggs, 1,365t milk.
Fishing
Commercial fishing and fish processing around the islands is mainly of skipjack tuna. Fish exports account for about one-third of total export earnings. Domestic seafood demand is served by small, local operations.
Production, in general, has fallen since a high in 1997 when the typical annual marine fish catch was 63,000t, to around 30,000t by 2004. Likewise there were 182,000 units of pearls and shells harvested in 1997 and only 54,000 by 2004.
The first black cultured pearls, produced over a seven-year period at a demonstration farm near Gizo, were auctioned in Australia in June 2004.
In 2004, the total marine fish catch was 36,488 tonnes and the total crustacean catch was 20 tonnes.
Forestry
Logging is one of the country's main economic lifelines, contributing around 18 per cent of GDP. The forests contain some 170,000 hectares of exploitable land having 13 million cubic metres of commercial timber. However, instead of the 250,000cum recommended by environmentalists as sustainable felling, felling described as 'unsustainable' by the Asian Development Bank, accelerated in 2004 as logging companies increased production ahead of new legislation aimed at curbing exploitation of the natural forests.
Timber imports in 2004 were US$448,000, while exports amounted to US$104.9 million.
Timber production in 2004 included 692,000 cubic metre (cum) roundwood, 12,000cum sawnwood, 554,000cum sawlogs and veneer logs, 138,000cum woodfuel.

Industry and manufacturing
The industrial sector accounts for around 5 per cent of GDP and employs some 5 per cent of the workforce.
Manufacturing activities include palm oil, rice milling, fish smoking, canning and freezing, saw milling, copra drying, food processing, tobacco, soft drinks, production of nails, detergents and soaps, wood and rattan furniture, fibreglass articles, boats, clothing, handicrafts, shell jewellery, buttons.
Most timber is exported as logs, but an increasing proportion is being sawn; the government hopes to develop wood processing to enable profitable marketing of sawn timber and veneers.

Tourism
Tourism in normal circumstances constitutes an important element of the economy, with diving and fishing being popular attractions. Prior to 2000, tourist arrivals were in excess of 15,000, but ethnic violence during 2000–03 precipitated an almost total collapse in numbers with only 1,245 arrivals in 2001, the lowest on record. The situation had sufficiently stabilised to see numbers begin to rise in 2004, especially from Australia and New Zealand, although poor air services remain an impediment. There has also been a revival of hotel construction and refurbishment.

Environment
The Solomon Islands was ranked second, after Indonesia, for coral reef fish species and the range and variety of its corals.
The main environmental problems are deforestation, soil erosion and major, possibly irreversible, destruction to coral reefs There is a lack of resources to control the activities of the logging companies.

Mining
The mining sector typically accounts for 1 per cent of GDP, and employs 1 per cent of the workforce.
Panning of alluvial gold produces some 50–100kg per annum.
Undeveloped mineral resources include small deposits of copper, lead, zinc, silver, nickel, cobalt, bauxite, phosphates and asbestos.
Bugotu Nickel Ltd is working on a feasibility study of the latteritic nickel deposits on Takata and San Jorge, Isabel Province. The nickel resource is estimated at 45 million tonnes.
Ross Mining of Australia opened the Gold Ridge gold mine, 45km from Majuro, with reserves of about three million ounces which will last over 10 years. The violence of the civil unrest caused the operations at the mine to be suspended; by early 2006 it had still not reopened.

Hydrocarbons
There are no hydrocarbon reserves and the Solomon Islands relies entirely on imported refined oil to meet domestic demand.

Energy
New Zealand contributed NZ$1 million towards restoring a regular power supply to the capital, after the civil unrest in 2003.

Banking and insurance
The ADB considers the banking sector to employ limited competition with strong participation by Australian financial institutions.
Central bank
Central Bank of Solomon Islands
Main financial centre
Honiara, on Guadalcanal Island

Time
GMT plus 11 hours

Geography
The Solomon Islands lie in the south-western Pacific Ocean, to the north-east of Australia and Papua New Guinea, its closest neighbour, and north of Vanuatu. The country comprises hundreds of mainly small islands, extending over an area of around 28,500sq kilometres. There are six main islands: Guadalcanal, where the capital, Honiara, is located, Choiseul, San Cristobal, Makira, New Georgia and Malaita. The islands are mountainous and forested, with active as well as dormant volcanoes.
Hemisphere
Southern

Climate
Warm and humid, equatorial with average temperatures from 22 degrees Celsius (C) (mountainous areas inland) to 28 degrees C (coastal areas). Rainfall averages about 3,500mm per annum, but varies greatly according to location and mostly falls Nov–Apr, when cyclones may occur as well.

Entry requirements
Passports
Required by all, valid for at least six months.

Visa
Visas required by all except nationals of most EU countries, North America, Australasia and some other countries. (For a list of countries for which prior approval is required, see www.commerce.gov.sb/Divisions/Immigration/Immigration_Requirements.htm.) Travellers with onward passage and adequate funds are issued on arrival with a visitor's permit for up to three months.

Currency advice/regulations
There are no restrictions on the import of local currency, but export is limited to SI$250, or on the import of foreign currencies, subject to declaration; re-export is limited to the amount imported.

Customs
Personal effects (including an allowance of alcoholic beverages and tobacco) are allowed duty-free up to SI$500. Import licences are required for most goods and specific licences are required for fruit, vegetables and animal products.

Prohibited imports
Weapons without a police permit, narcotics and pornography.

Health (for visitors)

Mandatory precautions
Vaccination certificate required for yellow fever if travelling from an infected zone.

Advisable precautions
Vaccination for diphtheria, tuberculosis, hepatitis A and B, polio, tetanus, typhoid. Malaria is a problem, especially in Honiara, and prophylaxis should be taken. Hookworm is endemic and any itchy rash should be checked by a physician. There is a rabies risk.

Hotels

There are over 60 hotels. Visitors are advised to book well in advance. Hotel tax of 10 per cent is added to bill. In addition to Honiara's three hotels, there are resorts, guesthouses and government resthouses of varying standards and quality scattered throughout the islands. Tipping is not customary or encouraged.

Public holidays (national)

Fixed dates
1 Jan (New Year's Day), 7 Jul (Independence Day), 25 Dec (Christmas Day), 26 Dec (National Day of Thanksgiving).
Each province celebrates their own public national holiday: 25 Feb (Choiseul), 2 Jun (Isable), 8 Jun (Temotu), 29 Jun (Central Island), 20 Jul (Rennell), 1 Aug (Guadalcanal), 3 Aug (Makira/Ulawa), 15 Aug (Malaita), 7 Dec (Western Province).

Variable dates
Good Friday, Easter Monday, Queen's Official Birthday (second Fri in Jun).

Working hours

Banking
Mon–Fri: 0830–1500.

Business
Mon–Fri: 0730/0800–1200, 1300–1630/1700; Sat: 0730/0800–1200.

Government
Mon–Fri: 0800–1200, 1300–1630.

Shops
Mon–Fri: 0800–1700; 0800–1200; Sat: 0800–1200. Many shops open Sat afternoon and Sun; Chinese stores often open at other times. There are several 24-hour stores in Honiara.

Telecommunications

Telephone/fax
Automatic telephone service available in Honiara, Auki, Gizo, Noro, Munda, Buala, Lata and Tulagi.
International services available 24 hours via TELECOM (Solomon Islands) satellite and cable links. Specialised systems such as private leased circuits and data links can be provided.

Postal services
There is no local delivery system.

Electricity supply

240/220V AC with flat three-pin plug fittings and bayonet-type sockets, typical of Australia.

Weights and measures

Officially, the metric system is in use.

Social customs/useful tips

Tipping is not customary, and visitors are strongly advised to refrain from the practice. Women should avoid wearing shorts and make sure their legs are adequately covered to avoid giving offence. The social structure of the Solomon Islands is extremely complex, with traditions, culture and even language varying from island to island and among villages on the same island.

Security

The security situation has improved since 2003, however resources are still limited and response times to calls for assistance may be slow. Attacks on foreign nationals are rare however personal security precausions should be taken if visiting the island of Malaita and rural Guadalcanal. Swearing is a crime and can lead to large civil fines and even jail.

Getting there

Air
National airline: Solomon Airlines.
International airport/s: Henderson International (HIR), 13km from Honiara; bank, duty free shop and car hire.
Airport tax: SI$40.

Surface
Water: Regular shipping links with Australia, New Zealand, Hong Kong, Japan, UK and Europe.

Getting about

National transport
Air: Solomon Airlines fly regular services from Henderson Airport to main islands and towns. Charter flights are available.
Road: Surfaced roads are concentrated on Guadalcanal and Malaita and few are properly maintained. Other roads, mostly in the rural areas, are coral or gravel surfaced, supplemented by dirt tracks. Terrain can be difficult.
Buses: Bus services operate in and around Honiara.
Water: Inter-island shipping services are operated by the government and also by private companies and missionaries. There are large passenger boats, and cargo vessels also carry passengers in varying degrees of comfort.

City transport
Taxis: Taxis are available in Honiara and Auki and can be booked in advance or hailed in the street. As they are not metered, it is advisable to agree the fare before the journey starts.

Car hire
Car hire is available in Honiara. Driving is on the left.

BUSINESS DIRECTORY

The addresses listed below are a selection only. While World of Information makes every endeavour to check these addresses, we cannot guarantee that changes have not been made, especially to telephone numbers and area codes. We would welcome any corrections.

Telephone area codes
Dialling code for Solomon Islands, IDD access code +677 followed by subscriber's number.

Useful telephone numbers
Police and fire: 23-666
Fire: 999
Ambulance: 25-566
Marine emergency: 21-535
Emergencies outside Honiara: 111
Directory enquiries: 101
Overseas operator: 102
Shipping and time: 107
Operator assistance: 100
Customs: 22-301
Immigration: 22-243

Chambers of Commerce
Solomon Islands Chamber of Commerce and Employers, PO Box 70, Honiara (tel: 23-342; fax: 21-851; e-mail: chamberc@solomon.com.sb).

Banking
Australia and New Zealand Banking Group Ltd (ANZ), PO Box 10, Honiara (tel: 21-111; fax: 26-937; e-mail: solomons@anz.com).

Development Bank of Solomon Islands, PO Box 911, Honiara (tel: 21-595; fax: 23-715; e-mail: dbsi@welkam.solomon.com.sb).

National Bank of Solomon Islands, PO Box 37, Honiara (tel: 21-874; fax: 23-478; e-mail: nbsi@welkam.solomon.com.sb).

Westpac Banking Corporation, 721 Mendana Avenue, PO Box 466, Honiara (tel: 21-222; fax: 24-957).

Central bank
Central Bank of Solomon Islands, PO Box 634, Honiara (tel: 21-791 fax: 23-513; e-mail: info@cbsi.com.sb).

Travel information
Guadalcanal Travel Service, Mendana Avenue, PO Box 114, Honiara (tel: 22-586; fax: 26-184; e-mail: gts@welkem.solomon.com.sb).

Henderson International Airport, PO Box G8, Honiara (tel: 36-720; fax: 36-775; e-mail: civilair@welkam.solomon.com.sb).

Solomon Islands Airlines, PO Box 23, Mendana Avenue, Honiara (tel: 20-031; fax: 20-232; e-mail: solair@welkam.solomon.com.sb).

Western Province Tourism Association, PO Box 56, Gizo (tel: 30-254; fax: 39-240)

Ministry of tourism
Ministry of Culture and Tourism, PO Box G26, Honiara (tel: 28-603; fax: 27-587; e-mail: commerce@commerce.gov.sb).

National tourist organisation offices
Solomon Islands Visitors Bureau, P.O.Box 321, Medana Avenue, Honiara (tel: 22-442; fax: 23-986; e-mail: info@sivb.com.sb).

Ministries
Ministry of Agriculture and Fisheries, PO Box G13, Honiara (tel: 21-327; fax: 21-955).

Ministry of Commerce, Industries and Employment, PO Box G26, Honiara (tel: 21-849; fax: 25-084).

Ministry of Education and Human Resources Development, PO Box G28, Honiara (tel: 23-900; fax: 20-485).

Ministry of Finance, PO Box 26, Honiara (tel: 23-700; fax: 20-392).

Ministry of Foreign Affairs, PO Box G10, Honiara (tel: 21-250; fax: 20-351).

Ministry of Forest Environment and Conservation, PO Box G24, Honiara (tel: 25-848; fax: 21-245).

Ministry of Health and Medical Services, PO Box 349, Honiara (tel: 20-830; fax: 20-085).

Ministry of Home Affairs, PO Box G11, Honiara (tel: 21-621; fax: 22-606).

Ministry of Justice and Legal Affairs, PO Box 404, Honiara (tel: 21-181; fax: 25-610).

Ministry of Lands and Housing, PO Box G38, Honiara (tel: 21-430; fax: 20-094).

Ministry of Mines and Energy, PO Box G37, Honiara (tel: 21-521; fax: 25-811).

Ministry of National Planning and Development, PO Box G30, Honiara (tel: 25-063; fax: 25-138).

Ministry of Police and National Security, PO Box G4, Honiara (tel: 22-208; fax: 25-949).

Ministry of Post and Telecommunication, PO Box G25, Honiara (tel: 21-821; fax: 21-472).

Ministry of Provincial Government and Rural Development, PO Box G35, Honiara (tel: 21-140; fax: 21-289).

Ministry of Transport, Works and Utilities, PO Box G8, Honara (tel: 26-560; fax: 26-458; e-mail: sidapp@pipolfastaem.gov.sb).

Ministry of Youth, Women, Sports and Recreation, PO Box G39, Honiara (tel: 25-490; fax: 25-686).

Office of the Prime Minister, PO Box G1, Honiara (tel: 22-202, 21-863; fax: 21-608, 25-470).

Other useful addresses
Controller of Customs and Excise, Customs and Excise Division, Ministry of National Planning and Development, PO Box G30, Honiara.

Foreign Investment Board, Ministry of Commerce, Industries and Employment, PO Box G26, Honiara (tel: 21-849; fax: 25-084).

Governor General, PO Box 252, Honiara (tel: 22-222, 21-777; fax: 23-335).

Investment Corporation of Solomon Islands Ltd, PO Box 570, Honiara (tel: 22-511; fax: 21-263).

Solomon Islands Ports Authority, PO Box 307, Honiara (tel: 22-646; fax: 23-994).

Solomon Islands Statistics Office, PO Box G6, Honiara (tel: 23-700).

Telekom Office, Mendana Avenue, Honiara (tel: 21-576; fax: 23-110).

Trading Co (Solomons) Ltd, Mendana Avenue, PO Box 114, Honiara (tel: 22-588).

Other news agencies: ABC Pacific Beat: www.radioaustralia.net.au/pacbeat

Pacific Magazine: www.pacificmagazine.net

Internet sites
Asia Business Connection (gateway site): http://asiabiz.com

Somalia

KEY FACTS

Official name: Jamhuriyadda ee Soomaaliya (Republic of Somalia)

Head of State: President Abdullahi Yusuf Ahmed (since 10 Oct 2004)

Head of government: Prime Minister Nur 'Adde' Hassan Hussein (appointed 24 Nov 2007)

Ruling party: None

Area: 738,000 square km

Population: 8.70 million (2007)*

Capital: Mogadishu

Official language: Somali

Currency: Somali shilling (SoSh) = 100 centesimi

Exchange rate: SoSh1,400.00 per US$ (Jul 2008)

GDP per capita: US$283 (2006)*

GDP real growth: 2.40% (2005)

Labour force: 4.20 million (2004)

Inflation: 100.00% (2003)

Balance of trade: -US$335.00 million (2004)*

Foreign debt: US$2.60 billion (2003)

* estimated figure

NOTA

Somalia is experiencing profound political crisis and instability. Travel to the country should be avoided unless absolutely necessary. Visitors should seek advice prior to departure, and register their presence with the diplomatic representatives of their own country on arrival.

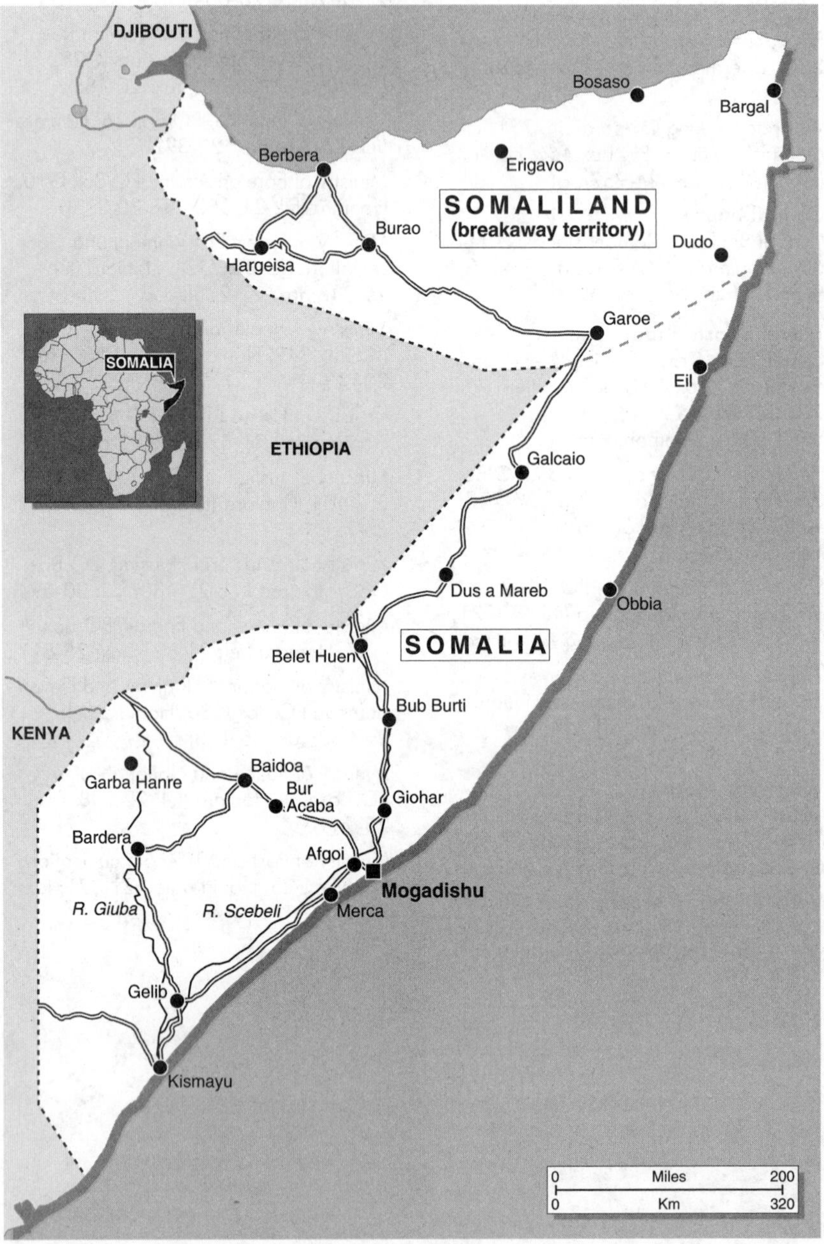

It's hard to keep up with who is in and who is out in politics in Somalia, and harder still to keep tabs on which clan or sub-clan the personal are members of, how they might relate to other clans and sub-clans, and what region they are from. Prime Minister Nur 'Adde' Hassan Hussein, for instance, is a member of the Abdgal sub-clan of the Hawiye clan, which is dominant in the capital, Mogadishu, as was his predecessor, Ali Mohamed Gedi. So the balance is the same. At the time of his appointment by President Abdullahi Yusuf Ahmed in

November 2007, he was described as 'a man who is not tainted by the civil and the Transitional Federal Government (TFG)'s political wars'. He has a reputation as a capable administrator and technocrat who had headed the Somali Red Crescent Society during a very difficult period in Somali history.

There is very little that can be said with any certainty about Somalia. When it became independent in 1961 it was with only two of the five parts of the Somali nation that had been split in colonial times. The two parts were the British and Italian Somalilands (ironically, the Italian bit in the north of Somalia is in the process of declaring its own independence from Somalia); the other three were the north-eastern area of Kenya (the Northern Frontier District as the British called it), the French territory of the Afars and Issas (now Djibouti) and the Ogaden region of Ethiopia.

In 1977 Somalia exported live animals, bananas and meat and meat products and under President Siad Barre there was a veneer of civilisation and visitors could go to the beach. By 2007, thirty years later, Somalia is known for its violence, its displaced people, its refugee camps, its floods, its droughts, its inability to come to any form of political settlement, and the pirates off its coast. The United Nations estimates that some 3.5 million people will need assistance at the end of 2008.

In June 2008, the 'latest' agreement to be signed, by Prime Minister Nur Adde and Sheikh Sharif Sheikh Ahmad, a senior Islamist leader, provided for the departure of Ethiopian troops within 120 days, a key component of any agreement. But then another top Islamist leader, Sheikh Hassan Dahir Aweys, rejected the UN-brokered agreement.

There are no reliable statistics on Somalia, they are all guesstimates. And depressing.

With a population of 11–12 million in 2006, and an income per capita estimated in 2002 to be US$122 (compared to US$515 in sub-Saharan Africa), the World Bank considers that Somalia is one of the poorest countries in the world. The United Nations Development Programme (UNDP)'s Human Development Index ranked Somalia 161 out of 163 countries in 2001. The civil conflict, continuing insecurity in many parts of the country, and poor access to services and infrastructure have made conditions worse than they were before the civil war. Developments in income poverty, education and health help demonstrate the deteriorated situation.

Poverty

Extreme poverty is estimated at 43 per cent, but is 10 percentage points higher for rural and nomadic populations. General poverty afflicts 73 per cent of households, but reaches 80 per cent in rural and nomadic populations. Income inequality is significant with the poorest 10 per cent of the population receiving only 1.5 per cent of total income. Households in the top 20 per cent of income distribution receive more than half of the total income.

There have been modest gains in education indicators in recent years, but all are still extremely low. Gross primary school enrolment of 22 per cent remains the lowest in the world. One in five Somalis is illiterate. Twice as many boys as girls attend primary and secondary school. Twice as many men as women are literate

Somalia's health indicators are also among the worst in Africa. Life expectancy is 47 years, and under-five and maternal mortality rates are a staggering 224 and 11 per 1,000 live births, respectively. A majority of the population (71 per cent) does not receive minimum dietary energy

Somalia has been without an effective central government since President Siad Barre was overthrown in 1991. Years of fighting between rival warlords and an inability to deal with famine and disease have led to the deaths of up to one million people.

A two-year United Nations' humanitarian effort primarily in the south was able to alleviate famine conditions, but having suffered significant casualties, the UN withdrew in 1995. Since then there has been very limited aid.

In the north, the self-proclaimed state of Somaliland and the region of Puntland run their own affairs. Somaliland, which is not recognised internationally, has enjoyed relative stability.

The economy

Agriculture used to be the most important sector, with livestock normally accounting for about 40 per cent of GDP and 65 per cent of export earnings. Livestock, hides, fish, charcoal and bananas were Somalia's principal exports; sugar, sorghum, corn and machined goods the principal imports. Somalia's small industrial sector, based on the processing of agricultural products, has largely been looted and sold as scrap metal.

Amazingly, and despite the seeming anarchy, Somalia's service sector has managed to survive and grow. Telecommunication firms provide wireless services in most major cities. In the absence of a formal banking sector, money exchange services have sprouted throughout the country, handling between US$500 million and one billion annually.

The ongoing civil disturbances and clan rivalries, however, have interfered with any broad-based economic development and international aid arrangements.

Donor support to Somalia has focused on humanitarian relief and development assistance. The World Bank has not had an active lending programme in Somalia since 1991 because of the political and financial crisis. The Bank has now signed a country re-engagement note under which it will help provide basic public goods, accelerate socio-economic recovery, and create an enabling environment for long-term institutional and policy change. In partnership with the UNDP, it will work to support macroeconomic data analysis and dialogue, create an enabling environment for the livestock and meat industry, prepare a plan to address

KEY INDICATORS — Somalia

	Unit	2003	2004	2005	2006	2007
Population	m	11.16	11.56	10.74	*9.50	*8.70
Gross domestic product (GDP)	US$bn	1.34	–	–	*2.39	–
GDP per capita	US$	120	0	*600	*283	0
GDP real growth	%	3.5	2.8	*2.4	–	–
Inflation	%	100.0	–	–	–	–
Exports (fob) (goods)	US$m	126.0	*241.0	–	–	–
Imports (cif) (goods)	US$m	343.0	*576.0	–	–	–
Balance of trade	US$m	-217.0	*-335.0	–	–	–
Foreign debt	US$bn	2.6	–	–	–	–
Exchange rate	per US$	2,620.00	–	1,375.00	–	–

* estimated figure

HIV/Aids issues and promote capacity building for skills development.

The Somaliland secessionists provide port facilities to land-locked Ethiopia and have established commercial ties with regional states. There is significant investment in commercial ventures, including airlines, telecommunications, hotels, fishery resources, and trade, partially funded by remittances from Somalis living and working abroad.

In September 2007, Transparency International ranked Somalia and Myanmar as the two most corrupt countries in the world.

Risk assessment

Politics	Poor
Economy	Poor
Reginal stability	Fair

COUNTRY PROFILE

Historical profile

Somalia was part of the Arab-controlled Indian Ocean trading network until the early sixteenth century. As external Arab influence waned prominent clans rose and assumed control of their regions. The country was divided into protectorates established by the British and Italians. In the nineteenth century much of the Ogaden Desert – ethnically part of Somalia – was annexed by the Ethiopian empire of Menelik I; the area has remained part of Ethiopia ever since.

1900 Somalia was controlled by the British in the north (British Somaliland Protectorate), and Italy in the south (Italian Somaliland).

1950–60 Italian Somaliland was a UN Trust Territory, under Italian administration.

1960 The northern and southern regions were united when granted independence from the UK and Italy. Aden Abdullah Osman Daar was elected president.

1967 Abdi Rashid Ali Shermarke won the presidential election.

1969 President Shermarke was assassinated in a coup d'état and the military leader, Mohammed Siad Barre, became president. The country was renamed the Somali Democratic Republic, political parties were banned and the National Assembly dissolved.

1970 Barre declared Somalia a socialist and one-party state under the Somali Revolutionary Socialist Party.

1974–75 A major drought effected thousands and caused widespread starvation.

1977 Ethnic Somalis in the Ogaden rebelled against Ethiopian control and war began when Somali troops invaded the territory.

1978 Abdullahi Yusuf Ahmed led a failed military coup against Barre.

1980s There were devastating droughts which caused widespread starvation throughout most of the decade.

1981 The president appointed members of his own Marehan clan to government posts, at the expense of other, Mijertyn and Isaq, clans.

1982 Disaffected clans, with Ethiopian military support, attacked government positions. Although the government repulsed the rebels, clashes continued throughout the 1980s.

1988 A peace agreement with Ethiopia ended the Ogaden war but civil tensions increased.

1989 As the security situation worsened, Barre offered to resign and hold free elections in 1990.

1991 President Barre fled after rebels entered Mogadishu and the state of Somalia collapsed. Numerous international efforts were made to resolve the situation but effective central government was lacking for almost a decade. War-lords controlled territories through violence and clan allegiances as civil society degenerate into fiefdoms of factional fighting. The self-styled Somaliland Republic (in the north), headed by Mohammed Ibrahim Egal, broke away from war-torn Somalia.

1992 After a period of intense conflict between the numerous clans, the US sent a force to protect the UN humanitarian aid effort and help restore order.

1993 The Addis Ababa Accords were signed. The UN began peace-keeping operations, taking over from US Marines. US Task Force Rangers launched a military offensive (later known as the Battle of Mogadishu) against General Aideed and the Somali National Alliance (SNA). Eighteen US troops, and up to 1,000 Somalis, were killed.

1994 The US withdrew all of its forces from Somalia.

1995 The remainder of the UN peacekeeping force withdrew.

1996 General Aideed died from gunshot wounds. His son, Hussein Aideed, replaced him as head of the clan-based gang.

1997 Twenty-six of Somalia's 28 factions signed the Cairo Declaration peace accord.

1998 The leaders of the north-eastern region of Puntland, including Abdullahi Yusuf Ahmed, declared the region autonomous.

1999 Inter-clan violence continued in central and southern Somalia. President Guelleh of Djibouti announced an international peace plan based on the participation of Islamic and civil groups rather than warlords.

2000 A four-month reconciliation conference in Djibouti ended when the transitional national government (TNG) elected a civilian as the country's first president since 1990 – Abd al Qasim Salad Hassan. Hussein Aideed, and other war lords, in Somalia, and Abdullahi Yusuf, president of Puntland, opposed the TNG.

2001 Militia loyal to Aideed attacked TNG forces. Jama Ali Jama deposed Abdullahi Yusuf as president of Puntland but was later overthrown by Abdullahi Yusuf who recaptured the presidency, with the help of Ethiopian forces. The president of Somaliland, Muhammad Haji Ibrahim Egal, died and was succeeded by Dahir Riyale Kahin.

2002 A cease-fire was agreed between 21 warring factions and the TNG.

2003 Dahir Riyale Kahin of the ruling United People's Party (UDUB) (Somaliland), won presidential and parliamentary elections. A peace conference, the Somali National Reconciliation Conference, was set up in Kenya

2004 In January, at peace talks, warlords and politicians signed a deal to set up a new parliament; the Transitional National Assembly (TNA) was inaugurated and for security reasons continued to be held in Kenya. Abdullahi Yusuf, (president of Puntland), won the TNA presidential elections held on 10 October. Abdullahi appointed Mohammed Ali Ghedi as prime minister. On the 26 December the south-Asian tsunami hit the region of Puntland, resulting in hundreds of deaths.

2005 A cabinet was formed in January. Authority within the country was maintained by rival warlords who controlled various tribal lands. In December the UN Food and Agricultural Organisation (FAO) warned that the worst harvests in 10 years in southern Somalia meant that up to two million people would need food aid. Poor rains were the main cause, the FAO predicting that the harvest would be as low as 25 per cent of the average. This meant that livestock too were dying from a lack of food and water.

2006 In January, the president and Sharif Hassan Sheikh Adan, the speaker of the parliament, agreed to work together to restore central government. Fighting broke out between forces of the Islamic Courts Union (ICU), which had restored some order to parts of the capital through the use of Sharia (Islamic law), and warlord militias in March. By 6 June, the ICU had seized power in the capital and by August were in control of most of central and southern Somalia. Sheikh Hassan Dihir Aweys was appointed head of the ICU, which was renamed Midowga Maxkamadaha Islaamiga (Supreme Islamic Courts Council) (SICC). In July, a prominent cabinet minister was killed as he left a mosque in Baidoa and around 40 government ministers resigned their posts. On 7 August, the prime minister dismissed the cabinet and, after a fortnight, nominated a new one. Mogadishu's international airport and seaport were re-opened in August. The transitional government and the SICC opened peace talks in September, but they came to nothing and fighting resumed in December. Ethiopian ground and air forces entered Somalia in support of the transitional government. The SICC was routed and, on 28 December, the transitional government took control of Mogadishu.

2007 In September, Transparency International ranked Somalia and Myanmar as the two most corrupt countries in the world. Fighting in the capital erupted as factions supporting the president and prime minister clashed over interests in oil exploration contracts, coming to a head in October. On 17 October the head of the World Food Programme UN humanitarian agency was kidnapped by armed raiders who stormed the UN compound in Mogadishu. The main market in Mogadishu, which provided trade of essential goods for around 85 per cent of residents and traders throughout the country, was destroyed by fire on 3 October. The fire began following a clash between government troops and rebels fighting around the former defence ministry building. The UN reported that 400,000 people were displaced from Mogadishu between July–October. Mohammed Ali Ghedi resigned as prime minister on 29 October. President Abdullahi Yusuf Ahmed appointed Professor Salim Aliyow Ibirow as acting prime minister until 24 November when Nur 'Adde' Hassan Hussein was appointed. On 4 December President Yusuf was flown to Nairobi for treatment, believed to be for complications arising from a liver transplant 13 years ago. As a result Prime Minister Nur Adde represented the President in talks in Ethiopia with US secretary of state, Condeleezza Rice. The talks discussed replacing Ethiopian troops in Somalia with an AU peacekeeping force. In the meantime, five ministers resigned from the cabinet. On 16 December the prime minister, Nur Adde, announced that he would be replacing the 30-member cabinet with a much smaller cabinet.

2008 The UN Security Council extended the AU-led mission to Somalia by six months on 20 February, and again on 20 August. Also on 20 August representatives of the Transitional Federal Government (TFG) and the Alliance for the Re-liberation of Somalia (The Alliance) signed an agreement to cease hostilities, the result of several months of talks in Djibouti.

Political structure

The self-styled republics of Somaliland and Puntland have their own elected governments (but are unrecognised internationally). In April 2002, a new state was declared in south-western Somalia.

Constitution

The Somali National Reconciliation Conference, held in Mbagathi, Nairobi, Kenya, began on 27 June 2003. On 5 July 2003, the Leaders Committee agreed that Somalia should adopt a federal system of government, with selection of the MPs being carried out by the signatories (political leaders) to the Declaration of Cessation of Hostilities signed in Eldoret, Kenya, on 27 October 2002, and by certain politicians, who were officially invited. If the government fails to complete the process of federalism throughout Somalia within a period of two-and-a-half years, parliament should withdraw its vote of confidence, necessitating the formation of a new transitional government to complete the process of federalism within one year.

Form of state

Federal republic

The executive

The president is elected by parliament. The prime minister is appointed by the president.

National legislature

In August 2004, a 275-seat transitional parliament was inaugurated in Nairobi, Kenya. Parliament serves a four-year term.

Legal system

At independence in 1960, Somalia had four legal systems: English common law, Italian law, Islamic Sharia and Somali customary law. In 1973, the Siad Barre regime introduced a unified civil code. There is no national judicial system.

Last elections

10 October 2004 (presidential election by the Transitional National Assembly in Kenya)

Results: Presidential: Abdullahi Yusuf Ahmed won 189 votes (out of 275); Abdullahi Ahmed Addou won 79 votes.

Next elections

2008

Political parties

There are no formal political parties. Warlords and their supporters wield most of the power. Political organisation largely reflects membership of clans and sub-clans.

Ruling party

None

Population

8.70 million (2007)*

Last census: February 1987: 7,114,431

Population density: 15 inhabitants per square km. Urban population: 28 per cent (1995–2001).

Annual growth rate: 2.3 per cent 1994–2004 (WHO 2006)

Internally Displaced Persons (IDP)

375,000 (UNHCR 2004)

Ethnic make-up

Somali (85 per cent), Bantu, Arabs and others (15 per cent).

Religions

Islam is the state religion (majority Sunni Muslims) (98 per cent), Christian minority (2 per cent).

Education

The UN Children's Fund (Unicef) supports 352 primary schools in central and southern Somalia, out of 418 that are operational. Additionally, Unicef has rehabilitated 35 schools, trained 2,300 teachers and initiated a school improvement programme. Several non-government organisations have concentrated on adult literacy programmes and civic education. Private education has recently been re-established in Somali, although school fees are proving to be out of reach of the ordinary Somali family. Somaliland expatriates residing in the United Arab Emirates (UAE) have initiated efforts to raise funds for the Amoud University. The University, established in 1997 in Boroma, is essentially a community project. In June 2003, Somalia opened its first medical college, the Benadir University Medical College (BUMC), since 1991. BUMC will be funded by donations from Somali physicians and by tuition fees. The education sector received only 12 per cent funding in the Consolidated Appeals Process (CAP), 2003. About 40 per cent of all teachers are unqualified and many have not completed their primary school education.

Literacy rate: 17.1 per cent, adult rate: 35 per cent, adult rate for the urban population; 10 per cent for rural and nomadic populations (2003).

Female adult literacy is estimated to be 52 per cent of the male rate.

Compulsory years: Six to 14.

Enrolment rate: Primary school enrolment increased by 29 per cent in 2002, compared to 2001, and there were 30 per cent more teachers. In 2003, one out of six children received formal primary education. Female primary school enrolment was 53 per cent of the male rate.

Health

The country's health services collapsed during the war and access to healthcare depends mostly on external assistance. Unicef remains the key provider of essential medical services and supplies to 123 maternal and child health centres, 174 health posts, and 16 hospitals.

Surveys in areas with high concentrations of displaced families show malnutrition rates as high as 40 per cent. Only 1.5 per

cent of one to two years old are vaccinated. In addition, Somalia has the highest incidence of tuberculosis in the world, while cholera is endemic in most areas. In March 2004, Somalia was removed from the UN list of countries with endemic polio, as no new cases had been reported in two years.
It is estimated that 31 per cent of the population have access to improved water facilities.
In 2003, 50 per cent of the urban population and 15 per cent of the rural population had access to health services.
There were cases of polio reported to the World Health Organisation – Global Polio Eradication Initiative (WHO – Polio Eradication) in 2006; the country had previously been free of the disease and its re-emergence was due to infected travellers. In a synchronised campaign with Ethiopia and Kenya, inoculation began for under fives by WHO – Polio Eradication and the country's health authorities in September 2006.
Life expectancy: 44 years, 2004 (WHO 2006)
Fertility rate/Maternal mortality rate: 6.3 births per woman, 2004 (WHO 2006)
Birth rate/Death rate: 46.4 births per 1,000 population; 17.6 deaths per 1,000 population (2003).
Child (under 5 years) mortality rate (per 1,000): 133 per 1,000 live births (World Bank)

Welfare
Insecurity continues to be the greatest threat to the lives and welfare of the population, who are highly dependent on external assistance. International aid is jeopardised by widespread factional fighting, the kidnapping of aid workers and also by the mining of all major roads in Northern Gedo, the area most in need of food aid. An estimated 400,000 Somalis are internally displaced.
Although the World Food Programme (WFP) supports the repatriation of refugees with a nine-month food supply or cash equivalent, more than 10 per cent of the population require emergency food assistance. In May 2003, the WFP distributed 1,355 tonnes of food around Somalia.

Main cities
Somalia: Mogadishu (capital, estimated population 1.2 million in 2004), Kismayu (209,300), Merca (179,700).
Somaliland: Hargeisa (241,200), Berbera (222,700), Burao (55,900), Erigavo (19,100).
Puntland: Bosaso (33,200), Garowe (22,800), Galkayo (20,100), Lasanod (16,000).

Languages spoken
Somali is one of the major languages of Africa and belongs to a set of languages called lowland Eastern Cushitic. It did not have a written form until the Latin script was adopted in 1972. Arabic, Italian and English (mainly for business) are also in use.
Arabic and English are to be the second official languages of the Transitional Federal Government of Somalia, as agreed on 5 July 2003 at the Somali National Reconciliation Conference.

Official language/s
Somali

Media
Press
Dailies: In Somalia, newspapers include Xog-Ogaal Qaran News (www.qarannews.com), Codka xoriyadda and Ayaamaha.
Dhambaal News (www.dhambaalnews.com) and Jamhuuriya (www.jamhuuriya.info) are based in Somaliland. In English, Somaliland Times (www.somalilandtimes.net) and the Awdal New Network (www.awdalnews.com) gives online news from Somaliland.
There are a number of internet news outlets aimed at the Somali diaspora including www.luuliyo.com, www.waagacusub.com, www.hiiraan.com, www.hormoodnews.com and www.banadir.com (with articles in English).
Weeklies: Publications include Dadka, Panorama, Republican (Hargeisa), Sanca and Xurmo.
Periodicals: Monthly publications include Ayaamaha and Himilo.

Broadcasting
Radio: In June 2007 the government ordered the closure of the three main radio stations in the capital (Shabelle Media Network, Horn Afrik and IQK). The order was rescinded four days later, reportedly after pressure from the US ambassador to Kenya.
The governments in the breakaway provinces of Somaliland and Puntland maintain a tight control on broadcasting in their areas. The Transitional Federal Government closed the Shabelle Media Network, Banadir Radio and Radio Simba on 12/13 November 2007, without explanation. The information minister said the stations had been 'carrying false reports and misrepresenting the activities of the security forces'. Critics claimed the government was closing down independent news outlets that did not report pro-government news.
There is no national, domestic broadcaster however the many independent radio stations provide the principal source of news for the population. Radio Magadishu is government-run with coverage limited to the capital. The FM stations Radio HornAfrk (www.hornafrik.com), Radio Shabelle (www.shabelle.net) and Radio Banaadir (www.radiobanadir.com) all broadcast in the capital. Radio Hargeisa (www.radiohargeysa.net) is Somaliland government-owned; the privately owned Radio Galkayo (www.radiogaalkacyo.com) and Voice of Peace broadcast in Puntland.
Television: Two private TV networks exist, Somali Telemedia Network (STN) and HornAfrk TV (www.hornafrik.com), broadcast international produced programmes. Somaliland National TV (SLNTV) is government-owned. Somali Broadcasting Corporation (SBC) is a private station in Puntland.

News agencies
There is no official agency but APA and Panapress report on Somali matters.

Economy
The state of Somalia is in suspended chaos and so is its economy. Without sustained peace and a working civil society the economy is all but defunct. Somalia is a failed state and while its GDP growth was 2.4 per cent in 2005, most of this is due to remittances from abroad. Somalia does not have an administration sufficiently in control to gather statistics for even superficial analyses. Wealth in the country is judged by ownership of livestock and land, one can only infer that trade is through barter of essential and subsistence items. The government of Somalia was resident in Kenya for several years before being forced to return and defend its legitimacy and sovereignty, in the face of Islamist insurgents who captured over half the country in 2006. With backing from the Ethiopian Army it regained control but has been unable to re-invigorate the economy.
The situation is complicated by the break-away Republic of Somaliland, which has become an autonomous zone with its own currency and government. Another autonomous region, the Puntland State of Somalia, has its own chaotic economic policy.
Somaliland represents the strongest local economy and has undergone something of a boom since it declared independence in 1991. The autonomous region has undergone a modest transformation with infrastructural improvements and an emergent business elite. Without international recognition, however, Somaliland cannot access funds from the IMF or World Bank or develop trade relations.
The Puntland State, where many Somalis wish to remain part of Somalia, faces many of the problems faced by Somalia

proper, including factional fighting and almost complete economic collapse.
International economic agencies are reluctant to invest in the country until it can achieve a measure of peace and the rule of law. Even so, a Coca-Cola bottling plant opened in 2004, becoming the largest investment the country had received since 1991.
In 2004, the UN estimated that at least US$5 billion would be needed to rebuild Somalia. Before the civil war, in the early 1990s, Somalia was agrarian with few natural resources.

External trade

While Somalia belongs to the African, Caribbean and Pacific Group of States (ACP Group) which has a trade agreement with the European Union, it does not have a central government authority that can provide evidence of abidance of international and official regulations. Nevertheless, less formal trade is undertaken with regional neighbours, while remittances provide the majority of foreign earnings.
The continuing need for the large-scale import of fuels and food results in an ongoing poor balance of trade.
There is an illegal trade in qat (called jaad in Somalia, an additive, mild hallucinogen) from Ethiopia and Yemen.

Imports

Principal imports are manufactures, petroleum products, foodstuffs and construction materials.

Main sources: Djibouti (31.0 per cent total, 2006), India (8.2 per cent), Kenya (8.1 per cent).

Exports

Principal exports are livestock, bananas, hides, fish, charcoal and scrap metal.

Main destinations: UAE (49.8 per cent total, 2006), Yemen (21.5 per cent), Oman (6.0 per cent).

Agriculture

Farming

Agriculture is the most important sector in the economy. It contributes about 65 per cent to GDP and employs 65 per cent of the working population. It is often badly affected by drought, as well as by the chaos of recent years.
Livestock, particularly camels, is the principal foreign exchange earner, accounting for 40 per cent of GDP. Exports are mainly to Arabian Gulf states and formerly to Saudi Arabia. A Saudi ban on the import of allegedly diseased Somali livestock has damaged the trade.
Much of the land is desert or semi-desert and only 13 per cent is cultivated, making food security a constant concern. Some crops are grown on the fertile land in the Juba and Scebali valleys, but the farmers have been displaced by nomads.
Subsistence farmers grow maize and sorghum. Wheat and rice are imported.
The most important cash crops are bananas, cotton and frankincense.
In 2004, the total marine fish catch was 26,300 tonnes and the total crustacean catch was 450 tonnes.
In August 2006, the Supreme Islamic Courts Council (SICC) issued a directive to halt the production of charcoal. Somalia lost 1.2 million hectares, or 14 per cent of its forest cover between 1990–2005 and has had a serious detrimental effect on the environment. The principal export of charcoal is to Gulf states, where wood from mango trees is highly favoured and a bag of charcoal can cost as much as US$15 each.

Industry and manufacturing

The industrial sector is small, contributing about 5 per cent to GDP and employing 8 per cent of the working population.
The principal industries are meat and fish processing, sugar refining, fruit and vegetable canning, textiles and leather goods. Many factories are idle, because foreign exchange shortages have cut off foreign inputs.

Tourism

There are no tourism facilities.

Mining

There are significant mineral resources, but they have not yet been commercially exploited. The most important regions include an area extending from the Ethiopian border to beyond Berbera in Somaliland and west of the River Scebali near Mogadishu. The former contains reserves of copper, gold, molybdenum and bismuth, while the latter contains iron, gold and apatite.
The country also contains reserves of uranium, marble, manganese, tin, beryl and columbite. Salt and gypsum were extracted commercially before the civil war began.

Hydrocarbons

There are no proven oil reserves, but there are indications of oil and gas potential. Exploration was conducted by oil majors until 1991, when they withdrew after the outbreak of the civil war. The Republic of Somaliland has invited international companies with exploration rights within its self-declared territories to return, but despite some interest, international investors appear to be waiting until legal issues arising from the existence of pre-1991 contracts can be settled. In August 2005, the new government announced that it would welcome approaches by foreign firms to, but warned against concluding exploration contracts with local administrations, which would not be recognised.
Somalia relies on imports for its fuel needs.
Downstream, Somalia has a single oil refinery with a capacity of 10,000 barrels per day (bpd), although it has not been in use for some years and is probably in a state of disrepair.
Somalia has one natural gas field with reserves of around 7 billion cubic metres, although political and economic chaos have prevented exploitation. Currently, there are no production or imports of natural gas.
Somalia does not produce or import coal.

Energy

Electricity generation amounts to under 100MW and is fuelled by diesel, which has to be imported. A monopoly of electricity generation and supply is owned by the Ente Nazionale Energia Elettrica (ENEE).

Financial markets

Stock exchange

the Nairobi Stock Exchange was formed in 1954. It became fully automated in December 2007. The NSE 20 share index is expected to be joined by an all-share index in 2008.

Banking and insurance

The first commercial bank to be established since 1990, the Universal Bank of Somalia (UBSOM), was launched on 22 January 2002. The bank is 51 per cent owned by Somalis and 49 per cent by overseas investors. UBSOM has links with 62 overseas banks in 72 countries.

Central bank

Central Bank of Somalia

Main financial centre

Mogadishu

Time

GMT plus three hours

Geography

Somalia lies on the east coast of Africa, with Ethiopia to the north-west and Kenya to the west. There is a short frontier with Djibouti in the north-east. Somalia has a long coastline of 3,200km on the Indian Ocean and the Gulf of Aden, forming the Horn of Africa.
The country is shaped like the number 7 with the northern top stretching west along the coast of the Gulf of Aden. Here the land is a desert plain that rises to the Ogo and Migiurtinia mountains fringing the coastline, – of which the highest peak is Surud Ad at 2,408 metres (m). Southwards, the land becomes more fertile savannah which eventually runs into an arid and extensive region of sand dunes and rugged plateau. There are few rivers, the largest are in the central and southern regions, the Webi Guiba and Webi Scebeli rise in Ethiopia and flow into the Indian

Ocean. The north has no permanently flowing rivers, the Daror and the Nugaaleed are intermittent streams.

Hemisphere

Northern

Climate

Tropical. Humid on coast, drier in north. Average temperatures 27–32 degrees Celsius (C) throughout year, but can reach 42 degrees C on coast. Dry seasons from January–February and August–September. Rainy seasons from March–June and October–December.

Dress codes

Lightweight clothes are required. Women should dress modestly.

Entry requirements

Passports

Required by all.

Visa

The civil war has disrupted consular services worldwide. Visas are required by the break-away territories of Somiland and Puntland and can be obtained at the port of entry. Travellers should contact their own ministry of foreign affairs for advice about local conditions and travelling to Somalia and breakaway provinces.

Currency advice/regulations

Import/export of only small amounts of local currency is allowed. Import of foreign currency is unlimited, but it must be declared on a form for which a small charge may be made. Currency transactions should be recorded at each exchange. Export of foreign currency is limited to the amount declared on arrival.

The Somali shilling is the unit of currency, except in Somaliland, which uses the Somaliland shilling. US dollars are accepted everywhere.

Health (for visitors)

Mandatory precautions

Yellow fever and cholera certificates if arriving from an infected area.

Advisable precautions

Hepatitis A and E are widespread and hepatitis B is hyper-endemic. Vacinations for meningococcal meningitis, yellow fever, cholera, typhoid and polio vaccinations are advisable. Malaria prophylaxis should be taken as risk exists throughout the country (two types of prophylaxis are recommended); anti-mosquito measures include mosquito repellents, nets and clothing covering the body, these offer protection against hepatitis B. Tap water must be treated as unsafe unless boiled and filtered. Eat only well cooked meals, preferably served hot; vegetables should be cooked and fruit peeled. Dairy products are unpasteurised and should be avoided.

A comprehensive medical pack and all medication is essential for the traveller as there is little to be found in the country. Medical insurance is essential, including emergency evacuation.

Credit cards

Credit cards are not accepted in Somalia.

Public holidays (national)

Fixed dates

1 Jan (New Year's Day), 1 May (Labour Day), 26 Jun (Independence Day), 1 Jul (Foundation Day).

Variable dates

Eid al Adha, Ashura, Birth of the Prophet, Eid al Fitr (three days).

Islamic year – 1429 (10 Jan 2008–28 Dec 2008): The Islamic year contains 354 or 355 days, with the result that Muslim feasts advance by 10–12 days against the Gregorian calendar. Dates of feasts vary according to the sighting of the new moon, so cannot be forecast exactly.

Working hours

Banking

Sat–Thu: 0800–1130.

Business

Sat–Thu: 0800–1230, 1630–1900.

Government

Sat–Thu: 0800–1400.

Shops

Sat–Thu: 0900–1300, 1600–2000.

Telecommunications

Mobile/cell phones

There are several GSM 900 and 900/1800 services available.

Electricity supply

220V AC, 50 cycles. The electricity system is poor.

Social customs/useful tips

Islamic customs should be respected. It is the convention to use the right hand when shaking hands and passing or receiving anything. Muslims are not permitted to drink alcohol or eat pork. Do not smoke or drink in public during Ramadan. Refusal of offered refreshment is considered discourteous. Shoes should be removed on entry to mosques.

Khat was banned by the Islamists in November 2006. It is a stimulant and commonly chewed by men, inducing a state of calm and sometimes causing aggressive behavior. It is grown in much of the Horn of Africa, including Kenya, and exported to Yemen.

Security

Any visit to Somalia should be undertaken only after a risk assessment has been carefully weighed; terrorism is a constant threat. Armed robbery and kidnapping by numerous bands of militia is endemic. Hargeisa, capital of the self-declared Republic of Somaliland is the only place that may offer a relatively secure environment in the country. Foreign nationals should register their presence with their respective diplomatic representatives.

Getting there

Air

National airline: Damal Airlines (based in the UAE) operates scheduled regional flights from eight airports in Somalia.

International airport/s: Mogadishu International (MGQ), 6.4km from city. This airport was re-opened on 15 July 2006.

Surface

Road: There are road links with Kenya in the south and Djibouti in the north. Four-wheel drive vehicles are recommended.

Main port/s: El Ma'an, Bassasso, Kismayu, Merca, Mogadishu.

Berbera is the economic lifeline for the self-declared Somaliland Republic.

Getting about

National transport

Air: Damal Airlines flies to nine towns throughout the country, including Mogadishu.

Road: Travel may be restricted and local enquiries should be made. There were good roads from Mogadishu to Kismayu (via Merca) and Baidoa in the southern part of the country, and to Hargeisa and Berbera in the north. However, since the civil strife began conditions have deteriorated. Most other routes are mainly tracks and gravel roads. Driving is on the right.

Water: Coastal shipping of both freight and passengers is extensive. The number of incidents of piracy off the Somali coast has increased sharply in the last few years.

City transport

Taxis: Fares are by negotiation and tipping is not usual. Taxis can be hired on a time basis.

Car hire

Car hire is available in Mogadishu although foreign visitor should avoid driving alone until the politicial situation in Somalia improves.

There are no traffic lights in the country except in Hargeisa in Somaliland. The condition of the roads makes driving difficult and night driving is dangerous due to the absence of lighting.

BUSINESS DIRECTORY

The addresses listed below are a selection only. While World of Information makes every endeavour to check these addresses, we cannot guarantee that changes have not been made, especially to telephone numbers and area codes. We would welcome any corrections.

Telephone area codes

It is unlikely that all landlines quoted are working.

The international direct dialling (IDD) code for Somalia is +252, followed by area code and subscriber's number: Mogadishu1Hargeisa2

Chambers of Commerce
Somalia Chamber of Commerce, Industry and Agriculture, PO Box 27, Via Asha, Mogadishu (tel: 281-866).

Somaliland Chamber of Commerce, Hargeisa (tel: 523-143; email: hargcham@yahoo.com; internet: www.somalilandchamberofcommerce.co m).

Banking
Commercial and Savings Bank of Somalia, PO Box 203, Juley Street 1st, Mogadishu (tel: 22-861, 22-959).

Central bank
Central Bank of Somalia, PO Box 11, Corso Somalia 55, Mogadishu, Somalia (tel: 215-241).

Travel information
Daallo Airlines, # 30 Street, Baraka Market, Mogadishu (tel: 215-301; fax: 216-248; email: daallo@globalsom.com; internet: www.daallo.com).

Damalair, PO Box 27449, Dubai UAE (tel :+ (+971-4) 271-5005; fax: (+971-4) 272-0890; email: airdamal@emirates.net.ae; internet: www.damalair.co.ae).

Somali Airlines (operations suspended), PO Box 726, Via Medina, Mogadishu.

Other useful addresses
Agricultural Development Corporation, PO Box 930, Mogadishu.

Livestock Development Agency of Somalia, PO Box 1759, Mogadishu.

National Petroleum Agency of Somalia, PO Box 573, Mogadishu.

Somali Broadcasting Service, Ministry of Information and National Guidance, Private Bag, Mogadishu (tel: 2455).

Statistical Department, PO Box 1742, Mogadishu (tel: 80-385).

Internet sites
Africa Business Network: www.ifc.org/abn

African Development Bank: www.afdb.org

Africa Online: www.africaonline.com

AllAfrica.com: http://allafrica.com

Puntland State of Somalia: http://members.tripod.com/~Puntland/

Somalia News: www.somalianews.com

Somaliland official website: www.somalilandgov.com

United Nations Somalia: www.unsomalia.org

Wakiil Business Centre: www.wakiil.com

South Africa

KEY FACTS

Official name: Republic of South Africa

Head of State: President Thabo Mbeki (ANC) (since 1999; re-elected Apr 2004)

Head of government: President Thabo Mbeki

Ruling party: African National Congress (ANC) (since 1994; re-elected Apr 2004)

Area: 1,127,200 square km

Population: 47.85 million (2007)

Capital: Cape Town (legislative); Johannesburg (financial); Tshwane (changed from Pretoria in July 2007) (administrative); Bloemfontein (judicial)

Official language: Afrikaans, English, Ndebele, Sesotho, Northern Sotho, SiSwati, Tsonga, Tswana, Venda, Xhosa, Zulu.

Currency: Rand (R) = 100 cents

Exchange rate: R7.55 per US$ (Jul 2008)

GDP per capita: US$5,906 (2007)

GDP real growth: 5.10% (2007)

Labour force: 19.14 million (2004)

Unemployment: 24.20% (2007)*

Inflation: 7.10% (2007)

Balance of trade: US$3.93 billion (2006)

Foreign debt: US$28.50 billion (2004)

Visitor numbers: 8.40 million (2006)*

* estimated figure

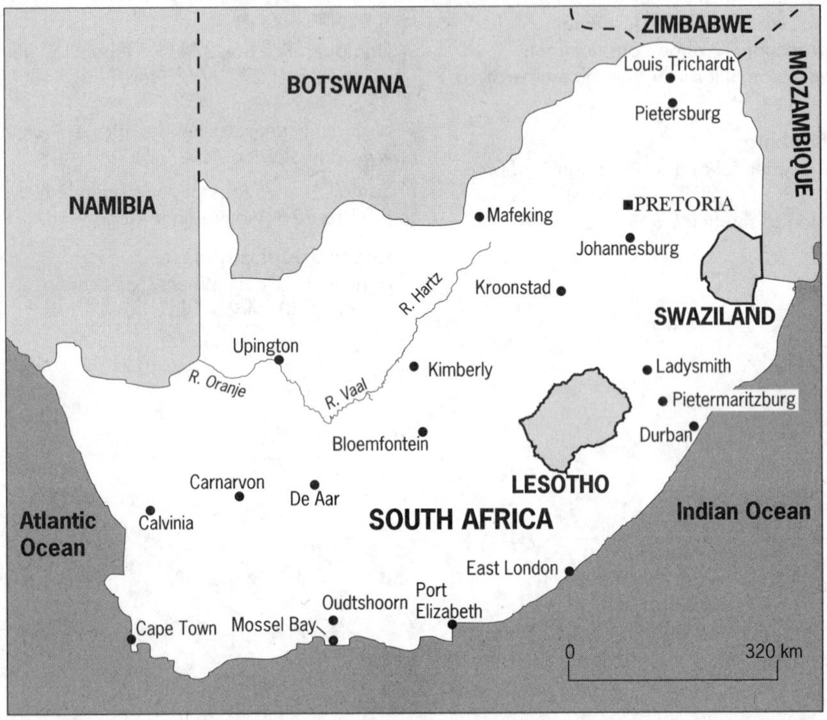

When Jakob Zuma was elected leader of the African Nation Congress (ANC) on 18 December 2007, the writing was on the wall for President Thabo Mbeki. Zuma had been dismissed as deputy president by Mbeki in 2005, on charges of fraud and corruption, and had been accused of rape. He is however, supported by the Youth League of the ANC and the party's left wing, as well as the trade union movement.

South Africa is the major economic driving force within the 14-nation southern African region. It absorbs a substantial share of their exports through the Southern African Customs Union (Sacu) – a long standing association of South Africa, Botswana, Namibia, Swaziland, and Lesotho.

Operations of South African companies are to be found not only in the southern African countries, but also in Zambia, Tanzania, Nigeria, Ghana, Mozambique and further north. The stock of South Africa's foreign direct investment (FDI) in the rest of Africa is around 10 per cent of its total stock up from 5 per cent in 2000. The peg of the currencies of Lesotho, Namibia and Swaziland to the rand within the Common Monetary Area contributes to the maintenance of low inflation across the region.

Unemployment still high

South Africa's economic fundamentals seem broadly under control. Gross domestic product (GDP) growth has not dipped below 3.0 per cent since 2002, reaching 5.4 per cent in 2006 and 5.1 per cent in 2007. Inflation, which peaked at 9.2 per cent in 2002, was 4.7 per cent in 2006, but back up to 7.1 per cent in 2007. The economy has registered its highest growth in 21 years, and this bodes well for achieving the government's objective of 4.5 per cent average annual growth over the next few years and its 6 per cent growth target by 2010.

With GDP per capita of US$5,906, South Africa is one of the few African countries to have joined the group of upper middle income countries. Its economy is larger than that of Malaysia, and is by far the largest in sub-Saharan Africa – about 40 per cent of total sub-Saharan African GDP – exerting major influence on total output, trade, and investment flows of the African continent. It dominates the southern African region, where it plays a vital role in the regional economic institutions, such as Sacu and the Southern African Development Community (SADC), and continental fora such as the New Partnership for Africa's Development (Nepad).

Services now account for most of South Africa's economy, surpassing the abundant mineral and energy resources that formed the core of the country's economic activity. Much of manufacturing is based on mining, and platinum has overtaken gold and diamond exports. In the post-apartheid era the government has focused on controlling the deficit while striving to step up spending on social programmes to combat inequality. The Central Bank has used tight macroeconomic policies to control inflation.

Despite the size of the economy and recent improvements in growth, South Africa continues to face major social challenges of widespread unemployment, poverty, and the continuing high prevalence of HIV/Aids. Unemployment remains very high – 26 per cent according to the narrow definition, 37 per cent according to the broad definition, including discouraged workers. South Africa's income aggregates hide extreme differences in incomes and wealth between the white and non-white populations. Thirteen per cent of the population lives in 'first world' conditions, while at the other extreme, about 22 million people live in developing country conditions. In this latter group only one-quarter of households have access to electricity and running water; only half have a primary school education; and over a third of the children suffer from chronic malnutrition.

The International Monetary Fund (IMF) says the main short-term risks arise from the possibility of deterioration in the external environment. A pronounced slowdown in global growth would reduce demand for South African exports, erode consumer and business confidence and dampen growth. Also, a weakening of global appetite for emerging market assets could put downward pressure on the rand with a potential adverse impact on growth.

On the monetary policy stance, some upside risks to the inflation outlook may be emerging. The prediction is for a period of increasing inflation with the inflation rate rising above five per cent before slowing down gradually.

Despite concerns over the appreciation of the rand, South Africa's flexible exchange rate has continued to serve the country well. The government plans to continue with the policy of building up international reserves when market conditions are favourable but otherwise not intervening in the foreign exchange market.

South Africa's share of world export markets has remained broadly constant since the mid- to late-1990s, but exports have declined in volume. Metals and commodities have benefited from higher world prices; manufacturing has performed more modestly and textiles very poorly. Indicators as to areas the government should look at point to the cost of investing and doing business in South Africa, education standards, availability of skilled labour, and the quality of infrastructure.

Privatisation

State-owned enterprises (SoEs) continue to play a significant role in the economy, and the authorities see them as a key vehicle for strengthening infrastructure and public service delivery. Privatisation does not at the moment seem a popular option. They account for 1.2 per cent of total employment, with combined assets the equivalent of 12.8 per cent of GDP and a turnover of 6.1 per cent of GDP. The major entities are Eskom (energy), Transnet (transportation), and Denel (defence). Over the next few years they and other SoEs will be major players in the further development of electricity, ports, the railways, roads and water resources. South Africa has de-emphasised the role of privatisation as a way of enhancing efficiency and will instead focus on the operational restructuring of the large SoEs, together with the sale of their non-core assets.

Significant progress has been made with broad based Black Economic Empowerment (BEE). This initiative uses several tools to achieve empowerment of the black population, including voluntary sector-specific 'charters' that set targets for a range of empowerment indicators, including percentage of black ownership, black participation in management, and skills development. Several sectors, significantly the mining industry, have made significant progress. Progress on land reform remains mixed. Against a target of 30 per cent of agricultural land under black ownership by 2015, to date only four per cent has been achieved. The programme includes land restitution (return of land lost due to racially discriminatory laws) and land redistribution (purchase of land by black individuals facilitated by government grants and loans).

Politics

After the British seized the Cape of Good Hope area in 1806, many of the Dutch settlers (Boers) trekked north to found their

KEY INDICATORS — South Africa

	Unit	2003	2004	2005	2006	2007
Population	m	46.09	44.56	46.89	47.48	47.85
Gross domestic product (GDP)	US$bn	165.60	214.70	241.93	257.28	282.63
GDP per capita	US$	3,624	4,500	5,160	5,418	5,906
GDP real growth	%	2.6	3.7	5.1	5.4	5.1
Inflation	%	5.8	1.4	3.4	4.7	7.1
Unemployment	%	31.0	26.2	26.0	25.6	24.3
Industrial output	% change	–	4.5	4.9	4.3	–
Agricultural output	% change	–	-1.7	4.9	-13.1	–
Coal output	mtoe	134.6	136.9	138.9	144,800.0	97.7
Exports (fob) (goods)	US$m	32,179.0	48,430.0	54,581.0	75,171.0	76,184.0
Imports (cif) (goods)	US$m	26,021.0	48,545.0	56,459.0	71,243.0	81,890.0
Balance of trade	US$m	6,158.0	115.0	-1,878.0	3,928.0	-5,705.0
Current account	US$m	-1,490.0	-5,330.0	-9,177.0	-16,602.0	-20,556.0
Total reserves minus gold	US$m	6,496.0	13,141.0	18,579.0	23,057.0	29,589.0
Foreign exchange	US$m	6,164.0	12,794.0	18,260.0	22,720.0	29,234.0
Exchange rate	per US$	7.56	6.45	7.23	7.04	6.83

own republics. The discovery of diamonds (1867) and gold (1886) spurred wealth and immigration and intensified the subjugation of the native inhabitants. The Boers resisted British encroachments, and were militarily defeated although their culture persists to this day. The resulting Union of South Africa operated under a policy of apartheid – the segregated development of the races. The 1990s brought an official end to racial segregation and separate development although it had already changed out of all recognition, and ushered in black majority rule.

The apartheid government eventually negotiated itself out of power, and the new leadership under Nelson Mandela, who worked in a limestone quarry while he served 26 years on Robben Island, South Africa's high security political jail, for his part in the struggle for independence, encouraged reconciliation, himself welcoming even his former jailers to his home. Now, diversity is a key feature of South Africa, where, as the British Broadcasting Corporation (BBC) reported, community leaders include rabbis and chieftains, rugby players and returned exiles, where traditional healers ply their trade around the corner from stockbrokers and where housing ranges from mud huts to palatial homes with swimming pools.

Thabo Mbeki was re-elected to a second 5-year term as president following elections in April 2004. The government is dominated by the African National Congress (ANC) which won 70 per cent of the votes (279 seats) in theparliamentary elections. His term ends in 2009.

He had taken over as president when Nelson Mandela stepped down in mid-1999. He was born in 1942 into one of the leading families active in black politics. Mbeki's father was a leading thinker in the South African Communist Party. He has said that he will not stand again in the elections due in 2009. Mbeki played a central role both in planning the armed insurrection that caused the first cracks in white rule and the talks that led to its end. He has mediated in African conflicts, including those in Côte d'Ivoire, Burundi and Democratic Republic of Congo.

Zimbabwe

But his trickiest mediation has been that of Zimbabwe and the intransigent Mr Mugabe. Criticised internationally for his 'quiet' diplomacy, and eventually in South Africa itself, it was not until mid-2008 that he was finally able to persuade Mr Mugabe to negotiate rather than dictate. Mugabe and his Zanu-PF ruling party lost the June 2008 elections, although Mugabe himself won the second round of the presidential election when his opponent, Morgan Tsvangirai, withdrew. In a last ditch bid, Mbeki pretty much took up residence in Harare, the capital of Zimbabwe, in mid-September, and on 11 September an historic power sharing deal was signed and Mr Mugabe and Mr Tsvangirai shook hands. The devil will be in the detail of the agreement, but Mr Mbeki could now go home.

Risk assessment

Politics	Good
Economy	Good
Regional stability	Good

COUNTRY PROFILE

Historical profile

The sudden, in political terms, change from white, minority ruled South Africa to black, majority ruled South Africa that happened in the early 1990s astonished and delighted the international community. The world had watched as Nelson Mandela walked to freedom on 11 February 1990; it watched again as long, snaking lines of South Africans patiently queued to vote in their first ever free election in April 1994, and it cheered when Nelson Mandela became president of sub-Saharan Africa's most developed nation on 10 May 1994. The anti-apartheid campaign had been one of the most successful campaigns ever – the economic sanctions, the boycott of wine and oranges, the sport's boycott (which perhaps hurt the white South Africans most of all), the 'Free Mandela' t-shirts, marches in London's Trafalgar Square, isolation at the United Nations, all contributed.

When F W de Klerk became prime minister in 1989, just three weeks before the September elections (in which the Nationalist Party (NP) lost 30 seats), few would have predicted that in five years there would be black majority rule. De Klerk pushed for 'talks about talks' between his ruling NP and Nelson Mandela's African National Congress (ANC); de Klerk wanted sanctions lifted immediately, Mandela wanted them kept in place until the ANC were certain change in South Africa had become irreversible. Whatever the differencies then, the road to a negotiated settlement had begun.

The change of presidents from Nelson Mandela to Thabo Mbeki in June 1999 served to convince South Africans that they had made it as a democratic nation.

1652 The Dutch East India Company set up a supply station which became Cape Town, supplying sailing ships to and from the Dutch East Indies (Indonesia).

1795 Britain took control of the Cape.

1806 The Cape Colony became British and settlement began in 1820.

1835 Mass treks by Afrikaners (Boers) moved inland, fighting the Ndebele and Zulus.

1899–1902 After many battles, the Boer War was eventually won by the British. With the signing of the Treaty of Vereeniging on 31 May 1902, all Boers became British subjects.

1910 The Union of South Africa was established from the former British colonies of Cape and Natal and the Boer republics of Transvaal and Orange Free State. South Africa became a self-governing dominion led by former Boer generals.

1912 The Native National Congress, the precursor to the African National Congress (ANC), was founded.

1913 The Land Act was introduced to prevent blacks, except those in Cape province, from buying land outside reserves.

1914 The National Party was founded.

1919 South West Africa (Namibia), formerly a German colony, came under South African administration.

1948 Apartheid (separateness) laws excluding non-whites from political and economic influence were applied by successive National Party governments.

1950 The population was classified by race. The Group Areas Act was passed to segregate blacks and whites. The South African Communist Party (SACP) was banned. The ANC responded with a campaign of civil disobedience led by Nelson Mandela.

1960 Apartheid laws were brutally enforced; the most notorious incident was the Sharpeville massacre. The ANC became the main black political organisation opposing the government and consequently was banned.

1961 South Africa was declared a republic and left the Commonwealth. Mandela launched the ANC's military wing which began a campaign of disruption and sabotage.

1964 Nelson Mandela, leader of the ANC, was jailed for life. The UN imposed sanctions against South Africa.

1976 More than 600 people were killed in the Soweto uprising.

1983 An interim constitution established power-sharing of three population groups (whites, Asians and mixed race (coloured)), effectively excluding participation of blacks.

1989 P W Botha (prime minister from 1978–83 and president from 1983–89) was replaced by F W de Klerk; he began a reform programme that started the dismantling of apartheid.

1990 Nelson Mandela was released from prison. The ban on the ANC was lifted. Namibia was granted independent.

1991 The last apartheid laws were repealed. Fighting broke out between the ANC and the Zulu Inkatha movement.
1993 A non-racial constitution was formulated through a multi-racial negotiating forum. A transitional Government of National Unity (GNU) was established replacing the three-chamber, racially-based parliament. On 24 April, Oliver Tambo, long-time anti-apartheid campaigner and former leader of the ANC died.
1994 In the first non-racial, fully democratic elections, the ANC won a majority of seats in parliament and Nelson Mandela became president. South Africa successfully reapplied for Commonwealth membership and took up its seat in the UN General Assembly for the first time in 20 years.
1996 The new constitution was adopted. A Truth and Reconciliation Commission (TRC) was set up. Those that perpetrated and suffered human rights abuse were allowed to record their experiences for mutual recognition.
1998 The TRC branded apartheid a crime against humanity and held the ANC accountable for numerous human rights abuses. South Africa intervened militarily in Lesotho to prevent civil war breaking out in the kingdom.
1999 Thabo Mbeki was elected president by the National Assembly. The ANC increased its share of the election vote and formed a coalition government with the mainly Zulu Inkatha Freedom Party (IFP).
2000 Despite President Mbeki's controversial views on Aids, South Africa played host to the 13th World Aids Conference in July. The Democratic Party, the New National Party (NNP) and the Federal Alliance merged to form the Democratic Alliance (DA), which won a quarter of the vote in local elections.
2001 It was proposed that the name of Pretoria be changed to the City of Tshwane and the Port Elizabeth to the Nelson Mandela Metropolitan Municipality. Legal action against the South African government by 39 multi-national pharmaceutical companies over the production of generic Aids drugs was dropped. This enabled South Africa, and many other poor countries, to import cheaper drugs to combat the epidemic. The DA collapsed after the NNP pulled out of the coalition. The government was cleared of unlawful conduct over allegations of corruption in arms deal with European firms. The High Court ruled that pregnant women must be given anti-retroviral drugs to prevent HIV transmission to their infants.
2002 The name of Northern Province was changed to Limpopo Province. The Organisation of African Unity (OAU) became the African Union (AU) with President Mbeki as the first chairman. Right-wing extremists were accused of bombing atrocities in Soweto; 17 were arrested.
2003 Walter Sisulu, a key veteran figure in the anti-apartheid struggle, died.
2004 The ruling ANC won a landslide victory in the general elections. On 23 April, Thabo Mbeki was elected unopposed for a second term as president. Black economic empowerment (BEE) legislation was enacted; its objective was to address economic inequalities such as the imbalance in ethnic ownership and lack of black opportunity and aspirations, caused during the decades of apartheid. Within ten years the government expects increased ownership and control of enterprises and assets by black people and black personnel in senior positions, and an increase in training and investment in black development. The legislation is binding on all public companies and government entities.
2005 On 14 June, Mbeki dismissed his deputy, Jacob Zuma, who was charged with corruption. Phumzile Mlambo-Ngcuka was named as his successor on 21 June. In December, a charge of rape was brought against Zuma.
2006 Zuma was aquitted of rape charges in May and reinstated as ANC deputy president. In September, the corruption charges against him were dismissed. In October, Johannesburg International Airport's name was changed to OR Tambo International Airport.
2007 Jacob Zuma was elected leader of the ANC on 18 December, replacing Tharbo Mbeki.
2008 The High Court ruled that Chinese South Africans would be re-classified as 'black' people so that they could benefit from government policies to help those previously disadvantaged under the old apartheid system. The controversial land reform bill was postponed in August. Government says that it still wants to redistribute around a third of white owned farmland by 2014.

Political structure

Constitution
The constitution was implemented in February 1997.
South Africa consists of a central government and nine provincial governments. The head of a province is called a premier.
The right to regional autonomy is enshrined in the constitution, subject to the principles of the national constitution.
Electoral system: list-system proportional representation based on universal adult suffrage, aged over 18.

Form of state
Federal republic

The executive
Executive powers are vested in the president, who is both Head of State and head of government, and is elected by the National Assembly for no more than two, five-year terms.
The president, must appoint all but two cabinet members from National Assembly members.

National legislature
The bicameral legislature consists of the National Assembly with between 350–400-members, elected by popular vote. Seats are apportioned to political parties dependent on their share of the vote.
The National Council of Provinces (NCOP) aligns national legislation that affects the provinces. The NCOP has 54 permanent members and 36 special delegates.
Both institutions serve for five year terms.

Legal system
Based on Roman-Dutch law and the constitution.
An anti-prejudice law was passed in 2000.

Last elections
23 April 2004 (presidential); 14 April 2004 (parliamentary).
Results: Presidential: Thabo Mbeki (ANC) was re-elected by the National Assembly unopposed.
Parliamentary: ANC won 69.69 per cent of the vote (279 seats out of 400); DA won 12.37 per cent (50 seats); Inkatha Freedom Party 6.97 per cent (28 seats). Turnout was 76.7 per cent.

Next elections
2009 (presidential and parliamentary)

Political parties

Ruling party
African National Congress (ANC) (since 1994; re-elected Apr 2004)

Main opposition party
Democratic Alliance (DA)

Population
47.85 million (2007)
Last census: October 2001: 44,819,778 (provisional)
Population density: 35 inhabitants per square km (2000). Urban population: 58 per cent of the total population (1995–2001).
Annual growth rate: 1.4 per cent 1994–2004 (WHO 2006)

Ethnic make-up
Black (75 per cent), white (13 per cent), coloured (9 per cent), Asian (3 per cent).

Religions
Christian (68 per cent), Islam (2 per cent), Hindu 1.5 per cent, indigenous beliefs and animist 28.5 per cent.

Education

Public expenditure on education amounts to 5.5 per cent of GDP.
Primary education begins at age six and lasts for six years. Junior secondary school lasts until age 15 when students may choose between an academic programme lasting a further three years at a senior secondary school or a vocational, technical course lasting two years in technical schools.
Government strategy for national schooling includes higher qualified teachers appointed to poorer schools and equalising school expenditure for all racial groups.
Literacy rate: 86 per cent adult rate; 92 per cent youth rate (15–24) (Unesco 2005).
Compulsory years: Six to 15
Enrolment rate: 133 per cent gross primary enrolment of relevant age group (including repeaters); 95 per cent gross secondary enrolment (World Bank).
Pupils per teacher: 45 in primary schools.

Health

Per capita total expenditure on health (2003) was US$669; of which per capita government spending was US$258, at the international dollar rate, (WHO 2006).
There are major national programmes in operation including the Integrated Nutrition Programme, the Polio and Measles Immunisation Campaign and Telemedicine (an interactive medical exchange based on information technology).
A R40 million (US$4.6 million) protocol signed between South Africa, Swaziland and Mozambique to control the spread of malaria lays the basis for a common programme of action in these countries.

HIV/Aids

South Africa has one of the highest HIV/Aids infection rates in the world and by January 2005 1.25 million sufferers had died of Aids, with over 1,000 Aids-related deaths recorded each day. An estimated 5.6 million people are HIV positive in South Africa which has the largest number of individuals living with the virus in a single country.
In March 2007, the government announced an ambitious five-year, US$6.4 billion, plan to fight HIV/Aids. It has set targets to halve infections by 2011, increase the availablity of anti-retroviral (ARV) drugs and introduce an internationally recognised benchmark assessment of progress.
The nationwide use of ARVs is seen by Aids groups as a significant weapon in the fight to limit the damage the disease inflicts on sufferers, their families and the community at large. The emergence of generic ARV drugs improved the overall situation however some provincial governments have a poor record of implementing treatment due to a lack of resources.
Former president Nelson Mandela publicly announced that his son had died of Aids in January 2005, saying, 'Let us give publicity to HIV/Aids and not hide it, because the only way of making it appear to be a normal illness, just like TB, like cancer, is always to come out and say somebody has died because of HIV.' In April 2004, Inkatha opposition leader, Mangosuthu Buthelezi, had announced that his son had also died of Aids.
South Africa is still in the process of addressing the deprivation wrought on black communities during the apartheid era including, poverty, poor primary healthcare, minimal education and families fractured by migratory work. This legacy has left women more vulnerable to the disease, and, by transmission, their children (20 per cent of children infected with HIV die of Aids before aged 5); in March 2007, 40 per cent of women aged 25–29 were HIV positive; there is a 2:1 ratio of female to male HIV infection (UNAids 2004). The number of orphans is growing, from 2.2 million (2003), to a projected 3.1 million or 18 per cent of all children by 2010. A local study reported in 2003 that life expectancy for women is expected to fall to 37 years by 2010, a drop of 17 years from 54 in 1999, male life expectancy will fall to 38 years at the same time. If this trend does not alter there will be noticeably fewer mid-adult women than men in the next two decades. By 2009 deaths by Aids-related illness is expected to exceed all other causes of death.
The South African pharmaceutical company, Aspen, was granted approval by US regulators to manufacture and supply antiretroviral drugs for local patients.
HIV prevalence: 21.5 per cent, aged 15–49 years
5.3 million adults and children living with HIV
27.9 per cent pregnant women (attending antenatal services) HIV positive
2.9 million women living with HIV
370,000 Aids deaths (adults and children) in 2003
(UNAids estimates, end 2003)
Life expectancy: 48 years, 2004 (WHO 2006)
Fertility rate/Maternal mortality rate: 2.8 births per woman, 2004 (WHO 2006)
Birth rate/Death rate: 18.9 births per 1,000 population; 18.4 deaths per 1,000 population (2003).
Population data issued by South Africa's Medical Research Council in March 2004 recorded a 44 per cent increase in adult deaths between 1998–2003, after population growth and improved registration had been factored in; deaths of women 20–49 increased by 168 per cent. It was concluded that this growth was due to Aids.
Child (under 5 years) mortality rate (per 1,000): 53 per 1,000 live births (World Bank)
Head of population per physician: 0.77 physicians per 1,000 people, 2004 (WHO 2006)

Welfare

The social assistance programme of the Department of Social Development provides benefits to approximately three million people comprising the elderly, persons with disabilities and children under the age of seven years. The government has emphasised the need to transform expensive institutional services into a more self-reliant approach towards individual and community care. Access to welfare grants is, however, limited. The State Maintenance Grants have been phased out and the availability of services for victims of violence across the country remains equally limited. Lack of an integrated approach towards allocations, capacity to spend and monitor the funds are some of the key problems relating to the distribution of poverty relief funds.

Main cities

Pretoria (Tswane Municipal Municipality is the central area) (capital, estimated population, 1.0 million (m) in 2005), Cape Town (Kaapstad (in Afrikaans) and iKapa (in Xhosa)) (legislative capital, 2.4m), Durban (eThekwini) (2.1m), Johannesburg (financial capital 1.5m), Soweto (1.0m), Port Elizabeth (848,400), East London (208,851), Benoni (359,491), Vereeniging (341,109), Bloemfontein (judicial capital, 328,311).

Languages spoken

Official language/s

Afrikaans, English, Ndebele, Sesotho, Northern Sotho, SiSwati, Tsonga, Tswana, Venda, Xhosa, Zulu.

Media

National news agency: PO Box 7766, Cotswold House, Greenacres Office Park, Cnr Victory & Rustenburg Roads, Victory Park, Johannesburg, 2000 (tel: 782-1600; fax: 782-1587/8; email: comms@sapa.org.za; internet: www.sapa.org.za).

Press

Press freedom is guaranteed by the constitution. The Freedom of Commercial Speech Trust plays an important role in industry self-regulation, forestalling government intervention.
Dailies: Newspapers published in major cities may be available throughout the country as reflect national and local news.

News 24 (www.news24.com) is a media organisation that has a number of Afrikaans titles: Die Burger, Volksblad, Rapport, Jou Geldsaka, Sondag, and NetAfrikaans among others.
From Cape Town, in English, Cape Argus (www.capeargus.co.za), the Cape Times (www.capetimes.co.za), and in Afrikaans Die Burger (www.dieburger.com).
From Johannesburg, in English, The Times (www.thetimes.co.za), which includes a business section and Sunday Times, Citizen (www.citizen.co.za), The Star (www.thestar.co.za) and Sowetan (www.sowetan.co.za). In Chinese China Express (www.sa-cnet.com) and China News (www.chinanews.co.za).
From Pretoria, in English, Pretoria News (www.pretorianews.co.za), Society News (www.societynews.co.za) and in Afrikaans Rekord (www.rekord.co.za).
From Durban, in English, Daily News (www.dailynews.co.za) and Post (www.thepost.co.za) (with Indian sections), in Zulu Isolezwe (www.isolezwe.co.za) and Ilanga (www.ilanganews.co.za).
Weeklies: In English, Daily Mail & Guardian (www.mg.co.za), is the leading independent newspaper, The Sunday Tribune (ww.sundaytribune.co.za), Sunday Independent (www.sunday.co.za), Sunday World (www.sundayworld.co.za) and Weekend Post (www.weekendpost.co.za). In Afrikaans Landbou Weekblad (www.landbou.com).
Business: Publications, in English, include Business Day (www.businessday.co.za) Financial Mail (http://free.financialmail.co.za), Cape Business News (www.cbn.co.za), Business Report (www.busrep.co.za), Guateng Business www.news24.com/Gauteng_Business/Home) and in Afrikaans Sake (www.news24.com/Sake/Home). Personal Finance (www.persfin.co.za) covers financial and investment issues. Destiny (www.mydestinymag.com) is a business magazine aimed at women

Broadcasting

The South African Broadcasting Corporation (SABC) is the state-owned national broadcaster.
Radio: There are numerous commercial radio stations particularly located around cities and large towns. Services are broadcast in various languages particular to local language spoken in the locale. SABC operates 20 regional and national services in 11 languages and an external radio service broadcasting in short wave to the African continent.
Other major commercial stations include SA FM (www.safm.co.za), East Coast Radio (www.ecr.co.za), Jacaranda FM (www.jacarandafm.com), Cape Talk (www.capetalk.co.za) and Radio Algoa (www.radioalgoa.com).
Television: SABC operates three national channels and two pay-to-view channels. Commercial stations with free-to-air television includes e.tv (www.etv.co.za) and pay-to-view M-Net (www.mnet.co.za) showing many internationally made programmes.
During an election period the media is monitored by the Independent Media Commission.

News agencies

SAPA (South African Press Association)
National news agency: PO Box 7766, Cotswold House, Greenacres Office Park, Cnr Victory & Rustenburg Roads, Victory Park, Johannesburg, 2000 (tel: 782-1600; fax: 782-1587/8; email: comms@sapa.org.za; internet: www.sapa.org.za).

Economy

South Africa has a highly diversified and open economy with well developed sectors in mining, agriculture, manufacturing and services providing a characteristically modern industrialised state. However, this sophisticated first-world economy runs in parallel with an alternative economy, of an historically segregated society characterised by poor infrastructure and a tendency to the informal, with high unemployment and low wages producing an uneven distribution of wealth. There has been a concerted effort to produce a more equitable structure but the economy is still split largely between the affluent white minority and the poorer black majority. Whites still own large tracts of fertile land and direct most of the industry and service sectors, while many blacks remain poor, landless and languishing in the country's shanty towns. The black middle class has begun to grow and assert itself as it becomes more affluent and demanding of the government. In turn, the government began a process of black economic empowerment (BEE), in 2005. To comply, public companies have to demonstrate the principles of BEE by favouring black employment and fostering their promotion within the organisation. Government contracts are awarded following a scrutiny of businesses to establish compliance. The lack of training during the apartheid period led to a lack of a pool of black managers and executives. Many major employers have now begun courses or backed scholarships to readdress the situation. Another aspect of BEE is black ownership of shares in companies, which has led to some criticism that only cronies of the ruling ANC are benefiting.
The economy is largely based on the country's abundant mineral and energy resources. Manufacturing is underpinned by the mining sector while gold and diamonds dominate exports. Foreign investors are attracted to the country's robust infrastructure, with developed transport, water and electricity networks. Dams have been built on the rivers and provide water for irrigation, industrial and household use. There are also developed professional services while the stock exchange is ranked world class.
The government has many social problems to tackle that hinder economic growth. Around half the population lives in poverty with limited access to health and education facilities and utilities. The HIV/Aids prevalence rate has risen to over 20 per cent of the population and has put a strain on, and will continue to hinder, future development. The estimated impact of HIV/Aids on the economy by 2006 ranged from 0.5–2.5 per cent of GDP, through lost productivity and higher production costs (including health costs). All of South Africa's key sectors have reported major detrimental effects.
Diversification away from the mining sector continues to show progress although an alarming exodus of young qualified whites is creating skilled manpower shortages. South Africa's tourism sector has expanded considerably since the end of the apartheid era but it still has a very long way to go before reaching its full potential.
The economy in 2005 was strong with GDP growth at 4.9 per cent, based largely on strong domestic demand due to growing disposable income, a large reduction in interest rates, and rising house and stock prices. Unemployment remained high at 26.7 per cent in 2005 and is not expected to fall in the near future. Increased employment opportunities are not increasing enough to satisfy the growing labour force, not only for the domestic workforce but also for migrant workers.
The South African Reserve Bank (SARB) has a flexible exchange rate policy that has given the country an impressive international reserve, thus improving South Africa's debt risk. Its long-term sovereign credit rating rose to BBB+ in August 2005.
The service sector provides 66 per cent of GDP, agriculture 3 per cent and industry 31 per cent, of which manufacturing is 19 per cent. In 2005, all sectors recorded a growth rate of just under 5 per cent.
In the short term, the economic outlook is expected to remain buoyant due to low interest rates and the government's moderately expansionist fiscal policy, and the helpful growth in the global economy. Nevertheless warnings from the IMF include a need to tackle the problem of high unemployment, widespread poverty and the large wealth disparity, which it felt

could be eased through labour market reforms and further trade liberalisation. Crime is still unacceptably high and social deprivation and HIV/Aids can only be ameliorated by social and economic progress through clearly defined and targetted programmes.

External trade

South Africa is a member of the Southern African Development Community (SADC), the objectives of which include reducing trade barriers, achieving regional development and economic growth and evolving common systems and institutions. Its currency, the rand, is also legal tender throughout the Common Monetary Area (CMA) (Swaziland, Lesotho and Namibia). With it immense mineral wealth, South Africa is the world's leading exporter of gold and platinum. It is also one of the leading world producer of diamonds, wine, railroad rolling stock, mining equipment and synthetic fuels. Exports provide almost 50 per cent of GDP and world commodity prices strongly affect the balance of trade.

Imports

Principal imports are machinery and equipment, vehicles, petroleum and natural gas, chemicals, scientific instruments and foodstuffs.

Main sources: Germany (12.5 per cent total, 2006), China (10.0 per cent), US (7.6 per cent).

Exports

Principal exports are gold (around 20 per cent of total), diamonds, metals and metal products, minerals, machinery and equipment. Other major exports are granite, asbestos, iron, manganese, chrome and titanium ore.

Main destinations: Japan (11.9 per cent total, 2006), US (11.5 per cent), UK (8.8 per cent).

Agriculture

Farming

South African agricultural is open to market forces and farmers take responsibility for production decisions, and pricing and distribution. The country has achieved self-sufficiency in staple grains, such as maize and wheat, and basic foodstuffs such as fresh milk and other dairy products, meat, vegetables and fruit. The agricultural sector accounted for 3.4 per cent of GDP in 2004, with a growth rate of 1.2 per cent. The sector employs around 13 per cent of the workforce.

LandCare is a key community support programme in the National Department of Agriculture which aims to promote sustainable land management practices and prevent land degradation in rural areas.

The government policy of forging partnerships to stimulate black empowerment is growing within the agricultural sector. Nevertheless land reforms to enable black farmers access to quality land has been slow with only 4 per cent redistributed by 2007 – of the 30 per cent planned for by 2014 – prompting a series of 'symbolic' property invasions, similar to those carried out in Zimbabwe.

South Africa has about 33 per cent of the southern hemisphere's deciduous fruit market in Europe. After minerals and metals, deciduous fruit is the country's largest export industry. The wine industry yields significant indirect benefits for the economy as a major employer and exporter. However, growth and competitiveness in the wine and tobacco industries is likely to be hampered by higher excise duty.

Oilseed production for bio-diesel offers a unique opportunity to facilitate such partnerships.

The controversial land reform bill was postponed in August 2008. Government says that it still wants to redistribute around a third of white owned farmland by 2014.

Crop production ('000 tonnes) for 2005 included: 14,707 tonnes (t) cereals in total, 2,034t wheat, 11,996t maize, 1,909t potatoes, 248t barley, 354t sorghum, 322t bananas, 691t sunflower seed, 779t apples, 343t pears, 1,559t citrus fruit, 1,700t grapes, 494t tomatoes, 172t pineapples, 370t oilcrops, 21,725t sugar cane, 5,447t fruit in total, 2,471t vegetables in total. Livestock production (tonnes) included: 1,887,802t meat in total, 643,000t beef, 140,000t pig meat, 122,000t lamb, 36,547t goat meat, 19,500t game meat, 925,255t poultry, 340,000t eggs, 2,552,000t milk, 1,500t honey, 75,600t cattle hides, 18,420t sheepskins, 44,156t greasy wool.

Fishing

The general policy towards fisheries has been the protection of marine ecology and the promotion and sustained utilisation of the sea and its resources.

South Africa is largely self-sufficient in white fish and has a substantial export surplus and is self-sufficient in canned fish. Some 10 per cent of the abalone yield and 25 per cent of rock lobster is marketed locally and the rest is exported, mainly to the Far East. Cultivation of oysters and mussels is growing steadily and the possibility of cultivating abalone is being researched.

Of domestic fishmeal demand of 260,000 tonnes per year (tpy), 60,000tpy is locally produced and the rest is imported.

Fishing quotas for foreign vessels are issued in terms of formal bilateral fisheries agreements. Of all the quota fish caught in South Africa's exclusive fishing zone (200 nautical miles offshore), foreign catches make up only 2.4 per cent. The figure does not include non-quota species such as tuna. Foreign boats are allocated quotas for hake, hose mackerel and squid.

In a meeting of African ministers in Namibia, held on 2 July, members discussed illegal and unregulated fishing, which is estimated to cost Africa US$1 billion per annum in lost revenue and the threat to stocks and local artisan fishing.

In 2004, the total marine fish catch was 866,928 tonnes and the total crustacean catch was 3,490 tonnes.

Forestry

About 7 per cent of the total land area is forested, with forest cover estimated at 8.9 million hectares (ha). About 27 per cent of the total land area is wooded. The country has extensive forest plantations and a large network of more than 200 protected areas covering nearly 5 per cent of the forest areas, including around 20 national parks. Deforestation accounts for around 1 per cent per annum or the equivalent of 8,000ha of forest cover.

Government policy has focussed on making South Africa self-sufficient in wood and wood products, taking into account the country's limited water supply and scarcity of suitable habitats. Industrial roundwood is produced in large quantities. The forestry industry is dependent on resources available from plantations and produces a wide range of wood and paper products. Although it produces and exports pulp and paper, significant volumes of paper are also imported.

Exports of forest materials amount to US$1.4 billion while imports amounted to US$633.7 million in 2004.

Timber production in 2004 included 33,159,400 cubic metre (cum) roundwood, 21,159,400cum industrial roundwood, 2,171,300cum sawnwood, 14,833,300cum pulpwood, 5,235,900cum sawlogs and veneer logs, 1,021,600cum wood-based panels, 12,000,000cum wood fuel; 200,600 tonnes (t) charcoal, 3,774,182t paper and paperboard (including 336,000t newsprint), 602,182t printing and writing paper, 1,709,000t paper pulp, 923,000t recovered paper.

Industry and manufacturing

South Africa is one of Africa's most industrialised countries and enjoys a strong resource base. Most of the raw materials and semi-manufactured goods required by industry are available from local sources. Only clothing and textiles, furniture (hardwoods), chemicals and transport equipment (components) still rely to a lesser extent on imports of raw materials or intermediate goods. Output is dominated by engineering and metal products, especially steel, and it has become a world leader in manufacturing railway

rolling stock, mining equipment and other machinery. Major steel companies include Iscor and Highveld Steel.
Other major growth areas are automobile production and the chemical industry. Although food and tobacco processing remain of great importance, their share of total output has fallen significantly. Food products, iron and steel and transport equipment together account for about a third of total gross manufacturing output. Other manufactures include paper and paper products, fabricated metal products, electrical and non-electrical machinery.
Industrial production accounted for 31.8 per cent of GDP, in 2004, of which 20 per cent was manufacturing; overall, services accounted for 64.9 per cent. All showed a growth increase of 3.2 per cent, 2.6 per cent and 4.1 per cent respectively.

Tourism
The tourism sector typically contributes up to 5 per cent of GDP and is an important source of foreign exchange. While visitor numbers increased in 2004, tourist spending fell by 7.4 per cent on the previous year, which led to a slight drop in employment. Estimates for 2005 show tourism contributing 3.9 per cent to GDP. The sector is expected to attract US$5.7 million or 14.1 per cent of total capital investment.
Europe constitutes the greater part of the overseas market (typically 65 per cent), followed by Asia (15 per cent), North America (12 per cent), Australasia (5 per cent), the Middle East (2 per cent) and the Indian Ocean Islands (1 per cent).
South Africa's tourism sector has expanded considerably since the end of the apartheid era but it still has a very long way to go before reaching its full potential. The country, which receives 52 per cent of the 13.4 million visitors to southern Africa each year, is positioning itself as the hub of a region-wide 'tourism park' wherein visitors will be able to move from one southern African country to another without going through formal borders. By pooling their resources and attractions together, southern African countries hope to emulate the islands of the Caribbean and increase tourist numbers. In the meantime, South Africa is steadily moving towards becoming the most popular conference destination in Africa.

Environment
In February 2008 South Africa announced that for the first time in 13 years it would begin a cull of elephants in a measure to control their numbers and reduce the impact that large herds have on the natural environment, other wildlife and human crops and habitation.

Mining
South Africa is the world's foremost producer and exporter of gold and platinum, and a significant exporter of diamonds, iron ore, asbestos, manganese ore, vanadium, ferro-chromium, chrome ore and granite.
International commodities traded in US dollars have all been affected by the rise in the rand since 2003 and most mining companies have experienced a drop in profits due to the disparity of expenses incurred in other currencies
A leading aluminium manufacturer, Alcan, has plans to build a smelter at Coega, near Port Elizabeth. Originally production would have reached 600,000 tonnes annually, however, in September 2005 plans were halted while a feasibility study was undertaken to facilitate a 900,000 tonnes processing plant. A smelter is expected to be operational by 2008.
The government has begun plans to introduce a state diamond trader company and producers such as UK-based, diamond company De Beers (founded in South Africa and the world's leading diamond trading company) would be required to forward a percentage of rough diamonds intended for export to the new Diamond Exchange and Export Centre (DEEC) for cutting and polishing by local craftsmen.
Diamonds, which had been exempt, are expected to be subject to a new export tax of 15 per cent following legislation due in 2006.
At least 40 per cent of the world's total recoverable gold reserves are in South Africa. Precious metals' producers will also be required to refine more of their output locally to provide more metals for South African design and manufacturing.
The mining sector only accounts for 6 per cent of GDP and South Africa sees value added diamond and gold processing as a source of added revenue and employment. The mining sector employs 6 per cent of the country's labour force and contributes up to one-third of the export revenue.

Hydrocarbons
South Africa's primary fuel is coal. It has over 49.5 billion tonnes of recoverable reserves – around 5 per cent of the world's total – and is the third largest net exporter globally.
It also had small reserves of oil but these were never enough to match its consumption. The majority of its oil is imported from the Middle East, with Iran and Saudi Arabia as the chief suppliers, however to reduce its dependency on this region South Africa has entered into agreement with Angola, Equatorial Guinea and Nigeria (the largest supplier of the African sources).
There has been much investment in synthetic fuels and South Africa is the world's largest producer of oil from coal and produces motor petroleum, distillates, kerosene and alcohols.
The country's oil refining capacity is over 468,500bpd, while oil consumption amounts to around 525,000bpd (2004). Refined products are sold in the local market and exported to East Africa and the Indian sub-continent. A 2002 joint venture by Sasol/Total for a US$123 million extension to its Natref refinery, increasing capacity by nearly 17,000bpd.
According to estimates, South Africa has 22.1 billion cubic metres of natural gas reserves. Production is estimated at around 1.4 billion cubic metres per annum, all of which is consumed locally.
US-based Forest Oil Corporation estimated the recoverable reserves at the Ibhubezi Prospect at 84.9 billion cubic metres, the production of which would be geared towards regional electrification. This has sparked further exploration around the western coast of South Africa. There is huge potential for South Africa to increase natural gas production.
Coal provides a significant source of foreign exchange. Most of South Africa's reserves are bituminous, with 45 per cent in ash content and only one per cent in sulphur content. Around 70 per cent of the recoverable reserves are located in three fields – Waterberg, Witbank and Highveld. Production levels were around 134.6 million tonnes of oil equivalent (toe) and 88.9 million toe is consumed domestically.

Energy
The bulk supply electricity company, Eskom, a self-financing, parastatal utility company, has an installed generating capacity of about 36,000MW. Largely through Eskom, South Africa supplies almost 60 per cent of the total electricity generated on the continent of Africa. Nevertheless, a third of South Africa's population does not have access to the national grid. Eskom is the fourth-largest power company in the world by capacity and is being restructured with a view to eventual privatisation.
In January 2008 electricity exports to southern African countries were suspended by Eskom, due to acute domestic shortages. Daily power cuts threatened the economy and government talks with the power company agreed that a lack of past investment had led to the shortabe in generating capacity and that there was an urgent need for reinvestment.
The government is hoping to expand private sector involvement in the

electrification drive, in the generation, transmission and distribution sectors. In October 2004 the government announced investment of US$26 billion until 2009, to improve the electricity infrastructure.

Eskom produces about 97 per cent of South Africa's electricity needs, with the balance made up by mines, industries and municipalities with their own small stations. It operates 17 coal-fired power stations, two hydroelectric, two pumped storage schemes, two gas turbine stations and the country's only nuclear power plant at Koeberg. Three inactive power stations will be re-commissioned at a cost of US$1.96 billion, with assistance from a foreign company skilled in such work to increase capacity. The 2,000MW nuclear power station, operated by Eskom and supervised by the Council for Nuclear Safety, is likely to remain the only nuclear facility for some time.

The extension of the electricity grid to less privileged, mainly rural, areas is a major priority of the government's energy policy. The emphasis is toward renewable energy resources such as solar energy and hydropower. The National Energy Council is investigating possibilities in this area. Renewable energy sources account for around 5 per cent of primary energy needs.

South Africa exports electricity to Botswana, Lesotho, Mozambique, Namibia, Swaziland and Zimbabwe. It also imports a small amount of electricity from neighbouring countries, mostly from Namibia, although the amount varies widely in accordance with the capacity of other countries to supply.

Financial markets

Stock exchange

After years of isolation, South Africa's financial markets have changed rapidly to adopt international standards and operate in a competitive global market. Since 1994, the Johannesburg Stock Exchange (JSE) has deregulated the market allowing the ownership of local brokers by foreign companies and banks. Anglo American dominates the JSE, with price changes in its stocks substantially affecting the market's indices. As such, the JSE is influenced to a significant extent by world gold prices. The South African Futures Exchange (Safex) was taken over by the JSE in 2001, following the approval of the country's competition regulators.

Among projects to continue improving efficiency and competitiveness is the creation of a paperless financial exchange, known as Strate (share transactions totally electronic). Strate is 50 per cent owned by the JSE, but is open to all electronic settlements including those not listed as JSE securities. Such improvements are vital if South Africa's financial markets are to cope with rapidly rising volumes and with competition from other emerging markets. The market response to Strate began as strong and positive.

The JSE broke through the 19,000 level for the first time in January 2006.

Banking and insurance

The financial services sector has changed rapidly since South Africa re-entered the global economy in the 1990s. Domestic banks have restructured and foreign banks compete fiercely in the commercial sector.

The South African Reserve Bank (SARB) (central bank) supervises the domestic and international activities of banks, discount houses and building societies. It issues the country's currency and is the custodian of South Africa's gold and foreign exchange reserves. It is responsible for the implementation of monetary policy which it formulates in conjunction with the finance ministry.

In May 2005, the UK's third largest bank, Barclays, purchased a 60 per cent share in South Africa's third largest, Absa. Bought for R33 billion (US$5.2 billion) it was the single largest foreign investment deal since apartheid ended.

Central bank

South African Reserve Bank (SARB)

Main financial centre

Johannesburg

Time

GMT plus two hours

Geography

South Africa occupies the southern extremity of the African continent. It is bordered by Namibia to the north-west, by Botswana and Zimbabwe to the north, by Mozambique to the north-east, and by Swaziland to the east; Lesotho is a 30,000 square km country isolated within South Africa's territory.

South Africa's coastline stretches over 2,500km from the Namibian border on the Atlantic coast in the west, around the Cape of Good Hope to the Mozambique border on the Indian Ocean coast in the east. The land along the coast is low-lying but quickly rises to mountainous escarpments that separate it from the high plateau of the interior. The highest region in South Africa is the Drakensberg Mountains in the east, which also straddle the border with Lesotho. Njesuthi is South Africa's tallest peak at 3,408 metres (m), although the Drakensberg's highest mountain is Thabana Ntlenyana (3,482m) in Lesotho.

The Kalahari desert in the north-east border region with Namibia and Botswana stretches for 900,000 square km. Much of the central plane is grassland and veld (savannah) that stretches to the coast in the east and is flanked in the west by highlands.

Hemisphere

Southern

Climate

There are regional variations due to relative elevations. The Cape coastal area is warm and temperate throughout the year with temperature ranges in Cape Town between 13–20 degrees Celsius (C); inland Pretoria and other high veld areas have temperature ranges of 13–22 degrees C and Johannesburg, slightly lower 11–19 degrees C. On the Natal coast humidity can be high during the summer, while the winters are drier with temperatures in Durban 17–24 degrees C. The highest temperatures are recorded in the Kalahari desert and the coldest are recorded in the remote Roggeveld Mountains in the west; the Drakensberg Mountains have snow on their peaks in winter.

Entry requirements

Passports

Required by all and must be valid for 30 days beyond date of departure.

Visa

Are not required by nationals listed at www.southafricahouse.com under Home Affairs then Visa exempt countries then foreign citizens then Visas, lastly see Who needs a visa. All other nationals must apply to the nearest South African consulate, see www.home-affairs.gov.za/forms.asp for a visa application form; visas must be applied for before arrival.

Business travellers should contact a South African consulate for further information. All visitors must have proof of return/onward passage, and may have to show evidence of sufficient funds for the intended stay.

Currency advice/regulations

Import of local currency is limited to R5,000 and export to R500 per person. Import of foreign currency is unlimited but must be declared; export is limited to the amount declared.

Travellers cheques (in major currencies) are widely accepted.

Customs

Personal items are duty-free.

Prohibited imports

Illegal drugs, pornography, firearms, ammunition, flick-knives and explosives.

Meat, dairy products and processed cheeses.

Plants and plant materials, honey, margarine and vetegable oils require an import permit.

Health (for visitors)
Mandatory precautions
Yellow fever vaccination certificate required if travelling from infected areas, (certificates are not valid until 10 days after immunisation).
Advisable precautions
Vaccinations are necessary for typhoid and hepatitis A and B; vaccination for hepatitis A is advisable. To avoid the risk of bilharzia, only use well-maintained, chlorinated swimming pools. Malaria exists throughout the year in certain areas of northern Transvaal, eastern low veld and northern Natal; prophylaxis should be taken for visits to these areas. Water precautions should be taken in rural areas. HIV/Aids is prevalent.

Hotels
A wide choice is available in main commercial centres. It is advisable to make reservations well in advance, especially during December and January, March and April.

Credit cards
Major credit and charge cards are widely accepted. ATMs are widely available.

Public holidays (national)
Fixed dates
1 Jan (New Year's Day), 21 Mar (Human Rights Day), 27 Apr (Freedom Day), 1 May (Worker's Day), 16 Jun (Youth Day), 9 Aug (National Women's Day), 24 Sep (Heritage Day), 16 Dec (Reconciliation Day), 25 Dec (Christmas Day), 26 Dec (Day of Goodwill).
Holidays that fall on Sunday are taken on Monday.
Variable dates
Good Friday, Family Day (on Easter Monday) (Mar/Apr)

Working hours
Banking
Mon–Fri: 0830–1530; Sat: 0830–1100. Some banks have extended hours.
Business
Mon–Fri: 0730/0830–1600/1700. Some businesses have extended hours.
Government
Mon–Fri: 0730/0830–1600/1700.
Shops
Mon–Fri: 0830–1700; Sat: 0830–1300. Certain shops are open on Sundays.

Telecommunications
Mobile/cell phones
There are GSM roaming facilities available, with coverage throughout most of the country.

Electricity supply
Usually 220/230V AC, but 220/250V in Port Elizabeth and 250V in Pretoria.

Social customs/useful tips
There are no particular taboos, but visitors should be mindful that in certain parts of the country strong racist attitudes still prevail. It is best not to get involved in political discussions.
Visitors should not photograph security institutions.

Security
Visitors should avoid visiting black townships without guidance from reliable local residents and without a trustworthy companion. Certain townships in the Pretoria-Witwatersrand-Vereeniging region and around the Cape Town, Durban and Pietermaritzburg regions should be avoided unless a visit is absolutely necessary – notably Thokoza, Sebokeng, Alexandra, Boipatong, Katlehong, Langa, Mitchell's Plain, Gugulethu, Khayelitsha, Crossroads, KwaMashu and Mpumulanga.
Periodic attacks on visitors to townships have occurred and the crime rate has soared as unemployment and politically-related violence have increased. Street crime is less of a problem in major urban areas, though care must be taken in central Johannesburg at night. Care must also be taken when visiting extreme right-wing strongholds such as Ventersdorp in the Western Transvaal. It is advisable not to carry unnecessary valuables, expensive jewellery and large amounts of money.
Crime in Johannesburg continues to escalate. Do not resist if confronted. Avoid walking in the streets alone after shopping. Use taxis at night and only those booked through a reputable hotel or among those listed in the official Johannesburg guide. Keep car doors locked while you are in the vehicle or when it is parked. If you are driving after dark, keep car doors locked and avoid slowing down.

Getting there
Air
National airline: South African Airways
International airport/s: OR Tambo International Airport (name changed from Johannesburg Intenational (JNB) in October 2006), serves as a hub for flights to other countries in the region. It is 24km from city, duty-free shop, bar, restaurant, bank, post office, shops, car hire; Cape Town International (CPT), 22km east of city, duty-free shop, car hire, bank, bar and restaurant; Durban International (DUR), 16km from city, duty-free shop, car hire, bank, bar and restaurant. Taxis and buses serve all airports.
Other airport/s: Bloemfontein (BFN), 10km east of the city; Port Elizabeth (PLZ), 25km from the city.
Airport tax: None

Surface
Road: Possible from Botswana, Lesotho, Namibia, Swaziland, Zimbabwe and Mozambique. Travellers are generally advised to check regulations and conditions regarding entry by road with the Automobile Association of South Africa.
The Maputo Corridor project includes a link from the Atlantic coast at Namibia's Walvis Bay across the Kalahari desert to join the South African road network, linking the western side of southern Africa with the Indian Ocean at Maputo, Mozambique. There is a toll road between Witbank in South Africa and Maputo.
Rail: There are services from Mozambique, Botswana, Zimbabwe and Namibia.
Water: Cruise ships call at some Indian Ocean islands.
Main port/s: Cape Town, Durban, Port Elizabeth and East London.

Getting about
National transport
Air: All major cities and towns are linked with regular, scheduled services. South African Airways, InterAir and Airlink fly domestic routes.
Road: Extensive network of tarred roads, including 51,000km linking main centres. There is a further 130,000km of untarred roads – some of the remoter sections can become impassable in wet weather.
Buses: Inter-city services are operated by Greyhound, Citiliner and other private companies. Vehicles are a good standard.
Rail: Network of some 24,000km with good services throughout the country. Reservations for express trains should be made well in advance. Two classes available, but visitors are advised to travel first class. Most long distance mainline trains have restaurant cars and all have sleeping accommodation (couchettes operated in both first- and second-class).
Named services include: Blue Train, a luxury service, running three times a week (Pretoria-Johannesburg-Cape Town; with sleeping accommodation, restaurant cars, air-conditioning, suites, staterooms available); Trans Orange, once a week (Durban-Cape Town); Trans Natal, daily (Durban-Johannesburg).
City transport
Taxis: Widely available in all towns. Taxis cannot be hailed in the street but must be booked or called from a rank. Fares within a city depend on distance and time, while longer distance fares are lower and should be agreed in advance. A 10 per cent tip is usual.
Buses, trams & metro: There are exstensive bus networks in all main towns. Fares in Cape Town and Johannesburg are zonal, with payment in cash or with ten-ride pre-purchase 'clipcards' from

kiosks. In Pretoria there are various pre-purchase ticket systems. In Durban conventional buses vie for passengers with minibuses and combi-taxis (both legal and illegal); also found in other South African towns. Although cheap and very fast, they should be used with care.

Trains: There are frequent local trains in the Cape Town and Pretoria and Johannesburg urban areas. All trains have first- and second-class accommodation.

Car hire

Self-drive and chauffeur-driven cars are widely available. An international driving licence is required unless visitor's national licence carries the photograph and signature of the holder.

Driving is on the left. Speed limits: built-up areas 60kph; country roads 100kph; declared freeways and some main roads 120kph. Heavy fines for speeding.

BUSINESS DIRECTORY

The addresses listed below are a selection only. While World of Information makes every endeavour to check these addresses, we cannot guarantee that changes have not been made, especially to telephone numbers and area codes. We would welcome any corrections.

Telephone area codes

The international dialling code (IDD) for South Africa is +27, followed by area code and subscriber's number:

Bloemfontein51Ladysmith361
Cape Town21Pietermaritzburg331
Durban31Port Elizabeth41
Johannesburg11Pretoria12

Chambers of Commerce

American Chamber of Commerce, 60 Fifth Street, PO Box 1132, Houghton 2041, Johannesburg (tel: 788-0265; fax: 880-1632; e-mail: administrator@amcham.co.za).

Bloemfontein Chamber of Business, 37 Kellner Street, PO Box 87, Bloemfontein 9300 (tel: 447-3368; fax: 447-5064; e-mail:bcci@intekom.co.za).

Cape Town Regional Chamber of Commerce and Industry, 19 Louis Gradner Street, PO Box 204, Cape Town 8000 (tel: 402-4300; fax: 402-4302; e-mail: info@capechamber.co.za).

Durban Chamber of Commerce & Industry, 190 Stanger Street, PO Box 1506, Durban 4000 (tel: 335-1000; fax: 332-1288; e-mail: chamber@durbanchamber.co.za).

Johannesburg Chamber of Commerce and Industry, Private Bag 34, Corner Empire Road and Owl Street, Auckland Park 2006, Johannesburg (tel: 726-5300; fax: 782-2000; e-mail: info@jcci.co.za).

Ladysmith Chamber of Commerce and Industry, PO Box 7, Ladysmith 3370 (tel: 631-0541; fax: 637-4407; e-mail: lcci@futurenet.co.za).

Pietermaritzburg Chamber of Business, Royal Show Grounds, Commercial Road, PO Box 11734, Dorpspruit 3206, Pietermaritzburg (tel: 345-2747; fax: 394-4151; e-mail: pcb@futurenet.co.za).

Port Elizabeth Regional Chamber of Commerce and Industry, 22 Grahamstown Road, PO Box 2221, North End 6056, Port Elizabeth (tel: 484-4430; fax: 487-1851; e-mail: info@pechamber.org.za).

Pretoria Chamber of Commerce and Industry, 852 Park Street, PO Box 40653, Arcadia 0007, Pretoria (tel: 342-3236; fax: 342-1486; e-mail: pcci@mweb.co.za).

South African Chamber of Business, 24 Sturdee Avenue, PO Box 213, Saxonwold 2132, Johannesburg (tel: 446-3800; fax: 446-3847; e-mail: info@sacob.co.za).

Banking

Absa Bank Ltd, 2nd Floor, ABSA Towers North, 180 Commissioner Street, Johannesburg 2001 (tel: 350-4000; fax: 350-3768).

International Bank of Southern Africa Ltd, 3rd Floor, Sunnyside Ridge Bldg, 32 Princess of Wales Terrace, Parktown, Johannesburg 2193 (tel: 644-3300, 643-6740, 643-6743; fax: 643-1122).

Nedcor Bank Ltd, 135 Rivonia Rd, Sandown, Sandton, Johannesburg 2001 (tel: 294-4444; fax: 295-5555).

South African Bank of Athens Ltd, Bank of Athens Building, 116 Marshall Street, Johannesburg 2001 (tel: 832-1211; fax: 838-1001, 833-7976).

Standard Bank of South Africa Ltd, 5 Simmonds Street, Johannesburg 2001 (tel: 636-9111; fax: 636-3544).

Central bank

South African Reserve Bank, 370 Church Street; PO Box 427, Pretoria 0001 (tel: 313-3911; fax: 313-3197; email: www.reservebank.co.za).

Travel information

Airlink, Bonaero Park, Johannesburg (tel: 961-1700; fax: 395-1076; internet: www.flyairlink.com)

Automobile Association of South Africa, Denis Paxton House, Alladale Road, Kyalami Midrand 1685; PO Box 596, Johannesburg 2000 (tel: 799-1000; fax: 799-1960; e-mail: aasa@aasa.co.za).

Blue Train Reservations, PO Box 2671, Joubert Park 2044 (tel: 334-8459; fax: 334-8464; e-mail: bluetrain@transnet.co.za).

Coach Services: Translux Express, PO Box 2383, Johannesburg 2000 (tel: 774-3333; fax: 774-3318); Greyhound Coach Lines, PO Box11229, Johannesburg 2000 (tel: 830-1301; fax: 830-1528); Intercape Mainliner, PO Box 618, Bellville 7535 (tel: 386-4400; fax: 386-2488).

Eastern Cape Tourism Board, PO Box 186, Bisho 5605 (tel: 635-2115; fax: 636-4019; e-mail: info@ectourism.co.za).

Free State Department of Environmental Affairs and Tourism, PO Box 264, Bloemfontein 9300 (tel: 403-3435; fax: 448-8361).

Gauteng Tourism Authority, The Rosebank Mall, Rosebank 2196 (tel: 327-2000; fax: 327-7000; e-mail: tourism@gauteng.net).

Interair South Africa, Private Bag 8, PO JHB Int'nl Airport 1627, Johannesburg (tel: 616-0636; fax: 616-0930; email: info@interair.co.za).

KwaZulu-Natal Tourism Authority, PO Box 2516, Durban 4000 (tel: 304-7144; fax: 305-6693; e-mail: info@tourism-kzn.org).

Mpumalanga TourismAuthority, PO Box 679, Nelspruit 1200 (tel: 752-7001; fax: 759-5441; e-mail: mtanlpsa@cis.co.za).

Northern Cape Tourism Board, Private Bag X5017, Kimberley 8300 (tel: 832-2657; fax: 831-2937; e-mail: tourism@northerncape.org.za).

Northern Province Tourism Board, PO Box 1309, Pietersburg 0700 (tel: 288-0099; fax: 288-0094; e-mail: ceo@greatnorth.co.za).

North-West Parks and Tourism Council, PO Box 4488, Mmabatho 2735 (tel: 386-1225; fax: 386-1158; e-mail: nwptb@iafrica.com).

Rovos Rail Reservations, Victoria Hotel, PO Box 2837, Pretoria 0001 (tel: 323-6052; fax: 323-0843).

South African Airways, Private Bag X13, JHB Int'nl Airport, 1627; Airways Park, 32 Jones Road, Kempton Park, Johannesburg International Airport (tel: 978-1000; fax: 978-3507; internet: www.flysaa.com).

South African National Parks, 643 Leyds Street, Muckleneuk, Pretoria; PO Box 787, Pretoria 0001 (tel: 343-1991; fax: 343-0905; e-mail: reservations@parks-sa.co.za).

Western Cape Tourism Board, Private Bag X9108, Cape Town 8000 (tel: 426-5639; fax: 426-5640; e-mail: info@capetourism.org).

Ministry of tourism
Ministry of Environmental Affairs and Tourism, Fedsure Forum Building, 315 Pretorius Street, Pretoria; Private Bag X447, Pretoria 0001 (tel: 310-3611; fax: 322-0082).

National tourist organisation offices
South African Tourism, Bojanala House, 12 Rivonia Road, Illovo 2196 (tel: 778-8000; fax: 778-8001; e-mail: info@southafrica.net; internet site: http://www.southafrica.net).

Ministries
NB For the following Ministry addresses: Pretoria (administrative), Cape Town (legislative).

Ministry of Agriculture and Land Affairs, Private Bag X250, Pretoria 0001 (tel: 319-6886; fax: 321-8558); Private Bag X9087, Cape Town 8000 (tel: 465-7690; fax: 465-6550).

Ministry of Arts, Culture, Science and Technology, Private Bag X727, Pretoria 0001 (tel: 337-8378; fax: 324-2687); Private Bag X9156, Cape Town 8000; (tel: 465-4850; fax: 461-1425).

Ministry of Communications, Private Bag X882, Pretoria 0001 (tel: 427-8111; fax: 362-6915); Private Bag X9151, Cape Town 8000 (tel: 462-1632; fax: 462-1646).

Ministry of Correctional Services, Private Bag X853, Pretoria 0001 (tel: 323-8803; fax: 323-4111); Private Bag X9131, Cape Town 8000 (tel: 462-2314; fax: 465-4375).

Ministry of Defence, Private Bag X427, Pretoria 0001 (tel: 355-6119; fax: 347-0118); PO Box 47, Cape Town 8000 (tel: 469-6070; fax: 465-5870).

Ministry of Education, Private Bag X603, Pretoria 0001 (tel: 312-5501; fax: 323-5989); Private Bag X9034, Cape Town 8000 (tel: 465-7350; fax: 461-4788).

Ministry of Environmental Affairs and Tourism, Private Bag X447, Pretoria 0001 (tel: 310-3611; fax: 322-0082); Private Bag X9154, Capetown 8000 (tel: 465-7240; fax: 465-3216).

Ministry of Finance, Private Bag X115, Pretoria 0001 (tel: 323-8911; fax: 323-3262); PO Box 29, Cape Town 8000 (tel: 464-6100; fax: 461-2934).

Ministry of Foreign Affairs, Private Bag X152, Pretoria 0001 (tel: 351-0005; fax: 351-0253); 120 Plein St, Cape Town 8001 (tel: 464-3700; fax: 465-6548).

Ministry of Health, Private Bag X399, Pretoria 0001 (tel: 328-4773; fax: 325-5526); Private Bag X9070, Cape Town 8000 (tel: 465-7407; fax: 465-1575).

Ministry of Home Affairs, Private Bag X741, Pretoria 0001 (tel: 326-8081; fax: 321-6491); Private Bag X9102, Cape Town 8000 (tel: 461-5818; fax: 461-2359).

Ministry of Housing, Private Bag X645, Pretoria 0001 (tel: 421-1311; fax: 341-8513); Private Bag X9029, Cape Town 8000 (tel: 465-7295; fax: 465-3610).

Ministry of Intelligence Services, PO Box 56450, Arcadia 0007(tel: 338-1800; fax: 323-0718); PO Box 51278, Waterfront 8002 (tel: 401-1800; fax: 461-4644).

Ministry of Justice and Constitutional Development, Private Bag X276, Pretoria 0001 (tel: 323-8581; fax: 321-1708); Private Bag X256, Cape Town 8000 (tel: 465-7506; fax: 465-2783).

Ministry of Labour, Private Bag X499, Pretoria 0001 (tel: 322-6523; fax: 320-1942); Private Bag X9090, Cape Town 8000 (tel: 461-6030; fax: 462-2832).

Ministry of Minerals and Energy, Private Bag X646, Pretoria 0001 (tel: 322-8695; fax: 322-8699); Private Bag X9111, Cape Town 8000 (tel: 462-2310; fax: 461-0859).

Ministry of Provincial and Local Government, Private Bag X802, Pretoria 0001 (tel: 334-0705; fax: 326-4478); Private Bag X9123, Cape Town 8000 (tel: 462-1441; fax: 461-0851).

Ministry of Public Enterprises, Private Bag X15, Hatfield 0028 (tel: 431-1000; fax: 342-7224); Private Bag X9079, Cape Town 8000 (tel: 461-6376; fax: 465-2381).

Ministry of Public Service and Administration, Private Bag X884, Pretoria 0001 (tel: 314-7911; fax: 328-6529); Private Bag X9148, Cape Town 8000 (tel: 465-5491; fax: 465-5484).

Ministry of Public Works, Private Bag X890, Pretoria 0001 (tel: 324-1510; fax: 325-6380); Private Bag X9155, Cape Town 8000 (tel: 462-4184; fax: 461-6962).

Ministry of Safety and Security, Private Bag X463, Pretoria 0001 (tel: 339-2800; fax: 339-2819); Private Bag X9080, Cape Town 8000 (tel: 465-7400; fax: 461-2073).

Ministry of Social Development, Private Bag X885, Pretoria 0001 (tel: 312-7637; fax: 321-2658); Private Bag X9153, Cape Town 8000 (tel: 465-4011; fax: 465-4469).

Ministry of Sport and Recreation, Private Bag X869, Pretoria 0001 (tel: 334-3100; fax: 321-8493); Private Bag X9149, Cape Town 8000 (tel: 465-5506; fax: 465-4402).

Ministry of Trade and Industry, Private Bag X274, Pretoria 0001 (tel: 322-7677; fax: 322-7851); Private Bag X9047, Cape Town 8000 (tel: 461-7191; fax: 465-1291).

Ministry of Transport, Private Bag X193, Pretoria 0001 (tel: 309-3131; fax: 328-3194); Private Bag X9129, Cape Town 8000 (tel: 465-7260; fax: 461-6845).

Ministry of Water Affairs and Forestry, Private Bag X313, Pretoria 0001 (tel: 36-8733; fax: 328-4254); Private Bag X9052, Cape Town 8000 (tel: 464-1500; fax: 465-3362).

Office of the President, Private Bag X1000, Pretoria 0001 (tel: 337-5100; fax: 321-8870); Private Bag X1000, Cape Town 8000 (tel: 464-2100; fax: 464-2123).

Other useful addresses
Association of Advertising Agencies (AAA), PO Box 2289, Parklands 2121 (tel: 781-2772; fax: 781-2796; e-mail: aaa@gem.co.za).

Afrikaanse Handelsinstituut (AHI) (Afrikaans Trade Institute), Lynnwood Galleries, 354 Rosemary Street, Lynnwood 0081; PO Box 35100, Menlopark 00101 (tel: 348-5440; fax: 348-8771; e-mail: pta@ahi.co.za).

Association of Marketeers (ASOM), 8 Sloane Street, Bryanston, Sandton; PO Box 98859, Sloane Park 2152, Bryanston (tel: 706-1633; fax: 706-4151; e-mail: asom@pixie.co.za).

Board on Tariffs and Trade, Fedlife Forum, Cnr Van der Walt and Pretorius Streets, Private Bag X753, Pretoria 0001 (tel: 322-8244; fax: 322-0149).

British High Commission, 255 Hill Street, Arcadia, Pretoria 0002 (tel: 483-1200; fax: 483-1302); 91 Parliament Street, Cape Town 8001 (tel: 461-7220; fax: 461-0017).

Chamber of Mines of South Africa, PO Box 61809, Marshalltown 2107 (tel: 498-7100; fax: 834-4251).

Chemical & Allied Industries Association, 15th Floor, Metal Box Centre, 25 Owl Street, Auckland Park 2006 (tel: 482-1671; fax: 726-8310).

Clothing Federation of South Africa, 42 van der Linde Street, Bedfordview 2008 (tel: 622-8125; fax: 622-8316).

COEGA Development Corporation, Libra Chambers, Cnr Oakworth Road and Carnarvon Place, Humerail, Port Elizabeth; Private Bag X13130, Humewood, Port Elizabeth 6013 (tel: 507-9111; fax: 585-5445; e-mail: info@coega.co.zu).

Government Communications and Information System (GCIS), 356 Vermeulen Street, Pretoria; Private Bag X745, Pretoria 0001 (tel: 314-2127; 325-2030; e-mail: govcom@gcis.pwv.gov.za; internet site: http://www.gcis.gov.za).

ICC Durban (international convention centre), 45 Ordnance Road, Durban 4001; PO Box 155, Durban 4000 (tel: 360-1000; fax: 360-1005; e-mail: mktg@icc.co.za).

Industrial Development Corporation of South Africa, 19 Fredman Drive, Sandton 2146; PO Box 784055, Sandton 2146 (tel: 269-3000; fax: 269-3116; e-mail: callcentre@idc.co.za).

Iscor Limited, Roger Dyason Road, Pretoria West; PO Box 450, Pretoria 0001 (tel: 307-3000; fax: 307-4721; e-mail: webmaster@iscor.com).

JSE Securities Exchange (stock exchange), 1 Exchange Square, 2 Gwen Lane, Sandown, Sandton 2196; Private Bag X991174, Sandton 2146 (tel: 520-7000; fax: 520-8584; e-mail: miscellaneous@jse.co.za).

South African Association for the Conference Industry (SAACI), PO Box, Kloof 3640 (tel 764-6977; fax: 764-6974; e-mail: sec@saaci.co.za).

South African Business Initiative for Reconstruction and Development, 17th Floor, Metal Box Centre, 25 Owl Street, Auckland Park 2092 (tel: 482-5100; fax: 482-5507).

South African Diamond Board, 5th Floor, SA Diamond Centre, 240 Commissioner Street, Johannesburg 2001 (tel: 334-8980/6; fax: 334-8898; e-mail: mabombol@sadb.co.za).

South African Embassy (USA), 3051 Massachusetts Avenue, NW Washington, DC (tel: (+1-202) 232-4400; fax: (+1-202) 265-1607; e-mail: safrica@southafrica.net).

South African Foreign Trade Organisation (SAFTO), Export House, 71 Maud Street, Sandton; PO Box 782706, Sandton 2146 (tel: 883-3737; fax: 883-6569; e-mail: safto@apollo.is.co.za).

South African Petroleum Industry Association, Trust Bank Centre, Adderley Street, Cape Town 8001; PO Box 7082, Roggebaai 8012 (tel: 419-8054; fax: 419-8058).

Statistics South Africa, Steyn's Building, 274 Schoeman Street, Pretoria 0002; Private Bag X44, Pretoria 0001 (tel: 310-8911; fax: 322-3374; e-mail: info@statssa.pwv.gov.za; internet site: www.statssa.gov.za/).

Trade and Investment South Africa, Rex Welsh House, Maud Street, Sandown, Sandton 2196; PO Box 782084, Sandton 2146 (tel: 884-2206; fax: 884-3236; e-mail: isa@isa.org.za).

US Embassy, 877 Pretorius Street, Pretoria; PO Box 9536, Pretoria 0001(tel: 342-1048; fax: 342-2244).

National news agency: PO Box 7766, Cotswold House, Greenacres Office Park, Cnr Victory & Rustenburg Roads, Victory Park, Johannesburg, 2000 (tel: 782-1600; fax: 782-1587/8; email: comms@sapa.org.za; internet: www.sapa.org.za).

Internet sites

African Development Bank: www.afdb.org

Africa Online: www.africaonline.com

AllAfrica.com: http://allafrica.com

International Finance Corporation: www.ifc.org/abn

Johannesburg Stock Exchange: www.jse.co.za/

Development Bank of South Africa: www.dbsa.org

Mbendi AfroPaedia (information on companies, countries, industries and stock exchanges in Africa): http://mbendi.co.za

Province of the North West Tourist Board: www.tourismnorthwest.co.za/

South African Development Community (SADC): www.sadcreview.com

South African Futures Exchange: www.safex.co.za/

South African yellow pages: www.ipages.co.za/

Trade Web: www.trade.co.za/

South Georgia

COUNTRY PROFILE

Historical profile

1775 Captain Cook landed and took formal possession of South Georgia and the South Sandwich Islands (SGSSI).
1904 A whaling station was established by the Norwegian C A Larsen.
1908 The UK government annexed SGSSI by Letters Patent as part of the Falkland Islands Dependencies and the islands came under UK administration.
1965 Leith Harbour, the last shore-based whaling station in South Georgia, was closed.
1982 Argentine military forces occupied South Georgia for 22 days. South Georgia and the South Sandwich Islands became overseas territories of the UK.
2001 The UK military garrison closed and was replaced by a British Antarctic Survey (BAS) base at King Edward Point. There is a science station for biological study on Bird Island.
2005 A revised version of the 2000 environment management plan was drafted and published on the British Antartic Survey's website. The new plan was published in 2006 and set out environmental policies for the next five years.
2006 Alan Huckle became Commissioner in July.
2007 HMS Nottingham, a destroyer class ship, became the South Atlantic patrol ship to maintain a British maritime presence in the South Atlantic around Ascension Island, St Helena, Tristan da Cunha, South Georgia, the South Sandwich Islands and the Falkland Islands.

Political structure

South Georgia and the South Sandwich Islands (SGSSI) are British overseas territories, legally distinct from the Falkland Islands but, for convenience, they are administered from the Falkland Islands. With no indigenous or permanent inhabitants, there is no need for representative government, but a separate constitution for the territory was promulgated in 1985. The governor of the Falkland Islands is also the commissioner for the SGSSI; in this capacity he consults the Falklands Executive Council on those matters relating to the territory which might affect the Falkland Islands.
Other administrative posts based in Stanley, Falkland Islands, include the assistant commissioner who is also director of the SGSSI Fisheries, a financial secretary and attorney general. The marine officer, based at King Edward Point, is responsible for customs, immigration, posts and fisheries liaison.

Population

20 (2004) (British Antarctic Survey (BAS) scientists)

Main cities

King Edward Point (administrative centre); Grytviken, formerly a whaling station on South Georgia, was the garrison town.

Languages spoken

Official language/s
English

Media

Press
Weeklies: The South Atlantic Remote Territories Media Association publishes an online newsletter which includes articles on South Georgia (www.sartma.com).

Economy

The South Georgia Environmental Management Plan was set out in 2000 and was revised in 2005, covering the period from 2006 to 2010. The British government is committed to providing a sustainable policy framework which conserves, manages and protects the rich natural environment, at the same time allowing for human activities and the generation of revenue.
Income is derived from fishing licences, fees for transshipping fish catches, tourist landing charges and the sale of postage stamps.

Agriculture

Fishing
Large-scale fishing began in 1969/70 by Soviet bloc countries. In 1993, the UK extended its territorial waters around the SGSSI from 19.3km (12 miles) to 321.8km (200 miles) and created the SGSSI Maritime Zone. In 1996, new laws opened fishing grounds with a licensing scheme. Approximately 100–200,000 tonnes of krill are caught around South Georgia each year. The SGSSI government applies conservation measures to the maritime zone, but has the right to impose additional measures if appropriate. There is satellite imagery surveillance of the fishing zone.
The toothfish total allowable catch (TAC) for the 2006/07 season was increased by 15 per cent by the SGSSI and approved by the Convention for the Conservation of Antarctic Marine Resources

KEY FACTS

Official name: South Georgia and the South Sandwich Islands (SGSSI)

Head of State: Queen Elizabeth II; represented by Commissioner Alan Edden Huckle (resides in Falkland Islands) (from July 2006)

Area: 3,755 square km

Population: 20 (2004) (British Antarctic Survey (BAS) scientists)

Capital: King Edward Point (administrative centre)

Official language: English

Currency: Falkland Islands pound or pound sterling (Fl£ or £) = 100 pence

Exchange rate: Fl£ or £0.51 per US$ (Jan 2007); (pegged to pound sterling)

Tourism
Visitors arrive mainly by tour ships, although an international airport is planned. The largest number cme from the US (32 per cent) , followed by the UK (25 per cent) and Germany (15 per cent). Extended walks, ie more than one kilometre from the landing site, are growing in popularity, as are visits to the nesting sites of the wandering albatross, especially Prion Island, which is carefully managed.

Environment
The South Georgia Environmental Plan 2005 (for the period 2006–10) was published on the British Antarctic website in January 2006.
South Georgia is the breeding ground for some 85 per cent of the world's southern fur seal population, as well as significant populations of elephant seals, albatrosses, petrels and penguins. In 1910, reindeer were introduced by Norwegian whaling companies.
The South Sandwich Islands represent a maritime ecosystem.

Hydrocarbons

Time
GMT minus two hours

Geography
South Georgia is an isolated, mountainous sub-Antarctic island, which lies in the South Atlantic Ocean, 2,150km east of Tierra del Fuego and about 1,390km east-south-east of the Falkland Islands. Surrounded by cold waters originating from the Antarctic, South Georgia has a harsher climate than expected from its latitude. More than 50 per cent of the island is covered by permanent ice with many large glaciers reaching the sea at the head of fjords. The main mountain range is the Allardyce Range, which has its highest point at Mount Paget (2,960m).
The South Sandwich Islands, which comprise a chain of active volcanic islands around 240km long, lie about 750km south-east of South Georgia. The climate is wholly Antarctic and in the late winter, the islands may be surrounded by pack ice.
Hemisphere
Southern

Climate
South Georgia and the South Sandwich Islands are prone to very sudden and unexpected changes of weather brought on by the Antarctic Convergence, where cold waters flowing up from Antarctica meet warm water from the north. The average temperature in summer is -2 degrees Centigrade.

Entry requirements
Only a limited number of visitors are allowed to land each year. All visitors must apply to the Office of the Commissioner, South Georgia and South Sandwich Islands, Government House, Stanley, Falkland Islands (tel: (+500) 27-433, fax: (+500) 27-434; e-mail: gov.house@horizon.co.fk) at least 60 days in advance of their journey for permission to land. Application forms can be obtained from the Commissioner's office or on-line from the official South Georgia government website (www.sgisland.org). Details of all places to be visited must be provided and there is a landing fee. There are no search-and-rescue facilities.
Passports
Passports must be valid for a minimum of six months.
Visa
Not required, but visitors must report to the Marine Officer at King Edward Point, Cumberland Bay East.

Health (for visitors)
Advisable precautions
There are no medical facilities available. Comprehensive medical emergency insurance is necessary as well as sufficient stocks of prescribed medication. Sunburn is a problem in this sub-polar region, sunblock should be applied regularly.
All of the historic buildings in the territory present a safety risk; they are storm damaged and flimsy, causing wind blown asbestos particles. Visitors should not approach within 200 metres of them without permission of the Marine Officer at King Edward Point.

Credit cards
The museum shop accepts VISA and Mastercard, but not American Express.

Working hours
Government
Mon–Fri (winter): 0900–1315, 1430–1730; Mon–Fri (summer): 1100–1315, 1630–1930.

Telecommunications
Postal services
A new post code for the islands has been issued through the Universal Postal Union: SIQQ 1ZZ.

Getting there
Air
There is currently no routine air access, but there are plans for an international airport.
Surface
The only access is by yacht or cruise ships.

Getting about
National transport
Road: There are no road links on the islands.

BUSINESS DIRECTORY

The addresses listed below are a selection only. While World of Information makes every endeavour to check these addresses, we cannot guarantee that changes have not been made, especially to telephone numbers and area codes. We would welcome any corrections.

Telephone area codes
There are no land lines on South Georgia. All communications are by either radio or mobile/cell phones

Ministries

Other useful addresses
British Antarctic Survey, High Cross, Madingley Rd, Cambridge CB3 OET, UK (tel: (+44-1223) 221-400; fax: (+44-1223) 362-616; e-mail: information@bas.ac.uk).
Licensing Officer SGSSI, Fisheries Department, Stanley, Falkland Islands (tel: (+500) 27-260; fax: (+500) 27-265; e-mail: fish.fig@horizon.co.fk).
Office of the Commissioner, South Georgia and South Sandwich Islands, Government House, Stanley, Falkland Islands (tel: (+500) 27-433, fax: (+500) 27-434; e-mail:gov.house@horizon.co.fk).
Project Atlantis (Environmental and educational resource) Dundee University, 23 Springfield, Dundee, Scotland DD1 4JE (tel: (+44) (0)1382 388-159; internet: www.atlantishome.org).

Internet sites
British Antarctic survey: www.antartic.ac.uk
British Geographical Survey: www.bgs.ac.uk
Government website: www.sgisland.org
Information for Yachts visiting South Georgia: www.rccpf.org.uk/ anc click on Index MAPS showing PUBLICATIONS.
South Atlantic Remote Territories Media Association: www.sartma.com
South Georgia Heritage Trust: www.sght.org
University of Dundee educational resource: www.atlantishome.org
UK Foreign and Commonwealth Office: www.fco.gov.uk

Spain

Spain celebrated the end of 2007 by triumphantly announcing that it had overtaken Italy in GDP per capita. In what was the run up to a general election, this was good news for Spanish prime minister, José Luis Rodríguez Zapatero. Spain saw a prolongation of the period of buoyant economic activity in 2007, with GDP growth of 3.8 per cent, only 0.1 per cent down on the previous year. In its report on the Spanish economy, Banco de Espana (BE) (Bank of Spain) noted that this performance was compatible with an easing of approximately 0.5 per cent in the contribution of national demand to growth, offset by a similar-sized improvement in the contribution of the external sector. However, following strong growth of 4.1 per cent in the first quarter of 2007, Spanish economic activity had gradually slowed to 3.5 per cent by the final quarter of 2007. In June 2008 the prestigious Organisation for Economic Co-operation and Development (OECD) lowered its growth forecasts for Spain for 2008 and 2009. In so doing the Paris-based agency was merely formalising what every Spanish businessman and housewife already knew to be the case. Things certainly weren't what they used to be as the housing market slumped into freefall.

Reality check

The OECD forecast Spanish gross domestic product (GDP) growth to be 1.6 per cent for 2008, down from an earlier forecast of 2.5 per cent. The forecast for 2009 was a growth rate of 1.1 per cent, down from an earlier 2.4 per cent. Were the OECD forecasts to be correct, Spain would under perform the euro zone for the first time since the currency bloc was established; the OECD forecast average euro zone growth at 1.7 per cent for 2008, and 1.4 per cent for 2009. Spanish economy minister, Pedro Solbes, described the OECD forecast as 'overly pessimistic'; in April 2008 the Spanish government had already cut its growth figure down to 2.1 per cent from an original 3.1 per cent. Sr Solbes considered the OECD had 'under-estimated' the impact of the

KEY FACTS

Official name: Reino de España (Kingdom of Spain)

Head of State: King Juan Carlos I (since 1975)

Head of government: Prime Minister José Luis Rodríguez Zapatero (PSOE) (since 2004; re-elected 12 Apr 2008)

Ruling party: Partido Socialista Obrero Español (PSOE) (Spanish Socialist Workers' Party) (since 2004; re-elected 9 Mar 2008)

Area: 504,782 square km, including the Balearic and Canary Islands, and the Ceuta and Melilla enclaves in North Africa

Population: 44.87 million (2007)

Capital: Madrid

Official language: Castilian Spanish, Catalan (in Catalonia including the Balearics), Basque (in the Basque provinces), Valencian (Province of Valencia), Galician (Galicia).

Currency: Euro (eur) = 100 cents

Exchange rate: eur0.63 per US$ (Jul 2008)

GDP per capita: US$32,067 (2007)

GDP real growth: 3.80% (2007)

Labour force: 21.77 million (2007)*

Unemployment: 8.20% (2007)

Inflation: 2.80% (2007)

Balance of trade: -US$85.59 billion (2005)

Foreign debt: US$1,217.77 billion (2004)

Visitor numbers: 58.50 million (2006)*

* estimated figure

government's economic stimulus measures. The most high profile of the measures was an across the board personal income tax rebate of 300 (US$330) (rising to 400 (US$440) in 2009) which it was hoped would inject some 6 billion (US$6.6 billion) into the economy, boosting consumer spending by 0.7 per cent in 2008 and by a further 1.0 per cent in 2009. According to Sr Solbes this single measure would add 0.2 per cent and 0.3 per cent respectively to GDP. The OECD's acting Chief Economist, Jorgen Elmeskov, had identified Spain – after Iceland – as the OECD member country most vulnerable to what he described as the 'head winds' generated by the global financial crisis. OECD secretary general, Angel Gurría, added that in Spain the construction sector was a more important component of the economy.

What was certainly the case was that Spaniards' confidence in the economy had plummeted since the beginning of 2008 as rocketing food and fuel prices, rising unemployment and the slump in property prices combined to send optimism to new lows. The last time Spain had been in recession was in 1993. A survey of consumer attitudes conducted by Spain's Sociological Research Institute found unemployment and the economy in general to be the two biggest issues of concern to the country. Of those answering the survey, 46.1 per cent described the situation in April 2008 as either 'bad' or 'very bad' – a nine point increase over March. More than half of the respondents considered that the situation had worsened over the previous 12 months, with 44.5 per cent expecting it to worsen even more over the following 12 months. A meagre 10 per cent thought that the economy would improve in that time.

In May the rise in oil prices pushed Spanish inflation to its highest level for 11 years, despite the manifest slowing down of the economy. The Instituto Nacional Estadístico (INE) (National Statistics Institute), which had given the annual growth figure for consumer prices to be 4.2 per cent in April 2008, put the figure for May 2008 at 4.8 per cent. Retail sales in April 2008 had fallen for the fifth month in a row. May sales were down by 3.5 per cent on a year earlier, in March the figure had been 5.5 per cent. While food sales in April rose by 1.2 per cent, all other items fell by 1.3 per cent. Purchases of household goods dropped by 5.8 per cent. At constant prices, and after correcting for the number of shopping days available, total sales dropped by 3.5 per cent in April.

The number of building permits issued for housing for the first quarter of 2008 dropped by almost 60 per cent, to a figure of 87,500. The March fall had been even more dramatic when the number of building permits issued dropped by 72 per cent. In the 'normal' years of Spain's construction boom the number of annual housing starts had reached some 800,000; estimates for 2008 were nearer 250,000 as Spanish property developers came to terms with a housing stock of some 600,000 unsold new homes. Spain's College of Property Registrars reported a drop of 29 per cent in property transactions in the first quarter of 2008. In March the INE reported a drop in existing home sales of 46 per cent. In recent years, residential construction has accounted for some 9 per cent of Spain's annual GDP, roughly twice the average figure among Europe's industrialised countries. To put the comparison into perspective, for some years Spain accounted for the construction of more new houses than Britain, France and Germany combined.

Paradise lost

In 2007, GDP growth had averaged 3.8 per cent, the result of some easing in domestic demand and an improvement in the contribution of net external demand to output growth. The BE noted that against this background, the slowing trajectory on which the Spanish economy embarked during 2008 was consistent with the tailing off of some of the impulses behind the buoyancy of spending in previous years, and with the maturing of the business cycle. With hindsight, the raising of interest rates by the European Central Bank (ECB), and the increasingly subdued rises in house prices had begun to temper consumption and residential investment decisions as early as 2006. The gradual loss of momentum in domestic demand continued in 2007, but was not reflected on a similar scale by GDP, owing to the offsetting effect of net external demand. The contribution of net exports to growth was forecast to carry on improving due to a lesser pace of imports. One, possibly the only, bright spot in the economic panorama was that investment in equipment ended the year at a rate of increase of close to 9 per cent, highlighting the still robust degree of business activity in late 2007 against a background of sound corporate earnings and a favourable demand outlook.

Spain's net borrowing continued to increase, albeit at a slacker pace than in previous years, reaching 9.5 per cent of GDP in 2007, mainly due to a marked and expected deterioration in the income balance. The tendency towards a gradual easing in investment by companies and, above all, by households was expected to reduce the current account deficit. The pace of employment generation reflected the gradual slowdown of activity in the second half of 2007, ending the year at a growth rate of 2.5 per cent. This trajectory has continued, somewhat more sharply, in the opening months of 2008. It has particularly affected employment in the construction industry and also, though to a lesser extent, in manufacturing activities, some of which are closely related to the construction branch. In contrast,

KEY INDICATORS **Spain**

	Unit	2003	2004	2005	2006	2007
Population	m	40.66	41.34	43.39	44.07	44.87
Gross domestic product (GDP)	US$bn	836.10	991.44	1,127.97	1,231.73	1,438.96
GDP per capita	US$	20,335	24,144	25,997	27,950	32,067
GDP real growth	%	2.5	2.7	3.5	3.9	3.8
Inflation	%	3.2	3.1	3.4	3.6	2.8
Unemployment	%	11.4	11.3	9.2	8.5	8.3
Coal output	mtoe	7.0	6.7	6.4	6.1	20.1
Exports (fob) (goods)	US$m	151,876	184,255	194,502	220,774	256,682
Imports (cif) (goods)	US$m	200,088	248,779	280,094	325,444	380,198
Balance of trade	US$m	-38,212	-64,524	-85,592	-104,670	-123,516
Current account	US$m	-23,676	-49,160	-83,001	-106,399	-145,275
Total reserves minus gold	US$m	19,788.0	12,389.0	9,678.0	10,822.0	11,480.0
Foreign exchange	US$m	17,513.0	10,481.0	8,594.0	10,088.0	10,792.0
Exchange rate	per US$	0.88	0.80	0.77	0.75	0.69

employment in services is proving far more resilient. Despite this loss of dynamism in the labour market, labour costs began to rise in 2007, when compensation per employee grew at a rate of 3.6 per cent, and have continued to do so in early 2008, with growth in wage settlements to February of 3.5 per cent. It is highly likely, once the effect of indexation clauses (for the deviation by inflation from its official target in 2007) is taken into account, that labour costs will rise by more than 4 per cent in 2008 for almost 70 per cent of private sector workers subject to a collective bargaining agreement. This development was considered unfortunate by the BE, given the cyclical changes facing the Spanish economy, as it may ultimately have an adverse effect on firms' hiring decisions, accentuating the unemployment situation.

The election

The terrorist bombings of 11 March 11 2004 not only managed to alter the course of Spanish politics but at the same time drive it from the international stage on which it had begun to take its place. An editorial in the *Wall St Journal* was less than complimentary about prime minister José Luis Rodríguez Zapatero's 'invisibility' internationally. Four years on, in the weeks before the 9 March 2008 elections, the polls were not able to give any clear predictions as to the outcome. In the event, Sr Zapatero (by Spanish custom he should be known as Sr Rodríguez, but somehow he is stuck with the more evocative name – which means 'cobbler') and his Partido Socialist Obrero de Espana (PSOE) (Spanish Workers' Socialist Party) won a slightly bigger victory with a 16 seat margin over their main rivals, the Partido Popular (PP). (Popular Party). The PSOE's win largely reflected national sentiment – in the four years since 2004, Spain had withdrawn its troops from Iraq and the government had put in place a number of 'liberal' social measures such as legalising gay marriages.

Perhaps surprisingly, the electorate appeared to have considered Mr Zapatero and his economic team, still headed up by Sr Solbes, to be the better bet to steer the national economy through tricky times. Equally surprisingly, the PSOE team were also considered a better bet to deal with the fraught question of Basque nationalism. Not long before the general election took place the Basque terrorist faction Euzkadi Ta Askatasuna (ETA), shot a retired Basque town councillor in the Basque town of Mondragón. ETA's stated aim is the establishment of a Marxist independent state comprising the Spanish Basque provinces of Vizcaya, Guipuzcoa, Alava, as well as the autonomous region of Navarra, and the south-western French Departments of Labourd, Basse-Navarra and Soule. Beneath this somewhat grandiose ambition lies a less attractive veneer of petty crime, drug dealing and delinquency. Sr Zapatero's efforts to resolve the Basque problem had been less than adroit, succeeding in little more than seeing ETA abandon – with fatal consequences – the 'permanent' ceasefire it had declared in mid-2007. Announcing the end of the ceasefire, ETA also vowed to 'act on all fronts in defence of the Basque Country'.

An equally fraught problem that had caused both political parties to make bold statements without too much conviction was that of immigration. Mariano Rajoy, the leader of the PP had claimed that the PSOE were 'soft' on immigrants. By European standards, Spain's 10 per cent immigrant population has yet to reach worrying proportions. But Spain has no tradition of dealing with immigration – the sight of Moroccan shop assistants or even waitresses in Catalonia is new. By focussing on immigration rather than on the more pressing question of the economy, Mr Rajoy may well have handed Mr Zapatero an electoral gift. In the Spring of 2007 immigration may have been exercising the politicians minds, but inflation and job security were what mattered most to the voters. Perhaps ironically, when questioned about the handling of immigration, voters appeared to have greater confidence in Mr Rajoy's more robust approach.

Franco goes

In late 2007 Mr Zapatero's government saw its controversial *Ley de la Memoria Historica* (*Law of Historical Memory*), reach the statute book. The law aimed to draw a line, if not heal, some of Spain's lingering differences and memories but, in the view of many, only succeeded in exacerbating an already fierce debate. In Spain the wounds opened by the Civil War had generally been left to heal themselves alone. Mr Rajoy's PP had accused the government of going against the spirit of democratic transition that had allowed Spain to put the past behind it. Relations between the two principal parties have always lacked the parliamentarian spirit seen in more northerly European democracies.

Risk assessment

Economy	Fair
Politics	Good
Regional stability	Good

COUNTRY PROFILE

Historical profile

The Spanish are descended from the Iberians, Celts, Romans and Arabs that conquered the peninsula up to the eighth century.

From around the eleventh century a Christian Reconquista (Reconquest) of territories lost to the Moors began in earnest. In the thirteenth century, Castilla and Aragón emerged as the two main kingdoms in the peninsula. In the fifteenth century, the kingdoms united, following the marriage of the princess of Castilla and the heir to the throne of Aragón, Isabella I and Ferdinand V. The Catholic Monarchs completed the Reconquista, united all of Spain and launched the Spanish Inquisition, which forced Catholicism on all of the population.

1492 Spain began colonising much of the Americas, beginning with Hispaniola (Haiti and the Dominican Republic), following Christopher Columbus' landings in the region.

1556 Spain took control of Melilla in Morocco.

1560s Spain colonised the Philippines.

1668 Spain took control of Ceuta in Morocco.

1702–14 The major European powers fought to install a new monarchy in Spain in the War of the Spanish Succession, following the death of Charles II in 1700. France eventually installed the grandson of Louis XIV, Philip of Anjou, as the King of Spain.

1778 Spain took control of Fernando Pó (Bioko, now part of Equatorial Guinea).

1808–13 The Spanish population, with help from Britain, fought against French rule in the War of Independence.

1868 The army revolted against the Spanish monarchy. A military government, led by General Juan Prim, took power. Prim offered the Spanish crown to the son of Italian king Victor Emmanuel II, Amadeo of Savoy.

1873 Prim was assassinated. Amadeo of Savoy left Spain after failing to get installed as the new king. The remnants of the government announced the creation of the First Spanish Republic.

1874 Attempts to introduce constitutional and political reforms to the Republic failed and the monarchy was restored.

1884 Spain took control of the Spanish Sahara (now Western Sahara); it became a province of Spain in 1934.

1885 Spain established the colony of Spanish Guinea in Central Africa, comprising Río Muni and Fernando Pó.

1898 Spain lost control of Cuba, Guam, the Philippines and Puerto Rico, after being defeated in Cuba by the US.

1912 Spain and France partitioned Morocco into protectorates. Spain established the Spanish Morocco protectorate.
1923 The war in Morocco and an economic recession resulted in an authoritarian government led by General Miguel Primo de Rivera, taking over Spain.
1926 The Spanish and French defeated the Moroccans, bringing the war to an end.
1930 After failing with economic and political reforms, Primo de Rivera resigned from government
1931 Republican parties won the municipal elections, which led the Spanish King, Alfonso XIII, to abdicate. The Second Republic was declared.
1936–39 Civil war broke out when the democratically elected Republican government was attacked in an attempted coup d'état. The Nationalist alliance composed of monarchists, right-wing parties and the army, led by Francisco Franco y Bahamonde, fought to take control of Spain. Fascist Germany and Italy, ignoring arms embargoes, supported Franco's forces with men and materials. The government, denied legitimate arms from other European sources, gained the backing of the Soviet Union and welcomed over 56,000 overseas volunteers to fight in the International Brigades.
1939 Nationalist forces won the Civil War. General Franco became Head of State, established a dictatorship, restricted individual liberties and severely repressed all challenges to his power.
1955 An isolated Spain was allowed to join the UN.
1956 Spain granted Morocco independence, but retained control of the Ceuta and Melilla enclaves in northern Morocco.
1958 Spain handed the Tarfaya enclave in West Africa over to Morocco.
1959 The Euskadi ta Azkatasuna (ETA) (Homeland and Freedom) group was formed with the aim of creating an independent Basque region.
1968 Spanish Guinea in West Africa gained independence and was renamed Equatorial Guinea.
1969 Spain withdraws from the Sidi Ifni enclave in West Africa, handing it over to Morocco.
1973 Prime Minister Admiral Luis Carrero Blanco was assassinated by ETA after the government had executed a number of Basque militants.
1975 General Franco died. Juan Carlos, grandson of the last King, Alfonso XIII, was crowned King Juan Carlos I and became Head of State. Spain withdrew from Western Sahara.
1977 Restrictions on political activity were lifted and free parliamentary elections were held. The Union de Centro Democrático (UCD) (Union of the Democratic Centre) coalition, led by Adolfo Sáurez González, won.
1978 A new constitution confirmed Spain as a parliamentary monarchy with freedom for political parties and enshrined the 'indissoluble unity of the Spanish nation'. It also recognised the right to autonomy of its 'nationalities and regions'.
1980s Referenda on regional autonomy in the Basque region and Catalonia began the process of devolution. Spain was divided into 17 regions, each with a president and parliament, plus the two self-governing enclaves on the north African coast (Moroccan) – Ceuta and Melilla.
1981 The paramilitary Guardia Civil (Civil Guard) attempted a coup d'état, holding members of the cabinet and parliament hostage. The coup was aborted when King Carlos demanded that the military must remain loyal to the crown and the constitution.
1982 The Partido Socialista Obrero Español (PSOE) (Spanish Socialist Workers' Party), under Felipe González, won the general election. Morocco laid claim to Ceuta, Melilla and the Canary Islands.
1983 A secret death squad known as the Grupo Antiterrorista de Liberacion (GAL) (Anti-Terrorist Group) was set up funded by the Interior Ministry in order to combat ETA. Between 1983 and 1987, 28 people are murdered by the GAL in what became known as Spain's 'dirty war'. Several of those killed later turned out to have no connection with ETA and revelations surrounding the death squads' activities later contributed to the downfall of the PSOE government.
1986 Spain joined the EU.
1986–96 The PSOE won the 1986, 1990 and 1993 parliamentary elections and Felipe González served four terms as prime minister.
1995 José María Aznar, leader of the opposition Partido Popular (PP) (Popular Party) survived an assassination attempt by ETA.
1996 Aznar became prime minister of a PP minority government.
1998 ETA announced a unilateral ceasefire. It was blamed for more than 800 deaths since its campaign of terror began in 1968.
2000 ETA called off its ceasefire. The PP won parliamentary elections.
2001 A new round of talks began between Britain and Spain on the future of Gibraltar.
2002 Euro currency replaced the peseta. An international incident occurred when 12 Moroccan soldiers landed on the desbuted tiny uninhabited Isla del Perejil (Parsley Island), close to the Spanish-controlled Ceuta enclave in Morocco. Spain re-occupied the island, to which Morocco lays claim and calls Leila. An sinking oil tanker severely polluted around 400km of Atlantic coastline in northern Spain.
2003 The Batasuna (Unity) party (previously the Herribatasuna party), believed to be the political organisation representing ETA, was banned. Government support for the US-lead coalition invasion of Iraq was opposed by an estimated 85 per cent of the population, causing a further deterioration in support for the PP.
2004 ETA announced a cease-fire in Catalonia. In March, 10 co-ordinated bombs exploded on four commuter trains in Madrid, during the morning rush hour, killing 191 people and injuring over 1,800. ETA denied responsibility; a gang of extremist Islamists, who later committed suicide in a bomb blast during a police raid, were identified as the culprits. The Madrid atrocity had an immediate effect on the electorate, who gave a victory to the opposition party, PSOE in the general elections. José Luis Rodríguez Zapatero (PSOE) was sworn in as prime minister on 7 April.
2005 In February, Spain voted in favour of the EU constitution, but the turnout was low at 42.3 per cent. In the Basque regional elections in April, the moderate nationalist ruling party lost ground to the Socialists but retained office. In June, at least 250,000 people marched in Madrid to protest against the government's intention to negotiate with ETA. In August, 17 Spanish troops serving with NATO forces in Afghanistan were killed in a helicopter crash. In September, Spain reinforced fences protecting its enclaves in North Africa, Ceuta and Melilla, after hundreds of would-be immigrants attempted to storm the territories. In November, Spain concluded an arms deal with Venezuela, despite protests from the US; Spain launched an investigation into allegations that CIA planes made secret stopovers on Spanish territory for purposes of extraordinary rendition, whereby foreign suspects were sent to another country for interrogation under less humane conditions but in actuality were likely to have been tortured by proxy.
2006 Spain agreed to write off most of the debt owed to it by Bolivia. ETA announced a complete cease-fire. In a local referendum residents of Catalonia voted by 73.9 per cent in favour of greater regional autonomy and self-government, plans are expected to include the right to spend tax revenues and more control over airports and immigration. The outcome promoted other regions, such as Galicia, Valancia, the Balearic islands and Andalusia to push for greater autonomy. The largest fraud case in Spain's history may have cost over 200,000 investors

US$5.4 billion; an estimated 1 per cent of the population had invested their savings in two unregulated and unprotected stamp trading companies that lacked government backed insurance policies. The companies traded worthless stamps with other crooked dealers in a scam that included embezzlement, money laundering and tax evasion. Authorities were concerned that the scandal risked damaging confidence in private investment in Spain. ETA exploded a car bomb in a Madrid airport car park, killing two people and ending a nine-month cease-fire. However ETA also claimed that its cease-fire was still in effect. Over 31,000 African migrants (six times the numbers arriving in 2005), lacking work permits, made the hazardous ocean journey, in open wooden boats, to the Canary Islands in an attempt to enter the EU for work and a better life.

2007 In January, Prime Minister Zapatero acknowledged that he had committed a 'clear error' in his prediction of peace with ETA 24 hours before the December bomb blast but did not give a reason for the failure of talks with ETA. In June ETA called off its 15-month ceasefire. On 4 October, Spanish police arrested 23 senior members of Batasuna. Of the 28 defendants on trial for the 2004 Madrid train bombings three were found guilty on 31 October and sentenced to thousands of years in prison while seven were acquitted, including the alleged mastermind.

2008 In the 9 March general election, the ruling PSOE won 169 seats, but was short of the 176 needed for an outright parliamentary majority. The opposition PP won 153 seats. The re-election of José Zapatero as prime minister was not a foregone conclusion. In the first round of voting in the Congress of Deputies, held on 9 April, with a majority of 176 votes required, he won only 168 with 158 against and 23 abstentions. In the second round, when only a relative majority was required, he won with 169 votes. He took office on 12 April and named a new cabinet with a majority of women members. The senate voted overwhelmingly to adopt the European Union's Lisbon Treaty on 15 July. Once King Juan Carlos has signed the treaty, Spain will become the 23rd EU state to ratify it.

Political structure

Constitution

The constitution dates from the advent of democracy in 1978. Most laws are debated and passed in Congress first, and then in the Senate, the upper house, which can send back amended bills. In case of emergency, the government may issue decrees. They are called Decree Laws if they require ratification by parliament. All laws require the king's ratification and come into force when published in the Official Bulletin.

There are 17 comunidades autónomas (autonomous regions): Andalucia, Aragón, Asturias, Baleares (Balearic Islands), Canarias (Canary Islands), Cantabria, Castilla-La Mancha, Castilla y León, Cataluñya, Comunidad Valencian, Extremadura, Galicia, La Rioja, Madrid, Murcia, Navarra, País Vasco (Basque country). Spain also has sovereignty of five communities on and off the coast of Morocco: the coastal ports of Ceuta and Melilla are administered as autonomous regions; the islands of Chafarinas, Peñon de Alhucemas and Peñon de Velez de la Gomera are under direct Spanish administration.

Autonomous regions have regional parliaments and governments with varying degrees of powers on local affairs. Three regions with a tradition of autonomy and their own language – the Basque country (Euskadi), Cataluñya and Galicia – have these wider powers. The Basque government, for example, raises its own taxes.

There is universal suffrage from age 18.

Form of state

Federal parliamentary democratic monarchy

The executive

The president of the government (prime minister) appoints the cabinet and has executive power. He is appointed by the head of state and his appointment must be ratified by the national legislature.

National legislature

The bicameral Las Cortes Generales (The General Courts) is the national legislature.

The Congreso de los Diputados (Congress of Deputies) is the lower house and has 350 members, directly elected every four years under proportional representation.

In the 248-member Senado (Senate) the upper house is composed of 208 senators who are chosen in direct elections in the 51 provinces. An additional 40 senators are appointed as regional representatives. Senators serve a four-year term.

Parties need to gain at least 3 per cent of the vote to gain representation in either house.

Legal system

The Spanish legal system is based on civil law. The Supreme Court is at the summit of the judiciary. There are also 16 Division High Courts, 50 Provincial High Courts and, below these, Courts of First Instance, District Courts, Municipal and Peace Courts. Spain does not accept compulsory jurisdiction by the International Court of Justice (ICJ).

Last elections

9 March 2008 (parliamentary)

Results: Parliamentary: PSOE won 43.64 per cent of the vote (169 seats out of 350); PP, 40.11 per cent (153); Izquierda Unida (UL) (United Left) 3.8 per cent (two), Convergència i Unió (CiU) (Convergence and Union) (coalition of two Catalán parties) 3.5 per cent (11), Esquerra Republicana de Cataluyna (ERC) (Catalan Republican Left) 1.17 per cent (three), Eusko Alberdi Jeltzalea-Partido Nacionalista Vasco (EAJ-PNV) (Basque Nationalist Party) 1.2 per cent (six); Coalición Canaria (CC) (Canary Island Coalition) 0.65 per cent (two); Bloque Nacionalista Galego (BNG) 0.82 per cent (two); Unión, Progreso y Democracia (UPD) (Union, Progress and Democracy) 1.2 per cent (one); Nafarroa Bai (NaBai) (Navarre Yes) 0.25 per cent (one).

Senate: PP won 101 seats (out of 264), PSOE 89, Entesa Catalana de Progrés (coalition of four parties from Catatonia) 12, EAJ-PNV 2, CiU 4, members appointed by regional legislatures 56.

Next elections

March 2012 (parliamentary)

Political parties

Ruling party

Partido Socialista Obrero Español (PSOE) (Spanish Socialist Workers' Party) (since 2004; re-elected 9 Mar 2008)

Main opposition party

Partido Popular (PP) (People's Party)

Population

44.87 million (2007)

Last census: November 2001: 40,847,371 (including offshore territories)

Population density: 79 inhabitants per square km. Urban population: 78 per cent (1995–2001).

Annual growth rate: 0.7 per cent 1994–2004 (WHO 2006)

Ethnic make-up

In addition to Spaniards, there are several minor groups, including Gypsies, Portuguese, Latin Americans and North Africans.

Religions

Roman Catholic (94 per cent), Islam, Protestant and Jewish.

Education

Primary schooling begins at the age of six and lasts for six years. Secondary schooling lasts until aged 16 (both of which are provided free). Final exams allow progression to higher secondary schools which teach either academic or vocational programmes. Teaching may be carried out in Spanish, Catalan, Basque, or Galician.

Private schools are responsible for the education of more than 30 per cent of children.

Higher education is only possible after successfully sitting an entrance exam.

There are some 20 state universities, four polytechnics, two independent universities and eight technical universities. The development of alternative forms of higher education have made access to established universities more selective. It has also been proposed that the present five-year university degree courses be reduced to three years.
Public expenditure on education typically amounts to 5 per cent of annual gross national income.
Literacy rate: 97.9 per cent, adult rates (2003)
Compulsory years: Six to 16
Enrolment rate: 109 per cent, gross primary enrolment of relevant age group (including repeaters); 120 per cent, gross secondary enrolment (World Bank).
Pupils per teacher: 15 in primary schools

Health

Per capita total expenditure on health (2003) was US$1,853; of which per capita government spending was US$1,321, at the international dollar rate, (WHO 2006).
As Spain's economy has grown, spending on healthcare has risen, reaching 7.5 per cent of GDP, spending just below the Organisation for Economic Co-operation and Development (OECD) average of 7.7 per cent on medical goods and services. Most of this expenditure is in the form of state funding at 71.4 per cent. Efforts are under way to cut the state's pharmaceutical bill, representing 20 per cent of total public health spending. Pre-paid healthcare plans amount to 14.1 per cent of the 28.6 per cent of GDP spent privately on health costs.
The health sector, under the authority of INSALUD, the National Institute of Health, includes hospitals, community health centres and emergency services. The social security health scheme covers all insured persons and their dependants.

HIV/Aids

HIV prevalence: 0.7 per cent aged 15–49 in 2003 (World Bank)
Life expectancy: 80 years, 2004 (WHO 2006)
Fertility rate/Maternal mortality rate: 1.3 births per woman, 2004 (WHO 2006)
Birth rate/Death rate: 10 births per 1,000 population; 9.5 deaths per 1,000 population (2003).
Child (under 5 years) mortality rate (per 1,000): 4.0 per 1,000 live births (World Bank)
Head of population per physician: 3.30 physicians per 1,000 people, 2003 (WHO 2006)

Welfare

The National Institute of Social Security oversees a national insurance scheme, which is compulsory for all employed and self-employed workers. It provides a range of benefits including those for sickness, maternity, accident insurance, retirement pensions and unemployment benefits. Contributions are paid by employees, employers and the state. The employed are classified in a series of professional and labour categories for the purpose of determining social security taxes. Each category has maximum and minimum contribution bases which are revised annually. The state pays retirement pensions from the age of 65 for men and women. Spain offers a special system of unemployment protection for casual workers in agriculture. The Rural Employment Plan combines employment policy measures and social welfare benefits. The benefit is granted to workers who have paid contributions under the Agricultural Social Security Scheme and is equivalent to 75 per cent of the national minimum wage payable for a maximum period of 180 days.

Main cities

Madrid (capital, estimated population 2.9 million in 2005), Barcelona (capital of Catalonia) (1.5 million), Valencia (741,100), Seville (685,393), Zaragoza (621,164), Málaga (525,662), Bilbao (344,236), Murcia (384,429), Córdoba (309,882), Las Palmas (Majorca) (354,863), Las Palmas (Grand Canary) (354,863).

Languages spoken

Castilian Spanish is the principal language; Catalán, Galician, Euskera (Basque), Aragonese and Asturian are also spoken. English and French are spoken in most business circles.

Official language/s

Castilian Spanish, Catalan (in Catalonia including the Balearics), Basque (in the Basque provinces), Valencian (Province of Valencia), Galician (Galicia).

Media

The constitution enshrines the right to free expression of thoughts, ideas and opinions.

Press

The printed media market is mature with a wide variety of respected titles backed up by a plethora of specialist publications. The media is largely free, although the government has closed down two Basque newspapers, Egin, in 1998 and Euskaldunon Egunkari in 2003, accusing them of being linked with the terrorist organisation ETA.
Concerns have been raised that media outlets has been unduly influenced by political pressure.
Ownership is largely concentrated in the control of a few large media groups; foreign investment has been redirected to focus on periodicals.
Dailies: There are over 100 newspapers published daily, although most have circulations of less than 100,000. The major dailies are published in Madrid but other cities have their own dailies, particularly in Catalonia and the Basque region. Most publish in Spanish or in regional languages; some are bilingual. Free-issue newspapers account for around 51 per cent of the market.
In Spanish, with the largest circulation El País (www.elpais.com) is socialist in character in a tabloid format and has regional and international editions, ABC (www.abc.es) is a centre-right paper, El Mundo (www.elmundo.es) is a conservative publication. Other newspapers with smaller circulations, from Barcelona La Vanguardia (www.lavanguardia.es) and El Periodico de Catalunya (www.elperiodico.com) with articles in Catalan; from Bilbao El Correo (www.elcorreodigital.com) and El Diario Montanes (www.eldiariomontanes.es); from Andalucia Diario de Cadiz (www.diariodecadiz.es),Cordoba (www.diariocordoba.com) and Metro (www.diariometro.es) Seville; from the Balearic Islands Diario de Ibiza (www.diariodeibiza.es) and Mallorca Confidencial (www.mallorcaconfidencial.com); from Canary Islands La Provincia (www.laprovincia.es) and El Dia (www.eldia.es); from La Coruna Xornal (www.xornal.com) with articles in Galacian; from Andoain Berria (www.berria.info) in Basque.
English, French and Germany newspapers are published in areas with large expatriate communities and tourist areas.
Weeklies: There are several general and special interest magazines and news magazines such as Cambio 16, Sábado Gráfico and El Tiempo (www.tiempodehoy.com). El Mundo has a Sunday edition called La Revista. In the Canary Islands Canarias 7 reports news items, Metropolitan from Barcelona. Ragazza (www.ragazza.orange.es) Inerviú (www.interviu.es) and Diez Minutos (www.diezminutos.orange.es) are tabloid magazines.
Business: In Spanish, Cinco Días (www.cincodias.com), Expansión (www.expansion.com), La Gaceta de los Negocios (www.negocios.com/gaceta), Agenda de la Empresa Andaluza (www.agendaempresa.com), Vigo Empresa (www.puertodevigo.com), El Economista (www.eleconomista.es), El Mundo Financiero (www.elmundofinanciero.com) and

Negocio (www.neg-ocio.com). Weekly financial publications in Spanish include Su Dinero, Levamte-El Mercantil Valencia (www.levante-emv.com) from Valencia and Actualidad Económic (www.actualidad-economica.com) from Madrid.
Periodicals: A number of specialist magazine exist including Planeta Humano and Qué, bi-monthly covering people and current affairs.

Broadcasting
National public radio and television services are provided by Radiotelevisión Española (RTVE) (www.rne.es), which is funded by state subsidies and advertising.
Radio: The public broadcaster Radio Nacional de España (RNE) (www.rne.es), provides four national services. There are several commercial networks, the largest of which is Cadena SER (www.cadenaser.com) with over 50 regional stations.
There are over 100 radio stations, which have a presence in every region, including overseas territories, providing services over the internet.
Television: Televisión Española (TVE) (www.rtve.es) broadcasts several channels, from popular local programmes such as long-running dramas to international imported shows and special interest programmes. There are another three private terrestrial channels and six regional public broadcasters with 10 channels between them, some in Catalan and Basque. Digital and satellite TV networks have expanded rapidly and the government has plans to discontinue free-to-air analogue signals by 2010. National commercial channels include Tele Cinco (www.telecinco.es), Antena 3 (www.antena3tv.com) and Cuatro (www.cuatro.com).

Advertising
All usual media are available although TV and public hoardings tend to be most popular method, although radio, newspaper and cinema advertising is also widespread.

Economy
Spain has a mixed economy with large agricultural and industrial sectors, as well as important tourism and banking industries. In the 1990s, emphasis was increasingly placed on regional development, with assistance from the EU. In addition, key objectives of industrial strategy were to improve the efficiency of public enterprises and to stem losses, often involving the privatisation of companies.
Since the Maastricht Treaty of 1992, economic policies have been primarily dictated by the financial guidelines laid down in the EU's Stability and Growth Pact (SGP). Spain has been a major net recipient of EU transfers. It received approximately US$10 billion in 2004, or about 1 per cent of Spain's GDP.
Despite its growing economy, Spain has not fully recovered from the economic transition that was necessary for EU membership. The unemployment rate in Spain is still relatively high, standing at around nine per cent in 2005, but down from 10.4 per cent in 2004. The rate is declining overall, but such high rates carry social and economic costs. With the government committed to labour market reforms, including a reduction in union powers and changes to the social security system, more social disquiet cannot be ruled out.
Spain has benefited much more than other countries from low eurozone interest rates. Low mortgage rates, together with jobs creation, have led to an unprecedented demand for property, with construction becoming the motor of economic growth. Structural reforms and a sound fiscal policy have also helped boost the economy's health.

External trade
As a member of the European Union, Spain operates within a communitywide free trade union, with tariffs sets as a whole. Internationally, the EU has free trade agreements with a number of nations and trading blocs worldwide.
While agriculture only provides less than 4 per cent of GDP, Spain produces Europe's largest supply of citrus and strawberries and is the world's leading olive oil, and third largest wine producer. Manufacturing includes textiles, food processing, naval engineering, vehicle assembly and machinery; new technology includes information technology and telecommunications.
Exports accounts for around 55 per cent of GDP, while tourism (Spain is a worldwide top tourist destination) provides the majority of foreign earnings.

Imports
Main imports include machinery and equipment, petroleum and natural gas, chemicals, semi-finished goods, foodstuffs, consumer goods, and medical instruments.
Main sources: Germany (14.2 per cent total, 2006), France (12.8 per cent), Italy (8.3 per cent).

Exports
Commodity exports include machinery, vehicles, pharmaceuticals, medicines, consumer goods and agricultural products: olive oil and wine.
Main destinations: France (18.7 per cent total, 2006), Germany (10.9 per cent), Portugal (8.9 per cent).

Agriculture
Farming
Fundamental reform to the Common Agricultural Policy (CAP) was introduced throughout most of the EU on 1 January 2005. The subsidies paid on farm output, which tended to benefit large farms and encourage overproduction, were replaced by single farm payments not conditional on production. This is expected to reward farms that maintain a healthy environment, food safety and animal welfare standards. The changes are also intended to encourage market conscious production and cut the cost of CAP to the EU taxpayer. Spain introduced this measure on 1 January 2006.
Spain is the world's largest producer of olive oil: the industry has been modernising, although olive groves, mainly located in Andalucia, typically suffer periodic drought and work is usually undertaken by low paid migrant workers. The revised CAP should benefit the region by limiting unsustainable growth.
Spain is now the third-largest wine producer in Europe after France and Italy, with a growing tendency towards the quality end of the wine market. EU restrictions limit the amount of land available for vineyards and, with domestic consumers developing a taste for wines of increased quality, the price of grapes and available vineyards has increased enormously. Newer regions are producing quality wines to rival those of the long established Rioja and Penedes denominaciones.
Cava, the Spanish wine made using the champagne method, is gaining a global reputation for quality and value. Notable among these are Ribera de Duero in Castilla y Leon, where the legendary Vega Sicilia wines are produced, and the Priorat denominaciones in Catalonia.
Crop production ('000) for 2005 included: 13,792 tonnes (t) cereals in total, 3,788t wheat, 3,951t maize, 2,592t potatoes, 4,448t barley, 263t treenuts, 4,867t citrus fruit, 5,880t grapes, 4,474t tomatoes, 1,007t oilcrops, 40t tobacco, 3,713t olives, 1,131t peaches and nectarines, 6,677t sugar beet, 953t chillies and peppers, 798t apples, 330t seed cotton, 96t cotton lint, 14,805t fruit in total, 12,348t vegetables in total. Livestock production ('000) included: 5,736t meat in total, 715t t beef, 3,310t pig meat, 2487t lamb and goat meat, 1,341t poultry, 726t eggs, 7,465t milk, 37t honey, 80t cattle hides; 120 tonnes cocoons, silk.

Fishing
As the owner of the largest fishing fleet in the EU, Spain is also the largest consumer of seafood and seafood products in the EU. Spain's total fish catch continues to decline as a result of depleted stocks and lower limits on catches in both EU and

non-EU waters. Spain's seafood trade is mainly conducted with other EU countries, Argentina, Morocco and Namibia.
In 2004, the total marine fish catch was 739,416 tonnes and the total crustacean catch was 17,453 tonnes.

Forestry

Forest and other wooded land accounts for about half the land area, with forest cover estimated at 14.3 million hectares (ha). Most of the forest is available for wood supply. The area of forest has been expanding strongly, at an annual average increase of 0.62 per cent per year. About 80 per cent of forest is privately owned, while the remaining area is mostly owned by municipalities. Forest and other wooded land accounts for 50 per cent of total land area. About 45 per cent of the forest is available for wood supply. The main species are Scots and Aleppo pine, oak, beech, chestnut, poplars and eucalyptus.
Imported raw materials including eucalyptus pulpwood and hardwood logs are used for all primary forest products. Spain is a net importer of paper and sawnwood, although part of the pulp production is exported.
Exports of forest material in 2004 amounted to US$2.6 billion, while imports amounted to US$5.0 billion.
Production ('000) in 2004 included 16,290 cubic metres (cum) roundwood, 14,235cum industrial roundwood, 3,730cum sawnwood, 7,795cum sawlogs and veneers, 5,520cum pulpwood, 4,754cum wood-based panels, 2,055cum wood fuel; 5,490 tonnes (t) paper and paperboard (including 310t newsprint), 1,205t printing and writing paper, 1,917t paper pulp, 3,650t recovered paper.

Industry and manufacturing

The industrial sector contributes approximately 34 per cent to GDP and employs over 29 per cent of the labour force.
Since joining the EU, Spain's industry and manufacturing sectors have undergone modernisation and restructuring, assisted by large levels of foreign direct investment (FDI). The automotive, telecommunications and chemical industries dominate the sector.
Industrial production grew by 3.3 per cent year-on-year in August 2005 but fell to 0.5 per cent growth in September.

Tourism

Since 1996, Spain has been ranked second, behind the US, for tourist earnings globally, and second, behind France, for tourist numbers. The tourism industry accounts for around 12 per cent of Spain's GDP and accounts for around 8 per cent of total employment.
Spain's reputation for economic sea-and-sand holidays is under seige from eastern Mediterranian resorts, so that the long-term emphasis is now on diversification with quality and variety, year-round tourism and short-break city holidays.
The tourism sector contracted by 13 per cent in the wake of the US-led invasion of Iraq in March 2003. Bomb attacks carried out by al-Qaeda against commuter trains in Madrid on 11 March 2004 were expected to have a negative impact on Spain's tourism industry. However, tourism sector growth was between 3 and 4 per cent in the first quarter of 2004.
Visitors from Germany and UK make up over 48 per cent of all tourists. Total tourist receipts for 2005 are expected to amount to eur184.3 million (US$245.6 million).

Mining

The mining sector contributes 1 per cent to GDP. Spain is the world's second-largest producer of natural stone, which accounts for 15 per cent of the total value of Spanish mining. Marble has become a particularly important source of foreign exchange earnings. Gold, silver and copper mining take place on a small scale. Spain also extracts lignite, iron ore, mercury, pyrites, zinc, lead, copper and tungsten. The traditional production of uranium ore in Spain ceased with the closure of Mina Fé in Salamanca.

Hydrocarbons

Spain is heavily dependent on imported oil, with Mexico and Russia as its largest suppliers. In 2005, Spain had only 158 million barrels of proven domestic oil reserves. Some 99 per cent of the 1.6 million barrels per day (bpd) consumed by Spain in 2004 were imported. Spain's largest domestic production comes from the Casablanca complex in the Mediterranean, which provides 6,500bpd. Spain's total crude oil refining capacity stood at 1.4 million bpd in 2004. Oil consumption relative to that of gas has fallen steadily in Spain over the past two decades. Spain is currently exploring the Atlantic Ocean and the Bay of Cadiz for oil deposits but results have so far been disappointing.
Natural gas production is limited and much of Spain's domestic demand is supplied by imports. Consumption levels in 2004 were at 27.3 billion cubic metres. At current rates of production, reserves should last another 25 years. Spain imports gas from Norway, via pipelines through France, and Algeria, via pipelines running through Morocco. In July 2001, Spain and Algeria agreed to build a second trans-Moroccan pipeline, the Medgaz pipeline, which is expected to be complete by 2008.
Environmental restrictions mean that coal, Spain's largest indigenous energy source, is being gradually phased out. Coal reserves totalled 728 million tonnes in 2005. Government coal subsidies are expected to decrease by some 4 per cent per year, which will make the price of Spanish coal uncompetititve in the open market. Production levels in 2004 were at 6.7 million tonnes of oil equivalent (toe), a decrease of 2 per cent on 2003 output. Consumption totalled 21.1 million toe in 2004, up 3 per cent on 2003. In July 2002, the EU ordered Spain to lower its coal production by 65 per cent by 2010. Production subsidies will last until 2008 if coal mines do not improve their economic viability.

Energy

Most of Spain's electricity is generated by conventional thermal power plants (52.3 per cent), followed by hydroelectricity (25.2 per cent), nuclear (14.9 per cent) and other renewables (7.6 per cent).
Spain's electricity generation and consumption has increased in recent years at more than double the rate recorded in Western Europe as a whole. Rising consumption has stretched Spain's capacity and has resulted in a number of major blackouts.
Since January 2003, consumers have been able to choose their own electricity supplier.
In January 2004, Spain signed an agreement with Portugal to work towards integrating their respective electricity markets.

Financial markets

Stock exchange

The Bolsa de Madrid is the fourth-largest stock exchange in the eurozone.

Banking and insurance

Central bank

Banco de España; European Central Bank (ECB).

Main financial centre

Madrid

Time

Mainland – GMT plus one hour (daylight saving: late March–October, GMT plus two hours) = mainland
Canaries – GMT (daylight saving, GMT plus one hour)

Geography

Spain is situated in south-western Europe. It occupies most of the Iberian peninsula, sharing it with Portugal to the west. The country includes the Balearic Islands in the Mediterranean Sea (200km south-east of Barcelona), the Canary Islands in the Atlantic Ocean and two small enclaves in Morocco. Mainland Spain is bounded to the north by the Cantabrian Sea, the Pyrenees and France, to the east by the

Mediterranean, and to the south by the Straits of Gibraltar and Morocco.
Mountains ranges, including the Pyrenees, run from the Atlantic in the north to the Mediterranean coast. Another band runs down the east to the Sierra Nevada in the south, which includes the largest mainland mountain Mulhacén at 3,482 metres (m). Land in the south is dry with many traditional olive groves. The flat central plateau (meseta) occupies much of the land around the capital, Madrid. The longest river, the Ebro, is 940km, beginning in the Cantabrian mountains of the north-east and flowing into the Mediterranean. The River Tagus runs for 716km through central Spain and 322km in Portugal.
The Canary Islands are rugged volcanic Atlantic Ocean outcrops. Of the 13 islands six are uninhabited. Pico de Teide, on Tenerife, at 3,718 metres is Spain's tallest mountain.

Hemisphere

Northern

Climate

Most of Spain has a Mediterranean climate with mild winters and hot summers, although the mountainous north is colder and wetter. Temperatures range from 40 degrees centigrade Celsius (C) to minus 15 degrees C.

Dress codes

Particular attention is paid to dress, although dress codes are not rigid. Most businessmen and male officials wear suits and ties during business hours.

Entry requirements

Passports

Are required by all non-EU visitors and must be valid for at least six months beyond the planned stay. EU visitors and nationals of Andorra, Liechtenstein, Malta, Monaco and Switzerland may use valid national ID cards.

Visa

Required by all; except nationals of EU and Schengen Accord signatory countries. Tourists from North America and Australasia may visit, visa-free, for up to 90 days. All other nationals, visiting for business purposes, should contact the nearest Spanish embassy for a visa application form. A Schengen visa application (offered in several languages) can be downloaded from http://europa.eu/abc/travel/ see 'documents you will need'.

Currency advice/regulations

The import of foreign and local currency is unlimited. Export of local currency is unlimited but amounts over eur6,000 must be declared. Export of foreign currencies over the equivalent of eur3,050 in bank notes and travellers cheques must be declared.
Travellers cheques are widely accepted.

Customs

Personal items are duty-free. There are no duties levied on alcohol and tobacco between EU member states, providing amounts imported are for personal consumption. The Canary Islands are not a member of the EU.

Health (for visitors)

Nationals of the European Economic Area (EEA) countries and Switzerland can access reduced cost and sometimes free medical treatment using a European Health Insurance Card (EHIC) while visiting the EEA. Exceptions include nationals of the 10 countries which joined the EU in 2004 whose EHIC is not valid in Switzerland. Applications for the EHIC should be made before travelling.

Mandatory precautions

None

Advisable precautions

Up-to-date tetanus and polio immunisations are recommended. Long-term visitors should consider hepatitis A immunisation. Tap water may not be safe to drink outside the major cities and visitors are advised to drink bottled mineral water.

Hotels

Hotels are classified from one- to five-star, plus a 'Grand De Luxe' category (pensions/hostels classified from one- to three-star). Paradores (national tourist inns) are also increasingly popular. Accommodation should be booked well in advance, especially during holiday season. NB: Term Residencia denotes establishments without dining-room facilities.

Credit cards

All major credit and charge cards are accepted. ATMs are widely available.

Public holidays (national)

Fixed dates

1 Jan (New Year's Day), 6 Jan (Epiphany), 1 May (Labour Day), 15 Aug (Assumption Day), 12 Oct (National Day), 1 Nov (All Saints' Day), 6 Dec (Constitution Day), 8 Dec (Immaculate Conception), 25 Dec (Christmas Day).

Variable dates

Good Friday (Mar/Apr).

Working hours

Executives rarely arrive in their offices before 0900. Many then go out for coffee, and again for a snack at 1200 to keep them going until a late lunch. Lunches, no earlier than 1400, and often preceded by a visit to a bar for an aperitivo, are abundant and lengthy. A business lunch, always accompanied by wine, coffee, brandy and cigars, can last from three to five hours. It is considered impolite to get down to business until after dessert.
Although many go home for lunch and a brief siesta, an increasing number of companies in big cities are abolishing the long lunch break. In December 2005 the government officially abolished the siesta when a law was published decreeing that lunch breaks would be one hour only, thereby allowing civil servants to finish work at 6pm.
In the hot summer months, most ministries and many companies close down for the day at 1400 or 1500. In August, many businesses close down completely.

Banking

Mon–Fri: 0830–1400. In some autonomous regions larger bank branches may open later in the afternoon and on Saturday morning, between Apr–Sep.

Business

Usually open Mon–Fri: 0900–1400 and 1630–1930.

Government

Vary considerably from region to region and according to time of year. In Madrid: Mon–Fri: generally 0900–1330 and 1500–1800; except Jul and Aug, 0830–1430 (1400 on Fri) with only skeleton staff remaining during afternoon.

Shops

Mon–Sat: 0930–1330, 1700–2030; Department stores and malls Mon–Sat: 1000–2200.

Telecommunications

Mobile/cell phones

There are 3G and 900/1800 GSM services.

Electricity supply

220V AC with round, two-pin plugs.

Social customs/useful tips

A ban on smoking in public places was introduced on the 1 January 2006.
Handshaking is the customary form of greeting. Although English is widely spoken, an effort to speak Spanish is appreciated. Business cards are frequently exchanged as a matter of courtesy.
Meals are taken later in Spain than in other European countries which means that people go to bed later and also generally go to work later. Dinner is after 2200 and people rarely go to bed before 2400. Leaving someone's home before 0100 can be taken as a sign of boredom. It is acceptable to telephone someone at home until 2400.
Spaniards generally use two surnames, the last being their mother's surname. When addressing someone, either personally or in correspondence, only the first of the surnames is used. Don is a widely used title of respect, and is used in conversation with the christian name only.
The tu (more intimate second person singular) form is today used widely, even on first acquaintance.

Entry into the EU in 1986 has slowly changed customs as Spaniards are keen to be seen as Europeans. However, they remain very attached to an informal and relaxed way of life and enjoyment is an important part of life. Each city and village has its annual festival which would not be complete without dance, songs, wine and a bullfight. Bullfighting remains popular despite a budding animal protection movement, and soccer remains by far the most popular sport. Family and friendship ties are of major importance and often a source of mutual favours. Regional origins also command loyalties. Spaniards, even children of migrants to big cities, constantly refer to their home province. In Catalonia Catalan is very much, and very proudly, the lingua franca, and it helps at least to be able to greet people in Catalan. This is less the case in the Basque country, where fewer people speak Basque, and is not an issue either in Valencia or in Galicia, both of which have their own languages, but where Castilain Spanish is the lingua franca for day-to-day purposes.

Security

A chronic drug problem, coupled with persistent unemployment and frequent amnesties for petty criminals, has caused an increase in petty crime in big cities. Mugging has become frequent, and often violent, in tourist areas. Many insurance companies no longer cover the theft of car radios.

Getting there

Air

National airline: Iberia.

International airport/s: Madrid Barajas (MAD), 13km north-east of Madrid. Facilities include banks, restaurants, duty-free and car hire. There are buses, taxis and a railway service to the city centre.

Continental and regional fights arrive at Alicante (ALC), 12km south-west of city; Barcelona (BCN) 10km south-west of city; Bilbao (BIO), 9km from city; Málaga (AGP) 8km south-west of city; Santiago de Compostela (SCQ), 10km north-east of city; Seville (SVQ), 12km east of city, Valencia (VLC), 10km west of city. Also on Balearic Islands: Palma de Mallorca (PMI), 9km south-east of Palma; on Canary Islands: Gran Canaria (LPA), 19km south of Las Palmas; Tenerife TCI Sur Reina Sofia (TFS), 61km south-west of Santa Cruz de Tenerife.

Airport tax: None

Surface

Road: There are several good quality toll motorways connecting Spain to France and Portugal.

Rail: Services radiate from the Madrid hub and express services connect to the pan-European network, through France. There are several services connecting Portugal.

Water: The are regular ferry and shipping services from UK (Plymouth-Santander), France (Marseilles-Alicante) and Algeria (Algiers-Alicante).

Main port/s: Barcelona, Valencia, Alicante, Málaga, Algeciras, Cádiz, La Coruña, Bilbao, Vigo.

Getting about

National transport

Air: Frequent services from Madrid to all major urban centres are operated by Iberia.

Road: Roads are based on radial routes centred on Madrid. They are often very busy during the holiday season. Good roads connect all main towns. There is a network of over 150,000km, including 2,000km of motorways (usually toll) mostly confined to coastal regions.

Buses: There are regular bus and coach services between main towns.

Rail: There are approximately 14,410km of track, of which about 11,500km is operated by Red Nacional de Ferrocarriles Españoles (RENFE) (National Network of Spanish Railroads) and the rest (narrow gauge) by Ferrocarriles Españoles de Via Estrecha (FEVE). A high-speed link between Madrid and Barcelona, operated by RENFE, opened in February. The train will take just over two and a half hours over the 550Km (342 miles).

Water: Regular steamer and hydrofoil services operated by Compañía Transmediterránea connect Balearic Islands with Barcelona, Valencia and Alicante. Also weekly ferry service to Las Palmas (Canary Islands) from Barcelona.

City transport

Taxis: Available in most major cities; all metered. Tend to have a distinct colour in each city. Tipping between 5–10 per cent.

Car hire

Available at competitive rates in most large towns. A national driving licence is normally all that is required. Drive on the right. Speed limits are 60kph in towns, 100kph on national highways, 120kph on motorways and 90kph on other roads. Traffic coming from right generally has priority. Seat belts must be worn in front seats. Spanish drivers tend to drive faster than their northern counterparts.

BUSINESS DIRECTORY

The addresses listed below are a selection only. While World of Information makes every endeavour to check these addresses, we cannot guarantee that changes have not been made, especially to telephone numbers and area codes. We would welcome any corrections.

Telephone area codes

The international direct dialling (IDD) code for Spain is +34 followed by area code and subscriber's number:

Alicante	96	León	987
Avilés	98	Madrid	91
Barcelona	93	Málaga	95
Bilbao	94	Salamanca	923
Cádiz	956	Santander	942
Cartagena	968	Seville	95
Castellón de la Plana	964	Tarragona	977
Ceuta	952	Valencia	96
Granada	958	Valladolid	983
Huelva	959	Vigo	986
La Coruña	981	Zaragoza	976

Chambers of Commerce

American Chamber of Commerce in Spain, 8 Tuset, 08006 Barcelona (tel: 415-9963; fax: 415-1198; e-mail: info@amchamspain.com).

Barcelona Cámara de Comercio, 452 Avenguda Diagonal, 08006 Barcelona (tel: 416-9300; fax: 416-9301).

Bilbao Cámara Oficial de Comercio, Industria y Navegación, 50 Almeda Recalde, 48008 Bilbao (tel: 470-6500; fax: 443-6171; e-mail: info@camarabilbao.com).

British Chamber of Commerce in Spain, 21 Calle Bruc, 08010 Barcelona (tel: 317-3220; fax: 302-4896; e-mail: britchamber@britchamber.com).

Consejo Superior de Cámaras de Comercio, Industria y Navegación de España, Calle Velazquez 157, 28002 Madrid (tel: 590-6900; fax: 590-6908; e-mail: csc@cscamaras.es).

Córdoba Cámara Oficial de Comercio e Industria, Pérez de Castro 1, 14003 Córdoba (tel: 296-199; fax: 202-106; e-mail: info@camaracordoba.com).

Franco-Spanish Chamber of Commerce and Industry, Calle Ruiz de Alarcon 7, 28014 Madrid (tel: 522-6742; fax: 523-3642; e-mail: lachambre@lachambre.es).

Las Palmas de Gran Canaria Cámara Oficial de Comercio, Industria y Navegación , León y Castillo 24, 35003 Las Palmas de Gran Canaria (tel: 391-045; fax: 362-350; e-mail: webmaster@cameraalp.es).

Madrid Cámara Oficial de Comercio e Industria, Calle Huertas 13, 28012 Madrid (tel: 538-3500; fax: 538-3677; e-mail: camaramadrid@camaramadrid.es).

Málaga Cámara Oficial de Comercio, Industria y Navegación, Cortina del Muelle 23, 29015 Málaga (tel: 221-1673; fax: 222-9894; e-mail: info@camaramalaga.com).

Mallorca, Ibiza y Formentera Cámara de Comercio, Estudio General 7, 07001 Palma de Mallorca (tel: 710-188; fax: 726-302; e-mail: ccinmallorca@camaras.org).

Sevilla Cámara Oficial de Comercio, Industria y Navegación, Plaza de la Contratación 8, 41004 Sevilla (tel: 211-005; fax: 225-619; e-mail: ccinsevilla@camaradesevilla.com).

Valencia Cámara de Comercio, Industria y Navegación, Poeta Querol 15, 46002 Valencia (tel: 103-900; fax: 531-742; e-mail: info@camaravalencia.com).

Zaragoza Cámara Oficial de Comercio e Industria, Calle Isabel La Catolica 2, 50071 Zaragoza (tel: 306-161; fax: 357-945; e-mail: cci@camarazaragoza.com).

Banking

Banco Atlántico SA, Diagonal 407 bis, Barcelona (tel: 237-1240).

Banco Bilbao Vizcaya Argentaria, Plaza de San Nicolás 4, 48005 Bilbao (tel: 424-4620).

Banco de la Exportación SA, Barcas 10, Valencia 2 (tel: 351-7862).

Banco de Sabadell, Plaza Sant Roc 20, 08201 Sabadell (tel: 726-2100).

Banco Español de Crédito (Banesto), Paseo de la Castellana 7, Madrid (tel: 338-1000).

Banco Internacional de Comercio, José Ortega y Gasset 56, 28006 Madrid (tel: 402-8362).

Banco Popular Español, Velázquez 34, 28001 Madrid (tel: 435-3620).

Banco Santander Central Hispano (BSCH) (established April 1999), Apartado de Correos 00045, Santander (tel: 221-200).

La Caixa de Catalunya, Avinguda Diagonal 621, Barcelona 08028 (tel 934-045000).

Confederación Española de Cajas de Ahorros (confederation of Spanish savings banks), Alcalá 27 Madrid 14 (tel: 232-7810).

Consejo Superior Bancario (central committee of Spanish banking), José Abascal 57, Madrid 9 (tel: 441-0611).

La Caixa de Barcelona (savings bank), Avinguda Diagonal 530, 08006 Barcelona (tel: 201-6666).

Central bank

Banco de España, Alcalá 48, 28014 Madrid (tel: 338-5000).

European Central Bank (ECB), Kaiserstrasse 29, D-60311 Frankfurt am Main, Germany (tel: (+49-69) 13-440; fax: (+49-69) 1344-6000; email: info@ecb.int).

Travel information

Federación Española de Hoteles, Orense 32, 28020 Madrid (tel: 556-7112; fax: 556-7361; e-mail: federahoteles@ipf.es).

Iberia, 130 Velazquez Madrid, (tel: 902-400-500 (bookings); www.iberia.com).

Instituto De Turismo De España (Turespaña) 6 Jose Lázaro Galdiano, 28071 Madrid (tel: 343-3500; internet: www.tourspain.es/en).

Ministry of tourism

Ministerio de Industria, Turismo y Comercio, José González de Galdiano 6, Madrid (tel: 343-3621; email: turespaña@turespaña.es

Ministries

Ministry for Development, P de la Castellana 67, 28071 Madrid (tel: 597-7000; fax: 597-8502).

Ministry of Economy, Finance and Trade, Alcalá 9, Madrid 28071 (tel: 595-8000).

Ministry of Education and Culture, Alcalá 34, 28071 Madrid (tel: 532-5089; fax: 532-5873).

Ministry of the Environment, Pza San Juan de la Cruz, 28071 Madrid (tel: 597-7000; fax: 597-6349).

Ministry of Foreign Affairs, Pza de la Provincia 1, 28071 Madrid (tel: 379-9549).

Ministry of Health and Consumer Affairs, P del Prado 18-20, 28071 Madrid (tel: 596-1000; fax: 429-3525).

Ministry of Industry and Energy, Paseo de la Castellana 160, Madrid 16 (tel: 349-4806).

Ministry of the Interior, P de la Castellana 5, 28071 Madrid (tel: 537-1000; fax: 537-1177).

Ministry of Justice, San Bernardo 45, 28071 Madrid (tel: 930-2000).

Ministry of Labour and Social Affairs, Agustín de Bethencourt 4, 28071 Madrid (tel: 553-6000; fax: 554-7528).

Ministry of Public Administrations, P de la Castellana 3, 28071 Madrid (tel: 586-1000; fax: 319-2448).

President's Office, Complejo de la Moncloa, 28071 Madrid (tel: 335-3535).

Other useful addresses

Agencia para el Desarrollo, Consejeria de Economia e Innocacion Tecnologica, Comunidad de Madrid (fax: 420-6456, 399-7451; e-mail: agencia.desarrollo@madrid.org).

Bolsa de Comercio de Valencia (stock exchange), Pascual y Genis 19, 46001 Valencia (tel: 352-1487).

Bolsa de Madrid (stock exchange), Palacio de la Bolsa, Plaza de la Lealtad 1 (tel: 232-8484).

Central de Reservas de los Paradores de España, Calle Velázquez 25, 28001 Madrid (tel: 435-9700/9744/9768/9814).

Confederación Española de Organizaciones Empresariales (Spanish confederation of employers' organisations), Diego de León 50, 28006 Madrid (tel: 262-4410).

Fira de Barcelona, Avenida Reina Maria Cristina s/n, 08004 Barcelona (tel: 423-3101; fax: 423-8651).

IFEMA (Feria de Madrid), Parque Ferial Juan Carlos 1, 28042 Madrid (tel: 722-5180/5000; fax: 722-5801; e-mail: infoifema@ifema.es).

Instituto Nacional de la Seguridad Social, Subdirección General de Relaciones Internacionales, Padre Damián 4, 28036 Madrid (tel: 450-1900).

Spanish Embassy (USA), 2375 Pennsylvania Avenue, NW, Washington DC 20037 (tel: (+1-202) 452-0100; fax: (tel: (+1-202) 833-5670; e-mail: spain@spainemb.org).

Internet sites

Andalucia: www.andalucia.com

Balearics: www.caib.es

Bank of Spain: www.bde.es

Barcelona: www.bcn.es

Basque Country: www.euskadi.net

Bilbao: www.bilbao.net

Canary Islands: www.gobcan.es

Current affairs: www.sispain.com

El Pais newspaper: www.elpais.es

Galicia: wwwxunta.es

Government spokesman: www.la-moncloa.es

Hotel reservations: www.red2000.com

Iberia: www.iberia.com

Madrid: www.munimadrid.es
Ministry of Tourism: www.tourspain.es
Paradores (hotels): www.parador.es
Renfe (national railways): www.renfe.es
Spain statistics: www.ine.es/welcoing.htm
Spanish Rail Service: www.spanish-rail.co.uk
Spanish Tourism: www.spain.info
Stock Exchange: www.bolsamadrid.es
Train information: www.renfe.es

Sri Lanka

KEY FACTS

Official name: Sri Lanka Prajathanthrika Samajavadi Janarajaya / Llankais Sananayaka socialisak kutiyarasa / Democratic Socialist Republic of Sri Lanka

Head of State: President Mahinda Rajapakse (UPFA) (since Nov 2005),

Head of government: Ratnasiri Wickremanayake (since Nov 2005)

Ruling party: Coalition government led by United People's Freedom Alliance (UPFA) (elected Apr 2004)

Area: 65,610 square km

Population: 19.93 million (2007)

Capital: Colombo (official capital); many governmental functions are centred in Sri Jayawardenepura, a suburb of Colombo.

Official language: Sinhala, Tamil, English

Currency: Rupee (Rs) = 100 cents

Exchange rate: Rs107.55 per US$ (Jul 2008)

GDP per capita: US$1,506 (2007)*

GDP real growth: 6.30% (2007)*

Labour force: 8 (2006)*

Unemployment: 7.60% (2006)*

Inflation: 19.70% (2007)

Balance of trade: -US$3.37 billion (2006)

Foreign debt: US$10.89 billion (2004)

* estimated figure

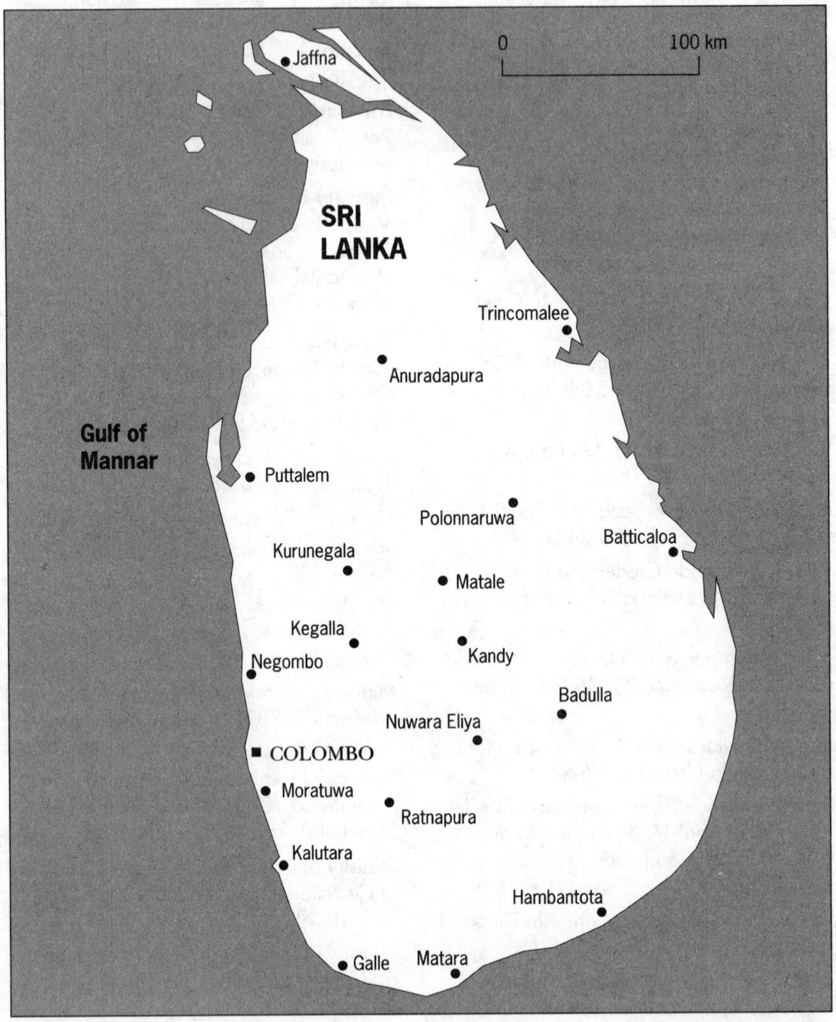

For three decades, Sri Lanka, the original serendipity, has been dogged by something approaching civil war, a civil war to which the world appears to have become largely indifferent. The name of Velupillai Prabrakharan rarely features in news bulletins outside Sri Lanka. For over 30 years Mr Prabrakharan has been the defining figure of Sri Lankan modern history. Mr Prabrakharan has been described as the self-styled Sun God of Sri Lanka's Tamil Hindu minority. The Tamils constitute less than 25 per cent of Sri Lanka's population. In that period, he and his henchmen have notched up a liturgy of assassinations, terror and civil war. The Tamil Tigers were using suicide bombing as a weapon long before al Qaeda and its adherents, using the method to assassinate Indian Prime Minister Rajiv Gandhi.

The overall objective of the Tigers is to create an independent Tamil state in the north of Sri Lanka. This is not a long-standing objective, emerging only in the 1980s in response to the Sri Lankan government's insensitive – even violent – response to Tamil wishes for greater autonomy. Mr Prabrakharan has, however, always been opposed to anything less than an independent Tamil state. It is not easy to distinguish between Mr Prabrakharan's desires for his Tamil people and what has become his apparent wish for self-aggrandisement. Loss of confidence in Mr Prabrakharan's leadership has caused eastern Tamils to revolt under a disaffected Tamil officer, Colonel Karuna. Although Mr Karuna had to take cover, the eastern Tamil stalemate has become an irritant and an embarrassment for Prabrakharan.

Resilient growth

The IMF notes that in the 1980s and 90s, Sri Lanka's economic growth averaged about 5 per cent, despite a 20 year civil war with various levels of intensity. In 2000–01, a significant slowdown in growth was associated with a widespread civil conflict. Following a ceasefire in 2002, the economy performed well with real GDP growth averaging 6.2 per cent despite a number of external and domestic shocks, including high international oil prices, increased competition for apparel exports following the end of the Multi-Fibre Arrangement (MFA), and the continuing conflict between the Liberation Tigers of Tamil Eelam (LTTE) and the government. The growth pick up in 2006 was supported by a relatively calm political environment and high external support for tsunami reconstruction.

Sustaining the current growth momentum and moving towards a higher economic growth path is possible but will be a challenge. In its Ten Year Horizon Development Framework, the government of Sri Lanka envisages attaining growth of about 8 per cent per annum, mainly through investments of about US$4.5 billion (about 17 per cent of GDP) in infrastructure projects in power, roads, water supply, and ports.

According to the Asian Development Bank (ADB) the apparently resurgent conflict has not had an impact on growth, driven by strong domestic demand and buoyant private sector activity, but global food and oil price increases, in combination with expansionary macroeconomic policies, has doubled inflation. Growth was forecast to decelerate over a two-year period, as the global slowdown began to affect key export markets, and as the government took steps to cool the economy. After expanding rapidly in 2006 the economy slowed in 2007, but still showed robust growth of an estimated 6.7 per cent. Several important characteristics emerge from these 2 years, which were marked by a renewed, and escalating, civil conflict. First, the economy has proven more resilient than expected by most observers (both local and international). Second, post-*tsunami* reconstruction, rising credit expansion, and public sector investment continued to fuel growth in construction, which now accounts for almost 7.4 per cent of GDP. Third, expansionary fiscal policies, largely negative real interest rates, and high remittances also substantially boosted aggregate demand. On the supply side, services remained strong (especially telecommunications, finance, international port services, and logistics), contributing 64 per cent of GDP growth in 2007 despite the conflict-related slowdown in tourism While tourism contributes only 1–2 per cent of GDP, the social costs of fewer tourists are high, as an estimated 300,000 jobs are linked to the industry. Agriculture fell back to its lacklustre performance of the past, unable to sustain the post-*tsunami* recovery of 2006. The garment industry, Sri Lanka's industrial mainstay, continued to weather difficult conditions. It grew by 7 per cent, increasing exports to the European Union (EU) by 24 per cent, taking advantage of the GSP Plus concessions granted in 2005, while its exports to the United States decreased by 3.4 per cent. Soaring global prices for fuel and food and high government bank borrowing were the main causes of the doubling of inflation in the Sri Lanka Consumer Price Index (SLCPI), from 9.6 per cent to 20.2 per cent. Inflation reached 5 percentage points higher than the targeted rate of the central bank.

Higher interest rates reduced private sector credit growth from 24 per cent to 20 per cent year on year. However, the central bank cautioned that the success of its policies to bring down inflation would depend on government borrowing being kept within limits set by the central bank. The ADB also noted that Sri Lanka's sharp rise in inflation also reflected global food and fuel price increases, with their impact increased by the depreciation of the currency against the US dollar. Due to the global wheat shortage, as elsewhere in Asia, wheat import prices rose by over 60 per cent (in Sri Lanka rupee terms) in 2007, causing bread prices to rise by almost 200 per cent.

The overall balance of payments improved considerably in 2007, recording a surplus of US$570 million. This was largely due to a US$500 million sovereign bond issue. The government securities market was liberalised to allow foreign investors to participate (resulting in a net inflow of US$470 million in 2007) and official foreign exchange reserves increased. The central bank continued to intervene in the foreign exchange market during the year to stabilise the Sri Lanka rupee; however, in sharp contrast to 2006, total net sales of foreign currencies amounted to only US$5 million for all of 2007, compared to US$453 million in 2006. In the first two months of 2008, net purchases of dollars by the central bank

KEY INDICATORS — Sri Lanka

	Unit	2003	2004	2005	2006	2007
Population	m	20.15	20.48	*19.62	19.77	*19.93
Gross domestic product (GDP)	US$bn	18.20	20.06	23.53	26.96	*30.01
GDP per capita	US$	925	989	*1,200	1,364	*1,506
GDP real growth	%	5.9	5.2	6.0	7.3	*6.3
Inflation	%	9.0	7.6	10.6	9.5	19.7
Industrial output	% change	–	5.2	6.0	7.2	–
Agricultural output	% change	–	-0.7	2.5	4.7	–
Exports (fob) (goods)	US$m	5,133.0	5,306.0	6,098.0	6,883.0	–
Imports (cif) (goods)	US$m	6,672.0	7,265.0	9,171.0	10,253.0	–
Balance of trade	US$m	-1,539.0	-1,959.0	-3,073.0	-3,370.0	–
Current account	US$m	-70.0	-640.0	-660.0	-1,434.0	-1,369.0
Total reserves minus gold	US$m	2,265.0	2,132.0	2,651.0	2,837.0	3,515.0
Foreign exchange	US$m	2,193.0	2,058.0	2,581.0	2,762.0	3,433.0
Exchange rate	per US$	96.86	101.19	108.45	107.82	108.90

* estimated figure

amounted to US$360 million, a result of considerable foreign inflows driven by the sharp easing of monetary policy in the US.

The government, for the second year, largely maintained its policy of not providing retail fuel subsidies. It is the only country in South Asia to have done so, saving the government the equivalent of approximately 0.7 per cent of GDP annually since 2006. However, global price changes are quickly catching up with domestic price adjustments. Despite the latest hike in January 2008, gasoline prices are only partially cross subsidising kerosene prices.

Risk assessment

Economy	Good
Politics	Fair
Regional stability	Good

COUNTRY PROFILE

Historical profile

Sri Lanka became an outpost of Buddhism after the religion had mostly disappeared in the rest of South Asia. Historic kingdoms included that centred around the central city of Kandy, which resisted Western encroachment until 1815.

1815 The British became the first colonial power to win control of the island, which became known as Ceylon. Tamils from India were brought over to work on the plantations.

1931 The right to vote was introduced by the colonial authorities, who also established a system of power-sharing with the people of Ceylon.

1948 Ceylon gained full independence from British rule.

1949 The right to vote was taken away from Indian Tamils.

1951 Solomon Bandaranaike left the ruling Ekshat Jathika Pakshaya (EJP) (United National Party) to form the Sri Lanka Nidahas Pakshaya (Sri Lanka Freedom Party) (SLFP).

1953 A decision by the EJP government to cut the rice ration in the slump following the Korean War saw riots assume insurrectionary proportions.

1956 Bandaranaike became prime minister. Sinhala was made the state language by Bandaranaike's SLFP government, sparking anti-Tamil pogroms.

1959–60 Bandaranaike was assassinated by a Buddhist monk in 1959. His widow, Sirimavo, was elected SLFP leader and prime minister the following year. She stepped up the nationalisation programme.

1964 A pact with India forced half a million Indian Tamil plantation workers to return to India.

1965 The EJP won elections and began attempts to reverse the nationalisation programme.

1970 Sirimavo Bandaranaike began what would be her second term as prime minister, which would last until 1977.

1971 A rural uprising led by the Marxist Janatha Vimukthi Peramuna (JVP) (People's United Liberation Front) was crushed.

1972 The country changed its name from Ceylon to Sri Lanka and Buddhism became the country's official religion.

1976 The main Tamil party, the Federal Party, and other Tamil groups, formed the Tamil United Liberation Front (TULF), calling for a separate Tamil state in the northern and eastern parts of the country. The Liberation Tigers of Tamil Eelam (LTTE, also known as the Tamil Tigers) was formed.

1977 A constitutional amendment was passed which established a presidential system of government from the end of the year. In elections, the TULF won all the seats in Tamil areas.

1978 J R Jayewardene became the country's first executive president. Continued violence and pressure from the Tamils led the government to recognise the Tamil language in the new constitution.

1983–84 Tamil terrorist activity and anti-Tamil pogroms broke out. The latter constituted the worst outbreak of violence for many years, sparking a state of emergency. India began training Tamil guerrillas. Conflicts developed in the north of the island between the army and the Tamil Tigers.

1985 The first attempts at peace talks with the LTTE failed.

1986 Violence continued to convulse the northern and eastern provinces. Sri Lanka's relations with India were severely strained by the violence. India mediated informally between TULF legislators, Tamil leaders and the Sri Lankan government.

1987 Following an accord with India, more than 7,000 Indian troops were sent to Sri Lanka to try to implement a peace accord. The government signed accords created new councils for Tamil areas in the north and east.

1989 Ranasinghe Premadasa was sworn in as president. The state of emergency which had been in force since May 1983 was repealed.

1990 Indian troops went home after losing more than 1,000 soldiers and failing to achieve their objectives. The LTTE controlled large parts of northern Sri Lanka.

1991 The LTTE was implicated in the assassination of Indian prime minister Rajiv Gandhi.

1993 President Premadasa was killed in an LTTE bomb attack.

1994 The Bahejana Nidasa Pakhsaya (People's Alliance) (PA), a left-wing nine-party coalition centred on the SLFP, won the legislative elections. The prime minister, Chandrika Bandaranaike Kumaratunga (SLFP), was elected president. She appointed her mother, Sirimavo Bandaranaike, as prime minister, for the third time.

1995 Peace talks with the LTTE collapsed and the LTTE resumed its bombing campaign. The government launched a major offensive, driving the LTTE out of its Jaffna stronghold.

1996 The LTTE bombed the capital, Colombo, leading to a nationwide state of emergency.

1998 Sri Lanka's fiftieth anniversary celebrations were marred by renewed fighting between the army and separatist LTTE in the north of the country. The Tamil Tigers bombed Sri Lanka's holiest Buddhist site and captured key northern towns in a large offensive.

1999 President Kumaratunga won her second and final term in office; she had been partially blinded in one eye in a terrorist bombing at an election rally .

2000 Government forces lost control to Tamil Tiger separatists, of a key military base in the north. Norway began mediation between the government and the LTTE. The general elections resulted in a hung parliament, with the PA dependent on two moderate Tamil-linked parties for support. Former prime minister (the world's first female head of government) Sirimavo Bandaranaike, had died soon after casting her vote. A Tamil Tiger proposed cease-fire was rejected by the government.

2001 The LTTE was declared a terrorist organisation by Britain and Canada. The LTTE destroyed half Air Lanka's fleet of airplanes at Colombo's airport. President Kumaratunga announced a snap general election, which were won by the opposition EJP.

2002 It was estimated that 64,000 people had been killed since the LTTE's armed struggle for independence began. A cease-fire, negotiated by Norway, came into effect, ending the civil war between the government and the LTTE. The ruling EJP won local elections, which were also billed as a referendum on peace plans. The ban on the LTTE was lifted as a prelude to peace talks at which the LTTE dropped its demand for independence in favour of regional autonomy with self-government.

2003 In April, the LTTE withdrew from peace talks and in November, it demanded interim executive powers over the north and east, where the Tamil population is concentrated. Peace talks stalled and fearing the break-up of Sri Lanka, the

president suspended parliament and deployed troops in Colombo as a state of emergency was declared.
2004 President Kumaratunga took the opportunity of the state of emergency to called snap general elections, which were won by the her party, the United People's Freedom Alliance (UPFA) and Mahinda Rajapakse became prime minister. On 26 December, an earthquake off the Indonesian island of Sumatra caused a tsunami that devastated coastal areas of north and eastern Sri Lanka; the final estimate was 35,322 dead or missing and 516,150 people displaced.
2005 Reconstruction of the coastal regions devastated by the tsunami was necessary in many areas under de facto control of the LTTE. The government planned to give the LTTE separatists a key role in the distribution of international aid and encourage peace talks in the process. However by June little aid had been provided and anger mounted in the stricken areas. The nationalist Janatha Vimukthi Peramuna (JVP) (People's United Liberation Front) pulled out of the government coalition in protest at the collaboration and reduced the government's working majority. The foreign minister, Lakshman Kadirgaamar was assassinated on 13 August. On 17 November, the presidential election was won by Mahinda Rajapakse (UPFA); Ratnasiri Wickremanayake was appointed prime minister on 21 November. It was reported officially that over 3,000 people died in the year in Tamil separatist violence (including the bloodshed caused by a factional rift within the LTTE) and many feared that the violence would escalate, as over 200,000 people were displaced due to insurgency actions and government response.
2006 The South Asia Free Trade Agreement (SAFTA) came into effect on 1 January, between Sri Lanka, Bhutan, Bangladesh, India, Maldives, Nepal and Pakistan. In May the EU added the LTTE to its list of terrorist organisations (a move that followed the US and India), and froze all LTTE financial assets held within the EU. Unicef accused the breakaway Tamil Tigers faction, led by Colonel Karuna, of abducting and recruiting children as soldiers. In June the number of dead attributed to the conflict since 1972 was quoted at 60,000. Peace talks bagan again in Geneva in October, amid increased violence that killed 372 government soldiers, 128 civilians and an unknown number of insurgents, since July. However, within a fortnight of the talks the leader of the LTTE said the truce was 'defunct'.
2007 A dissident faction of the opposition UNP crossed the floor to join the government in return for government posts. The president limited the number of disaffections so as to retain the UNP as the official opposition party and block the Marxist JVP from gaining that position. Three ministers resigned in protest at the accommodation of 18 legislators within the government, a number necessary to secure a majority in parliament. SP Thamilselvan, a leading political member of the Tamil Tigers, was killed in a government air raid on 2 November.
2008 On 2 January, the prime minister announced a formal ending to the 2002 cease-fire with the Tamil Tigers. In response the Japanese peace envoy said that Japanese aid (US$400 million in 2007 and US$9 billion since 1985) would have to be reconsidered as 'the termination of the ceasefire agreement may prompt the pursuit of a military solution of the conflict, with dire humanitarian consequences'. The government had been the sponsor of a devolution package and the Japanese position was that this should be pursued and offered to the Tamil Tigers.

Political structure

Constitution

The constitution dates from 1978, when a presidential system of government was established. Local authority is represented by 24 district councils in nine provinces and the Pradesiya Sabas (councils based on local administrative divisions). The devolution of power is limited, partly due to non-implementation, and partly due to the fact that Article 2 of the constitution stipulates a unitary state. Also politically significant is Article 9, which guarantees the 'foremost place' to Buddhism among faiths and stipulates the duty of the state to protect and sustain the religion. Both are obstacles to any scheme for devolution. Article 76 further stipulates that parliament may not 'abdicate or in any manner alienate its legislative power', complicating the creation of an autonomous Tamil entity.
The constitutional situation reflects events in 1987, when a peace accord was signed with India, which had intervened to protect the Tamil population. The Indo-Sri Lankan accord introduced a tier of government at provincial level, with elected provincial councils and certain powers delegated from the central government. Traditionally there are nine provinces, but the accord provided for the temporary merger of the Northern and Eastern Provinces (those regarded by Sri Lankan Tamils as their traditional homelands), pending a referendum for which the political conditions have not yet materialised.
The constitution provides the executive and security forces with sweeping powers on the declaration of a state of war. The Public Security Ordinance grants the armed forces wide powers of arrest and confiscation and allows home entry without a warrant once a war footing is declared. A two-thirds parliamentary majority is required for the removal of the president or amendment of the constitution.

Form of state

Socialist democratic republic

The executive

The president is directly elected for a six-year term and is head of state, head of the executive, head of government and head of the armed forces. No presidential incumbent may serve more than two terms. The president has the power to appoint or dismiss the prime minister (whose powers are relatively limited) and the cabinet and to dissolve parliament. After the election victory of the EJP in December 2001, President Kumaratunga agreed to delegate some of her extensive powers to the cabinet.

National legislature

There is a unicameral National State Assembly with a six-year term of office. Of the 225 members, 196 represent the 22 electoral districts and are elected by proportional representation. A further 29 seats are allocated on a proportional representation basis according to the overall national party results.

Legal system

The judiciary is formally independent of the executive. The Supreme Court has sole jurisdiction over interpretation of the constitution. It is also the final arbiter in settling charges against the president. The legal code reflects the system of English law inherited in 1948, with subsequent amendments in line with legal changes in the UK.

Last elections

2 April 2004 (parliamentary); 17 November 2005 (presidential).
Results: Parliamentary: President Chandrika Kumaratunga's United People's Freedom Alliance (UPFA) won 45.8 per cent of the vote (105 seats out of 225), Ekshat Jathika Pakshaya (EJP) (United National Party) 37.9 per cent (82), the Tamil National Alliance (TNA) 6.6 per cent (22) and the Jathika Hela Urumaya Party (National Heritage Party), led by Buddhist Monks, 6.1 per cent (nine).
Presidential: Prime Minister Mahinda Rajapakse (UPFA) 50.3 per cent of the vote, former prime minister Ranil Wickremesinghe (UNP) 48.4 per cent. Turnout was 73.7 per cent.

Next elections

2011 (presidential); 2010 (parliamentary).

Political parties
Ruling party
Coalition government led by United People's Freedom Alliance (UPFA) (elected Apr 2004)
Main opposition party
Ekshat Jathika Pakshaya (EJP) (United National Party)

Population
19.93 million (2007)
Last census: July 2001: 16,864,544 (provisional)
Population density: 295 inhabitants per square km (2000). Urban population: 23 per cent of the total (1995–2001).
Annual growth rate: 1.0 per cent 1994–2004 (WHO 2006)
Ethnic make-up
Sinhalese (74 per cent), Tamils (18 per cent), Moors (7 per cent), others (1 per cent).
Sri Lankan Tamils form the overwhelming majority in the Northern Province. The Eastern Province is ethnically mixed with three groups in sizeable numbers – Sri Lankan Tamils, mainly Tamil-speaking Moors (Muslims) and Sinhalese. Indian Tamils, descendants of those brought over by the British to work the tea plantations, are concentrated in the plantation districts of the Central Highlands. Elsewhere the Sinhalese are in the majority and make up about three-quarters of the total population.
Religions
Buddhism (69 per cent), Hinduism (16 per cent), Christian (8 per cent), Muslim (7 per cent). Sinhalese are predominantly Theravada Buddhists and Tamils are Hindus, while Arab and Malay descendants are mainly Muslims.

Education
Public investment in education amounts to 1.3 per cent of GDP. Universal primary education and gender parity, at this level, have been achieved.
Primary and junior secondary school are compulsory, lasting until aged 14. Senior secondary and collegiate schools are discretional and last until aged 18. All schooling until this age is provided free. Teaching is provided in English, Sinhala, Tamil and GCE exams at aged 16 must include a language subject in the student's mother tongue of Sinhalese or Tamil.
The education sector faces problems such as declining efficiency and quality of educational institutions and a shortage of teachers, nevertheless, standards are high and the importance allocated to education is evident in the high literacy rates.
Sri Lanka has received assistance from the World Bank, via the International Development Association (IDA). The ongoing Second General Education Project contributed a US$70.3 million for programmes based on improving enrolment, curriculum development and textbook provision. The Asian Development Bank has provided concessional loans to aid the North and East Community Restoration Development project to fund, among other programmes, educational facilities damaged during the internal conflict.
Literacy rate: 92 per cent adult rate; 97 per cent youth rate (15–24) (Unesco 2005).
Compulsory years: Five to 14
Enrolment rate: 110 per cent, gross primary enrolment of relevant age group (including repeaters); 74 per cent, gross secondary enrolment (World Bank).
Pupils per teacher: 28 in primary schools.

Health
Per capita total expenditure on health (2003) was US$121; of which per capita government spending was US$55, at the international dollar rate, (WHO 2006).
World Bank estimates show that the average life expectancy is higher than in most developing countries and the infant mortality rate is relatively low. Sri Lanka's social indicators showed steady improvement during the 1990s including a decline in the maternal mortality rate. There is increased access by the rural population to safe water (from 29 per cent to over 83 per cent) and sanitation (from 39 per cent to over 60 per cent). However, relevant sources indicate increased incidences of malaria and a high malnutrition rate for children under the age of five. The government's Samurdhi (Prosperity) Programme is assisting, particularly the most vulnerable groups, to reduce child malnutrition. Adolescent health services, nutrition and geriatric services and institutions are under strain. The use of traditional medicine (ayurveda) to supplement public healthcare is widespread.
HIV/Aids
HIV prevalence: 0.1 per cent aged 15–49 in 2003 (World Bank)
Life expectancy: 71 years, 2004 (WHO 2006)
Fertility rate/Maternal mortality rate: 1.9 births per woman, 2004 (WHO 2006); maternal mortality 30 per 100,000 live births (World Bank).
Birth rate/Death rate: 16 births and 6.5 deaths per 1,000 population (2003)
Child (under 5 years) mortality rate (per 1,000): 13 per 1,000 live births (World Bank)
Head of population per physician: 0.55 physicians per 1,000 people, 2004 (WHO 2006)

Welfare
Despite sustained government efforts to introduce various poverty reduction programmes such as direct income transfers and subsidies, about 21 per cent of the country's population are poor. However, estimates on the poverty level exclude the conflict-centered north-east, which has about 2.8 million people, 15 per cent of the total population.
For a number of years poor families have been able to benefit from a food stamps project which provides vouchers for food. A much more ambitious poverty alleviation scheme, the Janasaviya programme, begun in the mid-1990s, entitled families to a monthly payment for the purchase of specific consumer goods. The Prosperity Programme is another government sponsored poverty reduction scheme, introduced in 1994, which aims to provide social services and a social safety net to very poor households. Two projects, funded by the Asian Development Bank, are the Emergency Assistance for the Rehabilitation of North and East Sri Lanka, and the Eastern Province Coastal Community Development Project.
Old age, disability and death have been covered since 1958 by a social insurance programme funded from the Employees' Provident Fund (EPF). Employers pay 12 per cent of salaries to the EPF, the country's main social insurance fund, with a further 8 per cent taken from employees.
A social assistance programme for the unemployed – arguably the hallmark of a comprehensive welfare system – saw legislation introduced in 1995 in advance of a three-stage phasing in of the programme, aimed at families earning less than Rs1,000 (US$10.41) per month.

Main cities
Colombo (capital, estimated population 651,889 in 2005); many of the governmental functions are centered in Sri Jayawardenepura, a suburb of Colombo, 118,556), Dehiwala-Mount Lavinia (216,695), Moratuwa (185,581), Kandy (112,256), Jaffna (144,650).

Languages spoken
The national languages, Sinhala and Tamil, are widely spoken. English is commonly used in government and is spoken by about 10 per cent of the population.
Official language/s
Sinhala, Tamil, English

Media
The human rights watchdog, Amnesty International said that between 2006 and Februray 2008 at least 10 media workers had been killed and others abducted, detained or 'disappeared'. Tamil journalists working in the conflict areas of the north and east of the country were most at risk,

while Sinhalese journalists in the south faced official intimidation, especially if they reported on corruption.
Other news agencies: The Sinhalaya News Agency (www.news.sinhalaya.com).
Press
The government assumed wide powers to censor the press under a Public Security Ordinance in 2000. Media outlets are divided along language and ethnic lines and offer services in major languages only.
In March 2008 anti-terrorist police arrested five journalists, accusing them of links with the rebel Tamil Tigers. Campaigner for press freedom claimed that Sri Lanka was 'one of the most dangerous places for journalist to operate in'.
Dailies: In Singhala, Dinamina is government-owned, Lankadeepa (www.lankadeepa.lk) and Lakbima (www.lakbima.lk) are private.
In Tamil, Uthayan (www.uthayan.com), Virakesari (www. Virakesari.lk) and Thinakkural (www.thinakural.com) are privately owned.
In English, Daily News (www.newslk.com) is government-owned, The Island (www.island.lk), and Daily Mirror (www.dailymirror.lk) are private. There are a number of English online news outlets including (http://123srilanka.com), (www.lankatruth.com), (http://news.onlanka.com) and (www.srilankanewsfirst.com).
Weeklies: The Sunday Observer The Sunday Leader (www.thesundayleader.lk), Sunday Island and Sunday Times (www.sundaytimes.lk), are published weekly, together with Sinhalese and Tamil weeklies such as Virakesari Illustrated Weekly.
Business: Several newsletters of specific interest are published by various representative groups including Ceylon Commerce by the Ceylon Chamber of Commerce (www.chamber.lk), Industrial Ceylon by the Ceylon National Chamber of Industries, Business Lanka and Expo News by the Ministry of Trade and Shipping Information Service, Sri Lanka Ports News by the Sri Lanka Ports Authority, Clothing magazine by the Clothing Industry Training Institute and the Sri Lanka Investment News by the Greater Colombo Economic Commission. An Indian publication Business Today (www.business-today.com) is also widely read.
Periodicals: Some of the popular and useful periodicals include Explore Srilanka, Lanka Monthly Digest (www.lmd.lk) and the fashion magazine Satyn.
Broadcasting
Radio: The state-owned Sri Lanka Broadcasting Corporation (www.slbc.lk) transmits six services with commercial programmes in Sinhala, Tamil and English. ABC Radio is the largest commercial network with five national stations, MBC (www.maharaja.lk) has four radio channels. There are dozens of local, privately operated radio stations, mostly broadcasting in FM including TNL Rocks (www.tnlrocks.com) and Yes FM (www.yesfmonline.com). External services are broadcast, on short wave, by Colombo International Radio in over six languages to central Asia.
Television: The state controlled Sri Lanka Rupavahini Corporation (SLBC) (www.rupavahini.lk), which operates two channels and Independent Television Network (ITN) (www.itn.lk) one. Other private operators include Sirasa TV (www.sirasa.com), MTV (www.capitalmaharaja.com), Swanavahini (www.swarnavahini.lk) in Sinhala and Shakthi TV (www.webtv.lk) in Tamil.
Advertising
Press, cinema, commercial television and radio all accept advertising. Outdoor advertising is widespread; direct mail advertising must conform to a code of practice.

Economy
Sri Lanka has suffered large loss of life and considerable economic problems due to the civil war between government forces and the separatist Liberation Tigers of Tamil Eelan (LTTE), known as the Tamil Tigers, which broke out in 1983. The conflict has held back GDP growth by up to 2 per cent per annum. Inefficient infrastructure has been one of the main factors dragging down the competitiveness of Sri Lankan products and limiting the country's economic growth potential. Conflict in the north and east has limited the possibility of infrastructural development, while it has been a specific policy of the LTTE to sabotage infrastructural projects.
The sectoral mix reflects an agriculture-based economy that has made considerable progress in diversification.
Industry in Sri Lanka accounts for around a quarter of GDP. Tea, textiles, garments and precious gems number among the most prominent exports. The southern and western parts of the country, where most of the agriculture and industry are located, have not been directly affected by the war. Tourism is also an important contributor to the economy in these regions.
The economy has recovered since the disastrous year of 2001, when it shrank by 1.4 per cent. Growth, which returned in 2002, has exceeded five per cent in the following years, mainly fuelled by the services sector with strong growth in telecommunications, tourism and financial services. The services sector is the largest component of GDP, contributing around 55 per cent to GDP annually. There is a small but growing information technology sector.

External trade
Sri Lanka is a member of South Asia Association for Regional Co-operation, which operates a preferential trading arrangement that covers 6,000 products. In 2004 the South Asia Free Trade Area (Safta) was ratified, to be implemented between the seven member states (Bangladesh, Bhutan, India, Maldives, Nepal, Pakistan and Sri Lanka) by 2012.
Traditional plantation produce (tea, rubber and coconuts) had significant influence in export earnings, however clothing and leather product manufacturing is now the largest sector accounting for 39 per cent of total output followed by the production of food, beverages and tobacco at 22 per cent. The industrial sector also includes petrochemicals, plastics and processed rubber. There is a growing trade in information technology and software development. The export of precious gems are a modest but important export addition to foreign earnings.
Imports
Major imports are textile fabrics, mineral products, petroleum, foodstuffs, machinery and transport equipment.
Main sources: India (19.3 per cent total, 2006), China (10.4 per cent), Singapore (8.6 per cent).
Exports
Major exports are textiles and apparel, tea and spices, diamonds, emeralds, rubies, coconut products, rubber manufactures and fish.
Main destinations: US (27.6 per cent total, 2006), UK (11.3 per cent), India (9.3 per cent).

Agriculture
Farming
Sri Lanka's economy is becoming more service-oriented and less dependent on agriculture. By 2004, agriculture accounted for around 18 per cent of GDP (down from 30 per cent in 1980) and employed a third of the labour force. About 44 per cent of the land area is cultivated arable land.
The sector includes mostly large state-owned tea, rubber and coconut plantations and smaller holdings where rice, sugar cane, cassava, sweet potatoes, soya beans, other vegetables, cashew nuts, cocoa, castor, spices, chillies, onions and other crops are produced, sometimes at virtually subsistence level. Other agricultural products include spices, mainly cinnamon, and coffee. Sri Lanka is self-sufficient in rice, the main food crop. Livestock raised include buffaloes, goats, pigs, sheep and poultry.
Agricultural productivity on the small farms is low. The sector as a whole is

struggling against declining terms of trade, with a general decline in the price of commodities like coconut and rubber coupled with rising costs, particularly transport.

Plantation crops provide export earnings, although output has declined in recent years. Sri Lanka exports 44 per cent of its rubber output, with production increasingly shifting to crepe rubber and latex.

Tea is the most important agricultural export, although there is a lot of room for productivity gains. Smallholdings account for around 58 per cent of total output. The sector is showing signs of improvement. Private tea plantations owned by foreign investors are increasingly common and a number of new tea-blending units have become operational, helping to increase the added value of tea.

Production has matched the steady increase in world demand for spices. Sri Lanka produces over 85 per cent of the world's demand for cinnamon. Spice production accounted for 95.521 hectares of land in 2004.

Crop production in 2005 included: 3,172,220 tonnes (t) cereals in total, 3,126,000t rice, 220,000t cassava, 76,300t potatoes, 40,000t sweet potatoes, 600,000t plantains, 23,600t pulses, 1,950,000t coconuts, 50,000t chillies and peppers, 258,650t oilcrops, 4,390t tobacco, 94,700t natural rubber, 17,800t pepper spice, 21,180t various herbs and spices, 4,800t ginger, 1,015,000t sugar cane, 308,090t tea, 6,200t treenuts, 96,500t mangoes, 846,200t fruit in total, 557,000t vegetables in total. Livestock production included: 136,332t meat in total, 29,000t beef, 3,955t buffalo meat, 2,200t pig meat, 1,500t goat meat, 99,521t poultry, 52,053t eggs, 174,100t milk, 4,200t cattle hides.

Fishing

Around 90 per cent of the country's fishermen lost their livelihoods in the December 2004 tsunami. The government undertook to re-invest in boats and harbour infrastructure. Those unwilling to go back to sea will be retrained for onshore work, particularly in the building trade.

Fishing typically accounts for 2 per cent of GDP. Production includes prawns, shrimps, lobsters, crabs and sea cucumbers, for export and local consumption. The fisheries produce in the region of 200,000 tonnes of marine fish per year, 30,000 tonnes of freshwater fish and 10,000 tonnes of crustaceans.

New companies engaged in marine fishing qualify for a five-year tax holiday. Fishing activity has been affected both by higher petroleum prices and by the poor security situation.

In 2004, the total marine fish catch was 236,850 tonnes and the total crustacean catch was 15,320 tonnes.

Forestry

About 38 per cent of the land area (1.94 million hectares) is forested, and forestry accounts for 2 per cent of GDP, providing timber for local demand. Around 15 per cent of land area is subject to national protection. Forests of broadleaved, deciduous and evergreen are adapted to dry and monsoon seasons. Savannah and thorn woodland are found beside coastal areas populated by mangroves. Plantations account for around 316,000 hectares (ha) of forest cover and are established at a rate of 3,100ha per year. In the 1990s, Sri Lanka lost almost 20 per cent of its natural forest, at an average of 35,000ha per annum, so that only small fragments of tropical rainforest remain, each less than 10,000 hectares in area. Illegal logging has removed timber from unprotected forests, adding to the reduction. Some tropical timber plantations provide teak, eucalyptus, pine and mahogany, which are commercially farmed, with exports of timber and forestry products totalling US$33.7 million, and imports amounting to US$204.7 million, in 2004. Most paper is imported. Non-wood forest products harvested include bamboo, rattan, gums, resins and medicinal plants, cinnamon, cloves, nutmeg and cardamom.

Timber production in 2004 included 6,340,385 cubic metre (cum) roundwood, 694,000cum industrial roundwood, 61,000cum sawnwood, 117,000cum sawlogs and veneer logs, 21,500cum wood-based panels, 5,646,385cum woodfuel; 1,453 tonnes (t) charcoal, 24,500t paper and paperboard, 11,000t printing and writing paper, 21,000t paper pulp, 13,000t recovered paper.

Industry and manufacturing

Industry contributes around 27 per cent of GDP. One-third of manufacturing output, which accounts for around 15 per cent of GDP, is based on raw materials from the agricultural sector. There are 10 dedicated Export Processing Zones, mainly employing female labour.

A master plan for industrial development, co-ordinated with the Japanese International Co-operation Agency (JICA) and the United Nations Industrial Development Organisation (Unido), identifies electronics, information technology, rubber and plastics, machinery, footwear, textiles and apparel and agro-based industries as target sectors, with policy development responsibilities for these sectors shared between JICA and Unido.

Tourism

Since 2003, benefiting from the truce with the Tamil Tigers, the tourism sector has staged a recovery with visitor numbers passing the half million mark, and continuing to grow. There were 566,202 arrivals in 2004 and, despite the December 2004 tsunami, there was no fall-off in visitor numbers in the immediate aftermath and the sector held steady through the year. The main markets are Europe and the US, but since 2004 there has been a growth in the numbers of arrivals from other Asian countries and Australia. Tourism is expected to contribute 3.8 per cent to GDP in 2005.

Mining

Mining and quarrying account for around 2 per cent of GDP and employ 1 per cent of the workforce. Sri Lanka is rich in minerals such as ilmenite, plumbago, graphite, dolomite, kaolin, rutile, feldspar, quartz, mica, monazite, apatite, industrial clays and limestone. Precious and semi-precious stones, such as sapphires, rubies, catseyes, alexandrites, aquamarines, garnets, tourmalines, zircons, topaz, spinels, amethysts and moonstones provide increasing export income.

Hydrocarbons

Sri Lanka does not have any proven hydrocarbon reserves, but indications of possible deposits off the north and west have been detected and further explration is continuing. Sri Lanka consumes in excess of 75,000 barrels per day (bpd) of oil, all of which is imported. It is used for power generation and transport.

Sri Lanka does not produce or import gas and only imports a small amount of coal.

Energy

Sri Lanka has installed generating capacity of 2.1GW. Hydroelectric power is the principal source, but its contribution has declined in recent years from over 80 per cent to around 40 per cent in 2005. To overcome the unreliability of weather-dependent hydro-power and to extend coverage and meet the rising demand for electricity, generation is converting increasingly to fossil fuels, particularly coal, which have to be imported. Electricity demand is increasing by around 9 per cent per annum.

The government is planning seven new power generating projects, only two of which are hydro-electric.

Financial markets

Stock exchange

The Colombo Stock Exchange (CSE) is plagued by problems associated with the country's political instability. Poor political risk perceptions caused by the civil war, the much-anticipated general elections and the weakened coalition that finally resulted were thought responsible for much of the decline in the All Share Price Index (ASPI).

Banking and insurance
There are 26 commercial banks, but the sector is dominated by two state banks – Bank of Ceylon and People's Bank — which hold 55 per cent of market share. The government's deficit financing crowds out the private sector, meaning that banks have traditionally focussed on the public sector and reap high spreads from soaring interest rates. Meanwhile, deposit rates are low thanks to Sri Lanka's closed capital account and lack of competition among banks. This has created a perverse situation, where, although government security yields are higher than those from risky bank deposits, money keeps flowing into the banks.
The dominance of the two state banks is holding back development of the sector. Government-mandated lending policies mean that the two are effectively the industry's interest rate setters. Monopoly yields insulate the public banks from competitive problems that would otherwise be caused by managerial slack, poor asset bases and high costs. Organised resistance from unions and a desire to keep the banks' huge funds within the public sector have so far ruled out privatisation, although there are signs the government is amenable to gradual privatisation and an eventual stock market listing.

Central bank
Central Bank of Sri Lanka

Main financial centre
Colombo

Time
GMT plus 5 hours 30 minutes

Geography
Sri Lanka lies on the same continental shelf as India, from which it is separated by the shallow Palk Strait. The relief is dominated by the central highland massif, with an average elevation of over 1,500 metres, situated in the south central part of the island. This is surrounded by upland ridges and valleys which in the south-west of the island continue to the coast. The eastern region is an undulating plain with isolated hills and the north has flat, low and fertile plains intersected by ridges.

Hemisphere
Southern

Climate
Colombo and the south-west experience monsoon rains May–September; the likely temperature range is 22–31 degrees Celsius (C) with average annual rainfall of 2,240mm. The north-east experiences monsoon rains November–February; lower temperatures (down to 10 degrees C) occur inland at higher altitudes, with average rainfall of 1,000–1,500mm a year.

Dress codes
Men usually wear a lightweight or tropical suit and tie for business meetings, and women mostly dress conventionally. On social occasions, dress as for business meetings unless stipulated otherwise. Rainwear is needed, as are warmer clothes for the hilly areas, especially between November and February. Discreet dress in public places is appreciated.

Entry requirements

Passports
Passports are required by all, and must be valid for at least three months from the date of issue of visa.

Visa
Required by all; some exceptions exist, see www.slembassyusa.org/consular/visas.html for the full list of nationals who can enter, for one month without a visa, for tourist purposes, and who have return/onward passage. Free-of-charge visas are issued on arrival, at the port of entry.
Business visas must be obtained before arrival and are only issued for a 30-day stay (business travellers from SAARC countries may apply for a visa on arrival). All applications should be submitted with a letter from a sponsoring agency in Sri Lanka, plus a letter from the representative's company with their accreditation, a travel itinerary and a copy of onward/return passage. Visa applications may be referred to the relevant authorities in Sri Lanka, therefore adequate time should be included for processing.

Currency advice/regulations
The import of local currency is limited to Rs1,000; export is limited to Rs250. The import of Indian and Pakistani foreign currency is prohibited, all other foreign currency is unlimited but amounts over US$5,000 (or equivalent) must be declared; export of foreign currency is limited to the amount declared on arrival. Travellers cheques are accepted in banks.

Customs
Personal effects are allowed duty-free, however, valuable items (including jewellery) must be declared and must be re-exported on departure. Tobacco imports are not duty-free.

Prohibited imports
The import of firearms, ammunition, explosives, dangerous weapons, illegal drugs and pornography is strictly prohibited.
The export of antiques, rare books, palm leaf manuscripts, rare anthropological material and any wild animal (including ivory), bird or reptile, tea or rubber is prohibited.

Health (for visitors)
Medical facilities are adequate if limited. Immediate cash payment is often required by doctors and hospitals.

Mandatory precautions
A vaccination certificate for yellow fever is required if travelling from an infected area. Infants under one year are exempt.

Advisable precautions
Vaccinations for diphtheria, tuberculosis, hepatitis A and B, Japanese B encephalitis, polio, tetanus and typhoid are recommended. Malaria, dengue fever and chikungunya fever are caused by mosquitoes; precautions including mosquito repellents, nets and clothing covering the body should be used. There is a rabies risk. Water should be boiled and filtered before drinking. Fruit must be washed in such water and peeled.
Medical insurance, including emergency evacuation, is necessary.

Hotels
A 10 per cent service charge is added to hotel bills.

Credit cards
Major credit cards are widely accepted; charge cards have limited acceptance.

Public holidays (national)

Fixed dates
1 Jan (New Year's Day), 4 Feb (Independence Day), 13–14 Apr (Sinhala and Tamil New Year), 1 May (Labour Day), 17 Dec (Ramazan), 25 Dec (Christmas Day).

Variable dates
Good Friday, Tamil Thai Pongal Day (Jan), Mahasivarathri (Feb), Vesak (Buddha Purnima) (May), Diwali (Hindu, Oct/Nov), Eid al Adha, Birth of the Prophet Mohammed, Eid al Fitr.
Although not official public holidays, Poya holidays are observed on the day of each full moon.
Hindu, Muslim and Buddhist festivals are timed according to local sightings of various phases of the moon.

Working hours

Banking
Mon–Fri: 0900–1500.

Business
Mon–Fri: 0900–1700.

Government
Mon–Fri: 0830–1615.

Shops
Mon–Fri: 0900–1730; Sat: 0900–1300.

Telecommunications

Mobile/cell phones
GSM 900 and 1800 services cover much of the island, particularly in the east and populated areas.l

Electricity supply
230–240V AC, 50 cycles

Weights and measures
Metric system (local units also in use)

Social customs/useful tips
Alcoholic drinks are not served in hotels or restaurants on Poya (full moon) days. Footwear and headgear should be removed before entering Buddhist shrines; photographing statues of the Buddha is acceptable but not posing beside them; a yellow-robed Buddhist bhikku should not be asked to pose for photographs nor should visitors attempt to shake hands with him.
Filming with a video camera and other photography near military and government installations is prohibited.
Appointments should be made in advance. Punctuality is appreciated. Men shake hands on meeting and taking leave. Some people may prefer not to shake hands with those of the opposite sex.
The form of address is Mr or Mrs followed by family or surname, and people with an academic or professional title should be addressed by their full title.
Visitors should take note of local customs and take care to respect religious conventions. It is the convention to use the right and not the left hand when shaking hands and passing or receiving anything.
Restaurants usually add a service charge but further gratuities are optional.

Security
Visitors should avoid areas north of Puttalam, Anuradhapura and Nilaveli as well as the eastern side of the island south of Trincomalee including Batticaloa.
The areas once under conflict were heavily mined and travelling off main roads can be hazardous; warning notices are posted. Visitors must comply with any instruction issued at road blocks and security checks.
Registration with the relevant national embassy on arrival is highly advisable.

Getting there
Air
National airline: SriLankan Airlines
International airport/s: Colombo Bandaranaike International (CMB) in Katunayake, 29km north of Colombo, with duty-free shops, bar, restaurant, bank, post office and car hire. There are taxis, bus and rail links.
Airport tax: Departure tax: Rs1,000
Surface
Water: Ferry services to India have been suspended due to the ongoing insecurity situation. International shipping lines that maintain contacts with Sri Lanka may provide passenger services on cargo ships.
Main port/s: Colombo, Trincomalee, Galle, Kandasanturai.

Getting about
National transport
Air: There are airports in Batticaloa, Gal Oya, Palali and Trincomalee; the airport at Jaffna is currently closed.
Road: The extensive road network has 27,000km of road, 19,000km of which is surfaced. Over 90 per cent of all haulage is transported by roads.
Buses: Express services are available to all main destinations and should be booked in advance. Some services have air-conditioning.
Rail: An intercity express train runs between Colombo and Kandy. There are regular services linking Colombo to other main centres. Some services offer air-conditioning, dining cars and first-class accommodation. The service to Jaffna has been discontinued.
City transport
Taxis: Metered taxis are usually found in large towns, they may have yellow tops and red numbers on a white plate.
Air-conditioned taxis cost 10 per cent more. A 10 per cent tip is usual.
Car hire
Self-drive and chauffeur-driven car hire are available although chauffeur-driven cars are generally recommended. If driving, do not ignore 'no parking' signs (in Colombo vehicles parked illegally are destroyed by security forces suspecting a terrorist bomb). It is highly advisable to be aware of all traffic laws and parking restrictions. Driving is on the left.
Traffic is generally congested and the average rate of progress on roads nationwide is 30kph. Many roads are one-way only.
A national or international driving licence must be presented for local endorsement (on weekdays only) at the Automobile Association offices in Colombo.

BUSINESS DIRECTORY
The addresses listed below are a selection only. While World of Information makes every endeavour to check these addresses, we cannot guarantee that changes have not been made, especially to telephone numbers and area codes. We would welcome any corrections.

Telephone area codes
The international direct dialling code (IDD) for Sri Lanka is +94, followed by area code and subscriber's number:

Colombo Central	11	Moratuwa	11
Dehiwela	11	Negombo	31
Galle	91	Nuwara Eliya	52
Jaffna	21	Panadura	34
Kandy	81	Trincomalee	26
Kurunegala	37		

Useful telephone numbers
Police, fire and ambulance90
Emergency433-333
Accident service693-184/185
Directory enquiries161
International calls100
Speaking clock104

Chambers of Commerce
American Chamber of Commerce in Sri Lanka, Colombo Hilton Hotel, Lotus Road, Colombo 1 (tel: 233-6073; fax: 233-6072; e-mail: amcham@itmin.com).

Ceylon Chamber of Commerce, 50 Navam Mawatha, PO Box 274, Colombo 2 (tel: 245-2183; fax: 243-7477; e-mail: info@chamberlk).

Federation of Chambers of Commerce and Industry of Sri Lanka, 29 Gregory's Road, PO Box 2015, Colombo 7 (tel: 698-225; fax: 699-530; e-mail: info@fccisl.org).

National Chamber of Commerce of Sri Lanka, 450 DR Wijewardene Mawatha Street, PO Box 1375, Colombo 10 (tel: 268-9600; fax: 268-9596; e-mail: sg@nccsl.lk).

Banking
Bank of Ceylon, 4 Bank of Ceylon Mawatha, Colombo 1 (tel: 244-8348; fax: 244-8606).

Commercial Bank of Ceylon, 21 Bristol St, Colombo 1 (tel: 244-5010; fax: 244-9889; email: email@combank.net).

DFCC Bank, 73/5 Galle Road, Colombo 3 (tel: 244-0366; fax: 244-0376; email: dfcc@sri.lanka.net).

Hatton National Bank, 10 RA de Mel Mawatha, Colombo 3 (tel: 234-3473; fax: 244-0658).

National Development Bank, 40 Navam Mawatha, Colombo 2 (tel: 243-7701; fax: 244-0262).

Pan Asia Bank, 450 Galle Road, Colombo 3 (tel: 256-5564; fax: 256-5576; email: panasia@pabnk.lk).

People's Bank, 110 Sir James Peiris Mawatha, Colombo 2 (tel: 232-4188; fax: 244-7671).

Sampath Bank, PO Box 997, Sampath Centre Building, 110 Sir James Peiris Mawatha, Colombo 2 (tel: 230-0260; fax: 230-0143).

Seylan Bank, Ceylinco Seylan Towers, 90 Galle Road, Colombo 3 (tel: 243-7901; fax: 243-3072).

Union Bank of Colombo, World Trade Centre, Echelon Square, Colombo 1 (tel: 234-6346; fax: 234-6356).

Central bank
Central Bank of Sri Lanka, PO Box 590, 30 Janadhipathi Mawatha, Colombo 1 (tel: 247-7000; fax: 247-7712; e-mail: cbslgen@sri.lanka.net).

Travel information

Atlas Lanka (Pvt) Ltd, 86/1. Chatham Street, Colombo 1 (tel: 233-4255/6; fax 243-5292; email: atlaslka@sltnet.com).

Automobile Association of Ceylon, 40 Sir Macan Markar Mawatha, Galle Face, Colombo 3 (tel: 242-1528; fax: 244-6074).

Bandaranayake International Airport, Katunayake (tel: 225-2861; fax: 225-3187).

SriLankan Airlines, Level 22, East Tower, World Trade Centre, Echelon Square, Colombo 1 (tel: 733-5555; fax: 733-5122; internet: www.srilankan.aero).

Ministry of tourism

Ministry of Tourism, 64 Galle road, Colombo 03 (tel: 238-5241; fax: 239-9274; internet: www.slmts.slt.lk).

National tourist organisation offices

Sri Lanka Tourist Board, 80 Galle road, Colombo 03 (tel: 243-7059/60; fax: 244-0001; internet: www.srilankatourism.org).

Ministries

Ministry of Agriculture, Sampathapay, 82 Rajamalwatte Road, Battaramulla (tel: 288-6623).

Ministry of Aviation and Airports Developments, 64 Galle Road, Colombo 3.

Ministry of Buddha Sasana and Religious Affairs, 135 Anagarika Dharmapala Mawatha, Colombo 7 (tel: 232-9064; fax: 243-7992).

Ministry of Constitutional Affairs and Industrial Development, 73/1 Galle Road, Colombo 3 (tel: 232-7553; fax: 244-9402).

Ministry of Co-operative Development, 349 Galle Road, Colombo 3.

Ministry of Defence, 155 Baladaksha Mawatha, Colombo 3 (tel: 243-0860; fax: 254-1529).

Ministry of Development, Rehabilitation & Reconstruction of the East and Rural Housing Development, 43/89 Bristol Building, York Street, Colombo 1.

Ministry of Development, Rehabilitation & Reconstruction of the North and Tamil Affairs, North and East: 121 Park Road, Colombo 5.

Ministry of Education, Isurupaya, Sri Jayewardenepura Kotte, Battaramulla (tel: 286-5141; fax: 286-5162).

Ministry of Finance and Planning, Secretariat Building, Colombo 1 (tel: 243-3937; fax: 244-9823; email: minfi@boisrilanka.org).

Ministry of Fisheries and Aquatic Resources Development, Maligawatte, Colombo 10 (tel: 244-6183; fax: 254-1184).

Ministry of Foreign Affairs, Republic Building, Colombo 1 (tel: 232-5371; fax: 244-6091; email: for_min@sri.lanka.net).

Ministry of Forestry and Environment, Unity Plaza Building, Colombo 4 (tel: 258-8274; fax: 258-3290).

Ministry of Health, Suwasiripaya, 385 Wimalawasa Mawatha, Colombo 10 (tel/fax: 269-2694).

Ministry of Higher Education and IT Development, 18 Ward Place, Colombo 8.

Ministry of Information and Media, World Trade Centre, Echelon Square, Colombo 1.

Ministry of Internal & International Commerce, Muslim Religious Affairs, and Shipping Development, Insurance Building, Vauxhall Street, Colombo 2.

Ministry of Irrigation and Water Resources Management, 500 TB Jayah Mawatha, Colombo 10 (tel: 268-7491; fax: 269-4968).

Ministry of Justice, Superior Courts Complex Colombo 12 (tel: 232-9044; fax: 232-0785).

Ministry of Labour, Labour Secretariat, Kirula Road, Colombo 5 (tel: 258-8078; fax: 258-2938).

Ministry of Land Development and Minor Export Agriculture, Govijana Mandiraya, Rajamalwatte Road, Battaramulla.

Ministry of Estate Infrastructure and Livestock Developemnt, 45 St Michaels Road, Colombo 3.

Ministry of Mahaweli Development, 500 TB Jayah Mawatha, Colombo 10 (tel: 268-7491; fax: 268-7386).

Ministry of Plan Implementation, Sethsiripaya, Battaramulla (tel: 286-2721; fax: 286-2478).

Ministry of Ports Development and Development of the South, 45 Laden Bastian Road, Colombo 1 (tel: 242-1231; fax: 242-3485).

Ministry of Post and Telecommunications, Sethsiripaya, Battaramulla.

Ministry of Power and Energy, 80 Flower Road, Colombo 7.

Ministry of Public Administration, Home Affairs and Plantation Industries, Independence Square, Colombo 7 (tel: 269-6211; fax: 269-5279).

Ministry of Rural Industrial Development, Janakala Kendraya, Pelawatte, Battaramulla.

Ministry of Samurdhi, Rural Development, Parliamentary Affairs and Up-Country Development, 7A Reed Avenue, Colombo 7 (tel: 268-9589; fax: 268-8945).

Ministry of Science and Technology, 320 TB Jaya Mawatha, Colombo 10.

Ministry of Social Services and Housing Development for Fishing Community, Sethsiripaya, Battaramulla.

Ministry of Transport, 1 DR Wijewardana Mawatha, Colombo 10 (tel: 268-7105; fax: 269-4547).

Ministry of Urban Development, Construction and Public Utilities, Sethsiripaya, Battaramulla (tel: 286-2721; fax: 286-4765).

Ministry of Vocational Training, 475/32 Kotta Ropad, Rajagiriya.

Ministry of Womens Affairs, 177 Nawala Road, Colombo 5.

Other useful addresses

Board of Investment of Sri Lanka (BOI), World Trade Centre, Echelon Square, Colombo 1 (tel: 243-6639; fax: 244-7994; internet: www.boisrilanka.com/boihome/boi.htm).

British High Commission, 190 Galle Road, Colombo 3 (tel: 243-7336; fax: 243-0308; email: bhc@eureka.lk).

Colombo Plan, 28 St Michael's Road, Colombo 3 (tel: 256-4448; fax: 256-4531; email: cplan@slt.lk).

Colombo Stock Exchange, World Trade Centre, Echelon Square, Colombo 1 (tel: 244-6581; fax: 244-5279; internet: www.lanka.net/cse).

Sri Lanka Embassy (USA), 2148 Wyoming Avenue, NW, Washington DC 20008 (tel: (+1-202) 483-4025; fax: (+1-202) 232-7181; email: slembassy@starpower.net).

Sri Lanka Export Credit Insurance Corporation, Export Guarantee House, Colombo 2 (tel: 271-9410; fax: 271-9400; email: slecic@tradenetsl.lk).

Sri Lanka Export Development Board, 42 Navam Mawatha, Colombo 2 (tel: 230-0675; fax: 230-0715; email: serve@edbtradenetsl.lk).

Sri Lanka Importers', Exporters' and Manufacturers' Association, PO Box 12, Colombo 10 (tel: 269-6321; fax: 252-2524; email: sliema@isplanka).

Sri Lanka Tea Board, 574 Galle Road, Colombo 3 (tel: 258-2236; fax: 258-9132; email: tboard@sri.lanka.net).

US Embassy, 210 Galle Road, Colombo 3 (tel: 244-8007; fax: 243-7345; email: cdscmb@usia.gov).

Other news agencies: The Sinhalaya News Agency (www.news.sinhalaya.com).

Internet sites

InfoLanka (gateway site): www.infolanka.com

Sri Lanka Telecom directory: www.slt.lk

Tamilnet: www.tamilnet.com

Sudan

KEY FACTS

Official name: Jamhuryat es Sudan (Republic of Sudan)

Head of State: President Omar Hassan Ahmad al Bashir (took power 1993; elected 1996, re-elected 2000)

Head of government: President Omar Hassan Ahmad al Bashir

Ruling party: National Congress Party (NCP) (elected 2000)

Area: 2,505,813 square km

Population: 35.04 million (2005)

Capital: Khartoum

Official language: Arabic

Currency: Sudanese pound (S£) = 100 piastre (The pound was adopted on 9 Jan 2007; S£1 = 100 old Dinar)

Exchange rate: S£2.07 per US$ (Jul 2008)

GDP per capita: US$1,242 (2007)*

GDP real growth: 8.00% (2005)

Labour force: 13.80 million (2004)

Unemployment: 18.70% (2003)

Inflation: 8.50% (2005)

Oil production: 457,000 bpd (2007)

Balance of trade: -US$1.12 billion (2005)

Visitor numbers: 328,000 (2006)*

* estimated figure

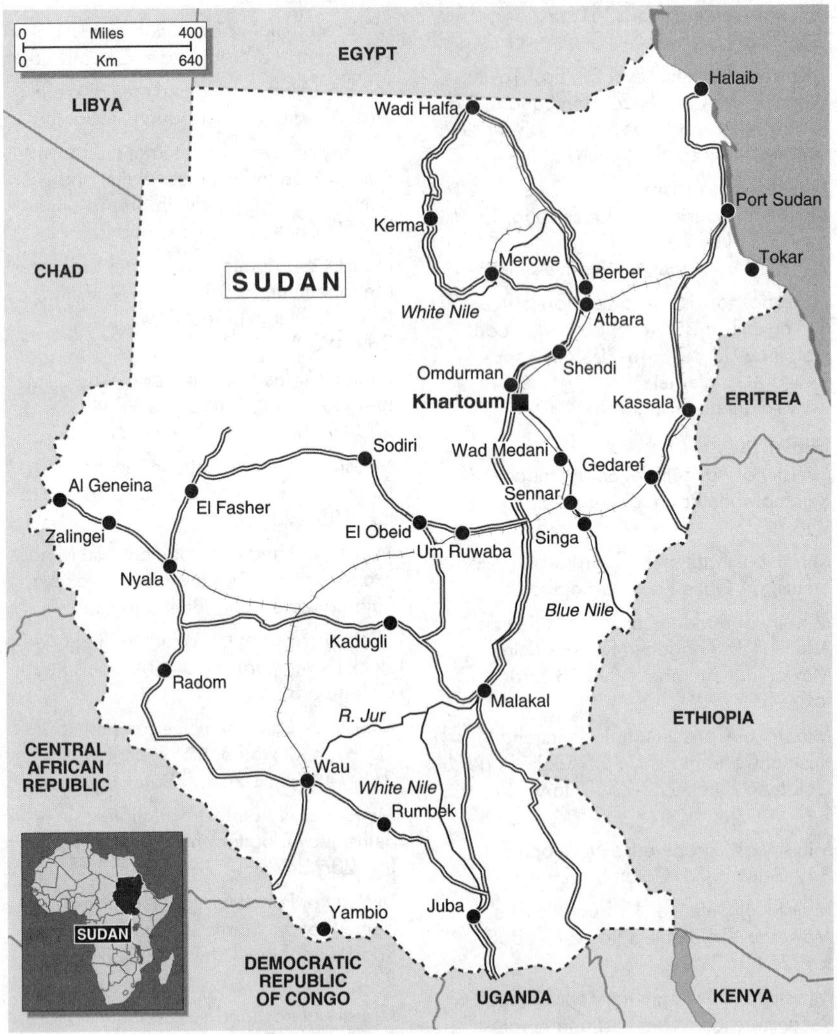

According to the International Monetary Fund (IMF) Sudan's economic performance in 2007 was mixed. Overall economic growth was strong and average inflation was relatively low. However, due partly to delays in implementing key public expenditure control measures, there was an accumulation of domestic arrears of about 2.8 per cent of gross domestic product (GDP). Bold actions were taken to rein-in tax exemptions, widen the tax base, and strengthen tax and budget administration. However, some structural benchmarks related to public financial management reforms were delayed. Looking ahead, the surge in oil prices provides an important opportunity to reduce domestic arrears. The recent hike in international oil prices suggests an additional 3.3 per cent of GDP in government revenue in 2008. However, only a portion of this can be used to clear central government domestic arrears, as oil revenues must be shared with the states.

Economic growth in 2007 remained strong by regional standards but moderated in relation relative to 2006. Real GDP growth in 2007 was estimated at about 10 per cent with non-oil growth at just under 8 per cent, compared with 11 and 10 per cent respectively in 2006. While oil production was higher than in 2006, it was less than projected. Sharp drops in foreign investment and private sector credit, the impact of regional floods, and lower-than projected agricultural output contributed to the slowdown in non-oil growth. Inflation at end-2007 was 8.8 per cent, somewhat higher than projected. Inflation surged to 20 per cent by end-March 2008, however, driven almost entirely by a rise in food prices (in line with a similar increase in world food prices).

The fiscal position on a cash basis improved in 2007, but delays in implementing expenditure controls led to the accumulation of some new domestic arrears. The fiscal deficit (on a cash basis) dropped from an annualised 6.0 per cent of GDP at end-March to an estimated 3.1 per cent by end-December – reflecting higher oil revenue and lower current expenditures (despite some 0.4 per cent of GDP in domestic arrears repayment).

The challenges of implementing the various peace agreements, disarmament, and fiscal decentralisation have also impacted fiscal performance. For example, central government transfers to the states quintupled between 2004 and 2007 – from 1.5 to 8 per cent of GDP, and from 8 to 34 per cent of total central government expenditures.

Higher oil prices and renewed exchange rate flexibility facilitated a rise in net international reserves (NIR) of the central bank, but at a slower rate than anticipated. NIR rose from US$563 million in May to an estimated US$981 million by end-December 2007 (1 month of imports). Despite higher oil prices, NIR also fell slightly in January 2008 to about US$940 million – possibly reflecting lower FDI and higher outward remittances.

The exchange rate has shown increasing flexibility since the end of the currency conversion in July, with the pound depreciating by over 2 per cent during August–December 2007. However, the shift to greater flexibility was accompanied by periods of unwarranted volatility, resulting in continued sales of foreign exchange by the central bank to smooth short-term turbulence. In real effective terms, the pound depreciated by about 2 per cent during 2007.

Oil exports rose by 54 per cent in volume terms and by 66 per cent in dollar terms (reflecting the surge in oil prices in the last five months of the year). Non-oil exports remained weak. Imports registered the smallest increase in five years – with a significant slowdown in machinery, transport equipment and crude materials. The overall current account deficit (on a cash basis) was 11.0 per cent of GDP for 2007, compared with 13.5 per cent in 2006. Notably, however, inflows of foreign exchange registered a sharp drop, due mainly to lower foreign direct investment and net private current transfers.

The economic outlook for 2008 envisages a resumption of non-oil growth to levels seen before the fiscal and financial difficulties of late 2006–early 2007. Overall real GDP growth is forecast at 8.3 per cent – encompassing 4.4 per cent real growth in the oil sector and 8.9 per cent growth in the non-oil sector. The resumption of strong activity in the non-oil sector hinges upon the repayment of domestic government arrears, and a related pick-up in private sector credit. The external current account is expected to improve, reflecting increased oil exports, but the overall balance of payments will also depend on developments in private transfers and FDI, which fell sharply in 2007. Conservative assumptions in this regard suggest room to rebuild net international reserves of the central bank to at least US$1.5 billion. Inflation is expected to increase in light of the projected rise in international commodity prices, but to remain within single digits for the year as a whole.

The official 2008 budget envisaged an overall fiscal deficit (cash and commitment) of 3.4 per cent of GDP. It did not anticipate the cash payment of domestic arrears accumulated in 2007, but rather a rescheduling of payments to the years 2009–10.

The surge in international oil prices that came after the budget was drawn up provides an important opportunity to reduce domestic arrears. Given the volatility of oil production and of the government's share during the past two years, the Sudanese authorities will keep the new baseline. However, in light of higher international oil prices, total oil revenues are projected to be higher-than-budgeted by about 3.3 per cent of GDP.

UNAMID - Unamuddle

In September 2007 Sudanese president, Omar El Bashir, had reluctantly agreed to a 26,000-strong hybrid UN-African Union (AU) (UNAMID) peacekeeping force to be deployed in Darfur. Hitherto, the Sudanese government had denounced any UN involvement in Darfur as neo-colonial. The Sudanese government finally agreed to a UN presence if there were not enough AU troops available. Cynics expressed the view that Sudan had only agreed to the arrangement because it was unlikely ever to become effective. In the event, the AU had some difficulty in mustering 26,000 men – the peacekeeping force never managed to number more than 15,000. The meeting of many key Darfur rebels in Arusha (Tanzania) in August 2007 under the aegis of the AU and UN had been supposed to arrive at a common negotiating position vis-à-vis Khartoum. Some Darfur rebel leaders boycotted the talks, and also boycotted the subsequent talks with the Khartoum government, which took place in Libya in October 2007. Meanwhile, violence continued in Darfur with accusations and counter accusations between Chad and Sudan of breach of each other's border in the area. This complicated the fate of

KEY INDICATORS — Sudan

	Unit	2003	2004	2005	2006	2007
Population	m	35.86	37.99	35.30	*36.22	*37.16
Gross domestic product (GDP)	US$bn	17.68	21.56	27.90	36.40	*46.16
GDP per capita	US$	493	617	790	*1,005	*1,242
GDP real growth	%	5.9	7.3	8.6	11.3	*10.5
Inflation	%	10.3	8.4	8.5	7.2	7.9
Oil output	'000 bpd	255.0	301.0	379.0	397.0	457.0
Exports (fob) (goods)	US$m	2,095.0	3,777.8	4,824.3	5,813.0	*8,866.3
Imports (cif) (goods)	US$m	1,476.0	3,586.2	5,946.0	7,105.0	–
Balance of trade	US$m	619.0	-191.6	-1,121.7	-1,292.0	–
Current account	US$m	-1,460.0	-1,450.0	-2,919.0	-5,489.0	*-5,432.0
Total reserves minus gold	US$m	847.5	1,626.1	2,449.8	1,659.9	1,377.9
Foreign exchange	US$m	847.2	1,626.1	2,449.7	1,659.9	1,377.9
Exchange rate	per US$	259.25	257.91	201.10	202.50	2.03

* estimated figure

millions of internally displaced people and refugees. According to some estimates, the Darfur conflict has cost more than 250,000 lives and displaced over 2.5 million people since it erupted in 2003. The wider international UN force was slow to deploy due to a lack of aviation, transport and logistical units. At root, Sudan remained divided: its 27 million northerners are mostly Arab and Muslim. The 8 million southerners are largely black: those that are not Christian are animist by religion.

Distraction

In July 2008, the International Criminal Court (ICC) decided to proceed with the indictment of Sudan's president Omar al Bashir for genocide. This was the first time that the court had sought an indictment for the crime of genocide, considered the most serious of all international crimes. Mr Omar al Bashir's indictment came as no surprise to the international community. Mr Omar al Bashir had hardly taken the ICC seriously; on the contrary he had promoted those suspected of war-crimes. Fears were expressed that an indictment would lead to a renewal of the genocide. Initially, these appeared unfounded.

Designer Darfur

2007 was nevertheless, for Sudan, a year of misguided mythology. The genocide that had characterised southern Sudan in the early part of the decade had virtually ceased, leaving a massive humanitarian problem as thousands of refugees continued to seek food and drink. For some time, the problems of Darfur had attracted high-profile international support. Hollywood stars such as George Clooney pitched in, observing that 'many governments have offered expressions of concern, but few have offered the most basic tools necessary to keep civilians safe and for peacekeepers to do their job. It is time for governments to put their helicopters where their mouths are'. Not just helicopters: the UNAMID force needs another 8,000 peacekeepers if it is to do its job properly. Taking things a stage further, US film mogul Steven Spielberg resigned as a consultant to the Beijing Olympic Games in protest at China's role as Sudan's largest trading partner. Meanwhile, common sense also prevailed: in an article in the London *Spectator* Justin Marozzi, who had just spent three months in Sudan, wrote: 'In what was simplified into a conflict between African farmers and Arab nomads, some 300,000 people were estimated to have been slaughtered when the killings were at their peak in 2003–04. Most of the killing (as well as the rapes and the pillaging) was attributed to the *Janjaweed*, the government supported mercenaries on horseback'. Appalling though the massacres were, the problem has moved on and any resolution now needs to confront a more complex state of affairs.

In the 2007 peace negotiations in the Nigerian capital of Abuja, two main rebel groups were invited to participate: The Justice and Equality Movement (JEM) and the Sudan People's Liberation Movement (SPLM). After lengthy discussions, the parties agreed to end the war which had, in one fashion or another, gone on for some 50 years. By 2008 the number of belligerent participants had grown staggeringly to well over 20, embracing the SLM-Unity, SLM-Mother, SLM-Minni, SLM-Free Will, SLM-Peace, with their adversaries, the JEM-Peace and the JEM-Unity without forgetting the JEM itself and the United Revolutionary Front. In his article, Mr Marozzi explained that the conflict had come to pit Arab against Arab, African against African, rebel versus rebel, bandits versus civilians and aid workers, *Janjaweed* versus peacekeepers, not to mention in the wider context, Sudan versus Chad. This is a far cry from the simplistic bad-guy government against good-guy rebels scenario often depicted by the so called 'Darfur Lobby'. The US based Save Darfur Coalition website invited readers to say if their 'mutual fund is supporting genocide'. A similar question is presented by the Divest for Darfur campaign.

In mid-2008, aid workers and diplomats alike were able to agree at least on one thing: the genocide had effectively ceased, to be replaced by a rather messy civil-war. UK journalist, Alex de Waal the co-author of *Darfur: a New History of a Long War* has written that 'In the current hyper-moralised debate over Sudan, anyone who questions Sudan's critics risks being called an apologist for Khartoum'.

China

The China National Petroleum Corporation (CNPC) is one of the longest established in Sudan, participating in a number of projects, often with a controlling interest. The pervasive presence of CNPC is unlike that of oil companies from other countries. The aims of CNPC and the Chinese government are exactly the same, driven by an overruling need to secure long term oil supplies. Sudan represents a major source of oil for China, explaining the massive investments that China has made in the country. China had gained primary ownership of Sudan's largest oil joint venture, the Greater Nile Petroleum Operating Company (GNPOC) in 2007. The GNPOC project represents almost half of CNPC's overseas oil production. In an article in the *Wall Street Journal*, CNPC acknowledged that national (Chinese) interests took precedence over company priorities. This unique link between nation and oil company has enabled China to strengthen CNPC's dominant role in the Sudanese oil industry by providing the government of Sudan with access to military weapons and, where appropriate, political support in the international arena.

Oil?

The US government agency, the Energy Information Administration (EIA), notes that Sudan's oil exports, which have increased sharply since the completion of the Greater Nile Oil Pipeline which transports oil between the inland oil fields and refineries in Khartoum and Port Sudan in 1999, account for 70 per cent of total export revenues. Additional growth in Sudan's hydrocarbon sector will likely occur with a refurbished infrastructure, which has seen little improvement since the beginning of the country's civil conflicts in 1955. As of January 2007, according to the minister of state for energy and mines, Sudan was considering joining the Organisation of Petroleum Exporting Countries (OPEC), but by mid-2008 had still not joined.

Sudan had proven oil reserves of 6.6 billion barrels at the end of 2007, dramatically up from an estimated 0.3 million barrels of proven oil reserves ten years ago at the end of 1997. The majority of Sudan's proven reserves are located in the south in the Muglad and Melut basins. The civil war has meant that oil exploration has mostly been limited to the central and south-central regions of the country. It is estimated that substantial potential reserves are held in north-west Sudan, the Blue Nile basin, and the Red Sea area in eastern Sudan.

In 2007, crude oil production averaged 457,000 barrels per day (bpd), up from 331,000bpd in 2006. According to Dr Angelina Teny, minister of state for mines and energy, Sudan plans to be producing one million bpd of crude oil by the end of 2008. In 2006, Sudan consumed 94,000bpd and exported approximately 320,000bpd of crude oil, with the majority of crude destined for Asian markets.

Risk assessment

Economy	Good
Politics	Poor
Regional stability	Fair

COUNTRY PROFILE

Historical profile

1821 The swamps of southern Sudan were unaffected by the Arab-controlled northern regions until the Turks defeated Egypt, conquered northern Sudan and opened the south to trade.
1869 After the opening of the Suez Canal, the British became involved in Sudan.
1881–85 Mohammed Ahmed, who proclaimed himself the long-looked-for Mahdi (the guided one), led his followers, the Muslim Sudanese, in a rebellion against Egyptian mis-rule; General Gordon was sent by Britain to quash the rebellion. In 1885, Gordon and the British army were massacred by the Mahdi's army at Khartoum. Sudan was ruled by the Mahdi for the next 17 years. The Mahdi united the tribes in a modern Islamic state.
1898 The Mahdi was defeated by the British and Anglo-Egyptian army.
1899 Sudan was ruled as an Anglo-Egyptian condominium until it achieved independence as a parliamentary republic in 1956.
1945 At the end of the Second World War, political parties emerged: the Umma Party was created by supporters of the Mahdi while the Ashiqqa Party was established by rivals of the Mahdi and eventually became the National Union Party (NUP).
1956 Sudan gained independence. With southern calls for a federation or even secession rejected, a civil war broke out between the largely Muslim north and the largely Christian/Animist south.
1958 A military coup led by General Ibrahim Abboud overthrew the civilian government of Prime Minister Abd Allah Khalil. Martial law was declared and Abboud proclaimed himself prime minister.
1962 Civil war began in the south, led by the Anya Nya movement.
1964 The 'October Revolution' overthrew Abboud and a national government was established.
1969 Colonel Jaafar Mohammed al Nimieri led the 'May Revolution' military coup, installing a revolutionary council.
1972 Nimieri became the country's first elected president and gave the southern provinces a degree of autonomy under the Addis Ababa agreement between the government and the Anya Nya, reducing the level of fighting.
1978 Oil was discovered in southern Sudan.
1983 The President increased the Islamisation campaign when the autonomy agreement was revoked and Sharia (Islamic law) was introduced. The Sudan People's Liberation Movement (SPLM) was established; its armed wing, the Sudan People's Liberation Army (SPLA) gained control of much of the south.
1985–86 Nimieri was ousted in a bloodless coup and after a brief period of military rule, Sadiq al Mahdi, the great-grandson of the Great Mahdi, became prime minister after elections in 1986.
1989 Sadiq al Mahdi was replaced following another bloodless coup by the National Salvation Revolution; Omar Hassan Ahmad al Bashir became chairman of the Revolutionary Command Council for National Salvation (RCCNS).
1992 The Sudanese pound was replaced as the currency by the Sudanese dinar.
1993 The RCCNS was abolished after Omar al Bashir was appointed president; Sudan returned to civilian rule, although with one political party exercising dominance – Al Muttamar al Watani (National Congress Party) (NCP), the country was not strictly a democracy.
1995 Egyptian President Mubarak accused Sudan of being involved in an attempt to assassinate him in Addis Ababa.
1996 The first presidential and legislative elections since 1989 were held; Omar al Bashir was elected president for a five-year term. Sanctions were imposed against Sudan by the UN for the country's failure to extradite three men suspected of involvement in the 1995 attempted assassination of Mubarak.
1997 The Khartoum Peace Agreement was ratified by the National Assembly. Peace talks between the SPLA and the government resumed in Nairobi.
1998–99 Voters in a referendum endorsed a new constitution. Sudan began to export oil. After a power struggle within the ruling NCP, between Bashir and Hassan al Turabi (a hardline Islamist and ideologue), the President imposed a state of emergency and dissolved the National Assembly.
2000 Omar al Bashir and the NCP were re-elected. Most opposition parties boycotted the elections.
2001 Hassan al Turabi, was arrested and his party, the National Islamic Front (NIF), was banned. The UN Security Council approved the lifting of sanctions imposed in 1996. The UN's World Food Programme estimated that three million people were facing famine.
2002 After peace talks in Kenya, the government and the SPLA signed the Machakos Protocol: the government accepted the right of the south to seek self-determination after a six-year interim period.
2003 Rebels in the western region of Darfur started an uprising by attacked government targets, claiming the region was being neglected by Khartoum. Hassan al Turabi, was released and the ban on the NIF was lifted. China and the Sudan announced a US$1 billion investment plan to enhance Sudan's oil infrastructure including increased capacity at the Khartoum refinery and construction of a 750-kilometre-long pipeline between the Kordofan oilfield and the coast.
2004 A campaign to quell the insurrection in Darfur began; thousands of people were displaced by the fighting. Army officers and opposition politicians, including al Turabi, were arrested over an alleged coup plot. Bashir agreed to grant autonomy to the south for six years, split the country's oil revenues with the southern provinces and allow the southerners to vote in a referendum of independence at the end of the six-year period. The conflict in the western region of Darfur between nomad Arab militia and black African villagers gained world attention. The government denied that it supported the Janjaweed militias, accused of systematic killings of African villagers, and said that there was no evidence of any atrocities.
2005 The government and the Sudan People's Liberation Army (SPLA) signed a peace agreement which ended a 22-year civil war. The agreement began a period of transition which is due to run until 2009, when parliamentary and state legislative elections are scheduled to take place. SPLA leader, John Garang, was appointed vice president for the six-year period of reconciliation, and a new constitution gave a large degree of autonomy to the south. Security forces arrested many members and top officials of the main opposition Umma Party (UP), because of planned celebrations marking an anti-government uprising in 1986. Sudan said it had found quantities of oil in its western region of Darfur. John Garang was killed in a helicopter crash; riots broke out in Khartoum, between black southern Sudanese and northern Arabs. Garang's deputy, Salva Kiir, was named his successor as vice president of national Sudan and president of southern Sudan. Chad declared 'a state of belligerence' with Sudan. In an effort to ease tensions between the two countries, President Obasanjo of Nigeria, as head of the African Union, attempted mediation between a Sudanese envoy and Chad's President Deby, but with little success.
2006 The AU extended the mandate for its peacekeeping force by a further 10 months. Chad broke-off diplomatic

relations with Sudan, following attacks on Chadian towns by Sudanese backed Chad rebels based in the Darfur region. A UN resolution was passed calling for a 20,000 international force of soldiers and police to be admitted to the Darfur region as peace-keepers. President Bashir remained uncompromising in its opposition to intervention. The UN envoy, Jan Pronk, was expelled for claiming that government troops had suffered defeats in southern Sudan.

2007 On 9 January 2007 the currency was changed from the dinar (in use since 1992), back to the pound; the exchange rate was set at S£1 to 100 old dinar. Old currency notes are due to be phased out by July 2007. At the second anniversary celebrations of the country's peace agreement the president and vice president had a public row concerning the lack of progress in implementing the terms of the agreement. Vice President Kiir accused the national government of supporting militia operating in the south, who had not been disarmed, and failing to share the wealth of resources found in the south. The African Union, for the second time, rejected President Bashir's bid to become head of the organisation. Other African leaders, the international community and aid agencies all lobbied to reject his candidacy because of the conflict in Darfur which had, in four years, killed over 200,000 people and displaced more than two million. An agreement was signed between Sudan, Chad and the Central African Republic in February whereby no shelter will be given to rebel movements from another country. The minister of humanitarian affairs, Ahmed Haroun and a Janjaweed leader, Ali Mohammed Ali Abd al Rahman (known as Ali Kushayb) were indited by the International Criminal Court for crimes against humanity, committed during attackes on the civilian population of Darfur. On 31 August, the UN voted for a united peacekeeping force to be sent to Sudan to bolster African Union (AU) troops already deployed in Darfur to protect civilians. An AU base, staffed by mostly Nigerian troops acting as military observers, was attacked by heavily armed rebels on 30 September; 10 soldiers were killed and the incident sparked international condemnation. Dissident members of the SLA, the Justice and Equality Movement (JEM), were blamed for the attack. On 7 October rebels burned down the AU-base town of Haskanita, which had been previously attacked. The UN Mission (Unmis) reported the town was under the control of government troops. The government announced a unilateral ceasefire in Darfur in advance of peace talks, despite two rebel groups boycotting the talks, which began in Libya on 27 October. The SLA-Unity and the JEM groups decided not to attend the talks after other, smaller rebel groups, had also been invited. The talks continued while representatives approached SLA-Unity and Jem to reconsider their decision. Meanwhile, in early November, the northern National Congress Party and southern Sudan People's Liberation Movement finally agreed to implement all provisions of the 2005 peace agreement. On 31 December the UN–AU Mission in Darfur (Unamid) began operations, replacing the AU forces.

2008 On 14 July the International Criminal Court (ICC) accused President al Bashir of genocide in Darfur and formally requested a warrant for his arrest. Sudan does not recognise the ICC and claimed the move was a 'foreign conspiracy'. On 21 July, the African Union (AU) called on the UN to suspend the war crimes accusation against President al Bashir, saying it would jeopardise the ongoing peace process.

Political structure

Constitution

A multi-party parliamentary system was introduced in 1986, comprising a five-member Supreme Council and a 360-member Majlis Watani (National Assembly).

In 1994, the government increased the number of states to 26. Each state has a wali (governor), legislative council and council of ministers. In March 2002, the government indicated that it would replace elections for the wali with a system of electoral colleges which would submit six possible candidates, giving the president the final decision on appointments. A new constitution was promulgated on 1 January 1999, allowing opposition political associations to register prior to the elections. Eligibility for voting was reduced from 18 to 17 years on 3 January 1999.

Form of state

Federal republic

The executive

The president has inherited most of the powers of the now disbanded Revolutionary Command Council of National Salvation (RCCNS), which assumed unified powers in the 1989 military coup. These include the right to override constitutional elections to the 26 state governorships. Executive power at the operational level resides with the cabinet, which includes both civilian and military representatives. In 2002, the government scrapped the two-term limitation to the presidency. The president is directly elected by universal suffrage.

National legislature

The Majlis Watani (National Assembly) was elected in December 2000, a year after it was suspended by presidential decree. Out of a total of 360 seats, 270 are directly elected for a four-year term in single-seat constituencies, 35 members represent women, 26 members represent university graduates and 29 are representatives of trade unions.

Legal system

Sharia (Islamic law) with an admixture of English common law operates officially at the federal level, although individual states choose whether or not it should apply at state level. In practice the legal system is split along political lines, with Sharia imposed universally in the north, but ineffective in the rebel-held south. The judiciary is in theory politically independent under the constitution introduced at the beginning of 1999. However, military or paramilitary elements influence the judiciary or operate direct extra-judicial military rule throughout the country.

Last elections

December 2000 (parliamentary and presidential)

Results: Presidential: Omar al Bashir was re-elected with 86.5 per cent of the vote. Parliamentary: the ruling National Congress Party (NCP) won 355 seats in the elections to the National Assembly.

Next elections

2009 (presidential and parliamentary)

Political parties

Ruling party

National Congress Party (NCP) (elected 2000)

Main opposition party

Umma Party (UP)

Population

35.04 million (2005)

Last census: September 1993: 24,940,683. The next election, scheduled for February 2008 was postponed to April.

Population density: Urban population: 37 per cent of the total population.

Annual growth rate: 2.2 per cent 1994–2004 (WHO 2006)

Internally Displaced Persons (IDP)

4.0 million (UNHCR 2004)

Ethnic make-up

Black (52 per cent), Arab (39 per cent), Beja (6 per cent). In the north and central regions the population consists mainly of Muslim Arabs and Nubians. In the south the people are socially, culturally and historically related to the peoples of east Africa.

Religions

Islam (Sunni Muslim) in the north (70 per cent); in the south traditional beliefs (25 per cent) and Christianity (5 per cent).

Education

Elementary education for those aged six to 12 years is free. Intermediate education starts at the age of 13 and lasts three years. Secondary education starts at 16 years and also lasts for three years. Students completing secondary education are eligible for university. There are five universities, two in Khartoum (one is a branch of Cairo University), an Islamic university at Omdurman and universities at Juba and Wad Medani.

Public expenditure on education typically amounts to 1 per cent of annual gross national income.

Unicef has voiced concerns at the low-level of public spending on education and at low enrolment and high dropout rates, calling for, among other things, significantly increased public spending, stronger teacher training and in particular the attention given to girls' education. Interventions to promote girls' education have resulted in an increase in the enrolment of girls by 5.7 per cent. The percentage of total girls' enrolment increased marginally from 45.3 per cent in 2000–01 to 45.6 per cent in 2001–02. Nationally, enrolment in primary schools increased by 5.8 per cent.

In 2002 Unicef undertook, with BRAC (an international NGO educational organisation specialising in providing schooling in poor rural areas), to provide 100 primary schools under the Village Girls Schools Project, in southern Sudan, within three years.

Literacy rate: 60 per cent adult rate; 79 per cent youth rate (15–24) (Unesco 2005).

Compulsory years: Six to 14.

Enrolment rate: 51 per cent gross primary enrolment of relevant age group (including repeaters); 21 per cent gross secondary enrolment (World Bank).

Pupils per teacher: 29 in primary schools.

Health

Per capita total expenditure on health (2003) was US$54; of which per capita government spending was US$23, at the international dollar rate, (WHO 2006).

Public health services are organised by the ministry of health. Some health care is provided free of charge. Total expenditure on health is about 3.5 per cent of GDP, of which government spending is about 19 per cent.

In August 2004 epidemiologists of the Global Polio Eradication Initiative announced that new cases of polio had been confirmed in the Darfur region of Sudan. The infection is believed to have spread from Northern Nigeria.

HIV/Aids

The conflict in southern Sudan has left many destitute; UN peacekeepers are expected to provide a buffer between the warring sides and when this happens UNAids will send in teams to ensure HIV/Aids is not an inevitable consequence of the peace-keepers' arrival and the sex-industry that usually develops in conflict zones.

HIV prevalence: 2.3 per cent aged 15–49 in 2003 (World Bank)

Life expectancy: 58 years, 2004 (WHO 2006)

Fertility rate/Maternal mortality rate: 4.3 births per woman, 2004 (WHO 2006)

Birth rate/Death rate: 36.5 births per 1,000 population; 9.6 deaths per 1,000 population (2003).

Child (under 5 years) mortality rate (per 1,000): 63 per 1,000 live births (World Bank)

Head of population per physician: 0.22 physicians per 1,000 people, 2004 (WHO 2006)

Welfare

Social insurance in Sudan is not provided through the government. There is no social security budget.

Main cities

Khartoum (capital, estimated population 1.7 million in 2005), Omdurman (3.0 million), Khartoum North (1.7 million), Port Sudan (504,868), Nyala (496,695), Kusti (306,721), Kassala (386,510), Wad Medani (315,105), Juba (198,527), Atbara (103,734).

Languages spoken

Arabic and English are used in business. African languages include Nilotic and Nilo-Hamitic. The government is considering eliminating the official teaching and use of English as part of its Islamisation programme.

Official language/s

Arabic

Media

The broadcast media is tightly constrained by censorship laws and statutory government ownership. There is a military censor permanently stationed in Sudan television to ensure the official line is always adopted. Print media enjoys a less restrictive regime but authorities have mechanism to control and influence items published, which had resulted in an unsurprising amount of self-censorship.

Press

Press restrictions have eased with increasing discussion of some domestic and foreign policy issues. Ownership of publications by individuals or political groups is banned. The board and chairman of a publication must be government-appointed, and 26 per cent of the publisher's equity goes to the government. The National Press and Publications Council (NPPC) has the power to suspend any publication. A wide variety of English and Arabic-language publications operate in the shadow of the government's information policy.

Dailies: Most newspapers are published in Khartoum. In Arabic, national publications include Al Ayaam (www.alayaam.net), Al Rayaam (www.rayaam.net), a mass circulation private newspaper; regional publications include Al Sahafah (www.alsahafa.info), Akhbar Al Youn (www.akhbaralyoumsd.net), Al Mshaheer (www.almshaheer.com), Al Sudani (www.alsudani.info). In English, leading independent include Khartoum Monitor and Sudan Vision. Online news is published by Sudan Tribune (www.sudantribune.com) and Sudan Online (www.sol-sd.com).

Weeklies: In Arabic, publications include Al Sudan al Jadid and Al Fajr (bi-weekly).

Periodicals: Periodicals include the Arabic political monthly magazine Addaraweesh (published in the UK) and the political newspaper Mehairah covering current affairs. Sudanow is government owned and Al Midan is the monthly organ of the Sudanese Communist party (www.midan.net).

Broadcasting

All broadcasting is controlled by the National Radio and Television Corporation based in Omdurman.

Radio: The government-owned The Sudan National Radio Corporation (www.sudanradio.info) broadcasts daily radio programmes in Amharic, Arabic, English, French, Somali and Tigrinya. The privately owned Mango 96 FM is a music station. The internationally funded Miraya radio station (www.mirayafm.org), is run by the UN, broadcasting in Arabic and English it is based in Juba.

Television: The government-owned Sudan National Broadcasting Corporation (SNBC) (www.srtc.gov.sd) has a monopoly for internal broadcasting. The government-owned Juba TV is based in the semi-autonomous south.

There are restrictions on satellite dish ownership, but satellite services are offered in tandem with domestic. A six-channel pan-Arab cable network offers CNN, Saudi Middle East Broadcasting Corporation (MEBC), Kuwait-TV and Dubai-TV.

Economy

Sudan's economy is predominantly agricultural. Subsistence farming is combined with cash crops such as gum arabic, sesame and cotton. Economic growth is being fuelled by oil production, but has resulted in little improvement to living standards which in the oil-producing south have deteriorated due to the effects of the prolonged civil war.

The expanding oil and gas reserves have been developmed largely with the assisstance of China. Sudan stands to become one of the world's leading oil producers. The Sudanese economy is undergoing rapid development, although this has been skewed towards the north. Oil production has boosted the trade balance with oil export revenues accounting for around 70 per cent of Sudan's total export earnings. The after effects off the civil war in the south, continuing US sanctions and poor infrastructure have been obstacles to growth. The development of the oil and gas sectors will inevitably transform the economic profile of Sudan. An escalating humanitarian crisis in Dafur in the West is attracting international scrutiny and is likely to put pressure on the government and economy. Hundreds of thousands have been displaced and farms have been left to deteriorate. Despite the social crisis, GDP has continued to grow to over nine per cent in 2006.

External trade

In 2005 the Greater Arab Free Trade Area (Gafta) was ratified by 17 members, including Sudan, creating an Arab economic bloc. A customs union was established whereby tariffs within Gafta will be reduced by a percentage each year, until none remain.

Around 70 per cent of total export revenue is generated by crude oil. In June 2007, Sudan was in negotiation to join the Organisation of Petroleum Exporting Countries (Opec).

Industrialisation is limited and although Sudan is considered a major source of minerals, exploration and commercialisation is underdeveloped.

Imports

Principal imports are foodstuffs, manufactured goods, refinery and transport equipment, medicines and chemicals, textiles and wheat.

Main sources: China (18.1 per cent total, 2006), Saudi Arabia (9.2 per cent), UAE (5.8 per cent).

Exports

Principal exports are crude oil and petroleum products, cotton, sesame, livestock, groundnuts, gum Arabic and sugar.

Main destinations: Japan (49.8 per cent total, 2006), China (32.1 per cent), Saudi Arabia (3.1 per cent).

Agriculture

Farming

Sudan is a semi-arid country and a large part is desert. Irrigated farmland constitutes about one-fifth of the total cultivated area, but produces about 50 per cent of total crop production. The traditional farming areas are semi-arid and used for livestock rearing, while export crops are grown in the irrigated areas, mostly in the Gezira area between the Blue and White Niles. The country is often racked by drought and famine.

Agriculture accounted for around 30 per cent of GDP in 2004. The majority of the population work on the land.

Principal export crops are cotton, oil seeds (mainly groundnuts and sesame) and gum arabic (used in soft drinks, baking, cosmetics, pharmaceuticals and other industrial applications), of which Sudan is the world's largest producer. Main food crops include sorghum (dura) and millet. Cotton is the main cash crop providing 45 per cent of agricultural export earnings, followed by gum arabic and sesame (21 per cent). Livestock-raising is of considerable importance, employing about 40 per cent of the population. Sudan is aiming to become self-sufficient in rice and tea production.

Sudan has attempted to tackle the problem of land usage. Government policy aims to increase the area of cultivable land (only about 10 per cent of the potential arable land is under cultivation) through the rehabilitation and expansion of existing irrigation schemes. A planting scheme has given precedence to food crops over land devoted to cotton production and export.

Crop production in 2005 included: 5,366,748 tonnes (t) cereals in total, 4,228,000t sorghum, *1,200,000t groundnuts in shell, 400,000t wheat, 663,000t millet, *16,000t potatoes, *15,748t rice, 137,000t yams, 272,000t pulses, *330,000t dates, 150,070t citrus fruit, 265,000t seed cotton, *700,000t tomatoes, 547,920t oilcrops, *195,000t mangoes, *5,500,000t sugar cane, *173,000t tea, 1,161,270t fruit in total, 1,866,700t vegetables in total.

* estimate

Estimated livestock production included: 714,675t meat in total, 325,000t beef, 41,175 camel meat, 144,000t lamb, 126,000t goat meat, 29,500t poultry, 47,000t eggs, 5,106,190t milk, 710t honey, 56,280t cattle hides, 24,250t goatskins, 22,500t sheepskins. 46,000t greasy wool.

Fishing

Sudan possesses vast freshwater and marine fishing potential. The freshwater sources comprise rivers and lakes. The Nile alone has an estimated potential output of 60,000 tonnes of fish a year, but the fisheries are barely exploited. Fishing on the Red Sea coastline is also under-exploited and is being encouraged with government assistance.

Over 95 per cent of the Sudanese catch of fish is obtained from inland fisheries on the Nile, its tributaries and associated swamp lands. Subsistence fishing is widespread, but the commercial sector is under-developed. Marine fishing is mainly carried out by artisanal fishermen in small boats.

Sudan exported around US$1 million of fish per annum before the war, but now exports only a small amount of dried and salted fish.

In 2004, the total marine fish catch was 5,000 tonnes.

Forestry

Sudan has 17 per cent forest cover, most of which is located in the mountains and the wooded savannahs. In 1990—2000, forest cover diminished by an average of 1.44 per cent per annum or around 960,000 hectares (ha) per year. Rapid deforestation is a result of demand for fuelwood. Sudan produces a large amount of industrial roundwood, mainly for posts and poles, and also produces sawnwood, although not enough to ensure self-sufficiency. Sudan's most important non-wood forest product is gum arabic. Sudan is also one of the world's main producers of olibanum resin.

Timber imports in 2004 were US$45.5 million, while exports amounted to US$1.7 million.

Timber production in 2004 included 19,654,780 cubic metre (cum) roundwood, 2,173,000cum industrial roundwood, 50,700cum sawnwood, 123,000cum sawlogs and veneer logs, 1,500cum wood-based panels, 17,481,780cum woodfuel; 849,878t charcoal.

Industry and manufacturing

The industrial sector contributed around 28 per cent to GDP in 2004 and employs 10 per cent of the workforce. The main activities are oil refining, agricultural products, textiles and leatherwares.

Tourism

The revival of tourism, which was destroyed by the civil war, is being planned. The sector is expected to contribute around one per cent to GDP in 2005.

Mining

The mining sector has played a relatively insignificant role in the country's economic development. Chromite, gypsum, gold, copper and iron ore are exploited on a commercial basis. Other mineral deposits include zinc, lead, talc, coal, nickel and tin, phosphate and uranium, but not in sufficient quantities to develop. If financial and infrastructural problems can be overcome, the sector could make a significant contribution to the economy.

Hydrocarbons

Sudan possesses proven oil reserves of around 635 barrels. In 2004, oil production was 343,000 barrels per day (bpd). Estimated oil reserves are at least 1.7 billion barrels and range up to 3 billion barrels. With more oil fields scheduled to come on stream, the government's aim has been to increase oil production to 500,000bpd by the end of 2005. Western oil companies have been deterred from investing in the Sudanese oil sector by US sanctions and the continuing instability, but Asian countries, principally China, India and Malaysia, have been very active, seeking to secure Sudanese oil for their own burgeoning reqirements. Sudan exports both crude and refined oil.

Sudan has several oil refineries and is adding to capacity. An agreement to build a new refinery in Port Sudan was signed in August 2005 with the Malaysian company Petronas.

Total gas reserves stand at around 105 billion cubic metres, but gas production is negligible. Sudan does not consume natural gas and none is imported. This could change if gas fields are developed, but investor interest in this sector is low.

Coal is neither produced nor imported.

Energy

Sudan has installed electricity generation capacity of 728MW. Generation, distribution and transmission are the responsibility of the state-owned National Electricity Corporation. Sixty per cent of electricity generation is produced by thermal power, mostly oil, and 40 per cent by hydroelectricity, although this varies according to rainfall. The Roseires dam on the Blue Nile produces a large proportion of Sudan's electricity, with installed capacity of 274MW. Hydroelectric sources are being expanded. New dams are under construction, including the Merowe dam and the Kajbar dam. The Merowe facility, which will have capacity of 1,000MW, is being built at the Nile's fourth cataract. The Kajbar Dam, which is located at the Nile's second cataract near the Egyptian border, will have a 300MW capacity. Both are highly controversial due to the impact they will have on regional water resources. The Kajbar dam is also facing opposition from Nubian groups, which are resisting the flooding and destruction of ancient Nubian archeological sites as well as forced resettlement.

Financial markets

Stock exchange

The first stock exchange opened in January 1995.

Banking and insurance

Central bank

Bank of Sudan

Main financial centre

Khartoum

Time

GMT plus two hours

Geography

Sudan lies in north-eastern Africa. It is the largest country in Africa and the ninth largest in the world. It lies entirely within the tropics and is bordered by Egypt and Libya in the north, Ethiopia, Eritrea and the Red Sea in the east, Kenya, Uganda and the Democratic Republic of Congo in the south and the Central African Republic and Chad in the west.

The River Nile and its tributaries, the White and Blue Niles, are the country's most important physical features. The Blue Nile, in particular, plays a vital economic role, supporting 40 per cent of the current irrigated area and with the potential to support 70 per cent of future irrigated land. The Blue Nile is prone to serious seasonal flooding.

The topographic features are a large, broad plain with mountains to the north-east along the coast of the Red Sea and in the south-eastern border region with Uganda and Kenya. This is the location of Mount Kinyeti (3,187 metres) the country's tallest peak.

Hemisphere

Northern

Climate

Tropical in the south, hot and dry in the north. In Khartoum, the hottest month is May (26–42 degrees Celsius (C)), the coldest is January (16–32 degrees C). The northern zone receives very little rainfall and is mainly desert. The south is mainly tropical while the central zone is semi-arid grassland.

From mid-April to the end of June the climate is extremely hot and dry. Sandstorms (haboobs) are frequent in desert areas between April and September. The rainy season extends from July to September. During this period road travel outside the cities is difficult. In Khartoum, the average temperature by day in the summer is 42 degrees C and 32 degrees C in the winter.

Dress codes

Formal clothing should be worn for business and social engagements. Lightweight clothing is essential at all times, although visitors should carry some warmer clothing if travelling to Sudan during the winter months (November to March). A light raincoat is needed during the months of July, August and September. Women should be aware of the fact that the north is predominantly Muslim and are advised to dress modestly.

Entry requirements

Passports

Required by all. Passports must be valid for six months from date of entry.

Visa

Required by all. For information see www.sudanembassy.org and follow the link to visa/passport.

Business visas require a letter of invitation from a sponsoring company giving purpose of visit, duration of stay, a commitment to financial responsibility and references, plus copies of commercial correspondence with entities in Sudan.

Visitors are required to register with the Aliens Department within three days of their arrival (hotels will do this). Once registered, they are not required to obtain an exit visa.

Contact the closest consulate for further information.

Prohibited entry

Nationals of Israel and holders of passports with Israeli travel stamps,

Currency advice/regulations

The import and export of local currency is prohibited. Import of foreign currency is unlimited but must be declared; export is limited to the amount declared.

Travellers cheques have limited acceptance.

Customs

Alcohol is strictly forbidden; products from Israel are prohibited.

Health (for visitors)

Mandatory precautions

Valid yellow fever and cholera certificates are required if travellers are arriving from infected areas, or travellers are intending to visit the south of Sudan.

Advisable precautions

Vaccinations for yellow fever, diphtheria, tetanus, polio, hepatitis A and typhoid are recommended. Other vaccinations that may be recommended are cholera, tuberculosis, hepatitis B and meningitis. There is a risk of rabies. Malaria is prevalent throughout the country. Anti-mosquito measures including repellents, nets and clothing that cover the body should be used (these will also provide protection against hepatitis B and yellow fever). Tap water must be treated as unsafe unless boiled and filtered (bottled water is available in the main cities). Eat only well cooked meals, preferably served hot; vegetables should be cooked and fruit peeled. Dairy products are unpasteurised and should be avoided. Use only well maintained, chlorinated, swimming pools as bilharzia can be contracted from streams and rivers.

Medical facilities are scarce outside Khartoum. A first aid kit that includes disposable syringes is a reasonable precaution. Medical insurance is essential, including emergency evacuation, and an adequate supply of personal medicines is necessary.

Hotels
Accommodation can be difficult to obtain outside Khartoum and Port Sudan. Advisable to book in advance. Service charge of 10 per cent is usual. Hotel bills are subject to 10 per cent sales tax.

Credit cards
Credit cards may be accepted but visitors should ensure that they have sufficient hard currency (preferably US dollars) to cover their expenses during their stay.

Public holidays (national)
Fixed dates
1 Jan (Independence Day), 30 Jun (Revolution Day), 25 Dec (Christmas Day).
Variable dates
Eid al Adha, Coptic Christmas (Jan), Islamic New Year, Birth of the Prophet, Coptic Easter (Mar/Apr, two days), Eid al Fitr (three days).
Islamic year – 1429 (10 Jan 2008–28 Dec 2008): The Islamic year contains 354 or 355 days, with the result that Muslim feasts advance by 10–12 days against the Gregorian calendar. Dates of feasts vary according to the sighting of the new moon, so cannot be forecast exactly.

Working hours
Banking
Sat–Thu: 0830–1200.
Business
Sat–Thu: 0800–1430.
Government
Sat–Thu: 0800/0830–1330/1400.
Shops
Sat–Thu: 0800–1330, 1730–2000.

Telecommunications
Mobile/cell phones
There are 900 and 900/1800 GSM services available in large urban areas only.

Electricity supply
240V AC

Social customs/useful tips
Visitors should address Sudanese males using the form Sayed (meaning Mr) with the first name only. There are a large number of local traditions and most Muslim customs are observed. Politeness and patience are more important than punctuality. Women are often not present at business or social gatherings. There is a ban on alcohol and gambling in the north.
Some souvenirs, such as cheetah skins, although available in the souks (markets) are banned by the Government.
Military establishments should not be photographed, nor should bridges, dams, rail and air transport facilities. Visitors should not attempt to photograph Sudanese people without permission or if they appear reluctant. Photography permits issued by the Tourist Information Office in Khartoum are often ignored by the authorities, who may confiscate film and camera. Most banks in Sudan are heavily fortified and resemble prisons as much as they do commercial institutions.
The Islamic legal and moral code, Sharia, is in operation in the north.

Security
Southern Sudan, the Nuba mountains, the Ethiopian and Eritrean borders and the Kassala area near the Eritrean border are all zones of military activity, (including the laying of anti-personnel landmines), and are insecure. There is banditry in Darfur state. Travel in these areas should be avoided unless work is absolutely essential. In general, no land borders into or out of Sudan can be crossed safely, with the exception of the Wadi Halfa crossing into Egypt. The political situation in Sudan is not stable and foreign nationals should contact their embassy, and keep in contact throughout their stay. Before embarking, visitors are advised to consult their embassy for an up-to-date appraisal of the situation, as well as brief themselves regarding developments in the wider region. Demonstrations should be avoided and British and US citizens may wish to keep a low profile.

Getting there
Air
National airline: Sudan Airways
International airport/s: Khartoum (KRT), 4km from city; duty-free shop and restaurant.
Airport tax: Departure tax: US$20, except transit passengers.
Surface
Road: There are road links, with varing degrees of accessibility, to all surrounding countries. Drivers wishing to enter Sudan by road must apply for permission in Khartoum or from overseas representatives. Applicants must list vehicle and passenger details, with supporting documents from a recognised motoring organisation, or a guarantee from a bank or registered business.
Most border crossings remain dangerous, with the exception of the relatively secure border with Egypt via Wadi Halfa.
Rail: A railway line runs from Cairo to the Aswan High Dam in Egypt; passengers can then take a river boat on to Wadi Halfa just inside the Sudanese border, and train to Khartoum.
Water: The only major harbour is Port Sudan on the Red Sea coast. International shipping lines that maintain contacts with Sudan may provide passenger services on cargo ships.
Sudan's River Transport Corporation (RTC) operates a Nile ferry from Aswan in Egypt to Wadi Halfa, the service can be is hindered by local conditions and circumstances.
Main port/s: Port Sudan.

Getting about
National transport
Travellers must obtain special permits to travel anywhere outside Khartoum. These are obtainable from the Passport and Immigration Office in Khartoum. Before travelling, it is advisable to check the security situation in the area. Visitors arriving in any town or city in Sudan must register with the police on arrival and show the necessary paperwork.
Permits are required to visit archaeological or historical sites. These can be obtained from the Department of Antiquities in Khartoum.
Air: Sudan Airways operates a regular service between Khartoum, Port Sudan and El Obeid and other larger towns. Small air taxi companies fly from Khartoum to main towns.
Road: Main tarred roads are the 1,186km route from Port Sudan to Khartoum, from Port Sudan to Kassala and on to Shavak, from Khartoum to Sennar and on to Malakal. Another 800km of tarred roads exist, but the rest of the country's 48,000km network is of very variable quality.
Buses: Scheduled coach services include Khartoum-Kosti, Khartoum-Omdurman, Khartoum-El Fasher, Juba-Nimule, Juba-Faradge.
Rail: A network links Khartoum with Port Sudan, Kassala, Wau, Nyala and Wadi Halfa, but not Juba. The condition of the network is very dilapidated and services can be very slow.
There are three-classes offered but only first class is suitable for business travel.
Water: There are ferries operating on the White and Blue Niles but may not offer a complete journey as underinvestment has left waterways in need of repair and redevelopment.
City transport
Taxis: Easily available in Khartoum and can be hailed, or taken from ranks. Fares are negotiatable and should be agreed before start of any journey.
Car hire
Available in main centres. A national or international driving licence is required.

BUSINESS DIRECTORY
The addresses listed below are a selection only. While World of Information makes every endeavour to check these addresses, we cannot guarantee that changes have not been made, especially to telephone numbers and area codes. We would welcome any corrections.

Telephone area codes
The international dialling code (IDD) for Sudan is +249, followed by area code and subscriber's number:

El Obeid	81	Khartoum North	85
Kassala	41		
Khartoum	11	Port Sudan City	31

Chambers of Commerce

Union of Sudanese Chambers of Commerce, Gamhoria Street, PO Box 81, Khartoum (email: chamber@sudanchamber.org).

Banking

Bank of Khartoum, PO Box 1008, Khartoum.

Farmers Commercial Bank, PO Box 1116, Kasr Avenue, Khartoum.

Tadamon Islamic Bank, PO Box 3154, Baladia Avenue, Khartoum.

Al-Baraka Bank, PO Box 3583, Al-Baraka Tower, Khartoum.

El Nilein Industrial Development Bank, PO Box 466, 1722 United Nations Square, Khartoum.

Central bank

Bank of Sudan, Al-Gamaa Avenue, PO Box 313, Khartoum, Sudan (email: sudanbank@sudanmail.net).

Travel information

River Transport Corporation, PO Box 284, Khartoum North.

Sudan Airways, SDC Building, Street 15, New Extension, PO Box 253, Khartoum.

Ministry of tourism

Ministry of Tourism and Wildlife, PO Box 22213, Khartoum (email: postmaster@sudan-tourism.gov.sd; internet: www.sudan-tourism.gov.sd).

Ministries

Ministry of Agriculture and Forests, Khartoum.

Ministry of Animal Welfare, Khartoum.

Ministry of Aviation, Khartoum.

Ministry of Culture and Information, Khartoum.

Ministry of Defence, Khartoum.

Ministry of Education, Khartoum.

Ministry of Energy and Mining, Khartoum.

Ministry of the Environment and Tourism.

Ministry of Finance & National Economy, Khartoum.

Ministry of Foreign Affairs, Khartoum.

Ministry of Health, Khartoum.

Ministry of Higher Education and Scientific Research, Khartoum.

Ministry of the Interior, Khartoum.

Ministry of National Industry, Khartoum.

Ministry of Public Services, Khartoum.

Ministry of Social Planning, Khartoum.

Ministry of Trade, Khartoum.

Ministry of Transport, Khartoum.

Other useful addresses

National Corporation for Antiquities and Museums, PO Box 178, Khartoum.

Sudanese Embassy (USA), 2210 Massachusetts Avenue, NW, Washington DC 20008 (tel: (+1-202) 338-8565; fax: (+1-202) 667-2406; email: info@sudanembassyus.org).

Internet sites

Africa Business Network: www.ifc.org/abn

AllAfrica.com: http://allafrica.com

African Development Bank: www.afdb.org

Africa Online: www.africaonline.com

Mbendi AfroPaedia (information on companies, countries, industries and stock exchanges in Africa): http://mbendi.co.za

The Sudan Page: www.sudan.net

Suriname

KEY FACTS

Official name: Republiek Suriname (Republic of Suriname)

Head of State: President Ronald Venetiaan (NF)

Head of government: President Ronald Venetiaan (since 2000; re-elected 2005)

Ruling party: Nieuwe Front voor Democratie (NF) (New Front for Democracy) coalition led by Nationale Partij Suriname (NPS) (National Party of Suriname) (since 2000; re-elected 2005)

Area: 163,265 square km

Population: 525,000 (2007)

Capital: Paramaribo (Parbo)

Official language: Dutch

Currency: Suriname dollar (Su$) = 100 cents

Exchange rate: Su$2.75 per US$ (Jul 2008)

GDP per capita: US$4,577 (2007)*

GDP real growth: 5.50% (2007)*

Labour force: 180,000 (2004)

Inflation: 6.40% (2007)*

Balance of trade: US$94.00 million (2006)*

Foreign debt: US$285.00 million (2004)

* estimated figure

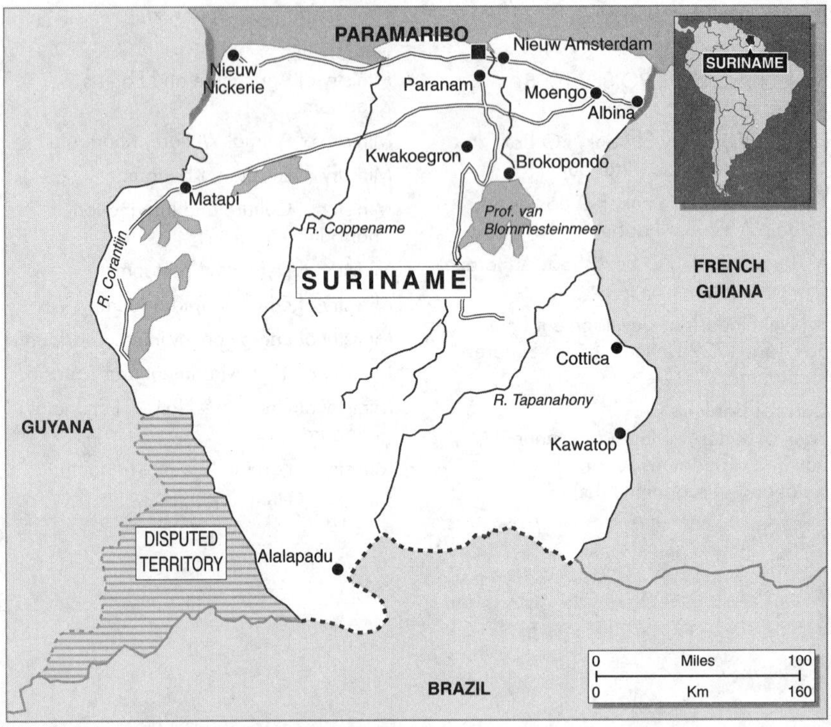

COUNTRY PROFILE

Historical profile

1602 Dutch traders arrived.

1651 British settlers and plantation owners arrived and set up first community and commercial estates using African slaves.

1652 Britain ceded territory to The Netherlands and gained New Amsterdam (New York) in exchange. Later referred to as Dutch Guiana.

1800s After slavery was abolished, indentured labourers from China and India, Java were brought in to work on plantations.

1916 The mining of bauxite began and gradually become the country's principal export.

1948 The country was renamed Suriname

1954 Suriname gained self-government from The Netherlands, which still controlled defence and foreign affairs.

1975 Full independence was granted. Johan Ferrier became president and Henck Arron of the Nationale Partij Suriname (NPS) (National Party of Suriname) became prime minister. Around 30 per cent of the population emigrated to The Netherlands.

1980 A military coup, led by Sergeant-Major Desi Bouterse, ousted first Prime Minister Arron and then President Ferrier, who was ultimately replaced by Henk Chin A Sen. Bouterse ruled through the National Military Council, imposing martial law, censorship and banning political parties.

1982 15 members of the opposition were killed by the army, which resulted in fiscal aid from The Netherlands and the US being halted.

1985 The ban on opposition parties was lifted and a new constitution, which included a strong military role, was devised.

1987 A democratically elected president and a 51-seat National Assembly were re-established. Elections were won by an opposition coalition. A National State Council of politicians and military was established, under the constitution, but with an ill-defined 'advisory' role did not achieve satisfactory government.

1990 Bouterse staged another coup and resumed power.

1991 A civilian government was elected. International aid was resumed. Bouterse retired from the army and founded the Nationale Democratische Partij (NDP) (National Democratic Party). Ronald Venetiaan was elected president.
1996 The nationalistic NDP won a majority of seats in the general elections and joined a coalition government. President Jules Wijdenbosch, an ally of Bouterse, named him special advisor and gave him diplomatic immunity from foreign drug smuggling charges.
1999 A poor economy resulted in widespread strikes, which brought down the government.
2000 Early elections were won by a coalition, Nieuwe Front voor Democratie (NF) (New Front for Democracy); Ronald Venetiaan became president. International relations with Guyana deteriorated over a disputed maritime boundary, including an area rich in oil.
2004 The Suriname guilder (fl) was converted to the Suriname dollar (Su$), at a rate of Su$1.00 per fll,000. The UN attempts to resolve the maritime dispute with Guyana.
2005 The ruling NF coalition narrowly won parliamentary elections. After two unsuccessful presidential elections, Ronald Venetiaan won in the third round.
2006 Major floods devastated homes of around 30,000 people in Upper Suriname. The country's long-term foreign currency, sovereign credit rating was raised from -B to B, as efforts to pay back loans were seen largely as successful. The EU provided eur20 million (US$15.4 million) to upgrade the country's infrastructure and reconstruct the banana industry.
2007 The Japanese agreed to finance the construction of the new fishery centre to international standards and capable of providing modern facilities for the enlarged fishing fleet. The UN ruled that both Suriname and Guyana should share the oil-rich offshore territory.
2008 In April, Desi Bouterse, the former dictator went on trail for the murder of 15 political opponents in 1982. On 2 July, a three-month US humanitarian mission was launched providing medical treatment and engineering projects in rural areas. Suriname joined the International Criminal Court (ICC) on 16 July.

Political structure

Form of state

Parliamentary democratic republic

The executive

The presidency is decided by an electoral colleges based in parliament, for a term of five years. The president is Head of State, head of government and commander-in-chief of the armed forces. During a term in office, the president is accountable to the national assembly. The president has wide executive power to appoint and dismiss ministers, enact laws and declare war (with the assent of the national assembly).
The political system is multi-party and numerous parties must form coalitions to come to power. To win the presidency, a coalition needs a two-thirds majority in the national assembly. Failing three rounds, the vote goes to the United People's Congress, which contains assembly members and local and regional councillors, which elects a president by a simple majority.

National legislature

The unicameral Nationale Assemblée (National Assembly) has 51 members, elected by proportional representation, for five-year terms.

Last elections

25 May 2005 (parliamentary)

Results: Parliamentary: the ruling Nieuwe Front voor Democratie (NF) (New Front for Democracy) coalition won 41.1 per cent of the vote (24 seats out of 51) and the National Democratic Party (NDP) (Nationale Democratische Partij) 23.1 per cent (15 seats); turnout was 65.5 per cent.

Next elections

May 2010 (parliamentary)

Political parties

Ruling party

Nieuwe Front voor Democratie (NF) (New Front for Democracy) coalition led by Nationale Partij Suriname (NPS) (National Party of Suriname) (since 2000; re-elected 2005)

Main opposition party

National Democratic Party (NDP) (Nationale Democratische Partij)

Population

525,000 (2007)

Last census: August 2004: 487,024 (provisional)

Population density: Three inhabitants per square km. Urban population: 75 per cent (1995—2001). Urban population growth rate: 1.3 per cent (2000–05).

Annual growth rate: 0.8 per cent 1994–2004 (WHO 2006)

Ethnic make-up

East Indian (37 per cent), Creole (31 per cent), Javanese (15 per cent), Black (10 per cent), Indian (3 per cent), Chinese (2 per cent).

Religions

Hindu (25 per cent), Protestant (25 per cent), Roman Catholic (23 per cent), Islam (20 per cent), traditional beliefs (5 per cent).

Education

Primary schooling begins at age 6 and last until aged 12. An exam deteremines the route either to a general lower secondary, or technical school. Advancement at age 16, following further exams, leads to either an academic, pre-university senior, or upper vocational, school.
Teaching may be delivered in either Dutch or English.
Higher education is provided through either a Univerisity, Institute, Academy, or Polytechnic College.

Literacy rate: 93 per cent adult rate.

Compulsory years: 7 to 12.

Enrolment rate: 92.18 per cent net primary; 2.93 per cent net secondary enrolments.

Pupils per teacher: 17 in primary schools.

KEY INDICATORS Suriname

	Unit	2003	2004	2005	2006	2007
Population	m	0.45	0.46	0.51	*0.52	*0.53
Gross domestic product (GDP)	US$bn	1.50	1.11	1.78	*2.14	*2.40
GDP per capita	US$	3,500	2,401	3,485	*4,136	*4,577
GDP real growth	%	3.8	4.6	5.5	*4.8	*5.5
Inflation	%	20.0	9.0	9.9	11.3	*6.4
Exports (fob) (goods)	US$m	445.0	881.0	1,211.5	1,391.0	1,359.0
Imports (cif) (goods)	US$m	300.0	853.0	1,189.1	1,297.0	1,185.3
Balance of trade	US$m	145.0	28.0	22.4	94.0	173.7
Current account	US$m	-140.0	-150.0	-193.0	110.4	184.9
Total reserves minus gold	US$m	105.8	129.4	125.8	215.3	400.9
Foreign exchange	US$m	94.7	118.0	115.5	204.9	390.4
Exchange rate	per US$	2,346.75	259.28	2.75	2.75	2.74

* estimated figure

Health
Per capita total expenditure on health (2003) was US$309; of which per capita government spending was US$142, at the international dollar rate, (WHO 2006).

HIV/Aids

HIV prevalence: 1.7 per cent aged 15–49 in 2003 (World Bank)

Life expectancy: 67 years, 2004 (WHO 2006)

Fertility rate/Maternal mortality rate: 2.6 births per woman, 2004 (WHO 2006)

Birth rate/Death rate: 19.4 births per 1,000 population; 6.8 deaths per 1,000 population (2003).

Child (under 5 years) mortality rate (per 1,000): 30 per 1,000 live births (World Bank)

Main cities
Paramaribo (Parbo) (capital, estimated population 254,147 in 2005), Lelydorp (16,016), Nieuw Nickerie (11,396).

Languages spoken
Sranan Tongo (Creole) is the lingua franca. English, Sarnami (Hindi), Javanese and Chinese are also spoken.

Official language/s

Dutch

Media
Press

Daily newspapers include De Ware Tijd (www.dwtonline.com) and De West (www.dewestonline.cq-link.sr) and a periodical Dagblad Suriname (www.dbsuriname.com).

Broadcasting

Radio: All stations broadcast programmes in Dutch with other local languages. Stichting Radio Omroep Suriname (SRS) is government-owned; commercial stations include Radio Paramaribo, Radio Apintie (www.apintie.fm), Radio Nickerie (RANI), Radio 10 (www.radio10.sr); ABC (www.abcsuriname.com) is a radio and TV broadcasting station.

Television: Government-owned commercial TV services include STVS (www.parbo.com/stvs) and ATV (http://www.atv.sr).

Economy
Suriname's economy grew between 3 and 5.9 per cent per year during the 2001–05 period. The rate of inflation has been greatly reduced and now stands at 9.9 per cent, down from a high of 58.6 per cent in 2000. The IMF forecasts growth for 2006 of 3.3 per cent.

Ronald Venetiaan's government began well. It increased taxes and attempted to control spending, but a large pay rise for civil servants threatened earlier gains in stabilising the economy.

The Netherlands government agreed to restart aid flows, which will allow Suriname to access international development financing.

Alcoa's US$65 million expansion to its Paranam alumina refinery, which was completed in 2005, is a boost to Suriname's economy.

Economic prospects for the medium-term depend on renewed commitment to responsible monetary and fiscal policies and to the introduction of structural reforms to liberalise markets and promote competition.

The Inter-American Development Bank estimated that in 2006 migrant workers sent some US$102 million to their families in Suriname.

External trade
As a member of the Caribbean Community and Common Market (Caricom), Suriname operates within the single market (Caribbean Single Market and Economy (CSME)), which became operational on 1 January 2006. Goods, services, businesses and money are free to move within CSME without barriers and tariffs.

Natural resources include a major world source of bauxite, rainforest timbers, gold, iron ore, seafood and agricultural products.

Imports

Principal imports are capital equipment, petroleum, foodstuffs, cotton and consumer goods

Main sources: US (29.3 per cent total, 2005), The Netherlands (17.5 per cent), Trinidad and Tobago (12.7 per cent), China (6.5 per cent), Japan (5.2 per cent)

Exports

Principal exports are aluminium oxide, crude oil, timber, shrimp and fish, rice and bananas.

Main destinations: Norway (23.5 per cent total, 2005), US (16.5 per cent), Canada (16.1 per cent), Belgium (9.7 per cent), France (7.9 per cent), UAE (7.3 per cent)

Agriculture
Just 0.5 per cent of Suriname's total landmass is accounted for by permanent crop and arable land, concentrated predominantly along the coastal plain. Despite the dearth of land devoted to agricultural activities, Suriname is self sufficient in most basic foodstuffs and the sector accounts for up to 10 per cent of total GDP. Some 20 per cent of the country's workforce is employed in the agricultural sector.

The staple food crop and most important agricultural export is rice, the farming of which is highly mechanised. Suriname exports 40,000 tonnes of rice annually to the EU. Other major crops include palm oil, coconuts, bananas, sugar, citrus fruits and coffee.

Crop production in 2005 included: 195,000 metric tonnes (t) rice, 4,300t cassava, 9,000t coconuts, 43,000t bananas, 11,843t plantains, 120,000t sugar cane, 1,496t oilcrops, 260t groundnuts, 17,152t citrus, 1,090t tomatoes, 3,450t watermelons, 74,081t fruit in total, 21,854t vegetables in total. Livestock production included: 9,179t meat in total, 2,000t beef, 1,450t pig meat, 57t lamb and goat meat, 5,671t poultry, 2,500t eggs, 8,500t milk, 86t honey.

The commercial fishing industry accounts for about 7 per cent of Surinam's total export earnings; the sector has grown in importance in recent years. Fishing for shellfish, in particular, has increased. The typical total fish catch is over 19,000mt, plus over 7,700mt of other seafood, per annum.

A new fishery centre, providing mooring facilities, an ice factory, freezing stations, fuel stop and workshops for the enlarged fishing fleet was underconstruction in January 2007, with finance provided by the Japanese government.

In 2004, the total marine fish catch was 18,647 tonnes and the total crustacean catch was 13,930 tonnes.

Suriname has vast forestry resources in relation to its size. Approximately 80 per cent of the country's total landmass is covered by forests and woodland, but just 2 per cent is exploited as access is limited.

Industry and manufacturing
Industrial activities in Suriname centre on the processing of agricultural produce (particularly timber), bauxite mining and timber processing. The sector contributes approximately 15 per cent to total GDP and employs one fifth of Suriname's labour force.

In 2003, Alcoa announced a US$65 million, 250,000 tonne expansion to its Paranam alumina refinery, which will increase capacity by approximately 12 per cent. The project was completed midway through 2005.

Tourism
The travel and tourism industry is growing in Suriname. Employment in the sector has risen to 4.9 per cent of the workforce and tourism now represents 5.4 per cent of the country's total GDP.

Ecotourism is growing in importance and has contributed to the permanent protection of 1.62 million ha of tropical forests.

Mining
In a typical year for the economy of Suriname the mining sector contributes approximately 12 per cent of total GDP. The sector also employs some 5 per cent of the country's total workforce.

One of the largest producers of bauxite in the world, Suriname's reserves stand at 600 million tonnes. The US imports 400,000 tonnes of alumina from

Suriname each year and it contributes up to 60 per cent of exports and 10–15 per cent of government income.
The deposits in the major mining areas, Moengo and Paranam, are maturing and were expected to reach the end of their life in 2006. Another, new production site opened in 2006, at Kaaimangrasie and Klaverblad, and are expected to last until 2010. Other reserves in the east, west and north of Suriname are expected to last until 2025.
Annual gold production is valued at US$25 million per annum, although 80 per cent of this is in the informal sector and much of the country's gold output is smuggled away into French Guiana. In 2004 Cambior, the Canadian mining company, began shipment of gold bars from their Rosebel Gold mine. It is expected that 220,000 ounces of gold will be produced in the first year valued at US$157 per ounce; the government will receive 2.2 per cent royalties from the mine.
Other commercially viable minerals include iron ore, copper, nickel, platinum and kaolin.
In 2006, a new bauxite mine opened, with reserves of an estimated 13.5 million tonnes.

Hydrocarbons
Exploration currently underway in the Saramacca oil region is expected to double proven reserves to 350 million barrels. A new onshore oil field began production in 2006. The new Calcutta field is estimated to contain 23 million barrels of crude oil, with further exploration expected to raise the estimation.
The country's only oil refinery produces diesel, heavy vacuum gas oil, fuel oil and bitumen. Staatsolie Maatschappij Suriname is a government-owned company that has exclusive rights to explore and produce hydrocarbons alone or in conjunction with other oil companies.
Staatsolie aims to develop the Tambaredjo oil field to produce 20,000 bpd.
After four years of contention, in 2007, a UN tribunal made a decision concerning the disputed oil-rich territory clamed by both Guyana and Suriname. The ruling declared that both countries were entitled to explore the region off the Atlantic coastline with Suriname being granted 17,871 square kilometres. An estimate of the recoverable oil is 2 billion cubic metres (15 billion barrels) and 1.19 trillion cubic metres of gas.
The disputed maritime area included an oil-rich concession granted to a Canadian company, with the agreement on both sides a surge in exploration by other oil companies is expected.
Suriname does not produce or import natural gas or coal.

Energy
Suriname's total installed electricity generation capacity is approximately 415MW. The Afobakka hydroelectric power station supplies electricity for the country's aluminium industry. Suriname Aluminum Company (Suralco) produces about 75MW of electricity for the Suriname government, roughly 75 per cent of the electricity needs of the capital city of Paramaribo.
In 2004, Suriname's State Energy Company signed a US$23.7 million deal with the Trinidad-based Royal Bank of Trinidad and Tobago to finance part of its local electricity projects estimated to cost US$100 million.

Banking and insurance
Suriname's banking sector has traditionally been highly indebted and needs reform. The government has equity stakes in six of Suriname's eight banks, including a 10 per cent stake in the largest bank, De Surinaamse Bank. Domestic borrowing is mostly undertaken by the government.
Central bank
Centrale Bank van Suriname
Main financial centre
Paramaribo.

Time
GMT minus three hours

Geography
Suriname is located on the northern coast of South America, facing the Atlantic Ocean. It is bordered by French Guiana to the east, Guyana to the west and Brazil to the south.
The terrain is hilly and most of the country is covered by tropical rain forests, except along a narrow strip of low-lying coastal plain. This area, which is swampy, is 80km at its widest and is home to most of the population. There is a 3,000km network of rivers, most of which flow northwards into the Atlantic Ocean. River travel is the main means of access into the forested interior. The most important rivers are the Corantijn, Suriname, Mariwijne and Coppename. A huge man-made lake, the WJ van Blommestein Meer, one of the largest reservoirs in the world, lies astride the Suriname river in the north-east of the country.
Hemisphere
Northern

Climate
Tropical but cooled by trade winds. Rain throughout the year but heaviest from November–January and from April–July. Average daily temperature remains fairly constant throughout the year at 27 degrees Celsius (C); daily range from 22–35 degrees C from May–October; slightly lower temperatures from November–April.

Entry requirements
Passports
Required by all, valid for six months from date of arrival.
Visa
Required by nationals of most countries; for current list of exceptions, see www.surinameembassy.org. All visitors must have return/onward passage. Business visas require a letter from the employing company explaining the purpose of visit, and the details of all the contacts in Suriname plus an itinerary.
Currency advice/regulations
Import and export of local currency is limited to Su$150. There are no restrictions on the import and export of foreign currencies, subject to declaration of amounts over US$10,000

Health (for visitors)
Mandatory precautions
Yellow fever vaccination certificate required if arriving from an infected area.
Advisable precautions
Yellow fever, typhoid and polio vaccinations. Malaria prophylaxis recommended and water precautions should be taken.

Hotels
Paramaribo and Nieuw Nickerie have a number of modern hotels but beds are limited. Service charge of 10 per cent is usual.

Public holidays (national)
Fixed dates
1 Jan (New Year's Day), 1 May (Labour Day), 1 Jul (Abolition of Slavery Day), 25 Nov (Independence Day), 25–26 Dec (Christmas).
Variable dates
Holi (Hindu, Mar), Good Friday, Easter Monday, Eid al Fitr.
In addition, Chinese, Jewish and Indian businesses will be closed for their own religious holidays.

Working hours
Banking
Mon–Fri: 0800–1500.
Business
Mon–Fri: 0730–1630.
Government
Mon–Fri: 0700–1500.
Shops
Mon–Fri: 0700/0730–1630; Sat: 0730–1300.

Electricity supply
110/127V and/or 220V AC, 60 cycles

Getting there
Air
National airline: Surinam Airways (SLM).
International airport/s:
Paramaribo-Johan Adolf Pengel

International Airport (PMB), 46km from city; duty-free shop, bank, cafeterias, car hire.
Airport tax: US$35, payable only in US dollars or euros.
Surface
Road: A coastal road links Paramaribo with Guyana (at Nieuw Nickerie) and French Guiana (at Albina).
Water: There are sea links with the US and Europe. Car ferry services run from French Guiana and Guyana.
Main port/s: Paramaribo.

Getting about
National transport
Most infrastructure has been on the country's narrow coastal plain, with links to the interior weak. Much of the sparsely-populated country is accessible only by air or river.
Air: Domestic flights to towns in the interior are operated from Zorg en Hoop airfield near Paramaribo by Surinam Airways and Gum Air. Charter services are available.
Road: There are over 4,000km of roads, of which around a quarter are paved. Coastal towns are linked by road from Nieuw Nickerie in the west, through Paramaribo, to Albina in the east. Roads in the interior are not surfaced and are poorly maintained.
Buses: Paramaribo and most towns have a local bus service. Bus routes link coastal towns but service is irregular and tends to be crowded.
Water: River transport is the main means of travel in the interior and in some coastal areas.
City transport
Taxis: Taxis are available, but scarce after 10 pm and on Sundays and holidays. They are not metered and fares should be agreed in advance of journey.
Car hire
Available in Paramaribo at the airport and through main hotels and the Tourist Information Office. International driving licences required.

BUSINESS DIRECTORY

Telephone area codes
The international dialling code (IDD) for Suriname is +597 followed by subscriber's number.

Chambers of Commerce
Suriname Chamber of Commerce & Industry, PO Box 139, Mr JC de Miranda Straat, Paramaribo (tel: 473-527; fax: 470-802; e-mail: chamber@sr.net).

Banking
De Surinaamse Bank NV, Henck Arronstraat 26-30, Paramaribo (tel: 471-100; fax: 477-835).

Finabank NV, Dr. S. Redmondstraat 55-61, Paramaribo.

Hakrinbank NV, Dr S. Redmondstraat 11-13, Paramaribo (tel: 477-722; fax: 472-066).

Landbouwbank NV, Lim A Postraat 28-30, Paramaribo (tel: 475-945, 475-101; fax: 410-821).

Nationale Ontwikkelingsbank (NOB), Coppenamelaan 160-162, Paramaribo (tel: 465-000; fax: 497-192).

RBTT Bank (Suriname), Kerkplein 1 Paramaribo (tel: 471-555; fax: 411-325).

Surinaamse Postspaarbank (SPSB), Knuffelsgracht 11-13, Paramaribo (tel: 472-256; fax: 472-952).

Surinaamse Volkscrediet Bank (VCB), Steenbakkerijstraat 2, Paramaribo (tel: 472-616; fax: 472-616).

Central bank
Centrale Bank van Suriname, PO Box 1081, Waterkant 16-20, Paramaribo (tel: 473-741; fax: 476-444; e-mail: info@cbvs.sr).

Travel information
Tourist Information Centre, Waterkant 1, Fort Zeelandia Complex, Paramaribo (tel: 479-200; fax: 477-786; e-mail: stsmktg@sr.net).

Ministry of tourism
Ministry of Transport, Communication and Tourism, Prins Hendrikstraat 26-28, Paramaribo (tel: 420-422; fax: 420-425; e-mail: odc@minctc.sr).

National tourist organisation offices
Suriname Tourism Foundation, Dr JF Nassylaan 2, Paramaribo; PO Box 656, Paramaribo (tel: 410-357; fax: 477-786; email: info@suriname-tourism.org).

Ministries
Ministry of Agriculture, Animal Husbandry and Fisheries, Cultuurtuinlaan, Paramaribo (tel: 474-177; fax: 470-301).

Ministry of Defence, Kwattaweg 29, Paramaribo (tel: 474-244; fax: 420-055).

Ministry of Economic Affairs, Kleine Waterstraat 4, Paramaribo (tel: 75-080).

Ministry of Education, Dr. F. Kaffiludistraat 117-123, Paramaribo (tel: 498-383; fax: 495-083).

Ministry of Finance, Onafhandelijkheidsplein 3, Paramaribo (tel: 472-619; fax: 476-314).

Ministry of Foreign Affairs, Gravenstraat 6-8, Paramaribo (tel: 471-209; fax: 410-851).

Ministry of Internal Affairs, Onafhankelijkheidsplein 2, Paramaribo (tel: 476-461; fax: 421-170).

Ministry of Labour, Wagenwegstraat 22, Paramaribo (tel: 477-045; fax: 410-465).

Ministry of Natural Resources, Mr. Dr. J.C. de Mirandastraat 13-15, Paramaribo (tel: 473-420; fax: 472-911).

Ministry of Planning and International Co-operation, Dr. S Redmondstraat 118, Paramaribo (tel: 473-628; fax: 421-056).

Ministry of Social Affairs and Housing, Waterkant 30-32, Paramaribo (tel: 472-610; fax: 470-516).

Ministry of Trade and Industry, Nieuwe Haven, Paramaribo (tel: 479-886; fax: 477-602).

Ministry of Transportation, Communications and Tourism, Prins Hendrikstraat 26-28, Paramaribo (tel: 420-422; fax: 470-425).

President of the Republic of Suriname, Onafhankelijkheidsplein, Paramaribo (tel: 472-841; fax: 475-266).

Vice President and Council of Ministers, Dr. S. Redmondstraat, 1e Etage, Paramaribo (tel: 474-805; fax: 472-917).

Other useful addresses
Algemene Aannemers Vereniging (AAV), Gravenstraat 73, Paramaribo (tel: 478-419; fax: 474-531).

Associatie van Surinaarns Bedrijfsleven (V.S.B.), Domineestraat 33 boven, Paramaribo (tel: 476-585; fax: 421-160).

Orde van Raadgavende Ingenieursbureaus in Suriname (ORIS), P.O. Box 1864, van Roosmalenstraat no. 30, Paramaribo (tel: 472-275, 474-381; fax: 474-408).

Stichting Planbureau Suriname, PO Box 172, Dr S. Redmondstraat 110, Paramaribo (tel: 473-146).

Vereniging Surinaams Bedrijfsleven (Suriname Trade and Industry Association), Prins Hendrikstraat 18, PO Box 111, Paramaribo (tel: 475-286/7; fax: 472-287).

Other news agencies: Caribbean Net News: www.caribbeannetnews.com

Internet sites
Economic Commission for Latin America and the Caribbean: http://www.eclac.cl

Inter-American Development Bank: http://www.iadb.org

Organisation of American States: http://www.oas.org

Republic of Suriname homepage: http://www.sr.net. srnet/InfoSurinam

Swaziland

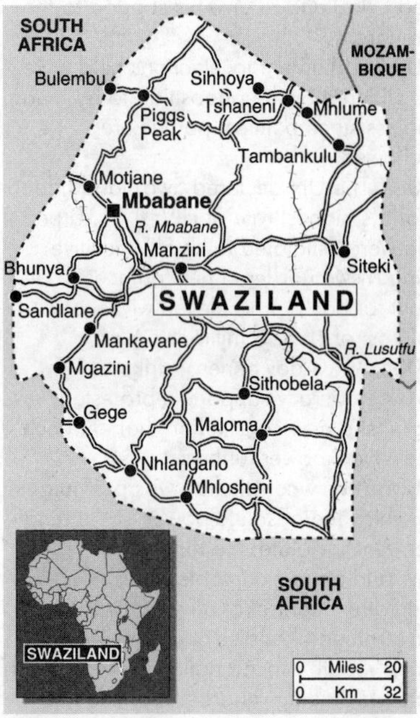

King Mswati celebrates his fortieth birth in 2008; there will be a joint party to celebrate 40 years of independence from the UK, to be held in lavish style in a football stadium. There will also be 'elections' in 2008 – to the *Liqoqo*, traditional tribal assembly – but there are no political parties and in a new constitution promulgated in 2006 the absolute power of the King remains inviolate; the King is above the law and not accountable to his people, with direct control of all security forces, governmental bodies and government posts. Mswati is either revered, and admired for having 13 wives, or blamed for his country's slide into poverty.

Given its location, it has always been said that Swaziland can, in the final analysis do little which runs counter to the interests of Pretoria. If it so chose, South Africa could at any time cut off the supply of food to Swaziland and its people would simply starve. Within this fragile context, Swaziland faces a serious socio-economic situation. Although it is classified as a lower-middle-income country, income distribution is highly skewed and 700,000 of the 1.1 million people live on less than US$1 a day. A growing fiscal deficit threatens macroeconomic stability and external viability, and concerns over governance, particularly the rule of law, are threatening to undermine social harmony and investor and donor sentiment. The humanitarian situation is difficult, with persistent high rates of HIV/Aids, unemployment, poverty, and food shortages.

Immediate change is unlikely. The mountainous kingdom of Swaziland is one of the world's last remaining absolute monarchies. King Mswati III rules by decrees which have the full force of law. His subjects live mainly in rural areas and maintain traditional ways of life.

Mswati has shown no enthusiasm for sharing power, but the banned opposition parties and trade unions have been vocal in their demands for greater democracy and limits on the king's power; their leaders have been arrested on several occasions. Some of the king's ministers privately concede the king has too much power. Judges, whose rulings he regularly overturns, say he has blatant disregard for the law. His profligate spending has turned international donors away and the country's external debt is now running at 35 per cent of gross domestic product. The king's national development company – a family enterprise – has an iron grip on all major business and owns one of the two national daily newspapers.

High inflation

The International Monetary Fund (IMF) says that while the rest of sub-Saharan Africa grew over the last decade, the Swazi economy stagnated and continues to register sluggish economic growth. GDP growth has fallen from an average of 2.5 per cent during 1980–94, but since then it has average less than 1.0 per cent primarily as a result of low agricultural productivity, repeated droughts, and declining domestic and foreign investment. Inflation is expected to be almost 13 per cent in 2008, driven by high food and fuel prices. Political change in South Africa has eroded some of Swaziland's advantage in attracting foreign capital, on which much growth has depended in the past. Any advantages it had as an investment location in southern Africa disappeared within a

KEY FACTS

Official name: Umbuso weSwatini (Kingdom of Swaziland)

Head of State: King Mswati III

Head of government: Prime Minister Themba Dlamini (appointed by the King) (since 2003)

Ruling party: Political parties are de facto banned

Area: 17,363 square km

Population: 1.16 million (2007)*

Capital: Mbabane (administrative capital); Lobamba (legislative capital and the seat of the monarchy)

Official language: English and siSwati

Currency: Lilangeni – plural Emalangeni (E) = 100 cents; at par with the South African Rand

Exchange rate: E7.55 per US$ (Jul 2008)

GDP per capita: US$2,523 (2007)

GDP real growth: 2.40% (2007)

Labour force: 416,000 (2004)

Unemployment: 30.20% (2004)

Inflation: 8.20% (2007)

Balance of trade: US$685.00 million (2006)

Foreign debt: US$470.00 million (2004)

Visitor numbers: 873,000 (2006)*

* estimated figure

few months of Nelson Mandela walking to freedom. The country is a landlocked 'island' within South Africa and Mozambique, about half the size of Holland. Its currency is pegged to the South African rand. It relies to a large extent on volatile revenues from the Southern African Customs Union (Sacu) and worker remittances from its citizens working in the South African mines substantially supplement domestically earned income. However, the income from Sacu will gradually decline as a new revenue sharing agreement between the member states is implemented.

Sugar and wood pulp remain important foreign exchange earners. Mining has declined in importance with only coal mines and stone quarries active. About nine-tenths of its imports and three-quarters of its exports are trade with South Africa.

Risk assessment

Politics	Poor
Economy	Poor
Regional stability	Fair

COUNTRY PROFILE

Historical profile

1903 After a period of rivalry between the British and the Boers, Swaziland became a British protectorate.
1963 Swaziland's first constitution was introduced.
1964 The first elections resulted in victory for the Imbokodvo National Movement (INM).
1967 Swaziland was granted internal self-government as a protected state. Sobhuza II was recognised as King and head of state; Prince Makhosini Dlamini, leader of the INM, was appointed prime minister.
1968 Independence was granted.
1973 The King revoked the Westminster-based constitution and banned political parties.
1978 The previous constitution was replaced with a system designed to accommodate both western and traditional styles of government. Political parties were banned.
1982 King Sobhuza II died.
1986 After a lengthy selection and training period, Crown Prince Makhosetive was chosen to succeed his father and he was crowned King Mswati III.
1992 Parliament was dissolved and Swaziland was governed by the Liqoqo (traditional tribal assembly).
1993 Democratic reforms led to the people directly electing some members of the Liqoqo.
1996 The King appointed a Constitutional Review Commission (CRC).
2000 The government put five critics of the government under house arrest and banned trade union meetings. The Swaziland Federation of Trade Unions (SFTU) met in South Africa and drew up the Nelspruit Declaration, demanding the formation of an interim government. The government amended the labour laws. Swaziland became eligible for African Growth and Opportunities Act (AGOA) benefits.
2001 A number of political activists were forced into exile in South Africa. Decree 2 was issued by King Mswati, giving the monarch power to overrule court decisions. It was soon repealed after the US threatened to end the country's benefits under AGOA.
2002 The Internal Security Bill was enacted, which made it illegal to display support for any political party. The Libyan leader, Colonel Muammar al Qadafi, visited Swaziland to give his support to the monarchy.
2003 Parliamentary elections held were considered by the opposition to be meaningless since political parties are outlawed.
2004 The UN declared Swaziland had the world's highest rate of HIV; 4 in 10 people were estimated to be HIV positive. King Mswati ordered new palaces to be built for each of his eleven wives, at a total cost of US$15 million.
2005 A two-day general strike by pro-democracy supporters protested against a new constitution that entrench the King's power further.
2006 A new constitution was promulgated in which the absolute power of the King remains inviolate; the King is above the law and not accountable to his people, with direct control of all security forces, governmental bodies and government posts. South African police shot at protestors blockading a border crossing into Swaziland; the protestors were demanding political reform.
2007 Six opposition members who took part in the border blockade were charged with sedition. Protests for democratic reforms were held in July.
2008 The opposition declared it would boycott upcoming elections in protest at the lack of multi-party elections.

KEY INDICATORS — Swaziland

	Unit	2003	2004	2005	2006	2007
Population	m	1.08	1.10	1.13	*1.15	*1.16
Gross domestic product (GDP)	US$bn	1.18	2.51	2.61	2.79	*2.94
GDP per capita	US$	1,091	2,172	2,316	*2,431	*2,523
GDP real growth	%	1.5	2.1	2.3	2.8	*2.4
Inflation	%	9.5	3.5	4.8	5.3	8.2
Industrial output	% change	–	1.8	1.7	1.3	–
Agricultural output	% change	–	1.8	1.7	4.7	–
Exports (fob) (goods)	US$m	820.0	1,878.0	1,889.0	1,877.0	–
Imports (cif) (goods)	US$m	938.0	1,350.0	1,423.0	1,192.0	–
Balance of trade	US$m	-118.0	528.9	466.0	685.0	–
Current account	US$m	89.4	51.7	86.4	98.1	*36.0
Total reserves minus gold	US$m	277.5	323.6	243.9	372.5	762.6
Foreign exchange	US$m	264.1	306.5	231.0	358.9	748.3
Exchange rate	per US$	7.56	6.46	7.23	7.23	6.83

* estimated figure

Political structure

Constitution

The constitution was promulgated in 1978. The country is run on a dual system. The traditional structure of Swaziland is headed by the Ingwenyama (the lion) (King), the Ndlovukazi (the she-elephant) (Queen Mother), and the more than 300 Chiefs who control the largely rural population. The other is the western-style central government, headed by the King, acting together with parliament, cabinet and civil service. Succession to the throne is governed by Swazi law and custom.
The draft of a proposed new constitution was written in 2003. However, it was available only in English and is also to be published in SiSwati during 2004, after which there is to be a further period of national consultation..
The Kingdom is divided into four regions.

Form of state

Absolute monarchy

The executive
Under the 1978 constitution, considerable executive power is vested in the monarch and exercised through a cabinet of ministers (all appointed by the monarch). Royal decrees carry the full force of law.
National legislature
There is a bi-cameral Libandla (legislature) consisting of the Senate (20 members appointed by the King; additional 10 members elected by the House of Assembly from among its own membership), and the Liqoqo (House of Assembly) (55 elective members, directly elected every five years (the first time in 1993), with voters electing one representative from each of the tinkhundla (traditional assemblies); 10 further members appointed by the King).
Legal system
The legal system is based on South African Roman-Dutch law in statutory courts and Swazi traditional law and custom in traditional courts. The Court of Appeal is the highest court in Swaziland. Court decisions are often overruled by the King.
Last elections
October 2003 (Liqoqo, traditional tribal assembly)
Results: Liqoqo: the elections were considered by the opposition to be meaningless since political parties are outlawed. Only one of the elected MPs has a political affiliation (former prime minister Obed Dlamini, a member of the Ngwane National Liberation Congress). Several other members of outlawed parties contested seats as independent candidates; turnout was low.
Next elections
2008 (Liqoqo, traditional tribal assembly)

Political parties
Ruling party
Political parties are de facto banned

Population
1.16 million (2007)*
Last census: October 1997: 929,718
Population density: 59 inhabitants per square km. Urban population: 27 per cent (1995–2001).
Annual growth rate: 1.0 per cent 1994–2004 (WHO 2006)
Ethnic make-up
Africans (97 per cent), Europeans (3 per cent).
Religions
Christianity (60 per cent), traditional beliefs (40 per cent).

Education
Although education is subsidised by government, free public education remains a distant goal. School drop-out rates for children of vulnerable households are increasing, with more than 10 per cent of school drop-outs in the first term due to families forced to use school fees to pay the rising costs of staple foods.
It is estimated that through the loss of parents, due to HIV/Aids, 10 per cent of households are headed by a child.
A survey in 2001 showed there were 728 schools in the country, of which 549 were primary and 179 were secondary/high schools. The University of Swaziland provides higher education. There is scope for vocational training, including nursing, although there are no training institutes for doctors and dentists.
Literacy rate: 82 per cent adult rate (2003)
Compulsory years: None.
Enrolment rate: 128 per cent boys, 121 per cent girls gross primary enrolment (including repeaters); 60 per cent gross secondary enrolment (Unicef 2004).
Pupils per teacher: 37 in primary schools; 20 in secondary schools.

Health
Per capita total expenditure on health (2003) was US$324; of which per capita government spending was US$185, at the international dollar rate, (WHO 2006).
HIV/Aids
Swaziland has the highest HIV/Aids rate in the world. In a 2005 antenatal survey of pregnant women aged 25–29 the prevalence rate was 56.3 per cent. The number of orphans of Aids is projected to be, by 2010, between 10–15 per cent of the population and the gender imbalance stark as the disease strikes down a disproportionate number of females.
In 2005 over US$6 million was provided by international donors to help fight the disease but a US$1.5 million anti-retroviral (ARV) drugs programme was cancelled when no government infrastructure was in place to establish an effective way of monitoring patients taking the ARV medication.
Food security in Swaziland is directly linked to the toll on its young, productive adults, during its longstanding HIV/Aids epidemic. UNAIDS estimates that the annual loss to GDP per capita due to Aids will be 1.2 per cent by 2010. Demographically, urban populations have fallen by 5 per cent as HIV sufferers return to their family farms to receive care.
Projections show that by 2010, Swaziland's population with be 25 per cent smaller than it should be on current population growth trends. HIV/Aids has already begun to reduce life expectancy, falling from 54 years in 1996 to 42.5 years in 2003.
HIV prevalence: 42.6 per cent in 2005 (UNAIDS)
Life expectancy: 37 years, 2004 (WHO 2006)
Fertility rate/Maternal mortality rate: 3.8 births per woman, 2004 (WHO 2006)
Birth rate/Death rate: 29 births and 21 deaths per 1,000 people (2003)
Child (under 5 years) mortality rate (per 1,000): 105 per 1,000 live births (2003); 10 per cent of children aged under five are malnourished (World Bank).
Head of population per physician: 0.16 physicians per 1,000 people, 2004 (WHO 2006)

Welfare
UN estimates show that 66 per cent of Swaziland's population live below the poverty line. The average unemployment rate is about 40 per cent, although this figure is higher in rural areas.
According to the UN World Food Programme in early 2002, some 144,000 people required food aid after a severe drop in agricultural production. The total food aid amounted to 17,720 tonnes.

Main cities
Mbabane (administrative capital, estimated population 81,594 in 2005), Lobamba (legislative capital and the seat of the monarchy), Manzini (36,594), Matsapha.

Languages spoken
Most Swazis are bi-lingual in English and SiSwati. In 2006 concern was expressed that teaching of SiSwati was less than English and that under 25 per cent of students who sat the 2005 Junior Certificate SiSwati examination passed; 92 per cent sitting the English language examination passed.
Official language/s
English and SiSwati
Media
Censorship extends to all radio and television output, excluding the Christian radio station. The print media is also restricted with the only privately owned newspaper reduced to commenting on news trivia while all adverse comments concerning the King are avoided.
Other news agencies: There is no official agency but APA (www.apanews.net) and Panapress (www.panapress.com) report on Swaziland matters.
Press
Dailies: In English, the privately owned Times of Swaziland (www.times.co.sz) is a tabloid style newspaper and The Swazi Observer (www.observer.org.sz) is an establishment newspaper.
Weeklies: Both dailies have weekend editions , Times of Swaziland Sunday, The Weekend Observer (www.observer.org.sz).
Periodicals: The Dzadze Family Magazine caters to women and consumer interests.

Broadcasting

Radio: The state-run Swaziland Broadcasting and Information Service operates three channels, the siSwati channel, the English channel and the Information service. The US-owned evangelical Trans World Radio (www.twr.org.za) has transmitters in Swaziland and broadcasts regionally.

Television: The state-run Swaziland Television Authority transmits most services in English with some in siSwati.

News agencies

Other news agencies: There is no official agency but APA (www.apanews.net) and Panapress (www.panapress.com) report on Swaziland matters.

Economy

In recent years, Swaziland's GDP has remained strong while inflation has remained in single-digit figures, indicating macroeconomic stability, although growth in GDP per capita is modest. Despite being classified as a middle-income country, the distribution of income is highly unequal and around two thirds of the population lives below the poverty line on less than US$1 per day.

HIV/Aids affects around a third of the population, with prevalence rates rising, resulting in a fall of life expectancy and economic strain. This along with severe droughts in the 2003/04 and 2004/05 seasons has resulted in the cry that the country is suffering a natural disaster.

Swaziland's economic relations with South Africa remain close and the lilangeni is pegged to the rand. Company income taxes are in line with South Africa, although the rate on three-month treasury bills is generally 2 per cent lower.

The government's economic plans include the National Development Strategy which seeks to ensure that by 2022 Swaziland will rank in the top 10 per cent of middle-income developing countries with sustainable economic development and political stability. However, agricultural output has dropped. The King's proflgate spending is also hindering social improvements.

External trade

Swaziland is a member of the Common Market for Eastern and Southern Africa (Comesa), and operates within a free trade zone with 13 of the 19 member states. It is a member of the Southern African Development Community (SADC), the objectives of which includes reducing trade barriers, achieving regional development and economic growth and evolving common systems and institutions and is a member of the Common Monetary Area (CMA) (South Africa, Lesotho and Namibia) where the South African rand is legal tender throughout.

Sugar and soft drinks concentrate are the leading export earners, with timber and derivative the next important exports. Coal and gold mining have declined and their share of exports are no longer significant. Garment manufacturing suffered from foreign competition following the end of the Multi-Fibre Agreement (MFA) in 2005, which saw world sales of Asian garments eliminate many markets for African manufacturers.

Imports

Principal imports are vehicles, machinery, foodstuffs, petroleum and chemicals.

Main sources: South Africa (95.6 per cent total, 2004), EU (0.9 per cent), (Japan 0.9 per cent), Singapore (0.3 per cent)

Exports

Principal exports are soft drink concentrates, sugar, wood pulp, citrus and canned fruit and garments.

Main destinations: South Africa (59.7 per cent total, 2004), EU (8.8 per cent), US (8.8 per cent), Mozambique (6.2 per cent)

Agriculture

Farming

The agricultural sector contributes around 13 per cent to GDP and employs half of the working population.

Sugar cane is the principal crop. 38,000 hectares of land are given over to it. With yields of 100 tonnes per hectare, Swaziland is one of the world's most efficient sugar producers. All sugar cane is grown under irrigation. The industry is regulated by the Swaziland Sugar Association (SSA). Sugar is Swaziland's highest export earner and accounts for 51 per cent of total agricultural production, 24 per cent of GDP, 13 per cent of total exports and 57 per cent of foreign exchange earnings. A third of sugar production is exported to the EU at advantageous prices, but a decision by the EU, announced in 2004, to reduce the subsidy bodes ill for continuing prosperity of the sector.

Commercial farming, on the 40 per cent of the land owned by individual (mainly non-Swazi) freeholders, is centred on sugar, citrus, pineapples, tobacco and cotton.

Most maize and cotton is grown by small-scale farmers on Swazi Nation Land (SNL) (60 per cent of the land).

Smallholders own 80 per cent of the livestock. The country's main food crops are maize, beans, groundnuts and sorghum. Food self-sufficiency declined in the 1990s and efforts to expand local fruit and vegetable production by the National Agricultural Marketing Board (Namboard) have had only a limited impact.

The 2008 maize harvest in 2008 is expected to be double 2007 when drought devastated the crop. However, the projected 64,000 tonnes will still mean that the total cereal import requirement in the 2008/09 marketing year (April/March) will be about 136,000 tonnes, according to a joint assessment by the UN Food and Agriculture Organisation (FAO) and the UN World Food Programme (WFP).

Estimated crop production for 2005 included: 71,070 tonnes (t) cereals in total, 70,000t maize, 6,000t potatoes, 2,300t sweet potatoes, 8,300t roots and tubers, 73,850t citrus fruit, 3,400t tomatoes, 32,000t pineapples, 1,870t oilcrops, 4,500,000t sugar cane, 6,500t seed cotton, 111,412t fruit in total, 10,700t vegetables in total. Estimated livestock production included: 20,616t meat in total, 12,500t beef, 1,133t pig meat, 1,854t goat meat, 5,000t poultry, 1,050t eggs, 37,500t milk, 1,200t cattle hides.

Forestry

Forests cover 8 per cent of total land area. The value of exports in 2004 amounted to US$62 million.

Timber production in 2004 included: 890,000 cubic metre (cum) roundwood, 330,000cum industrial roundwood, 102,000cum sawnwood, 260,000cum sawlogs and veneer logs, 8,000cum wood-based panels, 560,000cum woodfuel.

Industry and manufacturing

The industrial sector employs over a fifth of the workforce and in 2004 contributed around 46 per cent of GDP. It is traditionally centred on the agro-industries: sugar refining, fruit canning and woodpulp processing. The forest products sector is one of the world's main sources of unbleached pulp.

Starting with textile production, the modern industrial sector has grown rapidly, with the South African market its main outlet. The US's African Growth and Opportunities Act (AGOA) enabled Swazi textile producers to access lucrative US markets, although the US has threatened to withdraw these benefits unless the government undergoes democratic reform.

The textile industry was affected in 2005 by increasing competition following the ending of the Agreement on Textiles and Clothing and by reduction of exports caused by the stronger rand.

Other activities include brick manufacture and shoe production.

Tourism

Tourism is in the early stages of developement. It is a growing sector which is being actively developed by the government. It is expected to contribute 2.4 per cent to GDP in 2005. The main source of visitors in 2004 was South Africa, reflecting the strong rand, followed by other neighbouring countries,

Germany, the Netherlands, the UK and France.

Mining
Mining activity has declined due to the depletion of iron ore, diamonds, gold and tin and the closure of the Bulembu asbestos mine. Coal is mined for export to South Africa; around 600,000 tonnes of anthracite were produced in 2004. Mineral production accounts for around 2 per cent of GDP.

Hydrocarbons
There are no known oil or gas reserves. Swaziland is entirely dependent on imports. Swaziland has no refineries.
There are substantial reserves of high-quality anthracite coal, which is extracted at the Maloma colliery for export to South Africa. Swaziland's domestic low-quality coal requirements are met by imports from South Africa.

Energy
Swaziland relies on imports of electricity, as well as petroleum and coal, for most of its energy needs. 80 per cent of electricity is supplied by South Africa and twenty per cent by Mozambique. A feeder line connecting South Africa and Mozambique crosses Swaziland.
A hydroelectric station at Maguga Dam on the Komati river, has commenced operations, but has only a maximum output of 19 MW.
Distribution of electricity is unreliable and outages are common. To improve reliability and ease dependence on South Africa, development of power stations using Swaziland's own coal resources is under investigation.

Financial markets
Stock exchange
The Swaziland Stock Exchange (SSE) began operating in 1990, and the Securities Market started in 1998. The SSE is one of the world's smallest bourses.

Banking and insurance
In a report published in December 2002, the IMF praised Swaziland's 'well-developed banking system' and noted that in 2002 'banks' capitalisation, risk management and provisioning appeared to be sound and their non-performing loans were relatively low.' However, the future of the government-owned Swaziland Development and Savings Bank (SDSB) remains in doubt due to its high level of bad loans. The IMF has urged the government to privatise the bank.
Central bank
Central Bank of Swaziland
Main financial centre
Mbabane

Time
GMT plus two hours
Geography
Swaziland is a landlocked country that is surrounded on three sides by South Africa and on its forth side by Mozambique. It is one of the smallest country in Africa and is located on the eastern flank of the Drakensberg mountains extending to the Lubombo escarpment in the east.
These volcanic mountains produce a landscape of high veld with altitudes of 1,800 meters (m) in the north, south and west dropping down to middle veld of between 400–600m to the lowlands or bush veld at around 300m. There are five major rivers and their tributaries running through the country with large lakes and waterfalls and is a major habitat for rare birds and invertebrates.
Hemisphere
Southern

Climate
Temperatures range from about 7–10 Celsius (C) (with occasional frost) during April–September, to 20–30 C during August–January. The wettest months are December and March.
The mountainous high veld region to the north-west has a temperate climate with hot, wet summers and dry winters when the temperature rises during the day but with cold nights. The adjacent middle veld has a warm temperate climate, while further to the east lies the sub-tropical low veld, including the Lubombo plain and escarpment.

Entry requirements
Passports
Required by all.
Visa
Required by all; except citizens of UK, North America, Australasia and others listed at www.gov.sz, see Entry requirements under Tourism, Environment and Community. To stay over 60 days requires a visa extension, to be obtained from the immigration department.
Currency advice/regulations
The import and export of local and foreign currency is unlimited. It is advisable to exchange local currency before leaving Swaziland as the lilangeni is not readily accepted elsewhere.
Travellers cheques are widely accepted.

Health (for visitors)
Mandatory precautions
A yellow fever certificate is required if arriving from an infected area.
Advisable precautions
Vaccinations for diphtheria, tetanus, hepatitis A and typhoid are recommended. Other vaccinations that may be advised include tuberculosis, cholera and hepatitis B. There is a risk of rabies.
Anti-malaria prophylaxes are needed in all but the high elevations. There is a very high prevalence of HIV/Aids.
Water precautions are essential. Eat only cooked food, served hot; avoid dairy, pork and salads; all fruits should be peeled. To avoid bilharzia, use only well maintained, chlorinated swimming pools.
Any medicines required by the traveller should be brought into the country and it would be wise to have precautionary antibiotics if going outside major urban centres. A travel kit including a disposable syringe is a reasonable precaution.
Medical insurance is essential, including emergency evacuation.

Hotels
There is no official rating system. Accommodation is fairly scarce, especially during national holidays, so rooms should be booked well in advance. Bills generally include the service charge, but a 10 per cent tip is also usual. A 10 per cent government tax is added to the room rates.

Credit cards
Major credit and charge card are accepted.

Public holidays (national)
Fixed dates
1 Jan (New Year's Day), 19 Apr (King's Birthday), 25 Apr (National Flag Day), 1 May (Labour Day), 22 Jul (Birthday of the late King), 6 Sep (Independence Day), 25–26 Dec (Christmas).
Variable dates
Good Friday, Easter Monday, Ascension, Umhlanga/Reed Dance Day^ (Aug/Sep).
^ Dependent on local sightings of the moon.

Working hours
Banking
Mon–Fri: 0830–1300/1430; Sat: 0830–1100.
Business
Mon–Fri: 0800–1300, 1400–1700; Sat: 0815 or 0830–1230.
Government
Mon–Fri: 0800–1300, 1400–1700.

Telecommunications
Mobile/cell phones
There is a 900 GSM service throughout most of the country.

Electricity supply
230V AC, 50 Hz, with round, three-pin plugs.

Security
If you enter Swaziland from South Africa by road, on the N4, via the Oshoek border post, avoid travelling after dark as there is a risk of hijacking.

Getting there
Air
National airline: Royal Swazi National Airways
International airport/s: Matsapha (MTS), 9km south-west of Manzini, 40km from Mbabane; refreshments, currency exchange, car hire. There are no direct intercontinental flights, but regular services operate regionally, particularly from South Africa. Swazi Express provides a regional air service
Airport tax: Departures tax: E20
Surface
Road: There are tarred roads from Johannesburg and Durban and from Mozambique (Siteki-Lomahasha road). All Swazi border posts open daily throughout the year; hours of operation vary. Vehicles are subject to searches.
Rail: There is a rail service between Durban (South Africa) and Maputo (Mozambique) via Mpaka in the central eastern district of Lubombo.

Getting about
National transport
Road: The network is fairly well developed. An ongoing project improved the network with the provision of a dual carriageway and toll road between Manzini-Mbabane, which was opened in October 2003 and completed the Matspha-Mbabane-Ngwenya highway.
Buses: There is a good system that extends throughout the country.
Taxis: Minibus taxis run shorter routes than the buses, at slightly higher prices.
City transport
Taxis: Scarce. Best to order from hotel. A tip is usual.
Car hire
Self-drive cars are available at airport and city centre; a national driving licence is required. Driving is on the left and the maximum speed limit is 80kph.

BUSINESS DIRECTORY

The addresses listed below are a selection only. While World of Information makes every endeavour to check these addresses, we cannot guarantee that changes have not been made, especially to telephone numbers and area codes. We would welcome any corrections.

Telephone area codes
The international direct dialling code (IDD) for Swaziland is +268, followed by subscriber's number.

Chambers of Commerce
Swaziland Chamber of Commerce and Industry, PO Box 72, Mbabane (tel: 404-4408; fax: 404-5442; e-mail: chamber@dial.pipex.sz).

Banking
First National Bank of Swaziland Ltd, 2nd Floor, Sales House Building, Mbabane (tel: 404-5401/2/3; fax: 404-4735).

Nedbank (Swaziland) Limited, PO Box 68, Corner Plaza Mall Street and Bypass Road, Mbabane (tel: 404-3351/5; fax: 404-4060).

Standard Bank Swaziland Ltd, Standard House, Swazi Plaza, Mbabane (tel: 404-6930/1/2, 404-6599, 408-30/4; fax: 404-5899).

Swazibank, PO Box 336, Gwamile Street (tel: 404-2551; fax: 404-1241: email: vinahnkambule@swazibank.sz).

Central bank
Central Bank of Swaziland, PO Box 546, Warner Street, Mbabane (tel: 404-2000; fax: 404-0063; email: info@centralbank.org.sz).

Travel information
Hotels and Tourism Association of Swaziland, PO Box 462, Mbabane (tel: 404-2218; fax: 404-4516).

Royal Swazi National Airways, PO Box 939, Matsapa Airport, Manzini.

Swazi Express (charter airline), Matsapha (tel: 518-6840; fax: 518-7160; internet: www.swaziexpress.com).

Ministry of tourism
Ministry of Tourism, Environment and Communications, 2nd Floor, Income Tax Bld, Mhlambanyatsi Road; PO Box 2653, Mbabane (tel: 404-4556; fax: 404-5415).

National tourist organisation offices
Swaziland Tourism Authority, PO Box A1030, Mbabane (tel: 405-7510; internet: www.welcometoswaziland.com).

Ministries
Cabinet Office, PO Box 395, Mbabane (tel: 404-2251; fax: 404-3943).

Ministry of Agriculture and Co-operatives, PO Box 162, Mbabane (tel: 404-2731; fax: 404-4700).

Ministry of Broadcasting, Information and Tourism, PO Box 338, Mbabane (tel: 404-2761/9; fax: 404-2774).

Ministry of Defence, PO Box 1928, Mbabane (tel: 404-2809; fax: 404-2483).

Ministry of Economic Planning and Statistics, PO Box 602, Mbabane (tel: 404-3765; fax: 404-2157).

Ministry of Education, PO Box 39, Mbabane (tel: 404-2491; fax: 404-3880).

Ministry of Enterprise and Employment, PO Box 451, Mbabane (tel: 404-3201; fax: 404-4711); Trade Promotion Unit (tel: 404-5180).

Ministry of Finance, PO Box 443, Mbabane (tel: 404-8148; fax: 404-3187).

Ministry of Foreign Affairs and Trade, PO Box 518, Mbabane (tel: 404-2661; fax: 404-2669).

Ministry of Health and Social Welfare, PO Box 5, Mbabane (tel: 404-2431; fax: 404-2092).

Ministry of Home Affairs, PO Box 432, Mbabane (tel: 404-2941; fax: 404-4303).

Ministry of Housing and Urban Development, PO Box 1832, Mbabane (tel: 404-6035; fax: 404-4085).

Ministry of Justice and Constitutional Development, PO Box 924, Mbabane (tel: 404-3531; fax: 404-4796); Attorney General's Chambers, PO Box 578, Mbabane (tel: 404-2807).

Ministry of Natural Resources and Energy, PO Box 57, Mbabane (tel: 404-6244; fax: 404-2436); Geological Survey & Mines, PO Box 57, Mbabane (tel: 404-2411). Rural Water Supply, PO Box 961, Mbabane (tel: 404-1231).

Ministry of Public Service and Information, PO Box 338, Mbabane (tel: 404-2761; fax: 404-2774).

Ministry of Public Works and Transport, PO Box 58, Mbabane (tel: 404-2321; fax: 4042364); Civil Aviation (tel: 404-2420).

Prime Minister's Office, PO Box 395, Mbabane (tel: 404-2251; fax: 4043943). Deputy Prime Minister's Office, PO Box A33 Swazi Plaza (tel: 404-2723; fax: 404-4085).

Other useful addresses
Central Co-operative Union, PO Box 551, Manzini (tel: 505-2787; fax 505-5313; email: ccu.admin@africaonline.co.sz).

Central Statistics Office, PO Box 456, Mbabane (tel: 404-2151/4; fax: 404-2157).

Central Transport Administration, PO Box 378, Mbabane (tel: 404-2871; fax: 404-3002).

Civil Service Board, PO Box 158, Mbabane (tel: 404-2601).

Cotton Board, PO Box 230, Manzini (tel/fax: 505-2775).

Federation of Swaziland Employers, PO Box 777, Mbabane (tel: 404-0768; fax: 404-6107; email: fse@realnet.co.sz).

National Agricultural Marketing Board, PO Box 1713, Matsapha (tel: 518-5211; fax: 518-4088).

National Maize Corporation, PO Box 158, Manzini (tel: 518-7432; fax: 518-4461).

Parliament, King's Office (tel: 416-1080). Parliament Offices (tel: 416-1286).

Police Headquarters, PO Box 49, Mbabane (tel: 404-2051).

Posts and Telecommunications Corporation, PO Box 125, Mbabane (tel: 404-2341; fax: 404-3130).

Small Enterprise Development Co Ltd, Mbabane Industrial Sites, PO Box A186, Swazi Plaza (tel: 404-2811; fax: 404-0723).

Statistics Department, PO Box 456, Mbabane (tel: 404-2151; fax: 404-2157).

Swazi Business Growth Trust, PO Box 78, Eveni (tel: 404-4705; fax: 404-4783).

Swaziland Citrus Board, PO Box 343, Mbabane (tel: 404-3547).

Swaziland Commercial Board, PO Box 509, Mbabane (tel: 404-2930).

Swaziland Cotton Board, PO Box 230, Manzini (tel: 505-2775).

Swaziland Dairy Board, PO Box 2975, Manzini (tel: 505-8262).

Swaziland Electricity Board, PO Box 258, Mbabane (tel: 404-6668; fax: 404-2335).

Swaziland Embassy (USA), 1712 New Hampshire Ave, NW, Washington DC 20009 (tel: (1-202) 234-5002; fax: (1-202) 234-8059; e-mail: embassy@swaziland-usa.com).

Swaziland Industrial Development Company, PO Box 866, Mbabane (tel: 404-3391; fax: 404-5619).

Swaziland International Trade Fair, PO Box 877, Manzini (tel: 505-4242; fax: 505-2314).

Swaziland Investment Promotion Authority, PO Box 4194, Mbabane H100 (tel: 404-0470; fax: 404-3374; email: sipa@business-swaziland.com).

Swaziland National Housing Board, PO Box 798, Mbabane (tel: 404-5610; fax: 404-5224).

Swaziland Railway, PO Box 475, Mbabane (tel: 404-27211; fax: 404-7210).

Swaziland Sugar Association, PO Box 445, Mbabane (tel: 404-2646).

Swaziland Television Authority, PO Box A146, Swazi Plaza (tel: 404-3036; fax: 404-2093).

Tinkhundla Headquarters, PO Box A33, Swazi Plaza, Mbabane (tel: 404-2723; fax: 404-4058).

Water Services Corporation, PO Box 20 Mbabane (tel: 404-5584; fax: 404-5355).

Internet sites

Africa Business Network: www.ifc.org/abn

AllAfrica.com: http://allafrica.com

African Development Bank: www.afdb.org

Africa Online: www.africaonline.com

Mbendi AfroPaedia (information on companies, countries, industries and stock exchanges in Africa): http://mbendi.co.za

Simunye news service: www.swazis.org.uk/~news/

Swazi news: www.swazinews.co.sz/about.htm

Swazi Observer: www.swaziobserver.sz/

Swaziland Solidarity Campaign: www.swazis.org

Sweden

KEY FACTS

Official name: Konungariket Sverige (The Kingdom of Sweden)

Head of State: King Carl XVI Gustaf

Head of government: Prime Minister Fredrik Reinfeldt (Moderata) (since 5 Oct 2006)

Ruling party: Coalition led by Moderata Samlingspartiet (Moderata) (Moderate Coalition Party), with Centerpartiet) (Cp) (Centre Party), Folkpartiet Liberalerna (FpL) (Liberal People's Party) and Kristdemokraterna (KD) (Christian Democrats) (since Sep 2006)

Area: 448,964 square km

Population: 9.17 million (2007)*

Capital: Stockholm

Official language: Swedish

Currency: Swedish krona (SKr) = 100 öre

Exchange rate: SKr5.96 per US$ (Jul 2008)

GDP per capita: US$49,655 (2007)*

GDP real growth: 5.60% (2007)

Labour force: 4.59 million (2006)*

Unemployment: 1.70% (2007)

Inflation: 6.10% (2007)

Balance of trade: US$19.70 billion (2005)

Foreign debt: US$513.18 billion (2004)

* estimated figure

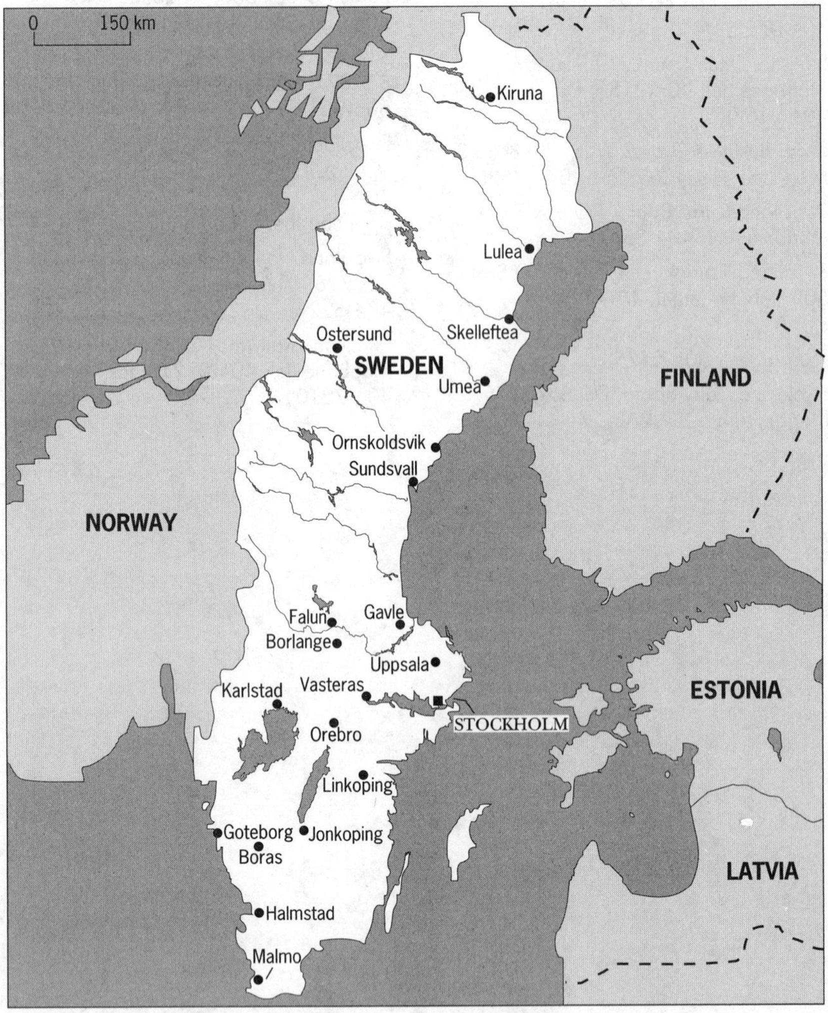

According to the Swedish ministry of finance, Sweden's gross domestic product (GDP) was expected to grow by 3.7 per cent in 2007 and by 3.3 per cent in 2008. Total unemployment, measured as the annual average, was forecast to decline from 8.4 per cent in 2006 to 6.7 per cent in 2007 and to 6.2 per cent in 2008. General government net lending was projected to be 2.3 per cent of GDP in 2007 and 2.2 per cent in 2008.

Rising employment, solid growth

Exports were set to grow at a brisk pace in 2007, though somewhat more slowly in line with less vigorous global growth and a stronger Swedish krona. While growth in investment was also likely to decelerate, high capacity utilisation and propitious financial prospects for businesses indicated that the level of investment would remain buoyant. Due to rapidly growing disposable income, rising employment and a solid initial wealth position, household consumption was projected to increase substantially. Spurred primarily by solid revenue growth, public consumption was also set to rise most rapidly in the local government sector.

Demand for labour was strong, the number of newly reported vacancies high and businesses were planning to hire more people. As a result, employment was expected to continue rising in 2007 and 2008. The labour supply was set to increase substantially in 2007, followed by slower growth. Partly owing to the reforms proposed by the Spring Fiscal Policy Bill, unemployed people would look for jobs more actively and efficiently than before. Open unemployment was likely to decrease substantially in 2007 and 2008. As a result of major cutbacks in labour market policy programmes in 2006, total unemployment – consisting of people who are either openly unemployed or participating in the programmes – was expected to decrease more than open unemployment in 2007.

Inflation was low and was expected to slow down in 2007 as the Swedish krona strengthened and energy prices declined. Owing to the strong demand for labour, resource utilisation in the labour market was expected to be tight in 2008. The likely result would be a gradual acceleration of wage growth and inflation in 2008 and 2009. Faced by rising wages and inflation, the Sveriges Riksbank (central bank) is expected to raise its repo rate during 2009. In short, the effect was expected to be a slowdown in employment and GDP growth in 2009 and 2010 to below the potential growth rate. The reforms that have been announced and adopted since the government took office were set to considerably impact upon rates of employment and GDP growth in the long run.

It is expected that Sweden's foreign-born population will increasingly be relied on as the main source of its labour supply, particularly in manual and low-paid jobs and a better integration of immigrants into the labour force is crucial. The immigrant population constitutes 10 per cent of the total, and is set to rise. There is a notable minority Muslim population. Sweden's car market is predicted to record robust growth, with new passenger-car registrations forecast to rise by 3.8 per cent annually over 2004–08.

Sweden's September 2006 election had marked a sea-change in Swedish politics as the Social Democratic Party (SDP)- led minority coalition was voted out of office after 12 years in government. Outgoing prime minister, Goran Persson, had been Europe's second-longest serving prime minister. The incoming centre-right Alliance – a coalition of former opposition parties, made up from the Moderata Samlingspartiet (Moderata) (Moderate Coalition Party), Centerpartiet (Cp) (Centre Party), the Folkpartiet Liberalerna (FpL) (People's Party Liberals) and the Kristdemokraterna (KD) (Christian Democrats) – had won a seven-seat majority. The new prime minister, Fredrik Reinfeldt of the Moderata, drew up an ambitious programme of reforms focused on tackling unemployment, introducing tax cuts and improving the education system. Mr Reinfeldt brought youth and energy to Swedish politics. Very much in the mold of former UK prime minister, Tony Blair, when he assumed leadership, he is credited with bringing unity to Sweden's political centre-right.

Social welfare and capitalism

This neutral and pacifist kingdom has a great tradition of generous social welfare combined with successful capitalism, with the economy following public-private partnership principles. Sweden ranks sixth out of 177 countries in the UN Human Development Index (HDI), which tracks the quality of countries' education and welfare provisions along with life expectancy. The HDI puts Sweden below Norway, Australia and Iceland but comfortably above the US, UK and Japan. The country has the lowest infant mortality rate, the highest level of female participation in parliament, the highest tax rate and a very high ranking quality of life.

Outlook

The economy is fundamentally robust but negative statistics have emerged regarding unemployment, a slowing of growth and a cut in interest rates. A cut in the overall corporate tax rate was announced in the 2008 autumn budget. Together with a reduction in the social contribution fees paid by companies, this will help strengthen business as Sweden's export-led economy starts to feel the effects of the global slowdown. Sweden's centre-right government under Prime Minister Fredik Reinfeldt feels that after spending the first half of its term in office on unpopular reforms, it is now in a position to put in place more popular measures such as tax cuts and increased welfare spending.

Risk assessment

Politics	Good
Economy	Good
Regional stability	Good

COUNTRY PROFILE

Historical profile

1389–1520 Having evolved from a feudal society, Sweden was ruled by Denmark.

1520 The Massacre of Stockhom occurred when the Danish King Kristian II, in an attempt to assert his supremacy, executed resisting Swedish noblemen, which led to a revolt, headed by Gustav Eriksson Vasa.

1523 King Kristian II was defeat by Vasa, who was crowned Gustav I. His victory heralded the start of Sweden's ascendancy in Europe.

1611 Gustav II Adolph (Gustavus Adolphus) became King. He engaged in expansionist policies that attempted to gain control of the Baltic trading routes and which brought him into conflict with neighbouring states.

KEY INDICATORS — Sweden

	Unit	2003	2004	2005	2006	2007
Population	m	8.85	8.99	9.04	9.11	*9.17
Gross domestic product (GDP)	US$bn	300.80	346.40	358.48	393.61	455.32
GDP per capita	US$	34,981	38,449	39,658	43,190	*49,655
GDP real growth	%	1.7	3.5	2.9	4.0	5.6
Inflation	%	2.1	1.1	0.8	1.5	1.7
Unemployment	%	4.8	5.4	5.8	7.0	6.1
Exports (fob) (goods)	US$m	100,939	121,700	134,904	148,756	–
Imports (cif) (goods)	US$m	82,317	97,970	115,203	127,341	–
Balance of trade	US$m	18,622	23,730	19,701	21,415	–
Current account	US$m	22,990	28,020	25,239	33,303	37,987
Total reserves minus gold	US$m	19,681.0	22,129.0	22,063.0	24,778.0	27,044.0
Foreign exchange	US$m	18,015.0	20,611.0	21,355.0	24,074.0	26,382.0
Exchange rate	per US$	7.96	7.35	7.02	6.83	6.52

* estimated figure

1629 Sweden fought to possess Prussia and Pomerania (now part of Germany) in the Thirty Years War.
1632 Gustav II was killed at the battle of Lutzen (in Saxony, now part of Germany) and was succeeded by his daughter, Kristina.
1654 Kristina abdicated after converting to Catholicism – an act that was unacceptable in Lutheran Sweden.
1700 Start of the Great Nordic War when Russia, Denmark, Norway and Poland formed an alliance against Sweden and its 15-year old King Karl XII in an attempt to retrieve some of their lost lands.
1700–1720 A succession of battles resulted in the loss of all Swedish lands in Germany, the Baltic provinces of Russia and much of Finland. Success against the Danes in Norway allowed Sweden to consolidate into easily defended borders.
1718 The power of the monarchy diminished and was vested in the Council of Aristocrats who depended on parliament for its authority.
1772 King Gustav III began reforms that strengthened the power of the monarchy. These developments resulted in an almost absolute monarchy.
1792 King Gustav III was assassinated by members of the Swedish nobility. Gustav IV Adolf became King.
1808–09 Sweden was defeated by the Russians. Finland, which was then part of Sweden, was ceded to Russia. King Gustav IV Adolf was replaced by Karl XIII in 1809.
1814 Sweden entered a union with Norway.
1905 The emergence of Norwegian nationalism led Norway to declare independence. A parliamentary form of government emerged in Sweden.
1920s The Sveriges Socialdemokratiska Arbetarparti (SSA) (Swedish Social Democratic Party) first came to power. Except for a brief period during 1936, the SSA stayed in power from 1932 to 1976.
1939–45 Sweden declared its neutrality during the Second World War, although German troops were transported through its territory to Norway. Sweden also supplied Nazi Germany with iron ore until 1943.
1952 Sweden became a founder member of the Nordic Council.
1959 Sweden became a founder member of the European Free Trade Area (EFTA) with Austria, Denmark, Norway, Portugal, Switzerland and the UK.
1969–71 Olof Palme (prime minister 1969–76 and 1982–86) introduced constitutional reforms. The bicameral legislature was replaced by a unicameral legislature, elected by proportional representation.
1975 A new constitution was promulgated; it reduced the power of the monarchy and limited its role to that of figurehead and ceremonial duties.
1976 A centre-right coalition government, the Centerpartiet (Cp) (Centre Party), and Moderata Samlingspartiet (Moderata) (Moderate Party) won the parliamentary election.
1978 The coalition government collapsed due to disagreement about economic problems and the building of a controversial nuclear power plant. The former coalition partner, Folkpartiet Liberalerna (FpL) (Liberal People's Party) formed a new government.
1979 The Cp won the parliamentary elections by a one seat majority.
1982 The SSA won the parliamentary elections. Olof Palme became prime minister again.
1986 Palme was assassinated in Stockholm by an unknown gunman.
1991 After parliamentary elections, Moderata formed the government with Carl Bildt as prime minister.
1994 The SSA won the general election. Sweden joined Nato's Partnership for Peace (PfP) military co-operation programme.
1995 Sweden joined the EU.
1996 Carlsson stepped down as the leader of the SSA and prime minister. Göran Persson replaced him.
1998 Following parliamentary elections the SSA formed a minority government. The reduced voto for the SSA was believed to be due to widespread anger at social expenditure cuts.
2002 The SSA won the parliamentary elections and continued to lead a minority government that relied on support from the Vänsterpartiet (Vp) (Left Party) and the Miljöpartiet de Gröna (MP) (Environmental Party the Greens).
2003 Foreign Minister Anna Lindh was stabbed to death in a Stockholm department store. In a referendum voters narrowly defeated the proposal to join the single European currency.
2004 The man who confessed to killing Anna Lindh was convicted of her murder and sentenced to life imprisonment, overturning a previous ruling which consigned him to a psychiatric hospital.
2006 In parliamentary elections the ruling SSA narrowly lost with 46.2 per cent against the opposition coalition, led by Moderata Samlingspartiet (M) (Moderate Coalition Party), which won with 48.1 per cent of the vote (178 seats in the 349 legislative assembly); turnout was 80.4 per cent. Fredrik Reinfeldt (Moderate) became prime minister.
2007 Ingmar Bergman died in July.
2008 An international conference was held on 29 May outside Stockholm, under the UN's auspices concerning the situation in Iraq. Around 100 countries took part discussing support and efforts to restore stability and rebuild a functioning economy.

Political structure

Constitution

The constitution consists of four separate documents: the Regeringsformen (Instrument of Government) passed in 1974, Successionsordningen (Act of Succession) dating from 1810, the Tryckfrihetsförordningen (Freedom of the Press Act) of 1949 (originating from 1766), and the Yttrandefrihetsgrundlagen (Freedom of Expression Act) of 1991.
There are 288 municipalities throughout the country, each with a popularly elected council. Immigrants, resident for three years, have the right to vote and run for office in local elections.
Universal suffrage is at aged 18. Voter turnout is traditionally high, between 85–90 per cent.
Under proportional representation 310 parliamentary seats are allocated on a constituency basis, in 28 multi-member constituencies; the remaining seats are divided nationally. To win parliamentary representation, a party must poll either 4 per cent overall – to receive a seat from the national allocation – or 12 per cent in any one constituency for a seat from the national remainder.

Form of state

Parliamentary democratic monarchy

The executive

Executive power is exercised by the Regeringen (cabinet) which is led by the prime minister (elected by parliament) and is responsible to parliament. The prime minister appoints members of the cabinet.

National legislature

Legislative power is vested in the unicameral Riksdag (parliament) (349 members directly elected for a four-year term). In the event of an early dissolution, the new parliament serves only the remainder of the previous parliament's term.

Legal system

The legal system is divided into the general courts and the general administrative courts. The general courts are composed of a Supreme Court (Högsta domstolen), six Courts of Appeal and 95 District Courts which are responsible for criminal cases involving individuals. The Supreme Court is the highest court in the land and is composed of 16 judges appointed by the government. The general administrative courts are responsible for cases involving public authorities and individuals.

Last elections

17 September 2006 (parliamentary).
Results: Parliamentary: a coalition led by Moderata Samlingspartiet (Moderata)

(Moderate Coalition Party) 26.1 per cent (97 seats) with Centerpartiet (Cp) (Centre Party) 7.9 per cent (29 seats), Folkpartiet Liberalerna (FpL) (People's Party Liberals) 7.5 per cent (28 seats) and Kristdemokraterna (KD) (Christian Democrats) 6.6 per cent (24 seats) narrowly won 130 out of 349 seats in the national legislature. The ruling Sveriges Socialdemokratiska Arbetarparti (SSA) (Swedish Social Democratic Party) won 35.2 per cent (130); Vänsterpartiet (Vp) (Left Party) 5.8 per cent (22 seats); Miljöpartiet de Gröna (MP) (Environmental Party the Greens) 5.2 per cent (19 seats). Turnout was 80.4 per cent.

Next elections
September 2010 (parliamentary)

Political parties

Ruling party
Coalition led by Moderata Samlingspartiet (Moderata) (Moderate Coalition Party), with Centerpartiet) (Cp) (Centre Party), Folkpartiet Liberalerna (FpL) (Liberal People's Party) and Kristdemokraterna (KD) (Christian Democrats) (since Sep 2006)

Main opposition party
Sveriges Socialdemokratiska Arbetarparti (SSA) (Swedish Social Democratic Party)

Population

9.17 million (2007)*

Last census: December 2000: 8,872,110

Population density: 20 inhabitants per square km. Urban population: 83 per cent (1995–2001).

Annual growth rate: 0.2 per cent 1994–2004 (WHO 2006)

Ethnic make-up
Native Swedes account for 88 per cent of the population. Around 50 per cent of all foreign nationals are from other Nordic countries (Denmark, Finland, Iceland and Norway).
Sweden has two minority groups of native inhabitants in the north: the Finnish speaking people of the north-east and an estimated 17,000 Sámi (Lapp) people.

Religions
About 90 per cent of the population belong to the Church of Sweden (Lutheran); there are 8 per cent other Protestants and 1 per cent Roman Catholics.

Education

Pre-school classes are offered to any six year old enrolled, the first (and compulsory) school begins at aged seven; both are free of charge and the majority are run by municipalities. In 2001–02 over one million pupils were enrolled (within both); independent schools accounted for 1 per cent of enrolments. The average number of pupils per school was 209, with an average of 108 pupils in independent schools. Many schools are now working with integrated age levels where children of different ages are taught together in the same class. Around three-quarters of all compulsory schools are connected to the Internet. At aged 16 students who have successfully completed their compulsory schooling progress to upper secondary school. Nearly all pupils continue to the upper secondary school. Each municipality has the right to establish its own upper secondary schools and a national curriculum provides a basis for further studies and basic eligibility for higher education.
Higher education is offered in 13 state-run universities and 23 university colleges. There are also three private universities: Chalmers University of Technology, the University College of Jönköping and the Stockholm School of Economics. Further education for adults (aged 20 years and over) is offered within the public adult education system through municipal adult education.

Literacy rate: 99 per cent, adult rate (2003)

Compulsory years: 7 to 16

Enrolment rate: 107 per cent gross primary enrolment, 140 per cent gross secondary enrolment: of relevant age groups (including repeaters and training for unemployed within the age group) (World Bank 2001).

Pupils per teacher: 12 in primary schools

Health

Per capita total expenditure on health (2003) was US$2,704; of which per capita government spending was US$2,305, at the international dollar rate, (WHO 2006).
Sweden has for many years actively worked with health promotion in line with the World Health Organisation's (WHO) European 'Health for All' policy. There is a close collaboration between the government and local and regional providers of public medical and healthcare services.
A governmental body, the National Public Health Committee, is responsible for providing many recommendations to the government, along with wide-ranging consultation, is being used as a basis for the future development of the healthcare system.
The public sector finances health services, through taxation, for the entire population although the Federation of Health Insurance Societies, (established in 1907), helps to promote a national compulsory system of health insurance.

HIV/Aids

HIV prevalence: 0.1 per cent aged 15–49 in 2003 (World Bank)

Life expectancy: 81 years, 2004 (WHO 2006)

Fertility rate/Maternal mortality rate: 1.7 births per woman, 2004 (WHO 2006)

Birth rate/Death rate: 9.7 births and 10.6 deaths per 1,000 people (2003)

Child (under 5 years) mortality rate (per 1,000): 2.8 per 1,000 live births (World Bank)

Head of population per physician: 3.28 physicians per 1,000 people, 2002 (WHO 2006)

Welfare

The Swedish social insurance system is managed by the state and is compulsory for everyone, providing means-tested and general benefits. The main goal of the social insurance is to provide protection against loss of income and is composed of sickness insurance, early retirement pensions, occupational injury insurance and old age pensions. The Social Services Act of 1982 regulates the welfare benefit system while the National Board of Health and Welfare (Socialstyrelsen) supervises the overall quality of social service provision.
A Social Insurance Act was introduced in 2001, dividing social insurance into two categories: a domicile-based insurance scheme, which provides guaranteed benefits, and a work-related insurance scheme, which safeguards against loss of income. These insurance systems are available to anyone living or working in Sweden. Social insurance is divided into 50 per cent going into pensions, 25 per cent to sickness and disability benefit and 15 per cent to families with children.
The pension system was reformed in 1998 and is composed of various components, including an income-related pension, a premium pension and a guaranteed pension. The premium pension allows a person to invest their own funds into part of the pension scheme. A state pension is guaranteed to all the population on a low income or without any income.

Main cities

Stockholm (capital, estimated population – excluding urban areas – 770,284 in 2005), Göteborg (480,461), Malmö (269,543), Uppsala (182,767).

Languages spoken

Finnish, Skäine and Sámi are spoken. English, and to a lesser extent German, are also widely spoken.

Official language/s
Swedish

Media

Other news agencies: TT (Tidnignarnas Telegrambyrå) 105 12 Stockholm, (tel: 692-2600; fax: 692-2855; email: redaktionen@tt.se). TT is a private independent agency.

Press

Dailies: In Swedish, the most influential nationals are either owned or run by political parties and trade unions. These include Aftonbladet (www.aftonbladet.se) (Social Democratic), Dagens Nyheter (www.dn.se) (Liberal, independent), Expressen(www.expressen.se) (Liberal), Göteborgs-Posten (www.gp.se) (Liberal), Svenska Dagbladet (www.svd.se) (Conservative) Sydsvenska Dagbladet (www.sydsvenskan.se) and Aktuellt I Politiken (www.aip.nu). In Finnish Ruotsin Suomalainen (www.ruotsinsuomalainen.com).

Regional publications in Swedish, include from Stockholm Kristdemokraten (www.kristdemokraten.com) Metro (www.metro.se), from GT (www.gt.se), from Malmo Kvallsposten (www.kvp.se) and SVT Sydnytt (www.svt.se/sydnytt) and from Uppsala Upplands Nyheter (www.upplandsnyheter.se) and Uppsalanytt (www.uppsalanytt.se).

Weeklies: Main Sunday newspapers and weekly publications include for men Café (www.cafe.se), Se och Hör (TV listings), Aftonbladet (www.aftonbladet.se) and Dagens Nyheter (www.dn.se).

Business: In Swedish, Affärsvärlden (www.affarsvarlden.se) is the oldest and most respected business magazine. Other publications include the weekly Ekonominyheterna (http://ekonominyheterna.se) an affiliate of Veckans Affärer, the daily Dagens Industri (http://di.se) and Finanstidningen (owned by the major media organisation Modern Times Group). Fri Kopenskap (www.fri-kopenskap.se) and Privata Affarer (www.privataaffarer.se) are published in Stockholm.

Periodicals: These include Galago (on culture), Grönköpings Veckoblad (www.gronkoping.nu) a literary magazine Moderna, Slitz (www.slitz.se) is a magazine for men. Two major women's magazine include Amelia (www.amelia.se), published fortnightly, which is Sweden's most popular and Vecko Revyn (www.veckorevyn.com) is a tabloid style publication.

Broadcasting

All broadcasting is overseen by Granskningsnamnden (Swedish Broadcasting Commission). State broadcasting is provided by Sveriges Television and Radio.

Radio: There are four national radio stations provided by Sveriges Radio (www.sr.se), with news broadcasts provided in 14 foreign languages. External services can by accessed via short wave, or on-demand through the internet, which also has archived and live transmissions. There are around commercial 100 radio stations some of which have drawn together to produce near-national networks. The largest stations and networks include Rix FM (www.rixfm.com), NRJ (www.nrj.se), Mix Megapol (www.mixmegapol.com) and Radio Match (www.radiomatch.com).

Television: All Swedish television will be provided by digital signals by 2008. Most homes have cable or satellite reception with dozens of channels on offer.

Sveriges Television (svt.se) has 2 major networks and a 24 hour news channel, as well as special interest programmes via satellite TV. There are four commercial TV channels including TV3 (www.tv3.se), TV4 (www.tv4.se), Kanal 5 (http://kanal5.se) and ZTV (www.ztv.se).

Advertising

Sophisticated and of a high standard, but tends to be expensive. All media are available except state radio and state television. The promotion of alcohol consumption is not allowed (except for light beers) and toys and confectionary during children's television, while tobacco advertising is restricted to the print media only.

Economy

The Swedish economic model, a 'third-way' between capitalism and socialism, was built upon a generous welfare system, a corporatist structure between government, industry and trade unions, and high levels of public sector employment. This was paid for by high rates of marginal income tax, wealth taxes and employer social security contributions. In the 1980s, the weakness of this approach became more apparent, culminating in the recession of 1990–93, when negative economic growth and rapidly increasing unemployment made it unsustainable. The government introduced a number of reforms and an austerity package which stabilised government finances and the economy gradually recovered.

In 2004 a booming export market helped generate a GDP increase of 3.5 per cent. In 2005 trade levelled off, GDP was down to 2.7 per cent growth. 2007 is predicted to bring similar increases of 2.7 per cent. Interest rates meanwhile are at historic lows.

Sweden largely escaped negative fall-out from the recent global market slump. Business investment climbed, with the telecommunications and car industries performing particularly well. Productivity has strengthened. Domestic consumption, supported by low interest rates, low inflation and higher real wages, remained robust.

These healthy figures have added up to notable current account surpluses. Public finances are in good order, with an estimated surplus of 0.7 per cent.

Nevertheless the warning that tempers the praise is that central government must remain in control of and limit the negative effects of long-term funding of welfare payments and pension plans for an ageing population.

Another concern is the rise in unemployment although a host of tax incentives and government policies have been recently announced to try to tackle the increase.

The OECD recommended that unemployment payment schemes should be overhauled and tertiary education shortened.

The IMF urged a streamlining of social security to eliminate disincentives to work, such as relatively high taxes for low earners. Measures such as these are intended to boost employment in general, while increasing the hours worked and overall productivity.

External trade

As a member of the European Union, Sweden operates within a communitywide free trade union, with tariffs sets as a whole, however it does not belong to the European Monetary Union and retains the krona as its currency. Internationally, the EU has free trade agreements with a number of nations and trading blocs worldwide. Over 50 per cent of all exports are traded with the EU.

Foreign trade accounts for 85 per cent of all trade and exports provide 45 per cent of GDP, of which, natural resources, forestry, mining and hydroelectric power provides 30 per cent; manufacturing, particularly of globally brands – Saab, Volvo, Ericsson, and AstraZeneca – provides the majority of the remainder.

Imports

Main imports include machinery, petroleum and derivatives, chemicals, vehicles, iron and steel, foodstuffs, consumer goods and clothing.

Main sources: Germany (18.0 per cent total, 2006), Denmark (9.7 per cent), Norway (8.5 per cent).

Exports

Major exports include vehicles, automotive and engineering parts and products (35 per cent of total), pharmaceuticals, paper products, pulp and timber, iron, steel and electricity.

Main destinations: Germany (9.9 per cent total, 2006), US (9.3 per cent), Norway (9.1 per cent).

Agriculture

Farming

Although Sweden is one of the biggest countries in Europe, its arable land amounts to only 2.8 million hectares (ha) constituting about 7 per cent of the total land area. Grain is harvested on 45 per cent of arable land. Agriculture contributes 2 per cent of GDP and employs less than 2 per cent of the total work force.

Dairy products, grains, sugarbeets and potatoes are produced. There are 1.7 million cows in the country. Over the past decade, cattle herd numbers have fallen while yields have risen.
Most farms are family concerns, in which the work is done by members of the family. Part-time farming, with income supplemented by other employment (eg forestry), has become a common feature. Restructuring and modernisation of equipment have resulted in fewer but larger farms. Farming is concentrated in the southern regions, where livestock farming predominates.
Sweden's adherence to the EU's Common Agricultural Policy (CAP) has brought some regulation of agriculture. Agricultural support policies have been adjusted to CAP, including production quotas and increased export subsidies. Import licences are required for certain agricultural commodities.
Fundamental reform to the CAP was introduced on 1 January 2005 in Sweden. The subsidies paid on farm output, which tended to benefit large farms and encourage overproduction, were replaced by single farm payments not conditional on production. This is expected to reward farms that provide and maintain a healthy environment, food safety and animal welfare standards. The changes are also intended to encourage market conscious production and cut the cost of CAP to the EU taxpayer.
Crop production in 2005 included: 5,059,900 tonnes (t) cereals in total, 2,250,100t wheat, 1,586,700t barley, 746,900t oats, 950,500t potatoes, 66,880t pulses, 20,086t tomatoes, 81,646t oilcrops, 2,400,000t sugar beet, 19,340t apples, 33,598t fruit in total, 310,249t vegetables in total. Livestock production included: 553,750t meat in total, 142,400t beef, 294,500t pig-meat, 18,500t game meat, 3,800t lamb and goat meat, 93,150t poultry, 92,300t eggs, 3,229,200t milk, 3,400t honey, 10,200t cattle hides, 2,160t sheepskins.

Fishing

The Swedish market for seafood is typically over 150,000 tonnes annually calculated on the basis of product weight. Estimated output from the domestic seafood processing sector amounts to around 85,000 tonnes per year. About 75 per cent of this amount is for the home market with marinated herring the most important product. Over half of the fishing industry is located in western Sweden. In addition to coastal and deep-sea fishing around the western coast, Sweden has an abundance of natural lakes, which can provide enough fish to meet domestic needs.
Most fish imports are from Norway and Denmark, which together typically account for 75 per cent of total Swedish imports, indicating the importance of the Scandinavian link in its seafood industry.
As the EU presses for radical reform to its Common Fisheries Policy (CFP), Sweden is expected to support its principles based on the ecosystem approach.
In 2004, the total marine fish catch was 261,520 tonnes and the total crustacean catch was 3,479 tonnes.

Forestry

Forest and other wooded land accounts for nearly 75 per cent of the land area, with forest cover estimated at 27.1 million hectares (ha). Approximately 23 million ha of forest area is available for wood supply.
The forest industry and forestry account for more than 4 per cent of Sweden's GDP, 12 per cent of industrial employment and 15 per cent of Sweden's exports. Sweden's pulp and paper industry is the third-largest in Europe after Germany and Finland. About one-third of Sweden's wood pulp and over half its paper and board are exported. Sweden accounts for more than 13 per cent of paper demand in the EU.
Following large scale divestiture, 52 per cent of forest land is owned privately, 24 per cent is owned by the state (primarily through Sveaskog AB) and 24 per cent through commercial companies.
Exports of forest material in 2004 amounted to US$12.9 billion, while imports amounted to US$2.2 billion.
Production in 2004 included 67,300,00 million cubic metres (cum) roundwood, 61,400,000cum industrial roundwood, 16,900,000cum sawnwood, 35,400,000cum sawlogs and veneers, 25,500,000cum pulpwood, 681,000cum wood-based panels, 5,900,000cum wood fuel; 11,589,000 tonnes (t) paper and paperboard (including 2,649,000t newsprint), 3,033,000t printing and writing paper, 12,464,000t paper pulp, 1,500,000t recovered paper.

Industry and manufacturing

The powerful industrial sector contributes 29 per cent of GDP and accounts for 75 per cent of all exports. It is a key reason why the Swedish people have one of the highest standards of living in the world.
Industrial strength was traditionally based on extensive reserves of iron, timber and the rivers and lakes that provided cheap energy, although in recent years hi-tech production has increased in significance. With such a small domestic market, industry has always had to look overseas for survival and it has profited from the development of a mature export culture.
The state is gradually decreasing its ownership in firms under its control. The government is committed to ending state subsidies for inefficient industries. As a result of this policy, traditional sectors, such as shipyards and the textile industry, have virtually ceased to exist. In other traditional industries, there has been drastic rationalisation and concentration on narrow segments of the market.
The industrial sector is based largely on indigenous resources (iron ore, timber and water-power). Major industries include motor vehicles, food processing, chemicals, iron and steel, transportation equipment, electrical and electronic equipment and forestry products. Sweden's industrial structure tends to be centred on large, capital-intensive companies, due to the nature of tax, social security and labour market regulations, which do not favour smaller firms.
Engineering is Sweden's main industrial sector, accounting for around a third of industrial output and for a similar proportion of exports. The country's main engineering companies include Ericsson, Electrolux, Volvo (owned by Ford), SKF, Saab, Scania and Sandvik. Manufacturing employs approximately 30 per cent of the workforce.
The Organisation for Economic Co-operation and Development (OECD) recently named Sweden as one of the leading countries in the Internet and other information technology (IT) markets, along with the US and Finland. In the same month, Sweden topped the International Data Corporation's (IDC) Information Society Index of 55 countries in the IT sector. IT remains an important contributor to the economy. Internet companies in Sweden are managing to survive the burst of the 'dotcom' bubble and the country is at the forefront of the development of mobile telephone Internet technology. Sweden is also beginning to lead the way in the biotechnology sector and has more biotech companies per capita than any other country.
Timber production accounts for just over a fifth of industrial output. Sweden has a large forestry sector supplying raw materials to industry and for export. With 57 per cent of the land area covered in forest, Sweden has the largest timber reserves in Western Europe.
Despite all its strengths, in 2005 a dark cloud formed over Swedish manufacturing. 10,000 workers were victims of redundancies, out of a total of 700,000. Jobs have been lost to countries with lower labour costs such as Asia and Eastern Europe. Another 5,000-8,000 job losses are expected to be announced next year. Business taxes are considered too high and Foreign Direct Investment (FDI) has dropped to zero this year.

Tourism
Tourism is an important part of the growing service sector in Sweden, with the industry accounting for 2.7 per cent of Sweden's GDP. Tourist arrivals numbered 10.4 million in 2004, a significant improvement on the previous year. Norway and Germany are the most frequent visitors. 100,000 people are employed in the industry, comprising 2.4 per cent of the workforce.

Mining
The mining sector typically accounts for 9 per cent of GDP and employs 0.5 per cent of the industrial workforce.
Sweden is rich in mineral deposits, the most important of which are iron ore, zinc, lead, copper, silver and pyrites. There are also large deposits of uranium, exploitation of which has been held back by environmental and political objections. Swedish companies focus on making high quality speciality iron and steel.
Sweden's share of total world iron ore output comes to around 2 per cent, making Sweden one of the largest iron ore exporters in Europe. Sweden's shares of the Western world's production of copper, lead and zinc concentrates amount to 1 per cent, 3.7 per cent and 3.3 per cent, respectively.

Hydrocarbons
Sweden is poor in hydrocarbon resources and has limited reserves. As a result, oil represents a large proportion of total Swedish imports. Swedish refineries have an annual capacity of 20 million tonnes. The largest, Scanraff, north of Göteborg on the west coast, has a capacity of over 200,000 barrels per day (bpd). Natural gas is imported in small quantities through a pipeline from Denmark across the Baltic Straits and is used in southern Sweden. In 2004 consumption of natural gas reached 0.8 billion cubic metres. Consumption of coal reached 2.4 million tonnes oil equivalent in the same year.

Energy
The Swedish are among the highest individual electricity consumers in the world. The government began a seven-year programme in 1997 to stimulate energy saving and development of alternative fuels in readiness for the controversial shutdown of the country's nuclear power industry. Currently nuclear power accounts for 50 per cent of electrical energy. In 1999, the Swedish government won legal backing for plans to close the first of the country's 12 nuclear reactors, heralding the dismantling of the nuclear industry. Unit one of the Barseback reactor closed in 1999; the closure of unit two followed in 2005. Sweden's remaining ten plants are expected to be shut down between 2012-2025.
Sweden has abundant renewable resources such as biofuels, water and wind power. There are over 200 major hydropower plants (more than 10 MW) and 2,000 smaller ones. Most hydroelectric plants are sited on the main northern rivers. Hydropower and biofuels combined generate 40 per cent of the nation's energy. Imported oil similarly provides 40 per cent of energy, with nuclear supplying the remaining 20 per cent. Manufacturing and district heating systems are replacing oil use with biofuels and electricity.

Financial markets
Stock exchange
Sweden's stock exchange was restructured in 2001 in an attempt to raise its profile on the international markets. Formally known as the Stockholm Exchange, it rebranded itself as the Stockholmsbörsen. In December 2001, the Stockholmsbörsen, which handled stocks and stock derivative trading, merged with OM Fixed Income Exchange, which deals in fixed income trading. The exchange is part of Norex, which comprises the stock exchanges of Copenhagen, Oslo, Stockholm and Iceland.
There are over 300 companies listed on the Stockholmsbörsen. Ericsson, the major mobile phone manufacturer, has market capitalisation of one-third of the value of all quoted companies and 28 per cent of share trading.

Banking and insurance
Liberalisation and increased openness has boosted the competitiveness of the Swedish financial sector. There have been serveral mergers between banking and insurance firms. There is a predominance of large corporations in the sector. More than 70 per cent of people in this sector are employed by firms with a payroll of more than 200.
Central bank
Sveriges Riksbank
Main financial centre
Stockholm

Time
GMT plus one hour (daylight saving, late March to late October, GMT plus two hours)

Geography
Sweden is situated in northern Europe. It occupies about 66 per cent of the Scandinavian peninsula and is bordered by Finland to the north-east and Norway to the west. Sweden has a long coastline, with the Baltic Sea and the Gulf of Bothnia to the east and the Skagerrak and Kattegat to the south-west.
Approximately 15 per cent of Sweden lies north of the Arctic Circle. There are thousands of lakes and islands. Around 54 per cent of the country is covered in coniferous forests. Agricultural land is located in the southern plains, where the population is most concentrated. The central region comprises lowlands. The west bordering Norway is mountainous, from which numerous rivers drain into the Gulf of Bothnia; the highest point in Sweden at 2,111m is Mount Kebnekaise.
Hemisphere
Northern

Climate
Because of the Atlantic gulf stream, Sweden has a milder climate than some other regions in the same latitude. The average winter temperature in the north, where there is always snow from December to March, is minus 13 degrees Celsius (C), in central Sweden minus 3 degrees C and in the south minus 1 degree C. In summer average temperatures are 13 degrees C in the north, 18 degrees C in central Sweden and 17 degrees C in the south.

Dress codes
Clothing to suit the climate is vital because of the extremes. Heavy coats, warm boots, gloves and ear protection are required in winter and light clothing in summer.
Swedes can be informal in business attire, but suits are worn at business meetings and for social events in the evening.

Entry requirements
Passports
Required by all, except nationals of countries which are signatories of the Schengen Accords, which includes most EU/EEA member states, who may visit on national IDs.
Visa
Required by all, except nationals of EU countries, Iceland, Norway, North America, Australasia and Japan, for up to three months. For those requiring a visa, a Schengen visa covers all entry needs; for business trips, an invitation from a business contact in Sweden and proof of occupation and travel funds should be included when applying. A Schengen visa application (offered in several languages) can be downloaded from http://europa.eu/abc/travel/ see 'documents you will need'.
Currency advice/regulations
There are no restrictions on the import and export of local or foreign currencies.
Customs
Personal items are duty-free.There are no duties levied on alcohol and tobacco between EU member states, providing amounts imported are for personal consumption.

Health (for visitors)
Nationals of the European Economic Area (EEA) countries and Switzerland can access reduced cost and sometimes free medical treatment using a European Health Insurance Card (EHIC) while visiting the EEA. Exceptions include nationals of the 10 countries which joined the EU in 2004, whose EHIC is not valid in Switzerland. Applications for the EHIC should be made before travelling.
Mandatory precautions
Vaccination certificates not required unless travelling from an infected area.
Advisable precautions
Up-to-date tetanus and polio immunisations are recommended.

Hotels
There is no official rating system in operation. There is a shortage of accommodation in major cities so reservations should be made well in advance.

Public holidays (national)
Fixed dates
1 Jan (New Year's Day), 6 Jan (Epiphany), 1 May (Labour Day), 6 June (National Day), 24–26 Dec (Christmas).
Variable dates
Good Friday, Easter Monday, Ascension Day, Whit Monday, Midsummer Holiday (fourth Sat in Jun), All Saints' Day (first Sat in Nov).

Working hours
Banking
Mon–Fri: 0930–1500 (larger branches open longer).
Business
Mon–Fri: 0830–1700 (often closed one hour earlier in summer).
Government
Mon–Fri 0900–1700.
Shops
Mon–Fri: 0900–1800 (closed 1400 or 1600 on Sat).

Telecommunications
Telephone/fax
Direct dialling throughout country and to most parts of the world. Shops displaying 'TELE' or 'TELEBUTIK' sign offer cheap international phone services (also telex and telefax).
There are some 5.7 million fixed telephone lines in Sweden. More people are switching to ISDN lines (of which there were 270,000), or exclusively using mobile phones.
Postal services
Good service. Stamps are available at most newspaper kiosks and tobacconists. The main post office in Stockholm opens daily from 0800–1800. Approximately 95 per cent of first class letters are delivered overnight. In 1993 Sweden became the first country in the world to completely liberalise the postal market. However, the state-owned postal service, Posten still accounts for 95 per cent of the total market for letters. The main competitor is City Mail, which operates mainly in the three largest cities.
Mobile/cell phones
Pay-as-you-go phones are extremely popular, and make up 44 per cent of all subscriptions. Telia accounts for 51 per cent of all mobile phone subscriptions, followed by Tele2 with 33 per cent and Europolitan with 16 per cent.
Internet/e-mail
The largest ISP's on the Swedish market are Telia, Tele2, Telenordia and Spray/BIP, which together control 77 per cent of the market.

Electricity supply
220V AC

Social customs/useful tips
Swedes appreciate punctuality. A gift of flowers is usual when visiting a business partner's home for the first time. Guests should not start drinking before their hosts have proposed their health.
Think twice before refusing to go to a sauna with a host, since such an invitation is seen as a gesture of confidence and friendship by your host. Business meetings are sometimes conducted in saunas.

Security
Sweden has very low rates of violent crime, but some districts in the major cities should be avoided, particularly at night and particularly by women. Car burglaries and drugs-related crimes are increasing.

Getting there
Air
National airline: Scandinavian Airlines System (SAS).
International airport/s: Stockholm-Arlanda (ARN), 45km north of capital; Stockholm-Västerås (VST), 5km east of Västerås; Göteborg-Landvetter (GOT), 25km east of Göteborg; Malmö-Sturup (MMX), 30km east of Malmö.
Airport tax: None
Surface
Road: Sweden can be reached by road from Denmark via the Øresund tunnel and bridge link between Copenhagen and Malmö. There is also road access from Norway and Finland.
Rail: Statens Jarnvagar (SJ) (State Railways) is the major rail company in Sweden. It runs international high-speed trains between either Stockholm/Göteborg-Copenhagen (Denmark) – journey time five hours/3.30 hours; Stockholm-Oslo – journey time 4.45 hours. These services offer business class accommodation.
Overnight trains with sleeping coaches are available between Berlin (Germany) and Malmö.
Water: There are ferry links with ports in northern and eastern Europe.

Getting about
National transport
Air: There are daily flights connecting all main towns, some by SAS and others by small local airlines.
Road: Sweden has a well-developed and maintained road network totalling about 420,000km, two-thirds of which are privately-managed, including unpaved forestry roads. Most private roads are open to the public. At least 95 per cent of traffic is carried by the national and municipal roads. There are around 20,000km of motorways.
Dipped headlights during the day are mandatory. The roads are snow-bound or icy during the winter months, when appropriate tyres are a requirement.
Buses: Efficient bus service, mainly controlled by the Statens Jarnvagar (SJ) (State Railways). Services integrated with rail service.
Rail: There are good, reliable rail links between most major cities and towns, especially in the south. Seats on express services must be booked in advance.
Water: There is an extensive ferry network in and around Sweden.
City transport
Taxis: Available in all major towns. If you order a taxi in advance there is an extra charge. Some taxi companies offer flat rates for travel within urban areas, and others have special fares for women travelling alone at night.
Gratuities for taxis are around 10 per cent.
Buses, trams & metro: All rail, bus and tram services have a unified ticketing system. Books of 20 travel coupons are available for purchase at Press Agency news-stands.
A city transfer service links Arland and Västerås airports with Stockholm city centre, with a journey time of about 40 minutes. The journey time from Västerås airport is around 75 minutes.
Trams run in the southern parts of Bromma and Lidingö.
Metro: The Tunnelbana serves many districts of Stockholm, with 100 stations marked by a blue T sign. The extended rail service includes outlying suburbs.
Car hire
Available at all airports and in most towns and cities.

BUSINESS DIRECTORY
The addresses listed below are a selection only. While World of Information makes every endeavour to check these addresses, we cannot guarantee that changes have not been made, especially

to telephone numbers and area codes. We would welcome any corrections.

Telephone area codes

The international direct dialling code (IDD) for Sweden is +46, followed by area code and subscriber's number:
Gävle26Malmö40
Göteborg31Norrköping11
Helsingborg42Oxelösund155
Jönköping36Stockholm8
Karlskrona455Sundsvall60
Karlstad54Umeå90
Luleå920Uppsala18

Useful telephone numbers

Police, fire and ambulance: 112

Chambers of Commerce

American Chamber of Commerce in Sweden, 3 Jakobs Torg, PO Box 16050, 10321 Stockholm (tel: 5061-2610; fax: 5061-2910; e-mail: amcham@chamber.se).

British Swedish Chamber of Commerce, 3 Jakobs Torg, PO Box 16050, 10321 Stockholm (tel: 5061-2617; fax: 5061-2915; e-mail: bscc@chamber.se).

Central Sweden Chamber of Commerce, 1 Linnévägen, PO Box 296, 80104 Gävle (tel: 662-080; fax: 662-099; e-mail: chamber@mhk.cci.se).

East Sweden Chamber of Commerce, 3 Nya Rådstugugatan, 60224 Norrköping (tel: 28-5030; fax: 13-7719; e-mail: info@east.cci.se).

Jönköping Chamber of Commerce, 11 Elmiavägen, 55454 Jönköping (tel: 301-430; fax: 129-579; e-mail: jncci@jn.wtc.se).

Mid Sweden Chambe of Commerce, 26 Kyrkogatan, 85232 Sundsvall (tel: 171-880; fax: 618-640; e-mail: sdl@mid-chamber.cci.se).

Southern Sweden Chamber of Commerce and Industry, 2 Skeppsbron, 21120 Malmö (tel: 690-2400; fax: 690-2490; e-mail: info@handelskammaaren.com).

Stockholm Chamber of Commerce, 9 Västra Trädsgårdsgatan, PO Box 16050, 10321 Stockholm (tel: 5551-0000; fax: 5663-1635; e-mail: info@chamber.se).

Swedish Chambers of Commerce, 9 Västra Trädsgårdsgatan, PO Box 16050, 10321 Stockholm (tel: 5551-0036; fax: 5663-1637; e-mail: info@chamber.se).

Uppsala Chamber of Commerce, Uppsala Science Park, 75183 Uppsala (tel: 502-950; fax: 554-458; e-mail: info@uppsala.chamber.se).

Wermland Chamber of Commerce, 6 Södra Kyrkogatan, 65224 Karlstad (tel: 221-480; fax: 221-490; e-mail: info@wermland.cci.se).

Western Sweden Chamber of Commerce and Industry, 18 Mässens Gata, PO Box 5253, 40225 Göteborg (tel: 835-900; fax: 835-936; e-mail: info@handelskammaren.net).

Banking

Götabanken, Sveavägen 14, 10377 Stockholm (tel: 790-4000) and Hamngatan 16, 40509 Gothenburg (tel: 625-000).

Handelsbanken, 20540 Malmö (tel: 245-000; fax: 236-134).

Nordea, Västra Trädgårdsgatan 17, 5 tr, 10571 Stockholm (tel: 614-8558; fax: 614-7530).

Skandinaviska Enskilda Banken, Kungsträdgårdsgatan 8, 10640 Stockholm (tel: 763-5000; fax: 242-394).

Svenska Bankforeningen (Swedish bankers' association), Regeringsgatan 42, Box 7603, 10394 Stockholm (tel: 243-300).

Svenska Handelsbanken, Kungsträdgårdog 2, 10670 Stockholm (tel: 701-1000; fax: 611-5071).

Svenska Sparbanksforeningen (Swedish savings banks' association), Drottninggatan 29, Box 16426, 10327 Stockholm (tel: 572-000).

SwedBank, Brunkebergstorg 8, 10534 Stockholm (tel: 790-1000).

Central bank

Sveriges Riksbank, Brunkebergstorg 11, SE-103 37 Stockholm (tel: 787-0000; fax: 210-531; e-mail: registratorn@riksbank.se).

Travel information

Kungliga Automobil Klubben (KAK), Blasieholmshamnen 6, 11148 Stockholm (tel: 678-0055; fax: 678-0068; e-mail: info@kak.se).

SJ AB (State Railways), 105 50 Stockholm (tel: 762 20 00; fax: 762 24 24; website: www.sj.se); on-line booking at www.swedenbooking.com).

Svenska Turistföreningen (Swedish Tourist Association), Stureplan 4, PO Box 25, 10120 Stockholm (tel: 463-2100; fax: 678-1958; info@stfturist.se).

Svensk Turism AB, Kammakargatan 39, Box 1158, 11181 Stockholm (tel: 762-7400; e-mail: info@svenskturism.se).

Scandinavian Airlines System (SAS), Frösundaviks Allé 1, 19587 Stockholm (tel: 797-0000; fax: 797-1603).

National tourist organisation offices

VisitSweden (The Swedish Travel and Tourism Council), Sveavögen 21, Box 3030, 103 61 Stockholm (tel: 789-1000; fax: 789-1031; e-mail: reception@visitsweden.com).

Ministries

All ministries in Sweden have the same address: S-10333 Stockholm (tel: 405-1000; fax: 723-1171).

Invest in Sweden Agency, S-10338 Stockholm (tel: 676-8876/0; fax: 676-8888).

National Board of Forestry, S-55183 Jönköping (tel: 155-600; fax: 190-740).

National Board of Trade, Box 1209, S-11182 Stockholm (tel: 791-0500; fax: 200-324).

National Electrical Safety Board, Box 1371, S-11193 Stockholm (tel: 453-9700; fax: 453-9710).

National Maritime Administration, S-60178 Norrköping (tel: 191-000; fax: 101-949).

National Post and Telecom Agency, Box 5398, S-10249 Stockholm (tel: 678-5500; fax: 678-5505).

Statistics Sweden, Karlavägen 100, S-11581 Stockholm (tel: 783-4000; fax: 661-5261).

Swedish Board of Agriculture, S-55182 Jönköping (tel: 155-000; fax: 190-546).

Swedish Board of Customs, Box 2267, S-10317 Stockholm (tel: 789-7300; fax: 208-012).

Swedish Civil Aviation Administration, S-60179 Norrköping (tel: 192-000; fax: 192-575).

Swedish Board for Investment and Technical Support, BITS, Box 7837, S-10398 Stockholm (tel: 678-5000; fax: 678-5050).

Swedish National Board of Fisheries, Lilla Bommen 6, S-40126 Göteborg (tel: 630-300; fax: 156-577).

Swedish National Board for Industrial and Technical Development (NUTEK), S-11786 Stockholm (tel: 681-9100; fax: 196-826).

Swedish National Road Administration, S-78187 Borlänge (tel: 75-000; fax: 84-640).

Swedish Nuclear Power Inspectorate, S-10658 Stockholm (tel: 698-8400; fax: 661-9086).

Swedish Patent Office, Box 5055, S-10242 Stockholm (tel: 782-2500; fax: 666-0286).

Swedish Standards Institution, Box 3295, S-10366 Stockholm (tel: 613-5200; fax: 411-7035).

Swedish Trade Council, PO Box 5513, S-11485 Stockholm (tel: 783-8500; fax: 662-9093).

Other useful addresses

British Embassy, Skarpögatan 6-8, Box 27819, 11593 Stockholm (tel:

671-9000; fax: 662-9989 (commercial section).

Federation of Commercial Agents of Sweden, Hantverkargatan 46, 11221 Stockholm (tel: 540-975).

Federation of Commercial Agents of Sweden, Western Division, Box 36059, 40013 Göteborg (tel: 192-045).

Federation of Swedish Industries, Storgatan 19, 11485 Stockholm (tel: 783-8000; fax: 662-3595).

Federation of Swedish Wholesalers and Importers, Grevgatan 34, Box 5512, 11485 Stockholm (tel: 635-280).

Handels Arbetsgivareorg (HAO) (commercial employers' confederation), Box 1720, 11187 Stockholm (tel: 762-7700).

Kungl Automobil Klubben (KAK) (Royal Automobile Club), S. Blasieholmshamnen 6, S-11148 Stockholm (tel: 678-0055; fax: 678- 0068).

Motormännens Riksförbund (Automobile Association), Sturegatan 32, PO Box 5855, 10248 Stockholm 5 (tel: 782-3800; fax: 666-0371).

SACO/SR (confederation of professional associations), Box 2206, 10315 Stockholm (tel: 225-200).

Sollentunamassan (organisers of trade fairs), Box 174, 19123 Sollentuna (tel: 925-900; fax: 929-774).

Stockholmsbörsen, SE-10578 Stockholm (tel: 405-6000; fax: 405-6001).

Stockholm Technical Fair (Stockholmsmassan AB), Alvsjo, 12580 Stockholm (tel: 749-4100; fax: 992-044).

Svenska Arbetsgivareforeningen (employers' confederation), Sodra Blasieholmshammen 4A, 10-330 Stockholm (tel: 762-6000; fax: 762-6290).

Sveriges Exportrad (Swedish Trade Council), PO Box 5513, 11485 Stockholm (tel: 783-8500; fax: 663-6706).

Swedish Embassy (USA), Suite 900, 1501 M Street, NW, Washington DC 20005 (tel: (+1-202) 467-2600; fax: (+1-202) 467-2699; e-mail: ambassaden.washington@foreign.ministry.se).

Swedish Institute, Box 7434, 10391 Stockholm (tel: 789-2000).

Swedish Trade Fair Foundation (Svenska Massan), Skanegatan 26, Box 5222, 40224 Göteborg (tel: 109-100; fax: 160-330).

TCO (central organisation of salaried employees), Box 5252, 10245 Stockholm (tel: 782-9100).

Tidningarnas Telegrambyrå (news agency), Kungsholmstorg 5, 10512 Stockholm (tel: 132-600; fax: 515-377).

Other news agencies: TT (Tidnignarnas Telegrambyrå) 105 12 Stockholm, (tel: 692-2600; fax: 692-2855; email: redaktionen@tt.se). TT is a private independent agency.

Internet sites

Export directory: http://www.swedishtrade.se/sed

Government of Sweden: http://www.sweden.gov.se

Invest in Sweden Agency: http://www.isa.se/

Statistics Sweden: http://www.scb.se/eng/index.asp

Swedish Statistics network: http://www.svenskstatistik.net/eng/index.htm

Virtual Sweden: http://www.sweden.se

Visit Sweden: http://www.visit-sweden.com

Switzerland

KEY FACTS

Official name: Schweizerische Eidgenossenschaft (German); Confédération Suisse (French); Confederazione Svizzera (Italian) (Swiss Confederation)

Head of State: Federal President Micheline Calmy-Rey (for 2007) (presidency rotates annually among ministers)

Head of government: Federal President Micheline Calmy-Rey

Ruling party: Four-party coalition led by the Schweizerische Volkspartei (SVP) (Swiss People's Party) (since 1999; re-elected 2003); with Sozialdemokratische Partei der Schweiz (SPS) (Social Democrat Party of Switzerland), the Freisinnig-Demokratische Partei der Schweiz (FDP) (Freethinking-Democratic Party of Switzerland) and the Christlich-Demokratische Volkspartei (CVP) (Christian Democratic People's Party)

Area: 41,293 square km

Population: 7.30 million (2007)*

Capital: Bern (German)/Berne (French)

Official language: German, French, Italian and Romansch

Currency: Swiss franc (Swf) = 100 centimes

Exchange rate: Swf1.02 per US$ (Jul 2008)

GDP per capita: US$58,084 (2007)*

GDP real growth: 3.10% (2007)

Labour force: 3.81 million (2006)*

Unemployment: 2.50% (2007)

Inflation: 0.80% (2007)

Balance of trade: US$4.84 billion (2005)

Foreign debt: US$839.55 billion (2004)

Visitor numbers: 7.86 million (2006)*

* estimated figure

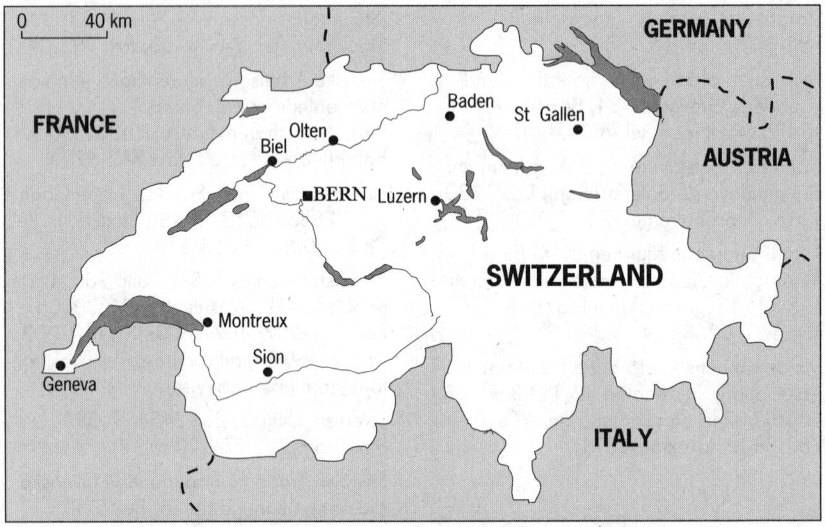

The Swiss were shocked in 2008 when two of their venerable banks – Credit Suisse and UBS – were forced into making heavy writedowns on their exposure to risky US credit. This was on top of the earlier scandal generated by neighbouring Liechtenstein's problems with the German tax authorities when Switzerland's Vontobel private bank became embroiled in the bank secrecy issue. Generally, though, the strengthening of the Swiss franc was once again pulling in the depositors. Some 12 per cent of Switzerland's GDP comes from the financial services sector.

According to the Paris based Organisation for Economic Co-operation and Development (OECD), Switzerland has been enjoying a vigorous economic expansion, which has benefited from buoyant financial market activity, strong foreign demand and, until recently, a depreciating currency. In the view of the OECD, some of the drivers of this growth may prove to be temporary, although large immigration flows, which have contributed to substantial job creation, are likely to make a longer-lasting contribution to the expansion of potential output. Supported by high levels of employment, GDP per capita is still among the highest in the OECD at US$58,034 in 2007. Yet economy-wide productivity is well below levels observed in leading countries, reflecting relatively weak productivity performance in sectors not exposed to international competition. While the general government's budget has swung into surplus in recent years, strong spending growth in social entitlement programmes poses risks for the capacity of fiscal policy to contribute to enhancing prosperity.

Switzerland has had a long-standing surplus on its current account. But over the past 15 years that surplus has surged to levels unmatched by nearly any other OECD country at any point. The OECD's key recommendation is that the authorities should prepare for a possible sharp increase in the value of the Swiss franc if and when investors engaged in the 'carry trade' unwind their positions. To that end they should examine labour, capital and product markets with a view to ensuring they are as flexible as possible and that factors are as mobile as possible, both geographically and sectorally. This will allow any necessary adjustment to a higher exchange rate to be smoothly accommodated.

The OECD also notes that Switzerland's fiscal institutions have been successful in keeping the overall level of taxation and spending at a moderate level, and the use of budget rules at different levels of government has improved the conduct of fiscal policy. However, in recent years the increase in spending, particularly on social programmes, has been considerable. Reform of these programmes is needed not only to guarantee budgetary sustainability, but also to free up public resources that can be put to better use in promoting growth. Retaining and reintegrating people with health problems in the workplace is called for in order to cope with the pressures on the labour supply that population ageing will create. Switzerland's tax system, in the view of the OECD, could be simplified in order to reduce the administrative burden placed on firms, especially small- and medium-sized enterprises and start-ups. In addition, tax-induced distortions to labour and capital allocation decisions should be eliminated in order to increase productivity growth.

Switzerland has not found it easy to adapt to a rapidly changing Europe. Unable to isolate itself from developments on the continent, it could not ignore wider trends towards globalisation. The nature and form of its relations with the European Union (EU) remained unresolved.

Politics by referenda

In a unique arrangement, Switzerland's government is not determined by a parliamentary majority but according to a four-party power-sharing arrangement established in 1959, known as the 'magic formula'. Any law can be overturned in a referendum, which must take place if, within three months, 50,000 voters sign a petition demanding one. Referenda can also take place if 100,000 voters sign a petition for a change to the constitution. To consider such matters and to vote on cantonal and communal issues, Swiss go to the polls a wearying four times a year. Switzerland is the world refrenda champion, accounting for more than half of all national referenda held globally. A referendum, held in June 2008, whereby Swiss communes could vote to limit naturalisation of foreigners in individual cases, was rejected.

Differences between the four main political parties, as well as frequent calls for referenda, add to difficulties in getting legislation passed. The SVP again won the highest number of votes (29 per cent) in the October 2007 general elections, but with no clear winner a coalition of four parties was formed. The SVP withdrew from the coalition after their leader, Christoph Blocher, was ousted from the Federal Council (cabinet) and replaced by Eveline Widmer-Schlumpf (also of the SVP). In 2008 the SVP gave an ultimatum to Widmer-Schlumpf and Samuel Schmid (another SVP minister) to resign from the federal council or be expelled from the SVP; they declined and remained as government ministers.

Outlook

In an interview with the London *Financial Times* in August 2008, the chairman of the Swiss National Bank (central bank), Jean-Pierre Roth, admitted that the country had not escaped a slow down, but '...we will probably have better economic growth than most off our neighbours because we still have very strong domestic demand...' and Switzerland '...is more globalised than the European economies, so we still benefit a lot from the dynamics of Asia'.

Risk assessment

Politics	Good
Economy	Good
Regional stability	Good

COUNTRY PROFILE

Historical profile

Switzerland was part of the Holy Roman Empire until 1499 when it gained independence. Switzerland's Roman connection remains strong. The Pope is still guarded by a 105-strong Swiss Guard, drawn largely from the Catholic cantons of central Switzerland.

1515 Switzerland declared its neutrality after nearly being defeated by the French and Venetians.

1648 The Peace of Westphalia concluded the Thirty Years' War in Europe and recognised Swiss independence.

1815 The Congress of Vienna restored independence to Switzerland after it had been annexed by France as part of the Napoleonic Empire during 1798–1803. The Congress laid down the principle of the perpetual neutrality of Switzerland.

1874 The modern constitution was inaugurated.

1914–18 Switzerland was neutral during the First World War.

1919–20 The Treaty of Versailles again recognised Switzerland's neutrality. In 1920, the country joined the League of Nations, but did not join its successor, the UN, when it was formed in 1945.

1939–45 Switzerland pursued a policy of neutrality during the Second World War, but refused refuge to Jews trying to escape German-occupied Europe and traded gold with the Nazis. Swiss banks also provided interest free credits to the Axis powers, which enabled Germany to finance its war effort.

1959 Switzerland was a founder member of the European Free Trade Agreement (EFTA).

1971 Women were granted the right to vote.

1986 The Swiss population rejected UN membership in a referendum.

1988 Switzerland's first female minister, Elisabeth Kopp, resigned from her post following accusations that she had violated official secrecy laws by tipping off her husband about an inquiry into his business affairs.

1992 In the referendum on Swiss membership of the European Economic Area (EEA), a free trade agreement between the EU and EFTA, opponents of the pact won with 50.3 per cent of the vote. Switzerland joined the World Bank and IMF.

KEY INDICATORS — Switzerland

	Unit	2003	2004	2005	2006	2007
Population	m	7.33	7.43	7.27	7.29	*7.30
Gross domestic product (GDP)	US$bn	315.23	359.46	366.51	387.98	423.94
GDP per capita	US$	43,000	49,305	50,387	53,245	*58,084
GDP real growth	%	-0.4	1.7	1.9	3.2	3.1
Inflation	%	0.6	0.8	1.2	1.4	0.8
Unemployment	%	3.9	3.4	3.4	3.4	2.5
Exports (fob) (goods)	US$m	100,000	138,164	150,053	167,251	200,109
Imports (cif) (goods)	US$m	96,000	122,617	145,218	162,213	187,076
Balance of trade	US$m	4,000	15,547	4,835	5,038	13,033
Current account	US$m	42,420	42,870	61,417	58,708	72,835
Total reserves minus gold	US$m	47,652.0	55,497.0	36,297.0	38,094.0	44,474.0
Foreign exchange	US$m	45,560.0	53,634.0	35,421.0	37,364.0	43,867.0
Exchange rate	per US$	1.32	1.24	1.25	1.20	1.15

* estimated figure

1998 Swiss banks agreed to a US$1.25 billion settlement with Jewish Holocaust survivors and families.
1999 Ruth Dreifuss became Switzerland's first female president. The Schweizerische Volkspartei (SVP) (Swiss People's Party) won the largest electoral victory for any party in Switzerland for over 80 years.
2001 The national airline, Swissair, went bankrupt.
2002 Switzerland joined the UN. An independent panel of historian concluded Swiss authorities new of the fate of Jewish refugees turned away in 1942 and that Swiss banking bolstered the economy of Nazi Germany, although not enough to have prolonged the Second World War. Abortion, within the first 12 weeks of a pregnancy, was made legal.
2003 In a referendum, nuclear energy was supported as a source of power and a moratorium on building new nuclear power plants was rejected. The SVP won the biggest share of the vote in the October parliamentary elections by increasing its vote to 27.7 per cent (a 5 per cent increase on the 1999 election), winning 55 seats in the 200-member National Council and making it the largest of the four governing parties in the coalition, which gave it extra seat in the cabinet at the expense of the Christlich-Demokratische Volkspartei (CVP) (Christian Democratic People's Party).
2004 Swiss banks began to informed EU tax departments on personal accounts held by EU taxpayers. Stem cell research was agreed, by referendum.
2005 New compliance, banking laws, introduced to curtail money laundering, and the EU-wide decline in personal tax rates led to a reduction in the flow of money into Switzerland's banks.
2006 Genetically modified crops were banned for five years. Tough, new asylum laws were introduced.
2007 Micheline Calmy-Rey was elected president and head of government for 2007. Violence broke out in October in Berne during a parliamentary election campaign of the ruling, anti-immigration party, SVP, when left-wing protesters began hurling rocks and bottles. The SVP went on to win the highest number of votes (29 per cent) in the October general elections. There was no clear winner and a coalition of four parties was formed. The SVP withdrew from the coalition after their leader, Christoph Blocher, was ousted from the Federal Council (cabinet) and replaced by Eveline Widmer-Schlumpf (SVP).
2008 Pascal Couchepin became federal president on 1 January. The SVP gave an ultimatum to Widmer-Schlumpf and Samuel Schmid (also an SVP minister) to resign from the federal council or be expelled from the SVP; she and Schmid remained as government ministers. A referendum, held in June, whereby Swiss communes could vote to limit naturalisation of foreigners in individual cases, was rejected. The SVP expelled Eveline Widmer-Schlumpf and Samuel Schmid from its list of members.

Political structure

Constitution
Switzerland's constitution dates back to 1874 and has been much amended over the years. It unites more than 3,000 communes and 26 cantons and half-cantons in a confederation which devolves considerable powers to local bodies.
Responsibility for determining and administering civil, penal and commercial law, foreign and trade issues, defence, communications, social insurance and energy is reserved for the federal government. The cantons and half-cantons, each of which have their own constitution and government, are responsible for the administration of federal law as well as their own cantonal laws. The communes have local autonomy over roads, local public utilities and the granting of citizenship.
Major issues are frequently decided by referendum. The constitution, or any of the country's federal laws, may only be amended by the passage of a proposal by national referendum. A national referendum may be called if a petition is signed by 50,000 people (on a legislative matter) or 100,000 people (on a constitutional matter). In some cantons, referenda may be necessary to approve all changes in cantonal legislation. The federal government, or its political opponents, may also initiate a referendum on any issue. Voter turnout averages 40–50 per cent. Since the constitution's inception, voters have been asked to approve over 148 amendments.

Form of state
Federal parliamentary democratic republic

The executive
The chief executive organ in the country is the Federal Council, whose seven members each hold a ministerial portfolio, and whose president and vice president are appointed each calendar year on a rotating basis from among its members.

National legislature
The bicameral Federal Assembly is made up of the Bundesversammlung, Assemblée Fédérale (Federal Assembly) consisting of the Standerat, Conseil des Etats, or Consiglio degli Stati (Council of States) with 46 seats elected by Cantons (local administrations) for terms of four years and the Nationalrat, Conseil National, or Consiglio Nazionale (National Council) with 200 seats popularly elected by proportional representation for terms of four years.
Members of the Federal Council are elected, usually for a four-year term, from among members of the Federal Assembly. The Federal Assembly supervises the army, the civil service and the administration of the law as well as electing the Federal Supreme Court, the Federal Tribunal of Insurance and the Federal Council.

Legal system
Customary law marginally influences the civil law system. Individual cantons elect and maintain their own magistracy. Each canton has justices of the peace, District Courts, Labour Courts, Courts for Tenancy, an Appeal Court, a Cassation Court and, for more important cases under penal law, a Jury Court. Apart from military courts, there are just two federal judicial authorities: the Federal Supreme Court and the Federal Tribunal of Insurance.

Last elections
21 October 2007 (parliamentary)
Results: Parliamentary: In parliamentary elections, the Schweizerische Volkspartei (SVP) (Swiss People's party) won 29 per cent of the vote (62 seats out of 200), the Sozialdemokratische Partei der Schweiz (SPS) (Social Democrat Party of Switzerland) 19.5 per cent (43), the Freisinnig-Demokratische Partei der Schweiz (FDP) (Freethinking-Democratic Party of Switzerland) 15.6 per cent (31), the Christlich-Demokratische Volkspartei (CVP) (Christian Democratic People's Party), and the Grüne Partei der Schweiz (GPS) (Green Party of Switzerland), 9.6 per cent (20). Turnout was 48.9 per cent.

Next elections
October 2007 (parliamentary)

Political parties

Ruling party
Four-party coalition led by the Schweizerische Volkspartei (SVP) (Swiss People's Party) (since 1999; re-elected 2003); with Sozialdemokratische Partei der Schweiz (SPS) (Social Democrat Party of Switzerland), the Freisinnig-Demokratische Partei der Schweiz (FDP) (Freethinking-Democratic Party of Switzerland) and the Christlich-Demokratische Volkspartei (CVP) (Christian Democratic People's Party)

Main opposition party
Grüne Partei der Schweiz (GPS) (Green Party of Switzerland)

Population
7.30 million (2007)*
Last census: December 2000: 7,204,055
Population density: 182 inhabitants per square km. Urban population: 67 per cent of the total population (1995–2001).

Annual growth rate: 0.4 per cent 1994–2004 (WHO 2006)
Ethnic make-up
Switzerland is dominated by Germans (65 per cent), French (18 per cent) and Italians (10 per cent). Foreigners comprise 19.7 per cent of the population. In a referendum held in September 2000, the Swiss voted against limiting the proportion of foreigners to 18 per cent.
Religions
Roman Catholic (46 per cent), Protestant (40 per cent).

Education

With no central ministry of education, each of the 26 Swiss cantons (semi-autonomous regions) have overall and exclusive responsibility for education. Private schools exist at the level of vocational secondary school but do not attract federate funding or canton control.
Most cantons set the number of compulsory years for primary schooling at six, some others set it at four or five; for lower secondary school most set the minimum years at three, and some at five or four; whichever cycle is used, overall, compulsory schooling lasts for nine years.
Teaching is given in the language of the canton.
At aged 16, students can go into upper level secondary schools (either private or state-run), which offer general or vocational programmes and last for between three and four years. General secondary education (Matura), offers academic study, preparing a student for university. Technical high schools provide a range of vocational and training programmes.
Typically 85 per cent of students complete upper secondary school.
Switzerland has 12 universities and higher education colleges. There are also a number of science universities and more than 20 polytechnics (Fachhochschulen).
In the 1990s, the cantons began a reform of the educational system to ensure that it provided the best means of maintaining a high degree of educated citizens.
Literacy rate: 99 per cent, adult rate (2003)
Compulsory years: Six to 15.
Enrolment rate: 97 per cent gross primary enrolment of relevant age group (including repeaters); 100 per cent gross secondary enrolment (World Bank).
Pupils per teacher: 19 in primary schools.

Health

Per capita total expenditure on health (2003) was US$3,776; of which per capita government spending was US$2,209, at the international dollar rate, (WHO 2006).
Healthcare services are entirely private and individuals are expected and, in some areas, obliged, to cover themselves with private health insurance policies. Each canton has responsibility for the provision of healthcare. The type of hospital a patient may be admitted to will depend on the level of health insurance the person holds.
HIV/Aids
HIV prevalence: 0.4 per cent aged 15–49 in 2003 (World Bank)
Life expectancy: 81 years, 2004 (WHO 2006)
Fertility rate/Maternal mortality rate: 1.4 births per woman, 2004 (WHO 2006); maternal mortality five per 100,000 live births (World Bank).
Birth rate/Death rate: 9.6 births and 8.8 deaths per 1,000 people (2003)
Child (under 5 years) mortality rate (per 1,000): 4.3 per 1,000 live births (World Bank)
Head of population per physician: 3.61 physicians per 1,000 people, 2002 (WHO 2006)

Welfare

Switzerland's comprehensive social welfare system is funded by the state, by employer contributions and by employee national insurance contributions. It is a legal requirement that all citizens residing for three months or more in Switzerland must take out minimum healthcare insurance.
Unemployment insurance is compulsory and many employees are also insured against accidents at work. Old age, disability and widow(er)s' pensions are paid out of compulsory contributions. The precise arrangements may differ in each canton.
Over 20 per cent of the federal budget is spent on social welfare. Some social security schemes have their own separate budgets.

Main cities

Bern/Berne/Bienne (capital, estimated population 119,250 in 2005), Zürich (332,800), Geneva/Genève (178,034), Basel/Basle (163,186), Lausanne (112,136).

Languages spoken

The national languages are German in central and eastern areas (64 per cent), French in the west (19 per cent) and Italian in the south (8 per cent).
Raeto-Romansch is spoken in the south-east (1 per cent). English is widely spoken.
There are two forms of German spoken. High German, or Hochdeutsch is only spoken in formal situations or used for written work; Swiss-German, or Schwyzertütsch is spoken by all in daily life in German-speaking Switzerland, using different dialects and is incomprehensible to all who speak High German.
Official language/s
German, French, Italian and Romansch

Media

Other news agencies: SDA+ATS (in German) (www.sda.ch).
Swiss Infor (operated by SRG SSR Idée Suisse in nine languages) (www.swissinfo.org).
Press
There is a decentralised press owing to regional variations in language and culture, producing a large number of publications with relatively small circulation. There are more than 600 newspapers in total and nearly 2,000 magazines.
Dailies: About 120 regional newspapers (75 per cent printed in German and 20 per cent in French). The most popular includes, 20 Minutten (www.20min.ch), a free publication with a tabloid style; from Zurich, Blick (www.blick.ch) and Tages Anzeiger (www.tagesanzeiger.ch); from Genéva, Le Temps (www.letemps.ch) and Tribune de Genéva (www.tdg.ch); from Lugano Corriere del Ticino (www.cdt.ch); from Bern Berner Zeitung (www.bauernzeitung.ch); from Lausanne, Le Matin (www.lematin.ch) and from Basel Basler Zeitung (www.baz.ch).
Weeklies: Many dailies have weekend editions including Sonntags Blick, Le Matin Dimanche and Sonntags Zeitung. A Swiss edition of a French magazine is l'Hebdo (www.hebdo.ch) is available in French speaking cantons.
Business: Daily newspapers include Neue Zürcher Zeitung (www.nzz.ch) from Zürich and is of international repute; Cash (www.cash.ch) for finance and Handelzeitung (www.handelszeitung.ch), Agefi (www.agefi.com). Others periodicals include Finanz und Wirtschaft (www.fuw.ch) (twice weekly) Swiss News (www.swissnews.ch) and Bilanz (www.bilanz.ch) (monthlies).
Periodicals: In German, The Panorama Journal (www.panoramajournal.ch) reports on events, sport and life in the Bern area; Der Schweizerische Beobachter (www.beobachter.ch), is a consumer magazine; Nebelspalter (www.nebelspalter.ch), is a satirical magazine; Pro (www.pro-helvetia.ch) is a Swiss Arts Council publication,
Broadcasting
A fee for reception of any radio or television signal is levied by Billag AG (www.billag.ch). The Federal Office of Communications (www.bakom.ch) has overall responsibility for broadcast media. Digital Audio Broadcasting (DAB) was underway in 2007 and expected to be fully implemented nationally within a few years.

The public broadcaster is SRG SSR Idée Suisse (www.srg-ssr.ch), which operates national radio and television stations, broadcasting in Swiss-German (www.drs.ch), French (www.rsr.ch), Italian (www.rtsi.ch) and Rumansch (www.rtr.ch).
Radio: Apart from the national networks provided by SRG SSR Idée Suisse, independent radio stations are typically exclusive to a city or region, including from Bern, Radio BE1 (www.radiobe1.ch), from Zürich, Energy Züri (www.energyzueri.ch) and Radio 24 (www.radio24.ch), and from Basel, Radio 105 (www.105.ch) and Radio X (www.radiox.ch).
SRG SSR Idée Suisse broadcasts an international service in nine languages.
Most radio stations provide services over the internet.
Television: There are over 80 local and regional TV stations providing services for all linguistic populations. Pay-for-view, satellite and cable television are available.

Advertising

The various languages adds to the expense of advertising, which on commercial TV is only allowed at specific times. Newspapers, cinemas and direct mail are widely used, but poster advertising is confined to selected sites. Information can be obtained from the Union Suisse d'Agences-Conseils en Publicité in Zürich. The main advertising media are newspapers and magazines..

Economy

Switzerland is one of the wealthiest countries in the world, with a well developed manufacturing sector as well as a highly skilled labour force, an important tourist industry and banking and insurance sectors.
The services sector dominates the economy with 64 per cent of GDP, followed by industry with 34 per cent and agriculture with 2 per cent. Within the services sector, tourism accounts for 6.3 per cent. Despite not being a member of the European Union (EU), the Swiss economy remains heavily dependent on the economic fortunes of the EU and the euro. Swiss exports are dominated by chemicals and machinery and electronic goods. The EU takes over 65 per cent of Swiss exports (20 per cent to Germany alone) and supplies 76 per cent of imports (over one-third from Germany).
After the wilderness years of the 1990s, the Swiss economy reached a 10-year high in 2000 with a three per cent rise in GDP, the result of robust domestic demand coupled with a strong growth in exports. GDP growth slowed from 1.3 per cent in 2001 to 0.1 per cent in 2002 and slowed even further to -0.4 per cent in 2003. This was due to capacity constraints, particularly a labour shortage, coupled with falls in external demand due to the global slowdown and a restrictive fiscal policy. It crept back up to 1.9 per cent in 2005. Inflation is traditionally low, usually less than one per cent; it reached 1.2 per cent in 2005, largely due to the sharp rise in the price of oil.
Switzerland's GNP is considerably higher than its GDP. The difference is net property income from abroad (interest, profit and rent), which is large because of the very high level of net external assets. This is the result of years of large current account surpluses.
Swiss banking is well known for its 'numbered accounts' and secrecy laws. But new, tougher laws on money laundering have led to a drop in foreign money as Switzerland becomes a less attractive destination for unaccounted-for monies. In June 2004, Switzerland, along with Andorra, Monaco, San Marino and Liechtenstein, agreed to put in place equivalent measures to those to be applied by the EU's member states as regards the taxation of income from savings. These measures, which came into effect in July 2005, have made Swiss banks even less attractive.

External trade

Although Switzerland has consistently rejected EU membership, it is a member of the European Economic Area (EEA), which gives it access into the EU's single market. It has a trade agreement with the EU on a number of measures including trade in processed agricultural goods, customs fraud and taxation.
Foreign trade accounts for almost 80 per cent all trade and exports provide 45 per cent of GDP, of which industry accounts for around 30 per cent. Over 60 per cent of exports are destined for the EU. Precision tools and equipment, pharmaceuticals and chemicals, electrical and electronic goods are important export items, while banking, insurance and tourism provides the greater part of foreign earnings.

Imports

Main imports are machinery, chemicals, vehicles, metals, agricultural produce and textiles.
Main sources: Germany (31.6 per cent total, 2005), Italy (10.5 per cent), France (10.0 per cent), US (5.6 per cent), The Netherlands (4.8 per cent), Austria (4.6 per cent), UK (4.4 per cent),

Exports

Principal exports include non- and electrical machinery, medical instruments, chemicals, pharmaceuticals, clocks and watches, textiles and clothing, metals, jewellery and foodstuffs.
Main destinations: Germany (19.4 per cent total, 2005), US (10.9 per cent), Italy (9.1 per cent), France (8.7 per cent), UK (5.4 per cent), Spain (4.1 per cent)

Agriculture

Farming

The agricultural sector contributes around 2.9 per cent to GDP and employs four per cent of the workforce, with activity concentrated on dairy farming. Agriculture is a state subsidised sector – approximately 75 per cent of a farmer's income is financed by subsidies. There are around 80,000 peasant farms of less than 20 hectares (ha) remaining, and of these barely half provide full-time occupations for their owners. Holdings of over 20ha number around 13,000. The average farm is less than 16ha in size. Pasture land totals some 8,500 square km, equivalent to a fifth of the total land area. A further 11,700 square km is given over to arable land, orchards and vineyards.
Farming is highly mechanised, with one of the highest tractor densities in the world. Farmers have use of large and expensive equipment through machinery syndicates.
Government fixing of minimum prices means that meat, sugar, vegetables and fruit are two or three times more expensive than in neighbouring countries, a situation which international agencies such as the World Trade Organisation are anxious to see rectified. There are protective customs barriers and other duties on imported goods as well as actual import restrictions, so that the domestic market remains highly protected, a significant factor in Switzerland's opposition to EU membership.
Crop production in 2005 included: 1,022,516 tonnes (t) cereals in total, 551,932t wheat, 126,228t maize, 505,150t potatoes, 246,813t barley, 152,000t grapes, 27,500t tomatoes, 26,750t oilcrops, 1,550,000t sugar beets, 263,000t apples, 550,955t fruit in total, 324,500t vegetables in total. Livestock production included: 435,220t meat in total, 134,300t beef, 233,000t pig meat, 5,770t lamb, 58,000t poultry, 34,400t eggs, 3,821,800t milk, 4,200t honey, 19,000t cattle hides, 1,390t sheepskins.

Fishing

Switzerland's fish industry, based on 123,000 hectares of lakes, is insignificant and declining. Untreated industrial and agricultural effluents are polluting fisheries, while canalisation, underground channelling of watercourses and the absence of suitable spawning grounds have contributed to the reduction of fish habitats.
There are more than 50 fish species found in Swiss waters, but only a few have been used by the fishing industry for food. Catches consist for the most part of lake

herring and perch together with various other types of whitefish. Catches of whitefish and perch have steadily declined.
Only around 5 per cent of the fish and fish products consumed within the country are obtained from domestic sources.

Forestry

Forest and other wooded land accounts for nearly a third of the land area, with forest cover estimated at 1.19 million hectares. 90 per cent of the forest area is available for wood supply. 4.5 million cubic metres of wood is produced annually There has been a steady rise in growing stock with afforestation accounting for an annual average increase of 4,000ha of forest covers between 1990 and 2000. More than two-thirds of the forest area is under public ownership.
Domestic consumption is 6.4 million cubic metres. Sensitivity about preserving the scenic environment is high. In light of acid rain damage, particularly in the north-west, as well as increased competition in the sector, the prospects for further growth in production appear limited.
The forest industry has to cope with high labour costs. Although paper production is sufficient to meet domestic demands, the industry is partly dependent on pulp imports. Per capita consumption of forest products remains above the European average.
Exports of forest material in 2004 amounted to US$2.0 billion, while imports amounted to US$2.2 billion.
Production in 2004 included 4,700,000 cubic metres (cum) roundwood, 3,700,000cum industrial roundwood, 1,505,000cum sawnwood, 3,200,000cum sawlogs and veneers, 500,000cum pulpwood, 897,000cum wood-based panels, 1,000,000cum woodfuel; 1,777,000 tonnes (t) paper and paperboard (including 361,000t newsprint), 620,000t printing and writing paper, 260,000t paper pulp, 1,163,000t recovered paper.

Industry and manufacturing

The industrial sector contributes approximately 30 per cent to GDP and employs about 33 per cent of the labour force. The well-developed export-oriented manufacturing sector is centred on the production of finished goods. Traditional industries include machines, tools, pharmaceuticals, textiles, watchmaking, food processing, chemicals and engineering. Among well-known Swiss companies are Nestlé and Novartis. There is an increasing emphasis on specialisation and the development of high technology products. Swiss companies spend 2.9 per cent of GDP on research and development, one of the highest figures in the world.
Switzerland is home to the world's biggest clock and watch industry, which produces about 8 per cent of annual export revenues.

Tourism

Tourism has traditionally been one of Switzerland's most reliable sources of foreign exchange, especially during the winter when the country becomes a popular destination for skiers. Visitor numbers declined in the wake of the 11 September 2001 terrorist attacks in the US and subsequently by the Iraq war and the Sars outbreak in 2003, which discouraged the important US and Japanese markets, but have improved since 2004. Germany continues to be the main source of visitors, followed by the US and the UK. The sector is expected to contribute 6.2 per cent to GDP in 2005.
China has designated Switzerland as an approved destination for its holidaying citizens. Chinese visitors could swell Switzerland's arrival numbers by millions.

Mining

Switzerland is not richly endowed with mineral deposits. Only rock salt and building materials are mined or quarried in significant quantities.

Hydrocarbons

Switzerland has no fossil energy resources apart from a small deposit of natural gas at Finsterwald and is dependent on imports to meet its energy requirements. Around 1.3 per cent of total energy consumption is of fossil fuels. Oil, gas and coal are all imported. Switzerland consumes around 260,000 barrels per day (bpd) of crude and refined oil. Around three billion cubic metres of natural gas are imported. Coal consumption, which is around 100,000 tonnes of oil equivalent, has declined in recent years, largely for environmental reasons.

Energy

Hydroelectricity is Switzerland's only natural energy resource and supplies 12 per cent of total energy requirements. Nuclear energy supplies about 38 per cent. Switzerland is one of Europe's largest per capita users of nuclear fuel and with public support (two referenda in 2003 sanctioned its use) does not intend to decrease its reliance on this form of energy production in the near future.
Switzerland is a net exporter of electricity but a net importer of energy, mainly in the form of petroleum and related products. Dependence on imported oil and gas is declining.

Financial markets

Stock exchange

The SWX Swiss Exchange took steps to internationalise in the late-1990s, with the opening of an overseas office in London in 1999, resulting in 27 per cent of the turnover in Swiss shares being transacted outside the country. In 2000, SWX launched the Virt-X, the first pan-European blue chip bourse, in conjunction with the UK's Tradepoint Financial Services (TFS). The exchange uses the Swiss market's trading platform, trading companies from Europe's leading stock market indices.

Banking and insurance

Switzerland is the world's biggest offshore private banking centre, but banking secrecy laws and a favourable taxation regime are coming under increasing scrutiny in the light of the dormant accounts scandal and the possibility of EU membership. Switzerland is a signatory of a new EU tax agreement, introduced in July 2005 in a number of non-EU countries. Switzerland will impose a withholding tax, up to 35 per cent, to be passed to the tax department of an EU citizen's country, but retaining the anonymity of the saver, instead of informing the relevant EU country about the amount of money in savings accounts and allowing tax to be levied from the home country.
Switzerland has also agreed to supply information on tax fraud, for criminal or civil trials, and notify EU member states about additional malpractices.
Were Switzerland to join the EU its competitive advantage in financial services would almost certainly be reduced.
Banking still remains the largest sector in the canton of Zürich, but the success of these operations lies increasingly with their non-Swiss business.
New banking rules were introduced in January 2003 requiring proof of identity, nationality and date of birth for the ultimate owners of bank accounts opened by financial intermediaries.

Central bank

Swiss National Bank (SNB)

Time

GMT plus one hour (daylight saving, late March to late October, GMT plus two hours)

Geography

Switzerland is a landlocked country bordered by Germany to the north, Austria to the east, Italy to the south and France to the west.
Located high in the Alpine region of western Europe, most of the country's land area is too mountainous to permit any great density of population, which means that most of the country's population reside in the low-lying urban areas. About half of the country's total land area is covered by rock, water or glaciers, or is

forested, and a further quarter is either under grass or cultivation.

Hemisphere
Northern

Climate
Geographic factors mean, inevitably, that Switzerland experiences particularly marked variations in weather. While winters are generally severe, especially at higher altitudes, summers tend to be warmer than in the countries to the north. Low-lying areas are often wet. Zürich is prone to a heavy atmosphere in certain wind conditions. Temperatures range from about minus 1 degrees Celsius (C) to 18 degrees C.

Dress codes
Business attire is formal. Warm clothing is essential from September to May, especially in the higher altitudes.

Entry requirements
Passports
Required by all, valid for three months beyond date of departure.

Visa
Required by all, except nationals of EU/EEA countries, Australasia, North America, Japan and some other countries. Contact the nearest embassy or consulate for details. A business visa for a citizen of a non-exempt country requires a letter of invitation from or evidence of correspondence with a Swiss company presented to the local Swiss embassy.

Currency advice/regulations
There are no restrictions on the import or export of local and foreign currencies.

Customs
Personal effects and gifts up to value of Swf300 are duty-free.

Health (for visitors)
Nationals of the European Economic Area (EEA) countries and Switzerland can access reduced cost and sometimes free medical treatment using a European Health Insurance Card (EHIC) while visiting the EEA. Exceptions include nationals of the 10 countries which joined the EU in 2004 whose EHIC is not valid in Switzerland. Applications for the EHIC should be made before travelling.

Mandatory precautions
Vaccination certificates are not usually required.

Advisable precautions
Medical insurance is advisable as treatment is expensive.

Hotels
Hotels keep a high standard throughout the country, and are classified by the Swiss Hotel Association from one- to five-star. A 15 per cent service is included on bill. Reservations should be made well in advance during the winter holiday season.

Credit cards
All major credit cards are accepted.

Public holidays (national)
Fixed dates
1 Jan (New Year's Day), 1 Aug (National Day), 25 Dec (Christmas).

Variable dates
Good Friday, Easter Monday, Ascension Day, Whit Monday.

Working hours
Banking
Regional variations but generally Mon–Fri: 0830–1630. Money exchange at any airport and larger railway stations daily until 2200.

Business
Mon–Fri: 0800–1200, 1330–1700.

Government
Mon–Fri: 0730–1145, 1330–1800, or 0800–1230, 1315–1730.

Shops
Mon–Fri: 0800–1215, 1330–1830 (in larger cities also during lunch hours but Mon morning often closed); Sat: 0830–1600.

Telecommunications
Mobile/cell phones
There are 3G, 900/1800 GSM services available.

Electricity supply
220V AC, 50Hz

Social customs/useful tips
Appointments should always be made before making visits. If the appointment cannot be kept, this should be communicated.
Hand-shaking is frequent. When invited to dinner in a private house, flowers or chocolates for the hosts are the usual gifts.
When drinks are served, it is customary to wait until all the party has been attended to, and then to raise the glass with a salute to each.
The Swiss are proud of their often colourful cultural traditions. Traditional costume is still worn daily in a few areas of the country, although in most areas, it is restricted to celebrations and tourist-related events.

Security
There are no special problems with security in Switzerland; normal precautions apply, especially in the cities.

Getting there
Air
There are regular flights by all major international airlines.
National airline: Swiss International Airlines (Swiss)
International airport/s: EuroAirport Basle-Mulhouse-Freiburg (BSL), 5km from Basle; Berne-Belp (BRN), 9km from city; Geneva International (GVA), 5km north of city; Zürich (ZRH), 9km north of city. Zürich and Geneva airports are directly linked to the national rail system.
Airport tax: None.

Surface
There are good road and rail links with all surrounding countries. It is advisable to book for rail travel beforehand.
Road: Major roads and tunnels link Switzerland to all neighbouring countries.
Water: There is limited access by water from France, Germany and Italy.

Getting about
National transport
Air: There are several daily flights linking Zürich, Geneva, Basle, Lugano and Berne.
Road: There is a road network of around 72,000km, including 17,000km of motorways. Roads are of good quality, but travel can be slow due to the terrain and the volume of traffic.
Rail: There are over 5,000km of track, practically all electrified. About 60 per cent is operated by Schweizerische Bundesbahnen (SBB) (Swiss Federal Railways) and the rest by about 120 small private companies. Rail journeys between major towns rarely exceed two or three hours.
In December 2007 the Lötschberg rail tunnel was opened between Bern and Valais cantons. It is estimated that the link will save up to an hour across the Alps. It will allow heavier trains, including 'piggy back' services for lorries.
Water: All the larger lakes are serviced by steamers operated by SBB.

City transport
A train from Zürich airport to the city centre takes about 12 minutes, while a taxi can take more than twice as long.
All local city transport is linked together on the same ticketing system. Tickets should be purchased before boarding from ticket dispensers by the stops.
Taxis: Widely available but they do not ply for hire. Zürich taxis have a higher tariff than elsewhere. A 15 per cent service charge is included; no tip required.
Buses, trams & metro: Good services in major towns. Tickets should be bought in advance from vending machines. Multi-journey tickets also available. Flat fare up to five stops.

Car hire
Self-drive and chauffeur-driven cars available in all main towns. A valid national or international driving licence is required, and insurance is compulsory. Speed limits are 50kph in built-up areas, 80kph on normal roads and 120kph on motorways. Further information can be obtained from the Touring Club Suisse (TCS) or the Automobil Club der Schweiz/Automobile Club Suisse (ACS).

BUSINESS DIRECTORY

The addresses listed below are a selection only. While World of Information makes every endeavour to check these addresses, we cannot guarantee that changes have not been made, especially to telephone numbers and area codes. We would welcome any corrections.

Telephone area codes

The international direct dialling (IDD) code for Switzerland is +41, followed by area code and subscriber's number:

Basel	61	Lucerne	41
Bern	31	Neuchâtel	32
Fribourg	26	St Gallen	71
Geneva	22	Winterthur	52
Lausanne	21	Zürich	1

Useful telephone numbers

Police: 117
Fire brigade: 118
Ambulance: 144
Motor breakdown service: 140
Swiss Air Rescue: 47-47-47
Emergency service of Touring Club of Switzerland: 35-80-00

Chambers of Commerce

American Swiss Chamber of Commerce,41 Talacker, 8001 Zurich (tel: 211-2454; fax: 211-9572; e-mail: info@amcham.ch).

Basel Chamber of Commerce, 67 Aeschenvorstadt, 4010 Basel (tel: 270-6060; fax: 270-6005; e-mail: hkbb@hkbb.ch).

Bern Chamber of Commerce and Industry, 1 Gutenbergstrasse, PO Box 5464, 3001 Bern (tel: 388-8787; fax: 382-8788; e-mail: info@bern-cci.ch).

British-Swiss Chamber of Commerce, 155 Freiestrasse, 8032 Zürich (tel: 422-3131; fax: 422-3244; e-mail: bscc@bscc.co.uk).

Fribourg Chamber of Commerce, Industry and Services, 37 Route du Jura, 1706 Fribourg (tel: 347-1220; fax: 347-1239; e-mail: cfcis@cci.ch).

Geneva Chamber of Commerce and Industry, 4 Boulevard du Théâtre, PO Box 5039, 1211 Genève 11 (tel: 819-9111; fax: 819-9100; e-mail: ccig@cci.ch).

St Gallen-Appenzell Chamber of Commerce and Industry, 16 Gallusstrasse, 9001 St Gallen (tel: 224-1010; fax: 224-1060; e-mail: sekretariat@ihk.ch).

Swiss Business Federation, 47 Hegibachstrasse, 8032 Zürich (tel: 421-3535; fax: 421-3434; e-mail: info@economiesuisse.ch).

Swiss Chambers of Commerce and Industry, 47 Avenue d'Ouchy, PO Box 315, 1001 Lausanne (tel: 613-3535; fax: 613-3505 e-mail: info@cci.ch).

Vaud Chamber of Commerce and Industry, 47 Avenue d'Ouchy, 1001 Lausanne (tel: 613-3535; fax: 613-3505; e-mail: cvci@cvci.ch).

Winterthur Chamber of Commerce, 15 Neumarkt, 8401 Winterthur (tel: 213-0763; fax: 213-0729; e-mail: info@haw.ch).

Zürich Chamber of Commerce, 5 BleicherwegPO Box 3058, 8022 Zürich (tel: 217-4050; fax: 217-4051; e-mail: direktion@zurichcci.ch).

Banking

Banque Cantonale de Genève, Quai de l'Ile 17, Case postale, 1211 Genéve 2 (tel: 317-2727; fax: 793-5960).

Banca della Svizzera Italiana, 2 Via Magatti, 6901 Lugano (tel: 587-111).

Bank Leu, Bahnhofstrasse 32, CH-8001 Zürich (tel: 219-1111).

Crédit Suisse, Paradeplatz 8, CH-8021 Zürich (tel: 215-1111).

Crédit Suisse, Pl Bel-Air 2, Case postale, 1211 Genève 70 (tel: 391-2111; fax: 391-2591).

Société de Banque Suisse, rue de la Confédération 2, Case postale, 1211 Genève 2 (tel: 375-7575; fax: 376-5024).

Swiss Bank Corporation, Aeschenvorstadt 1/Gartenstrasse 9, Basel (tel: 202-020).

Swiss Bankers' Association, Aeschenplatz 4, Postfach 4182, CH-4002 Basel (tel: 235-888).

Swiss Volksbank, Weltpoststrasse 5, 3015 Bern (tel: 328-111).

Union de Banques Suisses, Rue Rhone 8, Case postale, 1211 Genève 2 (tel: 388-1111; fax: 388-9652).

Union Bank of Switzerland, Bahnhofstrasse 45, CH-8000 Zürich (tel: 234-1111).

United European Bank, 11 Quai des Bergues, CP 2280, 1211 Genève (tel: 907-2111; fax: 732-3002).

Zürcher Kantonalbank, Bahnhofstrasse, PO Box 4039, 8022 Zürich (fax: 211-1525).

Central bank

Schweizerische Nationalbank, Börsenstrasse 15, 8022 Zürich (tel: 631-3111; fax: 631-3911; e-mail: snb@snb.ch).

Travel information

Automobile Club de Suisse (ACS), Wasserwerkgasse 39, 3000 Bern (tel: 328-3111; fax: 311-0310; e-mail: acszv@acs.ch).

Swiss Travel Centre, Grubenstrasse 12, 8045 Zürich (tel: 210-5500; fax: 210-5501; e-mail: information@stc.ch).

Touring Club Suisse (TCS), Chemin de Blandonnet 4, 1214 Vernier, Geneva (tel: 417-2727; fax: 417-2020; e-mail: info@tcs.ch).

National tourist organisation offices

Switzerland Tourism, Tödistrasse 7, 8002 Zürich (tel: 288-1111; fax: 288-1205; email: info@myswitzerland.com).

Ministries

Bundesamt für Statistik (BFS) (central statistics office), Schwarztorstrasse 96, CH-3003 Bern (tel: 323-6011; fax: 323-6061).

Federal Department of Finance, Bundesgasse 3, 3003 Bern (tel: 66-111).

Federal Department of Public Economy, Bundeshaus-Ost, 3003 Bern (tel: 612-111).

Federal Office for Industry, Crafts and Labour, Bundesgasse 8, CH-3003 Bern (tel: 612-944).

Swiss Federal Tax Administration, Eidgenössische Steuerverwaltung, Eigerstrasse 65, CH-3003 Bern (tel: 617-112).

Other useful addresses

British Embassy, Thunstrasse 50, CH-3005 Berne 15 (tel: 352-5021/6; fax: 352-0583).

Embassy of the United States of America, Jubilumstrasse 93, CH-3005 Berne (tel: 357-7011; fax: 357-7344).

Swiss Embassy (USA), 2900 Cathedral Avenue, NW, Washington DC 20008 (tel: (+1-202) 745-7900; fax: (+1-202) 387-2564; e-mail: vertretung@was.rep.admin.ch).

Swiss Federation of Commerce and Industry, Börsenstrasse 26, CH-8022 Zürich (tel: 221-2707).

SWX Swiss Exchange, Selnaustrasse 30, Postfach, CH-8021 Zürich (tel: 229-2111).

Union Suisse d'Agences-Conseils en Publicité (advertising), Kurfürstenstr 80, CH-8002 Zürich (tel: 202-6540).

Other news agencies: SDA+ATS (in German) (www.sda.ch).

Swiss Infor (operated by SRG SSR Idée Suisse in nine languages) (www.swissinfo.org).

Internet sites

Details of government departments: www.admin.ch/ch/e/index.html

Index of Swiss business and tourism: www.swissdir.ch

Swiss Federal Statistical office: www.admin.ch/bfs/eindex.htm

Syria

KEY FACTS

Official name: Jumhuriya al Arabya as Suriya (Syrian Arab Republic)

Head of State: President Bashar al Assad (since 2000)

Head of government: Prime Minister Mohammed Naji al Otari (since 2003)

Ruling party: Al-Jabha al-Wataniyyah at-Wahdwamiyyah (National Progressive Front) (NPF), a coalition of 10 parties led by Hizb al Ba'ath al Arabi al Ishtiraki (Ba'ath Party) (Arab Socialist Rebirth Party) (re-elected Apr 2007)

Area: 185,180 square km (plus 1,295 square km Israeli-controlled Golan Heights)

Population: 19.41 million (2007)*

Capital: Damascus

Official language: Arabic

Currency: Syrian pound (Syr£) = 100 piastres

Exchange rate: Syr£51.00 per US$ (Jul 2008)

GDP per capita: US$1,946 (2007)*

GDP real growth: 3.90% (2007)*

Labour force: 5.50 million (2006)*

Unemployment: 18.00% (2006) (Including a percentage of Iraqi refugees)

Inflation: 7.00% (2007)*

Oil production: 394,000 bpd (2007)

Balance of trade: -US$3.12 billion (2006)

Visitor numbers: 4.42 million (2006)*

Annual FDI: US$300.00 million (typical annual amount)

* estimated figure

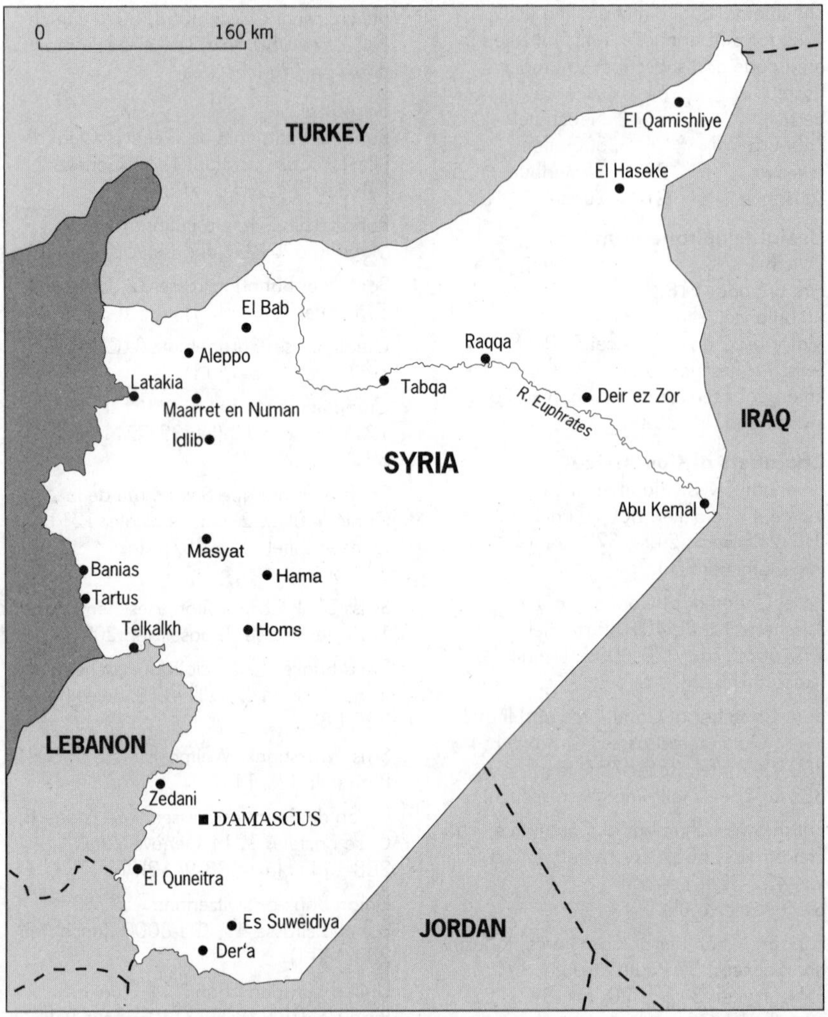

Syria's economy has been characterised by the International Monetary Fund (IMF) as a 'stable but stagnant' economy. This characterisation reflects to some degree the isolation of Syria from the major currents and shocks of the global economy and, some analysts have suggested, the failure of the narrowly based political establishment to adopt obvious and essential economic reforms. In consequence, under 50 years of Ba'ath rule, the economy has remained in a heavily regulated, old-fashioned and inefficient mode. In addition, the fact that the government of Syria is, to put it politely, quasi-totalitarian and riddled with large scale corruption even at the highest levels, does little to prepare the ground for economic reform.

Anaemic economic performance

In recent years the Syrian economy has managed only modest growth. Syria has had to cope with a number of extraneous factors, not least the effects of the Iraqi post-war situation. Conservative estimates put the number of Iraqi refugees in Syria at over one million, with some estimates suggesting a figure as high as 2 million. Disregarding the effects of the Iraq war and Syria's continued international political ostracisation, there remain a number of weaknesses that are inherent to the economy. These include the failure of a number of economic sectors to perform, low personal income, population growth pressures, declining oil production, low productivity and high unemployment and poor technical education and standards. Additionally, critical sectors of the economy are owned and run by private monopolies. The most obvious of these is the tobacco monopoly, which is the private fiefdom of the ruling Assad family and is not subject to any taxation or pricing controls.

Remarkably the 2006 war, between Israel and Hezbollah, hadleft Syria unaffected in terms of military damage. But the key effect of the war was to damage irrevocably Israel's previous reputation for military invincibility. This, in turn enhanced Syria's reputation if only by association: the Hezbollah leadership and tacticians who were overseeing the fighting are reportedly based in Damascus. Syria is also reported to provide substantial funding for Hezbollah.

The friends you keep

The first result of the 2006 war was to lower Syria's ranking on the axis of evil league table. The US Iraq Study Group reporting in late 2006 recommended that the US open face-to-face dialogue with Syria. In April 2007 US House Speaker Nancy Pelosi – a Democrat – made her way to Damascus in the face of White House opposition. Previously senior British diplomats were known to have been in Damascus. There were also reports that prior to the 2006 war direct negotiations had taken place between Syrian and Israeli representatives.

Flagging economy

According to the World Bank Syria is a lower middle-income country with a per capita income in 2007 of about US$1,946, a population of 19.4 million growing at about 2.6 per cent per annum and a labour force growing at the rapid rate of about 4 per cent per annum. The Bank notes that although Syria still enjoys strong macro-economic fundamentals (low inflation, moderate debt, and comfortable foreign assets reserves), growth performance has been weak in recent years reflecting declining oil production and continuous contraction in private investment since the mid-1990s. Following a decade of high growth in the 1990s, real economic growth averaged 1.25 per cent per annum between 1999 and 2003, well below the current population growth. Since 2004 gross domestic product (GDP) growth has picked up reaching 3.9 per cent in 2007; Syria's GDP is highly dependent on the oil and agriculture sectors, both subject to uncertainties due to changes in oil prices and rain dependency respectively. The oil sector provides half of the government's revenues and about two thirds of its export receipts. The agriculture sector, for its part, contributes to about 30 per cent of GDP and employment.

Oil

Oil exports and workers remittances are the main sources of foreign earnings and allow the country to finance its imports and achieve a current account surplus of 5 per cent of GDP. Oil reserves are expected to be depleted within 15 years. Without new discoveries, Syria will become a net importer in 2010 and run out of oil in the late 2020s.

Syria's oil output continues to decline in some measure due to technological problems but also to the depletion of reserves. Since peaking at 590,000 barrels per day (bpd) in 1996, it is estimated that Syria's average crude oil output fell to 394,000bpd in 2007, as older fields, especially Jebisseh and Omar, reach maturity. Oil production is expected to continue its decline over the next several years, while consumption rises, leading to a reduction in Syrian net oil exports. Reserves were 2.5 thousand million barrels at the end of 2007, compared to Iraq's 115.0 thousand million barrels.

Syria aims to reverse the trend toward declining oil exports through intensified oil exploration and production efforts, enhanced oil recovery (EOR) techniques, and a switch from oil-fired to natural-gas fired electric power plants.

New realities

The collapse of Syrian hegemony in Lebanon in 2005 brought home some uncomfortable new realities to Syria. One of these was the establishment of a UN commission of inquiry in April, under German prosecutor Detlev Mehlis, charged with investigating the assassination of Mr Hariri. The commission found that Mr Hariri's assassination was linked to his opposition to Syria's successful attempt to extend President Lahoud's term in office and his threat to continue this opposition. It also accused members of the Lebanese and Syrian military intelligence of being complicit in the crime. Moreover, Mr Mehlis had expressed a desire to question a number of high-ranking Syrian officials, including, according to Lebanese media sources, President Assad's brother-in-law, Asef Shawkat, who heads Syria's Military Intelligence. The commission later requested permission to question Assad himself, as well as Farouq al Shara, Syria's foreign minister until February 2006.

Son of Assad

Soon after taking office in 2000, President Bashar al Assad had raised expectations of political and economic reform in a country, still within the grip of a state of emergency going back to the 1960s. Political dialogue forums were established, outside the structures of the ruling National

KEY INDICATORS — Syria

	Unit	2003	2004	2005	2006	2007
Population	m	18.11	18.60	18.65	18.94	*19.41
Gross domestic product (GDP)	US$bn	21.90	25.05	*27.37	*34.92	*37.76
GDP per capita	US$	1,226	1,308	*1,468	*1,844	*1,946
GDP real growth	%	0.9	3.4	*2.9	*4.4	*3.9
Inflation	%	1.5	3.5	7.2	10.6	*7.0
Unemployment	%	–	10.8	12.5	18.0	–
Oil output	'000 bpd	594.0	536.0	469.0	417.0	394.0
Natural gas output	bn cum	–	5.2	5.4	5.5	5.3
Exports (fob) (goods)	US$m	5,593.0	5,355.0	5,557.0	7,205.0	–
Natural gas	US$m	5.2	–	–	–	–
Imports (cif) (goods)	US$m	5,001.0	7,109.0	7,880.0	10,325.0	–
Balance of trade	US$m	592.0	-1,754.0	-2,323.0	-3,120.0	–
Current account	US$m	750.0	-90.0	219.0	-2,133.0	-2,181.0
Exchange rate	per US$	50.21	11.22	52.21	52.21	51.10

* estimated figure

Progressive Front, allowing for the voice of dissidence while controlling its influence. Subsequently, however, with the collapse of Syrian rule in Lebanon and its virtual pariah status on the world scene, the regime cracked down on its internal critics. By May 2005, the last dialogue forum was disbanded. A much vaunted reform agenda, scheduled for release at a Ba'athist congress in June, failed to satisfy those hoping for meaningful change both inside and outside the country. The congress voted to relax the decades-old state of emergency but parliament did not ratify this until the end of 2006. Divisions within the government itself also made life difficult for President Bashar al Assad. In mid-2005, long-serving vice president, Abdul Halim Khaddam, unexpectedly resigned. Later, in December, from his new home in Paris, Khaddam gave an interview that included a call for the overthrow of President Assad and the accusation that Assad had directly threatened the life of former Lebanese prime minister Rafik Hariri. In September, interior minister Ghazi Kanaan was found dead in Damascus, apparently having committed suicide. Kanaan had recently been interviewed by the UN's commission of inquiry into the death of Hariri, causing speculation that Kanaan had given, or was about to give, evidence against the Assad government and had subsequently been silenced.

One major blot on otherwise improving international relations has been the bombing by Israel in September 2007 of what Israel claimed was a secret nuclear reactor. Satellite images published by the US in April 2008 appeared to show Syria's secret plutonium-producing nuclear reactor before its destruction by the Israelis, claiming North Korea had helped build it. The site was cleared before UN inspectors from the International Atomic Energy Agency (IAEA) visited the site on 22 June. The preliminary investigation declared the results inconclusive.

Outlook

The Hezbollah triumph has helped the Syrian government recover from its setbacks. Although the UN investigations into the assassination of Rafik Hariri will continue to dog Syria, the overall climate appears to have changed. It will be down to the Syrian government to decide how it wishes to take advantage of the changes in international relations that now confront it. A hopeful sign was the approval by the government, in 2006, of the recommendation of the US Iraq Study Group report that said countries bordering Iraq 'should form a support group to reinforce security and national reconciliation'.

Risk assessment

Politics	Poor
Economy	Fair
Regional stability	Poor

COUNTRY PROFILE

Historical profile

1943 Syria achieved independence with Shukri al Kuwatli as its first president.
1948 Syria contributed to a pan-Arab military force that failed to occupy the newly-created state of Israel.
1949 President al Kuwatli was overthrown in a military coup.
1955–59 After a five-year exile in Egypt, Shukri al Kuwatli returned to be president again. Syria moved towards greater economic and political co-operation with Egypt.
1963 The Hizb al Ba'ath al Arabiyah al Ishtiraki (Ba'ath) (Socialist Arab Rebirth Party) (founded in 1947) seized power.
1967 In the Six Day War, Israel seized the Golan Heights from Syria.
1970 Former air force commander and defence minister, Hafez al Assad, seized power in a bloodless coup.
1971 Al Assad was elected president. He was re-elected for four further seven-year terms in 1978, 1985, 1992 and 1999.
1973 In the 6 October War (also known as the Yom Kippur War), Egypt and Syria invaded Israel to reclaim some of the land lost in the Six Day War, but despite some early strategic gains for Egypt and Syria, Israel counter-attacked and repelled the invasion, re-conquering the Golan Heights from Syria.
1976 The Syrian army intervened in the Lebanese civil war to ensure that the Maronites remained in power.
1980 Start of the Iran-Iraq War – Syria backed Iran.
1981 Israel formally annexed the Golan Heights.
1982–87 Israel invaded Lebanon and attacked the Syrian army based there. After hostilities ended, Syrian forces remained in Lebanon.
1990 Syria participated in the US-led allied military operations against Iraq.
1991 Syria attended the Middle East peace conference in Madrid and held bilateral talks with Israel.
2000 Syrian-Israeli talks on the future of the Golan Heights were indefinitely postponed. President Hafez al Assad died and the Ba'ath party proposed his son Bashar al Assad as president, which was approved by referendum.
2001 The UN General Assembly voted Syria a two-year seat on the Security Council.
2002 The US declared Syria a state that formed part of the 'axis of evil'. Syria denied US allegations that it was acquiring weapons of mass destruction.
2003 Muhammed Naji al Otari was appointed prime minister. Syria denied US allegations that it was developing chemical weapons and helping fugitive Iraqis; the US threatened economic and diplomatic sanctions.
2004 The US imposed economic sanctions, citing Syria's support for terrorism and failing to stop militants entering Iraq. A UN Security Council resolution called for Syrian forces to leave Lebanon; Syria re-deployed some of its troops stationed around Beirut.
2005 Mass anti-Syrian protests in Beirut (Lebanon) followed the assassination of former Lebanese prime minister Rafik Hariri in a car bomb attack. The presidents of Syria and Lebanon bowed to pressure from the UN and US, as a full withdraw of Syrian troops from the Lebanon was achieved. The ruling Ba'ath party relaxed a number of laws that sanctioned some independent political parties, granted more press freedom and relaxed the state of emergency (that has been in place since 1963). UN investigators were allowed to question Syrian officials about the assassination of Rafik Hariri. Later, Interior Minister Ghazi Kanaan, accused of being involved in the murder of Hariri, was found dead, apparently of suicide. An official UN interim report implicated senior Syrian and Lebanese security officials in the killing of Hariri; Syria rejected the report. Following weeks of pressure, Syria agreed to allow five senior officials to be interviewed by the UN investigator, Detlev Mehlis.
2006 The Danish and Norwegian embassies in Damascus were attacked after worldwide Muslim condemnations of cartoons depicting the Prophet Mohammed were published in a Danish newspaper. Syria and Iraq restored diplomatic relations after a 25-year gap and became an increasingly safe haven for those fleeing the terror in Iraq.
2007 Parliamentary elections were held in April; the ruling Al-Jabha al-Wataniyyah at-Wahdwamiyyah (National Progressive Front) (NPF) coalition, under the leadership of Hizb al Ba'ath al Arabi al Ishtiraki (Ba'ath Party) (Arab Socialist Rebirth Party), won 178 seats, with approved independents winning the remaining 78 seats. In May, President Bashar al Assad was re-elected, unopposed, through a general referendum and won 97.62 per cent of the vote. Turnout was 95.86 per cent. Tough visa requirements were

imposed on Iraqis as the influx of refugees grew. In September, Israel bombed and destroyed what it claimed was a secret nuclear reactor.
2008 On 25 April the US published satellite images of Syria's secret plutonium-producing nuclear reactor before its destruction by the Israelis, claiming North Korea had helped build it. The site was cleared before UN inspectors from the International Atomic Energy Agency (IAEA) visited the site on 22 June. The preliminary investigation declared the results inconclusive. In August an agreement to improve diplomatic relations was reached for a common border to be formally demarcated between Lebanon and Syria.

Political structure

Constitution

The 1973 constitution was amended in 2000, reducing the minimum age of a president from 40 to 34 years.

Form of state

Socialist democratic republic that has been run by a military regime since 1963.

The executive

The president is Head of State, and has almost absolute power as the country is a one-party state with a disproportionate share of power in the hands of the Ba'ath Party and minority Alawite community. Presidential candidates are nominated by parliament and agreed by referendum for a seven-year term.
The president appoints and dismisses the vice presidents, the prime minister and the Council of Ministers. He holds the posts of commander-in-chief of the armed forces and secretary general of the Ba'ath Party. The Council of Ministers is headed by the prime minister and its members are appointed from the ruling party.

National legislature

The 250-member Majlis al Shaab (People's Assembly) is directly elected for a four-year term. The Ba'th Party is guaranteed 167 seats and therefore a majority. The assembly may not initiate laws; it may assess and may occasionally modifies those proposed by the executive branch.

Legal system

The judiciary is guaranteed independence under the constitution, however in practice, the Minister of Justice has the power to appoint, promote and transfer members of the judiciary and has undue influence. The legal system has separate religious and secular courts using Sharia (Islamic law) and a civil law code respectively.
Syria has not accepted compulsory International Court of Justice (ICJ) jurisdiction.

Last elections

22/23 April 2007 (parliamentary); 18 June 2000 (presidential)

Results: Parliamentary: the ruling Al-Jabha al-Wataniyyah at-Wahdwamiyyah (National Progressive Front) (NPF), a coalition of 10 parties led by Hizb al Ba'ath al Arabi al Ishtiraki (Ba'ath Party) (Arab Socialist Rebirth Party), won 172 seats (out of 250); 78 seats were won by independents. Turnout was 56.12 per cent.
Presidential: Bashar Al-Asad was elected president by referendum, with 97.29 per cent of the vote. He was nominated by the ruling Ba'ath party and ran unopposed.

Next elections

27 May 2007 (presidential); 2011 (parliamentary)

Political parties

Ruling party

Al-Jabha al-Wataniyyah at-Wahdwamiyyah (National Progressive Front) (NPF), a coalition of 10 parties led by Hizb al Ba'ath al Arabi al Ishtiraki (Ba'ath Party) (Arab Socialist Rebirth Party) (re-elected Apr 2007)

Main opposition party

Most political opposition is severely repressed and leading critics of the government are in exile.

Population

19.41 million (2007)*
Last census: September 1994: 13,782,315
Population density: 81 inhabitants per square km. Urban population: 52 per cent of the total (1995—2001).
Annual growth rate: 2.6 per cent 1994–2004 (WHO 2006)

Ethnic make-up

Arabs (90 per cent); Kurds, Armenians and Assyrians (10 per cent).

Religions

About 90 per cent of the population are Muslim with those of the Sunni denomination outnumbering Alawi (Shi'a) Muslims by about six to one. The remainder are Christian (8 per cent), Druze and Jewish (2 per cent). Religious freedom is provided by the constitution.

Education

Primary schooling lasts for six years. Secondary education, which begins at the age of 12, also lasts for six years and is divided into two three-year cycles. Students may either enter the general or the technical branches, although entry is selective and is based on the Intermediate Level Diploma (al Kafa'a) examination. The first cycle is introductory. Technical secondary education is divided into industrial and commercial tracks. There are agricultural and technical schools and four universities, at Damascus, Aleppo, Tishreen and Homs. All higher education institutions are state-controlled and state-financed.

Literacy rate: 83 per cent adult rate; 95 per cent youth rate (15–24) (Unesco 2005).
Compulsory years: Six to 12.
Enrolment rate: 101 per cent gross primary enrolment, of relevant age group (including repeaters); 43 per cent gross secondary enrolment (World Bank).
Pupils per teacher: 23 in primary schools.

Health

Per capita total expenditure on health (2003) was US$116; of which per capita government spending was US$56, at the international dollar rate, (WHO 2006).
Medical services are relatively well developed in larger towns and cities, but there is considerable variation in rural areas. Annual total expenditure on health is 5–6 per cent of GDP, of which government spending is 43–44 per cent.

HIV/Aids

HIV prevalence: 0.1 per cent aged 15–49 in 2003 (World Bank)
Life expectancy: 72 years, 2004 (WHO 2006)
Fertility rate/Maternal mortality rate: 3.3 births per woman, 2004 (WHO 2006); maternal mortality 110 deaths per 100,000 live births (World Bank)
Birth rate/Death rate: 29.5 births and five deaths per 1,000 people (2003).
Child (under 5 years) mortality rate (per 1,000): 16 per 1,000 live births (2003); 13 per cent of children aged under five are malnourished (World Bank).
Head of population per physician: 1.4 physicians per 1,000 people, 2001 (WHO 2006)

Welfare

The government maintains a basic range of social welfare provisions, including free healthcare for low-income groups, and is officially committed to improving the quality of state welfare provision as economic conditions allow. The government claims that the expansion of the private sector has led to more young children working. The labour and social affairs minister is responsible for enforcing minimum wage levels in the public and private sectors. The law does not protect temporary workers who are not subject to regulations on minimum wages.

Main cities

Damascus (capital, estimated population 1.7 million in 2005), Aleppo (Halab) (2.3 million), Homs (768,489).

Media

National news agency: SANA
Other news agencies: All4Syria (www.all4syria.org).

Press

Dailies: The state runs four national and many regional newspapers with news contained in them is provided by the Syrian Arab News Agency (SANA). In Arabic, Al Thawra (www.althawranews.net), has the largest circulation; Al Baath (http://albaath.online.fr) (official publication of the Ba'ath Party); Tishreen (www.tishreen.info) and in English Syria Times (http://syriatimes.tishreen.info). The first private, political daily newspaper to open since 1963 was Al Watan (www.al-watan.com).

Weeklies: In Arabic, Teshreen al Osboi a political magazine and Mawkef al Riyadhi (http://riadi.alwehda.gov.sy) covering sports news are government-run. Star Syria (www.star-sy.com) is a youth magazine.

Business: In Arabic, Al Iqtissad wal Nagl (www.aliqtisad.com) is a monthly magazine; Al-Iqtissadiya (www.iqtissadiya.com) for business and political news.

Periodicals: There are over 140 private magazines and others produced by government departments, state organisations, trade unions, political, professional and religious associations. In Arabic, Al Arabieh and Ayam Al Osrah (www.ayam-mag.com) are women's magazines; Al Maaloumatieh is a consumer magazine. In Arabic and English, Al Nashra al Ektisadyeh (www.dcc-sy.com) is published by the Chamber of Commerce. In Arabic and French, Ougarit (www.ougarit.org) (quarterly) and Maaber (www.maaber.org) for culture and literature. In English, Syria Today (www.syria-today.com) for current affairs.

Broadcasting

Radio: The state radio service, Radio Sout Al Sha'ab (www.rtv.gov.sy) broadcasts domestic and external programmes in Arabic, French, English, Russian, German, Spanish, Portuguese, Polish, Turkish and Bulgarian. Private radio stations all broadcasting from Damascus, include Farah FM (www.farah.fm), Rotana Style FM (www.rotana.net) and Syria Al Ghad (www.syriaalghad.com).

Television: Syrian television (www.rtv.gov.sy) operates two terrestrial channels and a satellite station. Many households are subscribed to satellite television providers and the only private station based in Syria, Al Sham, competes for audiences with pan-Arab and Western (generally for expatriate communities) TV satellite stations.

There are plans for further licensing of 24 private satellite television channels, by the Minster of Information.

Advertising

All advertising is controlled by the Arab Advertising Organisation (AAO). There are restrictions on advertising alcohol, cigarettes and the use of women in commercials. Advertising is available in the press, public cinemas, on commercial TV and outdoors public spaces in main centres but carry government and municipal taxes. Direct mail is also available.

Economy

The main sectors of an economy, which is struggling to emerge from decades of over-centralisation and stagnation, are agriculture and hydrocarbons. While agriculture accounts for around 20 per cent of GDP, involves a quarter of the population and ensures self-sufficiency in food, Syria has been dependent on its oil and gas reserves to sustain the economy. Hydrocarbons, which typically contribute 20 per cent to GDP, have been responsible for 65 per cent of exports and 50 per cent of government revenue. Production and exports , however, are falling as the existing fields decline. It is forecast that, in the absence of the discovery of significant new deposits in the meantime, Syria will become a net importer of oil by 2012 and run out of oil by 2020. Unless other sectoral activities are developed and foreign direct investment (FDI) attracted quickly, Syria could find itelf relegated to the status of a low-income country. For the present, Syria benefits from rising oil prices.

The government is attempting to diversify and modernise the economy, but there are obstacles to be overcome. The economy has for several decades been under tight state control and while the need to introduce market-based practices has been acknowledged since the nineties, restructuring has been slow, impeded by vested interests, corruption and bureaucratic inertia. A number of reforms have been introduced, but only in recent years has the process been pursued with any vigour and much remains to be done. Dismantling the centralised controls and rationalising of the regulatory system are essential to increase FDI, levels of which have been low and mainly from the oil and gas industry. The political uncertainty occasioned by Syria's international and regional relations, particularly US antagonism, add to the caution of potential investors. Recent reforms have stimulated growing interest, nevertheless, and there has been a growth in FDI from the Gulf states and Lebanon, themselves wary of investing in the West in current political climate.

As the pace of reform has increased, particularly in the banking sector,where private banking has been allowed, the economy has shown improvements. Exports of manufactured goods have increased, while the services sector has done well, due mainly to the expansion of tourism. Around three-quarters of visitors to Syria come from the Gulf states, but the government, recognising the contribution tourism makes to the economy, is seeking to expand the sector and to construct infrastructure more suitable to a wider market. Increased FDI is essential for further development, as is a more benign political environment. Tourism is already next only to agriculture and oil in importance to the economy.

The economy is not keeping pace with the growth in population. The official unemployment figure is 12.3 per cent, but is probably at least 20 per cent. Around 75 per cent of the population is below the age of 35, while 40 per cent are aged below 15. For those in work, pay is low. An important source of income is remittances from the huge number of Syrians working abroad; currency transfer by expatriates is also an important source of foreign exchange for the government. A third of the population is estimated to live in varying degrees of poverty.

External trade

In 2005 the Greater Arab Free Trade Area (Gafta) was ratified by 17 members, including Syria, creating an Arab economic bloc. A customs union was established whereby tariffs within Gafta will be reduced by a percentage each year, until none remain. It is also a signatory of the Euro-Mediterranean Partnership agreement, which provides for the introduction of free trade between the EU and 10 Mediterranean countries by 2012.

Foreign trade provides almost 70 per cent of GDP and over 65 per cent of all exports are oil and it derivatives and natural gas. As manufacturing only provides around 25 per cent of GDP, producing handicrafts and light manufacturers, its importance to exports is less than that of agriculture which exports livestock and cereals and the majority of the annual cotton lint harvest not used domestically for spinning and garment production.

Imports

Major imports are capital machinery and vehicles, food and livestock, appliances, chemicals, plastics, various yarns and paper.

Main sources: Russia (10.2 per cent total, 2006), China (6.5 per cent), Ukraine (5.3 per cent).

Exports

Main exports are crude oil, petroleum products, cotton, clothing, fruits, vegetables, wheat, meat and live animals.

Main destinations: Italy (19.6 per cent total, 2006), France (8.8 per cent), Saudi Arabia (8.7 per cent).

Agriculture

Farming

Agriculture remains a leading sector of the economy, contributing approximately 25 per cent to GDP and employing around a quarter of the labour force.

Agricultural land is mainly privately owned. Approximately 31 per cent of the total land is cultivated. Much of Syria is mountainous and part of the eastern part of the country is desert or semi-desert. The fertile areas include the coastal strip and the Euphrates and Kabur valleys. Intensification of farming in the rain-fed areas is ongoing; these areas account for more than 80 per cent of the total crop area. The al Thaura dam, built with Russian technology, brings irrigation to a vast area.

Main crops are cotton, wheat and barley. Wheat and barley together account for two-thirds of the cultivated area. Extreme fluctuations in grain production from year to year caused by rainfall variability have traditionally caused much hardship for the rural population. Cotton is the main cash crop. Other leading crops include vegetables, citrus fruits, olives, tobacco and sugar beet. Sheep and goats are grazed in many areas. Wool is also an important product.

Population growth in Syria is estimated at 3 per cent, and to ensure food security for its growing population, the government is focussing on a food self-sufficiency strategy, improving crop production technology and crop diversification. Farm production increased in the period 1993–2003 and Syria moved from being a food importer to food exporter.

Crop production in 2005 included: 5,620,317 (t) cereals in total, 4,668,750t wheat, 767,416t barley, *500,000t potatoes, 279,526t pulses, 736,500t citrus fruit, *920,000t tomatoes, 254,975t oilcrops, 203,000t treenuts, 620,000t olives, 1,150,000t sugar beets, 1,024,000t seed cotton, 310,000t grapes, 26,500t tobacco, 1,606,800t fruit in total, 2,639,400t vegetables in total. Livestock production included: *391,021t meat in total, *47,350t beef, 315t camel meat, *207,000t lamb, *5,120t goat meat, *130,621t poultry, *167,000t eggs, 1,917,820t milk, 1,940t honey, 14t cocoons, silk, *7,317t cattle hides, *34,500t sheepskins, 33,650t greasy wool.

* estimate

Fishing

Syria's small annual fish catch is mostly destined for the domestic market.

In 2004, the total marine fish catch was 2,785 tonnes and the total crustacean catch was 146 tonnes.

Forestry

Syria is lightly forested with less than 3 per cent of forest or woodland cover. In ancient times, Syria had extensive mountain forests but these have largely been cleared or degraded and only remnants of mixed coniferous forest remain. The predominant species include Abies cilicica, Pinus halipensis and Pinus brutia. Syria has established a moderately large area of plantations based on cypress, pine and eucalyptus species. The country has a modest network of protected areas – State Forest Protection Zones provide the most substantive forest conservation measures.

Syria produces very modest volumes of sawn timber, veneer, plywood and particleboard. The majority of demand for wood and paper products is met by imports. Exports in 2004 amounted to US$8.4 million while imports were values at US$362 million.

Industry and manufacturing

The industrial sector contributed 27.1 per cent to GDP in 2004, of which, 24.2 per cent was manufacturing; as a whole it employs around 20 per cent of the labour force. Industrial growth matched the trend in GDP, with a low rate of 0.9 in 2003 that jumped to 2.5 in 2004.

In the mid-1960s the government began a policy of rapid industrialisation, especially in the areas of iron and steel and other heavy industries. Factories turn out a wide range of products, including tractors and television sets. In 2007 the state-owned Handasieh, in partnership with the Iranian car manufacturer Khodro Iran began production of Syria's first, domestically built automobile.

Many of Syria's industries are agrarian-based, such as food processing and textiles. Sugar processing, an important activity, is mainly conducted by state-owned enterprises. The textile industry is the oldest-established, contributing approximately 15 per cent of export earnings. Other industries include cement, soap, glass, footwear, leather goods and brassware.

Tourism

Tourism is increasingly important, with Syria's magnificent castles and other historical sites attracting over one million tourists a year. Aleppo in the north has been designated a World Heritage Site. A peace agreement between Israel and its Arab neighbours, including Syria, is required for Syria to fully develop its tourist potential which derives from its close proximity to Western Europe, its Mediterranean coastline and its rich history and historical sites.

Tourism is geared to the Middle East market and is heavily concentrated in Damascus. Tourists are mainly Lebanese and Jordanian, although Syria is also popular with the French and citizens from the former Soviet Union. Tourists from other Arab countries account for some 75 per cent of total visitors. Iranian pilgrims are a significant tourist category who visit religious sites around Syria. American- and Canadian-Syrian visitors are also increasing.

In 2003 Syria joined the Euromed Heritage Programme, a computerisation project, sponsored by the EU, which focusses on cultural tourists of archaeology, arts and history, promoting sites through the internet.

The travel and tourism sector is expected to contribute US$5.4 billion or 2.1 per cent of GDP and employ around 6 per cent of the work force in 2005. Tourism is estimated to attract 7 per cent of total capital investment and generate around US$2.7 billion, or 24.1 per cent of in total exports.

Mining

The mining sector contributes up to 10 per cent to GDP and employs around 5 per cent of the working population. Syria has large phosphate deposits which are used in its growing fertiliser industry. Approximately 76 per cent of phosphate mined is exported, with 10 per cent used at the Homs fertiliser factory. Other mineral resources include gypsum.

Hydrocarbons

Proven oil reserves totalled 3.0 billion barrels in 2005 and are only expected to last until 2012.

Oil production was 496,000 barrels per day (bpd) in 2005. Crude oil accounts for up to 65 per cent of total export earnings, 20 per cent of GDP and 50 per cent of government revenue. Further exploration is under way with five blocks allocated to international companies, although in 2005 most Western oil exploration firms had begun to withdraw as no new finds had been made.

Due to Syria's alleged harbouring of terrorists, US sanctions are set to prohibit US investment in Syria's energy sector. This could result in a long-term decrease of production. The UN and Asia are taking a different line to the US on combat of terrorism, they seek to improve relations with the country and perhaps their investment will counter US sanctions.

Total gas reserves are estimated at 310 billion cubic metres (cum) and output was 46.6 billion cum in 2005. Syria is beginning to convert oil-fired electrical generating plants to gas, as oil stocks decline.

There are several pipelines either in operation, under construction or being planned to transport gas from the Egyptian fields in Sinai to Jordan, Lebanon and Syria – with a possible extension to Turkey and Europe.

A new, 32km gas pipeline, called GASYLE 1, connecting the Syrian Baniyas gas pipeline to the Deir al-Ammar-Beddawi power plant in northern Lebanon began operations in May 2005. It is expected to provide 1.5 million cum of gas per day.

In May 2004, significant gas discoveries were made in the northern central part of

Syria and is expected to allow Syria to expand its exports. The first oil joint venture between China and Syria was set up in July 2004. The joint venture is between the largest oil producer in China, China National Petroleum Corporation (CNPC) and the state-owned Syrian Petroleum Company (SPC). It is hoped that the establishment of the company – the Sino-Syrian Kawkab Oil Company (SSKOC) – will speed up CNPC's development of the Kbeibe oil field in the north-east of Syria.
In February 2004, Syria and Yemen signed a co-operation agreement in the field of oil, gas and mineral resources.
Syria does not produce any coal but imports around 2,000 tonnes of coke per annum.

Energy

The government is promoting the rapid development of gas production for electricity generation. Total installed capacity is scheduled to reach 6,000MW (including hydroelectric capacity of 1,700MW) with an increased capacity of 3,000MW by 2010.
From the 1990s onwards the power industry has been in crisis. Power cuts have been commonplace. The government attempted to address chronic under-capacity in power generation by awarding contracts to build four new power stations and existing power plants underwent modernisation.
A US$300 million electricity line links the grids of three countries – Jordan, Syria and Egypt
All new thermal plants are built to use gas, and existing oil-fired power stations have been converted to gas or combined oil and gas fuel to reduce the overall consumption of oil, freeing up to 150,000 barrels per day (bpd) of oil for export.
Factories and oil refineries are gradually expected to convert from fuel oil to natural gas.
Syria's main gas-fired power stations are located in Suwaidiyah (300MW), Deir ez Zor (120MW) and Thayyem (90MW). The General Organisation for Electricity's (GOE) national transmission system supplies all regions via 230kV and 66kV lines.

Financial markets

Stock exchange

In August 2004, Syria became a participant of the Arab Stock Exchange – established in Cairo. Legislation to establish a Syrian Stock Market is, by end-2005, being prepared in co-operation with stock markets in Amman and Istanbul.

Banking and insurance

A series of reforms since 2000 has included official approval of private banking, in joint ventures, with foreign equity limited to 49 per cent, to be sited in 'free zones'. A Monetary and Credit Council (MSC) was establishment to supervise and co-ordinate the activities of private banks. Restrictions on the trading of foreign currency and the need for a majority local partner will be a disincentive to a wider pool of potential participants.
Three Lebanese banks – Fransabank, Banque Européenne pour le Moyen Orient and Société Générale Libano-Européenne de Banque – opened branches in the free zones. Five other non-Syrian banks, including the Jordanian Arab Bank and Housing Bank for Trade and Finance (HBTF) were later given approval to begin trading.
The government has eased the ban on domestic nationals opening foreign currency accounts. Nevertheless this reform has been of limited benefit as it is still technically illegal to hold hard currency and most Syrians continue to channel their funds through Lebanese banks. The lack of domestic credit and the poor quality of Syria's banking sector represent a major hindrance to the development of the country's economy.

Central bank

Central Bank of Syria

Main financial centre

Damascus

Time

GMT plus two hour (daylight saving, April to October, GMT plus three hours)

Geography

Syria is bordered by Turkey to the north; by the Mediterranean Sea and northern Lebanon to the west; by Israel and Jordan to the south; and by Iraq to the east.
Western Syria contains a series of mountain ranges, lying parallel to the Mediterranean. The northern range is separated from Syria's coastline by a narrow plain. The highest peak is Jabal ash Shaykh (Mount Hermon) in the extreme south-west of the country. To the east of the mountains, the Euphrates River crosses partly cultivatable plains in the north, while the central and southern areas consist mainly of desert plains.

Hemisphere

Northern

Climate

Syria has a moderate Mediterranean climate, four distinct seasons, and cloudless blue skies for the greater part of the year. Temperatures in autumn and spring range between 20 and 25 degrees Celsius (C), 30–35 degrees C in summer (May–September) and 5 to 10 degrees C in winter. Winter is generally moderate but wet in the coastal region and cold inland; summer is hot and dry inland, hot and humid on the coast.

Dress codes

Lightweight clothing is needed during the hottest months (May–September). Both men and women should dress discreetly in public. For business meetings men should wear a suit and tie, women a two-piece suit or equivalent. On social occasions dress as for business meetings unless otherwise indicated.

Entry requirements

Passports

Passports are required by all and must be valid for at least a month from the date of visit. Passports that carry an Israeli visa are prohibited.

Visa

Required by all except Arab nationals. All visas should be acquired before travelling.

Business visas require a letter of introduction and full itinerary along with the application. Contact the nearest consulate for further details.
Visa extensions are needed for visits over 15 days and can only be obtained from the Syria Immigration and Passport Administration.

Prohibited entry

Nationals of Israel, holders of passports with evidence of travel in Israel.

Currency advice/regulations

The import and export of local and foreign currency is limited to US$5,000 (or equivalent).
Travellers cheques are not widely accepted.

Customs

Personal items are duty-free. Gold jewellery must be declared on arrival.

Prohibited imports

Firearms, ammunition; birds and bird products.

Health (for visitors)

Medical services are well developed and many doctors speak English.

Mandatory precautions

A certificate of vaccination against yellow fever is required if travelling from an infected area.

Advisable precautions

Typhoid, tetanus, hepatitis A and polio immunisations are recommended, and anti-malaria precautions should be taken. There is a risk of rabies.

Hotels

Rooms are in short supply, and it is essential to book in advance. At first-class and international hotels, it will be necessary to pay in foreign currency (Arab nationals and resident foreigners exempted).
Hotels in Damascus are located close to most tourist attractions.

Credit cards
Credit cards are accepted in main business areas – contact the card provider for more details. Charge cards are not accepted.
In 2003, the Real Estate Bank (REB) became the first Syrian bank to accept MasterCard and Visa cards issued abroad.

Public holidays (national)
Fixed dates
1 Jan (New Year's Day), 8 Mar (Revolution Day), 21 Mar (Mothers' Day), 17 Apr (Independence Day), 1 May (Labour Day), 6 May (Martyrs' Day), 6 Oct (Liberation War Day), 25 Dec (Christmas Day).
Holidays that fall at the weekend are taken later in lieu.
Variable dates
Eid al Adha (three days), Islamic New Year, Birth of the Prophet, Eid al Fitr (three days).
Islamic year – 1429 (10 Jan 2008–28 Dec 2008): The Islamic year contains 354 or 355 days, with the result that Muslim feasts advance by 10–12 days against the Gregorian calendar. Dates of feasts vary according to the sighting of the new moon, so cannot be forecast exactly.

Working hours
Friday is the weekend break.
Banking
Sat–Thu: 0800–1400; early closing Thu.
Business
Sat–Thu: 0830–1430.
Government
Sat–Thu: 0830/0900–1300/1400, 1600/1700–1900/2000.
Shops
Sat–Thu: 0930–1400, 1630–2100 (summer); Sat–Thu: 0930–1400, 1600–2000 (winter).

Telecommunications
Mobile/cell phones
Two networks exist: GSM 900 and 1800

Electricity supply
220V, 50Hz AC with European, two-pin plugs.

Weights and measures
Metric system (local units also in use).

Social customs/useful tips
Appointments should be made in advance. Punctuality is appreciated. It is conventional to shake hands on meeting and taking leave. Sometimes a conference visit is a way of doing business. The host may hold several conversations with guests at the same time. It is not customary to start talking business immediately. At meetings it is polite to drink coffee or tea, when offered. It is useful for business cards to have Arabic translations on the reverse side. A few words of Arabic will be appreciated.
Do not smoke or drink in public during Ramadan. Islamic customs should be respected. Shoes should be removed on entry to mosques. Women should dress modestly. It is the convention to use the right and not the left hand when shaking hands and passing or receiving anything.
Alcohol is available to visitors.
Do not photograph anything remotely connected with the armed forces, including radio transmission aerials, and remember that some Syrians, particularly in rural areas, may regard cameras with suspicion.
It is considered very impolite for men to sit next to women on buses.
The punishment for possession of drugs is life imprisonment. For drug trafficking, the death penalty applies.
Travellers cheques are generally accepted and it is advisable to take US dollars as well. Accommodation in all hotels must be paid in hard currency, except one-star hotels. Food, beverages, telephone calls etc can be paid in local currency. It is illegal to change money on the streets. Only change money in recognised exchange shops, banks and hotels.

Security
Visitors should keep in touch with developments in the Middle East as any increase in regional tension might affect travel advice. Visitors are advised to carry identity documents at all times. Avoid driving outside the main cities at night.

Getting there
Air
National airline: Syrianair
International airport/s: Damascus International (DAM), 29km south-east of city, with banking, refreshments and duty-free shop. A bus service operates every 30 mins from 0600-2300, into the city centre.
Aleppo (ALP) 10km from city, with banking, refreshments and duty-free shop.
Taxis are available from both airports, and fares should be negotiated beforehand. Journey time into Damascus city centre is 30 minutes, and 20 minutes into Aleppo.
Airport tax: International departures: Syr£200, excluding transit passengers.
Surface
Road: From Istanbul via Ankara the E5 road runs to Damascus via Aleppo. From the east a road runs from Iran via Iraq, and was considered excellent, however border crossings are currently suspended. From the south the road from Akaba, (the terminus of the E5) runs via Amman (Jordan), and includes stretches of motorway. Other roads include those from the Lebanon.
Service taxis are faster than buses and run between Damascus-Amman or Irbid (Jordan).
Rail: Routes link Syria with Istanbul and Ankara (Turkey) and Amman (Jordan). Sleeper-cars are available and all trains are air-conditioned.
There are rail lines running from northern Iraq to the Syrian coast, however services are currently suspended.
Water: Car ferries sail from Bodrum (Turkey), Rhodes, Heraklion, Santorini and Piraeus (Greece). Cruise ferries are run by Italian, Greek, Cypriot and Turkish companies, with sailings that vary from year to year. Passage may take up to three days. Ferries from Alexandria (Egypt) dock at the Lebanese port of Beirut – the distance to Damascus is shorter than any via Syrian port; visitors should check the viability of this route before travelling.
Main port/s: Latakia, Tartus and Banias.

Getting about
National transport
Air: There are internal flights by Syrianair between Damascus, Aleppo, Latakia, Qamishli and Deir Ez Zor.
Road: The 30,208km road network has some 22,500km of relatively good surfaced roads linking main centres.
Buses: Luxury couch services operate between major towns. Bus tickets, with assigned seats, should be bought prior to boarding. Qadmous, al Ahliah and al Ryan are private bus companies.
Minibuses serve smaller locations; they have no schedule and leave when full.
Microbuses are modern vans used on short routes between cities and on routes to small towns and villages. They are more comfortable than the minibuses and there is no standing room. Departures are more frequent but they are more expensive than the minibuses. Fares are usually paid on board.
Taxis: May be used to travel between cities as they are affordable; either negotiate a fare with the driver or check that the meter runs correctly. Long-haul service (shared) taxis are also available on the more popular routes, they cost more than microbuses but less than a personal taxi hire.
Rail: Two classes of rail service are available, with restaurant cars, sleeping carriages and air-conditioning. The railway links all the major cities and has a regular timetable, but it can be slow so it may not suit the business traveller.
City transport
Taxis: Yellow cabs in Damascus are expensive; always check the meter has been set. Fares are mostly by negotiation.
Drivers do not expect a tip.
In other cities, fares are set by government departments.

Buses, trams & metro: From airport to city centre.

Car hire

Private cars are rarely available, but taxis are reasonably priced.

BUSINESS DIRECTORY

The addresses listed below are a selection only. While World of Information makes every endeavour to check these addresses, we cannot guarantee that changes have not been made, especially to telephone numbers and area codes. We would welcome any corrections.

Telephone area codes

The international direct dialling (IDD) code for Syria is +963, followed by the area code and subscriber's number:

Aleppo21Lattakia41
Damascus11Raqqah22
Hassakah52Tartous43
Homs31Zabadani13

Chambers of Commerce

Federation of Syrian Chambers of Commerce, Mousa bin Nosair Street, PO Box 5909, Damascus (tel: 333-7344; fax: 333-1127; fax: syr-trade@mail.syr; internet: www.fedcommsyr.org).

Aleppo Chamber of Commerce, Amir Palace Hotel Building, Bab Jnein Street, PO Box 1261, Aleppo (tel: 223-8236; fax: 221-3493; e-mail: alepchmb@mail.sy).

Aleppo Chamber of Industry, PO Box 1859, Aleppo (tel: 362-0600; fax: 362-0040; e-mail: alpindus@net.sy).

Damascus Chamber of Commerce, 126 Mouawiah Street, Hariqa, PO Box 1040, Damascus (tel: 221-1339; fax: 222-5874; e-mail: dcc@net.net).

Damascus Chamber of Industry, Mouawiah Street, PO Box 1305, Damascus (tel: 221-5042; fax: 224-5981; e-mail: dci@mail.sy).

Damascus Countryside Chamber of Commerce, Bagdad Street, PO Box 5859, Damascus (tel: 231-5653; fax: 231-3798).

Hasakah Chamber of Commerce and Industry, PO Box 243, Hasakah (tel: 221-645; fax: 313-842).

Homs Chamber of Commerce and Industry, Abulauf Street, PO Box 440, Homs (tel: 469-440; fax: 464-247; e-mail: homschamber@homschamber.org).

Lattakia Chamber of Commerce and Industry, PO Box 124, Latakia (tel: 479-530; fax: 478-526; e-mail: lattakia@chamberlattakia.com).

Tartous Chamber of Commerce and Industry, PO Box 403, Tartous (tel: 329-852; fax: 329-728; e-mail: info@tarcci.com).

Banking

Agricultural Co-operative Bank; PO Box 4325, al Naanaa Garden, Damascus (tel: 221-3462, 222-139).

Commercial Bank of Syria (Banque Commerciale de Syrie) PO Box 933, Yousef Azmeh Square, Damascus (tel: 221-8890, 221-8891).

Industrial Bank; PO Box 7578, Almuhandiseen Building, Maisaloun Street, Damascus (tel: 222-8200).

Popular Credit Bank, PO Box 2841, Maisaloun Street, Damascus (tel: 222-7604, 221-8555).

Real Estate Bank, PO Box 2337, Y al Azme Square, Damascus (tel: 221-8602/3).

Central bank

Central Bank of Syria, PO Box 2254, 29 Ayar Street, Damascus (tel: 221-6581; fax: 245-5576).

Travel information

Silk Road Travel and Tourism, Fardoss Street, PO Box 12958, Damascus (tel: 223-0500/5; fax: 223-1138, 231-5555; email: hanano@silkroad-tours.com).

Syrianair, Syrian Arab Airlines, Youssef al Azmeh Square; PO Box 417, Damascus (tel: 223-1838, 223-2154; fax: 221-4923; internet: www.syriaair.com).

Ministry of tourism

Ministry of Tourism, rue Abou Firas al Hamadani, Damascus (tel: 221-0122; internet: www.syriatourism.org).

Ministries

Ministry of Electricity, PO Box 3386, Damascus (tel: 222-3086, 222-9654; fax: 222-9062).

Ministry of Health, Najmeh Suare, Parliament Street, Damascus (tel: 333-9602, 3333-3801, 331-1020; fax: 331-1114).

Other useful addresses

Arab Advertising Organisation, Moutanabbi Street, PO Box 2842, Damascus.

British Embassy, Kotob Building, 11 Mohd Kurd Ali Street, Malki PO Box 37, Damascus (tel: 371-2561/3).

Cotton Marketing Organisation, BP 729, Rue Bab al araj, Aleppo (tel: 238-486).

Director General of the Damascus International Fair, Kouwatli Street, Damascus (tel: 229-853/840/914).

General Organisation for Cement, PO Box 5265, Damascus (tel: 666-7000/3).

General Organisation for Chemicals and Foodstuffs, PO Box 893, Damascus (tel: 222-8521, 222-5421).

General Organisation for Engineering Industries, PO Box 3120, Damascus (tel: 212-1824/5).

General Organisation for Insurance (The Syrian Insurance Company), PO Box 22679, Damascus (tel: 221-8430/1; fax: 222-0494).

General Organisation for Machinery and Equipment, PO Box 3130, Damascus (tel: 221-8223, 221-8156; fax: 221-1118).

General Organisation for Metals and Building Materials, PO Box 3136, Damascus (tel: 442-0941, 442-0944, 442-0948; fax: 442-0947).

General Organisation for Sugar, PO Box 429, Homs.

General Organisation for the Textile Industries, BP 620, Rue Fardoss, Damascus (tel: 221-6200, 222-7158; fax: 221-6201).

General Organisation for Trading and Distribution, PO Box 15, Damascus (tel: 221-0396).

General Organisation of Free Zones, PO Box 2790, Damascus (tel: 219-137).

International Centre for Agricultural Research in the Dry Areas, Box 5466, Aleppo.

Public Establishment for Distribution and Exploitation of Electric Energy, PO Box 35199, Damascus (tel: 224-5926, 222-3086, 222-9654).

Public Establishment for Electricity Generation and Transmission, PO Box 3386, Damascus (tel: 212-9795, 211-9935; fax: 222-9062).

Syrian Embassy (USA), 2215 Wyoming Avenue, NW, Washington DC 20008 (tel: (+1-202) 232-6313; fax: (+1-202) 234-9548; email: info@syrianembassy.org).

Syrian Tourism Investment Forum, Damascus (tel: 223-9383; email: invest-souq@syriatourism.org; www.syriatourism.com).

National news agency: SANA

Other news agencies: All4Syria (www.all4syria.org).

Internet sites

Al Thawra newspaper: www.thawra.com

ArabNet: www.arab.net

Arabia Online: www.arabia.com

Ministry of Information: www.moi-syria.com

Museums with no borders www.discoverislamicart.org

Travel Information: www.visit-syria.com

Taiwan

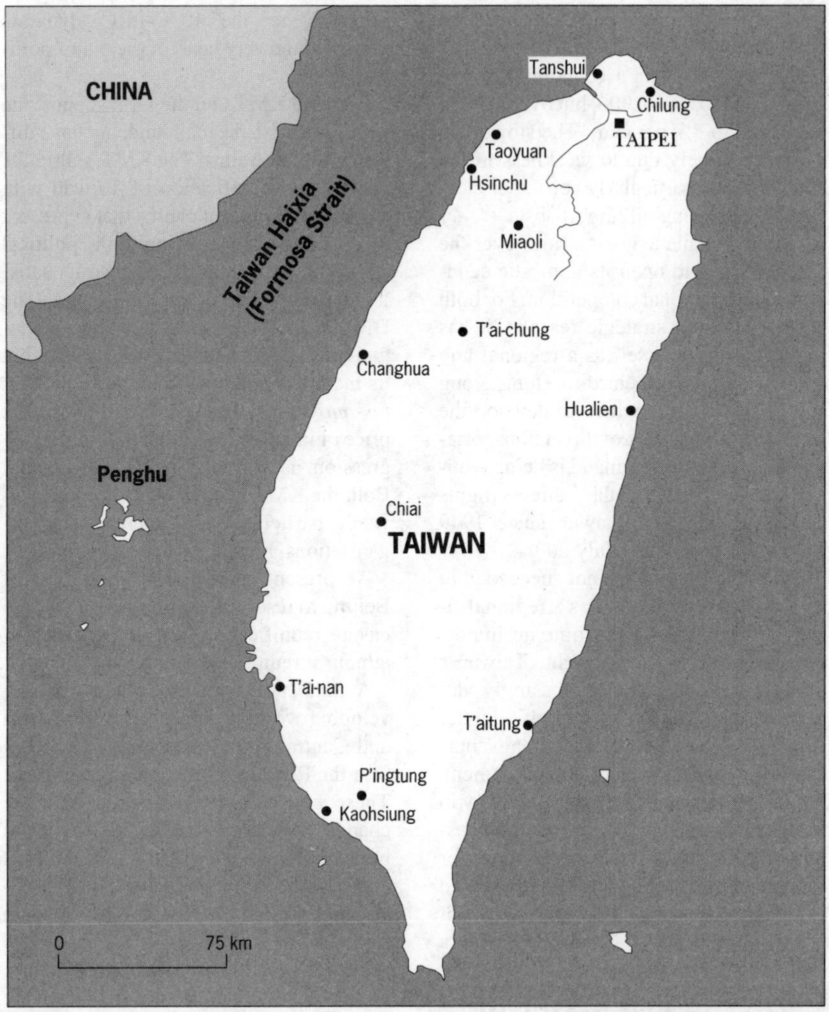

KEY FACTS

Official name: Chung-hua Min-kuo (Republic of China)

Head of State: President Ma Ying-jeou (Kuomintang) (took office 20 May 2008)

Head of government: Prime Minister Liu Chao-shiuan premier (Kuomintang) (appointed 20 May 2008)

Ruling party: Kuomintang (KMT) (Chinese Nationalist Party) (from 12 Jan 2008)

Area: 35,961 square km

Population: 23.08 million (2007)

Capital: Taipei

Official language: Mandarin Chinese

Currency: Taiwanese dollar (T$) = 100 cents

Exchange rate: T$30.35 per US$ (Jul 2008)

GDP per capita: US$16,606 (2007)

GDP real growth: 5.70% (2007)

Labour force: 10.46 million (2006)

Unemployment: 3.90% (2007)

Inflation: 1.80% (2007)

Balance of trade: US$15.82 billion (2005)

Foreign debt: US$86.73 billion (2005)

Visitor numbers: 3.52 million (2006)*

* estimated figure

According to the Asian Development Bank (ADB) in its *Asian Development Outlook 2008* publication, Taiwan's economic growth accelerated in 2007, as gross domestic product (GDP) rose to 5.7 per cent, one per cent more than the average recorded for the period 2003–06. According to the ADB, the momentum of growth was particularly strong in the second half of the year due to recovering private consumption and buoyant exports. For the year as a whole, exports were the principal demand side driver of the economy despite a drop in merchandise export growth from 12.9 per cent to 10.1 per cent as a percentage of total GDP. A drop in exports to the US of 0.9 per cent was compensated by strong demand from mainland China and other Asian markets. Some sort of equilibrium in overall trade was maintained as import growth also fell from 11.0 per cent to 8.0 per cent. The slowdown in external demand was responsible for limiting expansion in 2007.

Inflation rose from an annual rate of 1 per cent in the first quarter of 2007 to an estimated 4.5 per cent in the fourth. For the year as a whole, the ADB recorded that Taiwan's inflation rate had risen by 1.8 per cent, three times the rate of 0.6 per cent recorded for 2006. Annual core inflation rose to a decade high1.4 per cent. In view of the inflationary pressures evident in the economy, Taiwan's authorities saw fit to raise the base lending rate to an annual 4.31 per cent at the end of 2007. Resilient domestic demand looked likely to cushion the Taiwanese economy from the global downturn. Export growth was expected to slow to 6.0 per cent in 2008 but import growth looked likely to outpace export growth, at an annual 6.5 per cent. The main external risk for Taiwan was a sharper than anticipated slump in the US market; the hoped for bonanza of improved links with mainland China was also expected to take longer to materialise.

All change

Politics in Taiwan are rarely dull. In May 2007, Su Tseng-chang resigned and Chang Chun-hsiung was appointed as prime minister. But this still didn't prevent, in the 2008 parliamentary elections held on 12 January, the opposition Koumintang (of the Pan-Blue Coalition) taking power when they won 81 seats (out of 113), with 72 per cent of the vote. The ruling MCT (Pan-Green Coalition) only managed 27 seats and resulted in President Chen Shui-bian stepping down as leader of the MCT and being replaced by Frank Hsieh. On 22 March, in presidential elections, Ma Ying-Jeou (Kuomintang) won 58.46 per cent of the vote; Frank Hsieh (MCT) won 41.55 per cent. Ma Ying-jeou took office as president on 20 May; Vincent Siew became vice president and Liu Chao-shiuan prime minister.

Growth slows

The economic crisis that engulfed much of Asia in the late 1990's scarcely caused a ripple in the boardrooms of Taipei. The Taiwanese enjoy one of Asia's highest living standards (GDP per capita in 2007 was US$16,606). The Republic of China (ROC) (Taiwan) is a net exporter of capital to the region and Taiwanese companies are themselves seen with increasing frequency on the regional and global business stage. Furthermore, Taiwan's foreign exchange reserves are the third highest of any country in the world. It is one of Asia's powerhouses and a centre for hi-tech exports.

That said, Taiwan's economic growth slowed in 2005 and 2006, but by 2007 had recovered to 5.7 per cent. The slowdown had been largely due to weakness in the export sector, particularly consumer electronics, and rising oil import costs.

Taiwan has made great strides over the past ten years to open its domestic economy to international competition. For both commercial and strategic reasons, it has sought a role for itself as a regional hub and an alternative centre to Hong Kong and Shanghai from which to develop the Chinese market. Lack of direct transportation links with the mainland is being rectified as the first regular, direct flights between China and Taiwan since 1949 were inaugurated on 4 July 2008.

Although Taiwan has not succeeded in its bid to ensconce itself as a regional financial centre, it has become an important market in its own right. Taiwan's industry is becoming increasingly dependent on the export of higher value-added products and is a major purchaser of industrial plant and equipment. Major infrastructure projects underway in the telecommunications, energy and transportation sectors provide opportunities for foreign engineering and technology-based companies. An affluent and fashion conscious population of 22 million with a high propensity to spend, provides a growing consumer market. Increasingly, the younger generation takes its cue from Japan rather than the US.

ROC and PRC

In reality there is little separation between affairs of state and that of domestic political considerations in Taiwan. Varying approaches to the ROC-PRC dynamic remain at the very heart of the major political parties.

Both the KMT and the DPP support the *status quo* with the mainland, but have differing ultimate aims. The KMT's ultimate goal is the reunification of Taiwan with mainland China, but claims that at present this is not desirable owing to the political environment in the PRC, hence its satisfaction with the current *status quo*. The DPP on the other hand, advocates eventual official independence for Taiwan, but its members continue to embrace the *status quo* simply because they believe the price of independence, that is, Chinese aggression, is currently not worth paying. Both the KMT and the DPP promote Taiwan's participation in supranational organisations, however.

At present it remains the policy of Beijing to reserve the right 'to use force to ensure reunification' should peaceful attempts at reunification fail.

A number of countries, mostly in the developing world and particularly in Africa and Central America, continue to recognise the ROC officially and not the PRC. These however, are dwindling with the change of heart by Costa Rica when it broke diplomatic ties with Taiwan in June 2007. At the same time Taiwan had its application to join the United Nations again rejected.

Taiwan did achieve a minor victory, however, when it threatened to boycott the Beijing Olympics if China downgraded the island's status by calling it 'China-Taipei' instead of 'Chinese-Taipei' as defined by the International Olympic Committee (IOC). China had to back down and Taiwan went on to win medals in both the main and Paralympic games.

Outlook

The prospects for the Taiwanese economy are promising; the IMF forecasts healthy growth. It is important to note when evaluating the economy of the ROC that it is not, in pure terms, a developing economy. Owing to the hi-tech nature of the economy's output and its highly skilled workforce, it shares more in common with

KEY INDICATORS — **Taiwan**

	Unit	2003	2004	2005	2006	2007
Population	m	22.87	23.07	22.77	22.88	23.08
Gross domestic product (GDP)	US$bn	289.52	305.30	346.65	365.51	383.31
GDP per capita	US$	12,660	13,260	15,224	15,978	16,606
GDP real growth	%	3.2	5.7	4.0	4.9	5.7
Inflation	%	0.1	1.6	2.3	0.6	1.8
Unemployment	%	5.3	4.4	4.1	3.9	3.9
Exports (fob) (goods)	US$m	130,000	170,500	198,431	223,789	–
Imports (cif) (goods)	US$m	113,000	165,400	182,614	200,375	–
Balance of trade	US$m	17,000	5,100	15,817	23,414	–
Current account	US$m	29,270	19,010	16,019	24,661	31,701.0
Foreign debt	US$bn	62.7	80.0	87.8	91.6	–
Exchange rate	per US$	34.38	33.35	32.76	32.52	32.38

Organisation for Economic Co-operation and Development (OECD) countries than those of the developing world, hence the less explosive, yet steady rate of growth.

Risk assessment

Politics	Fair
Economy	Good
Reginal stability	Good

COUNTRY PROFILE

Historical profile

Before the arrival of the Europeans, the island was occupied by indigenous people and immigrants from mainland China.
1590 Portuguese navigators discovered Taiwan and called it Ilha Formosa, meaning 'beautiful island' in Portuguese. This is the origin of Taiwan's other name, Formosa.
1624 The Dutch arrived in Taiwan.
1629 The Spaniards, alarmed by growing Dutch control of Taiwan, arrived and occupied the northern part of the island.
1630 The Dutch formally settled on the island.
1630–62 The Dutch and Spanish fought for control of the island. The Spanish were defeated and driven out. The Dutch strengthened their control after the establishment of the Dutch East India Company and Taiwan became an important trading centre. Chinese resistance eventually grew so strong that the Dutch were driven off the island.
1700–1800 Chinese mass migration to the island took place.
1885 Taiwan was officially made a province of China.
1895 China ceded control of Taiwan to Japan following the Sino-Japanese war. The Japanese modernised the country, upgrading infrastructure, restoring the communications network and developing agriculture.
1945 After Japan's defeat in the Second World War, Taiwan became a province of the Republic of China, controlled by the Kuomintang (KMT) (Chinese Nationalist Party).
1949 The KMT was driven out of the mainland by the communist People's Liberation Army (PLA) led by Mao Zedong. President Chiang Kai-shek withdrew his forces to Taiwan. The KMT asserted that it, rather than the new People's Republic of China, constituted the rightful government of mainland China and that it would eventually resume control of all of China.
1954 The US signed a security agreement with the KMT pledging to protect Taiwan.
1971 The People's Republic of China replaced Taiwan as Chinese representatives at the UN.
1975 Chiang Kai-Shek died. His son, Chiang Ching-kuo, became president.
1987 Martial law and one-party rule were dismantled.
1988 The death of President Chiang Ching-kuo. Taiwan-born Lee Teng-hui became president.
1994 Nationwide local elections were held. The KMT retained its dominance of the political system, although the candidate of the opposition Min-chu Chin-pu Tang (MCT) (Democratic Progressive Party), Chen Shui-bian, was elected mayor of Taipei.
1995 The KMT lost ground to the MCT in the legislative elections.
1996 President Lee Teng-hui comfortably won Taiwan's first direct presidential elections.
1998 The KMT was re-elected, with an increased majority.
1999 Taiwan suffered its worst earthquake for nearly 100 years.
2000 Chen Shui-bian of the MCT won the presidential elections.
2001 The pro-independence MCT won the parliamentary elections; the KMT lost its majority for the first time in 50 years.
2002 Taiwan joined the World Trade Organisation. Laws were enacted to put the military under the control of the civilian cabinet. President Chen Shui-bian took over the leadership of the MCT.
2004 President Chen Shui-bian (MCT), was re-elected, having survived an assassination attempt on the eve of the elections. Constitutional changes and electoral reforms were introduced including reducing the number of seats in the legislative Yuan to 113; with a single-member district parallel voting system; the term of office for members of parliament increased to four years. Of the legislative Yuan seats, 73 are plurality seats (one for each district), six for aboriginal peoples and the remaining from party lists by proportional representation, of which 50 per cent must be allocated to women. Although President Chen's pro-independence Min-chu Chin-pu Tang (MCT) (Democratic Progressive Party) won the single largest number of seats in the general elections, it narrowly failed to take control of parliament.
2005 The China's National People's Congress passed an anti-secession law, enshrining Beijing's claim of sovereignty and its threat of military force in the event of Taiwan's formal independence; more than one million people took to the streets in Taiwan to express opposition to the law. The Supreme Court ruled that the disputed 2004 presidential elections were valid.
2006 Following the defeat of the MCT in local elections, Prime Minister Hsieh resigned and was replaced by Su Tseng-chang. President Chen abolished the National Unification Council. Corruption scandals involving the president's family and entourage led to unsuccessful opposition calls for a referendum on the president's suitability for office. Chen devolved some powers to the prime minister office. The president's wife appeared in court in December on corruption charges.
2007 In May, Su Tseng-chang resigned and Chang Chun-hsiung was appointed as prime minister. Costa Rica broke diplomatic ties with Taiwan in June; President Arias said his country wanted to attract more investment from China. In June Taiwan once again applied to join the UN; the application was rejected and hailed by China as in keeping with its 'One China' policy.
2008 In parliamentary elections held on 12 January the opposition Koumintang (of the Pan-Blue Coalition) won 81 seats (out of 113), with 72 per cent of the vote. The ruling MCT (Pan-Green Coalition) only managed 27 seats and resulted in President Chen Shui-bian stepping down as leader of the MCT. On 22 March, in presidential elections, Ma Ying-Jeou (Kuomintang) won 58.46 per cent of the vote; Frank Hsieh (MCT) won 41.55 per cent. Ma Ying-jeou took office as president on 20 May; Vincent Siew became vice president and Liu Chao-shiuan prime minister. In the first formal talks with China (they had been suspended since 1999) an agreement to allow 36 direct flights (18 each) a week between them; a further agreement allowed 3,000 tourists per day to visit each country. The first regular, direct flights between China and Taiwan since 1949 were inaugurated on 4 July.

Political structure

Constitution

The Legislative Yuan, presided over by the prime minister, is the highest government body. It is responsible for passing laws and drafting the budget. It is elected every three years and has the power to dismiss the prime minister.
The 29-member Control Yuan exercises powers of investigation, impeachment and censure over senior officials, including the grand justices of the Judicial Yuan and members of the Examination Yuan, and power of audit over central and local government finances. Its members are appointed by the president with the approval of the legislature.
The Examination Yuan supervises examinations for entry into public office and deals with personnel questions of the civil service.
The Kuo-min Ta-hui (National Assembly) passed a series of constitutional amendments in April 2000 which reduced itself to an ad hoc institution deprived of most

of its powers. The powers of initiating constitutional amendments, changing the national boundaries, impeaching the president or vice president and approving the appointment of senior officials, were transferred to the Legislative Yuan. The Kuo-min Ta-hui retains the functions of ratifying constitutional amendments and impeachment proceedings against the president.
The National Assembly is to convene for a month from no later than 31 May 2005 to vote on whether public referenda could be used to change the constitution, which means the abolition of the Assembly itself. Other constitutional amendments slated to go before the Assembly are plans to streamline the Legislative Yuan by halving the number of seats from 225 to 113, beginning from 2007, and the extension of legislators' terms from three to four years and whether it should hand over to grand justices the rights to impeach the president.

Form of state
Representative democracy

The executive
The president is directly elected for a four-year term. The president nominates a prime minister to head the Executive Yuan (cabinet), which is the highest administrative organ of the nation, and is responsible to the Legislative Yuan. The Executive Yuan consists of the ministries and commissions and 19 subordinate administrative organs of state.

National legislature
The Li fa Yuan (Legislative Yuan) is the highest legislative organ of state. The number of seats in the legislative Yuan was reduced to 113 in 2004; a single-member district parallel voting system was introduced; the term of office for members of parliament was increased from three to four years. Of the legislative Yuan seats 73 are plurality seats (one for each district), six for aboriginal peoples and the remaining from party lists by proportional representation, of which 50 per cent must be allocated to women

Legal system
The Judicial Yuan is the highest judicial organ of state. Justices are appointed by the president with the approval of the Control Yuan. Subordinate organs of the Judicial Yuan include the Supreme Court, the high courts, the district courts, the Administrative Court and the Commission on the Disciplinary Sanctions of Public Functionaries.

Last elections
12 January 2008 (parliamentary); 22 March 2008 (presidential).
Results: Parliamentary: KMT won 81 seats (out of 113), with 72 per cent of the vote; the MCT won 27 seats; 34 seats were allocated on a party list system and six seats were reserved for ethnic minorities.
Presidential: Ma Ying-Jeou (Kuomintang) won 58.46 per cent of the vote, Frank Hsieh (MCT) won 41.55 per cent; turnout was 76.33 per cent.

Next elections
2011 (parliamentary); 2011 (presidential).

Political parties

Ruling party
Kuomintang (KMT) (Chinese Nationalist Party) (from 12 Jan 2008)

Main opposition party
Min-chu Chin-pu Tang (MCT) (Democratic Progressive Party)

Population

23.08 million (2007)
Population density: 619 inhabitants per square km
Annual growth rate: 0.8 per cent (2003)

Ethnic make-up
Taiwan's population is mostly ethnic Han Chinese. A majority of these are local Taiwanese, who have language links to Fujian province across the Taiwan Strait. There is a powerful minority of immigrants that came from the mainland during the 1940s, as well as a Hakka minority.
Taiwan's non-Han aborigines (yuanchumin) are related to the Polynesian and Malay ethnic groups. They comprise dozens of distinct groups, including the Rukai tribe (about 8,000 strong) and the Clouded Leopard People. They have limited rights and may not sell or develop lands. Indigenous rights groups have campaigned to regain political and economic autonomy in the aboriginal territories that were demarcated during the Japanese occupation.

Religions
The majority of people are Buddhist or Taoist with Confucian influence. Most Chinese make no sharp distinction between Buddhism and Taoism in Taiwan, and most practise a hybrid of these two religions. About 2.5 per cent of the population are Christian.

Education

There are 2,600 primary schools with a total enrolment around two million students. Primary school lasts for six years before entry to junior high school, at aged 12, for three years. Dependent on exam results at aged 15, students may move on to either a senior vocational high school or a senior high school (for more academic courses which lead to entrance exams for higher education). There are 986 secondary schools and 188 vocational institutions.
All education is delivered in Chinese however English is a compulsory subject during the secondary cycles. Higher education is offered at colleges and universities from aged 18. The total number of universities and colleges is 150 and the gross enrolment of graduates aged between 18 and 21 years is nearly 70 per cent per cent.
Compulsory years: Six to 15.
Pupils per teacher: 19 in primary school.

Health

Taiwan's public health sector offers a universal health insurance system, the first in Asia to ensure equal access to care for the entire population. Total expenditure on health per capita is approaching developed country standards.
Taiwan has 700 hospitals and 17,000 clinics and an active pharmaceutical industry.
Life expectancy: 77 years (government statistics, 2004).
Fertility rate/Maternal mortality rate: 1.4 births per woman; maternal mortality 7.86 per 100,000 live births (Government statistics).
Birth rate/Death rate: 3.25 per 1,000 (Government statistics).
Child (under 5 years) mortality rate (per 1,000): 6.7 per 1,000 live births (2003)

Welfare

The welfare policy is not universal but is budgeted according to the county or city governments. There is provision for special subsidies and assistance to low-income earners and families, based on variations in regional income distribution for each fiscal year. Some low-income families with children qualify for an additional monthly subsidy.
The elderly comprise a growing proportion of the population. Pensioners (aged from 65 years) of Taipei City and County, Ilan, Hsinchu, Tainan, Chiayi City, Kaohsiung and Penghu counties benefit from organised pension systems. There is serious shortage of housing for elderly people, despite Taiwan's 350 retirement and nursing homes.

Main cities

Taipei (capital, estimated population 2.6 million in 2005), Kaohsiung (1.6 million), Taichung (1.0 million), Tainan (755,800), Panchiao (589,700).

Languages spoken

The second language spoken is Fukienese, a dialect of Mandarin, but very different to it, that is spoken in the Fujian province in China. Fukienese is also called Taiwanese. Other Chinese dialects spoken are Shanghaiese, Hakka and Cantonese. English is spoken only by the elite.

Official language/s
Mandarin Chinese

Media

National news agency: Central News Agency (www.cna.com.tw).

Press

Dailies: In Chinese, United Daily News (http://udn.com), China Times (http://news.chinatimes.com), Liberty Times (www.libertytimes.com.tw), Central Daily News () and the Taiwan Daily. In English, The China Post (www.chinapost.com.tw), Taiwan News (www.etaiwannews.com) and Taipei Times (www.taipeitimes.com). Local newspapers, in Chinese include Apple Daily (http://1-apple.com.tw), and Taiwan Shin Sheng Daily News (www.tssdnews.com.tw) from Taipei and Keng Sheng Daily News (www.ksnews.com.tw), from Hualien.

Business: In Chinese and English, Taiwan Economic News (http://cens.com) and CommonWealth (www.cw.com.tw) (monthly) specifically deal with business and financial news. Major newspapers have business sections and the government publishes Taiwan Journal (http://taiwanjournal.nat.gov.tw) with information on trade and statistics and Invest in Taiwan (http://investintaiwan.nat.gov.tw) with information on local industries.

Periodicals: In English and published by the government, Taiwan Panorama (www.taiwan-panorama.com) and Taiwan Review (http://taiwanreview.nat.gov.tw) are news and general interest monthlies.

Broadcasting

The Central Broadcasting System (CBS) is the national broadcaster for Taiwan.

Radio: The RTI (Radio Taiwan International) broadcasts nationally and to mainland China. External services are relayed worldwide in up to10 languages.

There are over 170 radio stations, which cater for specific musical genres. UFO Network is one of the most popular private radio station, others include Hit FM (www.hitfm.com.tw) and Kiss Radio Taiwan (www.kiss.com.tw). The only English language station is ICRT FM (www.uforadio.com.tw).

Television: There are three state-owned TV networks (www.pts.org.tw) but most households subscribe to cable TV.

Advertising

A full range of advertising opportunities are available.

Economy

During the 1980s and 1990s, Taiwan became one of the foremost of the regional 'tiger' economies, combining elements of the 'Asian Miracle' of state-guided development with a strong base of competitive, market-oriented small- and medium-sized enterprises. The latter enabled Taiwan to ride out the Asian crisis with relative equanimity as exporters enjoyed a devaluation-led boom.

In the second half of 2001, Taiwan fell into recession. Exports suffered the biggest blow as a result of the global decline in demand for high-tech and electronic produce, a sector that typically accounted for 50 per cent of Taiwan's overall exports. More workers were laid off as operations were shifted to mainland China. The high rate of capital flight to China also damaged the economy.

The foreign investment environment has been good, with joint ventures and direct investment in most sectors enabled since 1995. As part of its commitments as a WTO member, Taiwan, which joined in January 2002, agreed to liberalise its telecommunications market and has opened other sectors of the economy to foreign buyers. Taiwan is concerned that large foreign monopolies will erode the government's influential role and threaten domestic industries. Taiwan is looking to extend its cross-straits links and encourage trade with the mainland.

The economy began to recover in 2002, but was slowed briefly again by the outbreak of Severe Acute Respiratory Syndrome (Sars) in early 2003. Taiwan committed US$1.4 billion to offset the effects of the disease, with a successful outcome – GDP growth stabilised at 3.2 per cent in 2003 and continued to grow, reaching 5.7 per cent in 2004. Growth was slower in 2005 (4.1 per cent), due to high oil prices, a fall in exports and uncertainty in the high tech sector.

Taiwan is a creditor economy, holding one of the world's largest foreign exchange reserves.

External trade

Taiwan belongs to the 21-member Asia-Pacific Economic Co-operation (Apec) forum, which is a bloc of countries that border the Pacific with the aim of facilitating trade, economic growth and investment in the region.

The manufacturing sector accounts for 50 per cent of GDP. Taiwan is a global leading producer of hi-tech goods and the largest supplier of semi-conductors, telecommunication equipment, computers and monitors and optical disks (DVDs). Industrial production includes polycarbonates, refined petroleum and vehicle assembly. With few natural resources it has to import most of its energy needs and raw materials. Nevertheless, the balance of trade is kept level by the high volume of Taiwanese of exports.

Imports

Imports are dominated by raw materials, machinery and electrical equipment (around 45 per cent of total), coal, crude oil and natural gas.

Main sources: Japan (22.9 per cent total, 2006), China (12.2 per cent), US (11.6 per cent).

Exports

Main export commodities are electronics, computers and monitors, textiles, refined oil and derivatives, polycarbonates and vehicles.

Main destinations: China (22.7 per cent total, 2006), Hong Kong (15.7 per cent), US (14.7 per cent).

Agriculture

Farming

The agriculture sector contributes 2 per cent to GDP.Since accession to the WTO in 2002 Taiwan has refocussed its agricultural objectives. The workforce is being reduced by 4 per cent per year until it reaches 633,000 workers and the emphasis will be on quality food rather than quantity. Taiwan's farm plots are generally small, hindering cost-efficient management. Estimates show that 76 per cent of all farming households have less than one hectare (ha) of arable landand 80 per cent have members working part- or full-time in other occupations.

Rice is still the principal and most valuable crop (in quantiy and cultivated land), followed by betel nuts, pineapples, mangoes, sugar cane, watermelons, tea, bamboo shoots, pears, and peanuts. Industrial crops include cotton, hemp and jute.

Fishing

The fishing industry has gradually developed from small-scale coastal fishing to deep-sea commercial fishing. The deep-water fishing industry is large and expanding, supplemented by aquaculture. Eel is an important aquacultural product as are milkfish, tilapia, groupers, tiger prawn and oyster. Intense aqcuaculture has done some damage to the environment by drawing off huge amounts of water. This has caused land to cave in. The government is tackling the problem by encouraging the recycling of freshwater. The government has been actively engaged in international fishery management and has signed official or private fishery agreements with 29 countries.

The annual fish catch in Taiwan is typically 1.4 million tonnes.

In 2004, the total marine fish catch was 843,035 tonnes and the total crustacean catch was 25,289 tonnes.

Forestry

The timber industry is limited by inaccessibility, the poor quality of much of the forestry resources and by an official policy of conserving supplies. Taiwan's forested area covers around 2.1 million hectares, which is about half the land area. Forestry products include sawn timber, plywood, paper and fuel for local use.

Industry and manufacturing

The industrial sector contributes around 35 per cent to GDP, with manufacturing accounting for 95 per cent of industrial exports. Heavy industries include motor manufacturing, steel production and shipbuilding. Taiwan's main strength is its high-tech industry. In recent years, Taiwan has moved away from manufacturing electronic toys, deemed to be unhealthy for children, and focussed on electronic components. Most production is exported, accounting for an estimated 55 per cent of total exports and 20 per cent of GDP. The government is hoping to develop Taiwan into a green silicon island. In 2002, the Taiwan Industrial Technology Association (TITA) was set up to upgrade industries. TITA will spend US$571 million each year on developing industries such as optoelectronics, aerospace, chemicals, semiconductors, telecommunications and information technology (IT).

Many Taiwanese products have an important share in the global market and the communications industry has been boosted by the liberalisation of the global telecommunications industry.

The main concern for Taiwan's industry is that low-end and mid-range manufacturers are moving to China. To remain competitive, Taiwan needs to focus on developing integrated software design.

Tourism

Tourism contributed 2.78 per cent to GDP in 2004. In 2005, 3,378,000 arrivals were recorded, exceeding the government's target for the year. Of this total, 1,380,000 described themselves as tourists. The government recognises the economic importance of the sector and is actively promoting it and improving facilities. On 13 June 2008 an agreement was signed with Taiwan on 13 June to allow 3,000 tourists per day into each country from 18 July.

Mining

Mining accounts for less than 1 per cent of GDP. Taiwan has few exploitable mineral resources. Due to the depletion of local sources, nearly all of the rare earth and metallic mining products are imported. Over 20 types of minerals are mined in Taiwan, mainly marble, limestone, serpentine and gravel. Marble is Taiwan's most important mineral resource with reserves conservatively estimated at over 300 million tonnes. Marble, salt, sand and gravel constitute the most valuable mineral products. Taiwan also produces iron and steel from imported iron ore and iron scrap and processed products such as aluminium, copper, lead, nickel, tin and zinc from imported raw materials.

Taiwan has four gold-bearing mines with metal content estimated at 100 tonnes. Taiwan utilises its large trade surpluses to import gold.

Hydrocarbons

Taiwan is almost entirely reliant on energy imports. Approximately 99.5 per cent of oil and coal needs and over 80 per cent of natural gas requirements are imported. Taiwan had proven oil reserves of four million barrels in 2004 and produces around 8,000 barrels per day (bpd). Oil consumption is estimated at around one million bpd. Taiwan is dependent on imports from the Middle East ands West Africa. Oil accounts for 46 per cent of total primary energy consumption, mainly by industry. There are four refineries with a total refining capacity of 1.22 million bpd. Taiwan is laying claim to the potentially oil-rich Spratly Islands, an area of contention between Taiwan, Vietnam, China, Brunei, Malaysia and The Philippines. Taiwan has around eight billion cubic metres of gas reserves and produces around 890 million cubic metres per annum. Natural gas consumption amounts to around eight billion cubic metres per annum. Most of Taiwan's imports of liquefied natural gas (LNG) come from Indonesia and Malaysia. The government plans to triple LNG consumption by 2010 as part of its commitment to the environment. Taiwan has coal reserves of 98 million tonnes, but ceased production in 2000. Taiwan consumes 55 million tonnes of coal per annum. Most coal imports come from China, Indonesia and Australia. Coal is used for electricity generation, steel production, cement and petrochemical industries.

Energy

Taiwan has installed electricity generating capacity of around 34.5GW. The state-owned Taiwan Power Company (Taipower) operates 72 power stations. Taipower's output is 68 per cent thermally produced , 17 per cent nuclear and most of the rest by hydro-power. Privatisation of Taipower has been delayed and is expected to take place in 2006.

Independent power producers are allowed to provide up to 20 per cent of Taiwan's electricity under a law passed in 1994. Foreign investors are allowed to participate in the electricity sector.

In June 2004, plans were approved for a 4,000MW LNG-fired complex, the Tatan Power Plant, to be built by Taipower; it is expected to be completed in 2007, before the adjacent LNG terminal becomes operational in 2009, so the plant will run on coal until then. In addition, an 800MW coal-fired power plant at Changhua in central Taiwan will be built by Taipower for around US$1.4 billion and will come online in two stages during 2011.

Financial markets

A computerised over-the-counter (OTC) market, the Taisdaq, was introduced in 1994. Taiwan's financial markets are regulated by the Securities and Futures Commission.

Stock exchange

The Taiwan Stock Exchange (TSE) was opened to indirect foreign investment in 1984. Electronics companies have the largest share of the stock market. The stock exchange's dismal performance in 2001/02 was brought on by the downturn in electronic products that sent the Taiex index spiralling downwards.

Banking and insurance

Foreign banks have been allowed to compete in the Taiwanese market since 1989. In June 2001, the government passed a package of legislation to reform the financial sector. The most important part of this legislation is the financial holding company law, which allows banks, security houses, insurance companies, investment funds, and futures brokerages to be grouped under one entity.

Central bank

Central Bank of China

Main financial centre

Taipei

Offshore facilities

Offshore banking has also been available since 1984. Foreign banks are permitted to set up offshore banking units (OBUs) without first having established a branch in Taiwan.

Time

GMT plus eight hours

Geography

Taiwan is an island 395km long and 144km across. It has high mountains, rising out of the sea along its eastern shore. The western side is flat and fertile. Taipei is located at the northen end of the island and is the largest city.

Hemisphere

Northern

Climate

Subtropical with temperatures ranging from 33 degrees Celsius (C) in Jul–Aug to 12 degrees C in Jan–Feb. Average rainfall is 2,500mm per year, with typhoons from May–Oct and occasional snow in the mountains in Jan–Feb.

Entry requirements

Passports

Required by all and must be valid for six months from date of visit.

Visa

Required by all, except citizens of EU, North America, Australasia and some Asian countries. Visit www.boca.gov.tw for a full list of nationals from visa-exempt entry countries and application forms for those who must apply of a visa. Visa free (tourist) visits are limited to 30 days without extension. All business visits of less than six months may be undertaken on visitors visas. Applications require a business letter of intent and itinerary. All visitors must have return/onward passage.

Currency advice/regulations

All currencies imported must be declared in writing on arrival; re-convertion is allowed on production of exchange receipts. The import and export of foreign currency is unlimited; amounts over US$10,000 (or foreign equivalent) must be declared. Import and export of local currency is limited to T$8,000; permission must be obtain from the Ministry of Finance for export of amounts in excess of this.

Travellers cheques are accepted in banks and tourist venues.

Customs

All baggage must be itemised in writing. Personal effects are duty-free.

Prohibited imports

Illegal drugs, gambling aids (including mahjong sets), firearms and explosives, non-canned meat and fresh fruit. Communist propaganda and items originating from China, Cuba, North Korea and members of the CIS.

Health (for visitors)

Mandatory precautions

Vaccination certificate for either yellow fever or cholera if travelling from an infected area.

Advisable precautions

Inoculations and boosters should be current for diphtheria, tetanus, hepatitis A, polio and typhoid. Other vaccinations that may be recommended are cholera, tuberculosis, and Japanese B encephalitis and hepatitis B. Use malaria prophylaxis (which will also provide protection against dengue fever and hepatitis B) including mosquito repellents, sleeping nets and clothing that cover the body after dark. There is a risk of rabies in rural areas. Use only bottled or boiled water for drinks, washing teeth and making ice. Eat only well cooked meals, preferably served hot; vegetables should be cooked and fruit peeled. Dairy products are unpasteurised and should be avoided. Avoid pork and salad and food from street vendors. A full first-aid kit would be useful.

Locally manufactured Western proprietary medicines are easily obtainable, but visitors on regular medication should bring their own supplies – amounts for the length of the visit only.

Visitors should have medical insurance, including emergency evacuation.

Hotels

It is advisable to book hotel rooms in advance. Room facilities usually include TVs and refrigerators. Larger hotels will arrange transport to/from the airport. A 10 per cent service charge is added to the bill. Reasonably priced accommodation is available at Japanese-style hot springs resorts in the mountains.

Credit cards

Major credit and charge cards are accepted in most establishments.

Public holidays (national)

Fixed dates

1 Jan (Founding of the Republic of China), 28 Feb Memorial Day.

Holidays that fall on the weekend are taken on the next working days in lieu.

Variable dates

Chinese New Year (Jan/Feb, four days), Tomb Sweeping Day (Mar/Apr), Tuen Ng (Dragon Boat) Festival (May/Jun), Mid-Autumn Moon Festival (Sep/Oct). Religious and cultural festivals are determined by the Buddhist lunar calendar.

Working hours

Banking

Mon–Fri: 0900–1530; Sat: 0900–1200.

Business

Mon–Fri: 0830–1230, 1330–1730; Sat: 0830–1230.

Government

Mon–Fri: 0830–1230, 1330–1730; Sat: 0830–1230.

Shops

Sun–Sat: 0900–2200 (department stores 1100–2130).

Telecommunications

Mobile/cell phones

There are 900 and 1800 GSM service throughout most of the island.

Electricity supply

110V AC, 60 cycles

Weights and measures

Metric system (some Chinese units in use).

Social customs/useful tips

Shaking hands is the normal form of greeting. When addressing Chinese persons, the family or surname comes first. Business cards are usually exchanged and should be in both Chinese and English. They constitute an important part of the business culture, and Taiwanese expect visitors to carry cards. Cards using mainland (simplified) script are not advisable as this could cause offence.

Visitors should remember that Taiwanese of all backgrounds need to maintain 'face', this means that it is important not to embarrass your Taiwanese counterpart either privately or when in company. Rejection of gifts as small as cigarettes may cause offence, as a sign that the offerer is not considered wealthy. In general, however, the social environment in Taiwan is very liberal and visitors need not fear inadvertently causing offence.

When visiting people's homes, removing shoes is mandatory. The subject of death should be avoided in conversation as it is considered a bad omen.

Getting there

Air

An agreement was signed with China on 13 June 2008 to allow 36 direct flights (18 each) a week to start on 4 July. A further agreement will allow 3,000 tourists per day into each country from 18 July.

National airline: China Airlines (CAL). Taiwan's second carrier, Eva Air, is a major international carrier.

International airport/s: Taiwan Taoyuan International Airport (TTY) (formerly called Chiang Kai-Shek International), 40km south-west of Taipei, with duty-free shop, bar, restaurant, bank, post office, hotel reservations and shops; Kaohsiung International (KHH).

There are bus and taxi services to the closest cities.

Airport tax: None

Surface

Water: Regular ferry services run between Keelung and Kaohsiung ports (Taiwan) and Okinawa (Japan). There are also some sea links between Kaohsiung and Macao.

Main port/s: Keelung (including Suao), Hualien, Taichung.

Getting about

National transport

Air: Domestic air services are operated by China Airlines. Far Eastern Air Transport and seven other carriers connect most of the main cities.

Road: The road network covers 20,000km, most of it surfaced. A good highway links the main centres between Keelung and Kaohsiung. Bad terrain and one-way systems can make road travel difficult outside urban centres.

Buses: Extensive bus services cover coastal, cross-island and inland areas. Express coach services link Taipei, Kaohsiung and other main centres. Advance booking is recommended. Destinations are clearly marked in English at urban bus stations.

Rail: The railway extends the whole length of Taiwan, mainly along the west coast, including high-speed intercity trains. These services are good with air-conditioned express trains linking main centres. Urban train stations have destinations marked in English.

A US$17.8 billion high speed 345km rail system linking Taipei with the southern city of Kaohsiung (journey time 80 minutes) is expected to be operational by the end of 2006.

Water: There are ferry services from Kaohsiung and Chiayi to the Pescadores Islands, from Taitung to the Lanyu and Green Islands.

City transport

Rush-hour traffic in Taipei can be chaotic and stressful. Allow plenty of time for getting to and from the airport.

Taxis: Taxis are plentiful. Metered taxis are available in Taipei, and fares are metered by kilometres and delay time. Have the destination (and the return address) written in Chinese for the taxi driver's reference.

Tipping is not an established practice, though it is becoming more usual.

From Taiwan Taoyuan International Airport to city centre the journey time is 45–60 minutes.

Buses, trams & metro: An underground rail system and a Rapid Mass Transit System are under construction in Taipei and Kaohsiung. Construction of the Taipei system is expected to be fully completed by 2009; Kaohsiung in 2007.

Car hire

Self-drive car hire is available, although chauffeur-driven cars are recommended due to traffic conditions. An international driving licence is required. Driving is on the right-hand side of the road.

BUSINESS DIRECTORY

The addresses listed below are a selection only. While World of Information makes every endeavour to check these addresses, we cannot guarantee that changes have not been made, especially to telephone numbers and area codes. We would welcome any corrections.

Telephone area codes

The international direct dialling (IDD) code for Taiwan is +886 followed by the area code and subscriber's number:

Hualien	38	Taichung	4
Kaohsiung	7	Tainan	6
Keelung	32	Taipei	2
Pingtung	8		

Useful telephone numbers

Fire and ambulance: 119.

Police: 110.

English-speaking police: 311-9940, 311-9816 ext 264.

Ambulance: 721-6315.

Women's help-line 581-5469.

International calls: 100.

Directory enquiries: Chinese language 104 (long-distance: 105). English language 311-6796.

Chambers of Commerce

American Chamber of Commerce in Taipei, Chia Hsin Building, 96 Chungshan North Road, Section 2, Taipei 104 (tel: 2581-7089; fax: 2542-3376; e-mail: amcham@amcham.com.tw).

British Chamber of Commerce in Taiwan, Fu Key Building, 99 Ren Ai Road, Section 2, Taipei 106 (tel: 2356-0210; fax: 2356-0211; e-mail: info@bcctaipei.com).

Chinese National Association of Industry and Commerce, 390 Fu Hsing South Road, Taipei 106 (tel: 2707-0111; fax : 2701-7601; e-mail: webmaster@nfict.org).

European Chamber of Commerce Taipei, 285 Zhongxiao East Road, Section 4, Taipei (tel: 2740-0236; fax: 2772-0530; e-mail: ecct@ecct.com.tw).

Taiwan Chamber of Commerce, 158 Sung Chiang Road, Taipei 104 (tel: 2536-5455; fax: 2521-1980; e-mail: tcoc@tcoc.org.tw).

Banking

Bank of Taiwan, 120 Chungking S Road, Sec 2, Taipei (tel: 2314-7377; fax: 2331-5840).

Chang Hwa Commercial Bank, 23-1 Chang An E Rd, Sec 1, Taipei City (tel: 2523-0739; fax: 2523-0172).

Chiao Tung Bank, 91 Heng Yang Road, Taipei (tel: 2361-3000; fax: 2311-3263).

Citibank, PO Box 3343, Citicorp Center, 52 Minsheng E Road, Sec 4, Taipei City 105 (tel: 2715-5931; fax: 2712-7388).

First Commercial Bank, 30 Chungking S Road, Sec 1, Taipei 10036 (tel: 2311-111; fax: 2361-0036).

Hua Nan Commercial Bank, 38 Chungking S Road, Sec 1, Taipei (tel: 2371-3111; fax: 2371-5734).

International Commercial Bank of China, 100 Chi Lin Road, Taipei (tel: 2563-3156; fax: 2561-1216).

Shanghai Commercial & Savings Bank Ltd, 2 Min Chuan East Road, Section 1, Taipei City (tel: 2581-7111; fax: 2567-1921).

Standard Chartered Bank, 168 Tun Hwa North Rd, Taipei City 105 (tel: 2716-2621, 2717-2866; fax: 2716-4068).

Taipeibank, 50 Chungshan North Road, Section 2, Taipei City (tel: 2542-5656; fax: 2542-8870).

Taiwan Co-operative Bank, 77 Kuanchien Road, Taipei (tel: 2311-8811; fax: 2331-6567).

Central bank

Central Bank of China, 2 Roosevelt Road, Section 1, Taipei 100 (tel: 2393-6161; fax: 2357-1974; internet: www.cbc.gov.tw).

A computerised over-the-counter (OTC) market, the Taisdaq, was introduced in 1994. Taiwan's financial markets are regulated by the Securities and Futures Commission.

Travel information

China Airlines (CAL), 131 Nanking East Road, Section 3, Taipei 104 (tel: 2715-2626; fax: 2717-5120).

Taiwan Taoyuan International Airport, No 9, Hangjan S Rd, Dayuan Shiang, Taoyuan, Taiwan 33758 (tel: 2398-2143, 2398-3274; internet: www.cksairport.gov.tw)

Flight information (24 hours) (tel: 2398-2050).

Sungshan Domestic Airport Travel Information Service Centre (tel: 2349-1580).

Taiwan Visitors' Association, 5th Floor, 9 Ming Chuan East Road, Sec 2, Taipei (tel: 2594-3261; fax: 2594-3265).

Tourist Information Hot Line (tel: 2717-3737).

National tourist organisation offices

Tourism Bureau, 9F Floor, 280 Chung Hsiao East Road, Section 4; PO Box 1490, Taipei (tel: 2721-8541; fax: 2773-5487: internet www.taiwantourism.org).

Ministries

Ministry of Economic Affairs, 15 Foochow Street, Taipei (tel: 2321-2200; fax: 2391-9398).

Ministry of Education (MoE), 5 Chungshan S. Road, Taipei (tel: 2356-6051; fax: 2397-6920).

Ministry of Finance, 2 Aikuo West Road, Taipei (tel: 2322-8000; fax: 2321-1205).

Ministry of Foreign Affairs, 2 Chieh Shou Road, Taipei (tel: 2311-9292; fax: 2314-4972).

Ministry of the Interior (MoI), 5 Hsuchow Road, Taipei (tel: 2356-5000; fax: 2356-6201).

Ministry of Justice (MoJ), 130 Chungking S. Road, Sec. 1, Taipei (tel: 2314-6871; fax: 2389-6239).

Ministry of National Defence, Chiehshou Hall, Chungking S. Road, Taipei (tel: 2311-6117; fax: 2314-4221).

Ministry of Transportation and Communications, 2 Changasha Street, Section 1, Taipei (tel: 2349-2900; fax: 2389-6009).

Monetary Affairs Dept, Ministry of Finance, 2 Aikuo W Road, Taipei (tel: 2321-3836).

President's Office, 122 Chungking South Road, Section 1, Taipei (the First Bureau tel: 2311-3731; fax: 2314-0746; Protocol Section: 2311-5877; Spokesman's Office: 2331-1604).

Other useful addresses

Board of Foreign Trade, 1 Hukou St, Taipei (tel: 2351-0271; fax: 2351-3603).

British Trade and Cultural Office, 9th floor, Fu Key Building, 99 Jen Ali Road, Section 2, Taipei 10625 (tel: 2322-4242; fax: 2394-8673).

China External Trade Development Council (CETRA), 4-8th floor, International Trade Building, 333 Keelung Road, Sec 1, Taipei 10548 (tel: 2725-5200; fax: 2757-6653).

Chinese National Association of Industry & Commerce, 13th floor, 390 Fu Hsing South Rd, Sec 1, Taipei (tel: 2707-0111; fax: 2701-7601).

Chinese National Export Enterprises Association (CNEEA), 6th floor, 285 Nanking E. Road, Sec. 3, Taipei (tel: 2713-8153; fax: 2713-0115).

Chinese National Federation of Industries, 12th floor, 390 Fuhsing South Road, Section 1, Taipei (tel: 2703-3500; fax: 2703-3982).

Chinese Petroleum Corporation, 83 Chung-Hwa Road, Section 1, Taipei 10331 (tel: 2361-0221; fax: 2371-5944).

Council for Economic Planning and Development, 9/F, 87 Nanking East Road, Section 2, Taipei (tel: 2551-3522; fax: 2581-8549).

Directorate-General of Budgets, Accounting & Statistics, Executive Yuan, 1 Chung Hsiao East Road, Section 1, Taipei (internet: www.stat.gov.tw/).

Euro-Asia Trade Organisation, 3rd floor, 9 Roosevelt Road, Sec. 2, Taipei (tel: 2393-2115; fax: 2392-8393).

Government Information Office, Taipei (tel: 2322-8888).

Industrial Development Bureau, MOEA, 41-3 Hsinyi Road, Sec. 3, Taipei (tel: 2754-1255; fax: 2703-0160).

Industrial Development and Investment Centre, MOEA, 4 Chunghsiao W. Road, Sec 1, Taipei (tel: 2389-2111; fax: 2382-0497).

Industry of Free China, 9th Floor, 87 Nanking East Road, Section 2, Taipei (tel: 2543-5988).

International Co-operation Department, MOEA, 15 Foochow St., Taipei (tel: 2321-2200; fax: 2321-3275).

International Economic Co-operation Development Fund, 7th floor, 51 Chung-Ching S. Road, Sec. 2, Taipei (tel: 2396-6316; fax: 2396-9147).

International Telecommunications Administration (ITA), 28 Hangchou S. Rd, Sec. 1, Taipei (tel: 2344-3781).

International Trade Association of the R.O.C., 8th floor, 148 Chunghsiao E. Road, Sec. 4, Taipei (tel: 2772-6252; fax: 2752-2411).

Investment Commission, Ministry of Economic Affairs, 8th Floor, 7 Roosevelt Road, Sec 1, Taipei (tel: 2351-3151; fax: 2396-3970).

Securities and Exchange Commission, 12th Floor, Yangteh Building, 3 Nanhai Road, Taipei (tel: 2341-3191; fax: 2394-8249).

Taipei Economic and Cultural Representative Office (USA), 4201 Wisconsin Avenue, NW, Washington DC 20016 (tel: (+1-202) 895-1800; fax: (+1-202) 363-0999; email: contact@tecro-info.org).

Taipei World Trade Centre Exhibition Hall, 5 Hsinyi Road, Section 5, Taipei (tel: 2886-2725; fax: 2886-1314).

Taiwan Stock Exchange Corp, 85 Yen Ping S Road, Taipei (tel: 2311-4020; fax: 2311-4004).

Taiwan Textile Federation, 22 Ai-Kuo E. Road, Taipei (tel: 2341-7251; fax: 2392-3855).

World Trade Center Taichung, 60 Tienpao St, Taichung (tel: 2254-2271; fax: 2254-2341).

National news agency: Central News Agency (www.cna.com.tw).

Internet sites

Taiwan business directory: www.tbdo.anjes.com.tw

Taiwan business express: www.business.com.tw

Taiwan News, the Voice of Taiwan: www.eTaiwanNews.com

Taiwan Trade Point: www.tradepoint.anjes.com.tw

Tajikistan

KEY FACTS

Official name: Respublika i Tojikiston (Republic of Tajikistan)

Head of State: President Emomali Rakhmonov (leader since 1992; re-elected 1999)

Head of government: Prime Minister Akil Akilov (since 1999)

Ruling party: Hizbi Demokrati Khalkii Tajikistan (HDKT) (People's Democratic Party of Tajikistan) (re-elected Feb/Mar 2005)

Area: 143,100 square km

Population: 6.42 million (2007)*

Capital: Dushanbe

Official language: Tajik (Farsi)

Currency: Somoni (Sm) = 100 dirams

Exchange rate: Sm3.43 per US$ (Jul 2008)

GDP per capita: US$578 (2007)*

GDP real growth: 7.80% (2007)

Labour force: 2.72 million (2004)

Inflation: 13.10% (2007)

Balance of trade: -US$261.00 million (2006)

Foreign debt: US$896.00 million (2004)

* estimated figure

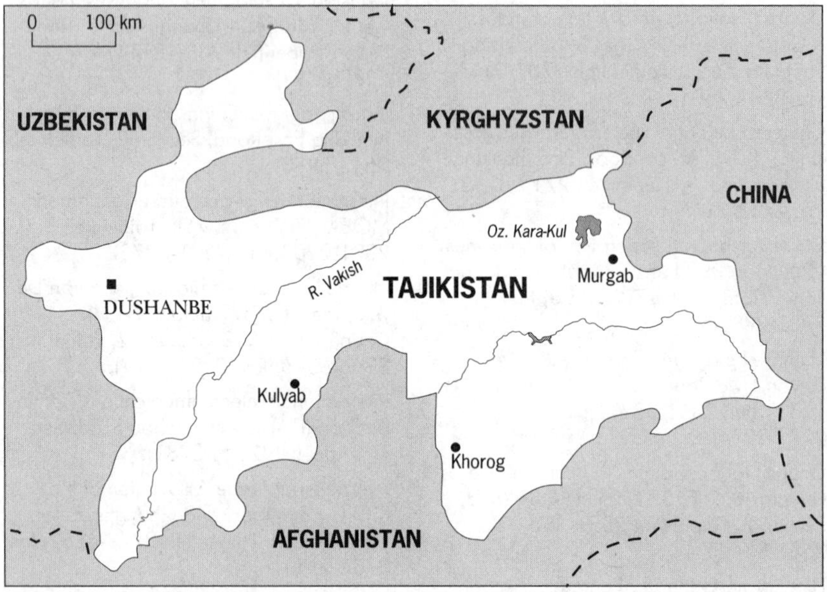

In 2007, Tajikistan's growth remained steady at 7.8 per cent, albeit slightly below the impressive average recorded over the years 2000–04. According to the Asian Development Bank (ADB) in its 2008 *Asian Development Outlook* this was largely due to the sluggish rate of agricultural reform, an indifferent business environment and unexpectedly high energy costs.

Mainstays underperform

According to the ADB, in 2007 the two traditional mainstays of the economy, aluminium and cotton failed to deliver. Aluminium output only rose by 1.5 per cent reflecting the higher price of imported natural gas from Uzbekistan and unexpected electricity shortages caused by lower hydropower generation. Cotton production fell by 4 per cent due to declining productivity. In compensation, industrial production doubled its growth rate to 9.9 per cent and non-cotton agricultural production rose to 6.5 per cent. The services sector growth rate rose by 8.0 per cent.

Tajikistan's inflation rate for 2007 was 13.1 per cent, but the year-end rate was much higher, at 19.7 per cent. Inflation was pushed up by higher food and fuel prices and strong consumer demand fuelled by increased worker remittances. The looming inflationary pressure caused the National Bank of Tajikistan to tighten its lending to the financial sector. The ADB considers that two main development challenges continue to confront the government in 2008. The maintenance of macroeconomic stability and continued economic diversification both need to be addressed if Tajikistan's high growth rates are to be maintained.

Like many transition states, Tajikistan's recent economic history has been one of contraction. But Tajikistan's case has been more severe than most. The country was already one of the poorest of the Soviet republics and the collapse of the Soviet Union meant that Tajikistan lost the subsidies that accounted for some 80 per cent of its income. It also lost its major markets. On top of this, Tajikistan's five-year civil war effectively destroyed its economy. The war caused many of its most qualified people to emigrate, and state spending to rise. In the twenty-first century, Tajik politics were dominated by events beyond its borders – namely unofficial competition between Russia and the US for influence in Central Asia. Having firmly committed to Russia in October 2004, Tajikistan remained within the Russian orbit.

Slowing growth, reasonable outlook

Tajikistan's gross domestic product (GDP) is one of the lowest in the former Soviet Union. While still below its level at the end of the Soviet era, (GDP) has grown strongly over the last ten years. The future of the economy and the potential for attracting foreign investment depends largely on Tajikistan's political stability and on the will to continue with economic reform, including the privatisation of state-own enterprises. Sixty per cent of the population lives below the poverty line. The country has one of the lowest per capita GDPs (US$578 in 2007) among the former Soviet republics, and the economy is heavily dependent on assistance from the IMF, Russia and, more recently, the United States. In late 2005, the IMF put Tajikistan on a list of 19 countries selected for 'one hundred per cent debt relief' each year.

Hundreds of thousands of Tajiks find work in Russia. Their remittances are vitally important to the economy, representing close to 12 per cent of GDP (according to the World Bank).

The United States assists Tajikistan on a broad range of issues, including democratic and economic reforms, counter-narcotics, counter-terrorism, non-proliferation and the training of army officers and border guards. In June 2005, US Government funded a US$36 million project to construct a Tajik-Afghan Bridge across the Pyanj River. It was opened in August 2007, linking the Tajik town of Nizhny Pyanj with Shir Khan Bandar in Afghanistan and extended the trans-Afghanistan road (Regional Road Corridor Improvement Project) through Central Asia. It is capable of carrying more than 1,000 cars daily.

Expensive legal battle

It is ironic that in a country where six out of ten people live below the poverty line, over US$50 million is being spent on lawyers. The case, in the London courts, centres on Tajik Aluminium Company (Talco) and profit-stripping that may or may not have been going on for years. In the meantime, Talco should produce more that US$1 billion worth of metal during 2008, while the lawyers bills keep on going up.

In another irony in 2008, in April the IMF demanded the return of a US$47 million loan following a false submission of data by Tajikistan.

Risk assessment

Politics	Fair
Economy	Fair
Regional stability	Fair

COUNTRY PROFILE

Historical profile

1916–17 The Central Asian republics joined in a violent uprising against Russian rule, which was suppressed. After the October Revolution in Russia, the Russian ruler, Lenin, gave the peoples of Central Asia the right of self-determination.
1920s Southern Tajikistan remained under the control of the Khan of Bukhara while northern Tajikistan was incorporated into Soviet-controlled Turkestan, which also included Uzbekistan, Kyrgyzstan, part of northern Turkmenistan and southern Kazakhstan. Soviet nationalities policy, under the direction of Stalin, saw Soviet rule enforced by Red Army troops who put down fierce Muslim resistance in Central Asia after the Russian civil war.
1924 Tajikistan was granted autonomous status in the Socialist Soviet Republic (SSR) of Uzbekistan.
1929 Tajikistan was detached from Uzbekistan and became a separate SSR.
1930s–80s The country underwent a period of agricultural collectivisation and industrialisation, which was unpopular with the population.
1989 Tajik became the official state language.
1990 Social and ethnic tensions erupted in violence in Dushanbe and along the Tajikistan-Kyrgyzstan border. A state of emergency was declared and Soviet troops were sent to Dushanbe to suppress pro-democracy protests. President Kahar Mahkamov resigned after being accused of supporting an attempted coup against the Soviet leader Mikhail Gorbachev.
1991 The collapse of the Soviet Union resulted in Tajikistan declaring independence. Rahmon Nabiyev was appointed president after winning Tajikistan's first direct presidential elections. Tajikistan joined the Commonwealth of Independent States (CIS), following the collapse of the Soviet Union.
1992 Anti-government demonstrations in Dushanbe turned into civil war between pro-government forces and Islamist and pro-democracy groups. Nabiyev was forced to resign and the CPT government collapsed. Pro-Communists massacred thousands of government supporters in Dushanbe. The CPT regained power and Imamali Rakhmonov became head of state.
1993 The Supreme Court returned the country to one-party rule after banning all political parties other than the ruling CPT. A CIS peace-keeping force was deployed along the Tajikistan-Afghan border to prevent armed incursions by Islamic guerrilla groups.
1994 A cease-fire between the government and the rebels was agreed. A presidential constitution was approved by national referendum. Rakhmonov won the presidential elections, which were deemed by international observers to be neither free nor fair.
1995 Rakhmonov supporters won the legislative elections, which took place without the participation of any of the opposition groups. Fighting erupted on the Afghan border.
1996 A UN-sponsored cease-fire between the government and Islamist rebels came into effect.

KEY INDICATORS — Tajikistan

	Unit	2003	2004	2005	2006	2007
Population	m	6.42	6.59	6.34	*6.38	*6.42
Gross domestic product (GDP)	US$bn	1.08	2.08	2.31	2.81	3.71
GDP per capita	US$	169	329	364	*441	*578
GDP real growth	%	6.0	10.6	6.7	7.0	7.8
Inflation	%	14.5	7.1	7.3	9.9	13.1
Industrial output	% change	–	14.3	6.7	8.0	–
Agricultural output	% change	–	11.3	6.7	8.0	–
Exports (fob) (goods)	US$m	710.0	1,096.9	1,108.1	1,267.0	*1,468.2
Imports (cif) (goods)	US$m	830.0	1,232.4	1,430.9	1,528.0	*2,455.4
Balance of trade	US$m	-120.0	-135.5	-322.8	-261.0	*-987.2
Current account	US$m	-20.0	-80.0	-58.0	-84.0	-351.0
Foreign debt	US$bn	–	–	–	–	–
Total reserves minus gold	US$m	111.9	157.5	168.2	175.1	–
Foreign exchange	US$m	111.0	156.2	162.7	171.6	–
Exchange rate	per US$	2.79	2.97	3.43	3.43	3.43

* estimated figure

1997 Opposition parties were legalised and as part of a peace treaty between the Tajikistan government and the Islamic United Tajik Opposition (UTO), the government agreed to give 30 per cent of its seats to opposition representatives, retaining 50 per cent for itself, and to give the remaining 20 per cent to independents.
1998 The government removed the ban on religious political parties. Rakhmonov pardoned all opposition leaders in exile. Tajikistan joined the CIS Customs Union.
1999 President Rakhmonov was re-elected for a third term. The UTO armed forces were integrated into the state army.
2000 A new bicameral parliament was set up. The elections were won by the Hizbi Demokrati Khalkii Tajikistan (HDKT) (People's Democratic Party of Tajikistan). The somoni replaced the Tajik rouble as the currency. Belarus, Kazakhstan, Kyrgyzstan, Russia and Tajikistan (formerly the Customs Five) established the Eurasian Economic Community (EEC).
2001 Tajikistan, China, Russia, Kazakhstan, Kyrgyzstan and Uzbekistan formed the Shanghai Co-operation Organisation (SCO). Rahmon Sanginov, a renegade warlord, declared one of the country's most wanted criminals, was killed in a gun battle with security forces.
2002 Tajikistan became the last Central Asian republic to join NATO's Partnership for Peace (PfP) programme. The number of border guards was doubled to prevent al Qaeda members from crossing the border with Afghanistan to escape US forces.
2003 Russian President Vladimir Putin announced an agreement to increase Russian military presence. President Rakhmonov's term in office was extended by two more consecutive seven-year terms, by referendum.
2004 A moratorium on the death penalty was introduced. Russia regained control of a former Soviet space monitoring centre at Nurek and opened a military base in Dushanbe.
2005 The ruling HDKT was re-elected. However, international observers said the elections had not reached acceptable international standards. Opposition leader, Mahmadruzi Iskandarov (Hizbi Demokrati (Democratic Party)), had been arrested and released in Moscow after an extradition request was dismissed, was kidnapped and transported to Tajikistan to be re-arrested; he was sentenced on terrorism and corruption charges and received a 23-year sentence.
2006 Incumbent Emomali Rakhmonov won 79 per cent of the vote for president; giving him his fourth term in office. The election was neither free nor fair according to international observers.
2007 In August, a bridge across the Pyanj River, built by the US army, linked the Tajik town of Nizhny Pyanj with Shir Khan Bandar and extended the trans-Afghanistan road (Regional Road Corridor Improvement Project) through Central Asia.
2008 The IMF demanded the return of a US$47 million loan in April, following a false submission of data by Tajikistan.

Political structure

Constitution

A presidential constitution was approved by national referendum in 1994. The constitution granted basic economic and political rights and guaranteed religious freedoms. It gave the president powers to appoint the chairs of regions, districts, cities, including Dushanbe, as well as of the Gorno-Badakshan Autonomous Region and the governor of the National Bank of Tajikistan (central bank), subject to the approval of deputies in parliament. The president also has powers of dismissal over these offices. In addition, the president gained the power to declare a state of martial law and issue decrees, as well as immunity from prosecution. Parliament has the power to impeach the president, subject to the findings of the Constitutional Court. If more than two-thirds of deputies vote in favour of impeachment, parliament may dismiss the president from office.

Form of state

Presidential socialist republic

The executive

The president, elected by universal suffrage every seven years, holds executive power. The government consists of the prime minister and cabinet and may present its resignation to the president if it declares it cannot function normally.
In 2003, voters in a referendum favoured allowing President Rakhmonov to run two further consecutive seven-year terms in office after 2006.

National legislature

There is a bicameral Majlisi Oli (supreme assembly) with a Majlisi Mamoyandogan (assembly of representatives, the lower house), which has 63 members who are elected for a five-year term. Of these, 22 are elected by proportional representation and 41 from single-seat constituencies. The Majlisi Milliy (national assembly) forms the second, upper chamber and has 33 members, eight of which are appointed by the president and the rest elected by local assemblies for a five-year term. The National Assembly functions only when convened and accordingly meets less frequently than the lower house.

Legal system

The judiciary is constitutionally independent from the legislature and executive. Courts include the Supreme Court, Constitutional Court, Military Court and High Economic Court. In addition there are district and city courts, as well as the Dushanbe City Court. Gorno-Badakshan Autonomous Region has its own court.
The president has powers to appoint and dismiss judges of all courts on petition of the minister of justice, except for judges appointed to the Supreme Court, High Economic Court and Constitutional Court. The latter is composed of seven judges elected from the legal profession, one of whom is a representative of Gorno-Badakshan Autonomous Region.

Last elections

13 March 2005 (second round parliamentary); 27 February 2005 (first round parliamentary); 6 November 2006 (presidential).
Results: Parliamentary (second round): the ruling HDKT was re-elected with 74 per cent of the vote (52 seats out of 63); the CPT 13 per cent (four); the RPT (8 per cent) (two).
Parliamentary (first round): the ruling HDKT won 49 seats out of 63, the CPT three, the Nahzati Islomi Tojikiston (NIT) (Islamic Renaissance of Tajikistan) two and independents six. Turnout was 88 per cent.
Presidential: Incumbent Emomali Rakhmonov won with 79 per cent of the vote.

Next elections

2010 (parliamentary); 2011 (presidential)

Political parties

Ruling party

Hizbi Demokrati Khalkii Tajikistan (HDKT) (People's Democratic Party of Tajikistan) (re-elected Feb/Mar 2005)

Main opposition party

Communist Party of Tajikistan (CPT)

Population

6.42 million (2007)*
Last census: January 2000: 6,127,000 (provisional)
Population density: 44 inhabitants per square km (2000).
Annual growth rate: 1.2 per cent 1994–2004 (WHO 2006)

Ethnic make-up

Tajik (69.1 per cent), Uzbek (25 per cent), Russian (2.7 per cent), with remaining minorities including Tatar and Kyrgyz groups. Tajikistan is the exception among the Central Asian republics in that its population is predominantly Persian rather than Turkic. The Tajiks are made up of a number of closely related ethnic groups which differ both anthropologically (inhabitants of the Pamir mountains in the north are tall, dark complexioned with light-coloured eyes; those from Kuliab are stocky and dark-skinned; northern Tajiks are fair-complexioned, brown- and black-eyed). Customs and rituals also differ.

Religions

The majority (80 per cent) of ethnic Tajiks and Uzbeks are Sunni Muslims; 5 per cent are Shi'a Muslims. Ethnic Badakhshanis belong to the Ismaili Muslim sect and have the Aga Khan as their spiritual leader. There are also Baptists and Bukhara Jews. There is no official religion.

Education

Public expenditure on education typically amounts to 3 per cent of GDP.

Primary education lasts four years, followed by eight years of secondary schooling which is divided into two cycles of five and three years in either general, technical or vocational education. Successful students may progress to either a university or institute of which there are 29 established.

In 2003, the Asian Development Bank (ADB) approved a US$7.5 million loan for education reforms to give about 90,000 children better access to quality education. About 300 schools, in pilot districts, which were damaged during the civil war and lacked maintenance, received funding for refurbishment and to provide textbooks and learning materials, plus pay for enhancing female teacher training.

The total cost of the project was US$9.38 million, 80 per cent of which was covered by the ADB's loan, while the government provided the balance of US$1.88 million.

Nationwide, the education system is suffering from an exodus of large numbers of qualified teachers to find better paid work. School attendance levels are also falling, as children are pressed into helping their families cope with the widespread poverty and social vulnerability. Gender imbalance is particularly marked at the upper secondary level, with the proportion of girls declining.

Literacy rate: 100 per cent adult rate; 100 per cent youth rate (15–24) (Unesco 2005).

Compulsory years: Seven to 16.

Enrolment rate: 85 per cent gross primary enrolment (ADB); 76 per cent gross secondary enrolment (Unicef).

Pupils per teacher: 24 in primary schools.

Health

Per capita total expenditure on health (2003) was US$71; of which per capita government spending was US$15, at the international dollar rate, (WHO 2006).

The structure of Tajikistan's health system has evolved from the Soviet model of healthcare with few structural changes. The state funds most of the healthcare services in the country. The health ministry runs national-level healthcare services, while local authorities administer most regional services.

State hospitals have limited supplies of free medicines. People have been increasingly forced to pay for their own healthcare, often buying their own medicines off the street.

The health budget each year has major shortfalls that are partially covered by international aid. The government has introduced more than 11 national and sectoral programmes, including those to combat tuberculosis, prevent HIV/Aids and improve reproductive health. The World Bank began a major rehabilitation project with an estimated expenditure of US$25 million in 2000–03 in the Soghd and Khatlon regions. The project aimed to rehabilitate 300 health posts, rural physician clinics and outpatient facilities.

Tajikistan has the youngest population of any former Soviet states, with 70 per cent aged under 30 years.

Tajikistan has substantial environmental problems that pose risks to human health. There is high risk of communicable disease with the breakdown of public health measures such as mosquito control and immunisation. Less than 50 per cent of the rural population have access to clean water. Tajikistan is one of the primary transfer points for the flow of drugs due to transparent border controls and poor custom regulations.

HIV/Aids

HIV prevalence: 0.1 per cent aged 15–49 in 2003 (World Bank)

Life expectancy: 63 years, 2004 (WHO 2006)

Fertility rate/Maternal mortality rate: 3.7 births per woman, 2004 (WHO 2006); maternal mortality 66.5 per 100,000 live births (World Bank).

Birth rate/Death rate: 32.8 births and 8.5 deaths per 1,000 people (2003).

Child (under 5 years) mortality rate (per 1,000): 76 per 1,000 live births (World Bank)

Head of population per physician: 2.03 physicians per 1,000 people, 2003 (WHO 2006)

Welfare

As the poorest of the CIS countries, a significant proportion of Tajikistan's population now faces severe social hardship, especially with most of the country's social welfare budget being spent on pensions. The country relies heavily on overseas assistance, highlighting the failure of the state to create a self-financing welfare system.

Main cities

Dushanbe (capital, estimated population 582,496 in 2005), Khujand (formerly Leninabad) (144,782).

Media

Despite a constitutionally guaranteed free press, the government has a heavy influence on all media outlets and has led to widespread self-censorship. Laws prohibit the dissemination of information containing state secrets, inciting racial discrimination and any form of ethnic or religious hatred.

National news agency: Khovar (in Russian) (www.khovar.tj).

Other news agencies: Avesta news agency (www.avesta.tj/en).

Press

Tajikistan does not possess any pulp mills or paper making industries and has to import all newsprint paper and printing equipment, which has resulted in significantly higher printing costs and an inability to produce daily newspapers. The UN considers this situation denies citizens access to current news.

Weeklies: The four official weeklies are not popular as they are concerned with published resolutions, government decision and official chronicles and lack any innovation. They have deplorable circulation figures of 700–2,000, of which 75 per cent are secured by subscription and only 25 per cent are sold retail.

Government-owned and published three times per week, Jumhuriyat and Sadio Mardumin Tajik, Khalq Ovozi in Uzbek and Narodnaya Gazeta in Russian. Private publications include Neru-i Sukhan and Tojikiston in Takik. Political parties publish Minbar-i Khalq (People's Democratic Party), Nido-i Ranjbar in Takik (Communist Party), Golos Tajikistana in Russian (Communist Party), Najot (Islamic Rebirth Party).

Broadcasting

The broadcasting law prohibits dissemination of information containing state secrets, inciting of racial discrimination and any form of ethnic or religious hatred.

Radio: The Government runs Tajik radio with two national networks and in the capital, Radio Sado i Dushanbe. There are two private stations, Asia Plus (www.asiaplus.tj) and Radio Vatan (www.vatan.tj) in the capital and Radio Tiroz (www.tiroz.tj) in Khujand.

External radios stations can be received including BBC, VOA and Voice of Free Tajikistan (run by national exiles).

Television: The state runs three regional networks, Tajik TV, Soghd TV and Khatlon TV. Safina TV (www.safina.tj) the only private operation.

Advertising
All media outlets accept advertising. Alcohol is banned from being advertised

Economy
Tajikistan's GDP per capita is one of the lowest in the countries of the former Soviet Union. Like many transition states, Tajikistan's economy in the aftermath of the break-up of the Soviet Union experienced severe contraction, but its transition has been more extreme than most. Already the poorest of the Soviet republics, Tajikistan was weakened further by the loss of subsidies (which accounted for up to 80 per cent of its income) and markets, but the five-year civil war effectively destroyed the economy. The war ravaged the limited infrastructure, led to the emigration of some of the most qualified and skilled workers and caused state spending to increase. Associated economic and weather problems have forced many to seek survival in the black economy. Government corruption and incompetence added to the problems caused by the break-up of the Soviet Union and the civil war.

Agriculture, particularly cotton, dominates the official economy. Industry is largely limited to the Tadaz aluminium smelter, the Nurek hydropower station and small obsolete light industry and food processing factories. Economic growth has become more broad-based in recent years, with about two-thirds of it coming from outside the cotton and aluminum industries. A rise in global cotton prices helped to finance imports.

With support from abroad, principally the IMF as well as Russia and the US, Tajikistan has begun to show encouraging signs of growth. GDP has grown annually at not less than six per cent for several years, although from a low base, still leaving most of the population in poverty. Remittances from migrant workers are important to the economy, as well as being crucial to the existence of the impoverished reipients.

Tajikistan is badly in need of foreign investment, but lack of foreign investor interest is not surprising given the country's recent political history and complex political balance.

In the medium term, the economy needs to continue to diversify to develop new sources of economic expansion. Sustaining growth in landlocked Tajikistan is also dependent on promoting mutually beneficial economic co-operation with neighbouring countries.

Tajikistan, located at the crossroads of Russia, Iran, Pakistan and China, has become a narcotics hub and a major transit route for opium produced in Afghanistan.

External trade
It belongs to the Eurasian Economic Community (EurAsec or EAEC), which was established in 2000 to promote a customs union between its six member states (Belarus, Kazakhstan, Kyrgyzstan, Russia, Tajikistan, and Uzbekistan), and among other objectives, to introduce standardised currency exchange and rules for trade in goods and service. The EAEC evolved out of the Commonwealth of Independent States (CIS) Customs Union and has begun the process of merging with the Central Asian Co-operation Organisation (CACO).

Tajikistan has the potential for mining gold, silver, uranium, antimony and tungsten, which are yet to be exploited commercially. About 75 per cent of all exports are produced by one aluminium smelter, Talco. Cotton is another important commodity and accounts for almost 10 per cent of exports. Both of these products are subject to world prices and Talco is an old soviet era factory, which along with the general infrastructure is in need of re-investment. Remittances are vital to the country's foreign earnings.

Imports
Main imports are electricity, petroleum and derivatives, aluminium oxide, machinery, equipment and foodstuffs.

Main sources: Russia (19.3 per cent total, 2005), Kazakhstan (12.7 per cent), Uzbekistan (11.5 per cent), Azerbaijan (8.6 per cent), China (7.0 per cent), Ukraine (6.2 per cent), Romania (4.6 per cent), Turkmenistan (4.0 per cent)

Exports
The main exports are aluminium, electricity, cotton and textiles, fruits and vegetable oil .

Main destinations: The Netherlands (46.6 per cent total, 2005), Turkey (15.8 per cent), Russia (9.1 per cent), Uzbekistan (7.3 per cent), Latvia (4.9 per cent), Iran (4.0 per cent)

Agriculture
Farming
Agriculture typically accounts for around 23 per cent of GDP and employs 42 per cent of the workforce.

Because of Tajikistan's mountainous nature, only 7 per cent of the land is suitable for farming. Tajikistan is a large net importer of different types of grain. The main agricultural areas are in the lower-lying regions of the south-west and the north-west – part of the Fergana basin.

During the Soviet era agriculture was the mainstay of the Tajikistan economy, particularly cotton and wheat. The sector is heavily dependent on irrigation, which covers about 75 per cent of arable land. Irrigation networks have become clogged or are otherwise in need of restoration.

Crops constitute about two-thirds, and animal husbandry one-third, of rural production. Cattle, sheep and goats are reared. Important products are cotton, grain, fruits, grapes, vegetables and tobacco leaves. Lack of processing and packing facilities and inefficient distribution mean that large amounts of the vegetable and fruit crops are wasted and that the country often fails even to meet its domestic needs.

Production was devastated by the civil war of 1992–97, and has only slowly recovered with increased production since hostilities ended. Farm machinery has suffered depreciation over the years without replacement, and the quality of seed varieties has fallen.

In a report published in early 2005 – The Curse of Cotton: Central Asia's destructive monoculture – the International Crisis Group (ICG) said that while the former Soviet cotton producing countries of Uzbekistan, Tajikistan and Turkmenistan continued to exploit their cotton growers there was little hope of improving economic development and tackling poverty. The cotton industry is vital to the economy of Tajikistan, yet while the industry continues to rely on cheap labour (including children), land ownership is uncertain, state intervention discourages competition and the rule of law is limited, there is little incentive for the powerful vested interests to reform the system.

In addition to the economic and social costs to the rural populations, the environmental costs of the monoculture have been devastating. The degradation of the Aral Sea in particular has lead to international concern.

Crop production in 2005 included: 859,100 tonnes (t) cereals in total, 630,000t wheat, 556,000t potatoes, 113,000t maize, 31,400t pulses, 209,800t tomatoes, 4,500t treenuts, 7,000t tobacco, 550,000t seed cotton, 54,957t oilcrops, 226,500t fruit in total, 862,700t vegetables in total,. Livestock production included: 45,500t meat in total, 24,000t beef, 18,700t lamb, 2,600t poultry, 5,600t eggs, 500,800t milk, 1,000t honey, 2,660t cattle hides, 2,400t sheepskins, 4,000t greasy wool.

Fishing
Fishing remains important for domestic consumption, but pollution and a lack of investment have reduced fish stocks drastically. Tibet stone loach is a common fish in Tajikistan where it is present up to 4,500 metres altitude, but is of no commercial importance. The typical annual fish catch is over 200 tonnes.

Forestry
The state-owned forestry and wooded land accounts for only 5 per cent of land area with forest cover estimated at over

400,000 hectares (ha). Most of the forests located between 1,000 and 3,000 metre altitude are protected. The main stock of the forests include coniferous and juniper species, which are not available for wood supply.
There are no large-scale primary forest industries and the relatively low per capita consumption of forest products is met mainly by imports from the Russian Federation.
Timber imports in 2004 were US$3.9 billion, while exports only amounted to US$80,000.

Industry and manufacturing
Industry contributes around 24 per cent to GDP.
Industrial production experienced a significant decline throughout the 1990s. The industrial sector is dominated by some 300 large state-owned enterprises in areas such as heavy industry, transport and wholesale trading and is mainly built around inefficient, labour-intensive production.
Aluminium is Tajikistan's key industrial sector. The country has one of the world's largest aluminium smelters, the state-owned Tadaz aluminium smelter, which has a capacity of 517,000 tonnes a year. Located at Tursunzade in western Tajikistan, the plant is a main source of revenue for the government.
Light industry accounts for around 45 per cent of the value of total industrial production. The main sectors are food processing (mainly dairy products, meat, fruit and cooking oil), tobacco, cotton cleaning, silk, textiles, knitted goods, footwear, tanning, carpet weaving and simple electronics.

Tourism
Tourism is undeveloped. The civil war in the nineties wrecked the tourist sector.Infrastructure was backward even before the civil war and has to be developed afresh. The importance of tourism to the economy is recognised and development is being encouraged, with attention to mountaineering, trekking and eco-tourism.

Environment
The Aral Sea is drying up due to the over-use of water from the two main rivers which feed into it and has lost 40 per cent of its water, dropping by up to 19 metres. This has resulted in desertification of the surrounding land. A UN study published in 2004 reported that there was no possibility of restoring the water and the need must be on preserving what is left.
The government has endorsed a 2004 joint strategy to resolve the demands of its water requirements with its neighbours.
Hundreds of thousands of people endured the worst winter since the 1960s without heat, electricity or running water before an appeal was made to the UN for aid in February 2008. As the first winter snows fell and temperatures dropped to -20 Celsius people began to overload the power system in an attempt to keep warm, while rivers in the mountains that fed the hydro-electric power stations froze and cut off supplies; domestic pipes froze and left millions without drinking water. The UN issued an appeal for US$25 million.

Mining
Tajikistan has an established history of mineral production. In the Soviet era, the country used to mine and process uranium amounting to around 500,000 tonnes per year of ore, but with demand falling in the post-Soviet era, uranium production ceased in the 1990s.
Tajikistan holds around 500,000 tonnes of antimony reserves, 6.2 million tonnes of mercury, 60,000 tonnes of silver and 150 tonnes of gold. Lack of modern equipment and techniques means that some resources are not exploited to full capacity. Antimony, bismuth and mercury have been mined, but most deposits are depleted and the mines closing down. Despite large silver reserves, only around one tonne of silver is produced every year.
There are significant deposits of world-class marble; also uranium, radium, arsenic, bismuth, mica and small amounts of potassium salts, molybdenum, sulphur, boron, common salt, carbonates, fluorite, quartz sand, asbestos, lead and zinc. Deposits of semi-precious stones include lapis lazuli, rubies, amethyst and ornamental quartz.

Hydrocarbons
Tajikistan has proven oil reserves of 12 million barrels. The state-owned energy company, Tajikneftegaz, is responsible for all oil exploration, drilling, and production and produces around 3,500 barrels per day of oil. Most of Tajikistan's oil demand needs are met by imports, with Uzbekistan supplying 70 per cent of oil imports. In total, the CIS accounts for over 97 per cent of Tajikistan's oil needs.
There are proven natural gas reserves of 5.6 billion cubic metres (cum). Tajikistan has a small natural gas extraction industry which meets only a fraction of the annual domestic requirement of 1.1 billion cum. Over 90 per cent of gas consumed in Tajikistan is imported, mainly from Uzbekistan. Gas is supplied via a pipeline running from Uzbekistan to Dushanbe, in exchange for use of a rail corridor and gas pipeline across north Tajikistan.
Tajikistan could have up to six billion tonnes of coal reserves, among of the largest coal deposits in Central Asia, but these have not been proven. There are six large coal fields, with that at Fan Yagnob estimated to contain two billion tonnes of reserves. Mostly brown coal is mined in Yagnob and Myonadu, besides coking coal at Nazarailok in the Karateginsk Valley in the east.

Energy
Tajikistan used to receive energy supplies from Russia in exchange for cotton and minerals. Since independence there have been chronic energy shortages due to a breakdown in communications and infrastructure, especially in the winter period and when water levels are low, given the country's dependence on hydroelectric power.
Tajikistan is a mountainous country with potential to produce hydroelectricity in significant amounts. Energy generation is extremely variable from year to year, depending on the level of rainfall. The electricity monopoly, Barki Tojik (Tajik Electricity), estimates that only 10 per cent of hydroelectric potential is being used.
Besides hydroelectric power, oil typically accounts for 23 per cent of energy consumption, natural gas for 17 per cent and coal for 1 per cent. Total generating capacity in Tajikistan is 4.4GW.
The grave investment deficit in power generation is not helped by the fact that production costs of electricity can run higher than market prices. Tajikistan is littered with incomplete power projects, including plans for a chain of nine power stations along the Vaksh river, discontinued because of the civil war.
Development of the Roghun hydropower station in eastern Tajikistan has been resumed. Work on the plant began in the 1980s, but construction was never completed due to a lack of funds. The plant will be the largest hydropower facility in Central Asia, possibly producing enough electricity to meet domestic needs.

Financial markets
Stock exchange
The Tajik commodity exchange was inaugurated in March 1996.

Banking and insurance
The banking sector remains extremely weak, with the five largest banks (which account for 85 per cent of total commercial bank credit and 90 per cent of deposits) handicapped by substantial non-performing loans. A law on Banks and Banking Activity in May 1998 introduced regulations which are close to international standards.
The restructuring of Agroinvestbank, the largest commercial bank, was completed in March 2004.
Central bank
National Bank of Tajikistan

Time
GMT plus five hours

Geography
Tajikistan is situated in the south-east of Central Asia. To the south of Tajikistan lies Afghanistan, Uzbekistan to the north and west, the People's Republic of China to the east and Kyrgyzstan to the north-east.
The terrain is almost entirely mountainous with more than one-half of the country above 3,000 metres. The main mountain ranges are the western Tian Shan in the north, the southern Tian Shan in the central region and the Pamirs in the south-east. The northern Pamirs are the highest mountains of Tajikistan, and of the former Soviet Union – Lenin Peak 7,134 metres and Ismail Samani Peak (formerly Communism Peak) 7,495 metres. There is a dense river network.

Hemisphere
Northern

Climate
Extreme continental; temperatures range between minus 20 degrees Celsius (C) and 0 degrees C in January, and from 0 degrees C to 30 degrees C in June, depending on altitude. From minus 5 degrees C to 35 degrees C in foothills, valleys and Dushanbe; sub-zero temperatures in the Pamir mountains. Rainfall between 150 and 250mm per annum.

Dress codes
Not overly formal but modest, particularly outside Dushanbe.

Entry requirements
Passports
Required by all, valid for at least six months after date of departure.

Visa
Required by all, except nationals of Russia, Belarus, Kazakstan and Kyrghyzstan. Visas may be obtained at Dushanbe airport by air travellers, but land travellers must obtain their visas in advance from the nearest Tajik embassies. All applications must be supported by a letter of invitation endorsed by the Ministry of Foreign Affairs. (For details, see www.traveltajikistan.com/visas).
A business visa requires, in addition to a letter of invitation from a local company or organisation, a business letter undertaking full financial responsibility for expenses incurred by the representative and a full itinerary.
Visitors must obtain special permission to visit Gorno-Badakhshan autonomous region.

Currency advice/regulations
There are no restrictions on the import of local and foreign currencies, but it must be declared on arrival. Export of local currency is prohibited. Foreign currency can be exported up to the amount declared on arrival.
Travellers cheques are not generally accepted. Tajikistan is a cash-only economy, although carrying large amounts of cash can be dangerous. US dollars are widely accepted.

Customs
Most personal effects may be imported duty-free, subject to declaration on arrival.

Health (for visitors)
A reciprocal health agreement for urgent medical treatment exists with the United Kingdom. Proof of UK residence will be required. Standards of healthcare are significantly below Western levels. Although emergency treatment can be very expensive, doctors and hospitals often expect immediate cash payment. Uninsured visitors requiring urgent medical evacuation may face extreme difficulties. Comprehensive travel and medical insurance, including evacuation by air ambulance, is essential.

Mandatory precautions
Vaccination certificates are required for yellow fever if travelling from an infected area. Visitors staying for longer than 90 days may be submitted to an Aids test, which carries the possibility of infection with HIV or other pathogens, given the lack of medical supplies in Tajikistan.

Advisable precautions
Water precautions are recommended: water purification tablets may be useful, or drink bottled water. The risk of water-borne diseases, including cholera, is high.
It is advisable to be in date for the following immunisations: polio and tetanus (both within 10 years), typhoid, hepatitis A, and tuberculosis. Anti-malarial precautions are also advisable. There has been a significant increase in the number of cases of diphtheria and professional advice should be sort to determine a suitable precaution.
Any medicines required should be taken by the visitor, and it would be wise to have precautionary antibiotics if going outside major urban centres. A travel kit including a disposable syringe is a reasonable precaution.

Hotels
Visitors are advised to use well-known travel operators with established contacts in Tajikistan. There is a lack of adequate hotel accommodation and there are very few hotels outside the two main towns, Dushanbe and Khodzhent.

Credit cards
Credit cards are not generally accepted.

Public holidays (national)
The Islamic year contains 354 or 355 days, with the result that Muslim feasts advance by 10–12 days against the Gregorian calendar. Dates of feasts vary according to the sighting of the new moon, so cannot be forecast exactly.
Tajikistan uses the Persian calendar, which differs from the Gregorian calendar: there are 31 days in each of the first six months of the Persian calendar, 30 days in each of the next five months and 29 days in the last month, except in leap year when it has 30 days.

Fixed dates
1 Jan (New Year's Day), 8 Mar (Women's Day), 20–22 Mar (Navruz/Persian New Year), 1 May (Labour Day), 9 May (Victory Day), 9 Sep (Independence Day), 6 Nov (Constitution Day), 9 Nov (National Reconciliation Day).

Variable dates
Eid al Adha, Eid al Fitr.

Working hours
Banking
Mon–Fri: 0800–1700.

Business
Mon–Fri: approximately 0900–1800 (appointments are best made in the morning).

Shops
No formal hours, but generally within 0800–2100.

Telecommunications
Mobile/cell phones
Limited 900/1800 GSM services exist particularly around Dushanbe.

Electricity supply
220V AC

Social customs/useful tips
The increasing influence of Islam is widely evident, particularly in rural areas. The Islamic faith can be traced back to the seventh century in Tajikistan and although religious activity was banned during the Soviet era it has begun to play a more important role in everyday life since the late 1980s. Closer links with Iran (Iranian television is beamed into Tajikistan) have been established since independence, although alcohol (generally vodka) is still freely available and consumed. Gratuities are becoming more customary, particularly in international hotels.
'Dushanbe' – Tajik for Monday – is named after the day when, for centuries, merchants have gathered at Dushanbe's famous oriental bazaar.

Security
The prevalence of light weapons and local warlords throughout the country mean that care should be taken at all times. Visitors should avoid demonstrations, crowds, or congregations of military personnel.
Visitors may have their movements, hotel rooms and correspondence (including telephone and fax) monitored by security

personnel. Taking photographs of military or otherwise strategically significant installations is not advised. There are periodic nightly curfews. Travel alone or on foot after dark is highly inadvisable. Car hire with a driver is advised rather than the use of public transport. Visitors are reminded to be vigilant and to dress down.

Getting there

Air

National airline: Tajikistan Airlines

International airport/s: Dushanbe (DYU), 3km south of city; restaurant, post office, chemist and left luggage.

There are bus services (nos 3 and 12), hours 0600–1800, and train services (lines 3 and 4), hours 0600–1900, between the airport and city centre, with a journey time of 20 minutes. Taxis operate between 0800—2000, journey time five minutes; as they are not metered the fare should be agreed in advance.

Airport tax: None.

Surface

There are border crossings with neighbouring countries, but not all of them may be open. It is advisable to check in advance.

Road: There are a few primary roads; secondary roads, particularly in mountain areas, are of poor quality. An all-weather road connects the capital Dushanbe to the Samarkand railhead (in Uzbekistan) to the north-west. Vehicles with Tajik licence plates may be refused entry into Uzbekistan.

On 26 August 2007, a bridge was opened across the Pyanj River, build by the US army (at a cost of US$37 million), linking the Tajik town of Nizhny Pyanj with Shir Khan Bandar in Afghanistan and extended the trans-Afghanistan road (Regional Road Corridor Improvement Project) through Central Asia.

The Regional Road Corridor Improvement Project, estimated at US$18 billion, to improve Central Asian roads, airports, railway lines and seaports and provide a vital transit route between Europe and Asia was agreed, on 3 November 2007. Six new transit corridors, between Afghanistan, Azerbaijan, China, Kazakhstan, Kyrgyzstan, Mongolia, Tajikistan and Uzbekistan, of mainly roads and rail links, will be constructed, or existing resources upgraded, by 2013. Half the costs with be provided by the Asian Development Bank and other multilateral organisations and the other half by participating countries.

Rail: Tajikistan is linked to the rail network of the former Soviet republics, with the main line running south from Dushanbe to the Uzbekistan border town of Termez and on to Samarkand, Tashkent and the Black Sea. A line running from Andizhan to Samarkand, both in Uzbekistan, cuts through the northern tip of Tajikistan.

Getting about

National transport

Air: There are flights between Dushanbe and Khorog, Khojand and Kulyab, but take-off is dependent on weather conditions and fuel availability.

Road: The road network is generally in a poor condition. Roads are often closed due to weather conditions. Road travel, especially in the east, can be impeded by checkpoints, from which soldiers or other armed groups may shoot if vehicles do not stop. Travel by road should only be undertaken during daylight hours, with the appropriate vehicle and with the utmost precautions.

Buses: Buses run between the main centres when weather conditions permit.

Rail: The railway system is not well-developed, with only around 500km of rail track. The north and south of the country are not linked by rail, because of the mountainous terrain. Passengers are advised to safeguard their possessions.

City transport

Taxis: Taxis can be found at prominent places in the cities. They can also be hailed in the street. It is advisable to use only officially-licensed taxis. As they are not metered, the fare should be agreed in advance. Before setting off, the passenger should be satisfied that the driver is clear about the destination.

Minibus taxis (marshrutkas) travel on fixed routes and stop on request, but they can be over-crowded.

Car hire

There are no international car hire companies operating in Tajikistan.

BUSINESS DIRECTORY

The addresses listed below are a selection only. While World of Information makes every endeavour to check these addresses, we cannot guarantee that changes have not been made, especially to telephone numbers and area codes. We would welcome any corrections.

Telephone area codes

The international direct dialling (IDD) code for Tajikistan is +992, followed by area code and subscriber's number:

Dushanbe 372

Useful telephone numbers

Police: 02

Fire: 01

Ambulance: 03

Chambers of Commerce

Tajikistan Chamber of Commerce and Industry, 21 Mazayeva Street, 734012 Dushanbe (tel: 279-519; fax: 211-480).

Banking

Agroinvestbank, Prospekt S Sherozi 21, Dushanbe (tel: 210-385; fax: 211-206).

Orienbank, 95/1 Rudaki Ave, Dushanbe (tel: 210-920; fax: 211-662).

Tajikbankbusiness (commercial bank), 29 Shotemur Street, 734025 Dushanbe (tel/fax: 210-634).

Tajikvnesheconombank (Tajikistan Bank for Foreign Economic Affairs), Dushanbe (tel: 233-571, 225-952).

Central bank

National Bank of Tajikistan, Prospekt Rudaki 107A, 734003 Dushanbe (tel: 600-3227; fax: 600-3235; e-mail: info@natbank.tajnet.com).

Travel information

Tajikistan Airlines, Titova Street 32/1, 734006 Dushanbe (tel: 212-247; fax: 510-041; e-mail: mop_gart@tajnet.com).

Tajikistan Republican Council of Tourism and Excursions, Sherozi Avenue 11, 734018 Dushanbe (tel: 332-770; fax: 334-420).

Travel Tajikistan, Proletarskaya 5/11, 734000 Dushanbe (tel: 247-673; fax: 217-184; e-mail: info@traveltajikistan.com).

National tourist organisation offices

National Tourism Company SAYOH, Pushkin Street 14, 734095 Dushanbe (tel: 234-233; fax: 217-184)

Ministries

Council of Ministers, Prospekt Rudaki 48, 734025 Dushanbe (tel: 232-903; fax: 228-120).

EU Co-ordinating Unit, c/o Ministry of External Economic Relations, Prospekt Rudaki 42, Dushanbe (tel: 222-403, 227-077; fax: 228-120).

Ministry of Agriculture, 46 Rudaki Ave, Dushanbe 734051 (tel: 276-249).

Ministry of Communications, 57 Rudaki Ave, 734025 Dushanbe (tel: 232-284; fax: 212-953; International Relations Department (tel: 216-010; fax: 510-277).

Ministry of Construction, 36 Kirova Street, Dushanbe 734025 (tel: 226-143).

Ministry of Economy and External Economic Affairs, 42 Rudaki Ave, 734025 Dushanbe (tel: 232-944).

Ministry of Finance, Prospekt Kuibysheva 3, 734025 Dushanbe (tel: 273-941; fax: 213-329).

Ministry of Foreign Affairs, 40 Rudaki Ave, 734051 Dushanbe (tel: 221-560, 232-971; fax: 227-051).

Ministry of Foreign Economic Relations, 42 Rudaki Ave, Dushanbe (tel: 232-971; fax: 232-964).

Ministry of Grain Products, 42 Rudaki Ave, Dushanbe 734051 (tel: 276-131).

Ministry of Industrial Afairs, 80 Rudaki Avenue, Dushanbe 734023 (tel: 232-249, 231-845; fax: 232-381).

Ministry of Information, Ulitsa Negmata Karabaeva 17, 734018 Dushanbe (tel: 335-851).

Ministry of Justice, 25 Rudaki Ave, 734025 Dushanbe (tel: 214-405; fax: 218-066).

Ministry of Trade and Material Resources, 37 Bokhtar Street, Dushanbe 734002 (tel: 273-434).

Prime Minister's Office, 80 Rudaki Ave, 734023 Dushanbe (tel: 211-871; fax; 215-110).

Other useful addresses

British Embassy, Gulyamov Street 67, Tashkent 700000, Uzbekistan (accredited to Tajikistan) (tel: (+998 71) 120-7852; fax: (+998 71) 120-6549).

State Statistical Committee (SSC), 17 Bokhtar Street, Dushanbe 734025 (tel: 276-882; fax: 275-408).

Tajikistan Embassy (USA), 1005 New Hampshire Avenue, Washington DC 20037 (tel: (+1-202) 223-6090; fax: (+1-202) 223-6091; e-mail: tajikistan@verizon.net).

Tajikistan (TDA) Office, c/o Tajik Bank Business, 23/2 Rudaki Avenue, 734620 Dushanbe (tel: 233-512; fax: 224-844).

Tajikvneshtorg (foreign trade organisation), Prospekt Lenina 41, 734051 Dushanbe (tel: 232-903; fax: 228-120).

National news agency: Khovar (in Russian) (www.khovar.tj).

Other news agencies: Avesta news agency (www.avesta.tj/en).

Internet sites

Tajikistan Privatisation Agency: http://privatization.tajikistan.com

Tajikistan Resource Page: http://www.eurasianet.org/resource/tajikistan/index.shtml

National Tourism Company: http://www.tajiktour.tajnet.com

Tanzania

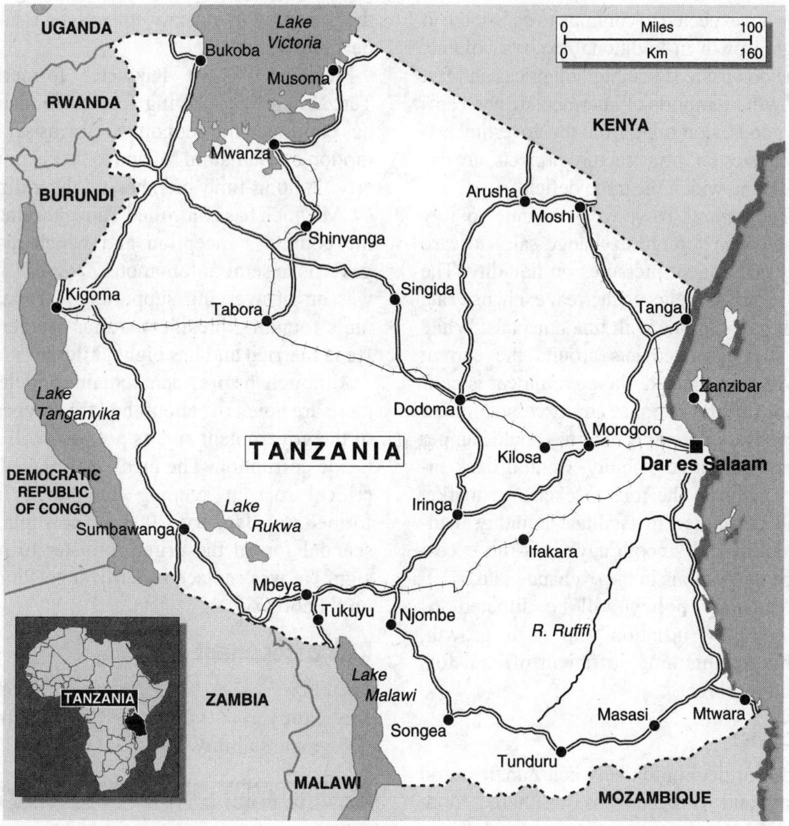

What a difference the sun makes, and good rains. Tanzania had a good harvest in 2007, and there was sufficient rain water to provide adequate levels for the hydro-dams that are the main source of electric power generation. Agriculture grew by 5 per cent in 2007, and, providing the weather is kind, is expected to expand by just over 5 per cent in 2008.

The 2008 edition of *African Economic Outlook* (AEO), published by te African Development Bank, reports that after GDP growth of 6.6 in 2007 the outlook is encouraging for the next years. Growth in 2008 is forecast to be 6.5 per cent, with 6.7 forecast for 2009. Dampeners could be the increase in fuel costs, the early 2008 political turmoil in Kenya (which has cut tourism revenue) and the private sector wage regulations announced in 2008.

The improved harvest in 2006/07 enabled the government to scale back food aid distribution, and to rebuild its strategic grain reserve (SGR) to around 130,000 tons by June 2007. A further 150,000 tons is expected in 2008. Other sectors that improved in 2007 were the tourism, real estate and business service sub-sectors. Industrial production, comprising manufacturing, mining, and quarrying and construction, grew by around 9.2 per cent in 2007. Further growth will depend on successfully overcoming infrastructure weaknesses, especially in transportation and energy.

Wages increase

The Labour Institutions Act of 2004 has allowed the government to set new sectoral minimum wages, which went into effect in January 2008. These range from Tsh85,000–Tsh350,000, compared to former minimum wages of Tsh48,000 for urban workers and Ts35,000 for rural workers. These are considered high by

KEY FACTS

Official name: Jamhuri ya Muungano wa Tanzania (United Republic of Tanzania)

Head of State: President Jakaya Kikwete (since 21 Dec 2005)

Head of government: Prime Minister Mizengo Pinda (appointed 8 Feb 2008)

Ruling party: Chama Cha Mapinduzi (CCM) (Party of the Revolution) (since 1977; re-elected 14 Dec 2005)

Area: 945,087 square km

Population: 38.96 million (2007)

Capital: Dodoma (official, legislative centre); Dar es Salaam (the former capital is the largest city and de factol commercial capital)

Official language: KiSwahili and English

Currency: Tanzania shilling (Tsh) = 100 senti (convertible with currencies of Kenya and Uganda)

Exchange rate: Tsh1,164.50 per US$ (Jul 2008)

GDP per capita: US$415 (2007)*

GDP real growth: 7.30% (2007)*

Labour force: 18.97 million (2004)

Inflation: 5.00% (2007)*

Balance of trade: -US$1.90 billion (2006)

Foreign debt: US$7.80 billion (2004)

* estimated figure

some sectors and the anticipated growth in sectoral output in 2008 will depend on how businesses cope.

The AEO notes that the government has emphasised the participation of the private sector as a key partner in Tanzania's development strategy. There is a high level of political support through the Tanzania Private Sector Foundation (chaired by President Jakaya Kikwete). The increased number of foreign direct investments (FDI) projects approved by the Tanzania Investment Centre (TIC) indicates that the strategy is having some success.

Under its first president, 'Mwalimu' (teacher) Julius Nyerere, Tanzania had endured many years of socialism which turned out to have been an economic disaster. In 1967 Nyerere issued the *Arusha Declaration*, which called for self-reliance through the creation of co-operative farm villages and the nationalisation of factories, plantations, banks and private companies. A decade later, despite financial and technical aid from the World Bank and sympathetic countries, the programme had completely failed due to inefficiency, corruption, resistance from peasants and the rise in the price of imported petroleum.

Tanzania remains one of the poorest countries in Africa with GDP per capita of US$336 in 2007. Sustained IMF-endorsed reforms have generated strong macroeconomic performance in Tanzania, while the poverty reduction strategy *Mkukuta*, pays particular attention to stimulating private investment, developing infrastructure, and building the human capacity necessary to develop a competitive economy.

The external sector is expected to continue benefiting from increased exports due to solid growth in the mining and manufacturing sectors, and a strong performance of traditional exports. Expanded road infrastructure, the abolition of many local taxes and facilitated access to inputs for production are expected to continue to contribute to high growth in traditional exports volume. The downside is that high oil prices and fast growth of imports of intermediate and capital goods, stemming from the government's initiatives on infrastructure projects, are expected to widen the trade deficit.

The central bank will continue to rely heavily on foreign exchange sales to ease any consequent pressures on liquidity. The government believes the real exchange rate is broadly in line with fundamentals. While moderate movements around the current level are expected, the government is conscious of the fact that any excessive future depreciations or appreciations could hamper macroeconomic stability. Central bank intervention in the foreign exchange market will be limited to facilitate liquidity management and smooth any short-run excessive fluctuations in the exchange rate.

Monetary policy will be directed towards low inflation and high growth, while maintaining sufficient official foreign reserves.

Politics

The political union between Zanzibar and mainland Tanzania has weathered more than four decades of change. Zanzibar has its own parliament and president, but a long standing political impasse between the Chama Cha Mapinduzi (CCM) and the Civic United Front (CUF) opposition in Zanzibar continues despite talks aimed at settling the dispute. It is to be hope the violence in Kenya following the December 2007 elections will serve as a warning on the need to work out any unresolved issues peacefully.

President Jakaya Kikwete, formerly Tanzania's long-serving foreign minister has continued the economic reforms set in motion by Benjamin Mkapa to tackle poverty. A long-time member of the ruling CCM which has controlled Tanzania since the country's inception and which also governs in semi-autonomous Zanzibar, he was an unswerving supporter of Tanzania's founding president, Julius Nyerere. He is married and has eight children.

Although the president remains popular, there are concerns about the effectiveness of the government and its political will to tackle corruption. The media has played a critical role in keeping the public informed. In January 2008, a corruption scandal forced the prime minister to resign. He was replaced by Mizengo Pinda on 8 February.

Risk assessment

Politics	Fair
Economy	Fair
Regional stability	Good

KEY INDICATORS — Tanzania

	Unit	2003	2004	2005	2006	2007
Population	m	35.89	36.58	37.50	*38.20	*38.96
Gross domestic product (GDP)	US$bn	10.10	11.35	12.61	14.20	*16.18
GDP per capita	US$	255	295	336	*372	*415
GDP real growth	%	5.2	6.3	6.8	6.7	*7.3
Inflation	%	4.6	4.6	4.4	7.2	*7.0
Industrial output	% change	–	10.1	11.2	8.6	–
Agricultural output	% change	–	6.0	5.3	3.8	–
Exports (fob) (goods)	US$m	1,691.0	1,248.0	1,664.1	1,759.0	2,226.6
Imports (cif) (goods)	US$m	2,682.0	1,972.0	2,661.5	3,661.0	4,860.6
Balance of trade	US$m	-911.0	-724.0	-997.4	-1,902.0	-2,634.1
Current account	US$m	-250.0	-620.0	-651.0	-1,110.0	-1,855.8
Total reserves minus gold	US$m	2,038.4	2,295.7	2,048.8	2,259.3	2,886.4
Foreign exchange	US$m	2,023.0	2,280.1	2,033.8	2,244.2	2,870.4
Exchange rate	per US$	1,017.70	1,089.33	1,282.00	1,282.00	1,158.00

* estimated figure

COUNTRY PROFILE

Historical profile

1832 The increasing importance of Zanzibar as a spice and slave trading centre led the Sultan of Oman to transfer his capital there from Muscat. Around this time, Britain signed a number of agreements with Oman to limit the potential threat to Britain's colonies from France. Meanwhile, Germany signed a number of 'friendship' treaties with local chiefs – treaties which formed the basis of the German East Africa Company which was established to exploit and colonise what became Tanganyika.

1886 The UK and Germany signed an agreement which gave Germany control of mainland Tanzania and the UK control of Zanzibar.

1918 After Germany's defeat in the First World War, the League of Nations mandated the territory to Britain.

1961 Tanganyika gained independence under Julius Nyerere and the Tanganyika Africa National Union (TANU).

1964 The United Republic of Tanzania was formed following the union of Tanganyika and Zanzibar.
1977 The new constitution established a real one-party state for the whole of Tanzania after the Tanganyika African National Union and Zanzibar's Afro-Shirazi Party merged to create Chama Cha Mapinduzi (CCM) (Party of the Revolution).
1979 Tanzania invaded Uganda, forcing its dictator, Idi Amin, to flee to Saudi Arabia.
1985 Nyerere stepped down as president and was replaced by the president of Zanzibar, Ali Hassan Mwinyi.
1992 The constitution was amended to allow multi-party politics.
1995 The first multi-party elections took place. Benjamin William Mkapa (CCM) was elected president and the CCM was re-elected to government. The Zanzibar opposition Civic United Front (CUF) refused to accept the election results in Zanzibar.
1999 A conciliation agreement was signed between the CCM and the CUF, bringing an end to four years of hostility. Julius Nyerere, the former president and founder figure of modern Tanzania, died.
2000 President Benjamin Mkapa was re-elected for a second term. The CCM was re-elected in the parliamentary elections. Because of unfair elections in Zanzibar, a re-run was held in 16 of its 50 constituencies; it was won by the ruling party, the CCM.
2001 There were clashes in Zanzibar between supporters of CUF and the police. The CCM and the opposition CUF signed a further agreement aimed at ending hostilities on Zanzibar.
2002 The African Development Bank (ADB) signed an agreement with the Deputy Minister for Finance, Alhaj Adbisalaam Issa Khatibu, for a loan of approximately US$47 million to partially finance the Dar es Salaam water supply and sanitation project.
2004 The presidents of Tanzania, Uganda and Kenya signed a protocol in Arusha over a proposed customs union.
2005 Jakaya Kikwete was elected president. The CCM retained an outright majority of seats in parliament elections.
2006 A challenge to the legality of the 1964 Act of Union was dismissed by the Zanzibar high court. The African Development Bank cancelled over US$640 million in debt by Tanzania.
2008 President Jakaya Kikwete was elected chairman of the African Union on 31 January. Governor of the central bank, Daudi Ballali, was sacked following an international audit found improper payments to local companies of over US$120 millions. A corruption scandal forced the president to dissolve his cabinet and the prime minister to resign. Mizengo Pinda was appointed as prime minister on 8 February.

Political structure

Constitution

The constitution was introduced in 1965 following the union of Zanzibar and Tanganyika in 1964. Zanzibar is partially autonomous, with 50 political constituencies.

The 1977 constitution established a one-party state for the whole of Tanzania after the two parties merged to create Chama Cha Mapinduzi (CCM) (Party of the Revolution).

Form of state

Republic

The executive

Executive power rests with the president, who is elected by direct popular vote for a five-year term. The president can serve a maximum of two terms.

One vice president is appointed by the president, as is the cabinet (in consultation with the prime minister), and the second vice president is the directly elected president of Zanzibar.

National legislature

The constitution provides for legislative power to be held by a unicameral National Assembly with members serving a term of five years, and for universal adult suffrage. The legislative body, the Bunge, has 274 members with 232 elected for a five-year term in single-seat constituencies. The president allocates 37 special seats to women and five seats are dedicated to members of the Zanzibar House of Representatives.

Legal system

The legal system is based on English common law, the 1977 Union and 1985 Zanzibari constitutions, as amended. The judiciary is relatively independent. A permanent Commission of Enquiry has wide powers to investigate abuses of power. In Zanzibar, Kadhis (Islamic courts) have jurisdiction over certain areas of law.

Last elections

14 December 2005 (presidential and parliamentary)

Results: Presidential: Jakaya Kikwete (CCM) won 80.28 per cent of the vote; Ibrahim Haruna Lipumba (CUF) won 11.68 per cent; and Freeman Mbowe (Chadema) 5.88 per cent.

Parliamentary: CCM won 70 per cent of the votes (275 seats out of 323); CUF won 14.3 per cent (31 seats); Chadema 8.2 per cent (11 seats). Turnout was 72 per cent.

Next elections

2010 (presidential and parliamentary)

Political parties

Ruling party

Chama Cha Mapinduzi (CCM) (Party of the Revolution) (since 1977; re-elected 14 Dec 2005)

Main opposition party

Chama Cha Wananchi (CUF) (Civic United Front).

Population

38.96 million (2007)

Last census: August 2002: 34,443,603 (provisional)

Annual growth rate: 2.3 per cent 1994–2004 (WHO 2006)

Ethnic make-up

About 98 per cent of the population is of indigenous African or Arab (Zanzibar) origin, with the remainder mainly from the Indian sub-continent. Those of Indian, Pakistani and Goan descent tend to work in the towns, mainly dominating the trading environment, but also moving into the industrial sector. The small population of Arab descent is mainly engaged in trade. There are about 10,000 Europeans.

Over 120 tribal groups exist in Tanzania, the most important of which are Sukuma (12 per cent of total population), Makonde (4 per cent), Chagga (4 per cent), Haya (3 per cent), Nyamwezi (3 per cent), Ha (3 per cent), Gogo (3 per cent) and Hehe (3 per cent).

Religions

Islam and Christianity are the main organised religions. However, many people adhere to ancient tribal and animist religions. The religious make-up is believed to be Christianity: 33 per cent, Islam: 33 per cent, traditional beliefs: 33 per cent and Hinduism: 1 per cent.

Education

In 2003, three million seven to 13-year-olds were not in school, most enrolled late and intake and transition rates remained very low. This was the a result of the introduction of 'user fees' during the 1990s, when more than two million Tanzanian children were prevented from entering school and the rate of illiteracy began rising at 2 per cent a year. The education system is beset with problems of poor quality and a lack of participation among enrolled students. This reversed the country's early success of the 1960s when the literacy rate was around 91 per cent (the highest in Africa). The root cause of the problem is the government's debt obligations which have forced it to cut back on education. By 2000, the government was spending twice as much per capita on debt repayments than on education.

In 2001, the government announced in 2001 that it would abolish primary school fees, and the World Bank announced US$150 million interest free credit to

expand school access and increase school retention at the primary level. During 2001, Tanzania enrolled 1,100,000 pupils in school, a 41 per cent increase over 779,000 in 2000.
The fees for secondary education, however, widened the gap between those participating in primary and secondary education. Parents must pay fees they cannot afford and teachers are under pressure to act as debt collectors to finance their schools. The situation is particularly dire in rural areas where schools are only able to recover around a third of fees. As a result, the education system is beset with problems of poor quality and a lack of participation among enrolled students. Oxfam, the main non-governmental organisation investing in Tanzanian education, estimates that in poorer schools there is only one desk for every 38 pupils and one textbook for every four children. Meanwhile, teachers are trying to cope with crumbling classrooms, falling salaries, worsening conditions and increasing class sizes.
Moreover, gross inequalities have developed between genders and classes, particularly in the fee-paying secondary schools. This has led to a progressive exclusion and marginalisation of adolescents and the most vulnerable children from basic family and community support.
Literacy rate: 77 per cent adult rate; 92 per cent youth rate (15–24) (Unesco 2005).
Compulsory years: Seven to 14.
Enrolment rate: 67 per cent gross primary enrolment; 6 per cent gross secondary enrolment; of relevant age groups (including repeaters) (World Bank).
Pupils per teacher: 37 in primary schools.

Health

Per capita total expenditure on health (2003) was US$29; of which per capita government spending was US$16, at the international dollar rate, (WHO 2006).
The public health sector has been increasingly deprived of funds in recent years due to the government's move towards privatisation of the health service sector. User fees, introduced in the 1990s to ease the government's fiscal problems, have denied pregnant women and the rural poor access to primary healthcare facilities and essential medicines. While the government claims that mothers and children under five years receive free healthcare, in reality it is very different, particularly for those suffering from HIV/Aids, mental health problems and other diseases. Moreover, medicines which are supposed to be free are often in short supply at state-run hospitals and the number of hospital beds per capita has declined since 1990.

HIV/Aids

On top of inadequate health service provision, HIV/Aids is a continuing problem with infection rates estimated at over 25 per cent in urban areas. Like many African countries, Tanzania cannot afford the expensive Western drugs needed to treat the effects of Aids and initiatives aimed at the promotion of safe sex are often poorly designed and ineffective.
In 2007, officials in Zanzibar released figures that showed the HIV/Aids rate had increase from 0.6 per cent in 2002, to 0.9 per cent of the population in 2006.
HIV prevalence: 8.8 per cent aged 15–49 in 2003 (World Bank)
Life expectancy: 48 years, 2004 (WHO 2006)
Fertility rate/Maternal mortality rate: 4.9 births per woman, 2004 (WHO 2006); maternal mortality 1,100 per 100,000 live births (World Bank)
Birth rate/Death rate: 39.5 births and 17.4 deaths per 1,000 people (2003)
Child (under 5 years) mortality rate (per 1,000): 104 per 1,000 live births (2003); 29.4 per cent of children aged under five were malnourished (World Bank).
Head of population per physician: 0.02 physicians per 1,000 people, 2002 (WHO 2006)

Welfare

Between 15 million and 18 million of the total population live below the World Bank poverty line. The state does not have the capacity to function as a welfare provider while its ability to increase poor adult literacy rates, especially among women, remains negligible. Rather than building up the capacity and efficiency of state institutions, multilateral and bilateral donors are contracting out welfare services to non-governmental organisations (NGOs), which have little accountability and whose impact is usually localised and short-term.

Main cities

Dodoma (capital, estimated population 168,706 in 2005), Dar es Salaam (former capital and de facto commercial capital, estimated population 2.6 million), Arusha (317,169), Mbeya (258,102), Morogoro (235,402), Mwanza (225,244), Zanzibar (219,954), Tanga (190,029).

Languages spoken

KiSwahili is the predominant language with English spoken by most people, especially in the main towns. English is the language most used in business.

Official language/s

KiSwahili and English

Media

The government allows private newspapers and private radio and television operators, although these organisations exercise a strong degree of self-censorship.
Media policies on Zanzibar are different from the mainland; there are no private broadcasters or newspapers although reception of both is received on the islands.
Other news agencies: The Guardian Limited (www.ippmedia.com).

Press

Dailies: A number of newspapers have English and KiSwahili editions including the government-owned Daily News and Harari Leo (www.dailynews-tsn.com), Nipashe and The Guardian (www.ippmedia.com); in KiSwahili, Majira (www.majira.co.tz), Tanzania Daima (www.freemedia.co.tz); in English This Day (www.thisday.co.tz).
Weeklies: Including Sunday papers, are Sunday News, Mzalendo (KiSwahili), Daily News on Saturday, East African, Express, Heko, Mfanyakazi, Shangwe, Sunday Mail, Sunday News, Sunday Observer, Sunday Times and Taifa Letu. The Government Gazette is a weekly, which lists official announcements.
Business: Publications include the weekly Business Times (www.businesstimes.co.tz) and The Express (www.theexpress.com).
Periodicals: A wide range is published. They include The African Review, published by the Department of Political Science of the University of Dar es Salaam; Foreign Trade News Bulletin published twice a year by the Ministry of Industry.
Weeklies
Some daily newspapers have Sunday editions. Other publications include The Arusha Times (www.arushatimes.co.tz), the Government Gazette, which lists official announcements and Taifa Letu.

Broadcasting

Radio: The public service Radio Tanzania Dar es Salaam (RTD) and Parapanda Radio Tanzania (PRT), an FM station geared to younger listeners, are adapting to the increasingly commercial media environment. RTD covers 85 per cent of the country with internal services in KiSwahili and external services in English. The Voice of Tanzania and Zanzibar broadcasts on three wavelengths in KiSwahili. The Voice of Tanzania-Zanzibar operates from Zanzibar.
There are many locally based FM radio stations, including Radio Free Africa (www.radiofreeafrica.co.tz), Radio One (www.ippmedia.com), Kiss FM (www.kissfmtz.net), Clouds FM (www.cloudsfm.co.tz) has a network of nine city stations include Zanzibar.
Television: Public service Televisheni ya Taifa (TVT) does not have complete

national coverage. Independent Television (ITV) (www.itv.co.tz) is a popular network, Coastal Television Network and Dar es Salaam Television and Star TV (www.startvtz.com) are private, while TV Zanzibar is state run.

News agencies

Other news agencies: The Guardian Limited (www.ippmedia.com).

Economy

The government's efforts to build an export-oriented economy have been accompanied by a policy of economic stabilisation, which entailed the devaluation of the shilling, austerity measures targeting inflation, and moves to cut state bureaucracy and loss-making public enterprises. The IMF and World Bank are keen to promote Tanzania as a success story since the country adopted their liberalising agenda of rolling back the corrupt state bureaucracy, breaking protectionist barriers, privatising parastatals and instituting policies to attract foreign investment. Economic fundamentals seem to support this idea. During the years 1997–2002, Tanzania achieved an average growth rate of 4.8 per cent as it developed its infrastructure and engaged in extensive infrastructural projects. Even with the level of growth at 6.3 per cent in 2004 and 4.1 per cent in 2005, Tanzania's development has not had many noticeable effects on the wider population, particularly the rural poor who make up around a third of the population. With the increase of the Aids prevalence rate to around 8 per cent, there will be an increasing strain on the economy, particularly with worsening social indicators. The growth figures, measured in Tanzanian shillings, hide the stagnation of GDP in dollar terms due to currency depreciation; the shilling fell by 20 per cent between 2001 and mid-2003. With a population growth rate of up to 3 per cent, GDP per capita is slowly edging up, albeit from a low level; GDP per capita increased from US$253 in 2002 to US$336 by 2005. The government's ability to commit funds for public services also diminished through trade liberalisation.

Uganda, Kenya and Tanzania signed the Common External Tariff (CET) agreement on 1 January 2005. This will eliminate many barriers to trade and develop common tariffs between the nations.

External trade

Tanzania is a member of the East African Economic Community (EAC) (with Kenya and Uganda), which operates a customs union with common external tariffs. It is also a member of the Southern African Development Community (SADC), the objectives of which include reducing trade barriers, achieving regional development and economic growth and evolving common systems and institutions.

Foreign earnings provided by tourism ranks second to agricultural exports, which accounts for around 50 per cent of all exports; coffee is the principal cash crop, along with cotton, sisal and tobacco. Mining produces gold, diamonds and tanzanite are more exports that have grown in importance since the mid-1990s.

Cloves are Zanzibar's principal export commodity, while manufacturing is limited to assembly of semi-finished goods and substitution industries.

Imports

Principal imports are consumer goods, machinery and transport equipment, industrial raw materials and crude oil.

Main sources: South Africa (9.8 per cent total, 2006), China (9.3 per cent), Kenya (7.8 per cent).

Exports

Main exports include, coffee, cashew nuts, cotton, manufactures and gold.

Main destinations: China (9.0 per cent total, 2005), India (8.9 per cent), The Netherlands (6.4 per cent).

Agriculture

Farming

The agricultural sector is the mainstay of the economy. It contributes around 45 per cent of GDP and over 50 per cent of export earnings. Approximately 70 per cent of the population are peasant farmers.

Land laws affecting ownership are complicated and hinder potential investors in agricultural activity. The government has expressed an interest in taking up land reform to attract the private sector.

Tanzania has more than 40 million hectares of arable land, but only six million are cultivated. Only 15 per cent of the country has access to water, and the crops are almost totally dependent on the weather. Coffee, cotton, sisal, tobacco, cashew nuts and tea are the most important crops.

There has been a serious decline in production of most crops. Coffee, cotton and sisal are among the crops which have declined and stagnated, although some export crops are showing signs of growth, including tobacco, tea, cashew nuts and horticulture.

The cashew nut sector has benefited from a return to a system where smallholders deal directly with the buyers. Tanzania supplies more than one-quarter of the global market.

Heavy cotton subsidies in the US have affected cotton production in Tanzania, following the liberalisation of the markets.

The effects of subsidies are also felt in traditional industries such as beef, wheat and dairy products and also in non-traditional markets like spices.

Crop production in 2005 included: 5,019,500 tonnes (t) cereals in total, 3,230,000t maize, 7,000,000t cassava, 2,000,000t sugar cane, 215,000t millet, *260,000t potatoes, *970,000t sweet potatoes, 800,000t sorghum, 680,000t rice, 150,0400t bananas, 600,000t plantains, 484,000t pulses, *370,000t coconuts, *65,000t oil palm fruit, 25,500t tea, *145,000t tomatoes, 154,320t oilcrops, *24,500t tobacco, *3,500t cocoa beans, *57,000t green coffee, 200,000t mangoes, *12,500t cloves, 142,500t fibre crops, 23,500t sisal, 330,000t seed cotton, 1,338,250t fruit in total, 1,193,100t vegetables in total.

* estimate

Estimated livestock production included: 364,207t meat in total, 246,330t beef, 17,000t game meat, 13,000t pig meat, 10,320t lamb, 30,600t goat meat, 46,957t poultry, 36,745t eggs, 944,000t milk, 27,000t honey, 48,300t cattle hides, 6,375t goatskins, 2,580t sheepskins, 3,820t greasy wool.

Fishing

Tanzania has extensive inland as well as marine fisheries, with the freshwater lakes and rivers accounting for over 80 per cent of production. Foreign vessels trawl Tanzania's exclusive economic zones and take their catches elsewhere for processing; the government wishes to attract some of this business to Tanzania. Nile perch and sardines make up over three-quarters of Tanzania's total fish exports. Tanzania exports around US$150 million of Nile perch and related products annually, 80 per cent of which are sold to the EU market. The industry is well-organised and gives employment to over 300,000 people. The government is encouraging domestic fish consumption by developing local fish markets.

In a meeting of African ministers in Namibia, held on 2 July, members discussed illegal and unregulated fishing, which is estimated to cost Africa US$1 billion per annum in lost revenue and the threat to stocks and local artisan fishing.

In 2004, the total marine fish catch was 46,360 tonnes and the total crustacean catch was 1,300 tonnes.

Forestry

Tanzania has around 33 million hectares of forests and woodlands. The forests have been under intense pressure from population growth and activities such as harvesting of fuelwood, agricultural demands, fires and illegal logging. The government is seeking to create the conditions for private investment in plantation and sustainable management by local communities.

Timber imports in 2004 were US$36.8 million, while exports amounted to US$12.4 million.
Timber production in 2004 included 23,819,209 cubic metre (cum) roundwood, 2,314,000cum industrial roundwood, 24,000cum sawnwood, 317,000cum sawlogs and veneer logs, 153,000cum pulpwood, 21,505,209cum woodfuel; 1,327,620 tonnes (t) charcoal, 25,000t paper and paperboard (including 8,000t newsprint), 6,000t printing and writing paper, 54,000t paper pulp.

Industry and manufacturing

The industrial and manufacturing sector accounts for 16.7 per cent of GDP and employs 5 per cent of the workforce. Typically, less than a fifth of industrial production is exported.
Most production is geared towards import substitution and the government has traditionally directed public investment towards the sugar and textile industries, tanneries, pulp and paper mills, the fertiliser industry, cement factories, and sisal and cashew nut processing industries. These are engaged in the processing of local minerals and agricultural raw materials for local consumption. Production also includes paper and pulp, cement, textiles and some light engineering.
Growth has been restricted by a lack of foreign exchange needed for the import of raw materials, spare parts and fuel. Foreign aid is aimed at rehabilitating existing industries, but the government is slowly gearing production towards export markets. The high cost of credit inhibits the development of the private sector which is characterised by small enterprises.
Industrial production increased by 8.4 per cent in 2003.
In November 2005, a US$6 billion Mini-Tiger Plan 2020 was launched. Designed to attract foreign direct investment, the scheme aims to expand Tanzania's manufacturing base and increase annual GDP by 2020 to US$40 billion.

Tourism

Tourism is Tanzania's fastest-growing industry. The sector is expected to contribute 4.3 per cent to GDP in 2005. Over 600,000 tourists visited Tanzania in 2004. The government's target is one million visitors by 2010. Tanzania is a comparatively expensive destination, which results in around 50 per cent of visitors entering on short trips from neighbouring countries rather than directly into Tanzania for longer and more lucrative stays. In June 2005, several tourism and travel organisations inaugurated a joint programme to investigate ways of attracting more visitors directly into the country. The government has made tourist visas available at the point of entry into Tanzania. The fact that Tanzania has only a small number of embassies abroad makes it difficult for tourists to obtain the necessary entry visas in advance.

Environment

There is concern about gold mining activities taking place in the Eastern Arc Mountains of Tanzania, which are said to be destroying the Amani nature reserve, a UNESCO-designated biosphere reserve and Balangai forest reserve.
It was revealed in January 2008 that a new genus of monkey, the Rungwecebus kipunji, (known locally as the kipunji) the first to be described since 1925, had been located in two remote forests – Rungwe-Livingstone Forest in the Southern Highlands and the Ndundulu Forest in the Udzungwa Mountains. The kipunji are threatened on two fronts – their habitat is at risk from loggers and they are often trapped and killed by farmers as they raid cultivated crops. It is estimated that there are around 1,000 Kipunji in existence.
The Rungwecebus kipunji is being considered for inclution on the International Union for Conservation of Nature and Natural Resources (IUCN) Red List of Threatened Species.

Mining

Tanzania is well-endowed with mineral sources, especially gold, base metals, diamonds and other gemstones. Mining accounts for around 2.3 per cent of GDP and is targeted to increase to 10 per cent by 2025.
Gold mining and production have expanded considerably in recent years. 50 tonnes were produced in 2004. Tanzania is the third largest gold producer in Africa. Gold has become a major export, mainly to the EU.
There is significant interest in the Kagera nickel-copper-cobalt belt, which runs north and east bordering with Burundi. There are considerable reserves of iron, tin, gypsum and kaolin. There is a large phosphate mine at Minjingu, supplying a fertiliser plant at Tanga.
Tanzania is also a significant producer of gems, including a diamond mine in Shinyanga and rubies from Longido. Other gemstones include sapphires and tanzanite, which is unique to Tanzania.

Hydrocarbons

Tanzania imports about 900,000 tonnes per year (tpy) of crude oil. Of this, 55–65 per cent is processed at the country's only refinery. The Tanzanian and Italian Petroleum Refinery (Tiper), based in Dar es Salaam, has a capacity of 750,000 tpy. There is scope for petroleum refining in Dar es Salaam, amounting to 14,900 barrels per day (bpd). More than 50 per cent of imported oil is consumed by vehicles, with industry consuming 25 per cent and the rest used commercially and in homes. Oil continues to account for over 50 per cent of export earnings. Exploration for oil has been taking place since 1980 without success, but exploration is still taking place.
Natural gas reserves were estimated at 28.2 billion cubic metres in 2003. Offshore reserves have been recently discovered at Songo Songo Island in the Indian Ocean, Kimbiji and Mnazi Bay near Mtwara. Ocelot and Trans Canada Pipelines (OTC) are developing the Songo Songo reserves and plan to build a pipeline to deliver gas to Dar es Salaam. The main hydrocarbons development concerns the Songo Songo gas field, which has reserves estimated at 35 billion cubic metres. The Songo Songo project aims to supply gas via pipeline to the Ubungo power plant in Dar es Salaam.
There are proven coal reserves of 200 million tonnes in Mchuchuma in south-west Tanzania near the northern tip of Lake Nyasa, but the only developed colliery is at Songwe-Kiwara with capacity of 100,000 tonnes per year. Studies indicate the Mchuchuma coal deposits could provide fuel for 400MW generating capacity for up to 35–40 years. The coals are bituminous and with low sulphur content.

Energy

Total installed electricity generating capacity is 882MW, of which about 60 per cent is hydroelectric and the remainder thermal (diesel and coal run). In July 2004, gas from the Songo Songo gas field, supplied through a 200km pipeline to Dar es Salaam, began to power the upgraded Ubungo electricity plant and producing 115MW. All power generated will be sold to Tanzania Electric Supply Company (Tanesco) through a 20-year purchase agreement.
Bio-mass fuel is still the principal energy source for most people in the country.
Tanzania has been implementing a rural electrification programme since 1967, but progress has been slow due to the very low population density and the high cost of supplying power to such a dispersed population.
Development plans are concentrated on further utilisation of the country's hydroelectric potential (estimated to be around 3,800MW), which is being developed with the aid of foreign investment. Mainly concentrated in south-west Tanzania and the Rufiji River basin. The Kihansi 180MW hydroelectric project supplements supplies from Mtera hydropower station.
Zanzibar will receive a new supply of electricity from the mainland, when a new US$45 million, marine power cable is

connected on the island of Pemba in 2009. Although the cable has only to travel 70km the depth of the channel is 800m but is will not expected to be an obstacle to fishing or commercial activities.

Financial markets

Stock exchange

Tanzania has a small stock market, the Dar-es-Salaam Stock Exchange (DSE), which operates for three half-sessions per week. In October 2002, the government allowed foreign participation in the DSE
The stock exchange is hampered by a lack of participation by foreign investors and the local investor community, which has few surplus funds and remains unconvinced of the value of investing in the stock market. Analysts have suggested that East Africa does not need three exchanges and proposed that Uganda and Tanzania merge their exchanges, especially after the creation of the EAC in late 1999.

Banking and insurance

Central bank

Bank of Tanzania

Main financial centre

Dar es Salaam

Time

GMT plus three hours

Geography

Tanzania consists of Tanganyika, on the African mainland, and the nearby islands of Zanzibar and Pemba. Tanganyika lies on the east coast of Africa, bordered by Uganda and Kenya to the north, by the Democratic Republic of Congo (DRC) to the west, and by Zambia, Malawi and Mozambique to the south. Zanzibar and Pemba are in the Indian Ocean about 40km (25 miles) off the coast of Tanganyika, north of Dar es Salaam.
Tanzania is by far the largest country in east Africa. It is divided into three major regions: the coastal plains and river valleys, the central plateau and basin country, and the southern highlands.
The northern coastal area is humid and rainy, with some of the lushest vegetation in Tanzania. Further south the rainfall decreases and the vegetation develops into a drier savanna woodland. Tanzania's major rivers cut across the coastal plains, creating fertile alluvial fans where cotton, sisal and tropical fruits are grown. A few miles inland from the ocean the vegetation switches to tropical savannah woodland.
The central plateau region occupies the major part of the country, wedged between the two rift valleys. The plateau is bordered by Lake Victoria in the north, the Rukwa Valley in the south, Lake Tanganyika and the Ruwenzori Mountains in the west, and the coastal plains in the east. The famous Serengeti Plains and the Masai Steppe are located in the north-east of this central region.
The southern highlands consist of a variety of mountain and hill formations and are sparsely populated.
The islands of Zanzibar and Pemba are located about 35km from the Tanzanian coast in the Indian Ocean. They are low-lying and coral ringed.

Hemisphere

Southern

Climate

Tropical, with variations according to altitude. Rainy seasons April–May and November–December. Warmer on coast, cooler in upland areas. Temperatures range from 23–30 degrees Celsius (C).
Climatically, Tanzania can be divided into two major zones, the wet and humid lowlands around Lake Victoria and the Indian Ocean, and the semi-arid plateau region.
The coastal area is almost always hot and humid with a rainy season that extends for more than 10 months. The most uncomfortable period is December–April when the temperature sometimes exceeds 32 degrees C, with humidity over 90 per cent. The coolest time of the year, and the best time to visit, is June–September when the temperature drops to 15–21 degrees C with relatively low humidity.
The central plateau has distinct wet and dry seasons with great seasonal variations in temperature. Heavy rains fall in March–May and light rains in November–December.
In Dar es Salaam the rainy seasons are usually March–May and November–December, but these can vary from year to year.

Dress codes

Men should wear a lightweight/tropical suit and tie, and women a lightweight suit or formal dress, for business meetings. Women's dress should be modest. On safari it is considered best to avoid bright colours as they may irritate the animals. Visitors to the highlands are advised to take warm clothing. A light raincoat and umbrella are useful during the rainy season.

Entry requirements

Passports

Required by all.

Visa

Required by all; with a few exceptions for citizens of some African states. Details can be found on the visa form, see www.tanzania.go.tz and link to visa. Business travellers should submit an application form with a letter of invitation from a local contact; or introduction by an employing company, detailing nature of business and itinerary.
All visitors must have proof of return/onward passage.

Currency advice/regulations

The import and export of local currency is illegal. The import and export of foreign currency is unlimited. A receipt for all money transactions should be obtained and kept until departure.
Travellers cheques are accepted in banks and bureaux de change.

Customs

Personal items are duty-free, however a custom's bond may be demanded for video and filming equipment, radios, tape recorders and musical instruments until re-exported. Firearms require a special permit.
The export of local handcraft must be accompanied by sales receipts on departure.
Visitors have to go through customs travelling to and from Zanzibar.

Health (for visitors)

Mandatory precautions

A yellow fever vaccination certificate if arriving from areas of known infection. Zanzibar authorities require yellow fever vaccination certificate if arriving from Tanzania.

Advisable precautions

Visitors should take precautions against all tropical diseases. Vaccinations for diphtheria, polio, tetanus, hepatitis A, typhoid and Yellow fever are recommended.
Other vaccinations that may be recommended are cholera, tuberculosis, hepatitis B and meningitis. There is a risk of rabies. HIV/Aids is prevalent.
Malaria is a countrywide problem, except at altitudes above 1,800 metres. Malaria prophylaxis should be taken.
A reasonable precaution could include a first aid kit with a sterile needle kit and disposable syringes.
All water should be regarded as potentially contaminated, use only bottled water (readily available in Dar es Salaam) or boiled and filtered water for drinking, brushing teeth, washing vegetables and reconstituting powdered milk. Local dairy products should be avoided as milk is unpasteurised; vegetables, meat and fish should be well cooked and eaten hot. Fruit should be peeled. Use only well maintained, chlorinated, swimming pools as bilharzia can be contracted from streams and rivers.
Medical insurance is essential, including emergency evacuation, and an adequate supply of personal medicines is necessary.

Hotels

Accommodation tends to be expensive and can be difficult to obtain, especially in Dar es Salaam, so reservations should be made well in advance and confirmation obtained. Bills must be settled with foreign exchange.

Credit cards

Tanzania has a cash economy and major credit cards are only accepted in larger hotels.

Public holidays (national)

Fixed dates

1 Jan (New Year's Day), 12 Jan (Zanzibar Revolution Day), 26 Apr (Union Day), 1 May (Labour Day), 7 Jul (Saba Saba/Industry Day), 8 Aug (Nane Nane/Farmers' Day), 14 Oct (Nyerere Day), 9 Dec (Independence and Republic Day), 25–26 Dec (Christmas).

Variable dates

Eid El Haj, Good Friday and Easter Monday (Mar/Apr), Maulid Day (Apr/May), Eid al Fitr.

Islamic year – 1429 (10 Jan 2008–28 Dec 2008): The Islamic year contains 354 or 355 days, with the result that Muslim feasts advance by 10–12 days against the Gregorian calendar. Dates of feasts vary according to the sighting of the new moon, so cannot be forecast exactly.

Working hours

Banking

Mon–Fri: 0800–1300; Sat: 0830–1300. In larger town branch opening hours may be extended Mon–Fri: 1400–1800.

Business

Mon–Fri: 0900–1230, 1500–1700.

Government

Mon–Fri: 0800–1230, 1400–1600.

Shops

Mon–Fri: 0800–1800.

Telecommunications

Mobile/cell phones

GSM services 900/1800/400 are available in populated areas only.

Electricity supply

230V AC, 50 cycles; with a variety of round and square three-pin plug sockets.

Weights and measures

The metric system is in use but UK weights and measures are still used in many industries, for example, building.

Social customs/useful tips

Patience is required when doing business in Tanzania. Visitors should use cameras only in private settings and tourist resorts otherwise permission must be sought. Visitors should be aware that bridges, railway stations and public buildings are regarded as security installations and should not be photographed. There are no restrictions on alcohol. Almost all business executives speak English.

Business visitors should address Tanzanians as Mr, Mrs or Ms. The term Ndugu is equivalent to comrade in English. The normal greeting when meeting an individual is Jambo. Handshaking is normal practice both on meeting and parting.

Tanzania has a large number of local traditions, although few will affect the business traveller or tourist. There are no particular taboos, but visitors should be aware of religious customs. Muslims should not be offered pork or ham and many do not drink alcohol. During the Islamic holy month of Ramadan, Muslims do not eat or drink during daylight hours.

Security

Street crime is a serious problem in Tanzania, especially in Dar es Salaam. Be alert at all times. Passports, traveller's cheques, wristwatches and cash are regularly stolen. Use hotel safe deposit boxes and do not carry too much cash.

Getting there

Air

National airline: Air Tanzania.

International airport/s: Dar es Salaam (DAR), 13km from city, duty-free shops, restaurant, bar, bank, shops, post office; Kilimanjaro International (JRO), 50km from Arusha (between Arusha and Moshi), bar, restaurant, post office, shops. Shuttle bus services run to town centres. Zanzibar (ZNZ), 8km from Kisauni. Taxis are available.

Airport tax: Zanzibar only, departure tax: US$25

Surface

Road: The Great North Road runs from Zambia through Tanzania to Kenya; the road is in good condition. Road links from Rwanda, Uganda, Mozambique and Malawi are less reliable.

Rail: The Tanzania-Zambia Railway Authority (Tazara), jointly owned and administered by the Tanzanian and Zambian governments, operates a 1,860km railway link between Dar es Salaam and Kapiri Mposhi (Zambia). Passenger services run twice a week; there are three classes, with sleeper carriages for first- and second-class passengers; bookings are recommended.

Water: Ferry services connect with ports in Burundi, the Democratic Republic of Congo and Zambia (on Lake Tanganyika), Kenya and Uganda (on Lake Victoria) and Malawi (on Lake Malawi).

Main port/s: Dar es Salaam, Mtwara, Tanga and Zanzibar

Getting about

National transport

Air: Air Tanzania operates services between Dar es Salaam, and Zanzibar and other major towns. Precision Air also operates scheduled domestic and regional flights.

ZanAir operates flights from Zanzibar.

There are charter companies that operate to isolated airfields, national parks and numerous towns.

Road: All-weather roads connect major centres, but minor roads are liable to be impassable in the rainy season except to four-wheel drive vehicles. There are roads from Songea to Makambako and from Mwanza to Musoma.

Buses: Express services link most centres. Routes include: Dar es Salaam-Songea; Dodoma-Moshi; Lindi-Tunduma; Lindi-Mtwara.

Some services may be unreliable.

Rail: There are seven lines run by the Tanzanian Railway Corporation, mostly radiating out from the Dar es Salaam to all regions in the north and west.

Water: Ferry services run from Dar es Salaam to Zanzibar and Pemba Islands every day. A number of steamer services run during the week on Lakes Tanganyika and Victoria. Two ferries operate on Lake Malawi on the Tanzanian side between Itungi port and Mbamba bay, passing through various small ports.

City transport

Taxis: It is advisable to use only authorised taxis, available in main towns. Taxis from hotels have fixed rates for journeys within Dar es Salaam. Fares in any other taxis are by negotiation and should be agreed before the journey. Taxi drivers do not expect tips.

Buses, trams & metro: Bus services operate within Dar es Salaam; a flat fare system operates but they are generally unreliable and overcrowded and unsuitable for business visitors.

Car hire

Car hire, with or without a driver, can be arranged through hotels or at the airport. It is advisable to get a four-wheel-drive if intending to go off main roads.

An international driving licence is necessary and driving is on the left.

BUSINESS DIRECTORY

The addresses listed below are a selection only. While World of Information makes every endeavour to check these addresses, we cannot guarantee that changes have not been made, especially to telephone numbers and area codes. We would welcome any corrections.

Telephone area codes

The international direct dialling (IDD) code for Tanzania is +255, followed by area code and subscriber's number:

Arusha	27	Mwanza	28
Dar es Salaam	22	Tanga	53
Kilimanjaro	27	Zanzibar	54
Moshi	55		

Chambers of Commerce

Arusha Chamber of Commerce, Industry and Agriculture, PO Box 141, Arusha (tel:

250-8556; fax: 250-4191; e-mail: tccia.arusha@cats-net.com).

Tanzania Chamber of Commerce, Industry and Agriculture, Twiga House, Samora Avenue, PO Box 9713, Dar es Salaam (tel: 212-1421; fax: 211-9437; e-mail: tccia.info@cats-net.com).

Zanzibar National Chamber of Commerce, Industry and Agriculture, Darajani, PO Box 1407, Zanzibar (tel: 223-3083; fax: 223-3349; e-mail: znzchamber@zitec.org).

Banking

Akiba Commercial Bank Limited, PO Box 669, TDFL Bldg (Phase II), Upanga Rd, Dar es Salaam (tel: 211-8340–4; fax: 211-4173).

Azania Bancorp Ltd, PO Box 9271, Samora Ave, Dar es Salaam (tel: 211-8026, 211-7998; fax: 223-6741).

Bank of Tanzania, PO Box 2939, 10 Mirambo Street, Dar es Salaam (tel: 211-0945–7, 211-0950–2; fax: 212-8151; 211-2671, 211-2573, 211-3325, 211-2537; email: info@bot-tz.org).

Citibank (T) Limited, PO Box 71625, Ali Hassan Mwinyi Road, Dar es Salaam (tel: 211-7575, 211-7601; fax: 211-3910, 211-7576).

CRDB Limited, PO Box 268, Maktaba St, Dar es Salaam (tel: 211-7442–7).

Diamond Trust Bank (T) Limited, PO Box 115, Jamhuri/Ali Hassan Mwinyi Rd, Dar es Salaam (tel: 211-4888–4892; fax: 211-4210).

Eurafrican Bank (T) Limited, PO Box 3054, NDC Development House, Kivukoni/Ohio Street, Dar es Salaam (tel: 211-0928, 211-1229, 211-0104; fax: 211-3740).

Exim Bank (T) Limited, PO Box 6649, 9 Samora Avenue, Dar es Salaam (tel: 211-9738; fax: 211-9737).

Habib African Bank Limited, PO Box 70086, India St, Dar es Salaam (tel: 211-1107/9).

International Bank of Malaysia (T) Limited, PO Box 9362, Haidery Plaza, Upanga/Kisutu St, Dar es Salaam (tel: 211-0518, 211-0520, 211-0571; fax: 211-0196).

Kenya Commercial Bank Ltd, PO Box 804, Audit House, 36 Upanga Road, Dar es Salaam (tel: 211-5386–8; fax: 211-5391).

Kenya Commercial Bank (T) Limited, PO Box 804, Peugot Hse, Dar es Salaam (tel: 211-5386–8; fax: 211-5391).

National Micro-Finance Bank Limited, PO Box 9213, Samora Ave, Dar es Salaam (tel: 211-6925–9, 211-6933, 211-0900, 211-8785; fax: 211-4058).

NBC Limited, PO Box 1863, NBC House, Sokoine Drive, Dar es Salaam (tel: 211-3914; fax: 211-2887).

Stanbic Bank Tanzania Ltd, PO Box 72647, Sukari House, Ohio Street/Sokoine Drive, Dar es Salaam (tel: 211-2195–2200; fax: 211-3742)

Standard Chartered Bank Tanzania Ltd, PO Box 9011, Ohio/Sokoine Drive, Dar es Salaam (tel: 211-7350–52, 211-3787, 211-7377; fax: 211-3770, 211-3775).

Tanzania Investment Bank, PO Box 9373, Samora Avenue, Dar es Salaam (tel: 2111708–13; fax: 211-3438) .

Tanzania Postal Bank, PO Box 9300, Mkwepu Street, Dar es Salaam (tel: 211-2358–60, 211-2385/9, 211-6409, 211-7748; fax: 223-8212).

Central bank

Bank of Tanzania, 10 Mirambo Street, PO Box 2939, Dar es Salaam (tel: 211-0945/6/7, 211-0951/2; fax: 211-3325; e-mail: info@hq.bot-tz.org).

Travel information

Air Tanzania, PO Box 543, ATC House; 2nd Floor, 773/40 Ohio Street, Dar es salaam, (tel: 211-8411; fax: 211-3114; email: bookings@airtanzania.com; internet: www.airtanzania.com).

Dar es Salaam International Airport, PO Box 19043, Dar es Salaam (tel: 284-4610/19; fax: 284-4343, 284-3022, 284-4209).

Kilimanjaro International Airport, PO Box 995, Arusha (tel: 222-2941; fax: 222-8553).

Precision Air, Along Nyerere-Pugu Road; PO Box 70770 (tel: 286-0701; fax: 286-0725; internet: www.precisionairtz.com).

Scandinavia Express, Nyerere Road, Vingunguti; PO Box 2414, Dar es Salaam (tel: 286-1947–9; fax: 286-1950; internet: www.scandinaviagroup.com).

Tanzanair, Azikiwe & Samora Ave/Airport International Terminal, PO Box 364, Dar es Salaam (tel: 230-232/4, 246-583; fax: 246-296).

Tanzania National Parks, PO Box 3134, Arusha (tel: 250-1930/1931; fax: 254-8216; email: tanapa@yako.habari.co.tz; internet: www.tanapa.com).

Tanzania Railways Corporation, PO Box 468, Dar es Salaam (tel: 211-0599, 211-0600; fax: 211-6525; internet: www.trctz.com).

Tanzania Zambia Railway Authority, Head Office, Nyerere Road; PO Box 2834, Dar es Salaam (tel: 286-5187; fax: 286-5334; internet: www.tazara.co.tz).

Zanair Ltd, PO Box 2113, Zanzibar (tel: 223-3670; internet: www.zanair.com).

Zanzibar Tourist Corporation, PO Box 216, Zanzibar (tel: 223-2344; fax: 223-3430).

National tourist organisation offices

Tanzania Tourist Board, IPS Building, 3rd Floor, PO Box 2485, Dar es Salaam (tel: 211-1244/5; fax: 211-6420; e-mail: safari@ud.co.tz).

Ministries

Ministry of Agriculture and Food Security, PO Box 9192, Dar es Salaam (tel: 286-2480/1; fax: 286-2077; email: psk@kilimo.go.tz).

Ministry of Energy and Minerals, PO Box 9152, Mkwepu Street, Dar es Salaam (tel: 211-7153–59; fax: 211-6719; email: madini@africaonline.co.tz).

Ministry of Finance, Tancot, PO Box 9111, Dar es Salaam (tel: 211-1174–79; fax: 213-8573).

Ministry of Industries and Trade, PO Box 9503, Lumumba Street, Dar es Salaam (tel: 218-1397, 218-0049/50; fax: 218-2481).

Office of the President, State House, Magogoni Road; PO Box 9120, Dar es Salaam (tel: 211-6679; fax: 211-3425).

Office of the President of Zanzibar (vice president), PO Box 776, Zanzibar (tel: 30-814; fax: 33-722).

Prime Minister's Office, Magogoni Road; PO Box 3021, Dar es Salaam (tel: 213-5076, 211-7249/50/51/52).

Other useful addresses

Board of External Trade, PO Box 5402, Dar es Salaam (tel: 233-524).

Board of Internal Trade, PO Box 883, Dar es Salaam (tel: 228-301).

British High Commission, Umoja House, Mirambo Street; PO Box 9200, Dar es Salaam (tel: 211-0101; fax: 211-0102).

Cashew Nut Authority of Tanzania, PO Box 533, Mtwara.

Coffee Authority of Tanzania, PO Box 732, Moshi (tel: 275-4190).

National Development Corporation, Development House, Kivukoni Front/Ohio Street, PO Box 2669, Dar es Salaam (tel: 211-2893, 211-1460/3; fax: 211-3618; e-mail: ndc@cats-net.com; internet: www.ndctz.com).

National Insurance Corporation of Tanzania Ltd, PO Box 9264, Dar es Salaam.

Presidential Parastatal Sector Reform Commission, 2nd Floor, Sukari House, Sokoine Drive/Ohio Street, PO Box 9252, Dar es Salaam (tel: 211-5482,

211-7988/9; fax: 211-3065/6, 212-2870; email: info@psrctz.com; internet: www.psrctz.com).

Radio Tanzania, PO Box 9191, Dar es Salaam.

Southern Paper Mills Co Ltd, (Marketing Dept) Tanzania Elimu Supplies Building, Bandari Road, Dar es Salaam (tel: 211-1602; fax: 211-3233).

State Mining Corporation, PO Box 4958, Dar es Salaam.

Tanzania Electric Supply Company Ltd (TANESCO), PO Box 9024, Dar es Salaam (tel: 211-2891; fax: 211-3836; email: mdtan@intafrica.com).

Tanzania Exporters' Association (TANEXA), c/o Sima International, PO Box 1175, Dar es Salaam.

Tanzania Harbours Authority, PO Box 9184, Dar es Salaam (internet: www.tanzaniaports.com).

Tanzania National Parks, PO Box 3134, Arusha (tel: 250-1930/1931; fax: 254-8216; email: tanapa@yako.habari.co.tz; internet: www.tanapa.com).

Tanzania Petroleum Development Corporation (TPDC), Managing Director, PO Box 2774, Dar es Salaam; Director of Exploration and Production, PO Box 5233, Dar es Salaam; email: tpdcexploration@raha.com); Director of Research & Corporate Services, PO Box 2774, Dar es Salaam.

Tanzania Railways Corporation, PO Box 468, Dar es Salaam.

Tanzania Revenue Authority, PO Bnox 11491, Dar es Salaam (tel: 211-9591/4; fax: 212-8593; email: trais@afsat.com).

Tanzanian Embassy (USA), 2139 R Street, NW, Washington DC 20008 (tel: (+202-1) 939-6129; fax: (+202-1) 797-7408; email: tanz-us@clark.net).

Television Zanzibar, PO Box 314, Zanzibar.

US Embassy, Laibon Road, PO Box 9123, Dar es Salaam.

Internet sites

Africa Business Network: www.ifc.org/abn

AllAfrica.com: http://allafrica.com

African Development Bank: www.afdb.org

Africa Online: www.africaonline.com

Mbendi AfroPaedia (information on companies, countries, industries and stock exchanges in Africa): http://mbendi.co.za

Official government website: www.tanzania.go.tz

Official Zanzibar Government website: www.zanzibargovernment.org

Tanzania Yellow pages: www.yellowpages.co.tz/

Terres Australes

COUNTRY PROFILE

Historical profile

1552–59 Saint Paul and Amsterdam Islands were sighted by survivors of a Portuguese expedition led by Ferdinand Magellan.
1772 Captain Marion Dufresne and ship's mate Crozet saw the group of islands, which became known as the Crozet Archipelago.
1772 Yves de Kerguelen sighted another archipelago, later named after him.
1840 Adélie Land, in Antarctica, was sighted and claimed by the French.
1924 A French government decree attached administration for the islands to the government of Madagascar (then a French colony).
1947 France established observation stations.
1955 Terres Australes et Antarctiques Francaises were accorded the status of an overseas French territory.
1959 The international community signed the Antarctic Treaty, establishing the legal framework for the management of Antarctica, banning any military activity within the Antarctic continent and guaranteeing the protection of its environment and wildlife.
1961 The Antarctic Treaty came into force.
1993 A co-operation agreement between the national institutes in charge of polar research in France and Italy agreed to construct a permanent scientific base, Concordia, approximately 1,000km from the French scientific base of Dumont d'Urville.
2000–01 Concordia was built and completed.
2002 Ten countries began working on a glacial project, the European Programme of Glaciology (EPICA), drilling to study the climate in the Antarctic during the last 500,000 years. Drilling reached 2,871 metres and collected ice samples from 520,000 years ago.
2003 The drilling reached the rock base of the Antarctic continent at a depth of 3,300 metres.
2004 The role of the administrateur supérieur was undertaken by a préfet, based in Saint Pierre on Réunion.
2005 Michel Champon took office as préfet. TAAF celebrated its fiftieth anniversary.
2007 Eric Pilloton was appointed préfet on 7 February. On 16 May, Nicolas Sarkozy became head of state and president of the French Republic.

Political structure

Terres Australes et Antarctiques Françaises (TAAF) (French Southern and Antarctic Territories) is a French Térritoire d'Outre Mer (TOM) (Overseas Territory), but is administered under two different international laws. France exercises full sovereignty over the southern islands, unanimously recognised by all nations.
Adélie Land (on mainland Antarctica) is administered according to the 1959 Antarctic Treaty, despite the US not recognising France's claim to the Land. The Antarctic Treaty is an international agreement which provides for broad scientific co-operation and demilitarisation of the Antarctic continent and restrained existing territorial claims without prejudicing the solution to the sovereignty problem.
The fully sovereign area is governed by one law and two main decrees. The law of 6 August 1955 confers administrative and financial autonomy on the TOM. The implementation decree of 13 January 1956 defines the TOM's financial system and the decree of 8 September 1956 provides for the TOM's administrative organisation.
The TOM is under the authority of a chief administrator, whose official residence is in Paris. The administrator is assisted by an advisory council, which meets twice a year and consists of seven members appointed for five-year terms. The council must be consulted on the TOM's draft budget and it is kept informed and consulted on any proposed new scientific missions or applications for concessions and commercial activities.
The TOM is divided into four districts, each under the authority of a district head appointed by the chief administrator:
Saint Paul and Amsterdam Islands – permanent settlement is Martin de Viviés.
Crozet Islands – settlement is Alfred Faure (Possession Island).
Kerguelen Islands – settlement is Port aux Français.
Adélie Land – settlement is Dumont D'Urville.

Population

310 (summer total) (150 winter total)
Annual growth rate: 0.0 per cent (2003)

Languages spoken

Official language/s
French

KEY FACTS

Official name: Le Territoire des Terres Australes et Antarctiques Françaises (TAAF) (French Southern and Antarctic Territories)

Head of State: President of France Nicolas Sarkozy, represented by Préfet Eric Pilloton (appointed 7 Feb 2007) (based in Saint Pierre, on Réunion)

Area: 439,797 square km consisting of: Kerguelen Archipelago 7,215 square km, Crozet Archipelago 115 square km, Amsterdam Island 54 square km, Saint Paul Islands 7 square km, Terre Adélie (in Antarctica) 432,000 square km

Population: 310 (summer total) (150 winter total)

Capital: Port-aux-Françaises (on Kerguelen)

Official language: French

Currency: Euro (eur) = 100 cents

Exchange rate: eur0.63 per US$ (Jul 2008)

Media
There are two publications issued by Terres Australes et Antarctiques Francaises (TAAF). A monthly official journal and a quarterly pamphlet of general interest see publications at www.taaf.fr.

Economy
The Terres Australes have no permanent population, but are temporarily inhabited by scientific reserch groups. Scientific activities are supported and developed by the Institut Français pour la Récherché et la Technologie Polaires (IFRTP) (French Institute for Polar Research and Technology) and the administration of the TOM is in charge of the logistics. Most of the TOM's economic activities centre around supporting the IFRTP. Fishing is the other main economic activity with fish landed by foreign ships exported to France and Réunion; others are philately and tourist cruises.

External trade
Crayfish and other fish are exported to France and Réunion.

Agriculture
Research has indicated the viability of large-scale farming of giant brown macrocystis, a type of seaweed.

Fishing
French vessels fish for crayfish off Amsterdam and Saint Paul. There is an agreement between France and Ukraine to fish for icefish and toothfish.
A research programme which has been carried out since 1970, has shown that trout adapt well to a sub-antarctic environment and the result of sea-ranching salmon was also a biological success.
There are estimated to be 60 to 120 million tons of krill in the TOM's coastal waters. Around Saint Paul and Amsterdam Islands, there are plentiful supplies of bull head fish, false cod, crayfish and cape lobster.

Tourism
The French research vessel, Marion Dufresne, conducts tourist cruises.

Hydrocarbons
A limited amount of oil drilling has been carried out.

Banking and insurance
Central bank
The Paris-based Institut d'Emission d'Outre-Mer (IEOM) provides all central banking services except foreign exchange reserves.

Time
GMT plus five hours

Geography
Terres Australes consists of several groups of islands in the southern Indian Ocean and a sector of Antarctica.
Adélie Land, a narrow segment of mainland Antarctica, is thick continental ice over barren rock. Les Îles Crozet consists of five large and 15 tiny islands, their combined area is over 330 square km. They are volcanic with black basalt geology and treeless terrain. Pic Marion-Dufresne (1,090 metres) is the highest point on Île de l'Est. The main island of Îles Kerguelen, in the southern Indian Ocean, is volcanic, its highest point is the glaciated Mount Ross. It has around 300 smaller islands forming an archipelago, which combined is 7,000 square km in area. Iles Saint-Paul et Amsterdam are small uninhabited volcanic islands.

Hemisphere
Southern

Climate
The climate of Iles Saint-Paul et Amsterdam is oceanic, damp and mild. The temperature averages 15 degrees Celsius (C). The climate is particularly extreme in the Crozet Archipelago – the islands lie at the centre of an area where tropical and antarctic air masses meet, causing deep depressions and cyclone-forming processes. The Îles Kerguelen have a cool, humid climate due to the proximity of the Antarctic continent. The summers last from December to March and are similar to those beyond the Arctic Circle. The winters from May to October are comparatively mild. The climate is unstable with constant winds, sometimes at a speed of 160kph. The temperature of the surrounding sea averages 4 degrees C.
Adélie Land's climate is harsh. The temperature of the coastal area never rises above 4 degrees C in summer and can fall to minus 37 degrees C in winter.

Entry requirements
Visa
Required by all, except citizens of EU, North America, Australasia and Japan, for stays up to one month; this includes business trips by representatives of overseas companies or organisations. For further exceptions, full details and a copy of the application form visit www.diplomatie.fr/venir/visas/ index.html. Proof of adequate funds for stay and return/onward ticket are necessary.

Currency advice/regulations

Health (for visitors)
Advisable precautions
Protective clothing is essential. Sunscreen should be applied and protective eyewear worn in summer in the Antarctic.

Weights and measures
The metric system is in use.

Getting there
Air
There are no air links to or between the bases.

Surface
Water: Relief ships bring new personnel and supplies. A charter vessel calls five times a year to the Antarctic islands and another calls twice a year to Adélie Land.

BUSINESS DIRECTORY

The addresses listed below are a selection only. While World of Information makes every endeavour to check these addresses, we cannot guarantee that changes have not been made, especially to telephone numbers and area codes. We would welcome any corrections.

Banking
Central bank
Institut d'Emission d'Outre-Mer (IEOM), 5 rue Roland Barthes, 75598 Paris Cedex 12, France (tel: (+33-1) 5344-4141; fax : (+33-1) 4347-5134; email: contact@ieom.fr).

Other useful addresses
Institut Français pour la Recherche et la Technologie Polaires (IFRTP), Technopole Brest Iroise, BP 75, 29280 Plouzane, France (tel: (+33-2) 9805-6500; fax: (+33-2) 9805-6555).

Terres Australes et Antarctiques Françaises (TAAF), 34 Rue des Renaudes, 75017 Paris (tel: (+33-1) 4053-4652; fax: (+33-1) 4766-9123).

Internet sites
French tourism: www.discoverfrance.net/Colonies/Antarctic.shtml

Information about antarctica: www.gdargaud.net/Antarctica/InfoAntarctica.html

Thailand

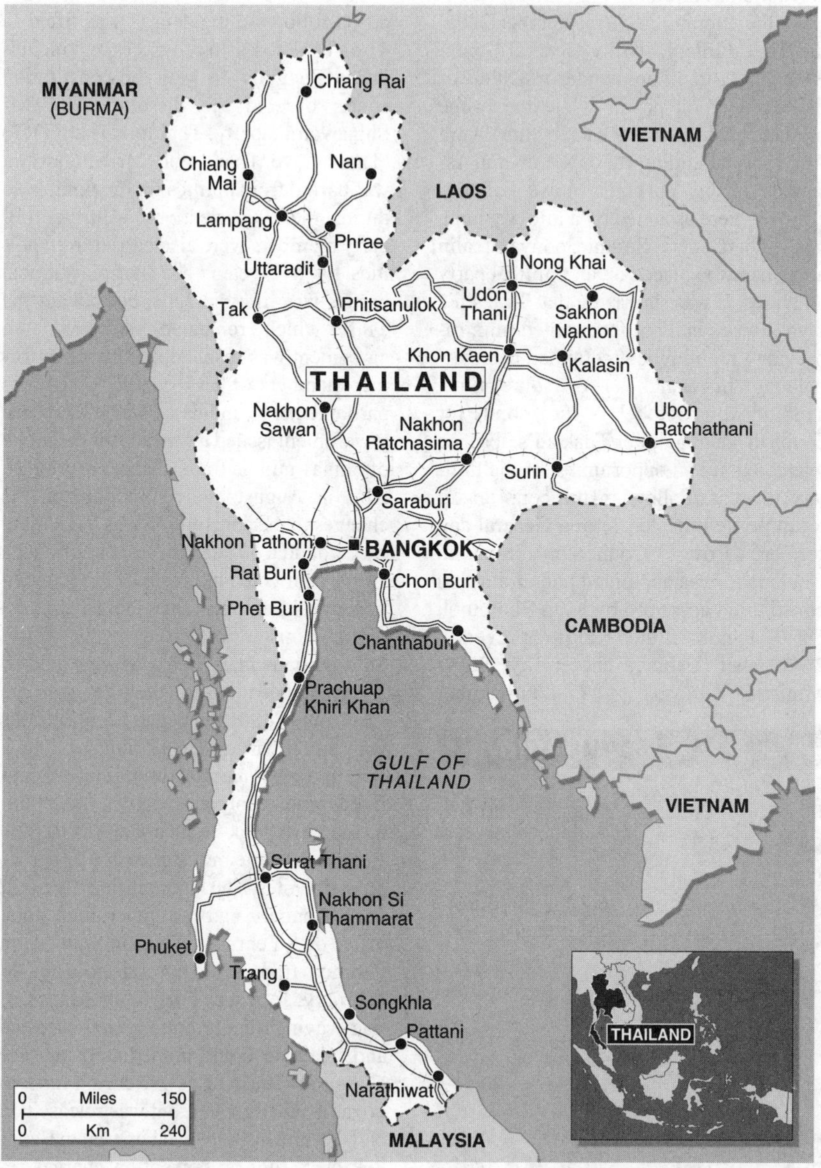

Embarrassingly, in September 2008 a Bangkok court ordered Thailand's Prime Minister Samak Sundaravej to resign after finding that he had violated the Thai constitution by accepting payment for appearing on two television shows while in office. By way of riposte, Mr Sundaravej's People's Power Party (PPP) announced that it would name him as his own replacement, a confusing move that appeared to go against the spirit of the court ruling.

The court ruling was a further step in the battle between PPP and supporters of exiled former prime minister Thaksin Shinawatra who at the time was in London seeking political asylum to avoid having to face corruption charges in Thailand. In 2007 and 2008 Thailand's courts had become a central part of the political scene as corruption charges against Mr Thaksin and his wife Pojaman began to surface. But Mr Thaksin was not alone in facing

KEY FACTS

Official name: Prathet Thai; Ratcha Anachak Thai (Kingdom of Thailand)

Head of State: King Bhumibol Adulyadej (Rama IX) (since 1946)

Head of government: Prime Minister Samak Sundaravej (from 2 Feb 2008)

Ruling party: Coalition led by Palang Prachachon (People's Power Party) (PPP), with Phak Chart Thai (Thai Nation Party) (TNP) and Phak Pua Paendin (For the Motherland Party) (FMP), Ruam Jai Thai Chat Pattana (Thais United National Development Party) (Thais United), Matchima Thipataya (Independent Democratic Party) (IDP) and Phracharaj (Royalist People's Party) (RPP) (from 2 Feb 2008)

Area: 514,000 square km

Population: 65.74 million (2007)

Capital: Bangkok

Official language: Thai

Currency: Baht (B) = 100 satang

Exchange rate: B33.31 per US$ (Jul 2008)

GDP per capita: US$3,737 (2007)*

GDP real growth: 4.80% (2007)*

Labour force: 36.43 million (2006)

Unemployment: 1.70% (2007)*

Inflation: 2.20% (2007)*

Oil production: 309,000 bpd (2007)

Balance of trade: US$2.25 billion (2006)

Foreign debt: US$51.00 billion (2004)

Visitor numbers: 13.88 million (2006)*

* estimated figure

charges – Mr Samak also faced three charges of corruption that had yet to reach the courts. Thailand's Constitutional Court was also weighing up charges against the PPP for election fraud in December 2008.

Political manoeuvrings, or shenanigans?

The February 2005 elections had produced a landslide victory for the incumbent, telecommunications magnate Thaksin Shinawatra, whose party won 400 out of a possible 500 seats. He is the patriarch of the country's richest family, owners of Shin Corporation, a company whose profits have climbed hugely during Thaksin's leadership. He was also the first leader to last for an entire electoral term – in the 1990s the country had eight different administrations. His success was attributed to his astute judgement, ambitious drive and self-marketing. His party, Thai Rak Thai, meaning Thais love Thais, has focussed on populist policies such as affordable healthcare, a village credit system and forgiveness of farmers' debt. These priorities were reached after extensively canvassing views from millions of poor Thai peasants.

While this was good news, concerns mounted about Thaksin's authoritarian streak. He was dismissive of inconvenient court judgements and watchdogs and blasé about the human cost of some of his more stringent crime crackdowns. He had used the country's Islamic uprisings to consolidate and tighten his grip over the nation.

A cabinet reshuffle in August 2005 had rewarded long-standing loyal politicians and was designed to improve the government's tarnished image, hit by a series of corruption scandals.

On the evening of 19 September 2006, the Thai military, led by General Sonthi Boonyaratglin, Commander-in-Chief of the Army, took power while the prime minister businessman Thaksin Shinawatra was away attending the UN General Assembly in New York. The powers of government were assumed by a military junta headed by General Sonthi Boonyaratkalin and a ban was placed on all political party activities. It was surprising that Thaksin's own sources had not forewarned him; rumours of an imminent coup had been circulating in Bangkok for some time. Traditionally October is the month for coups in Thailand, but Thaksin's absence was too good an opportunity for the military to miss. Following the coup an interim prime minister, retired General and former Privy Councillor Surayud Chulanont, was appointed and an interim constitution approved by King Bhumibol. On 8 October, the King approved a 26-member Cabinet chosen by Prime Minister Surayud. A 200-member Constitution Drafting Assembly was given 180 days to produce a draft constitution which would be put to the people in a referendum, after which an election would be held, supposedly before the end of 2007. The coup was the 18th in Thailand since it became a constitutional monarchy in 1932, but the first since 1991.

On 26 January 2007, martial law – imposed following the coup – was lifted in 41 of Thailand's 76 provinces and including in Bangkok. In May the constitution courts ordered the dissolution of Mr Shinawatra's party, Thai Rak Thai (TRT) (Thais Love Thais) and Mr Shinawatra was barred from politics for breaking laws during the 2006 elections; a further 110 party members were also barred from politics for five years. The ban on political parties was lifted in June, but not for the TRT, which remained dissolved. An agreement was reached in July when former members of TRT agreed to stand as parliamentary candidates of the PPP. The government issued a warrant for the arrest of Shinawatra on fraud charges in August. Also in August, the referendum on the changes to the constitution was held; there was around a 60 per cent turnout of which 70 per cent voted in favour of the proposition which, among other things, limits a prime minister to two terms in office. Snap parliamentary elections were held on 23 December in which the PPP won 233 seats (out of 480) and began coalition talks with minor parties. On 19 January 2008 a coalition agreement between the PPP and five minor political parties was announced. Samak Sundaravej (PPP) was elected as prime minister with 310 parliamentary votes. The King ratified the result on 29 January and the government took office on 2 February. Thaksin Shinawatra returned from self-imposed exile on 28 February, to a welcome of thousands of flag-waving supporters. He was arrested and taken to court immediately to face charges of abuse of power during his tenure as prime minister, but was released on bail. He and his wife went on trial in Bangkok on 8 July on corruption charges related to a Bangkok real estate deal. Shinawatra's wife was found guilty while he fled Thailand into exile in the UK in August.

Economy

By 2007 Thailand had put behind it the financial crisis of 1997 and 1998, when the banking system, burdened by non-performing loans of as much as 45 per cent of total lending, had become largely insolvent and 58 out of 91 finance

KEY INDICATORS — Thailand

	Unit	2003	2004	2005	2006	2007
Population	m	63.65	63.34	65.11	65.28	65.74
Gross domestic product (GDP)	US$bn	143.20	161.49	176.22	206.70	*245.66
GDP per capita	US$	2,037	2,521	2,707	3,166	*3,737
GDP real growth	%	6.8	6.1	4.5	5.1	*4.8
Inflation	%	1.4	2.7	4.5	4.6	*2.2
Unemployment	%	0.8	2.0	1.3	2.1	1.7
Industrial output	% change	–	8.0	7.5	5.8	–
Agricultural output	% change	–	-4.8	-5.0	4.8	–
Oil output	'000 bpd	217.0	218.0	276.0	286.0	309.0
Natural gas output	bn cum	19.6	20.3	21.4	24.3	25.9
Coal output	mtoe	5.4	5.8	5.9	5.4	8.9
Exports (fob) (goods)	US$m	75,430	96,107	109,216	128,220	151,130
Imports (cif) (goods)	US$m	64,564	84,983	106,054	125,975	125,170
Balance of trade	US$m	10,866	11,124	3,162	2,245	25,960
Current account	US$m	7,960	7,290	-7,852	2,174	14,923
Total reserves minus gold	US$m	41,077.0	48,664.0	50,691.0	65,291.0	85,221.0
Foreign exchange	US$m	40,965.0	48,498.0	50,502.0	65,147.0	85,110.0
Exchange rate	per US$	41.33	40.26	36.05	35.74	33.59

* estimated figure

companies had had to close their doors. Growth in 2007 was 4.8 per cent, despite the political uncertainties and imposition of capital controls in December 2006 (removed in March 2008), and proposed amendments to the Foreign Business Act. Net exports had provided the main support for growth while domestic demand had been weak. Inflation had fallen to 2.2 per cent (from 4.6 per cent in 2006). The baht appreciated by about 14 per cent against the dollar in 2006, but had slowed to a more manageable 4.6 per cent in 2007.

Industry was the fastest growing sector in 2007 and made the strongest contribution – 2.5 percentage points of total GDP growth. manufacturing increasedby 5.8 per cent, driven by export oriented activities. There were gains in cassava and palm oil production, as well as in fisheries. Exports of palm oil, rice and rubber were boosted by high word commodity prices. Tourism, however, fell owing to the riots. Employment rose by 1.6 per cent to 36.2 million, while the unemployment rate averaged 1.4 per cent according to government figures.

Faster growth is forecast in 2008 and 2009 for both consumption and investment. However, politics have a funny way of intervening in Thailand and investors need to feel secure, especially those that remember 1997.

Risk assessment

Politics	Poor
Economy	Fair
Regional stability	Fair

COUNTRY PROFILE

Historical profile

The modern Thai language originates from the Tai-speaking people who migrated south in the first millennium AD from the Chinese province of Yunnan, south of the Yangtze River.

1767 The former capital of Siam, Ayutthaya, fell to Burmese invaders.

1782 King Rama I – first of the Chakri dynasty – was crowned and founded the capital city Bangkok.

1851–68 King Mongkut (Rama IV) began a period of reform and modernisation while adroitly avoiding European colonisation. Treaties were signed with the US, Great Britain, France and Japan, among others. Barriers against traders were eliminated, allowing expansion.

1868–1910 Chulalongkorn, (Rama V) continued his father's programmes by modernising the legal and administrative systems, reforming the political structure and abolishing slavery. He also began construction of a railway network. Some Siam territories in Indochina were ceded to Britain and France.

1910 Vajiravudha (Rama VI) became King. He introduced compulsory education, among other reforms.

1925 Prajadhipok, the brother of Vajiravudha, became King.

1932 A group of students, led by Pibul Songgram and Pridi Phanomyang, in a bloodless coup d'état forced King Prajadhipok to replace absolute monarchy with a constitution monarchy and introduce parliamentary government. A new National Assembly was established.

1933 The first general elections were held.

1935 The King abdicated. A council of regency chose his 10-year old brother, Ananda, to be Rama VIII. He was studying in Switzerland at the time.

1938 Pibul Songgram became prime minister

1939 Siam was renamed Thailand.

1941–1946 Under the leadership of Pibul, Thailand allied itself with Japan and allowed Japanese troops to traverse the country. Thailand declared war on the US and Britain but the Thai ambassador in Washington withheld the official declaration and so technically the country remained neutral. Pridi Phanomyang led an American-backed anti-Japanese movement.

1945 Pridi became prime minister and Pibul was jailed briefly for war crimes.

1946 King Ananda returned for the second time from studying in Switzerland but died shortly after in mysterious circumstances. He was succeeded by his brother, Bhumipol Aduldej, the present King Rama IX, although he was not formally crowned until 1950. Inflation and corruption marred the government's reputation.

1947 Pibul led an army coup d'état and instituted a military dictatorship. Pibul was staunchly anti-Communist and under his rule the Chinese community, suspected of being Communist sympathisers, was harassed.

1950 Bhumibol Adulyadej became King and was crowned Rama IX. Thailand aligned itself with the US during the Cold War and sent troops to fight in the Korean War.

1957 Pibul was overthrown in a coup led by Field Marshal Sarit Thanarat.

1958 Sarit deposed his own premier, took power himself and imposed martial law and dissolved all political parties.

1973 Student riots destabilised the military government and free elections were held. The King appointed a civilian, Sanya Thammasak, as premier.

1974 A new constitution was introduced, legalising political parties.

1976 The military seized power and Admiral Sa'ngad Chaloryoo, annulled the 1974 constitution and re-introduced martial law. A new constitution was introduced. Thanin Kraivixien became prime minister, he imposed a harsh rule and kept unions under tight control while he carried out anti-Communist purges of the civil service and educational institutions.

1975 With the ending of the Vietnam War Thailand became the temporary home to many refugees from Indochina.

1977 Thanin was overthrown by General Kriangsak Chomanand.

1978 A new constitution was promulgated in which a bicameral National Assembly was established.

1991 Another military coup led by General Suchinda Krapayoon replaced Kriangsak.

1992 General Krapayoon resigned and elections were held. A coalition led by the Pak Prachatipat (PP) (Democratic Party) was victorious.

1995 The Phak Chart Thai (PCT) (Thai Nation Party) won the general election and formed a coalition government.

1997 The constitution was amended to allow the direct election of a prime minister for a four-year term. The baht fell sharply during the Asian financial crisis and led to bankruptcies and unemployment. Chuan Leekpai (PP) was elected prime minister; he worked closely with the IMF to reform the badly damaged economy.

2000 Thailand's first senate election was held. Subsequent rulings against the results by the Election Commission necessitated two further elections.

2001 Elections to the House of Representatives took place. Thaksin Shinawatra became prime minister and the Thai Rak Thai (TRT) (Thais Love Thais) formed a coalition government with the Phak Chart Patthana (PCP) (National Development Party).

2002 The PCT and the Phak Khwam Wang Mai (PKWM) (New Aspiration Party) joined the ruling coalition. Supachai Panitchpakdi became director general of the World Trade Organisation (WTO).

2004 A wave of terrorist attacks by separatist Islamic and ethnic Malays from southern provinces killed over 100 people. Over 100 Islamic insurgents were killed while attacking several police bases in the south and 85 Islamic detainees were killed while in custody following violence at a rally in the south. Many suffocated to death in the back of a police van; an enquiry concluded the tragedy was unforeseen. An outbreak of avian flu prompted the slaughter of millions of birds. Six provinces along the west coast of Thailand, including the tourist resorts of Phuket and Khao Lak, were devastated by a tsunami which swept the whole region on 26 December after an earthquake off

the coast of Sumatra. The final estimate for Thailand was 8,212 dead or missing and 6,000 people displaced.
2005 The ruling TRT party won a landslide victory in the general elections; Thaksin Shinawatra was the first Thai prime minister to win a second term in office. By mid-2005 it was estimated that over 1,000 people had been killed since 2004 in the violence in southern Thailand. There was a recurrence of avian flu.
2006 Snap general elections were called amid controversy concerning allegations of corruption against the prime minister. Opposition parties boycotted the elections, which were won by the ruling TRT with 57 per cent of the vote. Despite the victory, the prime minister was forced to step down, and his deputy, Chidchai Vanasatidya, became acting prime minister. The Supreme Administrative Court ruled that the general elections were invalid. The court's ruling prompted Shinawatra to resume his duties as prime minister. While abroad attending a UN General Assembly meeting Thaksin Shinawatra was deposed in a bloodless army coup. A ban was placed on all political party activities. Retired, ex-army general, Surayud Chulanont was sworn in as prime minister. Shinawatra resigned his leadership of TRT.
2007 Matial law was lifted in Bangkok and 41 (out of 76) provinces in January, two months after its imposition. Matial law continued in border regions and in the north in general. In May, the constitutional court ordered the dissolution of the TRT and barred TRT leader Thaksin Shinawatra from politics for breaking laws during the 2006 general elections; the court also barred a further 110 party members from politics for five years. The ban on political party activities that had been in place since September 2006 was lifted in June; the TRT remained dissolved. An agreement was reached in July when former members of TRT agreed to stand as parliamentary candidates of Palang Prachachon (PPP) (People's Power Party). The government issued a warrant for the arrest of Shinawatra on fraud charges in August. In August, a referendum agreed to changes to the constitution; there was around a 60 per cent turnout of which 70 per cent voted in favour of the proposition which, among other things, limits a prime minister to two terms in office. King Bhumibol Adulyadej celebrated his eightieth birthday in December. Although the king has few legal powers, he has been instrumental in calming relations between the military and civilian government and the people. In snap parliamentary elections held on 23 December the PPP won 233 seats (out of 480) and began coalition talks with minor parties.
2008 On 19 January a coalition agreement between the PPP and five minor political parties was announced. Samak Sundaravej (PPP) was elected as prime minister with 310 parliamentary votes; his closest rival, Abhisit Vejjajiva (DP) had 163. The King ratified the result on 29 January. The government took office on 2 February. Thaksin Shinawatra returned from self-imposed exile on 28 February, to a welcome of thousands of flag-waving supporters. He was arrested and taken to court immediately to face charges of abuse of power during his tenure as prime minister, but was released on bail. He and his wife went on trial in Bangkok on 8 July on corruption charges related to a Bangkok real estate deal. Shinawatra's wife was found guilty while he fled Thailand into exile in the UK in August.

Political structure

Constitution

Thailand is a constitutional monarchy, with the King as Head of State.
The 1997 constitution was suspended, following the 2006 military coup. A new constitution was agreed by referendum in August 2007, which included making just over half the senate seats to be elected and limiting the powers and privileges of the prime minister, by restricting the office to two terms, banning a prime minister from owning major holdings in private companies and making it easier to impeach a prime minister. Turnout for the referendum was 60 per cent.

Form of state

Constitutional monarchy

The executive

Executive power lies with the cabinet, headed by a prime minister for a term of four years, who must be an elected member of the House of Representatives.

National legislature

The bicameral, Rathasapha (National Assembly) consists of the Sapha Phuthaen Ratsadon (House of Representatives), with 480 seats, 400 of which are voted on in constituency elections and 80 are determined by proportional representation along party lines and the Wuthisapha (Senate) with 150-members, 74 of which are appointed and 76 are elected. General elections are held every four years.

Legal system

Courts follow the traditional pattern of courts of first instance, a court of appeal and a Supreme Court.

Last elections

23 December 2007 (parliamentary)
Results: Parliamentary: Palang Prachachon (People's Power Party) (PPP) won 233 seats (out of 480), the PP won 165, the Phak Chart Thai (Thai Nation Party) (TNP) won 37, Phak Pua Paendin (For the Motherland Party) (FMP) won 24, Ruam Jai Thai Chat Pattana (Thais United National Development Party) (Thais United) won 9, Matchima Thipataya (Independent Democratic Party) (IDP) won 7 and Phracharaj (Royalist People's Party) (RPP) won 5. Turnout was 85.38 per cent.

Next elections

December 2011 (parliamentary)

Political parties

Ruling party

Coalition led by Palang Prachachon (People's Power Party) (PPP), with Phak Chart Thai (Thai Nation Party) (TNP) and Phak Pua Paendin (For the Motherland Party) (FMP), Ruam Jai Thai Chat Pattana (Thais United National Development Party) (Thais United), Matchima Thipataya (Independent Democratic Party) (IDP) and Phracharaj (Royalist People's Party) (RPP) (from 2 Feb 2008)

Main opposition party

Pak Prachatipat (PP) (Democratic Party)

Population

65.74 million (2007)
Last census: April 2000: 60,617,200
Population density: 122 inhabitants per square km. Urban population: 20 per cent.
Annual growth rate: 1.0 per cent 1994–2004 (WHO 2006)

Ethnic make-up

Approximately 80 per cent of the population are Thais, 10 per cent Chinese and 5 per cent Malays. Other ethnic minorities include Laotian, Vietnamese, Kampuchean and a number of hill tribes.

Religions

Buddhist (85 per cent), Muslim (4 per cent), Christian (0.5 per cent), Hindu and Confucian.

Education

Primary schooling lasts for six years until students are aged 13 when they progress to the lower secondary school. At aged 16 students may either follow a general academic or vocational path in an upper secondary school.
There are 16 universities in Thailand, of which 12 are in Bangkok. There are also 21 recognised private colleges of higher education. Culturally, higher education is biased towards the social sciences and humanities, with science and technology accounting for only 22 per cent of total tertiary enrolment.
The education system in Thailand is undergoing major reforms. The main objective is the eventual decentralisation of education in the country as in 2001, policy was implemented through a central office, regional office, provincial office, then a district office. From August 2002 it will be administered through a central office, a local area education office and the school.

The government hopes to transform the learning process from a teacher-oriented system to a learner-oriented method. There are plans to introduce more technology in education.
Literacy rate: 93 per cent adult rate; 98 per cent youth rate (15–24) (Unesco 2005).
Compulsory years: Six to 16
Enrolment rate: 89 per cent gross primary enrolment; 59 per cent gross secondary enrolment, of relevant age groups (including repeaters), (World Bank).
Pupils per teacher: 21 in primary schools

Health

Per capita total expenditure on health (2003) was US$260; of which per capita government spending was US$160, at the international dollar rate, (WHO 2006).
It is estimated that only 10 per cent of the population have pre-paid health insurance plans. Improve access to healthcare has been promised by the government by implementing a standard B30 (US$0.70) per hospital visit rule across the country. There are fears, however, that the reduced cost will entail a fall in healthcare standards.
The government has as a central objective, the standardisation of healthcare throughout the country. Plans stress the need to reorganise and decentralise public health administration. Private sector healthcare is expanding faster than the public sector, with private healthcare expenditure currently estimated to be running at double the public sector level. Private hospitals (over 370) account for 25 per cent of all hospital beds.
The ministry of health provides free medical services to the poor in all government hospitals. Thailand has well over 1,000 public hospitals, over 13,000 specialised private clinics, over 8,000 health centres and an estimated 0.23 doctors per 1,000 of the population. The health of the Thai population has improved significantly over the last 20–30 years with life expectancy rising by 17 years, the infant mortality rate dropping by about two-thirds and the proportion of the population with access to safe drinking water more than trebling.
In 2004 avian flu broke out, killing nine people and prompting the slaughter of more than 100 million poultry.

HIV/Aids

In a region where conservative leaders have been reluctant to publicly endorse HIV/Aids prevention programmes, Thailand took the initiative in 1994 and introduced a full scale public education and condom distribution programme, so that by 2004 people newly testing HIV positive fell to 21,260, vastly less than the peak of 142,819 in 1991.
HIV prevalence: 1.5 per cent aged 15–49 in 2003 (World Bank)
Life expectancy: 70 years, 2004 (WHO 2006)
Fertility rate/Maternal mortality rate: 1.9 births per woman, 2004 (WHO 2006); maternal mortality 44 deaths per 100,000 (World Bank).
Birth rate/Death rate: 16.4 births and 6.9 deaths per 1,000 people (2003)
Child (under 5 years) mortality rate (per 1,000): 23 per 1,000 live births (2003); 18 per cent of children aged under five were malnourished (World Bank).

Welfare

The social insurance bill provides for cover during illness or accidents unrelated to work, maternity, disability, funeral expenses, child welfare, pensions and unemployment. The welfare system was radically restructured in 1997 with the introduction of a centralised Government Pension Fund (GPF) worth about B71 billion (US$1.57 billion), replacing the old civil service pension scheme with a privately managed autonomous entity.
The labour department of the Ministry of the Interior manages workers' security and welfare and oversees a compensation fund for workers. In 70 out of 73 provinces, employers with more than 20 workers are required by law to contribute to the compensation fund. This fund provides benefits to employees who suffer injury in the workplace, or who fall ill or die as a result of the performance of their work. On average, 60 per cent of the monthly wages will be paid. This amount should not fall below B2,000 (US$46) and should not exceed B9,000 (US$206). Medical expenses are also paid in the case of an injury and in the case of death, the funeral expenses will be covered by the employer.
The public welfare department (PWD) of the Ministry of the Interior provides welfare services to various groups of people such as children and the young, landless farmers, hill tribe minorities, the destitute, the disabled, the handicapped, the aged and those hit by disaster.
Thaksin Shinawatra has ambitious objectives to deal with social problems in Thailand. These include plans to establish family advisory centres and childcare clinics.
Child prostitution in Thailand has received strong international attention. Eradicating the trade in children and women is likely to be a slow process for Thailand, since anti-trafficking laws have been difficult to implement. Female unemployment in Thailand remains high, so many turn to prostitution to earn their living.

Main cities

Bangkok (Krung Thep – City of Angels) (capital, estimated population 7.0 million (m) in 2005), Samut Prakan (1.5m), Si Racha (1.8m), Khlong Luang (834,202), Chon Buri (573,423), Chiang Mai (168,135).

Languages spoken

Business is conducted in Thai. Chinese (mainly the Zhiu Zhou dialect from southern China) is spoken in major towns. Many senior government officials and businessmen speak some English which, along with French and German, is increasingly being used in tourist areas. Malay and indigenous languages are spoken.

Official language/s

Thai

Media

Much of terrestrial television and radio is controlled and operated by the government and military.
National news agency: Thai News Agency (MCOT)

Press

Dailies: In Thai, main newspapers includes the mass-circulation Daily News (www.dailynews.co.th) and Thairath (www.thairath.co.th); other local and regional publications include Thai Post (www.thaipost.net) and Matichon (www.matichon.co.th), principal in of a media network. In English, the principal example include The Bangkok Post (www.bangkokpost.co.th) and The Nation (www.nationmultimedia.com) and Chiang Mai (www.chiangmai-mail.com).
Weeklies: Daily newspapers produce weekend editions including, in Thai, Matichon.
Business: In Thai, Krungthep Turakij (www.bangkokbiznews.com), Manager (www.manager.co.th), Post Today (www.posttoday.com), Prachachat Turakij (www.matichon.co.th/prachachat), Siam Turakij (www.siamturakij.com) and Than Settikij (www.thannews.th.com); in English, Business Day (http://www.biz-day.com), Thailand News and Press Releases (www.thailand4.com) is a business media outlet.
Periodicals: Various international publications such as New York Times, Newsweek, The Economist and Asiaweek are sold by newsagents.

Broadcasting

Radio: The National Broadcasting Service of Thailand (NBT) (www.prd.go.th) operates a national network and external service which broadcasts in nine languages, including English. There are many commercial including MCOT (http://radio.mcot.net) and Bangkok FM (www.bangkokfm.com) and non-commercial radio stations, such as

KU Radio network (http://radio.ku.ac.th) operated by Kasetsart University and Army Radio (www.tv5.co.th).
Television: NBT operates Channel 11 (www.prd.go.th); Thailand Independent Television (TiTV) and Modernine TV (http://modernine.mcot.net) are government operated; TV5 (www.tv5.co.th) and BBTV (www.ch7.com) are operated by the Royal Thai Army. Thai TV3 (www.becnews.com) is commercial.

Advertising

Advertising is available in the press, on commercial radio and television, in cinemas and outdoors. Static and mobile loudspeakers are widely used. Tobacco advertising is banned, and alcohol advertising was banned in 2007. While the media is free to report and criticise government policies reporters exercise self-censorship regarding such issues as the monarchy, the military and the judiciary.

Economy

While maintaining its position as the world's leading rice exporter, Thailand has steadily diversified its economy. To broaden the traditional agrarian base, the government has long encouraged industrialisation, both generally, through a succession of five-year economic development plans, and specifically, by making incentives available to encourage investment from domestic and foreign sources. Thai governments have acknowledged that the prosperity of Thailand lies in its ability to cope successfully with an increasingly competitive world economy.

After a couple of years' growth exceeding six per cent per annum, Thailand suffered a setback in 2005 as a consequence of several unforeseeable occurrences – the tsunami of December 2004, which damaged the tourist sector, a recurrence of the avian flu outbreak, a prolonged drought, escalating oil prices and a further escalation of the unrest in the south. Inflation, which had doubled in 2004, has continued to rise, while trade and current account balances have worsened.

Exports account for around 65 per cent of GDP. Thailand's ability to maintain strong export growth depends on the economic performance of key markets, notably Japan, the USA and the EU. Thailand has a shortage of skilled labour and outdated technology and measures to support productivity and competitiveness will be needed to sustain growth.

In January 2007, the government began introducing new rules in foreign investment laws, which may force some foreign-owned Thai companies, particularly in service industries, to divest shares to become, if not wholly Thai-owned, then joint partnerships. The stock market fell sharply when the proposals were published. The government's attitude was that these measures brought Thailand's foreign direct investment into line with international practice.

External trade

Thailand belongs to the Association of South East Asian (Asean) Free Trade Area (Afta) and maintains a list of goods that have preferential import duties between members and a programme of tariff reductions due to be introduced in the next few years. It also belongs to the 21-member Asia-Pacific Economic Co-operation (Apec) forum, which is a bloc of countries that border the Pacific with the aim of facilitating trade, economic growth and investment in the region.

A diversified manufacturing sector provides 46 per cent of GDP and a wide range of export commodities from rice (Thailand is a world producer), rubber, steel, tin, vehicles, hi-tech electronic goods, garments, seafood and processed food and electricity.

Imports

Principal imports are capital goods, intermediate goods and raw materials, consumer goods and fuels.

Main sources: Japan (20.1 per cent total, 2006), China (10.4 per cent), US (6.7 per cent).

Exports

Principal exports are textiles and footwear, fishery products, rice, natural rubber, jewellery, vehicles and computers and electronic goods and electrical appliances.

Main destinations: US (15.0 per cent total, 2006), Japan (12.7 per cent), China (9.0 per cent).

Agriculture

Farming

Agriculture accounts for around 10 per cent of GDP and employs just over half of the workforce. The rise of the manufacturing industry has meant that agriculture's share of GDP is declining, although farming still provides income for the majority of the population.

About 39 per cent of the total land area is cultivated. Production has generally been increased by expansion of planted acreage, rather than productivity improvements such as irrigation or use of fertilisers. Yield per paddy is one of the lowest in south-east Asia.

Thailand is known as the rice bowl of Asia and is one of the world's leading net exporters of food. The principal rice-growing area is the Chao Phya river basin. Tapioca is mainly produced in the south-east, kenaf in the north-east and maize in the central plain. Thailand is the world's largest exporter of natural rubber. Over 90 per cent of the rubber is produced in the south and most of it is exported through Penang in Malaysia.. Other major crops include sugar, cassava, cotton, jute, tobacco, fruit (especially pineapples), beans, oilseeds and coffee.

Livestock raised includes pigs, cattle, sheep and poultry. Buffaloes, oxen, horses and elephants are used as draught animals.

Crocodiles are farmed for their skins.

Agricultural co-operatives are organised by farmers to help co-ordinate joint farming activities and to provide low interest credits to members. The co-operatives are regulated by the ministry of agriculture and co-operatives.

Crop production ('000) in 2005 included: 31,490 tonnes (t) cereals in total, 27,000t rice, 16,938t cassava, 4,180t maize, 2,000t bananas, 298t pulses, 1,500t coconuts, 5,250t oil palm fruit, 1,130t citrus fruit, 45t grapes, 270,000t tomatoes, 2,050t pineapples, 1,105t oilcrops, 70t tobacco, 60t green coffee, 1,800t mangoes, 3,020t natural rubber, 34t ginger, 49,572,000t sugar cane, 47t treenuts, 6t tea, 136t kapok fruit, 8,138t fruit in total, 3,380t vegetables in total; 400 tonnes cocoa beans.

Livestock production included: 1,896,859t meat in total, 115,000t beef, 62,314t buffalo meat, 682,500t pig meat, 930t goat meat, 1,035,800t poultry, 694,060t eggs, 900,000t milk, 3,500t honey, 5,000t cocoons, silk.

Fishing

Thailand is the world's main exporter of fish and seafood. Exports typically earn US$4 billion per year. Shrimp products account for over half of the export revenue. Canned tuna is another important export item, typically accounting for 15 per cent of export revenue. The government has focussed on upgrading the fishing industry by cutting production and improving product quality. Shrimp exporters are moving to create more ready-to-eat fish-based products.

In December 2004 Thailand complained to the WTO that the US imposition of import duties was a violation of free-trade agreements. The US imports US$1 billion worth of shrimp and has provisionally set at tariff of 5.56–10.25 per cent on imports it claims are being 'dumped' on US markets.

In 2004, the total marine fish catch was 2,267,116 tonnes and the total crustacean catch was 139,089 tonnes.

Forestry

Forests are estimated to cover 17 per cent of total land area, with a further 18 per cent subject of a reforestation programme following a rapid decrease in the 1980s. There has been a ban on logging in natural forests since 1989 and the government

has implemented a number of measures to protect the remaining forests and encourage plantation forest management. Exports of forest materials in 2004 amounted to US$941.3 million, while imports amounted to US$1.4 billion.
Production in 2004 included 28,685,240 cubic metres (cum) roundwood, 8,700,000cum industrial roundwood, 288,000 cum sawnwood, 2,900,000cum pulpwood, 300,000cum sawlogs and veneers, 685,000cum wood-based panels, 19,985,240cum wood fuel; 1,262,465 tonnes (t) charcoal, 3,420,000t paper and paperboard (including 120,000t newsprint), 920,000t printing and writing paper, 990,000t paper pulp, 819,000t recovered paper.

Industry and manufacturing

The industrial sector contributed around 44 per cent to GDP in 2004 and employs 15 per cent of the workforce. Manufacturing accounted for around 35 per cent of GDP and 80 per cent of exports.
The majority of industries are in the private sector and most registered factories are small undertakings, but there is a range of medium- and large-concerns.
Main industrial products include processed food, precious stones and jewellery, cement, sugar, refined oil, synthetic fibres, textiles, assembled vehicles and parts, paint, steel, paper, pharmaceuticals, galvanised iron sheet, plastics (including artificial flowers), electronics, electrical appliances, glass, tin ingots, condensed milk, tin plate, detergent, hydrochloric acid and caustic soda. The local processing of wood has been encouraged and exports of plywood, veneer, parquet, furniture, household utensils and paper products show significant growth potential.

Tourism

Tourism is Thailand's single most important foreign exchange earner. There were 11.8 million arrivals in 2004, the majority coming from Malaysia, Japan, the UK, the US and Germany. Despite adverse factors in 2005, notably the December 2004 tsunami, but also avian flu and higher fuel costs, as well as the unrest in the south, visitor numbers did not fall taking the year as a whole. Arrivals numbered around 12 million, an increase of 3 per cent. The projection for the year had been 13 million. There was a rise in tourists from Asian countries and the government intends to pay particular attention to the new Chinese market and to Japan.

Environment

Mining

Mining accounts for around 2.5 per cent of GDP and employs three per cent of the workforce.
Mining has been officially designated a priority economic sector eligible for preferential tax and promotional privileges from the Board of Investment. The Bank of Thailand sets guidelines for private commercial banks to extend loans to the sector at prime lending rates.
Although many reserves remain largely unexploited, Thailand has a rich variety of mineral resources, including antimony, fluorite, iron ore, lead, lignite, limestone, manganese, precious stones, tungsten and zinc.
Tin, which is produced in northern, central and southern Thailand, is the most important mining commodity in terms of revenue. It is estimated that only 30 out of 145 tin mines are still active in the country.
Thailand is the world's biggest gem exporter. Low cost labour has helped Thailand remain a leading exporter. China is expected to become a major competitor in gem production and export. While Thailand's gem industry is more developed, China's lower priced stones have already entered the market.

Hydrocarbons

Thailand had proven oil reserves of 580 million barrels in 2004 and produced 218,000 barrels per day (bpd), of which only around 100,000 bpd was crude oil. Consumption was 909,000 bpd, an increase of around nine per cent on 2003. Thailand is dependent on imports, but in the face of a surge in prices in 2005, the government is encouraging refiners to reduce their imports and increasing domestic production. Thailand has four refineries with a joint capacity of around 700,000 barrels per day.
Thailand had natural gas reserves of 430 billion cubic metres in 2004 and produced 20.3 billion cubic metres. Consumption was 28.7 billion cubic metres, an increase of 4.7 per cent on 2003 levels. Most of the output is used for electricity generation. The largest gas field is in Bongkot, in the Gulf of Thailand, and is operated by a subsidiary of the state-owned Petroleum Authority of Thailand (PTT). This field supplies up to 35 per cent of national demand. Domestic demand is increasing at a greater rate than production levels, so to fulfil its requirements Thailand has become a net importer of natural gas from Myanmar.
Thailand had coal reserves of 1.50 billion tonnes in 2004 and produced 5.8 million tonnes oil equivalent (mtoe). Consumption was 10.2 mtoe, an increase of 10.2 per cent in 2003. Thailand imports coal to meet domestic requirements.

Energy

Thailand had electricity generating capacity of around 26GW in 2005. It is estimated that Thailand will need a further 20GW over ten years to meet future demand. Most of the genration is supplied by natural gas. Electricity is imported from Laos and Malaysia and an interconnector with Cambodia is under construction.
Thailand is attempting to reduce its dependence on imported oil by developing use of indigenous natural gas, lignite and hydro-power.
Geothermal resources have been discovered in Chiang Mai, Mae Hong Son, Chiang Rai and Phrae provinces.

Financial markets

Stock exchange

The Stock Exchange of Thailand (SET) handles a daily turnover of B4–8 billion (US$95–191 million). Total capitalisation stood at US$50 billion in 2002, with 383 listed companies.

Banking and insurance

Thailand set up the Thai Asset Management Corporation (TAMC) in 2001 to take over bad loans in the banking sector. The high level of non-performing loans has prevented Thailand's banks from functioning properly. Banks have been reluctant to lend and this has made economic recovery difficult.
Internal reform also continued in 2001–02 as part of the ongoing restructuring drive. The implementation of risk management systems has been high on the agenda. Siam Commercial Bank, Thailand's most profitable bank is concentrating on upgrading technology and attracting more customers to its internet banking system. Thai Farmers Bank underwent major restructuring, splitting its branches into different departments and making them more customer-oriented.

Central bank

Bank of Thailand

Main financial centre

Bangkok

Time

GMT plus seven hours

Geography

Thailand is situated in the Indo-Chinese peninsula, sharing borders with Myanmar to the west and north, Laos to the east and north, Cambodia to the east and Malaysia to the south.
Thailand can be divided into four regions – the central alluvial plain, the semi-arid plateau of the north-east, the mountainous north and the southern peninsula. It covers an area of 513,115 square km, about the size of France, and measures 1,650km from north to south and 800km from west to east. It has a coastline of 2,400km.
Its narrowest part is the Kra Isthmus, which is about 64km wide, with the Gulf of

Thailand to the east and the Andaman Sea to the west.

Hemisphere

Northern

Climate

The climate varies from tropical savannah in the north and tropical monsoon in the south. There are three main seasons: hot (March–May), rainy (June–October) and cool (November–February). In Bangkok temperatures range from 25 degrees Celsius (C) in December to 34 degrees C in April and May.

Dress codes

Light, loose cotton clothing is advisable, although it should be modest. Sweaters may be needed in the evenings and during the cooler season. Businessmen wear shirts and ties, while jackets are worn for official functions or meetings with government officials; jackets and ties may be required for evening wear at larger hotels. Smart attire is also expected of businesswomen.

Entry requirements

Passports

Required by all and must be valid for six months beyond date of visit.

Visa

Required by all; a list of exceptions for certain nationals visiting as tourists are listed at www.thai-la.net, follow link to visa.

A business visitor must complete a non-immigrant visa application and produce a letter of invitation from a Thai company, printed on a company letterhead. The letter must include the host company's registration, stating the 'capital investment' and documentation of the payment of the last two years' taxes. Proof of visit for business purposes must also be furnished along with a letter of approval by the Thai Labour Department. Business visas are only valid for up to 90 days.

Extensions, for either tourist or business visas, may be granted by the Immigration Bureau in Thailand.

Prohibited entry

Entry is refused to nationals of Afghanistan unless in transit within three hours. Entry may be refused to persons of untidy appearance.

Currency advice/regulations

The import and export of foreign currency is unlimited. The import of local currency is unlimited; export of amounts greater than B50,000 require prior authorisation.

Travellers cheques are accepted in most banks.

Customs

Personal effects are allowed duty-free. Radio equipment requires a permit and cameras, computers and luxury jewellery must be declared at customs.

Export of images or statues of Buddha, antiques and archaeologically valuable items is only allowed with a certificate from the Department of Fine Arts. Articles exceeding B10,000 in value require a Certificate of Exportation.

Prohibited imports

Illegal drugs, pornographic material, firearms and ammunition. Live animals and meat, plants and plant material require a permit.

Health (for visitors)

Mandatory precautions

A vaccination certificate for yellow fever is required if travelling from an infected area.

Advisable precautions

Inoculations and boosters should be current for diphtheria, tetanus, hepatitis A, polio and typhoid. Other vaccinations that may be recommended are cholera, tuberculosis, and Japanese B encephalitis and hepatitis B. Use malaria prophylaxis (which will also provide protection against dengue fever and hepatitis B) including mosquito repellents, sleeping nets and clothing that cover the body after dark.

There is a risk of rabies in rural areas.

Use only bottled or boiled water for drinks, washing teeth and making ice. Eat only well cooked meals, preferably served hot; vegetables should be cooked and fruit peeled. Dairy products are unpasteurised and should be avoided.

Avoid pork and salad and food from street vendors. A full first-aid kit would be useful.

Locally manufactured Western proprietary medicines are easily obtainable, but visitors on regular medication should bring their own supplies – amounts for the length of the visit only.

Visitors should have medical insurance, including emergency evacuation.

Hotels

Choose a hotel in the district in which you are doing business. Most top hotels have good facilities for meetings and can arrange secretarial services if notified in advance. A 10 per cent service charge and 11 per cent tax are added to hotel bills, and it is customary to give small tips for good service.

Credit cards

Major credit and charge cards are widely accepted.

Public holidays (national)

Fixed dates

1 Jan (New Year), 6 Apr (Chakri Day), 13–16 Apr (Songkran/Thai New Year), 1 May (Labour Day), 5 May (Coronation Day), 9 Aug (Sin National Day), 12 Aug (Queen's Birthday), 23 Oct (Chulalongkorn Day), 5 Dec (King's Birthday), 10 Dec (Constitution Day).

Holidays falling on a weekend are taken on the following Monday/Tuesday.

Variable dates

Chinese New Year (Jan/Feb), Makha Bucha Day (Feb), Visakha Bucha Day (May), Asanha Bucha Day (Jul), Buddhist Lent Day (Jul), Naga Fire Ball (Oct), Loy Kratong (Nov).

Religious festivals are determined by the Buddhist lunar calendar.

Working hours

Banking

Mon–Fri: 0830–1530.

Business

Mon–Fri: 0830–1700. Sat: 0830–1200.

Government

Mon–Fri: 0830–1630.

Shops

Mon–Sun: 0900–1800/1900. Some shops are open 24 hours.

Telecommunications

Mobile/cell phones

There are 900, 1800 and 1900 GSM services throughout most of the country.

Electricity supply

220V AC, 50 cycles for domestic use, with plug fittings having two round or flat pins.

Weights and measures

Metric system (local units also in use).

Social customs/useful tips

Always carry business cards and give them to any new acquaintance when introduced. To show respect, offer and accept business cards with both hands, and always read the cards you receive before putting them down.

To the Thais face is very important and losing it can be disastrous, with little chance of social recovery; all dealings should be controlled, polite and respectful.

Thai business relationships, networks and associations can be extensive and visitors should expect to spend much time cultivating contacts.

Both men and women should dress in smart, lightweight casual wear. Shorts, bare shoulders, and sandals would be inappropriate in a business setting. Westerners are expected to shake hands and Thais are willing to accommodate this practice. Thai women, however, may still be reluctant to shake hands, and may prefer simply to exchange smiles on being introduced. Thais address each other and foreign visitors by their forename, prefixed by khun.

The head is considered the most esteemed part of the body and the feet the least, so visitors should take care not to touch someone's head (even accidentally) or show the soles of their feet.

Images of Buddha are held sacred and cannot be taken out of Thailand without official permission.
Shoes should be removed when entering a Thai house or Buddhist temple. Women must never touch a Buddhist monk, give things to him, or receive things from him, directly.
It is a criminal offence to make critical or defamatory comments about the King or other members of the Royal family, punishable by a sentence of three to 15 years.

Security
Experienced business visitors should not encounter any problems, particularly in central Bangkok. However, Thailand's position in the world drug trade, puts the gullible traveller at risk. It is advisable to lock all luggage and keep it in sight while travelling. Do not accept anything to be taken through customs on behalf of someone else.

Getting there
Air
National airline: Thai Airways International.
International airport/s: The Suvarnabhumi-Bangkok Airport (BKK) (opened in September 2006), 25km east of the city, is the central hub for Thai Airways and the country's principal commercial airport. Facilities include duty-free shopping, restaurants, entertainment, bank, post office, hotel reservations, car hire and business suites. There are train, bus and metered taxi services; limousines, either luxury or 4WD-SUV, are available. In March 2007 Don Muang, the original Bangkok international airport, was re-opened to ease congestion at Suvarnabhumi, caused mostly by the increase in traffic from low-cost airlines. Suvarnabhumi Airport is the world's second largest (after Hong Kong International Airport) single building and terminal (563,000 square metres), it took six years to build and cost around US$3 billion.
Chiang Mai International (CNX); Phuket International (HKT), 35km from Phuket; Hat Yai International (HDY), 9km from Hat Yai.
Other airport/s: Don Muang International, 30km north of Bangkok was decommissioned after the new Suvarnabhumi-Bangkok airport was opened in September 2006. It may re-open for udget airlines to use its facilities.
Airport tax: Departure tax: B700, excluding transit passengers.
Surface
Road: The Asian Highway runs from the northern region through Bangkok and on to southern Thailand, crossing the border with Malaysia and ending in Singapore. The Friendship Bridge in the north links Thailand and Laos.
Rail: There are daily rail services, including the Eastern and Oriental Express, between Singapore, Penang, Kuala Lumpur and Bangkok (including a ferry ride). Trains are air-conditioned with sleeper-coaches (journey time 48 hours). A service runs from Bangkok to Phnom Peng (Cambodia) and through to Saigon (Vietnam). The journey time is over 24 hours and the trains are more basic in facilities.
Water: Passenger liners occasionally visit. International shipping lines that maintain contacts with Thailand may provide passenger services on cargo ships. Limited ferry services are available from Cambodia, Laos and Malaysia.
Main port/s: Bangkok

Getting about
National transport
Considerable investment is earmarked for improving the country's transport facilities. In remote areas conditions are still uncertain, and banditry occurs in the north-west of the country.
Air: Thai Airways and Bangkok Airways operate domestic services to main centres.
Road: There are over 64,000km of national and provincial roads and highways, most of which are paved. Major highways are four-lanes. Toll roads exist around Bangkok.
Buses: Long-distance (air-conditioned) express coaches operate between main centres; local services are not generally recommended.
Rail: Thailand's railway network is controlled by the State Railway of Thailand (SRT), which is responsible for building, operating and maintaining Thailand's 4,600km of railway track.
Rail services are generally recommended: the system is equipped with modern rolling stock, including air-conditioned coaches, sleeping accommodation and restaurant cars on main express services. All main lines originate in Bangkok. Four main routes radiate from Bangkok's main station (Hualompong), with the track to the south extending to the Malaysian border.
Water: There are 1,110–1,600km of navigable inland waterways, depending on the season. Various types of ferries and passenger/cargo boats operate on rivers and in coastal areas.
City transport
Avoid rush-hour travel; hours-long traffic jams are routine in Bangkok, the fastest method of travel is either the metro or a motorbike taxi.
Taxis: Taxis have yellow number plates and, although they are metered, fares should be agreed in advance; a surcharge is imposed during traffic jams. Tipping is not customary.
Taxi drivers rarely understand English and it is best to have the name and address of one's destination written in Thai to show to the driver. There are air-conditioned limousine services provided by main hotels. Tuk tuks are motorised trishaws.
Buses, trams & metro: The metro consists of two networks, the underground and the over-ground. Tokens for single trips or cards for frequent travel are not interchangeable between the two networks, however work is underway to unify the system. The metro system is planned to be 91km long with three lines covering major areas of Bangkok by 2009.
Trains: The Bangkok Mass Transit System opened in 1999. The subway, a new mass transit system, opened on 3 July 2004.
Helicopter: Royal Orchid Sheraton jointly operates a helicopter service between the airport and the River City shopping complex next to the hotel, with a flight time of seven minutes. There is a five-minute walk by connecting bridge to the hotel.
Car hire
Chauffeur-driven car hire is available in Bangkok, Pattaya, Hat Yai, Phuket and Chiang Mai. It is not advisable to drive yourself in Bangkok. An international driving licence is required and driving is on the left. A driving licence is required to ride motorcycles.

BUSINESS DIRECTORY
The addresses listed below are a selection only. While World of Information makes every endeavour to check these addresses, we cannot guarantee that changes have not been made, especially to telephone numbers and area codes. We would welcome any corrections.

Telephone area codes
The international direct dialling code for Thailand is +66, followed by area code and subscriber's number:

Bangkok	2	Nakhon Ratchasima	44
Chiang Mai	53	Nakhon Sawan	56
Khon Kaen	43	Phuket	76
Lampang	54	Udon Thani	42

Useful telephone numbers
Metropolitan Mobile Police: 123, 191, 246-1338/42
Tourist Assistance Centre: 195, 281-5051
Capital Security Police: 123
Fire: 199, 246-0199
Ambulance: 252-2171/75
Directory (Bangkok): 13
Directory (provinces): 183
International calls: 100
Rail travel: 223-1431

Chambers of Commerce

American Chamber of Commerce in Thailand, Kian Gwan Building, 140 Wireless Road, Bangkok 10330 (tel: 251-9266; fax: 651-4472; e-mail: service@amchamthailand.com).

British Chamber of Commerce Thailand, 208 Wireless Road, Bangkok (tel: 651-5350; fax: 651-5354; e-mail: info@bccthai.com).

Chiang Mai Chamber of Commerce, Hillside Plaza and Condotel, Huai-Kaew Road, Chiang Mai 50300 (tel: 223-256; fax: 222-482).

Khon Kaen Chamber of Commerce, 359 Mittaphab Road, Khon Kaen 4000 (tel: 224-521; fax: 225-719; e-mail: info@kkchamber.com).

Nakhon Ratchasima Chamber of Commerce, 1818 Suranarai Road, Nakhon Ratchasima 30000 (tel: 296-120; fax: 296-124).

Phuket Chamber of Commerce, 1 Montree Road, Phuket 83000 (tel: 217-567; fax: 232-038; e-mail: cham,ber@phuket.ksc.co.th).

Thai Chamber of Commerce, 150 Rajabophit Road, Bangkok 10200 (tel: 225-0086; fax: 225-4913; e-mail: tcc@tcc.or.th).

Banking

Bangkok Bank PCL, 333 Silom Road, Bangkok (tel: 231-4333; fax: 236-8281/2).

Bangkok Bank of Commerce Ltd, 99 Surasak Road, Silom, Bangrak, Bangkok 10500 (tel: 234-9230, 235-5040/9; fax: 234-2939).

Bangkok Metropolitan Bank Ltd, 2 Chalermkhet 4 Street, Pomrab, Bangkok (tel: 223-0561; fax: 224-3768).

Bank of Agriculture and Agricultural Co-operatives, 469 Nakhon Sawan Road, Dusit, Bangkok 10300 (tel: 280-0180).

Bank of America NT & SA, 2/2 Wireless Road, Bangkok 10500 (tel: 251-6333; fax: 253-1905).

Bank of Asia PCL, 191 South Sathorn Road, Bangkok 10120 (tel: 287-2211/3; fax: 287-2973/4).

Bank of Ayuthaya Ltd, 1222 Rama III Road, Bangkok 10120 (tel: 296-2000, 683-1000; fax: 683-1304).

Bank of Toyko Ltd, 62 Silom Road, Bangkok (tel: 236-0119/9103; fax: 236-9110).

Chase Manhattan Bank, Siam Shopping Centre, 965 Rama I Road, Bangkok 10330 (tel: 252-1141).

Citibank NA, 127 Sathorn Tai Road, Bangkok (tel: 213-2441; fax: 213-2517).

Deutsche Bank, 21 Sathorn Tai Road, Bangkok (tel: 240-9401; fax: 240-9425).

Export-Import Bank of Thailand, Boon Pong Tower, 1193 Thanon Phahonyothin, Bangkok 10400 (tel: 271-3700, 278-0047; fax: 271-3204).

First Bangkok City Bank Ltd, 20 Yukhon Road 2, Pomrab, Bangkok (tel: 223-0501; fax: 225-3036).

Hongkong & Shanghai Banking Corporation, 64 Silom Road, Bangkok (tel: 267-3000; fax: 236-7687).

Import-Export Bank of Japan, 138 Silom Road, Bangkok 10500 (tel: 235-7373).

Industrial Finance Corp of Thailand, 1770 New Petchburi Road, Bangkapi, Bangkok 10320 (tel: 253-7111; fax: 253-9677).

International Commercial Bank of China, 36/12 PS Tower, Asoke, 21 Sukhumvit, Phrakhanong, Bangkok 10110 (tel: 259-2000; fax: 259-1330) .

Krung Thai Bank Ltd, 35 Sukhumvit Road, Bangkok (tel: 255-2222; fax: 255-9391/6).

Nakornthon Bank Ltd, 90 Sathonthanee Building, Sathorn Nua Road, Bangrak, Bangkok (tel: 233-2111; fax: 236-4226).

Siam Commercial Bank, 9 Rachadapisek Road, Bangkok (tel: 344-1111; fax: 937-7454).

Siam City Bank Public Company Limited, 1101 New Petchburi Road, Bangkok 10400 (tel: 208-5000/5043; fax: 253-1240).

Standard Chartered Bank, 990 Rama IV Road, Bangkok (tel: 636-1000; fax: 636-1198/9).

Thai Danu Bank Ltd, 393 Silom Road, Bangkok (tel: 233-9160/9; fax: 236-7939).

Thai Farmers Bank, 1 Thai farmers Lane, Rat Burana Road, Bangkok (tel: 470-1122; fax: 470-1571).

Thai Military Bank Ltd, 3000 Phahonyothin Rd, Bangkok 10900 (tel: 299-1111, 273-7020; fax: 273-7121/7124).

Central bank

Bank of Thailand, 273 Samsen Road, Bangkok 10200 (tel: 283-5353; fax: 280-0449).

Travel information

Police (Tourist) (to reports a theft for insurance purposes), 29/1 Soi Lang Suan, Ploenchit Road, Lumpini, Bangkok (tel: 255-2964/8).

Royal Automobile Association of Thailand, 151, Soi Aphaisongkram, Phaholyothin, 10900, Bangkok (tel: 511-2230/1).

Thai Airways, 89 Vibhavadi Rangsit Road, Bangkok 9 10900 (tel: 356-1111; fax: 356-2222; internet: www.thaiairways.com).

Thai Hotels Association, 203-209/2 Rajdamnoen Klang Avenue, Bangkok 10200 (tel: 281-9496, 281-9579; fax: 281-4188).

National tourist organisation offices

Tourism Authority of Thailand, Le Concorde Building, 202 Rachadapisek Road, Huai Khwang, Bangkok 10320 (tel: 694-1222; fax: 694-1329, 694-1221; internet: www.tourismthailand.org).

Ministries

Ministry of Agriculture and Co-operatives, Thanon Ratchadamnoen Nok, Bangkok 10200 (tel: 281-5955, 281-5939; fax: 280-1691).

Ministry of Commerce, Thanon Samamchai, Bangkok 10200 (tel: 282-6171/9; fax: 280-0775).

Ministry of Defence, Thanon Samamchai, Bangkok 10200 (tel: 225-0098, 222-1121; fax: 226-3115).

Ministry of Education, Wang Chan Kasem, Thanon Ratchadamnoen Nok, Bangkok 10300 (tel: 280-0306).

Ministry of Finance, Thanon Rama VI, Bangkok 10400 (tel: 273-9021; fax: 293-9408).

Ministry of Foreign Affairs, Sri Ayutthaya Road, Bangkok 10400 (tel: 643-5000; fax: 643-5180).

Ministry of Industry, Thanon Rama VI, Bangkok 10400 (tel: 202-3000; fax: 202-3048).

Ministry of the Interior, Thanon Atsadang, Bangkok 10200 (tel: 222-1141/55; fax: 223-8851).

Ministry of Justice, Thanon Rachadaphisek, Chatuchak, Bangkok 10900 (tel: 541-2284/91; fax: 541-2307).

Ministry of Labour and Social Welfare, Thanon Mitmaitri, Dindaeng, Bangkok 10400 (tel: 245-4782; fax: 246-1520).

Ministry of Public Health, Thanon Tiwanond, Amphoe Muang, Nonthaburi 11000 (tel: 591-8491; fax: 591-8492).

Ministry of Science, Technology and Environment, Thanon Rama VI, Ratchathewi, Bangkok 10400 (tel: 246-0064; fax: 246-5146).

Ministry of Transport and Communications, 38 Thanon Ratchadanoen Nok, Bangkok 10100 (tel: 283-3000; fax: 281-3959).

Ministry of University Affairs, 328 Thanon Si Ayutthaya, Khet Ratchathewi, Bangkok 10400 (tel: 246-0025, 246-1106/14; fax: 245-8636, 245-8930, 246-8883).

Other useful addresses

Advertising Association of Thailand, 12/14 Prachaniwet 1 Road, Lardyao, Chatuchak, Bangkok 10900 (tel: 591-6461; fax: 589-9470).

ASEAN Investment Promotion Agency, Board of Investment, 555 Vipavadee Rangsit, Chatuchak, Bangkok 10900 (tel: 537-8111; fax: 537-8177; web: www.boi.go.th).

ASEAN Secretariat, 70 A J1 Sisingamangaraja, Jakarta 12110, Indonesia (tel: 62(21)726-2991, 724-3372; fax: 724-3504, 739-8234; web: www.asean.or.id).

Bangkok Mass Transit Authority, 131 Tiumruammitr Road, Huay Kwang, Bangkok 10310 (tel: 246-0339, 246-0741/4, 246-0750/2).

British Embassy, Wireless Road, Bangkok (tel: 253-0191; fax: 255-8619, 255-9278).

Chiangmai Province Commercial Office, Chiangmai City Hall, Chotana Road, Muang District, Chiangmai 50300 (tel: 221-217; fax: 221-121).

Communications Authority of Thailand, 99 Chaeng Watthana Road, Bangkok 10002 (tel: 573-0099).

Customs Department, Atnarong Road, Klongtoey, Bangkok 10110 (tel: 249-0431, 671-7555/7).

Department of Export Promotion, 22/77 Rachadapisek Road, Bangkok 10900 (tel: 513-1909/15, 511-5066/77; fax: 512-1079, 513-1917).

Department of Foreign Trade, Samamchai Road, Bangkok 10110 (tel: 225-1315/29; fax: 224-7269, 225-4763).

Deparetment of Industrial Promotion,Thanon Rama VI, Ratchathewi, Bangkok 10400 (tel: 202-4415/6; fax: 246-0031)

Department of Local Administration, Thanon Asadang, Bangkok 10200 (tel: 222-3852, 222-8847; fax: 222-5858).

Department of Mineral Resources, Rama VI Road, Bangkok 10400 (tel: 246-0034, 246-1161/9).

Eastern Trader's Association for Exporting Fruit-Vegetable, 30/31-32 Trirat Road, Muang District, Chanthaburi 22000 (tel: 325-962; fax: 325-962).

Economic and Social Commission for Asia and the Pacific (ESCAP), United Nations Building, Bangkok (tel: 288-1234; fax: 288-1000).

Election Division, Department of Local Administration, Ministry of Interior, Thanon Asadang, Bangkok 10200 (tel: 221-5871; fax: 222-6886).

Export Promotion Centre-Chanthaburi, 30/31-32 Trirat Road, Chanthaburi 22000 (tel: 325-962/3; fax: 325-962).

Export Promotion Centre-Chiang Mai, 29/19 Singharaj Road, Chiang Mai 50200 (tel: 216-350/1, 221-376; fax: 215-307).

Export Promotion Centre-Hat Yai, 7-15 Jootee-Uthit 1 Road, Hat Yai, Songkla 90110 (tel: 234-349, 231-744; fax: 234-329).

Export Promotion Centre-Khon Kaen, 68/4 Kiang Muang Road, Khon Kaen 40000 (tel: 221-472; fax: 221-476).

Export Promotion Centre-Surat Thani, 148/59 Surat-Nakornsri Road, Bang Kung, Surat Thani , Bangkok 84000 (tel: 286-916; fax: 288-632).

Export Service Centre, Department of Commercial Relations, Ministry of Commerce, 22–77 Thanon Rachadaphisek–Ladprao, Bangkok 10900 (tel: 513-1905).

Federation of Nakhon Ratchasima Industries, 269 Friendship Highway, Tambon Kokgruad Muang District, Nakhon Ratchasima 30280 (tel: 251-028; fax: 251-033).

Federation of Southern Industries, Songkhla Chapter, 165 Southern Industrial Promotion Center Building, 3rd Floor, Karnchanawanitch, Haadyai District, Songkhla 90110 (tel: 211-905).

Federation of Thai Industries, Queen Sirikit National Convention Center, Zone C 4th Floor, 60 New Rachadapisek Road, Klongtoey, Bangkok 10110 (tel: 229-4255; fax: 229-4941).

Federation of Thai Industries, Chiangmai and Nearby Chapter, Northern Industrial Promotion Centre Building, 1st Floor, 158 Tung Hotel Road, Muang District, Chiangmai 50000 (tel: 304-346; fax: 246-353).

Federation of Thai Industries, Khon Kaen Chapter, 359/2 Mittaphab Road, Muang District, Khon Kaen 40000 (tel: 225-679; fax: 225-678).

Federation of Thai Industries, Surathani Chapter, 160/19 Surat-Punpin Road, Makhamtia, Muang District, Surathani 84000 (tel: 285-722).

Federation of Thai Udon Thani Industries and Nearby Chapter, 83/14 Watana Road, Muang District, Udon Thani 41000 (tel: 242-004; fax: 246-498).

Fishery Association of Thailand, 1575 Charoen Nakom Road, Bangkok 10600 (tel: 437-0158/62; fax: 437-1262).

Foreign Bankers Association, 19th Floor, Sathorn Thani Building 2, 92/55 North Sathorn Road, Silom Bangrak, Bangkok 10500 (tel: 236-4730, 236-7224; fax: 236-4731).

General Post Office, 1160 Thanon Jaroenkrung, Bangkok 10501 (tel: 233-1050).

Industrial Estate Authority of Thailand, 618 Nikhom Makkasan Road, Phayathai, Bangkok (tel: 253-0561).

Industrial Finance Corporation, 1770 New Petchaburi Road, Bangkok 10500 (tel: 253-7111, 253-9666; fax: 253-9677, 254-8098).

Lawyers Association, 26 Ratchadamnern Avenue, Bangkok 10220 (tel: 224-1873).

National Statistical Office, Lan Luang Road, Bangkok 10100 (tel: 281-3022; fax: 281-3815, 281-3848).

Northern Industrial Promotion Center, 158 Tung Hotel Road, Muang District, Chiangmai 50000 (tel: 245-361; fax: 248-315).

Northern Investment Promotion Office, 369/1 Charoenrat Road, Watgate, Muang District, Chiangmai 50000 (tel: 248-778; fax: 240-919).

Office of the Board of Investment, 555 Vibhavadi-Rangsit Road, (opposite Central Plaza Hotel), Chatuchak, Bangkok 10900 (tel: 537-8111, 537-8155; fax: 537-8177; email: head@boi.go.th).

Office of Foreign Trade, Sanambin Road, Suthep, Muang District, Chiangmai 50200 (tel: 274-672; fax: 277-901).

Office of the National Culture Commission, Thanon Ratchadapisek, Khet Huay Khwang, Bangkok 10310 (tel: 248-5839, 247-0013/19 (ext 201); fax: 248-5841, 248-5851, 248-5845).

Office of the National Economic and Social Development Board, 962 Krung Kasem, Bangkok 10100 (tel: 282-8434; fax: 282-0891).

Port Authority of Thailand, Thanon Sunthomkosa, (tel: 249-0362).

Prime Minister's Office, Government House, Thanon Nakhon Pathom, Bangkok 10300 (tel: 282-6543, 282-6877; fax: 282-8587, 282-8631).

Religious Affairs Department, Thanon Ratchamnoen Nok, Bangkok 10300 (tel: 281-6080 (ext 43, 74 or 40); fax: 281-5415).

Royal Thai Embassy (US), Suite 401, 1024 Wisconsin Avenue, NW, Washington DC 20007 (tel: (+1-202) 944-3600; fax: (+1-202) 944-3611; email: thai.wsn@thaiembdc.org).

Securities Exchange of Thailand, 32 Sinthon Building, Bangkok 10500 (tel: 250-0001/8).

Southern Industrial Economic Affairs Center, 3rd Floor, Songkhla Industrial Office

Building, Karnchanawanitch Road, Muang district, Songkhla 90000 (tel: 321-166; fax: 321-167).

Southern Industrial Promotion Center, Department of Industrial Promotion, 165 Karnchanawanitch, Muang District, Songkhla 90110 (tel: 211-905).

Stock Exchange of Thailand (SET), Sinthon Building, 2nd Floor, 132 Wireless Road, Bangkok 10330 (tel: 254-0960, 254-0969, 256-7100, 256-7109; fax: 254-7120, 256-3040).

Telephone Organisation of Thailand, 89/2 Moo 3 Chaeng Wattana, Bangkok 10002 (tel: 505-1000; fax: 574-9533).

Thai Bankers' Association, 4th Floor, Lake Rachada Office Complex, Building II, Rachadapisek Road, Bangkok 10110 (tel: 264-0883/7; fax: 264-0888).

Thai Mining Association, 79 Prachatipatai Road, Banpanthom, Pranakom, Bangkok 10200 (tel: 282-8947/9; fax: 280-3786, 282-7372).

Thai Petrochemical Industry and Trade Association, 175-177 Surawong Road, Bangkok 10500 (tel: 238-2956/9; fax: 236-3110).

Thai Rice Mill Association, 81 Soi Rong Nam Kheng, Charoenkrung Road, Samphanthawong, Bangkok 10100 (tel: 235-7863, 234-7295; fax: 234-7286).

Trade Statistics Centre, Department of Business Economics, Ratchadamnoen Klang, Bangkok 10200 (tel: 282-6393, 280-1727; fax: 280-0775, 280-0826).

National news agency: Thai News Agency (MCOT)

Internet sites

Airports of Thailand: www.airportthai.co.th

Board of Investment: www.boi.go.th

Commercial directory: www.sino.net.thai/commerce/thaiprod.htm

Eastern and Oriental Express: www.orient-express.com

Thailand government: www.thaigov.go.th

Thailand trade directory: www.sino.net/index.htm

Timor-Leste

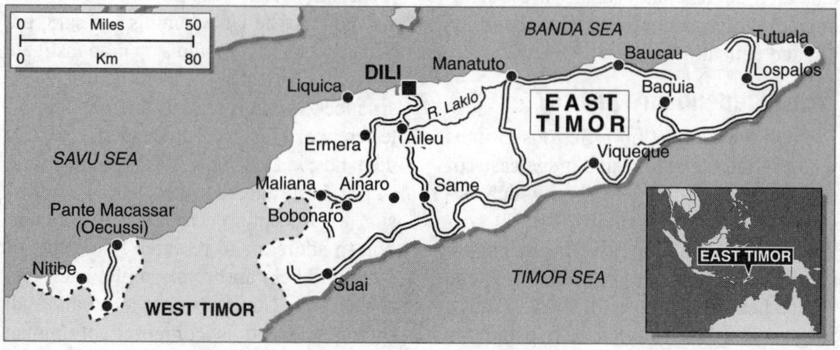

Two rounds of voting, in parliamentary and presidential elections, were held in Timor-Leste in 2007. Following the second round of voting, José Ramos-Horta was elected president. The parliamentary elections were less straightforward, as no single party gained a clear cut majority, obliging the president to invite the Alliance of Majority in Parliament (AMP) coalition lead by former president Xanana Gusmão to form a government. The appointment of the AMP government in August 2007 triggered violent protests in the country's east, as supporters of the former ruling party, Fretilin, voiced their protests at the election's outcome. Fretilin had polled the most votes but had been unable to put together a coalition that would have been able to defeat the AMP.

Weak economy

However violent the post election situation may have been, in comparison to 2006, 2007 was a tranquil year, as international security and police forces remained present to underpin the republic's law and order. For some five years, Timor-Leste's economy had shown indifferent growth rates. In 2007, inflation crept up to annual rate of 7 per cent although in 2007 the non-oil economy was estimated by the World Bank to have expanded sharply. Poor levels of job creation have caused unemployment to rise sharply. None the less, the economy grew by an estimated 7.8 per cent in 2007, excluding offshore oil and gas exploration activities.

The mainly Catholic, former Portuguese colony of Timor-Leste gained its independence in May 2002. Independence was hard-won, coming after 25 years of Indonesian rule established by means of an invasion in 1975. In 1999 the UN organised a referendum on the status of the region. Indonesia reacted to the majority vote for Timor-Leste independence with a campaign of violence and brutality. Between 1,000 –1,500 people were killed in skirmishes. The UN governed the country from 1999 with 10,000 troops and a UN peace-keeping presence remained after independence was won. In May 2005 the UN withdrew from the country.

On gaining independence from Indonesia Timor-Leste quickly became the land of acronyms: independence marked the end of the mandate of The United Nations Transitional Administration in Timor-Leste (UNTAET), to be replaced by the UN Mission of Support in Timor-Leste (UNMISET). This, in turn was succceeded by The United Nations Office in Timor-Leste (UNOTIL), which among other things, worked with the PNTL – the national police force. Following the unrest in April/May 2006, UNOTIL's mandate was extended until August 2006. UNOTIL was duly replaced by the more snappily named UN Integrated Mission to Timor-Leste (UNMIT), which focussed on policing functions and police training, political and community reconciliation, assistance for the national

KEY FACTS

Official name: República Democrática de Timor-Leste (Democratic Republic of Timor-Leste)

Head of State: President José Ramos-Horta (from 20 May 2007)

Head of government: Prime Minister José Ramos-Horta (Fretilin) (from 10 Jul 2006)

Ruling party: Frente Revolucionária do Timor-Leste Independente (Fretilin) (Revolutionary Front for Timor-Leste Independence) (elected 30 Aug 2001)

Area: 19,000 square km

Population: 1.04 million (2007)*

Capital: Díli

Official language: Portuguese and Tetum (Portuguese is the language of documentation).

Currency: US dollar (US$) = 100 cents (adopted as transitional currency, Jan 2000)

GDP per capita: US$440 (2007)*

GDP real growth: 19.80% (2007)*

Labour force: 422,000 (2006)

Inflation: 7.80% (2007)

Balance of trade: -US$133.00 million (2007)

* estimated figure

elections due in 2007 and humanitarian relief services. Despite the restoration of stability, the security situation in Timor-Leste had remained fragile in the lead up to the 2007 elections and beyond.

The economy recovers

The Timor-Leste economy suffered hugely from the internal strife of 1999, with GDP falling by 34 per cent in 1999. From 2000, the trend has been upwards although it is most definitely still officially a low-income country. Despite political turmoil Timor-Leste has restored macroeconomic stability by means of prudent fiscal policy. This does not mean the economy is strong. Forty per cent of the Timor-Leste population live in poverty and employment is low. Exports are the main drivers of the economy and include coffee, oil and gas. Agriculture employs three-quarters of the workforce. Though large it is not a developed sector, characterised as it is by subsistence farming.

Indonesia and Australia are the country's biggest markets. Investment is key for the country's future financial security. Reforms of the insurance, investment and land laws have been carried out in the hope of establishing a competitive business-friendly climate attractive to international enterprise. Remaining obstacles include poor infrastructure and administrative capacity. Timor-Leste wages are higher than in neighbouring countries, which is a disincentive to investment.

Timor-Leste had an annual per capita GDP of US$440 in 2007 according to the World Bank. Illiteracy is as high as 57 per cent. Timor-Leste's National Development Plan identifies governance, poverty reduction and better food security as development priorities. Targets include achieving an annual GDP growth rate of 5 per cent in the medium term and a 50 per cent reduction of the number of people living below the poverty line by 2015. Other development priorities include strengthening the judiciary and other institutions; creating an enabling environment for media, civil society and business; reducing unemployment and providing skills training and education.

Post-independence justice?

In 2000 the UN set up a Serious Crimes Unit (SCU) to examine and judge cases of war crimes, murder and rape which occurred during the turmoil of 1999. Although the operation was insufficiently resourced, the panel consisted of one Timor-Leste judge and two foreign judges. The UN convicted 75 people of crimes committed during the election period. More problematic however was the non-compliance of the Indonesians, who would not recognise the authority of the court nor hand over its suspects. Furthermore there was a lack of will for justice among top-level officials in Timor-Leste, who feared long-term damage in their relationship with Indonesia if they took an aggressive or insistent stance towards prosecutions. This reluctance contrasted with the stance of the Timor-Leste Church, which campaigned for justice, and with ordinary people, many of whom became tired of the delays and excuses.

The SCU wound up operations in late 2004. The UN has been highly critical of the impunity enjoyed by criminals. Indonesia itself brought 18 people to court – but no-one to justice. All were either acquitted, or had their sentences quashed. Over 300 people escaped investigation, the most significant being the high-ranking Indonesian General Wiranto.

In July 2005 the UN continued to apply pressure on the fledgling state, recommending international intervention in its justice system and continued efforts in prosecution. If this was not achieved within six months, the UN Commission said, the Security Council should step in to instigate prosecutions instead. There is official resistance to what is seen as international interference. However, in response to UN demands, in December 2004 Indonesia and Timor-Leste agreed to establish a Commission for Reception, Truth and Reconciliation to address and research the events of 1999 and help absorb ex-militia back into society. The Commission is located in Bali (Indonesia) and is composed of human rights and legal experts. There is some skepticism about whether this latest organisation will have any teeth.

Outlook

The IMF has recommended that Timor-Leste concentrate on education and health development. Also, the subsistence economy should be modernised and reformed into a market economy. Employment needs to improve and infrastructure needs to be extended. An agreement was signed with Australia in January 2006 that cleared the way for the start of oil and gas production in the Greater Sunrise field; if the project goes ahead, Timor-Leste will receive an equal share of the proceeds.

In 2008 the United Nation troops that had helped restored peace in 2005 and had since been in control of security began to transfer power to local police forces in January. President Ramos-Horta was shot and seriously wounded by rebel military forces that attacked his home on 11 February. There was a state of emergency until late March. In April, President Ramos-Horta returned from Australia, where he had received treatment for the gunshot wounds inflicted in February.

Risk assessment

Politics	Fair
Economy	Fair
Regional stability	Fair

KEY INDICATORS — Timor-Leste

	Unit	2003	2004	2005	2006	2007
Population	m	0.87	0.98	0.99	*1.01	*1.04
Gross domestic product (GDP)	US$bn	0.39	0.34	0.35	0.35	*0.46
GDP per capita	US$	346	357	354	*348	*440
GDP real growth	%	-3.0	1.0	2.3	-3.4	*19.8
Inflation	%	2.0	4.1	1.8	4.1	7.8
Exports (fob) (goods)	US$m	8.0	8.0	10.0	8.0	–
Imports (cif) (goods)	US$m	237.0	167.0	241.0	141.0	–
Balance of trade	US$m	-229.0	-159.0	-231.0	-133.0	–
Current account	US$m	40.0	119.0	-292.0	679.0	1,161.0
Total reserves minus gold	US$m	–	–	–	83.8	230.3
Foreign exchange	US$m	–	–	–	83.8	230.3
Exchange rate	per US$	1.00	1.00	1.00	1.00	1.00

* estimated figure

COUNTRY PROFILE

Historical profile

Before the arrival of the Portuguese and Dutch, Timor-Leste was linked by trade to China and India.

1512 Portuguese navigators landed and established Díli as the colonial capital. Sandalwood, honey, wax and slaves were exported.
1749 The eastern half of Timor-Leste became a Portuguese colony and remained so until the mid-1970s, when the Portuguese colonial empire disintegrated. The western half became part of the Dutch East Indies and later Indonesia.
1895 There were several uprisings against Portuguese rule.
1942 The Japanese invaded. Up to 60,000 people were killed during fighting between Australian and Japanese troops.
1945 The end of the Second World War saw the end of Japanese rule.
1974—75 A military coup in Portugal, led to a policy of decolonisation. The Portuguese governor and administration withdrew and the capital, Díli, was occupied by the Marxist Frente Revolucionária do Timor-Leste Independente (Fretilin) (Revolutionary Front for Timor-Leste Independence). Indonesian troops occupied the state, setting up a provisional government. An estimated 200,000 people died in the military crackdown and famine that followed.
1976 Timor-Leste was integrated into Indonesia, becoming the 27th Indonesian province however, this act was never officially recognised by the UN.
1985 The rebels suffered a setback when the Australian government recognised Indonesia's incorporation of Timor-Leste. Nevertheless Australia gave shelter to exiled Timorese dissidents.
1991 Portugal took Australia to the International Court of Justice (ICJ), on behalf of Timor-Leste, alleging Australia had failed to observe the rights of the Timorese to national self-determination, when it recognised Indonesia's occupation of Timor-Leste in 1975.
1992 Fretilin leader, Xanana Gusmão, was captured by Indonesian troops and convicted of subversion.
1995 The ICJ ruled it did not have jurisdiction in the matter of Australia actions concerning Timor-Leste.
1996 Bishop Carlos Belo and foreign minister-in-exile, José Ramos Horta, jointly won the Nobel Peace Prize.
1998 President Suharto of Indonesia was forced to step down. President B J Habibie considered offering Timor-Leste 'special status' and wider autonomy, but exiled Timorese leaders and Portugal rejected the idea.
1999 The UN Mission organised a referendum, which had a 98.5 per cent turnout, with 78.5 per cent of the population voting for independence. International military intervention halted Indonesian army atrocities and the Indonesian government agreed to grant Timor-Leste extensive autonomy. The first donor conference was held in Tokyo, Japan.
2000 The Lisbon, Portugal, donor conference was held. The UN Transitional Administration for East Timor (UNTAET) established the East Timor Transitional Administration (ETTA). A donor conference was held in Brussels in Belgium.
2001 Gusmão resigned as head of the interim parliament. Timor-Leste voted for an Assembleia Constituinte (Constituent Assembly) in their first democratic election run by the UN. Fretilin won 55 of the 88 seats in the constituent assembly. The ETTA was transformed into the East Timor Public Administration (ETPA) after the elections and Mari Alkatiri was sworn in as chief minister. The gradual reduction of the UNTAET peace-keeping force began.
2002 Timor-Leste became independent on 20 May with the independence hero, Xanana Gusmão as president and Mari Alkatiri as prime minister. Timor-Leste became a member of the World Bank Group and joined the UN.
2003 Former Indonesian military chief in Timor-Leste was sentenced to five years in jail for crimes against humanity by an Indonesian court, due to his failure to prevent attacks on civilians following the 1999 independence vote. The Australian parliament ratified the Timor Sea Treaty, which permitted the development of the Bayu-Undan gas field, the royalties from which will fund the country's economic development.
2004 A UN-backed tribunal issued a warrant for the arrest of the Indonesian presidential candidate, General Wiranto, for human rights abuses in Timor-Leste.
2005 Indonesia and Timor-Leste, recognised the location of their shared land border.
2006 Timor-Leste and Australia signed and agreement for the start of oil and gas production in the Greater Sunrise field with an equal share of the proceeds. Prime Minister Alkatiri resigned and was replaced by José Ramos-Horta.
2007 José Ramos-Horta won the presidential elections in May. General elections held in July did not produce a clear winner. The ruling Fretilin won 29 per cent of the vote (21 seats out of 88) and the newly formed Conselho Nacional de Reconstrução do Timor (CNRT) (National Congress for Timorese Reconstruction), led by former president Xanana Gusmão, won 24.1 per cent (18); either of these parties had to form a coalition to assume power. In August, in a move to break the political deadlock caused by the inconclusive general elections, the president appointed Xanana Gusmão (CNRT) as prime minister. Fretilin challenged the decision in court.
2008 The United Nation troops that had restored peace in 2005 and had since been in control of security began to transfer power to local police forces in January. President Ramos-Horta was shot and seriously wounded by rebel military forces that attacked his home on 11 February. Parliament extended the state of emergency by a further 30 days from 24 February. In April, President Ramos-Horta returned from Australia, where he had received treatment for the gunshot wounds inflicted in February.

Political structure

Constitution

The constitution, passed in 2001, became valid on 20 May 2002, when Timor-Leste gained independence.

Form of state

Democratic, sovereign, independent and unitary state.

The executive

The president of the republic is the head of state and supreme commander of the defence force, and is elected by universal suffrage. The term of office is five years and no president can serve more than two terms.

The Council of State is the political advisory body of the president, headed by the president. It comprises the speaker of the national parliament, the prime minister, five citizens elected by the national parliament and five citizens designated by the president for the period corresponding to the president's term of office.

National legislature

The National Parliament is a unicameral legislature created in 2001. It has between 52–65 members, serving for five years. Members are elected by a parallel–party list system. The parliament elects the prime minister. Some legislation may be vetoed by the president.

Legal system

The legal system is under reform, putting in place structures under the new constitution.

Since 2000, the International Development Law Organisation (IDLO) has delivered practical training programmes to Timor-Leste's judges and prosecutors as part of a USAID-funded project for upgrading the system of justice.

Amnesty International issued a report in March 2003 which claimed that Timor-Leste's legal framework was incomplete and that there was 'a lack of clarity among judicial and other relevant officials about existing applicable law'. Some of the main problems include a lack of public defenders, delayed processing of court cases and legislation that was inconsistent with international human rights law and standards. It said that these problems encouraged vigilante violence and a loss of confidence in the legal system among police officers.

Last elections

9 April/9 May 2007 (presidential); 1 July 2007 (parliamentary).

Results: Presidential: José Ramos Horta won 69.3 per cent of the vote; Francisco Guterres won30.7 per cent.

Parliamentary: the ruling Fretilin won 29 per cent of the vote (21 seats out of 88); the newly formed Conselho Nacional de Reconstrução do Timor (CNRT) (National Congress for Timorese Reconstruction) 24.1 per cent (18); the coalition of Associação Social-Democrata Timorense (ASDT) (Timorese Social Democratic Association) and Partido Social Democrata (PSD) (Social Democratic Party) 15.8 per cent (11); Partido Democrático (PD) (Democratic Party) 11.3 per cent (eight). Turnout was 80.5 per cent.

Next elections

2012 (parliamentary); 2012 (presidential).

Political parties

Ruling party

Frente Revolucionária do Timor-Leste Independente (Fretilin) (Revolutionary Front for Timor-Leste Independence) (elected 30 Aug 2001)

Main opposition party

Partido Democrático (PD) (Democratic Party)

Population

1.04 million (2007)*

Last census: July 2004: 924,642 (provisional)

Annual growth rate: 0.5 per cent 1994–2004 (WHO 2006)

Ethnic make-up

Before the arrival of the Europeans, peoples of Asia and Insulindia, mainly Malays, Makasare and Papuans, migrated to Timor-Leste.

Religions

Roman Catholic (91.4 per cent), Protestant (2.6 per cent), Muslim (1.7 per cent). There are also Buddhist and Hindu communities.

Education

Around 70 per cent of school age population attend primary school and 44 per cent are enrolled at secondary school. There is a shortage of teachers due to the fact that 80 per cent of Timor-Leste's teachers were Indonesian and the vast majority left following Indonesia's withdrawal. More than half the population is illiterate. The Roman Catholic Church is attempting to implement a literacy programme for the schools as the country needs to educate its people to manage the new nation's bureaucracy.

Health

Per capita total expenditure on health (2003) was US$125; of which per capita government spending was US$95, at the international dollar rate, (WHO 2006).

Life expectancy: 63 years, 2004 (WHO 2006)

Fertility rate/Maternal mortality rate: 7.8 births per woman, 2004 (WHO 2006)

Child (under 5 years) mortality rate (per 1,000): 87 deaths per 1,000 live births; 42.6 children aged under 5 are malnourished (World Bank).

Head of population per physician: 0.1 physicians per 1,000 people, 2004 (WHO 2006)

Main cities

Díli (capital, estimated population 59,069 in 2005), Los Palos (19,111).

Languages spoken

Tetum and Bahasa Indonesian/Malayu are the local languages. It is estimated that Portuguese is spoken by only 5 per cent of the population, with Tetum spoken by 82 per cent and Indonesian by 43 per cent. Although Tetum is widely spoken, it is an undeveloped language and only recently achieved a standardised grammar and spelling.

Official language/s

Portuguese and Tetum (Portuguese is the language of documentation).

Media

Press

There are two daily publication based in Timor Leste, Suara Timor Lorosae (www.suaratimorlorosae.com) and the Timor Post; periodicals include La'o Hamutuk (www.laohamutuk.org) a joint government and international organisations publication.

Broadcasting

Radio: Around 90 per cent of the public receive transmissions from the national public service provided by Radio Nacional de Timor Leste (RTL). There are two other radio stations, Radio Falintil/Voz da Esperanca is a community radio and Radio Timor Kmanek (RTK) is operated by the Catholic Church.

Television: Fewer residents have access to Televisão de Timor Leste (TTL), but programmes are broadcast for 24 hours a day in Tetum, Indonesian, English and Portuguese. Rural districts show three-hour videotaped summaries of the week's programming on projection screens.

Economy

Timor-Leste is primarily an agricultural economy with coffee as its main export. During the time of the Indonesian occupation (1975–99), it was heavily dependent on external transfers, with approximately 85 per cent of recurrent and capital expenditure coming from Indonesia. The public and private sectors collapsed during the conflicts which broke out in 1999, while GDP fell by 34 per cent and inflation spiralled out of control.

Between 2000–01, the economy made a recovery on the back of UN reconstruction and expatriate consumption, with growth rates of over 15.0 per cent. Large scale rebuilding of infrastructure means that since 1999 investment has accounted for a high level of national GDP – 30 per cent in 2004.

When UN officials left the country in 2002, the country went into recession and GDP contracted. This was not helped by delays in the implementation of development projects. Drought in 2003 and a surge in population pushed down per capita GDP.

The output of important food crops (excluding rice) has returned to pre-1999 levels. The improvement in food supply has helped to reduce inflation from 140 per cent in 2000 to 0.9 per cent in 2005. Timor-Leste still relies heavily on imports, including rice to feed its population. However, imports did fall by 34 per cent in 2004.

Despite extensive international aid and support, around 42 per cent of the country continues to live below the poverty line and is likely to remain impoverished as growth is unstable. The educated workers pre-1999 were mainly Indonesian and left the country with the onset of violence. The workforce is expanding rapidly due to a high fertility rate, but is largely unskilled. The country's main priorities in the medium-term are setting up a central bank with normal operations and strengthening the revenue base. The latter will be greatly helped by the development of offshore oil and gas fields, which will generate revenue when they come on stream by around 2009. This will help move the government away from dependence on external funding. The exploitation of hydrocarbons is likely to prompt rapid growth of Timor-Leste's economy, with per capita income set to rise from around US$378 in 2005 to US$1,000 or more by 2009. In January 2004, Portugal said it would give Timor-Leste US$63 million in aid over the following three years.

Timor-Leste needs to develop its regulatory framework and administrative capacity more quickly. There are plans for new investment, insurance and export laws which should help create a business climate attractive to investors. The non-oil private sector is underdeveloped: the economy is primarily dependent on subsistence agriculture and government activity. The offshore oil and gas reserves, however, promise to generate good GDP growth.

External trade
Timor Leste does not belong to the World Trade Organisation or other regional economic bloc. The country is the recipient of much foreign aid needed to repair and instigate development of not only the physical infrastructure but social and entrepreneurial structures as well.
Off-shore reserves of oil and natural gas have begun production and provide the majority of the country's income. Vanilla cultivation for export is being encouraged.

Imports
Principal imports include food, petroleum, building materials, vehicles and machinery.
Main sources: Indonesia (47.0 per cent total, 2006), Singapore (14.6 per cent), Australia (13.6 per cent), Japan (10.4 per cent).

Exports
Principal exports are oil and natural gas, coffee.
Main destinations: Australia (53.7 per cent total, 2006), US (23.9 per cent), Germany (3.9 per cent), Portugal (2.9 per cent).

Agriculture

Farming
In 2005 agriculture generated 21 per cent of GDP and supplied income for 95 per cent of villages. Prior to 1999, livestock had been a traditional source of income for Timor-Leste. Livestock has a large social and economic function: it is exchanged in marriage, and can be a source of cash income or a savings account. The majority of rural families hold livestock. An IMF vaccination programme in 2004–05 significantly reduced the incidence of disease among farm animals. Investment is required to recommence poultry and livestock farming.
Timor-Leste's agriculture has very low productivity due to a lack of technology, modern techniques and money.
The World Bank is encouraging diversification into horticultural products. Vegetables and rice could be grown commercially. The higher elevations in Timor-Leste are ideal for growing pineapples, oranges, mangoes, bananas and papaya.
Coffee is the principal source of foreign exchange for Timor-Leste. It is in the hands of about 45,000 growers with an average of only one hectare each. There are virtually no large scale farms. Wet processed Arabica beans fetch the highest price but the processing facilities were put out of action during the fighting. Arabica beans account for about 80 per cent of the annual harvest. All coffee is produced organically. Renewal and maintenance of the road infrastructure is necessary for the rehabilitation of the coffee industry.
Subsistence farming is giving way to a market economy. The government sees the country's farming future in goods with high margins such as cashew nuts, vanilla and cut flowers. The main priority for now, however, should be food security.
Estimate crop production in 2005 included: 135,608 tonnes (t) cereals in total, 70,175t maize, 41,525t cassava, 1,000t potatoes, 26,000t sweet potatoes, 65,433t rice, 4,500t pulses, 111,525t roots and tubers, 14,000t coconuts, 3,137t oilcrops, 100t cocoa beans, 14,000t green coffee, 425t various spices, 3,000t mangoes, 7,370t fruit in total, 18,225t vegetables in total. Estimated livestock production included: 28,873t meat in total, 1,100t beef, 570t buffalo meat, 10,080t pig meat, 240t goat meat, 1,840t poultry, 1,600t eggs, 375t milk, 400t honey.

Fishing
Although there are extensive rich fishing areas in the seas surrounding Timor-Leste, only traditional coastal fishing was practised as there was no established structure for offshore or deep-sea fishing. The government is contemplating establishing an exclusive economic zone for Timor-Leste and administering fishing and other activities in this area. Domestic fish consumption is very low. There are plans to promote the consumption of dried fish which could be more easily distributed from the coast to inner areas.
In 2004, the total marine fish catch was 344 tonnes.
A quarter of Timor-Leste's forested areas are in danger of degradation. Deforestation has caused landslides, and a worsening in soil and water quality. In recent years sandalwood, teak, ebony and redwood have been exploited at an unsustainable rate. The forestry sector, if responsibly managed, has potential for good revenue and significant employment opportunities.

Industry and manufacturing
The coffee industry is large and a service sector is developing in urban areas. The manufacturing industry in Timor-Leste is virutally non-existent. Priority areas for investment are industries processing raw materials from forests and marine and agricultural resources, and industries fabricating agricultural machinery, tools and small- and medium-sized fishing boats. The government is promoting the development of native handicrafts for export.

Tourism
Timor-Leste is looking to tourism to give impetus to the economy and its diversification. The sector is being built from scratch, the pre-independence conflict, during which tourism was not an option, having left the infrastructure in ruins.
Attention is being focussed in the initial phase on adventure and eco-tourists, who know what to expect and are prepared to rough it. The longer-term aim is to establish a niche market, exploiting local cultural features as well as the natural attractions, which will distinguish Timor-Leste from its regional competitors. Immediate problems are scarce accommodation, high prices, insufficient and expensive air connections and the perception that the country is still unsafe.
Measures to attract foreign investment have been adopted.

Mining
At the moment there is no significant mining activity. There are indications however that there could be economically interesting deposits of marble, granite, limestone and gold. The government is in the process of setting up a fiscal policy and regulatory framework, which would enable surveys and exploration to begin.

Hydrocarbons
In March 2003, Australia approved a treaty to allow multi-billion dollar oil and gas developments in the Timor Sea. The deal entitles Timor-Leste to 90 per cent of the production from the Joint Petroleum Development Area (JPDA) of the Timor Sea, which covers the Bayu-Undan, Greater Sunrise, Jahal and Kuda Tasi fields.
ConocoPhillips, the third-largest US oil and gas company received permission in June 2003 to develop the US$1.5 billion Bayu-Undan liquefied natural gas project in the Timor Sea. Production began in February 2004. The Bayu-Undan project is expected to earn US$100 million a year.
An agreement was signed with Australia in January 2006 that will finally clear the way for the start of oil and gas production in the Greater Sunrise field. Although the companies involved in the Greater Sunrise plan have yet to confirm they will go ahead, the field is reckoned to be worth a fortune. The agreement states that Timor-Leste and Australia will share the proceeds equally.

Energy
The national power system was managed by Indonesians who left during the violence of 1999. This left a lack of people technically capable of maintaining power supplies. Generating capacity is around 38.3MW. The government has been investing in electrical infrastructure. Rural areas still have very limited access to electricity and prices are high throughout the country.
Deforestation is a problem: more sustainable energy resources have to be found.

Banking and insurance
By 2005, the banking system consisted of four commercial banks, but most bank

deposits are invested abroad. The banking sector requires a stronger regulatory framework and more investment opportunities if it is to grow.
The Banking and Payments Authority (BPA) provides currency – US dollars – to the country's banks. It also supervises commercial banking, strives to ensure monetary stability and moderate inflation. In the future the BPA will develop into a central bank.

Time
GMT plus eight hours

Geography
The island of Timor is the largest and furthest east of the Lesser Sundar Islands in the Malay Archipelago, between the Indian and Pacific Oceans. Timor-Leste occupies the eastern part of the island, together with the Oecussi-Ambeno enclave in the north-west of the island. The island of Atauro, to the north of Dili, and the small, uninhabited island of Jaco off the eastern tip are also part of the territory. Indonesia, of which the rest of Timor island is a part, lies to the west and north, New Guinea to the east and Australia to the south.
The terrain is mountainous in the interior. The highest point is Mount Ramelau, which rises to 2,963m. A range of mountains runs the length of the country from east to west, dividing the hot northern coastal region from the milder south coastal plain and its rivers and swamps.
Hemisphere
Southern

Climate
The dry season is between July and October when it becomes very hot and dusty with the monsoon winds blowing off the deserts of Australia. Rainy season: Nov–Jun. Temperatures range from 15 degrees Celsius (C) in the mountains to 30 degrees C and above on the north coast. Humidity: 75—85 per cent. There is a risk of tropical cyclones.

Entry requirements
Passports
Required by all, valid for six months beyond date of departure.
Visa
Visas are not required in advance, but are issued to passport-holders on arrival for a fee of US$35 for visits up to 30 days and may be extended.
Currency advice/regulations
The import of currency is permitted, subject to declaration of amounts over US$5,000.

Health (for visitors)
Comprehensive medical and travel insurance is essential as medical services are severely limited. In the event of a medical emergency, evacuation to Australia is probably the only option for treatment, and insurance policies should cover this eventuality. Such treatment carried out locally will require immediate cash payment for doctors' and hospital services.
Advisable precautions
Malaria prophylaxis should be taken. Dengue fever and Japanese encephalitis are common throughout the island and tuberculosis is prevalent, while cholera and rabies may also be present.

Public holidays (national)
Fixed dates
1 Jan (New Year's Day), 1 May (Labour Day), 20 May (Independence Day), 15 Aug (Assumption Day), 30 Aug (Constitution Day), 20 Sep (Liberation Day), 1 Nov (All Saints' Day),12 Nov (Santa Cruz Day), 28 Nov (Independence Manifesto Day), 8 Dec (Immaculate Conception), 25 Dec (Christmas Day).
Variable dates
Good Friday

Working hours
Banking
Mon–Fri: 0930–1530.
Business
Mon–Fri: 0800–1700.
Government
Mon–Fri: 0800–1730.

Social customs/useful tips
Visitors should expect to pay all expenses in hard cash.

Getting there
Air
International airport/s: Nicolau Lobato International Airport (DIL), 5km west of Dili. It has limited commercial flights and few gound facilities. There are scheduled services to Western and Northern Australia.
Airport tax: US$10 departure tax.
Surface
The main land route into Timor-Leste from West Timor (Indonesia) is the border crossing at Motaain near the town of Batugede. Entry into the Oecussi-Ambeno enclave is through the border crossing at Oesilo. Travellers entering Timor-Leste from West Timor are issued with Timorese visas on arrival; Indonesian visas for entry into West Timor from Timor-Leste must be obtained in advance.
Water: There are weekly shipping services between Díli and Singapore, and Díli and Darwin, Australia.

Getting about
National transport
Outside the capital, infrastructure is extremely limited.

BUSINESS DIRECTORY
The addresses listed below are a selection only. While World of Information makes every endeavour to check these addresses, we cannot guarantee that changes have not been made, especially to telephone numbers and area codes. We would welcome any corrections.

Telephone area codes
The international direct dialling (IDD) code for Timor-Leste is +670, followed by the subscriber's number.

Banking
Central bank
Banking and Payments Authority of Timor-Leste, Avenida Bispo Medeiros, PO Box 59, Dili (tel: 331-3712; fax: 331-3713; e-mail: info@bancocentral.tl).

Travel information
National tourist organisation offices
Timor-Leste Government Tourism Office, Ministry of Development, Apartado 194, Edificio do Fomento, Rua Dom Aleixo Corte-Real, Dili (tel: 331-0371; fax: 333-9179; e-mail: info@turismotimorleste.com).

Ministries
Ministry of Foreign Affairs and Cooperation, GPA Building 1, Rua Avenida Presidente Nicolau Lobato, PO Box 6, Dili (tel: 333-9600; fax: 333-9025).

Ministry of Health, Edifício dos Serviços Centrais do Ministério da Saúde, Rua de Caicoli, PO Box 374, Dili (tel: 332-2467; fax: 332-5189; e-mail: ministerforhealthtl@yahoo.com).

Ministry of Justice, Avenida Jacinto Candido, Dili (e-mail: moj@mj.gov.tl).

Ministry of Planning and Finance, Building 5, Palaco do Governo, Dili (e-mail: itds@mopf.gov.tl).

Prime Minister's Office, Government Palace, Rua Avenida Presidente Nicolau Lobato, Dili (tel: 723-0140; fax: 332-2026; e-mail: mail@primeministerandcabinet.gov.tp).

Other useful addresses
Commission for Reception, Truth and Reconciliation in East Timor (CAVR), Comarca Balide, Dalan Balide, PO Box 144, Dili (tel: 331-1263; e-mail: info@cavr-timorleste.org).

Oil, Gas and Energy Directorate, Edificio do Fomento, Rua Dom Aleixo Corte-Real, PO Box 171, Dili (tel: 331-7142; fax: 331-7143; e-mail. emrd@gov.east-timor.org).

US Embassy, Praia de Coquieros, Dili (tel: 332-4684; fax: 331-3206).

Internet sites
East Timor Action Network: http://www.etan.org

Petroleum Transparency: http://www.transparency.gov.tl

Timor Leste government: http://www.timor-leste.gov.tl

Togo

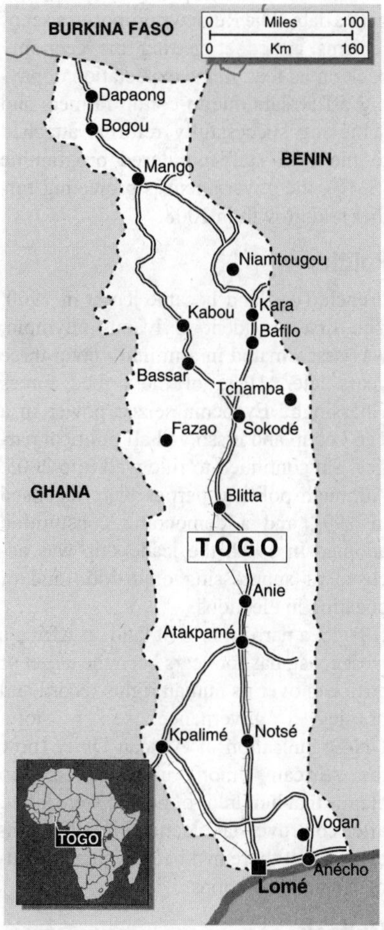

The elections in October 2007 were deemed by the Economic Community of West African States (Ecowas) monitors to have been 'free, fair and transparent...apart from some deficiencies'. The European Union (EU) observers said that the poll was carried out in 'transparent' and 'satisfactory' conditions. Nevertheless, the main opposition party, the Union des Forces de Changement (UFC) (Union of Forces for Change) challenged the results, charging that ballot boxes had been tampered with and fake election cards distributed. None of the other parties challenged the results.

The Rassemblement du Peuple Togolais (RPT) (Rally of the Togolese People) returned to power with 32.71 per cent of the vote (50 seats out of 81), the UFC 30.75 (27), and the Comité d'Action pour la Renouveau (CAR) (Action Committee for Renewal) 6.81 per cent (4). Turnout was 94.8 per cent. On 3 December, Komlan Mally was appointed prime minister

Togo's economic growth levelled off in the early 1980s with the fall in world demand for phosphates. Despite this major setback, Togo's relative prosperity was still the envy of many poorer landlocked neighbours in West Africa's Sahel zone.

This small sub-Saharan country's economy is today heavily dependent on both commercial and subsistence agriculture, which provides employment for 65 per cent of the labour force, although some basic foodstuffs must still be imported. Cocoa, coffee, and cotton generate about 40 per cent of export earnings, with cotton being the most important cash crop. Togo is still the world's fourth-largest producer of phosphate.

A decade-long effort, supported by the World Bank and the International Monetary Fund (IMF), to implement economic reform, encourage foreign investment, and bring revenues in line with expenditures has moved slowly. Real progress depends on increased openness in government financial operations, progress toward legislative elections, and continued support from foreign donors. Togo is working with donors to write a poverty reduction paper that could eventually lead to a debt reduction plan.

Togo has come under fire from international organisations for human rights abuses and is plagued by political unrest. While most bilateral and multilateral aid to Togo remains frozen, the European Union, which cut off aid in 1993 over the country's human rights record, initiated a partial resumption of co-operation and development aid in late 2004 based upon commitments by Togo to expand opportunities for political opposition and liberalise portions of the economy.

Eyadéma succession

President Gnassingbé Eyadéma finally died in February 2005 and was succeeded by his son Faure Gnassingbé, supported by the military. The succession, in direct contravention of the nation's constitution,

KEY FACTS

Official name: République Togolaise (Togolese Republic)

Head of State: President Faure Gnassingbé (RPT) (sworn in 4 May 2005)

Head of government: Prime Minister Komlan Mally (from 3 Dec 2007)

Ruling party: Rassemblement du Peuple Togolais (RPT) (Rally of the Togolese People) (since 1994; re-elected 2007)

Area: 56,000 square km

Population: 6.46 million (2007)*

Capital: Lomé

Official language: French

Currency: CFA franc (CFAf) = 100 centimes (Communauté Financière Africaine (African Financial Community) franc).

Exchange rate: CFAf413.80 per US$ (Jul 2008); CFAf655.95 per euro (pegged from Jan 1999)

GDP per capita: US$387 (2007)

GDP real growth: 2.10% (2007)

Labour force: 2.12 million (2004)

Inflation: 0.90% (2007)

Balance of trade: -US$441.00 million (2005)

Foreign debt: US$1.81 billion (2004)

* estimated figure

was challenged by popular protest and a threat of sanctions from regional and international leaders. Faure Gnassingbé Eyadéma reluctantly agreed to hold elections in April 2005. He was re-elected and in turn elected Edem Kodjo, the leader of a moderate opposition party, prime minister. Kodjo brought the leaders of two other opposition parties into government.

Political agreement

The Political Agreement signed in August 2006 by the RPT and the main opposition parties had led to the formation, in September 2006, of a Government of National Union run by Yawovi Agboyibor (CAR). The agreement also led to the establishment of a new electoral commission (Commission électorale nationale indépendante) (CENI) which organised the election on 14 October 2007. An important aspect of the Political Agreement concerning security was addressed by the National Assembly when it adopted a law regarding the reform of the army. This law ensures that the Togo Armed Forces stay outside the political arena and would not interfere in any political process.

Uneven economy

According to the World Bank Togo's economic performance has been uneven over the last several years. Periods of growth (1994–97) have tended to coincide with improved political conditions, better macroeconomic management, and the resumption of external aid. Conversely, Togo's periods of economic decline (1991–93, and 1998–2001, 2005–06) have coincided with political disruption, poor economic management, and the suspension of donor assistance. The government's success in stabilising the country's economy and fostering growth in 2003 and 2004, when GDP grew by around 3 per cent, was not pursued consistently in subsequent years. Togo's GDP growth rate fell to 2.1 per cent in 2007 after growing by 4.1 per cent in 2006.

The World Bank goes on to note that the phosphate sector reform that occurred through a joint venture agreement with the private sector in 2002 was a short-lived success, and the company has continued accumulating larger losses since then. Cotton production fell by 60 per cent in 2005 after the cotton para-statal failed to pay for the 2004 harvest. The government has since decided to put the company into liguidation and create a new company partly owned by producers as an interim step towards investment by a strategic private partner. Large amounts of domestic arrears have been partially repaid from the proceeds of a West African Economic and Monetary Union (WAEMU) money market loan taken in 2006 which attracted considerable interest and helped raise CFAf 36.3 billion (US$71 million).

According to the World Bank, Togo's economic decline has reduced living standards for large segments of the population. The Bank reports that poverty remains widespread, affecting some 70 per cent of the population. The survey shows that poverty has deepened in rural areas, and pockets of extreme poverty still exist in urban areas, including the capital, Lomé. To help the economy get into better shape and facilitate development partners re-engage in the country, a Public Expenditure Management and Financial Assessment Review (PEMFAR) and a Financial Sector Review were conducted in Togo in 2005. These two reviews showed that the country has been characterised by weak budget execution and monitoring, which has adversely affected transparency and efficiency, and the quality of public finance data. The Reviews proposed a set of reforms aimed at getting the economy back on its feet. In the expectation of paying off arrears due to cotton farmers and achieving successfully reforms attached to the IMF staff-monitored programme (SMP), the government is projecting further real growth in 2008.

KEY INDICATORS — Togo

	Unit	2003	2004	2005	2006	2007
Population	m	5.04	5.25	6.15	*6.30	*6.46
Gross domestic product (GDP)	US$bn	1.34	2.10	2.11	2.22	*2.50
GDP per capita	US$	265	375	343	*352	*387
GDP real growth	%	3.0	2.9	1.2	4.1	*2.1
Inflation	%	-0.9	1.2	6.8	2.2	*0.9
Agricultural output	% change	–	3.2	3.7	3.7	–
Exports (fob) (goods)	US$m	449.0	580.0	631.0	–	–
Imports (cif) (goods)	US$m	561.0	1,007.0	1,077.0	–	–
Balance of trade	US$m	-112.0	-427.0	-441.0	–	–
Current account	US$m	-220.0	-182.0	-234.0	-133.0	-160.0
Total reserves minus gold	US$m	182.5	323.3	194.6	374.5	438.1
Foreign exchange	US$m	181.8	322.7	194.1	373.9	437.5
Exchange rate	per US$	574.89	528.29	507.22	496.60	454.40

* estimated figure

Politics

French Togoland became Togo in 1960. The first president, Sylvanus Olympio, was assassinated in a military coup three years later. Head of the armed forces Gnassingbé Eyadéma seized power in a 1967 coup and dissolved all political parties. He continued to rule well into 2005. Although political parties were legalised in 1991 and a democratic constitution adopted in 1992, the leadership was accused of suppressing opposition and of cheating in elections.

Togo, a narrow strip of land on Africa's west coast, has for years been the target of criticism over its human rights record and political governance. A joint UN-Organisation of African Unity (now the African Union) investigation into claims that hundreds of people were killed after controversial elections in 1998 concluded that there had been systematic human rights violations.

Outlook

Improving Togo's business environment will be crucial for raising external competitiveness and attracting investment. The government pland upgrades of public infrastructure to alleviate constraints on the private sector (especially transport and energy). Making revenue administration more efficient and avoiding new arrears to suppliers should help restore business confidence. Additional reforms to develop the private sector include the adoption of a new investment code, a reduction in the relatively high corporate tax rate, steps to facilitate business registration, and judicial reform.

Risk assessment

Politics	Fair
Economy	Fair
Regional stability	Fair

COUNTRY PROFILE

Historical profile

1894 The country, then known as Togoland, became a German colony.
1914 Britain and France invaded and captured Togoland.
1922 Togoland was divided between Britain and France under a League of Nations mandate.
1930–50s The division of Togoland split the indigenous Ewe people, which led to the creation of a nationalist movement which demanded the unification of the two territories.
1956 British-ruled Togoland was incorporated into Ghana.
1960 The French section of Togoland gained independence as a republic under the presidency of Sylvanus Olympio.
1962 A proposed referendum on unification with Ghana was blocked by President Olympio.
1963 Olympio was executed in a coup by, a low ranking, Gnassingbé Eyadémaand. Nicolas Grunitzky was appointed president.
1967 Grunitzky was in turn ousted by Major General Gnassingbé Eyadéma.
1979 Eyadéma stood and won as the sole candidate in the presidential election.
1985 France intervened militarily to support the Eyadéma regime, following an attempted coup.
1985–1990 Political pressure for democratic rule increased.
1991 A new government headed by Joseph Koffigoh introduced a national conference to pave the way for multi-party elections. Much of the president's powers were stripped from him. The unrest that followed – orchestrated by the army, which backed Eyadéma – included spontaneous uprisings, a series of attacks on reformers, the prime minister's residence and the bombing of electoral material.
1992 The fragile democratic process of reforms faltered as a series of governments of national unity were imposed, through which much of Eyadéma's powers were re-gained. A new constitution was introduced. Parliamentary elections were postponed and a general strike lasting six months ensued.
1993 In January, representatives of both Germany and France failed to bridge the rift between the government and Eyadéma. The army opened fired on crowds that had gathered at the meeting, killing many and forcing the foreign representatives to hurriedly depart the country. After a series of delays, the country's first multi-party presidential elections were held. Eyadéma, standing for the Rassemblement du Peuple Togolais (RPT) (Rally of the Togolese People), was the only candidate as all other major parties boycotted the election. The EU suspended aid in protest at the abandonment of democractic elections.
1994 The RPT won the legislative elections, but needed the support of the Union Togolaise pour la Démocratie (UTD) (Togolese Union for Democracy) to form a majority. The Union des Forces de Changement (UFC) (Union of Forces for Change) boycotted the election.
1996 After winning three delayed by-elections, the RPT no longer required UTD's support.
1998 Opposition parliamentary members were arrested and held in detention. Human rights abuses escalated in the run-up the presidential elections, including extra-judicial executions. Eyadéma won the presidential election; the official results were strongly contested by opposition parties and criticised by the UN.
1999 An independent electoral commission (CENI), was formed, with equal representation of opposition and government. The parliamentary elections were boycotted by all opposition parties after the government unilaterally amended the electoral code and altered the representation on the CENI.
2001 The UN and the Organisation of African Unity (OAU) concluded there were hundreds of summary executions and torture in the run-up to the 1998 presidential election.
2002 The ruling RPT won the parliamentary elections; the main opposition parties boycotted the elections. The constitution was amended allowing unlimited terms in office for a president and required a one-year residency for an candidate – effectely barring the strongest opposition candidate, Gilchrist Olympio (UFC), (exiled son of Sylvanus Olympio, the first president of Togo, executed by Eyadéma).
2003 The opposition parties were unable to agree on a candidate to run against the the incumbent Eyadéma, who won the presidential elections, against allegations of widespread vote rigging.
2004 The French government resumed partial aid to Togo, suspended since 1998.
2005 President Gnassingbé Eyadéma died. Unconstitutionally, the armed forces conferred power on his son, Faure Gnassingbé, but after international pressure he stepped down and later won the presidential elections, against Emmanuel Bob Akitani of the opposition UFC; the opposition disputed the results and there were violent protests in the streets of the capital, Lomé. A clampdown by security forces provoked thousands of opposition supporters to flee to Benin or Ghana. The Constitutional Court confirmed the election of Faure Gnassingbé as president. Edem Kodjo was sworn in as prime minister.
2006 Reconciliation talks – that had been halted on the death of Gnassingbé Eyadéma – were resumed in Burkina Faso between the government and opposition leaders. The EU agreed to re-establish aid and trade if political and economic progress were undertaken. An agreement was reached with opposition parties, excluding Gilchrist Olympio and the UFC and President Faure Gnassingbé appointed Yawovi Agboyibo, who had helped broker the agreement, to the post of prime minister. Agboyibo's principal undertaking was preparing the country for parliamentary elections in 2007.
2007 Floods that devastated Togo during the summer left 20,000 people homeless at a cost of US$1.1 million. A request for urgent funds was issued as the UN warned of resulting water-borne disease outbreaks and locust infestations. Historic parliamentary elections, which included opposition political parties that had boycotted all elections since 1993 were held on 14 October. The RTP won 32.71 per cent of the vote (50 seats out of 81), the UFC 30.75 (27), and the Comité d'Action pour la Renouveau (CAR) (Action Committee for Renewal) 6.81 per cent (4). Turnout was 94.8 per cent. On 3 December, Komlan Mally was appointed prime minister.

Political structure

Constitution
In 2002 a new, democratic constitution, formally initiating Togo's fourth republic was instituted.
On the death of the president, the chairman of the National Assembly becomes interim president until elections are held.
The country is divided into préfectures, administered by préfects, and supervised by the interior ministry.

Form of state
Republic

The executive
Executive power is vested in the president, who is elected for a period of five years. The prime minister is the head of government and is selected by the president from the parliamentary majority. A Council of Ministers is appointed by the president and the prime minister.

National legislature
Legislative power is vested in the unicameral, 81-seat, L'Assemblé Nationale (National Assembly). Its members are elected by popular vote to serve five-year terms.

Legal system
Togo has a French-based court system.

Last elections
24 April 2005 (presidential); 14 October 2007 (parliamentary).

Results: Presidential: Faure Gnassingbé (RPT) won 60.2 per cent of the vote, Emmanuel Bob Akitani of the (UFC) 38.2 per cent, Nicolas Lawson of the Renewal and Redemption Party 1 per cent and Harry Olympio of the Rally for Support of Democracy and Development 0.6 per cent; turnout was 63.6 per cent.
Parliamentary: the RTP won 32.71 per cent of the vote (50 seats out of 81), the UFC 30.75 (27), and the Comité d'Action pour la Renouveau (CAR) (Action Committee for Renewal) 6.81 per cent (4). Turnout was 94.8 per cent.
Next elections
2012 (parliamentary); 2010 (presidential).

Political parties
Ruling party
Rassemblement du Peuple Togolais (RPT) (Rally of the Togolese People) (since 1994; re-elected 2007)
Main opposition party
Union des Forces de Changement (UFC) (Union of Forces for Change)

Population
6.46 million (2007)*
Last census: November 1981: 2,719,567
Population density: 77 inhabitants per square km. Urban population: 34 per cent (1995–2001).
Annual growth rate: 3.2 per cent 1994–2004 (WHO 2006)
Ethnic make-up
African (99 per cent), European (1 per cent).
Religions
Traditional beliefs (50 per cent), Christianity (35 per cent) (mostly Roman Catholic), Islam (15 per cent).

Education
Public expenditure on education is 4–5 per cent of GDP, of which per capita expenditure is 16–17 per cent per student.
Literacy rate: 60 per cent adult rate; 77 per cent youth rate (15–24) (Unesco 2005).
Compulsory years: Six to 15
Enrolment rate: 124 per cent gross primary enrolment, 36 per cent secondary enrolment; of relevant age groups (including repeaters) (World Bank).
Pupils per teacher: 46 in primary schools

Health
Per capita total expenditure on health (2003) was US$62; of which per capita government spending was US$15, at the international dollar rate, (WHO 2006).
HIV/Aids
The impact of HIV/Aids has yet to peak with deaths, orphans and HIV positive pregnant women all showing an increase. By the end of 2003 there were an estimated 10,000 deaths from Aids, although this number could be as high as 16,000; the difference may be due to underreporting or misdiagnosis.
Of the estimated 110,000 people living with HIV/Aids, 9,300, are children (aged 0–14) and 54,000 are women; and 9 per cent of pregnant women tested were positive for HIV in 2003, which bears out the UNAids message that women and children are typically more vulnerable to HIV/Aids in Africa.
Between 2001–03 the number of orphans (aged 0–17) rose from 8,700 to 9,300.
HIV prevalence: 4.1 per cent aged 15–49 in 2003 (World Bank)
Life expectancy: 54 years, 2004 (WHO 2006)
Fertility rate/Maternal mortality rate: 5.2 births per woman, 2004 (WHO 2006)
Birth rate/Death rate: 35.2 births and 11.5 deaths per 1,000 people (2003)
Child (under 5 years) mortality rate (per 1,000): 78 per 1,000 live births; 25 per cent of children aged under five are malnourished (World Bank).
Head of population per physician: 0.04 physicians per 1,000 people, 2004 (WHO 2006)

Main cities
Lomé (capital, estimated population 824,738 in 2005), Sokodé (76,732), Kara (48,570).

Languages spoken
Ewe and Kabyè are widely spoken.
Official language/s
French

Media
National news agency: Agence Togolaise de Presse (ATOP)
Other news agencies: République Togolaise (in French and English) (www.republicoftogo.com)
Le Togolais (in French) (www.letogolais.com)
Press
There is only one daily newspaper, in French, Togo Presse (www.editogo.tg) is national and state-owned. There are several weekly publications including Nouvelle Combat, Carrefour, Crocodile, Le Regard, Le Combat du Peuple, Motion d'Information, Le Togolais, Le Canard, Le Changement and Le Replublicain.
Broadcasting
Radio: As the most popular medium, particularly in rural areas, the state-operated Radio Togolaise, broadcasting in French and local languages, runs a national radio network, Radio Lomé (www.radiolome.tg) on FM. Other, external services, are provided by the French service RFI 1 Afrique (www.rfi.fr), VOA and BBC. There are many private commercial radio stations including Zephyr FM (www.zephyr.tg) and Africa No1 (www.africa1.com) from Lomé and Radio Maria Togo (www.radiomaria.tg) operated by the Catholic Church.
Television: All television stations are based in Lomé. The state-owned Télevision Togolaise (TVT) (www.tvt.tg) broadcasts mainly in French, with other local languages. There are several external services broadcasting locally including the French television channel TV5 (www.tv5.org), Euronews (www.euronews.net) and on cable, Media Plus and Canal Plus Horizon.
News agencies
National news agency: Agence Togolaise de Presse (ATOP)
Other news agencies: République Togolaise (in French and English) (www.republicoftogo.com)
Le Togolais (in French) (www.letogolais.com)

Economy
The economy has been heavily affected by the political instability of Togo. In 1993, the EU – Togo's principal donor source – suspended aid due to the deteriorating state of democracy and human rights violations by the then president, Gnassingbé Eyadéma. By 1994 Togo owed as much in foreign debt as the annual projected government revenue. The economy suffered a general strike in the late 1990s and GDP growth dropped to a negative. The government implemented macroeconomic reforms, tightening expenditure and improving measures to collect taxes and the economy has improved since 2001. Agricultural production has grown since 2002 with good harvests and climate conditions, achieving a government goal in food self-sufficiency. In recent years, GDP has grown by around 3 per cent. Inflation has been stable at under 3 per cent a year.
Subsistence agriculture, which employs two-thirds of the labour force, contributes around 40 per cent of GDP. The main agricultural products – cocoa, coffee and cotton – contribute around 35 per cent of foreign exchange earnings. Phosphate mining was a large revenue earner in the past, but the sector has declined by over 22 per cent, and lack of investment has hindered recovery. The reliance on primary production means that Togo is vulnerable to climatic problems and external economic shock in world commodity prices.
There have been no international aid programmes in Togo since 2003, although the EU resumed partial aid, for social welfare projects, in 2004 and the World Bank provides advisory assistance.

External trade

As a member of the Economic Community of West African States (Ecowas), which was set up to promote economic integration among members, Togo is also a member of the West African Economic and Monetary Union using the common currency, the CFA franc.

Cash crops include coffee, cocoa and cotton although phosphates provides the single largest share of foreign exchange. There are reserves of limestone and marble yet to be fully exploited. Togo is a regional hub for trading and transit, with re-exports if consumer goods to neighbouring, landlocked countries.

Imports

Principal imports are machinery and equipment, foodstuffs and petroleum products.

Main sources: France (17.8 per cent total, 2005), China (13.3 per cent), Côte d'Ivoire (6.5 per cent), Italy (4.5 per cent), Spain (4.3 per cent)

Exports

Principal exports are cotton, phosphates, coffee and cocoa.

Main destinations: Ghana (26.0 per cent total, 2005), Burkina Faso (18.2 per cent), Benin (11.5 per cent), Mali (7.3 per cent), India (5.8 per cent), Nigeria (4.0 per cent)

Agriculture

The agricultural sector contributes around 40 per cent to GDP and employs around 75 per cent of the workforce.

Traditional methods of cultivation still prevail despite attempts at rapid modernisation.

Self-sufficiency in basic foodstuffs is generally maintained except during drought years. The majority of farmers are smallholders who raise stock and grow maize, millet, yams, cassava, sorghum and rice.

Cotton, coffee and cocoa are the principal export earners.

Estimated crop production in 2005 included: 787,100 tonnes (t) cereals in total, 485,000t maize, 725,000t cassava, 180,000t sorghum, 570,000t yams, 115,000t oil palm fruit, 47,024t oilcrops, 1,800t tobacco, 8,500t cocoa beans, 13,500t green coffee, 185,000t seed cotton, 76,000t cotton lint, 2,520t various herbs and spices, 50,650t fruit in total, 136,000t vegetables in total. Livestock production included: 34,154t meat in total, 5,725t beef, 4,928t pig meat, 4,070t lamb, 3,731t goat meat, 4,500t game meat, 11,200t poultry, 6,440t eggs, 9,338t milk, 703t sheepskins.

In 2004, the total marine fish catch was 20,754 tonnes and the total crustacean catch was 12 tonnes.

Forestry

The majority of timber production is used in domestic fuel. The value of exports in 2004 amounted to US$689,000, while imports amounted to US$4.4 million.

The estimated production for 2004 included: 4,678,000 cubic metres (cum) roundwood, 254,000cum industrial roundwood, 13,000cum sawnwood, 44,000cum sawlogs and veneers, 4,424,000cum woodfuel; 179,900t charcoal.

Industry and manufacturing

The industrial sector, in 2004, contributed 22.8 per cent to GDP, of which 9.4 per cent was manufacturing, and employed 10 per cent of the workforce.

Activity is centred on the processing of agricultural commodities and the production of phosphoric acid, fertilisers and cement along with beverages, footwear, textiles and plastics.

Tourism

Tourism in 2005 is estimated to earn US$41.7 million or 1.8 per cent of gross GDP, employ 3.8 per cent of the workforce and attract US$50.6 million, or 10.2 per cent of all capital investment.

Togo has several distinct environments to offer the tourist, from Atlantic beach resorts to high savannah game parks and tropical forests. Facilities may be basic but should attract eco-tourists wishing to see some unspoiled African landscapes.

Mining

The mining sector contributes around 12 per cent to GDP and employs 5 per cent of the workforce. Mining production is concentrated on phosphates, marble and limestone, although the country has potential for commercial extraction of diamonds, gold and base metals. There are also known reserves of iron ore, bauxite, dolomite and chromite.

Phosphate mining is the second principal export earner after cotton. Reserves are estimated at over 60 million tonnes, mainly located around Lake Togo. There are environmental concerns about the high level of cadmium in Togolese phosphate rock. The possible development of safer but lower-grade carbo-phosphates is being explored. There are 200 identified base metal deposits, including the lead zinc prospect at Pagala which is licensed to Anglo American.

Hydrocarbons

Togo relies entirely on imported oil products, typically over 6,800 barrels per day (bpd) to supply its needs. The government has tried to attract foreign interest in offshore prospecting but the last exploration well was drilled in 1986 and foreign prospectors have not bidded for any offshore blocks, despite oil being found in the regional.

Currently there is no production or import of natural gas. However, with two pipeline projects currently underway so this is set to change. The US$260 million West African Gas Pipeline (WAGP) is currently under construction and will supply natural gas from Nigeria's Escravos field to Togo, Benin and Ghana. The 1,000km pipeline will be managed by Chevron Texaco.

Togo does not produce or import coal.

Energy

Togo is heavily dependent on imported fuel. Electricity is imported from the Akosombo and Nkong hydroelectric dams in Ghana.

Banking and insurance

Central bank

Banque Centrale des Etats de l'Afrique de l'Ouest (Central Bank of West African States).

Main financial centre

Lomé.

Time

GMT

Geography

Togo lies in West Africa, forming a narrow strip stretching north from a coastline around 50km wide on the Gulf of Guinea. It is bordered by Ghana to the west, by Benin to the east, and by Burkina Faso, to the north.

Togo is 550km long and varies in width from 40 to 130km. Much of the country is savannah, thicker in the south than the north, with deciduous forests in the central part. The terrain varies from the wide, rolling sandstone Oti Plateau in the north to the low, sandy coastal plain facing the ocean in the south. The narrow coastal strip is fringed by extensive inland lagoons and marshes; Lake Togo is in this area. Further inland are the Ouatchi Plateau and the Mono tableland. The Togo mountains straddle the country from the south-west to north-west; the average elevation is 700m. At the southern extremity of the range is Mount Agou, which at 986m is the highest point in Togo. The main rivers are the Mono, which with its tributaries drains the southern part of the country, and the Oti, which drains the northern plains.

Hemisphere

Northern

Climate

Tropical, mean annual temperature 28 degrees Celsius. Drier in the north. Two rainy seasons between April–June and September–October.

Entry requirements
Passports
Required by all, valid for six months beyond date of departure.
Visa
Required by all, except nationals of Benin, Burkina Faso, Côte d'Ivoire and Niger.
Currency advice/regulations
The import of local currency is restricted to CFAf1 million and export to CFAf25,000. Import of foreign currencies is restricted to CFAf1 million, subject to declaration on arrival, and export to the amount declared.
Health (for visitors)
Mandatory precautions
Yellow fever vaccination certificate required by all.
Advisable precautions
Malaria precautions and prophylaxes are essential. Hepatitis A and B, tetanus, typhoid and polio. There is an HIV/Aids risk and a rabies risk.
All water should be regarded as a potential health risk; only bottled or boiled water should be used for drinking, brushing teeth or making ice. Milk is unpasteurised and should be boiled and dairy products should be avoided. Only hot, cooked food and peeled fruit should be eaten. Medical insurance that includes evacuation is advised.

Hotels
High-standard hotels in Lomé, which should be booked well in advance. Ten per cent tip is usual.

Credit cards
Credit cards accepted.

Public holidays (national)
Fixed dates
1 Jan (New Year's Day), 13 Jan (Liberation Day), 27 Apr (Independence Day), 1 May (Labour Day), 21 Jun (Martyrs' Day), 15 Aug (Assumption Day), 1 Nov (All Saints' Day), 25 Dec (Christmas Day).
Variable dates
Easter Monday, Ascension Day, Whit Monday, Eid al Adha, Birth of the Prophet, Eid al Fitr.
Islamic year – 1429 (10 Jan 2008–28 Dec 2008): The Islamic year contains 354 or 355 days, with the result that Muslim feasts advance by 10-12 days against the Gregorian calendar. Dates of feasts vary according to the sighting of the new moon, so cannot be forecast exactly.

Working hours
Banking
Mon–Fri: 0730–1130, 1430–1600.
Business
Mon–Fri: 0700–1200, 1430–1730.
Government
Mon–Fri: 0700–1200, 1430–1730.
Shops
Mon–Fri: 0800–1200, 1430–1730; Sat: 0730–1230.

Telecommunications
Mobile/cell phones
A GSM 900 service is available in populated areas.

Electricity supply
220V AC, 50 cycles.

Social customs/useful tips
Business is conducted in French.

Security
Togo is relatively trouble-free, although visitors should be wary of the occasional car hijacking.

Getting there
Air
International airport/s: Gnassingbé Eyadéma International (LFW), 6km from Lomé; duty-free shop, restaurant, bank, post office, car hire. Taxis operate, from 0600 until the last flight, to the city centre.
Airport tax: None.
Surface
Road: A well-surfaced coastal road, which passes through Lomé, connects Togo with Ghana and Benin and thence to Nigeria. There is a road from Burkina Faso down to Lomé.
Main port/s: Lomé. Kpeme handles phosphate shipments.

Getting about
National transport
Air: Air Togo flies between Lomé, Sokodé, Mango, Lama-Kara, Niamtougou and Dapaong.
Road: Surfaced roads run from Lomé to the borders of neighbouring countries, along the coast west to Ghana and east to Benin, and northwards the length of Togo to Burkina Faso. Other roads may not be passable in the rainy season.
Rail: The main railway lines run from Lomé northwards to Blitta (midway between Atakpamé and Sokodé) and to Kpalimé, and eastwards to Aného.
Water: Ferries serve the ports along the coast.
City transport
Taxis: Readily available in Lomé, while shared taxis ply to other main towns; tipping is not usual.
Car hire
Available, but generally expensive. International driving licence required.

BUSINESS DIRECTORY

The addresses listed below are a selection only. While World of Information makes every endeavour to check these addresses, we cannot guarantee that changes have not been made, especially to telephone numbers and area codes. We would welcome any corrections.

Telephone area codes
The international direct dialling (IDD) code for Togo is +228, followed by subscriber's number.

Chambers of Commerce
Togo Chamber of Commerce, Agriculture and Industry, Angle Avenues de la Présidence et Georges Pompidou, PO Box 360, Lomé (tel: 221-2065; fax: 221-4730; e-mail: ccit@rdd.tg).

Banking
Banque Internationale pour l'Afrique au Togo, BP 346, 13 rue du Commerce, Lomé (tel: 221-3286; fax: 221-1019; e-mail: bia-togo@café.tg).

Banque Togolaise de Développement, BP 65, Place de L'Independance, Angle Avenues des Nîmes et Grunitzky, Lomé (tel 221-3641; fax: 221-4456; e-mail: togo_devbank.btd.tog).

Banque Togolaise pour le Commerce et l'Industrie, BP 363, 169 Boulevard du 13 Janvier, Lomé (tel: 221-4641; fax: 21-3265; e-mail: sda@btci.tg).

Ecobank-Togo, BP 3302, 20 Rue du Commerce, Lomé (tel: 222-6574; fax: 221-4237; e-mail: ecobanktg@ecobank.com).

Société Inter Africaine de Banque, BP 4874, 14 Rue du Commerce, Lomé (tel: 221-1341; fax: 221-5829; e-mail: siab@bibway.com).

Société Nationale d'Investissement et Fonds Annexes BP 2682, 11 Avenue du 24 Janvier, Lomé (tel: 221-6221; fax: 221-6225; e-mail: sni@ids.tg).

Union Togolaise de Banques, BP 359, Boulevard du 13 Janvier, Lomé (tel: 221-6411; fax: 221-2206; utbsdg@café.tg).

Central bank
Banque Centrale des Etats de l'Afrique de l'Ouest, Direction Nationale, BP 120, Rue des Nimes, Lomé (tel: 221-2512; fax: 221-7602).

Travel information
Ministry of tourism
Ministry of Culture, Tourism and Leisure, BP 3114, Lomé (tel: 221-5400; fax: 221-8927).

National tourist organisation offices
Office national togolais du tourism, BP 1289, Route d'Aného, Lomé, (tel: 221-4313; fax: 221-8927; e-mail: info@togo-tourisme.com).

Other useful addresses
Direction de la Statistique, BP 118, Lomé (tel: 270-662).

Direction des Professions Touristiques, BP 1289, Lomé (tel: 215-662, 214-313).

Kpeme Port Authority, OTP BP 362, Lomé (tel: 213-901; fax: 217-105).

Office des Produits Agricoles du Togo, BP 1334, Lomé (agency dealing with marketing, export, development) (tel: 214-471).

OPTT-Post Office and Telecommunications of Togo, Lomé (tel: 213-737; fax: 210-373).

Togo Embassy (USA), 2208 Massachusetts Avenue, NW, Washington DC 20008 (tel: (+1-202) 234-4212; fax: (+1-202) 232-3190).

National news agency: Agence Togolaise de Presse (ATOP)

Internet sites

Africa Business Network: http://www.ifc.org/abn

AllAfrica.com: http://allafrica.com

African Development Bank: http://www.afdb.org

Africa Online: http://www.africaonline.com

Mbendi AfroPaedia (information on companies, countries, industries and stock exchanges in Africa): http://mbendi.co.za

Republic of Togolais (in French): http://www.republicoftogo.com

Online Togo news: http://www.togodaily.com

Togo Official website: http://www.afrika.com/togo/html

Tokelau

KEY FACTS

Official name: Tokelau

Head of State: Queen Elizabeth II, represented by Governor General of New Zealand, Anand Satyanand (since 23 Aug 2006) and Administrator David Payton (appointed Oct 2006)

Head of government: Ulu-o-Tokelau Pio Tuia (from Feb 2008)

Area: 12 square km (three coral atolls: Nukunonu, Fakaofo, Atafu)

Population: 1,151 (19 October 2006, census result); some 6,000 Tokelauans live in New Zealand.

Capital: Each atoll has its own administrative centre

Official language: Tokelauan (English also spoken)

Currency: New Zealand dollar (NZ$) =100 cents; also Tala or Samoan dollar (S$)

Exchange rate: NZ$1.31 per US$ (Jul 2008)

GDP per capita: US$1,000 (2003)

Balance of trade: -US$225,000 (2003)

COUNTRY PROFILE

Historical profile

Tokelau's three atolls are believed to have been settled by people from Samoa, Cook Islands and Tuvalu.

1889 The Union Islands became a British protectorate.

1916 At the request of the inhabitants, the United Kingdom annexed the islands and included them within the Gilbert and Ellice Islands Colony (now Kiribati and Tuvalu).

1926 The British government transferred administrative control of the islands to New Zealand (NZ).

1946 The islands were renamed Tokelau Islands.

1948 The Tokelau Islands Act made NZ the formal administering authority.

1976 The islands were renamed Tokelau.

1994 Executive and administrative functions were delegated by NZ to the General Fono (or Council of Faipule when the General Fono is not in session).

1996 Subordinate legislative power was granted to the General Fono by the New Zealand Tokelau Amendment Act.

2001 Tokelau became responsible for its own public service.

2002 Neil Walter was appointed administrator.

2003 A new Principles of Partnership document was signed with NZ.

2004 The UN presented a Special Case Study on de-colonisation, urging Tokelau to become independent. The NZ premier Helen Clark visited and signed a three-year agreement on economic support. The General Fono agreed to explore an option of self-government in free association with NZ.

2005 A draft constitution was approved by the General Fono, and agreement was reached on the main elements of the Treaty of Free Association.

2006 A referendum on the Treaty of Free Association with NZ failed with less than the necessary two-thirds majority. Tokelau's status remained unchanged. David Payton was appointed administrator. Census results showed that the population on the three tiny atolls had had a 20 per cent drop of inhabitants over five years.

2007 A second referendum on the Treaty of Free Association, also failed to reach a two-thirds majority.

Political structure

Constitution

Under the 1948 Tokelau Islands Act (through which New Zealand was the formal administering authority), Tokelau is within the territorial boundaries of New Zealand and Tokelauans are New Zealand citizens.

The 1948 Act was amended and subordinate legislative power was granted to the General Fono by the Tokelau Amendment Act in 1996.

Form of state

Self-administering territory of New Zealand.

The executive

The Head of State is the British Monarch, who is represented by an administrator, appointed from New Zealand. The Ulu o Tokelau (head of government) is a position, which is rotated annually among the three Faipule (leaders) and holds executive power and presides over the Council for Ongoing Goverment (cabinet). The Council consists of the Faipule and Pulenuku (mayors) of each atoll. It has a mandate to manage government business but not to pass laws or introduce taxes.

National legislature

Each island atoll has a Council of Elders (Taupulega) which is the source of authority. The Taupulega delegates authority to the General Fono (parliament) on matters of taxes, law, national policy, budget and management. Parliament sits for three–four days, three–four times a year on the atoll which is home to the current Ulu o Tokelau (head of government). When not in session government business is executed through the Council of Ongoing Government.

The unicameral parliament comprises 20 members, elected by proportional representation between the three islands: Nukunonu six seats, Fakaofo and Atafu seven seats, elected by universal suffrage for a term of three years.

Legal system

The villages have the statutory power to enact their own laws covering village affairs.

Civil and criminal jurisdiction is exercised by commissioners and the New Zealand high court.

There is little crime apart from petty theft and there are no prisons. Punishment generally takes the form of public rebukes, fines or labour.

Last elections

January 2008 (General Fono)

Results: General Fono: all seats were won by independents.

Next elections

2011 (General Fono)

Political parties
There are no organised political parties.
Political situation
The voters in Tokelau decided to remain a territory of New Zealand, in the October 2007 referendum on independence, which fell 16 votes short, in the second United Nations-supervised ballot in less than two years. The government leader, Pio Tuia requested that everyone should accept the vote and not ask for another one. Some observers considered the huge expatriate community influenced the vote, which if full independence were attained, would have had an impact on their migration status in New Zealand.

Population
1,151 (19 October 2006, census result); some 6,000 Tokelauans live in New Zealand.
Last census: 19 October 2006: 1,152 (preliminary result)
Annual growth rate: -0.6 per cent (2003)
Ethnic make-up
The residents are mainly Polynesians, with close links to Samoa.
Religions
Christianity
Education
Each atoll has its own school with classes beginning at pre-school and carrying through to Year 10. The Year 11 class is hosted on a different atoll every five years and is made up of students combined from each atoll. After graduation from school, the top eight or 10 students are given a scholarship for further study overseas. Staff members are qualified teachers, usually from Samoa, Fiji and New Zealand.
Health
Tokelau has two doctors, one dentist, eight nurses and three midwives. Tokelau collaborates with the World Health Organisation (WHO) in health promotion projects. There are hospitals on Atafu, Fakaofo and Nukunono.
Life expectancy: 69 years (estimate 2003)
Main cities
Fakaofo (estimated population 540 in 2003), Atafu (140), Nukunonu (90).

Languages spoken
Official language/s
Tokelauan (English also spoken)
Media
Other news agencies: ABC Pacific Beat: www.radioaustralia.net.au/pacbeat
Pacific Magazine:
www.pacificmagazine.net

Press
There are online news outlets including Event Polynesia, with a sub-heading for Tokelau (www.eventpolynesia.com).
Broadcasting
Radio: There is only one radio station which broadcasts to each of the islands in AM and FM. External service include Pacific Island Radio (www.pacificislandsradio.com), Radio Australia (www.radioaustralia.net.au/pacbeat) and from New Zealand (www.accessradio.org.nz), which provides news for expatriate Tokelauns.
Television: There are no television broadcasts.
Economy
The economy is based on communal subsistence, agriculture and fishing. The atolls' size, isolation and lack of land-based resources allow little scope for economic development.
Sales of licences to fish for tuna, postage stamps, souvenir coins, handicrafts and remittances from migrant workers are the principal sources of foreign exchange.
Grants from New Zealand account for about 80 per cent of expenditure.
Funding from the New Zealand bilateral aid programme, the UN Development Programme (UNDP), the South Pacific Commission, the ILO and other international agencies has been the main source of development assistance.
Since 1982, the General Fono has collected a tax on the salaries of public servants unavailable for communal service (called the Community Services Levy) in order to subsidise copra and handicrafts producers, provide honoraria to members of island councils and supplement village projects.
Fees from fishing licences purchased by foreign companies operating within Tokelau's Exclusive Economic Zone raise up to US$700,000 annually.
New Zealand has been devolving powers to Tokelau under the 'Modern House of Tokelau' project, giving each village full responsibility for running all the public services on its atoll. New Zealand's annual subsidies to Tokelau amount to over US$15 million and the UNDP co-ordinates with New Zealand to provide development assistance. The trust fund to which New Zealand and Tokelau have been contributing, stood at over US$11 million at the end of 2004; the fund will be built up until 2009. Tokelauans fear that, without external assistance in future, they will be unable to sustain themselves.
In August 2004, the New Zealand government agreed a grant of nearly US$300,000 towards improving boat access to the islands and a study of improvements to telecommunications. It is estimated that Tokelau's shipping resources will be almost doubled by the funding.
External trade
Tokelau has a close link to New Zealand which provides a framework for international trade however Tokelau's isolation (28 hours by sea from its closest neighbour) hampers trade.
Imports
Imports are foodstuffs, building materials and fuel.
Main sources: New Zealand
Exports
Modest exports of stamps, copra and handicrafts.
Main destinations: New Zealand
Agriculture
The soil is thin and infertile and the land does not rise more than five metres above sea level. Rainfall is erratic and crops are subject to drought and storm damage. The main subsistence crops are coconut and breadfruit, supplemented by pulaka, ta'amu, pandanus, bananas, pawpaw, with experimental crops of cucumbers, tomatoes, beans, cabbage and watermelon. Estimated crop production in 2005 included: 3,000 tonnes (t) coconuts, 61t fruit in total, 300t roots and tubers, 390t oilcrops. Estimated livestock production included: 24t meat in total, 20t pig meat, 5t poultry and 8t eggs.
Fishing
Fishing for tuna, bonito, trevally and mullet supplies the main source of protein for the inhabitants. The clam industry is an area with some potential. The typical annual marine fish catch is 200t.
Industry and manufacturing
Main industries include copra production, woodwork and the manufacture of woven and plaited goods such as hats, mats, bags and fans. The copra industry suffers from volatile world prices.
Tourism
Tokelau is not a tourist destination, but it does attract a small number of visitors. Access is only by cargo vessel from Samoa once a month. The main accommodation is a small hotel. There is opportunity for swimming and snorkelling.
Hydrocarbons
Tokelau has no hydrocarbon reserves and imports all of its fuel needs from New Zealand.
Banking and insurance
The nearest commercial banking services are in Apia, Samoa, although savings facilities under the control of the administrative officer have been set up on each atoll.

Time
GMT minus 11 hours

Geography
Tokelau comprises three atolls (Atafu, Nukunonu and Fakaofo) lying about 480km (300 miles) north of Samoa in the Pacific Ocean.

Hemisphere
Southern

Climate
The average mean temperature is 28 degrees Celsius; warmest in May and coolest in July. Rainfall is heavy but irregular. Severe tropical storms are rare, but possible.

Entry requirements
Tokelau is a dependent territory of New Zealand. Passport and visa requirements are the same as for New Zealand.

Visa
Consent to visit Tokelau should be obtained in advance from the Councils of Elders (taupulega). This, together with visas and visitor and cruising permits, can be arranged through the Tokelau Apia Liaison Office in Samoa. Accommodation and a return ticket must be booked before arrival.

Currency advice/regulations
There are no restrictions on the import and export of local or foreign currencies.

Customs
Any firearms must be surrendered until departure.

Prohibited imports
Illegal drugs, plants or plant material, animals or by-products, biological specimens, artifacts made from endangered wildlife and weapons, such as flick knives, are prohibited.

Health (for visitors)

Mandatory precautions
Vaccination certificates required for yellow fever if travelling from infected area.

Advisable precautions
Vaccination for hepatitis A and B, tetanus, typhoid. Rabies is a risk.

Hotels
The Luana Liki Hotel can be found on the atoll of Nukunonu. There are no hotels on Atafu and Fakaofo, although accommodation can be arranged through local families prior to or upon arrival.

Telecommunications
In August 2004, New Zealand announced it would give a grant of US$300,000 some of which will go to fund a study of improvements in telecommunications. Tokelau has one of the smallest telecommunications networks in the world, and all provided by Telecommunications Tokelau Corporation (TeleTok), a community-owned corporation established in 1996.
Basic local, national and international telecommunications services are provided via a satellite link using the Australian Telstra-designed DAMA-Net.

Telephone/fax

Internet/e-mail

Social customs/useful tips
Visitors should be considerate of the island's customs, such as paying due respect to all older persons.
Atafu is officially a dry island. Atafu, Fakaofo and Nukunono have only one co-operative store each. Water is scarce everywhere.

Getting there

Air
There are no air services to Tokelau.

Surface
Water: Tokelau can only be reached by sea. The MV Tokelau carries cargo and passengers between Samoa and Tokelau, supplemented by two other vessels (Samoa Express and Lady Naomi), which ply the route less frequently. Private yachts are the only other means of reaching Tokelau. There are no harbour facilities and only small boats are able to pass through the surrounding reefs; these passes are too shallow for most yachts, which, like the cargo ships, have to anchor outside the reef, although conditions are often unsuitable for such anchorage.

Getting about

National transport
Road: There are no paved roads and few vehicles.
Water: There is a fortnightly catamaran passenger service, which runs between the atolls.

BUSINESS DIRECTORY

The addresses listed below are a selection only. While World of Information makes every endeavour to check these addresses, we cannot guarantee that changes have not been made, especially to telephone numbers and area codes. We would welcome any corrections.

Telephone area codes
The international direct dialling (IDD) code for Tokelau is +690 followed by subscriber's number.

Other useful addresses
Tokelau Apia Liaison Office, PO Box 865, Apia, Samoa (tel: (+685) 20-822; fax: 21-761; e-mail: maka@lesamoa.net).

Tokelau Council of Faipule, PO Box 865, Apia, Samoa (tel: (+685) 20-822; fax: 21-761; e-mail: falani.aukuso@clear.net.nz).

Other news agencies: ABC Pacific Beat: www.radioaustralia.net.au/pacbeat

Pacific Magazine: www.pacificmagazine.net

Internet sites
General information on Tokelau: www.dot.tk

Government of Tokelau: www.tokelau.org.nz

Tonga

COUNTRY PROFILE

Historical profile

Tonga's dynasty goes back to the tenth century.
1899 Under the Tripartite Treaty, Britain gained control of Germany's rights in Tonga, Niue, and the Solomon Islands in exchange for withdrawing its claim to Samoa.
1965 King Taufa'ahau Tupou IV was crowned.
1992 A Pro-Democracy Movement (PDM) emerged.
1994 The PDM formed the first political party, the People's Party (PP).
1996 In the general election, the PP won a majority of those seats open to popular vote.
1999 The Human Rights and Democracy Movement (HRDM) (formerly the Peoples' Party) won five of the popularly elected nine seats in the Legislative Assembly.
2000 Prince 'Ulukalala Lavaka Ata was appointed prime minister by the King.
2001 Tonga was removed from the Organisation for Economic Co-operation and Development (OECD) blacklist of countries acting as unfair tax havens or associated with money laundering after implementing legislative amendments tightening financial regulations.
2002 In parliamentary elections, the HRDM won seven of the nine elected seats.
2003 Changes to the constitution were made, giving greater powers to the King and increasing state control of the media.
2004 Royal Tongan Airlines (RTA) was declared bankrupt, with debts of over US$8.5 million and a lack of funds forced RTA to halt its inter-island services.
2005 In parliamentary elections, the HRDM won seven of the nine seats. The People's Democratic Party (PDP) was formed led by Teisina Fuko.
2006 Feleti Sevele (HRDM) became the first commoner as prime minister, after Prince Ulukalala Lavaka Ata resigned. Prince Tu'ipelehake and his wife Princess Kaimana died in a traffic accident in the US. King Taufa'ahau Tupou IV died. In an initial crowning ceremony Crown Prince Sia'osi Taufa'ahau Manumata'ogo Tuku'aho Tupou (known as Crown Prince Tupouto'a) was sworn in as King Sia'osi (Tongan for George) Tupou V. A pro-democracy demonstration turned into a riot that killed eight people, injured dozens and led to the arrest of over 100 demonstrators and the destruction of the central business district, including an arson attack on a supermarket owned by the prime minister. The King's formal coronation was postponed.
2007 In February a former member of parliament filed a criminal complaint against the prime minister, accusing him of provoking the 2006 riots by calling on government supporters to rally opposite the gathering of pro-democracy demonstrators. Tonga became the 151st member of the WTO in July.
2008 In parliamentary elections held on 23–24 April, the last to be held under the old constitution, pro-democracy candidates won a clean sweep. The HRDM won 28.36 per cent (four seats out of nine), independents won 41.09 per cent (three), the People's Democratic Party 13.97 per cent (two). Turnout was 48 per cent. On 29 July the King announced, three days before his enthronement, that he would relinquish the monarchy's traditional near-absolute power, changing the country's form of state to a constitutional monarchy by 2010, when a new, democratic parliament will be elected.

Political structure

Constitution

The constitution dates from 1875.
Changes to the constitution were made in October 2003, giving greater powers to the King and increasing state control of the media.

Form of state

Hereditary monarchy

The executive

Power lies with the King, who appoints the prime minister and the cabinet, which becomes the Privy Council when presided over by the King. The cabinet is comprised of at least two members each from the nobles and popularly elected blocs.
The prime minister if appointed for life.

National legislature

The Fale Alea (Legislative Assembly) is a unicameral chamber, with 30 members. Nine members are elected by popular vote for a three-year term, nine members are selected by 33 hereditary nobles, and 12 cabinet ministers sit ex officio, including two governors.
The legislative assembly is constituted not to allow political parties to gain power and challenge the monarchy.
In new reforms, to be introduced in 2010, 17 members of parliament will be popularly elected, four will be elected by the nobles and four will be appointed by the King.

KEY FACTS

Official name: Kingdom of Tonga

Head of State: King Sia'osi (George) Tupou V (since Sep 2006)

Head of government: Prime Minister Dr Feleti (Fred) Sevele (HRDM) (since 2005; re-confirmed Mar 2006)

Area: 748 square km (170 islands)

Population: 103,000 (2007)*

Capital: Nuku'alofa (on Tongatapu)

Official language: Tongan

Currency: Tongan dollar or Pa'anga (T$) = 100 seniti

Exchange rate: T$1.80 per US$ (Jul 2008)

GDP per capita: US$2,138 (2007)*

GDP real growth: -3.50% (2007)*

Labour force: 57,340 (2007)*

Unemployment: 13.30% (2004)

Inflation: 5.90% (2007)*

Balance of trade: -US$100.00 million (2006)

Foreign debt: US$81.00 million (2005)

Visitor numbers: 41,000 (2004)

* estimated figure

Last elections
23–24 April 2008 (parliamentary)
Results: Parliamentary: the HRDM won 28.36 per cent (four seats out of nine), independents won 41.09 per cent (three), the People's Democratic Party 13.97 per cent (two). Turnout was 48 per cent.
Next elections
2010 (parliamentary)

Political parties
The constitution does not allow political parties to form a government, but at the discretion of the monarch, some representatives may join the cabinet.
Ruling party
The pro-democracy Human Rights and Democracy Movement (HRDM)
Main opposition party
Political situation
Despite new reforms, which increases the amount of seats given to commoners from nine to 17, for nobles from nine to four and four appointed by the King, scheduled to be introduced in 2010, the government of Tonga shows little sign of willing acceptance. A protest, which turned into a riot in 2007, that killed eight people, injured dozens and led to the arrest of over 100 demonstrators; the destruction of the central business district was extensive, including an arson attack on a supermarket owned by the prime minister with damage estimated at US$200 million and over 350 people charged with rioting; a state of emergency in the capital was imposed, was all sparked by a parliamentary decision to hold elections that wouldn't be using new reforms. Added to which, around two weeks before the elections measures of censorship were introduce.
The Tonga Broadcasting Commission (TBC) was required to censor parliamentary candidates' political broadcasts and TBC broadcasters were prohibited from interviewing candidates on the grounds that they 'lacked the necessary training for objective coverage'. The Tonga Media Council stated that this would 'definitely have an impact'. Nevertheless, the elections results returned a clean sweep for pro-democracy parties.

Population
103,000 (2007)*
Last census: November 1996: 97,784
Population density: 139 inhabitants per square km. Urban population: 33 per cent (1995—2001).
Annual growth rate: 0.6 per cent 1994–2004 (WHO 2006)
Ethnic make-up
The population is mainly of Polynesian descent. Only about 300 inhabitants are of European origin.
Religions
The Wesleyan Methodist church is the major denomination.

Education
In June 2005, New Zealand and the World Bank announced their co-operation in a US$10 million project to improve the quality of education in Tonga.
Literacy rate: 98.5 per cent, adult rate (2003)
Compulsory years: 6 to 14.

Health
Per capita total expenditure on health (2003) was US$300; of which per capita government spending was US$255, at the international dollar rate, (WHO 2006).
In May 2004, a report ranked Tongans the second most obese people in the world. WHO have indicated that this may mask an underlying nutritional deficiency.

KEY INDICATORS — Tonga

	Unit	2003	2004	2005	2006	2007
Population	m	0.10	0.10	0.10	0.10	*0.10
Gross domestic product (GDP)	US$bn	0.24	0.19	0.22	0.22	*0.22
GDP per capita	US$	2,200	2,059	2,109	2,181	*2,138
GDP real growth	%	1.9	–	2.3	1.3	*-3.5
Inflation	%	10.0	11.0	9.7	7.0	*5.9
Industrial output	% change	–	-1.0	10.0	-0.2	–
Agricultural output	% change	–	-3.3	-3.0	-0.5	–
Exports (fob) (goods)	US$m	20,741.0	19,022.0	18,308.0	9,589.0	–
Imports (cif) (goods)	US$m	75,047.0	85,890.0	99,998.0	86,447.0	–
Balance of trade	US$m	-54,305.0	-66,868.0	-81,690.0	-76,858.0	–
Current account	US$m	-10,493.0	-15,164.0	-13,737.0	-15,423.0	*23.0
Total reserves minus gold	US$m	42.6	58.3	46.9	48.0	65.2
Foreign exchange	US$m	39.8	55.3	44.0	44.9	61.9

Life expectancy: 71 years, 2004 (WHO 2006)
Fertility rate/Maternal mortality rate: 3.4 births per woman, 2004 (WHO 2006)
Birth rate/Death rate: 24.5 births and 5.5 deaths per 1,000 people (2003)
Child (under 5 years) mortality rate (per 1,000): 15 per 1,000 live births (World Bank)
Head of population per physician: 0.34 physicians per 1,000 people, 2001 (WHO 2006)

Main cities
Nuku'alofa, on Tongatapu (capital, estimated population 22,779 in 2005).

Languages spoken
English is widely spoken. It is used in education and for administrative purposes.
Official language/s
Tongan

Media
Other news agencies: ABC Pacific Beat: www.radioaustralia.net.au/pacbeat
Pacific Magazine: www.pacificmagazine.net
Press
A constitutional amendment increased the power of the state to control the media with licensing laws and ownership rules. Publications in Tongan include Taimi o Vavau (The Tonga Times) (www.timesoftonga.com).
Weeklies: Weeklies are available in both English and Tongan covering local political and economic news. These include Ko e Kalonikali Tonga/Tonga Chronicle and Tonga Times (bi-weekly) in Tongan and English editions.
Taimi o Tonga is a bi-lingual weekly publication – the government banned Taimi o Tonga in 2003, following a March 2002 sedition charge which was later dropped; its licence was re-approved by the government in October 2004.
Periodicals: In Tongan and English, Matangi Tonga (www.matangitonga.to) and Eva, are quarterly magazines, Tonga Star (www.tongastar.com), is bi-monthly and provides critical analyses of the economic and political affairs. Others include Lao & Hia (fortnightly), Ofa ki Tonga (Christian publication, Ko e Tohi Fanongonongo and Taumu'a Lelei (Catholic publication) monthly.
Broadcasting
The public service broadcaster is the Tonga Broadcasting Commission (TBC) (www.Tonga-broadcasting.com), which does not accept advertising.
Radio: The national network, TBC, has three stations include Radio Tonga 1, Kool 90FM and FM103 (a 24 hour Radio Australia relay), broadcasts are in Tongan and English. Private local radio stations

include Milennium Radio (www.tongatapu.net.to), UCB Pacific (Christian service), Radio 2000 and Radio Nuku'alofa.
Television: TBC operates Television Tonga. There are several private TV stations including the Friendly Island Broadcasting Network, based in Vava'u, Tonfon TV, a pay-to-view service and OBN TV7 a popular channel that has it service suspended by the government in November 2006. A new channel, TelevisionTonga 2, was launched in 2008, broadcasting a range of programmes including sports, films and foreign programmes.
Advertising
Radio and newspaper advertising is accepted in Tongan and English.

Economy
Tonga is a small, open economy dependent on the export of agricultural produce (including coconut products), foreign aid and private remittances from abroad to offset its regular trade deficit.
One of the main problems facing Tonga is job creation. There are 2,000 school-leavers per year, but only 500 find jobs and few can emigrate. Unemployment and underemployment are creating social problems.
The collapse of Royal Tongan Airlines (RTA) in April 2004 had an adverse affect on the whole economy, as the only realistic means of arrival is by air. The collateral damage to tourist facilities and local economies of the outlying islands has resulted in recession for them.
Other areas of possible development include offshore oil, fish and vegetable canneries and coconut-based industries. Offshore banking is growing rapidly. Anti-corruption measures are a central part of the economic reform programme. Agriculture, one of the mainstays of Tonga's economy, picked up in 2003.
The economy will remain heavily dependent on foreign remittances from Tongans working abroad and due to the weakness of the Tongan currency, consumer price inflation will remain high.

External trade
Tonga is a member of the South Pacific Regional Trade and Economic Co-operation Agreement (Sparteca) along with 12 other regional nations, which allows products duty free access by Pacific Island Forum members to Australian and New Zealand markets (subject to the country of origin restrictions). Tonga became a member of the World Trade Organisation in 2005.
Remittances contribute the dominant proportion of foreign earnings. Tourism will grow in importance following an agreement by an international hotelier in 2007 to develop a resort and the growth in visiting cruise ships. Manufacturing and agriculture are underdeveloped while the importance of fishing is growing.
Imports
Main imports are foodstuffs, building materials, machinery and vehicles, fuels and chemicals.
Main sources: New Zealand (33.4 per cent total, 2005), Fiji (26.7 per cent), Australia (10.5 per cent), US (8.4 per cent)
Exports
Main exports are agricultural produce: squash, vanilla beans and root crops and tuna, seaweed and sea slugs.
Main destinations: Japan (41.5 per cent total, 2005), US (33.1 per cent), New Zealand (6.3 per cent)

Agriculture
Agriculture and fishing accounts for around 35 per cent of GDP and employs around half the labour force. The soil is generally fertile, but production can suffer from hurricane damage.
All land is held by the Crown and every adult male Tongan is entitled to a smallholding (alienation of land is forbidden). Two-thirds of the kingdom's families raise their own livestock (pigs and poultry) and subsistence crops of manioc, yams, breadfruit, watermelons, tomatoes, cassava, oranges and capsicum. Coconut, vanilla and bananas are produced for export, as is the tranquiliser ingredient, kava.
Cash crops include squash and vanilla crops and aloe vera, which has become a popular crop among farmers as it has a viable export market and there is a new processing plant in Nuku'alofa.
Estimated crop production in 2005 included: 58,000 tonnes (t) coconuts, 3,500t citrus, 3,700t taro, 130t vanilla, 9,000t cassava, 6,000t sweet potatoes, 4,400t yams, 7,564t oilcrops, 3,000t plantains, 15t coffee, 250t spices, 9,800t fruit in total, 26,550t vegetables in total.
Estimated livestock production included: 2,180t meat in total, 342 beef, 1,496t pig meat, 25t goat meat, 317t poultry, 28t eggs, 370t milk, 12t honey.
Fishing
Fishing provides additional food and export revenue. Seaweed is in big demand, particularly from Japanese buyers.
The typical annual marine fish catch is over 4,000t, plus over 300t of other seafood.
In 2004, the total marine fish catch was 1,213 tonnes and the total crustacean catch was 400 tonnes.
Forestry
Old coconut tree trunks fulfil up to 25 per cent of timber needs. In 2003 forest exports amounted to US$158,000 and imports amounted to US$2.6 million.
Production in 2003 included 2,100 cubic metres (cum) industrial roundwood, 2,009cum sawnwood, 91,000cum wood fuel.

Industry and manufacturing
The industrial sector accounts for 12.7 per cent of GDP and employs approximately 7.0 per cent of the workforce. There is a thriving small-industries centre on a mini-industrial area in Nuku'alofa where most of the more advanced products are made. Annual industrial production is almost US$20 million per annum.
Manufacturing accounts for 8 per cent of GDP and employs 5 per cent of the labour force. The wide range of products includes shoes, saddles, footballs, knitwear, wooden toys, corrugated iron, plastic piping, bicycle assembly, wire netting, paper, paint, biscuits and processed milk, pulp and passion fruit processing, dumper truck bodies and mini-excavators.

Tourism
Tourism is an important economic activity and foreign exchange earner, but still relatively underdeveloped. There is potential for expansion and efforts are being made to upgrade the infrastructure. Several hundred yachts visit the harbour annually, boosting the local economy by an estimated US$500,000 per annum. The main market is New Zealand, followed by Australia and the US.
Air visitor arrivals, which include holiday visitors, those visiting friends and relatives as well as those visiting for business or to attend a conference, rose by 10 per cent in 2003 to a record high of 40,110.
The sector was dealt a heavy blow in 2004 when Royal Tongan Airlines collapsed. This is particularly serious as the only realistic means of arrival is by air.
The Royal Tonga International Hotel opened in October 2007.

Mining
The US Geological Survey has found huge undersea sediment-filled basins that could hold oil deposits near Tonga, the Solomon Islands and Papua New Guinea. German and Russian researchers have discovered copper and zinc deposits off Tonga.

Hydrocarbons
Tonga has no hydrocarbon resources and is entirely dependent on imports from New Zealand. Tonga does not import gas or coal.

Banking and insurance
Main financial centre
Nuku'alofa.

Time
GMT plus 13 hours

Geography
Tonga (also known as the Friendly Islands) comprises 172 islands in the south-western Pacific Ocean, about 650km (400 miles) east of Fiji. The Tonga Islands are divided into three main groups – Tongatapu (southern group) Ha'apai (middle group) and Vava'u (northern group). Only 36 of the islands are permanently inhabited.
All are formed from limestone but with two different geological bases, either an uplifted coral foundation or an overlay of a volcanic base. The maximum height of any volcanic range is 1,033 metres, on Kao. Few islands have rivers or lakes and most rely on wells and rainwater for their supply.
Hemisphere
Southern

Climate
From May–November, temperatures are relatively cool and reach between 11–29 degrees Celsius (C). December–April is the wet season, with temperatures reaching 32°C and with high humidity. Average rainfall is 1,700mm per year, but varies from place to place.

Entry requirements
Passports
Required by all, and must be valid six months from date of entry.
Visa
Tourists and business persons listed at www.tongaconsulate.us/visa/visa4tim.htm l may enter for a period not exceeding 31 days providing the visitor holds onward/return passage and proof of adequate funds.
A one month extension is possible if permission is obtained locally from the principal immigration officer; a fee applies.
Currency advice/regulations
No restrictions on import and export of local and foreign currency.
Travellers cheques are accepted in banks and major hotels; Australian dollars and pounds sterling cheques will avoid additional exchange fees.
Customs
Personal items are duty-free. Imports from some countries may require an import licence or be subject to temporary control.
Prohibited imports
Illegal drugs and firearms. Quarantine is required for all imported live animals and plants.

Health (for visitors)
Mandatory precautions
Vaccination certificate for yellow fever if travelling from an infected area.
Advisable precautions
Inoculations and boosters should be current for tetanus, hepatitis A and typhoid. There may be a need for vaccinations for diphtheria, tuberculosis and hepatitis B. Insect repellent should be worn at all times, especially during the early morning and evening. There is a rabies risk.

Hotels
Information regarding various types of tourist accommodation is available in Nuku'alofa and throughout the islands from the Tonga Visitors' Bureau.

Credit cards
Credit and charge cards are accepted.

Public holidays (national)
Fixed dates
1 Jan (New Year's Day), 25 Apr (Anzac Day), 4 May (Crown Prince's Birthday), 4 Jun (Independence Day), 4 Jul (King Taufa'ahau Tupou IV's Birthday), 4 Nov (Constitution Day), 4 Dec (Tupou I Day), 25–26 Dec (Christmas).
Variable dates
Good Friday and Easter Monday (Mar/Apr).

Working hours
Sunday is widely observed as a day of rest, with work, sports and transport services forbidden.
Banking
Mon–Fri: 0930–1530; Sat: 0900–1200.
Business
Mon–Fri: 0800–1700; Sat: 0800–1200.
Government
Mon–Fri: 0830–1630.
Shops
Mon–Fri: 0800–1700; Sat: 0800–1200.

Telecommunications
Telephone/fax
The telephone system is fully automatic with 24-hour international communications.
Mobile/cell phones
There are GSM 900 service available on many inhabited islands.

Electricity supply
240V AC, with Australian style flat three-pin plugs.

Weights and measures
Metric system

Social customs/useful tips
It is customary to shake hands on meeting and taking leave. Business cards are exchanged after introduction. Appointments should be made in advance. Those meeting for the first time are addressed by their title and family name; Tongans address each other by their first name.
Gratuities are not encouraged or customary. Tongans appreciate modesty in dress, casual attire is recommended for most occasions. Beachware is only acceptable at the beach and not in general public. It is an offence to appear in public without a shirt. Drunkenness is frowned upon; alcohol consumption may be restricted.

Getting there
Air
National airline: Air Fiji has provided international access since Royal Tongan Airlines collapsed in 2004.
International airport/s: Fua'amotu International, Tongatapu (TBU), 15km south-east of Nuku'alofa; bank, duty-free shop and car hire. Taxis and buses available to centre.
Airport tax: International departures include a passenger service charge of T$25; not applicable for transit passengers.
Surface
Water: No regular passenger services to the kingdom, but berths may be available on cruise ships visiting Nuku'alofa and Vava'u.
Main port/s: Nuku'alofa (on Tongatapu), Neiafu (on Vava'u), Pangai (on Lifuka), Ha'apai.

Getting about
National transport
No public transport, shipping or air services operate into, out of, or on Tonga on Sundays.
Air: Airlines of Tonga (partly owned by Air Fiji), a new domestic carrier and Peau 'o Vava'u Airways operate inter-island flights.
Road: Total road network of about 400km with 80–90 per cent paved; over 190km are on Tongatapu.
Buses: Buses serve all parts of Tongatapu from Nuku'alofa.
Water: Various shipping lines operate inter-island ferry services. The principal service leaves Nuku'alofa in the afternoon and arrives the following morning in Ha'apia, at Hafeva then Pangia, then goes on to Vava'u; by mid afternoon it retraces its route back to Nuku'alofa. There is no need for advance bookings, schedules may change at short notice due to weather conditions. Charter yachts are available.
City transport
Taxis: Private taxis are for hire. Fares should be agreed before undertaking a journey.
Car hire
Self-drive or chauffeur-driven cars are available. International or national driving licence must be presented to the Police Traffic Department in Nuku'alofa to obtain local driving licence.
Speed limits of 40kph in country areas and slower through towns are enforced. Driving is on the left.

BUSINESS DIRECTORY
The addresses listed below are a selection only. While World of Information makes every endeavour to check these addresses, we cannot guarantee that changes have not been made, especially

to telephone numbers and area codes. We would welcome any corrections.

Telephone area codes
The international direct dialling (IDD) code for Tonga is +676 followed by subscriber's number.

Useful telephone numbers
Police: 992
Fire: 999
Ambulance: 933

Chambers of Commerce
Tonga Chamber of Commerce, Tungi Arcade, PO Box 1704, Nuku'alofa (tel: 25-168; email: chamber@kalianet.to).

Banking
Bank of Tonga, PO Box 924, Naku'alofa (tel: 23-933; fax: 23-634).

ANZ Bank, PO Box 910; Cnr Salote and Railway Roads, Nuku'alofa (tel: 24-944; fax: 23-870; email: anztonga@anz.com).

MBf Bank Limited, PO Box 3118; Nuku'alofa, Taufa'ahau Rd, Nuku'alofa (tel: 24-600; fax: 24-662; email: mbfbank@kalianet.to).

Tonga Development Bank; PO Box 126; Nuku'alofa, Fatafehi Rd, Nuku'alofa (tel: 23-333; fax: 23-775; email: tdevbank@tdb.to).

Westpac Bank Tonga, PO Box 924; Taufa'ahau Rd, Nuku'alofa, (tel: 23-933; fax: 23-634; email: westpactonga@westpac.com.au).

Central bank
National Reserve Bank of Tonga, Queen Salote Road, PO Box 25, Nuku'alofa, Tonga (tel: 24-057 fax: 24-201; e-mail: nrbt@reservebank.to).

Travel information
Flight information (0630-1930 hours Mon-Sat) (tel: 32-088).

Fua'amotu International Airport, Ministry of Civil Aviation, PO Box 845, Nuku'alofa (tel: 32-001; fax: 32-003).

Tourist information (tel: 32-060).

Peau Vava'u Limited (domestic airline), Taufa'ahau Road, Nuku'alofa (tel: 878-8896; fax: 28-637; email: administration@peauvavau.to).

National tourist organisation offices
Tonga Visitors' Bureau, PO Box 37, Nuku'alofa (tel: 23-507, 21-733; fax: 22-129; internet: www.vacations.tvb.gov.to).

Ministries
Ministry of Civil Aviation, PO Box 845, Nuku'alofa (tel: 32-001; fax: 32-003).

Ministry of Labour, Commerce and Industries, Salote Road, PO Box 110, Nuku'alofa (tel: 23-688; fax: 23-887).

Office of Prime Minister, Ministry of Agriculture, Fisheries and Forestry, Ministry of Marine, Nuku'alofa (tel: 21-300).

Other useful addresses
Asian Development Bank (ADB), South Pacific Regional Mission, La Casa di Andrea, Lini Highway; PO Box 127, Port Vila, Vanuatu (tel: (+678-2) 23-300; fax: (+678-2) 23-183; adbsprm@adb.org; internet: www.adb.org/SPRM).

Immigration Division, Ministry of Foreign Affairs, Government of Tonga, P O Box 352, Nuku'alofa (tel: 26-970, 26-969; fax: 26-971, 23-360).

Tonga Department of Statistics, PO Box 149, Nuku'alofa (email: dept@stats.gov.to; internet: www.spc.int/prism/country/to/stats).

Other news agencies: ABC Pacific Beat: www.radioaustralia.net.au/pacbeat

Pacific Magazine: www.pacificmagazine.net

Internet sites
Government of Tonga: http://pmo.gov.to

Tonga information website: www.tongatapu.net.to

Trinidad and Tobago

KEY FACTS

Official name: Republic of Trinidad and Tobago

Head of State: President George Maxwell Richards (since 2003; re-elected 11 Feb 2008)

Head of government: Prime Minister Patrick Manning (PNM) (since 2001; re-elected 2007)

Ruling party: People's National Movement (PNM) (since 2002 re-relected 2007)

Area: 5,128 square km

Population: 1.30 million (2007)*

Capital: Port-of-Spain

Official language: English

Currency: Trinidad and Tobago dollar (TT$) = 100 cents

Exchange rate: TT$6.21 per US$ (Jul 2008)

GDP per capita: US$15,905 (2007)*

GDP real growth: 5.50% (2007)*

Labour force: 618,000 (2006)

Unemployment: 7.00% (2006)

Inflation: 7.90% (2007)*

Oil production: 154,000 bpd (2007)

Balance of trade: US$3.15 billion (2005)*

Foreign debt: US$2.80 billion (2003)

* estimated figure

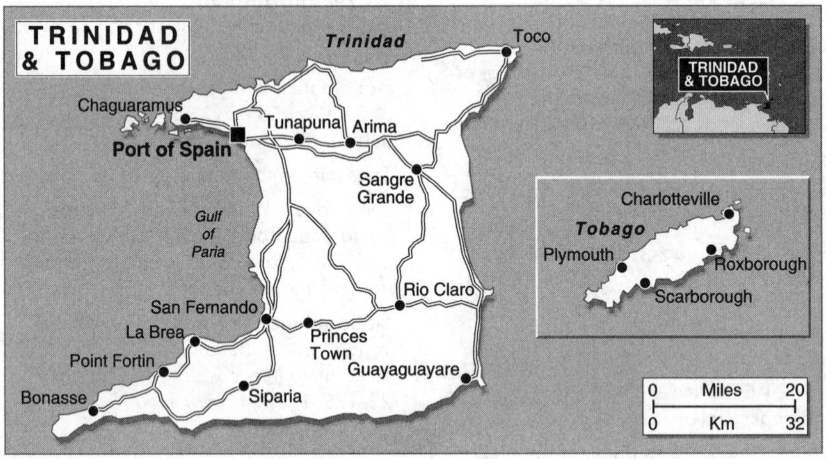

Trinidad's growth dropped in 2007 to 5.5 per cent from the healthy 12.0 per cent of 2006, according to the 2007–2008 edition of *Economic Survey of Latin America and the Caribbean* , published by the Economic Commission for Latin America and the Caribbean (ECLAC). The fall was principally down to a decline in growth in the energy sector, which makes up 43 per cent of GDP. The oil industry had grown by 20.6 per cent in 2006, but by only 4.4 per cent in 2007. Growth in 2006 was fuelled by the introduction of large-scale projects, while 2007 had technical difficulties at one of the major energy plants. As a result crude oil production dropped by 15.9 per cent, exports by 42.4 per cent and refining by 23.3 per cent.

Natural gas production grew by 4.1 per cent in 2007, compared to over 20 per cent in 2006. On top of this, as reported by consultancy firm Ryder Scott in August 2007, there has been no major new gas discovery since 2004. Unless this is addressed, Trinidad and Tobago will run out of gas by 2018. The government has reacted by providing fiscal incentives for new oil and gas exploration.

Non-energy sector growth was 6.7 per cent in 2007. Large increases in the cost of cement and steel suggest that this sector may be overheating. Agriculture declined by 5.9 per cent as workers are attracted to other sectors, and low investment in infrastructure.

Trinidad's flourishing private sector has led to the rapid growth of the middle class, an important stabilising factor in what is, in so many respects, a divided nation. Economic and social mobility are distinguishing characteristics of Trinidad and Tobago life, not matched elsewhere in the Caribbean or indeed in most developing oil economies.

In Trinidad and Tobago, political allegiance has long tended to follow ethnic lines. Afro-Trinidadians, who make up 40 per cent of the population largely support the People's National Movement (PNM), while Indo-Trinidadians, who are also roughly 40 per cent of the population generally support the United National Congress (UNC). After the incumbent UNC and the opposition PNM each won equal numbers of parliamentary seats (18) in the 36 member House of Representatives in the 2001 election, the then president and head of state, A N R Robinson, exercising discretionary powers, appointed Patrick Manning, head of the PNM, as Head of Government. Conflict between the UNC and the PNM inevitably followed, leading to a second round of general elections in 2002. In the 2002 election, the PNM won 20 seats in the House of Representatives and was then able to form a government. In March 2003, George Maxwell Richards succeeded Robinson as president and Head of State. The 5 November 2007 parliamentary elections were again won by the PNM with 26 seats (out of 41). The UNC won 15; turnout was 66 per cent. Patrick Manning retained the office of prime minister.

Vision 2020

A key priority for the PNM Government is its Vision 2020 programme under which Trinidad and Tobago aims to achieve developed country status by the year 2020. The government's development strategy allocates energy sector revenue towards upgrading and modernising economic infrastructure and expanding and diversifying the non-energy economy. The government is investing in technology parks with a view to establishing high tech industries in areas such as telecommunications and software development.

To achieve the goals set out in the Vision 2020 programme, Trinidad and Tobago needs to diversify its economy. This would require improvements in competitiveness and public service delivery of services. The Social and Economic Policy Framework 2006–08 defines as medium-term priorities of the government to expand educational opportunities at all levels, improve access to health and housing, strengthen security, and enhance the environment for private investment, while maintaining a stable macroeconomic policy framework.

Despite its booming economy, Trinidad and Tobago faces serious social problems including high murder rates, drug trafficking and ethnic tension between the two major cultural groups. Oil has given Trinidad and Tobago a healthy economy, with per capita GDP rising from US$6,758 in 2001 to almost US$16,000 in 2007. Although economic growth has remained strong, income distribution is uneven.

Trinidad and Tobago has the bulk of the Caribbean's oil and gas reserves; it is also the region's only significant hydrocarbon exporter. The largest oil producer in Trinidad and Tobago is BP Trinidad and Tobago (BPTT), owned by BP (70 per cent) and Repsol-YPF (30 per cent). BPTT controls some 50 per cent of Trinidad and Tobago's total crude oil production.

Corruption and incompetence

Manning's government has been the subject of allegations of incompetence, occasional corruption and unmasked nepotism. The prime minister came under heavy fire when he appointed his senator wife, Hazal Manning, to the post of minister of education. In addition, five members of his party have been under investigation on charges of administrative malpractice.

In 2006 former prime minister, Basdeo Panday (UNC) was sentenced to two years in prison when he was convicted of financial impropriety, for failing to declare monies held overseas, contrary to parliamentary rule. Subsequently, the Chief Justice, Satnarine Sharma, was accused of misconduct in public office by interfering in the outcome of the case. The matter had to be referred to the UK-based Privy Council for a judicial review. It was decided that the prosecution of Sharma should go forward. In a counter claim the Chief Justice accused the prime minister of attempting to have him removed from office. Panday's conviction resulted in him loosing his parliamentary seat.

On the policy front, the Manning government has been unable to halt the rapidly increasing level of crime in the country, though in fairness this problem has been growing for many years. Other policy measures include a reduction in income tax prompted by increasing oil and gas export revenues that have swelled the treasury and thus reduced the government's fiscal burden. Free university education has also been reintroduced.

Outlook

Trinidad and Tobago is in the fortunate position of having to decide how to spend it, not how to spend as little as possible. How to use the current energy windfall to support long-term economic growth, while at the same time expanding proven gas reserves will be the main challenge. The government is expected to continue to follow the basic elements of the Vision 2020 development plan, which includes continued expansion of public investment financed by energy revenue to fund infrastructure projects and social spending. Current data suggests that GDP growth for 2008 will be in the 5.5–6.0 per cent range.

Risk assessment

Politics	Fair
Economy	Good
Regional stability	Good

COUNTRY PROFILE

Historical profile

1498 Trinidad was sighted by a Spanish expedition led by Christopher Columbus.
1532 The island was colonised by the Spanish.
1595 Spanish colonisers were defeated by an English fleet under Sir Walter Raleigh.
1630s The Dutch settled on Tobago and created sugar plantations.
1763 Trinidad was occupied by France, with Spanish consent.
1781 The French seized Tobago.
1797 Trinidad was seized by the British during the Napoleonic wars.
1802 Trinidad was officially transferred to British sovereignty.
1814 Tobago became a British colony of the Windward Island group.
1834 Slavery was abolished and indentured workers were brought in from India to work on the sugar plantations.

KEY INDICATORS — Trinidad and Tobago

	Unit	2003	2004	2005	2006	2007
Population	m	1.21	1.26	1.29	*1.30	*1.30
Gross domestic product (GDP)	US$bn	10.50	12.54	16.21	18.17	*20.70
GDP per capita	US$	7,355	10,509	12,519	*13,996	*15,905
GDP real growth	%	6.7	9.1	7.9	12.0	*5.5
Inflation	%	3.7	3.7	6.9	8.3	*7.9
Unemployment	%	10.5	8.4	8.0	6.2	–
Oil output	'000 bpd	163.0	155.0	171.0	174.0	154.0
Natural gas output	bn cum	24.8	27.7	29.0	35.0	39.0
Exports (fob) (goods)	US$m	5,256.0	6,671.0	9,161.0	–	–
Imports (cif) (goods)	US$m	3,922.0	4,650.0	6,011.0	–	–
Balance of trade	US$m	1,334.0	2,021.0	3,150.0	–	–
Current account	US$m	1,351.0	1,447.0	3,594.0	4,654.0	*4,171.0
Total reserves minus gold	US$m	2,451.1	3,168.2	4,856.4	6,585.7	6,693.7
Foreign exchange	US$m	2,257.8	2,993.0	4,781.4	6,530.9	6,657.4
Exchange rate	per US$	6.15	6.15	6.31	6.33	6.30

* estimated figure

1889 Tobago was amalgamated with Trinidad and together the islands became a unified British colony.
1945 Universal suffrage was granted.
1956 Eric Williams founded the People's National Movement (PNM).
1958 Trinidad and Tobago became part of the British-sponsored West Indies Federation.
1959 Britain gave Trinidad and Tobago internal self-government with Williams as prime minister.
1962 When Jamaica opted to leave the Federation, Trinidad and Tobago followed, becoming independent within the Commonwealth.
1967 Trinidad and Tobago joined the Organisation of American States (OAS).
1968 Anglophone Caribbean states, including Trinidad and Tobago, formed the Caribbean Free Trade Area (Carifta), which became the Caribbean Community and Common Market (Caricom) in 1973.
1970 A state of emergency was declared after the army mutinied against the minority East Indian population.
1972 The state of emergency was lifted.
1976 On 1 August, Trinidad and Tobago became a republic within the Commonwealth. The PNM won the parliamentary elections. Ellis Clarke, previously the governor general, was sworn in as the country's first president and Eric Williams became prime minister.
1981 Eric Williams died and George Chambers became prime minister.
1986 The PNM lost power in the general election – its first defeat since 1957. The Tobago-based National Alliance for Reconstruction (NAR), led by Arthur Robinson, won a decisive victory.
1987 Noor Hassanali became president.
1990 More than 100 Islamic extremists staged an coup détat, blowing up the police headquarters, seizing parliament and holding Prime Minister Robinson and several senior officials hostage. The uprising was short-lived.
1991 The austere economic programme lost the NAR the general elections. The PNM took over and Patrick Manning became prime minister.
1995 The Asian-dominated United National Congress (UNC) won most seats in the general election and formed a coalition government with the support of the NAR. Basdeo Panday became prime minister.
1997 Arthur N R Robinson was elected president; when prime minister in 1989, he had proposed, to the UN, the commission of the International Criminal Court, which was unauguarted in 2002, to procecute individuals for genocide, crimes against humanity and war crimes.
1999 Trinidad and Tobago restored the death sentence.
2000 The ruling UNC narrowly won the general election with 19 seats (PNM 16 and NAR one). Three UNC members of parliament defected to the opposition and the government fell, in December.
2001 The result of general elections was a tie with the UNC and PNM both winning 18 out of 36 seats. President Robinson appointed Patrick Manning as prime minister, despite the UNC garnering a larger percentage of the vote. With a hung parliament little legislation was carried out.
2002 Prime Minister Manning finally called the third general election in three years in October and his PNM won with 20 seats.
2003 Maxwell Richards was inaugurated as president in March. Caroni, the state-owned sugar company closed with the loss of over 8,000 jobs.
2005 In April, Trinidad became the home of the Caribbean Court of Justice, a final court of appeal intended to replace the UK-based Privy Council.
2006 Former prime minister, Basdeo Panday was sentenced to two years in prison when he was convicted of financial impropriety, for failing to declare monies held overseas, contrary to parliamentary rule. Subsequently, the Chief Justice, Satnarine Sharma, was accused of misconduct in public office by interfering in the outcome of the case. The matter had to be referred to the UK-based Privy Council for a judicial review. It was decided that the prosecution of Sharma should go forward. In a counter claim the Chief Justice accused the prime minister of attempting to have him removed from office. Panday's conviction resulted in him loosing his parliamentary seat. A new, draft constitution was tabled in parliament for public consultation, in August. Proposed changes included an executive president and a diminished role for the prime minister as well as an alternative way of appointing a Chief Justice. The annual rate of inflation rose to 10 per cent in October. New, commercially viable oil and gas deposits were found off Trinidad in November. BWIA, the national airline, stopped operating on 31 December.
2007 Caribbean Airlines began operating on 1 January. A new petrochemical complex will be built on Trinidad, the contract worth US$1.1 billion was given to the German company MAN Ferrostaal in February. On 5 November, in parliamentary elections, the ruling PNM won 26 seats (out of 41) the UNC won 15; turnout was 66 per cent. Patrick Manning retained the office of prime minister.
2008 As the only candidate standing, President George Maxwell Richards was re-elected by an electoral college.

Political structure

Constitution

The constitution was adopted in 1976.

Form of state

Republic

The executive

Executive power is divided between the president, who is the head of state, and the prime minister, who is the head of government.

The president is elected every five years by an electoral college made up of members of both houses of parliament.

The prime minister, who has a cabinet composed of members of parliament, is usually the leader of the majority party in the House of Representatives.

National legislature

The parliament is bicameral. The House of Representatives has 36 members elected by universal suffrage for a five-year term. The Senate consists of 31 members appointed by the president: 16 on the prime minister's advice, six on the advice of the leader of the opposition and nine chosen exclusively by the president.

Legal system

An independent judiciary is guaranteed by the constitution. Foreign investors have the same rights as Trinidad and Tobago citizens.

The Supreme Court is the highest legal body. Civil trials are handled by a single judge in the high court without a jury. Decisions made by the high court can be presented for appeal to the three–judge court of appeal. Court of appeal decisions can be appealed to the regional Caribbean Court of Justice (CCJ), which was inaugurated on 16 April 2005, replacing the privy council in London as the highest court of appeal.

Last elections

14 February 2003 (presidential); 5 November 2007 (parliamentary).

Results: Presidential: Maxwell Richards was elected by the Electoral College comprised of members of both chambers of parliament.

Parliamentary: the People's National Movement (PNM) won 46 per cent of the vote (26 seats out of 41) and the United National Congress (UNC) won 29.8 per cent (15) and Congress of the People 22.7 per cent (but no seats); turnout was 66 per cent.

Next elections

2012 (parliamentary); 2008 (presidential).

Political parties

Ruling party

People's National Movement (PNM) (since 2002 re-relected 2007)

Main opposition party

United National Congress (UNC) (a breakaway faction the Congress of the People formed in 2007).

Population
1.30 million (2007)*
Last census: May 2000: 1,262,366
Population density: 251 inhabitants per square km. Urban population: 74 per cent (1995–2001).
Annual growth rate: 0.4 per cent 1994–2004 (WHO 2006)
Ethnic make-up
Black (43 per cent), East Indian (40 per cent), mixed (14 per cent), white (1 per cent), Chinese (1 per cent).
Religions
Roman Catholics (34 per cent), Hindus (30 per cent), Protestants (19 per cent), Muslims (10 per cent).

Education
Primary schooling lasts for seven years followed by secondary, academic and technical or vocational qualifications. World Bank estimates show that the total primary school enrolment of the relevant age group typically stood at 99 per cent for boys and 98 per cent for girls (including repetition rates) between 1994—2000. The number of pupils per primary school teacher is typically 25. Public expenditure on education typically amounted to 3.6 per cent of annual gross national income between 1994—97.
A new campus of the University of Trinidad and Tobago, costing US$100 million, opened in 2006 including a donation of US$10 million from British Petroleum (BP) towards construction of the university, which was founded as a charitable trust by the government.
Literacy rate: 99 per cent adult rate; 100 per cent youth rate (15–24) (Unesco 2005).
Compulsory years: Five to 11
Pupils per teacher: 25 in primary schools

Health
Per capita total expenditure on health (2003) was US$532; of which per capita government spending was US$201, at the international dollar rate, (WHO 2006).
Improved water sources are available to 86 per cent of the population.
HIV/Aids
The prevalence rate is relatively high, although the number of deaths due to Aids between 2001–03 did not increase significantly, from an estimated 1,500–1,900. There were 29,000 people living with HIV at the end of 2003, of which 700 were children (aged 0–14). Research among young adults (15-24) showed that 95 per cent knew that a healthy–looking person could be HIV positive, and 33 per cent knew of at least two prevention methods and three myths concerning the disease.
HIV prevalence: 0.1 per cent aged 15–49 in 2003 (World Bank)
Life expectancy: 70 years, 2004 (WHO 2006)
Fertility rate/Maternal mortality rate: 1.6 births per woman, 2004 (WHO 2006). Anaemia is common among 53 per cent of pregnant women.
Birth rate/Death rate: 8 deaths and 13 births per 1,000 people (World Bank)
Child (under 5 years) mortality rate (per 1,000): 17 per 1,000 live births (World Bank)

Welfare
Trinidad and Tobago operates social insurance and social assistance systems that were implemented in 1999. The 1999 law ensures state provision for employees, domestic and agricultural workers, but does not cover self-employed workers. Social assistance covers residents aged 65 or older or aged 40 years for those with special needs, based on a means-test.
Old age pensions are available to men aged 60–65 and above with 750 weeks of contribution and compulsory retirement. The state also operates a welfare system for benefits covering sickness, maternity, medical provision for workers and family allowance, including a food subsidy. Medical care is available in public hospitals and health offices and centres for recipients of means tested pensions.
Trinidad and Tobago is experiencing a rise in social problems related to young people, despite the economy's improved performance. Restricted access to the secondary education system and unemployment (which reached 30 per cent for the 15–19 age group in 2001), poverty and reduced family care have contributed to youth involvement in crime and drug abuse.

Main cities
Port of Spain (capital, estimated population 50,479 in 2005), San Fernando (centre of the oil industry) (75,246), Arima (33,539).
Scarborough (main town on Tobago, estimated population (16,807).

Languages spoken
Hindi is commonly spoken within the East Indian community.
Official language/s
English

Media
Press
Dailies: There are three national, daily newspapers, including Daily Express (www.trinidadexpress.com) and Trinidad Guardian (www.guardian.co.tt) and Newsday (www.newsday.co.tt); tabloids include TnT Mirror an important online news outlet Trinidad & Tobago News (www.trinidadandtobagonews.com) and Tobago News (www.thetobagonews.com).
Weeklies: Daily newspapers have weekend editions including Mirror Weekend and The Sunday Punch (politics and satire) plus a magazine The Bomb (politics).
Broadcasting
The state-owned Caribbean New Media Group (CNMG) operates radio and television stations.
Radio: Broadcasts may be in English, Hindi and Creole reflecting the islands ethnic diversity with programme contents produced for a variety of listening tastes. The majority of stations are located on Trinidad. CNMG operates four radio stations, Radio 730 AM, Vibe CT 105, Sandeet 106.1 and the most popular 95.1FM City Talk radio. Other private radio stations include i95.5 FM (www.i955fm.com) with news, WeFM (www.96wefm.com) and Power FM (www.power102fm.com).
Television: The commercial channel, TV6, has the largest audiences with a combination of local and foreign (mostly US) programmes. CNMG has two channels. Other channels include Gayelle (www.gayelletv.com) and NCC TV (www.ncctt.org), which are community TVs. Pay-to-view TV includes Jump TV (www.jumptv.com) and Media Zone (www.mediazone.com).
Advertising
Radio is most popular form of advertising, followed by the print media. There are not regulations governing product advertising beyond trademark use.

Economy
Trinidad and Tobago has traditionally been heavily dependent on the production of oil and natural gas, with its economy significantly influenced by the fluctuations of oil and gas prices. Since the steep rise in global oil prices, the economy has experienced a large energy windfall. According to a report by the Central Bank in 2007, annual GDP growth averaged 8 per cent between 2002–07 and budgets are expected to be around $US8 billion a year until 2012.
Despite these excellent figures the underlining fiscal position has deteriorated with a rapid rise in public spending, 2005–06, in an ambitious public investment programme and a widening non-energy deficit of around 15 per cent of GDP.
Trinidad and Tobago has the highest per capita income in the Caribbean and Latin America at US$12,625 in 2005 – Bermuda, in the Atlantic, notwithstanding.
The country is the only significant exporter of oil and gas of the Caribbean islands. The sector accounts for around 40 per cent of GDP. A heritage and stabilisation fund has been set up whereby 60 per cent of oil and gas revenue in excess of budgeted amounts will be automatically

deposited and only released through parliamentary appropriation. With the energy as a finite resource, a development strategy to strengthen the service sector, particularly tourism has been created.
The service sector already provides the major part of GDP, at 51 per cent. Trinidad and Tobago is a regional centre for the financial services and has the potential for growth in information technology, telecommunications and transport. The industrial sector, including the petrochemical industry, accounts for 48 per cent of GDP, of which manufacturing is 7 per cent, agriculture has a negligible provision, at less than 1 per cent.
The hydrocarbons sector remains one of the most attractive areas for foreign investment. In 2005 Trinidad and Tobago's fourth production module or 'train' came into production, increasing output by almost 50 per cent and producing 4.7 million tonnes per year, making it the world's largest train and Trinidad and Tobago the world's fifth largest exporter of liquefied natural gas (LNG).
The Inter-American Development Bank estimated that in 2006 migrant workers sent some US$110 million to their families in Trinidad and Tobago.

External trade

Trinidad and Tobago is a member of the Caribbean Community and Common Market (Caricom) and operates within the single market (Caribbean Single Market and Economy (CSME)), which became operational on 1 January 2006.
Natural gas has replaced oil as the principal export earner, mainly in the form of liquefied natural gas (LNG). The petrochemical sector produces oil derivatives including methanol, ammonia and urea. Natural gas has allowed the development of smelting iron and aluminium production. Manufacturing is dominated by food processing, tobacco and factory assemblies. Agriculture is losing its importance as the sugar industry has contracted.

Imports

Principal imports include machinery, transport equipment, manufactured goods, foodstuffs and live animals.
Main sources: US (29.5 per cent total, 2006), Brazil (15.6 per cent), Venezuela (6.6 per cent).

Exports

Principal exports include natural gas, crude oil and petroleum derivatives, iron and aluminium, processed food and beverages, tobacco products, sugar, cocoa, coffee, citrus and flowers.
Main destinations: US (59.5 per cent total, 2006), Spain (5.3 per cent), Jamaica (5.2 per cent).

Agriculture

Farming

About 23 per cent of the total land area is farmed. Although there is abundant rainfall, it is unevenly distributed, some areas becoming waterlogged, thereby curtailing production. Only 3 per cent of arable land is irrigated. About 60 per cent of the country's agriculture is in private hands and 40 per cent is controlled by the government.
The farming of major cash crops (sugar, coffee, cocoa and citrus fruits) has slumped owing to labour shortages, diseases and falling export demand. Output declined by 18 per cent in 2003 and by 20.2 per cent in 2004. Sugar production fell by 25.2 per cent in 2003 and by 42.7 per cent in 2004, due partly to poor quality canes and bad weather, as well as structural problems. Unfavourable weather also adversely affected coffee and cocoa production. Citrus production recovered in 2004 after a bad 2003.
The Agricultural Development Bank (ADB), which is primarily government-owned, provides loans to farmers and finances about 85 per cent of the country's agricultural development.
The Agricultural Development Corporation is charged with developing the agricultural sector. The sector is also the subject of an investment incentive programme, involving tax exemptions for approved projects. Other measures include a US$21 million four-year repair and rehabilitation programme for roads and more funding for water management and flood defence systems.
Crop production in 2005 included: 665,000 tonnes (t) sugar cane, 4,800t taro, 3,050t maize, 1,650t yautia, 1,050t cassava, 3,000t rice, 7,000t bananas, 4,650t plantains, 3,670t pulses, 18,000t coconuts, 13,900t citrus fruit, 4,500t pineapples, 2,340t oilcrops, 1,900t tomatoes, 2,200t eggplants, 200t tobacco, 1,350t cocoa beans, 540t green coffee, 68,685t fruit in total, 24,730t vegetables in total. Livestock production included: 61,700t meat in total, 765t beef, 2,925t pig meat, 410t lamb and goat meat, 57,600t poultry, 3,800t eggs, 10,500t milk, 44t honey.

Fishing

The country does not have a large commercial fishing industry, but relies on small private fishermen whose production does not meet domestic demand. The fishing sector is an important local source of food.
In 2004, the total marine fish catch was 9,001 tonnes and the total crustacean catch was 702 tonnes.

Forestry

Forests cover around one-third of the total land area. Deforestation accounted for an average annual loss of 0.9 per cent, equivalent of 2,000 hectares of forest cover, in 1990–2000. The country has a well-developed commercial forests industry, based primarily on the harvesting of teak and Caribbean pine. Some three-quarters of the wood is used for industrial purposes, and the rest is used for fuel and charcoal. It produces modest quantities of industrial round timber and sawn timber. Much of the domestic demand is met by imports of sawn timber, wood-based panels and paper products. Timber imports in 2004 were US$132.2 million, while exports amounted to US$1.7 million.
Timber production in 2004 included 85,856 cubic metre (cum) roundwood, 33,000cum sawnwood, 51,000cum sawlogs and veneer logs, 34,856cum woodfuel.

Industry and manufacturing

Trinidad and Tobago is the most industrialised of the Caribbean islands. The industrial sector typically contributes 44 per cent of GDP, of which manufacturing contributes 8 per cent. Development since the 1970s has centred on heavy export-oriented industries, which are geared towards maximising the country's energy resources.
The principal manufactured products include refined petroleum, petrochemicals, nitrogenous fertilisers, iron, steel, methanol, plastics, sugar, and various import-substitution products. The growth of the petrochemicals sector has helped offset the effects of a decline in the sugar industry.
Manufacturing output increased by 5 per cent in 2003 and by 6.6 per cent in 2004, partly as a result of more favourable international economic conditions, particularly in other CARICOM countries.

Tourism

Trinidad and Tobago is unusual in the Caribbean in not being dependent on tourism. The sector's contribution to GDP for 2005 is forecast at 2.4 per cent. The sector's potential as a means of economic diversification is recognised and the sector is being encouraged and promoted, especially in Tobago, where it is the only industry. Because Trinidad and Tobago is geographically less susceptible to the effects of hurricanes than many of its neighbours, its tourism receives a boost when other Caribbean nations endure harsh weather conditions. The sector provides employment for 34,000 people.
Visitor numbers, which had risen steadily until 2000, fell back for a couple of years due to conditions in the US. Recovery was delayed until 2003, when air arrivals rebounded to a record 409,007 arrivals. Overall figures were nonetheless down,

because cruise ship business collapsed from 104,000 passengers to 55,532, a trend which was repeated in 2004.
Whereas the stay-over market has benefited from increased air capacity, the decline in the cruise ship sector follows a reduction in services to the southern Caribbean.
Infrastructure is improving and air routes to Europe and the US are being expanded. The US is the principal market, followed by the Caribbean and the UK.

Mining
Trinidad and Tobago's mining sector revolves around the petroleum industry. Asphalt and pitch sand are extracted. Other minerals quarried include diorite, limestone, argillite clay and porcelainite. The world's largest supply of natural asphalt is found in La Brea on Trinidad.

Hydrocarbons
Trinidad and Tobago is well-endowed with oil and natural gas resources, which make a major contribution to the economy. The sector accounts for 25 per cent of GDP and 75 per cent of the country's export earnings. Rising world prices since 2003 encouraged increased exploration, reversing a decline in oil production. Trinidad and Tobago has proven reserves of 990 million barrels.
Natural gas has overtaken oil in importance to the economy. Trinidad and Tobago has proven reserves of 740 billion cubic metres. Liquefied natural gas (LNG) output has increased significantly, following completion in 2002 and 2003 of major facilities by the Atlantic LNG Company of Trinidad and Tobago (jointly-owned by the National Gas Company of Trinidad and Tobago, BP-Amoco, British Gas, Suez and Repsol). LNG is exported to the US and Spain for use in electricity, industry and petrochemical production. Trinidad and Tobago is expected to rank as the fifth largest producer of LNG in the world by 2006.
A pipeline from Trinidad and Tobago to Martinique and Guadeloupe, connecting several other Caribbean islands, is being planned.
Trinidad and Tobago does not produce or import coal.

Energy
The electricity sector was previously a state monopoly, but since 1994, a joint venture – Powergen – between the government, Amoco, and the Southern Electric Company of Atlanta, operates at a peak of 700MW but has capacity of 1,178MW.

Banking and insurance
The country has a number of international and domestic commercial banks including Citibank, Royal Bank and Scotia Bank.

Central bank
Central Bank of Trinidad and Tobago
Main financial centre
Port of Spain
Offshore facilities

Time
GMT minus four hours

Geography
Trinidad and Tobago lies in the Caribbean Sea off the eastern coast of Venezuela. Trinidad is the larger of the two islands, Tobago lies 32km north-east of Trinidad. The terrain of Trinidad is principally flat, although three ranges of higher land – peaking at almost 1,000 metres – cross the island from west to east.
Hemisphere
Northern

Climate
The islands have a humid, tropical climate with a rainy season from June to December, and an annual temperature range between 21 and 32 degrees Celsius.

Dress codes
Dress is generally informal and suited to the hot tropical climate. Men generally wear a shirt and tie for business meetings.

Entry requirements
Passports
Required by all, except nationals of Caricom countries, valid for six months beyond date of departure.
Visa
Required by all who are not exempt; a full list can be found at www.visittnt.com/General/things/visa.html. Business travellers should submit an employer's letter stating credentials with the visa application form.
Currency advice/regulations
There are no restrictions on the import of local and foreign currencies, subject to declaration on arrival. Export of local currency is limited to TT$200 and of foreign currency to TT$2,500 per annum.
Prohibited imports
Illegal drugs, weapons and explosives, specific animals (including monkeys and mongoose), animals that have died on transit, products used in relation to certain animals (such as used animal blankets and saddles) as well as dung may not be brought into Trinidad and Tobago.

Health (for visitors)
Mandatory precautions
Yellow fever vaccination certificate if arriving from infected area.
Advisable precautions
Yellow fever, hepatitis A, polio and tetanus vaccinations are advisable. Water precautions should be taken.

Hotels
A range of hotels is available in Trinidad and Tobago. They are generally expensive, although less so in Tobago. A 10 per cent tip is usual. A hotel room tax (in properties of 16 rooms or over) of 10 per cent has replaced value-added tax.
Book well in advance if arriving during Carnival time.

Credit cards
Credit cards are accepted.

Public holidays (national)
Fixed dates
1 Jan (New Year's Day), 30 Mar (Shouter Baptist Liberation Day), 30 May (Indian Arrival Day), 19 Jun (Labour Day), 1 Aug (Emancipation Day), 31 Aug (Independence Day), 24 Sep (Republic Day), 25–26 Dec (Christmas).
Variable dates
Good Friday, Easter Monday, Corpus Christi (May/Jun), Diwali (Hindu, Oct/Nov), Eid al Fitr.

Working hours
Carnival (two-day event immediately preceding Ash Wednesday) is usually taken as an unofficial holiday.
Banking
Mon–Thu: 0800–1400; Fri: 0800–1200, 1500–1700.
Business
Business hours are 0800–1600.
Government
Mon–Fri: 0815–1630.
Shops
Mon–Fri: 0800–1630; Sat: 0800–1200.
Supermarkets stay open later in the evenings and are open all day Saturday. Some open on Sunday. Some close on Thursday afternoon.

Telecommunications
Mobile/cell phones
GSM 850/1900 and 1800 services provide cover for most of the islands.

Electricity supply
Domestic: 115 and 230V AC, 60 cycles.
Industrial: 400V, 60 cycles three-phase.

Weights and measures
Metric system legally in use since 1981, but many traders continue to use the imperial system.

Social customs/useful tips
Both the social and business environment in Trinidad and Tobago are friendly and informal, and it is common to be on a first-name basis with people whom you have met before.

Security
The last major instance of political violence was in 1990, and the islands are generally a safe place to visit. The usual precautions against pickpockets should be taken in crowded areas.

Getting there
Air
National airline: Caribbean Airlines (replacing BWIA in early 2007 as the national airline).
International airport/s: Piarco International, 25km east of Port of Spain, Trinidad; duty-free shop, restaurant, bank, post office, car hire.
Crown Point International, 5km west of Scarborough, Tobago.
Airport tax: TT$100, payable in local currency only.
Surface
Water: There are ferry services to neighbouring islands. Cruise ships call at Port of Spain, Trinidad, and Scarborough, Tobago.
Main port/s: Chaguaramas, Point Lisas, Port of Spain, Point-à-Pierre (Trinidad); Scarborough (Tobago).

Getting about
National transport
Air: Tobago Express flies frequent 'airbridge' services throughout the day between Piarco and Crown Point airports. The journey takes about 25 minutes.
Road: There is an extensive road network of around 8,000km. Major highways run north-south and east-west. Traffic jams are common.
Buses: Cheap and generally crowded.
Water: The two islands are connected by ferries between Port of Spain (Trinidad) and Scarborough (Tobago). There are two fast catamaran ferries, with a journey time of around two hours. A daily car ferry takes over six hours and the passage can be uncomfortable.
City transport
Taxis: Shared, route taxis are widely used. Routes with standard fares operated by passenger cars bearing 'H' registration plates and two-coloured Maxi Taxis (yellow stripe in Port of Spain). Negotiate fares for regular taxis in advance. Limousine service available at airport.
Taxis can be hired by distance, by the hour or by the day.
Car hire
National driving licences of most countries accepted for a period of three months from arrival. Insurance required. Cars drive on left. The maximum speed limit is 80kph on highways.

BUSINESS DIRECTORY

The addresses listed below are a selection only. While World of Information makes every endeavour to check these addresses, we cannot guarantee that changes have not been made, especially to telephone numbers and area codes. We would welcome any corrections.

Telephone area codes
This international direct dialling code for Trinidad and Tobago is +1-868 followed by subscriber's number.

Useful telephone numbers
Police: 999, 623-5191
Fire: 990
Ambulance: 990, 625-3222/3

Chambers of Commerce
American Chamber of Commerce of Trinidad and Tobago, Trinidad Hilton Hotel and Conference Centre, Lady Young Road, Port of Spain (tel: 627-8570; fax: 627-7405; e-mail: inbox@amchamtt.com).

British-Caribbean Chamber of Commerce, Chamber Building, Columbus Circle, West Moorings, PO Box 499, Port of Spain (tel: 637-6966; fax: 637-7427; e-mail: info@britishcaribbean.com).

Caribbean Association of Industry and Commerce, Trinidad Hilton Hotel and Conference Centre, Lady Young Road, PO Box 442, Port of Spain (tel: 623-4830; fax: 623-6116; e-mail: caic@trinidad.net).

Greater Chaguanas Chamber of Industry and Commerce, Kibon House, 1 Endevour Road, Chaguanas (tel/fax: 671-5754; e-mail: admin@chaguanaschamber.com).

South Trinidad Chamber of Industry and Commerce, Cross Crossing Shopping Centre, Lady Hailes Avenue, PO Box 80, San Fernando (tel: 657-9077; fax: 652-5613; e-mail: execoffice@southchamber.com).

Trinidad and Tobago Chamber of Industry and Commerce, Chamber House, Columbus Circle, West Moorings, PO Box 499, Port of Spain (tel: 637-6966; fax: 637-7425; e-mail: chamber@chamber.org.tt).

Banking
Agricultural Development Bank of Trinidad and Tobago, PO Box 154, Port of Spain (tel: 623-6261/5, 625-6539; fax: 624-3087).

Bank of Commerce, PO Box 69, Port of Spain (tel: 627-9325/8; fax: 627-0904).

Bank of Nova Scotia, The Scotia Building, 56–58 Richmond Street, Port of Spain (tel: 625-3566/5222; fax: 623-0256).

Citibank, PO Box 1249, 12 Queen's Park East, Port of Spain (tel: 625-6445/9, 625-1046/9; fax: 624-8131; 625-6820).

Citicorp Merchant Bank, 12 Queen's Park East, Port of Spain (tel: 623-3344; fax: 624-8131).

CLICO Investment Bank, 1 Rust Street, St. Clair, Port of Spain (tel: 628-3628; fax 628-3639).

First Citizens Bank, Park & Henry Streets, Port of Spain (tel: 623-2423, 623-2576/8; fax: 627-5956).

Republic Bank Ltd, PO Box 1153, Port of Spain, Trinidad (tel: 625-3611, 623-0371; fax: 623-0371); Corner Wilson and Castries St, Scarborough, Tobago (tel: 639-2561).

Royal Merchant Bank & Finance Company, 7th Floor, 55 Independence Square, Port of Spain (tel: 625-3511, 624-5212).

The Royal Bank of Trinidad and Tobago, Head Office, Royal Court, 19-21 Park Street, Port of Spain (tel: 623-4291, 625-3764; fax: 624-4866).

Central bank
Central Bank of Trinidad and Tobago, Eric Williams Plaza, Independence Square, PO Box 1250, Port of Spain (tel: 625-4835; fax: 627-4696; e-mail: info@central-bank.org.tt).

Travel information
Caribbean Airlines, Sunjet House, 30 Edward Street, Port of Spain (tel: 669-3000; fax: 669-1680).

Piarco International Airport, Caroni North Bank Road, Piarco (tel: 669-8047; fax: 669-0228).).

Tourist Information Office, Crown Point Airport (tel: 639-0509; fax: 639-3566).

Tourist Information Office, Piarco Airport (tel: 669-5196; fax: 669-6045; e-mail: tourism-info@tdc.co.tt).

Trinidad and Tobago Automobile Association (TAA), 41 Woodford Street, Newtown, Port-of-Spain (tel: 622-7194; fax: 622-9079; e-mail: taa@tstt.net.tt).

Ministry of tourism
Ministry of Tourism, 51-55 Frederick Street, Port of Spain (tel: 624-1403; fax: 625-0437; e-mail: mintourism@tourism.gov.tt).

National tourist organisation offices
Tourism Development Company Ltd, Maritime Centre, 29 Tenth Avenue, Barataria (tel: 675-7034; fax: 675-7432; e-mail : info@tdc.co.tt).

Ministries
Ministry of Communications and Information Technology, Kent House, Long Circular Road, Maraval (tel: 628-1323; fax: 622-4783).

Ministry of Community Empowerment, Autorama Building, El Socorro Road, San Juan (tel: 675-6728; fax: 674-4021).

Ministry of Consumer Affairs, Agostini Compound, 3 Duncan Street, Port of Spain (tel: 623-7741; fax: 625-4737).

Ministry of Culture, Algico Building, Jerningham Avenue, Queen's Park East, Port of Spain (tel: 625-3012; fax: 625-3278).

Ministry of Education, Hayes Street, St Clair (tel: 622-2181; fax: 628-7818).

Ministry of Energy and Energy Industries, Level 9, Riverside Plaza, Corner Besson & Piccadilly Streets, Port of Spain (tel: 623-6708; fax: 623-2726).

Ministry of Enterprise Development, Level 15, Riverside Plaza, Corner Besson & Piccadilly Streets, Port of Spain (tel: 623-2931; fax: 627-8488).

Ministry of the Environment, Level 16, Eric Williams Finance Building, Independence Square, Port of Spain (tel: 627-9700; fax: 625-1585).

Ministry of Finance, Level 8, Eric Williams Finance Building, Independence Square, Port of Spain (tel: 627-9700; 627-6108).

Ministry of Food Production and Marine Resources, PO Box 389, St Clair Circle, St Clair (tel: 622-1221; 622-8202).

Ministry of Foreign Affairs, Knowsley Building, 1 Queen's Park West, Port of Spain (tel: 623-4116; fax: 627-0571).

Ministry of Health, Corner Duncan Street & Independence Square, Port of Spain (tel: 627-0012; fax: 623-9528).

Ministry of Housing and Settlements, NHA Building, Corner George Street & South Quay, Port of Spain (tel: 624-5058; fax: 625-2793).

Ministry of Human Development, Sacred Heart Building, 16-18 Sackville Street, Port of Spain (tel: 624-2000; fax: 625-7003).

Ministry of Infrastructure Development, Corner Richmond & London Streets, Port of Spain (tel: 625-1225; fax: 625-8070).

Ministry of Integrated Planning and Development, Level 14, Eric Williams Finance Building, Independence Square, Port of Spain (tel: 623-4308; fax: 623-8123).

Ministry of Labour, Manpower Development and Industrial Relations, Level 11, Riverside Plaza, Corner Besson & Piccadilly Streets, Port of Spain (tel: 623-4241; fax: 624-4091).

Ministry of Legal Affairs, 72-74 South Quay, Port of Spain (tel: 625-4586; fax: 625-9803).

Ministry of Local Government, Kent House, Long Circular Road, Maraval (tel: 628-1325; fax: 622-7410).

Ministry of National Security, Temple Court, 31-33 Abercromby Street, Port of Spain (tel: 623-2441; fax: 625-3925).

Ministry of Sport, ISSA Nicholas Building, Corner Frederick & Duke Streets, Port of Spain (tel: 625-5622; fax: 623-4507).

Ministry of Transport, Corner Richmond & London Streets, Port of Spain (tel: 625-1225; fax: 627-9886).

Office of The Attorney General, Cabildo Chambers, Corner Sackville & St Vincent Streets, Port of Spain (tel: 623-7010; fax: 625-0470).

Office of The Prime Minister, Whitehall, Maraval Road, Port of Spain (tel: 622-1625; fax: 622-0055).

Other useful addresses

Businessmen's Association of Trinidad and Tobago, PO Box 322, Time Plaza, Room 10, 28 Henry Street, Port of Spain (tel: 623-4568).

Caribbean Employers' Confederation, 43 Dundonald Street, Port of Spain (tel: 625-4723).

Caribbean Industrial Research Institute, O'Meara Industrial Estate, Macoya Road, Trincity, Arima (tel: 662-7161/4; fax: 663-4180).

Export Development Corporation, Export House, 10-14 Phillips Street, PO Box 582, Port of Spain (tel: 623-6022/3; fax: 625-0050).

Industrial Development Corporation, 10-12 Independence Square, PO Box 949, Port of Spain (tel: 623-7291/6, 623-7289).

Management Development Centre, Room 212, Salvatoria Building, PO Box 1301, Port of Spain (tel: 623-4951/3).

National Gas Company of Trinidad and Tobago Limited, Goodrich Bay Road, Point Lisas Industrial Estate, Point Lisas (tel: 636-4662; fax: 679-2384).

Petroleum Company of Trinidad and Tobago Limited (PETROTRIN), Administrative Building, Southern Main Road, Pointe-à-Pierre (tel: 658-4200, 658-4230; fax: 658-1315; e-mail: petroweb@petrotrin.com).

Reinsurance Company of Trinidad and Tobago, Trinre House, 52 Jerningham Avenue, Belmont, PO Box 1087, Port of Spain (tel: 623-6194/6602; fax: 624-4021).

Small Business Association of Trinidad and Tobago, Third Floor, MPU Building, 3 Besson Street, Port of Spain (tel: 624-3666).

Shipping Association of Trinidad and Tobago, Room 12a, 64-66 South Quay, Port of Spain (tel: 623-8570).

Telecommunications Services of Trinidad and Tobago Ltd (TSTT), 54 Frederick Street, PO Box 971, Port of Spain (tel: 624-5756/5703; fax: 625-4585; e-mail: tsttceo@tstt.net.tt).

Tobago House of Assembly, (Foreign Investment Proposals in Tobago), Bacolet Street, Scarborough.

Trinidad and Tobago Development Finance Co Ltd, PO Box 187, 8-10 Cipriani Boulevard, Port of Spain (tel: 623-4665/7, 625-4666/8; fax: 624-3563).

Trinidad and Tobago Embassy (USA), 1708 Massachusetts Avenue, NW, Washington DC (tel: (+1-202) 467-6490; fax: (+1-202) 785-3130; e-mail: embttgo@erols.com).

Trinidad and Tobago Export Trading Company Limited, Level 4 Long Circular Mall, Long Circular Road, St. James (tel: 622-7968; fax: 628-2349).

Trinidad and Tobago Manufacturers' Association, 8 Stanmore Avenue, Port of Spain (tel: 623-1029/31, fax: 623-1031).

Other news agencies: Cananews: www.cananews.net

Internet sites

Government website: http://www.gov.tt

Information on economic trends, investment opportunities, infrastructure, news and events: http://www.tidco.co.tt/

Petroleum Company of Trinidad and Tobago Ltd: http://www.petrotrin.com

Prime Minister's Office: http://www.opm.gov.tt

Statistics Office: http://www.cso.gov.tt

Telecommunications Services of Trinidad and Tobago Ltd: http://www.tstt.net.tt

Trinidad and Tobago company database: http://tradepoint.tidco.co.tt/ttcdbase/

Tristan da Cunha

KEY FACTS

Official name: Tristan da Cunha

Head of State: Head of State: Queen Elizabeth II, represented by Governor Andrew Gurr (since Nov 2007) (resides in St Helena)

Head of government: Administrator David Morley (from Sep 2008)

Area: 98 square km

Population: 284 (2005)*

Capital: Edinburgh of the Seven Seas

Official language: English

Currency: Pound sterling (£) = 100 pence

Exchange rate: £0.50 per US$ (Jul 2008)

GDP per capita: US$2,644 (2003)*

* estimated figure

COUNTRY PROFILE

Historical profile

1506 The island was sighted by the Portuguese admiral, Tristão da Cunha, on his way to the East Indies.

1810 The first settlers arrived but failed to establish a permanent community.

1816 The island was annexed by Britain and a garrison established to provide additional security for Napoleon who was incarcerated on St Helena.

1817 The garrison was withdrawn but Corporal Glass elected to stay on the island with his wife to guard the remaining stores and incidentally founded the community.

The community gradually developed during the nineteenth century and for a time became relatively prosperous with frequent calls by American whalers in the 1850s. The seven families represented four nations – Britain, Holland, US and Italy. With the decline of sail the island became increasingly isolated and impoverished; sometimes several years passed without a ship calling. The only contact with the outside world was provided by an irregular succession of pastors and a very occasional passing ship.

1938 The island became a dependency of St Helena.

1942 A garrison and radio/meteorological station was established.

1949 The island's extreme isolation ended with the establishment of the crawfish industry.

1950s An official currency, the British sterling, was introduced.

1961 The volcano erupted and the community was evacuated, returning some two years later to re-establish the settlement.

1981 The 1981 Nationality Act ended the islanders' British citizenship and right of abode.

1999 The Nationality Act came under review in the UK government's 'Partnership for Prosperity and Progress' White Paper.

2000 Development of the crawfish industry ended Tristan's dependence on the UK and gave the islanders economic confidence.

2001 The island was hit by a hurricane which inflicted considerable damage.

2003 A report said that the fishing industry had considerable potential for development, providing the necessary infrastructure was put in place.

2004 A new, long wheel-based type Land Rover fire engine, provided by the UK government, was delivered. Michael Clancy became governor.

2006 In Jun an oilrig ran aground on a reef on the south-east side of the island during a hurricane while being towed from South Africa to South America, although attempts were made to refloat the rig it was not until December that a foreign tugboat managed to refloat it. By September every home on the island had a telephone line, and a new satellite service allowed for broadband internet access and live television broadcasts.

2007 HMS Nottingham, a destroyer class ship, became the South Atlantic patrol ship to maintain a British maritime presence in the South Atlantic around Ascension Island, St Helena, Tristan da Cunha, South Georgia, the South Sandwich Islands and the Falkland Islands. David Morley became the resident administrator in September and Andrew Gurr became governor in November. In December the resident doctor urgently requested medical supplies to be delivered, due to an outbreak of acute viral induced asthma as medication was running out. No ship was scheduled to visit until January 2008, while a parachute drop was considered, it was the reassigned Royal Fleet Auxiliary ship HMS Gold Rover that finally re-supplied the island on 21 December.

2008 Plans to repair and refurbish the harbour were announced in January. Work to be undertaken by UK Royal Engineers with materials supplied through the European Development Fund and UK government. On 13 February the fish-processing factory burned down, which also destroyed the island's main electricity generator. Stand-by generators were only able to supply a limited amount of electricity to the population, despite delivery of another generator.

Political structure

Tristan is the only inhabited island, although there is a meteorological station on Gough Island, maintained by the South African navy.

Although technically under the jurisdiction of St Helena, the island effectively administers itself independently. Responsibility for it, as a British Overseas Territories, is divided between the British Foreign and Commonwealth Office (FCO) and the Department for International Development (DfID). The post of Minister for Overseas Territories within the FCO was created and an Overseas Territories Consultative Council set up.

In 2002, full British citizenship was granted to the inhabitants of Tristan da Cunha.

Constitution

Form of state

As a British Overseas Territory, Tristan da Cunha is a dependency of St Helena.

The executive

Executive authority is exercised by an administrator appointed by the FCO, who acts as chairman of the Island Council (three nominated members, eight elected, two ex-officio members; one member must be a woman), which meets six times a year. A chief islander is also elected, for three years.

National legislature

The legislative council has 15 members, with 12 non-partisan members elected by popular vote for a four-year term and three ex officio members.

Last elections

June 2005

Next elections

June 2009

Population

284 (2005)*

Last census: December 1988: 296

Population density: 3.0 inhabitants per sq km.

Ethnic make-up

English, Scottish, Irish, Dutch and Italian.

Main cities

Edinburgh of the Seven Seas (capital, estimated population 270 in 2003).

Languages spoken

Official language/s

English

Media

Press

News is published by the online newspaper Tristan Times (www.tristantimes.com) and the South Atlantic Remote Territories Media Association (www.sartma.com).

Broadcasting

The Tristan Broadcasting Service provides local and BBC World Service programmes on 93.5FM.

Radio: Atlantic FM was re-launched on 13 January 2008 providing a limited service with local news and information.

Economy

Tristan's economy is based on crawfish (rock lobster), philatelic sales and by sales of handicrafts which are increasingly imported ready-made.

Since the opening of the first crawfish cannery and freezing plant in 1949, the economy has been transformed from subsistence, sometimes near starvation level, to self-sufficiency.

The annual crawfish catch is limited to 340 tonnes, of which 145 tonnes comes from the main island and the balance from the fisheries around Gough, Nightingale and Inaccessible Islands. An agreement was signed with a New Zealand company for catching Patagonian toothfish. Revenue from the industry more than adequately covers the island's running costs and has allowed reserves to be built up. These provided a buffer against the decline in Far Eastern demand.

Other economic activities are hampered by poor access with only about 60 days per year suitable for landing. A new harbour has improved conditions and permits more regular visits particularly by small yachts. Tristan's fresh water is considered to have special properties and there are plans to develop a mineral water export business.

A hurricane in 2001 devastated the only settlement on the island and severely damaged its prosperity. The British government allocated US$106,000 to help the island recover from the disaster.

Plans for a new jetty are going ahead; this is urgently required for the future development of the tourism and fishing industries.

External trade

Imports

As a UK Overseas Territory, Tristan da Cunha is a member of the European Union's Association of Overseas Countries and Territories (OCT Association), and some EU regulations apply. Foreign earnings are generated by commercial fishing licences, with postage stamps, coins and handicrafts supplied by mail order.

Agriculture

Farming

The cultivated area is estimated at no more than 15 hectares. Potatoes are the main crop. Cattle, sheep and poultry are kept. Each married couple is allowed to graze seven sheep and two cows on settlement land, or any number on the plateau.

Each family grows potatoes on about an acre of ground. Potatoes were first introduced to the island in 1816 when the first settlers arrived and have been grown on the same land each year without rotation; they are easily grown in volcanic soil.

Fishing

Tristan da Cunha's fisheries zone is rich in unique species – rock lobsters, wreckfish, Tristan red scorpion fish, Tristan wrasse and Atlantic amberjack.

The economy is based on crawfish (rock lobster). Fish provide a major source of protein.

Hydrocarbons

Tristan da Cunha does not have any hydrocarbon reserves and relies entirely on imports of refined oil to meet domestic demands.

Time

GMT

Geography

The Tristan da Cunha archipelago comprises the main island as well as Inaccessible and Nightingale Islands. Gough Island, to the south-east, also comes under Tristan administration, combined their surface area is 201 square kilometres.

The main island of Tristan da Cunha is a single, almost circular, volcanic island that lies 2,400km west of Cape Town in the South Atlantic Ocean. It has only one relatively flat area, where the capital is located. Queen Mary's Peak (2,010 metres) is the highest mountain, at the centre of the island.

Inaccessible Island lies 32km west of Tristan; the three Nightingale Islands 35km south; and Gough Island (Diego Alvarez) 350km south, which has a manned weather station with seven personnel.

Hemisphere

Southern

Climate

Tristan da Cunha has a mild, temperate climate. Temperatures range from 3–25 degrees Celsius. The average annual rainfall is 1,700mm.

Entry requirements

Visa

None required, but visitors must have permission of the Island Council and Administrator to land; this is normally granted. All visitors must have onward/return passage, full medical insurance including emergency evacuation and sufficient funds for a visit. A small landing fee is charged.

Hotels

There is no hotel accommodation on the island.

Working hours

Government

Mon—Fri: 0830—1230, 1300—1630.

Telecommunications

Telephone/fax

The Administrator's office and the factory in Tristan have satellite communications by telephone and fax. Faxes are only available to the government.

A public satellite telephone provides an international service through a radio telephone link via Cape Town Radio.

Postal services

The international postal code for Tristan da Cunha is TDCU 1ZZ.

Internet/e-mail

Getting there

Air

Surface

Water: The harbour is too small for ships to berth. Passengers are normally ferried to land in small boats and landing is not guaranteed. Improvements to the harbour are vital to the economy.

The RMS St Helena makes an annual visit. The ship is operated under contract by Andrew Weir Shipping Ltd on behalf of the owners, St Helena Line Ltd.

Premier Fishing operates two fishing boats, the Kelso and the Edinburgh, which make irregular connections between Tristan and Cape Town.

The South African Navy operates the Agulhas to approximate sailing dates, mainly for official personnel.

Yachts call frequently and offer an alternative means of reaching the island, as does the occasional cruise ship.

BUSINESS DIRECTORY

The addresses listed below are a selection only. While World of Information makes every endeavour to check these addresses, we cannot guarantee that changes have not been made, especially to telephone numbers and area codes. We would welcome any corrections.

Telephone area codes

The international direct dialling (IDD) code for Tristan de Cunha is +874 (satellite) followed by subscriber's number.

Travel information

Travel information (for air travel and bookings on the RMS St Helena):

Passenger Services Department, Andrew Weir Shipping Ltd, Dexter House, 2 Royal Mint Court, London EC N4XX, UK (tel: (+44-207) 575-6480; fax: (+44-207) 575-6200; email: reservations@aws.co.uk; internet site: www.aws.co.uk).

Premier Fishing, PO Box 181, Cape Town 8000, South Africa. (tel: (+27-21) 419-0124).

St Helena Line, Andrew Weir Shipping (SA) Pty Ltd, 3rd Floor, BP Centre, Thibault Square, Cape Town, South Africa (tel: (+27-21) 425-1165; fax: (+27-21) 421-7485; email: sthelenaline@mweb.co.za).

Miss Kerry Yon, Solomon and Co plc, Jamestown, St Helena, South Atlantic (tel: (+290) 2523; fax: (+290) 2423; email: solco.shipping@helanta.sh).

Ministries

Administrator's Office, Edinburgh of the Seven Seas (e-mail: hmg@cunha.demon.co.uk).

Other useful addresses

The Tristan Resource Centre, Michael Swales, Denstone College, Uttoxeter, Staffs, UK (tel: (+44)-(0)1538) 703-322).

St Helena Desk Officer, Foreign and Commonwealth Office, Room, King Charles Street, London SW1A 2AH, UK (tel: (+44-(0)207) 270-2695).

Miles Apart (books, maps, videos on South Atlantic Islands), 5 Harraton House, Exning, Newmarket, Suffolk CB8 7HF, UK (tel: (+44-(0)1638) 577-627; fax: (+44-(0)1638) 577-874); 5929 Avon Drive, Bethesda, Maryland 20814, US (tel/fax: (+1-301) 571-8942; email: familycarter@msn.com).

Internet sites

Sartma (South Atlantic Remote Territories Media Association): www.sartma.com

Tristan Times: www.tristantimes.com

Tunisia

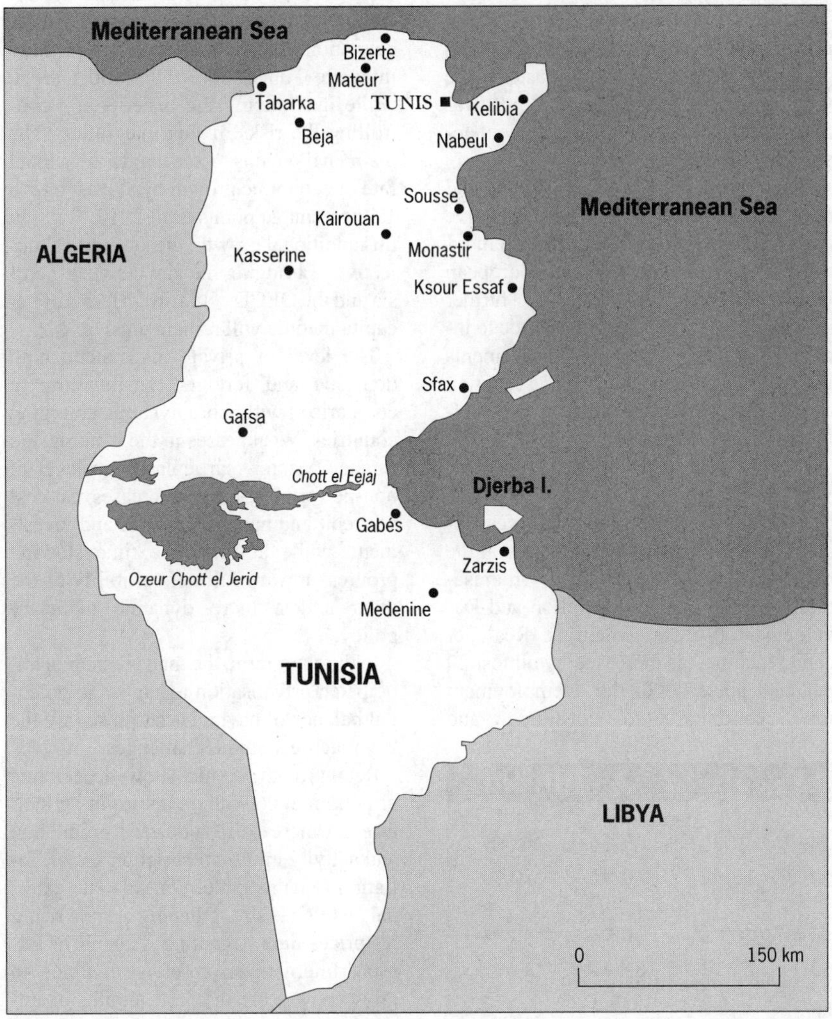

Tunisia generally enjoyed political stability and economic success in 2006. GDP for the year grew by an expected 6 per cent and investors were taking note of the good conditions. In November 2006 an offshore oilfield, funded by Chinese and Swedish investors, was opened up, ultimately planned to produce 150,000 barrels per day (bpd).

Exports also surged in 2006 with the electrical and mechanical sectors performing particularly well. Tourism, long an important component of foreign earnings, also brought in increasing revenues. Reforms continued to go ahead in the banking sector, with an emphasis on good governance and efficiency. State bank Banque du Sud was due to be privatised. Finance officials busied themselves with further liberalisation and privatisation measures designed to encourage overseas investors.

Tunisia's economic and structural problems include persistently high joblessness, a tangled bureaucracy and bloated state sector combined with a rampant black market.

Despite its small size and peaceful relations with the rest of the world, Tunisia did not escape the global fuss surrounding

KEY FACTS

Official name: Jumhuriya at Tunisiya (Republic of Tunisia)

Head of State: President Zine al Abidine Ben Ali (RCD) (since 1987; re-elected to a fourth five-year term Oct 2004)

Head of government: Prime Minister Mohamed Ghannouchi (since 1999)

Ruling party: Rassemblement Constitutionnel Démocratique (RCD) (Democratic Constitutional Rally) (re-elected Oct 2004)

Area: 164,150 square km

Population: 10.92 million (2007)

Capital: Tunis

Official language: Arabic

Currency: Dinar (D) = 1,000 millimes

Exchange rate: D1.16 per US$ (Jul 2008)

GDP per capita: US$3,397 (2007)*

GDP real growth: 6.30% (2007)*

Labour force: 3.50 million (2006)*

Unemployment: 13.90% (2006)

Inflation: 3.10% (2007)

Oil production: 98,000 bpd (2007)

Balance of trade: -US$2.81 billion (2006)

Foreign debt: US$20.60 billion (2006)*

Visitor numbers: 6.55 million (2006)*

* estimated figure

the headscarf. In October 2006 women walking the streets wearing an Islamic style headscarf were arrested in a new crackdown. The headdress, increasing in popularity, is seen as a sectarian and political statement and is frowned upon among public employers. The main opposition in Tunisia is Islamic and stands to benefit from any perceived illiberality towards Muslims.

Secular ideas

Tunisia has long been important in the Mediterranean. Close to vital shipping lanes, it is of some strategic significance. French colonial rule ended in 1956, and in 1957 the republic was proclaimed. Tunisia was led for three decades by Habib Bourguiba, who advanced secular ideas. These included emancipation for women – women's rights in Tunisia are among the most advanced in the Arab world, the abolition of polygamy and compulsory free education. Bourguiba insisted on an anti-Islamic fundamentalist line, but at the same time increased his own powers to become a virtual dictator. After 31 years, he was retired on grounds of senility and Zine al Abidine Ben Ali came into office. He will rule at least until 2014, provided he wins the 2009 election.

Although Tunisia has introduced some press freedoms and has freed a number of political prisoners, human rights groups say the authorities tolerate little dissent. None the less, Tunisia in recent years has sought to defuse rising pressures for a more open political society.

Unlike most of its near neighbours, Tunisia lacks significant hydrocarbon reserves. With no predominant natural resource, Tunisia has developed a diverse economy, with important agricultural, mining, energy, tourism, and manufacturing sectors. Governmental control of economic affairs, while still heavy has gradually lessened over the past decade with increasing privatisation, simplification of the tax structure, and a prudent approach to debt.

Progressive social policies have helped raise living conditions in Tunisia relative to the region. Tunisia is gradually removing barriers to trade with the European Union. Broader privatisation, further liberalisation of the investment code to increase foreign investment, improvements in government efficiency, and reduction of the trade deficit are among the challenges ahead.

Economy

Tunisia has made significant progress toward its objective of catching up with the economic level of the lower-tier Organisation for Economic Co-operation and Development (OECD) countries. Real per capita income has increased by almost 20 per cent since 2000, the unemployment rate continues to decline, and macroeconomic imbalances remain under control owing to the capacity of the fiscal, monetary, and exchange rate policies to respond rapidly to changing conditions and economic shocks.

Although the growing openness of the economy and market-oriented economic policies have had good results thus far, their benefits could be eroded unless reforms are continued and deepened. An acceleration of reforms is necessary to fully integrate Tunisia into the world market, while maximizing the benefits and controlling the risks of this integration. The main challenge is to accelerate the annual rate of economic growth by at least one to 1.5 percentage points until 2010. Without this additional growth, the authorities' objective of bridging the gap between Tunisia and the OECD countries in terms of per capita income will remain elusive.

The level of private investment, both domestic and foreign, remains low in comparison with more dynamic emerging countries. Weaknesses in the banking and financial sector, particularly the level of non-performing loans, increases the cost of credit and hampers growth and investment, while at the same time slowing progress toward full convertibility of the dinar and a more dynamic monetary policy.

In the short term, the management of anticipated privatisation receipts and potential balance of payments surpluses are the key macroeconomic challenges.

Real growth should show accelerated growth in 2006 with an upturn in agriculture, an increase in industrial production and activity in the construction sector. Inflation remains under control. The external position is strengthening despite rising oil prices and stagnating demand in Europe. International reserves continue to grow (now more than 3.5 months of imports of goods and services).

External debt remains high, although it was set to decline considerably in 2006 given the forecast for strong growth and assuming that a portion of privatisation receipts is used to reduce the external debt burden. The fiscal deficit remains under control despite the impact of higher oil prices. The authorities continued to allow retail petroleum prices to rise in 2005 and further increases were provided for in the 2006 budget. Tunisia's budget calculations were based on a crude oil price of US$60 a barrel and called for an increase in the fiscal deficit of one-half percentage point to 3.6 per cent of gross domestic product. Financing of the deficit was to be through domestic bond issues.

KEY INDICATORS — Tunisia

	Unit	2003	2004	2005	2006	2007
Population	m	9.90	9.92	10.92	*10.92	*10.92
Gross domestic product (GDP)	US$bn	25.00	28.18	28.96	30.96	*35.01
GDP per capita	US$	2,186	2,855	2,857	*3,044	*3,397
GDP real growth	%	4.7	5.8	4.0	5.5	*6.3
Inflation	%	2.2	3.6	2.0	4.5	3.1
Unemployment	%	14.7	13.9	14.2	13.9	–
Industrial output	% change	–	4.0	4.2	3.8	–
Agricultural output	% change	–	9.0	3.5	3.0	–
Oil output	'000 bpd	66.0	69.0	74.0	69.0	98.0
Exports (fob) (goods)	US$m	8,027.0	9,679.0	10,488.0	11,488.0	15,148.0
Imports (cif) (goods)	US$m	10,896.0	12,114.0	12,456.0	14,299.0	18,024.0
Balance of trade	US$m	-2,869.0	-2,434.0	-1,969.0	-2,811.0	-2,876.0
Current account	US$m	-738.0	-590.0	-304.0	-630.0	-904.0
Foreign debt	US$bn	13.6	–	19.6	*20.6	–
Total reserves minus gold	US$m	2,945.4	3,935.7	4,372.2	6,773.2	7,850.8
Foreign exchange	US$m	2,912.9	3,895.0	4,341.1	6,741.4	7,816.8
Exchange rate	per US$	1.28	1.25	1.32	1.30	1.23

* estimated figure

Outlook

The medium-term growth target is a 6.2 per cent for the period 2006–10 which the government expects will require an increase in investment of 1.4 percentage points of GDP, an improvement in national savings of 1.8 percentage points of GDP, with a contribution from the government of 1.2 percentage points and a gradual improvement in overall factor productivity. Foreign borrowing should decline in a context of ongoing fiscal consolidation, despite any increased recourse by the private sector to external borrowing to finance its investment.

Risk assessment

Politics	Poor
Economy	Good
Regional stability	Fair

COUNTRY PROFILE

Historical profile

670 The Arabs conquered Carthage.
1207–1574 After the Arab empire collapsed, Tunisia became part of the Moroccan empire of the Almohads before emerging as the independent Hafsid empire.
1600s The Hafsids were defeated by the Ottomans, who developed a system of rule by a local elite descended from the Turks, the Huseinid beys.
1700s Tunisia became a national monarchy.
1881 France invaded Tunisia from Algeria.
1883 Tunisia was declared a French protectorate.
1930s The Néo-Destour nationalist movement developed under Habib Bourguiba, who was jailed by the French.
1942–43 During the Second World War, German and Italian troops, who came to Tunisia to resist allied forces in Algeria, were driven out by the Allies in 1943.
1956 Tunisia gained independence from France under the leadership of Bourguiba.
1957 The monarchy was abolished and the Republic of Tunisia was declared.
1961–63 The Tunisian government demanded the withdrawal of French troops from Bizerte; fighting broke out between French and Tunisian forces. French forces left Bizerte following an agreement between the French and Tunisian governments in 1963.
1974 A constitutional amendment named Bourguiba 'President for Life'.
1981 The first multi-party parliamentary elections since independence were won by President Bourguiba's party in a landslide victory.
1982–85 The headquarters of the Palestinian Liberation Organisation (PLO) relocated from Beirut to Tunis, where it stayed until it moved to the Palestinian autonomous areas (Gaza and Jericho) in 1994. In 1985, Israel raided the headquarters in revenge for a PLO attack on a yacht in Larnaca, Cyprus.
1987 In conformation with the constitution, Prime Minister Zine al Abidine Ben Ali succeeded President Bourguiba, who was declared by his physicians mentally unfit to rule, due to senility.
1989 President Ben Ali won the presidential election; he was re-elected in 1994; both elections were uncontested.
1999 Ben Ali was re-elected for a third term in the first multi-party presidential elections. Mohamed Ghannouchi was appointed prime minister.
2000 Violence erupted in several towns and cities over increasing levels of poverty and price rises in certain basic commodities.
2002 An al Qaeda terrorist bomb killed 19 people in a synagogue in Djerba. A referendum agreed to abolish the three-term limit for incumbent presidents and to raise the age limit of an incumbent president from 70 to 75.
2004 Incumbent Zine al Abidine Ben Ali won 94.5 per cent of the presidential vote, Mohamed Bouchiha won 3.8 per cent. The ruling, Rassemblement Constitutionnel Démocratique (RCD) (Democratic Constitutional Rally), was re-elected with 91.6 per cent of the popular vote.
2005 A second parliamentary legislative body, the Chamber of Advisors, was inaugurated with 112 members, drawn from professional bodies, local officials and presidential appointees.
2006 The hijab, worn by women, was described by the president as 'a sectarian form of dress which had come into Tunisia uninvited', before a ban on its wearing in public places was introduced. The Mouvement des Démocrates Socialistes (MDS) (Movement of Democratic Socialists), the opposition party elected May Eljeribi as the first female political leader in Tunisia.
2007 The law banning the wearing of the hijab in state offices was lifted in October when the Administrative Court of Tunis deemed the law unconstitutional.
2008 In June UK-based Amnesty International accused Tunisia of illegal detentions and torture of suspects under its anti-terrorism policies.

Political structure

Constitution

The constitution was introduced in 1959. Parties must be officially recognised before they can contest elections. Legal opposition parties are guaranteed a minimum of 34 seats in the lower chamber of parliament.
Constitutional amendments in 2002, included unlimited terms of office for the president and a age limit of 75 years and gave the president control over voting procedures and immunity from prosecution for life.
A new second legislative chamber was also agreed.

Form of state

Republic

The executive

Executive power is held by the president, who is also Head of State, elected by universal suffrage for a five-year term. The president sets state policy; he may appoint and dismiss the prime minister. Cabinet members are proposed by the prime minister and endorsed by the president.
The president can serve unlimited terms of office, up to aged 75.

National legislature

The 182-member Chambre des Députés (Chamber of Deputies) is elected for a five-year term by universal adult suffrage. It includes 34 opposition members representing political opposition parties.
The 112-member Chambre des Conseillers (Chamber of Advisors) drawn from professional bodies, local officials and presidential appointees, are appointed for six-year terms.

Legal system

The legal system is based on the French civil law system and Islamic law. There is some judicial review of legislative acts in the Supreme Court.

Last elections

24 October 2004 (presidential and parliamentary)
Results: Presidential: Zine El Abidine Ben Ali was re-elected with 94.5 per cent of the vote, against 3.8 per cent for Mohamed Bouchiha (Popular Unity Party), 1 per cent for Mohamed Ali Halouani (Ettajdid Movement) and 0.8 per cent for Mounir Béji (Social Liberal Party). Turnout was 91.5 per cent.
Parliamentary: ruling RCD, won 152 seats out of 189, the MDS 14, the Popular Unity Party 11, the Unionist Democratic Union seven, the Ettajdid Movement three, and the Social Liberal Party two.

Next elections

2009 (presidential and parliamentary)

Political parties

Ruling party

Rassemblement Constitutionnel Démocratique (RCD) (Democratic Constitutional Rally) (re-elected Oct 2004)

Main opposition party

Mouvement des Démocrates Socialistes (MDS) (Movement of Democratic Socialists)

Population
10.92 million (2007)
Last census: September 2004: 9,932,400
Population density: 60 inhabitants per square km. Urban population: 65 per cent (2005 census); 20 per cent of the total population lives in Tunis.
Annual growth rate: 1.21 per cent (census 2004)
Ethnic make-up
Arab-Berber (98 per cent), European (1 per cent), other (1 per cent).
Religions
Islam is the state religion – observance is strong (98 per cent); Christianity (1 per cent); Jewish (1 per cent) – there has been a Jewish population on the southern island of Djerba for 2,000 years and there remains a small Jewish population in Tunis which is descended from those who fled Spain in the late fifteenth century.

Education
Education is free up to university level – the government typically spends as much as 20 per cent of its revenues on an extensive education system. Primary education begins aged six, and lasts for six years. Secondary education begins at 12 and lasts seven years. Registration at primary schools is 95 per cent (100 per cent of boys and 89 per cent of girls) – the highest in north Africa and the Middle East. A compulsory schooling period of nine years has been introduced, although some children still leave school at the age of 12, especially in rural areas. A stronger emphasis has been placed on scientific and technical subjects at secondary level.
Literacy rate: 73 per cent adult rate; 94 per cent youth rate (15–24) (Unesco 2005).
Compulsory years: Six to 16.
Pupils per teacher: 24 in primary schools.

Health
Per capita total expenditure on health (2003) was US$409; of which per capita government spending was US$187, at the international dollar rate, (WHO 2006).
State healthcare is provided free of charge to the families of employees paying social security contributions and at least nominal tax. This covers an estimated 70 per cent of the population. Free state healthcare is also available for those with any kind of disability. The discrepancy between urban and rural access to healthcare diminished during the 1990s, with most rural areas having at least basic health clinics.
There is a well-developed private healthcare sector, with private clinics in towns providing substantially better facilities than state hospitals. Many healthcare professionals have carried out at least part of their training abroad, mostly in France.
HIV/Aids
HIV prevalence: 0.1 per cent aged 15–49 in 2003 (World Bank)
Life expectancy: 72 years, 2004 (WHO 2006)
Fertility rate/Maternal mortality rate: 1.9 births per woman, 2004 (WHO 2006)
Child (under 5 years) mortality rate (per 1,000): 19 per 1,000 live births; 4 per cent of children under aged five are malnourished (World Bank).
Head of population per physician: 1.34 physicians per 1,000 people, 2004 (WHO 2006)

Welfare
The social security system provides pensions for the elderly and disabled, and welfare for orphans and the needy. A total of 945,500 employees, or 47.7 per cent of the workforce, are insured under the social security system. The scheme is financed by compulsory levies from employers and employees. There are no contributions from the state budget. The main social security institution is the Caisse Nationale de la Sécurité Sociale (CNSS) (National Social Security Organisation), which deals with about 45 per cent of outlay.
There is a graded scheme for contributions. The non-agricultural private sector pays most as a proportion of the employee's salary: 11.5 per cent paid by the employer and 6.25 per cent by the employee. In the public sector, where contributions are made to the Caisse Nationale de Retraite et de Prévoyance Sociale (CNRPS) (National Pension Fund), the employer pays 8 per cent and the employee 7 per cent. State pensions are paid to CNSS and CNRPS contributors.

Main cities
Tunis (capital, estimated population 767,564 in 2005), Sfax (229,622), Ariana (243,152), Ettadhamen (165,973), Sousse (192,008), Kairouan (149,122).

Languages spoken
French is the business language. The number of Tunisians speaking English is increasing.
Official language/s
Arabic

Media
The government maintains control of all media reporting by and encourages widespread self-censorship, with fines and imprisonment as ultimate sanctions.
National news agency: Tunisian News Agency (TAP) (in Arabic, French and English)

Press
The government uses mandatory pre-screening and controls the advertising revenue to censor 'unacceptable' publications. While the constitution guarantees freedom of expression, the Press Code gives allows wide-ranging powers to ban publications.
There are several independent newspapers and magazines, including two opposition party journals.
Dailies: In Arabic, Al Horria (www.tunisieinfo.com/alhorria), published by the RCD political party, Assabah (www.assabah.com.tn) and Essahafa (www.essahafa.info.tn). Publications from Tunis include Al Chourouk (www.alchourouk.com) and el Wahda (www.elwahda.org.tn).
In French, La Presse (www.lapresse.tn), published by the RCD political party, Le Renouveau (www.tunisieinfo.com/LeRenouveau).
Weeklies: In French, Réalités (www.realites.com.tn) and L'Observateur and L'Avenir. In Arabic, Ar Rai and Al Moustaqbal. Others are Dialogue, Al Tariq al Jadid and Al Mauqif. In English, Tunisia News is published in the Maghreb, on Saturdays.
Business: L'Economiste Maghrebin (www.leconomiste.com.tn), is published bi-monthly.
Periodicals: There are many magazines published in Arabic, French and one in Italian.
Broadcasting
Radio: Tunisian Radio (www.radiotunis.com), with four stations covering, news, youth, culture and live transmissions. Other private, commercial stations include Radio Mosaique FM (www.mosaiquefm.net), Jawhara FM (www.jawharafm.net) and the religious station Ezzitouna Radio.
Television: La Télévision Tunisienne (http://tunisiatv.com) is the national, state-run TV with two channels, Tunis 7 and Canal 21. The other domestic channel is Hannibal TV (www.hannibaltv.com.tn), with a wide variety of programmes. Pan-Arab channels are readily received.
News agencies
National news agency: Tunisian News Agency (TAP) (in Arabic, French and English)

Economy
International observers have commended Tunisia on its economic performance in the last few years. It has moved into the middle-income category, one of the few developing countries in the region to have achieved this, with a sovereign credit rating of BBB.

The economy has been under slow and steady reform since the 1980s, when the state had a greater influence and bearing on its direction. However, prudent economic and fiscal planning, coupled with a move towards a market economy, has produced sustained growth since the 1990s.
In 2004, GDP growth was 5.8 per cent, falling to 4.2 per cent in 2005, led by a strengthening service sector and bumper harvests in 2003 and 2004. Tourism and increased consumer confidence stimulated domestic demand and inflation rose to 3.6 per cent in 2004, but fell again in 2005 to 2.0 per cent.
Production in oil and gas has fallen and the government is attempting to diversify the economy further, into industry and manufacturing with a programme to enhance productivity in preparation for global competition.
The agricultural sector, which in official data includes output from fisheries, constituted 12.6 per cent of GDP, compared to 27.8 per cent for industry, of which manufacturing makes up 17.7 per cent and services 59.5 per cent, of which tourism makes up around 10 per cent of GDP. Agriculture has a significant bearing on the economy as it employs just under a quarter of the labour force. Mining makes up approximately 3 per cent of GDP. Remittances from over 600,000 Tunisians living abroad constitute a further important source of foreign exchange.
Tunisia is a country where 55 per cent of the population is aged less than 25 and a growing work force has led to an official unemployment rate of around 14 per cent, however with high underemployment this rate may not reflect the true nature of the jobless market.
The IMF has advised that an early repayment of the external debt would enhance Tunisia's sovereign risk ratings further.
The government is expected to consider tax reforms to remove the current complex system that includes too many exemptions and special regimes.
Tunisia has benefitted from proximity to its principal European market and has managed its economy with enough clear objectives to have achived sustained growth and progress.

External trade

In 2005 the Greater Arab Free Trade Area (Gafta) was ratified by 17 members, including Tunisia, creating an Arab economic bloc. A customs union was established whereby tariffs within Gafta will be reduced by a percentage each year, until none remain. It is also a signatory of the Euro-Mediterranean Partnership agreement, which provides for the introduction of free trade between the EU and 10 Mediterranean countries by 2012.
Despite natural resources including oil, natural gas, phosphate (Tunisia is the world's largest producer) and iron, foreign earnings are dominated by agriculture and tourism. The share of export trade in GDP is 100 per cent.

Imports

Main imports are cotton, machinery and electronic equipment, vehicles and hydrocarbons.
Main sources: France (24.9 per cent total, 2006), Italy (21.8 per cent), Germany (9.4 per cent).

Exports

Main export commodities are textiles, steelwork, phosphate, iron ore, manufactured and leather goods, agricultural products and hydrocarbons.
Main destinations: France (28.8 per cent total, 2006), Italy (20.4 per cent), Germany (8.5 per cent).

Agriculture

Farming

The government sees agriculture as a principal growth sector, however it is heavily influenced by the climate and rainfall. The principal area of cultivation is in north, along the Mediterranean coast, where ancient oil groves are still located. Major projects to augment irrigation are underway, with a new dam and reservoir supplying the north-east region and waterways being installed. In the desert south, oasis crops of dates are famous and exported throughout the region and Europe. In the central area rainfall directly affects crop production as a wet year will produce a good harvest; conversely, a dry year risks desertification.
The sector employs around 30 per cent of the population, and contributed 12.6 per cent of GDP in 2004, showing an annual growth of 9 per cent, a drop on the record 21.5 per cent in 2003 when rains produced bumper harvests.
The agricultural investment code offers tax and other financial advantages, while the Agence de Promotion des Investissements Agricoles (APIA) (Agency for the Promotion of Agricultural Investment) channels investment into agriculture. The Banque Nationale Agricole (BNA) provides medium- and long-term credit for agricultural development projects. Since all suitable land is already being farmed, government policy centres on improving yields through new farming techniques and making the most of water resources.
Rural depopulation, an inequitable land tenure system, drought, soil erosion, overgrazing and low producer prices remain the major constraints to development.
The country's 55 million olive trees occupy one-third of all arable land and olive oil, at over 70 per cent of production it is the most important agricultural export. Tunisia is the world's fourth, after Italy, Spain, Greece, largest exporter. In 2003 the harvest was 1.2 million tonnes about four times the typical annual yeald. Other main products from the sector are flour, sugar, tomato paste, milk, wine and animal feed.
The recent growth in organic food has encouraged over 240 operations, which have attracted international certification accredited to the EU, producing among others, olive oil and dates.
Crop production in 2005 included: 1,833,000 tonnes (t) cereals in total, 1,360,000t wheat, 435,000t barley, 380,000t potatoes, 93,624t pulses, 302,000t citrus fruit, 115,000t grapes, 920,000t tomatoes, 160,855t oilcrops, 3,500t tobacco, 700,000t olives, 16,965t various spices, 57,000t almonds, 125,000t dates, 257,000t chillies and peppers, 18,000t figs, 130,000t apples, 1,058,460t fruit in total, 2,200,430t vegetables in total. The estimated livestock production included: 250,015t meat in total, 55,000t beef, 55,000t lamb, 9,500t goat meat, 120,600t poultry, 83,000t eggs, 960,500t milk, 2,500t honey, 1,000t edible snails, 5,000t cattle hides, 7,800t sheepskins, 8,800t greasy wool.

Fishing

Most seafood production is for domestic consumption and the sector is relatively undeveloped, with extensive small-scale fishing using more traditional methods. The coastal areas around Sfax and the Kerkennah Islands, where the sea is very shallow, are well-known locally for their fishing industry. Total seafood production is typically around 80,000 tonnes, with some 20 per cent of this exported.
Catches typically include sardines, pilchards, tuna and whitefish. However, tuna fishing is diminishing as Mediterranean stocks decline.
In 2004, the total marine fish catch was 89,252 tonnes and the total crustacean catch was 7,308 tonnes.

Forestry

An arid climate, a fast-growing population and animal herds have put Tunisia's already limited woodland areas at serious risk. However efforts to reverse the trend have increased forests by 0.2 per cent or 1,000 hectares.
The oak forests of the country's north provide timber and cork.
Timber imports in 2004 were US$339.2 million, while exports amounted to US$77.4 million.
The estimated production for 2004 included: 2,351,308 cubic metres (cum) roundwood, 213,800cum industrial roundwood, 20,400cum sawnwood,

20,800cum sawlogs and veneers, 75,000cum pulpwood, 104,000cum wood-based panels, 2,137,508cum woodfuel; 203,420 tonnes (t) charcoal, 94,000t paper and paperboard, 38000t printing and writing paper, 10,000t paper pulp, 11,000t recovered paper.

Industry and manufacturing

The industrial sector is based primarily on processing domestic raw materials, notably phosphates and agricultural commodities, and textiles, including clothing and leather products. An industrial restructuring programme launched in the mid-1990s has seen high levels of public investment in upgrading businesses' competitiveness in preparation for the liberalisation of markets and European competition. The present strategy is to target specific types of products where relatively cheap labour, proximity to Europe and government incentives can combine to give Tunisia a price and quality advantage over other exporters. The programme has been particularly successful among small- and medium-sized enterprises (SMEs).

Industrial production increased by 4.2 per cent in 2004 and accounted for 27.8 per cent of GDP, of which manufacturing was 17.7, recording growth at 4.6 per cent.

Tourism

The tourism sector accounts for around 10 per cent of GDP. One of the country's highest net earners of foreign exchange, it has been an increasingly important source of employment. Over 80 per cent of visitors come from EU countries; the strong euro resulted in higher than expected number of tourist arrivals, up by 19 per cent, in 2004.

Tunisia is a member of the Euromed Heritage Programme, a computerisation project, sponsored by the EU, which focusses on cultural tourists of archaeology, arts and history, promoting sites through the internet.

Travel and tourism is expected to provide 8.8 per cent of GDP, employ 16.5 per cent of total employment and attract US$1.1 billion or 17 per cent of all capital investment in 2005. The industry it estimated to earn overall, US$2.9 billion or, 20 per cent of total exports.

The country has a wealth of archaeological sites, traditional habitats and sandy beaches to provide destinations to cater for the wishes of many different holidaymakers.

Mining

The mining sector contributes 3 per cent of GDP and employs 4 per cent of the working population. Tunisia is the world's fifth-largest source of phosphates although the quality of the rock mined is poor. Extraction (largely in Metlaoui and Gafsa) is geared increasingly towards local phosphate processing rather than exporting it in a raw state. Other important minerals mined include iron ore, salt, fluorspar, barytes, lead, zinc, potash and uranium. Foreign investment is being sought by the government for the mining industry.

Hydrocarbons

Total oil reserves stood at 600 million barrels in 2004; at current production levels, these should last until 2013. Although oil reserves are dwindling, production rose by 2.6 per cent from 66,000 barrels per day (bpd) in 2003 to 69,000bpd in 2003. Growing demand for petroleum has meant that Tunisia became a net importer of oil in 2000. The Tunisian government launched a campaign in 2004, to increase exploration levels for oil and gas. The government is investing US$687 in an attempt to attract further investment. Tunisia has one refinery at Bizerte with a small capacity of 32,000 bpd, therefore the country is reliant on imports of refined products to meet demand.

Tunisia's natural gas reserves amounts to over 97 billion cubic metres. To replace declining oil reserves, the government is promoting the natural gas sector; local production typically meets 80 per cent of domestic demand. However demand for natural gas is increasing at a greater pace than production and the government plans for around half of energy consumption to be natural gas in the long term. Tunisia and Libya began planning pipelines in 2003 to supply natural gas to southern and northern Tunisia; completion is expected in 2006.

Tunisia does not produce coal but imports around 118,000 short tonnes of coke per annum.

Energy

The state-owned electricity and gas company, Société Tunisienne de l'Electricité et du Gaz's (STEG) no longer has a monopoly on power generation, although the company retains its monopoly on distribution.

Emphasis is on expanding electricity production and distribution, and stepping up the oil and gas exploration programme. Demand for electricity is growing by 7 per cent per annum and around 95 per cent of homes have access to electricity. The government intends to add around 300MW of generating capacity every two to three years.

General Electric is to build a US$80 million, 240MW gas power station at Bir M'Cherga, bringing the STEG's capacity to 1,810MW, produced by five power stations (three gas and two thermal power).

Financial markets

Stock exchange

Tunisia's small Bourse des Valeurs Mobilières de Tunis (BVMT) (Tunis Stock Exchange) is state run. Large-scale privatisation could bring more foreign portfolio investment and the government offers significant tax incentives to encourage business to join the exchange but expansion has remain doggedly slow. The privatisation programme, mainly limited to small companies, may not spark the interest to heighten growth on the exchange, in the medium-term.

Despite modest investor interest, the Tunisian capital market is still mainly a retail market, with little activity from local financial institutions. While the number of stocks listed remains relatively few, and in the absence of a secondary market, the stock exchange cannot become a major vehicle for raising capital.

Banking and insurance

Tunisia aims to become the regional financial centre and is keen to build on its status as an economy with investment grade status. However, the banking sector is overcrowded, plagued by bad debts and dominated by the public sector.

The government is determined to rationalise the sector and the government has engaged in a modernisation programme, including privatisation and mergers in a process of consolidation in the sector. The capital base of many banks has improved with the injection of government funds into state-owned banks and the restructuring of non-performing loans.

Central bank

Banque Centrale de Tunisie

Main financial centre

Tunis

Time

GMT plus one hour

Geography

Tunisia is in North Africa, between Algeria to its west and Libya to its south-east. The north and eastern borders are a long, 1,148km Mediterranean coastline. It has two islands off its eastern coast, the larger of which, Ile de Jerba, is connected to the mainland by a 6km causeway, and is the location of Tunisia largest international airport. The other is the island chain of the Iles des Kerkennah.

The mainland has three distinct regions from the fertile north where most of the agricultural crops are grown, and where the Atlas mountains run down to the sea. The middle section is semi-arid desert that is wholly dependent on rainfall for its agricultural produce; the Sahara Desert occupies the southern region, and is largely unproductive. There are no major rivers, irrigation is supplied through rainwater dams and bore-holes.

Hemisphere

Northern

Climate

The northern coastal area has a Mediterranean climate with warm, rainy winters (December–March) and hot summers. The southern and inland area is hot and arid. Temperatures in Tunis range from 6–14 degrees Celsius (C) in January to 21–33 degrees C in August. The wettest month is January and the driest is July.

Dress codes

Formal attire should be worn for business meetings. Women should wear clothes that cover most of the body, including shoulders and legs. In the countryside, western dress and customs are rare and dress should be modest.

Entry requirements

Passports

Required by all, and must be valid for at least six months beyond date of visit.

Visa

Required by all; some exceptions, for visits up to three months, include citizens of US, EU, certain Arab, and many Commonwealth countries. A full list of exceptions can be found at www.tunisia.or.jp/ (see under visas). Business travellers from these countries may visit as a tourist without further reference. Those visitors, both business and tourist, not included on the list should contact the nearest Tunisian consulate for information and visa application form at least three weeks before departure.

Currency advice/regulations

Local currency may not be imported or exported; there are no restrictions on the import of foreign currency. However, the re-export of foreign cash is limited to the amount imported, and the re-conversion of dinars into foreign exchange may not exceed 30 per cent of any foreign currency converted during the visit, or D100, whichever is the greater. Therefore all currency forms should be retained.

Traveller's cheques are widely accepted, and preferably made up of sterling, euros or US dollars.

Customs

Personal items are duty-free and gifts to the value of D100 are allowed.

Antiques require an exit permit.

Prohibited imports

Firearms (except for hunting), explosives, narcotics, immoral or obscene publications, walkie-talkies and material deemed subversive.

Health (for visitors)

Mandatory precautions

Yellow fever vaccination certificate required if arriving from an infected area.

Advisable precautions

Immunisation is recommended against diphtheria, hepatitis, polio, tetanus and typhoid. Rabies is present. Water precautions should be taken outside main towns: boil tap water or drink mineral water and wash fresh foods carefully.

Hotels

Classified into five categories; a government hotel tax is added to the bill. Hotel and restaurant staff expect 10 per cent tip.

Credit cards

Major credit and charge cards are widely accepted. ATMs are common in town centres.

Public holidays (national)

Fixed dates

1 Jan (New Year's Day), 20 Mar (Independence Day), 21 Mar (Youth Day), 9 Apr (Martyrs' Day), 1 May (Labour Day), 25 Jul (Republic Day), 13 Aug (Women's Day), 7 Nov (New Era Day/Accession of President Ben Ali).

Many businesses close during July/August.

Variable dates

Eid al Adha (Tabaski, two days), Islamic New Year, Birth of the Prophet, Eid al Fitr (Korité, two days).

Islamic year – 1429 (10 Jan 2008–28 Dec 2008): The Islamic year contains 354 or 355 days, with the result that Muslim feasts advance by 10–12 days against the Gregorian calendar. Dates of feasts vary according to the sighting of the new moon, so canno be forecast exactly.

Working hours

The weekly day of rest is Sunday, not Friday as is usual in the Muslim world. Tunis is virtually closed down during August.

Banking

Mon–Fri (summer): 0730–1130; Mon–Thu (winter): 0800–1100 and 1400–1615, Fri (winter): 0800–1100 and 1300–1600.

Business

Mon–Sat (summer): 0830–1300; Mon–Fri (winter): 0830–1300, 1500–1745.

Government

Mon–Sat (summer): 0830–1300; Mon–Fri (winter): 0830–1300, 1500–1745. Government offices' opening hours may vary by half an hour.

Shops

Mon–Sat (summer): 0800–1200 and 1600–1900; Mon–Sat (winter): 0900–1300 and 1500–1900.

Telecommunications

Mobile/cell phones

There are 900 GSM services available, with coverage throughout the inhabited part of the country.

Electricity supply

220V AC, with round two-pin plugs.

Social customs/useful tips

The legacy of French rule is considerable in the towns and a rather formal attitude to courtesy prevails. Senior government or company officials should be addressed as Monsieur and government ministers as Monsieur le Ministre. It is customary to shake hands on meeting and taking leave. Business cards are exchanged after introduction.

Personal relationships are important in business, and time is usually spent in light conversation, over tea or coffee, before embarking on business matters. Regular visits and personal contact are vital in order to establish a relationship of confidence with agents and customers in Tunisia.

Hospitality is important. It is appropriate to present a small gift in appreciation of hospitality.

Islam affects society at every level. A statute passed in the first year of independence enforced equality of the sexes. Nevertheless, gatherings of men and women are usually separate, the sexes are separated in mosques, and only men may enter a cemetery to attend a funeral.

Alcohol is freely available in towns, although less common in rural areas. Strict Muslims will not drink alcohol, but many Tunisian men do, and it is acceptable for non-Muslim visitors to do so. The minimum drinking age is 21 years.

Mint tea or fresh lemon or orange juice are typical non-alcoholic drinks. It is polite to accept a drink when offered.

During Ramadan visitors are advised not to eat, drink or smoke in public during daylight hours.

Getting there

Air

National airline: Tunisair.

International airport/s: The two largest are Tunis-Carthage (TUN), 8km from the city, with flights by national airlines; travel time to the city is 15–30 minutes and Monastir (MIR) 9km from the city, accepting charter flights. Facilities in both include duty-free shopping, bank, restaurant and car hire.

Smaller airports for regional flights include Djerba-Zarzis (DJE), 9km from Houmek Souk; Sfax-el Maou (SFA), 7km west of city; Tozeur-Nefta (TOE), 10km from city; Tabarka (TBJ), 8km from city. All have duty-free shops and bus and taxi services.

Construction of a new international airport in Enfidha, 75km from Tunis, began in March 2005.

Airport tax: None

Surface

Road: Access is possible by road from Algeria and Libya.

Rail: Access by rail from Algeria.

Water: Passenger traffic comes mostly to Tunis-La Goulette. Regular passenger ferry services operate between Tunis and France, Italy and Malta.
Main port/s: Tunis-La Goulette, Sfax, Bizerte, Gabes, Sousse and Zarzis; of which Tunis-Goulette and Sfax are the largest.

Getting about

National transport

Air: Tuninter operates regular domestic services linking Tunis with Djerba, Monastir, Tozeur and Sfax. The air taxi company, Tunisavia, operates executive flights, from Tunis, throughout the country.
Road: The road network extends for around 19,000km, of which main national roads account for 10,800km. About 57 per cent of the network is paved. There is a 143km motorway between Tunis and Sousse.
Buses: Extensive long-distance services connect all major towns and cities.
Taxis: Long distance taxis (louages) operate between all main towns; these are considered the fastest method of road transport.
Rail: A 2,200km network links the main towns. There are two classes, some with air-conditioned, first-class accommodation. It is recommended purchasing a ticket in advance; those purchased onboard may be charged at a much higher price. It is an advantage to book in advance especially for air-conditioned trains.
Water: There are regular ferries from Sfax-Iles Kerkenna and Djerba island.

City transport

In 2004 work started on a major new bridge linking the Rades and La Goulette suburbs of Tunis, which is scheduled to be finished in 2007. Its capacity, estimated at 3,000 vehicles a day, will greatly increase traffic between northern and southern suburbs of the capital city.
Taxis: Taxis are available in all main towns and are fairly easy to obtain. Louage taxis have fares shared by several passengers. Taxis are metered, a surcharge is added at night.
Buses, trams & metro: The Société Nationale de Transports operates local buses with extensive services operating in all main towns.
The SMLT light-rail metro that runs four lines through Tunis has a focal point for all at Place de la République and connects to national and suburban lines.

Car hire

Cars are easy to hire at airports and hotels but are expensive and the condition of the cars vary. Roads are being improved but local driving is erratic. International driving permit required if national driving licence doesn't include a photograph. Traffic drives on the right; speed limits are 110kph on major highways and 50kph in towns. Permission must be obtained to drive in Saharan areas.

BUSINESS DIRECTORY

The addresses listed below are a selection only. While World of Information makes every endeavour to check these addresses, we cannot guarantee that changes have not been made, especially to telephone numbers and area codes. We would welcome any corrections.

Telephone area codes

The international direct dialling (IDD) code for Tunisia is +216 followed by subscriber's number.

Chambers of Commerce

American-Tunisian Chamber of Commerce and Industry, 10 Avenue Mosbah Jarbou, Rue 7116, El Manar 3, 2092 Tunis (tel: 7188-9780; fax: 7188-9880; e-mail: tacc@tacc.org.tn).

British-Tunisian Chamber of Commerce and Industry, 23 Rue de Jérusalem, 1002 Tunis (tel: 7180-2284; fax: 7180-1535; e-mail: tbcci@gnet.tn).

Cap Bon Chambre de Commerce et d'Industrie, 3 Rue de Fel, Cité Néapolis, PO Box 113, 8000 Nabeul (tel: 7228-7260; fax: 7228-7417; e-mail: cci.capbon@planet.tn).

Central Chambre de Commerce et d'Industrie, Rue Chédly Khaznadar, 4000 Sousse (7322-5044; fax: 7322-4227; e-mail: ccis.sousse@planet.tn).

French-Tunisian Chambre de Commerce et d'Industrie, 39 Rue 8301, 1002 Tunis (tel: 7184-4310; fax: 7184-5962; e-mail: ctfci@planet.tn).

North-Eastern Chambre de Commerce et d'Industrie, 46 Rue Ibn Khaldoun, 7000 Bizerte (tel: 7243-1044; fax: 7243-2379; e-mail: ccine.biz@gnet.tn).

North-Western Chambre de Commerce et d'Industrie, Hedi Chaker Street, 9000 Beja (tel: 7845-6261; fax: 7845-5789; e-mail: ccino.beja@gnet.tn).

Sfar Chambre de Commerce et d'Industrie, 10 Rue Tahar Sfar, PO Box794, 3018 Sfax (tel: 7429-6120; fax: 7429-6121; e-mail:ccis@planet.tn).

South-Eastern Chambre de Commerce et d'Industrie, 202 Avenue Farhat Hached, 6000 Gabes (tel: 7527-4900; fax: 7527-4688; e-mail: csise@gnet.tn).

South-Western Chambre de Commerce et d'Industrie, Rue des Roses, PO Box 46, 2100 Gafsa (tel: 7622-6650; fax: 7622-4150; e-mail: cciso@planet.tn).

Tunis Chambre de Commerce, 1 Rue des Entrepreneurs, 1000 Tunis (tel: 7135-0300; fax:7135-4744; e-mail: ccitunis@planet.tn).

Banking

Alubaf International Bank – Tunis, PO Box 51, Rue 8007 Montplaisir, 1002 Tunis (tel: 7178-3500 fax: 7179-3905, 7178-4343).

Amen Bank, Avenue Mohamed V, 1002 Tunis (tel: 7134-0511; fax: 7134-9909).

Banque Arabe Tuniso–Libyenne de Développment et de Commerce Extérieur, PO Box 102, 25 Avenue Kheireddine Pacha, 1002 Tunis (tel: 7178-1500; fax: 7178-2818).

Banque du Sud, 95 Avenue de la Liberté, 1002 Tunis (tel: 7184-9400, 7179-2400; fax: 7178-2663).

Banque Internationale Arabe de Tunisie SA, PO Box 520, 70-72 Avenue Habib Bourguiba, 1080 Tunis Cedex (tel: 7134-0722/0733, 7125-2655, ; fax: 7134-0680, 7134-7648).

Banque Nationale Agricole, Rue Hedi Nouira, 1001 Tunis (tel: 7183-1000/1200; fax: 7183-5388, 7183-2807).

Société Tunisienne de Banque SA, Rue Hedi Nouira, 1001 Tunis (tel: 7134-0477, 7125-8000; fax: 7134-0009, 7134-8400, 7134-0446).

Tunis International Bank, PO Box 81, 18 Avenue des Etats Unis D'Amerique, 1002 Tunis (tel: 7178-2411; fax: 7178-9970).

Central bank

Banque Centrale de Tunisie, 25 Rue Hédi Nouira, PO Box 777, 1080 Tunis (tel: 7134-0588; fax: 7134-0615; e-mail: boc@bct.gov.tn).

Travel information

Tunisair, Customer Service Unit, Boulevard du 7 Novembre 1987, 2035 L'Ariana, Tunis (tel: 7083-7000 ext: 2572/2510; fax: 7083-6839; reservations tel: 7194-1285; email: resaonline@tunisair.com.tn; internet: www.tunisair.com).

Tunisian Airports Office, Ministère des Technologies de la Communication et du Transport, Direction Générale de l'Aviation Civile, 13 Rue 8006 Montplaisir, 1002 Tunis (tel: 7179-4424; fax: 7179-4227).

Tunisavia, Boulvard de l'Environnement 2035, Aéroport Tunis-Carthage, Tunis (tel: 7128-0555, 7128-0521; email: siege@tunisavia.com.tn; internet: www.tunisavia.com.tn).

National tourist organisation offices

Tunisian National Tourism Office (ONTT), 1 Ave Mohamed V, 1001Tunis (tel: 7134-1077; fax: 7135-0997; email: info@tourismtunisia.com; internet: www.tourismtunisia.com).

Ministries

Ministry of Agriculture, 30 rue Alain Savery, 1002 Tunis Belvedere (tel: 7128-7133).

Ministry of Communication Technologies, Cabinet de Monsieur le Ministre, 3 bis, rue d'Angleterre, 1000 Tunis.

Ministry of Communications, Belvedere du 9 Avril 1938, 1030 Tunis (tel: 7133-6409; fax: 7135-4628).

Ministry of Economic Development, Direction Générale de la Privatisation, Place Ali Zouaoui, 1000 Tunis (tel: 7135-4467; fax: 7135-0975).

Ministry of Defence, 1008 Montfleury, Tunis (tel: 7156-0244).

Ministry of Education, Boulevard Bab Bnat, Tunis (tel: 71263850; fax: 7156-9307).

Ministry of Equipment and Housing, Av H Cherita –Cite Jardin, 1002 Tunis (tel: 7168-1802).

Ministry of Higher Education, 28 rue de Sousse, 1030 Tunis (tel: 7178-2947).

Ministry of Public Health, Bab Saadoun, Tunis (tel: 7126-0727).

Ministry of Vocational Training and Employment, 21 rue de Lybie – Lafayette, 1002 Tunis (tel: 7178-2432).

Other useful addresses

Agence de Promotion de L'Industrie, 63 rue de Syrie, 1002 Tunis-Belvédère (tel: 7179-2144; fax: 7178-2482).

Agricultural Investment Promotion Agency, 62 rue Alain Savary, 1003 Tunis Khadra, Tunis (tel: 7128-8400, 7128-8091; fax: 7178-2353).

American Embassy, Zone Nord-Est des Berges du Lac, Nord de Tunis, 2045, La Goulette, Tunisia (tel: 7110-7000; fax: 7196-2115).

American Express, c/o Carthage Tours, 59 avenue Habib Bourguiba, 1001 Tunis (tel: 7125-4304; fax: 7135-2740).

Arab League, avenue Khéreddine Pacha, Tunis.

British Embassy, 5 Place de la Victoire, 1000 Tunis (tel: 7124-5100, 7124-5324, 7134-1444; fax: 7135-1487; email: britishemb@planet.tn; internet: www.british-emb.intl.tn).

Central Post Office, rue Charles de Gaulle, Tunis.

CEPEX (agency for promotion of Tunisian exports), 28 rue v Gandhi, 1001 Tunis (tel: 7135-0043, 7135-0801; fax: 7135-3683; email: cepexedpuc@attmail.com).

Entreprise Tunisienne D'Activités Petrolières, 27 avenue Khéreddine Pacha, 1002 Tunis (tel: 7178-2288).

Export Promotion Centre, 28 rue Ghandi, 1001 Tunis (tel: 7135-0344; fax: 7135-3683).

Industrial Land Agency, 2 rue Badii Ezzamen, Cité Mahrajéne, 1002 Tunis-Belvédère, El Menza I (tel: 7179-7360, 7180-0616; fax: 7178-2303).

Institut National de Statistique, 27 rue de Liban, Tunis (tel: 7128-2500).

Maghreb Permanent Consultative Committee, 14 rue Yahia ibn Omar, Mutuelleville, Tunis.

National Sanitation Office, 32 rue Hedi Nouira, Tunis (tel: 7170-4000).

National Water Distribution Company, 67 rue Jawarhel ehru, Montfleury (tel: 7149-3700; fax: 7139-0561).

Office du Commerce de Tunisie, avenue Mohammed V, 1002 Tunis (tel: 7128-8673, 7128-8864, 7168-2903; fax: 7178-8974, 7178-4974).

Prime Ministry, Privatisation General Directorate, 4 Rue ibn Nadim Montplaisir, 1002 Tunis (tel: 7128-2467; fax: 7128-1675).

Tunisian Chemical Group, 5–7 rue Khartoum, 1002 Tunis (tel: 7178-4488).

Tunisian Electricity and Gas Company, 38 rue Kemal Ataturk, Tunis (tel: 7134-1311; fax: 7134-9981).

Tunisian Embassy (USA), 1515 Massachusetts Avenue, NW, Washington DC 20005, USA (tel: (+1-202) 862-1850; fax: (+1-202) 862-1858).

Tunisian External Communication Agency, 2 rue d'Algérie, 1001 Tunis (tel: 7165-1999, 7135-0202; fax: 7134-1902).

Union Tunisienne de l'Industrie, du Commerce et de l'Artisanat, 32 rue Charles de Gaulle, Tunis (tel: 7124-3711).

National news agency: Tunisian News Agency (TAP) (in Arabic, French and English)

Address: (tel: 7187-0657; fax: 7188-8999; email: desk.national@email.ati.tn; internet: www.tap.info.tn).

Internet sites

Information on Tunisia: www.tunisiaonline.com

www.investintunisia.tn

www.tunisie.com

Africa Business Network: www.ifc.org/abn

AllAfrica.com: http://allafrica.com

African Development Bank: www.afdb.org

Mbendi AfroPaedia (information on companies, countries, industries and stock exchanges in Africa): http://mbendi.co.za

Radio Tunisia: www.radiotunis.com

KEY FACTS

Official name: Türkiye Cumhuriyeti (Republic of Turkey)

Head of State: President Ahmet Necdet Sezer (since 16 May 2000)

Head of government: Prime Minister Recep Tayyip Erdogan (AKP) (appointed 11 Mar 2003)

Ruling party: Adalet ve Kalkinma Partisi (AKP) (Justice and Development Party) (elected 2002; re-elected July 2007)

Area: 779,452 square km

Population: 74.88 million (2007)

Capital: Ankara

Official language: Turkish

Currency: Yeni Turk Lirasi (New Turkish Lira) (YTL) = 100 kurus

Exchange rate: YTL1.18 per US$ (Jul 2008)

GDP per capita: US$9,629 (2007)

GDP real growth: 4.90% (2007)

Labour force: 24.57 million (2005); (24.7 million 2006)

Unemployment: 9.70% (2007)*

Inflation: 8.70% (2007)

Balance of trade: -US$47.04 billion (2006)

Foreign debt: US$183.40 billion (2006)

Visitor numbers: 18.92 million (2006)*

Annual FDI: US$19.90 billion (2006); (US$16.70 billion Jan–Nov 2007)

* estimated figure

Turkey

Following a prolonged legal standoff in the first half of 2008, in which Turkey's constitutional court had threatened to ban the ruling Adalet ve Kalkinma Partisi (AKP) (Justice and Development Party), like many others, credit rating agency Standard & Poor's breathed a sigh of relief and raised its outlook for Turkey from negative to stable.

In its 2008 survey of Turkey's economy, the Paris based Organisation for Economic Co-operation and Development (OECD) considers that in the past two decades Turkey's economy has successfully shifted to a growth strategy based on open and competitive markets. According to the OECD the recovery from the 2001 crisis introduced an unprecedented period of high growth. Turkey now finds itself in the difficult transition period between a successful exit from post-crisis recovery to a sustainable path of high growth. The main challenges that present themselves during this transition include the need to preserve the gains of fiscal consolidation, notably the prioritisation of expenditure programmes, and to avoid pro-cyclical policies. Also essential is the need to enable monetary policy and inflation targeting to support other policies, in particular structural policies. Finally, there remains the need to reduce the obstacles to formal employment in order to mobilise the productivity potential of the Turkish economy.

However, the OECD is well aware of the fact that achieving this transition is far from trivial, as witnessed by the nervousness of financial markets, increased exchange rate volatility, growing tensions in the economy, as well as a disappointing growth performance since mid-2007. A new, sustainable path of high growth is made difficult by internal as well as external political tensions. Decisive economic reforms will allow Turkey to exploit its comparative advantages and improve its resilience in the face of adverse international shocks.

After a succession of boom and bust cycles in 2001, according to the OECD, a fiscal, monetary and institutional reform package was implemented. Backed by the favourable international environment and by the opening of accession negotiations with the European Union (EU), average growth rates of almost 7 per cent in the period 2002–07 made a welcome beginning to the process of catching up with the OECD average. Large numbers of jobs were created in industry and services amid exits from agriculture, while inflation declined. A primary fiscal surplus of around 6 per cent of GDP was achieved for several years, and public debt was brought down and put on a sustainable path.

As already noted, in early 2008 political tensions arose in the domestic political environment, with a parallel deterioration of conditions in international financial markets. Turkey's interest rates increased significantly, inflation expectations accelerated further above targets, and the growth of Turkey's export markets slowed down. Consumer and business confidence weakened and macroeconomic projections for 2008 and 2009 are the weakest of the post 2001 period.

Shaken by the loss of its Middle Easter empire in the first World War, Turkey became a republic in 1923 and became a secular state during the rule of Kemal Ataturk in the 1920s. Until 1946 it was effectively a one-party state under the People's Republican Party, but free elections in1950 gave victory to the Democrat Party.

It is now one of the largest of the secular Muslim states. Turkey has always been relatively Western-oriented as a nation. Having joined the UN in 1945, Turkey went on to become an integral member of Nato from 1952 onwards. Traditionally a staunch ally of the United States, Turkey still seeks membership of the European Union (EU). In this respect Turkey has been more than patient. It first signed an association agreement with the (then) EEC in1963. Later, an agreement on Turkey's associate membership was signed in November 1970, before most of today's members had signed up. 2006 became an historic year for all the wrong reasons, as more countries appeared to be cooling on the idea of Turkey's full membership. In December 2006 the EU decided to suspend 8 of the 35 chapters on the agenda for Turkey's accession negotiations due to Turkey's failure to open its ports and airports to Cyprus, a necessary requirement to extend Turkey's customs union with the EU to the member states who joined in 2004.

The economy

Turkey has a three-year (from 2005) SDR6.66 billion (US$9.46 billion) Stand-By Arrangement with the International Monetary Fund (IMF). In Ankara in December 2005, the fund's first deputy managing director Anne Krueger said Turkey's economy continued to perform well. That is still largely the case, although at first glance there is something more Central American than European about Turkey's economy. In 2001 the economy actually contracted by a massive 7.5 per cent. Since then gross domestic product (GDP) growth has averaged around 7.00 per cent, registering 4.9 per cent in 2007, its lowest figure since 2001. More worrying are Turkey's inflation figures which are light years away from the European Central Bank and Maastricht Treaty guidelines. In 2006 inflation was 9.6 per cent and in 2007, 8.7 per cent. However, this figure is dramatically down on the 2001–03 average figure of over 40 per cent. The unemployment rate is currently around 10 per cent.

Although manufacturing overtook agriculture in the 1980s as the major contributor to GDP, the Turkish economy still retains a strong rural character with agriculture accounting for around 11 per cent of GDP and 39 per cent of employment. There is a substantial unregistered economy, with estimates of its value ranging from 20 per cent to 50 per cent of economic activity. Tax reforms including personal income tax, VAT, corporate tax and financial intermediation tax, aim to improve efficiency, reduce incentives to remain in the informal economy, and offset the expected structural decline in revenues as interest rates and revenues from financial intermediation taxes decline. Financial sector reforms include adoption of a new banking law, strengthening of banking regulatory and supervisory authority and restructuring and privatisation of state banks.

Elections

Abdullah Gül (AKP) was the sole candidate in the election in parliament in April for a new president. He narrowly failed to secure the necessary minimum 367 votes. The constitutional court invalidated the vote while demonstrators protested against Gül's Islamist background and the army threatened to intervene in defence of the secular constitution. Following the failure to secure an election in a second round in May, Gül withdrew his candidature. The government introduced measures to reform the constitution, including election of the president by the populace, but President Ahmet Necdet Sezer vetoed this amendment. In early general elections in July, called to break the presidential election deadlock, the ruling AKP won 46.76 per cent of the vote (341 seats, out of 550); the CHP won 20.64 per cent (110) and the MHP 14.33 per cent (71); Independents won 28 seats. In August, Abdullah Gül was elected as president.

Outlook

The economic outlook for Turkey is bright. The IMF forecasts continuing growth of 5 per cent. Strong growth will remain a feature of the Turkish economy so long as the country's drive towards full EU membership continues and increased levels of FDI flows in. However, this eventuality is by no means assured. Though Turkey struck a huge blow when it began the accession talks process in 2005, major European players such as Germany and France (particularly since the elections there are won by Mr Sarkozy), remain stringently opposed to Turkish EU membership.

KEY INDICATORS — Turkey

	Unit	2003	2004	2005	2006	2007
Population	m	71.08	72.02	72.97	73.92	74.88
Gross domestic product (GDP)	US$bn	242.23	301.95	362.46	528.69	663.42
GDP per capita	US$	3,313	4,251	5,062	7,760	9,629
GDP real growth	%	5.8	8.0	7.4	6.9	4.9
Inflation	%	24.5	10.6	8.2	9.6	8.7
Unemployment	%	10.5	9.3	10.3	9.9	*9.7
Industrial output	% change	–	8.8	8.6	7.4	–
Agricultural output	% change	–	2.0	5.7	2.9	–
Coal output	mtoe	10.5	10.2	12.8	12.6	31.0
Exports (fob) (goods)	US$m	50,000	66,896	76,887	91,937	115,306
Imports (cif) (goods)	US$m	70,000	90,726	109,658	138,973	162,033
Balance of trade	US$m	-20,000	-23,830	-32,771	-47,036	-46,727
Current account	US$m	-8,040	-15,570	-22,709	-32,193	-37,575
Foreign debt	US$bn	147.3	161.6	170.6	183.4	–
Total reserves minus gold	US$m	33,991.0	35,669.0	50,579.0	60,982.0	73,384.0
Foreign exchange	US$m	33,793.0	35,480.0	50,402.0	60,710.0	73,156.0
Foreign direct investment (FDI)	US$bn	–	9.8	20.2	19.9	–
Exchange rate	per US$	1,526,225	1,466,813	1.43	1.43	1.18

* estimated figure

Risk assessment

Politics	Fair
Economy	Fair
Regional integration	Fair

COUNTRY PROFILE

Historical profile

Founded by Constantine the Great in AD330, Turkey (or Asia Minor as it was known) was for more than 1,000 years the heartland of the Eastern Roman (Byzantine) empire. From the eleventh century, invasions from Central Asia led to the Islamic Turkification of the region, headed by the Ottomans, a name derived from their fourteenth century leader Osman Gazi, who had masterminded the comprehensive defeat of the Byzantines at the Battle of Baphaeon in 1301. The modern republic was established in the 1920s by nationalist leader Kemal Atatürk.

1453 The Ottomans gradually expanded their areas of territorial control, creating the Ottoman empire.

1500s–1800s The Ottoman empire attempted to widen its territorial control into the Mediterranean and Central Europe. This led to conflicts with the major European powers, including the Habsburgs and the Russians. Successive wars eventually undermined the Ottoman empire.

1914–18 Turkey fought in the First World War on the side of the Germans. The majority of Ottoman possessions came under British or French control after the War.

1920–22 Mustafa Kemal, renamed Atatürk (Father of all the Turks) in 1934, led the country in the War of National Liberation, following the dismemberment of the Ottoman empire by the entente powers at the end of the First World War.

1923 The Republic of Turkey was established; the independence of the Turkish state was recognised by the Treaty of Lausanne. Atatürk was elected as the Republic's first president. Sweeping changes were made in all areas – legal, political, social and economic. The Islamic legal codes were replaced by Western ones. Turkey is the only Muslim country where the principle of secularism is written into the constitution.

1925 Turkey adopted the Gregorian calendar. The fez (a conical, brimless hat), considered to be a sign of Ottoman backwardness, was prohibited.

1928 Islam ceased to by the State religion. The Arabic script was replaced by the Latin alphabet.

1930 Constantinople was officially renamed Istanbul.

1934 Women were given the vote.

1938 Atatürk died and was succeeded by Ismet Inonu.

1945 President Inonu kept Turkey out of the Second World War, except for the last four months, when it fought on the side of the Allies against Germany. Turkey joined the UN.

1950 The first open multi-party elections were won by the Democratic Party.

1952 Turkey joined NATO.

1960 The government was overthrown by a military coup.

1961 A constitution was approved by referendum, establishing a two-chamber parliament. Elections were held and civilian rule was restored.

1963 An agreement was signed with the European Economic Community (EEC).

1965 Suleyman Demirel became prime minister (he went on to occupy this office seven times).

1971 After a wave of strikes and unrest, there was a period of military supervision of government.

1973 Return to civilian rule.

1974 Turkey invaded northern Cyprus and 37 per cent of the island came under Turkish control, enforcing partition between north and south.

1978 The US lifted the trade embargo it had imposed on Turkey after the 1974 invasion.

1980 A military coup followed civil unrest and martial law was declared throughout the country.

1981 All political parties were disbanded.

1982 A new constitution was approved by referendum. It created a seven-year presidency and reduced parliament to a single house.

1983 New political parties were allowed, subject to strict rules. Turgut Ozal became president.

Northern Cyprus officially declared its independence as the Kuzey Kýbrýs Türk Cumhuriyeti (KKTC) (Turkish Republic of Northern Cyprus) and introduced its own government and legal system. The independence move was rejected by the international community and only Turkey recognised it as a state.

1984 The Kurdistan Workers' Party (PKK) launched a separatist guerrilla war in the south-east.

1987 Martial law ended, enabling Turkey to become a full and active member of the Organisation of Economic Co-operation and Development (OECD), in addition to becoming an associate member of the EEC.

1990 Turkey allowed the use of its bases for the launch of air strikes against Iraq by the US-led coalition in the war to drive Iraqi forces out of Kuwait.

1992 In an anti-PKK operation, Turkish troops entered Kurdish safe havens in Iraq. Turkey joined the Black Sea alliance.

1993 Following the death of Turgut Ozal, Süleyman Demirel became president. Tansu Ciller was appointed as Turkey's first female prime minister. The PKK declared a unilateral cease-fire in March but by July it had broken down.

1995 Turkey launched a major military offensive against the Kurds in northern Iraq. The Ciller coalition collapsed. Although the pro-Islamist Welfare Party (RP) won the elections, it lacked support to form a government. Two major centre-right parties formed an anti-Islamist coalition. Turkey entered the EU customs union.

1996 The centre-right coalition fell and Necmettin Erbakan was appointed prime minister, heading the first pro-Islamic government since 1923.

1997 The Erbakan coalition government collapsed and Mesut Yilmaz was appointed prime minister.

1998 Corruption allegations forced out the Yilmaz government and Bülent Ecevit was appointed prime minister.

1999 The PKK leader, Abdullah Ocalan, captured in Kenya, received a death sentence, later commuted to life imprisonment. Two earthquakes in the Izmit region killed over 17,000 people.

2000 After the failure of a move to change the constitution to allow Süleyman Demirel to stay in office, Ahmet Necdet Sezer was elected president.

2001 Parliament voted to change the constitution to bring it closer to the constitutions in EU countries.

2002 To meet EU conditions on opening membership talks, parliament voted for wide reforms. The Islamist Adalet ve Kalkinma Partisi (AKP) (Justice and Development Party) won a landslide victory in parliamentary elections. Abdullah Gül became prime minister. Constitutional changes allowed the AKP leader, previously disbarred from public office due to a criminal conviction, Recep Tayyip Erdogan, to run for parliament.

2003 Recep Tayyip Erdogan was appointed prime minister. Parliament adopted a package of human rights reforms including freedom of speech, giving the Kurdish language some rights and reducing the political role of the military.

2004 EU leaders agreed to open talks with Turkey's EU accession after Turkey agreed to recognise Cyprus as an EU member. The death penalty was banned.

2005 The new Turkish lira, Yeni Turk Lirasi (YTL), was introduced as six zeroes were dropped from the currency. EU accession negotiations commenced. The Blue Stream gas pipeline under the Black Sea from Russia to the Turkish port of Samsun opened.

2006 The Baku-Tbilisi-Ceyhan oil pipeline opened. Turkey's refusal to open its ports to Cypriot traffic caused deadlock in the EU accessions negotiations.

2007 In parliamentary elections for a new president, the sole candidate, Abdullah Gül (AKP), narrowly failed to secure the necessary minimum 367 votes in April. The constitutional court invalidated the vote, demonstrators protested against Gül's Islamist background and the army threatened to intervene in defence of the secular constitution. Following the failure to secure an election in a second round in May, Gül withdrew his candidature. The government introduced measures to reform the constitution, including election of the president by the populace, but the president vetoed this amendment. In early general elections in July, called to break the presidential election deadlock, the ruling AKP won 46.76 per cent of the vote (341 seats (out of 550); the CHP won 20.64 per cent (110) and the MHP 14.33 per cent (71); Independents won 28 seats. In August, Abdullah Gül was elected as president. The Turkish military launched air strikes against the Kurdish PKK inside Iraq.
2008 Parliament approved a relaxation of the headscarf ban for university students in February, thereby arousing the ire of secular Turks who claimed that it was the first step in changing modern Turkey and that it was a sign of creeping Islamic influence in political life. The ruling AKP risked a ban on its existence and loss of power when it were accused of undermining the secular constitution by introducing legislation that would create an Islamic state by stealth. The Constitutional Court denied the ban and fined the political party 50 per cent of its treasury funding for one year. An indictment was filed against 86 people for plotting to overthrow the government; they were alleged to belong to the ultra-nationalist and Kemalist group, Ergenekon.

Political structure

Constitution

A 1982 referendum approved a new constitution embodying considerable restrictions on personal liberty.
The constitution was amended in 1999 and 2001. The 1999 amendment was undertaken to ease the path of the privatisation programme while an amendment in October 2001 was aimed at redefining human rights in view of Turkey's aspirations to join the EU. In December 2002, three articles of the constitution were amended, allowing a person with a prison conviction (non-terrorist charge) to stand for parliament. Apart from these additions, the new constitution differs little from the 1926 version, promulgated by Kemal Atatürk, which enshrines Turkey as a secular, democratic and unitary republic.
Only political parties gaining more than 10 per cent of the national vote are entitled to parliamentary seats
Voting eligibility: universal direct suffrage over 18 years.

Form of state

Parliamentary democratic republic

The executive

Executive power rests with the president and council of ministers. The president is the head of state. The president, who serves a seven-year term, is elected by the parliament and appoints the prime minister, who in turn chooses the Council of Ministers. A National Security Council guides government policy in areas of security and law and order. It is chaired by the president and is composed of government ministers and armed forces commanders.

National legislature

Legislative power rests with the unicameral Türkiye Büyük Millet Meclisi (TGNA) (Turkish Grand National Assembly). The TGNA consists of 550 representatives elected directly by adult suffrage for five-year terms. Only political parties gaining over 10 per cent of the vote are eligible to sit in the TGNA.

Legal system

The legal system is based on European models and the 1982 constitution.
The court system is divided into three areas: civil, penal and administrative. The highest courts are the Appeal Court for civil and penal cases and the State Council for tax and administrative cases.

Last elections

22 July 2007 (parliamentary); 27 April, 6 May and 28 August 2007 (presidential).
Results: Parliamentary: The AKP won 46.76 per cent of the vote and 341 seats (out of 550); the CHP won 20.64 per cent (112) and the Milliyetçi Hareket Partisi (MHP) (Nationalist Movement Party) 14.33 per cent (70); Independents won 27 seats. Turnout was 84.2 per cent.
Presidential: (third round) Abdullah Gül (AKP) won 339 votes; Sabahattin Çakmakoglu (MHP) 70; Hüseyin Tayfun Içli (Demokratik Sol Partisi (DSP) (Democratic Left Party)) 13. National assembly member turnout 448.

Next elections

2007 (presidential); 2012 (parliamentary).

Political parties

Ruling party

Adalet ve Kalkinma Partisi (AKP) (Justice and Development Party) (elected 2002; re-elected July 2007)

Main opposition party

Cumhuriyet Halk Partisi (CHP) (Republican People's Party)

Population

74.88 million (2007)
Last census: October 2000: 67,803,927
Population density: 84 inhabitants per square km.
Annual growth rate: 1.6 per cent 1994–2004 (WHO 2006)

Ethnic make-up

Mainly ethnic Turks, with a large Kurdish minority and small numbers of Armenians, Greeks and Jews.

Religions

Muslim with a small Christian minority. Turkey is a secular state which guarantees complete freedom of worship to non-Muslims.

Education

Although complusory education is free, facilities are extremely limited, forcing a number of students to attend night school or take private tuition to improve their chances of gaining a place at one of Turkey's 29 universities.
Unicef has highlighted the problem of poor education figures for girls, particularly over the age of 11. In traditional families, it is generally not considered necessary to educate girls beyond primary school, so that less than 40 per cent of girls, aged 11–15, in rural areas are enrolled in secondary school. In 2003, a joint Unicef and government programme aimed at addressing the problem has resulted in new schools opened in areas of most need and transport for students who have to travel long distances. Female enrolment figures have slowly begun to rise.
Annual total public expenditure on education is 3–4 per cent of GDP, of which 49 per cent is spent on primary education, 20 per cent on secondary education and 31 per cent on tertiary education (Unicef 2004).
Literacy rate: 87 per cent adult rate; 96 per cent youth rate (15–24) (Unesco 2005).
Compulsory years: Six to 14
Enrolment rate: 105 per cent male, 96 per cent female, gross primary enrolment; 67 per cent male, 48 per cent female, gross secondary enrolment, of relevant age groups (including repeaters), (Unicef 2004).
Pupils per teacher: 23 in primary schools.

Health

Per capita total expenditure on health (2003) was US$528; of which per capita government spending was US$378, at the international dollar rate, (WHO 2006).
Healthcare is provided free of charge. Standards are low, leading many to seek medical services in private hospitals and abroad. Major differences exist in the availability and quality of medical care between major urban centres and eastern parts of the country. Family planning was introduced in the 1960s. Due to opposition from religious groups it did not

receive strong support and funding. Nevertheless, population growth has slowed from 2.0 per cent between 1975–2001 to 1.4 per cent 2001–05 (World Bank estimates).

Life expectancy: 71 years, 2004 (WHO 2006)

Fertility rate/Maternal mortality rate: 2.4 births per woman, 2004 (WHO 2006)

Birth rate/Death rate: 17.95 births per 1,000 population; 5.95 deaths per 1,000 population (World Bank).

Child (under 5 years) mortality rate (per 1,000): 33 per 1,000 live births; 8 per cent of children under aged five are malnourished (World Bank).

Head of population per physician: 1.35 physicians per 1,000 people, 2003 (WHO 2006)

Welfare

The social security system is based on three major organisations, the Social Insurance Institution (SSK), the Emekli Sandigi (government employees' retirement fund) and Bag-Kur for the self-employed.

Mass social security began in 1946 with the SSK giving limited benefits and has been gradually expanded. Membership is compulsory for all salaried employees except civil servants, who join Emekli Sandigi. Social insurance law provides for benefits covering work injury and occupational illness, sickness, maternity, old age, disability and death.

Main cities

Ankara (capital, estimated population 3.6 million (m) in 2005), Istanbul (10.1m), Izmir (2.5m), Bursa (1.5m), Adana (1.3m), Gaziantep (1.0m).

Media

National news agency: Anadolu Agency

Other news agencies: Anka News Agency (www.ankaajansi.com.tr) Turkish News Agency (www.turkishnewsagency.com)

Press

Dailies: There are several national and regional dailies including in Turkish Hürriyet (www.hurriyet.com.tr), Türkiye (www.turkiyegazetesi.com.tr) and Milliyet (www.milliyet.com.tr), are mass circulation newspapers, Yeni Asir (www.yeniasir.com.tr) and Sabah (www.sabah.com.tr), Aksam(www.aksam.com.tr), Posta (www.postagazetesi.net) and Today's Zaman (www.todayszaman.com) (with English online articles).

In English, the main publication is Turkish Daily News (www.turkishdailynews.com.tr) with The New Anatolian (www.thenewanatolian.com).

Weeklies: Some daily newspapers have weekend editions, such as Sunday's Zaman. Other magazines, in Turkish, include Aksiyon (www.aksiyon.com.tr), Aydinlik (www.aydinlik.com.tr), Yeni Mesaj (www.yenimesaj.com.tr) and Yeni Ümit (www.yeniumit.com.tr). In English Voices (www.voicesnewspaper.com) from Altinkum and Turkish Weekly (www.turkishweekly.net).

Business: In Turkish, Dünya Ekonomi Politika (www.dunyagazetesi.com.tr), (with English online articles), and Finansal Forum are important publications; others include Eko Haber (www.ekohaber.com.tr) and Referans (www.referansgazetesi.com). Ýktisat, Ýþletme ve Finans Dergisi (Journal of Economy, Business and Finance) is a monthly economic publication.

Periodicals: In Turkish, English, and French.Bizim Anadolu (www.bizimanadolu.com) is a monthly newspaper. The State Institute of Statistics (www.turkstat.gov.tr) publish yearbooks.

Broadcasting

The national broadcaster is the Türkiye Radyo ve Televizyon Kurumu (TRT) (www.trt.net.tr).

Radio: TRT (www.trt.net.tr) has six stations, providing a national, regional and local network, which includes news, education and cultural programmes, modern and traditional music and programmes for foreign tourists. There are numerous commercial radio stations based in all regions, including Kanal D (www.kanald.com.tr), Radio Sok (www.asyaradyo.com) (Adana), Radyo Marti (www.radyomarti.net) (Antalya), Radyo Net (www.vizeradyonet.com) (Ankara) and Metro FM (www.metrofm.com.tr) (Istanbul).

Television: TRT (www.trt.net.tr) operates four national channels. There are many subscriber cable and satellite television services available with programmes in Turkish, Kurdish and Arabic. Major TV networks include NTV MSNBC (www.ntv.com.tr), Pusula (www.pusula.tv), Samanyolu Haber TV (www.samanyoluhaber.com), Sky Turk (www.skyturk.tv) and Ulusal Kanal (www.ulusalkanal.com.tr).

Advertising

There are opportunities for radio, billboards and print media advertising. There are local codes of practice in operation, as well as statutory requirements.

Economy

Although the economy grew 7.4 per cent in 2005, it slowed to 5.0 per cent in 2006 due to severe weather and the impact of Avian Flu on tourist arrivals. Turkey has continued debt problems and a current account deficit which increased to US$23 billion in 2005, up from US$15.54 billion in 2004. The sharp rises in oil prices in 2005 accounted for much of the deficit, despite the small production generated by its own oil fields. It did not, however, deter the inflow of direct foreign investment of US$9.8 billion and an even larger amount of US$20.2 billion in 2006, due in large part to the privatisation of the electricity supply sector.

The government implemented a tightened monetary policy to stabilise the economy and bring down inflation to 8.2 per cent in 2005. After four straight years of reduction it began rising in 2006 to around 10.0 per cent. Unemployment was reduced to 9.9 per cent by 2006.

Both exports and imports rose in 2005, with the country's main foreign currency earners being textiles and tourism, followed by automotive exports, which generated US$10 billion in revenues.

The future prospect of Turkey joining the EU has improved investor prospects with a greater streamlined banking system and tax service.

External trade

Turkey is a member of the Economic Co-operation Organization (ECO), comprising 10 regional Central Asian countries. It is also a signatory of the Euro-Mediterranean Partnership agreement, which provides for the introduction of free trade between the EU and 10 Mediterranean countries by 2012.

Turkey has been in negotiation for entry to the European Union, which in 2007, reached the stage of candidate country. It has a customs union with EU but has yet to resolve the issue of Cypriot shipping docking in Turkey.

Turkey has also begun trade co-operation with its neighbours in the Black Sea Economic Co-operation Organisation (BSECO), which promotes trade and investment among the 11 member states.

Manufacturing, principally textiles and vehicle assembly, accounts for 20 per cent of GDP, while the share of foreign trade in GDP is 60 per cent. Turkey is the third largest exporter of tobacco.

Imports

Principal imports include hydrocarbons, machinery, chemicals, semi-finished goods, vehicles.

Main sources: Russia (12.7 per cent total, 2006), Germany (10.6 per cent), China (6.9 per cent).

Exports

Principal exports are textiles and clothing (over 35 per cent of total), agricultural products, tobacco, iron and steel, electrical and electronic equipment, chemical and industrial products, vehicles.

Main destinations: Germany (11.3 per cent total, 2006), UK (8.0 per cent), Italy (7.9 per cent).

Agriculture

Farming

Agriculture accounts for around 17 per cent of GDP, over 20 per cent of exports and employing about 45 per cent of the labour force. The sector is subsidised, with state support accounting for as much as 7.5 per cent of GDP.

The mainstays of Turkish agriculture are wheat and sheep, although there has been an increase in fruit and vegetable production as well as growth in regional crops such as tea, tobacco, cotton and hazelnuts. Turkey expects to become a leading cotton producer over the next 10 years.

Turkey is the world's largest producer of hazelnuts (70 per cent of the world supply). Production is dominated by Fiskorbirlik, the state-run hazelnut farmers' co-operative.

The GAP south-eastern Anatolian irrigation project, although incomplete, has already raised production and productivity considerably: according to official figures, wheat production nationally has jumped 64 per cent since 1985, barley production by 42 per cent and cotton production by almost 500 per cent. Rice, wheat, soyabeans and potatoes are now produced in more than minimal amounts for the first time. The project will irrigate some 1.8 million hectares (ha), 25 per cent of which will be given over to cotton production.

Turkey remains self-sufficient in food with agricultural exports including tobacco, cotton, dried fruit (hazelnuts, seedless raisins, figs, apricots), pulses (chickpeas and lentils), live sheep, goats, fresh fruits (applies and citrus fruits) and fresh tomatoes. Cereals, especially wheat and barley, are Turkey's most important crops.

Imports, particularly of dairy products and beef, are growing faster than exports. Significant quantities of rice and processed food products are also imported. Liberal trade policies have opened up markets for imports of both cotton and burley tobacco.

Crop production in 2005 included: 34,567,700 tonnes (t) cereals in total, 21,000,000t wheat, 3,500,000t maize, 9,000,000t barley, 4,170,000t potatoes, 525,000t rice, 1,558,300t pulses, 2,587,650t citrus fruit, 3,650,000t grapes, 9,700,000t tomatoes, 839,528t oilcrops, 140,716t tobacco, 850,000t olives, 2,290,000t seed cotton, 800,855t fibre crops, 13,500,000t sugar beets, 1,745,000t chillies and green peppers, 783,000t treenuts, 202,000t tea, 2,550,000t apples, 11,480,900t fruit in total, 25,395,111t vegetables in total.

Livestock production included: 1,647,035t meat in total, 367,000t beef, 272,000t lamb, 45,000t goat meat, 958,010t poultry, 830,000t eggs, 10,538,000t milk, 73,929t honey, 34,680t cattle hides, 48,160t sheepskins, 46,000t greasy wool, 169t cocoons, silk.

Fishing

Salt water fishing contributes to 77 per cent of the total fishery production, with 62 per cent of the catches obtained from the Black Sea. Anchovies remain the traditional catch with a potential for further processing. Fishery production also thrives on horse mackerel, whiting and bonito.

The main production area for inland fisheries is Lake Van, where gray mullets are mainly caught. The Atatürk Dam and other smaller dams, which were constructed under the Southeast Anatolian Project (GAP), have increased the potential for inland fisheries by over 9,000 tonnes.

Trout constitute more than 60 per cent of the total aquaculture production, 25 per cent of which is obtained from the Aegean Sea. Turkey mainly exports large quantities of canned tuna to the EU and other developed countries.

In 2004, the total marine fish catch was 472,766 tonnes and the total crustacean catch was 7,801 tonnes.

Forestry

Forest and other wooded land accounts for slightly more than a quarter of the total land area, with forest cover estimated at 10.2 million hectares (ha). Most of the forest is available for wood supply, although it is moderately used for fuel consumption. Only a small area of forest is owned by the state.

Turkey produces a significant quantity of industrial roundwood. Major forest industries rely on local resources for the production of sawnwood, particle board and plywood. The pulp and paper industry is able to meet domestic demand by imports.

Exports of forest material in 2004 amounted to US$238 million, while imports amounted to US$1.4 billion.

Timber production in 2004 included 16,503,000 cubic metre (cum) roundwood, 11,225,000cum industrial roundwood, 6,215,000cum sawnwood, 5,235,000cum sawlogs and veneer logs, 4,278,000cum pulpwood, 3,388,000cum wood-based panels, 5,278,000cum woodfuel; 1,643,000 tonnes (t) paper and paperboard (including 54,000t newsprint), 217,000t printing and writing paper, 278,000t paper pulp, 1,016,000t recovered paper.

Industry and manufacturing

Industry accounts for 25 per cent of GDP and employs approximately 18 per cent of the labour force.

There have been high levels of industrial growth since the mid-1970s, despite low levels of capital investment and plant utilisation. There has also been rapid development of light industry, general diversification and growth in exports of manufactured goods.

Main areas of specialisation include textiles, ready-to-wear clothes, ceramics and glass, iron and steel, chrome, chemicals and light consumer goods.

The industrial sector is still dominated by large state-owned industries. These State Economic Enterprises are mainly engaged in textiles, food processing, chemicals, metals and motor vehicle production. The food processing sector is growing rapidly and agricultural products continue to provide a large proportion of export revenue.

Turkey's non-state industrial sector is dominated by a number of family-run conglomerates. Koc Holding is the largest, with 108 companies operating in 10 core sectors. Koc produces one-third of Turkey's cars, most of its fridges and televisions and owns the biggest supermarket chain. Sabanci Holdings, which has 50 operating companies, is active in chemicals, textiles, cars, banking, and supermarkets. The third-largest conglomerate, Cukorova, is active in commercial vehicles, paper and mobile telephones, although it is concentrating its efforts on the finance sector. There are also dozens of smaller conglomerates with up to 33 companies.

The textile sector, once one of the engines of Turkish economic growth, is losing the interest of the major conglomerates that dominate Turkey's industrial structure.

Tourism

Tourism has grown rapidly in recent years and is a major contributor to the economy. The sector is the second largest earner of foreign currency after exports. 22 million tourists visited Turkey in 2004, far exceeding forecasts. Tourism is expected to contribute 5.5 per cent to GDP in 2005. Tourist activity is concentrated along the coasts of the Aegean and Mediterranean Seas, where the bulk of accommodation is concentrated. Cultural, mountain and winter tourism are being developed.

Mining

Substantial mineral reserves exist, including copper, zinc, lead, iron ore, coal and lignite. Deposits of borax, wolfram and chromite are internationally significant. Turkey is the world's second-largest producer of boron and a leading exporter of chrome. Etibank controls 60 per cent of all mining activity.

Hydrocarbons

Turkey has oil reserves of 300 million barrels. Turkey relies on importing and refining oil, notably from Russia as well as

Middle Eastern countries such as Libya and Algeria. Demand is growing by 2–3 per cent per year – slower than overall energy demand, as Turkey moves towards using gas to satisfy its energy needs.
The Baku-Tbilisi-Ceyhan oil pipeline opened in May 2005. The 1,760km pipeline carries oil from Azerbaijan's port of Baku through Georgia and then across Turkey to Ceyhan. The pipeline will have a one million barrels per day (bpd) capacity. It is estimated that transit fees will earn the Turkish government revenue of US$300 million a year.
Turkey has natural gas reserves of 8.5 billion cubic metres. Turkey supplies only 2 per cent of its domestic requirements and has to import natural gas for domestic use. Domestic energy demand is projected to grow five-fold by 2020 and gas imports are expected to rise considerably. Turkey's domestic gas consumption has quadrupled since 1992, reflecting government policy of increasing reliance on gas. Gas is cleaner, plentiful in neighbouring countries and allows Turkey to diversify energy sources and increase energy security. Turkey can charge transit fees, as well as bring neighbouring post-Soviet republics into its sphere of influence.
Turkey's coal reserves include 278 million tonnes of anthracite and bituminous coal (hard coal) and 8.3 billion tonnes of sub-bituminous and lignite coal. Despite the huge reserves, production levels have fallen as a result of a lack of investment in the industry. Around 40 per cent of Turkey's lignite is located in the Afsin-Elbistan basin of south-east Anatolia, while hard coal is mined only in one location – the Zonguldak basin of north-west Turkey. Turkish coal, which is used mainly for power generation, is generally of poor quality and highly polluting.

Energy
Turkey is a net energy importer (about 60 per cent of its energy requirements) and is Europe's fastest-growing energy market. Demand is not being met in a country that still experiences frequent blackouts and industrial losses as a result of the energy bottleneck. Total installed generating capacity is around 34,367 MW.
The electricity is generated by coal-fired plants and hydropower. There has been rapid expansion of hydroelectricity capacity with over 100 power plants in operation. There are plans to develop nuclear energy (possibly after 2010) as a source of electricity.

Financial markets
Stock exchange
The Istanbul Stock Exchange (ISE) was established in 1985.

Commodity exchange
The Istanbul Gold Exchange (IGE) includes silver and platinum spot trading.

Banking and insurance
Central bank
Türkiye Cumhuriyet Merkez Bankasi (TCMB) (Central Bank of the Republic of Turkey)

Time
GMT plus two hours (daylight saving, late March to late October, GMT plus three hours)

Geography
Turkey is mostly situated in Asia Minor on the Anatolian peninsula, which is bordered to the north-east by Georgia and Armenia, to the east by Iran, and to the south by Iraq and Syria. Part of the country reaches into Europe, occupying eastern Thrace (Trakiya), which is separated from the rest of Turkey by the inland Sea of Marmara and is bordered to the west by Greece and Bulgaria. Turkey has an extensive coastline with the Black Sea to the north, the Mediterranean Sea to the south and the Aegean Sea to the west. The Sea of Marmara links the Black Sea and the Aegean Sea.
Turkey is a mountainous country, over three-quarters of which exceeds 500m elevation and averages 1,130m. The highest point is Mount Ararat (Agri Dagi) in the east, reaching 5,165m. There are two major ranges: the North Anatolian mountains in the north and the Taurus mountains in the south. Many short, fast rivers flow down from the mountains, as well as the great Tigris and Euphrates rivers, which rise in the mountains of eastern Turkey, where practically all the water they carry down to the Persian Gulf is generated. There are numerous lakes, the largest of which is Lake Van to the east near the Iranian border.
Hemisphere
Northern

Climate
Coastal regions have a Mediterranean climate, with mild, moist winters and hot, dry summers. The interior plateau has low and irregular rainfall, cold and snowy winters and hot, almost rainless summers.
Ankara: 0–23 degrees Celsius (C) (Jan–Jul); annual rainfall 367mm. Istanbul: 5–23 degrees C (Jan–Jul); annual rainfall 723mm. Ismir: 8–27 degrees C (Jan–Jul); annual rainfall 700mm.

Dress codes
Although the population is predominantly Muslim, Turkey is a secular state and for the visitor daily life in cities and tourist areas is similar to that in Europe. However, in rural areas, standards are much more conservative and women should be cautious in their dress. They should wear clothing which covers most of the body and probably also a headscarf, or at least be able to cover their hair if the need arises. Topless bathing is illegal but tolerated on southern and Aegean tourist beaches.
Dress for formal occasions is conservative and men normally wear a dark business suit or formal dress. Ties are almost always worn for business meetings. Turkish women dress formally for most social occasions.

Entry requirements
Passports
Required by all, valid for at least three months from date of departure, with exception of nationals of Belgium, France, Germany, Greece, Italy, Luxmbourg, Malta, the Netherlands and Spain.
Visa
Required by all, except nationals of some EU and other European, Latin American, Middle East and Asian countries and New Zealand. Details of requirements for individual countries can be found at www.turkishconsulate.org.uk/en/visa.htm.
Currency advice/regulations
There are no restrictions on the import of local or foreign currencies. Visitors bringing in a large amount of foreign currency should have it recorded in their passports by the Turkish authorities. Export of local and foreign currencies is restricted to US$5,000. Currency exchange slips should be retained.
Travellers cheques can be cashed in banks, but cash in euros or US$ is preferred.
Customs
Personal effects and gifts up to the value of eur255.65 may be brought in duty-free. It is advisable to retain invoices and foreign currency exchange slips to cover value of purchases. Export of antiques is prohibited.

Health (for visitors)
Mandatory precautions
Cholera certificate required if travelling from an infected area.
Advisable precautions
Anti-malaria and anti-cholera precautions are advisable. Hepatitis and rabies are prevalent in all areas, and there have been outbreaks of cholera in eastern Turkey. Malaria tablets should be taken for travel to the Adana area and inoculation against cholera and typhoid for travel to the south-eastern region is advised. A tetanus booster if travelling to central and eastern Anatolia is recommended.
Tap water is unpalatable due to heavy chlorination. Bottled water is easily obtainable in food stores. Medicines are easy to purchase without prescription in local pharmacies. The location of a nearby

all-night pharmacy is displayed in any pharmacy window. Medical services are adequate in main city hospitals like Istanbul's American and German hospitals.

Hotels
Classified into five categories – deluxe and first- to fourth-class. Prices vary and many hotels reduce their rates between mid-Oct and mid-Apr. A service charge of 15 per cent usually added and tipping is extra; 18 per cent VAT is also added. Advance reservations are advisable. Tap water is safe in major hotels.

Credit cards
Access, Diners Club, Visa, American Express and Eurocard are accepted in most hotels, restaurants and shops, and can be used to withdraw money from automatic cash dispensers at banks.

Public holidays (national)
Fixed dates
1 Jan (New Year's Day), 23 Apr (National Sovereignty/Children's Day), 19 May (Atatürk Commemoration/Youth and Sports Day), 30 Aug (Victory Day), 29 Oct (Republic Day).
Variable dates
Eid al Adha (four days), Eid al Fitr (three days).
Islamic year – 1429 (10 Jan 2008–28 Dec 2008): The Islamic year contains 354 or 355 days, with the result that Muslim feasts advance by 10–12 days against the Gregorian calendar. Dates of feasts vary according to the sighting of the new moon, so cannot be forecast exactly.

Working hours
Banking
Mon–Fri: 0830–1230; 1330–1700.
Business
Mon–Fri: 0830–1200; 1300–1730.
Government
Mon–Fri: 0830–1230; 1330–1730.
Shops
Mon–Sat: 0900–1300; 1400–1900.
Many flower shops open late. Pharmacies display the location of one opening late. Many food shops open on Sun.

Telecommunications
Telephone/fax
Postal services
Mobile/cell phones
GSM 1800 and 900 services are available throughout most of the country.
Internet/e-mail

Electricity supply
220V AC, 50Hz (110V in parts of Istanbul).

Social customs/useful tips
Hospitality is very important. Turkey is a Muslim country and religion plays an important part in Turkish life. Practically all business entertaining is conducted in restaurants and clubs.
Personal contact is the key to doing business. Bureaucracy tends to be the greatest obstacle for foreigners. Information is most easily and efficiently obtained by going directly to the top of any organisation, government or private.
It is polite when visiting the home of a business associate to bring a gift of chocolates, flowers or cake. When entering you may be asked to take off your shoes and put on slippers. Do not be critical of Ataturk, the founder of the Republic, and avoid discussion of Kurds, Armenians and other minorities.

Security
Levels of petty crime in main cities are comparable to those in most Western European cities.
Ultra-leftist and Kurdish terrorists are active in Istanbul and other western cities but do not constitute more than a minor threat. Visitors to south-eastern Turkey are advised to travel only during daylight hours and on major roads. The police monitor checkpoints on roads throughout the south-eastern region. Drivers and all passengers in the vehicle should be prepared to provide identification if stopped at a checkpoint.

Getting there
Air
National airline: Turkish Airlines
International airport/s: Ankara-Esenboga (ESB), 35km north-east of the city; duty-free shop, bank, restaurants and bars.
Istanbul-Atatüürk (IST), 24km west of the city; duty-free shop, bank, restaurant, bar and car hire.
Istanbul-Sabiha Gökçen (SAW), 32km east of the city. With bank, duty-free shop, restaurants and business centre.
Airport tax: None
Surface
Road: Coach services are available from Austria, France, Germany and Switzerland, as well as a number of countries in the Middle East.
There are connecting routes from the CIS, Greece, Bulgaria and Iran. It is possible to select the northern route via Belgium, Germany, Austria or the southern route through Belgium, Austria and Italy with a car-ferry connection to Turkey.
Rail: Express rail services from Munich, Vienna, Budapest and Bucharest.
Connections are available from London (Liverpool Street) via the Hook of Holland and Cologne to Istanbul on the Istanbul Express, which also transports cars from other European cities.
Water: Turkish Maritime Lines (TML), the national shipping organisation, and several other cruise lines operate services to Turkey. There are ferry connections with Italy, Cyprus and Greece. For the one-day ferry from the Greek island of Rhodes to Marmaris, a visa is not required.

Getting about
National transport
Air: Turkish Airlines operate regular services between Istanbul, Izmir, Ankara and other major towns. Bodrum regional airport offers internal flights and connections to other nearby Mediterranean destinations. Travelling by air within Turkey is relatively inexpensive.
Road: The Tarsus-Pozanti-Ayrimi-Gaziantep (Tag) motorway connects the southern Antolian region with the rest of Turkey, providing a vital link for the future growth of the region. There has been an extensive road building and maintenance programme in operation since 1999 involving over 1,400km of motorway.
Buses: Many private companies operate day and night services between all cities. Services are generally quicker than trains and prices are competitively low.
Rail: There is 8,542km of rail track. Most major cities and towns are linked by regular rail services.
Water: There are steamship services between Istanbul and most major coastal towns. Car ferries that offer cabins are highly sought-after and should be booked in advance.
City transport
Taxis: Metered taxis available in major towns and cities. Also available are the much cheaper Dolmus taxis, which have fixed routes and carry 8–12 passengers. Tipping not customary. For longer journeys the fare should be agreed beforehand. Drivers rarely speak much English and may be new to the city, so advisable to carry a road map.
Buses, trams & metro: Metros run in three of Turkey's main cities — Ankara, Istanbul and Izmir — and are planned for Bursa and Adana.
Car hire
All international companies are represented. Available at main hotels, airports and travel agents but expensive. International driving licence preferred, but most foreign licences accepted. Driving is on the right.

BUSINESS DIRECTORY
The addresses listed below are a selection only. While World of Information makes every endeavour to check these addresses, we cannot guarantee that changes have not been made, especially to telephone numbers and area codes. We would welcome any corrections.

Telephone area codes

The international direct dialling code (IDD) for Turkey is +90, followed by area code and subscriber's number:

Adana	322	Istanbul (Thrace)	212
Ankara	312	Izmir	232
Bursa	224	Kayseri	352
Dlyarbakir	412	Konya	332
Gaziantep	342	Malatya	422
Istanbul (Anatolia)	216	Samsun	362

Chambers of Commerce

Adana Chamber of Commerce, 52 Abidinpasa Cadessi, Adana (tel: 352-0052; fax: 351-8009; e-mail: basanlik@adan-to.org.tr).

American-Turkish Business Association, Emlak Kredi Bloklari, Levent, 80620 Istanbul (tel: 270-6718; fax: 279-0031; e-mail: taba@taba.org.tr).

Ankara Chamber of Commerce, 2 Sogutozu Mahallesi, 06530 Ankara (tel: 285-7950; fax: 284-2314; info@atonet.org.tr).

British Chamber of Commerce in Turkey, 18 Mesrutiyet Cadessi, Galatasaray, 34435 Istanbul (tel: 249-0658; fax: 252-5551; e-mail: buscenter@bcct.org.tr).

Istanbul Chamber of Commerce, Resadiye Cadessi, Eminonu, 34378 Istanbul (tel: 455-6000; fax: 513-1565; e-mail: ito@ito.org.tr).

Izmir Chamber of Commerce, 126 Ataturk Cadessi , Pasaport, 35210 Izmir (tel: 441-7777; fax: 446-2251; e-mail: info@izto.org.tr).

Kayseri Chamber of Commerce, 6 Tennuri Sokak, 38040 Kayseri (tel: 222-4528; fax: 232-1069; e-mail: kaytic@kayserito.org.tr).

Konya Chamber of Commerce, 1 Vatan Cadessi, 42040 Konya (tel: 353-4850; fax: 353-0546; e-mail: kto@kto.org.tr).

Samsun Chamber of Commerce and Industry, Hancerli Mahallesi, 8 Abbasasa Sokak, 55020 Samsun (tel: 432-3626; fax: 432-9055; e-mail: samsuntso@samsuntso.org.tr).

Turkey Union of Chambers of Commerce, Industry, Maritime Trade and Commodity Exchanges, 149 Ataturk Bulvari, Bakanlyklar, Ankara (tel: 413-8000; fax: 418-3268; e-mail: info@tobb.org.tr).

Banking

Akbank, Sabanci Center, 80745 4.Levent, Istanbul (tel: 270-2666/0044; fax: 269-7383/8081).

Demirbank, Büyükdere Cadessi 122, 80280 Esentepe, Istanbul (tel: 275-1900; fax: 267-4794/2786).

Esbank, Eskisehir Bankasi, Mesrutiyet Cadessi 141, 80050 Tepebasi, Istanbul (tel: 251-7270; fax: 243-2396).

Garanti Bank, 63 Buyukdere Caddesi, Maslak 80670 Istanbul (tel/fax: 335-3535).

Koçbank, Barbaros Bulvari, Morbasan Sokak, Koza Is Merkezi C Blok, 80692 Besiktas, Istanbul (tel: 274-7777; fax: 267-2987).

Pamukbank, Büyükdere Cadessi 82, 80450 Gayrettepe, Istanbul (tel: 275-2424; fax: 275-8606).

Türkiye Is Bankasi, Atatürk Bulvari 191, 06684 Kavaklidere, Ankara (tel: 428-1140; fax: 425-0750/2).

Yapi ve Kredi Bankasi, Büyükdere Cadessi Yapi Kredi Plaza, A Blok, 80620 Levent, Istanbul (tel: 280-1111; fax: 280-1670/1).

Central bank

Türkiye Cumhuriyet Merkez Bankasy, Ystiklal Cadessi 10 Ulus, 06100 Ankara (tel: 310-3646; fax: 310-7434; e-mail: info@tcmb.gov.tr).

Travel information

Turkish Airlines, General Administration Building, Ataturk Airport Yesilkoy, Istanbul (tel: 463-6363; fax: 465-2121; e-mail: turkishairlines@thy.com).

Ministry of tourism

Ministry of Culture and Tourism, Atatürk Bulvari 29, 06050 Opera, Ankara (tel: 309-0850; fax: 312-4359; e-mail: kultur@kultur.gov.tr).

National tourist organisation offices

Tourism Information Office, Gazi Mustafa Kemal Bulvari 121, Ankara (tel: 488-7007; fax: 231-5572).

Ministries

President's Office, Cankaya, Ankara (tel: 468-5030; fax: 427-1330; internet site: www.cankaya.gov.tr).

Prime Minister's Office, Bakanliklar, Ankara (tel: 419-5896; fax: 417-0476: internet site: www.basbakanlik.gov.tr).

Ministry of Agriculture and Rural Affairs, Ataturk Bulvari 153, Ankara (tel: 417-6000; fax: 417-7168).

Ministry of Defence, Ankara (tel: 425-4596; fax: 418-1795).

Ministry of Education, Ataturk Bulvari, Ankara (tel: 419-1410; fax: 417-7027).

Ministry of Energy and Natural Resources, Inonu Bulvari 27, Ankara (tel: 212-6915; fax: 212-3816).

Ministry of the Environment, Eskisehir Yolu, Ankara (tel: 287 9965; fax: 285-2742).

Ministry of Finance, Ankara (tel: 425-0080; fax: 425-0058; internet site: www.maliye.gov.tr).

Ministry of Foreign Affairs, Balgat, Ankara (tel: 287-1665; fax: 287-8811).

Ministry of Forestry, Ataturk Bulvari 153, Ankara (tel: 417-6000; fax: 213-2610).

Ministry of Health, Sihhiye, Ankara (tel: 431-4820; fax: 431-4879).

Ministry of Industry and Trade, Eskisehir Yolu, Ankara (tel: 286-0365; fax: 285-4318).

Ministry of the Interior, Ankara (tel: 418-1368; fax: 418-1795).

Ministry of Justice, Ankara (tel: 419-6050; fax: 417-3954).

Ministry of Labour and Social Security, Inonu Bulvari, Ankara (tel: 212-9700; fax: 215-4962).

Ministry of Public Works and Housing, Vekaletler Cad 1, Ankara (tel: 417-9260; fax: 418-5540).

Ministry of Transport, Ankara (tel: 212-4416; fax: 212-4930).

Other useful addresses

Borsa Komiserligi (stock exchange), Menkul Kiymetler ve Kambiyo Borsasi, Rihtim Caddesi 245, 80030 Karakoy, Istanbul (tel: 298-2100; fax: 298-2500; internet site: http://www.ise.org).

British Consulate General Ankara, Merutiyet Caddesi No 34, Tepebasi, Beyoglu PK33, Ankara (tel: 293-7450; fax: 245-4989).

British Embassy, Sehit Ersan Caddesi 46/A, Cankaya, Ankara (tel: 468-6230/42; fax: 468-3214).

Customs Modernisation Project, Gümrük Müstesarligi, Anafartalar Cad No 6 Kat 14, 06100, Ulus, Ankara (tel: 306-8532, 306-8439; fax: 306-8535).

Director General of Mining, Ankara (tel: 287-9750; fax: 287-9152).

Director General of Press and Publications, Ankara (tel: 468-4967; fax: 468-4966).

Director General of State Water Affairs, Ankara (tel: 418-3415; fax: 418-3409).

Director General of Telecommunications, Ankara (tel: 313-1121; fax: 313-1919).

Embassy of the United States of America, 110 Ataturk Blvd, Ankara (tel: 426-5470, 468-6110; fax: 467-0057/19).

Export Promotion Centre (IGEME), Mithatpasa Cad No 60, Kisilay, Ankara (tel: 418-5351; internet site: http://www.igeme.org.tr).

General Directorate of Foreign Investment, Inönü Bulvari, 06510 Emek, Ankara (tel: 212-8914/5; fax: 212-8916).

Housing Development Administration, Project Implementation Unit, Bilkent Plaza, B1 Blok Kat 1, Bilkent 06530, Ankara (tel: 266-7764, 266-7774; fax: 266-7733).

Modern Tercume Burosu (translation service), Karanfil Sokak 21/4, Yenisehir, Ankara (tel: 417-8122).

Privatisation Administration, Ziya Gokalp Street No 80, Kurtulus 06600 Ankara (tel: 430-0194, 430-4560; fax: 430-6930; e-mail: hascili@oib.gov.tr).

State Institute of Statistics, Necatibey Caddesi 114, Ankara (tel: 417-6440; internet site: http://www.die.gov.tr/ENGLISH/index.html).

State Planning Organisation, Necatibey Caddesi 108, Ankara (tel: 417-6440; internet site: http://www.dpt.gov.tr).

Türk Argus Ajansi (translation service), Lamartin Caddesi 32/4 Taksim, Istanbul (tel: 250-5200).

Türk Haberler Ajansi (news agency), Turkocagi Caddesi 1/4, Cagaloglu, Istanbul (tel: 511-4200).

Turkish Embassy (USA), 2525 Massachusetts Avenue, NW, Washington DC 20008 (tel: (+1-202) 612-6700; fax: (+1- 202) 612-6744; e-mail: info@turkey.org).

Turkish International Co-operation Agency, Kizilirmak Cadessi 31, Kocatepe, Ankara (tel: 417-2790).

Türkiye Radyo Televizyon Kurumu, Nevzat Tandogan Caddesi 2, Kavaklidere, Ankara (tel: 428-2230; fax: 414-2767).

Türk Snayicileri ve Isadamlari Dernegi (association of Turkish industrialists and businessmen), Cumhuriyet Caddesi, 233/9-10 Harbiye, Istanbul (tel: 246-2412, 240-1205).

National news agency: Anadolu Agency

Other news agencies: Anka News Agency (www.ankaajansi.com.tr)

Turkish News Agency (www.turkishnewsagency.com)

Internet sites

Foreign Trade Secretariat: http://dtm.gov.tr

Republic of Turkey: http://www.turkey.org

State Institute of Statistics: http://www.die.gov.tr

Treasury Secretariat: http://www.treasury.gov.tr

Turkish Foreign Trade and Tourism Centre: http://www.turkex.com

Turkish highways: http://www.kgm.gov.tr/indexe.htm

Turkmenistan

KEY FACTS

Official name: Türkmenistan Jumhuriyati (Republic of Turkmenistan)

Head of State: President Gurbanguly Berdymukhamedov (from 14 Feb 2007)

Head of government: President Gurbanguly Berdymukhamedov

Ruling party: Democratic Party of Turkmenistan (DP) (one-party state)

Area: 488,100 square km

Population: 5.19 million (2007)*

Capital: Ashgabat

Official language: Turkmen

Currency: Manat (M) = 100 tennesi

Exchange rate: M14,267.50 per US$ (Jul 2008); (official, pegged)

GDP per capita: US$5,189 (2007)*

GDP real growth: 11.60% (2007)*

Labour force: 2.22 million (2004)

Unemployment: 60.00% (unofficial, 2004)* (no official unemployment)

Inflation: 6.40% (2007)

Oil production: 198,000 bpd (2007)

Balance of trade: US$2.00 billion (2005)

Foreign debt: US$1.18 billion (2004)

* estimated figure

Described in the London *Economist* as the North Korea of Central Asia, oil rich Turkmenistan's human rights record leaves a lot to be desired. The flickering optimism of 2006, with the death of former President Saparmurat Niyazov, self styled Father of all the Turkmen, did not last long. Despite some minor improvements following Mr Niyazov's replacement by the succinctly named Mr Gurbanguly Berdymukhamedov, in June 2008 UK based Amnesty International called the situation in Turkmenistan 'appalling'. The IEconomist quotes Michael Denison of Leeds University as saying that in Turkmenistan there is no tradition of political activism. As a result, there is no political pressure from below for political, and economic, reforms and greater liberties.

The economy grows, debt shrinks

The World Bank notes that rising with export revenues from its natural gas and oil exports, which together account for some 80 per cent of Turkmenistan's merchandise exports, Turkmenistan's current account has run a healthy surplus since 2000. Given that Turkmenistan's gas reserves are estimated to be the fourth largest in the world, this does not come as a total surprise. In 2005–06, Turkmenistan negotiated improved payment terms for its natural gas exports to Russia and Ukraine. The agreement with Russia, signed in the spring of 2003, is due to last for 25 years. A 30 year agreement with China, signed in the spring of 2006, for natural gas exports, will also help maintain Turkmenistan's foreign exchange revenue.

The continued accumulation of foreign exchange reserves has enabled Turkmenistan's debt to be reduced. By 2005, external debt was less than 60 per cent of the 2000 level. This impressive economic growth mask's Turkmenistan's very limited progress in economic reforms since independence. In Turkmenistan the state has maintained a pervasive presence in the economy. According to the World Bank, privatisation stalled in the late 1990s, with most large- and medium-scale enterprises, especially in the sectors considered by the authorities as essential to the economy, remaining in state hands. Commercial enterprises remain subject to mandatory state plans, and production resources are distributed by the state. Virtually all cotton and wheat crops are grown under the state order system and procured by the state at below-market prices, although some initial positive steps to initiate reforms of the state-order system for cotton have been introduced. Basic commodities such as water, energy, natural gas, and salt are either free or heavily cross-subsidised.

Somewhat surprisingly, Turkmenistan is one of the few countries in the world that has not yet introduced current account convertibility. The parallel market exchange rate is four to five times the official rate, which puts a brake on the prospects for private sector growth. Under former president Niyazov, a significant share of Turkmenistan's foreign exchange earnings was directed towards infrastructure and national prestige projects, some of which appear to have generated little economic return. The age and limited capacity of the natural gas pipeline network and the lack of alternative natural gas export routes has for some time constrained the natural gas export potential and makes exports vulnerable to disruptions. Since 2004 there have also been signs of increasing inflation, and the parallel market exchange rate has further depreciated.

Poverty prevails

According to the World Bank, the poverty picture is mixed. Absolute poverty, based on the US$2.15 per capita per day poverty line, is less than one per cent. But an estimated 45 to 50 per cent of the population consumed below the subsistence minimum in 2003, and 30 per cent of the population had a level of consumption below half the national average. The official jobless rate is zero, as the state guarantees employment for every Turkmen citizen. However, surveys indicate that unemployment is growing, especially among the younger generations. The policy of accelerated public sector wage increases – wages and salaries have been doubled three times in the past five years and were raised another 50 per cent in January 2005 – may be contributing to unemployment.

The oil and the gas

According to the US Energy Information Administration (EIA) Turkmenistan has proven oil reserves of roughly 600 million barrels based on estimates by the US based *Oil and Gas Journal*, although probable and possible oil reserves are over 2 billion barrels plus 6 billion barrels of undiscovered reserves. Most of the country's oilfields are situated in the South Caspian Basin and the Garashyzlyk onshore area in the west of the country. Turkmenistan's oil production has rebounded since it obtained independence from the Soviet Union, increasing from 110,000 barrels per day (bpd) in 1992 to approximately 214,000bpd in 2004 before trending down to 180,000 bpd in 2007. The government has frequently targeted higher oil production, but the oil sector struggles to meet its growth goals due to a shifting interest to gas production, lagging foreign investment in this sector, and heavy competition for investment within the Central Asian region. According to previous reports in 2007, Turkmenistan aims to produce 2.2 million bpd by 2030. The Turkmen government recently announced plans to produce 216,000bpd in 2008, though this amount is higher than the 190,000bpd projected by the EIA. Turkmenistan exports roughly 40 per cent of its production. Local consumption is estimated at 110,000bpd according to EIA and is subsidised by the Turkmen government. In February 2008, Mr Berdymukhamedov instituted a new retail fuel system providing transportation customers with free gasoline up to a specified allocation (120 litres per month for car owners) and charging a market rate, established by the government, for any amounts exceeding the quota.

Foreign investment is limited to joint ventures and production sharing agreements (PSAs) with Turkmenneft, the state-owned oil company, and has typically been concentrated on offshore oil projects in the Caspian Sea with a few small onshore fields by mid-sized international oil companies.

Many of the prime oil deposits are located in disputed areas of the Caspian Sea, and without an agreement between Iran, Azerbaijan and Turkmenistan on maritime borders, these fields will likely remain undeveloped. In 2007, Chevron began negotiations with Turkmenistan on the disputed Kyapaz-Serdar oil and gas field linking Turkmen and Azeri maritime borders in the Caspian Sea, and in February 2008, Buried Hill claimed that it signed a PSA with the Turkmen government to begin production from this field. The field holds an estimated 700 million barrels of reserves according to some press reports. Turkmenistan is currently in political discussions with Azerbaijan.

Gas production in Turkmenistan following the collapse of the Soviet Union was for some time locked in pricing disputes with Russia and other countries, which resulted in Russia cutting access to its pipelines. Since all of the pipelines connecting the region to world markets were owned by Gazprom, Russia's state owned gas company, and routed through Russia, Turkmen natural gas was squeezed out of the market. As a result, Turkmenistan's ability to attract investment for existing field development disappeared. The country's output dropped throughout the 1990s, from 57 billion cubic metres (bcm) per year in 1992 to 13bcm per year in 1998. In 1999, a Turkmen-Russian agreement took hold, and in 2000, production leapt to 43.8bcm before reaching an estimated 67.4bcm in 2007, making Turkmenistan the second largest gas producer after Russia in the former Soviet bloc. In May 2007, the chairman of Turkmengaz, Yashygeldy Kakayev, said the country's energy strategy is to almost

KEY INDICATORS — Turkmenistan

	Unit	2003	2004	2005	2006	2007
Population	m	5.59	5.74	5.02	5.10	*5.19
Gross domestic product (GDP)	US$bn	4.75	6.70	17.17	21.85	*26.91
GDP per capita	US$	850	2,469	3,418	4,280	*5,189
GDP real growth	%	10.0	7.5	9.0	11.1	*11.6
Inflation	%	5.0	5.9	10.7	8.2	*6.4
Oil output	'000 bpd	210.0	202.0	192.0	163.0	198.0
Natural gas output	bn cum	55.1	54.6	58.8	62.2	67.4
Exports (fob) (goods)	US$m	2,970.0	4,000.0	4,944.0	–	–
Imports (cif) (goods)	US$m	2,250.0	2,850.0	2,949.0	–	–
Balance of trade	US$m	720.0	1,150.0	1,995.0	–	–
Current account	US$m	450.0	520.0	875.0	3,351.0	4,525.0
Exchange rate	per US$	5,200.00	5,200.00	5,200.00	5,200.00	5,200.00

* estimated figure

double gas production to 120bcm in 2010 and more than triple production 240bcm by 2030. In early 2008, the Turkmen government announced that it plans to produce 73bcm of gas in 2008. Turkmenistan has proven natural gas reserves of approximately 2.83 trillion cubic metres (tcm) at the end of 2007, up from 2tcm in 2006 according to the *Oil and Gas Journal*. This ranks Turkmenistan among the top 12 countries in terms of natural gas reserves

Risk assessment

Politics	Poor
Economy	Good
Regional stability	Fair

COUNTRY PROFILE

Historical profile

Present-day Turkmenistan was divided three ways between Tsarist Russia and the Khanates of Bukhara and Khiva until 1881, when Russian troops captured Ashgabat and incorporated the country into Russian Turkestan. The fierce Turkmen tribes south of the Amu Darya River were subdued in 1885.

1917 Central Asian peoples were given the right of self-determination by Lenin after the October Revolution in Russia.

1916–21 Turkmens joined other Central Asians violently opposing a Russian decree conscripting them for non-combatant duties. They fought against the Bolsheviks during the Russian civil war. In 1921, Turkmenistan formed part of the Turkestan Autonomous Soviet Socialist republic (ASSR).

1924 Turkmenistan was given Union Republic status.

1920s–1930s The Soviet programme of agricultural collectivisation and secularisation saw an upsurge in armed resistance and popular uprisings in Turkmenistan.

1960s The completion of the Kara-Kum canal led to a rapid expansion in cotton production. The canal is around 800km long and carries water from the Amu Darya river westwards to Mary and Ashgabat.

1971 Muhammad Gapusov was appointed head of the Turkmenistan Communist Party.

1985 Saparmurad Niyazov replaced Gapusov.

1989 Agzybirlik (Unity), a democratic front led by Turkmenistani intellectuals, was formed, but was banned the following year.

1990 Turkmenistan's Supreme Soviet declared economic and political sovereignty from Moscow and elected Niyazov as its chairman (in effect, state president).

1991 Niyazov supported an attempted military coup against Soviet President Mikhail Gorbachev. Turkmenistan declared independence just before the collapse of the Soviet Union and joined the Commonwealth of Independent States (CIS).

1992 Turkmenistan adopted a new constitution, making the president head of government as well as head of state and giving him the option to appoint a prime minister. Niyazov was re-elected in a direct election in which he was the only candidate allowed to stand.

1993 The manat was introduced as the new national currency. The government began opening up the country to limited foreign investment in the country's oil and gas reserves.

1994 In parliamentary elections, all candidates were returned unopposed. In a referendum, President Niyazov's term of office was extended to 2002 without a new election.

1997 The private ownership of land was legalised.

1998 A natural gas pipeline to Iran was opened.

1999 Parliament made President Niyazov president for life. In parliamentary elections, all the elected officials had been approved by the President.

2001 President Niyazov declared that he wants to retire by 2010, when he will be aged 70.

2002 Turkmenistan became a full member of the Islamic Development Bank (IDB). The President renamed the months of the year after himself, his mother and his spiritual guide, the Ruhnama. He claimed to have escaped an attempt on his life.

2003 Russian oil producer, Gazprom, agreed to buy 60 billion cubic metres of gas from Turkmenistan annually. The President cancelled a 1993 dual citizenship agreement with Russia, which sparked a diplomatic row with Moscow.

2004 President Niyazov decreed that young men were forbidden to wear long hair or beards, listen to car radios or smoke in the street; the opera and ballet were also banned. An agreement on water resources was signed by the presidents of Turkmenistan and Uzbekistan. In Majlis elections all 50 seats were filled by candidates supporting the president.

2005 Amnesty International condemned Turkmenistan's human rights record.

2006 President Niyazov died. The State Security Council named Deputy Prime Minister Kurbanguli Berdymukhamedov as acting president.

2007 In the presidential election, Gurbanguly Berdymukhammedov won 89.2 per cent of the vote, beating five other candidates; turnout was 98.7 per cent. Berdymukhammedov was sworn into office in February. Turkmenistan Russia and Kazakhstan agreed to build a new gas pipeline north of the Caspian Sea to ensure gas to Russia.

2008 Gas supplies to Iran were cut in January, during one of the coldest winters in many years. Turkmenistan blamed a technical fault but required Iran to pay more for a resumed supply. The Persian Islamic calendar imposed by the previous president was dropped and the old version re-adopted.

Political structure

Constitution

Turkmenistan was the first Central Asian state to adopt a constitution (on 18 May 1992), which upholds political pluralism, separates legislative, executive and judicial powers and guarantees private ownership of property. However, adherence to the principles of the constitution is rare.

Turkmenistan is divided into five administrative regions: Ashkhabat, Turkmenbashi (formerly Krasnovodsk), Mary, Tashauz and Chardzhou.

Form of state

Republic

The executive

The president is head of state, head of government and Supreme Commander of the Armed Forces. The president is directly elected by universal adult suffrage for a maximum of two five-year terms, although in 1999, President Niyazov was nominated president for life by the Khalk Maslakhaty (People's Council). The president must ratify all parliamentary legislation and may legislate by decree; he has the option to appoint a prime minister at any time.

In 2001, President Niyazov announced that he would retire no later than 2010, when he will be 70. Presidential elections are supposed to be held in 2010 and will be open only for younger people who have already held office for five to 10 years and have been approved by the legislature; candidates must have lived in the country for 10 years.

National legislature

The 50-member Majlis (unicameral assembly) is directly elected for a five-year term by universal adult suffrage (over 18 years of age).

The Khalk Maslakhaty (People's Council) is the highest representative body in Turkmenistan. It consists of the president, deputies of the 50-member elected Majlis, cabinet ministers, Khalk Vekillen (who are elected by the citizens of each entrap or local authority), the Chairman of the Supreme Court, the Chairman of the Higher Economic Court, the Procurator General, the heads of the administration of velayats (regional administrations), mayors of municipal councils and the heads of villages which are administrative centres of

f entraps. The Khalk Maslakhaty meets infrequently.
The president appoints cabinet ministers and chairs sessions of the Khalk Maslakhaty, which is subordinate to the presidency.

Legal system
The legal system is based on civil law. Members of the Supreme Court, the highest judicial body, are appointed by the president. There is no judicial review of legislative acts or presidential decrees.

Last elections
11 February 2007 (presidential); 19 December 2004 (parliamentary).
Results: Parliamentary: DP won all 50 seats unopposed. Turnout was 76.9 per cent.
Presidential: Gurbanguly Berdymukhammedov won 89.2 per cent of the vote. Turnout was 98.7 per cent.

Next elections
2009 (parliamentary); 2012 (presidential).

Political parties

Ruling party
Democratic Party of Turkmenistan (DP) (one-party state)

Main opposition party
Opposition parties are banned.

Population

5.19 million (2007)*
Last census: January 1995: 4,483,251
Population density: 11 inhabitants per square km (2000). Urban population: 45 per cent (1994–2000).
Annual growth rate: 1.5 per cent 1994–2004 (WHO 2006)

Ethnic make-up
Turkmen (77 per cent), Russian (6.7 per cent), Uzbek (9.2 per cent) and Kazakh (2 per cent).

Religions
The majority of the population are Sunni Muslim (89 per cent). The remainder are predominately Eastern Orthodox Christians (9 per cent).
The government directly controls the hiring, promotion and sacking of Sunni Muslim and Eastern Orthodox clergy.
Turkmenistan has a tradition of Sufism or Islamic mysticism and hosts several important Sufi religious sites.

Education

Secondary specialised education lasts for three to four years. General higher education lasts for four years. The Academy of Sciences in Ashgabat was the Republic's principal college of higher education. However, funding problems meant that by October 2000 the Academy was closed.
According to the government, 20 per cent of the relevant age group participate in some form of tertiary education. Those doing so are forced to undergo family checks going back three generations, while overseas education is not sanctioned by the government.
Females constitute 53 per cent of students in secondary education, 38 per cent of students in higher education and 29 per cent of students in professional schools. Although there is equal opportunity for females in education, they are often disadvantaged in employment situations.
A series of reforms have taken place since independence, with the aim of reducing the costs of education in general and vocational education in particular. Vocational training schools provide training to general education graduates, or adults who are required to pay fees. Some schools, especially in the bigger cities, are able to make enough income to maintain or even expand their activities. However, as government spending on vocational training in rural areas was reduced in the late 1990s, a number of vocational schools closed.
The quality of education is widely regarded as poor at all levels, and the sector is likely to come under increasing pressures from budgetary cuts and high population growth in the region. In September 2000, President Niyazov announced the axing of 5,000 jobs in the education sector as part of his drive to control the government's budget. Combined with low wages in the sector, this move is likely to undermine morale and reduce Turkmenistan's relatively high education statistics.
Literacy rate: 98 per cent adult rate; 100 per cent youth rate (15–24) (Unesco 2005).
Enrolment rate: 90 per cent gross primary enrolment of relevant age group (including repeaters) (World Bank).

Health

Per capita total expenditure on health (2003) was US$221; of which per capita government spending was US$149, at the international dollar rate, (WHO 2006).
The healthcare system in Turkmenistan has suffered serious under-funding in recent years so that the benefits enjoyed by Turkmenis under the Soviet regime has been lost. Life expectancy has fallen to the lowest of any central Asean state. The president ordered nearly all higher education institutes to be closed and so stopped the training of new doctors and nurses. By the end of 2003, over 15,000 public medical workers had been sacked and free healthcare was abolished. Hospitals outside the capital were closed, leaving 55 per cent of the population, living in rural areas, forced to travel long distances for treatment.
The availability of prescription drugs is severely limited, although the privatisation of pharmacies has led to an increase in the supply of non-prescription drugs. There are no private hospitals or clinics in the region although some practitioners offer basic medical services.
Environmental hazards have contributed to widespread respiratory diseases, which prompted the government to ban smoking in public places. Nevertheless government policy on healthcare has ignored the need for Aids awareness, which is thought, by campaigners, to be an heavily underreported.

HIV/Aids
HIV prevalence: 0.1 per cent aged 15–49 in 2003 (World Bank)
Life expectancy: 60 years, 2004 (WHO 2006)
Fertility rate/Maternal mortality rate: 2.7 births per woman, 2004 (WHO 2006); maternal mortality 65 per 100,000 live births (World Bank).
Child (under 5 years) mortality rate (per 1,000): 79 deaths per 1,000 live births (World Bank).
Head of population per physician: 4.18 physicians per 1,000 people, 2002 (WHO 2006)

Welfare

The government has attempted to deliver social services during the transitional period, but significant fiscal constraints continue to impede the progress of universal social transfers in the long-run. Taxes collected by the state tax service go to the state budget and the social security fund.
The social security system is partly financed by payroll taxes set at 30 per cent of wages and voluntary contributions, while the government bears the full cost of social pensions and other subsidies as needed.
The state provides for different types of welfare payments, including pensions and several benefits related to disability, child-care, minimum social allowance, workers compensation, unemployment and family allowances. In 2001, the government decided to double public sector salaries.
Pensions are calculated on the number of years employed and the level of income. Pension benefits were doubled in 2003 following a presidential decree.
Maternity leave benefits are paid according to work experience and income. It is usually paid for 112 days. Workers' compensation benefits are paid at the rate of 6 per cent of salary in cases of unhealthy work conditions and 12 per cent of salary for severely harmful work conditions.
Those working in desert areas receive compensation at the rate of 10 per cent of their salary.
The government's human rights record remains extremely poor and it continues to commit serious human rights abuses.

Interference with citizens' privacy remains a problem. Domestic violence and discrimination against women are prevalent.

Main cities
Ashgabat (capital, estimated population 763,537 in 2005), Turkmenabat (Chärjew) (232,158), Dashhowuz (209,087).

Languages spoken
There is a 28 per cent population of Russian or Uzbek speakers. English is also spoken.

Official language/s
Turkmen

Media
The Turkmen government has an absolute monopoly of the media.

National news agency: Turkmen State News Service (TSNS): www.turkmenistan.ru

Other news agencies: News Central Asia: www.newscentralasia.net

Press
It has been reported that Turkmenistan is a very repressive climate for journalists, according to international observers, it controls not only printing presses but it monitors media outlets and imposes editorial policies.

In Turkmen, Turkmenistan is published six times a week, Watan is published three times a week, Galkynys is a weekly and represents the Democratic Party of Turkmenistan, Turkmen Dunyasi is a monthly and represents the Ashgabat-based World Turkmens Association. Edebiyat we Sungat is a literature and the arts magazine. In Russian the Neytralnyy Turkmenistan is published six times a week.

Broadcasting
Radio: Turkmen Radio operated two stations, Watan and Char Tarapdan (also in English) (assess may be by www.intervalsignals.net).

Television: There are four channels operated by Turkmenistan state television including TMT 1-2-3 and 4. TMT4 is multinational, transmitting in Turkmen, Russian, English and French. Imported programmes are routinely edited before public broadcasting.

Economy
Turkmenistan is a largely desert country, with over 80 per cent of its land mass covered by the Kara Kum desert. The majority of the population work in agriculture, principally nomadic cattle raising and intensive agriculture, and the hydrocarbons sector. Turkmenistan's economy is based on the production of raw materials, principally gas, oil and cotton, which together generate around 90 per cent of export revenues. Turkmenistan is the second-largest gas producer in the Commonwealth of Independent States (CIS), after the Russian Federation, and is among the 10 largest cotton exporters in the world. Since independence in 1991, the end of state subsidies from Moscow and galloping inflation have caused a huge drop in living standards.

The economy is dominated by the state, which accounts for around 80 per cent of annual output. A centrol control system is prevalent, with the state fixing prices, output targets and controlling the distribution, marketing and trade of most products. Progress on economic reform has been slow and promised wealth generated by massive natural gas reserves remains a distant prospect. Investors remain largely wary of Turkmenistan, whose economy is characterised by an inadequate legal framework, often contradictory laws, corruption and excessive bureaucracy.

Non-payment by neighbouring republics for gas exports has been one of Turkmenistan's biggest problems since independence and, combined with limited export routes, has undermined the ability to take advantage of rising energy prices. Turkmenistan is dependent on a gas pipeline owned by Russia's Gazprom, which has occasionally been closed down in order to maintain high prices for Russian gas exports. The bottleneck in gas exports, which account for around 60 per cent of export revenues, hampers Turkmenistan's access to vital hard currency markets.

Economic data are unreliable and policy-making is opaque. The government frequently lies about the state of the economy and public finances, attracting criticism from the IMF and the European Bank for Reconstruction and Development (EBRD) as well as the CIS. While the economy is certainly growing, the increase is at a lower rate than claimed by the government. In real terms, GDP is only around 40 per cent of its level in 1989, two years before independence. Life remains austere for many in Turkmenistan and over half the population lives below the poverty line.

Growth is driven by domestic investment – mostly state-led investments in oil and gas extraction, petrochemicals, electricity generation and transmission, textiles, and luxury housing. About 1.5 per cent of GDP is invested by foreign companies developing oil fields under production-sharing agreements.

In 2003, the government adopted the Strategy for Turkmenistan's Economic, Political and Cultural Development for the Period up to 2020, which sets production targets for all sectors, to be supported by state-led investments.

On 1 January 2008 local currency began to be exchanged for foreign currency at regulated commercial rates, beginning at 6,250 manat per US dollar. The measure overturned a ten-year ban on money exchange and is expected to promote foreign investment.

External trade
Turkmenistan is a member of the Economic Cooperation Organization (ECO), comprising 10 regional Central Asian countries.

National statistics are not published; exports are chiefly primary products, cotton and hydrocarbons. Manufacturing and the service sector are underdeveloped and therefore most industrial and community requirements are imported.

Imports
Principal imports are machinery and equipment, vehicles, chemicals, and foodstuffs.

Main sources: UAE (12.4 per cent total, 2005), Azerbaijan (10.9 per cent), US (9.4 per cent), Russia (8.9 per cent), Ukraine (7.4 per cent), Turkey (7.2 per cent), Iran (6.1 per cent), Germany (5.3 per cent), Kazakhstan (4.2 per cent)

Exports
The main exports are natural gas, crude oil, petrochemicals and cotton.

Main destinations: Ukraine (43.5 per cent total, 2005), Iran (15.0 per cent), Hungary (5.4 per cent)

Agriculture
Farming
Agriculture typically contributes around 20 per cent to GDP. The cultivated land area is around 32 million hectares (ha), with arable land accounting for 19 million ha. Cotton, a major export earner, is cultivated on over 750,000ha of arable land. Turkmenistan was the second largest producer of cotton in the former Soviet Union and the 10th largest producer in the world, with a high annual export earning of US$245 million in 1998 that fell to US$130 million by 2002.

In a report published in early 2005 – The Curse of Cotton: Central Asia's destructive monoculture – the International Crisis Group (ICG) said that while the former Soviet cotton producing countries of Uzbekistan, Tajikistan and Turkmenistan continued to exploit their cotton growers there was little hope of improving economic development and tackling poverty. The cotton industry is vital to the economy of Turkmenistan, yet while the industry continues to rely on cheap labour (including children), land ownership is uncertain, state intervention discourages competition and the rule of law is limited, there is little incentive for the powerful vested interests to reform the system.

The government has started to diversify production in the agricultural sector away from the cotton monoculture. This has

generated a small export surplus in cereal production and a growth of 18 per cent in wheat production. The 23 per cent rise in agricultural output could possibly signal self-sufficiency in grain production.
Turkmenistan is reliant on an inefficient Soviet irrigation system, which diverts water from the Amu Darya river and has contributed to the drying up of the Aral Sea. The irrigation system suffers from poor management and maintenance, with water losses of about 50 per cent, rising salinity and poor drainage.
An absence of storage and packaging facilities means that up to 30 per cent of the grain and cotton harvests are lost annually. Livestock accounts for around one-quarter of agricultural production, including the famous Karakul sheep.
Crop production in 2005 included: 2,834,000 tonnes (t) wheat, 120,000t rice, 160,000t potatoes, 170,000t grapes, 9,000t pulses, 277,500t tomatoes, 71,400t oilcrops, 1,000,000t seed cotton, 219,000t cotton lint, 3,000t tobacco, 269,000t fruit in total, 779,500t vegetables in total. Estimated livestock production included: 210,700t meat in total, 100,000t beef, 90,000t lamb, 14,000t poultry, 35,260t eggs, 1,400,000t milk, 8,000t honey, 10,450t cattle hides, 12,000t sheepskins, 20,000t greasy wool.

Fishing

Turkmenistan has considerable fishing resources, with estimated total reserves at 50,000 tonnes of Caspian Sea fish and 8,000 tonnes of inland water fish.
Turkmenbashi, on the Caspian Sea, provides an excellent base for accessing marine resources, being located near the main fishing grounds and remaining ice-free throughout the year. The typical annual fish catch is over 12,000 tonnes; the main fish type is kilka, although herring, shad, mullet and crayfish are also harvested.

Forestry

Less than 10 per cent of Turkmenistan has forest cover. All forested land is owned by the state. There is no large-scale forest industry and most wood products are imported from Russia.

Industry and manufacturing

Industry typically contributes around 45 per cent of GDP and employs 25 per cent of the workforce.
The sector is dominated by the processing of hydrocarbons and other raw materials. The sector is labour intensive and the use of energy and raw materials is wasteful.
There is some light engineering industry, which mainly concentrates on the production of cables. US-based Coca Cola has a plant in Turkmenistan. Gap, the multinational clothing retailer, in a joint venture with Turkmen, has a fully, vertically integrated jeans production facility, using locally produced cotton,

Tourism

The potential for tourism in Turkmenistan, a large part of which is desert, is limited. Attractions include a number of historical and cultural sites. Mountain and coastal resorts are being developed and hotel accommodation is expanding. Visitor numbers are modest at some 8,000 a year, but increasing slowly. Air connections are improving and Ashgabat Airport has been modernised.

Environment

The Aral Sea is drying up due to the overuse of water from the two main rivers which feed into it and has lost 40 per cent of its water, dropping by up to 19 metres. This has resulted in desertification of the surrounding land. A UN study published in 2004 reported that there was no possibility of restoring the water and the need must be on preserving what was is left.
The government has endorsed a 2004 joint strategy to resolve the demands of its water requirements with its neighbours.
An artificial lake (132 cubic metres deep, 3,460 square km in area) in the Kara Kum Desert is planned to be constructed by 2010 at a cost of US$6 billion. It will be situated at the Karashor valley and according to the government will prevent the 4,060 square km large lowlands from being flooded, stop desalinisation of the land and return the area to crop growing. Environmentalists claim it will undermine the agricultural sector and contribute to water loss.

Mining

There are large deposits of iodine-bromine, sodium sulphate, magnesium, sulphur, potassium and other salts in Turkmenistan. Prime deposits of ore and rock are located in Tourakyr, Bolshoy Balkhan, Kopet Dag, Badkhyz, Govurdak, Kugitang, Cheleken, Turkmenbashi peninsula, central and south-east Garagum and northern Turkmenistan. Of these, the Zulfagar alunite deposit in Badkhyz in the south contains several million tonnes of ore with a 50 per cent alunite content.
Turkmenistan has the third largest deposits of sulphur in the world, located in the Kara Kum desert. Deposits of industrial minerals, notably kaolin and building granite, are also exploited. Non-ferrous and rare metals are mined and used for the production of chemicals. Gold and platinum are also present.
Despite Turkmenistan's vast resources, mineral deposits are under-exploited and not used significantly in domestic industry. Turkmenistan has not traditionally extracted or processed any significant amounts of metal ores, although the government has shown interest in attracting foreign investment to build its own metal-producing facilities.

Hydrocarbons

Turkmenistan's oil reserves stood at 500 million barrels in 2004. It remains difficult to estimate Turkmenistan's potential oil reserves as much will depend on negotiations to define ownership and prospecting rights in the Caspian Sea. Oil production increased to 260,000 barrels per day (bpd) in 2004. The government plans to increase oil production to two million bpd by 2010, despite difficulties in meeting goals because of shortage of foreign investment.. Turkmenistan exported around 170,000 bpd in 2004. Turkmenistan has two oil refineries — Turkmenbashi and Chardzhou — with a combined capacity of 237,000bpd.
State-owned Turkmenneft accounts for 90.5 per cent of oil extraction and state-owned gas producer Turkmengaz produces another 3 per cent. The rest is produced by foreign companies in production-sharing arrangements.
Turkmenistan had proven natural gas reserves of 2.90 trillion cubic metres in 2004, making it one of the world's largest deposits, although the government claims the actual figure may be closer to 20 trillion cubic metres. Gas production was 55.6 billion cubic metres in 2004.
State-owned Turkmengaz accounts for 85 per cent of production.
In 1998, a natural gas pipeline to Iran was opened. A number of alternatives for further gas pipelines have been put forward, including a trans-Caspian pipeline (TCP), which would run across the Caspian to Azerbaijan through Georgia to Turkey, and an alternative pipeline south, through Afghanistan to Pakistan.
Turkmenistan does not produce or import coal.

Energy

Turkmenistan has an electricity generating capacity of 3.9GW and generates 60 per cent more electricity than it consumes. All power stations run on natural gas.
Turkmenistan is connected to Iranian power lines for export of electricity. Iran and Turkmenistan may exchange electricity during periods of peak energy consumption, usually summer in Turkmenistan and winter in Iran. Electricity is also exported to Kazakhstan.
Turkmenistan plans to sell electricity through Iran to other countries of the Economic Co-operation Organisation (ECO), which includes six former Soviet republics.
The government aims to increase electricity production to 25.5 billion by 2012, but reaching this target will require significant investment in energy infrastructure.

Financial markets

Commodity exchange

The State Commodity and Raw Materials (SC&RM) exchange trades commodities only.

Banking and insurance

The economic crisis of 1997–98 led to all banks in Turkmenistan becoming 'government commercial banks'. Prior to this move, Turkmenistan had 67 banks, two of which were state-owned banks (Vneshekonombank and Sberbank). Vneshekonombank has become one of the largest banks in Central Asia since its creation in 1991. The bank dominates import/export operations and is a key institution for the operation of foreign investment in Turkmenistan. Sberbank holds 95 per cent of all household deposits.
The banking sector is widely viewed as corrupt and inefficient, failing to channel funds effectively, and is constrained by the government's tight control of the credit and foreign exchange markets.

Central bank

Central Bank of Turkmenistan

Main financial centre

Ashgabat

Time

GMT plus five hours

Geography

Turkmenistan is the second largest Central Asian republic and shares lengthy borders with Iran to its south and Uzbekistan to its north and east. The country also borders Kazakhstan to the north-west and Afghanistan to the south-east. The Caspian Sea, where the major port of Turkmenbashi is located, is to the west. The Kara Kum desert comprises over 80 per cent of Turkmenistan's total area. The Kopet Dag mountains extend along Turkmenistan's southern border with Iran and Afghanistan.

Hemisphere

Northern

Climate

Temperatures in Ashgabat range between 0 and 40 degrees Celsius (C).
Turkmenistan can be very hot in the summer, with temperatures of 35 degrees C common and a maximum of up to 50 degrees C in some provinces. Winters in the Ashgabat area tend to be mild and temperatures do not usually fall below freezing. However, in mountainous southern areas it is not uncommon for temperatures as low as minus 33 degrees C to be recorded. Ashgabat is the southernmost capital city of the former Soviet republics, on the same latitude as San Francisco and Cordoba.

Dress codes

Smart clothes are required for business visitors.

Entry requirements

Passports

Required by all. Passports must be valid for six months after date of departure.

Visa

Required by all. Business visitors require a full itinerary and an invitation, certified by the Ministry of Foreign Affairs in Ashgabat, from a local, private individual or company to support their application. The Turkmen Chamber of Commerce can provide new business visitors with such a letter. For tourists, these can be obtained from authorised travel agents in Ashgabat. All visitors must provide evidence of sufficient funds for the visit and return/onwards passage.
For further information visit www.turkmenistanembassy.org.
All visa applications made overseas are referred to Ashgabat for a decision. This can take several weeks. There is an accelerated 24 hours service, but a supplementary fee is levied.
On arrival visitors must complete an immigration card and pay a US$10 immigration fee. The authorities retain one copy and the other must be handed back, by the visitor, on departure.
Visitors must register within three days of their arrival, excluding weekends and holidays, with the Turkmenistan State Registration Service. This is carried out by the inviting organisation or individual, and a registration fee is paid. Tourists should register with the State Committee of Turkmenistan for Tourism and Sports. Registration is for the period of the visa; three days before departure, visitors must de-register with the same authorities. Visitors not staying in Ashgabat should register at the local velayat office of their place of residence (there is no need to register both in Ashgabat and regionally).
Visitors transiting the country can be registered at entry and exit points if their stay is not longer than five days and they hold a valid transit visa. Transit visitors cannot change their visas in-country, and need to notify the authorities if they intend to vary their route through the country.

Currency advice/regulations

On 1 January 2008 local currency began to be exchanged for foreign currency at regulated commercial rates. The import of foreign currency is unlimited but must be declared; export is limited to the amount declared. Visitors should check with the central bank for up-to-date regulations.
Ensure you bring enough US dollars to cover all potential needs, Turkmenistan is a cash-only economy. Traveller's cheques and credit cards are not commonly accepted.

Customs

On arrival declare all foreign currency and valuable items such as jewellery, cameras, computers etc.

Prohibited imports

Firearms, illegal drugs and wool carpets.

Health (for visitors)

Mandatory precautions

Vaccination certificate required for yellow fever if travelling from an infected area.

Advisable precautions

Water precautions recommended: water purification tablets may be useful or drink bottled water.
It is advisable to be in date for the following immunisations: polio, diphtheria, tetanus, typhoid, hepatitis A, tuberculosis. Also hepatitis B if you are spending more than 6–8 working weeks in a year in the region.
Anti-malarial precautions are advisable. Inoculation against rabies is advisable if travelling to rural areas. It could be wise to have precautionary antibiotics if going outside major urban centres. A travel kit including a disposable syringe is a reasonable precaution. There is a shortage of routine medications and visitors should take all necessary medicines with them. Medical insurance, including emergency evacuation, is necessary.

Hotels

Rooms are often in short supply and expensive. It is advisable to book in advance through Intourist or other specialist travel agents. A number of major hotel renovations and new building projects have been undertaken in the centre of Ashgabat.

Credit cards

Credit cards are accepted.

Public holidays (national)

Fixed dates

1 Jan (New Year's Day), 12 Jan (Remembrance Day), 19 Feb (National Flag Day), 20 Mar (Novruz Bairam/Persian New Year), 9 May (Victory Day), 18 May (Constitution Day), 6 Oct (Remembrance Day), 27–28 Oct (Independence celebrations), 17 Nov (Students' Day), 12 Dec (Day of Neutrality).

Variable dates

Eid al Adha (Kurban Bairam), Eid al Fitr (Seker Bairam – three days).

Islamic year – 1429 (10 Jan 2008–28 Dec 2008): The Islamic year contains 354 or 355 days, with the result that Muslim feasts advance by 10–12 days against the Gregorian calendar. Dates of feasts vary according to the sighting of the new moon, so cannot be forecast exactly.

Working hours
Banking
Mon–Fri: 0930–1730.
Business
Mon–Fri: 0900–1800.
Government
Mon–Fri: 0900–1800.
Shops
Mon–Sat: 0900–1800.

Telecommunications
Mobile/cell phones
The usage of mobile phones is extremely limited; a GSM 900 services exist in Ashgabat, Mary and Turkmenabat.

Electricity supply
220V AC 50Hz. Round two-pin continental plugs are standard.

Social customs/useful tips
Gratuities are becoming more customary, particularly in international hotels. Visitors are advised to carry some form of identity at all times.

Security
It is unwise to venture out on the streets alone at night. Visitors should be vigilant and are advised to dress down. Keep expensive jewellery, watches and cameras out of sight.

Getting there
Air
National airline: Turkmenistan Airlines
International airport/s: Ashgabat Airport (ASB), 4km from city centre. The are limited services from UK, Germany, Russia and the Middle East.
Airport tax: Departure tax: US$25; nationals of CIS countries US$15.
Surface
Road: Primary roads are few; secondary roads, particularly in desert areas, are of poor quality.
There are border crossings with Iran, Afghanistan, Kazakhstan and Uzbekistan. A road links Chardhzhou and Mazar-e-Sharif in Afghanistan.
Rail: A railway service operates from Iran. It runs nearly 300km from the Iranian Silk Road city of Mashhad, crosses the Turkmen border at Sarakhs and joins the Soviet-era Turksib railway at Tedzhen. It gives Turkmenistan access to the Iranian Gulf port of Bandar Abbas.
Water: The only coastline is along the Caspian Sea.
Main port/s: Turkmenbashi, has ferry links to Baku (Azerbaijan).

Getting about
National transport
Air: Akhal Air Company (division of Turkmenistan Airlines) operates domestic services. Daily flights between Ashgabad and Mary.
Road: Roads are poorly maintained and sometimes dangerous. However, new highways are under construction.
Buses: Buses serve Turkmenbashi (formerly Krasnovodsk) and Mary.
Rail: There are lines between Ashgabat, Turkmenbashi, Dashgouz and Mary. Trains to Gushgi are currently prohibited to foreign visitors due to the proximity of the Afghan border.
City transport
Taxis: Volga taxis have a sign on top. Agree a price beforehand. It is safer to use officially marked taxis which should not be shared with strangers.
Car hire
A national licence with authorised translation, or an international driving permit, is required.

BUSINESS DIRECTORY

The addresses listed below are a selection only. While World of Information makes every endeavour to check these addresses, we cannot guarantee that changes have not been made, especially to telephone numbers and area codes. We would welcome any corrections.

Telephone area codes
The international direct dialling (IDD) code for Turkmenistan is +993, followed by area code and subscriber's number:
Ashgabat12
Mary522
Turkmenabad (Chardhzhou)378
Turkmenbashi (Krasnovodsk)243

Useful telephone numbers
Fire: 01
Police: 02
Ambulance: 03
Gas leak: 04

Chambers of Commerce
Turkmenistan Chamber of Commerce and Industry, 17 Karreyeva Street, Ashgabat 744000 (tel: 355-594; fax: 355-381; e-mail: asccitm@online.tm).

Banking
Daykhanbank, 60 Atabayeva St, Ashgabat (tel: 419-873, 419-875; fax: 419-868).

Garashsyzlyk, 30 A Shevchenko St, Ashgabat (tel: 354-875, 397-393; fax: 397-892).

International Joint-Stock Bank Garaguma, 3 K Kuliyeva St, Ashgabat (tel: 354-062, 475-269; fax: 353-854).

National Bank of Pakistan, Sheraton Turkmen Hotel, 7 Gorogly St, 744000 Ashgabat (tel: 350-465, 512-050; fax: 350-465).

Obabank, 51 Ostrovskogo, Ashgabat (tel: 346-968, 346-558; fax: 246-968).

Prezidentbank, (temporarily at:) 22 Bitarap Turkmenistan Str, Ashgabat (tel: 357-943; fax: 510-812).

The Savings Bank of Turkmenistan, 86 Prospect Mahtumkuly, 744000 Ashgabat (tel: 394-298, 395-4671; fax: 396-553).

Senagat, 42 Turkmenbashy Shayoly Prospect, Ashgabat (tel: 510-305, 350-694; fax: 510-571).

The State Bank for Foreign Economic Affairs of Turkmenistan (Turkmenvnesheconombank), 22 Asudalyk St, 744000 Ashgabat (tel: 235-0252; fax: 239-7982).

Central bank
Central Bank of Turkmenistan, 22 Bitarap Turkmenistan St, 744000, Ashkabad, (tel: 353-442; fax: 356-711; email: cbtmode@cat.glasnet.ru).

Travel information
Akhal Air Company, Ashgabat Airport, 744088 Ashgabat (tel: 225-6084/1052; fax: 229-0724, 225-4402).

DN Tours, Magtumguly Avenue 48/1, 744000 Ashgabat (tel: 270-438, 270-449; fax: 270-420; email: dntour@online.tm; internet: www.dntours.com).

Intourist, Hotel Ashgabat, Prospekt Makhtumkuli 74, 744023 Ashgabat (tel: 290-026).

Lufthansa Airport Office, Ashgabat Airport (tel: 510-697; fax: 510-728).

Turkmenintour, Ul Makhtumkhuli 74, Ashgabat (tel: 256-932, 255-191; fax: 293-169).

Turkmenistan Airlines, Ashgabat Airport (foreign economic relations) (tel: 290-766; fax: 254-402).

Ministry of tourism
National tourist organisation offices
State Committee of Turkmenistan for Tourism and Sport, 17-1984 Pushkin Street, 744000 Ashgabat, (tel: 354-777, 397-606, 396-740; internet: www.tourism-sport.gov.tm; www.turkmenistan.gov.tm; www.turkmens.com).

Ministries
Ministry of Agriculture, Ulitsa Azadi 63, Ashgabat 744000 (tel: 256-691; fax: 253-557).

Ministry of Automobile Transport, Ulitsa Baba Annanova 2, Ashgabat 744025 (tel: 474-992; fax: 470-391).

Ministry of Communications, Ulitsa Zhitnikova 36, Ashgabat 744000 (tel: 256-665).

Ministry of Construction, Ulitsa Alishera Navoi 56, Ashgabat 744000 (tel: 256-060).

Ministry of Construction Materials Industry, Ulitsa Steklozavodskaya 1, Ashgabat 744000 (tel: 251-560; fax: 251-913).

Ministry of Consumer Goods, Ulitsa Annadurdieva 52, Ashgabat 744000 (tel: 255-442; fax: 254-833).

Ministry of Economy and Finance, Borodinskaya Street no 2, Ashgabat 744000 (tel: 251-653; fax: 256-511).

Ministry of Energy and Industry, Ulitsa N Pomma 6, Ashgabat 744000 (tel: 254-921; fax: 291-670).

Ministry of Foreign Affairs, Prospect Lenina no 11, Ashgabat 744000 (tel: 251-463).

Ministry of Foreign Economic Relations, Ulitsa Kemine 92, Ashgabat 744000 (tel: 297-511; fax: 297-524).

Ministry of Health, Prospect Magtymguly 95, Ashgabat 744000 (tel: 251-063; fax: 255-032).

Ministry of Information, Ulitsa Chekhova 8, Ashgabat (tel: 297-572).

Ministry of Interior Affairs (tel: 251-328).

Ministry of Melioration and Water Resources, Ulitsa Seidi 1, Ashgabat 744000 (tel: 253-032; fax: 298-589).

Ministry of Oil and Gas Industry and Mineral Resources, 28 Gogolia Street, Ashgabat 744000 (tel: 293-827; fax: 510-443).

Ministry of Trade, Pervomayskovo Street no 1, Ashgabat 744000 (tel: 251-047; fax: 295-108).

Office of the President (tel: 254-534).

Other useful addresses

American Business Liaison, Gogol Street no 17, Ashgabat 74000 (tel: 253-386).

British Embassy, 301-308 Office Building, Ak Altin Plaza Hotel, Ashgabat (tel: 251-0861; fax: 632-510).

Central Asia Research Forum, School of Oriental and African Studies, Thornhaugh Street, London WC1H 0XG, UK (tel: (+44-(0)20) 7323-6300; fax: (+44-(0)20) 7436-3844).

Department of Investments, Cabinet of Ministers, Ashgabat (tel: 254-954; fax: 255-112).

EU-TACIS, 92 Kemine Street, Ashgabat (tel: 512-117, 251-020; fax: 511-721).

Kuvyat (state energy corporation), 6 Nurberdi Pomma Street, Ashgabat; Foreign Economic Relations (tel/fax: 254-921).

State Agency for Foreign Investment of Turkmenistan, 53 Azadi Street, Ashgabat 74400 (tel: 350-231; fax: 350-415).

State Committee on Statistics, 72 Magtymgyly Avenue, Ashgabat 744000 (tel: 294-265, 253-596; fax: 254-379).

State Commodity and Raw Materials Exchange, Magtumguly Street 3111, Ashgabat (tel: 254-321; fax: 510-304).

State Customs Office, 7 Stepan Razin, 7440225 Ashgabat (tel: 470-455; fax: 470-221).

State Railway of Turkmenistan, 7 Saparmirat Turkmenbashi Street, 744007 Ashgabat; Engineering Department (tel: 473-936; fax: 473-958); International Services (tel: 473-958; fax: 510-632).

State TV and radio, Prospekt Svobody 89, Ashgabat (tel: 251-515).

Turkmenistan Embassy (USA), 2207 Massachusetts Svenue, NW, Washington DC 20008 (tel: (1-202) 588-1500; fax: (1-202) 588-0697; e-mail: turkmen@earthlink.net).

Turkmenintorg Foreign Trade Organisation, Hivinskaya Str 1, 744000 Ashgabat (tel: 298-774/684/975, 297-521; fax: 298-774/955, 295-987).

National news agency: Turkmen State News Service (TSNS): www.turkmenistan.ru

Other news agencies: News Central Asia: www.newscentralasia.net

Internet sites

Turkmenistan Embassy, Washington, US: www.turkmenistanembassy.org

Turkmenistan Information Centre: www.turkmenistan.com

Turks and Caicos Islands

COUNTRY PROFILE

Historical profile

The first residents of the islands were Amerindians. There are claims that Christopher Columbus actually made his first landing (1492) in the Americas on Grand Turk, and not in the neighbouring Bahamas.

1512 Spanish explorer, Juan Ponce de León, arrived.

1678 British settlers came from Bermuda and set up a salt-panning industry.

1766 Having overridden French and Spanish claims to the islands, Britain appointed a colonial resident.

1799 The islands were annexed to the Bahamas.

1874–1962 The islands were administered from British ruled Jamaica, after which they became a Crown colony and were ruled from the Bahamas.

1972 When the Bahamas gained independence the islands gained their own governor.

1976 A constitution was adopted and the first independent elections were won by the pro-independence People's Democratic Movement (PDM).

1980 The PDM lost the general election to the Progressive National Party (PNP) which was committed to maintaining the status quo.

1982 Plans for independence were reversed.

1985 Chief Minister Norman Saunders, the minister for development and commerce, and a PNP member of the Legislative Council, were arrested and subsequently convicted in the US on drug trafficking charges.

1986 The constitution was suspended following allegations of corruption in local government and a commission of inquiry found the chief minister, Nathaniel Francis, and two of his ministers, unfit to govern. The governor assumed direct control of government and the Executive Council, and ruled through a special Advisory Council.

1988 The constitution was reinstated with revisions.

2002 Jim Poston became governor.

2003 The ruling PDM won the parliamentary election but in two by-elections, won by the opposition, the PNP gained a majority in parliament. Chief Minister Taylor resigned on 15 August and Michael Eugene Misick was sworn in on the same day.

2004 The EU's Savings Tax Directive was implemented.

2005 Richard Tauwhare was sworn in as governor.

2006 A new constitution revised the title of the chief minister to premier. A new minimum wage, for all workers, was introduced.

2007 On 9 February, the general elections were won by the ruling PNP with 60 per cent of the vote (13 out of 15 seats); the DPM won 40 per cent (two). Michael Misick continued as premier.

2008 Governor Tauwhare resigned and Deputy Governor Mahala Wynns became acting governor on 16 July. Gordon Wetherell became governor on 5 August.

Political structure

Constitution

The 1976 constitution was suspended in 1986, restored and revised in 1988 and amended in 1993. It provided for the exercise of a ministerial type of government, through a governor appointed by the British monarch, an Executive Council (ExCo) which had general control of government, and a Legislative Council (LegCo). A new constitution of August 2006 replaced the legislative council with a unicameral house of assembly of 21 members, 15 of whom are directly elected for a four-year term, four nominated from the cabinet, one ex-officio (the attorney-general) and the speaker. The cabinet consists of two ex-officio members (the financial secretary and the attorney-general), the premier and other ministers. The British monarch continues to be head of state, represented by a governor.

Voting: universal suffrage 18 years and over.

Form of state

Caribbean dependency status: overseas territory of the UK.

The executive

The head of state, Queen Elizabeth II, is represented by an appointed governor. The cabinet consists of two ex-officio members (the financial secretary and the attorney-general), the premier and other ministers.

National legislature

The unicameral house of assembly is composed of 21 members, 15 of whom are directly elected for a four-year term, four nominated from the cabinet, one ex-officio (the attorney-general) and the speaker.

KEY FACTS

Official name: Turks and Caicos Islands

Head of State: Queen Elizabeth II, represented by Governor Gordon Wetherell (sworn in 5 Aug 2008)

Head of government: Premier Michael Eugene Misick (since 2003; re-elected 9 Feb 2007)

Ruling party: Progressive National Party (PNP)

Area: 430 square km

Population: 21,151 (2006)*

Capital: Cockburn Town (on Grand Turk)

Official language: English

Currency: US dollar (US$) = 100 cents

GDP per capita: US$9,600 (2003)

GDP real growth: 4.90% (2003)

Labour force: 12,000 (2008)

Unemployment: 10.00% (2003)

Inflation: 4.00% (2003)

Balance of trade: -US$6.40 million (2003)

Visitor numbers: 155,600 (2003)

* estimated figure

Legal system
The legal system is based on laws of England and Wales, with a small number of laws adopted from Jamaica and The Bahamas.
Last elections
9 February 2007 (parliamentary)
Results: Parliamentary: the ruling PNP won 60 per cent of the vote (13 out of 15 seats); the DPM won 40 per cent (two).
Next elections
2011 (parliamentary)

Political parties
Ruling party
Progressive National Party (PNP)
Main opposition party
People's Democratic Movement (PDM)
Political situation

Population
21,151 (2006)*
Last census: August 2001: 19,886
Population density: 53 inhabitants per square km.
Annual growth rate: 3.2 per cent (2003)
Ethnic make-up
Afro-Caribbean (95 per cent)
Religions
Baptist (41 per cent), Methodist (19 per cent), Anglican (18 per cent), Seventh-Day Adventist (2 per cent).

Education
The school system is constrained by insufficient infrastructure and is poorly equipped to deal with children of immigrants for whom English is not a first language.
The UK government has a number of projects, which it is working on through the Department for International Development (DFID). By improving teaching methods, the government hopes that around 80 per cent of children will achieve levels in reading and mathematics acceptable to their age.
The primary and secondary curriculum is also under review with plans that it will be standardised.
Compulsory years: Four to 16
Enrolment rate: 94 per cent primary enrollment of relevant age group, 80.2 per cent secondary enrollment.

Health
The UK government has designed an ongoing programme of reforms to improve the health care system. Priorities include human resource development, greater access to financial resources and the prevention and control of HIV/Aids.
The hospital on the island of Grand Turk serves as a referral centre for all of the islands. There are nine community health care clinics throughout the islands.
HIV/Aids
HIV prevalence: Less than 1 per cent in 2004
Life expectancy: 77.7 years (estimate 2003)
Fertility rate/Maternal mortality rate: 4.61 births per woman

Welfare
There is a reciprocal health and welfare agreement with the UK, which entitles nationals of the Turks and Caicos islands to benefits such as income support, housing allowances and child benefits.

Main cities
Cockburn Town (capital, estimated population 5,000 in 2003) situated on Grand Turk island.

Main islands
Grand Turk (business centre), Providenciales (most tourism facilities), South Caicos (fishing and sailing), Salt Cay, Middle Caicos, North Caicos (natural bird sanctuary), Pine Cay and Parrot Cay.
Eight out of 30 islands are inhabited.

Languages spoken
Official language/s
English

Media
Press
There are no dailies but three weekly newspapers all published in . Turks and Caicos Weekly News (www.tcweeklynews.com), Turks and Caicos Free Press (www.tcifreepress.com) and the Turks and Caicos Sun (www.suntci.com). There is an online community newsletter (http://enews.tc). Times of the Island (www.timespub.tc) is a quarterly magazine.
Broadcasting
Radio: Radio Turks and Caicos (RTC) (http://tcimall.tc/rtc) broadcasts three channels. Private stations include the religious Radio Vision Christina (www.radiovision.net) and Power 92.5 (WIV) (www.power925fm.com).
Television: The Turks & Caicos Television, is based in Grand Turk, while WIV-TV is based in Providenciales, both are cable television services.
Multi-channel satellite television is received from the US and Canada.
Advertising
Advertising is possible through the print media and radio.

Economy
The economy is based on tourism and the financial services industry. The tourism sector is estimated to be worth over US$200 million each year. The 2008/09 budget announced the Turks and Caicos Islands' biggest budget deficit ever. The country is US$36 million in deficit and has forced the government to introduce heavy tax hikes to pay for what the government called a 'culture of over-spending' in government departments; the premier's office alone was shown to have spent US$11 million.
Rising tax rates include a new minimum business licence fee of US$500 per year (a three-fold increase), airport departure tax of US$55 (up from US$10) and a 50 per cent tax on wire transfer fees on overseas cash transfers. There are new customs service charges and an accommodation tax increase from 10 per cent to 15 per cent.

External trade
As a UK Overseas Territories the Turks and Caicos Islands is a member of the European Union's Association of Overseas Countries and Territories (OCT Association). It is also an associate member of the Caribbean Community and Common Market (Caricom) but does not operate within the single market (Caribbean Single Market and Economy (CSME)), which became operational on 1 January 2006.
Foreign earnings are provided by the offshore financial sector, tourism and fisheries. All capital goods and foodstuffs are imported.
Imports
Principal imports are food and beverages, tobacco, clothing, consumer goods, manufactures and construction materials.
Main sources: UK, US

KEY INDICATORS — **Turks and Caicos Islands**

	Unit	2003	2004	2005	2006	2007
Population	m	0.02	0.02	*0.02	0.02	–
Gross domestic product (GDP)	US$bn	0.23	–	–	–	–
GDP per capita	US$	9,600	–	–	–	–
GDP real growth	%	4.9	–	–	–	–
Exports (fob) (goods)	US$m	169.2	–	–	–	–
Imports (cif) (goods)	US$m	175.6	–	–	–	–
Balance of trade	US$m	-6.4	–	–	–	–
Exchange rate	per US$	1.0	1.0	1.00	1.0	1.0

Exports
Principal reported exports are lobster, fish, dried and fresh conch, and conch shells.
Main destinations: UK, US

Agriculture
Farming
The agricultural sector is limited to small-scale production for domestic consumption and accounts for around 2 per cent of GDP. The growing tourism sector has encouraged production of fruit and vegetables for hotels and restaurants.
Farming is confined to the rearing of livestock and the growing of maize, beans and some fresh fruit. A hydroponics facility has been developed at Providenciales.
Fishing
The fishing industry grew as the salt industry declined. Over-fishing, low prices and better paid jobs in the growing tourism industry in the 1990s led to a decline in fishing. However, as export prices started to improve, particularly for conch, and the government started to improve conservation techniques and encourage value-added processing, so the industry has rebounded.
Fishing for lobster and conch production accounts for just under 2 per cent of GDP. There is a commercial conch farm on Providenciales.
The typical total annual fish catch is over 1,300mt; shellfish, molluscs and cephalopods account for another 1,000mt per annum.

Industry and manufacturing
The manufacturing sector accounts for less than 1 per cent of GDP. Activity is confined to fish processing (mainly lobsters and conch) and construction work. A rice-milling and packaging plant, supplied with rice from Guyana, is the only significant industrial enterprise.
Construction activity has increased with new tourist and residential developments. The Turks and Caicos Investment Agency is promoting the islands as a location for manufacturing electronic goods.

Tourism
Tourism is the mainstay of the Turks and Caicos economy and continues to expand rapidly, despite the effects of recession in the US and the 2001 terrorist attacks in the US. The main factor influencing growth in the tourism sector has been promotion efforts and improved airline access from North America to Providenciales. 77 per cent of total arrivals come from the US. Wishing to diversify away from dependence on this market, promotions have targeted Europe and Asia. Resort and other facilities continue to be developed, together with a strategic tourism plan for 2004–07. A cruise terminal and pier project in Grand Turk was opened in 2006.

Hydrocarbons
The Turks and Caicos Islands do not produce any hydrocarbons. They rely entirely on imports of refined oil products. The Islands do not import either natural gas or coal.

Banking and insurance
Under an EU tax directive introduced in July 2005 in a number of associate and dependent EU countries, the Turks and Caicos began imposing a withholding tax to be passed to the relevant EU depositor's country but retaining the anonymity of the saver. Withholding taxes began at 15 per cent, and will rise to 35 per cent by 2011. Turks and Caicos has also agreed to supply information on tax fraud, for criminal or civil trials, and notify EU member states about additional malpractices.
Central bank
There is no central bank.
Main financial centre
Cockburn Town, Grand Turk.
Offshore facilities
The Financial Services Commission is an independent statutory body responsible for licensing and supervising all finance-related entities and registering companies.

Time
GMT minus five hours (daylight saving, April to October, GMT minus four hours)

Geography
The Turks and Caicos Islands (TCI) are a group of around 40 islands in the North Atlantic Ocean, split into two groups by a deep channel, which combined covers 500 square km of land. They are situated in the north of the Caribbean, 48km south of the Bahamas and 145km north of Haiti. The islands are limestone plateaux, no higher that 75 metres, most with lush green vegetation. Off their northern shore, TCI has the world's third largest coral reef system.
Hemisphere
Northern

Climate
Tropical, tempered by trade winds. Winter nights sometimes cool, summers are hot. Mean temperature range from 25–29 degrees Celsius.

Entry requirements
Passports
Required by all except visitors from North America who require birth certificate (or, a notarised copy) and photo ID (all US and Canadian nationals require a passport for re-entry to their country from January 2007). Proof of onward/return passage is required.

Visa
Not required except by citizens not found within the list given in www.turksandcaicostourism.com – Facts and General Information – Visas and Immigration. Further local information can be found at www.tcimall.tc/government or from the nearest British consulate.
Prohibited entry
Currency advice/regulations
The import and export of local and foreign currency is unrestricted.
Prohibited imports
Illegal drugs and pornography; firearms require a permit from the commissioner of police prior to arrival.

Health (for visitors)
Mandatory precautions
Yellow fever vaccination certificate required if arriving from an infected area.
Advisable precautions
Typhoid and polio vaccinations. Water precautions.

Hotels
Accommodation is available on Grand Turk, South, Middle and North Caicos, Salt Cay, Pine Cay, and Providenciales, reservations are necessary. There is an 8 per cent room tax and 10–15 per cent service charge added to bills.

Public holidays (national)
Fixed dates
1 Jan (New Year's Day), 12 Jun (Queen's Birthday), 25–26 Dec (Christmas).
Variable dates
Commonwealth Day (second Mon in Mar), Good Friday and Easter Monday (Mar/Apr), National Heroes' Day (last Mon in May), Emancipation Day (first Mon in Aug), National Youth Day (last Fri in Sep), Columbus Day (second Mon in Oct).

Working hours
Banking
Mon–Thu: 0830–1430; Fri: 0830–1230, 1430–1630.
Business
Mon–Fri: 0830–1600.
Government
Mon–Thu (winter): 0800–1230, 1400–1630; Fri: 0800–1230, 1400–1600.
Mon–Thu (summer): 0700–1130, 1300–1530; Fri: 0700–1130, 1300–1500.

Telecommunications
Mobile/cell phones
A GSM 850 service is available.

Electricity supply
120/240 V, 60 cycles

Weights and measures

Getting there

Air

International airport/s: Grand Turk (GDT); South Caicos International (XSC); Providenciales (PDS), duty-free shop, car-hire.

Airport tax: Departure tax: US$35.

Surface

Water: Cruise ships visit regularly.

Main port/s: Cockburn Harbour (South Caicos), Grand Turk, Providenciales.

Getting about

National transport

Air: Air Turks and Caicos serves Providenciales, South, Middle and North Caicos, Salt Cay and Grand Turk. Other scheduled and charter companies operate between the islands.

Road: Main roads on Grand Turk, South Caicos and Providenciales are surfaced.

Taxis: Taxis are unmetered and can be hired for the day, agree a price before travelling.

Water: There are scheduled ferries and island hoppers operating between most of the islands.

Car hire

Available on Grand Turk, Providenciales and South Caicos. National driving licence required, a flat tax of US$10 is levied on all hirings. Driving is on the left.

BUSINESS DIRECTORY

The addresses listed below are a selection only. While World of Information makes every endeavour to check these addresses, we cannot guarantee that changes have not been made, especially to telephone numbers and area codes. We would welcome any corrections.

Telephone area codes

The international direct dialling code (IDD) for Turks and Caicos Islands is +1 649 followed by subscriber's number.

Chambers of Commerce

Grand Turk Chamber of Commerce, PO Box 148, Grand Turk (tel: 946-2324; fax: 946-2504).

Banking

Bordier International Bank and Trust Ltd, PO Box 5, Caribbean Place, Providenciales (tel: 946-4535; fax: 946-4540; email: enquiries@bibt.com).

First Caribbean Bank, PO Box 258, Grand Turk (tel: 946-2831; Fax: 649 946 2695; email: care@firstcaribbeanbank.com).

Scotiabank International, Cherokee Road; PO Box 15, Providenciales (tel: 946-4750; fax: 946-4755; email: bns.turkscaicos@scotiabank.com).

Turks and Caicos Banking Co Ltd (private international banking services), PO Box 123, Harbour House, Front Street, Grand Turk (tel: 946-2368; fax: 946-2365; email: ajbf@turksandcaicosbanking.tc).

Central bank

None

Travel information

Air Turks and Caicos, PO Box 191; 1 InterIsland Plaza, Old Airport Road, Providenciales, (tel: 941-5481; fax: 946-4040; email: fly@airturksandcaicos.com).

SkyKing Airlines, PO Box 398, Providenciales (admin tel: 941-5464 ext 200 / 504; fax: 941-4264; email: cservices@skyking.tc; reservations: 941-3136; fax: 941-5127; email: res@skyking.tc; internet: http://skyking.tc).

Spirit Air (regional flights) 2800 Executive Way, Miramar, Florida 33025, USA (tel: (+1-954) 447-7965; fax: (+1-954) 447-7979; internet: www.spiritair.com).

National tourist organisation offices

Turks and Caicos Tourist Board, Front Street, PO Box 128, Grand Turk (tel: 946-2321/2; fax: 946-2733; email: tci.tourism@tciway.tc; internet: www.turksandcaicostourism.com).

Turks & Caicos Islands Tourist Board, Stubbs Diamond Plaza, Providenciales (tel: 946-4970, 491-5746; fax 941-5494).

Ministries

Governor's Office, Government House, Waterloo, Grand Turk (tel: 946-2309; fax: 946-2903; e-mail: govhouse@tciway.tc).

Main Government Offices, Cockburn Town, Grand Turk (tel: 946-2801).

Ministry of Education, Youth, Sports and Women's Affairs (tel: 946-2801, ext 142; fax: 946-1337; e-mail tci.sports@tciway.tc).

Ministry of Finance, Commerce and Development (tel: 946-2935, 946-2937; fax: 946-2557; e-mail: fsc@tciway.tc).

Ministry of Health and Education (tel: 946-2801; fax: 946-2722).

Other useful addresses

Development Board, PO Box 105, Hibiscus Square, Pond Street, Grand Turk (tel: 946-2058).

Financial Services Commission, Harry Francis Building, Pond Street, Grand Turk (tel: 946-2802; fax: 946-2821).

General Trading Company (Turks & Caicos) Ltd, PMBI, Cockburn Town, Grand Turk (tel: 946-2464).

Government Information Service (GIS), Government Square, Grand Turk (tel: 946-2301 ext 40505/40506; fax: 946-1120).

Immigration And Work Permits, Director Of Immigration, Immigration Department, Southbase, Grand Turk

(tel: 946-2939/2700; fax: 946-2924; email: iam@tciway.tc).

TCInvest, Hibiscus Square, Box 105, Grand Turk (tel: 946-2058; fax: 946-1464; email: tcinvest@tciway.tc; internet: www.tcinvest.tc).

Turks & Caicos Hotel Association, Third Turtle Inn, Providenciales (tel: 946-4230).

Turks Islands Importers Ltd (TIMCO), Front Street, PO Box 72, Grand Turk (tel: 946-2480).

Internet sites

Gateway Sites: www.turksandcaicos.tc

Local Information: www.tc/info.htm

Tuvalu

COUNTRY PROFILE

Historical profile

Tuvalu was formerly known as the Ellice (or Lagoon) Islands.
1892 A British protectorate was declared over the Ellice Islands and the group was linked administratively with the Gilbert Islands to the north.
1916 The UK annexed the protectorate, which was renamed the Gilbert and Ellice Islands colony.
1975 The Ellice Islands, under the old native name of Tuvalu (eight standing together), became a separate British dependency.
1978 Tuvalu became an independent country within the Commonwealth.
1987 The Tuvalu Trust Fund was established; it provides an average 15 per cent of the country's annual budget.
1989 A UN report on the greenhouse effect listed Tuvalu as one of the island groups which would completely disappear beneath the sea in the twenty-first century unless drastic action was taken.
1996 The 12-member parliament was forced out and Bikenibeu Paeniu became prime minister.
1998 Tomasi Puapua was appointed governor general.
1999 A no-confidence vote forced out Paeniu. Ionatana Ionatana was elected prime minister.
2000 Ionatana Ionatana died suddenly. Tuvalu was formally admitted to the UN.
2001 Parliament elected Faimalaga Luka as prime minister but later lost a no-confidence vote; Koloa Talake was elected as his replacement.
2002 Nine out of 15 MPs were re-elected but Prime Minister Talake and three ministers lost their seats. Parliament elected Saufatu Sopoanga was prime minister.
2003 The Sopoanga government lost its majority and ruled through a minority government. Faimalaga Luka was sworn in as governor general. The government regained its majority.
2004 During the first six months of the year, there were several very high 'king tides' associated with the new moon. At only four metres above sea level, at their highest points, the islands experienced seawater swamping of homes and agricultural land. Prime Minister Sopoanga lost a no-confidence vote; Deputy Prime Minister Maatia Toafa was elected prime minister.
2005 Filoimea Telito was sworn in as governor general. Tuvalu signed the Pacific Islands Air Service Agreement (PIASA), to become the eighth Forum Country to do so. PIASA is designed to ensure open skies policies with more viable routes for airlines in the Pacific.
2006 In general elections, eight out of 15 members of parliament lost their seats, including the entire cabinet. Maatia Toafa retained his seat but lost his post when Apisai Ielemia was selected as prime minister.
2008 In a referendum held in April, voters agreed to maintain a constitutional monarchy.

Political structure

Constitution

The constitution dates from 1978. The British sovereign is head of state, represented by a governor general with limited powers. The governor general's powers to veto government measures were abolished under a constitutional amendment in 1986. Each island is ruled by a traditional council of chiefs which runs services and determines development priorities.

Form of state

Constitutional monarchy and parliamentary democracy

The executive

The British monarch is titular Head of State, represented by a governor general, whose functions are largely ceremonial. The governor general is appointed on the advice of the prime minister, in consultation with parliament.
Executive power is exercised by a cabinet of five members and is led by the prime minister. The government is collectively accountable to parliament.

National legislature

The unicameral Fale i Fono (parliament) has 15 members, directly elected for four-year terms. Seven islands send two members each, with one from Nukulaelae (with the smallest population). The parliament has the power to make laws, it can remove the prime minister through a vote of no-confidence and can be dissolved early by the governor general in accordance with the constitution.

Last elections

3 August 2006 (parliamentary)
Results: Parliamentary: only non-partisans were elected (no political parties exist); eight out of 15 members of parliament lost their seats to new, younger opponents.

Next elections

2010 (parliamentary)

KEY FACTS

Official name: Tuvalu

Head of State: Queen Elizabeth II, represented by Governor General Filoimea Telito (sworn in 15 Apr 2005)

Head of government: Prime Minister Apisai Ielemia (since 16 Aug 2006)

Area: 26 square km (nine islands – five coral atolls and four reef islands)

Population: 11,992 (2007)*

Capital: Vaiaku in Funafuti administrative division

Official language: Tuvaluan, English

Currency: Australian dollar (A$) = 100 cents)

Exchange rate: A$1.02 per US$ (Jul 2008)

GDP per capita: US$2,020 (PPP, 2004)

GDP real growth: -4.00% (2004)

Labour force: 7,000 (2003)

Inflation: 5.64% (2005)

Balance of trade: -US$8.19 million (2004)

Visitor numbers: 1,377 (2003)

* estimated figure

Political parties
There are no organised political parties, although there are opposing political groupings.
Ruling party
Political situation
The politics of Tuvalu are dominated by the very real possibility that this collection of low-lying islands and atolls will disappear as global warming raises sea levels. In April 2008 the UN convention on climate change, noted that the government of Tuvalu had already appealed to the Australia and New Zealand governments for homes for 3,000 people in the short term and possible the whole population within the next few years. A new class of refugees are being created – those fleeing climate changes in their homelands. Tuvalu, along with the Maldives, had spent time and effort in convincing the UN Human Rights Council to acknowledge that climate change could undermine the human rights of the people of small islands. Nevertheless, progress towards implementation of the Kyoto Protocol on climate change has not been broad or thorough and the peoples of small islands are running out of time.

Population
11,992 (2007)*
Last census: November 2002: 9,561
Population density: 323 inhabitants per square km (2003)
Annual growth rate: 0.6 per cent 1994–2004 (WHO 2006)
Ethnic make-up
Tuvalu's population is Polynesian in origin.
Religions
Christianity, under which the Church of Tuvalu (Congregationalists) accounts for 97 per cent of the population.

Education
The vast distances between islands make the provision of education harder, as each small community requires a trained teacher. There is only one public, secondary school, located on the island of Vaitupu, where children reside for the academic year.
Compulsory years: Seven to 14.
Pupils per teacher: 19.5 (in primary schools); 12.2 (in secondary schools) (2005)

Health
Per capita total expenditure on health (2003) was US$74; of which per capita government spending was US$62, at the international dollar rate, (WHO 2006). Tuberculosis has been a long-term problem, which is monitored regularly and remedied under directly observed treatments (Dots), which has notably increased the rate of recoveries.
Life expectancy: 61 years, 2004 (WHO 2006)
Fertility rate/Maternal mortality rate: 3.7 births per woman, 2004 (WHO 2006)
Head of population per physician: 0.55 physicians per 1,000 people, 2002 (WHO 2006)

Main cities
Vaiaku in Funafuti administrative division (capital, estimated population 5,300 in 2003).

Languages spoken
Official language/s
Tuvaluan, English

Media
Other news agencies: ABC Pacific Beat: www.radioaustralia.net.au/pacbeat
Pacific Magazine: www.pacificmagazine.net
Press
The Tuvalu Echo is published fortnightly and the government publishes a newsletter Sikuleo o Tuvalu.
Broadcasting
The government operates Radio Tuvalu and the online Tuvalu-News (www.tuvalu-news.tv). Most residents receive foreign television satellite programmes.
Radio: Radio Tuvalu is a government-owned station.
Advertising
Adverts may be placed on radio and in the newspaper, plus through overseas based television services.

Economy
Tuvalu is a mere 26 square kilometres in size and has an economy to match. The small subsistence economy accounts for approximately 30 per cent of GDP. It is supplemented by copra exports and official transfers and investment income from overseas assets. Its smallness means that even a slight change in economic activity will affect GDP. In 2003 two construction projects (a hospital renovation and extention and a government office block) were almost equal to the total value of GDP for the previous year. As a result of these projects labour income rose by over 10 per cent in 2003, internal revenue collection was up (but fell by 12 per cent in 2004) and import duties declined by around 20 per cent in 2004, reflecting the decline in imports of construction materials.
Tuvalu has had to take its revenue where it can and when it was allocated .tv as its country-level domain (CLD) indicator it went into business with a California corporation to take advantage of it. The government sold its share in DotTV Corporation in 2001 for A$20 million (US$10 million) and continues to receive a small royalty.
Other sources of revenue are fishing licences for the exclusive economic zone and remittances from seafarers (some 20 per cent of GDP). The Tuvalu Maritime Training Institute is being upgraded over the period 2005–07. This is an important project as it not only boosts economic activity but also ensures the Institute retains its accreditation from the International Maritime Organisation. The government also anticipates a grant from Japan to rebuild the electricity generation and distribution system on Funatuti over 2005–06. The Tuvalu Trust Fund (TTF) invests in equities and is normally an important source of income. The government invests its budget surpluses in the TTF as a financial stockpile for years when it runs a deficit. A second fund, for the outer islands – the Falekaupule Trust Fund – has been provided with funds by a loan from the Asian Development Bank (ADB).
The ADB forecasts that the economy will pick up in 2005. A proposal to introduce a value added tax (VAT) is being considered. This will become important if the Pacific Island Countries Trade Agreement is ratified since Tuvalu will loose revenue on imports from the region.

External trade
Tuvalu is a member of the South Pacific Regional Trade and Economic Co-operation Agreement (Sparteca) along with 12 other regional nations, which allows products duty free access by Pacific Island Forum members to Australian and

KEY INDICATORS **Tuvalu**

	Unit	2003	2004	2005	2006	2007
Population	m	0.01	0.01	0.01	0.01	0.01
GDP real growth	%	3.0	-4.0	–	–	–
Inflation	%	2.5	2.8	–	–	–
Exports (fob) (goods)	US$m	–	1.0	–	–	–
Imports (cif) (goods)	US$m	–	9.2	–	–	–
Balance of trade	US$m	–	-8.2	–	–	–
Exchange rate	per US$	1.55	1.36	1.28	0	0

New Zealand markets (subject to the country of origin restrictions).
Most foreign earnings are provided by sales of stamps and coins by mail order and remittances.

Imports
Principal imports are food, animals, vehicles, mineral fuels, machinery and manufactured goods.
Main sources: Fiji (45.8 per cent total, 2006), Japan (18.8 per cent), China (18.1 per cent), Australia (7.7 per cent).

Exports
Copra and fish are the principal export commodities; coconut oil is exported to New Zealand.
Main destinations: Germany (62.1 per cent total, 2006), Italy (20.7 per cent), Fiji (7.0 per cent).

Agriculture

Farming
About 80 per cent of the population survive through subsistence agriculture.
Much of the soil is infertile, rainfall is variable and crops are liable to cyclone damage. Copra is the only export crop. Family smallholdings produce subsistence crops of pulaka, taro and other vegetables, bananas and coconuts. Agriculture is under threat from salinisation of the soil caused by rising ocean waters.
Estimated crop and livestock production in 2005 included: 1,600 tonnes (t) coconuts, 140t roots & tubers, 270t bananas, 208t oilcrops, 735t fruit in total, 530t vegetables in total; 138t meat in total, 93t pig meat, 45t poultry, 22t eggs, 3t honey.

Fishing
Fishing and exploitation of the sea are important to the economy, serving mainly local consumption. There is potential to increase income by negotiating fisheries agreements with other countries. The typical annual marine fish catch is 500t.

Industry and manufacturing

A small industry sector (baking, construction, boat building, coconut oil mill, soap making etc) serves local needs, some handicrafts are exported.

Tourism

There is no developed tourist industry owing to Tuvalu's remote location, infrequent flights and lack of amenities, although a Tourism Action Plan has been developed. Air access from Fiji has improved, but the number of visitors, mainly on official or other business and relatives, is small. There were 1,377 visitors in 2003, of whom only 184 were classified as holiday-makers.
Facilities, including the airport, the sole hotel and some guest houses, are concentrated on Funafuti. The other islands are relatively unspoilt, but are not easily accessible.

Environment

The government has publicly acknowledged the problem of the rising sea levels, but feels the situation has been exaggerated by the world media. Claims that the islands will be washed away by 2050 are debateable.

Mining

Tuvalu has no known mineral resources.

Hydrocarbons

There are no known hydrocarbons reserves. The UN Law of the Sea gave Tuvalu an exclusive economic zone of 12,949 square km for exploration.

Banking and insurance

The state-owned National Bank of Tuvalu (NBT) dominates the country's banking sector. Its monopoly position ensures that it remains in profit.
Tuvalu's currency is the Australian dollar and interest rates are determined by the Reserve Bank of Australia (RBA), so the government has little control over monetary policy. The royalty revenues generated by the '.tv' domain name (after the sale of the DotTV Corporation) have been lower than expected and are paid irregularly.

Central bank
National Bank of Tuvalu

Time

GMT plus 12 hours

Geography

Tuvalu is a scattered group of nine small atolls, extending about 560km (350 miles) from north to south in the western Pacific Ocean. Fiji lies to the south, Kiribati to the north and the Solomon Islands to the west. At their highest point, these islands are only four metres above sea level, and vulnerable to the rise in sea levels caused through global warming.

Hemisphere
Southern

Climate

Hot and humid, temperatures 26–32 degrees Celsius. Rainfall varies considerably, up to 3,000mm in a year, falling most heavily from November–February. Hurricanes possible.

Entry requirements

Passports
Required by all.

Visa
None required, however visitors must have return/onward tickets and sufficient funds for their stay.

Currency advice/regulations
No restrictions on import and export of local and foreign currency.

Customs
Personal effects allowed duty-free. There are quarantine regulations for plants and animals, and it is inadvisable to carry fruit or plant material. Certain goods may be subject to regulation or import licensing, such as arms, fireworks, drugs, motorcycles, jewellery.

Health (for visitors)

Health facilities are basic.

Mandatory precautions
Vaccination certificate for yellow fever required if travelling from an infected zone.

Advisable precautions
There is rabies risk. Vaccinations for diphtheria, tuberculosis, hepatitis A and B, polio, tetanus and typhoid are recommended.

Hotels

There is only one hotel, the government owned Vaiaku Lagi Hotel. Reservations should be made well in advance. Visitors may be asked to share rooms when there are accommodation shortages. Private guest houses are also available.
Tipping is optional and not expected.

Public holidays (national)

Fixed dates
1 Jan (New Year's Day), 15 May (Gospel Day) 12 Jun (Queen's Official Birthday), 5 Aug (National Children's Day), 1–2 Oct (Tuvalu Days, Anniversary of Independence), 25–26 Dec (Christmas).
Holidays that fall at the weekend are taken either on Friday or Monday.

Variable dates
Commonwealth Day (second Mon in Mar), Good Friday, Easter Monday.

Working hours

Banking
Mon–Thu: 0930–1300; Fri: 0830–1200.

Business
Mon–Fri: 0800–1600.

Government
Mon–Thu: 0730–1615; Fri: 0730–1245.

Shops
Mon–Sat: 0630–1730.

Electricity supply

240V AC (on island of Funafuti only)

Weights and measures

Imperial system (metric units allowed in some instances).

Social customs/useful tips

Tipping is not customary. In business an informal attitude prevails. It is customary to shake hands on meeting and taking leave. Sometimes business cards are exchanged after introduction. Business is conducted in English. Visitors should be perceptive to unfamiliar local customs. Alcohol is generally available, but there are some limitations on consumption outside licensed premises. The minimum drinking age is 20 years.

Getting there
Air
International airport/s: Funafuti International (FUN), east of Funafuti.
Airport tax: Departure tax: A$10; not applicable to transit passengers
Surface
Water: There are two government-owned ships that sail infrequently between Suva (Fiji) and Funafuti; sailing time is three days.

Getting about
National transport
Road: The only tar roads are on Funafuti. Elsewhere there are tracks. There is a limited number of vehicles, including some minibuses.
Water: An inter-island service is available which can be interupted by bad weather.
City transport
Taxis: There are a few taxis from the airport to the city centre. Hotels offer an airport pick-up service.

BUSINESS DIRECTORY

The addresses listed below are a selection only. While World of Information makes every endeavour to check these addresses, we cannot guarantee that changes have not been made, especially to telephone numbers and area codes. We would welcome any corrections.

Telephone area codes
The international direct dialling (IDD) code for Tuvalu is +688 followed by subscriber's number.

Useful telephone numbers
Police and fire: 20-726
Ambulance: 20-749

Chambers of Commerce
Tuvalu Chamber of Commerce, PO Box 27, Funafuti (tel: 208-46; fax: 208-29).

Banking
Development Bank of Tuvalu, PO Box 9, Vaiaku, Funafuti (tel: 201-99; fax: 208-50).

Central bank
National Bank of Tuvalu; PO Box 13, Vaiaku, Funafuti (tel: 208-03; fax: 208-02; e-mail: gmbt@tuvalu.tu).

Travel information
Air Fiji, 185 Victoria Parade, Suva, Fiji (tel: (+679) 331-5055; email: suvasales@airfiji.com.fi).

Air Marshall Islands, PO Box 1319, Majuro MH 96960, Republic of the Marshall Islands (tel: (+692) 625-3731; fax: (+692) 625-3730; email: amisales@ntamar.net; internet: www.airmarshallislands.com).

Funafuit International Airport, Vaiaku Funafuti (tel: 20-737, 20-057; email: travel@tuvalu.tv).

Funafuti International Airport, Department of Civil Aviation, Ministry of Works and Communication, Private Mail Bag, Funafuti (tel: 20-737, 20-725, 20-721; fax: 20-722).

South Pacific Tourism Organisation, Level 3, FNPF Place, 343-359 Victoria Parade; PO Box 13119, Suva, Fiji (tel: (+679) 330-4177; internet: www.spto.org).

Tuvalu Marine Department, Vaiaku, Funafuti, (tel: 20-055; fax: 20-722; email: danitaleli@yahoo.co.nz).

Ministry of tourism
National tourist organisation offices
Tuvalu Tourism Office, Private Mail Bag, Vaiaku, Funafuti (tel: 20-184, 20-480; fax: 20-829; lleneuoti@yahoo.com; internet: www.timelesstuvalu.com).

Ministries
Ministry of Commerce and Natural Resources, Vaiaku, Funafuti.

Ministry of Finance, Vaiaku, Funafuti (tel: 20-840).

Statistics Division, c/o Finance Ministry, Vaiaku, Funafuti (tel: 20-839).

Other useful addresses
Asian Development Bank (ADB), South Pacific Regional Mission, La Casa di Andrea, Lini Highway; PO Box 127, Port Vila, Vanuatu (tel: (+678-2) 3300; fax: (+678-2) 3183; email: adbsprm@adb.org; internet: www.adb.org/SPRM).

Broadcasting and Information Office, Vaiaku Funafuti.

Business Development Advisory Board, PO Box 9, Funafuti (tel: 20-850).

Department of Civil Aviation, Ministry of Works and Communications, Private Mail Bag, Funafuti (tel: 20-737, 20-725, 20-721; fax: 20-722).

Department of Commerce, PO Box 33, Funafuti (tel: 20-839).

UN Permanent Mission of Tuvalu, 800 Second Avenue, Suite 400 B, New York, NY 10017 (tel: (+1-212) 490-0534; fax: (+1 212) 808-4975; email: enele@onecommonwealth.org).

Other news agencies: ABC Pacific Beat: www.radioaustralia.net.au/pacbeat

Pacific Magazine: www.pacificmagazine.net

Internet sites
South Pacific Tourism Organisation: www.tuvalu.spto.org

Tuvalu home page: www.tuvaluislands.com

Uganda

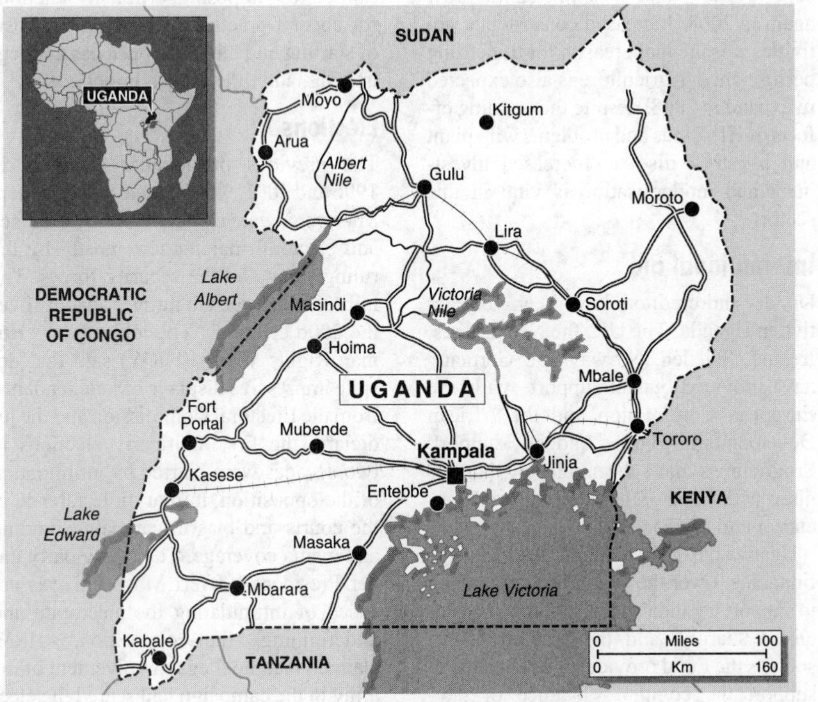

Once described, by Britain's war-time prime minister, Winston Churchill, as 'the Pearl of Africa' Uganda in 2008 was doing better than could have been imagined when President Museveni came to power in 1986. Some things don't change – Joseph Kony is still head of the Lords Resistance Army (LRA) (a cult-like group that for more than 20 years has been fighting to run the country along the lines of the biblical Ten Commandments) and still refusing to come to the peace table, this time not because he thinks he can win the battle, but because the International Criminal Court (ICC) has an arrest warrant out for him. And he doesn't think he can talk the ICC round as he might a fellow Ugandan.

For the last two decades, Uganda's economy has been characterised by high growth and low inflation. Growth in 2007 was 6.5 per cent, up on the 5.0 per cent of 2006. Inflation was steady at 6.8 per cent. Exports in 2007 were up by 42 per cent on 2006, driven mostly by increased diversification. Imports, however also showed a sharp increase, of 35 per cent, which was put down to improved foreign direct investment (FDI) in infrastructure projects.

The rain comes

Rainfall in Uganda during the 2007/08 growing season was normal and evenly distributed. Food production and cash crops were up and should help poverty reduction efforts as income and asset inequality decline. About 67 per cent of the labour force works in the agriculture sector.

Human rights

In the 1970s and early 1980s Uganda was notorious for its human rights abuses, first during the military dictatorship of Idi Amin from 1971–79 and then after the return to power of Milton Obote, who had been ousted by Amin. During this time up to half a million people were killed in state-sponsored violence. Since becoming president in 1986 Museveni has introduced democratic reforms and has been credited with substantially improving human rights, notably by reducing abuses by the army and the police. Never-the-less,

KEY FACTS

Official name: Republic of Uganda

Head of State: President Yoweri Kaguta Museveni (NRM) (since 1986; re-elected 23 Feb 2006)

Head of government: Prime Minister Apolo Nsimbabi (NRM) (since 1999)

Ruling party: National Resistance Movement (NRM)

Area: 236,036 square km

Population: 30.93 million (2005)

Capital: Kampala

Official language: English

Currency: Ugandan shilling (Ush) = 100 cents

Exchange rate: Ush1,630.00 per US$ (Jul 2008)

GDP per capita: US$309 (2007)*

GDP real growth: 6.50% (2007)*

Labour force: 13.76 million (2006)

Unemployment: 3.20% (2006)

Inflation: 6.80% (2007)

Balance of trade: -US$921.10 million (2005)

Foreign debt: US$4.82 billion (2004)

Visitor numbers: 539,000 (2006)*

* estimated figure

Uganda needs to strengthen and sustain measures introduced in recent years to improve governance and combat corruption in particular.

Despite economic and political challenges, the government has made notable improvements in social well being. Universal primary and secondary education programmes have been introduced, there are better health outcomes and continued reduction in HIV/Aids infection rates. But, the 2008 edition of the *African Economic Outlook* (AEO) deduces, further significant progress in poverty reduction will be difficult due to limited economic diversification and heavy dependence on subsistence agriculture.

Economic turnaround

Although Uganda has made considerable progress, none would deny that there is still a long way to go and the threat of further domestic and regional unrest cannot be dismissed. The tribal violence in Kenya in January 2008 was a sharp reminder or this. The foundation for the economic turnaround in Uganda was laid when the National Resistance Movement, under the leadership of President Yoweri Museveni, assumed control of the government in 1986. Uganda's annual average growth rate over the past decade of nearly 6.0 per cent is exceptional, given that Uganda is a landlocked country and has been buffeted by deteriorating terms of trade since the mid-1990s. The key challenge now is to sustain this growth so as to reduce poverty. The government is focussing on promoting productivity growth, reducing vulnerability to external shocks, diversifying the economy to high value added activities, and expanding private sector participation. Growth in 2008 was still below its potential because of infrastructure constraints, especially the energy deficit. Industrial output was up by almost 6 per cent in 2007, and is expected to grow again in 2008. Increased construction activities was the main reason for this strong performance. Agriculture is also expected to expand in 2008, despite the ongoing effects of HIV/Aids and problems with plant and livestock disease. Increased investment and modernisation is vital in this sector.

International aid

Donors and creditors have been very active in Uganda. The UK, the Netherlands, Ireland, Sweden, Norway and Germany have provided budget support, while the European Commission and the African Development Bank budget support. Programmes have been closely harmonised with those of the International Monetary Fund (IMF).

Uganda has no prolonged need for IMF financing. Over the years, Fund financing to support Uganda's reform efforts has declined sharply, and the amount of resources the Fund provides is not needed to support the country's balance of payments. In contrast, donor funds cover over one-half of public spending. There is a case for continued Fund engagement, possibly in a non-borrowing arrangement, which would provide for policy advice and a basis for continued donor support and to mobilise foreign private investment.

Transparency and accountability is essential for improving the business environment and promoting private sector growth. The authorities should curb corruption by imposing criminal sanctions for corrupt practices. Reducing the costs of starting and closing a business and registering land titles is also important.

Elections

The previous presidential elections in 1996 and 2001, which re-elected President Museveni, were characterised by violence and electoral malpractice, mostly by the ruling party and the security forces. The military continued to throw a shadow over the 2006 elections. The lobby group Human Rights Watch (HRW) said that despite impressive displays of independence from the Electoral Commission and the judiciary, the first multiparty elections in two decades were marred by intimidation of the opposition, military interference in the courts and bias in campaign funding and media coverage. The ruling party under President Yoweri Museveni was accused of intimidating the electorate and undermining the opposition. HRW claimed that the illegal involvement of the army in the campaign had scared the electorate, while the opposition had its hands tied by politically motivated criminal charges against its leaders. The Electoral Offences Squad investigated both the government and opposition parties for abuses, though accusations against the opposition were less serious. Museveni was only able to stand in these election because parliament had voted in 2005 to abolish a constitutional limit on presidential terms, thereby paving the way for Museveni to seek re-election.

Outlook

Despite isolated outbreaks of violence associated with a controversial development within a rain forest area, Uganda in 2007 and 2008 remained largely peaceful. In the north in former LRA territory, the United Nations High Commissioner for Refugees (UNHCR) estimated that as many as 500,000 refugees may have returned to their homes from displacement camps in neighbouring countries. After hosting the Commonwealth Head of Government Meeting (CHOGM) in Kampala in November 2007 Museveni will serve as Chairman of the Commonwealth until 2009.

KEY INDICATORS — Uganda

	Unit	2003	2004	2005	2006	2007
Population	m	24.49	25.52	28.82	29.85	30.93
Gross domestic product (GDP)	US$bn	6.30	6.83	8.73	9.49	*11.23
GDP per capita	US$	234	242	252	265	*309
GDP real growth	%	5.2	5.9	6.7	5.0	*6.5
Inflation	%	6.1	5.9	8.0	6.6	6.8
Industrial output	% change	–	5.6	9.1	3.4	–
Agricultural output	% change	–	5.2	5.1	5.0	–
Exports (fob) (goods)	US$m	498.0	705.3	862.5	1,187.6	1,686.2
Imports (cif) (goods)	US$m	1,151.0	1,460.3	1,783.6	2,215.6	2,982.5
Balance of trade	US$m	-653.0	-755.0	-921.1	-1,027.9	-1,296.4
Current account	US$m	-390.0	-130.0	-183.0	-379.0	-744.0
Total reserves minus gold	US$m	1,080.3	1,308.1	1,344.2	1,810.9	2,559.8
Foreign exchange	US$m	1,075.5	1,307.4	1,343.1	1,810.8	2,559.5
Exchange rate	per US$	1,898.50	1,810.30	1,810.50	1,810.50	1,706.70

* estimated figure

Risk assessment

Politics	Fair
Economy	Fair
Regional stability	Fair

COUNTRY PROFILE

Historical profile
1886–1890 The UK colonised Uganda.
1900 Bugunda in western Uganda became an autonomous region with its own constitutional monarchy.
1958 The UK allowed Uganda self-government.
1962 Uganda became an independent state within the Commonwealth.
1963 Uganda became a republic. Sir Edward Mutesa II, the King of Bugunda, became Uganda's first president.
1966 Milton Obote, the defence minister, seized power with the help of Colonel Idi Amin, second-in-command of the army. Obote repressed the Baganda and re-integrated Buganda.
1967 The constitutional role of kings was abolished, along with federal system of government.
1971 Obote was ousted by Idi Amin, who expelled the large Asian (mainly Indian) community and carried out purges in which thousands died. Asians had owned 90 per cent of Uganda's businesses and the economy collapsed.
1979 Tanzania invaded Uganda, causing Amin to flee to Saudi Arabia. Yusufu Lule was briefly appointed president before being replaced by Godfrey Binaisa.
1980 Obote won the presidential election and started to pursue liberal economic policies to obtain aid from western donors, and the economy began to improve.
1985 Ethnic feuding resulted in a coup removing Obote from power.
1986 Yoweri Museveni came to power at the head of the National Resistance Movement (NRM), which had waged a guerrilla war since 1981. He banned multi-party politics, saying they led to ethnic fighting.
1996 President Museveni was elected president for a five-year term.
1998 Uganda intervened in the Democratic Republic of Congo (DRC) on behalf of the rebels, against the Kabila government.
2001 President Museveni was re-elected. In legislative elections, the supporters of the 'No Party' Movement – formerly the NRM – secured a majority but over 50 MPs, including 10 ministers, lost their seats. President Museveni's cabinet was headed by incumbent Prime Minister Apolo Nsimbabi. A peace agreement was signed by Rwanda and Uganda in London.
2002 Over 400,000 people were evacuate from the war-zone at risk of brutal attacks on villages from the Lord's Resistance Army (LRA).
2003 The LRA announced a cease-fire, but as attacks continued an all-out offensive against the rebels was ordered. As Uganda withdrew the last of its troops from eastern DRC tens of thousands of DRC civilians fleeing fighting in their own country sought asylum in Uganda. Idi Amin died in Saudi Arabia.
2004 LRA rebels killed around 200 people at a camp for displaced persons in the north. President Museveni retired from the army at the rank of general. Faltering peace talks between the government and the LRA began.
2005 The constitution was amended which struck down the limit to presidential terms in office. Multi-party politics was restored by referendum. The International Criminal Court (ICC) issued arrest warrants for five commanders of the LRA including its leader, Joseph Kony. Opposition presidential candidate, Kizza Besgiye, was arrested after he returned from exile and accused of terrorism and unlawful possession of firearms. Uganda was ordered to pay compensation for rights abuses and plundering the DRC during its occupation in 2003 by the International Court of Justice (ICJ).
2006 Besigye was bailed allowing him to campaign in the presidential election, which was won by Yoweri Museveni. Kizza Besigye was acquitted of the charge against him. A cease-fire was agreed between government forces and the LRA. The UNHCR estimated that there were 1.5 million refugees of the long-running conflict in displacement camps in neighbouring countries; within two months, over 300,000 had returned to their homes.
2007 Racial violence erupted in April in Kampala, forcing police to protect Asian businesses and a Hindu temple in a conflict over a allowing development within an area of rain forest. Uganda and the DRC worked to defuse a border dispute in August. Severe flooding caused widespread damage in September.
2008 The LRA signed a permanent cease-fire during talks in Juba, Sudan. In April, Kony (leader of LRA) refused to sign the peace deal saying he did not understand the workings of the special court to be set up to try rebels. Peace negotiations resumed on 1 August but broke down within weeks. On 19 August the government rejected Kony's approach for talks to resume. Interior minister, Ruhaka Rugunda said after two years of negotiating there was nothing more to discuss and General Kony should have signed the peace agreement earlier.

Political structure
Between 1986 and 2006 parties were allowed under the 'no party' system, introduced after Museveni's accession to power, to exist but not to campaign, all parliamentary candidates running for elections as independents. The system was confirmed by referendum in 2000. Following another referendum in July 2005, party politics was re-introduced.

Constitution
An elected constituent assembly drafted a constitution which was promulgated on 8 October 1995. It retains the system of non-party government.
In July 2005, the Ugandan parliament voted for a constitutional amendment to allow President Yoweri Museveni to stay longer in office; he should stand down in 2006.

Form of state
Unitary republic

The executive
The president is elected for a five-year term. The president appoints a prime minister and a cabinet composed of representatives of a number of political parties.

National legislature
The Ugandan parliament has 292 members including 214 elected constituency representatives, 53 district women representatives, 10 Uganda People's Defence Forces (UPDF) representatives, five youth representatives, five representatives of disabled people and five workers' representatives.
The Movement system allows parties to exist in name but not to function. All candidates in parliamentary elections run as individuals.

Legal system
The legal system is based on English common law and the 1995 constitution.

Last elections
23 February 2006 (presidential and parliamentary).
Results: Presidential: Yoweri Museveni won 59.26 per cent of the votes; Kizza Besigne won 37.39 per cent. Turnout was 69.19 per cent.
Parliamentary: NRM won 205 seats (out of 333); FDC won 37 seats; Uganda People's Congress (UPC) nine seats; and Democratic Party (DP) eight seats. Turnout was 72 per cent.

Next elections
2011 (presidential and parliamentary).

Political parties

Ruling party
National Resistance Movement (NRM)

Main opposition party
Forum for Democratic Change (FDC).

Population
30.93 million (2005)
Last census: September 2002: 24,442,084

Population density: 114 inhabitants per square km; rural population per sq km of arable land: 349. Urban population: 15 per cent.
There is a high rural density in the south, in a belt from east to west. The north is sparsely populated.
Annual growth rate: 3.2 per cent 1994–2004 (WHO 2006)
Internally Displaced Persons (IDP)
1.6 million (UNHCR 2004)
Ethnic make-up
There are over 20 ethnic groups of which the Baganda, Banyankole and Basoga are the largest. Approximately 99 per cent of the population is of African descent and 1 per cent European or Asian.
Religions
Christianity (71 per cent), traditional beliefs (13 per cent), Islam (5 per cent), others (11 per cent).

Education

Unesco reported that a government's education programme launched in 1997, had successfully increased primary school enrolment from 2.5 million in 1997 to 6.5 million in 2001. The programme provided free primary education to four children including orphaned and disabled children from each household.
Primary school lasts for seven years and, having successfully undertaken exams, students then follow either an acedemic or vocational secondary schooling.
Literacy rate: 69 per cent adult rate; 80 per cent youth rate (15–24) (Unesco 2005).
Compulsory years: None.
Enrolment rate: 74 per cent gross primary; 12 per cent gross secondary; of relevant age groups, (including repeaters) (World Bank).
Pupils per teacher: 35 in primary schools.

Health

Per capita total expenditure on health (2003) was US$75; of which per capita government spending was US$23, at the international dollar rate, (WHO 2006).
The lack of resources and an extreme dependence on foreign aid has resulted in a high infant and maternal mortality rate and low immunisation coverage.
Improved water sources are available to 42 per cent of the population.
HIV/Aids
In 2005 there were an estimated 800,000 people living with HIV/Aids, with 100,000 new infections each year. Even though the prevalence has been falling – down to 6 per cent in 2005 from the high of 30 per cent in the early 1990s – those who are developing Aids is increasing and putting social and economic pressure on the country's resources. The number of people living longer with HIV has been rising due to anti-retroviral (ARV) drugs; there are over 65,000 patients currently receiving ARV medication. Since the beginning of the pandemic in Uganda, an estimated one million people have died of Aids and the government expects another to be treating over 50,000 Aids suffers each year.
Uganda was the first country in sub-Saharan Africa to show a decrease in the number of HIV positive sufferers, due to an extensive, long-term government initiative to combat the spread of the disease (one of the best instituted in Africa). UNAIDS granted US$250 million (2001–06) for government sponsored projects from the Global Fund to fight HIV/Aids, Tuberculosis and Malaria.
Rural areas have been badly hit with productivity and output in the agricultural sector significantly fallen as Aids has taken its toll of workers and those that curtail their time in the fields to care for the sick.
In April 2005, US researchers upheld findings of a 1997 Ugandan study that claimed the Aids drug Nevirapine was safe and effective. The use of the drug, to limit HIV mother-to-child infection, was embroiled in a politicised row in 2004 when it was claimed poor record keeping had invalidated the trial of the drug and that is was unsafe and causing thousands of severe side effects, including deaths.
A factory in Kampala, to open for production by January 2008, will produce three-in-one tablets of HIV/Aids anti-retorviral and anti-malaria medication. Domestic production reduces the need for and cost of imported drugs. Nevertheless, national distribution remains the largest impediment for healthworkers to manage in a country where only 41 per cent of HIV patients receive anti-retroviral drugs. Uganda has cut its HIV/Aids infection rate from 30 per cent in the 1990s to less than 10 per cent in 2007.
HIV prevalence: 4.1 per cent aged 15–49 in 2003 (World Bank)
Life expectancy: 49 years, 2004 (WHO 2006)
Fertility rate/Maternal mortality rate: 7.1 births per woman, 2004 (WHO 2006); maternal mortality rate 510 per 100,000 live births (World Bank).
Birth rate/Death rate: 46.6 births and 17 deaths per 1,000 people (2003).
Child (under 5 years) mortality rate (per 1,000): 81 per 1,000 live births (2003); 38 per cent of children aged under five are malnourished (World Bank).
Head of population per physician: 0.08 physicians per 1,000 people, 2004 (WHO 2006)

Welfare

The distribution of income in Uganda is less unequal than most countries in Africa, with the richest 20 per cent of the country owning 44.9 per cent of the national wealth while the bottom 20 per cent earning 7.1 per cent of the country's income. Around 10 per cent of the rural population lives under the national poverty line, while around 40 per cent of the urban population is classified as poor. The informal sector employs over 80 per cent of the urban population, implying a high degree of job insecurity and casual labour.

Main cities
Kampala (capital, estimated population 1.3 million in 2005), Gulu (138,946), Jinja (92,483).

Languages spoken
KiSwahili, Luganda and Luo are widely spoken.
Official language/s
English

Media

Press
The Media Council (http://mediavisionsite.com) regulates and censors information.
Dailies: The government publishes two newspapers, Bukedde (www.bukedde.co.ug) in Luganda and The New Vision (www.newvision.co.ug) in English. The Monitor (www.monitor.co.ug) and Red Pepper (www.redpepper.ug) (a tabloid) are independent and published in English.
Weeklies: The government publishes three regional newspapers, Orumuri (www.orumuri.co.ug) Rupiny (www.rupiny.co.ug) and Etop (www.etop.co.ug) in local languages. All daily newspapers have Sunday editions. The Observer Weekly (www.ugandaobserver.com) and Entatsi (in Runyakitara) are independent. .
Business: Apart from daily newspaper with business sections East African Business Week (http://www.busiweek.com) is based in Kampala.
Periodicals: In Luganda, Musizi is a Catholic monthly publication.
Broadcasting
The Uganda Communications Commission (www.ucc.co.ug) is responsible for the communications industry.
Radio: There has been a large expansion of services with many private local radio stations in operation. The public broadcaster is the Uganda Broadcast Corporation (UBC), with a national FM network with channels on Radio Uganda called Blue, Red, Green and Butebo, which provide programmes in English, KiSwahili and 20 local languages. Private stations include 95N9 Touch FM (www.touch.fm) and Arua One FM (www.aruaonefm.com) and the women's community radio Mama

FM (http://interconnection.org/umwa/community_radio.html).
Television: There are over a dozen channels broadcasting by terrestrial, cable and satellite. The state-owned UBC television service is a commercial service, broadcastings mainly in English, KiSwahili and Luganda. Most networks are privately-owned, including WBS Television (www.wbs-tv.com), which is centred on Kampala, as well as Multichoice, Nation TV and Pulse TV; Nkabi Broadcasting Services in based in Jinja. There are several Christian channels including Record Television Network, Top TV and Christian Life Ministries. Foreign channels are provided by Digital Satellite Television DSTV

Economy

Uganda's main problem is its reliance on coffee exports, which account for 70 per cent of export revenues and which have declined in unit value due to the depressed world coffee market. GDP has been growing annually by 5–6 per cent. Good macroeconomic indicators hide the fact that many Ugandans are not enjoying the fruits of growth, with a strong divide between the south-east and the troubled north and south-west. Inflation is high, having reached eight per cent in 2005. With monetary tools having a limited effect on macroeconomic indicators, fiscal policy plays an important role in achieving economic goals. Despite the government's attempts at fiscal sustainability, it faces problems with revenue collection and overspending which are largely linked to factors outside its control, such as droughts and depressed export prices.

External trade

Uganda is a member of the East African Economic Community (EAC) (with Kenya and Tanzania), which operates a customs union with common external tariffs.
Uganda is also a member of the Common Market for Eastern and Southern Africa (Comesa), and operates a free trade area with 13 of the 19 member states.
With ample, fertile land and good rainfalls agriculture provides the opportunity to cultivate a number of cash crops, including coffee, tea, tobacco, vanilla, cotton and cut flower (flown to European markets within hours of preparation). Industrial production is progressively replacing imports of construction materials, foodstuffs and household goods. Remittances are also an important source of foreign exchange.

Imports

Principal imports are capital equipment, vehicles, petroleum, medical supplies and cereals.
Main sources: Kenya (32.0 per cent total, 2005), UAE (8.6 per cent), South Africa (6.4 per cent), India (5.7 per cent), China (5.2 per cent), UK (4.4 per cent), US (4.1 per cent), Japan (4.0 per cent)

Exports

Principal exports are agricultural products, coffee (typically 70 per cent of total), tea, cotton, fish and fish products, horticultural products and gold.
Main destinations: Kenya (15.1 per cent total, 2005), Belgium (9.9 per cent), The Netherlands (9.7 per cent), France (7.1 per cent), Germany (5.1 per cent), Rwanda (4.0 per cent)

Re-exports

Gold, diamonds, coltan and niobium, mostly from neighbouring DRC.

Agriculture

Farming

Agriculture accounted for 32.2 per cent of GDP in 2004. Around 80 per cent of the population derive their livelihood from agriculture. The area under cultivation has only increased by one-third over the last 30 years.The situation has been worsened by irregular rainfall and climate change. This has eroded the farmers' confidence in applying improved technology to increase productivity, resulting in crop and livestock yields which have been ranked among the lowest in the world. Agricultural development is hampered by shortages of vital inputs, damage caused by civil war, low producer prices and corrupt purchasing bodies.
Uganda's varied climate allows the production of a wide range of produce. Around 75 per cent of Uganda's agricultural output is made up of food crop production, two-thirds of which is used for subsistence. Maize is one of the main food crops and is grown around Lake Victoria as a cash crop. The fertility of Ugandan land could make it a bread basket for East Africa, particularly if the effects of periodic droughts are ameliorated by adequate irrigation techniques.
Coffee is the main cash crop, providing around 70 per cent of agricultural export earnings. Most production is carried out on a small-scale basis. Rehabilitation of coffee holdings has been the main stimulus to economic growth in recent years. The government has encouraged planting of clone coffee which yields in a shorter period of around two years, is more disease resistant and gives higher yields. The private sector controls over 90 per cent of the coffee trade in Uganda. Liberalisation of the coffee market has meant that producers can sell coffee on the open market to the highest bidder, although the dismantling of state marketing boards has meant that they are more vulnerable to price fluctuations and have to deal with often unscrupulous middlemen. The formation of co-operatives has become a basis for reducing the adverse effects of liberalisation. There was concern in 2007 that the economic partnership agreement (EPA) between the EU and Africa, Caribbean and Pacific developing countries would have an adverse affect on coffee growers if the EU did not remove subsidies on its domestic coffee industries. Around 15,000 coffee farmers are certified as organic growers, out of a total number of one million growers. Uganda mostly grows Robusta coffee and has benefited from the political crisis in Côte d'Ivoire since 2002.
Cotton was once an important cash crop, but due to its labour intensiveness, relatively high cost of production and a poor marketing system, farmers looked towards growing non-traditional cash crops which have a readily available market. Cotton growing is being revived in some eastern areas, and production has been boosted by reforms in agricultural pricing and marketing regimes introduced in the 1990s. Sugar is grown on several vast estates and production is creeping up after collapsing completely in the early 1980s after then President Idi Amin forced Asians, who were the main sugar growers, to leave in 1972. Tobacco and tea are also important cash crops.
Exports of flowers increased by nearly 20 per cent in 2007 to a record US$32 million.
Estimated crop production in 2005 included: 2,625,000 tonnes (t) cereals in total, 1,350,000t maize, 5,500,000t cassava, 700,000t millet 573,000t potatoes, 2,650,000t sweet potatoes, 420,000t sorghum, 140,000t rice, 615,000t bananas, 9,900,000t plantains, 711,300t pulses, 139.270t oilcrops, 33,000t tobacco, 4,000t cocoa beans, 186,000t green coffee, 70t vanilla, 2,100t pepper spice, 1,600,000t sugar cane, 36,000t tea, 22,200t cotton lint, 10,567,650t fruit in total, 556,000t vegetables in total. Estimated livestock production included: 256,282t meat in total, 106,000t beef, 60,000t pig-meat, 5,782t lamb 28,800t goat meat, 37,700t poultry, 20,000t eggs, 700,000t milk, 300t honey, 14,847t cattle hides, 6,000t goatskins, 994mt sheepskins.

Fishing

Uganda's fishing industry is important, both for domestic consumption and export. The annual catch is typically around 220,000 tonnes, 40 per cent of which is exported. In 2004, the industry is estimated to have added US$100 million or six per cent to the nation's economy.
The fisheries industry is mostly based on inland capture fisheries from lakes Victoria, Albert, Edward, George and Kyoga. Lake Victoria is Uganda's most important fishery, supplying some 50 per cent of the national catch. Nile perch obtained from

Lake Victoria alone amount to 110,000 tonnes and remains the largest fish export item to the markets of Europe, Australia and South-East Asia. Estimates of Lake Kyoga put supplies at 30,000 tonnes, with the nature of the fishery shifting from a prolific Nile perch and tilapia fishery to increased supplies of mukene.

Forestry

Uganda is moderately forested with around 30 per cent forest cover and an additional 48 per cent of other wooded land. The majority of timber production is used in domestic fuel. There is a wide network of protected areas, including 50 parks and nature reserves. A large proportion of household energy needs are met by fuelwood. The sector produces sawnwood from local hardwood species and much of industrial roundwood is used for agricultural purposes. Paper is imported in large quantities.

Timber imports in 2004 were US$39 million, while exports amounted to US$1.8 billion.

Timber production in 2004 included 39,409,000 cubic metre (cum) roundwood, 3,175,000cum industrial roundwood, 264,000cum sawnwood, 1,055,000cum sawlogs and veneer logs, 2,500,000cum pulpwood, 4,600cum wood-based panels, 36,234,600cum woodfuel; 792,417t charcoal.

Industry and manufacturing

Industry accounts for around 21 per cent of GDP. The industrial sector is has seen relatively high levels of growth, particularly in food processing, tobacco, beverages, timber/paper and chemicals/soap.

Underutilisation of factory capacity and lack of foreign exchange tend to inhibit progress.

Other industries are textiles, cement, plastics, steel, metal products and brewing. Most of these are operating well below capacity mainly due to shortages of imported materials, spares and fuel, inadequate infrastructure and a lack of skilled manpower.

The building industry is hampered by a lack of finance and skilled manpower and most local building equipment factories still produce at only 50 per cent of their installed capacities. Consequently, many finished products, such as cement, sanitary ware, plumbing pipes and glass are imported.

The textile sector has failed to take advantage of the US's African Growth and Opportunity Act (AGOA), which gives the textile industries from qualifying countries like Uganda access to US markets. Manufacturers have been unable to raise capacity, so they cannot fulfill the demands of US customers. The sector's decline is due to a fall in cotton producton, which has been adversely affected by political instability in the cotton-growing northern regions.

Industrial production increased by 6.3 per cent in 2003.

Tourism

The government is investing heavily in tourism to build it up as major currency earner. Insecurity in parts of the country continues to be a handicap, but visitor numbers in 2004 increased by 68 per cent over the previous year, registering around 512,000 arrivals. The sector is expected to contribute 4.6 per cent to GDP in 2005.

In February 2008 the governments of Democratic Republic of Congo, Rwanda and Uganda agreed to joint measures to protect the mountain gorillas found within their shared border regions. Tourists visiting the area to view the endangered great apes raise a combined US$5 million for the countries concerned.

Environment

In February 2008 the governments of Democratic Republic of Congo, Rwanda and Uganda agreed to joint measures to protect the mountain gorillas found within their shared border regions. Tourists visiting the area to view the endangered great apes raise a combined US$5 million for the countries concerned. However, poaching and civil strife have dropped the numbers of gorillas to critically endangered levels, so that a 10-year conservation project which focuses of security and encouraging local people to preserve the animals and habitat is seen as the only hope for the gorilla's survival

Mining

Uganda has deposits of copper, cobalt and iron ore, as well as less viable fields of tungsten, beryl, columbo-tantalite, gold, bismuth, tin, limestone and phosphates. Uganda's mineral potential remains untested due to very little exploration to date.

Hydrocarbons

In March 2007, the Canadian oil company Heritage Oil announced that it had positive results from five oil wells dug in Uganda's western Rift Valley. No oil reserves information was given but the oil is considered to be of good quality. Heritage Oil and Energy Africa Uganda each has a 50 per cent interest in the area under exploration. If the oil reserves are found to support commercially viable levels of production, Uganda stands to benefit significantly, and notwithstanding proceeds from oil output, analysts estimate that investment could amount to US$60 million over 15 years.

The downstream industry is dependent on the importation of refined petroleum products and is the largest item of foreign exchange outflow. The majority of refined oil it consumes is imported from the Kenyan Mombassa Refinery. The development of the East African Community involving Uganda, Kenya and Tanzania will improve the pipeline infrastructure. A US$110 million pipeline from Kenya to Uganda is scheduled to begin construction in October 2006 and be completed in late 2007.

Neither natural gas nor coal is produced or imported.

Energy

Uganda relies on imported oil for around 50 per cent of its energy needs, the balance being provided by hydroelectricity. Nalubaale (Owen Falls) power station, operating since the mid-1950s, and its Kiira extension supply almost all of the electricity system's capacity of 380MW. Less than five per cent of the population has access to electricity, which due to growing demand of 30–40 MW per year, has to be rationed. After being dogged by controversy, a 250MW hydro-plant was inaugurated at Bujagali in August 2007 for completion in 2011–12. The scheme is a public-private partnership with the government, costing around US$750 million. It has World Bank assistance.

Financial markets

Stock exchange

The Kampala Stock Exchange (KSE) began trading in 1998.

Banking and insurance

Great efforts are being made to improve efficiency in the banking sector, including the placement of local banks under statutory management. However, Uganda's banking sector remains weak. In recent years, the Bank of Uganda's (BoU) (central bank) regulatory powers have been insufficient, with reports that troubled banks have failed to meet their reserve requirements.

In an effort to reverse the situation, the BoU increased the capital requirements of all banks and was granted power to close banks that failed to comply with a number of regulations. As a result, the ratio of non-performing loans to total assets has fallen and banking system profitability has improved. However, the BoU was forced to seize control of the Uganda Commercial Bank (UCB) after its privatisation due to fraudulent behaviour by the buyer. In 2002, an 80 per cent stake in UCB was sold to South Africa's Standard Bank Group.

The government is planning to increase the availability of credit to poor rural areas through micro-finance and a lighter regulatory framework.

Central bank
Bank of Uganda
Main financial centre
Kampala

Time
GMT plus three hours

Geography
Uganda is a landlocked country in East Africa, bordered by Sudan to the north, the Democratic Republic of Congo (DCR) to the west, Kenya to the east and Rwanda, Tanzania and Lake Victoria to the south.
The terrain is mainly plateau, stretching northwards from Lake Victoria and declining gradually from around 1,500m to 900m towards the Sudan border. Mountain ranges and volcanic hills ring the country. The highest point at 5,110m is Marherita Peak on snow-capped Mount Stanley. Lakes, swampland and rivers occupy around 20 per cent of the country. Lake Victoria occupies much of the south-easten corner of Uganda, stradding the borders with Kenya and Tanzania. In the west the frontier with the DRC passes through lakes Albert and Edward. The White Nile rises in Lake Victoria and travels north through Lakes Kyoga and Albert towards Sudan.
Much of the country is savannah and semi-desert, but there are equatorial forests in the central zone.
Hemisphere
Straddles the equator

Climate
Equatorial, tempered by high altitude. Temperatures are fairly constant throughout the year, hottest months December–February, June–August, with daytime range (in Kampala) of 27–29 degrees Celsius (C) compared with an annual average of 26 degrees C (night-time average 16 degrees C). Heaviest rainfall occurs March–May, October–November; April is wettest month (average fall for month 175 mm).

Dress codes
Lightweight clothing is advisable all year round. Senior officials tend to wear suits, local businessmen and government officials wear suits or safari suits. Light cotton dresses, skirts and blouses or lightweight suits are advised for women. A lightweight raincoat may be needed at any time of the year.

Entry requirements
Passports
Required by all, valid for six months from date of arrival.
Visa
Required by all, except nationals of COMESA and other countries listed on www.ugandaembassy.com/visa.htm (countries with reciprical visa-free entry).
Currency advice/regulations
Import and export of local currency is prohibited. There is no restriction on the import of foreign currency, subject to declaration on arrival, or on the export of foreign currency up to the amount declared on arrival.
Customs
Duty-free allowances are: one litre of spirits or wines, 500ml of perfume or toilet water, 225 grammes of tobacco products.
Prohibited imports
Game trophies require special permit.

Health (for visitors)
Mandatory precautions
A valid international certificate of vaccination against cholera is required for entry into and exit from Uganda. Vaccination must have taken place not less than seven days and no more than six months prior to entering the country. A valid international certificate of vaccination against yellow fever is also required for visitors arriving from infected areas. The certificate becomes valid 12 days after vaccination and lasts for 10 years.
Advisable precautions
There is a risk of malaria, typhoid is a risk outside main towns. Normal precautions for the tropics with regard to hygiene and drinking water should be taken. Bilharzia risk is present in the lakes and rivers and visitors are advised to swim only in well-maintained swimming pools. A mild form of dysentery is common. Rabies is a risk.
The Aids virus has reached epidemic proportions and precautions should be taken, including a travel kit with disposable syringe and needles. Any medicines required should be brought with the visitor and accompanied by their original packaging.
Medical facilities are limited and visitors should have sufficient insurance to ensure medical evacuation.

Hotels
Private and government-owned, variable standard, but available in all main centres. Should be booked in advance.

Credit cards
Most car hire firms and travel agencies refuse credit cards.

Public holidays (national)
Fixed dates
1 Jan (New Year's Day), 26 Jan (Liberation Day), 8 Mar (Women's Day), 1 May (Labour Day), 3 Jun (Martyrs Day), 9 Jun (National Heroes Day), 9 Oct (Independence Day), 25–26 Dec (Christmas).
Variable dates
Good Friday, Easter Monday, Ascension Day, Eid al Adha, Eid al Fitr.

Working hours
Banking
Mon–Fri: 0900–1400. Some bureaux de change open Sat and Sun.
Business
Mon–Fri: 0830–1245, 1400–1700.
Government
Mon–Fri: 0830–1245, 1400–1700.
Shops
Mon–Fri: 0830–1700; Sat: 0900–1600.

Telecommunications
Postal services
Not very reliable.
Mobile/cell phones
GSM 900 services are available throughout most of the country.

Electricity supply
240V AC, 50 cycles.

Social customs/useful tips
Appointments are essential for business meetings. Ugandans have a less urgent sense of time than Europeans, and appointments often run late, particularly if it is raining.
The customary form of greeting is to shake hands. Exchanging business cards is an established ritual.
Visitors should remember that an increasing number of Hindus and Muslims are engaged in commerce and local advice should be obtained if any entertainment is planned. There are many local traditions, but few will affect business visitors and tourists.

Security
There are still areas of the country that are not under secure government control. Rebel activity occasionally targets tourists, and visitors are advised to check with local embassies if they intend to travel away from the main urban centres or main road and rail routes. The government has stepped up its campaign against lawlessness.
Due to rebel raids, including activity spilling over from neighbouring countries, visitors are warned against travelling to certain destinations, particularly the northern and south-western regions, where the Mountains of the Moon and several game parks are located.

Getting there
Air
National airline: The government holds a 20 per cent in Victoria International Airlines, which has a limited number of southern African routes.
International airport/s: Entebbe (EBB), 35km from Kampala; duty-free shop, restaurant, bank, post office, car hire.
Airport tax: None
Surface
Road: There is road access from neighbouring countries, but the Sudanese

border crossing is not open to general traffic. There are daily bus services between Nairobi (Kenya) and Kampala.

Rail: There is a joint Kenyan-Ugandan rail link between Nairobi and Kampala, but it has been out of service for some time. Revival of the line is in prospect following transfer of control to a private company in November 2006.

Water: There are ferry services across Lake Victoria from Mwanza (Tanzania) and Kisumu (Kenya).

Getting about

National transport

Road: Uganda has a road network of around 35,000km. Most of the country is served by dirt roads of varying quality, but there are around 3,000km of surface roads connecting the main towns. Many major roads are in good condition.

Buses: Regular services scheduled include Entebbe-Kampala (journey time: 30–45 minutes). There are services between most main centres but they tend to be crowded. An interstate bus service between Kampala and Kigali (Rwanda) is frequently suspended due to military activity. Akamba Bus regularly travels between Kampala and Nairobi (Kenya).

Rail: Two Uganda-Kenya railway agreements were signed in April 2006. In Uganda a concession agreement covers the freight services of Uganda Railways Corporation (URC), while an Interface agreement covers matters common to the Kenya freight and passenger concession and the Uganda freight concession. The Rift Valley Railways Consortium (RVRC) will invest US$15 million over the first five years and a further US$75 million over the remainder of the agreement in Uganda and US$45 and US$300 million respectively in Kenya.

Water: Some freight and passenger transport is available on Lake Victoria.

City transport

Taxis: Available at airport and in Kampala at hotels, the railway station, main park and near major office blocks. The drive from Entebbe airport to Kampala city centre takes 45 minutes. Matatus (public taxis) are available within Kampala, its suburbs and in all major towns.

Car hire

Car hire is expensive. Services are available, mainly with driver, from a number of rental firms, and through independent taxi drivers. Driving is on the left. A valid international driving licence is required.

BUSINESS DIRECTORY

The addresses listed below are a selection only. While World of Information makes every endeavour to check these addresses, we cannot guarantee that changes have not been made, especially to telephone numbers and area codes. We would welcome any corrections.

Telephone area codes

The international direct dialling (IDD) code for Uganda is +256, followed by area code:

Entebbe	42	Lugazi	44
Fort Portal	483	Masaka	481
Jinja	43	Mbale	45
Kampala	41	Mbarara	485
Kasese	483	Tororo	45

Useful telephone numbers

Ambulance, fire, police: 999
Directory enquiries: 901
International hospital: 340-531, 345-768

Chambers of Commerce

Uganda National Chamber of Commerce and Industry, PO Box 3809, Kampala (tel: 225-8791; fax: 225-8793; e-mail: uncci@uol.co.ug).

Banking

Allied Bank International Uganda Ltd, PO Box 2750, 45 Jinja Road, Kampala (tel: 223-6535; fax: 223-0902; e-mail: allied@alliedbank.co.ug).

Bank of Baroda (Uganda) Ltd, PO Box 7197, 18 Kampala Road, Kampala (tel: 223-3680; fax: 225-8263; e-mail: bobho@spacenet.co.ug).

Barclays Bank of Uganda Ltd, PO Box 7101, 16 Kampala Road, Kampala (tel: 223-0972; fax: 225-9467; e-mail: uganda.barclays@barclays.com).

Cairo International Bank Ltd, PO Box 7052, 30 Kampala Road, Kampala (tel: 223-0136; fax: 223-0130; e-mail: cib@spacenetuganda.com).

Centenary Rural Development Bank Ltd, PO Box 1892, 7 Entebbe Road, Kampala (tel: 225-1276; fax: 225-1273; e-mail: info@centenarybank.co.ug).

Citibank Uganda Ltd, PO Box 7505, Centre Court, 4 Ternan Avenue, Nakasero, Kampala (tel: 234-0625; fax: 234-0624).

Crane Bank Ltd, PO Box 22572, 38 Kampala Road, Kampala (tel: 234-5345; fax: 223-1578; e-mail: cranebank@cranebanklimited.com).

Diamond Trust Bank (U) Ltd, PO Box 7155, 17/19 Kampala Rd, Kampala (tel: 225-9331; fax: 324-2286; e-mail: dtbu@spacenetuganda.com).

East African Development Bank, PO Box 7128, 4 Nile Avenue, Kampala (tel: 223-0021; fax: 225-9763; e-mail: dg@eadb.org).

Nile Bank Ltd, PO Box 2834, Spear House, 22 Jinja Road, Kampala (tel: 234-6904; fax: 225-7779; e-mail: comments@nilebank.co.ug).

Orient Bank Limited, PO Box 3072, 6 Kampala Road, Kampala (tel: 223-6012; fax: 234-8039; e-mail: mail@orient-bank.com).

Stanbic Bank Uganda Ltd, PO Box 7131, 45 Kampala Road, Kampala (tel: 223-1151; fax: 223-1116).

Standard Chartered Bank Uganda Ltd, PO Box 7111, 5 Speke Road, Kampala (tel: 225-8211; fax: 223-1473; e-mail: scb.uganda@standardchartered.com).

Tropical Africa Bank Ltd, PO Box 7292, 27 Kampala Road, Kampala (tel: 223-2857; fax: 221-2296; e-mail: admin@trafbank.com).

Central bank

Bank of Uganda, PO Box 7120, 37–43 Kampala Rd, Kampala (tel: 258-441; fax: 230-878; e-mail: info@boa.or.ug).

Travel information

Automobile Association of Uganda, 39 William Street, PO Box 10542, Kampala (tel: 225-0814; fax: 234-1245; e-mail: aau@africaonline.co.ug).

Eagle Aviation, Adam House, 11 Portal Avenue, PO Box 7392, Kampala (tel: 234-4292; fax: 234-4501;

e-mail: admin@flyeagleuganda.com).

East African Airlines, Pan Africa House, 3 Kimathi Avenue, PO Box 2389, Kampala (tel: 226-0625; fax: 234-9875;

e-mail: info@flyeastafrican.com).

Uganda Wildlife Authority, 7 Kira Road, PO Box 3530, Kampala; (tel: 234-6287; fax: 234-6291; e-mail: uwa@uwa.or.ug).

Ministry of tourism

Ministry of Tourism, Trade and Industry, Farmers House, Parliament Avenue, PO Box 7103, Kampala (tel: 234-3947; fax: 234-7286; e-mail: mintrade@mtti.co.ug).

National tourist organisation offices

Tourism Uganda, 13/15 Kimathi Avenue, Impala House, P.O.Box 7211, Kampala (tel: 234-2196; fax: 234-2188; e-mail: utb@visituganda.com).

Ministries

Ministry of Education and Sports, 17/19 Hannington Rd, PO Box 7063, Kampala (tel: 223-4451; fax: 223-44920; e-mail: pro@education.go.ug).

Ministry of Energy and Mineral Development, Amber House, 29-32 Kampala Road, PO Box 7270, Kampala (tel: 232-3355;fax: 223-0220; e-mail: psmemd@energy.go.ug).

Ministry of Finance, Planning and Economic Development, 2/12 Apollo Kaggwa Road, PO Box 8147, Kampala (tel: 270-7000; fax: 223-0163; e-mail: webmaster@finance.go.ug).

Ministry of Foreign Affairs, Parliament Building, PO Box 7048, Kampala (tel: 225-7525; fax: 225-6722; e-mail: mofa@starcom.co.ug).

Ministry of Gender, Labour and Social Development, Simbamanyo House, 2 Lumumba Avenue, PO Box 7136 , Kampala (tel: 234-7854; fax: 225-6374; e-mail: ps@mglsd.go.ug).

Ministry of Health, 6 Lourdel Road, PO Box 7272, Wandegeya, Kampala (tel: 234-0884; fax: 234-0887; e-mail: info@health.go.ug).

Ministry of Justice and Constitutional Affairs, 1 Parliament Avenue, PO Box 7183, Kampala (tel: 223-0538; fax: 225-4829; e-mail: info@justice.go.ug).

Ministry of Local Government, 1 Pilkington Road, PO Box 7037, Kampala (tel: 234-1224; fax: 225-8127; e-mail: info@molg.go.ug).

Ministry of Public Service, 12 Nakasero Hill Road, PO Box 7003, Kampala (tel: 225-5651; fax: 225-5643; e-mail: ps@publicservice.go.ug).

Ministry of Water, Lands and Environment, Century House, Parliament Avenue, PO Box 7096, Kampala (tel: 234-2931; fax: 223-0891; e-mail: mwle@mwle.go.ug).

Other useful addresses

British High Commission, Commercial Section, 120/12 Parliament Avenue, PO Box 7070, Kampala (tel: 225-7301; fax: 225-7304).

Civil Aviation Authority, PO Box 5536, Kampala (tel: 225-6874; fax: 225-6807).

Export Policy Analysis and Development Unit (EPADU), Impala House, PO Box 10951, Kampala (tel: 223-1390; fax: 223-1329).

Nile International Conference Centre, PO Box 3496, Kampala (tel: 225-8619; fax: 225-9130).

Privatisation Unit, Ministry of Finance and Economic Planning, IPS Building, 6th Floor, 14 Parliament Avenue, PO Box 10944, Kampala (tel: 225-6467; fax: 225-9997; e-mail: pmu@imul.com).

Public Enterprise Reform and Divestiture, IPS Building, PO Box 10944, Kampala (tel: 225-6467; fax: 225-9997).

Uganda Development Corporation, UDC Building, Parliament Avenue, PO Box 7042, Kampala (tel: 223-4383; fax: 224-1588).

Uganda Investment Authority, 28 Kampala Road, PO Box 7418, Kampala (tel: 225-1562; fax: 224-2903; e-mail: info@ugandainvest.com).

Uganda Railway Corporation, PO Box 7150, Kampala (tel: 225-8051; fax: 244-405).

Uganda Tea Corporation Ltd, Kasaku Estate, Jinja-Kampala Rd, PO Box 8955, Lugazi (tel: 48-230/45; fax: 223-0698).

Ugandan Embassy (US), 5911 16th Street, NW, Washington DC 20011 (tel: (+1-202) 726-7100; fax: (+1-202) 726-1727; e-mail: ugembassy@aol.com).

Internet sites

Africa Business Network: www.ifc.org/abn

African Development Bank: www.afdb.org

Africa Online: www.africaonline.com

AllAfrica.com: http://allafrica.com

Mbendi AfroPaedia (information on companies, countries, industries and stock exchanges in Africa): http://mbendi.co.za

Ukraine

KEY FACTS

Official name: Ukraina (Ukraine)

Head of State: President Viktor Yushchenko (sworn in 23 Jan 2005)

Head of government: Prime Minister Juliya Tymoshenko (BJT) (from 18 Dec 2007)

Ruling party: Coalition led by with Juliya Tymoshenko Blok (BJT) (Yulia Tymoshenko Bloc) with Nasha Ukrayina-Narodna Samooborona Blok (NU) (Our Ukraine-People's Self Defense bloc) (from 17 Oct 2007)

Area: 603,700 square km

Population: 46.12 million (2007)*

Capital: Kiev (Kyiv)

Official language: Ukrainian

Currency: Hryvna (H) = 100 kopiyka (plural hryvni)

Exchange rate: H3.67 per US$ (Jul 2008)

GDP per capita: US$3,046 (2007)*

GDP real growth: 7.30% (2007)*

Labour force: 22.30 million (2006)

Unemployment: 7.00% (2007)*

Inflation: 12.80% (2007)

Balance of trade: -US$5.19 billion (2006)

Foreign debt: US$54.29 billion (2006)

Visitor numbers: 18.94 million (2006)*

* estimated figure

At first sight, Ukraine in early 2008 looked to be in a strong economic position. Gross domestic product (GDP) had been 7.3 per cent in 2007 and the exchange rate against the US dollar remained unchanged. Ukraine joined the World Trade Organisation (WTO) on 6 February, another step towards international acceptance. The only blot on the economic horizon seemed to be the rate of growth of inflation, at 12.8 per cent in 2007.

Ukraine is the largest eastern European country after Russia, covering some 603,700 square kilometres. As the second largest of the former Soviet republics, Ukraine had one of the best chances of becoming a prosperous market economy when the USSR finally collapsed. It accounted for a quarter of the USSR's grain output, half of its sugar beet harvest and a third of its potato crop. In addition it possessed a highly skilled workforce.

Politics

When Viktor Yanukovych was declared the winner of the November 2004 presidential elections, his incensed rival, Viktor Yushchenko, rallied his supporters. It had been a hugely fraudulent poll and hundreds of thousands of pro-democracy activists marched peacefully in the streets for 10 days, demanding that a replacement ballot be held. This was the Orange Revolution, in which 20 per cent of the population participated.

Another election, this time not rigged, was held in December 2005, and sure enough the reformist Yushchenko (Narodnyi Soyuz Nasha Ukraina (NSNU) (People's Union Our Ukraine) won. He praised the country for setting 'an example for the millions of people who still cherish freedom and democracy'.

Political hopes – for reform, democracy and human rights – were pinned on the Orange Revolution, and to a certain extent these hopes have been dashed. The promised crackdown on corruption has not materialised although there has been progress on civil liberties and the country is no longer blacklisted by human rights groups.

A sort of game of musical prime ministers followed Yushchenko's victory as president in 2005. First Yuliya Tymoshenko was approved as prime minister, but was dismissed by Yushchenko and replaced with Yuri Yekhanurov. He was in turn sacked by parliament in 2006. But Yushchenko, unwilling to lose his prime minister refused to nominate another candidate and Yekhanurov remained in office. General elections followed (judged free and fair by international observers), in which the ruling NSNU lost ground to both the Partiya Regioniv (PR) (Party of the Regions) led by Viktor Yanukovich and the party created by the president's erstwhile colleague Juliya Tymoshenko of Blok Juliya Tymoshenko (BJT) (Yulia Tymoshenko Bloc). After months when the NSNU and VBJT failed to work out their differences, the PR, Komunistychna Partiya Ukrainy (KPU) (Communist Party of Ukraine) and the Sotsialistychna Partiya Ukrainy (SPU) (Socialist Party of Ukraine) formed a coalition government, which sparked disturbances in the parliamentary building. The NSNU announced it would become the main opposition party. President Yushchenko was forced to nominate his archrival, Viktor Yanukovych (PR), as prime minister or call another general election. The Yanukovych cabinet was later approved by parliament.

In 2007 after months of friction between the pro-Western president and the pro-Russian prime minister caused stalemate in the political process, parliament was dissolved by presidential decree and early elections were called for May. Prime Minister Yanukovych refused to obey the decree, pending a decision by the constitutional court on its legality, and the opposition mounted demonstrations. Finally in June, Yushchenko and Yanukovych agreed to early elections in September. The PR won 34.4 per cent of the vote (175 of 450 seats), BJT won 30.7 per cent (156 seats), Blok Nasha Ukrayina-Narodna Samooborona (NU) (Our Ukraine-People's Self Defense bloc) 14.2 per cent (72), KPU 5.39 per cent (27 seats) and (Narodnyi) Blok Lytvyna (BL) (Lytvyn Bloc) 3.96 per cent (20); turnout was 62.02 per cent. Juliya Tymoshenko (BJT) was proposed as prime minister in December. In the first vote, she lost by two votes and had to have her name resubmitted but was then finally re-elected on 18 December.

Economy

Ukraine's long-term economic prospects depend on building investor confidence through acceleration of market reforms, including addressing corruption. At first, quarrels among senior leaders, expensive social policies and unclear plans for privatisation, led to an incoherent policy and government malaise. Minimum pensions were increased to the levels of minimum wages. Wages for those employed by the state increased by 57 per cent.

After Russia, Ukraine was the most important economic component of the former Soviet Union. It generated more than one quarter of Soviet agricultural output. Its diversified heavy industry supplied the equipment and raw materials to industrial and mining sites in other regions of the USSR. This should have stood the country in good stead. Shortly after independence in December 1991, Ukraine liberalised most prices and erected a legal framework for privatisation; but widespread resistance to reform within the government and the legislature stalled the effort. Output by 1999 had fallen to less than 40 per cent of the 1991 level.

By 2008 the International Monetary Fund (IMF) was reporting that the economy had grown strongly since 2000, supported by a robust international environment, stabilising macroeconomic policies, including the de facto currency peg to the dollar and low fiscal deficits, as well as significant structural reforms. By many measures, Ukraine was also better insulated against shocks. Reserves had increased substantially and covered 170 per cent of short-term debt or four months of imports. The underlying fiscal position was strong with government debt only about 10 per cent of GDP, and the deficit, if maintained, would ensure fiscal sustainability under a wide range of scenarios.

However, over the last three years expansionary fiscal and incomes policies, rising terms of trade, surging capital inflows, and a credit boom have led to very strong domestic demand growth and a deteriorating current account position. Surging demand, along with rising food and gas prices, has raised inflation to unacceptably high levels.

Inflation

The rate of inflation has never been lower than 2 per cent and in August 2007 alone, it rose by 0.6 per cent. The inflation situation had strong regional variations, being much worse in Kiev, where it surged to 18.7 per cent for the first eleven months of 2007. It was set to deteriorate further, however. By April 2008 it had passed the 30 per cent mark, as the bickering continued between Prime Minister Juliya Tymoshenko's government and the office of President Viktor Yushchenko over economic policy and how to handle the problem. Inflation continued to rise by 3.1 per cent month-on-month (a 37.2 annualised rate), and although that was lower than the 3.8 per cent registered in March (which was a 9-year record) it was still higher than most analysts were expecting. Aided by an almost 50 per cent jump in food

KEY INDICATORS — Ukraine

	Unit	2003	2004	2005	2006	2007
Population	m	47.62	47.25	46.93	46.47	*46.12
Gross domestic product (GDP)	US$bn	49.50	64.95	86.04	106.47	140.48
GDP per capita	US$	1,250	1,366	1,833	2,291	*3,046
GDP real growth	%	8.5	12.1	2.7	7.1	7.3
Inflation	%	6.0	9.0	13.5	9.0	12.8
Unemployment	%	9.1	8.5	8.2	8.0	*7.0
Industrial output	% change	–	11.4	2.3	4.3	–
Agricultural output	% change	–	19.4	1.8	0.3	–
Natural gas output	bn cum	17.7	18.3	18.8	19.1	19.0
Coal output	mtoe	41.6	41.9	40.7	41.8	39.3
Exports (fob) (goods)	US$m	21,225.0	33,432.0	35,024.0	38,949.0	49,840.0
Imports (cif) (goods)	US$m	20,029.0	29,691.0	36,159.0	44,143.0	60,412.0
Balance of trade	US$m	1,196.0	3,741.0	-1,135.0	-5,194.0	-10,572.0
Current account	US$m	2,890.0	7,160.0	2,531.0	-1,617.0	-5,918.0
Foreign debt	US$bn	14.2	21.7	64.0	54.3	–
Total reserves minus gold	US$m	6,730.7	9,302.4	19,114.5	21,844.6	31,786.0
Foreign exchange	US$m	6,709.5	9,301.3	19,113.5	21,843.2	31,783.2
Exchange rate	per US$	5.33	5.32	5.06	5.06	5.06

* estimated figure

prices, the cumulative price rise for the first four months of 2008 was 13.1 per cent, 3.5 percentage points above the government's whole year 2008 target of 9.6 per cent.

A major part of the problem in addressing the inflation issue is the level of in-fighting in the government itself, with Tymoshenko under constant criticism from the Yushchenko camp. The government's policies have included raising wages and social benefits and paying compensation for lost Soviet-era savings. The economy – which had been growing in the 6 per cent to 7 per cent annual rate, continued to grow in the first quarter of 2008 (at a 6 per cent year-on-year rate) but by mid-2008 appeared to be slowing (although the bumper harvest expected for 2008 may provide some respite.

Risk assessment

Politics	Fair
Economy	Fair
Regional stability	Poor

COUNTRY PROFILE

Historical profile

1945 Following the end of the Second World War, the Soviet Union regained control of the lost areas of western Ukraine.

1954 Responsibility for the government of Crimea, an autonomous republic within Ukraine, was transferred from Russia to Ukraine as part of reforms initiated by Nikita Kruschev after Stalin's death.

1986 The Chernobyl nuclear reactor based in Ukraine exploded, causing widespread damage in both Ukraine and neighbouring Belarus.

1991 Under pressure from the opposition parties, in particular Narodniy Rukh Ukrayiny (Rukh) (People's Movement of Ukraine), the government gradually moved towards independence. Political power was transferred from the government of the former Soviet Union to Ukrainian national authorities in Kiev.

A majority voted for independence in a referendum, leading to a declaration of independence and the recognition of Ukraine as an independent state by the international community. Leonid Kravchuk won the presidential elections.

1992 Disagreements over economic policy saw the resignation of Ukraine's first prime minister, Vladimir Fokin, who was replaced by Leonid Kuchma.

1993 Arguments over economic policy and labour strikes led to the resignation of Kuchma and Yukhlym Zvyahilsky assumed the post.

1994 Kuchma returned as the main challenger to Kravchuk in the presidential elections, finally defeating Kravchuk in the run-off. Kuchma's attempts to swing the balance of power from parliament in favour of the presidency, in order to reduce the opposition to his economic programme, achieved mixed success.

1996 A new constitution gave the president the power to appoint a government formed by parliamentary deputies.

1997 Valeriy Pustovoitenko became prime minister.

1998 After elections, the Komunistychna Partiya Ukrainy (KPU) (Communist Party of Ukraine) emerged as the largest single party.

1999 Kuchma was re-elected president. He appointed reformist independent deputy Viktor Yuschenko as prime minister.

2000 Over 80 per cent of voters in a referendum supported President Kuchma's proposals for constitutional reform, designed to increase the powers of the presidency.

2001 Yushchenko's pro-reform government was toppled by the KPU-dominated parliament. Anatoly Kinakh became prime minister.

2002 In parliamentary elections, Viktor Yuschenko's Narodnyi Soyuz Nasha Ukraina (NSNU) (People's Union Our Ukraine) bloc gained the highest percentage of votes at 23.6 per cent. Russia, Ukraine, Kazakhstan and Belarus signed an economic union treaty.

2003 Mass demonstrations in Kiev demanded the resignation of President Kuchma. Ukraine and Russia signed an agreement on the joint use of the Kerch Strait and the status of the Azov Sea.

2004 Russian-backed Viktor Yanukovych won the presidential election and opposition supporters gathered in Kiev to protest against election fraud (the Orange Revolution) and the Supreme Court annulled the result. Viktor Yushchenko won the re-run election.

2005 Yushchenko was sworn in as president and Yuliya Tymoshenko was approved as prime minister. Yushchenko dismissed Tymoshenko and replaced her with Yuri Yekhanurov. Russia cut off gas supplies after Ukraine refused to agree to a four-fold price increase.

2006 Prime Minister Yekhanurov was sacked by parliament. Yushchenko, unwilling to lose his prime minister refused to nominate another candidate and Yekhanurov remained in office. In general elections (judged free and fair by international observers), the ruling NSNU lost ground to both the Partiya Regioniv (PR) (Party of the Regions) led by Viktor Yanukovich and the party created by the president's erstwhile colleague Juliya Tymoshenko of Blok Juliya Tymoshenko (BJT) (Yulia Tymoshenko Bloc). After months when the NSNU and VBJT failed to work out their differences, the PR, Komunistychna Partiya Ukrainy (KPU) (Communist Party of Ukraine) and the Sotsialistychna Partiya Ukrainy (SPU) (Socialist Party of Ukraine) formed a coalition government, which sparked disturbances in the parliamentary building. The NSNU announced it would become the main opposition party. President Yushchenko was forced to nominate his archrival, Viktor Yanukovych (PR), as prime minister or call another general election. The Yanukovych cabinet was later approved by parliament.

2007 Months of friction between the pro-Western president and the pro-Russian prime minister caused stalemate in the political process, resulting in a presidential decree dissolving parliament and early elections were called for May. Prime Minister Yanukovych refused to obey the decree, pending a decision by the constitutional court on its legality, as the opposition mounted demonstrations. Finally in June, Yushchenko and Yanukovych agreed to early elections in September. The PR won 34.4 per cent of the vote (175 of 450 seats), BJT won 30.7 per cent (156 seats), Blok Nasha Ukrayina-Narodna Samooborona (NU) (Our Ukraine-People's Self Defense bloc) 14.2 per cent (72), KPU 5.39 per cent (27 seats) and (Narodnyi) Blok Lytvyna (BL) (Lytvyn Bloc) 3.96 per cent (20); turnout was 62.02 per cent. Juliya Tymoshenko (BJT) was proposed as prime minister in December. In the first vote, she lost by two votes and had to have her name resubmitted but was elected on 18 December.

2008 Ukraine became a member of the WTO on 6 February. The government expected that the elimination of many export barriers would result in an expansion of the economy of as much as 1.7 per cent. The Russian state-owned gas producer Gazprom cut Ukraine's supplies by 25 per cent on 3 March 2008, claiming that debts of US$1.5 billion had not been paid. Ukraine claimed all outstanding money had been paid. Gas supplies were resumed when an agreement was reached on 13 March, whereby Gazprom supplies industrial customers directly and cuts out a Ukrainian intermediate supply company.

Political structure

Constitution

The 1996 constitution defines Ukraine as a sovereign, unitary state answerable to individual citizens, with the protection of citizens' rights as its foremost responsibility. The constitution forbids multiple nationality for Ukrainian citizens. The development and protection of the Ukrainian language is a constitutional obligation, but the constitution also guarantees free use of Russian and other minority languages, and requires the state to promote

the study of languages of 'international communication'.
The constitution recognises and guarantees the right to local self-government. Local government is based on 24 oblasts (regional divisions) and one autonomous republic (Crimea). The oblasts are further divided into rayons (districts).
The Autonomous Republic of Crimea is bound by the Ukrainian constitution and by acts of the Verkhovna Rada (Supreme Council). However, it has the power to legislate separately on matters such as transport, planning, land use and healthcare.
Constitutional changes agreed in December 2004, which entered into force in January 2006, have given more power to the parliament at the expense of the office of president. Following the parliamentary elections on 26 March 2006, the parliament now nominates the prime minister who must then be approved by the president, replacing the previous system under which the prime minister was nominated by the president and approved by the parliament.

Form of state
Presidential democratic republic

The executive
The highest executive authority rests with the president, who is directly elected for a five-year term and nominates the prime minister and regional governors, whose appointment are subject to the approval of parliament. The president has the power to appoint the cabinet, although parliament must approve it. Members of the cabinet do not necessarily need to be drawn from parliament. The president may rule by decree and did so in 1998, during deadlock in the legislature. Under normal circumstances, the prime minister shares some executive powers with the president and both can propose and approve legislation. This creates the potential for conflict between the two executive branches.

National legislature
The Verkhovna Rada (Supreme Council) (commonly called the Rada) is the legislature and its 450 members are elected for a five-year term: 225 by proportional representation and 224 in single-seat constituencies (in addition to the speaker). Only parties that obtain over 4 per cent of the vote are allocated PR seats. The Rada elects a speaker and plays an active role in proposing and enacting legislation.

Legal system
The legal system is based on a civil law code and, since the collapse of communism, has been engaged in an ongoing process of reform. The Constitutional Court is the highest interpreter of the constitution and is permitted to carry out judicial review of legislation. There are 18 Supreme Court judges, six each appointed for a nine-year non-renewable term by the president, parliament and a congress of Ukrainian judges.
The Supreme Court is the court of final appeal for civil and criminal cases originally heard in the lower courts. The Supreme Court's judges are appointed by a plenary session of existing judges. The lower courts are organised according to both geography and legal specialisation. The constitution encourages trial by jury and forbids the creation of emergency courts. Judges are granted legal immunity and can only be dismissed by a verdict of the Supreme or Constitutional Courts, or by an order of parliament.

Last elections
31 October/26 December 2004 (presidential); 30 September 2007 (parliamentary).
Results: Presidential (re-run): Viktor Yushchenko won 52 per cent of the vote and Viktor Yanukovych 44.2 per cent. Presidential (second round): Viktor Yanukovych, backed by Russia, won with 49.5 per cent of the vote, against pro-West Viktor Yushchenko with 46.6 per cent. Parliament passed a resolution declaring the presidential elections invalid. Presidential (first round): Prime Minister Viktor Yanukovych won 40.1 per cent of the vote against 39.2 per cent for former prime minister Viktor Yushchenko, 5.8 per cent for Oleksandr Moroz and 5 per cent for Petro Symonenko.
Parliamentary: The PR won 34.4 per cent of the vote (175 of 450 seats), BJT won 30.7 per cent (156 seats), Blok Nasha Ukrayina-Narodna Samooborona (NU) (Our Ukraine-People's Self Defense bloc) 14.2 per cent (72), Komunistychna Partiya Ukrainy (KPU) (Communist Party of Ukraine) 5.39 per cent (27 seats), (Narodnyi) Blok Lytvyna (BL) (Lytvyn Bloc) 3.96 per cent (20); turnout was 62.02 per cent.

Next elections
2009 (presidential); 2012 (parliamentary).

Political parties

Ruling party
Coalition led by with Juliya Tymoshenko Blok (BJT) (Yulia Tymoshenko Bloc) with Nasha Ukrayina-Narodna Samooborona Blok (NU) (Our Ukraine-People's Self Defense bloc) (from 17 Oct 2007)

Main opposition party
Partiya Regioniv (PR) (Party of the Regions)

Population

46.12 million (2007)*
Last census: December 2001: 48,457,102
Population density: 87 inhabitants per square km. Urban population: 67 per cent (2001 census).
Annual growth rate: -1.0 per cent 1994–2004 (WHO 2006)

Ethnic make-up
Ukrainian (72 per cent), Russian (22 per cent), Belarussian, Moldovan, Polish, Romanian and Tatar (in Crimea). Over 10 million ethnic Russians live in eastern Ukraine; Crimea is about 63 per cent Russian.

Religions
The principal religion is Christianity, of various denominations including Ukrainian Orthodox, Autocephalous Orthodox, and Ukrainian Greek Catholic (Uniate) Church. There is a small Jewish minority, and a Muslim minority mostly located in Crimea.

Education

The reversal of the Russian dominated education system is the primary aim of the government.
Literacy is almost universal in Ukraine, reflecting the high level of educational participation and high quality of teaching. Increased emphasis has also been placed on Ukrainian history, culture and literature.
Elementary schooling must begin by aged seven (parents may choose to enrol their children in school at aged six), and lasts until aged 10. This is followed by secondary basic education, which lasts until aged 15 when examinations determine academic upper secondary education until aged 18, or vocational education which lasts until aged 20.
Ukraine has large scientific and educational centres in Kiev, Odessa, Lviv, Kharkiv and Donetzk, with more than 200 higher educational institutes. There are 10 universities.
Literacy rate: 100 per cent adult rate; 100 per cent youth rate (15–24) (Unesco 2005).
Compulsory years: 6/7 to 16.
Enrolment rate: 78 per cent gross primary enrolment; 105 per cent gross secondary enrolment, of relvant age groups (including repeaters), (Unicef 2004)
Pupils per teacher: 21 in primary schools.

Health

Per capita total expenditure on health (2003) was US$305; of which per capita government spending was US$201, at the international dollar rate, (WHO 2006).
The precipitous economic decline since 1991 has significantly lowered living standards in Ukraine and adversely affected health. Although high soil fertility enables most Ukrainians to enjoy a sufficient diet, nutrition levels remain lower than optimum and high alcohol and tobacco consumption does little to improve matters. Moreover, lacking adequate funds, many health facilities have closed or reduced

their level of service since independence. Although the number of doctors is well above the Organisation for Economic Co-operation and Development (OECD) average, they lack the training, facilities and medicines to provide adequate preventative or primary healthcare. One result of this has been outbreaks of tuberculosis, which reached epidemic levels in the late 1990s.

HIV/Aids

HIV prevalence: 0.1 per cent aged 15–49 in 2003 (World Bank)

Life expectancy: 67 years, 2004 (WHO 2006)

Fertility rate/Maternal mortality rate: 1.1 births per woman, 2004 (WHO 2006)

Birth rate/Death rate: 10 births and 16.4 deaths per 1,000 population (2003)

Child (under 5 years) mortality rate (per 1,000): 15 per 1,000 live births (World Bank)

Head of population per physician: 2.95 physicians per 1,000 people, 2003 (WHO 2006)

Welfare

As part of its plan to reduce the fiscal deficit and meet IMF spending restrictions, the government has been forced to alter its social security structure.

More targetting of assistance to vulnerable groups is being planned, with reforms to family benefits, sickness benefits and the employment fund. A social insurance system provides benefits for old age pensions, sickness, maternity, work injury, and employee family allowances.

The pension system is being reformed, with preferential pensions being scaled down. The retirement age is 60 and 55 for men and women, with 25 or 20 years contributions, respectively. Reforms being enacted in 2004 intend to raise this and introduce additional voluntary and mandatory savings schemes. There are also plans to increase the pension age gradually.

The insurance scheme is funded by employee earnings of 1 per cent on wages up to H150 and 2 per cent on wages of H150 or more (capped at wage of H1,600 per month); employers pay 37 per cent of payroll and central and local governments provide subsidies as needed. There are an estimated 2.2 million Ukrainians who are eligible for extra social security payments as victims of the 1986 Chernobyl disaster.

Main cities

Kiev (Kyiv) (capital, estimated population 2.7 million (m) in 2005), Kharkiv (Kharkov) (1.5m), Odessa (1.0m), Dnepropetrovsk (1.0m), Donetsk (1.0m), Zaporizhzhya (822,931), Lviv (Lvov) (745,632); Sevastapol (349,827); Simferopol (350,616) and Yalta are the major centres of Crimea.

Languages spoken

Ukrainian, Polish and German are widely spoken in western Ukraine, while Russian is widely spoken in the east. Romanian, Bulgarian, Hungarian and Belarusian are also spoken.

Official language/s

Ukrainian

Media

National news agency: Ukrinform (Ukranian National News Agency)

Other news agencies: Unian: www.unian.net/eng

Interfax-Ukraine: www.interfax.com.ua/en

Press

Press freedom in the Ukraine has been described as partial, by the UK-based Freedom House, in 2007. Violence and intimidation of journalists is ongoing, perpetrated by politicos and criminals, while the legal system has not succeeded in finding those responsible for the death of prominent journalist Georgiy Gongadze in 2000.

Dailies: In Ukrainian, Fakty i Kommentarii (www.facts.kiev.ua), Segodnya (www.segodnya.ua) and Vecherniye Vesti are mass-circulations newspapers, others include Silski Visti (www.silskivisti.kiev.ua) and Kievshiye Vedomosti (www.kv.com.ua), Ukrayina Moloda (www.umoloda.kiev.ua) and Holos Ukrayiny (http://uamedia.visti.net/golos) the parliamentary newspaper.

In English, Den (www.day.kiev.ua), and online Ukryinska Pravda (www2.pravda.com.ua/en).

There are also local newspaper in provincial cities, including Oga (www.ogo.ua) from Rivne, Slovo (www.slovo.odessa.ua) from Odesa and in Russian, Zik (www.zik.com.ua) and Ekspres (www.expres.ua) from Lviv, and Gorod (www.gorod.donbass.com) from Donetsk in Russian.

Weeklies: Magazines in Ukrainian include Krytyka (http://krytyka.kiev.ua), Zerkalo Nedeli (www.zn.ua) comments on politics, and Ji (www.ji-magazine.lviv.ua), a cultural magazine. In English, The Ukrainian Observer (www.ukraine-observer.com) and Kyiv Post (www.kyivpost.com).

Business: In Ukrainian, Kontrakty (www.kontrakty.com.ua) and Delovaya Stolitsa (www.dsnews.com.ua) are newspapers. Finansovaya Ukraina covers financial news. In English, the Eastern Economist is published weekly.

Broadcasting

The Derzhkominform of Ukraine (state committee, for television and radio broadcasting) is responsible for providing transmission frequencies and dissemination of official information.

Radio: The government operated national service is Ukrayinsko Radio One with three stations (www.nrcu.gov.ua), plus Radio Ukraine International, with external transmissions. There are many private, commercial radio stations which are based regionally or in a city including Trand M Radio (www.trans-m-radio.com), from the Crimea, Shanson Radio (www.shanson.ua), from Kharkov, Melodia FM (www.melodia.ua), Planeta FM (http://planetafm.net), and Dovira FM (www.dovira.com.ua), from Kiev, Mama Radio (http://mama.odessa.fm) from Odessa.

Television: The government-operated network, National TV Company of Ukraine (www.1tv.com.ua), (known as UT1) operates three network channels, which broadcasts over 97 per cent of the territory. There are plans that by 2009 UT1 will acquire public broad broadcaster status and the government will forego its control of the network.

There are a number of commercial channels broadcasting via cable, satellite and terrestrial signals with a range in product content from entertainment, news, music, sports and culture. The most popular TV channel is Inter (http://intertv.com.ua) followed by Studio 1+1 (http://1plus1.tv).

Advertising

The advertising industry is dominated by television. There is a ban on the promotion and advertising of tobacco.

Economy

Despite its great potential for strong economic growth, Ukraine's economic development in the years following independence was poor. The transition years of the 1990s were marred by a lack of political consensus on how to best provide the conditions for a market economy. The re-election of President Kuchma in 1999 was followed by an acceleration of structural economic reforms and Ukraine's first annual GDP growth in 2000. Growth was maintained for several years, reaching 12.1 per cent in 2004, but the economy was set back by the upheavals of 2005, when growth fell to 2.6 per cent. By 2006, the economy was reviving with growth of 6.7 per cent.

Improvements in the economy and better investor confidence have brought about significant increases in foreign direct investment (FDI). Structural reforms are being pursued to attract more FDI, especially in the agricultural and high-tech sectors. New tax laws and a law introducing international mortgage lending have added improvements to the business environment.

The EU has become Ukraine's main trading partner since accession, but Russia retains its traditional importance. Ukraine exports steel to Russia and imports equipment, vehicle and chemical products from Russia. Ukraine is, in particular, reliant on Russia for its energy requirements, especially natural gas, the price of which has increased markedly since 2005, encouraging Ukraine to seek other sources.
Ukraine is an important transit route for Russian exports, including gas pipelines, to the West.
Ukraine became a member of the World Trade Organisation on 6 February 2008.

External trade
Following the break-up of the Soviet Union, trade was formalised with former republics through the Commonwealth of Independent States (CIS), however a free trade zone between members had not, by 2007, been implemented, due to differences in economic objectives, degrees of reforms and economic development. The Ukraine has declared its intentions of applying for membership of the European Union and has begun reforms necessary to align its economy with the EU.
As the world's fifth largest exporter of cereals, and sixth largest exporter of iron, primary industries are important to the economy. Over 30 per cent of all exports are traded to the EU and 25 per cent to Russia. Manufacturing reflects the Ukraine's historic role as an important manufacturing base of the former Soviet Union with production in heavy industry including steel making, shipbuilding, locomotive and aerospace industries, nuclear reactors and boilers, machinery and machine tools. Fees for oil transiting the country from Russia to Europe provide an important source of foreign earnings.

Imports
Principal imports include oil and natural gas (comprising around 30 per cent of all imports), vehicles, machinery, equipment, chemicals and plastics.
Main sources: Russia (30.6 per cent total, 2006), Germany (9.5 per cent), Turkmenistan (7.8 per cent).

Exports
Principal exports are ferrous and non-ferrous metals, fuel and petroleum products, chemicals, tools and machinery, transport equipment and cereals.
Main destinations: Russia (22.5 per cent total, 2006), Italy (6.5 per cent), Turkey (6.2 per cent).

Agriculture

Farming
Historically known as the 'bread basket' of the former Soviet Union, Ukraine used to produce 25 per cent of the total Soviet agricultural output. The agricultural sector, despite Ukraine's rich land resources (with one-third of the world's total acreage of black soil), went into decline for several years as a result of general inefficiency, late payments and a lack of finance for fuel, fertilisers and machinery.
In 2004, agriculture accounted for around 12 per cent of GDP, compared to 25 per cent at independence in 1991, but is gradually returning to positive growth.
Progress of agricultural sector reforms since 1992, including price and trade reforms, and agriculture-specific institutional reforms will have a significant impact on the future of agricultural production.
Economy-wide reforms will allow the sector to absorb technological advances more rapidly.
The main agricultural products are wheat, barley, potatoes, sugar beet and flax.
Ukraine is the world's largest producer of sugar beet.
The grain harvest in 2003 was at a record low due to extreme weather conditions and locust infestation, but the 2004 harvest was much improved.
Crop production in 2005 included: 37,394,000 tonnes (t) cereals in total, 18,700,000t wheat, 7,100,000t maize, 19,480,000t potatoes, 9,000,000t barley, 1,190,000t rye, 603,500t pulses, 370,000t grapes, 1,200,000t tomatoes, 2,122,250t oilcrops, 15,620,000t sugar beet, 91,240t treenuts, 700,000t apples, 730,000t oats, 1,890,600t fruit in total, 7,291,500t vegetables in total. Livestock production included: 1,579,500t meat in total, 556,000t beef, 510,000t pig meat, 15,500t lamb and goat meat, 470,000t poultry, 743,458t eggs, 13,803,500t milk, 60,502t honey, 103,000t cattle hides, 8,300t goatskins.

Fishing
The fishery sector is an elaborate organisational complex of oceanic fisheries, pond fish farms, co-operatives, scientific research and education as well as enterprises dealing with processing and the sale of fish products, stock protection and restoration. The sector typically employs more than 60,000 people. The Black Sea fishing industry is concentrated around the ports of Odessa, Mariupol, Sevastopol, Berdyansk and Izmail.
Ukraine has a potential capacity to harvest and rear between 700,000–800,000 tonnes (t) of fish, with an annual output of food fish products from vessels and coastal enterprises amounting to more than 600,000t. The country exports over a third of its fish catch and the industry makes a substantial contribution to the country's trade balance.
In 2004, the total marine fish catch was 157,804 tonnes and the total crustacean catch was 12,742 tonnes.

Forestry
Ukraine has mainly mixed and steppe forests, which account for one-sixth of the land area, with forest cover estimated at 9.5 million hectares (ha). Nearly two-thirds of the forest is available for wood supply, although consumption of forest products per capita is significantly below the European average. The state owns all the forest area.
The Zavarpattska and Polisia regions are the main centres for the forestry and paper industries. Apart from the smaller wood processing enterprises, most of the forest industry is privatised and caters to domestic demand. The industry is being modernised by improving the sawmills and other manufacturing operations.
Small quantities of roundwood and half-finished products are exported to the Middle East and European countries.
Wood pulp and paper, mainly from the Russian Federation are imported.
Exports of forest material in 2004 amounted to US$576 million, while imports amounted to US$644 million.
Production in 2004 included 14,861,800 cubic metres (cum) roundwood, 6,465,700cum industrial roundwood, 2,019,100cum sawnwood, 4,570,500cum sawlogs and veneers, 1,308,000cum wood-based panels, 8,396,000cum woodfuel; 701,914 tonnes (t) paper and paperboard (including 35,000t newsprint), 15,768t printing and writing paper, 68,000t paper pulp, 339,000t recovered paper.

Industry and manufacturing
The industrial sector, hich contributed around 37 per cent to GDP in 2004, is essentially divided into two. Most of the sector is concentrated on heavy industry, principally in metallurgy, mining and mechanical engineering. The iron and steel industry is the main earner of hard currency revenues. It is dominated by large companies, such as JSC Zaporozhstal, and the government has been reluctant to introduce privatisation and other reforms.
Ukraine has benefited from China's increasing demand for steel.
The high-technology industry, having been located in Ukraine in Soviet times, is modern and internationally competitive.

Tourism
The tourism sector is at an early stage of development, having to construct infrastructure practically from scratch after years of Soviet-era neglect. Ukraine's rich cultural and environmental resources offer considerable potential. Tourism is treated as an essential instrument in the modernisation of the economy, but its contribution is as yet modest. Around six million arrivals were recorded in 2004 and the sector

is expected to contribute 3.2 per cent of GDP in 2005.

Environment

Extensive pollution is one of the more persistent legacies of the Soviet regime when massive industrialisation was pursued at any cost. The most obvious example is the Chernobyl nuclear power explosion which increased rates of thyroid cancer, leukaemia and birth defects in the surrounding areas. All Ukraine's cities suffer from pollution, both in the air as well as rivers and agricultural land. The Lviv region has the most polluted water in the country. Only about 55 per cent of the Ukranian population has access to safe water.

Mining

The mining sector traditionally accounts for 10 per cent of GDP and employs 3 per cent of the workforce.

Ukraine possesses an estimated 5 per cent of the world's mineral reserves. It has the world's largest supply of titanium, the third-largest deposit of iron ore (more than 200 billion tonnes) and 30 per cent of the world's manganese ore. It also has deposits of mercury, uranium and nickel, and a small amount of gold.

The largest iron ore deposits are in the Krivoy Roj area, with estimated reserves of 18 billion tonnes, Kremenchuk with 4.5 billion tonnes and Kerch and Belozerskie in the Donetsk region. The manganese deposits around Nikopol are thought to be the largest in the world. Gold deposits containing an average of between five and six grammes of gold per tonne of ore exist in the Trans-Carpathian region. The area also contains deposits of zinc and lead.

Other natural resources present in Ukraine include salt, lime, limestone, china clay , sulphur (around Lviv) and granite. Phosphorus deposits of about 20 billion tonnes are also present.

Ukraine typically produces 50 million tonnes per year (tpy) of iron, 1,000 tpy of nickel and 500 tpy of uranium.

Hydrocarbons

Ukraine's proven oil and gas reserves were not exploited during the Soviet era, when other regions (Siberia and Central Asia) could be developed more cheaply. The country has large hydrocarbon reserves and an extensive network of pipelines carrying Russian oil and gas to Western Europe.

Ukraine has oil reserves of 395 million barrels, the majority of which are located in the Dnieper-Donetsk basin in the eastern part of Ukraine. 80 per cent of Ukraine's oil consumption is met by imports, mostly from Russia. Efforts to reduce dependence on Russian oil have included the construction of an international oil terminal at Odessa port.

Ukraine has natural gas reserves of 1.4 trillion cubic metres. Annual production was 17.2 billion cubic metres supplies little more than 20 per cent of total domestic consumption, with the remainder being imported from Russia and Turkmenistan.

A disagreement over prices led to Russia turning off its supply of gas to Ukraine in December 2005. An agreement was reached in January 2006, after pressure was put on both countries by the EU and others. The price per 1,000 cubic metres (cum) of gas from Russia was set at US$230 (up from US$50), but in a complex deal the Russian gas will be sold to Gazprom-owned Roskurenergo, which will mix this gas with cheaper gas from Turkmenistan, Uzbekistan and Kazakhstan and then sell it to Ukraine at US$95 per 1,000 cum.

Ukraine has 34.2 billion tonnes of coal reserves, but these are under-exploited. Ukraine is a net importer of coal. Reserves are set to last for the next 300 years.

Energy

Ukraine has 54.8GW of installed electricity capacity. There are four major thermal power stations and four nuclear power plants. The last working nuclear reactor at the Chernobyl plant was closed in December 2000. Thermal power, much of which is gas-fired, accounts for nearly 50 per cent of the electricity produced in Ukraine, while nuclear energy provides 40 per cent and hydroelectric plants supply the remainder .

A state-owned company, Enerhoatom, oversees the nuclear power plants. Lack of funding has meant that safety standards continue to be lax and strike action and power breakdowns are frequent.

A second reactor at the Khmelnitsky nuclear power plant was switched on in August 2004, the first new nuclear reactor since Chernobyl.

A five-year gas supply deal was reached in 2006. The price per 1,000 cubic metres (cum) of gas from Russia was set at US$230 (up from US$50) but in a complex deal the Russian gas is sold to Gazprom-owned Roskurenergo, which is mixed with cheaper gas from Turkmenistan, Uzbekistan and Kazakhstan and then sold to Ukraine at US$95 per 1,000cum.

Financial markets

Stock exchange

The Ukrainian Stock Exchange (USE) was founded in 1991. The Interbank Currency Exchange conducts secondary trading in government securities daily and has benefited from restructuring of government debt.

The Russian financial crisis of 1998 devastated the USE, with market capitalisation falling to under 5 per cent as a proportion of GDP. Recovery in dollar terms since has been muted due to the devaluation of the hryvna.

There are only 11 listed companies on the exchange, and trading volume is negligible. Total market capitalisation in 2003 was US$88.5 million.

Banking and insurance

There are seven domestic banks operating in the banking sector, two of which are state-owned and originate from the Soviet era. Foreign investors are permitted to participate in the banking sector, but are only granted a licence after at least a year of running an office in the country.

In February 2004, Ukraine was removed from the OECD Financial Action Task Force (FATF) list of non-co-operative countries on money-laundering after reforms had been implemented.

Central bank

National Bank of Ukraine

Time

GMT plus two hours (daylight saving, late March to late October, GMT plus three hours)

Geography

Ukraine is situated in Eastern Europe. The largest country entirely within Europe, Ukraine covers 603,700 square kilometres, stretching 2,000km from east to west and 1,000km from north to south. The Crimean peninsula in the south juts into the Black Sea, and has the Sea of Azov to the east.

In eastern Ukraine, the country is bordered by Russia to the east and north. In the western part of the country the northern border is with Belarus, and there are western borders with Poland and Slovakia. There are also short borders with Hungary, Romania and Moldova to the south-west, and a small salient of land south of Moldova which borders Bulgaria and has access to the Danube River delta.

The average height above sea level in Ukraine is only 175 metres, and most of the land area is composed of rolling steppes and wooded plains. About two-thirds of the country is covered by a thick layer of humus-rich soil, making it one of the most fertile regions in the world.

The only mountains are in the south on the Crimean peninsula (maximum height 1,545 metres) and the Carpathians in the west (maximum height 2,061 metres).

The main rivers are the Dnepr which drains the central regions of the country and flows into the Black Sea near Kherson and the Dnestr which flows through western Ukraine and Moldova before entering the Black Sea near Odessa.

Hemisphere

Northern

Climate

The moderate continental climate varies little across the country. The Black Sea resorts around Odessa and Yalta are usually warmer and drier than the rest of Ukraine. The average rainfall per year is 1,440mm, with the Crimea receiving only 400mm. Average temperatures in Kiev range from 20 degrees Celsius (C) in July to minus 7 degrees C in January. Average temperatures in Lviv in western Ukraine range from 16 degrees C in July, to minus 5 degrees C in January.

Dress codes

Business clothes are appropriate for meetings, including a suit or jacket with a tie for men and formal clothing for women.

Entry requirements

Passports

Required by all, valid for one month beyond departure date.

Visa

Required by all, except nationals of EU/EEA countries, North America, Japan, Switzerland, Andora, Vatican City, Monaco and San Marino. Letters of invitation are not required for either business or tourist visits by nationals of EU countries, US, Canada, Japan, Switzerland, Slovakia, or Turkey.

Currency advice/regulations

Import and export of local currency is restricted to H1,000; up to H5,000 may be exported subject to customs declaration. Import and export of foreign currencies is restricted to US$1,000 or, subject to customs declaration, up to US$10,000.

Customs

Small amount of personal goods, 200 cigarettes, 1 litre spirits, 2 litres wine and 10 litres beer are allowed duty free. There are strict regulations governing the export of antiques and items of historical interest. If in doubt seek prior permission from customs authorities.

Prohibited imports

Weapons, illegal drugs and certain pharmaceutical and communcations products are subject to import restrictions; licences are issued by the relevant government ministries.

Health (for visitors)

Mandatory precautions

Vaccination certificates if travelling from a cholera or yellow fever infected area. An HIV/Aids test is required for long-stay visitors only. A UK-issued certificate is usually accepted. All visitors entering Ukraine are required to purchase health insurance at the airport of entry and prior to passing through immigration control. British passport holders are exempt due to a reciprocal agreement between the Ukrainian and British governments.

Advisable precautions

It is advisable to be in date for the following immunisations: polio (within 10 years), tetanus (within 10 years), typhoid fever and hepatitis A (moderate risk only). There is a rabies risk. Any medicines required by the traveller should be imported and it is advisable to have precautionary antibiotics if travelling outside the major urban centres. However, there are restrictions on the import of some pharmaceuticals and visitors are advised to check with their local Ukrainian embassy prior to travel. A travel kit including a disposable syringe is a reasonable precaution.Water precautions are recommended (water purification tablets may be useful).

Hotels

Kiev has a shortage of hotels. It is worth booking rooms several weeks in advance through the Intourist travel agency.

Credit cards

Credit cards are not widely accepted.

Public holidays (national)

Fixed dates

1 Jan (New Year's Day), 7 Jan (Orthodox Christmas Day), 8 Mar (Women's Day), 1-2 May (Labour/May Days), 9 May (Victory Day), 28 Jun (Constitution Day), 24 Aug (Independence Day).

Variable dates

Orthodox Easter Monday, Orthodox Whit Monday.

Working hours

Banking

Mon–Fri: 0930–1730.
Open 24 hours at Kiev Borispol airport, but only until noon at Odessa.

Business

Mon–Fri: 0900–1800.

Government

Mon–Thu: 0700–1700; Fri: 0900–1200.

Shops

Mon–Sat: 0900–1900.

Social customs/useful tips

Tips are not expected at most cafes, although at more expensive restaurants a tip of between 5 and 10 per cent is appropriate.
Small gifts for your host are appreciated in the event of personal hospitality.
Handshaking is customary on meeting and on leaving. The formal mode of address, Pan (Mr) or Pani (Mrs) is usual even after several meetings. The use of business cards is widespread. It is important to be on time for meetings and appointments.
Referring to Ukraine as part of the Soviet Union or, even worse, as part of Russia, is a serious insult. The post-independence reaction to decades of 'Russification' led to strong nationalistic feelings, particularly in western Ukraine.

Security

Normal precautions should be taken when visiting Ukraine – avoid displaying large amounts of cash or expensive personal belongings. Avoid travelling alone at night in Kiev, particularly on the metro or in the city's parks.

Getting there

Air

National airline: Ukraine International Airlines

International airport/s: Kiev-Borispol International Airport (KBP), 27km from city centre; bank, post office, duty-free shop, car rental.

Other airport/s: Zhulhany Airport (IEV), 6km from Kiev.

Airport tax: None

Surface

Ukraine is included in the Pan-European Corridor 5 scheme. The project has some 3,270km of railways, linking Kiev in the Ukraine with western Europe via Italy, and 2,850 of new and upgraded roads.

Road: There are roads into Ukraine from all neighbouring countries.

Rail: There are links connecting Kiev and Lviv with all Commonwealth of Independent States member states. Direct rail connections are available to Warsaw in Poland, Budapest in Hungary and Bucharest in Romania.

Water: There are ferry services from Russia to the Crimean ports. Odessa and Yalta on the Black Sea have regular arrivals from Haifa, Istanbul, Limassol, Piraeus and Port Said. Riverboats from Odessa go to a number of Central European cities via the Danube.

Main port/s: The main Crimean ports are Yalta and Sevastopol, with Kerch the main port for the Sea of Azov. Izmail is the main Danube River port, and Odessa is the largest Black Sea port.

Getting about

National transport

Air: The main airports for domestic air traffic are Borispol International and Zhulany, from which there are connections to Chernivitsi, Dniepropetrovsk, Donetsk, Ivano-Frankivsk, Kharkov, Lugansk, Lviv, Mariupol, Odessa, Simferopol, Uzhgorod and Zaporizhzhya. Services during the winter months are often subject to cancellation or delay.

Road: There is an extensive road network comprising approximately 172,00km of road, with around 29,000km of these being main or national roads. Many roads are poorly surfaced and in need of modernisation.

Buses: Ukraine has an extensive bus network, with routes to every city and most smaller towns.

Taxis: Using taxis for long-distance journeys is an option as they are reasonably cheap. Payment is usually requested in hard currency. Agree a price before setting off.

Rail: The Ukrainian rail network links the major cities, most of which are at least one night's travel apart. There are three types of sleeper carriage: the spalny vahon is the first class compartment for two people; the kupe or kupeyny is the second class compartment for four people; and the platskart is the third class open carriage with groups of six bunks in each alcove, with more beds along the aisles – avoid the platskart unless absolutely necessary.

It is advisable to pre-book tickets before arriving in Ukraine. Foreigners can usually buy rail tickets from separate offices with English-speaking clerks, although the price will be slightly higher.

Although journey times are slower than air, rail travel is more reliable during the winter months.

Water: Passenger transport is available on the Dnepr and Dnestr rivers, which traverse large areas of the country, but price increases, lack of spare parts and cheaper land-based transport have caused a sharp decline in services.

City transport

Taxis: In most cities there are metered official taxis, unofficial 'gypsy cabs' with negotiated fares and fixed route, fixed price shared taxis and minibus services.

Car hire

International agencies are represented in the main cities, in addition to local agencies, offering a range of vehicles. Car hire is relatively cheap.

Speed limits are 60kph (37mph) in built-up areas, 90kph (55mph) in open areas and 110kph (69mph) on motorways. An international driving permit is required. It is illegal to drive having consumed any amount of alcohol.

BUSINESS DIRECTORY

The addresses listed below are a selection only. While World of Information makes every endeavour to check these addresses, we cannot guarantee that changes have not been made, especially to telephone numbers and area codes. We would welcome any corrections.

Telephone area codes

The international direct dialling code (IDD) for Ukraine is + 380, followed by area code and subscriber's number:

Dnepropetrovsk	56	Odessa	48
Donetsk	62	Sevastopol	69
Kharkov	57	Simferopol	65
Kiev	44	Yalta	65
Lviv	32		

Useful telephone numbers

Fire brigade: 01
Militia (Police): 02
Hospital enquiries: 003
Directory enquiries: 09
Address enquiries: 061
Lost property office: 229-7844
Paid enquiries service: 009
Railway timetable: 09
River port: 416-1268
Taxi: 058
Taxi enquiries: 225-0396
Time: 060

Chambers of Commerce

American Chamber of Commerce in Ukraine, 42 Shovkovychna Street, 01601 Kiev (tel: 490-5800; fax: 490-5801; e-mail: acc@amcham.ua).

British-Ukrainian Chamber of Commerce, 34a Grushevskogo Street, 01021 Kiev (tel: 410-5720; fax: 230-2151; e-mail: administrator@bucc.com.ua).

Crimea Chamber of Commerce and Industry, 45 Sevastopolskaya Street, 95013 Simferopol (e-mail: cci@cci.crimea.ua).

Dnipropetrovsk Chamber of Commerce and Industry, 4 Shevchenko Street, 49044 Dnipropetrovsk (tel: 236-2258; fax: 236-2259; e-mail: miv@dcci.dp.ua).

Donetsk Chamber of Commerce and Industry, 12 Dzerzinskogo Avenue, 83000 Donetsk (e-mail: dcci@dtpp.donetsk.ua).

Kharkov Chamber of Commerce and Industry, 3a Kartsarskaya Street, 61012 Kharkov (e-mail: info@kcci.kharkov.ua).

Kiev Chamber of Commerce and Industry, 55 Bogdana Khmelnitskogo Street, 01054 Kiev (tel: 246-8301; fax: 246-9966; e-mail: info@kiev-chamber.org.ua).

Lviv Chamber of Commerce and Industry, 14 Stryisky Park, 79011 Lviv (e-mail: lcci@cscd.lviv.ua).

Odessa Chamber of Commerce and Industry, 47 Bazarna Street, 65011 Odessa (tel: 728-6610; e-mail: orcci@orcci.odessa.ua).

Sevastopol Chamber of Commerce and Industry, 34 Bolshaya Morskaya Street, 99011 Sevastopol (e-mail: stpp@optima.com.ua).

Ukrainian Chamber of Commerce & Industry, 33 Velyka Zhytomyrska, 01601 Kiev (tel: 272-2911; fax: 272-3353; e-mail: ucci@ucci.org.ua).

Banking

Aggio Joint Stock Bank, 9 Leskova Street, 252011 Kiev (tel: 295-0305; fax 295-3164).

Commercial Bank (Ekspobank), 2-4 Volodarskogo Street, 254025 Kiev (tel: 216-1676; fax: 216-6073).

First Ukrainian International Bank (under full management of Bank Mees and Hpe Pierson NV, ABN/AMRO), 8 Prorizna Street, 252034 Kiev (tel: 224-2187; fax: 224-2055).

Gradobank, 1 Dimitrova Street, 252650 Kiev (tel: 261-9191; fax: 268-1530).

Inki Bank, 10/2 Mechnikova Street, 252023 Kiev (tel: 294-9219; fax: 290-6292).

Legbank Commercial Bank for Light Industry, 8/10 Esplanadna (Kuybysheva) Street, 252601 Kiev (tel: 220-6125; fax: 220-8684).

Ukreximbank, 8 Kreshchatyk Street, Kiev (tel: 226-3363; fax: 229-8082).

Ukrainian Bank for Foreign Economic Affairs, 8 Kreshchatyk Street, 252001 Kiev (tel: 293-1698).

Ukrainian Financial Group Joint Stock Commercial Bank, 7 Vokzalnaya Street, 252032 Kiev (tel: 245-4560; fax: 245-4587).

Central bank

National Bank of Ukraine, 9 Institutska Street, Kiev 01601 (tel: 253-0180; fax: 230-2033; e-mail: info@bank.gov.ua).

Travel information

Ukraine International Airlines, 63A Bogdana Khmelnytskogo Street, 01054 Kiev (tel: 461-5656 ; fax: 216-7994; e-mail: uia@ps.kiev.ua).

Ukrainian Travel Information System, 29A, Electrikov Street, 04176 Kiev (tel/fax: 537-2727; e-mail: info@utis.com.ua)

Ministry of tourism

Ministry of Culture and Tourism, 19 Ivana Franka Street, 01601 Kiev (tel: 235-2378; fax: 235-3257; e-mail: info@mincult.gov.ua).

National tourist organisation offices

State Tourism Administration of Ukraine, 36 Yaroslaviv Val Street, 01034 Kiev (tel: 212-4215; fax: 212-4277; e-mail: info@tourism.gov.ua).

Ministries

Ministry of Agriculture and Foodstuffs, 24 Kreshchatyk Street, 252001 Kiev (tel: 226-2772; fax: 229-8756).

Ministry of the Coal Industry, 4 Bohdana Khmelnitskoho Street, 252001 Kiev (tel: 226-2273, 228-0372; fax: 228-2131).

Ministry of Communications, 22 Kreshchatyk Street, Kiev (tel: 226-2140; fax: 228-6141).

Ministry of Culture, 19 Ivana Franka Street, 252030 Kiev (tel: 224-4911, 226-2645, 226-2902; fax: 225-3257).

Ministry of Defence, 6 Povitroflotsky Avenue, 252168 Kiev (tel: 224-7152; fax: 226-2015).

Ministry of Education, 10 Peremogy Avenue, 252135 Kiev (tel: 216-7210, 216-7763, 216-1575; fax: 274-1049).

Ministry of Engineering, the Defence Industry and Conversion, 6 Pushkinska Street, 252034 Kiev (tel: 229-0390; fax: 228-7653).

Ministry of Environment Protection, 5 Kreshchatyk Street, 252001 Kiev (tel: 226-2428, 228-0644; fax: 229-8383).

Ministry of Finance, 12/2 Hrushevskoho Street, 252008 Kiev (tel: 226-2044; fax: 293-2178).

Ministry of Foreign Affairs, 1 Mihaylivska Square, 252018 Kiev (tel: 226-3379, 293-1581; fax: 226-3169, 293-3302).

Ministry of Foreign Economic Relations, 8 Lvivska Square, 254655 Kiev (tel: 212-3005; fax: 212-5259).

Ministry of Forestry, 5 Kreshchatyk Street, 252001 Kiev (tel: 226-3253, 226-2735, 228-5666; fax: 228-7794).

Ministry of Health, 7 Hrushevskoho Street, 252021 Kiev (tel: 293-6194; fax: 293-6975).

Ministry of Industry, 34 Kreshchatyk Street, 252001 Kiev (tel: 226-2623; fax: 227-4104).

Ministry of Information, 2 Prorizna Street, 252601 Kiev (tel: 226-2871).

Ministry of Internal Affairs, 10 Bogomoltsa Street, 252021 Kiev (tel: 291-3333, 226-3317; fax: 291-3182).

Ministry of Justice, 13 Karl Marx Street, 252001 Kiev (tel: 226-2416; fax: 226-2416).

Ministry of Labour, 28 Pushkinska Street, 252004 Kiev (tel: 226-2445, 226-2639, 226-3215; fax: 224-5905).

Ministry for Nationalities, Migration and Cults Issues, 21/8 Instytutska Street, 252021 Kiev (tel: 293-5335; fax: 293-3531).

Ministry of Power Engineering and Electrification, 30 Kreshchatyk Street, 252001 Kiev (tel: 224-9388; fax: 224-4021).

Ministry for Protection of the Population against the Consequences of Chernobyl, 8 Lvivska Square, 254655 Kiev (tel: 212-5049; fax: 212-5069).

Ministry of Social Welfare, 26-28 Kudriavka Street, 252053 Kiev (tel: 222-5555, 226-2401; fax: 212-2535).

Ministry of Statistics, 3 Shota Rustaveli Street, 252023 Kiev (tel: 226-2021, 227-7057; fax: 227-0783, 227-4266).

Ministry of Transport, 51 Horkoho Street, 252005 Kiev (tel: 226-2266, 227-1029, 227-7087; fax: 227-7351).

Ministry of Youth and Sports Issues, 42 Esplanadna Street, 252023 Kiev (tel: 220-0200, 220-1461; fax: 220-1294).

Ukrainian Ministry for Economics and Issues of European Integration, 12/2 Hrushevskoho Street, 252008 Kiev (tel: 293-4005, 293-9329; fax: 293-6371).

Other useful addresses

British Embassy, 9 Desyatinna, 01025 Kiev (tel: 462-0011/15; fax: 462-0013; internet: wwwbritemb-ukraine.net).

Cabinet of Ministers, 12/2 Hrushevskoho Street, 252001 Kiev (tel: 226-3263; fax: 293-2093).

Committee for Standardisation, Methodology and Certification, 10 Kypska Street, 252021 Kiev (tel: 226-2971).

EBRD Kiev Office, c/o National Hotel, 5 Lipska Street, 252021 Kiev 21 (tel: 291-8847, 291-8977; fax: 291-6246).

EU Co-ordination Unit – TACIS Programme, Agency for International Co-operation and Investment, 1 Mihailivska Ploscha, 252018 Kiev (tel: 212-8312; fax: 230-2513).

European Centre for Macroeconomic Analysis of Ukraine, Kiev (tel & fax: 228-3283; e-mail: ecman@gv.kiev.va).

Foreign Trade Organisation (UKRIMPEX), 22 Vorovsky Street, 252054 Kiev (tel: 216-2174; fax: 216-1926, 216-2996).

International Finance Corporation Field Office, Suite 7, 28-A Lyuteranska Street, 252024 Kiev (tel: 293-4857, 293-8341; fax: 293-0539).

Kiev City Administration, 36 Khreshchatyk Street, Kiev (tel: 220-8065; fax: 228-4718).

Kiev Universal Commodity Exchange (KUCE), 1 Kudryashova Street, 252035 Kiev (tel: 276-7129, 244-0143, fax: 276-7129).

Soros International Economic Advisory Group, Kiev (tel: 296-9877; fax: 269-5263).

State Ukrainian Property Fund, 18/9 Kutuzova Street, 252133 Kiev (tel: 296-6963; fax: 296-6984).

Ukrainian Association of Industrialists and Entrepreneurs, 34 Kreshchatik Street, 252001 Kiev (tel: 224-3122, 228-3069; fax: 226-3152).

Ukrainian Embassy (USA), Suite 711, 3350 M Street, NW, Washington DC 20007 (tel: (+1-202) 333-0606; fax: (+1-202) 333-0606; e-mail: vmar@aol.com).

Ukrainian Exchange (commodities and stock exchange), 15 Proreznaya Street, 252601 Kiev (tel: 228-6481; fax: 229-6376).

Ukrainian League of Enterprises with Foreign Capital, 19A Lyuteranska Street, 252073 Kiev (tel: 229-3544; fax: 229-8739).

Ukrainian National News Agency (UKRINFORM), 8-16b Khemlnitski Street, 252601 Kiev (tel: 226-2469, 229-0143; fax: 229-2439/8007, 228-1659).

Ukrainian Universal Commodity Exchange, 1 Academika Glushkova Avenue, 252085 Kiev (tel: 261-6333, 261-6375; fax: 261-6362).

UKRINTERENERGO (State Foreign Trade Company), 27 Komintern Street, 252032 Kiev (tel: 291-7296; fax: 220-1885).

World Bank Field Office, Suite 2/3, 26 Shovkovychna Street, 252024 Kiev (tel: 293-1110, 293-4045; fax: 293-4236).

National news agency: Ukrinform (Ukranian National News Agency)

Other news agencies: Unian: www.unian.net/eng

Interfax-Ukraine: www.interfax.com.ua/en

Internet sites

Ukraine gateway site:
http://www.brama.com

Ukraine Embassy, London:
http://www.ukrainet.org

Ukraine Embassy, Washington:
http://www.ukremb.com

General information:
http://www.bizukraine.com

Tourism and travel:
http://www.ukraine.com

Ukraine International Airlines:
http://www.ukraine international.com

History and culture:
http://www:uazone.net

News on Ukraine:
http://www.infoukes.com

Travel and tourism:
http://www.travel.kyiv.org

United Arab Emirates

KEY FACTS

Official name: Al Imarat al Arabiyya al Muttahida (United Arab Emirates) (UAE)

Head of State: President Sheikh Khalifa bin Zaid al Nahayan (ruler of Abu Dhabi) (since Nov 2004)

Head of government: Prime Minister Sheikh Mohammed bin Rashed al Maktoum (ruler of Dubai) (from 4 Jan 2006)

Ruling party: There are no official political parties

Area: 83,600 square km

Population: 4.49 million (2007)*

Capital: Abu Dhabi (federal capital); Dubai (commercial capital)

Official language: Arabic

Currency: Dirham (Dh) = 100 fils

Exchange rate: Dh3.67 per US$ (fixed)

GDP per capita: US$42,934 (2007)*

GDP real growth: 7.40% (2007)

Labour force: 2.97 million (2006)

Unemployment: 2.40% (2001; last published figure)

Inflation: 11.00% (2007)*

Oil production: 2.92 million bpd (2007)

Balance of trade: US$42.95 billion (2005)

Foreign debt: US$39.10 billion (2006)

* estimated figure

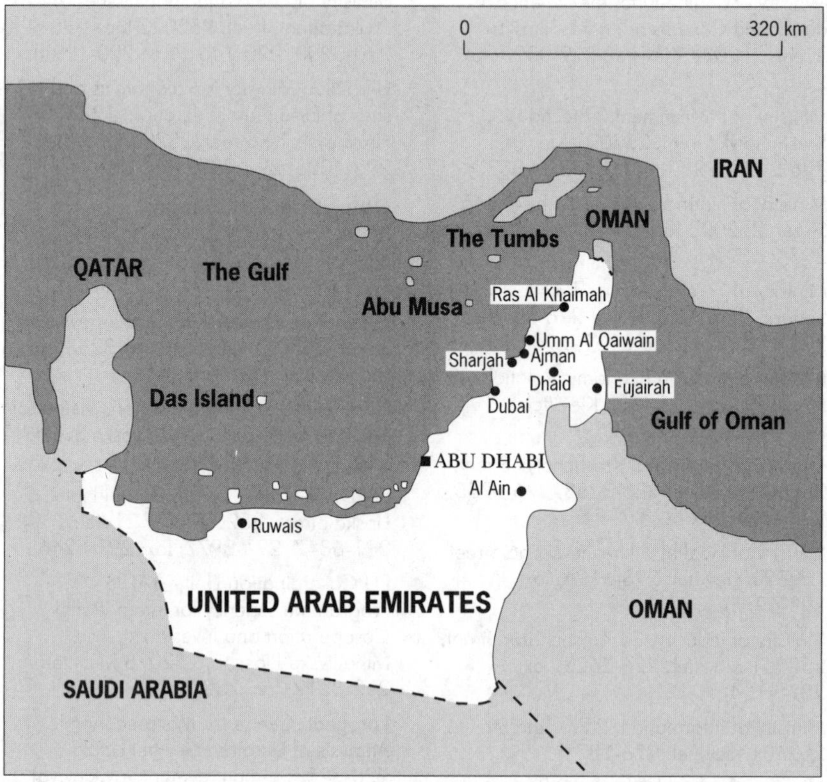

The United Arab Emirates (UAE) economy expected 7.8 per cent growth in 2008, mostly on the strength of the contributions of its rising non-oil sectors such as real estate, construction and finance. At the beginning of 2008, the UAE economy was the second largest in the Arab world. 'As long as there is strong demand for oil and gas and the oil prices average US$60 to US$80 a barrel the UAE economy will be in good shape,' said the UAE Central Bank Governor, Sultan Yasser al Suweidi. Mr al Suweidi predicted that the UAE economy may only register 6.6 per cent growth in 2008 in the light of a slump in oil prices. However, with oil hovering around US$99 a barrel in mid-2008, there was no immediate threat of a sudden decline in prices. According to preliminary reports released by the UAE ministry of economy, the country's GDP grew 16.48 per cent at current prices in 2007, primarily because of the expansion of the oil and gas sector and the growth of non-oil segments including real estate.

Figures from an International Monetary Fund (IMF) report showed that the UAE GDP increased by 16.7 per cent to Dh730 billion (US$198.9 billion) in 2007. The country's trade balance surplus reached Dh178 billion (US$48.5 billion), with exports rising to Dh664 billion (US$180.8 billion), 39.4 per cent of which was from crude oil exports. The volume of the UAE's foreign trade stood at Dh1.151 trillion (US$313.6 billion) in 2007, accounting for 158 per cent of the country's GDP.

Ranking success

The UAE rose to 8th position in the Foreign Direct Investment Confidence Index (FDICI) a destination for foreign direct investment (FDI), while ranking 15th out of 141 countries in the Inward FDI Performance Index for 2006 according to the

2007 *World Investment Report*. In 2007 the UAE had acquired the highest number of new investment projects in the region, rising from 88 in 2002 to 282 in 2006; with total FDI in the country valued at Dh70 billion (US$19 billion). This figure had risen to around Dh75 billion (US$20.4 billion) in 2007. The UAE ranked No 37 globally on the Davos World Competitiveness Index for 2007/2008, and first on the Arab World Competitiveness Index. The country came 23rd globally on the Business Competitiveness Index (BCI) for 2008 released by the World Economic Forum. It was also ranked first in the Cargo sector of the Gulf region reflecting the advanced services provided by its ports.

The UAE's industrial sector achieved an impressive growth of 19.7 per cent in 2007, contributing 12.4 per cent to national GDP. This sector has thus emerged as the second largest contributor to the UAE economy behind the oil industry. Tourism has contributed Dh19 billion (US$5.2 billion) to the economy during the past 10 years as reported by the Global Association of the Exhibition Industry. Eight million tourists travel to the UAE, twice the number of inhabitants; this figure was expected to reach 10 million by 2010. The number of hotels exceeds 450, with an annual occupancy rate of about 97 per cent. The UAE's airports handled around 38 million travellers in 2006, affirming their operational success and highlighting the adoption of the most advanced services. The figure was expected to increase by 55.4 per cent to 240 million travellers by 2015. Furthermore, the UAE's, air transport services ranked a very high 4th out of all the countries assessed by the Davos World Competitiveness Index in 2007/08.

The World Economic Research Centre has also awarded the UAE an 'A' ranking in terms of low levels of political and security risks for investment. The country was also commended for its currency level, as the UAE enjoys a low debt-to-GDP ratio. Government liquidity level has so far been able to bridge the deficit in foreign debt. The World Bank has ranked the UAE first in Middle East and north African countries in terms of managing counterfeiting and corruption and in the efficiency of its regulatory framework and government.

The UAE was set up in 1971 following British withdrawal from the Gulf under the East of Suez overall withdrawal. Under the revised arrangements, British responsibility for the defence and foreign relations of the Sheikhdoms was ended. The initial federation had only six members, the emirate of Ras al Khaimah joining in February 1972. Two states have an over-riding importance in the UAE – Abu Dhabi and Dubai. Despite their historic rivalries, the two have managed to agree on the broad lines of UAE policy, while pursuing very different development agendas.

An outward-oriented development strategy, good macroeconomic management and a business-friendly environment have all contributed to continuing high growth in the UAE in recent years

Diversifying economy

Dubai became the financial services centre of the Middle East, in competition with Bahrain, when it officially opened the Dubai International Financial Exchange (DFIX). The DFIX forms part of the Dubai International Financial Centre (DIFC), established in 2002. Both of these projects were the brainchild of the then *de facto* Emir of Dubai, Sheikh Mohammed bin Rashid al Maktoum. Sheikh Mohammed succeeded his brother Sheikh Maktoum bin Rashed al Maktoum as Emir of Dubai and prime minister and vice president of the UAE in January 2006.

The UAE sits on about 10 per cent of the world's proven oil reserves and also has the fifth largest gas reserves in the world. About 30 per cent of its GDP is based on oil exports, although recent developments in Dubai and elsewhere in the country have seen large strides taken in the financial and petrochemical sectors.

There have been several projects to diversify its economy and to reduce the UAE's dependence on oil and natural gas revenues. The non-oil sectors of the UAE's economy presently contribute as much as 70 per cent of the UAE's total GDP, and about 30 per cent of its total exports. The federal government has invested heavily in sectors such as aluminum production, tourism, aviation, re-export commerce and telecommunications. As part of its strategy to further expand its tourism industry, the UAE is building new hotels, restaurants and shopping centres, and expanding airports and duty-free zones. Dubai accounts for about 85 per cent of the Emirates' re-export trade. The UAE has been a member of the World Trade Organisation (WTO) since 1995, and has one of the most open economies in the region.

The oil and gas

UAE had proven crude oil reserves of 97.8 billion barrels at the end of 2007, or slightly less than 8 per cent of the world total. Production was 2.92 thousand barrels per day (bpd) Abu Dhabi holds 94 per cent of this amount, or about 92.2 billion barrels. Dubai contains an estimated 4.0 billion barrels, followed by Sharjah and Ras al Khaimah, with 1.5 billion and 100 million barrels of oil, respectively.

Dubai's production has been falling in recent years due to the decline of its modest reserves. Most of the UAE's oil fields have been producing since the 1960s or early 1970s. Proven oil reserves in Abu Dhabi have roughly doubled in the last

KEY INDICATORS — United Arab Emirates

	Unit	2003	2004	2005	2006	2007
Population	m	3.17	3.34	4.68	4.23	*4.49
Gross domestic product (GDP)	US$bn	80.40	70.96	130.26	163.30	*192.60
GDP per capita	US$	19,048	22,017	27,831	38,613	*42,934
GDP real growth	%	4.6	5.7	8.5	9.4	*7.4
Inflation	%	3.2	3.8	7.8	9.2	*11.0
Oil output	'000 bpd	2,520.0	2,667.0	2,751.0	2,969.0	2,915.0
Natural gas output	bn cum	44.4	45.8	46.6	47.4	49.2
Exports (fob) (goods)	US$m	60,800.0	69,480.0	103,100.0	–	–
Imports (cif) (goods)	US$m	51,955.0	45,660.0	60,150.0	94,670.0	–
Balance of trade	US$m	8,845.0	23,820.0	42,950.0	–	–
Current account	US$m	6,860.0	16,140.0	20,532.0	35,942.0	*41,666.0
Total reserves minus gold	US$m	15,087.8	18,529.9	21,010.3	27,617.4	77,238.8
Foreign exchange	US$m	14,731.5	18,209.0	20,867.7	27,511.9	77,161.9
Exchange rate	per US$	3.67	3.67	3.67	3.67	3.67

* estimated figure

decade, mainly due to significant increases in rates of recovery. Abu Dhabi has continued to identify new finds, especially offshore, and to discover new oil-rich structures in existing fields.

Under the UAE's constitution, each emirate controls its own oil production and resource development. Although Abu Dhabi joined OPEC in 1967 (four years before the UAE was formed), Dubai does not consider itself part of OPEC or bound by its quotas.

UAE's natural gas reserves of 215.07 trillion cubic feet (Tcf) (end 2007) are the world's fifth largest after Russia, Iran, Qatar, and Saudi Arabia. The largest reserves of 198.5Tcf are located in Abu Dhabi. Sharjah, Dubai, and Ras al Khaimah contain smaller reserves of 10.7Tcf, 4.0Tcf, and 1.2Tcf, respectively. In Abu Dhabi, the non-associated Khuff natural gas reservoirs beneath the Umm Shaif and Abu al Bukhush oil fields rank among the world's largest.

According to the US Energy Information Administration (EIA) the past few years have seen the UAE embark on a massive, multi-billion dollar programme of investment in its natural gas sector including a shift toward natural gas-fired power plants and the transformation of the Taweelah commercial district into a natural gas-based industrial zone. An ambitious plan, the Dolphin Project, to connect the natural gas grids of Qatar (including the Energy Gas Processing Plant in Ras Laffan) the UAE and Oman was opened in 2008. Most of the UAE's increased natural gas needs in the next decade are to be satisified with imported natural gas from Qatar. Much of the natural gas development in the UAE itself involves the extraction of natural gas liquids (NGLs) and reinjection of the gas to maintain pressure in oilfields.

Dynastic musical chairs

With the death of founding president Sheikh Zaid in November 2004, a new member of the al Nahayan clan stepped forward to inherit not only the family emirate of Abu Dhabi but also the virtually hereditary presidency of the UAE itself. A similar change took place in January 2006, when Sheikh Mohammed became the ruler of the emirate of Dubai, and the UAE's vice president and prime minister.

Democratic reform, sort of, some time

In December 2005, President Sheikh Khalifa announced plans to institute a partially-elected advisory council. Khalifa also stated that suffrage would be limited to a small number of electors who would in turn be chosen by the country's seven emirs. No date was given for the election and political parties will remain banned.

Also in December, the Emirate of Abu Dhabi held its first ever elections for its Chamber of Commerce and Industry. Women were also allowed to vote and two seats were reserved for women candidates.

Outlook

The UAE has remained violence-free in a region hyper-charged in the wake of the US-led invasion of Iraq. There have been no reports of Islamist terrorism or politically inspired attacks on the UAE's large expatriate population. There is also little to suggest so far that the country's citizens are agitating for democratic reform. The combination of public quiescence and restricted political freedom look set to continue as long as economic prosperity continues.

Risk assessment

Politics	Fair
Economy	Good
Regional stability	Good

COUNTRY PROFILE

Historical profile

1498 The Portuguese occupied the region.
1633 The Dutch turned the Portuguese out of their trading posts, to be ousted in their turn, by the British.
1820 Britain and a number of rulers in the Gulf signed a treaty to combat piracy. This began a series of agreements which led to the area becoming known as the Trucial Coast, comprising the Trucial states (Abu Dhabi, Dubai, Sharjah, Ras al Khaimah, Umm al Qaiwain, Fujairah and Ajman).
1892 Exclusive Agreements between the Trucial States and Britain were signed, which effectively gave the British control over foreign affairs, while each emirate retained control over internal affairs.
1952 The seven emirates formed a Trucial council to promote increased co-operation.
1958 Oil was discovered off Abu Dhabi.
1962 Oil was exported for the first time from Abu Dhabi.
1966 Oil was discovered off Dubai.
1968 Britain announced its intention to withdraw from the Gulf by 1971. A British plan to form a single state consisting of Bahrain, Qatar and the Trucial States did not take place.
1971 The independence of Bahrain and Qatar was negotiated. Iran occupied the islands of Greater and Lesser Tumb and Abu Musa. Abu Dhabi, Dubai, Sharjah, Fujairah, Umm al Qaiwain and Ajman formed the United Arab Emirates (UAE), a loose federation; Sheikh Zayed bin Sultan al Nahayan (ruler of Abu Dhabi) was elected president of the federation. Ras al Khaimah's ruler did not join at this point since he optimistically hoped that successful oil exploration would enable him to stick out for a better deal.
1972 Ras al-Khaimah joined the federation; the Federal National Council (FNC) was created as a 40-member consultative body, appointed by the seven rulers of the UAE.
1980s The UAE supported Iraq during the Iran-Iraq war.
1981 The UAE became a founding member of the Gulf Co-operation Council (GCC). The GCC's inaugural meeting was held in Abu Dhabi.
1991 The UAE joined the US-led alliance against Iraq. The Bank of Credit and Commerce International (BCCI), in which the Abu Dhabi royal family owned a 77.4 per cent stake, collapsed.
1992 Iran insisted that visitors to the islands of Abu Musa and Greater and Lesser Tumb must have Iranian visas.
1993 Abu Dhabi sued BCCI's executives for damages.
1994 A court in Abu Dhabi convicted 11 of the 12 former BCCI executives accused of fraud. They were given prison sentences and ordered to pay compensation.
1996 Iran's dispute with the UAE over the islands of Abu Musa and the Tumbs was further fuelled by Iran when it built an airport on Abu Musa and a power station on Greater Tumb. Two BCCI executives were cleared of fraud charges on appeal.
1998 Diplomatic relations with Iraq were restored – the UAE had severed them at the outbreak of the Gulf War.
1999 The GCC reiterated its support for the UAE over the three disputed islands of Greater and Lesser Tumb and Abu Musa.
2001 Six thousand prisoners were pardoned by the President on humanitarian grounds.The government ordered financial institutions to freeze the assets of 62 organisations and individuals suspected of funding terrorist movements.
2002 The UAE and Oman signed a final agreement delineating their entire 1,000km border.
2003 The minister of higher education said that the employment of women graduates was an important factor for the UAE.
2004 President Sheikh Zayed bin Sultan al Nahyan died. Sheikh Khalifa bin Zaid al Nahayan succeeded his father as ruler of Abu Dhabi, followed by the Federal

National Council (FNC) electing him as president of the UAE.
2005 A new terminal for Abu Dhabi International Airport was opened. Sheikh Zayed announced plans to elect half of the 40 members of the FNC, by a limited number of citizens.
2006 Sheikh Maktoum bin Rashed al Maktoum, ruler of Dubai, vice president and prime minister of the UAE, died. He was succeeded by Sheikh Mohammed bin Rashid al Maktoum. The state-owned company, Dubai Ports, purchased the UK shipping line P&O, which in turn controlled the management company of six of the largest ports in the US, which sparked a US national controversy concerning border security. Dubai Ports was forced to sell its assets to American International Group within weeks. The working week was changed to bring it into line with Western nations. Elections to the FNC were held; of the more than 300,000 people eligible to vote, only 6,595 were chosen by the authorities and given the right to vote and of these 1,163 were women.
2007 Sheikh Mohammed bin Rashed al Maktoum, the ruler of Dubai, donated US$10 billion to fund an educational foundation, set up to improve the standard of education in the Middle East. The Burj Dubai, still under construction, became the world's tallest skyscraper. It is due to be completed in September 2009 when Burj Dubai will be 693m tall and have 160 floors.
2008 On 1 January, a common market was created by Bahrain, Kuwait, Oman, Qatar, Saudi Arabia and UAE, the six wealthiest Gulf states. Citizens of these countries are now allowed to travel between and live in any of the six states, where they may find employment, buy properties and businesses and use the educational and health facilities freely. On 1 February the Emir of Dubai, Sheikh Mohammed bin Rashid al Maktoum, issued a decree appointing his son Sheikh Hamdan bin Mohammed bin Rashid al Maktoum as crown prince of the Emirate.

Political structure

Constitution

Highest government authority is vested in the Supreme Council of Rulers, which consists of the rulers of the seven emirates — Abu Dhabi, Dubai, Sharjah, Ras al Khaimah, Umm al Qaiwain, Fujairah and Ajman — which comprise the UAE. It is responsible for most internal and external affairs. Abu Dhabi and Dubai hold the power of veto on the Supreme Council. The Supreme Council meets four times a year, and elects the president and vice president (each for terms of five years). The president appoints the prime minister and the Council of Ministers.
The 40 members of the Federal National Council (FNC), drawn proportionately from each emirate, are appointed by the rulers.
The individual emirates have retained a great degree of autonomy and all local powers which are not specifically reserved for the federal government belong to them. Since 1971, the president has been the ruler of Abu Dhabi and the prime minister and vice president the ruler of Dubai, suggesting that elections are a matter of form and that in fact the two emirates with the largest economic and political muscle tend to dominate the federation.
A constitutional amendment in 1996 removed the word 'interim' from the constitution and designated Abu Dhabi the capital of the UAE.

Form of state

Federal monarchy

The executive

The Head of State is president for a term of seven years, chosen by the seven, hereditary rulers of the Emirates who make up the membership of the Federal Supreme Council (FSC).
The president, vice president and FSC comprise the executive branch. The FSC convenes four-times annually to set policies and sanction federal legislation. Within the FSC, Abu Dhabi and Dubai have effective veto power.

National legislature

The Federal National Council (FNC) has consultative functions only, with no legislative powers.
The FNC has 40 members, half of whom are appointed by the seven emirates (Abu Dhabi and Dubai appoint eight members each, Sharjah and Ras al Khaimah appoint six members each and Ajman, Fujairah and Umm al Qaiwain appoint four members each), to serve two-year terms. The other 20 members are elected by a specially chosen constituency of 7,000 people, selected by local governments.

Legal system

The federal courts, which consist of the Union Supreme Court and primary tribunals, were established by law in 1979. The former primary tribunals in Abu Dhabi, Sharjah, Ajman and Fujairah became federal primary tribunals and the former primary tribunals of other towns became circuits of the federal primary tribunals. The law applied is Sharia (Islamic Law).

Last elections

4 Nov 2004 (president and vice president; voting open only to members of the Federal Supreme Council); 6 December 2006 (half the members of the Federal National Council (FNC)

Results: Presidential: Sheikh Khalifa bin Zayed al Nahyan (ruler of Abu Dhabi) was elected.
FNC: all non-partisans were chosen.

Next elections

2011 (president and vice president; open only to members of the Federal Supreme Council); 2010 FNC (expected all members to be elected).

Political parties

Party political activity is not officially permitted in the UAE.

Ruling party

There are no official political parties

Population

4.49 million (2007)*

Last census: December 1995: 2,411,041

Population density: 30 inhabitants per square km.

Annual growth rate: 6.4 per cent 1994–2004 (WHO 2006)

Ethnic make-up

UAE nationals make up a fifth of the population. Around 80 per cent of the population are expatriates, with those from the Indian subcontinent accounting for about 40 per cent of the population. The second largest group is Iranians, who make up about 17 per cent. Non-UAE Arabs make up about 13 per cent and Westerners about 5 per cent.
Abu Dhabi is dominated by the Bani Yas tribe of which the al Bu Falasah is the most important section (to which the al Maktoums of Dubai belong).

Religions

The majority are Sunni Muslims; about 20 per cent are Shi'a Muslims. Many expatriates from the Indian subcontinent are Christian. The constitution guarantees full religious rights to all. The Apostolic Vicariate of Arabia is in Abu Dhabi.

Education

Primary education is compulsory and is followed by three years' preparatory education which qualifies students for general or technical secondary education. The language of instruction is English.
General secondary education lasts for three years. It consists of a common first year followed by specialisation in science or the humanities. At aged eighteen, students take an examination for progression to higher education.
Technical secondary education lasts for six years following primary school and comprises three main streams: technical, agricultural and commercial in both preparatory and secondary cycles. At aged eighteen, a Technical Secondary Diploma is awarded.
Secondary education is also offered in religious institutions.

Higher education is offered in public and private universities and Higher Colleges of Technology. These include the United Arab Emirates (UAE) University, and the Dubai University College, (a private college).
Emirate and federal politics can at times threaten academic standards. Education is allocated some 20 per cent of the federal budget.
Literacy rate: 77 per cent adult rate; 91 per cent youth rate (15–24) (Unesco 2005).
Compulsory years: 6 to 12.
Enrolment rate: 89 per cent gross primary enrolment; 80 per cent gross secondary enrolment, of relevant age groups (including repeaters) (World Bank).
Pupils per teacher: 16 in primary schools.

Health
Per capita total expenditure on health (2003) was US$623; of which per capita government spending was US$465, at the international dollar rate, (WHO 2006).
Life expectancy: 77 years, 2004 (WHO 2006)
Fertility rate/Maternal mortality rate: 2.5 births per woman, 2004 (WHO 2006); maternal mortality 3 per 100,000 live births (World Bank).
Child (under 5 years) mortality rate (per 1,000): 7.0 per 1,000 live births; 7 per cent of children aged under five are malnourished (World Bank).
Head of population per physician: 2.02 physicians per 1,000 people, 2001 (WHO 2006)

Welfare
There is an extensive and generous welfare system in the UAE, in many ways a model of a successful welfare state. However, this reflects the unique characteristics of the UAE – no social security contributions are levied on employers or employees, and there is no personal taxation. Many services remain free, and there are numerous grants, loans, and subsidies.

Main cities
Abu Dhabi (federal capital estimated population 535,097 in 2005), Dubai (commercial capital, 1.3 million), Sharjah (570,299), Ajman (256,554), Ras al Khaimah (107,662), Umm al Qaiwain (40,629).

Media
Dubai is the hub of the UAE's media industry and the dedicated Dubai Media City, which assures clients freedom of speech, is growing as an important regional centre attracting distinguished international media outlets.
National news agency: Emirates News Agency
Other news agencies: DPM News Agency: www.dpmnewsagency.com
Press
While the press is largely independent, in November 2007, Reporters Without Frontiers reported that press freedom in the UAE was bound by widespread self-censorship which eschewed any criticism of the government to avoid prosecution.
Dailies: Most newspapers are published in either Abu Dhabi or Dubai. Newspapers in Arabic that comment on news and politics include Al-Bayan (www.albayan.ae), Akhbar Al Arab (www.akhbaralarab.co.ae), also has economic and sports editions, Emarat al Youm (www.emaratalyoum.com), Al Khaleej (www.alkhaleej.co.ae). In English newspaper include Emirates Today (www.emiratestodayonline.com), Gulf News (www.gulf-news.com), Khaleej Times (www.khaleejtimes.com) and 7 Days (www.7days.ae).
Weeklies: In Arabic, Al Azmina Al Arabia (www.alazmina.info), bi-weekly for politics, culture and economics, Al-Sada (www.e-sada.com) is a magazine for women. In English, The Dubai Life (www.thedubailife.com) and Time Out Dubai (ww.timeoutdubai.com/dubai), covers entertainment and consumer items.
Business: In English monthly publications include the monthly Capital (www.capital-me.com), and UAE Banking & Business Review (www.sterlingp.ae) and Gulf Business (www.gulfbusiness.com) monthly magazine. The CPI Financial services published an online newsletter concerning banking and the financial services (www.cpifinancial.net).
Periodicals: There are over 30 magazines in Arabic and English. Al Shindagah (www.alshindagah.com), published six times a year and Review (www.sterlingp.ae) covers current affairs, Al Shumookh (www.alshumookh.net) monthly magazine lists cultural events.
Broadcasting
The state-owned Emirates Media Incorporated (EMI) operates three satellite TV channels and seven radio stations, four publications and five interactive internet websites.
Radio: Each Emirate has its own radio station, although most are located in either Abu Dhabi or Dubai. There are general interest music and news radio stations, broadcasting throughout the Emirates, while some are dedicated to religious texts or programmes for immigrant populations. Apart from EMI (www.emi.co.ae), another national network is the popular commercial Arabian Radio Network (ARN) (www.arnonline.com), including in English, Dubai 92.
A shortwave world service broadcasts to North America, Asia and Europe.
Television: Of the six TV networks based in UAE, three are pan-Arabic. The state-owned, Dubai Media Incorporated (DMI) produces a number of local TV programmes and operates four domestic channels (http://www.dubaitv.gov.ae), which provides programmes of information, entertainment, religion, culture, news and politics. In 2007 tests were undertaken by DMI to evaluate the viability of mobile digital video broadcasting. MBC (http://www.mbc.net) operates a four channels include the Al Arabiya News Channel (www.alarabiya.net). The private and independent satellite broadcaster Showtime Arabia (www.showtimearabia.com), based in Dubai, which operates over 30 channels showing imported programmes, by subscription. Residents also have a choice of hundreds of regional channels broadcasting via foreign satellite or cable TV companies. Many commercial channels broadcast foreign programmes in English with Arabic subtitles.
Residents have a choice of hundreds of regional channels broadcasting via satellite or cable. Many commercial channels broadcast foreign programmes in English with Arabic subtitles.
There are two local TV stations operating from Ajman (www.ajmantv.com) and Sharjah (www.sharjahtv.ae).
Advertising
The UAE is the region's marketing gateway. Dual English and Arabic usage is common on signs and in many publications.

Economy
The UAE has a buoyant economy, underpinned by vast oil and gas resources. GDP, boosted by rising oil prices and investor confidence, grew by 8.5 per cent in 2005. Abu Dhabi and Dubai account for approximately 60 per cent and 25 per cent respectively of overall GDP. Abu Dhabi, which possesses over 90 per cent of the oil wealth, is financially dominant, providing almost 75 per cent of federal revenues and grants to smaller emirates. Oil accounts for 30 per cent of GDP, but successful efforts are being made to diversify the economy. Dubai, for example, has developed a range of manufacturing industries, financial services and tourism, and is emerging, because of its favourable tax regime, as an important international diamond centre. Overseas companies and foreign direct investment have been attracted to the UAE by the creation of a dozen free trade zones, which offer special advances, while enabling the UAE to expand its non-oil exports.

The leading non-oil sectors are manufacturing (including Dubai's state-owned aluminium smelter, Dubal), commerce and government services (each contributing around 15 per cent to GDP), real estate (14 per cent), construction (12 per cent) and transport and communications (9 per cent). The UAE has made good progress in privatising small agricultural enterprises and has broadened the programme to include larger-scale industrial projects and public utilities.
The US company, General Electric (GE) formed a joint venture development fund with the Abu Dhabi investment company, Mubadala, to provide US$8 billion for financing Middle Eastern and African projects in clean energy, water and oil and gas.

External trade

In 2005 the Greater Arab Free Trade Area (Gafta) was ratified by 17 members, including the United Arab Emirates creating an Arab economic bloc. A customs union was established whereby tariffs within Gafta will be reduced by a percentage each year, until none remain. It also belongs to the Gulf Cooperation Council, which negotiates bilateral free trade agreements on behalf of members.
Hydrocarbons account for 80 per cent of GDP and the share of foreign trade in GDP is almost 150 per cent. Since 2000 the government has encouraged new manufacturing enterprises in metal processing, furniture and jewellery making and food processing. However, the service sector achieves more foreign earnings than any other except oil and natural gas, through tourism, financial services and banking and transport. The Dubai Ports Authority is one of the largest container handling bodies in the world.

Imports

Main imports are machinery and vehicles, pearls and precious stones, chemicals and food.
Main sources: US (11.4 per cent total, 2006), China (10.9 per cent), India (9.8 per cent).

Exports

Main exports are crude oil (45 per cent total), natural gas, pearls and precious stones, electronic equipment and vehicles.
Main destinations: Japan (25.6 per cent total, 2005), South Korea (10.2 per cent), Thailand (5.8 per cent).

Re-exports

Aluminium, from Dubai.

Agriculture

Farming

Agriculture contributes around 4 per cent to GDP and employs 8 per cent of the workforce. A harsh climate and sandy soil make self-sufficiency in food production an unlikely prospect. The northern Emirates of Ras al Khaimah, Fujairah (on the western Gulf of Onan coast) and Ajman supply 25 per cent of local demand. Ajman is the most productive and has been a focal region for agricultural development. Ras al Khaimah and Fujairah produce a more diverse selection of agricultural produce as a result of the higher rainfall they receive. Very few nationals still work on farms, where labour is mostly from Bangladesh and Baluchistan in south-west Pakistan.
Government farm subsidies are generous. Many farms are supported through funding available on easy credit terms, seed allocations and technical advice on fertilisation, irrigation, mechanisation and marketing of crops. Earth-moving and wells are free, and seeds, fertilisers and insecticides are half the market price. Abu Dhabi gives land to its citizens without charge, as well as underwriting other Emirates' grants of land to other UAE citizens via its financing of the federal budget. The main state-funded agricultural research centres and extension services are at al Dhafra, Liwa and Madina Zayed. The Arid Lands Research Centre operates experimental vegetable greenhouses on Saadiyat Island near Abu Dhabi town. The UAE is self-sufficient in various winter vegetables and excess crops of vegetables are sometimes dumped in the desert, due to a lack of processing facilities. The government already buys crops at 'favourable' prices, before selling them at discounted rates in the market.
Water shortages and soil salinity are constant problems. Agriculture is dependent on fast depleting underground aquifers. When these run dry, irrigation will depend almost entirely on desalinated water.
The country's largest dairy farm at Digdagga has a herd of Friesians producing meat and milk for local consumption.
Estimated crop production in 2005 included: 7,500 tonnes (t) potatoes, 760,000t dates, 16,500t citrus fruit, 240,000t tomatoes, 20,000t eggplants, 4,500t mangoes, 786,571t fruit in total, 506,492t vegetables in total. Estimated livestock production included: 89,840t meat in total, 9,750t beef, 15,390t camel meat, 13,500t lamb, 15,000t goat meat, 36,000t poultry, 17,000t eggs, 98,390t milk, 1,900t goatskins, 2,250t sheepskins.

Fishing

Catches cover over 80 per cent of domestic consumption. The UAE ranks fourth in the Arab world in the volume of its annual catch. Around 20 fishing ports and 25 repair workshops have been established along the coastline in Dubai, Sharjah and Ras al Khaimah. Over 15,000 tonnes of fish are imported to supplement domestic sources.
In 2004, the total marine fish catch was 89,330 tonnes and the total crustacean catch was 420 tonnes.

Forestry

The UAE has around 3.8 per cent forest cover, almost all of which is plantation. The government has initiated a long-term programme of afforestation. Abu Dhabi's western region now has about 5,000 hectares of mature tree plantations, including 120 million tamarind, tamarisk, acacia, neem and cork trees, as well as some 30 million date palms.
Timber imports in 2004 were US$620.6 million, while exports amounted to US$55.4 million.

Industry and manufacturing

The industrial sector typically accounts for under 20 per cent of GDP and employs 45 per cent of the workforce. Non-oil industry, particularly manufacturing and re-exports, is concentrated in free trade zones.
The government is placing increased emphasis on the expansion of non-oil manufacturing, such as cement, building materials, aluminium, fertilisers, foodstuffs, garments, furniture, plastics, fibreglass and processed metals.
Most non-oil export production is located on Dubai. Dubai has intensified efforts to promote foreign investment and attract regional and global capital. In April 2002, the Dubai Authority for Investment and Development (DAID) was set up to grant concessions, franchises and incentives and to issue licences to large investors. The DAID is authorised to set up, own and develop investment companies on its own or with other organisations.
Dubai's largest manufacturing enterprise, the state-owned Dubai Aluminium Company (Dubal), is expanding production from 536,000 tonnes in 2001 to 710,000 tonnes by 2007. Dubal is based in the thriving free trade area, the Jebel Ali Free Zone. Dubai is also keen to develop information technology (IT); the Dubai Internet City was set up in 2001. IT spending in the UAE was estimated at US$550 million to US$600 million during the first six months of 2004, putting spending for the full year on course to surpass the 2003 total of US$1.1 billion.
Abu Dhabi is planning to develop an industrial base, including petrochemicals, steel and aluminium. A seven-year, US$100 billion investment programme was initiated in 2005. It will be mainly government funded, but it is hoped to attract private private sector and foreign direct investment.

Tourism

Dubai is the largest tourism market in the Emirates, attracting both business travellers and an increasing number of leisure

tourists. Tourism is a key element in Dubai's development strategy. With the aim of making Dubai a major tourist destination, investment has been poured into infrastructure, including hotels, a new conference centre, a cruise terminal and, with a view to becoming an aviation hub, airport and airline fleet expansion. The annual growth rate in visitors to Dubai is typically between 10–15 per cent. Tourism is expected to contribute 1.2 per cent to GDP in 2005.
Shortage of prime building land has not deterred planners. The Palm (previously known as the Palm Islands) is a US$3 billion scheme, involving the construction of two man-made islands off the Dubai coast, each in the shape of a palm tree.

Mining
The development of non-hydrocarbon minerals plays a role in the government's policy of diversification away from dependence on the oil sector. Limestone, gypsum and dolerite are exploited. Celestite is known to exist but has not yet been extracted.
Copper is known to exist in Fujairah and Ras al Khaimah. There is also thought to be talc in Fujairah, chromium in Sharjah, Ajman, Fujairah and Ras al Khaimah, and manganese throughout the northern Emirates. Mineral studies are being undertaken in the Madah region of Fujairah, in Al-Siji in Sharjah and in the Masfouyt and Manama areas of Ajman. Ras al Khaimah already has two quarries, four cement companies and further downstream factories, with annual cement production of 2.3 million tonnes.

Hydrocarbons
The UAE is one of the world's largest producers of crude oil and natural gas, which account for around 30 per cent of GDP. Oil reserves total 97.8 billion barrels, with production at around 2.7 million barrels per day (bpd). Approximately 94 per cent is held by Abu Dhabi; Dubai holds just under 4 per cent, with 4 billion barrels, while Sharjah and Ras al Khaimah hold 1.5 billion and 100 million barrels respectively. Under the constitution, each emirate is responsible for its own production and resource development. Refinery capacity in the UAE is 645,000 bpd, an increase of around two-thirds over the past decade. A 300,000 bpd refinery is projected for construction at Fujairah.
Gas reserves total 6.06 trillion cubic metres, the world's fifth-largest, with production of around 46 billion cubic metres. Abu Dhabi holds 92.5 per cent of the total reserves, with 5.0 per cent in Sharjah, 1.9 per cent in Dubai and 0.5 per cent in Ras al Khaimah. Reserves are expected to last for another 150–170 years.
Coal is neither produced or imported in the UAE.

Energy
Electricity generation capacity is estimated at 5.8GW. The government is seeking to open up the sector with limited privatisation in order to inject new capital and increase capacity to meet soaring demand. Abu Dhabi is leading the way, with the creation of new independent power and water projects and joint ventures with minority interests held by foreign firms. The Abu Dhabi government has rejected full privatisation of the water and power sector.
The UAE is participating in a US$1 billion project to build a regional power grid linking the GCC countries. The UAE will join the regional grid, along with Oman, as part of the second phase of the project after it has connected all the power stations in the Emirates. The first phase, linking Saudi Arabia, Bahrain, Kuwait and Qatar, is scheduled for completion in 2009.

Financial markets
Stock exchange
There are two stock markets in the UAE: the Abu Dhabi Stock Market (ADSM) and the Dubai Financial Market (DFM). The stock exchanges are likely to experience strong growth in the future, particularly in corporate bonds. This will be strengthened by Dubai's intention to tap the markets for funds to help with infrastructure development. The DIFC bourse does not impose currency restrictions or limit the involvement of international portfolio investors.

Banking and insurance
Financial services constitute a key sector throughout the Emirates, with Dubai at the leading edge and hoping to overtake Bahrain as the Gulf's leading financial centre. The UAE's banking sector has attracted more foreign interest than other Gulf states due to its liberal banking regime and low level of taxation.
Development of the sector is focussed on the Dubai International Financial Sector (DIFC), which was launched in February 2001 as a link between the financial markets of Africa, Asia, the Middle East and the West. The DIFC has concentrated on the development of asset management, administration, reinsurance and Islamic finance in an attempt to develop a niche market.
Continuing large-scale infrastructure projects, growing prospects in the tourism industry and the creation of an automated stock exchange all represent considerable opportunities for banks. WTO membership, effective from 2003, obliges the UAE authorities to admit new foreign banks and help to increase competition in the sector. On the downside, the UAE's banking sector lacks transparency, although the OECD's Financial Action Task Force (FATF) declared the UAE's performance in 2002 as 'satisfactory'.
Sometimes the UAE's banking sector has attracted the wrong sort of attention, with money laundering being a particular blight on the banking sector. The 11 September 2001 terrorist attacks in the US focussed attention on the UAE, particularly its informal money transfer system known as hawala, in which funds are transferred from one country to another via a broker. The lack of paperwork and the fact that no money physically crosses borders has made hawala a channel for terrorist financing. In November 2002, the central bank tightened regulations on hawala brokers by introducing a certification system, which required brokers to provide details of their overseas clients and to notify the authorities if there are any suspicious transactions.
The merger of Emirates Bank International (EBI) and the National Bank of Dubai (NBK) was announced in March 2007. The new bank, Emirates NDB, will dominate banking in the UAE and be the largest bank by assets in the Gulf region.

Central bank
Central Bank of the United Arab Emirates

Time
GMT plus four hours

Geography
The UAE is bordered by Oman to the east, Saudi Arabia to the west and south, Qatar to the north, and by a coastline of approximately 650km on the southern shore of the Gulf. Much of the land is sand desert or salt flats. Six of the Emirates lie on the Arabian Gulf coast. Fujairah, the seventh, lies on the Gulf of Oman. The region is one of shallow seas and offshore islands and coral reefs. The UAE's two coasts are divided by the Hajjar Mountains stretching through the Musandam Peninsula to the Straits of Hormuz.

Hemisphere
Northern

Climate
Summer temperatures are hot, reaching 49 degrees Celsius (C) in the shade, while January, the coldest winter month, sees temperatures ranging from three to 28 degrees C. Humidity, particularly on the coast, can be extreme. Average annual rainfall is very low, ranging between 100mm and 200mm.

Dress codes
A lightweight suit or lightweight jacket and trousers are advised. A tie is de rigueur at business meetings but a jacket need not be worn. Long-sleeved shirts should be

worn at business and official meetings. In public places, women should dress discretely and men should wear shirts and long trousers. Bikinis are allowed on certain beaches.

Entry requirements

Passports

Required by all.

Visa

Required by all, except citizens of EU, North America, Australasia, Japan and a few other Asian countries, for visits up to one month. For a full list of exceptions visit www.uae-embassy.org and follow the link from Travel to UAE to consular services where a visa application form can also be found. All visits for those requiring a visa must be arranged through a sponsor such as tour operator or UAE resident or company. The sponsor organises a visa and will provide a letter of invitation, giving details of the sponsor's residency permit, and a copy of their passport. Visas for business visits are arranged by invitation only. Company credentials must be provided including a trading licence to a sponsor who arranges the visa and will meet the traveller at the airport.

Prohibited entry

Israeli nationals and holders of passports with Israeli visas stamped in them.

Currency advice/regulations

The import and export of local and foreign currency is limited to Dh40,000 (or equivalent). Amounts in excess of this must be declared on entry.

Travellers cheques are widely accepted.

Customs

Personal effects are duty-free. Small quantities of alcohol are allowed entry (non-Muslims only).

Prohibited imports

Firearms and ammunition require a special permit. Illegal drugs (drug trafficking is a capital offence), poppy seeds in all forms, religious propaganda, commercial loose pearls, raw seafood and fruit and vegetables from cholera infected areas are prohibited.

Health (for visitors)

Mandatory precautions

None.

Advisable precautions

Inoculations and boosters should be current for hepatitis A, polio, tetanus and typhoid. There may be a need for vaccinations for tuberculosis, hepatitis B and diphtheria. Anti-malaria precautions are recommended if travelling to the border with Oman, in the east.

NB Some drugs normally taken under a doctor's supervision are classified as narcotics in the UAE. A doctor's prescription should be carried along with any medication that is brought into the country. If suspected of being under the influence of drugs or alcohol, individuals may be required to submit to blood and/or urine tests and may be subject to prosecution.

Hotels

Excellent standards throughout the UAE, and rooms are generally in adequate supply although advance booking is always advisable.

A 20 per cent tax is included in all bills.

Credit cards

Major credit and charge cards are widely accepted.

Public holidays (national)

Fixed dates

1 Jan (New Year's Day), 6 Aug (Sheikh Zayed's Accession), 2 Dec (National Day).

Variable dates

Eid al Adha (three days), Islamic New Year, Birth of the Prophet, Ascension of the Prophet, Eid al Fitr (two days).

Islamic year – 1429 (10 Jan 2008–28 Dec 2008): The Islamic year has 354 or 355 days, with the result that Muslim feasts advance by 10–12 days against the Gregorian calendar each year. Dates of the Muslim feasts vary according to sightings of the new moon, so cannot be forecast exactly.

Working hours

Working hours may vary between Emirates and change from summer to winter. The working week was altered in 2006, to bring it into line with Western nations, although a two-day weekend was not made compulsory for the private sector.

During Ramadan, the Muslim holy month of fasting, working hours are reduced with most people working during daylight hours 0900–1300.

Banking

Mon–Thu: 0800–1300, 1500/1600–1800/1900; Fri: 0800–1300.

Business

Mon–Thu: 0800–1300, 1500/1600–1800/1900; Fri: 0830–1300. Some businesses operate on Saturday.

Government

Mon–Fri: 0700–1430.

Shops

Sat–Thu: 0930–1300, 1630–2130; Fri: 1400/1500–2100. Shopping centres general do not close during the day.

Telecommunications

Mobile/cell phones

There is a 900 GSM service operating throughout the territory – there are plans for 3G and 900/1800 services in the future.

Electricity supply

240/415V AC (Abu Dhabi) and 220/380V AC (Northern Emirates), with three-pin round or flat type plug fittings.

Weights and measures

Metric system (imperial system and local units also used).

Social customs/useful tips

Pork should not be eaten in the presence of Muslims. It is discourteous to eat, drink or smoke in front of Muslims in daylight hours during Ramadan (when it is illegal to do so in public).

Avoid using the term 'Mohammedan'.

Avoid asking personal questions, especially about wives.

Always shake hands on meeting and leaving. You may find the handshake lasts longer than in the West, but this is a sign of friendship. If you have made a good impression, the handshake on departure will be longer than that on arrival.

If coffee is served it is courteous to accept it. Cups will generally be refilled automatically unless the cup is shaken from side to side as it is returned to the server. To take only one cup of coffee is an insult, and to take three or more is considered greedy in some quarters – if in doubt follow the example of your host.

Most restaurants and hotels have bars and licensed restaurants, although a licence, which lays down a monthly quota, is required for purchase for consumption at home. Licences are not issued to Muslims.

Security

Visitors should keep in touch with developments in the Middle East as any increase in regional tension might affect travel advice.

The level of street crime has been traditionally far lower than in the West because of the severity of the penalties imposed. The influx of expatriate workers since the early 1970s has encouraged incidents of theft. Murder and violent crimes such as mugging and rape remain rare. Generally speaking the UAE has a very low incidence of crime.

Getting there

Air

Air Arabia, the Middle East's first low-fare airline, is headquartered in Sharjah and flies within the region and to the Indian subcontinent.

National airline: Etihad Airways and the airline Emirates are owned by the governments of Abu Dhabi and Dubai respectively.

International airport/s: Abu Dhabi International Airport (AUH); 35km from city. Expansion with a new terminal has increased facilities with duty-free shop, bar, bank, hotel reservations, post office, shops, car hire.

Dubai International (DXB), 4km from city, with duty-free shop, bar, bank, hotel reservations, post office, shops, car hire.

Sharjah International (SHJ), 10km from city, with duty-free shop, bar, restaurant, bank (restricted hours), hotel reservations. Ras al Khaimah International (RKT).
Other airport/s: Al Ain is Abu Dhabi's second airport 23km from the oasis of Al Ain. Fujairah has an airport.
Airport tax: None
Surface
Road: Road links are through Oman and Saudi Arabia. Buses run between Dubai and Muscat.
Water: Passenger services run between Sharjah and Bandar-é Abbas in Iran.

Getting about
National transport
Air: There are several daily services between Dubai and Abu Dhabi. There are numerous airstrips thoughout the region for charter hire flights.
Road: Good, surfaced roads along the coast links of all the Emirates.
City transport
Taxis: Taxis are plentiful and English is widely understood if not spoken.
Metered taxis are available in Abu Dhabi and the rounding-up of the charge is typical for a tip. It is advisable to negotiate fares in advance in other Emirates as taxis are not usually metered.
City traffic in Dubai has become very congested and it is advisable to allow plenty of time to reach a destination. Taxis on stands outside hotels charge more than those flagged in the street. Fixed fares are available for pre-paid journeys from Dubai airport to the city.
Some hotels offer a courtesy pick-up service; others offer the service but charge. A limousine can be booked through the hotel.
Car hire
Personal and chauffeur-driven car hire is available. International licences are acceptable only for short-term visitors and requirements should be checked on arrival. Driving is on the right, with speed limits of 60kph in towns and 80–100kph elsewhere.

BUSINESS DIRECTORY

The addresses listed below are a selection only. While World of Information makes every endeavour to check these addresses, we cannot guarantee that changes have not been made, especially to telephone numbers and area codes. We would welcome any corrections.

Telephone area codes
The international direct dialling (IDD) code for The United Arab Emirates is +971 followed by the area code:

Abu Dhabi	2	Fujairah	9
Ajman	6	Ras Al-Khaimah	7
Al-Ain	3	Sharjah	6
Dubai	4	Umm Al-Quwain	6

Useful telephone numbers
Directory enquiries: 180
Operator: 100
Call enquiries: 160
Call bookings: 150
Police (Abu Dhabi): 461-461

Chambers of Commerce
Abu Dhabi Chamber of Commerce and Industry, PO Box 662, Abu Dhabi (tel: 621-4000; fax: 621-5867; e-mail: service@adcci-gov.ae).

American Business Council (Dubai and Northern Emirates), PO Box 9281, Dubai (tel: 331-4735; fax: 331-4227; e-mail: amchamdx@emirates.net.ae).

American Business Group (Abu Dhabi), PO Box 43710, Abu Dhabi (tel: 626-2086; fax: 626-2087; e-mail: abgroup@emirates.net.ae).

Ajman Chamber of Commerce and Industry, PO Box 662, Ajman (tel: 742-2177; fax: 742-7591; e-mail: ajmchmbr@emirates.net.ae).

British Business Group (Abu Dhabi), PO Box 43635, Abu Dhabi (tel: 457-234; fax: 450-605; e-mail: bbgauh@emirates.net.ae).

British Business Group (Dubai and Northern Emirates), PO Box 9333, Dubai (tel: 397-0303; fax: 397-0939; e-mail: britbiz@emirates.net.ae).

Dubai Chamber of Commerce and Industry, PO Box 1457, Dubai (tel: 228-1181; fax: 221-1646; e-mail: dcciinfo@dcci.org).

Federation of UAE Chambers of Commerce and Industry, PO Box 3014, Abu Dhabi (tel: 621-4144; fax: 633-9210; e-mail: fcciauh@emirates.net.ae).

Federation of UAE Chambers of Commerce and Industry, PO Box 8886, Dubai (tel: 221-2977; fax: 223-5498; e-mail: fccidxb@emirates.net.ae).

French Business Group (Abu Dhabi), PO Box 73390, Abu Dhabi (tel: 674-1137; fax: 678-6650; e-mail: fbgad@emirates.net.ae).

Fujairah Chamber of Commerce and Industry, PO Box 738, Fujairah (tel: 222-2400; fax: 222-1464; e-mail: fujccia@emirates.net.ae).

Ras Al-Khaimah Chamber of Commerce and Industry, PO Box 87, Ras Al-Khaimah (tel: 233-3511; fax: 233-0233; e-mail: rkchmbr@emirates.net.ae).

Sharjah Chamber of Commerce and Industry, PO Box 580, Sharjah (tel: 568-8888; fax: 568-1119; e-mail:scci@sharjah.gov.ae).

Umm Al-Quwain Chamber of Commerce and Industry, PO Box 436, Umm Al-Quwain (tel: 765-1111; fax: 765-7056; e-mail: uaqcci@emirates.net.ae).

Banking
Abu Dhabi Commercial Bank, Al-Salam Street, PO Box 939, Abu Dhabi.

Arab Bank for Investment & Foreign Trade, PO Box 46733, Abu Dhabi.

Commercial Bank of Dubai Ltd, PO Box 2668, Dubai.

Emirates NDB (result of merger between Emirates Bank International and National Bank of Dubai in 2007), PO Box 2923, Dubai..

HSBC, UAE Omeir bin Yussuf Bld, Airport Road; PO Box 242 Abu Dhabi (tel: 633-2200; fax: 633-1564; internet: www.uae.hsbc.com).

Mashreq Bank, P.O. Box 1250, Omar Ibn Al Khatab Rd, Next to Al Ghurair Retail City, Deira, Dubai.

National Bank of Abu Dhabi, PO Box 4, Abu Dhabi.

National Bank of Fujairah, PO Box 786, Abu Dhabi..

National Bank of Sharjah, PO Box 4, Sharjah.

National Bank of Umm Al-Qawain, PO Box 17888, Al-Ain.

RakBank (National Bank of Ras Al-Khaimah), PO Box 5300, Oman Street, Al-Nakheel, Ras Al-Khaimah (tel: 228-1127; fax: 228-3238; email: nbrakho@emirates.net.ae).

Union National Bank, PO Box 865, Abu Dhabi.

Central bank
Central Bank of the United Arab Emirates, Al Bainunah Street; PO Box 854, Abu Dhabi (tel: 665-2220; fax: 666-7494; internet: www.centralbank.ae).

Travel information
Abu Dhabi International Airport, PO Box 28, Abu Dhabi (tel: 575-7500; fax: 575-7285; internet: www.dcaauh.gov.ae).

Abu Dhabi National Hotels Company, PO Box 6806, Abu Dhabi.
Air Arabia, Um Tarafa Area, Al Arouba Street, Rolla, Sharjai (call centre tel: 558-0000; internet: www.airarabia.com)

Dubai Airport (internet: www.dubaiairport.com).

Dubai Tourism P.O.Box 594, Dubai (tel: 223-0000; fax: 223-0022; internet: http://dubaitourism.co.ae).

Emirates Group, Emirates Headquarters, Near Clock Tower, Dubai (tel: 295-1111; internet: www.emirates.com).

Gulf Air, Hamdan St/Airport Road, Abu Dhabi.

Oman Air, PO Box 1058, Central Post Office Seeb International Airport, Muscat, Oman.

Qatar Airways, Almana Tower, Airport Road, PO Box 22550, Doha, Qatar.

Ras Al-Khaimah National Travel Agency, Ras Al-Khaimah.

Ministry of tourism
Department of Tourism and Commerce Marketing, PO Box 594, Dubai (tel: 223-0000; fax: 223-0022; e-mail: info@dubaitourism.co.ae; internet: www.dubaitourism.co.ae).

Ministries
Ministry of Agriculture & Fisheries, PO Box 213, Abu Dhabi.

Ministry of Communication, PO Box 900, Abu Dhabi.

Ministry of Defence, PO Box 2838, Dubai.

Ministry of Economy & Commerce, PO Box 901, Abu Dhabi.

Ministry of Education and Youth, PO Box 295, Abu Dhabi.

Ministry of Electricity & Water, PO Box 629, Abu Dhabi.

Ministry of Finance & Industry, PO Box 433, Abu Dhabi.

Ministry of Foreign Affairs, PO Box 1, Abu Dhabi.

Ministry of Health, PO Box 848, Abu Dhabi.

Ministry of Higher Education & Scientific Research, PO Box 45253, Abu Dhabi.

Ministry of Information & Culture, PO Box 17, Abu Dhabi.

Ministry for the Interior, PO Box 398, Abu Dhabi.

Ministry for Justice and Islamic Affairs & Awqaf, PO Box 2272, Abu Dhabi.

Ministry for Labour & Social Affairs, PO Box 809, Abu Dhabi.

Ministry of Petroleum & Mineral Resources, PO Box 59, Abu Dhabi.

Ministry of Planning, PO Box 904, Abu Dhabi.

Ministry of Public Works & Housing, PO Box 878, Abu Dhabi.

Ministry of State for Cabinet Affairs, PO Box 899, Abu Dhabi..

Minister of State for Supreme Council Affairs, PO Box 545, Abu Dhabi.

Ministry of Youth & Sports, PO Box 539, Abu Dhabi.

Other useful addresses
Abu Dhabi Company for Onshore Oil Operations (ADCO), PO Box 270, Abu Dhabi.

Abu Dhabi Gas Liquifaction Co Ltd, PO Box 3500, Abu Dhabi.

Abu Dhabi National Oil Co (ADNOC), PO Box 898, Abu Dhabi.

Abu Dhabi Water and Electricity Authority, ADWEA Building, Al Falah Street, PO Box 6120, Abu Dhabi.

Ajman Independent Studios, PO Box 442, Ajman.

Arab Monetary Fund (headquarters), PO Box 2818, Abu Dhabi.

British Embassy, Khalid Bin-Walid Street; PO Box 248, Abu Dhabi (tel: 610-1111; fax: 610-1585.

British Embassy, Al-Seef; PO Box 65, Dubai (tel: 309-4445; fax: 309-4302).

Department of Information, Dubai Municipality, PO Box 67, Dubai.

Dubai International Trade Centre, PO Box 9292, Dubai.

Dubai TV, PO Box 1695, Dubai.

Executive Council of Dubai (runs the emirate's political and financial affairs)

Jebel Ali Free Zone Authority, PO Box 3258, Dubai.

Gulf Arab Marketing & Exhibition Co (GAME), PO Box 610, Abu Dhabi.

Ports Authority of Dubai, PO Box 3258, Dubai.

Ports Authority of Sharjah, PO Box 510, Sharjah.

UAE Embassy (USA), 1010 Wisconsin Avenue, NW, Washington DC 20007 (tel: +1-202) 672-1050; fax: (tel: +1-202) 672-1082).

UAE Radio & TV Dubai, PO Box 2765, Dubai.

UAE Television & Broadcasting Corporation, PO Box 17, Abu Dhabi.

UAE TV Sharjah, PO Box 111, Sharjah.

National news agency: Emirates News Agency

Other news agencies: DPM News Agency: www.dpmnewsagency.com

Internet sites
Arab Net: www.arab.net

Arabia OnLine: www.arabia.com

Dubai Tourism: http://dubaitourism.co.ae

Etisalat web portal: http://ecompany.ae

UAE Government: www.government.ae

UAE information: www.uae.org.ae

UAE interact: www.uaeinteract.com

Yellow Pages: www.uae-ypages.com

United Kingdom

KEY FACTS

Official name: The United Kingdom of Great Britain and Northern Ireland (UK)

Head of State: Queen Elizabeth II (crowned 2 Jun 1953)

Head of government: Prime Minister Gordon Brown (since 27 Jun 2007)

Ruling party: Labour Party (since 1997; re-elected May 2005)

Area: 244,103 square km

Population: 60.84 million (2007)*

Capital: London

Official language: English; English and Welsh in Wales; English and Scottish Gaelic in Scotland.

Currency: Pound sterling (£) = 100 pence

Exchange rate: £0.50 per US$ (Jul 2008)

GDP per capita: US$45,575 (2007)*

GDP real growth: 3.10% (2007)*

Labour force: 31.10 million (2006)*

Unemployment: 5.40% (2007)

Inflation: 2.30% (2007)

Oil production: 1.64 million bpd (2007)

Balance of trade: -US$119.37 billion (2005); -US$11.05 billion (February 2006)

Foreign debt: US$6,785.92 billion (2004)

Visitor numbers: 30.70 million (2006)*

Annual FDI: US$534.30 billion (cumulative, 1995–2004, OECD); US$78.50 billion (OECD, 2004)*

* estimated figure

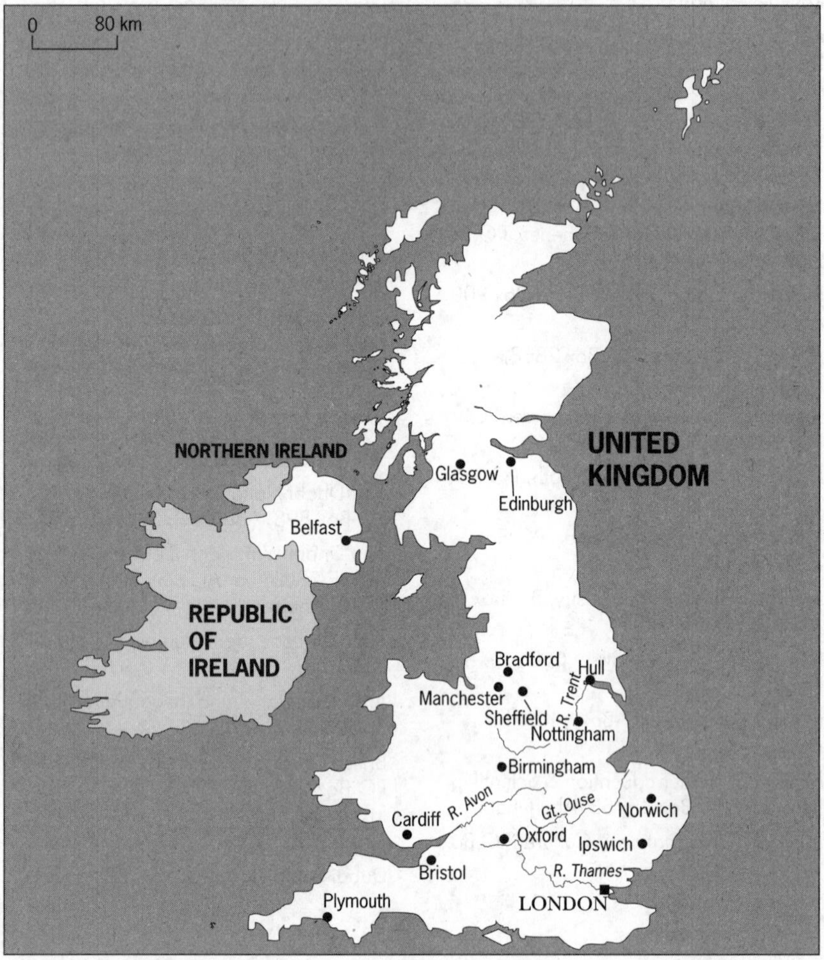

On 27 June 2008, Britain's prime minister Gordon Brown ought to have been celebrating his first year in office. In fact, he was more likely to have been wishing he had never been 'anointed' as Labour's leader following the departure from office of his nemesis, Tony Blair. Nicknamed 'phoney Tony' for his manipulation of the truth, Mr Blair had none-the-less supervised 10 years of increasing prosperity in the United Kingdom, winning three general elections in the process.

Accentuate the positive...

Where Mr Blair was a politician to his fingertips, and a communicator par excellence, Mr Brown appeared to be a hopeless communicator, simply unable to judge the mood of the moment. As the London *Economist* noted, an inability to communicate is a failing in any leader: 'for Mr Brown this weakness has proved catastrophic' it said. Mr Brown's honeymoon with an electorate that in any event had never selected him as its leader, was short-lived. Spurning glamorous overseas holidays, he opted to spend his first summer vacation (in 2007) in the UK. Thus he was able to take charge of dealing with the 2007 outbreak of foot and mouth disease by cutting short his holiday. This in itself did not adversely concern a UK electorate who, for the most part, were on holiday themselves.

Mr Brown's first serious misjudgement was to appear to be preparing for a general election in the autumn of 2007, presumably to consolidate his grip on power. Having set his party's preparations in motion, Mr Brown then changed his mind and called off the election 'that never was'. His decision seemed to be dictated by disarming opinion polls that, following his opponent, David Cameron's showing at the autumn Conservative Party conference, had begun to suggest that he might lose the election he had once sought to call. .

This volte-face did not smack of firm government. To make matters worse, Mr Brown denied that his decision had anything to do with Mr Cameron's increasing popularity, thereby hinting at his own electoral cowardice and Mr Cameron's growing confidence. To make matters worse, Mr Brown's personality did little to endear him to Britain's demanding electorate. His emergence as a control freak appeared to combine with a reputation for paranoia, neither helped by an inability to be succinct. A son of the manse, the tie-clad Mr Brown rarely looked relaxed or confident, prompting potential voters to wonder how on earth his party allowed him to become prime minister in the first place. That Mr Brown lacks charisma, poise and presence might be overlooked by voters. But his apparent lack of any political nouse cannot be easily overcome.

Goodbye Prudence

Initially, the financial crisis that enveloped the UK and the USA much more comprehensively than most other economies did not appear to be insurmountable. However, as the year wore on, the similarities in the structure, if not in the scale of the two economies began to make themselves apparent. By mid-2008 a survey conducted by the British Chambers of Commerce (BCC) suggested that there was 'a real risk of recession in the coming months' due to a 'menacing deterioration in UK prospects'. Mr Brown and his hapless chancellor of the exchequer (minister of finance), Alistair Dowling, were perhaps unfortunate in that the sub-prime in the US crisis and its aftermath neatly coincided with a rapid deterioration in the UK's terms of trade as fuel and food prices continued their inexorable rise. But Mr Brown was hoist by his own petard; throughout his ten years as chancellor of the exchequer, he had avidly promoted his image as the 'steady pair of hands' the UK economy needed. Having gone to some lengths to claim the credit for the UK's apparent prosperity, Mr Brown could not have it both ways when the economy headed south. For 10 years it was Mr Brown who had promised the UK electorate an end to boom and bust, promising voters that 'we will not build the new Jerusalem' on a mountain of debt'. An internal memo by investment bank ABN AMRO said: 'The UK looks more vulnerable to a housing (ie valuation) correction that the US. The degree of overvaluation looks more acute, nearing 50 per cent in the UK compared to 25 per cent in the USA'. It appeared as though Mr Bown's constant companion, 'prudence', had finally been given her marching orders.

In April 2008 the Bank of England's Monetary Policy Committee (MPC) voted to reduce the official Bank Rate paid on commercial bank reserves by 0.25 percentage points to 5.0 per cent. Consumer Price Index (CPI) inflation had risen to 2.5 per cent in February 2008 and the Bank's MPC expected inflation to rise further over the rest of the year, reflecting the continuing impact of higher energy and food prices, as well as the recent depreciation of sterling on import costs. Even if commodity prices remained at their current high levels, inflation was expected to fall back but to ensure that the inflation rate met the 2 per cent target in the medium term, the MPC needed to balance two risks. On the upside, above-target inflation this year could raise inflation expectations so that, in the absence of some margin of spare capacity, inflation would remain above the target. On the downside, the disruption in financial markets could lead to a slowdown in the economy that was sufficiently sharp to pull inflation below the target.

Balancing the risks

In the Bank of England's judgement, the balance of these risks to the inflation outlook in the medium term justified a cut in the bank rate in April 2008. Credit conditions had tightened and the availability of credit appeared to be worsening. While the depreciation seen in sterling would inevitably encourage exports, the prospects for output growth abroad continued to deteriorate. United Kingdom business surveys suggested that growth had begun to moderate and that a margin of spare capacity would emerge during the rest of the year. It was thought that this should help to keep domestic inflationary pressures in check in the medium term. Against that background, the Committee judged that a reduction in Bank Rate of 0.25 percentage points to 5.0 per cent was necessary to meet the 2 per cent target for CPI inflation in the medium term. The previous change in the Bank Rate had been a reduction of 0.25 percentage points to 5.25 per cent on 7 February 2008.

Gloomy outlook, undervalued assets

The Bank of England noted that fears that the macroeconomic outlook was worsening, particularly in the United States, were

KEY INDICATORS — United Kingdom

	Unit	2003	2004	2005	2006	2007
Population	m	59.42	59.51	60.22	60.53	*60.84
Gross domestic product (GDP)	US$bn	1,743.44	2,140.90	2,230.61	2,402.00	2,772.57
GDP per capita	US$	29,493	35,460	37,042	39,680	*45,575
GDP real growth	%	2.2	3.1	1.9	2.9	3.1
Inflation	%	1.3	1.3	2.0	2.3	2.3
Unemployment	%	5.0	4.8	4.8	5.4	5.4
Oil output	'000 bpd	2,245.0	2,029.0	1,808.0	1,636.0	1,636.0
Natural gas output	bn cum	102.7	95.9	88.0	80.0	72.4
Coal output	mtoe	17.2	15.3	12.5	11.3	10.4
Exports (fob) (goods)	US$m	305,000	349,310	381,790	447,580	442,280
Imports (cif) (goods)	US$m	376,282	455,380	501,160	590,470	617,800
Balance of trade	US$m	-71,282	-106,070	-119,370	-142,890	-175,520
Current account	US$m	-36,630	-47,040	-58,731	-92,566	-115,240
Total reserves minus gold	US$m	41,850.0	45,340.0	38,480.0	40,700.0	48,960.0
Foreign exchange	US$m	35,150.0	39,480.0	35,870.0	38,890.0	47,500.0
Exchange rate	per US$	0.59	0.55	0.51	0.51	0.49

weighing heavily on market sentiment and were impeding the functioning of interbank markets. Even investors with long holding periods were holding back from buying assets that they considered undervalued, because of the possibility of further price falls in the short term. The economic impact of these losses would be reduced to the extent that banks revealed losses promptly and raised new capital where necessary, rather than relying only on shrinking their balance sheets. In this respect, the level of capital raising and sales of illiquid loan portfolios by some banks offered a degree of reassurance.

In early 2008 a total reduction of 0.75 per cent in the bank rate was anticipated by the end of 2008. following an initial reduction of 0.25 per cent at the April 2008 meeting. In the United States, short-term rates had fallen, and there too a policy rate reduction of at least 25 basis points had been expected in April 2008. However, short-term rates in the euro area had risen, perhaps reflecting high inflation out-turns and the tone of comments from the European Central Bank. Longer term nominal and real rates had fallen in both the United States and the euro area, but had actually risen in the United Kingdom.

A further factor the Bank of England had to take into account was that the sterling effective exchange rate had depreciated further, to a little below the range it had occupied for most of the past ten years. Relative interest rate movements could account for much of the movement in sterling from the onset of financial market turbulence in August 2007 to the end of the year, but not the sharp fall over the first four months of 2008. According to the Bank of England sterling's depreciation appeared to be a symptom of both a change in the perceived risks around the UK economic outlook and the need for some rebalancing of the composition of aggregate demand.

There had been an increasing contrast between official measures of recent activity in the UK and forward-looking indicators of the outlook for the economy. The former suggested that growth had slowed little as yet, but the latter looked less robust. The office of national statistics (ONS) had reported an unrevised estimate of 0.6 per cent for GDP growth in the fourth quarter of 2007. The broad pattern of estimated demand growth had also remained unchanged, with weak growth in final domestic demand offset by stockpiling and net trade. But it now seemed less likely that an involuntary stock cycle had been triggered. First, part of the slowdown in consumption growth in the fourth quarter had been accounted for by unusual weakness in net spending on tourism, which was known to be poorly measured; consumption of goods and services, excluding tourism spending, was estimated to have grown by 0.4 per cent, supported by slightly above average growth in real post-tax labour income. Second, business investment was now estimated to have increased by 1.8 per cent in the fourth quarter, whereas the previous estimate had suggested that it had fallen by 0.5 per cent.

Mixed signals

Nevertheless, the Bank of England noted that indicators of output in the first quarter of 2008 pointed to stronger growth than expected at the time of the Bank's February Inflation Report. Manufacturing output had risen by 0.4 per cent in February and industrial production as a whole increased by 0.3 per cent. None the less, it remained unclear whether consumption was slowing as much as had been expected. Official retail sales data had been much stronger than earlier indications and price discounting did not seem to be behind the robust volume increase. The low readings from consumer confidence surveys seemed more consistent with the retail activity surveys than with the official data. Car sales were surprisingly strong in March 2008.

The housing market, however, had weakened further, with house prices falling about 1.5 per cent (on the average of the lenders' indices) in the first quarter. The benchmark Halifax index had fallen 2.5 per cent in March, but this had a record of being particularly volatile from month to month. The number of mortgage approvals for house purchase and net reservations, as measured by the Home Builders Federation survey balance, had also fallen.

Future developments in the housing market and the evolution of domestic demand would be influenced by the terms and availability of credit. According to the Bank's Credit Conditions Survey (CCS), there had been a widespread reduction in the availability of secured credit in the first quarter, with significant further reductions expected in the second quarter. Lenders had been withdrawing 100 per cent mortgage offers and expecting borrowers to provide a larger fraction of equity in exchange for more favourable borrowing terms.

The implications of a weakening housing market for consumption were uncertain. Housing equity withdrawal was likely to fall back sharply. But it was unclear how far this would reduce consumer spending rather than resulting in a fall in the net acquisition of financial assets by those who would otherwise have traded down..

Tightening credit conditions were also likely to affect corporate investment. The Bank's CCS had reported a significant reduction in the availability of credit to the corporate sector in the first quarter of 2008, with further tightening expected in the second quarter. A preliminary analysis of the 2008 Budget suggested that its implications for the outlook for growth and inflation were limited.

According to the ONS Labour Force Survey (LFS), employment had increased by over 150,000 in the three months to January, accompanied by a further fall in unemployment, and there had been a further rise in vacancies in February. However, total hours worked had fallen a little; also, employment had hardly changed in late 2007 according to the Workforce Jobs measure. The CIPS/NTC employment surveys had picked up slightly in March, but still suggested that employment growth would be muted. There was also some uncertainty about the supply of workers from abroad. The supposition was that there was a drop in net inward migration; surprisingly, it proved difficult to count workers who moved back and forth between the United Kingdom and their home countries.

Inflation inflates

A number of critical cost pressures had also intensified. Manufacturers' input prices in February had been almost 20 per cent higher than twelve months earlier, the highest inflation rate since measurement began in 1986. Annual imported goods price inflation had reached 8 per cent, its highest rate since 1995.Annual manufacturing output price inflation, excluding duty, although no higher in February than January, still remained at its highest level since the early 1990s.

CPI inflation rose to 2.5 per cent in February. Gas and electricity prices accounted for much of the increase since the end of 2007, and looked likely to make a further contribution as the price cuts of spring 2007 dropped out of the twelve-month comparison. The short-term outlook was for a gradual rise in CPI inflation, with a high probability of temporarily reaching or exceeding 3 per cent later in 2008. There were several near-term upside risks. First, domestic energy prices looked almost certain to increase more than expected, given the upward movement of wholesale gas futures. Second, the depreciation of sterling would increase pressures on prices. For the majority of the Bank of England's 'wise men', the outlook and the balance of risks warranted a reduction in Bank Rate of 0.25 percent. The previous two months in 2008 had in fact seen a further inflationary impetus from higher oil prices and an even weaker pound. Inflationary pressures were spreading well beyond the energy and food sectors, fuelled by higher inflation expectations. There also existed the risk that a premature cut in the bank rate would also fuel inflation expectations.

CPI inflation was 2.5 per cent in March 2008, some 0.75 of a percentage point higher than six months earlier.

In 2007 and early 2008 price inflation of imported goods rose to its highest since 1995, partially reflecting the depreciation of sterling. The scale and duration of any rise in inflation was uncertain, however. Businesses early in the supply chain appeared to have passed some of the cost increases through into higher output prices, and many businesses' pricing intentions remained high. Consumer-facing businesses found it less easy to pass on cost increases to their customers, perhaps reflecting weaker consumer demand. Those businesses not able to pass on the cost increases might instead attempt to push down on other costs, especially pay. But employees were likely to press for higher wages to compensate. Pay growth remained subdued, despite quite strong employment growth. Mid-2008 saw some public service unions beginning to flex their pay demand muscles.

Demand down

According to the Bank of England, domestic demand growth moderated in the final quarter of 2007 on the back of a sharp slowdown in consumers' expenditure growth. The official estimate of retail spending suggested a resilient first quarter, but surveys of retailers were more pessimistic. Housing market activity weakened further and house prices fell as mortgages became harder to obtain. Increased inflation would inevitably eat into household incomes, dampening household spending. Tighter credit and widening uncertainty would do little for business investment prospects, a fear that was already beginning to become reality in late-2007. Property investment, both domestic and commercial, was expected to fall sharply. Government spending made a moderate contribution to nominal domestic demand growth in 2007. According to the fiscal plans set out in the Labour government's 2008 Budget, the public sector's contribution to demand growth looked set to decline over the forecast period, reflecting reduced government revenues. Both pay and prices are likely to be influenced by expectations of future inflation. Measures of short-term household inflation expectations rose again, broadly in line with the recent and prospective movements in consumer price inflation. But some longer-term indicators of inflation expectations have also edged up. If expectations were to remain elevated, then that would pose an upside risk to inflation in the medium term.

The oil runs out – slowly

The UK is the largest producer of oil and natural gas in the EU. However, after years of being a net exporter of both fuels, the UK became a net importer of natural gas in 2004. Government estimates also predict that the country will become a net importer of oil by the end of the decade. Production from UK oil and natural gas fields peaked in the late 1990s and has declined steadily over the past several years, as the discovery of new reserves has not kept pace with the maturation of existing fields. In response, the government has begun a three-pronged approach to address the predicted domestic shortfalls: first, increasing domestic production through efficiency gains and the exploitation of marginal fields; second, establishing necessary import infrastructure, such as liquefied natural gas (LNG) receiving terminals and transnational pipelines; and thirdly, investing in energy conservation and renewables.

According to the *Oil and Gas Journal* (OGJ), the UK had 3.6 billion barrels of proven crude oil reserves at the end of 2007, the most of any EU member country. The UK consumed 1.69 million barrels per day (bpd) of oil in 2007. The importance of oil to the UK economy has declined slightly over the past two. Total oil production in the UK was 1.64 million bpd in 2007. The UK government expected oil production in the country to continue to decline, reaching 1.38 million bpd by 2009. Reasons for this decline include: the overall maturity of the country's oil fields, the application of new crude oil extraction technologies that lead to fields being exhausted at a quicker rate, and increasing costs as production shifts to more remote and inhospitable regions.

According to the OGJ, the UK also held an estimated 14.55 trillion cubic feet (Tcf) of proven natural gas reserves at the end of In order to take advantage of its domestic reserves, the UK government has encouraged the use of natural gas, including its substitution for coal and oil in industrial consumption and electricity production. As a result, natural gas consumption in the UK reached 91.4 billion cubic metres (bcm) in 2007. In 2004, the UK became a net importer of natural gas for the first time since 1996.

Production of natural gas reached 72.4 bcm in 2007. The UK is the fourth-largest producer of natural gas in the world, behind Russia, the United States and Canada. Most of the leading oil companies in the UK are also the leading natural gas producers, including BP, Shell and Total. The major gas distribution companies in the UK, such as Centrica and BG Group, also have a presence in this production sector. Like the oil industry, smaller independents have been able to acquire some maturing assets from larger operators, who find it difficult to profitably operate these older, declining fields.

Outlook

Surprisingly – or perhaps intentionally – the Bank of England in its April 2008 assessment of the UK economy avoided using the descriptive 'stagflation'. As the bank's governor, Mervyn King, entered his second term, his earlier remarks that the UK's 'non-inflationary consistently expansionary' (NICE) era would not last for ever, appeared, in one respect at least, to hit the mark. In other respects, Mr King's remarks appeared to be misleading, simply because the economic storm that looked likely to engulf the UK's economy was worse than even Mr King probably expected. The combination of rising inflation and sagging economic activity was a hard mix to overcome. On the monetary front the Bank of England had little room for manoeuvre. On the fiscal front, Prime Minister Brown had resorted, in mid-2008 to spend his short summer vacation (in the UK again) re-writing the strictly 'prudent' rules he had originally drawn up for government borrowing.

Risk assessment

Economy	Fair
Politics	Good
Regional stability	Good

COUNTRY PROFILE

Historical profile

After a thousand year period of Roman, Saxon and Viking occupation, feudal England was invaded by the Normans in

1066. The Norman-ruled Kingdom eventually emerged as an organised English state, headed by a monarch. Wales was united with England in 1536, while the 1707 Act of Union united England and Scotland as part of the United Kingdom (UK) of Great Britain. Ireland was united with Great Britain in 1801. By the eighteenth century, Great Britain had emerged as a major industrial, colonial and military power.
1837–1901 The long reign of Queen Victoria saw the British Empire at the height of its power.
1914—1918 Great Britain called on all its colonies and dominions to help it fight along side its allies, France and Russia, in the First World War against Germany and its allies.
1916 An uprising in Dublin by Irish republicans was put down after a few days and its leaders were either executed or interned.
1922 The Irish Free State (Eire) was created in southern Ireland. The remaining six north-eastern counties of Ireland remained part of Great Britain.
1939 Britain declared war on Germany in September, having failed to limit its expansionist policies and after Germany had invaded Poland.
1939–45 In the Second World War, Britain was a major member of the allied forces, along with the US and the Soviet Union against the Axis powers of Germany, Italy and Japan.
1945 Facing near economic collapse as a result of the war, the UK began to relinquish control of its colonies and its role in the world as the prime power declined.
1945—51 The Labour Party was elected into government. Led by Prime Minister Clement Attlee, the government implemented reforms to education, healthcare, housing and the social security system.
1953 Queen Elizabeth II was crowned on 2 June.
1969 The start of 'The Troubles' in Northern Ireland as violence between the Catholic civil rights movement and the Unionists, who perceived it as republicanism, intensified.
1973 The UK joined the European Economic Community.
1979 Following a decade marred by economic stagnation and endemic inflation, the Conservative Party gained a parliamentary majority in the general election, and Margaret Thatcher, leader of the party, became the UK's first woman prime minister.
1979–1990 Thatcher's radical domestic policies, including privatisation and local government reforms, did not prevent her securing two further election victories, in addition to gaining a victory in the 1982 Falklands conflict.
1990 Introduction of the community charge and a loss of party confidence stemming from her vociferous opposition to the European Community finally led to Thatcher being replaced by John Major as leader of the Conservative Party and prime minister.
1992 The Treaty on European Union (the Maastricht Treaty) was signed. The Treaty harmonised legislation in key areas of European Union (EU) social policy, immigration and finance, although the UK successfully opted out of the Social Chapter. The UK was forced out of the European Exchange Rate Mechanism (ERM) after the pound dropped below the permitted parity with the deutschmark. The Conservatives won the general election.
1997 The Labour Party, under the leadership of Tony Blair, won an overwhelming victory in the general election.
1998 The UK and Irish governments attempted to bring to an end the problems in Northern Ireland through the signing of the Good Friday Peace Agreement. The political settlement established a precedent for Ireland's direct involvement in Northern Ireland's affairs, with cross-border co-operation and the decommissioning of paramilitary arms.
1999 Scotland's first legislature for 300 years and Wales' first for 600 years were opened in June. Power and conditional authority were also devolved in Northern Ireland in December.
2000 Nationwide cases of foot and mouth broke out; four million cattle were culled and compensation payments totalled £1.1 billion (US1.5 billion).
2001 The Labour Party won a second landslide parliamentary victory.
2003 British forces joined a US-led invasion of Iraq.
2004 The Iraq Survey Group concluded Iraq did not possess weapons of mass destruction. A UK inquiry into the quality of intelligence used to justify UK participation in the Iraq war found no evidence of 'deliberate distortion or culpable negligence' by the government.
2005 The Labour Party won its third term in office but with a significantly reduced majority. Four bombs exploded (on three underground trains and a bus) during the morning rush hour in London, killing 52 people and injuring over 700.
2006 Police investigated allegations of peerages being purchased through financial donations to the Labour Party. Strict flight restrictions were imposed on international travellers following police raids foiling an alleged plot to crash up to 10 airplanes departing the UK for the US. Aleksandr Litvinenko, former Russian security service officer and outspoken critic of Russia's ruling elite was poisoned by radioactive thallium in London. Police traced the source to Russia but authorities refused to extradite the prime suspect.
2007 A large-scale withdrawal of troops from Iraq was announced. In Northern Ireland, following elections in March, in which the DUP won 36 seats (out of 108) and Sinn Féin won 28 seats, the two parties agreed to share power, ending direct rule from London. The Scottish National Party took office after winning Scotland's general election. Prime Minister Tony Blair resigned and was replaced, unopposed, by Gordon Brown. In the wettest July since records began in 1766 around 129mm fell and caused widespread flooding across central England. From May–July 387mm fell, double the 186mm average, and caused serious flooding in the north of England. The cost of flooding was estimated at £6 billion (US$12 billion).
2008 The Labour party suffered its worst election results in local elections since 1970s. In August the governor of the Bank of England warned that the UK's economy would not grow (2008–09) and while inflation was at 4.4 per cent (over double the government target of 2 per cent) as commodity prices rose steeply, interest rates were unlikely to be reduced before the end of the year. In foreign exchange markets the pound sterling dropped against the US dollar and against other currencies was at its worst since 1997.

Political structure

Constitution

There is no formal written constitution, instead constitutional law is based on legal precedent and legislation both within the UK and from EU supranational institutions. Power within the UK is partially devolved to Scotland, Wales and Northern Ireland. Local councils operate at the level of metropolitan boroughs, counties, districts and parishes, delivering a number of public services such as education and policing, although their powers, particularly regarding taxation and spending, are circumscribed by central government.

Form of state

Parliamentary democratic monarchy

The executive

The monarch is head of state. The monarchy is governed by convention and may not participate in politics or government affairs. It has, however, by unspoken agreement three rights: to be consulted, to encourage and to warn.

The monarch, in regard to democratic principles, accedes to the results of the popular vote and appoints the winner of any general election, and only in extreme circumstances may a monarch dismiss the government.

While government ministers act nominally in the name of the Crown, almost all

power rests with the prime minister as head of government and his cabinet of ministers (part of the executive but drawn from the legislature).
The prime minister chooses and chairs the cabinet, who are members of the political party which typically has most seats in the House of Commons. The cabinet consists of around 20 ministers, although its exact composition is not fixed and there are some ministers without portfolio. Secretaries of state are ministers who head specific government departments. Major figures of importance in the cabinet include the chancellor of the exchequer (responsible for economic management), the foreign secretary (foreign policy) and the home secretary (responsible for law and order). Other ministers deal on a functional basis with trade and industry, health, energy, transport and so on. Cabinet ministers head departments of civil servants and have junior ministers (who do not, as a rule, have a seat in the cabinet) to assist them. These ministries are effectively the executive arm of central government, implementing decisions of the cabinet and parliament.

National legislature
The parliament is based on two chambers, the House of Commons (lower house – with 646 members of parliament (MPs)) and the House of Lords (upper house – with 713 members: 595 life peers, 92 hereditary peers and 26 Church of England archbishops and bishops).
There are no fixed dates for general elections, although they must be held at least every five years. MPs are elected in a simple majority system (first-past-the-post) in single member constituencies.
The government is in the process of reforming the House of Lords (upper house). All but 10 per cent of the hereditary peers were removed from the Lords in 1999. Life peers are appointed by the Crown at the behest of the prime minister and new appointments generally include retired politicians, businessmen and academics. The government is planning further reform of the Lords, including the introduction of directly-elected members. No date has been set for the next round of reforms.
Parliament meets to consider government policies, pass laws and raise taxation for the purposes of government. Laws, known as bills before their successful passage through parliament, must be passed by the House of Commons. The House of Lords can suggest amendments to, or refuse to pass, most (but not budget) bills. The House of Commons is ultimately under no obligation to accept the Lords' amendments. It can overrule a House of Lords' refusal to pass a bill as a last resort.
Devolution of power to Scotland and Wales took place in 1999 and was Scotland's first legislature for 300 years and Wales' first for 600 years. Elections to the 129-member Scottish Parliament and the 60-member Welsh Assembly are conducted under a system of proportional representation. The Scottish Parliament may raise taxes, however the Welsh Assembly must seek funds from Westminster.

Legal system
The judiciary is independent of both the legislature and executive. The legal system in Scotland and Northern Ireland differs from that in England and Wales.
In England and Wales around 300 county courts deal with minor civil cases. Magistrates courts deal with minor criminal cases. Civil and criminal appeals from these courts are heard by crown courts, which sit in about 90 venues. Scotland and Northern Ireland have slightly different judicial systems. The main purpose of a crown court is to try the more important criminal cases. The High Court of Justice is the main civil court, divided into three sections: Chancery Division, Queens Bench Division and the Family Division.
The ultimate court of appeal and the supreme judicial authority for the UK (excluding Scottish criminal cases appeal) is the House of Lords. When sitting as a court of appeal, it consists of the Lord Chancellor, together with the Law Lords (formally called the Lords of Appeal in Ordinary) and deals only with appeals based on points of law.
Since the signing of the Single European Act in 1988, the European Court of Justice (ECJ) has supreme jurisdiction over some aspects of UK law, although this is not often exercised.

Last elections
5 May 2005 (parliamentary).
Results: Parliamentary: Labour won 35.22 per cent of the vote (356 seats out of 646); Conservatives won 32.33 per cent (198 seats); Liberal Democrats 22.05 per cent (62 seats); Democratic Unionist Party (DUP) 0.89 per cent (nine seats); Scottish National Party (SNP) 1.52 per cent (six seats); Sinn Féin 0.64 per cent (five seats); Social Democratic and Labour Party (SDLP) 0.46 per cent (three seats); Plaid Cymru 0.64 per cent (three seats); Ulster Unionist Party (UUP) 0.47 per cent (one seat); Respect 0.25 per cent (one seat); and independents 0.50 per cent (two seats). Turnout was 61.3 per cent.

Next elections
2010 (parliamentary).

Political parties

Ruling party
Labour Party (since 1997; re-elected May 2005)

Main opposition party
Conservative Party

Population
60.84 million (2007)*
Last census: April 2001: 58,789,187
Population density: 247 inhabitants per square km. Urban population: 90 per cent (1995–2001).
Annual growth rate: 0.3 per cent 1994–2004 (WHO 2006)

Ethnic make-up
The English, Scots, Welsh and Irish peoples combined make up over 90 per cent of the population of the UK; the largest ethnic minorities are those of Caribbean or African descent (875,000 people). The next largest ethnic groups are Indians (840,255 people) and Pakistani and Bangladeshis (639,390 people). Ethnic minority groups represent just under 6 per cent of the population.

Religions
Church of England (25 million (baptised)), Roman Catholic (4.12 million), Muslim (1.5 million), Presbyterian (1.1 million), Methodist (800,000), Sikh (500,000), Hindu (320,000), Jewish (285,000).

Education

The UK has a devolved education system. Alongside the state system are independent schools, often denominational, which are financed by fees, endowments and the state. Pre-school education is not state-funded; it is available for ages two to five, through playgroups and nursery schools. There is a national curriculum and assessment targets for all primary schools and a minimum attainment is set for all children.
The usual age for transfer to secondary schools is 11 in England, Wales and Northern Ireland and 12 in Scotland. About 90 per cent of state secondary school pupils in England, Wales and Scotland attend comprehensive schools, which provide a wide range of secondary education for most children of all abilities. In other areas, the grammar school system has been retained alongside the comprehensive system, with admission through some form of testing at the age of 10 or 11.
All children are tested at the ages of 7, 11 and 14 years, and take General Certificate of Secondary Education (GCSE) or Scottish Certificate of Education (SCE) examinations at 15–16 years. Students can then opt to study at further education institutions for a range of academic and vocational qualifications, such as Advanced level (A-level) or the National Vocational Qualification (NVQ).
Tertiary education typically starts at aged 18, when students go on to university or colleges of higher education. UK higher education has expanded so that first

degrees and further post-graduate qualifications are taken at over 162 universities and other colleges of higher education.
Compulsory years: 5 to 16 in England, Wales and Scotland; 4 to 16 in Northern Ireland.
Enrolment rate: 101 per cent gross primary enrolment of relevant age group (including repeaters); 158 per cent gross secondary enrolment; 59 per cent tertiary enrolment (World Bank).
Pupils per teacher: 19 in primary schools

Health

Per capita total expenditure on health (2003) was US$2,389; of which per capita government spending was US$2,047, at the international dollar rate, (WHO 2006).
The National Health Service (NHS) benefits from major government spending, with UK citizens provided with free treatment. Most people are required to pay an initial fee for some aspects of treatment such as eye tests, dental care and prescriptions. The NHS accounts for 85 per cent of total healthcare provision in the UK.
The service provided by the NHS is generally of high quality, but delays for many non-urgent operations have encouraged people to take out private health insurance policies. Private health cover is becoming increasingly common as a company benefit.
In May 2004 a World Health Organisation report on obesity stated 22 per cent of UK adults were obese.
Latest figures show 83 per cent of children were immunised against measles before aged one year. Many parents have withdrawn their infants from the programme and questioned the efficacy of the triple MMR (measles, mumps and rubella) vaccine, following a hotly contested report that claimed the onset of autism and the MMR vaccination were linked.
The government announced that it would take measures to prohibit visitors or 'health tourists' from accessing NHS services, limiting treatment to accidents and emergency cases only.
In 2003/04 the government introduced treatment centres to undertake routine medical and surgical services – such as cataract removal operations – aimed at reducing waiting lists. Overseas providers were hired to provide all the necessary treatment, outside the administration of local health authorities. This has provided competition for the NHS, to match the provision of treatment at a reduced cost with speedier flow-through.

HIV/Aids

HIV prevalence: 0.2 per cent aged 15–49 in 2003 (World Bank)
Life expectancy: 79 years, 2004 (WHO 2006)
Fertility rate/Maternal mortality rate: 1.7 births per woman, 2004 (WHO 2006)
Birth rate/Death rate: 12 births and 11 deaths per 1,000 people (World Bank)
Child (under 5 years) mortality rate (per 1,000): 5.3 per 1,000 live births (World Bank)

Welfare

The UK has long-established social security and welfare systems. Jobseekers Allowance is provided to most of those registered as unemployed. Additional benefits are paid to families on low incomes or with special needs, for example through the Family Credit Scheme. There is also a wide range of allowances for disabled people. The Housing Benefit Scheme is administered by local authorities and provides assistance with rent and other payments.

Pensions

The UK has an ageing population, with the number of over 65 year-olds projected to outnumber the numbers below 16 years by 2008. The number of those past retirement age is expected to peak at around 15 million in the 2030s. Bills for healthcare and pensions are set to rise significantly, while revenue from income tax falls. Government policy is to actively encourage private pension schemes for all employees, and most people now entering the labour market do not expect to receive a sufficient state pension on retirement. Private pension schemes allow retirement at any time between age 50 and 75.
The State Retirement Pension is paid to men at age 65 and women at age 60, although for women this age is starting to increase with the state retirement age to be equalised at age 65 by April 2020.
A report published in October 2004 found that state pensions were underfunded, and that 9–12 million people (or 40 per cent of the workforce) were not saving enough for their retirement.
In March 2005 the unfunded public workers' pensions liability was estimated at £690 billion (US$1.2 trillion) or 1.5 times the net public sector debt. The government has begun taking action to alleviate the problem but much more will be required and may include some combination of higher taxes, compulsory savings and/or an increase in the retirement age over 65.
In April 2005 the Pension Protection Fund (PPF) began operation. The fund is aimed at workers who lose their pension when their employer declares bankruptcy. The scheme is an insurance plan, to which all final salary pension schemes must belong. Pension schemes pay fees for each member into a fund and when a business collapses the employees should receive at least 90 per cent of the sum they were due when they retire and retired members should receive 100 per cent of the sum. Critics claim this measure will discourage businesses from running final salary pensions, if they are to shoulder yet another financial burden, and that one large enterprise that collapsed could overwhelm the fund.

Main cities

England: London (capital, estimated population 7.5 million in 2004), Birmingham (963,234), Liverpool (457,219), Sheffield (434,468), Leeds (442,921), Bristol (421,795), Manchester (386,849), Leicester (331,731),
Scotland: Edinburgh (capital) (464,290), Glasgow (Scotland) (1.2 million), Aberdeen (198,784), Dundee (153,539).
Wales: Cardiff (capital) (297,997), Swansea (169,412), Newport (116,186), Wrexham (43,079).
Northern Ireland: Belfast (capital) (258,902), Londonderry (Derry) (87,878).

Languages spoken

Other communities such as Indian, Pakistani, Jewish and Chinese maintain their languages.
In 2004 the Bòrd na Gàidhlig (the Bòrd) was established, as a statutory body, working to secure the status of Gaelic as an official language of Scotland.

Official language/s

English; English and Welsh in Wales; English and Scottish Gaelic in Scotland.

Media

National news agency: PA Group

Press

The Press Complaints Commission (www.pcc.org.uk) monitors ethical guidelines required by British media.
There are over 2,000 newspapers published in the UK. All major newspapers are in English. The impact of the internet has led all major national news corporations to invest in online editions.
Dailies: Of the 10 daily newspapers published in England, tabloid readership is the greatest, with the most popular, The Sun typically selling three million copies. The biggest selling broadsheet is The Daily Telegraph with around 900,000 copies sold daily. Broadsheets by popularity include The Daily Telegraph (www.telegraph.co.uk), The Times (www.timesonline.co.uk), The Guardian (www.guardian.co.uk) and The Independent (www.independent.co.uk). A free issue newspaper in London Metro (www.metro.co.uk) rivals some of the tabloid newspaper circulations.
Influential newspapers in Scotland include the Daily Record (www.dailyrecord.co.uk)

and The Herald (www.theherald.co.uk); in Wales Western Mail (http://icwales.icnetwork.co.uk); in Northern Ireland Belfast Telegraph (www.belfasttelegraph.co.uk) and The Irish News (www.irishnews.com).
There are a number of evening newspapers distributed in major cities including the London Evening Standard (www.thisislondon.co.uk), Manchester Evening News (www.manchestereveningnews.co.uk), Bristol Evening Post (www.epost.co.uk) and The South Wales Evening Post (www.thisissouthwales.co.uk).
Weeklies: Most daily newspapers publish Sunday editions. There are numerous speciality magazines targeting women and men, young and old; the National Magazine Company (www.natmags.co.uk) publishes several of these magazines. Those with serious comment on general interest, with national and international circulation, include Prospect (www.prospect-magazine.co.uk), The Spectator (www.spectator.co.uk) and New Statesman (www.newstatesman.com). Topics can be exclusive, such as The New Musical Express NME (www.nme.com), or technology or aimed at ethnic groups, others can be regional and some international. Satirical publications include Private Eye (www.private-eye.co.uk) and Viz (www.viz.co.uk). There are two tabloid magazines with large circulations Hello (www.hellomagazine.com) and Heat (www.heatworld.com).
Business: There are a large number of publications covering all aspects of business, some with international circulation, the most prestigious are The Financial Times (www.ft.com) a daily newspaper and The Economist (www.economist.com) a weekly magazine. Others include The Business (http://info.thebusiness.co.uk), Independent Business Today (www.ibpl.co.uk) is a newsletter published by the Institute of Independent Business, Financial News (www.efinancialnews.com), and Investors Chronicle (www.investorschronicle.co.uk) (weekly). Other regional publications include Business Brief Channel Islands, London Business Matters, Business and Finance in Scotland and Business Scotsman (http://business.scotsman.com).
The Bank of England (www.bankofengland.co.uk/publications) regularly publishes news on the British economy. The Shariah Investor (www.shariahinvestor.com) has articles concerning Islamic banking.
Periodicals: Which (www.which.co.uk) is an influential consumer monthly magazine.

Broadcasting
Public broadcasting is provided by the British Broadcasting Corporation (BBC), a behemoth in the area of worldwide broadcasting. Services are paid for by a licence fee levied against any owner of a television set.
Radio: The BBC operates the largest national network with 11 stations targeting differing audiences, including the World Service, which broadcasts in over 30 languages worldwide. Digital and live online and podcast services are available (www.bbc.co.uk/radio). There is also a BBC local radio network covering the four countries with programmes in English, Welsh and Gaelic.
Private, commercial radio stations thrive throughout the country, although the BBC typically garners the highest listening audiences for both age-related programming and general audience ratings. Popular commercial services include Virgin Radio (www.virgin.com), Classic FM (www.classicfm.co.uk), Talk Sport (www1.talksport.net) and Independent Radio News (IRN) (www.irn.co.uk).
Television: Digital television services are due to be fully implemented by 2012, when all analogue services will be suspended. A number of service providers are transmitting programmes in high definition.
There are five national terrestrial television channels in operation – BBC1 and BBC2 (www.bbc.co.uk), ITV1 (www.itv.com), Channels 4 (www.channel4.com) and 5 (www.channel5.com). All channels commission their own productions and transmit a range of genre programmes.
Free-to-air digital services are provided by all national channels, and some by pay-to-view satellite and cable TV providers. BBC Wales and Channel 4 Wales called S4C provide services in the Welsh language.
Major cable, digital and satellite systems are growing, particularly the Sky network (www.sky.com) and Virgin (www. virgin.com), which includes news and sports channels.

Advertising
There is a highly developed advertising industry covering all forms of media. Numerous terrestrial and digital commercial TV channels accept advertisements subject to principles set by the Advertising Standards Agency (and limited to and average 7–15 minutes per hour). Radio advertising is also effective (limited to 9–12 minutes per hour). The majority of newspapers and magazines carry advertising and relatively high circulation figures make this a particularly useful form of promotion.
Newspapers account for around 30 per cent of the media market compared to 40 per cent for television. Cinemas carry short advertisements and posters. Billboards and public transport are also widely used.
There is a ban on tobacco, and advertising limits on food and drinks for children.

Economy
The UK is a major financial centre and one of the world's largest exporters of financial services. The economy is large, open and mixed and characterised by an export-oriented manufacturing sector. The UK it is the third richest country in Europe and a member of the G8, a bloc of the wealthiest countries worldwide. This status is in no small measure based on its financial and service industries including insurance, banking and financial transaction services; the London Stock exchange is Europe's oldest and largest trading forum and globally second only to Wall Street.
Successive governments have conformed to macroeconomic policies that have led to higher GDP per capita, employment and disposable income levels. The macroeconomic policies have provided the flexibility to shield the economy from external shocks and benefit from globalisation, while providing stability in private and business confidence. Nevertheless, the openness of UK economy is at risk from global changes that can be swift, strong and adverse and require equally swift management to avoid a shock.
The government implemented a period of significant expansion, increasing public spending in 2001, which provided beneficial stimulus but also resulted in a greater fiscal deficit and rising public debt. However, a reversal in the deficit began in 2005/06 as the windfall energy-price related revenue and a booming financial sector provided an increase in GDP.
The service sector accounts for 72 per cent of GDP, industry 27 per cent and agriculture I per cent.
In 2005, GDP growth was 1.9 per cent, down from 3.3 per cent in 2004; growth in 2006 is estimated to be 2.7 per cent and marks 10 years of continued growth which is not seen, by the IMF, as at risk of contracting within the next few years. The consumer price index (CPI) inflation rate is projected to remain within 0.5 per cent of an annual 2.0 per cent for the next few years.
In September 2007 the UK bank Northern Rock was the first bank to have a run on its funds since the nineteenth century. The government committed £55 billion, (US$110 billion) in loan guarantees as it announced that 100 per cent of lenders' money would be secured. In December the pound sterling fell to a record low against the Euro following analysts' worries concerning the UK's inflation and economic growth. On 18 February 2008,

after weeks of attempting to find a private buyer, the government finally took the Northern Rock bank into public ownership. Plans to return the bank to viability will include reducing the workforce by anywhere between 1,000–3,000 jobs.

External trade

As a member of the European Union, the UK operates within a communitywide free trade union, with tariffs sets as a whole. Internationally, the EU has free trade agreements with a number of nations and trading blocs worldwide.

The sector that produces the biggest share of export earnings is banking and financial services, with international banking rated as one of the best and most profitable globally. Despite the declined in heavy industry and manufacturing output has been maintained by hi-tech industries in aerospace and telecommunications, pharmaceuticals and niche manufacturing that accounts for 25 per cent of GDP. The UK is still a major exporter of hydrocarbons, but became a net importer of oil and natural gas in 2004. The first liquefied natural gas (LNG) plant opened for imports in 2005.

In October 2007, Scotch whisky was awarded greater protection from foreign copies by British consumer laws. Scotch whisky exports are worth around US$4 billion to the Scottish economy annually and the regulation is seen as a vital measure to protect the integrity of the product.

Imports

Main imports are vehicles, consumer goods, capital machinery, raw materials, fuels and foodstuffs.

Main sources: Germany (12.1 per cent total, 2006), US (8.0 per cent), France (6.6 per cent).

Exports

Main exports are manufactured goods, fuels, chemicals and pharmaceuticals, food, beverages and tobacco.

Main destinations: US (13.2 per cent total, 2006), France (11.9 per cent), Germany (11.1 per cent).

Agriculture

Farming

Agriculture contributes one per cent to GDP, employs 2 per cent of the workforce and meets over two-thirds of domestic food consumption needs. The sector is highly efficient and is a significant exporter of agricultural produce, fertilisers and foodstuffs. The farming industry remains stuck in long-term recession. The National Farmers' Union (NFU), which represents a third of UK farmers, estimated that by 2005 British farmers owed the banks £12 billion (US$22.6 billion), the highest debt level in 20 years, and the average wage for full time farmers was estimated at £15,000 (US$28,282) per annum.

Setbacks have included Bovine Spongiform Encephalopathy (BSE) in the mid 1990s, resulting in the death of nearly 200,000 diseased cattle and the destruction 4.5 million asymtomatic cattle; extensive flooding in 2000; and the foot-and-mouth outbreak of 2001 which resulted in the culling of over 4 million animals. Government policy is to keep the agricultural industry competitive by reducing subsidies and allowing market forces to determine a farm's viability.

There was another outbreak of the foot and mouth disease on 3 August 2007 in the south of England. A three kilometre protection zone and a 10km surveillance zone were imposed while tests were carried out to find the source of the infection. The outbreak was tracked back to biological research facilities close to the first farm outbreak. On 22 September, the first case of the insect bourn virus, Bluetongue, was confirmed. The disease was found on a farm in the eastern region of England and was confirmed to be the same strain as found in outbreaks in western Europe, particularly the Netherlands.

UK membership of the EU has created policy disputes between the farmers' organisations, the UK government and the EU. Most of UK agriculture is governed by the EU's Common Agricultural Policy (CAP), which was reformed fundamentally on 1 January 2005. The subsidies paid on farm output, which tended to benefit large farms and encourage overproduction, were replaced by single farm payments not conditional on production. This was expected to reward farms that provided and maintain a healthy environment, food safety and animal welfare standards. The changes were also intended to encourage market conscious production and cut the cost of CAP to the EU taxpayer.

Crop production in 2005 included: 21,146,000 tonnes (t) cereals in total, 14,950,000t wheat, 1,914,000t rapeseed, 5,545,000t barley, 6,300,000t potatoes, 536,000t oats, 28,000t flax fibre, 860,000t pulses, 747,620t oilcrops, 7,500,000t sugar beet, 160,000t apples, 281,050t fruit in total, 2,659,813t vegetables in total. Livestock production included: 3,343,030t meat in total, 747,000t beef, 704,000t pig-meat, 310,000t lamb, 1,572,950t poultry, 567,900t eggs, 14,577,000t milk, 7,000t honey, 66,000t cattle hides, 62,000t sheepskins, 62,000t greasy wool.

Fishing

Once an important contribution to the economy, the UK's fishing industry is in decline. The total annual marine catch is typically 750,000 tonnes. Cod stocks in the North Sea, Skagerrak, Irish Sea and waters west of Scotland have been in decline for a number of years.

In 2004, the total marine fish catch was 522,063 tonnes and the total crustacean catch was 55,304 tonnes.

Forestry

Forests cover 24,000 square kilometres, accounting for nearly 10 per cent of total land use. Careful management and replanting programmes mean that forests in the UK are growing by almost 130 square kilometres per annum. Much of the forest plantations have been in the form of non-indigenous coniferous trees, such as the Norwegian Spruce, but in 2005 the government announced a change in policy in favour deciduous woodlands.

The UK typically produces around 7.5 million cubic metres of timber per annum. The UK is far from being self-sufficient in timber or wood products, importing up to 90 per cent of its requirements.

The UK is one of the largest markets for forest products in Europe, with consumption per capita remaining around the European average. Most of the internal demand for pulp and sawnwood is met by imports, although the paper industry depends on the large domestic supply of recovered paper.

Exports of forest products in 2004 amounted to US$2.6 billion, while imports amounted to US$11.2 billion.

Timber production in 2004 included 8,273,000 cubic metre (cum) roundwood, 8,042,000cum industrial roundwood, 2,782,343cum sawnwood, 5,030,000cum sawlogs and veneer logs, 2,617,000cum pulpwood, 3,533,000cum wood-based panels, 231,000cum woodfuel; 6,240,000 tonnes (t) paper and paperboard (including 1,117,000t newsprint), 1,515,000t printing and writing paper, 344,000t paper pulp, 7,616,991t recovered paper.

Industry and manufacturing

The manufacturing industry is centred in northern England and the Midlands. Heavy industry and mining have steadily declined since the nineteenth century industrial revolution, but more rapidly in recent decades. Regions where heavy industry and manufacturing were once important typically have lower GDP per capita and higher unemployment than in the south-east. Northern England, the Midlands and Wales were dealt several blows between the late 1990s and 2002 as foreign-owned plants, notably in the vehicle manufacturing sector, closed, causing tens of thousands of redundancies. The sector's contribution to GDP has fallen in the last twenty years from over 40 per to around 25 per cent.

The government's involvement in industry has decreased since the 1980s. Policy has focused on small- and medium-sized enterprises (SMEs) and on the development

of high-tech industry. The government has reformed its subsidies system to the larger industries, including the phased abolition of subsidies to ship-building operations.
The long-awaited turnaround in manufacturing investment has been delayed by rising oil and commodity prices pushing up costs and putting pressure on profit margins.

Tourism
Tourism is firmly established as one of the UK's top industries. The sector, which employs around one million people, is expected to contribute four per cent to GDP in 2005.. The UK ranks fifth in the international tourism earnings league behind the US, Spain, France and Italy.
Around 26 million arrivals were recorded in 2004, a number that matched the previous high of 25.7 million in 1998. Scotland accounted for the largest growth at 20 per cent against 12 per cent for the rest of the UK.

Mining
The UK is a significant producer of zinc, lead and limestone. There are also deposits of silver, copper, gold, iron ore and potash. Lead and tin production typically reach 2,000 tonnes per annum. Potash production is around 890,000 tonnes, placing UK in the top 10 producers in the world. An estimated 14.6 million tonnes of sandstone, 104.6 million tonnes of sand/gravel and 95.7 million tonnes of limestone are also produced.

Hydrocarbons
The UK has proven oil reserves of 4.5 billion barrels of oil and produces 730 million barrels per annum. Since production peaked in 1999 there has been a steady fall, underscoring the rapid rundown in the UK's domestic oil supplies. Around 2.3 million barrels per day (bpd) were produced in 2005, but it could be half that amount by 2010.
UK has proven gas reserves of 20.8 trillion cubic metres (cum) and produces 95.9 billion cum. Gas production peaked in 2000, but consumption has continued to grow, due mainly to its use in electricity generation. In 2005, the UK became a net importer of gas for the first time in decades.
The UK has estimaated coal reserves of 1.5 billion tonnes and produces around 28.2 million tonnes (less than 10 per cent of that mined in 1900). Imports amounted to 31.9 million tonnes.
The Office of Gas and Electricity Markets (Ofgem), the official regulator of the oil and gas industries, is charged with securing gas and electricity supplies and regulating markets to allow for competition and restrict business monopolies.

Energy
The UK has almost 80GW of installed electricity capacity, 77 per cent of which is thermal, 15 per cent nuclear, five per cent hydroelectric and two per cent renewable.
The net power generation is over 377 billion kilowatt hours (bkwh), while electricity consumption is over 400 bkwh. The bulk of UK imported electricity comes from France.
The largest producer of power is British Energy (BE), which operates eight nuclear power stations and generates about 20 per cent of the total electricity supply for the UK. There are 33 reactors; construction of the last new reactor, the 1188MW Sizewell B in East Anglia, was completed in 1994.
The government approved the development of three large offshore windfarms, at an estimated US$10 billion, in 2003. It is expected that when they become operational in 2010 they will generate as much electrical capacity as six nuclear power stations and five per cent of total power needs. The UK is reported to have Europe's best wind resources.
Wave power became the latest provider of electricity to the national grid, when the Pelamis project off the coast of Orkney delivered its first supply in 2004.

Financial markets
Stock exchange
The London Stock Exchange (LSE) is Europe's oldest and largest trading forum with a £2.8 trillion traded (US$5.2 trillion) in 2004. Almost 1,000 new companies were admitted to the lists since 2003. Two leading European exchanges the Deutsche Borse, in December 2004, and Euronext, in February 2005, made bids of takeover but both were rejected.

Banking and insurance
The UK's high street banks have been very profitable since the mid-1990s, despite being the focus of criticism. The UK banking sector is generally regarded as highly concentrated, but the rise of internet and telephone banking has put renewed pressure on high street banks.
One consequence has been the decision by several leading banks to reduce the number of small branches in areas of low population density.
It is not yet clear whether a radical switch to internet banking will appeal to customers, or whether the combined (so-called 'clicks and mortar') approach will prove more successful). There is evidence that cost-cutting among British banks has given them a better chance of breaking into European markets. Likewise, to compete in a tighter market, banks are being forced into mergers and take-overs. In 2004 the Banco Santander Central Hispano successful bid for the Abbey National Bank in a £8.5bn (US$15.6 billion) deal that created the world's eighth largest and Europe's fourth largest banking group.
Independent financial centres within the UK, Jersey, Guernsey, and the Isle of Man, are adhering to a new EU tax agreement, which was introduced in July 2005. They are imposing a withholding tax, up to 35 per cent, to be passed to the tax department of an EU citizen's country, while retaining the anonymity of the saver, instead of informing the relevant EU country about the amount of money in savings accounts and allowing tax to be levied from the home country.
They also supply information on tax fraud, for criminal or civil trials, and notify EU member states about additional malpractices.

Central bank
Bank of England. Monetary policy and the Exchange Equalisation Account is managed by the Bank of England. In 1997, the government authorised the Bank of England to set interest rates independently.

Main financial centre
The City of London. Edinburgh is the nation's second largest centre.

Time
GMT (daylight saving, late March to late October, GMT plus one hours)

Geography
The UK consists of a major island (divided into England, Wales and Scotland) together with the northern part of the island of Ireland and a number of other smaller islands, including the Channel Islands, the Isle of Man (both dependencies of the Crown) and other islands which are part of the main countries constituting the UK.
There are extensive, though not particularly high, mountain and hill ranges in Wales, Scotland and parts of England.
The rest of the country includes flatlands (as in East Anglia) and more gently rolling agricultural land.

Hemisphere
Northern

Climate
The climate is temperate, with a reasonable amount of rainfall. Very hot summers or very cold winters, such as are found on continental Europe, are rare. The temperature rarely goes above 25 degrees Celsius (C), or much below zero, except in mountainous regions such as the Scottish highlands. Rainfall is around 75mm per month on average, although it is higher in Scotland at up to an average of 280mm per month. The wettest month is usually November.

Dress codes
In general, British dress codes follow the conventional North American or European pattern. A suit and tie for men and smart attire for women are advisable at most business occasions.

Entry requirements
Passports
Required by all and must be valid for at least six months after the intended departure date.
Visa
Visas are required by all, except nationals of North America, Australasia, Japan and other EU members. For further exceptions and advice visit www.ukvisas.gov.uk (includes application forms). All visas must be applied for before travelling.
Currency advice/regulations
The import and export of local and foreign currencies is unlimited.
Travellers cheques are widely accepted.
Customs
Personal items are duty-free. There are no duties levied on alcohol and tobacco between EU member states, providing amounts imported are for personal consumption.
Prohibited imports
Illegal drugs, pornography, offensive weapons, counterfiet goods, meat and dairy products.
Firearms require a permit, to be obtained before arrival.

Health (for visitors)
Nationals of the European Economic Area (EEA) countries and Switzerland can access reduced cost and sometimes free medical treatment using a European Health Insurance Card (EHIC) while visiting the EEA. Exceptions include nationals of the 10 countries which joined the EU in 2004 whose EHIC is not valid in Switzerland. Applications for the EHIC should be made before travelling.
Mandatory precautions
There are no mandatory vaccination certificates required, although evidence of good health may be requested if travelling from areas infected with, for instance, yellow fever.
Advisable precautions
There are no major health hazards for foreign visitors. It is recommended that visitors have up-to-date tetanus immunisation.

Hotels
Classified from one- to five-star by AA and RAC (automobile associations), with five being the best. Rating system in Northern Ireland – A star, A, B star, B, C and D. Prices usually includes a 10–15 per cent service charge, but tipping is also expected.

Credit cards
Major credit and charge cards are widely accepted. ATMs are widely available.

Public holidays (national)
Fixed dates
1 Jan (New Year's Day), 2 Jan (Scotland only), 17 Mar (St Patrick's Day) and 12 Jul (Battle of the Boyne, Northern Ireland only), 25–26 Dec (Christmas).
Holidays that fall on the weekend are taken on the following Monday/Tuesday in lieu.
Variable dates
Good Friday, Easter Monday, May Day Bank Holiday (first Mon in May), Spring Bank Holiday (last Mon in May) and Summer Bank Holiday (last Mon in Aug).
Scotland has an additional public holiday (first Mon in Aug).

Working hours
Banking
Mon–Fri: 0900–1500/1630. Some banks open Saturday morning and there are variations in hours in Scotland and Northern Ireland.
Business
Mon–Fri: usually 0900–1700.
Government
0900–1700 (Mon–Fri). As flexible working hours are often adopted in government departments, it is advisable to make an appointment before a visit.
Shops
Mon–Sat: generally 0900–1730. An increasing number of shops are also taking advantage of Sunday shopping hours (a maximum of 6 hours) and are open 1000–1600 or 1100–1700.

Telecommunications
Mobile/cell phones
There are 3G, 900 and 1800 GSM services throughout the country and surrounding islands.

Electricity supply
230V AC with flat three-pin plugs.

Social customs/useful tips
A reasonable degree of punctuality is required by those in business. Business cards are usually exchanged at meetings. Gifts are not usually offered to business acquaintances, although when visiting a private home it may be appropriate to take chocolates or wine.
There are few unusual or particularly strict laws. Alcoholic drinks are not allowed into some sporting fixtures, notably soccer matches. Smoking is banned in Scotland and actively discouraged in the rest of the UK in many public places and is banned on all transport services.

Security
Street crime is still much less prevalent in the UK than, for instance, the USA. The police, with a few exceptions, remain unarmed. The number of firearms used in criminal activity is relatively low, although it has increased in recent years.

Getting there
Air
National airline: There are no state-owned airlines, but BA (British Airways) is internationally recognised.
International airport/s: London Heathrow (LHR), 24km west of London is the principal UK airport.
Other satellite airports serve regional cities that provide short-haul international flights. London City (LCY) 10km east of city; London Gatwick (LGW), 46km south of London; London Stansted (STN), 55km north-east of London.
Channel Islands: Guernsey (GCI), 6km south-west of St Peter Port; Jersey (JER), 8km west of St Helier.
Northern Ireland: Belfast International (BFS), 29km north-west of city.
Scotland: Aberdeen (ABZ), 11km north-west of city; Edinburgh (EDI), 11km west of city; Glasgow (Int) (GLA), 14km west of city.
Wales: Cardiff (Int) (CWL), 19km south-west of city.
The Heathrow Express connects Heathrow Airport to west London's Paddington station. Services run, every 15 minutes, between 05.00 and 23.45. The slower London underground connects, initially via the Piccadilly Line, to all mainline stations and city centre.
An extensive airbus service operates from Heathrow airport to the city, including Victoria coach station, Russell Square and Liverpool Street Station.
Rapid train services are available from other London airports to the city centre.
Other airport/s: London Luton (LTN), 51.2km north-west of London; Birmingham International (Int) (BHX), 13km east of city; Bournemouth Int (BOH), Bristol Int (BRS), East Midlands Int (EMA), Humberside Int (HUY), Leeds Bradford Int (LBA), Liverpool John Lennon (LPL), 11km south of Liverpool; Manchester Int (MAN); Newcastle Int (NCL), 8km north-west of Newcastle; Norwich (NWI), Plymouth City (PLH), Southampton Int (SOU), Teeside Int (MME).
Airport tax: All taxes are generally paid within the price of an airline ticket, however a doubling of an environmental tax on all flights leaving the UK may mean passengers are required to pay before boarding.
Surface
Road: There are major road links to all parts of the UK and from the Republic of Ireland to Northern Ireland.
Rail: The newly restored St Pancras International railway station was opened on 6 November 2007; the station is the

London terminus for Eurostar, Britain's first high speed train service to Europ. Eurostar connects Paris and Brussels via the channel tunnel, which carries foot and vehicle passengers and freight. The scheduled service operates everyday except Christmas day.

Water: Regular ferry and hovercraft connections with the continent and Ireland.

Main port/s: The main ports are London, Liverpool, Grimsby, Southampton, Milford Haven, Tees and Hartlepool, Dover, Felixstowe, Larne and Holyhead.

Getting about

National transport

Air: Most major cities are linked by regular flights to 21 main commercial airports. A number of small, 'no-frills' airlines have introduced domestic flights that can be very cheap if booked early enough, including connections to Ireland and Scotland and other regional cities.

Road: There is an extensive network of about 370,000km, including 2,800km of motorway, linking all major cities and towns. The M25 circles London as a hub linking other motorways in a network. Traffic can be heavy on these routes, especially as road haulage (wholly in the private sector) use them extensively. Major towns and cities are connected by trunk roads (A roads). Note that roads in rural areas (B roads) can be slow and winding.

Information on planning motorway journeys can be obtained through: www.trafficengland.com

Buses: Express buses between towns and cities are fully in the private sector. Urban and local buses are often still run by local authorities, although private companies operate some routes. For details of services contact www.traveline.org.uk/.

Rail: There is a network of about 18,400km, with relatively expensive first- and second-class services. All principal towns in the UK are connected by regular inter-city services.

Regional companies operate network services. It is advisable to book tickets in advance. These can be obtained on-line (www.thetrainline.com). For more information on UK train services and fare prices, contact: National Rail Enquiries on 0845 748 4950.

Water: There are public and private ferry and car ferry links between Hampshire and the Isle of Wight. Services also provide links with the isles of Scotland, subject to weather conditions, and Northern Ireland. Inshore and inland waterways, are under the control of the British Waterways Board.

City transport

Taxis: Available in all major cities and towns. Taxis can be hailed in the street, at taxi ranks or contacted by telephone. Taxis may charge extra – over and above the metered charge – depending on the number of passengers, the size of luggage items, for journeys at night and at weekends and for journeys exceeding 8km. Tipping is usually in the region of 10 per cent.

Buses, trams & metro: Extensive network linking all parts of the capital. Central London buses are the only ones still formally protected from private competition. Good bus services are also available in all other major towns. London is served by an extensive underground rail (metro) system. Reliable metro services also operate in Glasgow, Liverpool, Manchester (Metrolink Rapid Transit Tram) and Newcastle (Tyne and Wear Metro).

Ferry: There are passenger and car ferry services across the Thames in London and the Mersey in Liverpool.

Car hire

Widely available at airports and in main towns. All major international hire firms are represented. International driving licence or full national licence required. Driving is on the left. Speed limits: motorways/dual carriageways maximum 70mph (113kph), normal roads 40-70mph (64-97kph) (signposted) and built-up areas 30 or 40mph (48 or 64kph) (signposted). Speed cameras are in operation on motorways and other roads and imposed fines are usually forwarded as per car rental agreements.

BUSINESS DIRECTORY

The addresses listed below are a selection only. While World of Information makes every endeavour to check these addresses, we cannot guarantee that changes have not been made, especially to telephone numbers and area codes. We would welcome any corrections.

Telephone area codes

The international direct dialling (IDD) code for United Kingdom is +44, followed by area code and subscriber's number. When dialling from within the UK, add a 0 in front of the area codes below.

Aberdeen	1224	London	20
Belfast	2890 2	Manchester	161
Birmingham	121	Newcastle	191
Cambridge	1223	Nottingham	115
Cardiff	2920	Oxford	1865
Coventry	2476	Perth	1738
Dundee	1382	Plymouth	1752
Edinburgh	131	Portsmouth	2392
Exeter	1392	Sheffield	114
Glasgow	141	Southampton	2380
Liverpool	151	Swansea	1792

Useful telephone numbers

Emergency services999

Directory enquiries (BT, fee service) 118-500

International directory enquiries (BT, fee service)118-505

Chambers of Commerce

Birmingham Chamber of Industry and Commerce, 75 Harbourne Road, Birmingham B15 3DH (tel: 454-6171; fax: 455-8670; email: info@birminghamchamber.org.uk).

British Chambers of Commerce, 50 Broadway, St James Park, London SW1H 0RG (tel: 7152-4046; fax: 7565-2049).

Cardiff Chamber of Commerce, Trade and Industry, St David's House East, Wood Street, Cardiff CF10 1ES (tel: 2034-8280; fax: 2037-7653; email: enquiries@cardiffchamber.co.uk).

Edinburgh Chamber of Commerce, 27 Melville Street, Edinburgh EH3 7JF (tel: 477-7000; fax: 477-7002; email: information@ecce.org).

Leeds Chamber of Commerce, 102 Wellington Street, Leeds LS1 4LT (tel: 0113-247-0000; fax: 0113-247-111; email: info@leedschamber.co.uk).

London Chamber of Commerce and Industry, 33 Queen Street, London EC4R 1AP (tel: 7248-4444; fax: 7489-0391; email: lc@londonchamber.co.uk).

Manchester Chamber of Commerce and Industry, Churchgate House, 56 Oxford Street, Manchester M60 7HJ (tel: 237-4102; fax: 237-3277; email: info@mcci.org.uk).

Sheffield Chamber of Commerce and Industry, Albion House, Savile Street, Sheffield S4 7UD (tel: (0)114-201-8888; fax: (0)114-272-0950; email: info@scci.org.uk).

Banking

Abbey National, 2 Triton Square, Regent's Place, London NW1 3AN (tel: 7612-4000; fax: 7612-4230; email: investor@abbeynational.com).

Bank of Scotland, The Mound, Edinburgh EH1 1YZ (tel: 470-7777; fax: 243-5640).

Barclays Bank, 54 Lombard Street, London EC3P 3AH (tel: 7699-5000; fax: 7699-2680).

British Bankers' Association, Pinners Hall, 105-108 Old Broad Street London EC2N 1EX (tel: 7216-8800; fax: 7216-8811).

Chartered Institute of Bankers in Scotland, Drumsheugh House, 38b Drumsheugh Gardens, Edinburgh EH3 7SW (tel: 473-7777; fax:473-7788; email: info@ciobs.org.uk).

Clydesdale Bank, 30 St Vincent Place, Glasgow G1 2HL (tel: 248-7070; fax: 223-2559).

Halifax Plc, Trinity Road, Halifax HX1 2RG (tel: 01422-333-333; fax: 01422-391-777).

HSBC, 10 Lower Thames Street, London EC3R 6AE (tel: 7260-0500; fax: 7260-0501).

Lloyds TSB, 71 Lombard Street, London EC3P 3BS (tel: 7626-1500; fax: 7356-1731).

National Westminster Bank, 135 Bishopsgate, London EC2M 3UR (tel: 7375-5000; fax: 7375-5050).

Royal Bank of Scotland, 36 St Andrew Square, Edinburgh EH2 2YB (tel: 556-8555; fax: 557-6565).

Central bank

Bank of England, Threadneedle Street, London EC2R 8AH (tel: 7601-4444; fax: 7601-5460; internet: www.bankofengland.co.uk).

Travel information

Aberdeen Airport, Dyce, Aberdeen AB21 7DU (tel: 1224-722-331; fax: 1224-775-845; email: glal@baa.com).

Belfast International Airport, Aldergrove, Belfast BT 29 4AB (tel: 448-4848; fax: 448-4849; email: info.desk@bial.co.uk).

Birmingham International Airport, Birmingham B26 3QJ (tel: 767-5511; fax: 782-8802; email: custsrvs@bhx.co.uk).

BA, Waterside, PO Box 365, Harmondsworth, Middlesex (tel: 8738-5100; fax: 8738-9838).

Cardiff International Airport, Rhoose CF62 3BD (tel: 1446-711-111; fax: 1446-711-675; email: info@cial.co.uk).

Edinburgh Airport, Edinburgh EH12 9DN (tel: 333-1000; fax: 344 3470; email: glal@baa.com).

Gatwick Airport, West Sussex RH6 0NP (tel: 0870-000-2468; fax: 1293-503-794; email: gatwick_feedback@baa.com).

Glasgow Airport, Paisley, Renfrewshire PA3 2SW (tel: 887-1111; fax: 848-4769; email: glal@baa.com).

Heathrow Airport, 234 Bath Road, Harlington, Middlesex UB3 5AP (tel: 0870-0000-123; fax: 8745-4290; email: lhr1feedback@baa.com).

London City Airport, Royal Docks, London, E16 2PX (customer services tel: 7646-0088; internet: www.londoncityairport.com).

Manchester Airport, Manchester M90 1QX (tel: 489-3000; fax: 489-3813; email: info@manchesterairport.co.uk).

Northern Ireland Tourist Board, 59 North Street, Belfast BT1 1NB (tel: 231-221; fax: 240-960; email: info@nitb.com).

Passport Office, Globe House, 89 Ecclestone Square, London SW1V 1PN (tel: 0870-521-0410; fax: 7271-8403; email: london@ukpa.gov.uk).

Glasgow Prestwick International Airport, Aviation, Prestwick, Ayrshire KA9m 2PL (tel: 1292-511-000; fax: 1292-511-010; email: info@gpia.co.uk).

Stansted Airport, Essex CM24 1QW (tel: 0870-0000-303; fax: 1279-662-066; email: stansted_feedback@baa.com).

VisitScotland, 23 Ravelston Terrace, Edinburgh EH4 3TP (tel: 332-2433; fax: 343-1513; email: info@visitscotland.com).

Wales Tourist Board, Brunel House, 2 Fitzalan Road, Cardiff CF24 0UY (tel: 499-909; fax: 485-031; email: info@visitwales.com).

Ministry of tourism

Department of Culture, Media and Sport, 2-4 Cockspur Street, London SW1Y 5DH (tel: 7211 6200; email: enquiries@culture.gov.uk)

National tourist organisation offices

VisitBritain, Thames Tower, Blacks Road, Hammersmith, London W6 9EL (tel: 8563-3000; fax: 8563-3234; email: comments@englishtourism.org.uk).

Ministries

Cabinet Office, 70 Whitehall, London SW1A 2AS (tel: 7270-1234).

Department of Culture, Media and Sport, 2-4 Cockspur Street, London SW1Y 5DH (tel: 7211-6000; e-mail: enquiries@culture.gov.uk)

Department of Education and Skills, Sanctuary Building, Great Smith Street, London SW1P 3BT (tel: 0870-000-2288; fax: 01928-79-4248; e-mail: info@dfes.gov.uk).

Department of Environment, Food and Rural Affairs, Nobel House, 17 Smith Square, London SW1P 3JR (tel: 7238-6000; fax: 7238-6591).

Department of Health, Richmond House, 79 Whitehall, London SW1A 2NS (tel: 7210-4850; e-mail: dhmail@doh.gsi.gov.uk).

Department of International Development, 94 Victoria Street, London SW1E 5JL (tel: 7917-7000; fax: 7917-0019; e-mail: enquiry@dfid.gov.uk).

Department of Trade and Industry, 1 Victoria Street, London SW1H OET (tel: 7215-5000; e-mail: dti.enquiries@dti.gsi.gov.uk).

Department of Transport, Local Government and Regions, Eland House, Bressenden Place, London SW1E 5DU (tel: 7944-3000).

Department of Work and Pensions, Richmond House, 79 Whitehall, London SW1A 2NS (tel: 7238-0800; fax: 238-0763; peo@dwp.gsi.gov.uk).

Foreign and Commonwealth Office, King Charles Street, London SW1A 2AH (tel: 7270-1500).

Home Office, 50 Queen Annes Gate, London SW1H 9AT (tel: 7273-4000; fax: 7273-2065; e-mail: public.enquiries@homeoffice.gti.gov.uk).

Lord Chancellor's Department, Selborne House, 54-60 Victoria Street, London SW1E 6QW (tel: 7210-8500; e-mail: general.enquiries.@lcdhq.gsi.gov.uk).

Ministry of Defence, Main Building, Horse Guards Avenue, London SW1A 2HB (tel: 0870-607-4455).

Northern Ireland Office, 11 Millbank, London SW1P 4PN (tel: 7210-3000; fax: 7210-0249; e-mail: press.nio@nics.gov.uk).

Prime Ministers Office, 10 Downing Street, London SW1A 2AA (tel: 7270-3000).

Scotland Office, Dover House, London SW1A 2AU (tel: 7270-6754; fax: 7270-6812; e-mail: scottish.secretary@scotland.gov.uk).

Treasury, Parliament Street, London SW1P 3AG (tel: 7270-4558; fax: 7270-5244; e-mail: public.enquiries@hm-treasury.gov.uk).

Wales Office, Gwydyr House, London SW1A 2ER (e-mail: wales.office@wales.gsi.gov.uk).

Other useful addresses

Aberdeen Exhibition and Conference Centre, Bridge of Don, Aberdeen (tel: 1224-824-824; fax:1224-825-276; email: aecc@aecc.co.uk).

Advertising Standards Authority, 2 Torrington Place, London WC1E 7HW (tel: 7580-5555; fax: 7631-3051; email: inquiries@asa.org.uk).

BBC Television, Television Centre, Wood Lane, London W12 7RJ (tel: 8743-8000; fax: 8749-7520; email: info@bbc.co.uk).

British Council, 10 Spring Gardens, London SW1A 2BN (tel: 7930-8466; fax: 7389-6347; email: general.enquiries@britishcouncil.org).

British Embassy (USA), 3100 Massachusetts Avenue, NW, Washington DC 20008 (tel: (+1-202) 588-7800; fax: (+1-202) 5588-7870).

British Sky Broadcasting Group (BSkyB), 6 Centaurs Business Park, Grant Way, Isleworth TW7 5QD (tel: 7705-3000; fax: 7705-3060).

British Waterways Board, Willow Grange, Church Road, Watford WD17 4QA (tel:

01923-201-120; email: enquiries.hq@britishwaterways.co.uk).

Chartered Institute of Marketing, Moor Hall, Cookham, Maidenhead, Berkshire SL6 9QH (tel: 1628-427-500; fax: 1628-427-499; email: info@cim.co.uk).

Confederation of British Industry (CBI), Centre Point, 103 New Oxford Street, London WC1A 1DU (tel: 7395-8247; fax: 7240-1578; email: enquiry.desk@cbi.org.uk).

Crown Estate, 16 Carlton House Terrace, London SW1Y 5AH (tel: 7210-4377; fax: 7210-4236; email: pr@crownestate.co.uk).

Customs and Excise, New King's Beam House, 22 Upper Ground, London SE1 9PJ (tel: 7620-1313; fax: 7865-4975; email: enquiries.lon@hmce.gsi.gov.uk).

Design Council, 34 Bow Street, London WC2E 7DL (tel: 7420-5200; fax: 7420-5300; email: info@designcouncil.org.uk).

Guild of Registered Tourist Guides, The Guild House, 52d Borough High Street, London SE1 1XN (tel: 7403-1115; fax: 7378-1705; email: guild@blue-badge.org.uk).

Independent Television News (ITN), 200 Gray's Inn Road, London WC1X 8HF (tel: 7833-3000; fax: 7430-4868; email: info@itn.co.uk).

Institute of Export, Export House, Minerva Business Park, Lynch Wood, Peterborough PE2 6FT (tel: 1733-404-400; fax: 1733-404-444; email: institute@export.org.uk).

Institute of Linguists, Saxon House, 48 Southwark Street, London SE1 1UN (tel: 7940-3100; fax: 7940-3101; email: info@iol.org.uk).

ITV Network Centre, 200 Gray's Inn Road, London WC1X 8HF (tel: 7843-8000; fax: 7843-8158; email: info@itv.co.uk).

Kings Hall Exhibition and Conference Centre, Balmoral, Belfast (tel: 028-9066-5225; fax: 028-9066-1264; email: info@kingshall.co.uk).

London Stock Exchange, Old Broad Street, London EC2N 1HP (tel: 7797-1000; email: enquiries@londonstockexchange.com).

National Exhibition Centre, Birmingham B40 1NT (tel: 780-4141; fax: 780-2517; email: centre-exhibitions@necgroup.co.uk).

Office for National Statistics, 1 Drummond Gate, London SW1V 2QQ (tel: 7233-9233; fax: 7533-6262; email: info@statistics.gov.uk).

Press Complaints Commission, 1 Salisbury Square, London EC4Y 8JB (tel: 7353-1248; fax: 7353-8355; email: pcc@pcc.org.uk).

Scottish Exhibition and Conference Centre, Exhibition Way, Fenniston Street, Glasgow G3 8YW (tel: 248-3000; fax: 226-3423; email: info@secc.co.uk).

Trades Union Congress (TUC), Congress House, 23-28 Great Russell Street, London WC1B 3LS (tel: 7636-4030; fax: 7636-0632; email: info@tuc.org.uk).

National news agency: PA Group

Internet sites

Bank of England: www.bankofengland.co.uk

British Airways: www.british-airways.com

British Chambers of Commerce: www.britishchambers.org.uk/internet_home_page.htm

Confederation of British Industry: www.cbi.org.uk

Department of Trade and Industry: www.dti.gov.uk

Eurostar Train: www.eurostar.com

Kelly's Directory (search engine for UK industry): www.kellys.reedinfo.co.uk

UK export (database of British exporters): www.export.co.uk

UK Online (UK government gateway): www.ukonline.gov.uk

UK trade information: www.ukinfo.com

UK yellow pages: www.yell.co.uk

United States of America

KEY FACTS

Official name: United States of America

Head of State: President George Walker Bush (Republican) (since 2001; re-elected Nov 2004)

Head of government: President George W Bush

Ruling party: Republican Party

Area: 9,300,000 square km

Population: 301.97 million (2007)*

Capital: Washington DC

Official language: There is no official language declared in the constitution. English is the de facto working language and Spanish is the second, widely spoken, unofficial language.

Currency: US dollar (US$) = 100 cents

GDP per capita: US$45,845 (2007)

GDP real growth: 2.20% (2005); 0.6% (Q1 2007)*

Labour force: 151.40 million (2006)

Unemployment: 4.60% (2007)

Inflation: 2.80% (2007)*

Oil production: 6.88 million bpd (2007)

Balance of trade: -US$778.94 billion (2005)

Foreign debt: US$3,700.00 billion (2006)

Visitor numbers: 51.10 million (2006)*

* estimated figure

If 2007 was not one of the greatest years in US history, 2008 did not look like being much of an improvement. As the end of the Bush presidency approached, it was more and more apparent that not only had it been a failed presidency, it had been a presidency that had been less than straight with the American people. In the space of eight years George W Bush had left behind his folksy Texan approach to become one of the most controversial and divisive presidents in American history.

Obama's rise

The bright spot of an otherwise depressing year was the re-activation of political interest and activity brought about by the Democratic Party's selection of its presidential candidate. In what had once been expected to be a shoe-in for Senator Hillary Clinton, the wife of former President Bill Clinton, the challenge of Illinois senator, Barack Obama, eventually proved impossible to overcome. Senator Obama, and his 'Yes we can!' slogan appeared to offer the electorate the possibility of a new start, outside a tired political framework that voters had begun to dislike and distrust. One European newspaper described Obama's selection as 'the political theatre surrounding his bid to become America's first black president'. In contrast, the Republican Party's selection of Senator McCain proceeded in a more predictable manner, as the candidate endeavoured to distance himself from the Bush years while retaining the support of Republican loyalists. President Bush remained virtually invisible throughout Senator John McCain's campaign.

By mid-2008 the two presidential candidates were running neck and neck in the polls. Although the electorate appeared to view Mr McCain as the better bet as supreme military commander, Mr Obama made it clear from the outset that he would establish a schedule for a military withdrawal from Iraq. He also attached greater importance to winning the war against the Taliban in Afghanistan, a view that in mid-2008 was rapidly gaining currency both in North America and in Europe. If elected president, Mr Obama has said he would set a 16 month timetable for withdrawal from Iraq, with some troops to be repositioned to Afghanistan.

The vice presidency

In mid-2008 both parties were also engaged in the process of selecting a vice president. For different reasons the choice of vice presidential candidate in 2008 was likely to be of greater importance than in previous years. Not least, the eventual choice would offer voters an insight into the way the final campaign and electoral platform might shape up. Again for quite different reasons, both parties appeared to be close to selecting a female candidate. In the case of the Republican Party, this was seen as a tidy corrective to the hard-line, 'macho' militaristic policies that had proved so disastrous under Bush. The three front runners in mid-2008 were Carly Fiorina, the former chief executive of Hewlett-Packard. Once described as the most powerful woman in US business, Ms Fiorina had become a close advisor of Senator McCain. While Ms Fiorina had proved that she could operate in a male-dominated world, she lacked political experience. This was certainly not the case with another republican vice presidential possible, Alaska governor, Sarah Palin. A favourite among more conservative republicans, and a former beauty queen to boot, Ms Palin was once described as 'America's hottest governor'. Ms Palin held a lot of valuable electoral cards: a youthful mother of five and member of the National Rifle Association, she offered a useful antidote to the 72 year old McCain. Coming up on the rails as a potential Republican veep candidate, was Secretary of State Condoleeza Rice. Both female and black, in theory Ms Black ticked a number of the right boxes for Mr McCain. However, unelected, she was generally perceived as uncharismatic and had proved to be an ineffectual secretary of state. Her unmarried status had inevitably generated rumours, and her intellectual prowess (not to mention her membership of a chamber orchestra) did little to endear her to the Republican heartlands. Furthermore, it was generally accepted that her closeness to a discredited President Bush was a severe liability.

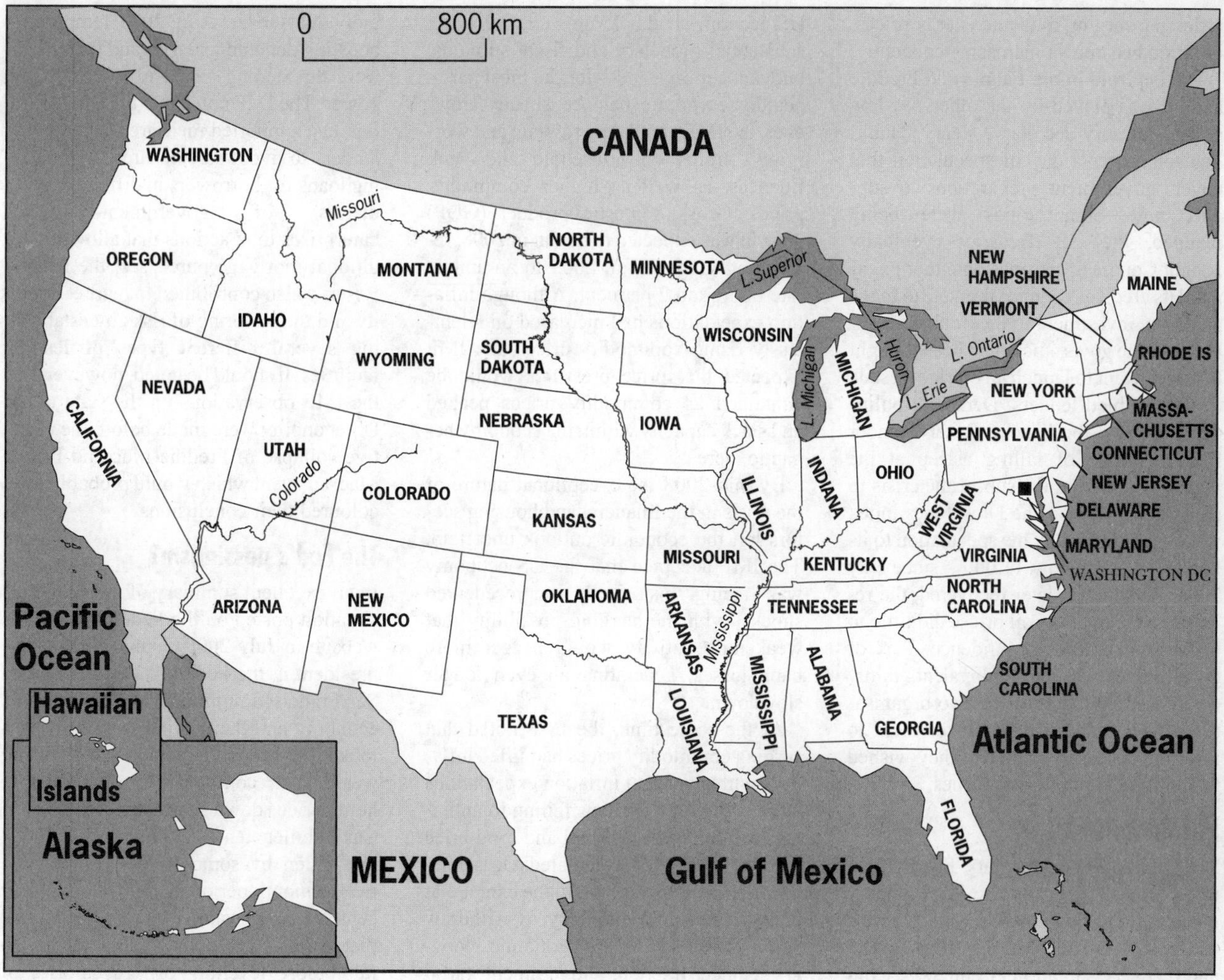

The Democrats' alternative to Republican front-runner Governor Palin was also a female state governor, Kathleen Sebelius of Kansas. Aged 60 and representing an essentially Republican heartland, Ms Sebelius was an obvious counterpoint to Senator Obama. Ms Sebelius was challenged by Missouri Senator Claire McCaskill, who had been a close advisor and strong supporter of Obama on the campaign trail. Missouri also promised to be a key state in the presidential election. Hovering in the wings remained Senator Hillary Clinton, whose choice would have healed the inevitable divisions within the Democrat Party following the bruising election campaign, but who brought with her considerable political baggage which many saw as an electoral handicap. Mrs Clinton had surprised many Democrats by the speed of her decision actively to support Barack Obama. While the vice presidential selection was a high profile affair for the Democrats, for the Republicans it had actuarial overtones, for the simple reason that given Senator McCain's age, a Republican vice president was more likely to become president. Governor Palin looked the most likely to bring both political insight combined with youth and even excitement to the campaign.

Fannie Mae and Freddie Mac

Originally created by President Roosevelt as part of the New Deal, and later privatised by President Johnson, the Federal National Mortgage Corporation (Fannie Mae) and the Federal Home Mortgage Corporation (Freddie Mac) are responsible for more than 40 per cent of outstanding mortgages in the US. In mid-July 2008 the shares of both billion dollar organisations plunged, as questions about their financial health began to become more persistent. It had become common knowledge that technically both organisations were insolvent. A Freddie or Fannie backed mortgage was tantamount to a state-backed loan: were the borrower to default, it was Freddie or Fannie who were left on the hook. As US real-estate prices continued to head south, mortgage defaults had begun to spread well beyond the sub-prime sector, the collapse of which had caused the world's banks to falter and its stock markets to fall. More and more lenders to prime borrowers were having recourse to the two guarantors. As US banks found themselves struggling in late-2007 and the first half of 2008, so the supply of mortgages also dried up, placing an even greater strain on Fannie and Freddie. Although the two institutions had managed to fill the vacuum created by the virtual collapse of the private securitisation market, the cash drain eventually proved too much; the only source available for more cash was the US Treasury. As the Federal Reserve had already pointed out, housing and credit markets looked likely to remain troubled, and commodity prices seemed certain to rise further. These factors are likely to weigh on the outlook for some time. In addition, reflecting surging food and energy prices, inflation became an increasing concern.

The key role in the Fannie and Freddie bailout was played by the otherwise low profile treasury secretary, Henry 'Hank' Paulson. After a day of speculation that covert government preparations to support both organisations were being planned, the US Treasury eventually sought Congress' permission either to expand its credit or even for the state to make an equity investment in the troubled institutions. The government had been thought to be reluctant to launch an outright rescue of the troubled lenders. Democrat politicians accused the Federal Reserve under Ben Bernanke of falling asleep at the wheel by allowing the sub-prime crisis to reach crisis levels. The Dow Jones index was sent tumbling by the speculation to its lowest level – below 11,000 – since July 2006. Although it later recovered, the relentless rise in crude oil prices did little to boost stockholder's confidence. Part of the problem was the ambivalent, thinly capitalised structure of the two organisations. This made it difficult for them to raise the necessary capital if they wished to continue as public companies.

IMF optimism?

The International Monetary Fund (IMF) in its annual report on the US economy noted that the slowdown in activity in the United States had been less than feared, and recovery should begin in 2009. Considering the severity of the shocks that had buffeted it, the IMF considered that the US economy had held up well, following substantial monetary and fiscal stimulus, buoyant exports, and – for the most part – healthy corporate balance sheets. However, the IMF noted the growing, and worrying, strains on household and bank finances, as well as higher commodity prices. Gross domestic product (GDP) growth was expected to be flat in 2008, recovering gradually in 2009 to an annual rate of around 2 per cent. Although inflation expectations had increased on relentlessly rising commodity prices, the IMF expected that price pressures would be contained as commodity prices peaked and slack capacity within the economy began to increase.

By mid-2008 the exceptional nature of the crisis in the financial and housing sectors left the economic outlook uncertain. The IMF accepted that the US economy was facing historically unprecedented shocks, with the nagging possibility that weakening activity would trigger more bank losses, generating an even longer slowdown.

At the same time, the IMF noted that surging commodity prices had lifted inflation, with signs that inflation expectations were edging up. Perhaps failing to anticipate the full extent of fuel and food price increases, the IMF anticipated a lessening of inflationary pressures, to the extent that it could become necessary to withdraw stimulus quickly as the economic recovery gained traction. Government fiscal stimulus was timely as tax rebate cheques were sent to low- and middle-income individuals in late April 2008, temporarily boosting demand when oil and food prices were threatening to eat in to purchasing power. The IMF noted that the administration had supported measures encouraging lenders to avoid foreclosures by modifying loans for borrowers in difficulty. Regulators of government-sponsored enterprises took actions that allow for additional mortgage purchases; the Federal Reserve also contributed to market liquidity and the lowering of risks by establishing several different types of lending facilities. It should be noted, however, that the IMF observations on the state of the US economy were made before the effective collapse of Freddie Mac and Fannie Mae, an event which would probably have coloured their conclusions.

The Fed's pessimism?

In an excellent summary of the economic situation posted on the Federal Reserve's website in July 2008, John Fernald, vice president at the Federal Reserve Bank of San Francisco, summarised the state of the economy and the inevitably gloomy outlook. Mr Fernald noted that housing wealth had continued to plunge, with home prices down sharply over 2007. The Case-Shiller ten-city home-price index had fallen by some 15 per cent over a twelve month period, and by about 20 per cent since its peak. Mr Fernald estimated that prices have considerably further to fall before levelling off. Inventories of both new and existing homes – measured as the supply of homes on the market relative to the current monthly sales pace – were very high. Falling prices and an overhang of home supply also created what Mr Fernald described as a drag on new home construction.

As everyone from Ushuaia to Ulan Bator had discovered, mounting losses on securities tied to sub-prime and other mortgages had helped spark the global financial turmoil and financial market stress still remained high throughout the world. However, on a more positive note, Mr Fernald expressed the view that business surveys did not suggest a major deterioration in overall conditions. For example, the Institute for Supply Management surveys purchasing and supply executives each month. For both manufacturing and non-manufacturing, these diffusion indices are currently close to 50, which is below their typical values. Hence, in Mr Fernald's view of things (which was apparently shared by the Federal Reserve) current readings appear consistent with slightly below-trend growth.

KEY INDICATORS — United States of America

	Unit	2003	2004	2005	2006	2007
Population	m	288.40	293.47	296.47	299.08	301.97
Gross domestic product (GDP)	US$bn	10,819.81	11,667.51	12,455.83	13,194.70	13,843.83
GDP per capita	US$	37,312	39,934	41,960	44,118	45,845
GDP real growth	%	3.0	4.4	3.2	2.8	2.2
Inflation	%	2.3	2.7	3.4	3.2	2.8
Unemployment	%	6.1	5.5	5.1	4.6	4.6
Oil output	'000 bpd	7,454.0	7,241.0	6,830.0	6,871.0	6,879.0
Natural gas output	bn cum	549.5	542.9	525.7	524.1	54.6
Coal output	mtoe	551.3	567.2	576.2	595.1	573.7
Exports (fob) (goods)	US$m	724,006	811,080	898,460	1,026,850	1,153,270
Imports (cif) (goods)	US$m	1,305,648	1,473,120	1,677,400	1,861,410	1,964,590
Balance of trade	US$m	-581,642	-662,040	-778,940	-834,550	-811,330
Current account	US$m	-530,670	-665,940	-791,504	-811,483	-738,636
Total reserves minus gold	US$m	74,890.0	75,890.0	54,080.0	54,850.0	59,520.0
Foreign exchange	US$m	39,720.0	42,720.0	37,840.0	40,940.0	45,800.0

In contrast, falling employment suggests more deterioration in economic conditions. However, it appeared that there were some contradictions. Over 2007, employment in goods-producing industries (mainly construction and manufacturing) had fallen by about 3.5 per cent. In previous recessions, job losses have always been more severe. Employment growth in services-producing industries had slowed, but employment remained above its year-ago level. In February, household spending appeared quite weak. For example, the year-on-year growth rate of non-durables consumption – a category that includes food, apparel and gasoline – had slowed to levels comparable to the 2001 recession. The non-durables category omits the purchases of durable goods, which tend to be volatile, as well as services, where the monthly data are likely to be less reliable.

From March 2008, however, consumer spending increased significantly. Some of the May increase undoubtedly reflected the effect of the US$50 billion tax stimulus payments. In Mr Fernald's view, although the increases in March and April might have reflected consumers spending early – knowing that they would soon be receiving a stimulus check – it could also have reflected entrenched resilience on the part of US consumers. Perhaps predictably, vehicle sales plummeted in the first half of 2008, reflecting petrol pump prices that had risen above US$4.00 per gallon, as well as tighter credit conditions. Business capital investment expenditure appeared to be holding up. Orders and shipments for non-defence capital goods excluding aircraft – such as durable equipment goods – were edging steadily up.

Growth in the second quarter of 2008 was close to the forecast trend, after two anaemic quarters. The continuing and intensifying negative pressures from housing and credit markets, combined with rising commodity prices, are likely to depress activity for some time. Mr Fernald expected the governmental fiscal stimulus programme to help support growth. A more solid recovery should take root in 2009, reflecting some waning of the drags on the economy. In particular, housing should begin to stabilise, credit conditions should gradually ease, and energy and food prices are expected to level off. In addition, the earlier policy easing by the Federal Reserve should provide some cushion for the economy.

The Michigan survey of households showed higher long-term inflation expectations. However, there was some evidence that the Michigan survey responses were highly sensitive to the current inflation rate, so it is likely that this measure will come down once oil and food prices stop rising. In contrast, the Survey of Professional Forecasters sees the same long-term inflation trend as they've been seeing since the late 1990s. And inflation compensation five-to-ten years ahead, derived from a comparison of nominal and inflation-indexed government securities, has come down from its highs earlier this year. In mid-2008 the markets pared back expectations about the pace of monetary-policy tightening. In June 2008, markets thought the federal funds rate would rise steadily over the course of 2008. They had by June 2008 come to expect only one rate increase during the rest of the year.

Foreign relations

One of the obvious attractions of Senator Obama as potential president was the possibility, or the hope, that a black president might be able completely to recast US foreign relations. Under the Bush presidency, either by default, neglect or sheer incompetence, the US relationship with the rest of the world had taken something of a battering. The miscalculations that had done so much damage to the US reputation and its former prestige were legion. For all the wrong reasons, names such as Guantánamo and Abu Ghraib and previously little known terms such as 'secret rendition' and 'water boarding' had entered a wider world lexicon.

While Senator McCain appeared to be offering a 'Bush lite' foreign policy, Senator Obama in the run up to the election was advocating a policy of engagement, one of meeting with and listening to both allies and potential foes. This would not only include dialogue with countries such as Syria, left out to dry by the Bush administration, but also with North Korea and even Cuba. Come the day, practical military considerations may overcome senator Obama's instincts, but as the son of a Kenyan, he is obviously well placed to further US relations in Africa – possibly the only 'success' of the Bush administration.

Energy matters

The United States had 29.4 billion barrels of proved oil reserves as of 31 December 2007, the eleventh highest in the world. These reserves were concentrated overwhelmingly (over 80 per cent) in four states: Texas (with 22 per cent of total US oil reserves), Louisiana (20 per cent), Alaska (20 per cent) and California (18 per cent). US proven oil reserves have declined more than 17 per cent since 1990, with the largest single-year decline (1.6 billion barrels) occurring in 1991.

US crude oil production, which declined following the oil price collapse of late-1985/early-1986, levelled off in the mid-1990s, and began falling again following the sharp decline in oil prices of late-1997/early-1998. During 2007, the United States produced around 6.9 million barrels per day (bpd) of oil, of which 5.4 million bpd was crude oil, 1.8 million bpd was natural gas liquids and 0.4 million bpd was other liquids. This compares to the 10.6 million bpd averaged during 1985.

Overall, the top suppliers of crude oil to the United States are Canada (1.6 million bpd), Mexico (1.6 million bpd), Saudi Arabia (1.5 million bpd), Venezuela (1.3 million bpd) and Nigeria (1.0 million bpd). The United States consumed an average of about 20.7 million bpd of oil during 2007, down from the peak of 20.8 million bpd in 2005. Of this, motor gasoline consumption was 9.1 million bpd (or 44 per cent of the total), distillate fuel oil consumption was 4.1 million bpd (20 per cent), jet fuel consumption was 1.6 million bpd (8 per cent), and residual fuel oil consumption was 0.9 million bpd (4 per cent).

As of 31 December 2007, the US had estimated natural gas reserves of 5.98 trillion cubic metres (Tcm), or about 3.4 per cent of world reserves (6th in the world). Natural gas consumption for 2007 was about 6.53 Tcm. More than 80 per cent of US natural gas imports come from Canada, mainly from the western provinces of Alberta, British Columbia and Saskatchewan. Overall, the United States depends on natural gas for about 22 per cent of its total primary energy requirements (oil accounts for around 41 per cent and coal for 23 per cent).

Outlook

For the future of US foreign policy and the shape and nature of its relationships with the rest of the world, much will depend on the outcome of the 2008 presidential election. Senator McCain is less likely to effect any major changes either in the direction or the priorities of foreign policy. Senator Obama's pronouncements have often sounded fresh and encouraging. It remains to be seen whether, if he is elected, Obama will be able to exert sufficient pressure to achieve his objectives. Not all the blame for the vicissitudes of the US economy can be laid at George Bush's feet. But the very presence of a new face in the White House should generate some optimism, even if unable to rein in the inflationary pressures. Both candidates were less than forthcoming over how the paradoxical, but frightening, poverty levels of over 30 million US citizens are ever going to be addressed.

Risk assessment

Politics	Good
Economy	Fair
Regional stability	Good

COUNTRY PROFILE

Historical profile

The first inhabitants of North America included the Pueblo people in New Mexico, the Apache in Texas, the Navajo in Arizona, Colorado and Utah, and the Hopi in Arizona, the Crow in Montana, the Cherokee in North Carolina and Mohawks and Iroquois in New York State.

1565–07 The Spanish, French and British founded settlements across North America.

1619 The first African slaves were brought into North America by the British.

1700s As the eighteenth century progressed, an increasing number of European settlers arrived. British attempts to assert authority over its 13 North American colonies led to conflicts with the French and the indigenous population. In order to recoup losses after winning the conflict the British imposed higher taxes, which led to civil unrest and the first stirrings of an independence movement.

1776 Independence from Britain was declared by the colonies.

1781 Rebel states set up a loose confederation, codified in Articles of Confederation, after defeating the British at the Battle of Yorktown.

1783 The British accepted the loss of their colonies under the Treaty of Paris.

1787 The 'founding fathers' drew up the constitution, which created a federal structure for the United States of America.

1788 The constitution came into effect.

1789 George Washington was elected the first US president.

1800s During the nineteenth century, populations expanded across the plains to the west coast. By 1850, a combination of land purchases, war and diplomacy had created much of the modern-day US. After 1850, immigrants began arriving from all over the world, mainly attracted by the industrial jobs in the north. The south remained committed to agriculture and the use of slaves.

1860 When the abolitionist Abraham Lincoln became president, the south seceded from the north and civil war was declared in 1861.

1865 The north won the civil war, but after Lincoln's assassination blacks in the south remained disenfranchised and segregated.

1898 The US's emergence as a world power was demonstrated when Spain lost control of its colonies in Cuba, Guam, the Philippines and Puerto Rico, after being defeated in Cuba by the US.

1914 The US declared its neutrality at the start of the First World War.

1917 The US declared war on Germany after a torpedo attack on the passenger vessel Lusitania a year earlier. Over one million US troops had served on the Allied side by the time the war ended in 1918.

1929 The Wall Street crash resulted in a lengthy economic recession referred to as the 'Great Depression'.

1941 After remaining neutral at the outbreak of the Second World War in 1939, the US declared war on the Axis powers following the Japanese air attack on Pearl Harbour.

1944 The US led the Allied liberation of Nazi-occupied Western Europe.

1945 Following the victory in Europe, the US dropped two atomic bombs on the Japanese cities of Hiroshima and Nagasaki, ending the Pacific War.

1947–50s The US's Marshall Plan was instrumental in the rebuilding of post-war Western Europe and Japan, providing financial aid. The Cold War emerged between the capitalist US and Western Europe and the communist Soviet Union and its Eastern European bloc.

1950–53 The US led a UN military force against communist North Korea after it had invaded South Korea. When the Chinese intervened on the side of the North Koreans the war became attritional. A cease-fire was signed in 1953.

1962 Tensions between the Soviet Union and the US reached a climax during the Cuban missile crisis.

1963 John F Kennedy, the youngest-ever US president, was assassinated in Dallas, Texas in November.

1964–73 The US was embroiled in the Vietnam War. The US government provided South Vietnam with military assistance against communist North Vietnam, but was forced to withdraw in 1973 when the war was lost and there was mounting domestic opposition to the high number of casualties.

1974 President Richard Nixon, who was elected in 1969, was forced to resign over the Watergate scandal involving a break-in at Democrat headquarters; tape recordings made in the White House showed he had sanctioned the burglary and subsequent cover-up.

1970s and 1980s was a period of great technological advancement and declining industrialisation when US corporations became worldwide leaders and US brands in computers, fast-food and entertainment became global brands. The collapse of the Soviet Union by 1991 left the US as the world's sole superpower.

1979 Iranian students attacked the US embassy in Tehran and held 63 hostages for 444 days. A failed military rescue mission in 1980 damaged the chances of incumbent Jimmy Carter winning the 1980 presidential election.

1980 Ronald Reagan became president. As a conservative popularist his policies were based on reducing federal services and tax cuts, particularly for high income earners, later dubbed Reagonomics.

1989 US troops invaded Panama to oust General Manuel Noriega from power.

1991 In the first Gulf War, a US-led coalition forced Iraq to withdraw from Kuwait.

1992 The Democratic candidate Bill Clinton defeated the Republican incumbent, George Bush, in the presidential election.

1995 A bomb in Oklahoma killed over 160 people; it was the worst case involving domestic terrorists in US history.

1996 Clinton was re-elected as president.

1999 The US led a NATO military campaign against Yugoslavia in response to Serbian violence towards ethnic Albanians in the Kosovo region.

2000 George W Bush was elected president but only after controversial vote counting was declared valid by Florida's Supreme Court.

2001 On 11 September, two passenger jets were flown into the twin towers of the World Trade Centre in New York, demolishing both towers. A third jet was crashed into the Pentagon in Washington. In all, 3,025 people died in the attacks. President Bush declared a 'war on terrorism'. The US launched military action in Afghanistan against the Taliban and Osama bin Laden's al Qaeda group, blamed for being behind the terrorist attacks of 11 September. The giant energy provider Enron declared bankruptcy when massive accountancy frauds were discovered.

2002 Bush described Iran, Iraq and North Korea as part of an 'axis of evil'. A multi-billion dollar accounting fraud in WorldCom was the biggest failure in US business history. The Department of Homeland Security was formed with a remit to protect the US against terrorist attacks. The US deployed troops to Kuwait after UN weapons inspectors failed to find sufficient evidence that Iraq had destroyed its alleged weapons of mass destruction.

2003 The space shuttle Columbia broke-up on re-entry killing its crew of seven astronauts. A US-led coalition

invaded Iraq. Within two months President Bush declared that 'major combat operations in Iraq have ended'.
2004 The US restored diplomatic relations with Libya after a break of 24 years. Former president, Ronald Reagan died. A Senate report declared the war on Iraq was based on 'flawed' information. Institutional failings in intelligence agencies and the government were held to be responsible for the failure to prevent the 11 September 2001 attack. George W Bush was re-elected president.
2005 New Orleans was destroyed by hurricane Katrina; hundreds of people died and thousands made homeless. A federal judge ruled that it was 'unconstitutional to teach Intelligent Design as an alternative to evolution in a public school science classroom'.
2006 Millions of people protested at proposed sanctions aimed at criminalising illegal immigration. The Supreme Court ruled that it would be unconstitutional for Guantanamo Bay prisoners to be tried by military tribunals. The Democratic Party won control of both houses of parliament, in what was seen as a vote against the limited successes in the Iraq war. Former president Gerald Ford died. The US trade deficit set a fifth consecutive year record high of US$763.6 billion, of which US$232.5 billion was with China alone.
2007 President Bush dispatched a further 20,000 troops to Iraq, specifically to police Baghdad and congress approved more funding for the campaign. The collapse of the sub-prime loans market had a knock-on effect on all major US banks with total losses estimated at US$500 billion. A credit squeeze began and spread abroad.
2008 The annualised inflation rate in June was 5 per cent higher when compared with a year earlier. The Senate approved the appointment of General David Petraeus as head of US Central Command on 10 July, with responsibility for US operations in Iraq and Afghanistan. In primary presidential elections John McCain became the Republican Party's nomination and after a long campaign, Barack Obama became the Democratic Party's candidate, beating Hillary Clinton. In July the government was forced to extend lines of credit for Fanny Mae and Freddy Mac (institutions mandated by the US Congress to provide funding to the housing market), to meet their financial obligations.

Political structure

Constitution
The constitution of 17 September 1787 came into effect on 4 March 1789. The constitution strictly separates powers between the executive (presidential administration), legislature (Congress – Senate and House of Representatives) and judiciary (Supreme Court).

Form of state
Federal presidential democratic republic

The executive
The president, elected for a maximum of two terms of four years by an electoral college of representatives elected from each state, wields executive power. The president is both the chief of state and head of government.

National legislature
Legislative power is vested in a bicameral Congress consisting of a 435-member House of Representatives, elected for a two-year term, and a 100-member Senate, one-third of whose members are elected every two years.

Legal system
The legal system is based on English common law. There are judicial reviews of legislative acts. The US accepts compulsory International Court of Jurisdiction (ICJ) authority, although only with reservations. The nine justices of the Supreme Court are appointed for life by the president, with confirmation by the Senate.

Last elections
2 November 2004 (presidential); 7 November 2006 (legislative).

Results: Presidential: George W Bush (Republican) won 50.89 per cent of the vote (286 electoral votes); and John Kerry (Democrat) 48 per cent (252 electoral votes).
House of Representatives: Democratic Party won 52.0 per cent of the vote (233 seats out of 435); Republican Party won 45.6 per cent (202 seats).
Senate (33 seats out of 100): Democratic Party 53.8 per cent of the vote (22 seats); Republican Party 42.4 per cent (nine seats); and independents (two seats). (Full senate: Democratic Party 49 seats; Republican Party 49 seats; independents two seats.)

Next elections
November 2008 (presidential and legislative).

Political parties

Ruling party
Republican Party

Main opposition party
Democratic Party

Population
301.97 million (2007)*

Last census: April 2000: 281,421,906

Population density: 31 inhabitants per square km. Urban population: 77 per cent.

Annual growth rate: 1.0 per cent 1994–2004 (WHO 2006)

Ethnic make-up
The US has the fourth-largest population in the world and contains a varied social and ethnic mix.
The US is not following the trend of an ageing population as seen in many OECD countries. All categories of ages show an increase, except the 5–13 years old, which declined by 380,000 in 2003–04. This growth in population indicates a high rate of immigration rather than a fertility rate no greater than 2.0 per cent. Approximately 22 per cent of the population is under 14 years of age. Some 20 per cent of the total population claim British ancestry, 20 per cent German and 18 per cent Irish ancestry.
In January 2003, the Census Bureau announced that Hispanics (Latinos) (13 per cent of the population) had overtaken blacks (12 per cent) as the largest minority group. In July it also reported that the legal Latino population grew by 4.6 million people between 2000–03, accounting for half the nation's total population growth during the period. The Asian population is also growing (around 4 per cent). Native Americans and native Alaskans combined are less than 1 per cent of the population.

Religions
There are some 90 religious organisations in the US with over 50,000 members each. There are approximately 86 million Protestants, 58 million Catholics, six million Jews and over six million members of other faiths. The total number of members of religious groups is estimated to be about 156 million. In the southern United States, the 'bible belt' stretches from California to Florida where the Baptist Church and Evangelism is strong. Numerous protestant sects can be found, each with their own unique outlook.

Education
Under a federal system, each state sets its own educational cycles; each year is a grade, from 1–12. Whichever cycle is adopted it incorporates 12 years. Education is mainly funded at local and state levels with policy set by the local school boards and state education authorities. Some federal funding is available to meet special needs. Schooling is generally compulsory from the age of six (states vary) to 16 years. Pupils at elementary and high schools (up to age 18) generally pay no tuition fees; further education establishments in general charge tuition fees. There is no state assistance for either tuition or living expenses for most university and undergratuate students, although loans are available. Some grant assistance is provided for students from low income and disadvantaged categories and scholarships are available on a competitive and special category basis.

High school graduates who decide to continue their education may enter a technical or vocational institution, a two-year college, or a four-year college or university.
The latest census reports that there are over 32 million elementary school children and over 15 million in high school; combined the projected number is expected to exceed 53 million, a figure not reached since the baby boomers swelled numbers in the early 1960s. The majority of high school students go on to college. Altogether, the system caters for over 72 million individuals in education.
Educational expenditure is typically around 7 per cent of the annual GDP. Elementary and secondary schools spent about 60 per cent of this total, and colleges and universities accounted for the remaining 40 per cent.
Compulsory years: 6 to 16
Enrolment rate: 101 per cent gross primary enrolment; 95.5 per cent gross secondary enrolment, of relevant age groups (including repeaters). (Unicef 2004).
Pupils per teacher: 16 in primary schools.

Health

Per capita total expenditure on health (2003) was US$5,711; of which per capita government spending was US$2,548, at the international dollar rate, (WHO 2006). Prepaid plans account for 64 per cent of private spending on health.
Healthcare is largely a private-sector concern. Exceptions include the extensive Medicare programme for the elderly and the lesser Medicaid programme for those on welfare. Some emergency hospital treatment is free of charge for the poor.
Health expenditure of 13 per cent of GDP is greater than the Organisation of Economic Co-operation and Development (OECD) average of 8 per cent.
Most people have private health insurance, either as a job benefit or paid for by themselves and is becoming a major financial burden, both for individuals and for the companies who pay for employee health schemes. The premiums for family coverage is over US$9,000 per annum; and for those in worker's health schemes, an employee's share averaged US$2,084, for family cover. The number of Americans without health insurance in 2004 rose for the fourth year in succession, to 45.8 million, some 15.7 per cent of the population, according to the Census Bureau.
The rise in health insurance costs (double digits for three consecutive years from 2000) has left employers with a growing insurance premium, which in turn has led many to pass on these costs directly to employees, or closing down their schemes entirely. This loss has prompted an alliance, which may have political ramifications, as companies and workers align themselves to challenge the power of the 'medical industrial complex' of private insurance companies, the pharmaceutical industry and the large private hospitals.
In May 2004 a report on obesity ranked US citizens the most obese in the developed world, with 31 per cent of adults grossly fat and of the rest, two out of three are merely overweight. Obesity rates have doubled in number since 1980.

HIV/Aids

HIV prevalence: 0.6 per cent aged 15–49 in 2003 (World Bank)
Life expectancy: 78 years, 2004 (WHO 2006)
Fertility rate/Maternal mortality rate: 2.0 births per woman, 2004 (WHO 2006)
Child (under 5 years) mortality rate (per 1,000): 7.0 per 1,000 live births; 1 per cent of children aged under five are malnourished (World Bank).

Welfare

Income security programmes are in general a mixture of federal and state funding and vary from state to state. The major programmes are unemployment compensation, housing subsidies for low income families and individuals, food stamps, child nutrition, payments to the disabled and family support payments. While states provide some limited form of income security, federal government policy concentrates on encouraging recipients back to work. In addition, the federal government makes social security payments to one in six Americans, either aged or disabled.

Pensions

Medicare trustees, in 2004, reported that the finance for the programme, set up to pay retirees, was deeply underfunded. Retirement payments are made from current revenue and the US$72 billion obligation (inluding the social security pension), to expected numbers of retirees, will outstrip assets and budgets by 2014, leaving the government to either make up the shortfall with tax increases or cut the pension benefits.
A trend by private companies to convert defined benefit and final salary schemes into defined contribution schemes (with uncertain benefits) has increased, with 75 per cent conversion in two decades, and US underfunding of defined benefit schemes estimated at US$278.6 billion. One of the largest providers of a defined benefit pension – United Airlines – has proposed transfering assets to the Pensions Benefit Guaranty Corporation (PBGC), a federal insurer, and divesting itself of a costly legacy. Worry has been expressed that if this and other businesses do likewise it could bankrupt the PBGC and require a government bail out costing tens of billions of dollars.

Main cities

Washington (capital, estimated population 558,891 in 2005), New York (8.2 million (m)), Los Angeles (3.9m), Chicago (2.9m), Houston (2.0m), Philadelphia (1.5m), Phoenix (1.4m), San Diego (1.3m), San Antonio (1.2m), Dallas (1.2m).

Languages spoken

There is no official language declared in the constitution. English is the de facto working language and Spanish is the second, widely spoken, unofficial language.

Official language/s

There is no official language declared in the constitution. English is the de facto working language and Spanish is the second, widely spoken, unofficial language.

Media

The Constitution guarantees both press and broadcasters freedom of speech, subject to the laws of libel and slander, although even in the latter cases, there are well established public interest defences to these charges.
The law that prevents dual ownership of broadcast and print media outlets was scrapped by the Federal Communications Commission (www.fcc.gov) in December 2007. Media entities will now be able to own both TV channels and newspapers in 20 US cities, but only if there are already eight independently owned media businesses existing in the market concerned, and any TV channel to be purchased is not one of the top four rated stations.

Press

Dailies: There are over 1,500 daily newspapers, published in either the morning or evening and mostly serving a city, state or region. The majority of newspapers are published in English, while some serve ethnic communities and are published in other languages. The main national dailies include USA Today (www.usatoday.com), New York Times (www.nytimes.com), Washington Post (www.washingtonpost.com), Los Angeles Times (www.latimes.com), Christian Science Monitor (www.csmonitor.com), Boston Globe (www.boston.com), distributed nationally in main centres. Other major publications include the Philadelphia Enquirer (www.philly.com), Baltimore Sun (www.baltimoresun.com), Chicago Sun-Times (www.suntimes.com), San Francisco Chronicle (www.sfgate.com), Detroit Free Press (www.freep.com), Chicago Tribune(www.chicagotribune.com), Atlanta Journal (www.ajc.com) and Houston Chronicle (www.chron.com).

Tabloid daily newspapers include Daily News (www.nydailynews.com) and the New York Post (www.nypost.com).
Weeklies: There are around 8,000 national magazines, mostly published in English and widely read including Time (www.time.com), Newsweek (www.newsweek.com) and US News & World Report (www.usnews.com). The Nation (www.thenation.com), is an independent political magazine. Condé Nast (www.condenast.com) publishes over 30 speciality magazines targeting women, men, young and old and special interest groups.
Business: The Wall Street Journal (http://online.wsj.com), the premier financial and business daily, is published in four regional editions. Major business magazines include BarronsWeekly, publicated by the Wall Street Journal Business Week (www.businessweek.com), Forbes (www.forbes.com) and Fortune (http://money.cnn.com with a link to Fortune). Others business news is carried by Market Watch (www.marketwatch.com), Investor's Business Daily (www.investorsbusinessdaily.com) and Washington Business Journal (http://washington.bizjournals.com). Business magazines which target ethnic groups include black entrepreneurs, Black Enterprise (www.blackenterprise.com), Minority Business Entrepreneur (www.mbemag.com) and Hispanic groups, Enterprise (http://hol.hispaniconline.com).
Periodicals: The Harvard Political Review (http://hprsite.squarespace.com) is an independent political magazines published four times a year. The New Yorker (www.newyorker.com) is an influential literary monthly magazine.

Broadcasting

Radio: Virtually all US households have a radio and there are several national networks with numerous local stations offering a variety of programmes to cater for all tastes. Clear Channel (www.clearchannel.com) is the largest commercial network with over 1,200 stations. CBS Radio (www.cbsradio.com) and ABC Radio Network (http://abcradionetworks.com) provide premium quality radio programmes to its own stations and affiliates (privately-owned stations that broadcast programmes made by others).
Regional networks include Keystone Broadcasting (www.keystonebroadcasting.com), Sheridan Broadcasting Network (SBN), which operates the American Urban Radio Networks (www.aurnol.com), of radio stations and affiliates targeting black American audiences and the non-commercial National Public Radio (www.npr.org), which has member stations broadcasting news, talk and cultural shows. In Spanish, the Hispanic radio network (http://especiales.univision.com), broadcasts in major cities nationwide.
External radio services are provided in over 40 languages to all parts of the world by the Voice of America radio network (www.voanews.com).
Television: Virtually all US households have a television set and 60 per cent have cable TV.
With the rapid growth in new technology in digital and satellite broadcasting the dominance of the four major commercial TV broadcasting networks has decreased. New mediums have allowed a wider variety of programmes to be seen at times dictated by the audience and caused steep erosion in viewer numbers for the traditional broadcast stations. Cable TV services include Fox Entertainment Group (www.fox.com), CNN 24-hour news (www.cnn.com) by Turner Broadcasting, MTV (www.mtv.com) broadcasting music and programmes for the young and the pay-TV HBO (www.hbo.com). In the large cities, cable viewers may have 50 or more channels to choose from, allowing advertisers to target their audience. Since viewer ratings determine success all networks compete fiercely with each other for viewers and advertising revenue. The four major networks are Columbia Broadcasting System (CBS) (www.cbs.com), National Broadcasting Corporation (NBC) (www.nbc.com), Capital Cities/ABC (ABC) (http://abc.go.com) and Fox. The a national public broadcasting network PBS (www.npr.org), supported by donations from the government and 'pledges' from viewers.
Business television channels include CNBC (www.cnbc.com), Bloomburg (www.bloomberg.com) and, in October 2007, a newly opened Fox Business Network (www.foxbusiness.com), which was launched to challenge CNBC.
Most broadcasting is in English, but there are also TV and radio stations serving local ethnic communities in their own languages. The Hispanic community is relatively well served in Florida, California and New York City.
Worldwide US government services are provided by VOA, International Broadcasting Bureau (http://ibb7-2.ibb.gov).

Advertising

The US is the world leader in mass advertising, utilising all forms of media. Television advertising, the primary medium, is highly competitive with huge budgets and professional presentations. Advertising requirements for high ratings can terminate TV shows regardless of their worth and advertisers may influence policy in other media outlets.

Economy

The US economy is the largest in the world and drives global growth. A World Bank report published in December 2007 stated that almost 50 per cent of the World's total GDP was produced between the US, China, Japan, Germany and India.
However, it took a battering in 2005–06 due to several severe hurricanes, high energy prices and a monetary squeeze. The current account deficit reached an all-time high of US$902 billion (third quarter 2006) or 6.1 per cent of nominal GDP (2006).
Americans are the world's greatest spenders and keep the global economy buoyant, they are also the worst of any G7 country at saving, with gross national saving (GNS) at 13.4 per cent of GDP, which is four percentage points less than the average G7 and 13 percentage points less than Japan's GNS.
Productivity was strong in 2005/06 giving positive tax revenues but high fuel bills and a cooling housing market was seen as a factor limiting GDP growth.
The unemployment rate has fallen from a high of 6.1 per cent in 2004 to 3.4 per cent in 2005 and 4.6 per cent in 2006.
The US economy is dominated by its service industries, which generate over half its GDP; financial institutions are the largest single industry contributor. IT, arts and entertainment products, incorporating intellectual property, are an important component of exports. Manufacturing accounts for less than 25 per cent of GDP, with exports consisting of machinery, such as transport, aerospace and defence equipment and electrical goods as well as chemicals and food.
The IMF has underlined the critical role that the US plays in globalisation and calls on the administration to challenge the calls for protectionist measures. The benefits to all economies, including the US, of a free trade global economy could be threatened if the US begins a period of isolation and insulation.
In the first quarter of 2007 the US sub-prime mortgage market began to collapse as banks began to write-off billions of dollars as high risk groups with poor credit ratings who were given housing loans defaulted. As the crisis grew the international repercussions included many central banks world-wide providing emergency funds for troubled financial institutions with holdings in the US mortgage market. Major banks lost billions of dollars as interest rates rose and they began to restrict lending in a credit crunch that rapidly spread.

External trade
The USA is a member of the North American Free Trade Agreement (Nafta) since it became operational in 1994, under which it has tri-lateral trade agreements with Canada and Mexico. Nafta has FTAs with a number of regional trading blocs.
Around 30 per cent of all exports are achieved through Nafta.
The US is the leading global exporter of a number of products including wheat and corn, liquefied natural gas, aluminium, sulphur, phosphates, salt and is the third largest exporter of rice. It is reliant on imported hydrocarbons, but is the world's largest producer of electricity. It has a full range of manufacturing industries, which provides around 20 per cent of GDP, from hi-tech semiconductors and telecommunications to automotive and aerospace assembly fabrication, from pharmaceutical and petrochemical production to metal processing, mineral extraction and foodstuff production including cheese, soya beans and tobacco. The service sector, including financial services, is an important source of foreign earnings with the New York Stock Exchange on par with the London Stock Exchange as the global leaders, has grown in importance and in 2006 provided over 75 per cent of GDP.

Imports
Principal imports are consumer goods (over 30 per cent of total), oil and natural gas, industrial supplies, agricultural products, capital goods, (over 30 per cent), computers, telecommunications equipment, vehicles and parts, office machines and electric generating and distribution machinery.
Main sources: Canada (16.4 per cent total, 2006), China (15.5 per cent), Mexico (10.7 per cent).

Exports
Main exports are telecommunications and computers equipment (around 50 per cent of total), agricultural products (wheat, corn, rice soya beans, tobacco), industrial materials (aluminium, pig iron, ferroalloys), manufactured goods, vehicles, aircrafts, banking and financial service.
Main destinations: Canada (22.2 per cent total, 2006), Mexico (12.9 per cent), Japan (5.8 per cent).

Agriculture
Farming
Agriculture accounts for just 2 per cent of total GDP and employs approximately 3 per cent of the country's workforce. However, despite its relatively small contribution to total US GDP, the agricultural sector continues to account for half of the world's corn production and over 20 per cent of world grain output. The US is the world's largest agricultural exporter and exports account for about 25 per cent of farmers' receipts.
Capital-intensive farming techniques produce dairy products, potatoes, fruit, vegetables and poultry for urban markets in the north-eastern states; wheat, barley, maize, oats, soya beans, fodder crops, pigs and cattle in the mid-west and central plains; cotton, tobacco, peanuts, citrus fruits, rice and sugar cane in the south; cattle and sheep in the central and western states; apples, berries and nuts in the Pacific north-west; and vines, apples, citrus fruits, peaches, tomatoes, olives, cotton and rice in California.
In October 2007, subsidies for cotton growers were declared illegal by the WTO, following an official complaint by Brazil that such payments constituted unfair trade. Brazil reserved the right to impose sanctions against the US, which could amount to US$4 billion.
The estimated crop production ('000) for 2005 included: 364,020 tonnes (t) cereals in total, 57,106t wheat, 280,228t maize, 19,111t potatoes, 10,102t rice, 25,804t sugar cane, 24,724t sugar beets, 82,820t soya beans, 2,097t pulses, 9,848t sorghum, 10,317t citrus fruit, 4,254t apples, 6,415t grapes, 12,766t tomatoes, 17,945t oilcrops, 290t tobacco, 12,574t seed cotton, 5,042t cotton lint, 1,296t treenuts, 25,873t fruit in total, 39,185t vegetables in total. Livestock production ('000) included: 39,556t meat in total, 11,310t beef, 9,401t pig meat, 86t sheep, 18, 538t poultry, 5,329t eggs, 80,150t milk, 82t honey, 1,046t cattle hides, 8t sheepskins, 18t greasy wool.

Fishing
The fishing industry is well established in the United States and the sector is highly developed on both the Pacific and Atlantic coasts.
Total seafood exports typically amount to over US$3 billion, mainly comprising ground fish (38 per cent), salmon (18 per cent), herring, lobster, shrimps, squid and crab. The top US export markets include Japan (37 per cent), Canada (21 per cent) and the EU (18 per cent). Shrimps account for approximately 36 per cent of total fish and seafood imports.
In 2004, the total marine fish catch was 3,521,398 tonnes and the total crustacean catch was 335,409 tonnes.

Forestry
One third of the total land area – 225.9 million hectares (ha) – of the Unites States is covered in forested land. Forests and other wooded areas are mainly concentrated in the east and west of the central plain.
The major part of the forest is classed as semi-natural, with less than a tenth remaining undisturbed, located mainly in Alaska and the west. About nine-tenths of the forest is available for wood supply.
The government owns nearly two fifths of forest and other wooded land, while the remainder is shared among private individuals and institutions, forest industries and some by indigenous peoples.
Forestry is widespread and about half domestic timber needs are met by Oregon and Washington states, with the south-east producing increasing quantities of softwood for pulp. About 30 per cent of global industrial roundwood comes from the US. The US produces and consumes large quantities of sawn timber, wood-based panels and paper. It is also the largest importer and the second-largest exporter, of forest products.
Exports of forest material in 2004 amounted to US$31.3 billion, while imports amounted US$15.7 billion.
Timber production ('000) in 2004 included 458,310 cubic metre (cum) roundwood, 414,702cum industrial roundwood, 87,436cum sawnwood, 234,673cum sawlogs and veneer logs, 171,024cum pulpwood, 44,262cum wood-based panels, 43,608cum woodfuel; 930 tonnes (t) charcoal, 83,612t paper and paperboard (including 5,097t newsprint), 21,126t printing and writing paper, 53,646t paper pulp, 43,102t recovered paper.

Industry and manufacturing
The industrial sector remains a relatively significant contributor to the US economy. The sector employs over 20 per cent of the total workforce and contributes approximately 22 per cent to total GDP. The manufacturing sector has declined in significance over recent years as the services sectors have expanded.
There has been a shift in the manufacturing sector away from 'smokestack' industries, such as cars, primary metals and heavy machinery, towards high-technology industries, such as aerospace, communications equipment, electronic components and computers. Food, printing and publishing and textiles and clothing are also important.

Tourism
The tourism industry accounts for over 10 per cent of total US GDP. Approximately 12 per cent of the country's total employment is accounted for by the sector.
Florida, California and New York are the top three destinations for international travellers to the US. Of all visitors flying to the US, about 40 per cent arrive through either Miami International, Los Angeles or New York JFK.
The Trade Industry Association of America (TIA) has lobbied the US government to minimise the disruption stricter security measures (put in place as a result of the

9/11attacks) have on international tourists to America.

Environment
The US is not a signatory to the Kyoto Protocol.

Mining
The mining sector contributes approximately 4 per cent to total US GDP and employs approximately 4 per cent of the total US workforce.
While there are economically exploitable reserves of virtually every mineral within the US, these are insufficient to meet the needs of the economy in almost all circumstances. The country is 100 per cent dependent on imports for its consumption of bauxite, graphite and manganese among others. Mineral resources include ores of iron, copper (about 13 per cent of worldwide production), lead (17 per cent of worldwide production), gold (15 per cent), silver (12 per cent) and nickel.
The US accounts for approximately 17 per cent of worldwide aluminium production.

Hydrocarbons
Total proven oil reserves currently stand at 29.4 billion barrels (end-2007). Some 80 per cent of proven reserves located in just four states: Texas, Louisiana, Alaska and California.
Oil production amounts to 6.9 million barrels per day (bpd), the vast majority of which was crude oil. US oil production has fallen sharply since the mid-1980s due to a decline in oil prices. In the period 2000–02, oil production was at a 50-year low. However, production has increased as more deepwater oil wells in the Gulf of Mexico and onshore oil fields in Alaska have come on-stream. Oil production suffered considerably following Hurricane Katrina and other severe storms in the Gulf of Mexico during the summer and autumn months of 2005. Several refineries as well as oil platforms were damaged.
The US has estimated proven natural gas reserves of 5.9 trillion cubic metres (end-2007). Gas production was 545.9 billion cubic metres while consumption was 652.9 billion cubic metres. Net imports amount to approximately 99 billion cubic metres. The vast majority of natural gas imports come from Canada, approximately 94 per cent of total gas imports.
US coal reserves account for over a quarter of the world's total reserves (28.6 per cent), estimated at 243 billion tonnes. The US produces 587.2 million tonnes of oil equivalent (end 2007). The states with the largest coal production include Wyoming, West Virginia and Kentucky. More than 90 per cent of US coal output is consumed by the electricity sector. There is a trend towards consumption of coal with lower sulphur content in order to meet environmental targets for sulphur dioxide emissions.

Energy
Total annual electricity generation is typically around 4,000 billion KW.
Coal-fired power stations account for approximately 50 per cent of generation, nuclear 21 per cent, gas 16 per cent, hydroelectricity 7 per cent, oil 2 per cent and other sources 1 per cent. In 2007 the US consumed 192.1 million tonnes of oil equivalent in nuclear energy.
US power demand is increasing rapidly, with the government forecasting 1.8 per cent average annual growth in electricity sales between 2000–20. This increase will require a significant addition in generating capacity and the government forecasts that 1,300 new power plants will be needed between 2002 and 2020.
Privately owned local monopolies regulated by state public utility commissions account for 80 per cent of electricity sales.
Coal inputs for electricity generation have risen and are expected to continue to grow, as are those of natural gas.

Financial markets
Stock exchange
The New York Stock Exchange (NYSE), the largest equities marketplace in the world, is home to some 2,800 companies valued at about US$15 trillion in market capitalisation. The Chicago Board of Trade is the largest of 11 commodity and financial futures exchanges. The National Association of Securities Dealers Automated Quotation System (Nasdaq) is a computer-based over-the-counter market in securities.

Banking and insurance
The banking and financial services industry in the US is noted for its complicated regulations, which are overseen by numerous federal and state authorities with overlapping jurisdictions.
Regulatory agencies include the Federal Reserve, the Federal Deposit Insurance Corporation (FDIC), the Securities and Exchange Commission, the Comptroller of the Currency, the Department of Justice and state bank departments. Depositors in banks or savings and loan associations which are members of the FDIC or Federal Savings and Loan Insurance Corporation have their deposits guaranteed to a limit of US$100,000 by the government's system of deposit insurance.

Central bank
Federal Reserve System

Time
There are six time zones
Eastern Standard Time – GMT minus five hours (daylight saving, minus four hours)
Central Standard Time – GMT minus six hours (daylight saving, minus five hours)
Mountain Standard Time – GMT minus seven hours (daylight saving, minus six hours)
Pacific Standard Time – GMT minus eight hours (daylight saving, minus seven hours)
Alaska Time – GMT minus eight hours (no daylight saving)
Hawaii Time – GMT minus 10 hours (no daylight saving)
Daylight saving from March (from 2007, previously daylight saving started in April) to November

Geography
The US is about half the size of Russia and covers a total area of about nine million square km. It stretches from the North Atlantic Ocean to the North Pacific Ocean.
The US has borders with Canada (8,893km) (including 2,477km Alaska/Canada), Cuba 29km (US Naval Base at Guantanamo Bay) and Mexico (3,326km).
The western part of the country is dominated by the two major mountain ranges, the Rockies and Sierras. In the eastern US, the lower Appalachian and Allegheny mountains provide the western boundary to the coastal plain. The lowest point is Death Valley, -86 metres; the highest point is Mount McKinley, 6,194 metres.
The central part of the country, the mid-west, is a vast plain, much of it flat and featureless; this is the breadbasket of the US.
Alaska has mountains and broad river valleys. Hawaii is rugged and volcanic.
The Everglades in southern Florida comprise the world's largest marsh at 5,659 square kilometres (2,185 square miles), however, it only averages a depth of 150mm.

Hemisphere
Northern

Climate
The size of the land area and the natural mountain barriers give a wide range of climates. It is tropical in Hawaii and Florida, arctic in Alaska, semi-arid in the great plains west of the Mississippi River and arid in the Great Basin of the south-west. California (especially the south) has a Mediterranean-style climate with mild winters and hot summers. The south and Gulf of Mexico areas have a semi-tropical climate. The east coast and the mid-west are invariably very cold in winter and very hot in summer. Snow can be heavy at times, but most cities are equipped for swift snow removal from major streets and the transportation system can cope fairly well in poor weather. Most buildings, cars and public transport are well heated or air-conditioned, according to the season.

Dress codes
There are no overriding dress codes. In the Wall Street financial district of New York and other financial centres, business suits are de rigueur, while on the west coast, senior executives might wear anything from suits or sports jackets and trousers to jeans and T-shirts. The more normal business attire would be a business suit, shirt and tie. Despite the reputation US businessmen have for flashy dressing, formal colours are more acceptable, with dark suits, dark socks and sombre ties being the most acceptable form.

Entry requirements
Passports
Required by all.
Extensive information can be gained through http://travel.state.gov.
The US has introduced machine-readable passport (MRP) technology to enhance security measures, screening visitors into and out of the US.
Visitors who do not possess MRP passports are required to apply for a visa for entry.
For Canadian citizens only, under the Nexus programme entry may be achieved using a Nexus photo-identification card.
All arrivals, including US citizens, travelling between Canada, Mexico, Central and South America, the Caribbean and Bermuda through land borders or by sea (including ferries) must have a passport or other biometric, secure documentation as proof of identity since, 23 January 2008.
Visa
Extensive information can be gained through http://travel.state.gov.
Visas are required by all, with some exceptions under the Visa Waiver Program (VWP). This reciprocal programme allows citizens of, among others, most of the EU, Australasia and Japan entry without a visa if they possess a machine readable passport (MRP) and have a return/onward ticket, entry for business and tourist visits up to 90 days.
All citizens of visa-free countries who do not have a MRP must apply for a visa. All other visitors must apply for a visa.
Currency advice/regulations
The import and export of local and foreign currencies is allowed. Amounts over US$10,000 (or foreign equivalent) must be declared.
Gold coins, medals and bullion may be imported unless originating from embargoed countries.
Travellers cheques, in US dollars, are widely accepted.
Customs
Personal items are duty-free. National alcohol allowances may be in excess of state allowances and may result in excess amount being taxed or confiscated.
Certain firearms and ammunition are allowed with a customs permit, obtained in advance.
Prohibited imports
Illegal drugs (personal medication requires a doctor's certificate); soil, plant and animal products (including endangered species); meat, poultry (fresh, dried or canned) and live fish (unless certified disease-free), their eggs (unless canned, pickled or smoked); Cuban cigars (purchased in any country); wildlife and endangered species (including hunting trophies, shells and crafted items); fireworks and hazardous material; some South American pre-Columbian artefacts; merchandise from embargoed countries and counterfeit items.
These prohibitions apply to transit passengers.

Health (for visitors)
Mandatory precautions
No vaccination certificates are required, however, visitors from countries where cholera or yellow fever is rife, or where an outbreak of infectious disease occurred within six months of arrival, will require vaccination certificates.
Advisable precautions
There are no major health hazards for visitors, and no inoculations or vaccinations are necessary.
All personal medicines must have a physician's certificate declaring their prescribed use. As health costs can be extremely high medical insurance, including emergency evacuation, is necessary.

Hotels
Major hotels have toll-free telephone numbers (with an 800 area code) for reservations. Unless a deposit has been paid, a hotel room will often not be held after 1700/1800, even when the hotel is notified of late arrival. Check-out times vary from 1000–1300 and short extensions can be arranged. Visitors may be charged for overstaying check-out time without making arrangements. Most good hotels have restaurant facilities, bars, free parking and swimming pools. Many hotels provide courtesy transport or an airport bus service.
Road-side motels are numerous and relatively inexpensive.

Credit cards
Major credit and charge cards are widely accepted. A credit card is essential for car hire and usually necessary for hotel bookings.

Public holidays (national)
Fixed dates
1 Jan (New Year's Day), 4 Jul (Independence Day), 11 Nov (Veterans' Day), 25 Dec (Christmas Day).
Any holiday falling on Saturday is taken on Friday before; holidays falling on a Sunday are taken on Monday following.
Variable dates
Martin Luther King's Birthday (third Mon in Jan), Washington's Birthday (third Mon in Feb), Memorial Day (last Mon in May), Labour Day (first Mon in Sep), Columbus Day (second Mon in Oct), Thanksgiving Day (fourth Thu in Nov).
Statutory and public holidays are fixed by state legislation and vary considerably between states.

Working hours
Most offices remain closed on the Friday following Thanksgiving. Working hours vary considerably depending on the industry.
Banking
0900–1500 (Mon-Fri).
Business
0900–1700 (Mon-Fri).
Government
0830–1730 (Mon-Fri).
Shops
0930–1800 (Mon-Fri); 1200–1700 (Sun).

Telecommunications
Courier services
Mobile/cell phones
GSM 850 and 1900 services are available throughout most of the country.

Electricity supply
110–120V AC, 60 cycles single phase, with flat two-point plug fittings.

Weights and measures
Units of measurement used in the US are in general the same as the imperial system. Short ton = hundredweight = 45.4 kilograms, one pound = 0.45 kilogram; one gallon = 3.79 litres, one pint = 0.47 litre. Conversion to metric system is taking place very slowly and on a voluntary basis, with the US Metric Board co-ordinating the process.

Social customs/useful tips
People are likely to use first names in discussions with you. They are also likely to refer to someone else by their surname only. Neither of these usages is considered impolite.
The main cultural role model in the US is that of the pioneer, the isolated man or woman battling against the odds, the story of someone rising from a deprived background to become rich and/or famous. This has led to an admiration for hard work, free enterprise and determination. Gun ownership by civilians is considered, by many, to be a part of American heritage.

Security
The US has a reputation for crime and violence. New York, Baltimore, Chicago, Detroit, Washington and Los Angeles

have a high rate of robbery. Washington, Detroit, Baltimore, Dallas, Houston, Philadelphia, Atlanta and Los Angeles have high murder rates.
However, much of the trouble is concentrated in parts of each city and avoiding these neighbourhoods will considerably reduce any risk. Elementary precautions should prevent visitors having too much trouble. Avoid walking in deserted streets, and try to walk on the street-side rather than next to buildings. Always be aware of the kind of neighbourhood it is. At night, except in lively and well-lit areas, call a taxi to collect you rather than walking to look for a one.
Although the risk of being mugged is often exaggerated (and crime figures have been falling since the mid-1990s), it is recommended not to resist a robbery attempt. Keep your valuables (especially expensive jewellery) out of sight.

Getting there

Air

International airport/s: The US is accessible by air from all continents and a vast number of countries. Some of the busiest international airports are La Guardia (LGA) (New York), Los Angeles (LAX), Miami International Airport (MIA), O'Hare International Airport (ORD), Hartsfield-Jackson Atlanta Airport (ATL); other important international airports include those in Boston (Logan Airport), Dallas-Fort Worth, Philadelphia, Houston, San Francisco, Washington Dulles International and John F Kennedy Airport (Newark).
Airport tax: Departure taxes are included in the price of a ticket, although local airport departure tax may be charged if the ticket was purchased outside the US.
There is a national programme that allows airports to impose a passenger facility charge of up to US$4.5.

Surface

Road: The US has land borders with Mexico in the south and Canada in the north and there are plenty of efficient overland border crossings between the US and these countries. Border crossings are strictly controlled.
Rail: There are limited passenger services from Mexico, crossing the border at either Yuma, El Paso or Del Rio. Rail links from Canada include Vancouver–Seattle, Toronto–Chicago and Montréal–New York, although these are not all direct and without layovers. Some rail lines run up to the border with Canada, in Michigan
Water: The US has numerous sea and inland water ports and is well served by the international shipping lines.

Getting about

National transport

Inter-state transport can be variable, however the US is generally perceived to have one of the most advanced transport structures in the world, including metro systems in most major cities and sufficient national bus networks. Transport by ferries and helicopters is also widely available. Nevertheless, the easiest and quickest method of crossing great distances in the US is by air.
Air: A highly developed network of airline services connects most towns of importance. Fare systems have been deregulated, leading to sharp competition.
Road: There is a comprehensive network of highways (interstate) that bisect the counrty from the east to west coast and from the borders with Canada through to Mexico. During the winter even the interstates can be closed or slowed by snow. There is an extensive secondary road system.
Buses: A wide network of air-conditioned long-distance buses link all major cities, but smaller cities and rural areas are generally not well served by public transport. Greyhound is the main bus system in the US and plays an important transport role in most parts of the country.
Rail: Around 245,000km of grade one railroad links approximately 500 stations. Most long-distance trains are air-conditioned and equipped with dining and sleeper carriages. Amtrak is generally comfortable and runs a popular shuttle service between New York and Washington; the New York to Boston route is also well travelled. Much of the national network is in need of new equipment, however, and in terms of time and cost, rail travel compares poorly to air travel on most inter-city routes.
Water: Ferries supply connections for national Highways across the Mississippi at various places.

City transport

Most cities have a good public transport network including a mixture of buses, suburban trains and subways. At night, taxis are the safer option for travel. Fares vary in different cities. Public transport is woefully inadequate in Los Angeles and the cable cars of San Francisco are a special treat. Commuter rail services throughout the US are usually safe and reliable.
Most cities have severe parking problems in downtown areas and it is more convenient to travel by public transport or taxi.
Taxis: It is wise to confirm the approximate cost when entering a cab.
In Los Angeles, taxis do not cruise streets looking for passengers, but there are taxi stands at airports, major hotels, and train and bus terminals.
Taxi fares in Washington DC are based on the unmetered zone system with a basic fare and each zone charged extra; drivers may stop and pick up several passengers following the same general route. Enquire in advance how many zones you will ride.
Buses, trams & metro: There are bus services in all main cities. Many hotels have courtesy bus services to and from airports.
In New York City buses are slower than the subway, and especially crowded during rush hours, but the routes are more varied and the stops more frequent, usually every two blocks. The subway is the fastest way to get around. Trains are identified by number or letter which are displayed on the front and sides of the cars. Some are local and some express so be sure the train you board stops where you need to get off. If travelling after 2200, wait for the train in the areas marked for off-peak hours.
A subway connects downtown Chicago and O'Hare International Airport with fast and frequent services from Terminal 2; from the city, the Dearborn Street subway runs to the airport.
Union Station is the transport hub in Washington DC. Connections between Metrorail and Metrobus are available at all Metrorail stations.
Ferry: There are commuter ferries across Boston, San Francisco and New York harbours.

Car hire

Car hire is widely available in major cities. A valid overseas or international driving licence and an international credit card are required. Other methods of payment may not be accepted. Driving is on the right. States are free to set their own speed limits: Montana has no day-time limit but at night the limit is 55mph; 75mph in Kansas, Nevada and Wyoming; 70mph in California, Missouri, Oklahoma, South Dakota and Texas.
For further information on state highways see www.us-highways.com with links to other relevant sites.

BUSINESS DIRECTORY

The addresses listed below are a selection only. While World of Information makes every endeavour to check these addresses, we cannot guarantee that changes have not been made, especially to telephone numbers and area codes. We would welcome any corrections.

Telephone area codes

The international direct dialling code (IDD) for the United States of America is +1, followed by area code and subscriber's number:

Alaska	907

Albuquerque	505	Manhattan	212
Atlanta	404	Newark	201
Austin	512	Montana	406
Boston	617	Oklahoma City	405
Chicago	312		
Denver	303	Philadelphia	215
Des Moines	515	Phoenix	602
Detroit	313	Pittsburgh	412
Hawaii	808	Portland	503
Houston	713	Sacramento	916
Kansas City	816	St Louis	314
Indianapolis	317	St Paul	612
Las Vegas	702	Salt Lake City	801
Los Angeles	213	San Francisco	415
Louisville	502	Seattle	206
Memphis	901	Washington DC	202
Miami	305		
New Orleans	504	Wichita	316
New York	718		

Useful telephone numbers
Emergency services: 911

Chambers of Commerce
British-American Business Council, 52 Vanderbilt Avenue, 20th Floor, New York NY 10017 (tel: 661-5660; fax: 661-1886; e-mail: info@babc.org).

United States Chamber of Commerce, 1615 H Street, NW, Washington DC 20062 (tel: 659-6000; e-mail: intl@uschambers.com).

Banking
Bank of America, 555 California Street, San Francisco, California, 94104 (tel: 415-622-3456; fax: 510-675-8170).

Bankers Trust, 280 Park Avenue, New York, New York, 10017 (tel: 212-250-2500; fax: 212-250-4029).

Chase Manhattan, 1 Chase Manhattan Plaza, New York, New York, 10081 (tel: 212-552-2222).

Chemical Bank, 270 Park Avenue, New York, New York, 10017 (tel: 212-270-6000; fax: 212-682-3761).

Citibank, 399 Park Avenue, New York, New York, 10043 (tel: 212-559-1000; fax: 212-223-2681).

First National Bank of Chicago, 1 First National Plaza, Chicago, Illinois, 60670 (tel: 312-732-4000; fax: 312-732-5965).

Inter-American Development Bank, 1300 New York Avenue NW, Washington DC 20577 (tel: 202-623-3900; fax: 202-623-2360).

Morgan Guaranty Trust, 60 Wall Street, New York, New York, 10260 (tel: 212-483-2323; fax: 212-233-2623).

Nations Bank, 100 North Tryon Street, Charlotte, North Carolina, 28255 (tel: 704-386-5000; 704-386-0645).

Central bank
Federal Reserve System, 20th Street and Constitution Avenue, NW, Washington DC 20551 (tel: (202) 452-3000; fax: (202) 452-3819).

Travel information
Amtrak (tel: 1-800-872-7245; internet: www.amtrak.com).

California Tourism, PO Box 1499, Sacramento, CA 95812-1499 (1-916-444-4429; internet: www.visitcalifornia.com).

Greyhound Lines Inc, PO Box 660362, MS 470 Dallas, TX 75266- 0362 (tel: 789-7000; internet: www.greyhound.com).

John F Kennedy International Airport, Building 14, Jamaica, New York 11430, (tel: 244-4444; internet: www.kennedyairport.com).

LaGuardia Airport Hangar 7 Center, Third Floor, Flushing, New York 11371 (tel: 533-3400; fax: 533-3421; internet: www.laguardiaairport.com).

Los Angeles International Airport, 1 World Way, Los Angeles, Ca 90045 (tel: 646-5252; internet: www.lawa.org/lax).

Metropolitan Transportation Authority, 347 Madison Avenue, New York, NY 10017-3739 (internet: www.mta.nyc.ny.us).

Miami International Airport, PO Box 592075, Miami, Florida 33159 (tel: 876-7000; fax: 876-7398; internet: www.miami-airport.com).

O'Hare International Airport, PO Box 66142 Chicago, Illinois 60666 (tel: 686-3700, 686-2200; fax: 686-3573; internet: www.ohare.com).

Visit Florida, Welcome Center, The Capitol, West Entrance, Tallahassee FL 32301 (tel: 488-6167; fax: 414-2560; internet: www.visitflorida.com).

National tourist organisation offices

Ministries
Department of Agriculture, 1400 Independence Avenue, SW, Washington DC 20250 (tel: 720-3631; internet: www.usda.gov).

Department of Commerce, 1401 Constitution Avenue, NW, Washington DC 20230 (tel: 482-2000; fax: 482-2741; internet: www.commerce.gov).

Department of Defence, The Pentagon, Washington DC 20301-1950 (tel: 692-7100; fax: 428-1982; internet: www.defenselink.mil).

Department of Education, Federal Office Bld 6, 400 Maryland Ave, Washington DC 20202 (tel: 401-3000; fax: 401-0596; internet: www.ed.gov).

Department of Energy, 1000 Independence Avenue, SW, Washington DC 20585 (tel: 586-5000; fax: 586-4403; internet: www.energy.gov).

Department of Health and Human Services, 200 Independence Ave, SW, Room 615F, Washington DC 20201 (tel: 690-7000; fax: 690-7203; internet: www.hhs.gov).

Department of Homeland Security, 3801 Nebraska Avenue, NW, Washington DC 20528 (tel: 282-8000; fax: 282-8401; internet: www.dhs.gov).

Department of Housing and Urban Development, 451 7th Street, SW, Room 10000 Washington DC 20410 (tel: 708-0417; fax: 619-8365; internet: www.hud.gov).

Department of the Interior, 1949 C Street, NW Washington DC 20240 (tel: 208-7351; fax: 208-6956; internet: www.doi.gov).

Department of Justice, 950 Pennsylvania Ave, NW Washington DC 20530-0001 (tel: 514-2001; fax: 307-6777; internet: www.justice.gov).

Department of Labor, 200 Constitution Ave, NW Washington DC 20210 (tel: 693-6000; fax: 693-6111; internet: www.dol.gov).

Department of State, 2201 C Street, NW Washington, DC 20520-0001 (tel: 647-5291; fax: 647-7120; internet: www.state.gov).

Department of Transportation, 400 7th Street, SW Washington DC 20570 (tel: 366-1111; fax: 366-7202; internet: www.dot.gov).

Department of the Treasury, 1500 Pennsylvania Ave, NW Washington DC 20220; (tel: 622-1100; fax: 622-0073; www.untreas.gov).

Office of the President, The White House, 1600 Pennsylvania Ave, Washington DC 20500 (tel: 456-1414; fax: 456-2461; internet: www.whitehouse.gov).

Other useful addresses
British Embassy, 3100 Massachusetts Avenue NW, Washington DC 20008-3600 (tel: 588 6500; fax: 588 7850; internet: www.britainusa.com).

Consumer Product Safety Commission, 4330 East West Highway, Bethseda, MD 20814 (tel: 504-7923; fax: 504-0124; internet: www.cpsc.gov).

Council of Economic Advisers, The White House, 1600 Pennsylvania Avenue NW Washington, DC 20500 (tel: 456-1414).

Environmental Protection Agency, Areil Rios Bld, 1220 Pennsylvania Ave NW, Washington DC 20460 (tel: 814-5000; internet: www.epa.gov).

Federal Trade Commission, 600 Pennsylvania Avenue, NW, Washington DC 20580 (tel: 382-4357; internet: www.ftc.gov).

New York Stock Exchange, 11 Wall Street, New York, NY 10005 (tel: 656-3000; internet: www.nyse.com).

Office of Science and Technology Policy, Executive Office of the President, 725 17th Street, Room 5228 Washington DC 20502 (tel: 456-7116; internet: www.ostp.gov)

Office of the United States Trade Representative, 600 17th Street, NW Washington DC 20508 (tel: 395-7360; internet: www.ustr.gov).

Securities and Exchange Commission, 100 F Street, NE, Washington DC 20549 (tel: 551-6551; internet: www.sec.gov).

United States Information Agency, 301 Fourth Street, SW, Washington DC 20547 (internet: http://usinfo.state.gov).

Other news agencies: UPI (United Press International):www.upi.com

Associated Press: www.ap.org

Voice of America: www.voanews.com

Internet sites

Alamo Rent A Car: www.alamo.com

American Airlines: www.aa.com

American Chamber of Commerce: www.amcham.com

American Stock Exchange: www.amex.com

Big Book (information on 16m businesses):www.bigbook.com

Big yellow pages (business and residential information):www.bigyellow.com

Continental Airlines: www.flycontinental.com.

Delta Airlines: www.delta.com

Export and Trade Information: www.stat.usa.gov

Federal Agencies: www.fedworld.gov

Lookup USA (locate addresses and telephone numbers of US businesses): www.infousa.com

Northwest Airlines: www.nwa.com

Southwest Airlines: www.southwest.com

Trade US: www.tradeUS.com

United Airlines: www.ual.com
US Bureau of Census: www.census.gov
US Customs and Border Protection www.cbp.gov
US Department of Commerce: www.commerce.gov
US Government gateway site: firstgov.gov/
US Office of Insular affairs: www.doi.gov/oia
US International Trade Administration: www.ita.doc.gov/ita_home

US Virgin Islands

KEY FACTS

Official name: Virgin Islands of the United States

Head of State: George W Bush

Head of government: Governor John deJongh (from 1 Jan 2007)

Ruling party: Democratic Party of the Virgin Islands (affiliated to the US Democratic Party) (re-elected Nov 2006)

Area: 355 square km

Population: 122,600 (2004)

Capital: Charlotte Amalie (on St Thomas)

Official language: English

Currency: US dollar (US$) = 100 cents

GDP per capita: US$15,500 (2004)

GDP real growth: 2.00% (2002, latest published)

Labour force: 43,930 (2004)

Unemployment: 6.20% (2004)

Inflation: 2.20% (2003)

Visitor numbers: 2.61 million (2005)

COUNTRY PROFILE

Historical profile

1493 The islands were first sighted by Columbus.
1494–1670 The indigenous Carib and Arawak Indian population endured various waves of European invasions and settlement, including African slaves who were used on sugar cane plantations.
1670 The islands of St John and St Thomas were colonised by Denmark.
1733 Denmark purchased St Croix from France.
1917 Denmark sold the islands to the US for US$25 million.
1927 US citizenship was granted to the islands' population.
1931 The Virgin Islands were placed under the administration of the US State Department.
1936 Universal suffrage and local government were provided for under the Organic Act.
1954 The USVI became an unincorporated territory of the United States, under a revised Organic Act, which introduced a form of constitution, with a governor appointed by the president of the US and an elected 15-member unicameral legislature (senate).
1970 A governor was elected for the first time, following the 1968 Elective Governor Act, which also included an elected government for the islands.
1973 The United States Virgin Islands (USVI) elected a non-voting delegate to the US House of Representatives for the first time.
1989 Hurricane Hugo caused total disruption to the power system
1995 Damage to the power system occurred when Hurricane Marilyn hit the islands. The US Federal government transferred control of Water Island to the territorial government.
1998 Governor Charles W Turnbull was elected. There were three serious hurricanes that tore through the West Indies and between them killed over 9,700 people: Bonnie, George and Mitch. However there was less damage inflicted in US Virgin territories due to reconstruction after previous hurricanes, which required buildings to be built to withstand Category 2 storms.
2002 Charles Turnbull was re-elected governor and the Democrats won a majority in the parliamentary election.
2006 In the November gubernatorial elections, the Democrat, John deJongh won 49 per cent of the vote.
2007 Governor John deJongh took office on 1 January. In September an area along the coastline of St John was reserved by the Trust for Public Land to be included in the US Virgin Islands National Park, giving it its largest expansion ever.
2008 In January, a 30-member Constitutional Convention began work on drafting a new constitution. It was the fourth time since 1965 that a new constitution has been envisaged, with previous work stalled over the lack of federal voting rights.

Political structure

Constitution
USVI is an unincorporated territory of the United States and only certain parts of the US constitution apply. Power is delegated from the US Congress.
Citizens are unable to vote in US federal or presidential elections. However US Virgin Islanders are entitled to vote in presidential primary elections and to send one, non-voting, member to the US House of Representatives for a two-year term.

Form of state
Overseas territory of the United States of America

The executive
Executive authority is exercised by the governor (elected for a four-year term by popular vote) who makes other executive appointments with the concurrence of the legislature.

National legislature
The unicameral legislature, the Senate, has 15 members elected by popular vote in two multi-seat constituencies; its measures are subject to the governor's approval.

Legal system
The legal system is based on US laws.

Last elections
7 November 2006 (gubernatorial); 4 November 2004 (Senate)

Results: Governor: John deJongh (Democrat) won 49 per cent of the vote, Kenneth Mapp (independent), his nearest rival, won 27 per cent.
Senate: The Democratic Party of the Virgin Islands (Dem) won 10 of the 15 seats in the Senate and the Independent Citizens Movement (ICM) won 4, the remaining seat going to an independent candidate.

Next elections
November 2010 (governor and parliamentary)

Political parties
Ruling party
Democratic Party of the Virgin Islands (affiliated to the US Democratic Party) (re-elected Nov 2006)
Political situation
The economic downturn in the US has had a knock-on effect on the islands. The undercapitalised Virgin Islands Community Bank was sold to FirstBank Virgin Islands in an emergency deal, before a deadline would have resulted in the Federal Deposit Insurance Corporation taking the bank into receivership.
Since then the US House of Representatives has passed a plan to stimulate the economy, including measures to expand mortgage loan opportunities for families at risk of home repossession. It also has islander taxpayers receiving a tax rebate of between US$300–US$600 per person, plus US$300 per child. The money is expected to strengthen the local economy and encourage consumer spending.

Population
122,600 (2004)
Last census: April 2000: 108,612
Population density: 352 inhabitants per square km. Urban population: 46 per cent (1994–2000).
Annual growth rate: 3 per cent (2003)
Ethnic make-up
Descendants of former African slaves form the majority (80 per cent) of the population. Whites make up a further 15 per cent. Almost three-quarters (74 per cent) of inhabitants are West Indians (45 per cent Virgin Islands-born, 29 per cent from elsewhere in the Caribbean). Puerto Ricans make up 5 per cent of the population.
Religions
Various Christian denominations predominate, (Baptist, Roman Catholic and Episcopalian).

Education
Compulsory years: Five to 16 years

Health
Life expectancy: 78.3 years (estimate 2003)
Fertility rate/Maternal mortality rate: 2.2 births per woman (World Bank)
Child (under 5 years) mortality rate (per 1,000): 8.3 per 1,000 live births (World Bank).

Main cities
Charlotte Amalie (on St Thomas, capital, estimated population 17,500 in 2005), Christiansted and Frederiksted on St Croix (6,300). The third major island and the least populous is St John (Cruz Bay).

Languages spoken
Spanish and Creole are also spoken.

Official language/s
English

Media
Press
Dailies: The two major dailies are Virgin Islands Daily News (www.virginislandsdailynews.com) and St Croix Avis. Other publications include an independent community newspaper St John Times.
The island is served by on-line news services (www.onepaper.com). The St Croix Source provides an alternative news and information source for and about the St Croix community. It is the sister publication of St Thomas Source and St John Source.
Weeklies: Tradewinds St John Newspaper (www.stjohntradewindsnews.com) is published and distributed weekly on St John, as well as to international subscribers. Since 1972, Tradewinds Newspaper has been the island authority. A general tourist publication, St Thomas This Week Magazine, is available on-line (www.st-thomas.com/week).
Business: Publications include Virgin Islands Business Journal.
Broadcasting
Television services are provided by US commercial broadcasters. WSVI TV 8 (Channel 8) (www.wsvi.tv) is an ABC affiliate and WVGN TV 14 (Channel 11) (www.wvgn.com) is an NBC affiliate; both channels broadcast syndicated US shows. There are several radio stations located on both islands and are identified by their call signs, a few are networked such as VI Radio (www.viradio.com). Most broadcast music while a few are news, talk and religious radio stations.

Economy
Tourism is the main economic activity, accounting for some 80 per cent of GDP. Financial services are increasing in importance. Agriculture makes little contribution to the economy. St John, the smallest island, with a population of about 5,000, has the strongest economy in the group.

External trade
As an unincorporated territory of the USA the US Virgin Islands are not part of the American Free Trade Agreement (Nafta), despite its heavy reliance on imports and aid from the US. Trade with the US is either directly by air and sea, or indirect via Puerto Rico.
The principal foreign exchange earner is tourism. Hovensa, on St Croix, is one of the world's largest oil refineries; and manufacturing is the next strongest sector producing refined oil and petroleum products and rum. There is a growing financial services sector and USVI has become the home to a number of foreign sales offices.
Imports
Main imports are crude oil, foodstuffs, consumer goods and building materials.
Main sources: US, Puerto Rico
Exports
Main exports refined petroleum products, rum, petrochemicals, clocks and watches.
Main destinations: US and Puerto Rico.

Agriculture
The agricultural sector contributes around 1 per cent to GDP. The US Virgin Islands are mainly hilly with little flat land. The poor quality of the soil and lack of rain precludes large-scale cultivation. Small quantities of sorghum, fruit and vegetables are produced on St Croix and St Thomas. Cattle are the main agricultural product; a special breed of Senepol cattle hardened to the hot temperatures was developed on St Croix for meat export.
Livestock production in 2005 included 730 tonnes (t) meat in total, 520t beef, 105t pig meat, 33t lamb and goat meat, 72t poultry, 160t eggs, 1,960t milk.
There is some commercial fishing, mainly of lobsters, but fishing is mostly for game, not commercial purposes. The typical total fish catch is over 300t, plus over 36t of other seafood, per annum.

Industry and manufacturing
The industrial sector contributes around 17 per cent to GDP. Manufacturing is better developed here than in much of the Caribbean; it is small-scale and export-based (mainly to the US). Manufacturers have the right to stamp 'Made in America' on their products. The main activities are rum distilling (3–4 million gallons per year), watch/clock assembly, ethanol refining, woollen textiles and garments.
The largest single employer is the Hovensa oil refinery on St Croix, which

KEY INDICATORS — US Virgin Islands

	Unit	2003	2004	2005	2006	2007
Population	m	0.12	0.12	–	–	–
Gross domestic product (GDP)	US$bn	2.40	–	–	–	–
GDP per capita	US$	19,000	–	–	–	–
Exchange rate	per US$	1.00	1.00	1.00	0.00	0.00

has a capacity of around 500,000 barrels per day (bpd).

Tourism
The tourism sector forms the mainstay of the economy, accounting for 80 per cent of GDP and employment. Visitor numbers declined due to the 11 September 2001 terrorist attacks in the US, and again in 2007–08 when the sub-prime mortgage crisis hit the US. The cruise ship business was particularly affected, especially following the withdrawal of calls to St Croix in 2002.The sector recovered in 2003 and 2004 and saw a record 2,623,327 visitors, with cruise ship passengers accounting for nearly two million of these, over 10 per cent up on 2003.

Hydrocarbons
The US Virgin Islands do not produce any hydrocarbons. They rely entirely on crude imports from Trinidad and Tobago. The largest refinery in the western hemisphere and one of the world's biggest, with a capacity of around 500,000 barrels per day (bpd), is located on St Croix. Less than a quarter of oil imports is consumed locally, the rest being re-exported as refined oil products, mainly to the US.
The US Virgin Islands do not import natural gas; around 283,000 short tonnes of coal per annum are imported.

Banking and insurance
Central bank
Federal Reserve System

Time
GMT minus four hours

Geography
The US Virgin Islands consist of four main inhabited islands (St Croix, St Thomas, St John and Water Island) and about 50 smaller, mostly uninhabited, islands. They are situated at the eastern end of the Greater Antilles, about 64km (40 miles) east of Puerto Rico in the Caribbean Sea. These islands are volcanic in origin and have mountainous interiors.
Hemisphere
Northern

Climate
Sub-tropical with a mean annual temperature of 26 degrees Celsius. Low levels of humidity. Rainy season runs May–November.

Entry requirements
Passports
Required by all.
From 23 January 2007, all travellers arriving by air from Canada, Mexico, Central and South America, the Caribbean and Bermuda must have a biometric passport. For Canadian citzens only, under the Nexus programme entry may be achieved using an Air Nexus Card, which includes a retinal-scan.
From 23 January 2008, all arrivals, including US citizens, travelling between Canada, Mexico, Central and South America, the Caribbean and Bermuda through land borders or by sea (including ferries) must have a passport or other biometric, secure documentation as proof of identity.
Visa
US entry requirements apply; visas required by all with some exceptions under the Visa Waiver Program (VWP). This reciprocal programme allows citizens of, among others, the EU, Australasia and Japan entry without a visa if they possess a MRP and have a return/onward ticket, for business and tourist visits up to 90 days. All citizens of visa-free countries who do not have a MRP must apply for a visa. All other visitors must apply for a visa.
For all information on visas see http://travel.state.gov/visa and follow link to Visa Types for Temporary Visitors for specific business visas and extended stays.
Currency advice/regulations
The import of local and foreign currency is unrestricted; amounts over US$10,000 (or equivalent) must be declared.
Customs
Personal items are duty-free. Alcohol and gifts are not duty-free.
Certain firearms and ammunition are allowed with a customs permit, obtained in advance.
Prohibited imports
Illegal drugs (personal medication requires a doctor's certificate); soil, plant and animal products (including endangered species); meat, poultry (fresh, dried or canned) and live fish (unless certified disease-free), their eggs (unless canned, pickled or smoked); Cuban cigars (purchased in any country); wildlife and endangered species (including hunting trophies, shells and crafted items); fireworks and hazardous material; some South American pre-Columbian artefacts; merchandise from embargoed countries and counterfeit items.
These prohibitions apply to transit passengers.

Health (for visitors)
Mandatory precautions
Yellow fever vaccination certificate if arriving from infected area.
Advisable precautions
Health insurance is strongly advised.
Adopt precautions when drinking water in rural areas. There is a bilharzia (schistosomiasis) risk when swimming – chlorinated pools are safe. Visitors should consider immunisation against hepatitis A.

Hotels
Advisable to book in advance, especially in winter months. There is an 8 per cent hotel tax. A 15 per cent tip is usual.

Public holidays (national)
Fixed dates
1 Jan (New Year's Day), 6 Jan (Three Kings' Day), 19 Jan (Martin Luther King Day), 3 Jul (Emancipation Day), 4 Jul (US Independence Day), 25 Jul (Hurricane Supplication Day), 17 Oct (Virgin Islands Thanksgiving Day), 1 Nov (D Hamilton Jackson Day), 11 Nov (Veterans' Day), 25 Dec (Christmas Day).
Variable dates
President's Day (second Mon in Feb), Maundy Thursday, Good Friday, Easter Monday, Memorial Day (fourth Mon in May), Labour Day (first Mon in Sep), Columbus Day (second Mon in Oct), US Thanksgiving Day (fourth Thu in Nov).

Working hours
Banking
Mon–Fri: 0900–1430; Fri: 0900–1400, 1530–1700.
Business
Mon–Fri: 0900–1700
Government
Mon–Fri: 0800–1700.
Shops
Mon–Sat: 0900–1700. Some Sunday opening when cruise ships are in port.

Telecommunications
Telephone/fax
Postal services
Mobile/cell phones
There are GSM service available.
Internet/e-mail

Electricity supply
110/120V AC, 60 Hz

Weights and measures

Getting there
Air
International airport/s: St Thomas-Cyril E. King (STT), 3km west of Charlotte Amalie, duty-free shop, bar, restaurant, bank, shops, car hire. St Croix-Alexander Hamilton (STX), 14km south-west of Christiansted.
Airport tax: None
Surface
Water: Regular ferry service with the British Virgin Islands.
Main port/s: Charlotte Amalie (St Thomas), Christiansted, Frederiksted, South Shore cargo port (St Croix).

Getting about
National transport
Air: There are frequent services between St Thomas and St Croix (by Sunaire Express).
Road: Throughout the islands there are around 800km of well maintained roads.

Buses: Public service on all main routes and group tours available.
Water: Regular ferry service between St Thomas and St John and the British Virgin Islands.

City transport

Taxis: Widely available; fixed-rate system applies but is not always strictly adhered to.
Higher charges are made for extra passengers, luggage and at night. Taxi vans usually carry multiple passengers; private taxis can be arranged for extra cost.

Car hire

A wide selection of cars is available. National licences are accepted and required. Traffic drives on the left. Speed limit is 35kph in towns and 55kph elsewhere.

BUSINESS DIRECTORY

The addresses listed below are a selection only. While World of Information makes every endeavour to check these addresses, we cannot guarantee that changes have not been made, especially to telephone numbers and area codes. We would welcome any corrections.

Telephone area codes

The international direct dialling code (IDD) for the US Virgin Islands is +1 340 followed by the subscriber's number.

Chambers of Commerce

St Croix Chamber of Commerce, PO Box 4369, Kingshill, St Croix 00851 (tel: 773-1435; fax: 773-8172; e-mail: stcroixchamber@vipowernet.net; internet: www.stxchamber.org).
St Thomas-St John Chamber of Commerce, 6 Main Street, PO Box 324, Charlotte Amalie, St Thomas 00804 (tel: 776-0100; fax: 776-0588; e-mail: chamber@islands.vi).

Banking

Banco Popular de Puerto Rico, Church St, Christiansted, St Croix, VI 00820.
First Virgin Islands Federal Savings Bank, 50 Kronprindesens Gade, Charlotte Amalie, St Thomas, VII 00803 (tel: 776-9494).

Central bank

Federal Reserve System, 20th Street and Constitution Avenue, NW, Washington DC 20551 (tel: (202) 452-3000; fax: (202) 452-3819).

Travel information

National tourist organisation offices

USVI Department of Tourism, PO Box 6400, St Thomas, VI 00804 (tel: 800-372; internet: www.usvitourism.vi).

Other useful addresses

Department of Economic Development and Agriculture (responsible for promotion and development of tourism), PO Box 6400, St Thomas 00804 (tel: 774-8784).
Industrial Development Commission, PO Box 3499, St Croix (tel: 773-6499); PO Box 6400, St Thomas (tel: 774-8784).
Office of the Governor, Government House, 21–22 Kongens Gade, Charlotte Amalie, St Thomas, VI 00801 (tel: 774-0001).
St Croix Hotel and Tourism Association, PO Box 24238, Gallows Bay, St Croix, USVI 00824 (tel: 773-7117; fax: 773-5883, e-mail: hax@noc.usvi.net).
St Thomas and St John Hotel Association, 4-D Contant, St Thomas, USVI 00803 (tel: 774-6835).
Virgin Islands Port Authority, Cyril E King Airport, St Thomas, VI 00801 (tel: 774-1629).

Internet sites

Tourist information: www.here.vi
US Office of Insular Affairs: www.doi.gov/oia
US Virgin Islands Guide: www.usvi.net/

Uruguay

KEY FACTS

Official name: República Oriental del Uruguay (Oriental Republic of Uruguay)

Head of State: President Tabaré Vázquez (Frente Amplio) (sworn in 1 Mar 2005)

Head of government: President Tabaré Vázquez

Ruling party: Frente Amplio (FA) (Broad Front) coalition (since 2004)

Area: 176,215 square km

Population: 3.45 million (2007)*

Capital: Montevideo

Official language: Spanish

Currency: Peso Uruguayo (Ur$) = 100 centavos

Exchange rate: Ur$19.15 per US$ (Jul 2008)

GDP per capita: US$5,274 (2005)

GDP real growth: 6.00% (2005)

Labour force: 1.55 million (2004)

Unemployment: 13.10% (2004)

Inflation: 4.70% (2005)

Balance of trade: US$28.20 million (2005)

Visitor numbers: 1.75 million (2006)*

* estimated figure

The World Bank praises what it terms Uruguay's 'cautious macro-economic management' grounded on favourable external conditions. As a result, Uruguay was able to overcome the 2002 crisis and recover its standing in terms of its gross domestic product (GDP). The Bank notes that Uruguay's economic achievements have been considerable, in that it succeeded in consolidating a sound fiscal situation, reducing inflation, doubling exports while diversifying its product markets. As a result, it became able to access international capital markets.

Four years of growth

According to the United Nations Economic Commission for Latin America and the Caribbean (ECLAC/CEPAL), in 2007, Uruguay enjoyed its fourth consecutive year of economic expansion, achieving a growth rate of about 7.5 per cent thanks to increases in both external and domestic demand. This higher demand, together with supply limitations in some sectors and upward trends in world commodity markets, led to inflationary pressure in the country's economy (8.6 per cent in the 12 months to November 2007). For the year as a whole it is estimated that the value of goods and services exports will be up 14 per cent and imports by 10 per cent, so the balance of payments current-account deficit should stand at about 1 per cent of GDP. If current conditions in local and international markets continue, economic growth in 2008 should be close to 6.5 per cent. According to the World Bank, during the first semester of 2007, poverty levels fell by 25 per cent while the percentage of people in a situation of extreme poverty is currently under 2 per cent. Similarly, unemployment fell from around 20 per cent by the end of 2002 to 12.2 per cent in 2005 and to 10.7 per cent by mid-2006; the figure was 9.7 per cent in July 2007, showing a continuing downward trend.

The IMF agrees

The International Monetary Fund (IMF) broadly concurs with ECLAC's positive assessment of the Uruguyan economy, observing that since 2002, GDP growth has averaged 7 per cent, inflation has remained moderate, and poverty rates have declined considerably, remaining among the lowest in the region. Renewed market access and strong foreign direct investment (FDI) have also resulted in a substantial increase in international reserves. Strong primary fiscal surpluses have helped reduce debt ratios and debt management operations have improved the structure of Uruguay's debt. Key reforms have been implemented since the crisis, including a comprehensive tax reform, bank restructuring and improved supervision. However, according to the IMF, important elements of the government's reform agenda, which would further reduce vulnerabilities and help sustain high growth, still need to be implemented.

With strong domestic demand, in the view of the IMF, real GDP growth could reach 5.25 per cent in 2007. Higher growth and the recovery of the energy sector from the 2006 dip improved fiscal prospects in 2007, with a 4 per cent of GDP primary surplus target likely to be met or surpassed. Inflation, however, had been rising and was likely to exceed the target range of 4.5 –6.5 per cent.

The authorities stressed that the rise in inflation is largely due to temporary factors (drought in 2006 has given way to floods in 2007) and likely to decline in the months ahead. Underlying inflation has steadily increased – with one measure of core inflation above the target range. The latest survey shows expected inflation near seven per cent by the end of 2007, and declining to within the target range in 2008.

Political changes

Tabaré Vážquez, the country's first left-wing president, began his five-year term in March 2005. The event was billed as something of a fête for Latin America's left-wing leaders. Hugo Chávez, Venezuela's radical nationalist president, Bolivia coca growers' leader Evo Morales and the Cuban foreign minister all attended the ceremony in Montevideo. The make-up of the ruling coalition – Frente Amplio, Encuentro Progresista and Nueva Mayoría (FA Coalition) – with its selection of communists, hard line trade union leaders and former guerrilla fighters, at first sight appeared to constitute a shift to the hard left of the Uruguayan political spectrum. Vázquez's vow to form a 'government of change' in his inaugural address only increased expectations of a radical transformation. However, the government's approach, particularly to economic policy, has remained consistent with mainstream left-of-centre thinking. The EP-FA has a working majority in both chambers of the Uruguayan Parliament. However, tensions between the moderate and radical wings of the EP - FA coalition have resulted in dilution of some elements of the government's ambitious program of economic and social reforms. Nonetheless, Vazquez's alliance has acquired a loyal following in the main urban centres, as well as among younger voters seeking to break away from the traditional parties.

The Frente Amplio (FA) (Broad Front) coalition has a working majority in both chambers of the Uruguayan Parliament. However, tensions between the moderate and radical wings of the coalition have resulted in dilution of some elements of the government's ambitious programme of economic and social reforms. Nonetheless, Vázquez's alliance has acquired a loyal following in the main urban centres, as well as among younger voters seeking to break away from the traditional parties.

Risk assessment

Economics	Good
Politics	Good
Regional stability	Good

COUNTRY PROFILE

Historical profile

1516 Spanish explorer Juan Díaz de Solis was killed by indigenous people while he was navigating the Rio de la Plata. His death discouraged European exploration for more than a century afterwards.
In the seventeenth century, the Portuguese began colonising Uruguay.
1726 The Spanish founded Montevideo and took over Uruguay.
1776 Uruguay became part of the vice royalty of La Plata, which was run from Buenos Aires in Argentina.
1808 The defeat of the Spanish monarchy by Napoleon weakened La Plata, leading to a rebellion in Uruguay which overthrew the vice royalty. The Uruguayans resisted Argentine and Brazilian invaders.
1825 Uruguay achieved formal independence from Spain.
1830 A constitution was approved.
1838–65 Uruguay became embroiled in civil war between the conservative Colorados (reds) and the liberal Blancos (whites).
1865–70 Uruguay joined Argentina and Brazil and fought a war against Paraguay, which was eventually defeated.
1904 The Colorados and Blancos fought their last civil war. The Blancos became the Partido Nacional (PN) (National Party)

KEY INDICATORS **Uruguay**

	Unit	2003	2004	2005	2006	2007
Population	m	3.40	3.43	3.40	*3.43	*3.45
Gross domestic product (GDP)	US$bn	10.93	13.14	16.88	19.32	*22.95
GDP per capita	US$	3,210	3,543	5,274	*6,036	*7,172
GDP real growth	%	2.5	12.0	6.6	7.0	*7.0
Inflation	%	19.5	9.2	4.7	6.4	8.1
Unemployment	%	16.9	13.1	12.2	10.8	–
Exports (fob) (goods)	US$m	2,127.0	3,145.0	3,758.0	3,699.0	5,063.0
Imports (cif) (goods)	US$m	2,107.0	2,992.2	3,729.9	4,701.0	5,554.3
Balance of trade	US$m	20.0	152.8	28.2	-1,002.0	-491.3
Current account	US$m	-87.3	3.1	24.3	-369.2	-184.0
Total reserves minus gold	US$m	2,083.0	2,508.0	3,074.0	3,085.0	4,114.0
Foreign exchange	US$m	2,079.0	2,507.0	3,068.0	3,084.0	4,114.0
Exchange rate	per US$	28.35	28.70	24.49	24.49	21.68

* estimated figure

and the Colorados the Partido Colorado (PC).
1903–07 and 1911–16 President José Batlle y Ordonez (Colorado party), introduced the welfare state, extended the right to vote to women, disestablished the Roman Catholic Church and abolished the death penalty.
1933 A military coup led to the abolition of opposition parties.
1951 A new constitution replaced the post of president with a nine-member council.
1962–73 The Tupamaros guerrillas engaged in a campaign of insurgency.
1973–85 A military dictatorship took power, unleashing a campaign of harsh repression.
1984 Violent protests erupted against military rule. The military dictatorship agreed to step down and return the country to constitutional government.
1985 Julio María Sanguinetti, a Colorado, was installed as president after democratic elections
1989 Luis Alberto Lacalle won the presidential election. An amnesty for human rights abusers endorsed by referendum.
1994 Sanguinetti won the presidential election.
1999 Jorge Batlle Ibañez (PC) was elected president.
2000 A commission was set up to investigate 'disappearances' under the military regime.
2002 The financial crisis that began in Asia and weakened many economies in Latin America, particularly Argentina, prompted Batlle to introduce fiscal measures including tax increases to prevent the crisis spilling into Uruguay. Banks were closed to stop the mass withdrawal of savings and a general strike was called.
2003 The government managed to restructure almost half of its US$11 billion foreign debt, pushing the repayment dates back five years. A referendum rejected proposals for the sale of state oil assets to foreign investment.
2004 The World Bank approved a US$6.80 million grant to promote energy efficient goods and service. Left-wing, Tabaré Vázquez (Frente Amplio) won the presidential elections and the Frente Amplio (FA) (Broad Front) coalition party won the parliamentary elections with 52 out of the 99 seats in the Chamber of Deputies and 17 out of 31 seats in the Senate.
2005 Tabaré Vázquez was sworn in as president and restored diplomatic relations with Cuba and signed an energy deal with Venezuela.
2006 Argentina attacked the building of two US$1 billion-plus pulp mills, by Finnish company, Botnia, on its border with Uruguay, claiming they would pollute the river ecosystem, but the International Court of Justice (ICJ) rejected the claim. Uruguay paid back its US$1.1 billion debt to the International Monetary Fund.
2007 Montevideo became the home of the new parliament of Mercosur, South America's leading trading bloc. Argentine environmentalists, in a flotilla of dinghies and skiffs, invaded the new port being built for the paper mills in August.
2008 The industry minister announced on 23 June that a natural gas and oil field had been found offshore in Uruguayan waters. However, until drilling takes place the field's production and profitability are only speculative.

Political structure

Constitution

The constitution dates from 1967, with a period of suspension during military rule between 1973 and 1985. Voting is by secret ballot and is obligatory for all citizens aged 18 and over. The electorate has to vote in support of a single party list for president, mayors and legislators. A reform to permit cross-party voting for the different positions was defeated at a referendum in 1994.

Form of state

Presidential democratic republic

The executive

Executive power is vested in the president, who is directly elected every five years, usually in October or November. The president is assisted by a vice president and an appointed council of ministers. The president has the power to veto parliamentary resolutions, but the veto can be overturned by a three-fifths majority of Congress.

National legislature

The bicameral Asamblea General (General Assembly) comprises the Cámara de Diputados (Chamber of Deputies) with 99 members and the Cámara de Senadores (Chamber of Senators (Senate)) with 31 members, plus the vice president. Both chambers are elected by proportional representation and members serve for five-year terms.

Legal system

The legal system is based on Spanish civil law. Written law is passed by parliament and promulgated by the president. The ultimate source of the law is the constitution.

Judicial power is exercised by the Supreme Court of Justice which has five members elected by Congress. The Court nominates all other judges and officials.

Last elections

31 October 2004 (presidential and parliamentary)

Results: Presidential: Tabaré Vázquez (Frente Amplio) won 50.7 per cent of the vote, Jorge Larrañaga (PN) 34.1 per cent and Guillermo Stirling (PC) 10.3 per cent. Turnout was 89.6 per cent.
Parliamentary: (Chamber of Deputies) the Frente Amplio (FA) (Broad Front) won 50.4 per cent (52 seats out of 99), the Partido Nacional-Blancos (PN) (National-White Party) won 34.3 per cent (35), the Partido Colorado (PC) (Colorado Party) 10.4 per cent (10) and the Partido Independiente (PI) (Independent Party) 1.8 per cent (two). Senate: FA 17 seats (out of 32), PN 11, PC three.

Next elections

2009 (presidential and parliamentary)

Political parties

Ruling party

Frente Amplio (FA) (Broad Front) coalition (since 2004)

Main opposition party

Partido Nacional-Blancos (PN) (National-White Party)

Population

3.45 million (2007)*

Last census: May 1996: 3,163,763

Population density: 19 inhabitants per square km. Urban population: 92 per cent (2002).

Annual growth rate: 0.7 per cent 1994–2004 (WHO 2006)

Ethnic make-up

Around 90 per cent are of European descent, with approximately one-quarter of the population of Italian origin. Minorities are black and mestizo (mixed race), but there are no pure Indian groups.

Religions

The majority of Uruguayans are Roman Catholic (66 per cent) with a small minority of Protestants (2 per cent) and Jews (1 per cent). Secular traditions are strong and a third of the population have no professed religious faith.

Education

All education, including university tuition, is provided free of charge. The curriculum is the same in both public and private schools. Secondary education is available from aged 12 and divided into two three-year courses. Technical studies are offered in technical schools and last between two and seven years. There are five universities and enrolment in tertiary education is typically 30 per cent.

Literacy rate: 98 per cent adult rate; 99 per cent youth rate (15–24) (Unesco 2005).

Compulsory years: Six to 14

Enrolment rate: 109.5 per cent gross primary enrolment; 98.5 per cent gross seconday enrolment, of relevant age groups (including repeaters) (Unicef 2004).

Pupils per teacher: 20 in primary schools

Health
Per capita total expenditure on health (2003) was US$824; of which per capita government spending was US$224, at the international dollar rate, (WHO 2006).
HIV/Aids
HIV prevalence: 0.3 per cent aged 15–49 in 2003 (World Bank)
Life expectancy: 75 years, 2004 (WHO 2006)
Fertility rate/Maternal mortality rate: 2.3 births per woman, 2004 (WHO 2006); maternal mortality 26 per 100,000 live births (World Bank).
Child (under 5 years) mortality rate (per 1,000): 12 per 1,000 live births (World Bank)
Head of population per physician: 3.65 physicians per 1,000 people, 2002 (WHO 2006)

Welfare
Uruguay maintains one of the most comprehensive systems of social security in Latin America, including free education, state medical care, pensions and unemployment benefits. Social security spending accounts for around 15 per cent of GDP.
The largest welfare expenditure is the payment of old age pensions. The long tradition of healthcare provision and a relatively low mortality rate have produced an ageing population. The pension age is low (with sometimes less than 30 years' service required). There are some 800,000 old-age pensioners out of a total population of three million and compared to a workforce of only one million, producing one of the highest ratios of pensioners to workers in the world.
There is widespread and vociferous opposition to any modification of the social security system. Many of the welfare benefits, including a workers' charter stipulating maximum hours, minimum wages and paid holidays, date from the beginning of the twentieth century.
Social security is covered by the state budget with about 50 per cent of contributions coming from tax revenues. Despite attempts by the government to raise the percentage derived from taxes, the remaining 50 per cent is still split roughly equally between contributions from workers and employers. Almost 90 per cent of the population is covered for all benefits.
Housewives, who are ineligible for retirement benefit, only receive separate pensions after their husbands have died.
Benefits include: a retirement pension at 60 for men, 55 for women or after 30 years of recognised service; an invalidity pension after 10 years of recognised service; an early retirement pension for citizens fulfilling political duties; free maternity care for working women and workers' wives; and sick pay of up to three months for all workers. Unemployment pay of up to six months is provided for all workers who have paid contributions for a year or more. This can reach up to 75 per cent of nominal salary. All medical costs are met by the state during the six-month period.

Main cities
Montevideo (capital, estimated population 1.4 million in 2005), Salto (103,622), Paysandú (80,352), Las Piedras (72,617), Rivera (69,681).

Languages spoken
Business languages: English and Portuguese. French and Italian are also widely spoken.
Official language/s
Spanish

Media
Press
Dailies: In Spanish, national newspapers, mostly published in Montevideo, include El País (www.elpais.com.uy), Diario Cambio (www.diariocambio.com.uy), El Telégrafo (www.eltelegrafo.com), La República (www.larepublica.com.uy), and Ultimas Noticias (www.ultimasnoticias.com.uy) an evening newspaper.
Weeklies: In Spanish, there are many magazines, the biggest of which is Brecha (www.brecha.com.uy), Juventud (www.chasque.apc.org/juventud) is a youth magazine, Guambia (www.guambia.com.uy) is a satirical weekly.
In English, the Uruguay Daily News (www.uruguaydailynews.com) has an online news digest.
Business: In Spanish, the leading weekly publications are Crónicas Económicas (www.cronicas.com.uy) and Búsqueda (Search), while El Observador (www.observador.com.uy) is a business-oriented newspaper. Económico (www.redtercermundo.org.uy/tm_economico/) is a monthly publication.
Periodicals: There are numerous periodicals and a few trade publications. The government's official journal Diario Oficial (www.impo.com.uy) is a monthly publication.
Broadcasting
The government-owned, national broadcaster is Servicio Oficial de Defusión Radiotelevisión y Espectáculos (SODRE) (www.sodre.gub.uy).
Radio: The public radio network has four stations broadcasting cultural, news, educational and entertainment programmes. There are more than 100 private, commercial radio stations, all broadcasting in Spanish, located throughout the country. From Montevideo, Radio Monte Carlo (www.radiomontecarlo.com.uy), Radio El Espectador (/www.espectador.com), Radio Sarandí (www.radiosarandi.com.uy) and 1410 AM Libre (www.1410amlibre.com.uy) transmit news and entertainment programmes.
Television: Over 70 per cent of households own television sets.
The public television channel TV Nacional Uruguay known as TNU (www.tnu.com.uy) broadcasts news, documentaries and cultural programmes nationally. Commercial TV stations include Teledoce (www.teledoce.com), Saeta TV Canal 10 (www.canal10.com.uy) and Monte Carlo TV canal 4 (www.canal4.com.uy) broadcasts foreign Spanish language shows, as well as dubbed US TV shows, and TV Ciudad (www.teveciudad.org.uy) broadcasting cultural shows.
There are pay-for-view television services available through (www.paysandu.com).
Advertising
Television advertising claims nearly half of all media advertising expenditure, while around 25 per cent is spent in the print media. Less than 20 per cent goes to radio advertising. Advertising placement fees, in particular on radio and television, are high by regional standards.

Economy
Following three successive contractions, in 2000, 2001 and 2002, Uruguay's economy has grown in every year since 2003. GDP grew by 12 per cent in 2004, but fell to six per cent in 2005. The annual rate of inflation, which reached almost 20 per cent in 2003, fell to around six per cent by 2006.
Uruguay has a highly centralised economy. Approximately 17 per cent of the labour force is employed by the state. The economy is among the most developed in Latin America with one of the highest per capita incomes in the region, at over US$5,810 in 2006. The economy is largely driven by services (a major feature of which is the well-run offshore financial sector), industry and commodity exports. Tourism plays a small but increasingly important role.
Uruguay has always been cause for concern, placed between Latin America's two largest economies, Brazil and Argentina. It depends on the Argentine and Brazilian markets for its agricultural exports, exposing it to fluctuations in their economies. In 2001 and 2002, the two markets dried up and the Uruguayan economy went into a period of recession, from which it began to emerge in 2003.
Uruguay has traditionally been seen as a haven within South America, attracting large amounts of flight capital from neighbouring countries. For years, Argentinians have been storing money in Uruguay's

banks, mostly due to a lack of confidence in their own financial system.

A left-wing president was elected in March 2005, the first in Uruguay's history. Despite the fears of many external observers, the government of Tabaré Ramón Vázquez Rosas has toned down its leftist electoral rhetoric since coming to power.

In June 2005 Uruguay signed a new deal with the IMF worth US$1.1 billion that will run for three years. Under the terms of the new programme, an inflation target of 3.5 is to be reached by 2008 and annual average growth is expected to be in the region of 4 per cent.

The new government has also stated that it sees a viable role for private capital in the economy over the next few years, but state-run monopolies in sectors such as water, telecommunications and energy will not be sold off. Privatisation of these enterprises would be politically impossible, as the vast majority of Uruguay's 3.5 million population is fervently opposed to privatisation.

The Inter-American Development Bank estimated that in 2006 migrant workers sent some US$115 million to their families in Uruguay.

External trade

As a member of Mercosur, the world's fourth largest free-trade zone, Uruguay (along with Argentina, Brazil and Paraguay), has access to a market of over 200 million consumers. The EU and Mercosur have been in negotiations to create a mutual free trade zone since 2004. Uruguay is also an associate member of the Andean Community (AC), when Mercosur negotiated a free trade area with AC.

Foreign trade accounts for around 50 per cent of GDP. Almost 90 per cent of productive land is used for animal husbandry and agriculture is the largest exporting sector. Processed meat (fresh, canned and frozen) and animal products accounts for around 50 per cent of manufacturing activity.

Imports

Main imports are fuels, capital machinery, chemicals and plastics, vehicles, electrical and electronic equipment.

Main sources: Argentina (18.9 per cent total, 2005), Brazil (18.5 per cent), Paraguay (14.0 per cent), US (8.6 per cent), China (6.2 per cent)

Exports

Main exports are meat, rice, wine, raw hides and skins, wool, fish and dairy products.

Main destinations: US (18.6 per cent total, 2005), Brazil 15.0 per cent), Mexico (6.9 per cent), Argentina (6.1 per cent), Spain (4.1 per cent), Germany (4.0 per cent)

Agriculture

Farming

Though agricultural production accounts for approximately 6 per cent of total GDP, agricultural-related products make up more than half of the country's exports. The sector also employs around 11 per cent of Uruguay's workforce.

Traditional exports have been hit by protectionism and tough competition from the EU. An outbreak of foot-and-mouth disease throughout the region also affected Uruguayan meat exports, although by 2003 the situation was under control and trade had resumed.

The sector is also an important supplier of raw materials (sugar, oilseeds, etc) to industry. It is expanding more rapidly than industry.

Livestock rearing forms the basis of the sector with cattle and sheep being produced for domestic consumption and for export (as meat, wool, hides and skins). Poultry and pigs are largely produced for the home market but exports of dairy products are increasing in importance. Exports of butter and cheese to Mercosur countries are substantial.

There is virtual self-sufficiency in food, although imports of wheat are required at times of low harvests.

Principal crops are wheat (mainly grown on mixed farms), rice (the main export crop, grown almost entirely in the north-east), sugar cane and beet, maize, barley, sorghum, linseed, sunflower seed, vegetables (mainly grown by smallholders) and citrus fruits (mainly oranges and tangerines).

The estimated crop production for 2005 included: 2,580,560 tonnes (t), 1,262,600t rice, 532,600t wheat, 250,000t maize, 377,000t soya beans, 136,345t potatoes, 100,000t sorghum, 406,500t barley, 242,177t citrus fruit, 147,057t grapes, 60,000t tomatoes, 72,478t apples, 142,619t oilcrops, 3,000t tobacco, 181,500t sugar cane, 508,495t fruit in total, 205,429t vegetables in total. Livestock production included: 602,451t meat in total, 496,498t beef, 16,000t pig meat, 26,504t lamb, 54,219t poultry, 36,248t eggs, 1,500,000t milk, 13,200t honey, 66,419t cattle hides, 9,863t sheepskins.

Fishing

The fishing industry typically generates US$80 million in exports per annum. Uruguay suffers from water pollution from its meat and leather industries, which has hit the fishing sector in previous years. If this problem can be permanently erradicated the prospects for the fishing industry will improve markedly.

In 2004, the total marine fish catch was 109,907 tonnes and the total crustacean catch was 2,762 tonnes.

Forestry

Uruguay has approximately 1.2 million hectares of forested land, which constitutes 5 per cent of the country's total landmass.

Assisted by fiscal incentives, forestry has become a dynamic sector, attracting both foreign and domestic investment. Local forest resources produce modest quantities of sawn timber and pulp with most of paper products imported.

It is estimated that 1.7 million tonnes of timber per year could be exported, but improvements and remodelling of existing facilities and infrastructure would be needed in order to transport the timber.

Export of forest materials in 2004 amounted to US$131 million, while imports total US$63 million.

Production in 2004 included: 6,399,152 cubic metres (cum) roundwood, 2,132,000cum industrial roundwood, 1,637,000cum pulpwood, 230,000cum sawnwood, 485,000cum sawlogs and veneers, 4,267,152cum wood fuel, 117,655 (t) charcoal, 96,000t paper and paperboard, 56,000t printing and writing paper, 41,000t paper pulp, 17,000t recovered paper.

Industry and manufacturing

Uruguay's industrial sector has been in recession in recent years and has suffered significant reductions in investment. The industry still accounts for a sizeable percentage of the workforce, though this is now falling.

Government industrial policy has promoted export operations, based mainly on agricultural processing and related labour-intensive industries. Although traditional key sectors are still meat processing and packing and while the wool industry and fisheries still have priority, attention has turned to other sectors such as textiles and leather. The penetration of new markets has been a key feature of plans to stimulate manufacturing industry and exports.

Despite a number of new trade agreements with Mercosur, the US and Mexico, industry still suffers deep-seated structural problems. These have included high levels of debt, obsolete machinery and poor investment.

Tourism

Tourism is of considerable importance to Uruguay's economy, accounting for just under 10 per cent of total GDP and employing 10.7 per cent of the country labour force.

The travel and tourism industry suffered a major decline in previous years following the economic crisis in Argentina, which, along with Brazil, is its most important market. However, the sector is now recovering and visitor numbers are rising, which has, in turn, resulted in an increase in capital investment in the sector.

Mining

Mining and quarrying combined make up less than 1 per cent of Uruguay's total GDP. The country has few known mineral reserves and is wholly dependent on imports for raw materials ranging from oil to aluminium.

There are known deposits of iron ore, gold, manganese, copper, zinc and lead. Regulations in 1990 opened up the sector to foreign investment but very few foreign companies are active. Argentina has been the main purchaser of sand from Uruguay while Spain, South Africa and the US have purchased semi-precious stones and granite. Japan and Argentina are also important markets for granite exports. However, most mine production is consumed domestically.

Hydrocarbons

With no proven oil reserves of its own and a significant demand for oil, Uruguay relies heavily on imports. The country has only one oil refinery, situated near Montevideo, which outputs 50,000 barrels per day (bpd).

Uruguay has looked increasingly to Venezuela to supply it with oil. In a deal struck in August 2005 the Venezuelan government agreed to supply Uruguay with 43,600 bpd of crude oil.

The National Administration of Fuel, Alcohol and Portland Cement (ANCAP), a state enterprise, has a monopoly on oil importing and refining. Intermittent oil exploration is carried out but results have been disappointing so far.

The importance of natural gas in the country's energy sector will increase with the construction of new pipelines and distribution systems. The government is hoping to increase gas usage to be 30 per cent of primary energy consumption, however the country's economic problems have hindered this target. Currently only small quantities are being imported.

There are known deposits of low-grade coal although no coal is produced and Uruguay relies on imports of approximately two million tonnes per annum.

Energy

Uruguay has approximately 2,100 megawatts (MW) of instilled electricity generating capacity. About half of the country's energy needs are produced domestically and the shortfall is covered by imports, predominantly from Argentina and Brazil. The 1,890MW hydropower plant at Salto Grande (built with Argentina), the 300MW Palmar plant, and two plants on the Rio Negro are sufficient to meet local demand and provide surplus for export.

Financial markets

Stock exchange

The Uruguayan stock market is the Bolsa de Montevideo, which runs an electronic listing system, the Bolsa Electrónica de Valores del Uruguay SA (Bevsa). Owing to the low levels of privatisation in Uruguay, there are few companies listed and many do not trade actively. Liquidity has traditionally been thin, with a high proportion of family businesses concentrating shares among a small number of people and eliminating speculators. However, the government's reforms to the state sector through a series of capital injections have helped improve liquidity levels.

Banking and insurance

Uruguay's banking and financial services sector continues to be dominated by three public banks. The Banco Central del Uruguay (BCU), which does not offer private credit, the Banco de la República Oriental de Uruguay (BROU) and the Banco Hipotecario de Uruguay (BHU) are the kingpins of the financial system.

The BROU is multi-purpose and is the largest credit provider, offering 40 per cent of overall private credit in Uruguay and receiving 33 per cent of deposits. The Banco Hipotecario specialises in mortgage lending.

In 2003, the Banco Comercial, the Banco de Montevideo and the Banco la Caja Obrera merged into a new institution, the Nuevo Banco Comercial.

A new Bank of the South, with a headquarters in Venezuela, will be launched in 2008 to provide an alternative source of development funding for the participating countries. Assets of US$7 billion will underpin its operations.

Central bank

Banco Central del Uruguay

Main financial centre

Montevideo

Time

GMT minus three hours (daylight saving, GMT minus two hours, is determined by presidential decree)

Geography

Uruguay has an area of 176,215 square km and is bordered by Argentina to the west, by Brazil in the north and by the Atlantic and the wide River Plate estuary to the south-east. The largest river, the Uruguay, runs along the border with Argentina.

About 95 per cent of the country is rolling grassland, with few hills above 300 metres. The highest point is the Cerro Catedral at 514 metres. Only about 6 per cent of the land is naturally forested.

The River Negro (Río Negro), the main tributary of the River Uruguay, cuts across the centre of the country, separating the two main ranges of hills, the Cuchilla de Haedo and the Cuchilla Grande. Artificial lakes on the Rio Negro cover 1,199 square km.

Hemisphere

Southern

Climate

The climate is temperate and rainfall is abundant, with an average of about 100 days of rain a year. In January, the hottest summer month, average temperatures range between 21 degrees Celsius (C) on the coast and 26 degrees C inland. In July the average temperatures are between 11 degrees C on the coast and 13 degrees C in the interior, with temperatures occasionally falling to freezing point at night.

Dress codes

Clothing is mostly informal, but jackets and ties or suits for men and skirts for women are usual for business. Uruguayans generally wear more conservative colours than their neighbours in Brazil and Argentina.

Entry requirements

Passports

Required by all except nationals of Argentina, Bolivia, Brazil, Chile, Colombia, Costa Rica, Dominican Republic, Ecuador, Guatemala, Honduras, Paraguay, Peru and the US. Nationals from these countries need a national identity card.

Visa

Required by all except nationals of EU, US, Canada, Japan, Norway, Switzerland, most Latin American countries and certain others for visits up to three months. A Tourist Card will be issued when travellers enter the country (usually given to airline passengers before landing), and must be kept until departure.

Business travellers from the countries mentioned above do not require visas. All other business visitors must have a letter of authorisation from their company or organisation.

The visitor is advised to check with the nearest consulate to determine the validity of their status before travelling.

Currency advice/regulations

The import and export of local and foreign currency is unrestricted.

Travellers cheques, in US dollars (US$50 and US$100 denominations only) are readily accepted. All other currency cheques have very limited acceptance.

Customs

Personal effects are allowed in duty-free, precious jewels and gold (worth more than US$500) must be declared.

Prohibited imports

Precious jewels, gold, firearms, pornography, subversive literature, inflammable articles, acids, illegal drugs, plants, seeds, and foodstuffs as well as some antiquities and business equipment must be declared.

Health (for visitors)
Mandatory precautions
None
Advisable precautions
A typhoid vaccination may be necessary. Water precautions should be taken outside Montevideo.
Excellent health care is available but foreign visitors must pay the full cost.

Hotels
Graded into four classes by the National Tourism Bureau – de luxe, 1, 2A and 2B. There is a 20 per cent value added tax on hotel bills. Service charge is normally included – if not, usually 10 per cent tip.

Credit cards
Major credit and charge cards are readily accepted. ATMs may not accepted foreign cards.

Public holidays (national)
Fixed dates
1 Jan (New Year's Day), 6 Jan (Epiphany), 1 May (Labour Day), 19 Jun (Birth of General Artigas), 18 Jul (Constitution Day), 25 Aug (Independence Day), 12 Oct (Discovery of America Day), 2 Nov (All Souls' Day), 25 Dec (Christmas Day).
Variable dates
Carnival (two days, Feb), Holy Wednesday–Good Friday (Easter–three days, Mar/Apr), Landing of the 33 Patriots (third Mon Apr), Battle of Las Piedras (third Mon May),

Working hours
Banking
Mon–Fri: 1000–1400; summer variations may apply in certain areas.
Business
Mon–Fri: 0830–1200, 1430–1830.
Government
From mid-Mar to mid-Dec: Mon–Fri: 0900–1600. From mid-Dec to mid-Mar: Mon–Fri: 0730–1330.
Shops
Mon–Sat: 0830–1230/1300, 1530/1600–1900/2000; Sun 0830–1200 food shops only.

Telecommunications
Mobile/cell phones
There are 850/1900, 1900 and 1800 GSM services available throughout most of the country.

Electricity supply
220V AC, 50 cycles

Social customs/useful tips
Punctuality is expected and business cards are essential. Uruguay's population is mostly of Italian or Spanish descent, and maintains many European customs, ranging from diet to dress. There is a long tradition of liberal legislation in contrast to many South American countries. Divorce and gambling, for example, are both legal. There is provision in the law for duels in matters of honour, something which much of the population considers an anachronism but which is nevertheless invoked from time to time.

Security
Residents consider the capital relatively safe to walk around at night compared with other South American cities.

Getting there
Air
National airline: Pluna (Primeras Líneas Uruguayas de Navegación Aérea)
International airport/s: Montevideo-Carrasco International (MVD), 19km from city; duty-free shops, bar, restaurant, bank, post office and car hire.
Airport tax: Departure tax: US$26; Buenos Aires only US$14. Not applicable to transit passengers.
Surface
Road: There are a number of border crossings from Brazil, the crossing from Argentina is preferable by car-ferry. A US$176 million programme to improve primary highways is under way.
Water: There are high-speed ferries and a night-ferry service from Buenos Aires–Montevideo (internet: www.buquebus.com). There are also services from Colonia (160km west of Montevideo) to Buenos Aires by ferry and a hydrofoil service (three times daily).
A port departure tax may be levied.
Main port/s: Montevideo River Plate (Rio Plate) harbour includes all the country's main port facilities, served by worldwide cargo lines.

Getting about
National transport
Air: The only internal destinations currently offered are domestic legs of international flights.
Road: Ninety per cent of roads are paved and while urban roads are good, rural roads are only fair. The highway network radiates from Montevideo towards the borders of Brazil and Argentina.
Buses: ONDA, CITA and COT run fast and frequent lines, connecting most towns across the country (routes include: Montevideo-Punta del Este and Montevideo-Paysandú).
Rail: The slow rail system only connects a few villages and is under threat of closure.
Water: Scheduled river services do not exist.
City transport
Taxis: Taxis are widely available in towns and from airports. They can be hailed in the street. Fares are metered, with higher charges for extra passengers and between 0000–0600. They can be hired on a time basis, in which case fares should be negotiated in advance. A 10 per cent tip is usual.
Buses, trams & metro: An extensive bus service links all the capital's suburbs. There is an airport bus to the city centre, travelling time 35 minutes.
Car hire
International driving licence must be accompanied by two photographs; traffic conditions within Montevideo can be difficult and chauffeur-driven cars are recommended. A driving permit for 90 days can be obtained from Montevideo town hall.

BUSINESS DIRECTORY

The addresses listed below are a selection only. While World of Information makes every endeavour to check these addresses, we cannot guarantee that changes have not been made, especially to telephone numbers and area codes. We would welcome any corrections.

Telephone area codes
The international dialling code (IDD) for Uruguay is +598 followed by area code and subscriber's number:

Canelones	33	Minas	44
Florida	352	Montevideo	2
Las Piedras	2	Paysandú	72
Maldonado	42	Punta del Este	42
Mercedes	53	San José de Carrasco	2

Useful telephone numbers
Emergency: 911
Emergency, outside Montevideo: 02911
Roadside assistance: 1707

Chambers of Commerce
American-Uruguayan Chamber of Commerce, Plaza Independencia 831, Edificio Plaza Mayor, 11100 Montevideo (tel: 908-9186; fax: 908-9187; email: info@ccuruguayusa.com).

British-Uruguayan Cámara de Comercio, Avenida Libertador Brigadier General Lavalleja 1641, Piso2, Oficina 201, CP 11.100

Montevideo (tel: 908-0349; fax: 908-0936; email: camurbri@netgate.com.uy).

Uruguay Cámara Nacional de Comercio y Servicios, Rincón 454, 11000 Montevideo (tel: 916-1277; fax: 916-1243; email: info@cncs.com.ny).

Banking
Banco de la República Oriental del Uruguay, Cerrito No. 351 Casa Central, Montevideo.

Banco Exterior, Sarandi No. 402, 11000 Montevideo.

Banco Holandés Unido, Sucursal Montevideo, 25 de Mayo No. 501, 11000 Montevideo.

Banco Pan de Azucar, Rincón No. 518/528, 11000 Montevideo .

Banco Santander, Cerrito No. 449, 11000 Montevideo.

Banco Sudameris, Rincón No. 500, Montevideo.

Banco Surinvest, Rincón No. 530, Montevideo.

Banesto-Banco Uruguay, 25 de Mayo No. 401, 11000 Montevideo.

Citibank, Cerrito No. 455, Montevideo.

Discount Bank (Latin America), Rincón No. 390, Montevideo.

The First National Bank of Boston, Zabala No. 1463, 11000 Montevideo.

ING Bank S.A., Misiones No. 352/60, Montevideo.

Lloyds Bank (BOLSA), Zabala No. 1500, Montevideo.

Nuevo Banco Comercial (NBC), Cerrito No. 400, 11100 Montevideo.

Central bank

Banco Central del Uruguay, Diagonal Fabini 777, 11100 Montevideo. (tel/fax: 1967; e-mail: info@bcu.gub.uy).

Travel information

Pluna Airlines, Administration Head Offices, Miraflores 1445, Carrasco (tel: 604-2244; fax: 604-2260; email: info@pluna.aero; internet: www.pluna.com.uy).

Ministry of tourism

Ministerio de Turismo del Uruguay (Ministry of Tourism), Rambla 25 de Agosto de 1825 esq, Yacaré, S/N (plano), Montevideo (tel: 188-5100; internet: www.turismo.gub.uy).

Ministries

Ministerio de Defensa Nacional (National Defence), Edificio 'Gral.Artigas', Avda. 8 de Octubre 2628, Montevideo.

Ministerio de Economía y Finanzas (Economy and Finance), Colonia 1089, P3, Montevideo.

Ministerio de Educación y Cultura (Education and Culture), Reconquista 535, Montevideo.

Ministerio de Ganadería, Agricultura y Pesca (Livestock, Agriculture and Fisheries), Constituyente 1476 Montevideo.

Ministerio de Industria, Energía y Minería (Industry, Energy and Mines), Rincón 747, Montevideo.

Ministerio del Interior (Home Office), Mercedes 993, Montevideo.

Ministerio de Relaciónes Exteriores (Foreign Affairs), Av 18 de Julio 1205, Montevideo.

Ministerio de Salud Pública (Public Health), Av 18 De Julio 1892, Montevideo. Ministerio de Trabajo y Seguridad Social (Labour and Social Security), Juncal 1511, Montevideo.

Ministerio de Transporte y Obras Públicas (Transport and Public Works), Rincón 561, Montevideo.

Ministerio de Vivienda, Ordenamiento Territorial y Medio Ambiente (Housing, Territorial Regulation and Environment), Zabala 1427, Montevideo.

Oficina de Planeamiento y Presupuesto (OPP) (Planning and Budget Office), Dr Luis A de Herrera 3350, Montevideo.

Other useful addresses

Aero Consultora Uruguaya, Florida 1280-202, Montevideo.

Asociación de Importadores y Mayoristas de Almacén, Ed de la Bolsa de Comercio, Rincón 454, Montevideo.

British Embassy, Calle Marco Bruto 1073, Montevideo (tel: 622-3630; fax: 622-7815; email: bemonte@internet.com.uy).

Comisión Para el Desarrollo de la Inversión (Committee for Investment Development), Plaza Independencia 776, P1 11100 Montevideo.

Cenci (Centro de Estadísticas Naciónales y Comercio Internacional del Uruguay) Misiones 136, 1 Montevideo.

Comisión Sectorial para el Mercosur, Paysandú esq, Florida, Montevideo.

Compañía Uruguaya de Exportaciónes S.A. (Comurex), Misiones 1372 Oficina 303, Montevideo.

Dirección General de Comercio Exterior (Bureau of Foreign Affairs), Cuareim 1384, P2 11100 Montevideo.

Dirección General de Estadísticas y Censos (DGEC), Cuareim 2052, Montevideo.

Dirección Nacional de Aduanas, Rbla. 25 de Agosto esq. Yacaré, Montevideo.

Export Trade Uruguay S.A., Caramurú 6092, Montevideo.

International Trade Consortium SRL, Rio Negro 1394, P.3, Montevideo.

Laboratorio Tecnológico del Uruguay, Av Italia 6201, Montevideo.

Latin American Integration Association, Cebollati 1461, Casilla de Correo 577, Montevideo.

Unidad Asesora de Promoción Industrial, Rincón 723, P.2, Montevideo.

Unión de Exportadores, Rincón 454, P.2, Montevideo.

Uruguayan Embassy (USA), 1913 'I' Street, NW, Washington DC 20006 (tel: (1-202) 331-1313; fax: (1-202) 331-8142; e-mail: uruwashi@uruwashi.org).

Other news agencies: Mercopress (in English): www.mercopress.com

Internet sites

El Observador Económico (Spanish): http://www.observador.com.uy

El Pais digital edition (Spanish): http://www.diarioelpais.com.edicion

Crónicas Económicas: http://www.cronicas.com.uy

Montevideo Free Zone (Zona France de Montevideo): http://www.zfm.com

Uzbekistan

KEY FACTS

Official name: Ozbekiston Respublikasy (Republic of Uzbekistan)

Head of State: President Islam Abduganievich Karimov (since 1991; re-elected 23 Dec 2007)

Head of government: Prime Minister Shavkat Mirziyayev (appointed 11 Dec 2003)

Ruling party: Coalition government: Chalk Demokratik Partijasi (CDP) (People's Democratic Party) and independents

Area: 447,400 square km

Population: 27.37 million (2007)*

Capital: Tashkent

Official language: Uzbek

Currency: Sum (Sum) = tiyin

Exchange rate: Sum1,313.44 per US$ (Jul 2008)

GDP per capita: US$815 (2007)*

GDP real growth: 9.50% (2007)*

Labour force: 14.44 million (2006)*

Unemployment: 0.60% (official, 2004); 30.00% (underemployment, 2005)*

Inflation: 12.30% (2007)*

Oil production: 114,000 bpd (2007)

Balance of trade: US$3.99 billion (2006)

Foreign debt: US$4.51 billion (2005)

* estimated figure

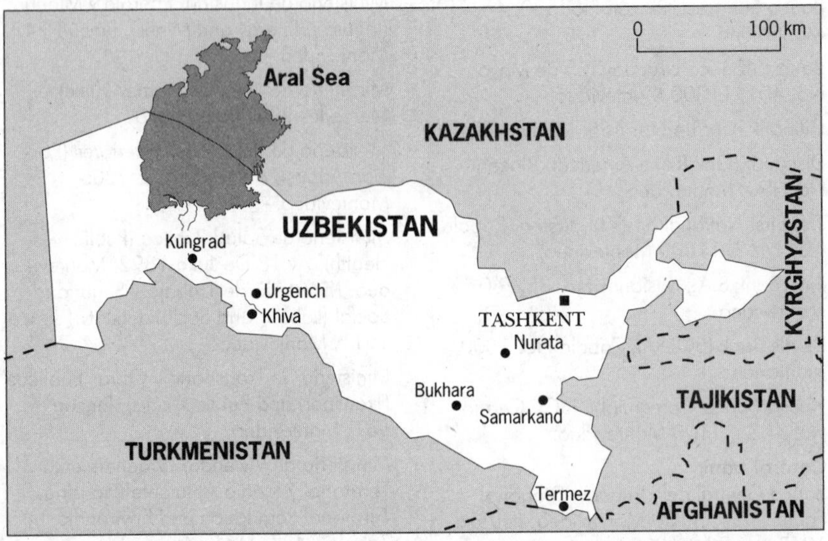

Uzbekistan's economy grew by a respectable 9.5 per cent in 2007, largely driven by the industry and services sectors with growth levels of 12.1 and 26.6 per cent respectively. According to the Asian Development Bank (ADB) in its *Asian Development Outlook* for 2008 Uzbekistan's high growth levels were helped by high commodity prices and buoyant external demand. The only negative in the equation was the inflationary pressure that the high growth levels were likely to generate.

Gas flow

Higher gas production enabled Uzbekistan to boost gas export volumes by some 18 per cent to an estimated US$14.5 billion, at an export gas price that had increased by over 40 per cent in the year. The growth in the services sector was also largely due to the gas industry, as billing for gas transit grew and infrastructure construction activity intensified. Inflationary pressure arose from a number of sources including an increase in the money supply, public sector wage increases and general election activities. Official data sources appeared to underestimate consumer price inflation at 7 per cent, which contrasted sharply with estimates by the International Monetary Fund (IMF) at a more alarming 12.3 per cent. In the view of the ADB Uzbekistan's generally benign economic outlook may deter the government from undertaking necessary economic reforms. In addition to the gas bonanza, Uzbekistan has benefited from high gold prices as one of the metal's largest producers and exporters.

Election farce

Uzbekistan's autocratic ruler Islam Karimov tightened his grip on power when, in a December 2007 election condemned by opposition activists as illegal and a 'farce', he was re-elected president. According to the UK's *The Guardian* Mr Karimov won an overwhelming victory despite being ineligible to stand as a candidate, having already served two consecutive presidential terms. Election officials claimed that Mr Karimov's first term began in 2000 – despite the fact that he has ruled Uzbekistan for 18 years, first as a Communist party boss, and then, after independence, as president.

Despite Western pressure, Karimov has outlawed opposition parties, harassed and imprisoned dissidents, and, despite his own promises, failed to take meaningful steps to stop the routine use of torture against perceived opponents. Scores of dissidents have been executed after sham trials. He appears to be increasingly reliant on his national security service chief, Rustam Inoyatov.

Mr Karimov presides over a particularly authoritarian regime under which dissidents are locked up, and a strange and depressing silence blankets the capital, Tashkent. Before the elections, the secret police arrested dozens of opposition activists and put them in jail. Others were placed under house arrest. The Organisation for Security and Co-operation in Europe (OSCE) sent a tiny election observation mission, saying that 'due to the apparent limited nature of the competition' it saw no point in conducting comprehensive monitoring. According to *The Guardian* activists say that the Karimov regime has become more brutally repressive since the massacre in the eastern city of Andijan in May 2005, when government soldiers killed almost 1,000 people. The official death toll was put at 187 – with Karimov blaming Islamist extremists and the West for the uprising. The revolt prompted Karimov to expel US troops, based in the country since 2001, and to forge a new strategic partnership with Russia.

Uzbekistan has the largest population of any of the former Soviet republics, most recently counted at 27.37 million (2007 estimate). Its strategic situation is important, explaining why both the US and the European Union (EU) during the 1990s courted Uzbekistan. However, its strategic importance emerged more forcefully after the 9/11 terror attacks on New York and the Pentagon. US intelligence and military forces used former Soviet military bases in Uzbekistan to mount their campaign to oust the Taliban government in Afghanistan, and have maintained a presence in the predominantly Muslim country, although they were asked to leave after the regime became deeply suspicious of their on-going activities.

The economy drifts

The World Bank has said that any evaluation of Uzbekistan's economic performance is complicated by the fact that official economic statistics are sometimes unreliable. According to official data, Uzbekistan recorded one of the smallest recessions at the start of the transition, and since the mid-1990s has been growing at around 5 per cent on average, with growth accelerating to over 7 per cent in 2004, 2005 and 2006; it jumped to 9 per cent in 2007. However, at times there have been questions over the reliability of official growth estimates and underlying source data. Private sector activity remains subdued or hidden in the large informal sector. Moreover, growth in recent years was driven by net exports, while domestic consumption has lagged. As a result, economic growth has not led to a significant improvement in living standards. Gross domestic product per capita in 2007 was US$815, representing a modest improvement over the US$358 recorded in 2001. Household survey data reveal that around a quarter of the population is poor (defined as consuming less than the minimum amount of calories needed per day), and around 46 per cent of the population live on less than US$2.15 per day.

The Bank goes on to report that formal employment generation has also been disappointing, and a growing number of Uzbeks have sought employment abroad, particularly in neighbouring Kazakhstan or in Russia. However, compared to other low income countries, Uzbekistan's non-monetary social indicators such as levels of literacy and school enrolment tend to be favourable, reflecting the legacy of Soviet investment in social infrastructure, but also post-independence efforts, particularly in education.

Uzbekistan's external position has been strong since 2003. Thanks in part to the recovery of world market prices of gold and cotton, the country's key export commodities. Foreign exchange reserves, including gold, have more than doubled to over US$3 billion.

Reflecting the government's 'gradual' approach to reform, the pace of transition to a market economy in Uzbekistan has remained slow and uneven. Among the structural reform measures adopted in recent years have been price increases and strengthened payment discipline in the energy sector; conversion of agricultural co-operatives into family leasehold farms; tax and expenditure cuts; easing of the registration, inspection, penalty, and licensing regimes for businesses; and steps towards introducing a mandatory and fully-funded second pillar of the pension system.

Extensive state controls over the economy continue to hinder the functioning of markets and the development of the private sector. Privatisation, particularly large scale, has been limited. Private property rights suffer from repeated violations by state enforcement organs, and the overall business climate remains unfriendly. The financial sector is also hampered by the dominance of a few large state banks and the use of commercial banks as enforcers of tax discipline and collectors of commercial information. Financial sector stability is impaired by the legacy of directed lending. In agriculture, farmers remain subject to state directives under which they are required to grow crops chosen by the government and must surrender the harvest of the key crops – cotton and wheat – at below-market prices to the state. The trade regime, both domestic and external, remains restrictive, and cross-border shuttle trade and domestic trade have been suppressed by administrative measures.

KEY INDICATORS — Uzbekistan

	Unit	2003	2004	2005	2006	2007
Population	m	26.85	26.80	26.24	26.98	*27.37
Gross domestic product (GDP)	US$bn	9.90	11.96	13.67	17.03	*22.31
GDP per capita	US$	386	375	521	631	*815
GDP real growth	%	3.2	7.1	7.0	7.3	*9.5
Inflation	%	10.0	8.8	21.0	14.2	*12.3
Industrial output	% change	–	5.0	5.0	7.4	–
Agricultural output	% change	–	10.1	6.2	6.2	–
Oil output	'000 bpd	166.0	152.0	126.0	125.0	114.0
Natural gas output	bn cum	53.6	55.8	55.7	55.4	58.5
Exports (fob) (goods)	US$m	3,065.0	3,700.0	4,749.0	5,615.0	–
Imports (cif) (goods)	US$m	2,554.0	2,820.0	3,667.0	3,994.0	–
Balance of trade	US$m	511.0	880.0	1,082.0	1,621.0	–
Current account	US$m	780.0	80.0	1,949.0	3,198.0	5,298.0
Foreign debt	US$bn	4.6	4.7	4.5	–	–
Exchange rate	per US$	975.00	1,020.00	1,241.10	1,241.10	1,287.50

* estimated figure

Governance is undermined by lack of government accountability, restrictions on access to information and development of civil society, few possibilities for citizens to comment and participate in policy making, and – as elsewhere in the region – significant corruption. The World Bank notes that as a result Uzbekistan's economic potential remains significantly underutilised. The pace, quality, and sustainability of economic growth must be improved to generate employment for the country's growing population, raise per capita incomes, and alleviate social tensions. While its landlocked location and long distance to major markets impose constraints on Uzbekistan's economic development, the main obstacles to growth in Uzbekistan are policy-related.

Oil and gas

Uzbekistan sits on large oil and natural gas reserves but faces challenges in getting those reserves to world markets. Uzbekistan is reluctant to export its resources through Russian-controlled pipelines, and so must seek to obtain capital and political support for pipelines either through Iran or through Turkey

Uzbekistan contains 600 million barrels of proven oil reserves.The majority of the known oil fields in Uzbekistan are found in the Bukhara-Khiva region, including the Kokdumalak field, which accounts for about 70 per cent of the country's oil production.

The US Energy Information Administration (EIA) reports that after consistent oil production declines since 1998, Uzbekistan has made agreements with foreign oil companies, especially ones from China, to develop small oil fields. Uzbekistan is attempting to privatise Uzbekneftegaz but its desire to maintain holding control over the company may thwart its plans to attract foreign investors. Also the Uzbek government's pledge to increase tax levels by roughly 30 per cent, year-over year, is hindering foreign investment.

Uzbekistan has three refineries – at Fergana, Alty-Arik, and Bukhara – with a total refining capacity of 222,000bpd. The Bukhara refinery, which was the first refinery built in the Commonwealth of Independent States since the break up of the Soviet Union and cost in excess of US$400 million, currently has a capacity of 50,000bpd, although it is expected to expand to 100,000bpd and refine both crude oil and gas condensate. Due to the country's decline in oil production in recent years, Uzbek refineries are operating well below their rated capacity.

Estimated natural gas reserves were 61.6 trillion cubic feet (Tcf) at the end of 2007. Uzbekistan produces natural gas from 52 fields in the country, with 12 major deposits – including Shurtan, Gazli, Pamuk, Khauzak – accounting for over 95 per cent of Uzbekistan's natural gas production. These deposits are concentrated in two general areas: the Amu Dar'ya Basin and in the Mubarek area of the southwest part of the country.

Uzbek natural gas production increased to 58.5 billion cubic metres (bcm) in 2007, from 55.4bcm in 2007 for the year. Uzbekistan is the second largest natural gas producer in the CIS (after Russia). However, Uzbekistan's natural gas fields were heavily exploited in the 1960s and 1970's by the Soviet Union, and as a result several older fields, such as Uchkyr and Yangikazgan, are beginning to decline in production. In order to offset those declines, Uzbekistan is speeding up development at existing fields, such as Garbi and Shurtan, as well as developing new fields and exploring for new reserves.

Risk assessment

Politics	Poor
Economy	Fair
Regional stability	Fair

COUNTRY PROFILE

Historical profile

1865–1876 The Russians took Tashkent and made it the capital of Turkestan, incorporating vast areas of Central Asia. They annexed the emirate of Bukhara and the khanates of Samarkand, Khiva and Kokand
1917 Following the October Revolution in Russia, the Tashkent Soviet was established.
1920 The Tashkent Soviet ousted the emir of Bukhara and the other khans.
1921 Uzbekistan became part of the Turkestan Autonomous Soviet Socialist Republic (ASSR).
1924 The Uzbek Soviet Socialist Republic (SSR) was formed from the Turkestan ASSR, the Bukharan People's Soviet Republic and the Khorezmian People's Soviet Republic; it was given Union Republic status in the Union of Soviet Socialist Republics (USSR).
1930s The Uzbek capital was transferred from Samarkand to Tashkent.
1944 The Soviet leader, Stalin, deported 160,000 Meskhetian Turks from Georgia to Uzbekistan.
1950s–80s Cotton production was boosted as the government undertook major irrigation projects on Uzbekistan's rivers and lakes. The country's water levels were drastically reduced.
1984 Thousands of Uzbek officials were arrested on corruption charges over the 'cotton affair' when millions of roubles went missing as a result of invented crop yields.
1989 Islam Karimov became the leader of the Communist Party of Uzbekistan. Ethnic violence broke out against the Meskhetian Turks and other minorities in the Ferghana Valley. Birlik (Unity), a nationalist movement, was founded.
1990 The Communist Party of Uzbekistan declared economic and political sovereignty and Islam Karimov became president.
1991 Independence from the USSR was declared. Uzbekistan joined the Commonwealth of Independent States (CIS). The first presidential elections were won by Islam Karimov; only a few opposition groups were allowed to field candidates.
1992 President Karimov banned the political parties Birlik and Erk (Freedom) Democratic Party and members of the opposition were arrested.
1994 Uzbekistan signed an economic integration treaty with Russia and an economic, military and social co-operation treaty with Kazakhstan and Kyrgyzstan.
1995 The ruling Chalk Demokratik Partijasi (CDP) (People's Democratic Party), formerly the Communist Party of Uzbekistan, won the elections. A referendum extended President Karimov's term of office until the year 2000.
1996 Uzbekistan, Kazakhstan and Kyrgyzstan agreed to create a single economic market.
1999 The president blamed bomb blasts in Tashkent on the IMU. A declaration of jihad was broadcast by the IMU from a radio station in Iran, demanding the resignation of the Uzbek leadership. The IMU, operating from mountain hideouts, attacked government forces (the first of many future cross-border incursions).
2000 President Karimov was re-elected. Uzbekistan is accused of widespread torture by US-based Human Rights Watch.
2001 The Shanghai Co-operation Organisation (SCO) was formed between Tajikistan, China, Russia, Kazakhstan, Kyrgyzstan and Uzbekistan. The US military were allowed to bases its troops and use Uzbekistan airspace for the US-led military operation in Afghanistan.
2002 A referendum agreed to the unicameral parliament increasing to two chambers and increasing a president's term in office from five to seven years. A long-standing border dispute with Kazakhstan was resolved.
2003 The Birlik movement and the opposition Erk party were allowed to hold official meetings; other political parties were

denied registration. President Karimov dismissed Otkir Sultanov due to the worst cotton harvest ever and appointed Shavkat Mirziyayev as prime minister.
2004 The European Bank for Reconstruction and Development (EBRC) cut aid due to the country's poor record on economic reform and human rights. Trading practices were restricted and sparked violent street protests in the eastern city of Kokland. An agreement with Turkmenistan on water resources was signed. Opposition parties were barred from taking part in parliamentary elections.
2005 After elections the government was formed by the ruling party, CDP, and independents. Violence erupted in Andijan after gunmen released inmates from prison and troops opened fire on demonstrators. The death toll was disputed; eyewitnesses said hundreds had been killed and the government only 180. 15 men were convicted of organising the violence and sentenced to 14–20 years in jail.
2006 Two opposition leaders were jailed for eight years for 'economic crimes' for criticising the crackdown in Andijan. Russia agrees to help in the development of Uzbekistan's gas and oil resources.
2007 President Islam Karimov was elected to a third term in office in December. The result was heavily criticised by international human rights observers for an election that was not considered free or fair.
2008 Igor Vorontsov, the representative of Human Rights Watch, was expelled. A 525km gas-pipeline between Uzbekistan and China began construction in July; when completed it is expected to carry 30 billion cubic metres per year.

Political structure

Constitution

The constitution was adopted in December 1992. It guarantees respect for all citizens, regardless of language, custom or tradition, and forbids any group or individual to exercise power on behalf of the people of Uzbekistan except for the elected president and legislature. The creation of a state ideology and censorship of the media are also contrary to the constitution; however, media censorship is still practised.
The autonomous region of Karakalpakstan has its own constitution, but is subject to the laws of Uzbekistan. Karakalpakstan has the right to withdraw from Uzbekistan depending on support via a referendum.
On 8 December 1992, Uzbekistan became the second Central Asian state to adopt a post-independence constitution. The already considerable powers of the president were increased, giving him the right to appoint regional governors who report directly to him. The constitution also included guarantees of freedom, of conscience and of travel, and a statement that the country should be a secular democracy. President Karimov has pointed to the Turkish state as his country's model. On 27 January 2002, a nationwide referendum agreed with the extension of the president's constitutional term in office from five to seven years and authorised the election of a bicameral parliament.

Form of state

Secular, (theoretically) democratic and presidential republic.

The executive

The president is head of state, holds supreme executive power and is directly elected for no more than two consecutive terms. A January 2002 referendum approved a two-year extension of the president's constitutional term of office from five to seven years (it was originally due to expire in 2005 and has been extended to 2007).
The president appoints the prime minister and ministers, subject to confirmation by the legislature, appoints the judges of the lower courts and the governors of the regions.
The Cabinet of Ministers is the government of the country; it is subordinate to the president.

National legislature

A January 2002 referendum approved increasing the country's parliament from a one-chamber legislature to two.
From December 2004, parliament comprises a lower house (Legislative Assembly with 120 seats, elected for a term of five years), responsible for formulating legislation and considering ministerial nominations, and an upper house (Senate), which will be responsible for approving legislation. President Islam Karimov selects 16 of the Senate's 100 representatives, with the remaining 84 elected from the ranks of regional, district and city legislative councils for each of the country's 12 regions, the city of Tashkent and the autonomous Republic of Karakalpakstan.

Legal system

Judicial power is nominally independent of government, but as the judges of the higher courts are selected from among lower court judges, who are themselves appointed by the president, there is in practice significant political control over the system.
The three highest courts are the Constitutional Court, the Supreme Court and the High Commercial Court. The first rules on the validity of legislation and on disputes between the government of Uzbekistan and the Karakalpakstan autonomous region. The second is the highest court of appeal for criminal and civil cases initiated in the lower courts. The third is the highest court of arbitration for civil cases initiated in the lower courts.

Last elections

26 December 2004/9 January 2005 (parliamentary); 23 December 2007 (presidential).
Results: Parliamentary: The Liberal-Democratic Party won 34 per cent of the vote (41 seats out of 120); CDP won 23.4 per cent (28 seats); Fidokorlar Milliy Demokratik Partiyasi (Fidokorlar National-Democratic Party) 18 seats; Milliy Tiklanish Demokratik Partiyasi (National Renaissance Democratic Party) 11 seats; Adolat Sotsial Demokratik Partiyasi (Adolat Social-Democratic Party) 10 seats; and initiative-group candidates 12 seats. Presidential: Islam Karimov won 90.77 per cent of the vote, no other candidate won more than 3.3 per cent. Turnout was 90.6 per cent.

Next elections

December 2014 (presidential); 2009 (parliamentary).

Political parties

In 1997, legislation came into force prohibiting parties based on ethnic or religious lines, or those advocating war or subversion of the constitutional order.
As a result of amendments to the Law on Elections in August 2003, only registered political parties and voters' initiative groups have the right to field candidates for election.

Ruling party

Coalition government: Chalk Demokratik Partijasi (CDP) (People's Democratic Party) and independents

Main opposition party

All parties in the Supreme Assembly are loyal to the president. The banned O'zbekiston Erk Demokratik Partiyasi (OEDP) (Erk Democratic Party) is considered to be the main opposition party to the Karimov regime.

Political situation

Population

27.37 million (2007)*
Last census: January 1989: 19,810,077
Population density: 60 inhabitants per square km. Urban population: 37 per cent (1995-2001).
Annual growth rate: 1.5 per cent 1994–2004 (WHO 2006)

Ethnic make-up

Uzbek (72 per cent), Russian (8 per cent), Tajik (7 per cent), Kazakh (4 per cent), others (9 per cent). There is a Korean minority estimated at 7 per cent. The Uzbeks are the second most numerous Turkic people in the world after the Turks themselves.

Religions

Muslim (88 per cent, mostly Sunni); Christian Eastern Orthodox (9 per cent).

Education
Although Uzbekistan's overall literacy rate is high, the government is implementing a long-term programme of transition from Cyrillic to Latin script, and in the short-term there is likely to be some changes in the literacy rate.
Primary education begins at aged six and last until aged 10. General secondary education lasts until aged 15, when students may choose between a technical, vocational or academic course for two years. From aged 17, specialised secondary schools offer advanced vocational or academic two-year courses.
There are 16 universities and 42 research institutes in the country, including the state-run Tashkent Islamic University.
The government initiated a National Programme for Personnel Training, giving high priority to introducing new educational technologies and attracting international donors. The reform programme replaced existing schools and it is estimated that seven million pupils will enrol in these new schools, and in sharp contrast with the past, 90 per cent (an unprecedented amount in the New Independent States) of these pupils are expected to enrol in vocational education and training.
In February 2005 a report by the International Crisis Group alleged that thousands of children are forced out of school to work in cotton fields. Uzbekistan is the world's fifth largest cotton producer and during the harvest season children of all ages are used to pick the cotton. Pay for this work may be denied and refusal to work may lead to expulsion from school.
Literacy rate: 99 per cent adult rate; 100 per cent youth rate (15–24) (Unesco 2005).
Compulsory years: Six to 15
Enrolment rate: 100 per cent gross primary school enrolment rate in 2000, 94 per cent at secondary level and 36 per cent at tertiary level.
Pupils per teacher: 21 in primary schools.

Health
Per capita total expenditure on health (2003) was US$159; of which per capita government spending was US$68, at the international dollar rate, (WHO 2006).
Healthcare standards were fairly uniform across the former Soviet Union, but the breakdown in trade and economic crises have brought about a severe shortage of medicines and equipment.
According to a presidential decree in 1999, private healthcare institutions, were exempted from tax in order to facilitate investment in medical equipment; it also included a programme for the development of medical treatment centres in villages over 2001–05. The government also plans to make premises and funds available for private healthcare institutions.
HIV/Aids
HIV prevalence: 0.1 per cent aged 15–49 in 2003 (World Bank)
Life expectancy: 66 years, 2004 (WHO 2006)
Fertility rate/Maternal mortality rate: 2.7 births per woman, 2004 (WHO 2006); maternal mortality 21 per 100,000 live births (World Bank).
Birth rate/Death rate: 23 births and 6 death per 1,000 people (World Bank)
Child (under 5 years) mortality rate (per 1,000): 57 per 1,000 live births; 7.9 per cent of children aged under five are malnourished (World Bank).
Head of population per physician: 2.74 physicians per 1,000 people, 2003 (WHO 2006)

Welfare
Social spending is relatively high compared to most other transitional countries. Social assistance is channelled through traditional local structures using the national Malhalla foundation, which is responsible for meeting the needs of the poor. The Malhalla collects information on the claimants' needs independently of the state. Wages in the agricultural sector have tended to fall behind the national average as a result of high taxes, contributing to increased risks of civil unrest. Expenditure on the social safety net continues to account for 3.5 per cent of GDP and benefits are usually increased in line with wages rather than with official inflation.
There is a comprehensive system of benefits for sickness, disability, maternity and unemployment, as well as a combined state and private pension scheme. However, many of these payments are linked to the declining minimum wage, with the result that those depending on benefits are likely to drop below the poverty line. There are special payments to veterans of the Soviet war in Afghanistan. The government also provides benefits through budget subsidies for housing maintenance and public utilities.

Main cities
Tashkent (capital, estimated population 2.2 million in 2005), Namangan (423,161), Samarkand (374,900), Andizhan (343,232), Bukhara (276,333), Nukus (226,983), Karshi (232,904), Fergana (205,159).

Media
Although the Uzbek Constitution guarantees press freedom, the state maintains tight control of the media with routine harassment of journalists. The government has control of much of the printing and distribution infrastructure. A law, pass in 2007, holds all media outlets responsible for the objectivity of their output and, as such, self-censorship is widespread.
National news agency: Jahon Information Agency
Other news agencies: UzA (Uzbekistan National News Agency): www.uza.uz/en
Press
Dailies: In Uzbek, Hurriyat (www.hurriyat.uz), a government-owned publication, Khalq Sozi has a Russian editionNarodnoe Slovo (www.narodnoeslovo.uz), Uzbekistan Ovozi and Tashkent Hakikati. In Russian, Pravda Vostoka (), Zerkalo XXI (www.zerkalo21.uz). In English, Good Morning and Ovozi Times.
Weeklies: In Uzbek, Mohiyat.
Business: Russian language publications include Review (www.review.uz), Business Partner Uzbekistana and Business-vestnik Vostoka) (Bvv) (Business News of the East) and Kommercheskij Vestnik (Commercial News). In English, publications include Business Partner and Business Review.
Broadcasting
The National Television and Radio Company (MTRK) (www.mtrk.uz) has a network of four TV channels and five radio stations.
Radio: MTRK national stations include radios' Uzbekistan, Yoshlar (the youth station), Mashal, Tashkent and Oltin Zamin. Private, commercial radio stations include Oriat FM (www.oriat.uz), Uzbegim Taronasi (www.fm101.uz), Radio Grand (www.grand.uz) and Radio Sezam FM.
Television: MTRK operates four channels, Uzbekistan, Yoshlar, Sport and Tashkent. There are two national and four, privately run TV stations, located in cities around the country including Bagdad TV and Muloqot from the Fergana region, Bekabad from the Tashket region, Aloqa AK from the Syrdarya region and Samarkand TV and Orbita TV.

Economy
Following independence in 1991, Uzbekistan faced the loss of subsidies from Russia and contracting regional markets, but by following a more cautious restructuring approach, emerged from the transition period in better shape than other states in the region. Uzbekistan was fortunate in being self-sufficient in oil and gas as well as agricultural products. Agriculture is the most important economic activity, employing nearly half the workforce and contributing around 45 per cent to GDP. Growth remains largely dependent on cotton, which accounts for a quarter of foreign exchange earnings. Oil, gas and gold are also major exports.
The government's medium-term objective has been to liberalise trade, attract

foreign investment and realise the benefits of currency convertibility. The government introduced a gradual economic liberalisation programme and pledged to privatise 'non-strategic' state-owned industries, rationalise the financial sector and attempt to attract much-needed foreign investment in an effort to increase know-how and economic efficiency. The government's ability to find buyers for medium- and large-scale enterprises, such as the oil and gas company Uzbekneftegaz and the telecommunications company Uzbektelecom, ultimately depends on the pace of economic reform and asking prices. Many analysts suspect the government has traditionally inflated the latter in order to delay the privatisation programme, a process which will expose the inefficiencies of Uzbekistan's company base and lead to a period of politically sensitive labour shedding.
In recent years, international financial organisations have become wary of lending to Uzbekistan, although the Asian Development Bank has provided financial aid as part of a development programme. In 2004, the European Bank for Reconstruction and Development withdrew aid because of Uzbekistan's poor record on economic reform and human rights and its failure to meet key economic targets.

External trade

Uzbekistan is a member of the Economic Cooperation Organization (ECO), comprising 10 regional Central Asian countries. It belongs to the Eurasian Economic Community (EurAsec or EAEC), which was established in 2000 to promote a customs union between its six member states (Belarus, Kazakhstan, Kyrgyzstan, Russia, Tajikistan, and Uzbekistan), and among other objectives, to introduce standardised currency exchange and rules for trade in goods and service. The EAEC evolved out of the Commonwealth of Independent States (CIS) Customs Union and has begun the process of merging with the Central Asian Co-operation Organisation (CACO). By August 2007 negotiations for Uzbekistan's membership of the World Trade Organisation was still ongoing.
Cotton is the single largest export item, however limited facilities only allow 15 per cent of annual production to be processed; it is the second largest exporter of cotton (after China). Other primary products exported include gold, oil and natural gas.

Imports

Principal imports are machinery and equipment (around 50 per cent of total), foodstuffs, chemicals and metals.
Main sources: Russia (27.6 per cent total, 2006), South Korea (15.5 per cent), China (10.3 per cent).

Exports

Principal exports are cotton (over 40 per cent of total), gold and precious stones, hydrocarbons, mineral fertilisers, ferrous metals, textiles, food products and vehicles.
Main destinations: Russia (23.8 per cent total, 2006), Poland (11.7 per cent), China (10.4 per cent).

Agriculture

Farming

The agricultural sector contributed around 31 per cent to GDP in 2004 and employs around a third of the working population. Only 9 per cent of the land is suitable for cultivation.
Over 1,500 farms operate on a co-operative basis. Family farms dominate 99 per cent of the cotton sector and 93 per cent of the corn sector.
Cotton is the main crop, around a million tonnes a year being produced, three-quarters of it for export. In a report published in early 2005 – The Curse of Cotton: Central Asia's destructive monoculture – the International Crisis Group (ICG) said that while the former Soviet cotton producing countries of Uzbekistan, Tajikistan and Turkmenistan continued to exploit their cotton growers there was little hope of improving economic development and tackling poverty. The cotton industry is vital to the economy of Uzbekistan, yet while the industry continues to rely on cheap labour (including children), land ownership is uncertain, state intervention discourages competition and the rule of law is limited, there is little incentive for the powerful vested interests to reform the system.
In addition to the economic and social costs to the rural populations, the environmental costs of the monoculture have been devastating. The degradation of the Aral Sea in particular has lead to international concern.
Crop production in 2005 included: 5,745,000 tonnes (t) wheat, 152,000t rice, 154,500t maize, 500,000t grapes, 339,766t oilcrops, 20,000t jute, 16,000t treenuts, 18,000t sesame seeds, 11,100t pulses, 850,000t potatoes, 1,200,000t tomatoes, 3,770,000t seed cotton, 1,250,000t cotton lint, 500,000t apples, 20,000t tobacco, 1,276,000t fruit in total, 3,572,300t vegetables in total. Livestock production included: 551,000t meat in total, 450,000t beef, 13,000t pig meat, 70,000t lamb, 16,000t poultry, 104,250t eggs, 4, 300,000t milk, 2,500t honey, 17,000t cocoons (silk), 45,600t cattle hides, 7,200t sheepskins, 16,000t greasy wool.

Forestry

Only 8 per cent of Uzbekistan is forested and commercial exploitation is for domestic purposes only as fuel. There is low production of industrial roundwood, because the government has placed restrictions on harvesting due to the poor condition of forests.
Timber imports in 2004 were US$53.8 million, while exports amounted to US$2.7 million.
Timber production in 2004 included 6,399,152 cubic metre (cum) roundwood, 2,132,000cum industrial roundwood, 230,000cum sawnwood, 485,000cum sawlogs and veneer logs, 1,637,000cum pulpwood, 4,267,152cum woodfuel; 117,655 tonnes (t) charcoal, 11,000t paper and paperboard.

Industry and manufacturing

Industry contributed around 25 per cent to GDP in 2004 and employs 18 per cent of the working population.
Main industries include chemical and gas production, heavy engineering, specialising in machinery for the cotton-growing and textile industries, aircraft construction, metal works, textiles and cotton derivatives, canned foods and nitrogenised fertilisers.

Tourism

Uzbekistan, situated on the route of the ancient Silk Road, is a country rich in historical and cultural heritage, giving it considerable tourist potential. Infrastructure is improving and attractions, including skiing, are being developed.

Environment

The Aral Sea had been drying up due to the overuse of water from the two main rivers which feed into it, with the loss of up to 50 per cent of its water. This resulted in desertification of the surrounding land. However, by 2006, a World Bank funded project had begun a reversal, as building works on the river Syr Darya, in Kazakhstan, increased the level of water in the northern section of the Aral Sea. Work continues to allow more water into the southern section and directly benefit Uzbekistan.
Uzbekistan has numerous environmental problems, more than half of irrigated land is heavily salinated and eroded. Surface and underground water sources used for human consumption in parts of the country have also been polluted by industrial and communal discharges.

Mining

Uzbekistan is rich in unexplored mineral deposits – its potential mineral wealth amounts to a value of US$3,000 billion. There are around 100 deposits of various metals, including gold, silver, uranium, zinc, copper and tungsten, which need developing. Uzbekistan is the

fourth-largest uranium producer in the world.
Uzbekistan is the ninth-largest gold producer in the world. Its commercial reserves are associated with open-cast mines of the Muruntau field in the Kyzylkum desert in central Uzbekistan, which have been developed by the main state gold producer Kyzylkumredmetzoloto (Navoi Integrated Mining and Metallurgical Plant) since 1967. Its annual output amounts to 55–60 tonnes, producing 70 per cent of Uzbekistan's total gold production.
The Zarafshan-Newmont joint-venture between Uzbekistan and the US mining company Newmont, set up in 1995, processes about 200 million tonnes of low-grade ore, previously regarded as waste, from the Muruntau open gold pit. The project is due to end in 2012.
Dzhetymtau, located in the Kyzylkum desert is estimated to hold reserves of 400 tonnes of gold and 350,000 tonnes of tungsten ores.
There are silver deposits in the central Kyzylkum region, which also contain gold, platinum group metals, cobalt and nickel, which can be recovered as by-products.
Uzbekistan is the only producer of enriched uranium in the former Soviet Union. All output is exported, since Uzbekistan has no nuclear reactors.
Uzbekistan's proven uranium reserves are around 80,000 tonnes, while estimated reserves are around 178,000 tonnes.
Sugraly is one of Central Asia's biggest uranium fields and holds an estimated 38,000 tonnes of uranium.
Kyzylkumredmetzoloto (Kyzylkum Precious Metals and Gold) is Uzbekistan's only uranium producer and exporter.
Uzbekistan possesses considerable reserves of lead and zinc.
Copper production in Uzbekistan averages 80,000 tonnes per year, principally from the Kalmakir open mine, with the remainder mined at the Sari Checku open pit. The ore is processed at the Almalyk concentrator.
Uzbekistan produces over 100,000 tonnes per year of feldspar, about one-third of the output of the former Soviet Union. The non-ferrous metal industry includes the mining of bismuth, tungsten and molybdenum. Other natural resources include rock salt, potassium salts, anthracite, graphite, ozokerite, sulphur, quartz, limestone, gypsum, bentonites and semi-precious stones.

Hydrocarbons

Uzbekistan had proved oil reserves of 600 million barrels in 2004 and produced 152,000 barrels per day (bpd). Production meets domestic demand of 131,000 bpd. Thereare three refineries —at Fergana, Alty-Arik and Bukhara with total capacity of 222,000 bpd.
Uzbekistan had proved reserves of natural gas of 1.86 trillion cubic metres in 2004 and is the tenth-largest natural gas producer in the world. Gas production was 55.8 billion cubic metres in 2004.
Principal oil and gas fields include Kuanish, Shakhpakthy and Chembar.
Other fields have been discovered in the Mamangan and Ferghana regions.
Whereas neighbouring Kazakhstan, Azerbaijan and increasingly Turkmenistan have signed numerous multi-million and even multi-billion dollar oil and gas production agreements with foreign energy companies, external involvement in the Uzbekistani sector only began in 2004, when agreements were signed with Russian and Chinese companies. The industry is almost entirely state-controlled, with 14 companies grouped around Uzbekneftegaz (Uzbek Oil and Gas), which is responsible for all aspects of exploration, production, distribution and processing in the hydrocarbons sector.
Uzbekistan has abundant reserves of coal, about one-third of which is highly valued anthracite, but production has rapidly declined and the industry is in need of modernisation. Production meets nearly all domestic needs of around one million tonnes per annum.

Energy

The energy sector is almost entirely state-controlled. Natural gas provides most of the necessary energy for local power generation facilities. Uzbekistan is the largest electricity producer among the Central Asian republics and a net exporter of electricity, supplying regional countries, such as Tajikistan.
Uzbekistan is part of the Central Asian power distribution system along with Kyrgyzstan, southern Kazakhstan, Tajikistan and Turkmenistan. In May 2002, the Uzbekistan government signed an agreement with the interim Afghan government to supply 30MW of electricity to northern Afghanistan.
Uzbekistan has 37 electric power plants with an overall capacity of over 11.2GW. There are hydroelectric power plants on the Syr Darya, Narin and Chirchik rivers, and thermal power stations at Syr Darya, Tashkent, Novo-Angren, Tachiatasch and Ferghana. Hydroelectric plants produce 15 per cent of Uzbekistan's electricity and thermal—powered plants 85 per cent.
Work began on the construction of five hydro-electric power plants in 2002. The largest is the Topalang hydroelectric power station in southern Uzbekistan, which will produce 175MW of electricity annually when fully constructed.

Financial markets

Stock exchange

The Republican Stock Exchange (RSE) 'Tashkent' opened in 1994. It houses a securities exchange, real estate traders, the national investment fund and the national securities depositary. It does not trade all joint-stock companies each month and therefore market capitalisation varies widely.

Banking and insurance

Three state-owned banks dominate the banking sector: Bank Asaka, National Bank of Uzbekistan (NBU) and Narodny Bank.

Central bank

National Bank of Uzbekistan (NBU)

Main financial centre

Tashkent

Time

GMT plus five hours

Geography

Uzbekistan is located in the heart of Central Asia. The fourth-largest republic in the former Soviet Union, Uzbekistan measures approximately 925km from north to south and 1,400km from west to east at its widest points. The republic has a short border with Afghanistan to the south, Kazakhstan lies to the north, Kyrgyzstan and Tajikistan to the east and south-east and Turkmenistan to the south-west.
The western region, including the Karakalpakstan oblast, marks the eastern fringe of the Turkmen desert. The Kyzylkum desert covers most of the area between Tashkent and the Aral Sea. The western reaches of the Tien Shan mountain range protrude from Kyrgyzstan and Tajikistan into south-eastern Uzbekistan. The fertile Ferghana Valley runs from the north-eastern finger of Uzbekistan, east of Tashkent, across the border into Kyrgyzstan. Half of the Aral Sea lies within Uzbekistan, the other half in Kazakhstan.
There are two main rivers. The Amu Darya, which enters from Afghanistan at Termez and runs along the border with Turkmenistan before turning north at Khiva and flowing into the southern end of the Aral Sea. The Syr Darya flows from the Tien Shan mountains northwards, east of Tashkent and into Kazakhstan, eventually reaching the northern end of the Aral Sea.

Hemisphere

Northern

Climate

Uzbekistan comprises mostly desert and semi-desert, with extreme continental temperatures: the average stands at minus 8 degrees Celsius (C) in January and 26 degrees C in June. Temperatures in Tashkent vary from minus 1 degree C in January to 29–40 degrees C or more in summer. Rainfall averages between 80 and 90mm per annum on the plains and 890 to 1,000mm per annum in the mountains.

Dress codes
Smart clothes are required for business visitors. Otherwise dress is not overly formal but modest, particularly outside Tashkent.

Entry requirements
Passports
Passports are required by all and must be valid for at least six months after the intended date of departure.
Visa
Required by all. Business travellers must obtain an invitation from a local company or organisation exceptions include nationals of the US, UK, Austria, Belgium, France, Germany, Italy, Japan, Spain and Switzerland who may apply directly. The Uzbek contact should submit a visa support letter to the Ministry of Foreign Affairs in Tashkent before the visitor applies for a visa. When an approval to visit has been agreed a confirmation is sent by the ministry to the embassy and the visitor should contact a consular section to ensure that a visa issuance confirmation of the Ministry of Foreign Affairs is in place before submitting their application.
To download a visa application see www.uzbekembassy.org and consular section, see visa information for further details.
Travellers on visitor's visas whose stay in Uzbekistan exceeds three days are required to register with the Local Department of the Ministry of Internal Affairs within three working days of arrival. Hotel administration should take care of such registration automatically.
Transit visas issued in other CIS countries are no longer recognised.
Currency advice/regulations
The import and export of local currency is unlimited. The import of foreign currency is unlimited but must be declared on arrival; export is limited to the amount declared. However, proof of legal exchange to local currency must be provided for re-export for imported sums of over US$2,000; retain all currency exchange receipts.
Travellers cheques have limited acceptance.
Customs
Personal items are duty-free, goods to the value of US$10,000 can be imported for personal use; valuable items such as jewellery, cameras, computers must be declared.
The export of antiques and art objects is subject to duty and a special permit from the Ministry of Culture, a certificate stating the age of the item(s) should be obtained when purchased.
Prohibited imports
Firearms, ammunition, illegal drugs, anti-Uzbek propaganda, fruit or vegetables, precious metals, gem stones and furs.

Health (for visitors)
Mandatory precautions
Vaccination certificates are required for yellow fever if travelling from an infected area.
Advisable precautions
Vaccinations for diphtheria, tetanus, hepatitis A and typhoid are recommended. Other vaccinations that may be advised include tuberculosis and hepatitis B. A non-malignant malaria occasionally occurs in the border area of Afghanistan and Tajikistan, visitors should avoid being bitten by using anti-mosquito sprays and long clothing. There is a risk of rabies.
Water precautions are recommended using water purification tablets or drinking bottled water.
Any medicines required by the traveller should be brought into the country and it would be wise to have precautionary antibiotics if going outside major urban centres. A travel kit including a disposable syringe is a reasonable precaution.
Medical insurance is essential, including emergency evacuation.

Hotels
Advisable to book in advance through Uzbektourism or other specialist travel agents.

Credit cards
Credit cards are not widely accepted outside Tashkent's top hotels and restaurants.

Public holidays (national)
Fixed dates
1 Jan (New Year's Day), 8 Mar (Women's Day), 20–22 Mar (Nawruz/Persian New Year), 1 May (Labour Day), 9 May (Victory Day), 1 Sep (Independence Day), 18 Nov (Flag Day), 8 Dec (Constitution Day).
Variable dates
Eid al Adha, Persian New Year, Birth of the Prophet, Eid al Fitr.
Islamic year – 1429 (10 Jan 2008–28 Dec 2008): The Islamic year contains 354 or 355 days, with the result that Muslim feasts advance by 10–12 days against the Gregorian calendar. Dates of feasts vary according to the sighting of the new moon, so cannot be forecast exactly.

Working hours
Banking
Mon–Fri: 0900–1800; Sat: 0900–1500. Banks at Tashkent airport are open only at arrival of international flights.
Business
Mon–Fri: 0800–1300, 1400–1700. Business hours generally include Saturday mornings.
Government
Mon–Fri: 0800–1300, 1400–1700. Some government offices are open Saturday mornings.
Shops
Mon–Fri: 0800–2000/2100. Shops are closed for lunch for one hour at any time between 1100 and 1500.

Telecommunications
Mobile/cell phones
There are 900 and 900/1800 GSM services located in highly populated areas only.

Electricity supply
220V AC, with round two-pin plugs.

Social customs/useful tips
Business is conducted formally. Appointments are essential when business cards are exchanged.
Personal relationships are the key to doing business in Uzbekistan, with the hierarchy confined to a small group of influential families. Establishing contact within that group can be vital.
Gratuities are illegal.
The giving of small gifts is widely practised, not as bribes but as social niceties. Uzbek hospitality is renowned. It may be regarded as insulting to decline an invitation to a private function. Offering basic food is considered insulting. It is polite to see a visitor off at a train station. If travelling on public transport, make sure to give up your seat to the old, parents with children and the disabled. Superstitions are taken somewhat seriously: for example, do not give an even number of flowers, as this is funereal; do not greet people in a doorway – this is considered unlucky.
Local customs of note are ram butting and wrestling, and wedding ceremonies in September which take place in the street.
Alcohol is available and smoking is widespread.

Security
Terrorist bombings in Tashkent have prompted many Western governments to advise their citizens not to visit Uzbekistan unless absolutely necessary. Visitors should alert their presence to their own embassies on arrival and take all precautions and advice given regarding safety measures.
It is unwise to venture out on the streets alone at night. Dress inconspicuously, as wealthy-looking foreigners can be a target for muggers. Identification should be carried at all times, and visitors should avoid photographing official buildings. If taking photographs in the vicinity of police or

soldiers, it is best to ask their permission first.

Since 1999, there has been an increasing terrorist and kidnapping threat in the north-east of the country, especially in the Ferghana Valley and mountainous regions on the Kyrgyz and Tajik borders. Visitors should register with the Uzbek authorities before entering these areas. Outbreaks of violence can lead to strong reactions from the Uzbekistani army, including wide-spread road blocks and the closure of some destinations. If stopped by police, visitors should remain calm and polite.

Getting there

Air

National airline: Uzbekistan Airlines

International airport/s: Tashkent International airport (TAS), 11km from city centre. Facilities include duty-free shops, bureau de change, left luggage, restaurants and bar. There are taxis, trains and trolley buses to the city (journey time 10–20 minutes).

Airport tax: Departure tax: US$10

Surface

There are border crossings with Afghanistan, Kazakhstan, Kyrgyzstan, Tajikistan and Turkmenistan, however not all are open and available to international travellers. Check with local authorities before making an abortive trip.

Road: Primary roads along trade routes are being upgraded to increase access for freight. Secondary roads are in poor condition especially in desert areas such as the borders with Turkmenistan and the western borders with Kazakhstan.

The Regional Road Corridor Improvement Project, estimated at US$18 billion, to improve Central Asian roads, airports, railway lines and seaports and provide a vital transit route between Europe and Asia was agreed, on 3 November 2007. Six new transit corridors, between Afghanistan, Azerbaijan, China, Kazakhstan, Kyrgyzstan, Mongolia, Tajikistan and Uzbekistan, of mainly roads and rail links, will be constructed, or existing resources upgraded, by 2013. Half the costs with be provided by the Asian Development Bank and other multilateral organisations and the other half by participating countries.

Rail: Tashkent is the hub of rail services in Central Asia. Lines run west to Ashgabat (Turkmenistan), south to Samarkand and on to Dushanbe (Tajikistan), east to Bishkek (Kyrgyzstan) and Almaty (Kazakhstan) and north to Moscow (Russia). The distances involved do not make this the most convenient means of travel, services are few and slow, and tickets must be purchased with hard currency, preferably US dollars.

Getting about

National transport

Air: Uzbekistan Airways has scheduled flights to many cities and towns around the country providing a realistically quick method of getting around the country. Tashkent, Bukhara, Samarkand and Urgench are all served by internal flights.

Road: The road network is deteriorating and many published statistics on paved and unpaved roads are often a decade out-of-date. Driving can be hazardous for the visitor and it is recommended that arrangements should be made to use a local driver and a four-wheel drive vehicle, particularly if travelling to the Tien Shan mountain ranges. Tashkent roads are relatively well maintained with street lighting. Outside the city however the risks of driving, especially at night, include livestock and farm vehicles (often animal-drawn). There are security checkpoints at the city limits of Tashkent and other towns throughout the country. A permit is necessary if travelling to Termez and other areas of the Surkhandarya region. The permit can be applied for in Tashkent and usually takes five days to process. Uzbekistan has a large highway police force, and drivers are frequently stopped for minor infractions or document checks.

Buses: Routes between the main cities are served by modern air-conditioned coach services which are reliable but infrequent. Other regional services are irregular and often used for transporting goods and livestock.

Rail: Tashkent, Samarkand and Bukhara are all connected by an electrified network. Some other routes are in varying states of disrepair, and long-distance travel by train should be avoided.

City transport

Taxis: In each city there are official taxis (with sign on top) and unofficial taxis. Agree rates in advance when using the official taxis. A few dollars are sufficient for a local journey in an unofficial taxi. In Tashkent it is safer to use official taxis or hire cars. Taxis can be hired for an hour, a day or a week.

Buses, trams & metro: An underground railway, trolleybus service and buses provide a comprehensive network in Tashkent.

Car hire

The are very few car hire facilities; a national licence with authorised translation or international driving permit is required.

BUSINESS DIRECTORY

The addresses listed below are a selection only. While World of Information makes every endeavour to check these addresses, we cannot guarantee that changes have not been made, especially to telephone numbers and area codes. We would welcome any corrections.

Telephone area codes

International direct dialling code (IDD) for Uzbekistan is +998, followed by area code and subscriber's number:

Bukara	65	Samarkand	66
Ferghana	73	Tashkent	71

Useful telephone numbers

Police: 02

Fire: 01

Ambulance: 03

Chambers of Commerce

American Chamber of Commerce in Uzbekistan, 41 Buyok Turon Street, Tashkent 700000 (tel: 120-6077; fax: 120-7077; e-mail: office@amcham-uzbekistan.org).

Uzbekistan Chamber of Commodity Producers and Entrepreneurs, 6 Bukhoro Street, Tashkent 700047 (tel: 133-0699; fax: 133-3799; e-mail: root@ptp.co.uz).

Banking

Bank Asaka (specialised state joint stock commercial), 67 Nukus Str, 700015 Tashkent (tel: 120-8111; fax: 120-8173).

Narodny Bank (People's Bank), Tashkent.

National Bank for Foreign Economic Activity of the Republic of Uzbekistan, 101 Amir Temur St, 700084 Tashkent (tel: 137-6077; fax: 133-3200).

Pakhta Bank, 79A Nukus St, Apar 1–2, Tashkent 700015 (tel: 120-5855; fax: 120-7712).

Ravnak Bank, 2 Furkat St, Tashkent 700021 (tel: 144-0753; fax: 144-1091).

Tadbirkorbank, 52 S Azimov St, Tashkent (133-1875; fax: 133-8100).

Uzbekistan-Turkish Bank, No.15/B Drujba Naradov Street, Tashkent (tel: 173-8323, 173-8324; fax: 120-6362).

Uzpromstroybank, 3 Shahrisabzskaya St, Tashkent 700000 (tel: 120-4528; 120-4520).

Central bank

Central Bank of Uzbekistan (CBU), Prospekt Uzbekistana 6, Tashkent 700001 (tel: 133-6829; fax: 136-7704).

Travel information

Sairam Tourism, 13A Movarounnahr St, Tashkent 700060 (tel: 133-7411; fax: 120-6937; internet: www.sairamtour.com).

Tashkent Intourist, 69A Navoi St, Tashkent (tel: 144-1294, 144-0278, fax: 144-0776).

Uzbekistan Airways, 41 Movaraunnakhr Street, Tashkent 700060 (tel: 255-1850; fax: 255-6822; internet: www.uzairways.com).

National tourist organisation offices
Uzbektourism, 47 Khorezm St, 700047 Tashkent (tel: 133-3854; fax: 136-7948; internet: www.uzbektourism.uz).

Ministries
Ministry of Agriculture, 4 Navoi St, 700004 Tashkent (tel: 114-1353, 141-0020; fax: 141-0053).

Ministry of Communication, 1 Alexei Tolstoi St, 700000 Tashkent (tel: 133-8503; fax: 133-1695).

Ministry for Cultural Affairs, 30 Navoi St, 700129 Tashkent (tel: 139-4957).

Ministry of Defence, 100 Academician Abdullaev St, 700000 Tashkent (tel: 133-6667).

Ministry of Energy and Electrification, 6 Horezm St, 700000 Tashkent (tel: 133-6128; fax: 136-2700).

Ministry of Finance, 5 Mustaqillik Sq, 700078 Tashkent (tel: 1391943; fax: 144-5643).

Ministry of Foreign Affairs, 9 Uzbekistan Ave, 700029 Tashkent (tel: 133-6475; fax: 139-4348; internet: http://jahon.mfa.uz).

Ministry of Foreign Economic Relations, Elyor Madjidovich Ganiev, 75 Buyuk Ipak Yuli St, 700077 Tashkent (tel: 1670734, 168-9256, 134-4480; fax: 168-7231, 168-7477).

Ministry of Health, 12 Navoi St, 700012 Tashkent (tel: 141-1680; fax: 141-1641).

Ministry of Higher and Special Secondary Education, 6 Mustaqillik Sq, 700078 Tashkent (tel: 139-4808; fax: 139-4329).

Ministry of Internal Affairs, 1 Herman Lopatin St, 700029 Tashkent (tel: 158-3614; fax: 133-8934).

Ministry of Justice, 5 Hamza St, 700047 Tashkent (tel: 133-5039; fax: 133-5176).

Ministry of Labour, 4 Abai St, 700195 Tashkent (tel: 141-7628; fax: 139-7821).

Ministry of Land Improvement and Water Economy, 5a Abdulla Qodiri St, 700128 Tashkent (tel: 141-1353; fax: 141-4924).

Ministry of Public Education, 5 Mustaqillik Sq, 700078 Tashkent (tel: 139-4214; fax: 139-1173).

Ministry of Social Security, 20a Abdulla Avioni St, 700100 Tashkent (tel: 153-5371).

Other useful addresses
British Embassy, 67 Gulyamov St, Tashkent 700000 (tel: 120-6574; fax: 120-6430; email: brit@emb.uz).

Business-Vestnik Vostoka (BVV) (English newspaper) (32 Matbuotchilar St, Tashkent (tel: 133-9593; email: bvv@bvv.bcc.com.uz).

Cabinet of Ministers, 5 Mustakillik Maidoni, Tashkent (tel: 139-8188; fax: 139-8121).

Central Asia Research Forum, School of Oriental and African Studies, Thornhaugh St, London WC1H 0XG, UK (tel: (+44) 171-323-6300; fax: (+44) 171-436-3844).

EU Co-ordinating Unit, Tarasa Chevchenka St Dom 4, 700029 Tashkent (tel: 138-4018, 156-3479, 156-0417; fax: 132-0652).

Foreign Investment Agency, 4th Floor, 16A Navoi Street, Tashkent (tel: 141-5541, 141-5752; fax: 189-1201).

Government House, 700008 Tashkent (tel: 139-8295; fax: 139-8601).

National Agency for Telecommunications and Postal Services, 1 Tolstoy Street, Tashkent (tel: 133-6503, 133-6645; fax: 139-8732).

National Association of Gold Mining and Diamond Processing Companies, 26 Turaqorghan Thoroughfare, 700019 Tashkent (tel: 148-0720; fax: 144-2603).

National Joint Stock Corporation for Construction in the City of Tashkent, 16a Uzbekistan Ave, 700027 Tashkent (tel: 133-9033; fax: 136-4788).

SME Development Agency, 89 Gargarin St. Samarkand, PO Box 703029 (tel: 124-2966; fax: 131-0107; email: ravshan@samarkand.silk.glas.apc.org).

State Company for Television and Radio Broadcasting, 69 Navoi St, 700011 Tashkent (tel: 133-8106; fax: 144-0021).

State Committee on Agriculture and Construction of the Republic of Uzbekistan, 6 Abai St, 700011 Tashkent (tel: 144-0084/5).

State Committee on Forecasting and Statistics of the Cabinet of Ministers, 45a Uzbekistanskii Ave, 700008 Tashkent (tel: 139-8216, 139-8669; fax: 167-2509, 167-7816).

State Committee on Forests, 49a Uzbekistan Ave, 700017 Tashkent (tel: 145-9180).

State Committee on Geology and Mineral Resources, 11 Taras Shevchenko St, 700060 Tashkent (tel: 133-7206; fax: 156-0283).

State Committee on Precious Metals, 26 Turk-Kurganskiy Proezd, 700019 Tashkent (tel: 148-0720, 148-0663; fax: 144-2603, 148-0481).

State Committee for Privatisation (GKI), Mustaqillik Maydoni 6, Tashkent (tel: 139-8768; fax: 139-8548).

State Committee on the Protection of Nature, 5a Abdulla Qodyri St, 700000 Tashkent (tel: 141-0442; fax: 141-3990).

State Committee on Science and Technology, 29 Hadicha Syleimonova St, 700017 Tashkent (tel: 139-1843; fax: 139-1243).

State Committee for Television and Radio, Ulitsa Khoremzskaya 49, Tashkent (tel: 144-3287).

State Corporation on Industrial and Civil Engineering Construction, 17 Proletar St, 700060 Tashkent (tel: 133-7725; fax: 133-1041).

State Corporation of Local Industries, 5 Mustaqillik Sq, 700078 Tashkent (tel: 139-1058; fax: 139-4853).

State Joint-Stock Association on Trade, 6 Mustaqillik Sq, 700078 Tashkent (tel: 139-4971; fax: 139-1282).

State Property Committee of the Republic of Uzbekistan, Prospekt Uzbekistanskij 55, 700003 Tashkent (fax: 113-94617; 139-2236).

Embassy of Uzbekistan (USA) 1746 Massachusetts Avenue, NW Washington 20036-1903 (tel: (+1-202) 887-5300; fax: (+1-202) 293-6804; internet: www.uzbekistan.org).

Uzbek Information Agency (state news agency), Ulitsa Khamza 2, Tashkent (tel: 139-4982, 133-1622).

Uzbekinvest, 5 Mustaqillik Sq, 700078 Tashkent (tel: 139-1989; fax: 189-1538, 144-5186).

Uzbekiston Ovozi Times (English newspaper), 32 Matbuotchilar St, Tashkent (tel: 133-2036, 133-3855; fax: 133-7914).

Uzbekneftgas (national corporation of the oil and gas industry), 21 Akhunbabaev St, 700047 Tashkent (tel: 133-5757; fax: 132-1062).

Uzbek Post Office, 1 Tolstoy Street, Tashkent (tel: 133-5747; fax: 136-0921).

National news agency: Jahon Information Agency

Other news agencies: UzA (Uzbekistan National News Agency): www.uza.uz/en

Internet sites
The Times of Central Asia: www.times.kg
News and commercial information: www.uzreport.com

General and government information: www.uzland.uz

Regional news and links: www.eurasianet.org

Vanuatu

KEY FACTS

Official name: Ripablik blong Vanuatu (Republic of Vanuatu)

Head of State: President Kalkot Mataskelekele (since 16 Aug 2004)

Head of government: Prime Minister Ham Lini (from 11 Dec 2004)

Ruling party: National unity government, a coalition of 10 political parties coalition led by Vanua'aku Pati (Our Land Party) with National Unity Party (VP/NUP) (since Aug 2004)

Area: 11,880 square km (82 islands)

Population: 229,000 (2007)*

Capital: Port Vila (on Efate)

Official language: Bislama (Ni-Vanuatu Pidgin), English, French

Currency: Vatu (V) = 100 centimes

Exchange rate: V95.48 per US$ (Jul 2008)

GDP per capita: US$1,989 (2008)

GDP real growth: 5.00% (2007)*

Inflation: 3.90% (2007)*

Balance of trade: -US$57.80 million (2004)

Foreign debt: US$68.60 million (2003)

* estimated figure

COUNTRY PROFILE

Historical profile

Human settlement dates back to around 4,000 BC.
1606 Portuguese explorers, Luis Váez de Torres and Pedro Ferdinand de Queirós arrived on the island they called Espiritu Santo, at Big Bay.
1792 Captain Cook explored the islands in 1792, calling the group the New Hebrides.
1887 The islands were administered as a joint French-British naval commission.
1906 An Anglo-French Condominium was established. Over half the male population was conscripted as indentured workers into Australia. The native population dropped dramatically, falling to 45,000 by 1935.
1938 A new religion emerged called the John Frum Cargo cult.
1956 The John Frum Cargo religious cult was recognised by the authorities.
1960s An independence movement, NaGriamel, grew; it advocated the return of land to the native Ni-Vanuatu.
1971 Over 36 per cent of the land was owned by foreigners, NaGriamel petitioned the United Nations to prevent further sales to non-indigenous people.
1977 The UK, France and local representatives agreed independence plans.
1980 The leader of NaGriamel attempted to gain independence for Espiritu Santo, but the insurrection was put down and the entire state of New Hebrides gained independence on 30 July, under the new name Vanuatu. The first prime minister was (Anglican Priest) Walter Lini.
1981 Vanuatu joined the United Nations.
1995 A coalition government of the Union des Partis Moderés (UPM) (Union of Moderate Parties) (Francophone) and the National United Party (NUP) (Anglophone) took office and Serge Vohor became prime minister.
1998 Donald Kalpokas formed a coalition government, comprising his Vanua'atu Party (VP) (Party of Our Land) and the NUP.
1999 John Bernard Bani was elected president. Parliament elected Barak Sopé prime minister ousting Donald Kalpokas.
2001 Sopé and his government were ousted following a no-confidence vote. A new government was formed with a coalition of the UPM and the VP, with Edward Natapei as prime minister.
2002 An earthquake struck Vanuatu, causing US$700,000 of damage. The UPM won the parliamentary elections.
2004 Cyclone Ivy caused flooding in many areas and some 1,000 people were evacuated to temporary shelters in Port Vila. In snap elections no clear majority was achieved, the VP, NUP, Vanuatu Republican Party (VRP), National Community Association (NCA) and People's Progressive Party (PPP) formed a coalition government. Alfred Masing Nalo was elected president by an electoral college, but the supreme court removed him and after several attempts to resolve the matter, Kalkot Mataskelekele finally became president. Serge Vohor became prime minister and formed a government of national unity. Vohor was ousted in a no-confidence motion and Ham Lini Vanuaroroa was elected prime minister.
2005 The active volcano Maroum, on Ambae, erupted and forced thousands of people to be evacuated.
2006 In March, disagreement over a decision to transfer the kava monopoly to government control resulted in the dismissal of the agriculture minister.
2007 Tribal violence, between rival islanders from Ambryn and Tanna, who had migrated to the capital of Port Vila, broke out when the death of one sorcerer had been attributed to another. Three deaths followed the fighting and a temporary state of emergency was imposed.
2008 Vanuatu completed the domestic requirements of the Pacific Island Countries Trade Agreement (PICTA) in February.

Political structure

Constitution

The constitution created a republic, headed by a president with ceremonial powers only. The president is elected by a two-thirds majority in an electoral college from members of parliament and presidents of regional councils including Shefa, Sanma, Penama, Tafea, Malampa and Torba. The president serves a five-year term.

A Malvatumauri (National Council of Chiefs) advises the government on matters of custom, land tenure and the preservation of Vanuatu's traditions. Members of the council are hereditary peers and may not sit in parliament unless given leave to and elected by their peers.

Form of state

Republic

The executive
The executive consists of a Council of Ministers headed by the prime minister who is elected by parliament from among its members. The prime minister and the 12 co-members of the Council of Ministers oversee the administration of the 13 government ministries.
The president, who is head of state, is elected for a five-year term by an electoral college made up of the members of parliament and the presidents of the six provincial governments. A two-thirds majority is required.
National legislature
The 52-member parliament is elected by universal adult suffrage for a four-year term in multi-seat constituencies.
Legal system
Based on English law.
Last elections
13/16 August 2004 (presidential); 6 July 2004 (parliamentary).
Results: Parliamentary: Vanua'aku Pati (VP) (Party of Our Land); Parti national uni (National United Party) (NUP) alliance won 18 seats (out of 52); Union des Partis Moderés (UPM) (Union of Moderate Parties) won nine seats; Parti Républican de Vanuatu (Vanuatu Republican Party) (VRP) four seats; Confédération Verte (Green Confederation) (GC) three seats; Parti progressiste populaire (People's Progressive Party) (PPP) three seats; Parti progressite mélanésien (Melanesian Progressive Party) (MPP) two seats; Association de la communauté nationale (National Community Association) (NCA) two seats; Parti de l'Action Populaire (People's Action Party) (PAP) one seat; Namangi Aute one seat; and independents nine seats.
Parliamentary election of presidential: Kalkot Mataskelekele won 49 out of 56 electoral college votes; Willie David Saul won seven.
Next elections
18 September 2008 (parliamentary)

Political parties
Ruling party
National unity government, a coalition of 10 political parties coalition led by Vanua'aku Pati (Our Land Party) with National Unity Party (VP/NUP) (since Aug 2004)
Main opposition party
Political situation
Who owns and who has the right to determine the fate of either tribal or public land has created problems for the government. On the one hand the government wishes to take up partnerships with foreign companies and provide land for commercial endeavours to develop the islands. On the other hand, local people consider traditional lands to be in the ownership of all the community and are not in the government's purview to sell or lease.

Population
229,000 (2007)*
Last census: November 1999: 186,678
Population density: 15 inhabitants per square km. Urban population: 22 per cent (1995–2001).
Annual growth rate: 2.1 per cent 1994–2004 (WHO 2006)
Ethnic make-up
The great majority of the population is Melanesian in origin, with around 5 per cent of European descent.
Religions
About 80 per cent of the population is Christian, although animism is still in evidence, and the cargo cult remains on Tanna Island. There have been localised secessionist movements in Santo, Malekula, Ambrym, Aoba, Pentecost and Maewo.
Education
In November 2003, the EU awarded a grant of eur8 million to 14 pacific countries to be used to enhance basic education, and in the case of Vanuatu, to extend compulsory schooling to eight years.
Literacy rate: 53 per cent adult rate in 2004
Compulsory years: Six to 12.
Enrolment rate: 117 per cent gross primary enrolment; 28.5 per cent gross secondary enrolment, of relevant age groups (including repeaters) (Unicef 2004).
Health
Per capita total expenditure on health (2003) was US$110; of which per capita government spending was US$81, at the international dollar rate, (WHO 2006).
HIV/Aids
In August 2004, Vanuatu had two confirmed HIV/Aids cases.
Life expectancy: 68 years, 2004 (WHO 2006)
Fertility rate/Maternal mortality rate: 4.0 births per woman, 2004 (WHO 2006)
Child (under 5 years) mortality rate (per 1,000): 31 per 1,000 live births (World Bank)
Main cities
Port Vila, on Efate (capital, estimated population 37,735 in 2005), Luganville (Santo) (12,846).
Languages spoken
English is spoken by 60 per cent of the population and French by 40 per cent. There are 115 indigenous languages.
Official language/s
Bislama (Ni-Vanuatu Pidgin), English, French
Media
Other news agencies: ABC Pacific Beat: www.radioaustralia.net.au/pacbeat
Pacific Magazine: www.pacificmagazine.net
Press
In English, the only daily is Vanuatu Daily Post (www.dailypost.com.vu), other weeklies are Port Vila Presse (www.news.vu/en), The Vanuatu Independent (www.independent.vu), Nasara (), and in Bislama Ni-Vanuatu.
Broadcasting
The state-owned Vanuatu Broadcasting and Television Corporation (VBTC) is responsible for public transmissions.
Radio: The VBTC operates Radio Vanuatu AM and Nambawan FM, in Bislama, English and French. External services by RFI

KEY INDICATORS — Vanuatu

	Unit	2003	2004	2005	2006	2007
Population	m	0.21	0.21	0.22	*0.22	*0.23
Gross domestic product (GDP)	US$bn	0.28	0.32	0.37	0.41	*0.46
GDP per capita	US$	1,150	1,484	1,692	*1,851	*1,989
GDP real growth	%	2.4	3.0	6.8	7.2	*5.0
Inflation	%	3.0	2.8	1.2	2.1	*3.9
Exports (fob) (goods)	US$m	22.0	34.2	38.0	37.7	–
Imports (cif) (goods)	US$m	93.0	92.0	131.2	147.6	–
Balance of trade	US$m	-71.0	-57.8	-93.2	-109.9	–
Current account	US$m	-20.0	-10.0	-67.0	-55.4	*-60.0
Total reserves minus gold	US$m	43.8	61.8	67.2	104.7	119.6
Foreign exchange	US$m	38.8	56.5	62.2	99.3	113.8
Exchange rate	per US$	122.56	111.79	107.34	107.34	100.00

* estimated figure

Radio France, BBC and Radio Australia are received. Laef FM is a religious radio station.
Television: VBTC operates Television Blong Vanuatu, the only public service. Cable and satellite services are available including Vanuatu TV (http://vanuatu.tv).

Economy
The majority of Vanuatu's population is engaged in subsistence agriculture.
Vanuatu's main export, copra, is a commodity subject to wide fluctuations in price on the world market. However, steps have been taken to reduce dependence on it by developing exports of cocoa, timber, beef and fish. Earnings from tourism and the tax-free financial centre help offset trade deficits and provide employment. The financial sector opened in 1971 and is an important foreign exchange earner.
Since the mid-1990s, macroeconomic performance has deteriorated rapidly due to structural problems, external factors and political instability. GDP growth stagnated in much of the late 1990s, recovering to 2.7 per cent in 2000, then falling again in 2001 and 2002, until it picked up in 2003 to 2.4 per cent and 3.0 per cent in 2004. Inflation has generally been stable at between 2–4 per cent.
The problems afflicting the Vanuatu economy arise from its narrow export base, which made it vulnerable in the Asian crisis, and currency devaluations in competing economies such as Fiji, the Solomon Islands and Papua New Guinea. The volatility of coalition governments in the recent past has deterred foreign investors who were already put off by the country's poor infrastructure and a lack of skills and education.
The tourism sector is recognised by the government as a key sector in its economic development to provide employment opportunities for its young and rapidly growing population. Although bureaucracy is one of the issues facing new investment, there have been some successful investment proposals approved by the Vanuatu Foreign Investment Board, which have centred on the tourism, international finance and agricultural sectors.
Vanuatu's beef industry has been a success, mainly due to access to export markets, since domestic demand for beef is not sufficient to keep the enterprise going.
Overall economic growth is low, in contrast to population growth, which is estimated to be growing by 2.6 per cent per year.
In April 2004, a new US$1.4 million five-year plan for Australian aid was agreed between the two countries.

External trade
Vanuatu is a member of the South Pacific Regional Trade and Economic Co-operation Agreement (Sparteca) along with 12 other regional nations, which allows products duty free access by Pacific Island Forum members to Australian and New Zealand markets (subject to the country of origin restrictions). It is also a member of the Melanesian Spearhead Group (with Fiji, Papua New Guinea and the Solomon Islands) as a sub-regional trade group, whereby customs tariffs have been harmonised and a free trade agreement is in negotiation.
Agriculture provides 80 per cent of commodity exports, however tourism is the largest export earner. A new sector in financial services has been introduced by the government.

Imports
Principal imports are machinery and equipment, live animals and foodstuffs, vehicles and fuels.
Main sources: Australia (20.0 per cent total, 2006), Japan (19.2 per cent), Singapore (11.7 per cent).

Exports
Main exports are copra, beef, timber, kava and tuna.
Main destinations: Thailand (59.0 per cent total, 2006), India (16.5 per cent), Japan (11.3 per cent).

Agriculture
Farming
The agricultural sector accounts for around 20 per cent of GDP, employs 70 per cent of the workforce and provides up to 80 per cent of the country's exports.
Agricultural production and livestock rearing is mainly carried out by smallholding farmers. More than 90 per cent of all the fruit and vegetables consumed in Vanuatu are imported.
Around 41 per cent of the land area is cultivatable, although only half is utilised. The soil is generally fertile and rainfall adequate, although crops can be subject to cyclone damage. The sector is hampered by a general lack of capital and investment, technical skills as well as the isolation of farmers.
Copra is Vanuatu's main export crop, accounting for approximately one-third of total export earnings and 6 per cent of GDP. Copra prices had been falling up to 2004 when world prices rose at a time when the Vanuatu Commodities Marketing Board (VCMB) opened up the market to competitive buyers in 2003. Output of copra reached 36,000 tonnes in 2004, and the sector has made a move towards coconut oil processing with exports generating US$9.3 million. In 2003 a new mechanised coconut-desiccating factory opened, in the northern region, capable of processing 24,000 coconuts per day. It is projected that this plant will produce 44 tonnes of coconut oil and 118 tonnes of coconut meat per day expanding export markets.
Kava, used for manufacturing tranquilliser drugs, has become an important export commodity, although production was scaled back due to plant disease and medical concerns over the substance's effects on the liver. Australia and New Zealand lifted a ban on kava after finding that these claims could not be substantiated, although in early 2006 Australia was considering banning the import as it was having an adverse affect on Aborigine communities.
Cattle rearing and forestry are becoming increasingly important foreign exchange earners.
Crop production in 2005 included: 315,000 tonnes (t) coconuts, 700t maize, 14,300t bananas, 1,000t cocoa beans, 110t spices, 42,500t roots and tubers, 2,450t groundnuts, 22,000t fruit in total, 41,685t oilcrops, 10,800t vegetables. Estimated livestock production included: 6,640t meat in total, 3,300t beef, 2,805t pig meat, 26t goat meat, 500t poultry, 320t eggs, 3,000t milk.

Fishing
An experimental project to seed reefs with trochus raised in hatcheries is under way (the shells are collected and sold as buttons). Investment project permits have been issued for fish farming.
The typical annual fish catch is over 27,000t, with 850t other seafood and 100,000 units pearls and shells.
In 2004, the total marine fish catch was 64,996 tonnes and the total crustacean catch was 29,741 tonnes.

Forestry
Access only by sea to exploitable forests has limited timber production. The government is working to achieve certification by the International Tropical Timber Organisation (ITTO) to prove that the country's forests are being sustainably managed. This would increase the added value of timber products.
In 2004 forest exports amounted to US$3.1 million, and imports amounted to US$1.4 million.
Timber production in 2004 included 119,000 cubic metre (cum) roundwood, 28,000cum sawnwood, 28,000cum sawlogs and veneer logs, 2,500,000cum pulpwood, 91,000cum woodfuel.

Industry and manufacturing
The industrial sector accounts for approximately 12 per cent of GDP and employs 5 per cent of the workforce. Manufacturing contributes about 5 per cent of GDP.
Main industries include copra processing, meat canning, fish processing, soft drinks bottling, furniture making, timber production, metalwork and handicrafts for the growing tourist market.

Japan has played an important part in helping to improve regional commercial centres for transporting and distributing agricultural products and other goods, providing investment for wharves on Tanna and Malekula Islands.
Industrial production increased by 1 per cent in 2003.

Tourism
Tourism is the main source of foreign exchange. The sector passed through a difficult period after its best year in 2000, when 57, 591 visitors were recorded and the sector accounted for 40 per cent of GDP. Affected in 2001 by the general downturn in tourist activity, arrivals fell to 53,300. The decline continued in 2002, due to a high exchange rate, competition from other Pacific destinations and cyclones. Aided by improving air connections and increased cruise ship tours, the sector began to recover slowly in 2003, but took off again in 2004 with a record 60,611 visitors. Australia continues to be the main market.
In July 2008 Unesco granted Roi Mata Domain World Heritage status.

Mining
While Vanuatu has mineral resources, including precious metals, these have yet to be exploited. In 2006, the government signed an agreement with a Swiss-American company to exploit the manganese spoil left over at an abandoned mine on Efate. Hundreds of jobs are expected to be created.

Hydrocarbons
Vanuatu does not have any hydrocarbon reserves. Refined oil is imported to meet domestic requirements. The government is encouraging renewable energy companies to invest in Vanuatu.

Energy
Vanuatu has around 32MW of installed generating capacity, entirely based on refined oil imports.
In 2000, Vanuatu became the first country in the Asia-Pacific region to attempt to base its entire economy on renewable energy. It plans to reach that goal by 2020, with electricity generated by geothermal heat, wind and solar power and locally manufactured hydrogen-based fuels, which could also be exported.

Banking and insurance
The introduction in 1983 of the International Companies Act helped Vanuatu to develop as an offshore banking centre, attracting some 100 banks. Following the 11 September 2001 terrorist attacks in the US, the US cut off all direct financial dealing with Vanuatu. The aim was to block all financial transactions that could be linked to terrorists, although Vanuatu was not considered to be a haven for terrorist assets. Vanuatu complied with the requirements of the OECD and was removed from the list of nations with 'tax havens' in 2003.

Central bank
Reserve Bank of Vanuatu

Main financial centre
Port Vila

Time
GMT plus 11 hours

Geography
Vanuatu comprises an irregular archipelago of about 80 islands in the south-west Pacific Ocean, spread over a distance of about 900km (560 miles) from north to south. The islands lie about 1,000km (600 miles) west of Fiji and 400km (250 miles) north-east of New Caledonia.
Most islands are mountainous and volcanic in origin. The capital and second largest town are on the islands if Efate and Espiritu Santo, respectively. Mount Tabwemasana, on Espiritu Santo, (height 1,877 metres) is the highest peak in the archipelago.

Hemisphere
Southern

Climate
Temperatures can range from 16–33 degrees Celsius and rainfall varies from 1,000–2,000mm per annum. Cyclones may occur from December to April.

Entry requirements
Passports
Required by all and must be valid for six months from date of arrival.

Visa
Required by all except citizens of the Commonwealth, EU, and the US for stays of up to 30 days. For a full list of exceptions see www.vanuatu.discoverparadise.org and follow link to resources to travel tips then to Visa Requirements. All travellers must hold onward/return tickets and sufficient funds for their stay.
A visa application can be downloaded from the above internet address (and follow links) and must be forwarded to the Principal Immigration Officer, The Immigration Department, Port Vila, Vanuatu, PMB 014 and must be approved before entry.

Prohibited entry
Anyone whose demeanour is not considered acceptable is prohibited entry.

Currency advice/regulations
The import and export of local and foreign currency is unrestricted.
Travellers cheques are widely accepted.

Customs
Personal items are duty-free. All goods of commercial value must be declared.

Prohibited imports
Firearms, ammunitions, illegal drugs, animals, plants and goods carried on behalf of other persons.

Health (for visitors)
Mandatory precautions
Vaccination certificate for yellow fever if travelling from an infected area.

Advisable precautions
Vaccinations for diphtheria, tetanus, hepatitis A and typhoid are recommended. Other vaccinations that may be advised include tuberculosis and hepatitis B. Malaria prophylaxes are required including mosquito nets, insect sprays and long clothing at night. Sunscreen is highly recommended, even in winter.
Any medicines required by the traveller should be brought into the country. Medical insurance is essential, including emergency evacuation.

Hotels
A 10 per cent tax is added to hotel bills.

Credit cards
Major credit cards are widely accepted. ATMs are available in most banks.

Public holidays (national)
Fixed dates
1 Jan (New Year's Day), 21 Feb (Father Lini Day), 5 Mar (Custom Chief's Day), 1 May (Labour Day), 24 Jul (Children's Day), 30 Jul (Independence Day), 15 Aug (Assumption Day), 5 Oct (Constitution Day), 29 Nov (Unity Day), 25–26 Dec (Christmas).

Variable dates
Good Friday, Easter Monday, Ascension Day.

Working hours
Banking
Mon–Fri: 0830–1500.

Business
Mon–Fri: 0800–1100, 1300–1700.

Government
Mon–Fri: 0730–1700.

Shops
Mon–Fri: 0730–1630/1700 (large supermarkets open until 1930). Sat: 0800–1200. Some shops open Sun morning.

Telecommunications
Telephone/fax
Domestic and international telecommunications are operated by Telecom Vanuatu. Formed in 1989, this is jointly owned by the government of Vanuatu and British and French telecommunications companies. A domestic firm, Communication Services (Vanuatu) Ltd, was granted a telecommunications licence in 1999.

Mobile/cell phones
There is a 900 GSM service in operation.

Internet/e-mail

Electricity supply
220V AC, 50 Hz with flat, three-pin plugs.

Weights and measures
Metric system

Social customs/useful tips
Tipping and bartering are not considered polite behaviour. It is customary to shake hands on meeting and taking leave.
An informal attitude prevails in business. Sometimes business cards are exchanged after introduction. Business is often conducted in Pidgin, English or French.

Getting there
Air
National airline: Air Vanuatu
International airport/s: Port Vila-Bauerfield (VLI), 6km from Port Vila (on Efate); duty-free shop, currency exchange, hotel reservations, post office, car hire and business lounge.
Airport tax: Departure tax: V2,500, included in ticket price.
Surface
Main port/s: Port Vila and Luganville (Santo)

Getting about
National transport
Air: VanAir operates inter-island services to 16 destinations from Port Vila-Bauerfield airport. A V400 service charge is imposed at every airport for any domestic flight.
Road: There are some 150km of surfaced road on Efate, and 100km on Espiritu Santo, which are passable in dry weather.
Buses: Privately run minivans operate unscheduled and unspecified routes around the islands.
Water: Inter-island sea links are unscheduled but generally good.
City transport
Taxis: Taxi services are plentiful and metered. Journey time from the airport to the city centre is about 10 minutes.
Buses, trams & metro: Buses serve the whole of Port Vila. Journey time from airport to city centre is 10 minutes.

Car hire
Car hire is available in Port Vila and Luganville. International, French and UK licences are acceptable.

BUSINESS DIRECTORY

The addresses listed below are a selection only. While World of Information makes every endeavour to check these addresses, we cannot guarantee that changes have not been made, especially to telephone numbers and area codes. We would welcome any corrections.

Telephone area codes
The international direct dialling code (IDD) for Vanuatu is +678 followed by subscriber's number.

Useful telephone numbers
Police: 22-222
Fire: 22-333
Ambulance: 22-100

Chambers of Commerce
Vanuatu Chamber of Commerce and Industry, PO Box 189, Port Vila (tel: 27-543; fax: 27-542; e-mail: vancci@vanuatu.com.vu).

Banking
ANZ Bank (Vanuatu) Ltd, Private Mail Bag 003, Port Vila (tel: 22-536; fax: 22-814).

Banque d'Hawaii (Vanuatu) Ltd, PO Box 29, Lini Highway, Port Vila (tel: 22-412; fax: 23-579).

European Bank Ltd, PO Box 65, International Bldg, Kumul Highway, Port Vila (tel: 27-700; fax: 22-884).

National Bank of Vanuatu, PO Box 249, Air Vanuatu House, Rue de Paris, Port Vila (tel: 22-201; fax: 22-761).

Central bank
Reserve Bank of Vanuatu, PMB 62, Port Vila, Vanuatu (tel: 23-333; fax: 24-231).

Travel information
Air Vanuatu, Air Vanuatu House, Rue de Paris, Port Vila (tel: 23-838; 23-878; fax: 23-250, 26-591; internet: www.airvanuatu.com).

Bauerfield Port Vila International Airport, Civil Aviation Department, PMB 068, Port Vila (tel: 22-993, 22-819; fax: 23-783).

The Principal Immigration Officer, PMB 014, Port Vila.

Tour Vanuatu, PO Box 409, Port Vila (tel: 22-733; fax: 23-442).

National tourist organisation offices
National Tourism Office of Vanuatu, PO Box 209, Port Vila (tel: 22-515, 22-685; fax: 23-889; internet site: http://www.vanuatutourism.com).

Ministries
Ministry of Finance and Housing, PO Box 31, Port Vila (tel: 22-951).

Ministry of Postal Services, Telecommunications and Meteorology, Private mail Bag 011, Port Vila (tel: 25-059; fax: 23-142).

Ministry of Trade, Co-operatives, Energy and Industry, Port Vila (tel: 23-979).

Prime Minister's Office, Private Mail Bag 053, Port Vila (tel: 22-413).

Other useful addresses
Asian Development Bank (ADB), South Pacific Regional Mission, La Casa di Andrea, Fr Dr W H Lini Highway; PO Box 127, Port Vila (tel: 23-300; fax: 23-183; email: adbsprm@adb.org; internet: http://www.adb.org/SPRM).

Department for Foreign Affairs, Port Vila (tel: 22-913, 22-347; fax: 23-142).

The Immigration Department, Port Vila, PMB 014, (tel: 22-354; fax: 25-492).

Other news agencies: ABC Pacific Beat: www.radioaustralia.net.au/pacbeat

Pacific Magazine: www.pacificmagazine.net

Internet sites
Investment promotion authority: www.investinvanuatu.com

Telephone directory (worldwide): www.teldir.com

Vanuatu government: www.vanuatu.gov.vu

Vanuatu online: www.vol.com.vu

Vanuatu portal: Vatu.com

Vanuatu Broadcasting and Television Corporation: www.vbtc.com.vu

Vatican City (The Holy See)

COUNTRY PROFILE

Historical profile

1917 The Code of Canon Law was devised. The Law provides codified information and rules on the operations of the Catholic Church.
1922 Achilles Ratti became Pope Pius XI.
1929 The Pope was instrumental in defining the Vatican's position within Italy, which was confirmed by the signing of the Lateran Treaty, when the Vatican City State was formed as a separate state.
1939 When Pius XI died, Eugenio Pacelli became Pope Pius XII, the 261st Pope.
1958 After Pius XII died, Pope John XXIII was elected.
1963 Second Vatican Council assembled (the first council sat in 325 AD), to debate the role of the Church in the modern world, particularly regarding church administration, doctrine and discipline. Foremost in the 16 decrees issued were the reforms in the format of the mass and the liturgy, adoption of local languages instead of Latin for services, and the promotion of ecumenicalism within Christian churches.
1964 Paul VI, appointed Pope in 1963, made the first-ever papal visit to Israel.
1965 Paul VI made the first papal trip to the Western hemisphere, with a visit to the UN headquarters in New York. The Vatican published a document that proclaimed the Jews were not to blame for the death of Jesus Christ.
1967 The Apostolic Constitution was ratified.
1974 The Vatican intervened in Italian politics by urging voters to reject, in a referendum, a recently passed law that made divorce legal.
1978 John Paul I was elected Pope, but died one month later, which made his the shortest reign as Pope. A Polish national, Karol Jozef Wojtyla, succeeded him as John Paul II.
1981 An assassination attempt was made on Pope John Paul II's life. The Vatican intervened in Italian politics by urging voters to reject in a referendum a recently passed law that made abortion legal.
1983 A new and revised Code of Canon Law was introduced.
1993 The Vatican officially recognised Israel as an independent state.
1998 The commandant of the Pope's Swiss Guard and his wife were murdered by a fellow Guardsman. Commandant Alois Estermann protected John Paul II from an assassination attempt in 1981. It was the first murder case in the Holy See within living memory.
1999 The Istituto per le Opere di Religione (IOR) (the Institute for Religious Works, otherwise known as the Bank of the Holy See or the Vatican Bank) was sued in the US for helping to conceal in 1945 Nazi-era assets looted from Holocaust survivors and Nazi sympathisers from Croatia.
2000 Pope John Paul II apologised for anti-Semitism by Christians throughout the ages and called for the formation of an independent Palestinian state.
2001 Pope John Paul II appointed 44 new cardinals. The Pope issued a worldwide apology to victims of sexual abuse by Roman Catholic priests and other officers of the Church.
2002 The Pope sent an envoy, Cardinal Roger Etchegaray, to the Middle East to help with the Israeli-Palestinian peace process. The Capuchin friar, Padre Pio, was canonised. After the Vatican ordered that management of Padre Pio's sanctuary in the south-eastern town of San Giovanni Rotondo should be taken from the local Capuchins and given to the regional archdiocese, the town's residents barricaded the entrance to the shrine.
2003 The Vatican hosted a closed-door seminar of top officials and international medical experts on the problem of pedophilia within the Church
2004 The Vatican library, which housed nearly two million books and manuscripts, adopted radio frequency identification (RFID) tags.
2005 Pope John Paul II, aged 84, who had been suffering from Parkinson's disease and severe arthritis, died on 2 April. Joseph Cardinal Ratzinger was elected Pope and chose the name Benedictus XVI. The Pope intervened in Italian politics by successfully urging a boycott of a referendum on Italy's fertility laws. A diplomatic row between the Vatican and Israel broke out when Israel demanded to know why the Pope did not mention Israeli victims during a speech deploring terrorism. The Vatican published a new policy document on homosexuality and the clergy, sparking controversy among liberal and conservative Catholics alike.
2006 The Vatican announced that it wanted to join the Schengen borderless zone. This would allow exchange of information, joint operations and preventative measures to ensure security throughout the Schengen countries. The Vatican excommunicated two bishops consecrated

KEY FACTS

Official name: Stato della Cittá del Vaticano (Vatican City State). Santa Sede (The Holy See) – the head organisation of the Roman Catholic Church – operates from the territory of the Vatican City State.

Head of State: Pope Benedict XVI (inaugurated 24 Apr 2005)

Head of government: Archbishop Giovanni Lajolo, President of the Pontifical Commission for the State of Vatican City (appointed 2006); Cardinal Tarcisio Bertone (appointed 2006), Secretary of State of The Holy See, handles diplomatic and political activity.

Area: 0 0.44 square km

Population: 880 (2004)

Capital: Vatican City

Official language: Latin; Italian is most commonly spoken.

Currency: Vatican City Lira and Euro (VCL and eur)

Exchange rate: VCL and eur0.63 per US$ (Jul 2008); (the Vatican City State has its own currency which, by agreement with the Italian state, is also legal tender in Italy; its value is pegged to that of the euro).

by the breakaway Chinese Catholic Church in an act considered illegal by the church authorities in The Holy See. In a speech given at the university of Regensburg in Germany, the Pope quoted a fourteenth century Byzantine emperor who seemed to say that the teachings of the Prophet Mohammed, 'spread by the sword' were 'evil and inhuman'. This caused a serious international storm of controversy among Muslims. It took a number of apologies by the Vatican and the Pope to lessen the tension.
2007 On 6 November, a meeting was held between Pope Benedict and the monarch of Saudi Arabia, King Abdullah. The meeting was the first between the two leaders and concerned Middle East conflict and inter-faith dialogue.

Political structure

The Vatican City and the Holy See are two different entities: the Vatican is the physical state, while the Holy See is a non-geographical sovereign entity. The Holy See participates in a number of international organisations, such as the UN, as an observer. Italy is in charge of defending the city state, although the Pope's personal guards, the Swiss Guards, belong to the Vatican City.
The Vatican City State employs 1,534 people. It is a sovereign country recognised as a separate subject under international law. The Pope is its absolute monarch and chief of state, but its general administration is overseen by an executive called the Pontifical Commission, appointed by the Pope and headed by a president. The Pope plays little part in the Commission's administration. The Commission runs a police force and post office, has a railway station and issues car licence plates. The term 'Vatican' is commonly used to describe the residence of the Pope – the Apostolic Palace.
The Holy See is exclusively made up of ecclesiastical dignitaries, being the head organisation of the Roman Catholic Church and consisting of the Pope and the Roman Curia. It operates from the territory of the Vatican City State and constitutes a sovereign institution with the status of a subject of international law. The Curia is headed by the Secretariat of State which is presided over by a Cardinal who assumes the title of Secretary of State. The Cardinal Secretary of State is the person primarily responsible for the diplomatic and political activity of The Holy See, in some circumstances representing the person of the Supreme Pontiff himself.
Central offices of The Holy See are: Secretariat of State (two sections), nine congregations, three tribunals, 11 pontifical councils, the Apostolic Chamber, the Administration of the Patrimony of the Apostolic See (APSA) (sometimes referred to as the Vatican Bank), Prefecture of the Economic Affairs of The Holy See, Prefecture of the Papal Household, Office of the Liturgical Celebrations of the Supreme Pontiff, The Holy See Press Office, Vatican Information Service, Central Office of Church Statistics, five pontifical commissions and committees, nine institutions linked to The Holy See, the Synod of Bishops and six pontifical academies. In addition to these central offices, there are 118 pontifical representations to nations and to international organisations. There are 2,674 people working in the Roman Curia: 755 ecclesiastics, 344 religious and 1,575 lay people. There are about 1,000 retired persons.
The Pope is elected for life by a Conclave composed of members of the College of Cardinals. Pope John Paul II changed the rules to make a simple majority sufficient to elect a Pope if no-one has the traditional two-thirds majority after 30 rounds of voting. The College of Cardinals consists of 183 cardinals, of which 117 are electors. Suffrage is limited to cardinals less than 80 years old.
After the Pope's death, the chamberlain becomes acting head of state. An official nine-day mourning period, known as the novemdiales, follows the death of the Pope. The Pope's body lies in state in St Peter's Basilica in the Clementine Chapel until the funeral, which takes place between four and six days following the Pope's death. A Conclave, consisting of all the Cardinals under 80 years, meets to elect the next pope no less than 15 days, and no more than 20 days, after the death of the Pope.

Constitution

In 2001, a new basic law, incorporating constitutional amendments adopted since the creation of the Vatican City State under the 1929 Lateran Treaty with Italy, entered into force. It replaced the 1967 document Regimini Ecclesiae Universae as the Vatican's constitutional text. It distinguishes between the legislative, executive and judicial branches, continuing to vest absolute authority over all three branches in the Pope as supreme pontiff and sovereign.

Form of state

Theocratic state, non-hereditary, elected monarchy (Bishop of Rome and Pope)

The executive

The Pope is the ex officio Head of the State and head of government of Vatican City. He has absolute monarchy powers with total control of legislative, executive and judicial power. He appoints his own advisors. The appointments include president of the Pontifical Commission for the State of Vatican City (head of government).
When a Pope is unable to perform his duties important decisions on the confirmation of bishops, doctrinal issues and the promulgation of laws within the Catholic Church are left in abeyance.
The Roman Curia is the administrative organisation that oversees the Roman Catholic Church, together with the Pope, providing the necessary organisation and objectives of the church.

Population

880 (2004)
Last census: July 2000: 798 (provisional)
Population density: 1,595 inhabitants per square km.
Annual growth rate: 0.9 per cent (2003)

Ethnic make-up

Italians and Swiss.

Religions

Roman Catholic.

Main cities

Vatican City (capital)

Languages spoken

Mainly Italian and Latin.

Official language/s

Latin; Italian is most commonly spoken.

Media

Quite apart from the hundreds of publications worldwide, which proclaim the policies and pronouncements of the Catholic Church, there are powerful transmitters that broadcast directly to a global audience.
National news agency: Agenzia Fides

Press

The only daily newspaper is L'Osservatore Romano (www.vatican.va see news services), with weekly editions published in several languages.
The official bulletin of the Holy See is Acta Apostolicae Sedis, which is published periodically and on papal pronouncements.

Broadcasting

Radio: Vatican Radio (www.radiovaticana.org) broadcasts in over 40 languages, with modern facilities for podcasts and interactive blogs. It broadcasts from a centre at Santa Maria di Galeria, which has diplomatic privileges similar to a foreign embassy.
Television: Centro Televisivo Vaticano (CTV) (www.vatican.va) provides live broadcasts of religious and papal matters, with footage for foreign news broadcasters; it acts as a press centre for broadcast journalists.

Economy

The main sources of income are The Holy See's book of real estate and from an internationally diversified portfolio of stocks and bonds.
Other income includes Obolo di San Pietro (Peter's Pence) (voluntary annual

contributions from dioceses), the sale of postage stamps, tourist mementoes and publications, and fees for admission to museums. The Istituto per le Opere di Religione (IOR) (Bank of The Holy See) collects money from residents.
No special agreements exist between the EU and The Holy See.
The 2004 Peter's Pence collection totalled US$51.7 million. The money was used for charitable purposes – to help the populations of countries struck by calamities and to aid Roman Catholic works in countries suffering strife. Following a series of sex scandals in the US involving clergymen, analysts predict that the Peter's Pence collection for 2005 will be significantly less than 2004's.

Tourism
Tourism and tourist numbers for the Holy See are difficult to ascertain as there is no practical border between the Holy See and Italy; however it is estimated that there are some 18 million visitors each year. Up to 100,000 people attend the Pope's annual Easter Message.

Banking and insurance
The Vatican's banking sector has been embroiled in a number of trans-national controversies over the past three decades. The IOR acknowledged 'moral involvement' in the collapse of the Italian private bank, the Banco Ambrosiano, in 1982 and paid US$241million to creditors. Roberto Calvi, who headed the Banco Ambrosiano, fled Italy pending a trial for corruption and was found dead in London in June 1982. Five people, all alleged to have Mafia ties, were charged in Rome with Calvi's murder in April 2005.
In 1999, survivors of Nazi-run concentration camps filed a law suit claiming that the IOR helped conceal assets looted from camp victims by the then pro-Nazi Croatian government.

Central bank
Istituto per le Opere di Religione (IOR) (Bank of The Holy See); European Central Bank (ECB).

Time
GMT plus one hour (daylight saving, late March to late October, GMT plus two hours)

Geography
The State of the Vatican City (The Holy See) is situated entirely within the city of Rome, Italy.

Hemisphere
Northern

Climate
Mediterranean, with hot summers and mild winters. Temperatures range from 4–30 Celsius (C).

Dress codes
Dress should be modest — no shorts or sundresses. Lightweight clothing for summer; medium-weight and light topcoat for winter.

Entry requirements
No formal regulations exist, however visitors must adhere to Italian entry requirements before entry to the city.
Italy: no visa requirements for citizens of Europe, the Americas, Australasia and some Asian countries, visiting for up to 90 days. For a full list, and further information for those citizens not included on the list of visa-free travel, see www.ambwashingtondc.esteri.it and see consular services. A Schengen visa application (offered in several languages) can be downloaded from www.eurovisa.info/ApplicationForm.htm.

Currency advice/regulations
The euro is legal tender alongside the Vatican City Lira.

Health (for visitors)
As for Italy, where no special immunisations are needed.

Public holidays (national)

Fixed dates
1 Jan (New Year's Day), 6 Jan (Epiphany), 25 April (Liberation Day), 1 May (Labour Day), 2 Jun (National Day), 15 Aug (Assumption Day), 1 Nov (All Saints' Day), 8 Dec (Immaculate Conception), 25–26 Dec (Christmas).

Variable dates
Easter Monday

Working hours

Business
Mon–Fri: 0830–1245 and 1630–2000.

Getting there

Air
A heliport is used by Vatican City officials and visiting dignitaries.
A low-cost charter airline was launched 27 August 2007 to carry pilgrims from Rome to Lourdes and other holy sites including the Holy Land, Santiago di Compostela, Fatima and places in Poland and Mexico.
International airport/s: Rome, served by Leonardo da Vinci (Fiumicino) (FCO), 35km from the Vatican City.

Surface
By road or rail through Rome. There is a speed limit of 30kph in the Vatican City.

Getting about

National transport
Rail: The Vatican City has its own small railway which runs into Italy. It covers 862 metres before leaving the City.

BUSINESS DIRECTORY

Telephone area codes
The international direct dialling (IDD) code for Vatican City is +39 followed by the area code 066982; this is complete in itself, giving access to a central switchboard/operator.

Banking

Central bank
Istituto per le Opere di Religione (IOR), 00120 Città del Vaticano, Rome (tel: 83-354; fax: 85-195); European Central Bank (ECB), Kaiserstrasse 29, D-60311 Frankfurt am Main, Germany (tel: +49(69)13-440; fax: +49(69)1344-6000).

Other useful addresses
Agenzia Fides, Palazzo di Propaganda Fide, Via di Propaganda 1c, 00187 Rome (tel: 6988-0115; fax: 6988-0107; email: fides@fides.va; internet: www.fides.org).

American Embassy, Via Delle Terme Deciane 26, 00153 Rome (tel: 646-741; fax: 5730-0682; e-mail: Usinb.holysee@agora.it).

Annuario Pontificio, Palazzo Apostolico, 00120 Città del Vaticano (tel: 698-3064); Press Room, Via della Conciciazione, 54, 00193 Roma (tel: 698-3466).

Apostolic Nunciature (UK), 54 Parkside, Wimbledon, London SW19 5NE, UK (tel: (+44-20) 8946-1410; fax: (+44-20) 8947-2494; email: gb nuntius@eaglenet.co.uk).

Apostolic Nunciature (USA), 3339 Massachusetts Ave, NW, Washington, DC 20008, (+1-202) 333-7121; fax: (+1-202) 337-4036).

British Embassy, Via dei Condotti 91, 00187 Rome (tel: 6992-3561; fax: 6994-0684).

Centro Televisivo Vaticano, Palazzo Belvedere, 00120 Vatican City (tel: 698-5467).

Prefecture of the Economic Affairs of the Holy See, Palazzo delle Congregazioni, Largo del Colonnato 3, 00193 Rome (tel: 84-263; fax: 85-011).

Radio Vaticana, Palazzo Pio, Piazza Pia 3, 00120 Roma (tel: 6988-3551; fax: 6988-3237).

Secretariat of State, Palazzo Apostolico, 00120 Vatican City (tel: 6982).

National news agency: Agenzia Fides

Internet sites
Vatican City: www.vatican.va
Vatican Facts: www.vaticanfacts.com

Agenzia Internazionale Fides: www.fides.org

Venezuela

KEY FACTS

Official name: República Bolivariana de Venezuela (Bolivarian Republic of Venezuela)

Head of State: President Hugo Chávez Frías (MVR) (since 2000, re-elected 4 Dec 2005)

Head of government: President Hugo Chávez Frías

Ruling party: Movimiento V República (Quinta) (Fifth Republic Movement) (re-elected Dec 2005)

Area: 916,490 square km

Population: 27.50 million (2007)

Capital: Caracas

Official language: Spanish

Currency: Bolívar fuerte (Bf) = 100 céntimos

Exchange rate: Bf2.15 per US$ (Jul 2008); (the Bolívar fuerte pegged at US$2.15 – official rate)

GDP per capita: US$8,596 (2007)*

GDP real growth: 8.40% (2007)*

Labour force: 12.50 million (2006)

Unemployment: 9.10% (2007)*

Inflation: 18.70% (2007)

Oil production: 2.61 million bpd (2007)

Balance of trade: US$32.98 billion (2006)

Foreign debt: US$35.57 billion (2004)

Visitor numbers: 770,000 (2006)*

Annual FDI: US$1.52 billion (2004)

* estimated figure

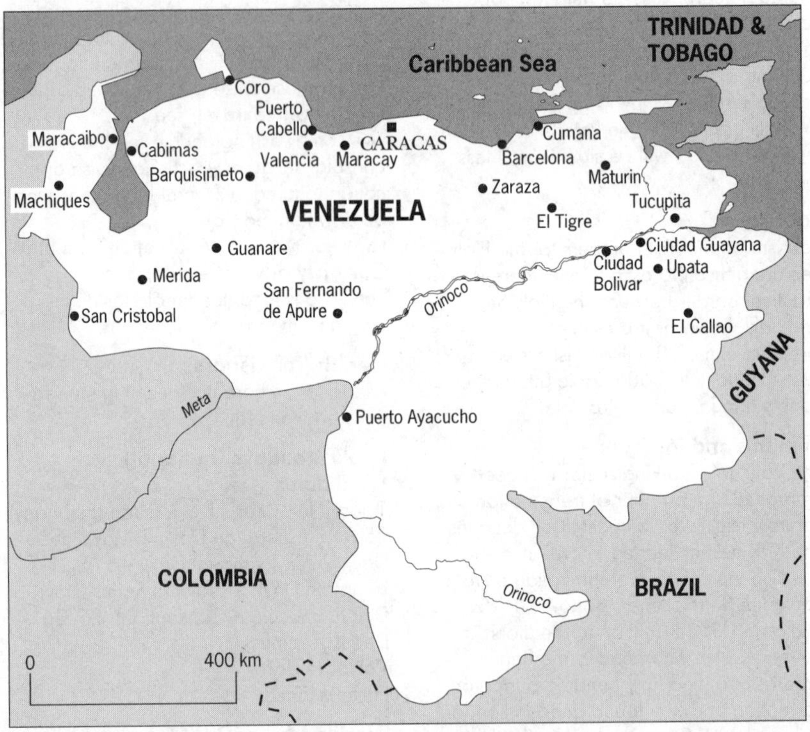

The December 2007 rejection by Venezuela's electorate of President Hugo Chávez' proposed constitutional reforms represented not only a major reversal for the controversial president, but also for those theorists that saw Chávez' grip on power inexorably increasing. As 2007 ended there were signs that the Chávez social revolution, despite its claims, had actually contributed to heightened social inequality, food shortages and higher inflation. On top of the referendum rejection, the nationalisation of Venezuela's oil production had resulted in lower output.

The poor get poorer

Despite the spin churned out by both the Chávez administration itself as well as its apologists that President Chávez' first priority in government has been the eradication of poverty, neither official statistics nor any respected independent estimates support the spin. Francisco Rodríguez the former chief economist of the Venezuelan National Assembly and Assistant Professor of Economics and Latin American studies at the US Wesleyan University, writing in the US *Foreign Affairs* summed up the situation gloomily. The percentage of underweight babies born in Venezuela rose from 8.4 per cent in 1999 to 9.1 per cent in 2006. During the same period the percentage of households without access to running water rose from 7.2 per cent to 9.4 per cent. This empirical analysis was confirmed by the government's own figures: the average share of the budget devoted to health, education and housing under Chávez in his first eight years in office, 25.12 per cent, was almost exactly the same as in the previous eight years at 25.08 per cent. Worse, the welfare expenditure in 2007 was actually lower than it was in 1992, the last year of the much maligned Carlos Andrés Pérez administration.

Until 2006, most Venezuelans had given Mr Chávez the benefit of the doubt, crediting him with satisfactory stewardship of the economy as in many cases their personal situation appeared to be improving. Theirs not to reason why until, by late 2007, polls suggested that for a majority of voters the situation had reversed and their personal situations, and their perception of the national situation, had worsened. The differential between official and black-market exchange rates had passed the 200 per cent mark, prices for staple foodstuffs were increasing and basic foodstuffs such as milk and beans had become scarce.

Professor Rodríguez attributes what by early 2008 was beginning to look like a crisis to the mismanagement of the economy by Chávez appointees. He points out that despite the unprecedented rise in oil revenues of 2007 (which continued in 2008) the Venezuelan government has managed to pursue even more expansionary economic policies, increasing government expenditure by over 130 per cent, and Venezuela's liquidity by an astonishing 218 per cent. Summing up the situation, Professor Rodríguez acknowledged that the government's expansionary policies had been acceptable during Venezuela's recession, but that their continuation after the recession had ended was ill-advised. They allowed the Chávez administration to achieve what most economists would have considered impossible, running a budget deficit in the middle of an oil price boom. Interestingly, Prof Rodríguez compares the policies and performance of the Chávez regime with the populist macroeconomics of the 1970s and the 1980s. Prof Rodríguez gives is a glimpse of the obvious, that the Chávez' regime's high profile public relations machine – which included close economic and political ties with Cuba, visits to Belarus and receptions from London's politically naïve mayor, Ken Livingstone – had succeeded in diverting attention from Venezuela's own problems.

According to the United Nations Economic Commission for Latin America and the Caribbean (ECLAC/CEPAL), Venezuela's GDP growth for 2007 was estimated to be over 8 per cent, largely due to the increased strength of internal demand. GDP rose by 8.4 per cent in the first three quarters of 2007, boosted by growth in the non-oil sector (9.9 per cent). The oil industry was down by 6.1 per cent. The strongest sectors were commerce (18.3 per cent), communications (23.2 per cent) and financial services (22.2 per cent), while construction grew by only 12.5 per cent during the same period. On the demand side, there were increases in consumption (16.5 per cent) and investment (22.7 per cent), reflecting growth in the volume of imports (31.1 per cent), but export volumes continued to fall (down 3.9 per cent). For 2008, the authorities estimate GDP growth at about 6 per cent, an exchange rate holding steady at 2,150 bolívares to the US$, and annual inflation averaging 11 per cent.

Nationalisation

Following the enactment of an enabling law by the executive branch in February 2007, the government implemented a number of policy measures. In January, it announced the nationalisation of two public-service companies: Electricidad de Caracas SA and Compañía Anónima Nacional de Teléfonos de Venezuela (CANTV). As of 1 May, Petróleos de Venezuela, SA (PDVSA) acquired controlling stakes in the strategic partnerships operating in the Orinoco oil belt. Foreign oil firms operating in Venezuela were to pay higher taxes on profits under the laws approved by parliament. The oil companies face a 50 per cent tax when a barrel of crude is priced at US$70 or more, rising to 60 per cent when the average prices top US$110.

The new laws represented a further attempt by President Chávez to obtain greater control over Venezuela's oil. In 2006, he had enacted laws requiring foreign oil firms to hand over at least a 60 per cent share of their Venezuelan operations. The country had also begun nationalising its electricity, telecommunications and natural gas industries as part of a drive toward 'twenty-first century socialism', whatever that was. Income from the new tax was likely to reach US$9bn a year, according to oil minister Rafael Ramirez, a figure which began to look conservative as oil prices continued to rise. Some analysts considered that the move would make foreign firms think carefully before making any further investments in Venezuela. The tax came months after President Chávez's nationalisation drive forced out two of the world's largest energy companies: ExxonMobil and ConocoPhillips. Exxon was seeking US$12bn in compensation from Venezuela after its oilfields were nationalised in 2007. In 2007 President Chavez also announced the immediate nationalisation of Venezuela's entire cement industry, claiming that his government could not allow private companies to export cement that was needed to tackle a severe housing shortage.

In May 2007, the government decided not to renew the operating licence of the privately owned opposition channel RCTV, which had operated for many years. President Chávez's announcements of the re-nationalisation of the telecommunications and power sectors sent shock waves through the Venezuelan stock exchange (Bolsa de Valores de Caracas (BVC)) and others across the region The BVC index fell by an impressive 18.66 per cent. Firms to be targeted by the looming change in legal status saw their shares particularly affected by the news. Joining

KEY INDICATORS **Venezuela**

	Unit	2003	2004	2005	2006	2007
Population	m	25.33	25.51	*26.43	*26.96	*27.50
Gross domestic product (GDP)	US$bn	85.50	109.32	143.44	184.25	*236.39
GDP per capita	US$	3,350	4,148	*5,427	*6,834	*8,596
GDP real growth	%	-13.0	17.3	10.3	10.3	*8.4
Inflation	%	34.1	21.7	15.9	13.6	18.7
Oil output	'000 bpd	2,987.0	2,980.0	3,007.0	2,824.0	2,613.0
Natural gas output	bn cum	29.4	28.1	28.9	28.7	28.5
Coal output	mtoe	5.1	6.6	6.2	5.9	0.1
Exports (fob) (goods)	US$m	19,708.0	38,748.0	55,487.0	65,210.0	69,165.0
Imports (cif) (goods)	US$m	7,578.0	17,318.0	23,955.0	32,226.0	45,463.0
Balance of trade	US$m	12,130.0	21,430.0	31,532.0	32,984.0	23,702.0
Current account	US$m	11,450.0	14,510.0	25,534.0	27,167.0	20,001.0
Total reserves minus gold	US$m	16,035.0	18,375.0	23,919.0	29,417.0	24,196.0
Foreign exchange	US$m	15,546.0	17,867.0	23,454.0	28,933.0	23,686.0
Exchange rate	per US$	2,124.20	1,887.70	3,796.20	2,140.00	2,147.30

* estimated figure

national figures condemning Chávez's apparent ambitions, opposition leader Manuel Rosales criticised the president's ruling style as despotic warning that Venezuela was moving closer towards a Marxist state. In October 2007, Venezuela's National Assembly had adopted the constitutional reform proposed by the President. The new constitution was submitted to the referendum of December 2007, but was not approved by the electorate. Among the most controversial measures had been moves to strip the central bank of its independence, changes to the country's territorial structure which would have implications for budgetary outlays, the indefinite re-election of the president, the creation of the legal concept of popular power, and changes in provisions relating to ownership.

Rattle those sabres

March 2008 saw the Organisation of American States (OAS) approve a resolution condemning a Colombia raid into Ecuador which resulted in the death of 24 Colombian Fuerzas Armadas Revolucionarias de Colombia-Ejército del Pueblo (Farc) guerrillas. The resolution was approved after talks in which the United States was the hemisphere's only nation explicitly supporting the Colombian position. While the resolution allowed both Colombia and Ecuador to save face and begin to repair relations, it failed to address some of the broader implications of Colombia's raid; foremost among which was the exaggerated support for Colombia's guerrillas expressed by President Chávez. Raising the ante, Mr Chávez had mobilised his armed forces in response to the raid, pledging war with Colombia if it tried a similar foray into Venezuelan territory. Venezuela's troop movements included the reported deployment of 10 tank battalions to the Colombian border. In response, Colombia reiterated that it did not plan to send troops to its border in a response to Venezuela's action. Venezuela's mobilisation also drew a predictable rebuke from the Bush administration, which has portrayed Colombia as an ally in need of a trade deal.

Mr Chávez dismissed the Washington portrayal of Venezuelan policy, preferring to portray the dispute as a struggle between the combined forces of Ecuador and Venezuela, two like-minded governments, and Colombia, the largest recipient of American military aid in Latin America. Colombia could claim a major tactical victory against the Farc, having killed Raúl Reyes, a commander believed to be the group's second in command and obtained, through the capture of a lap top computer, substantial information about Venezuela's support for the Farc. Soon after the raid, President Chávez appeared to be backtracking. A hastily arranged meeting of Messrs Chávez and Colombian President Alvaro Uribe in the Dominican Republic under the auspices of the regional Rio Group saw a peace deal between Colombia and Venezuela signed.

Thanks to the oil

Venezuela is one of the world's largest exporters of crude oil and the largest in the Western Hemisphere. According to the US Energy Information Administration (EIA) in 2006, Venezuela was the sixth-largest net oil exporter in the world. The oil sector accounts for more than three-quarters of total Venezuelan export revenues, about half of total government revenues, and around one-third of total gross domestic product (GDP). According to the US based *Oil and Gas Journal* (OGJ), Venezuela had 80.0 billion barrels of proven oil reserves in 2007, the largest amount in South America. Venezuela is a significant supplier of crude oil to the world market: in 2006, Venezuela had net oil exports of 2.2 million barrels per day (bpd), sixth-largest in the world and the largest in the Western Hemisphere. In recent years, crude oil production in the country has fallen, mostly due to natural decline at existing oil fields. Despite this, the government has tabled ambitious plans to double production.

Venezuela nationalised its oil industry in 1975–76, creating Petróleos de Venezuela SA (PdVSA), the country's state-run oil and natural gas company. Along with being Venezuela's largest employer, the EIA reports that PdVSA accounts for about one-third of the country's GDP, 50 per cent of the government's revenue and 80 per cent of Venezuela's exports earnings. In recent years, the Venezuelan government has reduced PdVSA's previous autonomy and amended the rules regulating the country's hydrocarbons sector. An example of this trend was the November 2004 appointment of Rafael Rodriguez, the energy minister, as chairman of PdVSA.

The EIA reports that in 2001, Venezuela enacted a new Hydrocarbons Law that superseded the previous 1943 Hydrocarbons Law and 1975 Nationalisation Law. Under the 2001 law, royalties paid by private companies increased from 1–17 per cent to 20–30 per cent. Further, the law guaranteed PdVSA a majority share of any new projects. Finally, the law stipulated that all future foreign investment would be in the form of joint ventures (JV) with PdVSA, or in other forms of strategic associations. In August 2003, Venezuela's ministry of energy and mines (MEM) transferred PdVSA's 32 operating contracts, the four strategic associations, and the risk exploration contracts to its subsidiary Corporación Venezolana de Petróleo (CVP). Legislation in 2006 later increased the royalty and income tax rates on the four strategic associations to 33.3 per cent and 50 per cent, respectively.

In 2007, Venezuela completed the transition of the four strategic associations to new structures in alignment with the 2001 law. PdVSA increased its holdings in the four projects to an average of 78 per cent, up from 40 per cent. Of the six companies involved in the projects, two reduced their holdings to allow space for the enlarged PdVSA share (Total and Statoil), two maintained their previous stakes (Chevron, BP), and two exited completely from the projects (ConocoPhillips and ExxonMobil).

It remained unclear how these events would influence foreign investment in Venezuela's oil sector. Most of the foreign oil companies have accepted the contract changes. Several factors that could influence oil company decisions include high world oil prices, increasing efficiency of operations (especially the strategic associations), and a desire to maintain access to Venezuela's large oil reserves. The EIA's view is that the future of foreign investment in Venezuela could shift to the national oil companies.

The EIA also notes that Venezuela's actual level of oil production is difficult to determine, with the country and independent industry analysts offering differing estimates. Most industry analysts and the EIA estimate that Venezuela produced around 2.8 million bpd of oil in 2006. These estimates conclude that at the end of 2007 it had still not fully recovered from the strikes of 2002–03. Another factor that complicates comparisons of Venezuelan oil production estimates are methodological and classification issues.

Risk assessment

Politics	Poor
Economy	Poor (despite the figures)
Regional stability	Fair

COUNTRY PROFILE

Historical profile

1498 Christopher Columbus landed at the mouth of the Orinoco River on 2 August.

1499 Alonso de Ojeda first saw Lake Maracaibo and called the area 'little Venice', or Venezuela, after the houses the local inhabitants built on stilts.
1520s Spanish colonisation began. The most exploitable resource was cocoa.
1567 Caracas was founded.
1620 By this time cocoa had become the principal export. Production attracted many Spanish immigrants.
1749 First rebellion against Spanish rule.
1810–21 Simón Bolívar defeated the Spanish army in a long war and created Greater Colombia out of Venezuela, Colombia, Ecuador, Bolivia and Peru.
1823 The last battles for independence gained Venezuela its freedom from Spanish control.
1830 Bolívar died, José Antonio Paez assumed the presidency.
1859–63 A civil war erupted in a power struggle between conservative centralists and federalists forces, which was won by the liberal federalists.
1870–88 General Antonio Guzmán ruled the country, increasing its international prestige, and developed the country's colonial bureaucracy into a modern state and commercial outpost of the industrialising countries around the North Atlantic.
1908–1935 General Juan Vicente Gómez ruled the country, instituting a harsh policy of repression while developing Venezuela into an oil-based, technocratic economy. The influence of foreign petroleum interests on domestic policies increased with the increase in direct foreign investment.
1935–41 General Eleazar Lopez Contreras became president and began a policy of liberal capitalist democracy.
1945 After decades of rule by dictators, political violence erupted in Caracas. A coup led by a group of young military men and Rómulo Ernesto Betancourt Bello (Acción Democrática (AD) (Democratic Action)), set up a new government committed to democracy and social and land reforms. Foreign powers were suspicious of the government's left-wing credentials until Betancourt announced prompt elections would be held, acceptable reforms implemented and no radical action would be taken against foreign oil interests.
1947 A new constitution that provided for a popular vote, by secret ballot, to elect a president was promulgated. Romulo Gallegos Freire (AD) became the first Venezuelan president to be elected by democratic vote.
1948 The government was overthrown in a military coup d'état backed by conservative elements opposed to the reforms. A succession of juntas formed governments.
1952 Marcos Evangelista Pérez Jiménez seized power and became the next dictator president.
1953 The United States of Venezuela was renamed the Bolivian Republic of Venezuela.
1958 Pérez Jiménez was deposed by the military and a governing council allowed free elections, in which Betancourt (AD) was elected president. A pact between the main parties, including the AD and the Partido Demócrata Cristiano de Venezuela (Copei) (Christian Democrat Party of Venezuela), agreed to share power and maintain a pluralistic democracy. Moderate economic reforms, with regard for US interests, were slowly introduced.
1969 Rafael Caldera Rodríguez became Venezuela's first Copei president and managed to achieve a degree of political and economic stability.
1973 Venezuela joined the Andean Community, which also included Ecuador, Colombia, Peru and Bolivia.
1974–79 Carlos Andrés Pérez Rodríguez (AD) held presidential office and used massive oil revenues to nationalise industries and diversify the economy.
1979–84 The election of President Herrera (Copei) coincided with a downturn in global oil prices which led to a series of problems, including rising corruption, capital flight, economic stagnation and high levels of external debt.
1988 Presidential and legislative elections were held in December. Pérez became the first former president to be re-elected.
1989 Public protests against the government's austerity programme, which involved drastic government spending cut-backs in order to stabilise the economy, broke out around the country. The first-ever direct elections of state governors were held.
1992 Lieutenant Colonel Hugo Rafael Chávez Frías led an unsuccessful coup attempt against President Pérez.
1993 Ramon Jose Velasquez became interim president as Pérez was prosecuted on charges of corruption.
1995 Rafael Caldera was elected president.
1996 Ex-president Pérez was convicted of embezzlement and corruption.
1998 The presidential election was won by Hugo Chávez of the Movimiento V República (Quinta) (Fifth Republic Movement), with more than 56 per cent of the vote.
1999 President Chávez's government began his 'Bolívarian Revolution' that included a unicameral national assembly, a new constitution, reduced civilian control of the military and an increased control by government of the economy. A referendum approved all the amendments. Torrential rains caused severe flooding in the north, in December, killing approximately 30,000 people.
2000 In the first elections under the new constitution Chávez was re-elected president. His coalition won 99 out of 165 assembly seats but not enough to rule unfettered. The assembly granted him the right to legislate by decree.
2001 There were calls for the president's resignation after he passed 49 laws under his special powers of decree, regarding land redistribution and the oil sector.
2002 Civil unrest interrupted oil exports. President Chávez was briefly ousted from power. Other Latin American countries refused to recognise Pedro Carmona Estanga as interim president and Chávez's supporters counter-demonstrated until he was reinstated. Chávez formally resumed his presidency. Nearly one-half of state-owned oil company PdVSA's employees walked off the job on 2 December in protest against the rule of President Chávez. The strike severely affected PdVSA, practically bringing the company's operations to a halt. PdVSA fired 18,000 workers following the strike, draining the company of technical knowledge and expertise. Industry analysts speculate that the strike did permanent damage to PdVSA's production capacity and remains the contributing factor to the decline in production in following years.
2003 The government imported petrol from Brazil as oil facilities were strike-bound.
2004 The electoral authority ruled that opponents of Chávez had collected enough signatures for a referendum on whether President Chávez should serve his remaining term in office. Chávez won 58 per cent of the vote.
2005 Land reforms, including land distribution, were introduced. President Chávez and Fidel Castro signed several trade and co-operation agreements. The Petrocaribe Alliance was created to supply 13 Caribbean states, including Cuba, directly with cheaper Venezuelan oil. Not only was it intended to cut the energy bills of the small island economies, but also to reduce US influence in the region. National assembly elections were boycotted by the opposition and Chávez loyalists made big gains. Quinta won 60 per cent of the vote (116 out of 167 seats).
2006 Parliament approved a new flag, with an eighth star for the province of Guayana Esequiba (a disputed border region with Guyana). Venezuela signed a US$3 billion arms deal with Russia, for jet fighters and helicopters. Venezuela became the fifth country to join the trading group Mercosur, which has a market of around 250 million people and accounts for almost 75 per cent of South America's GDP. In presidential elections, incumbent, Hugo Chávez won a third term in office, with 62 per cent of the vote; his

opponent, Manuel Rosales, won 38 per cent. Turnout was 75 per cent.
2007 Jorge Rodríguez replaced José Vicente Rangel as vice president in January. President Chavez announced key energy and telecommunications companies were to be nationalised. The national assembly granted Chávez the right to legislate by decree until mid-2008. Several oil projects in the Orinoco Belt were nationalised in May. Exxon Mobil and ConocoPhilips refused to relinquish their majority control of their Orinoco Belt oil operations. Following protests constitutional reforms were voted on in a referendum held on 2 December, they were narrowly rejected by 51 to 49 per cent.
2008 On 1 January a new currency, the Bolívar fuerte (Bf) was introduced at a rate of Bf1 to old B1,000. President Chávez was instrumental in the release of six hostages held by the Colombian Fuerzas Armadas Revolucionarias de Colombia-Ejército del Pueblo (Farc) (Revolutionary Armed Forces of Colombia-Peoples' Army). He also advised Colombian President Uribe that Farc should be considered insurgents instead of terrorists. Colombia took pre-emptive, cross-border strikes against Farc terrorists hiding out in Venezuela and Ecuador, killing over a dozen including the senior Farc leader Raul Reyes. Following the incursion troops were mobilised along the border and on 3 March, Venezuela expelled Colombian diplomats. Relations improved later after Ingrid Betancourt was freed from her Farc captors and President Uribe visited Venezuela for talks.

Political structure

Venezuela sends 12 deputies to the Latin American Parliament and five to the Andean Parliament.

Constitution

A new constitution was promulgated in 1999 which set out to strengthen civil and human rights, extended a presidential term from five to six years, with one consecutive re-election, revised impeachment mechanism and limited emergency powers. The bicameral parliament was replace with a single chamber when the senate was abolished, but popular participation by the people was to be encouraged through referenda. A stronger government involvement in economics included a ban on the privatization of the country's oil reserves.

Form of state

Federal presidential republic

The executive

Executive power rests with the president who is elected by popular, direct, universal suffrage for a six-year term, with one consecutive, renewable term.

National legislature

Asamblea Nacional (National Assembly) has 167 members, who serve 5-year terms (for a maximum three terms). Of these, 99 are elected by popular vote, 65 are elected through party-list proportional representation, and three are reserved for indigenous peoples.

Legal system

The Supreme Court appoints judges in consultation with civil society groups.

Last elections

December 2005 (parliamentary); 15 August 2004 (recall referendum); 3 December 2006 (presidential).

Results: Presidential: Incumbent, Hugo Rafael Chávez Fríaz (MVR) won 62 per cent of the vote; Manuel Rosales won 38 per cent. Turnout of 62 per cent.
Parliament: Qunita won 60.0 per cent (116 out of 167 seats), Por la Democracia Social (DS) (For Social Democracy) 8.2 per cent (18), Patria para Todos (PT) (Fatherland for All) 6.8 per cent (10), Partido Comunista de Venezuela (PCV) (Communist Party of Venezuela) 2.7 per cent (7); all other parties less than two seats. Opposition parties boycotted the election, turnout was 25.26 per cent and abstentions 74.74 per cent.

Next elections

2012 (presidential); 2009 (parliamentary).

Political parties

Ruling party

Movimiento V República (Quinta) (Fifth Republic Movement) (re-elected Dec 2005)

Main opposition party

Acción Democrática (AD) (Democratic Action) boycotted the 2005 election and has no parliamentary seats.

Population

27.50 million (2007)

Last census: October 2001: 23,054,210
Population density: 28 inhabitants per square km. Urban population: 87 per cent (2002).
Annual growth rate: 2.0 per cent 1994–2004 (WHO 2006)

Ethnic make-up

Mestizo (67 per cent), White (21 per cent), Black (10 per cent), Indian (2 per cent).

Religions

Roman Catholic (96 per cent), Protestant (2 per cent).

Education

Pre-primary (one year) and basic education lasts until aged 15. Exams then determine whether students progress onto an academic course for two years or a vocational course for three years. Many institutes of higher education have a selection procedure and often run preparatory courses as part of the admission process. Professional courses last for three years, catering for the industrial, farming, commercial and health sectors.
Universities, institutes, two ecclesiastic university institutes and three military institutes, provide higher education. Institutes and University Colleges generally provide for short courses of study lasting between two and three years. Long courses lasting for five to six years are also available. The universities are both public and private. National public universities are both autonomous and experimental institutions.
Literacy rate: 93 per cent adult rate; 98 per cent youth rate (15–24) (Unesco 2005).
Compulsory years: Five to 17
Enrolment rate: 91 per cent gross primary enrolment; 40 per cent gross seconday enrolment of relevant age groups (including repeaters).
Pupils per teacher: 21 in primary schools

Health

Per capita total expenditure on health (2003) was US$231; of which per capita government spending was US$102, at the international dollar rate, (WHO 2006).
Venezuela has achieved significant long-term advances with regard to health in hospital care but preventive and primary health care remains on a very small scale. Venezuela is vulnerable to natural disasters, the most frequent of which are floods with concurrent landslides, and there is also a risk of earthquakes. The Ministry of Family has assisted non-governmental organisations (NGOs) and community-based groups to participate in social programmes at a household level. The armed forces, which are already active in a social welfare programme known as Bolivar 2000, were used in the fight against a dengue epidemic in 2001.

HIV/Aids

HIV prevalence: 0.7 per cent aged 15–49 in 2003 (World Bank)
Life expectancy: 75 years, 2004 (WHO 2006)
Fertility rate/Maternal mortality rate: 2.7 births per woman, 2004 (WHO 2006); maternal mortality 60 per 100,000 live births (World Bank).
Birth rate/Death rate: 4 deaths per 24 births per 1,000 people; infant mortality 19 per 1,000 live births (World Bank).
Child (under 5 years) mortality rate (per 1,000): 18 per 1,000 live birth; 4 per cent of children under aged five are malnourished (World Bank).
Head of population per physician: 1.94 physicians per 1,000 people, 2001 (WHO 2006)

Welfare

Venezuela operates a social insurance system covering employees in private and

public employment, unemployed and family members.
The welfare system of benefits covers sickness, maternity, work injury, unemployment and family allowances. Pensioners are also covered for medical benefits. Sickness benefits are covered for up to 52 weeks. Maternity benefit is payable up to six months before and after confinement. Workers' medical benefits include free general and specialist care and hospitalisation. Unemployment benefit covers 60 per cent of the average weekly salary of the last 50 weeks and is paid for up to 13 weeks after waiting for one month following loss of employment. Unemployed persons are entitled to transportation subsidy, training and guidance services.

Pensions

A new system of private pensions was introduced in 1998. In 1999, Venezuela moved away from a pay-as-you-go pension system to one based on 'individual capitalisation funds', along the lines of the Chilean model. Under the mandatory pay-as-you-go system all participants receive pensions in proportion to their contributions, amounting to 12–13 per cent of base salary, and on the basis of the accumulation of the individual fund. The government pays for any deficiency between the accumulated value of the individual capitalised fund and the minimum amount of pension.
Full pensions are paid at aged 60, provided 240 months of contributions have been paid. At the age of 60, the employee has the option of either buying a life annuity from an insurance company, or withdrawing fixed monthly amounts from their individual capitalisation account.
A disability pension is available with 250 weeks of contribution, plus 30 per cent of workers' average earnings, payable after six months of disability.

Main cities

Caracas (capital, estimated population 1.8 million (m) in 2005), Maracaibo (1.8m), Valencia (1.3m), Barquisimeto (869,352), Ciudad Guayana (704,045), Petare (518,800), Maracay (406,812), Ciudad Bolívar (308,469).

Languages spoken

Spanish is spoken by the majority of the population. Indian dialects are spoken by about 200,000 Amerindians in the remote interior.

Official language/s

Spanish

Media

National news agency: ABN (Agencia Bolicariana de Noticias)

Press

Dailies: In Spanish, El Nacional (www.el-nacional.com), Ultimas Noticias (www.ultimasnoticias.com.ve), 2001 (www.2001.com.ve) is a tabloid, El Mundo (www.elmundo.com.ve) is an evening edition, El Universal (www.eluniversal.com), which has an English language edition called Daily News (http://english.eluniversal.com).
Weeklies: There are also numerous periodicals including El Carabobeño (www.el-carabobeno.com) with supplements and the monthly Producto (www.producto.com.ve).
Business: The magazine Dinero (www.dinero.com.ve) is a national publication; Reporte is a newspaper from Caracas.

Broadcasting

The president broadcasts a weekly programme on the public radio and TV services.
Radio: There are over 280 radio stations and all broadcast in Spanish. The state broadcaster, Radio Nacional de Venezuela (www.rnv.gov.ve) operates 15 radio stations in a nationwide network. Private commercial stations include Union Radio Noticias (www.unionradio.com.ve) and Fama FM (www.fama.fm).
The news agency ABN has recordings of National Assembly sessions online, (www.abn.info.ve), in Spanish.
Television: Venezolana de Television (www.vtv.gob.ve) is government run while all others are private and commercial and all broadcast in Spanish. Around 96 per cent of households have a TV set.
Private TV networks include Televen (www.televen.com), Venevision (www.venevision.net) with imported programmes, Globovision (www.globovision.com) a 24-hour news channel and Telsur (www.telesurtv.net) a pan-Latin station.
Radio Caracas Television (RCTV) had its licence withdrawn in May 2007.

Advertising

Television accounts for around 60 per cent of advertising expenditure.

Economy

The economy has performed inconsistently in recent years. Following a period of stagflation (a decline in real GDP coupled with inflation) in 2002 and 2003, the economy improved markedly in 2004 on the back of an increase in the price of oil. Real GDP growth of 17.3 per cent was achieved in 2004, only to fall sharply to 5.6 per cent in 2005. High inflation, peaking at 34.1 per cent in 2003, but falling to 15.9 per cent by 2005, continues to be a serious problem.
Venezuela's economic performance is largely dependent on oil, which in a typical year accounts for over 40 per cent of government revenues and up to 30 per cent of total GDP. While oil has generated growth, it has also distorted the economy and prevented diversification. Furthermore, volatile international oil prices have had damaging political repercussions.
An on-going restructuring programme has not generated enough foreign investment to diversify the economy. Domestic investment has been curtailed by high interest rates and a general feeling of insecurity created by President Chávez's unpredictability and opposition attempts to undermine the political order through economic sabotage.
President Chávez's hawkish approach to oil prices suggests that, like his predecessors, he believes that oil revenues will enable Venezuela to avoid the type of structural changes that have taken place in the rest of the region.
In December 2005, for the first time since President Chávez came to power, a multilateral institution gave the go-ahead for a substantial loan to Venezuela. The Inter-American Development Bank (IADB) agreed to lend US$768 million, a large portion of which was earmarked for development of the hydroelectric infrastructure.
In July 2006 Venezuela became the fifth country to join the trading group Mercosur, which now has a market of around 250 million people and accounts for almost 75 per cent of South America's GDP. In early 2007 President Chavez announced that key energy and telecommunications companies were to be nationalised.
The IADB estimated that in 2006 migrant workers sent some US$300 million to their families in Venezuela.

External trade

Venezuela is a member of the South American Community of Nations, (a tariff free, common market) and in October 2007 President Chavez announced that Venezuela would join Mercosur (economic bloc and free trade area) in December.
The export of petroleum plays an overwhelming influence on the economy and provides a trade surplus. Other commodities include heavy industrial products, manufactures and agricultural products.

Imports

Principal imports are raw materials, machinery and equipment, vehicles, consumer goods and construction materials.
Main sources: US (31.6 per cent total, 2005), Colombia (11.0 per cent), Brazil (9.1 per cent), Mexico (6.9 per cent)

Exports

Principal exports are petroleum, aluminium, steel, iron ore, chemicals and

plastics, agricultural products, fish, tobacco and basic manufactures.
Main destinations: US (51.2 per cent total, 2005), The Netherlands Antilles (7.3 per cent), Canada (2.4 per cent)

Agriculture

Farming

Land use is divided between arable land (3 per cent), permanent crops cultivation (1 per cent), meadows and pastures (20 per cent), forest and woodland (50 per cent) and other use (26 per cent). The country is subject to periodic droughts.
Venezuela's main arable centres are Acarigua, El Tigre, Maracay, Valencia and Barquisimeto.
The agricultural sector is not hugely important to the economy of Venezuela, constituting just 5 per cent of total GDP. There has been little investment in modern farm technology. Inefficient marketing, poor farm management and scant irrigation are all features of the Venezuelan agricultural industry.
The major crops are rice, maize, sorghum, sugar cane, coffee (the main export crop), cocoa and cotton. Tropical fruits, cassava, beans, groundnuts and other vegetables are staple crops for small farmers. Poultry and pig-farming are of growing importance with small quantities of meat exported. Beef production has, however, slumped due to the smuggling of cattle to Colombia (where prices are higher), and cheap imports.
Throughout the 1990s, the government liberalised agricultural imports through lowering tariffs and removing quantitative restrictions in the form of import licences. The overall aim was to boost agricultural efficiency and to refocus production on areas where the country has a comparative advantage.
An agricultural programme is under way, involving the improvement and irrigation of 350,000 hectares of existing agricultural land and the use of about one million new hectares for cultivation. The programme aims to increase output of cereals, sugar and oilseeds (to reduce dependence on imports), and promote crop diversification.
Since the election of Hugo Chávez as president in 1999, the government has introduced land reform measures designed to bring disused agricultural land into production and redistribute land to the rural poor. The measures have been resisted by the land-owning oligarchy in the countryside, particularly cattle ranchers. The national government accelerated its land reform programme and continued to expropriate local agribusinesses throughout 2005.
Crop production in 2005 included: 3,565,150 tonnes (t) cereals in total, 2,050,000t maize, 8,800,000t sugar cane, 520,000t cassava, 350,000t potatoes, 950,000t rice, 565,000t sorghum, 430,000t plantains, 520,000t bananas, 581,100t citrus fruit, 195,000t tomatoes, 170,000t coconuts, 315,000t oil palm fruit, 17,000t cocoa beans, 70,000t green coffee, 94,548t oilcrops, 2,320,600t fruit in total, 1,488,250 vegetables in total. Livestock production included: 1,216,550t meat in total, 405,000t beef, 118,000t pig meat, 7,550t lamb and goat meat, 686,000t poultry, 147,500t eggs, 1,268,000t milk, 90t honey, 48,250t cattle hides,

Fishing

Since coming to power President Chávez has passed legislation that regulates the activities of large trawlers in order to protect small fishing communities.
Generally, the fishing industry has seen good growth, owing to an increase in the tuna catch. The overall typical fish catch is in the region of 435,000mt, including 318,000mt marine fish and 79,000mt shellfish.
In 2004, the total marine fish catch was 356,210 tonnes and the total crustacean catch was 29,190 tonnes.

Forestry

Approximately half of Venezuela's total landmass is covered with forests and woodland, the majority of which are in the south and east of the country. The forestry sector remains undeveloped and around half the country's wood-derived products are imported.
Exports of forest materials in 2004 amounted to US$98.3 million, while imports constituted US$394.5 million.
Timber production in 2004 included 4,319,092 cubic metre (cum) roundwood, 1,526,000cum industrial roundwood, 947,000cum sawnwood, 805,000cum sawlogs and veneer logs, 721,000cum pulpwood, 233,000cum wood-based panels, 3,793,092cum woodfuel; 386,462 tonnes (t) charcoal, 723,000t paper and paperboard, 275,000t printing and writing paper, 142,000t paper pulp, 211,000t recovered paper.

Industry and manufacturing

Over time heavy industries have arisen with the intention of using local materials as inputs including the refining of aluminium (an increasingly significant export), petrochemicals (ammonia, sulphuric acid, fertilisers, plastics etc) and cement and steel production.
Import-dependent industries include motor vehicle assembly, tyres, rubber, pharmaceuticals, electrical goods and machinery. The traditional home market industries are beverages, textiles, food processing, ceramics and paper/pulp.
Major state enterprises include Sidor (steel), Venalum and Alcasa (aluminium) and Pequiven (petrochemicals). Venezuela's aluminium industry is inefficient and heavily indebted.
Manufacturing production remains highly concentrated, with around 10 per cent of all firms accounting for 75 per cent of output. Joint ventures involving state, domestic and foreign private capital were developed in the 1990s to expand the petrochemical and aluminium industries.
Manufacturing increased in 2004, on the wave of a general economic upswing in the economy during the year. In the first seven months of the 2004 calender year the manufacturing sector expanded by 38 per cent more than the same seven month period in 2003.

Tourism

The travel and tourism industry of Venezuela has been hampered by the political and economic stability in the country.
Though capital investment in the sector has risen to represent almost 12 per cent of total capital investment in the economy, employment in the sector is down, as is the industry's percentage contribution to total GDP.

Mining

Venezuela is endowed with a significant range of mineral resources. However, these deposits remain largely undeveloped. The sectors of the industry retaining the most importance include iron ore, bauxite, gold, diamond and nickel laterites. Other sources include zinc, copper, lead, silver, manganese, titanium, nickel, marble, sulphur, phosphates, mercury and uranium.
At present, the mining industry contributes just 1 per cent of the country's total GDP.
The government reformed its mining law in 1999, converting mining contracts signed with Corporacion Venezolana de Guayana (CVG) into mining concessions. The government eliminated exploration and surface taxes in the first three years of a concession.
Several foreign investment and joint ventures have propped up the sector. Venezuelan, Canadian and US companies have combined to exploit the extensive kimberlite sills in the region of Guaniamo and aid in the marketing of diamonds.
Nickel is mined at Loma de Niquel. The main mineral exploited is iron ore; reserves are estimated at 2,800 million tonnes, 80 per cent high-grade. The largest deposits are located at Cerro Bolívar and San Isidro. Estimated reserves of bauxite at Los Pijiguaos typically amount to some four billion tonnes of high-grade ore.
In September President Chávez suggested that the Las Cristinas gold mining region

would be re-nationalised at some point in the future. Crystallex, a Canadian mining company operating in the region and currently planning to build the what would be the largest gold mine in Venezuela, saw a sharp decline in its share price on the back of the news.

Hydrocarbons

Venezuela continues to be one of the world's most important oil exporters. The country is endowed with the most extensive proven oil reserves in the Western Hemisphere and the petroleum industry is the mainstay of the economy.

Total proven conventional oil reserves are estimated at 77.2 billion barrels, which should last at least 65 years at present production levels. This figure does not include significant extra-heavy and bitumen deposits, which are thought to be as high as 270 billion barrels.

Production is restricted by Venezuela's OPEC quota, which was officially set at 2.3 million barrels per day (bpd) in 2002. An opposition-led general strike in 2002 shut down the country's oil industry, causing oil output to fall to under 400,000bpd. By 2003, the strike in the oil sector had ended and oil production was rising to near normal levels. About 58 per cent of oil exports are destined for the US, which has become increasingly reliant on Venezuelan oil in recent years; Venezuela accounts for around 12 per cent of the US's oil supply.

By 2004, there were large proven natural gas reserves estimated at 4.2 trillion cubic metres, the eighth-largest in the world. Production of natural gas was 28.1 billion cubic metres in 2004. An estimated 60 per cent of gas production is consumed by the oil industry, 10 per cent is used for power generation, 6 per cent for petrochemical production and the rest is consumed by industrial and commercial customers in urban areas. The gas infrastructure consists of over 3,000 miles of pipeline and private companies are planning to extend the network, possibly to neighbouring countries such as Colombia and Brazil.

Exploitation of gas reserves is a priority, although output has slowly fallen year-by-year since the mid-1990s.

Venezuela is the second largest producer of coal in Latin America, after Colombia, and has 479 million tonnes of coal reserves (2004). PdVSA operates, through joint ventures between its subsidiary Carbozulia and foreign companies, four mines with production at 6.6 million tonnes of oil equivalent (2004). Domestic consumption is only around 15,000 tonnes per annum and most of Venezuela's mainly bituminous coal is exported to markets in North and South America and Europe. The government intends to increase production to around 18 million tonnes per annum by 2008.

Energy

Venezuela has an electricity generation capacity of 21.3 gigawatts (GW). Approximately 62 per cent of total electricity generated is hydroelectric, with traditional thermal sources constituting the remainder.

Almost half of Venezuela's electricity generating capacity is provided by the 10GW Raul Leoni hydroelectric dam on the Caroní River.

Venezuela's grid is connected to that of Colombia, enabling the country to export surplus electricity. However, there have been serious electricity shortages in recent years due to low rainfall and electricity theft, which is estimated to account for a quarter of Venezuelan energy consumption.

The electricity sector is dominated by the state-owned Electrificación de Caroni (EDELCA). Cadafe, which includes Cadela, Elecentro, Eleoriente, Eleoccidente, Desurca, and Semda, is the second-largest state-owned electricity company.

The Caruachia dam project began operations in early 2003 and will increase Venezuela's electricity generating capacity by 11 per cent, providing 2.2GW of power when it is completed in 2010. Another dam, the 2.2GW Tocoma hydroelectric dam, is scheduled for completion by 2010. In December 2005 the Inter-American Development Bank (IADB) approved a US$768 million loan for Venezuela, US$750 million of which is to be devoted to the construction and operation of the Tocoma dam.

Financial markets

Stock exchange

The Bolsa de Valores de Caracas (BCV) (Caracas Stock Exchange) is the largest stock exchange in the country. The Comisión Nacional de Valores (CNV) (National Securities Commission) authorises bond issues and the public share offerings of domestic and foreign companies, but foreign shares can be traded on the exchange only if the government has given prior authorisation. Shares are not widely traded as the major domestic companies are privately held. Latin American fund managers invest on average 2 per cent of their total portfolios in Venezuela, compared to an average of 30 per cent in Mexico and 15 per cent in Argentina.

Banking and insurance

With the bankruptcy of the second biggest bank in the country, Banco Latino, in 1994, the Venezuelan banking and financial services system went into meltdown. About a third of Venezuela's banks subsequently went into insolvency as depositors panicked, closing accounts and forcing under-capitalised banks to close. Since then, the financial sector in Venezuela has undergone a vigorous restructuring, ensuring that the banks of today are well capitalised with relatively clean balance sheets.

The government has been able to recuperate its losses through the privatisation of several leading banks, and Venezuela's financial system is largely controlled by foreign interests. Foreign participation in Venezuela's banking system rose to around 70 per cent of total banking assets. As elsewhere in Latin America, it was the Spanish banks which had the most influence in the banking system, with Spanish Grupo Santander taking the lead in buying indigenous banks.

In 2006, Venezuela's banking superintendent privately told several of the country's large banks that President Chávez intends to place official government representatives on their governing boards. In August 2008, President Chavez began plans to nationalise the Commercial Bank of Venezuela, owned by the Spanish Grupo Santander.

A new Bank of the South, (South America) with a headquarters in Venezuela, has plans to be launched in 2008, to provide an alternative source of development funding for the participating countries. Assets of US$7 billion will underpin its operations.

Central bank

Banco Central de Venezuela

Main financial centre

Caracas

Time

GMT minus four and a half hours (from 9 December 2007)

Geography

Venezuela is on the north coast of South America, bordered by Colombia to the west, Guyana to the east and Brazil to the south.

Venezuela is a mountainous country. A spur of the Andes reaches into the north-west and is home to Pico Bolivar, at 5,007m the highest point in Venezuela. In the south-east, bordering on Brazil, are the densely-forested Guiana Highlands, which make up around half of the country's terrain. The Angel Falls, the highest waterfall in world, is in the Guiana Highlands. The centre of the country, between the mountain ranges and opening to the Caribbean Sea, are plains (llanos) and coastal lowlands. The Orinoco, Venezuela's biggest river, rises in the Guiana Highlands, draining most of the country on its way to the north-eastern coast and culminating in an extensive delta, which is marshy and thickly wooded.

Hemisphere

Northern

Climate

Tropical, hot and humid, with more moderate temperatures in highlands.

Dry season from December–April, with mean temperature in Caracas 19 degrees Celsius (C), rising to 28 degrees C during the day; nights are cool. Rainy season from May–November, with mean daytime temperature in Caracas 23 degrees C.

Entry requirements

Passports

Required by all, valid for six months from date of arrival.

Visa

Required by all, except nationals of EU/EEA countries, North America, Australasia, Japan, some South American, Asian and other countries for up to 90 days. For a full list of exemptions and other details, visit www.embavenez-us.org

Currency advice/regulations

There are no restrictions on the import and export of local or foreign currencies

Health (for visitors)

Mandatory precautions

None (yellow fever vaccination certificates may be required by visitor leaving for other countries).

Advisable precautions

Yellow fever, cholera, typhoid, polio vaccinations. Malaria prophylaxis recommended for visits to some rural areas. Rabies is present and dengue fever is becoming more common. There are occasional outbreaks of viral encephalitis.

In north-central regions, to avoid the risk of Bilharzia use only chlorinated swimming pools for bathing.

Bottled water is advisable for new visitors. Unwashed raw foods and undercooked meats are not safe to eat.

Healthcare facilities are good in main cities, but the cost is high and therefore medical insurance is recommended.

Hotels

The selection of first-rate hotels is rather limited. Good standard in Caracas and main centres. Graded into classes by Tourism Department on a one- to five-star basis. Booking in advance is essential. There are some seasonal variations of rates. There is a 10 per cent tourist tax.

Public holidays (national)

Fixed dates

1 Jan (New Year's Day), 19 Apr (Emancipation Day), 1 May (Labour Day), 24 Jun (Battle of Carabobo), 5 Jul (Independence Day), 24 Jul (Simon Bolívar Day), 15 Aug (Assumption Day), 12 Oct (Spanishness Day), 1 Nov (All Saints' Day), 25 Dec (Christmas Day).

Variable dates

Epiphany (first Mon in Jan), Carnival (Feb), Maundy Thursday, Good Friday, Immaculate Conception (Dec).

Working hours

Banking

Mon–Fri: 0830–1130, 1400–1630.

Business

Mon–Fri: 0800–1800 (with long lunch break from noon to 1430).

Government

Mon–Fri: range from 0730–1530 to 0930–1730; long lunch break from noon to 1430.

Shops

Mon–Sat: 0900–1300, 1500–1900.

Telecommunications

Postal services

There is an efficient service to Europe and the US.

Mobile/cell phones

A GSM 900 network is limited to coverage in Caracas and main towns.

Electricity supply

110V AC, 60 cycles

Social customs/useful tips

The normal form of greeting is a handshake or an abrazo, a cross between a handshake and a hug. Luncheons are frequently heavy. Wine in restaurants tends to be expensive.

Public services are inefficient and it is advisable to hire professional help to carry out official transactions.

Punctuality is not a strong point and the traffic is often blamed for delays. Business meetings may be cancelled or rescheduled at the last moment.

There is no numbering system for streets in Caracas, and many street names are not marked. Directions are given by building or residence name and the neighbourhood or urbanización.

Security

Carry identification at all times as police make spot checks and a person without identification may be detained.

Beware of pickpockets. If unlucky enough to be robbed, do not argue as criminals can quickly become violent. Many Caracas residents carry handguns for personal defence and are prepared to use them.

Getting there

Air

National airline: Aeropostal.

International airport/s: Caracas-Maiquetía International (MQV), 22km north of city, duty-free shopping, bank, restaurants, post office and car hire. Journey time to city by bus 45 minutes running every hour. Taxis are located at a rank.

Other airport/s: Maracaibo-La Chinita (MAR), 17km from city, restaurant, car hire.

Airport tax: US$16.

Surface

Road: It is possible to cross from Colombia by the Caribbean Coastal Highway, or by the Pan-American Highway via San Cristobal. The only road from Brazil (via Santa Elena de Uairen) is very rough and is difficult in the rainy season. There is no direct access from Guyana.

Main port/s: Guanta, La Guaira, Maracaibo, Puerto Cabello.

Getting about

National transport

Air: Several carriers operate services to many destinations in Venezuela. Overbooking is common and it is advisable to arrive at the airport well before minimum check-in time. Cancellations and schedule changes are also likely to occur. Unlimited travel tickets are available.

Road: Roads between main cities are of a high standard, but there are maintenance problems. The road from Caracas to Maiquetía International Airport is closed indefinitely due a collapsed bridge. There are around 36,000km of surfaced roads, including 17,000km motorways and 13,000km highways. The Pan-American Highway runs from Caracas, via Valencia and Barquisimeto, to the Colombian border. Other main highways include: Valencia-Puerto Cabello; Coro-La Ceiba; Caracas-Ciudad Bolívar.

Buses: There are frequent services between major cities. It is advisable to book in advance. Buses are overcrowded, tend to break down and traffic jams are a problem.

Rail: A very limited service available (Barquisimeto-Puerto Cabello; around four trains per day). The first new line since 1937, connecting Caracas and Cua, was inaugurated in October 2006.

City transport

Taxis: Taxis are not metered and it is advisable to agree the fare before travelling. Higher fares are charged for late night journeys. Outside Caracas fares can be expensive for long trips. Licensed taxis are white with yellow number plates and can be hailed in the street. A fleet of black Ford Explorers operates from Caracas airport. Visitors should avoid taxi touts and unlicensed taxis, especially at the airport. Taxis from reliable companies can be booked through the hotels, some of which run their own limousine services. Shared taxis (por puestos) are widely used.

Buses, trams & metro: The metro reaches main points all along the Valley of Caracas. It is fast, cheap, clean, comfortable and safe, although pickpockets abound. It links with the metrobus services.

Car hire

Most international rental car companies are available in main towns and at airports. National or international licence accepted. A credit card is required. Insurance cover is recommended.

BUSINESS DIRECTORY

The addresses listed below are a selection only. While World of Information makes every endeavour to check these addresses, we cannot guarantee that changes have not been made, especially to telephone numbers and area codes. We would welcome any corrections.

Telephone area codes

The international direct dialling (IDD) code for Venezuela is +58, followed by area code and subscriber's number:

Barquisimeto	251	Maturin	291
Caracas	212	Merida	274
Ciudad Bolivar	285	Puerto Cabello	242
Cumana	293	San Cristobal	276
Maracaibo	261	Valencia	241
Maracay	243		

Chambers of Commerce

American-Venezuelan Cámara de Comercio, Torre Credival, 2da Avenida de Campo Alegre, Caracas (tel: 263-0833; fax: 263-1829; e-mail: vanamcham@venamcham.org).

British-Venezuelan Chamber of Commerce, Avenida Francisco de Miranda, Multicentro Empresarial del Este, Caracas (tel: 267-3112; fax: 263-0362; e-mail: britcham@ven.net).

Caracas Cámara de Comercio, Calle Andrés Eloy Blanco 215, Los Caobos, Caracas (tel: 571-3222; fax: 571-0050; e-mail: comercioccs@cantv.net).

Valencia Cámara de Comercio, Avenida Bolivar Norte, Edificio Cámara de Comercio, Valencia (tel: 857-5109; fax: 857-5147; e-mail: camaracomercio@cantv.net).

Venezualan Federación de Cámaras y Asociaciones de Comercio y Producción, Avenida El Empalme, Urbanizacion El Bosque, PO Box 2568, Caracas (tel: 731-1711, 731-0246; e-mail: direje@fedecamaras.org.ve).

Banking

Banco Industrial de Venezuela, Av Universidad Esquina de Traposos, Zona postal 1010, Apartado postal 2054, Caracas (tel: 545-9222/541-8622; fax: 545-8315).

Banco Mercantil, Av Andrés Bello No 1, Edif Mercantil, Aportado postal 789, Caracas 1010-A (tel: 541-4320, 541-6666; fax: 507-1239, 574-3216; e-mail: mercan24@bancomercantil.com; internet site: http://www.bancomercantil.com).

Banco Provincial, Av Este 'O', San Bernardo, Zona postal 1010-A, Apartado postal 1269, Caracas (tel: 574-5611, 574-6611; fax: 574-9408, 574-2065).

Central bank

Banco Central de Venezuela, Avenida Urdaneta esq Las Carmelitas, Apartado 2017, Caracas 1010 (tel: 801-5111; fax: 861-1649; e-mail: biblio@bcv.org.ve).

Travel information

Caracas-Maiquetía Airport, Ed Vargas, Maiquetia 1161 (tel: 303-1329; fax: 355-1224; e-mail: consejo_admin@iaaim.com.ve).

Ministry of tourism

Ministry of Tourism, Edificio Mintur, Avda Francisco de Miranda con Avda Principal de La Floresta, Caracas (tel: 208-4511; e-mail: webmaster@mintur.gob.ve).

National tourist organisation offices

Inatur (National Institute of Tourism), Edificio Mintur, Avda Francisco de Miranda con Avda Principal de La Floresta, Caracas (tel/fax: 286-3016; fax: 286-3016; e-mail: gpminatur@gmail.com).

Ministries

Ministry of Agriculture and Livestock, Torre Este, Piso 14, Caracas (tel: 509-0445; fax: 574-2432).

Ministry of Defence, Fuerta Tiuna, Conejo Blanco, Caracas 1090 (tel: 622-2745; fax: 662-4078).

Ministry of Education, Esquina de Salas, Edificio Sede Del Ministerio de Educación, Caracas (tel: 564-0672; fax: 564-0379).

Ministry of Energy, Torre Oeste, Parque Central, Piso 16, Caracas (tel: 507-6604; fax: 571-3953).

Ministry of the Environment, Torre Sur, Centro Simon Bolivar, Piso 25, Caracas (tel: 481-6275; fax: 483-1148).

Ministry of Family Affairs, Torre Oeste, Parque Central, Piso 51, Caracas (tel: 575-3690; fax: 573-7481).

Ministry of Finance, Edif Banco la Guaira, Piso 12, Av Mexico, Caracas (tel: 509-8281; fax: 509-7831).

Ministry of Foreign Affairs, Conde a Carmelitas, Torre M.R.E., Piso 2, Caracas 1010 (tel: 862-4484; fax: 861-0894).

Ministry of Foreign Trade, Centro Comercial los Cedros, Mezzanina 3, Avda Libertador, Caracas (tel: 762-2777; fax: 762-3883).

Ministry of Health and Social Security, Edif, Sur, Centro Simón Bolívar, Caracas (tel: 483-1566).

Ministry of Home Affairs, Esquina de Carmelitas, Caracas 1010 (tel: 483-4334; fax: 861-1967).

Ministry of Housing (tel: 509-8676; fax: 509-8437).

Ministry of Industrial Development, Edif Sur, Piso 9, Centro Simón Bolívar, Caracas (tel: 419-296; fax: 483-2607).

Ministry of Justice, Torre Norte, Centro Simón Bolívar, Piso 25 (tel: 483-1170; fax: 483-7515).

Ministry of Labour, Torre Sur, Piso 5, Centro Simón Bolívar, Caracas (tel: 483-1881; fax: 483-5940).

Ministry of Planning, Parque Central, Torre Oeste, Piso 26, Caracas (tel: 507-7902; fax: 573-2834).

Ministry of Public Works and Commercial Affairs, Centro Simón Bolívar, Torre Sur, Piso 6, Caracas (tel: 483-2124-; fax: 412-553).

Ministry of Trade and Industry, Av Libertador Centro Comercial Los Cedros, Piso 2, Caracas (tel: 531-0026; fax: 762-9869).

Ministry of Transport and Communications, Torre Este, Parque Central, Piso 50, Caracas (tel: 509-10761; fax: 509-1769).

Ministry of Urban Development, Torre Oeste, Parque Central, Piso 51, Caracas (tel: 574-5349; fax: 571-1767).

President's Office, Palacio de Miraflores, Avenida Urdeneta, Caracas 1010 (tel: 861-0811; fax: 861-1101).

Other useful addresses

Asociación Nacional de Comerciantes e Industriales, Plaza Panteón Norte 1, Apdo 33, Caracas.

CVG Bauxita de Venezuela S.A. (Raw Material for Aluminun), Av. La Estancia, Edif, Diamen, Piso 2, Chuao, Caracas (tel: 922-311, 916-187, 916-487; fax: 918-176).

British Embassy, Edificio Torre Las Mercedes, 3 Piso, Avenida La Estancia, Chuao, Caracas 1060 (tel: 911-255, 993-4111, 926-542, 914-253; fax: 993-9989).

Caracas Stock Exchange (fax: 952-2640; internet site: http://www.caracasstock.com).

Central Information Office (OCI), Parque Central, Torre Oeste, Piso 18, Caracas (tel: 572-7110; fax: 572-2675).

The Commission for State Reform, Torre Oeste, Piso 38, Parque Central, Caracas (tel: 507-8934/8931; fax: 572-3178).

Conapri (National Council for Investment Promotion), Centro Banavén, PB, Local 4,

Chuao, Caracas (tel: 923-801; fax: 926-498).

Consejo Venezolana de la Industria, Edif Cámara de Industriales, Esq de Puente Anauco, Caracas.

Corporación Venezolana de Guayana (CVG) (Main Company), Edif. de Administración, Via Caracas, Puerto Ordaz, Ciudad Guayana, C.P. 80915, Edo. Bolivar (tel: 303-333; fax: 226-300, 225-311).

CVG Ferrominera del Orinoco AA (Iron), Av La Estancia, Chuao, Edif, Torre Las Mercedes, Piso 9, Caracas 1070-A (tel: 911-166; fax: 911-639).

Fondo de Inversiones de Venezuela (Privatisation Programme Information), Torre Financiera del Banco Central de Venezuela, Piso 20, Esq de Santa Capilla, Avda Urdaneta, Caracas (tel: 806-5974; fax: 819-169).

PdVSA (Petróleos de Venezuela), Avda Liberator, La Campina, Apdo 169, Caracas 1010-A (tel: 708-1111; fax: 708-4661).

CVG Siderúrgica del Orinoco CA SIDOR. (Aluminium, Iron and Steel), Av La Estancia, Chuao, Edif. General de Seguros, Caracas, 1070-A (tel: 912-333, 911-462).

Superintendencia de Inversiones Extranjeras (SIEX – Superintendency of Foreign Investment), Apdo 213, Edif La Perla, Piso 3, Bolsa a Mercaderes, Caracas (tel: 483-6666; fax: 484-4368, 481-7919).

Unión Patronal Venezolana de Comercio, Edif General Urdaneta, Piso 2, Marrón a Pelota, Apdo 6578, Caracas.

US Embassy, Avda Principal de la Floresta, Esq Francisco de Miranda, La Floresta, Caracas (tel: 285-3111; fax: 285-0336).

Venezuelan Embassy (USA), 1099 30th Street, NW, Washington DC 20007 (tel: (+1-202) 342-2214; fax: (+1-202) 342-6820;

e-mail: despacho@embavenez-us.org).

National news agency: ABN (Agencia Bolicariana de Noticias)

Internet sites

Venezuela Export Directory: http://www.ddex.com/

Venezuela trade: http://www.trade-venezuela.com

Vietnam

KEY FACTS

Official name: Cong Hoa Xa Hoi Chu Nghia Viet Nam (The Socialist Republic of Vietnam) (SRV)

Head of State: President Nguyen Minh Triet (since 27 Jun 2006)

Head of government: Prime Minister Nguyen Tan Dung (appointed 27 Jun 2006)

Ruling party: Dang Cong San Viet Nam (DCSV) (Communist Party of Vietnam)

Area: 329,556 square km

Population: 85.59 million (2007)*

Capital: Hanoi

Official language: Vietnamese

Currency: Dong (D) = 100 xu

Exchange rate: D16,775.00 per US$ (Jul 2008)

GDP per capita: US$818 (2007)*

GDP real growth: 8.50% (2007)*

Labour force: 44.58 million (2006)

Unemployment: 4.30% (2006; urban rate only)

Inflation: 8.30% (2005); 27.04% (July 2008)

Oil production: 340,000 bpd (2007)

Balance of trade: -US$4.65 billion (2005)

Foreign debt: US$15.50 billion (2006)

Visitor numbers: 3.58 million (2006)*

* estimated figure

Vietnam's Tenth Communist Party Congress, in April 2006, produced a number of changes in the Party leadership, including a new president, vice resident and prime minister, two new deputy prime minister positions, and the appointment of ten new ministers or equivalent heads of agencies. Nong Duc Manh retained the key position of General Secretary. Vietnam's National Assembly had become increasingly active and influential in setting national priorities in recent years, as members became increasingly prepared to criticise the government openly.

Dissent?

The more active and critical role of the National Assembly in reviewing legislation and policies and Vietnam's more exigent media have certainly contributed to a greater degree of openness in Vietnam, but none the less dissent can still be met with serious punishment. Individuals can receive long prison terms on loose charges, such as espionage or 'undermining national security' and making propaganda against the state. Despite an occasionally looser official attitude on questions of religious freedom, a number of high-profile arrests and trials in early 2007 focussed on Vietnam's one-party political system and its clumsy management of diverse political views.

Strained resources

Vietnam's economy managed to maintain its high growth level in 2007, with gross domestic product (GDP) growing at 8.5 per cent, the third consecutive year that growth was over 8 per cent. According to the Asian Development Bank (ADB) in its 2008 *Asian Development Outlook* Vietnam's accession to the World Trade Organisation (WTO) at the beginning of 2007 provided an important stimulus to economic growth as well as to much needed market oriented economic reforms. The ADB considered that the sustained level of rapid growth has strained resources; this has reportedly shown itself in an import surge, infrastructure bottlenecks, skilled labour shortages and – importantly – inflationary pressures, which lead to an annual rate of inflation of over 19 per cent by March 2008 (the rate for 2007 as a whole was 8.3 per cent). This was the highest rate in over a decade. A tightened fiscal policy was likely to contain inflation in 2009, by which time it was expected to have dropped to 10.2 per cent. Measures introduced to contain inflation were expected to slow economic growth in the medium term. None the less, the ADB considered that the medium and long term economic prospects to be good.

Changing times

Vietnam is going through some interesting social changes as the older generations of Vietnamese who grew up knowing war as a routine, daily event are replaced by a younger, less ideologically conscious generation. Despite government efforts to introduce some sort of uniformity between north and south, it was in the south of the country that private industry continues to flourish, for the most part in the hands of the minority Hao community. The Hao are of Chinese origin, dislike working with their hands and are for the most part located in the south. Even though power is centred in the north, south Vietnam has always been more prosperous – and less disciplined – than the north. Reacting to the pressure to conform, many Hao decided to leave; the refugees that travelled in their thousands from Vietnam into neighbouring countries and as far afield as Australia were really the Hao people.

Vietnam had declared independence from French colonial rule in 1945. But it was not until 1954, after a bitter struggle between the Vietnamese, led by future president Ho Chi Min, that the French finally relinquished their claims.

In April 2005, Vietnam had marked the 30th anniversary of the defeat of South Vietnam by the Dang Cong San Viet Nam (DCSV) (Communist Party of Vietnam)-led North Vietnam. The victory in 1975 brought to an end 18 years of fighting between the US-backed South Vietnam and the Soviet and Chinese-backed North. The fighting, which saw US combat troops enter the war in 1965 and remain until 1973, cost the lives of an estimated 3–4 million

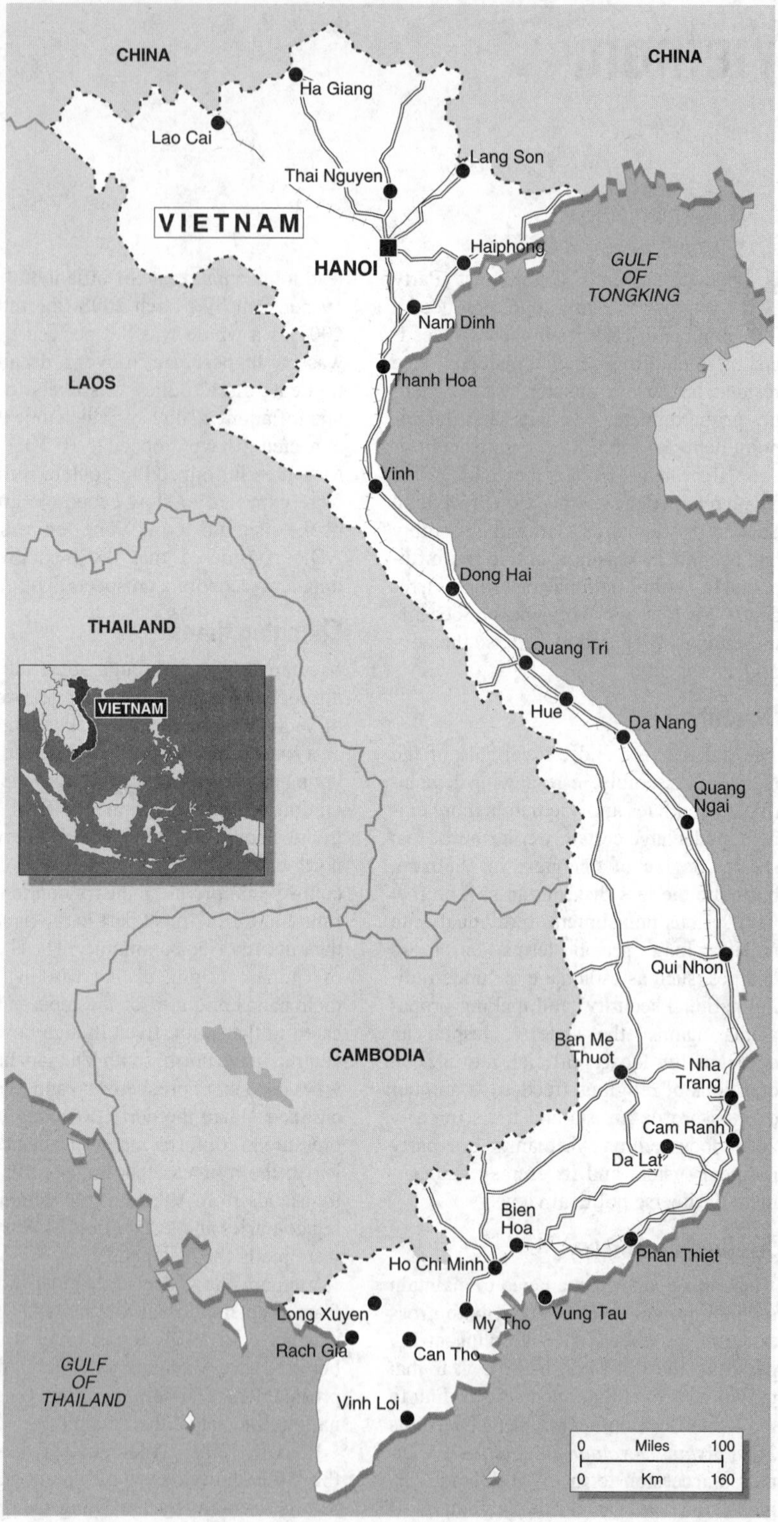

Vietnamese, as well as 58,000 US servicemen.

The first official visit by a Vietnamese leader to the US since the end of the Vietnam War took place in 2005. Prime Minister Phan Van Khai visited the White House and held talks with US president, George W Bush. Trade links between the two countries have been growing since the 1990s but relations remain strained over a number of points including the fate of 1,800 US servicemen classified as Missing in Action (MIA) since the Vietnam War, and US criticism of Vietnam's human rights record. in 2007 the US agreed to fund a study into eliminating the high levels of Agent Orange (a highly toxic defoliant) used by the US military during the Vietnam War from storage sites. Economic matters

Reflecting the economic ascendancy of the south, economic development has varied geographically, some areas recording high growth rates and vastly improved living standards, but others experiencing near stagnation. Ho Chi Minh City (the largest city in south Vietnam with 8.2 million people) and the surrounding provinces constitute the power-house of economic development with GDP per capita reaching nearly US$2,000, more than double the national average. Ho Chi Minh City and the surrounding provinces attract nearly around two-thirds of Vietnam's total foreign direct investment (FDI). Total (disbursed – i e actually materialising) FDI in 2006 reached a record US$4 billion. Total approved FDI in 2006 was US$10.2 billion, also a record. The largest investors by nation in Vietnam are Taiwan, Singapore, South Korea, Japan, and Hong Kong. The top five destinations for Vietnam's exports in 2006 were the US, EU, Japan, Australia and China. When the countries of the EU are counted individually, Australia was Vietnam's third largest export market in the calendar year 2006 after US and Japan.

The State Bank of Vietnam estimates remittances from overseas Vietnamese in 2006 were US$3.8 billion. Seventy per cent of remittances come from the United States, followed by Australia, Canada and Germany. The government of Vietnam estimates that there are 2.7 million Vietnamese residing overseas of which 1.2 million are in the United States.

Goods and services exports now constitute over 70 per cent of GDP, well more than double the 30 per cent share recorded in the mid-1990s. Crude oil alone accounted for 21 per cent of total merchandise export revenues in 2006. Other major export items include textiles, garments and footwear, seafood, timber products, rice, rubber, coffee, cashews, pepper and coal.

Vietnam's major imports are machinery and spare parts, refined petroleum products, urea, steel ingots, pharmaceuticals, textile and garment inputs, plastics and chemicals. The top five sources of imports in 2006 were China, Singapore, Taiwan, Japan, and Korea.

Oil

Vietnam had 3.4 thousand million barrels of proven oil reserves at the end of 2007. Crude oil production averaged 340,000 barrels per day (bpd) in 2007. Although it is a significant oil producer, Vietnam remains reliant on imports of petroleum products due to its lack of refining capacity. The planned development of several new oil fields in coming years is expected to increase Vietnamese production as exploration continues to yield new discoveries.

In addition to its oil, Vietnam also had proven gas reserves of 7.77 trillion cubic feet (Tcf) at ehe end of 2007. Vietnam's natural gas production and consumption have been rising rapidly since the late 1990s, with further increases expected as additional fields come on stream. Natural gas is currently produced entirely for domestic consumption. The Cuu Long basin offshore from the Mekong Delta in southern Vietnam, a source of associated gas from oil production, is the largest Vietnamese natural gas production area.

Politics

June 2006 session of the National Assembly confirmed the new political leadership, including new pesident (Nguyen Minh Triet), prime minister (Nguyen Tan Dung) and key cabinet ministers. The new leadership includes some relatively younger ministers and is considered a significant generational change. Generational changes are important in Vietnam, often representing the introduction of very different mindsets into the political process.

Administration and policy implementation is the responsibility of government ministries. The principal ministries may appear to be hardworking and systematic but often demonstrate surprising lethargy and even corruption. Bureaucrats can often show an exasperating vagueness about time and schedules; decision-making processes can be slow and opaque. A sign of the importance of generation change is the fact that talented young Vietnamese seeking career opportunities Vietnam's expanding economy and increasingly important private sector no longer see Party membership as essential to personal advancement.

Outlook

Vietnam looks set to continue to expand its economy at an impressive rate. Ironically, Vietnam is actually underperforming as long as it fails to address the problems of economic reform and bureaucracy. These problems are the lingering legacy of a four-decade war, which will be remedied by the new ideas that come with generational change.

Risk assessment

Politics	Fair
Economy	Good
Regional stability	Good

COUNTRY PROFILE

Historical profile

The Red River (Song Hong) Delta in the north is considered the 'Cradle of the Nation'. It was from here in the tenth century that the Nam Tien Movement was begun by General Le Han. The southward expansion occurred because of the need to seek new ricelands.

The Vietnamese expanded south, during the fourteenth to eighteenth centuries, conquering the Cham people and Mekong Delta.

1428 After a long period of rule by successive Chinese rulers, Vietnam gained independence from the Ming dynasty's control. The Le dynasty ruled until 1527.

1680 The Portuguese, Dutch, English and French established trading posts in Vietnam.

1771–1802 The Tai Son Rebellion years. The Tai Son brothers wrested control from the ruling Nguyen family. They aimed to seize the wealth of the rich and aid the poor. Most of the members of the Nguyen family were killed except for Nguyen Anh, the nephew of a Nguyen lord.

1802 Vietnam was unified under the leadership of Nguyen Anh who recaptured much of Vietnam from the Tai Son brothers.

1830–40 The Nguyen dynasty tried to rid Vietnam of French missionaries by forcing the Christian movement underground and executing priests. In response, the missionaries appealed to the French government for military intervention in Vietnam.

1859 The French began their attack on the region, capturing the city of Danang.

1861 The French captured Saigon (now Ho Chi Minh city).

1862 Vietnam agreed to the Treaty of Saigon that gave the French control of three provinces and the island of Poulo Condore, free passage of French ships and freedom for the missionaries.

1883 French rule began over the whole country as part of the Indochina territory that included Cambodia. Under colonial rule, transportation and communications improved but the standard of living among the Vietnamese people remained low. Their suffering contributed to rising nationalist sentiment.

1930 A revolutionary, Ho Chi Minh, formed the Indochinese Communist Party (ICP) to fight against French rule.

1940 The French administration was replaced by Japanese occupation during the war.

1945 The Japanese were expelled by the ICP and French forces. A war of independence against France began.

1954 At a peace conference in Geneva, Vietnam was divided at the seventeenth parallel into communist Democratic

KEY INDICATORS — Vietnam

	Unit	2003	2004	2005	2006	2007
Population	m	81.77	83.03	83.18	*84.40	*85.59
Gross domestic product (GDP)	US$bn	39.20	45.21	53.05	60.99	*70.02
GDP per capita	US$	455	535	638	*723	*818
GDP real growth	%	7.2	7.7	8.4	8.2	*8.5
Inflation	%	4.0	7.7	8.3	7.5	8.3
Oil output	'000 bpd	372.0	427.0	392.0	367.0	340.0
Natural gas output	bn cum	2.4	4.2	5.2	7.0	7.7
Coal output	mtoe	10.7	14.8	18.3	21.8	–
Exports (fob) (goods)	US$m	20,176.0	23,720.0	32,230.0	39,826.0	48,561.0
Imports (cif) (goods)	US$m	25,227.0	26,310.0	36,880.0	44,891.0	58,921.0
Balance of trade	US$m	-5,051.0	-2,590.0	-4,650.0	-5,155.0	-10,360.0
Current account	US$m	-1,840.0	-2,020.0	218.0	-244.0	-6,722.0
Total reserves minus gold	US$m	6,224.2	7,041.5	9,050.9	13,384.1	23,602.4
Foreign exchange	US$m	6,222.0	7,041.0	9,050.0	13,382.5	23,594.8
Exchange rate	per US$	15,524	15,746	16,047	16,073	16,040

* estimated figure

Republic of Vietnam (north) and American-backed Republic of Vietnam (south). North Vietnam sponsored a growing guerrilla movement (Viet Cong) in the south, which aimed to re-unite Vietnam.
1964 US armed forces began their official intervention in support of South Vietnam after the US Gulf of Tonkin resolution. The US was committed to South Vietnam.
1967 The US military presence totalled nearly 500,000 troops.
1968 The Communists launched an attack on South Vietnam. This 'Tet Offensive' targetted five major cities. The Communists were forced to retreat within weeks. The US bombing campaign against North Vietnam ended and US troops in South Vietnam were reduced.
1973 The Paris peace accords were signed, temporarily ending hostilities between the US and North Vietnam.
1975 US troops withdrew.
1976 North and South Vietnam were combined to form the Socialist Republic of Vietnam. Saigon was renamed Ho Chi Minh City.
1979 Vietnamese troops invaded Cambodia overthrowing the Pol Pot regime and instituting their own puppet government; Chinese troops invaded Vietnam but were defeated. During this time Vietnam established close relationships with the Soviet Union, which was necessary for its economic development.
1986 Economic reform began with the adoption of the doi moi (renovation) reforms.
1992 The state constitution was introduced, which allowed for some liberalisation of the Vietnamese economy.
1993 Full western aid resumed.
1995 Vietnamese and American rapprochement began. Vietnam joined the Association of Southeast Asian Nations (Asean).
1997 Tran Duc Luong was elected president by the National Assembly, and Phan Van Khai was appointed prime minister.
2000 Vietnam and the US signed an agreement enabling normal trading relations between the two countries.
2001 Nong Duc Manh was appointed secretary general of the Dang Cong San Viet Nam (DCSV) (Communist Party of Vietnam). The bilateral trade agreement between Vietnam and the US came into effect.
2002 Russia closed its naval base in Cam Ranh. Vietnam signed an accord with Russia to construct a US$100 million hydroelectric power station in Vietnam's central highlands. DCSV members won most seats in the National Assembly elections. President Tran Duc Luong was reappointed for a second term by the National Assembly.
2004 Vietnam's first human deaths from bird flu was followed within the year by another 30. The first US commercial flight since 1973 landed in Ho Chi Minh City.
2005 Prime Minister Phan Van Khai, the first Vietnamese leader since the end of the Vietnam War, visited the US.
2006 Nguyen Minh Triet and Nguyen Tan Dung replaced Tran Duc Luong and Phan Van Khai as president and prime minister seen as a move towards a younger leadership. A trade agreement was with the US was concluded, opening the way for Vietnam to membership of the World Trade Organisation (WTO).
2007 Vietnam join the WTO in January, after a 12-year accession process. In May, in elections for the National Assembly the coalition Vietnamese Fatherland Front (led by the Communist Party) won 492 seats (out of 493). The US agreed to fund a study into eliminating the high levels of Agent Orange (a highly toxic defoliant) used by the US military during the Vietnam War from storage sites. Prime Minister Dung was re-appointed in July and promised to implement economic reforms.
2008 In July petrol prices were increased by 31 per cent as the government moved to cut back on subsidies. Vietnam is the world largest producer of black pepper (around a third of global production) and while the crop was down from 90,300 tonnes to 87,000 tonnes, world prices jumped by 28 per cent and the total exports were US$166 million, with an average price of US$3,530 per tonne.

Political structure

Constitution

Vietnam has adopted, in broad terms, a Marxist-Leninist political ideology. A number of its political systems are derived from those of China and the former USSR. The political structure is dominated throughout by the Dang Cong San Viet Nam (DCSV) (Communist Party of Vietnam).
Under the 1992 state constitution, the DCSV continues to be ultimately responsible for policy, but the government assumed greater administrative and executive responsibility.
Twenty-four amendments to the 1992 constitution were passed in December 2001. The most important gave equality to the private sector of the economy.
Local government is vested in elected provincial, municipal and district councils.

Form of state

Socialist republic

The executive

Executive power is officially exercised by a Western-style council of ministers under a prime minister. However, in practice, there is a two-way balance with the presidency and party. The president is elected by the National Assembly for a five-year term. Between sessions of the National Assembly, affairs of state are dealt with by the president and the National Assembly's standing committee, the council of state. In any case, membership of the Council of Ministers generally coincides with that of the Politburo and Secretariat of the DCSV, and executive decisions may, de facto, be taken by the DCSV even without the co-operation of the government.
The DCSV's 166-member Central Committee meets once or twice a year and is responsible for selecting the Politburo, which has 17 members. The Politburo oversees the DCSV's daily functions and has the power and authority to issue directives to the government. It is the highest policy-making body.

National legislature

The Council of Ministers is responsible to and appointed by the legislative Quoc Hoi (National Assembly), itself elected to a five-year term by universal adult suffrage (voting is mandatory).
The Quoc Hoi is the highest representative and legislative body of the people of Vietnam and the only institution with the authority to enact the constitution, codes and laws and elect the president and vice president, prime minister, president of the supreme people's court and procurator general, among other high officials.
The National Assembly, which is dominated by the ruling DCSV, meets twice a year in plenary session for about two to three weeks at a time. The Assembly's principal purpose is the (generally automatic) approval of Politburo decisions and DCSV-inspired legislation.

Legal system

Vietnam applied French law in the colonial period, but assumed a legal system based on the Soviet mould after the communist takeover. The country has a civil law system, but much of the law is underdeveloped and in the process of being innovated, for example in the case of foreign investment. Civil cases involving such matters as family law are distinguished from 'economic' cases, which include disputes arising from trade, investment and payments involving foreign entities. 'Economic' cases are dealt with by a separate arbitration system, in which the Vietnam International Arbitration Centre (VIAC) is a prominent body. The People's Supreme Court is Vietnam's highest court. Under it are People's Courts for each province, municipality and district. The legal system is in the process of being reformed.

Last elections

20 May 2007 (parliamentary); 27 June 2006 (presidential)

Results: Presidential: Nguyen Minh Triet won 94.12 per cent of the vote (464 votes out of 498) by parliament.
Parliamentary: DCSV won 447 of 498 seats; non-party candidates won 51 seats; and self-appointed candidates three.
Turnout was 99.7 per cent.

Next elections
September 2007 (presidential); 2012 (parliamentary)

Political parties

Ruling party
Dang Cong San Viet Nam (DCSV) (Communist Party of Vietnam)

Main opposition party
Vietnam has no opposition parties.

Population

85.59 million (2007)*

Last census: April 1999: 76,323,173

Population density: 239 people per square km. Urban population: 25 per cent.

Annual growth rate: 1.5 per cent 1994–2004 (WHO 2006)

Ethnic make-up
Vietnamese (84 per cent) and Chinese (2 per cent). The remainder are Khmers, Chams and members of some 51 ethnic groups.

Religions
Although the country is officially atheist, many Vietnamese profess to being Buddhists. Christians are a significant minority (five million, mostly Catholics), followed by Caodaists, Hoa Hao Buddhists, Muslims and Hindus. There is a religious revival in Vietnam.

Education

Primary school lasts until age 11. Secondary school education is divided into lower secondary and upper secondary school lasting for four and three years, respectively. There is also provision for technical and vocational secondary education. Universities, specialised colleges, community and junior colleges provide higher education. There are currently over 100 higher education institutions. Distance education is offered in two open universities and other provincial centres.
The Ministry of Labour, Invalids and Social Affairs is expected to build a vocational training school in each province and a job training centre in each district by 2005. Since 1998, the state has invested US$12 million to upgrade infrastructure in job training centres and set up 39 new vocational schools. Trainees at vocational schools have annually increased by 20 per cent. Vietnam will provide vocational training to 1.3 million people annually, including 200,000 technicians, until 2010. As a result, the number of untrained workers will be reduced by 1.6 per cent by that year.
Public expenditure on education typically amounts to 3 per cent of annual gross national income.

Literacy rate: 90 per cent, adult rate (Unesco 2005)

Compulsory years: Six to 14.

Enrolment rate: 105.6 per cent gross primary enrolment; 67.1 per cent gross secondary enrolment, of relevant age groups (including repeaters) (World Bank 2004).

Pupils per teacher: 28, in primary schools.

Health

Per capita total expenditure on health (2003) was US$164; of which per capita government spending was US$46, at the international dollar rate, (WHO 2006).
The government has sought to improve the country's deteriorating healthcare system, which suffers from chronic underfunding and resultant shortages of medicine and equipment, recruitment problems and low staff morale. In 2001, an agreement was signed by the International Finance Corporation to invest US$8 million to establish a foreign-owned, Western-style hospital in Ho Chi Minh City. The new hospital will have modern equipment and advanced medical facilities. It is the first hospital project to be partly funded by private investors and reflects the government's promotion of investment in Vietnam's healthcare system.
The parlous state of Vietnam's healthcare system today dates back to the end of the war in 1975. Although on paper the results are impressive, including the establishment of 9,000 communal clinics and the training of an additional 23,000 doctors to give a ratio of approximately 40 doctors per 10,000 population, the reality is that many clinics are not equipped or stocked and are given inadequate budgets. Many doctors prefer to concentrate their efforts on the more remunerative private treatment of better-off patients.
This difference between private and public expenses partly reflects the system of health fees introduced in the 1990s to supplement the health budget. The new charges (from which civil servants and war veterans are exempt) backfired, resulting in lower bed-occupancy rates – in some cases drops of 40 per cent were registered.
In 2004, avian flu broke out twice killing 20 people and prompting the slaughter of more than 100 million poultry.

HIV/Aids
The official number of HIV/Aids cases by March 2006 was 104,000, however, some estimates put the real figure at three times this number. Young people, between 15–24 years, account for 40 per cent of the overall infection rate. The government has allocated US$6.7 million and the Asian Development Bank (ADB) allocated US$20 million for a programme, implemented over a five-year period, targetted specifically at the young. In 2004 the US included Vietnam in a list of 15 countries to benefit from a US$15 billion fund, at the beginning of in a five-year aid programme.

HIV prevalence: 0.4 per cent aged 15–49 in 2003 (World Bank)

Life expectancy: 71 years, 2004 (WHO 2006)

Fertility rate/Maternal mortality rate: 2.3 births per woman, 2004 (WHO 2006)

Birth rate/Death rate: 12.7 births and six deaths per 1,000 people (2003).

Child (under 5 years) mortality rate (per 1,000): 19 per 1,000 live births (2003); 37 per cent of children aged under five are malnourished (World Bank).

Head of population per physician: 0.53 physicians per 1,000 people, 2001 (WHO 2006)

Welfare

Vietnam's transition to a market economy has increased problems of unemployment and the availability of social security benefits. The country has about 46.6 million people of working age, accounting for 59 per cent of the total population. Vietnam aims to create 1.4 million jobs annually in the period between 2001–05. The country also plans to reduce unemployment to 5 per cent and increase working time in rural areas.
Although there are social security systems for the victims of war, the collapse of the co-operative system has affected benefits in rural areas. With the introduction of a new Labour Code in 1994, and the Law on Co-operatives in 1996, the Vietnamese government declared its willingness to provide social insurance to workers in all economic sectors. The Vietnam Social Security Organisation, founded in 1995, has a social insurance scheme covering both state and private employees for benefits including retirement, survivorship, sickness, maternity and compensation for work related injuries. The pension scheme is supported by 10 per cent and 5 per cent contributions from the employer and the employee, respectively.
The Ministry of Public Security has undertaken education programmes aimed at halting the increase in the traffic, to China each year, estimated at thousands of women, and young girls aged under 18 – who account for one in six cases.

Main cities

Hanoi (capital, estimated population 1.2 million (m) in 2005), Ho Chi Minh City (formerly Saigon) (3.4m), Hai Phong City (2.6m), Da Nang City (450,909), Bien

Hoa (514,450), Hue (275,307), Vung Tau (259,869), Phan Thiet (228,299).

Languages spoken

The Vietnamese alphabet is an adaptation from the Roman, using tonal marks. French is spoken in official circles and some English is spoken in business circles, especially in the south. Business is usually conducted in Vietnamese or English, although many executives speak French and Russian, and a few speak Chinese.

English and French are officially taught in secondary schools.

Official language/s

Vietnamese

Media

The Ministry of Culture and Information retains firm control of press and broadcasting and laws circumscribe journalists' ability to report freely.

National newş agency: VNA (Vietnam News Agency)

Press

Dailies: In Vietnamese and most with English versions, Nhân Dân (www.nhandan.com.vn), is the Communist Party newspaper, Tuoi Tre (www.tuoitre.com.vn) has a wide circulation among the young, Quân D?i Nhân Dân (www.qdnd.vn/qdnd), is the army's newpaper.

In English, Viet Nam News (vietnamnews.vnanet.vn), Saigon Giai Phong (www.saigon-gpdaily.com.vn), is the communist newspaper in Ho Chi Minh City. In French Le Courrier du Vietnam (http://lecourrier.vnagency.com.vn).

Weeklies: In English the Vietnam Courier is a communist publication and Doanh Nghiep is published by the Union of Co-operatives.

Business: In Vietnamese Tin Nhanh Chúng Khoán (www.tinnhanhchungkhoan.vn), with stock exchange details, Nghien Cuu Kinh Te (www.ie.netnam.vn) a bi-monthly, academic, Economic Studies Review publication.

In English, the Vietnam Investment Review (www.vir.com.vn), is a weekly circulated in Vietnam, and distributed throughout Asia, Europe and the US, coupled to the online business news outlet (http://english.vietnamnet.vn). The Saigon Times Weekly (www.saigontimesweekly.saigonnet.vn) is another weekly. Monthlies include Vietnam Economic Times (www.vneconomy.com.vn/eng) with analysis and business tips, and Vietnam Business Forum (http://vibforum.vcci.com.vn), a Chamber of Trade and Commerce publication.

Periodicals: Several commercial periodicals that have recently begun publishing, in Vietnamese, to an international standard include Nha Dep a women's magazine, Dinh Cao (Sports and Fitness), M (Fashion) and Phu Nu The Gioi (Woman's World). Other popular publications include Tuoi Tre (youth), and Lao Dong (Labour).

Broadcasting

Radio: The national radio service, Voice of Vietnam (VOV) (www.vov.org.un) has two networks with six channels broadcasting a wide variety of show including news, current affairs culture and music and an external service with programmes in many languages including English, French and Russian. There are other radio stations, some commercial, operating regionally including Hanoi Radio (www.htv.org.vn), The Voice of Ho Chi Minh (www.voh.com.vn) and Lamp Dong Radio (www.lamdong.gov.vn).

Television: The national broadcaster is Vietnam Television (VTV) (www.vtv.org.vn) with nine channels and is available via satellite. VTV also operates the country's largest cable network VCTV (www.vctv.com.vn) and a direct-to-home (DTH) satellite service which supplies the nine free-to-air channels, nine subscription channels and around 40 international channels. Ho Chi Minh city also has a TV station (HTV) (www.htv.com.vn) with domestic and foreign programmes.

Advertising

As television is the dominant medium it carries the majority of advertising which is regulated by legislation. Advertising content is heavily regulated, while tobacco, liquor and beer are banned and foreign products may require a licence from a relevant ministry to advertise.

Economy

Vietnam is a medium-sized country with a population of 83.6 million, split between a more Western-oriented, relatively infrastructure-rich south and the more highly populated but relatively impoverished north. Although the number of people living below the poverty line dropped below 40 per cent during the 1990s, and has fallen still further in recent years, Vietnam remains one of the world's poorest countries, with a GDP per capita of only US$618 in 2005 (up from US$535 in 2004).

The initial reform policies, collectively known as doi moi (change to the new), aimed to move from a centrally planned to a multi-sectoral economy based on market principles, with the objective of doubling Vietnam's GDP between 1991 and 2000. Deeper reform has been very slow, as some of the more conservative members of the Communist Party have wanted to maintain the state-controlled economy. Full privatisation on the Western model is not envisaged.

GDP grew by 7.5 per cent in 2005. Vietnam's growth is the fastest in south-east Asia, but it trails China, South Korea, Taiwan and Thailand when they were at similar stages of development. Vietnam's economic expansion was led by exports of clothing to the US. The industrial and construction sectors account for 40 per cent of the economy and the services sector, which is growing by around six per cent per annum, for around 38 per cent. Agriculture, forestry and fisheries account for the remaining 22 per cent of GDP, expanding at around three per cent.

Vietnam aims to become an industrialised country by the year 2020.

The official inflation rate in July (2008) was 27.04 per cent and was the largest year-on-year increase since 1991. The government increased the price of petrol by over 30 per cent, with analysts warning that the consumer price index may exceed 30 per cent by the end of the year. The Asian Development Bank revised its growth projection of 6.5 per cent in 2008, from the 7 per cent previously forecast.

External trade

Vietnam belongs to the Association of South East Asian (Asean) Free Trade Area (Afta) and maintains a list of goods that have preferential import duties between members. There is a programme of tariff reductions due to be introduced in the next few years. It joined the World Trade Organisation in January 2007 and has an FTA with the US.

Exports accounts for over 60 per cent of GDP and its share of GDP is around 150 per cent. Vietnam is the world's second-largest rice exporter (after Thailand); other exports include coffee, tea and rubber, as well as manufactured goods such as textiles, clothes and footwear. A growing hydrocarbon sector is providing increasing foreign exchange.

A large increase in imports in 2007 led to a trade deficit in the third quarter of US$7.6bn. The imports included heavy machinery for a number of large infrastructure projects. According to the ministry of industry and trade machinery imports increased by 55 per cent (to US$7.2bn) over the same period in 2006, steel imports rose by 66.5 per cent (to US$2.65bn) and feed imports by 51 per cent (to US$897m).

Imports

Principal imports include capital machinery and equipment, vehicles, fertiliser, steel products, raw cotton, grain, cement and raw materials.

Main sources: China (16.5 per cent total, 2006), Singapore (14.0 per cent), Taiwan (10.7 per cent).

Exports
Principal exports include crude oil, rice, sea food, coffee, rubber, tea, garments and shoes.
Main destinations: US (19.7 per cent total, 2006), Japan (13.1 per cent), Australia (9.2 per cent), China (7.6 per cent).

Agriculture
Farming
Agriculture accounts for around 22 per cent of GDP and employs 67 per cent of the workforce. Agricultural goods, including forestry and fishery products, account for more than 50 per cent of total export revenues.
About 15–18 per cent of the total land area is cultivated arable. In the south especially, climate and soils are ideal for rice production. Considerable losses can be sustained from typhoons, flooding and drought.
In the south, 60 per cent of the land is privately farmed; in the north, 95 per cent of farms have been turned into substantial collectives. A contract system on the land spurred a marked improvement in agricultural production.
Record exports of almost 90,000 tonnes of pepper, in 2004, showed a 32 per cent increase on 2003 figures and confirmed Vietnam as the world's largest exporter. The value of the 2004 exports amount to US$133.7 million even though the average world price declined by US$54.4 per tonne.
Ambitious plans include increased use of fertilisers, development of irrigation systems and resettlement of small farmers. Farmers have boosted rice production by planting high-yield varieties and using more modern farming techniques; government credit of about US$100 million was used mainly in the Mekong Delta. Half of Vietnam's rice is grown along the Mekong Delta.
Other main food crops include sugar cane, coconut, soya beans, silk, rubber, coffee, tea, tobacco, jute. Livestock raised includes pigs, buffaloes, cattle, sheep, goats, horses and poultry.
The Vietnam National Rubber Corporation development plans for the rubber industry will increase the area under cultivation from 250,000 hectares (ha) to 700,000ha. VNRC estimates 1.7 million ha of total natural land is available for rubber cultivation. The private sector is expected to take a 30–50 per cent share in the development of the industry.
The Vietnam National Coffee Corporation (Vinacaphe) has increased the total area of coffee cultivation to around 200,000ha, principally in the central highlands. Much cultivation in the coffee-growing highlands is under—reported due to a special tax regime. Annual production is thought to be as high as 40,000 tonnes and the government plans to increase production to 100,000 tonnes per year (tpy) by 2010.
Avian flu broke out twice in 2004 and prompted the slaughter of millions of birds.
Crop production in 2005 included: 39,841,000 tonnes (t) cereals in total, 36,341,000t rice, 3,500,000t maize, 5,700,000t cassava, 1,550,000t sweet potatoes, 1,250,000t bananas, 255,000t pulses, 940,000t coconuts, 572,500t citrus fruit, 317,123t oilcrops, 26,500t tobacco, 835,000t treenuts, 990,000t green coffee, 112,000t fibre crops, 450,000t natural rubber, 97,000t pepper spice, 91,800t various herbs and spices, 15,000,000t sugar cane, 110,000t tea, 5,440,500t fruit in total, 7,991,000t vegetables in total. Livestock production included: 2,740,052t meat in total, 121,000 beef, 103,200t buffalo meat, 2,100,000t pig meat, 9,150t goat meat, 388,200t poultry, 225,000t eggs, 196,000t milk, 11,000 honey, 3,000t cocoons, silk, 20,300t cattle hides.

Fishing
Fishing has traditionally been an important source of export earnings. The sector is facing severe depletion of inshore stocks. Coastal waters were typically overfished by the poorly equipped Vietnamese fleet, whose boats could only stay at sea for short periods of time. Poor infrastructure and processing technology is compounded by a lack of skills required for deep-water fishing on the part of fishermen.
Main fish products are shrimp, freshwater fish, catfish, dried squid and tuna.
In 2004, the total marine fish catch was 1,333,811 tonnes and the total crustacean catch was 166,689 tonnes.

Forestry
About 50 per cent of the total land area is forested. Forestry is developing, with 12–15 per cent of the removed volume of timber classified as industrial wood.
Legal exploitation from around one million hectares (ha) of plantations produces a domestic supply of approximately three million cubic metres of wood annually, but insufficient for the processing industry. The industry is estimated to have the potential to approach a turnover of US$1 billion annually, especially following the relaxation of import licences and quotas for domestic processors importing wood. The domestic industry is likely to remain dependent on felled and imported wood of dubious legal status at least over the medium-term. In the longer term, a government replanting programme designed to add five million ha of forest cover by 2010 should change this.
Timber imports in 2004 were US$568.7 million, while exports amounted to US$134.8 million.
Timber production in 2004 included 26,487,000 cubic metre (cum) roundwood, 5,237,000cum industrial roundwood, 2,900,000cum sawnwood, 2,737,000cum sawlogs and veneer logs, 1,850,000cum pulpwood, 117,000cum wood-based panels, 21,250,000cum woodfuel; 108,000 tonnes (t) charcoal, 887,000t paper and paperboard (including 35,000t newsprint), 70,000t printing and writing paper, 709,800t paper pulp, 175,000t recovered paper.

Industry and manufacturing
Industry contributed 40 per cent to GDP in 2004 and employs 10 per cent of the workforce.
The heavy industrial base is mostly located in the north, and in the past was adversely affected by conflicts with China. The economy's leading industries were incorporated into the state sector following the Communist takeover and despite limited 'equitisation' (distribution of shares to the public and employees), most remain in state hands. They include oil and gas, food and foodstuff processing, synthetic yarns and fabrics, textiles, engineering, cement, fertilisers, glass, rubber products, tobacco, chemicals, paper and steel. Of some 6,000 state-owned enterprises, only 400 have been equitised, while 2,000 have been organised into 17 'general corporations' (akin to conglomerates) and 77 'special corporations', tending to reinforce monopoly conditions.
Since the doi moi reforms of the 1980s, the government has been prioritising lighter, export-oriented and labour-intensive industries. Most of the government's special industrial zones have not yet been fully occupied, and much industry outside the 'legacy' sectors of command-economy industrialisation has been affected by ambivalent sentiment among foreign direct investors.

Tourism
Vietnam is developing as a tourist destination. More facilities are becoming available, although quality and infrastructure, such as roads and power, are inadequate, especially compared to competitors in the region. Visitor numbers have improved year-on-year, despite the presence of Sars. There were 3.43 million arrivals in 2005, an increase of 15.4 per cent on 2004. The main markets are China, the US, Taiwan, Japan, Hong Kong, Thailand, France, UK and Canada. Tourism is expected to contribute 2.2 per cent to GDP in 2005.

Mining

Vietnam is believed to possess a wide range of minerals. The sector is relatively undeveloped, owing to lack of investment and a discouraging legislative environment.

Mining is largely concentrated in the north. Commercially significant quantities of iron ore, apatite, chromite, rubies and gold exist. There are reserves of manganese, titanium ore, bauxite, tin, copper, zinc, lead, nickel, graphite and mica.

Other minerals include phosphates, salt, tin, chromium, wolfram, silver, antimony, pirit, kaolin and limestone.

Vietnam imports a number of metals, including steel.

Hydrocarbons

Vietnam had proven oil reserves of around 3 billion barrels in 2004 and produced 427,000 barrels per day (bpd). The largest oil fields are Back Ho, Rang Dong, Hang Ngoc and Dai Hung. Vietnam has no refinery capacity and has to import petroleum products. A refinery is being built at Dung Quat and a second is planned for Nghi Son. Vietnam is a net exporter of oil, exporting around 193,000 bpd in 2004.

Upstream activities in the oil sector are largely controlled by the government-owned Vietnam Oil and Gas Corporation (PetroVietnam). This is the only firm licensed to conduct petroleum activities. Operations conducted by foreign investors must be conducted in co-operation with PetroVietnam.

Vietnam had proven natural gas reserves of 240 billion cubic metres (cum) in 2004 and produced 20.3 billion cum. Production and consumption are set to increase as new fields come into production. Current production is absorbed by the domestic market. Domestic gas consumption is expected to increase to an annual 10 billion cubic metres by 2010.

Vietnam had coal reserves of 150 million tonnes in 2004, mostly anthracite, located in the north of Vietnam, where the province of Quang Ninh holds a significant proportion. Coal is the principal source of commercial energy, meeting about half of Vietnam's annual primary energy needs. Production totalled 14.8 million tonnes oil equivalent in 2004, up 38.6 per cent on 2003 output. Vietnam exports around five million tonnes of coal, mainly to China and Japan.

Energy

Vietnam has installed electricity generating capacity of around 8.5GW, supplied mainly by hydro-power and coal-fired thermal plants. Domestic demand is increasing faster than supply. Vietnam imports electricity from China and is seeking other sources, including Laos. The government plans to add over 1,000MW annually over 2002–10. A mixture of additional gas, coal-fired and hydroelectric plants are planned, together with a nuclear station.

Work has begun on creating a national electricity grid, which is due for completion in 2020.

Financial markets

Stock exchange

The Securities Trading Centre (STC), is located in Ho Chi Minh City; Saigon Commercial Bank (Sacombank) was the first bank to be listed. In July 2006 there were 41 stocks listed, by March 2007, the number had grown to 195, while the market capitalisation of companies had increased from US$400 million to US$22 billion (January 2006–March 2007).

The State Capital Investment Corporation (SCIC) and the US-based Morgan Stanley Investment Bank agreed in March 2007, to form a securities joint venture; the first in Vietnam's Communist-ruled economy. The investment banking service is expected to be in operation by October 2007. SCIC was created in 2005 to undertake capital ownership of the over 5,000 state-run companies, which account for 70 per cent of government tax revenue.

Banking and insurance

VietcomBank regulates matters relating to exchange control and is responsible for all transactions involving foreign exchange, including bills of exchange, foreign remittances, traveller's cheques and foreign currencies.

In 2005 the government decided that VietcomBank was to be the first state bank to be offered for partial privatisation and ostensibly to operate on purely commercial principles. In preparation for public ownership VietcomBank reduced its portfolio of state enterprised down to 50 per cent and reported a first-half year gross profit of US$82 million in 2005, up by 41 per cent on the previous year. The decision to part-privatise was based on the government's need to sustain economic growth.

There are four large state banks, which account for around 70 per cent of total lending, of which 60 per cent of loans are awarded to state entities and some are of dubious financial viability. Official figures for bad debt levels do not exist but officials in the state bank estimate it could be as high as 20 per cent.

Central bank

State Bank of Vietnam

Main financial centre

Hanoi

Time

GMT plus seven hours

Geography

Vietnam is bordered to the north by the People's Republic of China, to the west and south-west by Laos and Cambodia and to the east by the South China Sea. The country has 3,200km of coastline, 1,150km of land border with China and 1,650km of land border with Laos.

The country is broad in the north and south and narrow in its central region. There are two main cultivated areas, the Red River Delta (15,000 square km) in the north and the Mekong Delta (60,000 square km) in the south. Three-quarters of the country consists of mountains and hills, the highest point being Phan Si Pan mountain in the Hoang Lien Son range in the far north-west of Vietnam.

Hemisphere

Northern

Climate

Located in the tropical monsoon zone, Vietnam's climate is hot and humid with abundant seasonal rainfall.

In the north, climatic changes occur in four seasons: spring (January–April) brings light rain and constant humidity; summer (May to July) is very hot, humid and rainy; autumn (August–October) brings drier weather but sometimes includes storms; winter (October–early January) is cooler.

In the centre and the south it is hot year round and there are only two seasons: a rainy season (May–October) and a dry season (October–April).

Average annual temperatures in Hanoi are 29 degrees Celsius (C) in the hot season and 17 degrees C in the cold season; Hue in central Vietnam: 29 degrees C and 21 degrees C; Ho Chi Minh City: 30 degrees C and 24 degrees C.

The average annual rainfall in Hanoi is 1,680mm; Hue: 2,890mm; Ho Chi Minh City: 1979mm.

Dress codes

In Hanoi in the summer (officially from 15 April to 15 October), no jackets are required even for the most formal occasions. In winter, a jacket is more usual but a bush jacket is acceptable even when the weather is warm.

In the south, informal tropical-weight clothing is all that is needed at any time of the year. A jacket and tie is not necessary. In the highlands, where it is cooler, a bush jacket is acceptable any time.

Entry requirements

Passports

Required by all and must be valid for one month beyond the date of departure.

Visa

Required by all. Tourist visas are issued for visits up to one month long and can be extend when in Vietnam.

Business visas are issued only after authorities in Vietnam have approved sponsorship by a local company or organisation. If the business visitor does not have a local sponsor, assistance can be obtained from the embassy.
For a list of embassies worldwide where applications may be obtained see www.mofa.gov.vn/en, see Countries and Regions.
All visitors must retain the yellow portion of the immigration arrival-departure card, to be surrendered to authorities when leaving.

Currency advice/regulations
The import and export of local currency is prohibited. The import of foreign currency is unlimited, but amounts over US$3,000 (or equivalent) should be declared on arrival; export is limited to the amount declared.
Major hard currency may be freely traded however outside cities and main towns they are less likely to be accepted.
Travellers cheques (in US dollars) are widely accepted in banks and hotels.

Customs
Personal items are duty-free.
Antiques cannot be exported. Caution is advised when purchasing souvenirs made of ivory, silver, gold and stone, as you may require a permit from customs to take them out of Vietnam.

Prohibited imports
Firearms, anti-government propaganda, pornography and illegal drugs; drug smuggling is a capital offence.

Health (for visitors)

Mandatory precautions
Vaccination certificate required for yellow fever if travelling from an infected area.

Advisable precautions
Vaccinations for diphtheria, tetanus, hepatitis A, cholera and typhoid are recommended. Other vaccinations that may be advised include tuberculosis, hepatitis B, and Japanese encephalitis. Malaria prophylaxes are required including mosquito nets, insect sprays and long clothing at night.
Use only bottled or boiled water for drinks, washing teeth and making ice. Eat only well cooked meals, preferably served hot; vegetables should be cooked and fruit peeled. Avoid pork and salad and food from street vendors. A full first-aid kit, including disposable syringes, would be useful. Any medicines required by the traveller should be brought into the country. Medical insurance is essential, including emergency evacuation.

Hotels

Redevelopment and expansion has increased hotel accommodation in both Ho Chi Minh City and Hanoi where the standard of hotel accommodation is equal to Western hotels. Provincial town also have adequate facilities.
Tipping is discretionary; it is not a Vietnamese tradition although staff in restaurants and hotels may expect to be tipped.

Credit cards

Are accepted in more outlets but only in main towns and cities; where ATMs can be found.

Public holidays (national)

Fixed dates
1 Jan (New Year's Day), 30 Apr (Liberation of Ho Chi Minh City/Saigon), 1 May (May Day), 2 Sep (National Day).

Variable dates
Tet Nguyen Dan (Vietnamese New Year) (Jan/Feb – three days)

Working hours

Banking
Mon–Fri: 0730/0800–1130, 1300–1600.

Business
Mon–Sat: 0730–1130, 1230–1630 in summer (15 Apr to 15 Oct); 0800–1200, 1230–1630 in winter (16 Oct to 14 Apr).

Government
Mon–Sat: 0730–1130, 1230–1630 in summer; 0800–1200, 1230–1630 in winter.

Shops
Many small privately owned shops stay open seven days a week, often until late at night.

Telecommunications

Mobile/cell phones
There are 900 and 900/1800 GSM services available throughout most of the country.

Electricity supply

Electric current is 220V, 50Hz with round two-pin plug. Electricity supplies can be problematic, laptop computers should be protected by a surge suppressor.

Social customs/useful tips

Business is conducted slowly with many familiarisation meetings. Be patient with language difficulties and red tape. The combination of Confucian interaction norms and communist bureaucracy may create large amounts of the latter.
Most Vietnamese names consist of a family name, a middle name and a given name, in that order. The given name is used in address but to do so without a title is considered as expressing either great intimacy between friends or arrogance of the sort a superior would use with his or her inferior. The titles, Bac or Ong (Mr) (in increasing seniority), Ba (Mrs), Co or Chi (Miss) precedes a Vietnamese given name (sometimes full name). Wives may retain their own names and children take their father's family name. The middle name may be common to all the male members of a family.
It is rude to show the soles of the feet/shoes. Do not touch anyone's head, not even that of a child. When handing over or receiving anything, the right hand should generally be used. On formal occasions it is considered polite to use both hands. Etiquette for male visitors is to shake hands with a man but not with a woman, unless she offers her hand.
Shoes must be removed before entering any religious building. It is also customary to remove shoes before entering a Vietnamese home, but in modern residences the requirement is no longer observed.

Security

Most visits to Vietnam are trouble-free and serious or violent crimes against foreigners are rare. There have been some reports of aggravated theft and assault in areas frequented by tourists in Ho Chi Minh City, prompting the city police chief, Nguyen Chi Dung, to say that tourists who were robbed would receive an apology from the police.
Outside Hanoi and Ho Chi Minh City, the provision of prompt consular assistance is difficult because of poorly developed infrastructure throughout Vietnam, meaning travel and health insurance are well advised. Travel is restricted near military installations and in some border areas. Unexploded mines, bombs and shells are a hazard in former battlefield areas.

Getting there

Air

National airline: Vietnam Airlines (formerly Hang Khong Vietnam and the General Civil Aviation Administration of Vietnam).

International airport/s: Tan Son Nhat (SGN), 7km from Ho Chi Minh City, facilities include a café, duty-free shopping, VIP services, business lounge, currency exchange, limousine service and car rental with driver.
A new terminal, to handle up to 15 million passengers a year and at cost of US$240 million, was begun in 2004. The first phase of construction is expected to be completed by 2007.
Noi Bai (HAN), 38km from Hanoi, facilities include a café, duty-free shopping and currency exchange.
Danang International Airport, five-minutes drive to Danang City.
Metered taxis are available at all airports.

Airport tax: International departures US$14, excluding transit passengers.

Surface

Road: There is overland access to Vietnam via China (Quang Ninh and Lang Son border crossings in the north), Cambodia (Moc Bai) and Laos (Lao Bao).

Status of overland routes should be checked, as passage has not always been practicable.

Rail: Hanoi and Nanning, in China's Guangxi province, are linked by rail. China and Vietnam have also started a second cross-border rail service. The 761km rail link between Hanoi and Kunming, the capital of Yunnan (south-west China), and which runs through the northern Vietnamese border town of Lao Cai, is being upgraded with work expected to be completed by 2008. There is rail connection linking Hanoi with Pingxiang in China's Guangxi province via the Dong Dang border point in Lang Son province, 200km north of Hanoi. Construction of a new line linking Phnom Penh and Ho Chi Minh City is underway. This project is part of the Asian Development Bank's (ADB) Greater Mekong sub-regional co-operation scheme as part of the Trans-Asia railway.

Services include air-conditioned day and overnight sleeping carriages and restaurant cars.

Water: There are daily and weekly ferry services along the Mekong River from Phnom Penh (Cambodia) to Chau Doc and Can Tho.

Main port/s: Ho Chi Minh City, Haiphong, and Danang.

Getting about

National transport

Air: Vietnam Airlines, provides regular scheduled services between Hanoi, Hue, Danang and Ho Chi Minh City. Flights should be booked well in advance.

Road: There is a 88,000km road network in relatively good condition; roads are better in the south. The coastal Route 1 between Hanoi and Ho Chi Minh City can become impassable in heavy rain. A four-wheel drive vehicle is advisable outside the major centres.

Rail: There is over 2,650km rail network in various degrees of maintenance. The main line between Hanoi-Ho Chi Minh City (travel time 30 hrs minimum) is efficient with first class accommodation with air-conditioning, sleeper carriages and restaurant cars. Long-distance trains are more reliable and comfortable, as well as offering a faster service. Fares for foreigners are comparable to internal air fares.

Water: There are several local ferry services including hydrofoils between Mong Cai and Cat Ba and motorboats between Phu Quoc and Rach Gia.

City transport

Taxis: Taxis serving the hour-long route between downtown Hanoi and the city's airport will typically be ancient and non-air-conditioned vehicles. In Ho Chi Minh City, taxis are modern. Tipping is discretionary; taxi drivers do not expect to be tipped. Taxis and motorbikes are a faster form of hired transport. When travelling by taxi it may be advisable to note down the registration number of the driver (displayed on the rear side of the vehicle), for security reasons.

In Hanoi, cycle-rickshaws (the famous cyclo) are available, but slow and best for sightseeing.

Car hire

Personal car hire is not allowed, all hire vehicles come with a driver; hiring can be from half a day to over a week. A four-wheel-drive vehicle is required outside major cities.

BUSINESS DIRECTORY

The addresses listed below are a selection only. While World of Information makes every endeavour to check these addresses, we cannot guarantee that changes have not been made, especially to telephone numbers and area codes. We would welcome any corrections.

Telephone area codes

The international direct dialling code (IDD) for Vietnam is +84, followed by area code and subscriber's number:

Da Nang	51	Ho Chi Minh City	8
Haiphong	31	Lang Son	25
Hanoi	4	Lao Cai	20

Useful telephone numbers

English-language directory enquiries: 108
Police: 113
Fire: 114
Ambulance: 115

Chambers of Commerce

American Chamber of Commerce in Vietnam - Hanoi, Press Club, 59A Ly Thai To Street, Hanoi (tel: 934-2790; fax 934-2787; e-mail: info@amchamhanoi.com).

American Chamber of Commerce in Vietnam - Ho Chi Minh City, New World Hotel, 76 Le Lai Street, Ho Chi Minh City (tel: 824-3562; fax: 824-3572; e-mail: amcham@hcm.vnn.vn).

British Business Group Vietnam - Hanoi, Metropole Hotel, 56 Ly Thai To Street, Hanoi (tel: 936-2420; fax: 936-2419; e-mail: eurochamhanoi@hn.vnn.vn).

British Business Group Vietnam - Ho Chi Minh City, 25 Le Duan Boulevard, Ho Chi Minh City (tel: 829-8430; fax: 822-5172; e-mail: bbgv.hcmc@hcm.fpt.vn).

Vietnam Chamber of Commerce and Industry, 9 Dao Duy Anh Street, Hanoi (tel: 574-3084; fax: 574-2020; e-mail: vcci@hn.vnn.vn).

Banking

ANZ International Merchant Banking Division, 14 Le Thai To Street, Hanoi (tel: 825-8190; fax: 825-8188/9).

Bank of America, 27 Ly Thuong Kiet St, Hanoi (tel: 824-9316; fax: 824-9322).

Crédit Lyonnais, Han Man Officetel, 65 Nguyen du St., Quan 1, Ho Chi Minh City (tel: 299-226; fax: 296-465).

Indovina Bank Ltd (first joint-venture bank), 36 Ton That Dam, D1, Ho Chi Minh City (tel: 822-4995, 823-0130; fax: 823-0131).

Thai Military Bank, Unit 113, 1 Floor, Saigon Trade Center, No. 37 Ton Due Thang Street, Ben Nghe Ward, District 1, Ho Chi Minh City (tel: 910-0606, 910-1388/90; fax: 910-0505).

Industrial and Commercial Bank of Vietnam, 108 Tran Hung Dao, Hanoi (tel: 942-1066, 942-1186; fax: 942-1143).

Central bank

State Bank of Vietnam, 49 Ly Thai To Street, Hoan Kiem District, Hanoi (tel: 825-8388; fax: 825-8385; internet: www.sbv.gov.vn).

Travel information

Ben Thanh Tourist Service, 165 Pham Ngui Lao Street, 1st District, Ho Chi Minh City (tel: 886-0635; fax: 836-1953).

Cathay Pacific Airways, 58 Dong Khoi Road, District 1, Ho Chi Minh City (tel: 822-3203; fax: 822-2679); also at 27 Ly Thuong Kiet Street, Hanoi (tel: 824-9427; fax: 822-2679).

Quang Nam-Da Nang Tourist Company (Da Nang Tourism), 68 Bach Dang Street, Da Nang (tel: 822-112, 821-423, 822-213).

Thua Thien-Hue Tourist Company, No. 9 Ngo Quyen Street, Hue City (tel: 83-288, 82-369).

Sasco Travel (for limousine service), Sasco Building, Tan Son Nhat Airport, Ho Chi Minh City (tel: 848-7142; fax: 848-7141; internet: www.sascotravel.com.vn).

Viet Value Travel Ltd (for car hire), 4th Floor ILU Building, 18 Yen Phu, Ba Dinh, Hanoi (tel: 715-0753; fax: 715-0754; email: vietvaluetravel@yahoo.com; internet: http://vietvaluetravel.com).

Vietnamtourism, 30A Ly Thuong Kiet Street, Hanoi (tel: 825-5552, 826-4148; fax: 855-7583).

Vietnam Airlines (formerly Hang Khong Vietnam and the General Civil Aviation Administration of Vietnam), Gailem Airport, Hanoi (tel: 827-2643; fax: 827-2291).

National tourist organisation offices
Vinatour, 54 Nguyen Du, Hanoi (tel: 942-4490; 942-3997; fax: 942-2707; internet: www.vinatour.com.vn).

Vinatour, 28 Le Thi Hong Gam, District 1, Ho Chi Minh City, (tel: 217- 925, 297-026; fax: 299-868; email: vinatour-saigonoffice@saigonnet.vn).

Ministries
Ministry of Agriculture and Rural Development, 6 Ngoc Ha Street, Hanoi; International Relations Department (tel: 845-9670/71/72; fax: 845-4319).

Ministry of Construction, 37 Le Dai Hanh Street, Hanoi; International Relations Department (tel: 825-5497; fax: 825-2153).

Ministry of Culture and Information, 51-53 Ngo Quyen, Hanoi.

Ministry of Education & Training, 49 Dai Co Viet Street, Hanoi; International Relations Department (tel: 869-4961; fax: 826-3243).

Ministry of Energy, 18 Tran Nguyen Han, Hanoi.

Ministry of Finance, 8 Phgan Huy Chu Street, Hanoi; International Relations Section (tel: 826-2061, 824-0437; fax: 826-2266).

Ministry of Fisheries, 57 Ngoc Khanh, Hanoi.

Ministry of Foreign Affairs, 1 Ton That Dam Street, Hanoi; International Organisation Department (tel: 845-6525, 845-5900; fax: 845-9205).

Ministry of Forestry, 123 Lo Duc, Hanoi.

Ministry of Health, 138 Duong Giang Vo, Hanoi.

Ministry of Industry, 7 Trang Thi Street, Hanoi (fax: 826-9033); International Relations Department (tel: 826-7988, 825-9887).

Ministry of Justice, 25a Cat Linh Street, Hanoi; Internatinal Relations Department (tel: 843-0931; fax: 825-4835).

Ministry of Labour, War Invalids and Social Affairs, 2 Dinh Le Street, Hanoi; International Relations Department (tel: 826-9534; fax: 824-8036).

Ministry of Marine Products, 57 Ngoc Khanh Street, Hanoi; International Relations Department (tel: 832-5607; fax: 832-6702).

Ministry of National Defence, 28A Dien Bien Phy Street, Hanoi (tel: 826-8101; fax: 845-7195); International Relations Department, 33 A Pham Ngu Lao Street, Hanoi (tel: 825-3646).

Ministry of Planning and Investment (background information on aid-financed projects), 2 Hoanag Van Thu, Hanoi; External Economic Relations Department (tel: 845-8241 (ext 3505); fax: 823-0161).

Ministry of Public Health, 138 A Giango Vo, Hanoi; International Relations Department (tel: 844-2463, 846-4050; fax: 846-4051).

Ministry of Sciences, Technology and Environment, 39 Tran Hung Dao Street, Hanoi; International Relations Department (tel: 826-3388; fax: 825-2733).

Ministry of Trade, 31 Trang Tien Street, Hanoi; (tel: 826-2522; fax: 826-4696).

Ministry of Transport, 80 Tran Hung Dao Street, Hanoi; International Relations Department (tel: 825-3301; fax: 825-5851).

Office of the National Assembly, 35 Ngo Quyen, Hanoi (tel: 252-861).

Other useful addresses
ASEAN Investment Promotion Agency, Ministry of Planning and Investment, c/o ASEAN Vietnam, 7 Chu Van An Street, Hanoi (fax: 843-5758).

ASEAN Secretariat, 70 A Jl Sisingamangaraja, Jakarta 12110, Indonesia (tel: (+62-21) 726-2991, 724-3372; fax: (+62-21) 724-3504, 739-8234).

Asian Development Bank, Vietnam Resident Mission, c/o State Bank of Vietnam, Room 401, 16 Tong Dan Street, Hanoi (tel: 824-5908; fax: 824-6171).

British Consulate General, 25 Le Duan, District 1, Ho Chi Minh City (tel: 829-2433; fax: 822-5740).

British Embassy, 31 Hai Ba Trung, Hanoi (tel: 825-2510; fax: 826-5762).

British Embassy Commercial Office, 100 Tue Tinh Street, Hanoi (tel: 822-6875, 822-9455, 822-9457; fax: 822-9457).

Commerical and Tourist Services Centre, 1 Ba Trieu Street, Hanoi (tel: 826-8499; fax: 826-5388).

Department General for Post and Telecomunication, 18 Nguyen Du Street, Hanoi; International Relations Department (tel: 822-6622; fax: 822-6590).

Electricity of Vietnam (EVN), 18 Tran Nguyen Han Street, Hanoi (tel: 826-3725; fax: 824-9462).

Foreign Trade & Investment Development Centre, 92-96 Nguyen Hue Ave, District 1, Ho Chi Minh City (tel: 822-2982; fax: 822-2983).

Investip (will provide business contacts), 1 bis Yet Kieu Street, Hanoi (tel: 826-4707; fax: 826-6185).

The National Oil Service Company of Vietnam, 2 Le Loi Street, Vung Tau Srv, Ho Chi Minh City (tel: 897-562; fax: 897-664).

Petrovietnam, 22 Ngo Quyen Street, Hanoi; International Relations Department (tel: 825-2526; fax: 826-5942).

Saigon Shipping Company (Saigonship), 9 Nguyen Cong Tru Street, District 1, Ho Chi Minh City (tel: 896-316, 896-302; fax: 825-067).

State Committee for Co-operation and Investment Consultancy Service Centre (will provide business contacts), 56 Quoc Tu Giam Street, Hanoi (tel: 825-4970; fax: 825-9271).

Tea Estate Agencies Ltd, 31 Nguyen Gia Thieu Street, Hanoi (tel: 822-8556; fax: 822-7923).

US Embassy, 7 Lang Ha, Dong Da District, Hanoi (tel: 843-1500).

Vietnam Civil Aviation, Gia Lam Airport, Hanoi; International Relations Department (tel: 827-2241).

Vietnam Fund Management Co Ltd (investment into Vietnamese companies and projects), 3 Trieu Viet Vuong Street, Hanoi (tel: 822-8632, 826-6315; fax: 822-8648); 4 Dong Khoi, District 1, Ho Chi Minh City (tel: 829-1074, 829-7206; fax: 823-0685).

Vietnam National Foreign Trade Corporation (TRANSAF), 46 Ngo Quyen, Hanoi.

Vietnamese Embassy (US), Suite 400, 1233 20th Street, NW, Washington DC 20036 (tel: (+1-202) 861-0737; fax: (+1-202) 202-861-0917; email: info@vietnamembassy-usa.org).

National news agency: VNA (Vietnam News Agency)

Internet sites
Asian Development Bank: www.adb.org/vrm

General Statistics Office (GSO): www.gso.gov.vn

Vietnam Access (trade fairs and business opportunities): http://vietnamaccess.com

Vietnam Business Journal: www.viam.com

Wallis and Futuna

KEY FACTS

Official name: Wallis and Futuna

Head of State: President of France Nicolas Sarkozy, represented by Administrateur Supérieur Philippe Paolantoni (from 28 Jul 2008)

Head of government: President of the Territorial Assembly Pesamino Taputai (DD) (from 11 Apr 2007)

Ruling party: Coalition of various political parties and independent members, of which non are dominant (since 2007)

Area: 144 square km – Wallis (or Uvea): 77.6km; Futuna: 64.4km

Population: 16,025 (2006)*

Capital: Mata Utu (on Wallis)

Official language: Wallisian, Futunian, French

Currency: Comptoirs Français du Pacifique franc (CFPf) = 100 centimes

Exchange rate: CFPf92.21 per US$ (Jan 2007); (pegged CFPf119.25 per euro)

GDP per capita: US$3,800 (2004)

Balance of trade: -US$50,000 (2003)

* estimated figure

COUNTRY PROFILE

Historical profile

1616 The islands of Futuna and Alofi were sighted by two Dutch navigators, Willem Cornelius van Schouten and Jacob le Maire, who re-named them the Hoorn Islands.
1767 Samuel Wallis, the English navigator, sighted the island of Uvea, and renamed it Wallis.
1820 The Takumasiva royal dynasty was restored in the kingdom of Uvea (Wallis).
1837 The first European settlers were French, led by missionaries.
1842 Wallis was granted French protection following a local rebellion.
1887 Queen Amelia of Uvea signed a treaty, establishing an official French protectorate.
1888, The Kings of Alo and Sigave (Futuna and Alofi) signed a treaty, establishing an official French protectorate.
1924 The protectorates were annexed and became an official French colony
1942 US forces used Wallis as a strategic air base during the Second World War.
1959 Following a referendum, Wallis and Fortuna voted to become a Térritoire d'Outre-Mer (TOM) (Overseas Territory).
1959 Tomasi Kulimoetoke II became the Lavelua (King of Uvea), ending a period of instability within the royal family.
1961 Wallis and Futuna became a TOM and adopted the French constitution.
1999 Sagato Alofi became the the Tuiagaifo (King of Alo); Pasilio Keletaona became the Keletaona (King of Sigave).
2002 The ruling right-wing Rassemblement pour la République (RPR) (Rally for the Republic) and its affiliates retained a majority in the Territorial Assembly elections. Christian Job was appointed administrateur supérieur, replacing Alain Waquet. Wallis and Futuna's only newspaper, the weekly Te Fenua Fo'ou, closed down after being subjected to threats and raids from the local (traditional) authorities.
2004 Xavier de Furst was appointed administrateur supérieur.
2006 Richard Didier was appointed administrateur supérieur, Préfet.
2007 Parliamentary elections were held on 1 April. Pesamino Teputai became president of the territorial assembly on 11 April. Tomasi Kulimoetoke II, the King of Uvea, died on 7 May. On 16 May, Nicolas Sarkozy became head of state and president of the French Republic.
2008 Kapiliele (Gabriel) Faupala was chosen by members of the traditional council of ministers to succeed the late King Tomasi, who had designated him to follow him as king. Philippe Paolantoni was appointed administrateur supérieur on 28 July.

Political structure

Constitution

28 September 1958 (French Fifth Republic)
In 1961, Wallis and Futuna became a Térritoire d'Outre-Mer (TOM) (Overseas Territory) of France.
Wallis and Futuna is administered by an administrator (administrateur supérieur) appointed by France and is represented in the French parliament by a deputy and a senator.
The islands are divided into three administrative districts based on the ancient kingdoms: Uvea (Wallis), Alo (Futuna) and Sigave (Futuna).
Wallis and Futuna is the only French territory where a native system of monarchy has been allowed to survive. There are three traditional kings: the Lavelua (King of Uvea), the Tuiagaifo (King of Alo) and the Keletaona (the title of King of Sigave depends on family heritage, and therefore, he has the title of Tui Sigave, Tamolevai or Keletaona).
In Uvea, there is a kivalu, the equivalent of a prime minister, who is appointed by the King.

Form of state

Térritoire d'Outre-Mer (TOM) (Overseas Territory) of France

The executive

The President of the French Republic is the head of state, represented by an appointed administrateur supérieur, Préfet (supreme administrator) who exercises executive power with the right of veto over some of the territorial assembly decisions.

National legislature

Local affairs are conducted by an elected Territorial Assembly with legislative powers (20 members elected by proportional representation for five years – 13 members are elected from Wallis and seven from Futuna) and traditional councils of rulers and leaders. The administrator has veto power over many of the Assembly's decisions.

Legal system

French law is applied while the traditional kings deal with customary law.

Last elections

1 April 2007 (territorial assembly)

Results: Parliamentary: Union pour un Mouvement Populaire (UMP) (Union for a Popular Movement) won four seats (out of 20); Divers Droite (DD) (Various Right groups) won seven seats; Parti Socialiste (PS) (Socialist Party) four seats; Divers Gauche (DG) (Various Left groups) one seat; and unlisted candidates four seats. Turnout was 74.98 per cent.

Next elections
2012 (territorial assembly)

Political parties

Ruling party
Coalition of various political parties and independent members, of which non are dominant (since 2007)

Main opposition party

Population

16,025 (2006)*

Last census: July 2003: 14,944

Population density: 55 inhabitants per square km.

Annual growth rate: 1 per cent (2003)

Ethnic make-up
Polynesian

Religions
Roman Catholic

Education

Compulsory education is provided free-of-charge. Primary education is either provided by public funds or by Roman Catholic missionaries. Secondary education is pubically provided.

Compulsory years: Five to 14

Health

Healthcare is publically funded. There is a 60-bed hospital on Wallis and a 23-bed hospital on Futuna; severe emergency medical cases are evacuation to New Caledonia or Australia.

Life expectancy: 73 (estimate 2003)

Child (under 5 years) mortality rate (per 1,000): 21 per 1,000 live births.

Welfare

While there is no social security benefits offered to the general community, the state assist in the care of old aged pensioners.

Main cities

Mata Utu, on Wallis (capital, estimated population 1,187 in 2005).

Languages spoken

Official language/s
Wallisian, Futunian, French

Media

The islands maintain international and local contacts for news and information through electronic media.

Press

Broadcasting

Radio: The French RFO (http://wallisfutuna.rfo.fr) service provides overseas radio programmes for broadcasting.

Economy

The economy is based on subsistence agriculture and fishing. Licensing of fishing rights, import taxes, remittances from migrant workers and grants from France are the other sources of income.

External trade

As a Téritoire d'Outre-Mer (TOM) of France, Wallis and Futuna is integrated as an outermost region of the European Union and EU trade agreements may apply.

Imports
Principal imports are chemicals, machinery, vehicles and consumer goods.

Main sources: France (97 per cent total, 2004), Australia (2 per cent), New Zealand (1 per cent)

Exports
Exports are copra, chemicals and construction materials.

Main destinations: Italy (40 per cent total, 2004), Croatia (15 per cent), US (14 per cent), Denmark (13 per cent)

Agriculture

Farming
Approximately 80 per cent of the labour force depend on agriculture for their livelihood. The soil of the main islands is volcanic and rainfall is adequate.
Estimated crop production in 2005 included: 2,300 tonnes (t) coconuts, 2,400t cassava, 1,600t taro, 4,100t bananas, 18t tobacco, 8,667t fruit in total, 615t vegetables in total, 50t citrus fruit, 500t yams, 299t oilcrop. Estimated livestock production included: 379t meat in total, 3t beef, 315t pig meat, 15t goat meat, 46t poultry, 33t eggs, 30t milk, 11t honey.

Fishing
Tuna is fished for local consumption. Licensing of fishing rights to Japan and South Korea provide an important source of revenue.
The typical annual fish catch, for local consumption, is 300t with 4t other seafood.

Forestry
Timber is logged for local consumption and some pine reafforestation has been undertaken.

Industry and manufacturing

Industrial activity is limited to handicrafts.

Hydrocarbons

Banking and insurance

The only bank is Banque de Wallis et Futuna (a subsidiary of BNP, the French multinational bank).

Central bank
The Paris-based Institut d'Emission d'Outre-Mer (IEOM) provides all central banking services except foreign exchange reserves.

Time

GMT plus twelve hours

Geography

Wallis and Futuna consists of two islands groups – Wallis Island (also known as Uvea) and 22 islets on the surrounding reef, and, to the south-east, Futuna (or Hooru), comprising the two small islands of Futuna and Alofi. Combined, the area of the islands is 274 square kilometres and are 230km apart. They are north-east of Fiji and west of Samoa.
The islands are volcanic with the tallest peak, Mont Singavi (on Futuna) at 765 metres. The main islands had lush rain forests covering them but have been seriously denuded since wood is the major source of fuel. Deforestation has resulted in soil erosion particularly on Futuna. Alofi has no source of fresh water and does not have any permanent settlements.

Hemisphere
Southern

Climate

Hot and humid, although May–October can be dry and cooler. Rainy season from November to April. Average temperature 27 degrees Celsius.

Entry requirements

Passports
Required by all except certain French nationals.

Visa
Required by all, except citizens of EU, North America, Australasia and Japan, for stays up to one month; this includes business trips by representatives of foreign entities with an invitation from a local company or organisation. Proof of adequate funds for stay, an itinerary, a guarantee of repatriation if necessary and return/onward ticket are also required.
For further exceptions, full details and a copy of the application form visit www.diplomatie.gouv.fr and follow the link Getting to France to Getting a Visa.

Currency advice/regulations
As there are only two banks in the country (none at the airport), it is advisable to enter the country with cash, the most practical being the local currency, Comptoirs Français du Pacifique franc (CFPf). Travellers cheques can be exchanged at the banks, but each transaction is accompanied by a large commission; the banks will give advances on Visa or MasterCard.

Health (for visitors)

Mandatory precautions
Vaccination certificates required for yellow fever if travelling from an infected area.

Advisable precautions
Vaccinations for diphtheria, tuberculosis, hepatitis A and B, polio, tetanus and typhoid are recommended. Rabies risk.

Hotels
There are only four hotels with 26 rooms available, all located in Mata Utu on Wallis. Holiday residences are available.

Public holidays (national)
Fixed dates
1 Jan (New Years Day), 28 Apr (Saint Pierre Chanel), 1 May (Labour Day), 8 May (Victory Day 1945), 14 Jul (National Day), 29 Jul (Territory Day), 1 Nov (All Saints Day), 11 Nov (Armistice Day), 25 Dec (Christmas).
Holidays that fall at the weekend are not taken in lieu.
Variable dates
Good Friday (Mar/Apr), Ascension (Apr/May) Assumption (Aug).

Working hours
Banking
Mon–Fri: 0730–1545.
Business
Mon–Fri: 0730–1130, 1330–1730. Sat: 0730–1130.
Government
Mon–Fri: 0730–1130, 1215–1600.
Shops
Mon–Fri: 0730–1100, 1400–1800. Half-day Sat and Sun.

Telecommunications
Telephone/fax
Communications are by satellite, although a limited radio link is maintained.

Electricity supply
220V, 50 Hz with round, either two or three pin-plugs.

Weights and measures
Metric system

Getting there
Air
Scheduled but only weekly flights are via either New Caledonia or Fiji, provided by Aircalin. Book well in advance.
National airline: Wallis and Futuna is planning to set up its own airline.
International airport/s: Wallis Hihifo Airport (WLS), 6km from Mata Utu; bureau de change, bars, VIP lounge, duty-free, pharmacy, tourist help desk.
Surface
Water: There are no regular passengership services to the islands.
Main port/s: Mata Utu; Leava

Getting about
National transport
There is no public transport or taxis.
Road: There are surfaced roads in Mata Utu and a road network links the main towns on Wallis.
Buses: Minibus services operate on Wallis.
Car hire
Car hire is available on Wallis.

BUSINESS DIRECTORY

The addresses listed below are a selection only. While World of Information makes every endeavour to check these addresses, we cannot guarantee that changes have not been made, especially to telephone numbers and area codes. We would welcome any corrections.

Telephone area codes
The international direct dialling (IDD) code for Wallis and Futuna is +681 followed by the subscriber's number .

Banking
Banque de Wallis et Futuna, PO Box 59, Mata Utu (tel: 722-124; fax: 722-156; internet: www.bnpparibas.com).

Central bank
Institut d'Emission d'Outre-Mer (IEOM), 5 rue Roland Barthes, 75598 Paris Cedex 12, France (tel : (+33 1) 5344-4141; fax : (+33 1) 4347-5134; e-mail: contact@ieom.fr).

Travel information
Aircalin, 8 Rue Frédéric Surleau, BP 3736, Noumea 98846 New Caledonia (tel: (+687) 265-500; fax: (+687) 265-561).

Aircalin, BP 49, Matu Utu, 98600 Wallis (tel: 720-000; fax: 722-711; internet: www.aircalin.com).

Aircalin, BP 50, 98620 Futuna (tel: 723-204; fax: 723-439).

Wallis Hihifo Airport, BP 1, Mata Utu 98600 (tel: 721-200; fax: 721-203; email: aviation.sna@wallis.co.nc).

Other useful addresses
Service des Postes et Télécommunications, BP 00 98600, Mata Utu (tel: 720-700; fax: 722-500; e-mail: spt.get@wallis.co.nc).

Internet sites
Wallis and Futuna (in French): www.wallis.co.nc

Yemen

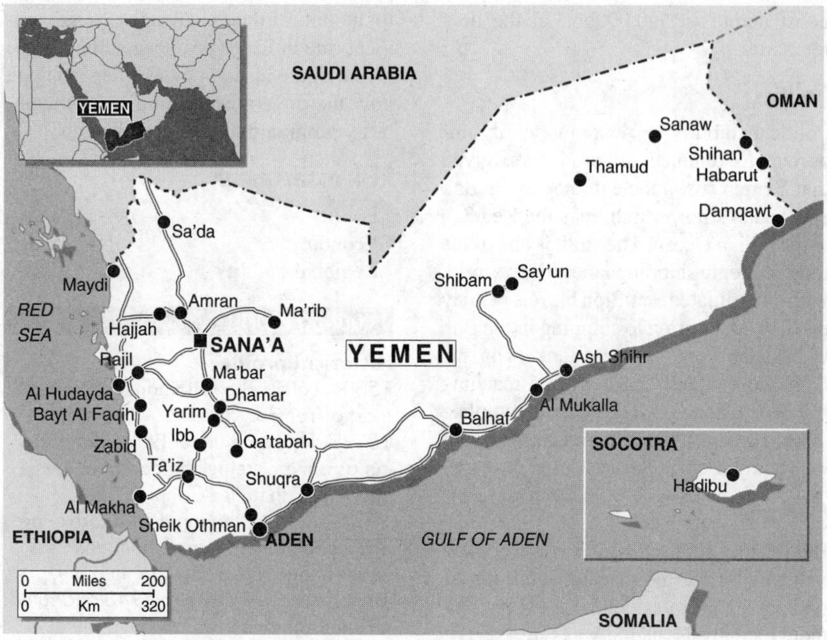

A September 2008 bomb attack in Sana'a, Yemen's capital, lead Yemeni authorities to believe that al Qaeda was responsible for the attack. A US State Department spokesman said the the explosions bore the hallmarks of an al Qaeda attack. Some unconfirmed reports said that Islamic Jihad in Yemen – which is affiliated with al Qaeda – had claimed responsibility for the attack. The rising profile of al Qaeda in Yemen has for some time been something of an unresolved challenge for Yemen's government. Low living standards have offered al Qaeda a happy hunting ground for recruitment as public anger over widespread poverty remains unchecked. Yemen ranks 153 out of 177 countries in the 2007 UNDP Human Development Index. With an estimated 35 per cent of the population living below the poverty line, the food price increases of 2007 and 2008 have further aggravated the situation. Estimates quoted by the World Bank put the number of Yemenis who have fallen below the poverty line in the last year at some 6 per cent of the population.

Mixed macroeconomics

Overall growth for 2007 was estimated at 3.1 per cent, just down on the 3.2 per cent recorded in 2006. The main positive economic outcome was the reduction in the inflation rate from 18.3 per cent recorded in 2006 to 12.4 per cent in 2007. A slower decline in oil production combined with high prices was expected to help Yemen's economic growth rate to improve to an annual 4.2 per cent. Rising inflation looked likely to be the main concern in 2008, as the annualised rate for 2008 rose to 27 per cent, making it unlikely that the rate for the whole year would drop below

Yemen's long-standing President, Ali Abdullah Saleh, was re-elected to another seven-year term in September 2006, with 77 per cent of the vote. It was the first time Mr Saleh had faced a serious challenge since coming to power 28 years ago. His main opponent, former oil minister Faisal al-Shamlan, received 21.8 per cent of the votes. International monitors said the vote was fair despite protests from the opposition that it was illegal. Roughly five million of the 9.2 million eligible Yemenis cast ballots, the electoral commission said. It was only the second presidential vote since north and south Yemen united in 1990. The election was being seen as a test of the government's commitment to tackling corruption.

KEY FACTS

Official name: Jamhuriya al Yamaniya (Republic of Yemen)

Head of State: President Ali Abdullah Saleh (GPC) (since 1999; re-elected Sep 2006)

Head of government: Prime Minister Ali Mohamed Mujawar (GPC) (appointed 31 Mar 2007)

Ruling party: Al Mutammar al Shabi al Am (GPC) (General People's Congress)

Area: 527,968 square km

Population: 22.29 million (2007)*

Capital: Sana'a

Official language: Arabic

Currency: Rial (YR) = 100 fils

Exchange rate: YR198.95 per US$ (Jul 2008)

GDP per capita: US$972 (2007)*

GDP real growth: 3.10% (2007)*

Labour force: 5.76 million (2006)

Unemployment: 30.00% (2006)

Inflation: 12.40% (2007)*

Oil production: 336,000 bpd (2007)

Balance of trade: US$2.26 billion (2005)

Foreign debt: US$5.30 billion (2006)

Visitor numbers: 382,000 (2006)*

* estimated figure

Economic and social challenges

Yemen is one of the least developed countries in the world with a per capita GDP of US$972 in 2007; 42 per cent of the people live in poverty and one in five is malnourished. Yemen's 15 million population, which is predominantly rural, faces enormous economic and social challenges. Among the major problems are limited access to basic services and a very high fertility rate estimated at 6.7 per cent.

Most of Yemen's growth is due to a surge in world oil prices, rather than any expansion on the non-oil sector. Inflation appears to be out of government control, public sector reform has stalled, and continued fighting between the government and Islamist and tribal dissidents has deterred many investors. This fighting has also helped to hold back a potentially budding tourist sector.

The oil

Yemen's economy is highly dependent on oil production, with the country's oil exports accounting for 70 per cent of government revenues. Production in 2007 was 336,000 barrels per day (bpd), most of which was exported, primarily to Asian markets, including China, India, and Thailand. Recent high oil prices have increased Yemen's hard currency receipts. However, high oil prices have also increased the country's expenditures on petroleum product subsidies, which cost hundreds of millions of dollars per year and constitute a heavy burden on the country's budget – 8 per cent of GDP in 2006.

Yemen had proven crude oil reserves of 2.8 thousand million barrels at the end of 2007. Yemen's production is likely to decrease, in part, according to Yemen's Petroleum Exploration and Production Authority (PEPA), this is due to declining production in Masila and Marib, the country's two largest fields. Despite these declines, Yemen has optimistic plans to boost output to 500,000bpd in the next few years.

Politics

Political stability in Yemen is vitally important to regional oil producers, given that Yemen sits at the entrance to the Bab el Mandab strait, which links the Red Sea to the Indian Ocean. The strait is one of the most strategic shipping lanes in the world, with an estimated 3 million barrels per day oil flow. Disruption to shipping in the Bab el Mandab could prevent tankers in the Gulf and the Gulf of Aden from reaching the Suez Canal/Sumed pipeline complex, instead diverting them at great cost around the southern tip of Africa.

Outlook

Before the 2006 elections Ali Abdullah Saleh had indicated that he would not be running in the presidential elections, although analysts had always (correctly) predicted a last minute change of heart. President Saleh ruled the Yemen Arab Republic (North Yemen) from 1978–90 and has since ruled as president of the united Republic of Yemen. There had been some speculation that his son, Colonel Ahmad Ali Abdullah Saleh, might run for office. The younger Saleh is currently commander of the elite Republican Guard and, since 1997, an MP.

Kidnappings, and now bombings, are becoming more frequent in Yemen, and can be expected to increase further until the government finds a way to engage constructively with tribal elements of the population. Zaidi militants are also likely to mount further challenges to government rule in Saada province, although the extent of the insurgency will depend upon how the government administers its amnesty programme for ex-combatants.

Risk assessment

Politics	Fair
Economy	Fair
Regional stability	Fair

KEY INDICATORS — Yemen

	Unit	2003	2004	2005	2006	2007
Population	m	19.70	20.30	20.47	21.62	*22.29
Gross domestic product (GDP)	US$bn	11.10	12.83	15.19	19.11	*21.66
GDP per capita	US$	558	518	586	884	*972
GDP real growth	%	3.1	2.7	3.7	3.2	*3.1
Inflation	%	10.7	12.5	11.8	18.3	*12.4
Oil output	'000 bpd	454.0	429.0	426.0	390.0	336.0
Natural gas output	bn cum	–	–	–	–	–
Exports (fob) (goods)	US$m	3,400.0	4,468.0	6,379.8	7,316.4	–
Imports (cif) (goods)	US$m	2,900.0	3,734.0	4,124.1	5,926.1	–
Balance of trade	US$m	500.0	734.0	2,255.7	1,390.3	–
Current account	US$m	130.0	130.0	246.0	206.0	-924.0
Total reserves minus gold	US$m	4,986.9	5,664.8	6,115.4	7,511.5	7,715.4
Foreign exchange	US$m	4,982.0	5,613.5	6,096.6	7,504.4	7,715.4
Exchange rate	per US$	177.95	184.78	198.48	198.48	198.90

* estimated figure

COUNTRY PROFILE

Historical profile

1500s–1600s The Ottomans controlled most of Yemen.

1839 Aden came under British rule, serving as a major refuelling port after the opening of the Suez Canal in 1869.

1918–62 The Ottoman empire broke up and north Yemen gained independence under Imam Yahya. His son, Imam Ahmad succeeded him in 1948 and ruled until his death in 1962. A coup d'état overthrew his son and the Yemen Arab Republic (YAR), was established by the military. A civil war between royalists, supported by Saudi Arabia, and republicans, backed by Egypt ensued.

1967 British withdrew from Aden as local resistance to their presence grew steadily more violent. A communist state in the south was established, comprising Aden and the former protectorate of South Arabia. It was officially known as the People's Democratic Republic of Yemen (PDRY). A nationalisation programme began.

1970s–80s The YAR and the PDRY were in conflict. Ali Abdullah Saleh became president of the YAR in 1978. President Ali Nasser Mohammed of the PDRY fled the country in 1986, after thousands died in political conflict.

1990 The YAR and the PDRY were unified and became the Republic of Yemen, with Ali Abdullah Saleh as president.

1991 A constitution was adopted. Yemen's support for Iraq in the Gulf War, led to around a million migrant workers from other gulf states being evicted and returning home.

1993 Democratic elections (the first in the Arabian Peninsula) led to a three-party coalition comprising the former ruling party of the YAR, General People's Congress (GPC), led by Ali Abdullah Saleh, the former ruling party of the PDRY,

Yemeni Socialist Party (YSP), led by al Beedh, and a mainly northern Islamic tribal grouping, the Congregation for Reform (Islah). Disputes within the coalition resulted in an escalating political crisis.
1994 The constitution was amended. In spite of the signing of a conciliation agreement, a series of military confrontations broke out, leading to a full-scale civil war between northern and southern forces. Unity was restored and President Saleh was re-elected by parliament. A coalition government was formed, comprising the GPC and Islah, with the YSP and other smaller parties in opposition.
1995 Yemen and Eritrea clashed over the Hanish islands in the Red Sea.
1997 The ruling GPC won the first election since the 1994 civil war.
1998 Eritrea and Yemen accepted the ruling of the Permanent Court of Arbitration in the Hague that Yemen should have the island of Greater Hanish.
2000 Yemen and Saudi Arabia signed a treaty resolving a 65-year dispute over land and sea boundaries. The US naval vessel, USS Cole, was damaged in a suicide attack in Aden; a bomb exploded at the British Embassy.
2001 A referendum approved the extension of the president's term of office by two years to seven years and the parliamentary term by two years to six years. In response to the attack on New York, President Saleh told US President Bush that Yemen would join the fight against terrorism.
2002 Jarallah Omar, secretary general of the opposition party, YSP, was assassinated by an Islamic militant. Yemen expelled more than 100 foreign Islamic scholars, suspected of being al Qaeda members. The supertanker Limburg was badly damaged in an explosion off the coast of Yemen.
2003 The ruling GPC was re-elected. The 10 chief suspects in the bombing of the USS Cole escaped from custody in Aden.
2004 Government troops fought with followers of Hussein al Houthi, the leader of an insurrection in the north. Fifteen men were sentenced on terror charges, some for bombing the supertanker Limburg, and two more for bombing the USS Cole. Government troops killed Hussein al Houthi
2005 More fighting between government forces and al Houthi supporters caused over 200 deaths. The World Health Organisation confirmed 83 cases of polio; Yemen had been free of the disease. A agreement with the northern insurgents was reached.
2006 Over 625 supporters of the al Houthi uprising were freed from prison under an amnesty. In presidential elections Ali Abdullah Saleh was re-elected.
2007 Dozens of followers of al Houthi were killed in clashes with government troops. Ali Mohamed Mujawar was appointed prime minister in March. Addul Malik al Houthi agreed to a ceasefire in June. A volcano erupted on the tiny island of al Tair in September. The island, 140km from Yemen, had a small military base which was destroyed during the eruption. Citizens were banned from carrying firearms in the capital and demonstrations without permits were banned.
2008 More violence broke out between supporters loyal to Addul Malik al Houthi and security forces in January. Bomb attacks were carried out against local police and official buildings as well as foreign businesses, embassies and tourist targets.

Political structure

Constitution

The constitution was adopted in 1991 and was amended in 1994 and 2001. Voting eligibility: 18 years.
A 2001 referendum approved the extension of the president's and parliament's terms of office from five to seven years, and from four to six years, respectively.

Form of state

Republic

The executive

Power is vested in the post of president, who is the Head of State.
The president is elected by popular vote from at least two candidates, endorsed by parliament. He sets a national agenda and is empowered to rule by decree in the case of parliament's absence, call for parliamentary elections, appoint a prime minister to form a government, call for general referenda and form the National Defence Council.
The president can serve a maximum of two, seven-year terms.
The prime minister, in consultation with the president, selects the cabinet to assist in the duties of the executive branch.

National legislature

The bicameral parliament is composed of an upper house, the Consultative Council, and a lower house, the House of Representatives.
The House of Representatives, with 301 elected members who serve six-year terms, has legislative powers.
The Shura, Consultative Council, is composed of 111 members, appointed by the president, and serves only as advisory body.
There are 17 administrative provinces (11 in the north and six in the south).

Legal system

An independent judiciary was established under the constitution. It is based on Sharia (Islamic law), Turkish law, English common law and local tribal customary law. The Supreme Court is based in the capital.

Last elections

20 September 2006 (presidential); 27 April 2003 (parliamentary)
Results: Parliamentary: GPC won 58.01 per cent of the votes (238 seats out of 301); Islah won 22.55 per cent (46 seats); Yemen Socialist Party 3.84 per cent (eight seats). Turnout was 75.98 per cent.
Presidential: Ali Abdullah Saleh won 77.17 per cent of the vote; Faisal Bin Shamlan won 21.81 per cent. Turnout was 65.16 per cent.

Next elections

2009 (parliamentary); 2013 (presidential)

Political parties

Ruling party

Al Mutammar al Shabi al Am (GPC) (General People's Congress)

Main opposition party

At tajammu al yemeni lil Islah (Islah) (Yemeni Congregation for Reform)

Population

22.29 million (2007)*
Last census: December 1994: 14,587,807
Population density: 30 inhabitants per square km. Urban population: 25 per cent (1995–2001).
Annual growth rate: 3.4 per cent 1994–2004 (WHO 2006)

Ethnic make-up

Arabs form 96 per cent of the population. There are ethnic tensions between Arabs and Afro-Arab and South Asian minorities. European communities are concentrated in the major metropolitan areas.

Religions

Muslim (more than 99 per cent), including Shi'ite, Sunni and Zaydi (members of a Shi'ite subsect). Small number of Jews.

Education

Primary education begins at the age of six and lasts for nine years.
Secondary education is provided for academic and vocational courses both lasting three years. The first year comprises a common curriculum, with the option to choose either the scientific or literary subjects for the remaining two years. There are some technical secondary schools, three vocational training centres, a Veterinary Training School and several agricultural secondary schools. There are also religious institutions, which concentrate on Islamic education. Higher education is provided by the University of Sana'a (1970), the University of Aden (1973) and the University of Science and Technology, Sana'a.
Literacy rate: 49 per cent adult rate; 68 per cent youth rate (15–24) (Unesco 2005).

Compulsory years: Six to 15.
Enrolment rate: 70 per cent gross primary enrolment; 34 per cent gross secondary enrolment, of relevant age groups (including repeaters) (World Bank).
Pupils per teacher: 30 in primary schools.

Health
Per capita total expenditure on health (2003) was US$89; of which per capita government spending was US$37, at the international dollar rate, (WHO 2006).
There were cases of polio reported to the World Health Organisation – Global Polio Eradication Initiative in 2006; the country had previously been free of the disease and its re-emergence was due to infected travellers.
HIV/Aids
HIV prevalence: 0.1 per cent aged 15–49 in 2003 (World Bank)
Life expectancy: 59 years, 2004 (WHO 2006)
Fertility rate/Maternal mortality rate: 6.0 births per woman, 2004 (WHO 2006); maternal mortality 350 per 100,000 live births (World Bank).
Child (under 5 years) mortality rate (per 1,000): 82 per 1,000 live births; 46 per cent of children under aged five are malnourished (World Bank).
Head of population per physician: 0.33 physicians per 1,000 people, 2004 (WHO 2006)

Main cities
Sana'a (San'a) (capital, estimated population 2.4 million in 2005), Aden (507,355), Ta'iz (596,672), Hodeida (548,433), Ibb (225,611).

Media
National news agency: Saba (Yemen News Agency)
Press
Dailies: In Arabic, the government-owned national newspaper is Al Thawra (www.althawranews.net), other regional private publications include Al Ayyam (www.al-ayyam.info) and 14 October (www.14october.com), from Aden, Akhbar al Youm (www.alshomoa.net), Al Thaqafiah (www.y.net.ye/althaqafiah) and Al Shoura from Sanna.
In English, the Yemen Times (http://yementimes.com) is a widely read newspaper, Yemen Observer (www.yobserver.com) is an independent English online newspaper covering current events.
Weeklies: In Arabic, publications include 26 September (www.26september.info), Al Ray News (www.raynews.net), and Ektissad ws Aswaq (www.ekwas.net) on economics, news and analysis.

Broadcasting
High rates of illiteracy has effectively left radio and television as primary sources of news and information for the domestic population.
Radio: The state-run Yemen Radio (www.yemenradio.net) has two networks, from the capital and Aden.
Television: The only terrestrial TV network is Yemen Television with two channels. There is satellite TV with nine international and pan-Arab networks available, including the government-owned Yemen Satellite Channel, offering a wide variety of programmes.

Economy
Although GDP per capita rose to US$586 in 2005, from US$518 in 2004, Yemen's population remains among the poorest in the world with 40 per cent of the population living below the national poverty line. One of the challenges facing Yemen has been to reduce its dependence on its rapidly depleting oil reserves by turning to non-oil sectors and to attract private investment.
Privatisation, liberalisation and opening the economy to the world market system have resulted in an enhanced international position for Yemen. International investors, including Gulf Co-operation Council (GCC) sources, in co-operation with the EU, Japan, the US and the World Bank/IMF, have combined to develop an improving economic position.
Industry, in 2004, was 37.5 per cent of GDP, of which 4.9 per cent was manufacturing, while agricultural production contributed 13.8 per cent.
Reform measures were incorporated into the 2005 budget and macroeconomic indicators were used for the first time, nevertheless the IMF in its appraisal of the economy considers Yemen 'at a crossroads'. The government has the challenge of rapidly declining oil revenue against the need to promote growth and diversity. Progress and structural reforms have begun and while the short-term outlook is manageable, without a long-term strategy, including prioritising and sequencing, the fiscal momentum is unlikely to be sustained.

External trade
In 2005 the Greater Arab Free Trade Area (Gafta) was ratified by 17 members, including Yemen, creating an Arab economic bloc. A customs union was established whereby tariffs within Gafta will be reduced by a percentage each year, until none remain.
Crude oil dominates the export market but reserves are diminishing. A new liquefied natural gas (LNG) export plant began construction in 2005, with production expected to begin in 2009.
The coffee harvest was replaced by the cultivation of qat (an additive, mild hallucinogen), trafficked illegally to the Horn of Africa.
Imports
Main imports are foodstuffs, live animals, vehicles, machinery and equipment.
Main sources: UAE (20.6 per cent total, 2006), Saudi Arabia (10.2 per cent), Switzerland (8.4 per cent).
Exports
Crude and refined oil and derivatives, seafood, fruit and vegetables, tobacco products and animal hides.
Main destinations: India (24.9 per cent total, 2006), China (22.6 per cent), Thailand (14.3 per cent).

Agriculture
With its fertile soil and relatively high levels of rainfall, Yemen possesses the best climatic conditions for agriculture on the Arabian peninsula. Due to its mountainous terrain, terrace agriculture is common practice. In the east and north, herding is the chief activity. In southern Yemen, fertile areas are severely limited and confined to the wadis, comprising only 1 per cent of the total land area.
Agriculture employs nearly 70 per cent of the total workforce and generated 13.8 per cent of GDP in 2004. The main crops are sorghum, wheat, barley, maize, millet, sesame, cotton, coffee, vegetables, dates, fruit, tobacco and qat (a legal narcotic).
The cultivation of qat, a widely used mild narcotic shrub dominates production. It is estimated that up to 25 per cent of irrigated land is given over to qat, which generates a value added equivalent of 25 per cent of GDP.
Cereals, fruit and vegetables account for 75 per cent of output, but annual imports of grain are still required. Cereal yields are low and the climate is more suitable for fruit production. Private sector trading companies have invested in agriculture in Tihama and Marib, concentrating on bananas and citrus fruits.
Drought in some places and floods in others, plus general manpower shortages remain serious problems. The Marib Dam provides irrigation and for a region adjacent to the desert (Empty Quarter).
Estimated crop production in 2005 included: 559,210 tonnes (t) cereals in total, 107,322t wheat, 72,962t millet, 33,472t maize, 222,400t potatoes, 311,982t sorghum, 99,000t bananas, 60,800t pulses, 201,620t citrus fruit, 169,000t grapes, 200,438t tomatoes, 11,242t oilcrops, 11,900t tobacco, 33,300t dates, 11,600t green coffee, 73,800t papayas, 646,220t fruit in total, 736,643t vegetables in total. Estimated livestock production included: 202,584t meat in total, 59,800t beef, 3,184t camel

meat, 30,300t lamb, 26,000t goat meat, 87,300t poultry, 31,980t eggs, 263,788t milk, 681t honey, 11,169t cattle hides, 5,200t goatskins, 6,000t sheepskins, 6,838t greasy wool.

Fishing

Fisheries are one of Yemen's greatest potential sources of wealth after oil. There are some fish exports to Europe and the Middle East.

In 2004, the total marine fish catch was 239,860 tonnes and the total crustacean catch was 3,200 tonnes.

Industry and manufacturing

The industrial sector contributed 37.5 per cent of GDP, of which manufacturing was 4.9 per cent in 2004. The sector employs around 10 per cent of the working population. Excluding the petroleum sector, industry accounts for only 4 per cent of GDP.

Heavy industry is mostly government-owned while the private sector is encouraged to participate in joint ventures and light industries including food processing, clothing, textiles, leather goods, jewellery, cosmetics, mineral water, fertilisers and cigarettes.

Fish processing is a growth area.

Industrial production increased by 5.0 per cent, and manufacturing by 5.3 per cent, in 2004.

Tourism

The government has been seeking to develop tourism as a potential source of revenue. The country has a moderate climate all-year-round and an ancient civilisation which would prove of great interest to visitors. However, with the rise of terriorist activities tourism has been hampered.

Travel and tourism, in 2005, is expected to contribute around US$253 million or 1.9 per cent of GDP and 13 per cent of total exports, and employ 8.6 per cent of all workers. Around US$283 million or 12.8 per cent of total capital investment is expected to be invested in the sector in 2005.

Environment

Yemen has water shortages, especially in the increasingly urbanised areas around Sana'a and other cities.

Mining

Salt is mined at Salif, where deposits total 25 million tonnes. Gypsum and marble are extracted. There are also deposits of zinc, lead, iron, sulphur, gold, silver, copper and nickel.

Hydrocarbons

In 2004, oil reserves stood at 4 billion barrels. Oil production was 420,000 barrels per day (bpd). Over 80 per cent of total oil production is exported. Exploration is ongoing, and in August 2003 a new field of four wells was announced, although the quality of oil has yet to be determined.

Downstream, Yemen has a refining capacity of 130,000bpd with two refineries at Aden (120,000bpd) and Marib (10,000bpd).

Reserves of natural gas were estimated at 478 billion cubic metres in 2004. Yemen does not exploit this resource yet, it could be used for power generation and industry in the future, although two-thirds of its reserves is earmarked for export. A US$5 billion liquefied natural gas (LNG) project was scheduled to come on line by 2006, but ExxonMobil left the consortium in 2002. The project found Chinese and Indian backers and is expected to be completed by 2009 and will involve construction of gas-gathering facilities, a pipeline to the Gulf of Aden and an LNG plant. An estimated 6.2 million tonnes of LNG will be exported per annum. A second pipeline will carry gas for local consumption to Sana'a.

Yemen neither produces nor imports coal.

In February 2004, Syria and Yemen signed a co-operation agreement in the field of oil, gas and mineral resources.

Energy

Installed electricity generating capacity is estimated at 810MW, all of it produced by oil-fired power stations. Yemen has power problems and expansion of electricity is a major priority. Plans include thermal power stations and grid extension.

Banking and insurance

Domestic banks are burdened by red tape and private sector credit is crowded out by the state, although the government has announced a reform programme to develop the financial sector.

Central bank

Central Bank of Yemen

Main financial centre

Sana'a

Time

GMT plus three hours

Geography

Yemen is situated in the south of the Arabian peninsula, bordered to the north by Saudi Arabia, to the east by Oman, to the south by the Gulf of Aden, and to the west by the Red Sea. The islands of Perim and Kamaran at the southern end of the Red Sea and the island of Socotra at the entrance to the Gulf of Aden are also part of the Republic.

Hemisphere

Northern

Climate

The semi-desert coastal plain known as the Tihama is hot, humid and dusty. The highlands, which are agreeable in summer but cold in winter, enjoy most of the unreliable rainfall (March–April and July–September).

Entry requirements

Passports

Required by all, valid for six months from date of departure.

Visa

Required by all, except nationals of Iraq, Jordan and Syria.

Tourist visas, valid for visits up to two months, require a confirmation letter from a tour company and proof of return/onward passage. Business visas, valid for visits up to two months, require a letter from the applicant's company explaining the purpose of the visit and the nature of business and proof of return/onward passage. Visas valid for six months may be issued to business travellers proposing to make several jouneys, in which case a letter of invitation from a Yemeni company is also required.

Prohibited entry

Israeli nationals or holders of passports with Israeli visas or other indication of a visit to Israel are denied entry or transit facilities.

Currency advice/regulations

The import and export of local currency by non-residents is prohibited. There are no restrictions on the import of foreign currencies, subject to declaration of amounts over US$3,000; export of foreign currencies is restricted to the amount imported and declared.

Customs

600 cigarettes, 60 cigars or 450g of tobacco; two bottles of alcohol; one bottle of perfume, perfumed water or eau de cologne; gifts to a value of YR100,000; and gold ornaments up to 350 grams are allowed duty-free.

Prohibited imports

Firearms, illegal drugs, pornographic literature and all products of Israeli origin are prohibited.

Health (for visitors)

Mandatory precautions

Certificate of vaccination against yellow fever if travelling from infected area.

Advisable precautions

Vaccinations against typhoid and polio are recommended, also anti-malaria precautions (malaria has been endemic in Tihama).

Water precautions are essential; water and milk should be boiled. Local dairy products should be avoided as milk is unpasteurised; vegetables, meat and fish should be well cooked and eaten hot. Use only well maintained, chlorinated swimming pools as bilharzia can be contracted from streams and rivers. Gastric upsets common.

Hotels
Sana'a has several first-class hotels. It is advisable to book in advance. The major hotels have good restaurants.

Credit cards
Major credit cards are acceptable.

Public holidays (national)
Fixed dates
1 May (Labour Day), 22 May (Unity Day), 26 Sep (Revolution Day), 14 Oct (National Day), 30 Nov (Independence Day).
Variable dates
Eid al Adha (four days), Eid al Fitr (four days), Islamic New Year, Birth of the Prophet.
Islamic year – 1429 (10 Jan 2008–28 Dec 2008): The Islamic year contains 354 or 355 days, with the result that Muslim feasts advance by 10–12 days against the Gregorian calendar. Dates of feasts vary according to the sighting of the new moon, so cannot be forecast exactly.

Working hours
Banking
Sat–Wed: 0800–1200, Thu: 0800–1130 (closed Fri); in summer: Sat–Wed: 0730–1130, Thu: 0730–1100 (closed Fri).
Business
Sat–Wed: 0800–1230, 1600–1900; Thu: 0800–1200 (closed Fri).
Government
Sat–Thu: 0900–1300.
Shops
Sun-Thu: 0800-1300, 1600-2100.

Telecommunications
Telephone/fax
The telephone directory is in Arabic. For help, ask the telephone operator at your hotel or ring 18 (English spoken).
Mobile/cell phones
There are GSM 900 services available in the south and west of the country.

Electricity supply
Generally 220V AC, with two-pin plug fittings.

Weights and measures
Metric system

Social customs/useful tips
Islamic culture and customs are strictly observed, but visitors are allowed to drink alcohol in hotels or private homes.

Security
Visitors should keep in touch with developments in the Middle East as any increase in regional tension might affect travel advice.

Getting there
Air
National airline: Yemenia (Yemen Airways)
International airport/s: Sana'a International (SAH), 13km north of Sana'a, with duty-free shop, restaurant, bank, car hire; Aden International (ADE), 11km north-east of Aden.
Airport tax: None.
Surface
There are road connections from Saudi Arabia and Oman, but driving to Yemen is advised against.
Main port/s: Aden, Hodeidah and Mukalla

Getting about
National transport
Internal travel may be affected by local night-time curfews and military check points.
Air: Regular scheduled services link Sana'a, Aden, Hodeida, Ta'iz and Marib.
Road: There are metalled roads between main centres.
Buses: There are scheduled services between all main centres.
City transport
Most hosts will send a car to the airport to meet guests.
Taxis: Taxis have yellow licence plates and wait on ranks outside the major hotels and terminals.
Fare is by negotiation and there is a minimum charge system in cities. Always agree the fare before setting off; the hotel will advise what the price should be as the starting point for negotiation. A fixed fare is charged between Sana'a airport and the city centre.
Dahabs (shared taxis) are minibuses which ply set routes in the city. Prices are fixed between destinations and are reasonably cheap.
Buses, trams & metro: Buses wait outside the airport.
Car hire
Available in Sana'a and other main centres.

BUSINESS DIRECTORY
The addresses listed below are a selection only. While World of Information makes every endeavour to check these addresses, we cannot guarantee that changes have not been made, especially to telephone numbers and area codes. We would welcome any corrections.

Telephone area codes
The international direct dialling (IDD) code for Yemen is +967, followed by the area code and subscriber's number:

Aden	2	Sana'a	1
Almahra	5	Taiz	4
Amran	7	Yarim	4
Hodeidah	3	Zabid	3

Chambers of Commerce
Aden Chamber of Commerce, Queen Arwa Road, PO Box 473, Crater, Aden (tel: 221-176; fax: 255-660; e-mail: cciaden@y.net.ye).

Federation of Yemen Chambers of Commerce and Industry, Al-Qiyadah Road, PO Box 16992, Sana'a (tel: 265-038; fax: 261-269; e-mail: fucci@y.net.ye).

Hadhramout Chamber of Commerce and Industry, Mukalla Main Street, PO Box 8302, Mukalla (tel: 353-258; fax: 303-437; e-mail: hdramoutchamber@y.net.ye).

Hodeidah Chamber of Commerce and Industry, Liberty Squaret, PO Box 3370, Hodeidah (tel: 217-401; fax: 211-528; e-mail: hodcii@y.net.ye).

National Chamber of Commerce and Industry, PO Box 5029, Crater, Aden (tel: 51203; fax: 232-412).

Sana'a Chamber of Commerce and Industry, Airport Road, PO Box 195, Sana'a (tel: 232-361; fax: 232-412; e-mail: sanaacomyemen@y.net.ye).

Ta'iz Chamber of Commerce and Industry, Chamber Street, PO Box 5029, Taiz (tel: 210-581; fax: 212-335; e-mail: taizchamber@y.net.ye).

Banking
Arab Bank Plc, PO Box 5130, Madram Street, Maala, Aden (tel: 242-099, 240-043; fax: 242-098).

Credit Agricole Indosuez, PO Box 651, Al Ma'ala Main St, Aden (tel: 247-4024; fax: 247-282).

International Bank of Yemen YSC, PO Box 819, al Maidan - Crater, Off Queen Arwa Rd, Crater, Aden (tel: 255-795; fax: 252-016).

National Bank of Yemen, PO Box 5, Crater, Aden (tel: 252-875, 253-327; fax: 252-875).

Watani Bank for Trade and Investment, PO Box 4424, Queen Arwa St, Agaba, Aden (tel: 2506-1017; fax: 250-618).

Yemen Bank for Reconstruction and Development, PO Box 239, Aden (tel: 252-104, 254-046; fax: 252-141).

Yemen Commercial Bank, PO Box 4230, Aden (tel: 255-813, 253-384; fax: 255-428).

Central bank
Central Bank of Yemen, PO Box 59, Ali Abdulmoghni Street, Sana'a (tel: 274-310 fax: 274-057; e-mail: info@centralbank.gov.ye).

Travel information
Sana'a International Airport, PO Box 1438, Sana'a (tel/fax: 250-819).

Yemenia (Yemen Airways), PO Box 1183, Sana'a (tel: 201-822; fax: 201-821; e-mail: info@yemenia.com).

Ministry of tourism

Ministry of Culture and Tourism, Al-Hasabah, PO Box 129, Sana'a (tel: 235-112; fax: 235-113; e-mail: yementpb@y.net.ye).

National tourist organisation offices

General Tourism Development Authority, Al-Hasabah, PO Box 129, Sana'a (tel: 252-319; fax: 252-316; e-mail: gtda@gtda.gov.ye).

Tourism Promotion Board, Al-Hasabah, PO Box 5607, Sana'a (tel: 251-033; fax: 251-034; e-mail: ytpb@yementourism.com).

Ministries

Ministry of Agriculture and Water Resources, PO Box 2805 (tel: 200-999; fax: 209-509).

Ministry of Civil Service and Administration Reform, PO Box 1992, Sana'a (tel: 200-404; fax: 274-456).

Ministry of Communications, PO Box 17045, Sana's (tel: 271-100; fax: 251-150).

Ministry of Construction, PO Box 1180, Sana'a (tel: 202-288; fax: 274-145).

Ministry of Culture and Tourism (tel: 200-002; fax: 252-316).

Ministry of Defence (tel: 250-330; fax: 251-559).

Ministry of Economy, Supply & Trade, PO Box 1704, Sana'a (tel: 202-471).

Ministry of Education (tel: 274-548; fax: 274-558).

Ministry of Electricity and Water, PO Box 11422, Sana'a (tel: 250-143; fax: 251-554).

Ministry of Finance, PO Box 190, Sana'a (tel: 260-375; fax: 263-040).

Ministry of Fishery Wealth, PO Box 19179, Sana'a (tel: 262-866; fax: 263-165).

Ministry of Foreign Affairs, PO Box 1994, Sana'a (tel: 202-555; fax: 209-540).

Ministry of Higher Education and Scientific Research, PO Box 11327, Sana'a (tel: 200-463; fax: 262-001).

Ministry of Housing and Urban Planning, PO Box 1445, Sana'a (tel: 262-614; fax: 215-613).

Ministry of Immigrants Affairs, PO Box 1299, Sana'a (tel: 215-666; fax: 263-027).

Ministry of Industry, PO Box 607, Sana'a (tel: 252-339; fax: 252-366).

Ministry of Information (tel: 200-050; fax: 282-050).

Ministry of the Interior and Security (tel: 252-701; fax: 251-529).

Ministry of Justice (tel: 252-158; fax: 252-138).

Ministry of Labour and Vocational Training, PO Box 60, Sana'a (tel: 274-922; fax: 274-107).

Ministry of Legal Affairs, PO Box 1292, Sana'a (tel: 262-047; fax: 262-047).

Ministry of Local Government, PO Box 2198, Sana'a (tel: 250-626; fax: 251-513).

Ministry of Oil and Mineral Resources, PO Box 81, Sana'a (tel: 202-312; fax: 202-314).

Ministry of Planning and Development, PO Box 175, Sana'a (tel: 250-118; fax: 251-503).

Ministry of Provision and Trade, PO Box 804, Sana'a (tel: 252-337; fax: 251-366).

Ministry of Public Health, PO Box 274160, Sana'a (tel: 252-222; fax: 244-143).

Ministry of Securities and Social Affairs (tel: 262-809; fax: 209-547).

Ministry of State for Cabinet Affairs (tel: 200-677; fax: 209-518).

Ministry of State for Foreign Affairs, PO Box L994, Sana'a (tel: 202-544; fax: 209-540).

Ministry of State for House of Deputies Affairs (tel: 200-671; fax: 209-518).

Ministry of Transport, PO Box 2781 (tel: 260-904; fax: 263-169).

Ministry of Tourism, PO Box 129, Sana'a (tel: 252-319; fax: 260-186).

Ministry of WAQF and Guidance (tel: 274-438; fax: 274-17).

Ministry of Youth and Sport, PO Box 2701, Sana'a (tel: 215-653; fax: 263-181).

Other useful addresses

British Consulate-General, PO Box 6304, Khormaksar, Aden (tel: 232-712; fax: 231-256).

British Embassy, PO Box 1287, Sana'a (tel: 264-081; fax: 263-059).

Central Planning Organisation, PO Box 175, Sana'a (tel: 250-1018).

Foreign Trade Corporation, PO Box 77, Sana'a (tel: 72-058).

General Post Office, Liberation (Tahreer) Square, (tel: 71-401/2).

Ports and Marine Affairs Corporation, PO Box 3183, Hodeidah.

Republic of Yemen Embassy (USA), Suite 705, 2600 Virginia Avenue, NW, Washington DC 20037 (tel: (+1-202) 965-4760; fax: (+1-202) 337-2017; e-mail: information@yemenembassy.org).

United Nations Development Programme, PO Box 551 Sana'a (tel: 70-593/70-596).

National news agency: Saba (Yemen News Agency)

Internet sites

ArabNet: http://www.arab.net/welcome.html

Arabia.On.Line: http://www.arabia.com

Embassy of the Republic Yemen, Washington DC: http://www.yemenembassy.org

Yemen gateway site: http://www.al-bab.com/yemen/Default.htm

Yemen Times On-line: http://www.yementimes.com

Zambia

KEY FACTS

Official name: Republic of Zambia

Head of State: President Levy Mwanawasa (MMD) (since 2001; re-elected 28 Sep 2006)

Head of government: President Levy Mwanawasa

Ruling party: Movement for Multi-party Democracy (MMD) (since 1991, re-elected 28 Sep 2006)

Area: 752,614 square km

Population: 12.16 million (2007)*

Capital: Lusaka

Official language: English

Currency: Kwacha (K) = 100 ngwee

Exchange rate: K3,380.00 per US$ (Jul 2008)

GDP per capita: US$918 (2007)*

GDP real growth: 5.20% (2007)*

Labour force: 4.47 million (2004)

Unemployment: 50.00% (2006)

Inflation: 10.60% (2007)*

Balance of trade: US$631.00 million (2006)

Foreign debt: US$502.00 million (2006) (US$7.2 billion given in debt relief in 2006)

* estimated figure

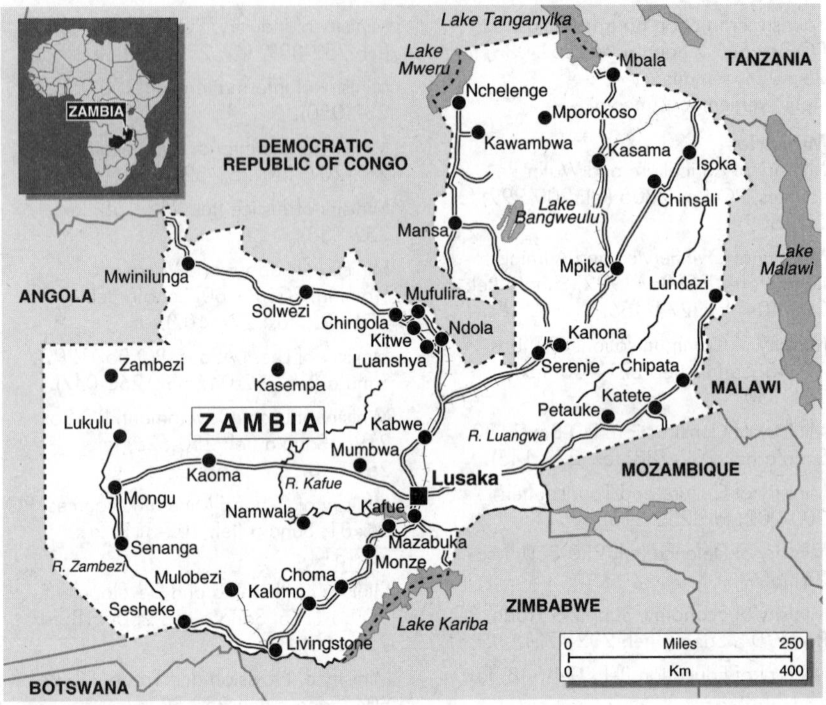

President Levy Mwanawasa will be missed by his fellow Zambians, and not only because his death will mean an election, and elections in Africa can be tricky affairs. There is no obvious successor to Mwanawasa, but there are a number of names to go into the hat. He will also be missed for his quiet authority and honesty. He was one of few African leaders to raise his voice against the leadership and policies of Robert Mugabe (whom he had likened to a 'sinking titanic') in Zimbabwe. He described what was happening in Zimbabwe as 'embarrassing to the region and the continent'. He was considered by the international community to be at the forefront of the fight against corruption.

The ruling Movement for Multi-party Democracy (MMD) has no party vice president who would have an automatic right to replace Mwanawasa. This may lead to party bickering and a break-away faction, which would play into the hands of opposition leader Michael Sato of the Patriotic Front (PF). Sata had come second in the 2006 presidential elections, although his party in the parliamentary elections held at the same time had won only one seat (out of 159). Hakainde Hichilema of the United Democratic Alliance Coalition (UDA) came third in the elections and will stand again. It remains to be seen whether Rupiah Banda will be the sole representative of the MMD to stand against Sato and Hichilema. Mwanawasa' widow, Maureen, was reported to have suggested that finance minister, Mandu Magandi, should succeed her husband rather than Banda.

The territory of Northern Rhodesia was administered by the South Africa Company from 1891 until it was taken over by the UK in 1923. During the 1920s and 1930s, advances in mining spurred development and immigration. The name was changed to Zambia upon independence in 1964, under President Kenneth Kaunda. In the 1980s and 1990s, declining copper prices and a prolonged drought hurt the economy. Elections in 1991 brought an end to one-party rule. The new president was Frederick Chiluba. His presidency ushered in an era that will mostly be remembered for its corruption. In the 2001 elections, Levy Mwanawasa defeated Chiluba and his first action was to launch a far-reaching anti-corruption campaign in 2002, which resulted in the prosecution of Chiluba and many of his supporters.

Modest improvements

The World Bank reports that during the last three decades, macroeconomic instability, incomplete policy implementation, and inefficient state-owned enterprises have had a seriously negative effect on Zambia's frail economy. This has been compounded by a collapse in copper prices, oil price shocks, and the continuing contraction of food production. As a result, and also reflecting ill-advised economic policies, per capita income dropped by nearly 5 per cent annually between 1974 and 1990. When Levy Mwanawasa defeated Frederick Chiluba he set in train a series of economic reforms.

In macroeconomic terms, much has changed. In some measure this is due to a series of ambitious market-orientated reforms. Gross domestic product (GDP) per capita has risen from US$355 annually in 2001 to US$918 in 2007. GDP growth in 2007 was 5.2 per cent. Zambia's GDP growth has averaged over 5.0 per cent annually since 2003. Inflation, which was over 20 per cent annually in 2001–03, appears to be falling, down to 10.6 per cent in 2007 from 18.3 per cent in 2005. In December 2005, the International Monetary Fund (IMF) approved relief for Zambia on all outstanding debt to the IMF incurred before 1 January 2005. This amounted to approximately US$577 million.

The medium-term development strategy for Zambia is to reduce poverty through strong economic growth and economic diversification driven by the private sector. The strategy targets real growth of at least 5 per cent a year, single-digit inflation by 2007, and a strengthened international reserve position. These reforms are urgently needed if the Zambian government is to create an environment more conducive to private sector development. Implementation of the reform agenda is now key.

IMF and World Bank aid

The IMF is collaborating with the World Bank in many areas of Zambia's development. In some areas the Fund leads and its analyses serve as inputs into World Bank policy formulation and advice; these include macroeconomic stability, fiscal, monetary and exchange rate policies. The Fund and the Bank share responsibility in the areas of trade, the financial sector, public expenditure management, including debt management, and economic governance. The Bank takes the lead in the social sectors, including health, education, social protection, water and sanitation, agriculture and rural development, private sector development including regulatory issues and the environment.

Diversification

A central element of the Mwanawasa government's economic policies has been diversification away from reliance on copper revenues – even though the fortunes of the copper industry are currently in a bull phase. The drivers are investments in private sector operations. However, investment remains at less than 6 per cent of GDP in the context of annual population growth of 3 per cent.

Another challenge is to attract new investment that will ensure diversified sources of growth. Long term, copper cannot be the mainstay of the Zambian economy. It will continue to be extremely important, but by the nature of that industry, growth in the main accrues to those who finance it. It can create only so much employment, it is the kind of growth that, while good for the economy, is not as broad based as Zambia needs. It is not the type of growth that improves people's lives. The main areas for which the World Bank and government agencies are seeking investments are agriculture and tourism, both offer broad based growth that is sustainable in the long haul. All that is required is the infrastructure to open up the country.

The copper crisis years are over. Copper prices are in an upswing. But the core problem remains: Zambia is not in control of the final destiny of its copper mining industry. Prices are set on the London Metal Exchange and in many of the years since independence have been even lower than pre-Independence levels.

Zambia is still a major producer, but mines in the landlocked country have to contend with high transport costs, ageing infrastructure and growing competition from Australia and Chile and even closer to home. Canadian companies are fast-tracking developments in the Democratic Republic of the Congo (DRC), Australians are looking in Botswana.

Influenced by the bull phase of the industry, the mining companies disagree. There are good years left, technology is good, the challenge is to keep costs down. Industrial sources say prices will hold 'for at least four years' and 'more optimistic forecasts are over exuberant'. Zambia's production 'high' is 700,000 tonnes per year, 450,000 tonnes were produced over 2004. A new 'Copperbelt', to the West, centred on Solwezi, has improved Zambia's production by 25 per cent over two years, and is expected to increase by a further 60 per cent within six.

The Chinese question

In the run up to the September 2006 presidential elections, the question of the Chinese presence in Zambia loomed large in the campaign of presidential candidate Michael Sata of the eventual runners up,

KEY INDICATORS — Zambia

	Unit	2003	2004	2005	2006	2007
Population	m	10.85	11.00	11.60	*11.87	*12.16
Gross domestic product (GDP)	US$bn	4.80	5.39	7.27	10.89	*11.16
GDP per capita	US$	447	448	627	*917	*918
GDP real growth	%	3.1	5.0	5.2	6.2	*5.2
Inflation	%	21.5	18.0	18.3	9.0	10.6
Industrial output	% change	–	10.6	9.8	6.7	–
Agricultural output	% change	–	4.3	-0.6	-0.6	–
Exports (fob) (goods)	US$m	1,117.0	1,548.0	2,127.0	3,375.0	4,593.7
Imports (cif) (goods)	US$m	1,633.0	1,519.0	2,068.0	2,744.0	3,610.6
Balance of trade	US$m	-516.0	29.0	55.0	631.0	983.1
Current account	US$m	-650.0	-620.0	-730.0	-12.0	-743.0
Foreign debt	US$bn	6.5	7.3	7.2	0.5	0.5
Total reserves minus gold	US$m	247.7	337.1	559.8	719.7	1,090.0
Foreign exchange	US$m	247.2	312.2	544.0	706.4	1,080.2
Exchange rate	per US$	4,502.50	4,757.11	4,245.00	4,103.80	3,840.00

* estimated figure

the Patriotic Front (PF). Mr Sata was quoted as saying that Zambia should restore relations with Taiwan, which he referred to as a 'sovereign state'. Recognition of Taiwan would mean cutting ties with China, which has invested some US$300 million in Zambia, mostly in the copper industry and businesses related to the copper industry. Reflecting his country's sensitivity over Mr Sata's remarks, the Chinese ambassador to Lusaka Li Baodong was quoted by the state owned *Zambia Daily Mail* as saying that Chinese investors had put on hold further investments in the country 'until the uncertainty surrounding our bilateral relations with Zambia is cleared'. In the event, Mr Mwanawasa won the election comfortably, taking 42.98 per cent of the vote against Mr Sata's 29.37 per cent. However, in 2008, the same questions will arise – what will Mr Sato do about the Chinese presence in Zambia if he wins the presidency? The Chinese are even more entrenched in Zambia than they were at the time of the 2006 elections. There has even been a visit by Chinese President Hu Jintao, who in February 2007 visited Zambia to inaugurate a large mining investment zone .

Outlook

Much depends on this election. Zambia has been quietly moving along, avoiding the problems encountered by its neighbours and near-neighbours, including the failed economies in Zimbabwe and the Democratic Republic of the Congo (DRC), and violence in Kenya, and the DRC. If it can come through this election unscathed, Zambia will have done well.

Risk assessment

Politics	Good
Economy	Fair
Regional stability	Good

COUNTRY PROFILE

Historical profile

In the sixteenth century, people from the Luba and Lunda around the Congo River set up small kingdoms in Zambia.
Portuguese explorers visited the region in the late eighteenth century. Migration and slave-trading by the Portuguese and Arabs led to instability in the region.
1851 British missionary David Livingstone visited central Africa.
1880s British settlers followed Livingstone and the British South Africa Company, headed by British imperialist and financier, Cecil John Rhodes, opened its first copper mine at Broken Hill (later Kabwe) in 1908.
1924 The colony was put under direct British rule.
1953–63 Northern Rhodesia (later Zambia) was part of the British-sponsored Federation of Rhodesia and Nyasaland.
1960 The United National Independence Party (UNIP) was formed by Kenneth Kaunda to campaign for independence and the dissolution of white minority rule.
1964 Zambia gained independence under the presidency of Kenneth Kaunda. The government supported Marxist rebels in Mozambique, independence movements in Rhodesia (later Zimbabwe) and the African National Congress (ANC) in South Africa. This led to internal security problems and financial difficulties as Zambia's colonial neighbours attempted to destabilise the country.
1964–1970s Key enterprises and land were nationalised.
1972 Zambia became a one-party state with UNIP as the only legal party.
1975 The Tanzania-Zambia Railway Authority (Tazara) opened, linking the Zambian Copperbelt to the Tanzanian port of Dar es Salaam, reducing the country's dependence on Rhodesia and South Africa for port access.
1976 Zambia gave support to Rhodesia's bid for independence and its eventual transformation from white minority rule into Zimbabwe.
1989 Zambia began a programme of austerity measures to stabilise the economy, following a long-term fall in the price of Zambia's chief export, copper.
1990 Food riots heightened calls for an end to one-party rule.
1991 Multi-party elections were held in which Kaunda was defeated by Frederick Chiluba and the Movement for Multi-party Democracy (MMD).
1996 The MMD and President Chiluba were re-elected in a landslide victory.
1999 There was a spate of Angolan terrorist attacks in Lusaka. The Indeni Oil Refinery in Ndola was sabotaged.
2000 Kaunda resigned as leader of UNIP.
2001 Even though the MMD voted to change the constitution and allow the president to run for a third term in office, Chiluba announced he would not stand. The MMD was re-elected although the opposition said the elections were flawed.
2002 Levy Mwanawasa (MMD) was inaugurated as president; the opposition filed a petition to have the result of the presidential election nullified, alleging vote-rigging by the ruling party. The government said it would not accept genetically modified (GM) maize to help alleviate severe food shortages.
2003 Former president Frederick Chiluba's immunity from prosecution was removed and he was arrested and charged on 59 counts, including corruption and abuse of office.
2004 The court case against Chiluba was dropped but he was quickly re-arrested and charged, with embezzling US$488,000 from state funds.
2005 The World Bank approved a US$3.8 billion debt relief package, which wrote off over 50 per cent of Zambia's debt. The IMF and Japanese government also cancelled outstanding debt worth around US$577 million and US$692 million respectively. Drought caused widespread hunger and an appeal for food for millions of citizens was made by President Mwanawasa.
2006 President Mwanawasa suffered a minor stroke. The government announced that as a result of the US$4 billion of debt relief, healthcare for people living in the rural areas would be provided free of charge. Incumbent Levy Mwanawasa (MMD) won 43.0 per cent of the vote for president, beating Michael Sata (PF) with 29.4 per cent and Hakainde Hichilema (United Democratic Alliance (UDA)) with 25.3 per cent. In parliamentary elections, the MMD won 72 out of 150 directly elected seats; the next largest bloc, the PF, won 44, in coalition with the United Party for National Development (UPND) with 2; the UDA won 27; other parties won one seat each and two seats were not contested due to the death of candidates. It was announced that the first deposits of oil and gas had been found in the border region with Angola (Africa's second largest oil producer).
2007 In February, a large mining investment zone was inaugurated by Chinese President Hu Jintao. In May, the UK High Court ruled that former president Chiluba had conspired, along with four aides, to defraud Zambia of around US$46 million.
2008 On 29 June, President Mwanawasa had a mild stroke and was admitted to hospital, while attending the African Union summit in Egypt. He was later flown to France for specialist treatment where he died on 19 August. Vice president Rupiah Banda took over as interim leader; according to the constitution an election must be held within 90 days. There was no obvious successor; Mwanawasa was reported to have said that the next president should come from a different province from previous presidents Kaunda (Northern), Chiluba (Luapula) and himself (Central), although his wife, Maureen was said to be considering her position.

Political structure

Constitution

In November 1991, Zambia's one-party state was replaced by a multi-party democratic system based on a new constitution.

In 1995 the ruling Movement for Multi-party Democracy (MMD) revised the constitution. The Zambia Law Association criticised the new constitution on the grounds that it allows parliament to make retrospective laws and that a president could be elected on receiving the highest number of votes cast even if these amounted to less than 50 per cent. It also condemned amendments to the Bill of Rights of the 1991 Constitution without a referendum. A controversial Bill passed by President Chiluba on 28 May 1996 made further amendments to the constitution: future presidential candidates must be second-generation Zambians.

Form of state
Republic

The executive
Executive power is held by the president elected by universal suffrage for a five-year term. The constitution provides for a cabinet appointed from within parliament and gives it extra powers. The president does not have the right to declare martial law. The president must obtain parliamentary approval to impose a state of emergency longer than seven days.

National legislature
The unicameral National Assembly has 150 members elected in single seat constituencies and eight members appointed by the president, for a five-year terms.

Legal system
The president appoints judges and nominates the chief justice. Courts include the Supreme Court of Zambia and the High Court.

Last elections
28 September 2006 (presidential and legislative)
Results: Presidential: Levy Mwanawasa (MMD) won 43.0 per cent of the vote, Michael Sata (PF) won 29.4 per cent and Hakainde Hichilema (UDA) won 25.3 per cent.
Parliamentary: Movement for Multi-party Democracy (MMD) won 27.5 per cent of the vote (69 seats out of 159); United Party for National Development (UPND) 23.3 per cent (49 seats); Forum for Democracy and Development (FDD) 15.3 per cent (12 seats); United National Independence Party (UNIP) 10.4 per cent (13 seats); Heritage Party 7.4 per cent (4 seats); Patriotic Front 2.8 per cent (1 seat); Zambia Republican Party 5.5 per cent (1 seat); non-partisan 1; appointed members 8; Speaker 1.

Next elections
30 October 2008 (presidential, after the death of former president, Levy Mwanawasa); 2011 (presidential and legislative)

Political parties
Ruling party
Movement for Multi-party Democracy (MMD) (since 1991, re-elected 28 Sep 2006)
Main opposition party
United Party for National Development (UPND)

Population

12.16 million (2007)*
Last census: October 2000: 9,885,591
Population density: 13 inhabitants per square km. Urban population: 40 per cent.
Annual growth rate: 2.1 per cent 1994–2004 (WHO 2006)
Ethnic make-up
There are 73 ethnic groups in Zambia. The largest single group, comprising 34 per cent of the population, is the Bemba (north-east and Copperbelt areas). Other important groups include the Tonga of the southern province with 16 per cent of the population; the Nyanja of the eastern provinces (14 per cent) who are well represented in the capital, Lusaka; and the Lozi (9 per cent) of the west.
The European population live and work mostly in the urban areas, or on the farmlands along the railway lines. A high proportion of the Asian community is to be found on the Copperbelt and other urban centres.
Religions
Christian, Muslim and indigenous beliefs. Approximately 70 per cent of the population is Christian (mainly Roman Catholic and Protestant).

Education

The HIV/Aids crisis in sub-Saharan Africa has not only undermined public investment in education but has also contributed to the shortage of trained teachers, in 2001 815 primary school teachers, or 45 per cent of teachers trained that year, died of Aids. This has resulted in declining literacy rates and low levels of school enrolment. Enrolment rates for the richest households are more than one-third higher than for the poorest households.
A first cycle primary education begins at age seven, lasting until age 11, then three years in a second cycle primary school prepares children for exams to determine progression to a junior secondary school for two years until aged 16 when successfully completed exams allow progression into senior secondary school for the last two years. There are two universities that provide higher education and several specialist institutions providing professional and vocational training.
The government has developed a strong education sector reform through the Basic Education Sub-sector Investment Programme (Bessip), which has set a target of universal primary school enrolment for just under half a million children by 2005. Annual government expenditure during the first phase of the reform amounted to US$56 million, excluding contributions from international donors for the projects. The scheme aims to construct 2,000 additional classrooms and improve training in rural schools. Zambia spends typically less than 3 per cent of GDP on education.
Literacy rate: 80 per cent adult rate; 89 per cent youth rate (15–24) (Unesco 2005).
Compulsory years: Seven to 13.
Enrolment rate: 89 per cent gross primary enrolment; 27 per cent gross secondary enrolment, of relevant age groups (including repeaters) (World Bank).
Pupils per teacher: 39 in primary schools.

Health

Per capita total expenditure on health (2003) was US$51; of which per capita government spending was US$26, at the international dollar rate, (WHO 2006).
Healthcare is provided free in state-funded hospitals and commercially in private sector clinics. Rural health care is rudimentary and frequently provided only by missionary hospitals and clinics. State funding cut-backs have led to severe shortages of medical equipment and staff. Many medical posts are unfilled for lack of funds. The government is keen to encourage private investment in hospitals and believes foreign investment provides the key to the redevelopment of the health sector.
Improved water sources are available to 64 per cent of the population.
HIV/Aids
Zambia has one of the highest rates of HIV in Africa. It is estimated that 42 per cent of hospital beds are occupied by HIV/Aids sufferers. The World Bank reported that the Aids epidemic would radically reduce the rate of population growth; it fell from 2.8 per cent annually in 1990–97 to 1.5 per cent in 2003.
The impact on households is severe, with children often kept from attending school in order to help with harvesting of subsistence crops. Studies show that around 55 per cent of households affected by HIV/Aids are unable to pay school fees. Households affected by HIV/Aids have on average 30–35 per cent less income than those who are not affected. Around 60 per cent of families of Aids sufferers endure food shortages and malnutrition as a direct result of the disease.
Nationally HIV/Aids also poses a significant economic threat, with a projected annual loss in GDP growth per capita of 1.15 per cent forecast for the period

2000–10. Government spending on intervention plans was budgeted at US$560 million between 2002–05, of which US$88 million was allocated to antiretroviral treatment and US$126 million to hospital treatment. Zambia, as one of the poorest countries in the world, has been identified as in need of international aid to fight the disease.

A disturbing aspect of the disease that has been identified since 2001 is the gender disparity that has developed. Whereas the highest risk group was previously sexually active males, now women in general and young women in particular lead the male rates — by over 10 per cent in urban areas and over 5 per cent in rural areas. A UN taskforce studying this shift in the demographics has identified socio-economic forces that have left females vulnerable to the disease.

HIV prevalence: 15.6 per cent aged 15–49 in 2003 (World Bank)

Life expectancy: 40 years, 2004 (WHO 2006)

Fertility rate/Maternal mortality rate: 5.5 births per woman, 2004 (WHO 2006); maternal mortality 6.5 per l,000 (World Bank).

Child (under 5 years) mortality rate (per 1,000): 102 per 1,000 live births; 28.1 per cent of children aged under 5 arre malnourished (World Bank).

Head of population per physician: 0.12 physicians per 1,000 people, 2004 (WHO 2006)

Welfare

Zambia is one of the poorest countries in the world, with an estimated 80 per cent of its 11 million people living in desperate poverty. In December 2003 the statistics office stated that 'the food basket... was K528,529 for a family of six. The same family on average was expected to live on K758,961 for all their basic needs'.

The government provides some basic welfare for pensioners, children and people affected by disasters.

The Pension Scheme Regulation Act of 1996 provides a regulatory framework for private pension schemes. The Zambia National Provident Fund (ZNPF) was successfully transformed into the National Pension Scheme Authority (Napsa) in early 2000. The weaknesses of ZNPF, which included poor benefits, delays in payment and ineffective record keeping were critically examined to overcome similar problems for the Napsa. The economic difficulties in Zambia and the low retirement age of 55 made it necessary for Napsa to begin with modest benefits. The scheme offers three principal benefits namely retirement, invalidity and survivors' benefits. Additionally, it provides a funeral grant.

The scheme is based on the principle of social insurance and requires compulsory financial contributions from both employees and their employers at a rate of 5 per cent each. Retirement benefit is paid on the basis of a minimum contributory period of 15 years. The scheme is basic to allow the development of private occupational pension schemes.

Main cities

Lusaka (capital, estimated population 1.3 million in 2004), Ndola (349,300), Kitwe (306,200), Kabwe (219,600), Chingola (151,100), Mufulira (131,500), Luanshya (125,300), Livingstone (111,200).

Languages spoken

English is the usual medium for business. There are 73 identified African languages, all Bantu, of which seven are recognised as official vernaculars – Tonga, Lozi, Bemba, Kaonde, Luvale, Lunda and Nyanja. Zambian traders usually have a working knowledge of English.

Official language/s

English

Media

Freedom of the press is constrained by legal provisions, which have led to self-censorship.

National news agency: Zambia News Agency

Press

Since 1996 readership has been falling and prices have risen by 500 per cent so that newspapers have become a luxury item for most Zambians. Most newspapers are distributed in the capital and Copperbelt towns, while the rest of the country receives copies 1–3 days after publication.

Dailies: The government owns two newspapers, Times of Zambia (www.times.co.zm) and Zambia Daily Mail (www.daily-mail.co.zm); The Post (www.postzambia.com) is privately owned.

Weeklies: Dailies publish Sunday papers including Sunday Mail and Sunday Times; independent publications include The Monitor and National Mirror (church owned).

Business: Publications include The Lusaka Times (www.lusakatimes.com) and the Zambia Daily Mail have sections on business and the economy. Periodicals include The Zambian Marketer and Development Zambia published by (www.langmead.com).

Periodicals: Langmead and Baker (www.langmead.com) publishes several magazines aimed at various special interest groups.

Broadcasting

The state-run Zambia National Broadcasting Corporation (ZNBC) is the dominant organisation in broadcasting.

Radio: ZNBC has four networks with two broadcasting in English, one in local languages and the fourth which carries commercials.

Radio Phoenix (www.radiophoenix.co.zm) is a national commercial radio network; there are a number of local commercial radio stations in operation including Q-FM and Mazabuka Community Radio and Breeze FM (www.breezefm.makeni.net). There are several religious content radio stations.

Television: ZNBC operates the only public terrestrial network with one channel. There is no Zambian based satellite operation, although the MultiChoice Zambia services can be received from South Africa.

News agencies

National news agency: Zambia News Agency

Economy

Zambia's main economic zone follows the rail-line southwards from the Copperbelt, around Ndola and Kitwe, through Lusaka, the capital, to Victoria Falls. This area has been subject to urbanisation, although the rest of the country is relatively sparsely inhabited. Approximately 52 per cent of GDP output is from the services sector, 27 per cent from industry and 21 per cent from agriculture.

The main economic activity is mining, with copper making up 58 per cent of exports and cobalt around 19 per cent. Economic restructuring since 1991 has focused on the development of non-copper sectors, which have subsequently recorded growth. However, this has not stopped falling incomes, increased poverty, rising unemployment, increased debt and a growing informal sector. Two-thirds of Zambians, mainly in rural areas, face expenditure limits well below the cost of their basic needs and over a third spend at least 85 per cent of their income on food, making them vulnerable to price fluctuations caused by food shortages. Zambia also faces high inflation and a widening current account deficit, which are worsened by the continuing depreciation of the kwacha.

Full donor support and free market reform have had little impact on poverty and the economy still depends on the volatile price of copper, while agricultural output is severely restricted by climatic change. Despite this, the economy has managed to grow in recent years to 5.1 per cent in 2005. Unemployment is a significant problem with half the population unemployed. In 2006, inflation was brought down to around nine per cent, after being in double digits for several decades. The IMF and Japanese have cancelled outstanding debt worth around US$577 million and US$692 million respectively.

External trade
Zambia is a member of the East African Economic Community (EAC) (with Kenya and Tanzania), which operates a customs union with common external tariffs. It is a member of the Common Market for Eastern and Southern Africa (Comesa), and operates a free trade area with 13 of the 19 member states. It is also a member of the Southern African Development Community (SADC), the objectives of which include reducing trade barriers, achieving regional development and economic growth and evolving common systems and institutions.
Zambia is one of the world's largest recipients of international aid.
There are valuable reserves in minerals copper, lead, zinc, cobalt and gemstones. Agricultural produce are also important exports along with electricity.

Imports
Principal imports are petroleum and derivatives, capital machinery, electricity, fertiliser, foodstuffs and clothing.
Main sources: South Africa (47.1 per cent total, 2006), UAE (10.4 per cent), Zimbabwe (5.7 per cent).

Exports
Principal exports are copper, cobalt, electricity, tobacco, vegetables, flowers and cotton.
Main destinations: Switzerland (39.8 per cent total, 2006), South Africa (11.0 per cent), Thailand (7.7 per cent).

Agriculture

Farming
About 10 per cent of Zambia's 600 million hectares is arable land but only around 30 million hectares are under cultivation. There are more than 300,000 smallholders, mostly subsistence farmers, earning cash from growing mainly cotton and tobacco. About 500 highly mechanised commercial farms and estates account for 40 per cent of marketed crops and animal produce. The country has abundant perennial and underground water resources. Power generated by hydroelectric installations has been extended to some farming areas. In the wetter northern part of the country, tea and coffee thrive at the higher altitudes, with maize and millet at lower levels. The climate of the central province suits maize, soya beans, cotton and tobacco. The south and west are drier and suit sorghum, tobacco, cotton and groundnuts.
Agriculture accounts for approximately 21 per cent of GDP. Most state-run farms have been privatised. One problem that the industry faces is that much of the land is under tribal authority and difficult to access. In order to tackle this problem, the government has set up areas of virgin land, such as the Tazara Corridor Services (Tazcor), which are open for investment.
Government policy has long been to achieve self-sufficiency in food production, increase exports and improve the supply of inputs to peasant farmers. Measures have included a wide range of production incentives, comprising preferential tax and loan rates, the encouragement of foreign investment and improvements in producer prices. The 2004 budget included a proposal to give away land to local and foreign investors.
Official policy has also encouraged new crops for export which include coffee, flowers and exotic vegetables for European markets. In contrast to these successful new crops, cashew nut production has failed to penetrate European markets.
Regional integration means that farmers are finding foreign competition difficult as high production costs, high taxation levels and cheap imports continue to undermine their competitiveness. The country is marginally self-sufficient in food with maize surpluses in times of good weather.
Estimated crop production in 2005 included: 1,161,000 tonnes (t) maize, 1,800,000t sugar cane, 950,000t cassava, 135,000t wheat, 53,000t sweet potatoes, 19,000t sorghum, 12,000t rice, 17,000t pulses, 25,000t tomatoes, 25,640t oilcrops, 4,800t tobacco, 4,100t green coffee, 4,160t various spices, 750t tea, 22,000t cotton lint, 101,200t fruit in total, 267,400t vegetables in total. Estimated livestock production included: 127,074t meat in total, 40,800t beef, 11,000t pig meat, 546t lamb, 4,728t goat meat, 33,500t game meat, 36,500t poultry, 46,400t eggs, 64,200t milk, 200t honey, 5,355t cattle hides.

Fishing
Annual commercial fish production is estimated at 70,000 tonnes. The sector suffers due to infrastructural difficulties, including lack of input supply, such as nets and boats, poor transport and storage facilities. The private sector has stepped up investment in fish marketing and distribution, fish farming and manufacturing of nets and boats.
The Department of Fisheries in Zambia and the Department of National Parks and Wildlife Management in Zimbabwe, with the co-operation of Norway and Denmark, have undertaken a project to facilitate the sustainable utilisation of the shared fisheries resources on Lake Kariba.

Forestry
Forest and other wooded land accounts for 42 per cent and 37 per cent of the total land area respectively. Although nearly half of Zambia's land area is covered by forest, there are only a few commercially exploitable tree species. It is estimated that forests cover some 31.2 million hectares (ha), with most being open savannah woodlands and miombo woodland comprising around 80 per cent of the country's vegetation. There are large networks of protected areas constituting 32 per cent of the forests with around 20 national parks and more than 30 game management areas.
Charcoal is a significant cooking and heating fuel in rural areas but, in some regions, woodland has been ravaged and a severe shortage of charcoal is expected unless there is government sponsored replanting. There is some export of sawn timber, while most of the demand for paper products is met by imports.
Timber imports in 2004 were US$21.2 million, while exports amounted to US$3 million.
Timber production in 2004 included 8,053,000 cubic metre (cum) roundwood, 157,000cum sawnwood, 319,000cum sawlogs and veneer logs, 17,900cum wood-based panels, 7,219,000cum woodfuel; 1,041,000t charcoal.

Industry and manufacturing
Industry contributes around 27 per cent to GDP in 2004. The sector employs 8 per cent of the labour force.
Macroeconomic stabilisation and divestiture of state assets has led to a severe contraction in these sectors of the economy. The government is no longer willing to subsidise the industrial and manufacturing sector. This change contrasts vividly with policy in the 1960s and 1970s whereby vast copper profits were used to establish one of the largest parastatal economies in Africa.
Targetted sectors for development include agriculture-derived processed products and non-traditional exports such as textiles, chemicals and engineering products.
Industrial production increased by 5.1 per cent in 2003.

Tourism
Tourism is a growing sector, forecast to account for some 4.5 per cent of GDP in 2005 and generate over 55,000 jobs. Infrastructure remains underdeveloped, including air connections. The cost of air fuel is a serious problem. Nevertheless, visitor numbers continue to grow, rising from 577,526 in 2003 to 610,109 in 2004. The collapse of neighbouring Zimbabwe's tourist industry has benefitted the Zambian tourism, as visitors discover that the Victoria Falls can be viewed from the Zambian side. The government recognises the sector's importance and is aiming to attract a million visitors annually by 2010.

Mining

Zambia has enormous mineral wealth, with major deposits of copper, cobalt, lead, zinc, emeralds, aquamarine, amethyst and tourmaline. It also has small reserves of selenium, manganese, tin, nickel, iron, gold, silver and diamonds.
The mining sector contributes around a fifth of GDP and employs around 10 per cent of the workforce. Copper and its by-products, mostly cobalt, account for around 90 per cent of mining production and mining exports. Zambia is also the second largest producer of cobalt (9,000 tons in 2004) after the Democratic Republic of Congo (DRC) (11,000 tons in 2004) and has one of the world's largest reserves. Substantial amounts of cobalt can be recovered from the copper slag heaps, for which Canada's Colossus Resources obtained a 25-year contract with the Zambia Consolidated Copper Mines (ZCCM) signed in 2000. The Nkana and Mufulira cobalt mines and refineries produce 1,800 tonnes per year (tpy) of cobalt. The Nkana and Nchanga mines produce more than half of Zambia's copper and 70 per cent of its cobalt.
In August 2002, Anglo American decided to formally quit its mining operations at the Konkola Copper Mines (KCM), which sought a new strategic equity partner. Anglo American's withdrawal followed nine years of negotiations over the privatisation of the mines and two years of operation. The decision was prompted by the drop in KCM's assets and high running costs (including US$350 million expenditure on upgrading facilities), while world metal prices were at the time low. The government pledged to keep the mines open and finally in August 2004 a formal agreement with Vedanta Resources Plc was announced whereby Vedanta Resources acquired a 51 per cent controlling stake in KCM for US$48.2 million in cash. Vedanta plans to expand production from the current (2005) 2 million tonnes per year (tpy) to 6 million tpy.
There is very little mining activity outside the Copperbelt although base metal exploration has continued in other regions. Zambia is prospecting for chromium, nickel, tin, tantalite and iron ore. The government allows private sector purchase and export of gemstones. Mining companies can retain 50 per cent of foreign exchange earnings.
Zambia contains approximately a quarter of the world's gem emeralds and accounts for an estimated 20 per cent of output of rough emeralds. Other gemstones mined on a smaller scale include amethysts in the Southern Province near Lake Kariba and Kalomo. Deposits of aquamarine and tourmaline are mined for the jewellery trade. Production of gemstones is estimated to be worth US$200 million annually.

Hydrocarbons

Zambia has no known oil or gas reserves and the country is dependent on imported fuel supplies. The 1,710km Tazama pipeline from Dar es Salaam, Tanzania, supplies oil to the Indeni refinery at Ndola. Oil imports are significant, accounting for about one-fifth of the total import bill, although imports have been cut back steadily since the mid-1980s in order to save foreign exchange. With Zambia's deal to buy crude oil directly from Iran oil prices in Zambia are likely to drop.
Zambia does not import natural gas.
Most coal is locally produced at the Maamba Collieries, which has reserves of over 50 million tonnes. Due to a variety of problems production has never exceeded 800,000 tonnes per year (tpy), compared with a rated capacity of 1.2 million tpy. The Maamba Collieries were privatised, with an 80 per cent share sold to Benicon Limited, in 1998. Zambia uses coal in the mining transformation process. All coal produced is consumed domestically and fulfils all domestic demand.

Energy

Almost 70 per cent of total domestic energy needs are met by hydroelectricity, mostly from plants at Kafue Gorge, Kariba North and Livingstone, which, together with several smaller hydroelectric and diesel plants, have a capacity of 1,700MW. The national demand for power is about 1,000MW, of which 70 per cent is accounted for by the mining industry. However, only 10 per cent of the population has access to electricity.
The Zambian Electricity Supply Company (Zesco) is the national electricity authority responsible for transmission and distribution. It is up for privatisation, although divestment has been delayed due to ongoing political disputes and its lengthy reorganisation in preparation for privatisation.
Zambia also owns the Central African Power Corporation (CAPC) with Zimbabwe. CAPC operates the two Kariba power stations. The country is able to export power to Zimbabwe, Botswana, Namibia and Tanzania and is connected to the Democratic Republic of Congo (DRC) (from which Zambia has imported electricity) and South Africa.
In September 2004, Zesco signed a memorandum of understanding with Farab International of Iran for construction of the US$100 million Itezhi-tezhi hydropower plant on the Kafue River, in Zambia's southern province, which will have a capacity of 120 megawatts.

Financial markets

Stock exchange

The Lusaka Stock Exchange (LuSE) was launched in 1994. There has been a slow response from foreign investors, despite Zambia's complete relaxation of controls on foreign exchange.
The Exchange performed relatively wel in 2004. The All Share Index ended the year 447.46 compared to 371.99 in 2003. The upward trend was as a result of significant gains recorded in Chilanga Cement, Farmers House and National Breweries Plc. This was as a result of increasing investor awareness, the favourable results these companies have been reporting, and the reduction in interest rates, which have made the capital market an attractive investment forum.
The Exchange recorded share volumes of 327,429,911 (against 820,43,079 in 2003) and a turnover of K47, 560,824,870 (K14, 064,081,461in 2003).

Banking and insurance

Zambia's banking sector has undergone a period of crisis and change. The liberalisation of the economy during the 1990s gave rise to the launch of a number of banks. Poor management and over-banking led to the closure of a number of these banks, prompting a wave of concern among investors and depositors who lost money.
In March 2003 the government first directed the Zambia Privatisation Agency (ZPA) to privatise the main state owned commercial bank, Zambia National Commercial Bank. 49 per cent of its shares were to be sold to a qualified investor with management rights, 25.8 per cent were to be offered to the Zambian public through the Zambia Privatisation Trust Fund (ZPTF), 25 per cent were to be retained by the government and the existing minority shareholders, who held 0.2 per cent, were to retain their shares. The ZPA called for tenders to be received by September 2005.
The largest commercial banks, Barclays Bank of Zambia and Standard Chartered Bank Zambia, are foreign-owned. However, since January 1972 all foreign-owned banks have been required to incorporate locally.
There are several state-owned development banks and other private financial institutions. The Development Bank of Zambia offers medium- and long-term loans and business consultancy services.The Agricultural Finance Company and Zambia Agricultural Development Bank were merged and renamed the Lima Bank. The government-owned Zambia State Insurance Corporation (ZSIC) is the major insurance company in Zambia.

Other development banks include the state-owned Zambia National Building Society.

Central bank

Bank of Zambia

Main financial centre

Lusaka

Time

GMT plus two hours

Geography

Zambia is landlocked, bordered to the south by Zimbabwe and the Caprivi Strip (an extension of Namibia); to the south-east by Mozambique; to the east by Malawi; to the north-east by Tanzania; to the north and north-west by the Democratic Republic of Congo (DRC); and to the west by Angola.

About nine-tenths of the country is a high rolling plateau (900–1,200 metres above sea level) covered by savannah bush and woodland. The only relief from the monotony of the plateau is the Zambezi and Luangwa rift system. The Luapula River, part of the Congo River system, cuts into the northern part of the plateau.

Zambia takes its name from the Zambezi River. At 2,655km long, this is the third longest river in Africa.

Hemisphere

Southern

Climate

Altitude governs Zambia's climate and it is generally cooler than its neighbours. There are three distinct seasons: cool and dry from May to August; hot and dry from September to October; and rainy from November to April. Rainfall varies widely across the country. The average temperature is 16 degrees Celsius (C) in the winter and 24 degrees C in summer.

The Zambezi and Luangwa river valleys can remain hot and humid all year, typical of tropical lowlands. They are particularly uncomfortable in the rainy season.

Dress codes

The contrast between morning, midday and evening temperatures means that a sweater is often required in the early morning and after sunset between April and September. A light raincoat or umbrella is useful during the wet season from November to April.

Dress is generally informal. Lightweight suits can be worn for most of the year; during the hot season tropical suits are preferable. Tailored safari suits are popular. A hat and sunglasses are useful for protection against the sun.

Most women wear cotton or other lightweight dresses during the day and evening. Warm dresses and lightweight coats are needed during the coldest season, June to August.

Entry requirements

Passports

Required by all; it must be valid for six months beyond the date of stay and with sufficient space for a visa.

Visa

Required by all, exceptions include those listed on the Visa Application Instructions (items 4 and 5) and for tourist visits only, see www.zambiaembassy.org. Tourist visas can be obtained at all border crossings, fees will be levied in cash, usually sterling or dollars (exact amounts as change may not be available).

All business visits require a visa, obtained in advance. Applications should include an invitation from a local company or organisation giving brief details of the nature of business, a full itinerary and proof of onward/return passage.

Currency advice/regulations

The import and export of local currency is limited to K100. The import of foreign currency is unlimited but must be declared, and bank notes with denominations over US$5,000 (or equivalent) must be recorded with customs; export is limited to the amount declared. Retain all official currency exchange forms and receipts (they are also necessary for purchase of domestic airline tickets). Use only authorised banks and bureaux de change for currency conversions.

Travellers cheques, in major currencies, are widely accepted.

Health (for visitors)

Mandatory precautions

A yellow fever and cholera vaccination certificate is required if arriving from an infected area.

Advisable precautions

Vaccinations for diphtheria, tetanus, polio, hepatitis A and typhoid are recommended. Other vaccinations that may be appropriate are tuberculosis, hepatitis B, meningitis, cholera and yellow fever (if travelling to the remote border region with DRC and Angola).

A malignant malaria is present (falciparum, which is resistant to chloroquine) from November to May throughout the country and all year in the Zambezi valley. Use malaria prophylaxis including mosquito repellents, sleeping nets and clothing that fully cover the body after dark. Rabies is a risk. Bilharzia is present, use only well-maintained and chlorinated swimming pools. HIV/Aids is prevalent.

All water for drinking, brushing teeth or making ice should be sterilised when outside of the main cities. Bottled water is available. Milk is pasteurised and therefore safe. Vegetables should be cooked and fruit peeled.

Take all prescription medicines; ensure that medical insurance includes evacuation.

Hotels

Several good quality hotels are available. Hotels are graded from one to five stars by the Hotels Board. A service charge of 10 per cent, plus 10 per cent sales tax are added to all bills. Room charges must be settled in foreign currency. Some hotels require a deposit to cover the room rate and an element for food and drink to be converted to Kwacha on arrival. Tipping is not customary in Zambia but is acceptable.

Credit cards

Major credit cards are accepted in most hotels and tourist facilities. ATMs exist in larger branches in city centres only.

Public holidays (national)

Fixed dates

1 Jan (New Year's Day), 12 Mar (Youth Day), 1 May (Labour Day), 25 May (African Day), 24 Oct (Independence Day), 25 Dec (Christmas Day).

Holidays that fall on the weekend are taken on Monday.

Variable dates

Good Friday and Easter Monday (Mar/Apr), Heroes' Day and Unity Day (first Mon and Tue of Jul), Farmers' Day (first Mon of Aug).

Working hours

Banking

Mon–Fri: 0815–1430. Some larger branches open 0816–1030 on first and last Sat of month.

Business

Mon–Fri: 0800–1230, 1400–1630.

Government

Mon–Fri: 0800–1300, 1400–1700.

Shops

Privately owned: Mon–Fri: 0800–1700, Sat: 0800–1300; state-owned: Mon–Sat: 0800–1800, Sun: 0800–1200.

Note: There are wide variations outside city centres.

Telecommunications

Mobile/cell phones

There are 900 GSM services available in large towns and cities.

Electricity supply

230V AC

Social customs/useful tips

Visitors normally entertain business guests in hotels or restaurants, while residents prefer to entertain informally at home or at their clubs. Temporary membership of clubs can normally be obtained on an introduction from friends.

Security

The stealing of cheques has become a problem in Zambia. Visitors are advised to carry travellers' cheques in small denominations and to cash only sufficient for current needs. There has also been a rise in violent crime due to the economic decline and care must be taken when travelling after dark. It is not regarded as advisable to travel by car between Lusaka and the Copperbelt after dark.

Getting there

Air

International airport/s: Lusaka International (LUN), 26km from city; duty-free shop, bar, restaurant, bank, shops, car hire; Livingstone International Airport (LVI).

Airport tax: International departures: US$25, in cash, excluding transit passengers. Domestic departures: K12,000.

Surface

Road: There are tarred roads from Zimbabwe, Botswana, Namibia (Caprivi Strip), Democratic Republic of Congo (DRC), Tanzania and Malawi; motorists should check border post hours, and regulations concerning their vehicles. A customs bond may be required for the import of cars.

During the rainy season many rural roads are impassable. It is not advisable to travel by car between Lusaka and the Copperbelt after dark.

A road bridge across the River Zambezi between Namibia and Zambia opened in May 2004.

Rail: The Tanzania Zambia Railway Authority (Tazara) railway links Zambia to Tanzania – the connection is at Kapiri Mposhi.

Zambia Railways Limited (ZRL) connects with Democratic Republic Congo and Zimbabwe where lines run on to Mozambique, South Africa and Botswana.

Water: Services include ferries across the Zambezi river from Botswana (Kazungula) and across Lake Tanganyika from Burundi (Bujumbura) and from Tanzania (Kigoma).

Getting about

National transport

Air: There are regular flights from Lusaka, south to Livingstone and to the Copperbelt in the north. There are several flights a week from Lusaka to other centres including Mfuwe in the Luangwa valley. Charter companies also operate and are in heavy demand. There is a total of around 150 airfields and airstrips.

Road: The total network is almost 40,000km, of which about 6,500km are main roads. Surfaced roads link main centres. During the rainy season many rural roads are impassable.

Buses: Eagle Travel runs regular coach services to numerous locations including tourist sites. Non-tourist services can be irregular and crowded.

Rail: There are three main lines running from Livingstone-Lusaka, Lusaka-Copperbelt and Kapiri Mposhi to the northern border with Tanzania.

There is an overnight train from Livingstone-Lusaka with sleeping carriages, running three time a week. And day-time services that take many more hours, as they stop at more stations along the line. All lengthy trips should be booked at least one week in advance.

The total network is over 2,000km and in need of investment, which through joint ventures, was agreed in 2006 between the governments of Zambia and China. New and refurbished lines, and rolling stock will provide more access to the Indian Ocean through Tanzania and Mozambique.

City transport

Taxis: These are available between airports and hotels and within town centres. They are generally unmetered.

Buses, trams & metro: A number of privately-owned companies run domestic services over a number of routes. Buses are irregular and crowded, especially during the rush hour.

Car hire

Car hire usually comes with a driver; on special request, firms may offer self-drive vehicles. The Zambia Tourist Board has authorised over 16 car-hire firms serving mainly Lusaka, Livingstone and the Copperbelt which are the major urban and tourist centres.

BUSINESS DIRECTORY

The addresses listed below are a selection only. While World of Information makes every endeavour to check these addresses, we cannot guarantee that changes have not been made, especially to telephone numbers and area codes. We would welcome any corrections.

Telephone area codes

The international direct dialling (IDD) code for Zambia is +260, followed by the area code and subscriber's number:

Chingola	2	Livingstone	3
Chipata	6	Luanshya	2
Choma	3	Lusaka	1
Kabwe	2	Mongu	7
Kasama	4	Ndola	2
Kitwe	2	Solwezi	8

Chambers of Commerce

Livingstone Chamber of Commerce and Industry, 29 Airport Road, PO Box 60648, Livingstone (tel/fax: 323-656; email: denmar@zamtel.zm).

Lusaka Chamber of Commerce and Industry, Farmers House, Cairo Rod, PO Box 37997, Lusaka (tel: 221-266; fax: 224-114; email: luschamb@zamnet.zm).

Zambia Association of Chambers of Commerceand Industry, Showgrounds, Great East Road, PO Box 30844, Lusaka (tel: 255-046; fax: 253-007; email: zacci@zamnet.zm).

Banking

Barclays Bank of Zambia, Cairo Rd, PO Box 31936, Lusaka (tel: 228-858/66; fax: 222-519, 226-185).

Cavmont Merchant Bank Ltd, Fourth Floor, Tazara House, Independence Avenue, PO Box 38474, Lusaka (tel: 224 280; fax: 221 643; e-mail: info@cavmont.com.zm).

Citibank, Citibank House, PO Box 30037, Lusaka (tel: 229-025/6/7/8; fax: 226-264).

Indo Zambia Bank, 686 Cairo Rd, PO Box 35411, Lusaka (tel: 225-080, 222-622; fax: 225-090).

Investrust Bank Plc, Investrust House, Plot 4527/8, Freedom Way, PO Box 32344, Lusaka (tel: 238-733; fax: 237 060; e-mail: inquiries@investrustbank.co.zm).

Stanbic Bank, Cairo Rd, Woodgate House, PO Box 31955, Lusaka (tel: 229-071/3, 229-285/6; fax: 221-152, 225-380).

Standard Chartered Bank, PO Box 32238, Lusaka (tel: 229-242; fax: 222-092).

Union Bank, Zimco House, PO Box 34940, Lusaka (tel: 229-397/8; fax: 221-866).

Zambia National Commercial Bank, Cairo Rd, PO Box 33611, Lusaka (tel: 228-979, 221-355; fax: 224-006).

Central bank

Bank of Zambia, Bank Square, Cairo Road, PO Box 30080, Lusaka 10101 (tel: 228-888 fax: 221-722; internet: www.boz.zm).

Travel information

Lusaka International Airport, National Airports Corporation Limited, PO Box 30175, Lusaka (tel/fax: 271-359; email: naclaps@zamnet.zm; internet: www.lun.aero).

Tourism Council of Zambia, PO Box 36561, Lusaka (tel: 251-666; fax: 251-501; e-mail: tcz@zamnet.zm; internet: www.zambiatourism.com).

Zambian Airways, Head Office, Lusaka International Airport; PO Box 34777, Lusaka, (tel: 271-230; fax: 271-054; internet: www.zambianairways.com).

Zambian Express, Lusaka (tel: 222-060, 238-162/65; fax: 238-166; e-mail: zamex@zamnet.zm).

Ministry of tourism

Ministry of Tourism, PO Box 30575, Lusaka (tel: 227-645; fax: 225-174).

National tourist organisation offices
Zambia National Tourist Board (ZNTB), Tourist Centre, Mosi-oa-Tunya Road, PO Box 60342, Livingstone (tel: 321-404/5; fax: 321-487; e-mail: zntblive@zamnet.zm); Century House, Cairo Road, Lusaka Square, PO Box 30017, Lusaka (tel: 229-087/90; fax: 225-174; e-mail: zntb@zamnet.zm).

Ministries
Ministry of Agriculture, Food and Fisheries, Mulungushi House, Box RW 50291, Lusaka (tel: 251-537/233; fax: 252-029).

Ministry of Commerce, Trade and Industry, Kwacha House Annex, PO Box 31968/34373, Lusaka (tel: 228-301, 221-184; fax: 226-673).

Ministry of Communication and Transport, PO Box 50065, Lusaka (tel: 251-444/938/740/759; fax: 002-601, 253-260).

Ministry of Community Development and Social Services, Fidelity House, PO Box 31958, Lusaka (tel: 227-840, 228-321; fax: 225-327).

Ministry of Defence, PO Box RW 17X, Lusaka (tel: 251-211, 254-667; fax: 254-670, 221-339, 253-875).

Ministry of Education, PO Box 50093, Lusaka (tel: 227-636; fax: 222-396).

Ministry of Energy and Water Development, Ministerial Headquarters, Lusaka (tel: 263-870; fax: 252-339).

Ministry of Environment and Natural Resources, Mulungushi House, PO Box 30055, Lusaka (tel: 252-711, 250-186; fax: 252-952).

Ministry of Finance, PO Box RW 50062, Lusaka (tel: 250-544, 227-668; fax: 250-501).

Ministry of Foreign Affairs, PO Box 50069, Lusaka (tel: 262-666; fax: 250-634/240, 252-867).

Ministry of Health, PO Box 30205, Lusaka (tel: 227-745, 223-435; fax: 223-435).

Ministry of Home Affairs, PO Box 50997, Lusaka (tel: 254-261/362; fax: 224-656, 254-669).

Ministry of Information and Broadcasting Services, PO Box 50200, Lusaka (tel: 251-766, 253-965; fax: 254-013, 252-391, 250-524).

Ministry of Labour and Social Security, PO Box 32186, Lusaka (tel: 227-640).

Ministry of Lands, Mulungushi House, PO Box 30069, Lusaka (tel: 252-288; fax: 250-130).

Ministry of Legal Affairs, PO Box 50106, Lusaka (tel: 251-588; fax: 253-695).

Ministry of Local Government and Housing, PO Box 34204, Lusaka (tel: 253-077; fax: 252-680).

Ministry of Mines and Minerals Development, PO Box 31969, Lusaka (tel: 252-990; fax: 251-224).

Ministry of Science, Technical Education and Vocational Training, PO Box 50464, Lusaka (tel: 229-673; fax: 252-951).

Ministry of Sports, Youth and Child Development, 4th Floor, Memaco House, Sapele Rd, Lusaka (tel: 227-168; fax: 223-996).

Ministry of Works and Supply, PO Box 50236, Lusaka (tel: 253-266; fax: 222-360).

Other useful addresses
British High Commission, 5210 Independence Avenue; PO Box 50050, 15101 Ridgeway, Lusaka (tel: 251-133; fax: 253-798; email: BHC-lusaka@fco.gov.uk).

Central Statistics Office, PO Box 31908, Lusaka.

Chilanga Cement plc, Kafue Road, PO Box 32639, Lusaka (tel: 225-2853, 701-297; fax: 252-853, 252-655).

Export Board of Zambia, PO Box 30064, Third Floor, State Lottery Building, Cairo Road, North End, Lusaka (tel: 228-106/7; fax: 222-509).

Lusaka Stock Exchange Ltd, Lusaka (tel: 228-594, 228-391; fax: 228-608, 225-969; e-mail: luse@zamnet.zm).

Metal Marketing Corp of Zambia, PO Box 35570, 10101 Lusaka (tel: 228-131/140).

National Air Charters, PO Box 33650, 10101 Lusaka (tel: 229-154, 228-274).

National Commission for Development Planning, PO Box 50268, Lusaka.

National Import & Export Corporation, PO Box 30282, 10101 Lusaka (tel: 228-018).

Nitrogen Chemicals, PO Box 360226, Kafue (tel: 311-531/5; fax: 311-313).

Zambia Consolidated Copper Mines Ltd (ZCCM), 5309 Dedan Kimathi Road, PO Box 30048, Lusaka (tel: 229-115; fax: 221-057).

Zambia Electricity Supply Corporation Ltd (Zesco), PO Box 33304, Stand 6949 Great East Road, Lusaka 10101 (tel: 223-970, 239-343, 225-074; fax: 223-971, 237-601, 239-343, 222-753).

Zambian Embassy (USA), 2419 Massachusetts Avenue, NW, Washington DC 20008 (tel: (+1-202) 265-9717; fax: (+1-202) 332-0826; e-mail: info@zambiainfo.org).

Zambia Industrial & Commercial Copper Industry Service Bureau, PO Box 22100, Kitwe.

Zambia Investment Centre, 5th Floor, Ndeke House, Haile Selassie Avenue, PO Box 34580, Lusaka (tel: 252-130, 252-152; fax: 252-150; e-mail: invest@zamnet.zm).

Zambia National Broadcasting Corporation, PO Box 50015, 10101 Lusaka (tel: 229-648).

Zambia National Oil Company Limited (ZNOC), Lusaka (tel: 222-135; fax: 220-144, 221-265).

Zambia Privatisation Agency (ZPA), Privatisation House, Nasser Road, PO Box 30819, Lusaka (tel: 227-851, 223-859, 227-791; fax: 225-270; e-mail: zpa@zamnet.zm).

Zambia Railways Ltd (ZRL), PO Box 80935, Kabwe (tel: 223-822, 222-201/209; fax: 228-023/025).

Zambia Telecommunications Co Ltd, Lusaka (tel: 611-111, 612-399; fax: 613-055, 615-855).

National news agency: Zambia News Agency

Address: (internet: www.zana.gov.zm).

Internet sites
Africa Business Network: www.ifc.org/abn

African Development Bank: www.afdb.org

Africa Online: www.africaonline.com

AllAfrica.com: http://allafrica.com

Mbendi AfroPaedia (information on companies, countries, industries and stock exchanges in Africa): http://mbendi.co.za

Office of the President: www.statehouse.gov.zm

Zambian Express: www.africa-insites.com

Zambian gateway website: www.zamnet.zm

Zambian Statistical Office: www.zamstats.gov.zm

Zimbabwe

KEY FACTS

Official name: Republic of Zimbabwe

Head of State: President Robert Gabriel Mugabe (Zanu-PF) (since 1980; re-elected 2002)

Head of government: President Robert Gabriel Mugabe

Ruling party: Zimbabwe African National Union-Patriotic Front (Zanu-PF) (re-elected 31 Mar 2005)

Area: 391,109 square km

Population: 11.73 million (2007)*

Capital: Harare

Official language: English, Shona and Ndebele

Currency: Zimbabwe dollar (Z$) = 100 cents

Exchange rate: Z$27,719.00 per US$ (Jul 2008, official) (street rate Z$75 billion to US$1 July 2008)

GDP per capita: US$55 (2007)*

GDP real growth: -6.00% (2007)*

Labour force: 5.94 million (2004)

Unemployment: 80.00% (2007)

Inflation: 11250000.00% (Jun 2008); (the official statistician declared that with the lack of goods in the shops it was impossible to determine an accurate inflation rate)

Balance of trade: -US$269.00 million (2005)

Foreign debt: US$3.90 billion (2006)

Visitor numbers: 2.29 million (2006)*

* estimated figure

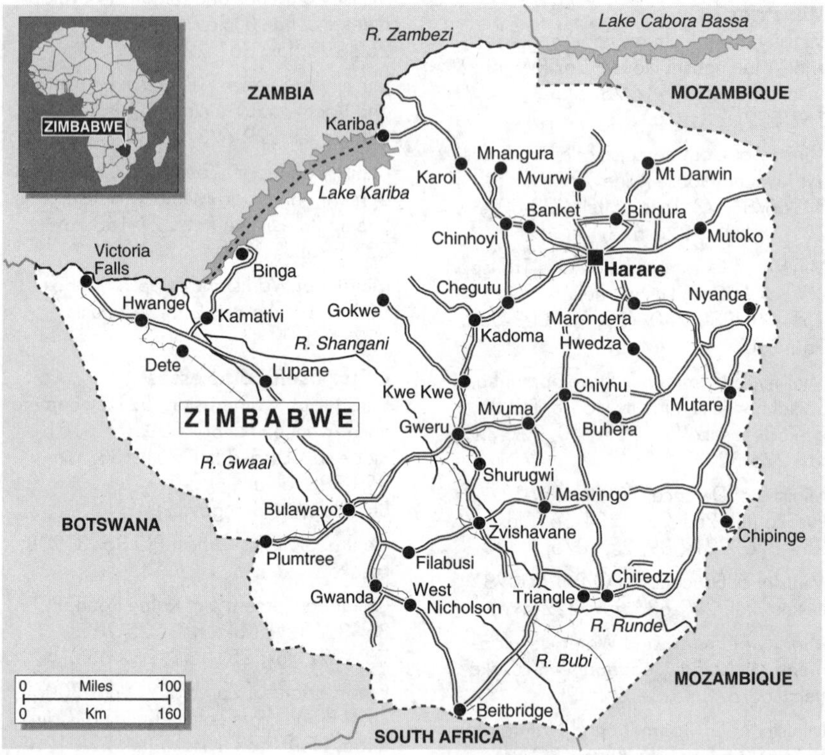

Zimbabwe is in economic and social ruins. The country no longer has an economy to speak of, millions face food shortages and at least 80 per cent of the population do not have a job. Once one of the richest countries in Africa, Zimbabwe has, in a few years, descended into economic chaos, coupled with increasing political restlessness and crisis in 2008. This follows years of government mismanagement and corruption, with much of the blame being laid on the policies of the octogenarian president, Robert Mugabe.

There has been soaring inflation during 2007 and 2008, which has compounded a dramatic drop in production. Retailers have been raising their prices several times during the course of a day, and for even the smallest of transactions such as buying a coffee, it can take suitcases full of bank notes just to make a payment. It is thought that 20 per cent of the population are infected with HIV, and life expectancy has plummeted. Poverty has increased, and more than half the population survives on less than the equivalent of US$1 a day, while life expectancy has dropped to just 35, according to the UN. Aid agencies have been warning that upwards of four million are at risk of severe hunger. At least 30 per cent of the population have emigrated and now live outside of Zimbabwe, and government policies have led to massive internal displacement and homelessness.

The country has descended from bread basket to basket case in a matter of years. Only an improved political situation is likely to improve conditions. Although a September 2008 political agreement between the main parties could represent a major improvement, there is still a very long way to go.

Economic implosion

Government policies have been blamed for the severe economic implosion which Zimbabwe is experiencing. The figures are depressing beyond belief, with inflation rising spectacularly. An already staggering inflation rate of 1,200 per cent at the end of 2006, was estimated pessimistically by the IMF to rise to 5,000 per cent by the end of 2007. In reality, inflation has continued to rise, above and way beyond these pessimistic figures: in February 2008, it was estimated to be running at the unheard of rate of 165,000 per cent, and 2.2 million per cent in July. However, by August 2008, this was estimated to have soared yet further to the incredible rate of 11.25 million per cent. The official government statistician declared at the time that with the lack of goods in the shops, it had become impossible to determine an accurate inflation rate.

As inflation continued to rise through 2008, the central bank printed ever higher value bank notes. In May 2008, the largest value bank note was Z$500,000, but less than two months later, by mid-July, a Z$100 billion dollar note had been issued. By the end of July, however, the central bank's governor, Gideon Gono, finally proclaimed that he was no longer prepared to continue to print ever higher value notes. In a bid to get to grips with the woeful economic crisis, the bank redenominated the currency, knocking ten zero's off the value of existing notes, turning Z$10 billion into Z$1, although that will still be insufficient to buy a loaf of bread. In September, in yet another sign that authorities were failing to control the economy and a thriving black market, acceptance of foreign currencies as a form of payment was licensed for an initial experimental period of 18 months.

The destruction of commercial large scale farming was the initial cause of Zimbabwe's economic woes. The government's land reform programme redistributed commercial (white owned) farmland to indigenous inexperienced and would-be farmers, many of whom were Robert Mugabe's cronies. This reduced the number of large scale farming units from about 3,200 in 2000 to about 250 partially operational units by 2005. This has led to the loss of property and incomes of more than 300,000 farmers and workers, as well as the crucial rural social infrastructure which farmers also provided. In the process, much of the country's on-farm infrastructure has also been removed, stolen or vandalised. In 2005, commercial agricultural output was estimated at between just 5 and 20 per cent of 2000 levels. With ongoing economic problems since then, and with the political crisis through 2007 and 2008, it is likely that these figures will have worsened further. The Commercial Farmers Union has recently described commercial output as a disaster.

External trade

The documented collapse of commercial agricultural production is mirrored by declines in other sectors. Zimbabwe has some of the world's largest reserves of minerals, including coal and asbestos, with valuable ores in platinum, copper, nickel, gold, iron and chromite. Minerals are now the country's main export commodity, and such as it is, the mainstay of the economy. However, the political and economic situation has discouraged foreign direct investment, and mineral production has not been maintained or grown, with mining companies warning that the sector is close to collapse. Gold production, for example, has dropped from a potential 30 tonnes, to a projection of just 4 tonnes in 2008. Mineral production has also suffered from investor scepticism, as well as raw material shortages and a major skills drain.

Despite the parlous state of the economy and continuing political uncertainty, Chinese interests have been assiduously investing in Africa, and have not avoided Zimbabwean commercial interests. It is thought that they have backed the government diplomatically and financially. Zimbabwe has seen, for example, active Chinese investment in the minerals sector, among others.

Tourism was a vital export earner, but visitor numbers have declined dramatically as Zimbabwe has increasingly been viewed as a pariah state: repressive regimes attract few visitors. The perception from the most important markets, such as the US, UK and Australia, is that Zimbabwe is unsafe, and this has been compounded by government travel warnings to this effect.

Zimbabwe is a member of the Common Market for Eastern and Southern Africa (Comesa), but does not operate a free trade area with the other member states as the economy has been too weak to maintain the union. It is also a member of the Southern Africa Development Community (SADC), the objectives of which include reducing trade barriers, achieving regional economic development and growth and evolving some common systems and institutions.

It remains to be seen how the economy will respond to the government's last ditch attempts to gain economic control. The situation changes by the day, and the economy looks bleak in the short term, while the implications of a political resolution reached in September 2008 are still being deciphered.

Politics

Robert Mugabe played a key role in ending white rule in Rhodesia, and he and his Zimbabwe African National Union-Patriotic Front (Zanu-PF) party have dominated Zimbabwe's politics since independence in 1980. Robert Mugabe has been strong and ruthless, anti-Western, suspicious of capitalism and deeply intolerant of dissent and opposition. As Zimbabwe's economy has been ruined and the country left bleeding, political strife and repression have become more commonplace under his rule.

KEY INDICATORS — Zimbabwe

	Unit	2003	2004	2005	2006	2007
Population	m	13.51	14.71	*11.73	*11.73	*11.73
Gross domestic product (GDP)	US$bn	4.60	4.70	*4.55	*1.44	*0.64
GDP per capita	US$	359	496	*388	*123	*55
GDP real growth	%	-13.1	-4.8	*-5.3	*-5.4	*-6.0
Inflation	%	431.7	282.4	237.8	1,016.7	*10,453.0
Industrial output	% change	–	-3.5	-11.7	–	–
Agricultural output	% change	–	-2.9	-10.0	–	–
Coal output	mtoe	1.9	2.1	2.6	1.8	–
Exports (fob) (goods)	US$m	1,225.0	1,409.0	1,644.0	–	–
Imports (cif) (goods)	US$m	1,914.0	1,599.0	1,913.0	–	–
Balance of trade	US$m	-689.0	-190.0	-269.0	–	–
Current account	US$m	410.0	-310.0	-511.0	*-333.0	*-116.0
Foreign debt	US$bn	3.9	4.7	4.0	3.9	–
Exchange rate	per US$	438.72	4,303.28	17,694.15	250.00	30,000.00

* estimated figure

The main challenge in recent years to Zanu-PF has come from the opposition Movement for Democratic Change (MDC). The MDC says that its members have been killed, tortured and harassed by Zanu-PF supporters, while Robert Mugabe has claimed that the MDC is no more than a political tool of the West. The party has however, been weakened by political infighting, which first led to a split in 2005, with both factions claiming presidency of the MDC. Morgan Tsvangirai is seen as the most powerful leader within the MDC, with the other faction being led by Arthur Mutambara.

Senate elections in 2005 led to a sweeping Zanu-PF victory, with very low voter turnout of only around 20 per cent. However, 2008 brought a new parliamentary and presidential electoral campaign, and along with it widespread unrest and political violence, much of which was perpetrated by the ruling Zanu-PF party and the ruthless Joint Operations Command, led by the powerful former spymaster Emerson Mnangagwa. A huge government spending spree ahead of elections increased national debt 65-fold from Z$25,000 billion to a massive Z$1,600,000 billion (US$34 billion)This was considered a desperate measure by the government to secure votes and Mugabe's re-election.

Despite concerns over the credibility of the election on 29 March, and amid re-counts and confusion as results were delayed, the Electoral Commission eventually started releasing results in mid-April, which confirmed a slim MDC parliamentary victory. It also appeared that their leader, Morgan Tsvangirai, had won the first round of the presidential election, but without the outright majority required to secure the presidency.

A second round of voting ensued. The following campaign involved a stepping up of opposition crackdown, and against voters with the temerity to support Morgan Tsvangirai. Diplomats who tried to investigate the violence were attacked, and NGOs who attempted to feed the victims of Mugabe's disastrous policies were banned, in an apparent bid to hide the humanitarian disaster and political thuggery from the outside world. Eventually Morgan Tsvangirai's nerve failed amid death threats and the murders of at least 65 MDC supporters and members, and displacement of upwards of 25,000 people. With Tsvangirai's announcement that he would no longer contest the presidential election, he effectively handed victory to Robert Mugabe, who won 90 per cent of the vote in June's second round. Criticised for his weakness, there was a danger that he could not again be seen as an effective leader, either of the MDC, or the country.

Despite claiming that MDC would never rule Zimbabwe, Robert Mugabe however, had found that he had been fighting from an ever tighter corner. His own Zanu-PF party has been riven by splits and defections, and the African Union and SADC had started to ratchet up the critical rhetoric of Robert Mugabe's regime both in advance of the second round of presidential voting, and following Robert Mugabe's proclaimed victory. The regime was becoming increasingly isolated internationally, which reduced Robert Mugabe's political options.

Forced into negotiations with the opposition MDC, which were mediated by South Africa's President Thabo Mbeki, the two main political parties announced a power-sharing agreement on 12 September. Both parties rushed to claim victory – Zanu-PF claiming Mugabe still retains power, and MDC arguing that his influence has been cut. However, the terms of this agreement are still unfolding, and the implications for Zimbabwe and its people are still being deciphered.

Never-the-less, the agreement could herald the beginning of the end of Robert Mugabe's brutal regime. Although he will still head the cabinet, the deal contains elements which may reduce his power and could lead to the dismantling of his 28 year regime

Outlook

It remains to be seen how the economy will respond to both the power-sharing agreement and the government's recent last ditch attempts to regain economic control.

However, if the political agreement re-establishes effective rule of law and political pluralism, and if Zimbabwe is able to successfully combat corruption, then there could yet be hope for Zimbabwe's social and economic woes to reduce. Unwavering Chinese investment interest, although uncomfortable for the West, could play a part in this. Foreign aid will also play a major role, and although it is as yet unclear how the international community will respond financially to the new political agreement, aid flows will increase dramatically as the international community seeks to rebuild this failed nation. Other than feeding the starving, improvements will be needed in availability of health care and educational opportunities, and the economy will require substantial rebuilding; it is hard to make a dependable estimate about how long any of this might take.

Risk assessment

Politics	Poor
Economy	Poor
Regional stability	Fair

COUNTRY PROFILE

Historical profile

In the eleventh century, the Shona people of Great Zimbabwe began trading with the Swahili traders on the Mozambique coast. Great Zimbabwe became southern Africa's richest and most powerful nation. In the 1500s, as Great Zimbabwe began to decline, the various Shona tribes broke up into autonomous states. Alliances between Shona states led to the formation of the Rozwi state.

1830–1890 European venturers and missionaries explored much of the south. Cecil John Rhodes was one who gained great wealth from the diamonds found in the area.

1834 The Ndebele people, push out of present day South Africa, invaded and established the Ndebele state.

1889 Rhodes founder of the British South Africa Company (BSA) and was granted the territories that today comprise Zimbabwe, under a British mandate as Southern Rhodesia.

1890 White migration began as settlers arrived.

1893 The BSA crushed a Ndebele uprising.

1922 The white minority voted to become a self-governing British dominion.

1930s Opposition to colonial rule began to grow.

1953 The Central African Federation (CAF) was created, merging Southern Rhodesia (Zimbabwe), Northern Rhodesia (Zambia) and Nyasaland (Malawi).

1960s The Zimbabwe African People's Union (Zapu, mainly Ndebele) and the Zimbabwe African National Union (Zanu mainly Shona) were formed.

1963 The CAF collapsed after Zambia and Malawi elected to become separate independent states.

1964 Ian Smith of the Rhodesian Front (RF) became prime minister. He gained independence from Britain with an electoral system that would preserve white minority rule.

1965 The RF made a unilateral declaration of independence (UDI). Despite international sanctions, Smith managed to keep his regime intact until 1980, with the support of apartheid South Africa and Portugal's colonialist regime in Mozambique. Zapu and Zanu began a campaign of guerrilla warfare.

1976 Although Zanu and Zapu formed the Patriotic Front (PF) alliance, co-operation between the two remained limited. The civil war continued and intensified towards the end of the 1970s.
1979 A new constitution, favourable to the PF, was drawn up at Lancaster House in the UK.
1980 Robert Mugabe's Zanu party won the general election and Zimbabwe gained independence from Britain. Mugabe became prime minister. Opposition leader Joshua Nkomo was appointed to the cabinet.
1982 Nkomo was sacked after Mugabe accused him of plotting to overthrow the government. Zapu was largely destroyed by the North Korean-trained Fifth Brigade which Mugabe sent into Matabeleland. According to the Catholic church a systematic campaign of terror was carried out against the rural population.
1987 Zanu and Zapu put their differences behind them and merged to form the Zimbabwe African National Union-Patriotic Front (Zanu-PF). Mugabe changed the constitution and became executive president.
1997 The economy crashed due to concerns about compensation payments to former guerrillas and the consequences of seizing 1,480 of mostly white-owned farms. Mass, violent demonstrations ensued.
1998 A national general strike due to soaring food prices, gained 80 per cent commitment. Mugabe decided, without consulting parliament, to intervene in the war in Democratic Republic of Congo (DRC) by sending troops.
2000 So-called 'squatters' seized hundreds of white-owned farms in a campaign of intimidation. Mugabe lost a referendum vote for constitutional amendments. Zanu-PF won the parliamentary election by a narrow majority, against the Movement for Democratic Change's (MDC). Protests in Harare, against rises in food prices and demanding Mugabe's resignation, turned into riots.
2001 The finance minister declared that foreign reserves had run out. The World Bank and IMF cut aid due to ongoing land seizure programme. A list of 2,030 white-owned farms required to be handed over under the new land-acquisition law, was published.
2002 New legislation outlawed criticism of the president and gave sweeping powers to the police to maintain public order. The EU imposed sanctions on 20 members of the Zimbabwean government, including the president, after its team of election observers was expelled. Robert Mugabe was re-elected in controversial circumstances. His opponent, Morgan Tsvangirai, was arrested on trumped up charges of treason. Zimbabwe was suspended from the Commonwealth. The opposition failed in its legal challenge to the election results. Media freedom was curtailed.
2003 The currency was devalued by 93 per cent. The US imposed economic sanctions on President Mugabe and 76 other high-ranking government officials, freezing their assets and barring Americans from conducting business with them. Zimbabwe withdrew from The Commonwealth after it refused to end Zimbabwe's suspension, citing Mugabe's election-rigging and persecution of dissidents.
2004 After their plane was impounded in Harare, 70 mercenaries planning a coup in Equatorial Guinea, were detained and charged. Canaan Banana, Zimbabwe's first black president, died.
2005 The ruling Zanu-PF was re-elected, with an increased majority; the opposition MDC claimed the elections were rigged. Thousands of shanty homes and businesses were demolished by the government, and around 200,000 people made homeless. The government passed a number of constitutional amendments, including the re-introduction of a 66-seat upper house (Senate). Treason charges against Morgan Tsvangirai, leader of the opposition, were dropped. Elections to the upper house were held and as expected the ruling Zanu-PF won 43 out of 50 seats. The Consumer Council reported that the cost of buying groceries increased almost 10-fold during the year; bread rose by some 1,157 per cent.
2006 Annual inflation rate was 1,042.9 per cent, rose by 129 percentage points in one month. The Zimbabwe dollar was devalued by 60 per cent; at the same time the central bank dropped three zeros from the currency as new bank notes were issued. The annual inflation rate reached 1,204.6 per cent.
2007 The annunal rate of inflation was 1,593.6 per cent, in January, having jumped by 45.4 per cent in one month. In February, the central bank governor stated the informal exchange rate was Z$9,000–10,000 per US$1. By March, the unconfirmed inflation rate was 2,200 per cent. On 1 July, the inflation rate was estimated by domestic bank officials to be 15,000 per cent. On 1 August, a new Z$200,000 bank note was introduced in an attempt to tackle Zimbabwe's hyper-inflation. Inflation jumped to 7,638 per cent in July, despite government orders to shopkeepers to cut prices. Unemployment was estimated at 80 per cent. In September, Constitutional Amendment Bill number 18 was passed by parliament. A final compromise between the ruling Zanu-PF and the opposition MDC had agreed a redrawing of electoral boundaries and an increased number of parliamentary members; the amendment also agreed that the next presidential election would be held in 2008 to coincide with parliamentary elections, and parliament be allowed to chose Mugabe's successor should he retire mid-term (which, as Zanu-PF holds a majority, in effect allows Mugabe to pick his own successor). The Bill was signed into law on 30 October. British Airways, the last foreign long-haul airline flying to Zimbabwe, flew its last flight out of Harare on 28 October. The RBZ raised the maximum limit on cheques accepted for clearing to Z$500 million. Former prime minister Ian Smith, who had declared UDI in 1965, died on 20 November. Robert Mugabe was endorsed as the Zanu-PF presidential candidate in December. The official inflation rate was 8,000 per cent, in December but the official statistician declared that with the lack of goods in the shops it was impossible to determine an accurate inflation rate. President Mugabe suspended the attorney general on 16 December.
2008 A new Z$10 million note was introduced on 25 January 2008, valued at around US$3.90 on the black market. The new notes, officially called bearer cheques, were introduced in an attempt to stabilise the economy. The official inflation rate was 100,000 per cent in January; the black-market exchange rate was Z$7.5 million to US$1. Around three million people have left the country in search of work abroad while about 80 per cent of the population live in poverty. The Mutambara faction of the MDC announced that they would form a united front with Simba Makoni, the former finance minister to oppose Mugabe in the presidential elections. By mid-March the unoffical rate for a US$ had reached between Z$30 million and Z$35 million (compared to the official rate of around Z$31,250). In parliamentary elections held on 29 March, the opposition MDC won 51.3 per cent (109 seats out of 210), the ruling Zanu-PF won 45.9 per cent (97), independents 2.25 per cent (one). By-elections, due to the death of candidates, in three seats will be held at a later date. The RBZ introduced a Z$50 million note on 3 April and increased the maximum withdrawal limit to Z$5 billion per day. A re-count of 23 parliamentary seats in April confirmed an overall win for the MDC. The result of the presidential election was withheld until a 'verification and collation' process was completed by the electoral commission. While President Mugabe was out of the country attending a UN summit on the ongoing global food crisis he banned international aid groups and non-governmental agencies from distributing food until they had re-applied for

permits. Almost three weeks before the 27 June presidential elections international observers from Human Rights Watch stated there was a 'campaign of violence' which had 'extinguished any hope of free and fair run-off presidential elections'. Senior officials loyal to Robert Mugabe were linked to violent incidents and with torture camps run by Zanu-PF. African criticism of the violence during the presidential election was voiced by a troika of observer states (Tanzania, Angola and Swaziland – from the Southern African Development Community (SADC)), which was monitoring the hustings. It stated that violence was 'escalating throughout Zimbabwe'. The official rebuttal claimed the statement was biased. On 22 June Morgan Tsvangirai pulled out of the presidential election, citing the violence perpetrated against his supporters. The US announced that it would not recognise the result of the 27 June run-off presidential election, stating that a credible victory could not be claimed by Mugabe while opposition members were being killed. Tsvangirai called on the African Union and SADC to intervene and resolve the situation. Nelson Mandela, in a speech at an official dinner to celebrate his 90th birthday, condemned the violence and criticised the condition of Zimbabwe as a 'failure of leadership'. Mugabe claimed victory on 28 June and was inaugurated on 29 June for his sixth term in office. Thabo Mbeki held talks in Harare with President Mugabe on 5 July. Morgan Tsvangirai refused to attend the talks saying that by attending talks held at State House he would be acknowledging Mugabe's presidency. In May, the central bank issued a Z$500 million banknote to ease the cash shortage. The official inflation rate in June was just over 11,250,000 per cent. A new, Z$100 billion note was introduced on 19 July. On 22 July Mugabe and Tsvangirai shook hands and signed a Memorandum of Understanding (MoU) that could lead the way to a lasting political settlement, although initially all that had been agreed was in effect 'talks about talks'. Parliament was opened on 26 August, five months after the disputed polls. Opposition MPs heckled President Mugabe as he gave his opening speech. MDC chairman, Lovemore Moyo was elected speaker of parliament on 25 August.

Political structure

Constitution

The constitution was first instigated in 1979, based on articles agreed in the Lancaster House accord. An amendment in 1987 resulted in the appointment of an executive president as Head of State.

The election laws were amended in January 2002 to ban independent election monitors and deny voting rights to Zimbabweans living abroad.

Further amendments to the constitution, in 2005, included the re-introduction of an upper house – the Senate. The Senate has 66 members – 50 members elected for five-year terms (five from each of the 10 provinces), 10 traditional chiefs and six members appointed by the president.

Constitutional Amendment Bill number 18 became law on 30 October 2007. Under the Bill the next presidential election would be brought forward to 2008 so as to coincide with the parliamentary elections. Seats in the lower house were increased from 150 to 210, and in the Senate from 84 to 93. The most controversial admendment was to allow Mugabe to choose his successor, which would be voted on by the then Zanu-PF-dominated parliament.

Form of state

Republic

The executive

Executive power is vested in the president (elected by universal suffrage every six years), vice presidents and cabinet. Both the vice presidents and cabinet are appointed by the president.

National legislature

Legislative power is vested in the parliament, comprising a 150-member House of Assembly (lower house) and a 66-member Senate (upper house), both elected for five years. The lower house is made up of 120 directly elected members; 20 seats are given to presidential appointees including eight reserved for provincial governors; 10 seats are for representatives of tribal chiefs, chosen by their peers. The Senate comprises 50 members elected by popular vote for five-year terms. Six seats are reserved for presidential appointees and 10 seats are for representatives of tribal chiefs.

Legal system

Based on the constitution and English common law.

Last elections

29 March (parliamentary and presidential – first round); 27 June 2008 (presidential runoff).

Results: Parliamentary (house of assembly): MDC won 51.3 per cent (109 seats out of 210), Zanu-PF won 45.9 per cent (97), Independent 2.25 per cent (one). (Senate) MDC 30 seats, Zanu-PF 30. Presidential (runoff): Robert Mugabe (the only candidate) won 90 per cent of the vote; turnout was 42.4 per cent.

Next elections

29 March 2008 (presidential, parliamentary and council)

Political parties

Ruling party

Zimbabwe African National Union-Patriotic Front (Zanu-PF) (re-elected 31 Mar 2005)

Main opposition party

Movement for Democratic Change (MDC)

Population

11.73 million (2007)*

Last census: August 2002: 11,631,657

Population density: 29 inhabitants per square km. Urban population: 36 per cent (1995–2001).

Annual growth rate: 1.1 per cent 1994–2004 (WHO 2006)

Internally Displaced Persons (IDP)

100,000–200,000 (UNHCR 2004)

Ethnic make-up

Shona (75 per cent) (including the Zezuru clan (18 per cent) and the Karanga clan (22 per cent)); Ndebele (18 per cent); white (1 per cent). There are several minor ethnic groups, and a small number of inhabitants of Asian or mixed racial descent.

Religions

Dual Christian/indigenous beliefs (50 per cent), Christian (25 per cent), indigenous beliefs (24 per cent).

Education

The educational system was one of the best in the region with universal primary school enrolment and secondary education reaching about 50 per cent of those eligible.

The worsening public finances has put the country's education facilities at risk as the government rationalises non-military expenditure. With increases in education levies of between 400 per cent and 2,000 per cent in 2003–04, impoverished families are increasingly unable to find the money to send their children to school. Primary enrolment has declined from 93 per cent in 2000 to 65 per cent in 2003. When schools reassembled for the winter term 2004, they were forced to turn away 800,000 orphans because President Mugabe's government has run out of money to pay their fees.

Literacy rate: 90 per cent adult rate; 98 per cent youth rate (15–24) (Unesco 2005).

Compulsory years: Five to 12.

Enrolment rate: 95.0 per cent gross primary enrolment; 44.5 per cent gross secondary enrolment, of relevant age groups (including repeaters) (World Bank).

Pupils per teacher: 37 in primary schools.

Health

Per capita total expenditure on health (2003) was US$132; of which per capita government spending was US$47, at the international dollar rate, (WHO 2006).

The state of Zimbabwe's healthcare was mixed in the 1990s. Spending on private healthcare (such as private household expenditure and insurance) averaged 3.7 per cent of GDP.
Estimates in 2002 showed that 24 per cent of health workers' posts were vacant and 73 per cent of health facilities had no drugs.
In 2005 the UK gave over US$17.9 million to UN and non-governmental agencies (NGO) to provide food for five million people affected by food shortages. Around US$1 million was allocated to help those who had returned to their rural homes after being evicted under the government's Operation Murambatsvina.
An outbreak of polio in Namibia and a related disease in Botswana, in June 2006, prompted an international alert for increased vigilance in surrounding countries.

HIV/Aids

The UN stated, in April 2005, that one million children have been made orphans and another 160,000 would lose a parent in 2005. Unicef called on donor countries to look beyond the political administration of Zimbabwe and focus on the victims of the disease. Only US$14 is contributed for each Zimbabwean compared to US$68 for citizens of neighbouring Namibia or US$111 in Mozambique. With one of the highest infection rates in the region, with an estimated 1.8 million people HIV positive in 2003 Zimbabwe's sick can ill-afford international neglect. Poor governance, profligacy and the politicisation of relief by President Mugabe has left donors averse to giving more. The HIV prevalence rate for females aged 15–24 years is 33 per cent and the incidence of mother-to-child transmission of HIV/Aids is 12 per cent, and these pose another serious impediment to Zimbabwe's embattled population.

HIV prevalence: 24.65 per cent aged 15–49 in 2003 (World Bank)
Life expectancy: 36 years, 2004 (WHO 2006)
Fertility rate/Maternal mortality rate: 3.4 births per woman, 2004 (WHO 2006); maternal mortality 400 per 100,000 live births (World Bank).
Child (under 5 years) mortality rate (per 1,000): 78 per 1,000 live births; 13 per cent of children under aged five are malnourished (World Bank).
Head of population per physician: 0.16 physicians per 1,000 people, 2004 (WHO 2006)

Welfare

Many companies operated some form of social security plan for their employees, which usually included medical aid but the deteriorating economy has curtailed welfare measures. Workers may individually contribute to private insurance and medical aid funds.

Main cities

Harare (capital, estimated population 1.5 million in 2005), Bulawayo (717,670), Chitungwiza (346,582), Mutare (168,112), Gweru (146,339), Epworth (115,787).

Languages spoken

Local languages, Shona and Ndebele spoken by the majority of the population, are written languages and are taught in schools.

Official language/s

English, Shona and Ndebele

Media

The Ministry of Information and Publicity exerts tight control of the media. The Access to Information law makes it an offence to report on Zimbabwe unless state-registered; only Zimbabwean citizens or residents of the country are eligible for registration. Foreign journalists are only allowed into the country to cover specific, usually non-political events. Through these measures press freedom has been seriously curtailed. Not only are there repressive laws, but violence by either supporters or members of Zanu-PF, have effectively silenced reporters and distorted news and views. In 2007, the Freedom House annual survey showed Zimbabwe had earned the lowest possible score for political rights and civil liberties including, press freedom.
Other news agencies: ZimOnline (from South Africa): www.zimonline.co.za
Zimbabwe Daily News online (from UK): www.zimdaily.com
The Zimbabwe Times (from US): www.thezimbabwetimes.com
Jeune Afrique (in French): www.jeuneafrique.com

Press

Spiralling costs have pushed up the price of production and publications and caused serious falls in circulation numbers.
Dailies: Government-owned newspapers include The Herald (www.herald.co.zw), and The Chronicle (www.chronicle.co.zw), published in Bulawayo. The Daily Mirror (www.zimmirror.co.zw) is independent. A newspaper, critical of the Mugabe government,The Daily News and its weekend edition, was suspended and in February 2008 the owner newspaper group applied for re-instatement.
Weeklies: There are more newspapers published at the weekend than daily, including The Zimbabwe Independent (www.thezimbabweindependent.com),The Standard (www.thezimbabwestandard.com), The Saturday Mirror and The Sunday Mirror (www.zimmirror.co.zw).
Business: The privately owned The Financial Gazette (www.fingaz.co.zw) is a weekly newspaper, published in Harare. Daily newspapers have sections given over to business and economics. The Farmer a weekly covers agricultural matters.

Broadcasting

The national, Zimbabwe Broadcasting Corporation (ZBC) is state-run.
Radio: For most Zimbabweans radio is the only source of information and news. ZBC operates four services – Radio 1 (in English), 2 (in Shona and Ndebele) 4 (an educational channel) and Radio 3 is a commercial station aimed at the young. There are no private radio stations although Zimbabwe is targeted by a number of overseas broadcasts. The Voice of the People (VOP) (www.vopradio.co.zw), operated by former staff of ZBC, broadcasts from Madagascar.
Television: ZBC operates one TV channel. Satellite TV is available from South Africa.

News agencies

Other news agencies: ZimOnline (from South Africa): www.zimonline.co.za
Zimbabwe Daily News online (from UK): www.zimdaily.com
The Zimbabwe Times (from US): www.thezimbabwetimes.com
Jeune Afrique (in French): www.jeuneafrique.com

Economy

The Zimbabwean economy is in ruins. The economy at the domestic level has stagnated and at the international level is constrained by hyperinflation and the black market. Every year since 1999 has seen negative growth and accelerating inflation. During that period, economic life has become characterised by food shortages, a collapsing currency, lack of foreign exchange, and hyperinflation. By 2008 the economy was in serious hyper-inflation with a new Z$10 million note introduced on 25 January, valued at around US$3.90 on the black market. The new notes, officially called bearer cheques, were introduced in an attempt to stabilise the economy. Around three million people have left the country in search of work abroad while about 80 per cent of the population live in poverty. In May 2008, the central bank issued a Z$500 million banknote to ease the cash shortage and in July the official annual inflation rate was 2,200,000 per cent while the informal exchange rate was Z$75 billion per US$1.
Zimbabwe was largely self-sufficient agriculturally in the 1990s. The government's programme of land resettlement –

dispossessing white farmers and allocating their lands to black Zimbabweans, who were largely inexperienced as farmers – has since 2001 resulted in the decline of the sector to the point that, not only has Zimbabwe's capacity to produce for the export market, especially tobacco, been impaired, but the country can no longer feed itself. Foodstuffs began disappearing from the markets in 2004 and Zimbabwe has become dependent on imports and international aid.

Minerals now constitute the main export commodities and are the mainstay of the economy. Zimbabwe has the second-largest reserves of platinum, which is easy to extract and has lower production costs than the first-ranking South Africa. Gold-mining accounts for around 50 per cent of mineral output and is a major export commodity; in early 2007, the mining companies warned that the sector was on the verge of collapse. The mineral reserves have attracted the attention of the Chinese, who are assiduously investing in Africa, and may have backed the government diplomatically and financially and allowed it to repay IMF US$120 million loan in August 2005.

In his bi-annual monetary policy speech in October 2007, the governor of the Reserve Bank of Zimbabwe (RBZ), Gideon Gono, announced a rise in the bank's main lending rate to 800 per cent, from 650 per cent.

External trade

Zimbabwe is a member of the Common Market for Eastern and Southern Africa (Comesa), but does not operate a free trade area with the other member states as the economy is too weak to maintain the union. It is also a member of the Southern African Development Community (SADC), the objectives of which include reducing trade barriers, achieving regional development and economic growth and evolving common systems and institutions.

Zimbabwe has some of the world's largest reserves in minerals including coal and asbestos with ores in platinum, copper, nickel, gold, iron and chromite. However, the political situation has discouraged virtually all direct foreign investment and mining production has not been maintained or grown. Traditional exports in tobacco have dropped dramatically since 2000, from 237,000 tonnes to 50,000 tonnes in 2006; cotton is the primary agricultural export.

Zimbabwe, in 2007, was in the grip of hyperinflation and trade was severely hampered as the currency lost its value at home and abroad and all goods imported had to be paid for in hard currencies. A lack of foreign exchange led to a critical shortage of imported fuel and electricity. The grey economy, with trade in black market goods, began to grow accordingly.

Tourism was a vital export earner, but the sector contracted due to the poor image of Zimbabwe abroad. Remittances, especially in US dollars, have become a necessity for trade within the country. Exports still exist, both primary and manufactured, but intermittent energy supplies hamper production.

Imports

Main imports are petroleum, machinery and vehicles, other manufactures, chemicals and food.

Main sources: South Africa (46.8 per cent total, 2006), China (6.0 per cent), Botswana (4.9 per cent).

Exports

Main exports are cotton, timber, chrome alloy, gold, ferroalloys and some textiles.

Main destinations: South Africa (31.5 per cent total, 2006), Zambia (7.8 per cent), China (6.2 per cent).

Agriculture

Farming

Agriculture used to be the dominant sector of the economy. Since 1999 government policy has skewed typical patterns.Whereas Zimbabwe was almost self-sufficient in food with annual exports of around US$70 million, in 2004, imports of food were estimated at US$280 million, in addition to the immense aid provided through the World Food Programme. Since 2000, the government has appropriated white-owned farm property with little or no compensation. Over 200,000 black agricultural workers lost their jobs when corporate and white-owned farms were confiscated and the land given to 124,000 black families. The government has not sought to combine land transfers with the necessary capital and expertise to run the farms and this has resulted in the virtual destruction of the commercial farming sector. The agricultural sector is now firmly small scale, poorly invested, subsistence farming. It is estimated that 85 per cent of Zimbabwe households rely on farm wages for food and other needs.

In June 2004, President Mugabe's government said that, in future, all land would be owned by the state and then leased back to farmers.

Concerted measures employed to ensure increased agricultural production are hampered by a lack of farm machinery and foreign exchange to purchase the necessary equipment.

It is estimated that the country has to import 250,000 tonnes of maize to meet expected shortfalls.

Estimated crop production in 2005 included: 1,187,300 metric tonnes (t) cereals in total, 900,000t maize, 190,000t cassava, 140,000t wheat, 25,000t barley, 84,000t soya beans, 3,290,000t sugar cane 265,000t seed cotton, 90,770t oilcrops, 65,000 tobacco leaves, 85,000t bananas, 22,000t tea, 1,752t pepper spice, 225,250t fruit in total, 161,775t vegetable in total. Estimated livestock production included: 207,063t meat in total, 96,750t beef, 27,500t pig meat, 12,840t goat meat, 32,000t game meat, 36,607t poultry, 22,000t eggs, 248,000t milk, 8,600t cattle hides, 2,140t goatskins.

Fishing

Despite the existence of five major flood plains, the country has little fishery potential. There are no natural lakes of any significant size and large man-made reservoirs are primarily used for hydro-electric and farming purposes.

Lake Kariba accounts for approximately 80 per cent of the country's total fish production. The industrial fishery thrives on fresh water sardines (kapenta) which were introduced to the lake from Lake Tanganyika. Lake Kariba also supports an artisanal gillnet fishery, which is based on 40 indigenous species near the lake's shores. This type of activity is important for the local economy, as most of the land available along the shore is unsuitable for crop cultivation.

The catch from reservoirs other than Lake Kariba is typically estimated at 2,000 tonnes per year. The bulk of the catch from these small reservoirs is not usually marketed but kept for domestic consumption. The catch from small dams typically constitutes another 2,000 tonnes, while rivers and fish farms are estimated to yield 1,000 tonnes of fish.

Forestry

Timber production is primarily used for fuelwood, which provides three-quarters of domestic energy supplies. The country's main exported forest product is sandalwood.

Timber imports in 2004 were US$42 million, while exports amounted to US$30 million.

Timber production in 2004 included 9,107,000 cubic metre (cum) roundwood, 992,400cum industrial roundwood, 397,000cum sawnwood, 786,000cum sawlogs and veneer logs, 94,000cum pulpwood, 8,115,200cum woodfuel; 80,000 tonnes (t) paper and paperboard.

Industry and manufacturing

Zimbabwe's industrial sector was one of the most advanced and diversified in sub-Saharan Africa. Since 2000, the sector has been undermined by capital flight, a lack of foreign exchange, an overvalued exchange rate, severe fuel shortages and the constant threat of forced nationalisation. The largely liberalised textile sector is also struggling against competition from countries such as South Africa where subsidies and tariffs operate as barriers to free trade.

Other problems include a lack of capacity which can only be improved with increased foreign investment. As supporters of the Zanu-PF begin to attack foreign companies operating in Zimbabwe, prospects for industrial expansion are bleak. Successful and successive general stikes were called through 2004–05 to register the growing plight of low wages.

Zimbabwe's heavy industries are also facing hard times, despite being targetted by the government as essential to developing import substitutes, which would reduce the loss in foreign exchange. In recent years, Zimbabwe has experienced an expansion in the chemicals and cement sectors.

Growth in industrial production in 2004 was a negative -3.5 per cent in 2004.

Tourism

Tourism has stagnated as Zimbabwe is becoming increasingly viewed as a pariah state. Repressive regimes do not attract much tourism and Zimbabwe is losing much foreign exchange from this potentially lucrative industry. The continuing perception in important markets, such as the US, UK and Australia is that Zimbabwe is unsafe, compounded by government travel warnings. Hotels have become dependent on NGOs for business, but this is threatened by proposed government legislation to curb NGO activity.

Government statistics are unreliable. The World Travel and Tourism Council regards the country as one of the lowest ranked for contributions to national GDP – 1.4 per cent in 2005. The sector may grow, but not from Western foreign tourists. The expectation is that tourism will decline by around 3.3 per cent between 2006–15. The tourist sector is estimated to have attracted 8.4 per cent of total capital investment but this is a 2.6 per cent fall on previous years.

A symptom of the sector's malaise is the collapse of Victoria Falls as a centre, since tourists find that they can view the falls from Zambia, where tourism has benefited considerably from its neighbour's troubles.

Zimbabwe is courting the fledgling Asian market, especially China, which has granted Approved Destination Status to the country.

Mining

The mining sector accounts for around 8 per cent of GDP and employs 5 per cent of the workforce. Many minerals, including chromite, copper and nickel ores, iron ore, tin ore, gold ore, phosphate rock, limestone and iron pyrites are converted to downstream products. The main exceptions are coal, phosphate rock, pyrites and limestone, which, along with a substantial proportion of iron, steel, copper and asbestos production are sold on the domestic market. Import substitution is encouraged. However, high fuel prices have increased costs markedly.

The government's policy on land and assets tenure has left foreign companies concerned that their assets could be seized without cause or warning. The 'economic empowerment provisions' require companies to sell a 20 per cent stake to local black investors and 30 per cent by 2015.

Illegal trade in gold has risen due to the low prices paid to small gold producers. In July 2006 Jack Murehwa (Chamber of Mines) said gold mining had shrunk from 24 tonnes a year to 11 because 'the government-set price was below the current market rates'.

Legislation to be agreed late in 2007 may force mining firms to give the government a free 25 per cent stake, as well as 26 per cent to Zimbabweans, to be paid for out of earnings.

Hydrocarbons

There are no proven oil deposits in Zimbabwe. Zimbabwe has no refining capacity and traditionally imports its oil from South Africa. The National Oil Company of Zimbabwe (Noczim) is responsible for supplying the country with oil, but supplies are unreliable due to a high fuel prices and its inability to pay its bills.

Coal is for domestic use only. Around 60 per cent of coal production is used for electricity generation. The Wankie Coal Company (WCC) is the country's only coal producer and is 40 per cent owned by the government. Annual production is typically around four million tonnes.

There are no proven natural gas deposits in Zimbabwe.

Energy

Coal provides 60 per cent of local electricity generating capacity with wood, oil and hydroelectric power providing the rest. Zimbabwe continues to face problems relating to the rising cost of oil and electricity imports. This has resulted in severe debts within the electricity sector and continual threats to the power supply.

Emphasis is on developing local energy resources, particularly coal and hydropower. Projects under way involve expansion of the huge Hwange coal field, including two new thermal power stations, and the building of hydroelectric stations on the Zambezi River.

The Zimbabwe Electricity Supply Authority (Zesa), which oversees generation, transmission and distribution of electricity, has plans for a number of projects aimed at rehabilitating existing power generators, as well as creating new ones. Zimbabwe is keen to co-operate with neighbouring states and will be largely helped by the growing ties within the Southern African Development Community (SADC). The government also has ambitious, and probably unrealistic, plans to provide hundreds of rural districts with electricity through solar power to provide lighting as well as helping rural industries.

Financial markets

Stock exchange

Zimbabwe's first stock exchange was formed in 1896, but lasted just six years. The current Zimbabwe Stock Exchange (ZSE) was founded in 1946 and was located in Bulawayo. In 1974, the Zimbabwe Stock Exchange Act was promulgated and the ZSE was relocated to Harare.

Banking and insurance

Before the economic crisis that began in 2000, Zimbabwe had a sophisticated banking system. Performance has been adversely affected by the macroeconomic environment, including the government's foreign exchange regime, negative interest rates and the high level of domestic borrowing.

The banking sector comprises the Reserve Bank of Zimbabwe (RBZ) (central bank), five commercial banks, four merchant banks, five finance houses (mainly engaged in hire purchase), two discount houses serving the money market, three building societies and the Post Office Savings Bank. In addition, state-owned corporations invest and lend for specific development purposes.

Central bank

Reserve Bank of Zimbabwe

Main financial centre

Harare

Time

GMT plus two hours

Geography

Zimbabwe is a landlocked country in southern central Africa. It is bounded by the Limpopo river and South Africa to the south, by the Zambezi river and Zambia to the north, by Mozambique to the east and by Botswana to the west.

The country falls into three geographical areas: the high veld, the low veld and the Eastern Highlands. The high veld comprises the major part of the country extending across the central area and rising gradually from the south-west to the north-east, with an average altitude of 1,200 metres. The two main cities, Harare (altitude 1,472 metres) and Bulawayo (

altitude 1,343 metres) lie in this area. The low veld comprises the Sabi-Limpopo valleys in the south and the Zambezi valley in the north including the spectacular Victoria Falls that form the border with Zambia. Further east the Zambezi is dammed for electricity generation at Kariba, forming a 250km long lake. The Eastern Highlands borders Mozambique and contains two ranges, the Chimanimani Mountains, with peaks reaching 2,436 metres, and the Inyanga Mountains, with peaks up to 2,595 metres.

Hemisphere

Southern

Climate

Most of the country is semi-tropical with day temperatures of 30 degrees Celsius (C), or slightly above on hot days in the rainy season, but falling as low as 0 degrees C at night in the dry winter season. Rainfall is largely confined to the months November to March and is subject to wide annual variations with considerable influence on agricultural production. Heavier rain falls in the Eastern Highlands.

Dress codes

Business dress is generally formal, suits or jacket with a tie and trousers for men. Many hotels and restaurants require smart casual attire, particularly in the evening, with some insisting on jacket and tie, thus excluding denim jeans. Women normally dress conservatively in European style.

Entry requirements

Passports

Required by all.

Visa

Are required by all, except citizens of countries with reciprocal visa-free entry, see www.zimbabweembassy-uk.com and follow link to Consular, then Visa Requirements then Category A, B or C for further information.

Contact the consular section of the nearest embassy for further advice and requirements for a visa, and confirmation the visitor requires a visa. All visitors must have an onward/return ticket and sufficient money for their stay.

Currency advice/regulations

The import and export of local currency is limited to Z$15,000. The import of foreign currency is unlimited but must be declared in writing; export is limited to the amount declared.

The new Zimbabwe dollar went into circulation on 21 August 2006, whereby three zeros were dropped (Z$1,000,000 became Z$1,000). The new notes are now the only legal tender.

Travellers cheques are accepted in banks and major hotels.

Customs

Personal items are duty-free.

Agricultural plant material including seeds and bulbs and fresh meat require an import licence.

Prohibited imports

Illegal drugs, honey, pornographic literature, assault knives and imitation firearms.

Health (for visitors)

Mandatory precautions

Yellow fever vaccination certificate if travelling from an infected area.

Advisable precautions

Vaccinations for diphtheria, tetanus, polio, hepatitis A and typhoid are recommended. Other vaccinations that may be advised include tuberculosis and hepatitis B and cholera. HIV/Aids is prevalent.

Anti-malarial prophylaxis is necessary for the Zambezi valley throughout the year and elsewhere from November–June. Bilharzia is endemic, to avoid the risk, only use well maintained, chlorinated swimming pools. Water precautions are necessary, use only boiled or bottled water. Local dairy products should be avoided as milk is unpasteurised; vegetables, meat and fish should be well cooked and eaten hot. Fruit should be peeled. Sun-screen should be used regularly.

Medical services are poor throughout the country and the services of private doctors may be charged in full before treatment begins. Medical insurance is essential, including emergency evacuation, and an adequate supply of personal medicines is necessary.

A reasonable precaution could include a first aid kit with a sterile needle kit and disposable syringes.

Hotels

Several hotels of various standards are available in the main cities, rated from one to five stars by the Tourist Board. Most of the larger ones are air-conditioned. The government imposes a bed tax per person per night, and it is usual to tip 10 per cent.

Credit cards

Major credit and charge cards are widely accepted. Hyperinflation has led to long queues while clients make several withdrawals at ATMs that were designed to issue a maximum of 40 bank notes.

Public holidays (national)

Fixed dates

1 Jan (New Year's Day), 18 Apr (Independence Day), 1 May (Labour Day), 25 May (Africa Day), 22 Dec (Unity Day), 25–26 Dec (Christmas).

Holidays that fall on the weekend are given in lieu.

Variable dates

Good Friday, Easter Monday, Heroes' Day and Defence Force's Day (third Mon and Tue Aug)

Working hours

Banking

Mon–Fri: 0830–1500, (Wed) 0830–1300; Sat: 0830–1130.

Business

Mon–Fri: 0745/0830–1600/1700.

Government

Mon–Fri: 0745/0830–1600/1700.

Shops

Mon–Fri: 0800–1300, 1400–1700; Wed half day. Sat: 0800–1200.

Telecommunications

Mobile/cell phones

There are 900 GSM services available in main towns and cities.

Electricity supply

220V 50Hz with either UK style flat, or round, three-pin plugs.

Social customs/useful tips

Zimbabweans generally rise early and go to bed early, particularly on weekdays. Punctuality is generally appreciated in business circles. Hospitality, particularly for meals, is widely offered and may be freely reciprocated. The formal address (Mr, Mrs or Miss with surname) is usual and a given-name terms are only adopted on closer acquaintance. The giving or receiving of gifts, other than between personal friends, is not customary. No particular proscriptions apply to eating, drinking or smoking and there are no particular religious observances or taboos. Tipping (for example, 10 per cent of a restaurant bill) is common.

It is unwise to photograph major government buildings, military personnel or equipment without prior official permission. Photographers should bring their own film as it is not generally available locally.

Security

Physical attacks, car-jacking and credit card fraud are increasing problems. Foreign nationals who are perceived to be wealthy could be targetted by criminals operating in the vicinity of hotels, restaurants and shopping malls in Harare and other major tourist areas. Caution should be exercised at all times.

Visitors should make two photocopies of the biographic page of their passport; one copy should be retained at home and the other carried at all times for identification purposes.

Getting there

Air

British Airways stopped flying to Harare after its flight to London on 28 October 2007.

National airline: Air Zimbabwe
International airport/s: Harare International Airport (HRE), 12km from city; post office, restaurant, duty-free shop and bank/bureau de change.
Bulawayo Airport (BUQ), 24km from city.
Other airport/s: Victoria Falls Airport (VFA); Kariba Airport (KAB).
Airport tax: Departure tax varies depending on the destination; all taxes have to be paid in US dollars. To and from UK US$52, to South Africa US$31, to China US$11, to Dubai US$8.
Surface
Road: Direct routes from Zambia via Victoria Falls, Kariba and Chirundu. Entry from South Africa at Beitbridge and from Botswana at Plumtree. There are three main routes from Mozambique in the east. Most of the border posts are closed from 1800 to 0600 hours every day although specific hours vary.
Rail: There are regular services to Zambia via the Victoria Falls and from Botswana via Bulawayo. There is a rail connection from Beira and Maputo (Mozambique). Rail travel from South Africa was suspended in 1999.

Getting about
National transport
Air: Regular inexpensive daily flights to all major destinations.
Road: Network of over 85,000km, of which about one-quarter are classed as main or secondary roads and half are surfaced with gravel. Good roads connect major towns. Nationwide petrol shortages may impede travel.
Buses: Good inter-city network operated by Express Motorways Africa Ltd, Zimbabwe Omnibus Company, plus numerous local operators. Express coach services from Harare to Bulawayo, Mutare, Kariba, Chipinge, Masvingo. Advisable to book in advance.
Rail: National Railways of Zimbabwe operate services between Harare and Gweru, Bulawayo, Victoria Falls, Mutare, Masvingo, Chinhoyi and intermediate towns (there are also certain places served by branch lines). Two classes – some trains carry restaurant cars and couchette sleeping accommodation. (NB Bedding is charged). Advisable to book tickets (and bedding) in advance. The system is badly rundown and lacks investment.
Water: Ferries cross Lake Kariba.
City transport
Taxis: These are not usually hailed in the street, they are available at ranks near main hotels. A 10 per cent tip is usual.
Buses, trams & metro: Urban services in some centres can be sporadic.
Car hire
Self-drive cars are available in main cities and at Harare airport, although their condition may not be well maintained. However, they are a useful method of transport as most main intercity roads tend to be of good quality, always maintain an adequate supply of fuel as shortages may leave a traveller stranded. Traffic drives on the left and a foreign or international driving licence is acceptable during short visits.

BUSINESS DIRECTORY

The addresses listed below are a selection only. While World of Information makes every endeavour to check these addresses, we cannot guarantee that changes have not been made, especially to telephone numbers and area codes. We would welcome any corrections.

Telephone area codes
The international direct dialling code (IDD) for Zimbabwe is + 263, followed by area code and subscriber's number:

Bulawayo	9	Harare	4
Chiredze	31	Mutare	20

Chambers of Commerce
Zimbabwe National Chamber of Commerce, 115 Nelson Mandela Avenue, PO Box 1934, Harare (tel: 799-692; fax: 799-695; e-mail: info@zncc.co.zw).

Banking
Barclays Bank of Zimbabwe Ltd, PO Box 1279, Barclay House, Jason Moyo Avenue/First Street, Harare (tel: 758-280/1/2/3; fax: 752-913).

First Merchant Bank of Zimbabwe, PO Box 2786, FMB House, 67 Samora Machel Avenue, Harare (tel: 703-071, 727-294; fax: 250-682).

Merchant Bank of Central Africa, PO Box 3200, 14th Floor, Old Mutual Centre, Third Street, Jason Moyo Avenue, Harare (tel: 738-081; fax: 708-005).

NMB Bank, PO Box 2564, 1st Floor, Unity Court, Corner 1st Street/Union Avenue, Harare (tel: 759-651/9, 759-601/6; fax: 759-648).

Stanbic Bank Zimbabwe Ltd, PO Box 300, Stanbic Bank Centre, 59 Samora Machel Avenue, Harare (tel: 759-480/3, 759-471/9, 759-479; fax: 749-030).

Standard Chartered Bank Zimbabwe Ltd, PO Box 373, John Boyne House, 38 Speke Ave, Harare (tel: 752-864; fax: 758-076).

Zimbabwe Banking Corporation Ltd, PO Box 3198, Zimbank House, 46 Speke Avenue, Harare (tel: 757-471/94; fax: 757-497, 751-741).

Central bank
Reserve Bank of Zimbabwe, PO Box 1283, 80 Samora Machel Avenue, Harare (tel: 703-000; fax: 707-800; e-mail: rbzmail@rbz.co.zw).

Travel information
Air Zimbabwe, PO Box AP1, Harare Airport, Harare (tel: 575-111; fax: 575-068).

National tourist organisation offices
Zimbabwe Tourism Authority, 9th Floor, Kopje Plaza, 1 Jason Moyo Avenue, Cnr Jason Moyo/Rotten Row, PO Box CY286, Causeway, Harare (tel: 758-730/34, 752-570, 758-712/14; fax: 758-726/28; e-mail: mktg@ztazim.org; zta@africaonline.co.zw; internet site: http://www.tourismzimbabwe.co.zw).

Ministries
Ministry of Agriculture, Ngungunyana Building 1, Borrowdale Road, P Bag 7701, Causeway, Harare (tel: 706-081, 700-596; fax: 734-646).

Ministry of Defence, Munhumutapa Building, Samora Machel Avenue, P Bag 7713, Causeway, Harare (tel: 700-155, 728-271).

Ministry of Education, Ambassador House, Union Avenue, PO Box CY121, Causeway, Harare (tel: 734-051, 734-067; fax: 734-075).

Ministry of Environment and Tourism, 14th Floor Karigamombe Centre, 53 Samora Machel Avenue, P Bag, 7753, Causeway, Harare (tel: 794-455, 704-701; fax: 794-450).

Ministry of Finance, Munhumutapa Building, Samora Machel Avenue, P Bag, 7705, Causeway, Harare (tel: 794-571, 796-191; fax: 792-750).

Ministry of Foreign Affairs, Munhumutapa Building, Samora Machel Avenue, PO Box 4240, Harare (tel: 727-005, 794-681; fax: 706-293).

Ministry of Health and Child Welfare, Kaguvi Building, 4th Street, PO Box CY198, Causeway, Harare (tel: 730-011, 794-411; fax: 793-634).

Ministry of Higher Education: Old Mutual Centre, 1st Floor, 3rd Street/J Moyo Avenue, PO Box UA 275, Union Avenue, Harare (tel: 702-361, 796-441; fax: 790-923, 728-730).

Ministry of Home Affairs, 11th Floor, Mukwati Building, P Bag 505D, Harare (tel: 723-653, 703-642; fax: 728-768).

Ministry of Industry and International Trade, 13th Floor, Mukwati Building, 4th Street/Livingston Avenue, P Bag 7708, Causeway, Harare (tel: 702-731, 729-801).

Ministry of Information, Posts and Telecommunications, 8th-11th Floor, Linquenda House, Baker Avenue, PO Box CY1276 & CY825, Causeway, Harare (tel: 703-891, 706-891; fax: 735-640).

Ministry of Justice, Legal and Parliamentary Affairs, Corner House, Leopold

Takawira Street, P Bag 7704, Causeway, Harare (tel: 790-902, 790-905; fax: 790-901).

Ministry of Lands and Water Development, Ngungunyana Building, 1 Borrowdale Road, P Bag 7701, Causeway, Harare (tel: 706-081, 700-596).

Ministry of Local Government, Rural and Urgan Development, 16th-20th Floors, Mukwati Building, P Bag 7706, Causeway, Harare (tel: 790-601, 728-601).

Ministry of Mines, Zimre Centre, L Takawira Street/Union Avenue, P Bag 7709, Causeway, Harare (tel: 732-881, 732-885; fax: 790-704).

Ministry of National Affairs, Employment Creation and Co-operatives, Zanu PF Building, Rotten Row/Samora Machel Avenue, PO Box 4530, Harare (tel: 734-691, 730-893; fax: 735-338).

Ministry of National Security, Chaminuka Building, 5th Street, Causeway, Harare (tel: 795-965).

Ministry of Public Construction and National Housing, Corner L Takawira Street & H Chitepo Avenue, PO Box CY441, Causeway, Harare (tel: 704-561, 704-021; fax: 702-271).

Ministry of Public Service, Labour and Social Welfare, 12th Floor Compensation House, Central Avenue/4th Street, P Bag 7707, Causeway, Harare (tel: 790-871, 796-451).

Ministry of Sports Recreation and Culture, Pax House, 89 Union Avenue, Harare (tel: 707-411, 794-450; fax: 707-580).

Ministry of Transport and Energy, 4th Floor Atlas House, 62 Robert Mugabe Road, Private Bag 7742, Causeway, Harare (tel: 706-446, 706-161; fax: 708-225, 752-923).

Office of the President and Cabinet, Munhumutapa Building, Samora Machel Avenue/3rd Street, Private Bag 7700, Causeway, Harare (tel: 707-091, 707-098; fax: 734-644, 792-044).

Parliament of Zimbabwe, Baker Avenue Box 8055, Causeway, Harare (tel: 729-722, 795-548).

Other useful addresses

Agricultural Marketing Authority (AMA), Royal Mutual House, 45 Baker Avenue, PO Box 8094, Harare (tel: 730-944).

Attorney-General's Office, Corner House, Leopold Takawira Street, P.Bag 7704, Causeway, Harare (tel: 790-902, 790-905).

British Embassy, 7th Floor, Corner House, Cnr Samora Machel Avenue-Leopold Takawira Street; PO Box 4490, Harare (tel: 772-990, 774-700; fax: 774-605; email: consular.harare@fco.gov.uk).

Chamber of Mines of Zimbabwe, 4 Central Avenue, PO Box 712, Harare (tel: 702-843; fax: 707-983).

Cold Storage Commission (CSC), Josiah Chinamano Road, Bulawayo (tel: 68-961; fax: 67-522).

Commercial Farmers' Union, Agriculture House, PO Box 1241, Leopold Takawira Street, Harare (tel: 791-881).

Confederation of Zimbabwe Industries, Industry House, 109 Rotten Row, PO Box 3794, Harare (tel: 739-833; fax: 702-873).

Cotton Marketing Board (CMB), Kurima House, 89 Baker Avenua, Harare (tel: 739-061; fax: 66-429).

Dairy Marketing Board (DMB), Dolphin House, Leopold Takawira Street, Harare (tel: 705-700).

Grain Marketing Board (GMB), Kurima House, 89 Baker Avenue, Harare (tel: 732-011; fax: 732-019).

Minerals Marketing Corporation of Zimbabwe, Globe House, 51 Jason Moyo Avenue, PO Box 2628, Harare (tel: 703-402, 705-862; fax: 722-441).

Parliament of Zimbabwe, Baker Avenue Box 8055, Causeway, Harare (tel: 729-722, 795-548).

Zimbabwe Broadcasting Corporation (ZBC), Broadcasting Centre, Pockets Hill, PO Box HG444, Highlands, Harare (tel: 486-670, 481-252/9; fax: 498-613).

Zimbabwean Embassy (USA), 1608 New Hampshire Avenue, NW, Washington DC 20009 (tel: (+1-202) 332-7100; fax: (+1-202) 483-9326; e-mail: zimemb@erols.com).

Zimbabwe International Trade Fair, Zift, PO Famona, Bulawayo (tel: 64-911).

Zimbabwe Investment Centre, 109 Rotten Row, PO Box 5950, Harare (tel: 757-931/5; fax: 757-937).

Zimbabwe State Trading Corporation, Globe House, 51 Jason Moyo Avenue, Harare (tel: 729-353).

Zimbabwe Stock Exchange, PO Box UA234, 8th Floor, Southampton House, Union Avenue, Harare (tel: 736-861; fax: 791-045).

Zimbabwe Tourist Development Corporation, PO Box 8052, Causeway, Harare (tel: 793-666).

Internet sites

Africa Business Network: www.ifc.org/abn

AllAfrica.com: www.allafrica.com

African Development Bank: www.afdb.org

Africa Online: www.africaonline.com

Mbendi AfroPaedia (information on companies, countries, industries and stock exchanges in Africa): http://mbendi.co.za

The world in 2008

According to the respected Stockholm International Peace Research Institute the four year period between 2003 and 2007 was probably the first time in human history that no inter-state conflicts were recorded. However, the optimism that began in 1989 with the fall of the Berlin Wall took something of a knock in 2008, when military skirmishes over Abkhazia and South Ossetia between Georgia and Russia came close to triggering a wider conflict, with worrying Cold War overtones.

There'll be some changes made

What was certain was that in late 2007 and early 2008 the world's geo-political balance seemed to be undergoing something of a change. Some of that process could be easily understood: it was clear that China was becoming the world's economic superpower, and that India was not lagging far behind. It was equally clear that the need for food security was beginning to run headlong into the equally urgent need for energy security, as food crops were abandoned for more profitable bio-fuel cultivation. That this shift resulted in exaggerating already high food costs on top of rising fuel costs, thereby returning inflation to the agenda of world concerns had certainly not been foreseen.

> We are asking our planet to somehow absorb a massive increase in economic activity on top of an already existing degree of environmental stress...

Other aspects of the changes taking place were less easily understood. As inflation became a global worry, so did the status of the world's financial institutions. The credit crunch resulting from dubious lending and financial re-packaging exercises started to take its toll. US economic policy under Bush had adhered for the most part to the unregulated principles of Ronald Reagan. Until Reagan, the US had broadly followed the ideas of John Kenneth Galbraith who, having originally, and wholeheartedly, embraced the New Deal of Franklin Roosevelt, later converted to the ideas of the British economist John Maynard Keynes who put forward the theory that the State should intervene in the face of serious recessions and imbalances. Under George W Bush inequality in the US had reached levels which, some observers considered, had not been seen since the 1929 depression. As it reached the end of eight years at the helm, the Bush administration could only look around in disbelief at the tattered ruins of its economic and foreign policy. Surprisingly, in mid-2008 the Republican and Democratic presidential candidates were neck and neck in the election race as the Republicans distanced themselves from Bush and the Democrats sought to define new policies that a battered electorate could respond to.

The end in sight

The inevitable focus of US foreign policy remained Iraq, as a bruised Bush administration tried to salvage some self-respect from its post-war policies, or the disastrous lack of them. A cornerstone of the administration's revised policy was the agreement to accept a specific date for the complete withdrawal of US forces from Iraq: the end of 2011. The White House hope was that agreement on this could be reached before the United Nations mandate for the presence of US forces in Iraq was due to expire at the end of 2008. In late 2007 the administration had still hoped to reach agreement with the Iraqi government by mid-2008, but the questions of immunity for US troops and contractors and the extension of the authority to arrest and detain Iraqis remained to be resolved. By mid-2008 agreement had already been reached on most aspects of the agreement following a number of concessions by the US. The radically improved security situation in most parts of Iraq had given the Iraqi government greater confidence in its dealings with the US coalition.

The Petraeus effect

Much of the credit for the improved security situation was given to US General David Petraeus who oversaw the strategy known as the 'surge' which saw the average number of attacks, for the most part carried out by al-Qaeda led insurgents, reduced from 180 per day in 2007 to 25 per day by mid 2008. US forces had withdrawn from 14 of Iraq's 18 provinces with 11 of those provinces transferred to Iraqi control. Al Qaeda's presence in Iraq was largely confined to the region of Mesopotamia.

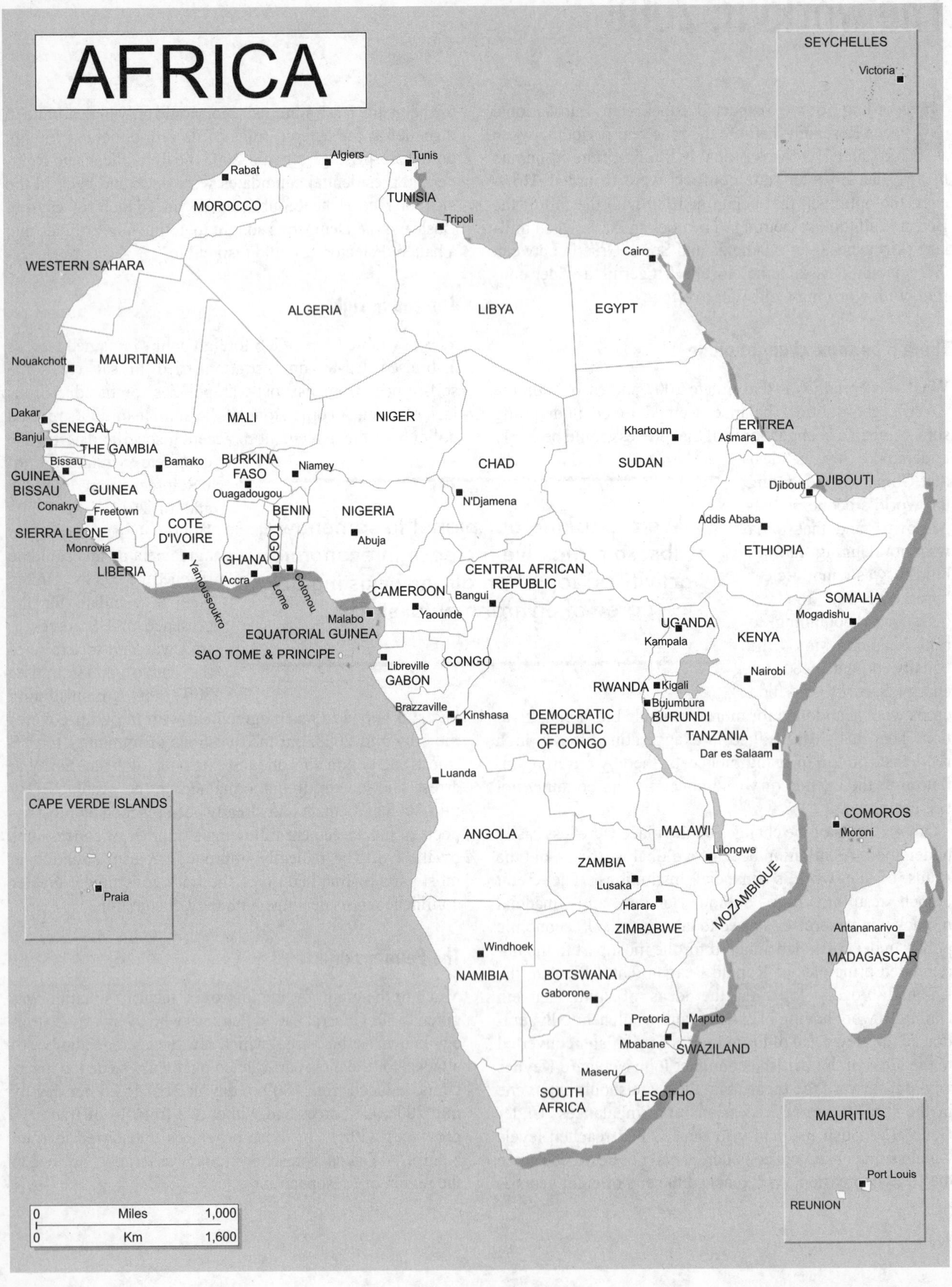
AFRICA
SEYCHELLES
Victoria
Algiers
Tunis
Rabat
TUNISIA
MOROCCO
Tripoli
Cairo
WESTERN SAHARA
ALGERIA
LIBYA
EGYPT
Nouakchott
MAURITANIA
Dakar
SENEGAL
Banjul
THE GAMBIA
Bissau
GUINEA BISSAU
Bamako
MALI
NIGER
BURKINA FASO
Niamey
Ouagadougou
CHAD
Khartoum
SUDAN
ERITREA
Asmara
Djibouti
DJIBOUTI
GUINEA
Conakry
Freetown
SIERRA LEONE
COTE D'IVOIRE
BENIN
NIGERIA
N'Djamena
Addis Ababa
ETHIOPIA
Monrovia
LIBERIA
Yamoussoukro
GHANA
TOGO
Accra
Lome
Cotonou
Abuja
CENTRAL AFRICAN REPUBLIC
Bangui
CAMEROON
Yaounde
Malabo
EQUATORIAL GUINEA
SAO TOME & PRINCIPE
SOMALIA
Mogadishu
UGANDA
Kampala
KENYA
Libreville
GABON
CONGO
Nairobi
RWANDA
Kigali
Bujumbura
BURUNDI
Brazzaville
Kinshasa
DEMOCRATIC REPUBLIC OF CONGO
TANZANIA
Dar es Salaam
Luanda
CAPE VERDE ISLANDS
Praia
ANGOLA
COMOROS
Moroni
MALAWI
Lilongwe
ZAMBIA
Lusaka
MOZAMBIQUE
Harare
ZIMBABWE
Antananarivo
MADAGASCAR
Windhoek
NAMIBIA
BOTSWANA
Gaborone
Pretoria
Maputo
Mbabane
SWAZILAND
Maseru
LESOTHO
SOUTH AFRICA
MAURITIUS
Port Louis
REUNION
0 Miles 1,000
0 Km 1,600

Africa

As is generally the case, Africa only featured occasionally in the world's headlines in 2007 and 2008. When it did, it was generally bad, rather than good, news. The good news was the Bush administration's undertaking to increase aid to Africa to US$8.9 billion by 2010, double the 2004 figure. The bad news was that this aid figure for an entire continent of over 900 million people for a period of two years was less than 10 per cent of the amount paid by the Bush administration to rescue the insurance giant AIG.

Zimbabwe starves

The plight of Zimbabwe's starving people – by mid-2008 the annual inflation rate had risen to an unbelievable 11 million per cent – was for the most part pushed off the news pages by the apparent collapse of Western financial structures. For years Africa's struggling governments had been on the receiving end of trite advice from the smartly dressed representatives of the IMF and the EU, exhorting them to abandon the socialist policies long dear to their leaders in favour of the principles of the free market. Setting the irony of the situation to one side, it had become hard to explain to the millions of Africans living on less than a dollar a day why it was that the bailout of a US Insurance company was ten times more important than feeding Africa's hungry. Public ownership, the *bête noire* of the International Monetary Fund had, it seemed, become the answer to a capitalist maiden's prayer.

> ...by mid-2008 the annual inflation rate [for Zimbabwe] had risen to an unbelievable 11 million per cent

The gestation period for the agreement signed by Messrs Mugabe and Tsvangirai represented not the legitimate cut and thrust of the democratic process, but the failing efforts of an obsessive tyrant to cling on to power. The process of resolving Zimbabwe's dire problems could have been under way at least nine months earlier, had it not been for Mugabe's fear of the unknown. In this case the 'unknown' should certainly have included the accountability of Mugabe and his cronies not just for the deaths caused to his political opponents, but also to the thousands of Zimbabweans who had died from starvation or from lack of basic medication and hospital treatment. But, as long as Mugabe retained control of the army, there was little prospect of closure.

The crisis in the Darfur province of Sudan remained unresolved largely because of China's unwillingness to endorse UN engagement. China's involvement in Africa isn't purely about business – politics are on the table, too. There are now only five African countries left that recognise Taiwan – the rest have cut ties with the island in support of China's *One China* policy. Chinese involvement in African politics has included threats of withdrawing investment in Zambia if the opposition won an election, and heel-dragging in the UN on the issue of bringing troops to Darfur to stop the killing.

The China syndrome

Once the largest oil exporter in Asia, China became a net importer of oil in 1993.

This apparently insatiable demand for energy to feed its booming economy has resulted in it searching out and securing oil supplies from a number of African countries including Sudan, Chad, Nigeria, Angola, Algeria, Gabon, Equatorial Guinea and the Republic of Congo. Angola accounts for half of China's oil imports from Africa, according to the World Bank. In the first ten months of 2005, Chinese official sources say, Chinese companies invested a total of US$175 million in African countries, primarily on oil exploration projects and infrastructure. In 2007, the state-owned Chinese energy company CNOOC Ltd. announced that it would buy a 45 per cent stake in an offshore oil field in Nigeria, for US$2.27 billion. In less than a decade China has become a major factor in the development and exploitation of Africa's oil resources.

Currencies (units per US$) – Africa

	Unit	Jan 2004	Jan 2005	Jan 2006	Jan 2007	Jan 2008
Algeria	Algerian dinar	72.54	72.10	72.74	77.71	67.21
Angola	Readjusted kwanza	78.83	85.72	89.21	80.28	75.10
Benin	CFA franc	520.05	482.58	544.07	507.22	454.40
Botswana	Pula	4.43	4.27	5.41	6.18	6.50
Burkina Faso	CFA franc	520.05	482.58	544.07	507.22	454.40
Burundi	Burundi franc	1,060.00	1,060.00	1,035.95	1,000.15	1,139.23
Cameroon	CFA franc	520.05	482.58	544.07	507.22	454.40
Cape Verde	Cape Verde escudo	108.95	81.15	92.10	85.50	75.50
Central African Republic	CFA franc	520.05	482.58	544.07	507.22	454.40
Chad	CFA franc	520.05	482.58	544.07	507.22	454.40
Comoros	Comoros franc	454.33	361.94	408.05	380.41	340.80
Congo	CFA franc	520.05	482.58	544.07	507.55	454.40
Democratic Republic of Congo	Congolese franc	378.00	440.50	461.50	530.00	556.50
Côte d'Ivoire	CFA franc	520.05	482.58	544.07	507.22	454.40
Djibouti	Djibouti franc	175.00	175.85	174.25	174.70	175.47
Egypt	Egyptian pound	6.17	6.07	5.76	5.71	5.54
Equatorial Guinea	CFA franc	520.05	482.58	544.07	507.22	454.40
Eritrea	Nakfa	8.55	13.50	13.50	13.50	13.24
Ethiopia	Ethiopian birr	8.55	8.60	8.72	8.85	9.09
Gabon	CFA franc	520.05	482.58	544.07	507.22	454.40
Gambia	Dalasi	29.50	29.50	28.30	28.25	22.00
Ghana	Ghana Cedi	8,850.00	9,000.00	9,062.50	9,098.50	(d) 0.95
Guinea	Guinean franc	2,005.00	2,805.00	4,025.00	5,556.00	4,242.70
Guinea-Bissau	CFA franc	520.05	482.58	544.07	507.22	454.40
Kenya	Kenya shilling	76.00	78.65	74.00	69.55	62.95
Lesotho	Maloti	6.68	5.63	6.36	7.23	6.84
Liberia	Liberian dollar	1.00	47.00	57.00	58.00	59.15
Libya	Libyan dinar	1.31	1.25	1.33	1.28	1.22
Madagascar	Franc Malgache	5,700.00	9,275.00	2,087.00	2,030.00	1,786.00
Malawi	Kwacha	107.00	108.00	124.10	139.45	139.40
Mali	CFA franc	520.05	482.58	544.07	507.22	454.40
Mauritania	Ouguiya	264.61	261.64	268.17	270.80	252.54
Mauritius	Mauritius rupee	26.20	28.18	30.30	32.57	28.80
Morocco	Moroccan dirham	8.78	8.24	9.08	8.59	7.83
Mozambique	Metical	23,352.50	18,603.50	24,636.00	(b) 24.19	23.75
Namibia	Namibian dollar	6.68	5.63	6.36	7.23	6.83
Niger	CFA franc	520.05	482.58	544.07	507.22	454.40
Nigeria	Naira	139.55	133.15	130.75	128.16	118.04
Réunion	Euro	0.79	0.74	0.83	0.77	0.69
Rwanda	Rwanda franc	556.55	554.05	540.75	549.20	545.10
São Tomé and Príncipe	Dobra	8,700.00	9,040.00	7,755.00	6,780.00	14,101.00
Senegal	CFA franc	520.05	482.58	544.07	507.22	454.40
Seychelles	Seychelles rupee	5.50	5.52	5.52	5.49	8.02
Sierra Leone	Leone	2,450.00	2,455.00	2,910.74	2,970.11	2,989.20
Somalia	Somali shilling	2,620.00	3,068.00	2,070.00	1,375.00	1,397.00
South Africa	Rand	6.68	5.63	6.36	7.23	6.83
Sudan	Sudanese dinar	259.80	250.63	238.20	230.29	(f) 2.03
Swaziland	Lilangeni	6.68	5.63	6.36	7.23	6.83
Tanzania	Tanzania shilling	1,057.54	1,040.00	1,135.50	1,282.00	1,158.00
Togo	CFA franc	520.05	482.58	544.07	507.22	454.40
Tunisia	Tunisian dinar	1.21	1.20	1.34	1.32	1.23
Uganda	Ugandan shilling	1,937.00	1,737.50	1,865.50	1,810.00	1,706.70
Zambia	Kwacha	4,550.00	4,700.00	4,475.00	1,245.00	3,840.00
Zimbabwe	Zimbabwe dollar	(a) 824.00	5,729.27	(c) 26,003.40	100,000.00	(e) 3,000,000.00

(a) Currency auction rate; (b) metical re-denominated 1 Jul 2006; (c) dollar devalued by 60 per cent, three zeros removed from new bank notes issued 1 Aug 2006; (d) Ghana cedi re-denominated 3 Jul 2007; (e) Zimbabwe dollar devalued by 99.9 per cent 6 Sep 2007; (f) Sudanese pound (S£) replaced dinar at rate of S£1 to 100 dinar, Jan 2007.

Key indicators 2006/07

	Population (m)	Area ('000 sq km)	GDP per capita (US$)	Inflation (%)	GDP real growth (%)	Balance of trade (US$m)
Algeria	34.40	2,381.70	3,825	4.6	(b) 2.0	24,350
Angola	16.30	1,246.70	3,757	21.0	(b) 15.3	7,640
Benin	7.85	112.60	962	3.0	4.2	-573
Botswana	1.56	582.00	7,888	7.1	5.4	310
Burkina Faso	13.31	274.00	508	-0.2	4.2	-597
Burundi	7.79	27.80	128	8.4	3.6	-183
Cameroon	18.85	475.40	1,095	0.9	3.3	241
Cape Verde	0.49	4.03	2,891	4.4	6.9	-352
Central African Republic	4.27	623.00	402	0.9	4.2	32
Chad	9.49	1,284.00	747	-0.9	0.6	2,240
Comoros	0.63	2.20	691	3.0	-0.1	-240
Congo	3.54	342.00	2,158	2.6	-1.6	3,370
Democratic Republic of Congo	61.05	2,345.40	166	17.0	6.3	-423
Côte d'Ivoire	18.75	322.50	1,045	2.1	1.6	2,110
Djibouti	0.76	23.20	1,099	5.0	5.2	-263
Egypt	73.57	1,001.50	1,739	10.9	7.1	-9,100
Equatorial Guinea	1.20	28.10	8,702	4.5	12.4	5,090
Eritrea	4.67	125.00	281	9.0	1.3	-681
Ethiopia	77.17	1,251.30	252	17.0	11.4	-2,810
Gabon	1.43	267.70	7,887	5.0	5.5	2,350
Gambia	1.58	11.30	411	5.0	7.0	-57
Ghana	21.97	239.50	676	10.0	6.4	-2,540
Guinea	9.95	245.90	473	22.8	1.5	104
Guinea-Bissau	1.66	36.10	206	3.7	2.5	-11
Kenya	34.65	582.70	845	9.7	6.9	-2,250
Lesotho	2.45	30.40	665	6.0	5.1	-578
Liberia	3.75	111.40	195	11.2	9.4	-87
Libya	6.08	1,775.50	9,372	6.7	6.8	19,970
Madagascar	18.60	592.00	431	10.3	6.3	-739
Malawi	13.38	118.50	264	8.0	7.4	-470
Mali	11.99	1,241.20	517	2.5	2.5	-1,530
Mauritania	2.96	1,030.70	931	7.2	7.2	-573
Mauritius	1.26	1.90	5,520	10.7	4.6	795
Morocco	30.73	711.00	2,389	2.0	2.2	-10,290
Mozambique	20.50	799.40	369	7.9	7.0	-497
Namibia	2.06	824.30	3,584	6.7	4.4	-578
Niger	13.70	1,267.00	313	0.1	3.2	-392
Nigeria	143.85	923.80	1,159	5.5	6.4	25,150
Réunion	0.79	2.50	–	–	–	–
Rwanda	9.39	26.30	353	9.4	6.0	-229
São Tomé and Príncipe	0.17	0.90	880	18.6	7.0	-31
Senegal	12.23	196.20	910	5.9	5.0	-1,350
Seychelles	0.09	0.50	8,581	5.7	5.2	264
Sierra Leone	5.74	72.30	290	11.7	6.9	-148
Somalia	8.69	738.00	(b) 283	(c) 100.0	(d) 2.4	-335
South Africa	47.85	1,127.20	5,906	7.1	5.1	-1,880
Sudan	37.16	2,505.80	1,242	7.9	10.5	-1,120
Swaziland	1.16	17.40	2,523	8.2	2.4	466
Tanzania	38.96	945.10	415	7.0	7.3	-992
Terres Australes	(a) 0.00	439.80	–	–	–	–
Togo	6.46	56.00	387	0.9	2.1	-441
Tunisia	10.92	164.20	3,397	3.1	6.3	-1,970
Uganda	30.93	236.00	309	6.8	6.7	-921
Zambia	12.16	752.60	918	10.6	5.2	55
Zimbabwe	11.73	391.10	55	10453.0	-6.0	-269

(*) estimate (a) 310 people total, 150 winter only; latest figures: (b) 2006; (c) 2003; (d) 2005

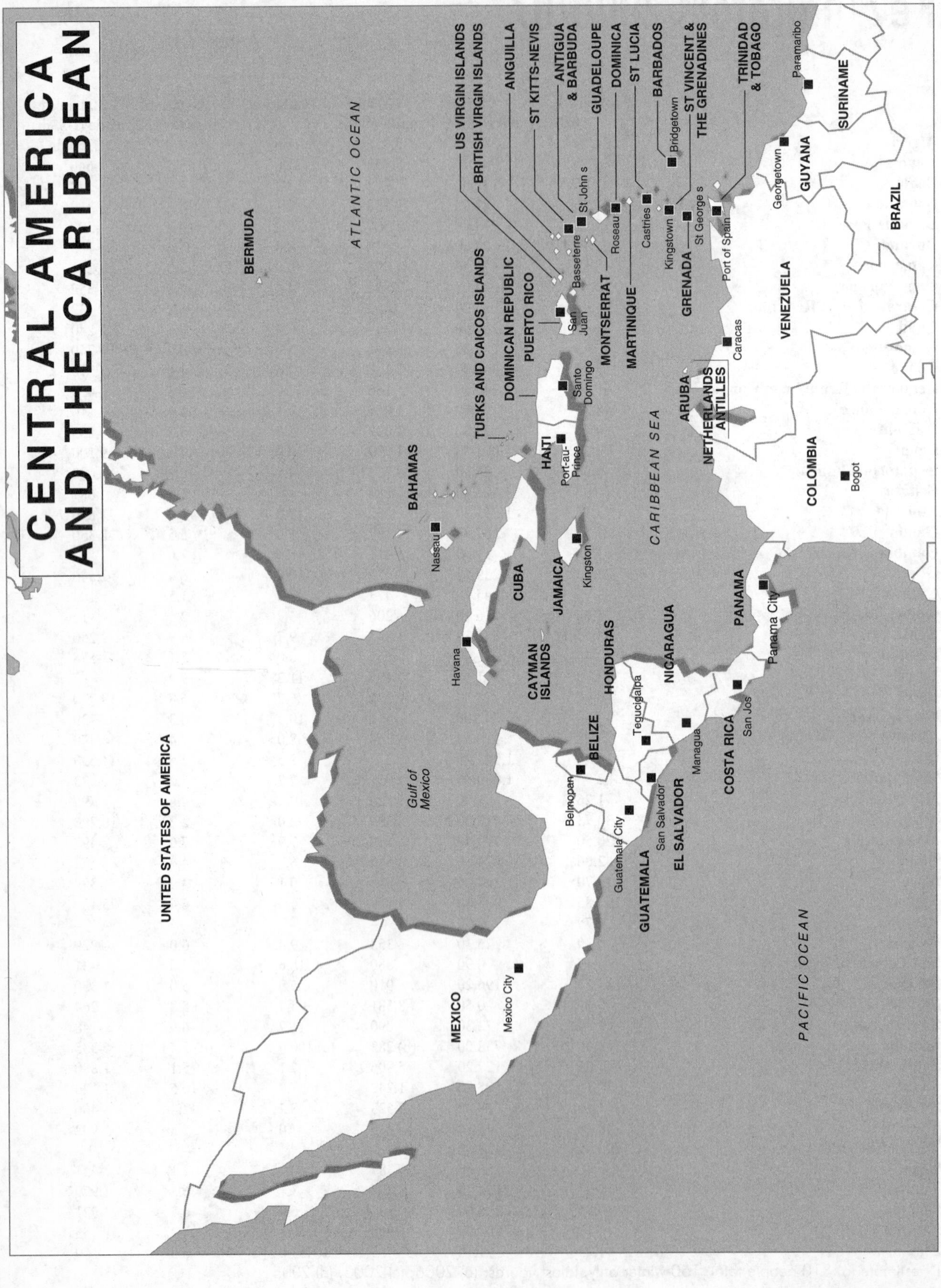
CENTRAL AMERICA AND THE CARIBBEAN
ATLANTIC OCEAN
BERMUDA
US VIRGIN ISLANDS
BRITISH VIRGIN ISLANDS
ANGUILLA
ST KITTS-NEVIS
ANTIGUA & BARBUDA
GUADELOUPE
DOMINICA
ST LUCIA
BARBADOS
ST VINCENT & THE GRENADINES
TRINIDAD & TOBAGO
Paramaribo
SURINAME
Georgetown
GUYANA
BRAZIL
Bridgetown
St John s
Basseterre
Roseau
Castries
Kingstown
St George s
Port of Spain
TURKS AND CAICOS ISLANDS
DOMINICAN REPUBLIC
PUERTO RICO
San Juan
MONTSERRAT
MARTINIQUE
GRENADA
VENEZUELA
Caracas
Santo Domingo
ARUBA
NETHERLANDS ANTILLES
BAHAMAS
HAITI
Port-au-Prince
CARIBBEAN SEA
COLOMBIA
Bogot
Nassau
CUBA
JAMAICA
Kingston
PANAMA
Panama City
Havana
CAYMAN ISLANDS
HONDURAS
NICARAGUA
Tegucigalpa
BELIZE
Belmopan
Managua
San Jos
COSTA RICA
Gulf of Mexico
UNITED STATES OF AMERICA
EL SALVADOR
San Salvador
Guatemala City
GUATEMALA
PACIFIC OCEAN
Mexico City
MEXICO

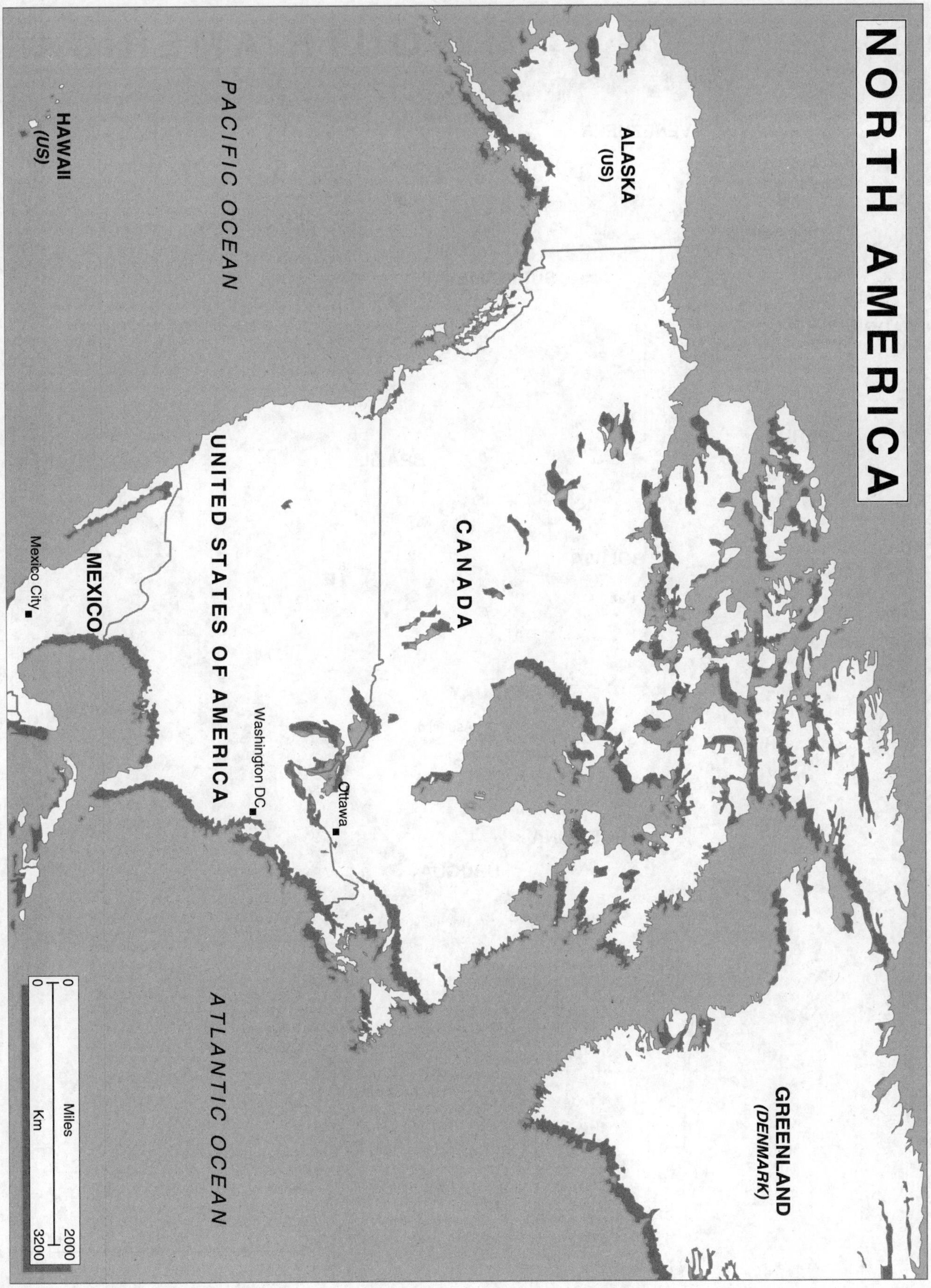
NORTH AMERICA
ALASKA
(US)
PACIFIC OCEAN
HAWAII
(US)
CANADA
UNITED STATES OF AMERICA
MEXICO
Mexico City
Washington DC
Ottawa
ATLANTIC OCEAN
GREENLAND
(DENMARK)
0 Miles 2000
0 Km 3200

SOUTH AMERICA
Caracas
VENEZUELA
GUYANA
Georgetown
Paramaribo
Cayenne
FRENCH GUIANA
Bogot
COLOMBIA
SURINAME
Quito
ECUADOR
PERU
BRAZIL
Lima
BOLIVIA
Bras lia
La Paz
PACIFIC OCEAN
PARAGUAY
Asunci n
CHILE
ARGENTINA
ATLANTIC OCEAN
URUGUAY
Santiago
Buenos Aires
Montevideo
Islas Malvinas (Argentina)
Claimed by UK as Falkland Islands
0
Miles
1000
0
Km
1600

America...

If it is true that there can be no power without a strong economy, then by September 2008 the US was probably ready to start looking for a new role in the world. Admittedly the US still outspent, by a long chalk, all the possible pretenders to its crown. But that 'spend' risked appearing pointless if it was no longer backed up by a cogent and enforceable foreign policy.

When in 2008 the US financial authorities decided to bail out the country's two largest mortgage lenders, Fannie Mae and Freddie Mac, some observers suggested that it was the end of the myth of free markets; when, later in the year, the investment bank Lehman Brothers filed for bankruptcy, and in a fire sale Merrill Lynch was sold to Bank of America, others more drily observed that the myth of free markets had ended with the original creation of the two mortgage giants. Despite owning US$600 billion in assets, Lehman brothers became a victim of the US 'sub-prime' banking crisis. After a dramatic weekend in which two of capitalisms icons had virtually disappeared, Wall Street's attention promptly switched to another failing giant, the world's largest insurance group AIG which played an even bigger role in the financial markets as its activities stretched to derivatives, mortgages, hedge funds and corporate loans. Within hours the US Federal Reserve, backed by the Treasury Department, had announced that it would grant the insurance group a loan of US$85 billion.

What was certain was that the successful candidate [for the US presidency] would be running a demoralised and weakened country.

The financial meltdown also distracted US voters from the autumn presidential election. In a close run election, it was not easy for voters to set aside party politics and assess the candidates on their merits – or their lack of them. Senator Obama's promises to free US politics from a Washington straitjacket appeared to have been countered by Senator McCain's surprise choice of Sarah Palin as running mate. What was certain was that the successful candidate would be running a demoralised and weakened country.

...South of the border

The May 2008 incursion of Colombian troops into Ecuador in successful pursuit of Fuerzas Armadas Revolucionarias Colombianas' (FARC) guerrillas marked the re-opening of the fault-line in South American politics between those republics sympathising with the views of Venezuela's maverick president Hugo Chávez and those retaining some sort of relationship with Washington. In September 2008, the same fault line showed itself just as violently – this time in Bolivia – when heightening violence between the leaders of the country's prosperous eastern provinces and government troops clashed, causing the deaths of 15 people. The conflict provoked an emergency meeting of the newly formed Union of South American Nations (UNASUR) called in Santiago by Chilean president Michelle Bachelet against a background of sharply deteriorating relations between the governments of Bolivia and Venezuela and Washington.

Since July 2008 Bolivia's left-wing president Evo Morales had managed to lose control of half his country as the governors of Bolivia's eastern provinces of Beni, Pando and Tarija not only demanded greater autonomy, but also sought to prevent President Morales from re-writing the constitution. At the heart of the dispute was Morales planned referendum to grant him a second consecutive term as president, grant Bolivia's indigenous majority greater power and transfer terrain to landless peasants. Accusing the United States of sponsoring the unrest, President Morales expelled the US ambassador. In a show of ideological solidarity, President Chávez followed suit accusing the US Ambassador in Bolivia of trying to help organise a coup attempt against Morales. Raising the ante further, Chávez threatened to deploy the Venezuelan army to Bolivia if his ally Morales were overthrown: an offer that Bolivia declined. Washington retaliated by expelling the Venezuelan ambassador to the US and declaring the Bolivian ambassador 'persona non grata'.

Currencies (units per US$) – Americas

	Unit	Jan 2004	Jan 2005	Jan 2006	Jan 2007	Jan 2008
Argentina	Peso	2.93	2.97	2.91	3.08	3.14
Belize	Belize dollar	1.97	1.98	1.97	1.97	1.97
Bolivia	Peso Boliviano	7.80	8.04	8.04	7.99	7.64
Brazil	Real	2.89	2.66	2.22	2.14	1.78
Chile	Chilean peso	592.55	555.75	528.75	539.90	498.75
Colombia	Colombian peso	2,779.70	2,352.50	2,289.70	2,218.60	1,998.60
Costa Rica	Colón	418.67	458.60	487.45	517.94	498.86
Ecuador	US dollar	1.00	1.00	1.00	1.00	1.00
El Salvador	Colón	1.00	1.00	1.00	1.00	1.00
French Guiana	Euro	0.79	0.74	0.83	0.77	0.69
Guatemala	Quetzal	8.02	7.75	7.65	7.69	7.60
Guyana	Guyana dollar	179.00	179.00	190.00	201.69	204.20
Honduras	Lempira	17.74	18.63	18.86	18.90	18.89
Mexico	Mexican peso	11.24	11.15	10.78	10.97	10.82
Nicaragua	Gold Cordóba	15.43	16.20	16.37	18.03	18.86
Panama	Balboa	1.00	1.00	1.00	1.00	1.00
Paraguay	Guarani	6,100.00	6,115.00	6,130.00	5,680.71	4,685.00
Peru	New sol	3.46	3.28	3.35	3.19	2.97
Suriname	Suriname dollar	2,515.00	(b) 2.74	2.74	2.75	2.74
Uruguay	Peso Uruguayo	29.32	26.41	24.08	24.49	21.68
Venezuela	BolGreek Centuryívar	2,851.74	2,578.29	2,602.56	(c) 2147.5	2,147.30
NORTH AMERICA						
Canada	Canadian dollar	1.29	1.20	1.16	1.17	1.02
United States of America	US dollar	1.00	1.00	1.00	1.00	1.00
CARIBBEAN						
Anguilla	EC dollar	2.67	2.70	2.70	2.70	2.70
Antigua	EC dollar	2.67	2.70	2.70	2.70	2.70
Aruba	Aruba guilder	1.79	1.79	1.79	1.79	1.79
Bahamas	Bahamian dollar	1.00	1.00	1.00	1.00	1.00
Barbados	Barbados dollar	1.99	2.00	2.00	2.00	2.00
Bermuda	Bermuda dollar	1.00	1.00	1.00	1.00	1.00
British Virgin Islands	US dollar	1.00	1.00	1.00	1.00	1.00
Cayman Islands	Cayman Islands dollar	0.82	0.82	0.82	0.82	0.82
Cuba	Cuban peso	21.00	(b) 1.00	1.00	0.82	0.82
Dominica	EC dollar	2.67	2.70	2.70	2.70	2.70
Dominican Republic	Dominican Republic peso	33.70	28.50	31.45	33.75	33.37
Grenada	EC dollar	2.67	2.70	2.70	2.77	2.70
Guadeloupe	Euro	0.79	0.74	0.83	0.77	0.69
Haiti	Gourde	40.00	36.00	42.15	37.65	36.75
Jamaica	Jamaican dollar	59.80	61.00	62.53	67.13	71.28
Martinique	Euro	0.79	0.74	0.83	0.77	0.69
Montserrat	EC dollar	2.67	2.70	2.70	2.70	2.70
The Netherlands Antilles	Netherlands Antilles guilder	1.78	1.79	1.79	1.79	1.79
Puerto Rico	US dollar	1.00	1.00	1.00	1.00	1.00
St Kitts Nevis	EC dollar	2.67	2.70	2.70	2.70	2.70
St Lucia	EC dollar	2.67	2.70	2.70	2.70	2.70
St Vincent	EC dollar	2.67	2.70	2.70	2.70	2.70
Trinidad and Tobago	Trinidad and Tobago dollar	6.15	6.23	6.28	6.31	6.30
Turks and Caicos Islands	US dollar	1.00	1.00	1.00	1.00	1.00
US Virgin Islands	US dollar	1.00	1.00	1.00	1.00	1.00

(a) Suriname guilder replaced with dollar 1 Jan; (b) Cuban dollar converts to US dollar.

Key indicators 2006/07

	Population (m)	Area ('000 sq km)	GDP per capita (US$)	Inflation (%)	GDP real growth (%)	Balance of trade (US$m)
Argentina	39.36	2,766.90	6,606	8.8	7.5	12,810
Belize	0.31	23.00	4,098	3.0	2.2	-287
Bolivia	9.83	1,098.60	1,342	8.7	4.2	481
Brazil	189.34	8,512.00	6,938	3.6	5.4	44,760
Chile	16.58	756.60	(c) 8857	4.4	5.0	10,180
Colombia	47.52	1,138.90	3,611	5.5	7.0	1,600
Costa Rica	4.44	51.10	5,905	9.4	6.8	-2,130
Ecuador	13.34	270.70	3,218	2.2	1.9	462
El Salvador	7.31	21.40	2,857	3.8	4.6	-3,380
French Guiana	0.20	91.00	–	–	–	–
Guatemala	13.31	108.90	2,532	6.8	5.7	-5,390
Guyana	0.76	215.00	1,365	12.2	5.4	-94
Honduras	7.51	112.10	1,635	6.9	6.3	-1,540
Mexico	105.37	1,958.20	8,479	3.9	3.3	-7,590
Nicaragua	6.05	148.00	945	11.8	3.7	-1,314
Panama	3.34	77.10	5,904	4.1	11.2	-1,320
Paraguay	6.03	407.00	1,802	8.1	6.4	175
Peru	28.07	1,285.20	3,886	1.8	9.0	5,160
Suriname	0.53	164.00	4,577	6.4	5.5	23
Uruguay	3.45	176.20	7,172	8.1	7.0	28
Venezuela	27.50	916.50	8,596	18.7	8.4	31,530
NORTH AMERICA						
Canada	32.93	9,976.10	43,485	2.1	2.6	53,790
United States of America	301.97	9,300.00	48,845	2.8	2.2	-778,940
CARIBBEAN						
Anguilla	(a) - 0.01	0.01	(c) 9,711	2.4	12.0	115,54
Antigua	0.83	0.03	13,092	3.4	6.1	-332
Aruba	0.12	0.02	(d) 21800	(d) 2.4	(e) 2.5	-795
Bahamas	0.33	13.90	19,895	1.9	4.5	-1,210
Barbados	0.28	0.40	13,605	5.5	4.2	-1390
Bermuda	0.07	0.01	(c) 80,676	(e) 3.1	(e) 2.5	487
British Virgin Islands	0.02	0.15	(d) 16,000	(e) 1.9	(c) 7.2	–
@Key inds-all = Cayman Islands0.050.30(c) 46,500(e) 7.0(c) 6.5841.7						
Cuba	11.40	110.90	4,051	2.8	6.5	-4,530
Dominica	0.07	0.80	4,333	2.7	0.9	-82
Dominican Republic	8.78	48.40	4,147	6.1	8.5	-3,480
Grenada	0.11	0.34	5,571	3.7	3.1	-202
Guadeloupe	0.44	1.80	(e) 7,900	–	–	–
Haiti	8.63	27.80	630	9.0	3.2	-921
Jamaica	2.69	11.00	4,172	9.3	1.4	-2,580
Martinique	0.40	1.10	–	–	–	–
Montserrat	(b) - 0.001	0.01	–	–	–	-21
Netherlands Antilles	0.19	0.80	(e) 17,270	(e) 3.2	(e) 0.7	-2310
Puerto Rico	3.96	8.90	19,600	12.4	1.2	–
St Kitts Nevis	0.05	0.30	10,143	4.5	3.3	-123
St Lucia	0.17	0.60	5,689	1.9	5.0	-304
St Vincent	0.12	0.40	5,229	6.1	(e) 2.2	-118
Trinidad and Tobago	1.30	5.10	15,905	7.9	5.5	3,150
Turks and Caicos Islands	(c) 0.02	0.43	–	–	–	–
US Virgin Islands	(c) 0.12	0.40	–	–	–	–

(*) estimate (a) 13,677 people; (b) 9,341 people; latest figures: (c) 2006; (d) 2004; (e) 2005

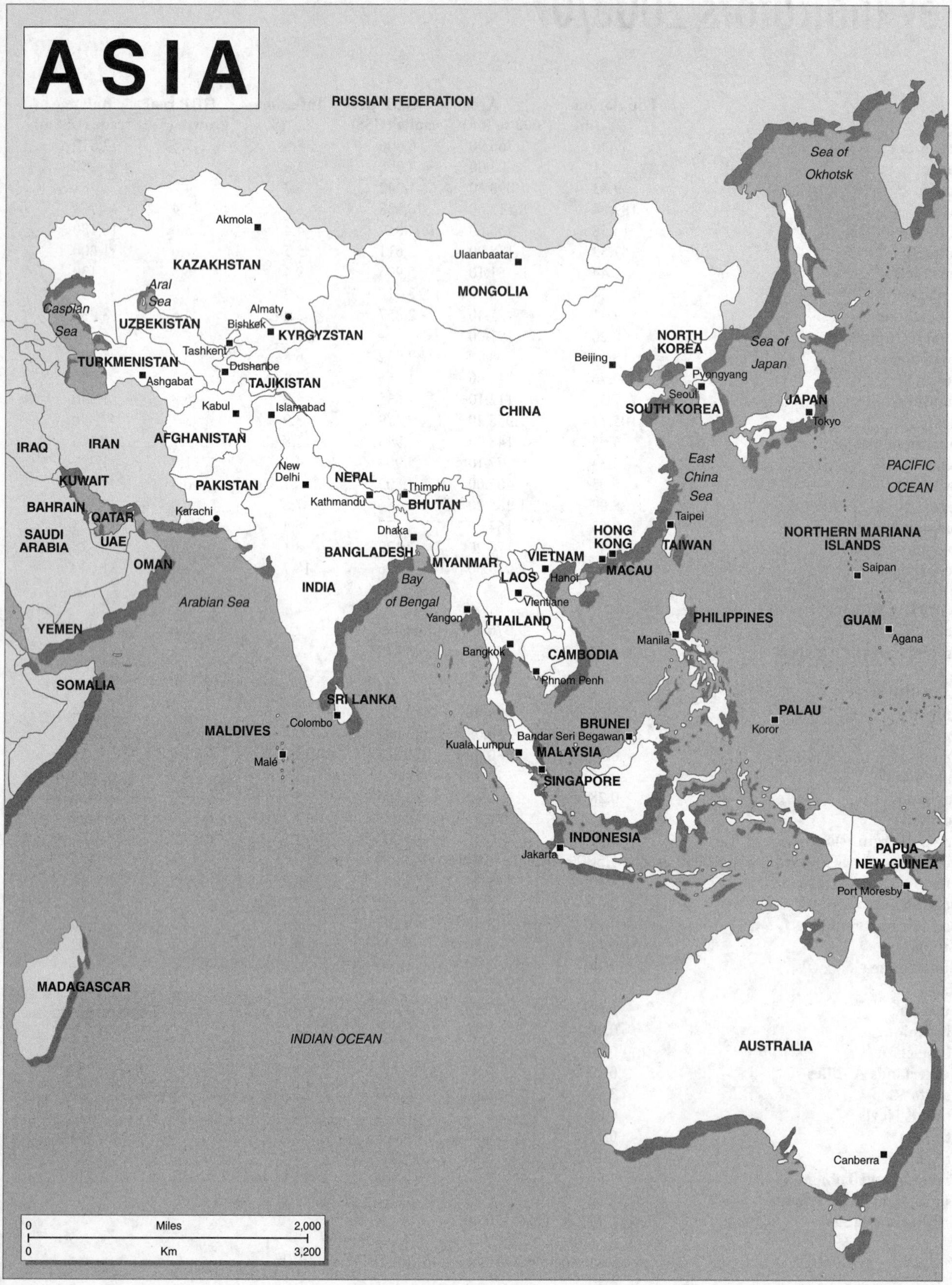
ASIA
RUSSIAN FEDERATION
Sea of Okhotsk
Akmola
KAZAKHSTAN
Ulaanbaatar
MONGOLIA
Aral Sea
Caspian Sea
Almaty
UZBEKISTAN
Bishkek
KYRGYZSTAN
Tashkent
TURKMENISTAN
Dushanbe
Ashgabat
TAJIKISTAN
Kabul
Islamabad
AFGHANISTAN
IRAQ
IRAN
KUWAIT
BAHRAIN
QATAR
SAUDI ARABIA
UAE
OMAN
YEMEN
SOMALIA
PAKISTAN
Karachi
New Delhi
NEPAL
Kathmandu
Thimphu
BHUTAN
Dhaka
BANGLADESH
INDIA
Arabian Sea
Bay of Bengal
MYANMAR
Yangon
CHINA
Beijing
NORTH KOREA
Pyongyang
Seoul
SOUTH KOREA
Sea of Japan
JAPAN
Tokyo
East China Sea
PACIFIC OCEAN
Taipei
TAIWAN
HONG KONG
MACAU
VIETNAM
Hanoi
LAOS
Vientiane
THAILAND
Bangkok
CAMBODIA
Phnom Penh
PHILIPPINES
Manila
NORTHERN MARIANA ISLANDS
Saipan
GUAM
Agana
PALAU
Koror
SRI LANKA
Colombo
MALDIVES
Malé
BRUNEI
Bandar Seri Begawan
Kuala Lumpur
MALAYSIA
SINGAPORE
INDONESIA
Jakarta
PAPUA NEW GUINEA
Port Moresby
MADAGASCAR
INDIAN OCEAN
AUSTRALIA
Canberra
0 Miles 2,000
0 Km 3,200

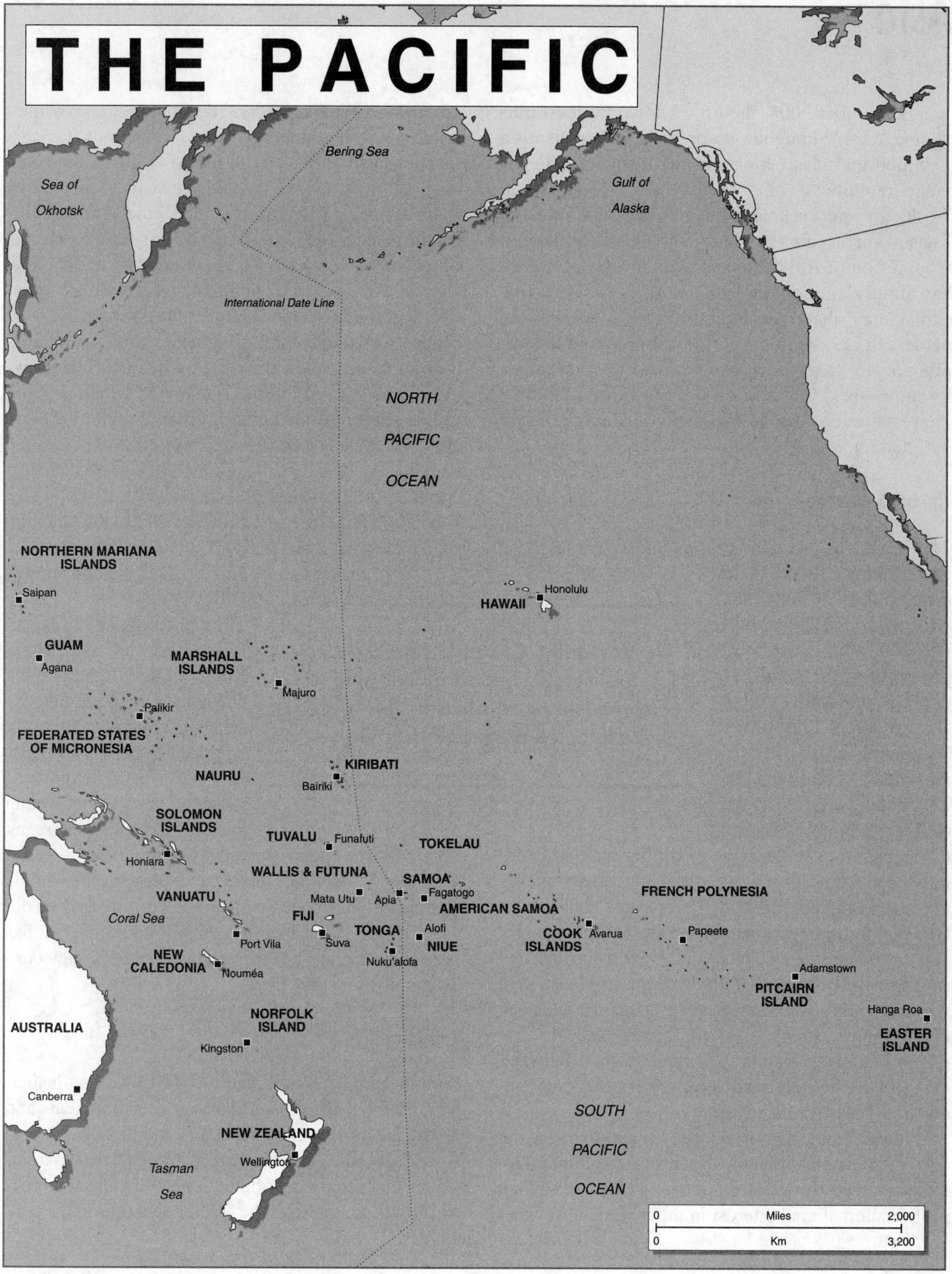
THE PACIFIC
Bering Sea
Sea of
Okhotsk
Gulf of
Alaska
International Date Line
NORTH
PACIFIC
OCEAN
NORTHERN MARIANA
ISLANDS
Saipan
HAWAII
Honolulu
GUAM
Agana
MARSHALL
ISLANDS
Majuro
Palikir
FEDERATED STATES
OF MICRONESIA
KIRIBATI
NAURU
Bairiki
SOLOMON
ISLANDS
TUVALU
Funafuti
TOKELAU
Honiara
WALLIS & FUTUNA
SAMOA
VANUATU
Mata Utu
Apia
Fagatogo
AMERICAN SAMOA
FRENCH POLYNESIA
Coral Sea
FIJI
TONGA
Alofi
NIUE
COOK
ISLANDS
Avarua
Papeete
Port Vila
Suva
NEW
CALEDONIA
Nouméa
Nuku'alofa
Adamstown
PITCAIRN
ISLAND
Hanga Roa
EASTER
ISLAND
NORFOLK
ISLAND
AUSTRALIA
Kingston
Canberra
SOUTH
PACIFIC
OCEAN
NEW ZEALAND
Wellington
Tasman
Sea
0
Miles
2,000
0
Km
3,200

Asia

In September 2008, the little known (at least outside Asia) Shanghai Co-operation Organisation which includes China and the former Asian soviet republics of Kazakhstan, Kyrgyzstan, Tajikistan and Turkmenistan – as well as China and Russia – refused to go along with Russia's planned recognition of Abkhazia and South Ossetia. Russia had simply not done its homework: however much China may share the Kremlin's diffidence about perceived US dominance, it is not prepared to simply go along with Russian efforts to re-create a bi-polar world that will do little to further China's interests, even less so those of its Central Asian neighbours.

The bank says 'no!'

This view was just as swiftly endorsed by the Asian Development Bank (major shareholder: China PR) with a prompt award of a US$40 million grant to repair some of the immediate damage inflicted by Russian troops, a high profile Asian rebuff to Russian ambitions. Following the undoubted success of the Beijing Olympic Games, China began to settle down to coping with an economy that risked overheating and the reality of depressed economies in both Europe and the US, its two major trading groups. Despite a frighteningly fast economic growth rate, and a trade surplus that runs into the trillions of dollars, China still has a long way to go before it lifts its per capita income to developed country status. Current figures indicate that China's per capita income is between US$1,000-US$2,000, still a far cry from average income in Western countries.

Although China had successfully stage-managed the games, intractable problems such as the continued internal pressure for greater political freedom and high profile international interest in the treatment of Tibet promised China's leaders an invigorating winter. There can be no doubt that China's economy has seen spectacular growth, and is likely to do so for some time; at the same time there is a growing concern that its large ageing population will become a drag on lifting the standard of living of the country as a whole. As China strives to create a large domestic middle class, the effect of its ageing population on economic expansion is going to become significant. The working, and hence revenue generating segment of the population, is going to bear the increasing burden of a fast growing older – non-productive – segment, which is going to live longer due to better nutrition, health care and other effective socio-economic policies.

Ironically, China's 'one child' policy succeeded in bringing some measure of control into its explosive population growth; but it has also reduced the potential size of the workforce able to meet its obligations to the elderly. This phenomenon is not restricted to China. Throughout Asia, in Japan, Korea, Taiwan, and Hong Kong similar demographic challenges will confront governments that are often ill equipped to deal with them. It is never easy for governments to ensure that young and old alike enjoy the rising benefits of the country's impressive progress. Such had been the White House preoccupation with the Middle East 'mess' that inadequate time and effort has been devoted by the White House to Asia. The simple fact has been that Asia has not loomed large in US policy considerations for some time.

Ironically, China's 'one child' policy succeeded in bringing some measure of control into its explosive population growth

Kim Jong ill?

Further north, rumours that the North Korean leader, Kim Jong Il had suffered a stroke raised both fears and hopes. Fears that his successors might throw North Korea's de-nuclearisation programme further in to reverse, hopes that a negotiated settlement might be possible that encompasses the further demands of the US.

Currencies (units per US$) – Asia

	Unit	Jan 2004	Jan 2005	Jan 2006	Jan 2007	Jan 2008
Afghanistan	Afghani	43.00	43.00	43.00	49.18	49.53
Australia	Australian dollar	1.33	1.28	1.31	1.28	1.16
Bangladesh	Taka	58.88	59.69	65.73	70.23	68.59
Bhutan	Ngultrum	45.63	43.47	43.97	44.43	39.34
Brunei	Brunei dollar	1.70	1.63	1.69	1.54	1.45
Cambodia	Riel	3,990.00	3,846.00	4,120.00	4,025.00	3,950.00
China	Renminbi yuan	8.28	8.28	(a) 8.09	7.80	7.37
Fiji	Fijian dollar	1.72	1.65	1.71	1.68	1.55
Hong Kong	Hong Kong dollar	7.76	7.77	7.76	7.80	7.79
India	Rupee	45.63	43.47	43.97	44.43	39.35
Indonesia	Rupiah	8,422.50	9,282.50	10,290.00	9,130.00	9,327.50
Japan	Yen	107.17	102.47	113.34	120.35	113.35
Kazakhstan	Tenge	143.25	129.96	133.69	125.33	120.75
North Korea	Won	2.20	900.00	900.00	142.45	142.45
South Korea	Won	1,191.50	1,035.20	1,041.50	940.05	930.10
Kyrgyzstan	Som	43.88	40.91	40.85	38.25	34.54
Laos	New kip	7,882.00	7,842.00	10,425.00	8,271.00	9,401.50
Macao	Pataca	7.97	8.01	7.99	8.03	8.03
Malaysia	Ringgit	3.80	3.80	3.77	3.51	3.32
Maldives	Rufiyaa	12.80	12.80	12.80	12.80	12.80
Marshall Islands	US dollar	1.00	1.00	1.00	1.00	1.00
Federated States of Micronesia	US dollar	1.00	1.00	1.00	1.00	1.00
Mongolia	Tugrik	1,126.00	1,209.00	1,215.00	1,165.00	1,169.30
Myanmar	Kyat	6.42	6.42	6.42	6.42	6.42
Nepal	Rupee	73.00	69.55	70.34	71.08	62.95
New Zealand	New Zealand dollar	1.52	1.38	1.44	1.45	1.29
Pakistan	Rupee	57.39	59.43	59.67	60.97	61.14
Papua New Guinea	Kina	3.27	3.10	3.02	2.96	2.75
Philippines	Peso	55.52	56.13	56.04	49.00	41.21
Samoa	Tala	2.78	2.68	2.72	2.70	2.54
Singapore	Singapore dollar	1.70	1.63	1.69	1.54	1.45
Sri Lanka	Rupee	96.95	104.48	101.33	108.45	108.90
Taiwan	Taiwanese dollar	33.95	31.69	33.19	32.76	32.38
Tajikistan	Tajik rouble	2.79	2.79	3.18	3.43	3.43
Thailand	Baht	39.62	38.85	41.07	36.05	33.59
Timor-Leste	US dollar	1.00	1.00	1.00	1.00	1.00
Turkmenistan	Manat	5,200.00	5,200.00	5,200.00	5,200.00	5,200.00
Uzbekistan	Sum	980.00	1,058.00	1,140.86	1,241.10	1,287.50
Vietnam	New dong	15,642.00	15,773.00	15,892.50	16,047.00	16,040.00

Key indicators 2006/07

	Population (m)	Area ('000 sq km)	GDP per capita (US$)	Inflation (%)	GDP real growth (%)	Balance of trade (US$m)
Afghanistan	(*) 25.80	647.50	(*) 323	(*) 13	(*) 5.5	-3,400
Australia	(*) 20.98	7,682.30	(*) 43,312	2.3	3.9	-13,670
Bangladesh	(*) 159.01	144.00	(*) 455	(*) 8.4	(*) 5.6	-3,110
Bhutan	(*) 2.33	47.00	(*) 2012	(*) 4.9	(*) 22.4	–
Brunei	(*) 0.39	5.80	32,167	(*) 0.4	(*) 0.4	2,870
Cambodia	(*) 14.34	181.00	(*) 600	(*) 5.9	(*) 9.6	-1,020
China	(*) 1321.05	9,597.10	(*) 2,461	(*) 4.7	(*) 11.4	134,190
Fiji	0.87	18.30	(*) 3,921	4.8	(*) -4.4	-742
Hong Kong	(*) 6.97	1.10	(*) 29650	2.0	(*) 6.3	-7,630
India	(*) 1123.97	3,287.60	(*) 978	6.4	9.2	-51,550
Indonesia	(*) 224.94	1,919.40	(*) 1925	6.4	(*) 6.3	22,370
Japan	(*) 127.76	377.70	(*) 34312	1.3	2.1	93,960
Kazakhstan	13.89	2,717.30	2,715	6.9	9.4	6,786
North Korea	23.11	122.40	–	–	–	-1,380
South Korea	48.55	99.10	19,751	2.5	5.1	33,470
Kyrgyzstan	(*) 5.25	198.50	(*) 713	10.2	8.2	-419
Laos	(*) 6.14	236.80	(*) 656	4.5	(*) 7.5	-457
Macao	0.54	(a)	36,357	5.6	27.3	-610
Malaysia	(*) 26.84	330.40	(*) 6948	2.1	6.3	24,950
Maldives	0.34	0.30	3,040	5.0	6.6	-494
Federated States of Micronesia	(*) 0.11	0.70	2,172	3.3	-3.2	-119
Mongolia	(*) 2.63	1,565.00	(*) 1486	9.0	(*) 9.9	-122
Myanmar	(*) 57.64	676.60	(*) 235	34.4	(*) 5.5	383
Nepal	(*) 24.06	147.20	(*) 400	6.4	(*) 2.5	-1,370
New Zealand	(*) 4.24	268.70	(*) 30,226	2.4	(*) 2.9	-2,360
Pakistan	158.17	803.90	(*) 909	7.7	(*) 6.4	-6,180
Papua New Guinea	(*) 6.32	462.80	(*) 685	(*) 4.3	(*) 4.3	1,080
Philippines	(*) 88.71	300.40	(*) 1625	2.8	7.3	-7,550
Samoa	(*) 0.19	2.80	2,101	(*) 2.6	(*) 6.0	-175
Singapore	(*) 4.59	0.60	(*) 35,163	2.1	7.7	16,500
Sri Lanka	(*) 19.93	65.60	(*) 1506	19.7	(*) 6.3	-3,070
Solomon Islands	(*) 0.51	27.50	(*) 704	6.3	(*) 5.4	–
Taiwan	23.08	36.00	16,606	1.8	5.7	15,820
Tajikistan	(*) 6.42	143.10	(*) 578	13.1	7.8	-323
Thailand	(*) 65.74	514.00	(*) 3737	(*) 2.2	(*) 4.8	3,160
Timor-Leste	(*) 1.04	19.00	(*) 440	7.8	(*) 19.8	-231
Turkmenistan	(*) 5.19	488.10	(*) 5189	(*) 6.4	(*) 11.6	2,000
Uzbekistan	(*) 27.37	447.40	(*) 815	(*) 12.3	(*) 9.5	1,080
Vietnam	(*) 85.59	329.60	(*) 818	8.3	(*) 8.5	-4,650

(*) estimate (a) area 29.2 square km

Europe

Russia's apparent overreaction to Georgia's attempt to take advantage of the distraction offered by the opening of the Beijing Olympic Games was seen by many observers as the beginning of a new cold war. Miscalculation had appeared to be the order of the day. If Georgia had misjudged the Russian response, so Russia misjudged not only the Chinese response, but that of most of Asia as symbolised in the Asian Development Bank's (major shareholder China PR) prompt award of a US$40 million grant to repair some of the immediate damage inflicted by Russian troops.

Paranoid Russia

But, as one observer, writing in the Paris based *International Herald Tribune* observed, Vladimir Putin 'is not Stalin or even Alexander 1st' and 'Germany is no longer the Germany of Bismarck, let alone Hitler' and 'France is not the France of Napoleon'. Relations between the US and Russia were no better, as US Secretary of State Condoleezza Rice warned that the Kremlin's attempts to rebuild Russia had taken a 'Dark turn', and that a 'paranoid, aggressive impulse' from the Russian past was reappearing. Ms Rice went further, criticising Russia for using its role as Europe's major energy supplier as 'a political weapon against some of its neighbours'. Ms Rice looked certain to increase Russia's paranoia as she widened the US criticism of Russia to attack the core policy of the Medvedev-Putin administration: 'What has become clear is that the legitimate goal of rebuilding Russia has taken a dark turn, with the rollback of personal freedoms, the arbitrary enforcement of the law, the pervasive corruption at various levels of Russian society and the paranoid, aggressive impulse which has manifested itself before in Russian history'.

Steinmeier's emancipation

Russia's disproportionate response to Georgian attacks resulted in disagreement between Russia and virtually every European political and defence organisation, including the EU, Nato and the Organisation for Security and Co-operation in Europe (OSCE). European security, and the continent's relationship with the US, looked like coming in to sharper focus with the advent of the 2009 German general election. The joker in the electoral pack was the German coalition's foreign minister, Social Democrat Frank-Walter Steinmeier. Mr Steinmeier had announced that one of his goals would be 'emancipating' Germany and Europe from the United States, preferring to steer an 'equidistant' policy between Russia and the US. Mr Steinmeier is a close political ally of former Chancellor Gerhard Schroeder. The German business community, conscious of the country's reliance on Russia for its energy needs, is wary of any overtly pro-Russian stance. This stance, described by one observer as an 'institutionalised comfort zone' is Mr Steinmeier's home ground. According to Christian Democrat spokesman Karl Theodor von Guttenberg, Mr Steinmeier had 'failed to emancipate himself from Schroeder. And the thing about Schroeder is that nobody can miss the raven sitting on his shoulder which speaks with a Russian accent'. Appeasement had been energetically promoted by Mr Stenmeier's mentor. Since resigning as Chancellor, Mr Schoeder has pursued a business career largely spent promoting Russian business interests in Europe.

Mr Steinmeier had announced that one of his goals would be 'emancipating' Germany and Europe from the United States

Sarko's false start

The tensions between Russia and Georgia, in many respects an EU protégé, placed the hyperactive French President Nicholas Sarkozy centre stage in his role as EU president for the second half of 2008. Mr Sarkozy got off to a false start when he naively accepted Russian assurances that they would withdraw all their troops from Georgia immediately. The initial agreement had to be revisited as Mr Sarkozy made a second visit to Moscow some weeks later. The EU had been unable to adopt a genuinely unified position over the Russian invasion of Georgia as key members of the 27 nation organisation, lead by Germany, appeared more preoccupied with their winter gas supplies than with taking a stand against Russian belligerence.

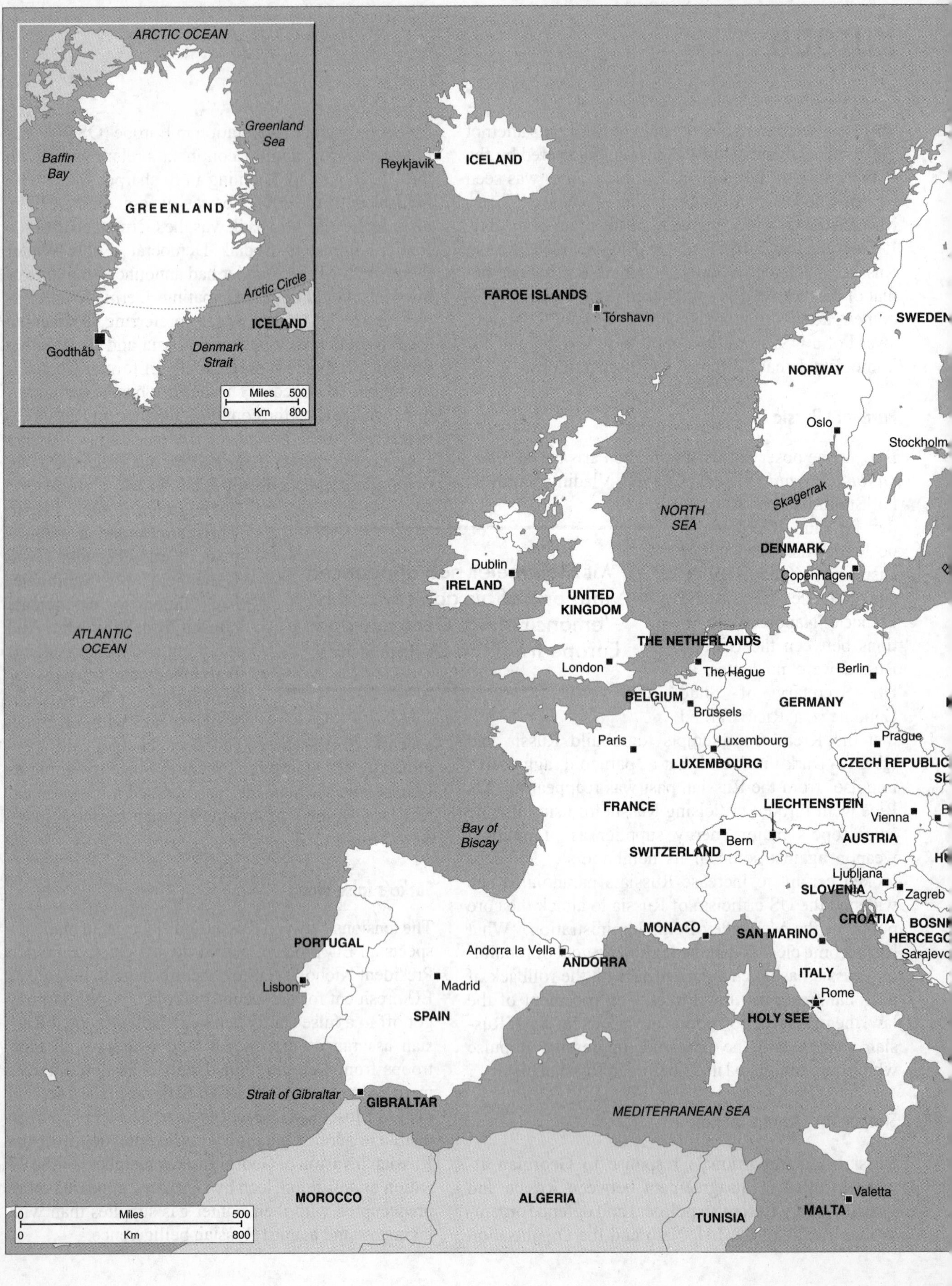
ARCTIC OCEAN
Greenland Sea
Baffin Bay
GREENLAND
Arctic Circle
ICELAND
Godthåb
Denmark Strait
0 Miles 500
0 Km 800
Reykjavik
ICELAND
FAROE ISLANDS
Tórshavn
SWEDEN
NORWAY
Oslo
Stockholm
Skagerrak
NORTH SEA
DENMARK
Copenhagen
Dublin
IRELAND
UNITED KINGDOM
ATLANTIC OCEAN
THE NETHERLANDS
London
The Hague
Berlin
BELGIUM
Brussels
GERMANY
Paris
Luxembourg
Prague
LUXEMBOURG
CZECH REPUBLIC
FRANCE
LIECHTENSTEIN
Vienna
Bay of Biscay
Bern
AUSTRIA
SWITZERLAND
Ljubljana
SLOVENIA
Zagreb
CROATIA
MONACO
SAN MARINO
PORTUGAL
Andorra la Vella
ANDORRA
Sarajevo
ITALY
Lisbon
Madrid
Rome
SPAIN
HOLY SEE
Strait of Gibraltar
GIBRALTAR
MEDITERRANEAN SEA
Valetta
MOROCCO
ALGERIA
TUNISIA
MALTA
0 Miles 500
0 Km 800

AND
allinn
ONIA
LATVIA
NIA
nius
Minsk
BELARUS
RUSSIA
Moscow
Kiev
UKRAINE
MOLDOVA
Kishinev
ROMANIA
Bucharest
BULGARIA
Sofia
je
NIA
BLACK SEA
GEORGIA
Tbilisi
Yerevan
ARMENIA
AZERBAIJAN
Baku
CASPIAN SEA
KAZAKHSTAN
ARAL SEA
UZBEKISTAN
TURKMENISTAN
IRAN
Ankara
TURKEY
Athens
SYRIA
IRAQ
Lefkosia
CYPRUS
LEBANON

Currencies (units per US$) – Europe

	Unit	Jan 2004	Jan 2005	Jan 2006	Jan 2007	Jan 2008
Albania	Lek	106.40	92.35	102.35	96.73	83.21
Andorra	Euro	0.79	0.74	0.83	0.77	0.69
Armenia	Dram	558.14	484.00	444.10	367.25	301.12
Austria	Euro	0.79	0.74	0.83	0.77	0.69
Azerbaijan	New manat	4,923.00	4,915.50	4,608.50	(c) 0.87	0.85
Belarus	Belarus rouble	2,162.50	2,176.00	152.50	2,142.00	2,156.50
Belgium	Euro	0.79	0.74	0.83	0.77	0.69
Bosnia-Herzegovina	Bosnian marka	1.56	1.44	1.65	1.51	1.35
Bulgaria	Lev	1.55	1.51	1.62	1.48	1.35
Croatia	Kuna	6.06	5.63	6.16	5.70	5.06
Cyprus	Cyprus pound	0.47	0.43	0.48	0.45	0.40
Czech Republic	Czech koruna	25.68	22.33	24.56	21.50	18.28
Denmark	Danish krone	5.90	5.47	6.19	5.76	5.17
Estonia	Kroon	12.41	11.51	12.98	12.10	10.83
Faroe Islands	Faroese krone	5.90	5.47	6.19	5.76	5.17
Finland	Euro	0.79	0.74	0.83	0.77	0.69
France	Euro	0.79	0.74	0.83	0.77	0.69
Georgia	Lari	2.11	1.82	1.79	1.71	1.59
Germany	Euro	0.79	0.74	0.83	0.77	0.69
Gibraltar	Gibraltar pound	0.56	0.52	0.57	0.51	0.49
Greece	Euro	0.79	0.74	0.83	0.77	0.69
Greenland	Danish krone	5.90	5.47	6.20	5.76	5.17
Hungary	Forint	207.42	180.73	207.05	195.85	176.03
Iceland	Icelandic krona	70.90	61.48	60.96	70.78	62.93
Ireland	Euro	0.79	0.74	0.83	0.77	0.69
Italy	Euro	0.79	0.74	0.83	0.77	0.69
Kosovo	Euro	–	–	–	–	0.69
Latvia	Lat	0.53	0.51	0.58	0.54	0.48
Liechtenstein	Swiss franc	1.24	1.14	1.29	1.25	1.15
Lithuania	Lit	2.74	2.54	2.86	2.67	2.39
Luxembourg	Euro	0.79	0.74	0.83	0.77	0.69
Macedonia	Macedonian denar	49.05	46.45	50.76	47.12	42.43
Malta	Maltese lira	0.34	0.32	0.36	0.33	0.30
Moldova	Moldovan leu	13.10	12.38	12.58	13.03	0.69
Monaco	Euro	0.79	0.74	0.83	0.77	0.69
Montenegro	Euro	0.79	0.74	0.83	0.77	0.69
The Netherlands	Euro	0.79	0.74	0.83	0.77	0.69
Norway	Norwegian krone	6.65	6.06	6.59	6.45	5.53
Poland	Zloty	3.74	2.99	13.25	2.99	2.49
Portugal	Euro	0.79	0.74	0.83	0.77	0.69
Romania	New leu	32,596.00	28,979.20	(b) 2.95	2.67	2.45
Russia	Rouble	29.24	27.72	28.46	26.57	24.68
San Marino	Euro	0.79	0.74	0.83	0.77	0.69
Serbia	Dinar	54.29	58.30	70.73	61.46	54.20
Slovakia	Slovak koruna	32.64	28.50	32.26	26.95	23.23
Slovenia	Euro	187.79	176.28	198.40	239.64	(d) 0.69
Spain	Euro	0.79	0.74	0.83	0.77	0.69
Sweden	Swedish krone	7.20	6.65	7.73	7.02	6.52
Switzerland	Swiss franc	1.24	1.14	1.29	1.25	1.15
Turkey	New Turkish lira	1,405,000.00	(a) 1.35	1.33	1.43	1.18
Ukraine	Hryvna	5.33	5.31	5.05	5.06	5.06
United Kingdom	UK pound	0.56	0.52	0.57	0.51	0.49
The Holy See	Euro	0.79	0.74	0.83	0.77	0.69
Euro	Single currency from 1 Jan 2002	0.79	0.74	0.83	0.77	0.69

(a) new Turkish lira from 1 Jan 2005; (b) new leu from 1 Jul 2005; (c) new manat from 1 Jan 2006; (d) euro adopted, tolar pegged to euro at rate of T239.64, 1 Jan 2007).

Key indicators 2006/07

	Population (m)	Area ('000 sq km)	GDP per capita (US$)	Inflation (%)	GDP real growth (%)	Balance of trade (US$m)
Albania	(*) 3.17	28.80	(*) 3,210	(*) 3.4	(*) 6	-1,820
Andorra	(f) 0.07	0.73	(g) 38,800	3.9	(g) 3.5	–
Armenia	(*) 3.47	29.80	7,974	4.4	13.8	-588
Austria	(*) 8.28	83.90	(*) 45,181	2.2	3.4	3,430
Azerbaijan	(*) 8.55	86.60	(*) 3,663	16.0	23.3	3,300
Belarus	(*) 9.65	208.00	(*) 4,641	8.4	(*) 8.2	-527
Belgium	10.66	30.50	42,557	1.8	2.7	5,240
Bosnia and Hercegovina	(*) 3.98	51.10	(*) 3,712	1.3	5.8	-4,950
Bulgaria	7.64	111.00	5,186	7.5	6.2	-5,400
Croatia	4.44	56.50	11,576	2.9	5.8	-9,290
Cyprus	(*) 0.78	9.30	(*) 27,326	2.1	2.1	-4,290
Czech Republic	(*) 10.27	78.90	(*) 17,070	2.8	6.5	-1,740
Denmark	(*) 5.45	43.10	(*) 57,261	(*) 1.7	1.8	10,260
Estonia	1.34	45.10	21,278	6.6	7.1	-1,840
Faroe Islands	0.05	1.40	–	5.5	–	–
Finland	(*) 5.26	338.10	(*) 46,602	1.6	4.4	32,200
France	(*) 61.68	544.00	(*) 41,511	1.6	1.8	-32,140
Georgia	(*) 4.37	69.70	(*) 2,355	9.2	12.4	-1,210
Germany	82.20	357.00	40,154	2.2	2.5	189,240
Gibraltar	0.03	(d)	(f) 38,322	(f) 2.8	10.8	-194
Greece	11.12	132.00	(*) 28,278	3.0	(*) 4.0	-34,250
Greenland	0.06	2,166.10	20,000	2.3	(h) 2.3	–
Hungary	(*) 10.06	93.00	(*) 13765	(*) 7.9	(*) 1.3	-1,990
Iceland	0.31	103.10	63,830	5.3	3.8	-1480
Ireland	(*) 4.32	70.30	59,924	2.9	(*) 5.3	37,650
Italy	58.67	301.30	35,872	2.0	1.5	6,000
Latvia	(*) 2.28	64.60	(*) 11,985	(*) 10.1	(*) 10.2	-2,970
Liechtenstein	(a) 0.04	0.20	***25,000	1.0	–	–
Lithuania	3.38	65.20	(*) 11,354	5.8	(*) 8.8	-2,840
Luxembourg	0.48	2.60	(*) 104,673	2.3	(*) 5.4	-4,210
Macedonia	(*) 2.05	25.70	3,647	2.2	(*) 5.0	-1,190
Malta	(*) 0.41	0.40	(*) 18,089	0.7	3.8	-1,200
Moldova	4.26	34.00	861	11.9	7.0	-1,191
Monaco	(b) 0.03	(e)	–	–	–	–
Montenegro	(*) 0.66	14.00	(*) 3,800	3.4	(*) 7.5	–
Netherlands	(*) 16.62	41.50	(*) 46,261	(*) 3.2	(*) 3.5	46,950
Norway	(*) 4.67	324.00	(*) 83,,923	2.5	3.5	50,140
Poland	(*) 38.14	312.70	(*) 11,041	2.5	6.5	-4,310
Portugal	10.62	92.10	21,019	7.7	1.9	-20,860
Romania	(*) 21.56	237.50	(*) 7,697	2.5	6.5	-9,620
Russia	(*) 6,0142.10	17,075.00	(*) 9,075	9.0	8.1	118,270
San Marino	(c) (g) 0.03	0.01	–	–	–	–
Serbia	(*) 7.45	102.20	(*) 5,596	6.8	7.3	-6,030
Slovakia	5.41	49.00	13,857	2.8	10.4	-2,450
Slovenia	2.03	20.30	22,933	3.6	6.0	-1,270
Spain	44.87	504.80	32,067	2.8	3.8	-8,559
Sweden	(*) 9.17	449.00	(*) 49,655	1.7	5.6	19,700
Switzerland	(*) 7.3	41.30	(*) 58,084	0.8	3.1	4,840
Turkey	74.88	779.50	9,629	8.7	4.9	-32,770
Ukraine	(*) 46.12	603.70	(*) 3,046	12.8	7.3	-1,140
United Kingdom	(*) 60.84	244.10	(*) 45,575	2.3	2.3	-119,370

(*) estimate (a) 35,322; (b) 32,000 (c) 30,368; area 5.8 square km; (d) area 5.8 square km; latest figures: (e) area 1.8 square km; (f) 2005; (g) 2006

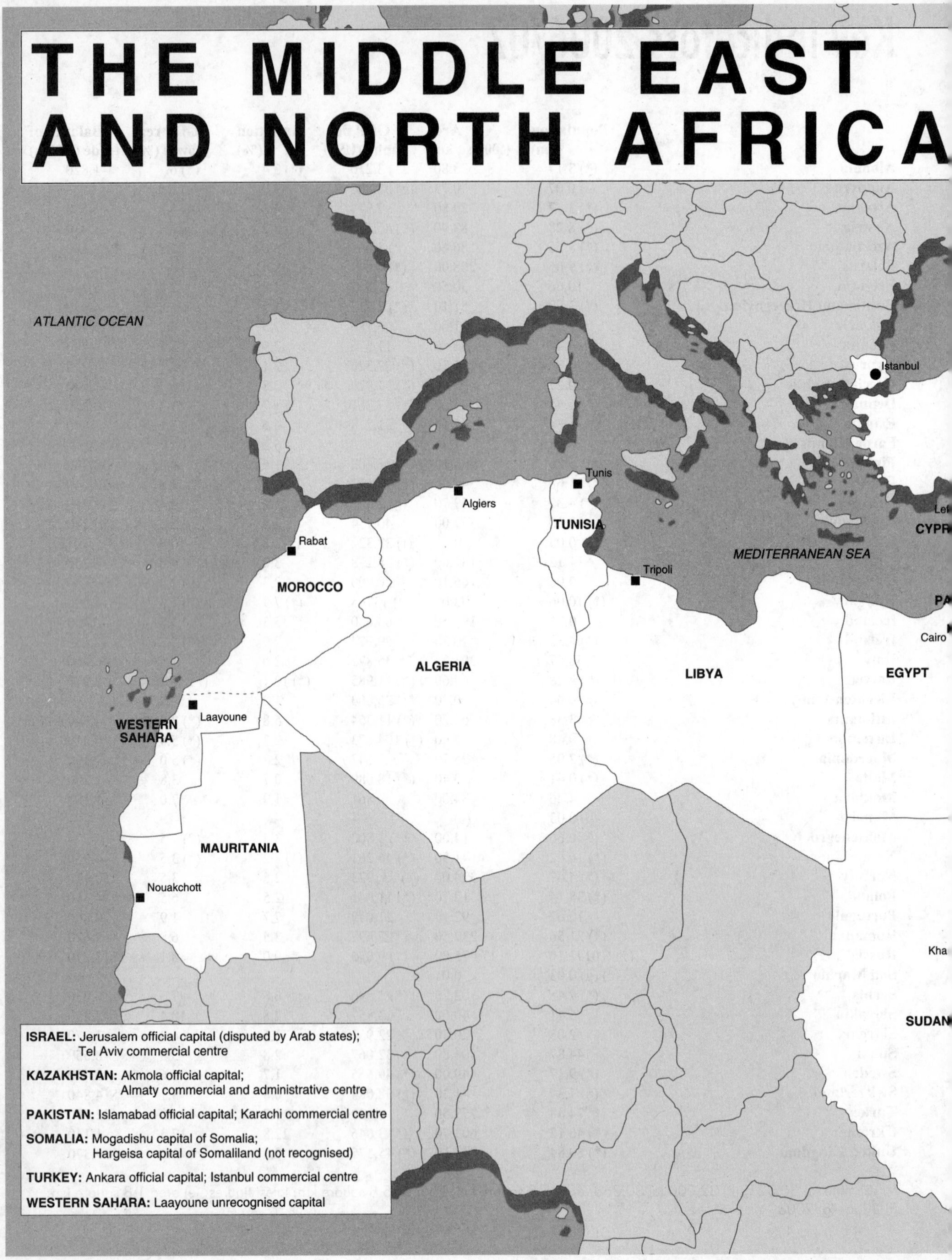
THE MIDDLE EAST
AND NORTH AFRICA
ATLANTIC OCEAN
MEDITERRANEAN SEA
Istanbul
Tunis
Algiers
TUNISIA
Rabat
Tripoli
MOROCCO
Cairo
ALGERIA
LIBYA
EGYPT
Laayoune
WESTERN SAHARA
MAURITANIA
Nouakchott
SUDAN
ISRAEL: Jerusalem official capital (disputed by Arab states); Tel Aviv commercial centre
KAZAKHSTAN: Akmola official capital; Almaty commercial and administrative centre
PAKISTAN: Islamabad official capital; Karachi commercial centre
SOMALIA: Mogadishu capital of Somalia; Hargeisa capital of Somaliland (not recognised)
TURKEY: Ankara official capital; Istanbul commercial centre
WESTERN SAHARA: Laayoune unrecognised capital

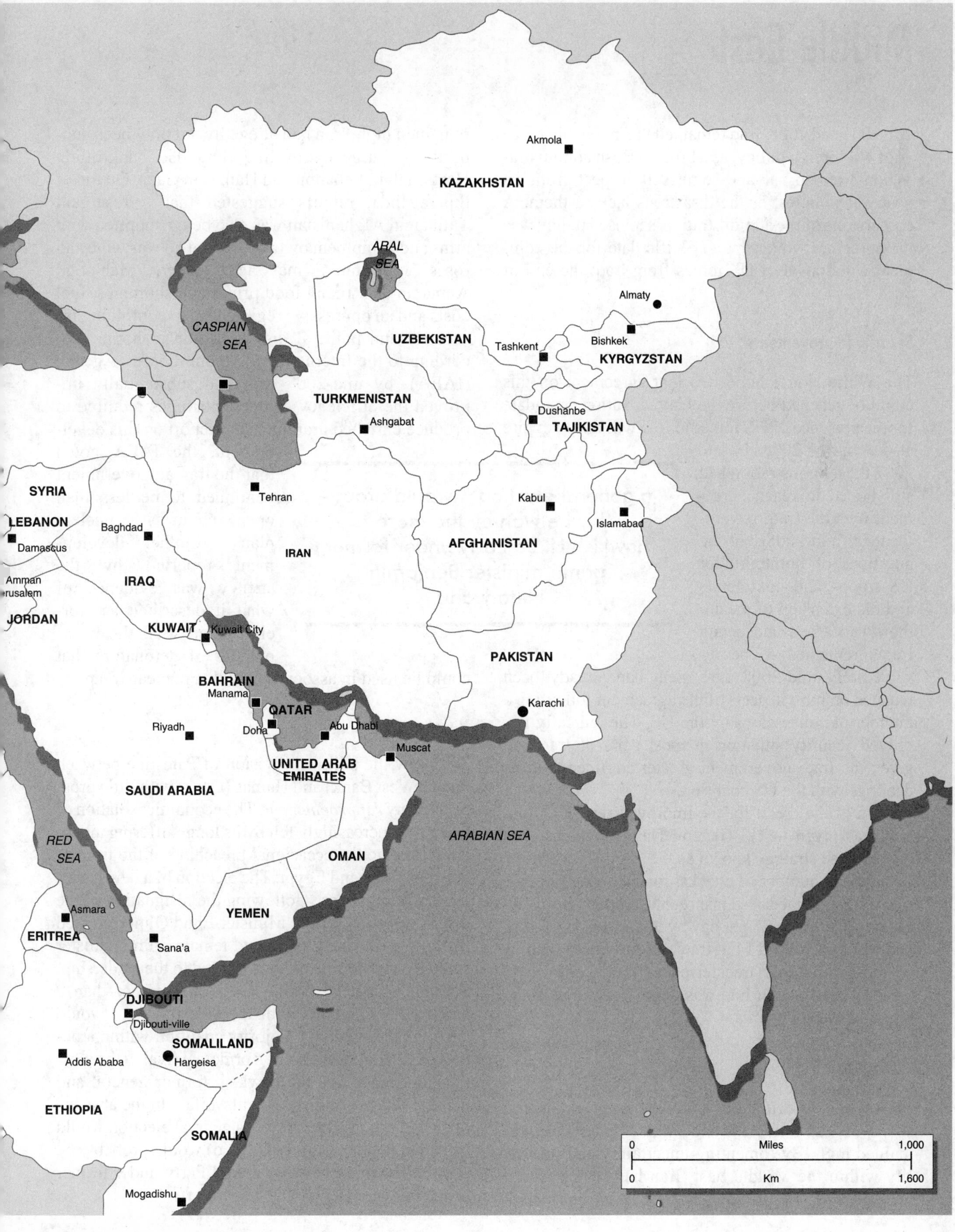
Akmola
KAZAKHSTAN
ARAL SEA
Almaty
CASPIAN SEA
UZBEKISTAN
Tashkent
Bishkek
KYRGYZSTAN
TURKMENISTAN
Dushanbe
Ashgabat
TAJIKISTAN
SYRIA
Tehran
Kabul
LEBANON
Baghdad
Islamabad
Damascus
IRAN
AFGHANISTAN
Amman
rusalem
IRAQ
JORDAN
KUWAIT
Kuwait City
PAKISTAN
BAHRAIN
Manama
QATAR
Karachi
Riyadh
Doha
Abu Dhabi
Muscat
UNITED ARAB EMIRATES
SAUDI ARABIA
RED SEA
ARABIAN SEA
OMAN
Asmara
YEMEN
ERITREA
Sana'a
DJIBOUTI
Djibouti-ville
SOMALILAND
Addis Ababa
Hargeisa
ETHIOPIA
SOMALIA
Mogadishu
0
Miles
1,000
0
Km
1,600

Middle East

In 2007 and 2008, Iraq remained the inevitable focus of US foreign policy, as a bruised Bush administration tried to salvage some self respect from its post-war policies, or the disastrous lack of them. A cornerstone of the administration's revised policy was the agreement to accept a specific date for the complete withdrawal of US forces from Iraq: the end of 2011.

Security improvements

The White House hope was that agreement on this could be reached before the United Nations mandate for the presence of US forces in Iraq was due to expire at the end of 2008. In late 2007 the administration had still hoped to reach agreement with the Iraqi government by mid-2008, but the questions of immunity for US troops and contractors and the extension of the authority to arrest and detain Iraqis remained to be resolved. By mid-2008 agreement had already been reached on most aspects of the agreement following a number of concessions by the US. The radically improved security situation in most parts of Iraq had given the Iraqi government greater confidence in its dealings with the US coalition.

a general election ...would probably be won by the more hawkish Likud Party under former prime minister Benjamin Netanyahu.

Much of the credit for the improved security situation was given to US General David Petraeus who oversaw the strategy known as the 'surge' which saw the average number of attacks, for the most part carried out by al Qaeda-led insurgents, reduced from 180 per day in 2007 to 25 per day by mid-2008. US forces had withdrawn from 14 of Iraq's 18 provinces with 11 of those provinces transferred to Iraqi control. Al Qaeda's presence in Iraq was largely confined to the region of Mesopotamia.

Nuclear Iran?

Meanwhile, speculation as to the true extent and scope of Iran's nuclear and military objectives remained high. By fomenting uncertainty and insecurity within the Middle East, Iran had long ensured that the crude oil price on which its ambitions rested, remained high. Iran had allegedly not only been supporting insurgency in Iraq, but also bankrolling Hezbollah in Lebanon and Hamas in Gaza. On top of this agenda, reports suggested that a resurgent Taliban in Afghanistan was also being supplied with arms and equipment by Iran. But not all was wine and roses for Iran's maverick leader, Mahmoud Ahmadinejad: rising food prices and shortages, fuel costs and an oppressive regime lead to continuing insecurity and political dissatisfaction at home. According to the International Atomic Energy Agency (IAEA), by mid-2008 Iran had substantially improved the efficiency of the centrifuges required to produce enriched uranium. In it report on this development, the IAEA noted that the Iranian government continued to be less than open about its nuclear plans. Another development reported by the agency was evidence of what it described as 'foreign expertise' in the development of detonators that could be used in association with a nuclear weapon.

New Israeli broom

2007 saw the political division of Palestine between Fatah (West Bank) and Hamas (Gaza) with little prospect of any *rapprochement*. The economic isolation of Gaza was increasingly felt by its long-suffering inhabitants despite the occasional breaching of the frontier between Gaza and Egypt. The election of a new leader for the Kadima party following the resignation of the disgraced Israeli Prime Minister Ehud Olmert looked likely to give Israel its second female prime minister since Golda Meir in 1974. If elected to the leadership, Foreign Minister Livni – a diplomat rather than a hawk in negotiations with the Palestinians – would have to put together a majority coalition within a period of 120 days. Ms Livni's principal rival in the election for leader was the hawkish former general and current defence minister Shaul Mofaz. In the absence of any coalition government, a general election would be called, which (polls suggested) would probably be won by the more hawkish Likud Party under former prime minister Benjamin Netanyahu.

Currencies (units per US$) – Middle East

	Unit	Jan 2004	Jan 2005	Jan 2006	Jan 2007	Jan 2008
Afghanistan	Afghani	43.00	43.00	43.00	49.18	49.53
Algeria	Algerian dinar	72.53	72.10	72.74	71.71	67.21
Bahrain	Bahraini dinar	0.38	0.38	0.38	0.38	0.37
Cyprus	Cyprus pound	0.47	0.43	0.48	0.45	0.40
Djibouti	Djibouti franc	175.00	175.85	174.25	174.70	175.47
Egypt	Egyptian pound	6.17	6.07	5.76	5.71	5.54
Iran	Rial	(o) 8,303.00	8,793.00	9,035.00	9,230.00	9,332.00
Iraq	New Iraqi dinar	(o) 0.31	(a) 1,462.5	1,469.60	1,314.65	1,216.70
Israel	Shekel	4.40	4.32	4.60	4.22	3.99
Jordan	Jordanian dinar	0.71	0.71	0.71	0.71	0.71
Kazakhstan	Tenge	143.25	129.96	133.69	125.33	120.75
Kuwait	Kuwaiti dinar	0.29	0.29	0.29	0.29	0.27
Kyrgyzstan	Som	43.88	40.91	40.85	38.25	34.54
Lebanon	Lebanese pound	1,514.00	1,513.50	1,503.50	1,512.00	1,512.00
Libya	Libyan dinar	1.31	1.25	1.33	1.28	1.22
Mauritania	Ouguiya	264.61	261.64	268.17	270.80	252.54
Morocco	Moroccan dirham	8.78	8.24	9.08	8.59	7.83
Oman	Rial	0.39	0.39	0.39	0.39	0.38
Pakistan	Rupee	57.39	59.43	59.67	60.97	61.14
Palestine	Dinar (Jordanian)	0.71	0.71	0.71	0.71	0.71
	New shekel (Israeli)	4.40	4.32	4.60	4.22	3.99
Qatar	Riyal	3.64	3.64	3.64	3.64	3.64
Saudi Arabia	Riyal	3.75	3.75	3.75	3.75	3.74
Somalia	Somali shilling	2,620.00	3,068.00	2,070.00	1,375.00	1,397.00
Sudan	Sudanese pound	259.80	250.63	238.20	230.24	(c) 2.03
Syria	Syrian pound	48.83	52.21	52.21	52.21	51.10
Tajikistan	Tajik rouble	2.79	2.79	3.18	3.43	3.43
Tunisia	Tunisian dinar	1.21	1.20	1.34	1.32	1.23
Turkey	New Turkish lira	1,405,000.00	(b) 1.35	1.33	1.43	1.18
Turkmenistan	Manat	(o) 5200.00	5,200.00	5,200.00	5,200.00	5,200.00
United Arab Emirates	Dirham	3.67	3.67	3.67	3.67	3.67
Uzbekistan	Sum	980.00	1,058.00	1,140.86	1,241.10	1,287.50
Yemen	Rial	178.01	185.71	193.46	198.48	198.90

(o) Official rate; (a) new Iraqi dinar; (b) new Turkish lira from 1 Jan 2005; (c) Sudanese pound (S£) replaced dinar at rate of S£1 to 100 dinar, Jan 2007.

Key indicators 2006/07

	Population (m)	Area ('000 sq km)	GDP per capita (US$)	Inflation (%)	GDP real growth (%)	Balance of trade (US$m)
Afghanistan	(*) 25.80	647.50	(*) 323	(*) 13.0	(*) 5.5	-3,400
Algeria	34.40	2,381.70	3,825	4.6	(b) 2.0	24,350
Bahrain	(*) 0.76	0.70	(*) 25,731	(*) 3.4	(*) 6.6	1,530
Cyprus	(*) 0.78	9.30	(*) 27,326	2.1	2.1	-4,290
Djibouti	0.76	23.20	1,099	5.0	5.2	-263
Egypt	73.57	1,001.50	1,739	10.9	7.1	-9,100
Iran	(*) 70.88	1,648.20	(*) 4,149	(*) 17.5	(*) 5.8	10,960
Iraq	(*) 27.50	434.90	1,063	(*) 12.3	(*) 5.0	-1,790
Israel	(*) 7.21	20.80	(*) 22,475	0.5	5.3	-4,030
Jordan	(*) 5.73	91.90	(*) 2,794	(*) 5.4	(*) 5.7	-5,020
Kazakhstan	13.89	2,717.30	2,715	6.9	9.4	6,786
Kuwait	(*) 3.31	17.80	(*) 33,634	(*) 4.9	(*) 4.6	32,300
Kyrgyzstan	(*) 5.25	198.50	(*) 713	10.2	8.2	-419
Lebanon	(*) 3.75	10.50	(*) 6,569	(*) 4.0	4.0	-6,090
Libya	6.08	1,775.50	9,372	6.7	6.8	19,970
Mauritania	2.96	1,030.70	931	7.2	7.2	-573
Morocco	30.73	711.00	2,389	2.0	2.2	-10,290
Oman	(*) 2.57	320.00	(*) 15,584	(*) 5.5	(*) 6.4	10,660
Pakistan	158.17	803.90	(*) 909	7.7	(*) 6.4	-6,180
Palestine	(*) 4.00	6.30	(*) 1,258	6.9	-8.0	–
Qatar	(*) 0.93	11.40	(*) 72,849	(*) 13.8	(*) 14.2	18,190
Saudi Arabia	(*) 24.29	2,149.70	(*) 15,481	(*) 4.1	(*) 4.1	123,310
Somalia	8.69	738.00	(b) 283	(c) 100.0	(d) 2.4	-335
Sudan	37.16	2,505.80	1,242	7.9	10.5	-1,120
Syria	(*) 19.41	185.20	(*) 1,946	(*) 7.0	(*) 3.9	-2,320
Tajikistan	(*) 6.42	143.10	(*) 578	13.1	7.8	-323
Tunisia	10.92	164.20	3,397	3.1	6.3	-1,970
Turkey	74.88	779.50	9,629	8.7	4.9	-32,770
Turkmenistan	(*) 5.19	488.10	(*) 5,189	(*) 6.4	(*) 11.6	2,000
United Arab Emirates	(*) 4.49	83.60	(*) 42,934	(*) 11.0	(*) 7.4	42,950
Uzbekistan	(*) 27.37	447.40	(*) 815	(*) 12.3	(*) 9.5	1,080
Yemen	(*) 22.29	528.00	(*) 972	(*) 12.4	(*) 3.1	2,260

(*) estimate

US Embassies

Albania
2100 S Street NW
Washington, DC 20008
Phone: (202) 223-4942
Fax: (202) 628-7342
E-mail: info@albaniaembassy.org
www.albaniaembassy.org

Afghanistan
2341 Wyoming Ave. NW
Washington, DC 20008
Phone: (202) 483-6410
Fax: (202) 483-6488
E-mail: Info@embassyofafghanistan.org
www.embassyofafghanistan.org

Algeria
2118 Kalorama Rd. NW
Washington, DC 20008
Phone: (202) 265-2800
Fax: (202) 667-2174
E-mail: ambassadoroffice@yahoo.com
www.algeria-us.org

Andorra
2 United Nations Plaza
25th Floor
New York, NY 10017

Angola
1615 M Street NW
Suite 900
Washington, DC 20036
Phone: (202) 785-1156
Fax: (202) 785-1258
E-mail: angola@angola.org
www.angola.org

Antigua & Barbuda
3216 New Mexico Ave. NW
Washington, DC 20016
Phone: (202) 362-5122
Fax: (202) 332-3171

Argentina
1600 New Hampshire Ave NW
Washington, DC 20009
Phone: (202) 238-6400
Fax: (202) 332-3171
E-mail: info@embajadaargentinaeeuu.org
www.embajadaargentinaeeuu.org

Armenia
2225 R Street
Washington, DC 20008
Phone: (202) 319-1976
Fax: (202) 319-2982
E-mail: armpublic@speakeasy.net
www.armeniaemb.org

Australia
1601 Massachusetts Ave. NW
Washington, DC 20036
Phone: (202) 797-3000
Fax: (202) 797-3168
www.austemb.org

Austria
3524 International Court NW
Washington, DC 20008-3035
Phone: (202) 895-6700
Fax: (202) 895-6750

Azerbaijan
2741 34th Street NW
Washington, DC 20008
Phone: (202) 337-3500
Fax: (202) 337-5911
E-mail: azerbaijan@azembassy.com
www.azembassy.com

Bahamas
2220 Massachusetts Ave. NW
Washington, DC 20008
Phone: (202) 319-2660
Fax: (202) 319-2668

Bahrain
3502 International Drive NW
Washington, DC 20008
Phone: (202) 342-0741
Fax: (202) 362-2192
E-mail: info@bahrainembassy.org
www.bahrainembassy.org

Bangladesh
3510 International Drive NW
Washington, DC 20008
Phone: (202) 244-2745
Fax: (202) 244-5366
E-mail: bdenq@bangladoot.org
www.bangladoot.org

Barbados
2144 Wyoming Ave. NW
Washington, DC 20008
Phone: (202) 939-9200
Fax: (202) 332-7467

Botswana
1531-3 New Hampshire Avenue NW
Washington, DC 20036
Phone: (202) 244-4990
Fax: (202) 244-4164
www.botswanaembassy.org

Belarus
1619 New Hampshire Avenue NW
Washington, DC 20009
Phone: (202) 986-1606
Fax: (202) 986-1805
E-mail: embassy@capu.net
www.belarusembassy.org

Belgium
3330 Garfield Street NW
Washington, DC 20008
Phone: (202) 333-6900
Fax: (202) 333-3079
E-mail: washington@diplobel.org
www.diplobel.us

Belize
2535 Massachusetts Avenue
Washington, DC 20008
Phone: (202) 332-9636
Fax: (202) 332-6888
E-mail: belize@oas.org
www.embassyofbelize.org

Benin
2124 Kalorama Road NW
Washington, DC 20008
Phone: (202) 232-6656
Fax: (202) 265-1996

Bhutan
2 UN Plaza
27th Floor
New York, NY 10017
Phone: (212) 826-1919
Fax: (212) 826-2998

Bolivia
3014 Massachusetts Avenue NW
Washington, DC 20008
Phone: (202) 483-4410
Fax: (202)328-3712
www.bolivia-usa.org

Bosnia & Herzegovina
2109 E Street NW
Washington, DC 20037
Phone: (202) 337-1500
Fax: (202) 337-1502
E-mail: info@bhembassy.org
www.bhembassy.org

Brazil
3006 Massachusetts Avenue NW
Washington, DC 20008
Phone: (202) 238-2700
Fax: (202) 238-2827
E-mail: webmaster@brasilemb.org
www.brasilmg.org

Brunei Darussalam
3520 International Court NW
Washington, DC 20008
Phone: (202) 237-1838
Fax: (202) 885-0560
E-mail: info@bruneiembassy.org
www.bruneiembassy.org

Bulgaria
1621 22nd Street NW
Washington, DC 20008
Phone: (202) 387-0174
Fax: (202) 234-7993
E-mail: office@bulgaria-embassy.org
www.bulgaria-embassy.org

Burkina Faso
2340 Massachusetts Avenue NW
Washington, DC 20008
Phone: (202) 332-5577
Fax: (202) 667-1882
E-mail: bf@burkinaembassy-usa.org
www.burkinaembassy-usa.org

Burundi
2233 Wisconsin Avenue NW
Suite 212
Washington, DC 20007
Phone: (202) 342-2574
Fax: (202) 342-2578
E-mail: burundiembassy@erols.com
www.burundiembassy-usa.org

Cambodia
4500 16th Street NW
Washington, DC 20011
Phone: (202) 726-7742
Fax: (202) 726-8381
E-mail: mail@embassyofcambodia.org
www.embassyofcambodia.org

Cameroon
2349 Massachusetts Avenue NW
Washington, DC 20008
Phone: (202) 265-8790
Fax: (202) 387-3826
E-mail: cdm@ambacam-usa.org

Canada
501 Pennsylvania Avenue NW
Washington, DC 20001
Phone: (202) 682-1740
Fax: (202) 682-7726
E-mail: webmaster@canadianembassy.org
www.canadianembassy.org

Cape Verde
3415 Massachusetts Avenue NW
Washington, DC 20007
Phone: (202) 965-6820
Fax: (202) 965-1207
E-mail: ambacvus@sysnet.net
www.capeverdeusa.org

Central African Republic
1618 22nd Street NW
Washington, DC 20008
Phone: (202) 483-7800
Fax: (202) 332-9893

Chad
2002 R Street NW
Washington, DC 20009
Phone: (202) 462-4009
Fax: (202) 265-1937
E-mail: info@chadembassy.org
www.chadembassy.org

Chile
1732 Massachusetts Avenue NW
Washington, DC 20036
Phone: (202) 785-1746
Fax: (202) 887-5579
www.chile-usa.org

China
2300 Connecticut Avenue NW
Washington, DC 20036
Phone: (202) 328-2500
Fax: (202) 588-0032
E-mail: chinaembassy_us@fmprc.gov.cn
www.china-embassy.org

Colombia
2118 Leroy Place NW
Washington, DC 20008
Phone: (202) 387-8338
Fax: (202) 232-8643
E-mail: emwas@colombiaemb.org
www.colombiaemb.org

Comoros
420 E 50th Street
New York, NY 10022
Phone: (212) 750-1637
Fax: (212) 983-4712

Congo, Republic of
4891 Colorado Avenue NW
Washington, DC 20011
Phone: (202) 726-5500
Fax: (202) 726-1860
E-mail: info@embassyofcongo.org
www.embassyofcongo.org

Congo, Democratic Republic of
1726 M Street NW
Washington, DC 20011
Phone: (202) 234-7690
Fax: (202) 234-2609

Costa Rica
2114 S Street NW
Washington, DC 20008
Phone: (202) 234-2945
Fax: (202) 265-4795
E-mail: embassy@costarica-embassy.org
www.costarica-embassy.org

Cote d'Ivoire
2424 Massachusetts Avenue NW
Washington, DC 20008
Phone: (202) 797-0300

Croatia
2343 Massachusetts Avenue NW
Washington, DC 20008
Phone: (202) 588-5899
Fax: (202) 588-8936
E-mail: webmaster@croatiaemb.org
www.croatiaemb.org

Cuba
2630 and 2639 16th Street NW
Washington, DC 20009
Phone: (202) 797-8518
Fax: (202) 986-7283
E-mail: cubaseccion@igc.apc.org
http://embacu.cubaminrex.cu

Cyrus
2211 R Street NW
Washington, DC 20008
Phone: (202) 462-5772
Fax: (202) 483-6710
E-mail: cypembwash@earthlink.net
www.cyprusembassy.net

Denmark
3200 Whitehaven Street NW
Washington, DC 20008
Phone: (202) 234-4300
Fax: (202) 328-1470
E-mail: wasamb@wasamb.um.dk
www.denmarkemb.org

Djibouti
1156 15th Street NW
Suite 515
Washington, DC 20005
Phone: (202) 331-0270
Fax: (202) 331-0302

Dominica
3216 New Mexico Avenue NW
Washington, DC 20016
Phone: (202) 364-6781
Fax: (202) 364-6791
E-mail: embdomdc@aol.com

Dominican Republic
1715 22nd Street NW
Washington, DC 20008
Phone: (202) 332-6280
Fax: (202) 265-8057
E-mail: embdompreusa@msn.com
www.domrep.org

Ecuador
2535 15th Street NW
Washington, DC 20009
Phone: (202) 234-7200
Fax: (202) 667-3482
E-mail: mecauwaa@erols.com
www.ecuador.org

Egypt
3521 International Court NW
Washington, DC 20008
Phone: (202) 895-5400
Fax: (202) 244-4319
E-mail: embassy@egyptembdc.org
www.egyptembassy.us

El Salvador
2308 California Street NW
Washington, DC 20008
Phone: (202) 265-9671
E-mail: cbartoli@elsalvador.org
www.elsalvador.org

Equatorial Guinea
2020 16th Street NW
Washington, DC 20009
Phone: (202) 518-5700
Fax: (202) 518-5252

Eritrea
1708 New Hampshire Avenue NW
Washington, DC 20009
Phone: (202) 319-1991
Fax: (202) 319-1304
E-mail: freweini@embassyeritrea.org

Czech Republic
3900 Spring of Freedom Street NW
Washington, DC 20008
Phone: (202) 274-9100
Fax: (202) 966-8540
E-mail: washington@embassy.mzv.cz
www.mzv.cz/washington

Estonia
1730 M Street NW
Suite 503
Washington, DC 20036
Phone: (202) 274-9100
Fax: (202) 588-0108
E-mail: info@estemb.org
www.estemb.org

Ethiopia
3506 International Drive NW
Washington, DC 20036
Phone: (202) 364-1200
Fax: (202) 686-9551
E-mail: info@ethiopianembassy.org
www.ethiopianembassy.org

Fiji
2233 Wisconsin Avenue NW
Suite 240
Washington, DC 20007
Phone: (202) 337-8320
Fax: (202) 337-1996
E-mail: info@fijiembassydc.com
www.fijiembassydc.com

Finland
3301 Massachusetts Avenue NW
Washington, DC 20008
Phone: (202) 298-5800
Fax: (202) 298-6030
E-mail: info@finland.org
www.finland.org

France
4101 Reservoir Road NW
Washington, DC 20007
Phone: (202) 944-6000
Fax: (202) 944-6072
E-mail: info@amb-wash.fr
www.info-france-usa.org

Gabon
2034 20th Street NW
Suite 200
Washington, DC 20009
Phone: (202) 797-1000
Fax: (202) 332-0668

Gambia
155 15th Street NW
Suite 1000
Washington, DC 20005
Phone: (202) 785-1399
Fax: (202) 785-1430
E-mail: info@gambiaembassy.us
www.gambiaembassy.us

Georgia
1615 New Hampshire Avenue NW
Suite 300
Washington, DC 20009
Phone: (202) 387-2390
Fax: (202) 393-4537
E-mail: embassy@georgiaemb.org
www.georgiaemb.org

Germany
4645 Reservoir Road NW
Washington, DC 20007-1998
Phone: (202) 298-4000
Fax: (202) 298-4249
www.germany-info.org

Ghana
3512 International Drive NW
Washington, DC 20008
Phone: (202) 686-4520
Fax: (202) 686-4527
E-mail: ghtrade@cais.com
www.ghana-embassy.org

Greece
2221 Massachusetts Avenue NW
Washington, DC 20008
Phone: (202) 939-1300
Fax: (202) 393-1324
www.greekembassy.org

Grenada
1701 New Hampshire Avenue NW
Washington, DC 20009
Phone: (202) 265-2561
Fax: (202) 265-2468
www.grenadaembassyusa.org

Guatemala
2220 R Street NW
Washington, DC 20008
Phone: (202) 745-4952
Fax: (202) 745-1908
E-mail: info@guatemala-embassy.org
www.guatemala-embassy.org

Guinea
2112 Leroy Place NW
Washington, DC 20008
Phone: (202) 986-4300

Guinea-Bissau
15929 Yukon Lake
Rockville, MD 20855
Phone: (301) 947-3958.

Guyana
2490 Tracy Place NW
Washington, DC 20008
Phone: (202) 265-6900
Fax: (202) 232-1297
E-mail: guyanaembassy@hotmail.com
www.guyana.org/govt/embassy.html

Haiti
2311 Massachusetts Avenue NW
Washington, DC 20008
Phone: (202) 332-4090
Fax: (202) 745-7215
E-mail: embassy@haiti.org
www.haiti.org

Holy See, The (Vatican City)
3339 Massachusetts Avenue NW
Washington, DC 20008
Phone: (202) 333-7121

Honduras
3007 Tilden Street NW
Suite 4M
Washington, DC 20008
Phone: (202) 966-7702
Fax: (202) 966-9751
E-mail: embhondu@aol.com
www.hondurasemb.org

Hungary
3910 Shoemaker Street NW
Washington, DC 20008
Phone: (202) 362-6730
Fax: (202) 966-8135
E-mail: office@huembwas.org
www.huembwas.org

Iceland
1156 15th Street NW
Suite 1200
Washington, DC 20005-1704
Phone: (202) 362-6730
Fax: (202) 265-6656
E-mail: icemb.wash@utn.stjr.is
www.iceland.org

India
2107 Massachusetts Avenue NW
Washington, DC 20008
Phone: (202) 939-7000
Fax: (202) 265-4351
www.indianembassy.org

Indonesia
2020 Massachusetts Avenue NW
Washington, DC 20036
Phone: (202) 775-5200
Fax: (202) 775-5365
www.embassyofindonesia.org

Iran
2209 Wisconsin Avenue NW
Washington, DC 20007
Phone: (202) 965-4990
Fax: (202) 965-1073
www.daftar.org/Eng/default.asp?lang=org

Iraq
1801 P Street NW
Washington, DC 20036
Phone: (202) 483-7500
Fax: (202) 462-5066
www.iraqembassy.org

Ireland
2234 Massachusetts Avenue NW
Washington, DC 20008
Phone: (202) 462-3939
Fax: (202) 232-5993
E-mail: ireland@irelandemb.org
www.irelandemb.org

Israel
3514 International Drive NW
Washington, DC 20008
Phone: (202) 364-5500
Fax: (202) 364-5423
E-mail: ask@israelemb.org
www.israelemb.org

Italy
3000 Whitehaven Street NW
Washington, DC 20008
Phone: (202) 612-4400
Fax: (202) 518-2154
www.italyemb.org

Jamaica
1520 New Hampshire Avenue NW
Washington, DC 20036
Phone: (202) 452-0660
Fax: (202) 452-0081
www.embassyofjamaica.org

Japan
2520 Massachusetts Avenue NW
Washington, DC 20008
Phone: (202) 238-6700
Fax: (202) 328-2187
www.embjapan.org

Jordan
3504 International Drive NW
Washington, DC 20008
Phone: (202) 966-2664
Fax: (202) 966-3110
E-mail: HKJEmbassyDC@aol.com
www.jordanembassyus.org

Kazakhstan
1401 16th Street NW
Washington, DC 20036
Phone: (202) 232-5488
Fax: (202) 232-5845
E-mail: kazak@intr.net
www.kazakhembus.com

Kenya
2249 R Street NW
Washington, DC 20008
Phone: (202) 387-3101
Fax: (202) 462-3829
E-mail: info@kenyaembassy.com
www.kenyaembassy.com

Korea
2450 Massachusetts Avenue NW
Washington, DC 20008
Phone: (202) 939-5600
Fax: (202) 797-0595
www.koreaembassyusa.org

Kuwait
2940 Tilden Street NW
Washington, DC 20008
Phone: (202) 966-0702
Fax: (202) 364-2868

Kyrgyzstan
2360 Massachusetts Avenue NW
Washington, DC 20008
Phone: (202) 395-7550
Fax: (202) 338-5139
E-mail: consul@kyrgysembassy.org

Laos
2222 S Street NW
Washington, DC 20008
Phone: (202) 332-6416
Fax: (202) 332-4923
www.laoembassy.com

Latvia
4325 17th Street NW
Washington, DC 20011
Phone: (202) 726-8213
Fax: (202) 726-6785
E-mail: embassy@latvia-USA.org
www.latvia-usa.org

Lebanon
2560 28th Street NW
Washington, DC 20008
Phone: (202) 939-6300
Fax: (202) 939-6324
E-mail: info@lebanonembassyus.org
www.lebanonembassyus.org

Lesotho
2511 Massachusetts Avenue NW
Washington, DC 20008
Phone: (202) 797-5533
Fax: (202) 234-6815
E-mail: lesothoembassy@verizon.net
www.lesothoemb-usa.gov.is

Liberia
5201 16th Street NW
Washington, DC 20011
Phone: (202) 723-0437
Fax: (202) 723-0436
E-mail: info@embassyofliberia.org
www.embassyofliberia.org

Lithuania
2622 16th Street NW
Washington, DC 20009-4202
Phone: (202) 234-5860
Fax: (202) 328-0466
E-mail: admin@ltembassyus.org
www.ltembassyus.org

Luxembourg
2200 Massachusetts Avenue NW
Washington, DC 20008
Phone: (202) 265-4171
Fax: (202) 328-8270
E-mail: infos@luxemnourg-usa.org
www.luxembourg-usa.org

Macedonia
1101 30th Street NW
Suite 302 Washington, DC 20007
Phone: (202) 337-3063
Fax: (202) 337-3093
E-mail: usoffice@macedoniaembassy.org
www.macedoniaembassy.org

Madagascar
2374 Massachusetts Avenue NW
Washington, DC 20008
Phone: (202) 265-5525
E-mail: malagasy@embassy.org
www.embassy.org/madagascar

Malawi
2408 Massachusetts Avenue NW
Washington, DC 20008
Phone: (202) 797-10007

Malaysia
3516 International Court NW
Washington, DC 20008
Phone: (202) 572-9700
Fax: (202) 483-7661
E-mail: malwashdc@kln.gov.my
www.myperwakilan.mjf.gov.my

Mali
2130 R Street NW
Washington, DC 20008
Phone: (202) 332-2249
Fax: (202) 332-6603
E-mail: info@maliembassy.us
www.maliembassy.us/new_site

Malta
2107 Connecticut Avenue NW
Washington, DC 20008
Phone: (202) 462-3611
Fax: (202) 387-5470
E-mail: Malta_Embassy@compuserve.com
www.foreign.gov.mt/org/ministry/missions/washington2

Marshall Islands
2433 Massachusetts Avenue NW
Washington, DC 20008
Phone: (202) 234-5414
Fax: (202) 232-3236
E-mail: info@rmiembassyus.org
www.rmiembassyus.org

Mauritania
2129 Leroy Place NW
Washington, DC 20008
Phone: (202) 232-5700
Fax: (202) 319-2623
E-mail: hyoussouf@comcast.net
www.ambanm-dc.org/newsite

Mauritius
4301 Connecticut Avenue NW
Suite 441
Washington, DC 20008
Phone: (202) 244-1491
Fax: (202) 966-0983
E-mail: MAURITUS.EMBASSY@prodigy.net
www.maurinet.com/embasydc.html

Mexico
1911 Pennsylvania Avenue NW
Washington, DC 20006
Phone: (202) 728-1600
Fax: (202) 728-1698
E-mail: mexembusa@sre.gob.mx
www.embassyofmexico.org

Micronesia
1725 N Street NW
Washington, DC 20036
Phone: (202) 223-4383
Fax: (202) 223-4391
E-mail: fsm@fsmembassy.org
www.fsmembassy.org

Moldova
2101 S Street NW
Washington, DC 20008
Phone: (202) 667-1130
Fax: (202) 667-1204
www.embassyrm.org

Mongolia
2833 M Street NW
Washington, DC 20007
Phone: (202) 333-7117
Fax: (202) 298-9227
E-mail: esyam@mongolianembassy.us
www.mongolianembassy.us

Morocco
1601 21st Street NW
Washington, DC 20009
Phone: (202) 462-7979
Fax: (202) 265-0161

Mozambique
1990 M Street NW
Suite 570
Washington, DC 20036
Phone: (202) 293-7146
Fax: (202) 835-0245
E-mail: embamoc@aol.com
www.embamoc-usa.org

Myanmar
2300 S Street NW
Washington, DC 20008
Phone: (202) 332-9044
Fax: (202) 332-0946
E-mail: info@mewashingtondc.com
www.mewashingtondc.com

Namibia
1605 New Hampshire Avenue NW
Washington, DC 20008
Phone: (202) 986-0540
Fax: (202) 986-0443
www.namibiaembassyusa.org

Nepal
2131 Leroy Place NW
Washington, DC 20008
Phone: (202) 667-4550
Fax: (202) 667-5534
E-mail: nepali@erols.com

Netherlands
4200 Linnean Avenue NW
Washington, DC 20008
Phone: (202) 244-5300
Fax: (202) 362-3430
www.netherlands-embassy.org

New Zealand
37 Observatory Circle
Washington, DC 20008
Phone: (202) 328-4800
Fax: (202) 667-5227
E-mail: nz@nzemb.org
www.nzemb.org

Nicaragua
1627 New Hampshire Avenue NW
Washington, DC 20009
Phone: (202) 939-6570
Fax: 9202) 939-6542

Niger
2204 R Street NW
Washington, DC 20008
Phone: (202) 483-4224
Fax: (202) 483-3169
E-mail: ambassadeniger@hotmail.com
www.pngembassy.org

Nigeria
1333 16th Street NW
Washington, DC 20036
Phone: (202) 986-8400
Fax: (202) 462-7124
www.nigeriaembassyusa.org

Norway
2720 34th Street NW
Washington, DC 20008
Phone: (202) 333-6000
Fax: (202) 337-0870
www.norway.org

Oman
2535 Belmont Road NW
Washington, DC 20008
Phone: (202) 387-1980
Fax: (202) 745-4933
www.omani.info

Pakistan
3517 International Court
Washington, DC 20008
Phone: (202) 243-6500
Fax: (202) 686-1534
E-mail: info@embassyofpakistan.org
www.embassyofpakistan.org

Palau
1150 18th Street
Suite 750
Washington, DC 20036
Phone: (202) 452-6814
Fax: (202) 452-6281
E-mail: info@palauembassy.com
www.palauembassy.com

Panama
2862 McGill Terrance NW
Washington, DC 20008
Phone: (202) 483-1407
Fax: (202) 483-8413
E-mail: info@embassyofpanama.org
www.embassyofpanama.org

Papua New Guinea
1779 Massachusetts Avenue NW
Suite 805
Washington, DC 20036
Phone: (202) 745-3680
Fax: (202) 234-4508
E-mail: info@pngembassy.org

Paraguay
2400 Massachusetts Avenue NW
Washington, DC +20008
Phone: 202) 483-6960
Fax: (202) 234-4508
E-mail: secretaria@embaparuse.gov.py
www.embaparusa.gov.py

Peru
1700 Massachusetts Avenue NW
Washington, DC 20036
Phone: (202) 833-9860
Fax: (202) 659-8124
E-mail: webmaster@embassyofperu.us
www.Peruvianembassy.us

Philippines
1600 Massachusetts Avenue NW
Washington, DC 20036
Phone: (202) 467-9300
Fax: (202) 467-9417
www.philippineembassy-usa.org

Poland
2640 16th Street NW
Washington, DC 20009
Phone: (202) 234-3800
Fax: (202) 328-6271
E-mail: polemb.info@earthlink.net

Portugal
2125 Kalorama Road NW
Washington, DC 20008
Phone: (202) 328-8610
Fax: (202) 462-3726
E-mail: portugal@portugalemb.org
www.portugalemb.org

Qatar
2555 M Street NW
Suite 200
Washington, DC 20037
Phone: (202) 274-1600
Fax: (202) 237-0061
E-mail: info@qatarembassy.org
www.qatarembassy.net

Romania
1607 23rd Street NW
Washington, DC 20008
Phone: (202) 332-4848
Fax: (202) 232-4748
E-mail: romania1@roembus.org
www.roembus.org

Russia
2650 Wisconsin Avenue NW
Washington, DC 20007
Phone: (202) 298-5700
Fax: (202) 298-5735
www.russianembassy.org

Rwanda
1714 New Hampshire Avenue NW
Washington, DC 20009
Phone: (202) 232-2882
Fax: (202) 232-4544
E-mail: rwandaemb@rwandemb.org
www.rwandemb.org

Saint Kitts/Nevis
3216 New Mexico Avenue NW
Washington, DC 20016
Phone: (202) 686-2636
Fax: (202) 686-5740
E-mail: info@embshn.com
www.embassy.gov.kn/default.asp?

Saint Lucia
3216 New Mexico Avenue NW
Washington, DC 20016
Phone: (202) 364-6792
Fax: (202) 364-6723

Saint Vincent & The Grenadines
3216 New Mexico Avenue NW
Washington, DC 20016
Phone: (202) 365-6730
Fax: (202) 364-6736
E-mail: mail@embsvg.com
www.embsvg.com

Saudi Arabia
601 New Hampshire Avenue NW
Washington, DC 20037
Phone: (202) 337-4076
E-mail: info@saudiembassy.net
www.saudiembassy.net

Senegal
2112 Wyoming Avenue NW
Washington, DC 20008
Phone: (202) 234-+0540
Fax: (202) 332-6315
E-mail: erahayu@senegalembassy-us.org
www.senegalembassy-us.org

Serbia/Montenegro/Yugoslavia
2134 Kalorama Road NW
Washington, DC 20008
Phone: (202) 332-0333
Fax: (202) 332-3933
www.serbiaembusa.org

Seychelles
800 2nd Avenue
Suite 400
New York , NY 10017
Phone: (212) 687-9766
Fax: (212) 972-1786

Sierra Leone
1701 19th Street NW
Washington, DC 20009
Phone: (202) 939-9261
Fax: (202) 483-1793
www.embassyofsierraleone.org

Singapore
3501 International Place NW
Washington, DC 20008
Phone: (202) 537-3100
Fax: (202) 537-0876
E-mail: singemb@bellatlantic.net
www.gov.sg/mfa/washington

Slovak Republic
3523 International Court NW
Washington, DC 20008
Phone: (202) 237-1054
Fax: (202) 237-6438
E-mail: info@slovakembassy-us.org
www.slovakembassy-us.org

Slovenia
1525 New Hampshire Avenue NW
Washington, DC 20036
Phone: (202) 667-5363
Fax: (202) 667-4563
www.gov.si/mzz/dkp/vwa

South Africa
3051 Massachusetts Avenue NW
Washington, DC 20008
Phone: (202) 232-4400
Fax: (202) 265-1607
E-mail: info@saembassy.org
www.saembassy.org

Spain
2375 Pennsylvania Avenue NW
Washington, DC 20037
Phone: (202) 452-0100
Fax: (202) 833-5670
E-mail: spain@spainemb.org
www.spainemb.org

Sri Lanka
2148 Wyoming Avenue NW
Washington, Dc 20008
Phone: (202) 483-4025
Fax: (202) 232-7181
E-mail: slembassy@starpower.net
www.slembassyusa.org

Sudan
2210 Massachusetts Avenue NW
Washington, DC 20008
Phone: 202) 338-8565
Fax: (202) 667-2406
E-mail: info@sudanembassy.org
www.sudanembassy.org

Suriname
4301 Connecticut Avenue NW
Suite 460
Washington, DC 20008
Phone: (202) 244-7488
Fax: (202) 244-5878
www.surinameembassy.org

Swaziland
3400 International Drive NW
Washington, DC 20008

Sweden
2900 K M Street NW
Washington, DC 20005
Phone: (202) 467-2600
Fax: (202) 467-2656
E-mail: embassaden.washington@foreign.minstry.se
www.swedenabroad.se

Switzerland
2900 Cathedral Avenue NW
Washington, DC 20008
Phone: (202) 745-7900
Fax: (202) 387-2564
E-mail: vertretung@was.rep.admin.ch
www.swissemb.org

Syria
2215 Wyoming Avenue NW
Washington, Dc 20008
Phone: (202) 745-7900
Fax: (202) 234-9458
E-mail: info@syrembassy.org
www.syrianembassy.us

Taiwan
4201 Wisconsin Avenue NW
Washington, DC 20016
Phone: (202) 895-1800
Fax: (202) 966-0825
www.roc-taiwan.org/us/mp.asp?

Tanzania
2139 R Street NW
Washington, DC 20008
Phone: (202) 939-6125
Fax: (202) 797-7408
E-mail: balozi@tanzaniaembassy-us.org
www.tanzaniaembassy-us.org

Thailand
1024 Wisconsin Avenue
Suite 401
Washington, DC 20007
Phone: (202) 944-3600
Fax: (202) 944-3611
E-mail: thai.wsn@thaiembdc.org
www.thaiembdc.org

Togo
2208 Massachusetts Avenue NW
Washington, DC 20008
Phone: (202) 234-4212
Fax: (202) 232-3190

Tonga
800 2nd Avenue
Suite 400 B
New York, NY 10017

Trinidad & Tobago
1708 Massachusetts Avenue NW
Washington, DC 20036
Phone: (202) 467-6490
Fax: (202) 785-3130
E-mail: embttgo@erols.com
http://ttembassy.cjb.net

Tunisia
1515 Massachusetts Avenue NW
Washington, DC 20005
Phone: (202) 862-1850
Fax: (202) 862-1858
http://tuniaiaembassy.org

Turkey
2525 Massachusetts Avenue NW
Washington, DC 20005
Phone: (202) 612-6700
Fax: (202) 612-6744
E-mail: info@turkey.org
www.turkey.org

Turkmenistan
2207 Massachuestts Avenue NW
Washington, DC 20008
Phone: (202) 588-1500
Fax: (202) 588-0697
E-mail: turkmen@earthlink.net
www.turkmenistanembassy.org

Uganda
5911 16th Street NW
Washington, DC 20011
Phone: (202) 726-7100
Fax: (202) 726-1727
E-mail: ugembassy@aol.com
www.ugandaembassy.com

Ukraine
3350 M Street NW
Washington, DC 20007
Phone: (202) 333-0606
Fax: (202) 333-0817
www.mfa.gov.ua/usa/en

United Arab Emirates
3522 International Court NW
Suite 400
Washington, DC 20008
Phone: (202) 243-2400
Fax: (202) 243-2432
http://uae-embassy.org

United Kingdom
3100 Massachusetts Avenue NW
Washington, DC 20008
Phone: (202) 588-6500
Fax: (202) 588-7870
www.britainusa.com

Uruguay
1913 I Street NW
Washington, DC 20006
Phone: (202) 331-1313
Fax: (202) 331-8142
E-mail: uruwashi@uruwashi.org
www.uruwashi.org

Uzbekistan
1746 Massachusetts Avenue NW
Washington, DC 20036
Phone: (202) 887-5300
Fax: (202) 293-6804
E-mail: emb@uzbekistan.org
www.uzbekistan.org

Venezuela
1099 30th Street NW
Washington, DC 20007
Phone: (202) 342-2214
Fax: (202) 342-6820
E-mail: prensa@embavenez-us.org
www.embavenez-us.org

Vietnam
1233 20th Street NW
Suite 400
Washington, DC 20037
Phone: (202) 861-0737
Fax: (202) 861-0917
E-mail: info@vietnamembassy-usa.org
www.vietnamembassy-usa.org

Western Samoa
800 2nd Avenue
Suite 400D
New York, NY 10017
Phone: (212) 599-6196
Fax: (212) 599-0797

Yemen
2319 Wyoming Avenue NW
Washington, DC 20008
Phone: (202) 965-4760
Fax: (202) 337-2017
E-mail: info@yemenembassy.org
www.yemenembassy.org

Zambia
2419 Massachusetts Avenue NW
Washington, DC 20008
Phone: (202) 265-9717
Fax: (202) 332-0826
E-mail: info@zambiainfo.org
www.zambiaembassy.org

Zimbabwe
1608 New Hampshire Avenue NW
Washington, DC 20009
Phone: (202) 332-7100
Fax: (202) 483-9326
E-mail: zimemb@erols.com
www.zimebassy-usa.org

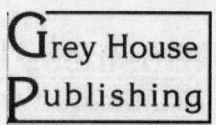

The Encyclopedia of Emerging Industries

*Published under an exclusive license from the Gale Group, Inc.

The fifth edition of the *Encyclopedia of Emerging Industries* details the inception, emergence, and current status of nearly 120 flourishing U.S. industries and industry segments. These focused essays unearth for users a wealth of relevant, current, factual data previously accessible only through a diverse variety of sources. This volume provides broad-based, highly-readable, industry information under such headings as Industry Snapshot, Organization & Structure, Background & Development, Industry Leaders, Current Conditions, America and the World, Pioneers, and Research & Technology. Essays in this new edition, arranged alphabetically for easy use, have been completely revised, with updated statistics and the most current information on industry trends and developments. In addition, there are new essays on some of the most interesting and influential new business fields, including Application Service Providers, Concierge Services, Entrepreneurial Training, Fuel Cells, Logistics Outsourcing Services, Pharmacogenomics, and Tissue Engineering. Two indexes, General and Industry, provide immediate access to this wealth of information. Plus, two conversion tables for SIC and NAICS codes, along with Suggested Further Readings, are provided to aid the user. *The Encyclopedia of Emerging Industries* pinpoints emerging industries while they are still in the spotlight. This important resource will be an important acquisition to any business reference collection.

"This well-designed source…should become another standard business source, nicely complementing Standard & Poor's Industry Surveys. It contains more information on each industry than Hoover's Handbook of Emerging Companies, is broader in scope than The Almanac of American Employers 1998-1999, but is less expansive than the Encyclopedia of Careers & Vocational Guidance. Highly recommended for all academic libraries and specialized business collections." –Library Journal

Hardcover ISBN 978-1-59237-242-3, 1,400 pages, $325.00

Encyclopedia of American Industries

*Published under an exclusive license from the Gale Group, Inc.

The Encyclopedia of American Industries is a major business reference tool that provides detailed, comprehensive information on a wide range of industries in every realm of American business. A two volume set, Volume I provides separate coverage of nearly 500 manufacturing industries, while Volume II presents nearly 600 essays covering the vast array of services and other non-manufacturing industries in the United States. Combined, these two volumes provide individual essays on every industry recognized by the U.S. Standard Industrial Classification (SIC) system. Both volumes are arranged numerically by SIC code, for easy use. Additionally, each entry includes the corresponding NAICS code(s). The *Encyclopedia's* business coverage includes information on historical events of consequence, as well as current trends and statistics. Essays include an Industry Snapshot, Organization & Structure, Background & Development, Current Conditions, Industry Leaders, Workforce, America and the World, Research & Technology along with Suggested Further Readings. Both SIC and NAICS code conversion tables and an all-encompassing Subject Index, with cross-references, complete the text. With its detailed, comprehensive information on a wide range of industries, this resource will be an important tool for both the industry newcomer and the seasoned professional.

"Encyclopedia of American Industries contains detailed, signed essays on virtually every industry in contemporary society. ... Highly recommended for all but the smallest libraries." -American Reference Books Annual

Two Volumes, Hardcover ISBN 978-1-59237-244-7, 3,000 pages, $650.00

Encyclopedia of Global Industries

*Published under an exclusive license from the Gale Group, Inc.

This fourth edition of the acclaimed *Encyclopedia of Global Industries* presents a thoroughly revised and expanded look at more than 125 business sectors of global significance. Detailed, insightful articles discuss the origins, development, trends, key statistics and current international character of the world's most lucrative, dynamic and widely researched industries – including hundreds of profiles of leading international corporations. Beginning researchers will gain from this book a solid understanding of how each industry operates and which countries and companies are significant participants, while experienced researchers will glean current and historical figures for comparison and analysis. The industries profiled in previous editions have been updated, and in some cases, expanded to reflect recent industry trends. Additionally, this edition provides both SIC and NAICS codes for all industries profiled. As in the original volumes, *The Encyclopedia of Global Industries* offers thorough studies of some of the biggest and most frequently researched industry sectors, including Aircraft, Biotechnology, Computers, Internet Services, Motor Vehicles, Pharmaceuticals, Semiconductors, Software and Telecommunications. An SIC and NAICS conversion table and an all-encompassing Subject Index, with cross-references, are provided to ensure easy access to this wealth of information. These and many others make the *Encyclopedia of Global Industries* the authoritative reference for studies of international industries.

"Provides detailed coverage of the history, development, and current status of 115 of "the world's most lucrative and high-profile industries." It far surpasses the Department of Commerce's U.S. Global Trade Outlook 1995-2000 (GPO, 1995) in scope and coverage. Recommended for comprehensive public and academic library business collections." -Booklist

Hardcover ISBN 978-1-59237-243-0, 1,400 pages, $495.00

The Directory of Mail Order Catalogs, 2008

Published since 1981, *The Directory of Mail Order Catalogs* is the premier source of information on the mail order catalog industry. It is the source that business professionals and librarians have come to rely on for the thousands of catalog companies in the US. Since the 2007 edition, *The Directory of Mail Order Catalogs* has been combined with its companion volume, *The Directory of Business to Business Catalogs*, to offer all 13,000 catalog companies in one easy-to-use volume. Section I: Consumer Catalogs, covers over 9,000 consumer catalog companies in 44 different product chapters from Animals to Toys & Games. Section II: Business to Business Catalogs, details 5,000 business catalogs, everything from computers to laboratory supplies, building construction and much more. Listings contain detailed contact information including mailing address, phone & fax numbers, web sites, e-mail addresses and key contacts along with important business details such as product descriptions, employee size, years in business, sales volume, catalog size, number of catalogs mailed and more. Three indexes are included for easy access to information: Catalog & Company Name Index, Geographic Index and Product Index. *The Directory of Mail Order Catalogs*, now with its expanded business to business catalogs, is the largest and most comprehensive resource covering this billion-dollar industry. It is the standard in its field. This important resource is a useful tool for entrepreneurs searching for catalogs to pick up their product, vendors looking to expand their customer base in the catalog industry, market researchers, small businesses investigating new supply vendors, along with the library patron who is exploring the available catalogs in their areas of interest.

"This is a godsend for those looking for information." –Reference Book Review

Softcover ISBN 978-1-59237-202-7, 1,700 pages, $350/$250 Library | Online Database $495.00

Sports Market Place Directory, 2008

For over 20 years, this comprehensive, up-to-date directory has offered direct access to the Who, What, When & Where of the Sports Industry. With over 20,000 updates and enhancements, the *Sports Market Place Directory* is the most detailed, comprehensive and current sports business reference source available. In 1,800 information-packed pages, *Sports Market Place Directory* profiles contact information and key executives for: Single Sport Organizations, Professional Leagues, Multi-Sport Organizations, Disabled Sports, High School & Youth Sports, Military Sports, Olympic Organizations, Media, Sponsors, Sponsorship & Marketing Event Agencies, Event & Meeting Calendars, Professional Services, College Sports, Manufacturers & Retailers, Facilities and much more. The Sports Market Place Directory provides organization's contact information with detailed descriptions including: Key Contacts, physical, mailing, email and web addresses plus phone and fax numbers. *Sports Market Place Directory* provides a one-stop resources for this billion-dollar industry. This will be an important resource for large public libraries, university libraries, university athletic programs, career services or job placement organizations, and is a must for anyone doing research on or marketing to the US and Canadian sports industry.

"Grey House is the new publisher and has produced an excellent edition...highly recommended for public libraries and academic libraries with sports management programs or strong interest in athletics." -Booklist

Softcover ISBN 978-1-59237-348-2, 1,800 pages, $225.00 | Online Database $479.00

Food and Beverage Market Place, 2008

Food and Beverage Market Place is bigger and better than ever with thousands of new companies, thousands of updates to existing companies and two revised and enhanced product category indexes. This comprehensive directory profiles over 18,000 Food & Beverage Manufacturers, 12,000 Equipment & Supply Companies, 2,200 Transportation & Warehouse Companies, 2,000 Brokers & Wholesalers, 8,000 Importers & Exporters, 900 Industry Resources and hundreds of Mail Order Catalogs. Listings include detailed Contact Information, Sales Volumes, Key Contacts, Brand & Product Information, Packaging Details and much more. *Food and Beverage Market Place* is available as a three-volume printed set, a subscription-based Online Database via the Internet, on CD-ROM, as well as mailing lists and a licensable database.

"An essential purchase for those in the food industry but will also be useful in public libraries where needed. Much of the information will be difficult and time consuming to locate without this handy three-volume ready-reference source." –ARBA

3 Vol Set, Softcover ISBN 978-1-59237-198-3, 8,500 pages, $595 | Online Database $795 | Online Database & 3 Vol Set Combo, $995

The Grey House Performing Arts Directory, 2007

The Grey House Performing Arts Directory is the most comprehensive resource covering the Performing Arts. This important directory provides current information on over 8,500 Dance Companies, Instrumental Music Programs, Opera Companies, Choral Groups, Theater Companies, Performing Arts Series and Performing Arts Facilities. Plus, this edition now contains a brand new section on Artist Management Groups. In addition to mailing address, phone & fax numbers, e-mail addresses and web sites, dozens of other fields of available information include mission statement, key contacts, facilities, seating capacity, season, attendance and more. This directory also provides an important Information Resources section that covers hundreds of Performing Arts Associations, Magazines, Newsletters, Trade Shows, Directories, Databases and Industry Web Sites. Five indexes provide immediate access to this wealth of information: Entry Name, Executive Name, Performance Facilities, Geographic and Information Resources. *The Grey House Performing Arts Directory* pulls together thousands of Performing Arts Organizations, Facilities and Information Resources into an easy-to-use source – this kind of comprehensiveness and extensive detail is not available in any resource on the market place today.

"Immensely useful and user-friendly … recommended for public, academic and certain special library reference collections." –Booklist

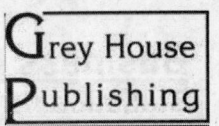

Softcover ISBN 978-1-59237-138-9, 1,500 pages, $185.00 | Online Database $335.00

New York State Directory, 2008/09

The New York State Directory, published annually since 1983, is a comprehensive and easy-to-use guide to accessing public officials and private sector organizations and individuals who influence public policy in the state of New York. *The New York State Directory* includes important information on all New York state legislators and congressional representatives, including biographies and key committee assignments. It also includes staff rosters for all branches of New York state government and for federal agencies and departments that impact the state policy process. Following the state government section are 25 chapters covering policy areas from agriculture through veterans' affairs. Each chapter identifies the state, local and federal agencies and officials that formulate or implement policy. In addition, each chapter contains a roster of private sector experts and advocates who influence the policy process. The directory also offers appendices that include statewide party officials; chambers of commerce; lobbying organizations; public and private universities and colleges; television, radio and print media; and local government agencies and officials.

"This comprehensive directory covers not only New York State government offices and key personnel but pertinent U.S. government agencies and non-governmental entities. This directory is all encompassing... recommended." -Choice

New York State Directory - Softcover ISBN 978-1-59237-358-1, 800 pages, $145.00
New York State Directory with *Profiles of New York* – 2 Volumes, Softcover ISBN 978-1-59237-359-8, 1,600 pages, $225.00

The Grey House Homeland Security Directory, 2008

This updated edition features the latest contact information for government and private organizations involved with Homeland Security along with the latest product information and provides detailed profiles of nearly 1,000 Federal & State Organizations & Agencies and over 3,000 Officials and Key Executives involved with Homeland Security. These listings are incredibly detailed and include Mailing Address, Phone & Fax Numbers, Email Addresses & Web Sites, a complete Description of the Agency and a complete list of the Officials and Key Executives associated with the Agency. Next, *The Grey House Homeland Security Directory* provides the go-to source for Homeland Security Products & Services. This section features over 2,000 Companies that provide Consulting, Products or Services. With this Buyer's Guide at their fingertips, users can locate suppliers of everything from Training Materials to Access Controls, from Perimeter Security to BioTerrorism Countermeasures and everything in between – complete with contact information and product descriptions. A handy Product Locator Index is provided to quickly and easily locate suppliers of a particular product. This comprehensive, information-packed resource will be a welcome tool for any company or agency that is in need of Homeland Security information and will be a necessary acquisition for the reference collection of all public libraries and large school districts.

"Compiles this information in one place and is discerning in content. A useful purchase for public and academic libraries." –Booklist

Softcover ISBN 978-1-59237-196-6, 800 pages, $195.00 | Online Database $385.00

The Grey House Safety & Security Directory, 2008

The Grey House Safety & Security Directory is the most comprehensive reference tool and buyer's guide for the safety and security industry. Arranged by safety topic, each chapter begins with OSHA regulations for the topic, followed by Training Articles written by top professionals in the field and Self-Inspection Checklists. Next, each topic contains Buyer's Guide sections that feature related products and services. Topics include Administration, Insurance, Loss Control & Consulting, Protective Equipment & Apparel, Noise & Vibration, Facilities Monitoring & Maintenance, Employee Health Maintenance & Ergonomics, Retail Food Services, Machine Guards, Process Guidelines & Tool Handling, Ordinary Materials Handling, Hazardous Materials Handling, Workplace Preparation & Maintenance, Electrical Lighting & Safety, Fire & Rescue and Security. Six important indexes make finding information and product manufacturers quick and easy: Geographical Index of Manufacturers and Distributors, Company Profile Index, Brand Name Index, Product Index, Index of Web Sites and Index of Advertisers. This comprehensive, up-to-date reference will provide every tool necessary to make sure a business is in compliance with OSHA regulations and locate the products and services needed to meet those regulations.

"Presents industrial safety information for engineers, plant managers, risk managers, and construction site supervisors…" –Choice

Softcover ISBN 978-1-59237-205-8, 1,500 pages, $165.00

The Grey House Transportation Security Directory & Handbook

This is the only reference of its kind that brings together current data on Transportation Security. With information on everything from Regulatory Authorities to Security Equipment, this top-flight database brings together the relevant information necessary for creating and maintaining a security plan for a wide range of transportation facilities. With this current, comprehensive directory at the ready you'll have immediate access to: Regulatory Authorities & Legislation; Information Resources; Sample Security Plans & Checklists; Contact Data for Major Airports, Seaports, Railroads, Trucking Companies and Oil Pipelines; Security Service Providers; Recommended Equipment & Product Information and more. Using the *Grey House Transportation Security Directory & Handbook*, managers will be able to quickly and easily assess their current security plans; develop contacts to create and maintain new security procedures; and source the products and services necessary to adequately maintain a secure environment. This valuable resource is a must for all Security Managers at Airports, Seaports, Railroads, Trucking Companies and Oil Pipelines.

"Highly recommended. Library collections that support all levels of readers, including professionals/practitioners; and schools/organizations offering education and training in transportation security." -Choice

Softcover ISBN 978-1-59237-075-7, 800 pages, $195.00

The Grey House Biometric Information Directory

This edition offers a complete, current overview of biometric companies and products – one of the fastest growing industries in today's economy. Detailed profiles of manufacturers of the latest biometric technology, including Finger, Voice, Face, Hand, Signature, Iris, Vein and Palm Identification systems. Data on the companies include key executives, company size and a detailed, indexed description of their product line. Information in the directory includes: Editorial on Advancements in Biometrics; Profiles of 700+ companies listed with contact information; Organizations, Trade & Educational Associations, Publications, Conferences, Trade Shows and Expositions Worldwide; Web Site Index; Biometric & Vendors Services Index by Types of Biometrics; and a Glossary of Biometric Terms. This resource will be an important source for anyone who is considering the use of a biometric product, investing in the development of biometric technology, support existing marketing and sales efforts and will be an important acquisition for the business reference collection for large public and business libraries.

"This book should prove useful to agencies or businesses seeking companies that deal with biometric technology. Summing Up: Recommended. Specialized collections serving researchers/faculty and professionals/practitioners." -Choice

Softcover ISBN 978-1-59237-121-1, 800 pages, $225.00

The Environmental Resource Handbook, 2008/09

The Environmental Resource Handbook is the most up-to-date and comprehensive source for Environmental Resources and Statistics. Section I: Resources provides detailed contact information for thousands of information sources, including Associations & Organizations, Awards & Honors, Conferences, Foundations & Grants, Environmental Health, Government Agencies, National Parks & Wildlife Refuges, Publications, Research Centers, Educational Programs, Green Product Catalogs, Consultants and much more. Section II: Statistics, provides statistics and rankings on hundreds of important topics, including Children's Environmental Index, Municipal Finances, Toxic Chemicals, Recycling, Climate, Air & Water Quality and more. This kind of up-to-date environmental data, all in one place, is not available anywhere else on the market place today. This vast compilation of resources and statistics is a must-have for all public and academic libraries as well as any organization with a primary focus on the environment.

"…the intrinsic value of the information make it worth consideration by libraries with environmental collections and environmentally concerned users." –Booklist

Softcover ISBN 978-1-59237-195-2, 1,000 pages, $155.00 | Online Database $300.00

The Rauch Guide to the US Adhesives & Sealants, Cosmetics & Toiletries, Ink, Paint, Plastics, Pulp & Paper and Rubber Industries

The Rauch Guides save time and money by organizing widely scattered information and providing estimates for important business decisions, some of which are available nowhere else. Within each Guide, after a brief introduction, the ECONOMICS section provides data on industry shipments; long-term growth and forecasts; prices; company performance; employment, expenditures, and productivity; transportation and geographical patterns; packaging; foreign trade; and government regulations. Next, TECHNOLOGY & RAW MATERIALS provide market, technical, and raw material information for chemicals, equipment and related materials, including market size and leading suppliers, prices, end uses, and trends. PRODUCTS & MARKETS provide information for each major industry product, including market size and historical trends, leading suppliers, five-year forecasts, industry structure, and major end uses. Next, the COMPANY DIRECTORY profiles major industry companies, both public and private. Information includes complete contact information, web address, estimated total and domestic sales, product description, and recent mergers and acquisitions. *The Rauch Guides* will prove to be an invaluable source of market information, company data, trends and forecasts that anyone in these fast-paced industries.

"An invaluable and affordable publication. The comprehensive nature of the data and text offers considerable insights into the industry, market sizes, company activities, and applications of the products of the industry. The additions that have been made have certainly enhanced the value of the Guide." –Adhesives & Sealants Newsletter of the Rauch Guide to the US Adhesives & Sealants Industry

Paint Industry: Softcover ISBN 978-1-59237-127-3 $595 | Plastics Industry: Softcover ISBN 978-1-59237-128-0 $595 | Adhesives and Sealants Industry: Softcover ISBN 978-1-59237-129-7 $595 | Ink Industry: Softcover ISBN 978-1-59237-126-6 $595 | Rubber Industry: Softcover ISBN 978-1-59237-130-3 $595 | Pulp and Paper Industry: Softcover ISBN 978-1-59237-131-0 $595 | Cosmetic & Toiletries Industry: Softcover ISBN 978-1-59237-132-7 $895

Research Services Directory: Commercial & Corporate Research Centers

This ninth edition provides access to well over 8,000 independent Commercial Research Firms, Corporate Research Centers and Laboratories offering contract services for hands-on, basic or applied research. Research Services Directory covers the thousands of types of research companies, including Biotechnology & Pharmaceutical Developers, Consumer Product Research, Defense Contractors, Electronics & Software Engineers, Think Tanks, Forensic Investigators, Independent Commercial Laboratories, Information Brokers, Market & Survey Research Companies, Medical Diagnostic Facilities, Product Research & Development Firms and more. Each entry provides the company's name, mailing address, phone & fax numbers, key contacts, web site, e-mail address, as well as a company description and research and technical fields served. Four indexes provide immediate access to this wealth of information: Research Firms Index, Geographic Index, Personnel Name Index and Subject Index.

"An important source for organizations in need of information about laboratories, individuals and other facilities." –ARBA

Softcover ISBN 978-1-59237-003-0, 1,400 pages, $465.00

International Business and Trade Directories

Completely updated, the Third Edition of *International Business and Trade Directories* now contains more than 10,000 entries, over 2,000 more than the last edition, making this directory the most comprehensive resource of the worlds business and trade directories. Entries include content descriptions, price, publisher's name and address, web site and e-mail addresses, phone and fax numbers and editorial staff. Organized by industry group, and then by region, this resource puts over 10,000 industry-specific business and trade directories at the reader's fingertips. Three indexes are included for quick access to information: Geographic Index, Publisher Index and Title Index. Public, college and corporate libraries, as well as individuals and corporations seeking critical market information will want to add this directory to their marketing collection.

"Reasonably priced for a work of this type, this directory should appeal to larger academic, public and corporate libraries with an international focus." –Library Journal

Softcover ISBN 978-1-930956-63-6, 1,800 pages, $225.00

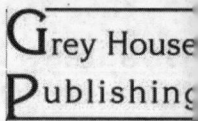

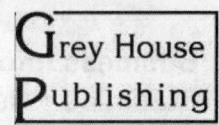

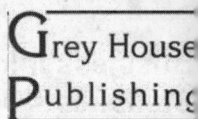

The Encyclopedia of Warrior Peoples & Fighting Groups

Many military groups throughout the world have excelled in their craft either by fortuitous circumstances, outstanding leadership, or intense training. This new second edition of *The Encyclopedia of Warrior Peoples and Fighting Groups* explores the origins and leadership of these outstanding combat forces, chronicles their conquests and accomplishments, examines the circumstances surrounding their decline or disbanding, and assesses their influence on the groups and methods of warfare that followed. Readers will encounter ferocious tribes, charismatic leaders, and daring militias, from ancient times to the present, including Amazons, Buffalo Soldiers, Green Berets, Iron Brigade, Kamikazes, Peoples of the Sea, Polish Winged Hussars, Teutonic Knights, and Texas Rangers. With over 100 alphabetical entries, numerous cross-references and illustrations, a comprehensive bibliography, and index, the *Encyclopedia of Warrior Peoples and Fighting Groups* is a valuable resource for readers seeking insight into the bold history of distinguished fighting forces.

"Especially useful for high school students, undergraduates, and general readers with an interest in military history." –Library Journal

Hardcover ISBN 978-1-59237-116-7, 660 pages, $135.00 | Ebook ISBN 978-1-59237-172-3 www.gale.com/gvrl/partners/grey.htm

The Encyclopedia of Invasions & Conquests, From the Ancient Times to the Present

This second edition of the popular *Encyclopedia of Invasions & Conquests*, a comprehensive guide to over 150 invasions, conquests, battles and occupations from ancient times to the present, takes readers on a journey that includes the Roman conquest of Britain, the Portuguese colonization of Brazil, and the Iraqi invasion of Kuwait, to name a few. New articles will explore the late 20th and 21st centuries, with a specific focus on recent conflicts in Afghanistan, Kuwait, Iraq, Yugoslavia, Grenada and Chechnya. In addition to covering the military aspects of invasions and conquests, entries cover some of the political, economic, and cultural aspects, for example, the effects of a conquest on the invade country's political and monetary system and in its language and religion. The entries on leaders – among them Sargon, Alexander the Great, William the Conqueror, and Adolf Hitler – deal with the people who sought to gain control, expand power, or exert religious or political influence over others through military means. Revised and updated for this second edition, entries are arranged alphabetically within historical periods. Each chapter provides a map to help readers locate key areas and geographical features, and bibliographical references appear at the end of each entry. Other useful features include cross-references, a cumulative bibliography and a comprehensive subject index. This authoritative, well-organized, lucidly written volume will prove invaluable for a variety of readers, including high school students, military historians, members of the armed forces, history buffs and hobbyists.

"Engaging writing, sensible organization, nice illustrations, interesting and obscure facts, and useful maps make this book a pleasure to read." –ARBA

Hardcover ISBN 978-1-59237-114-3, 598 pages, $135.00 | Ebook ISBN 978-1-59237-171-6 www.gale.com/gvrl/partners/grey.htm

Encyclopedia of Prisoners of War & Internment

This authoritative second edition provides a valuable overview of the history of prisoners of war and interned civilians, from earliest times to the present. Written by an international team of experts in the field of POW studies, this fascinating and thought-provoking volume includes entries on a wide range of subjects including the Crusades, Plains Indian Warfare, concentration camps, the two world wars, and famous POWs throughout history, as well as atrocities, escapes, and much more. Written in a clear and easily understandable style, this informative reference details over 350 entries, 30% larger than the first edition, that survey the history of prisoners of war and interned civilians from the earliest times to the present, with emphasis on the 19th and 20th centuries. Medical conditions, international law, exchanges of prisoners, organizations working on behalf of POWs, and trials associated with the treatment of captives are just some of the themes explored. Entries are arranged alphabetically, plus illustrations and maps are provided for easy reference. The text also includes an introduction, bibliography, appendix of selected documents, and end-of-entry reading suggestions. This one-of-a-kind reference will be a helpful addition to the reference collections of all public libraries, high schools, and university libraries and will prove invaluable to historians and military enthusiasts.

"Thorough and detailed yet accessible to the lay reader. Of special interest to subject specialists and historians; recommended for public and academic libraries." - Library Journal

Hardcover ISBN 978-1-59237-120-4, 676 pages, $135.00 | Ebook ISBN 978-1-59237-170-9 www.gale.com/gvrl/partners/grey.htm

The Encyclopedia of Rural America: the Land & People

History, sociology, anthropology, and public policy are combined to deliver the encyclopedia destined to become the standard reference work in American rural studies. From irrigation and marriage to games and mental health, this encyclopedia is the first to explore the contemporary landscape of rural America, placed in historical perspective. With over 300 articles prepared by leading experts from across the nation, this timely encyclopedia documents and explains the major themes, concepts, industries, concerns, and everyday life of the people and land who make up rural America. Entries range from the industrial sector and government policy to arts and humanities and social and family concerns. Articles explore every aspect of life in rural America. *Encyclopedia of Rural America*, with its broad range of coverage, will appeal to high school and college students as well as graduate students, faculty, scholars, and people whose work pertains to rural areas.

"This exemplary encyclopedia is guaranteed to educate our highly urban society about the uniqueness of rural America. Recommended for public and academic libraries." -Library Journal

Two Volumes, Hardcover, ISBN 978-1-59237-115-0, 800 pages, $250.00

The Religious Right, A Reference Handbook

Timely and unbiased, this third edition updates and expands its examination of the religious right and its influence on our government, citizens, society, and politics. From the fight to outlaw the teaching of Darwin's theory of evolution to the struggle to outlaw abortion, the religious right is continually exerting an influence on public policy. This text explores the influence of religion on legislation and society, while examining the alignment of the religious right with the political right. A historical survey of the movement highlights the shift to "hands-on" approach to politics and the struggle to present a unified front. The coverage offers a critical historical survey of the religious right movement, focusing on its increased involvement in the political arena, attempts to forge coalitions, and notable successes and failures. The text offers complete coverage of biographies of the men and women who have advanced the cause and an up to date chronology illuminate the movement's goals, including their accomplishments and failures. This edition offers an extensive update to all sections along with several brand new entries. Two new sections complement this third edition, a chapter on legal issues and court decisions and a chapter on demographic statistics and electoral patterns. To aid in further research, *The Religious Right*, offers an entire section of annotated listings of print and non-print resources, as well as of organizations affiliated with the religious right, and those opposing it. Comprehensive in its scope, this work offers easy-to-read, pertinent information for those seeking to understand the religious right and its evolving role in American society. A must for libraries of all sizes, university religion departments, activists, high schools and for those interested in the evolving role of the religious right.

" Recommended for all public and academic libraries." - Library Journal

Hardcover ISBN 978-1-59237-113-6, 600 pages, $135.00 | Ebook ISBN 978-1-59237-226-3 www.gale.com/gvrl/partners/grey.htm

From Suffrage to the Senate, America's Political Women

From Suffrage to the Senate is a comprehensive and valuable compendium of biographies of leading women in U.S. politics, past and present, and an examination of the wide range of women's movements. Up to date through 2006, this dynamically illustrated reference work explores American women's path to political power and social equality from the struggle for the right to vote and the abolition of slavery to the first African American woman in the U.S. Senate and beyond. This new edition includes over 150 new entries and a brand new section on trends and demographics of women in politics. The in-depth coverage also traces the political heritage of the abolition, labor, suffrage, temperance, and reproductive rights movements. The alphabetically arranged entries include biographies of every woman from across the political spectrum who has served in the U.S. House and Senate, along with women in the Judiciary and the U.S. Cabinet and, new to this edition, biographies of activists and political consultants. Bibliographical references follow each entry. For easy reference, a handy chronology is provided detailing 150 years of women's history. This up-to-date reference will be a must-purchase for women's studies departments, high schools and public libraries and will be a handy resource for those researching the key players in women's politics, past and present.

"An engaging tool that would be useful in high school, public, and academic libraries looking for an overview of the political history of women in the US." –Booklist

Two Volumes, Hardcover ISBN 978-1-59237-117-4, 1,160 pages, $195.00 | Ebook ISBN 978-1-59237-227-0 www.gale.com/gvrl/partners/grey.htm

An African Biographical Dictionary

This landmark second edition is the only biographical dictionary to bring together, in one volume, cultural, social and political leaders – both historical and contemporary – of the sub-Saharan region. Over 800 biographical sketches of prominent Africans, as well as foreigners who have affected the continent's history, are featured, 150 more than the previous edition. The wide spectrum of leaders includes religious figures, writers, politicians, scientists, entertainers, sports personalities and more. Access to these fascinating individuals is provided in a user-friendly format. The biographies are arranged alphabetically, cross-referenced and indexed. Entries include the country or countries in which the person was significant and the commonly accepted dates of birth and death. Each biographical sketch is chronologically written; entries for cultural personalities add an evaluation of their work. This information is followed by a selection of references often found in university and public libraries, including autobiographies and principal biographical works. Appendixes list each individual by country and by field of accomplishment – rulers, musicians, explorers, missionaries, businessmen, physicists – nearly thirty categories in all. Another convenient appendix lists heads of state since independence by country. Up-to-date and representative of African societies as a whole, An African Biographical Dictionary provides a wealth of vital information for students of African culture and is an indispensable reference guide for anyone interested in African affairs.

"An unquestionable convenience to have these concise, informative biographies gathered into one source, indexed, and analyzed by appendixes listing entrants by nation and occupational field." –Wilson Library Bulletin

Hardcover ISBN 978-1-59237-112-9, 667 pages, $135.00 | Ebook ISBN 978-1-59237-229-4 www.gale.com/gvrl/partners/grey.htm

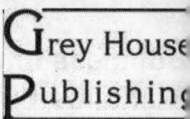

American Environmental Leaders, From Colonial Times to the Present

A comprehensive and diverse award winning collection of biographies of the most important figures in American environmentalism. Few subjects arouse the passions the way the environment does. How will we feed an ever-increasing population and how can that food be made safe for consumption? Who decides how land is developed? How can environmental policies be made fair for everyone, including multiethnic groups, women, children, and the poor? *American Environmental Leaders* presents more than 350 biographies of men and women who have devoted their lives to studying, debating, and organizing these and other controversial issues over the last 200 years. In addition to the scientists who have analyzed how human actions affect nature, we are introduced to poets, landscape architects, presidents, painters, activists, even sanitation engineers, and others who have forever altered how we think about the environment. The easy to use A–Z format provides instant access to these fascinating individuals, and frequent cross references indicate others with whom individuals worked (and sometimes clashed). End of entry references provide users with a starting point for further research.

"Highly recommended for high school, academic, and public libraries needing environmental biographical information." –Library Journal/Starred Review

Two Volumes, Hardcover ISBN 978-1-59237-119-8, 900 pages $195.00 | Ebook ISBN 978-1-59237-230-0
www.gale.com/gvrl/partners/grey.htm

World Cultural Leaders of the Twentieth & Twenty-First Centuries

World Cultural Leaders of the Twentieth & Twenty-First Centuries is a window into the arts, performances, movements, and music that shaped the world's cultural development since 1900. A remarkable around-the-world look at one-hundred-plus years of cultural development through the eyes of those that set the stage and stayed to play. This second edition offers over 120 new biographies along with a complete update of existing biographies. To further aid the reader, a handy fold-out timeline traces important events in all six cultural categories from 1900 through the present time. Plus, a new section of detailed material and resources for 100 selected individuals is also new to this edition, with further data on museums, homesteads, websites, artwork and more. This remarkable compilation will answer a wide range of questions. Who was the originator of the term "documentary"? Which poet married the daughter of the famed novelist Thomas Mann in order to help her escape Nazi Germany? Which British writer served as an agent in Russia against the Bolsheviks before the 1917 revolution? A handy two-volume set that makes it easy to look up 450 worldwide cultural icons: novelists, poets, playwrights, painters, sculptors, architects, dancers, choreographers, actors, directors, filmmakers, singers, composers, and musicians. *World Cultural Leaders of the Twentieth & Twenty-First Centuries* provides entries (many of them illustrated) covering the person's works, achievements, and professional career in a thorough essay and offers interesting facts and statistics. Entries are fully cross-referenced so that readers can learn how various individuals influenced others. An index of leaders by occupation, a useful glossary and a thorough general index complete the coverage. This remarkable resource will be an important acquisition for the reference collections of public libraries, university libraries and high schools.

"Fills a need for handy, concise information on a wide array of international cultural figures."-ARBA

Two Volumes, Hardcover ISBN 978-1-59237-118-1, 900 pages, $195.00 | Ebook ISBN 978-1-59237-231-7
www.gale.com/gvrl/partners/grey.htm

Political Corruption in America: An Encyclopedia of Scandals, Power, and Greed

The complete scandal-filled history of American political corruption, focusing on the infamous people and cases, as well as society's electoral and judicial reactions. Since colonial times, there has been no shortage of politicians willing to take a bribe, skirt campaign finance laws, or act in their own interests. Corruption like the Whiskey Ring, Watergate, and Whitewater cases dominate American life, making political scandal a leading U.S. industry. From judges to senators, presidents to mayors, *Political Corruption in America* discusses the infamous people throughout history who have been accused of and implicated in crooked behavior. In this new second edition, more than 250 A–Z entries explore the people, crimes, investigations, and court cases behind 200 years of American political scandals. This unbiased volume also delves into the issues surrounding Koreagate, the Chinese campaign scandal, and other ethical lapses. Relevant statutes and terms, including the Independent Counsel Statute and impeachment as a tool of political punishment, are examined as well. Students, scholars, and other readers interested in American history, political science, and ethics will appreciate this survey of a wide range of corrupting influences. This title focuses on how politicians from all parties have fallen because of their greed and hubris, and how society has used electoral and judicial means against those who tested the accepted standards of political conduct. A full range of illustrations including political cartoons, photos of key figures such as Abe Fortas and Archibald Cox, graphs of presidential pardons, and tables showing the number of expulsions and censures in both the House and Senate round out the text. In addition, a comprehensive chronology of major political scandals in U.S. history from colonial times until the present. For further reading, an extensive bibliography lists sources including archival letters, newspapers, and private manuscript collections from the United States and Great Britain. With its comprehensive coverage of this interesting topic, *Political Corruption in America: An Encyclopedia of Scandals, Power, and Greed* will prove to be a useful addition to the reference collections of all public libraries, university libraries, history collections, political science collections and high schools.

"...this encyclopedia is a useful contribution to the field. Highly recommended." - CHOICE
"Political Corruption should be useful in most academic, high school, and public libraries." Booklist

Two Volumes, Hardcover ISBN 978-1-59237-297-3, 500 pages, $195.00

Religion and Law: A Dictionary

This informative, easy-to-use reference work covers a wide range of legal issues that affect the roles of religion and law in American society. Extensive A–Z entries provide coverage of key court decisions, case studies, concepts, individuals, religious groups, organizations, and agencies shaping religion and law in today's society. This *Dictionary* focuses on topics involved with the constitutional theory and interpretation of religion and the law; terms providing a historical explanation of the ways in which America's ever increasing ethnic and religious diversity contributed to our current understanding of the mandates of the First and Fourteenth Amendments; terms and concepts describing the development of religion clause jurisprudence; an analytical examination of the distinct vocabulary used in this area of the law; the means by which American courts have attempted to balance religious liberty against other important individual and social interests in a wide variety of physical and regulatory environments, including the classroom, the workplace, the courtroom, religious group organization and structure, taxation, the clash of "secular" and "religious" values, and the relationship of the generalized idea of individual autonomy of the specific concept of religious liberty. Important legislation and legal cases affecting religion and society are thoroughly covered in this timely volume, including a detailed Table of Cases and Table of Statutes for more detailed research. A guide to further reading and an index are also included. This useful resource will be an important acquisition for the reference collections of all public libraries, university libraries, religion reference collections and high schools.

Hardcover ISBN 978-1-59237-298-0, 500 pages, $135.00

Human Rights in the United States: A Dictionary and Documents

This two volume set offers easy to grasp explanations of the basic concepts, laws, and case law in the field, with emphasis on human rights in the historical, political, and legal experience of the United States. Human rights is a term not fully understood by many Americans. Addressing this gap, the new second edition of *Human Rights in the United States: A Dictionary and Documents* offers a comprehensive introduction that places the history of human rights in the United States in an international context. It surveys the legal protection of human dignity in the United States, examines the sources of human rights norms, cites key legal cases, explains the role of international governmental and non-governmental organizations, and charts global, regional, and U.N. human rights measures. Over 240 dictionary entries of human rights terms are detailed—ranging from asylum and cultural relativism to hate crimes and torture. Each entry discusses the significance of the term, gives examples, and cites appropriate documents and court decisions. In addition, a Documents section is provided that contains 59 conventions, treaties, and protocols related to the most up to date international action on ethnic cleansing; freedom of expression and religion; violence against women; and much more. A bibliography, extensive glossary, and comprehensive index round out this indispensable volume. This comprehensive, timely volume is a must for large public libraries, university libraries and social science departments, along with high school libraries.

"...invaluable for anyone interested in human rights issues ... highly recommended for all reference collections."
- American Reference Books Annual

Two Volumes, Hardcover ISBN 978-1-59237-290-4, 750 pages, $225.00

The Comparative Guide to American Elementary & Secondary Schools, 2008

The only guide of its kind, this award winning compilation offers a snapshot profile of every public school district in the United States serving 1,500 or more students – more than 5,900 districts are covered. Organized alphabetically by district within state, each chapter begins with a Statistical Overview of the state. Each district listing includes contact information (name, address, phone number and web site) plus Grades Served, the Numbers of Students and Teachers and the Number of Regular, Special Education, Alternative and Vocational Schools in the district along with statistics on Student/Classroom Teacher Ratios, Drop Out Rates, Ethnicity, the Numbers of Librarians and Guidance Counselors and District Expenditures per student. As an added bonus, *The Comparative Guide to American Elementary and Secondary Schools* provides important ranking tables, both by state and nationally, for each data element. For easy navigation through this wealth of information, this handbook contains a useful City Index that lists all districts that operate schools within a city. These important comparative statistics are necessary for anyone considering relocation or doing comparative research on their own district and would be a perfect acquisition for any public library or school district library.

"This straightforward guide is an easy way to find general information. Valuable for academic and large public library collections." –ARBA

Softcover ISBN 978-1-59237-223-2, 2,400 pages, $125.00 | Ebook ISBN 978-1-59237-238-6 www.gale.com/gvrl/partners/grey.htm

The Complete Learning Disabilities Directory, 2008

The Complete Learning Disabilities Directory is the most comprehensive database of Programs, Services, Curriculum Materials, Professional Meetings & Resources, Camps, Newsletters and Support Groups for teachers, students and families concerned with learning disabilities. This information-packed directory includes information about Associations & Organizations, Schools, Colleges & Testing Materials, Government Agencies, Legal Resources and much more. For quick, easy access to information, this directory contains four indexes: Entry Name Index, Subject Index and Geographic Index. With every passing year, the field of learning disabilities attracts more attention and the network of caring, committed and knowledgeable professionals grows every day. This directory is an invaluable research tool for these parents, students and professionals.

"Due to its wealth and depth of coverage, parents, teachers and others… should find this an invaluable resource." -Booklist

Softcover ISBN 978-1-59237-207-2, 900 pages, $145.00 | Online Database $195.00 | Online Database & Directory Combo $280.00

Educators Resource Directory, 2007/08

Educators Resource Directory is a comprehensive resource that provides the educational professional with thousands of resources and statistical data for professional development. This directory saves hours of research time by providing immediate access to Associations & Organizations, Conferences & Trade Shows, Educational Research Centers, Employment Opportunities & Teaching Abroad, School Library Services, Scholarships, Financial Resources, Professional Consultants, Computer Software & Testing Resources and much more. Plus, this comprehensive directory also includes a section on Statistics and Rankings with over 100 tables, including statistics on Average Teacher Salaries, SAT/ACT scores, Revenues & Expenditures and more. These important statistics will allow the user to see how their school rates among others, make relocation decisions and so much more. For quick access to information, this directory contains four indexes: Entry & Publisher Index, Geographic Index, a Subject & Grade Index and Web Sites Index. *Educators Resource Directory* will be a well-used addition to the reference collection of any school district, education department or public library.

"Recommended for all collections that serve elementary and secondary school professionals." –Choice

Softcover ISBN 978-1-59237-179-2, 800 pages, $145.00 | Online Database $195.00 | Online Database & Directory Combo $280.00

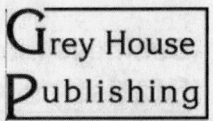

Profiles of New York | Profiles of Florida | Profiles of Texas | Profiles of Illinois | Profiles of Michigan | Profiles of Ohio | Profiles of New Jersey | Profiles of Massachusetts | Profiles of Pennsylvania | Profiles of Wisconsin | Profiles of Connecticut & Rhode Island | Profiles of Indiana | Profiles of North Carolina & South Carolina | Profiles of Virginia | Profiles of California

The careful layout gives the user an easy-to-read snapshot of every single place and county in the state, from the biggest metropolis to the smallest unincorporated hamlet. The richness of each place or county profile is astounding in its depth, from history to weather, all packed in an easy-to-navigate, compact format. Each profile contains data on History, Geography, Climate, Population, Vital Statistics, Economy, Income, Taxes, Education, Housing, Health & Environment, Public Safety, Newspapers, Transportation, Presidential Election Results, Information Contacts and Chambers of Commerce. As an added bonus, there is a section on Selected Statistics, where data from the 100 largest towns and cities is arranged into easy-to-use charts. Each of 22 different data points has its own two-page spread with the cities listed in alpha order so researchers can easily compare and rank cities. A remarkable compilation that offers overviews and insights into each corner of the state, each volume goes beyond Census statistics, beyond metro area coverage, beyond the 100 best places to live. Drawn from official census information, other government statistics and original research, you will have at your fingertips data that's available nowhere else in one single source.

"The publisher claims that this is the 'most comprehensive portrait of the state of Florida ever published,' and this reviewer is inclined to believe it...Recommended. All levels." –Choice on Profiles of Florida

Each Profiles of... title ranges from 400-800 pages, priced at $149.00 each

America's Top-Rated Cities, 2008

America's Top-Rated Cities provides current, comprehensive statistical information and other essential data in one easy-to-use source on the 100 "top" cities that have been cited as the best for business and living in the U.S. This handbook allows readers to see, at a glance, a concise social, business, economic, demographic and environmental profile of each city, including brief evaluative comments. In addition to detailed data on Cost of Living, Finances, Real Estate, Education, Major Employers, Media, Crime and Climate, city reports now include Housing Vacancies, Tax Audits, Bankruptcy, Presidential Election Results and more. This outstanding source of information will be widely used in any reference collection.

"The only source of its kind that brings together all of this information into one easy-to-use source. It will be beneficial to many business and public libraries." –ARBA

Four Volumes, Softcover ISBN 978-1-59237-349-9, 2,500 pages, $195.00 | Ebook ISBN 978-1-59237-233-1
www.gale.com/gvrl/partners/grey.htm

America's Top-Rated Smaller Cities, 2008/09

A perfect companion to *America's Top-Rated Cities*, *America's Top-Rated Smaller Cities* provides current, comprehensive business and living profiles of smaller cities (population 25,000-99,999) that have been cited as the best for business and living in the United States. Sixty cities make up this 2004 edition of America's Top-Rated Smaller Cities, all are top-ranked by Population Growth, Median Income, Unemployment Rate and Crime Rate. City reports reflect the most current data available on a wide-range of statistics, including Employment & Earnings, Household Income, Unemployment Rate, Population Characteristics, Taxes, Cost of Living, Education, Health Care, Public Safety, Recreation, Media, Air & Water Quality and much more. Plus, each city report contains a Background of the City, and an Overview of the State Finances. *America's Top-Rated Smaller Cities* offers a reliable, one-stop source for statistical data that, before now, could only be found scattered in hundreds of sources. This volume is designed for a wide range of readers: individuals considering relocating a residence or business; professionals considering expanding their business or changing careers; general and market researchers; real estate consultants; human resource personnel; urban planners and investors.

"Provides current, comprehensive statistical information in one easy-to-use source... Recommended for public and academic libraries and specialized collections." –Library Journal

Two Volumes, Softcover ISBN 978-1-59237-284-3, 1,100 pages, $195.00 | Ebook ISBN 978-1-59237-234-8
www.gale.com/gvrl/partners/grey.htm

Profiles of America: Facts, Figures & Statistics for Every Populated Place in the United States

Profiles of America is the only source that pulls together, in one place, statistical, historical and descriptive information about every place in the United States in an easy-to-use format. This award winning reference set, now in its second edition, compiles statistics and data from over 20 different sources – the latest census information has been included along with more than nine brand new statistical topics. This Four-Volume Set details over 40,000 places, from the biggest metropolis to the smallest unincorporated hamlet, and provides statistical details and information on over 50 different topics including Geography, Climate, Population, Vital Statistics, Economy, Income, Taxes, Education, Housing, Health & Environment, Public Safety, Newspapers, Transportation, Presidential Election Results and Information Contacts or Chambers of Commerce. Profiles are arranged, for ease-of-use, by state and then by county. Each county begins with a County-Wide Overview and is followed by information for each Community in that particular county. The Community Profiles within the county are arranged alphabetically. *Profiles of America* is a virtual snapshot of America at your fingertips and a unique compilation of information that will be widely used in any reference collection.

A Library Journal Best Reference Book "An outstanding compilation." –Library Journal

Four Volumes, Softcover ISBN 978-1-891482-80-9, 10,000 pages, $595.00

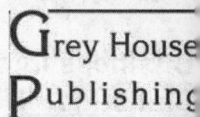

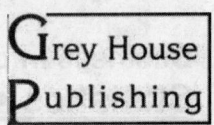

Ancestry in America: A Comparative Guide to Over 200 Ethnic Backgrounds

This brand new reference work pulls together thousands of comparative statistics on the Ethnic Backgrounds of all populated places in the United States with populations over 10,000. Never before has this kind of information been reported in a single volume. Section One, Statistics by Place, is made up of a list of over 200 ancestry and race categories arranged alphabetically by each of the 5,000 different places with populations over 10,000. The population number of the ancestry group in that city or town is provided along with the percent that group represents of the total population. This informative city-by-city section allows the user to quickly and easily explore the ethnic makeup of all major population bases in the United States. Section Two, Comparative Rankings, contains three tables for each ethnicity and race. In the first table, the top 150 populated places are ranked by population number for that particular ancestry group, regardless of population. In the second table, the top 150 populated places are ranked by the percent of the total population for that ancestry group. In the third table, those top 150 populated places with 10,000 population are ranked by population number for each ancestry group. These easy-to-navigate tables allow users to see ancestry population patterns and make city-by-city comparisons as well. This brand new, information-packed resource will serve a wide-range or research requests for demographics, population characteristics, relocation information and much more. *Ancestry in America: A Comparative Guide to Over 200 Ethnic Backgrounds* will be an important acquisition to all reference collections.

"This compilation will serve a wide range of research requests for population characteristics ... it offers much more detail than other sources." –Booklist

Softcover ISBN 978-1-59237-029-0, 1,500 pages, $225.00

Weather America, A Thirty-Year Summary of Statistical Weather Data and Rankings

This valuable resource provides extensive climatological data for over 4,000 National and Cooperative Weather Stations throughout the United States. Weather America begins with a new Major Storms section that details major storm events of the nation and a National Rankings section that details rankings for several data elements, such as Maximum Temperature and Precipitation. The main body of Weather America is organized into 50 state sections. Each section provides a Data Table on each Weather Station, organized alphabetically, that provides statistics on Maximum and Minimum Temperatures, Precipitation, Snowfall, Extreme Temperatures, Foggy Days, Humidity and more. State sections contain two brand new features in this edition – a City Index and a narrative Description of the climatic conditions of the state. Each section also includes a revised Map of the State that includes not only weather stations, but cities and towns.

"Best Reference Book of the Year." –Library Journal

Softcover ISBN 978-1-891482-29-8, 2,013 pages, $175.00 | Ebook ISBN 978-1-59237-237-9 www.gale.com/gvrl/partners/grey.htm

Crime in America's Top-Rated Cities

This volume includes over 20 years of crime statistics in all major crime categories: violent crimes, property crimes and total crime. *Crime in America's Top-Rated Cities* is conveniently arranged by city and covers 76 top-rated cities. Crime in America's Top-Rated Cities offers details that compare the number of crimes and crime rates for the city, suburbs and metro area along with national crime trends for violent, property and total crimes. Also, this handbook contains important information and statistics on Anti-Crime Programs, Crime Risk, Hate Crimes, Illegal Drugs, Law Enforcement, Correctional Facilities, Death Penalty Laws and much more. A much-needed resource for people who are relocating, business professionals, general researchers, the press, law enforcement officials and students of criminal justice.

"Data is easy to access and will save hours of searching." –Global Enforcement Review

Softcover ISBN 978-1-891482-84-7, 832 pages, $155.00

The Complete Directory for People with Disabilities, 2008

A wealth of information, now in one comprehensive sourcebook. Completely updated, this edition contains more information than ever before, including thousands of new entries and enhancements to existing entries and thousands of additional web sites and e-mail addresses. This up-to-date directory is the most comprehensive resource available for people with disabilities, detailing Independent Living Centers, Rehabilitation Facilities, State & Federal Agencies, Associations, Support Groups, Periodicals & Books, Assistive Devices, Employment & Education Programs, Camps and Travel Groups. Each year, more libraries, schools, colleges, hospitals, rehabilitation centers and individuals add *The Complete Directory for People with Disabilities* to their collections, making sure that this information is readily available to the families, individuals and professionals who can benefit most from the amazing wealth of resources cataloged here.

"No other reference tool exists to meet the special needs of the disabled in one convenient resource for information." –Library Journal

Softcover ISBN 978-1-59237-194-5, 1,200 pages, $165.00 | Online Database $215.00 | Online Database & Directory Combo $300.00

The Complete Learning Disabilities Directory, 2008

The Complete Learning Disabilities Directory is the most comprehensive database of Programs, Services, Curriculum Materials, Professional Meetings & Resources, Camps, Newsletters and Support Groups for teachers, students and families concerned with learning disabilities. This information-packed directory includes information about Associations & Organizations, Schools, Colleges & Testing Materials, Government Agencies, Legal Resources and much more. For quick, easy access to information, this directory contains four indexes: Entry Name Index, Subject Index and Geographic Index. With every passing year, the field of learning disabilities attracts more attention and the network of caring, committed and knowledgeable professionals grows every day. This directory is an invaluable research tool for these parents, students and professionals.

"Due to its wealth and depth of coverage, parents, teachers and others... should find this an invaluable resource." -Booklist

Softcover ISBN 978-1-59237-207-2, 900 pages, $145.00 | Online Database $195.00 | Online Database & Directory Combo $280.00

The Complete Directory for People with Chronic Illness, 2007/08

Thousands of hours of research have gone into this completely updated edition – several new chapters have been added along with thousands of new entries and enhancements to existing entries. Plus, each chronic illness chapter has been reviewed by a medical expert in the field. This widely-hailed directory is structured around the 90 most prevalent chronic illnesses – from Asthma to Cancer to Wilson's Disease – and provides a comprehensive overview of the support services and information resources available for people diagnosed with a chronic illness. Each chronic illness has its own chapter and contains a brief description in layman's language, followed by important resources for National & Local Organizations, State Agencies, Newsletters, Books & Periodicals, Libraries & Research Centers, Support Groups & Hotlines, Web Sites and much more. This directory is an important resource for health care professionals, the collections of hospital and health care libraries, as well as an invaluable tool for people with a chronic illness and their support network.

"A must purchase for all hospital and health care libraries and is strongly recommended for all public library reference departments." –ARBA

Softcover ISBN 978-1-59237-183-9, 1,200 pages, $165.00 | Online Database $215.00 | Online Database & Directory Combo $300.00

The Complete Mental Health Directory, 2008/09

This is the most comprehensive resource covering the field of behavioral health, with critical information for both the layman and the mental health professional. For the layman, this directory offers understandable descriptions of 25 Mental Health Disorders as well as detailed information on Associations, Media, Support Groups and Mental Health Facilities. For the professional, The Complete Mental Health Directory offers critical and comprehensive information on Managed Care Organizations, Information Systems, Government Agencies and Provider Organizations. This comprehensive volume of needed information will be widely used in any reference collection.

"... the strength of this directory is that it consolidates widely dispersed information into a single volume." –Booklist

Softcover ISBN 978-1-59237-285-0, 800 pages, $165.00 | Online Database $215.00 | Online & Directory Combo $300.00

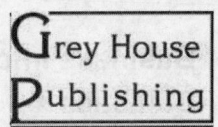

The Comparative Guide to American Hospitals, Second Edition

This new second edition compares all of the nation's hospitals by 24 measures of quality in the treatment of heart attack, heart failure, pneumonia, and, new to this edition, surgical procedures and pregnancy care. Plus, this second edition is now available in regional volumes, to make locating information about hospitals in your area quicker and easier than ever before. The Comparative Guide to American Hospitals provides a snapshot profile of each of the nations 4,200+ hospitals. These informative profiles illustrate how the hospital rates when providing 24 different treatments within four broad categories: Heart Attack Care, Heart Failure Care, Surgical Infection Prevention (NEW), and Pregnancy Care measures (NEW). Each profile includes the raw percentage for that hospital, the state average, the US average and data on the top hospital. For easy access to contact information, each profile includes the hospital's address, phone and fax numbers, email and web addresses, type and accreditation along with 5 top key administrations. These profiles will allow the user to quickly identify the quality of the hospital and have the necessary information at their fingertips to make contact with that hospital. Most importantly, *The Comparative Guide to American Hospitals* provides easy-to-use Regional State by State Statistical Summary Tables for each of the data elements to allow the user to quickly locate hospitals with the best level of service. Plus, a new 30-Day Mortality Chart, Glossary of Terms and Regional Hospital Profile Index make this a must-have source. This new, expanded edition will be a must for the reference collection at all public, medical and academic libraries.

"These data will help those with heart conditions and pneumonia make informed decisions about their healthcare and encourage hospitals to improve the quality of care they provide. Large medical, hospital, and public libraries are most likely to benefit from this weighty resource."-Library Journal

Four Volumes Softcover ISBN 978-1-59237-182-2, 3,500 pages, $325.00 | Regional Volumes $135.00 | Ebook ISBN 978-1-59237-239-3 www.gale.com/gvrl/partners/grey.htm

Older Americans Information Directory, 2008

Completely updated for 2008, this sixth edition has been completely revised and now contains 1,000 new listings, over 8,000 updates to existing listings and over 3,000 brand new e-mail addresses and web sites. You'll find important resources for Older Americans including National, Regional, State & Local Organizations, Government Agencies, Research Centers, Libraries & Information Centers, Legal Resources, Discount Travel Information, Continuing Education Programs, Disability Aids & Assistive Devices, Health, Print Media and Electronic Media. Three indexes: Entry Index, Subject Index and Geographic Index make it easy to find just the right source of information. This comprehensive guide to resources for Older Americans will be a welcome addition to any reference collection.

"Highly recommended for academic, public, health science and consumer libraries…" –Choice

1,200 pages; Softcover ISBN 978-1-59237-357-4, $165.00 | Online Database $215.00 | Online Database & Directory Combo $300.00

The Complete Directory for Pediatric Disorders, 2008

This important directory provides parents and caregivers with information about Pediatric Conditions, Disorders, Diseases and Disabilities, including Blood Disorders, Bone & Spinal Disorders, Brain Defects & Abnormalities, Chromosomal Disorders, Congenital Heart Defects, Movement Disorders, Neuromuscular Disorders and Pediatric Tumors & Cancers. This carefully written directory offers: understandable Descriptions of 15 major bodily systems; Descriptions of more than 200 Disorders and a Resources Section, detailing National Agencies & Associations, State Associations, Online Services, Libraries & Resource Centers, Research Centers, Support Groups & Hotlines, Camps, Books and Periodicals. This resource will provide immediate access to information crucial to families and caregivers when coping with children's illnesses.

"Recommended for public and consumer health libraries." –Library Journal

Softcover ISBN 978-1-59237-150-1, 1,200 pages, $165.00 | Online Database $215.00 | Online Database & Directory Combo $300.00

The Directory of Drug & Alcohol Residential Rehabilitation Facilities

This brand new directory is the first-ever resource to bring together, all in one place, data on the thousands of drug and alcohol residential rehabilitation facilities in the United States. The Directory of Drug & Alcohol Residential Rehabilitation Facilities covers over 1,000 facilities, with detailed contact information for each one, including mailing address, phone and fax numbers, email addresses and web sites, mission statement, type of treatment programs, cost, average length of stay, numbers of residents and counselors, accreditation, insurance plans accepted, type of environment, religious affiliation, education components and much more. It also contains a helpful chapter on General Resources that provides contact information for Associations, Print & Electronic Media, Support Groups and Conferences. Multiple indexes allow the user to pinpoint the facilities that meet very specific criteria. This time-saving tool is what so many counselors, parents and medical professionals have been asking for. *The Directory of Drug & Alcohol Residential Rehabilitation Facilities* will be a helpful tool in locating the right source for treatment for a wide range of individuals. This comprehensive directory will be an important acquisition for all reference collections: public and academic libraries, case managers, social workers, state agencies and many more.

"This is an excellent, much needed directory that fills an important gap…" –Booklist

Softcover ISBN 978-1-59237-031-3, 300 pages, $135.00

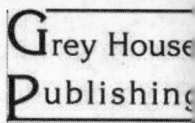

Canadian Almanac & Directory, 2008

The Canadian Almanac & Directory contains sixteen directories in one – giving you all the facts and figures you will ever need about Canada. No other single source provides users with the quality and depth of up-to-date information for all types of research. This national directory and guide gives you access to statistics, images and over 100,000 names and addresses for everything from Airlines to Zoos - updated every year. It's Ten Directories in One! Each section is a directory in itself, providing robust information on business and finance, communications, government, associations, arts and culture (museums, zoos, libraries, etc.), health, transportation, law, education, and more. Government information includes federal, provincial and territorial - and includes an easy-to-use quick index to find key information. A separate municipal government section includes every municipality in Canada, with full profiles of Canada's largest urban centers. A complete legal directory lists judges and judicial officials, court locations and law firms across the country. A wealth of general information, the *Canadian Almanac & Directory* also includes national statistics on population, employment, imports and exports, and more. National awards and honors are presented, along with forms of address, Commonwealth information and full color photos of Canadian symbols. Postal information, weights, measures, distances and other useful charts are also incorporated. Complete almanac information includes perpetual calendars, five-year holiday planners and astronomical information. Published continuously for 160 years, *The Canadian Almanac & Directory* is the best single reference source for business executives, managers and assistants; government and public affairs executives; lawyers; marketing, sales and advertising executives; researchers, editors and journalists.

Hardcover ISBN 978-1-59237-220-1, 1,600 pages, $315.00

Associations Canada, 2008

The Most Powerful Fact-Finder to Business, Trade, Professional and Consumer Organizations

Associations Canada covers Canadian organizations and international groups including industry, commercial and professional associations, registered charities, special interest and common interest organizations. This annually revised compendium provides detailed listings and abstracts for nearly 20,000 regional, national and international organizations. This popular volume provides the most comprehensive picture of Canada's non-profit sector. Detailed listings enable users to identify an organization's budget, founding date, scope of activity, licensing body, sources of funding, executive information, full address and complete contact information, just to name a few. Powerful indexes help researchers find information quickly and easily. The following indexes are included: subject, acronym, geographic, budget, executive name, conferences & conventions, mailing list, defunct and unreachable associations and registered charitable organizations. In addition to annual spending of over $1 billion on transportation and conventions alone, Canadian associations account for many millions more in pursuit of membership interests. *Associations Canada* provides complete access to this highly lucrative market. *Associations Canada* is a strong source of prospects for sales and marketing executives, tourism and convention officials, researchers, government officials - anyone who wants to locate non-profit interest groups and trade associations.

Hardcover ISBN 978-1-59237-277-5, 1,600 pages, $315.00

Financial Services Canada, 2008/09

Financial Services Canada is the only master file of current contacts and information that serves the needs of the entire financial services industry in Canada. With over 18,000 organizations and hard-to-find business information, Financial Services Canada is the most up-to-date source for names and contact numbers of industry professionals, senior executives, portfolio managers, financial advisors, agency bureaucrats and elected representatives. Financial Services Canada incorporates the latest changes in the industry to provide you with the most current details on each company, including: name, title, organization, telephone and fax numbers, e-mail and web addresses. *Financial Services Canada* also includes private company listings never before compiled, government agencies, association and consultant services - to ensure that you'll never miss a client or a contact. Current listings include: banks and branches, non-depository institutions, stock exchanges and brokers, investment management firms, insurance companies, major accounting and law firms, government agencies and financial associations. Powerful indexes assist researchers with locating the vital financial information they need. The following indexes are included: alphabetic, geographic, executive name, corporate web site/e-mail, government quick reference and subject. *Financial Services Canada* is a valuable resource for financial executives, bankers, financial planners, sales and marketing professionals, lawyers and chartered accountants, government officials, investment dealers, journalists, librarians and reference specialists.

Hardcover ISBN 978-1-59237-278-2, 900 pages, $315.00

Directory of Libraries in Canada, 2008/09

The Directory of Libraries in Canada brings together almost 7,000 listings including libraries and their branches, information resource centers, archives and library associations and learning centers. The directory offers complete and comprehensive information on Canadian libraries, resource centers, business information centers, professional associations, regional library systems, archives, library schools and library technical programs. *The Directory of Libraries in Canada* includes important features of each library and service, including library information; personnel details, including contact names and e-mail addresses; collection information; services available to users; acquisitions budgets; and computers and automated systems. Useful information on each library's electronic access is also included, such as Internet browser, connectivity and public Internet/CD-ROM/subscription database access. The directory also provides powerful indexes for subject, location, personal name and Web site/e-mail to assist researchers with locating the crucial information they need. *The Directory of Libraries in Canada* is a vital reference tool for publishers, advocacy groups, students, research institutions, computer hardware suppliers, and other diverse groups that provide products and services to this unique market.

Hardcover ISBN 978-1-59237-279-9, 850 pages, $315.00

Canadian Environmental Directory, 2008 /09

The Canadian Environmental Directory is Canada's most complete and only national listing of environmental associations and organizations, government regulators and purchasing groups, product and service companies, special libraries, and more! The extensive Products and Services section provides detailed listings enabling users to identify the company name, address, phone, fax, e-mail, Web address, firm type, contact names (and titles), product and service information, affiliations, trade information, branch and affiliate data. The Government section gives you all the contact information you need at every government level – federal, provincial and municipal. We also include descriptions of current environmental initiatives, programs and agreements, names of environment-related acts administered by each ministry or department PLUS information and tips on who to contact and how to sell to governments in Canada. The Associations section provides complete contact information and a brief description of activities. Included are Canadian environmental organizations and international groups including industry, commercial and professional associations, registered charities, special interest and common interest organizations. All the Information you need about the Canadian environmental industry: directory of products and services, special libraries and resource, conferences, seminars and tradeshows, chronology of environmental events, law firms and major Canadian companies, *The Canadian Environmental Directory* is ideal for business, government, engineers and anyone conducting research on the environment.

Softcover ISBN 978-1-59237-224-9, 900 pages, $315.00

Canadian Parliamentary Guide, 2008

An indispensable guide to government in Canada, the annual *Canadian Parliamentary Guide* provides information on both federal and provincial governments, courts, and their elected and appointed members. The Guide is completely bilingual, with each record appearing both in English and then in French. The Guide contains biographical sketches of members of the Governor General's Household, the Privy Council, members of Canadian legislatures (federal, including both the House of Commons and the Senate, provincial and territorial), members of the federal superior courts (Supreme, Federal, Federal Appeal, Court Martial Appeal and Tax Courts) and the senior staff for these institutions. Biographies cover personal data, political career, private career and contact information. In addition, the Guide provides descriptions of each of the institutions, including brief historical information in text and chart format and significant facts (i.e. number of members and their salaries). The Guide covers the results of all federal general elections and by-elections from Confederations to the present and the results of the most recent provincial elections. A complete name index rounds out the text, making information easy to find. No other resources presents a more up-to-date, more complete picture of Canadian government and her political leaders. A must-have resource for all Canadian reference collections.

Hardcover ISBN 978-1-59237-310-9, 800 pages, $184.00

FREE CD-ROM

Grey House Publishing

PO Box 860 ◆ 185 Millerton Road ◆ Millerton, NY 12546
(800) 562-2139 ◆ (518) 789-8700 ◆ FAX (518) 789-0556
www.greyhouse.com ◆ e-mail: books@greyhouse.com

FREE CD-ROM WITH YOUR PURCHASE

Nations of the World, 2009 – CD-Rom

With your FREE CD-Rom, you can quickly and easily view and print out Country Reports as ready-to-use resources – right from PDF files – great for all types of users. Just attach this coupon to your payment and we'll ship your CD-Rom at no cost.

FREE CD-ROM COUPON

☐ I have enclosed my payment for *Nations of the World, 2009*. Send my FREE CD-Rom to the address below.

Name: _____ Invoice#: _____

Company Name: _____

Address: _____

City:_____ State: _____ Zip Code: _____

Telephone Number: _____ Fax Number: _____

Authorization Signature: _____ Date: _____

FREE CD-ROM

Grey House Publishing

PO Box 860 ◆ 185 Millerton Road ◆ Millerton, NY 12546
(800) 562-2139 ◆ (518) 789-8700 ◆ FAX (518) 789-0556
www.greyhouse.com ◆ e-mail: books@greyhouse.com

FREE CD-ROM WITH YOUR PURCHASE

Nations of the World, 2009 – CD-Rom

With your FREE CD-Rom, you can quickly and easily view and print out Country Reports as ready-to-use resources – right from PDF files – great for all types of users. Just attach this coupon to your payment and we'll ship your CD-Rom at no cost.

FREE CD-ROM COUPON

☐ I have enclosed my payment for *Nations of the World, 2009*. Send my FREE CD-Rom to the address below.

Name: _____ Invoice#: _____

Company Name: _____

Address: _____

City:_____ State: _____ Zip Code: _____

Telephone Number: _____ Fax Number: _____

Authorization Signature: _____ Date: _____

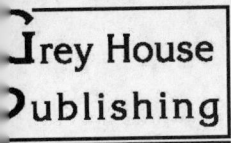